I0813544

חומש קורן שלם עם רש״י ואונקלוס

THE KOREN SHALEM ḤUMASH WITH RASHI AND ONKELOS

TRANSLATION AND COMMENTARY BY RABBI LORD JONATHAN SACKS

SECOND EDITION

KOREN

THE MAGERMAN EDITION

חומש קורן שלם עם רש״י ואונקלוס

THE KOREN SHALEM ḤUMASH WITH RASHI AND ONKELOS

TRANSLATION AND COMMENTARY BY

Rabbi Lord Jonathan Sacks זצ״ל

KOREN PUBLISHERS JERUSALEM

The Koren Shalem Ḥumash with Rashi and Onkelos
Translation and commentary by Rabbi Lord Jonathan Sacks
The Magerman Edition
Second Hebrew-English Edition

Koren Publishers Jerusalem Ltd.
POB 4044, Jerusalem 91040, ISRAEL
POB 8531, New Milford, CT 06776-8531, USA

www.korenpub.com

The publication of this book was made possible
through the generous support of *The Jewish Book Trust.*

Hardcover, ISBN 978-965-7765-17-3

Printed in PRC

Second printing

KH3

We have been blessed in our lives, by virtue of our philanthropic endeavors, to meet some of the most amazing and beautiful souls in the Jewish world. The pinnacle of those blessings was the time we shared with Rabbi Lord Jonathan Sacks and his wife, Lady Elaine Sacks.

As a part of the project to support the new translation of the Tanakh, along with Rabbi Sacks' new translation of and commentary on the Ḥumash, we were blessed with the opportunity to spend a few *Shabbatot* with Lord and Lady Sacks, to hear Rabbi Sacks speak in our community, and to have him spend time celebrating *ḥagim* with our community's children at school events. Learning from Rabbi Sacks is a privilege and a pleasure he has shared with the world through his publications and public speaking. Spending time with Rabbi Sacks – the man, the beautiful *neshama* – is more rare, and those experiences we had with him in our home and in our community, at Shabbat meals and on Shabbat afternoon walks, are priceless experiences we will never forget.

Rabbi Lord Jonathan Sacks was the authentic Torah voice for our generation, simultaneously steeped in Torah tradition and deeply engaged with people of all faiths. He succinctly understood and eloquently conveyed both the particular Jewish identity of our sacred writings as well as their universal relevance.

We pray that this unique, traditional, painstakingly researched and annotated translation of and commentary on the Ḥumash enlivens Torah for *klal Yisrael*, unites us in our traditions, inspires us with new, and old, ways of thinking, and ultimately brings us closer to the Redemption.

Debra and David Magerman
Philadelphia, Pennsylvania

CONTENTS

VAYIKRA/LEVITICUS
Parasha · Haftara

BEMIDBAR/NUMBERS
Parasha · Haftara

DEVARIM/DEUTERONOMY

Parasha · Haftara

THE TEN COMMANDMENTS

SPECIAL HAFTAROT

PUBLISHER'S PREFACE
THE KOREN ḤUMASH

The publication of the new *Koren Ḥumash* with commentary by Rabbi Lord Jonathan Sacks is a time of celebration, but one that is bittersweet. Its publication close to his fourth yahrzeit is a reminder that his living presence is no longer with us, but also that his Torah lives on and continues to grow in influence. Rabbi Sacks' enthusiasm, joyful scholarship, erudition, and penetrating insight permeated all his writings, conveying to us and to future generations that our Torah is a limitless source of wisdom, faith, and moral clarity. We were well into this ambitious endeavor when he went into the hospital, from which he fully expected to return.

I cannot write a preface for him; no one can. But his many books on Ḥumash – the *Covenant & Conversation* series, and those exploring leadership, ethics, spirituality, life-changing ideas, and belief – speak for themselves. These works, alongside his astonishing range of books, articles, and lectures – all of which have marshalled to complete Rabbi Sacks' commentary – reveal the depth, breadth, and relevance of the Torah's messages for the current age. The Torah is, as the Rabbis teach, "betrothed" to the Jewish people; yet it also contains the blueprint for a healthy and holy society that has universal relevance. Rabbi Sacks was our guide through the bewildering thickets of modernity, our guide to a fresh and refreshing engagement with Torah, and we gratefully follow the path he has charted for us.

His passing leaves a void which no one in this generation fills. We hope these writings will engage, provoke, and inspire the next generation of Torah scholars, teachers, laypeople, and indeed all God-seekers.

In the best of circumstances, the creation of this Ḥumash would be a collaboration of many. It is my privilege to thank them.

This project, the sister project of *The Koren Tanakh* which was published two years ago, has been sponsored by our friends Debra and David Magerman of Philadelphia and Jerusalem. With continual encouragement and no lack of patience, they shared the vision that animated both Rabbi Sacks and Koren, and enabled us to create this work you hold in your hands. For my colleagues at Koren, we thank you; for the many future generations who will read and use this Ḥumash weekly, we are forever in your debt.

We thank the family of Rabbi Sacks, Lady Elaine Sacks and her children Joshua, Dina, and Gila, for their encouragement and commitment, particularly after his passing. The leadership of The Rabbi Sacks Legacy, its chief executive, and my friends, Joanna Benarroch and Alan Sacks, provided encouragement during the awful days of 2020 and 2021, when we felt leaderless, and they continue to be valued and cherished partners.

Jessica Sacks' scholarship and erudition is not simply hereditary but unique to her, and she engaged with her uncle's writings with compassion and dedication. Rabbi Reuven Ziegler oversaw the entire project, and Dayan Ivan Binstock of the London Beth Din reviewed the Ḥumash.

Management of the editorial side was led by Gila Chitiz and Ashirah Firszt, and the production and design side was led by Rabbi Avishai Magence and Caryn Meltz; the typography was designed by Esther Be'er and Tomi Mager. I would also like to acknowledge Dr. Joel B. Wolowelsky for the initial commentary drafts, Rabbi Julian Sinclair, Yaffa Aranoff, Dr. Yoel Finkelman, and Tani Bednarsh for their review and comments, Debbie Ismailoff and Ita Olesker for copyediting, Rabbi Yedidya Naveh for authoring and translating the haftara commentary, Rabbi Yinon Chen, Tali Simon, Doron Chitiz, and Avichai Gamdani for proofreading, Eliyahu Misgav for cover design, and Gila Chitiz, Tani Bednarsh, and Elchanan Spitz for creating a database of books, essays, articles, and broadcasts of Rabbi Sacks.

Rabbi Sacks taught: "In Judaism we not only learn to live; we live to learn. In study, we make Torah real in the mind so that we can make it actual in the world." We pray that this masterful commentary on the Torah will allow countless people to ascend to ever greater heights in *living* and *learning*, to internalize the Torah's relevance to the individual and to society, and to help heal our fractured world.

Matthew Miller, Publisher
Jerusalem, Tishrei 5785 (October 2024)

Rabbi Sacks intended that this Ḥumash be his flagship project, one in which he could incorporate many of his timeless messages and ideas. "Traditional commentaries," he wrote of the Haggada, "are usually close readings of individual words and phrases rather than reflections on the meaning of the whole. That is a classic Jewish response, and I have not hesitated to do likewise.... But it is the great themes, the overarching principles, that are often neglected or taken for granted." These great themes – freedom and responsibility, love and justice, the meaning of the covenant between God and humanity and God and Israel – were for Rabbi Sacks the lifeblood of Judaism, and their text is the Torah as we read it week by week.

After translating the Ḥumash for *The Koren Tanakh*, Rabbi Sacks began writing his commentary, beginning with the book of Exodus. Regretfully, he was unable to see it to completion. The Ḥumash editorial team at Koren, led by Rabbi Sacks' niece Jessica Sacks, compiled the rest of the Ḥumash commentary from his vast array of books, articles, commentaries, and lectures. The work was always done with Rabbi Sacks' intention for the Ḥumash commentary as our guiding light, mission statement, and purpose. Great care was taken to present his invaluable ideas and messages in his own words, only adapting and reshaping them to preserve his style in the new format. We pray that we have managed to bring Rabbi Sacks' words alive through the Torah and his dream project to fruition. May this work allow his beautiful Torah to enlighten and inspire all of us for generations to come.

Targum Onkelos

The text of the Targum, including its vocalization and punctuation, is reprinted with permission of the Shetilei Zeitim Institute through the generosity and assistance of its publisher, Rabbi Yosef Iraqi Hacohen, and Adam Bin Nun. This highly accurate version of the text reflects the ancient tradition of reading the Targum publicly, as is still practiced today in Yemenite communities.

It is appropriate to mention that the punctuation according to this tradition is at times at odds with the punctuation typically dictated by the cantillation marks. According to the Yemenite tradition, there is a pause after the *tevir* cantillation mark as opposed to the more common custom of pausing after the *tipeḥa* cantillation mark which follows the *tevir*. We have chosen to follow this recognized Yemenite tradition for punctuation.

The Targum is presented in the Koren Siddur typeface, to distinguish it from the Hebrew text of the Torah. We have marked in gray instances where the Targum's translation is not literal but explicatory. Of course, any translation is itself a form of commentary, and sometimes the boundary between literal and allegorical translation can be blurry. We have attempted a conservative approach, marking only words whose content cannot be said to be denoted by any parallel word or phrase in the original Hebrew.

Rashi

Rashi's commentary on the Torah is one of the most important and widely published works of Jewish scholarship in existence. For the past thousand years, Jews around the world have studied and taught the Torah to their students with the close help of Rashi's comments. Because of the numerous manuscripts and printed editions of the commentary in circulation over the centuries, and because of the habit of later students to emend and add to Rashi's original text, there has never been any universally accepted, authoritative version of the commentary's text. In this edition, we have attempted to present Rashi's commentary with all later additions and textual corruptions removed.

In placing before the readers our new edition of Rashi's text, we have not presumed to reach the pinnacle of critical and philological accuracy. But we have worked hard to provide a text that is as clear and precise as possible. We worked with three types of textual witnesses: (1) manuscripts of Rashi's commentary, such as the Weimar, Vienna, and Munich codices; (2) early printed versions of the commentary, such as the Rome, Reggio di Calabria, Guadalajara, and Venice editions, all from the fifteenth century; and (3) influential printed editions published over the centuries, such as that of Avraham Berliner from

◀ the nineteenth

the nineteenth century, and the Ariel Humash and Bar Ilan University's "Keter" edition, both published recently. But our chief source was the Leipzig Manuscript (MS Leipzig 1) from the thirteenth century. Experts have long considered this manuscript to be the most authoritative version of Rashi's commentary on the Torah, and with God's help, we have succeeded in many instances in learning from it the most correct version of the text. For this we are indebted to the Institute of Microfilmed Hebrew Manuscripts at the National Library of Israel.

Alongside the effort to arrive at the most correct version of the text, we invested great effort in vocalizing and punctuating Rashi's commentary, providing a finished product that is considerably more accessible to the modern reader than past editions. We owe a special thanks for this to our stellar team of copyeditors, Rabbi Karmiel Cohen and Rabbi Yinon Chen. In places where Rashi cites a given midrashic story but quotes it only in part, we have provided the complete quote ourselves, in the same font but without vocalization. See for example Rashi on Leviticus 10:2.

Rashi's commentary is presented in the modern typeface "Koren Rashi," which was designed by the late Eliyahu Koren himself before his death. Design for this typeface placed emphasis on beauty, legibility, and closeness in form to standard Hebrew "square" lettering. "Koren Rashi" is unique in that it occasionally features multiple glyphs for the same letter to help readers' eyes to flow (see for example the letter ת in the phrase תלתל כתית). The typeface is based on the style of calligraphy characteristic of Sephardic manuscripts from the fifteenth century.

It is our hope that the Targum Onkelos and Rashi texts presented here, incorporating both historical accuracy and modern readability, will enhance both the study and appreciation of these works.

Haftarot

Following the Ḥumash section we have printed the haftarot according to the various customs of the Ashkenazim, Sepharadim, and Yemenites, Chabad. Chabad follows the Ashkenazi custom unless indicated otherwise. We included a short commentary for each haftara, originally written in Hebrew by Rabbi David Nativ (for Koren's Ḥumash Yisrael) and translated by Rabbi Yedidya Naveh. The commentary for the special haftarot was composed especially for this volume by Rabbi Yedidya Naveh. We hope that these commentaries provide the reader with the context to appreciate the significance of the words of the prophets and their depth and timeless teachings.

TORAH READINGS FOR SPECIAL DAYS

Rosh Ḥodesh	Numbers 28:1–15, p. 1155
Fast Days	Exodus 32:11–14, p. 641 Continues with Exodus 34:1–10, p. 651
Ninth of Av	Shaḥarit: Deuteronomy 4:25–40, p. 1251 Minḥa: See Fast Days, above.
Ḥanukka – Day 1	Ashkenazim: Numbers 7:1–17, p. 981 Sepharadim: Numbers 6:22–7:17, p. 979
Ḥanukka – Days 2–7	Read the offering for the respective day, Numbers 7:18–53, p. 985 On Rosh Ḥodesh, read the Rosh Ḥodesh reading from the first Torah scroll, and the Ḥanukka reading from the second Torah scroll.
Ḥanukka – Day 8	Numbers 7:54–8:4, p. 989
Purim	Exodus 17:8–16, p. 509
Purim on Shabbat (in Walled Cities)	Exodus 17:8–16, p. 509 *Haftara*: Same as Shabbat Zakhor.

TORAH READINGS FOR FESTIVALS

Pesaḥ – Day 1	Exodus 12:21–51, p. 465 On Shabbat, Sepharadim read Exodus 12:14–51, p. 463 *Maftir*: Numbers 28:16–25, p. 1159
Day 2	Leviticus 22:26–23:44, p. 871 In Israel: *Revi'i* (second Torah scroll): Numbers 28:19–25, p. 1159 In the Diaspora: *Maftir*: Same as Day 1
Day 3	Exodus 13:1–16, p. 473 *Revi'i* (second Torah scroll): Numbers 28:19–25, p. 1159
Day 4	Exodus 22:24–23:19, p. 557 (If it falls on a Sunday, Sepharadim read the passage for Day 3.) *Revi'i* (second Torah scroll): Numbers 28:19–25, p. 1159
Day 5	Exodus 34:1–26, p. 651 (If it falls on a Monday, Sepharadim read the passage for Day 4.) *Revi'i* (second Torah scroll): Numbers 28:19–25, p. 1159
Day 6	Numbers 9:1–14, p. 1003 *Revi'i* (second Torah scroll): Numbers 28:19–25, p. 1159
Shabbat Ḥol HaMoed Pesaḥ	Exodus 33:12–34:26, p. 649 *Maftir*: Numbers 28:19–25, p. 1159

Day 7	Exodus 13:17–15:26, p. 479 *Maftir*: Numbers 28:19–25, p. 1159
Day 8 (Diaspora)	Deuteronomy 15:19–16:17, p. 1341 On Shabbat: Deuteronomy 14:22–16:17, p. 1331 *Maftir*: Numbers 28:19–25, p. 1159
Shavuot – Day 1	Exodus 19:1–20:23, p. 521 *Maftir*: Numbers 28:26–31, p. 1159
Day 2 (Diaspora)	Deuteronomy 15:19–16:17, p. 1341 On Shabbat: Deuteronomy 14:22–16:17, p. 1331 *Maftir*: Same as Day 1
Rosh HaShana – Day 1	Genesis 21:1–34, p. 133 *Maftir*: Numbers 29:1–6, p. 1161
Day 2	Genesis 22:1–24, p. 139 *Maftir*: Same as Day 1
Yom Kippur – Shaḥarit	Leviticus 16:1–34, p. 819 *Maftir*: Numbers 29:7–11, p. 1163
Minḥa	Leviticus 18:1–30, p. 833
Sukkot – Day 1	Leviticus 22:26–23:44, p. 871 *Maftir*: Numbers 29:12–16, p. 1163
Day 2	Israel: Numbers 29:17–19, p. 1165 Diaspora: Same as Day 1
Day 3	Israel: Numbers 29:20–22, p. 1165 Diaspora: Numbers 29:17–25, p. 1165
Day 4	Israel: Numbers 29:23–25, p. 1165 Diaspora: Numbers 29:20–28, p. 1165
Day 5	Israel: Numbers 29:26–28, p. 1165 Diaspora: Numbers 29:23–31, p. 1165
Day 6	Israel: Numbers 29:29–31, p. 1165 Diaspora: Numbers 29:26–34, p. 1165
Hoshana Rabba	Israel: Numbers 29:32–34, p. 1165 Diaspora: Numbers 29:26–34, p. 1165
Shabbat Ḥol HaMoed Sukkot	Exodus 33:12–34:26, p. 649 *Maftir*: Read the offering for the respective day (in the Diaspora adding the offering for the previous day).
Shemini Atzeret (Diaspora)	Deuteronomy 15:19–16:17, p. 1341 On Shabbat: Deuteronomy 14:22–16:17, p. 1331 *Maftir*: Numbers 29:35–30:1, p. 1167
Simḥat Torah (Israel and Diaspora)	First Torah scroll: Deuteronomy 33:1–34:12, p. 1485 Second Torah scroll: Genesis 1:1–2:3, p. 3 Third Torah scroll (*Maftir*): Numbers 29:35–30:1, p. 1167

BLESSINGS BEFORE AND AFTER READING THE TORAH (ASHKENAZI CUSTOM)

Before reading the Torah, the Oleh says:

בָּרְכוּ Bless the LORD, the blessed One.

Cong: בָּרוּךְ Bless the LORD, the blessed One, for ever and all time.

Oleh: בָּרוּךְ Bless the LORD, the blessed One, for ever and all time.

Blessed are You, LORD our God, King of the Universe,
who has chosen us from all peoples and has given us His Torah.
Blessed are You, LORD, Giver of the Torah.

After the reading, the Oleh recites:

Oleh: בָּרוּךְ Blessed are You, LORD our God, King of the Universe,
who has given us the Torah of truth, and everlasting life He has planted in our midst.
Blessed are You, LORD, Giver of the Torah.

BLESSINGS BEFORE AND AFTER READING THE HAFTARA

Before reading the haftara, the person called up for maftir recites:

בָּרוּךְ Blessed are You, LORD our God, King of the Universe, who chose good prophets and was pleased with their words, spoken in truth. Blessed are You, LORD, who chooses the Torah, His servant Moses, His people Israel, and the prophets of truth and righteousness.

After the haftara, the person called up for maftir recites the following blessings:

בָּרוּךְ Blessed are You, LORD our God King of the Universe, Rock of all worlds, righteous for all generations, the faithful God who says and does, speaks and fulfills, all of whose words are truth and righteousness. You are faithful, LORD our God, and faithful are Your words, not one of which returns unfulfilled, for You, God, are a faithful (and compassionate) King. Blessed are You, LORD, faithful in all His words.

רַחֵם Have compassion on Zion for it is the source of our life, and save the one grieved in spirit swiftly in our days. Blessed are You, LORD, who makes Zion rejoice in her children.

שַׂמְּחֵנוּ Grant us joy, LORD our God, through Elijah the prophet Your servant, and through the kingdom of the house of David Your anointed – may he soon come and gladden our hearts. May no stranger sit on his throne, and may others no longer inherit his glory, for You took an oath to him by Your holy name that his light would never be extinguished. Blessed are You, LORD, Shield of David.

On Shabbat, including Shabbat Ḥol HaMo'ed Pesaḥ, say:

עַל הַתּוֹרָה For the Torah, for divine worship, for the prophets, and for this Sabbath day which You, LORD our God, have given us for holiness and rest, honor and glory – for all these we thank and bless You, LORD our God, and may Your name be blessed by the mouth of all that lives, continually, for ever and all time. Blessed are You, LORD, who sanctifies the Sabbath.

ברכות התורה (מנהג אשכנזים)

Before קריאת התורה*, the* עולה *says:*

עולה: בָּרְכוּ אֶת יהוה הַמְבֹרָךְ.

קהל: בָּרוּךְ יהוה הַמְבֹרָךְ לְעוֹלָם וָעֶד.

עולה: בָּרוּךְ יהוה הַמְבֹרָךְ לְעוֹלָם וָעֶד.

בָּרוּךְ אַתָּה יהוה, אֱלֹהֵינוּ מֶלֶךְ הָעוֹלָם,
אֲשֶׁר בָּחַר בָּנוּ מִכָּל הָעַמִּים וְנָתַן לָנוּ אֶת תּוֹרָתוֹ.
בָּרוּךְ אַתָּה יהוה, נוֹתֵן הַתּוֹרָה.

After קריאת התורה*, the* עולה *says:*

בָּרוּךְ אַתָּה יהוה, אֱלֹהֵינוּ מֶלֶךְ הָעוֹלָם,
אֲשֶׁר נָתַן לָנוּ תּוֹרַת אֱמֶת וְחַיֵּי עוֹלָם נָטַע בְּתוֹכֵנוּ.
בָּרוּךְ אַתָּה יהוה, נוֹתֵן הַתּוֹרָה.

ברכות ההפטרה

Before reading the הפטרה*, the person called up for* מפטיר *says:*

בָּרוּךְ אַתָּה יהוה אֱלֹהֵינוּ מֶלֶךְ הָעוֹלָם אֲשֶׁר בָּחַר בִּנְבִיאִים טוֹבִים, וְרָצָה בְדִבְרֵיהֶם הַנֶּאֱמָרִים בֶּאֱמֶת.
בָּרוּךְ אַתָּה יהוה, הַבּוֹחֵר בַּתּוֹרָה וּבְמֹשֶׁה עַבְדּוֹ וּבְיִשְׂרָאֵל עַמּוֹ וּבִנְבִיאֵי הָאֱמֶת וָצֶדֶק.

After the הפטרה*, the person called up for* מפטיר *says the following blessings:*

בָּרוּךְ אַתָּה יהוה, אֱלֹהֵינוּ מֶלֶךְ הָעוֹלָם, צוּר כָּל הָעוֹלָמִים, צַדִּיק בְּכָל הַדּוֹרוֹת, הָאֵל הַנֶּאֱמָן, הָאוֹמֵר וְעוֹשֶׂה, הַמְדַבֵּר וּמְקַיֵּם, שֶׁכָּל דְּבָרָיו אֱמֶת וָצֶדֶק. נֶאֱמָן אַתָּה הוּא יהוה אֱלֹהֵינוּ וְנֶאֱמָנִים דְּבָרֶיךָ, וְדָבָר אֶחָד מִדְּבָרֶיךָ אָחוֹר לֹא יָשׁוּב רֵיקָם, כִּי אֵל מֶלֶךְ נֶאֱמָן (וְרַחֲמָן) אָתָּה. בָּרוּךְ אַתָּה יהוה, הָאֵל הַנֶּאֱמָן בְּכָל דְּבָרָיו.

רַחֵם עַל צִיּוֹן כִּי הִיא בֵּית חַיֵּינוּ, וְלַעֲלוּבַת נֶפֶשׁ תּוֹשִׁיעַ בִּמְהֵרָה בְיָמֵינוּ. בָּרוּךְ אַתָּה יהוה, מְשַׂמֵּחַ צִיּוֹן בְּבָנֶיהָ.

שַׂמְּחֵנוּ יהוה אֱלֹהֵינוּ בְּאֵלִיָּהוּ הַנָּבִיא עַבְדֶּךָ, וּבְמַלְכוּת בֵּית דָּוִד מְשִׁיחֶךָ, בִּמְהֵרָה יָבוֹא וְיָגֵל לִבֵּנוּ. עַל כִּסְאוֹ לֹא יֵשֶׁב זָר, וְלֹא יִנְחֲלוּ עוֹד אֲחֵרִים אֶת כְּבוֹדוֹ, כִּי בְשֵׁם קָדְשְׁךָ נִשְׁבַּעְתָּ לּוֹ שֶׁלֹּא יִכְבֶּה נֵרוֹ לְעוֹלָם וָעֶד. בָּרוּךְ אַתָּה יהוה, מָגֵן דָּוִד.

On שבת*, including* שבת חול המועד פסח*, say:*

עַל הַתּוֹרָה וְעַל הָעֲבוֹדָה וְעַל הַנְּבִיאִים וְעַל יוֹם הַשַּׁבָּת הַזֶּה, שֶׁנָּתַתָּ לָּנוּ יהוה אֱלֹהֵינוּ לִקְדֻשָּׁה וְלִמְנוּחָה, לְכָבוֹד וּלְתִפְאָרֶת. עַל הַכֹּל יהוה אֱלֹהֵינוּ אֲנַחְנוּ מוֹדִים לָךְ וּמְבָרְכִים אוֹתָךְ, יִתְבָּרַךְ שִׁמְךָ בְּפִי כָּל חַי תָּמִיד לְעוֹלָם וָעֶד. בָּרוּךְ אַתָּה יהוה, מְקַדֵּשׁ הַשַּׁבָּת.

On Yom Tov and on Shabbat Ḥol HaMo'ed Sukkot, say (adding on Shabbat the words in parentheses):

עַל הַתּוֹרָה For the Torah, for Divine worship, for the prophets,
(for this Sabbath day) and for this day of

On Pesaḥ: the Festival of Matzot
On Shavuot: the Festival of Shavuot
On Sukkot: the Festival of Sukkot
On Shemini Atzeret and Simḥat Torah: the Festival of Shemini Atzeret

which You, LORD our God, have given us (for holiness and rest), for joy and gladness, honor and glory –
for all these we thank and bless You, LORD our God,
and may Your name be blessed by the mouth of all that lives,
continually, for ever and all time.
Blessed are You, LORD, who sanctifies (the Sabbath), Israel and the festivals. (Amen.)

BLESSINGS BEFORE AND AFTER READING THE TORAH (SEPHARDIC CUSTOM)

Before reading the Torah, the Oleh says:

Oleh: The LORD is with you *Cong:* May the LORD bless you

Oleh: בָּרוּךְ Bless the LORD, the blessed One.

Cong: בָּרוּךְ Bless the LORD, the blessed One, for ever and all time.

Oleh: בָּרוּךְ Bless the LORD, the blessed One, for ever and all time.
Blessed are You, LORD our God, King of the Universe,
who has chosen us from all peoples and has given us His Torah.
Blessed are You, LORD, Giver of the Torah.

After the reading, the Oleh recites:

Oleh: Blessed are You, LORD our God, King of the Universe,
who has given us His Torah, the Torah of truth, and everlasting life He has planted in our midst.
Blessed are You, LORD, Giver of the Torah.

On יום טוב *and on* שבת חול המועד סוכות*,*
say (adding on שבת *the words in parentheses):*

עַל הַתּוֹרָה וְעַל הָעֲבוֹדָה וְעַל הַנְּבִיאִים (בשבת: וְעַל יוֹם הַשַּׁבָּת הַזֶּה), וְעַל יוֹם

בפסח: חַג הַמַּצּוֹת הַזֶּה

בשבועות: חַג הַשָּׁבוּעוֹת הַזֶּה

בסוכות: חַג הַסֻּכּוֹת הַזֶּה

בשמיני עצרת ובש״ת: (הַ)שְּׁמִינִי חַג (הָ)עֲצֶרֶת הַזֶּה

שֶׁנָּתַתָּ לָּנוּ, יהוה אֱלֹהֵינוּ (בשבת: לִקְדֻשָּׁה וְלִמְנוּחָה)
לְשָׂשׂוֹן וּלְשִׂמְחָה, לְכָבוֹד וּלְתִפְאָרֶת.
עַל הַכֹּל יהוה אֱלֹהֵינוּ אֲנַחְנוּ מוֹדִים לָךְ וּמְבָרְכִים אוֹתָךְ.
יִתְבָּרַךְ שִׁמְךָ בְּפִי כָּל חַי תָּמִיד לְעוֹלָם וָעֶד.
בָּרוּךְ אַתָּה יהוה, מְקַדֵּשׁ (בשבת: הַשַּׁבָּת וְ)יִשְׂרָאֵל וְהַזְּמַנִּים. (אָמֵן.)

ברכות התורה (מנהג ספרדים)

Before קריאת התורה*, the* עולה *says:*

עולה: יהוה עִמָּכֶם קהל: יְבָרֶכְךָ יהוה

עולה: (רַבָּנָן) בָּרְכוּ אֶת יהוה הַמְבֹרָךְ.

קהל: בָּרוּךְ יהוה הַמְבֹרָךְ לְעוֹלָם וָעֶד.

עולה: בָּרוּךְ יהוה הַמְבֹרָךְ לְעוֹלָם וָעֶד.

בָּרוּךְ אַתָּה יהוה, אֱלֹהֵינוּ מֶלֶךְ הָעוֹלָם,
אֲשֶׁר בָּחַר בָּנוּ מִכָּל הָעַמִּים, וְנָתַן לָנוּ אֶת תּוֹרָתוֹ.
בָּרוּךְ אַתָּה יהוה, נוֹתֵן הַתּוֹרָה.

After the reading, the עולה *recites:*

בָּרוּךְ אַתָּה יהוה, אֱלֹהֵינוּ מֶלֶךְ הָעוֹלָם,
אֲשֶׁר נָתַן לָנוּ (אֶת) תּוֹרָתוֹ תּוֹרַת אֱמֶת, וְחַיֵּי עוֹלָם נָטַע בְּתוֹכֵנוּ.
בָּרוּךְ אַתָּה יהוה, נוֹתֵן הַתּוֹרָה.

BLESSINGS BEFORE AND AFTER READING THE HAFTARA

Before reading the haftara, the person called up for maftir recites:

בָּרוּךְ Blessed are You, Lord our God, King of the Universe, who chose good prophets and was pleased with their words, spoken in truth. Blessed are You, Lord, who chose the Torah, His servant Moses, His people Israel, and the prophets of truth and righteousness.

After reading the haftara, he recites:

גֹּאֲלֵנוּ Our Redeemer, the Lord of hosts is His name, Holy One of Israel *Isaiah 47*

בָּרוּךְ Blessed are You, Lord our God, King of the Universe, Rock of all worlds, righteous for all generations, the faithful God who says and does, speaks and fulfills, all of whose words are truth and righteousness. You are faithful, Lord our God, and faithful are Your words, not one of which returns unfulfilled, for You, God, are a faithful (and compassionate) King. Blessed are You, Lord, faithful in all His words.

רַחֵם Have compassion on Zion for it is the source of our life, and save the one grieved in spirit swiftly in our days. Blessed are You, Lord, who makes Zion rejoice in her children.

שַׂמְּחֵנוּ Grant us joy, Lord our God, through Elijah the prophet Your servant, and through the kingdom of the house of David Your anointed – may he soon come and gladden our hearts. May no stranger sit on his throne, and may others no longer inherit his glory, for You took an oath to him by Your holy name that his light would never be extinguished. Blessed are You, Lord, Shield of David.

On Shabbat, including Shabbat Ḥol HaMo'ed Pesaḥ, say:

עַל הַתּוֹרָה For the Torah, for divine worship, for the prophets, and for this Sabbath day which You, Lord our God, have given us for holiness and rest, honor and glory – for all these we thank and bless You, Lord our God, and may Your name be blessed by the mouth of all that lives, continually, for ever and all time. Blessed are You, Lord, who sanctifies the Sabbath.

On Yom Tov and on Shabbat Ḥol HaMo'ed Sukkot, say
(adding on Shabbat the words in parentheses):

עַל הַתּוֹרָה For the Torah, for Divine worship, for the prophets,
(for this Sabbath day) and for this day of

On Pesaḥ: the Festival of Matzot
On Shavuot: the Festival of Shavuot
On Sukkot: the Festival of Sukkot
On Shemini Atzeret and Simḥat Torah: the Festival of Shemini Atzeret

which You, Lord our God, have given us (for holiness and rest), for joy and gladness, honor and glory –
for all these we thank and bless You, Lord our God,
and may Your name be blessed by the mouth of all that lives,
continually, for ever and all time.
Blessed are You, Lord, who sanctifies (the Sabbath), Israel and the festivals. (Amen.)

ברכות ההפטרה

Before reading the הפטרה, *the person called up for* מפטיר *recites:*

בָּרוּךְ אַתָּה יהוה אֱלֹהֵינוּ מֶלֶךְ הָעוֹלָם אֲשֶׁר בָּחַר בִּנְבִיאִים טוֹבִים, וְרָצָה בְדִבְרֵיהֶם הַנֶּאֱמָרִים בֶּאֱמֶת. בָּרוּךְ אַתָּה יהוה, הַבּוֹחֵר בַּתּוֹרָה וּבְמֹשֶׁה עַבְדּוֹ וּבְיִשְׂרָאֵל עַמּוֹ וּבִנְבִיאֵי הָאֱמֶת וְהַצֶּדֶק.

After reading the הפטרה, *he recites:*

גֹּאֲלֵנוּ יהוה צְבָאוֹת שְׁמוֹ, קְדוֹשׁ יִשְׂרָאֵל: ישעיה מז

בָּרוּךְ אַתָּה יהוה, אֱלֹהֵינוּ מֶלֶךְ הָעוֹלָם, צוּר כָּל הָעוֹלָמִים, צַדִּיק בְּכָל הַדּוֹרוֹת, הָאֵל הַנֶּאֱמָן, הָאוֹמֵר וְעוֹשֶׂה, מְדַבֵּר וּמְקַיֵּם, כִּי כָל דְּבָרָיו אֱמֶת וָצֶדֶק. נֶאֱמָן אַתָּה הוּא יהוה אֱלֹהֵינוּ וְנֶאֱמָנִים דְּבָרֶיךָ, וְדָבָר אֶחָד מִדְּבָרֶיךָ אָחוֹר לֹא יָשׁוּב רֵיקָם, כִּי אֵל מֶלֶךְ נֶאֱמָן (וְרַחֲמָן) אָתָּה. בָּרוּךְ אַתָּה יהוה, הָאֵל הַנֶּאֱמָן בְּכָל דְּבָרָיו.

רַחֵם עַל צִיּוֹן כִּי הִיא בֵּית חַיֵּינוּ, וְלַעֲלוּבַת נֶפֶשׁ תּוֹשִׁיעַ בִּמְהֵרָה בְיָמֵינוּ. בָּרוּךְ אַתָּה יהוה, מְשַׂמֵּחַ צִיּוֹן בְּבָנֶיהָ.

שַׂמְּחֵנוּ יהוה אֱלֹהֵינוּ בְּאֵלִיָּהוּ הַנָּבִיא עַבְדֶּךָ, וּבְמַלְכוּת בֵּית דָּוִד מְשִׁיחֶךָ, בִּמְהֵרָה יָבוֹא וְיָגֵל לִבֵּנוּ. עַל כִּסְאוֹ לֹא יֵשֵׁב זָר, וְלֹא יִנְחֲלוּ עוֹד אֲחֵרִים אֶת כְּבוֹדוֹ, כִּי בְשֵׁם קָדְשְׁךָ נִשְׁבַּעְתָּ לּוֹ שֶׁלֹּא יִכְבֶּה נֵרוֹ לְעוֹלָם וָעֶד. בָּרוּךְ אַתָּה יהוה, מָגֵן דָּוִד.

On שבת, *including* שבת חול המועד פסח, *say:*

עַל הַתּוֹרָה וְעַל הָעֲבוֹדָה וְעַל הַנְּבִיאִים וְעַל יוֹם הַשַּׁבָּת הַזֶּה, שֶׁנָּתַתָּ לָּנוּ יהוה אֱלֹהֵינוּ לִקְדֻשָּׁה וְלִמְנוּחָה, לְכָבוֹד וּלְתִפְאָרֶת. עַל הַכֹּל יהוה אֱלֹהֵינוּ אֲנַחְנוּ מוֹדִים לָךְ וּמְבָרְכִים אוֹתָךְ, יִתְבָּרַךְ שִׁמְךָ בְּפִי כָּל חַי תָּמִיד לְעוֹלָם וָעֶד. בָּרוּךְ אַתָּה יהוה, מְקַדֵּשׁ הַשַּׁבָּת. אָמֵן.

On יום טוב *and on* שבת חול המועד סוכות, *say (adding on* שבת *the words in parentheses):*

עַל הַתּוֹרָה וְעַל הָעֲבוֹדָה וְעַל הַנְּבִיאִים (בשבת: וְעַל יוֹם הַשַּׁבָּת הַזֶּה),
וְעַל יוֹם

בפסח: חַג הַמַּצּוֹת הַזֶּה
בשבועות: חַג הַשָּׁבוּעוֹת הַזֶּה
בסוכות: חַג הַסֻּכּוֹת הַזֶּה
בשמיני עצרת ובש״ת: (הַ)שְּׁמִינִי חַג (הָ)עֲצֶרֶת הַזֶּה

שֶׁנָּתַתָּ לָּנוּ, יהוה אֱלֹהֵינוּ (בשבת: לִקְדֻשָּׁה וְלִמְנוּחָה)
לְשָׂשׂוֹן וּלְשִׂמְחָה, לְכָבוֹד וּלְתִפְאָרֶת.
עַל הַכֹּל יהוה אֱלֹהֵינוּ אֲנַחְנוּ מוֹדִים לָךְ וּמְבָרְכִים אוֹתָךְ.
יִתְבָּרַךְ שִׁמְךָ בְּפִי כָּל חַי תָּמִיד לְעוֹלָם וָעֶד.
בָּרוּךְ אַתָּה יהוה, מְקַדֵּשׁ (בשבת: הַשַּׁבָּת וְ)יִשְׂרָאֵל וְהַזְּמַנִּים. (אָמֵן.)

בראשית
GENESIS

THE BOOK OF GENESIS

Genesis, the book of Bereshit, is as its name suggests, about beginnings: the birth of the universe, the origins of humanity, and the first chapters in the story of the people that would be known as Israel. It tells of how this people began, first as an individual, Avraham, who heard a call to leave his home and begin a journey, then as a family; it closes as the extended family stands on the threshold of becoming a nation. The journey turns out to be unexpectedly complicated and fraught with setbacks. In a sense, it continues till today. This is part of what makes Genesis so vivid. We can relate to its characters and their dilemmas. We are part of their world, as they are of ours. This is our story; this is where we came from; this is our journey.

But this is not all Genesis is. Rambam makes the fundamental point that *reshit* does not mean "beginning" in the sense of "first of a chronological sequence." For that, Biblical Hebrew has other words. *Reshit* implies the most significant element, the part that stands for the whole, the foundation, the principle. Genesis is Judaism's foundational work, a philosophy of the human condition under the sovereignty of God.

This is a difficult point to understand, because there is no other book quite like it. It is not myth. It is not history in the conventional sense, a mere recording of events. Nor is it theology: Genesis is less about God than about human beings and their relationship with God. The theology is almost always implicit rather than explicit. What Genesis is, in fact, is *philosophy written in a deliberately non-philosophical way*. It deals with all the central questions of philosophy: what exists (ontology), what can we know (epistemology), are we free (philosophical psychology), and how we should behave (ethics). But it does so in a way quite unlike the philosophical classics from Plato to Wittgenstein. To put it at its simplest: Philosophy is *truth as system*. Genesis is *truth as story*. It is a unique work, philosophy in the narrative mode.

So we learn about what exists by way of a story about creation. We learn about knowledge through a tangled tale of the first man, the first woman, a serpent, and a tree. We begin to understand human freedom and its abuse through the story of Kayin. We learn how to behave through the lives of Avraham and Sara and their children. It is this that has helped to make Tanakh the most widely read and influential book in the history of civilization. Only the gifted few can fully understand a philosophical classic, but everyone can relate to a story.

Everyone can understand Genesis, yet not understand at the same level; that is another feature of the book. Each of its stories has layer upon layer of meaning and significance, which we only grasp after repeated readings. Our understanding of the book grows as we grow. Each age adds insights, commentaries, and interpretations of its own. The book's literary style allows it to be read afresh in each generation. Only stories have this depth, this ambiguity, this principled multiplicity of meanings.

Torah is God's book of humanity, and each of us is a chapter in its unfinished story. Its words form our covenant with Heaven. And as we listen and respond, we add our voice to the unbroken conversation between the Jewish people and its destiny.

Parashat Bereshit

1 1 2 When God began creating heaven and earth, the earth was void and desolate,

רש"י

א א| בְּרֵאשִׁית. אָמַר רַבִּי יִצְחָק: לֹא הָיָה צָרִיךְ לְהַתְחִיל אֶת הַתּוֹרָה אֶלָּא מֵ"הַחֹדֶשׁ הַזֶּה לָכֶם" (שמות יב, ב) שֶׁהִיא מִצְוָה רִאשׁוֹנָה שֶׁנִּצְטַוּוּ יִשְׂרָאֵל. וּמַה טַּעַם פָּתַח בִּ"בְרֵאשִׁית" – מִשּׁוּם "כֹּחַ מַעֲשָׂיו הִגִּיד לְעַמּוֹ לָתֵת לָהֶם נַחֲלַת גּוֹיִם" (תהלים קיא, ו), שֶׁאִם יֹאמְרוּ אֻמּוֹת הָעוֹלָם לְיִשְׂרָאֵל: לִסְטִים אַתֶּם שֶׁכְּבַשְׁתֶּם אַרְצוֹת שִׁבְעָה גוֹיִם, הֵם אוֹמְרִים לָהֶם: כָּל הָאָרֶץ שֶׁל הַקָּדוֹשׁ בָּרוּךְ הוּא הִיא, הוּא בְּרָאָהּ וּנְתָנָהּ לַאֲשֶׁר יָשַׁר בְּעֵינָיו, בִּרְצוֹנוֹ נְתָנָהּ לָהֶם, וּבִרְצוֹנוֹ נְטָלָהּ מֵהֶם וּנְתָנָהּ לָנוּ:
בְּרֵאשִׁית בָּרָא. אֵין הַמִּקְרָא הַזֶּה אוֹמֵר אֶלָּא דָּרְשֵׁנִי, כְּמוֹ שֶׁדְּרָשׁוּהוּ רַבּוֹתֵינוּ ז"ל: בִּשְׁבִיל הַתּוֹרָה שֶׁנִּקְרֵאת "רֵאשִׁית דַּרְכּוֹ" (משלי ח, כב), וּבִשְׁבִיל יִשְׂרָאֵל שֶׁנִּקְרְאוּ "רֵאשִׁית תְּבוּאָתֹה" (ירמיה ב, ג). וְאִם בָּאתָ לְפָרְשׁוֹ כִּפְשׁוּטוֹ, כָּךְ פָּרְשֵׁהוּ: בְּרֵאשִׁית בְּרִיאַת שָׁמַיִם וָאָרֶץ, וְהָאָרֶץ הָיְתָה תֹהוּ וָבֹהוּ וְחֹשֶׁךְ, וַיֹּאמֶר אֱלֹהִים יְהִי אוֹר. וְלֹא בָּא הַמִּקְרָא לְהוֹרוֹת סֵדֶר הַבְּרִיאָה לוֹמַר שֶׁאֵלּוּ קָדְמוּ, שֶׁאִם בָּא לְהוֹרוֹת כָּךְ, הָיָה לוֹ לִכְתֹּב: בָּרִאשׁוֹנָה בָּרָא אֶת הַשָּׁמַיִם וְגוֹ', שֶׁאֵין לְךָ 'רֵאשִׁית' בַּמִּקְרָא שֶׁאֵינוֹ דָּבוּק לַתֵּבָה שֶׁל אַחֲרָיו, כְּמוֹ: "בְּרֵאשִׁית מַמְלֶכֶת יְהוֹיָקִם" (שם כז, א), "רֵאשִׁית מַמְלַכְתּוֹ" (בראשית י, י), "רֵאשִׁית דְּגָנְךָ" (דברים יח, ד). אַף כָּאן אַתָּה אוֹמֵר: "בְּרֵאשִׁית בָּרָא אֱלֹהִים" וְגוֹ' כְּמוֹ: 'בְּרֵאשִׁית בְּרֹא', וְדוֹמֶה לוֹ: "תְּחִלַּת דִּבֶּר ה' בְּהוֹשֵׁעַ", כְּלוֹמַר תְּחִלַּת דִּבּוּרוֹ שֶׁל הַקָּדוֹשׁ בָּרוּךְ הוּא בְּהוֹשֵׁעַ, "וַיֹּאמֶר ה' אֶל הוֹשֵׁעַ" וְגוֹ' (הושע א, ב). וְאִם תֹּאמַר, לְהוֹרוֹת בָּא שֶׁאֵלּוּ תְּחִלָּה נִבְרְאוּ, וּפֵרוּשׁוֹ: 'בְּרֵאשִׁית הַכֹּל בָּרָא אֵלּוּ', וְיֵשׁ לְךָ מִקְרָאוֹת שֶׁמְּקַצְּרִים לְשׁוֹנָם וּמְמַעֲטִים תֵּבָה אַחַת, כְּמוֹ: "כִּי לֹא סָגַר דַּלְתֵי בִטְנִי" (איוב ג, י) וְלֹא פֵרֵשׁ מִי הַסּוֹגֵר, וּכְמוֹ: "יִשָּׂא אֶת חֵיל דַּמֶּשֶׂק" (ישעיה ח, ד) וְלֹא פֵרֵשׁ מִי יִשָּׂאֶנּוּ, וּכְמוֹ: "אִם יַחֲרוֹשׁ בַּבְּקָרִים" (עמוס ו, יב) וְלֹא פֵרֵשׁ 'אִם יַחֲרוֹשׁ אָדָם בַּבְּקָרִים', וּכְמוֹ: "מַגִּיד מֵרֵאשִׁית אַחֲרִית" (ישעיה מו, י) וְלֹא פֵרֵשׁ 'מַגִּיד מֵרֵאשִׁית דָּבָר אַחֲרִית דָּבָר' – אִם כֵּן תְּמַהּ עַל עַצְמְךָ שֶׁהֲרֵי הַמַּיִם קָדְמוּ, שֶׁהֲרֵי כְּתִיב: "וְרוּחַ אֱלֹהִים מְרַחֶפֶת עַל פְּנֵי הַמָּיִם" (להלן פסוק ב), וַעֲדַיִן לֹא גִּלָּה הַמִּקְרָא בְּרִיַּת הַמַּיִם מָתַי הָיְתָה, לָמַדְתָּ שֶׁקָּדְמוּ לָאָרֶץ, וְעוֹד שֶׁהַשָּׁמַיִם מֵאֵשׁ וּמַיִם נִבְרְאוּ, עַל כָּרְחֲךָ לֹא לִמֵּד הַמִּקְרָא בְּסֵדֶר הַמֻּקְדָּמִים וְהַמְאֻחָרִים כְּלוּם: **בָּרָא אֱלֹהִים.** וְלֹא אָמַר 'בָּרָא ה'', שֶׁבַּתְּחִלָּה עָלָה בְּמַחֲשָׁבָה לִבְרֹאתוֹ בְּמִדַּת הַדִּין, וְרָאָה שֶׁאֵין מִתְקַיֵּם, וְהִקְדִּים מִדַּת רַחֲמִים וְשִׁתְּפָהּ לְמִדַּת הַדִּין, וְהַיְינוּ דִּכְתִיב: "בְּיוֹם עֲשׂוֹת ה' אֱלֹהִים אֶרֶץ וְשָׁמָיִם" (להלן ב, ד):

ב| **תֹהוּ וָבֹהוּ.** תֹּהוּ לְשׁוֹן תְּמַהּ וְשִׁמָּמוֹן, שֶׁאָדָם תּוֹהֶה וּמִשְׁתּוֹמֵם עַל

as He is called merciful, so you be merciful. The prophets described the Almighty by all the various attributes: long-suffering, abounding in kindness ... powerful and so on – to teach us that these qualities are good and righteous and that a human being should cultivate them, and thus imitate God as far as we can. (*Hilkhot Deot* 1:11)

Implicit in the first chapter of Genesis is a momentous challenge: Just as God is creative, so you be creative. What is more, it tells us how to be creative – namely, in three stages. The first is the stage of saying, "Let there be." What is truly creative is not science or technology per se, but the word. Because we can speak, we can think and therefore imagine a world different from the one that currently exists. Creation begins with the creative word, the idea, the vision, the dream. The first stage in creation is imagination.

The second stage is for us the most difficult. "And there was...." It is one thing to conceive an idea, another to execute it. Between the intention and the fact, the dream and the reality, lies struggle, opposition, and the fallibility of the human will. It is all too easy, having tried and failed, to conclude that nothing ultimately can be achieved, that the world is as it is, and that all human endeavor is destined to end in failure. Yet Judaism holds the opposite, that though creation is difficult, laborious, and fraught with setbacks, we are summoned to it as our essential human vocation: "It is not for you to complete the work," said R. Tarfon, "but neither are you free to desist from it" (Avot 2:16). There is a

פרשת בראשית

א א ב בְּרֵאשִׁ֖ית בָּרָ֣א אֱלֹהִ֑ים אֵ֥ת הַשָּׁמַ֖יִם וְאֵ֥ת הָאָֽרֶץ׃ וְהָאָ֗רֶץ הָיְתָ֥ה תֹ֙הוּ֙ א

אונקלוס

א א בְּקַדְמִין בְּרָא יְיָ, יָת שְׁמַיָּא וְיָת אַרְעָא: ב וְאַרְעָא, הֲוָת צָדְיָא

BERESHIT

The Book of Books starts with the beginning of beginnings: the creation of the universe and life. The story is told from two different perspectives, first as cosmology (the origins of matter), then as anthropology (the birth of humanity).

The first narrative (Gen. 1:1–2:3) emphasizes harmony and order. God creates the universe in six days and dedicates the seventh as a day of holiness and rest. The second (2:4–3:24) focuses on humanity, not as a biological species but as persons-in-relation. God fashions man, sees that "it is not good for man to be alone" (2:18), and then fashions the woman. The serpent tempts them; they sin and are banished from the garden.

From then on, the human drama unfolds as tragedy. Kayin murders his brother. By the end of the *parasha*, God sees "how great man's wickedness was upon the earth" (6:5) and "regretted that He had made man on earth" (6:6). God creates order; man creates chaos. The question that remains to challenge us is: which will prevail?

1:1 בְּרֵאשִׁית בָּרָא אֱלֹהִים *When God began creating* – Rashi begins his commentary: "Rabbi Yitzḥak said: The Torah should have begun with the verse, 'This month shall be to you the beginning of months' (Ex. 12:2), which was the first mitzva given to Israel." To understand a book, one needs to know to which genre it belongs. What Rashi is succinctly saying in his enigmatic question is that the Torah is not a book of history, even though it includes history. It is not a book of science, even though the first chapter of Genesis is the necessary prelude to science, representing as it does the first time people saw the universe as the product of a single creative will, and therefore as intelligible rather than capricious and mysterious. The Torah is, first and last, a book about how to live.

Rashi gives one answer to his question. I would suggest an additional one. Jewish ethics is not confined to law. It includes virtues of character, general principles, and role models. It is conveyed not only by commandments but also by stories. And so the book of how to live opens with the most fundamental question of all. As the psalm (8:4) puts it: "What are mortals, that You should be mindful of them?"

1:1 אֵת הַשָּׁמַיִם וְאֵת הָאָרֶץ *Heaven and earth* – The Torah begins with the universal, and only later, in chapter 12, Parashat Lekh Lekha, does it narrow in on the particular. As far as Plato was concerned, knowledge starts with the particular – this tree, this person; looking at these you begin to realize that what is interesting is not this tree but tree-ness, not this person, but the universal things that make a person a person. Following Plato, Western thought has not been interested in the particular or parochial. It considers truth to be universal and eternal or not truth at all. Judaism is structurally unique – it is the only world religion ever to believe in a universal God, the God of all peoples, times, and places, and at the same time to believe in a particular way of life that not all people have to follow, because there is more than one way to find God. The structure we see in Genesis – first universal, then particular – recurs repeatedly in our prayers and our thought. It is a basic form of the Jewish mind.

LET THERE BE ...

Just as God is called gracious, so you be gracious. Just

there was darkness on the face of the deep, and the spirit of God moved over
3 4 the waters. God said, "Let there be light." And there was light. God saw the
5 light: it was good; and God separated the light from the darkness. And God
called the light "day," and the darkness He called "night." There was evening,
and there was morning – one day.
6 Then God said, "Let an expanse stretch through the water; let it separate water
7 from water." So God made the expanse, and it separated the water beneath the

רש״י

בֹּהוּ שֶׁבָּהּ: **תֹהוּ.** אישטורדישו״ן בְּלַעַז: **בֹהוּ.** לְשׁוֹן רֵיקוּת וְצָדוּ: **עַל פְּנֵי תְהוֹם.** עַל פְּנֵי הַמַּיִם שֶׁעַל הָאָרֶץ: **וְרוּחַ אֱלֹהִים מְרַחֶפֶת.** כִּסֵּא הַכָּבוֹד עוֹמֵד בָּאֲוִיר וּמְרַחֵף עַל פְּנֵי הַמַּיִם בְּרוּחַ פִּיו שֶׁל הַקָּדוֹשׁ בָּרוּךְ הוּא וּבְמַאֲמָרוֹ, כְּיוֹנָה הַמְרַחֶפֶת עַל הַקֵּן, אקוביטי״ר בְּלַעַז:

ד **וַיַּרְא אֱלֹהִים אֶת הָאוֹר כִּי טוֹב וַיַּבְדֵּל.** אַף בָּזֶה אָנוּ צְרִיכִים לְדִבְרֵי אַגָּדָה, רָאָהוּ שֶׁאֵינוֹ כְּדַאי לְהִשְׁתַּמֵּשׁ בּוֹ רְשָׁעִים וְהִבְדִּילוֹ לַצַּדִּיקִים לֶעָתִיד לָבֹא. וּלְפִי פְּשׁוּטוֹ, כָּךְ פָּרְשֵׁהוּ: רָאָהוּ כִּי טוֹב וְאֵין נָאֶה לוֹ וְלַחֹשֶׁךְ שֶׁיִּהְיוּ מִשְׁתַּמְּשִׁים בְּעִרְבּוּבְיָא, וְקָבַע לָזֶה תְּחוּמוֹ בַּיּוֹם וְלָזֶה תְּחוּמוֹ בַּלַּיְלָה:

ה **יוֹם אֶחָד.** לְפִי סֵדֶר לְשׁוֹן הַפָּרָשָׁה הָיָה לוֹ לִכְתֹּב: יוֹם רִאשׁוֹן, כְּמוֹ שֶׁכָּתוּב בִּשְׁאָר הַיָּמִים: שֵׁנִי, שְׁלִישִׁי, רְבִיעִי. לָמָּה כָּתַב "אֶחָד"? עַל שֵׁם שֶׁהָיָה הַקָּדוֹשׁ בָּרוּךְ הוּא יָחִיד בְּעוֹלָמוֹ, שֶׁלֹּא נִבְרְאוּ הַמַּלְאָכִים עַד יוֹם שֵׁנִי. כָּךְ מְפֹרָשׁ בִּבְרֵאשִׁית רַבָּה (ג, ח):

ו **יְהִי רָקִיעַ.** יֶחֱזַק הָרָקִיעַ, שֶׁאַף עַל פִּי שֶׁנִּבְרְאוּ שָׁמַיִם בְּיוֹם רִאשׁוֹן, עֲדַיִן לַחִים הָיוּ, וְקָרְשׁוּ בַּשֵּׁנִי מִגַּעֲרַת הַקָּדוֹשׁ בָּרוּךְ הוּא בְּאָמְרוֹ: "יְהִי רָקִיעַ", וְזֶהוּ שֶׁכָּתוּב: "עַמּוּדֵי שָׁמַיִם יְרוֹפָפוּ" (איוב כו, יא) כָּל יוֹם רִאשׁוֹן, וּבַשֵּׁנִי – "וְיִתְמְהוּ מִגַּעֲרָתוֹ" (שם), כְּאָדָם שֶׁמִּשְׁתּוֹמֵם וְעוֹמֵד מִגַּעֲרַת הַמְאַיֵּם עָלָיו: **בְּתוֹךְ הַמָּיִם.** בְּאֶמְצַע הַמַּיִם, שֶׁיֵּשׁ הֶפְרֵשׁ בֵּין מַיִם הָעֶלְיוֹנִים לָרָקִיעַ כְּמוֹ בֵּין הָרָקִיעַ לַמַּיִם שֶׁעַל הָאָרֶץ. הָא לָמַדְתָּ שֶׁהֵם תְּלוּיִים בְּמַאֲמָרוֹ שֶׁל מֶלֶךְ:

ז **וַיַּעַשׂ אֱלֹהִים אֶת־הָרָקִיעַ.** תִּקְּנוֹ עַל עָמְדוֹ וְהִיא עֲשִׂיָּתוֹ, כְּמוֹ: "וְעָשְׂתָה אֶת צִפָּרְנֶיהָ" (דברים כא, יב):

comes not from God but from an independent force: Satan, the Devil, Lucifer, the Prince of Darkness, and the many other names given to the force that is not God but is opposed to Him and those who worship Him. This idea, which has surfaced in sectarian forms in each of the Abrahamic monotheisms, as well as in secular totalitarianisms, is one of the most dangerous in all of history. It divides humanity into the unshakably good and the irredeemably evil, giving rise to a long history of bloodshed and barbarism of the kind we see being enacted today in many parts of the world in the name of holy war against the greater and lesser Satan. Dualism is not monotheism, and the Sages, who called it *shetei reshuyot*, "two powers" or "two domains" (Berakhot 33b), were right to reject it utterly. In the words of historian Jeffrey Russel, dualism "denied the unity and omnipotence of God in order to preserve His perfect goodness." Further, it allows people to commit "altruistic evil": evil committed in a sacred cause, in the name of high ideals. Dualism resolves complexity. But monotheism requires the ability to handle complexity. God who creates light brings back the darkness also. "There was evening, and there was morning – one day."

1:6 **וִיהִי מַבְדִּיל** *Let it separate* – The narrative of creation is tightly structured. For three days, God creates domains – light and dark, sea and sky, sea and dry land. Order is a matter of distinction and separation; the verb *lehavdil*, to separate and divide, appears five times in Genesis 1. For the next three days, He populates those domains with their appropriate contents: the sun, moon, and stars, fish and birds, land animals and man. The seventh day, the Sabbath, is the apotheosis of creation: an enduring symbol of the world at peace with itself and its maker, the first thing in the Torah to be called holy.

ג וָבֹהוּ וְחֹשֶׁךְ עַל־פְּנֵי תְהוֹם וְרוּחַ אֱלֹהִים מְרַחֶפֶת עַל־פְּנֵי הַמָּיִם: וַיֹּאמֶר
ד אֱלֹהִים יְהִי־אוֹר וַיְהִי־אוֹר: וַיַּרְא אֱלֹהִים אֶת־הָאוֹר כִּי־טוֹב וַיַּבְדֵּל
ה אֱלֹהִים בֵּין הָאוֹר וּבֵין הַחֹשֶׁךְ: וַיִּקְרָא אֱלֹהִים ׀ לָאוֹר יוֹם וְלַחֹשֶׁךְ
קָרָא לָיְלָה וַיְהִי־עֶרֶב וַיְהִי־בֹקֶר יוֹם אֶחָד:
ו וַיֹּאמֶר אֱלֹהִים יְהִי רָקִיעַ בְּתוֹךְ הַמָּיִם וִיהִי מַבְדִּיל בֵּין מַיִם לָמָיִם:
ז וַיַּעַשׂ אֱלֹהִים אֶת־הָרָקִיעַ וַיַּבְדֵּל בֵּין הַמַּיִם אֲשֶׁר מִתַּחַת לָרָקִיעַ

אונקלוס

וְרֵיקָנְיָא, וַחֲשׁוֹכָא עַל אַפֵּי תְהוֹמָא, וְרוּחָא מִן קֳדָם יי, מְנַשְּׁבָא
עַל אַפֵּי מַיָּא: ג וַאֲמַר יי יְהֵי נְהוֹרָא, וַהֲוָה נְהוֹרָא: ד וַחֲזָא יי, יָת נְהוֹרָא
אֲרֵי טָב, וְאַפְרֵישׁ יי, בֵּין נְהוֹרָא וּבֵין חֲשׁוֹכָא: ה וּקְרָא יי לִנְהוֹרָא
יְמָמָא, וְלַחֲשׁוֹכָא קְרָא לֵילְיָא, וַהֲוָה רְמַשׁ וַהֲוָה צְפַר יוֹם חַד:
ו וַאֲמַר יי, יְהֵי רְקִיעָא בִּמְצִיעוּת מַיָּא, וִיהֵי מַפְרֵישׁ, בֵּין מַיָּא
לְמַיָּא: ז וַעֲבַד יי יָת רְקִיעָא, וְאַפְרֵישׁ, בֵּין מַיָּא דְּמִלְּרַע לִרְקִיעָא,

lovely rabbinic phrase: *Maḥashava tova HaKadosh barukh Hu metzarefa lemaase* (Tosefta, Pe'ah 1:4). This is usually translated as "God considers a good intention as if it were the deed." I translate it differently: "When a human being has a good intention, God joins in helping it become a deed," meaning, He gives us the strength, if not now, then eventually, to turn it into achievement. If the first stage in creation is imagination, the second is will.

Finally: "God saw…was good." This is the hardest of the three stages of creation to understand. But Genesis makes clear that to see that someone is good and to say so is a creative act. There may be some few individuals who are inescapably evil, but they are few. Within almost all of us is something positive and unique but which is all too easily injured, and which grows only when exposed to the sunlight of someone else's recognition and praise. To see the good in others and let them see themselves in the mirror of our regard is to help someone grow to become the best they can be. "Greater," says the Talmud, "is one who causes others to do good than one who does good himself" (Bava Batra 9a). To help others become what they can be is to give birth to creativity in someone else's soul. This is done not by criticism but by searching out the good in others, and helping them see it, own it, and live it.

"God saw…it was good" – this too is part of the work of creation, the subtlest and most beautiful of all. When we recognize the goodness in someone, we do more than create it; we help it become creative. This is what God does for us, and what He calls us to do for others.

1:4 כִּי־טוֹב *It was good – Tov,* "good," is a moral word. The Torah in Genesis 1 is telling us something radical. The reality to which Torah is a guide (the word "Torah" itself means guide, instruction, or law) is *moral* and *ethical*. The question Genesis seeks to answer is not "How did the universe come into being?" but "How then shall we live?" This is the Torah's most significant paradigm shift. The universe that God made and that we inhabit is not about power or dominance but about *tov* and *ra*, good and evil. For the first time, here, religion is ethicized. God, we are told, cares about justice, compassion, faithfulness, loving-kindness, the dignity of the individual, and the sanctity of life.

1:4 וַיַּבְדֵּל אֱלֹהִים בֵּין הָאוֹר וּבֵין הַחֹשֶׁךְ *God separated the light from the darkness* – "I am the Lord; there is no other, forming light, creating darkness, making peace, creating evil" (Is. 45:7). The first act of creation inspired the single most emphatic rejection of dualism in the Bible. Dualism is the view that there is not one force operative in the universe but two: a force of good and a force of evil. Evil, in this worldview,

8 expanse from the water above. And so it was. God called the expanse "heavens."
There was evening, and there was morning – a second day.
9 Then God said, "Let the water beneath the heavens be gathered to one place,
10 and let dry ground appear." And so it was. God called the dry ground "earth,"
11 and the gathered waters He called "seas." And God saw: it was good. Then
God said, "Let the earth produce vegetation: seed-bearing plants and trees of
12 all the kinds on earth that grow seed-bearing fruit." And so it was. The earth
produced vegetation: plants bearing seeds, each of its kind, and trees bearing
13 fruit containing seeds, each of its kind. And God saw: it was good. There was
evening, and there was morning – a third day.
14 Then God said, "Let there be lights in the heavens' expanse to separate day
15 from night and to serve for signs and seasons, days and years. They shall be

רש״י

מֵעַל לָרָקִיעַ. ׳עַל הָרָקִיעַ׳ לֹא נֶאֱמַר אֶלָּא ״מֵעַל״, לְפִי שֶׁהֵן תְּלוּיִין בָּאֲוִיר. וּמִפְּנֵי מָה לֹא נֶאֱמַר ׳כִּי טוֹב׳ בַּשֵּׁנִי? לְפִי שֶׁלֹּא נִגְמְרָה מְלֶאכֶת הַמַּיִם עַד יוֹם שְׁלִישִׁי וַהֲרֵי הִתְחִיל בָּהּ בַּשֵּׁנִי, וְדָבָר שֶׁלֹּא נִגְמַר אֵינוֹ בִּמְלוֹאוֹ וְטוּבוֹ, וּבַשְּׁלִישִׁי שֶׁנִּגְמְרָה מְלֶאכֶת הַמַּיִם וְהִתְחִיל וְגָמַר מְלָאכָה אַחֶרֶת, כָּפַל בּוֹ ׳כִּי טוֹב׳ שְׁנֵי פְעָמִים (להלן פסוקים י, יב): אַחַת לִגְמַר מְלֶאכֶת הַשֵּׁנִי וְאַחַת לִגְמַר מְלֶאכֶת הַיּוֹם:

ח **וַיִּקְרָא אֱלֹהִים לָרָקִיעַ שָׁמָיִם.** שָׂא מַיִם, שָׁם מַיִם, אֵשׁ וּמַיִם שֶׁעֵרְבָן זֶה בָּזֶה וְעָשָׂה מֵהֶם שָׁמַיִם:

ט **יִקָּווּ הַמַּיִם.** שֶׁהָיוּ שְׁטוּחִים עַל פְּנֵי כָּל הָאָרֶץ, וְהִקְוָם בָּאוֹקְיָנוֹס, הוּא הַיָּם הַגָּדוֹל שֶׁבְּכָל הַיַּמִּים:

י **קָרָא יַמִּים.** וַהֲלֹא יָם אֶחָד הוּא? אֶלָּא אֵינוֹ דּוֹמֶה טַעַם דָּג הָעוֹלֶה מִן הַיָּם בְּעַכּוֹ לְטַעַם דָּג הָעוֹלֶה מִן הַיָּם בְּאַסְפַּמְיָא:

יא **תַּדְשֵׁא הָאָרֶץ דֶּשֶׁא עֵשֶׂב.** לֹא דֶשֶׁא לְשׁוֹן עֵשֶׂב וְלֹא עֵשֶׂב לְשׁוֹן דֶּשֶׁא, וְלֹא הָיָה לְשׁוֹן הַמִּקְרָא לוֹמַר: ׳תַּעֲשִׂיב הָאָרֶץ׳, שֶׁמִּינֵי דְשָׁאִין מְחֻלָּקִין, כָּל אֶחָד לְעַצְמוֹ נִקְרָא עֵשֶׂב פְּלוֹנִי, וְאֵין לָשׁוֹן לַמְדַבֵּר לוֹמַר דֶּשֶׁא פְּלוֹנִי, שֶׁלְּשׁוֹן דֶּשֶׁא הוּא לְבִישַׁת הָאָרֶץ כְּשֶׁהִיא מִתְמַלֵּאת בִּדְשָׁאִים: **תַּדְשֵׁא.** תִּתְמַלֵּא וְתִתְכַּסֶּה לְבוּשׁ עֲשָׂבִים. בִּלְשׁוֹן לַעַז נִקְרָא דֶּשֶׁא אירבידי״ן, כֻּלָּן בְּעִרְבּוּבְיָא, וְכָל שֹׁרֶשׁ לְעַצְמוֹ נִקְרָא עֵשֶׂב: **מַזְרִיעַ זֶרַע.** שֶׁיְּגַדֵּל בּוֹ זַרְעוֹ לִזְרֹעַ מִמֶּנּוּ בְּמָקוֹם אַחֵר: **עֵץ פְּרִי.** שֶׁיְּהֵא טַעַם הָעֵץ כְּטַעַם הַפְּרִי. וְהִיא לֹא עָשְׂתָה כֵּן, אֶלָּא וַתּוֹצֵא הָאָרֶץ עֵץ עֹשֶׂה פְּרִי, וְלֹא הָעֵץ פְּרִי, לְפִיכָךְ כְּשֶׁנִּתְקַלֵּל אָדָם עַל עֲוֹנוֹ נִפְקְדָה גַּם הִיא עַל עֲוֹנָהּ וְנִתְקַלְּלָה: **אֲשֶׁר זַרְעוֹ בוֹ.** הֵן גַּרְעִינֵי כָּל פְּרִי שֶׁמֵּהֶן הָאִילָן צוֹמֵחַ כְּשֶׁנּוֹטְעִין אוֹתוֹ:

יב **וַתּוֹצֵא הָאָרֶץ וְגוֹ׳.** אַף עַל פִּי שֶׁלֹּא נֶאֱמַר ׳לְמִינֵהוּ׳ בִּדְשָׁאִין בְּצִוּוּיָן, שָׁמְעוּ שֶׁנִּצְטַוּוּ הָאִילָנוֹת עַל כָּךְ וְנָשְׂאוּ קַל וָחֹמֶר בְּעַצְמָן, כַּמְפֹרָשׁ בָּאַגָּדָה בִּשְׁחִיטַת חֻלִּין (חולין ס ע״א):

יד **יְהִי מְאֹרֹת וְגוֹ׳.** מִיּוֹם רִאשׁוֹן נִבְרְאוּ, וּבָרְבִיעִי צִוָּה עֲלֵיהֶם לְהִתָּלוֹת בָּרָקִיעַ, וְכֵן כָּל תּוֹלְדוֹת שָׁמַיִם וָאָרֶץ נִבְרְאוּ מִיּוֹם רִאשׁוֹן וְכָל אֶחָד וְאֶחָד נִקְבַּע בַּיּוֹם שֶׁנִּגְזַר עָלָיו, הוּא שֶׁכָּתוּב (לעיל פסוק א): ״אֵת הַשָּׁמַיִם״ – לְרַבּוֹת תּוֹלְדוֹתֵיהֶם, ״וְאֵת הָאָרֶץ״ – לְרַבּוֹת תּוֹלְדוֹתֶיהָ: **יְהִי מְאֹרֹת.** חָסֵר וָי״ו כְּתִיב, עַל שֶׁהוּא יוֹם מְאֵרָה לִפֹּל אַסְכָּרָה בַּתִּינוֹקוֹת, הוּא שֶׁשָּׁנִינוּ: בָּרְבִיעִי הָיוּ מִתְעַנִּים עַל אַסְכָּרָה שֶׁלֹּא תִּפֹּל בַּתִּינוֹקוֹת (תענית כז ע״ב): **לְהַבְדִּיל בֵּין הַיּוֹם וּבֵין הַלָּיְלָה.** מִשֶּׁנִּגְנַז הָאוֹר הָרִאשׁוֹן, אֲבָל בְּשִׁבְעַת יְמֵי בְרֵאשִׁית שִׁמְּשׁוּ הָאוֹר וְהַחֹשֶׁךְ הָרִאשׁוֹנִים זֶה בַּיּוֹם וְזֶה בַּלַּיְלָה: **וְהָיוּ לְאֹתֹת.** כְּשֶׁהַמְּאוֹרוֹת לוֹקִין סִימָן רַע הוּא לָעוֹלָם, שֶׁנֶּאֱמַר: ״וּמֵאֹתוֹת הַשָּׁמַיִם אַל תֵּחָתּוּ״ (ירמיה י, ב), בַּעֲשׂוֹתְכֶם רְצוֹן הַקָּדוֹשׁ בָּרוּךְ הוּא אֵין אַתֶּם צְרִיכִים לִדְאֹג מִן הַפֻּרְעָנוּת: **וּלְמוֹעֲדִים.** עַל שֵׁם הֶעָתִיד, שֶׁעֲתִידִים יִשְׂרָאֵל לְהִצְטַוּוֹת עַל הַמּוֹעֲדוֹת, וְהֵם נִמְנִים לְמוֹלַד הַלְּבָנָה: **וּלְיָמִים.** שִׁמּוּשׁ הַחַמָּה חֲצִי יוֹם וְשִׁמּוּשׁ הַלְּבָנָה חֶצְיוֹ, הֲרֵי יוֹם שָׁלֵם: **וְשָׁנִים.** לְסוֹף שְׁלֹשׁ מֵאוֹת וְשִׁשִּׁים וַחֲמִשָּׁה יָמִים יִגְמְרוּ מַהֲלָכָתָן בִּשְׁנֵים עָשָׂר מַזָּלוֹת הַמְשָׁרְתִים אוֹתָם, וְהִיא שָׁנָה:

טו **וְהָיוּ לִמְאוֹרֹת.** עוֹד זֹאת יְשַׁמְּשׁוּ, שֶׁיָּאִירוּ לָעוֹלָם:

science, both as human wisdom and as an insight into the divine wisdom evident in the cosmos. The Babylonian Talmud sees the study of astronomy, for those who are capable of it, as a religious duty. There is a blessing to be

ח וּבֵין הַמַּיִם אֲשֶׁר מֵעַל לָרָקִיעַ וַיְהִי־כֵן: וַיִּקְרָא אֱלֹהִים לָרָקִיעַ שָׁמָיִם
וַיְהִי־עֶרֶב וַיְהִי־בֹקֶר יוֹם שֵׁנִי:
ט וַיֹּאמֶר אֱלֹהִים יִקָּווּ הַמַּיִם מִתַּחַת הַשָּׁמַיִם אֶל־מָקוֹם אֶחָד וְתֵרָאֶה
י הַיַּבָּשָׁה וַיְהִי־כֵן: וַיִּקְרָא אֱלֹהִים ׀ לַיַּבָּשָׁה אֶרֶץ וּלְמִקְוֵה הַמַּיִם קָרָא
יא יַמִּים וַיַּרְא אֱלֹהִים כִּי־טוֹב: וַיֹּאמֶר אֱלֹהִים תַּדְשֵׁא הָאָרֶץ דֶּשֶׁא עֵשֶׂב
מַזְרִיעַ זֶרַע עֵץ פְּרִי עֹשֶׂה פְּרִי לְמִינוֹ אֲשֶׁר זַרְעוֹ־בוֹ עַל־הָאָרֶץ וַיְהִי־
יב כֵן: וַתּוֹצֵא הָאָרֶץ דֶּשֶׁא עֵשֶׂב מַזְרִיעַ זֶרַע לְמִינֵהוּ וְעֵץ עֹשֶׂה־פְּרִי
יג אֲשֶׁר זַרְעוֹ־בוֹ לְמִינֵהוּ וַיַּרְא אֱלֹהִים כִּי־טוֹב: וַיְהִי־עֶרֶב וַיְהִי־בֹקֶר
יוֹם שְׁלִישִׁי:
יד וַיֹּאמֶר אֱלֹהִים יְהִי מְאֹרֹת בִּרְקִיעַ הַשָּׁמַיִם לְהַבְדִּיל בֵּין הַיּוֹם וּבֵין
טו הַלַּיְלָה וְהָיוּ לְאֹתֹת וּלְמוֹעֲדִים וּלְיָמִים וְשָׁנִים: וְהָיוּ לִמְאוֹרֹת בִּרְקִיעַ

אונקלוס

ובין מיא, דמעל לרקיעא, והוה כן: ח וקרא יי, לרקיעא שמיא, והוה רמש והוה צפר יום תנין: ט ואמר יי, יתכנשון מיא, מתחות שמיא לאתר חד, ותתחזי יבשתא, והוה כן: י וקרא יי ליבשתא ארעא, ולבית כנישת מיא קרא ימי, וחזא יי ארי טב: יא ואמר יי, תדאית ארעא דתאה, עסבא דבר זרעיה מזדרע, אילן פירין, עביד פירין לזניה, דבר זרעיה ביה על ארעא, והוה כן: יב ואפיקת ארעא, דתאה, עסבא דבר זרעיה מזדרע לזנוהי, ואילן עביד פירין, דבר זרעיה ביה לזנוהי, וחזא יי ארי טב: יג והוה רמש והוה צפר יום תליתי: יד ואמר יי, יהון נהורין ברקיעא דשמיא, לאפרשא, בין יממא ובין ליליא, ויהון לאתין ולזמנין, ולממני בהון יומין ושנין: טו ויהון לנהורין ברקיעא

1:12 לְמִינֵהוּ *Each of its kind* – The key recurring word is *leminehem, lemino, lemina.* God creates plants, animals, birds, fish *leminehem,* according to their different kinds. The essence of Genesis 1 is ordered diversity. This is the priestly way of seeing the world, one which we will see expressed most clearly in the book of Leviticus. For the priest, the moral life is something we learn by honoring the distinctions God has taught us to see in the structure of reality. There is milk, a sign of life, and meat, a sign of death. There is plant life and there is animal life. There are brothers and others. Each has its boundaries that must be respected. That is sacred ontology and it creates an ethic of holiness. Its theoretical foundations lie here in Genesis 1.

1:14 וְהָיוּ לְאֹתֹת וּלְמוֹעֲדִים *To serve for signs and seasons* – Nature is something we can observe and learn from. "He who knows how to calculate the cycles and planetary courses, but does not, of him Scripture says, '[They] feast… never once turning to look at the LORD's workings, never once noticing the work of His hands' (Is. 5:12). How do we know that it is one's duty to calculate the cycles and planetary courses? Because it is written, 'For this will be your wisdom and understanding in the eyes of the peoples' (Deut. 4:6). What wisdom and understanding is in the sight of the peoples? Say, that is the science of cycles and planets" (Shabbat 75a).

The Sages attached religious dignity and integrity to

16 lights in the heavens' expanse, shining upon the earth." And so it was. God
made the two great lights – the greater light to rule by day and the lesser light
17 to rule by night – and the stars. God set them in the heavens' expanse to shine
18 upon the earth, to rule by day and by night and to separate light from darkness.
19 And God saw that it was good. There was evening, and there was morning – a
fourth day.
20 Then God said, "Let the water teem with swarms of living creatures, and let
21 birds fly over the earth across the heavens' expanse." So God created the great
sea serpents, and all the kinds of crawling, living things that swarm in the water,
and all the kinds of winged, flying creatures. And God saw that it was good.
22 God blessed them, saying: "Be fertile and multiply and fill the waters of the
23 seas, and let flying creatures multiply on earth." There was evening, and there
was morning – a fifth day.

רש״י

טז **הַמְּאֹרֹת הַגְּדֹלִים.** שָׁוִים נִבְרְאוּ, וְנִתְמַעֲטָה הַלְּבָנָה עַל שֶׁקִּטְרְגָה וְאָמְרָה: אִי אֶפְשָׁר לִשְׁנֵי מְלָכִים שֶׁיִּשְׁתַּמְּשׁוּ בְּכֶתֶר אֶחָד: **וְאֵת הַכּוֹכָבִים.** עַל יְדֵי שֶׁמִּעֵט אֶת הַלְּבָנָה, הִרְבָּה צְבָאֶיהָ לְהָפִיס דַּעְתָּהּ:

כ **נֶפֶשׁ חַיָּה.** שֶׁיְּהֵא בָּהּ חִיּוּת: **שֶׁרֶץ.** כָּל דָּבָר חַי שֶׁאֵינוֹ גָּבוֹהַּ מִן הָאָרֶץ קָרוּי שֶׁרֶץ, בָּעוֹף – כְּגוֹן זְבוּבִים, בַּשְּׁקָצִים – כְּגוֹן נְמָלִים וְחִפּוּשִׁית וְתוֹלָעִים, וּבַבְּרִיּוֹת – כְּגוֹן חֹלֶד וְעַכְבָּר וְחֹמֶט וְכַיּוֹצֵא בָּהֶם, וְכָל הַדָּגִים:

כא **הַתַּנִּינִם.** דָּגִים גְּדוֹלִים שֶׁבַּיָּם. וּבְדִבְרֵי אַגָּדָה: הוּא לִוְיָתָן וּבֶן זוּגוֹ, שֶׁבְּרָאָם זָכָר וּנְקֵבָה וְהָרַג אֶת הַנְּקֵבָה וּמְלָחָהּ לַצַּדִּיקִים לֶעָתִיד לָבֹא, שֶׁאִם יִפְרוּ וְיִרְבּוּ לֹא יִתְקַיֵּם הָעוֹלָם בִּפְנֵיהֶם: **נֶפֶשׁ הַחַיָּה.** נֶפֶשׁ שֶׁיֵּשׁ בָּהּ חִיּוּת:

כב **וַיְבָרֶךְ אֹתָם.** לְפִי שֶׁמְּחַסְּרִים אוֹתָם וְצָדִין מֵהֶן וְאוֹכְלִין אוֹתָם, הֻצְרְכוּ לִבְרָכָה. וְאַף הַחַיּוֹת הֻצְרְכוּ לִבְרָכָה, אֶלָּא מִפְּנֵי הַנָּחָשׁ הֶעָתִיד לִקְלָלָה, לְכָךְ לֹא בֵּרְכָן, שֶׁלֹּא יְהֵא הוּא בַּכְּלָל: **פְּרוּ.** לְשׁוֹן פְּרִי, כְּלוֹמַר עֲשׂוּ פֵּרוֹת:

humanity with His image. Thus, science and monotheism come hand in hand. We need science to understand the universe, and we need religion to guide our way within it, from the world as it is to the world as it ought to be.

1:21 כָּל־נֶפֶשׁ הַחַיָּה הָרֹמֶשֶׂת *All the kinds of crawling, living things* – God delights in diversity. The Rabbis sensed it when they said, "Even those creatures you hold superfluous in the world, such as the flies and fleas and gnats, they too are part of the creation of the world. Through all does the Holy One, blessed be He, make manifest His mission, even through the serpent, even through the gnat, even through the frog" (Bereshit Rabba 10:8). Biodiversity is a source of wonder to the psalmist:

How many are Your works, Lord.
You made them all in wisdom;
The earth is full of Your creations.
(Ps. 104:24)

1:22 וַיְבָרֶךְ אֹתָם אֱלֹהִים *God blessed them* – God's first blessings are not addressed to Adam, but to animals. Rambam warns us against an anthropocentric view of reality. "The universe does not exist for man's sake, but each being exists for its own sake and not because of some other thing" (*Guide for the Perplexed* III:13). To be sure, humanity with its unique capacity for moral choice is the focus of the Torah's concerns; but Genesis sets forth a view of nature which is not man-centered – but God-centered.

טז הַשָּׁמַ֔יִם לְהָאִ֖יר עַל־הָאָ֑רֶץ וַֽיְהִי־כֵֽן׃ וַיַּ֣עַשׂ אֱלֹהִ֔ים אֶת־שְׁנֵ֥י הַמְּאֹרֹ֖ת
הַגְּדֹלִ֑ים אֶת־הַמָּא֤וֹר הַגָּדֹל֙ לְמֶמְשֶׁ֣לֶת הַיּ֔וֹם וְאֶת־הַמָּא֤וֹר הַקָּטֹן֙
יז לְמֶמְשֶׁ֣לֶת הַלַּ֔יְלָה וְאֵ֖ת הַכּוֹכָבִֽים׃ וַיִּתֵּ֥ן אֹתָ֛ם אֱלֹהִ֖ים בִּרְקִ֣יעַ הַשָּׁמָ֑יִם
יח לְהָאִ֖יר עַל־הָאָֽרֶץ׃ וְלִמְשֹׁל֙ בַּיּ֣וֹם וּבַלַּ֔יְלָה וּֽלֲהַבְדִּ֔יל בֵּ֥ין הָא֖וֹר וּבֵ֣ין
יט הַחֹ֑שֶׁךְ וַיַּ֥רְא אֱלֹהִ֖ים כִּי־טֽוֹב׃ וַֽיְהִי־עֶ֥רֶב וַֽיְהִי־בֹ֖קֶר י֥וֹם רְבִיעִֽי׃
כ וַיֹּ֣אמֶר אֱלֹהִ֔ים יִשְׁרְצ֣וּ הַמַּ֔יִם שֶׁ֖רֶץ נֶ֣פֶשׁ חַיָּ֑ה וְעוֹף֙ יְעוֹפֵ֣ף עַל־הָאָ֔רֶץ
כא עַל־פְּנֵ֖י רְקִ֥יעַ הַשָּׁמָֽיִם׃ וַיִּבְרָ֣א אֱלֹהִ֔ים אֶת־הַתַּנִּינִ֖ם הַגְּדֹלִ֑ים וְאֵ֣ת
כָּל־נֶ֣פֶשׁ הַֽחַיָּ֣ה ׀ הָֽרֹמֶ֡שֶׂת אֲשֶׁר֩ שָׁרְצ֨וּ הַמַּ֜יִם לְמִֽינֵהֶ֗ם וְאֵ֨ת כָּל־ע֤וֹף
כב כָּנָף֙ לְמִינֵ֔הוּ וַיַּ֥רְא אֱלֹהִ֖ים כִּי־טֽוֹב׃ וַיְבָ֧רֶךְ אֹתָ֛ם אֱלֹהִ֖ים לֵאמֹ֑ר פְּר֣וּ
כג וּרְב֗וּ וּמִלְא֤וּ אֶת־הַמַּ֙יִם֙ בַּיַּמִּ֔ים וְהָע֖וֹף יִ֥רֶב בָּאָֽרֶץ׃ וַֽיְהִי־עֶ֥רֶב וַֽיְהִי־
בֹ֖קֶר י֥וֹם חֲמִישִֽׁי׃

אונקלוס

דִשְׁמַיָּא, לְאַנְהָרָא עַל אַרְעָא, וַהֲוָה כֵן: טז וַעֲבַד יי, יָת תְּרֵין נְהוֹרַיָּא
רַבְרְבַיָּא, יָת נְהוֹרָא רַבָּא לְמִשְׁלַט בִּימָמָא, וְיָת נְהוֹרָא זְעֵירָא לְמִשְׁלַט
בְּלֵילְיָא, וְיָת כּוֹכְבַיָּא: יז וִיהַב יָתְהוֹן, יי בִּרְקִיעָא דִשְׁמַיָּא, לְאַנְהָרָא
עַל אַרְעָא: יח וּלְמִשְׁלַט בִּימָמָא וּבְלֵילְיָא, וּלְאַפְרָשָׁא, בֵּין נְהוֹרָא
וּבֵין חֲשׁוֹכָא, וַחֲזָא יי אֲרֵי טָב: יט וַהֲוָה רְמַשׁ וַהֲוָה צְפַר יוֹם רְבִיעָי:

כ וַאֲמַר יי, יִרְחֲשׁוּן מַיָּא, רְחֵישׁ נַפְשָׁא חַיְתָא, וְעוֹפָא יְפָרַח עַל אַרְעָא,
עַל אַפֵּי רְקִיעַ שְׁמַיָּא: כא וּבְרָא יי, יָת תַּנִּינַיָּא רַבְרְבַיָּא, וְיָת כָּל נַפְשָׁא
חַיְתָא דְרָחֲשָׁא, דְּאַרְחִישׁוּ מַיָּא לִזְנֵיהוֹן, וְיָת כָּל עוֹפָא דְּפָרַח לִזְנוֹהִי,
וַחֲזָא יי אֲרֵי טָב: כב וּבָרֵיךְ יָתְהוֹן, יי לְמֵימַר, פּוּשׁוּ וּסְגוֹ, וּמְלוֹ יָת מַיָּא
בְּיַמְמַיָּא, וְעוֹפָא יִסְגֵּי בְּאַרְעָא: כג וַהֲוָה רְמַשׁ וַהֲוָה צְפַר יוֹם חֲמִישָׁי:

recited on seeing "one of the sages of the nations of the world." For the Sages to institute a blessing – a religious act of thanksgiving – over Greek and Roman scholars showed a remarkable open-mindedness to wisdom whatever its source. The heavenly bodies are intended not just to exist, but also as "signs" to be studied, to help us navigate in time and space. The Rambam sees science as a way to the love and awe of God.

1:21 אֶת הַתַּנִּינִם הַגְּדֹלִים *The great sea serpents* – In Ugaritic mythology, the god of the sky does battle with the god of the sea, a "great sea serpent," and out of his victory establishes dry land, usually over the dead body of his victim. But in Genesis there is no myth. God speaks and the universe comes into being. Genesis 1 is the beginning of the end of the mythic imagination. No longer is the universe seen as unpredictable. It is the work of a single, rational creative will. This is what will make science possible: science was born when people stopped telling stories about nature and instead observed it. Nor is the God of Genesis – as were the gods of myth – at best indifferent, at worst actively hostile to human beings. Genesis speaks of a God who endows

24 Then God said, "Let the land produce every kind of living thing: all the different
species of cattle, crawling things and wild animals of the earth." And so it was.
25 God made the different kinds of wild animals of the earth, and cattle, and all
the species of creature that creep upon land. And God saw that it was good.
26 Then God said, "Let us make humankind in our image, our likeness, that they
may rule over the fish of the sea and the flying creatures of the heavens, the
cattle and all the earth, and every living creature that moves upon the earth."
27 So God created humankind in His image: in the image of God He created him;
28 male and female He created them. God blessed them, saying, "Be fertile and
multiply. Fill the earth and subdue it. Rule over the fish of the sea, and the
flying creatures of the heavens, and every living thing that moves upon the

רש"י

כד **תּוֹצֵא הָאָרֶץ.** הוּא שֶׁפֵּרַשְׁתִּי (לעיל פסוק יד) שֶׁהַכֹּל נִבְרָא מִיּוֹם רִאשׁוֹן וְלֹא הֻצְרְכוּ אֶלָּא לְהוֹצִיאָם: **נֶפֶשׁ חַיָּה.** שֶׁיֵּשׁ בָּהּ חִיּוּת: **וָרֶמֶשׂ.** הֵם שְׁרָצִים שֶׁהֵם נְמוּכִים וְרוֹמְשִׂים עַל הָאָרֶץ, וְנִרְאִים כְּאִלּוּ נִגְרָרִין שֶׁאֵין הִלּוּכָן נִכָּר, כָּל לְשׁוֹן רֶמֶשׂ וְשֶׁרֶץ בִּלְשׁוֹנֵנוּ קונמוברי"ש:

כה **וַיַּעַשׂ.** תִּקֵּן לְצִבְיוֹנָן בְּקוֹמָתָן:

כו **נַעֲשֶׂה אָדָם.** עַנְוְתָנוּתוֹ שֶׁל הַקָּדוֹשׁ בָּרוּךְ הוּא לָמַדְנוּ מִכָּאן, לְפִי שֶׁהָאָדָם בִּדְמוּת הַמַּלְאָכִים וְיִתְקַנְּאוּ בוֹ, לְפִיכָךְ נִמְלַךְ בָּהֶם. וּכְשֶׁהוּא דָּן אֶת הַמְּלָכִים הוּא נִמְלָךְ בְּפַמַּלְיָא שֶׁלּוֹ, שֶׁכֵּן מָצִינוּ בְּאַחְאָב שֶׁאָמַר לוֹ מִיכָה: "רָאִיתִי אֶת ה' יֹשֵׁב עַל כִּסְאוֹ וְכָל צְבָא הַשָּׁמַיִם עֹמֵד עָלָיו מִימִינוֹ וּמִשְּׂמֹאלוֹ" (מלכים א' כב, יט), וְכִי יֵשׁ יָמִין וּשְׂמֹאל לְפָנָיו? אֶלָּא אֵלּוּ מַיְמִינִים לִזְכוּת וְאֵלּוּ מַשְׂמְאִילִים לְחוֹבָה, וְכֵן: "בִּגְזֵרַת עִירִין פִּתְגָמָא וּמֵאמַר קַדִּישִׁין שְׁאֵלְתָא" (דניאל ד, יד), אַף כָּאן בְּפַמַּלְיָא שֶׁלּוֹ נָטַל רְשׁוּת. אָמַר לָהֶם: יֵשׁ בָּעֶלְיוֹנִים כִּדְמוּתִי, אִם אֵין בַּתַּחְתּוֹנִים כִּדְמוּתִי הֲרֵי יֵשׁ קִנְאָה בְּמַעֲשֵׂה בְרֵאשִׁית: **נַעֲשֶׂה אָדָם.** אַף עַל פִּי שֶׁלֹּא סִיְּעוּהוּ בִּיצִירָתוֹ, וְיֵשׁ מָקוֹם לַמִּינִים לִרְדּוֹת, לֹא נִמְנַע הַכָּתוּב מִלְּלַמֵּד דֶּרֶךְ אֶרֶץ וּמִדַּת עֲנָוָה, שֶׁיְּהֵא הַגָּדוֹל נִמְלָךְ וְנוֹטֵל רְשׁוּת מִן הַקָּטָן. וְאִם כָּתַב 'אֶעֱשֶׂה אָדָם' לֹא לָמַדְנוּ שֶׁהָיָה מְדַבֵּר עִם בֵּית דִּינוֹ, אֶלָּא עִם עַצְמוֹ. וּתְשׁוּבַת הַמִּינִים כָּתַב בְּצִדּוֹ: "וַיִּבְרָא אֱלֹהִים אֶת הָאָדָם", וְלֹא כָתַב 'וַיִּבְרְאוּ': **בְּצַלְמֵנוּ.** בִּדְפוּס שֶׁלָּנוּ: **כִּדְמוּתֵנוּ.** לְהָבִין וּלְהַשְׂכִּיל: **וְיִרְדּוּ בִדְגַת הַיָּם.** יֵשׁ בַּלָּשׁוֹן הַזֶּה לְשׁוֹן רִדּוּי וּלְשׁוֹן יְרִידָה, זָכָה – רוֹדֶה בַּחַיּוֹת וּבַבְּהֵמוֹת, לֹא זָכָה – נַעֲשֶׂה יָרוּד לִפְנֵיהֶם וְהַחַיָּה מוֹשֶׁלֶת בּוֹ:

כז **וַיִּבְרָא אֱלֹהִים אֶת הָאָדָם בְּצַלְמוֹ.** בִּדְפוּס הֶעָשׂוּי לוֹ, שֶׁהַכֹּל נִבְרָא בְּמַאֲמָר וְהוּא בַּיָּדַיִם, שֶׁנֶּאֱמַר: "וַתָּשֶׁת עָלַי כַּפֶּכָה" (תהלים קלט, ה) נַעֲשָׂה בְחוֹתָם כְּמַטְבֵּעַ הָעֲשׂוּיָה עַל יְדֵי רֹשֶׁם, שֶׁקּוֹרִין קוי"ן בְּלַעַ"ז, וְכֵן הוּא אוֹמֵר: "תִּתְהַפֵּךְ כְּחֹמֶר חוֹתָם" (איוב לח, יד): **בְּצֶלֶם אֱלֹהִים בָּרָא אוֹתוֹ.** פֵּרֵשׁ לְךָ שֶׁאוֹתוֹ צֶלֶם הַמְּתֻקָּן לוֹ צֶלֶם דְּיוֹקַן יוֹצְרוֹ הוּא: **זָכָר וּנְקֵבָה בָּרָא אֹתָם.** וּלְהַלָּן הוּא אוֹמֵר: "וַיִּקַּח אַחַת מִצַּלְעֹתָיו" וְגוֹ' (להלן ב, כא)! מִדְרַשׁ אַגָּדָה, שֶׁבְּרָאוֹ שְׁנֵי פַרְצוּפִים בִּבְרִיאָה רִאשׁוֹנָה, וְאַחַר כָּךְ חִלְּקוֹ. וּפְשׁוּטוֹ שֶׁל מִקְרָא: כָּאן הוֹדִיעֲךָ שֶׁנִּבְרְאוּ שְׁנֵיהֶם בַּשִּׁשִּׁי, וְלֹא פֵּרֵשׁ לְךָ כֵּיצַד בְּרִיָּתָן, וּפֵרֵשׁ לְךָ בְּמָקוֹם אַחֵר:

כח **וְכִבְשֻׁהָ.** חָסֵר וָי"ו, לְלַמֶּדְךָ שֶׁהַזָּכָר כּוֹבֵשׁ אֶת הַנְּקֵבָה שֶׁלֹּא תְּהֵא יַצְאָנִית. וְעוֹד לְלַמֶּדְךָ, שֶׁהָאִישׁ שֶׁדַּרְכּוֹ לִכְבֹּשׁ מְצֻוֶּה עַל פְּרִיָּה וּרְבִיָּה וְלֹא הָאִשָּׁה:

and Ḥava is the phrase "Be fertile and multiply" experienced not just as a blessing but as a command. Bringing children into the world thus presupposes moral responsibility, for one might have chosen otherwise. That responsibility for those one has brought into existence extends to caring for them in their dependency, and to ensuring that they will have a world to inherit.

1:28 **מִלְאוּ אֶת־הָאָרֶץ וְכִבְשֻׁהָ** *Fill the earth and subdue it* – Rabbi Joseph Soloveitchik, in *The Lonely Man of Faith*, noted that in the phrase "and subdue it" we receive our mandate to be masters of our environment. As a result of developments over time – in knowledge, control, medical technology, education, and our range of resources and facilities – we are able to address problems in ways that previous generations were

כד וַיֹּאמֶר אֱלֹהִים תּוֹצֵא הָאָרֶץ נֶפֶשׁ חַיָּה לְמִינָהּ בְּהֵמָה וָרֶמֶשׂ וְחַיְתוֹ־
כה אֶרֶץ לְמִינָהּ וַיְהִי־כֵן: וַיַּעַשׂ אֱלֹהִים אֶת־חַיַּת הָאָרֶץ לְמִינָהּ וְאֶת־
הַבְּהֵמָה לְמִינָהּ וְאֵת כָּל־רֶמֶשׂ הָאֲדָמָה לְמִינֵהוּ וַיַּרְא אֱלֹהִים כִּי־טוֹב:
כו וַיֹּאמֶר אֱלֹהִים נַעֲשֶׂה אָדָם בְּצַלְמֵנוּ כִּדְמוּתֵנוּ וְיִרְדּוּ בִדְגַת הַיָּם וּבְעוֹף
הַשָּׁמַיִם וּבַבְּהֵמָה וּבְכָל־הָאָרֶץ וּבְכָל־הָרֶמֶשׂ הָרֹמֵשׂ עַל־הָאָרֶץ:
כז וַיִּבְרָא אֱלֹהִים ׀ אֶת־הָאָדָם בְּצַלְמוֹ בְּצֶלֶם אֱלֹהִים בָּרָא אֹתוֹ זָכָר
כח וּנְקֵבָה בָּרָא אֹתָם: וַיְבָרֶךְ אֹתָם אֱלֹהִים וַיֹּאמֶר לָהֶם אֱלֹהִים פְּרוּ וּרְבוּ
וּמִלְאוּ אֶת־הָאָרֶץ וְכִבְשֻׁהָ וּרְדוּ בִּדְגַת הַיָּם וּבְעוֹף הַשָּׁמַיִם וּבְכָל־חַיָּה

אונקלוס

כד וַאֲמַר יי, תַּפֵּיק אַרְעָא, נַפְשָׁא חַיְתָא לִזְנַהּ, בְּעִיר וּרְחֵישׁ, וְחַיַּת
אַרְעָא לִזְנַהּ, וַהֲוָה כֵן: כה וַעֲבַד יי יָת חַיַּת אַרְעָא לִזְנַהּ, וְיָת בְּעִירָא
לִזְנַהּ, וְיָת, כָּל רִחְשָׁא דְּאַרְעָא לִזְנוֹהִי, וַחֲזָא יי אֲרֵי טָב: כו וַאֲמַר יי,
נַעְבֵּיד אֱנָשָׁא, בְּצַלְמַנָא כִּדְמוּתַנָא, וְיִשְׁלְטוּן בְּנוּנֵי יַמָּא וּבְעוֹפָא
דִּשְׁמַיָּא, וּבִבְעִירָא וּבְכָל אַרְעָא, וּבְכָל רִחְשָׁא דְּרָחֵישׁ עַל אַרְעָא:
כז וּבְרָא יי יָת אָדָם בְּצַלְמֵיהּ, בִּצְלֵם אֱלֹהִים בְּרָא יָתֵיהּ, דְּכַר וְנֻקְבָּא
בְּרָא יָתְהוֹן: כח וּבָרֵיךְ יָתְהוֹן יי, וַאֲמַר לְהוֹן יי, פּוּשׁוּ וּסְגוּ, וּמְלוֹ יָת
אַרְעָא וּתְקוּפוּ עֲלַהּ, וּשְׁלוּטוּ, בְּנוּנֵי יַמָּא וּבְעוֹפָא דִשְׁמַיָּא, וּבְכָל חַיְתָא

MAN IN GOD'S IMAGE

Genesis 1:26–27 is not so much a metaphysical statement about the nature of the human person as it is *a political protest against the very basis of hierarchical, class- or caste-based societies,* whether in ancient or modern times.

The phrase "in the image of God" would not have been unfamiliar to the first readers of the Torah; they knew it well. It was commonplace in the first civilizations, Mesopotamia and ancient Egypt, that certain people were said to be in the image of God. These were the kings of the Mesopotamian city-states and the pharaohs of Egypt. Nothing could have been more radical than to say that not just kings and rulers are God's image. We all are. In some fundamental sense we are all equal in dignity and ultimate worth, for we are all in God's image regardless of color, culture, or creed, physical form or mental ability. Today the idea is still daring; how much more so must it have been in an age of absolute rulers with absolute power.

Momentous ideas made the West what it is, ideas like human rights, the abolition of slavery, the equal worth of all, and justice based on the principle that right is sovereign over might. All of these ultimately derived from the statement in the first chapter of the Torah that we are made in God's image and likeness. No other text has had a greater influence on moral thought, nor has any other civilization ever held a higher vision of what we are called on to be.

1:26 נַעֲשֶׂה אָדָם *Let us make humankind* – There are several understandings of this enigmatic first-person plural. The view put forth by Rabbi Samson Raphael Hirsch is striking. According to Hirsch, "us" refers to the rest of creation. Before making mankind, with its potential for disrupting nature, God invites nature itself to give its assent. The implied condition is that man will use nature only in the service of God, its maker. To exploit nature rapaciously for our own ends is *ultra vires*. It breaks the condition on which man was made.

1:28 פְּרוּ וּרְבוּ *Be fertile and multiply* – All of nature shares with God the property of being creative, of bringing new life into being, but only humanity shares with God the moral choice of bringing new life into the world. Only for Adam

29 earth." Then God said, "I give you all these seed-bearing plants on the face of
30 the earth and every tree with seed-bearing fruit. They shall be yours to eat. And
to all the beasts of the earth and birds of the heavens and everything that crawls
over the earth and has within it living spirit – I give every green plant for food."
31 And so it was. Then God saw all that He had made: and it was very good. There
was evening, and there was morning – the sixth day.
2 1/2 So the heavens and the earth were finished, and all their vast array. On the
seventh day God finished the work that He had done, and on the seventh day
3 He rested from all the work that He had done. God blessed the seventh day and
sanctified it, because on it He rested from all His work, from all that God had
created and done.

רש״י

כט-ל **לָכֶם יִהְיֶה לְאָכְלָה וּלְכָל חַיַּת הָאָרֶץ.** הִשְׁוָה לָהֶם הַכָּתוּב בְּהֵמוֹת וְחַיּוֹת לְמַאֲכָל, וְלֹא הִרְשָׁה לְאָדָם וּלְאִשְׁתּוֹ לְהָמִית בְּרִיָּה וְלֶאֱכֹל בָּשָׂר, אַךְ כָּל יֶרֶק עֵשֶׂב יֹאכְלוּ יַחַד כֻּלָּם. וּכְשֶׁבָּאוּ בְּנֵי נֹחַ, הִתִּיר לָהֶם בָּשָׂר, שֶׁנֶּאֱמַר: "כָּל רֶמֶשׂ אֲשֶׁר הוּא חַי וְגוֹ׳ כְּיֶרֶק עֵשֶׂב" שֶׁהִתַּרְתִּי לְאָדָם הָרִאשׁוֹן "נָתַתִּי לָכֶם אֶת כֹּל" (להלן ט, ג):

לא **יוֹם הַשִּׁשִּׁי.** הוֹסִיף הֵ״א בַּשִּׁשִּׁי בִּגְמַר מַעֲשֵׂה בְרֵאשִׁית, לוֹמַר שֶׁהִתְנָה עִמָּהֶם עַל מְנָת שֶׁיְּקַבְּלוּ עֲלֵיהֶם יִשְׂרָאֵל חֲמִשָּׁה חֻמְשֵׁי תוֹרָה. דָּבָר אַחֵר, "יוֹם הַשִּׁשִּׁי", כֻּלָּם תְּלוּיִים וְעוֹמְדִים עַד יוֹם הַשִּׁשִּׁי, הוּא שִׁשִּׁי בְּסִיוָן הַמּוּכָן לְמַתַּן תּוֹרָה:

ב ב **וַיְכַל אֱלֹהִים בַּיּוֹם הַשְּׁבִיעִי.** רַבִּי שִׁמְעוֹן אוֹמֵר: בָּשָׂר וָדָם שֶׁאֵינוֹ יוֹדֵעַ עִתָּיו וּרְגָעָיו צָרִיךְ לְהוֹסִיף מֵחוֹל עַל הַקֹּדֶשׁ, הַקָּדוֹשׁ בָּרוּךְ הוּא שֶׁיּוֹדֵעַ עִתָּיו וּרְגָעָיו, נִכְנַס בּוֹ כְּחוּט הַשַּׂעֲרָה, וְנִרְאָה כְּאִלּוּ כִּלָּה בּוֹ בַּיּוֹם. דָּבָר אַחֵר: מֶה הָיָה הָעוֹלָם חָסֵר? מְנוּחָה, בָּאת שַׁבָּת בָּאת מְנוּחָה, כָּלְתָה וְנִגְמְרָה הַמְּלָאכָה:

ג **וַיְבָרֶךְ וַיְקַדֵּשׁ.** בֵּרְכוֹ בַּמָּן, שֶׁכָּל יְמוֹת הַשָּׁבוּעַ יוֹרֵד לָהֶם עֹמֶר לַגֻּלְגֹּלֶת, וּבַשִּׁשִּׁי לֶחֶם מִשְׁנֶה. וְקִדְּשׁוֹ בַּמָּן שֶׁלֹּא יָרַד בּוֹ מָן כְּלָל, וְהַמִּקְרָא כָּתוּב עַל הֶעָתִיד: **אֲשֶׁר בָּרָא אֱלֹהִים לַעֲשׂוֹת.** הַמְּלָאכָה שֶׁהָיְתָה רְאוּיָה לַעֲשׂוֹת בַּשַּׁבָּת כָּפַל וַעֲשָׂאָהּ בַּשִּׁשִּׁי, כְּמוֹ שֶׁמְּפֹרָשׁ בִּבְרֵאשִׁית רַבָּה (יא, ט):

The Sabbath was and remains a revolutionary idea. Many ancient religions had their holy days. But none had a day on which it was forbidden to work. Rabbinic tradition says that when the Torah was first translated into Greek, the translators changed this sentence to make it comprehensible. Instead of "On the seventh day God finished the work that He had done," the translators wrote, "On the sixth day…." It is as if they knew that the Greeks could understand that in six days God made the universe but not that on the seventh He made rest – that rest itself is a creation. Rest is the creation which allows us to enjoy all other creations. Just as clear space surrounds a page or frames a picture, so clear time is the frame in which we set our work, giving it the dignity of art.

2:3 **אֲשֶׁר בָּרָא אֱלֹהִים לַעֲשׂוֹת** *That God had created and done* – "Because on it He rested from all His work, from all that God had created." The sentence should finish there. In fact, though, there is one extra word in the Hebrew, *laasot*, translated here "and done," but which literally means "to do, to make, to function."

Ibn Ezra and Abrabanel interpret it to mean "[He had created it] in such a way that it would continue to create itself." God as we see Him in Genesis 2 is a gardener, not a mechanic, one who plants systems that grow. It is a universe impossible to predict in detail, one that gives rise to agencies that are themselves creative. Without stretching the text too far, we might say that *laasot* means, quite simply, "to evolve."

כט הָרֹמֵשׂ עַל־הָאָרֶץ: וַיֹּאמֶר אֱלֹהִים הִנֵּה נָתַתִּי לָכֶם אֶת־כָּל־עֵשֶׂב ׀
זֹרֵעַ זֶרַע אֲשֶׁר עַל־פְּנֵי כָל־הָאָרֶץ וְאֶת־כָּל־הָעֵץ אֲשֶׁר־בּוֹ פְרִי־עֵץ
ל זֹרֵעַ זָרַע לָכֶם יִהְיֶה לְאָכְלָה: וּלְכָל־חַיַּת הָאָרֶץ וּלְכָל־עוֹף הַשָּׁמַיִם
וּלְכֹל ׀ רוֹמֵשׂ עַל־הָאָרֶץ אֲשֶׁר־בּוֹ נֶפֶשׁ חַיָּה אֶת־כָּל־יֶרֶק עֵשֶׂב לְאָכְלָה
לא וַיְהִי־כֵן: וַיַּרְא אֱלֹהִים אֶת־כָּל־אֲשֶׁר עָשָׂה וְהִנֵּה־טוֹב מְאֹד וַיְהִי־עֶרֶב
וַיְהִי־בֹקֶר יוֹם הַשִּׁשִּׁי:
ב א ב וַיְכֻלּוּ הַשָּׁמַיִם וְהָאָרֶץ וְכָל־צְבָאָם: וַיְכַל אֱלֹהִים בַּיּוֹם הַשְּׁבִיעִי מְלַאכְתּוֹ
ג אֲשֶׁר עָשָׂה וַיִּשְׁבֹּת בַּיּוֹם הַשְּׁבִיעִי מִכָּל־מְלַאכְתּוֹ אֲשֶׁר עָשָׂה: וַיְבָרֶךְ
אֱלֹהִים אֶת־יוֹם הַשְּׁבִיעִי וַיְקַדֵּשׁ אֹתוֹ כִּי בוֹ שָׁבַת מִכָּל־מְלַאכְתּוֹ
אֲשֶׁר־בָּרָא אֱלֹהִים לַעֲשׂוֹת:

אונקלוס

דְּרָחֵשׁ עַל אַרְעָא: כט וַאֲמַר יי, הָא יְהָבִית לְכוֹן, יָת כָּל עִסְבָּא דְּבַר זַרְעֵיהּ מִזְדְּרַע, דְּעַל אַפֵּי כָל אַרְעָא, וְיָת כָּל אִילָן, דְּבֵיהּ פֵּירֵי אִילָנָא דְּבַר זַרְעֵיהּ מִזְדְּרַע, לְכוֹן יְהֵי לְמֵיכַל: ל וּלְכָל חַיַּת אַרְעָא, וּלְכָל עוֹפָא דִּשְׁמַיָּא, וּלְכֹל דְּרָחֵישׁ עַל אַרְעָא, דְּבֵיהּ נַפְשָׁא חַיְתָא, יָת כָּל יָרוֹק עִסְבָּא לְמֵיכַל, וַהֲוָה כֵן: לא וַחֲזָא יי יָת כָּל דַּעֲבַד, וְהָא תַקִּין לַחֲדָא, וַהֲוָה רְמַשׁ וַהֲוָה צְפַר יוֹם שְׁתִיתָי: ב א וְאִשְׁתַּכְלָלוּ, שְׁמַיָּא וְאַרְעָא וְכָל חֵילֵיהוֹן: ב וְשֵׁיצִי יי בְּיוֹמָא שְׁבִיעָאָה, עֲבִידְתֵיהּ דַּעֲבַד, וְנָח בְּיוֹמָא שְׁבִיעָאָה, מִכָּל עֲבִידְתֵיהּ דַּעֲבַד: ג וּבָרֵיךְ יי יָת יוֹמָא שְׁבִיעָאָה, וְקַדֵּישׁ יָתֵיהּ, אֲרֵי בֵיהּ נָח מִכָּל עֲבִידְתֵיהּ, דִּבְרָא יי לְמֶעְבַּד:

unable to do. Our attitudes to situations such as old age and disability evolve with our expanded possibilities. The more we are active and not passive, the more we can shape our circumstances rather than be shaped by them, the more dignified is our existence.

1:31 טוֹב מְאֹד *Very good* – Seven times in Genesis 1 the word "good" appears, the last with the addition of the word "very," meaning that the universe is not just good in its individual elements but also in their complex interaction. Natural (or scientific) law, moral law, and religious or ritual law are all part of the same phenomenon: the God-given, law-governed structure of reality. When this is honored by human beings, there is order. When it is violated, there is chaos and violence.

THE SEVENTH DAY

The Hebrew text until this point is precisely structured around the number seven, in ways not always apparent in translation. The word "good" appears seven times. The word "God" appears thirty-five times. The words "heavens" and "earth" each appear twenty-one times. The words "light" and "day" occur seven times in the first paragraph. The first verse contains seven words, the second fourteen words. This paragraph, describing the seventh day, contains thirty-five words, and so on. The passage as a whole contains 67 x 7 words. The entire passage is structured like a fractal, so that the sevenfold motif of the text as a whole is mirrored at lower levels of magnitude. The Sabbath, then, is woven into the pattern of creation.

naked? Have you eaten from the tree from which I commanded you not to eat?"
12 The man said, "The woman You put here with me – she gave me fruit from the
13 tree and I ate." Then the LORD God said to the woman, "What is this you have
14 done?" The woman said, "The serpent beguiled me and I ate." And the LORD
God said to the serpent, "Because you have done this, you are accursed more
than all the animals and all wild beasts. You will creep on your belly and dust
15 will you eat all the days of your life. I will plant hostility between you and the
woman, between your children and hers. And man will strike your head, and
16 you will strike his heel." To the woman He said, "I will make your pain
in pregnancy searingly great; in sorrow will you bear children. You will long for
17 your husband, but he will rule over you." To Adam He said, "Because

רש"י

הֲמִן הָעֵץ. בִּתְמִיָּה:

יב **אֲשֶׁר נָתַתָּה עִמָּדִי.** כָּאן כָּפַר בַּטּוֹבָה:

יג **הִשִּׁיאַנִי.** הִטְעַנִי, כְּמוֹ: "אַל יַשִּׁיא אֶתְכֶם חִזְקִיָּהוּ" (דברי הימים ב׳ לב, טו):

יד **כִּי עָשִׂיתָ זֹּאת.** מִכָּאן שֶׁאֵין מְהַפְּכִים בִּזְכוּתוֹ שֶׁל מֵסִית, שֶׁאִלּוּ שְׁאָלוֹ: לָמָּה עָשִׂיתָ זֹאת? הָיָה לוֹ לְהָשִׁיב: דִּבְרֵי הָרַב וְדִבְרֵי הַתַּלְמִיד, דִּבְרֵי מִי שׁוֹמְעִין?: **מִכָּל הַבְּהֵמָה וּמִכֹּל חַיַּת הַשָּׂדֶה.** אִם מִבְּהֵמָה נִתְקַלֵּל, מֵחַיָּה לֹא כָּל שֶׁכֵּן?! הֶעֱמִידוּ רַבּוֹתֵינוּ מִדְרָשׁ זֶה בְּמַסֶּכֶת בְּכוֹרוֹת (דף ח ע"א) לְלַמֵּד שֶׁיְּמֵי עִבּוּרוֹ שֶׁל נָחָשׁ שֶׁבַע שָׁנִים: **עַל גְּחֹנְךָ תֵלֵךְ.** רַגְלַיִם הָיוּ לוֹ וְנִקְצְצוּ:

טו **וְאֵיבָה אָשִׁית.** אַתָּה לֹא נִתְכַּוַּנְתָּ אֶלָּא שֶׁיָּמוּת אָדָם, שֶׁיֹּאכַל הוּא תְּחִלָּה וְתִשָּׂא אֶת חַוָּה, וְלֹא בָּאתָ לְדַבֵּר אֶל חַוָּה תְּחִלָּה אֶלָּא לְפִי שֶׁהַנָּשִׁים קַלּוֹת לְהִתְפַּתּוֹת וְיוֹדְעוֹת לְפַתּוֹת בַּעְלֵיהֶן, לְפִיכָךְ "וְאֵיבָה אָשִׁית": **יְשׁוּפְךָ.** יְכַתֶּתְךָ, כְּמוֹ: "וָאֶכֹּת אֹתוֹ" (דברים ט, כא), וְתַרְגּוּמוֹ: "וְשַׁפִּית יָתֵיהּ": **וְאַתָּה תְּשׁוּפֶנּוּ עָקֵב.** לֹא יְהֵא לְךָ קוֹמָה, וּתְשָׁכֶנּוּ בַּעֲקֵבוֹ וְאַף מִשָּׁם תְּמִיתֶנּוּ. וּלְשׁוֹן 'תְּשׁוּפֶנּוּ' כְּמוֹ: "נָשַׁף בָּהֶם" (ישעיה מ, כד), כְּשֶׁהַנָּחָשׁ בָּא לְנְשֹׁךְ הוּא נוֹשֵׁף כְּמִין שְׁרִיקָה, וּלְפִי שֶׁהַלָּשׁוֹן נוֹפֵל עַל הַלָּשׁוֹן כָּתַב לְשׁוֹן נְשִׁיפָה בִּשְׁנֵיהֶם:

טז **עִצְּבוֹנֵךְ.** זֶה צַעַר גִּדּוּל בָּנִים: **וְהֵרֹנֵךְ.** זֶה צַעַר הָעִבּוּר: **בְּעֶצֶב תֵּלְדִי בָנִים.** זֶה צַעַר הַלֵּדָה: **וְאֶל אִישֵׁךְ תְּשׁוּקָתֵךְ.** לְתַשְׁמִישׁ, וְאַף עַל פִּי כֵן אֵין לָךְ מֵצַח לְתָבְעוֹ בַּפֶּה אֶלָּא "הוּא יִמְשָׁל בָּךְ", הַכֹּל מִמֶּנּוּ וְלֹא מִמֵּךְ: **תְּשׁוּקָתֵךְ.** תַּאֲוָתֵךְ, כְּמוֹ: "וְנַפְשׁוֹ שׁוֹקֵקָה" (ישעיה כט, ח):

peace. Yeshayahu is the classic instance of this, foreseeing a time when "nation shall not raise sword against nation" (2:4), and, in a reversal of the conflicts that emerge from our story, the world will be in a state of *shalom*, the integrated diversity that constitutes peace.

3:16 אֶל־אִישֵׁךְ תְּשׁוּקָתֵךְ וְהוּא יִמְשָׁל־בָּךְ *You will long for your husband but he will rule over you* – The word "longing," *teshuka*, appears only twice elsewhere in Tanakh, in God's warning to Kayin about the danger of the violent anger he is feeling toward Hevel: "Sin is crouching at the door; it *longs to have you*, but you must rule over it" (Gen. 4:7), and much later, in Song of Songs: "I am my beloved's, and his longing is for me" (7:11). This is a fine instance of intertextuality. In both places in Genesis, longing is about the dangerous power of passion. It will cause Ḥava to be subservient to her husband and Kayin to be a slave to his emotions. In Song of Songs, *teshuka* is benign because it is mutual. In no other book in Tanakh do woman and man – and thus Israel and God – stand on such equal terms (the dominant voice in the Song is the woman). Longing, desire, passion – these are dangerously labile emotions. Yet the Judaic answer is not that state beloved of the Greek philosophers, namely *ataraxia*, serenity, affectlessness, the "therapy of desire," nor is it the *nirvana* of the Eastern mystics. In Judaism, joy, exhilaration, strong emotion, and above all, love – "with all your heart, with all your soul, and with all your might" – are all part of the religious life. If we master our desires, they need not master us.

כִּי עֵירֹם אָתָּה הֲמִן־הָעֵץ אֲשֶׁר צִוִּיתִיךָ לְבִלְתִּי אֲכָל־מִמֶּנּוּ אָכָלְתָּ׃
יב וַיֹּאמֶר הָאָדָם הָאִשָּׁה אֲשֶׁר נָתַתָּה עִמָּדִי הִוא נָתְנָה־לִּי מִן־הָעֵץ
יג וָאֹכֵל׃ וַיֹּאמֶר יהוה אֱלֹהִים לָאִשָּׁה מַה־זֹּאת עָשִׂית וַתֹּאמֶר הָאִשָּׁה
יד הַנָּחָשׁ הִשִּׁיאַנִי וָאֹכֵל׃ וַיֹּאמֶר יהוה אֱלֹהִים ׀ אֶל־הַנָּחָשׁ כִּי עָשִׂיתָ
זֹּאת אָרוּר אַתָּה מִכָּל־הַבְּהֵמָה וּמִכֹּל חַיַּת הַשָּׂדֶה עַל־גְּחֹנְךָ תֵלֵךְ
טו וְעָפָר תֹּאכַל כָּל־יְמֵי חַיֶּיךָ׃ וְאֵיבָה ׀ אָשִׁית בֵּינְךָ וּבֵין הָאִשָּׁה וּבֵין זַרְעֲךָ
טז וּבֵין זַרְעָהּ הוּא יְשׁוּפְךָ רֹאשׁ וְאַתָּה תְּשׁוּפֶנּוּ עָקֵב׃ אֶל־
הָאִשָּׁה אָמַר הַרְבָּה אַרְבֶּה עִצְּבוֹנֵךְ וְהֵרֹנֵךְ בְּעֶצֶב תֵּלְדִי בָנִים וְאֶל־
יז אִישֵׁךְ תְּשׁוּקָתֵךְ וְהוּא יִמְשָׁל־בָּךְ׃ וּלְאָדָם אָמַר כִּי שָׁמַעְתָּ

אונקלוס

אֲרֵי עַרְטִלַּאי אַתְּ, הֲמִן אִילָנָא, דְּפַקֵּידְתָּךְ, בְּדִיל דְּלָא לְמֵיכַל מִנֵּיהּ אֲכַלְתָּא: יב וַאֲמַר אָדָם, אִתְּתָא דִּיהַבְתְּ עִמִּי, הִיא, יְהַבַת לִי מִן אִילָנָא וַאֲכָלִית: יג וַאֲמַר יי אֱלֹהִים, לְאִתְּתָא מָא דָא עֲבַדְתְּ, וַאֲמַרַת אִתְּתָא, חִוְיָא אַטְעְיַנִי וַאֲכָלִית: יד וַאֲמַר יי אֱלֹהִים לְחִוְיָא אֲרֵי עֲבַדְתְּ דָּא, לִיט אַתְּ מִכָּל בְּעִירָא, וּמִכָּל חֵיוַת בָּרָא, עַל מְעָךְ תֵּיזֵיל, וְעַפְרָא תֵּיכוֹל כָּל יוֹמֵי חַיָּיךְ: טו וּדְבָבוּ אֲשַׁוֵּי, בֵּינָךְ וּבֵין אִתְּתָא, וּבֵין בְּנָךְ וּבֵין בְּנַהָא, הוּא יְהֵי דְּכִיר מָא דַּעֲבַדְתְּ לֵיהּ מִלְּקַדְמִין, וְאַתְּ תְּהֵי נָטַר לֵיהּ לְסוֹפָא: טז לְאִתְּתָא אֲמַר, אַסְגָּאָה אַסְגֵּי צַעֲרִיכִי וְעִדּוּיַכִי, בְּצַעַר תְּלִידִין בְּנִין, וּלְוָת בַּעְלִיךְ תְּהֵי תֵּיאוּבְתִּיךְ, וְהוּא יִשְׁלוֹט בִּיךְ: יז וּלְאָדָם אֲמַר, אֲרֵי קַבֵּילְתָּא

3:12 הָאִשָּׁה אֲשֶׁר נָתַתָּה עִמָּדִי *The woman You put here* – Adam blames the woman. The woman blames the serpent. The result is that they are both punished and exiled from Eden. Genesis is a set of variations on the theme of family, and none runs smoothly. With Adam and Ḥava comes conflict. With each successive generation, new tensions arise. This is the great power of the Book of Books and the reason why it has never lost its hold on the human imagination: It is about us, people we can recognize and identify with. The real dramas are not the ones fought in court or in the battlefield. They are the ones fought and resolved in the home, between parents and children, between siblings, between husbands and wives. No literature more systematically expresses the dignity of the personal, the high moral drama of everyday life with its defensiveness, its petty betrayals, its self-deception.

Families are not ideal worlds. They are significant precisely because they are real worlds with people we know and trust. Working out our tensions with them, we learn how to resolve our tensions with society. And yes, they have their share of pain. It is the pain of life lived in relationship. Without it we could not learn to love.

3:15 בֵּין זַרְעֲךָ וּבֵין זַרְעָהּ *Between your children and hers* – And yet, in the prophet Yeshayahu's vision:

> A baby will play at the cobra's hole,
> and an infant's hand
> will explore the viper's nest.
> There will be no wrong or violence
> on all My holy mountain,
> for knowledge of the Lord will fill the earth
> as waters cover the ocean. (Is. 11:8–9)

By the eighth century BCE the prophets of Israel had become the first people in history to envisage a world at

you listened to your wife and ate of the tree from which I commanded you
not to eat – cursed will be the land on your account. By painful toil you will
18 eat from it all the days of your life. It will sprout thorns and thistles for you,
19 and you shall eat plants of the field. By the sweat of your brow will you eat
bread until you return to the land, for from there you were taken. You are
20 dust, and you will return to dust." Then the man named his wife Ḥava, for she
21 would become the mother of all life. Then the LORD God made garments of
skins for Adam and his wife and clothed them.
22 The LORD God then said, "Now that man has become like one of us, knowing REVI'I
good and evil, he must not be allowed to reach out his hand and take also from

רש״י

יז) **אֲרוּרָה הָאֲדָמָה בַּעֲבוּרֶךָ.** מַעֲלָה לְךָ דְּבָרִים אֲרוּרִים, כְּגוֹן זְבוּבִים וּפַרְעוֹשִׁים וּנְמָלִים. מָשָׁל לְיוֹצֵא לְתַרְבּוּת רָעָה וְהַבְּרִיּוֹת מְקַלְּלוֹת שָׁדַיִם שֶׁיָּנַק מֵהֶם:

יח) **וְקוֹץ וְדַרְדַּר תַּצְמִיחַ לָךְ.** הָאָרֶץ, כְּשֶׁתִּזְרָעֶנָּה מִינֵי זְרָעִים תַּצְמִיחַ קוֹץ וְדַרְדַּר, קוֹנְדָּס וְעַכָּבִיּוֹת, וְהֵן נֶאֱכָלִין עַל יְדֵי תִקּוּן: **וְאָכַלְתָּ אֶת עֵשֶׂב הַשָּׂדֶה.** וּמַה קְּלָלָה הִיא זוֹ? וַהֲלֹא בִּבְרָכָה נֶאֱמַר לוֹ: "הִנֵּה נָתַתִּי לָכֶם אֶת כָּל עֵשֶׂב זֹרֵעַ זֶרַע" וְגוֹ׳ (לעיל א, כט)? אֶלָּא מָה אָמוּר כָּאן בָּרֹאשׁ הָעִנְיָן: "אֲרוּרָה הָאֲדָמָה בַּעֲבוּרֶךָ בְּעִצָּבוֹן תֹּאכְלֶנָּה", וְאַחַר הָעִצָּבוֹן: "וְקוֹץ וְדַרְדַּר תַּצְמִיחַ לָךְ", כְּשֶׁתִּזְרָעֶנָּה קִטְנִית אוֹ יַרְקוֹת גִּנָּה, הִיא תַּצְמִיחַ לְךָ קוֹצִים וְדַרְדָּרִים וּשְׁאָר עִשְׂבֵי שָׂדֶה, וְעַל כָּרְחֲךָ תֹּאכְלֵם:

יט) **בְּזֵעַת אַפֶּיךָ.** לְאַחַר שֶׁתִּטְרַח בּוֹ הַרְבֵּה:

כ) **וַיִּקְרָא הָאָדָם.** חָזַר הַכָּתוּב לְעִנְיָנוֹ הָרִאשׁוֹן: "וַיִּקְרָא הָאָדָם שֵׁמוֹת" (לעיל ב, כ), וְלֹא הִפְסִיק אֶלָּא לְלַמֶּדְךָ שֶׁעַל יְדֵי קְרִיאַת שֵׁמוֹת נִזְדַּוְּגָה לוֹ חַוָּה, כְּמוֹ שֶׁכָּתוּב: "וּלְאָדָם לֹא מָצָא עֵזֶר כְּנֶגְדּוֹ" (שם), לְפִיכָךְ "וַיַּפֵּל... תַּרְדֵּמָה" (שם, כא), וְעַל יְדֵי שֶׁכָּתַב: "וַיִּהְיוּ שְׁנֵיהֶם עֲרוּמִּים" (שם, כה) סָמַךְ לוֹ פָּרָשַׁת הַנָּחָשׁ, לְהוֹדִיעֲךָ שֶׁמִּתּוֹךְ שֶׁרָאָה עֶרְוָתָהּ וְרָאָה אוֹתָם עֲסוּקִים בְּתַשְׁמִישׁ נִתְאַוָּה לָהּ, וּבָא עֲלֵיהֶם בְּמַחֲשָׁבָה וּבְמִרְמָה: **חַוָּה.** נוֹפֵל עַל לְשׁוֹן 'חַיָּה' שֶׁמְּחַיָּה אֶת וְלָדוֹתֶיהָ, כַּאֲשֶׁר תֹּאמַר: "מֶה הֹוֶה לָאָדָם" (קהלת ב, כב) בִּלְשׁוֹן 'הָיָה':

כא) **כָּתְנוֹת עוֹר.** יֵשׁ דִּבְרֵי אַגָּדָה אוֹמְרִים: חֲלָקִים כְּצִפֹּרֶן מְדֻבָּקִין עַל עוֹרָן. וְיֵשׁ אוֹמְרִים: דָּבָר הַבָּא מִן הָעוֹר, כְּגוֹן צֶמֶר אַרְנָבִים שֶׁהוּא רַךְ וְחַם, וְעָשָׂה לָהֶם כָּתְנוֹת מִמֶּנּוּ:

כב) **הָיָה כְּאַחַד מִמֶּנּוּ.** הֲרֵי הוּא יָחִיד בַּתַּחְתּוֹנִים כְּמוֹ שֶׁאֲנִי יָחִיד בָּעֶלְיוֹנִים, וּמַה הִיא יְחִידוּתוֹ? "לָדַעַת טוֹב וָרָע", מַה שֶּׁאֵין כֵּן בַּבְּהֵמָה וּבַחַיָּה: **וְעַתָּה פֶּן יִשְׁלַח יָדוֹ וְגוֹ׳.** וּמִשֶּׁיִּחְיֶה לְעוֹלָם הֲרֵי הוּא קָרוֹב לְהַטְעוֹת הַבְּרִיּוֹת אַחֲרָיו וְלוֹמַר אַף הוּא אֱלוֹהַּ. וְיֵשׁ מִדְרְשֵׁי אַגָּדָה, אֲבָל אֵין מְיֻשָּׁבִין עַל פְּשׁוּטוֹ:

3:21 **וַיַּעַשׂ יהוה אֱלֹהִים לְאָדָם וּלְאִשְׁתּוֹ כָּתְנוֹת עוֹר וַיַּלְבִּשֵׁם** *God made garments of skins for Adam and his wife and clothed them* – The first-century sage Rabbi Meir read the *ayin* of the word *or*, "skins," as an *alef* – and thus interprets the phrase "garments of skins" as "garments of light" (Bereshit Rabba 20:12). For Adam now saw that physical being, "nakedness," was not simply a source of shame. There is a spiritual dimension to the physical relationship between husband and wife. At one level it is the most animal of desires, but at another it is as close as we come to the principle of divine creativity itself, namely, that love creates life. It is only when we relate to one another as persons possessed of non-negotiable dignity that we respond to the "image of God" in the other.

In a sense, the whole of Judaism – or at least *mitzvot bein adam lehavero*, "the commands between us and our fellow human beings" – is an extended commentary on this idea. The rules of justice, mercy, charity, compassion, regard for the poor, love for the neighbor and the stranger, delicacy of speech, and sensitivity to the easily injured feelings of others are all variants on the theme of respect for the human other as an image and likeness of the Divine Other. It is when Ḥava receives her name that God robes the couple in garments of light.

3:22 **פֶּן יִשְׁלַח יָדוֹ... וָחַי לְעֹלָם** *He must not be allowed to... live forever* – For better or worse, mankind has attained a new

לְקוֹל אִשְׁתֶּךָ וַתֹּאכַל מִן־הָעֵץ אֲשֶׁר צִוִּיתִיךָ לֵאמֹר לֹא תֹאכַל מִמֶּנּוּ
יח אֲרוּרָה הָאֲדָמָה בַּעֲבוּרֶךָ בְּעִצָּבוֹן תֹּאכֲלֶנָּה כֹּל יְמֵי חַיֶּיךָ: וְקוֹץ וְדַרְדַּר
יט תַּצְמִיחַ לָךְ וְאָכַלְתָּ אֶת־עֵשֶׂב הַשָּׂדֶה: בְּזֵעַת אַפֶּיךָ תֹּאכַל לֶחֶם עַד
שׁוּבְךָ אֶל־הָאֲדָמָה כִּי מִמֶּנָּה לֻקָּחְתָּ כִּי־עָפָר אַתָּה וְאֶל־עָפָר תָּשׁוּב:
כ כא וַיִּקְרָא הָאָדָם שֵׁם אִשְׁתּוֹ חַוָּה כִּי הִוא הָיְתָה אֵם כָּל־חָי: וַיַּעַשׂ יהוה
אֱלֹהִים לְאָדָם וּלְאִשְׁתּוֹ כָּתְנוֹת עוֹר וַיַּלְבִּשֵׁם:
כב וַיֹּאמֶר ׀ יהוה אֱלֹהִים הֵן הָאָדָם הָיָה כְּאַחַד מִמֶּנּוּ לָדַעַת טוֹב ג רביעי
וָרָע וְעַתָּה ׀ פֶּן־יִשְׁלַח יָדוֹ וְלָקַח גַּם מֵעֵץ הַחַיִּים וְאָכַל וָחַי לְעֹלָם:

אונקלוס

לְמֵימַר אִתְּתָךְ, וַאֲכַלְתְּ מִן אִילָנָא, דְּפַקֵּידְתָּךְ לְמֵימַר, לָא תֵיכוֹל מִנֵּיהּ, לִיטָא אַרְעָא בְּדִילָךְ, בְּעָמַל תֵּיכְלִנַּהּ, כֹּל יוֹמֵי חַיָּךְ: יח וְכוּבִין וְאָטְדִין תַּצְמַח לָךְ, וְתֵיכוֹל יָת עִסְבָּא דְּחַקְלָא: יט בְּזֵיעֲתָא דְּאַפָּךְ תֵּיכוֹל לַחְמָא, עַד דְּתִתּוּב לְאַרְעָא, דְּמִנַּהּ אִתְבְּרֵיתָא, אֲרֵי עַפְרָא אַתְּ, וּלְעַפְרָא תְּתוּב: כ וּקְרָא אָדָם, שׁוּם אִתְּתֵיהּ חַוָּה, אֲרֵי, הִיא הֲוָת אִמָּא דְּכָל בְּנֵי אֲנָשָׁא: כא וַעֲבַד יי אֱלֹהִים, לְאָדָם וּלְאִתְּתֵיהּ, לְבוּשִׁין דִּיקָר עַל מְשַׁךְ בִּסְרְהוֹן וְאַלְבֵּשִׁנּוּן: כב וַאֲמַר יי אֱלֹהִים, הָא אָדָם הֲוָה יְחִידָאי בְּעָלְמָא מִנֵּיהּ, לְמִדַּע טָב וּבִישׁ, וּכְעַן דִּלְמָא יוֹשֵׁיט יְדֵיהּ, וְיִסַּב אַף מֵאִילַן חַיַּיָּא, וְיֵיכוֹל וְיֵיחֵי לְעָלַם:

3:19 בְּזֵעַת אַפֶּיךָ *By the sweat of your brow* – The Jewish liturgy for Saturday night – the time that recalls the expulsion from Eden – culminates in a hymn to the values of work and the family (Ps. 128): "You shall eat the fruit of your labor; you shall be happy and thriving." Work has spiritual value. How so?

When the Holy One, blessed be He, told Adam, "Cursed will be the land on your account … it will sprout thorns and thistles," Adam wept. He said, "Master of the Universe, am I and my donkey to eat in the same manger?" But when he heard the words "By the sweat of your brow will you eat bread," he was consoled (Pesaḥim 118a).

Labor elevates man, for by it he *earns* his food. Animals find sustenance; only mankind creates it. As the thirteenth-century commentator Rabbeinu Baḥya put it, "The active participation of man in the creation of his own wealth is a sign of his spiritual greatness." The "thorns and thistles" are a curse; work itself is not a curse, but a blessing.

3:19 עָפָר אַתָּה וְאֶל עָפָר תָּשׁוּב *You are dust, and you will return to dust* – Until this point, death has not entered Adam's consciousness, but now he is brought face-to-face with it. It is now, too, that Adam remembers God's words to the woman. She will give birth to children – in pain, to be sure, but she will bring new life into the world. Suddenly Adam knows that though we die, if we are privileged to have children, something of us will live on: our genes, our influence, our example, our ideals. That is our immortality. But this cannot be achieved alone.

Until he became aware of his mortality, Adam could think of his wife as a mere *ezer kenegdo* – as an assistant, not an equal. Now he knows otherwise. Without her, he cannot have children – and children are to be his share in eternity. With this awareness he ceases to think of her as an assistant. She is a person in her own right – more even than he, for it is she, not he, who will actually give birth. In this respect she is more like God than he can be, for God is He-who-brings-new-life-into-being. It is now that he turns to his wife and for the first time sees her as a person, giving her a personal name, Ḥava, meaning, "she who gives life."

2 "With the LORD's help I have made a man." Later, she gave birth to his brother
3 Hevel. Hevel became a shepherd, while Kayin was a worker of the land. Time
4 passed, and Kayin brought fruit of the land as an offering to the LORD. Hevel
too brought an offering: fat portions from the firstborn of his flock. The LORD
5 looked favorably on Hevel and his offering, but upon Kayin and his offering He
6 did not look with favor. Kayin became very angry, and his face downcast. The
7 LORD said to Kayin, "Why are you angry; why is your face downcast? If you act
well, will you not be uplifted? If you fail to act well, sin is crouching at the door;
8 it longs to have you, but you must rule over it." Then Kayin said to his brother

רש״י

אָחִיו אֶת הָבֶל. שְׁלֹשָׁה 'אֶתִים' רִבּוּיִים הֵם, מְלַמֵּד שֶׁתְּאוֹמָה נוֹלְדָה עִם קַיִן, וְעִם הֶבֶל נוֹלְדוּ שְׁתַּיִם, לְכָךְ נֶאֱמַר: "וַתֹּסֶף": **רֹעֵה צֹאן.** לְפִי שֶׁנִּתְקַלְּלָה הָאֲדָמָה, פֵּרַשׁ לוֹ מֵעֲבוֹדָתָהּ:

ג **מִפְּרִי הָאֲדָמָה.** מִן הַגָּרוּעַ, וְיֵשׁ אַגָּדָה שֶׁאוֹמֶרֶת זֶרַע פִּשְׁתָּן הָיָה:

ד **וַיִּשַׁע.** וַיִּפֶן, וְכֵן: "שְׁעֵה מֵעָלָיו" (איוב יד, ו) פְּנֵה מֵעָלָיו: **וַיִּשַׁע.** יָרְדָה אֵשׁ וְלִחֲכָה מִנְחָתוֹ:

ה **לֹא שָׁעָה.** לֹא פָּנָה, וְכֵן: "אַל יִשְׁעוּ" (שמות ה, ט) אַל יִפְנוּ:

ז **הֲלֹא אִם תֵּיטִיב.** כְּתַרְגּוּמוֹ פֵּרוּשׁוֹ: **לַפֶּתַח חַטָּאת רֹבֵץ.** לְפֶתַח קִבְרְךָ חֶטְאֲךָ שָׁמוּר: **וְאֵלֶיךָ תְּשׁוּקָתוֹ.** שֶׁל חַטָּאת, הוּא יֵצֶר הָרָע, תָּמִיד שׁוֹקֵק וּמִתְאַוֶּה לְהַכְשִׁילְךָ: **וְאַתָּה תִּמְשָׁל בּוֹ.** אִם תִּרְצֶה תִּתְגַּבֵּר עָלָיו:

ח **וַיֹּאמֶר קַיִן אֶל הֶבֶל.** נִכְנַס עִמּוֹ בְּדִבְרֵי רִיב וּמַצָּה לְהִתְעוֹלֵל עָלָיו וּלְהָרְגוֹ. וְיֵשׁ בָּזֶה מִדְרְשֵׁי אַגָּדָה, אַךְ זֶה יִשּׁוּבוֹ שֶׁל מִקְרָא:

rain, victory in battle, or restoring past imperial glories. This is the exact opposite of what the Torah views as true faith: humility in the face of God, respect for the integrity of creation, and reverence for human life – the only thing that bears the image of God.

4:7 **וְאַתָּה תִּמְשָׁל־בּוֹ** *But you must rule over it* – We can rephrase this a little more technically nowadays. Kayin is experiencing a rush of emotion to the amygdala, the so-called reptile brain with its fight-or-flight reactions, including anger. God is urging him to use his prefrontal cortex, more rational and deliberative, capable of thinking beyond the immediacy of me, here, now. The choice – God is saying – is in your hands. You are free to do what you choose. But actions have consequences. You cannot overeat and take no exercise, and at the same time stay healthy. You cannot act selfishly and win the respect of other people. You cannot allow injustices to prevail and sustain a cohesive society. You cannot let rulers use power for their own ends without destroying the basis of a free and gracious social order. There is nothing mystical about these ideas. They are eminently intelligible. But they are also, and inescapably, moral. Neuroscience has shown us where in the brain the battle for freedom is fought, but it has not shown us freedom itself. This we can know only introspectively, from within. Sin is crouching at the door. But we can rule over our own minds.

4:8 **וַיֹּאמֶר קַיִן אֶל הֶבֶל אָחִיו** *Kayin said to his brother Hevel* – The verse contains fractured syntax. It says, "Then Kayin said," but it does not say *what* he says. To turn it into a coherent sentence, translations usually add words not in the original, or paraphrase the verb from "said" to "talked with" or "had words with." In so doing, however, they completely miss the point of the verse. Style mirrors substance. The fractured syntax represents fractured relationship. The conversation breaks down. "Then Kayin said" – but his speech gets no further, and there is nothing but tension and silence. When words fail, violence begins.

Violence, Alan Brien once wrote, is the repartee of the

ב וַתֹּסֶף לָלֶדֶת אֶת־אָחִיו אֶת־הָבֶל וַיְהִי־הֶבֶל רֹעֵה צֹאן וְקַיִן הָיָה עֹבֵד
ג אֲדָמָה: וַיְהִי מִקֵּץ יָמִים וַיָּבֵא קַיִן מִפְּרִי הָאֲדָמָה מִנְחָה לַיהוָה:
ד וְהֶבֶל הֵבִיא גַם־הוּא מִבְּכֹרוֹת צֹאנוֹ וּמֵחֶלְבֵהֶן וַיִּשַׁע יהוה אֶל־
ה הֶבֶל וְאֶל־מִנְחָתוֹ: וְאֶל־קַיִן וְאֶל־מִנְחָתוֹ לֹא שָׁעָה וַיִּחַר לְקַיִן מְאֹד
ו וַיִּפְּלוּ פָּנָיו: וַיֹּאמֶר יהוה אֶל־קָיִן לָמָּה חָרָה לָךְ וְלָמָּה נָפְלוּ פָנֶיךָ:
ז הֲלוֹא אִם־תֵּיטִיב שְׂאֵת וְאִם לֹא תֵיטִיב לַפֶּתַח חַטָּאת רֹבֵץ וְאֵלֶיךָ
ח תְּשׁוּקָתוֹ וְאַתָּה תִּמְשָׁל־בּוֹ: וַיֹּאמֶר קַיִן אֶל־הֶבֶל אָחִיו וַיְהִי בִּהְיוֹתָם

אונקלוס

ב וְאוֹסֵיפַת לְמֵילַד, יָת אֲחוּהִי יָת הָבֶל, וַהֲוָה הֶבֶל רָעֵי עָנָא,
וְקַיִן, הֲוָה פָּלַח בְּאַרְעָא: ג וַהֲוָה מִסּוֹף יוֹמִין, וְאַיְתִי קַיִן, מֵאִבָּא
דְאַרְעָא, קֻרְבָּנָא קֳדָם יי: ד וְהֶבֶל אַיְתִי אַף הוּא, מִבַּכִּירֵי עָנֵיהּ
וּמִשַּׁמִּינֵיהוֹן, וַהֲוָת רַעֲוָא מִן קֳדָם יי, בְּהֶבֶל וּבְקֻרְבָּנֵיהּ: ה וּבְקַיִן
וּבְקֻרְבָּנֵיהּ לָא הֲוָת רַעֲוָא, וּתְקֵיף לְקַיִן לַחֲדָא, וְאִתְכְּבִישׁוּ אַפּוֹהִי:

ו וַאֲמַר יי לְקַיִן, לְמָא תְּקֵיף לָךְ, וּלְמָא אִתְכְּבִישׁוּ אַפָּךְ: ז הֲלָא
אִם תּוֹטֵיב עוּבָדָךְ יִשְׁתְּבֵיק לָךְ, וְאִם לָא תוֹטֵיב עוּבָדָךְ, לְיוֹם
דִּינָא חֶטְאָךְ נְטִיר, עָתִיד לְאִתְפְּרָעָא מִנָּךְ אִם לָא תְתוּב, וְאִם
תְּתוּב יִשְׁתְּבֵיק לָךְ: ח וַאֲמַר קַיִן לְהֶבֶל אֲחוּהִי, וַהֲוָה בְּמִהְוֵיהוֹן

4:2 הָבֶל *Hevel* – Hevel's name is, among other things, the keyword of the Book of Ecclesiastes; as the King James version translates: "Vanity of vanities; all is vanity." *Hevel* has also been translated as "meaningless, pointless, futile, useless." These translations miss the point. *Hevel* is a word for "breath." Jews speak of the soul, or the spiritual dimension of humankind, in language drawn from the act of breathing. In Hebrew, words for soul – such as *nefesh, ruaḥ, neshama* – are all types of breath. *Hevel* means a shallow, fleeting, ephemeral breath. Ecclesiastes is a sustained meditation on mortality. All the wealth and glory even the greatest accumulate means nothing, because all that separates us from non-existence is a mere breath. Kayin, in contrast, means not only "to make" but also "to acquire, to possess, to own." The Hebrew word *Baal*, the name of the chief Canaanite god, has the same range of meanings: "to own, to possess, to exercise power over someone or something." That for the Bible is the ultimate idolatry. The earth belongs to God. God does not sanctify the will to power. This, as the Bible understands it, is the fundamental conflict within the human condition: the struggle between the *will to power* and the *will to life.*

Hevel represents mortal human life – a mortality that comes less from sin than from the fact that we are embodied souls in a physical world subject to deterioration and decay. All that separates us from the grave is the breath God breathed into us (Gen. 2:7). We are *hevel*, mere breath. But it is God's breath. Life is holy.

4:5 וַיִּחַר לְקַיִן מְאֹד *Kayin became very angry* – The reason God rejects Kayin's offering becomes clear in Kayin's reaction. Imagine the following: You offer someone a gift. Politely, they refuse it. How do you respond? There are two possibilities. You can ask yourself, "What did I do wrong?" or you can be angry with the intended recipient. If you respond in the first way, you were genuinely trying to please the other person. If the second, it becomes retrospectively clear that your concern was not with the other but with yourself. You were trying to assert your own dominance by putting the other in your debt. That is what sacrifices were in the pagan world: attempts to appease, placate, or bribe the gods, thereby coercing or manipulating them into doing one's will – whether sending

Hevel – and when they were in the field, Kayin rose up against his brother
9 Hevel and killed him. The LORD asked Kayin, "Where is your brother, Hevel?"
10 "I do not know," he said. "Am I my brother's keeper?" He said, "What is it you
have done? The voice of your brother's blood cries out to Me from the land!
11 Now you are cursed, more so than the land that has opened its mouth to receive
12 your brother's blood from your hand. When you work the land, it will no longer
13 grant you its powers. You will be a fugitive wanderer over the land." Kayin said
14 to the LORD, "My sin is more than I can bear. You have banished me today from
the face of the land, and from Your face too I will be hidden. I will be a fugitive
15 wanderer over the land, and whoever finds me will kill me." The LORD said to
him, "Whoever then kills Kayin will suffer vengeance seven times over." Then
16 the LORD put a mark on Kayin so that none who found him would kill him. So
Kayin departed from the LORD's presence and lived in the land of Nod, east
17 of Eden. Kayin knew his wife, and she conceived and gave birth to Ḥanokh.

רש"י

ט **אי הבל אחיך.** להכנס עמו בדברי נחת, אולי ישיב: אני הרגתיו וחטאתי לך: **לא ידעתי.** נעשה כגונב דעת העליונה: **השמר אחי.** לשון תמה הוא, וכן כל ה"א הנקודה בחטף פתח:

י **דמי אחיך.** דמו ודם זרעיותיו. דבר אחר, שעשה בו פצעים הרבה, שלא היה יודע מהיכן נפשו יוצאה:

יא-יב **מן האדמה.** יותר ממה שנתקללה היא כבר בעונה, וגם בזו הוסיפה לחטוא "אשר פצתה את פיה לקחת את דמי אחיך" וגו', והנני מוסיף לה קללה אצלך: "לא תסף תת כחה": **נע ונד.** אין לך רשות לדור במקום אחד:

יג **גדול עוני מנשוא.** בתמיה, אתה טוען עליונים ותחתונים ועוני אי אפשר לטעון?!:

טו **לכן כל הרג קין.** זה אחד מן המקראות שקצרו דבריהם ורמזו ולא פרשו: "לכן כל הרג קין" לשון גערה, כה יעשה לו, כך וכך ענשו, ולא פרש ענשו: **שבעתים יקם.** איני רוצה להנקם מקין עכשיו, לסוף שבעה דורות אני נוקם נקמתי ממנו, שיעמד למך מבני בניו ויהרגהו. וסוף המקרא שאמר: "שבעתים יקם", והיא נקמת הבל מקין, הוא למדנו שתחלת מקרא לשון גערה היא שלא תהא בריה מזיקתו. וכיוצא בו: "ויאמר דוד... כל מכה יבסי ויגע בצנור" (שמואל ב' ה, ח) ולא פרש מה יעשה לו, אבל דבר הכתוב ברמז: כל מכה יבוסי ויגע בצנור ויקרב אל השער ויכבשנו, "ואת העורים" וגו', וגם אותם יכה על אשר אמרו העור והפסח: לא יבא דוד אל תוך הבית; המכה את אלו אני אעשנו ראש ושר. כאן קצר דבריו, ובדברי הימים (א' יא, ו) פרש: "יהיה לראש ולשר": **וישם ה' לקין אות.** חקק לו אות משמו במצחו:

טז **ויצא קין.** יצא בהכנעה כגונב דעת העליונה: **בארץ נוד.** בארץ שכל הגולים נדים שם: **קדמת עדן.** שם גלה אביו כשגרש מגן עדן, שנאמר: "וישכן מקדם לגן עדן" (לעיל ג, כד) את שמירת דרך מבוא הגן – יש לך ללמד שהיה אדם שם. ומצינו רוח מזרחית קולטת בכל מקום את הרוצחים: "אז יבדיל משה וגו' מזרחה שמש" (דברים ד, מח). דבר אחר, "בארץ נוד", כל מקום שהולך היתה הארץ מזדעזעת מתחתיו, והבריות אומרות: סורו מעליו, זהו שהרג את אחיו:

the God of peace, hated in the name of the God of love, and practiced cruelty in the name of the God of compassion. When this happens, God speaks, sometimes in a still, small voice almost inaudible beneath the clamor of those claiming to speak on His behalf. What He says at such times is: *Not in My Name.*

ט בַּשָּׂדֶה וַיָּקָם קַיִן אֶל־הֶבֶל אָחִיו וַיַּהַרְגֵהוּ: וַיֹּאמֶר יהוה אֶל־קַיִן
י אֵי הֶבֶל אָחִיךָ וַיֹּאמֶר לֹא יָדַעְתִּי הֲשֹׁמֵר אָחִי אָנֹכִי: וַיֹּאמֶר מֶה
יא עָשִׂיתָ קוֹל דְּמֵי אָחִיךָ צֹעֲקִים אֵלַי מִן־הָאֲדָמָה: וְעַתָּה אָרוּר
אָתָּה מִן־הָאֲדָמָה אֲשֶׁר פָּצְתָה אֶת־פִּיהָ לָקַחַת אֶת־דְּמֵי אָחִיךָ
יב מִיָּדֶךָ: כִּי תַעֲבֹד אֶת־הָאֲדָמָה לֹא־תֹסֵף תֵּת־כֹּחָהּ לָךְ נָע וָנָד תִּהְיֶה
יג יד בָאָרֶץ: וַיֹּאמֶר קַיִן אֶל־יהוה גָּדוֹל עֲוֺנִי מִנְּשֹׂא: הֵן גֵּרַשְׁתָּ אֹתִי
הַיּוֹם מֵעַל פְּנֵי הָאֲדָמָה וּמִפָּנֶיךָ אֶסָּתֵר וְהָיִיתִי נָע וָנָד בָּאָרֶץ וְהָיָה
טו כָל־מֹצְאִי יַהַרְגֵנִי: וַיֹּאמֶר לוֹ יהוה לָכֵן כָּל־הֹרֵג קַיִן שִׁבְעָתַיִם יֻקָּם
טז וַיָּשֶׂם יהוה לְקַיִן אוֹת לְבִלְתִּי הַכּוֹת־אֹתוֹ כָּל־מֹצְאוֹ: וַיֵּצֵא קַיִן
יז מִלִּפְנֵי יהוה וַיֵּשֶׁב בְּאֶרֶץ־נוֹד קִדְמַת־עֵדֶן: וַיֵּדַע קַיִן אֶת־אִשְׁתּוֹ

אונקלוס

בְּחַקְלָא, וְקָם קַיִן, עַל הֶבֶל אֲחוּהִי וְקַטְלֵיהּ: ט וַאֲמַר יי לְקַיִן, אָן הֶבֶל
אֲחוּךְ, וַאֲמַר לָא יְדַעְנָא, הֲנָטַר אֲחִי אֲנָא: י וַאֲמַר מָא עֲבַדְתָּא,
קָל דַּם זַרְעִין דַּעֲתִידִין לְמִפַּק מִן אֲחוּךְ, קָבְלִין קֳדָמַי מִן אַרְעָא:
יא וּכְעַן לִיט אַתְּ, מִן אַרְעָא דִּפְתַחַת יָת פֻּמַּהּ, וְקַבִּילַת, יָת דְּמָא
דַּאֲחוּךְ מִן יְדָךְ: יב אֲרֵי תִפְלַח בְּאַרְעָא, לָא תוֹסִיף לְמִתַּן חֵילַהּ
לָךְ, מְטַלְטַל וְגָלֵי תְּהֵי בְאַרְעָא: יג וַאֲמַר קַיִן קֳדָם יי, סַגִּי חוֹבִי
מִלְּמִשְׁבַּק: יד הָא תָרֵיכְתָּא יָתִי יוֹמָא דֵין, מֵעַל אַפֵּי אַרְעָא, וּמִן
קֳדָמָךְ לֵית אֶפְשָׁר לְאִטְּמָרָא, וְאֵיהֵי, מְטַלְטַל וְגָלֵי בְּאַרְעָא, וִיהֵי כָּל
דְּיִשְׁכְּחִנַּנִי יִקְטְלִנַּנִי: טו וַאֲמַר לֵיהּ יי, לְכֵן כָּל קָטוֹלָא קַיִן, לְשִׁבְעָא
דָרִין יִתְפְּרַע מִנֵּיהּ, וְשַׁוִּי יי לְקַיִן אָתָא, בְּדִיל דְּלָא לְמִקְטַל יָתֵיהּ
כָּל דְּיִשְׁכְּחִנֵּיהּ: טז וּנְפַק קַיִן מִן קֳדָם יי, וִיתֵיב בַּאֲרַע גָּלֵי וּמְטַלְטַל
דַּהֲוָת עֲבִידָא עֲלוֹהִי מִלְּקַדְמִין כְּגִנְּתָא דְעֵדֶן: יז וִידַע קַיִן יָת אִתְּתֵיהּ,

inarticulate. If we can speak together, we will be able to live together. Speech heals hate; silence incubates it. Such is the verdict of Jewish narrative and law.

THE FIRST MURDER

That the Bible is preoccupied by violence is evident at the outset and it is a central theme in Genesis.

"If you act well, will you not be uplifted? If you fail to act well, sin is crouching at the door." This is God's warning to Kayin as soon as he feels the stirrings of anger. We have a disposition to do wrong, for we are driven by our desires. Other people also have desires. Sometimes both cannot be satisfied. The other stands in my way. So I am faced with a choice. Do I regard the other as an obstacle to be overridden or removed? Or do I recognize his or her integrity as another person with the same desires and rights as mine? Kayin chooses the first, and kills Hevel. Challenged by God, he replies, "Am I my brother's keeper?" meaning: "Am I responsible for his fate?" The road from denial of responsibility to violence and murder is slippery and short.

This, however, is not all. The first murder follows directly from the offerings brought by Kayin and Hevel, the first recorded act of worship. The connection between religion and violence is struck at the start.

Too often in the history of religion, people have killed in the name of the God of life, waged war in the name of

18 He built a city, naming it Ḥanokh after his son. Ḥanokh had a son Irad, and
Irad had a son Meḥuyael. Meḥiyael had a son Metushael, and Metushael had
19 a son Lemekh. Lemekh married two women, one named Ada and the other HAMISHI
20 Tzila. Ada gave birth to Yaval. He was the ancestor of those who live in tents
21 and raise livestock. His brother's name was Yuval. He was the ancestor of all
22 those who play the lyre and the pipe. Tzila, too, had a son, Tuval-Kayin, who
forged all kinds of bronze and iron tools. Tuval-Kayin's sister was Naama.
23 Lemekh said to his wives: "Ada and Tzila, listen to my voice; wives of Lemekh,
heed my words. I killed a man for wounding me, killed a boy for bruising
24 me. If Kayin will be avenged seven times, then Lemekh, seventy-seven."
25 Adam knew his wife again, and she gave birth to a son and named him Shet,
"because God has granted me another child in place of Hevel," for Kayin had

רש״י

יז **וַיְהִי.** קַיִן בֹּנֶה עִיר, וַיִּקְרָא שֵׁם הָעִיר לְזֵכֶר בְּנוֹ חֲנוֹךְ:

יח **וְעִירָד יָלַד.** יֵשׁ מָקוֹם שֶׁהוּא אוֹמֵר בְּזָכָר ׳הוֹלִיד׳ וְיֵשׁ מָקוֹם שֶׁהוּא אוֹמֵר ׳יָלַד׳, שֶׁהַלֵּדָה מְשַׁמֶּשֶׁת שְׁתֵּי לְשׁוֹנוֹת, לֵדַת הָאִשָּׁה נייסטר״א בְּלַעַז, וּזְרִיעַת תּוֹלְדוֹת הָאִישׁ אינייינדרי״ר בְּלַעַז; כְּשֶׁהוּא אוֹמֵר ׳הוֹלִיד׳ בִּלְשׁוֹן הִפְעִיל, מְדַבֵּר בְּלֵדַת הָאִשָּׁה, פְּלוֹנִי הוֹלִיד אֶת אִשְׁתּוֹ בֵּן אוֹ בַת, כְּשֶׁהוּא אוֹמֵר ׳יָלַד׳ מְדַבֵּר בִּזְרִיעַת הָאִישׁ:

יט **וַיִּקַּח לוֹ לֶמֶךְ.** לֹא הָיָה לוֹ לְפָרֵשׁ כָּל זֶה, אֶלָּא לְלַמְּדֵנוּ מִסּוֹף הָעִנְיָן שֶׁקִּיֵּם הַקָּדוֹשׁ בָּרוּךְ הוּא הַבְטָחָתוֹ שֶׁאָמַר: ״שִׁבְעָתַיִם יֻקַּם קָיִן״, עָמַד לֶמֶךְ לְאַחַר שֶׁהוֹלִיד בָּנִים וְעָשָׂה דּוֹר שְׁבִיעִי וְהָרַג אֶת קַיִן. זֶהוּ שֶׁאָמַר: ״כִּי אִישׁ הָרַגְתִּי לְפִצְעִי״ וְגוֹ׳: **שְׁתֵּי נָשִׁים.** כָּךְ הָיָה דַּרְכָּן שֶׁל דּוֹר הַמַּבּוּל, אַחַת לִפְרִיָּה וּרְבִיָּה וְאַחַת לְתַשְׁמִישׁ. זוֹ שֶׁהִיא לְתַשְׁמִישׁ מַשְׁקָהּ כּוֹס שֶׁל עִקָּרִין כְּדֵי שֶׁתֵּעָקֵר, וּמְקֻשֶּׁטֶת כְּכַלָּה וּמַאֲכִילָהּ מַעֲדַנִּים, וַחֲבֶרְתָּהּ נְזוּפָה וַאֲבֵלָה כְּאַלְמָנָה, וְזֶהוּ שֶׁפֵּרֵשׁ אִיּוֹב (כד, כא): ״רֹעֶה עֲקָרָה לֹא תֵלֵד וְאַלְמָנָה לֹא יְיֵטִיב״, כְּמוֹ שֶׁמְּפֹרָשׁ בְּאַגָּדַת ׳חֵלֶק׳. **עָדָה.** הִיא שֶׁל פְּרִיָּה וּרְבִיָּה, עַל שֵׁם שֶׁמְּגֻנָּה עָלָיו וּמוּסֶרֶת מֵאֶצְלוֹ, ״עָדָה״ תַּרְגּוּם שֶׁל סוּרָה: **צִלָּה.** הִיא שֶׁל תַּשְׁמִישׁ, עַל שֵׁם שֶׁיּוֹשֶׁבֶת תָּמִיד בְּצִלּוֹ. דִּבְרֵי אַגָּדָה הֵם בִּבְרֵאשִׁית רַבָּה (כג, ב):

כ **אֲבִי יֹשֵׁב אֹהֶל וּמִקְנֶה.** הוּא הָיָה הָרִאשׁוֹן לְרוֹעֵי בְּהֵמוֹת בַּמִּדְבָּרוֹת, וְיוֹשֵׁב אֹהָלִים חֹדֶשׁ כָּאן וְחֹדֶשׁ כָּאן; כְּשֶׁכָּלֶה הַמִּרְעֶה לְצֹאנוֹ בְּמָקוֹם זֶה הוֹלֵךְ וְתוֹקֵעַ אָהֳלוֹ בְּמָקוֹם אַחֵר. וּמִדְרַשׁ אַגָּדָה: בּוֹנֶה בָּתִּים לַעֲבוֹדָה זָרָה, כְּמָה דְּאַתְּ אָמַר: ״סֵמֶל הַקִּנְאָה הַמַּקְנֶה״ (יחזקאל ח, ג), וְכֵן אָחִיו ״תֹּפֵשׂ כִּנּוֹר וְעוּגָב״ לְזַמֵּר לַעֲבוֹדָה זָרָה:

כב **תּוּבַל קַיִן.** לְשׁוֹן תַּבְלִין, תִּבֵּל וְהִתְקִין אֻמָּנוּתוֹ שֶׁל קַיִן לַעֲשׂוֹת כְּלֵי זַיִן לָרוֹצְחִים: **לֹטֵשׁ כָּל חֹרֵשׁ נְחֹשֶׁת וּבַרְזֶל.** מְחַדֵּד אֻמָּנוּת נְחֹשֶׁת וּבַרְזֶל, כְּמוֹ: ״יִלְטוֹשׁ עֵינָיו לִי״ (איוב טז, ט). ׳חֹרֵשׁ׳ אֵינוֹ לְשׁוֹן פֹּעֵל, אֶלָּא לְשׁוֹן פּוֹעֵל, שֶׁהֲרֵי נָקוּד קָמַץ (צירי) וְטַעְמוֹ לְמַטָּה, כְּלוֹמַר מְחַדֵּד וּמְתַקֵּן כָּל כְּלֵי אֻמָּנוּת נְחֹשֶׁת וּבַרְזֶל: **נַעֲמָה.** הִיא אִשְׁתּוֹ שֶׁל נֹחַ. בִּבְרֵאשִׁית רַבָּה (כג, ג):

כג-כד **שְׁמַעַן קוֹלִי.** שֶׁהָיוּ נָשָׁיו פּוֹרְשׁוֹת מִמֶּנּוּ מִתַּשְׁמִישׁ לְפִי שֶׁהָרַג אֶת קַיִן וְאֶת תּוּבַל קַיִן בְּנוֹ, שֶׁהָיָה לֶמֶךְ סוּמָא וְתוּבַל קַיִן מוֹשְׁכוֹ, וְרָאָה אֶת קַיִן וְנִדְמָה לוֹ כְּחַיָּה, וְאָמַר לְאָבִיו לִמְשֹׁךְ בַּקֶּשֶׁת, וַהֲרָגוֹ. וְכֵיוָן שֶׁיָּדַע שֶׁהוּא קַיִן זְקֵנוֹ הִכָּה כַּף אֶל כַּף וְסָפַק אֶת בְּנוֹ בֵּינֵיהֶן וַהֲרָגוֹ. וְהָיוּ נָשָׁיו פּוֹרְשׁוֹת מִמֶּנּוּ וְהוּא מְפַיְּסָן: ״שְׁמַעַן קוֹלִי״ לְהִשָּׁמַע לִי; וְכִי ״אִישׁ״ אֲשֶׁר ״הָרַגְתִּי, לְפִצְעִי״ הוּא נֶהֱרַג? וְכִי אֲנִי פְּצַעְתִּיו מֵזִיד שֶׁיְּהֵא הַפֶּצַע קָרוּי עַל שְׁמִי? ״וְיֶלֶד״ אֲשֶׁר הָרַגְתִּי, ״לְחַבֻּרָתִי״ נֶהֱרַג? כְּלוֹמַר עַל יְדֵי חַבּוּרָתִי? בִּתְמִיָּה; וַהֲלֹא שׁוֹגֵג אֲנִי, לֹא זֶהוּ פִּצְעִי וְלֹא זֶהוּ חַבּוּרָתִי. פֶּצַע – מַכַּת חֶרֶב אוֹ חֵץ, נברידור״א בְּלַעַז: **כִּי שִׁבְעָתַיִם יֻקַּם קָיִן.** קַיִן שֶׁהָרַג מֵזִיד נִתְלָה לוֹ עַד שִׁבְעָה דּוֹרוֹת, אֲנִי שֶׁהָרַגְתִּי שׁוֹגֵג כָּל שֶׁכֵּן שֶׁיִּתָּלֶה לִי שְׁבִיעִיּוֹת הַרְבֵּה: **שִׁבְעִים וְשִׁבְעָה.** לְשׁוֹן רִבּוּי שְׁבִיעִיּוֹת אָחַז לוֹ, כָּךְ דָּרַשׁ רַבִּי תַּנְחוּמָא (יא). וּמִדְרַשׁ בְּרֵאשִׁית רַבָּה: לֹא הָרַג לֶמֶךְ כְּלוּם, וְנָשָׁיו פּוֹרְשׁוֹת מִמֶּנּוּ מִשֶּׁקִּיְּמוּ פְּרִיָּה וּרְבִיָּה, לְפִי שֶׁנִּגְזְרָה גְּזֵרָה לְכַלּוֹת זַרְעוֹ שֶׁל קַיִן לְשִׁבְעָה דוֹרוֹת, אָמְרוּ: מָה אָנוּ יוֹלְדוֹת לַבֶּהָלָה? לְמָחָר הַמַּבּוּל בָּא וְשׁוֹטֵף אֶת הַכֹּל. וְהוּא אוֹמֵר לָהֶן: ״וְכִי אִישׁ הָרַגְתִּי לְפִצְעִי״? וְכִי אֲנִי הָרַגְתִּי אֶת הֶבֶל שֶׁהוּא אִישׁ בְּקוֹמָה וְיֶלֶד בְּשָׁנִים שֶׁיְּהֵא זַרְעִי כָּלֶה בְּאוֹתוֹ עָוֹן? וּמַה קַּיִן שֶׁהָרַג, נִתְלוּ לוֹ שִׁבְעָה דוֹרוֹת, אֲנִי שֶׁלֹּא הָרַגְתִּי לֹא כָּל שֶׁכֵּן שֶׁיִּתָּלוּ לִי שְׁבִיעִיּוֹת הַרְבֵּה? וְזֶהוּ קַל וָחֹמֶר שֶׁל שְׁטוּת, אִם כֵּן אֵין הַקָּדוֹשׁ בָּרוּךְ הוּא גּוֹבֶה אֶת חוֹבוֹ וּמְקַיֵּם אֶת דְּבָרוֹ:

כה **וַיֵּדַע אָדָם וְגוֹ׳.** בָּא לוֹ לֶמֶךְ אֵצֶל אָדָם הָרִאשׁוֹן וְקָבַל עַל נָשָׁיו.

וַתַּהַר וַתֵּלֶד אֶת־חֲנוֹךְ וַיְהִי בֹּנֶה עִיר וַיִּקְרָא שֵׁם הָעִיר כְּשֵׁם בְּנוֹ
יח חֲנוֹךְ: וַיִּוָּלֵד לַחֲנוֹךְ אֶת־עִירָד וְעִירָד יָלַד אֶת־מְחוּיָאֵל וּמְחִיָּיאֵל
יט יָלַד אֶת־מְתוּשָׁאֵל וּמְתוּשָׁאֵל יָלַד אֶת־לָמֶךְ: וַיִּקַּח־לוֹ לֶמֶךְ שְׁתֵּי חמישי
כ נָשִׁים שֵׁם הָאַחַת עָדָה וְשֵׁם הַשֵּׁנִית צִלָּה: וַתֵּלֶד עָדָה אֶת־יָבָל
כא הוּא הָיָה אֲבִי יֹשֵׁב אֹהֶל וּמִקְנֶה: וְשֵׁם אָחִיו יוּבָל הוּא הָיָה אֲבִי
כב כָּל־תֹּפֵשׂ כִּנּוֹר וְעוּגָב: וְצִלָּה גַם־הִוא יָלְדָה אֶת־תּוּבַל קַיִן לֹטֵשׁ
כג כָּל־חֹרֵשׁ נְחֹשֶׁת וּבַרְזֶל וַאֲחוֹת תּוּבַל־קַיִן נַעֲמָה: וַיֹּאמֶר לֶמֶךְ לְנָשָׁיו
עָדָה וְצִלָּה שְׁמַעַן קוֹלִי נְשֵׁי לֶמֶךְ הַאְזֵנָּה אִמְרָתִי כִּי אִישׁ הָרַגְתִּי
כד לְפִצְעִי וְיֶלֶד לְחַבֻּרָתִי: כִּי שִׁבְעָתַיִם יֻקַּם־קָיִן וְלֶמֶךְ שִׁבְעִים וְשִׁבְעָה:
כה וַיֵּדַע אָדָם עוֹד אֶת־אִשְׁתּוֹ וַתֵּלֶד בֵּן וַתִּקְרָא אֶת־שְׁמוֹ שֵׁת כִּי שָׁת־לִי

אונקלוס

וְעַדִּיאַת וִילֵידַת יָת חֲנוֹךְ, וַהֲוָה בָּנֵי קַרְתָּא, וּקְרָא שְׁמַהּ דְּקַרְתָּא,
כְּשׁוּם בְּרֵיהּ חֲנוֹךְ: יח וְאִתְיְלֵיד לַחֲנוֹךְ יָת עִירָד, וְעִירָד, אוֹלֵיד יָת
מְחוּיָאֵל, וּמְחִיָּיאֵל, אוֹלֵיד יָת מְתוּשָׁאֵל, וּמְתוּשָׁאֵל אוֹלֵיד יָת לָמֶךְ:
יט וּנְסֵיב לֵיהּ לֶמֶךְ תַּרְתֵּין נְשִׁין, שׁוּם חֲדָא עָדָה, וְשׁוּם תִּנְיֵיתָא צִלָּה:
כ וִילֵידַת עָדָה יָת יָבָל, הוּא הֲוָה, רִבְּהוֹן, דְּיָתְבֵי מַשְׁכְּנִין וּמָרֵי בְּעִיר:
כא וְשׁוּם אֲחוּהִי יוּבָל, הוּא הֲוָה, רִבְּהוֹן, דְּכָל דִּמְנַגַּן עַל פּוּם נִבְלָא
יָדְעֵי זְמַר כִּנָּרָא וַאֲבוּבָא: כב וְצִלָּה אַף הִיא, יְלֵידַת יָת תּוּבַל קַיִן, הוּא
הֲוָה, רִבְּהוֹן, דְּכָל דְּיָדְעֵי עֲבִידַת נְחָשָׁא וּבַרְזְלָא, וַאֲחָתֵיהּ דְּתוּבַל
קַיִן נַעֲמָה: כג וַאֲמַר לֶמֶךְ לִנְשׁוֹהִי, עָדָה וְצִלָּה שְׁמַעָא קָלִי, נְשֵׁי לֶמֶךְ,
אַצִּיתָא לְמֵימְרִי, לָא גְבָרָא קְטֵלִית דְּבְדִילֵיהּ אֲנָא סָבֵיל חוֹבִין לְמֶמֶת,
וְאַף לָא עוּלֵימָא חַבֵּילִית דִּבְדִילֵיהּ יִשְׁתֵּיצֵי זַרְעִי: כד אֲרֵי שִׁבְעָא דָרִין
אִתְלִיאוּ לְקָיִן, הֲלָא לְלֶמֶךְ בְּרֵיהּ שִׁבְעִין וְשִׁבְעָא: כה וִידַע אָדָם עוֹד
יָת אִתְּתֵיהּ, וִילֵידַת בַּר, וּקְרַת יָת שְׁמֵיהּ שֵׁת, אֲרֵי אֲמַרַת, יְהַב לִי

4:19 לֶמֶךְ *Lemekh* – Among Lemekh's family's prodigious achievements, only his song, which tells us of the violence becoming endemic in human society, earns more than a few words. The Hebrew Bible is uninterested in *Homo sapiens* the biological species. It is even relatively uninterested in *Homo faber*, the tool-making, environment-changing life-form. And so it passes over, in short order, Yaval, "the ancestor of those who live in tents and raise livestock," Yuval, "the ancestor of all those who play the lyre and the pipe," and Tuval-Kayin, who "forged all kinds of bronze and iron tools." It is interested exclusively in *Homo religious*, the first humans to hear and respond to the divine voice.

4:24 **וְלֶמֶךְ שִׁבְעִים וְשִׁבְעָה** *Lemekh, seventy-seven* – Early societies, René Girard has argued, did not yet have a legal system – laws, courts, prisons, and punishments – to enforce order. Instead they practiced reciprocity, the rule of tit for tat. They acted generously to others until they encountered a hostile response. They then did to the others what the others had done to them.

The trouble with this strategy is that it gives rise to potentially endless cycles of retaliation. It begins with a single act of murder. This sets in motion a blood feud, vendetta, or clan war. Short of mass assassination, there is no natural end to this cycle of retaliation.

15 ten years, and then he died. Mahalalel lived sixty-five years and had a
16 son, Yered. After Yered was born, Mahalalel lived eight hundred and thirty years
17 and had other sons and daughters. Altogether, Mahalalel lived eight hundred
18 and ninety-five years, and then he died. Yered lived one hundred
19 and sixty-two years and had a son, Ḥanokh. After Ḥanokh was born, Yered
20 lived eight hundred years and had other sons and daughters. Altogether, Yered
21 lived nine hundred and sixty-two years, and then he died. Ḥanokh
22 lived sixty-five years and had a son, Metushelaḥ. Ḥanokh walked faithfully with
God for three hundred years after Metushelaḥ was born, and had other sons
23 and daughters. Altogether, Ḥanokh lived for three hundred and sixty-five years.
24 Ḥanokh walked faithfully with God and then he was no more, for God took
25 him. Metushelaḥ lived one hundred and eighty-seven years and had SHEVI'I
26 a son, Lemekh. After Lemekh was born, Metushelaḥ lived seven hundred and
27 eighty-two years and had other sons and daughters. Altogether, Metushelaḥ
28 lived nine hundred and sixty-nine years, and then he died. Lemekh
29 lived one hundred and eighty-two years and had a son. He named him Noaḥ,
saying, "This one will bring us comfort after all our labor and the sorrow of
30 our hands on the land the Lord has cursed." After Noaḥ was born, Lemekh

רש״י

כד **ויתהלך חנוך.** צדיק היה וקל בדעתו לשוב להרשיע, לפיכך מהר הקדוש ברוך הוא וסלקו והמיתו קודם זמנו, וזהו ששנה הכתוב במיתתו, לכתב: "ואיננו" בעולם למלאות שנותיו: **כי לקח אתו.** לפני זמנו, כמו: "הנני לקח ממך את מחמד עיניך" (יחזקאל כד, טז):

כח **ויולד בן.** שממנו נבנה העולם:

כט **זה ינחמנו.** ינח ממנו את עצבון ידינו. עד שלא בא נח לא היה להם כלי מחרשה והוא הכין להם, והיתה הארץ מוציאה קוצים ודרדרים כשזורעים חטים, מקללתו של אדם הראשון, ובימי נח נחה, וזה 'ינחמנו' – ינח ממנו. ואם לא תפרשהו כך, אין טעם הלשון נופל על השם, ואתה צריך לקרות שמו מנחם:

5:29 **זה ינחמנו** *This one will bring us comfort* – There is something not quite right here. The root *n-ḥ-m* (for "comfort") does not yield the name Noaḥ but *Menaḥem*. The name Noaḥ comes from the word that means "to rest." Complex resonances are being set up. Noaḥ is the man who rests when he should act, for when disaster threatens the world he saves himself and his family, no one else. The text also contains a wordplay lost in translation. Noaḥ's Hebrew name, the two letters *nun-ḥet*, is an exact reversal of the word *ḥet-nun*, "grace, favor," a key word in the story: "Noaḥ found *favor* in the Lord's sight" (Gen. 6:8). Noaḥ's grace is ambivalent, his life a reversal. Most significantly, the word used by Lemekh at Noaḥ's birth, *nun-ḥet-mem*, reappears later in the story with the opposite meaning to that which Lemekh intended: "The Lord saw how great man's wickedness was upon the earth, and that his thoughts constantly inclined toward evil. Then the Lord regretted [*vayinaḥem*] that He had made man on earth, and His heart was touched with sorrow" (6:5–6). *Nun-ḥet-mem* turns out to be a contronym. It means "relief" but also "regret," comfort but also discomfort. Noaḥ does bring relief from man's work, but it is the release found in death. Not only does Noaḥ fail to lift God's curse upon the land, he lives through the worst curse of all. Noaḥ's greatness is also his weakness. Avraham is to begin his service of God by moving, leaving home, and traveling to a distant land. Noaḥ's gift is that, living through a time of widespread evil, he is not

טו שָׁנָה וַיָּמֹת׃ וַיְחִי מַהֲלַלְאֵל חָמֵשׁ שָׁנִים וְשִׁשִּׁים שָׁנָה
טז וַיּוֹלֶד אֶת־יָרֶד׃ וַיְחִי מַהֲלַלְאֵל אַחֲרֵי הוֹלִידוֹ אֶת־יֶרֶד שְׁלֹשִׁים שָׁנָה
יז וּשְׁמֹנֶה מֵאוֹת שָׁנָה וַיּוֹלֶד בָּנִים וּבָנוֹת׃ וַיִּהְיוּ כָּל־יְמֵי מַהֲלַלְאֵל חָמֵשׁ
יח וְתִשְׁעִים שָׁנָה וּשְׁמֹנֶה מֵאוֹת שָׁנָה וַיָּמֹת׃ וַיְחִי־יֶרֶד שְׁתַּיִם
יט וְשִׁשִּׁים שָׁנָה וּמְאַת שָׁנָה וַיּוֹלֶד אֶת־חֲנוֹךְ׃ וַיְחִי־יֶרֶד אַחֲרֵי הוֹלִידוֹ
כ אֶת־חֲנוֹךְ שְׁמֹנֶה מֵאוֹת שָׁנָה וַיּוֹלֶד בָּנִים וּבָנוֹת׃ וַיִּהְיוּ כָּל־יְמֵי־יֶרֶד
כא שְׁתַּיִם וְשִׁשִּׁים שָׁנָה וּתְשַׁע מֵאוֹת שָׁנָה וַיָּמֹת׃ וַיְחִי חֲנוֹךְ
כב חָמֵשׁ וְשִׁשִּׁים שָׁנָה וַיּוֹלֶד אֶת־מְתוּשָׁלַח׃ וַיִּתְהַלֵּךְ חֲנוֹךְ אֶת־הָאֱלֹהִים
אַחֲרֵי הוֹלִידוֹ אֶת־מְתוּשֶׁלַח שְׁלֹשׁ מֵאוֹת שָׁנָה וַיּוֹלֶד בָּנִים וּבָנוֹת׃
כג כד וַיְהִי כָּל־יְמֵי חֲנוֹךְ חָמֵשׁ וְשִׁשִּׁים שָׁנָה וּשְׁלֹשׁ מֵאוֹת שָׁנָה׃ וַיִּתְהַלֵּךְ
כה חֲנוֹךְ אֶת־הָאֱלֹהִים וְאֵינֶנּוּ כִּי־לָקַח אֹתוֹ אֱלֹהִים׃ וַיְחִי שביעי
כו מְתוּשֶׁלַח שֶׁבַע וּשְׁמֹנִים שָׁנָה וּמְאַת שָׁנָה וַיּוֹלֶד אֶת־לָמֶךְ׃ וַיְחִי
מְתוּשֶׁלַח אַחֲרֵי הוֹלִידוֹ אֶת־לֶמֶךְ שְׁתַּיִם וּשְׁמוֹנִים שָׁנָה וּשְׁבַע מֵאוֹת
כז שָׁנָה וַיּוֹלֶד בָּנִים וּבָנוֹת׃ וַיִּהְיוּ כָּל־יְמֵי מְתוּשֶׁלַח תֵּשַׁע וְשִׁשִּׁים שָׁנָה
כח וּתְשַׁע מֵאוֹת שָׁנָה וַיָּמֹת׃ וַיְחִי־לֶמֶךְ שְׁתַּיִם וּשְׁמֹנִים
כט שָׁנָה וּמְאַת שָׁנָה וַיּוֹלֶד בֵּן׃ וַיִּקְרָא אֶת־שְׁמוֹ נֹחַ לֵאמֹר זֶה יְנַחֲמֵנוּ
ל מִמַּעֲשֵׂנוּ וּמֵעִצְּבוֹן יָדֵינוּ מִן־הָאֲדָמָה אֲשֶׁר אֵרְרָהּ יהוה׃ וַיְחִי־לֶמֶךְ

אונקלוס

שְׁנִין, וּמִית: טו וַחֲיָא מַהֲלַלְאֵל, שִׁתִּין וַחֲמֵשׁ שְׁנִין, וְאוֹלֵיד יָת יָרֶד: טז וַחֲיָא מַהֲלַלְאֵל, בָּתַר דְּאוֹלֵיד יָת יֶרֶד, תַּמְנֵי מְאָה וּתְלָתִין שְׁנִין, וְאוֹלֵיד בְּנִין וּבְנָן: יז וַהֲווֹ כָּל יוֹמֵי מַהֲלַלְאֵל, תַּמְנֵי מְאָה וְתִשְׁעִין וַחֲמֵשׁ שְׁנִין, וּמִית: יח וַחֲיָא יֶרֶד, מְאָה וְשִׁתִּין וְתַרְתֵּין שְׁנִין, וְאוֹלֵיד יָת חֲנוֹךְ: יט וַחֲיָא יֶרֶד, בָּתַר דְּאוֹלֵיד יָת חֲנוֹךְ, תַּמְנֵי מְאָה שְׁנִין, וְאוֹלֵיד בְּנִין וּבְנָן: כ וַהֲווֹ כָּל יוֹמֵי יֶרֶד, תְּשַׁע מְאָה וְשִׁתִּין וְתַרְתֵּין שְׁנִין, וּמִית: כא וַחֲיָא חֲנוֹךְ, שִׁתִּין וַחֲמֵשׁ שְׁנִין, וְאוֹלֵיד יָת מְתוּשְׁלַח: כב וְהַלֵּיךְ חֲנוֹךְ בְּדַחַלְתָּא דַּייָ, בָּתַר דְּאוֹלֵיד יָת מְתוּשֶׁלַח, תְּלָת מְאָה שְׁנִין, וְאוֹלֵיד בְּנִין וּבְנָן: כג וַהֲווֹ כָּל יוֹמֵי חֲנוֹךְ, תְּלָת מְאָה וְשִׁתִּין וַחֲמֵשׁ שְׁנִין: כד וְהַלֵּיךְ חֲנוֹךְ בְּדַחַלְתָּא דַּייָ, וְלַיְתוֹהִי, אֲרֵי לָא אֲמֵית יָתֵיהּ יְיָ: כה וַחֲיָא מְתוּשֶׁלַח, מְאָה וּתְמָנַן וּשְׁבַע שְׁנִין, וְאוֹלֵיד יָת לָמֶךְ: כו וַחֲיָא מְתוּשֶׁלַח, בָּתַר דְּאוֹלֵיד יָת לֶמֶךְ, שְׁבַע מְאָה וּתְמָנַן וְתַרְתֵּין שְׁנִין, וְאוֹלֵיד בְּנִין וּבְנָן: כז וַהֲווֹ כָּל יוֹמֵי מְתוּשֶׁלַח, תְּשַׁע מְאָה וְשִׁתִּין וּתְשַׁע שְׁנִין, וּמִית: כח וַחֲיָא לֶמֶךְ, מְאָה וּתְמָנַן וְתַרְתֵּין שְׁנִין, וְאוֹלֵיד בַּר: כט וּקְרָא יָת שְׁמֵיהּ, נֹחַ לְמֵימַר, דֵּין, יְנַחֲמִנַּנָא מֵעוּבָדַנָא וּמִלֵּיאוּת יְדַנָא, מִן אַרְעָא, דְּלַטַהּ יְיָ: ל וַחֲיָא לֶמֶךְ,

lived five hundred and ninety-five years and had other sons and daughters.
31 Altogether, Lemekh lived seven hundred and seventy-seven years, and then
32 he died. After Noaḥ was five hundred years old, Noaḥ had three sons:
6 1 Shem, Ḥam, and Yefet. Humans began to multiply on earth, and daughters
2 were born to them. When the sons of God saw that the daughters of man were
3 lovely, they began to take whomever they chose to be wives to them. Then the
LORD said, "My spirit will not forever judge man; he is of flesh. His life shall be
4 but one hundred and twenty years." In those days the Nefilim were on earth,
and later also, for the sons of God had gone to the daughters of man and had
children with them. These were the heroes of old, men of legends.
5 The LORD saw how great man's wickedness was upon the earth, and that his MAFTIR
6 thoughts constantly inclined toward evil. Then the LORD regretted that He had

רש״י

לב **בֶּן חֲמֵשׁ מֵאוֹת שָׁנָה.** אָמַר רַבִּי יוּדָן: מַה טַּעַם כָּל הַדּוֹרוֹת הוֹלִידוּ לְמֵאָה שָׁנָה וְזֶה לַחֲמֵשׁ מֵאוֹת? אָמַר הַקָּדוֹשׁ בָּרוּךְ הוּא: אִם רְשָׁעִים הֵם יֹאבְדוּ בַּמַּיִם וְרַע לְצַדִּיק זֶה, וְאִם צַדִּיקִים הֵם אַטְרִיחַ עָלָיו לַעֲשׂוֹת תֵּבוֹת הַרְבֵּה, כָּבַשׁ אֶת מַעְיָנוֹ וְלֹא הוֹלִיד עַד חֲמֵשׁ מֵאוֹת שָׁנָה, כְּדֵי שֶׁלֹּא יְהֵא יֶפֶת הַגָּדוֹל שֶׁבְּבָנָיו רָאוּי לָעֳנָשִׁין לִפְנֵי הַמַּבּוּל, דִּכְתִיב: "כִּי הַנַּעַר בֶּן מֵאָה שָׁנָה יָמוּת" (ישעיה סה, כ) – רָאוּי לָעֹנֶשׁ לֶעָתִיד, וְכֵן לִפְנֵי מַתַּן תּוֹרָה: **אֶת שֵׁם אֶת חָם וְאֶת יָפֶת.** וַהֲלֹא יֶפֶת הַגָּדוֹל הוּא! אֶלָּא בַּתְּחִלָּה אַתָּה דּוֹרֵשׁ אֶת שֶׁהוּא צַדִּיק, וְנוֹלַד כְּשֶׁהוּא מָהוּל, וְשֶׁאַבְרָהָם יָצָא מִמֶּנּוּ וְכוּ׳. בִּבְרֵאשִׁית רַבָּה (כו, ג):

ו ב **בְּנֵי הָאֱלֹהִים.** בְּנֵי הַשָּׂרִים וְהַשּׁוֹפְטִים. דָּבָר אַחֵר, "בְּנֵי הָאֱלֹהִים", הֵם הַשָּׂרִים הַהוֹלְכִים בִּשְׁלִיחוּתוֹ שֶׁל מָקוֹם, אַף הֵם הָיוּ מִתְעָרְבִים בָּהֶם. כָּל 'אֱלֹהִים' שֶׁבַּמִּקְרָא לְשׁוֹן מָרוּת, וְזֶה יוֹכִיחַ: "וְאַתָּה תִּהְיֶה לּוֹ לֵאלֹהִים" (שמות ד, טז), "רְאֵה נְתַתִּיךָ אֱלֹהִים" (שם ז, א): **כִּי טֹבֹת הֵנָּה.** אָמַר רַבִּי יוּדָן: "טבת" כְּתִיב, מִשֶּׁהָיוּ מְטִיבִין אוֹתָהּ מְקֻשֶּׁטֶת לִכָּנֵס לַחֻפָּה, הָיָה גָּדוֹל נִכְנָס וּבוֹעֲלָהּ תְּחִלָּה: **מִכֹּל אֲשֶׁר בָּחָרוּ.** אַף בְּעוּלַת בַּעַל, אַף הַזָּכָר וְהַבְּהֵמָה:

ג **לֹא יָדוֹן רוּחִי בָאָדָם.** לֹא יִתְרַעֵם וְיָרִיב רוּחִי עָלַי בִּשְׁבִיל הָאָדָם: **לְעֹלָם.** לְאֹרֶךְ יָמִים; הִנֵּה רוּחִי נָדוֹן בְּקִרְבִּי אִם לְהַשְׁחִית וְאִם לְרַחֵם, לֹא יִהְיֶה מָדוֹן זֶה בְּרוּחִי לְעֹלָם, כְּלוֹמַר לְאֹרֶךְ יָמִים: **בְּשַׁגַּם הוּא בָשָׂר.** כְּמוֹ 'בְּשֶׁגַּם', כְּלוֹמַר בִּשְׁבִיל שֶׁגַּם זֹאת בּוֹ שֶׁהוּא בָּשָׂר וְאַף עַל פִּי כֵן אֵינוֹ נִכְנָע לְפָנַי, וּמָה אִם יִהְיֶה אֵשׁ אוֹ דָּבָר קָשֶׁה. כַּיּוֹצֵא בּוֹ: "עַד שַׁקַּמְתִּי דְּבוֹרָה" (שופטים ה, ז) כְּמוֹ 'שֶׁקַּמְתִּי', וְכֵן: "שָׁאַתָּה מְדַבֵּר עִמִּי" (שם ו, יז) כְּמוֹ 'שֶׁאַתָּה', אַף 'בְּשַׁגַּם' כְּמוֹ 'בְּשֶׁגַּם': **וְהָיוּ יָמָיו וְגוֹ׳.** עַד מֵאָה וְעֶשְׂרִים שָׁנָה אַאֲרִיךְ לָהֶם אַפִּי, וְאִם לֹא יָשׁוּבוּ – אָבִיא עֲלֵיהֶם מַבּוּל. וְאִם תֹּאמַר, מִשֶּׁנּוֹלַד יֶפֶת עַד הַמַּבּוּל אֵינוֹ אֶלָּא מֵאָה שָׁנָה? אֵין מֻקְדָּם וּמְאֻחָר בַּתּוֹרָה, כְּבָר הָיְתָה הַגְּזֵרָה גְּזוּרָה עֶשְׂרִים שָׁנָה קֹדֶם שֶׁהוֹלִיד נֹחַ תּוֹלָדוֹת, וְכֵן מָצִינוּ בְּסֵדֶר עוֹלָם (סוף פכ״ח). יֵשׁ מִדְרְשֵׁי אַגָּדָה רַבִּים בְּ"לֹא יָדוֹן", אֲבָל זֶה עִקָּרוֹ פְּשׁוּטוֹ:

ד **הַנְּפִלִים.** עַל שֵׁם שֶׁנָּפְלוּ וְהִפִּילוּ אֶת הָעוֹלָם, וּבִלְשׁוֹן עִבְרִית לְשׁוֹן עֲנָקִים הוּא: **בַּיָּמִים הָהֵם.** בִּימֵי דוֹר אֱנוֹשׁ וּבְנֵי קַיִן: **וְגַם אַחֲרֵי כֵן.** אַף עַל פִּי שֶׁרָאוּ בְּאָבְדָן שֶׁל דּוֹר אֱנוֹשׁ, שֶׁעָלָה אוֹקְיָנוֹס וְהֵצִיף שְׁלִישׁ הָעוֹלָם, לֹא נִכְנַע דּוֹר הַמַּבּוּל לִלְמֹד מֵהֶם: **אֲשֶׁר יָבֹאוּ.** הָיוּ יוֹלְדוֹת עֲנָקִים כְּמוֹתָם: **הַגִּבֹּרִים.** לִמְרֹד בַּמָּקוֹם: **אַנְשֵׁי הַשֵּׁם.** אוֹתָם שֶׁנִּקְּבוּ בְּשֵׁמוֹת: עִירָד מְחוּיָאֵל מְתוּשָׁאֵל, שֶׁנִּקְרְאוּ עַל שֵׁם אָבְדָן, שֶׁנִּמּוֹחוּ וְהֻתָּשׁוּ. דָּבָר אַחֵר, אַנְשֵׁי שִׁמָּמוֹן, שֶׁשִּׁמְּמוּ אֶת הָעוֹלָם:

ו **וַיִּנָּחֶם ה׳ כִּי עָשָׂה.** נֶחָמָה הָיְתָה לְפָנָיו שֶׁבְּרָאוֹ בַּתַּחְתּוֹנִים, שֶׁאִלּוּ הָיָה מִן הָעֶלְיוֹנִים הָיָה מַמְרִידָן, בִּבְרֵאשִׁית רַבָּה (כז, ד): **וַיִּתְעַצֵּב.** הָאָדָם "אֶל לִבּוֹ" שֶׁל מָקוֹם, עָלָה בְּמַחֲשַׁבְתּוֹ שֶׁל מָקוֹם לְהַעֲצִיבוֹ, זֶהוּ תַּרְגּוּם אוּנְקְלוֹס. דָּבָר אַחֵר, "וַיִּנָּחֶם", נֶהֶפְכָה מַחֲשַׁבְתּוֹ שֶׁל מָקוֹם מִמִּדַּת רַחֲמִים לְמִדַּת הַדִּין, עָלָה בְּמַחֲשָׁבָה לְפָנָיו מַה לַּעֲשׂוֹת בָּאָדָם שֶׁעָשָׂה בָּאָרֶץ, וְכֵן כָּל לְשׁוֹן נִחוּם שֶׁבַּמִּקְרָא לְשׁוֹן נִמְלָךְ מַה לַּעֲשׂוֹת: "וּבֶן אָדָם וְיִתְנֶחָם" (במדבר כג, יט), "וְעַל עֲבָדָיו יִתְנֶחָם" (דברים לב, לו), "וַיִּנָּחֶם ה׳ עַל הָרָעָה" (שמות לב, יד), "נִחַמְתִּי כִּי הִמְלַכְתִּי" (שמואל א׳ טו, יא), כֻּלָּם לְשׁוֹן מַחֲשָׁבָה אַחֶרֶת הֵם. "וַיִּתְעַצֵּב אֶל לִבּוֹ" – נִתְאַבֵּל עַל אָבְדַן מַעֲשֵׂה יָדָיו, כְּמוֹ: "נֶעֱצַב הַמֶּלֶךְ עַל בְּנוֹ" (שמואל ב׳ יט, ג). וְזוֹ כָּתַבְתִּי לִתְשׁוּבַת הַמִּינִים: גּוֹי אֶחָד שָׁאַל אֶת רַבִּי יְהוֹשֻׁעַ בֶּן קָרְחָה, אָמַר לוֹ: אֵין אַתֶּם מוֹדִים שֶׁהַקָּדוֹשׁ בָּרוּךְ הוּא רוֹאֶה אֶת הַנּוֹלָד? אָמַר לוֹ: הֵן. אָמַר לוֹ: וְהָא כְתִיב: "וַיִּתְעַצֵּב אֶל לִבּוֹ"? אָמַר לוֹ: נוֹלַד לְךָ בֵּן זָכָר מִיָּמֶיךָ? אָמַר לוֹ: הֵן. אָמַר לוֹ: וּמֶה עָשִׂיתָ? אָמַר לוֹ: שָׂמַחְתִּי וְשִׂמַּחְתִּי אֶת הַכֹּל. אָמַר לוֹ: וְלֹא הָיִיתָ יוֹדֵעַ שֶׁסּוֹפוֹ לָמוּת? אָמַר לוֹ: בִּשְׁעַת חֶדְוְתָא חֶדְוְתָא,

אַחֲרֵי הוֹלִידוֹ אֶת־נֹחַ חָמֵשׁ וְתִשְׁעִים שָׁנָה וַחֲמֵשׁ מֵאוֹת שָׁנָה וַיּוֹלֶד
לא בָּנִים וּבָנוֹת: וַיְהִי כָּל־יְמֵי־לֶמֶךְ שֶׁבַע וְשִׁבְעִים שָׁנָה וּשְׁבַע מֵאוֹת שָׁנָה
לב וַיָּמֹת: וַיְהִי־נֹחַ בֶּן־חֲמֵשׁ מֵאוֹת שָׁנָה וַיּוֹלֶד נֹחַ אֶת־שֵׁם
ו א אֶת־חָם וְאֶת־יָפֶת: וַיְהִי כִּי־הֵחֵל הָאָדָם לָרֹב עַל־פְּנֵי הָאֲדָמָה וּבָנוֹת
ב יֻלְּדוּ לָהֶם: וַיִּרְאוּ בְנֵי־הָאֱלֹהִים אֶת־בְּנוֹת הָאָדָם כִּי טֹבֹת הֵנָּה וַיִּקְחוּ
ג לָהֶם נָשִׁים מִכֹּל אֲשֶׁר בָּחָרוּ: וַיֹּאמֶר יהוה לֹא־יָדוֹן רוּחִי בָאָדָם לְעֹלָם
ד בְּשַׁגַּם הוּא בָשָׂר וְהָיוּ יָמָיו מֵאָה וְעֶשְׂרִים שָׁנָה: הַנְּפִלִים הָיוּ בָאָרֶץ
בַּיָּמִים הָהֵם וְגַם אַחֲרֵי־כֵן אֲשֶׁר יָבֹאוּ בְּנֵי הָאֱלֹהִים אֶל־בְּנוֹת הָאָדָם
וְיָלְדוּ לָהֶם הֵמָּה הַגִּבֹּרִים אֲשֶׁר מֵעוֹלָם אַנְשֵׁי הַשֵּׁם:
ה וַיַּרְא יהוה כִּי רַבָּה רָעַת הָאָדָם בָּאָרֶץ וְכָל־יֵצֶר מַחְשְׁבֹת לִבּוֹ רַק מפטיר
ו רַע כָּל־הַיּוֹם: וַיִּנָּחֶם יהוה כִּי־עָשָׂה אֶת־הָאָדָם בָּאָרֶץ וַיִּתְעַצֵּב

אונקלוס

בָּתַר דְּאוֹלִיד יָת נֹחַ, חֲמֵשׁ מְאָה וְתִשְׁעִין וַחֲמֵשׁ שְׁנִין, וְאוֹלִיד
בְּנִין וּבְנָן: לא וַהֲווֹ כָּל יוֹמֵי לֶמֶךְ, שְׁבַע מְאָה וְשַׁבְעִין וּשְׁבַע שְׁנִין,
וּמִית: לב וַהֲוָה נֹחַ, בַּר חֲמֵשׁ מְאָה שְׁנִין, וְאוֹלִיד נֹחַ, יָת שֵׁם יָת
חָם וְיָת יָפֶת: ו א וַהֲוָה כַּד שָׁרִיאוּ בְּנֵי אֲנָשָׁא, לְמִסְגֵּי עַל אַפֵּי
אַרְעָא, וּבְנָתָא אִתְיְלִידָא לְהוֹן: ב וַחֲזוֹ בְּנֵי רַבְרְבַיָּא יָת בְּנָת
אֲנָשָׁא, אֲרֵי שַׁפִּירָן אִנִּין, וּנְסִיבוּ לְהוֹן נְשִׁין, מִכָּל דְּאִתְרְעִיאוּ:
ג וַאֲמַר יְיָ, לָא יִתְקַיַּם דָּרָא בִּישָׁא הָדֵין קֳדָמַי לְעָלַם, בְּדִיל דְּאִנּוּן
בִּסְרָא וְעוֹבָדֵיהוֹן בִּישִׁין, אַרְכָּא יְהִיב לְהוֹן, מְאָה וְעֶסְרִין שְׁנִין
אִם יְתוּבוּן: ד גִּבָּרַיָּא, הֲווֹ בְאַרְעָא בְּיוֹמַיָּא הָאִנּוּן, וְאַף בָּתַר כֵּן,
דְּעָאלִין בְּנֵי רַבְרְבַיָּא לְוָת בְּנָת אֲנָשָׁא, וִילִידָן לְהוֹן, אִנּוּן גִּבָּרַיָּא,
דְּמֵעָלְמָא אֲנָשִׁין דִּשְׁמָא: ה וַחֲזָא יְיָ, אֲרֵי סְגִיאַת, בִּישַׁת אֲנָשָׁא
בְּאַרְעָא, וְכָל יִצְרָא מַחְשְׁבָת לִבֵּיהּ, לְחוֹד בִּישׁ כָּל יוֹמָא: ו וְתָב יְיָ
בְּמֵימְרֵיהּ, אֲרֵי עֲבַד יָת אֲנָשָׁא בְּאַרְעָא, וַאֲמַר בְּמֵימְרֵיהּ לְמִתְבַּר

affected by it. He is unmoved. But he is also unable to grow. Noaḥ ("rest") stands still.

6:6 וַיִּנָּחֶם יהוה *The Lord regretted* – Having made human beings in His image, God sees the first man and woman disobey the first command, and the first human child commit the first murder. Within a short space of time "the earth had become…full of violence." God "saw how great man's wickedness was upon the earth." We then read one of the most searing sentences in religious literature. "The Lord regretted that He had made man on earth, and His heart was touched with sorrow" (Gen. 6:6). The *parasha* that started with the beginnings of creation ends with God's regret. It is now that the real story of the Torah – the faltering move toward the society we still seek to build – begins.

7 made man on earth, and His heart was touched with sorrow. The LORD said,
“I will erase My creation, humankind, from the face of the land – man, even
animals and creeping things, even birds of the heavens – for I regret having
8 made them.” But Noaḥ found favor in the LORD’s sight.

The haftara for Parashat Bereshit is on page 1500.
On Erev Rosh Ḥodesh Marḥeshvan read the haftara on page 1636.

רש״י

בִּשְׁעַת אֶבְלָא אֶבְלָא. אָמַר לוֹ: כָּךְ מַעֲשֶׂה לִפְנֵי הַקָּדוֹשׁ בָּרוּךְ הוּא, אַף עַל פִּי שֶׁגָּלוּי לְפָנָיו שֶׁסּוֹפָן לַחֲטֹא וּלְאַבְּדָן לֹא נִמְנַע מִלְּבָרְאָן, בִּשְׁבִיל הַצַּדִּיקִים הָעֲתִידִים לַעֲמֹד מֵהֶם:

ז **וַיֹּאמֶר ה׳ אֶמְחֶה אֶת הָאָדָם.** הוּא עָפָר וְאָבִיא עָלָיו מַיִם וְאֶמְחֶה אוֹתוֹ, לְכָךְ נֶאֱמַר לְשׁוֹן מְחוּי: **מֵאָדָם עַד בְּהֵמָה.** אַף הֵם הִשְׁחִיתוּ דַרְכָּם. דָּבָר אַחֵר, הַכֹּל נִבְרָא בִּשְׁבִיל הָאָדָם, וְכֵיוָן שֶׁהוּא כָּלֶה מַה צֹּרֶךְ בְּאֵלּוּ: **כִּי נִחַמְתִּי כִּי עֲשִׂיתִם.** חָשַׁבְתִּי מַה לַּעֲשׂוֹת עַל אֲשֶׁר עֲשִׂיתִים:

אֶל־לִבּֽוֹ׃ ז וַיֹּ֣אמֶר יהוה אֶמְחֶ֨ה אֶת־הָאָדָ֤ם אֲשֶׁר־בָּרָ֙אתִי֙ מֵעַל֙ פְּנֵ֣י
הָֽאֲדָמָ֔ה מֵֽאָדָם֙ עַד־בְּהֵמָ֔ה עַד־רֶ֖מֶשׂ וְעַד־ע֣וֹף הַשָּׁמָ֑יִם כִּ֥י נִחַ֖מְתִּי
כִּ֥י עֲשִׂיתִֽם׃ ח וְנֹ֕חַ מָ֥צָא חֵ֖ן בְּעֵינֵ֥י יהוֽה׃

The הפטרה *for* פרשת בראשית *is on page 1501.*
On ערב ראש חודש מרחשוון *read the* הפטרה *on page 1637.*

אונקלוס

תְּקְפְּהוֹן כִּרְעוּתֵיהּ: ז וַאֲמַר יְיָ, אֶמְחֵי יָת אֱנָשָׁא דִּבְרֵיתִי מֵעַל אַפֵּי
אַרְעָא, מֵאֱנָשָׁא עַד בְּעִירָא, עַד רִחְשָׁא וְעַד עוֹפָא דִּשְׁמַיָּא,
אֲרֵי תָּבִית בְּמֵימְרִי אֲרֵי עֲבַדְתִּנּוּן: ח וְנֹחַ, אַשְׁכַּח רַחֲמִין קֳדָם יְיָ:

11 12 and Yefet. The earth had become corrupt in God's sight, full of violence. And
when God saw how corrupt the earth had become, all flesh corrupting its ways
13 upon the earth, God said to Noaḥ, "The end of all flesh has come
before Me, for the earth is full of violence because of them. I am about to
14 destroy them, along with all the earth. So make yourself an ark of cypress wood.
15 Make it with compartments and coat it in pitch inside and out. This is how you
shall make it: the ark shall be three hundred cubits long, fifty cubits wide, and
16 thirty cubits high. Make a window for the ark, and taper the latter to within a
cubit of the top. Put a door in the side of the ark and make lower, middle, and

רש״י

יא **וַתִּשָּׁחֵת.** לְשׁוֹן עֶרְוָה וַעֲבוֹדָה זָרָה, כְּמוֹ: "פֶּן תַּשְׁחִתוּן" (דברים ד, טז), "כִּי הִשְׁחִית כָּל בָּשָׂר" (להלן פסוק יב): **וַתִּמָּלֵא הָאָרֶץ חָמָס.** גָּזֵל:

יב **כִּי הִשְׁחִית כָּל בָּשָׂר.** אֲפִלּוּ בְּהֵמָה חַיָּה וָעוֹף נִזְקָקִין לְשֶׁאֵינָן מִינָן:

יג **קֵץ כָּל בָּשָׂר.** כָּל מָקוֹם שֶׁאַתָּה מוֹצֵא זְנוּת, אַנְדַּרְלָמוּסְיָא בָּאָה לָעוֹלָם וְהוֹרֶגֶת טוֹבִים וְרָעִים: **כִּי מָלְאָה הָאָרֶץ חָמָס.** לֹא נֶחְתַּם גְּזַר דִּינָם אֶלָּא עַל הַגָּזֵל: **אֶת הָאָרֶץ.** כְּמוֹ מִן הָאָרֶץ, וְדוֹמֶה לוֹ: "כְּצֵאתִי אֶת הָעִיר" (שמות ט, כט) מִן הָעִיר. "חָלָה אֶת רַגְלָיו" (מלכים א׳ טו, כג) מִן רַגְלָיו. דָּבָר אַחֵר, "אֶת הָאָרֶץ", עִם הָאָרֶץ, שֶׁאַף שְׁלֹשָׁה טְפָחִים שֶׁל עֹמֶק הַמַּחֲרֵשָׁה נִמּוֹחוּ וְנִטַּשְׁטְשׁוּ:

יד **עֲשֵׂה לְךָ תֵּבַת.** הַרְבֵּה רֶוַח וְהַצָּלָה לְפָנָיו, וְלָמָּה הִטְרִיחוֹ בְּבִנְיָן זֶה? כְּדֵי שֶׁיִּרְאוּהוּ אַנְשֵׁי דּוֹר הַמַּבּוּל עָסוּק בָּהּ מֵאָה וְעֶשְׂרִים שָׁנָה וְשׁוֹאֲלִין אוֹתוֹ: מַה זֹּאת לְךָ? וְהוּא אוֹמֵר לָהֶם: עָתִיד הַקָּדוֹשׁ בָּרוּךְ הוּא לְהָבִיא מַבּוּל לָעוֹלָם, אוּלַי יָשׁוּבוּ: **עֲצֵי גֹפֶר.** כָּךְ שְׁמוֹ. וְלָמָּה מִמִּין זֶה? עַל שֵׁם גָּפְרִית שֶׁנִּגְזַר עֲלֵיהֶם לִמָּחוֹת בּוֹ: **קִנִּים.** מְדוֹרִים מְדוֹרִים לְכָל בְּהֵמָה וְחַיָּה: **בַּכֹּפֶר.** זֶפֶת בִּלְשׁוֹן אֲרַמִּי. וּמָצִינוּ בַּתַּלְמוּד 'כְּפְרָא'. בְּתֵבָתוֹ שֶׁל מֹשֶׁה, עַל יְדֵי שֶׁהָיוּ הַמַּיִם תָּשִׁים, דַּיָּהּ בְּחֹמֶר מִבִּפְנִים וְזֶפֶת מִבַּחוּץ, וְעוֹד כְּדֵי שֶׁלֹּא יָרִיחַ רֵיחַ רַע שֶׁל זֶפֶת, אֲבָל כָּאן מִפְּנֵי חֹזֶק הַמַּיִם זִפְּתָהּ מִבַּיִת וּמִחוּץ:

טז **צֹהַר.** יֵשׁ אוֹמְרִים חַלּוֹן, וְיֵשׁ אוֹמְרִים אֶבֶן טוֹבָה הַמְּאִירָה לָהֶם: **וְאֶל אַמָּה תְּכַלֶּנָּה מִלְמַעְלָה.** כְּסוּיָהּ מְשֻׁפָּע וְעוֹלֶה עַד שֶׁהוּא קָצָר מִלְמַעְלָה וְעוֹמֵד עַל אַמָּה, כְּדֵי שֶׁיָּזוּבוּ הַמַּיִם לְמַטָּה מִכָּאן וּמִכָּאן: **בְּצִדָּהּ תָּשִׂים.** שֶׁלֹּא יִפְּלוּ גְשָׁמִים בָּהּ:

the water will not be sufficient to save humankind. So why should it matter what source of illumination Noaḥ had in the ark during those tempestuous days? What is the lesson for the generations?

I would like to offer a midrashic speculation. The answer, I suggest, lies in the history of the Hebrew language. Throughout the biblical era, the word *teva* meant an ark. More generally, it meant "box." However, by the time of the Midrash, *teva* had come also to mean "word."

It seems to me that the Rabbis of the Midrash were not so much commenting on Noaḥ and the ark as they were reflecting on a fundamental question of Torah. Where and what is the *tzohar*, the brightness, the source of illumination? Does it come solely from within, or also from without? Does the Torah come with a window or a precious stone?

There are certainly those who believed that Torah is self-sufficient, illuminated by a precious stone that generates its own light. There are, however, other views. Most famously, Rambam believed that a knowledge of science and philosophy – a window to the outside world – was essential to understanding God's word. He made the radical suggestion, in the *Mishneh Torah* (*Hilkhot Yesodei HaTorah* 2:2), that it was precisely these forms of study that were the way to the love and fear of God.

Science, which allows us to understand the world as God's work, and humanities, which explore the human person as God's image, have an honorable place within the Jewish worldview. They have religious dignity; they are the gift of God. *We need to open a series of windows so that the world can illuminate our understanding of Torah, and so that the Torah, in turn, may guide us as we seek to make our way through the world.*

יא
יב וַתִּשָּׁחֵת הָאָרֶץ לִפְנֵי הָאֱלֹהִים וַתִּמָּלֵא הָאָרֶץ חָמָס: וַיַּרְא אֱלֹהִים
אֶת־הָאָרֶץ וְהִנֵּה נִשְׁחָתָה כִּי־הִשְׁחִית כָּל־בָּשָׂר אֶת־דַּרְכּוֹ עַל־
יג הָאָרֶץ: וַיֹּאמֶר אֱלֹהִים לְנֹחַ קֵץ כָּל־בָּשָׂר בָּא לְפָנַי
יד כִּי־מָלְאָה הָאָרֶץ חָמָס מִפְּנֵיהֶם וְהִנְנִי מַשְׁחִיתָם אֶת־הָאָרֶץ: עֲשֵׂה
לְךָ תֵּבַת עֲצֵי־גֹפֶר קִנִּים תַּעֲשֶׂה אֶת־הַתֵּבָה וְכָפַרְתָּ אֹתָהּ מִבַּיִת
טו וּמִחוּץ בַּכֹּפֶר: וְזֶה אֲשֶׁר תַּעֲשֶׂה אֹתָהּ שְׁלֹשׁ מֵאוֹת אַמָּה אֹרֶךְ הַתֵּבָה
טז חֲמִשִּׁים אַמָּה רָחְבָּהּ וּשְׁלֹשִׁים אַמָּה קוֹמָתָהּ: צֹהַר ׀ תַּעֲשֶׂה לַתֵּבָה
וְאֶל־אַמָּה תְּכַלֶּנָּה מִלְמַעְלָה וּפֶתַח הַתֵּבָה בְּצִדָּהּ תָּשִׂים תַּחְתִּיִּם

אונקלוס

יא וְאִתְחַבַּלַת אַרְעָא קֳדָם יְיָ, וְאִתְמְלִיאַת אַרְעָא חֲטוֹפִין: יב וַחֲזָא
יְיָ, יָת אַרְעָא וְהָא אִתְחַבַּלַת, אֲרֵי חַבִּילוּ כָּל בִּסְרָא, אֱנָשׁ אוֹרְחֵיהּ
עַל אַרְעָא: יג וַאֲמַר יְיָ לְנֹחַ, קִצָּא דְּכָל בִּסְרָא עָאל לִקְדָמַי, אֲרֵי
אִתְמְלִיאַת אַרְעָא, חֲטוֹפִין מִן קֳדָם עוֹבָדֵיהוֹן בִּישַׁיָּא, וְהָאֲנָא
מְחַבֵּילְהוֹן עִם אַרְעָא: יד עֲבֵיד לָךְ תֵּיבְתָא דְּאָעִין דְּקַדְרוֹס, מְדוֹרִין
תַּעֲבֵיד יָת תֵּיבְתָא, וְתַחְפֵּי יָתַהּ, מִגָּיו וּמִבָּרָא בְּכֻפְרָא: טו וְדֵין,
דְּתַעֲבֵיד יָתַהּ, תְּלָת מְאָה אַמִּין, אָרְכָּא דְּתֵיבְתָא, חַמְשִׁין אַמִּין
פּוּתְיַהּ, וּתְלָתִין אַמִּין רוּמַהּ: טז נְהוֹר תַּעֲבֵיד לְתֵיבְתָא, וּלְאַמְּתָא
תְּשַׁכְלְלִנַּהּ מִלְעֵילָא, וְתַרְעַהּ דְּתֵיבְתָא בְּסִטְרַהּ תְּשַׁוֵּי, מְדוֹרִין אַרְעָאִין,

6:11 וַתִּשָּׁחֵת הָאָרֶץ... וַתִּמָּלֵא הָאָרֶץ חָמָס *Corrupt... full of violence* – It was Thomas Hobbes (1588–1679) who – without referring to the flood – gave it its best explanation. Before there were political institutions: a stable ruler, an effective government, and enforceable laws, people would be in a state of permanent and violent chaos as they competed for scarce resources – "a war of every man against every man." There would be "continual fear, and danger of violent death; and the life of man, solitary, poor, nasty, brutish, and short." Such situations exist today in a whole series of failed or failing states. That is precisely the Torah's description of life before the flood. When there is no rule of law to constrain individuals, the world is filled with violence.

6:14 עֲשֵׂה לְךָ תֵּבַת עֲצֵי־גֹפֶר *Make yourself an ark of cypress wood* – Noaḥ's ark, his *teva*, contrasts with the *teva*, or "basket," in which Moshe is saved as a child. Moshe, who three times in his early years intervenes when he sees injustice, is the antitype of Noaḥ, the exemplum of obedience to authority.

6:16 צֹהַר תַּעֲשֶׂה לַתֵּבָה *Make a window* – There is a difficulty understanding what *tzohar* means, since the word does not appear anywhere else in Tanakh. Everyone agrees that it is referring to a source of illumination. It will give light within the ark itself. But what exactly is it? Rashi quotes a midrash in which two Rabbis disagree as to its meaning: "Some say this was a window; others say that it was a precious stone that gave light to them" (Bereshit Rabba 31:11). The precious stone had the miraculous quality of being able to generate light within the darkness.

It remains fascinating to ask why the Rabbis of the Midrash would spend time on a question that has no practical relevance. There will be – God promised this in this *parasha* – no further flood. There will be no new Noaḥ. In any future threat to the existence of the planet, an ark floating on

17 upper decks. And I – I am about to bring floodwaters over the earth to destroy
all flesh that has within it the breath of life under the heavens. Everything on
18 earth will die. But I will establish My covenant with you, and you will enter the
19 ark – you, your sons, your wife, and your sons' wives with you. And you shall
take two of each living creature, male and female, into the ark to keep alive with
20 21 you. Of every kind of bird, animal, and wild beast, bring two to keep alive. As
for you, take all the food to be eaten and store it: it will be for food for you and
7 22 1 for them." Noaḥ did so: all that God commanded him, he fulfilled. Then the SHENI
Lord said to Noaḥ, "Enter the ark, you and all your household, for I have seen
2 you alone to be righteous before Me in this generation. Take seven and seven
of every pure animal, seven pairs, and two of every animal that is not pure, of
3 each kind a pair. Also take seven pairs of each kind of bird, male and female, to
4 keep their kind alive across the earth. For in seven days' time I will send rain on
the earth for forty days and forty nights, and I will wipe from the face of the

רש״י

תַּחְתִּיִּם שְׁנִיִּם וּשְׁלִשִׁים. שָׁלֹשׁ עֲלִיּוֹת זוֹ עַל גַּב זוֹ, עֶלְיוֹנִים לָאָדָם, אֶמְצָעִיִּים לְמָדוֹר הַבְּהֵמוֹת, תַּחְתִּיִּים לַזֶּבֶל:

יז **וַאֲנִי הִנְנִי מֵבִיא.** הִנְנִי מוּכָן לְהַסְכִּים עִם אוֹתָם שֶׁזֵּרְזוּנִי כְּבָר: "מָה אֱנוֹשׁ כִּי תִזְכְּרֶנּוּ" (תהלים ח, ה): **מַבּוּל.** שֶׁבִּלָּה אֶת הַכֹּל, שֶׁבִּלְבֵּל אֶת הַכֹּל, שֶׁהוֹבִיל אֶת הַכֹּל מִן הַגָּבוֹהַּ לַנָּמוּךְ. וְזֶהוּ שֶׁתִּרְגֵּם אוּנְקְלוֹס: "טוֹפָנָא", שֶׁהֵצִיף אֶת הַכֹּל וֶהֱבִיאָם לְבָבֶל שֶׁהִיא עֲמוּקָה, לְכָךְ נִקְרֵאת 'שִׁנְעָר', שֶׁכָּל מֵתֵי מַבּוּל נִנְעֲרוּ לְשָׁם:

יח **וַהֲקִמֹתִי אֶת בְּרִיתִי.** בְּרִית הָיָה צָרִיךְ עַל הַפֵּרוֹת שֶׁלֹּא יֵרָקְבוּ וְיֵעָפְשׁוּ, וְשֶׁלֹּא יַהַרְגוּהוּ רְשָׁעִים שֶׁבַּדּוֹר: **אַתָּה וּבָנֶיךָ וְאִשְׁתְּךָ.** הָאֲנָשִׁים לְבַד וְהַנָּשִׁים לְבַד, מִכָּאן שֶׁנֶּאֶסְרוּ בְּתַשְׁמִישׁ הַמִּטָּה:

יט **וּמִכָּל הָחַי.** אֲפִלּוּ שֵׁדִים: **שְׁנַיִם מִכֹּל.** מִן הַפָּחוּת שֶׁבָּהֶם לֹא פָּחֲתוּ מִשְּׁנַיִם, אֶחָד זָכָר וְאֶחָד נְקֵבָה:

כ **מֵהָעוֹף לְמִינֵהוּ.** אוֹתָן שֶׁדָּבְקוּ בְּמִינֵיהֶם וְלֹא הִשְׁחִיתוּ דַּרְכָּם; וּמֵאֲלֵיהֶן בָּאוּ, וְכָל שֶׁהַתֵּבָה קוֹלַטְתּוֹ הִכְנִיס בָּהּ:

כב **וַיַּעַשׂ נֹחַ.** זֶה בִּנְיַן הַתֵּבָה:

ז א **רָאִיתִי צַדִּיק.** וְלֹא נֶאֱמַר 'צַדִּיק תָּמִים', מִכָּאן שֶׁאוֹמְרִים מִקְצַת שִׁבְחוֹ שֶׁל אָדָם בְּפָנָיו וְכֻלּוֹ שֶׁלֹּא בְּפָנָיו:

ב **הַטְּהוֹרָה.** הָעֲתִידָה לִהְיוֹת טְהוֹרָה לְיִשְׂרָאֵל, לָמַדְנוּ שֶׁלָּמַד נֹחַ תּוֹרָה: **שִׁבְעָה שִׁבְעָה.** כְּדֵי שֶׁיַּקְרִיב מֵהֶם קָרְבָּן בְּצֵאתוֹ:

ג **גַּם מֵעוֹף הַשָּׁמַיִם וְגוֹ'.** בַּטְּהוֹרִים דִּבֵּר הַכָּתוּב, וְיִלָּמֵד סָתוּם מִן הַמְפֹרָשׁ:

ד **כִּי לְיָמִים עוֹד שִׁבְעָה.** אֵלּוּ שִׁבְעַת יְמֵי אֶבְלוֹ שֶׁל מְתוּשֶׁלַח הַצַּדִּיק, שֶׁחָס הַקָּדוֹשׁ בָּרוּךְ הוּא עַל כְּבוֹדוֹ וְעִכֵּב אֶת הַפֻּרְעָנוּת. צֵא וַחֲשֹׁב שְׁנוֹתָיו שֶׁל מְתוּשֶׁלַח וְתִמְצָא שֶׁהֵם כָּלִים בִּשְׁנַת שֵׁשׁ מֵאוֹת שָׁנָה לְחַיֵּי נֹחַ: **כִּי לְיָמִים עוֹד.** מַהוּ "עוֹד"? זְמַן אַחַר זְמַן זֶה, נוֹסָף עַל מֵאָה וְעֶשְׂרִים שָׁנָה: **אַרְבָּעִים יוֹם.** כְּנֶגֶד יְצִירַת הַוָּלָד, שֶׁקִּלְקְלוּ לְהַטְרִיחַ לְיוֹצְרָם לָצוּר צוּרַת מַמְזֵרִים:

perfect only relative to the low standard then prevailing. Had he lived in the generation of Avraham, they claim, he would have been insignificant. Others say the opposite: if in a wicked generation Noaḥ was righteous, how much greater he would have been in a generation with role models like Avraham.

The argument, it seems to me, turns on whether Noaḥ's isolation is part of his character – he is a loner – or merely a necessary tactic in that time and place. If he is naturally a loner, he would not gain by the presence of heroes like Avraham. He would be impervious to influence, whether for good or bad. If he is not a loner by nature but merely by circumstance, then in another age he would seek out kindred spirits and become greater still.

יז שְׁנִיִּם וּשְׁלִשִׁים תַּעֲשֶׂהָ: וַאֲנִי הִנְנִי מֵבִיא אֶת־הַמַּבּוּל מַיִם עַל־הָאָרֶץ
לְשַׁחֵת כָּל־בָּשָׂר אֲשֶׁר־בּוֹ רוּחַ חַיִּים מִתַּחַת הַשָּׁמָיִם כֹּל אֲשֶׁר־בָּאָרֶץ
יח יִגְוָע: וַהֲקִמֹתִי אֶת־בְּרִיתִי אִתָּךְ וּבָאתָ אֶל־הַתֵּבָה אַתָּה וּבָנֶיךָ וְאִשְׁתְּךָ
יט וּנְשֵׁי־בָנֶיךָ אִתָּךְ: וּמִכָּל־הָחַי מִכָּל־בָּשָׂר שְׁנַיִם מִכֹּל תָּבִיא אֶל־הַתֵּבָה
כ לְהַחֲיֹת אִתָּךְ זָכָר וּנְקֵבָה יִהְיוּ: מֵהָעוֹף לְמִינֵהוּ וּמִן־הַבְּהֵמָה לְמִינָהּ
כא מִכֹּל רֶמֶשׂ הָאֲדָמָה לְמִינֵהוּ שְׁנַיִם מִכֹּל יָבֹאוּ אֵלֶיךָ לְהַחֲיוֹת: וְאַתָּה
קַח־לְךָ מִכָּל־מַאֲכָל אֲשֶׁר יֵאָכֵל וְאָסַפְתָּ אֵלֶיךָ וְהָיָה לְךָ וְלָהֶם לְאָכְלָה:
ז כב א וַיַּעַשׂ נֹחַ כְּכֹל אֲשֶׁר צִוָּה אֹתוֹ אֱלֹהִים כֵּן עָשָׂה: וַיֹּאמֶר יהוה לְנֹחַ שני
בֹּא־אַתָּה וְכָל־בֵּיתְךָ אֶל־הַתֵּבָה כִּי־אֹתְךָ רָאִיתִי צַדִּיק לְפָנַי בַּדּוֹר
ב הַזֶּה: מִכֹּל ׀ הַבְּהֵמָה הַטְּהוֹרָה תִּקַּח־לְךָ שִׁבְעָה שִׁבְעָה אִישׁ וְאִשְׁתּוֹ
ג וּמִן־הַבְּהֵמָה אֲשֶׁר לֹא טְהֹרָה הִוא שְׁנַיִם אִישׁ וְאִשְׁתּוֹ: גַּם מֵעוֹף
הַשָּׁמַיִם שִׁבְעָה שִׁבְעָה זָכָר וּנְקֵבָה לְחַיּוֹת זֶרַע עַל־פְּנֵי כָל־הָאָרֶץ:
ד כִּי לְיָמִים עוֹד שִׁבְעָה אָנֹכִי מַמְטִיר עַל־הָאָרֶץ אַרְבָּעִים יוֹם וְאַרְבָּעִים

אונקלוס

תִּנְיָנִין וּתְלִיתָאִין תַּעְבְּדִנַּהּ: יז וַאֲנָא, הָאֲנָא מַיְתֵי יָת טוֹפָנָא מַיָּא עַל אַרְעָא, לְחַבָּלָא כָּל בִּסְרָא, דְּבֵיהּ רוּחָא דְּחַיֵּי, מִתְּחוֹת שְׁמַיָּא, כֹּל דִּבְאַרְעָא יְמוּת: יח וַאֲקִים יָת קְיָמִי עִמָּךְ, וְתֵיעוֹל לְתֵיבְתָא, אַתְּ, וּבְנָךְ, וְאִתְּתָךְ וּנְשֵׁי בְנָךְ עִמָּךְ: יט וּמִכָּל דְּחַי, מִכָּל בִּסְרָא, תְּרֵין מִכּוֹלָא, תַּעֵיל לְתֵיבְתָא לְקַיָּמָא עִמָּךְ, דְּכַר וְנֻקְבָּא יְהוֹן: כ מֵעוֹפָא לִזְנוֹהִי, וּמִן בְּעִירָא לִזְנַהּ, מִכֹּל, רִחְשָׁא דְּאַרְעָא לִזְנוֹהִי, תְּרֵין מִכּוֹלָא, יֵיעֲלוּן לְוָתָךְ לְקַיָּמָא: כא וְאַתְּ סַב לָךְ, מִכָּל מֵיכַל דְּמִתְאֲכִיל, וְתִכְנוֹשׁ לְוָתָךְ, וִיהֵי לָךְ, וּלְהוֹן לְמֵיכַל: כב וַעֲבַד נֹחַ, כְּכֹל, דְּפַקֵּיד יָתֵיהּ, יי כֵּן עֲבַד: ז א וַאֲמַר יי לְנֹחַ, עוֹל אַתְּ וְכָל אֱנָשׁ בֵּיתָךְ לְתֵיבְתָא, אֲרֵי יָתָךְ חֲזֵיתִי, זַכַּאי קֳדָמַי בְּדָרָא הָדֵין: ב מִכָּל בְּעִירָא דָּכְיָא, תִּסַּב לָךְ, שִׁבְעָא שִׁבְעָא דְּכַר וְנֻקְבָּא, וּמִן בְּעִירָא, דְּלֵיתַהָא דָּכְיָא, תְּרֵין דְּכַר וְנֻקְבָּא: ג אַף מֵעוֹפָא דִּשְׁמַיָּא, שִׁבְעָא שִׁבְעָא דְּכַר וְנֻקְבָּא, לְקַיָּמָא זַרְעָא עַל אַפֵּי כָל אַרְעָא: ד אֲרֵי לִזְמַן יוֹמִין עוֹד שִׁבְעָא, אֲנָא מַחֵית מִטְרָא עַל אַרְעָא, אַרְבְּעִין יְמָמִין,

7:1 אֹתְךָ רָאִיתִי צַדִּיק *I have seen you alone to be righteous* – Noaḥ is a good man in a bad age. But his influence on the life of his contemporaries is, apparently, nonexistent. It is reasonable to assume that these two facts – Noaḥ's righteousness and his lack of influence on his contemporaries – are intimately related. Noaḥ preserves his virtue by separating himself from his environment. That is how, in a world gone mad, he stays sane.

The famous debate among the Sages as to whether the phrase "perfect" or "a person of integrity in his generation" (Gen. 6:9) is praise or criticism may well be related to this. Some say that perfect "in his generation" means that he was

5 earth every living creature I have made." Noaḥ did all that the LORD commanded
6 him. Noaḥ was six hundred years old when the floodwaters came upon the
7 earth. Noaḥ, with his sons, his wife, and his sons' wives, came into the ark to
8 escape the waters of the flood. The pure animals, the animals that were not
9 pure, the birds, and all that walked the earth came two by two to Noaḥ into the
10 ark, male and female, as God had commanded Noaḥ. Thus, after seven days the
11 floodwaters came upon the earth. In the six hundredth year of Noaḥ's life, in
the second month, on the seventeenth of the month – on that day, all the
12 wellsprings of the great deep burst, and the heavens' floodgates opened. The
13 rain fell on the earth for forty days and forty nights. On that very day, Noaḥ, his
sons, Shem, Ḥam, and Yefet, Noaḥ's wife, and his sons' three wives entered the
14 ark. With them came every kind of wild beast, every kind of animal, every
creeping, crawling creature of the land, every kind of flying creature, every bird,
15 and each winged thing. They came to Noaḥ, to the ark, two by two, of all flesh
16 that had within it the breath of life. They came, male and female of all flesh,
17 as God had commanded him. Then the LORD shut him in. For forty days the SHELISHI

רש"י

ה **וַיַּעַשׂ נֹחַ.** זֶה בִּיאָתוֹ לַתֵּבָה:

ז **נֹחַ וּבָנָיו.** הָאֲנָשִׁים לְבַד וְהַנָּשִׁים לְבַד, לְפִי שֶׁנֶּאֶסְרוּ בְּתַשְׁמִישׁ הַמִּטָּה מִפְּנֵי שֶׁהָעוֹלָם שָׁרוּי בְּצַעַר: **מִפְּנֵי מֵי הַמַּבּוּל.** אַף נֹחַ מִקְּטַנֵּי אֲמָנָה הָיָה, מַאֲמִין וְאֵינוֹ מַאֲמִין שֶׁיָּבֹא הַמַּבּוּל, וְלֹא נִכְנַס לַתֵּבָה עַד שֶׁדְּחָקוּהוּ הַמַּיִם:

ט **בָּאוּ אֶל נֹחַ.** מֵאֲלֵיהֶן: **שְׁנַיִם שְׁנַיִם.** כֻּלָּם הֻשְׁווּ בְּמִנְיָן זֶה, מִן הַפְּחוּתוּת הָיוּ שְׁנַיִם:

יא **בַּחֹדֶשׁ הַשֵּׁנִי.** רַבִּי אֱלִיעֶזֶר אוֹמֵר: זֶה מַרְחֶשְׁוָן, רַבִּי יְהוֹשֻׁעַ אוֹמֵר: זֶה אִיָּר: **נִבְקְעוּ.** לְהוֹצִיא מֵימֵיהֶן: **תְּהוֹם רַבָּה.** מִדָּה כְּנֶגֶד מִדָּה, הֵם חָטְאוּ בְּ"רַבָּה רָעַת הָאָדָם" (לעיל ו, ה) וְלָקוּ בִּ"תְהוֹם רַבָּה":

יב **וַיְהִי הַגֶּשֶׁם עַל הָאָרֶץ.** וּלְהַלָּן (פסוק יז) הוּא אוֹמֵר: "וַיְהִי הַמַּבּוּל"? אֶלָּא כְּשֶׁהוֹרִידָן הוֹרִידָן בְּרַחֲמִים שֶׁאִם יַחְזְרוּ יִהְיוּ גִּשְׁמֵי בְרָכָה, כְּשֶׁלֹּא חָזְרוּ הָיוּ לְמַבּוּל: **אַרְבָּעִים יוֹם וְגוֹ'.** אֵין יוֹם רִאשׁוֹן מִן הַמִּנְיָן, לְפִי שֶׁאֵין לֵילוֹ עִמּוֹ, שֶׁהֲרֵי כָּתוּב: "בַּיּוֹם הַזֶּה נִבְקְעוּ כָּל מַעְיְנוֹת" (לעיל פסוק יא), נִמְצְאוּ אַרְבָּעִים יוֹם כָּלִים בְּכ"ח בְּכִסְלֵו לְרַבִּי אֱלִיעֶזֶר, שֶׁהֶחֳדָשִׁים נִמְנִין כְּסִדְרָן אֶחָד מָלֵא וְאֶחָד חָסֵר, הֲרֵי שְׁנֵים עָשָׂר מִמַּרְחֶשְׁוָן וְעֶשְׂרִים וּשְׁמוֹנָה מִכִּסְלֵו:

יג **בְּעֶצֶם הַיּוֹם הַזֶּה.** לִמֶּדְךָ הַכָּתוּב שֶׁהָיוּ בְּנֵי דוֹרוֹ אוֹמְרִים: אִלּוּ אָנוּ רוֹאִים אוֹתוֹ נִכְנָס לַתֵּבָה אָנוּ שׁוֹבְרִין אוֹתָהּ וְהוֹרְגִין אוֹתוֹ. אָמַר הַקָּדוֹשׁ בָּרוּךְ הוּא: אֲנִי מַכְנִיסוֹ לְעֵינֵי כֻלָּם, וְנִרְאֶה דְּבַר מִי יָקוּם:

יד **צִפּוֹר כָּל כָּנָף.** דָּבוּק הוּא, צִפּוֹר שֶׁל כָּל מִין כָּנָף, לְרַבּוֹת חֲגָבִים:

טז **וַיִּסְגֹּר ה' בַּעֲדוֹ.** הֵגֵן עָלָיו שֶׁלֹּא יִשְׁבְּרוּהָ, הִקִּיף הַתֵּבָה דֻּבִּים וַאֲרָיוֹת וְהָיוּ הוֹרְגִים בָּהֶם. וּפְשׁוּטוֹ שֶׁל מִקְרָא, סָגַר כְּנֶגְדּוֹ מִן הַמַּיִם, וְכֵן כָּל

his contemporaries or to God? We cannot be sure. The text is suggestive but not conclusive.

The Torah sets a high standard for the moral life. It is not enough to be righteous if that means turning our backs on a society that is guilty of wrongdoing. We must take a stand. We must protest. We must register dissent even if the probability of changing minds is small. That is because the moral life is a life we share with others. We are, in some sense, responsible for the society of which we are a part. There are times when each of us must lead.

Hasidim used to call Noaḥ a *tzaddik im peltz*, "a righteous man in a fur coat." There are two ways of keeping warm on a cold day. You can wear a fur coat or light a fire. Wear a fur coat and you warm only yourself. Light a fire and you warm others. Jews are supposed to light a fire.

ה לַיְלָה וּמָחִיתִי אֶת־כׇּל־הַיְקוּם אֲשֶׁר עָשִׂיתִי מֵעַל פְּנֵי הָאֲדָמָה׃ וַיַּעַשׂ
ו נֹחַ כְּכֹל אֲשֶׁר־צִוָּהוּ יהוה׃ וְנֹחַ בֶּן־שֵׁשׁ מֵאוֹת שָׁנָה וְהַמַּבּוּל הָיָה מַיִם
ז עַל־הָאָרֶץ׃ וַיָּבֹא נֹחַ וּבָנָיו וְאִשְׁתּוֹ וּנְשֵׁי־בָנָיו אִתּוֹ אֶל־הַתֵּבָה מִפְּנֵי
ח מֵי הַמַּבּוּל׃ מִן־הַבְּהֵמָה הַטְּהוֹרָה וּמִן־הַבְּהֵמָה אֲשֶׁר אֵינֶנָּה טְהֹרָה
ט וּמִן־הָעוֹף וְכֹל אֲשֶׁר־רֹמֵשׂ עַל־הָאֲדָמָה׃ שְׁנַיִם שְׁנַיִם בָּאוּ אֶל־נֹחַ
י אֶל־הַתֵּבָה זָכָר וּנְקֵבָה כַּאֲשֶׁר צִוָּה אֱלֹהִים אֶת־נֹחַ׃ וַיְהִי לְשִׁבְעַת
יא הַיָּמִים וּמֵי הַמַּבּוּל הָיוּ עַל־הָאָרֶץ׃ בִּשְׁנַת שֵׁשׁ־מֵאוֹת שָׁנָה לְחַיֵּי־נֹחַ
בַּחֹדֶשׁ הַשֵּׁנִי בְּשִׁבְעָה־עָשָׂר יוֹם לַחֹדֶשׁ בַּיּוֹם הַזֶּה נִבְקְעוּ כׇּל־מַעְיְנוֹת
יב תְּהוֹם רַבָּה וַאֲרֻבֹּת הַשָּׁמַיִם נִפְתָּחוּ׃ וַיְהִי הַגֶּשֶׁם עַל־הָאָרֶץ אַרְבָּעִים
יג יוֹם וְאַרְבָּעִים לָיְלָה׃ בְּעֶצֶם הַיּוֹם הַזֶּה בָּא נֹחַ וְשֵׁם־וְחָם וָיֶפֶת בְּנֵי־נֹחַ
יד וְאֵשֶׁת נֹחַ וּשְׁלֹשֶׁת נְשֵׁי־בָנָיו אִתָּם אֶל־הַתֵּבָה׃ הֵמָּה וְכׇל־הַחַיָּה
לְמִינָהּ וְכׇל־הַבְּהֵמָה לְמִינָהּ וְכׇל־הָרֶמֶשׂ הָרֹמֵשׂ עַל־הָאָרֶץ לְמִינֵהוּ
טו וְכׇל־הָעוֹף לְמִינֵהוּ כֹּל צִפּוֹר כׇּל־כָּנָף׃ וַיָּבֹאוּ אֶל־נֹחַ אֶל־הַתֵּבָה שְׁנַיִם
טז שְׁנַיִם מִכׇּל־הַבָּשָׂר אֲשֶׁר־בּוֹ רוּחַ חַיִּים׃ וְהַבָּאִים זָכָר וּנְקֵבָה מִכׇּל־
יז בָּשָׂר בָּאוּ כַּאֲשֶׁר צִוָּה אֹתוֹ אֱלֹהִים וַיִּסְגֹּר יהוה בַּעֲדוֹ׃ וַיְהִי הַמַּבּוּל שלישי

אונקלוס

וְאַרְבְּעִין לֵילָוָן, וְאֶמְחֵי, יָת כׇּל יְקוּמָא דַּעֲבָדִית, מֵעַל אַפֵּי אַרְעָא: ה וַעֲבַד נֹחַ, כְּכֹל דְּפַקְדֵיהּ יי: ו וְנֹחַ, בַּר שֵׁית מְאָה שְׁנִין, וְטוֹפָנָא הֲוָה, מַיָּא עַל אַרְעָא: ז וְעָאל נֹחַ, וּבְנוֹהִי, וְאִתְּתֵיהּ וּנְשֵׁי בְנוֹהִי, עִמֵּיהּ לְתֵיבְתָא, מִן קֳדָם מֵי טוֹפָנָא: ח מִן בְּעִירָא דָּכְיָא, וּמִן בְּעִירָא, דְּלֵיתַהָא דָּכְיָא, וּמִן עוֹפָא, וְכֹל דְּרָחֵישׁ עַל אַרְעָא: ט תְּרֵין תְּרֵין, עָאלוּ עִם נֹחַ, לְתֵיבְתָא דְּכַר וְנֻקְבָּא, כְּמָא דְּפַקֵּיד יי יָת נֹחַ: י וַהֲוָה לִזְמַן שִׁבְעָא יוֹמִין, וּמֵי טוֹפָנָא, הֲווֹ עַל אַרְעָא: יא בִּשְׁנַת שֵׁית מְאָה שְׁנִין לְחַיֵּי נֹחַ, בְּיַרְחָא תִּנְיָנָא, בְּשִׁבְעַת עַסְרָא יוֹמָא לְיַרְחָא, בְּיוֹמָא הָדֵין, אִתְבְּזַעוּ כׇּל מַבּוּעֵי תְּהוֹם רַבָּא, וְכַוֵּי דִּשְׁמַיָּא אִתְפְּתַחָא: יב וַהֲוָה מִטְרָא נָחֵית עַל אַרְעָא, אַרְבְּעִין יְמָמִין, וְאַרְבְּעִין לֵילָוָן: יג בִּכְרַן יוֹמָא הָדֵין עָאל נֹחַ, וְשֵׁם וְחָם וָיֶפֶת בְּנֵי נֹחַ, וְאִתַּת נֹחַ, וּתְלָת נְשֵׁי בְנוֹהִי, עִמְּהוֹן לְתֵיבְתָא: יד אִנּוּן וְכׇל חַיְתָא לִזְנַהּ, וְכׇל בְּעִירָא לִזְנַהּ, וְכׇל רִחְשָׁא, דְּרָחֵישׁ עַל אַרְעָא לִזְנוֹהִי, וְכׇל עוֹפָא לִזְנוֹהִי, כֹּל צִפַּר כׇּל דְּפָרַח: טו וְעָאלוּ עִם נֹחַ לְתֵיבְתָא, תְּרֵין תְּרֵין מִכׇּל בִּסְרָא, דְּבֵיהּ רוּחָא דְּחַיֵּי: טז וְעָאלַיָּא, דְּכַר וְנֻקְבָּא מִכׇּל בִּסְרָא עָאלוּ, כְּמָא דְּפַקֵּיד יָתֵיהּ יי, וְאַגֵּין יי בְּמֵימְרֵיהּ עֲלוֹהִי: יז וַהֲוָה טוֹפָנָא,

7:5 וַיַּעַשׂ נֹחַ כְּכֹל אֲשֶׁר צִוָּהוּ יהוה *Noaḥ did all that the Lord commanded him* – Noaḥ is the only person in Tanakh called a *tzaddik*, "righteous." Yet Noaḥ's righteousness is turned inward. He has no influence on his contemporaries. Is he, after the flood, haunted by guilt? Does he think of the lives he might have saved if only he had spoken out, whether to ▶

flood came upon the earth. The waters swelled, lifting the ark so that it rose
18 above the land. The waters surged, swelling enormously on the earth, and the
19 ark began to drift on the surface of the water. The waters surged ever more,
20 until all the high mountains beneath all the heavens were covered. Fifteen
21 cubits above them the waters surged as the mountains were covered. All flesh
that moved upon the earth perished – birds, animals, wild beasts, and all the
22 creatures that swarm on the earth, and all humankind. Everything on dry land
23 that had breath of life in its nostrils died. Every living thing on the face of the
earth was wiped out: from humans to animals, from creeping creatures to
winged birds of the heavens, all were wiped from the earth. Only Noaḥ and
24 those with him in the ark survived. For one hundred fifty days, the waters
8 1 surged over the earth. Then God remembered Noaḥ and all the wild beasts and
animals with him in the ark. God sent a wind over the earth, and the waters
2 began to subside. The wellsprings of the deep and heavens' floodgates closed,
3 and the heavens' rains were reined in. The water steadily receded from the
4 earth, and by the end of one hundred fifty days, the water had abated. In the
seventh month, on the seventeenth day of the month, the ark came to rest on
5 the mountains of Ararat. The water continued to abate until the tenth month,

רש״י

'בְּעַד' שֶׁבַּמִּקְרָא לְשׁוֹן 'כְּנֶגֶד' הוּא: "בְּעַד כָּל רֶחֶם" (להלן כ, יח), "בַּעֲדֵךְ וּבְעַד בָּנַיִךְ" (מלכים ב' ד, ד), "עוֹר בְּעַד עוֹר" (איוב ב, ד), "מָגֵן בַּעֲדִי" (תהלים ג, ד), "הִתְפַּלֵּל בְּעַד עֲבָדֶיךָ" (שמואל א' יב, יט), כְּנֶגֶד עֲבָדֶיךָ:

יז| **וַתָּרָם מֵעַל הָאָרֶץ.** מְשֻׁקַּעַת הָיְתָה בַּמַּיִם אַחַת עֶשְׂרֵה אַמָּה, כִּסְפִינָה טְעוּנָה שֶׁמְּשֻׁקַּעַת מִקְצָתָהּ בַּמַּיִם, וּמִקְרָאוֹת שֶׁלְּפָנֵינוּ יוֹכִיחוּ:

יח| **וַיִּגְבְּרוּ.** מֵאֲלֵיהֶן:

כ| **חֲמֵשׁ עֶשְׂרֵה אַמָּה מִלְמַעְלָה.** לְמַעְלָה שֶׁל גֹּבַהּ כָּל הֶהָרִים לְאַחַר שֶׁהֻשְׁווּ הַמַּיִם לְרָאשֵׁי הֶהָרִים:

כב| **נִשְׁמַת רוּחַ חַיִּים.** נְשָׁמָה שֶׁל רוּחַ חַיִּים: **אֲשֶׁר בֶּחָרָבָה.** וְלֹא דָּגִים שֶׁבַּיָּם:

כג| **וַיִּמַח.** לְשׁוֹן וַיִּפְעַל הוּא וְאֵינוֹ לְשׁוֹן וַיִּפָּעֵל, וְהוּא מִגִּזְרַת 'וַיִּפֶן' 'וַיִּבֶן'. כָּל תֵּבָה שֶׁסּוֹפָהּ הֵ"א, כְּגוֹן בָּנָה, מָחָה, קָנָה, כְּשֶׁהוּא נוֹתֵן וָי"ו יוּ"ד בְּרֹאשָׁהּ נָקוּד בְּחִירִיק תַּחַת הַיּוּ"ד: **אַךְ נֹחַ.** לְבַד נֹחַ, זֶהוּ פְּשׁוּטוֹ. וּמִדְרַשׁ אַגָּדָה, גּוֹנֵחַ וְכוֹהֶה דָּם מִטֹּרַח הַבְּהֵמוֹת וְהַחַיּוֹת. וְיֵשׁ אוֹמְרִים שֶׁאִחֵר מְזוֹנוֹת לָאֲרִי וְהִכִּישׁוֹ, וְעָלָיו נֶאֱמַר: "הֵן צַדִּיק בָּאָרֶץ יְשֻׁלָּם" (משלי יא, לא):

ח א| **וַיִּזְכֹּר אֱלֹהִים.** זֶה הַשֵּׁם מִדַּת הַדִּין הוּא, וְנֶהֶפְכָה לְמִדַּת רַחֲמִים עַל יְדֵי תְּפִלַּת הַצַּדִּיקִים. וְרִשְׁעָתָן שֶׁל רְשָׁעִים הוֹפֶכֶת מִדַּת רַחֲמִים לְמִדַּת הַדִּין, שֶׁנֶּאֱמַר: "וַיַּרְא ה' כִּי רַבָּה רָעַת הָאָדָם וְגוֹ' וַיֹּאמֶר ה' אֶמְחֶה" (לעיל ו, ה-ז), וְהוּא שֵׁם מִדַּת רַחֲמִים: **וַיִּזְכֹּר אֱלֹהִים אֶת נֹחַ וְגוֹ'.** מַה זָּכַר לָהֶם לַבְּהֵמוֹת? זְכוּת שֶׁלֹּא הִשְׁחִיתוּ דַּרְכָּם קֹדֶם לָכֵן, וְשֶׁלֹּא שִׁמְּשׁוּ בַּתֵּבָה: **וַיַּעֲבֵר אֱלֹהִים רוּחַ.** רוּחַ תַּנְחוּמִין וַהֲנָחָה עָבְרָה לְפָנָיו: **עַל הָאָרֶץ.** עַל עִסְקֵי הָאָרֶץ: **וַיָּשֹׁכּוּ.** כְּמוֹ: "כְּשֹׁךְ חֲמַת הַמֶּלֶךְ" (אסתר ב, א), לְשׁוֹן הֲנָחַת חֵמָה:

ב| **וַיִּסָּכְרוּ מַעְיְנֹת.** כְּשֶׁנִּפְתְּחוּ כְּתִיב: "כָּל מַעְיְנוֹת" (לעיל ז, יא) וְכָאן אֵין כְּתִיב 'כָּל', לְפִי שֶׁנִּשְׁתַּיְּרוּ מֵהֶם אוֹתָן שֶׁיֵּשׁ בָּהֶם צֹרֶךְ לָעוֹלָם, כְּגוֹן חַמֵּי טְבֶרְיָא וְכַיּוֹצֵא בָּהֶן: **וַיִּכָּלֵא.** וַיִּמָּנַע, כְּמוֹ: "לֹא תִכְלָא רַחֲמֶיךָ" (תהלים מ, יב), "לֹא יִכָּלֵה מִמֵּךְ" (להלן כג, ו):

ג| **מִקְצֵה חֲמִשִּׁים וּמְאַת יוֹם.** הִתְחִילוּ לַחְסֹר, וְהוּא אֶחָד בְּסִיוָן, כֵּיצַד? בְּעֶשְׂרִים וְשִׁבְעָה בְּכִסְלֵו פָּסְקוּ הַגְּשָׁמִים, הֲרֵי שְׁלֹשָׁה מִכִּסְלֵו וְעֶשְׂרִים וְתִשְׁעָה מִטֵּבֵת הֲרֵי שְׁלֹשִׁים וּשְׁנַיִם, וּשְׁבָט וַאֲדָר וְנִיסָן וְאִיָּר מֵאָה וּשְׁמוֹנָה עָשָׂר, הֲרֵי מֵאָה וַחֲמִשִּׁים:

ד| **בַּחֹדֶשׁ הַשְּׁבִיעִי.** סִיוָן, וְהוּא שְׁבִיעִי לְכִסְלֵו שֶׁבּוֹ פָּסְקוּ הַגְּשָׁמִים: **בְּשִׁבְעָה עָשָׂר יוֹם.** מִכָּאן אַתָּה לָמֵד שֶׁהָיְתָה הַתֵּבָה מְשֻׁקַּעַת בַּמַּיִם אַחַת עֶשְׂרֵה אַמָּה, שֶׁהֲרֵי כְּתִיב: "בָּעֲשִׂירִי בְּאֶחָד לַחֹדֶשׁ נִרְאוּ רָאשֵׁי הֶהָרִים", זֶה אָב שֶׁהוּא עֲשִׂירִי לְמַרְחֶשְׁוָן לִירִידַת גְּשָׁמִים, וְהֵם הָיוּ גְּבוֹהִים

אַרְבָּעִים יוֹם עַל־הָאָרֶץ וַיִּרְבּוּ הַמַּיִם וַיִּשְׂאוּ אֶת־הַתֵּבָה וַתָּרָם מֵעַל
יח הָאָרֶץ׃ וַיִּגְבְּרוּ הַמַּיִם וַיִּרְבּוּ מְאֹד עַל־הָאָרֶץ וַתֵּלֶךְ הַתֵּבָה עַל־פְּנֵי
יט הַמָּיִם׃ וְהַמַּיִם גָּבְרוּ מְאֹד מְאֹד עַל־הָאָרֶץ וַיְכֻסּוּ כָּל־הֶהָרִים הַגְּבֹהִים
כ אֲשֶׁר־תַּחַת כָּל־הַשָּׁמָיִם׃ חֲמֵשׁ עֶשְׂרֵה אַמָּה מִלְמַעְלָה גָּבְרוּ הַמָּיִם
כא וַיְכֻסּוּ הֶהָרִים׃ וַיִּגְוַע כָּל־בָּשָׂר ׀ הָרֹמֵשׂ עַל־הָאָרֶץ בָּעוֹף וּבַבְּהֵמָה
כב וּבַחַיָּה וּבְכָל־הַשֶּׁרֶץ הַשֹּׁרֵץ עַל־הָאָרֶץ וְכֹל הָאָדָם׃ כֹּל אֲשֶׁר נִשְׁמַת־
כג רוּחַ חַיִּים בְּאַפָּיו מִכֹּל אֲשֶׁר בֶּחָרָבָה מֵתוּ׃ וַיִּמַח אֶת־כָּל־הַיְקוּם ׀
אֲשֶׁר ׀ עַל־פְּנֵי הָאֲדָמָה מֵאָדָם עַד־בְּהֵמָה עַד־רֶמֶשׂ וְעַד־עוֹף הַשָּׁמַיִם
כד וַיִּמָּחוּ מִן־הָאָרֶץ וַיִּשָּׁאֶר אַךְ־נֹחַ וַאֲשֶׁר אִתּוֹ בַּתֵּבָה׃ וַיִּגְבְּרוּ הַמַּיִם
ח א עַל־הָאָרֶץ חֲמִשִּׁים וּמְאַת יוֹם׃ וַיִּזְכֹּר אֱלֹהִים אֶת־נֹחַ וְאֵת כָּל־הַחַיָּה ו
וְאֶת־כָּל־הַבְּהֵמָה אֲשֶׁר אִתּוֹ בַּתֵּבָה וַיַּעֲבֵר אֱלֹהִים רוּחַ עַל־הָאָרֶץ
ב וַיָּשֹׁכּוּ הַמָּיִם׃ וַיִּסָּכְרוּ מַעְיְנֹת תְּהוֹם וַאֲרֻבֹּת הַשָּׁמָיִם וַיִּכָּלֵא הַגֶּשֶׁם
ג מִן־הַשָּׁמָיִם׃ וַיָּשֻׁבוּ הַמַּיִם מֵעַל הָאָרֶץ הָלוֹךְ וָשׁוֹב וַיַּחְסְרוּ הַמַּיִם
ד מִקְצֵה חֲמִשִּׁים וּמְאַת יוֹם׃ וַתָּנַח הַתֵּבָה בַּחֹדֶשׁ הַשְּׁבִיעִי בְּשִׁבְעָה־
ה עָשָׂר יוֹם לַחֹדֶשׁ עַל הָרֵי אֲרָרָט׃ וְהַמַּיִם הָיוּ הָלוֹךְ וְחָסוֹר עַד הַחֹדֶשׁ

אונקלוס

ארבעין יומין על ארעא, וסגיאו מיא, ונטלו ית תיבתא, ואתרמת מעל ארעא: יח ותקיפו מיא, וסגיאו לחדא על ארעא, ומהלכא תיבתא על אפי מיא: יט ומיא, תקיפו, לחדא לחדא על ארעא, ואתחפיאו, כל טוריא רמיא, דתחות כל שמיא: כ חמש עסרי אמין מלעילא, תקיפו מיא, ואתחפיאו טוריא: כא ומית, כל בסרא דרחיש על ארעא, בעופא ובבעירא ובחיתא, ובכל רחשא דרחיש על ארעא, וכל אנשא: כב כל, דנשמת רוח חיין באפוהי, מכל דביבשתא מיתו: כג ומחא, ית כל יקומא דעל אפי ארעא, מאנשא עד בעירא עד רחשא ועד עופא דשמיא, ואתמחיאו מן ארעא, ואשתאר ברם נח, ודעמיה בתיבתא: כד ותקיפו מיא על ארעא, מאה וחמשין יומין: ח א ודכיר יי ית נח, וית כל חיתא וית כל בעירא, דעמיה בתיבתא, ואעבר יי רוחא על ארעא, ונחו מיא: ב ואסתכרו מבועי תהומא, וכוי דשמיא, ואתכלי מטרא מן שמיא: ג ותבו מיא, מעל ארעא אזלין ותיבין, וחסרו מיא, מסוף, מאה וחמשין יומין: ד ונחת תיבתא בירחא שביעאה, בשבעת עסרא יומא לירחא, על טורי קרדו: ה ומיא, הוו אזלין וחסרין, עד ירחא

רש״י

על ההרים חמש עשרה אמה, וחסרו מיום אחד בסיון עד אחד באב חמש עשרה אמה לששים יום, הרי אמה לארבעה ימים, נמצא שבששה עשר של סיון לא חסרו אלא ארבע אמות, ונחה התבה ליום המחרת, למדת שהיתה משקעת אחת עשרה אמה במים שעל ראשי ההרים:

6 and on the first day of the tenth month, the mountaintops became visible. After
7 forty days Noaḥ opened the window he had made in the ark and sent a raven
8 forth. It flew to and fro until the water on the earth had dried. After that he sent
9 forth a dove to see whether the water had subsided from the face of the land. But
the dove found no resting place to plant its foot, and so it returned to him, to the
ark, for water still covered the face of the earth completely. He reached out his
10 hand and brought the dove back to him, into the ark. Then he waited another
11 seven days, and again he sent the dove forth from the ark. The dove came back
to him in the evening – and in its beak was a freshly picked olive leaf. Noaḥ knew
12 then that the water had subsided from the earth. He waited another seven days
13 and again sent forth the dove – and it returned to him no more. So it was that,
by the first day of the first month of Noaḥ's six hundred and first year, the water
on the earth dried up. Noaḥ removed the covering of the ark and saw that the
14 face of the land was dry. By the twenty-seventh day of the second month, the
15 16 earth had dried completely. Then God said to Noaḥ, "Leave the ark – REVI'I
17 you, and your wife, your sons, and your sons' wives with you. And every living

רש"י

ה **בעשירי... נראו ראשי ההרים.** זה אב שהוא עשירי למרחשון שהתחיל הגשם. ואם תאמר, הוא אלול ועשירי לכסלו שפסק הגשם, כשם שאתה אומר "בחדש השביעי" סיון והוא שביעי להפסקה – אי אפשר לומר כן, על כרחך שביעי אי אתה מונה אלא להפסקה, שהרי לא כלו ארבעים יום של ירידת גשמים ומאה וחמשים של תגברת המים עד אחד בסיון. ואם אתה אומר שביעי לירידה אין זה סיון. והעשירי אי אפשר למנות אלא לירידה, שאם אתה אומר להפסקה והוא אלול, אי אתה מוצא "בראשון באחד לחדש חרבו המים מעל הארץ" (להלן פסוק יג), שהרי מקץ ארבעים יום משנראו ראשי ההרים שלח את העורב, ועשרים ואחת יום הוחיל בשליחות היונה, הרי ששים יום משנראו ראשי ההרים עד שחרבו פני האדמה. ואם תאמר באלול נראו, נמצא שחרבו במרחשון, והוא קורא אותו ראשון?! ואין זה אלא תשרי שהוא ראשון לבריאת עולם, ולרבי יהושע הוא ניסן:

ו **מקץ ארבעים יום.** משנראו ראשי ההרים: **את חלון התבה אשר עשה.** לצהר, ולא זה פתח התבה העשוי לביאה ויציאה:

ז **יצוא ושוב.** הולך ומקיף סביבות התבה, ולא הלך בשליחותו, שהיה חושדו על בת זוגו, כמו ששנינו באגדת 'חלק' (סנהדרין קח ע"ב): **עד יבשת המים.** פשוטו כמשמעו. אבל מדרש אגדה: מוכן היה העורב לשליחות אחרת בעצירת גשמים בימי אליהו, שנאמר: "והערבים מביאים לו לחם ובשר" (מלכים א' יז, ו):

ח **וישלח את היונה.** לסוף שבעה ימים, שהרי כתיב (להלן פסוק י): "ויחל עוד שבעת ימים אחרים", מכלל זה אתה למד שאף בראשונה הוחיל שבעה ימים: וישלח. אין זה לשון שליחות אלא לשון שלוח, שלחה ללכת לדרכה, ובזו יראה אם קלו המים, שאם תמצא מנוח לא תשוב אליו:

י **ויחל.** לשון המתנה, וכן: "לי שמעו ויחלו" (איוב כט, כג), והרבה יש במקרא:

יא **טרף בפיה.** אומר אני שזכר היה, לכך הוא קוראהו פעמים לשון זכר ופעמים לשון נקבה, לפי שכל יונה שבמקרא לשון נקבה, כמו: "כיוני הגאיות כלם המות" (יחזקאל ז, טז), וכן: "כיונה פותה" (הושע ז, יא): **טרף.** חטף. ומדרש אגדה לשון מזון, ודרשו "בפיה" לשון מאמר, אמרה: יהיו מזונותי מרורין כזית זו ובידו של הקדוש ברוך הוא ולא יהו מתוקים כדבש ובידי בשר ודם:

יב **וייחל.** הוא לשון 'ויחל' (לעיל פסוק י), אלא שזה לשון ויפעל וזה לשון ויתפעל, 'ויחל' וימתן, 'וייחל' ויתמתן:

יג **בראשון.** לרבי אליעזר הוא תשרי ולרבי יהושע הוא ניסן: **חרבו.** נעשה כמין טיט, שקרמו פניה של מעלה:

יד **יבשה.** נעשית גריד כהלכתה. **בשבעה ועשרים,** וירידתן בחדש השני בשבעה עשר, אלו אחד עשר ימים שהחמה יתרה על הלבנה, שמשפט דור המבול שנה תמימה היה:

טז **אתה ואשתך וגו'.** איש ואשתו, כאן התיר להם תשמיש המטה:

ו הָעֲשִׂירִ֑י בָּעֲשִׂירִי֙ בְּאֶחָ֣ד לַחֹ֔דֶשׁ נִרְא֖וּ רָאשֵׁ֥י הֶהָרִֽים׃ וַיְהִ֕י מִקֵּ֖ץ
ז אַרְבָּעִ֣ים י֑וֹם וַיִּפְתַּ֣ח נֹ֔חַ אֶת־חַלּ֥וֹן הַתֵּבָ֖ה אֲשֶׁ֥ר עָשָֽׂה׃ וַיְשַׁלַּ֖ח אֶת־
ח הָעֹרֵ֑ב וַיֵּצֵ֤א יָצוֹא֙ וָשׁ֔וֹב עַד־יְבֹ֥שֶׁת הַמַּ֖יִם מֵעַ֥ל הָאָֽרֶץ׃ וַיְשַׁלַּ֥ח אֶת־
ט הַיּוֹנָ֖ה מֵאִתּ֑וֹ לִרְאוֹת֙ הֲקַ֣לּוּ הַמַּ֔יִם מֵעַ֖ל פְּנֵ֥י הָאֲדָמָֽה׃ וְלֹא־מָצְאָה֩
הַיּוֹנָ֨ה מָנ֜וֹחַ לְכַף־רַגְלָ֗הּ וַתָּ֤שָׁב אֵלָיו֙ אֶל־הַתֵּבָ֔ה כִּי־מַ֖יִם עַל־פְּנֵ֣י
י כָל־הָאָ֑רֶץ וַיִּשְׁלַ֤ח יָדוֹ֙ וַיִּקָּחֶ֔הָ וַיָּבֵ֥א אֹתָ֛הּ אֵלָ֖יו אֶל־הַתֵּבָֽה׃ וַיָּ֣חֶל
יא ע֔וֹד שִׁבְעַ֥ת יָמִ֖ים אֲחֵרִ֑ים וַיֹּ֛סֶף שַׁלַּ֥ח אֶת־הַיּוֹנָ֖ה מִן־הַתֵּבָֽה׃ וַתָּבֹ֨א
אֵלָ֤יו הַיּוֹנָה֙ לְעֵ֣ת עֶ֔רֶב וְהִנֵּ֥ה עֲלֵה־זַ֖יִת טָרָ֣ף בְּפִ֑יהָ וַיֵּ֣דַע נֹ֔חַ כִּי־קַ֥לּוּ
יב הַמַּ֖יִם מֵעַ֥ל הָאָֽרֶץ׃ וַיִּיָּ֣חֶל ע֔וֹד שִׁבְעַ֥ת יָמִ֖ים אֲחֵרִ֑ים וַיְשַׁלַּח֙ אֶת־הַיּוֹנָ֔ה
יג וְלֹא־יָסְפָ֥ה שׁוּב־אֵלָ֖יו עֽוֹד׃ וַ֠יְהִי בְּאַחַ֨ת וְשֵׁשׁ־מֵא֜וֹת שָׁנָ֗ה בָּרִאשׁוֹן֙
בְּאֶחָ֣ד לַחֹ֔דֶשׁ חָרְב֥וּ הַמַּ֖יִם מֵעַ֣ל הָאָ֑רֶץ וַיָּ֤סַר נֹ֨חַ֙ אֶת־מִכְסֵ֣ה הַתֵּבָ֔ה
יד וַיַּ֕רְא וְהִנֵּ֥ה חָרְב֖וּ פְּנֵ֥י הָאֲדָמָֽה׃ וּבַחֹ֨דֶשׁ הַשֵּׁנִ֔י בְּשִׁבְעָ֧ה וְעֶשְׂרִ֛ים
טו י֖וֹם לַחֹ֑דֶשׁ יָבְשָׁ֖ה הָאָֽרֶץ׃ וַיְדַבֵּ֥ר אֱלֹהִ֖ים אֶל־נֹ֥חַ לֵאמֹֽר׃ ז רביעי
טז יז צֵ֖א מִן־הַתֵּבָ֑ה אַתָּ֕ה וְאִשְׁתְּךָ֛ וּבָנֶ֥יךָ וּנְשֵֽׁי־בָנֶ֖יךָ אִתָּֽךְ׃ כָּל־הַחַיָּ֨ה

אונקלוס

עֲסִירָאָה, בַּעֲסִירָאָה בְּחַד לְיַרְחָא, אִתְחֲזִיאוּ רֵישֵׁי טוּרַיָּא: ו וַהֲוָה, מִסּוֹף אַרְבְּעִין יוֹמִין, וּפְתַח נֹחַ, יָת כַּוַּת תֵּיבְתָא דַּעֲבַד: ז וְשַׁלַּח יָת עוֹרְבָא, וּנְפַק מִפַּק וְתָאֵיב, עַד דִּיבִישׁוּ מַיָּא מֵעַל אַרְעָא: ח וְשַׁלַּח יָת יוֹנָה מִלְּוָתֵיהּ, לְמִחְזֵי אִם קַלּוּ מַיָּא, מֵעַל אַפֵּי אַרְעָא: ט וְלָא אַשְׁכַּחַת יוֹנָה מְנָח לְפַרְסַת רַגְלַהּ, וְתָבַת לְוָתֵיהּ לְתֵיבְתָא, אֲרֵי מַיָּא עַל אַפֵּי כָל אַרְעָא, וְאוֹשֵׁיט יְדֵיהּ וְנַסְבַהּ, וְאָעֵיל יָתַהּ, לְוָתֵיהּ לְתֵיבְתָא: י וְאוֹרֵיךְ עוֹד, שִׁבְעָא יוֹמִין אָחֳרָנִין, וְאוֹסֵיף, שַׁלַּח יָת יוֹנָה מִן תֵּיבְתָא: יא וַאֲתָת לְוָתֵיהּ יוֹנָה לְעִדָּן רַמְשָׁא, וְהָא טְרַף זֵיתָא תְּבִיר מַחֵית בְּפֻמַּהּ, וִידַע נֹחַ, אֲרֵי קַלּוּ מַיָּא מֵעַל אַרְעָא: יב וְאוֹרֵיךְ עוֹד, שִׁבְעָא יוֹמִין אָחֳרָנִין, וְשַׁלַּח יָת יוֹנָה, וְלָא אוֹסֵיפַת לְמִתַּב לְוָתֵיהּ עוֹד: יג וַהֲוָה, בְּשִׁית מְאָה וְחַדָא שְׁנִין, בְּקַדְמָאָה בְּחַד לְיַרְחָא, נְגוֹבוּ מַיָּא מֵעַל אַרְעָא, וְאַעְדִּי נֹחַ יָת חוֹפָאָה דְּתֵיבְתָא, וַחֲזָא, וְהָא נְגוֹבוּ אַפֵּי אַרְעָא: יד וּבְיַרְחָא תִּנְיָנָא, בְּעַסְרִין וְשִׁבְעָא, יוֹמָא לְיַרְחָא, יְבֵישַׁת אַרְעָא: טו וּמַלֵּיל יי עִם נֹחַ לְמֵימַר: טז פּוּק מִן תֵּיבְתָא, אַתְּ, וְאִתְּתָךְ, וּבְנָךְ וּנְשֵׁי בְנָךְ עִמָּךְ: יז כָּל חַיְתָא

8:16 צֵא מִן־הַתֵּבָה *Leave the ark* – There are many midrashic comments on Noaḥ and his place in the history of faith, but one is unrivaled in its sharpness:

Once the waters had abated, Noaḥ should have left the ark. However, Noaḥ said to himself, "I entered with God's permission, as it says, 'Enter the ark' (Gen. 7:1). Shall I now leave without permission?" The Holy One, blessed be He, said to him, "Is it permission, then, that you are seeking? Very well, then, here is permission," as it is said, "[Then God said to Noaḥ,] Leave the ark" (8:16).

thing with you – birds, animals, and all wild beasts that walk the earth – bring
them out with you. Let them swarm again on the earth and be fertile and
18 multiply upon it." So Noaḥ came out with his sons, his wife, and his sons' wives.
19 Every beast, creeping thing, winged creature, everything that creeps across the
20 earth, emerged from the ark by families. Then Noaḥ built an altar to the LORD
and, taking of each of the kinds of pure animals and pure birds, sacrificed burnt
21 offerings on the altar. The LORD smelled the fragrant aroma and said in His
heart, "Never again will I curse the land because of man; the devisings of the
human heart are evil from its youth. And never again will I destroy all life as I

רש״י

יז **הוצא.** כְּתִיב, 'הַיְצֵא' קְרִי. "הַיְצֵא" – אֱמֹר לָהֶם שֶׁיֵּצְאוּ, "הוֹצֵא" – אִם אֵינָן רוֹצִים לָצֵאת הוֹצִיאֵם אַתָּה: **וְשָׁרְצוּ בָאָרֶץ.** וְלֹא בַתֵּבָה, מַגִּיד שֶׁאַף הַבְּהֵמָה וְהָעוֹף נֶאֶסְרוּ בְּתַשְׁמִישׁ:

יט **לְמִשְׁפְּחֹתֵיהֶם.** קִבְּלוּ עֲלֵיהֶם עַל מְנָת לְדָבֵק בְּמִינָן:

כ **מִכֹּל הַבְּהֵמָה הַטְּהֹרָה.** אָמַר: לֹא צִוָּה לִי הַקָּדוֹשׁ בָּרוּךְ הוּא לְהַכְנִיס מֵאֵלּוּ שִׁבְעָה שִׁבְעָה אֶלָּא כְּדֵי לְהַקְרִיב קָרְבָּן מֵהֶם:

כא **מִנְּעֻרָיו.** 'מִנְּעָרָיו' כְּתִיב, מִשֶּׁנִּנְעַר לָצֵאת מִמְּעֵי אִמּוֹ נִתַּן בּוֹ יֵצֶר הָרָע:

"Noahide" laws, but the principle is essentially the same. God no longer makes maximal demands: He makes minimal ones. This is what contemporary philosophers call a "thin" morality, the basic requirements of human conduct as such.

God does not condemn humankind; He does not hold it guilty or incapable of good. Rather, He lowers His requirements to the level at which an acceptable degree of virtue is humanly achievable. Enough, He seems to say, that you honor the sanctity of life and the basic human decencies.

But that is not the end of the story. If it were, the Torah would merely be one work of moral philosophy among many others, articulating the "thin" principles universal to the human condition. Instead it makes a surprising move. God asks one individual – eventually a family, a tribe, a collection of tribes, a nation – to serve as an exemplary role model, to be as it were a living case study in what it is to live closely and continuously in the presence of God. In Lon Fuller's terms, in his book *The Morality of Law*, the covenant of Noaḥ is "the morality of duty" – the minimum standard, the kind of thing you enact as law. The covenant of Avraham is "the morality of aspiration," the ideals at which we aim: Avraham is a role model of life at its best.

God, we are reminded, also loves those He does not choose for that morality of aspiration. They are part of His covenant with humanity – part of the covenant of the morality of duty. It is inscribed into the terms of the covenant itself that God sets His image on everyone.

8:21 **יֵצֶר לֵב הָאָדָם** *The devisings of the human heart* – Reading the story closely, it seems that God created humans in the faith that they would *naturally* choose the right and the good. They would not need to eat the fruit of the Tree of Knowledge of good and evil; calculation, reflection, decision – all the things we associate with knowledge – would not be necessary. They would act as God wanted them to act, because they had been created in His own image.

It did not turn out that way. Adam and Ḥava sinned, Kayin committed murder, and within a few generations the world was reduced to chaos. Everything else in the universe was *tov*, "good." But "the devisings of the human heart" – the *yetzer* – are not.

We now know the neuroscience behind this. We have a prefrontal cortex that evolved to allow humans to think and act reflectively, considering the consequences of their deeds. But this is slower and weaker than the amygdala (what the Jewish mystics called the *nefesh habehemit*, the animal soul), which produces, even before we have had time to think,

אֲשֶׁר־אִתְּךָ מִכָּל־בָּשָׂר בָּעוֹף וּבַבְּהֵמָה וּבְכָל־הָרֶמֶשׂ הָרֹמֵשׂ עַל־
יח הָאָרֶץ הוֹצֵא אִתָּךְ וְשָׁרְצוּ בָאָרֶץ וּפָרוּ וְרָבוּ עַל־הָאָרֶץ: וַיֵּצֵא־נֹחַ הַיְצֵא
יט וּבָנָיו וְאִשְׁתּוֹ וּנְשֵׁי־בָנָיו אִתּוֹ: כָּל־הַחַיָּה כָּל־הָרֶמֶשׂ וְכָל־הָעוֹף כֹּל
כ רוֹמֵשׂ עַל־הָאָרֶץ לְמִשְׁפְּחֹתֵיהֶם יָצְאוּ מִן־הַתֵּבָה: וַיִּבֶן נֹחַ מִזְבֵּחַ
לַיהוה וַיִּקַּח מִכֹּל ׀ הַבְּהֵמָה הַטְּהֹרָה וּמִכֹּל הָעוֹף הַטָּהֹר וַיַּעַל עֹלֹת
כא בַּמִּזְבֵּחַ: וַיָּרַח יהוה אֶת־רֵיחַ הַנִּיחֹחַ וַיֹּאמֶר יהוה אֶל־לִבּוֹ לֹא אֹסִף
לְקַלֵּל עוֹד אֶת־הָאֲדָמָה בַּעֲבוּר הָאָדָם כִּי יֵצֶר לֵב הָאָדָם רַע מִנְּעֻרָיו

אונקלוס

דְּעִמָּךְ מִכָּל בִּסְרָא, בְּעוֹפָא וּבִבְעִירָא, וּבְכָל רִחְשָׁא, דְּרָחֵישׁ עַל
אַרְעָא אַפֵּיק עִמָּךְ, וְיִתְיַלְדוּן בְּאַרְעָא, וְיִפְשׁוּן וְיִסְגּוֹן עַל אַרְעָא:
יח וּנְפַק נֹחַ, וּבְנוֹהִי, וְאִתְּתֵיהּ וּנְשֵׁי בְנוֹהִי עִמֵּיהּ: יט כָּל חַיְתָא, כָּל
רִחְשָׁא וְכָל עוֹפָא, כֹּל דְּרָחֵישׁ עַל אַרְעָא, לְזַרְעֳיָתְהוֹן, נְפַקוּ מִן
תֵּיבְתָא: כ וּבְנָא נֹחַ, מַדְבְּחָא קֳדָם יי, וּנְסֵיב, מִכֹּל בְּעִירָא דָּכְיָא,
וּמִכֹּל עוֹפָא דְּכֵי, וְאַסֵּיק עֲלָוָן עַל מַדְבְּחָא: כא וְקַבֵּיל יי בְּרַעֲוָא
יָת קֻרְבָּנֵיהּ, וַאֲמַר יי בְּמֵימְרֵיהּ, לָא אוֹסֵיף, לְמִלְטַט עוֹד יָת אַרְעָא
בְּדִיל חוֹבֵי אֲנָשָׁא, אֲרֵי, יִצְרָא לִבָּא דַּאֲנָשָׁא, בִּישׁ מִזְּעוּרֵיהּ,

> R. Yehuda bar Ilai said: If I had been there, I would have broken down the ark and taken myself out. (*Tanḥuma*, Noaḥ 13–14)

To understand this midrash, one must read the story of the flood carefully, with an ear to the pace of the narrative. The story begins rapidly. God announces the imminent destruction of life on earth. He orders Noaḥ to build an ark, specifying its precise measurements. Details follow as to what Noaḥ must take with him. The rain comes; the earth is flooded; Noaḥ and those with him are the sole survivors. The rain ceases and the water abates.

We expect to read next that Noaḥ emerges. Instead the narrative slows down, and for fourteen verses almost nothing happens. The water recedes. The ark comes to rest. Noaḥ opens a window and sends out a raven. Then he sends out a dove. He waits seven days and sends it out again. It returns with an olive leaf. Another seven days pass. He sends the dove a third time. This time it does not return, but Noaḥ still does not step out onto dry land. Eventually God Himself says, "Leave the ark," and only then does Noaḥ do so. The midrash is unmistakable in its note of exasperation. When it comes to rebuilding a shattered world, you do not wait for permission.

THE NOAHIDE COVENANT

The story of the first eight chapters of Genesis is tragic but simple: creation, followed by de-creation, followed by re-creation. God creates order. Humans then destroy that order to the point where "the earth had become… full of violence," with "all flesh corrupting its ways upon the earth" (Gen. 6:11–12). God brings a flood that wipes away all life, until – with the exception of Noaḥ, his family, and other animals – the earth has returned to the state it was in at the beginning of the Torah, when "the earth was void and desolate, there was darkness on the face of the deep, and the spirit of God moved over the waters" (1:2). Now, God begins again.

This is the point at which the Torah confronts what Christianity is later to call "original sin," but in a quite different way. God makes a covenant with all humanity, based on the prohibition of murder ("One who sheds the blood of man….") The Sages were eventually to identify seven

22 have done. As long as earth and time endure – sowing time and harvest, cold
9 1 and heat, summer, winter, day, and night will not cease." Then God blessed

רש״י

לֹא אֹסִף, וְלֹא אֹסִף. כָּפַל הַדָּבָר לִשְׁבוּעָה, הוּא שֶׁכָּתוּב (ישעיה נד, ט): "אֲשֶׁר נִשְׁבַּעְתִּי מֵעֲבֹר מֵי נֹחַ", וְלֹא מָצִינוּ בָּהּ שְׁבוּעָה אֶלָּא זוֹ שֶׁכָּפַל דְּבָרָיו וְהִיא שְׁבוּעָה, וְכֵן דָּרְשׁוּ חֲכָמִים בְּמַסֶּכֶת שְׁבוּעוֹת (דף לו ע״א):

כב עֹד כָּל יְמֵי הָאָרֶץ וְגוֹ׳ לֹא יִשְׁבֹּתוּ. שֵׁשׁ עִתִּים הַלָּלוּ, שְׁנֵי חֳדָשִׁים לְכָל אֶחָד וְאֶחָד, כְּמוֹ שֶׁשָּׁנִינוּ: חֲצִי תִּשְׁרֵי וּמַרְחֶשְׁוָן וַחֲצִי כִּסְלֵו – זֶרַע, חֲצִי כִּסְלֵו וְטֵבֵת וַחֲצִי שְׁבָט – קֹר וְכוּ׳, בְּבָבָא מְצִיעָא (דף קו ע״ב): קֹר. קָשֶׁה מֵחֹרֶף: וָחֹרֶף. עֵת זֶרַע שְׂעוֹרִים וְקִטְנִיּוֹת הַחֲרִיפִין לְהִתְבַּשֵּׁל מַהֵר, וְהוּא חֲצִי שְׁבָט וַאֲדָר וַחֲצִי נִיסָן: קַיִץ. הוּא זְמַן לְקִיטַת תְּאֵנִים וּזְמַן שֶׁמְּיַבְּשִׁין אוֹתָן בַּשָּׂדוֹת, וּשְׁמוֹ קַיִץ, כְּמוֹ: "וְהַלֶּחֶם וְהַקַּיִץ לֶאֱכוֹל הַנְּעָרִים" (שמואל ב׳ טז, ב): חֹם. הוּא סוֹף יְמוֹת הַחַמָּה, חֲצִי אָב וֶאֱלוּל וַחֲצִי תִּשְׁרֵי, שֶׁהָעוֹלָם חַם בְּיוֹתֵר, כְּמוֹ שֶׁשָּׁנִינוּ בְּמַסֶּכֶת יוֹמָא (דף כט ע״א) שִׁלְהֵי קַיְטָא קָשֵׁי מִקַּיְטָא: וְיוֹם וָלַיְלָה לֹא יִשְׁבֹּתוּ. מִכְּלָל שֶׁשָּׁבְתוּ כָּל יְמוֹת הַמַּבּוּל, שֶׁלֹּא שִׁמְּשׁוּ הַמַּזָּלוֹת וְלֹא נִכַּר בֵּין יוֹם וָלַיְלָה: לֹא יִשְׁבֹּתוּ. לֹא יִפְסְקוּ כָּל אֵלֶּה מִלְּהִתְנַהֵג כְּסִדְרָן:

the other will receive a jail sentence of ten years. If both inform, they will be sentenced to five years each. If both stay silent, they will be found guilty of the lesser offense and be sentenced to a year in prison.

It does not take long to work out that for each, the optimal decision is to inform. The result, however, is that they both receive a five-year sentence, whereas if they had both stayed silent, they would have received only one year. The Prisoner's Dilemma establishes the paradoxical, but deeply significant, fact that two people, each pursuing their own self-interest, generate an outcome which is bad for them, both individually and collectively.

What people suspected, and were eventually able to prove, is that the Prisoner's Dilemma yields its paradoxical result only if it is played once. If it is played over and over – the so-called "iterated Prisoner's Dilemma" – the parties eventually learn that they are doing themselves, as well as the other person, harm. Once they discover this, they learn to cooperate.

At this point, game theory provided sociobiologists with an answer to a question that had long puzzled Darwinians, including Charles Darwin himself. In the struggle for survival, the fittest wins. Despite this, all human societies value altruistic behavior, and some forms of it can be found in nonhuman species.

In the late 1970s, a competition was announced to find the computer program that did best at playing the iterated Prisoner's Dilemma against itself and other opponents. The winning program was devised by Anatol Rapoport, and was called Tit-for-Tat. It was dazzlingly simple: it began by cooperating, and then repeated the last move of its opponent, working on the rule of "What you did to me, I will do to you," or "measure for measure." This was the first time scientific proof had been given for any moral principle.

What is fascinating about this chain of discoveries is that it precisely mirrors the central principle of the covenant God made with Noaḥ: "One who sheds the blood of man – by man shall his blood be shed" (Gen. 9:6). This is measure for measure (in Hebrew, *midda keneged midda*), or retributive justice: as you do, so shall you be done to.

In 1989, however, Martin Nowak produced a program that beats Tit-for-Tat. He called it Generous. It overcame one weakness of Tit-for-Tat, namely that when you meet a particularly nasty opponent, you get drawn into a potentially endless and destructive cycle of retaliation, which is bad for both sides. Generous avoided this possibility by randomly but periodically forgetting the last move of its opponent, thus allowing the relationship to begin again. What Nowak had produced, in fact, was a computer simulation of *forgiveness*.

After the flood, God vows: "Never again will I curse the land because of man; the devisings of the human heart are evil from its youth. And never again will I destroy all life as I have done" (8:21). This is the principle of divine compassion.

There is, then, an objective basis for morality. It rests on two key ideas: justice and forgiveness, or what the Sages called *middat hadin* and *middat haraḥamim*. Without these, no group can survive.

כב וְלֹא־אֹסִף עוֹד לְהַכּוֹת אֶת־כָּל־חַי כַּאֲשֶׁר עָשִׂיתִי׃ עֹד כָּל־יְמֵי הָאָרֶץ
ט א זֶרַע וְקָצִיר וְקֹר וָחֹם וְקַיִץ וָחֹרֶף וְיוֹם וָלַיְלָה לֹא יִשְׁבֹּתוּ׃ וַיְבָרֶךְ אֱלֹהִים

אונקלוס

וְלָא אוֹסֵיף עוֹד, לְמִמְחֵי יָת כָּל דְּחַי כְּמָא דַּעֲבַדִית: כב עוֹד כָּל
יוֹמֵי אַרְעָא, זְרוּעָא, וּחְצָדָא, וְקוֹרָא וְחוּמָא, וְקֵיטָא וְסִתְוָא, וְיֵימָם
וְלֵילֵי לָא יִבְטְלוּן: ט א וּבָרֵיךְ יְיָ,

the fight-or-flight reactions without which humans before civilization would simply not have survived.

The problem is that these reactions can be deeply destructive. Often they lead to violence. It is not that we only do evil. Empathy and compassion are as natural to us as are fear and aggression. The problem is that fear lies just beneath the surface of human interaction, and it can overwhelm all our other instincts.

Daniel Goleman calls this an *amygdala hijack*. "Emotions make us pay attention right now – this is urgent – and give us an immediate action plan without having to think twice." Impulsive action is often destructive because it is undertaken without thought of consequences. Therefore, Rambam argued, many of the laws of the Torah constitute a training in virtue simply by making us think before we act.

8:21 רַע מִנְּעֻרָיו *Evil from its youth* – A new principle enters the relationship between God and humanity. Where earlier the wickedness of the human heart was a reason to destroy the earth, it now becomes a reason *not* to destroy it. Divine justice has given way to divine compassion. In making His covenant with Noaḥ, *God rejects rejection*.

8:22 עֹד כָּל־יְמֵי הָאָרֶץ *As long as earth and time endure* – The real subject of the Torah is not our faith in God, which is often faltering, but His unfailing faith in us. *The Torah is not man's book of God. It is God's book of man.* God never stops believing in us, loving us, and hoping for the best from us. There are moments when He almost despairs. Yet – God has patience. God has forgiveness. God has compassion. God has love. For centuries, theologians and philosophers have been looking at religion upside down. The real phenomenon at its heart, the mystery and the miracle, is not our faith in God, but God's faith in us.

There may be times in our lives – certainly there have been in mine – when the sun disappears and we enter the cloud of black despair. King David knew these feelings well. They are the theme of several psalms. People can be brutal to one another. There are some who, having suffered pain themselves, find relief in inflicting it on others. You can lose faith in humanity, or in yourself, or both. At such times, the knowledge that God has faith in us is transformative, redemptive. As David said in Psalms: *Were my father and my mother to forsake me, the Lord would take me in* (27:10).

We may lose heart; God never will. We may despair; God will give us hope. God believes in us even if we don't believe in ourselves. We may sin and disappoint and come short again and again, but God never ceases to forgive us when we fail and lift us when we fall.

As long as God's faith endures, dawn will continue to follow dark, spring follow winter. Have faith in God's faith in us and you will find the path from darkness to light.

THE NOAHIDE COVENANT: "OBJECTIVE" MORALITY

The two great principles of the Noahide covenant happen also to be the first two principles to have been established by computer simulation. The Prisoner's Dilemma imagines the following scenario: Police arrest two men on suspicion of a serious crime. They do not have enough evidence to convict them; at most they have evidence sufficient to prove them guilty of a lesser offense. Their aim is to get them to inform on one another. They therefore put them in separate rooms, with no possible communication between them, and offer them a deal. If one informs and the other stays silent, the informant will go free, and

10 you and your descendants after you, and with every living creature that is with
you – the birds, the animals, and all the wild beasts of earth that are with you,
11 everything that left the ark, every living creature on earth. I will establish My
covenant with you, that never again may all life be destroyed by the waters of a
12 flood; never again will there be a flood to destroy the earth." God said, "This is
the sign of the covenant I am making between Me and you – and every living
13 creature with you – for all generations to come. I have laid down My bow in the
14 clouds to be the sign of the covenant between Me and the earth. Whenever I
15 bring clouds over the earth and the rainbow appears in the clouds, I will
remember My covenant that binds Me and you and every living creature of all
16 flesh so that never again will the waters become a flood to destroy all life. The
rainbow will be there in the cloud, and I will see it, remembering the eternal
covenant between God and every living creature, all flesh upon the earth."

רש״י

י **חַיַּת הָאָרֶץ אִתְּכֶם.** הֵם הַמִּתְהַלְּכִים עִם הַבְּרִיּוֹת: **מִכֹּל יֹצְאֵי הַתֵּבָה.** לְהָבִיא שְׁקָצִים וּרְמָשִׂים: **לְכֹל חַיַּת הָאָרֶץ.** לְהָבִיא הַמַּזִּיקִין שֶׁאֵינָן בִּכְלַל "הַחַיָּה אֲשֶׁר אִתְּכֶם", שֶׁאֵין הִלּוּכָן עִם הַבְּרִיּוֹת:

יא **וַהֲקִמֹתִי.** אֶעֱשֶׂה קִיּוּם לִבְרִיתִי, וּמַהוּ קִיּוּמוֹ? אוֹת הַקֶּשֶׁת, כְּמוֹ שֶׁמְּסַיֵּם וְהוֹלֵךְ:

יב **לְדֹרֹת עוֹלָם.** נִכְתַּב חָסֵר, שֶׁיֵּשׁ דּוֹרוֹת שֶׁלֹּא הֻצְרְכוּ לְאוֹת לְפִי שֶׁצַּדִּיקִים גְּמוּרִים הָיוּ, כְּמוֹ דּוֹרוֹ שֶׁל חִזְקִיָּהוּ מֶלֶךְ יְהוּדָה וְדוֹרוֹ שֶׁל רַבִּי שִׁמְעוֹן בֶּן יוֹחַאי:

יד **בְּעַנְנִי עָנָן.** כְּשֶׁתַּעֲלֶה בְמַחֲשָׁבָה לְפָנַי לְהָבִיא חֹשֶׁךְ וַאֲבַדּוֹן לָעוֹלָם:

טז **בֵּין אֱלֹהִים וּבֵין כָּל נֶפֶשׁ חַיָּה.** בֵּין מִדַּת הַדִּין שֶׁל מַעְלָה וּבֵינֵיכֶם; שֶׁהָיָה לוֹ לִכְתֹּב: 'בֵּינִי וּבֵין כָּל נֶפֶשׁ חַיָּה', אֶלָּא זֶהוּ מִדְרָשׁוֹ: כְּשֶׁתָּבֹא מִדַּת הַדִּין לְקַטְרֵג עֲלֵיכֶם לְחַיֵּב אֶתְכֶם, אֲנִי רוֹאֶה אֶת הָאוֹת וְנִזְכָּר:

The second is *the integrity of the created world.* If we read the chapter carefully we see that *five times* God insists that the covenant of Noaḥ is not merely with humanity, but with all life on earth.

The third lies in the symbol of the covenant, the rainbow. Rabbi Samson Raphael Hirsch suggests that this sign represents the white light of God refracted into the infinite shadings of the spectrum (commentary on Gen. 9:14). This is what I have called the dignity of difference: unity in heaven creates diversity here on earth.

These three dimensions define the covenant of fate. Note that the covenant of fate *precedes* the covenant of faith, because faith is particular, but fate is universal. Without these foundations of human solidarity, we cannot survive.

covenants of faith. But the covenant of Noaḥ says nothing about faith. The world has been almost destroyed by a flood. All mankind, all life, with the exception of Noaḥ's ark, has shared the same fate. There is a famous prophecy in Isaiah 11 that one day, "wolf will lie down beside lamb." So far it has only happened once: in Noaḥ's ark. Why there? Not because they were friends, but because otherwise they would drown. That is a covenant of fate.

In the Noahide covenant God is saying: Never again will I destroy the world. But I cannot promise that *you* will never destroy it because I have given you free will. All I can do is teach you *how* not to destroy the world.

This code, the covenant of Noaḥ, has three dimensions. The first, as we have seen, is *the sanctity of human life.*

י וְאֶת־זַרְעֲכֶם אַחֲרֵיכֶם׃ וְאֵת כָּל־נֶפֶשׁ הַחַיָּה אֲשֶׁר אִתְּכֶם בָּעוֹף
בַּבְּהֵמָה וּבְכָל־חַיַּת הָאָרֶץ אִתְּכֶם מִכֹּל יֹצְאֵי הַתֵּבָה לְכֹל חַיַּת הָאָרֶץ׃
יא וַהֲקִמֹתִי אֶת־בְּרִיתִי אִתְּכֶם וְלֹא־יִכָּרֵת כָּל־בָּשָׂר עוֹד מִמֵּי הַמַּבּוּל
יב וְלֹא־יִהְיֶה עוֹד מַבּוּל לְשַׁחֵת הָאָרֶץ׃ וַיֹּאמֶר אֱלֹהִים זֹאת אוֹת־הַבְּרִית
אֲשֶׁר־אֲנִי נֹתֵן בֵּינִי וּבֵינֵיכֶם וּבֵין כָּל־נֶפֶשׁ חַיָּה אֲשֶׁר אִתְּכֶם לְדֹרֹת
יג עוֹלָם׃ אֶת־קַשְׁתִּי נָתַתִּי בֶּעָנָן וְהָיְתָה לְאוֹת בְּרִית בֵּינִי וּבֵין הָאָרֶץ׃
יד טו וְהָיָה בְּעַנְנִי עָנָן עַל־הָאָרֶץ וְנִרְאֲתָה הַקֶּשֶׁת בֶּעָנָן׃ וְזָכַרְתִּי אֶת־בְּרִיתִי
אֲשֶׁר בֵּינִי וּבֵינֵיכֶם וּבֵין כָּל־נֶפֶשׁ חַיָּה בְּכָל־בָּשָׂר וְלֹא־יִהְיֶה עוֹד הַמַּיִם
טז לְמַבּוּל לְשַׁחֵת כָּל־בָּשָׂר׃ וְהָיְתָה הַקֶּשֶׁת בֶּעָנָן וּרְאִיתִיהָ לִזְכֹּר בְּרִית
עוֹלָם בֵּין אֱלֹהִים וּבֵין כָּל־נֶפֶשׁ חַיָּה בְּכָל־בָּשָׂר אֲשֶׁר עַל־הָאָרֶץ׃

אונקלוס

וְעִם בְּנֵיכוֹן בָּתְרֵיכוֹן: י וְעִם כָּל נַפְשָׁא חַיְתָא דְּעִמְּכוֹן, בְּעוֹפָא בִּבְעִירָא, וּבְכָל חֵיוַת אַרְעָא עִמְּכוֹן, מִכֹּל נָפְקֵי תֵיבוּתָא, לְכֹל חֵיוַת אַרְעָא: יא וַאֲקֵים יָת קְיָמִי עִמְּכוֹן, וְלָא יִשְׁתֵּיצֵי כָּל בִּסְרָא, עוֹד מִמֵּי טוֹפָנָא, וְלָא יְהֵי עוֹד, טוֹפָנָא לְחַבָּלָא אַרְעָא: יב וַאֲמַר יי, דָּא אָת קְיָם דַּאֲנָא יָהֵיב, בֵּין מֵימְרִי וּבֵינֵיכוֹן, וּבֵין, כָּל נַפְשָׁא חַיְתָא דְּעִמְּכוֹן, לְדָרֵי עָלְמָא: יג יָת קַשְׁתִּי, יְהַבִית בַּעֲנָנָא, וּתְהֵי לְאָת קְיָם, בֵּין מֵימְרִי וּבֵין אַרְעָא: יד וִיהֵי, בְּעַנָּנוּתִי עֲנָנָא עַל אַרְעָא, וְתִתַּחְזֵי קַשְׁתָּא בַּעֲנָנָא: טו וְדָכִירְנָא יָת קְיָמִי, דְּבֵין מֵימְרִי וּבֵינֵיכוֹן, וּבֵין, כָּל נַפְשָׁא חַיְתָא בְּכָל בִּסְרָא, וְלָא יְהֵי עוֹד מַיָּא לְטוֹפָנָא, לְחַבָּלָא כָּל בִּסְרָא: טז וּתְהֵי קַשְׁתָּא בַּעֲנָנָא, וְאֶחְזֵינַהּ, לְמִדְכַּר קְיָם עָלַם, בֵּין מֵימְרָא דַּיי, וּבֵין כָּל נַפְשָׁא חַיְתָא, בְּכָל בִּסְרָא דְּעַל אַרְעָא:

9:10 לְכֹל חַיַּת הָאָרֶץ *Every living creature on earth* – The concept of the covenant with Noaḥ tells us that, prior to our particular commitments to this faith or that, this culture, nation, civilization or that, we are human beings, cast together in a fate which grows more interconnected with every passing century, each passing year. We have a duty, not just to ourselves, our families and friends, but also to the ever-widening concentric circles – community, society, humanity – of which we are a part. We are responsible for what we could do, but did not, to alleviate the human condition. To be sure, these responsibilities are not open-ended; we can't do it all. We have limited time, energy, and resources, and those with whom we are most closely bound in a web of obligations have a right to expect that we will give them priority. But what applies to a community applies to society, and ultimately to the world: We are worth what we are willing to share. Each of us has a contribution to make, and "whether we do much or we do little, what matters is that our heart is turned to Heaven" (Menaḥot 110a).

9:13 לְאוֹת בְּרִית *The sign of the covenant* – When we read Genesis and Exodus superficially, it seems as if the covenants of Noaḥ, Avraham, and Sinai are the same sort of thing. But they are not. The covenants of Avraham and Sinai are

17 So said God to Noaḥ: "This is the sign of the covenant that I have established
between Me and all flesh that is on earth."
18 Noaḥ's sons who came out from the ark were Shem, Ḥam, and Yefet. Ḥam SHISHI
19 was the father of Kenaan. These three were Noaḥ's sons; and from them all
20 the world branched out. Noaḥ began to be a man of the land, and he planted
21 a vineyard. He drank some of the wine, became drunk, and lay uncovered
22 in his tent. Ḥam, father of Kenaan, saw his father's nakedness and told his
23 two brothers who were outside. Shem and Yefet then took a cloak and put it
over both their shoulders. They walked backward and covered their father's
nakedness, averting their faces so as not to see the nakedness of their father.
24 Noaḥ woke from his wine and realized what his youngest son had done to him.
25 He said, "Cursed be Kenaan! The lowest of slaves shall he be to his brothers."
26 Then he said, "Blessed be the LORD, God of Shem; Kenaan shall be his slave.

רש״י

יז) **זאת אות הַבְּרִית.** הֶרְאָהוּ הַקֶּשֶׁת וְאָמַר לוֹ: הֲרֵי הָאוֹת שֶׁאָמַרְתִּי:

יח) **וְחָם הוּא אֲבִי כְנָעַן.** לָמָּה הֻצְרַךְ לוֹמַר כָּאן? לְפִי שֶׁהַפָּרָשָׁה עֲסוּקָה וּבָאָה בְּשִׁכְרוּתוֹ שֶׁל נֹחַ שֶׁקִּלְקֵל בָּהּ חָם וְעַל יָדוֹ נִתְקַלֵּל כְּנַעַן, וַעֲדַיִן לֹא כָתַב תּוֹלְדוֹת חָם וְלֹא יָדַעְנוּ שֶׁכְּנַעַן בְּנוֹ, לְפִיכָךְ הֻצְרַךְ לוֹמַר כָּאן: "וְחָם הוּא אֲבִי כְנָעַן":

כ) **וַיָּחֶל.** עָשָׂה עַצְמוֹ חֻלִּין, שֶׁהָיָה לוֹ לַעֲסֹק תְּחִלָּה בִּנְטִיעָה אַחֶרֶת: **אִישׁ הָאֲדָמָה.** אֲדוֹנֵי הָאֲדָמָה, כְּמוֹ: "אִישׁ נָעֳמִי" (רות א, ג): **וַיִּטַּע כָּרֶם.** כְּשֶׁנִּכְנַס לַתֵּבָה הִכְנִיס עִמּוֹ זְמוֹרוֹת וְיִחוּרֵי תְאֵנִים:

כא) **אָהֳלֹה.** "אָהֳלָה" כְּתִיב, רֶמֶז לַעֲשָׂרָה שְׁבָטִים שֶׁנִּקְרְאוּ עַל שֵׁם שׁוֹמְרוֹן שֶׁנִּקְרֵאת אָהֳלָה, שֶׁגָּלוּ עַל עִסְקֵי יַיִן, שֶׁנֶּאֱמַר: "הַשֹּׁתִים בְּמִזְרְקֵי יַיִן" (עמוס ו, ו): **וַיִּתְגַּל.** לְשׁוֹן וַיִּתְפַּעֵל:

כב) **וַיַּרְא חָם אֲבִי כְנַעַן.** יֵשׁ מֵרַבּוֹתֵינוּ אוֹמְרִים, כְּנַעַן רָאָה וְהִגִּיד לְאָבִיו, לְכָךְ הֻזְכַּר עַל הַדָּבָר וְנִתְקַלֵּל: **וַיַּרְא... אֵת עֶרְוַת אָבִיו.** יֵשׁ אוֹמְרִים סֵרְסוֹ, וְיֵשׁ אוֹמְרִים רְבָעוֹ:

כג) **וַיִּקַּח שֵׁם וָיֶפֶת.** אֵין כְּתִיב 'וַיִּקְחוּ' אֶלָּא "וַיִּקַּח", לִמֵּד עַל שֵׁם שֶׁנִּתְאַמֵּץ בַּמִּצְוָה יוֹתֵר מִיֶּפֶת, לְכָךְ זָכוּ בָנָיו לְטַלִּית שֶׁל צִיצִית, וְיֶפֶת זָכָה לִקְבוּרָה לְבָנָיו, שֶׁנֶּאֱמַר: "אֶתֵּן לְגוֹג מְקוֹם שָׁם קֶבֶר" (יחזקאל לט, יא). וְחָם שֶׁבִּזָּה אֶת אָבִיו, נֶאֱמַר בְּזַרְעוֹ: "כֵּן יִנְהַג מֶלֶךְ אַשּׁוּר אֶת שְׁבִי מִצְרַיִם וְאֶת גָּלוּת כּוּשׁ נְעָרִים וּזְקֵנִים עָרוֹם וְיָחֵף וַחֲשׂוּפַי שֵׁת" וְגוֹ' (ישעיה כ, ד): **וּפְנֵיהֶם אֲחֹרַנִּית.** לָמָּה נֶאֱמַר פַּעַם שְׁנִיָּה? לְלַמֵּד שֶׁכְּשֶׁקָּרְבוּ אֶצְלוֹ וְהֻצְרְכוּ לַהֲפֹךְ עַצְמָם לְכַסּוֹתוֹ, הָפְכוּ פְּנֵיהֶם אֲחוֹרַנִּית:

כד) **בְּנוֹ הַקָּטָן.** הַפָּסוּל וְהַבָּזוּי, כְּמוֹ: "הִנֵּה קָטֹן נְתַתִּיךָ בַּגּוֹיִם בָּזוּי" (ירמיה מט, טו; עובדיה א, ב):

כה) **אָרוּר כְּנָעַן.** אַתָּה גָּרַמְתָּ לִי שֶׁלֹּא אוֹלִיד בֵּן רְבִיעִי אַחֵר לְשַׁמְּשֵׁנִי, אָרוּר בִּנְךָ הָרְבִיעִי לִהְיוֹת מְשַׁמֵּשׁ אֶת זַרְעָם שֶׁל אֵלּוּ הַגְּדוֹלִים שֶׁהֻטַּל עֲלֵיהֶם טֹרַח עֲבוֹדָתִי מֵעַתָּה. וּמָה רָאָה חָם שֶׁסֵּרְסוֹ? אָמַר לָהֶם לְאֶחָיו: אָדָם הָרִאשׁוֹן שְׁנֵי בָנִים הָיוּ לוֹ, וְהָרַג זֶה אֶת זֶה בִּשְׁבִיל יְרֻשַּׁת הָעוֹלָם, וְאָבִינוּ יֵשׁ לוֹ שְׁלֹשָׁה בָנִים וְעוֹדֶנּוּ מְבַקֵּשׁ בֵּן רְבִיעִי:

כו) **בָּרוּךְ ה׳ אֱלֹהֵי שֵׁם.** שֶׁעָתִיד לִשְׁמֹר הַבְטָחָתוֹ לְזַרְעוֹ לָתֵת לָהֶם אֶת אֶרֶץ כְּנַעַן: **וִיהִי.** לָהֶם כְּנַעַן לְמַס עוֹבֵד:

The great religious challenge is: can I see a trace of God in the face of a stranger?

9:23 **עֶרְוַת אֲבִיהֶם** *The nakedness of their father* – The opening of the *parasha* was full of expectation; no one else in the Torah receives such accolades as Noaḥ. Yet the last scene of his life is full of pathos. The decorousness of Shem and Yefet's behavior cannot hide from us the embarrassment they feel at knowing that their father – the sole human being worthy of rescue during the flood – has become debased. Noaḥ's end – drunk, disheveled, an embarrassment to his children – eloquently tells us that if you save yourself while doing nothing to save the world, you do not even save yourself. Noaḥ, so the narrative seems to suggest, could not live with the guilt of survival.

יז וַיֹּאמֶר אֱלֹהִים אֶל־נֹחַ זֹאת אוֹת־הַבְּרִית אֲשֶׁר הֲקִמֹתִי בֵּינִי וּבֵין כָּל־
בָּשָׂר אֲשֶׁר עַל־הָאָרֶץ׃
יח וַיִּהְיוּ בְנֵי־נֹחַ הַיֹּצְאִים מִן־הַתֵּבָה שֵׁם וְחָם וָיָפֶת וְחָם הוּא אֲבִי ח ששי
יט כ כְנָעַן׃ שְׁלֹשָׁה אֵלֶּה בְּנֵי־נֹחַ וּמֵאֵלֶּה נָפְצָה כָל־הָאָרֶץ׃ וַיָּחֶל נֹחַ אִישׁ
כא הָאֲדָמָה וַיִּטַּע כָּרֶם׃ וַיֵּשְׁתְּ מִן־הַיַּיִן וַיִּשְׁכָּר וַיִּתְגַּל בְּתוֹךְ אָהֳלֹה׃
כב כג וַיַּרְא חָם אֲבִי כְנַעַן אֵת עֶרְוַת אָבִיו וַיַּגֵּד לִשְׁנֵי־אֶחָיו בַּחוּץ׃ וַיִּקַּח שֵׁם
וָיֶפֶת אֶת־הַשִּׂמְלָה וַיָּשִׂימוּ עַל־שְׁכֶם שְׁנֵיהֶם וַיֵּלְכוּ אֲחֹרַנִּית וַיְכַסּוּ
כד אֵת עֶרְוַת אֲבִיהֶם וּפְנֵיהֶם אֲחֹרַנִּית וְעֶרְוַת אֲבִיהֶם לֹא רָאוּ׃ וַיִּיקֶץ
כה נֹחַ מִיֵּינוֹ וַיֵּדַע אֵת אֲשֶׁר־עָשָׂה לוֹ בְּנוֹ הַקָּטָן׃ וַיֹּאמֶר אָרוּר כְּנָעַן עֶבֶד
כו עֲבָדִים יִהְיֶה לְאֶחָיו׃ וַיֹּאמֶר בָּרוּךְ יְהוָה אֱלֹהֵי שֵׁם וִיהִי כְנַעַן עֶבֶד לָמוֹ׃

אונקלוס

יז וַאֲמַר יי לְנֹחַ, דָּא אָת קְיָם דַּאֲקֵימִית בֵּין מֵימְרִי, וּבֵין כָּל בִּסְרָא דְּעַל אַרְעָא: יח וַהֲווֹ בְנֵי נֹחַ, דִּנְפַקוּ מִן תֵּיבְתָא, שֵׁם וְחָם וָיֶפֶת, וְחָם, הוּא אֲבוּהִי דִּכְנָעַן: יט תְּלָתָא אִלֵּין בְּנֵי נֹחַ, וּמֵאִלֵּין אִתְבַּדַּרוּ בְּכָל אַרְעָא: כ וְשָׁרִי נֹחַ גְּבַר פָּלַח בְּאַרְעָא, וּנְצַב כַּרְמָא: כא וּשְׁתִי מִן חַמְרָא וּרְוִי, וְאִתְגַּלִּי בְּגוֹ מַשְׁכְּנֵיהּ: כב וַחֲזָא, חָם אֲבוּהִי דִּכְנַעַן, יָת עֶרְיְתָא דַּאֲבוּהִי, וְחַוִּי לִתְרֵין אֲחוֹהִי בְּשׁוּקָא: כג וּנְסֵיב שֵׁם וָיֶפֶת יָת כְּסוּתָא, וְשַׁוִּיאוּ עַל כְּתַף תַּרְוֵיהוֹן, וַאֲזַלוּ מַחְזְרִין, וְכַסִּיאוּ, יָת עֶרְיְתָא דַּאֲבוּהוֹן, וְאַפֵּיהוֹן מַחְזְרִין, וְעֶרְיְתָא דַּאֲבוּהוֹן לָא חֲזוֹ: כד וְאִתְּעַר נֹחַ מֵחַמְרֵיהּ, וִידַע, יָת דַּעֲבַד לֵיהּ בְּרֵיהּ זְעֵירָא: כה וַאֲמַר לִיט כְּנָעַן, עֲבֵד פָּלַח יְהֵי לַאֲחוֹהִי: כו וַאֲמַר, בְּרִיךְ יי אֱלָהֵיהּ דְּשֵׁם, וִיהֵי כְנַעַן עַבְדָּא לְהוֹן:

9:17 הַבְּרִית אֲשֶׁר הֲקִמֹתִי *The covenant that I have established* – Vowing never again to destroy all life – though not guaranteeing that humanity might not do so of its own accord – God has begun the world again, this time with Noaḥ in place of Adam, father of a new start to the human story. Genesis 9 is therefore parallel to Genesis 1. In both there is a keyword, repeated seven times, but it is a different word. In Genesis 1 the word is *tov*, "good." In Genesis 9, the word is *brit*, "covenant."

The terms of the human condition have changed. God acknowledges now that "the devisings of the human heart are evil from its youth" (Gen. 8: 21), despite the fact that we were created in God's image. The difference is that there is only one God. If there were only one human being, he or she might live at peace with the world. But we know that this could not be the case because *lo tov* – "it is not good – for man to be alone" (2:18). We are social animals. And when one human being thinks he or she has godlike powers vis-à-vis another human being, the result is violence. Therefore, thinking yourself godlike, if you are human, all too human, is very dangerous indeed.

When we call something *good*, we are speaking about how it is in itself. But when we speak of *covenant*, we are talking about relationships. A covenant is a moral bond between persons. God teaches Noaḥ – and through him all humanity – that we should think, *not of ourselves but of the human other*, as being in the image of God. That is the only way to save ourselves from violence and self-destruction.

27 May God enlarge Yefet, and let him dwell in the tents of Shem; Kenaan shall be
28 29 his slave.” After the flood Noaḥ lived three hundred and fifty years. Noaḥ lived
a total of nine hundred and fifty years, and he died.
10 1 These are the descendants of Noaḥ’s sons, Shem, Ḥam, and Yefet; after the
2 flood, children were born to them. Yefet’s sons were Gomer, Magog, Madai,
3 Yavan, Tuval, Meshekh, and Tiras. Gomer’s sons were Ashkenaz, Rifat, and
4 5 Togarma. Yavan’s sons were Elisha, Tarshish, Kitim, and Dodanim. From
these the seagoing nations spread out to their territories, each with its own
6 language, by their clans and their nations. Ḥam’s sons were Kush, Mitzrayim,
7 Put, and Kenaan. Kush’s sons were Seva, Ḥavila, Savta, Raama, and Savtekha.
8 Raama’s sons were Sheva and Dedan. Kush was the father of Nimrod, the first
9 mighty warrior on earth. He was a mighty hunter before the Lord, which is
10 why people still say, “Like Nimrod, a mighty hunter before the Lord.” His
kingdom began with Babylon, Erekh, Akad, and Kalneh in the land of Shinar.
11 12 From that land, Ashur went out and built Nineveh, Reḥovot Ir, Kalaḥ, and
13 Resen between Nineveh and Kalaḥ; that is the great city. Mitzrayim fathered
14 the Ludim, Anamim, Lehavim and Naftuḥim, Patrusim, Kasluḥim – from
15 whom the Philistines descended – and the Kaftorim. Kenaan fathered
16 17 Tzidon, his firstborn, and Ḥet, and the Jebusites, Amorites, and Girgashites, the
18 Hivites, Arkites, and Sinites, the Arvadites, Zemarites, and Hamatites. Later,

אונקלוס

כז יַפְתֵּי יי לְיֶפֶת, וְיַשְׁרֵי שְׁכִינְתֵּיהּ בְּמַשְׁכְּנֵי שֵׁם, וִיהֵי כְנַעַן עַבְדָּא לְהוֹן: כח וַחֲיָא נֹחַ בָּתַר טוֹפָנָא, תְּלָת מְאָה וְחַמְשִׁין שְׁנִין: כט וַהֲווֹ כָּל יוֹמֵי נֹחַ, תְּשַׁע מְאָה וְחַמְשִׁין שְׁנִין, וּמִית: י א וְאִלֵּין תּוֹלְדָת בְּנֵי נֹחַ, שֵׁם חָם וָיֶפֶת, וְאִתְיְלִידוּ לְהוֹן, בְּנִין בָּתַר טוֹפָנָא: ב בְּנֵי יֶפֶת, גּוֹמֶר וּמָגוֹג, וּמָדַי וְיָוָן וְתוּבָל, וּמֶשֶׁךְ וְתִירָס: ג וּבְנֵי גּוֹמֶר, אַשְׁכְּנַז וְרִיפַת וְתוֹגַרְמָה: ד וּבְנֵי יָוָן אֱלִישָׁה וְתַרְשִׁישׁ, כִּתִּים וְדוֹדָנִים: ה מֵאִלֵּין, אִתְפָּרַשׁוּ, נְגָוַת

רש״י

כז יַפְתְּ אֱלֹהִים לְיֶפֶת. מְתֻרְגָּם: ״יַפְתֵּי״, יַרְחִיב: וְיִשְׁכֹּן בְּאָהֳלֵי שֵׁם. יַשְׁרֶה שְׁכִינָתוֹ בְּיִשְׂרָאֵל. וּמִדְרַשׁ חֲכָמִים, אַף עַל פִּי שֶׁ״יַּפְתְּ אֱלֹהִים לְיֶפֶת״, שֶׁבָּנָה כֹּרֶשׁ שֶׁהָיָה מִבְּנֵי יֶפֶת בַּיִת שֵׁנִי, לֹא שָׁרְתָה בּוֹ שְׁכִינָה; וְהֵיכָן שָׁרְתָה? בְּמִקְדָּשׁ רִאשׁוֹן שֶׁבָּנָה שְׁלֹמֹה שֶׁהָיָה מִבְּנֵי שֵׁם: וִיהִי כְנַעַן עֶבֶד. אַף מִשֶּׁיִּגְלוּ בְּנֵי שֵׁם יִמָּכְרוּ לָהֶם עֲבָדִים מִבְּנֵי כְנַעַן:

י ב וְתִירָס. זוֹ פָּרַס:

ח לִהְיוֹת גִּבֹּר. לְהַמְרִיד כָּל הָעוֹלָם עַל הַקָּדוֹשׁ בָּרוּךְ הוּא בַּעֲצַת דּוֹר הַפַּלָּגָה:

ט גִּבֹּר צַיִד. צָד דַּעְתָּן שֶׁל בְּרִיּוֹת בְּפִיו וּמַטְעָן לִמְרֹד בַּמָּקוֹם: לִפְנֵי ה׳. מִתְכַּוֵּן לְהַקְנִיטוֹ עַל פָּנָיו: עַל כֵּן יֵאָמַר. עַל כָּל אָדָם מַרְשִׁיעַ בְּעַזּוּת פָּנִים, יוֹדֵעַ רִבּוֹנוֹ וּמִתְכַּוֵּן לִמְרֹד בּוֹ, יֵאָמֵר: זֶה כְּנִמְרֹד גִּבּוֹר צַיִד:

יא מִן הָאָרֶץ. כֵּיוָן שֶׁרָאָה אַשּׁוּר אֶת בָּנָיו שׁוֹמְעִין לְנִמְרוֹד וּמוֹרְדִין בַּמָּקוֹם לִבְנוֹת הַמִּגְדָּל, יָצָא מִתּוֹכָם:

יב הָעִיר הַגְּדֹלָה. הִיא נִינְוֵה, שֶׁנֶּאֱמַר: ״וְנִינְוֵה הָיְתָה עִיר גְּדוֹלָה לֵאלֹהִים״ (יונה ג, ג):

יג לְהָבִים. שֶׁפְּנֵיהֶם דּוֹמִים לְלַהַב:

יד וְאֶת פַּתְרֻסִים וְאֶת כַּסְלֻחִים אֲשֶׁר יָצְאוּ מִשָּׁם פְּלִשְׁתִּים. מִשְּׁנֵיהֶם יָצְאוּ, שֶׁהָיוּ פַּתְרוּסִים וְכַסְלוּחִים מַחֲלִיפִין מִשְׁכַּב נְשׁוֹתֵיהֶם אֵלּוּ לָאֵלּוּ, וְיָצְאוּ מֵהֶם פְּלִשְׁתִּים:

יח וְאַחַר נָפֹצוּ. מֵאֵלֶּה נָפוֹצוּ מִשְׁפָּחוֹת הַרְבֵּה:

כז כח יַפְתְּ אֱלֹהִים לְיֶפֶת וְיִשְׁכֹּן בְּאָהֳלֵי־שֵׁם וִיהִי כְנַעַן עֶבֶד לָמוֹ: וַיְחִי־נֹחַ
כט אַחַר הַמַּבּוּל שְׁלֹשׁ מֵאוֹת שָׁנָה וַחֲמִשִּׁים שָׁנָה: וַיְהִי כָּל־יְמֵי־נֹחַ תְּשַׁע
מֵאוֹת שָׁנָה וַחֲמִשִּׁים שָׁנָה וַיָּמֹת:
י א וְאֵלֶּה תּוֹלְדֹת בְּנֵי־נֹחַ שֵׁם חָם וָיָפֶת וַיִּוָּלְדוּ לָהֶם בָּנִים אַחַר הַמַּבּוּל:
ב ג בְּנֵי יֶפֶת גֹּמֶר וּמָגוֹג וּמָדַי וְיָוָן וְתֻבָל וּמֶשֶׁךְ וְתִירָס: וּבְנֵי גֹּמֶר אַשְׁכְּנַז
ד ה וְרִיפַת וְתֹגַרְמָה: וּבְנֵי יָוָן אֱלִישָׁה וְתַרְשִׁישׁ כִּתִּים וְדֹדָנִים: מֵאֵלֶּה
ו נִפְרְדוּ אִיֵּי הַגּוֹיִם בְּאַרְצֹתָם אִישׁ לִלְשֹׁנוֹ לְמִשְׁפְּחֹתָם בְּגוֹיֵהֶם: וּבְנֵי
ז חָם כּוּשׁ וּמִצְרַיִם וּפוּט וּכְנָעַן: וּבְנֵי כוּשׁ סְבָא וַחֲוִילָה וְסַבְתָּה וְרַעְמָה
ח וְסַבְתְּכָא וּבְנֵי רַעְמָה שְׁבָא וּדְדָן: וְכוּשׁ יָלַד אֶת־נִמְרֹד הוּא הֵחֵל
ט לִהְיוֹת גִּבֹּר בָּאָרֶץ: הוּא־הָיָה גִבֹּר־צַיִד לִפְנֵי יְהוָה עַל־כֵּן יֵאָמַר
י כְּנִמְרֹד גִּבּוֹר צַיִד לִפְנֵי יְהוָה: וַתְּהִי רֵאשִׁית מַמְלַכְתּוֹ בָּבֶל וְאֶרֶךְ וְאַכַּד
יא וְכַלְנֵה בְּאֶרֶץ שִׁנְעָר: מִן־הָאָרֶץ הַהִוא יָצָא אַשּׁוּר וַיִּבֶן אֶת־נִינְוֵה
יב וְאֶת־רְחֹבֹת עִיר וְאֶת־כָּלַח: וְאֶת־רֶסֶן בֵּין נִינְוֵה וּבֵין כָּלַח הִוא הָעִיר
יג הַגְּדֹלָה: וּמִצְרַיִם יָלַד אֶת־לוּדִים וְאֶת־עֲנָמִים וְאֶת־לְהָבִים וְאֶת־
יד נַפְתֻּחִים: וְאֶת־פַּתְרֻסִים וְאֶת־כַּסְלֻחִים אֲשֶׁר יָצְאוּ מִשָּׁם פְּלִשְׁתִּים
טו טז וְאֶת־כַּפְתֹּרִים: וּכְנַעַן יָלַד אֶת־צִידֹן בְּכֹרוֹ וְאֶת־חֵת: וְאֶת־
יז הַיְבוּסִי וְאֶת־הָאֱמֹרִי וְאֵת הַגִּרְגָּשִׁי: וְאֶת־הַחִוִּי וְאֶת־הַעַרְקִי וְאֶת־
יח הַסִּינִי: וְאֶת־הָאַרְוָדִי וְאֶת־הַצְּמָרִי וְאֶת־הַחֲמָתִי וְאַחַר נָפֹצוּ מִשְׁפְּחוֹת

אונקלוס

עַמְמַיָּא בְּאַרְעֲתְהוֹן, גְּבַר לְלִישָּׁנֵיהּ, לְזַרְעֲיָתְהוֹן בְּעַמְמֵיהוֹן: ו וּבְנֵי חָם, כּוּשׁ וּמִצְרַיִם וּפוּט וּכְנָעַן: ז וּבְנֵי כוּשׁ, סְבָא וַחֲוִילָה, וְסַבְתָּא וְרַעְמָה וְסַבְתְּכָא, וּבְנֵי רַעְמָה שְׁבָא וּדְדָן: ח וְכוּשׁ אוֹלֵיד יָת נִמְרוֹד, הוּא שָׁרִי, לְמֶהֱוֵי גְּבַר בְּאַרְעָא: ט הוּא הֲוָה גִּבַּר תַּקִּיף קֳדָם יְיָ, עַל כֵּן יִתְאֲמַר, כְּנִמְרוֹד, גִּבַּר תַּקִּיף קֳדָם יְיָ: י וַהֲוָת רֵישׁ מַלְכוּתֵיהּ בָּבֶל, וְאֶרֶךְ וְאַכַּד וְכַלְנֵה, בְּאַרְעָא דְּבָבֶל: יא מִן אַרְעָא הַהִיא נְפַק אַתּוּרָאָה, וּבְנָא יָת נִינְוֵה, וְיָת רְחוֹבוֹת קַרְתָּא וְיָת כָּלַח: יב וְיָת רֶסֶן, בֵּין נִינְוֵה וּבֵין כָּלַח, הִיא קַרְתָּא רַבְּתָא: יג וּמִצְרַיִם, אוֹלֵיד, יָת לוּדָאֵי וְיָת עֲנָמָאֵי, וְיָת לְהָבָאֵי וְיָת נַפְתּוּחָאֵי: יד וְיָת פַּתְרוּסָאֵי וְיָת כַּסְלוּחָאֵי, דִּנְפַקוּ מִתַּמָּן, פְּלִשְׁתָּאֵי וְיָת קַפֻּטְקָאֵי: טו וּכְנַעַן, אוֹלֵיד, יָת צִידוֹן בְּכְרֵיהּ וְיָת חֵת: טז וְיָת יְבוּסָאֵי וְיָת אֱמוֹרָאֵי, וְיָת גִּרְגָּשָׁאֵי: יז וְיָת חִוָּאֵי וְיָת עַרְקָאֵי וְיָת אַנְתּוּסָאֵי: יח וְיָת אַרְוָדָאֵי וְיָת צְמָרָאֵי וְיָת חֲמָתָאֵי, וּבָתַר כֵּן אִתְבַּדַּרוּ, זַרְעֲיָת

3 there. They said to each other, "Come, let us make bricks, let us bake them
4 thoroughly." They used bricks for stone and tar for mortar. And they said,
"Come, let us build ourselves a city and a tower that reaches the heavens, and
make a name for ourselves. Otherwise we will be scattered across the face of

רש״י

ג אִישׁ אֶל רֵעֵהוּ. אֻמָּה לְאֻמָּה, מִצְרַיִם לְכוּשׁ וְכוּשׁ לְפוּט וּפוּט לִכְנַעַן: **הָבָה.** הַזְמִינוּ עַצְמְכֶם. כָּל 'הָבָה' לְשׁוֹן הַזְמָנָה הוּא, שֶׁמְּכִינִים עַצְמָן וּמִתְחַבְּרִים לִמְלָאכָה אוֹ לְעֵצָה אוֹ לְמַשָּׂא. הָבָה – הַזְמִינוּ, אפרייליי״ר בְּלַעַז: **לְבֵנִים.** שֶׁאֵין אֲבָנִים בְּבָבֶל, שֶׁהִיא בִּקְעָה: **וְנִשְׂרְפָה לִשְׂרֵפָה.** כָּךְ עוֹשִׂין הַלְּבֵנִים שֶׁקּוֹרִים טיוול״ש, שׂוֹרְפִים אוֹתָן בְּכִבְשָׁן: **לַחֹמֶר.** לָטוּחַ הַקִּיר:

As after so many other technological advances, they immediately conclude that they now have the power of gods. They are no longer subject to nature. They have become its masters. They will storm the heavens. Their man-made environment – the city with its ziggurat or artificial mountain – will replicate the structure of the cosmos, but here they will rule, not God. It is a supreme act of hubris, but one committed time and again in history.

11:4 **עִיר וּמִגְדָּל** *A city and a tower* – These towers – of which the remains of at least thirty have been discovered – were man-made "holy mountains," the mountain being the place where heaven and earth most visibly meet. Inscriptions on several of these buildings, decoded by archaeologists, refer, as does the Torah, to the idea that their top "reaches heaven." The largest – the great ziggurat of Babylon to which the Torah refers – was a structure of seven stories, three hundred feet high, on a base of roughly the same dimensions.

The pride of the people of Bavel lies in their newfound technological ability to construct buildings of unprecedented grandeur. They do not realize that the greatest creative power is language – a message signaled in the opening verses of the Torah with the grand simplicity of the repeated formula "God said… and there was." What is holy for the Torah is not power, but the use to which we put it, and this is intrinsically linked to language – the medium in which we frame our ideals, construct imaginative possibilities, and call others to join us in realizing them. The word is prior to the work. With great poetic justice, it is not a technical problem that causes the builders to abandon the project, but rather the loss of the ability to communicate.

empires. We have historical evidence dating back to the neo-Assyrians who asserted their supremacy by insisting that their language was the only one to be used by the nations and populations they had defeated. In other words, this is an attempt to frustrate the natural process which has already been described in the previous chapter, which talked about the emergence of seventy languages and human diversity.

The great nineteenth-century commentator Rabbi Naftali Tzvi Yehuda Berlin questions the apparent repetition: "the same language, the same words." "The same words," Berlin suggests, means "they all had the same opinions," they were of like mind. There is nothing dangerous in this initially. They all want to build a city and a tower. The danger lies in the future. Having built a cosmopolis, a total and totalizing man-made environment, the risk is that they will impose a man-made uniformity on all who live there. There will be no freedom of speech, no dignity of dissent. Any disagreement will be held to endanger the necessary unity of the *polis*, the city-state (*Haamek Davar* on Gen. 11:4). Berlin, who taught in the yeshiva of Volozhin in Belarus, died in 1893, before the Russian Revolution, but in retrospect his words were prophetic. Bavel was, he implied, the first totalitarianism.

11:3 **וְנִשְׂרְפָה לִשְׂרֵפָה** *Let us bake them thoroughly* – The men on the plain at Shinar make a technological discovery. They learn how to make bricks by pouring clay into molds, drying it in the sun, and eventually firing it in kilns. This gives them the first processed (as opposed to entirely natural) building material in history, enabling the construction of buildings on a larger scale and reaching greater heights than hitherto.

ג וַיִּמְצְאוּ בִקְעָה בְּאֶרֶץ שִׁנְעָר וַיֵּשְׁבוּ שָׁם׃ וַיֹּאמְרוּ אִישׁ אֶל־רֵעֵהוּ הָבָה
נִלְבְּנָה לְבֵנִים וְנִשְׂרְפָה לִשְׂרֵפָה וַתְּהִי לָהֶם הַלְּבֵנָה לְאָבֶן וְהַחֵמָר הָיָה
ד לָהֶם לַחֹמֶר׃ וַיֹּאמְרוּ הָבָה ׀ נִבְנֶה־לָּנוּ עִיר וּמִגְדָּל וְרֹאשׁוֹ בַשָּׁמַיִם

אונקלוס

וְאַשְׁכַּחוּ בִקְעֲתָא, בְּאַרְעָא דְּבָבֶל וִיתִיבוּ תַמָּן: ג וַאֲמַרוּ גְּבַר לְחַבְרֵיהּ, הַבוּ נִרְמֵי לִבְנִין, וְנוֹקֵידִנּוּן בְּנוּרָא, וַהֲוָת לְהוֹן לְבֵינְתָא לְאַבְנָא, וְחֵימָרָא, הֲוָה לְהוֹן לְשִׁיעַ: ד וַאֲמַרוּ, הַבוּ נִבְנֵי לַנָא קַרְתָּא, וּמִגְדְּלָא וְרֵישֵׁיהּ מָטֵי עַד צֵית שְׁמַיָּא,

in itself, and *very* good in relation to all else. The goodness of the world in Genesis 1 is ontological and ecological. It depends on respect for boundaries – in a word, *order*.

The opposite of order is Bavel – "confusion." The builders of the tower defy the principle stated in the book of Psalms: "The heavens are the Lord's; but He has granted the earth to mankind" (Ps. 115:16). The Hebrew word *avera*, like its English equivalent, "transgression," means "straying across a boundary, entering forbidden territory." It is a failure to engage in *havdala*, knowing the difference between one thing and another and what belongs where. Aspiring to make their home in heaven, the builders of Bavel fail to honor the distinction between man and God.

Their punishment precisely fits the crime. By creating disorder, they inherit disorder, an inability to communicate with one another and thus engage in the collaborative activity on which all human achievement depends. By dishonoring language – God creates the world with words, because words create order, classifying and labeling distinctions – their language is dishonored. By aspiring to reach heaven by technological prowess rather than moral conduct, the builders of Bavel discover that not only do we fail to reach heaven, we also lose our compact nature, our unity, on earth.

Bavel is a profound commentary on the human desire to take the place of God. The word "responsibility" comes from the word "response." It implies the existence of an Other who has legitimate claims on my conduct, for or to whom I am accountable. The Hebrew equivalent, *aḥrayut*, derives from the word *aḥer*, meaning "other." Responsibility is intrinsically relational. H. Richard Niebuhr defines the biblical ethic of responsibility as the principle "God is acting in all actions upon you. So respond to all actions upon you as to respond to His action." In other words, your life is a personal communication from God, who awaits your reply.

Bavel represents the failure of ontological responsibility, the idea that we are accountable to something or someone beyond ourselves. Fired by technological progress, the men on the plain of Shinar attempt to construct a self-sufficient universe in which man is accountable only to himself. "The possession of unlimited power," wrote Lord Acton of the later city-state of Athens, "corrodes the conscience, hardens the heart, and confounds the understanding of monarchs.... It is bad to be oppressed by a minority, but it is worse to be oppressed by a majority.... The philosophy that was then in the ascendent taught them that there is no law superior to that of the State – the lawgiver is above the law. It followed that the sovereign people had a right to do whatever was within its power, and was bound by no rule of right or wrong but its own judgment of expediency."

The result was that "the emancipated people ... became a tyrant." Responsibility is *response*-ability: accountability to an authority beyond us, in the here and now. The alternative, from Bavel to Nazi Germany and Soviet Communism, is a story of human blood shed on the altar dedicated to the greater glory of humankind.

11:1 וַיְהִי כָל הָאָרֶץ שָׂפָה אֶחָת וּדְבָרִים אֲחָדִים *The whole world spoke ... the same words* – Perhaps the whole land, not the whole world. The whole land was of one speech and a shared vocabulary: an enforced shared speech by imperial conquest. This describes the practice of the world's first

5 the earth." But the LORD came down to see the city and the tower being built
6 by the children of men. The LORD said, "If, as one people with one language,
they have begun to do this, nothing they plan to do will be impossible for them.
7 Let us go down and confuse their language so that one will not understand the
8 speech of another." From there the LORD scattered them all over the earth,
9 and they abandoned the building of the city. That is why it was called Bavel,
because it was there that the LORD confused the language of all the earth; and
from there the LORD scattered them all across the face of the earth.

רש״י

ד **פֶּן נָפוּץ.** שֶׁלֹּא יָבִיא עָלֵינוּ שׁוּם מַכָּה לַהֲפִיצֵנוּ מִכָּאן:

ה **וַיֵּרֶד ה׳ לִרְאֹת.** לֹא הֻצְרַךְ לְכָךְ, אֶלָּא לְלַמֵּד לַדַּיָּנִים שֶׁלֹּא יַרְשִׁיעוּ הַנִּדּוֹן עַד שֶׁיִּרְאוּ וְיָבִינוּ. מִדְרַשׁ רַבִּי תַּנְחוּמָא (יח): **בְּנֵי הָאָדָם.** אֶלָּא בְּנֵי מִי? שֶׁמָּא בְּנֵי חֲמוֹרִים וּגְמַלִּים?! אֶלָּא בְּנֵי אָדָם הָרִאשׁוֹן שֶׁכָּפָה אֶת הַטּוֹבָה וְאָמַר: "הָאִשָּׁה אֲשֶׁר נָתַתָּה עִמָּדִי" (לעיל ג, יב), אַף אֵלּוּ כָּפוּ בַּטּוֹבָה לִמְרֹד בְּמִי שֶׁהִשְׁפִּיעָם טוֹבָה וּמִלְּטָם מִן הַמַּבּוּל:

ו **הֵן עַם אֶחָד.** כָּל טוֹבָה זוֹ יֵשׁ עִמָּהֶם, שֶׁעַם אֶחָד הֵם וְשָׂפָה אַחַת לְכֻלָּם, וְדָבָר זֶה הֵחֵלּוּ לַעֲשׂוֹת: **הַחִלָּם.** כְּמוֹ 'אָמְרָם' 'עֲשׂוֹתָם', לְהַתְחִיל הֵם לַעֲשׂוֹת: **לֹא יִבָּצֵר.** בִּתְמִיָּה. "יִבָּצֵר" לְשׁוֹן מְנִיעָה כְּתַרְגּוּמוֹ, וְדוֹמֶה לוֹ: "יִבְצֹר רוּחַ נְגִידִים" (תהלים עו, יג):

ז **הָבָה נֵרְדָה.** בְּבֵית דִּינוֹ נִמְלַךְ מֵעַנְוְתָנוּתוֹ יְתֵרָה: **הָבָה.** מִדָּה כְּנֶגֶד מִדָּה, הֵם אָמְרוּ: "הָבָה נִבְנֶה", וְהוּא כְּנֶגְדָּם מָדַד וְאָמַר: "הָבָה נֵרְדָה": **וְנָבְלָה.** וּנְבַלְבֵּל, נוּ"ן מְשַׁמֵּשׁ בִּלְשׁוֹן רַבִּים, וְהֵ"א אַחֲרוֹנָה יְתֵרָה כְּהֵ"א שֶׁל 'נֵרְדָה': **לֹא יִשְׁמְעוּ.** זֶה שׁוֹאֵל לְבֵנָה וְזֶה מֵבִיא טִיט, וְזֶה עוֹמֵד עָלָיו וּפוֹצֵעַ אֶת מֹחוֹ:

ח **וַיָּפֶץ ה׳ אֹתָם מִשָּׁם.** בָּעוֹלָם הַזֶּה. מַה שֶּׁאָמְרוּ "פֶּן נָפוּץ" (לעיל פסוק ד) נִתְקַיֵּם עֲלֵיהֶם, הוּא שֶׁאָמַר שְׁלֹמֹה: "מְגוֹרַת רָשָׁע הִיא תְבוֹאֶנּוּ" (משלי י, כד):

ט **וּמִשָּׁם הֱפִיצָם.** לִמֵּד שֶׁאֵין לָהֶם חֵלֶק לָעוֹלָם הַבָּא. וְכִי אֵי זוֹ קָשָׁה, שֶׁל דּוֹר הַמַּבּוּל אוֹ שֶׁל דּוֹר הַפַּלָּגָה? אֵלּוּ לֹא פָּשְׁטוּ יָד

When human beings try to become more than human, they quickly become less than human. Only when God is God can man be man. That means keeping heaven and earth distinct, organizing the latter only under the conscious sovereignty of the former. Without this there is little to prevent human beings from sacrificing the many for the sake of the few, or the few for the sake of the many. Humility in the presence of divine order is our last, best safeguard against mankind arrogating to itself power without restraint, might without right. Bavel means chaos, confusion, and the loss of that order which is a precondition of both nature – the world God creates – and culture – the world we create.

11:7 **וְנָבְלָה שָׁם שְׂפָתָם** *Confuse their language* – The story is shot through with literary devices: inversions, word plays, ironies, and puns. It is chiastic, beginning and ending with the same words, *kol haaretz* ("The whole world/the earth"). In the middle comes the word *shamayim*, "the heavens." There is a lot of assonance: *sham, shem, shamayim*. One of the most masterly effects is that the two keywords, *l-v-n*, "brick," and *n-v-l*, "confuse," are precise inversions of one another. As so often in the Torah, literary technique is closely related to the moral or spiritual message being conveyed. In this case the wordplay draws attention to the phenomenon of inversion itself. The results of human behavior are often the opposite of what was intended. The builders want to concentrate humanity in one place: "Let us build ourselves a city.... Otherwise we will be scattered across the face of the earth" (Gen. 11:4). The result is that they are dispersed: "From there the LORD scattered them all over the earth" (11:8). They want to "make a name" for themselves, and they do, but the name they make – Bavel – becomes an eternal symbol of confusion.

11:9 **וּמִשָּׁם הֱפִיצָם יהוה** *From there the LORD scattered them* – When, at the end of the Bavel story, God "confused the language" of the builders, He is not creating a new state of affairs but restoring the old. *When a single culture is imposed on all, suppressing the diversity of languages and traditions, this*

ה וְנַֽעֲשֶׂה־לָּ֖נוּ שֵׁ֑ם פֶּן־נָפ֖וּץ עַל־פְּנֵ֥י כָל־הָאָֽרֶץ׃ וַיֵּ֣רֶד יהוה לִרְאֹ֥ת אֶת־
ו הָעִ֖יר וְאֶת־הַמִּגְדָּ֑ל אֲשֶׁ֥ר בָּנ֖וּ בְּנֵ֥י הָאָדָֽם׃ וַיֹּ֣אמֶר יהוה הֵ֣ן עַ֤ם אֶחָד֙
וְשָׂפָ֤ה אַחַת֙ לְכֻלָּ֔ם וְזֶ֖ה הַחִלָּ֣ם לַעֲשׂ֑וֹת וְעַתָּה֙ לֹֽא־יִבָּצֵ֣ר מֵהֶ֔ם כֹּ֛ל אֲשֶׁ֥ר
ז יָֽזְמ֖וּ לַעֲשֽׂוֹת׃ הָ֚בָה נֵֽרְדָ֔ה וְנָבְלָ֥ה שָׁ֖ם שְׂפָתָ֑ם אֲשֶׁר֙ לֹ֣א יִשְׁמְע֔וּ אִ֖ישׁ
ח שְׂפַ֥ת רֵעֵֽהוּ׃ וַיָּ֨פֶץ יהוה אֹתָ֛ם מִשָּׁ֖ם עַל־פְּנֵ֣י כָל־הָאָ֑רֶץ וַֽיַּחְדְּל֖וּ לִבְנֹ֥ת
ט הָעִֽיר׃ עַל־כֵּ֞ן קָרָ֤א שְׁמָהּ֙ בָּבֶ֔ל כִּי־שָׁ֛ם בָּלַ֥ל יהוה שְׂפַ֣ת כָּל־הָאָ֑רֶץ
וּמִשָּׁם֙ הֱפִיצָ֣ם יהוה עַל־פְּנֵ֖י כָּל־הָאָֽרֶץ׃

אונקלוס

וְנַעֲבֵיד לַנָא שׁוּם, דִּלְמָא נִתְבַּדַּר עַל אַפֵּי כָל אַרְעָא: ה וְאִתְגְּלִי יי, לְאִתְפְּרָעָא עַל עוֹבָד קַרְתָּא וּמִגְדְּלָא, דִּבְנוֹ בְּנֵי אֲנָשָׁא: ו וַאֲמַר יי, הָא עַמָּא חַד וְלִישָׁן חַד לְכֻלְּהוֹן, וְדֵין דְּשָׁרִיאוּ לְמֶעְבַּד, וּכְעַן לָא יִתְמְנַע מִנְּהוֹן, כֹּל דְּחַשִּׁיבוּ לְמֶעְבַּד: ז הָבוּ נִתְגְּלֵי, וּנְבַלְבֵּיל תַּמָּן לִישָׁנְהוֹן, דְּלָא יִשְׁמְעוּן, אֱנָשׁ לִישַׁן חַבְרֵיהּ: ח וּבַדַּר יי יָתְהוֹן, מִתַּמָּן עַל אַפֵּי כָל אַרְעָא, וְאִתְמְנַעוּ מִלְּמִבְנֵי קַרְתָּא: ט עַל כֵּן, קְרָא שְׁמַהּ בָּבֶל, אֲרֵי תַמָּן, בַּלְבֵּיל יי לִישַׁן כָּל אַרְעָא, וּמִתַּמָּן בַּדַּרִנּוּן יי, עַל אַפֵּי כָל אַרְעָא:

11:4 פֶּן־נָפוּץ *Otherwise we will be scattered* – The people are attempting to frustrate God's command in Genesis 1, "Be fruitful and multiply. Fill the earth." They attempt to concentrate in a city. Throughout the Torah we find a critique of urban civilization. The first city is founded by the first murderer, following the first fratricide. The city is born in blood. The people of Sedom do not like strangers. They do not see them as protected by law – nor even by the conventions of hospitality. There is a clear suggestion of sexual depravity and potential violence. There is also the idea of a crowd, a mob. People in a crowd can commit crimes they would not dream of doing on their own. Not by accident are the patriarchs and matriarchs not city dwellers.

In Bavel, human life is cheap. (When the tower was being built, said the Sages, if a person fell and died, no one noticed. If a brick fell, they wept.) In Egypt, entire populations – among them, eventually, the children of Israel – can be pressed into service as a labor force to build pyramids, temples, and monuments, many of which still stand today.

The Tanakh is not opposed to cities as such. In a sense, the Torah project is to sustain strong face-to-face communities even within cities. The antitype of the dehumanizing city is Jerusalem, home of the Divine Presence. But that, at this stage of history, lies long in the future.

11:4 עַל פְּנֵי כָל הָאָרֶץ *Across the face of the earth* – The essence of Genesis 1 is ordered diversity. By attempting to suppress the individuality of the nations they conquer and their distinct languages, the Mesopotamians, the builders of Bavel, transgress that set of harmonious boundaries created by God: biodiversity in Genesis 1, human diversity in Genesis 10.

11:5 וַיֵּרֶד יהוה *The Lord came down* – The world of myth, against which Judaism is a sustained protest, is one in which boundaries are not observed. To the Judaic mind this is paganism, and it is never morally neutral. God creates order; man creates chaos – and the result is inevitably destructive.

The most fundamental boundary is the one created first: the differentiation between "heaven" and "earth." Defying this boundary is the sin of the builders of the tower. Their aspiration to "reach the heavens" is laughable, and indeed the Torah makes a joke of it. They think that their construction – three hundred feet high – has reached the heavens, whereas God has to "come down" to look at it.

10 These are the descendants of Shem. When Shem was one hundred years old, he
11 had a son, Arpakhshad, two years after the flood. After Arpakhshad was born,
12 Shem lived five hundred years and had other sons and daughters. When
13 Arpakhshad was thirty-five years old, he had a son, Shelaḥ. After Shelaḥ was
born, Arpakhshad lived four hundred and three years and had other sons and
14 15 daughters. When Shelaḥ was thirty years old, he had a son, Ever. After
Ever was born, Shelaḥ lived four hundred and three years and had other sons
16 and daughters. Ever lived thirty-four years and then had a son, Peleg.
17 After Peleg was born, Ever lived four hundred and thirty years and had other
18 sons and daughters. Peleg lived thirty years and then had a son, Reu.
19 After Reu was born, Peleg lived two hundred and nine years and had other
20 sons and daughters. Reu lived thirty-two years and then had a son,
21 Serug. After Serug was born, Reu lived two hundred and seven years and had
22 other sons and daughters. Serug lived thirty years and then had a son,
23 Naḥor. After Naḥor was born, Serug lived two hundred years and had other
24 sons and daughters. Naḥor lived twenty-nine years and then had
25 a son, Teraḥ. After Teraḥ was born, Naḥor lived one hundred and nineteen
26 years and had other sons and daughters. Teraḥ lived seventy years and
27 fathered Avram, Naḥor, and Haran. These are the descendants of Teraḥ. Teraḥ

אונקלוס

י אִלֵּין תּוֹלְדָת שֵׁם, שֵׁם בַּר מְאָה שְׁנִין, וְאוֹלֵיד יָת אַרְפַּכְשָׁד, תַּרְתֵּין שְׁנִין בָּתַר טוֹפָנָא: יא וַחֲיָא שֵׁם, בָּתַר דְּאוֹלֵיד יָת אַרְפַּכְשָׁד, חֲמֵשׁ מְאָה שְׁנִין, וְאוֹלֵיד בְּנִין וּבְנָן: יב וְאַרְפַּכְשַׁד חֲיָא, תְּלָתִין וַחֲמֵשׁ שְׁנִין, וְאוֹלֵיד יָת שָׁלַח: יג וַחֲיָא אַרְפַּכְשַׁד, בָּתַר דְּאוֹלֵיד יָת שֶׁלַח, אַרְבַּע מְאָה וּתְלָת שְׁנִין, וְאוֹלֵיד בְּנִין וּבְנָן: יד וְשֶׁלַח חֲיָא תְּלָתִין שְׁנִין, וְאוֹלֵיד יָת עֵבֶר: טו וַחֲיָא שֶׁלַח, בָּתַר דְּאוֹלֵיד יָת עֵבֶר, אַרְבַּע מְאָה וּתְלָת שְׁנִין, וְאוֹלֵיד בְּנִין וּבְנָן: טז וַחֲיָא עֵבֶר, תְּלָתִין וְאַרְבַּע שְׁנִין, וְאוֹלֵיד יָת פָּלֶג: יז וַחֲיָא עֵבֶר, בָּתַר דְּאוֹלֵיד יָת פֶּלֶג, אַרְבַּע מְאָה וּתְלָתִין שְׁנִין, וְאוֹלֵיד בְּנִין וּבְנָן: יח וַחֲיָא פֶלֶג תְּלָתִין שְׁנִין, וְאוֹלֵיד יָת רְעוּ: יט וַחֲיָא פֶלֶג, בָּתַר דְּאוֹלֵיד יָת רְעוּ, מָאתַן וּתְשַׁע

רש״י

בָּעִקָּר וְאֵלּוּ פָּשְׁטוּ יָד בָּעִקָּר לְהִלָּחֵם בּוֹ, וְאֵלּוּ נִשְׁטְפוּ וְאֵלּוּ לֹא נֶאֶבְדוּ מִן הָעוֹלָם! אֶלָּא שֶׁדּוֹר הַמַּבּוּל הָיוּ גַּזְלָנִים וְהָיְתָה מְרִיבָה בֵּינֵיהֶם, וְאֵלּוּ הָיוּ נוֹהֲגִים אַהֲבָה וְרֵעוּת בֵּינֵיהֶם, שֶׁנֶּאֱמַר: "שָׂפָה אֶחָת וּדְבָרִים אֲחָדִים" (לעיל פסוק א). לָמַדְתָּ שֶׁשְּׂנוּאוּי הַמַּחֲלֹקֶת וְגָדוֹל הַשָּׁלוֹם:

י **שֵׁם בֶּן מְאַת שָׁנָה.** כְּשֶׁהוֹלִיד אֶת אַרְפַּכְשַׁד שְׁנָתַיִם אַחַר הַמַּבּוּל:

is an assault on our God-given differences, and the result is tyranny and oppression. The Torah is showing us how – and why – the unity of God coexists with the diversity of humankind.

י אֵלֶּה תּוֹלְדֹת שֵׁם שֵׁם בֶּן־מְאַת שָׁנָה וַיּוֹלֶד אֶת־אַרְפַּכְשָׁד שְׁנָתַיִם
יא אַחַר הַמַּבּוּל: וַיְחִי־שֵׁם אַחֲרֵי הוֹלִידוֹ אֶת־אַרְפַּכְשָׁד חֲמֵשׁ מֵאוֹת
יב שָׁנָה וַיּוֹלֶד בָּנִים וּבָנוֹת: וְאַרְפַּכְשַׁד חַי חָמֵשׁ וּשְׁלֹשִׁים שָׁנָה
יג וַיּוֹלֶד אֶת־שָׁלַח: וַיְחִי אַרְפַּכְשַׁד אַחֲרֵי הוֹלִידוֹ אֶת־שֶׁלַח שָׁלֹשׁ שָׁנִים
יד וְאַרְבַּע מֵאוֹת שָׁנָה וַיּוֹלֶד בָּנִים וּבָנוֹת: וְשֶׁלַח חַי שְׁלֹשִׁים
טו שָׁנָה וַיּוֹלֶד אֶת־עֵבֶר: וַיְחִי־שֶׁלַח אַחֲרֵי הוֹלִידוֹ אֶת־עֵבֶר שָׁלֹשׁ שָׁנִים
טז וְאַרְבַּע מֵאוֹת שָׁנָה וַיּוֹלֶד בָּנִים וּבָנוֹת: וַיְחִי־עֵבֶר אַרְבַּע
יז וּשְׁלֹשִׁים שָׁנָה וַיּוֹלֶד אֶת־פָּלֶג: וַיְחִי־עֵבֶר אַחֲרֵי הוֹלִידוֹ אֶת־פֶּלֶג
יח שְׁלֹשִׁים שָׁנָה וְאַרְבַּע מֵאוֹת שָׁנָה וַיּוֹלֶד בָּנִים וּבָנוֹת: וַיְחִי־
יט פֶלֶג שְׁלֹשִׁים שָׁנָה וַיּוֹלֶד אֶת־רְעוּ: וַיְחִי־פֶלֶג אַחֲרֵי הוֹלִידוֹ אֶת־רְעוּ
כ תֵּשַׁע שָׁנִים וּמָאתַיִם שָׁנָה וַיּוֹלֶד בָּנִים וּבָנוֹת: וַיְחִי רְעוּ
כא שְׁתַּיִם וּשְׁלֹשִׁים שָׁנָה וַיּוֹלֶד אֶת־שְׂרוּג: וַיְחִי רְעוּ אַחֲרֵי הוֹלִידוֹ אֶת־
כב שְׂרוּג שֶׁבַע שָׁנִים וּמָאתַיִם שָׁנָה וַיּוֹלֶד בָּנִים וּבָנוֹת: וַיְחִי
כג שְׂרוּג שְׁלֹשִׁים שָׁנָה וַיּוֹלֶד אֶת־נָחוֹר: וַיְחִי שְׂרוּג אַחֲרֵי הוֹלִידוֹ אֶת־
כד נָחוֹר מָאתַיִם שָׁנָה וַיּוֹלֶד בָּנִים וּבָנוֹת: וַיְחִי נָחוֹר תֵּשַׁע
כה וְעֶשְׂרִים שָׁנָה וַיּוֹלֶד אֶת־תָּרַח: וַיְחִי נָחוֹר אַחֲרֵי הוֹלִידוֹ אֶת־תֶּרַח
כו תְּשַׁע־עֶשְׂרֵה שָׁנָה וּמְאַת שָׁנָה וַיּוֹלֶד בָּנִים וּבָנוֹת: וַיְחִי־
כז תֶרַח שִׁבְעִים שָׁנָה וַיּוֹלֶד אֶת־אַבְרָם אֶת־נָחוֹר וְאֶת־הָרָן: וְאֵלֶּה
תּוֹלְדֹת תֶּרַח תֶּרַח הוֹלִיד אֶת־אַבְרָם אֶת־נָחוֹר וְאֶת־הָרָן וְהָרָן

אונקלוס

שְׁנִין, וְאוֹלֵיד בְּנִין וּבְנָן: כ וַחֲיָא רְעוּ, תְּלָתִין וְתַרְתֵּין שְׁנִין, וְאוֹלֵיד יָת שְׂרוּג: כא וַחֲיָא רְעוּ, בָּתַר דְּאוֹלֵיד יָת שְׂרוּג, מָאתַן וּשְׁבַע שְׁנִין, וְאוֹלֵיד בְּנִין וּבְנָן: כב וַחֲיָא שְׂרוּג תְּלָתִין שְׁנִין, וְאוֹלֵיד יָת נָחוֹר: כג וַחֲיָא שְׂרוּג, בָּתַר, דְּאוֹלֵיד יָת נָחוֹר מָאתַן שְׁנִין, וְאוֹלֵיד בְּנִין וּבְנָן:

כד וַחֲיָא נָחוֹר, עֶסְרִין וּתְשַׁע שְׁנִין, וְאוֹלֵיד יָת תָּרַח: כה וַחֲיָא נָחוֹר, בָּתַר דְּאוֹלֵיד יָת תֶּרַח, מְאָה וּתְשַׁע עֶסְרֵי שְׁנִין, וְאוֹלֵיד בְּנִין וּבְנָן: כו וַחֲיָא תֶרַח שַׁבְעִין שְׁנִין, וְאוֹלֵיד יָת אַבְרָם, יָת נָחוֹר וְיָת הָרָן: כז וְאִלֵּין תּוֹלְדָת תֶּרַח, תֶּרַח אוֹלֵיד יָת אַבְרָם, יָת נָחוֹר וְיָת הָרָן, וְהָרָן

Parashat Lekh Lekha

12 1 The Lord said to Avram, "Go – from your land, your birthplace, and your

רש״י

יב א-בו לֵךְ לְךָ. לַהֲנָאָתְךָ וּלְטוֹבָתְךָ, וְשָׁם אֶעֶשְׂךָ לְגוֹי גָּדוֹל, וְכָאן אִי אַתָּה זוֹכֶה לְבָנִים; וְעוֹד, שֶׁאוֹדִיעַ טִבְעֲךָ בָּעוֹלָם:

a question, but there is always an answer, for if we could understand God we would know that the world is as it is because it would be less good were it otherwise. There is a palace. Therefore there are no flames.

The faith of Avraham begins in the refusal to accept either answer. Suppose both God and evil exist? Suppose there are both the palace and the flames?

It is in that cry, that sacred discontent, that Avraham's journey begins. At the heart of reality is a contradiction between order and chaos, and it has no resolution at the level of thought. It can be resolved only at the level of action, only by making the world other than it is. To be a Jew is to have the courage to refuse easy answers; to reject either consolation or despair. God exists; therefore life has a purpose. Evil exists; therefore we have not yet achieved that purpose. Until then we must travel, just as Avraham and Sara traveled, to begin the task of shaping a different kind of world.

What haunts us about the midrash is not just Avraham's question, but God's reply. He says, in effect, "I am here," without explaining the flames. He does not attempt to put out the fire. It is as if, instead, He were calling for help. God made the building. Man set it on fire. Only man can put out the flames. Avraham asks God, "Where are You?" God replies, "I am here; where are you?" Man asks God, "Why did You abandon me?" So begins a dialogue between earth and heaven, which has not ceased for four thousand years. In these questions, which only the other can answer, God and man find one another. Perhaps only together can they extinguish the flames.

12:1 לֶךְ־לְךָ *Go* – In Hebrew the suggestive phrase is *Lekh lekha* – literally, "Go for yourself," or possibly "Go to yourself." A more midrashic interpretation takes the phrase to mean "Go *with* yourself" – meaning, by traveling from place to place you will extend your influence not over one land but many:

> When the Holy One said to Avraham, "Go – from your land, your birthplace, and your father's house" what did Avraham resemble? A jar of scent with a tight-fitting lid put away in a corner so that its fragrance could not go forth. As soon as it was moved from that place and opened, its fragrance began to spread. So the Holy One said to Avraham, "Avraham, many good deeds are in you. Travel about from place to place, so that the greatness of your name will go forth in My world." (Bereshit Rabba 39:2)

Avraham is commanded to leave his place in order to testify to the existence of a God not bounded by place – Creator and sovereign of the entire universe. Avraham and Sara are to be like perfume, leaving a trace of their presence wherever they go. Implicit in this midrash is the idea that the fate of the first Jews already prefigured that of their descendants, who would be scattered throughout the world in order to spread knowledge of God throughout the world. Unusually, exile is seen here not as punishment but as a necessary corollary of a faith that sees God everywhere. *Lekh lekha* means "Go with yourself" – your beliefs, your way of life, your faith.

12:1 לֶךְ־לְךָ מֵאַרְצְךָ *Go – from your land* – There is another interpretation of the phrase *Lekh lekha*: "Go by yourself." Only a person willing to stand alone, singular and unique, can worship the God who is alone, singular and unique. Only one able to leave behind the natural sources of identity – home, family, culture and society – can encounter God

פרשת לך לך

יב א וַיֹּאמֶר יהוה אֶל־אַבְרָם לֶךְ־לְךָ מֵאַרְצְךָ וּמִמּוֹלַדְתְּךָ וּמִבֵּית אָבִיךָ

אונקלוס

יב א וַאֲמַר יי לְאַבְרָם, אִיזֵיל לָךְ, מֵאַרְעָךְ וּמִיַּלָּדוּתָךְ וּמִבֵּית אֲבוּךְ,

LEKH LEKHA

In response to the call of God, Avraham and Sara begin their journey to a new land and a new kind of faith, which will become the context of the entire Jewish drama thereafter.

Avraham's life is a culmination of all that has gone before. The first four dramas of Genesis dealt with the evasion and abdication of responsibility. Adam denies personal responsibility. Kayin denies moral responsibility. Noaḥ fails the test of collective responsibility. Bavel was a rejection of ontological responsibility (see ch. 11, "The Tower of Bavel"). Avraham represents the turning point, offering a counterpoint to the previous failures.

The first words of God to Avraham, as we shall see, are a call to personal responsibility. By entering into battle, in Genesis 14, to rescue (not his brother, but his brother's son) Lot, Avraham exercises *moral* responsibility. Unlike Kayin, he *is* his brother's keeper. As the drama builds in the next *parasha*, he will display collective and finally ontological responsibility in the greatest trial of all.

AVRAHAM'S CALL

Tradition offers several explanations of how Avraham and Sara's journey began. According to one, Avraham was the iconoclast who broke his father's idols. According to another, he was the philosopher who, seeing people worship the sun and the stars, asked, "But who created *them*?" But the Midrash contains a third and altogether more radical reading:

> The Lord said to Avram: "Go…." To what may this be compared? To a man who was traveling from place to place when he saw a palace in flames. He wondered, "Is it possible that the palace lacks an owner?" The owner of the palace looked out and said, "I am the owner of the palace." So Avraham our father said, "Is it possible that the world lacks a ruler?" The Holy One, blessed be He, looked out and said to him, "I am the ruler, the sovereign of the universe." (*Midrash HaGadol*, Bereishit 12:1)

This is a deeply enigmatic passage. Avraham sees a palace. The world has order, and therefore it has a creator. But the palace is in flames. The world is full of *dis*order, of evil, violence, and injustice. Now, no one builds a building and then deserts it. If there is a fire, there must be someone to put it out. The building must have an owner. If so, where is he? That is the question, and it gives Avraham no peace. With this we arrive at the starting point of Jewish faith. Faith is born not in the answer but in the question, not in harmony but in dissonance. If God created the world, then why does He allow man to destroy the world? Can God have made the world only to abandon it?

From time immemorial to the present, there have always been two ways of seeing the world. The first view says there is no God. There are contending forces, chance and necessity – the chance that produces variation, and the necessity that gives the strong victory over the weak. From this perspective, the evolution of the universe is inexorable and blind, and therefore we never know *why*. There is no why. There is no palace. There are only flames.

The second view insists that there is a God. All that exists or transpires does so because He willed it. Therefore, all injustice is an illusion. Perhaps the world itself is an illusion. When the innocent suffer, it is to teach them to find faith through suffering, the soul's strength through the body's torments. Evil is the cloak that masks the good. There is

2 father's house – to the land that I will show you. I will make you a great nation,
and I will bless you and make your name great. You will become a blessing.
3 And I will bless those who bless you, and those who curse you I will curse. And
4 through you, all the families of the earth will be blessed." So Avram went, as the
Lord had told him, and with him went Lot. Avram was seventy-five years old

רש"י

וְאֶעֶשְׂךָ לְגוֹי גָּדוֹל. לְפִי שֶׁהַדֶּרֶךְ גּוֹרֶמֶת לִשְׁלֹשָׁה דְּבָרִים: מְמַעֶטֶת פְּרִיָּה וּרְבִיָּה, וּמְמַעֶטֶת אֶת הַמָּמוֹן, וּמְמַעֶטֶת אֶת הַשֵּׁם; לְכָךְ הִזְקִיק לְשָׁלֹשׁ בְּרָכוֹת הַלָּלוּ, שֶׁהִבְטִיחוֹ עַל הַבָּנִים וְעַל הַמָּמוֹן וְעַל הַשֵּׁם: **וַאֲבָרֶכְךָ.** בְּמָמוֹן. בְּרֵאשִׁית רַבָּה (לט, יח): **וֶהְיֵה בְּרָכָה.** הַבְּרָכוֹת נְתוּנוֹת בְּיָדְךָ. עַד עַכְשָׁיו הָיוּ בְּיָדִי, בֵּרַכְתִּי לְאָדָם וְנֹחַ, וּמֵעַכְשָׁיו אַתָּה תְּבָרֵךְ אֶת אֲשֶׁר תַּחְפֹּץ. בְּרֵאשִׁית רַבָּה (שם). דָּבָר אַחֵר, "וְאֶעֶשְׂךָ לְגוֹי גָּדוֹל", זֶה שֶׁאוֹמְרִים אֱלֹהֵי אַבְרָהָם; "וַאֲבָרֶכְךָ", זֶה שֶׁאוֹמְרִים אֱלֹהֵי יִצְחָק; "וַאֲגַדְּלָה שְׁמֶךָ", זֶה שֶׁאוֹמְרִים אֱלֹהֵי יַעֲקֹב. יָכוֹל יִהְיוּ חוֹתְמִין בְּכֻלָּן? תַּלְמוּד לוֹמַר: "וֶהְיֵה בְּרָכָה", בְּךָ חוֹתְמִין וְלֹא בָּהֶם: **מֵאַרְצְךָ.** וַהֲלֹא כְּבָר יָצָא מִשָּׁם עִם אָבִיו וּבָא עַד חָרָן? אֶלָּא כָּךְ אָמַר לוֹ: הִתְרַחֵק עוֹד וְצֵא מִבֵּית אָבִיךָ: **אֲשֶׁר אַרְאֶךָּ.** לֹא גִּלָּה לוֹ הָאָרֶץ מִיָּד, כְּדֵי לְחַבְּבָהּ בְּעֵינָיו וְלָתֵת לוֹ שָׂכָר עַל כָּל דִּבּוּר וְדִבּוּר. כַּיּוֹצֵא בוֹ: "אֶת בִּנְךָ אֶת יְחִידְךָ אֲשֶׁר אָהַבְתָּ" (להלן כב, ב), כַּיּוֹצֵא בוֹ: "עַל אַחַד הֶהָרִים אֲשֶׁר אֹמַר אֵלֶיךָ" (שם), כַּיּוֹצֵא בוֹ: "וּקְרָא אֵלֶיהָ אֶת הַקְּרִיאָה אֲשֶׁר אָנֹכִי דֹּבֵר אֵלֶיךָ" (יונה ג, ב):

ג **וְנִבְרְכוּ בְךָ.** יֵשׁ אַגָּדוֹת רַבּוֹת, וְזֶהוּ פְּשׁוּטוֹ: אָדָם אוֹמֵר לִבְנוֹ תְּהֵא כְּאַבְרָהָם. וְכֵן כָּל 'וְנִבְרְכוּ בְךָ' שֶׁבַּמִּקְרָא, וְזֶה מוֹכִיחַ: "בְּךָ יְבָרֵךְ יִשְׂרָאֵל לֵאמֹר יְשִׂמְךָ אֱלֹהִים כְּאֶפְרַיִם וְכִמְנַשֶּׁה" (להלן מח, כ):

associated with the founder of a new faith. They are the kind of attributes to which any of us could aspire. None of us can be an Avraham, but all of us can take him as a role model.

Avraham is the paradigm of an unheroic hero, one who (in Rambam's lovely phrase) "does what is right because it is right" (*Hilkhot Teshuva* 10:2) and not for the sake of popularity or fame. As the founder of Judaism, Avraham gives us a vision of what it is to live directly and immediately in the presence of God, who knows our thoughts, our hopes, our fears, our dreams. This involves a radically new kind of heroism: the heroism of decency and goodness, integrity and faithfulness, the humble, unostentatious heroism of being willing to live by one's convictions though all the world thinks otherwise, being true to the call of eternity, not the noise of now.

12:3 **וְנִבְרְכוּ בְךָ כֹּל מִשְׁפְּחֹת הָאֲדָמָה** *All the families of the earth will be blessed* – Half promise, half command. Avraham, unlike Adam and Noaḥ, is not a symbol of humanity as a whole. He is an individual singled out for a particular destiny. His children, too, become a people singled out for a particular destiny. Why Avraham is chosen, we never discover. That is one of the great enigmas of the Tanakh. *But to what end he is chosen*, we discover at the very beginning: to be a blessing. Not to his family or to God alone, but to all the peoples on earth. Somehow he will enrich the lives of others, of cultures and faiths very different from his own. Some will bless him for this, others will curse him. That much is known in advance. But the lives of his descendants will be peculiarly interwoven with the history of many nations, and they will leave their mark, hopefully for blessing, on many cultures. This has been a recurring theme of Jewish experience.

12:4 **כַּאֲשֶׁר דִּבֶּר אֵלָיו יהוה** *As the Lord had told him* – Avraham is a new human type: the person whose life is a response to the call of God. Until now, with the exception of Noaḥ, we have encountered human beings for whom God's command is a constraint from which they try to break free, by violence in the case of Kayin and the generation of the flood, by hubris in the case of the builders of Bavel. Avraham is different. For him, the command is life itself. God speaks; Avraham listens and acts, without resistance on the one hand, and with pride on the other. His life is an answer to God's question; his existence is lived in the conscious presence of the divine will.

With Avraham a new faith is born: the faith of responsibility, in which the divine command and the human act meet and give birth to a new and blessed order, built on the principles of righteousness and justice. Judaism is supremely a religion of freedom – not freedom in the modern sense,

ב אֶל־הָאָ֖רֶץ אֲשֶׁ֥ר אַרְאֶֽךָּ׃ וְאֶֽעֶשְׂךָ֙ לְג֣וֹי גָּד֔וֹל וַאֲבָרֶכְךָ֔ וַאֲגַדְּלָ֖ה שְׁמֶ֑ךָ
ג וֶהְיֵ֖ה בְּרָכָֽה׃ וַאֲבָֽרְכָה֙ מְבָ֣רְכֶ֔יךָ וּמְקַלֶּלְךָ֖ אָאֹ֑ר וְנִבְרְכ֣וּ בְךָ֔ כֹּ֖ל מִשְׁפְּחֹ֥ת
ד הָאֲדָמָֽה׃ וַיֵּ֣לֶךְ אַבְרָ֗ם כַּאֲשֶׁ֨ר דִּבֶּ֤ר אֵלָיו֙ יהוה וַיֵּ֥לֶךְ אִתּ֖וֹ ל֑וֹט וְאַבְרָ֕ם

אונקלוס

לְאַרְעָא דְּאַחֲזֵינָךְ: ב וְאַעְבְּדִנָּךְ לְעַם סַגִּי, וַאֲבָרְכִנָּךְ, וַאֲרַבֵּי שְׁמָךְ, וּתְהֵי
מְבָרַךְ: ג וַאֲבָרֵיךְ מְבָרְכָךְ, וּמְלַטְטָךְ אֵלוּט, וְיִתְבָּרְכוּן בְּדִילָךְ, כָּל זַרְעִית
אַרְעָא: ד וַאֲזַל אַבְרָם, כְּמָא דְּמַלֵּיל עִמֵּיהּ יְיָ, וַאֲזַל עִמֵּיהּ לוֹט, וְאַבְרָם,

who stands above and beyond nature. Avraham's children are summoned to be the people that defy the laws of nature because they refuse to define themselves as the products of nature. That is not to say that economic or biological or psychological forces have no part to play in human behavior. They do. But with sufficient imagination, determination, discipline, and courage we can rise above them. Avraham does. So, at most times, will his children.

Lekh Lekha in this sense means being prepared to take an often lonely journey: "Go by yourself." To be a child of Avraham is to have the courage to be different, to challenge the idols of the age, whatever the idols and whichever the age. In an era of polytheism, that meant seeing the universe as the product of a single creative will – and therefore not meaningless but coherent, meaningful. When power was worshipped, it meant constructing a society that cared for the powerless, the widow, orphan, and stranger. During centuries in which the mass of mankind was sunk in ignorance, it meant honoring education as the key to human dignity and creating schools to provide universal literacy. In ages of radical individualism like today, it means knowing that we are not what we own but what we share; not what we buy but what we give. To be a Jew is to be willing to hear the still, small voice of eternity urging us to travel, move, go on ahead, continuing Avraham's journey toward that unknown destination at the far horizon of hope.

12:1 מֵאַרְצְךָ וּמִמּוֹלַדְתְּךָ וּמִבֵּית אָבִיךָ *From your land, your birthplace, and your father's house* – The call to Avraham is a counter-commentary to the three great determinisms of the modern world. Karl Marx held that behavior is determined by structures of power in society, among them the ownership of land. Therefore God said, "Go from your land." Spinoza believed human conduct is given by the instincts we acquire at birth (what we now might call genetic determinism). Therefore God said, "Go from your birthplace." Freud held that we are shaped by early experiences in childhood. Therefore God said, "Go from your father's house." Avraham is the refutation of determinism. There are structures of power, but we can stand outside them. There are genetic influences on our behavior, but we can master them. We are shaped by our parents, but we can go beyond them. Avraham's journey is as much psychological as geographical. Like the Israelites in Moshe's day, he is traveling to freedom.

12:1 אֶל־הָאָרֶץ אֲשֶׁר אַרְאֶךָּ *To the land that I will show you* – Rashi, following an ancient exegetic tradition, translates God's opening words as "Journey for yourself" (Gen. 12:1). According to him, God is saying, "Travel for your own benefit and good. There I will make you into a great nation; here you will not have the merit of having children." In His first words to Avraham, God is already intimating that what seems like a sacrifice is, in the long run, not so. Sometimes we have to give up our past in order to acquire a future. "Go for yourself" – believe in what you can become.

12:2 וֶהְיֵה בְּרָכָה *You will become a blessing* – There has never been anyone like Avraham, yet the Torah is exceptionally understated in its account of him. Leaving aside midrashic interpretations, the Torah's presentation of Avraham does not fit any conventional image of the religious hero. To be sure, he is a man of exemplary virtue. But if we were asked to characterize him with adjectives, the words that spring to mind – gentle, kind, gracious – are not those usually

5 when he left Ḥaran. Avram took Sarai his wife, and Lot his nephew, and all the
wealth they had acquired and the people they had gathered in Ḥaran. They set
6 out to go to the land of Canaan, and they entered the land of Canaan. Avram
traveled through the land to the region of Shekhem, to the Oak of Moreh. The
7 Canaanites were then in the land. Then the LORD appeared to Avram and said,
"To your descendants I will give this land." There he built an altar to the LORD,
8 who had appeared to him. And from there he moved on to the hills east of Beit
El, and pitched his tent with Beit El to the west and Ai to the east. There he
9 built an altar to the LORD and called on the name of the LORD. Then Avram
journeyed on, traveling toward the Negev.
10 There was a famine in the land. Avram went down to Egypt to stay there for
11 a while because the famine in the land was severe. And as his arrival in Egypt
drew close, he said to Sarai his wife, "I know what a beautiful woman you are.

רש״י

ה **אשר עשו בחרן.** שהכניסום תחת כנפי השכינה, אברהם מגייר את האנשים ושרה מגיירת הנשים, ומעלה עליהם הכתוב כאלו עשאום. ופשוטו של מקרא: עבדים ושפחות שקנו להם, כמו: "עשה את כל הכבד הזה" (להלן לא, א), "וישראל עשה חיל" (במדבר כד, יח) לשון קונה וכונס:

ו **ויעבר אברם בארץ.** נכנס לתוכה: **עד מקום שכם.** להתפלל על בני יעקב כשיבאו לשכם: **אלון מורה.** הוא שכם. הראהו הר גרזים והר עיבל ששם קבלו ישראל שבועת התורה: **והכנעני אז בארץ.** היה הולך וכובש את ארץ ישראל מזרעו של שם, שבחלקו של שם נפלה כשחלק נח את הארץ לבניו, שנאמר: "ומלכי צדק מלך שלם" (להלן יד, יח), לפיכך "ויאמר - אל אברם - לזרעך אתן את הארץ הזאת" (להלן פסוק ז), עתיד אני להחזירה לבניך שהם מזרעו של שם:

ז **ויבן שם מזבח.** על בשורת הזרע ועל בשורת ארץ ישראל:

ח **ויעתק משם.** אהלו: **מקדם לבית אל.** במזרחה של בית אל, נמצאת בית אל במערבו, הוא שנאמר: "בית אל מים": **אהלה.** אהלה כתיב, בתחלה נטה את אהל אשתו ואחר כך את שלו. בראשית רבה (לט, טו): **ויבן שם מזבח.** נתנבא שעתידין בניו להכשל שם על עון עכן והתפלל עליהם:

ט **הלוך ונסוע.** לפרקים, יושב כאן חדש או יותר ונוסע משם ונוטה אהלו במקום אחר, וכל מסעיו "הנגבה", ללכת לדרומה של ארץ ישראל, והוא בחלקו של יהודה שנטלו בדרומה של ארץ ישראל, והוא לצד ירושלים, הר המוריה. בראשית רבה (לט, טז):

י **רעב בארץ.** באותה הארץ לבדה, לנסותו אם יהרהר אחר דבריו של הקדוש ברוך הוא, שאמר לו ללכת אל ארץ כנען ועכשו מסיאו לצאת ממנה:

יא **הנה נא ידעתי.** מדרש אגדה: עד עכשיו לא הכיר בה מתוך צניעות שבשניהם, ועכשיו הכיר בה על ידי מעשה. דבר אחר, מנהג העולם שעל ידי טורח הדרך אדם מתבזה, וזאת עמדה ביפיה. ופשוטו של מקרא: הנה נא הגיעה שעה שיש לדאג על יפיך; ידעתי זה ימים כי יפת מראה את, ועכשיו אנו באים בין אנשים שחורים ומכוערים, אחיהם של כושים, ולא הרגלו באשה יפה. ודומה לו: "הנה נא אדני סורו נא" (להלן יט, ב):

of God. Yet none has been more honest about the failings of even the greatest. God does not ask us to be perfect. He asks us, instead, to take risks in pursuit of the right and the good, and to acknowledge the mistakes we will inevitably make. In Judaism, the moral life is about learning and growing, knowing that even the greatest have failings and even the worst have saving graces. It calls for humility about ourselves and generosity toward others. This unique blend of idealism and realism is morality at its most demanding and mature.

ה בֶּן־חָמֵשׁ שָׁנִים וְשִׁבְעִים שָׁנָה בְּצֵאתוֹ מֵחָרָן: וַיִּקַּח אַבְרָם אֶת־שָׂרַי
אִשְׁתּוֹ וְאֶת־לוֹט בֶּן־אָחִיו וְאֶת־כָּל־רְכוּשָׁם אֲשֶׁר רָכָשׁוּ וְאֶת־הַנֶּפֶשׁ
ו אֲשֶׁר־עָשׂוּ בְחָרָן וַיֵּצְאוּ לָלֶכֶת אַרְצָה כְּנַעַן וַיָּבֹאוּ אַרְצָה כְּנָעַן: וַיַּעֲבֹר
אַבְרָם בָּאָרֶץ עַד מְקוֹם שְׁכֶם עַד אֵלוֹן מוֹרֶה וְהַכְּנַעֲנִי אָז בָּאָרֶץ:
ז וַיֵּרָא יהוה אֶל־אַבְרָם וַיֹּאמֶר לְזַרְעֲךָ אֶתֵּן אֶת־הָאָרֶץ הַזֹּאת וַיִּבֶן שָׁם
ח מִזְבֵּחַ לַיהוה הַנִּרְאֶה אֵלָיו: וַיַּעְתֵּק מִשָּׁם הָהָרָה מִקֶּדֶם לְבֵית־אֵל
וַיֵּט אָהֳלֹה בֵּית־אֵל מִיָּם וְהָעַי מִקֶּדֶם וַיִּבֶן־שָׁם מִזְבֵּחַ לַיהוה וַיִּקְרָא
ט בְּשֵׁם יהוה: וַיִּסַּע אַבְרָם הָלוֹךְ וְנָסוֹעַ הַנֶּגְבָּה:
י וַיְהִי רָעָב בָּאָרֶץ וַיֵּרֶד אַבְרָם מִצְרַיְמָה לָגוּר שָׁם כִּי־כָבֵד הָרָעָב בָּאָרֶץ:
יא וַיְהִי כַּאֲשֶׁר הִקְרִיב לָבוֹא מִצְרָיְמָה וַיֹּאמֶר אֶל־שָׂרַי אִשְׁתּוֹ הִנֵּה־נָא

אונקלוס

בַּר שַׁבְעִין וְחַמֵשׁ שְׁנִין, בְּמִפְקֵיהּ מֵחָרָן: ה וּדְבַר אַבְרָם יָת שָׂרַי
אִתְּתֵיהּ וְיָת לוֹט בַּר אֲחוּהִי, וְיָת כָּל קִנְיָנְהוֹן דִּקְנוֹ, וְיָת נַפְשָׁתָא
דְּשַׁעֲבִידוּ לְאוֹרָיְתָא בְּחָרָן, וּנְפָקוּ, לְמֵיזַל לְאַרְעָא דִּכְנַעַן, וַאֲתוֹ
לְאַרְעָא דִּכְנָעַן: ו וַעֲבַר אַבְרָם בְּאַרְעָא, עַד אֲתַר שְׁכֶם, עַד מֵישַׁר
מוֹרֶה, וּכְנַעֲנָאָה בְּכֵן בְּאַרְעָא: ז וְאִתְגְּלִי יי לְאַבְרָם, וַאֲמַר, לִבְנָךְ,
אֶתֵּין יָת אַרְעָא הָדָא, וּבְנָא תַמָּן מַדְבְּחָא, קֳדָם יי דְּאִתְגְּלִי לֵיהּ:

ח וְאִסְתַּלַּק מִתַּמָּן לְטוּרָא, מִמַּדְנַח, לְבֵית אֵל וּפְרַסֵיהּ לְמַשְׁכְּנֵיהּ,
בֵּית אֵל מִמַּעַרְבָא וְעַי מִמַּדִנְחָא, וּבְנָא תַמָּן מַדְבְּחָא קֳדָם יי, וְצַלִּי
בִּשְׁמָא דַּיי: ט וּנְטַל אַבְרָם, אָזֵיל וְנָטֵיל לְדָרוֹמָא: י וַהֲוָה כַּפְנָא בְּאַרְעָא,
וּנְחַת אַבְרָם לְמִצְרַיִם לְאִתּוֹתָבָא תַמָּן, אֲרֵי תְּקֵיף כַּפְנָא בְּאַרְעָא:
יא וַהֲוָה, כַּד קְרֵיב לְמֵיעַל לְמִצְרָיִם, וַאֲמַר לְשָׂרַי אִתְּתֵיהּ, הָא כְעַן

the ability to do what we *like*, but in the ethical sense of the ability to choose to do what we *should*, to become co-architects with God of a just and gracious social order. The former leads to a culture of rights, the latter to a culture of responsibilities: to *freedom as responsibility*.

12:10 וַיֵּרֶד אַבְרָם מִצְרַיְמָה *Avram went down to Egypt* – In an extraordinary series of observations on Parashat Lekh Lekha, Ramban (Rabbi Moshe ben Naḥman Girondi, or Naḥmanides) delivers harsh criticisms of Avraham and Sara. The first has to do with Avraham's decision, after arriving at the land of Canaan, to leave and go to Egypt because "there was a famine in the land" (Gen. 12:10). According to Ramban (commentary on Gen. 12:10, based on Zohar, Tazria, 52a), Avraham should have stayed in Canaan; he should have had faith in God that He would sustain him despite the famine. Avraham's decision to leave was not his only error; he also put Sara in a position in which she was compelled to tell a lie. In saying that she was Avraham's sister and not his wife, she was taken into Pharaoh's harem where she might have been forced into adultery. This is a very harsh judgment, made more so by Ramban's further assertion that it was because of this lack of faith that Avraham's children were sentenced to exile in Egypt centuries later.

No religion has held a higher view of humanity than the book that tells us we are each in the image and likeness

12 When the Egyptians see you, they will say, 'She is his wife'; they will kill me
13 and keep you alive. Please, say you are my sister. Then I will be treated well for
14 your sake, and because of you my life will be spared." When Avram came to SHENI
Egypt, the Egyptians saw the woman, saw that she was very beautiful indeed.
15 And when Pharaoh's officials saw her, they praised her to Pharaoh, and the
16 woman was taken into Pharaoh's palace. He treated Avram well for her sake:
he acquired flocks, herds, donkeys, male and female servants, she-donkeys,
17 and camels. But the LORD struck Pharaoh and his household with terrible
18 afflictions because of Avram's wife Sarai. Pharaoh summoned Avram and said,
19 "What have you done to me? Why did you not tell me she was your wife? Why
did you say 'She is my sister,' so that I took her as a wife? Now – here is your
20 wife. Take her. Go." Pharaoh gave orders to his men about him, and they sent
13 1 him on his way, together with his wife and all that he had. Then Avram went
up from Egypt to the Negev with his wife and all he had, and with him went
2 3 Lot. And Avram had become very wealthy in cattle, silver, and gold. From the
Negev he continued on his journey to Beit El, to the site between Beit El and
4 Ai where his tent had previously been, and where he had first made an altar.
5 There Avram called on the name of the LORD. Lot, who went with Avram, had SHELISHI
6 flocks, herds, and tents as well, and the land could not support them living
together; so many were their possessions that they were unable to live side by

רש״י

יג **לְמַעַן יִיטַב לִי בַעֲבוּרֵךְ.** יִתְּנוּ לִי מַתָּנוֹת:

יד **וַיְהִי כְּבוֹא אַבְרָם מִצְרָיְמָה.** הָיָה לוֹ לוֹמַר 'כְּבוֹאָם מִצְרַיְמָה', אֶלָּא לִמֵּד שֶׁהִטְמִין אוֹתָהּ בְּתֵבָה, וְעַל יְדֵי שֶׁתָּבְעוּ אֶת הַמֶּכֶס פָּתְחוּ וְרָאוּ אוֹתָהּ:

טו **וַיְהַלְלוּ אֹתָהּ אֶל פַּרְעֹה.** הִלְּלוּהָ בֵּינֵיהֶם לוֹמַר, הֲגוּנָה זוֹ לַמֶּלֶךְ:

טז **וּלְאַבְרָם הֵיטִיב.** פַּרְעֹה בַּעֲבוּרָהּ:

יז **וַיְנַגַּע.** בְּמַכַּת רָאתָן לָקָה שֶׁהַתַּשְׁמִישׁ קָשֶׁה לוֹ. בִּבְרֵאשִׁית רַבָּה (מא, ב): **עַל דְּבַר שָׂרַי.** עַל פִּי דִבּוּרָהּ, אוֹמֶרֶת לַמַּלְאָךְ הַךְ, וְהוּא מַכֶּה:

יט **קַח וָלֵךְ.** לֹא כַּאֲבִימֶלֶךְ שֶׁאָמַר לוֹ: "הִנֵּה אַרְצִי לְפָנֶיךָ" (להלן כ, טו), אֶלָּא אָמַר לוֹ: לֵךְ וְאַל תַּעֲמֹד, שֶׁהַמִּצְרִים שְׁטוּפֵי זִמָּה הֵם, שֶׁנֶּאֱמַר: "וְזִרְמַת סוּסִים זִרְמָתָם" (יחזקאל כג, כ):

כ **וַיְצַו עָלָיו.** עַל אוֹדוֹתָיו, לְשַׁלְּחוֹ וּלְשָׁמְרוֹ: **וַיְשַׁלְּחוּ.** כְּתַרְגּוּמוֹ: "וְאַלְוִיאוּ":

יג א-ב **כָּבֵד מְאֹד.** טָעוּן מַשָּׂאוֹת: **וַיַּעַל אַבְרָם... הַנֶּגְבָּה.** לָבֹא לִדְרוֹמָהּ שֶׁל אֶרֶץ יִשְׂרָאֵל, כְּמוֹ שֶׁאָמַר לְמַעְלָה: "הָלוֹךְ וְנָסוֹעַ הַנֶּגְבָּה" (לעיל יב, ט) לְהַר הַמּוֹרִיָּה, וּמִכָּל מָקוֹם כְּשֶׁהוּא הוֹלֵךְ מִמִּצְרַיִם לְאֶרֶץ כְּנַעַן מִדָּרוֹם לַצָּפוֹן הוּא מְהַלֵּךְ, שֶׁאֶרֶץ מִצְרַיִם בִּדְרוֹמָהּ שֶׁל אֶרֶץ יִשְׂרָאֵל, כְּמוֹ שֶׁמּוֹכִיחַ בַּמַּסָּעוֹת וּבִגְבוּלֵי הָאָרֶץ:

ג **וַיֵּלֶךְ לְמַסָּעָיו.** כְּשֶׁחָזַר הָיָה לָן בָּאַכְסַנְיוֹת שֶׁלָּן בָּהֶן כְּשֶׁהָלַךְ לְשָׁם. לִמֶּדְךָ דֶּרֶךְ אֶרֶץ שֶׁלֹּא יְשַׁנֶּה אָדָם מֵאַכְסַנְיָה שֶׁלּוֹ. דָּבָר אַחֵר, בַּחֲזָרָתוֹ פָּרַע הַקָּפוֹתָיו: **מִנֶּגֶב.** אֶרֶץ מִצְרַיִם בִּדְרוֹמָהּ שֶׁל אֶרֶץ כְּנַעַן:

ד **אֲשֶׁר עָשָׂה שָׁם בָּרִאשֹׁנָה.** וַאֲשֶׁר קָרָא "שָׁם אַבְרָם בְּשֵׁם ה'". וְגַם יֵשׁ לוֹמַר "וַיִּקְרָא שָׁם" עַכְשָׁיו "בְּשֵׁם ה'":

ה **הַהֹלֵךְ אֶת אַבְרָם.** מִי גָּרַם לוֹ שֶׁהָיָה לוֹ זֹאת? הִלּוּכוֹ עִם אַבְרָם:

ו **וְלֹא נָשָׂא.** לֹא הָיְתָה יְכוֹלָה לְהַסְפִּיק מִרְעֶה לְמִקְנֵיהֶם: **וְלֹא נָשָׂא אֹתָם.** לָשׁוֹן קָצָר הוּא וְצָרִיךְ לְהוֹסִיף עָלָיו, כְּמוֹ: 'וְלֹא נָשָׂא אוֹתָם מִרְעֵה הָאָרֶץ', לְפִיכָךְ כָּתַב: "וְלֹא נָשָׂא" בִּלְשׁוֹן זָכָר:

יב יָדַעְתִּי כִּי אִשָּׁה יְפַת־מַרְאֶה אָתְּ: וְהָיָה כִּי־יִרְאוּ אֹתָךְ הַמִּצְרִים וְאָמְרוּ
יג אִשְׁתּוֹ זֹאת וְהָרְגוּ אֹתִי וְאֹתָךְ יְחַיּוּ: אִמְרִי־נָא אֲחֹתִי אָתְּ לְמַעַן יִיטַב־
יד לִי בַעֲבוּרֵךְ וְחָיְתָה נַפְשִׁי בִּגְלָלֵךְ: וַיְהִי כְּבוֹא אַבְרָם מִצְרָיְמָה וַיִּרְאוּ שני
טו הַמִּצְרִים אֶת־הָאִשָּׁה כִּי־יָפָה הִוא מְאֹד: וַיִּרְאוּ אֹתָהּ שָׂרֵי פַרְעֹה
טז וַיְהַלְלוּ אֹתָהּ אֶל־פַּרְעֹה וַתֻּקַּח הָאִשָּׁה בֵּית פַּרְעֹה: וּלְאַבְרָם הֵיטִיב
בַּעֲבוּרָהּ וַיְהִי־לוֹ צֹאן־וּבָקָר וַחֲמֹרִים וַעֲבָדִים וּשְׁפָחֹת וַאֲתֹנֹת וּגְמַלִּים:
יז וַיְנַגַּע יהוה ׀ אֶת־פַּרְעֹה נְגָעִים גְּדֹלִים וְאֶת־בֵּיתוֹ עַל־דְּבַר שָׂרַי אֵשֶׁת
יח אַבְרָם: וַיִּקְרָא פַרְעֹה לְאַבְרָם וַיֹּאמֶר מַה־זֹּאת עָשִׂיתָ לִּי לָמָּה לֹא־
יט הִגַּדְתָּ לִּי כִּי אִשְׁתְּךָ הִוא: לָמָה אָמַרְתָּ אֲחֹתִי הִוא וָאֶקַּח אֹתָהּ לִי
כ לְאִשָּׁה וְעַתָּה הִנֵּה אִשְׁתְּךָ קַח וָלֵךְ: וַיְצַו עָלָיו פַּרְעֹה אֲנָשִׁים וַיְשַׁלְּחוּ
יג א אֹתוֹ וְאֶת־אִשְׁתּוֹ וְאֶת־כָּל־אֲשֶׁר־לוֹ: וַיַּעַל אַבְרָם מִמִּצְרַיִם הוּא
ב וְאִשְׁתּוֹ וְכָל־אֲשֶׁר־לוֹ וְלוֹט עִמּוֹ הַנֶּגְבָּה: וְאַבְרָם כָּבֵד מְאֹד בַּמִּקְנֶה
ג בַּכֶּסֶף וּבַזָּהָב: וַיֵּלֶךְ לְמַסָּעָיו מִנֶּגֶב וְעַד־בֵּית־אֵל עַד־הַמָּקוֹם אֲשֶׁר־
ד הָיָה שָׁם אָהֳלֹה בַּתְּחִלָּה בֵּין בֵּית־אֵל וּבֵין הָעָי: אֶל־מְקוֹם הַמִּזְבֵּחַ
ה אֲשֶׁר־עָשָׂה שָׁם בָּרִאשֹׁנָה וַיִּקְרָא שָׁם אַבְרָם בְּשֵׁם יהוה: וְגַם־לְלוֹט שלישי
ו הַהֹלֵךְ אֶת־אַבְרָם הָיָה צֹאן־וּבָקָר וְאֹהָלִים: וְלֹא־נָשָׂא אֹתָם הָאָרֶץ

אונקלוס

יְדַעְנָא, אֲרֵי, אִתְּתָא שַׁפִּירַת חֵיזוּ אַתְּ: יב וִיהֵי, אֲרֵי יֶחֱזוֹן יָתִיךְ מִצְרָאֵי, וְיֵימְרוּן אִתְּתֵיהּ דָּא, וְיִקְטְלוּן יָתִי וְיָתִיךְ יְקַיְּמוּן: יג אֵימַרִי כְּעַן דַּאֲחָתִי אַתְּ, בְּדִיל דְּיֵיטַב לִי בְּדִילִיךְ, וְתִתְקַיַּם נַפְשִׁי בְּפִתְגָּמַיְכִי: יד וַהֲוָה, כַּד עָאל אַבְרָם לְמִצְרָיִם, וַחֲזוֹ מִצְרָאֵי יָת אִתְּתָא, אֲרֵי שַׁפִּירָא הִיא לַחְדָּא: טו וַחֲזוֹ יָתַהּ רַבְרְבֵי פַרְעֹה, וְשַׁבַּחוּ יָתַהּ לְפַרְעֹה, וְאִדְּבַרַת אִתְּתָא לְבֵית פַּרְעֹה: טז וּלְאַבְרָם אוֹטֵיב בְּדִילַהּ, וַהֲווֹ לֵיהּ עָן וְתוֹרִין וּחְמָרִין, וְעַבְדִּין וְאַמְהָן, וַאֲתָנָן וְגַמְלִין: יז וְאַיְתִי יי עַל פַּרְעֹה, מַכְתָּשִׁין רַבְרְבִין וְעַל אֱנָשׁ בֵּיתֵיהּ, עַל עֵיסַק שָׂרַי אִתַּת אַבְרָם: יח וּקְרָא פַרְעֹה לְאַבְרָם, וַאֲמַר, מָא דָּא עֲבַדְתְּ לִי, לְמָא לָא חַוֵּיתָ לִי, אֲרֵי אִתְּתָךְ הִיא: יט לְמָא אֲמַרְתְּ אֲחָת הִיא, וּדְבַרִית יָתַהּ, לִי לְאִתּוּ, וּכְעַן, הָא אִתְּתָךְ דְּבַר וְאִיזֵיל: כ וּפַקֵּיד עֲלוֹהִי, פַּרְעֹה גֻּבְרִין, וְאַלְוִיאוּ יָתֵיהּ, וְיָת אִתְּתֵיהּ וְיָת כָּל דְּלֵיהּ: יג א וּסְלֵיק אַבְרָם מִמִּצְרַיִם, הוּא, וְאִתְּתֵיהּ וְכָל דְּלֵיהּ, וְלוֹט עִמֵּיהּ לְדָרוֹמָא: ב וְאַבְרָם תַּקִּיף לַחְדָּא, בִּבְעִירָא, בְּכַסְפָּא וּבְדַהֲבָא: ג וַאֲזַל לְמַטְלָנוֹהִי, מִדָּרוֹמָא וְעַד בֵּית אֵל, עַד אַתְרָא, דִּפְרַסֵיהּ תַּמָּן לְמַשְׁכְּנֵיהּ בְּקַדְמֵיתָא, בֵּין בֵּית אֵל וּבֵין עָי: ד לַאֲתַר מַדְבְּחָא, דַּעֲבַד תַּמָּן בְּקַדְמֵיתָא, וְצַלִּי תַמָּן, אַבְרָם בִּשְׁמָא דַיי: ה וְאַף לְלוֹט, דַּאֲזַל עִם אַבְרָם, הֲווֹ עָן וְתוֹרִין וּמַשְׁכְּנִין: ו וְלָא סוֹבָרַת יָתְהוֹן, אַרְעָא

7 side. A dispute broke out between Avram's herdsmen and those of Lot; and
8 the Canaanites and the Perizzites were then too living in the land. Avram said
to Lot, "Please, let there be no friction between me and you, and between my
9 herdsmen and yours, for we are brothers. The whole land lies before you; please
separate yourself from me. If you go to the left, I will go to the right; if you go to
10 the right, I will go to the left." Lot raised his eyes and saw that the whole plain
of the Jordan up to Tzoar was well watered. It was like the garden of the LORD,
like the land of Egypt; this was before the LORD destroyed Sedom and Amora.
11 So Lot chose for himself the entire plain of the Jordan. He traveled eastward,
12 and the two men separated. Avram settled in the land of Canaan while Lot
13 settled in the cities of the plain, pitching his tent near Sedom. But the people of
14 Sedom were evil, great sinners against the LORD. After Lot had separated from
him, the LORD said to Avram, "Raise your eyes and look around from where
15 you are to the north, south, east, and west. All the land you see I will give to you
16 and your descendants forever. I will make your descendants like the dust of the

רש״י

ז **וַיְהִי רִיב.** לְפִי שֶׁהָיוּ רוֹעָיו שֶׁל לוֹט רְשָׁעִים וּמַרְעִים בְּהֶמְתָּם בִּשְׂדוֹת אֲחֵרִים, וְרוֹעֵי אַבְרָם מוֹכִיחִים אוֹתָם עַל הַגָּזֵל, וְהֵם אוֹמְרִים: נִתְּנָה הָאָרֶץ לְאַבְרָם, וְלוֹ אֵין יוֹרֵשׁ וְלוֹט יוֹרְשׁוֹ, וְאֵין זֶה גָּזֵל; וְהַכָּתוּב אוֹמֵר: ״וְהַכְּנַעֲנִי וְהַפְּרִזִּי אָז יֹשֵׁב בָּאָרֶץ״, וְלֹא זָכָה בָּהּ אַבְרָם עֲדַיִן:

ח **אֲנָשִׁים אַחִים.** קְרוֹבִים. וּמִדְרַשׁ אַגָּדָה, דּוֹמִין בְּקַלַסְתֵּר פָּנִים:

ט **אִם הַשְּׂמֹאל וְאֵימִנָה.** בְּכָל אֲשֶׁר תֵּשֵׁב לֹא אֶתְרַחֵק מִמְּךָ וְאֶעֱמֹד לְךָ לְמָגֵן וּלְעֵזֶר. וְסוֹף דָּבָר הֻצְרַךְ לוֹ, שֶׁנֶּאֱמַר: ״וַיִּשְׁמַע אַבְרָם כִּי נִשְׁבָּה אָחִיו״ וְגוֹ׳ (להלן יד, יד): **וְאֵימִנָה.** אַיְמִין אֶת עַצְמִי, כְּמוֹ ״וְאַשְׂמְאִילָה״ – אַשְׂמְאִיל אֶת עַצְמִי. וְאִם תֹּאמַר, הָיָה לוֹ לִנָּקֵד וְאַיְמִינָה, כָּךְ מָצִינוּ בְּמָקוֹם אַחֵר: ״אִם אִשׁ לְהֵמִין״ (שמואל ב׳ יד, יט) וְאֵין נָקוּד ׳לְהַיְמִין׳:

י **כִּי כֻלָּהּ מַשְׁקֶה.** אֶרֶץ נַחֲלֵי מַיִם: **לִפְנֵי שַׁחֵת ה׳ אֶת סְדֹם וְאֶת עֲמֹרָה.** הָיָה אוֹתוֹ מִישׁוֹר ״כְּגַן ה׳״ – לָאִילָנוֹת; ״כְּאֶרֶץ מִצְרַיִם״ – לִזְרָעִים: **בֹּאֲכָה צֹעַר.** עַד צוֹעַר. וּמִדְרַשׁ אַגָּדָה דּוֹרְשׁוֹ לִגְנַאי, עַל שֶׁהָיוּ שְׁטוּפֵי זִמָּה בָּחַר לוֹ לוֹט בִּשְׁכוּנָתָם. בְּמַסֶּכֶת הוֹרָיוֹת (דף י ע״ב):

יא **כִּכַּר.** מִישׁוֹר, כְּתַרְגּוּמוֹ: **מִקֶּדֶם.** נָסַע מֵאֵצֶל אַבְרָם וְהָלַךְ לוֹ לְמַעֲרָבוֹ שֶׁל אַבְרָם, נִמְצָא נוֹסֵעַ מִמִּזְרָח לְמַעֲרָב. וּמִדְרַשׁ אַגָּדָה, הִסִּיעַ עַצְמוֹ מִקַּדְמוֹנוֹ שֶׁל עוֹלָם, אָמַר: אִי אֶפְשִׁי לֹא בְּאַבְרָם וְלֹא בֵּאלֹהָיו:

יב **וַיֶּאֱהַל.** נָטָה אֹהָלִים לְרוֹעָיו וּלְמִקְנֵהוּ ״עַד סְדֹם״:

יג **וְאַנְשֵׁי סְדֹם רָעִים.** וְאַף עַל פִּי כֵן לֹא נִמְנַע לוֹט מִלִּשְׁכֹּן עִמָּהֶם. וְרַבּוֹתֵינוּ לָמְדוּ מִכָּאן: ״שֵׁם רְשָׁעִים יִרְקָב״ (משלי י, ז): **רָעִים.** בְּגוּפָם: **וְחַטָּאִים.** בְּמָמוֹנָם: **לַה׳ מְאֹד.** יוֹדְעִים רִבּוֹנָם וּמִתְכַּוְּנִים לִמְרֹד בּוֹ:

יד **אַחֲרֵי הִפָּרֶד לוֹט.** כָּל זְמַן שֶׁהָרָשָׁע עִמּוֹ הָיָה הַדִּבּוּר פּוֹרֵשׁ מִמֶּנּוּ:

טז **אֲשֶׁר אִם יוּכַל אִישׁ.** כְּשֵׁם שֶׁאִי אֶפְשָׁר לֶעָפָר לִמָּנוֹת, כָּךְ זַרְעֲךָ לֹא יִמָּנֶה:

Amora will be destroyed. Twice the text stresses the wickedness of their inhabitants. The people are "evil" and "great sinners."

None of this is apparent to Lot at the time. We imagine him standing on a hilltop surveying the panorama. He has no way of knowing the character of the people in the towns he sees, nor what will be their ultimate fate. Evidently Lot's character failure lies in the fact that he "raised his eyes and saw." Like Ḥava when she saw that the fruit of the Tree of Knowledge was "enticing to the eyes" (Gen. 3:6), Lot judges by appearances. The children of the covenant follow sound, not sight, the voice of God in the depths of the soul, not the seductive surfaces of the visible. So Avraham loses his first potential heir.

ז לָשֶׁבֶת יַחְדָּו כִּי־הָיָה רְכוּשָׁם רָב וְלֹא יָכְלוּ לָשֶׁבֶת יַחְדָּו׃ וַיְהִי־רִיב
בֵּין רֹעֵי מִקְנֵה־אַבְרָם וּבֵין רֹעֵי מִקְנֵה־לוֹט וְהַכְּנַעֲנִי וְהַפְּרִזִּי אָז יֹשֵׁב
ח בָּאָרֶץ׃ וַיֹּאמֶר אַבְרָם אֶל־לוֹט אַל־נָא תְהִי מְרִיבָה בֵּינִי וּבֵינֶךָ וּבֵין
ט רֹעַי וּבֵין רֹעֶיךָ כִּי־אֲנָשִׁים אַחִים אֲנָחְנוּ׃ הֲלֹא כָל־הָאָרֶץ לְפָנֶיךָ הִפָּרֶד
י נָא מֵעָלָי אִם־הַשְּׂמֹאל וְאֵימִנָה וְאִם־הַיָּמִין וְאַשְׂמְאִילָה׃ וַיִּשָּׂא־לוֹט
אֶת־עֵינָיו וַיַּרְא אֶת־כָּל־כִּכַּר הַיַּרְדֵּן כִּי כֻלָּהּ מַשְׁקֶה לִפְנֵי ׀ שַׁחֵת יהוה
יא אֶת־סְדֹם וְאֶת־עֲמֹרָה כְּגַן־יהוה כְּאֶרֶץ מִצְרַיִם בֹּאֲכָה צֹעַר׃ וַיִּבְחַר־לוֹ
לוֹט אֵת כָּל־כִּכַּר הַיַּרְדֵּן וַיִּסַּע לוֹט מִקֶּדֶם וַיִּפָּרְדוּ אִישׁ מֵעַל אָחִיו׃
יב אַבְרָם יָשַׁב בְּאֶרֶץ־כְּנָעַן וְלוֹט יָשַׁב בְּעָרֵי הַכִּכָּר וַיֶּאֱהַל עַד־סְדֹם׃
יג יד וְאַנְשֵׁי סְדֹם רָעִים וְחַטָּאִים לַיהוה מְאֹד׃ וַיהוה אָמַר אֶל־אַבְרָם אַחֲרֵי
הִפָּרֶד־לוֹט מֵעִמּוֹ שָׂא־נָא עֵינֶיךָ וּרְאֵה מִן־הַמָּקוֹם אֲשֶׁר־אַתָּה שָׁם
טו צָפֹנָה וָנֶגְבָּה וָקֵדְמָה וָיָמָּה׃ כִּי אֶת־כָּל־הָאָרֶץ אֲשֶׁר־אַתָּה רֹאֶה לְךָ
טז אֶתְּנֶנָּה וּלְזַרְעֲךָ עַד־עוֹלָם׃ וְשַׂמְתִּי אֶת־זַרְעֲךָ כַּעֲפַר הָאָרֶץ אֲשֶׁר ׀ אִם־

אונקלוס

לְמִתַּב כַּחְדָא, אֲרֵי הֲוָה קִנְיָנְהוֹן סַגִּי, וְלָא יְכִילוּ לְמִתַּב כַּחְדָא: ז וַהֲוָת מַצּוּתָא, בֵּין רָעַן בְּעִירֵיהּ דְּאַבְרָם, וּבֵין רָעַן בְּעִירֵיהּ דְּלוֹט, וּכְנַעֲנָאָה וּפְרִזָּאָה, בְּכֵן יָתֵיב בְּאַרְעָא: ח וַאֲמַר אַבְרָם לְלוֹט, לָא כְעַן תְּהֵי מַצּוּתָא בֵּינָא וּבֵינָךְ, וּבֵין רָעֲוָתִי וּבֵין רָעֲוָתָךְ, אֲרֵי גֻּבְרִין אַחִין אֲנַחְנָא: ט הֲלָא כָל אַרְעָא קֳדָמָךְ, אִתְפָּרַשׁ כְּעַן מִלְּוָתִי, אִם אַתְּ לְצִפּוּנָא אֲנָא לְדָרוֹמָא, וְאִם אַתְּ לְדָרוֹמָא וְאַצְפְּנָךְ: י וּזְקַף לוֹט יָת עֵינוֹהִי, וַחֲזָא יָת כָּל מֵישַׁר יַרְדְּנָא, אֲרֵי כֻלֵּיהּ בֵּית שַׁקְיָא, קֳדָם דְּחַבֵּיל יי, יָת סְדוֹם וְיָת עֲמוֹרָה, כְּגִנְּתָא דַּיי כְּאַרְעָא דְמִצְרַיִם, מָטֵי צוֹעַר: יא וּבְחַר לֵיהּ לוֹט, יָת כָּל מֵישַׁר יַרְדְּנָא, וּנְטַל לוֹט בְּקַדְמֵיתָא, וְאִתְפָּרַשׁוּ, גְּבַר מִלְּוָת אֲחוּהִי: יב אַבְרָם יְתֵיב בְּאַרְעָא דִכְנָעַן, וְלוֹט, יְתֵיב בְּקִרְוֵי מֵישְׁרָא, וּפְרַס עַד סְדוֹם: יג וְאֲנָשֵׁי סְדוֹם, בִּישִׁין בְּמָמוֹנְהוֹן וְחַיָּבִין בְּגוּיַתְהוֹן, קֳדָם יי לַחֲדָא: יד וַיי אֲמַר לְאַבְרָם, בָּתַר דְּאִתְפְּרַשׁ לוֹט מֵעִמֵּיהּ, זְקוֹף כְּעַן עֵינָךְ וַחֲזִי, מִן אַתְרָא דְּאַתְּ תַּמָּן, לְצִפּוּנָא וּלְדָרוֹמָא וּלְמַדִּנְחָא וּלְמַעַרְבָא: טו אֲרֵי יָת כָּל אַרְעָא, דְּאַתְּ חָזֵי לָךְ אֶתְּנִנַּהּ, וְלִבְנָךְ עַד עָלְמָא: טז וַאֲשַׁוֵּי יָת בְּנָךְ סַגִּיאִין כְּעַפְרָא דְּאַרְעָא, כְּמָא דְּלֵית אֶפְשַׁר

13:10 וַיִּשָּׂא־לוֹט אֶת־עֵינָיו *Lot raised his eyes* – Lot chooses the good land with evil inhabitants. Evidently, he puts the material before the moral and spiritual. This alone is sufficient to tell us that, as far as the covenant is concerned, he is not a child of Avraham.

The text goes out of its way to emphasize this, using a prolepsis – telling us in advance things we would not otherwise discover until later. The verse links Sedom with Egypt, the full significance of which we will not realize until the book of Exodus. We are told that in the future, Sedom and

earth: if anyone could count the dust of the earth, then could your descendants
17 be counted. Get up and walk through the length and breadth of the land, for
18 to you shall I give it." So Avram took his tent and came to settle by the Oaks of
Mamre, in Ḥevron. There he built an altar to the Lord.
14 1 In the days of Amrafel, king of Shinar, Aryokh, king of Elasar, Kedorlaomer, REVI'I
2 king of Eilam, and Tidal, king of Goyim, they all waged war against Bera, king
of Sedom, Birsha, king of Amora, Shinav, king of Adma, and Shemever, king of
3 Tzevoyim, and the king of Bela – that is, Tzoar. These had all come together in
4 Siddim Valley – now the Dead Sea; for twelve years they had served
5 Kedorlaomer, but in the thirteenth year they had rebelled. In the fourteenth
year Kedorlaomer and his allied kings came and defeated the Refaim in
6 Ashterot Karnayim, the Zuzim in Ham, the Eimim in Shaveh Kiryatayim, and
the Horites in the hill country of Se'ir as far as Eil Paran by the wilderness.
7 Then they swung back and came to Ein Mishpat – that is, Kadesh – conquering
the whole territory of the Amalekites, as well as the Amorites living in Ḥatzetzon
8 Tamar. Then the kings of Sedom, Amora, Adma, Tzevoyim, and Bela – that is,
9 Tzoar – marched out and drew up their battle lines in Siddim Valley against
Kedorlaomer, king of Eilam, Tidal, king of Goyim, Amrafel, king of Shinar, and
10 Aryokh, king of Elasar: four kings battling five. The Siddim Valley was riddled

רש״י

יח | **מַמְרֵא.** שֵׁם אָדָם:

יד א | **אַמְרָפֶל.** הוּא נִמְרוֹד, שֶׁאָמַר לְאַבְרָהָם: פֹּל לְתוֹךְ כִּבְשַׁן הָאֵשׁ: **מֶלֶךְ גּוֹיִם.** מָקוֹם יֵשׁ שֶׁשְּׁמוֹ 'גּוֹיִם' עַל שֵׁם שֶׁנִּקְבְּצוּ שָׁמָּה מִכַּמָּה אֻמּוֹת וּמְקוֹמוֹת, וְהִמְלִיכוּ אִישׁ עֲלֵיהֶם וּשְׁמוֹ תִּדְעָל. בְּרֵאשִׁית רַבָּה (מב, ד):

ב | **בֶּרַע.** רַע לַשָּׁמַיִם וְרַע לַבְּרִיּוֹת: **בִּרְשַׁע.** שֶׁנִּתְעַלָּה בְּרֶשַׁע: **שִׁנְאָב.** שׂוֹנֵא אָבִיו שֶׁבַּשָּׁמַיִם: **שֶׁמְאֵבֶר.** שָׂם אֵבֶר לָעוּף וְלִקְפֹּץ וְלִמְרֹד בְּהַקָּדוֹשׁ בָּרוּךְ הוּא: **בֶּלַע.** שֵׁם הָעִיר:

ג | **עֵמֶק הַשִּׂדִּים.** כָּךְ שְׁמוֹ, עַל שֵׁם שֶׁהָיוּ בּוֹ שָׂדוֹת הַרְבֵּה: **הוּא יָם הַמֶּלַח.** לְאַחַר זְמַן נִמְשַׁךְ הַיָּם לְתוֹכוֹ וְנַעֲשָׂה יָם הַמֶּלַח. וּמִדְרַשׁ אַגָּדָה אוֹמֵר, שֶׁנִּתְבַּקְּעוּ הַצּוּרִים סְבִיבוֹתָיו וְנִמְשְׁכוּ יְאוֹרִים לְתוֹכוֹ:

ד | **שְׁתֵּים עֶשְׂרֵה שָׁנָה עָבְדוּ.** חֲמִשָּׁה מְלָכִים הַלָּלוּ "אֶת כְּדָרְלָעֹמֶר":

ה | **וּבְאַרְבַּע עֶשְׂרֵה שָׁנָה.** לְמָרְדָן: **בָּא כְדָרְלָעֹמֶר.** לְפִי שֶׁהוּא הָיָה בַּעַל הַמַּעֲשֶׂה נִכְנַס בְּעָבִי הַקּוֹרָה: **וְהַמְּלָכִים אֲשֶׁר אִתּוֹ.** אֵלֶּה שְׁלֹשָׁה מְלָכִים: **זוּזִים.** הֵם זַמְזֻמִּים (דברים ב, כ):

ו | **בְּהַרְרָם.** בְּהָר שֶׁלָּהֶם: **אֵיל פָּארָן.** כְּתַרְגּוּמוֹ: "מֵישַׁר". וְאוֹמֵר אֲנִי שֶׁאֵין 'אַיִל' לְשׁוֹן מִישׁוֹר, אֶלָּא מִישׁוֹר שֶׁל פָּארָן 'אַיִל' שְׁמוֹ, וְשֶׁל מַמְרֵא 'אֵלוֹנֵי' שְׁמוֹ, וְשֶׁל יַרְדֵּן 'כִּכָּר' שְׁמוֹ, וְשֶׁל שִׁטִּים 'אָבֵל' שְׁמוֹ, "אָבֵל הַשִּׁטִּים" (במדבר לג, מט), וְכֵן "בַּעַל גָּד" (יהושע יא, יז) 'בַּעַל' שְׁמוֹ, וְכֻלָּם מְתֻרְגָּמִין "מֵישַׁר" וְכָל אֶחָד שְׁמוֹ עָלָיו: **עַל הַמִּדְבָּר.** אֵצֶל הַמִּדְבָּר, כְּמוֹ: "וְעָלָיו מַטֵּה מְנַשֶּׁה" (במדבר ב, כ):

ז | **עֵין מִשְׁפָּט הִוא קָדֵשׁ.** עַל שֵׁם הֶעָתִיד, שֶׁעֲתִידִים מֹשֶׁה וְאַהֲרֹן לְהִשָּׁפֵט שָׁם עַל עִסְקֵי אוֹתוֹ הָעַיִן, וְהֵם מֵי מְרִיבָה. וְאוּנְקְלוֹס תִּרְגְּמוֹ כִּפְשׁוּטוֹ, מָקוֹם שֶׁהָיוּ בְּנֵי הַמְּדִינָה מִתְקַבְּצִים שָׁם לְכָל מִשְׁפָּט: **שְׂדֵה הָעֲמָלֵקִי.** עֲדַיִן לֹא נוֹלַד עֲמָלֵק, וְנִקְרָא עַל שֵׁם הֶעָתִיד: **בְּחַצְצֹן תָּמָר.** הוּא עֵין גֶּדִי, מִקְרָא מָלֵא בְּדִבְרֵי הַיָּמִים (ב׳ כ, ב) בִּיהוֹשָׁפָט:

ט | **אַרְבָּעָה מְלָכִים אֶת הַחֲמִשָּׁה.** וְאַף עַל פִּי כֵן נִצְּחוּ הַמּוּעָטִים, לְהוֹדִיעֲךָ שֶׁגִּבּוֹרִים הָיוּ, וְאַף עַל פִּי כֵן לֹא נִמְנַע אַבְרָהָם מִלִּרְדֹּף אַחֲרֵיהֶם:

יז יוּכַל אִישׁ לִמְנוֹת אֶת־עֲפַר הָאָרֶץ גַּם־זַרְעֲךָ יִמָּנֶה: קוּם הִתְהַלֵּךְ
יח בָּאָרֶץ לְאָרְכָּהּ וּלְרָחְבָּהּ כִּי לְךָ אֶתְּנֶנָּה: וַיֶּאֱהַל אַבְרָם וַיָּבֹא וַיֵּשֶׁב
בְּאֵלֹנֵי מַמְרֵא אֲשֶׁר בְּחֶבְרוֹן וַיִּבֶן־שָׁם מִזְבֵּחַ לַיהוָה:

יד א וַיְהִי בִּימֵי אַמְרָפֶל מֶלֶךְ־שִׁנְעָר אַרְיוֹךְ מֶלֶךְ אֶלָּסָר כְּדָרְלָעֹמֶר מֶלֶךְ יא רביעי
ב עֵילָם וְתִדְעָל מֶלֶךְ גּוֹיִם: עָשׂוּ מִלְחָמָה אֶת־בֶּרַע מֶלֶךְ סְדֹם וְאֶת־
בִּרְשַׁע מֶלֶךְ עֲמֹרָה שִׁנְאָב ׀ מֶלֶךְ אַדְמָה וְשֶׁמְאֵבֶר מֶלֶךְ צביים וּמֶלֶךְ צְבוֹיִם
ג בֶּלַע הִיא־צֹעַר: כָּל־אֵלֶּה חָבְרוּ אֶל־עֵמֶק הַשִּׂדִּים הוּא יָם הַמֶּלַח:
ד שְׁתֵּים עֶשְׂרֵה שָׁנָה עָבְדוּ אֶת־כְּדָרְלָעֹמֶר וּשְׁלֹשׁ־עֶשְׂרֵה שָׁנָה מָרָדוּ:
ה וּבְאַרְבַּע עֶשְׂרֵה שָׁנָה בָּא כְדָרְלָעֹמֶר וְהַמְּלָכִים אֲשֶׁר אִתּוֹ וַיַּכּוּ אֶת־
רְפָאִים בְּעַשְׁתְּרֹת קַרְנַיִם וְאֶת־הַזּוּזִים בְּהָם וְאֵת הָאֵימִים בְּשָׁוֵה
ו קִרְיָתָיִם: וְאֶת־הַחֹרִי בְּהַרְרָם שֵׂעִיר עַד אֵיל פָּארָן אֲשֶׁר עַל־הַמִּדְבָּר:
ז וַיָּשֻׁבוּ וַיָּבֹאוּ אֶל־עֵין מִשְׁפָּט הִוא קָדֵשׁ וַיַּכּוּ אֶת־כָּל־שְׂדֵה הָעֲמָלֵקִי
ח וְגַם אֶת־הָאֱמֹרִי הַיֹּשֵׁב בְּחַצְצֹן תָּמָר: וַיֵּצֵא מֶלֶךְ־סְדֹם וּמֶלֶךְ עֲמֹרָה
וּמֶלֶךְ אַדְמָה וּמֶלֶךְ צביים וּמֶלֶךְ בֶּלַע הִוא־צֹעַר וַיַּעַרְכוּ אִתָּם מִלְחָמָה צְבוֹיִם
ט בְּעֵמֶק הַשִּׂדִּים: אֵת כְּדָרְלָעֹמֶר מֶלֶךְ עֵילָם וְתִדְעָל מֶלֶךְ גּוֹיִם וְאַמְרָפֶל
י מֶלֶךְ שִׁנְעָר וְאַרְיוֹךְ מֶלֶךְ אֶלָּסָר אַרְבָּעָה מְלָכִים אֶת־הַחֲמִשָּׁה: וְעֵמֶק

אונקלוס

לִגְבַר, לְמִמְנֵי יָת עַפְרָא דְּאַרְעָא, אַף בְּנָךְ לָא יִתְמְנוֹן: יז קוּם הַלֵּיךְ
בְּאַרְעָא, לְאָרְכַּהּ וּלְפְתָיַהּ, אֲרֵי לָךְ אֶתְּנִנַּהּ: יח וּפְרַס אַבְרָם, וַאֲתָא,
וִיתֵיב, בְּמֵישְׁרֵי מַמְרֵא דִּבְחֶבְרוֹן, וּבְנָא תַמָּן מַדְבְּחָא קֳדָם יְיָ:
יד א וַהֲוָה, בְּיוֹמֵי אַמְרָפֶל מַלְכָּא דְּבָבֶל, אַרְיוֹךְ מַלְכָּא דְּאֶלָּסָר,
כְּדָרְלָעֹמֶר מַלְכָּא דְּעֵילָם, וְתִדְעָל מַלְכָּא דְּעַמְמֵי: ב עֲבַדוּ קְרָבָא,
עִם בֶּרַע מַלְכָּא דִּסְדוֹם, וְעִם בִּרְשַׁע מַלְכָּא דַּעֲמוֹרָה, שִׁנְאָב מַלְכָּא
דְּאַדְמָה, וְשֶׁמְאֵבֶר מַלְכָּא דִּצְבוֹיִם, וּמַלְכָּא דְּבֶלַע הִיא צוֹעַר: ג כָּל
אִלֵּין אִתְכַּנַּשׁוּ, לְמֵישַׁר חַקְלַיָּא, הוּא אֲתַר יַמָּא דְּמִלְחָא: ד תַּרְתָּא
עַסְרֵי שְׁנִין, פְּלַחוּ יָת כְּדָרְלָעֹמֶר, וּתְלָת עַסְרֵי שְׁנִין מְרַדוּ: ה וּבְאַרְבַּע
עַסְרֵי שְׁנִין אֲתָא כְדָרְלָעֹמֶר, וּמַלְכַיָּא דְּעִמֵּיהּ, וּמְחוֹ יָת גִּבָּרַיָּא
דִּבְעַשְׁתְּרַת קַרְנַיִם, וְיָת תַּקִּיפַיָּא דִּבְהָמְתָא, וְיָת אֵימְתָנֵי, דִּבְשָׁוֵה
קִרְיָתַיִם: ו וְיָת חוֹרָאֵי דִּבְטוּרָא דְּשֵׂעִיר, עַד מֵישַׁר פָּארָן, דִּסְמִיךְ עַל
מַדְבְּרָא: ז וְתָבוּ, וַאֲתוֹ, לְמֵישַׁר פְּלוּג דִּינָא הִיא רְקַם, וּמְחוֹ, יָת כָּל חֲקַל
עֲמַלְקָאָה, וְאַף יָת אֱמוֹרָאָה, דְּיָתֵיב בְּעֵין גֶּדִי: ח וּנְפַק מַלְכָּא דִּסְדוֹם
וּמַלְכָּא דַּעֲמוֹרָה, וּמַלְכָּא דְּאַדְמָה וּמַלְכָּא דִּצְבוֹיִם, וּמַלְכָּא דְּבֶלַע
הִיא צוֹעַר, וְסַדַּרוּ עִמְּהוֹן קְרָבָא, בְּמֵישַׁר חַקְלַיָּא: ט עִם כְּדָרְלָעֹמֶר
מַלְכָּא דְּעֵילָם, וְתִדְעָל מַלְכָּא דְּעַמְמֵי, וְאַמְרָפֶל מַלְכָּא דְּבָבֶל,
וְאַרְיוֹךְ מַלְכָּא דְּאֶלָּסָר, אַרְבְּעָא מַלְכִין לָקֳבֵיל חַמְשָׁא: י וּמֵישַׁר

with tar pits, and when the kings of Sedom and Amora tried to flee, they fell
11 into them. The others fled to the mountains. The victors seized all the
12 possessions of Sedom and Amora and all the food, and they left, taking with
them – since he had been living in Sedom – Avram's nephew, Lot, and his
13 possessions. A fugitive came and reported this to Avram the Hebrew, who was
then living near the Oaks of Mamre the Amorite, a kinsman of Avram's allies,
14 Eshkol and Aner. When Avram heard that his own kinsman had been taken
captive, he marshaled the three hundred eighteen trained men born in his
15 household, and went in pursuit as far as Dan. He divided his forces against the

רש"י

י) **בארת בארת חמר.** בארות הרבה היו שם שנוטלין משם אדמה לטיט של בנין. ומדרש אגדה, שהיה הטיט בהם, ונעשה נס למלך סדום שיצא משם, לפי שהיו באמות מקצתן שלא היו מאמינין שנצל אברהם מאור כשדים מכבשן האש, וכיון שיצא זה מן החמר האמינו באברהם למפרע: **הרה נסו.** להר נסו. 'הרה' כמו 'להר', כל תבה שצריכה למ"ד בתחלתה הטיל לה ה"א בסופה. ויש חלוק בין 'הרה' ל'ההרה', שה"א שבסוף התבה עומדת במקום למ"ד שבראשה, אבל אינה עומדת במקום למ"ד ונקודה פתח תחתיה, והרי 'הרה' כמו 'להר' או כמו 'אל הר' ואינו מפרש לאיזה הר, אלא כאשר מצא תחלה, וכשהוא נותן ה"א בראשה לכתב 'ההרה', 'המדברה', פתרונו כמו 'אל ההר' או כמו 'להר', ומשמע לאותו הר הידוע ומפרש בפרשה:

יב) **והוא ישב בסדם.** מי גרם לו זאת? ישיבתו בסדום:

יג) **ויבא הפליט.** זה עוג שפלט מן המלחמה, וזהו: "נשאר מיתר הרפאים" (דברים ג, יא) – 'נשאר' שלא הרגוהו אמרפל וחבריו כשהכו הרפאים בעשתרת קרנים. תנחומא (חקת כה). ובראשית רבה: זה עוג שפלט מדור המבול, וזהו "מיתר הרפאים", שנאמר: "הנפלים היו בארץ" וגו' (לעיל ו, ד), ומתכון שיהרג אברם וישא את שרה: **העברי.** שבא מעבר הנהר: **בעלי ברית אברם.** שכרתו עמו ברית:

יד) **וירק.** כתרגומו: "וזריז", וכן: "והריקתי אחריכם חרב" (ויקרא כו, לג), אזדיין בחרבי עליכם, וכן: "אריק חרבי" (שמות טו, ט), וכן: "והרק חנית וסגר" (תהלים לה, ג): **חניכיו.** שחנכו למצות, והוא לשון התחלת כניסת האדם או כלי לאמנות שהוא עתיד לעמד בה. וכן: "חנך לנער" (משלי כב, ו), "חנכת המזבח" (במדבר ז, י), "חנכת הבית" (תהלים ל, א), ובלעז קורין לו אנשיני"ר: **שמנה עשר וגו'.** רבותינו אמרו: אליעזר לבדו היה, והוא מנין גימטריא של שמו: **עד דן.** שם תשש כחו, שראה שעתידים בניו להעמיד שם עגל:

טו) **ויחלק עליהם.** לפי פשוטו סרס המקרא: 'ויחלק הוא ועבדיו עליהם לילה' כדרך הרודפים שמתפלגים אחר הנרדפים כשבורחים זה לכאן וזה לכאן: **לילה.** כלומר, אחר שחשכה לא נמנע מלרדפם.

gathered" (Gen. 12:5), which may refer to converts they had made but may equally merely refer to their servants, they attract no disciples.

He lives among people whose beliefs and practices are alien to his own, yet he does not reprimand them, except when the servants of Avimelekh, a king with whom he had made a treaty, seize one of the wells he has dug (21:25). He holds them to the standards of simple, human morality, not those of divine ethics or holiness.

When his nephew Lot chooses to live among the people of Sedom, *about whom the Tanakh* says that they "were evil, great sinners against the LORD" (13:13), Avraham does not criticize him. Nor does he condemn them. To the contrary, he now fights a battle on their behalf. When, in the next *parasha*, he hears that God is planning to punish them, he will plead for them, in one of the most audacious prayers in the Tanakh: "Shall the judge of all the earth not do justice?" (18:25).

Avraham does not seek to impose his views on others. Yet his contemporaries sense that there is something special, Godly, about him. Malki Tzedek, king of Shalem, salutes him with the words "Blessed be Avram by God Most High, Maker of heaven and earth" (14:19). The Hittites say to him, "You are a prince of God in our midst" (23:6). Avraham impresses his contemporaries by the way he lives, not the way he forces, or even urges, others to live.

הַשִּׂדִּים בֶּאֱרֹת חֵמָר וַיָּנֻסוּ מֶלֶךְ־סְדֹם וַעֲמֹרָה וַיִּפְּלוּ־שָׁמָּה
יא וְהַנִּשְׁאָרִים הֶרָה נָּסוּ׃ וַיִּקְחוּ אֶת־כָּל־רְכֻשׁ סְדֹם וַעֲמֹרָה וְאֶת־כָּל־
יב אָכְלָם וַיֵּלֵכוּ׃ וַיִּקְחוּ אֶת־לוֹט וְאֶת־רְכֻשׁוֹ בֶּן־אֲחִי אַבְרָם וַיֵּלֵכוּ וְהוּא
יג יֹשֵׁב בִּסְדֹם׃ וַיָּבֹא הַפָּלִיט וַיַּגֵּד לְאַבְרָם הָעִבְרִי וְהוּא שֹׁכֵן בְּאֵלֹנֵי
יד מַמְרֵא הָאֱמֹרִי אֲחִי אֶשְׁכֹּל וַאֲחִי עָנֵר וְהֵם בַּעֲלֵי בְרִית־אַבְרָם׃ וַיִּשְׁמַע
אַבְרָם כִּי נִשְׁבָּה אָחִיו וַיָּרֶק אֶת־חֲנִיכָיו יְלִידֵי בֵיתוֹ שְׁמֹנָה עָשָׂר וּשְׁלֹשׁ
טו מֵאוֹת וַיִּרְדֹּף עַד־דָּן׃ וַיֵּחָלֵק עֲלֵיהֶם ׀ לַיְלָה הוּא וַעֲבָדָיו וַיַּכֵּם וַיִּרְדְּפֵם

אונקלוס

חַקְלַיָּא, בֵּירָן בֵּירָן מַסְּקָן חֵימָרָא, וַעֲרַקוּ, מַלְכָּא דִסְדוֹם וַעֲמוֹרָה וּנְפַלוּ
תַמָּן, וּדְאִשְׁתְּאָרוּ לְטוּרָא עֲרַקוּ: יא וּשְׁבוֹ, יָת כָּל קִנְיָנָא דִסְדוֹם וַעֲמוֹרָה,
וְיָת כָּל מֵיכַלְהוֹן וַאֲזַלוּ: יב וּשְׁבוֹ יָת לוֹט וְיָת קִנְיָנֵיהּ, בַּר אֲחוּהִי דְאַבְרָם
וַאֲזַלוּ, וְהוּא יָתֵיב בִּסְדוֹם: יג וַאֲתָא מְשֵׁיזְבָא, וְחַוִּי לְאַבְרָם עִבְרָאָה,
וְהוּא שָׁרֵי בְּמֵישְׁרֵי מַמְרֵא אֱמוֹרָאָה, אֲחוּהִי דְאֶשְׁכּוֹל וַאֲחוּהִי דְעָנֵר,
וְאִנּוּן אֱנָשׁ קְיָמֵיהּ דְאַבְרָם: יד וּשְׁמַע אַבְרָם, אֲרֵי אִשְׁתְּבִי אֲחוּהִי, וְזָרֵיז
יָת עוּלֵימוֹהִי יְלִידֵי בֵיתֵיהּ, תְּלָת מְאָה וּתְמָנַת עֲסַר, וּרְדַף עַד דָּן: טו
וְאִתְפְּלֵיג עֲלֵיהוֹן לֵילְיָא, הוּא וְעַבְדּוֹהִי וּמְחָנוּן, וּרְדַפִנּוּן

14:14 וַיָּרֶק אֶת חֲנִיכָיו *He marshaled* – Leaders lead. That does not mean to say that they do not follow. But what they follow is different from what most people follow. They do not conform for the sake of conforming. They follow an inner voice, a call. They have a vision, not of what is, but of what might be. They think outside the box. They march to a different tune.

To be a Jew is to be willing to challenge the prevailing consensus when, as so often happens, nations slip into worshipping the old gods. We make a mistake when we think of idols in terms of their physical appearance – statues, figurines, icons. In that sense they belong to ancient times we have long outgrown. Instead, the right way to think of idols is in terms of what they represent. They symbolize power. That is what Ra was for the Egyptians, what Baal was for the Canaanites, what Zeus was for the Greeks, and what missiles and bombs are for terrorists and rogue states today.

Power allows us to rule over others without their consent. Judaism is a sustained critique of power. It is about how a nation can be formed on the basis of shared commitment and collective responsibility. It is about how to construct a society that honors the human person as the image and likeness of God. It is about a vision, never fully realized but never abandoned, of a world based on justice and compassion. Here Avraham stands up to power in defense of his nephew. We notice that he himself is a force to be reckoned with, but his military prowess and leadership are only used here, once, in defense of others.

14:14 וַיִּרְדֹּף *He… went in pursuit* – The unique structure of biblical spirituality – its calibrated tension between the universality of justice and the particularity of love – is the most compelling way I know of giving religious expression to *both* our common humanity *and* our religious differences.

Consider the life of Avraham. Readers of the Tanakh are so familiar with his story that they often fail to notice how strange it is. Here is the father of monotheism, yet in the biblical text itself Avraham breaks no idol, challenges no polytheist, and establishes no new religious movement. Other than an ambiguous hint that Avraham took with him on his journey "the people (literally, 'souls') they had

captors at night and defeated them, pursuing them to Ḥova, north of Damascus.
16 He recovered all the plunder, as well as his kinsman Lot and his possessions,
17 the women, and the other survivors as well. When he returned from defeating
Kedorlaomer and the kings with him, the king of Sedom came out to greet him
18 at Shaveh Valley – that is, the Valley of the King. And Malki Tzedek, king of
19 Shalem, offered bread and wine. He was a priest of God Most High, and he
blessed Avram, saying: "Blessed be Avram by God Most High, Maker of heaven
20 and earth, and blessed be God Most High who delivered your foes into your
21 hand." Then Avram gave him a tenth of everything. And the king of Sedom said ḤAMISHI
22 to Avram, "Give me the people, and keep the possessions for yourself." But
Avram said to the king of Sedom, "I raise my hand in oath to the LORD, God
23 Most High, Maker of heaven and earth, that I will not accept anything of yours,
not even a thread or a shoe strap, so that you never shall say, 'I made Avram
24 rich.' I will accept nothing but what my young men have eaten and the share
that belongs to the men who went with me – Aner, Eshkol, and Mamre; let
15 1 them have their share." After these events the word of the LORD came

רש"י

וּמִדְרַשׁ אַגָּדָה, שֶׁנֶּחְלַק הַלַּיְלָה, וּבַחֲצוֹת רִאשׁוֹן שֶׁלּוֹ נַעֲשָׂה לוֹ הַנֵּס, וַחֲצִיוֹ הַשֵּׁנִי נִשְׁמַר וּבָא לַחֲצוֹת לַיְלָה שֶׁל מִצְרַיִם: **עַד חוֹבָה.** אֵין מָקוֹם שֶׁשְּׁמוֹ 'חוֹבָה', וְדָן קוֹרֵא 'חוֹבָה' עַל שֵׁם עֲבוֹדָה זָרָה שֶׁעֲתִידָה לִהְיוֹת שָׁם:

יז **עֵמֶק שָׁוֵה.** כָּךְ שְׁמוֹ, כְּתַרְגּוּמוֹ: "לְמֵישַׁר מְפַנַּא", פָּנוּי מֵאִילָנוֹת וּמִכָּל מִכְשׁוֹל: **עֵמֶק הַמֶּלֶךְ.** "בֵּית רֵיסָא דְמַלְכָּא" (אונקלוס), בֵּית רִיס אֶחָד, שֶׁהוּא שְׁלֹשִׁים קָנִים, שֶׁהָיָה מְיֻחָד לַמֶּלֶךְ לְשַׂחֵק שָׁם. וּמִדְרַשׁ אַגָּדָה, עֵמֶק שֶׁהֻשְׁווּ שָׁם כָּל הָאֻמּוֹת וְהִמְלִיכוּ אֶת אַבְרָהָם עֲלֵיהֶם לִנְשִׂיא אֱלֹהִים וּלְקָצִין:

יח **וּמַלְכִּי צֶדֶק.** מִדְרַשׁ אַגָּדָה, הוּא שֵׁם בֶּן נֹחַ: **לֶחֶם וָיָיִן.** כָּךְ עוֹשִׂים לִיגִיעֵי מִלְחָמָה, וְהֶרְאָה לוֹ שֶׁאֵין בְּלִבּוֹ עָלָיו עַל שֶׁהָרַג אֶת בָּנָיו. וּמִדְרַשׁ אַגָּדָה, רָמַז לוֹ עַל הַמְּנָחוֹת וְעַל הַנְּסָכִים שֶׁיַּקְרִיבוּ שָׁם בָּנָיו:

יט **קֹנֵה שָׁמַיִם וָאָרֶץ.** כְּמוֹ: עֹשֵׂה שָׁמַיִם וָאָרֶץ, עַל יְדֵי עֲשִׂיָּתוֹ קְנָאָן לִהְיוֹת שֶׁלּוֹ:

כ **אֲשֶׁר מִגֵּן.** אֲשֶׁר הִסְגִּיר, וְכֵן: "אֲמַגֶּנְךָ יִשְׂרָאֵל" (הושע יא, ח): **וַיִּתֶּן לוֹ.** אַבְרָם: **מַעֲשֵׂר מִכֹּל.** אֲשֶׁר לוֹ, לְפִי שֶׁהָיָה כֹּהֵן:

כא **תֶּן לִי הַנֶּפֶשׁ.** מִן הַשְּׁבִי שֶׁלִּי שֶׁהִצַּלְתָּ, הַחֲזֵר לִי הַגּוּפִים לְבַדָּם:

כב **הֲרִמֹתִי יָדִי.** לְשׁוֹן שְׁבוּעָה, מֵרִים אֲנִי אֶת יָדִי לְאֵל עֶלְיוֹן, וְכֵן: "בִּי נִשְׁבַּעְתִּי" (להלן כב, טז) – נִשְׁבָּע אֲנִי. וְכֵן: "נָתַתִּי כֶּסֶף הַשָּׂדֶה קַח מִמֶּנִּי" (להלן כג, יג) – נוֹתֵן אֲנִי לְךָ כֶּסֶף הַשָּׂדֶה וְקָחֵהוּ מִמֶּנִּי:

כג **אִם מִחוּט וְעַד שְׂרוֹךְ נַעַל.** אֲעַכֵּב לְעַצְמִי מִן הַשְּׁבִי: **וְאִם אֶקַּח מִכָּל אֲשֶׁר לָךְ.** אִם תֹּאמַר לָתֵת לִי שָׂכָר מִבֵּית גְּנָזֶיךָ: **וְלֹא תֹאמַר וְגוֹ'.** שֶׁהַקָּדוֹשׁ בָּרוּךְ הוּא הִבְטִיחַנִי לְעַשְּׁרֵנִי, שֶׁנֶּאֱמַר: "וַאֲבָרֶכְךָ וַאֲגַדְּלָה שְׁמֶךָ" (לעיל יב, ב):

כד **הַנְּעָרִים.** עֲבָדַי אֲשֶׁר הָלְכוּ אִתִּי, וְעוֹד "עָנֵר אֶשְׁכֹּל וּמַמְרֵא" וְגוֹ'; אַף עַל פִּי שֶׁעֲבָדַי נִכְנְסוּ לַמִּלְחָמָה, שֶׁנֶּאֱמַר: "וַיִּרְדֹּף עַד דָּן" (לעיל פסוק יד), וְעָנֵר וַחֲבֵרָיו יָשְׁבוּ עַל הַכֵּלִים לִשְׁמֹר. וּמִמֶּנּוּ לָמַד דָּוִד שֶׁאָמַר: "כְּחֵלֶק הַיֹּרֵד בַּמִּלְחָמָה וּכְחֵלֶק הַיֹּשֵׁב עַל הַכֵּלִים יַחְדָּו יַחֲלֹקוּ" (שמואל א' ל, כד), וּלְכָךְ נֶאֱמַר: "וַיְהִי מֵהַיּוֹם הַהוּא וָמָעְלָה וַיְשִׂמֶהָ לְחֹק וּלְמִשְׁפָּט" (שם פסוק כה), וְלֹא נֶאֱמַר 'וָהָלְאָה', לְפִי שֶׁכְּבָר נִתַּן הַחֹק בִּימֵי אַבְרָהָם:

טו א **אַחַר הַדְּבָרִים הָאֵלֶּה.** כָּל מָקוֹם שֶׁנֶּאֱמַר 'אַחַר' – סָמוּךְ, 'אַחֲרֵי' – מֻפְלָג. בְּרֵאשִׁית רַבָּה (מד, ה). אַחַר שֶׁנַּעֲשָׂה לוֹ נֵס זֶה שֶׁהָרַג אֶת הַמְּלָכִים, וְהָיָה דּוֹאֵג וְאוֹמֵר: שֶׁמָּא קִבַּלְתִּי שָׂכָר עַל כָּל צִדְקוֹתַי?

טז עַד־חוֹבָה אֲשֶׁר מִשְּׂמֹאל לְדַמָּשֶׂק: וַיָּשֶׁב אֵת כָּל־הָרְכֻשׁ וְגַם אֶת־
יז לוֹט אָחִיו וּרְכֻשׁוֹ הֵשִׁיב וְגַם אֶת־הַנָּשִׁים וְאֶת־הָעָם: וַיֵּצֵא מֶלֶךְ־סְדֹם
לִקְרָאתוֹ אַחֲרֵי שׁוּבוֹ מֵהַכּוֹת אֶת־כְּדָרְלָעֹמֶר וְאֶת־הַמְּלָכִים אֲשֶׁר
יח אִתּוֹ אֶל־עֵמֶק שָׁוֵה הוּא עֵמֶק הַמֶּלֶךְ: וּמַלְכִּי־צֶדֶק מֶלֶךְ שָׁלֵם הוֹצִיא
יט לֶחֶם וָיָיִן וְהוּא כֹהֵן לְאֵל עֶלְיוֹן: וַיְבָרְכֵהוּ וַיֹּאמַר בָּרוּךְ אַבְרָם לְאֵל
כ עֶלְיוֹן קֹנֵה שָׁמַיִם וָאָרֶץ: וּבָרוּךְ אֵל עֶלְיוֹן אֲשֶׁר־מִגֵּן צָרֶיךָ בְּיָדֶךָ
כא וַיִּתֶּן־לוֹ מַעֲשֵׂר מִכֹּל: וַיֹּאמֶר מֶלֶךְ־סְדֹם אֶל־אַבְרָם תֶּן־לִי הַנֶּפֶשׁ חמישי
כב וְהָרְכֻשׁ קַח־לָךְ: וַיֹּאמֶר אַבְרָם אֶל־מֶלֶךְ סְדֹם הֲרִמֹתִי יָדִי אֶל־יהוה
כג אֵל עֶלְיוֹן קֹנֵה שָׁמַיִם וָאָרֶץ: אִם־מִחוּט וְעַד שְׂרוֹךְ־נַעַל וְאִם־אֶקַּח
כד מִכָּל־אֲשֶׁר־לָךְ וְלֹא תֹאמַר אֲנִי הֶעֱשַׁרְתִּי אֶת־אַבְרָם: בִּלְעָדַי רַק
אֲשֶׁר אָכְלוּ הַנְּעָרִים וְחֵלֶק הָאֲנָשִׁים אֲשֶׁר הָלְכוּ אִתִּי עָנֵר אֶשְׁכֹּל
טו א וּמַמְרֵא הֵם יִקְחוּ חֶלְקָם: אַחַר | הַדְּבָרִים הָאֵלֶּה הָיָה יב

אונקלוס

עַד חוֹבָה, דְּמִצִּפּוּנָא לְדַמָּשֶׂק: טז וַאֲתֵיב, יָת כָּל קִנְיָנָא, וְאַף יָת לוֹט אֲחוּהִי וְקִנְיָנֵיהּ אֲתֵיב, וְאַף יָת נְשַׁיָּא וְיָת עַמָּא: יז וּנְפַק מַלְכָּא דִסְדוֹם לְקַדָּמוּתֵיהּ, בָּתַר דְּתָב, מִלְּמִמְחֵי יָת כְּדָרְלָעֹמֶר, וְיָת מַלְכַיָּא דְעִמֵּיהּ, לְמֵישַׁר מְפַנָּא, הוּא בֵּית רֵיסָא דְמַלְכָּא: יח וּמַלְכִּי צֶדֶק מַלְכָּא דִירוּשְׁלֶם, אַפֵּיק לְחֵים וַחֲמַר, וְהוּא מְשַׁמֵּישׁ קֳדָם אֵל עִלָּאָה: יט וּבָרְכֵיהּ וַאֲמַר, בְּרִיךְ אַבְרָם לְאֵל עִלָּאָה, דְּקִנְיָנֵיהּ שְׁמַיָּא וְאַרְעָא: כ וּבְרִיךְ אֵל עִלָּאָה, דִּמְסַר סָנְאָךְ בִּידָךְ, וִיהַב לֵיהּ חַד מִן עַסְרָא מִכּוֹלָא: כא וַאֲמַר מַלְכָּא דִסְדוֹם לְאַבְרָם, הַב לִי נַפְשָׁתָא, וְקִנְיָנָא סַב לָךְ: כב וַאֲמַר אַבְרָם לְמַלְכָּא דִסְדוֹם, אֲרֵימִית יְדִי בִּצְלוֹ קֳדָם יי אֵל עִלָּאָה, דְּקִנְיָנֵיהּ שְׁמַיָּא וְאַרְעָא: כג אִם מִחוּטָא וְעַד עַרְקַת מְסָנָא, וְאִם אֶסַּב מִכָּל דְּלָךְ, וְלָא תֵימַר, אֲנָא עַתָּרִית יָת אַבְרָם: כד בַּר מִדַּאֲכַלוּ עוּלֵימַיָּא, וְחוּלָק גֻּבְרַיָּא, דַּאֲזַלוּ עִמִּי, עָנֵר אֶשְׁכּוֹל וּמַמְרֵא, אִנּוּן יְקַבְּלוּן חוּלָקְהוֹן: טו א בָּתַר פִּתְגָמַיָּא הָאִלֵּין, הֲוָה

14:18 מַלְכִּי צֶדֶק מֶלֶךְ שָׁלֵם *Malki Tzedek, king of Shalem* – The God who appears to Avraham also appears to Malki Tzedek, king of Shalem, described as "a priest of God Most High" though not party to the Abrahamic covenant. He appears to Avimelekh, king of the Philistines, and to Lavan, Yaakov's high-handed father-in-law. Even an Egyptian Pharaoh can relate to the Divine. After Yosef has interpreted his dream, Pharaoh says, "Could we find another like him, a man who has within him the spirit of God?"

The Torah seems to delight in this discovery of godliness outside the Abrahamic covenant. When, in the early centuries CE, the Sages said that the righteous of every nation have a share in the World to Come, they were doing no more than making explicit a view implicit in the Torah throughout, that Israel has no monopoly on virtue or wisdom or grace.

to Avram in a vision, saying: "Do not be afraid, Avram. I am your shield. Your
2 reward shall be very great." But Avram said, "My Lord God, what will You have
given me if I remain childless, and the one who will take charge of my household
3 is Eliezer of Damascus?" Avram said, "You have given me no children. A man
4 of my household will be my heir." Then the word of the Lord came to him:
"That man will not be your heir; one who comes forth from your own loins will
5 be your heir." He took him outside and said, "Look at the heavens and count
the stars – if indeed you can count them." He said to him, "That is how your
6 descendants will be." And because Avram put his trust in the Lord, He

רש"י

לְכָךְ אָמַר לוֹ הַמָּקוֹם: "אַל תִּירָא": **אָנֹכִי מָגֵן לָךְ.** מִן הָעֹנֶשׁ, שֶׁלֹּא תֵּעָנֵשׁ עַל כָּל אוֹתָן נְפָשׁוֹת שֶׁהָרַגְתָּ. וּמַה שֶּׁאַתָּה דוֹאֵג עַל קִבּוּל שְׂכָרְךָ – "שְׂכָרְךָ הַרְבֵּה מְאֹד":

ב **הוֹלֵךְ עֲרִירִי.** מְנַחֵם בֶּן סָרוּק פֵּרְשׁוֹ לְשׁוֹן יוֹרֵשׁ, וְחָבֵר לוֹ: "עֵר וְעֹנֶה" (מלאכי ב, יב). 'עֲרִירִי' – בְּלֹא יוֹרֵשׁ, כַּאֲשֶׁר תֹּאמַר: "וּבְכָל תְּבוּאָתִי תְשָׁרֵשׁ" (איוב לא, יב) – תַּעֲקֹר שָׁרָשֶׁיהָ, כָּךְ לְשׁוֹן עֲרִירִי – חֲסַר בָּנִים, וּבְלַעַז דישאנפנטי"ן. וְלִי נִרְאֶה, "עֵר וְעֹנֶה" מִגִּזְרַת "וְלִבִּי עֵר" (שיר השירים ה, ב), וַ'עֲרִירִי' לְשׁוֹן חֻרְבָּן, וְכֵן: "עָרוּ עָרוּ" (תהלים קלז, ז), וְכֵן: "עָרוֹת יְסוֹד" (חבקוק ג, יג), וְכֵן: "עַרְעֵר תִּתְעַרְעַר" (ירמיה נא, נח), וְכֵן: "כִּי אַרְזָה עֵרָה" (צפניה ב, יד): **וּבֶן מֶשֶׁק בֵּיתִי.** כְּתַרְגּוּמוֹ, כָּל בֵּיתִי נִזּוֹן עַל פִּיו, כְּמוֹ: "וְעַל פִּיךָ יִשַּׁק" (להלן מא, מ), אַפּוֹטְרוֹפּוֹס שֶׁלִּי; וְאִלּוּ הָיָה לִי בֵּן, הָיָה בְּנִי מְמֻנֶּה עַל שֶׁלִּי: **דַּמֶּשֶׂק.** לְפִי הַתַּרְגּוּם מִדַּמֶּשֶׂק הָיָה; וּלְפִי מִדְרַשׁ אַגָּדָה, שֶׁרָדַף הַמְּלָכִים עַד דַּמֶּשֶׂק. וּבַתַּלְמוּד שֶׁלָּנוּ (יומא כח ע"ב) דּוֹרְשׁוֹ נוֹטָרִיקוֹן: דּוֹלֶה וּמַשְׁקֶה מִתּוֹרַת רַבּוֹ לַאֲחֵרִים:

ג **הֵן לִי לֹא נָתַתָּה זָרַע.** וּמַה תּוֹעֶלֶת בְּכָל אֲשֶׁר תִּתֵּן לִי?:

ה **וַיּוֹצֵא אֹתוֹ הַחוּצָה.** לְפִי פְשׁוּטוֹ, הוֹצִיאוֹ מֵאָהֳלוֹ לַחוּץ לִרְאוֹת הַכּוֹכָבִים. וּלְפִי מִדְרָשׁוֹ, אָמַר לוֹ: צֵא מֵאִצְטַגְנִינוּת שֶׁלְּךָ, שֶׁרָאִיתָ בַּמַּזָּלוֹת שֶׁאֵינְךָ עָתִיד לְהַעֲמִיד בֵּן – אַבְרָם אֵין לוֹ בֵּן, אֲבָל אַבְרָהָם יֵשׁ לוֹ בֵּן; שָׂרַי לֹא תֵלֵד, אֲבָל שָׂרָה תֵּלֵד – אֲנִי קוֹרֵא לָכֶם שֵׁם אַחֵר וְיִשְׁתַּנֶּה הַמַּזָּל. דָּבָר אַחֵר, הוֹצִיאוֹ מֵחֲלָלוֹ שֶׁל עוֹלָם וְהִגְבִּיהוֹ לְמַעְלָה מִן הַכּוֹכָבִים; וְזֶהוּ לְשׁוֹן הַבָּטָה, מִלְמַעְלָה לְמַטָּה:

ו **וְהֶאֱמִן בַּה'.** לֹא שָׁאַל לוֹ אוֹת עַל זֹאת, אֲבָל עַל יְרֻשַּׁת הָאָרֶץ שָׁאַל לוֹ אוֹת וְאָמַר לוֹ: "בַּמָּה אֵדַע" (להלן פסוק ח): **וַיַּחְשְׁבֶהָ לּוֹ צְדָקָה.** הַקָּדוֹשׁ בָּרוּךְ הוּא חֲשָׁבָהּ לְאַבְרָהָם לִזְכוּת וְלִצְדָקָה עַל הָאֱמוּנָה שֶׁהֶאֱמִין בּוֹ. דָּבָר

religious life so decisively in order to hand on to them what they find precious. *Avraham and Sara have a child because they so nearly do not have a child.* Judaism has never taken its children for granted, because Jews have known what it is like to be an Avraham or Sara.

Let us not treat the future lightly. When God promises Avraham that his reward will be very great, he replies: "My Lord God, what will You have given me if I remain childless?" That is the question eternity asks of us. What meaning will our lives and the lives of our ancestors have if they are not lent immortality by our continuity, by our bringing it about that we have Jewish grandchildren? If we would only remember the many miracles it took to bring us to this hour, we would willingly do our duty to ensure that the next generation stays Jewish, and the generation after that. Jewish continuity is the greatest gift we can bring to the future and the past.

15:2 **דַּמֶּשֶׂק אֱלִיעֶזֶר** *Eliezer of Damascus* – The reference to Eliezer has taken on a new intelligibility in the light of ancient documents from the Nuzi archives, which show that it was a well-established practice in Avraham's day for childless individuals to adopt someone, even a slave, as a son. He would then have all the attendant duties and rights of a natural son and heir. Whether or not Avraham has adopted his slave Eliezer, it is clear that with the departure of Lot, there is no one else he can look to.

15:6 **וְהֶאֱמִן בַּיהוה** *Avram put his trust in the Lord* – The Hebrew word *emuna* is usually translated as "faith" or "belief." But like many words which lie at the center of a unique way of life, it defies exact translation. When Avraham, old and childless, is told that he will have as many descendants as the stars of the sky, he "put his trust in [*vehe'emin*] God," who

דְּבַר־יהוה אֶל־אַבְרָם בַּמַּחֲזֶה לֵאמֹר אַל־תִּירָא אַבְרָם אָנֹכִי מָגֵן לָךְ
ב שְׂכָרְךָ הַרְבֵּה מְאֹד׃ וַיֹּאמֶר אַבְרָם אֲדֹנָי יֱהוִה מַה־תִּתֶּן־לִי וְאָנֹכִי
ג הוֹלֵךְ עֲרִירִי וּבֶן־מֶשֶׁק בֵּיתִי הוּא דַּמֶּשֶׂק אֱלִיעֶזֶר׃ וַיֹּאמֶר אַבְרָם הֵן
ד לִי לֹא נָתַתָּה זָרַע וְהִנֵּה בֶן־בֵּיתִי יוֹרֵשׁ אֹתִי׃ וְהִנֵּה דְבַר־יהוה אֵלָיו
ה לֵאמֹר לֹא יִירָשְׁךָ זֶה כִּי־אִם אֲשֶׁר יֵצֵא מִמֵּעֶיךָ הוּא יִירָשֶׁךָ׃ וַיּוֹצֵא
אֹתוֹ הַחוּצָה וַיֹּאמֶר הַבֶּט־נָא הַשָּׁמַיְמָה וּסְפֹר הַכּוֹכָבִים אִם־תּוּכַל
ו לִסְפֹּר אֹתָם וַיֹּאמֶר לוֹ כֹּה יִהְיֶה זַרְעֶךָ׃ וְהֶאֱמִן בַּיהוה וַיַּחְשְׁבֶהָ לּוֹ

אונקלוס

פִּתְגָמָא דַּיי עִם אַבְרָם, בִּנְבוּאָה לְמֵימַר, לָא תִדְחַל אַבְרָם, מֵימְרִי תְּקוֹף לָךְ, אַגְרָךְ סַגִּי לַחֲדָא: ב וַאֲמַר אַבְרָם, יי אֱלֹהִים מָא תִתֵּין לִי, וַאֲנָא אָזֵיל דְּלָא וְלַד, וּבַר פַּרְנָסָא הָדֵין דִּבְבֵיתִי, הוּא דַּמְשְׂקָאָה אֱלִיעֶזֶר: ג וַאֲמַר אַבְרָם, הָא לִי, לָא יְהַבְתְּ וְלַד, וְהָא בַּר בֵּיתִי יָרֵית יָתִי: ד וְהָא פִתְגָמָא דַּיי עִמֵּיהּ לְמֵימַר, לָא יֵירְתִנָּךְ דֵּין, אֱלָהֵין בַּר דְּתוֹלִיד, הוּא יֵירְתִנָּךְ: ה וְאַפֵּיק יָתֵיהּ לְבָרָא, וַאֲמַר אִסְתַּכִּי כְעַן לִשְׁמַיָּא, וּמְנִי כּוֹכְבַיָּא, אִם תִּכּוֹל לְמִמְנֵי יָתְהוֹן, וַאֲמַר לֵיהּ, כְּדֵין יְהוֹן בְּנָךְ: ו וְהֵימִין בְּמֵימְרָא דַּיי, וְחַשְׁבַהּ לֵיהּ

15:1 אַל תִּירָא אַבְרָם *Do not be afraid, Avram* – It is after he faces the sword to save Lot that God tells Avram, "I am your shield." Each year we tell the story of Avraham's call from God to leave his home and travel to "the land that I will show you." I call that the journey into insecurity. Life has been highly insecure for Jews for four thousand years. We are still on that journey. A lot of people are struck by the history of Jewish suffering. I am always struck by the history of Jewish recovery from suffering. What gives a people the strength to keep going? It is that feeling that you can face the future without fear if you know you are not alone. It is that famous line in Psalm 23: "Though I walk through the valley of the shadow of death, I fear no evil, for You are with me." That, I think, is the positive reason for faith in the twenty-first century. We can handle anything so long as we have the humility to know that we are answerable to something much greater than ourselves.

THE PROMISE OF CHILDREN

The first recorded words of man to God in the history of the covenant are a plea for there to be future generations. The first Jew fears he will be the last.

According to the Torah, had nature taken its course, Sara would not have had a child and there would be no Jewish people. If Avraham had had his way and been content with Yishmael, there would have been no Jewish people. If – Yitzḥak having been born – the word from Heaven telling Avraham to stay his hand had been delayed, there would have been no Jewish people. On such slender avoidance of the probable does Jewish continuity rest.

It is as if, from the beginning, a message is being woven into our being. To move from one generation to the next requires a series of miracles. At every stage in the transition from Avraham and Sara to Yitzḥak, continuity seems impossible. Nature is against it. Prediction rules otherwise. At times even Heaven itself seems to decree against it. We are Jews today by virtue of miracles. How then do we survive?

The story of Avraham and Sara and their longing for a child, the promises, the delay, the hope, the despair, the torments and trials, could have no other effect than to create, at the very beginning of Jewish time, a focus bordering on an obsession with Jewish children.

No people can have cared more for their children, invested more energy in them and shaped the whole of their

15 with great wealth. As for you, you will join your ancestors in peace; you will be
16 buried in ripe old age. And the fourth generation will return here, for the guilt of
17 the Amorites is not yet resolved." And when the sun set and it was very dark, a
18 smoking furnace appeared and a blazing torch passed between these pieces. On
that day the LORD made a covenant with Avram: "To your descendants I will give
19 this land, from the River of Egypt to the great river Euphrates, the land of the
20 Kenites, the Kenizzites, the Kadmonites, the Hittites, the Perizzites, the Refaim,

רש"י

ברכש גדול. בממון גדול, כמו שנאמר: "וינצלו את מצרים" (שמות יב, לו):

טו **ואתה תבוא אל אבתיך.** ולא תראה כל אלה: **אל אבתיך.** אביו עובד עבודה זרה והוא מבשרו שיבא אליו?! למדך שעשה תרח תשובה: **תקבר בשיבה טובה.** בשרו שיעשה ישמעאל תשובה בימיו, ולא יצא עשו לתרבות רעה בימיו, ולפיכך מת חמש שנים קדם זמנו, ובו ביום מרד עשו:

טז **ודור רביעי.** לאחר שיגלו למצרים יהיו שם שלשה דורות, והרביעי ישובו לארץ הזאת, לפי שבארץ כנען היה מדבר עמו וכרת ברית זו, כדכתיב: "לתת לך את הארץ הזאת לרשתה" (לעיל פסוק ז). וכן היה: יעקב ירד למצרים, צא וחשב דורותיו – יהודה פרץ וחצרון, וכלב בן חצרון מבאי הארץ היה: **כי לא שלם עון האמרי.** להיות משתלח מארצו עד אותו זמן, שאין הקדוש ברוך הוא נפרע מאמה עד שתתמלא סאתה, שנאמר: "בסאסאה בשלחה תריבנה" (ישעיה כז, ח):

יז **ויהי השמש באה.** כמו: "ויהי הם מריקים שקיהם" (להלן מב, לה), "ויהי הם קברים איש" (מלכים ב' יג, כא), כלומר, ויהי דבר זה: **השמש באה.** שקעה: **ועלטה היה.** חשך היום: **והנה תנור עשן וגו'.** רמז לו שיפלו המלכיות בגיהנם: **באה.** טעמו למעלה, לכך הוא מבאר שבאה כבר. ואם היה טעמו למטה בא"ף, היה מבאר כשהיא שוקעת; ואי אפשר כן, שהרי כבר כתב: "ויהי השמש לבוא" (לעיל פסוק יב), והעברת תנור עשן לאחר מכאן היתה, נמצא שכבר שקעה. וזה חלוק בכל תבה לשון נקבה שיסודה שתי אותיות, כשהטעם למעלה לשון שעבר הוא, כגון זה, וכגון: "ורחל באה" (להלן כט, ט), "קמה אלמתי" (להלן לז, ז), "הנה שבה יבמתך" (רות א, טו), וכשהטעם למטה הוא לשון הוה, דבר שנעשה עכשיו והולך, כמו: "באה עם הצאן" (להלן כט, ו), "קמה באמה" (מיכה ז, ו), "ובבקר היא שבה" (אסתר ב, יד):

יח **לזרעך נתתי.** אמירתו של הקדוש ברוך הוא כאלו היא עשויה: **הנהר הגדל.** לפי שהוא דבוק לארץ ישראל קראהו גדול, אף על פי שהוא מאחר בארבעה נהרות היוצאים מעדן, שנאמר: "והנהר הרביעי הוא פרת" (לעיל ב, יד); משל הדיוט: עבד מלך – מלך, הדבק לשחור וישתחוו לך:

יט **את הקיני.** עשר אמות יש כאן, ולא נתן להם אלא שבעה גוים, והשלשה אדום ומואב ועמון, והם קיני קנזי קדמני, ועתידים להיות ירשה לעתיד, שנאמר: "אדום ומואב משלוח ידם ובני עמון משמעתם" (ישעיה יא, יד):

is written, "*There was a famine in the land*" [Gen. 12:10], and of Israel it is written, "*For two years now there has been famine in the land*" [45:6]. Of Avraham: "*Avram went down to Egypt*" [12:10]. Of Israel: "*Our ancestors went down to Egypt*" [Num. 20:15]. Of Avraham: "*To stay there for a while*" [Gen. 12:10]. Of Israel: "*We have come to stay for a while in your land*" [47:4]. (Bereshit Rabba 40:6)

And so on through a long series of linguistic and substantive parallels between Avraham's fate and the later experience of the Israelites. The exiles of Avraham, Yitzḥak, and Yaakov are, in other words, prefigurations of what is now foretold explicitly in *brit bein habetarim,* the covenant between the pieces. It is as if the patriarchs and matriarchs of the Jewish people had *rehearsed in advance* the fate of their children, not necessarily knowing they were doing so, but nonetheless *laying the foundations of future hope.* The Israelites, exiled and enslaved, would be liberated and redeemed, not only because God said so, but because He had *done so* in the past. He had already shown, several times in different ways, that He was with the ancestors of the nation, protecting them and bringing them safely back.

טו בִּרְכֻשׁ גָּדוֹל: וְאַתָּה תָּבוֹא אֶל־אֲבֹתֶיךָ בְּשָׁלוֹם תִּקָּבֵר בְּשֵׂיבָה
טז טוֹבָה: וְדוֹר רְבִיעִי יָשׁוּבוּ הֵנָּה כִּי לֹא־שָׁלֵם עֲוֺן הָאֱמֹרִי עַד־הֵנָּה:
יז וַיְהִי הַשֶּׁמֶשׁ בָּאָה וַעֲלָטָה הָיָה וְהִנֵּה תַנּוּר עָשָׁן וְלַפִּיד אֵשׁ אֲשֶׁר עָבַר
יח בֵּין הַגְּזָרִים הָאֵלֶּה: בַּיּוֹם הַהוּא כָּרַת יהוה אֶת־אַבְרָם בְּרִית לֵאמֹר
לְזַרְעֲךָ נָתַתִּי אֶת־הָאָרֶץ הַזֹּאת מִנְּהַר מִצְרַיִם עַד־הַנָּהָר הַגָּדֹל נְהַר־
יט כ פְּרָת: אֶת־הַקֵּינִי וְאֶת־הַקְּנִזִּי וְאֵת הַקַּדְמֹנִי: וְאֶת־הַחִתִּי וְאֶת־הַפְּרִזִּי

אונקלוס

בְּקִנְיָנָא סַגִּי: טו וְאַתְּ, תִּתְכְּנֵישׁ לְוָת אֲבָהָתָךְ בִּשְׁלָם, תִּתְקְבַר בְּסֵיבוּ טָבָא: טז וְדָרָא רְבִיעָאָה יְתוּבוּן הָלְכָא, אֲרֵי לָא שְׁלִים, חוֹבָא דֶּאֱמוֹרָאָה עַד כְּעַן: יז וַהֲוָה שִׁמְשָׁא עָאלַת, וְקַבְלָא הֲוָה, וְהָא תַנּוּר דְּתָנַן וּבְעוֹר דְּאִישָׁא, עֲדָא, בֵּין פַּלְגַיָּא הָאִלֵּין: יח בְּיוֹמָא הַהוּא, גְּזַר יְיָ, עִם אַבְרָם קְיָם לְמֵימַר, לִבְנָךְ, יְהַבִית יָת אַרְעָא הָדָא, מִנַּהֲרָא דְּמִצְרַיִם, עַד נַהֲרָא רַבָּא נַהֲרָא פְרָת: יט יָת שַׁלְמָאֵי וְיָת קְנִזָּאֵי, וְיָת קַדְמוֹנָאֵי: כ וְיָת חִתָּאֵי וְיָת פְּרִזָּאֵי

the Temple. Three of them wept. But R. Akiva gave them a message of consolation. The prophets, he said, foresaw this day of destruction, and it has come to pass. But they also foresaw a later day when the city would be rebuilt. Since one vision has come true, so will the other. The day will come when Zekharya's prophecy will be fulfilled: "Old men and old women will sit in the squares of Jerusalem… and the city squares will be full and alive with young boys and girls playing" (Zech. 8:4–5). Nineteen hundred years later, one Sabbath afternoon in Jerusalem, I lived to see R. Akiva's hope come true. *If only he had known*, I thought. If only R. Akiva had known how long it would take, how many exiles, expulsions, persecutions, pogroms, blood libels, inquisitions, and Crusades Jews would first have to endure. If only he had known of the Holocaust and its millions of innocent victims gassed and turned to ashes. Would he not have wept? Would he still have kept his faith? In that moment of truth I knew the answer. Yes, *all the more would he have held to his faith*, knowing that God could not have led this people so long through the valley of the shadow of death without one day bringing them to the city of peace.

15:14 וְאַחֲרֵי־כֵן יֵצְאוּ בִּרְכֻשׁ גָּדוֹל *Afterward… with great wealth* – One of the most striking facts about the patriarchal families is that they all experience exile. Avraham and Yitzḥak are both forced, through famine, to travel to the land of the Philistines. Yaakov suffers exile twice, once to escape Esav, a second time to be rejoined with his son Yosef. In none of these is exile the result of sin, and it is the first instance that provides the interpretive clue to the rest. It occurs earlier in our *parasha*, almost immediately after God's call to Avraham to leave his land, birthplace, and father's house: "There was a famine in the land. Avram went down to Egypt" (Gen. 12:10). He senses danger, fearing that the Egyptians will kill him and take Sarai into the royal harem. Sarai, saying that she is Avraham's sister, is indeed taken into Pharaoh's palace, which is then visited by a series of plagues. Pharaoh then sends the couple away.

The episode seems to disturb the narrative logic of the patriarchal story. Why, if God wants Avraham to go to the land of Canaan, does He force him to leave almost as soon as he has arrived? Midrash Rabba, an early rabbinic commentary, linking that episode with what is foretold here, gives what is undoubtedly the correct answer:

> The Holy One, blessed be He, said to our father Avraham, "Go forth and tread a path for your children." For you find that everything written in connection with Avraham is written in connection with his children. Of Avraham it

16 21 the Amorites, the Canaanites, the Girgashites, and the Jebusites." 1 Sarai,
Avram's wife, had borne him no children; but she had an Egyptian maidservant
2 named Hagar. Sarai said to Avram, "The LORD has kept me from having
children. Come now to my maid. Perhaps through her I might build a family."
3 And Avram listened to Sarai. So it was that, after living in Canaan for ten years,
Avram's wife Sarai took Hagar, her Egyptian maidservant, and gave her to her
4 husband Avram to be his wife. He came to Hagar and she conceived. And when
she realized that she was pregnant, she began to look upon her mistress with
5 contempt. Sarai said to Avram, "The abuse I suffer is your fault. I laid my servant
in your arms and now that she knows she is pregnant, she looks upon me with
6 contempt. Let the LORD judge between me and you!" Avram said to Sarai,
"Your maid is in your own hands. Do with her whatever you think best." Sarai

רש״י

כ **וְאֶת הָרְפָאִים.** אֶרֶץ עוֹג, שֶׁנֶּאֱמַר בָּהּ: ״הַהוּא יִקָּרֵא אֶרֶץ רְפָאִים״ (דברים ג, יג):

טז א **שִׁפְחָה מִצְרִית.** בַּת פַּרְעֹה הָיְתָה, כְּשֶׁרָאָה נִסִּים שֶׁנַּעֲשׂוּ לְשָׂרָה, אָמַר: מוּטָב שֶׁתְּהֵא בִתִּי שִׁפְחָה בְּבַיִת זֶה וְלֹא גְבִירָה בְּבַיִת אַחֵר:

ב **אוּלַי אִבָּנֶה מִמֶּנָּה.** לִמֵּד עַל מִי שֶׁאֵין לוֹ בָּנִים שֶׁאֵינוֹ בָּנוּי אֶלָּא הָרוּס: **אִבָּנֶה מִמֶּנָּה.** בִּזְכוּת שֶׁאַכְנִיס צָרָתִי לְבֵיתִי: **לְקוֹל שָׂרָי.** לְרוּחַ הַקֹּדֶשׁ שֶׁבָּהּ:

ג **וַתִּקַּח שָׂרַי.** לְקָחַתָּהּ בִּדְבָרִים: אַשְׁרַיִךְ שֶׁזָּכִית לִדָּבֵק בְּגוּף קָדוֹשׁ כָּזֶה: **מִקֵּץ עֶשֶׂר שָׁנִים.** מוֹעֵד הַקָּבוּעַ לְאִשָּׁה שֶׁשָּׁהֲתָה עֶשֶׂר שָׁנִים וְלֹא יָלְדָה לְבַעֲלָהּ, חַיָּב לִשָּׂא אַחֶרֶת: **לְשֶׁבֶת אַבְרָם וגו׳.** מַגִּיד שֶׁאֵין יְשִׁיבַת חוּצָה לָאָרֶץ עוֹלָה לוֹ מִן הַמִּנְיָן, לְפִי שֶׁלֹּא נֶאֱמַר לוֹ: ״וְאֶעֶשְׂךָ לְגוֹי גָּדוֹל״ (לעיל יב, ב) עַד שֶׁיָּבֹא לְאֶרֶץ יִשְׂרָאֵל:

ד **וַיָּבֹא אֶל הָגָר וַתַּהַר.** מִבִּיאָה רִאשׁוֹנָה: **וַתֵּקַל גְּבִרְתָּהּ בְּעֵינֶיהָ.** אָמְרָה: שָׂרָה זוֹ אֵין סִתְרָהּ כְּגִלּוּיָהּ, מַרְאָה עַצְמָהּ כְּאִלּוּ הִיא צַדֶּקֶת וְאֵינָהּ צַדֶּקֶת, שֶׁלֹּא זָכְתָה לְהֵרָיוֹן כָּל הַשָּׁנִים הַלָּלוּ, וַאֲנִי נִתְעַבַּרְתִּי מִבִּיאָה רִאשׁוֹנָה:

ה **חֲמָסִי עָלֶיךָ.** חָמָס הֶעָשׂוּי לִי, עָלֶיךָ אֲנִי מַטִּילָה הָעֹנֶשׁ; כְּשֶׁהִתְפַּלַּלְתָּ לְהַקָּדוֹשׁ בָּרוּךְ הוּא: ״מַה תִּתֶּן לִי וְאָנֹכִי הוֹלֵךְ עֲרִירִי״ (לעיל טו, ב) לֹא הִתְפַּלַּלְתָּ אֶלָּא עָלֶיךָ, וְהָיָה לְךָ לְהִתְפַּלֵּל עַל שְׁנֵינוּ וְהָיִיתִי אֲנִי נִפְקֶדֶת עִמָּךְ. וְעוֹד, דְּבָרֶיךָ אַתָּה חוֹמֵס מִמֶּנִּי, שֶׁאַתָּה שׁוֹמֵעַ בִּזְיוֹנִי וְשׁוֹתֵק: **אָנֹכִי נָתַתִּי שִׁפְחָתִי וגו׳ בֵּינִי וּבֵינֶיךָ.** כָּל ׳בֵּינְךָ׳ שֶׁבַּמִּקְרָא חָסֵר וְזֶה מָלֵא, קְרִי בֵּיהּ: ׳וּבֵינֶיךָ׳, שֶׁהִכְנִיסָה עַיִן הָרָע בְּעִבּוּרָהּ שֶׁל הָגָר וְהִפִּילָה עֻבָּרָהּ. הוּא שֶׁהַמַּלְאָךְ אוֹמֵר לְהָגָר: ״הִנָּךְ הָרָה״ (להלן פסוק יא), וַהֲלֹא כְּבָר הָרְתָה, וְהוּא מְבַשֵּׂר לָהּ שֶׁתַּהַר?! אֶלָּא מְלַמֵּד שֶׁהִפִּילָה הֵרָיוֹן הָרִאשׁוֹן:

ו **וַתְּעַנֶּהָ שָׂרָי.** הָיְתָה מְשַׁעְבֶּדֶת בָּהּ בְּקֹשִׁי:

despite the fact that Avraham, Sara, and Yitzḥak are the heroes of the story as a whole, in the two crucial scenes in the desert our imaginative sympathies are with Hagar and her child. That is what gives the story its counter-intuitive depth.

16:6 וַתְּעַנֶּהָ שָׂרָי *Sarai treated her harshly* – Note the characterization of the key figures, especially Avraham and Sara. No reader can fail to sense the harsh light in which Sara is portrayed in her relationship with Hagar and Yishmael. Having proposed the idea of Hagar sleeping with Avraham, she

by the father. Here the order is reversed. The result, happy for Sara and Yitzḥak, is tragic for Hagar and Yishmael.

Peeling away the layers of this complex and subtle text, we will discover another story altogether. The rabbis heard discordant notes in the narrative, and realized that it is conveying a different and surprising message. Only a superficial reading yields the conclusion: Yitzḥak chosen, Yishmael rejected. In fact, here, at the first *generational* succession in the Abrahamic covenant, the Torah contains not only a narrative but also a counter-narrative. *Yishmael is not vilified.* As we shall see,

כא וְאֶת־הָרְפָאִים׃ וְאֶת־הָאֱמֹרִי וְאֶת־הַכְּנַעֲנִי וְאֶת־הַגִּרְגָּשִׁי וְאֶת־
טז א הַיְבוּסִי׃ וְשָׂרַי אֵשֶׁת אַבְרָם לֹא יָלְדָה לוֹ וְלָהּ שִׁפְחָה מִצְרִית יג
ב וּשְׁמָהּ הָגָר׃ וַתֹּאמֶר שָׂרַי אֶל־אַבְרָם הִנֵּה־נָא עֲצָרַנִי יהוה מִלֶּדֶת
בֹּא־נָא אֶל־שִׁפְחָתִי אוּלַי אִבָּנֶה מִמֶּנָּה וַיִּשְׁמַע אַבְרָם לְקוֹל שָׂרָי׃
ג וַתִּקַּח שָׂרַי ׀ אֵשֶׁת אַבְרָם אֶת־הָגָר הַמִּצְרִית שִׁפְחָתָהּ מִקֵּץ עֶשֶׂר
שָׁנִים לְשֶׁבֶת אַבְרָם בְּאֶרֶץ כְּנָעַן וַתִּתֵּן אֹתָהּ לְאַבְרָם אִישָׁהּ לוֹ לְאִשָּׁה׃
ד ה וַיָּבֹא אֶל־הָגָר וַתַּהַר וַתֵּרֶא כִּי הָרָתָה וַתֵּקַל גְּבִרְתָּהּ בְּעֵינֶיהָ׃ וַתֹּאמֶר
שָׂרַי אֶל־אַבְרָם חֲמָסִי עָלֶיךָ אָנֹכִי נָתַתִּי שִׁפְחָתִי בְּחֵיקֶךָ וַתֵּרֶא כִּי
ו הָרָתָה וָאֵקַל בְּעֵינֶיהָ יִשְׁפֹּט יהוה בֵּינִי וּבֵינֶיךָ׃ וַיֹּאמֶר אַבְרָם אֶל־שָׂרַי
הִנֵּה שִׁפְחָתֵךְ בְּיָדֵךְ עֲשִׂי־לָהּ הַטּוֹב בְּעֵינָיִךְ וַתְּעַנֶּהָ שָׂרַי וַתִּבְרַח

אונקלוס

וְיָת גִּבָּרַיָּא: כא וְיָת אֱמוֹרָאֵי וְיָת כְּנַעֲנָאֵי, וְיָת גִּרְגָּשָׁאֵי וְיָת יְבוּסָאֵי:
טז א וְשָׂרַי אִתַּת אַבְרָם, לָא יְלֵידַת לֵיהּ, וְלַהּ, אַמְתָא מִצְרֵיתָא
וּשְׁמַהּ הָגָר: ב וַאֲמַרַת שָׂרַי לְאַבְרָם, הָא כְעַן, מַנְעַנִי יי מִלְּמֵילַד,
עוּל כְּעַן לְוָת אַמְתִי, מָאִם אֶתְבְּנֵי מִנַּהּ, וְקַבֵּיל אַבְרָם לְמֵימַר שָׂרָי:
ג וּדְבָרַת, שָׂרַי אִתַּת אַבְרָם, יָת הָגָר מִצְרֵיתָא אַמְתַהּ, מִסּוֹף עֲסַר
שְׁנִין, לְמִתַּב אַבְרָם בְּאַרְעָא דִּכְנָעַן, וִיהַבַת יָתַהּ, לְאַבְרָם בַּעְלַהּ לֵיהּ
לְאִתּוּ: ד וְעָאל לְוָת הָגָר וְעַדִּיאַת, וַחֲזָת אֲרֵי עַדִּיאַת, וְקַלַּת רִבּוֹנְתַהּ
בְּעֵינַהָא: ה וַאֲמַרַת שָׂרַי לְאַבְרָם דִּין לִי עֲלָךְ, אֲנָא, יְהַבִית אַמְתִּי לָךְ, וַחֲזָת
אֲרֵי עַדִּיאַת, וְקַלִּית בְּעֵינַהָא, יְדִין יי בֵּינָא וּבֵינָךְ: ו וַאֲמַר אַבְרָם לְשָׂרַי,
הָא אַמְתִּיךְ בִּידִיךְ, עֲבִידִי לַהּ דְּתַקִּין בְּעֵינַיכִי, וְעַנִּיתַהּ שָׂרַי, וַעֲרַקַת

HAGAR

This is the first story of sibling rivalry in Avraham's family, and it begins with heartache. Avram has been promised countless children. Yet the years pass and still he and Sara have no child. In despair, Sara proposes an arrangement. Hagar is to become a surrogate mother. Then as now it is a procedure fraught with potential conflict.

Hagar does conceive, and this alters the relationship between the two women. Hagar "began to look upon her mistress with contempt." As the bearer of Avraham's child, she is no longer content to be treated as a servant. Sara notices the change and reacts angrily. Uncharacteristically, Avraham shrugs off the dilemma. "Your maid is in your own hands. Do with her whatever you think best." Sara ill-treats Hagar, who flees into the desert. There she is met by an angel who tells her to go back. She returns and Yishmael is born.

In the next chapter, God appears to Avraham and reaffirms His covenant with him, adding for the first time a command: circumcision. Avraham is to undergo this operation. So is Yishmael. It will become the sign of the covenantal family. The revelation, however, contains a twist. Despite the fact that Avraham now has a son, God tells him he will have another, born to him by Sara. A year later, Yitzḥak is born.

The message seems clear. Just as Avraham was chosen out of all humankind, so is Yitzḥak. But this is not a straightforward story. Yitzḥak is not the firstborn. Yishmael is. What we seem to have here is a *displacement narrative*. In almost all societies where birth order has a bearing on rank, the oldest (usually male) child succeeds to the role occupied

7 treated her harshly – and Hagar ran away from her. An angel of the Lord found
8 her near a spring of water in the desert, the spring by the road to Shur. He said,
"Hagar, maidservant of Sarai, where have you come from and where are you
9 going?" She said, "I am running away from my mistress Sarai." The angel of the
Lord said to her, "Go back to your mistress; submit yourself under her hand."
10 And the angel of the Lord added: "I will greatly multiply your descendants;
11 they will be too many to count." Said the angel of the Lord: "You are pregnant
and will give birth to a son. You shall name him Yishmael, for the Lord has
12 heard your affliction. He will become a wild donkey of a man; his hand will be
against everyone, and everyone's hand against him. He will live up against all
13 his brothers." She gave a name to the Lord who had spoken to her: "You are
the God who sees me," for she said: "Have I not here seen Him who sees me?"
14 That is why the well is called Be'er Laḥai Ro'i. It is still there between Kadesh
15 and Bered. So Hagar bore Avram a son, and Avram gave the name Yishmael to

רש"י

ח **אֵי מִזֶּה בָאת.** מֵהֵיכָן בָּאת. יוֹדֵעַ הָיָה, אֶלָּא לִתֵּן לָהּ פֶּתַח לִכָּנֵס עִמָּהּ בִּדְבָרִים. וּלְשׁוֹן "אֵי מִזֶּה", אַיֵּה הַמָּקוֹם שֶׁתֹּאמַר עָלָיו "מִזֶּה" אֲנִי בָּאָה:

ט **וַיֹּאמֶר לָהּ מַלְאַךְ וְגוֹ'.** עַל כָּל אֲמִירָה הָיָה שָׁלוּחַ לָהּ מַלְאָךְ אַחֵר, לְכָךְ נֶאֱמַר 'מַלְאָךְ' בְּכָל אֲמִירָה וַאֲמִירָה:

יא **הִנָּךְ הָרָה.** כְּשֶׁתָּשׁוּבִי תַּהֲרִי, כְּמוֹ: "הִנָּךְ הָרָה" (שופטים יג, ה) דְּאֵשֶׁת מָנוֹחַ: **וְיֹלַדְתְּ בֵּן.** כְּמוֹ 'וְיוֹלֶדֶת'. וְדוֹמֶה לוֹ: "יֹשַׁבְתְּ בַּלְּבָנוֹן מְקֻנַּנְתְּ בָּאֲרָזִים" (ירמיה כב, כג): **וְקָרָאת שְׁמוֹ.** צִוּוּי הוּא, כְּמוֹ שֶׁאוֹמֵר לַזָּכָר: "וְקָרָאתָ אֶת שְׁמוֹ יִצְחָק" (להלן יז, יט):

יב **פֶּרֶא אָדָם.** אוֹהֵב מִדְבָּרוֹת לָצוּד חַיּוֹת, כְּמוֹ שֶׁכָּתוּב: "וַיֵּשֶׁב בַּמִּדְבָּר וַיְהִי רֹבֶה קַשָּׁת" (להלן כא, כ): **יָדוֹ בַכֹּל.** לִסְטִים: **וְיַד כֹּל בּוֹ.** הַכֹּל שׂוֹנְאִין אוֹתוֹ וּמִתְגָּרִין בּוֹ: **וְעַל פְּנֵי כָל אֶחָיו יִשְׁכֹּן.** שֶׁיִּהְיֶה זַרְעוֹ גָּדוֹל:

יג **אַתָּה אֵל רֳאִי.** נָקוּד חֲטַף קָמָץ מִפְּנֵי שֶׁהוּא שֵׁם דָּבָר, אֱלוֹהַּ הָרְאִיָּה, שֶׁרוֹאֶה בְּעֶלְבּוֹן שֶׁל עֲלוּבִין: **הֲגַם הֲלֹם.** לְשׁוֹן תְּמִיהָ, וְכִי סְבוּרָה הָיִיתִי שֶׁאַף הֲלוֹם בַּמִּדְבָּרוֹת רָאִיתִי שְׁלוּחוֹ שֶׁל מָקוֹם, "אַחֲרֵי רֹאִי" אוֹתָם בְּבֵיתוֹ שֶׁל אַבְרָהָם שֶׁשָּׁם הָיִיתִי רְגִילָה לִרְאוֹת מַלְאָכִים? וְתֵדַע שֶׁהָיְתָה רְגִילָה לִרְאוֹתָם, שֶׁהֲרֵי מָנוֹחַ רָאָה אֶת הַמַּלְאָךְ פַּעַם אַחַת וְאָמַר: "מוֹת נָמוּת" (שופטים יג, כב), וְזוֹ רָאֲתָה אַרְבָּעָה זֶה אַחַר זֶה וְלֹא חָרְדָה:

יד **בְּאֵר לַחַי רֹאִי.** כְּתַרְגּוּמוֹ: "דְּמַלְאָךְ קַיָּמָא אִתַּחְזִי עֲלַהּ":

טו **וַיִּקְרָא אַבְרָם שֵׁם וְגוֹ'.** אַף עַל פִּי שֶׁלֹּא שָׁמַע אַבְרָהָם דִּבְרֵי הַמַּלְאָךְ שֶׁאָמַר: "וְקָרָאת שְׁמוֹ יִשְׁמָעֵאל" (לעיל פסוק יא), שָׁרְתָה רוּחַ הַקֹּדֶשׁ עָלָיו וּקְרָאוֹ יִשְׁמָעֵאל:

hero worship. Rabbi Tzvi Hirsch Chajes explains that the tendency of Midrash to make the heroes seem perfect and the villains completely evil is entirely for educational reasons. It is difficult to teach ethics through stories whose characters are fraught with complexity and ambiguity. The moral life is not something we understand in depth all at once. As children we hear stories of heroes and villains. We learn basic distinctions: right and wrong, good and bad, permitted and forbidden. As we grow, though, we begin to realize how difficult some decisions are. Do I go to Egypt? Do I stay in Canaan? Do I show compassion to my servant's child despite the risk that he may be a bad influence on my child who has been chosen by God for a sacred mission? Anyone who thinks such decisions are easy is not yet morally mature. So the best way of teaching ethics is to do so by way of stories that can be read at different levels at different times in life. When we first read the story we may think that the wild Yishmael is something quite different from the righteous Avraham. As we return to the story again and again, however, we begin to realize that the complexities of the son are bound up with the complexities of the father.

ז מִפָּנֶיהָ׃ וַיִּמְצָאָהּ מַלְאַךְ יְהוָה עַל־עֵין הַמַּיִם בַּמִּדְבָּר עַל־הָעַיִן בְּדֶרֶךְ
ח שׁוּר׃ וַיֹּאמַר הָגָר שִׁפְחַת שָׂרַי אֵי־מִזֶּה בָאת וְאָנָה תֵלֵכִי וַתֹּאמֶר
ט מִפְּנֵי שָׂרַי גְּבִרְתִּי אָנֹכִי בֹּרַחַת׃ וַיֹּאמֶר לָהּ מַלְאַךְ יְהוָה שׁוּבִי אֶל־
י גְּבִרְתֵּךְ וְהִתְעַנִּי תַּחַת יָדֶיהָ׃ וַיֹּאמֶר לָהּ מַלְאַךְ יְהוָה הַרְבָּה אַרְבֶּה
יא אֶת־זַרְעֵךְ וְלֹא יִסָּפֵר מֵרֹב׃ וַיֹּאמֶר לָהּ מַלְאַךְ יְהוָה הִנָּךְ הָרָה וְיֹלַדְתְּ
יב בֵּן וְקָרָאת שְׁמוֹ יִשְׁמָעֵאל כִּי־שָׁמַע יְהוָה אֶל־עָנְיֵךְ׃ וְהוּא יִהְיֶה פֶּרֶא
יג אָדָם יָדוֹ בַכֹּל וְיַד כֹּל בּוֹ וְעַל־פְּנֵי כָל־אֶחָיו יִשְׁכֹּן׃ וַתִּקְרָא שֵׁם־יְהוָה
הַדֹּבֵר אֵלֶיהָ אַתָּה אֵל רֳאִי כִּי אָמְרָה הֲגַם הֲלֹם רָאִיתִי אַחֲרֵי רֹאִי׃
יד טו עַל־כֵּן קָרָא לַבְּאֵר בְּאֵר לַחַי רֹאִי הִנֵּה בֵין־קָדֵשׁ וּבֵין בָּרֶד׃ וַתֵּלֶד
הָגָר לְאַבְרָם בֵּן וַיִּקְרָא אַבְרָם שֶׁם־בְּנוֹ אֲשֶׁר־יָלְדָה הָגָר יִשְׁמָעֵאל׃

אונקלוס

מִן קֳדָמַהָא: ז וְאַשְׁכְּחַהּ, מַלְאֲכָא דַייָ, עַל עֵינָא דְּמַיָּא בְּמַדְבְּרָא, עַל עֵינָא בְּאוֹרְחָא דְחַגְרָא: ח וַאֲמַר, הָגָר, אַמְתַהּ דְּשָׂרַי, מְנָן אַתְּ אָתְיָא וּלְאָן אַתְּ אָזְלָא, וַאֲמַרַת, מִן קֳדָם שָׂרַי רִבּוֹנְתִי, אֲנָא עָרְקָא: ט וַאֲמַר לַהּ מַלְאֲכָא דַייָ, תּוּבִי לְוָת רִבּוֹנְתִיךְ, וְאִשְׁתַּעְבִּידִי תְּחוֹת יְדַהָא: י וַאֲמַר לַהּ מַלְאֲכָא דַייָ, אַסְגָּאָה אַסְגֵּי יָת בְּנַיְכִי, וְלָא יִתְמְנוּן מִסְּגֵי: יא וַאֲמַר לַהּ מַלְאֲכָא דַייָ, הָא אַתְּ מְעַדְּיָא וּתְלִידִין בַּר, וְתִקְרַן שְׁמֵיהּ יִשְׁמָעֵאל, אֲרֵי קַבֵּיל יְיָ צְלוֹתִיךְ: יב וְהוּא יְהֵי מָרוֹד בַּאֲנָשָׁא, הוּא יְהֵי צְרִיךְ לְכוֹלָּא, וְאַף אֱנָשָׁא יְהוֹן צְרִיכִין לֵיהּ, וְעַל אַפֵּי כָל אֲחוֹהִי יִשְׁרֵי: יג וְצַלִּיאַת בִּשְׁמָא דַייָ דְּאִתְמַלַּל עִמַּהּ, אֲמַרַת אַתְּ הוּא אֱלָהָא חָזֵי כּוֹלָּא, אֲרֵי אֲמַרַת, אַף הָכָא, שָׁרִיתִי חָזְיָא בָּתַר דְּאִתְגְּלִי לִי: יד עַל כֵּן קְרָא לְבֵירָא, בֵּירָא דְּמַלְאַךְ קַיָּמָא אִתַּחְזִי עֲלַהּ, הָא הִיא בֵּין רְקַם וּבֵין חַגְרָא: טו וִילֵידַת הָגָר, לְאַבְרָם בַּר, וּקְרָא אַבְרָם שׁוּם בְּרֵיהּ, דִּילֵידַת הָגָר יִשְׁמָעֵאל:

later blames Avraham: "*The abuse I suffer is your fault*" (Gen. 16:5). Avraham, for his part, seems caught helplessly in the tension between the two women.

The Hebrew text uses a significant word to describe Sara's treatment of Hagar: *vate'ane'a*, literally, she "oppressed" her. The Hebrew verb is the same as will later be used to describe the Egyptians: they "oppressed" the Israelites (Ex. 1:11–12). It also appears in Deuteronomy in the text of remembrance to be recited by the Israelites on bringing first fruits to the Temple ("The Egyptians dealt cruelly with us and *oppressed* us … and the Lord … saw our *oppression*, our toil and our enslavement," Deut. 26:6–7). Hagar is herself an Egyptian (Gen. 16:3). There is a subtle hint here that the experience of the Israelites at the hands of the Egyptians will mirror the Egyptian Hagar's experience at the hands of Sara. This unmistakably qualifies the simple stereotype: Israelites good, Egyptians bad.

16:12 **פֶּרֶא אָדָם** *A wild donkey of a man* – On this, Ramban writes: "Our mother [Sara] transgressed in this affliction, as did Avraham by allowing her to do so. So God heard her [Hagar's] affliction and gave her a son who would be *a wild donkey of a man* to afflict the seed of Avraham and Sara with all kinds of affliction" (commentary on Gen. 16:6).

No one in the Torah is portrayed as perfect. No religious literature was ever further from hagiography, idealization, and

11 you: every male among you shall be circumcised. You must circumcise the
flesh of your foreskin – this shall be the sign of the covenant between Me and
12 you. Throughout the generations, every male among you shall be circumcised
at the age of eight days, including the slave born in your household, including
13 one acquired from a stranger not descended from you. All must be circumcised
– those born in your household, those acquired with your money – and My
14 covenant in your flesh will be a covenant everlasting. Any uncircumcised male,
whose foreskin has not been circumcised, shall be severed from his people; he
15 has broken My covenant." God then said to Avraham, "As for
16 Sarai your wife, you shall no longer call her Sarai. Her name will be Sara. I will
bless her and give you a son by her. I will bless her so that she shall birth nations;
17 kings of peoples shall descend from her." Avraham fell on his face and laughed.
"Can a hundred-year-old man become a father?" he said to himself. "Can Sara,
18 at ninety, bear a child?" To God Avraham said, "If only Yishmael might live
19 before You!" God said, "Nonetheless, Sara your wife will bear you a son, and
you shall name him Yitzḥak. I will establish My covenant with him as an

רש״י

אֲשֶׁר תִּשְׁמְרוּ... הִמּוֹל לָכֶם" וְגוֹ': **בֵּינִי וּבֵינֵיכֶם.** אוֹתָם שֶׁל עַכְשָׁיו: **וּבֵין זַרְעֲךָ אַחֲרֶיךָ.** הָעֲתִידִין לְהִוָּלֵד אַחֲרֶיךָ: **הִמּוֹל.** כְּמוֹ 'לְהִמּוֹל', כְּמוֹ שֶׁאַתָּה אוֹמֵר 'עֲשׂוֹת' כְּמוֹ 'לַעֲשׂוֹת':

יא **וּנְמַלְתֶּם.** כְּמוֹ 'וּמַלְתֶּם', וְהַנּוּ"ן בּוֹ יְתֵרָה לִיסוֹד הַנּוֹפֵל בּוֹ לִפְרָקִים, כְּמוֹ נוּ"ן שֶׁל 'נוֹשֵׁךְ' וְנוּ"ן שֶׁל 'נוֹשֵׂא'. 'וּנְמַלְתֶּם' כְּמוֹ 'וּנְשָׂאתֶם' (להלן מה, יט), אֲבָל 'יִמּוֹל' לְשׁוֹן יִפָּעֵל, כְּמוֹ: יֵעָשֶׂה, יֵאָכֵל:

יב **יְלִיד בָּיִת.** שֶׁיְּלָדַתּוּ הַשִּׁפְחָה בַּבַּיִת: **וּמִקְנַת כֶּסֶף.** שֶׁקְּנָאוֹ מִשֶּׁנּוֹלַד:

יג **הִמּוֹל יִמּוֹל יְלִיד בֵּיתְךָ.** כָּאן כָּפַל עָלָיו וְלֹא אָמַר לִשְׁמוֹנָה יָמִים, לְלַמֶּדְךָ שֶׁיֵּשׁ יְלִיד בַּיִת נִמּוֹל לְאֶחָד, וּכְמוֹ שֶׁמְּפֹרָשׁ בְּמַסֶּכֶת שַׁבָּת (דף קלה ע״ב):

יד **וְעָרֵל זָכָר.** כָּאן לִמֵּד שֶׁהַמִּילָה בְּאוֹתוֹ מָקוֹם שֶׁהוּא מַבְדִּיל בֵּין זָכָר לִנְקֵבָה: **אֲשֶׁר לֹא יִמּוֹל.** מִשֶּׁיַּגִּיעַ לִכְלַל עֳנָשִׁין – "וְנִכְרְתָה". אֲבָל אָבִיו אֵין עָנוּשׁ עָלָיו כָּרֵת, אֲבָל עוֹבֵר בַּעֲשֵׂה: **וְנִכְרְתָה הַנֶּפֶשׁ.** הוֹלֵךְ עֲרִירִי וּמֵת קֹדֶם זְמַנּוֹ:

טו **לֹא תִקְרָא אֶת שְׁמָהּ שָׂרָי.** דְּמַשְׁמַע שָׂרַי לִי וְלֹא לַאֲחֵרִים, "כִּי שָׂרָה" סְתָם "שְׁמָהּ", שֶׁתְּהֵא שָׂרָה עַל כֹּל:

טז **וּבֵרַכְתִּי אֹתָהּ.** וּמַה הִיא הַבְּרָכָה? שֶׁחָזְרָה לְנַעֲרוּתָהּ, שֶׁנֶּאֱמַר: "הָיְתָה לִּי עֶדְנָה" (להלן יח, יב): **וּבֵרַכְתִּיהָ.** בַּהֲנָקַת שָׁדַיִם כְּשֶׁנִּצְרְכָה לְכָךְ, בַּיּוֹם מִשְׁתֶּה יִצְחָק, שֶׁהָיוּ מְרַנְנִים עֲלֵיהֶם שֶׁהֵבִיאוּ אֲסוּפִי מִן הַשּׁוּק וְאוֹמְרִים בְּנֵנוּ הוּא, וְהֵבִיאָה כָּל אַחַת בְּנָהּ עִמָּהּ וּמִנִּקְתָּה לֹא הֵבִיאָה, וְהִיא הֵנִיקָה אֶת כֻּלָּם. הוּא שֶׁנֶּאֱמַר: "הֵינִיקָה בָנִים שָׂרָה" (להלן כא, ז). בְּרֵאשִׁית רַבָּה רְמָזוֹ בְּמִקְרָאת (נג, ט):

יז **וַיִּפֹּל אַבְרָהָם עַל פָּנָיו וַיִּצְחָק.** זֶה תִּרְגֵּם אוּנְקְלוֹס לְשׁוֹן שִׂמְחָה: 'וַחֲדִי', וְשֶׁל שָׂרָה לְשׁוֹן מָחוֹךְ (להלן יח, יב), לָמַדְתָּ שֶׁאַבְרָהָם הֶאֱמִין וְשָׂמַח, וְשָׂרָה לֹא הֶאֱמִינָה וְלִגְלְגָה, וְזֶהוּ שֶׁהִקְפִּיד הַקָּדוֹשׁ בָּרוּךְ הוּא עַל שָׂרָה וְלֹא הִקְפִּיד עַל אַבְרָהָם: **הַלְּבֶן.** יֵשׁ תְּמִיהוֹת שֶׁהֵן קִיּוּמוֹת, כְּמוֹ: "הֲנִגְלֹה נִגְלֵיתִי" (שמואל א׳ ב, כז), "הֲרוֹאֶה אַתָּה" (שמואל ב׳ טו, כז), אַף זוֹ קִיֶּמֶת, וְכָךְ אָמַר בְּלִבּוֹ: הֲנַעֲשָׂה חֶסֶד זֶה לְאַחֵר, מַה שֶּׁהַקָּדוֹשׁ בָּרוּךְ הוּא עוֹשֶׂה לִי?: **וְאִם שָׂרָה הֲבַת תִּשְׁעִים שָׁנָה.** הָיְתָה כְּדַאי לֵילֵד? וְאַף עַל פִּי שֶׁדּוֹרוֹת הָרִאשׁוֹנִים הָיוּ מוֹלִידִין בְּנֵי חֲמֵשׁ מֵאוֹת שָׁנָה, בִּימֵי אַבְרָהָם נִתְמַעֲטוּ הַשָּׁנִים כְּבָר וּבָא תַּשּׁוּת כֹּחַ לָעוֹלָם; וְצֵא וּלְמַד מֵעֲשָׂרָה דּוֹרוֹת שֶׁמִּנֹּחַ וְעַד אַבְרָהָם שֶׁמִּהֲרוּ תוֹלְדוֹתֵיהֶן בְּנֵי שְׁלֹשִׁים וּבְנֵי שִׁבְעִים:

יח **לוּ יִשְׁמָעֵאל יִחְיֶה.** הַלְוַאי שֶׁיִּחְיֶה יִשְׁמָעֵאל, אֵינִי כְּדַאי לְקַבֵּל מַתַּן שָׂכָר כָּזֶה: **יִחְיֶה לְפָנֶיךָ.** יִחְיֶה בְּיִרְאָתֶךָ, כְּמוֹ: "הִתְהַלֵּךְ לְפָנַי" (לעיל פסוק א) – "פְּלַח קֳדָמַי":

יט **אֲבָל.** לְשׁוֹן אֲמִתַּת דְּבָרִים, וְכֵן: "אֲבָל אֲשֵׁמִים אֲנַחְנוּ" (להלן מב, כא), "אֲבָל בֵּן אֵין לָהּ" (מלכים ב׳ ד, יד): **וְקָרָאתָ אֶת שְׁמוֹ יִצְחָק.** עַל שֵׁם הַצְּחוֹק; וְעַל שֵׁם עֲשָׂרָה נִסְיוֹנוֹת, וְתִשְׁעִים שָׁנָה שֶׁל שָׂרָה, וּשְׁמוֹנָה יָמִים שֶׁנִּמּוֹל, וּמֵאָה שָׁנָה שֶׁל אַבְרָהָם: **אֶת בְּרִיתִי.** בְּרִית הַמִּילָה תְּהֵא מְסוּרָה לְזַרְעוֹ:

יא בֵּינִי וּבֵינֵיכֶם וּבֵין זַרְעֲךָ אַחֲרֶיךָ הִמּוֹל לָכֶם כָּל־זָכָר: וּנְמַלְתֶּם
יב אֵת בְּשַׂר עָרְלַתְכֶם וְהָיָה לְאוֹת בְּרִית בֵּינִי וּבֵינֵיכֶם: וּבֶן־שְׁמֹנַת
יָמִים יִמּוֹל לָכֶם כָּל־זָכָר לְדֹרֹתֵיכֶם יְלִיד בָּיִת וּמִקְנַת־כֶּסֶף מִכֹּל
יג בֶּן־נֵכָר אֲשֶׁר לֹא מִזַּרְעֲךָ הוּא: הִמּוֹל ׀ יִמּוֹל יְלִיד בֵּיתְךָ וּמִקְנַת
יד כַּסְפֶּךָ וְהָיְתָה בְרִיתִי בִּבְשַׂרְכֶם לִבְרִית עוֹלָם: וְעָרֵל ׀ זָכָר אֲשֶׁר לֹא־
יִמּוֹל אֶת־בְּשַׂר עָרְלָתוֹ וְנִכְרְתָה הַנֶּפֶשׁ הַהִוא מֵעַמֶּיהָ אֶת־בְּרִיתִי
טו הֵפַר: וַיֹּאמֶר אֱלֹהִים אֶל־אַבְרָהָם שָׂרַי אִשְׁתְּךָ לֹא־תִקְרָא
טז אֶת־שְׁמָהּ שָׂרָי כִּי שָׂרָה שְׁמָהּ: וּבֵרַכְתִּי אֹתָהּ וְגַם נָתַתִּי מִמֶּנָּה לְךָ בֵּן
יז וּבֵרַכְתִּיהָ וְהָיְתָה לְגוֹיִם מַלְכֵי עַמִּים מִמֶּנָּה יִהְיוּ: וַיִּפֹּל אַבְרָהָם עַל־
פָּנָיו וַיִּצְחָק וַיֹּאמֶר בְּלִבּוֹ הַלְּבֶן מֵאָה־שָׁנָה יִוָּלֵד וְאִם־שָׂרָה הֲבַת־
יח תִּשְׁעִים שָׁנָה תֵּלֵד: וַיֹּאמֶר אַבְרָהָם אֶל־הָאֱלֹהִים לוּ יִשְׁמָעֵאל יִחְיֶה
יט לְפָנֶיךָ: וַיֹּאמֶר אֱלֹהִים אֲבָל שָׂרָה אִשְׁתְּךָ יֹלֶדֶת לְךָ בֵּן וְקָרָאתָ אֶת־
שְׁמוֹ יִצְחָק וַהֲקִמֹתִי אֶת־בְּרִיתִי אִתּוֹ לִבְרִית עוֹלָם לְזַרְעוֹ אַחֲרָיו:

אונקלוס

בֵּין מֵימְרִי וּבֵינֵיכוֹן, וּבֵין בְּנָךְ בָּתְרָךְ, מִגְּזַר לְכוֹן כָּל דְּכוּרָא: יא וְתִגְזְרוּן, יָת בִּסְרָא דְּעֻרְלַתְכוֹן, וִיהֵי לְאָת קְיָם, בֵּין מֵימְרִי וּבֵינֵיכוֹן: יב וּבַר תְּמָנְיָא יוֹמִין, יִגְּזַר לְכוֹן, כָּל דְּכוּרָא לְדָרֵיכוֹן, יְלִיד בֵּיתָא, וּזְבִין כַּסְפָּא מִכֹּל בַּר עַמְמִין, דְּלָא מִבְּנָךְ הוּא: יג מִגְזַר יִגְּזַר, יְלִיד בֵּיתָךְ וּזְבִין כַּסְפָּךְ, וּתְהֵי קְיָמִי, בְּבִסְרְכוֹן לִקְיָם עָלָם: יד וַעֲרַל דְּכוּרָא, דְּלָא יִגְּזַר יָת בִּסְרָא דְּעֻרְלְתֵיהּ, וְיִשְׁתֵּיצֵי, אֱנָשָׁא הַהוּא מֵעַמֵּיהּ, יָת קְיָמִי אַשְׁנִי: טו וַאֲמַר יְיָ לְאַבְרָהָם, שָׂרַי אִתְּתָךְ, לָא תִקְרֵי יָת שְׁמַהּ שָׂרָי, אֲרֵי שָׂרָה שְׁמַהּ: טז וַאֲבָרֵיךְ יָתַהּ, וְאַף אֶתֵּין מִנַּהּ, לָךְ בַּר, וַאֲבָרְכִנַּהּ וּתְהֵי לִכְנִשָׁן, וּמַלְכִין דְּשַׁלְטִין בְּעַמְמַיָּא מִנַּהּ יְהוֹן: יז וּנְפַל אַבְרָהָם, עַל אַפּוֹהִי וַחֲדִי, וַאֲמַר בְּלִבֵּיהּ, הַלְּבַר מְאָה שְׁנִין יְהֵי וְלַד, וְאִם שָׂרָה, הֲבַת תִּשְׁעִין שְׁנִין תְּלִיד: יח וַאֲמַר אַבְרָהָם קֳדָם יְיָ, לְוַי יִשְׁמָעֵאל יִתְקַיַּם קֳדָמָךְ: יט וַאֲמַר יְיָ, בְּקֻשְׁטָא שָׂרָה אִתְּתָךְ, תְּלִיד לָךְ בַּר, וְתִקְרֵי יָת שְׁמֵיהּ יִצְחָק, וַאֲקֵים יָת קְיָמִי עִמֵּיהּ, לִקְיָם עָלַם לִבְנוֹהִי בָּתְרוֹהִי:

17:10 הִמּוֹל לָכֶם כָּל־זָכָר *Every male among you shall be circumcised* – As the incident in Egypt exemplified (Gen. 12:10–17), sexual relationships are the test of a society's morals. Do I respect other people as persons in their own right, or do I see them as means to my ends, instruments of my pleasure? Do I relate to you in freedom and dignity, or do I simply use you? The nature of the sexual encounter will – not immediately, but eventually – affect all other social relationships. Marriage is the moralization of sex, and the breakdown of marriage is the beginning of the disintegration of society, a fact that virtually every civilization has learned too late. The sign of the covenant, therefore, will be circumcision, because man needs to be reminded in one place more than others of the binding force of moral obligation.

20 everlasting covenant for his descendants after him. As for Yishmael – I have
heard you. I will bless him and make him fertile and multiply him exceedingly.
He will become father of twelve princes, and I will make of him a great nation.
21 But I will establish My covenant with Yitzḥak, whom Sara will bear to you this
22 time next year." When He finished speaking with him, God went up from
23 Avraham. On that very day, Avraham took his son Yishmael, along with all
those born in his house or acquired with money, every male in Avraham's
household, and circumcised the flesh of their foreskins as God had instructed
24 25 him. Avraham was ninety-nine years old when he was circumcised, and his son MAFTIR
26 Yishmael was thirteen. That very day, Avraham and his son Yishmael were
27 circumcised; and all the men of his household, whether home-born or acquired
from strangers, were circumcised together with him.

The haftara for Parashat Lekh Lekha is on page 1504.

רש״י

כ| **שְׁנֵים עָשָׂר נְשִׂיאִם.** כַּעֲנָנִים יִכְלוּ, כְּמוֹ: "נְשִׂיאִים וְרוּחַ" (משלי כה, יד):

כב| **מֵעַל אַבְרָהָם.** לָשׁוֹן נְקִיָּה הוּא כְּלַפֵּי שְׁכִינָה, וְלָמַדְנוּ שֶׁהַצַּדִּיקִים מֶרְכַּבְתּוֹ שֶׁל מָקוֹם:

כג| **בְּעֶצֶם הַיּוֹם.** בּוֹ בַּיּוֹם שֶׁנִּצְטַוָּה, בַּיּוֹם וְלֹא בַּלַּיְלָה, לֹא נִתְיָרֵא לֹא מִן הַגּוֹיִם וְלֹא מִן הַלֵּיצָנִים, וְשֶׁלֹּא יִהְיוּ אוֹיְבָיו וּבְנֵי דוֹרוֹ אוֹמְרִים: אִלּוּ רְאִינוּהוּ לֹא הִנַּחְנוּהוּ לָמוּל וּלְקַיֵּם מִצְוָתוֹ שֶׁל מָקוֹם: **וַיָּמָל.** לְשׁוֹן וַיִּפְעַל:

כד| **בְּהִמֹּלוֹ.** בְּהִפָּעֲלוֹ, כְּמוֹ: "בְּהִבָּרְאָם" (לעיל ב, ד): **בְּהִמֹּלוֹ בְּשַׂר עָרְלָתוֹ.** בְּאַבְרָהָם לֹא נֶאֱמַר 'אֵת' לְפִי שֶׁלֹּא הָיָה חָסֵר אֶלָּא חִתּוּךְ בָּשָׂר, שֶׁכְּבָר נִתְמַעֵךְ עַל יְדֵי תַּשְׁמִישׁ, אֲבָל יִשְׁמָעֵאל שֶׁהָיָה יֶלֶד הֻזְקַק לַחְתֹּךְ עָרְלָה וְלִפְרֹעַ הַמִּילָה, לְכָךְ נֶאֱמַר בּוֹ 'אֵת' (להלן פסוק כה):

כו| **בְּעֶצֶם הַיּוֹם הַזֶּה.** שֶׁמָּלְאוּ לְאַבְרָהָם תִּשְׁעִים וָתֵשַׁע שָׁנָה וּלְיִשְׁמָעֵאל שְׁלֹשׁ עֶשְׂרֵה שָׁנִים, "נִמּוֹל אַבְרָהָם וְיִשְׁמָעֵאל בְּנוֹ":

What are we to make of all this? Undoubtedly, one theme is miraculous birth. Sara, like Rivka and Raḥel after her, is infertile, so the children born to them are marked as divine gifts, in a strong sense, God's children.

But there is also a counter-theme, moving in the opposite direction. The patriarchs and prophets move in the real world, not a world of magic and myth and larger-than-life legend. Avraham begins a journey, but it is beset by obstacles. He receives a promise, but its fulfillment is long delayed and fraught with diversions and false turns.

Avraham's journey, like that of Moshe and the Israelites in a later generation, takes longer than they or we expect. There is no sudden transition from here to the Promised Land, from starting point to destination. Taking Genesis literally, the universe might be made in seven days, but anything in the human world that involves profound change takes time. *Faith is the ability to live with delay without losing trust in the promise; to experience disappointment without losing hope, to know that the road between the real and the ideal is long and yet be willing to undertake the journey.*

Jews are often restless and impatient: in the Talmud they are described (by a Sadducee) as an *ama peziza*, a "rash people" (Shabbat 88a). Yet none has waited longer – for freedom and equality, for the return to the land, and for the Messiah. To wait without despair, to hope and keep on hoping: that is the faith of Avraham and Sara's children, the faith that they themselves lived. And though it was shot through with disappointments, and though they themselves sometimes gave expression to their doubts and fears, it did not prove in vain. Jews kept faith alive. Faith kept the Jewish people alive.

כ וּֽלְיִשְׁמָעֵאל֮ שְׁמַעְתִּיךָ֒ הִנֵּ֣ה ׀ בֵּרַ֣כְתִּי אֹת֗וֹ וְהִפְרֵיתִ֥י אֹת֛וֹ וְהִרְבֵּיתִ֥י
כא אֹת֖וֹ בִּמְאֹ֣ד מְאֹ֑ד שְׁנֵים־עָשָׂ֤ר נְשִׂיאִם֙ יוֹלִ֔יד וּנְתַתִּ֖יו לְג֥וֹי גָּדֽוֹל׃ וְאֶת־
בְּרִיתִ֖י אָקִ֣ים אֶת־יִצְחָ֑ק אֲשֶׁר֩ תֵּלֵ֨ד לְךָ֤ שָׂרָה֙ לַמּוֹעֵ֣ד הַזֶּ֔ה בַּשָּׁנָ֖ה
כב כג הָאַחֶֽרֶת׃ וַיְכַ֖ל לְדַבֵּ֣ר אִתּ֑וֹ וַיַּ֣עַל אֱלֹהִ֔ים מֵעַ֖ל אַבְרָהָֽם׃ וַיִּקַּ֨ח אַבְרָהָ֜ם
אֶת־יִשְׁמָעֵ֣אל בְּנ֗וֹ וְאֵ֨ת כָּל־יְלִידֵ֤י בֵיתוֹ֙ וְאֵת֙ כָּל־מִקְנַ֣ת כַּסְפּ֔וֹ כָּל־
זָכָ֕ר בְּאַנְשֵׁ֖י בֵּ֣ית אַבְרָהָ֑ם וַיָּ֜מָל אֶת־בְּשַׂ֣ר עָרְלָתָ֗ם בְּעֶ֨צֶם֙ הַיּ֣וֹם הַזֶּ֔ה
כד כַּאֲשֶׁ֛ר דִּבֶּ֥ר אִתּ֖וֹ אֱלֹהִֽים׃ וְאַ֨בְרָהָ֔ם בֶּן־תִּשְׁעִ֥ים וָתֵ֖שַׁע שָׁנָ֑ה בְּהִמֹּל֖וֹ מפטיר
כה בְּשַׂ֥ר עָרְלָתֽוֹ׃ וְיִשְׁמָעֵ֣אל בְּנ֔וֹ בֶּן־שְׁלֹ֥שׁ עֶשְׂרֵ֖ה שָׁנָ֑ה בְּהִ֨מֹּל֔וֹ אֵ֖ת בְּשַׂ֥ר
כו כז עָרְלָתֽוֹ׃ בְּעֶ֨צֶם֙ הַיּ֣וֹם הַזֶּ֔ה נִמּ֖וֹל אַבְרָהָ֑ם וְיִשְׁמָעֵ֖אל בְּנֽוֹ׃ וְכָל־אַנְשֵׁ֤י
בֵיתוֹ֙ יְלִ֣יד בָּ֔יִת וּמִקְנַת־כֶּ֖סֶף מֵאֵ֣ת בֶּן־נֵכָ֑ר נִמֹּ֖לוּ אִתּֽוֹ׃

The הפטרה *for* פרשת לך לך *is on page 1505.*

אונקלוס

כ וְעַל יִשְׁמָעֵאל קַבֵּילִית צְלוֹתָךְ, הָא בָּרֵיכִית יָתֵיהּ, וְאַפֵּישֵׁית יָתֵיהּ, וְאַסְגֵּיתִי יָתֵיהּ לַחְדָא לַחְדָא, תְּרֵי עֲסַר רַבְרְבִין יוֹלֵיד, וְאֶתְּנִנֵּיהּ לְעַם סַגִּי: כא וְיָת קְיָמִי אֲקִים עִם יִצְחָק, דִּתְלֵיד לָךְ שָׂרָה לְזִמְנָא הָדֵין, בְּשַׁתָּא אָחֳרַנְתָּא: כב וְשֵׁיצִי לְמַלָּלָא עִמֵּיהּ, וְאִסְתַּלַּק יְקָרָא דַיְיָ, מֵעִלָּווֹהִי דְּאַבְרָהָם: כג וּדְבַר אַבְרָהָם יָת יִשְׁמָעֵאל בְּרֵיהּ, וְיָת כָּל יְלִידֵי בֵיתֵיהּ וְיָת כָּל זְבִינֵי כַסְפֵּיהּ, כָּל דְּכוּרָא, בֶּאֱנָשֵׁי בֵּית אַבְרָהָם, וּגְזַר יָת בְּסַר עָרְלַתְהוֹן, בִּכְרַן יוֹמָא הָדֵין, כְּמָא דְמַלֵּיל עִמֵּיהּ יְיָ: כד וְאַבְרָהָם, בַּר תִּשְׁעִין וּתְשַׁע שְׁנִין, כַּד גְּזַר בִּסְרָא דְעָרְלְתֵיהּ: כה וְיִשְׁמָעֵאל בְּרֵיהּ, בַּר תְּלָת עֶסְרֵי שְׁנִין, כַּד גְּזַר, יָת בִּסְרָא דְעָרְלְתֵיהּ: כו בִּכְרַן יוֹמָא הָדֵין, אִתְגְּזַר אַבְרָהָם, וְיִשְׁמָעֵאל בְּרֵיהּ: כז וְכָל אֱנָשֵׁי בֵיתֵיהּ יְלִידֵי בֵיתָא, וּזְבִינֵי כַסְפָּא מִן בְּנֵי עַמְמַיָּא, אִתְגְּזַרוּ עִמֵּיהּ:

17:20 שְׁנֵים־עָשָׂר נְשִׂיאִם *Twelve princes* – Note the extraordinary length to which the text goes to insist that *Yishmael will be blessed by God*. This is stated four times, the first and last times to Hagar, the second and third to Avraham himself (Gen. 16:9–12; 17:20; 21:13, 18). The first, above in 16:10, *repeats to Hagar the promise God made to Avraham*, that his children would be too numerous to count (15:5). The handmaid will be blessed just as Avraham, the "knight of faith," will be. Here, the promise of "twelve princes" reminds us of Yaakov's twelve sons, each of whom becomes a tribe. The phrase "a great nation" likewise echoes God's promise to Avraham (12:2). He is being promised by God that, although Yitzḥak will continue the covenant, Yishmael will, in worldly terms, be no less great, perhaps greater. Certainly he will have a share in Avraham's blessing.

17:21 וְאֶת־בְּרִיתִי אָקִים אֶת־יִצְחָק *I will establish My covenant with Yitzḥak* – By the time the *parasha* ends, we have heard four promises of children and seen three prospective heirs, Lot, Eliezer, and Yishmael, fail to fit the specification. Lot makes his home among evildoers. Eliezer is not part of the patriarchal family. Yishmael will become "a wild donkey of a man: his hand will be against everyone, and everyone's hand against him" (Gen. 16:12).

Parashat Vayera

18 1 The LORD appeared to him by the Oaks of Mamre as he was sitting at the
2 entrance to his tent in the heat of the day. Avraham looked up and saw three
men standing nearby. The moment he saw them, he ran from the opening of

רש"י

יח א| **וַיֵּרָא אֵלָיו.** לְבַקֵּר אֶת הַחוֹלֶה. אָמַר רַבִּי חָמָא בַּר חֲנִינָא: יוֹם שְׁלִישִׁי לְמִילָתוֹ הָיָה, וּבָא הַקָּדוֹשׁ בָּרוּךְ הוּא וְשָׁאַל בּוֹ: **בְּאֵלֹנֵי מַמְרֵא.** הוּא שֶׁנָּתַן לוֹ עֵצָה עַל הַמִּילָה, לְפִיכָךְ נִגְלָה עָלָיו בְּחֶלְקוֹ: **יֹשֵׁב.** 'יָשַׁב' כְּתִיב, בִּקֵּשׁ לַעֲמֹד, אָמַר לוֹ הַקָּדוֹשׁ בָּרוּךְ הוּא: שֵׁב, וְאַתָּה סִימָן לְבָנֶיךָ שֶׁעָתִיד אֲנִי לְהִתְיַצֵּב בַּעֲדַת הַדַּיָּנִים וְהֵן יוֹשְׁבִים: **פֶּתַח הָאֹהֶל.** לִרְאוֹת אִם יֵשׁ עוֹבֵר וָשָׁב, וְיַכְנִיסֵם בְּבֵיתוֹ: **כְּחֹם הַיּוֹם.** הוֹצִיא הַקָּדוֹשׁ בָּרוּךְ הוּא חַמָּה מִנַּרְתִּיקָהּ שֶׁלֹּא לְהַטְרִיחוֹ בְּאוֹרְחִים, וּלְפִי שֶׁרָאָהוּ מִצְטַעֵר שֶׁלֹּא הָיוּ אוֹרְחִים בָּאִים, הֵבִיא הַמַּלְאָכִים עָלָיו בִּדְמוּת אֲנָשִׁים:

ב| **וְהִנֵּה שְׁלֹשָׁה אֲנָשִׁים.** אֶחָד לְבַשֵּׂר אֶת שָׂרָה וְאֶחָד לַהֲפֹךְ אֶת סְדוֹם וְאֶחָד לְרַפְּאוֹת אֶת אַבְרָהָם, שֶׁאֵין מַלְאָךְ אֶחָד עוֹשֶׂה שְׁתֵּי שְׁלִיחֻיּוֹת, תֵּדַע לְךָ שֶׁכֵּן כָּל הַפָּרָשָׁה הוּא מַזְכִּירָן בִּלְשׁוֹן רַבִּים, "וַיֹּאכֵלוּ" (להלן פסוק ח), "וַיֹּאמְרוּ אֵלָיו" (שם פסוק ט), וּבַבְּשׂוֹרָה נֶאֱמַר: "וַיֹּאמֶר שׁוֹב אָשׁוּב" (שם פסוק י), וּבַהֲפִיכַת סְדוֹם הוּא אוֹמֵר: "כִּי לֹא אוּכַל לַעֲשׂוֹת דָּבָר" (להלן יט, כב), "לְבִלְתִּי הָפְכִּי" (שם פסוק כח). וּרְפָאֵל שֶׁרִפֵּא אֶת אַבְרָהָם הָלַךְ מִשָּׁם לְהַצִּיל אֶת לוֹט, הוּא שֶׁנֶּאֱמַר: "וַיְהִי כְהוֹצִיאָם אֹתָם הַחוּצָה וַיֹּאמֶר הִמָּלֵט עַל נַפְשֶׁךָ" (שם פסוק יז), לָמַדְתָּ שֶׁהָאֶחָד הָיָה מַצִּיל: **נִצָּבִים עָלָיו.** לְפָנָיו, אֲבָל לָשׁוֹן נְקִיָּה הוּא כְּלַפֵּי הַמַּלְאָכִים: **וַיַּרְא.** מַהוּ "וַיַּרְא... וַיַּרְא" שְׁנֵי פְעָמִים? הָרִאשׁוֹן כְּמַשְׁמָעוֹ, וְהַשֵּׁנִי לְשׁוֹן הֲבָנָה – נִסְתַּכֵּל שֶׁהָיוּ נִצָּבִים בְּמָקוֹם אֶחָד וְהֵבִין שֶׁלֹּא הָיוּ רוֹצִים לְהַטְרִיחוֹ, וְקָדַם הוּא וְרָץ לִקְרָאתָם. בְּבָבָא מְצִיעָא (דף פו ע"ב): כְּתִיב "נִצָּבִים עָלָיו" וּכְתִיב "וַיָּרָץ לִקְרָאתָם", כַּד חַזְיוּהּ דַּהֲוָה שָׁרֵי וְאָסַר, פִּרְשׁוּ הֵימֶנּוּ. מִיָּד – "וַיָּרָץ לִקְרָאתָם":

For Rambam, on the other hand, "the general statement that the Lord appeared to Avraham is followed by the description of the way in which that appearance of the Lord took place, namely, that Avraham first saw three men; he ran and spoke to them" (*Moreh Nevukhim* II:42). Our verse, in that case, is a chapter heading. First the Torah states, in general terms, that God appeared to Avraham, then it describes how: in a vision of three men. Verse 1 is a superscription to the chapter as a whole, not a separate incident.

Rashi's explanation is different. The previous chapter has told of Avraham's circumcision at the age of ninety-nine. Following the midrashic assumption that God's conduct is a model for ours, Rashi infers that God's appearance in the first verse is "to visit the sick" (commentary on Gen. 18:1), teaching us the mitzva by divine example. Normally, a divine appearance is a prelude to an act of communication, but here, not so. God "appeared" without saying anything. There are times – visiting the sick – when mere presence is enough.

the forces of nature as gods. They worshipped power and the powerful. Avraham knows, however, that God is not *in* nature but *beyond* nature. There is only one thing in the universe on which He has set His image: the human person, *every* person, powerful and powerless alike.

Avraham knows the paradoxical truth that to live the life of faith is to see the trace of God in the face of the stranger. It is easy to receive the Divine Presence when God appears as God. What is difficult is to sense the Divine Presence when it comes disguised as three anonymous passersby. Avraham knows that serving God and offering hospitality to strangers are not two things but one. That, we are to understand, is Avraham's greatness.

18:1 **וַיֵּרָא אֵלָיו יהוה... כְּחֹם הַיּוֹם** *The LORD appeared to him... in the heat of the day* – What was the content of this revelation? According to the reading explained above ("The Three Visitors"), God appears to tell Avraham of His plan to destroy Sedom; the intervening passage is an interruption.

פרשת וירא

יח א וַיֵּרָא אֵלָיו יְהוָה בְּאֵלֹנֵי מַמְרֵא וְהוּא יֹשֵׁב פֶּתַח־הָאֹהֶל כְּחֹם הַיּוֹם׃ טו
ב וַיִּשָּׂא עֵינָיו וַיַּרְא וְהִנֵּה שְׁלֹשָׁה אֲנָשִׁים נִצָּבִים עָלָיו וַיַּרְא וַיָּרָץ לִקְרָאתָם

אונקלוס

יח א וְאִתְגְּלִי לֵיהּ יְיָ, בְּמֵישְׁרֵי מַמְרֵא, וְהוּא, יָתֵיב בִּתְרַע מַשְׁכְּנָא
כְּמֵיחַם יוֹמָא: ב וּזְקַף עֵינוֹהִי וַחֲזָא, וְהָא תְּלָתָא גֻּבְרִין, קָיְמִין עִלָּווֹהִי, וַחֲזָא, וּרְהַט לְקַדָּמוּתְהוֹן

VAYERA

God appears to Avraham. Three strangers pass by. Avraham engages in a momentous dialogue with God about justice. Lot, with his wife and two of his daughters, is rescued from the destruction of Sedom. Eventually, the promised child, Yitzḥak, is born to Sara. The *parasha* ends with the great test of *akedat Yitzḥak* (the binding of Yitzḥak).

In Lekh Lekha we saw Avraham accept *personal* and *moral* responsibility. Now we see him accept *collective* responsibility. He prays for the inhabitants of Sedom, even though he knows they are sinful, on the grounds that there may be innocent, righteous people among them. They are not his kin, not part of his specific covenant with God, but they are human beings, and Avraham feels the imperative of praying, even arguing with God, on their behalf.

In contrast to the builders of Bavel, he also demonstrates *ontological* responsibility, the duty of human beings to respond to the otherness, and the command, of God. This is the basis of the greatest of his trials, his willingness to sacrifice even his son if God so commands it. Avraham knows that we are but "dust and ashes" (Gen. 18:27) in the face of the Infinite. His task is to obey the will of Heaven on earth, encapsulated in the words "to keep the way of the Lord, by doing what is right and just" (18:19).

THE THREE VISITORS

The interpretation of this chapter hinges upon the way we translate the word *Adonai* in Avraham's appeal: "*Adonai*, if I have found favor in your sight, please do not pass your servant by." *Adonai* can be a reference to one of the names of God. It can also be read as "my lords" or "sirs." In the first case, Avraham would be addressing God: "Please God, do not leave. Stay while I serve the visitors." In the second, he would be speaking to the passersby, asking them not to pass by but to stay, rest, and eat. (The sentence shifts between singular and plural because, in this reading, Avraham is addressing the men collectively, but specifically directing his words to the one he takes to be their leader or senior.)

Normally, differences of interpretation of biblical narrative have no halakhic implications. They are matters of legitimate disagreement. This case of Avraham's addressee is unusual, however, because if we translate *Adonai* as "Lord" it is a holy name, and both the writing of the word by a scribe, and the way we treat a parchment or document containing it, have special stringencies in Jewish law. If, by contrast, we translate it as "my lords" or "sirs," it has no special sanctity. Jewish law rules that in the later scene with Lot, *adonai* is read as "sirs," but in the case of Avraham it is read as "Lord."

This is an extraordinary fact, because it suggests that *Avraham actually interrupts God as He is about to speak, asking Him to wait while he attends to the visitors.* Faced with a choice between listening to God and offering hospitality to what seem to be human beings, Avraham chooses the latter. God accedes to his request, and waits while Avraham brings the visitors food and drink, before engaging him in dialogue about the fate of Sedom.

What the passage is telling us is something of immense profundity. The idolaters of Avraham's time worshipped

3 his tent to greet them, and bowed down low to the ground. He said, "My Lord,
4 if I have found favor in your sight, please do not pass your servant by. Let a little
5 water be brought so that you can wash your feet and rest under the tree. Since
you are passing by your servant, let me bring a morsel of bread so that you can
be refreshed before you go on your way." They replied, "Do just as you say."
6 Avraham rushed to Sara in the tent and said, "Hurry – three *se'a* of fine flour;
7 knead it and bake bread." Avraham himself ran to the herd and took a tender
8 choice calf and gave it to the young man, who hurried to prepare it. He brought
curds and milk and the calf that had been prepared, and set them before them,
9 standing by them as they ate, under the tree. They asked him, "Where is your
10 wife Sara?" "There, in the tent," he replied. Then one of them said, "I will return
to you this time next year, and your wife Sara will have a son." Sara was listening
11 at the opening of the tent behind him. Avraham and Sara were already old,

רש״י

ג **וַיֹּאמַר אֲדֹנָי אִם נָא וְגוֹ׳.** לַגָּדוֹל שֶׁבָּהֶם אָמַר, וּקְרָאָם כֻּלָּם אֲדוֹנִים, וְלַגָּדוֹל אָמַר: "אַל נָא תַעֲבֹר", וְכֵיוָן שֶׁלֹּא יַעֲבֹר הוּא יַעַמְדוּ חֲבֵרָיו עִמּוֹ, וּבְלָשׁוֹן זֶה הוּא חוֹל. דָּבָר אַחֵר, קֹדֶשׁ הוּא, וְהָיָה אוֹמֵר לְהַקָּדוֹשׁ בָּרוּךְ הוּא לְהַמְתִּין לוֹ עַד שֶׁיָּרוּץ וְיַכְנִיס אֶת הָאוֹרְחִים, וְאַף עַל פִּי שֶׁכָּתוּב אַחַר "וַיָּרָץ לִקְרָאתָם", הָאֲמִירָה קֹדֶם לָכֵן הָיְתָה, וְדֶרֶךְ הַמִּקְרָאוֹת לְדַבֵּר כֵּן, כְּמוֹ שֶׁפֵּרַשְׁתִּי אֵצֶל "לֹא יָדוֹן רוּחִי בָאָדָם" (לעיל ו, ג) שֶׁנִּכְתַּב אַחַר "וַיּוֹלֶד נֹחַ" (לעיל ה, לב), וְאִי אֶפְשָׁר לוֹמַר אֶלָּא אִם כֵּן קֹדֶם הַגְּזֵרָה עֶשְׂרִים שָׁנָה. וּשְׁתֵּי הַלְּשׁוֹנוֹת בִּבְרֵאשִׁית רַבָּה (מח, י; מט, ז):

ד **יֻקַּח נָא.** עַל יְדֵי שָׁלִיחַ, וְהַקָּדוֹשׁ בָּרוּךְ הוּא שִׁלֵּם לְבָנָיו עַל יְדֵי שָׁלִיחַ, שֶׁנֶּאֱמַר: "וַיָּרֶם מֹשֶׁה אֶת יָדוֹ וַיַּךְ אֶת הַסֶּלַע" (במדבר כ, יא): **וְרַחֲצוּ רַגְלֵיכֶם.** כְּסָבוּר שֶׁהֵם עַרְבִיִּים שֶׁמִּשְׁתַּחֲוִים לַאֲבַק רַגְלֵיהֶם, וְהִקְפִּיד שֶׁלֹּא לְהַכְנִיס עֲבוֹדָה זָרָה לְבֵיתוֹ. אֲבָל לוֹט שֶׁלֹּא הִקְפִּיד הִקְדִּים לִינָה לִרְחִיצָה, שֶׁנֶּאֱמַר: "וְלִינוּ וְרַחֲצוּ רַגְלֵיכֶם" (להלן יט, ב): **תַּחַת הָעֵץ.** תַּחַת הָאִילָן:

ה **וְסַעֲדוּ לִבְּכֶם.** בַּתּוֹרָה בַּנְּבִיאִים וּבַכְּתוּבִים מָצִינוּ דְּפִתָּא סַעֲדְתָּא דְּלִבָּא. בַּתּוֹרָה: "וְסַעֲדוּ לִבְּכֶם", בַּנְּבִיאִים: "סְעָד לִבְּךָ פַּת לֶחֶם" (שופטים יט, ה), בַּכְּתוּבִים: "וְלֶחֶם לְבַב אֱנוֹשׁ יִסְעָד" (תהלים קד, טו). אָמַר רַבִּי חָמָא: 'לְבַבְכֶם' אֵין כְּתִיב כָּאן אֶלָּא 'לִבְּכֶם', מַגִּיד שֶׁאֵין יֵצֶר הָרָע שׁוֹלֵט בַּמַּלְאָכִים: **אַחַר תַּעֲבֹרוּ.** אַחַר כֵּן תֵּלֵכוּ: **כִּי עַל כֵּן עֲבַרְתֶּם.** כִּי הַדָּבָר הַזֶּה אֲנִי מְבַקֵּשׁ מִכֶּם מֵאַחַר שֶׁעֲבַרְתֶּם עָלַי לִכְבוֹדִי. "כִּי עַל כֵּן" – כְּמוֹ: 'עַל אֲשֶׁר', וְכֵן כָּל 'כִּי עַל כֵּן' שֶׁבַּמִּקְרָא: "כִּי עַל כֵּן בָּאוּ בְּצֵל קֹרָתִי" (להלן יט, ח), "כִּי עַל כֵּן רָאִיתִי פָנֶיךָ" (להלן לג, י), "כִּי עַל כֵּן לֹא נְתַתִּיהָ" (להלן לח, כו), "כִּי עַל כֵּן יָדַעְתָּ חֲנֹתֵנוּ" (במדבר י, לא):

ו **קֶמַח סֹלֶת.** סֹלֶת לְעוּגוֹת, קֶמַח לַעֲמִילָן שֶׁל טַבָּחִים לְכַסּוֹת אֶת הַקְּדֵרָה לִשְׁאֹב אֶת הַזֻּהֲמָא:

ז **בֶּן בָּקָר רַךְ וָטוֹב.** שְׁלֹשָׁה פָרִים הָיוּ, כְּדֵי לְהַאֲכִילָן שָׁלֹשׁ לְשׁוֹנוֹת בְּחַרְדָּל: **אֶל הַנַּעַר.** זֶה יִשְׁמָעֵאל, לְחַנְּכוֹ בְּמִצְוֹת:

ח **וַיִּקַּח חֶמְאָה וְגוֹ׳.** וְלֶחֶם לֹא הֵבִיא, לְפִי שֶׁפֵּרְסָה שָׂרָה נִדָּה, שֶׁחָזַר לָהּ אֹרַח כַּנָּשִׁים אוֹתוֹ הַיּוֹם, וְנִטְמֵאת הָעִסָּה: **חֶמְאָה.** שֻׁמַּן הֶחָלָב שֶׁקּוֹלְטִין מֵעַל פָּנָיו: **וּבֶן הַבָּקָר אֲשֶׁר עָשָׂה.** אֲשֶׁר תִּקֵּן. קַמָּא קַמָּא שֶׁתִּקֵּן אַמְטֵי וְאַיְתֵי קַמַּיְהוּ: **וַיֹּאכֵלוּ.** נִרְאוּ כְּמוֹ שֶׁאָכְלוּ, מִכָּאן שֶׁלֹּא יְשַׁנֶּה אָדָם מִן הַמִּנְהָג:

ט **וַיֹּאמְרוּ אֵלָיו.** נָקוּד עַל אי״ו, וְתַנְיָא, רַבִּי שִׁמְעוֹן בֶּן אֶלְעָזָר אוֹמֵר: כָּל מָקוֹם שֶׁהַכְּתָב רַבֶּה עַל הַנְּקֻדָּה אַתָּה דּוֹרֵשׁ הַכְּתָב, וְכָאן נְקֻדָּה רַבָּה עַל הַכְּתָב וְאַתָּה דּוֹרֵשׁ הַנְּקֻדָּה, שֶׁאַף לְשָׂרָה שָׁאֲלוּ: אַיּוֹ אַבְרָהָם? לִמְּדָנוּ שֶׁיִּשְׁאַל אָדָם בְּאַכְסַנְיָא שֶׁלּוֹ לָאִישׁ עַל הָאִשָּׁה וְלָאִשָּׁה עַל הָאִישׁ. בְּבָבָא מְצִיעָא (דף פז ע״א) אוֹמְרִים: יוֹדְעִים הָיוּ מַלְאֲכֵי הַשָּׁרֵת שָׂרָה אִמֵּנוּ הֵיכָן הָיְתָה, אֶלָּא לְהוֹדִיעַ שֶׁצְּנוּעָה הָיְתָה כְּדֵי לְחַבְּבָהּ עַל בַּעְלָהּ. אָמַר רַבִּי יוֹסֵי בְּרַבִּי חֲנִינָא: כְּדֵי לְשַׁגֵּר לָהּ כּוֹס שֶׁל בְּרָכָה: **הִנֵּה בָאֹהֶל.** צְנוּעָה הִיא:

י **כָּעֵת חַיָּה.** כָּעֵת הַזֹּאת לַשָּׁנָה הַבָּאָה, וּפֶסַח הָיָה, וְלַפֶּסַח הַבָּא נוֹלַד יִצְחָק, מִדְּלָא קָרֵינַן כְּעֵת חַיָּה: **כָּעֵת חַיָּה.** כָּעֵת הַזֹּאת שֶׁתְּהֵא חַיָּה לָכֶם, שֶׁתִּהְיוּ כֻּלְּכֶם שְׁלֵמִים וְקַיָּמִים: **שׁוֹב אָשׁוּב.** לֹא בִּשְּׂרוֹ הַמַּלְאָךְ שֶׁיָּשׁוּב אֵלָיו, אֶלָּא בִּשְׁלִיחוּתוֹ שֶׁל מָקוֹם אָמַר לוֹ, כְּמוֹ: "וַיֹּאמֶר לָהּ מַלְאַךְ ה׳ הַרְבָּה אַרְבֶּה" (לעיל טז, י) וְהוּא אֵין בְּיָדוֹ לְהַרְבּוֹת, אֶלָּא בִּשְׁלִיחוּתוֹ שֶׁל מָקוֹם אָמַר לָהּ, אַף כָּאן בִּשְׁלִיחוּתוֹ שֶׁל מָקוֹם אָמַר לוֹ: **וְהוּא אַחֲרָיו.** הַפֶּתַח הָיָה אַחַר הַמַּלְאָךְ:

יא **חָדַל לִהְיוֹת.** פָּסַק מִמֶּנָּה דֶּרֶךְ נָשִׁים – נִדּוֹת:

ג מִפֶּתַח הָאֹהֶל וַיִּשְׁתַּחוּ אָרְצָה: וַיֹּאמַר אֲדֹנָי אִם־נָא מָצָאתִי חֵן בְּעֵינֶיךָ
ד אַל־נָא תַעֲבֹר מֵעַל עַבְדֶּךָ: יֻקַּח־נָא מְעַט־מַיִם וְרַחֲצוּ רַגְלֵיכֶם וְהִשָּׁעֲנוּ
ה תַּחַת הָעֵץ: וְאֶקְחָה פַת־לֶחֶם וְסַעֲדוּ לִבְּכֶם אַחַר תַּעֲבֹרוּ כִּי־עַל־כֵּן
ו עֲבַרְתֶּם עַל־עַבְדְּכֶם וַיֹּאמְרוּ כֵּן תַּעֲשֶׂה כַּאֲשֶׁר דִּבַּרְתָּ: וַיְמַהֵר אַבְרָהָם
הָאֹהֱלָה אֶל־שָׂרָה וַיֹּאמֶר מַהֲרִי שְׁלֹשׁ סְאִים קֶמַח סֹלֶת לוּשִׁי וַעֲשִׂי
ז עֻגוֹת: וְאֶל־הַבָּקָר רָץ אַבְרָהָם וַיִּקַּח בֶּן־בָּקָר רַךְ וָטוֹב וַיִּתֵּן אֶל־הַנַּעַר
ח וַיְמַהֵר לַעֲשׂוֹת אֹתוֹ: וַיִּקַּח חֶמְאָה וְחָלָב וּבֶן־הַבָּקָר אֲשֶׁר עָשָׂה וַיִּתֵּן
ט לִפְנֵיהֶם וְהוּא עֹמֵד עֲלֵיהֶם תַּחַת הָעֵץ וַיֹּאכֵלוּ: וַיֹּאמְרוּ אֵלָיו אַיֵּה
י שָׂרָה אִשְׁתֶּךָ וַיֹּאמֶר הִנֵּה בָאֹהֶל: וַיֹּאמֶר שׁוֹב אָשׁוּב אֵלֶיךָ כָּעֵת חַיָּה
וְהִנֵּה־בֵן לְשָׂרָה אִשְׁתֶּךָ וְשָׂרָה שֹׁמַעַת פֶּתַח הָאֹהֶל וְהוּא אַחֲרָיו:
יא וְאַבְרָהָם וְשָׂרָה זְקֵנִים בָּאִים בַּיָּמִים חָדַל לִהְיוֹת לְשָׂרָה אֹרַח כַּנָּשִׁים:

אונקלוס

מִתְּרַע מַשְׁכְּנָא, וּסְגִיד עַל אַרְעָא: ג וַאֲמַר, יְיָ, אִם כְּעַן אַשְׁכַּחִית רַחֲמִין קֳדָמָךְ, לָא כְעַן תִּעְבַּר מֵעַל עַבְדָּךְ: ד יִסַּבוּן כְּעַן זְעֵיר מַיָּא, וְאַסְחוּ רַגְלֵיכוֹן, וְאִסְתְּמִיכוּ תְּחוֹת אִילָנָא: ה וְאֶסַּב פִּתָּא דִּלְחֶמָא, וּסְעוּדוּ לִבְּכוֹן בָּתַר כֵּן תִּעְבְּרוּן, אֲרֵי עַל כֵּן עֲבַרְתּוּן עַל עַבְדְּכוֹן, וַאֲמַרוּ, כֵּן תַּעְבֵּיד כְּמָא דְמַלֵּילְתָּא: ו וְאוֹחִי אַבְרָהָם, לְמַשְׁכְּנָא לְוָת שָׂרָה, וַאֲמַר, אוֹחַאי, תְּלָת סְאִין קִמְחָא סָלְתָּא, לוּשִׁי וְעַבִידִי גְּרִיצָן: ז וּלְבֵית תּוֹרֵי רְהַט אַבְרָהָם, וּנְסֵיב בַּר תּוֹרֵי, רַכִּיךְ וְטָב וִיהַב לְעוּלֵימָא, וְאוֹחִי לְמֶעְבַּד יָתֵיהּ: ח וּנְסֵיב שְׁמַן וַחֲלַב, וּבַר תּוֹרֵי דַּעֲבַד, וִיהַב קֳדָמֵיהוֹן, וְהוּא מְשַׁמֵּישׁ עִלָּוֵיהוֹן, תְּחוֹת אִילָנָא וַאֲכַלוּ: ט וַאֲמַרוּ לֵיהּ, אָן שָׂרָה אִתְּתָךְ, וַאֲמַר הָא בְמַשְׁכְּנָא: י וַאֲמַר, מְתָב אֲתוּב לְוָתָךְ כְּעִדָּן דְּאַתּוּן קַיָּמִין, וְהָא בְרָא לְשָׂרָה אִתְּתָךְ, וְשָׂרָה שְׁמַעַת, בִּתְרַע מַשְׁכְּנָא וְהוּא אֲחוֹרוֹהִי: יא וְאַבְרָהָם וְשָׂרָה סִיבוּ, עָאלוּ בְיוֹמִין, פְּסַק מִלְּמֶהֱוֵי לְשָׂרָה, אוֹרַח כִּנְשַׁיָּא:

18:4 וְהִשָּׁעֲנוּ תַּחַת הָעֵץ *Rest under the tree* – Unbeknown to Avraham, these passersby are angels, bringing news that Sara will have a child, Yitzḥak, first child of the covenant. At the dawn of Jewish time, an association is being struck: God shows kindness to those who show kindness to strangers. The Hebrew letter *bet*, with which the Torah begins, also means "house." It is open at one side, signaling graphically that a Jewish home is one that is open to visitors and strangers. From the story of Avraham the Rabbis derive the rule – no mere figure of speech but meant categorically – that *gedola hakhnassat orḥim mikabbalat pnei haShekhina*, "greater is hospitality than welcoming the Divine Presence" (Shabbat 127a; Shevuot 35b).

18:8 עֹמֵד עֲלֵיהֶם *Standing by them* – Using a very literal reading of the verses, Rabbi Shalom of Belz notes that in verse 2, the visitors are spoken of as standing *above* Avraham (*nitzavim alav*), while in verse 8, Avraham is described as standing *above them* (*omed aleihem*). At first, the visitors were higher than Avraham because they were angels and he a mere human being. But when he gave them food and drink and shelter, he stood even higher than the angels (cited in *Peninei Ḥasidut* on Gen. 18:2).

12 advanced in years; the way of women no longer visited Sara. So Sara laughed to
herself, saying, "Now that I am worn out, can I have this pleasure? With my
13 lord an old man?" Then the LORD said to Avraham, "Why did Sara laugh and
14 say, 'Can I really have a child, now that I am old?' Is anything beyond the LORD's
powers? At the due time next year I will return to you, and Sara will have a son."
15 Sara, because she was afraid, denied it: "I did not laugh," she said. But He said, SHENI
16 "Not so. You laughed." The men got up to leave and looked down toward
17 Sedom. Avraham accompanied them to see them on their way. The LORD said,
18 "Shall I hide from Avraham what I am about to do? Avraham is about to become
a great and mighty nation, and through him all the nations on earth will be
19 blessed. For I have chosen him so that he may direct his children and his
household after him to keep the way of the LORD by doing what is right and

רש״י

יב **בְּקִרְבָּהּ לֵאמֹר.** מִסְתַּכֶּלֶת בְּמֵעֶיהָ: אֶפְשָׁר הַקְּרָבַיִם הַלָּלוּ טוֹעֲנִין וָלָד? הַשָּׁדַיִם הַלָּלוּ שֶׁצָּמְקוּ מוֹשְׁכִין חָלָב? תַּנְחוּמָא (שופטים יח): **עֶדְנָה.** צַחְצוּחַ בָּשָׂר, וּלְשׁוֹן מִשְׁנָה: "מַשִּׁיר אֶת הַשֵּׂעָר וּמְעַדֵּן אֶת הַבָּשָׂר". דָּבָר אַחֵר, לְשׁוֹן עִדָּן, זְמַן וֶסֶת נִדּוּת:

יג **הַאַף אֻמְנָם.** הֲגַם אֱמֶת "אֵלֵד": **וַאֲנִי זָקַנְתִּי.** שִׁנָּה הַכָּתוּב מִפְּנֵי הַשָּׁלוֹם, שֶׁהֲרֵי הִיא אָמְרָה: "וַאדֹנִי זָקֵן":

יד **הֲיִפָּלֵא.** כְּתַרְגּוּמוֹ, "הֲיִתְכַּסֵּי", וְכִי שׁוּם דָּבָר מֻפְלָא וּמֻפְרָד וּמְכֻסֶּה מִמֶּנִּי מִלַּעֲשׂוֹת כִּרְצוֹנִי? **לַמּוֹעֵד.** לְאוֹתוֹ מוֹעֵד הַמְּיֻחָד שֶׁקָּבַעְתִּי לְךָ אֶתְמוֹל, "לַמּוֹעֵד הַזֶּה בַּשָּׁנָה הָאַחֶרֶת" (לעיל יז, כא):

טו **כִּי יָרֵאָה. כִּי צָחָקְתְּ.** הָרִאשׁוֹן מְשַׁמֵּשׁ לְשׁוֹן 'דְּהָא', שֶׁהוּא נוֹתֵן טַעַם לַדָּבָר: וַתְּכַחֵשׁ שָׂרָה לְפִי שֶׁיָּרֵאָה. וְהַשֵּׁנִי מְשַׁמֵּשׁ בִּלְשׁוֹן 'אֶלָּא': וַיֹּאמֶר, לֹא כִּדְבָרֵךְ הוּא, אֶלָּא צָחָקְתְּ; שֶׁאָמְרוּ רַבּוֹתֵינוּ: 'כִּי' מְשַׁמֵּשׁ בְּאַרְבַּע לְשׁוֹנוֹת, אִי, דִּלְמָא, אֶלָּא, דְּהָא:

טז **וַיַּשְׁקִפוּ.** כָּל הַשְׁקָפָה שֶׁבַּמִּקְרָא לְרָעָה, חוּץ מֵ"הַשְׁקִיפָה מִמְּעוֹן קָדְשְׁךָ" (דברים כו, טו), שֶׁגָּדוֹל כֹּחַ מַתְּנוֹת עֲנִיִּים שֶׁהוֹפֵךְ מִדַּת הָרֹגֶז לְרַחֲמִים: **לְשַׁלְּחָם.** לְלַוּוֹתָם, כִּסְבוּר אוֹרְחִים הֵם:

יז **הַמְכַסֶּה אֲנִי.** בִּתְמִיָּה, מָה שֶׁאֲנִי עֹשֶׂה בִּסְדוֹם?! לֹא יָפֶה לִי לַעֲשׂוֹת דָּבָר זֶה שֶׁלֹּא מִדַּעְתּוֹ! אֲנִי נָתַתִּי לוֹ אֶת הָאָרֶץ הַזֹּאת וַחֲמִשָּׁה כְּרַכִּין הַלָּלוּ שֶׁלּוֹ הֵן, שֶׁנֶּאֱמַר: "גְּבוּל הַכְּנַעֲנִי מִצִּידֹן... בֹּאֲכָה סְדֹמָה וַעֲמֹרָה" וְגוֹ' (לעיל י, יט), קָרָאתִי אוֹתוֹ אַבְרָהָם, "אַב הֲמוֹן גּוֹיִם" (לעיל יז, ה), וְאַשְׁמִיד אֶת הַבָּנִים וְלֹא אוֹדִיעַ לָאָב שֶׁהוּא אוֹהֲבִי?!:

יח **וְאַבְרָהָם הָיוֹ יִהְיֶה.** מִדְרַשׁ אַגָּדָה, "זֵכֶר צַדִּיק לִבְרָכָה" (משלי י, ז), הוֹאִיל וְהִזְכִּירוֹ בֵּרְכוֹ. וּפְשׁוּטוֹ, וְכִי מִמֶּנּוּ אֲנִי מַעְלִים? וַהֲרֵי הוּא חָבִיב לְפָנַי לִהְיוֹת לְגוֹי גָּדוֹל וּלְהִתְבָּרֵךְ בּוֹ כָּל גּוֹיֵי הָאָרֶץ:

יט **כִּי יְדַעְתִּיו.** לְשׁוֹן חִבָּה, כְּמוֹ: "מוֹדַע לְאִישָׁהּ" (רות ב, א), "הֲלֹא בֹעַז מֹדַעְתָּנוּ" (שם ג, ב), "וָאֵדָעֲךָ בְּשֵׁם" (שמות לג, יז). וְאָמְנָם עִקַּר לְשׁוֹן כֻּלָּם אֵינוֹ אֶלָּא לְשׁוֹן יְדִיעָה, שֶׁהַמְחַבֵּב אֶת הָאָדָם מְקָרְבוֹ אֶצְלוֹ וְיוֹדְעוֹ וּמַכִּירוֹ. וְלָמָּה יְדַעְתִּיו? "לְמַעַן אֲשֶׁר יְצַוֶּה", לְפִי שֶׁהוּא מְצַוֶּה אֶת בָּנָיו עָלַי לִשְׁמֹר דְּרָכַי. וְאִם תְּפָרְשֵׁהוּ כְּתַרְגּוּמוֹ: יָדַעְנָא בֵּהּ דִּי יְפַקֵּד, ... אֶת בָּנָיו וְגוֹ', אֵין 'לְמַעַן' נוֹפֵל עַל הַלָּשׁוֹן: **יְצַוֶּה.** לְשׁוֹן הֹוֶה, כְּמוֹ: "כָּכָה יַעֲשֶׂה אִיּוֹב" (איוב א, ה): **לְמַעַן הָבִיא.** כָּךְ הוּא מְצַוֶּה לְבָנָיו: שִׁמְרוּ דֶּרֶךְ ה' כְּדֵי שֶׁיָּבִיא ה' עַל אַבְרָהָם וְגוֹ'; 'עַל בֵּית אַבְרָהָם' לֹא נֶאֱמַר אֶלָּא "עַל אַבְרָהָם", לָמַדְנוּ כָּל הַמַּעֲמִיד בֵּן צַדִּיק כְּאִלּוּ אֵינוֹ מֵת:

even if it involves argument with Heaven itself. And it begins here with Avraham, the man empowered by God to argue with God so that justice might be seen to be done.

18:19 **לַעֲשׂוֹת צְדָקָה וּמִשְׁפָּט** *By doing what is right and just* – The Bible tells us very little about Avraham that might explain why he is chosen for the mission he undertakes. It does not call him righteous, as it does in the case of Noaḥ. It does not portray him as a miracle worker, as it does Moshe. The only place in the Bible to explain why Avraham is chosen is this verse. He is chosen because he will hand his way of life on to future generations.

The words of this explanation imply three things about what it is to be an heir of Avraham. On the most basic

יב וַתִּצְחַק שָׂרָה בְּקִרְבָּהּ לֵאמֹר אַחֲרֵי בְלֹתִי הָיְתָה־לִּי עֶדְנָה וַאדֹנִי זָקֵן:
יג וַיֹּאמֶר יְהוָה אֶל־אַבְרָהָם לָמָּה זֶּה צָחֲקָה שָׂרָה לֵאמֹר הַאַף אֻמְנָם
יד אֵלֵד וַאֲנִי זָקַנְתִּי: הֲיִפָּלֵא מֵיְהוָה דָּבָר לַמּוֹעֵד אָשׁוּב אֵלֶיךָ כָּעֵת חַיָּה
טו וּלְשָׂרָה בֵן: וַתְּכַחֵשׁ שָׂרָה ׀ לֵאמֹר לֹא צָחַקְתִּי כִּי ׀ יָרֵאָה וַיֹּאמֶר ׀ לֹא שני
טז כִּי צָחָקְתְּ: וַיָּקֻמוּ מִשָּׁם הָאֲנָשִׁים וַיַּשְׁקִפוּ עַל־פְּנֵי סְדֹם וְאַבְרָהָם הֹלֵךְ
יז עִמָּם לְשַׁלְּחָם: וַיהוָה אָמָר הַמְכַסֶּה אֲנִי מֵאַבְרָהָם אֲשֶׁר אֲנִי עֹשֶׂה:
יח יט וְאַבְרָהָם הָיוֹ יִהְיֶה לְגוֹי גָּדוֹל וְעָצוּם וְנִבְרְכוּ־בוֹ כֹּל גּוֹיֵי הָאָרֶץ: כִּי
יְדַעְתִּיו לְמַעַן אֲשֶׁר יְצַוֶּה אֶת־בָּנָיו וְאֶת־בֵּיתוֹ אַחֲרָיו וְשָׁמְרוּ
דֶּרֶךְ יְהוָה לַעֲשׂוֹת צְדָקָה וּמִשְׁפָּט לְמַעַן הָבִיא יְהוָה עַל־אַבְרָהָם

אונקלוס

יב וְחַיְּיכַת שָׂרָה בִּמְעָהָא לְמֵימַר, בָּתַר דְּסֵיבִית תְּהֵי לִי עוּלֵימוּ, וְרִבּוֹנִי סִיב: יג וַאֲמַר יי לְאַבְרָהָם, לְמָא דְנָן חַיְּיכַת שָׂרָה לְמֵימַר, הַבְקֻשְׁטָא, אוֹלֵיד וַאֲנָא סֵיבִית: יד הֲיִתְכַּסֵּא מִן קֳדָם יי פִּתְגָמָא, לִזְמַן, אֲתוּב לְוָתָךְ, כְּעִדָּן דְּאַתּוּן קַיָּמִין וּלְשָׂרָה בַר: טו וְכַדִּיבַת שָׂרָה לְמֵימַר, לָא חַיְּיכִית אֲרֵי דְּחֵילַת, וַאֲמַר לָא בְּרַם חַיֵּיכְתְּ: טז וְקָמוּ מִתַּמָּן גֻּבְרַיָּא, וְאִסְתַּכִּיאוּ עַל אַפֵּי סְדוֹם, וְאַבְרָהָם, אָזֵיל עִמְּהוֹן לְאַלְוָאֵיהוֹן: יז וַיי אֲמַר, הַמְכַסֵּי אֲנָא מֵאַבְרָהָם, דַּאֲנָא עָבֵיד: יח וְאַבְרָהָם, מִהְוָא יְהֵי, לְעַם סַגִּי וְתַקִּיף, וְיִתְבָּרְכוּן בְּדִילֵיהּ, כָּל עַמְמֵי אַרְעָא: יט אֲרֵי גְלֵי קֳדָמַי, בְּדִיל דִּיפַקֵּיד, יָת בְּנוֹהִי וְיָת אֱנָשׁ בֵּיתֵיהּ בָּתְרוֹהִי, וְיִטְּרוּן אוֹרְחָן דְּתָקְנָן קֳדָם יי, לְמֶעְבַּד צְדַקְתָּא וְדִינָא, בְּדִיל, דְּיַיְתֵי יי עַל אַבְרָהָם,

AVRAHAM INTERCEDES FOR SEDOM

This is a turning point in the history of the spirit. How can finite, fallible human beings challenge God Himself, and this, not in opposition to faith, but as part of the life of faith itself? How, in our *parasha*, can Avraham, who describes himself as mere "dust and ashes" (Gen. 18:27), confront "the judge of all the earth" (18:25), challenging God's verdict on the people of Sedom?

The answer is given by the Torah itself. It is clear that this speech of God's is an invitation to Avraham to speak. "Shall I hide from Avraham what I am about to do?" asks God. Not only does He invite Avraham to speak; He even signals in advance the words He wants Avraham to use – "right" (*tzedek/tzedaka*) and "just" (*mishpat*). These constitute "the way of the Lord" (18:19) that God wants Avraham to teach his children.

Avraham responds by using precisely these words in his challenge. He uses the root *tz-d-k* seven times. He uses the root *sh-p-t* twice, at the beginning and end of the key sentence: "Shall the judge [*hashofet*] of all the earth not do justice [*mishpat*]?" (18:25).

God wants Avraham and his descendants to be agents of justice. *For justice to be done and seen to be done, both sides must be heard.* There must be not only an advocate for the prosecution but also for the defense. That is what God wants of Avraham: to be the defense attorney for the people of Sedom; to argue their case; to be the voice of the other side. And that is precisely what Avraham does.

God needs humanity to become His partner in the administration of justice. He needs to hear a dissenting voice. No judge, however omniscient and infallible, can execute justice in the absence of counterargument. That is why Judaism – the religion for which justice is central – is a religion of argument and debate, for the sake of Heaven,

just, that the LORD may bring about for Avraham what He spoke of for him."
20 Then the LORD said, "The outcry against Sedom and Amora is great, and their
21 sin is very grave. I shall go down now and see if they have really done as much
22 as the outcry that has reached Me. If not, I will know." The men turned from
there and went toward Sedom, while Avraham still stood before the LORD.
23 Then Avraham stepped forward and said: "Would You really sweep away the
24 righteous with the wicked? What if there are fifty righteous people in the city?
Would You really sweep it away and not spare the place for the sake of the fifty
25 righteous people in it? Far be it from You to do such a thing – to kill the
righteous with the wicked, treating the righteous like the wicked. Far be it from
26 You! Shall the judge of all the earth not do justice?" The LORD said, "If I find

רש״י

כ **וַיֹּאמֶר ה׳.** אֶל אַבְרָהָם: זַעֲקַת סְדֹם וְגוֹ׳. **כִּי רָבָּה.** כָּל ׳רַבָּה׳ שֶׁבַּמִּקְרָא הַטַּעַם בַּבֵּי״ת, לְפִי שֶׁהֵן מְתֻרְגָּמִין ׳גְּדוֹלָה׳ אוֹ ׳גָּדְלָה וְהוֹלֶכֶת׳, אֲבָל זֶה טַעְמוֹ לְמַעְלָה בָּרֵי״שׁ לְפִי שֶׁמְּתֻרְגָּם ׳גָּדְלָה׳ כְּבָר, כְּמוֹ שֶׁפֵּרַשְׁתִּי: "וַיְהִי הַשֶּׁמֶשׁ בָּאָה" (לעיל טו, יז), "הִנֵּה שָׁבָה יְבִמְתֵּךְ" (רות א, טו):

כא **אֵרְדָה נָּא.** לִמֵּד לַדַּיָּנִים שֶׁלֹּא יִפְסְקוּ דִּינֵי נְפָשׁוֹת אֶלָּא בִּרְאִיָּה, הַכֹּל כְּמוֹ שֶׁפֵּרַשְׁתִּי בְּפָרָשַׁת הַפַּלָּגָה (לעיל יא, ה). דָּבָר אַחֵר, "אֵרְדָה נָּא" לְסוֹף מַעֲשֵׂיהֶם: **הַכְּצַעֲקָתָהּ.** שֶׁל מְדִינָה: **הַבָּאָה אֵלַי עָשׂוּ.** וְהֵן עוֹמְדִים בְּמִרְדָּם – "כָּלָה" אֲנִי עוֹשֶׂה בָּהֶם, "וְאִם לֹא" יַעַמְדוּ בְּמִרְדָּם – "אֵדְעָה" מָה אֶעֱשֶׂה, לְהִפָּרַע מֵהֶם בְּיִסּוּרִין, וְלֹא אֲכַלֶּה אוֹתָם. וְכַיּוֹצֵא בּוֹ מָצִינוּ בְּמָקוֹם אַחֵר: "וְעַתָּה הוֹרֵד עֶדְיְךָ מֵעָלֶיךָ וְאֵדְעָה מָה אֶעֱשֶׂה לָּךְ" (שמות לג, ה). וּלְפִיכָךְ יֵשׁ הֶפְסֵק נְקֻדַּת פָּסֵק בֵּין ׳עָשׂוּ׳ לְ׳כָלָה׳ כְּדֵי לְהַפְרִידָם תֵּבָה מֵחֲבֶרְתָּהּ. וְרַבּוֹתֵינוּ דָּרְשׁוּ: "הַכְּצַעֲקָתָהּ", צַעֲקַת רִיבָה אַחַת שֶׁהָרְגוּ מִיתָה מְשֻׁנָּה עַל שֶׁנָּתְנָה מָזוֹן לְעָנִי, כַּמְּפֹרָשׁ בְּ׳חֵלֶק׳ (סנהדרין קט ע״ב):

כב **וַיִּפְנוּ מִשָּׁם.** מִמָּקוֹם שֶׁאַבְרָהָם לִוָּם שָׁם: **עוֹדֶנּוּ עֹמֵד וְגוֹ׳.** וַהֲלֹא לֹא הָלַךְ לַעֲמֹד לְפָנָיו, אֶלָּא הַקָּדוֹשׁ בָּרוּךְ הוּא בָּא אֶצְלוֹ וְאָמַר לוֹ: "זַעֲקַת סְדֹם וַעֲמֹרָה" וְגוֹ׳ (לעיל פסוק כ), וְהָיָה לוֹ לִכְתֹּב: ׳וַה׳ עוֹדֶנּוּ עוֹמֵד עַל אַבְרָהָם׳? אֶלָּא תִּקּוּן סוֹפְרִים הוּא זֶה:

כג **וַיִּגַּשׁ אַבְרָהָם.** מָצִינוּ הַגָּשָׁה לַמִּלְחָמָה: "וַיִּגַּשׁ יוֹאָב" וְגוֹ׳ (דברי הימים א׳ יט, יד); הַגָּשָׁה לְפִיּוּס: "וַיִּגַּשׁ אֵלָיו יְהוּדָה" (להלן מד, יח); וְהַגָּשָׁה לִתְפִלָּה: "וַיִּגַּשׁ אֵלִיָּהוּ הַנָּבִיא" (מלכים א׳ יח, לו); וּלְכָל אֵלֶּה נִכְנַס אַבְרָהָם: לְדַבֵּר קָשׁוֹת וּלְפִיּוּס וְלִתְפִלָּה: **הַאַף תִּסְפֶּה.** הֲגַם תִּסְפֶּה. וּלְתַרְגּוּם שֶׁל אוּנְקְלוֹס שֶׁתִּרְגְּמוֹ לְשׁוֹן רֹגֶז, כָּךְ פֵּרוּשׁוֹ: הַאַף יַשִּׂיאֲךָ שֶׁתִּסְפֶּה צַדִּיק עִם רָשָׁע?:

כד **חֲמִשִּׁים צַדִּיקִם.** עֲשָׂרָה צַדִּיקִים לְכָל כְּרַךְ וּכְרַךְ, חֲמִשָּׁה מְקוֹמוֹת יֵשׁ.

כה **חָלִלָה לְּךָ.** וְאִם תֹּאמַר, לֹא יַצִּילוּ הַצַּדִּיקִים אֶת הָרְשָׁעִים, לָמָּה תָּמִית הַצַּדִּיקִים? חֻלִּין הוּא לָךְ! יֹאמְרוּ: כָּךְ הִיא אֻמָּנוּתוֹ, שׁוֹטֵף הַכֹּל, צַדִּיקִים וּרְשָׁעִים; כָּךְ עָשִׂיתָ לְדוֹר הַמַּבּוּל וּלְדוֹר הַפַּלָּגָה: **כַּדָּבָר הַזֶּה.** לֹא הוּא וְלֹא כַּיּוֹצֵא בּוֹ: **חָלִלָה לָּךְ.** לָעוֹלָם הַבָּא: **הֲשֹׁפֵט כָּל הָאָרֶץ.** נָקוּד בַּחֲטַף פַּתָּח הֵ״א שֶׁל ׳הֲשֹׁפֵט׳, לְשׁוֹן תְּמִיָּה, וְכִי מִי שֶׁהוּא שׁוֹפֵט לֹא יַעֲשֶׂה מִשְׁפַּט אֱמֶת?!:

What then, for Judaism, is the connection between religion, law, and morality? Is "justice" by definition what the "judge" decides, or is He bound by a code that exists outside Him? The answer is that law, as portrayed in the Torah, is *covenantal*. It is born in the mutual agreement of God and humanity to engage in constructing a society on the foundations of compassion, righteousness, and justice. God and man come together to form a covenant which binds both to a morality that each recognizes as righteous and just, much as two partners come together to form a marriage which both recognize as imposing obligations. Neither God nor man arbitrarily invent morality, just as neither husband nor wife invent marriage. By entering into a covenant, both agree to bind themselves to one another within its terms. Thus love is translated into a moral relationship whose terms are law.

כ אֵת אֲשֶׁר־דִּבֶּר עָלָיו: וַיֹּאמֶר יהוה זַעֲקַת סְדֹם וַעֲמֹרָה כִּי־רָבָּה
כא וְחַטָּאתָם כִּי כָבְדָה מְאֹד: אֵרֲדָה־נָּא וְאֶרְאֶה הַכְּצַעֲקָתָהּ הַבָּאָה אֵלַי
כב עָשׂוּ ׀ כָּלָה וְאִם־לֹא אֵדָעָה: וַיִּפְנוּ מִשָּׁם הָאֲנָשִׁים וַיֵּלְכוּ סְדֹמָה
כג וְאַבְרָהָם עוֹדֶנּוּ עֹמֵד לִפְנֵי יהוה: וַיִּגַּשׁ אַבְרָהָם וַיֹּאמַר הַאַף תִּסְפֶּה
כד צַדִּיק עִם־רָשָׁע: אוּלַי יֵשׁ חֲמִשִּׁים צַדִּיקִם בְּתוֹךְ הָעִיר הַאַף תִּסְפֶּה
כה וְלֹא־תִשָּׂא לַמָּקוֹם לְמַעַן חֲמִשִּׁים הַצַּדִּיקִם אֲשֶׁר בְּקִרְבָּהּ: חָלִלָה לְּךָ
מֵעֲשֹׂת ׀ כַּדָּבָר הַזֶּה לְהָמִית צַדִּיק עִם־רָשָׁע וְהָיָה כַצַּדִּיק כָּרָשָׁע
כו חָלִלָה לָּךְ הֲשֹׁפֵט כָּל־הָאָרֶץ לֹא יַעֲשֶׂה מִשְׁפָּט: וַיֹּאמֶר יהוה אִם־

אונקלוס

יָת דְּמַלֵּיל עֲלוֹהִי: כ וַאֲמַר יְיָ, קְבִילַת, סְדוֹם וַעֲמוֹרָה אֲרֵי סְגִיאַת, וְחוֹבַתְהוֹן, אֲרֵי תְקֵיפַת לַחֲדָא: כא אֶתְגְּלֵי כְעַן וְאֶדּוּן, הַכִקְבִילַתְהוֹן, דַּעֲאלַת לִקְדָמַי, עֲבַדוּ אַעֲבֵיד עִמְּהוֹן גְּמִירָא אִם לָא תָּיְבִין, וְאִם תָּיְבִין לָא אֶתְפְּרַע: כב וְאִתְפְּנִיאוּ מִתַּמָּן גֻּבְרַיָּא, וַאֲזַלוּ לִסְדוֹם, וְאַבְרָהָם, עַד כְּעַן מְשַׁמֵּישׁ בִּצְלוֹ קֳדָם יְיָ: כג וּקְרֵיב אַבְרָהָם וַאֲמַר, הַבִרְגַז תְּשֵׁיצֵי, זַכָּאָה עִם חַיָּבָא: כד מָאִם אִית, חַמְשִׁין זַכָּאִין בְּגוֹ קַרְתָּא, הַבִרְגַז תְּשֵׁיצֵי וְלָא תִשְׁבּוֹק לְאַתְרָא, בְּדִיל, חַמְשִׁין זַכָּאִין דִּבְגַוַּהּ: כה קֻשְׁטָא אִנּוּן דִּינָךְ, מִלְּמֶעְבַּד כְּפִתְגָּמָא הָדֵין, לְשֵׁיצָאָה זַכָּאָה עִם חַיָּבָא, וִיהֵי זַכָּאָה כְּחַיָּבָא, קֻשְׁטָא אִנּוּן דִּינָךְ, הֲדַיָּן כָּל אַרְעָא, בְּרַם יַעֲבֵיד דִּינָא: כו וַאֲמַר יְיָ, אִם

level, it means that we are the guardians of our children's future. We must ensure that they have a world to inherit. Today that means political, economic, and environmental sustainability.

Second, education – directing our children and our household after us – is a sacred task. Teach children to love, and they will have hope. Teach them to hate, and they will have only anger and the desire for revenge. Thinking about the past leads to war. Thinking about the future helps us to make peace.

Third, what is the end goal of this education? How are we to keep the way of the Lord? By doing what is right and just. That is the test. If religious people do what is right and just, they are keeping the way. If they do not, then somehow they have lost their way.

18:24 צַדִּיקִם בְּתוֹךְ הָעִיר *Righteous people in the city* – Rabbi Samson Raphael Hirsch once asked whom Avraham might have had in mind when he asked God to spare Sedom if it contained ten righteous people. What would it have been like to be righteous in such a corrupt civilization? He answered that such a person would not be "one who keeps to his own four walls." He would instead be one who "is to be found 'in the midst of the city' – *betokh ha'ir* – and in lively connection with everything and everybody." Even in Sedom, to be righteous is not to be segregated. It is to be a participant in society, challenging it where it needs to be challenged, but not abandoning it.

18:25 הֲשֹׁפֵט כָּל־הָאָרֶץ לֹא יַעֲשֶׂה מִשְׁפָּט *Shall the judge of all the earth not do justice?* – Perhaps the single greatest contribution of Israel to the religious heritage of mankind is what is often called ethical monotheism: the idea that God is not merely the author of the moral law but is Himself bound by it. It is this that gives rise to some of the most awe-inspiring passages in the Tanakh in which Moshe, Yirmeyahu, Iyov, and others argue with God on the basis of the shared code of justice and mercy which binds both creature and Creator, reaching a climax in this question of Avraham's.

fifty righteous people in the city of Sedom, I will spare the whole place for their
27 sake." Then Avraham spoke up again and said, "Now that I have dared to speak
28 to the Lord, though I am mere dust and ashes, what if the righteous are five less
than fifty? Will You destroy the whole city for the lack of five people?" He said,
29 "If I find forty-five there, I will not destroy it." He spoke to Him yet again,
saying, "What if only forty are found there?" He said, "I will refrain for the sake
30 of the forty." Then he said, "Please, may the Lord not be angry, but let me speak.
What if only thirty are found there?" He answered, "I will refrain if I find thirty
31 there." "Now that I have dared to speak to the Lord," he said, "what if only
twenty are found there?" He said, "I will not destroy, for the sake of the twenty."
32 Then he said, "Please, may the Lord not be angry, but let me speak just once
more. What if only ten are found there?" He said, "I will not destroy, for the
33 sake of the ten." When the Lord had finished speaking with Avraham, He left.
19 1 And Avraham went back to his place. The two angels arrived at Sedom in the SHELISHI
evening, while Lot was sitting in the city gate. Lot saw them, and rose to greet

רש״י

כו **אִם אֶמְצָא בִסְדֹם וְגוֹ׳.** לְפִי שֶׁסְּדוֹם הָיְתָה מֶטְרוֹפּוֹלִין וַחֲשׁוּבָה מִכֻּלָּם, תָּלָה בָהּ הַכָּתוּב:

כח **הֲתַשְׁחִית בַּחֲמִשָּׁה.** וַהֲלֹא הֵן תִּשְׁעָה לְכָל כְּרַךְ, וְאַתָּה צַדִּיקוֹ שֶׁל עוֹלָם תִּצְטָרֵף עִמָּהֶם:

כט **אוּלַי יִמָּצְאוּן שָׁם אַרְבָּעִים.** וְיִמָּלְטוּ אַרְבָּעָה הַכְּרַכִּים. וְכֵן שְׁלֹשִׁים יַצִּילוּ שְׁלֹשָׁה מֵהֶם, אוֹ עֶשְׂרִים יַצִּילוּ שְׁנַיִם מֵהֶם, אוֹ עֲשָׂרָה יַצִּילוּ אֶחָד מֵהֶם:

לא **הוֹאַלְתִּי.** רָצִיתִי, כְּמוֹ: "וַיּוֹאֶל מֹשֶׁה" (שמות ב, כא):

לב **אוּלַי יִמָּצְאוּן שָׁם עֲשָׂרָה.** עַל הַפָּחוֹת לֹא בִקֵּשׁ, אָמַר: דוֹר הַמַּבּוּל הָיוּ שְׁמוֹנָה, נֹחַ וּבָנָיו וּנְשֵׁיהֶם, וְלֹא הִצִּילוּ עַל דּוֹרָם. וְעַל תִּשְׁעָה עַל יְדֵי צֵרוּף כְּבָר בִּקֵּשׁ וְלֹא מָצָא:

לג **וַיֵּלֶךְ ה׳ וְגוֹ׳.** כֵּיוָן שֶׁנִּשְׁתַּתֵּק הַסָּנֵגוֹר הָלַךְ לוֹ הַדַּיָּן: **וְאַבְרָהָם שָׁב לִמְקֹמוֹ.** נִסְתַּלֵּק הַדַּיָּן נִסְתַּלֵּק הַסָּנֵגוֹר, וְהַקָּטֵגוֹר מְקַטְרֵג, לְפִיכָךְ "וַיָּבֹאוּ שְׁנֵי הַמַּלְאָכִים סְדֹמָה" (להלן יט, א), לְהַשְׁחִית.

יט א **וַיָּבֹאוּ שְׁנֵי.** וְהַשְּׁלִישִׁי שֶׁבָּא לְבַשֵּׂר אֶת שָׂרָה, כֵּיוָן שֶׁעָשָׂה שְׁלִיחוּתוֹ נִסְתַּלֵּק לוֹ: **הַמַּלְאָכִים.** וּלְהַלָּן (לעיל יח, ב) קְרָאָם 'אֲנָשִׁים'; כְּשֶׁהָיְתָה שְׁכִינָה עִמָּהֶם קְרָאָם 'אֲנָשִׁים'. דָּבָר אַחֵר, אֵצֶל אַבְרָהָם שֶׁכֹּחוֹ גָּדוֹל וְהָיוּ הַמַּלְאָכִים תְּדִירִין אֶצְלוֹ כַּאֲנָשִׁים, קְרָאָם 'אֲנָשִׁים', וְאֵצֶל לוֹט קְרָאָם 'מַלְאָכִים': **בָּעֶרֶב.** וְכִי כָּל כָּךְ שָׁהוּ הַמַּלְאָכִים מֵחֶבְרוֹן לִסְדוֹם? אֶלָּא מַלְאֲכֵי רַחֲמִים הָיוּ וּמַמְתִּינִים שֶׁמָּא יוּכַל אַבְרָהָם לְלַמֵּד עֲלֵיהֶם סָנֵגוֹרְיָא: **וְלוֹט יֹשֵׁב בְּשַׁעַר סְדֹם.** 'יָשַׁב' כְּתִיב, אוֹתוֹ הַיּוֹם מִנּוּהוּ שׁוֹפֵט עַל הַשּׁוֹפְטִים: **וַיַּרְא לוֹט וְגוֹ׳.** מִבֵּית אַבְרָהָם לָמַד לְחַזֵּר עַל הָאוֹרְחִים:

our way,' they replied [to Lot, when he begged them to respect his visitors]. Then they said, 'This fellow came here as a migrant and now he is setting himself up as a judge! We will treat you worse than them'" (19:9).

The third comes when, telling his daughters' husbands that they must escape because the city is about to be destroyed, "his sons-in-law thought him laughable" (19:14). Lot's elaborate new identity is about to come crashing down about him. He has not been accepted in this place. Sedom hates strangers, they still consider Lot a stranger, and his sons-in-law regard him as a fool.

Yet despite this, he hesitates. He has invested too much of himself into the project of making his home among the people of the plain. Now he faces the ultimate existential question: "Who am I?" Having tried so hard to become one of them, he finds it almost impossible to tear himself away.

The lives of Lot and Avraham exemplify for all time the contrast between ambivalence and the security that

אֶמְצָא בִסְדֹם חֲמִשִּׁים צַדִּיקִם בְּתוֹךְ הָעִיר וְנָשָׂאתִי לְכָל־הַמָּקוֹם
כז בַּעֲבוּרָם׃ וַיַּעַן אַבְרָהָם וַיֹּאמַר הִנֵּה־נָא הוֹאַלְתִּי לְדַבֵּר אֶל־אֲדֹנָי
כח וְאָנֹכִי עָפָר וָאֵפֶר׃ אוּלַי יַחְסְרוּן חֲמִשִּׁים הַצַּדִּיקִם חֲמִשָּׁה הֲתַשְׁחִית
בַּחֲמִשָּׁה אֶת־כָּל־הָעִיר וַיֹּאמֶר לֹא אַשְׁחִית אִם־אֶמְצָא שָׁם אַרְבָּעִים
כט וַחֲמִשָּׁה׃ וַיֹּסֶף עוֹד לְדַבֵּר אֵלָיו וַיֹּאמַר אוּלַי יִמָּצְאוּן שָׁם אַרְבָּעִים
ל וַיֹּאמֶר לֹא אֶעֱשֶׂה בַּעֲבוּר הָאַרְבָּעִים׃ וַיֹּאמֶר אַל־נָא יִחַר לַאדֹנָי
וַאֲדַבֵּרָה אוּלַי יִמָּצְאוּן שָׁם שְׁלֹשִׁים וַיֹּאמֶר לֹא אֶעֱשֶׂה אִם־אֶמְצָא
לא שָׁם שְׁלֹשִׁים׃ וַיֹּאמֶר הִנֵּה־נָא הוֹאַלְתִּי לְדַבֵּר אֶל־אֲדֹנָי אוּלַי יִמָּצְאוּן
לב שָׁם עֶשְׂרִים וַיֹּאמֶר לֹא אַשְׁחִית בַּעֲבוּר הָעֶשְׂרִים׃ וַיֹּאמֶר אַל־נָא
יִחַר לַאדֹנָי וַאֲדַבְּרָה אַךְ־הַפַּעַם אוּלַי יִמָּצְאוּן שָׁם עֲשָׂרָה וַיֹּאמֶר לֹא
לג אַשְׁחִית בַּעֲבוּר הָעֲשָׂרָה׃ וַיֵּלֶךְ יהוה כַּאֲשֶׁר כִּלָּה לְדַבֵּר אֶל־אַבְרָהָם
יט א וְאַבְרָהָם שָׁב לִמְקֹמוֹ׃ וַיָּבֹאוּ שְׁנֵי הַמַּלְאָכִים סְדֹמָה בָּעֶרֶב וְלוֹט טז שלישי
יֹשֵׁב בְּשַׁעַר־סְדֹם וַיַּרְא־לוֹט וַיָּקָם לִקְרָאתָם וַיִּשְׁתַּחוּ אַפַּיִם אָרְצָה׃

אונקלוס

אֶשְׁכַּח בִּסְדוֹם, חַמְשִׁין זַכָּאִין בְּגוֹ קַרְתָּא, וְאֶשְׁבּוֹק לְכָל אַתְרָא בְּדִילְהוֹן: כז וַאֲתֵיב אַבְרָהָם וַאֲמַר, הָא כְעַן שָׁרֵיתִי לְמַלָּלָא קֳדָם יי, וַאֲנָא עֲפַר וּקְטַם: כח מָאִם, יַחְסְרוּן, חַמְשִׁין זַכָּאִין חַמְשָׁא, הַתְחַבֵּיל בְּחַמְשָׁא יָת כָּל קַרְתָּא, וַאֲמַר לָא אֲחַבֵּיל, אִם אַשְׁכַּח תַּמָּן, אַרְבְּעִין וְחַמְשָׁא: כט וְאוֹסֵיף עוֹד, לְמַלָּלָא קֳדָמוֹהִי וַאֲמַר, מָאִם, יִשְׁתַּכְחוּן תַּמָּן אַרְבְּעִין, וַאֲמַר לָא אַעֲבֵיד גְּמִירָא, בְּדִיל אַרְבְּעִין: ל וַאֲמַר, לָא כְעַן, יִתְקַף רֻגְזָא דַּיי וַאֲמַלֵּיל, מָאִם, יִשְׁתַּכְחוּן תַּמָּן תְּלָתִין, וַאֲמַר לָא אַעֲבֵיד גְּמִירָא, אִם אַשְׁכַּח תַּמָּן תְּלָתִין: לא וַאֲמַר, הָא כְעַן אַסְגֵּיתִי לְמַלָּלָא קֳדָם יי, מָאִם, יִשְׁתַּכְחוּן תַּמָּן עַסְרִין, וַאֲמַר לָא אֲחַבֵּיל, בְּדִיל עַסְרִין: לב וַאֲמַר, לָא כְעַן, יִתְקַף רֻגְזָא דַּיי וַאֲמַלֵּיל בְּרַם זִמְנָא הָדָא, מָאִם, יִשְׁתַּכְחוּן תַּמָּן עַסְרָא, וַאֲמַר לָא אֲחַבֵּיל, בְּדִיל עַסְרָא: לג וְאִסְתַּלַּק יְקָרָא דַּיי, כַּד שֵׁיצִי, לְמַלָּלָא עִם אַבְרָהָם, וְאַבְרָהָם תָּב לְאַתְרֵיהּ: יט א וְעָאלוּ, תְּרֵין מַלְאֲכַיָּא לִסְדוֹם בְּרַמְשָׁא, וְלוֹט יָתֵיב בִּתְרַעָא דִסְדוֹם, וַחֲזָא לוֹט וְקָם לְקַדָּמוּתְהוֹן, וּסְגֵיד עַל אַפּוֹהִי עַל אַרְעָא:

Lot's sense of belonging, however, is either naivete or self-deception. The text makes this clear at three points. The first is the attempted sexual assault on Lot's visitors (Gen. 19:4–5). Evidently the people of Sedom do not take kindly to strangers. This is the first hint that perhaps Lot is also, in their eyes, a stranger.

The second indication is brutally explicit: "'Get out of

LOT IN SEDOM

Having chosen to put down roots in the Jordan Valley and the cities of the plain, Lot and his family become profoundly assimilated. His daughters marry local men; Lot rises to public position. Sedom is where Lot sees himself as belonging – so much so that the visitors have to drag him away physically.

2 them, bowing with his face to the ground. He said, "Please, my lords, turn aside
to your servant's house, stay the night, wash your feet, and then go on your way
early in the morning." "No," they said, "we will spend the night in the square."
3 But he was so insistent that they followed him to his house and came in. He
4 made a feast for them and baked unleavened bread, and they ate. They had not
yet gone to bed when all the townsmen, the men of Sedom – young and old, all
5 the people from every quarter – surrounded the house. They called to Lot,
"Where are the men who came to you tonight? Bring them out to us so that we
6 may know them." Lot went out to speak to them, shutting the door behind him,
7 8 and said, "My brothers, please do not do this evil. I have two daughters who
have never known a man. Let me bring them out to you; you may do what you
like with them. But do not do anything to these men, for they have come under
9 the protection of my roof." "Get out of our way," they replied. "This fellow came

רש"י

ב **הנה נא אדני.** הנה נא אתם אדונים לי אחר שעברתם עלי. דבר אחר, "הנה נא", צריכים אתם לתת לב על הרשעים הללו שלא יכירו בכם; וזו היא עצה נכונה: "סורו נא" וגו' – עקמו את הדרך לביתי דרך עקלתון, שלא יכירו שאתם נכנסים שם, לכך נאמר "סורו". בראשית רבה (נ, ד): **ויאמרו לא.** לאברהם אמרו: "כן תעשה" (לעיל יח, ה), מכאן שמסרבין לקטן ואין מסרבין לגדול: **כי ברחוב נלין.** הרי 'כי' משמש בלשון 'אלא', שאמרו: לא נסור אל ביתך אלא ברחובה של עיר נלין:

ג **ויסרו אליו.** עקמו את הדרך לצד ביתו: **ומצות אפה.** פסח היה:

ד **טרם ישכבו ואנשי העיר אנשי סדם.** כך נדרש בבראשית רבה (נ, ה): "טרם ישכבו ואנשי העיר" היו בפיהם של מלאכים, שהיו שואלים ללוט: מה טיבם ומעשיהם? והוא אומר להם: רבם רשעים. עודם מדברים בהם, ו"אנשי סדם נסבו" וגו'. ופשוטו של מקרא: ואנשי העיר, אנשי רשע, נסבו על הבית; על שהיו רשעים נקראים "אנשי סדם", כמו שאמר הכתוב: "ואנשי סדם רעים וחטאים" (לעיל יג, יג): **כל העם מקצה.** מקצה העיר עד הקצה, שאין אחד מוחה בידם, שאפלו צדיק אחד אין בהם:

ה **ונדעה אתם.** במשכב זכור, כמו: "אשר לא ידעו איש" (להלן פסוק ח):

ח **האל.** כמו 'האלה': **כי על כן באו.** כי הטובה הזאת תעשו לכבודי על אשר "באו בצל קרתי", "בטלל שריתי", תרגום של 'קורה' – שריתא:

ט **גש הלאה.** כשאמר להם על הבנות, אמרו לו: "גש הלאה", לשון נחת. ועל שאתה מליץ על האורחין, אמרו לו: איך מלאך לבך? "האחד בא לגור" – אדם נכרי יחידי אתה בינינו שבאת לגור, "וישפט שפוט" – נעשית מוכיח אותנו [ור' יוסף בר' שמעון (קרא) אומר הלא "גש הלאה" אינו אלא לשון דחיה ודחיפה, כמו "קרב אליך אל תגש בי" (ישעיה סה, ה) וכמו "ואת האש זרה הלאה" (במדבר יז, ב)

justifies it with the words "If war breaks out they may join our enemies and fight against us" (1:10). In the eyes of the Egyptians, they are not citizens but aliens, just as the people of Sedom see Lot. The Israelites, for their part, "acquired holdings" in Egypt (Gen. 47:27), implying that they intend to make it their home. It is not easy for Moshe to get them to leave. In the end they are "driven out" by the Egyptians (Ex. 12:39), just as Lot is physically dragged by the angels from Sedom (Gen. 19:16).

Sadly, this has often been the fate of Jews. Facing danger, they were slow to see it – in Spain in the fifteenth century, in Europe in the twentieth. How could a country to which they had contributed so much turn against them? How could they, who had lived there for so long, not be accepted? This delay – the recurrence of Lot's ambivalence – was fraught with risk. The people of history was sometimes deaf to the warning signals of history. This too, tragically, is part of the Passover story, and it begins with Lot in Sedom. Rashi's comment is profound: without knowing it, Lot is living through the first Passover.

ב וַיֹּאמֶר הִנֶּה נָּא־אֲדֹנַי סוּרוּ נָא אֶל־בֵּית עַבְדְּכֶם וְלִינוּ וְרַחֲצוּ רַגְלֵיכֶם
ג וְהִשְׁכַּמְתֶּם וַהֲלַכְתֶּם לְדַרְכְּכֶם וַיֹּאמְרוּ לֹּא כִּי בָרְחוֹב נָלִין: וַיִּפְצַר־בָּם
מְאֹד וַיָּסֻרוּ אֵלָיו וַיָּבֹאוּ אֶל־בֵּיתוֹ וַיַּעַשׂ לָהֶם מִשְׁתֶּה וּמַצּוֹת אָפָה
ד וַיֹּאכֵלוּ: טֶרֶם יִשְׁכָּבוּ וְאַנְשֵׁי הָעִיר אַנְשֵׁי סְדֹם נָסַבּוּ עַל־הַבַּיִת מִנַּעַר
ה וְעַד־זָקֵן כָּל־הָעָם מִקָּצֶה: וַיִּקְרְאוּ אֶל־לוֹט וַיֹּאמְרוּ לוֹ אַיֵּה הָאֲנָשִׁים
ו אֲשֶׁר־בָּאוּ אֵלֶיךָ הַלָּיְלָה הוֹצִיאֵם אֵלֵינוּ וְנֵדְעָה אֹתָם: וַיֵּצֵא אֲלֵהֶם
ז ח לוֹט הַפֶּתְחָה וְהַדֶּלֶת סָגַר אַחֲרָיו: וַיֹּאמַר אַל־נָא אַחַי תָּרֵעוּ: הִנֵּה־
נָא לִי שְׁתֵּי בָנוֹת אֲשֶׁר לֹא־יָדְעוּ אִישׁ אוֹצִיאָה־נָּא אֶתְהֶן אֲלֵיכֶם
וַעֲשׂוּ לָהֶן כַּטּוֹב בְּעֵינֵיכֶם רַק לָאֲנָשִׁים הָאֵל אַל־תַּעֲשׂוּ דָבָר כִּי־עַל־
ט כֵּן בָּאוּ בְּצֵל קֹרָתִי: וַיֹּאמְרוּ ׀ גֶּשׁ־הָלְאָה וַיֹּאמְרוּ הָאֶחָד בָּא־לָגוּר

אונקלוס

ב וַאֲמַר בְּבָעוּ כְעַן רִבּוֹנַי, זוּרוּ כְעַן, לְבֵית עַבְדְּכוֹן וּבִיתוּ וְאַסְחוּ רַגְלֵיכוֹן, וְתַקְדְּמוּן וּתְהָכוּן לְאוֹרַחְכוֹן, וַאֲמַרוּ לָא, אֱלָהֵין בִּרְחוֹבָא נְבִית: ג וְאַתְקֵיף בְּהוֹן לַחְדָּא, וְזָרוּ לְוָתֵיהּ, וְעָאלוּ לְבֵיתֵיהּ, וַעֲבַד לְהוֹן מִשְׁתְּיָא, וּפַטִּיר אֲפָא לְהוֹן וַאֲכַלוּ: ד עַד לָא שְׁכִיבוּ, וְאֱנָשֵׁי קַרְתָּא, אֱנָשֵׁי סְדוֹם אַקִּיפוּ עַל בֵּיתָא, מֵעוּלֵימָא וְעַד סָבָא, כָּל עַמָּא מִסּוֹפֵיהּ: ה וּקְרוֹ לְלוֹט וַאֲמַרוּ לֵיהּ, אָן גֻּבְרַיָּא, דַּאֲתוֹ לְוָתָךְ בְּלֵילְיָא, אַפֵּיקִנּוּן לְוָתַנָא, וְנֵדַע יָתְהוֹן: ו וּנְפַק לְוָתְהוֹן, לוֹט לְתַרְעָא, וְדַשָּׁא אֲחַד בַּתְרוֹהִי: ז וַאֲמַר, בְּבָעוּ כְעַן אַחַי לָא תַבְאֲשׁוּן: ח הָא כְעַן לִי תַּרְתֵּין בְּנָן, דְּלָא יְדַעוּנִין גְּבַר, אַפֵּיק כְּעַן יָתְהוֹן לְוָתְכוֹן, וַעֲבִידוּ לְהוֹן, כִּדְתָקֵין בְּעֵינֵיכוֹן, לְחוֹד, לְגֻבְרַיָּא הָאִלֵּין לָא תַעְבְּדוּן מִדַּעַם, אֲרֵי עַל כֵּן עָאלוּ בִּטְלַל שָׁרִיתִי: ט וַאֲמַרוּ קְרַב לְהַלְאָה, וַאֲמַרוּ חַד אֲתָא לְאִתּוֹתָבָא

was Passover. How could Lot have the foresight to know that the date of the angels' visit would one day become the festival of Passover? And why should he be observing its laws generations before it became a reality?

Rashi is hinting that Lot's experience in Sedom will be repeated in Egypt, this time on a national scale. Like Lot, the Israelites will settle in their new home and grow affluent. Rabbi Joseph Soloveitchik made an insightful comment about the opening of the book of Exodus (*Divrei Hashkafa*, 41–43). The first verse reads, "And these are the names of the sons of Yisrael who came (*haba'im*) to Egypt" (Ex. 1:1). The Hebrew verb appears in the present tense rather than the past. In fact, the Israelites had come generations before, but in the eyes of the Egyptians it was as if they had just arrived. The new Pharaoh, announcing his program of persecution,

comes from knowing who one is and why. Lot, who has tried to become someone else, finds himself regarded by his neighbors as an alien, an arriviste, an interloper. To his own sons-in-law he is "laughable." Avraham lives a different kind of life. He fights a war on behalf of his neighbors. He prays for them. But he lives apart, true to his faith, his mission, and his covenant with God. Yet even as he calls himself a "migrant and a visitor" (23:4), the Hittites see him as "a prince of God in our midst" (23:6). That equation has not changed. Non-Jews respect Jews who respect Judaism. They are embarrassed by Jews who are embarrassed by Judaism. Never be ambivalent about who and what you are.

19:3 מַצּוֹת *Unleavened bread* – Lot makes matzot. On this, Rashi makes a strange comment: *Pesaḥ haya,* he writes. It

here as a migrant and now he is setting himself up as a judge! We will treat you
worse than them." They pressed hard against Lot and moved forward to break
10 down the door. But the men inside reached out and pulled Lot back into the
11 house and shut the door behind him. Then they struck the men at the door,
young and old, with blindness so that they wore themselves out trying in vain
12 to find the door. The visitors said to Lot, "Who else do you have here – children-
in-law, sons, daughters, or anyone else in the city? Bring them out of here,
13 because we are about to destroy this place. So great is the outcry against them
14 before the LORD that He has sent us to destroy it." Lot went out and spoke to
his sons-in-law, the men who were betrothed to his daughters, and told them,
"Get up and leave this place: the LORD is about to destroy the city!" But his
15 sons-in-law thought him laughable. As dawn was breaking, the angels hurried
Lot. "Get up," they said. "Take your wife and your two daughters here, or you
16 will be swept away amid the city's sin." Still he hesitated. So the men seized
him, his wife, and his two daughters by the hand and led them safely outside
17 the city, for the LORD had mercy upon him. As soon as they had brought them

רש״י

וּכְמוֹ ״וְהִגְלֵיתִי אֶתְכֶם מֵהָלְאָה לְדַמָּשֶׂק״ (עמוס ה, כז) שֶׁאַף כָּאן לוֹט הָיָה מִתְחַבֵּט לִפְנֵיהֶם עַל הָאַכְסְנָאִים, וְהֵם אוֹמְרִים לוֹ: קְרַב הַלְאָה אַל תִּפְגַּע בָּנוּ; שֶׁאִם אַתָּה אוֹמֵר קְרַב אֵלֵינוּ וּשְׁמַע דְּבָרֵינוּ הוּא, מַה צּוֹרֶךְ לְדָבָר זֶה? וַהֲלֹא לוֹט קָרוֹב אֲלֵיהֶם עוֹמֵד, כְּמוֹ שֶׁמָּצִינוּ ״וַיֵּצֵא אֲלֵהֶם לוֹט הַפֶּתְחָה״ (לעיל פסוק ו)! אֶלָּא עַל כָּרְחֲךָ לְשׁוֹן הַרְחָקָה הוּא, כְּלוֹמַר, לֵךְ מֵעִמָּנוּ. וְהוֹדָה הַמּוֹרֶה לִדְבָרָיו]: הַדֶּלֶת. הַסּוֹבֶבֶת לִנְעֹל וְלִפְתֹּחַ:

יא פֶּתַח. הוּא הֶחָלָל שֶׁבּוֹ נִכְנָסִין וְיוֹצְאִין: בַּסַּנְוֵרִים. מַכַּת עִוָּרוֹן: מִקָּטֹן וְעַד גָּדוֹל. הַקְּטַנִּים הִתְחִילוּ בָּעֲבֵרָה תְּחִלָּה, שֶׁנֶּאֱמַר: ״מִנַּעַר וְעַד זָקֵן״ (לעיל פסוק ד), לְפִיכָךְ הִתְחִילָה הַפֻּרְעָנוּת מֵהֶם:

יב עֹד מִי לְךָ פֹה. פְּשׁוּטוֹ שֶׁל מִקְרָא, מִי יֵשׁ לְךָ עוֹד בָּעִיר הַזֹּאת חוּץ מֵאִשְׁתְּךָ וּבְנוֹתֶיךָ שֶׁבַּבַּיִת: חָתָן וּבָנֶיךָ וּבְנֹתֶיךָ. אִם יֵשׁ לְךָ חָתָן אוֹ בָּנִים וּבָנוֹת, ״הוֹצֵא מִן הַמָּקוֹם״: וּבָנֶיךָ. בְּנֵי בְּנוֹתֶיךָ הַנְּשׂוּאוֹת.

וּמִדְרַשׁ אַגָּדָה, ״עֹד״ – מֵאַחַר שֶׁעוֹשִׂין נְבָלָה כָּזֹאת, ״מִי לְךָ״ פִּתְחוֹן פֶּה לְלַמֵּד סָנֵגוֹרְיָא עֲלֵיהֶם, שֶׁכָּל הַלַּיְלָה הָיָה מֵלִיץ עֲלֵיהֶם טוֹבוֹת. קְרֵי בֵּיהּ: ׳מִי לְךָ פֶּה׳:

יד חֲתָנָיו. שְׁתֵּי בָּנוֹת נְשׂוּאוֹת הָיוּ לוֹ בָּעִיר: לֹקְחֵי בְנֹתָיו. שֶׁאוֹתָן שֶׁבַּבַּיִת אֲרוּסוֹת לָהֶם:

טו וַיָּאִיצוּ. כְּתַרְגּוּמוֹ ׳וּדְחִיקוּ׳, מִהֲרוּהוּ: הַנִּמְצָאֹת. הַמְזֻמָּנוֹת לְךָ בַּבַּיִת לְהַצִּילָם. וּמִדְרַשׁ אַגָּדָה יֵשׁ, וְזֶה יִשּׁוּבוֹ שֶׁל מִקְרָא: תִּסָּפֶה. תִּהְיֶה כָלֶה; ״עַד תֹּם כָּל הַדּוֹר״ (דברים ב, יד) מְתֻרְגָּם: ״עַד דְּסָף״:

טז וַיִּתְמַהְמָהּ. כְּדֵי לְהַצִּיל אֶת מָמוֹנוֹ: וַיַּחֲזִיקוּ. אֶחָד מֵהֶם הָיָה שָׁלִיחַ לְהַצִּילוֹ, וַאֲחֵרוֹ לַהֲפֹךְ אֶת סְדוֹם, לְכָךְ נֶאֱמַר: ״וַיֹּאמֶר הִמָּלֵט״ (להלן פסוק יז) וְלֹא נֶאֱמַר ׳וַיֹּאמְרוּ׳:

יז הִמָּלֵט עַל נַפְשֶׁךָ. דַּיֶּךָ לְהַצִּיל נְפָשׁוֹת, אַל תָּחוּס עַל הַמָּמוֹן: אַל

(Gen. 19:26). Festinger called this syndrome "post-decision dissonance." He predicted that the more important the issue, the longer the person delays a decision, and the harder it is to reverse, the more he or she will agonize over whether they have made the right choice. They have second thoughts; they need reassurance; they "look back."

called cognitive dissonance. According to Festinger, the need to avoid dissonance and the unbearable tension it creates is fundamental to human beings. It is this tension that Lot cannot resolve – and which is signaled by the *shalshelet* over "he hesitated."

Festinger's theory also explains the behavior of Lot's wife, who "looked back – and was turned into a pillar of salt"

וַיִּשְׁפֹּט שָׁפוֹט עַתָּה נָרַע לְךָ מֵהֶם וַיִּפְצְרוּ בָאִישׁ בְּלוֹט מְאֹד וַיִּגְּשׁוּ
י לִשְׁבֹּר הַדָּלֶת׃ וַיִּשְׁלְחוּ הָאֲנָשִׁים אֶת־יָדָם וַיָּבִיאוּ אֶת־לוֹט אֲלֵיהֶם
יא הַבָּיְתָה וְאֶת־הַדֶּלֶת סָגָרוּ׃ וְאֶת־הָאֲנָשִׁים אֲשֶׁר־פֶּתַח הַבַּיִת הִכּוּ
יב בַּסַּנְוֵרִים מִקָּטֹן וְעַד־גָּדוֹל וַיִּלְאוּ לִמְצֹא הַפָּתַח׃ וַיֹּאמְרוּ הָאֲנָשִׁים
אֶל־לוֹט עֹד מִי־לְךָ פֹה חָתָן וּבָנֶיךָ וּבְנֹתֶיךָ וְכֹל אֲשֶׁר־לְךָ בָּעִיר הוֹצֵא
יג מִן־הַמָּקוֹם׃ כִּי־מַשְׁחִתִים אֲנַחְנוּ אֶת־הַמָּקוֹם הַזֶּה כִּי־גָדְלָה צַעֲקָתָם
יד אֶת־פְּנֵי יהוה וַיְשַׁלְּחֵנוּ יהוה לְשַׁחֲתָהּ׃ וַיֵּצֵא לוֹט וַיְדַבֵּר ׀ אֶל־חֲתָנָיו ׀
לֹקְחֵי בְנֹתָיו וַיֹּאמֶר קוּמוּ צְּאוּ מִן־הַמָּקוֹם הַזֶּה כִּי־מַשְׁחִית יהוה
טו אֶת־הָעִיר וַיְהִי כִמְצַחֵק בְּעֵינֵי חֲתָנָיו׃ וּכְמוֹ הַשַּׁחַר עָלָה וַיָּאִיצוּ
הַמַּלְאָכִים בְּלוֹט לֵאמֹר קוּם קַח אֶת־אִשְׁתְּךָ וְאֶת־שְׁתֵּי בְנֹתֶיךָ
טז הַנִּמְצָאֹת פֶּן־תִּסָּפֶה בַּעֲוֺן הָעִיר׃ וַיִּתְמַהְמָהּ ׀ וַיַּחֲזִיקוּ הָאֲנָשִׁים בְּיָדוֹ
וּבְיַד־אִשְׁתּוֹ וּבְיַד שְׁתֵּי בְנֹתָיו בְּחֶמְלַת יהוה עָלָיו וַיֹּצִאֻהוּ וַיַּנִּחֻהוּ
יז מִחוּץ לָעִיר׃ וַיְהִי כְהוֹצִיאָם אֹתָם הַחוּצָה וַיֹּאמֶר הִמָּלֵט עַל־נַפְשֶׁךָ

אונקלוס

וְהָא דָאֵין דִּינָא, כְּעַן, נַבְאֵישׁ לָךְ מִדִּילְהוֹן, וְאַתְקִיפוּ בְּגֻבְרָא בְּלוֹט לַחֲדָא, וּקְרִיבוּ לְמִתְבַּר דַּשָּׁא: י וְאוֹשִׁיטוּ גֻבְרַיָּא יָת יְדֵיהוֹן, וְאַעִילוּ יָת לוֹט, לְוָתְהוֹן לְבֵיתָא, וְיָת דַּשָּׁא אֲחַדוּ: יא וְיָת גֻּבְרַיָּא דִּבְתְרַע בֵּיתָא, מְחוֹ בְּשַׁבְרִירַיָּא, מִזְּעֵירָא וְעַד רַבָּא, וּלְאִיאוּ לְאַשְׁכָּחָא תַּרְעָא: יב וַאֲמַרוּ גֻבְרַיָּא לְלוֹט, עוֹד מָא לָךְ הָכָא, חַתְנָא וּבְנָךְ וּבְנָתָךְ, וְכֹל דִּלָךְ בְּקַרְתָּא, אַפֵּיק מִן אַתְרָא: יג אֲרֵי מְחַבְּלִין אֲנַחְנָא, יָת אַתְרָא הָדֵין, אֲרֵי סְגִיאַת קְבִילַתְהוֹן קֳדָם יְיָ, וְשַׁלְחַנָא יְיָ לְחַבָּלוּתַהּ:

יד וּנְפַק לוֹט, וּמַלֵּיל עִם חַתְנוֹהִי נָסְבֵי בְנָתֵיהּ, וַאֲמַר קוּמוּ פּוּקוּ מִן אַתְרָא הָדֵין, אֲרֵי מְחַבֵּיל יְיָ יָת קַרְתָּא, וַהֲוָה כְּמָחֵיךְ בְּעֵינֵי חַתְנוֹהִי: טו וּכְמִסַּק צַפְרָא הֲוָה, וּדְחִיקוּ מַלְאֲכַיָּא בְּלוֹט לְמֵימַר, קוּם דְּבַר יָת אִתְּתָךְ, וְיָת תַּרְתֵּין בְּנָתָךְ דְּאִשְׁתְּכַחָא מְהֵימְנָן עִמָּךְ, דִּלְמָא תִלְקֵי בְּחוֹבֵי קַרְתָּא: טז וְאִתְעַכַּב וְאַתְקִיפוּ גֻבְרַיָּא בִּידֵיהּ וּבִיד אִתְּתֵיהּ, וּבִיד תַּרְתֵּין בְּנָתֵיהּ, בִּדְחַס יְיָ עֲלוֹהִי, וְאַפְּקוּהִי וְאַשְׁרְיוּהִי מִבָּרָא לְקַרְתָּא: יז וַהֲוָה כַּד אַפֵּיק יָתְהוֹן לְבָרָא, וַאֲמַר חוּס עַל נַפְשָׁךְ,

19:16 וַיִּתְמַהְמָהּ *He hesitated* – The Torah does not have a word for ambivalence. It does, however, have a tune for it. This is the rare note known as the *shalshelet*.

The *shalshelet* is an unusual note, going up and down, up and down, as if unable to move forward to the next note. The sixteenth-century commentator Rabbi Yosef Ibn Kaspi (in his commentary on Gen. 19:16) best defined what it was meant to convey: namely, a psychological state of uncertainty and indecision. We discussed the nature of Lot's indecision above (see "Lot in Sedom"). The graphic notation of the *shalshelet* itself looks like a streak of lightning, a "zigzag movement" (*tenua meuvetet*), a mark that goes repeatedly backward and forward. It conveys frozen motion. Lot is a prime example of what Leon Festinger

out, one said, "Run for your life. Do not look back. Do not stop anywhere in
18 the plain. Flee to the mountains or you will be swept away." But Lot said to
19 them, "No, my lords, please. Your servant has found favor in your eyes, and you
have done me great kindness in saving my life. But I cannot flee to the
20 mountains; the disaster would overtake me, and I would die. There is a town
here close enough for refuge. It is small. Let me flee there – is it not small? – so
21 that I might survive." "Very well," he said, "I will grant this request also; I will REVI'I
22 not overthrow the town of which you speak. But hurry. Flee there, because I
23 cannot do anything until you reach it." That is why the town is called Tzoar. By
24 the time Lot reached Tzoar, the sun had risen over the land. Then the LORD
rained down sulfur and fire on Sedom and Amora. Out of the heavens it came
25 from the LORD. He overthrew those cities, and the whole plain, and all the
26 cities' inhabitants, and the vegetation on the land. But Lot's wife looked back –

רש"י

תביט אחריך. אתה הרשעת עמהם ובזכות אברהם אתה נצול, אינך כדאי לראות בפרענותם ואתה נצול: **בכל הככר.** ככר הירדן: **ההרה המלט.** אצל אברהם ברח שהיה יושב בהר, שנאמר: "ויעתק משם ההרה" (לעיל יב, ח), ואף עכשיו היה יושב שם, שנאמר: "עד המקום אשר היה שם אהלה בתחלה" (לעיל יג, ג); ואף על פי שכתוב: "ויאהל אברם" וגו' (שם יח), אהלים הרבה היו לו ונמשכו עד חברון: **המלט.** לשון השמטה, וכן כל המלטה שבמקרא אשמוצי"ר בלעז, וכן: "והמליטה זכר" (ישעיה סו, ז), שנשמט העובר מן הרחם, "כצפור נמלטה" (תהלים קכד, ז), "לא יכלו מלט משא" (ישעיה מו, ב), להשמיט משא הרעי שבנקביהם:

יח **אל נא אדני.** רבותינו אמרו שזה קדש, שנאמר בו: "להחיות את נפשי" (להלן פסוק יט) – מי שיש בידו להמית ולהחיות, ותרגומו "בבעו כען ה'": **אל נא.** אל תאמרו אלי להמלט ההרה: **נא.** לשון בקשה:

יט **פן תדבקני הרעה.** כשהייתי אצל אנשי סדום היה הקדוש ברוך הוא רואה מעשי ומעשה בני עירי והייתי נראה צדיק וכדאי להנצל, וכשאבא אצל צדיק אני כרשע. וכן אמרה הצרפית לאליהו: "באת אלי להזכיר את עוני" (מלכים א' יז, יח) – עד שלא באת אצלי היה הקדוש ברוך הוא רואה מעשי ומעשה עמי ואני צדקת ביניהם, ומשבאת אצלי, לפי מעשיך אני רשעה:

כ **העיר הזאת קרבה.** ישיבתה קרובה, ולא נתמלאת סאתה עדין. ומה היא קריבתה? מדור הפלגה, שנתפלגו האנשים והתחילו להתישב איש איש במקומו, והיא היתה בשנת מות פלג, ומשם עד כאן חמשים ושתים שנה, שפלג מת בשנת ארבעים ושמנה לאברהם. כיצד? פלג חי אחרי הולידו את רעו מאתים ותשע שנה, מהם כלו שלשים ושתים כשנולד שרוג ומשרוג עד שנולד נחור שלשים, הרי ששים ושתים, ומנחור עד שנולד תרח עשרים ותשע, הרי תשעים ואחת, ומשם עד שנולד אברהם שבעים, הרי מאה ששים ואחת, תן להם ארבעים ושמנה, הרי מאתים ותשע, ואותה שנה היתה שנת הפלגה. וכשנחרבה סדום היה אברהם בן תשעים ותשע שנה, הרי מדור הפלגה עד כאן חמשים ושתים שנה. וצוער אחרה ישיבתה אחרי ישיבת סדום וחברותיה שנה אחת, הוא שנאמר: "אמלטה נא", 'נא' בגימטריא חמשים ואחת: **הלא מצער הוא.** עוונותיה מועטין ויכול אתה להניחה "ותחי נפשי" בה, זהו מדרשו. ופשוטו של מקרא, הלא עיר קטנה היא ואנשים בה מעט, אין לך להקפיד אם תניחנה "ותחי נפשי" בה:

כא **גם לדבר הזה.** לא דייך שאתה נצל אלא אף כל העיר אציל בגללך: **הפכי.** הופך אני, כמו "עד באי" (להלן מח, ה), "אחרי ראי" (לעיל טז, יג), "מדי דברי בו" (ירמיה לא, יט):

כב **כי לא אוכל לעשות.** זה ענשן של מלאכים על שאמרו: "כי משחתים אנחנו" (לעיל פסוק יג) ותלו הדבר בעצמן, לפיכך לא זזו משם עד שהזקקו לומר שאין הדבר ברשותן: **כי לא אוכל.** לשון יחיד, מכאן אתה למד שהאחד הופך והאחד מציל, שאין שני מלאכים נשלחים לדבר אחד: **על כן קרא שם העיר צוער.** על שם "והיא מצער" (לעיל פסוק כ):

כד **וה' המטיר.** כל מקום שנאמר "וה'" – הוא ובית דינו: **המטיר על סדם.** בעלות השחר, כמו שנאמר: "וכמו השחר עלה" (לעיל פסוק טו). שעה שהלבנה עומדת ברקיע עם החמה, לפי שהיו מהם עובדים לחמה ומהם ללבנה, אמר הקדוש ברוך הוא: אם אפרע מהם ביום יהיו עובדי לבנה אומרים, אלו לבנה מושלת לא היינו חרבין; ואם אפרע מהם בלילה יהיו עובדי החמה אומרים, אלו היה ביום

אַל־תַּבִּ֣יט אַחֲרֶ֔יךָ וְאַל־תַּעֲמֹ֖ד בְּכׇל־הַכִּכָּ֑ר הָהָ֥רָה הִמָּלֵ֖ט פֶּן־תִּסָּפֶֽה׃
יח יט וַיֹּ֥אמֶר ל֖וֹט אֲלֵהֶ֑ם אַל־נָ֖א אֲדֹנָֽי׃ הִנֵּה־נָ֠א מָצָ֨א עַבְדְּךָ֜ חֵן֮ בְּעֵינֶ֒יךָ֒
וַתַּגְדֵּ֣ל חַסְדְּךָ֗ אֲשֶׁ֤ר עָשִׂ֙יתָ֙ עִמָּדִ֔י לְהַחֲי֖וֹת אֶת־נַפְשִׁ֑י וְאָנֹכִ֗י לֹ֤א אוּכַל֙
כ לְהִמָּלֵ֣ט הָהָ֔רָה פֶּן־תִּדְבָּקַ֥נִי הָרָעָ֖ה וָמַֽתִּי׃ הִנֵּה־נָ֠א הָעִ֨יר הַזֹּ֧את קְרֹבָ֛ה
לָנ֥וּס שָׁ֖מָּה וְהִ֣וא מִצְעָ֑ר אִמָּלְטָ֨ה נָּ֜א שָׁ֗מָּה הֲלֹ֛א מִצְעָ֥ר הִ֖וא וּתְחִ֥י
כא נַפְשִֽׁי׃ וַיֹּ֣אמֶר אֵלָ֔יו הִנֵּה֙ נָשָׂ֣אתִי פָנֶ֔יךָ גַּ֖ם לַדָּבָ֣ר הַזֶּ֑ה לְבִלְתִּ֛י הׇפְכִּ֥י רביעי
כב אֶת־הָעִ֖יר אֲשֶׁ֥ר דִּבַּֽרְתָּ׃ מַהֵר֙ הִמָּלֵ֣ט שָׁ֔מָּה כִּ֣י לֹ֤א אוּכַל֙ לַעֲשׂ֣וֹת דָּבָ֔ר
כג עַד־בֹּאֲךָ֖ שָׁ֑מָּה עַל־כֵּ֛ן קָרָ֥א שֵׁם־הָעִ֖יר צֽוֹעַר׃ הַשֶּׁ֖מֶשׁ יָצָ֣א עַל־הָאָ֑רֶץ
כד וְל֖וֹט בָּ֥א צֹֽעֲרָה׃ וַֽיהֹוָ֗ה הִמְטִ֧יר עַל־סְדֹ֛ם וְעַל־עֲמֹרָ֖ה גׇּפְרִ֣ית וָאֵ֑שׁ
כה מֵאֵ֥ת יְהֹוָ֖ה מִן־הַשָּׁמָֽיִם׃ וַיַּהֲפֹךְ֙ אֶת־הֶעָרִ֣ים הָאֵ֔ל וְאֵ֖ת כׇּל־הַכִּכָּ֑ר
כו וְאֵת֙ כׇּל־יֹשְׁבֵ֣י הֶעָרִ֔ים וְצֶ֖מַח הָאֲדָמָֽה׃ וַתַּבֵּ֥ט אִשְׁתּ֖וֹ מֵאַחֲרָ֑יו

אונקלוס

לָא תִסְתַּכֵּי לַאֲחוֹרָךְ, וְלָא תְקוּם בְּכָל מֵישְׁרָא, לְטוּרָא אִשְׁתֵּיזֵב דִּלְמָא תִלְקֵי: יח וַאֲמַר לוֹט לְהוֹן, בְּבָעוּ יְיָ: יט הָא כְעַן, אַשְׁכַּח עַבְדָּךְ רַחֲמִין בְּעֵינָךְ, וְאַסְגֵּיתָא טֵיבוּתָךְ, דַּעֲבַדְתְּ עִמִּי, לְקַיָּמָא יָת נַפְשִׁי, וַאֲנָא, לֵית אֲנָא יָכֵיל לְאִשְׁתֵּיזָבָא לְטוּרָא, דִּלְמָא תְעָרְעִנַּנִי בִּשְׁתָּא וַאֲמוּת: כ הָא כְעַן, קַרְתָּא הָדָא קְרִיבָא, לִמְעִרַק לְתַמָּן וְהִיא זְעֵירָא, אֶשְׁתֵּיזֵב כְּעַן לְתַמָּן, הֲלָא זְעֵירָא, הִיא וְתִתְקַיַּם נַפְשִׁי: כא וַאֲמַר לֵיהּ, הָא נְסֵיבִית אַפָּךְ, אַף לְפִתְגָּמָא הָדֵין, בְּדִיל, דְּלָא לְמֶהְפַּךְ יָת קַרְתָּא דְּבָעֵיתָא עֲלַהּ: כב אוֹחִי אִשְׁתֵּיזֵב לְתַמָּן, אֲרֵי לָא אִכּוּל לְמֶעְבַּד פִּתְגָּמָא, עַד מֵיתָךְ לְתַמָּן, עַל כֵּן, קְרָא שְׁמַהּ דְּקַרְתָּא צוֹעַר: כג שִׁמְשָׁא נְפַק עַל אַרְעָא, וְלוֹט עָאל לְצוֹעַר: כד וַייָ, אַמְטַר עַל סְדוֹם, וְעַל עֲמוֹרָה גָּפְרֵיתָא וְאִישָׁתָא, מִן קֳדָם יְיָ מִן שְׁמַיָּא: כה וַהֲפַךְ יָת קִרְוַיָּא הָאִלֵּין, וְיָת כָּל מֵישְׁרָא, וְיָת כָּל יָתְבֵי קִרְוַיָּא, וְצִמְחָה דְּאַרְעָא: כו וְאִסְתַּכִּיאַת אִתְּתֵיהּ מִבָּתְרוֹהִי,

רש"י

כְּשֶׁהַחַמָּה מוֹשֶׁלֶת לֹא הָיִינוּ חֲרֵבִין, לְכָךְ כְּתִיב: "וּכְמוֹ הַשַּׁחַר עָלָה", וְנִפְרַע מֵהֶם בְּשָׁעָה שֶׁהַחַמָּה וְהַלְּבָנָה מוֹשְׁלִים: **הִמְטִיר... גׇּפְרִית וָאֵשׁ.** בַּתְּחִלָּה מָטָר וְנַעֲשָׂה גׇּפְרִית וָאֵשׁ: **מֵאֵת ה'.** דֶּרֶךְ מִקְרָאוֹת לְדַבֵּר כֵּן, כְּמוֹ: "נְשֵׁי לֶמֶךְ" (לעיל ד, כג) וְלֹא אָמַר 'נָשַׁי'; וְכֵן אָמַר דָּוִד: "קְחוּ עִמָּכֶם אֶת עַבְדֵי אֲדֹנֵיכֶם" (מלכים א' א, לג) וְלֹא אָמַר 'אֶת עֲבָדַי'; וְכֵן בַּאֲחַשְׁוֵרוֹשׁ: "בְּשֵׁם הַמֶּלֶךְ" (אסתר ח, ח) וְלֹא אָמַר 'בִּשְׁמִי'; אַף כָּאן אָמַר: "מֵאֵת ה'" וְלֹא אָמַר 'מֵאִתּוֹ': **מִן הַשָּׁמָיִם.** הוּא שֶׁאָמַר הַכָּתוּב: "כִּי בָם יָדִין עַמִּים" וְגוֹ' (איוב לו, לא). כְּשֶׁבָּא לְיַסֵּר הַבְּרִיּוֹת מֵבִיא עֲלֵיהֶם אֵשׁ מִן הַשָּׁמַיִם כְּמוֹ שֶׁעָשָׂה לִסְדוֹם, וּכְשֶׁבָּא לְהוֹרִיד הַמָּן – מִן הַשָּׁמַיִם, "הִנְנִי מַמְטִיר לָכֶם לֶחֶם מִן הַשָּׁמָיִם" (שמות טז, ד):

כה **וַיַּהֲפֹךְ אֶת הֶעָרִים וְגוֹ'.** אַרְבַּעְתָּן יוֹשְׁבוֹת בְּסֶלַע אֶחָד וַהֲפָכָן מִלְמַעְלָה לְמַטָּה, שֶׁנֶּאֱמַר: "בַּחַלָּמִישׁ שָׁלַח יָדוֹ" וְגוֹ' (איוב כח, ט):

כו **וַתַּבֵּט אִשְׁתּוֹ מֵאַחֲרָיו.** מֵאַחֲרָיו שֶׁל לוֹט:

19:26 **וַתַּבֵּט אִשְׁתּוֹ מֵאַחֲרָיו** *Lot's wife looked back – To mend the past, first you have to secure the future.* I learned this from Holocaust survivors. Many of them did not speak about those years, even to their spouses or their children,

27 and she was turned into a pillar of salt. Avraham rose early the next morning
28 and returned to the place where he had stood before the LORD. He looked
down toward Sedom and Amora and all the land of the plain, and he saw thick
29 smoke rising from the land like smoke from a kiln. So it was, that when God
destroyed the cities of the plain, He remembered Avraham and brought Lot
30 out of the overthrow that overturned the cities where Lot had lived. Lot went
up from Tzoar and settled in the hills together with his two daughters because
31 he was afraid to stay in Tzoar. He and his two daughters settled in a cave. The
elder said to the younger, "Our father is old, and there is no man left on earth
32 to come to us in the normal way of the world. Let us get our father drunk with
wine and then sleep with him, so that we may raise a new generation through
33 our father." That night they gave their father wine to drink. Then the elder
daughter went in and slept with him. He was unaware when she lay down and
34 when she arose. The next day, the elder said to the younger, "Last night I slept
with my father. Let us get him to drink wine again tonight, then you go in and
35 sleep with him. So may we preserve our family line through our father." So that

רש"י

וַתְּהִי נְצִיב מֶלַח. בַּמֶּלַח חָטְאָה וּבַמֶּלַח לָקְתָה, אָמַר לָהּ: תְּנִי מְעַט מֶלַח לָאוֹרְחִים הַלָּלוּ, אָמְרָה לוֹ: אַף הַמִּנְהָג הָרַע הַזֶּה אַתָּה בָּא לְהַנְהִיג בַּמָּקוֹם הַזֶּה?!:

כח **קִיטֹר.** תִּמּוּר שֶׁל עָשָׁן, טורק"א בְּלַעַ"ז: **כִּבְשָׁן.** חֲפִירָה שֶׁשּׂוֹרְפִין בָּהּ אֶת הָאֲבָנִים לְסִיד, וְכֵן כָּל 'כִּבְשָׁן' שֶׁבַּתּוֹרָה:

כט **וַיִּזְכֹּר אֱלֹהִים אֶת אַבְרָהָם.** מַה הִיא זְכִירָתוֹ שֶׁל אַבְרָהָם עַל לוֹט? נִזְכַּר, שֶׁהָיָה יוֹדֵעַ שֶׁשָּׂרָה אִשְׁתּוֹ שֶׁל אַבְרָהָם, וְשָׁמַע שֶׁאָמַר אַבְרָהָם בְּמִצְרַיִם עַל שָׂרָה: "אֲחוֹתִי הִיא" (לעיל יב, יט) וְלֹא גִּלָּה הַדָּבָר, שֶׁהָיָה חָס עָלָיו, לְפִיכָךְ חָס הַקָּדוֹשׁ בָּרוּךְ הוּא עָלָיו:

ל **כִּי יָרֵא לָשֶׁבֶת בְּצוֹעַר.** לְפִי שֶׁהָיְתָה קְרוֹבָה לִסְדוֹם:

לא **אָבִינוּ זָקֵן.** וְאִם לֹא עַכְשָׁיו אֵימָתַי? שֶׁמָּא יָמוּת אוֹ יִפְסֹק מִלֵּדָה: **וְאִישׁ אֵין בָּאָרֶץ.** סְבוּרוֹת הָיוּ שֶׁכָּל הָעוֹלָם נֶחֱרַב כְּמוֹ בְּדוֹר הַמַּבּוּל. בְּרֵאשִׁית רַבָּה (נא, ח):

לג **וַתַּשְׁקֶיןָ וְגוֹ'.** יַיִן נִזְדַּמֵּן לָהֶן בַּמְּעָרָה לְהוֹצִיא מֵהֶן שְׁתֵּי אֻמּוֹת: **וַתִּשְׁכַּב אֶת אָבִיהָ.** וּבַצְּעִירָה כְּתִיב: "וַתִּשְׁכַּב עִמּוֹ" (להלן פסוק לה). צְעִירָה לְפִי שֶׁלֹּא פָּתְחָה בִּזְנוּת אֶלָּא אֲחוֹתָהּ לִמְּדַתָּה, חִסֵּךְ עָלֶיהָ הַכָּתוּב וְלֹא פֵּרֵשׁ גְּנוּתָהּ, אֲבָל בְּכִירָה שֶׁפָּתְחָה בִּזְנוּת פִּרְסְמָהּ הַכָּתוּב בִּמְפֹרָשׁ. "וּבְקוּמָהּ" שֶׁל בְּכִירָה נָקוּד, הֲרֵי הוּא כְּאִלּוּ לֹא נִכְתַּב, לוֹמַר שֶׁבְּקוּמָהּ יָדַע, וְאַף עַל פִּי כֵן לֹא נִשְׁמַר לֵיל שֵׁנִי מִלִּשְׁתּוֹת:

and what is yours is yours." The Talmud (Sanhedrin 109a ff.) describes a city where, though no individual breaks the rules, there is no compassion, and so no safety for the vulnerable.

In the book of Isaiah, the prophet's prescription for escaping the fate of Sedom is clearly stated: "Seek justice. Correct what is cruel. Rule justice for orphans. Fight the widows' cause" (Is. 1:17).

The point is that it is not the responsibility of any particular group within society, but of everyone. That is what citizenship in a covenantal society is: co-responsibility for justice, equity, kindness, and compassion. A free society, implies the Bible, is a moral society, for if there is corruption and injustice, there will no longer be social cohesion. The powerful will oppress the powerless. The rich will be at best indifferent to, at worst exploitative of, the plight of the poor. Each will seek his or her own advantage rather than the common good. Society will become demoralized, people will not rally to its defense, and if it does not fall, like Sedom, to an enemy without, it will implode from within.

כז וַתְּהִי נְצִיב מֶלַח׃ וַיַּשְׁכֵּם אַבְרָהָם בַּבֹּקֶר אֶל־הַמָּקוֹם אֲשֶׁר־עָמַד
כח שָׁם אֶת־פְּנֵי יְהוָה׃ וַיַּשְׁקֵף עַל־פְּנֵי סְדֹם וַעֲמֹרָה וְעַל כָּל־פְּנֵי אֶרֶץ
כט הַכִּכָּר וַיַּרְא וְהִנֵּה עָלָה קִיטֹר הָאָרֶץ כְּקִיטֹר הַכִּבְשָׁן׃ וַיְהִי בְּשַׁחֵת
אֱלֹהִים אֶת־עָרֵי הַכִּכָּר וַיִּזְכֹּר אֱלֹהִים אֶת־אַבְרָהָם וַיְשַׁלַּח אֶת־לוֹט
ל מִתּוֹךְ הַהֲפֵכָה בַּהֲפֹךְ אֶת־הֶעָרִים אֲשֶׁר־יָשַׁב בָּהֵן לוֹט׃ וַיַּעַל
לוֹט מִצּוֹעַר וַיֵּשֶׁב בָּהָר וּשְׁתֵּי בְנֹתָיו עִמּוֹ כִּי יָרֵא לָשֶׁבֶת בְּצוֹעַר
לא וַיֵּשֶׁב בַּמְּעָרָה הוּא וּשְׁתֵּי בְנֹתָיו׃ וַתֹּאמֶר הַבְּכִירָה אֶל־הַצְּעִירָה
לב אָבִינוּ זָקֵן וְאִישׁ אֵין בָּאָרֶץ לָבוֹא עָלֵינוּ כְּדֶרֶךְ כָּל־הָאָרֶץ׃ לְכָה נַשְׁקֶה
לג אֶת־אָבִינוּ יַיִן וְנִשְׁכְּבָה עִמּוֹ וּנְחַיֶּה מֵאָבִינוּ זָרַע׃ וַתַּשְׁקֶיןָ אֶת־
אֲבִיהֶן יַיִן בַּלַּיְלָה הוּא וַתָּבֹא הַבְּכִירָה וַתִּשְׁכַּב אֶת־אָבִיהָ וְלֹא־יָדַע
לד בְּשִׁכְבָהּ וּבְקוּמָהּ׃ וַיְהִי מִמָּחֳרָת וַתֹּאמֶר הַבְּכִירָה אֶל־הַצְּעִירָה
הֵן־שָׁכַבְתִּי אֶמֶשׁ אֶת־אָבִי נַשְׁקֶנּוּ יַיִן גַּם־הַלַּיְלָה וּבֹאִי שִׁכְבִי עִמּוֹ
לה וּנְחַיֶּה מֵאָבִינוּ זָרַע׃ וַתַּשְׁקֶיןָ גַּם בַּלַּיְלָה הַהוּא אֶת־אֲבִיהֶן יָיִן

אונקלוס

וַהֲוָת קָמָא דִמְלַחָא: כז וְאַקְדֵּים אַבְרָהָם בְּצַפְרָא, לְאַתְרָא, דְשַׁמֵּישׁ תַּמָּן בִּצְלוֹ קֳדָם יי: כח וְאִסְתְּכִי, עַל אַפֵּי סְדוֹם וַעֲמוֹרָה, וְעַל כָּל אַפֵּי אֲרַע מֵישְׁרָא, וַחֲזָא, וְהָא סְלֵיק תְּנָנָא דְאַרְעָא, כִּתְנָנָא דְאַתּוּנָא: כט וַהֲוָה, כַּד חַבֵּיל יי יָת קִרְוֵי מֵישְׁרָא, וּדְכִיר יי יָת אַבְרָהָם, וְשַׁלַּח יָת לוֹט מִגּוֹ הֲפֵיכְתָא, כַּד הֲפַךְ יָת קִרְוַיָּא, דַּהֲוָה יָתֵיב בְּהוֹן לוֹט: ל וּסְלֵיק לוֹט מִצּוֹעַר וִיתֵיב בְּטוּרָא, וְתַרְתֵּין בְּנָתֵיהּ עִמֵּיהּ, אֲרֵי דְחֵיל לְמִתַּב בְּצוֹעַר, וִיתֵיב בִּמְעַרְתָּא, הוּא וְתַרְתֵּין בְּנָתֵיהּ: לא וַאֲמַרַת רַבְּתָא, לִזְעֵירְתָּא אֲבוּנָא סִיב, וּגְבַר לֵית בְּאַרְעָא לְמֵיעַל עֲלַנָא, כְּאוֹרַח כָּל אַרְעָא: לב אִיתָא נַשְׁקֵי יָת אֲבוּנָא, חַמְרָא וְנִשְׁכּוֹב עִמֵּיהּ, וּנְקַיֵּים מֵאֲבוּנָא בְּנִין: לג וְאַשְׁקִיאָה יָת אֲבוּהוֹן, חַמְרָא בְּלֵילְיָא הוּא, וְעָאלַת רַבְּתָא וּשְׁכֵיבַת עִם אֲבוּהָא, וְלָא יְדַע בְּמִשְׁכְּבַהּ וּבְמִקְמַהּ: לד וַהֲוָה בְּיוֹמָא דְבָתְרוֹהִי, וַאֲמַרַת רַבְּתָא לִזְעֵירְתָּא, הָא שְׁכֵיבִית רַמְשִׁי עִם אַבָּא, נַשְׁקֵינֵיהּ חַמְרָא אַף בְּלֵילְיָא, וְעוּלִי שְׁכוּבִי עִמֵּיהּ, וּנְקַיֵּים מֵאֲבוּנָא בְּנִין: לה וְאַשְׁקִיאָה, אַף בְּלֵילְיָא הַהוּא, יָת אֲבוּהוֹן חַמְרָא,

19:29 הַהֲפֵכָה בַּהֲפֹךְ אֶת הֶעָרִים *The overthrow that overturned the cities* – This language will be echoed in the opening chapter of Isaiah, describing the "overturning" of Judah, which, but for God's sparing of a few survivors "would have been like Sedom" (Is. 1:7, 9). What is the sin of Sedom that causes its utter destruction? The Mishna (Avot 5:14) summarizes the ethos of the city: "What is mine is mine,

sometimes for as long as forty or fifty years. Only when they had secured the future did they allow themselves to look back at the past. Only when they had built a life did they permit themselves to remember death. I think the Holocaust survivors knew that if they turned and looked back, they, like Lot's wife who disobeyed the angels, would be reduced to the salt of tears.

night they got their father to drink wine again, and the younger went and slept
36 with him. And he was unaware when she lay down and when she arose. And so
37 both of Lot's daughters became pregnant by their father. The elder had a son,
38 whom she named Moav. He is the ancestor of the Moabites of today. The
younger also had a son, whom she named Ben Ami. And he is the ancestor of
20 1 the Amonites of today. Avraham then journeyed on to the Negev
region, settling between Kadesh and Shur. For a while he lived as a stranger in
2 Gerar. There Avraham said of his wife Sara, "She is my sister." Avimelekh, king
3 of Gerar, sent for Sara and took her as his own. But God came to Avimelekh in
a dream one night and told him, "You will die because of the woman you have
4 taken. She is already married." Avimelekh had not gone near her, so he said,
5 "Lord, would You destroy an innocent nation? Did he not tell me, 'She is my
sister'? Did she not say, 'He is my brother'? I have acted from an innocent heart,
6 with clean hands." Then, in the dream, God said to him, "I too knew that you
acted from an innocent heart, and so I kept you from sinning against Me. That
7 is why I did not let you touch her. But now, give back the man's wife. He is a
prophet. He will pray for you and you will live. But if you do not give her back,
8 know that you and all your people are to die." Early the next morning, Avimelekh
9 summoned all his servants and told them all this – they were very afraid. Then
Avimelekh summoned Avraham and said, "What have you done to us? What

רש״י

לו **וַתַּהֲרֶיןָ.** אַף עַל פִּי שֶׁאֵין הָאִשָּׁה מִתְעַבֶּרֶת מִבִּיאָה רִאשׁוֹנָה, אֵלּוּ שָׁלְטוּ בְּעַצְמָן וְהוֹצִיאוּ עֶרְוָתָן לַחוּץ וְעִבְּרוּ מִבִּיאָה רִאשׁוֹנָה:

לז **מוֹאָב.** זוֹ שֶׁלֹּא הָיְתָה צְנוּעָה פֵּרְשָׁה שֶׁמֵּאָבִיהָ הוּא, אֲבָל צְעִירָה קְרָאַתּוּ בְּלָשׁוֹן נְקִיָּה, וְקִבְּלוּ שָׂכָר בִּימֵי מֹשֶׁה, שֶׁנֶּאֱמַר בִּבְנֵי עַמּוֹן: "וְאַל תִּתְגָּר בָּם" (דברים ב, יט) כְּלָל, וּבְמוֹאָב לֹא הִזְהִיר אֶלָּא שֶׁלֹּא יִלָּחֵם בָּם, אֲבָל לְצַעֲרָן הִתִּיר לוֹ:

כ א **וַיִּסַּע מִשָּׁם אַבְרָהָם.** כְּשֶׁרָאָה שֶׁחָרְבוּ הַכְּרַכִּים וּפָסְקוּ הָעוֹבְרִים וְהַשָּׁבִים נָסַע לוֹ מִשָּׁם. דָּבָר אַחֵר, לְהִתְרַחֵק מִלּוֹט שֶׁיָּצָא עָלָיו שֵׁם רָע שֶׁבָּא עַל בְּנוֹתָיו:

ב **וַיֹּאמֶר אַבְרָהָם.** כָּאן לֹא נָטַל רְשׁוּת, אֶלָּא עַל כָּרְחָהּ שֶׁלֹּא בְּטוֹבָתָהּ, לְפִי שֶׁכְּבָר לְקָחָהּ לְבֵית פַּרְעֹה עַל יְדֵי כֵן: **אֶל שָׂרָה אִשְׁתּוֹ.** עַל שָׂרָה אִשְׁתּוֹ. כַּיּוֹצֵא בוֹ: "אֶל הִלָּקַח אֲרוֹן וְגוֹ' וְאֶל חָמִיהָ" (שמואל א׳ ד, כא), שְׁנֵיהֶם בִּלְשׁוֹן 'עַל':

ד **לֹא קָרַב אֵלֶיהָ.** הַמַּלְאָךְ מְנָעוֹ, כְּמָה שֶׁנֶּאֱמַר: "לֹא נְתַתִּיךָ לִנְגֹּעַ אֵלֶיהָ" (להלן פסוק ו): **הֲגוֹי גַּם צַדִּיק תַּהֲרֹג.** אַף אִם הוּא צַדִּיק תַּהַרְגֶנּוּ? שֶׁמָּא כָּךְ דַּרְכְּךָ לְאַבֵּד אֻמּוֹת חִנָּם? כָּךְ עָשִׂיתָ לְדוֹר הַמַּבּוּל וּלְדוֹר הַפַּלָּגָה, אַף אֲנִי אוֹמֵר שֶׁהֲרַגְתָּם עַל לֹא דָבָר כְּשֵׁם שֶׁאַתָּה אוֹמֵר לְהָרְגֵנִי:

ה **גַּם הוּא.** לְרַבּוֹת עֲבָדִים וְגַמָּלִים וַחֲמָרִים שֶׁלָּהּ, אֶת כֻּלָּם שָׁאַלְתִּי וְאָמְרוּ לִי: אָחִיהָ הוּא: **בְּתָם לְבָבִי.** שֶׁלֹּא דִמִּיתִי לַחֲטֹא: **וּבְנִקְיֹן כַּפַּי.** נָקִי אֲנִי מִן הַחֵטְא, שֶׁלֹּא נָגַעְתִּי בָּהּ:

ו **יָדַעְתִּי כִּי בְתָם לְבָבְךָ וְגוֹ׳.** אֱמֶת שֶׁלֹּא דִמִּיתָ מִתְּחִלָּה לַחֲטֹא, אֲבָל נִקְיוֹן כַּפַּיִם אֵין כָּאן שֶׁלֹּא מִמְּךָ הָיָה שֶׁלֹּא נָגַעְתָּ בָּהּ, אֶלָּא אֲנִי חָשַׂכְתִּי אוֹתְךָ מֵחֵטְא: **לֹא נְתַתִּיךָ.** לֹא נָתַתִּי לְךָ כֹּחַ, וְכֵן: "וְלֹא נְתָנוֹ אֱלֹהִים לְהָרַע" (להלן לא, ז), וְכֵן: "וְלֹא נְתָנוֹ אָבִיהָ לָבוֹא" (שופטים טו, א) – לֹא נָתַן לוֹ מָקוֹם:

ז **הָשֵׁב אֵשֶׁת הָאִישׁ.** וְאַל תְּהֵא סָבוּר שֶׁתִּתְגַּנֶּה בְּעֵינָיו וְלֹא יְקַבְּלֶנָּה, אוֹ שֶׁיִּשְׂנָאֲךָ וְלֹא יִתְפַּלֵּל עָלֶיךָ: **כִּי נָבִיא הוּא.** וְיוֹדֵעַ שֶׁלֹּא נָגַעְתָּ בָּהּ, לְפִיכָךְ "וְיִתְפַּלֵּל בַּעַדְךָ":

לו וַתָּקָם הַצְּעִירָה וַתִּשְׁכַּב עִמּוֹ וְלֹא־יָדַע בְּשִׁכְבָהּ וּבְקֻמָהּ: וַתַּהֲרֶיןָ שְׁתֵּי
לז בְנוֹת־לוֹט מֵאֲבִיהֶן: וַתֵּלֶד הַבְּכִירָה בֵּן וַתִּקְרָא שְׁמוֹ מוֹאָב הוּא אֲבִי־
לח מוֹאָב עַד־הַיּוֹם: וְהַצְּעִירָה גַם־הִוא יָלְדָה בֵּן וַתִּקְרָא שְׁמוֹ בֶּן־עַמִּי
כ א הוּא אֲבִי בְנֵי־עַמּוֹן עַד־הַיּוֹם: וַיִּסַּע מִשָּׁם אַבְרָהָם יז
ב אַרְצָה הַנֶּגֶב וַיֵּשֶׁב בֵּין־קָדֵשׁ וּבֵין שׁוּר וַיָּגָר בִּגְרָר: וַיֹּאמֶר אַבְרָהָם
אֶל־שָׂרָה אִשְׁתּוֹ אֲחֹתִי הִוא וַיִּשְׁלַח אֲבִימֶלֶךְ מֶלֶךְ גְּרָר וַיִּקַּח אֶת־
ג שָׂרָה: וַיָּבֹא אֱלֹהִים אֶל־אֲבִימֶלֶךְ בַּחֲלוֹם הַלָּיְלָה וַיֹּאמֶר לוֹ הִנְּךָ מֵת
ד עַל־הָאִשָּׁה אֲשֶׁר־לָקַחְתָּ וְהִוא בְּעֻלַת בָּעַל: וַאֲבִימֶלֶךְ לֹא קָרַב אֵלֶיהָ
ה וַיֹּאמַר אֲדֹנָי הֲגוֹי גַּם־צַדִּיק תַּהֲרֹג: הֲלֹא הוּא אָמַר־לִי אֲחֹתִי הִוא
וְהִיא־גַם־הִוא אָמְרָה אָחִי הוּא בְּתָם־לְבָבִי וּבְנִקְיֹן כַּפַּי עָשִׂיתִי זֹאת:
ו וַיֹּאמֶר אֵלָיו הָאֱלֹהִים בַּחֲלֹם גַּם אָנֹכִי יָדַעְתִּי כִּי בְתָם־לְבָבְךָ עָשִׂיתָ
זֹּאת וָאֶחְשֹׂךְ גַּם־אָנֹכִי אוֹתְךָ מֵחֲטוֹ־לִי עַל־כֵּן לֹא־נְתַתִּיךָ לִנְגֹּעַ
ז אֵלֶיהָ: וְעַתָּה הָשֵׁב אֵשֶׁת־הָאִישׁ כִּי־נָבִיא הוּא וְיִתְפַּלֵּל בַּעַדְךָ וֶחְיֵה
ח וְאִם־אֵינְךָ מֵשִׁיב דַּע כִּי־מוֹת תָּמוּת אַתָּה וְכָל־אֲשֶׁר־לָךְ: וַיַּשְׁכֵּם
אֲבִימֶלֶךְ בַּבֹּקֶר וַיִּקְרָא לְכָל־עֲבָדָיו וַיְדַבֵּר אֶת־כָּל־הַדְּבָרִים הָאֵלֶּה
ט בְּאָזְנֵיהֶם וַיִּירְאוּ הָאֲנָשִׁים מְאֹד: וַיִּקְרָא אֲבִימֶלֶךְ לְאַבְרָהָם וַיֹּאמֶר

אונקלוס

וְקָמַת זְעֵירְתָא וּשְׁכִיבַת עִמֵּיהּ, וְלָא יְדַע בְּמִשְׁכְּבַהּ וּבְמִקִימַהּ: לו וְעַדִּיאָה, תַּרְתֵּין בְּנָת לוֹט מֵאֲבוּהוֹן: לז וִילֵידַת רַבְּתָא בַּר, וּקְרָת שְׁמֵיהּ מוֹאָב, הוּא אֲבוּהוֹן דְּמוֹאֲבָאֵי עַד יוֹמָא דֵין: לח וּזְעֵירְתָא אַף הִיא יְלֵידַת בַּר, וּקְרָת שְׁמֵיהּ בַּר עַמִּי, הוּא, אֲבוּהוֹן דִּבְנֵי עַמּוֹן עַד יוֹמָא דֵין: כ א וּנְטַל מִתַּמָּן אַבְרָהָם לַאֲרַע דָּרוֹמָא, וִיתֵיב בֵּין רְקַם וּבֵין חַגְרָא, וְאִתּוֹתַב בִּגְרָר: ב וַאֲמַר אַבְרָהָם, עַל שָׂרָה אִתְּתֵיהּ אֲחָתַת הִיא, וּשְׁלַח, אֲבִימֶלֶךְ מַלְכָּא דִגְרָר, וּדְבַר יָת שָׂרָה: ג וַאֲתָא מֵימַר מִן קֳדָם יי, לְוָת אֲבִימֶלֶךְ בְּחֶלְמָא דְלֵילְיָא, וַאֲמַר לֵיהּ, הָא אַתְּ מָאִית עַל עֵיסַק אִתְּתָא דִּדְבַרְתָּא, וְהִיא אֲתַת גְּבַר: ד וַאֲבִימֶלֶךְ, לָא קְרֵיב לְוָתַהּ, וַאֲמַר, יי, הַעַם אַף זַכַּאי תִּקְטוֹל: ה הֲלָא הוּא אֲמַר לִי אֲחָתַת הִיא, וְהִיא אַף הִיא אֲמָרַת אֲחִי הוּא, בְּקַשִּׁיטוּת לִבִּי, וּבְזַכָּאוּת יְדַי עֲבַדִית דָּא: ו וַאֲמַר לֵיהּ יי בְּחֶלְמָא, אַף קֳדָמַי גְּלֵי אֲרֵי בְקַשִּׁיטוּת לִבָּךְ עֲבַדְתְּ דָּא, וּמְנָעִית אַף אֲנָא, יָתָךְ מִלְּמֶחְטֵי קֳדָמַי, עַל כֵּן לָא שְׁבַקְתָּךְ לְמִקְרַב לְוָתַהּ: ז וּכְעַן, אֲתֵיב אִתַּת גֻּבְרָא אֲרֵי נְבִיָּא הוּא, וִיצַלֵּי עֲלָךְ וְתֵיחֵי, וְאִם לֵיתָךְ מְתִיב, דַּע אֲרֵי מְמָת תְּמוּת, אַתְּ וְכָל דִּלָךְ: ח וְאַקְדִּים אֲבִימֶלֶךְ בְּצַפְרָא, וּקְרָא לְכָל עַבְדּוֹהִי, וּמַלֵּיל, יָת כָּל פִּתְגָּמַיָּא הָאִלֵּין קֳדָמֵיהוֹן, וּדְחִילוּ גֻּבְרַיָּא לַחֲדָא: ט וּקְרָא אֲבִימֶלֶךְ לְאַבְרָהָם, וַאֲמַר

wrong have I done you? Why have you brought such onerous guilt upon me
10 and my kingdom? You have done to me that which should never be done. What
11 were you thinking of," asked Avimelekh, "that you did such a thing?" Avraham
replied, "I thought, 'There is no fear of God in this place. They will kill me
12 because of my wife.' Besides, she really is my sister. She is the daughter of my
13 father though not of my mother, and she became my wife. When God made
me wander from my father's house, I said to her, 'Do me this kindness: wherever
14 we go, say of me, "He is my brother."'" Avimelekh gave Avraham sheep, cattle,
15 and male and female slaves, and returned his wife Sara to him. Avimelekh said,
16 "Here is my land. Live wherever you wish." To Sara he said, "I am giving your

רש״י

ט | **מעשים אשר לא יעשו.** מכה אשר לא הרגלה לבא על בריה באה לנו על ידך – עצירת כל נקבים של זרע ושל קטנים ורעי ואזנים וחטם:

יא | **רק אין יראת אלהים.** אכסנאי שבא לעיר, על עסקי אכילה ושתיה שואלין אותו או על עסקי אשתו שואלין אותו, אשתך היא או אחותך היא?:

יב | **אחתי בת אבי היא.** ובת אב מתרת לבן נח, שאין אב לגוי; וכדי לאמת דבריו השיבם כן. ואם תאמר, והלא בת אחיו היתה! בני בנים הרי הם כבנים והרי היא בתו של תרח, וכך הוא אומר ללוט: "כי אנשים אחים אנחנו" (לעיל יג, ח): **אך לא בת אמי.** הרן מאם אחרת היה:

יג | **ויהי כאשר התעו אתי וגו׳.** אונקלוס תרגם מה שתרגם; ויש ליישבו עוד דבר דבור על אפניו: כשהוציאני הקדוש ברוך הוא מבית אבי להיות משוטט ונד ממקום למקום וידעתי שאעבר במקום רשעים, "ואמר לה זה חסדך": **כאשר התעו.** לשון רבים. ואל תתמה, כי הרבה מקומות לשון אלהות ולשון מרות קרוי בלשון רבים: "אשר הלכו אלהים" (שמואל ב׳ ז, כג), "אלהים חיים" (דברים ה, כג), "אלהים קדשים" (יהושע כד, יט), וכל לשון 'אלהים' לשון רבים. וכן: "ויקח אדני יוסף" (להלן לט, כ), "ואדני האדנים" (דברים י, יז), "אדני הארץ" (להלן מב, לג); וכן: "בעליו עמו" (שמות כב, יד), "והועד בבעליו" (שם כא, כט). ואם תאמר, מהו לשון 'התעו'? כל הגולה ממקומו ואינו מיושב קרוי 'תועה', כמו: "ותלך ותתע" (להלן כא, יד), "תעיתי כשה אבד" (תהלים קיט, קעו), "יתעו לבלי אכל" (איוב לח, מא), יצאו ויתעו לבקש אכלם: **אמרי לי.** עלי, וכן: "וישאלו אנשי המקום לאשתו" (להלן כו, ז) על אשתו, וכן: "ואמר פרעה לבני ישראל" (שמות יד, ג), "פן יאמרו לי אשה הרגתהו" (שופטים ט, נד):

יד | **ויתן לאברהם.** כדי שיתפיס ויתפלל עליו:

טו | **הנה ארצי לפניך.** אבל פרעה אמר לו: "הנה אשתך קח ולך" (לעיל יב, יט), לפי שנתירא, שהמצרים שטופי זמה:

טז | **ולשרה אמר.** אבימלך לכבודה, כדי לפיסה: הנה עשיתי לך כבוד זה, נתתי ממון לאחיך שאמרת עליו "אחי הוא", הנה הכבוד

overall pattern (see ch. 38 and commentary there).

Finally there is the sixth episode, when Potifar's wife attempts to seduce Yosef. Failing, she accuses him of rape and has him imprisoned.

In other words, there is a continuing theme in Genesis 12–50, a contrast between the people of the Abrahamic covenant and their neighbors, but it is not about idolatry, but rather about adultery, promiscuity, seduction, rape, and sexually motivated violence.

This gives us an entirely new way of thinking about Abrahamic faith. *Emuna*, the Hebrew word normally translated as "faith," does not mean a body of dogma, a set of principles, or a cluster of beliefs often held on non-rational grounds. *Emuna* means faithfulness, loyalty, fidelity, honoring your commitments, and acting in such a way as to inspire trust. It has to do with relationships, first and foremost with marriage.

When a society loses faith, eventually it loses the very idea of a sexual ethic, and the result in the long term is violence and the exploitation of the powerless by the powerful. Women suffer. Children suffer. There is a breakdown of trust where it matters most. So it was in the days of the patriarchs. Sadly, so it is today. Judaism, by contrast, is the sanctification of relationship, of the love between husband and wife which is as close as we will ever get to understanding God's love for us.

לוֹ מֶה־עָשִׂיתָ לָּנוּ וּמֶה־חָטָאתִי לָךְ כִּי־הֵבֵאתָ עָלַי וְעַל־מַמְלַכְתִּי
י חֲטָאָה גְדֹלָה מַעֲשִׂים אֲשֶׁר לֹא־יֵעָשׂוּ עָשִׂיתָ עִמָּדִי: וַיֹּאמֶר אֲבִימֶלֶךְ
יא אֶל־אַבְרָהָם מָה רָאִיתָ כִּי עָשִׂיתָ אֶת־הַדָּבָר הַזֶּה: וַיֹּאמֶר אַבְרָהָם
כִּי אָמַרְתִּי רַק אֵין־יִרְאַת אֱלֹהִים בַּמָּקוֹם הַזֶּה וַהֲרָגוּנִי עַל־דְּבַר אִשְׁתִּי:
יב וְגַם־אָמְנָה אֲחֹתִי בַת־אָבִי הִוא אַךְ לֹא בַת־אִמִּי וַתְּהִי־לִי לְאִשָּׁה:
יג וַיְהִי כַּאֲשֶׁר הִתְעוּ אֹתִי אֱלֹהִים מִבֵּית אָבִי וָאֹמַר לָהּ זֶה חַסְדֵּךְ אֲשֶׁר
תַּעֲשִׂי עִמָּדִי אֶל כָּל־הַמָּקוֹם אֲשֶׁר נָבוֹא שָׁמָּה אִמְרִי־לִי אָחִי הוּא:
יד וַיִּקַּח אֲבִימֶלֶךְ צֹאן וּבָקָר וַעֲבָדִים וּשְׁפָחֹת וַיִּתֵּן לְאַבְרָהָם וַיָּשֶׁב לוֹ
טו אֵת שָׂרָה אִשְׁתּוֹ: וַיֹּאמֶר אֲבִימֶלֶךְ הִנֵּה אַרְצִי לְפָנֶיךָ בַּטּוֹב בְּעֵינֶיךָ
טז שֵׁב: וּלְשָׂרָה אָמַר הִנֵּה נָתַתִּי אֶלֶף כֶּסֶף לְאָחִיךְ הִנֵּה הוּא־לָךְ כְּסוּת

אונקלוס

לֵיהּ, מָא עֲבַדְתְּ לַנָא וּמָא חֲטֵית לָךְ, אֲרֵי אֵיתִיתָא עֲלַי, וְעַל מַלְכוּתִי חוֹבָא רַבָּא, עוֹבָדִין דְּלָא כַשְׁרִין לְאִתְעֲבָדָא, עֲבַדְתְּ עִמִּי: י וַאֲמַר אֲבִימֶלֶךְ לְאַבְרָהָם, מָא חֲזֵיתָא, אֲרֵי עֲבַדְתָּא יָת פִּתְגָּמָא הָדֵין: יא וַאֲמַר אַבְרָהָם, אֲרֵי אֲמָרִית, לְחוֹד לֵית דַּחַלְתָּא דַּיְיָ, בְּאַתְרָא הָדֵין, וְיִקְטְלֻנַּנִי עַל עֵיסַק אִתְּתִי: יב וּבְרַם בִּקְשׁוֹטָא, אֲחָתִי בַת אַבָּא הִיא, בְּרַם לָא בַת אִמָּא, וַהֲוָת לִי לְאִתּוּ: יג וַהֲוָה כַּד טְעוֹ עַמְמַיָּא בָּתַר עוֹבָדֵי יְדֵיהוֹן, יָתִי קָרֵיב יְיָ לְדַחַלְתֵיהּ מִבֵּית אַבָּא, וַאֲמָרִית לַהּ, דֵּין טֵיבוּתִיךְ, דְּתַעְבְּדִין עִמִּי, לְכָל אֲתַר דִּנְהָךְ לְתַמָּן, אֵימָרִי עֲלַי אֲחִי הוּא: יד וּדְבַר אֲבִימֶלֶךְ עָן וְתוֹרִין, וְעַבְדִּין וְאַמְהָן, וִיהַב לְאַבְרָהָם, וַאֲתֵיב לֵיהּ, יָת שָׂרָה אִתְּתֵיהּ: טו וַאֲמַר אֲבִימֶלֶךְ, הָא אַרְעִי קֳדָמָךְ, בִּדְתָקֵין בְּעֵינָךְ תִּיב: טז וּלְשָׂרָה אֲמַר, הָא יְהָבִית, אֲלַף סִלְעִין דִּכְסַף לַאֲחוּיִךְ, הָא הוּא לִיךְ כְּסוּת דִּיקָר, חֲלָף דִּשְׁלַחִית דְּבַרְתִּיךְ,

20:11 וַהֲרָגוּנִי עַל דְּבַר אִשְׁתִּי *They will kill me because of my wife* – This theme appears no less than six (possibly even seven) times in Genesis. Whenever a member of the covenantal family leaves his or her own space and enters the wider world of their contemporaries, they encounter a world of sexual depravity.

Three times, Avraham (Gen. 12 and 20) and Yitzḥak (Gen. 26) are forced to leave their homes because of famine. On all three occasions, the husband fears he will be killed so that the local ruler can take his wife into his harem. All three times they put forward the story that their wife is actually their sister. At worst this is a lie, at best a half-truth. In all three cases the local ruler (Pharaoh, Avimelekh), protests their behavior when the truth becomes known. Clearly, the fear of death is real or the patriarchs would not be party to deception.

In the fourth case, Lot in Sedom (Gen. 19), the people cluster round Lot's house demanding that he bring out his two visitors so that they can be raped. Lot offers them his virgin daughters instead. Only swift action by the visitors – angels – who smite the people with blindness saves Lot's family from violence.

In the fifth case (Gen. 34), Shekhem, a local prince, rapes and abducts Dina when she "went out to visit some of the local girls," leading Shimon and Levi to practice deception and bloodshed in the course of rescuing her.

Then comes a marginal case, the story of Yehuda and Tamar, more complex than the others and not part of the

brother a thousand pieces of silver. This will allay the suspicions of everyone
17 who is with you. You are fully vindicated." Then Avraham prayed to God, and
God healed Avimelekh, his wife, and his female slaves so they could again have
18 children, for the LORD had prevented all the women in Avimelekh's household
21 1 from bearing children, because of Sara, Avraham's wife. The LORD
remembered Sara as He had said He would, and acted for Sara as He had
2 promised. Sara became pregnant and bore a son to Avraham in his old age at the
3 very time God had promised. Avraham named his newborn son, whom Sara
4 had borne him, Yitzḥak. And when Yitzḥak his son was eight days old, Avraham
5 circumcised him as God had commanded. Avraham was one hundred years old HAMISHI
6 when his son Yitzḥak was born to him. Sara said, "God has brought me laughter;
7 all those who hear will laugh with me." Then she said, "Who would have told
8 Avraham, 'Sara will nurse children'? Yet I have borne a son in his old age." The
child grew and was weaned; on the day Yitzḥak was weaned, Avraham held a
9 great feast. But Sara saw the son whom Hagar the Egyptian had borne Avraham

רש״י

הַזֶּה לָךְ "כְּסוּת עֵינַיִם לְכֹל אֲשֶׁר אִתָּךְ" – יְכַסֶּה עֵינֵיהֶם שֶׁלֹּא יְקִלּוּךְ, שֶׁאִלּוּ הֲשִׁיבוֹתִיךְ רֵיקָנִית יֵשׁ לָהֶם לוֹמַר, לְאַחַר שֶׁנִּתְעַלֵּל בָּהּ הֶחֱזִירָהּ, עַכְשָׁיו שֶׁהֻצְרַכְתִּי לְבַזְבֵּז מָמוֹן וּלְפַיְּסֵךְ, יוֹדְעִים יִהְיוּ שֶׁעַל כָּרְחִי הֲשִׁיבוֹתִיךְ וְעַל יְדֵי נֵס: **וְאֵת כֹּל.** וְעִם כָּל בָּאֵי עוֹלָם: **וְנֹכָחַת.** יְהֵא לָךְ פִּתְחוֹן פֶּה לְהִתְוַכֵּחַ וּלְהַרְאוֹת דְּבָרִים נִכָּרִים הַלָּלוּ. וּלְשׁוֹן 'הוֹכָחָה' בְּכָל מָקוֹם בֵּרוּר דְּבָרִים, וּבְלַעַז אשפרובי"ר. וְאוּנְקְלוֹס תִּרְגֵּם בְּפָנִים אֲחֵרִים, וּלְשׁוֹן הַמִּקְרָא כָּךְ הוּא נוֹפֵל עַל תַּרְגּוּמוֹ שֶׁל אוּנְקְלוֹס: הִנֵּה הוּא לָךְ כְּסוּת שֶׁל כָּבוֹד עַל הָעֵינַיִם שֶׁלִּי שֶׁשָּׁלְטוּ בָּךְ וּבְכָל אֲשֶׁר אִתָּךְ, וְעַל כֵּן תִּרְגֵּם: "וַחֲזֵית יָתִיךְ וְיָת כָּל דְּעִמִּיךְ". וְיֵשׁ מִדְרְשֵׁי אַגָּדָה, אֲבָל יִשּׁוּב לְשׁוֹן הַמִּקְרָא פֵּרַשְׁתִּי:

יז **וַיֵּלֵדוּ.** כְּתַרְגּוּמוֹ "וְאִתְרְוַחוּ", נִפְתְּחוּ נִקְבֵיהֶם וְהוֹצִיאוּ, וְהִיא לֵדָה שֶׁלָּהֶם:

יח **בְּעַד כָּל רֶחֶם.** כְּנֶגֶד כָּל פֶּתַח: **עַל דְּבַר שָׂרָה.** עַל פִּי דִּבּוּרָהּ שֶׁל שָׂרָה:

כא א **וַה׳ פָּקַד אֶת שָׂרָה.** סָמַךְ פָּרָשָׁה זוֹ לְכָאן, לְלַמֶּדְךָ שֶׁכָּל הַמְבַקֵּשׁ רַחֲמִים עַל חֲבֵרוֹ וְהוּא צָרִיךְ לְאוֹתוֹ דָּבָר הוּא נַעֲנֶה תְּחִלָּה, שֶׁנֶּאֱמַר: "וַיִּתְפַּלֵּל" וְגוֹ׳ (לעיל כ, יז) וַה׳ פָּקַד אֶת שָׂרָה", שֶׁפָּקַד כְּבָר קֹדֶם שֶׁרִפֵּא אֶת אֲבִימֶלֶךְ: **פָּקַד.** בְּהֵרָיוֹן: **כַּאֲשֶׁר דִּבֵּר.** בְּלֵדָה. וּמַה הִיא אֲמִירָה וְהֵיכָן הוּא דִּבּוּר? אֲמִירָה: "וַיֹּאמֶר אֱלֹהִים אֲבָל שָׂרָה אִשְׁתְּךָ" וְגוֹ׳ (לעיל יז, יט), דִּבּוּר: "הָיָה דְבַר ה׳ אֶל אַבְרָם" (לעיל טו, א) בִּבְרִית בֵּין הַבְּתָרִים, שָׁם נֶאֱמַר: "לֹא יִירָשְׁךָ זֶה" וְגוֹ׳ (שם ד), וְהֵבִיא הַיּוֹרֵשׁ מִשָּׂרָה: **וַיַּעַשׂ ה׳** לְשָׂרָה כַּאֲשֶׁר דִּבֵּר. לְאַבְרָהָם:

ב **לַמּוֹעֵד אֲשֶׁר דִּבֶּר אֹתוֹ.** "דְּמַלֵּיל יָתֵיהּ", אֶת הַמּוֹעֵד דִּבֶּר וְקָבַע כְּשֶׁאָמַר לוֹ: "לַמּוֹעֵד אָשׁוּב אֵלֶיךָ" (לעיל יח, יד), שָׂרַט לוֹ שְׂרִיטָה בַּכֹּתֶל, אָמַר לוֹ: כְּשֶׁתַּגִּיעַ חַמָּה לִשְׂרִיטָה זוֹ בַּשָּׁנָה הָאַחֶרֶת – תֵּלֵד:

ו **יִצְחַק לִי.** יִשְׂמַח עָלַי. וּמִדְרַשׁ אַגָּדָה, הַרְבֵּה עֲקָרוֹת נִפְקְדוּ עִמָּהּ, הַרְבֵּה חוֹלִים נִתְרַפְּאוּ בּוֹ בַּיּוֹם, הַרְבֵּה תְּפִלּוֹת נַעֲנוּ עִמָּהּ, וְרֹב שְׂחוֹק הָיָה בָּעוֹלָם:

ז **מִי מִלֵּל לְאַבְרָהָם.** לְשׁוֹן שֶׁבַח וַחֲשִׁיבוּת, רְאוּ מִי הוּא וְכַמָּה הוּא גָּדוֹל, שׁוֹמֵר הַבְטָחָתוֹ, וּמַבְטִיחַ וְעוֹשֶׂה: **מִלֵּל.** שִׁנָּה הַכָּתוּב וְלֹא אָמַר 'דִּבֶּר', גִּימַטְרִיָּא שֶׁלּוֹ מֵאָה, כְּלוֹמַר לְסוֹף מֵאָה לְאַבְרָהָם "הֵינִיקָה בָנִים שָׂרָה". וּמַהוּ 'בָּנִים' לְשׁוֹן רַבִּים? בְּיוֹם הַמִּשְׁתֶּה הֵבִיאוּ הַשָּׂרוֹת בְּנֵיהֶן עִמָּהֶן, שֶׁהָיוּ אוֹמְרוֹת: לֹא יָלְדָה שָׂרָה, אֶלָּא אֲסוּפִי הֵבִיאָה מִן הַשּׁוּק – וְהֵנִיקָה אוֹתָם:

ח **וַיִּגָּמַל.** לְסוֹף עֶשְׂרִים וְאַרְבָּעָה חֹדֶשׁ: **מִשְׁתֶּה גָדוֹל.** שֶׁהָיוּ שָׁם גְּדוֹלֵי הַדּוֹר, שֵׁם וָעֵבֶר וַאֲבִימֶלֶךְ:

ט **מְצַחֵק.** לְשׁוֹן עֲבוֹדָה זָרָה, שֶׁנֶּאֱמַר: "וַיָּקֻמוּ לְצַחֵק" (שמות לב, ו); לְשׁוֹן רְצִיחָה, "יָקוּמוּ נָא הַנְּעָרִים וִישַׂחֲקוּ לְפָנֵינוּ" (שמואל ב׳ ב, יד); לְשׁוֹן גִּלּוּי עֲרָיוֹת, כְּמוֹ: "לְצַחֶק בִּי" (להלן לט, יז). הָיָה מֵרִיב עִם יִצְחָק עַל הַיְרֻשָּׁה וְאוֹמֵר: אֲנִי בְּכוֹר וְנוֹטֵל פִּי שְׁנַיִם, וְיוֹצְאִים לַשָּׂדֶה וְנוֹטֵל קַשְׁתּוֹ וְיוֹרֶה בּוֹ חִצִּים, כְּמָה דְּאַתְּ אָמַר: "כְּמִתְלַהְלֵהַּ הַיֹּרֶה זִקִּים וְגוֹ׳ וְאָמַר הֲלֹא מְשַׂחֵק אָנִי" (משלי כו, יח-יט):

יז עֵינַיִם לְכֹל אֲשֶׁר אִתָּךְ וְאֵת־כֹּל וְנֹכָחַת׃ וַיִּתְפַּלֵּל אַבְרָהָם אֶל־הָאֱלֹהִים
יח וַיִּרְפָּא אֱלֹהִים אֶת־אֲבִימֶלֶךְ וְאֶת־אִשְׁתּוֹ וְאַמְהֹתָיו וַיֵּלֵדוּ׃ כִּי־עָצֹר
עָצַר יהוה בְּעַד כָּל־רֶחֶם לְבֵית אֲבִימֶלֶךְ עַל־דְּבַר שָׂרָה אֵשֶׁת
כא א אַבְרָהָם׃ וַיהוה פָּקַד אֶת־שָׂרָה כַּאֲשֶׁר אָמָר וַיַּעַשׂ יהוה לְשָׂרָה יח
ב כַּאֲשֶׁר דִּבֵּר׃ וַתַּהַר וַתֵּלֶד שָׂרָה לְאַבְרָהָם בֵּן לִזְקֻנָיו לַמּוֹעֵד אֲשֶׁר־
ג דִּבֶּר אֹתוֹ אֱלֹהִים׃ וַיִּקְרָא אַבְרָהָם אֶת־שֶׁם־בְּנוֹ הַנּוֹלַד־לוֹ אֲשֶׁר־
ד יָלְדָה־לּוֹ שָׂרָה יִצְחָק׃ וַיָּמָל אַבְרָהָם אֶת־יִצְחָק בְּנוֹ בֶּן־שְׁמֹנַת יָמִים
ה כַּאֲשֶׁר צִוָּה אֹתוֹ אֱלֹהִים׃ וְאַבְרָהָם בֶּן־מְאַת שָׁנָה בְּהִוָּלֶד לוֹ אֵת חמישי
ו יִצְחָק בְּנוֹ׃ וַתֹּאמֶר שָׂרָה צְחֹק עָשָׂה לִי אֱלֹהִים כָּל־הַשֹּׁמֵעַ יִצְחַק־לִי׃
ז וַתֹּאמֶר מִי מִלֵּל לְאַבְרָהָם הֵינִיקָה בָנִים שָׂרָה כִּי־יָלַדְתִּי בֵן לִזְקֻנָיו׃
ח וַיִּגְדַּל הַיֶּלֶד וַיִּגָּמַל וַיַּעַשׂ אַבְרָהָם מִשְׁתֶּה גָדוֹל בְּיוֹם הִגָּמֵל אֶת־יִצְחָק׃
ט וַתֵּרֶא שָׂרָה אֶת־בֶּן־הָגָר הַמִּצְרִית אֲשֶׁר־יָלְדָה לְאַבְרָהָם מְצַחֵק׃

אונקלוס

וחזית יתיך וית כל דעמיך, ועל כל מא דאמרת אתוכחת: יז וצלי אברהם קדם יי, ואסי יי, ית אבימלך וית אתתיה, ואמהתיה ואתרוחו: יח ארי מיחד אחד יי, באפי כל פתח ולדא לבית אבימלך, על עיסק שרה אתת אברהם: כא א ויי, דכיר ית שרה כמא דאמר, ועבד יי, לשרה כמא דמליל: ב ועדיאת וילידת שרה לאברהם, בר לסיבתוהי, לזמנא, דמליל יתיה יי: ג וקרא אברהם, ית שום בריה דאתיליד ליה, דילידת ליה שרה יצחק: ד וגזר אברהם ית יצחק בריה, בר תמניא יומין, כמא דפקיד יתיה יי: ה ואברהם בר מאה שנין, כד אתיליד ליה, ית יצחק בריה: ו ואמרת שרה, חדוא, עבד לי יי, כל דשמע יחדי לי: ז ואמרת, מהימן דאמר לאברהם וקיים, דתוניק בנין שרה, ארי ילידית בר לסיבתוהי: ח ורבא רביא ואתחסיל, ועבד אברהם משתיא רבא, ביומא דאתחסיל יצחק: ט וחזת שרה, ית בר הגר מצריתא, דילידת לאברהם מחייך:

21:3 יִצְחָק *Yitzḥak* – The name Yitzḥak means "he will laugh." Yitzḥak, the first Jewish child, hints at the fact that though we may suffer many trials, we will eventually know the laughter of joy. Jewish history has often been written in tears, but that is neither its essence nor its destiny.

21:9 מְצַחֵק *Mocking* – Literally, "laughing." The verb *tz-ḥ-k* is a recurring motif in the story of Avraham and Sara. It appears seven times in the narrative (Gen. 17:17; 18:12, 13, 15; 21:6 – twice – and 21:9), and in the Pentateuch the sevenfold repetition of a word is always significant. It signals a keyword around which the text is thematized.

Avraham "laughs" when he hears the news that he and Sara will have a son (17:17). So does Sara (18:12), for which she is rebuked by God. The name Yitzḥak, as we have seen, means "he will laugh." When he is born, Sara says, "God has brought me laughter; all those who hear will laugh with me" (21:6). *Tzḥok* has a whole range of senses, from *joy* to *disbelief*

▶

10 mocking. She said to Avraham, “Drive out that slave woman and her son, for
the son of that slave woman must not share the inheritance with my son, with
11 12 Yitzḥak.” This distressed Avraham greatly because of his son. But God told
Avraham, “Do not be distressed about the boy or about your slave. Listen to
whatever Sara tells you, because it is through Yitzḥak that your descendants
13 will be reckoned. But I will make the slave’s son too into a nation, because he is
14 your child.” Early the next morning Avraham took bread and a skin of water
and gave them to Hagar. He placed them on her shoulder, and together with
the child, he sent her away. She went wandering in the Be’er Sheva desert.
15 When the water in the skin was all gone, she cast the child away under one of
16 the bushes and went and sat down at a distance, about a bowshot away, saying,
“I cannot watch the child die.” Sitting there, at a distance, she raised her voice

רש״י

י **עִם בְּנִי עִם יִצְחָק.** מִכֵּיוָן שֶׁהוּא בְּנִי אֲפִלּוּ אִם אֵינוֹ הָגוּן כְּיִצְחָק, אוֹ הָגוּן כְּיִצְחָק אֲפִלּוּ אֵינוֹ בְּנִי, אֵין זֶה כְּדַאי לִירַשׁ עִמּוֹ, קַל וָחֹמֶר ״עִם בְּנִי עִם יִצְחָק״, שֶׁשְּׁתֵּיהֶם בּוֹ:

יא **עַל אוֹדֹת בְּנוֹ.** שֶׁיָּצָא לְתַרְבּוּת רָעָה. וּפְשׁוּטוֹ, עַל שֶׁאוֹמֶרֶת לוֹ לְשַׁלְּחוֹ:

יב **שְׁמַע בְּקֹלָהּ.** לָמַדְנוּ שֶׁהָיָה אַבְרָהָם טָפֵל לְשָׂרָה בִּנְבִיאוּת:

יד **לֶחֶם וְחֵמַת מַיִם.** וְלֹא כֶּסֶף וְזָהָב, לְפִי שֶׁהָיָה שׂוֹנְאוֹ עַל שֶׁיָּצָא לְתַרְבּוּת רָעָה: **וְאֶת הַיֶּלֶד.** אַף הַיֶּלֶד ״שָׂם עַל שִׁכְמָהּ״, שֶׁהִכְנִיסָה בּוֹ שָׂרָה עַיִן רָעָה, וַאֲחָזַתּוּ חַמָּה וְלֹא יָכֹל לֵילֵךְ בְּרַגְלָיו: **וַתֵּלֶךְ וַתֵּתַע.** חָזְרָה לְגִלּוּלֵי בֵּית אָבִיהָ:

טו **וַיִּכְלוּ הַמַּיִם.** לְפִי שֶׁדֶּרֶךְ חוֹלִים לִשְׁתּוֹת הַרְבֵּה:

טז **מִנֶּגֶד.** מֵרָחוֹק: **כִּמְטַחֲוֵי קֶשֶׁת.** כִּשְׁתֵּי טִיחוֹת, וְהוּא לְשׁוֹן יְרִיַּת חֵץ. בִּלְשׁוֹן מִשְׁנָה: ״שֶׁהִטִּיחַ בְּאִשְׁתּוֹ״, עַל שֵׁם שֶׁהַזֶּרַע יוֹרֶה כַּחֵץ. וְאִם תֹּאמַר, הָיָה לוֹ לִכְתֹּב ׳כִּמְטַחֵי קֶשֶׁת׳! מִשְׁפַּט הַוָּי״ו לִכָּנֵס לְכָאן, כְּמוֹ: ״בְּחַגְוֵי הַסֶּלַע״ (שיר השירים ב, יד) מִגִּזְרַת: ״וְהָיְתָה אַדְמַת יְהוּדָה לְמִצְרַיִם לְחָגָּא״ (ישעיה יט, יז) וּמִגִּזְרַת: ״יָחוֹגּוּ וְיָנוּעוּ כַּשִּׁכּוֹר״ (תהלים קז, כז), וְכֵן: ״קַצְוֵי אֶרֶץ״ (שם סה, ו) מִגִּזְרַת ׳קָצֶה׳: **וַתֵּשֶׁב מִנֶּגֶד.** כֵּיוָן שֶׁקָּרַב לָמוּת הוֹסִיפָה לְהִתְרַחֵק:

There is a moral reason for this complexity, and it is fundamental. Violence between groups begins in the in-group/out-group dichotomy. I identify with my side, and am suspicious of the other side. In situations of stress, sympathy for the other side can come to seem like a kind of betrayal. It is this that the Yishmael story is challenging. At the first critical juncture for the covenantal family – the birth of its first children – we feel for Sara and Yitzḥak. She is the first Jewish mother, and he the first Jewish child. *But we also feel for Hagar and Yishmael.* We enter their world, see through their eyes, empathize with their emotions. That is how the narrative is written, to enlist our sympathy. We weep with them, feeling their outcast state. *As does God.* Yishmael means “he whom God has heard.” For it is God who hears their tears, comforts them, saves them from death, and gives them His blessing.

The story of *akedat Yitzḥak* is notable for its complete absence of emotion. God commands, Avraham obeys. Throughout the ordeal Avraham says nothing to God except for one word at the beginning and the end: *Hineni,* “Here I am” (22:1, 11).

By contrast, the episode involving Hagar and Yishmael is saturated with emotion. Hagar weeps: She “went and sat down at a distance, about a bowshot away, saying, ‘I cannot watch the child die.’ Sitting there, at a distance, she raised her voice and wept” (21:16). Yishmael weeps: “God heard the boy crying” (21:17). There is a pathos here that is rare in biblical prose. There can be no doubt that the narrative is written to enlist our sympathy in a way it does not in the case of Yitzḥak. We *identify* with Hagar and Yishmael; we are *awed* by Avraham and Yitzḥak. The latter is a religious drama, the former a human one, and its very humanity gives it power.

י וַתֹּאמֶר לְאַבְרָהָם גָּרֵשׁ הָאָמָה הַזֹּאת וְאֶת־בְּנָהּ כִּי לֹא יִירַשׁ בֶּן־הָאָמָה
יא הַזֹּאת עִם־בְּנִי עִם־יִצְחָק: וַיֵּרַע הַדָּבָר מְאֹד בְּעֵינֵי אַבְרָהָם עַל אוֹדֹת
יב בְּנוֹ: וַיֹּאמֶר אֱלֹהִים אֶל־אַבְרָהָם אַל־יֵרַע בְּעֵינֶיךָ עַל־הַנַּעַר וְעַל־אֲמָתֶךָ
כֹּל אֲשֶׁר תֹּאמַר אֵלֶיךָ שָׂרָה שְׁמַע בְּקֹלָהּ כִּי בְיִצְחָק יִקָּרֵא לְךָ זָרַע:
יג יד וְגַם אֶת־בֶּן־הָאָמָה לְגוֹי אֲשִׂימֶנּוּ כִּי זַרְעֲךָ הוּא: וַיַּשְׁכֵּם אַבְרָהָם ׀
בַּבֹּקֶר וַיִּקַּח־לֶחֶם וְחֵמַת מַיִם וַיִּתֵּן אֶל־הָגָר שָׂם עַל־שִׁכְמָהּ וְאֶת־
טו הַיֶּלֶד וַיְשַׁלְּחֶהָ וַתֵּלֶךְ וַתֵּתַע בְּמִדְבַּר בְּאֵר שָׁבַע: וַיִּכְלוּ הַמַּיִם מִן־
טז הַחֵמֶת וַתַּשְׁלֵךְ אֶת־הַיֶּלֶד תַּחַת אַחַד הַשִּׂיחִם: וַתֵּלֶךְ וַתֵּשֶׁב לָהּ מִנֶּגֶד
הַרְחֵק כִּמְטַחֲוֵי קֶשֶׁת כִּי אָמְרָה אַל־אֶרְאֶה בְּמוֹת הַיָּלֶד וַתֵּשֶׁב מִנֶּגֶד

אונקלוס

י וַאֲמַרַת לְאַבְרָהָם, תָּרֵיךְ, אַמְתָא הָדָא וְיָת בְּרַהּ, אֲרֵי לָא יֵירַת בַּר אַמְתָא הָדָא, עִם בְּרִי עִם יִצְחָק: יא וּבְאֵישׁ פִּתְגָּמָא, לַחֲדָא בְּעֵינֵי אַבְרָהָם, עַל עֵיסַק בְּרֵיהּ: יב וַאֲמַר יי לְאַבְרָהָם, לָא יִבְאַשׁ בְּעֵינָךְ עַל עוּלֵימָא וְעַל אַמְתָךְ, כֹּל דְּתֵימַר לָךְ, שָׂרָה קַבֵּיל מִנַּהּ, אֲרֵי בְיִצְחָק, יִתְקְרוֹן לָךְ בְּנִין: יג וְאַף יָת בַּר אַמְתָא לְעַמָּא אֲשַׁוֵּינֵיהּ, אֲרֵי בְרָךְ הוּא: יד וְאַקְדֵּים אַבְרָהָם בְּצַפְרָא, וּנְסֵיב לַחְמָא וְרָקְבָא דְמַיָּא, וִיהַב לְהָגָר, שַׁוִּי עַל כַּתְפַּהּ, וְיָת רַבְיָא וְשַׁלְּחַהּ, וַאֲזַלַת וּטְעָת, בְּמַדְבַּר בְּאֵר שָׁבַע: טו וּשְׁלִימוּ מַיָּא מִן רָקְבָא, וּרְמַת יָת רַבְיָא, תְּחוֹת חַד מִן אִילָנַיָּא: טז וַאֲזַלַת וִיתֵיבַת לַהּ מִקָּבֵיל, אַרְחֵיקַת כְּמֵיגַד בְּקַשְׁתָּא, אֲרֵי אֲמַרַת, לָא אֶחֱזֵי בְּמוֹתֵיהּ דְּרַבְיָא, וִיתֵיבַת מִקָּבֵיל,

to *disdain*. In a later chapter it even has sexual undertones: "enjoying himself (with his wife)" (26:8). At this point the text is deliberately ambiguous, leaving it to us, the readers, to decide whether Sara is right to take offense (Yishmael is mocking) or wrong (he is sharing in the general celebration).

Sara's judgment, however, is unambiguous, her tone dismissive: "Drive out that *slave woman* and her son, for the son of that slave woman must not share the inheritance with my son, with Yitzḥak" (21:10). Not only does she not dignify either mother or child by calling them by name; her language has changed since chapter 16. Then she called Hagar a "maid" (*shifḥa*). Now she has become a "slave" (*ama*).

21:13 כִּי זַרְעֲךָ הוּא *Because he is your child* – The text makes a fine distinction between biological and ascribed identity. Yishmael, says God to Avraham, "*is* your child" (Gen. 21:13) while "it is through Yitzḥak that *your descendants will be reckoned*" (21:12). The former promises worldly greatness, the latter covenantal *responsibility*. Yet God recognizes that Yishmael *remains Avraham's son and will be blessed accordingly*.

THE BANISHMENT OF YISHMAEL

In general, the Hebrew Bible is highly reticent in telling us about people's emotional states. The scenes involving Hagar, however, are etched with emotional intensity.

To understand the significance of this, we have to realize that Genesis 21, the sending away of Yishmael, is parallel to Genesis 22, *akedat Yitzḥak*. In both, Avraham undergoes a trial involving the potential loss of a son. Yishmael and Yitzḥak, the two children, are both only dimly aware of what is happening. In both, they are about to die until Heaven intervenes, in the first case by providing a well of water, in the second, a ram to be offered as a sacrifice in Yitzḥak's place. The similarities serve to highlight the differences.

▶

24
25 you." Avraham said, "I swear." Then Avraham rebuked Avimelekh for the well
26 of water that Avimelekh's servants had seized. But Avimelekh said, "I do not
know who has done this. You did not tell me; I had not heard about it until
27 today." Avraham then brought sheep and cattle and gave them to Avimelekh,
28 and the two of them forged a covenant. Avraham set apart seven ewe lambs
29 from the flock. Avimelekh asked him, "What is the meaning of these seven
30 ewe lambs you have set apart?" He replied, "Accept these seven lambs from me
31 as testimony that I dug this well." That is why that place is called Be'er Sheva,
32 because there the two men swore an oath. Thus they made a pact at Be'er
Sheva. And then Avimelekh and Pikhol, commander of his troops, returned to
33 the land of the Philistines. Avraham planted a tamarisk tree in Be'er Sheva, and
34 there he called on the name of the LORD, the Everlasting God. Avraham stayed
on in the land of the Philistines for many days.
22 1 After these things, God tested Avraham. "Avraham!" He said. And Avraham SHEVI'I

SHEVI'I

רש״י

כה **וְהוֹכִחַ.** נִתְוַכַּח עִמּוֹ עַל כָּךְ:

ל **בַּעֲבוּר תִּהְיֶה לִּי.** זֹאת, "לְעֵדָה" – לְשׁוֹן עֵדוּת שֶׁל נְקֵבָה, כְּמוֹ: "וְעֵדָה הַמַּצֵּבָה" (להלן לא, נב): **כִּי חָפַרְתִּי אֶת הַבְּאֵר.** מְרִיבִים הָיוּ עָלֶיהָ רוֹעֵי אֲבִימֶלֶךְ וְאוֹמְרִים: אֲנַחְנוּ חֲפַרְנוּהָ; אָמְרוּ בֵּינֵיהֶם, כָּל מִי שֶׁיִּתְרָאֶה עַל הַבְּאֵר וְיַעֲלוּ הַמַּיִם לִקְרָאתוֹ שֶׁלּוֹ הִיא, וְעָלוּ לִקְרַאת אַבְרָהָם:

לג **אֶשֶׁל.** רַב וּשְׁמוּאֵל, חַד אָמַר: פַּרְדֵּס לְהָבִיא מִמֶּנּוּ פֵּרוֹת לְאוֹרְחִים בַּסְּעוּדָה; וְחַד אָמַר: פֻּנְדָּק לְאַכְסַנְיָא וּבוֹ כָּל מִינֵי פֵּרוֹת. וּמָצִינוּ לְשׁוֹן נְטִיעָה בְּאֹהָלִים, שֶׁנֶּאֱמַר: "וְיִטַּע אָהֳלֵי אַפַּדְנוֹ" (דניאל יא, מה): **וַיִּקְרָא שָׁם וְגוֹ׳.** עַל יְדֵי אוֹתוֹ אֵשֶׁל הִקְרָא שְׁמוֹ שֶׁל הַקָּדוֹשׁ בָּרוּךְ הוּא אֱלוֹהַּ לְכָל הָעוֹלָם; לְאַחַר שֶׁאוֹכְלִים וְשׁוֹתִים אוֹמֵר לָהֶם: בָּרְכוּ לְמִי שֶׁאֲכַלְתֶּם מִשֶּׁלּוֹ; סְבוּרִים אַתֶּם שֶׁמִּשֶּׁלִּי אֲכַלְתֶּם? מִשֶּׁל מִי שֶׁאָמַר וְהָיָה הָעוֹלָם אֲכַלְתֶּם:

לד **יָמִים רַבִּים.** מְרֻבִּים עַל שֶׁל חֶבְרוֹן; בְּחֶבְרוֹן עָשָׂה עֶשְׂרִים וְחָמֵשׁ שָׁנָה וְכָאן עֶשְׂרִים וָשֵׁשׁ, שֶׁהֲרֵי בֶּן שִׁבְעִים וְחָמֵשׁ שָׁנָה הָיָה בְּצֵאתוֹ מֵחָרָן, אוֹתָהּ שָׁנָה "וַיָּבֹא וַיֵּשֶׁב בְּאֵלֹנֵי מַמְרֵא" (לעיל יג, יח), שֶׁלֹּא מָצִינוּ קֹדֶם לָכֵן שֶׁנִּתְיַשֵּׁב אֶלָּא שָׁם, שֶׁבְּכָל מְקוֹמוֹתָיו הָיָה כְּאוֹרֵחַ חוֹנֶה וְנוֹסֵעַ וְהוֹלֵךְ, שֶׁנֶּאֱמַר: "וַיַּעֲבֹר אַבְרָם" (לעיל יב, ו), "וַיַּעְתֵּק מִשָּׁם" (שם פסוק ח), "וַיְהִי רָעָב בָּאָרֶץ וַיֵּרֶד אַבְרָם מִצְרַיְמָה" (שם פסוק י), וּבְמִצְרַיִם לֹא עָשָׂה אֶלָּא שְׁלֹשָׁה חֳדָשִׁים, שֶׁהֲרֵי שִׁלְּחוּ פַּרְעֹה, מִיָּד "וַיֵּלֶךְ לְמַסָּעָיו" (לעיל יג, ג) עַד "וַיָּבֹא וַיֵּשֶׁב בְּאֵלֹנֵי מַמְרֵא אֲשֶׁר בְּחֶבְרוֹן" (שם פסוק יח), שָׁם יָשַׁב עַד שֶׁנֶּהֶפְכָה סְדוֹם, מִיָּד "וַיִּסַּע מִשָּׁם אַבְרָהָם" (לעיל כ, א) מִפְּנֵי בּוּשָׁה שֶׁל לוֹט, וּבָא לְאֶרֶץ פְּלִשְׁתִּים, וּבֶן תִּשְׁעִים וְתֵשַׁע שָׁנָה הָיָה, שֶׁהֲרֵי בַּשְּׁלִישִׁי לְמִילָתוֹ בָּאוּ אֶצְלוֹ הַמַּלְאָכִים, הֲרֵי עֶשְׂרִים וְחָמֵשׁ שָׁנָה, וְכָאן כְּתִיב: "יָמִים רַבִּים" – מְרֻבִּים עַל הָרִאשׁוֹנִים, וְלֹא בָא הַכָּתוּב לִסְתֹּם אֶלָּא לְפָרֵשׁ, וְאִם הָיוּ מְרֻבִּים עֲלֵיהֶם שְׁתֵּי שָׁנִים אוֹ יוֹתֵר הָיָה מְפָרְשָׁם, עַל כָּרְחֲךָ אֵינָם יְתֵרִים יוֹתֵר מִשָּׁנָה, הֲרֵי עֶשְׂרִים וְשֵׁשׁ שָׁנָה. מִיָּד יָצָא מִשָּׁם וְחָזַר לְחֶבְרוֹן, וְאוֹתָהּ שָׁנָה קָדְמָה לִפְנֵי עֲקֵדָתוֹ שֶׁל יִצְחָק שְׁתֵּים עֶשְׂרֵה שָׁנִים. כָּךְ שְׁנוּיָה בְּסֵדֶר עוֹלָם:

כב א **אַחַר הַדְּבָרִים הָאֵלֶּה.** יֵשׁ מֵרַבּוֹתֵינוּ אוֹמְרִים: אַחַר דְּבָרָיו שֶׁל שָׂטָן שֶׁהָיָה מְקַטְרֵג וְאוֹמֵר: מִכָּל סְעוּדָה שֶׁעָשָׂה אַבְרָהָם לֹא הִקְרִיב לְפָנֶיךָ פַּר אֶחָד אוֹ אַיִל אֶחָד. אָמַר לוֹ: כְּלוּם עָשָׂה אֶלָּא בִּשְׁבִיל בְּנוֹ, אִלּוּ הָיִיתִי אוֹמֵר לוֹ: זְבַח אוֹתוֹ לְפָנַי, לֹא הָיָה מְעַכֵּב. וְיֵשׁ אוֹמְרִים: אַחַר דְּבָרָיו שֶׁל יִשְׁמָעֵאל שֶׁהָיָה מִתְפָּאֵר עַל יִצְחָק, שֶׁמָּל בֶּן שְׁלֹשׁ עֶשְׂרֵה שָׁנָה וְלֹא מִחָה. אָמַר לוֹ יִצְחָק: בְּאֵבֶר אֶחָד אַתָּה מְיָרְאֵנִי, אִלּוּ אָמַר לִי הַקָּדוֹשׁ בָּרוּךְ הוּא: זְבַח עַצְמְךָ לְפָנַי, לֹא הָיִיתִי מְעַכֵּב:

He redeemed them from slavery. Therefore they cannot be turned into permanent slaves: "For they are My servants whom I brought out from Egypt: they cannot be sold as slaves" (Lev. 25:42).

כד עִמָּדִי וְעִם־הָאָרֶץ אֲשֶׁר־גַּרְתָּה בָּהּ: וַיֹּאמֶר אַבְרָהָם אָנֹכִי אִשָּׁבֵעַ:
כה וְהוֹכִחַ אַבְרָהָם אֶת־אֲבִימֶלֶךְ עַל־אֹדוֹת בְּאֵר הַמַּיִם אֲשֶׁר גָּזְלוּ עַבְדֵי
כו אֲבִימֶלֶךְ: וַיֹּאמֶר אֲבִימֶלֶךְ לֹא יָדַעְתִּי מִי עָשָׂה אֶת־הַדָּבָר הַזֶּה וְגַם־
כז אַתָּה לֹא־הִגַּדְתָּ לִּי וְגַם אָנֹכִי לֹא שָׁמַעְתִּי בִּלְתִּי הַיּוֹם: וַיִּקַּח אַבְרָהָם
כח צֹאן וּבָקָר וַיִּתֵּן לַאֲבִימֶלֶךְ וַיִּכְרְתוּ שְׁנֵיהֶם בְּרִית: וַיַּצֵּב אַבְרָהָם אֶת־
כט שֶׁבַע כִּבְשֹׂת הַצֹּאן לְבַדְּהֶן: וַיֹּאמֶר אֲבִימֶלֶךְ אֶל־אַבְרָהָם מָה הֵנָּה
ל שֶׁבַע כְּבָשֹׂת הָאֵלֶּה אֲשֶׁר הִצַּבְתָּ לְבַדָּנָה: וַיֹּאמֶר כִּי אֶת־שֶׁבַע כְּבָשֹׂת
תִּקַּח מִיָּדִי בַּעֲבוּר תִּהְיֶה־לִּי לְעֵדָה כִּי חָפַרְתִּי אֶת־הַבְּאֵר הַזֹּאת:
לא לב עַל־כֵּן קָרָא לַמָּקוֹם הַהוּא בְּאֵר שָׁבַע כִּי שָׁם נִשְׁבְּעוּ שְׁנֵיהֶם: וַיִּכְרְתוּ
בְרִית בִּבְאֵר שָׁבַע וַיָּקָם אֲבִימֶלֶךְ וּפִיכֹל שַׂר־צְבָאוֹ וַיָּשֻׁבוּ אֶל־אֶרֶץ
לג פְּלִשְׁתִּים: וַיִּטַּע אֵשֶׁל בִּבְאֵר שָׁבַע וַיִּקְרָא־שָׁם בְּשֵׁם יְהוָה אֵל עוֹלָם:
לד וַיָּגָר אַבְרָהָם בְּאֶרֶץ פְּלִשְׁתִּים יָמִים רַבִּים:
כב א וַיְהִי אַחַר הַדְּבָרִים הָאֵלֶּה וְהָאֱלֹהִים נִסָּה אֶת־אַבְרָהָם וַיֹּאמֶר אֵלָיו יט שביעי

אונקלוס

עִמִּי, וְעִם אַרְעָא דְּאִתּוֹתַבְתְּ בַּהּ: כד וַאֲמַר אַבְרָהָם, אֲנָא אֲקַיֵּים: כה וְאוֹכַח אַבְרָהָם יָת אֲבִימֶלֶךְ, עַל עֵיסַק בֵּירָא דְמַיָּא, דַּאֲנַסוּ עַבְדֵי אֲבִימֶלֶךְ: כו וַאֲמַר אֲבִימֶלֶךְ, לָא יְדַעִית, מַאן עֲבַד יָת פִּתְגָמָא הָדֵין, וְאַף אַתְּ לָא חַוֵּית לִי, וְאַף אֲנָא, לָא שְׁמַעִית אֱלָהֵין יוֹמָא דֵין: כז וּדְבַר אַבְרָהָם עָן וְתוֹרִין, וִיהַב לַאֲבִימֶלֶךְ, וּגְזַרוּ תַּרְוֵיהוֹן קְיָם: כח וַאֲקֵים אַבְרָהָם, יָת שְׁבַע, חוּרְפָן דְּעָן בִּלְחוֹדֵיהוֹן: כט וַאֲמַר אֲבִימֶלֶךְ לְאַבְרָהָם, מָא אִנּוּן, שְׁבַע חוּרְפָן אִלֵּין, דַּאֲקֵימְתָּא בִּלְחוֹדֵיהוֹן: ל וַאֲמַר, אֲרֵי יָת שְׁבַע חוּרְפָן, תְּקַבֵּיל מִן יְדִי, בְּדִיל דִּתְהֵי לִי לְסָהֲדוּ, אֲרֵי חֲפַרִית יָת בֵּירָא הָדָא: לא עַל כֵּן, קְרָא, לְאַתְרָא הַהוּא בְּאֵר שָׁבַע, אֲרֵי, תַּמָּן קַיִּימוּ תַּרְוֵיהוֹן: לב וּגְזַרוּ קְיָם בִּבְאֵר שָׁבַע, וְקָם אֲבִימֶלֶךְ, וּפִיכֹל רַב חֵילֵיהּ, וְתָבוּ לַאֲרַע פְּלִשְׁתָּאֵי: לג וּנְצַב נִצְבָּא בִּבְאֵר שָׁבַע, וְצַלִּי תַמָּן, בִּשְׁמָא דַייָ אֱלָהּ עָלְמָא: לד וְאִתּוֹתַב אַבְרָהָם, בַּאֲרַע פְּלִשְׁתָּאֵי יוֹמִין סַגִּיאִין: כב א וַהֲוָה, בָּתַר פִּתְגָמַיָּא הָאִלֵּין, וַייָ, נַסִּי יָת אַבְרָהָם, וַאֲמַר לֵיהּ,

AKEDAT YITZḤAK

Throughout Tanakh, the gravest sin is child sacrifice. The Torah and Prophets denounce it in the strongest terms. Mesha king of Moab uses it in his campaign against Israel (II Kings 3:26–27). How can the Torah regard as Avraham's supreme achievement that he was willing to do what the worst of idolaters do?

To answer this fully, we must consider an overriding theme of the Torah as a whole. First principle: God owns the land of Israel. That is why He can command the return of property to its original owners in the Jubilee year: "The land shall not be sold in perpetuity, for the land is Mine. You are merely migrants and visitors to Me" (Lev. 25:23).

Second principle: God owns the children of Israel since

2 replied, "Here I am." Then God said, "Take your son, your only one, the one
whom you love – Yitzḥak – and go to the land of Moria. There, offer him up as
3 a burnt offering on one of the mountains, the one that I will show you." Early
the next morning Avraham rose and saddled his donkey. With him he took two
of his young men and Yitzḥak his son. He cut wood for the offering and set
4 out toward the place of which God had told him. On the third day Avraham
5 looked up and, in the distance, he saw the place. He told his young men, "Stay
here with the donkey. I and the boy will go there and worship. Then we will

רש״י

הִנֵּנִי. כָּךְ הִיא עֲנִיָּתָם שֶׁל חֲסִידִים, לְשׁוֹן עֲנָוָה הוּא וּלְשׁוֹן זִמּוּן:

ב **קַח נָא.** אֵין 'נָא' אֶלָּא לְשׁוֹן בַּקָּשָׁה, אָמַר לוֹ: בְּבַקָּשָׁה מִמְּךָ עֲמֹד לִי בָּזוֹ, שֶׁלֹּא יֹאמְרוּ: הָרִאשׁוֹנוֹת לֹא הָיָה בָּהֶן מַמָּשׁ: **אֶת בִּנְךָ.** אָמַר לוֹ: שְׁנֵי בָנִים יֵשׁ לִי. אָמַר לוֹ: "אֶת יְחִידְךָ". אָמַר לוֹ: זֶה יָחִיד לְאִמּוֹ וְזֶה יָחִיד לְאִמּוֹ. אָמַר לוֹ: "אֲשֶׁר אָהַבְתָּ". אָמַר לוֹ: שְׁנֵיהֶם אֲנִי אוֹהֵב. אָמַר לוֹ: "אֶת יִצְחָק". וְלָמָּה לֹא גִּלָּה לוֹ מִתְּחִלָּה? שֶׁלֹּא לְעַרְבְּבוֹ פִּתְאוֹם וְתָזוּחַ דַּעְתּוֹ עָלָיו וְתִטָּרֵף, וּכְדֵי לְחַבֵּב עָלָיו אֶת הַמִּצְוָה וְלִתֵּן לוֹ שָׂכָר עַל כָּל דִּבּוּר וְדִבּוּר: **אֶרֶץ הַמֹּרִיָּה.** יְרוּשָׁלַיִם. וְכֵן בְּדִבְרֵי הַיָּמִים (ב׳ ג, א): "לִבְנוֹת אֶת בֵּית ה׳ בִּירוּשָׁלַיִם בְּהַר הַמּוֹרִיָּה". וְרַבּוֹתֵינוּ פֵּרְשׁוּ, עַל שֵׁם שֶׁמִּשָּׁם הוֹרָאָה יוֹצְאָה לְיִשְׂרָאֵל. וְאוּנְקְלוֹס תִּרְגְּמוֹ עַל שֵׁם עֲבוֹדַת הַקְּטֹרֶת שֶׁיֵּשׁ בּוֹ מוֹר נֵרְדְּ וּשְׁאָר בְּשָׂמִים: **וְהַעֲלֵהוּ.** לֹא אָמַר לוֹ 'שְׁחָטֵהוּ', לְפִי שֶׁלֹּא הָיָה חָפֵץ הַקָּדוֹשׁ בָּרוּךְ הוּא לְשָׁחֲטוֹ אֶלָּא לְהַעֲלֵהוּ לָהָר לַעֲשׂוֹתוֹ עוֹלָה, וּמִשֶּׁהֶעֱלָהוּ אָמַר לוֹ הוֹרִידֵהוּ: **אַחַד הֶהָרִים.** הַקָּדוֹשׁ בָּרוּךְ הוּא מַתְהֶא הַצַּדִּיקִים וְאַחַר כָּךְ מְגַלֶּה לָהֶם, וְכָל זֶה כְּדֵי לְהַרְבּוֹת שְׂכָרָן, וְכֵן: "אֶל הָאָרֶץ אֲשֶׁר אַרְאֶךָּ" (לעיל יב, א), וְכֵן בְּיוֹנָה: "וּקְרָא אֵלֶיהָ אֶת הַקְּרִיאָה" (יונה ג, ב):

ג **וַיַּשְׁכֵּם.** נִזְדָּרֵז לַמִּצְוָה: **וַיַּחֲבֹשׁ.** הוּא בְּעַצְמוֹ, וְלֹא צִוָּה לְאֶחָד מֵעֲבָדָיו, שֶׁהָאַהֲבָה מְקַלְקֶלֶת הַשּׁוּרָה: **אֶת שְׁנֵי נְעָרָיו.** יִשְׁמָעֵאל וֶאֱלִיעֶזֶר, שֶׁאֵין אָדָם חָשׁוּב רַשַּׁאי לָצֵאת לַדֶּרֶךְ בְּלֹא שְׁנֵי אֲנָשִׁים, שֶׁאִם יִצְטָרֵךְ הָאֶחָד לִנְקָבָיו וְיִתְרַחֵק יִהְיֶה הַשֵּׁנִי עִמּוֹ: **וַיְבַקַּע.** "וַצְלַח", כְּמוֹ: "וְצָלְחוּ הַיַּרְדֵּן" (שמואל ב׳ יט, יח), לְשׁוֹן בִּקּוּעַ, פינדר״א בְּלַעַז:

ד **בַּיּוֹם הַשְּׁלִישִׁי.** לָמָּה אֵחַר מִלְּהַרְאוֹתוֹ מִיָּד? כְּדֵי שֶׁלֹּא יֹאמְרוּ: הֱמָמוֹ וְעִרְבְּבוֹ פִּתְאוֹם וְטָרַף דַּעְתּוֹ, וְאִלּוּ הָיָה לוֹ שָׁהוּת לְהִמָּלֵךְ אֶל לִבּוֹ לֹא הָיָה עוֹשֶׂה: **וַיַּרְא אֶת הַמָּקוֹם.** רָאָה עָנָן קָשׁוּר עַל הָהָר:

ה **עַד כֹּה.** כְּלוֹמַר, דֶּרֶךְ מוּעָט לַמָּקוֹם אֲשֶׁר לְפָנֵינוּ. וּמִדְרַשׁ אַגָּדָה, אֶרְאֶה הֵיכָן הוּא מַה שֶּׁאָמַר לִי הַמָּקוֹם: "כֹּה יִהְיֶה זַרְעֶךָ" (לעיל טו, ה):

In ancient times, and in antiquity in Greece and Rome, the basic social unit was not the individual but the family, under the absolute rule of its male head. The Torah was a radical break with this mindset. Monotheism was more than simply the belief in one God. Because each human was in His image, and because each could be in direct relationship with Him, the individual was suddenly given significance – not just fathers but also mothers, and not just parents but also children. No longer were they fused into a single unit, with a single controlling will. They were each to become persons in their own right, with their own identity and integrity.

First separate, then connect. That seems to be the Jewish way. That is how God created the universe, by first separating domains – day and night, upper and lower waters, sea and dry land – then allowing them to be filled. And that is how we create real personal relationships. By separating and leaving space for the other. Parents should not seek to control children. Spouses should not seek to control one another. It is the carefully calibrated distance between us in which relationship allows each party to grow.

Changes like this do not happen overnight, and they do not happen without wrenching dislocations. That is what is happening at both ends of the Avraham story. At the beginning of his mission, Avraham is told to separate himself from his father, and toward the end he is told to separate himself, in different ways, from each of his two sons. God tells him to listen to Sara and send Yishmael away. God tells him to sacrifice Yitzḥak, "your son, your only one, the one whom you love." These painful episodes are extreme representations – the agonizing birth pangs – of a new way of thinking about humanity.

ב אַבְרָהָם וַיֹּאמֶר הִנֵּנִי: וַיֹּאמֶר קַח־נָא אֶת־בִּנְךָ אֶת־יְחִידְךָ אֲשֶׁר־
אָהַבְתָּ אֶת־יִצְחָק וְלֶךְ־לְךָ אֶל־אֶרֶץ הַמֹּרִיָּה וְהַעֲלֵהוּ שָׁם לְעֹלָה
ג עַל אַחַד הֶהָרִים אֲשֶׁר אֹמַר אֵלֶיךָ: וַיַּשְׁכֵּם אַבְרָהָם בַּבֹּקֶר וַיַּחֲבֹשׁ
אֶת־חֲמֹרוֹ וַיִּקַּח אֶת־שְׁנֵי נְעָרָיו אִתּוֹ וְאֵת יִצְחָק בְּנוֹ וַיְבַקַּע עֲצֵי עֹלָה
ד וַיָּקָם וַיֵּלֶךְ אֶל־הַמָּקוֹם אֲשֶׁר־אָמַר־לוֹ הָאֱלֹהִים: בַּיּוֹם הַשְּׁלִישִׁי וַיִּשָּׂא
ה אַבְרָהָם אֶת־עֵינָיו וַיַּרְא אֶת־הַמָּקוֹם מֵרָחֹק: וַיֹּאמֶר אַבְרָהָם אֶל־
נְעָרָיו שְׁבוּ־לָכֶם פֹּה עִם־הַחֲמוֹר וַאֲנִי וְהַנַּעַר נֵלְכָה עַד־כֹּה וְנִשְׁתַּחֲוֶה

אונקלוס

אַבְרָהָם וַאֲמַר הָאֲנָא: ב וַאֲמַר, דְּבַר כְּעַן, יָת בְּרָךְ יָת יְחִידָךְ דִּרְחֵימְתָּא יָת יִצְחָק, וְאִיזֵיל לָךְ, לַאֲרַע פֻּלְחָנָא, וְאַסֵּיקְהִי קֳדָמַי תַּמָּן לַעֲלָתָא, עַל חַד מִן טוּרַיָּא, דְּאֵימַר לָךְ: ג וְאַקְדֵּים אַבְרָהָם בְּצַפְרָא, וְזָרֵיז יָת חֲמָרֵיהּ, וּדְבַר, יָת תְּרֵין עוּלֵימוֹהִי עִמֵּיהּ, וְיָת יִצְחָק בְּרֵיהּ, וְצַלַּח אָעֵי לַעֲלָתָא, וְקָם וַאֲזַל, לְאַתְרָא דַּאֲמַר לֵיהּ יְיָ: ד בְּיוֹמָא תְּלִיתָאָה, וּזְקַף אַבְרָהָם יָת עֵינוֹהִי, וַחֲזָא יָת אַתְרָא מֵרָחִיק: ה וַאֲמַר אַבְרָהָם לְעוּלֵימוֹהִי, אוֹרִיכוּ לְכוֹן הָכָא עִם חֲמָרָא, וַאֲנָא וְעוּלֵימָא, נִתְמְטֵי עַד כָּא, וְנִסְגּוֹד

Third principle: God is the ultimate owner of all that exists. That is why we must make a blessing over anything we enjoy (Berakhot 35a).

This is the jurisprudential basis of the whole of Jewish law. God created the universe. Therefore, God is the ultimate owner of the universe. The legal term for this is "eminent domain." God has the right to prescribe the conditions under which we may benefit from the universe. It is to establish this legal fact – not to tell us about the cosmology of the Big Bang – that the Torah begins with the story of creation.

In the ancient world, up to and including the time of the Roman Empire, children were considered the legal property of their parents. They had no rights. Under the Roman principle of *patria potestas*, a father could do whatever he wished with his child, including putting him to death. Infanticide was well known in antiquity.

It is this principle that underlies the entire practice of child sacrifice, which was widespread throughout the pagan world. The Torah is horrified by child sacrifice, which it sees as the worst of all sins. It therefore seeks to establish, in the case of children, what it establishes in the case of the universe as a whole, the land of Israel, and the people of Israel. We do not own our children. We are merely their guardians on God's behalf.

Only the most dramatic event could establish an idea so revolutionary and unprecedented in the ancient world. That is what the story of *akedat Yitzḥak* is about. When the angel calls to Avraham, "Do not lift your hand against the boy… for you have not withheld from Me your son" (Gen. 22:12), this is what it means. God does not want Avraham to sacrifice his child. God wants him to renounce ownership of his child – then to "do nothing to him." The story of the *akeda* is a polemic against the idea, universal to all pagan cultures, that children are the property of their parents.

22:2 לֶךְ־לְךָ *Go* – God's words "go (*lekh lekha*) to the land of Moria" inevitably remind us of God's first summons: "Go (*Lekh lekha*) from your land, your birthplace, and your father's house" (Gen. 12:1). These are the only two places in which this phrase occurs in the Torah. Avraham's last trial echoes his first. Note that the first trial meant that Avraham had to abandon his father, thereby looking as if he were neglecting his duties as a son. So, whether as a father to his sons or as a son to his father, Avraham is commanded to act in ways that seem the exact opposite of what we would expect and how we should behave. This is too strange to be accidental. Essentially, what we are seeing in these events is *the birth of the individual.*

6 come back to you." Avraham took the wood for the offering and placed it on
Yitzḥak his son. He himself took the fire and the knife. The two of them walked
7 together. Then Yitzḥak said to his father, Avraham, "Father?" Avraham said,
"Here I am, my son." Yitzḥak said, "Here is the fire and the wood, but where is
8 the lamb for the burnt offering?" And Avraham replied, "God will see to a lamb
9 for an offering, my son." The two of them walked on together. They came to
the place of which God had spoken. There Avraham built an altar and arranged
the wood. Then he bound Yitzḥak his son and laid him on the altar on top of
10 the wood. Avraham reached out his hand and took hold of the knife to slay his
11 son. But an angel of the LORD called out to him from the heavens, "Avraham!
12 Avraham!" He said, "Here I am." "Do not lift your hand against the boy; do
nothing to him, for now I know that you fear God: for you have not withheld
13 from Me your son, your only one." Avraham looked up and saw a ram caught in
a thicket by its horns. Avraham went, took hold of the ram, and offered it up as
14 a burnt offering in place of his son. And Avraham named the place The LORD
Will See. To this day it is said, "On the mountain of the LORD, He will be seen."

רש״י

וְנָשׁוּבָה. נִתְנַבֵּא שֶׁיָּשׁוּבוּ שְׁנֵיהֶם:

ו **הַמַּאֲכֶלֶת.** סַכִּין, עַל שֵׁם שֶׁאוֹכֶלֶת אֶת הַבָּשָׂר, כְּמָה דְּתֵימָא: "וְחַרְבִּי תֹּאכַל בָּשָׂר" (דברים לב, מב), וְשֶׁמַּכְשֶׁרֶת בָּשָׂר לַאֲכִילָה. דָּבָר אַחֵר, זֹאת נִקְרֵאת מַאֲכֶלֶת, עַל שֵׁם שֶׁיִּשְׂרָאֵל אוֹכְלִים מַתַּן שְׂכָרָהּ: **וַיֵּלְכוּ שְׁנֵיהֶם יַחְדָּו.** אַבְרָהָם שֶׁהָיָה יוֹדֵעַ שֶׁהוֹלֵךְ לִשְׁחֹט אֶת בְּנוֹ, הָיָה הוֹלֵךְ בִּרְצוֹן וְשִׂמְחָה כְּיִצְחָק שֶׁלֹּא הָיָה מַרְגִּישׁ בַּדָּבָר:

ח **יִרְאֶה לוֹ הַשֶּׂה.** כְּלוֹמַר, יִרְאֶה וְיִבְחַר לוֹ הַשֶּׂה, וְאִם אֵין שֶׂה – "לְעֹלָה בְּנִי". וְאַף עַל פִּי שֶׁהֵבִין יִצְחָק שֶׁהוּא הוֹלֵךְ לְהִשָּׁחֵט, "וַיֵּלְכוּ שְׁנֵיהֶם יַחְדָּו" בְּלֵב שָׁוֶה:

ט **וַיַּעֲקֹד.** יָדָיו וְרַגְלָיו מֵאֲחוֹרָיו. הַיָּדַיִם וְהָרַגְלַיִם בְּיַחַד הִיא עֲקֵדָה, וְהוּא לְשׁוֹן 'עֲקֻדִּים' (להלן ל, לט) שֶׁהָיוּ קַרְסֻלֵּיהֶם לְבָנִים, מָקוֹם שֶׁעוֹקְדִים אוֹתָן בּוֹ הָיָה נִכָּר:

יא **אַבְרָהָם אַבְרָהָם.** לְשׁוֹן חִבָּה הוּא, שֶׁכּוֹפֵל אֶת שְׁמוֹ:

יב **אַל תִּשְׁלַח.** לִשְׁחֹט. אָמַר לוֹ: אֶלָּא לְחִנָּם בָּאתִי לְכָאן? אֶעֱשֶׂה בּוֹ חֲבָלָה וְאוֹצִיא מְעַט דָּם! אָמַר לוֹ: "אַל תַּעַשׂ לוֹ מְאוּמָה": **כִּי עַתָּה יָדַעְתִּי.** מֵעַתָּה יֵשׁ לִי מַה אָשִׁיב לַשָּׂטָן וְלָאֻמּוֹת, הַתְּמֵהִים מַה הִיא חִבָּתִי אֶצְלְךָ, יָדַעְתִּי לִי פִּתְחוֹן פֶּה עַכְשָׁיו, שֶׁרוֹאִים "כִּי יְרֵא אֱלֹהִים אַתָּה":

יג **וְהִנֵּה אַיִל.** מוּכָן הָיָה לְכָךְ מִשֵּׁשֶׁת יְמֵי בְרֵאשִׁית: **אַחַר.** אַחֲרֵי שֶׁאָמַר לוֹ הַמַּלְאָךְ: "אַל תִּשְׁלַח יָדְךָ" רָאָהוּ כְּשֶׁהוּא נֶאֱחָז, וְהוּא שֶׁמְּתַרְגְּמִינַן: "וּזְקַף אַבְרָהָם יָת עֵינוֹהִי בָּתַר אִלֵּין": **בַּסְּבַךְ.** אִילָן: **בְּקַרְנָיו.** שֶׁהָיָה רָץ אֵצֶל אַבְרָהָם, וְהַשָּׂטָן סוֹבְכוֹ וּמְעַרְבְּבוֹ בָּאִילָנוֹת: **תַּחַת בְּנוֹ.** מֵאַחַר שֶׁכָּתוּב: "וַיַּעֲלֵהוּ לְעֹלָה" לֹא חָסֵר הַמִּקְרָא כְּלוּם, מַהוּ "תַּחַת בְּנוֹ"? עַל כָּל עֲבוֹדָה שֶׁעָשָׂה מִמֶּנּוּ הָיָה מִתְפַּלֵּל וְאוֹמֵר: יְהִי רָצוֹן שֶׁתְּהֵא זוֹ כְּאִלּוּ הִיא עֲשׂוּיָה בִּבְנִי, כְּאִלּוּ בְּנִי שָׁחוּט, כְּאִלּוּ דָּמוֹ זָרוּק, כְּאִלּוּ בְּנִי מֻפְשָׁט, כְּאִלּוּ הוּא נִקְטָר וְעָשׂוּי דֶּשֶׁן:

up something he loves. He has shown this time and time again. *The trial is to see whether Avraham can live with what seemed to be a clear contradiction between God's word now, and God's word previously – God's promise.*

Faith is not certainty; it is the courage to live with uncertainty. Avraham has what the poet John Keates called "Negative Capability – that is, when a man is capable of being in uncertainties, mysteries, doubts, without any irritable reaching after fact and reason." He knows the promises will come true; he can live with the uncertainty of not knowing how or when.

ו וְנָשׁ֥וּבָה אֲלֵיכֶֽם׃ וַיִּקַּ֨ח אַבְרָהָ֜ם אֶת־עֲצֵ֣י הָעֹלָ֗ה וַיָּ֙שֶׂם֙ עַל־יִצְחָ֣ק בְּנ֔וֹ
ז וַיִּקַּ֣ח בְּיָד֔וֹ אֶת־הָאֵ֖שׁ וְאֶת־הַֽמַּאֲכֶ֑לֶת וַיֵּלְכ֥וּ שְׁנֵיהֶ֖ם יַחְדָּֽו׃ וַיֹּ֨אמֶר
יִצְחָ֜ק אֶל־אַבְרָהָ֤ם אָבִיו֙ וַיֹּ֣אמֶר אָבִ֔י וַיֹּ֖אמֶר הִנֶּ֣נִּֽי בְנִ֑י וַיֹּ֗אמֶר הִנֵּ֤ה
ח הָאֵשׁ֙ וְהָ֣עֵצִ֔ים וְאַיֵּ֥ה הַשֶּׂ֖ה לְעֹלָֽה׃ וַיֹּ֙אמֶר֙ אַבְרָהָ֔ם אֱלֹהִ֞ים יִרְאֶה־לּ֥וֹ
ט הַשֶּׂ֛ה לְעֹלָ֖ה בְּנִ֑י וַיֵּלְכ֥וּ שְׁנֵיהֶ֖ם יַחְדָּֽו׃ וַיָּבֹ֗אוּ אֶֽל־הַמָּקוֹם֮ אֲשֶׁ֣ר אָֽמַר־
ל֣וֹ הָאֱלֹהִים֒ וַיִּ֨בֶן שָׁ֤ם אַבְרָהָם֙ אֶת־הַמִּזְבֵּ֔חַ וַֽיַּעֲרֹ֖ךְ אֶת־הָעֵצִ֑ים וַֽיַּעֲקֹד֙
י אֶת־יִצְחָ֣ק בְּנ֔וֹ וַיָּ֤שֶׂם אֹתוֹ֙ עַל־הַמִּזְבֵּ֔חַ מִמַּ֖עַל לָעֵצִֽים׃ וַיִּשְׁלַ֤ח אַבְרָהָם֙
יא אֶת־יָד֔וֹ וַיִּקַּ֖ח אֶת־הַֽמַּאֲכֶ֑לֶת לִשְׁחֹ֖ט אֶת־בְּנֽוֹ׃ וַיִּקְרָ֨א אֵלָ֜יו מַלְאַ֤ךְ
יב יהוה֙ מִן־הַשָּׁמַ֔יִם וַיֹּ֖אמֶר אַבְרָהָ֣ם ׀ אַבְרָהָ֑ם וַיֹּ֖אמֶר הִנֵּֽנִי׃ וַיֹּ֗אמֶר אַל־
תִּשְׁלַ֤ח יָֽדְךָ֙ אֶל־הַנַּ֔עַר וְאַל־תַּ֥עַשׂ ל֖וֹ מְא֑וּמָה כִּ֣י ׀ עַתָּ֣ה יָדַ֗עְתִּי כִּֽי־יְרֵ֤א
יג אֱלֹהִים֙ אַ֔תָּה וְלֹ֥א חָשַׂ֛כְתָּ אֶת־בִּנְךָ֥ אֶת־יְחִידְךָ֖ מִמֶּֽנִּי׃ וַיִּשָּׂ֨א אַבְרָהָ֜ם
אֶת־עֵינָ֗יו וַיַּרְא֙ וְהִנֵּה־אַ֔יִל אַחַ֕ר נֶאֱחַ֥ז בַּסְּבַ֖ךְ בְּקַרְנָ֑יו וַיֵּ֤לֶךְ אַבְרָהָם֙
יד וַיִּקַּ֣ח אֶת־הָאַ֔יִל וַיַּעֲלֵ֥הוּ לְעֹלָ֖ה תַּ֥חַת בְּנֽוֹ׃ וַיִּקְרָ֧א אַבְרָהָ֛ם שֵֽׁם־הַמָּק֥וֹם

אונקלוס

וּנְתוּב לְוָתְכוֹן: ו וּנְסֵיב אַבְרָהָם יָת אָעֵי דַעֲלָתָא, וְשַׁוִּי עַל יִצְחָק בְּרֵיהּ, וּנְסֵיב בִּידֵיהּ, יָת אִישָׁתָא וְיָת סַכִּינָא, וַאֲזַלוּ תַּרְוֵיהוֹן כַּחְדָא: ז וַאֲמַר יִצְחָק, לְאַבְרָהָם אֲבוּהִי וַאֲמַר אַבָּא, וַאֲמַר הָאֲנָא בְרִי, וַאֲמַר, הָא אִישָׁתָא וְאָעַיָּא, וְאָן אִמְּרָא לַעֲלָתָא: ח וַאֲמַר אַבְרָהָם, קֳדָם יי גְּלֵי אִמְּרָא, לַעֲלָתָא בְּרִי, וַאֲזַלוּ תַּרְוֵיהוֹן כַּחְדָא: ט וַאֲתוֹ, לְאַתְרָא דַּאֲמַר לֵיהּ יי, וּבְנָא תַמָּן אַבְרָהָם יָת מַדְבְּחָא, וְסַדַּר יָת אָעַיָּא, וַעֲקַד יָת יִצְחָק בְּרֵיהּ, וְשַׁוִּי יָתֵיהּ עַל מַדְבְּחָא, עֵיל מִן אָעַיָּא: י וְאוֹשֵׁיט אַבְרָהָם יָת יְדֵיהּ, וּנְסֵיב יָת סַכִּינָא, לְמִכֵּס יָת בְּרֵיהּ: יא וּקְרָא לֵיהּ, מַלְאֲכָא דַּיי מִן שְׁמַיָּא, וַאֲמַר אַבְרָהָם אַבְרָהָם, וַאֲמַר הָאֲנָא: יב וַאֲמַר, לָא תוֹשֵׁיט יְדָךְ לְעוּלֵימָא, וְלָא תַעֲבֵיד לֵיהּ מִדְּעַם, אֲרֵי כְעַן יְדַעְנָא, אֲרֵי דָחֲלָא דַּיי אַתְּ, וְלָא מְנַעְתָּא, יָת בְּרָךְ יָת יְחִידָךְ מִנִּי: יג וּזְקַף אַבְרָהָם יָת עֵינוֹהִי בָּתַר אִלֵּין, וַחֲזָא וְהָא דִכְרָא, אֲחִיד בְּאִילָנָא בְּקַרְנוֹהִי, וַאֲזַל אַבְרָהָם וּנְסֵיב יָת דִּכְרָא, וְאַסְּקֵיהּ לַעֲלָתָא חֲלַף בְּרֵיהּ: יד וּפְלַח וְצַלִּי אַבְרָהָם, תַּמָּן בְּאַתְרָא

22:8 אֱלֹהִים יִרְאֶה לּוֹ הַשֶּׂה לְעֹלָה בְּנִי *God will see to… my son* – Avraham's elusive statements to the servants and to Yitzḥak are usually taken as diplomatic evasions. I believe, however, that Avraham means exactly what he says. He is living the contradiction. He believes that the God who has promised him a son will not allow him to sacrifice that son. But he does not know how the contradiction between God's promise and His command will resolve itself.

The trial is *not* to see whether Avraham has the courage to sacrifice his son. The practice was commonplace in the ancient world, and completely abhorrent to Judaism. The trial is *not* to see whether Avraham has the strength to give

15 Then the angel of the LORD called to Avraham from the heavens a second
16 time and said, "By My own Self I swear, says the LORD, that because you
17 have done this and have not withheld your son, your only one, I will bless
you greatly and make your descendants as many as the stars of the heavens,
as the sand on the seashore. Your descendants will possess their enemies'
18 gate, and through your descendants will all nations of the earth be blessed,
19 because you have listened to My voice." Avraham returned to his young men,
and together they set out and went to Be'er Sheva, and Avraham stayed on in
Be'er Sheva.
20 Some time later, Avraham was told, "Milka too has had children with your MAFTIR
21 brother Naḥor: Utz, his firstborn, his brother Buz, Kemuel, father of Aram,
22 23 Kesed, Ḥazo, Pildash, Yidlaf, and Betuel." Betuel had a daughter Rivka. Milka
24 bore these eight sons to Avraham's brother Naḥor. His concubine, named
Reuma, also had children: Tevaḥ, Gaḥam, Taḥash, and Maakha.

The haftara for Parashat Vayera is on page 1504.

רש״י

יד **ה׳ יִרְאֶה.** פְּשׁוּטוֹ כְּתַרְגּוּמוֹ: ה׳ יִבְחַר וְיִרְאֶה לוֹ אֶת הַמָּקוֹם הַזֶּה לְהַשְׁרוֹת בּוֹ שְׁכִינָתוֹ וּלְהַקְרִיב כָּאן קָרְבָּנוֹת: **אֲשֶׁר יֵאָמֵר הַיּוֹם.** שֶׁיֹּאמְרוּ לִימֵי הַדּוֹרוֹת עָלָיו: בְּהַר זֶה יֵרָאֶה הַקָּדוֹשׁ בָּרוּךְ הוּא לְעַמּוֹ: **הַיּוֹם.** הַיָּמִים הָעֲתִידִים, כְּמוֹ ׳עַד הַיּוֹם הַזֶּה׳ שֶׁבְּכָל הַמִּקְרָא, שֶׁדּוֹרוֹת הַבָּאִים הַקּוֹרְאִים אֶת הַמִּקְרָא אוֹמְרִים עַל יוֹם שֶׁעוֹמְדִים בּוֹ: ׳הַיּוֹם הַזֶּה׳. וּמִדְרַשׁ אַגָּדָה, ״ה׳ יִרְאֶה״ עֲקֵדָה זוֹ לִסְלֹחַ לְיִשְׂרָאֵל בְּכָל שָׁנָה וּלְהַצִּילָם מִן הַפֻּרְעָנוּת, כְּדֵי שֶׁיֵּאָמֵר הַיּוֹם הַזֶּה בְּכָל דּוֹרוֹת הַבָּאִים: בְּהַר ה׳ נִרְאֶה אֶפְרוֹ שֶׁל יִצְחָק צָבוּר וְעוֹמֵד לְכַפָּרָה:

יז **בָּרֵךְ אֲבָרֶכְךָ.** אַחַת לָאָב וְאַחַת לַבֵּן: **וְהַרְבָּה אַרְבֶּה.** אַחַת לָאָב וְאַחַת לַבֵּן:

יט **וַיֵּשֶׁב אַבְרָהָם בִּבְאֵר שָׁבַע.** לֹא יְשִׁיבָה מַמָּשׁ, שֶׁהֲרֵי בְּחֶבְרוֹן הָיָה יוֹשֵׁב. שְׁתֵּים עֶשְׂרֵה שָׁנִים לִפְנֵי עֲקֵדָתוֹ שֶׁל יִצְחָק יָצָא מִבְּאֵר שֶׁבַע וּבָא לוֹ לְחֶבְרוֹן, כְּמוֹ שֶׁנֶּאֱמַר: ״וַיָּגָר אַבְרָהָם בְּאֶרֶץ פְּלִשְׁתִּים יָמִים רַבִּים״ (לעיל כא, לד), מְרֻבִּים מִשֶּׁל חֶבְרוֹן הָרִאשׁוֹנִים, וְהֵם עֶשְׂרִים וָשֵׁשׁ שָׁנָה כְּמוֹ שֶׁפֵּרַשְׁנוּ לְמַעְלָה:

כ **אַחֲרֵי הַדְּבָרִים הָאֵלֶּה וַיֻּגַּד וגו׳.** בְּשׁוּבוֹ מֵהַר הַמּוֹרִיָּה הָיָה אַבְרָהָם מְהַרְהֵר וְאוֹמֵר: אִלּוּ הָיָה בְּנִי שָׁחוּט כְּבָר הָיָה הוֹלֵךְ בְּלֹא בָּנִים, הָיָה לִי לְהַשִּׂיאוֹ אִשָּׁה מִבְּנוֹת עָנֵר אֶשְׁכּוֹל וּמַמְרֵא; בִּשְּׂרוֹ הַקָּדוֹשׁ בָּרוּךְ הוּא שֶׁנּוֹלְדָה רִבְקָה בַּת זוּגוֹ. וְזֶהוּ ״הַדְּבָרִים הָאֵלֶּה״, הִרְהוּרֵי דְּבָרִים שֶׁהָיוּ עַל יְדֵי הָעֲקֵדָה: **גַּם הִוא.** אַף הִיא הִשְׁוַת מִשְׁפְּחוֹתֶיהָ לְמִשְׁפְּחוֹת אַבְרָהָם שְׁתֵּים עֶשְׂרֵה, מָה אַבְרָהָם, שְׁבָטִים שֶׁיָּצְאוּ מִיַּעֲקֹב שְׁמוֹנָה בְּנֵי הַגְּבִירוֹת וְאַרְבָּעָה בְּנֵי שְׁפָחוֹת, אַף אֵלּוּ שְׁמוֹנָה בְּנֵי גְבִירוֹת וְאַרְבָּעָה בְּנֵי פִילֶגֶשׁ:

כג **וּבְתוּאֵל יָלַד אֶת רִבְקָה.** כָּל הַיִּחוּסִין הַלָּלוּ לֹא נִכְתְּבוּ אֶלָּא בִּשְׁבִיל פָּסוּק זֶה:

sacrifice has a victim. Yitzḥak may not have died physically, but the text seems to make him disappear, literarily, through three scenes in which his presence is central. He should be there to greet and be greeted by the two servants on his safe return from Mount Moria. He should be there to mourn his departed mother, Sara. Yet only Avraham is mentioned. Yitzḥak should be there to at least discuss, with his father and his father's servant, his future wife. Yet the arrangement is made between Avraham and his servant with no mention of Yitzḥak's wishes. Yitzḥak does not die on the mountain, but something in him does die – only to be revived when he marries. Then "he took Rivka as his wife, and he loved her; and Yitzḥak was comforted..." (Gen. 24:67). Here, as the *parasha* ends, Rivka quietly enters the narrative, hinting toward the first stage in Yitzḥak's healing.

טו הַהוּא יהוה ׀ יִרְאֶה אֲשֶׁר יֵאָמֵר הַיּוֹם בְּהַר יהוה יֵרָאֶה: וַיִּקְרָא
טז מַלְאַךְ יהוה אֶל־אַבְרָהָם שֵׁנִית מִן־הַשָּׁמָיִם: וַיֹּאמֶר בִּי נִשְׁבַּעְתִּי
נְאֻם־יהוה כִּי יַעַן אֲשֶׁר עָשִׂיתָ אֶת־הַדָּבָר הַזֶּה וְלֹא חָשַׂכְתָּ אֶת־בִּנְךָ
יז אֶת־יְחִידֶךָ: כִּי־בָרֵךְ אֲבָרֶכְךָ וְהַרְבָּה אַרְבֶּה אֶת־זַרְעֲךָ כְּכוֹכְבֵי הַשָּׁמַיִם
יח וְכַחוֹל אֲשֶׁר עַל־שְׂפַת הַיָּם וְיִרַשׁ זַרְעֲךָ אֵת שַׁעַר אֹיְבָיו: וְהִתְבָּרְכוּ
יט בְזַרְעֲךָ כֹּל גּוֹיֵי הָאָרֶץ עֵקֶב אֲשֶׁר שָׁמַעְתָּ בְּקֹלִי: וַיָּשָׁב אַבְרָהָם
אֶל־נְעָרָיו וַיָּקֻמוּ וַיֵּלְכוּ יַחְדָּו אֶל־בְּאֵר שָׁבַע וַיֵּשֶׁב אַבְרָהָם בִּבְאֵר
שָׁבַע:
כ וַיְהִי אַחֲרֵי הַדְּבָרִים הָאֵלֶּה וַיֻּגַּד לְאַבְרָהָם לֵאמֹר הִנֵּה יָלְדָה מִלְכָּה מפטיר
כא גַם־הִוא בָּנִים לְנָחוֹר אָחִיךָ: אֶת־עוּץ בְּכֹרוֹ וְאֶת־בּוּז אָחִיו וְאֶת־
כב קְמוּאֵל אֲבִי אֲרָם: וְאֶת־כֶּשֶׂד וְאֶת־חֲזוֹ וְאֶת־פִּלְדָּשׁ וְאֶת־יִדְלָף וְאֵת
כג בְּתוּאֵל: וּבְתוּאֵל יָלַד אֶת־רִבְקָה שְׁמֹנָה אֵלֶּה יָלְדָה מִלְכָּה לְנָחוֹר
כד אֲחִי אַבְרָהָם: וּפִילַגְשׁוֹ וּשְׁמָהּ רְאוּמָה וַתֵּלֶד גַּם־הִוא אֶת־טֶבַח וְאֶת־
גַּחַם וְאֶת־תַּחַשׁ וְאֶת־מַעֲכָה:

The הפטרה *for* פרשת וירא *is on page 1505.*

אונקלוס

ההוא, אמר קדם יי הכא יהון פלחין דריא, בכן יתאמר ביומא הדין, בטורא הדין אברהם קדם יי פלח: טו וקרא, מלאכא דיי לאברהם, תנינות מן שמיא: טז ואמר, במימרי קיימית אמר יי, ארי, חלף דעבדתא ית פתגמא הדין, ולא מנעתא ית ברך ית יחידך: יז ארי ברכא אברכנך, ואסגאה אסגי ית בנך ככוכבי שמיא, וכחלא, דעל כיף ימא, ויירתון בנך, ית קרוי סנאיהון: יח ויתברכון בדיל בנך, כל עממי ארעא, חלף, דקבילתא למימרי: יט ותב אברהם לות עולימוהי, וקמו, ואזלו כחדא לבאר שבע, ויתיב אברהם בבאר שבע: כ והוה, בתר פתגמיא האלין, ואתחוא לאברהם למימר, הא, ילידת מלכה אף היא, בנין לנחור אחוך: כא ית עוץ בכריה וית בוז אחוהי, וית קמואל אבוהי דארם: כב וית כשד וית חזו, וית פלדש וית ידלף, וית בתואל: כג ובתואל אוליד ית רבקה, תמניא אלין ילידת מלכה, לנחור אחוהי דאברהם: כד ולחינתיה ושמה ראומה, וילידת אף היא ית טבח וית גחם, וית תחש וית מעכה:

22:23 רִבְקָה *Rivka* – What happens to Yitzḥak after the *akeda*? As soon as the angel has stopped Avraham from sacrificing his son, Yitzḥak drops out of the picture. The text tells us that Avraham returns to the two servants who accompanied them on the way, but there is no mention of Yitzḥak.

What does this mean? We can only speculate. But if silences mean something, they suggest that *even an arrested*

PARASHAT ḤAYEI SARA

23 1 Sara's lifetime – the years of Sara's life – were one hundred and twenty-seven.
2 Sara died in Kiryat Arba – that is, Ḥevron – in the land of Canaan. And Avraham
3 came to mourn for Sara and to weep for her. Then Avraham rose from beside
4 his dead and spoke to the Hittites. He said, "I am a migrant and a visitor among

רש"י

כג א וַיִּהְיוּ חַיֵּי שָׂרָה מֵאָה שָׁנָה וְעֶשְׂרִים שָׁנָה וְשֶׁבַע שָׁנִים. לְכָךְ נִכְתַּב 'שָׁנָה' בְּכָל כְּלָל וּכְלָל, לוֹמַר לְךָ שֶׁכָּל אֶחָד נִדְרָשׁ לְעַצְמוֹ: בַּת מֵאָה כְּבַת עֶשְׂרִים לְחֵטְא, מַה בַּת עֶשְׂרִים לֹא חָטְאָה שֶׁהֲרֵי אֵינָהּ בַּת עֳנָשִׁין, אַף בַּת מֵאָה בְּלֹא חֵטְא, וּבַת עֶשְׂרִים כְּבַת שֶׁבַע לְיֹפִי: שְׁנֵי חַיֵּי שָׂרָה. כֻּלָּן שָׁוִין לְטוֹבָה:

ב בְּקִרְיַת אַרְבַּע. עַל שֵׁם אַרְבָּעָה עֲנָקִים שֶׁהָיוּ שָׁם: אֲחִימַן שֵׁשַׁי וְתַלְמַי וַאֲבִיהֶם. דָּבָר אַחֵר, עַל שֵׁם אַרְבָּעָה זוּגוֹת שֶׁנִּקְבְּרוּ שָׁם, אִישׁ וְאִשְׁתּוֹ: אָדָם וְחַוָּה, אַבְרָהָם וְשָׂרָה, יִצְחָק וְרִבְקָה, יַעֲקֹב וְלֵאָה:

וַיָּבֹא אַבְרָהָם. מִבְּאֵר שֶׁבַע "לִסְפֹּד לְשָׂרָה וְלִבְכֹּתָהּ". וְנִסְמְכָה מִיתַת שָׂרָה לַעֲקֵדַת יִצְחָק, לְפִי שֶׁעַל יְדֵי בְּשׂוֹרַת הָעֲקֵדָה שֶׁנִּזְדַּמֵּן בְּנָהּ לִשְׁחִיטָה וְכִמְעַט שֶׁלֹּא נִשְׁחַט, פָּרְחָה נִשְׁמָתָהּ וּמֵתָה:

ד גֵּר וְתוֹשָׁב אָנֹכִי עִמָּכֶם. גֵּר מֵאֶרֶץ אַחֶרֶת וְנִתְיַשַּׁבְתִּי עִמָּכֶם. וּמִדְרַשׁ אַגָּדָה: אִם תִּרְצוּ – הֲרֵינִי גֵּר, וְאִם לָאו – אֶהְיֶה תּוֹשָׁב וְאֶטְּלֶנָּה מִן הַדִּין, שֶׁאָמַר לִי הַקָּדוֹשׁ בָּרוּךְ הוּא: "לְזַרְעֲךָ אֶתֵּן אֶת הָאָרֶץ הַזֹּאת" (לעיל יב, ז): אֲחֻזַּת קֶבֶר. אֲחֻזַּת קַרְקַע לְבֵית הַקְּבָרוֹת:

in a land where they would be strangers, abandon every conventional form of security, and have the faith to believe that by living by the standards of righteousness and justice, they would be taking the first step to establishing a nation, a land, a faith and a way of life that would be a blessing to all humankind.

Surviving whatever fate threw at them, however much it seemed to derail their mission, Avraham and Sara knew that what makes a life satisfying is not external but internal, a sense of purpose, mission, of starting something that would be continued by those who came after them, of bringing something new into the world by the way they lived their lives. What mattered was the inside, not the outside; their faith, not their often-troubled circumstances.

Faith helps us to find the "why" that allows us to bear almost any "how." The serenity of Sara's (and later, Avraham's) death is eternal testimony to how they lived.

23:3 **וַיָּקָם אַבְרָהָם** *Then Avraham rose* – Avraham's grief is described in a mere five Hebrew words. Then immediately we read, "And Avraham rose from beside his dead." From here on, he engages in a flurry of activity with two aims in mind: first to buy a plot of land in which to bury Sara, second to find a wife for his son.

We have observed two people in the Torah who look back, one by implication, the other explicitly. Noaḥ ends his life drunk. The Torah does not say why but we can guess. He has lost an entire world. It is not hard to imagine this righteous man overwhelmed by grief as he replays in his mind all that has happened, wondering whether he might have done something to save more lives or avert the catastrophe.

Lot's wife, against the instruction of the angels, does look back as the cities of the plain disappear under fire and brimstone and the anger of God. Immediately she is turned into a pillar of salt, unable to move on.

Against the background of these two stories, Avraham sets a different precedent. He marks his loss, and then he rises from it. Avraham hears the future calling to him.

23:4 **גֵּר וְתוֹשָׁב** *A migrant and a visitor* – This is the first time we encounter the phrase *ger vetoshav*. It is no mere formulaic utterance; Avraham is acknowledging his legal lack of standing. As a stranger and temporary resident, he has no entitlement to own land. He depends on the goodwill of

פרשת חיי שרה

כג א וַיִּהְיוּ חַיֵּי שָׂרָה מֵאָה שָׁנָה וְעֶשְׂרִים שָׁנָה וְשֶׁבַע שָׁנִים שְׁנֵי חַיֵּי שָׂרָה׃
ב וַתָּמָת שָׂרָה בְּקִרְיַת אַרְבַּע הִוא חֶבְרוֹן בְּאֶרֶץ כְּנָעַן וַיָּבֹא אַבְרָהָם
ג לִסְפֹּד לְשָׂרָה וְלִבְכֹּתָהּ׃ וַיָּקָם אַבְרָהָם מֵעַל פְּנֵי מֵתוֹ וַיְדַבֵּר אֶל־בְּנֵי־
ד חֵת לֵאמֹר׃ גֵּר־וְתוֹשָׁב אָנֹכִי עִמָּכֶם תְּנוּ לִי אֲחֻזַּת־קֶבֶר עִמָּכֶם

אונקלוס

כג א וַהֲווֹ חַיֵּי שָׂרָה, מְאָה וְעֶסְרִין וּשְׁבַע שְׁנִין, שְׁנֵי חַיֵּי שָׂרָה: ב וּמִיתַת שָׂרָה, בְּקִרְיַת אַרְבַּע, הִיא חֶבְרוֹן בְּאַרְעָא דִּכְנָעַן, וַאֲתָא אַבְרָהָם, לְמִסְפְּדָה דְּשָׂרָה וּלְמִבְכַּהּ: ג וְקָם אַבְרָהָם, מֵעַל אַפֵּי מִיתֵיהּ, וּמַלֵּיל עִם בְּנֵי חִתָּאָה לְמֵימַר: ד דַּיָּר וְתוֹתָב אֲנָא עִמְּכוֹן, הַבוּ לִי אַחְסָנַת קְבוּרָא עִמְּכוֹן,

ḤAYEI SARA

By the time the *parasha* begins, Avraham has received two promises – both stated five times. The first is of a land (12:7; 13:14–17; 15:7; 15:18–21; 17:7–8), the second of children (12:2; 13:16; 15:5; 17:4–5; 22:17). Both are remarkable promises. The land in its length and breadth will be Avraham's and his children's as "an everlasting possession." Avraham will have as many children as the dust of the earth, the stars of the sky, and the sand on the seashore. What, though, is the reality at the time Sara dies? Avraham owns no land and has only one son, unmarried, to be the bearer of the covenant.

Ḥayei Sara contains three narratives. First comes the death of Sara, and Avraham's purchase of a burial plot for her, the first part of the Holy Land to be owned by the people of the covenant. Next is the search for a wife for Yitzḥak, the first Jewish child. Finally, we hear of the last period of Avraham's life, and of his death. A land: Israel. And children: Jewish continuity. The astonishing fact is that today, four thousand years later, they remain the dominant concerns of Jews throughout the world – the safety and security of Israel as the Jewish home, and the future of the Jewish people. Avraham's hopes and fears are ours.

The *parasha*, then, tells a difficult story. Yes, Avraham will have a land. He will have countless children. But these things will not happen soon, or suddenly, or easily. Nor will they occur without human effort. The future will happen, but it is we – inspired, empowered, given strength by the promise – who must bring it about.

THE YEARS OF SARA'S LIFE

A well-known comment by Rashi on the apparently superfluous phrase "the years of Sara's life" states: "The word 'years' is repeated [in the Hebrew] and without a number to indicate that they were all equally good." How could anyone say that the years of Sara's life were equally good? Twice, first in Egypt, then in Gerar, she was taken against her wishes into a royal harem.

There were the years when, despite God's repeated promise of many children, she was infertile, unable to have even a single child. There was the time when she persuaded Avraham to take her handmaid, Hagar, and have a child by her, which caused her great strife of the spirit. These things constituted a life of uncertainty and decades of unmet hopes.

Nietzsche was one of the most brilliant thinkers of the modern age, and also one of the most dangerous. Yet one of his most famous remarks is both profound and true: *He who has a why in life can bear almost any how*. Avraham and Sara are among the supreme examples in all history of what it is to have a "why" in life. The entire course of their lives came as a response to a call – a divine call to live

5 you. Sell me a burial site here so that I can bury my dead." The Hittites answered
6 Avraham, "Hear us, my lord. You are a prince of God in our midst. Bury your
dead in the choicest of our tombs. None of us will refuse you his tomb to bury
7 your dead." Avraham rose and bowed down to the Hittites, the people of the
8 land, and said to them, "If you are willing to allow me to bury the dead that lies
before me, then hear me and intercede on my behalf with Efron son of Tzoḥar.
9 Let him sell me the cave of Makhpela that he owns, at the edge of his field. Ask
10 him to sell it to me at the full price as a burial site in your midst." Efron was
sitting among the Hittites. Efron the Hittite answered Avraham in the hearing
11 of all the Hittites who had come to the city gate. He said, "No, my lord, hear
me. I give you the field and I give you the cave that is in it. In the presence of my
12 people, I give it to you. Bury your dead." Avraham bowed down again before

רש״י

ו **לֹא יִכְלֶה.** לֹא יִמְנַע, כְּמוֹ: "לֹא תִכְלָא רַחֲמֶיךָ" (תהלים מ, יב), וּכְמוֹ: "וַיִּכָּלֵא הַגֶּשֶׁם" (לעיל ח, ב):

ח **נַפְשְׁכֶם.** רְצוֹנְכֶם: **וּפִגְעוּ לִי.** לְשׁוֹן בַּקָּשָׁה, כְּמוֹ: "אַל תִּפְגְּעִי בִי" (רות א, טז):

ט **הַמַּכְפֵּלָה.** בַּיִת וַעֲלִיָּה עַל גַּבָּיו. דָּבָר אַחֵר, שֶׁכְּפוּלָה בְּזוּגוֹת: **בְּכֶסֶף מָלֵא.** שָׁלֵם, כָּל שָׁוְיָהּ:

י **וְעֶפְרוֹן יֹשֵׁב.** כְּתִיב חָסֵר, אוֹתוֹ הַיּוֹם מִנּוּהוּ שׁוֹטֵר עֲלֵיהֶם; מִפְּנֵי חֲשִׁיבוּתוֹ שֶׁל אַבְרָהָם שֶׁהָיָה צָרִיךְ לוֹ, עָלָה לִגְדֻלָּה: **לְכֹל בָּאֵי שַׁעַר עִירוֹ.** שֶׁכֻּלָּן בָּטְלוּ מִמְּלַאכְתָּן וּבָאוּ לִגְמֹל חֶסֶד לְשָׂרָה:

יא **לֹא אֲדֹנִי.** לֹא תִקְנֶה אוֹתָהּ בְּדָמִים: **נָתַתִּי לָךְ.** הֲרֵי הִיא כְּמוֹ שֶׁנְּתַתִּיהָ לְךָ:

humiliating, encounter. The Hittites say one thing and mean another. As a group they say, "Bury your dead in the choicest of our tombs" (Gen. 23:6). Efron, the owner of the field Avraham wants to buy, says: "Hear me. I give you the field and I give you the cave that is in it. In the presence of my people, I give it to you. Bury your dead" (23:11).

As the narrative makes clear, this elaborate generosity is a façade for some extremely hard bargaining. Avraham knows he is "a migrant and a visitor among you" (Gen. 23:4), meaning, among other things, that he has no right to own land. That is the force of their reply which, stripped of its overlay of courtesy, means: "Use one of our burial sites. You may not acquire your own."

Avraham is not deterred. He insists that he wants to buy his own. Efron's reply – "It is yours. I give it to you" – is in fact the prelude to a demand for a highly inflated price. Finally, however, Avraham fulfills his wish. The transfer of ownership is recorded in precise legal prose (23:17–20) to signal that, at last, Avraham owns part of the land. It is a small part: one field and a cave. A burial place, bought at great expense. That is as much of the divine promise of the land as Avraham will see in his lifetime.

23:6 **נְשִׂיא אֱלֹהִים אַתָּה בְּתוֹכֵנוּ** *You are a prince of God in our midst* – This is the first instance, and the classic example, of *kiddush Hashem* in the Torah. Noaḥ's righteousness was turned inward. He had no influence on his contemporaries. Lot chose the way of assimilation. He tried to merge into the society, Sedom, in which he had chosen to live. Avraham is different. He fights for his neighbors and prays for them but he does not become like them. He lives out the principle that has been the Jewish imperative ever since: be true to your faith and a blessing to others regardless of their faith. What is the result? When Avraham comes before the Hittites, they say to him: "You are a prince of God in our midst."

ה וְאֶקְבְּרָה מֵתִי מִלְּפָנָי׃ וַיַּעֲנוּ בְנֵי־חֵת אֶת־אַבְרָהָם לֵאמֹר לוֹ׃ שְׁמָעֵנוּ ׀
אֲדֹנִי נְשִׂיא אֱלֹהִים אַתָּה בְּתוֹכֵנוּ בְּמִבְחַר קְבָרֵינוּ קְבֹר אֶת־מֵתֶךָ
ז אִישׁ מִמֶּנּוּ אֶת־קִבְרוֹ לֹא־יִכְלֶה מִמְּךָ מִקְּבֹר מֵתֶךָ׃ וַיָּקָם אַבְרָהָם
ח וַיִּשְׁתַּחוּ לְעַם־הָאָרֶץ לִבְנֵי־חֵת׃ וַיְדַבֵּר אִתָּם לֵאמֹר אִם־יֵשׁ אֶת־
נַפְשְׁכֶם לִקְבֹּר אֶת־מֵתִי מִלְּפָנַי שְׁמָעוּנִי וּפִגְעוּ־לִי בְּעֶפְרוֹן בֶּן־צֹחַר׃
ט וְיִתֶּן־לִי אֶת־מְעָרַת הַמַּכְפֵּלָה אֲשֶׁר־לוֹ אֲשֶׁר בִּקְצֵה שָׂדֵהוּ בְּכֶסֶף
י מָלֵא יִתְּנֶנָּה לִּי בְּתוֹכְכֶם לַאֲחֻזַּת־קָבֶר׃ וְעֶפְרוֹן יֹשֵׁב בְּתוֹךְ בְּנֵי־חֵת
וַיַּעַן עֶפְרוֹן הַחִתִּי אֶת־אַבְרָהָם בְּאָזְנֵי בְנֵי־חֵת לְכֹל בָּאֵי שַׁעַר־עִירוֹ
יא לֵאמֹר׃ לֹא־אֲדֹנִי שְׁמָעֵנִי הַשָּׂדֶה נָתַתִּי לָךְ וְהַמְּעָרָה אֲשֶׁר־בּוֹ לְךָ
יב נְתַתִּיהָ לְעֵינֵי בְנֵי־עַמִּי נְתַתִּיהָ לָּךְ קְבֹר מֵתֶךָ׃ וַיִּשְׁתַּחוּ אַבְרָהָם לִפְנֵי

אונקלוס

וְאֶקְבַּר מִיתִי מִן קֳדָמָי: ה וַאֲתִיבוּ בְנֵי חִתָּאָה, יָת אַבְרָהָם לְמֵימַר לֵיהּ: ו קַבֵּיל מִנַּנָא רִבּוֹנַנָא, רַב קֳדָם יי אַתְּ בֵּינַנָא, בִּשְׁפַר קִבְרָנָא, קְבַר יָת מִיתָךְ, אֱנָשׁ מִנַּנָא, יָת קִבְרֵיהּ, לָא יִמְנַע מִנָּךְ מִלְּמִקְבַּר מִיתָךְ: ז וְקָם אַבְרָהָם, וּסְגִיד לְעַמָּא דְּאַרְעָא לִבְנֵי חִתָּאָה: ח וּמַלֵּיל עִמְּהוֹן לְמֵימַר, אִם אִית רַעֲוָא נַפְשְׁכוֹן, לְמִקְבַּר יָת מִיתִי מִן קֳדָמַי, קַבִּילוּ מִנִּי, וּבְעוֹ לִי מִן עֶפְרוֹן בַּר צוֹחַר: ט וְיִתֵּין לִי, יָת מְעָרַת כָּפֵילְתָּא דְּלֵיהּ, דְּבִסְטַר חַקְלֵיהּ, בִּכְסַף שְׁלִים, יִתְּנַהּ לִי, בֵּינֵיכוֹן לְאַחְסָנַת קְבוּרָא: י וְעֶפְרוֹן יָתֵיב בְּגוֹ בְנֵי חִתָּאָה, וַאֲתֵיב עֶפְרוֹן חִתָּאָה יָת אַבְרָהָם קֳדָם בְּנֵי חִתָּאָה, לְכֹל, עָאלֵי תְּרַע קַרְתֵּיהּ לְמֵימַר: יא לָא רִבּוֹנִי קַבֵּיל מִנִּי, חַקְלָא יְהַבִית לָךְ, וּמְעָרְתָא דְּבֵיהּ לָךְ יְהַבְתַּהּ, לְעֵינֵי בְנֵי עַמִּי, יְהַבְתַּהּ לָךְ קְבַר מִיתָךְ: יב וּסְגֵיד אַבְרָהָם, קֳדָם

The fate of Avraham's family, we now discover, will be not temporary but permanent – permanently temporary. They will know no certainty, have no fixed and unconditional home, even in the land of promise. Avraham has been told, in a dark vision of exile, that his offspring will be "migrants in a land not their own" (Gen. 15:13). That, we thought, meant Egypt. It turns out to mean Israel as well. This is the central, haunting irony of the Pentateuch. Even at their greatest moments, the people of the covenant will be strangers at home. This is how they will learn to make strangers feel at home.

23:4 תְּנוּ לִי אֲחֻזַּת קֶבֶר *Sell me a burial site* – Avraham undergoes a lengthy bargaining process with the Hittites to buy a field with a cave in which to bury Sara. It is a tense, even the Hittites even to begin the conversation with the cave's owner, Efron.

Reading this for the first time, we assume that the text represents Israel's prehistory. Genesis is about the promise, not the fulfilment. One day, this will change. Israel will become a nation with its own land. Time passes. Israel goes into exile. It is redeemed from slavery. Moshe leads the people out of Egypt on their way to the land. There, we cannot but expect, the people will find a home. At last, they will own the land. They will no longer be as Avraham was. Then, in one of the great paradigm-shifting moments of the Bible, the twenty-fifth chapter of Leviticus turns this expectation on its head: "The land shall not be sold in perpetuity, for the land is Mine. You are merely migrants and visitors to Me" (Lev. 25:23).

13 the people of the land and said to Efron in their hearing, "Please, would that
you would hear me. I give you the money for the field. Take it from me so that
14 15 I can bury my dead there." Efron answered Avraham and said to him, "My lord,
hear me. A piece of land worth four hundred silver shekel – what is that between
16 you and me? Bury your dead." Avraham heard Efron. He weighed out for him
the price he had mentioned in the Hittites' hearing: four hundred silver shekel
17 at the merchants' standard rate. So Efron's field in Makhpela near Mamre – the SHENI
18 field, its cave, and all the trees within the field's borders – passed to Avraham as
his possession, in the presence of all the Hittites who had come to the city gate.
19 Avraham then buried Sara his wife in the cave in the field of Makhpela near
20 Mamre – that is, Ḥevron – in the land of Canaan. Thus the field and its cave
24 1 passed from the Hittites to Avraham as a burial site. Avraham was
2 old, advanced in years, and the Lord had blessed him in all things. And
Avraham said to the senior servant of his household, who was in charge of all
3 he had, "Place your hand under my thigh. I want you to swear by the Lord,
God of heaven and earth, that you will not take a wife for my son from among
4 the daughters of the Canaanites among whom I live. Instead, go to my land and

רש״י

יג **אַךְ אִם אַתָּה לוּ שְׁמָעֵנִי.** אַתָּה אוֹמֵר לִי לִשְׁמֹעַ לְךָ וְלִקַּח חִנָּם, וַאֲנִי אִי אֶפְשִׁי בְּכָךְ. **אַךְ אִם אַתָּה לוּ שְׁמָעֵנִי.** הַלְוַאי וְתִשְׁמָעֵנִי: **נָתַתִּי.** דוֹנֵא״י בְּלַעַ״ז, מוּכָן הוּא אֶצְלִי וְהַלְוַאי נְתַתִּיו לְךָ כְּבָר:

טו **בֵּינִי וּבֵינְךָ.** בֵּין שְׁנֵי אוֹהֲבִים כָּמוֹנוּ ״מַה הִיא״ – חֲשׁוּבָה לִכְלוּם, אֶלָּא הַנַּח אֶת הַמֶּכֶר ״וְאֶת מֵתְךָ קְבֹר״:

טז **וַיִּשְׁקֹל אַבְרָהָם לְעֶפְרֹן.** חָסֵר וָי״ו, לְפִי שֶׁאָמַר הַרְבֵּה וַאֲפִלּוּ מְעַט לֹא עָשָׂה, שֶׁנָּטַל מִמֶּנּוּ שְׁקָלִים גְּדוֹלִים שֶׁהֵן קַנְטָרִין, שֶׁנֶּאֱמַר: ״עֹבֵר לַסֹּחֵר״, שֶׁמִּתְקַבְּלִים כְּשֶׁקֶל בְּכָל מָקוֹם, וְיֵשׁ מָקוֹם שֶׁשִּׁקְלֵיהֶן גְּדוֹלִים שֶׁהֵן קַנְטָרִין, צנטינא״ש בְּלַעַ״ז:

יז-יח **וַיָּקָם שְׂדֵה עֶפְרוֹן.** תְּקוּמָה הָיְתָה לוֹ שֶׁיָּצָא מִיַּד הֶדְיוֹט לְיַד מֶלֶךְ. וּפְשׁוּטוֹ שֶׁל מִקְרָא: וַיָּקָם הַשָּׂדֶה וְהַמְּעָרָה אֲשֶׁר בּוֹ וְכָל הָעֵץ לְאַבְרָהָם לְמִקְנָה וְגוֹ׳: **בְּכֹל בָּאֵי שַׁעַר עִירוֹ.** בְּקֶרֶב כֻּלָּם וּבְמַעֲמַד כֻּלָּם הִקְנָהוּ לוֹ:

כד א **בֵּרַךְ אֶת אַבְרָהָם בַּכֹּל.** ׳בַּכֹּל׳ עוֹלֶה בְּגִימַטְרִיָּא ׳בֵּן׳, וּמֵאַחַר שֶׁהָיָה לוֹ בֵּן הָיָה צָרִיךְ לְהַשִּׂיאוֹ אִשָּׁה:

ב **זְקַן בֵּיתוֹ.** לְפִי שֶׁהוּא דָּבוּק נָקוּד ׳זְקַן׳: **תַּחַת יְרֵכִי.** לְפִי שֶׁהַנִּשְׁבָּע צָרִיךְ לִטֹּל בְּיָדוֹ חֵפֶץ שֶׁל מִצְוָה כְּגוֹן סֵפֶר תּוֹרָה אוֹ תְּפִלִּין, וְהַמִּילָה הָיְתָה מִצְוָה רִאשׁוֹנָה לוֹ, וּבָאָה לוֹ עַל יְדֵי צַעַר וְהָיְתָה חֲבִיבָה עָלָיו, וּנְטָלָהּ:

THE SERVANT'S TEST

Avraham does not tell his servant (unnamed in the text but traditionally identified as Eliezer) to look for any specific traits of character. He simply tells him to find someone from his own extended family. Eliezer, however, formulates a test: "By this I will know that You have shown kindness (*ḥesed*) to my master." His use of the word *ḥesed* here is no accident, for it is the very characteristic he is looking for in the future wife of the first Jewish child, Yitzḥak, and he finds it in Rivka. *Ḥesed*, what I define as "love as deed," is central to the Jewish value system.

Ḥesed – providing shelter for the homeless, food for the hungry, or assistance to the poor; visiting the sick, comforting mourners, and providing a dignified burial for all – became constitutive of Jewish life. During the many centuries of exile and dispersion, Jewish communities were built around these needs. There were *ḥevrot*, "friendly societies," for each of them.

יג עַם־הָאָֽרֶץ׃ וַיְדַבֵּר אֶל־עֶפְרוֹן בְּאָזְנֵי עַם־הָאָרֶץ לֵאמֹר אַךְ אִם־אַתָּה
לוּ שְׁמָעֵנִי נָתַתִּי כֶּסֶף הַשָּׂדֶה קַח מִמֶּנִּי וְאֶקְבְּרָה אֶת־מֵתִי שָֽׁמָּה׃
יד טו וַיַּעַן עֶפְרוֹן אֶת־אַבְרָהָם לֵאמֹר לֽוֹ׃ אֲדֹנִי שְׁמָעֵנִי אֶרֶץ אַרְבַּע מֵאֹת
טז שֶׁקֶל־כֶּסֶף בֵּינִי וּבֵינְךָ מַה־הִוא וְאֶת־מֵתְךָ קְבֹֽר׃ וַיִּשְׁמַע אַבְרָהָם
אֶל־עֶפְרוֹן וַיִּשְׁקֹל אַבְרָהָם לְעֶפְרֹן אֶת־הַכֶּסֶף אֲשֶׁר דִּבֶּר בְּאָזְנֵי בְנֵי־
יז חֵת אַרְבַּע מֵאוֹת שֶׁקֶל כֶּסֶף עֹבֵר לַסֹּחֵֽר׃ וַיָּקָם ׀ שְׂדֵה עֶפְרוֹן אֲשֶׁר שני
בַּמַּכְפֵּלָה אֲשֶׁר לִפְנֵי מַמְרֵא הַשָּׂדֶה וְהַמְּעָרָה אֲשֶׁר־בּוֹ וְכָל־הָעֵץ
יח אֲשֶׁר בַּשָּׂדֶה אֲשֶׁר בְּכָל־גְּבֻלוֹ סָבִֽיב׃ לְאַבְרָהָם לְמִקְנָה לְעֵינֵי בְנֵי־חֵת
יט בְּכֹל בָּאֵי שַֽׁעַר־עִירֽוֹ׃ וְאַחֲרֵי־כֵן קָבַר אַבְרָהָם אֶת־שָׂרָה אִשְׁתּוֹ אֶל־
כ מְעָרַת שְׂדֵה הַמַּכְפֵּלָה עַל־פְּנֵי מַמְרֵא הִוא חֶבְרוֹן בְּאֶרֶץ כְּנָֽעַן׃ וַיָּקָם
הַשָּׂדֶה וְהַמְּעָרָה אֲשֶׁר־בּוֹ לְאַבְרָהָם לַאֲחֻזַּת־קָבֶר מֵאֵת בְּנֵי־
כד א חֵֽת׃ וְאַבְרָהָם זָקֵן בָּא בַּיָּמִים וַיהוָה בֵּרַךְ אֶת־אַבְרָהָם כ
ב בַּכֹּֽל׃ וַיֹּאמֶר אַבְרָהָם אֶל־עַבְדּוֹ זְקַן בֵּיתוֹ הַמֹּשֵׁל בְּכָל־אֲשֶׁר־לוֹ
ג שִׂים־נָא יָדְךָ תַּחַת יְרֵכִֽי׃ וְאַשְׁבִּיעֲךָ בַּיהוָה אֱלֹהֵי הַשָּׁמַיִם וֵאלֹהֵי
הָאָרֶץ אֲשֶׁר לֹא־תִקַּח אִשָּׁה לִבְנִי מִבְּנוֹת הַכְּנַעֲנִי אֲשֶׁר אָנֹכִי יוֹשֵׁב
ד בְּקִרְבּֽוֹ׃ כִּי אֶל־אַרְצִי וְאֶל־מוֹלַדְתִּי תֵּלֵךְ וְלָקַחְתָּ אִשָּׁה לִבְנִי לְיִצְחָֽק׃

אונקלוס

עמא דארעא: יג ומליל עם עפרון, קדם עמא דארעא למימר, ברם, אם עבדת לי טיבו קביל מני, אתין, כספא דמי חקלא סב מני, ואקבר ית מיתי תמן: יד ואתיב עפרון, ית אברהם למימר ליה: טו רבוני קביל מני, ארע שויא ארבע מאה סלעין דכסף, בינא ובינך מא היא, וית מיתך קבר: טז וקביל אברהם מן עפרון, ותקל אברהם לעפרון, ית כספא, דמליל קדם בני חתאה, ארבע מאה סלעין דכסף, מתקבל סחורה בכל מדינה: יז וקם חקל עפרון, דבכפילתא, דקדם ממרא, חקלא ומערתא דביה, וכל אילני דבחקלא, דבכל תחומיה סחור סחור: יח לאברהם לזבינוהי לעיני בני חתאה, בכל עאלי תרע קרתיה: יט ובתר כן קבר אברהם ית שרה אתתיה, במערת, חקל כפילתא, על אפי ממרא היא חברון, בארעא דכנען: כ וקם חקלא, ומערתא דביה, לאברהם לאחסנת קבורא, מן בני חתאה: כד א ואברהם סיב, עאל ביומין, ויי, בריך ית אברהם בכולא: ב ואמר אברהם, לעבדיה סבא דביתיה, דשליט בכל דליה, שו כען ידך תחות ירכי: ג ואקיים עלך, במימרא דיי אלהא דשמיא, ואלהא דארעא, דלא תסב אתתא לברי, מבנת כנענאי, דאנא יתיב ביניהון: ד אלהין לארעי, ולילדותי תיזיל, ותסב אתתא לברי ליצחק:

5 birthplace, and there find a wife for Yitzḥak my son." The servant asked, "What
if the woman does not want to come back with me to this land? Shall I bring
6 your son back to the land from which you came?" Avraham said to him, "Be
7 sure not to take my son back there. The Lord, God of the heavens, took me
from my father's house and from the land of my birth. He spoke to me and
swore to me, 'To your descendants I will give this land.' He will send His angel
8 before you, and there you will find a wife for my son. But if the woman does not
want to come back with you, then you will be released from this oath to me.
9 Just do not take my son back there." So the servant placed his hand under his
10 master Avraham's thigh and swore this by an oath to him. The servant then SHELISHI
took ten of his master's camels, laden with all his master's bounty, and set out
11 to Aram Naharayim, to the city of Naḥor. By the well outside the city, he had
the camels kneel. It was evening, the time when the women came out to draw
12 water. "Lord, God of my master Avraham," he said, "please, grant me success

רש״י

ז **ה׳ אֱלֹהֵי הַשָּׁמַיִם אֲשֶׁר לְקָחַנִי מִבֵּית אָבִי.** וְלֹא אָמַר ׳וֵאלֹהֵי הָאָרֶץ׳ וּלְמַעְלָה (לעיל פסוק ג) אָמַר: ״וְאַשְׁבִּיעֲךָ״ וְגוֹ׳. אָמַר לוֹ: עַכְשָׁיו הוּא אֱלֹהֵי הַשָּׁמַיִם וֵאלֹהֵי הָאָרֶץ, שֶׁהִרְגַּלְתִּיו בְּפִי הַבְּרִיּוֹת, אֲבָל כְּשֶׁלְּקָחַנִי מִבֵּית אָבִי הָיָה אֱלֹהֵי הַשָּׁמַיִם וְלֹא אֱלֹהֵי הָאָרֶץ, שֶׁלֹּא הָיוּ בָּאֵי עוֹלָם מַכִּירִים בּוֹ: **מִבֵּית אָבִי.** מֵחָרָן: **וּמֵאֶרֶץ מוֹלַדְתִּי.** מֵאוּר כַּשְׂדִּים: **וַאֲשֶׁר דִּבֶּר לִי.** לְצָרְכִּי, כְּמוֹ: ׳אֲשֶׁר דִּבֶּר עָלַי׳. וְכֵן כָּל ׳לִי׳ וְ׳לוֹ׳ וְ׳לָהֶם׳ הַסְּמוּכִים אֵצֶל דִּבּוּר מְפֹרָשִׁים בִּלְשׁוֹן ׳עַל׳, וְתַרְגּוּם שֶׁלָּהֶם: ׳עֲלַי׳ ׳עֲלוֹהִי׳ ׳עֲלֵיהוֹן׳, שֶׁאֵין נוֹפֵל אֵצֶל דִּבּוּר לְשׁוֹן ׳לִי׳ וְ׳לוֹ׳ וְ׳לָהֶם׳, אֶלָּא ׳אֵלַי׳ ׳אֵלָיו׳ ׳אֲלֵיהֶם׳, וְתַרְגּוּם שֶׁלָּהֶם: ׳עִמִּי׳ ׳עִמֵּיהּ׳ ׳עִמְּהוֹן׳. אֲבָל אֵצֶל אֲמִירָה נוֹפֵל ׳לִי׳ וְ׳לוֹ׳ וְ׳לָהֶם׳: **וַאֲשֶׁר נִשְׁבַּע לִי.** בֵּין הַבְּתָרִים:

ח **וְנִקִּיתָ מִשְּׁבֻעָתִי.** וְקַח לוֹ אִשָּׁה מִבְּנוֹת עָנֵר אֶשְׁכּוֹל וּמַמְרֵא: **רַק אֶת בְּנִי וְגוֹ׳.** ׳רַק׳ מִעוּט הוּא – בְּנִי אֵינוֹ חוֹזֵר, אֲבָל יַעֲקֹב בֶּן בְּנִי סוֹפוֹ לַחֲזֹר:

י **מִגְּמַלֵּי אֲדֹנָיו.** נִכָּרִין הָיוּ מִשְּׁאָר גְּמַלִּים, שֶׁהָיוּ יוֹצְאִין זְמוּמִין מִפְּנֵי הַגָּזֵל שֶׁלֹּא יִרְעוּ בִּשְׂדוֹת אֲחֵרִים: **וְכָל טוּב אֲדֹנָיו בְּיָדוֹ.** שְׁטַר מַתָּנָה כָּתַב לְיִצְחָק עַל כָּל אֲשֶׁר לוֹ, כְּדֵי שֶׁיִּקְפְּצוּ לִשְׁלֹחַ לוֹ בִּתָּם: **אֲרַם נַהֲרַיִם.** בֵּין שְׁתֵּי נְהָרוֹת יוֹשֶׁבֶת:

יא **וַיַּבְרֵךְ הַגְּמַלִּים.** הִרְבִּיצָם:

it can change lives. Wordsworth was right when he wrote in his poem "Tintern Abbey" that the "best portion of a good man's [and woman's] life" is their "little, nameless, unremembered acts / Of kindness and of love."

24:12 וַיֹּאמַ֓ר *He said* – The masoretic tradition has placed a *shalshelet* over this word, the musical note meant to convey a psychological state of uncertainty and indecision (see note on Gen. 19:16). The commentators identify multiple sources of ambivalence at this point. The Midrash, however, offers the most insightful explanation: Eliezer has mixed feelings about the mission itself. Until that point, says the Midrash (Bereshit Rabba 59:9), he had been "sitting and weighing whether his own daughter was suitable for Yitzḥak." He hoped, in other words, that one way or another, Avraham's estate would pass to him.

There are two cues that led the Midrash to this hypothesis. The first is that when Avraham first spoke to God about his childlessness, he said: "My Lord God, what will You have given me if I remain childless, and the one who will take charge of my household is Eliezer of Damascus?" (Gen. 15:2). Eliezer, at that time, was Avraham's putative

ה וַיֹּאמֶר אֵלָיו הָעֶבֶד אוּלַי לֹא־תֹאבֶה הָאִשָּׁה לָלֶכֶת אַחֲרַי אֶל־הָאָרֶץ
ו הַזֹּאת הֶהָשֵׁב אָשִׁיב אֶת־בִּנְךָ אֶל־הָאָרֶץ אֲשֶׁר־יָצָאתָ מִשָּׁם: וַיֹּאמֶר
ז אֵלָיו אַבְרָהָם הִשָּׁמֶר לְךָ פֶּן־תָּשִׁיב אֶת־בְּנִי שָׁמָּה: יהוה ׀ אֱלֹהֵי
הַשָּׁמַיִם אֲשֶׁר לְקָחַנִי מִבֵּית אָבִי וּמֵאֶרֶץ מוֹלַדְתִּי וַאֲשֶׁר דִּבֶּר־לִי
וַאֲשֶׁר נִשְׁבַּע־לִי לֵאמֹר לְזַרְעֲךָ אֶתֵּן אֶת־הָאָרֶץ הַזֹּאת הוּא יִשְׁלַח
ח מַלְאָכוֹ לְפָנֶיךָ וְלָקַחְתָּ אִשָּׁה לִבְנִי מִשָּׁם: וְאִם־לֹא תֹאבֶה הָאִשָּׁה
לָלֶכֶת אַחֲרֶיךָ וְנִקִּיתָ מִשְּׁבֻעָתִי זֹאת רַק אֶת־בְּנִי לֹא תָשֵׁב שָׁמָּה:
ט וַיָּשֶׂם הָעֶבֶד אֶת־יָדוֹ תַּחַת יֶרֶךְ אַבְרָהָם אֲדֹנָיו וַיִּשָּׁבַע לוֹ עַל־הַדָּבָר
י הַזֶּה: וַיִּקַּח הָעֶבֶד עֲשָׂרָה גְמַלִּים מִגְּמַלֵּי אֲדֹנָיו וַיֵּלֶךְ וְכָל־טוּב אֲדֹנָיו שלישי
יא בְּיָדוֹ וַיָּקָם וַיֵּלֶךְ אֶל־אֲרַם נַהֲרַיִם אֶל־עִיר נָחוֹר: וַיַּבְרֵךְ הַגְּמַלִּים מִחוּץ
יב לָעִיר אֶל־בְּאֵר הַמָּיִם לְעֵת עֶרֶב לְעֵת צֵאת הַשֹּׁאֲבֹת: וַיֹּאמַר ׀ יהוה
אֱלֹהֵי אֲדֹנִי אַבְרָהָם הַקְרֵה־נָא לְפָנַי הַיּוֹם וַעֲשֵׂה־חֶסֶד עִם אֲדֹנִי

אונקלוס

ה וַאֲמַר לֵיהּ עַבְדָּא, מָאִם לָא תֵיבֵי אִתְּתָא, לְמֵיתֵי בַּתְרַי לְאַרְעָא הָדָא, הַאֲתָבָא אָתֵיב יָת בְּרָךְ, לְאַרְעָא דִּנְפַקְתָּא מִתַּמָּן: ו וַאֲמַר לֵיהּ אַבְרָהָם, אִסְתְּמַר לָךְ, דִּלְמָא תְתֵיב יָת בְּרִי לְתַמָּן: ז יְיָ אֱלָהָא דִּשְׁמַיָּא, דִּדְבַרְנִי, מִבֵּית אַבָּא וּמֵאֲרַע יַלְדוּתִי, וּדְמַלֵּיל לִי, וּדְקַיֵּים לִי לְמֵימַר, לִבְנָךְ, אֶתֵּין יָת אַרְעָא הָדָא, הוּא, יִשְׁלַח מַלְאֲכֵיהּ קֳדָמָךְ, וְתִסַּב אִתְּתָא, לִבְרִי מִתַּמָּן: ח וְאִם לָא תֵיבֵי אִתְּתָא לְמֵיתֵי בָּתְרָךְ, וּתְהֵי זַכָּא, מִמּוֹמָתִי דָא, לְחוֹד יָת בְּרִי, לָא תְתֵיב לְתַמָּן: ט וְשַׁוִּי עַבְדָּא יָת יְדֵיהּ, תְּחוֹת, יַרְכָּא דְּאַבְרָהָם רִבּוֹנֵיהּ, וְקַיֵּים לֵיהּ, עַל פִּתְגָּמָא הָדֵין: י וּדְבַר עַבְדָּא, עַסְרָא גַמְלִין, מִגַּמְלֵי רִבּוֹנֵיהּ וַאֲזַל, וְכָל טוּב רִבּוֹנֵיהּ בִּידֵיהּ, וְקָם, וַאֲזַל, לַאֲרַם דְּעַל פְּרָת לְקַרְתָּא דְנָחוֹר: יא וְאַשְׁרֵי גַמְלַיָּא, מִבָּרָא לְקַרְתָּא עִם בֵּירָא דְמַיָּא, לְעִדָּן רַמְשָׁא, לְעִדָּן דְּנָפְקָן מְלַיְתָא: יב וַאֲמַר יְיָ, אֱלָהֵיהּ דְּרִבּוֹנִי אַבְרָהָם, זַמִּין כְּעַן קֳדָמַי יוֹמָא דֵין, וַעֲבֵיד טֵיבוּ, עִם רִבּוֹנִי

Ḥesed also added a word to the English language. In 1535, Myles Coverdale published the first-ever translation of the Hebrew Bible into English. It was when he came to this word that he realized that there was no word in English which captured its meaning. It was then that, to translate it, he coined the word "loving-kindness."

Ḥesed is what leads Eliezer to choose Rikva to become the first Jewish bride. It brings redemption to the world and

Through *ḥesed,* Jews humanized fate as, they believed, God's *ḥesed* humanizes the world. As God acts toward us with love, so we are called on to act lovingly to one another. The world does not operate solely on the basis of impersonal principles like power or justice, but also on the deeply personal basis of vulnerability, attachment, care, and concern, recognizing us as individuals with unique needs and potentialities.

13 today and show kindness to my master Avraham. I am standing here by the
14 spring and the daughters of the townspeople are coming out to draw water. If I
say to a young woman, 'Please lower your jar so that I can drink,' and she replies,
'Drink, and I will water your camels also,' let her be the one You have chosen
for Your servant Yitzḥak. By this I will know that You have shown kindness to
15 my master." Before he had even finished speaking, Rivka, daughter of Betuel
son of Milka, the wife of Avraham's brother Naḥor, came out with her jar on
16 her shoulder. The young woman was very beautiful, a virgin whom no man had
17 known. She went down to the spring, filled her jar, and came up. The servant
18 ran to meet her and said, "Please let me sip a little water from your jar." She said,
"Drink, my lord," and quickly lowered her jar to her hand and let him drink.
19 When she had let him drink his fill, she said, "I will draw water for your camels,
20 too, until they have had enough to drink." Quickly she emptied her jar into the
trough and ran back to the well to draw more water; she drew for all his camels.
21 The man stood gazing at her, silently wondering whether the LORD had made

רש״י

יד **אֹתָהּ הֹכַחְתָּ.** רְאוּיָה הִיא לוֹ, שֶׁתְּהֵא גּוֹמֶלֶת חֲסָדִים וּכְדַאי לִכָּנֵס בְּבֵיתוֹ שֶׁל אַבְרָהָם. וּלְשׁוֹן 'הוֹכַחְתָּ' בֵּרַרְתָּ, אפרובי״ט בְּלַעַז: **וּבָהּ אֵדַע.** לְשׁוֹן תְּחִנָּה, הוֹדַע לִי בָּהּ: **כִּי עָשִׂיתָ חֶסֶד.** אִם תִּהְיֶה מִמִּשְׁפַּחְתּוֹ וְהוֹגֶנֶת לוֹ אֵדַע כִּי עָשִׂיתָ חֶסֶד:

טז **בְּתוּלָה.** מִמְּקוֹם בְּתוּלִים: **וְאִישׁ לֹא יְדָעָהּ.** שֶׁלֹּא כְּדַרְכָּהּ. לְפִי שֶׁבְּנוֹת הַגּוֹיִם מְשַׁמְּרוֹת מְקוֹם בְּתוּלֵיהֶן וּמַפְקִירוֹת עַצְמָן מִמָּקוֹם אַחֵר, הֵעִיד עַל זוֹ שֶׁנְּקִיָּה מִכֹּל:

יז **וַיָּרָץ הָעֶבֶד לִקְרָאתָהּ.** לְפִי שֶׁרָאָה שֶׁעָלוּ הַמַּיִם לִקְרָאתָהּ: **הַגְמִיאִינִי.** לְשׁוֹן גְּמִיעָה, הומי״ר בְּלַעַז:

יח **וַתֹּרֶד כַּדָּהּ.** מֵעַל שִׁכְמָהּ:

יט **עַד אִם כִּלּוּ.** הֲרֵי 'אִם' מְשַׁמֵּשׁ בִּלְשׁוֹן 'אֲשֶׁר': **אִם כִּלּוּ.** "דִּיסַפְּקוּן", שֶׁזּוֹ הִיא גְּמַר שְׁתִיָּתָן כְּשֶׁשָּׁתוּ דֵּי סִפְקָן:

כ **וַתְּעַר.** לְשׁוֹן נְפִיצָה, וְהַרְבֵּה יֵשׁ בִּלְשׁוֹן מִשְׁנָה: "הַמְעָרֶה מִכְּלִי אֶל כְּלִי" (עבודה זרה עב ע״ח), וּבַמִּקְרָא יֵשׁ לוֹ דּוֹמֶה: "אַל תְּעַר נַפְשִׁי" (תהלים קמא, ח), "אֲשֶׁר הֶעֱרָה לַמָּוֶת נַפְשׁוֹ" (ישעיה נג, יב): **הַשֹּׁקֶת.** אֶבֶן חֲלוּלָה שֶׁשּׁוֹתִים בָּהּ הַגְּמַלִּים:

כא **מִשְׁתָּאֵה.** לְשׁוֹן שְׁאִיָּה, כְּמוֹ: "שָׁאוּ עָרִים", "תִּשָּׁאֶה שְׁמָמָה" (ישעיה ו, יא): **מִשְׁתָּאֵה.** מִשְׁתּוֹמֵם וּמִתְבַּהֵל עַל שֶׁרָאָה דְּבָרוֹ קָרוֹב לְהַצְלִיחַ, אֲבָל אֵינוֹ יוֹדֵעַ אִם מִמִּשְׁפַּחַת אַבְרָהָם הִיא אִם לָאו. וְאַל תִּתְמַהּ בְּתָי״ו שֶׁל "מִשְׁתָּאֵה", שֶׁאֵין לְךָ תֵּבָה שֶׁתְּחִלַּת יְסוֹדָהּ שִׁי״ן וּמְדַבֶּרֶת בִּלְשׁוֹן מִתְפַּעֵל שֶׁאֵין תָּי״ו מַפְרִידָהּ בֵּין שְׁתֵּי אוֹתִיּוֹת שֶׁל עִקַּר הַיְסוֹד, כְּגוֹן: "מִשְׁתָּאֵה", "מִשְׁתּוֹלֵל" (שם נט, טו) מִגִּזְרַת 'שׁוֹלֵל', "וַיִּשְׁתּוֹמֵם" (שם פסוק טז) מִגִּזְרַת 'שְׁמָמָה', "וְיִשְׁתַּמֵּר חֻקּוֹת עָמְרִי" (מיכה ו, טז) מִגִּזְרַת 'וַיִּשְׁמֹר', אַף כָּאן "מִשְׁתָּאֵה" מִגִּזְרַת 'תִּשָּׁאֶה'. וּכְשֵׁם שֶׁאַתָּה מוֹצֵא לְשׁוֹן מְשׁוֹמֵם בְּאָדָם נִבְהָל וְנֶאֱלָם וּבַעַל מַחֲשָׁבוֹת, כְּמוֹ: "עַל יוֹמוֹ נָשַׁמּוּ אַחֲרֹנִים"

someone you know has recently been bereaved, visit them and give them comfort. If you know of someone who has lost their job, do all you can to help them find another. The Sages called this "imitating God." It is the test by which the servant unerringly recognizes our second founding mother.

24:20 **וַתָּרָץ עוֹד** *And ran back* – Yitzḥak is the most passive of the patriarchs. Rivka is his opposite – initiating, full of energy. It is the people not like us who make us grow. When building a team, we need to recognize where we are weak and surround ourselves by people who are strong in those areas. Often this applies in family life as well. Marriage is the supreme embodiment of openness to otherness. It was and is the single greatest source of beauty in ordinary lives – moral beauty. It is a song scored for two different voices in complex harmony.

יג אַבְרָהָם: הִנֵּה אָנֹכִי נִצָּב עַל־עֵין הַמָּיִם וּבְנוֹת אַנְשֵׁי הָעִיר יֹצְאֹת
יד לִשְׁאֹב מָיִם: וְהָיָה הַנַּעֲרָ אֲשֶׁר אֹמַר אֵלֶיהָ הַטִּי־נָא כַדֵּךְ וְאֶשְׁתֶּה
וְאָמְרָה שְׁתֵה וְגַם־גְּמַלֶּיךָ אַשְׁקֶה אֹתָהּ הֹכַחְתָּ לְעַבְדְּךָ לְיִצְחָק וּבָהּ
טו אֵדַע כִּי־עָשִׂיתָ חֶסֶד עִם־אֲדֹנִי: וַיְהִי־הוּא טֶרֶם כִּלָּה לְדַבֵּר וְהִנֵּה רִבְקָה
יֹצֵאת אֲשֶׁר יֻלְּדָה לִבְתוּאֵל בֶּן־מִלְכָּה אֵשֶׁת נָחוֹר אֲחִי אַבְרָהָם וְכַדָּהּ
טז עַל־שִׁכְמָהּ: וְהַנַּעֲרָ טֹבַת מַרְאֶה מְאֹד בְּתוּלָה וְאִישׁ לֹא יְדָעָהּ וַתֵּרֶד
יז הָעַיְנָה וַתְּמַלֵּא כַדָּהּ וַתָּעַל: וַיָּרָץ הָעֶבֶד לִקְרָאתָהּ וַיֹּאמֶר הַגְמִיאִינִי
יח נָא מְעַט־מַיִם מִכַּדֵּךְ: וַתֹּאמֶר שְׁתֵה אֲדֹנִי וַתְּמַהֵר וַתֹּרֶד כַּדָּהּ עַל־יָדָהּ
יט וַתַּשְׁקֵהוּ: וַתְּכַל לְהַשְׁקֹתוֹ וַתֹּאמֶר גַּם לִגְמַלֶּיךָ אֶשְׁאָב עַד אִם־כִּלּוּ
כ לִשְׁתֹּת: וַתְּמַהֵר וַתְּעַר כַּדָּהּ אֶל־הַשֹּׁקֶת וַתָּרָץ עוֹד אֶל־הַבְּאֵר לִשְׁאֹב
כא וַתִּשְׁאַב לְכָל־גְּמַלָּיו: וְהָאִישׁ מִשְׁתָּאֵה לָהּ מַחֲרִישׁ לָדַעַת הַהִצְלִיחַ

אונקלוס

אַבְרָהָם: יג הָא אֲנָא קָאֵים עַל עֵינָא דְמַיָּא, וּבְנָת אֱנָשֵׁי קַרְתָּא, נָפְקָן לְמִמְלֵי מַיָּא: יד וּתְהֵי עוּלֵימְתָא, דְּאֵימַר לַהּ אַרְכִּינִי כְעַן קֻלְּתִיךְ וְאֶשְׁתֵּי, וְתֵימַר אִשְׁתְּ, וְאַף גַּמְלָךְ אַשְׁקֵי, יָתַהּ זַמֵּינְתָּא לְעַבְדָּךְ לְיִצְחָק, וּבַהּ אֵדַע, אֲרֵי עֲבַדְתְּ טֵיבוּ עִם רִבּוֹנִי: טו וַהֲוָה הוּא, עַד לָא שֵׁיצִי לְמַלָּלָא, וְהָא רִבְקָה נָפְקַת, דְּאִתְיְלִידַת לִבְתוּאֵל בַּר מִלְכָּה, אִתַּת נָחוֹר אֲחוּהִי דְּאַבְרָהָם, וְקֻלְּתַהּ עַל כִּתְפַּהּ: טז וְעוּלֵימְתָא, שַׁפִּירָא לְמִחְזֵי לַחְדָּא, בְּתוּלְתָּא, וּגְבַר לָא יְדָעַהּ, וּנְחָתַת לְעֵינָא, וּמְלַת קֻלְּתַהּ וּסְלֵיקַת: יז וּרְהַט עַבְדָּא לְקַדָּמוּתַהּ, וַאֲמַר, אַשְׁקִינִי כְעַן, זְעֵיר מַיָּא מִקֻּלְּתִיךְ: יח וַאֲמַרַת אִשְׁתְּ רִבּוֹנִי, וְאוֹחִיאַת, וַאֲחֵיתַת קֻלְּתַהּ, עַל יְדַהּ וְאַשְׁקִיתֵיהּ: יט וְשֵׁיצִיאַת לְאַשְׁקָיוּתֵיהּ, וַאֲמַרַת, אַף לְגַמְלָךְ אֱמְלֵי, עַד דִּיסְפְּקוּן לְמִשְׁתֵּי: כ וְאוֹחִיאַת, וּנְפַצַת קֻלְּתַהּ לְבֵית שִׁקְיָא, וּרְהַטַת עוֹד, לְבֵירָא לְמִמְלֵי, וּמְלַת לְכָל גַּמְלוֹהִי: כא וְגַבְרָא שָׁהֵי בַהּ מִסְתַּכַּל, שָׁתֵיק, לְמִדַּע, הַאַצְלַח

heir. The second is that when Avraham charges his servant with the mission to find a wife for his son, Eliezer replies, "What if (*ulai*) the woman does not want to come back with me to this land?" (24:5). As Ibn Ezra notes, the word *ulai* is not neutral (commentary on Psalms 116:16). It signifies an emotional involvement in the outcome: one wishes for the eventuality to either come to pass or not come to pass. Eliezer's "what if" may be an unconscious expression of the fact that, with half his mind, he wants the mission to fail. This would once again place him or his daughter in a position to be Avraham's heir. It is therefore with profoundly mixed feelings that he prays for the woman who is to be God's choice of Yitzḥak's wife to appear.

24:19 גַּם לִגְמַלֶּיךָ אֶשְׁאָב *I will draw water for your camels, too* – While fulfilling the stranger's request for water, Rivka identifies a need he has not mentioned and meets that as well. "Someone else's physical needs are my spiritual obligation," a Jewish mystic taught. The truths of religion are exalted, but its duties are close at hand.

Jewish ethics is refreshingly down-to-earth. If someone is in need, give. If someone is lonely, invite them home. If

22 his journey successful. When the camels had finished drinking, the man took
a gold ring weighing a half shekel and two gold bracelets for her arms weighing
23 ten shekel, and he asked, "Whose daughter are you? Please tell me, is there
24 room in your father's house for us to spend the night?" She answered him, "I
25 am the daughter of Betuel, the son Milka bore to Naḥor." She added, "We
have plenty of straw and fodder, as well as room for you to spend the night."
26 27 The man bowed low, prostrating himself to the LORD. He said, "Blessed be REVI'I
the LORD, God of my master Avraham, who has not withheld His kindness
and faithfulness from my master. As for me – the LORD has guided me on the
28 way to the house of my master's close family." The young woman ran and told
29 all this to her mother's household. Rivka had a brother named Lavan; he ran
30 outside to the man at the spring. He had seen the ring, and the bracelets on
his sister's arms, and had heard his sister Rivka tell what the man had said to
her. He came up to the man who was still standing by the camels at the spring,
31 and said, "Come. The LORD bless you! Why are you standing outside? I have
32 made room in the house and prepared a place for the camels." So the man
entered the house, the camels were unloaded, straw and fodder were brought
for the camels, and water was brought for him and his men to wash their feet.
33 Food was set before him to eat, but he said, "I will not eat until I have said
34 what I have to say." "Speak, then," said Lavan. "I am Avraham's servant," he

רש״י

(איוב יח, כ), ״שֹׁמּוּ שָׁמַיִם״ (ירמיה ב, יב), ״אֶשְׁתּוֹמַם כְּשָׁעָה חֲדָה״ (דניאל ד, טז), כָּךְ תְּפָרֵשׁ לְשׁוֹן ׳שְׁאִיָּה׳ בְּאָדָם בָּהוּל וּבַעַל מַחֲשָׁבוֹת. וְאוּנְקְלוֹס תִּרְגֵּם לְשׁוֹן ׳שְׁהִיָּה׳, ״וְגַבְרָא שָׁהֵי״, שׁוֹהֶא וְעוֹמֵד בְּמָקוֹם אֶחָד לִרְאוֹת ״הַהִצְלִיחַ ה׳ דַּרְכּוֹ״. וְאֵין לְתַרְגֵּם ׳שָׁתֵי׳, שֶׁהֲרֵי אֵינוֹ לְשׁוֹן שְׁתִיָּה, שֶׁאֵין אָלֶ״ף נוֹפֶלֶת בִּלְשׁוֹן שְׁתִיָּה: **מִשְׁתָּאֵה לָהּ.** מִשְׁתּוֹמֵם עָלֶיהָ, כְּמוֹ: ״אִמְרִי לִי אָחִי הוּא״ (לעיל כ, יג), ״אַנְשֵׁי הַמָּקוֹם לְאִשְׁתּוֹ״ (להלן כו, ז):

כב **בֶּקַע.** רֶמֶז לְשִׁקְלֵי יִשְׂרָאֵל בֶּקַע לַגֻּלְגֹּלֶת (שמות לח, כו): **וּשְׁנֵי צְמִידִים.** רֶמֶז לִשְׁנֵי לוּחוֹת מְצֻמָּדוֹת: **עֲשָׂרָה זָהָב מִשְׁקָלָם.** רֶמֶז לַעֲשֶׂרֶת הַדִּבְּרוֹת שֶׁבָּהֶן:

כג **וַיֹּאמֶר בַּת מִי אַתְּ.** לְאַחַר שֶׁנָּתַן לָהּ שְׁאָלָהּ, לְפִי שֶׁהָיָה בָּטוּחַ בִּזְכוּתוֹ שֶׁל אַבְרָהָם שֶׁהִצְלִיחַ הַקָּדוֹשׁ בָּרוּךְ הוּא דַּרְכּוֹ: **לָלִין.** לִינָה אַחַת, ׳לִין׳ שֵׁם דָּבָר, וְהִיא אָמְרָה ״לָלוּן״ (להלן פסוק כה), כַּמָּה לֵינוֹת אַתָּה יָכוֹל לָלוּן אֶצְלֵנוּ:

כד **בַּת בְּתוּאֵל.** הֱשִׁיבַתּוּ עַל רִאשׁוֹן רִאשׁוֹן וְעַל אַחֲרוֹן אַחֲרוֹן:

כה **מִסְפּוֹא.** כָּל מַאֲכַל הַגְּמַלִּים קָרוּי ׳מִסְפּוֹא׳, כְּגוֹן עָצָה וּשְׂעוֹרִים:

כז **בַּדֶּרֶךְ.** דֶּרֶךְ הַמְזֻמָּן, דֶּרֶךְ הַיָּשָׁר, בְּאוֹתוֹ דֶּרֶךְ שֶׁהָיִיתִי צָרִיךְ. וְכֵן כָּל בֵּי״ת וְלָמֶ״ד וְהֵ״א הַמְשַׁמְּשִׁים בְּרֹאשׁ הַתֵּבָה וּנְקוּדִים בְּפַתָּח, מְדַבְּרִים בַּדָּבָר הַפָּשׁוּט שֶׁנִּזְכַּר כְּבָר בְּמָקוֹם אַחֵר, אוֹ שֶׁהוּא מְבֹרָר וְנִכָּר בְּאֵיזוֹ הוּא מְדַבֵּר:

כח **לְבֵית אִמָּהּ.** דֶּרֶךְ הַנָּשִׁים הָיְתָה לִהְיוֹת לָהֶן בַּיִת לֵישֵׁב בּוֹ לִמְלַאכְתָּן, וְאֵין הַבַּת מַגֶּדֶת אֶלָּא לְאִמָּהּ:

כט **וַיָּרָץ.** לָמָּה וַיָּרָץ וְעַל מָה רָץ? ״וַיְהִי כִּרְאֹת אֶת הַנֶּזֶם״ (בפסוק הבא), אָמַר: עָשִׁיר הוּא זֶה, וְנָתַן עֵינָיו בַּמָּמוֹן:

ל **עַל הַגְּמַלִּים.** לְשָׁמְרָן, כְּמוֹ: ״וְהוּא עֹמֵד עֲלֵיהֶם״ (לעיל יח, ח) לְשַׁמְּשָׁם:

לא **פִּנִּיתִי הַבַּיִת.** מֵעֲבוֹדָה זָרָה:

לב **וַיְפַתַּח.** הִתִּיר זְמָם שֶׁלָּהֶם, שֶׁהָיָה סוֹתֵם אֶת פִּיהֶם שֶׁלֹּא יִרְעוּ בַּדֶּרֶךְ בִּשְׂדוֹת אֲחֵרִים:

לג **עַד אִם דִּבַּרְתִּי.** הֲרֵי ׳אִם׳ מְשַׁמֵּשׁ בִּלְשׁוֹן ׳אֲשֶׁר׳ וּבִלְשׁוֹן ׳כִּי׳, כְּמוֹ: ״עַד כִּי יָבֹא שִׁילֹה״ (להלן מט, י), וְזֶהוּ שֶׁאָמְרוּ חֲכָמִים: ׳כִּי׳ מְשַׁמֵּשׁ בְּאַרְבַּע לְשׁוֹנוֹת, וְהָאֶחָד ׳אִי׳ וְהוּא ׳אִם׳:

כב יְהוָה דַּרְכּוֹ אִם־לֹא: וַיְהִי כַּאֲשֶׁר כִּלּוּ הַגְּמַלִּים לִשְׁתּוֹת וַיִּקַּח הָאִישׁ
נֶזֶם זָהָב בֶּקַע מִשְׁקָלוֹ וּשְׁנֵי צְמִידִים עַל־יָדֶיהָ עֲשָׂרָה זָהָב מִשְׁקָלָם:
כג וַיֹּאמֶר בַּת־מִי אַתְּ הַגִּידִי נָא לִי הֲיֵשׁ בֵּית־אָבִיךְ מָקוֹם לָנוּ לָלִין:
כד כה וַתֹּאמֶר אֵלָיו בַּת־בְּתוּאֵל אָנֹכִי בֶּן־מִלְכָּה אֲשֶׁר יָלְדָה לְנָחוֹר: וַתֹּאמֶר
כו אֵלָיו גַּם־תֶּבֶן גַּם־מִסְפּוֹא רַב עִמָּנוּ גַּם־מָקוֹם לָלוּן: וַיִּקֹּד הָאִישׁ
כז וַיִּשְׁתַּחוּ לַיהוָה: וַיֹּאמֶר בָּרוּךְ יְהוָה אֱלֹהֵי אֲדֹנִי אַבְרָהָם אֲשֶׁר לֹא־ רביעי
עָזַב חַסְדּוֹ וַאֲמִתּוֹ מֵעִם אֲדֹנִי אָנֹכִי בַּדֶּרֶךְ נָחַנִי יְהוָה בֵּית אֲחֵי אֲדֹנִי:
כח כט וַתָּרָץ הַנַּעֲרָ וַתַּגֵּד לְבֵית אִמָּהּ כַּדְּבָרִים הָאֵלֶּה: וּלְרִבְקָה אָח וּשְׁמוֹ
ל לָבָן וַיָּרָץ לָבָן אֶל־הָאִישׁ הַחוּצָה אֶל־הָעָיִן: וַיְהִי ׀ כִּרְאֹת אֶת־הַנֶּזֶם
וְאֶת־הַצְּמִדִים עַל־יְדֵי אֲחֹתוֹ וּכְשָׁמְעוֹ אֶת־דִּבְרֵי רִבְקָה אֲחֹתוֹ לֵאמֹר
כֹּה־דִבֶּר אֵלַי הָאִישׁ וַיָּבֹא אֶל־הָאִישׁ וְהִנֵּה עֹמֵד עַל־הַגְּמַלִּים עַל־
לא הָעָיִן: וַיֹּאמֶר בּוֹא בְּרוּךְ יְהוָה לָמָּה תַעֲמֹד בַּחוּץ וְאָנֹכִי פִּנִּיתִי הַבַּיִת
לב וּמָקוֹם לַגְּמַלִּים: וַיָּבֹא הָאִישׁ הַבַּיְתָה וַיְפַתַּח הַגְּמַלִּים וַיִּתֵּן תֶּבֶן
לג וּמִסְפּוֹא לַגְּמַלִּים וּמַיִם לִרְחֹץ רַגְלָיו וְרַגְלֵי הָאֲנָשִׁים אֲשֶׁר אִתּוֹ: ויישם וַיּוּשַׂם
לד לְפָנָיו לֶאֱכֹל וַיֹּאמֶר לֹא אֹכַל עַד אִם־דִּבַּרְתִּי דְּבָרָי וַיֹּאמֶר דַּבֵּר: וַיֹּאמַר

אונקלוס

יי, אוֹרְחֵיהּ אִם לָא: כב וַהֲוָה, כַּד סְפִיקוּ גַּמְלַיָּא לְמִשְׁתֵּי, וּנְסֵיב גֻּבְרָא קְדָשָׁא דְּדַהֲבָא, תִּקְלָא מַתְקְלֵיהּ, וּתְרֵין שֵׁירִין עַל יְדַהָא, מַתְקַל עֲסַר סִלְעִין דִּדְהַב מַתְקַלְהוֹן: כג וַאֲמַר בַּת מַאן אַתְּ, חַוַּאי כְּעַן לִי, הַאִית בֵּית אֲבוּיךְ, אֲתַר כָּשַׁר לַנָא לִמְבָת: כד וַאֲמַרַת לֵיהּ, בַּת בְּתוּאֵל אֲנָא, בַּר מִלְכָּה, דִּילֵידַת לְנָחוֹר: כה וַאֲמַרַת לֵיהּ, אַף תִּבְנָא אַף כִּסְּתָא סַגִּי עִמַּנָא, אַף אֲתַר כָּשַׁר לִמְבָת: כו וּכְרַע גֻּבְרָא, וּסְגֵיד קֳדָם יי: כז וַאֲמַר, בְּרִיךְ יי אֱלָהֵיהּ דְּרִבּוֹנִי אַבְרָהָם, דְּלָא מְנַע טֵיבוּתֵיהּ, וְקֻשְׁטֵיהּ מִן רִבּוֹנִי, אֲנָא, בְּאוֹרַח תַּקְנָא דַּבְּרַנִי יי, בֵּית אֲחוּהִי דְּרִבּוֹנִי: כח וּרְהַטַת עוּלֵימְתָא, וְחַוִּיאַת לְבֵית אִמַּהּ, כְּפִתְגָּמַיָּא הָאִלֵּין: כט וּלְרִבְקָה אֲחָא וּשְׁמֵיהּ לָבָן, וּרְהַט לָבָן לְוָת גֻּבְרָא, לְבָרָא לְעֵינָא: ל וַהֲוָה כַּד חֲזָא יָת קְדָשָׁא, וְיָת שֵׁירַיָּא עַל יְדֵי אֲחָתֵיהּ, וְכַד שְׁמַע, יָת פִּתְגָּמֵי, רִבְקָה אֲחָתֵיהּ לְמֵימַר, כְּדֵין מַלֵּיל עִמִּי גֻּבְרָא, וַאֲתָא לְוָת גֻּבְרָא, וְהָא, קָאֵים עִלָּוֵי גַּמְלַיָּא עַל עֵינָא: לא וַאֲמַר, עוּל בְּרִיכָא דַּיי, לְמָא אַתְּ קָאֵים בְּבָרָא, וַאֲנָא פַּנֵּיתִי בֵיתָא, וַאֲתַר כָּשַׁר לְגַמְלַיָּא: לב וְעָאל גֻּבְרָא לְבֵיתָא, וּשְׁרָא מִן גַּמְלַיָּא, וִיהַב תִּבְנָא וְכִסְּתָא לְגַמְלַיָּא, וּמַיָּא לְאַסְחָאָה רַגְלוֹהִי, וְרַגְלֵי גֻּבְרַיָּא דְּעִמֵּיהּ: לג וְשַׁוִּיאוּ קֳדָמוֹהִי לְמֵיכַל, וַאֲמַר לָא אֵיכוֹל, עַד דַּאֲמַלֵּיל פִּתְגָּמָי, וַאֲמַר מַלֵּיל: לד וַאֲמַר,

35 said. "The Lord has blessed my master greatly, and he has prospered. He has
given him sheep and cattle, silver and gold, male and female servants, camels
36 and donkeys. My master's wife Sara bore my master a son in her old age, and he
37 committed to his son all that is his. My master made me swear, saying, 'You
must not take a wife for my son from among the daughters of the Canaanites in
38 whose land I live. Instead you must go to my father's house and family and
39 there find a wife for my son.' I asked my master, 'What if the woman does not
40 want to come back with me?' He answered, 'The Lord before whom I have
walked will send His angel with you to make your journey a success, so that
41 you may find a wife for my son from my family and father's house. You are
released from this vow only if you come to my family and they refuse to give
42 her to you. Then you are released from my vow.' Today, when I came to the
spring, I said, 'Lord, God of my master Avraham, if You will, please grant
43 success to this journey on which I have come. I am standing here by a spring of
water. The woman who comes out to draw water, to whom I say, "Please let me
44 sip a little water from your jar," and who says to me, "Drink, and I will also draw
for your camels" – let her be the one the Lord has chosen for my master's son.'

רש״י

לו וַיִּתֶּן לוֹ אֶת כָּל אֲשֶׁר לוֹ. שְׁטַר הַמַּתָּנָה בְּיָדִי:

לז-לח לֹא תִקַּח אִשָּׁה לִבְנִי מִבְּנוֹת הַכְּנַעֲנִי. אִם לֹא תֵלֵךְ תְּחִלָּה אֶל בֵּית אָבִי וְלֹא תֹאבֶה לָלֶכֶת אַחֲרֶיךָ:

לט אֻלַי לֹא תֵלֵךְ הָאִשָּׁה. 'אֵלַי' כְּתִיב, בַּת הָיְתָה לוֹ לֶאֱלִיעֶזֶר, וְהָיָה מְחַזֵּר לִמְצֹא עִלָּה שֶׁיֹּאמַר לוֹ אַבְרָהָם לִפְנוֹת אֵלָיו לְהַשִּׂיאוֹ בִּתּוֹ. אָמַר לוֹ אַבְרָהָם: בְּנִי בָּרוּךְ וּבִתְּךָ אָרוּר, וְאֵין אָרוּר מִדַּבֵּק בְּבָרוּךְ:

מב וָאָבֹא הַיּוֹם. הַיּוֹם יָצָאתִי וְהַיּוֹם בָּאתִי; מִכָּאן שֶׁקָּפְצָה לוֹ הָאָרֶץ. אָמַר רַבִּי אַחָא: יָפָה שִׂיחָתָן שֶׁל עַבְדֵי אָבוֹת לִפְנֵי הַמָּקוֹם מִתּוֹרָתָן שֶׁל בָּנִים, שֶׁהֲרֵי פָּרָשָׁה שֶׁל אֱלִיעֶזֶר כְּפוּלָה בַּתּוֹרָה, וְהַרְבֵּה גּוּפֵי תוֹרָה לֹא נִתְּנוּ אֶלָּא בִּרְמִיזָה:

Rivka" (Gen. 26:35). Yaakov, by contrast, "obeyed his father and mother" by going to find a wife from his mother's family (28:7).

These episodes raise the question of the role of parental authority in marriage. To what extent is Avraham's initiative in choosing, or getting his servant to choose, a wife for his son normative? Does a parent have a right, in Judaism, to determine who their child will marry?

This issue was much debated in the Middle Ages, an era in which parental authority, as well as respect for age and tradition, were far stronger than they are now. Normally it was expected that a child would act in accordance with the will of his or her parents in all things. Strikingly, the halakhists did not follow this line. Writing in the thirteenth century, Rabbi Shlomo Ibn Adret (Rashba, 1235–1310) argued that getting married is a positive commandment. As the wishes of God take precedence over those of human beings, parental wishes cannot override the desire of a child to marry and fulfill the mitzva. Since the child wants to do God's will, he is not bound to do his parents' will if it collides with his own in the choice of a marriage partner. As for Yitzḥak, Rashba argues that he was unique. Yitzḥak was a "perfect offering," a child of special sanctity; having been offered at the altar, he was not allowed to leave the land of Israel – in contrast to Avraham and Yaakov, both of whom traveled to Egypt. Had this not been so, says Rashba, he would certainly have undertaken the journey himself to choose a wife (*Teshuvot Hameyuḥasot LehaRamban*, 272). As it is, the text is explicit

לה עֶבֶד אַבְרָהָם אָנֹכִי: וַיהוָה בֵּרַךְ אֶת־אֲדֹנִי מְאֹד וַיִּגְדָּל וַיִּתֶּן־לוֹ צֹאן
לו וּבָקָר וְכֶסֶף וְזָהָב וַעֲבָדִם וּשְׁפָחֹת וּגְמַלִּים וַחֲמֹרִים: וַתֵּלֶד שָׂרָה אֵשֶׁת
לז אֲדֹנִי בֵן לַאדֹנִי אַחֲרֵי זִקְנָתָהּ וַיִּתֶּן־לוֹ אֶת־כָּל־אֲשֶׁר־לוֹ: וַיַּשְׁבִּעֵנִי
אֲדֹנִי לֵאמֹר לֹא־תִקַּח אִשָּׁה לִבְנִי מִבְּנוֹת הַכְּנַעֲנִי אֲשֶׁר אָנֹכִי יֹשֵׁב
לח בְּאַרְצוֹ: אִם־לֹא אֶל־בֵּית־אָבִי תֵּלֵךְ וְאֶל־מִשְׁפַּחְתִּי וְלָקַחְתָּ אִשָּׁה
לט מ לִבְנִי: וָאֹמַר אֶל־אֲדֹנִי אֻלַי לֹא־תֵלֵךְ הָאִשָּׁה אַחֲרָי: וַיֹּאמֶר אֵלָי יְהוָה
אֲשֶׁר־הִתְהַלַּכְתִּי לְפָנָיו יִשְׁלַח מַלְאָכוֹ אִתָּךְ וְהִצְלִיחַ דַּרְכֶּךָ וְלָקַחְתָּ
מא אִשָּׁה לִבְנִי מִמִּשְׁפַּחְתִּי וּמִבֵּית אָבִי: אָז תִּנָּקֶה מֵאָלָתִי כִּי תָבוֹא אֶל־
מב מִשְׁפַּחְתִּי וְאִם־לֹא יִתְּנוּ לָךְ וְהָיִיתָ נָקִי מֵאָלָתִי: וָאָבֹא הַיּוֹם אֶל־הָעָיִן כא
וָאֹמַר יְהוָה אֱלֹהֵי אֲדֹנִי אַבְרָהָם אִם־יֶשְׁךָ־נָּא מַצְלִיחַ דַּרְכִּי אֲשֶׁר
מג אָנֹכִי הֹלֵךְ עָלֶיהָ: הִנֵּה אָנֹכִי נִצָּב עַל־עֵין הַמָּיִם וְהָיָה הָעַלְמָה הַיֹּצֵאת
מד לִשְׁאֹב וְאָמַרְתִּי אֵלֶיהָ הַשְׁקִינִי־נָא מְעַט־מַיִם מִכַּדֵּךְ: וְאָמְרָה אֵלַי

אונקלוס

עַבְדָּא דְאַבְרָהָם אֲנָא: לה וַיְיָ, בָּרֵיךְ יָת רִבּוֹנִי, לַחֲדָא וּרְבָא, וִיהַב לֵיהּ, עָן וְתוֹרִין וּכְסַף וּדְהַב, וְעַבְדִּין וְאַמְהָן, וְגַמְלִין וַחֲמָרִין: לו וִילֵידַת, שָׂרָה אִתַּת רִבּוֹנִי בַּר לְרִבּוֹנִי, בָּתַר דְּסֵיבַת, וִיהַב לֵיהּ יָת כָּל דְּלֵיהּ: לז וְקַיֵּים עֲלַי רִבּוֹנִי לְמֵימַר, לָא תִסַּב אִתְּתָא לִבְרִי, מִבְּנָת כְּנַעֲנָאֵי, דַּאֲנָא יָתֵיב בְּאַרְעֲהוֹן: לח אֱלָהֵין לְבֵית אַבָּא, תֵּיזֵיל וּלְזַרְעִיתִי, וְתִסַּב אִתְּתָא לִבְרִי: לט וַאֲמָרִית לְרִבּוֹנִי, מָאִם, לָא תֵיתֵי אִתְּתָא בָּתְרָי: מ וַאֲמַר לִי, יְיָ דִּפְלַחִית קֳדָמוֹהִי, יִשְׁלַח מַלְאֲכֵיהּ עִמָּךְ וְיַצְלַח אוֹרְחָךְ, וְתִסַּב אִתְּתָא לִבְרִי, מִזַּרְעִיתִי וּמִבֵּית אַבָּא: מא בְּכֵן תְּהֵי זַכָּא מִמּוֹמָתִי, אֲרֵי תְהָךְ לְזַרְעִיתִי, וְאִם לָא יִתְּנוּן לָךְ, וּתְהֵי זַכָּא מִמּוֹמָתִי: מב וַאֲתֵיתִי יוֹמָא דֵין לְעֵינָא, וַאֲמָרִית, יְיָ אֱלָהֵיהּ דְּרִבּוֹנִי אַבְרָהָם, אִם אִית כְּעַן רַעֲוָא קֳדָמָךְ לְאַצְלָחָא אוֹרְחִי, דַּאֲנָא אָזֵיל עֲלַהּ: מג הָא אֲנָא קָאֵים עַל עֵינָא דְמַיָּא, וּתְהֵי עוּלֵימְתָא דְּתִפּוֹק לְמִמְלֵי, וְאֵימַר לַהּ, אַשְׁקִינִי כְעַן זְעֵיר מַיָּא מִקֻּלְּתִיךְ: מד וְתֵימַר לִי

24:34 עֶבֶד אַבְרָהָם אָנֹכִי *I am Avraham's servant* – Eliezer repeats the Torah's first detailed description of a marriage arrangement. The highly involved narrative is striking. Yitzḥak takes no part in the process. There is no indication that his father consults him, that he gives his consent to the arrangement, or that his views were taken into account in any way. Only after Rivka arrives do we hear of his reaction in a few brief words.

This is consistent with the general impression we have of Yitzḥak as a figure in the shadow of Avraham, who does what his father does rather than strike out in any new direction of his own.

The Torah's next presentation of marriage will be different. Esav and Yaakov each choose their own wives. Yet once again there is an emphasis on parental wishes. Esav chooses wives who become "a source of bitter sorrow to Yitzḥak and

45 Before I had even finished speaking to myself, Rivka came out with her jar on
her shoulder. She went down to the spring and drew water, and I asked her,
46 'Please, let me drink.' She immediately lowered her jar and said, 'Drink, and I
47 will also water your camels.' So I drank, and she gave the camels water too. I
asked her, 'Whose daughter are you?' She said, 'The daughter of Betuel son of
Naḥor, whom Milka bore to him.' So I placed a ring on her nose and bracelets
48 on her arms. I bowed low and prostrated myself to the LORD, and blessed the
LORD, God of my master Avraham, who led me on the right way to take the
49 daughter of my master's brother for his son. Now, if you are willing to show
kindness and faithfulness to my master, tell me; and if not, tell me that, so that
50 I may move on, right or left." Lavan and Betuel answered, "This is surely from
51 the LORD: there is nothing for us to say to you, bad or good. Here is Rivka in
front of you. Take her; go. Let her be the wife of your master's son, as the LORD
52 has spoken." When Avraham's servant heard these words, he bowed down to
53 the ground before the LORD. The servant brought out gold and silver jewelry HAMISHI
and clothes and gave them to Rivka. He also gave costly gifts to her brother and
54 her mother. Then he and his men ate and drank and spent the night there.
When they got up the next morning he said, "Send me on my way to my master."
55 But her brother and her mother replied, "Let the young woman stay with us a
56 year or ten months. Then she may go." "Do not delay me," he said, "now that

רש"י

מד **גם אתה.** 'גם' לרבות אנשים שעמו: **הכיח.** ברר והודיע, וכן כל הוכחה שבמקרא ברור דבר:

מה **טרם אכלה.** טרם שאני מכלה, וכן כל לשון הוה, פעמים שהוא מדבר בלשון עבר, ויכול לכתב 'טרם כליתי', ופעמים שמדבר בלשון עתיד; כמו: "כי אמר איוב" (איוב א, ה) הרי לשון עבר, "ככה יעשה איוב" (שם) הרי לשון עתיד, ופרוש שניהם לשון הוה: כי אומר היה איוב: "אולי חטאו בני" וגו' (שם) והיה עושה כך:

מז **ואשאל... ואשם.** שנה הסדר, שהרי הוא תחלה נתן ואחר כך שאל, אלא שלא יתפשוהו בדבריו ויאמרו: היאך נתת לה ועדין אינך יודע מי היא?:

מט **על ימין.** מבנות ישמעאל: **על שמאל.** מבנות לוט, שהיה יושב לשמאלו של אברהם. בבראשית רבה (ס, ט):

נ **ויען לבן ובתואל.** רשע היה וקפץ להשיב לפני אביו: **לא נוכל דבר אליך.** למאן בדבר הזה, לא על ידי תשובת דבר רע ולא על ידי תשובת דבר הגון ונכר, לפי שמה' יצא הדבר לפי דבריך שזמנה לך:

נב **וישתחו ארצה.** מכאן שמודים על בשורה טובה:

נג **ומגדנת.** מגדים, שהביא עמו מיני פרות של ארץ ישראל:

נד **וילינו.** כל לינה שבמקרא לינת לילה אחד:

נה **ויאמר אחיה ואמה.** ובתואל היכן היה? רוצה היה לעכב ובא מלאך והמיתו: **ימים.** שנה, כמו: "ימים תהיה גאלתו" (ויקרא כה, כט), שכך נותנין לבתולה זמן שנים עשר חדש לפרנס עצמה בתכשיטיה: **או עשור.** עשרה חדשים. ואם תאמר, 'ימים' ממש, אין דרך המבקשים לבקש דבר מועט, ואם לא תרצה – תן לנו מרבה מזה:

in assuring us that once Rivka has entered Yitzḥak's life, "he loved her."

24:55 **תשב הנער אתנו ימים או עשור** *Let the young woman stay... or ten months* – This is one of the longest chapters in

גַּם־אַתָּה שְׁתֵה וְגַם לִגְמַלֶּיךָ אֶשְׁאָב הִוא הָאִשָּׁה אֲשֶׁר־הֹכִיחַ יְהוָה
מה לְבֶן־אֲדֹנִי׃ אֲנִי טֶרֶם אֲכַלֶּה לְדַבֵּר אֶל־לִבִּי וְהִנֵּה רִבְקָה יֹצֵאת וְכַדָּהּ
מו עַל־שִׁכְמָהּ וַתֵּרֶד הָעַיְנָה וַתִּשְׁאָב וָאֹמַר אֵלֶיהָ הַשְׁקִינִי נָא׃ וַתְּמַהֵר
וַתּוֹרֶד כַּדָּהּ מֵעָלֶיהָ וַתֹּאמֶר שְׁתֵה וְגַם־גְּמַלֶּיךָ אַשְׁקֶה וָאֵשְׁתְּ וְגַם
מז הַגְּמַלִּים הִשְׁקָתָה׃ וָאֶשְׁאַל אֹתָהּ וָאֹמַר בַּת־מִי אַתְּ וַתֹּאמֶר בַּת־
בְּתוּאֵל בֶּן־נָחוֹר אֲשֶׁר יָלְדָה־לּוֹ מִלְכָּה וָאָשִׂם הַנֶּזֶם עַל־אַפָּהּ
מח וְהַצְּמִידִים עַל־יָדֶיהָ׃ וָאֶקֹּד וָאֶשְׁתַּחֲוֶה לַיהוָה וָאֲבָרֵךְ אֶת־יְהוָה אֱלֹהֵי
אֲדֹנִי אַבְרָהָם אֲשֶׁר הִנְחַנִי בְּדֶרֶךְ אֱמֶת לָקַחַת אֶת־בַּת־אֲחִי אֲדֹנִי
מט לִבְנוֹ׃ וְעַתָּה אִם־יֶשְׁכֶם עֹשִׂים חֶסֶד וֶאֱמֶת אֶת־אֲדֹנִי הַגִּידוּ לִי וְאִם־
נ לֹא הַגִּידוּ לִי וְאֶפְנֶה עַל־יָמִין אוֹ עַל־שְׂמֹאל׃ וַיַּעַן לָבָן וּבְתוּאֵל וַיֹּאמְרוּ
נא מֵיְהוָה יָצָא הַדָּבָר לֹא נוּכַל דַּבֵּר אֵלֶיךָ רַע אוֹ־טוֹב׃ הִנֵּה־רִבְקָה
נב לְפָנֶיךָ קַח וָלֵךְ וּתְהִי אִשָּׁה לְבֶן־אֲדֹנֶיךָ כַּאֲשֶׁר דִּבֶּר יְהוָה׃ וַיְהִי כַּאֲשֶׁר
נג שָׁמַע עֶבֶד אַבְרָהָם אֶת־דִּבְרֵיהֶם וַיִּשְׁתַּחוּ אַרְצָה לַיהוָה׃ וַיּוֹצֵא הָעֶבֶד חמישי
כְּלֵי־כֶסֶף וּכְלֵי זָהָב וּבְגָדִים וַיִּתֵּן לְרִבְקָה וּמִגְדָּנֹת נָתַן לְאָחִיהָ וּלְאִמָּהּ׃
נד וַיֹּאכְלוּ וַיִּשְׁתּוּ הוּא וְהָאֲנָשִׁים אֲשֶׁר־עִמּוֹ וַיָּלִינוּ וַיָּקוּמוּ בַבֹּקֶר וַיֹּאמֶר
נה שַׁלְּחֻנִי לַאדֹנִי׃ וַיֹּאמֶר אָחִיהָ וְאִמָּהּ תֵּשֵׁב הַנַּעֲרָ אִתָּנוּ יָמִים אוֹ עָשׂוֹר

אונקלוס

אף את אשת, ואף לגמלך אמלי, היא אתתא, דזמין יי לבר רבוני: מה אנא עד לא שיציתי למללא בלבי, והא רבקה נפקת וקלתה על כתפה, ונחתת לעינא ומלת, ואמרית לה אשקיני כען: מו ואוחיאת, ואחיתת קלתה מנה, ואמרת אשת, ואף גמלך אשקי, ושתיתי, ואף גמליא אשקיאת: מז ושאילית יתה, ואמרית בת מאן את, ואמרת, בת בתואל בר נחור, דילידת ליה מלכה, ושויתי קדשא על אפה, ושיריא על ידהא: מח וכרעית וסגידית קדם יי, ובריכית, ית יי אלהיה דרבוני אברהם, דדברני באורח קשוט, למסב, ית בת אחוהי דרבוני לבריה: מט וכען, אם איתיכון עבדין, טיבו וקשוט, עם רבוני חוו לי, ואם לא, חוו לי, ואתפני על ימינא או על סמאלא: נ ואתיב לבן ובתואל ואמרו, מן קדם יי נפק פתגמא, לית אנחנא יכלין, למללא עמך ביש או טב: נא הא רבקה קדמך דבר ואיזיל, ותהי אתתא לבר רבונך, כמא דמליל יי: נב והוה, כד שמע, עבדא דאברהם ית פתגמיהון, וסגיד על ארעא קדם יי: נג ואפיק עבדא, מנין דכסף ומנין דדהב ולבושין, ויהב לרבקה, ומגדנין, יהב לאחוהא ולאמה: נד ואכלו ושתיאו, הוא, וגבריא דעמיה ובתו, וקמו בצפרא, ואמר שלחוני לות רבוני: נה ואמר אחוהא ואמה, תתיב עולימתא עמנא, עדן בעדן או עסרא

the Lord has made my journey a success. Let me leave so that I may go back
57 58 to my master." They replied, "Let us call the young woman and ask her." So
they called Rivka and asked her, "Will you go with this man?" She replied, "I
59 will." So they sent their sister Rivka on her way, together with her nurse and
60 Avraham's servant and his men. They blessed Rivka and said to her, "Our sister,
may you grow into thousands of myriads, and may your descendants possess
61 their enemies' gates." Then Rivka set off with her maids, riding on camels
62 and following the man. The servant took Rivka and went. Yitzḥak was just
coming back from the direction of Be'er Laḥai Ro'i, for he was then living in the
63 Negev. He had gone out in the field toward evening to meditate. Looking up,
64 he saw – there were camels approaching. Rivka too looked up – and saw

רש״י

נז **ונשאלה את פיה.** מכאן שאין משיאין את האשה אלא מדעתה:

נח **ותאמר אלך.** מעצמי, ואף אם אינכם רוצים:

ס **את היי לאלפי רבבה.** את וזרעך תקבלו אותה ברכה שנאמר לאברהם בהר המוריה: "הרבה ארבה את זרעך" וגו' (לעיל כב, יז), יהי רצון שיהא אותו הזרע ממך ולא מאשה אחרת:

סב **מבוא באר לחי ראי.** שהלך להביא הגר לאברהם אביו שישאנה:
יושב בארץ הנגב. קרוב לאותו באר, שנאמר: "ארצה הנגב וישב בין קדש ובין שור" (לעיל כ, א), ושם היה הבאר, שנאמר: "הנה בין קדש ובין ברד" (לעיל טז, יד):

סג **לשוח.** לשון תפלה, כמו "ישפך שיחו" (תהלים קב, א):

during which the baby is named and blessed. The blessing given to Rivka by her family is a traditional part of this service.

24:63 לִפְנוֹת עָרֶב *Toward evening* – The three patriarchs are traditionally associated with the three daily prayer services respectively. My predecessor as chief rabbi, the late Lord Jakobovits of blessed memory, used to point out that the position of the sun at the times of the various services mirrors the stories of the patriarchs themselves. In the morning, the sun is in the east – and Avraham, who "rose early" (Gen. 19:27) to meet God, began his life in the east, in Ur Kasdim, namely Mesopotamia. In the early afternoon, the sun is overhead in the middle of the sky – reminding us of Yitzḥak, who spent his entire life within the land of Canaan, later to become the land of Israel. In the evening, when Yaakov "chanced upon" God (28:11), the sun is in the west, as was Yaakov, who ended his life in the west, in exile in Egypt.

24:63 לָשׂוּחַ בַּשָּׂדֶה *To meditate* – The word *siḥa* means not only meditation but also, and primarily, conversation. When the Talmud says, in the context of Yitzḥak, *ein siḥa ela tefilla*, we could translate this phrase as "conversation is a form of prayer" – and in a profound sense, it is so.

Prayer is a conversation between heaven and earth. But conversation is also a prayer – for in true conversation, I open myself up to the reality of another person. I enter his or her world. I begin to see things from a perspective not my own. In the touch of two selves, both are changed.

How appropriate, therefore, is the fact that Yitzḥak is seen praying immediately prior to his first encounter with the woman who was to become his wife. Avraham and Yaakov are alone when they pray. Yitzḥak is just about to meet the woman with whom he will share his life. For him, prayer is the prelude to a human relationship. Our openness to God shapes and is shaped by our openness to other people. Love of God is, or should be, interwoven with our love for human beings.

In prayer we do not simply speak; God, and the traditions of Jewish faith, speak through us. The very words we use are not our own, but those of thousands of years of our people's history, distilling the response to innumerable encounters with God. We become a channel through which

נו אַחַר תֵּלֵךְ: וַיֹּאמֶר אֲלֵהֶם אַל־תְּאַחֲרוּ אֹתִי וַיהוָה הִצְלִיחַ דַּרְכִּי
נז שַׁלְּחוּנִי וְאֵלְכָה לַאדֹנִי: וַיֹּאמְרוּ נִקְרָא לַנַּעֲרָ וְנִשְׁאֲלָה אֶת־פִּיהָ:
נח וַיִּקְרְאוּ לְרִבְקָה וַיֹּאמְרוּ אֵלֶיהָ הֲתֵלְכִי עִם־הָאִישׁ הַזֶּה וַתֹּאמֶר אֵלֵךְ:
נט וַיְשַׁלְּחוּ אֶת־רִבְקָה אֲחֹתָם וְאֶת־מֵנִקְתָּהּ וְאֶת־עֶבֶד אַבְרָהָם וְאֶת־
ס אֲנָשָׁיו: וַיְבָרְכוּ אֶת־רִבְקָה וַיֹּאמְרוּ לָהּ אֲחֹתֵנוּ אַתְּ הֲיִי לְאַלְפֵי רְבָבָה
סא וְיִירַשׁ זַרְעֵךְ אֵת שַׁעַר שֹׂנְאָיו: וַתָּקָם רִבְקָה וְנַעֲרֹתֶיהָ וַתִּרְכַּבְנָה עַל־
סב הַגְּמַלִּים וַתֵּלַכְנָה אַחֲרֵי הָאִישׁ וַיִּקַּח הָעֶבֶד אֶת־רִבְקָה וַיֵּלַךְ: וְיִצְחָק
סג בָּא מִבּוֹא בְּאֵר לַחַי רֹאִי וְהוּא יוֹשֵׁב בְּאֶרֶץ הַנֶּגֶב: וַיֵּצֵא יִצְחָק לָשׂוּחַ

אונקלוס

יַרְחִין, בָּתַר כֵּן תֵּיזֵיל: נו וַאֲמַר לְהוֹן לָא תְאַחֲרוּן יָתִי, וַיי אַצְלַח אוֹרְחִי, שַׁלְּחוּנִי, וְאֵהָךְ לְוָת רִבּוֹנִי: נז וַאֲמַרוּ נִקְרֵי לְעוּלֵימְתָא, וְנִשְׁמַע מָא דְּהִיא אָמְרָא: נח וּקְרוֹ לְרִבְקָה וַאֲמַרוּ לַהּ, הֲתֵיזְלִין עִם גֻּבְרָא הָדֵין, וַאֲמַרַת אֵיזֵיל: נט וְשַׁלַּחוּ, יָת רִבְקָה אֲחָתְהוֹן וְיָת מֵינִקְתַּהּ, וְיָת עַבְדָּא דְּאַבְרָהָם וְיָת גֻּבְרוֹהִי: ס וּבָרִיכוּ יָת רִבְקָה וַאֲמַרוּ לַהּ, אֲחָתַנָא, אַתְּ הֲוַאי לְאַלְפִין וּלְרִבְוָן, וְיֵירְתוּן בְּנַיְכִי, יָת קִרְוֵי סָנְאֵיהוֹן: סא וְקָמַת רִבְקָה וְעוּלֵימָתַהָא, וּרְכִיבָא עַל גַּמְלַיָּא, וַאֲזַלָא בָּתַר גֻּבְרָא, וּדְבַר עַבְדָּא, יָת רִבְקָה וַאֲזַל: סב וְיִצְחָק עָאל בְּמֵיתוֹהִי, מִבֵּירָא דְּמַלְאַךְ קַיָּמָא אִתַּחְזִי עֲלַהּ, וְהוּא יָתֵיב בַּאֲרַע דָּרוֹמָא: סג וּנְפַק יִצְחָק, לְצַלָּאָה

Marriage is a paradigm of faith. Because the word "faith" – *emuna* – entered Europe through Christianity, itself a product of Hellenistic as well as Hebraic culture, it was assumed to suggest a form of knowledge. In Biblical Hebrew it has no such connotation. *Emuna* means many things – trust, loyalty, fidelity, strength, firmness, affirmation, caring. All these things have to do not with knowledge but with the relationship between persons. They are about willingness to make a binding commitment in the conscious presence of uncertainty. Faith is a marriage; marriage is an act of faith. It is the redemption of loneliness so that we can face the future without fear. Anyone who has had the privilege of a happy marriage knows that it is the most important and beautiful thing in life.

24:60 וַיְבָרְכוּ אֶת־רִבְקָה *They blessed Rivka* – There has long been a custom among Sephardim – increasingly adopted by Ashkenazim – to mark the birth of a daughter with a special ceremony known as *zeved habat* ("the gift of a daughter"),

the Torah. As with the purchase of the cave of Makhpela, so here: acquiring a daughter-in-law will take much money and hard negotiation. The servant, on arriving in the vicinity of Avraham's family, immediately finds the girl, Rivka, before he has even finished praying for God's help. Securing her family's agreement is another matter. He brings out gold, silver, and clothing for the girl. He gives her brother and mother costly gifts. The family has a celebratory meal. But when the servant wants to leave, brother and mother say, "Let the young woman stay with us." Lavan, Rivka's brother, plays a role not unlike that of Efron: the show of generosity and concern conceals a tough, even exploitative, determination to make a profitable deal.

24:58 אֵלֵךְ *I will* – Rivka's family hesitates to send her out into the unknown. She does not hesitate. It is fitting, for this is what a marriage is: a journey across an unknown land, with nothing to protect you from the elements except one another. It may not be much, but it is everything.

65 Yitzḥak. She jumped down from the camel and asked the servant, "Who is that
man walking in the field toward us?" The servant replied, "That is my master."
66 And she took her veil and covered herself. The servant told Yitzḥak all he had
67 done. And Yitzḥak brought her into the tent of his mother Sara. He took Rivka
as his wife, and he loved her. And Yitzḥak was comforted after his mother's
death.
25 1 2 Avraham took another wife, whose name was Ketura. She bore him Zimran, SHISHI
3 Yokshan, Medan, Midyan, Yishbak, and Shuaḥ; Yokshan was the father of
Sheva and Dedan. The sons of Dedan were Ashurim, Letushim, and Leumim.
4 The sons of Midyan were Eifa, Efer, Ḥanokh, Avida, and Eldaa; all these were
5 6 descendants of Ketura. Avraham left all that was his to Yitzḥak – while he was
still living he gave gifts to the sons of his concubines and sent them eastward,
7 away from his son Yitzḥak, to the land of the East. These are the days, the years of
8 Avraham's life: he lived one hundred and seventy-five years. Avraham breathed

רש״י

סד **וַתֵּרֶא אֶת יִצְחָק.** רָאֲתָה אוֹתוֹ הָדוּר וְתָוְהָה מִפָּנָיו: **וַתִּפֹּל.** הִשְׁמִיטָה עַצְמָהּ לָאָרֶץ, כְּתַרְגּוּמוֹ: "וְאִתְרְכִינַת", הִטַּת עַצְמָהּ לָאָרֶץ וְלֹא הִגִּיעָה עַד הַקַּרְקַע, כְּמוֹ: "הַטִּי נָא כַדֵּךְ" (לעיל פסוק יד) "אַרְכִּינִי", "וַיֵּט שָׁמַיִם" (שמואל ב׳ כב, י; תהלים יח, י) "וְאַרְכֵּין", לְשׁוֹן מֻטֶּה לָאָרֶץ, וְדוֹמֶה לוֹ: "כִּי יִפֹּל לֹא יוּטָל" (תהלים לז, כד), כְּלוֹמַר, אִם יֻטֶּה לָאָרֶץ לֹא יַגִּיעַ עַד הַקַּרְקַע:

סה **וַתִּתְכָּס.** לְשׁוֹן מִתְפַּעֵל, כְּמוֹ: "וַתִּקָּבֵר" (להלן לה, ח), "וַתִּלָּכֵד" (שמואל א׳ ד, כא), "וַתִּשָּׁבֵר" (שם ד, יח):

סו **וַיְסַפֵּר הָעֶבֶד.** גִּלָּה לוֹ נִסִּים שֶׁנַּעֲשׂוּ לוֹ, שֶׁקָּפְצָה לוֹ הָאָרֶץ וְשֶׁנִּזְדַּמְּנָה לוֹ רִבְקָה בִּתְפִלָּתוֹ:

סז **הָאֹהֱלָה שָׂרָה אִמּוֹ.** וַיְבִאֶהָ הָאֹהֱלָה וְנַעֲשֵׂית דֻּגְמַת שָׂרָה אִמּוֹ, כְּלוֹמַר, וַהֲרֵי הִיא שָׂרָה אִמּוֹ, שֶׁכָּל זְמַן שֶׁשָּׂרָה קַיֶּמֶת הָיָה נֵר דָּלוּק מֵעֶרֶב שַׁבָּת לְעֶרֶב שַׁבָּת וּבְרָכָה מְצוּיָה בָּעִסָּה וְעָנָן קָשׁוּר עַל הָאֹהֶל, וּמִשֶּׁמֵּתָה פָּסְקוּ, וּכְשֶׁבָּאת רִבְקָה חָזְרוּ. בְּרֵאשִׁית רַבָּה (ס, טז): **אַחֲרֵי אִמּוֹ.** דֶּרֶךְ אֶרֶץ, כָּל זְמַן שֶׁאִמּוֹ שֶׁל אָדָם קַיֶּמֶת כָּרוּךְ הוּא אֶצְלָהּ, וּמִשֶּׁמֵּתָה – הוּא מִתְנַחֵם בְּאִשְׁתּוֹ:

כה א **קְטוּרָה.** זוֹ הָגָר, וְנִקְרֵאת קְטוּרָה עַל שֵׁם שֶׁנָּאִים מַעֲשֶׂיהָ כִּקְטֹרֶת, וְשֶׁקָּשְׁרָה פִּתְחָהּ, שֶׁלֹּא נִזְדַּוְּגָה לְאָדָם מִיּוֹם שֶׁפֵּרְשָׁה מֵאַבְרָהָם:

ג **אַשּׁוּרִם וּלְטוּשִׁם.** שֵׁם רָאשֵׁי אֻמּוֹת. וְתַרְגּוּם שֶׁל אוּנְקְלוֹס אֵין לִי לְיַשְּׁבוֹ עַל לְשׁוֹן הַמִּקְרָא:

ה **וַיִּתֵּן אַבְרָהָם וְגוֹ׳.** אָמַר רַבִּי נְחֶמְיָה: בְּרָכָה וּדְיָיתִיקִי נָתַן לוֹ. שֶׁאָמַר לוֹ הַקָּדוֹשׁ בָּרוּךְ הוּא לְאַבְרָהָם: "וֶהְיֵה בְּרָכָה" (לעיל יב, ב), הַבְּרָכוֹת מְסוּרוֹת בְּיָדְךָ לְבָרֵךְ אֶת מִי שֶׁתִּרְצֶה, וְאַבְרָהָם מְסָרָן לְיִצְחָק:

ו **הַפִּילַגְשִׁים.** חָסֵר כְּתִיב, שֶׁלֹּא הָיְתָה אֶלָּא פִּילֶגֶשׁ אַחַת, הִיא הָגָר הִיא קְטוּרָה. נָשִׁים בִּכְתֻבָּה, פִּילַגְשִׁים בְּלֹא כְתֻבָּה, כִּדְאָמְרִינַן בְּסַנְהֶדְרִין בְּנָשִׁים וּפִילַגְשִׁים דְּדָוִד: **נָתַן אַבְרָהָם מַתָּנֹת.** פֵּרְשׁוּ רַבּוֹתֵינוּ, שֵׁם טֻמְאָה מָסַר לָהֶם:

ז **מְאַת שָׁנָה וְשִׁבְעִים שָׁנָה וְחָמֵשׁ שָׁנִים.** בֶּן מֵאָה כְּבֶן שִׁבְעִים, וּבֶן שִׁבְעִים כְּבֶן חָמֵשׁ בְּלֹא חֵטְא:

24:64 וַתִּשָּׂא רִבְקָה אֶת עֵינֶיהָ וַתֵּרֶא אֶת יִצְחָק *Rivka too looked up – and saw Yitzḥak* – The great transformative experiences – love, a sudden sense of beauty, an upsurge of happiness – happen unpredictably and leave us, in Wordsworth's famous phrase, "surprised by joy."

25:1 קְטוּרָה *Ketura* – The Sages identify Ketura with Hagar. It is not unusual for people in the Torah to have more than one name; Yitro, Moshe's father-in-law, has seven. Hagar is called Ketura, tradition has it, because "her acts gave forth fragrance like incense (*ketoret*)" (Bereshit Rabba 51:4).

סד בַּשָּׂדֶה לִפְנוֹת עָרֶב וַיִּשָּׂא עֵינָיו וַיַּרְא וְהִנֵּה גְמַלִּים בָּאִים: וַתִּשָּׂא
סה רִבְקָה אֶת־עֵינֶיהָ וַתֵּרֶא אֶת־יִצְחָק וַתִּפֹּל מֵעַל הַגָּמָל: וַתֹּאמֶר אֶל־
הָעֶבֶד מִי־הָאִישׁ הַלָּזֶה הַהֹלֵךְ בַּשָּׂדֶה לִקְרָאתֵנוּ וַיֹּאמֶר הָעֶבֶד הוּא
סו אֲדֹנִי וַתִּקַּח הַצָּעִיף וַתִּתְכָּס: וַיְסַפֵּר הָעֶבֶד לְיִצְחָק אֵת כָּל־הַדְּבָרִים
סז אֲשֶׁר עָשָׂה: וַיְבִאֶהָ יִצְחָק הָאֹהֱלָה שָׂרָה אִמּוֹ וַיִּקַּח אֶת־רִבְקָה וַתְּהִי־
לוֹ לְאִשָּׁה וַיֶּאֱהָבֶהָ וַיִּנָּחֵם יִצְחָק אַחֲרֵי אִמּוֹ:
כה א ב וַיֹּסֶף אַבְרָהָם וַיִּקַּח אִשָּׁה וּשְׁמָהּ קְטוּרָה: וַתֵּלֶד לוֹ אֶת־זִמְרָן וְאֶת־ כב ששי
ג יָקְשָׁן וְאֶת־מְדָן וְאֶת־מִדְיָן וְאֶת־יִשְׁבָּק וְאֶת־שׁוּחַ: וְיָקְשָׁן יָלַד אֶת־
ד שְׁבָא וְאֶת־דְּדָן וּבְנֵי דְדָן הָיוּ אַשּׁוּרִם וּלְטוּשִׁם וּלְאֻמִּים: וּבְנֵי מִדְיָן
ה עֵיפָה וָעֵפֶר וַחֲנֹךְ וַאֲבִידָע וְאֶלְדָּעָה כָּל־אֵלֶּה בְּנֵי קְטוּרָה: וַיִּתֵּן אַבְרָהָם
ו אֶת־כָּל־אֲשֶׁר־לוֹ לְיִצְחָק: וְלִבְנֵי הַפִּילַגְשִׁים אֲשֶׁר לְאַבְרָהָם נָתַן
אַבְרָהָם מַתָּנֹת וַיְשַׁלְּחֵם מֵעַל יִצְחָק בְּנוֹ בְּעוֹדֶנּוּ חַי קֵדְמָה אֶל־אֶרֶץ
ז קֶדֶם: וְאֵלֶּה יְמֵי שְׁנֵי־חַיֵּי אַבְרָהָם אֲשֶׁר־חָי מְאַת שָׁנָה וְשִׁבְעִים שָׁנָה

אונקלוס

בְּחַקְלָא לְמִפְנֵי רַמְשָׁא, וּזְקַף עֵינוֹהִי וַחֲזָא, וְהָא גַּמְלַיָּא אָתַן: סד וּזְקַפַת רִבְקָה יָת עֵינַהָא, וַחֲזָת יָת יִצְחָק, וְאִתְרְכִינַת מֵעַל גַּמְלָא: סה וַאֲמָרַת לְעַבְדָּא, מַאן גַּבְרָא דֵּיכִי דִּמְהַלֵּיךְ בְּחַקְלָא לְקַדָּמוּתַנָא, וַאֲמַר עַבְדָּא הוּא רִבּוֹנִי, וּנְסֵיבַת עֵיפָא וְאִתְכַּסִּיאַת: סו וְאִשְׁתַּעִי עַבְדָּא לְיִצְחָק, יָת כָּל פִּתְגָמַיָּא דַּעֲבַד: סז וְאַעֲלַהּ יִצְחָק לְמַשְׁכְּנָא, וַחֲזָא וְהָא תַקְּנִין עוֹבָדַהָא כְּעוֹבָדֵי שָׂרָה אִמֵּיהּ, וּנְסֵיב יָת רִבְקָה, וַהֲוָת לֵיהּ לְאִתּוּ וְרַחֲמַהּ, וְאִתְנַחַם יִצְחָק בָּתַר אִמֵּיהּ: כה א וְאוֹסֵיף אַבְרָהָם, וּנְסֵיב אִתְּתָא וּשְׁמַהּ קְטוּרָה: ב וִילֵידַת לֵיהּ, יָת זִמְרָן וְיָת יָקְשָׁן, וְיָת מְדָן וְיָת מִדְיָן, וְיָת יִשְׁבָּק וְיָת שׁוּחַ: ג וְיָקְשָׁן אוֹלֵיד, יָת שְׁבָא וְיָת דְּדָן, וּבְנֵי דְדָן, הֲווֹ, לְמַשְׁרְיָן וְלִשְׁכוּנִין וְלִנְגָון: ד וּבְנֵי מִדְיָן, עֵיפָה וָעֵפֶר וַחֲנוֹךְ, וַאֲבִידָע וְאֶלְדָּעָה, כָּל אִלֵּין בְּנֵי קְטוּרָה: ה וִיהַב אַבְרָהָם, יָת כָּל דִּלֵיהּ לְיִצְחָק: ו וְלִבְנֵי לְחֵינָתָא דִּלְאַבְרָהָם, יְהַב אַבְרָהָם מַתְּנָן, וְשַׁלְּחִנּוּן, מֵעַל יִצְחָק בְּרֵיהּ בְּעוֹד דְּהוּא קַיָּם, קִדּוּמָא לַאֲרַע מַדִּנְחָא: ז וְאִלֵּין, יוֹמֵי, שְׁנֵי חַיֵּי אַבְרָהָם דַּחֲיָא, מְאָה וְשַׁבְעִין

attend to the presence of God, listening as well as speaking, opening myself up to a reality other and infinitely vaster than my own, and I become a different person as a result. It is not monologue but dialogue. That is prayer as *siḥa*.

flows the energy of Jewish history – the force of creation and the drive toward redemption. While the prayer lasts, we make those energies our own.

A genuine human conversation is a preparation for, and a microcosmic version of, the act of prayer. For in prayer I

his last and died in his ripe old age, aged and satisfied, and was gathered to his
9 people. His sons, Yitzḥak and Yishmael, buried him in the cave of Makhpela,
10 near Mamre, in the field of Efron son of Tzoḥar the Hittite – the field Avraham
had bought from the Hittites. There Avraham was buried with Sara his wife.
11 After Avraham's death, God blessed Yitzḥak his son, who was then living near
Be'er Laḥai Ro'i.
12 These are the descendants of Avraham's son Yishmael, whom Sara's SHEVI'I
13 maidservant, Hagar the Egyptian, bore to Avraham. The names of Yishmael's
sons, in the order of their birth, are: Nevayot – Yishmael's firstborn, Kedar,
14 Adbe'el, Mivsam, Mishma, Duma, Massa, Ḥadad, Teima, Yetur, Nafish, and MAFTIR
15, 16 Kedma. These were Yishmael's sons, and these are their names by their villages
17 and encampments: twelve princes and their tribes. These were the years of
Yishmael's life: he lived one hundred and thirty-seven years. He breathed his

רש״י

ט **יצחק וישמעאל.** מכאן שעשה ישמעאל תשובה והוליך את יצחק לפניו, והיא "שיבה טובה" (לעיל טו, טו) שנאמרה באברהם:

יא **ויהי אחרי מות אברהם ויברך וגו׳.** נחמו תנחומי אבלים. דבר אחר, אף על פי שמסר הקדוש ברוך הוא את הברכות לאברהם, נתירא לברך את יצחק, מפני שצפה את עשו יוצא ממנו. אמר: יבא בעל העולם ויברך את אשר ייטב בעיניו. ובא הקדוש ברוך הוא וברכו:

יג **בשמתם לתולדתם.** סדר לדתן זה אחר זה:

טז **בחצריהם.** כרכים שאין להם חומה, כתרגומו: "בפצחיהון", שהם מפצחים, לשון פתיחה, כמו: "פצחו ורננו" (תהלים צח, ד):

יז **ואלה שני חיי ישמעאל וגו׳.** אמר רבי חייא בר אבא: למה נמנו שנותיו של ישמעאל? כדי ליחס בהם שנותיו של יעקב. משנותיו של ישמעאל למדנו ששמש יעקב בבית עבר ארבע עשרה שנה כשפרש

continue what you began, is to achieve a satisfaction in life that cannot be destroyed by circumstance. To be happy does not mean that you have everything you want or everything you were promised. It means, simply, to have done what you were called on to do, to have made a beginning, and then to have passed on the baton to the next generation.

25:9 **יצחק וישמעאל בניו** *His sons, Yitzḥak and Yishmael* – Until now, we have assumed that the two half-brothers have lived in total isolation from one another. Yet the Torah places them together at the funeral without a word of explanation.

There is an extraordinary midrash, in Pirkei DeRabbi Eliezer (30), which tells of how Avraham twice visited his son Yishmael after his banishment. On the first occasion, Yishmael was not at home. His wife, not knowing Avraham's identity, refused the stranger bread and water. Yishmael, continues the midrash, divorced her and married a woman named Fatima. This time, when Avraham visited, again not disclosing his identity, the woman gave him food and drink. The midrash then says, "Avraham stood and prayed before the Holy One, blessed be He, and Yishmael's house became filled with all good things. When Yishmael returned, his wife told him about it, and Yishmael knew that his father still loved him." Father and son were reconciled.

This hidden story of Ḥayei Sara has immense consequence for our time. Jews and Muslims both trace their descent from Avraham – Jews through Yitzḥak, Muslims through Yishmael. The fact that both sons stand together at their father's funeral tells us that they too were reunited. Yes, there was conflict and separation, but that was the beginning, not the end. There is hope for the future in this story of the past. Avraham loved both his sons, and, in the end, is laid to rest by both.

ח וְחָמֵשׁ שָׁנִים: וַיִּגְוַע וַיָּמָת אַבְרָהָם בְּשֵׂיבָה טוֹבָה זָקֵן וְשָׂבֵעַ וַיֵּאָסֶף
ט אֶל־עַמָּיו: וַיִּקְבְּרוּ אֹתוֹ יִצְחָק וְיִשְׁמָעֵאל בָּנָיו אֶל־מְעָרַת הַמַּכְפֵּלָה
י אֶל־שְׂדֵה עֶפְרֹן בֶּן־צֹחַר הַחִתִּי אֲשֶׁר עַל־פְּנֵי מַמְרֵא: הַשָּׂדֶה אֲשֶׁר־
יא קָנָה אַבְרָהָם מֵאֵת בְּנֵי־חֵת שָׁמָּה קֻבַּר אַבְרָהָם וְשָׂרָה אִשְׁתּוֹ: וַיְהִי
אַחֲרֵי מוֹת אַבְרָהָם וַיְבָרֶךְ אֱלֹהִים אֶת־יִצְחָק בְּנוֹ וַיֵּשֶׁב יִצְחָק עִם־
בְּאֵר לַחַי רֹאִי:
יב וְאֵלֶּה תֹּלְדֹת יִשְׁמָעֵאל בֶּן־אַבְרָהָם אֲשֶׁר יָלְדָה הָגָר הַמִּצְרִית שִׁפְחַת שביעי
יג שָׂרָה לְאַבְרָהָם: וְאֵלֶּה שְׁמוֹת בְּנֵי יִשְׁמָעֵאל בִּשְׁמֹתָם לְתוֹלְדֹתָם בְּכֹר
יד טו יִשְׁמָעֵאל נְבָיֹת וְקֵדָר וְאַדְבְּאֵל וּמִבְשָׂם: וּמִשְׁמָע וְדוּמָה וּמַשָּׂא: חֲדַד
טז וְתֵימָא יְטוּר נָפִישׁ וָקֵדְמָה: אֵלֶּה הֵם בְּנֵי יִשְׁמָעֵאל וְאֵלֶּה שְׁמֹתָם מפטיר
יז בְּחַצְרֵיהֶם וּבְטִירֹתָם שְׁנֵים־עָשָׂר נְשִׂיאִם לְאֻמֹּתָם: וְאֵלֶּה שְׁנֵי חַיֵּי

אונקלוס

וחמש שנין: ח ואתנגיד ומית אברהם, בסיבו טבא סיב וסבע, ואתכניש לעמיה: ט וקברו יתיה, יצחק וישמעאל בנוהי, במערת כפילתא, בחקל, עפרון בר צוחר חתאה, דעל אפי ממרא: י חקלא, דזבן אברהם מן בני חתאה, תמן, אתקבר אברהם ושרה אתתיה: יא והוה, בתר דמית אברהם, ובריך יי ית יצחק בריה, ויתיב יצחק, עם בירא דמלאך קימא אתחזי עלה: יב ואלין, תולדת ישמעאל בר אברהם, דילידת, הגר מצריתא, אמתה דשרה לאברהם: יג ואלין, שמהת בני ישמעאל, בשמהתהון לתולדתהון, בכריה דישמעאל נביות, וקדר ואדבאל ומבשם: יד ומשמע ודומה ומשא: טו חדד ותימא, יטור נפיש וקדמה: טז אלין אנון, בני ישמעאל ואלין שמהתהון, בפצחיהון ובכרכיהון, תרי עסר רברבין לאמיהון: יז ואלין, שני חיי

AVRAHAM'S DEATH

This is a deeply serene description of old age and dying. There is also an earlier verse, no less moving: "Avraham was old, advanced in years, and the Lord had blessed him in all things" (Gen. 24:1).

Whether we think of children or the land – the two key divine promises to Avraham and Sara – the reality they saw fell far short of what they might have felt entitled to expect. Yet – in Ḥayei Sara, Avraham does two things: he buys the first plot in the land of Canaan, and he arranges for the marriage of Yitzḥak. One field and a cave; one child, Yitzḥak, married and with children, was enough for Avraham to die in peace.

Lao-Tzu, the Chinese sage, said that a journey of a thousand miles begins with a single step. To that Judaism adds, "It is not for you to complete the work but neither are you free to desist from it" (Avot 2:16). The meaning is clear. If you ensure that your children will continue to live for what you have lived for, then you can have faith that they will continue your journey until eventually they reach the destination. Avraham is able to die serenely because he has faith in God and faith that others would complete what he began. The same is surely true of Sara.

To place your life in God's hands, to have faith that whatever happens to you happens for a reason, to know that you are part of a larger narrative, and to believe that others will

last and died, and was gathered to his people. The Ishmaelites dwelt from Ḥavila
18 to Shur, up against Egypt, all the way to Assyria, settling up against all their
brothers.

The haftara for Parashat Ḥayei Sara is on page 1508.

רש״י

מֵאָבִיו קֹדֶם שֶׁבָּא אֵצֶל לָבָן, שֶׁהֲרֵי כְּשֶׁפֵּרַשׁ יַעֲקֹב מֵאָבִיו מֵת יִשְׁמָעֵאל, שֶׁנֶּאֱמַר: ״וַיֵּלֶךְ עֵשָׂו אֶל יִשְׁמָעֵאל״ וְגוֹ׳ (להלן כח, ט), כְּמוֹ שֶׁמְּפֹרָשׁ בְּסוֹף ׳מְגִלָּה נִקְרֵאת׳ (מגילה יז ע״א): **וַיִּגְוַע.** לֹא נֶאֶמְרָה ׳גְּוִיעָה׳ אֶלָּא בַּצַּדִּיקִים:

יח| **נָפָל.** שָׁכַן, כְּמוֹ: ״וּמִדְיָן וַעֲמָלֵק וְכָל בְּנֵי קֶדֶם נֹפְלִים בָּעֵמֶק״ (שופטים ז, יב). כָּאן הוּא אוֹמֵר לְשׁוֹן נְפִילָה, וּלְהַלָּן הוּא אוֹמֵר: ״עַל פְּנֵי כָל אֶחָיו יִשְׁכֹּן״ (לעיל טז, יב), עַד שֶׁלֹּא מֵת אַבְרָהָם – ״יִשְׁכֹּן״, מִשֶּׁמֵּת אַבְרָהָם – ״נָפָל״:

יִשְׁמָעֵ֔אל מְאַ֣ת שָׁנָ֔ה וּשְׁלֹשִׁ֥ים שָׁנָ֖ה וְשֶׁ֣בַע שָׁנִ֑ים וַיִּגְוַ֣ע וַיָּ֔מָת וַיֵּאָ֖סֶף
יח אֶל־עַמָּֽיו׃ וַֽיִּשְׁכְּנ֨וּ מֵֽחֲוִילָ֜ה עַד־שׁ֗וּר אֲשֶׁר֙ עַל־פְּנֵ֣י מִצְרַ֔יִם בֹּאֲכָ֖ה
אַשּׁ֑וּרָה עַל־פְּנֵ֥י כָל־אֶחָ֖יו נָפָֽל׃

The הפטרה *for* פרשת חיי שרה *is on page 1509.*

אונקלוס

יִשְׁמָעֵאל, מְאָה וּתְלָתִין וּשְׁבַע שְׁנִין, וְאִתְנְגִיד וּמִית, וְאִתְכְּנִישׁ
לְעַמֵּיהּ: יח וּשְׁרוֹ מֵחֲוִילָה עַד חַגְרָא, דְּעַל אַפֵּי מִצְרַיִם, מָטֵי לְאַתּוּר,
עַל אַפֵּי כָל אֲחוֹהִי שְׁרָא:

Parashat Toledot

25 19 This is the story of Yitzḥak, son of Avraham: Avraham was Yitzḥak's father.
20 When Yitzḥak was forty he married Rivka, daughter of Betuel the Aramean

רש"י

יט **ואלה תולדת יצחק.** יעקב ועשו האמורים בפרשה; ועל ידי שכתב הכתוב: "יצחק בן אברהם" הזקק לומר: "אברהם הוליד את יצחק", לפי שהיו ליצני הדור אומרים: מאבימלך נתעברה שרה, שהרי כמה שנים שהתה עם אברהם ולא נתעברה הימנו. מה עשה הקדוש ברוך הוא? צר קלסתר פניו של יצחק דומה לאברהם, והעידו הכל: אברהם הוליד את יצחק. וזהו שכתוב כאן: "יצחק בן אברהם", שהרי עדות יש ש"אברהם הוליד את יצחק":

כ **בן ארבעים שנה.** שהרי כשבא אברהם מהר המוריה נתבשר שנולדה רבקה, ויצחק היה בן שלשים ושבע שנה, שהרי בו בפרק מתה שרה, ומשנולד יצחק עד שמתה שרה שלשים ושבע שנים היו – בת תשעים היתה כשנולד, ובת מאה עשרים ושבע שנה היתה כשמתה, שנאמר: "ויהיו חיי שרה" וגו' (לעיל כג, א), הרי ליצחק שלשים ושבע שנים. ובו בפרק נולדה רבקה. המתין לה עד שתהא ראויה לביאה שלש שנים ונשאה: **בת בתואל מפדן ארם אחות לבן.** וכי עדין לא נכתב שהיא בת בתואל ואחות לבן ומפדן ארם? אלא להגיד שבחה, שהיתה בת רשע ואחות רשע ומקומה אנשי רשע, ולא למדה ממעשיהם: **מפדן ארם.** על שם ששני ארם היו, ארם נהרים וארם צובה, קורא אותו 'פדן', לשון: "צמד בקר" (שמואל א' יא, ז) תרגום: "פדן תורין". ויש פותרים 'פדן ארם' כמו "שדה ארם" (הושע יב, יג), שבלשון ישמעאל קורין לשדה 'פדן':

it in the Ḥumash: Hagar and Yishmael, alone in the heat of the desert, without water, about to die. The comparison is deliberate. Just as there, so here, our sympathies are being enlisted on behalf of the elder son.

The real doubt, however, lies in the way the text describes Yaakov's conduct. Whatever else the covenant is, we feel, it cannot be *this*: a blessing taken by deceit, a destiny acquired by disguise. Did God not say of Avraham, "For I have chosen him so that he may direct his children and his household after him to keep the way of the Lord by doing what is right and just" (Gen. 18:19)? Righteousness, justice, integrity, truth – these are key words of covenantal ethics, and we strain to see how they could be applied to Yaakov's conduct toward his blind father. Besides which, Yitzḥak may be deceived, but is God? The idea is absurd. Had God wanted the blessing to go to Yaakov, not Esav, He would have told that to Yitzḥak, as He told Avraham about Yitzḥak and Yishmael. There is just enough discord to make us wonder if we have read the story correctly. In the end we will discover that our unease was justified and that nothing in the story is as it seems – but only at the end. The suspense is maintained until the final scene, many years and two *parashot* later. Even then, only the most careful listening reveals the unexpected truth.

25:19 **אַבְרָהָם הוֹלִיד אֶת יִצְחָק** *Avraham was Yitzḥak's father* – The first half of the sentence tells us that Yitzḥak was Avraham's son. Why then does the text repeat, "Avraham was Yitzḥak's father"? The Sages offer a possible explanation (Bava Metzia 87a). Immediately prior to the story of Yitzḥak's birth, in Genesis 20, we are told that Sara was taken into the harem of Avimelekh, king of Gerar. Gossip may have suggested that Avraham was infertile, that Yitzḥak's true father was Avimelekh. Hence the double emphasis of our verse: not only was Avraham Yitzḥak's father, but also everyone could see this because father and son looked exactly alike.

The Sages link this idea to another detail in the text: Avraham and Sara are the first people in the Torah described as being old (Gen. 24:1), despite the fact that many previously mentioned biblical characters lived to a much greater age.

Until Avraham, people did not age. But people who saw Avraham would say, "That is Yitzḥak," and people who saw Yitzḥak would say, "That is Avraham," and so Avraham prayed to grow old, and this is the meaning of [the phrase] "Avraham was old" (Sanhedrin 103b).

Yitzḥak is the least individuated of the patriarchs; in some places his story directly echoes that of his father.

פרשת תולדת

כה יט וְאֵלֶּה תּוֹלְדֹת יִצְחָק בֶּן־אַבְרָהָם אַבְרָהָם הוֹלִיד אֶת־יִצְחָק: כ וַיְהִי יִצְחָק כג
בֶּן־אַרְבָּעִים שָׁנָה בְּקַחְתּוֹ אֶת־רִבְקָה בַּת־בְּתוּאֵל הָאֲרַמִּי מִפַּדַּן אֲרָם

אונקלוס

יט וְאִלֵּין, תּוֹלְדָת יִצְחָק בַּר אַבְרָהָם, אַבְרָהָם אוֹלֵיד יָת יִצְחָק:
כ וַהֲוָה יִצְחָק בַּר אַרְבְּעִין שְׁנִין, כַּד נְסֵיב יָת רִבְקָה, בַּת בְּתוּאֵל אֲרַמָּאָה, מִפַּדַּן אֲרָם,

TOLEDOT

Toledot tells the story of Yitzḥak and Rivka's twin sons, Yaakov and Esav, who struggle in the womb and seem destined to clash throughout their lives and those of their descendants. It contains two great passages: the birth and childhood of the boys, and the scene in which Yaakov, at Rivka's behest, dresses in Esav's clothes and takes his blessing from their father Yitzḥak. Between them is a narrative about Yitzḥak and Rivka traveling to Gerar because of famine, very similar to that told about Avraham and Sara in Genesis 20.

The *parasha* contains themes of similarity and difference – the almost seamless continuity between Avraham and Yitzḥak followed by the conflict and rivalry between Yitzḥak's two very different sons. On the surface, the stories of Yitzḥak and Yishmael and of Yaakov and Esav are about sibling rivalry and the displacement of the elder by the younger. Beneath the surface, however, the Sages heard a counter-narrative telling the opposite story: *the birth of the younger does not displace the older*. We are led to ask – what if the Torah understands, as did Freud and René Girard, and as did Greek and Roman myth, that sibling rivalry is the most primal form of violence? And what if, rather than endorsing it, it set out to undermine it, subvert it, challenge it, and eventually replace it with another, quite different way of understanding our relationship with God and with the human Other? What if, in this regard, Genesis is a more profound, multi-leveled, transformative text than we have taken it to be? These questions are central to our reading of Parashat Toledot.

YAAKOV AND ESAV

Nowhere are narrative and counter-narrative more subtly interwoven than in the story of Yaakov and Esav. It is a work of awesome brilliance and, once we have understood its hidden message, it is clear that it is intended as a forceful refutation of sibling rivalry, the major source of conflict in the stories of Genesis. Its significance, set at the very center of the book, is unmistakable. Once we have decoded the mystery of Yaakov, our understanding of covenant and identity will be changed forever.

The surface narrative is a paradigm, almost a caricature, of the trope of displacement – a story of the younger child displacing the older as heir to power. From Avraham to Menashe and Efrayim, this theme punctuates the book of Genesis. The first time we see the twins, at their birth, the younger Yaakov is already clinging to the heels of the firstborn Esav.

Yet, reading this parasha, we cannot but identify with Esav, not Yaakov. We feel their father's shock – "Yitzḥak was seized with a violent fit of trembling" (Gen. 27:33) – as he realizes that his younger son has deceived him. We empathize with Esav, whose first thought is not anger against his brother but simple love for Yitzḥak: "Bless me, me too, my father" (27:34). Then comes Yitzḥak's helplessness – "What then can I do for you, my son?" (27:37) – and Esav's weeping, all the more poignant given what we know of him, that he is strong, a hunter, a man not given to tears. The scene of the two together, robbed of what should have been a moment of tenderness and intimacy – son feeding father, father blessing son – is deeply affecting. There is only one other scene like

21 of Padan Aram, sister of Lavan the Aramean. And Yitzḥak pleaded with the
LORD on behalf of his wife, for she was childless. The LORD granted his plea
22 and Rivka became pregnant. But the children clashed within her. She said, "If
23 this is so, why am I living?" So she went to inquire of the LORD. The LORD said
to her, "Two nations are inside your womb; two peoples are to part from you.
24 People will overpower people, and the greater shall the younger serve." When
25 the time came for her to give birth, there were twins in her womb. The first
came out red. His whole body was like a hairy cloak, so they named him Esav.

רש"י

כא **ויעתר.** הרבה והפציר בתפלה: **ויעתר לו.** נתפצר לו ונתפתה לו. ואומר אני, כל לשון 'עתר' לשון הפצרה וריבוי הוא, וכן: "ועתר ענן הקטרת" (יחזקאל ח, יא) – מרבית עלית העשן, וכן: "והעתרתם עלי דבריכם" (שם לה, יג), וכן: "ונעתרות נשיקות שונא" (משלי כז, ו) – דומות למרבות והנם למשא, אינקריסמנ"ט בלעז: **לנכח אשתו.** זה עומד בזוית זו ומתפלל, וזו עומדת בזוית זו ומתפללת: **ויעתר לו.** ולא לה, שאין דומה תפלת צדיק בן רשע לתפלת צדיק בן צדיק, לפיכך לו ולא לה:

כב **ויתרצצו.** על כרחך המקרא הזה אומר דרשני, שסתם מה היא רציצה זו וכתב: "אם כן למה זה אנכי". רבותינו דרשוהו לשון ריצה: כשהיתה עוברת על פתחי תורה של שם ועבר יעקב רץ ומפרכס לצאת, עוברת על פתח עבודה זרה ועשו מפרכס לצאת. דבר אחר, מתרוצצים זה עם זה ומריבים בנחלת שני עולמות: **ותאמר אם כן.** גדול צער העבור, "למה זה אנכי" מתאוה ומתפללת על הריון: **ותלך לדרש.** לבית מדרשו של שם: **לדרש את ה'.** להגיד לה מה תהא בסופה:

כג **ויאמר ה' לה.** על ידי שליח, לשם אמר ברוח הקדש והוא אמר לה: **שני גוים בבטנך.** 'גיים' כתיב, אלו אנטונינוס ורבי, שלא פסקו מעל שלחנם לא צנון ולא חזרת לא בימות החמה ולא בימות הגשמים: **ושני לאמים.** אין 'לאם' אלא מלכות: **ממעיך יפרדו.** מן המעים הם נפרדים, זה לרשעו וזה לתמו: **מלאם יאמץ.** לא ישוו בגדלה, כשזה קם זה נופל, וכן הוא אומר: "אמלאה החרבה" (יחזקאל כו, ב) – לא נתמלאה צר אלא מחרבנה של ירושלים:

כד **וימלאו ימיה.** אבל בתמר כתיב: "ויהי בעת לדתה" (להלן לח, כז), שלא מלאו ימיה כי לשבעה חדשים ילדתם: **והנה תומם.** חסר. ובתמר "תאומים" מלא, לפי ששניהם צדיקים, אבל כאן אחד צדיק ואחד רשע:

כה **אדמוני.** סימן הוא שיהא שופך דמים: **כלו כאדרת שער.** מלא שער כטלית של צמר המלאה שער, פלוקיד"א בלעז: **ויקראו שמו עשו.** הכל קראו לו כן, לפי שהיה נעשה ונגמר בשערו כבן שנים הרבה:

down to you" (Gen. 27:29). Not so. The oracle will continue to unfold in unexpected ways.

25:23 **וְרַב יַעֲבֹד צָעִיר** *The greater will the younger serve* – The word *et*, signaling the object of the verb, is missing here (as noted by Radak and Rabbi Yosef Ibn Kaspi). Normally in Biblical Hebrew, the subject precedes the verb, and the object follows – but not always. Thus, while the phrase told to Rivka might mean "the older shall serve the younger," it could also mean "the younger shall serve the older." This reading, though it leans on poetic rather than conventional use of grammar, is supported by the unusual musical notation (*tipḥa-merkha-sof pasuk* in place of the normal *merkha-tipḥa-sof pasuk*).

What is more, *rav* and *tza'ir* are not opposites. The opposite of *tza'ir* ("younger") is *bekhir* ("older" or "firstborn"). *Rav* does not mean "older." It means "great" or possibly "chief." This linking of two terms as if they were polar opposites, when in fact they are not, further destabilizes the meaning. Who was the *rav*? The elder? The leader? The chief? The more numerous?

These ambiguities are not accidental, but integral to the text. The subtlety is such that we do not notice them at first, but later, when the narrative does not turn out as expected, we are forced to go back and notice what at first we missed: that the words Rivka heard may mean "the greater will serve the younger" or "the younger will serve the greater," and that the identities of the two are not at all obvious.

כא אֲחוֹת לָבָן הָאֲרַמִּי לוֹ לְאִשָּׁה: וַיֶּעְתַּר יִצְחָק לַיהוה לְנֹכַח אִשְׁתּוֹ
כב כִּי עֲקָרָה הִוא וַיֵּעָתֶר לוֹ יהוה וַתַּהַר רִבְקָה אִשְׁתּוֹ: וַיִּתְרֹצְצוּ הַבָּנִים
בְּקִרְבָּהּ וַתֹּאמֶר אִם־כֵּן לָמָּה זֶּה אָנֹכִי וַתֵּלֶךְ לִדְרֹשׁ אֶת־יהוה:
כג וַיֹּאמֶר יהוה לָהּ שְׁנֵי גיים בְּבִטְנֵךְ וּשְׁנֵי לְאֻמִּים מִמֵּעַיִךְ יִפָּרֵדוּ וּלְאֹם גוֹיִם
כד מִלְאֹם יֶאֱמָץ וְרַב יַעֲבֹד צָעִיר: וַיִּמְלְאוּ יָמֶיהָ לָלֶדֶת וְהִנֵּה תוֹמִם
כה בְּבִטְנָהּ: וַיֵּצֵא הָרִאשׁוֹן אַדְמוֹנִי כֻּלּוֹ כְּאַדֶּרֶת שֵׂעָר וַיִּקְרְאוּ שְׁמוֹ עֵשָׂו:

אונקלוס

אֲחָתֵיהּ, דְּלָבָן אֲרַמָּאָה לֵיהּ לְאִתּוּ: כא וְצַלִּי יִצְחָק קֳדָם יי לָקֳבֵיל
אִתְּתֵיהּ, אֲרֵי עַקְרָא הִיא, וְקַבֵּיל צְלוֹתֵיהּ יי, וְעַדִּיאַת רִבְקָה אִתְּתֵיהּ:
כב וְדָחֲקִין בְּנַיָּא בִּמְעַהָא, וַאֲמַרַת אִם כֵּן, לְמָא דְנַן אֲנָא, וַאֲזַלַת
לְמִתְבַּע אֻלְפָן מִן קֳדָם יי: כג וַאֲמַר יי לַהּ, תְּרֵין עַמְמִין בִּמְעַכִי,
וְתַרְתֵּין מַלְכְוָן, מִמְּעַכִי יִתְפָּרְשָׁן, וּמַלְכוּ מִמַּלְכוּ תִּתַּקַּף, וְרַבָּא
יִשְׁתַּעְבַּד לִזְעֵירָא: כד וּשְׁלִימוּ יוֹמַהָא לְמֵילַד, וְהָא תְיוֹמִין בִּמְעַהָא:
כה וּנְפַק קַדְמָאָה סָמוֹק, כֻּלֵּיהּ כִּגְלִים דִּסְעַר, וּקְרוֹ שְׁמֵיהּ עֵשָׂו:

Sensitive to this, the Rabbis told a profound psychological story. The close physical resemblance between Avraham and Yitzḥak refuted the charge of those who said Avraham was not the real father. At first, indeed, he looked like his clone. Eventually, however, Avraham has to pray for the deed to be undone. It is the space we make for otherness that makes love something other than narcissism and parenthood something greater than self-replication. We are each in God's image but no one else's.

25:22 **וַתֵּלֶךְ לִדְרֹשׁ אֶת יהוה** *So she went to inquire of the Lord* – The Netziv made the sharp observation that Rivka's "relationship with Yitzḥak was not the same as that between Sara and Avraham or Raḥel and Yaakov. When they had a problem, they were not afraid to speak about it. Not so with Rivka" (*Haamek Davar* on Gen. 24:65).

The Netziv senses a distance from the very first moment when Rivka sees Yitzḥak "had gone out in the field…to meditate" (Gen. 24:63), at which point she "took her veil and covered herself" (24:65). He comments, "She covered herself out of awe and a sense of inadequacy, as if she felt she was unworthy to be his wife, and from then on this trepidation was fixed in her mind."

Their relationship, suggests the Netziv, was never casual, candid, and communicative. The result is, at a series of critical moments, a failure of communication. It seems likely that Rivka never informs Yitzḥak of the oracle she hears before the twins, Esav and Yaakov, are born. The consequences of this silence will continue to unfold throughout the children's lives.

25:23 **שְׁנֵי גוֹיִם בְּבִטְנֵךְ** *Two nations are inside your womb* – This is a rare example in the Torah of an oracle as opposed to a prophecy. Oracles – a familiar form of supernatural communication in the ancient world – were normally obscure and cryptic, unlike the normal form of Israelite prophecy. This may well be the technical meaning of the phrase "she went to inquire of the Lord," which puzzled the medieval commentators.

The scene reminds us of the Delphic oracle in *Oedipus Rex* who tells Laius that he will be killed by his son. The story begins with the end, and the tension lies in waiting to see how it comes to pass. Nowhere else does the Tanakh come so close to Greek tragedy; fate and tragedy belong together, which is what makes this passage so unexpected, so *unbiblical*. The Torah rejects the idea of inescapable fate, a preordained future. Yet these verses set up an expectation, shaping the way we interpret all that follows. The story that begins with the words "The greater will the younger serve" seems destined to end with Yitzḥak's blessing to Yaakov, given against his intentions: "Be lord over your brothers, and may your mother's sons bow

26 Then his brother emerged, his hand grasping Esav's heel, so he named him
27 Yaakov. Yitzḥak was sixty years old when they were born. The boys grew up.
Esav became a skilled hunter, a man of the field, while Yaakov was an innocent
28 man who stayed among the tents. Yitzḥak loved Esav because he ate of his game,
29 but Rivka loved Yaakov. Once when Yaakov was cooking a stew, Esav came in
30 exhausted from the field. He said to Yaakov, "Let me gulp down some of that
31 red stuff. I am starved!" – that is how he came to be named Edom. Yaakov said,
32 "First sell me your birthright." And Esav said, "Look, I am about to die. What
33 use to me is a birthright?" But Yaakov said, "Swear to me first." So he swore, and
34 sold Yaakov his birthright. Yaakov then gave Esav bread and lentil stew. He ate,
drank, got up, and left. Thus – Esav disdained his birthright.

רש״י

כו **בַּעֲקֵב עֵשָׂו.** סִימָן שֶׁאֵין זֶה מַסְפִּיק לִגְמֹר מַלְכוּתוֹ עַד שֶׁזֶּה עוֹמֵד וְנוֹטְלָהּ הֵימֶנּוּ: **וַיִּקְרָא שְׁמוֹ יַעֲקֹב.** הַקָּדוֹשׁ בָּרוּךְ הוּא. דָּבָר אַחֵר, אָבִיו קָרָא לוֹ יַעֲקֹב עַל שֵׁם אֲחִיזַת הֶעָקֵב: **בֶּן שִׁשִּׁים שָׁנָה.** עֶשֶׂר שָׁנִים מִשֶּׁנִּשָּׂאָהּ עַד שֶׁנַּעֲשֵׂית בַּת שְׁלֹשׁ עֶשְׂרֵה שָׁנָה וּרְאוּיָה לְהֵרָיוֹן, וְעֶשֶׂר שָׁנִים הַלָּלוּ צִפָּה וְהִמְתִּין לָהּ כְּמוֹ שֶׁעָשָׂה אָבִיו לְשָׂרָה (לעיל טז, ג). כֵּיוָן שֶׁלֹּא נִתְעַבְּרָה יָדַע שֶׁהִיא עֲקָרָה וְהִתְפַּלֵּל עָלֶיהָ. וְשִׁפְחָה לֹא רָצָה לִשָּׂא, לְפִי שֶׁנִּתְקַדֵּשׁ בְּהַר הַמּוֹרִיָּה לִהְיוֹת עוֹלָה תְמִימָה:

כז **וַיִּגְדְּלוּ הַנְּעָרִים וַיְהִי עֵשָׂו.** כָּל זְמַן שֶׁהָיוּ קְטַנִּים לֹא הָיוּ נִכָּרִים בְּמַעֲשֵׂיהֶם וְאֵין אָדָם מְדַקְדֵּק בָּהֶם מַה טִּיבָם. כֵּיוָן שֶׁנַּעֲשׂוּ בְּנֵי שְׁלֹשׁ עֶשְׂרֵה שָׁנָה, זֶה פֵּרַשׁ לְבָתֵּי מִדְרָשׁוֹת וְזֶה פֵּרַשׁ לַעֲבוֹדָה זָרָה: **יֹדֵעַ צַיִד.** לָצוּד וּלְרַמּוֹת אֶת אָבִיו בְּפִיו, וְשׁוֹאֵל: אַבָּא, הֵיאַךְ מְעַשְּׂרִין אֶת הַמֶּלַח? הֵיאַךְ מְעַשְּׂרִין אֶת הַתֶּבֶן? כְּסָבוּר אָבִיו שֶׁהוּא מְדַקְדֵּק בַּמִּצְוֹת: **אִישׁ שָׂדֶה.** כְּמַשְׁמָעוֹ, אָדָם בָּטֵל, וְצוֹדֶה בְּקַשְׁתּוֹ חַיּוֹת וְעוֹפוֹת: **תָּם.** אֵינוֹ בָקִי בְּכָל אֵלֶּה, כְּלִבּוֹ כֵּן פִּיו. מִי שֶׁאֵינוֹ חָרִיף לְרַמּוֹת קָרוּי 'תָּם': **יֹשֵׁב אֹהָלִים.** אָהֳלוֹ שֶׁל שֵׁם וְאָהֳלוֹ שֶׁל עֵבֶר:

כח **בְּפִיו.** כְּתַרְגּוּמוֹ, בְּפִיו שֶׁל יִצְחָק. וּמִדְרָשׁוֹ, בְּפִיו שֶׁל עֵשָׂו, שֶׁהָיָה צָד אוֹתוֹ וּמְרַמֵּהוּ בִּדְבָרָיו:

כט **וַיָּזֶד.** לְשׁוֹן בִּשּׁוּל, כְּתַרְגּוּמוֹ: **וְהוּא עָיֵף.** בִּצְוָחָה, כְּמָה דְּתֵימַר: "כִּי עָיְפָה נַפְשִׁי לְהֹרְגִים" (ירמיה ד, לא):

ל **הַלְעִיטֵנִי.** אֶפְתַּח פִּי וּשְׁפֹךְ הַרְבֵּה לְתוֹכָהּ, כְּמוֹ שֶׁשָּׁנִינוּ: "אֵין אוֹבְסִין אֶת הַגָּמָל אֲבָל מַלְעִיטִין אוֹתוֹ" (שבת קנה ע״ב): **מִן הָאָדֹם הָאָדֹם.** עֲדָשִׁים אֲדֻמּוֹת, וְאוֹתוֹ הַיּוֹם מֵת אַבְרָהָם שֶׁלֹּא יִרְאֶה אֶת עֵשָׂו בֶּן בְּנוֹ יוֹצֵא לְתַרְבּוּת רָעָה, וְאֵין זוֹ "שֵׂיבָה טוֹבָה" שֶׁהִבְטִיחוֹ הַקָּדוֹשׁ בָּרוּךְ הוּא (לעיל טו, טו), לְפִיכָךְ קִצֵּר הַקָּדוֹשׁ בָּרוּךְ הוּא חָמֵשׁ שָׁנִים מִשְּׁנוֹתָיו, שֶׁיִּצְחָק חַי מֵאָה וּשְׁמוֹנִים שָׁנָה וְזֶה מֵאָה וְשִׁבְעִים וְחָמֵשׁ שָׁנָה, וּבִשֵּׁל יַעֲקֹב עֲדָשִׁים לְהַבְרוֹת אֶת הָאָבֵל. וְלָמָּה עֲדָשִׁים? שֶׁדּוֹמוֹת לְגַלְגַּל, שֶׁהָאֲבֵלוּת גַּלְגַּל שֶׁחוֹזֵר בָּעוֹלָם:

לא **מִכְרָה כַיּוֹם.** כְּתַרְגּוּמוֹ: "כְּיוֹם דִּלְהֵן", כַּיּוֹם שֶׁהוּא בָּרוּר כָּךְ מְכֹר לִי מְכִירָה בְּרוּרָה: **בְּכֹרָתְךָ.** לְפִי שֶׁהָעֲבוֹדָה בַּבְּכוֹרוֹת, אָמַר יַעֲקֹב: אֵין רָשָׁע זֶה כְּדַאי שֶׁיַּקְרִיב לְהַקָּדוֹשׁ בָּרוּךְ הוּא:

לב **הִנֵּה אָנֹכִי הוֹלֵךְ לָמוּת.** אָמַר עֵשָׂו: מַה טִּיבָהּ שֶׁל עֲבוֹדָה זוֹ? אָמַר לוֹ: כַּמָּה אַזְהָרוֹת וַעֲנָשִׁין וּמִיתוֹת תְּלוּיִין בָּהּ, כְּאוֹתָהּ שֶׁשָּׁנִינוּ (תענית יז ע״ב): אֵלּוּ הֵן שֶׁבְּמִיתָה, שְׁתוּיֵי יַיִן וּפְרוּעֵי רֹאשׁ. אָמַר: אֲנִי הוֹלֵךְ לָמוּת עַל יָדָהּ, אִם כֵּן מַה חֵפֶץ לִי בָּהּ?:

לד **וַיִּבֶז עֵשָׂו.** הֵעִיד הַכָּתוּב עַל רִשְׁעוֹ שֶׁבִּזָּה עֲבוֹדָתוֹ שֶׁל מָקוֹם:

that it is unbreakable. Whatever happens, a parent is still a parent, and a child is still a child. The bond may be deeply damaged, but it is never broken beyond repair.

Unconditional love is not uncritical, but it is unbreakable. That is how we should love our children – for it is how God loves us.

25:34 **וַיִּבֶז עֵשָׂו אֶת־הַבְּכֹרָה** *Esav disdained his birthright* – Yaakov drives a hard bargain: my stew for your birthright. Esav agrees and in a staccato succession of five consecutive verbs – literally: "he ate, drank, got up, left, despised his birthright" – reveals his character: mercurial, impetuous, no match for the subtle Yaakov.

כו וְאַחֲרֵי־כֵן יָצָא אָחִיו וְיָדוֹ אֹחֶזֶת בַּעֲקֵב עֵשָׂו וַיִּקְרָא שְׁמוֹ יַעֲקֹב וְיִצְחָק
כז בֶּן־שִׁשִּׁים שָׁנָה בְּלֶדֶת אֹתָם׃ וַיִּגְדְּלוּ הַנְּעָרִים וַיְהִי עֵשָׂו אִישׁ יֹדֵעַ
כח צַיִד אִישׁ שָׂדֶה וְיַעֲקֹב אִישׁ תָּם יֹשֵׁב אֹהָלִים׃ וַיֶּאֱהַב יִצְחָק אֶת־עֵשָׂו
כט כִּי־צַיִד בְּפִיו וְרִבְקָה אֹהֶבֶת אֶת־יַעֲקֹב׃ וַיָּזֶד יַעֲקֹב נָזִיד וַיָּבֹא עֵשָׂו
ל מִן־הַשָּׂדֶה וְהוּא עָיֵף׃ וַיֹּאמֶר עֵשָׂו אֶל־יַעֲקֹב הַלְעִיטֵנִי נָא מִן־הָאָדֹם
לא הָאָדֹם הַזֶּה כִּי עָיֵף אָנֹכִי עַל־כֵּן קָרָא־שְׁמוֹ אֱדוֹם׃ וַיֹּאמֶר יַעֲקֹב מִכְרָה
לב כַיּוֹם אֶת־בְּכֹרָתְךָ לִי׃ וַיֹּאמֶר עֵשָׂו הִנֵּה אָנֹכִי הוֹלֵךְ לָמוּת וְלָמָּה־זֶּה לִי
לג בְּכֹרָה׃ וַיֹּאמֶר יַעֲקֹב הִשָּׁבְעָה לִּי כַּיּוֹם וַיִּשָּׁבַע לוֹ וַיִּמְכֹּר אֶת־בְּכֹרָתוֹ
לד לְיַעֲקֹב׃ וְיַעֲקֹב נָתַן לְעֵשָׂו לֶחֶם וּנְזִיד עֲדָשִׁים וַיֹּאכַל וַיֵּשְׁתְּ וַיָּקָם וַיֵּלַךְ
וַיִּבֶז עֵשָׂו אֶת־הַבְּכֹרָה׃

אונקלוס

כו וּבָתַר כֵּן נְפַק אֲחוּהִי, וִידֵיהּ אֲחִידָא בְּעִקְבָא דְעֵשָׂו, וּקְרָא שְׁמֵיהּ
יַעֲקֹב, וְיִצְחָק, בַּר שִׁתִּין שְׁנִין כַּד יְלֵידַת יָתְהוֹן: כז וּרְבִיאוּ עוּלֵימַיָא,
וַהֲוָה עֵשָׂו, גְּבַר, נַחְשִׁרְכָן גְּבַר נָפֵיק חֲקַל, וְיַעֲקֹב גְּבַר שְׁלִים,
מְשַׁמֵּישׁ בֵּית אֻלְפָנָא: כח וּרְחֵים יִצְחָק, יָת עֵשָׂו אֲרֵי מִצֵּידֵיהּ הֲוָה
אָכֵיל, וְרִבְקָה רְחֵימַת יָת יַעֲקֹב: כט וּבַשֵּׁיל יַעֲקֹב תַּבְשִׁילָא, וַעֲאַל
עֵשָׂו, מִן חַקְלָא וְהוּא מְשַׁלְהֵי: ל וַאֲמַר עֵשָׂו לְיַעֲקֹב, אַטְעֵימְנִי כְעַן מִן
סִמּוֹקָא סָמְקָא הָדֵין, אֲרֵי מְשַׁלְהֵי אֲנָא, עַל כֵּן קְרָא שְׁמֵיהּ אֱדוֹם:
לא וַאֲמַר יַעֲקֹב, זַבֵּין כְּיוֹם דִּלְהֵין, יָת בְּכֵירוּתָךְ לִי: לב וַאֲמַר עֵשָׂו, הָא
אֲנָא אָזֵיל לִמְמָת, וּלְמָא דְנָן לִי בְּכֵירוּתָא: לג וַאֲמַר יַעֲקֹב, קַיֵּים לִי
כְּיוֹם דִּלְהֵין, וְקַיֵּים לֵיהּ, וְזַבֵּין יָת בְּכֵירוּתֵיהּ לְיַעֲקֹב: לד וְיַעֲקֹב יְהַב
לְעֵשָׂו, לְחֵים וְתַבְשִׁיל דִּטְלוֹפְחִין, וַאֲכַל וּשְׁתִי, וְקָם וַאֲזַל, וְשָׁט עֵשָׂו
יָת בְּכֵירוּתָא:

25:28 **ויאהב יצחק את־עשו** *Yitzhak loved Esav* – Is it conceivable that Yitzhak loves Esav merely because he has a taste for wild game? He surely knows that his elder son is a man of mercurial temperament who lives in the emotions of the moment. Even if this does not trouble him, the next episode involving Esav clearly will: "When Esav was forty years old, he married Yehudit daughter of Be'eri the Hittite, and Basmat daughter of Eilon the Hittite. These were a source of bitter sorrow to Yitzhak and Rivka" (Gen. 26:34–35). Esav has made himself at home among the Hittites and all they represented in terms of religion, culture, and morality.

Yet Yitzhak clearly *does* love Esav. The Sages gave an explanation. They interpreted the phrase "skilled hunter" as meaning that Esav trapped and deceived Yitzhak. He pretended to be more religious than he was (*Tanhuma,* Toledot 8, quoted by Rashi on Gen. 25:27). There is, though, a quite different explanation, closer to the plain sense of the text: Yitzhak *loves Esav because Esav is his son, and that is what fathers do.* They love their children unconditionally. That does not mean that Yitzhak cannot see the faults in Esav's character. But it does mean that Yitzhak knows that *a father must love his son because he is his son.* Yitzhak is teaching us a fundamental lesson in parenthood.

To take seriously the idea, central to Judaism, of *Avinu Malkeinu,* that our King is first and foremost our parent, is to invest our relationship with God with the most profound emotions. God wrestles with us, as does a parent with a child. We wrestle with Him as a child does with his or her parents. The relationship is sometimes tense, conflictual, even painful, yet what gives it its depth is the knowledge

26 1 Another famine afflicted the land, apart from the earlier famine in Avraham's
2 days, and Yitzḥak went to Avimelekh, king of the Philistines, in Gerar. The
Lord had appeared to him: "Do not go down to Egypt," He had said. "Stay in
3 the land I tell you of. Bide in this land and I will be with you and bless you, for
I am going to give all these lands to you and your descendants, fulfilling the
4 oath I swore to Avraham your father. I will make your descendants as many as
the stars of the heavens, and I will give them all these lands. All the nations of
5 the earth will bless themselves by your descendants, because Avraham listened
to My voice and kept My charge: My commandments, My statutes, and My
6 7 laws." So Yitzḥak now settled in Gerar. The men of the place inquired after his SHENI
wife; "She is my sister," he said. He was terrified to say "She is my wife." "The
men of the place might kill me for Rivka," he thought, "she is so beautiful."
8 When he had already been there for some time, Avimelekh, king of the
Philistines, looked down from a window and saw Yitzḥak enjoying himself
9 with his wife Rivka. Avimelekh summoned Yitzḥak. "She is your wife," he said.
"Why did you say, 'She is my sister'?" Yitzḥak replied, "I thought I might die
10 because of her." "What is this you have done to us?" said Avimelekh. "One of
the people might have slept with your wife, and you would have brought guilt
11 upon us." Avimelekh then issued an order to all the people: "Whoever touches

רש״י

כו ב| **אַל תֵּרֵד מִצְרָיְמָה.** שֶׁהָיָה דַּעְתּוֹ לָרֶדֶת מִצְרַיִם כְּמוֹ שֶׁיָּרַד אָבִיו בִּימֵי הָרָעָב. **אַל תֵּרֵד מִצְרָיְמָה.** שֶׁאַתָּה עוֹלָה תְמִימָה וְאֵין חוּצָה לָאָרֶץ כְּדַאי לְךָ:

ג| **הָאֵל.** כְּמוֹ ׳הָאֵלֶּה׳:

ד| **וְהִתְבָּרֲכוּ בְזַרְעֲךָ.** אָדָם אוֹמֵר לִבְנוֹ: יְהֵא זַרְעֲךָ כְּזַרְעוֹ שֶׁל יִצְחָק. וְכֵן בְּכָל הַמִּקְרָא, וְזֶה אָב לְכֻלָּן: ״בְּךָ יְבָרֵךְ יִשְׂרָאֵל לֵאמֹר״ וְגוֹ׳ (להלן מח, כ). וְאַף לְעִנְיַן הַקְּלָלָה מָצִינוּ כֵּן: ״וְהָיְתָה הָאִשָּׁה לְאָלָה״ (במדבר ה, כז), שֶׁהַמְקַלֵּל שׂוֹנְאוֹ אוֹמֵר: תְּהֵא כִּפְלוֹנִית; וְכֵן: ״וְהִנַּחְתֶּם שִׁמְכֶם לִשְׁבוּעָה לִבְחִירַי״ (ישעיה סה, טו), שֶׁהַנִּשְׁבָּע אוֹמֵר: אֱהֵא כִּפְלוֹנִי אִם עָשִׂיתִי כָּךְ וְכָךְ:

ה| **שָׁמַע אַבְרָהָם בְּקֹלִי.** כְּשֶׁנִּסִּיתִי אוֹתוֹ: **וַיִּשְׁמֹר מִשְׁמַרְתִּי.** גְּזֵרוֹת לְהַרְחָקָה עַל אַזְהָרוֹת שֶׁבַּתּוֹרָה, כְּגוֹן שְׁנִיּוֹת לָעֲרָיוֹת וּשְׁבוּת לַשַּׁבָּת: **מִצְוֹתַי.** דְּבָרִים שֶׁאִלּוּ לֹא נִכְתְּבוּ רְאוּיִין הֵם לְהִצְטַוּוֹת, כְּגוֹן גָּזֵל וּשְׁפִיכוּת דָּמִים: **חֻקּוֹתַי.** דְּבָרִים שֶׁיֵּצֶר הָרָע וְאֻמּוֹת הָעוֹלָם מְשִׁיבִים עֲלֵיהֶם, כְּגוֹן אֲכִילַת חֲזִיר וּלְבִישַׁת שַׁעַטְנֵז, שֶׁאֵין טַעַם בַּדָּבָר אֶלָּא הַמֶּלֶךְ גָּזַר חֻקּוֹ עַל עֲבָדָיו: **וְתוֹרֹתָי.** לְהָבִיא תּוֹרָה שֶׁבְּעַל פֶּה, הֲלָכָה לְמֹשֶׁה מִסִּינַי:

ז| **לְאִשְׁתּוֹ.** עַל אִשְׁתּוֹ, כְּמוֹ: ״אִמְרִי לִי אָחִי הוּא״ (לעיל כ, יג):

ח| **כִּי אָרְכוּ.** אָמַר: מֵעַתָּה אֵין לִי לִדְאֹג מֵאַחַר שֶׁלֹּא אֲנָסוּהָ עַד עַכְשָׁיו, וְלֹא נִזְהַר לִהְיוֹת נִשְׁמָר: **וַיַּשְׁקֵף אֲבִימֶלֶךְ.** רָאָהוּ מְשַׁמֵּשׁ מִטָּתוֹ:

י| **אַחַד הָעָם.** הַמְיֻחָד בָּעָם, זֶה הַמֶּלֶךְ: **וְהֵבֵאתָ עָלֵינוּ אָשָׁם.** אִם שָׁכַב, כְּבָר הֵבֵאתָ אָשָׁם עָלֵינוּ:

26:6 **וַיֵּשֶׁב יִצְחָק בִּגְרָר** *So Yitzḥak now settled in Gerar* – This story reads almost like a replay of Genesis 20, a generation later. In both cases the couple pass themselves off as brother and sister. The deception is discovered. Avimelekh is indignant, explanations are made, and the moment passes. In both cases Avimelekh promises the patriarchs security. Yet in both cases, there is a troubled aftermath, as we shall see.

כו א וַיְהִי רָעָב בָּאָרֶץ מִלְּבַד הָרָעָב הָרִאשׁוֹן אֲשֶׁר הָיָה בִּימֵי אַבְרָהָם
ב וַיֵּלֶךְ יִצְחָק אֶל־אֲבִימֶלֶךְ מֶלֶךְ־פְּלִשְׁתִּים גְּרָרָה: וַיֵּרָא אֵלָיו יהוה
ג וַיֹּאמֶר אַל־תֵּרֵד מִצְרָיְמָה שְׁכֹן בָּאָרֶץ אֲשֶׁר אֹמַר אֵלֶיךָ: גּוּר בָּאָרֶץ
הַזֹּאת וְאֶהְיֶה עִמְּךָ וַאֲבָרְכֶךָּ כִּי־לְךָ וּלְזַרְעֲךָ אֶתֵּן אֶת־כָּל־הָאֲרָצֹת
ד הָאֵל וַהֲקִמֹתִי אֶת־הַשְּׁבֻעָה אֲשֶׁר נִשְׁבַּעְתִּי לְאַבְרָהָם אָבִיךָ: וְהִרְבֵּיתִי
אֶת־זַרְעֲךָ כְּכוֹכְבֵי הַשָּׁמַיִם וְנָתַתִּי לְזַרְעֲךָ אֵת כָּל־הָאֲרָצֹת הָאֵל
ה וְהִתְבָּרְכוּ בְזַרְעֲךָ כֹּל גּוֹיֵי הָאָרֶץ: עֵקֶב אֲשֶׁר־שָׁמַע אַבְרָהָם בְּקֹלִי
ו ז וַיִּשְׁמֹר מִשְׁמַרְתִּי מִצְוֹתַי חֻקּוֹתַי וְתוֹרֹתָי: וַיֵּשֶׁב יִצְחָק בִּגְרָר: וַיִּשְׁאֲלוּ שני
אַנְשֵׁי הַמָּקוֹם לְאִשְׁתּוֹ וַיֹּאמֶר אֲחֹתִי הִוא כִּי יָרֵא לֵאמֹר אִשְׁתִּי
ח פֶּן־יַהַרְגֻנִי אַנְשֵׁי הַמָּקוֹם עַל־רִבְקָה כִּי־טוֹבַת מַרְאֶה הִוא: וַיְהִי כִּי־
אָרְכוּ־לוֹ שָׁם הַיָּמִים וַיַּשְׁקֵף אֲבִימֶלֶךְ מֶלֶךְ פְּלִשְׁתִּים בְּעַד הַחַלּוֹן
ט וַיַּרְא וְהִנֵּה יִצְחָק מְצַחֵק אֵת רִבְקָה אִשְׁתּוֹ: וַיִּקְרָא אֲבִימֶלֶךְ לְיִצְחָק
וַיֹּאמֶר אַךְ הִנֵּה אִשְׁתְּךָ הִוא וְאֵיךְ אָמַרְתָּ אֲחֹתִי הִוא וַיֹּאמֶר אֵלָיו
י יִצְחָק כִּי אָמַרְתִּי פֶּן־אָמוּת עָלֶיהָ: וַיֹּאמֶר אֲבִימֶלֶךְ מַה־זֹּאת עָשִׂיתָ
יא לָּנוּ כִּמְעַט שָׁכַב אַחַד הָעָם אֶת־אִשְׁתֶּךָ וְהֵבֵאתָ עָלֵינוּ אָשָׁם: וַיְצַו
אֲבִימֶלֶךְ אֶת־כָּל־הָעָם לֵאמֹר הַנֹּגֵעַ בָּאִישׁ הַזֶּה וּבְאִשְׁתּוֹ מוֹת יוּמָת:

אונקלוס

כו א וַהֲוָה כַפְנָא בְּאַרְעָא, בַּר מִכַּפְנָא קַדְמָאָה, דַּהֲוָה בְּיוֹמֵי אַבְרָהָם,
וַאֲזַל יִצְחָק, לְוָת אֲבִימֶלֶךְ מַלְכָּא דִּפְלִשְׁתָּאֵי לִגְרָר: ב וְאִתְגְּלִי לֵיהּ יְיָ,
וַאֲמַר לָא תֵיחוֹת לְמִצְרַיִם, שְׁרִי בְּאַרְעָא, דְּאֵימַר לָךְ: ג דּוּר בְּאַרְעָא
הָדָא, וִיהֵי מֵימְרִי בְּסַעֲדָךְ וַאֲבָרְכִנָּךְ, אֲרֵי לָךְ וְלִבְנָךְ, אֶתֵּין יָת כָּל
אַרְעָתָא הָאִלֵּין, וַאֲקִים יָת קְיָמָא, דְּקַיֵּימִית לְאַבְרָהָם אֲבוּךְ: ד וְאַסְגֵּי
יָת בְּנָךְ כְּכוֹכְבֵי שְׁמַיָּא, וְאֶתֵּין לִבְנָךְ, יָת כָּל אַרְעָתָא הָאִלֵּין, וְיִתְבָּרְכוּן
בְּדִיל בְּנָךְ, כָּל עַמְמֵי אַרְעָא: ה חֲלָף, דְּקַבֵּיל אַבְרָהָם לְמֵימְרִי, וּנְטַר
מַטְּרַת מֵימְרִי, פִּקּוֹדֵי קְיָמַי וְאוֹרָיָתָי: ו וִיתֵיב יִצְחָק בִּגְרָר: ז וּשְׁאִילוּ,
אֲנָשֵׁי אַתְרָא עַל עֵיסַק אִתְּתֵיהּ, וַאֲמַר אֲחָת הִיא, אֲרֵי דְּחֵיל לְמֵימַר
אִתְּתִי, דִּלְמָא יִקְטְלֻנַּנִי, אֲנָשֵׁי אַתְרָא עַל רִבְקָה, אֲרֵי שַׁפִּירַת חֵיזוּ
הִיא: ח וַהֲוָה, כַּד סְגִיאוּ לֵיהּ תַּמָּן יוֹמַיָּא, וְאִסְתְּכִי, אֲבִימֶלֶךְ מַלְכָּא
דִּפְלִשְׁתָּאֵי, מִן חֲרַכָּא, וַחֲזָא, וְהָא יִצְחָק מְחַיֵּיךְ, עִם רִבְקָה אִתְּתֵיהּ:
ט וּקְרָא אֲבִימֶלֶךְ לְיִצְחָק, וַאֲמַר בְּרַם הָא אִתְּתָךְ הִיא, וְאֵיכְדֵין אֲמַרְתְּ
אֲחָת הִיא, וַאֲמַר לֵיהּ יִצְחָק, אֲרֵי אֲמַרִית, דִּלְמָא אֶתְקְטֵיל עֲלַהּ:
י וַאֲמַר אֲבִימֶלֶךְ, מָא דָא עֲבַדְתְּ לַנָא, כִּזְעֵיר פּוֹן, שְׁכִיב, דִּמְיַחַד
בְּעַמָּא עִם אִתְּתָךְ, וְאֵיתֵיתָא עֲלַנָא חוֹבָא: יא וּפַקֵּיד אֲבִימֶלֶךְ, יָת
כָּל עַמָּא לְמֵימַר, דְּיַנְזֵיק, לְגַבְרָא הָדֵין, וּלְאִתְּתֵיהּ אִתְקְטָלָא יִתְקְטִיל:

12 this man or his wife shall be put to death." Yitzḥak planted crops in that land,
13 and that year he reaped a hundredfold because the LORD had blessed him. The SHELISHI
man became rich; he prospered more and more until he became very wealthy.
14 He had flocks and herds and a large retinue of servants, and the Philistines
15 envied him. So the Philistines stopped up all the wells that his father's servants
16 had dug in the time of his father Avraham, filling them with earth. Avimelekh
said to Yitzḥak, "Move away from us. You have become much too powerful for
17 18 us." So Yitzḥak left and camped in the valley of Gerar and settled there. And he
reopened the wells that had been dug in the time of his father Avraham, which
the Philistines had stopped up after Avraham died, and gave them the same
19 names his father had given them. Yitzḥak's servants dug in the valley and
20 discovered a well of fresh water, but the shepherds of Gerar quarreled with

רש"י

יב **בָּאָרֶץ הַהִוא.** אַף עַל פִּי שֶׁאֵינָהּ חֲשׁוּבָה כְּאֶרֶץ יִשְׂרָאֵל עַצְמָהּ, כְּאֶרֶץ שִׁבְעָה גוֹיִם: **בָּאָרֶץ הַהִוא בַּשָּׁנָה הַהִוא.** הָאָרֶץ קָשָׁה וְהַשָּׁנָה קָשָׁה: **בַּשָּׁנָה הַהִוא.** אַף עַל פִּי שֶׁאֵינָהּ כְּתִקְנָהּ, שֶׁהָיְתָה שְׁנַת רְעָבוֹן: **מֵאָה שְׁעָרִים.** שֶׁאֲמָדוּהָ כַּמָּה רְאוּיָה לַעֲשׂוֹת, וְעָשְׂתָה עַל אַחַת שֶׁאֲמָדוּהָ מֵאָה. וְרַבּוֹתֵינוּ אָמְרוּ: אֹמֶד זֶה לְמַעַשְׂרוֹת הָיָה:

יג **כִּי גָדַל מְאֹד.** שֶׁהָיוּ אוֹמְרִים: זֶבֶל פִּרְדוֹתָיו שֶׁל יִצְחָק וְלֹא כַּסְפּוֹ וּזְהָבוֹ שֶׁל אֲבִימֶלֶךְ:

יד **וַעֲבֻדָּה רַבָּה.** פְּעֻלָּה רַבָּה, בִּלְשׁוֹן לַעַז אוברינ"א. 'עֲבוֹדָה' מַשְׁמָע עֲבוֹדָה אַחַת, 'עֲבֻדָּה' מַשְׁמָע פְּעֻלָּה רַבָּה:

טו **סִתְּמוּם פְלִשְׁתִּים.** מִפְּנֵי שֶׁאָמְרוּ: תַּקָּלָה הֵם לָנוּ מִפְּנֵי הַגְּיָסוֹת הַבָּאוֹת עָלֵינוּ. "טַמּוּנִין פְּלִשְׁתָּאֵי", לְשׁוֹן סְתִימָה, וּבִלְשׁוֹן מִשְׁנָה: "מְטַמְטֵם אֶת הַלֵּב" (פסחים מב ע"א):

יז **בְּנַחַל גְּרָר.** רָחוֹק מִן הָעִיר:

יח **וַיָּשָׁב וַיַּחְפֹּר.** אֶת הַבְּאֵרוֹת אֲשֶׁר חָפְרוּ בִּימֵי אַבְרָהָם אָבִיו וּפְלִשְׁתִּים סִתְּמוּם קֹדֶם שֶׁנָּסַע יִצְחָק מִגְּרָר, חָזַר וַחֲפָרָן:

of the place – did not. They do not even simply ask him to move on. The act of "stopping up" the wells harms them more than it harms Yitzḥak. It robs them of a resource that will, in any case, become theirs, once the famine ends and Yitzḥak returns home.

More than hate destroys the hated, it destroys the hater. In this too, Yitzḥak and the Philistines are a portent of what will eventually happen to the Israelites in Egypt. By the time of the plague of locusts, we read:

> Pharaoh's officials then said to him, "How long must we leave this man to ensnare us? Send the people forth to serve the LORD their God. Do you not yet know that Egypt is being destroyed?" (Ex. 10:7)

In effect they said to Pharaoh: "You may think you are harming the Israelites. In fact you are harming us." This is the self-destructive nature of hate.

26:18 **כְּשֵׁמֹת אֲשֶׁר־קָרָא לָהֶן אָבִיו** *The same names his father had given them* – Yitzḥak does not strive to be original. He "reopened the wells that had been dug in the time of his father Avraham, which the Philistines had stopped up after Avraham died, and *gave them the same names*." He is content to be a link in the chain of generations, faithful to what his father started.

Yitzḥak represents the faith of persistence, the courage of continuity. He is the first Jewish child, and he represents the single greatest challenge of being a Jewish child: to continue the journey our ancestors began, rather than drifting from it, thereby bringing the journey to an end before it has reached its destination. And Yitzḥak, because of that faith, is able to achieve the most elusive of goals, namely peace – because he never gives up. When one effort fails, he begins again. So it is with all great achievement: one part originality, nine parts persistence.

יב וַיִּזְרַע יִצְחָק בָּאָרֶץ הַהִוא וַיִּמְצָא בַּשָּׁנָה הַהִוא מֵאָה שְׁעָרִים וַיְבָרְכֵהוּ
יג יד יְהוָה: וַיִּגְדַּל הָאִישׁ וַיֵּלֶךְ הָלוֹךְ וְגָדֵל עַד כִּי־גָדַל מְאֹד: וַיְהִי־לוֹ מִקְנֵה־ שלישי
טו צֹאן וּמִקְנֵה בָקָר וַעֲבֻדָּה רַבָּה וַיְקַנְאוּ אֹתוֹ פְּלִשְׁתִּים: וְכָל־הַבְּאֵרֹת
אֲשֶׁר חָפְרוּ עַבְדֵי אָבִיו בִּימֵי אַבְרָהָם אָבִיו סִתְּמוּם פְּלִשְׁתִּים וַיְמַלְאוּם
טז עָפָר: וַיֹּאמֶר אֲבִימֶלֶךְ אֶל־יִצְחָק לֵךְ מֵעִמָּנוּ כִּי־עָצַמְתָּ מִמֶּנּוּ מְאֹד:
יז יח וַיֵּלֶךְ מִשָּׁם יִצְחָק וַיִּחַן בְּנַחַל־גְּרָר וַיֵּשֶׁב שָׁם: וַיָּשָׁב יִצְחָק וַיַּחְפֹּר ׀
אֶת־בְּאֵרֹת הַמַּיִם אֲשֶׁר חָפְרוּ בִּימֵי אַבְרָהָם אָבִיו וַיְסַתְּמוּם פְּלִשְׁתִּים
אַחֲרֵי מוֹת אַבְרָהָם וַיִּקְרָא לָהֶן שֵׁמוֹת כַּשֵּׁמֹת אֲשֶׁר־קָרָא לָהֶן אָבִיו:
יט כ וַיַּחְפְּרוּ עַבְדֵי־יִצְחָק בַּנָּחַל וַיִּמְצְאוּ־שָׁם בְּאֵר מַיִם חַיִּים: וַיָּרִיבוּ רֹעֵי

אונקלוס

יב וּזְרַע יִצְחָק בְּאַרְעָא הַהִיא, וְאַשְׁכַּח, בְּשַׁתָּא הַהִיא עַל חַד מְאָה בִּדְשַׁעֲרוּהִי, וּבָרְכֵיהּ יְיָ: יג וּרְבָא גֻּבְרָא, וַאֲזַל אָזֵיל סָגֵי וְרָבֵי, עַד דִּרְבָא לַחְדָּא: יד וַהֲווֹ לֵיהּ גֵּיתֵי עָנָא וְגֵיתֵי תוֹרֵי, וּפָלְחָנָא סַגִּי, וְקַנִּיאוּ בֵּיהּ פְּלִשְׁתָּאֵי: טו וְכָל בֵּירֵי, דַּחֲפַרוּ עַבְדֵי אֲבוּהִי, בְּיוֹמֵי אַבְרָהָם אֲבוּהִי, טַמּוֹנִין פְּלִשְׁתָּאֵי, וּמְלוֹנִין עַפְרָא: טז וַאֲמַר אֲבִימֶלֶךְ לְיִצְחָק, אִיזֵיל מֵעִמַּנָא, אֲרֵי תְקֵיפְתָּ מִנַּנָא לַחְדָּא: יז וַאֲזַל מִתַּמָּן יִצְחָק, וּשְׁרָא בְּנַחְלָא דִּגְרָר וִיתֵיב תַּמָּן: יח וְתָב יִצְחָק, וַחֲפַר יָת בֵּירֵי דְּמַיָּא, דַּחֲפַרוּ בְּיוֹמֵי אַבְרָהָם אֲבוּהִי, וְטַמּוֹנִין פְּלִשְׁתָּאֵי, בָּתַר דְּמִית אַבְרָהָם, וּקְרָא לְהוֹן שְׁמָהָן, כִּשְׁמָהָן, דַּהֲוָה קָרֵי לְהוֹן אֲבוּהִי: יט וַחֲפַרוּ עַבְדֵי יִצְחָק בְּנַחְלָא, וְאַשְׁכַּחוּ תַמָּן, בֵּיר דְּמַיִין נָבְעִין: כ וּנְצוֹ רָעֲוָתָא

STOPPING UP THE WELLS

Centuries later, Pharaoh will say, at the beginning of the book of Exodus, "You see that the Israelite people are many and *more powerful* than we. Come, let us deal wisely with them in case they increase, and if war breaks out they may join our enemies and fight against us and escape from the land" (Ex. 1:9–10). The same word, *atzum*, "power/powerful," is Avimelekh's stated reason for sending Yitzḥak away now: "You have become much too powerful for us." Our passage signals the birth of one of the deadliest of human phenomena, antisemitism.

Amy Chua's thesis, in her book *World on Fire*, is that any conspicuously successful minority will attract envy that may deepen into hate and provoke violence. All three conditions are essential. The hated group must be *conspicuous*, for otherwise it would not be singled out. It must be *successful*, for otherwise it would not be envied. And it must be a *minority*, for otherwise it would not be attacked.

More specifically, according to Hannah Arendt (in part 1 of *The Origins of Totalitarianism*), what gives rise to antisemitism is the phenomenon of "wealth without power." Antisemitism is a complex, protean phenomenon because antisemites must be able to hold together two beliefs that seem to contradict one another: Jews are so powerful that they should be feared, and at the same time so powerless that they can be attacked without fear. Emotions are not rational; there is a world of difference between *rationality* and *rationalization*. "Wealth without power" precisely describes the position of Yitzḥak among the Philistines.

The Philistines do not ask Yitzḥak to share his water with them. They do not ask him to teach them how he (and his father) discovered a source of water that they – residents

Yitzḥak's shepherds, claiming that the water was theirs. So he called the well
21 Esek, because they contended with him there. They dug another well, and
22 there was a quarrel about that too; so he called it Sitna. He moved on from
there and dug another well, and this time they did not quarrel over it; so he
named this one Reḥovot. "Now the LORD has given us space," he said, "and we
23 24 will flourish in the land." From there he went up to Be'er Sheva. That night the REVI'I
LORD appeared to him and said, "I am the God of your father Avraham. Do not
be afraid, for I am with you. I will bless you and multiply your descendants for
25 the sake of Avraham My servant." Yitzḥak built an altar there and called on the
name of the LORD. There he pitched his tent, and there his servants dug a well.
26 Avimelekh came to him from Gerar, with Aḥuzat his advisor and Pikhol the
27 commander of his troops. Yitzḥak said to them, "Why have you come to me?
28 You hate me; you sent me away from you." They said, "We have seen clearly
that the LORD is with you, so we say: Let there be a pact between you and us.
29 Let us make a covenant with you that you will do us no harm, just as we did not
touch you, just as we have done you nothing but good and we sent you on your
30 way in peace. And now – the LORD bless you." Yitzḥak made them a feast, and ḤAMISHI
31 they ate and drank. Early in the morning they rose and exchanged oaths, and

רש"י

כ) **עֵשֶׂק.** עַרְעָר: **הִתְעַשְּׂקוּ.** נִתְעַשְּׂקוּ עִמּוֹ עָלֶיהָ בִּמְרִיבָה וְעַרְעָר:

כא) **שִׂטְנָה.** נויישמנ"ט:

כב) **וּפָרִינוּ בָאָרֶץ.** כְּתַרְגּוּמוֹ: "וְנִפּוּשׁ בְּאַרְעָא":

כו) **וַאֲחֻזַּת מֵרֵעֵהוּ.** "סִיעַת מֵרָחֲמוֹהִי", סִיעָה מֵאוֹהֲבָיו. וְיֵשׁ מִתְמַהּ עַל תָּי"ו שֶׁבַּ'אֲחֻזַּת' וְאַף עַל פִּי שֶׁאֵינָהּ תֵּבָה דְּבוּקָה לַחֲבֶרְתָּהּ, יֵשׁ דֻּגְמָתָהּ בַּמִּקְרָא: "הָבָה לָּנוּ עֶזְרָת מִצָּר" (תהלים ס, יג), "וּשְׁכֻרַת וְלֹא מִיָּיִן" (ישעיה נא, כא). וְיֵשׁ פּוֹתְרִים 'מֵרֵעֵהוּ' הַמֵּ"ם מִיסוֹד הַתֵּבָה, כְּמוֹ "שְׁלֹשִׁים מֵרֵעִים" (שופטים יד, יא) דְּשִׁמְשׁוֹן, כְּדֵי לַעֲשׂוֹת 'וַאֲחֻזַּת' תֵּבָה דְּבוּקָה, וּמְתַרְגְּמִין "סִיעַת רָחֲמוֹהִי": **אֲחֻזַּת.** לְשׁוֹן קְבוּצָה וַאֲגֻדָּה, שֶׁנֶּאֱחָזִים יַחַד:

כח) **רָאוֹ רָאִינוּ.** רָאוֹ בְּאָבִיךָ, רָאִינוּ בְּךָ: **תְּהִי נָא אָלָה בֵּינוֹתֵינוּ.** תְּהִי הָאָלָה אֲשֶׁר בֵּינוֹתֵינוּ מִימֵי אָבִיךָ, תְּהִי גַּם עַתָּה בֵּינֵינוּ וּבֵינֶךָ:

כט) **לֹא נְגַעֲנוּךָ.** כְּשֶׁאָמַרְנוּ לְךָ: "לֵךְ מֵעִמָּנוּ" (לעיל פסוק טז): **אַתָּה.** גַּם אַתָּה עֲשֵׂה לָנוּ כֵן:

the Kaplan hospital, allied to the Medical School of the Hebrew University. Israel Belkind, one of the founders of the settlement in 1890, called it Reḥovot precisely because of this verse: "He named this one Reḥovot, [saying,] 'Now the LORD has given us space… and we will flourish in the land.'"

I find it moving that Yitzḥak, who undergoes so many trials, from the *akeda* (the binding of Yitzḥak) when he was young, to the rivalry between his sons when he is old and blind, carries a name that means "He will laugh." Perhaps the name – given to him by God Himself before Yitzḥak was born – means what the psalm means when it says, "May those who sowed in tears reap in joy" (126:5). Faith means the courage to persist through all the setbacks, all the grief, never giving up, never accepting defeat. For at the end, despite the opposition, the envy, and the hate, lie the broad spaces, Reḥovot, and the laughter, Yitzḥak: the serenity of the destination after the storms along the way.

גְּרָר עִם־רֹעֵי יִצְחָק לֵאמֹר לָנוּ הַמָּיִם וַיִּקְרָא שֵׁם־הַבְּאֵר עֵשֶׂק כִּי
כא הִתְעַשְּׂקוּ עִמּוֹ׃ וַיַּחְפְּרוּ בְּאֵר אַחֶרֶת וַיָּרִיבוּ גַּם־עָלֶיהָ וַיִּקְרָא שְׁמָהּ
כב שִׂטְנָה׃ וַיַּעְתֵּק מִשָּׁם וַיַּחְפֹּר בְּאֵר אַחֶרֶת וְלֹא רָבוּ עָלֶיהָ וַיִּקְרָא שְׁמָהּ
כג רְחֹבוֹת וַיֹּאמֶר כִּי־עַתָּה הִרְחִיב יְהוָה לָנוּ וּפָרִינוּ בָאָרֶץ׃ וַיַּעַל מִשָּׁם רביעי
כד בְּאֵר שָׁבַע׃ וַיֵּרָא אֵלָיו יְהוָה בַּלַּיְלָה הַהוּא וַיֹּאמֶר אָנֹכִי אֱלֹהֵי אַבְרָהָם
אָבִיךָ אַל־תִּירָא כִּי־אִתְּךָ אָנֹכִי וּבֵרַכְתִּיךָ וְהִרְבֵּיתִי אֶת־זַרְעֲךָ בַּעֲבוּר
כה אַבְרָהָם עַבְדִּי׃ וַיִּבֶן שָׁם מִזְבֵּחַ וַיִּקְרָא בְּשֵׁם יְהוָה וַיֶּט־שָׁם אָהֳלוֹ
כו וַיִּכְרוּ־שָׁם עַבְדֵי־יִצְחָק בְּאֵר׃ וַאֲבִימֶלֶךְ הָלַךְ אֵלָיו מִגְּרָר וַאֲחֻזַּת
כז מֵרֵעֵהוּ וּפִיכֹל שַׂר־צְבָאוֹ׃ וַיֹּאמֶר אֲלֵהֶם יִצְחָק מַדּוּעַ בָּאתֶם אֵלָי
כח וְאַתֶּם שְׂנֵאתֶם אֹתִי וַתְּשַׁלְּחוּנִי מֵאִתְּכֶם׃ וַיֹּאמְרוּ רָאוֹ רָאִינוּ כִּי־הָיָה
יְהוָה ׀ עִמָּךְ וַנֹּאמֶר תְּהִי נָא אָלָה בֵּינוֹתֵינוּ בֵּינֵינוּ וּבֵינֶךָ וְנִכְרְתָה
כט בְרִית עִמָּךְ׃ אִם־תַּעֲשֵׂה עִמָּנוּ רָעָה כַּאֲשֶׁר לֹא נְגַעֲנוּךָ וְכַאֲשֶׁר עָשִׂינוּ
ל עִמְּךָ רַק־טוֹב וַנְּשַׁלֵּחֲךָ בְּשָׁלוֹם אַתָּה עַתָּה בְּרוּךְ יְהוָה׃ וַיַּעַשׂ לָהֶם חמישי
לא מִשְׁתֶּה וַיֹּאכְלוּ וַיִּשְׁתּוּ׃ וַיַּשְׁכִּימוּ בַבֹּקֶר וַיִּשָּׁבְעוּ אִישׁ לְאָחִיו וַיְשַׁלְּחֵם

אונקלוס

דִּגְרָר, עִם רָעֲוָתָא דְּיִצְחָק, לְמֵימַר דִּילַנָא מַיָּא, וּקְרָא שְׁמַהּ דְּבֵירָא עֵשֶׂק, אֲרֵי אִתְעַסַּקוּ עִמֵּיהּ: כא וַחֲפַרוּ בֵּיר אָחֳרִי, וּנְצוֹ אַף עֲלַהּ, וּקְרָא שְׁמַהּ שִׂטְנָה: כב וְאִסְתַּלַּק מִתַּמָּן, וַחֲפַר בֵּיר אָחֳרִי, וְלָא נְצוֹ עֲלַהּ, וּקְרָא שְׁמַהּ רְחוֹבוֹת, וַאֲמַר, אֲרֵי כְעַן, אַפְתִּי יְיָ, לַנָא וְנִפּוּשׁ בְּאַרְעָא: כג וּסְלֵיק מִתַּמָּן לִבְאֵר שָׁבַע: כד וְאִתְגְּלִי לֵיהּ יְיָ בְּלֵילְיָא הַהוּא, וַאֲמַר, אֲנָא, אֱלָהֵיהּ דְּאַבְרָהָם אֲבוּךְ, לָא תִדְחַל אֲרֵי בְּסַעְדָּךְ מֵימְרִי, וַאֲבָרְכִנָּךְ וְאַסְגֵּי יָת בְּנָךְ, בְּדִיל אַבְרָהָם עַבְדִּי: כה וּבְנָא תַמָּן מַדְבְּחָא, וְצַלִּי בִּשְׁמָא דַייָ, וּפְרַסֵיהּ תַּמָּן לְמַשְׁכְּנֵיהּ, וּכְרוֹ תַּמָּן עַבְדֵי יִצְחָק בֵּירָא: כו וַאֲבִימֶלֶךְ, אֲתָא לְוָתֵיהּ מִגְּרָר, וְסִיעַת מֵרַחֲמוֹהִי, וּפִיכֹל רַב חֵילֵיהּ: כז וַאֲמַר לְהוֹן יִצְחָק, מָדֵין אֲתֵיתוּן לְוָתִי, וְאַתּוּן סְנֵיתוּן יָתִי, וְשַׁלַּחְתּוּנִי מִלְּוָתְכוֹן: כח וַאֲמַרוּ, מִחְזָא חֲזֵינָא אֲרֵי הֲוָה מֵימְרָא דַייָ בְּסַעְדָּךְ, וַאֲמַרְנָא, תִּתְקַיַּם כְּעַן מוֹמָתָא, דַּהֲוָת בֵּין אֲבָהָתָנָא בֵּינָנָא וּבֵינָךְ, וְנִגְזַר קְיָם עִמָּךְ: כט אִם תַּעֲבֵיד עִמַּנָא בִּישָׁא, כְּמָא דְּלָא אַנְזֵיקְנָךְ, וּכְמָא דַּעֲבַדְנָא עִמָּךְ לְחוֹד טָב, וְשַׁלַּחְנָךְ בִּשְׁלָם, אַתְּ כְּעַן בְּרִיכָא דַייָ: ל וַעֲבַד לְהוֹן מִשְׁתְּיָא, וַאֲכַלוּ וּשְׁתִיאוּ: לא וְאַקְדִּימוּ בְּצַפְרָא, וְקַיִּימוּ גְּבַר לַאֲחוּהִי, וְשַׁלְּחִנּוּן

26:22 רְחֹבוֹת *Reḥovot* – How fitting it is that the town that today carries the name Yitzḥak gave the site of this third well is the home of the Weizmann Institute of Science, the Faculty of Agriculture of the Hebrew University, and

32 Yitzḥak sent them on their way. They parted from him in peace. That day,
Yitzḥak's servants came and told him about the well that they had dug; they
33 said, "We have found water." He named it Shiva, which is why the town is called
34 Be'er Sheva to this day. When Esav was forty years old, he married
Yehudit daughter of Be'eri the Hittite, and Basmat daughter of Eilon the Hittite.
27 35 1 These were a source of bitter sorrow to Yitzḥak and Rivka. When
Yitzḥak had grown old, when his eyes had grown so dim that he could not see,
he summoned his elder son Esav. "My son," he said. Esav replied, "Here I am."
2 3 He said, "I am old, and I do not know when I will die. So now, take your weapons,
4 your quiver and bow, and go out into the field and hunt me some game. Then
make me delicious food, prepared in the way that I love, and bring it to me to eat
5 so that my soul may bless you before I die." When Yitzḥak was speaking to Esav
his son, Rivka was listening. Esav went out into the field to hunt game to bring
6 back. And Rivka said to her son Yaakov, "I overheard your father say to your
7 brother Esav, 'Fetch me some game and make me delicious food so that I may
8 eat and give you my blessing before the Lord before I die.' Now, my son, listen
9 carefully to my instructions. Go to the flock and bring me two choice young
10 goats. I will make them into delicious food, in the way he loves. Then take it to

רש״י

לג **שִׁבְעָה.** עַל שֵׁם הַבְּרִית:

לד **בֶּן אַרְבָּעִים שָׁנָה.** עֵשָׂו נִמְשַׁל לַחֲזִיר, שֶׁנֶּאֱמַר: "יְכַרְסְמֶנָּה חֲזִיר מִיָּעַר" (תהלים פ, יד); הַחֲזִיר הַזֶּה כְּשֶׁהוּא שׁוֹכֵב פּוֹשֵׁט טְלָפָיו לוֹמַר: רְאוּ שֶׁאֲנִי טָהוֹר, כָּךְ אֵלּוּ גּוֹזְלִים וְחוֹמְסִים וּמַרְאִים עַצְמָם כְּשֵׁרִים. כָּל אַרְבָּעִים שָׁנָה הָיָה עֵשָׂו צָד נָשִׁים תַּחַת בַּעְלֵיהֶן וּמְעַנֶּה אוֹתָן; כְּשֶׁהָיָה בֶּן אַרְבָּעִים אָמַר: אַבָּא בֶּן אַרְבָּעִים שָׁנָה נָשָׂא אִשָּׁה, אַף אֲנִי כֵּן:

לה **מֹרַת רוּחַ.** לְשׁוֹן: "מַמְרִים הֱיִיתֶם" (דברים ט, כד), כָּל מַעֲשֵׂיהֶן הָיוּ לְעִצָּבוֹן "לְיִצְחָק וּלְרִבְקָה", שֶׁהָיוּ עוֹבְדוֹת עֲבוֹדָה זָרָה:

כז א **וַתִּכְהֶיןָ.** בַּעֲשָׁנָן שֶׁל אֵלּוּ. דָּבָר אַחֵר, כְּדֵי שֶׁיִּטֹּל יַעֲקֹב אֶת הַבְּרָכוֹת:

ב **לֹא יָדַעְתִּי יוֹם מוֹתִי.** אָמַר רַבִּי יְהוֹשֻׁעַ בֶּן קָרְחָה: אִם מַגִּיעַ אָדָם לְפֶרֶק אֲבוֹתָיו יִדְאַג חָמֵשׁ שָׁנִים לִפְנֵי כֵן וְחָמֵשׁ לְאַחַר כֵּן, וְיִצְחָק הָיָה בֶּן מֵאָה וְעֶשְׂרִים וְשָׁלֹשׁ, אָמַר: שֶׁמָּא לְפֶרֶק אִמִּי אֲנִי מַגִּיעַ וְהִיא מֵתָה בַּת מֵאָה וְעֶשְׂרִים וְשֶׁבַע, וַהֲרֵינִי בְּחָמֵשׁ שָׁנִים סָמוּךְ לְפִרְקָהּ, לְפִיכָךְ "לֹא יָדַעְתִּי יוֹם מוֹתִי", שֶׁמָּא לְפֶרֶק אִמָּא שֶׁמָּא לְפֶרֶק אַבָּא:

ג **תֶּלְיְךָ.** חַרְבְּךָ שֶׁדֶּרֶךְ לְתָלוֹתָהּ: **שָׂא נָא.** לְשׁוֹן הַשְׁחָזָה, כְּאוֹתָהּ שֶׁשָּׁנִינוּ: "אֵין מַשְׁחִיזִין אֶת הַסַּכִּין אֲבָל מַשִּׂיאָהּ עַל גַּבֵּי חֲבֶרְתָּהּ" (ביצה כח ע״א), חַדֵּד סַכִּינְךָ וּשְׁחֹט יָפֶה, שֶׁלֹּא תַּאֲכִילֵנִי נְבֵלָה: **וְצוּדָה לִּי.** מִן הַהֶפְקֵר וְלֹא מִן הַגָּזֵל:

ה **לָצוּד צַיִד לְהָבִיא.** מַהוּ "לְהָבִיא"? אִם לֹא יִמְצָא צַיִד – יָבִיא מִן הַגָּזֵל:

ז **לִפְנֵי ה׳.** בִּרְשׁוּתוֹ, שֶׁיַּסְכִּים עַל יָדִי:

ט **וְקַח לִי.** מִשֶּׁלִּי הֵם וְאֵינָם גָּזֵל, שֶׁכָּךְ כָּתַב לָהּ יִצְחָק בִּכְתֻבָּתָהּ לִטֹּל שְׁנֵי גְּדָיֵי עִזִּים בְּכָל יוֹם. בְּרֵאשִׁית רַבָּה (סה):

27:4 כַּאֲשֶׁר אָהַבְתִּי *Prepared in the way that I love* – This is not Yitzḥak's physical appetite speaking. It is his wish to be filled with the smell and taste he associates with his elder son, so that he can bless him in a mood of focused love. We will hear this in the wording of the blessing he gives, which is imbued with his son's particular scent, that of "a field the Lord has blessed" (Gen. 27:27).

לב יִצְחָק וַיֵּלְכוּ מֵאִתּוֹ בְּשָׁלוֹם: וַיְהִי ׀ בַּיּוֹם הַהוּא וַיָּבֹאוּ עַבְדֵי יִצְחָק
לג וַיַּגִּדוּ לוֹ עַל־אֹדוֹת הַבְּאֵר אֲשֶׁר חָפָרוּ וַיֹּאמְרוּ לוֹ מָצָאנוּ מָיִם: וַיִּקְרָא
לד אֹתָהּ שִׁבְעָה עַל־כֵּן שֵׁם־הָעִיר בְּאֵר שֶׁבַע עַד הַיּוֹם הַזֶּה: וַיְהִי
עֵשָׂו בֶּן־אַרְבָּעִים שָׁנָה וַיִּקַּח אִשָּׁה אֶת־יְהוּדִית בַּת־בְּאֵרִי
לה הַחִתִּי וְאֶת־בָּשְׂמַת בַּת־אֵילֹן הַחִתִּי: וַתִּהְיֶיןָ מֹרַת רוּחַ לְיִצְחָק
כז א וּלְרִבְקָה: וַיְהִי כִּי־זָקֵן יִצְחָק וַתִּכְהֶיןָ עֵינָיו מֵרְאֹת וַיִּקְרָא כד
ב אֶת־עֵשָׂו ׀ בְּנוֹ הַגָּדֹל וַיֹּאמֶר אֵלָיו בְּנִי וַיֹּאמֶר אֵלָיו הִנֵּנִי: וַיֹּאמֶר הִנֵּה־
ג נָא זָקַנְתִּי לֹא יָדַעְתִּי יוֹם מוֹתִי: וְעַתָּה שָׂא־נָא כֵלֶיךָ תֶּלְיְךָ וְקַשְׁתֶּךָ
ד וְצֵא הַשָּׂדֶה וְצוּדָה לִּי צידה: וַעֲשֵׂה־לִי מַטְעַמִּים כַּאֲשֶׁר אָהַבְתִּי צָיִד
ה וְהָבִיאָה לִּי וְאֹכֵלָה בַּעֲבוּר תְּבָרֶכְךָ נַפְשִׁי בְּטֶרֶם אָמוּת: וְרִבְקָה
שֹׁמַעַת בְּדַבֵּר יִצְחָק אֶל־עֵשָׂו בְּנוֹ וַיֵּלֶךְ עֵשָׂו הַשָּׂדֶה לָצוּד צַיִד לְהָבִיא:
ו וְרִבְקָה אָמְרָה אֶל־יַעֲקֹב בְּנָהּ לֵאמֹר הִנֵּה שָׁמַעְתִּי אֶת־אָבִיךָ מְדַבֵּר
ז אֶל־עֵשָׂו אָחִיךָ לֵאמֹר: הָבִיאָה לִּי צַיִד וַעֲשֵׂה־לִי מַטְעַמִּים וְאֹכֵלָה
ח וַאֲבָרֶכְכָה לִפְנֵי יְהוָה לִפְנֵי מוֹתִי: וְעַתָּה בְנִי שְׁמַע בְּקֹלִי לַאֲשֶׁר אֲנִי
ט מְצַוָּה אֹתָךְ: לֶךְ־נָא אֶל־הַצֹּאן וְקַח־לִי מִשָּׁם שְׁנֵי גְּדָיֵי עִזִּים טֹבִים
י וְאֶעֱשֶׂה אֹתָם מַטְעַמִּים לְאָבִיךָ כַּאֲשֶׁר אָהֵב: וְהֵבֵאתָ לְאָבִיךָ וְאָכָל

אונקלוס

יִצְחָק, וַאֲזַלוּ מִלְּוָתֵיהּ בִּשְׁלָם: לב וַהֲוָה בְּיוֹמָא הַהוּא, וַאֲתוֹ עַבְדֵי יִצְחָק, וְחַוִּיאוּ לֵיהּ, עַל עֵיסַק בֵּירָא דַּחֲפַרוּ, וַאֲמַרוּ לֵיהּ אַשְׁכַּחְנָא מַיָּא: לג וּקְרָא יָתַהּ שִׁבְעָה, עַל כֵּן שְׁמָהּ דְּקַרְתָּא בְּאֵר שֶׁבַע, עַד יוֹמָא הָדֵין: לד וַהֲוָה עֵשָׂו בַּר אַרְבְּעִין שְׁנִין, וּנְסֵיב אִתְּתָא יָת יְהוּדִית, בַּת בְּאֵרִי חִתָּאָה, וְיָת בָּשְׂמַת, בַּת אֵילוֹן חִתָּאָה: לה וַהֲוָאָה מְסָרְבָן וּמַרְגְּזָן, עַל מֵימַר יִצְחָק וְרִבְקָה: כז א וַהֲוָה כַּד סִיב יִצְחָק, וְכָהֲיָא עֵינוֹהִי מִלְּמֶחֱזֵי, וּקְרָא, יָת עֵשָׂו בְּרֵיהּ רַבָּא, וַאֲמַר לֵיהּ בְּרִי, וַאֲמַר לֵיהּ הָאֲנָא: ב וַאֲמַר, הָא כְעַן סֵיבִית, לֵית אֲנָא יָדַע יוֹמָא דְּאָמוּת: ג וּכְעַן סַב כְּעַן זֵינָךְ, סַיְפָךְ וְקַשְׁתָּךְ, וּפוֹק לְחַקְלָא, וְצוּד לִי צֵידָא: ד וַעֲבֵיד לִי תַּבְשִׁילִין, כְּמָא דִּרְחֵימִית, וְאַעֵיל לִי וְאֵיכוֹל, בְּדִיל, דִּתְבָרְכִנָּךְ נַפְשִׁי עַד לָא אֲמוּת: ה וְרִבְקָה שְׁמַעַת, כַּד מַלֵּיל יִצְחָק, עִם עֵשָׂו בְּרֵיהּ, וַאֲזַל עֵשָׂו לְחַקְלָא, לְמֵצַד צֵידָא לְאֵיתָאָה: ו וְרִבְקָה אֲמָרַת, לְיַעֲקֹב בְּרַהּ לְמֵימַר, הָא שְׁמַעִית מִן אֲבוּךְ, מְמַלֵּיל, עִם עֵשָׂו אֲחוּךְ לְמֵימַר: ז אַיְתָא לִי צֵידָא, וַעֲבֵיד לִי תַּבְשִׁילִין וְאֵיכוֹל, וַאֲבָרְכִנָּךְ, קֳדָם יי קֳדָם מוֹתִי: ח וּכְעַן בְּרִי קַבֵּיל מִנִּי, לְמָא דַּאֲנָא מְפַקְדָא יָתָךְ: ט אֵיזֵיל כְּעַן לְעָנָא, וְסַב לִי מִתַּמָּן, תְּרֵין, גַּדְיֵי עִזִּין טָבִין, וְאַעֲבֵיד יָתְהוֹן תַּבְשִׁילִין, לַאֲבוּךְ כְּמָא דִּרְחֵים: י וְתַעֵיל לַאֲבוּךְ וְיֵיכוֹל,

11 your father to eat so that he may give you his blessing before he dies." Yaakov
said to Rivka his mother, "My brother Esav is hairy, but I have smooth skin.
12 What if my father touches me? I will look to him like a fraud and bring upon
13 myself not a blessing but a curse." But his mother replied, "Your curse will be
14 on me, my son. Do as I say. Go; fetch them for me." So he went, took the goats,
and brought them to his mother, and his mother prepared delicious food in the
15 way his father loved. Then Rivka took her elder son Esav's best clothes, which
16 were with her in the house, and put them on Yaakov, her younger son. She put
17 the goatskins on his hands and the smooth part of his neck. She then handed
18 her son Yaakov the delicious food and bread that she had prepared. He went in
to his father; "My father," he said. His father replied, "Here I am. Who are you,
19 my son?" Yaakov said to his father, "I am Esav your firstborn. I have done as you
asked. Please sit up and eat some of my game so that your soul may bless me."
20 Yitzḥak asked his son, "How did you find it so quickly, my son?" He replied,
21 "The Lord your God brought it about for me." Then Yitzḥak said to Yaakov,
"Come close and let me feel you, my son, to know – are you really my son
22 Esav?" Yaakov came close to Yitzḥak his father, who felt him and said, "The
23 voice is the voice of Yaakov, but the hands are the hands of Esav." He did not

רש״י

יא| אִישׁ שָׂעִר. בַּעַל שֵׂעָר:

יב| יְמֻשֵּׁנִי. כְּמוֹ: "מְמַשֵּׁשׁ בַּצָּהֳרַיִם" (דברים כח, כט):

טו| הַחֲמֻדֹת. הַנְּקִיּוֹת, "דַּכְיָתָא". דָּבָר אַחֵר, שֶׁחָמַד אוֹתָן מִן נִמְרוֹד: אֲשֶׁר אִתָּהּ בַּבָּיִת. וַהֲלֹא כַּמָּה נָשִׁים הָיוּ לוֹ וְהוּא מַפְקִיד אֵצֶל אִמּוֹ? אֶלָּא שֶׁהָיְתָה בְּקִיאָה בְּמַעֲשֵׂיהֶן וְחוֹשֶׁדֶן:

יט| אָנֹכִי. הַמֵּבִיא לְךָ, וְעֵשָׂו הוּא בְּכוֹרֶךָ: עָשִׂיתִי. כַּמָּה דְבָרִים אֲשֶׁר דִּבַּרְתָּ אֵלָי: שְׁבָה. לְשׁוֹן מֵסֵב עַל הַשֻּׁלְחָן, לְכָךְ מְתֻרְגָּם "אִסְתְּחַר":

כא| גְּשָׁה נָּא וַאֲמֻשְׁךָ. אָמַר בְּלִבּוֹ: אֵין דֶּרֶךְ עֵשָׂו לִהְיוֹת שֵׁם שָׁמַיִם שָׁגוּר בְּפִיו, וְזֶה אוֹמֵר: "כִּי הִקְרָה ה׳ אֱלֹהֶיךָ" (לעיל פסוק כ):

כב| קוֹל יַעֲקֹב. שֶׁמְּדַבֵּר בִּלְשׁוֹן תַּחֲנוּנִים, "קוּם נָא" (לעיל פסוק יט), אֲבָל עֵשָׂו בִּלְשׁוֹן קַנְטוּרְיָא דִּבֵּר, "יָקֻם אָבִי" (להלן פסוק לא):

after all, not just a matter of relationships within the family. It is about God and destiny and spiritual vocation. It is about the future of an entire people, since God has repeatedly told Avraham that he will be the ancestor of a great nation who will be a blessing to humanity as a whole.

Rivka is not Lady Macbeth. This is the woman whom Avraham's servant chose to be the wife of his master's son because she is kind, because at the well she gave water to a stranger and to his camels also. If she has no other way of ensuring that the blessing will go to one who will cherish it and live it, then in this case, she must reason, the end justifies the means. This is one way of reading the story, and it is taken by many of the commentators. As the narrative continues, however, a more complex picture is to emerge.

27:22 וְהַיָּדַיִם יְדֵי עֵשָׂו *But the hands are the hands of Esav* – Three times, Yitzḥak expresses doubts – giving Yaakov three opportunities to admit the truth. He does not. Far from glossing over the morally ambiguous nature of Yaakov's conduct, the text goes out of its way to emphasize it.

The deception is possible only because Yitzḥak cannot see. The text at this point is almost an essay on the senses.

יא בעבר אשר יברכך לפני מותו: ויאמר יעקב אל־רבקה אמו הן עשו
יב אחי איש שער ואנכי איש חלק: אולי ימשני אבי והייתי בעיניו
יג כמתעתע והבאתי עלי קללה ולא ברכה: ותאמר לו אמו עלי
יד קללתך בני אך שמע בקלי ולך קח־לי: וילך ויקח ויבא לאמו ותעש
טו אמו מטעמים כאשר אהב אביו: ותקח רבקה את־בגדי עשו בנה
טז הגדל החמדת אשר אתה בבית ותלבש את־יעקב בנה הקטן: ואת
יז ערת גדיי העזים הלבישה על־ידיו ועל חלקת צואריו: ותתן את־
יח המטעמים ואת־הלחם אשר עשתה ביד יעקב בנה: ויבא אל־אביו
יט ויאמר אבי ויאמר הנני מי אתה בני: ויאמר יעקב אל־אביו אנכי
עשו בכרך עשיתי כאשר דברת אלי קום־נא שבה ואכלה מצידי
כ בעבור תברכני נפשך: ויאמר יצחק אל־בנו מה־זה מהרת למצא
כא בני ויאמר כי הקרה יהוה אלהיך לפני: ויאמר יצחק אל־יעקב
כב גשה־נא ואמשך בני האתה זה בני עשו אם־לא: ויגש יעקב אל־
כג יצחק אביו וימשהו ויאמר הקל קול יעקב והידים ידי עשו: ולא

אונקלוס

בדיל, דיברכנך קדם מותיה: יא ואמר יעקב, לרבקה אמיה, הא
עשו אחי גבר סערן, ואנא גבר שעיע: יב מאם ימושנני אבא,
ואיהי בעינוהי כמתלעב, ואיתי עלי, לוטין ולא ברכן: יג ואמרת
ליה אמיה, עלי אתאמר בנבואה דלא ייתון לוטיא עלך ברי,
ברם, קביל מני ואיזיל סב לי: יד ואזל ונסיב, ואיתי לאמיה, ועבדת
אמיה תבשילין, כמא דרחים אבוהי: טו ונסיבת רבקה, ית לבושי
עשו, ברה רבא דכיתא, דעמה בביתא, ואלבישת ית יעקב ברה
זעירא: טז וית, משכי דגדי בני עזי, אלבישת על ידוהי, ועל שעיעות
צוריה: יז ויהבת ית תבשיליא, וית לחמא דעבדת, בידא דיעקב
ברה: יח ועאל לות אבוהי ואמר אבא, ואמר האנא, מאן את ברי:
יט ואמר יעקב לאבוהי, אנא עשו בכרך, עבדית, כמא דמלילתא
עמי, קום כען אסתחר, ואכול מצידי, בדיל דתברכנני נפשך:
כ ואמר יצחק לבריה, מא דין, אוחיתא לאשכחא ברי, ואמר, ארי
זמין, יי אלהך קדמי: כא ואמר יצחק ליעקב, קרב כען ואמושנך
ברי, האת דין, ברי עשו אם לא: כב וקריב יעקב, לות יצחק
אבוהי ומשיה, ואמר, קלא קליה דיעקב, וידיא ידי עשו: כג ולא

27:10 בעבר אשר יברכך *So that he may give you his blessing* – Rivka has watched the twins grow up. She knows that Esav is a hunter, a man of violence. She has seen that he is impetuous, a man of impulse rather than calm reflection. She has seen him sell his birthright for a bowl of soup. No one who despises his birthright can be the trusted guardian of a covenant intended for eternity.

The blessing, she perceives, has to go to Yaakov. This is,

recognize him, because his hands were hairy like those of his brother Esav. And
24 he blessed him. "Are you really my son Esav?" he asked. He replied, "I am."
25 "Then serve me and let me eat some of my son's game so that my soul may bless
26 you." He served him food and he ate, he brought him wine and he drank. Then
27 Yaakov's father Yitzhak said to him, "Come close and kiss me, my son." So he
came close and kissed him, and Yitzhak smelled the smell of his clothes and
blessed him, saying: "The smell of my son is the smell of a field the LORD has
28 blessed. God endow you with dew of heaven, the cream of the land, much grain SHISHI
and wine. May peoples serve you; may nations bow down to you. Be lord over
your brothers, and may your mother's sons bow down to you. A curse on those
30 who curse you; on those who bless you, blessing." Yitzhak had finished blessing
Yaakov, and Yaakov had just left his father Yitzhak, when his brother Esav came
31 back from the hunt. He too had prepared delicious food and brought it to his
father. And he said to his father, "Let my father sit up and eat some of his son's
32 game so that your soul may bless me." "Who are you?" asked his father Yitzhak.
33 "I am your son, your firstborn, Esav," he replied. Yitzhak was seized with a
violent fit of trembling. "Who then was it that hunted game and brought it to
me? I ate it all before you came, and I blessed him – and he will be blessed."
34 When Esav heard his father's words, he burst into a loud and bitter cry. He said

רש״י

כד **וַיֹּאמֶר אָנִי.** לֹא אָמַר ׳אֲנִי עֵשָׂו׳, אֶלָּא ״אָנִי״:

כז **וַיָּרַח.** וַהֲלֹא אֵין רֵיחַ רַע יוֹתֵר מִשֶּׁטֶף הָעִזִּים? אֶלָּא מְלַמֵּד שֶׁנִּכְנְסָה עִמּוֹ גַּן עֵדֶן: **כְּרֵיחַ שָׂדֶה אֲשֶׁר בֵּרֲכוֹ ה׳.** שֶׁנָּתַן בּוֹ רֵיחַ טוֹב, וְזֶהוּ שְׂדֵה תַּפּוּחִים. כָּךְ דָּרְשׁוּ רַבּוֹתֵינוּ זִכְרוֹנָם לִבְרָכָה:

כח **וְיִתֶּן לְךָ.** יִתֵּן וְיַחֲזֹר וְיִתֵּן. בְּרֵאשִׁית רַבָּה (סו, ג). וּלְפִי פְּשׁוּטוֹ מוּסָף לְעִנְיָן רִאשׁוֹן: רֵיחַ בְּנִי אֲשֶׁר נָתַן לְךָ הַקָּדוֹשׁ בָּרוּךְ הוּא כְּרֵיחַ שָׂדֶה וְגוֹ׳, וְעוֹד יִתֶּן לְךָ מִטַּל הַשָּׁמַיִם וְגוֹ׳ כְּמַשְׁמָעוֹ. וּמִדְרְשֵׁי אַגָּדָה יֵשׁ הַרְבֵּה לְכַמָּה פָּנִים:

כט **בְּנֵי אִמֶּךָ.** וְיַעֲקֹב אָמַר לִיהוּדָה: ״בְּנֵי אָבִיךָ״ (להלן מט, ח), לְפִי שֶׁהָיוּ לוֹ בָּנִים מִכַּמָּה אִמָּהוֹת, וְכָאן שֶׁלֹּא נָשָׂא אֶלָּא אִשָּׁה אַחַת אָמַר: ״בְּנֵי אִמֶּךָ״: **אֹרְרֶיךָ אָרוּר וּמְבָרֲכֶיךָ בָּרוּךְ.** וּבְבִלְעָם הוּא אוֹמֵר: ״מְבָרֲכֶיךָ בָּרוּךְ וְאֹרְרֶיךָ אָרוּר״ (במדבר כד, ט)? הַצַּדִּיקִים – תְּחִלָּתָם יִסּוּרִים וְסוֹפָן שַׁלְוָה, וְאוֹרְרֵיהֶם וּמְצַעֲרֵיהֶם קוֹדְמִים לִמְבָרְכֵיהֶם, לְפִיכָךְ יִצְחָק הִקְדִּים קִלְלַת אוֹרְרִים לְבִרְכַּת מְבָרְכִים; וְהָרְשָׁעִים – תְּחִלָּתָם שַׁלְוָה וְסוֹפָן יִסּוּרִין, לְפִיכָךְ בִּלְעָם הִקְדִּים בְּרָכָה לִקְלָלָה:

ל **יָצֹא יָצָא.** זֶה יוֹצֵא וְזֶה בָּא:

לג **וַיֶּחֱרַד.** כְּמַשְׁמָעוֹ, לְשׁוֹן תְּמִיָּה. וּמִדְרָשׁוֹ, רָאָה גֵּיהִנָּם פְּתוּחָה מִתַּחְתָּיו: **מִי אֵפוֹא.** לָשׁוֹן לְעַצְמוֹ, מְשַׁמֵּשׁ עִם כַּמָּה דְּבָרִים: ״אֵיפוֹא״ – אַיֵּה פֹה, מִי הוּא וְאֵיפֹה הוּא הַצָּד צַיִד? **וָאֹכַל מִכֹּל.** מִכָּל טְעָמִים שֶׁבִּקַּשְׁתִּי לִטְעֹם טָעַמְתִּי בּוֹ: **גַּם בָּרוּךְ יִהְיֶה.** שֶׁלֹּא תֹּאמַר, אִלּוּלֵי שֶׁרִמָּה יַעֲקֹב לְאָבִיו לֹא נָטַל אֶת הַבְּרָכוֹת, לְכָךְ הִסְכִּים וּבֵרְכוֹ מִדַּעְתּוֹ:

27:27). He *hears* his voice ("The voice is the voice of Yaakov, but the hands are the hands of Esav"). Eventually, Yitzhak trusts the evidence of taste, touch, and smell over sound, and gives Yaakov the blessing.

כד הִכִּירוֹ כִּי־הָיוּ יָדָיו כִּידֵי עֵשָׂו אָחִיו שְׂעִרֹת וַיְבָרְכֵהוּ׃ וַיֹּאמֶר אַתָּה זֶה
כה בְּנִי עֵשָׂו וַיֹּאמֶר אָנִי׃ וַיֹּאמֶר הַגִּשָׁה לִּי וְאֹכְלָה מִצֵּיד בְּנִי לְמַעַן תְּבָרֶכְךָ
כו נַפְשִׁי וַיַּגֶּשׁ־לוֹ וַיֹּאכַל וַיָּבֵא לוֹ יַיִן וַיֵּשְׁתְּ׃ וַיֹּאמֶר אֵלָיו יִצְחָק אָבִיו
כז גְּשָׁה־נָּא וּשְׁקָה־לִּי בְּנִי׃ וַיִּגַּשׁ וַיִּשַּׁק־לוֹ וַיָּרַח אֶת־רֵיחַ בְּגָדָיו וַיְבָרְכֵהוּ
כח וַיֹּאמֶר רְאֵה רֵיחַ בְּנִי כְּרֵיחַ שָׂדֶה אֲשֶׁר בֵּרֲכוֹ יהוה׃ וְיִתֶּן־לְךָ הָאֱלֹהִים כה ששי
כט מִטַּל הַשָּׁמַיִם וּמִשְׁמַנֵּי הָאָרֶץ וְרֹב דָּגָן וְתִירֹשׁ׃ יַעַבְדוּךָ עַמִּים וְיִשְׁתַּחֲוֻ
לְךָ לְאֻמִּים הֱוֵה גְבִיר לְאַחֶיךָ וְיִשְׁתַּחֲווּ לְךָ בְּנֵי אִמֶּךָ אֹרְרֶיךָ אָרוּר
ל וּמְבָרְכֶיךָ בָּרוּךְ׃ וַיְהִי כַּאֲשֶׁר כִּלָּה יִצְחָק לְבָרֵךְ אֶת־יַעֲקֹב וַיְהִי אַךְ
לא יָצֹא יָצָא יַעֲקֹב מֵאֵת פְּנֵי יִצְחָק אָבִיו וְעֵשָׂו אָחִיו בָּא מִצֵּידוֹ׃ וַיַּעַשׂ
גַּם־הוּא מַטְעַמִּים וַיָּבֵא לְאָבִיו וַיֹּאמֶר לְאָבִיו יָקֻם אָבִי וְיֹאכַל מִצֵּיד
לב בְּנוֹ בַּעֲבֻר תְּבָרְכַנִּי נַפְשֶׁךָ׃ וַיֹּאמֶר לוֹ יִצְחָק אָבִיו מִי־אָתָּה וַיֹּאמֶר
לג אֲנִי בִּנְךָ בְכֹרְךָ עֵשָׂו׃ וַיֶּחֱרַד יִצְחָק חֲרָדָה גְּדֹלָה עַד־מְאֹד וַיֹּאמֶר
מִי־אֵפוֹא הוּא הַצָּד־צַיִד וַיָּבֵא לִי וָאֹכַל מִכֹּל בְּטֶרֶם תָּבוֹא וָאֲבָרְכֵהוּ
לד גַּם־בָּרוּךְ יִהְיֶה׃ כִּשְׁמֹעַ עֵשָׂו אֶת־דִּבְרֵי אָבִיו וַיִּצְעַק צְעָקָה גְּדֹלָה

אונקלוס

אִשְׁתְּמוֹדְעֵיהּ, אֲרֵי הֲוָאָה יְדוֹהִי, כִּידֵי, עֵשָׂו אֲחוּהִי סַעֲרָנִין, וּבָרְכֵיהּ: כד וַאֲמַר, אַתְּ דֵּין בְּרִי עֵשָׂו, וַאֲמַר אֲנָא: כה וַאֲמַר, קָרֵיב לִי וְאֵיכוֹל מִצֵּידָא דִּבְרִי, בְּדִיל דִּתְבָרְכִנָּךְ נַפְשִׁי, וְקָרֵיב לֵיהּ וַאֲכַל, וְאַעֵיל לֵיהּ חַמְרָא וּשְׁתִי: כו וַאֲמַר לֵיהּ יִצְחָק אֲבוּהִי, קְרַב כְּעַן וְשַׁק לִי בְּרִי: כז וּקְרֵיב וְנַשֵּׁיק לֵיהּ, וַאֲרַח, יָת רֵיחַ לְבוּשׁוֹהִי וּבָרְכֵיהּ, וַאֲמַר, חֲזֵי רֵיחָא דִבְרִי, כְּרֵיחַ חַקְלָא, דְּבָרְכֵיהּ יְיָ: כח וְיִתֵּין לָךְ יְיָ, מִטַּלָּא דִשְׁמַיָּא, וּמִטּוּבָא דְּאַרְעָא, וְסַגִּיּוּת עֲבוּר וַחֲמַר: כט יִפְלְחֻנָּךְ עַמְמִין, וְיִשְׁתַּעְבְּדוּן לָךְ מַלְכְּוָן, הֱוֵי רַב לַאֲחָךְ, וְיִסְגְּדוּן לָךְ בְּנֵי אִמָּךְ, לִיטָךְ יְהוֹן לִיטִין, וּבָרִיכָךְ יְהוֹן בְּרִיכִין: ל וַהֲוָה, כַּד שֵׁיצִי יִצְחָק לְבָרָכָא יָת יַעֲקֹב, וַהֲוָה, בְּרַם מִפַּק נְפַק יַעֲקֹב, מִן קֳדָם יִצְחָק אֲבוּהִי, וְעֵשָׂו אֲחוּהִי, עָאל מִצֵּידֵיהּ: לא וַעֲבַד אַף הוּא תַּבְשִׁילִין, וְאַעֵיל לַאֲבוּהִי, וַאֲמַר לַאֲבוּהִי, יְקוּם אַבָּא וְיֵיכוֹל מִצֵּידָא דִּבְרֵיהּ, בְּדִיל דִּתְבָרְכִנַּנִי נַפְשָׁךְ: לב וַאֲמַר לֵיהּ, יִצְחָק אֲבוּהִי מַאן אַתְּ, וַאֲמַר, אֲנָא, בְּרָךְ בֻּכְרָךְ עֵשָׂו: לג וּתְוַהּ יִצְחָק תִּוְהָא רַבָּא עַד לַחֲדָא, וַאֲמַר, מַאן הוּא דֵיכִי, דְּצָד צֵידָא וְאַעֵיל לִי, וַאֲכַלִית מִכּוֹלָא, עַד לָא תֵיעוֹל וּבָרֵיכְתֵּיהּ, אַף בְּרִיךְ יְהֵי: לד כַּד שְׁמַע עֵשָׂו יָת פִּתְגָמֵי אֲבוּהִי, וּצְוַח צְוָחָא, רַבָּא

Deprived of one (sight), Yitzḥak uses the other four. He *tastes* the food, *touches* Yaakov's hands (which Rivka has covered with goatskins), and *smells* his clothes ("The smell of my son is the smell of a field the Lord has blessed," Gen.

35 to his father, "Bless me, me too, my father!" "Your brother came in deceit and
36 took your blessing," he replied. Esav said, "Is he not rightly named Yaakov?
Twice he has supplanted me. He took my birthright and now he has taken my
37 blessing." And then, "Do you not have any blessing left for me?" Yitzḥak
answered Esav, "I have made him lord over you and given him all his brothers
as servants. I have endowed him with grain and wine. What then can I do for
38 you, my son?" Esav said to his father, "Have you only one blessing, father? Bless
39 me, me too, my father!" And Esav wept aloud. His father Yitzḥak answered him
and said: "Of the cream of the land your home shall be, of the dew of heaven

רש״י

לה **בְּמִרְמָה.** בְּחָכְמָה:

לו **הֲכִי קָרָא שְׁמוֹ.** לְשׁוֹן תֵּמַהּ הוּא, כְּמוֹ: "הֲכִי חָחִי חַתָּה" (להלן כט, טו), שֶׁמָּא לְכָךְ נִקְרָא שְׁמוֹ יַעֲקֹב, עַל שֵׁם סוֹפוֹ, שֶׁהוּא עָתִיד לְעָקְבֵנִי. תַּנְחוּמָא (תנחומא ישן כג): לָמָּה חָרַד יִצְחָק? אָמַר: שֶׁמָּא עָוֹן יֵשׁ בִּי שֶׁבֵּרַכְתִּי קָטָן לִפְנֵי גָּדוֹל וְשִׁנִּיתִי סֵדֶר הַיַּחַס, הִתְחִיל עֵשָׂו מְצַעֵק: "וַיַּעְקְבֵנִי זֶה פַעֲמַיִם", אָמַר לוֹ אָבִיו: מֶה עָשָׂה לְךָ? אָמַר לוֹ: "אֶת בְּכֹרָתִי לָקָח". אָמַר: בְּכָךְ הָיִיתִי מֵצֵר וְחָרֵד שֶׁמָּא עָבַרְתִּי עַל שׁוּרַת הַדִּין, עַכְשָׁיו לַבְּכוֹר בֵּרַכְתִּי, "גַּם בָּרוּךְ יִהְיֶה": **וַיַּעְקְבֵנִי.** כְּתַרְגּוּמוֹ: "וּכְמַנִי" חַכְמַנִי. "וְחָרַב" (דברים יט, יח) – "וּכְמַן". וְיֵשׁ מְתַרְגְּמִין: "וְחַכְמַנִי", נִתְחַכֵּם לִי: **אָצַלְתָּ.** לְשׁוֹן הַפְרָשָׁה, כְּמוֹ: "וַיָּאצֶל" (במדבר יא, כה):

לז **הֵן גְּבִיר.** בְּרָכָה זוֹ שְׁבִיעִית הִיא וְהוּא עוֹשֶׂה אוֹתָהּ רִאשׁוֹנָה? אֶלָּא אָמַר לוֹ: מַה תּוֹעֶלֶת לְךָ בִּבְרָכָה? אִם תִּקְנֶה נְכָסִים שֶׁלּוֹ הֵם, שֶׁהֲרֵי גְּבִיר שַׂמְתִּיו לָךְ, וּמַה שֶּׁקָּנָה עֶבֶד קָנָה רַבּוֹ!: **וּלְכָה אֵפוֹא מָה אֶעֱשֶׂה.** אַיֵּה אֵיפֹה אֲבַקֵּשׁ מַה לַּעֲשׂוֹת לְךָ?:

לח **הַבְרָכָה אַחַת.** הֵ"א זוֹ מְשַׁמֶּשֶׁת לְשׁוֹן תְּמִיָּה, כְּמוֹ: "הַבְּמַחֲנִים" (במדבר יג, יט), "הַשְּׁמֵנָה הִוא" (שם כ), "הַכְּמוֹת נָבָל" (שמואל ב׳ ג, לג):

לט **מִשְׁמַנֵּי הָאָרֶץ וְגוֹ׳.** זוֹ אִיטַלְיָא שֶׁל יָוָן:

verse tells us that "after Avraham's death, God blessed his son Yitzḥak, who then lived near Be'er Laḥai Roi" (25:11). On this, the Midrash says that even after his father's death, Yitzḥak continued to live near Hagar and treated her with respect (Midrash Aggada and Bereshit Rabbati ad loc.).

It seems that Yitzḥak, who himself was almost sacrificed, never forgets how Hagar and her son – his half-brother Yishmael – were sent away. The Midrash says that Yitzḥak reunited Hagar with Avraham after Sara's death. The biblical text tells us that Yitzḥak and Yishmael stood together at Avraham's grave (25:9). Somehow the divided family is reunited, seemingly at the instigation of Yitzḥak.

If this is so, then Yitzḥak's love for Esav is simply explained. It is as if Yitzḥak has said: I know what Esav is. He is strong, wild, unpredictable, possibly violent. It is impossible that he should be the person entrusted with the covenant and its spiritual demands. *But he, too, is my child.* I refuse to sacrifice him, as my father almost sacrificed me. I refuse to send him away, as my parents sent Hagar and Yishmael away. My love for my son is unconditional. I do not ignore who or what he is. But I will love him anyway, even if I do not love everything he does – because that is how God loves us, unconditionally, even if He does not love everything we do. I will bless him. I will hold him close. And I believe that one day that love may make him a better person than he might otherwise have been.

In this one act of loving Esav, Yitzḥak redeems the pain of two of the most difficult moments in his father Avraham's life: the sending away of Hagar and Yishmael and *akedat Yitzḥak*. A silence surrounds Yitzḥak in the text from the moment of the *akeda*. Esav here prompts him to voice an answer: "Have you only one blessing, father?" No. A parent has a blessing for every child. The past need not be repeated. Love can heal both the lover and the loved.

27:39 **מִשְׁמַנֵּי הָאָרֶץ** *Of the cream of the land* – The "cream of the land" and the "dew of heaven" are plentiful enough, Yitzḥak implies, for there to be enough for both sons. More significant is his qualification of Yaakov's supremacy. It will last, he says, only as long as he does not misuse it. If he acts

לה וּמָרָה עַד־מְאֹד וַיֹּאמֶר לְאָבִיו בָּרְכֵנִי גַם־אָנִי אָבִי׃ וַיֹּאמֶר בָּא אָחִיךָ
לו בְּמִרְמָה וַיִּקַּח בִּרְכָתֶךָ׃ וַיֹּאמֶר הֲכִי קָרָא שְׁמוֹ יַעֲקֹב וַיַּעְקְבֵנִי זֶה
פַעֲמַיִם אֶת־בְּכֹרָתִי לָקָח וְהִנֵּה עַתָּה לָקַח בִּרְכָתִי וַיֹּאמַר הֲלֹא־אָצַלְתָּ
לז לִּי בְּרָכָה׃ וַיַּעַן יִצְחָק וַיֹּאמֶר לְעֵשָׂו הֵן גְּבִיר שַׂמְתִּיו לָךְ וְאֶת־כָּל־
אֶחָיו נָתַתִּי לוֹ לַעֲבָדִים וְדָגָן וְתִירֹשׁ סְמַכְתִּיו וּלְכָה אֵפוֹא מָה אֶעֱשֶׂה
לח בְּנִי׃ וַיֹּאמֶר עֵשָׂו אֶל־אָבִיו הַבְרָכָה אַחַת הִוא־לְךָ אָבִי בָּרְכֵנִי גַם־אָנִי
לט אָבִי וַיִּשָּׂא עֵשָׂו קֹלוֹ וַיֵּבְךְּ׃ וַיַּעַן יִצְחָק אָבִיו וַיֹּאמֶר אֵלָיו הִנֵּה מִשְׁמַנֵּי

אונקלוס

וּמְרִירָא עַד לַחֲדָא, וַאֲמַר לַאֲבוּהִי, בָּרֵיכְנִי אַף לִי אַבָּא: לה וַאֲמַר, עָאל אֲחוּךְ בְּחָכְמָא, וְקַבֵּיל בִּרְכְתָךְ: לו וַאֲמַר, יָאוּת קְרָא שְׁמֵיהּ יַעֲקֹב, וְחַכְּמַנִי דְּנָן תַּרְתֵּין זִמְנִין, יָת בְּכֵירוּתִי נְסֵיב, וְהָא כְעַן קַבֵּיל בִּרְכְתִי, וַאֲמַר, הֲלָא שְׁבַקְתְּ לִי בִּרְכָן: לז וַאֲתֵיב יִצְחָק וַאֲמַר לְעֵשָׂו, הָא רַב, שַׁוִּיתֵיהּ עֲלָךְ וְיָת כָּל אֲחוֹהִי, יְהַבִית לֵיהּ לְעַבְדִּין, וּבַעֲבוּר וּבַחֲמַר סְעַדְתֵּיהּ, וְלָךְ כְּעַן, מָא אַעֲבֵיד בְּרִי: לח וַאֲמַר עֵשָׂו לַאֲבוּהִי, הֲבִרְכְתָא חֲדָא הִיא לָךְ אַבָּא, בָּרֵיכְנִי אַף לִי אַבָּא, וַאֲרִים עֵשָׂו, קָלֵיהּ וּבְכָא: לט וַאֲתֵיב, יִצְחָק אֲבוּהִי וַאֲמַר לֵיהּ, הָא, מְטוּבָא

27:38 **הַבְרָכָה אַחַת הִוא לְךָ אָבִי** *Have you only one blessing, father?* – There is a humanity here that defies all stereotypes and conventional categorizations. Esav is a child loved by his father and loving him in return. This is so striking that, despite the generally negative evaluation of Esav in the midrashic literature, this fact shines through: "R. Shimon ben Gamliel said: No man ever honored his father as I did mine, yet I found that Esav honored his father even more than I did" (Devarim Rabba 1:15).

There is at times a tendency on the part of the Midrash to separate biblical characters into the wholly good and wholly bad, and for this there are good pedagogic reasons, as Rabbi Tzvi Hirsch Chajes points out (*Mavo HaAggadot*). To serve effectively as role models, biblical heroes must be seen as consistently heroic, non-heroes as systematic villains.

Yet beneath this overlay of midrash, the Torah teaches a different and equally important message: Even heroes have their faults and non-heroes their virtues, and these virtues are important to God. "The Holy One, blessed be He, does not withhold the reward of any creature," said the Sages (Pesaḥim 118a). The Esav who emerges from the Torah has none of Avraham's faith, Yitzḥak's steadfastness, or Yaakov's persistence. He is carved of an altogether coarser grain. But he is not without his humanity, his filial loyalty, and a decent if quick-tempered disposition.

This too is part of the Torah's message. Just as we cannot predict God's actions in advance ("I will be what I will be," Ex. 3:14; "I will be gracious to whom I choose to be gracious, and will show mercy to whom I decide to show mercy," Ex. 33:19), so we cannot predict in advance where God's image will shine in the affairs of mankind. The loss of Yitzḥak's blessing could have been framed as a just consequence of Esav's sale of the birthright. Instead the text, at this moment, directs our feelings toward nothing but compassion.

"BLESS ME TOO"

Yitzḥak knows the pain of the displacement narrative. We recall that when Yitzḥak and Rivka first met, "Yitzḥak was just coming back from the direction of Be'er Laḥai Ro'i" (Gen. 24:62). We had encountered this place only once before. It is where the angel appeared to Hagar when, pregnant, she fled from Sara who was treating her harshly (16:14). An ingenious midrash says that when Yitzḥak heard that Avraham sent his servant to find a wife for him, he said to himself, "Can I live with a wife while my father lives alone? I will go and return Hagar to him" (*Midrash HaGadol* on Gen. 24:62). A later

40 above. By your sword you will live, and your brother you will serve; but when
41 you break loose, you will throw off his yoke from your neck." Esav resented
Yaakov because of the blessing his father had given him. "The days of mourning
for my father are approaching," he said to himself, "and then I will kill my
42 brother Yaakov." When Rivka was told what her elder son Esav had said, she
summoned her younger son Yaakov and said, "Your brother Esav is consoling
43 himself with the thought of killing you. Now, my son, listen to me. Flee at once
44 to my brother Lavan in Ḥaran. Stay with him a while, until your brother's rage
45 subsides. When your brother is no longer angry with you and has forgotten
what you did to him, I will send word to you to come back. Why should I lose
46 you both in one day?" Rivka then said to Yitzḥak, "I loathe my life because of

רש״י

מ **וְעַל חַרְבְּךָ.** כְּמוֹ: 'בְּחַרְבְּךָ', יֵשׁ 'עַל' שֶׁהוּא בִּמְקוֹם אוֹת בֵּית, כְּגוֹן "עֲמַדְתֶּם עַל חַרְבְּכֶם" (יחזקאל לג, כו) 'בְּחַרְבְּכֶם', "עַל צִבְאֹתָם" (שמות ו, כו) 'בְּצִבְאֹתָם': **וְהָיָה כַּאֲשֶׁר תָּרִיד.** לְשׁוֹן צַעַר, כְּמוֹ: "אָרִיד בְּשִׂיחִי" (תהלים נה, ג), כְּלוֹמַר, כְּשֶׁיַּעַבְרוּ יִשְׂרָאֵל עַל הַתּוֹרָה וְיִהְיֶה לְךָ פִּתְחוֹן פֶּה לְהִצְטַעֵר עַל הַבְּרָכוֹת שֶׁנָּטַל – "וּפָרַקְתָּ עֻלּוֹ" וְגוֹ':

מא **יִקְרְבוּ יְמֵי אֵבֶל אָבִי.** כְּמַשְׁמָעוֹ, שֶׁלֹּא אֲצַעֵר אֶת אַבָּא. וּמִדְרַשׁ אַגָּדָה לְכַמָּה פָּנִים יֵשׁ:

מב **וַיֻּגַּד לְרִבְקָה.** בְּרוּחַ הַקֹּדֶשׁ הֻגַּד לָהּ מַה שֶּׁעֵשָׂו מְהַרְהֵר בְּלִבּוֹ: **מִתְנַחֵם.** נִחָם עַל הָאַחְוָה לַחְשֹׁב מַחֲשָׁבָה אַחֶרֶת לְהִתְנַכֵּר לְךָ "לְהָרְגֶךָ". וּמִדְרַשׁ אַגָּדָה, כְּבָר אַתָּה מֵת בְּעֵינָיו וְשָׁתָה עָלֶיךָ כּוֹס תַּנְחוּמִים. לְשׁוֹן אַחֵר לִפְשׁוּטוֹ, לְשׁוֹן תַּנְחוּמִים, מִתְנַחֵם הוּא עַל הַבְּרָכוֹת בַּהֲרִיגָתְךָ:

מד **אֲחָדִים.** מוּעָטִים:

מה **לָמָּה אֶשְׁכַּל.** אֶהְיֶה שְׁכוּלָה מִשְּׁנֵיכֶם; הַקּוֹבֵר אֶת בָּנָיו קָרוּי 'שַׁכּוּל', וְכֵן יַעֲקֹב אָמַר: "כַּאֲשֶׁר שָׁכֹלְתִּי שָׁכָלְתִּי" (להלן מג, יד): **גַּם שְׁנֵיכֶם.** אִם יָקוּם עָלֶיךָ וְאַתָּה תַּהַרְגֶנּוּ יַעַמְדוּ בָּנָיו וְיַהַרְגוּךָ. וְרוּחַ הַקֹּדֶשׁ נִזְרְקָה בָּהּ וְנִתְנַבְּאָה שֶׁבְּיוֹם אֶחָד יָמוּתוּ, כְּמוֹ שֶׁמְּפֹרָשׁ בְּ'הַמְקַנֵּא לְאִשְׁתּוֹ' (סוטה יג ע"א):

being intellectually abused. As a teenager I heard these words from a renowned anthropologist on the BBC: "Far from being the basis of the good society, the family, with its narrow privacy and tawdry secrets, is the source of all our discontents."

What kind of family did this lecturer grow up in? I wondered at the time. It did not sound like any I knew. I saw honest men and women building a life together, caring for their children and working to give them chances they never had. "Haven in a heartless world" is what Christopher Lasch called his book on the subject.

Families are not fairy tales whose last line is "and they all lived happily ever after." They are places of conflict and stress. But they are also places where we learn to resolve those conflicts by honest communication, mutual understanding, and forgiveness. The family is where we learn the grammar of emotional intelligence by not giving up when the going gets tough. It is our ongoing seminar on the meaning of loyalty.

Families are where love is written not in poetry but in prose. There is a beauty, undemonstrative, unselfconscious, that lives in a thousand small gestures of listening, caring, helping, giving, for no ulterior motive other than the fact that here we are "we," not "I."

The discord in Rivka's sons' lives, from the womb and into adulthood, makes her question the value of her own. Her *yamim aḥadim* of separation from Yaakov will, as it turns out, be long. But Yaakov hopes to build his own family. For him, years will pass *keyamim aḥadim*, as but a few days, "so great was his love for [Raḥel]" (29:20). It is worth taking a risk for this. We can face the future without fear when we sense we will not face it alone.

מ הָאָרֶץ יִהְיֶה מוֹשָׁבֶךָ וּמִטַּל הַשָּׁמַיִם מֵעָל: וְעַל־חַרְבְּךָ תִחְיֶה וְאֶת־
מא אָחִיךָ תַּעֲבֹד וְהָיָה כַּאֲשֶׁר תָּרִיד וּפָרַקְתָּ עֻלּוֹ מֵעַל צַוָּארֶךָ: וַיִּשְׂטֹם
עֵשָׂו אֶת־יַעֲקֹב עַל־הַבְּרָכָה אֲשֶׁר בֵּרֲכוֹ אָבִיו וַיֹּאמֶר עֵשָׂו בְּלִבּוֹ יִקְרְבוּ
מב יְמֵי אֵבֶל אָבִי וְאַהַרְגָה אֶת־יַעֲקֹב אָחִי: וַיֻּגַּד לְרִבְקָה אֶת־דִּבְרֵי עֵשָׂו
בְּנָהּ הַגָּדֹל וַתִּשְׁלַח וַתִּקְרָא לְיַעֲקֹב בְּנָהּ הַקָּטָן וַתֹּאמֶר אֵלָיו הִנֵּה
מג עֵשָׂו אָחִיךָ מִתְנַחֵם לְךָ לְהָרְגֶךָ: וְעַתָּה בְנִי שְׁמַע בְּקֹלִי וְקוּם בְּרַח־לְךָ
מד אֶל־לָבָן אָחִי חָרָנָה: וְיָשַׁבְתָּ עִמּוֹ יָמִים אֲחָדִים עַד אֲשֶׁר־תָּשׁוּב חֲמַת
מה אָחִיךָ: עַד־שׁוּב אַף־אָחִיךָ מִמְּךָ וְשָׁכַח אֵת אֲשֶׁר־עָשִׂיתָ לּוֹ וְשָׁלַחְתִּי
מו וּלְקַחְתִּיךָ מִשָּׁם לָמָה אֶשְׁכַּל גַּם־שְׁנֵיכֶם יוֹם אֶחָד: וַתֹּאמֶר רִבְקָה

אונקלוס

דְּאַרְעָא יְהֵי מוֹתְבָךְ, וּמִטַּלָּא דִשְׁמַיָּא מִלְּעֵילָא: מ וְעַל חַרְבָּךְ תֵּיחֵי, וְיָת אֲחוּךְ תִּפְלַח, וִיהֵי כַּד יְעִבְרוּן בְּנוֹהִי עַל פִּתְגָּמֵי אוֹרָיְתָא, וְתַעְדֵּי נִירֵיהּ מֵעַל צַוְּרָךְ: מא וּנְטַר עֵשָׂו דְּבָבוּ לְיַעֲקֹב, עַל בִּרְכְתָא, דִּבָרְכֵיהּ אֲבוּהִי, וַאֲמַר עֵשָׂו בְּלִבֵּיהּ, יִקְרְבוּן יוֹמֵי אֶבְלֵיהּ דְּאַבָּא, וְאֶקְטוֹל יָת יַעֲקֹב אֲחִי: מב וְאִתְחַוָּא לְרִבְקָה, יָת פִּתְגָּמֵי עֵשָׂו בְּרַהּ רַבָּא, וּשְׁלַחַת, וּקְרָת לְיַעֲקֹב בְּרַהּ זְעֵירָא, וַאֲמַרַת לֵיהּ, הָא עֵשָׂו אֲחוּךְ, כָּמֵין לָךְ לְמִקְטְלָךְ: מג וּכְעַן בְּרִי קַבֵּיל מִנִּי, וְקוּם אִיזֵיל לָךְ, לְוָת לָבָן אֲחִי לְחָרָן: מד וְתֵיתֵיב עִמֵּיהּ יוֹמִין זְעֵירִין, עַד דִּתְתוּב חֵמְתָא דַּאֲחוּךְ: מה עַד דִּיתוּב רֻגְזָא דַאֲחוּךְ מִנָּךְ, וְיִתְנְשֵׁי יָת דַּעֲבַדְתְּ לֵיהּ, וְאֶשְׁלַח וְאַדְבְּרִנָּךְ מִתַּמָּן, לְמָא אֶתְכֵּול, אַף תַּרְוֵיכוֹן יוֹמָא חַד: מו וַאֲמַרַת רִבְקָה

harshly, Esav will "throw off his yoke" from his neck. For the first time, a doubt enters our understanding of the brothers' respective fates. Until now we have been led to believe that the narrative has reached closure. The elder (Esav) will serve the younger (Yaakov). Now, it is suddenly less clear. Perhaps Esav will not serve Yaakov after all. Perhaps Yaakov will misuse his power and Esav will rebel – a small incongruity, but a significant one.

27:40 וְהָיָה כַּאֲשֶׁר תָּרִיד *But when you break loose* – Many years later, the brothers are to meet again after a long estrangement (Gen. 32–33). Yaakov will be terrified of the encounter. He will bow down to Esav seven times. He will call him "my lord." He will refer to himself as "your servant." The roles will have been reversed. The blessing Yitzḥak gives Esav here casts a new light on the ambiguity of the oracle to Rivka in verse 23. Does older serve younger, or does younger serve older? It is an example of one of the most remarkable of all the Torah's narrative devices – the power of the future to transform our understanding of the past. Sometimes it is only later that we understand now. New situations retrospectively disclose new meanings in the text. This is the essence of Midrash.

27:44 וְיָשַׁבְתָּ עִמּוֹ יָמִים אֲחָדִים *Stay with him a while* – *Yamim aḥadim*, literally, "a few days." To Yaakov, Rivka explains her need for this separation with a rhetorical question: "Why should I lose you both in one day?" (Gen. 27:45). To Yitzḥak she uses another, more heartrending still: "If Yaakov marries a Hittite woman like them … why should I go on living?" (27:46).

I remember the first time I heard the idea of the family

these Hittite women. If Yaakov marries a Hittite woman like them, one of the
28 1 women of the land, why should I go on living?" So Yitzḥak called Yaakov to
him. He blessed him and charged him: "You are not to marry a Canaanite
2 woman. Go at once to Padan Aram, to the house of your mother's father Betuel,
3 and there marry a daughter of your mother's brother Lavan. May El Shaddai
bless you, make you fertile, and multiply you so that you become a community
4 of peoples. May He grant Avraham's blessing to you and your descendants, that
you may possess the land where you live as a stranger, which God gave to
5 Avraham." Then Yitzḥak sent Yaakov on his way. He went toward Padan Aram, SHEVI'I
to Lavan son of Betuel the Aramean, brother of Rivka, Yaakov and Esav's
6 mother. Esav learned that Yitzḥak had blessed Yaakov and sent him to Padan
Aram to find a wife, and that when he blessed him, he commanded him not to
7 marry a Canaanite woman, and that Yaakov had obeyed his father and mother MAFTIR
8 and had gone to Padan Aram. Esav realized then that the Canaanite women

רש״י

מו **קַצְתִּי בְחַיַּי.** מָאַסְתִּי בְּחַיַּי:

כח ב **פַּדֶּנָה.** כְּמוֹ ׳לְפַדַּן׳: **בֵּיתָה בְתוּאֵל.** לְבֵית בְּתוּאֵל, כָּל תֵּבָה שֶׁצְּרִיכָה לָמֶ״ד בִּתְחִלָּתָהּ הִטִּיל לָהּ הֵ״א בְּסוֹפָהּ:

ג **וְאֵל שַׁדַּי.** מִי שֶׁדַּי בְּבִרְכוֹתָיו לַמִּתְבָּרְכִין מִפִּיו יְבָרֵךְ אוֹתְךָ:

ד **אֶת בִּרְכַּת אַבְרָהָם.** שֶׁאָמַר לוֹ: ״וְאֶעֶשְׂךָ לְגוֹי גָּדוֹל״ (לעיל יב, ב), ״וְהִתְבָּרְכוּ בְזַרְעֲךָ״ (לעיל כב, יח) – יִהְיוּ אוֹתָן בְּרָכוֹת אֲמוּרוֹת בִּשְׁבִילְךָ, מִמְּךָ יֵצֵא אוֹתוֹ הַגּוֹי וְאוֹתוֹ הַזֶּרַע הַמְבֹרָךְ:

ה **אֵם יַעֲקֹב וְעֵשָׂו.** אֵינִי יוֹדֵעַ מַה מְּלַמְּדֵנוּ:

ז **וַיִּשְׁמַע יַעֲקֹב.** מְחֻבָּר לָעִנְיָן שֶׁל מַעְלָה: ״וַיַּרְא עֵשָׂו כִּי בֵרַךְ יִצְחָק״ וְגוֹ׳ וְכִי שִׁלַּח אוֹתוֹ פַּדֶּנָה אֲרָם וְכִי שָׁמַע יַעֲקֹב אֶל אָבִיו וְהָלַךְ פַּדֶּנָה אֲרָם וְכִי רָעוֹת בְּנוֹת כְּנַעַן, וְהָלַךְ גַּם הוּא אֶל יִשְׁמָעֵאל:

will show you" (Gen. 13:1) than famine forces him to leave. Throughout the Tanakh the land of Israel is never a simple destination, a place at which you simply arrive. It is indeed a geographical location, a country on the map, but it is more than that. It is the place we travel toward, symbol of a not-yet-realized future. That future, mapped out in greater detail in the book of Deuteronomy and in the visionary images of the prophets, is the perfect society: what Judaism is to call the Messianic age.

28:8 **וַיַּרְא עֵשָׂו** *Esav realized* – We learned before this story began, in Gen. 26:34, of the distress Esav's marriages cause his parents. Esav only learns of it now, indirectly. The failures of communication in this family have cost them dearly. Yitzḥak never did intend to give the blessing of the covenant to Esav. He intended to give each child the blessing that suited him. Why did Rivka not understand this? Because she and her husband did not communicate.

Now let us count the consequences of the deceit. Yitzḥak, old and blind, feels betrayed by Yaakov. He "was seized with a violent fit of trembling" (Gen. 27:33) when he realized what had happened, saying to Esav, "Your brother came in deceit" (27:35). Esav likewise feels betrayed and feels such violent hatred toward Yaakov that he vows to kill him. Rivka is forced to send Yaakov into exile, thus depriving herself for more than two decades of the company of the son she loves. As for Yaakov, the consequences last a lifetime, resulting in strife between his wives and between his children. "Few and hard have been the years of my life" (47:9), he says to Pharaoh as an old man. Four lives are scarred by one act which was not necessary in the first place.

אֶל־יִצְחָק קַצְתִּי בְחַיַּי מִפְּנֵי בְּנוֹת חֵת אִם־לֹקֵחַ יַעֲקֹב אִשָּׁה מִבְּנוֹת־
כח א חֵת כָּאֵלֶּה מִבְּנוֹת הָאָרֶץ לָמָּה לִּי חַיִּים: וַיִּקְרָא יִצְחָק אֶל־יַעֲקֹב
ב וַיְבָרֶךְ אֹתוֹ וַיְצַוֵּהוּ וַיֹּאמֶר לוֹ לֹא־תִקַּח אִשָּׁה מִבְּנוֹת כְּנָעַן: קוּם לֵךְ
פַּדֶּנָה אֲרָם בֵּיתָה בְתוּאֵל אֲבִי אִמֶּךָ וְקַח־לְךָ מִשָּׁם אִשָּׁה מִבְּנוֹת לָבָן
ג אֲחִי אִמֶּךָ: וְאֵל שַׁדַּי יְבָרֵךְ אֹתְךָ וְיַפְרְךָ וְיַרְבֶּךָ וְהָיִיתָ לִקְהַל עַמִּים:
ד וְיִתֶּן־לְךָ אֶת־בִּרְכַּת אַבְרָהָם לְךָ וּלְזַרְעֲךָ אִתָּךְ לְרִשְׁתְּךָ אֶת־אֶרֶץ
ה מְגֻרֶיךָ אֲשֶׁר־נָתַן אֱלֹהִים לְאַבְרָהָם: וַיִּשְׁלַח יִצְחָק אֶת־יַעֲקֹב וַיֵּלֶךְ שביעי
פַּדֶּנָה אֲרָם אֶל־לָבָן בֶּן־בְּתוּאֵל הָאֲרַמִּי אֲחִי רִבְקָה אֵם יַעֲקֹב וְעֵשָׂו:
ו וַיַּרְא עֵשָׂו כִּי־בֵרַךְ יִצְחָק אֶת־יַעֲקֹב וְשִׁלַּח אֹתוֹ פַּדֶּנָה אֲרָם לָקַחַת־
לוֹ מִשָּׁם אִשָּׁה בְּבָרְכוֹ אֹתוֹ וַיְצַו עָלָיו לֵאמֹר לֹא־תִקַּח אִשָּׁה מִבְּנוֹת
ז ח כְּנָעַן: וַיִּשְׁמַע יַעֲקֹב אֶל־אָבִיו וְאֶל־אִמּוֹ וַיֵּלֶךְ פַּדֶּנָה אֲרָם: וַיַּרְא עֵשָׂו מפטיר

אונקלוס

לְיִצְחָק, עֲקִית בְּחַיַּי, מִן קֳדָם בְּנָת חִתָּאָה, אִם נָסֵיב יַעֲקֹב, אִתְּתָא מִבְּנָת חִתָּאָה כְּאִלֵּין מִבְּנָת אַרְעָא, לְמָא לִי חַיִּין: כח א וּקְרָא יִצְחָק, לְיַעֲקֹב וּבָרֵיךְ יָתֵיהּ, וּפַקְדֵיהּ וַאֲמַר לֵיהּ, לָא תִסַּב אִתְּתָא מִבְּנָת כְּנָעַן: ב קוּם אִיזֵיל לְפַדַּן דַּאֲרָם, לְבֵית בְּתוּאֵל אֲבוּהָא דְּאִמָּךְ, וְסַב לָךְ מִתַּמָּן אִתְּתָא, מִבְּנָת לָבָן אֲחוּהָא דְּאִמָּךְ: ג וְאֵל שַׁדַּי יְבָרֵיךְ יָתָךְ, וְיַפְּשִׁנָּךְ וְיַסְגֵּינָךְ, וּתְהֵי לִכְנִשַׁת שִׁבְטִין: ד וְיִתֵּין לָךְ יָת בִּרְכְתָא דְּאַבְרָהָם, לָךְ וְלִבְנָךְ עִמָּךְ, לְמֵירְתָךְ יָת אֲרַע תּוֹתָבוּתָךְ, דִּיהַב יי לְאַבְרָהָם: ה וּשְׁלַח יִצְחָק יָת יַעֲקֹב, וַאֲזַל לְפַדַּן דַּאֲרָם, לְוָת לָבָן בַּר בְּתוּאֵל אֲרַמָּאָה, אֲחוּהָא דְּרִבְקָה, אִמֵּיהּ דְּיַעֲקֹב וְעֵשָׂו: ו וַחֲזָא עֵשָׂו, אֲרֵי בָרֵיךְ יִצְחָק יָת יַעֲקֹב, וְשַׁלַּח יָתֵיהּ לְפַדַּן דַּאֲרָם, לְמִסַּב לֵיהּ מִתַּמָּן אִתְּתָא, בְּדִבְרֵיךְ יָתֵיהּ, וּפַקֵּיד עֲלוֹהִי לְמֵימַר, לָא תִסַּב אִתְּתָא מִבְּנָת כְּנָעַן: ז וְקַבֵּיל יַעֲקֹב, מִן אֲבוּהִי וּמִן אִמֵּיהּ, וַאֲזַל לְפַדַּן דַּאֲרָם: ח וַחֲזָא עֵשָׂו,

28:4 בִּרְכַּת אַבְרָהָם *Avraham's blessing* – We now see that Yitzḥak fully understands the nature of his two sons. He loves Esav but this does not blind him to the fact that Yaakov will be the heir of the covenant. Therefore Yitzḥak has prepared two sets of blessings, one for Esav, the other for Yaakov. He blesses Esav (Gen. 27:28–29) with the gifts he feels he will appreciate: wealth and power. The covenantal blessings that God gave Avraham and Yitzḥak are completely different. They are about *children* and a *land*. It is this blessing that Yitzḥak gives Yaakov here. This is the blessing Yitzḥak intended for Yaakov all along.

Yaakov's blessing has nothing to do with wealth or power. It has to do with the children he will teach to be heirs of the covenant, and the land where his descendants will seek to create a society based on the covenant of law and love.

Each of us has a blessing that is our own. That is true not just of Yitzḥak but also of Yishmael, not just of Yaakov but also of Esav. The moral could not be more powerful. Never seek your brother's blessing. Be content with your own.

28:4 לְרִשְׁתְּךָ אֶת אֶרֶץ מְגֻרֶיךָ *The land where… you live as a stranger* – Avraham's blessing, now passed on to Yaakov, is the promise of a future sovereignty neither will live to see. No sooner does Avraham arrive in the land "that I

▶

9 displeased his father Yitzḥak. So Esav went to Yishmael and took Maḥalat,
daughter of Avraham's son Yishmael, a sister of Nevayot, to be his wife, with his
other wives.

The haftara for Parashat Toledot is on page 1510.
On Erev Rosh Ḥodesh Kislev read the haftara on page 1636.

רש״י

ט **אֲחוֹת נְבָיוֹת.** מִמַּשְׁמַע שֶׁנֶּאֱמַר: "בַּת יִשְׁמָעֵאל" אֵינִי יוֹדֵעַ שֶׁהִיא "אֲחוֹת נְבָיוֹת"? אֶלָּא לָמַדְנוּ שֶׁמֵּת יִשְׁמָעֵאל מִשֶּׁיְּעָדָהּ לְעֵשָׂו קֹדֶם נִשּׂוּאִין, וְהִשִּׂיאָהּ נְבָיוֹת אָחִיהָ. וְלָמַדְנוּ שֶׁהָיָה יַעֲקֹב בְּאוֹתוֹ הַפֶּרֶק בֶּן שִׁשִּׁים וְשָׁלֹשׁ שָׁנִים, שֶׁהֲרֵי יִשְׁמָעֵאל בֶּן שִׁבְעִים וְאַרְבַּע שָׁנִים הָיָה כְּשֶׁנּוֹלַד יַעֲקֹב – אַרְבַּע עֶשְׂרֵה שָׁנָה הָיָה גָּדוֹל יִשְׁמָעֵאל מִיִּצְחָק, "וְיִצְחָק בֶּן שִׁשִּׁים שָׁנָה בְּלֶדֶת אֹתָם" (לעיל כה, כו), הֲרֵי שִׁבְעִים וְאַרְבַּע – וּשְׁנוֹתָיו הָיוּ מֵאָה וּשְׁלֹשִׁים וָשֶׁבַע, שֶׁנֶּאֱמַר: "וְאֵלֶּה שְׁנֵי חַיֵּי יִשְׁמָעֵאל" וְגוֹ' (לעיל כה, יז), נִמְצָא יַעֲקֹב כְּשֶׁמֵּת יִשְׁמָעֵאל בֶּן שִׁשִּׁים וְשָׁלֹשׁ שָׁנִים הָיָה. וְלָמַדְנוּ מִכָּאן שֶׁנִּטְמַן בְּבֵית עֵבֶר אַרְבַּע עֶשְׂרֵה שָׁנָה וְאַחַר כָּךְ הָלַךְ לְחָרָן, שֶׁהֲרֵי לֹא שָׁהָה בְּבֵית לָבָן לִפְנֵי לֵדָתוֹ שֶׁל יוֹסֵף אֶלָּא אַרְבַּע עֶשְׂרֵה שָׁנָה, שֶׁנֶּאֱמַר: "עֲבַדְתִּיךָ אַרְבַּע עֶשְׂרֵה שָׁנָה בִּשְׁתֵּי בְנֹתֶיךָ וְשֵׁשׁ שָׁנִים בְּצֹאנֶךָ" (להלן לא, מא), וּשְׂכַר הַצֹּאן מִשֶּׁנּוֹלַד יוֹסֵף הָיָה, שֶׁנֶּאֱמַר: "וַיְהִי כַּאֲשֶׁר יָלְדָה רָחֵל אֶת יוֹסֵף" וְגוֹ' (להלן ל, כה). וְכָתוּב: "וְיוֹסֵף בֶּן שְׁלֹשִׁים שָׁנָה" (להלן מא, מו) כְּשֶׁמָּלַךְ, וּמִשָּׁם עַד שֶׁיָּרַד יַעֲקֹב לְמִצְרַיִם תֵּשַׁע שָׁנִים, שֶׁבַע שֶׁל שָׂבָע וּשְׁתַּיִם שֶׁל רָעָב, וְיַעֲקֹב אָמַר לְפַרְעֹה: "יְמֵי שְׁנֵי מְגוּרַי שְׁלֹשִׁים וּמְאַת שָׁנָה" (להלן מז, ט). צֵא וַחֲשֹׁב אַרְבַּע עֶשְׂרֵה שָׁנָה שֶׁלִּפְנֵי לֵדַת יוֹסֵף וּשְׁלֹשִׁים שֶׁל יוֹסֵף וְתֵשַׁע מִשֶּׁמָּלַךְ עַד שֶׁבָּא יַעֲקֹב, הֲרֵי חֲמִשִּׁים וְשָׁלֹשׁ, וּכְשֶׁפֵּרַשׁ מֵאָבִיו הָיָה בֶּן שִׁשִּׁים וְשָׁלֹשׁ, הֲרֵי מֵאָה וְשֵׁשׁ עֶשְׂרֵה, וְהוּא אוֹמֵר: "שְׁלֹשִׁים וּמְאַת שָׁנָה", הֲרֵי חֲסֵרִים אַרְבַּע עֶשְׂרֵה שָׁנִים. הָא לָמַדְתָּ שֶׁאַחַר שֶׁקִּבֵּל הַבְּרָכוֹת נִטְמַן בְּבֵית עֵבֶר אַרְבַּע עֶשְׂרֵה שָׁנָה: **עַל נָשָׁיו.** הוֹסִיף רִשְׁעָה עַל רִשְׁעָתוֹ, שֶׁלֹּא גֵּרַשׁ אֶת הָרִאשׁוֹנוֹת:

ט כִּ֥י רָע֖וֹת בְּנ֣וֹת כְּנָ֑עַן בְּעֵינֵ֖י יִצְחָ֥ק אָבִֽיו׃ וַיֵּ֥לֶךְ עֵשָׂ֖ו אֶל־יִשְׁמָעֵ֑אל וַיִּקַּ֡ח
אֶת־מָחֲלַ֣ת ׀ בַּת־יִשְׁמָעֵ֨אל בֶּן־אַבְרָהָ֜ם אֲח֧וֹת נְבָי֛וֹת עַל־נָשָׁ֖יו ל֥וֹ
לְאִשָּֽׁה׃

The הפטרה *for* פרשת תולדות *is on page 1511.*
On ערב ראש חודש כסלו *some read the* הפטרה *on page 1637.*

אונקלוס

אֲרֵי בִּישָׁן בְּנָת כְּנָעַן, בְּעֵינֵי יִצְחָק אֲבוּהִי: ט וַאֲזַל עֵשָׂו לְוָת יִשְׁמָעֵאל,
וּנְסֵיב, יָת מָחֲלַת בַּת יִשְׁמָעֵאל בַּר אַבְרָהָם, אֲחָתֵיהּ דִּנְבָיוֹת, עַל
נְשׁוֹהִי לֵיהּ לְאִתּוּ:

Such is the human price we pay for a failure to communicate. The Torah is exceptionally candid about such matters, which is what makes it so powerful a guide to life: real life, among real people with real problems. Communication matters. For us, speech is life. Life is relationship. And human relationships only exist because we can speak. We can tell other people our hopes, our fears, our feelings and thoughts.

Parents and leaders must establish a culture in which honest, open, respectful communication takes place, one that involves not just speaking but also listening. Without it, tragedy is waiting in the wings.

Parashat Vayetze

28 10 11 Yaakov left Be'er Sheva and journeyed toward Ḥaran. In time he chanced upon
a certain place and decided to spend the night there, because the sun had set.
He took some stones of the place and put them under his head, and in that
12 place lay down to sleep. And he dreamed: He saw a ladder set upon the ground,
whose top reached the heavens. On it, angels of God went up and came down.

רש״י

י **וַיֵּצֵא יַעֲקֹב.** על ידי שבשביל שרעות בנות כנען בעיני יצחק אביו הלך עשו אל ישמעאל, הפסיק הענין בפרשתו של יעקב וכתב: "וירא עשו כי ברך" וגו׳ (לעיל פסוק ו), ומשגמר – חזר לענין הראשון: **וַיֵּצֵא.** לא היה צריך לכתב אלא 'וילך יעקב חרנה', ולמה הזכיר יציאתו? אלא מגיד שיציאת צדיק מן המקום עושה רושם, שבזמן שהצדיק בעיר הוא הודה הוא זיוה הוא הדרה; יצא משם, פנה הודה פנה זיוה פנה הדרה, וכן: "ותצא מן המקום" (רות א, ז) האמור בנעמי ורות: **וַיֵּלֶךְ חָרָנָה.** יצא ללכת לחרן:

יא **וַיִּפְגַּע בַּמָּקוֹם.** לא הזכיר הכתוב באיזה מקום, אלא במקום הנזכר במקום אחר, הוא הר המוריה שנאמר בו: "וירא את המקום מרחק" (לעיל כב, ד): **וַיִּפְגַּע.** כמו: "ופגע ביריחו" (יהושע טז, ז), "ופגע בדבשת" (שם יט, יא). ורבותינו פרשו לשון תפלה, כמו: "ואל תפגע בי" (ירמיה ז, טז), ולמדנו שתקן תפלת ערבית. ושנה הכתוב ולא כתב 'ויתפלל', ללמדך שקפצה לו הארץ, כמו שמפרש בפרק 'גיד הנשה' (חולין צא ע״ב): **כִּי בָא הַשֶּׁמֶשׁ.** היה לו לכתב: 'ויבא השמש וילן שם', "כי בא השמש" משמע ששקעה לו חמה פתאום שלא בעונתה, כדי שילין שם: **וַיָּשֶׂם מְרַאֲשֹׁתָיו.** עשאן כמין מרזב סביב לראשו מפני חיות רעות. התחילו מריבות זו עם זו, זאת אומרת: עלי יניח צדיק את ראשו, וזאת אומרת: עלי יניח, מיד עשאן הקדוש ברוך הוא אבן אחת, וזהו שנאמר: "ויקח את האבן אשר שם מראשתיו" (להלן פסוק יח): **וַיִּשְׁכַּב בַּמָּקוֹם הַהוּא.** לשון מעוט – באותו מקום שכב, אבל ארבע עשרה שנים ששמש בבית עבר לא שכב בלילה, שהיה עוסק בתורה:

leave-taking – are dramatized by taking three steps forward, and at the end, three steps back. There is a basic shape – a deep grammar – of prayer; the inspiration for this is Yaakov's vision.

Prayer is a ladder. The first stage is the climb, the second is standing in heaven, and the third is bringing a fragment of heaven down to earth. For Yaakov realizes when he wakes from his vision that God is in *this* place. Heaven is not somewhere else, but is here – even if we are alone and afraid – if only we realize it.

28:11 **וַיִּפְגַּע בַּמָּקוֹם** *He chanced upon a certain place* – Later, in rabbinic Hebrew, the word *hamakom*, "the Place," came to mean "God." Hence in a poetic way the phrase *vayifga bamakom* could be read as "Yaakov chanced upon, had an unexpected encounter with, God." On the basis of this passage the Sages assert that "Yaakov instituted the evening prayer" (Berakhot 26b). Avraham, who instituted Shaḥarit, sought God before God sought him. Yitzḥak's prayer, Minḥa, is described as a *siḥa*, literally, a conversation or dialogue. There are two parties to a dialogue – Yitzḥak represents the religious experience as conversation between the word of God and the word of mankind. Yaakov's prayer is very different. He does not initiate it. His thoughts are elsewhere – on Esav from whom he is escaping, and on Lavan to whom he is journeying. Into this troubled mind comes a vision of God and the angels and a stairway connecting earth and heaven. He has done nothing to prepare for it. It is unexpected. Yaakov literally "chances upon" God as we can sometimes encounter a familiar face among a crowd of strangers. This is a meeting brought about by God, not man. That is one reason why Yaakov's prayer, Maariv, could not be made the basis of a regular obligation. None of us knows when the presence of God will suddenly intrude into our lives.

פרשת ויצא

כח י א וַיֵּצֵא יַעֲקֹב מִבְּאֵר שָׁבַע וַיֵּלֶךְ חָרָנָה: וַיִּפְגַּע בַּמָּקוֹם וַיָּלֶן שָׁם כִּי־בָא כו
הַשֶּׁמֶשׁ וַיִּקַּח מֵאַבְנֵי הַמָּקוֹם וַיָּשֶׂם מְרַאֲשֹׁתָיו וַיִּשְׁכַּב בַּמָּקוֹם הַהוּא:
יב וַיַּחֲלֹם וְהִנֵּה סֻלָּם מֻצָּב אַרְצָה וְרֹאשׁוֹ מַגִּיעַ הַשָּׁמָיְמָה וְהִנֵּה מַלְאֲכֵי

אונקלוס

י וּנְפַק יַעֲקֹב מִבְּאֵר שָׁבַע, וַאֲזַל לְחָרָן: יא וַעֲרַע בְּאַתְרָא, וּבָת תַּמָּן אֲרֵי עָאל שִׁמְשָׁא, וּנְסֵיב מֵאַבְנֵי אַתְרָא, וְשַׁוִּי אִיסָדוֹהִי, וּשְׁכֵיב בְּאַתְרָא הַהוּא: יב וַחֲלַם, וְהָא סֻלְמָא נְעִיץ בְּאַרְעָא, וְרֵישֵׁיהּ מָטֵי עַד צֵית שְׁמַיָּא, וְהָא מַלְאֲכַיָּא דַייָ, סָלְקִין וְנָחֲתִין בֵּיהּ: יג וְהָא

VAYETZE

Yaakov leaves home in flight from Esav, only to find himself in a fraught relationship with Lavan, his uncle, with whom he takes refuge. He falls in love with Lavan's younger daughter Raḥel, and agrees to work the seven years to earn her hand in marriage. When the wedding eventually takes place, Yaakov wakes the next morning to discover that Lavan has substituted the elder, Leah, in place of Raḥel. Yaakov later marries Raḥel as well, but there is tension between the sisters. Leah, unloved, is blessed with children; Raḥel, loved, is not. Interwoven with this is another tension between Yaakov and Lavan – about flocks, wages, and ownership – which eventually leads Yaakov to flee again, this time homeward.

Parashat Vayetze is framed by these two journeys. Yaakov, we see, is the man whose deepest spiritual encounters happen when he is on a journey, fleeing from one danger to another, alone and afraid at the dead of night.

THE VISION OF THE LADDER

The two encounters in this *parasha* and the next – the ladder and the wrestling match (Gen. 32:24) – provide us with powerful metaphors for spiritual life. Here we see it represented as climbing a ladder, rung by rung. Each day, week, month, or year, when we study and understand more, we come a little closer to heaven, learning to stand above the fray, rise above our reactive emotions, and begin to sense the complexity of the human condition. That is faith as a ladder.

The Zohar (I, 201b) identifies the ladder in Yaakov's vision with prayer: we who pray stand on earth, yet our prayers reach heaven. I would like to suggest that this primal vision does not merely give us a paradigm of prayer. Its impact extends to influence the very *structure* of Jewish liturgy. A close study of the liturgy reveals a prevalent symmetrical three-part structure, A-B-A, which has the following form: (a) ascent, (b) standing in the Presence, (c) descent. For example, Shaharit, the morning service, begins with (a) *Pesukei DeZimra*, a series of psalms which constitute a preparation for prayer. It moves on to (b) prayer-proper: the *Shema* with its three blessings, and the *Amida*, standing prayer. It ends with (c) a series of concluding hymns including *Ashrei*, itself a key element of *Pesukei DeZimra*. The threefold pattern of Shaḥarit is repeated in microcosm in the structure of the *Amida*. It too follows a three-part pattern: (a) *shevaḥ*, praise, the first three blessings; (b) *bakasha*, request, the middle blessings, and (c) *hodaya*, thanks or acknowledgment, the last three blessings.

Shevaḥ is a preparation. On this ladder of words, thoughts, and emotions, we move from the world around us, perceived by the senses, to an awareness of that which lies beyond the world. *Bakasha*, the central section, is standing in the Presence itself. *Hodaya* is leave-taking. We slowly make our way back to our mundane concerns, the arena of actions and interactions within which we live. The spiritual form of the first and last actions – entry and

13 The LORD stood over him there and said, "I am the LORD, the God of Avraham
your father, and the God of Yitzḥak. The land on which you lie I will give to you
14 and your descendants. Your descendants shall be like the dust of the earth, and
you will spread out to the west, the east, the north, and the south. Through you
15 and your descendants, all the families of the earth will be blessed. I am with
you. I will protect you wherever you go and I will bring you back to this land,
16 for I will not leave you until I have done what I have spoken of to you." Then
Yaakov awoke from his sleep and said, "Truly, the LORD is in this place – and I
17 did not know it!" He was afraid and said, "How full of awe is this place! This is
18 none other than the House of God, and this the gate of the heavens!" Yaakov

רש"י

יב **עֹלִים וְיֹרְדִים.** עוֹלִים תְּחִלָּה וְאַחַר כָּךְ יוֹרְדִים? מַלְאָכִים שֶׁלִּוּוּהוּ בָּאָרֶץ אֵין יוֹצְאִים חוּצָה לָאָרֶץ, וְעָלוּ לָרָקִיעַ, וְיָרְדוּ מַלְאֲכֵי חוּצָה לָאָרֶץ לְלַוּוֹתוֹ:

יג **נִצָּב עָלָיו.** לְשָׁמְרוֹ: **וֵאלֹהֵי יִצְחָק.** אַף עַל פִּי שֶׁלֹּא מָצִינוּ בַּמִּקְרָא שֶׁיִּחֵד הַקָּדוֹשׁ בָּרוּךְ הוּא שְׁמוֹ עַל הַצַּדִּיקִים בְּחַיֵּיהֶם לִכְתֹּב 'אֱלֹהֵי פְלוֹנִי', מִשּׁוּם שֶׁנֶּאֱמַר: "הֵן בִּקְדֹשָׁו לֹא יַאֲמִין" (איוב טו, טו), כָּאן יִחֵד שְׁמוֹ עַל יִצְחָק, לְפִי שֶׁכָּהוּ עֵינָיו וְכָלוּא בַּבַּיִת וַהֲרֵי הוּא כְּמֵת, וְיֵצֶר הָרָע פָּסַק מִמֶּנּוּ. תַּנְחוּמָא (תולדות ז): **שֹׁכֵב עָלֶיהָ.** קִפֵּל הַקָּדוֹשׁ בָּרוּךְ הוּא כָּל אֶרֶץ יִשְׂרָאֵל תַּחְתָּיו, כְּדֵי שֶׁתְּהֵא נוֹחָה לְכָבֵשׁ לְבָנָיו:

יד **וּפָרַצְתָּ.** וְחָזַקְתָּ, כְּמוֹ: "וְכֵן יִפְרֹץ" (שמות א, יב):

טו **אָנֹכִי עִמָּךְ.** לְפִי שֶׁהָיָה יָרֵא מֵעֵשָׂו וּמִלָּבָן: **עַד אֲשֶׁר אִם עָשִׂיתִי.** 'אִם' מְשַׁמֵּשׁ בִּלְשׁוֹן 'כִּי': **דִּבַּרְתִּי לָךְ.** לְצָרְכְּךָ וְעָלֶיךָ, מַה שֶּׁהִבְטַחְתִּי לְאַבְרָהָם עַל זַרְעוֹ לְךָ הִבְטַחְתִּי וְלֹא לְעֵשָׂו, שֶׁלֹּא אָמַרְתִּי לוֹ: 'כִּי יִצְחָק יִקָּרֵא לְךָ זָרַע' אֶלָּא "כִּי בְיִצְחָק" (לעיל כא, יב) וְלֹא כָּל יִצְחָק. וְכֵן כָּל 'לִי' וּ'לְךָ' וְ'לוֹ' וְ'לָהֶם' הַסְּמוּכִים אֵצֶל דִּבּוּר מְשַׁמְּשִׁים לְשׁוֹן 'עַל', וְזֶה יוֹכִיחַ, שֶׁהֲרֵי עִם יַעֲקֹב לֹא דִּבֵּר קֹדֶם לָכֵן:

טז **וְאָנֹכִי לֹא יָדָעְתִּי.** שֶׁאִם יָדַעְתִּי לֹא יָשַׁנְתִּי בְּמָקוֹם קָדוֹשׁ כָּזֶה:

יז **כִּי אִם בֵּית אֱלֹהִים.** אָמַר רַבִּי אֶלְעָזָר בְּשֵׁם רַבִּי יוֹסֵי בֶּן זִמְרָא: הַסֻּלָּם הַזֶּה עוֹמֵד בִּבְאֵר שֶׁבַע וְשִׁפּוּעוֹ מַגִּיעַ כְּנֶגֶד בֵּית הַמִּקְדָּשׁ, שֶׁבְּאֵר שֶׁבַע עוֹמֵד בִּדְרוֹמוֹ שֶׁל יְהוּדָה, וִירוּשָׁלַיִם בִּצְפוֹנוֹ בַּגְּבוּל שֶׁבֵּין יְהוּדָה וּבִנְיָמִין, וּבֵית אֵל הָיָה בַּצָּפוֹן שֶׁל נַחֲלַת בִּנְיָמִין בַּגְּבוּל שֶׁבֵּין בִּנְיָמִין וּבֵין בְּנֵי יוֹסֵף; נִמְצָא סֻלָּם שֶׁרַגְלָיו בִּבְאֵר שֶׁבַע וְרֹאשׁוֹ בְּבֵית אֵל מַגִּיעַ אֶמְצַע שִׁפּוּעוֹ נֶגֶד יְרוּשָׁלַיִם. וּלְפִי שֶׁאָמְרוּ רַבּוֹתֵינוּ שֶׁאָמַר הַקָּדוֹשׁ בָּרוּךְ הוּא, צַדִּיק זֶה בָּא לְבֵית מְלוֹנִי וְיִפָּטֵר בְּלֹא לִינָה?, וְעוֹד אָמְרוּ, יַעֲקֹב קְרָאוֹ בֵּית אֵל, וְזוֹ לוּז הִיא וְלֹא יְרוּשָׁלַיִם, וּמֵהֵיכָן לָמְדוּ לוֹמַר כֵּן? אֲנִי אוֹמֵר שֶׁנֶּעֱקַר הַר הַמּוֹרִיָּה וּבָא לְכָאן, וְזוֹ הִיא קְפִיצַת הָאָרֶץ הָאֲמוּרָה בִּשְׁחִיטַת חֻלִּין (חולין צא ע"ב), שֶׁבָּא בֵּית הַמִּקְדָּשׁ לִקְרָאתוֹ עַד בֵּית אֵל, וְזֶהוּ "וַיִּפְגַּע בַּמָּקוֹם" (לעיל פסוק יא): **מַה נּוֹרָא.** תַּרְגּוּם: "מָה דְּחִילוּ אַתְרָא הָדֵין". 'דְּחִילוּ' שֵׁם דָּבָר הוּא, כְּמוֹ 'סוּכְלְתָנוּ' 'וּכְסוּ לְמִלְבַּשׁ': **וְזֶה שַׁעַר הַשָּׁמָיִם.** מְקוֹם תְּפִלָּה לַעֲלוֹת תְּפִלָּתָם הַשָּׁמַיְמָה. וּמִדְרָשׁוֹ, שֶׁבֵּית הַמִּקְדָּשׁ שֶׁל מַעְלָה מְכֻוָּן כְּנֶגֶד בֵּית הַמִּקְדָּשׁ שֶׁל מַטָּה:

may lose faith in us, and though we may even lose faith in ourselves, God never loses faith in us. God is there, beside us, within us, urging us to stand and move on, for there is a task to do that we have not yet done and that we were created to fulfill. As for Yaakov, so for us, it feels in such a moment as if we are waking from sleep and realizing, as if for the first time, that "truly, the LORD is in this place." The place has not changed, but we have. Suddenly, with a certainty that is unmistakable, we know that we are not alone, that God is there and has been all along.

28:17 **זֶה שַׁעַר הַשָּׁמָיִם** *This the gate of the heavens* – "The house of God" came to refer to the synagogue, for prayer is "the gate of the heavens."

Prayer has two dimensions, one mysterious, the other not. There are too many cases of prayers being answered for us to deny that it makes a difference to our fate. I once heard the following story. A man in a Nazi concentration camp lost the will to live – and in the death camps, if you lost the will to live, you died. That night he poured out his heart in prayer. The next morning, he was transferred to work in the

יג אֱלֹהִים עֹלִים וְיֹרְדִים בּוֹ: וְהִנֵּה יהוה נִצָּב עָלָיו וַיֹּאמַר אֲנִי יהוה אֱלֹהֵי
אַבְרָהָם אָבִיךָ וֵאלֹהֵי יִצְחָק הָאָרֶץ אֲשֶׁר אַתָּה שֹׁכֵב עָלֶיהָ לְךָ אֶתְּנֶנָּה
יד וּלְזַרְעֶךָ: וְהָיָה זַרְעֲךָ כַּעֲפַר הָאָרֶץ וּפָרַצְתָּ יָמָּה וָקֵדְמָה וְצָפֹנָה וָנֶגְבָּה
טו וְנִבְרְכוּ בְךָ כָּל־מִשְׁפְּחֹת הָאֲדָמָה וּבְזַרְעֶךָ: וְהִנֵּה אָנֹכִי עִמָּךְ וּשְׁמַרְתִּיךָ
בְּכֹל אֲשֶׁר־תֵּלֵךְ וַהֲשִׁבֹתִיךָ אֶל־הָאֲדָמָה הַזֹּאת כִּי לֹא אֶעֱזָבְךָ עַד
טז אֲשֶׁר אִם־עָשִׂיתִי אֵת אֲשֶׁר־דִּבַּרְתִּי לָךְ: וַיִּיקַץ יַעֲקֹב מִשְּׁנָתוֹ וַיֹּאמֶר
יז אָכֵן יֵשׁ יהוה בַּמָּקוֹם הַזֶּה וְאָנֹכִי לֹא יָדָעְתִּי: וַיִּירָא וַיֹּאמַר מַה־נּוֹרָא
יח הַמָּקוֹם הַזֶּה אֵין זֶה כִּי אִם־בֵּית אֱלֹהִים וְזֶה שַׁעַר הַשָּׁמָיִם: וַיַּשְׁכֵּם

אונקלוס

יְקָרָא דַייָ, מְעַתַּד עִלָּווֹהִי וַאֲמַר, אֲנָא יְיָ, אֱלָהֵיהּ דְּאַבְרָהָם אֲבוּךְ, וֵאלָהֵיהּ דְּיִצְחָק, אַרְעָא, דְּאַתְּ שָׁכֵיב עֲלַהּ, לָךְ אֶתְּנִנַּהּ וְלִבְנָךְ: יד וִיהוֹן בְּנָךְ סַגִּיאִין כְּעַפְרָא דְאַרְעָא, וְתִתְקַף, לְמַעְרְבָא וּלְמַדִּנְחָא וּלְצִפּוּנָא וּלְדָרוֹמָא, וְיִתְבָּרְכוּן בְּדִילָךְ, כָּל זַרְעֲיַת אַרְעָא וּבְדִיל בְּנָךְ: טו וְהָא מֵימְרִי בְּסַעֲדָךְ, וְאַטְּרִנָּךְ בְּכֹל אֲתַר דִּתְהָךְ, וַאֲתִיבִנָּךְ, לְאַרְעָא הָדָא, אֲרֵי לָא אֶשְׁבְּקִנָּךְ, עַד דְּאַעֲבֵיד, יָת דְּמַלֵּילִית לָךְ: טז וְאִתְּעַר יַעֲקֹב מִשֵּׁינְתֵיהּ, וַאֲמַר, בְּקֻשְׁטָא יְקָרָא דַייָ, שְׁרֵי בְּאַתְרָא הָדֵין, וַאֲנָא לָא הֲוֵיתִי יָדַע: יז וּדְחֵיל וַאֲמַר, מָא דְּחִילוּ אַתְרָא הָדֵין, לֵית דֵּין אֲתַר הֶדְיוֹט, אֱלָהֵין אֲתַר דְּרַעֲוָא בֵיהּ מִן קֳדָם יְיָ, וְדֵין תְּרַע קֳבֵיל שְׁמַיָּא: יח וְאַקְדֵּים

28:12 וַיַּחֲלֹם *And he dreamed* – Not a nightmare but an epiphany. Yaakov signifies God's encounter with us – unplanned, unexpected – the vision, the voice, the call we can never know in advance but which leaves us transformed.

28:14 כַּעֲפַר הָאָרֶץ... וְנִבְרְכוּ בְךָ כָּל מִשְׁפְּחֹת הָאֲדָמָה *Like the dust of the earth.... all the families of the earth will be blessed* – Avraham, who described himself as "dust and ashes" (Gen. 18:27), was an *Ivri*, a Hebrew, one who wanders from place to place, whose sole security is his faith. To be a Jew has often meant just that. But he also bequeathed through Yaakov that half promise, half command: "You will become a blessing" (12:2). Avraham and Yaakov, unlike Adam and Noaḥ, are not symbols of humanity as a whole. They are individuals singled out for a particular destiny. Their children become a people singled out for a particular destiny. Why Avraham was chosen, we never discover. That is one of the great enigmas of the Bible. But to what end he was chosen, we discover at the very beginning: to be a blessing. Not to his family or to God alone; somehow he will enrich the lives of others, of cultures and faiths very different from his own. The lives of his descendants will be peculiarly interwoven with the history of many nations, and they will leave their mark, hopefully for blessing, on many cultures.

28:16 וְאָנֹכִי לֹא יָדָעְתִּי *And I did not know it* – At times we may feel utterly alone. We are not. Rav Naḥman of Breslav, who knew what it was to be broken-hearted, used to say, "A person needs to cry to his Father in the heavens with a powerful voice from the depths of his heart. Then God will listen to his voice and turn to his cry. And it may be that from this act itself, all doubts and obstacles that are keeping him back from true service of God will fall from him and be completely nullified" (*Likkutei Maharan* 2:46).

That is our heritage from Yaakov: the knowledge that we may fall, but we fall into the arms of God. Though others

rose early the next morning, took the stone he had placed under his head, set it
19 up as a pillar, and poured oil on top of it. He named the place Beit El; the town
20 was originally called Luz. Yaakov then made a vow. "If God will be with me," he
said, "protecting me on this journey I am taking, giving me bread to eat and
21 clothes to wear, and if I return in peace to my father's house, then the LORD will
22 be my God. This stone I set up as a pillar will become a house of God, and of all
29 1 that You give me I will dedicate a tenth to You." Yaakov began traveling again SHENI
2 and came to the land of the people of the East. There he saw a well in a field.
Three flocks of sheep were lying beside it because this was the well from which
3 the flocks were watered. The top of it was covered with a large stone. When all

רש״י

כ-כא **אם יהיה אלהים עמדי.** אם ישמר לי הבטחות הללו שהבטיחני להיות עמדי, כמו שאמר לי: "והנה אנכי עמך" (לעיל פסוק טו): **ושמרני.** כמו שאמר לי: "ושמרתיך בכל אשר תלך" (שם): **ונתן לי לחם לאכל.** כמו שאמר: "כי לא אעזבך" (שם), והמבקש לחם הוא קרוי נעזב, שנאמר: "ולא ראיתי צדיק נעזב וזרעו מבקש לחם" (תהלים לז, כה): **ושבתי.** כמו שאמר לי: "והשבתיך אל האדמה" (לעיל פסוק טו): **בשלום.** שלם מן החטא, שלא אלמד מדרכי לבן: **והיה ה׳ לי לאלהים.** שיחול שמו עלי מתחלה ועד סוף, שלא ימצא פסול בזרעי כמו שאמר: "אשר דברתי לך" (שם); והבטחה זו הבטיח לאברהם, שנאמר: "להיות לך לאלהים ולזרעך אחריך" (לעיל יז, ז):

כב **והאבן הזאת.** כך תפרש וי"ו זו של 'והאבן': אם תעשה לי את אלה ואף אני אעשה זאת: **והאבן הזאת אשר שמתי מצבה וגו׳.** כתרגומו: "אהי פלח עלה קדם ה׳". וכן עשה בשובו מפדן ארם כשאמר לו: "קום עלה בית אל" (להלן לה, א), מה נאמר שם? "ויצב יעקב מצבה וגו׳ ויסך עליה נסך" (שם יד):

כט א **וישא יעקב רגליו.** משנתבשר בשורה טובה והובטח בשמירה, נשא לבו את רגליו ונעשה קל ללכת. כך מפורש בבראשית רבה (ע, ח):

ב **ישקו העדרים.** משקים הרועים את העדרים, והמקרא דבר בלשון קצרה:

ג **ונאספו.** רגילים היו להאסף, לפי שהיתה האבן גדולה:

giving a tenth of one's income to charity. We worship God spiritually by helping His creations physically. That is why, when the Temple was destroyed and the sacrifices came to an end, *tzedaka* became a substitute:

> R. Dostai son of R. Yannai taught: Consider the difference between the Holy One and a king of flesh and blood. If a man brings a present to the king, it may or may not be accepted. Even if it is accepted, it remains doubtful whether the man will be admitted into the king's presence. Not so with the Holy One. A person who gives even a small coin to a beggar is deemed worthy of being admitted to behold the Divine Presence, as it is written, "I shall behold Your face through charity, and when I awake, shall be satisfied with Your likeness" (Ps. 17:15). (Bava Batra 10a)

Charity is a form of prayer, a preliminary to prayer. To know God is to act with justice and compassion, to recognize His image in other people, and to hear the silent cry of those in need. The mishnaic Sage R. Yehuda bar Ilai gave this poetic expression:

> There are ten strong things in the world: Rock is strong, but iron breaks it. Iron is strong, but fire melts it. Fire is strong, but water extinguishes it. Water is strong, but the clouds carry it. The clouds are strong, but the wind drives them. The wind is strong, but man withstands it. Man is strong, but fear weakens him. Fear is strong, but wine removes it. Wine is strong, but sleep overcomes it. Sleep is strong, but death stands over it. What is stronger even than death? Acts of charity. For it is written, "*Tzedaka* delivers from death" (Prov. 10:2). (Bava Batra 10a)

This is why, when Yaakov swears his allegiance to God, worship and charity are two inseparable sides of the same commitment.

יַעֲקֹב בַּבֹּקֶר וַיִּקַּח אֶת־הָאֶבֶן אֲשֶׁר־שָׂם מְרַאֲשֹׁתָיו וַיָּשֶׂם אֹתָהּ מַצֵּבָה
יט וַיִּצֹק שֶׁמֶן עַל־רֹאשָׁהּ: וַיִּקְרָא אֶת־שֵׁם־הַמָּקוֹם הַהוּא בֵּית־אֵל וְאוּלָם
כ לוּז שֵׁם־הָעִיר לָרִאשֹׁנָה: וַיִּדַּר יַעֲקֹב נֶדֶר לֵאמֹר אִם־יִהְיֶה אֱלֹהִים
עִמָּדִי וּשְׁמָרַנִי בַּדֶּרֶךְ הַזֶּה אֲשֶׁר אָנֹכִי הוֹלֵךְ וְנָתַן־לִי לֶחֶם לֶאֱכֹל וּבֶגֶד
כא כב לִלְבֹּשׁ: וְשַׁבְתִּי בְשָׁלוֹם אֶל־בֵּית אָבִי וְהָיָה יהוה לִי לֵאלֹהִים: וְהָאֶבֶן
הַזֹּאת אֲשֶׁר־שַׂמְתִּי מַצֵּבָה יִהְיֶה בֵּית אֱלֹהִים וְכֹל אֲשֶׁר תִּתֶּן־לִי עַשֵּׂר
כט א ב אֲעַשְּׂרֶנּוּ לָךְ: וַיִּשָּׂא יַעֲקֹב רַגְלָיו וַיֵּלֶךְ אַרְצָה בְנֵי־קֶדֶם: וַיַּרְא וְהִנֵּה שני
בְאֵר בַּשָּׂדֶה וְהִנֵּה־שָׁם שְׁלֹשָׁה עֶדְרֵי־צֹאן רֹבְצִים עָלֶיהָ כִּי מִן־הַבְּאֵר
ג הַהִוא יַשְׁקוּ הָעֲדָרִים וְהָאֶבֶן גְּדֹלָה עַל־פִּי הַבְּאֵר: וְנֶאֶסְפוּ־שָׁמָּה

אונקלוס

יַעֲקֹב בְּצַפְרָא, וּנְסֵיב יָת אַבְנָא דְּשַׁוִּי אִיסָדוֹהִי, וְשַׁוִּי יָתַהּ קָמָא,
וַאֲרִיק מִשְׁחָא עַל רֵישַׁהּ: יט וּקְרָא, יָת שְׁמֵיהּ דְּאַתְרָא הַהוּא בֵּית אֵל,
וּבְרַם, לוּז שְׁמַהּ דְּקַרְתָּא מִלְּקַדְמִין: כ וְקַיֵּים יַעֲקֹב קְיָם לְמֵימַר, אִם יְהֵי
מֵימְרָא דַּיי בְּסַעְדִי, וְיִטְּרִנַּנִי בְּאוֹרְחָא הָדָא דַּאֲנָא אָזֵיל, וְיִתֵּין לִי לְחֵים,
לְמֵיכַל וּכְסוּ לְמִלְבַּשׁ: כא וְאֵתוּב בִּשְׁלָם לְבֵית אַבָּא, וִיהֵי מֵימְרָא
דַּיי, לִי לֶאֱלָהּ: כב וְאַבְנָא הָדָא, דְּשַׁוֵּיתִי קָמָא, תְּהֵי דַּאֲיהֵי פָּלַח עֲלַהּ
קֳדָם יי, וְכֹל דְּתִתֵּין לִי, חַד מִן עַסְרָא אַפְרְשִׁנֵּיהּ קֳדָמָךְ: כט א וּנְטַל
יַעֲקֹב רַגְלוֹהִי, וַאֲזַל לַאֲרַע בְּנֵי מַדִּנְחָא: ב וַחֲזָא וְהָא בֵירָא בְּחַקְלָא,
וְהָא תַמָּן, תְּלָתָא עֶדְרִין דְּעָן רְבִיעִין עֲלַהּ, אֲרֵי מִן בֵּירָא הַהִיא,
מַשְׁקַן עֶדְרַיָּא, וְאַבְנָא רַבְּתָא עַל פֻּמָּא דְבֵירָא: ג וּמִתְכַּנְשִׁין לְתַמָּן

camp kitchen. There he was able, when the guards were not looking, to steal some potato peelings. It was these peelings that kept him alive. I heard this story from his son.

There is, however, a second dimension which is non-mysterious. Less than prayer changes the world, it changes us. In prayer, we escape from the prison of the self and see the world, including ourselves, from the outside. Prayer is where the relentless first-person singular, the "I," falls silent for a moment.

When Yaakov wakes from his sleep he says, "Truly, the Lord is in this place *ve'anokhi lo yadati*." *Lo yadati* means "I did not know"; *anokhi* means, again, "I," which in this sentence is superfluous. To translate it literally we would have to say, "And I, I did not know it!" How, asks Rabbi Pinchas Horowitz (*Panim Yafot*), do we come to know that "the Lord is in this place"? By *ve'anokhi lo yadati* – not knowing the I.

Sometimes it takes a great crisis to make us realize how self-centered we have been. The only question strong enough to endow existence with meaning is not "What do I need from life?" but "What does life need from me?" That is the question we hear when we truly pray. More than an act of speaking, prayer is an act of listening – to what God wants from us, here, now. More than prayer changes God, it changes us. It lets us see, feel, know that "the Lord is in this place." How do we reach that awareness? By moving beyond the first-person singular, so that for a moment, like Yaakov, we can say, "I know not the I." In the silence of the "I," we meet the "Thou" of God.

28:22 עַשֵּׂר אֲעַשְּׂרֶנּוּ לָךְ *I will dedicate a tenth* – Yaakov itemizes his side of the agreement – the commitment that "the Lord will be my God" – into two resolutions: "This stone … will become a house of God" and "of all that You give me I will dedicate a tenth to You." This second promise is later to find expression in the *maasrot* dedicated to the Levites and the poor, and eventually in *maaser kesafim*, the practice of

the flocks were gathered there, the stone would be rolled from the mouth of
the well and the sheep watered. The stone would then be put back in place on
4 top of the well. Yaakov asked the shepherds, "Brothers, where are you from?"
5 "We are from Ḥaran," they replied. He asked, "Do you know Lavan son of
6 Naḥor?" "We know him," they said. He asked, "Is he well?" "He is well," they
7 said, "and look, here is his daughter Raḥel coming with the sheep." "Look," he
said, "it is still broad daylight. It is not yet time to gather in the animals. Water
8 the flocks and take them back to pasture." But they said, "We cannot do that
until all the flocks are gathered and the stone is rolled from the top of the well.
9 Only then can we water the flocks." While he was still talking with them, Raḥel
10 came with her father's sheep; she was a shepherdess. When Yaakov saw Raḥel,
daughter of his mother's brother Lavan, with Lavan's sheep, he stepped forward,
rolled the stone from the top of the well, and watered his uncle Lavan's sheep.
11 12 And Yaakov kissed Raḥel – and wept aloud. And Yaakov told Raḥel that he was
13 related to her father: he was Rivka's son. She ran to tell her father. When Lavan
heard the news about Yaakov, his sister's son, he ran to meet him. He embraced

רש״י

וְגָלֲלוּ. וְגוֹלְלִין, וְתַרְגּוּמוֹ: ״וּמְגַנְדְּרִין״. כָּל לְשׁוֹן הֹוֶה מִשְׁתַּנֶּה לְדַבֵּר בִּלְשׁוֹן עָתִיד וּבִלְשׁוֹן עָבָר, לְפִי שֶׁכָּל דָּבָר הַהֹוֶה תָּמִיד כְּבָר הָיָה וְעָתִיד לִהְיוֹת: **וְהֵשִׁיבוּ.** ״וּמְתִיבִין״:

ו **בָּאָה עִם הַצֹּאן.** הַטַּעַם בָּאלֶ״ף, וְתַרְגּוּמוֹ: ״אָתְיָא״; ״וְרָחֵל בָּאָה״ (להלן פסוק ט) הַטַּעַם לְמַעְלָה בַּבֵּי״ת וְתַרְגּוּמוֹ: ״אֲתָת״, הָרִאשׁוֹן לְשׁוֹן ׳עוֹשָׂה׳ וְהַשֵּׁנִי לְשׁוֹן ׳עָשְׂתָה׳:

ז **הֵן עוֹד הַיּוֹם גָּדוֹל.** לְפִי שֶׁרָאָה אוֹתָם רוֹבְצִים, כְּסָבוּר שֶׁרוֹצִים לֶאֱסֹף הַמִּקְנֶה הַבַּיְתָה וְלֹא יִרְעוּ עוֹד. אָמַר לָהֶם: ״הֵן עוֹד הַיּוֹם גָּדוֹל״, אִם שְׂכִירִים אַתֶּם – לֹא הִשְׁלַמְתֶּם פְּעֻלַּת הַיּוֹם, וְאִם הַבְּהֵמוֹת שֶׁלָּכֶם – אַף עַל פִּי כֵן ״לֹא עֵת הֵאָסֵף הַמִּקְנֶה״ וְגוֹ׳. בְּרֵאשִׁית רַבָּה (ע, יא):

ח **לֹא נוּכַל.** לְהַשְׁקוֹת, לְפִי שֶׁהָאֶבֶן גְּדוֹלָה: **וְגָלֲלוּ.** זֶה מְתֻרְגָּם: ״וִיגַנְדְּרוּן״, לְפִי שֶׁהוּא לְשׁוֹן עָתִיד:

י **וַיִּגַּשׁ יַעֲקֹב וַיָּגֶל.** כְּאָדָם שֶׁמַּעֲבִיר אֶת הַפְּקָק מֵעַל פִּי צְלוֹחִית, לְהוֹדִיעֲךָ שֶׁכֹּחוֹ גָּדוֹל:

יא **וַיֵּבְךְּ.** לְפִי שֶׁצָּפָה בְּרוּחַ הַקֹּדֶשׁ שֶׁאֵינָהּ נִכְנֶסֶת עִמּוֹ לַקְּבוּרָה. דָּבָר אַחֵר, לְפִי שֶׁבָּא בְּיָדַיִם רֵיקָנִיּוֹת, אָמַר: אֱלִיעֶזֶר עֶבֶד אֲבִי אַבָּא הָיוּ בְּיָדָיו נְזָמִים וּצְמִידִים וּמִגְדָּנוֹת, וַאֲנִי אֵין בְּיָדִי כְּלוּם. לְפִי שֶׁרָדַף אֱלִיפַז בֶּן עֵשָׂו בְּמִצְוַת אָבִיו אַחֲרָיו לְהָרְגוֹ, וְהִשִּׂיגוֹ, וּלְפִי שֶׁגָּדַל אֱלִיפַז בְּחֵיקוֹ שֶׁל יִצְחָק מָשַׁךְ יָדוֹ. אָמַר לוֹ: מָה אֶעֱשֶׂה לְצִוּוּיוֹ שֶׁל אַבָּא? אָמַר לוֹ יַעֲקֹב: טֹל מַה שֶּׁבְּיָדִי, וְהֶעָנִי חָשׁוּב כַּמֵּת:

יב **כִּי אֲחִי אָבִיהָ הוּא.** קָרוֹב לְאָבִיהָ, כְּמוֹ: ״אֲנָשִׁים אַחִים אֲנָחְנוּ״ (לעיל יג, ח). וּמִדְרָשׁוֹ: אִם לְרַמָּאוּת הוּא בָּא – גַּם אֲנִי אָחִיו בְּרַמָּאוּת, וְאִם אָדָם כָּשֵׁר הוּא – גַּם אֲנִי ״בֶּן רִבְקָה״ אֲחוֹתוֹ הַכְּשֵׁרָה: **וַתַּגֵּד לְאָבִיהָ.** אִמָּהּ מֵתָה וְלֹא הָיָה לָהּ לְהַגִּיד אֶלָּא לוֹ:

יג **וַיָּרָץ לִקְרָאתוֹ.** כְּסָבוּר מָמוֹן הוּא טָעוּן, שֶׁהֲרֵי עֶבֶד הַבַּיִת בָּא לְכָאן בַּעֲשָׂרָה גְּמַלִּים טְעוּנִין: **וַיְחַבֵּק.** כְּשֶׁלֹּא רָאָה עִמּוֹ כְּלוּם אָמַר: שֶׁמָּא זְהוּבִים הֵבִיא וַהֲרֵי הֵם בְּחֵיקוֹ: **וַיְנַשֶּׁק לוֹ.** אָמַר: שֶׁמָּא מַרְגָּלִיּוֹת הֵבִיא וַהֲרֵי הֵם בְּפִיו:

29:13 וַיְחַבֶּק־לוֹ וַיְנַשֶּׁק־לוֹ *Embraced and kissed him* – In age after age, Jews sought refuge from those who, like Esav, sought to kill them. The nations who gave them refuge seemed at first to be benefactors. But they demanded a price. As we shall see (ch. 30, "An Aramean Sought My Father's Death"), Lavan's behavior is the paradigm of antisemites through the ages.

כָל־הָעֲדָרִים וְגָלְלוּ אֶת־הָאֶבֶן מֵעַל פִּי הַבְּאֵר וְהִשְׁקוּ אֶת־הַצֹּאן
ד וְהֵשִׁיבוּ אֶת־הָאֶבֶן עַל־פִּי הַבְּאֵר לִמְקֹמָהּ: וַיֹּאמֶר לָהֶם יַעֲקֹב אַחַי
ה מֵאַיִן אַתֶּם וַיֹּאמְרוּ מֵחָרָן אֲנָחְנוּ: וַיֹּאמֶר לָהֶם הַיְדַעְתֶּם אֶת־לָבָן
ו בֶּן־נָחוֹר וַיֹּאמְרוּ יָדָעְנוּ: וַיֹּאמֶר לָהֶם הֲשָׁלוֹם לוֹ וַיֹּאמְרוּ שָׁלוֹם וְהִנֵּה
ז רָחֵל בִּתּוֹ בָּאָה עִם־הַצֹּאן: וַיֹּאמֶר הֵן עוֹד הַיּוֹם גָּדוֹל לֹא־עֵת הֵאָסֵף
ח הַמִּקְנֶה הַשְׁקוּ הַצֹּאן וּלְכוּ רְעוּ: וַיֹּאמְרוּ לֹא נוּכַל עַד אֲשֶׁר יֵאָסְפוּ
ט כָּל־הָעֲדָרִים וְגָלְלוּ אֶת־הָאֶבֶן מֵעַל פִּי הַבְּאֵר וְהִשְׁקִינוּ הַצֹּאן: עוֹדֶנּוּ
י מְדַבֵּר עִמָּם וְרָחֵל ׀ בָּאָה עִם־הַצֹּאן אֲשֶׁר לְאָבִיהָ כִּי רֹעָה הִוא: וַיְהִי
כַּאֲשֶׁר רָאָה יַעֲקֹב אֶת־רָחֵל בַּת־לָבָן אֲחִי אִמּוֹ וְאֶת־צֹאן לָבָן אֲחִי
אִמּוֹ וַיִּגַּשׁ יַעֲקֹב וַיָּגֶל אֶת־הָאֶבֶן מֵעַל פִּי הַבְּאֵר וַיַּשְׁקְ אֶת־צֹאן לָבָן
יא יב אֲחִי אִמּוֹ: וַיִּשַּׁק יַעֲקֹב לְרָחֵל וַיִּשָּׂא אֶת־קֹלוֹ וַיֵּבְךְּ: וַיַּגֵּד יַעֲקֹב לְרָחֵל
יג כִּי אֲחִי אָבִיהָ הוּא וְכִי בֶן־רִבְקָה הוּא וַתָּרָץ וַתַּגֵּד לְאָבִיהָ: וַיְהִי כִשְׁמֹעַ
לָבָן אֶת־שֵׁמַע ׀ יַעֲקֹב בֶּן־אֲחֹתוֹ וַיָּרָץ לִקְרָאתוֹ וַיְחַבֶּק־לוֹ וַיְנַשֶּׁק־לוֹ

אונקלוס

כָּל עֶדְרַיָּא, וּמְגַנְדְּרִין יָת אַבְנָא מֵעַל פֻּמָּא דְבֵירָא, וּמַשְׁקַן יָת עָנָא, וּמְתִיבִין יָת אַבְנָא, עַל פֻּמָּא דְבֵירָא לְאַתְרַהּ: ד וַאֲמַר לְהוֹן יַעֲקֹב, אַחַי מְנָן אַתּוּן, וַאֲמַרוּ, מֵחָרָן אֲנַחְנָא: ה וַאֲמַר לְהוֹן, הַיְדַעְתּוּן יָת לָבָן בַּר נָחוֹר, וַאֲמַרוּ יָדְעִין: ו וַאֲמַר לְהוֹן הַשְׁלָם לֵיהּ, וַאֲמַרוּ שְׁלָם, וְהָא רָחֵל בְּרַתֵּיהּ, אָתְיָא עִם עָנָא: ז וַאֲמַר, הָא עוֹד יוֹמָא סַגִּי, לָא עִדָּן לְמִכְנַשׁ בְּעִיר, אַשְׁקוֹ עָנָא וְאִיזִילוּ רְעוֹ: ח וַאֲמַרוּ לָא נִכּוֹל, עַד דְּיִתְכַּנְשׁוּן כָּל עֶדְרַיָּא, וִיגַנְדְּרוּן יָת אַבְנָא, מֵעַל פֻּמָּא דְבֵירָא, וְנַשְׁקֵי עָנָא: ט עַד דְּהוּא מְמַלֵּיל עִמְּהוֹן, וְרָחֵל אֲתָת, עִם עָנָא דִּלְאֲבוּהָא, אֲרֵי רָעְיָתָא הִיא: י וַהֲוָה, כַּד חֲזָא יַעֲקֹב יָת רָחֵל, בַּת לָבָן אֲחוּהָא דְאִמֵּיהּ, וְיָת עָנָא דְּלָבָן אֲחוּהָא דְאִמֵּיהּ, וּקְרֵיב יַעֲקֹב, וְגַנְדַּר יָת אַבְנָא מֵעַל פֻּמָּא דְבֵירָא, וְאַשְׁקִי, יָת עָנָא דְּלָבָן אֲחוּהָא דְאִמֵּיהּ: יא וּנְשֵׁיק יַעֲקֹב לְרָחֵל, וַאֲרֵים יָת קָלֵיהּ וּבְכָא: יב וְחַוִּי יַעֲקֹב לְרָחֵל, אֲרֵי בַּר אֲחָת אֲבוּהָא הוּא, וַאֲרֵי בַּר רִבְקָה הוּא, וּרְהַטַת וְחַוִּיאַת לַאֲבוּהָא: יג וַהֲוָה כַּד שְׁמַע לָבָן, יָת שֵׁימַע יַעֲקֹב בַּר אֲחָתֵיהּ, וּרְהַט לְקַדָּמוּתֵיהּ וְגָפֵיף לֵיהּ וְנַשֵּׁיק לֵיהּ,

29:10 כַּאֲשֶׁר רָאָה יַעֲקֹב אֶת־רָחֵל *When Yaakov saw Raḥel* – Notice the sharp contrast with the earlier scene at which Avraham's servant sought a wife for his master's son at a well. Here it is Yaakov, not the woman, who is active. Rolling the stone off the well is a feat of considerable strength, as well as a daring defiance of local custom, not attributes we have hitherto associated with the quiet son of Yitzḥak. Evidently, Yaakov is seized with strong emotion. He kisses Raḥel; he weeps. The text at least raises the possibility that he has performed his act of bravado to impress her with both his strength and his kindness. It may be love at first sight.

and kissed him and brought him to his house. Yaakov told Lavan all that had
14 happened. Lavan said to him, "You are truly of my own bones, my own flesh."
15 And Yaakov stayed with him for a month. Then Lavan said to him, "If you are
my brother, does that mean you should work for me for nothing? Tell me what
16 your hire should be." Lavan had two daughters. The elder was called Leah and
17 the younger Raḥel. Leah had sensitive eyes; Raḥel was beautiful and lovely.
18 And Yaakov was in love with Raḥel, so he said, "I will work for you seven years SHELISHI
19 for your younger daughter Raḥel." Lavan replied, "Better that I give her to you
20 than to some other man. Stay on with me." So Yaakov worked for Raḥel seven
years. But so great was his love for her that they seemed to him but a few days.
21 Then Yaakov said to Lavan, "Give me my wife – my time is done, let me come
22 23 to her." So Lavan brought together all the local people and made a feast. In the
evening he took his daughter Leah and brought her in to him, and he came to
24 25 her. Lavan also gave his servant Zilpa to his daughter Leah as her maid. Then
came morning – and it was Leah. Yaakov said to Lavan, "What is this you have

רש״י

וַיְסַפֵּר לְלָבָן. שֶׁלֹּא בָּא אֶלָּא מִתּוֹךְ אֹנֶס אָחִיו, וְשֶׁנָּטְלוּ מָמוֹנוֹ מִמֶּנּוּ:

יד **אַךְ עַצְמִי וּבְשָׂרִי.** מֵעַתָּה אֵין לִי לְאָסְפְּךָ הַבַּיְתָה, הוֹאִיל וְאֵין בְּיָדְךָ כְּלוּם, אֶלָּא מִפְּנֵי קֻרְבָה אֲטַפֵּל בְּךָ חֹדֶשׁ יָמִים, וְכֵן עָשָׂה, וְאַף זוֹ לֹא לְחִנָּם, שֶׁהָיָה רוֹעֶה צֹאנוֹ:

טו **הֲכִי אָחִי אַתָּה.** לְשׁוֹן תְּמִיהָ, וְכִי בִּשְׁבִיל שֶׁאָחִי אַתָּה תַּעַבְדֵנִי חִנָּם?: **וַעֲבַדְתַּנִי.** כְּמוֹ 'וְתַעַבְדֵנִי'. וְכֵן כָּל תֵּבָה שֶׁהִיא לְשׁוֹן עָבָר, הוֹסֵף וָי"ו בְּרֹאשָׁהּ וְהִיא הוֹפֶכֶת הַתֵּבָה לְהַבָּא:

יז **רַכּוֹת.** שֶׁהָיְתָה סְבוּרָה לַעֲלוֹת בְּגוֹרָלוֹ שֶׁל עֵשָׂו וּבוֹכָה, שֶׁהָיוּ הַכֹּל אוֹמְרִים: שְׁנֵי בָּנִים לְרִבְקָה וּשְׁתֵּי בָּנוֹת לְלָבָן, הַגְּדוֹלָה לַגָּדוֹל וְהַקְּטַנָּה לַקָּטָן: **תֹּאַר.** הוּא צוּרַת הַפַּרְצוּף, לְשׁוֹן: "יְתָאֲרֵהוּ בַשֶּׂרֶד" (ישעיה מד, יג), קונפא"ס בְּלַעַז: **מַרְאֶה.** הוּא זִיו קְלַסְתֵּר:

יח **אֶעֱבָדְךָ שֶׁבַע שָׁנִים.** הֵם "יָמִים אֲחָדִים" שֶׁאָמְרָה לוֹ אִמּוֹ: "וְיָשַׁבְתָּ עִמּוֹ יָמִים אֲחָדִים" (לעיל כז, מד), וְתֵדַע שֶׁכֵּן הוּא, שֶׁהֲרֵי כְּתִיב: "וַיִּהְיוּ בְעֵינָיו כְּיָמִים אֲחָדִים" (להלן פסוק כ): **בְּרָחֵל בִּתְּךָ הַקְּטַנָּה.** כָּל הַסִּימָנִים הַלָּלוּ לָמָּה? לְפִי שֶׁיּוֹדֵעַ בּוֹ שֶׁהוּא רַמַּאי, אָמַר לוֹ: "אֶעֱבָדְךָ בְּרָחֵל", וְשֶׁמָּא תֹּאמַר רָחֵל אַחֶרֶת מִן הַשּׁוּק, תַּלְמוּד לוֹמַר: "בִּתְּךָ", וְשֶׁמָּא תֹּאמַר אַחְלִיף לְלֵאָה שְׁמָהּ וְאֶקְרָא שְׁמָהּ רָחֵל, תַּלְמוּד לוֹמַר: "הַקְּטַנָּה". וְאַף עַל פִּי כֵן לֹא הוֹעִיל:

כא **מָלְאוּ יָמָי.** שֶׁאָמְרָה לִי אִמִּי. וְעוֹד, "מָלְאוּ יָמַי", שֶׁהֲרֵי אֲנִי בֶּן שְׁמוֹנִים וְאַרְבַּע שָׁנָה, וְאֵימָתַי אַעֲמִיד שְׁנֵים עָשָׂר שְׁבָטִים? וְזֶהוּ שֶׁאָמַר: "וְאָבוֹאָה אֵלֶיהָ", וַהֲלֹא קַל שֶׁבַּקַּלִּים אֵינוֹ אוֹמֵר כֵּן! אֶלָּא לְהוֹלִיד תּוֹלָדוֹת אָמַר כֵּן:

כה **וַיְהִי בַבֹּקֶר וְהִנֵּה הִיא לֵאָה.** אֲבָל בַּלַּיְלָה לֹא הָיְתָה לֵאָה, לְפִי שֶׁמָּסַר יַעֲקֹב סִימָנִים לְרָחֵל, וּכְשֶׁרָאֲתָה שֶׁמַּכְנִיסִין לוֹ לֵאָה, אָמְרָה: עַכְשָׁיו תִּכָּלֵם אֲחוֹתִי. עָמְדָה וּמָסְרָה לָהּ אוֹתָן סִימָנִים:

this in one of its most beautiful lines: "So Yaakov worked for Raḥel seven years. But so great was his love for her that they seemed to him but a few days" (Gen. 29:20). He is oblivious to both labor and time. Not before and not afterward do we find in the Torah such romantic passion.

29:25 **וְהִנֵּה־הִוא לֵאָה** *And it was Leah* – Lavan has made it impossible for Yaakov to backtrack. He has invited "all the

her eyes in desiring the forbidden fruit (Gen. 3:6). Shmuel, seeing the sons of Yishai, among whom God has told him is Israel's future king, initially chooses Eliav, who looks the part. He is told by God that he has judged wrongly: "Do not consider his appearance or height, for I have rejected him. The LORD does not look at the things man looks at. Man looks at the outward appearance, but the LORD looks at the heart" (1 Sam. 16:7). Yet Yaakov is deeply in love. The Torah tells us

יד וַיְבִיאֵהוּ אֶל־בֵּיתוֹ וַיְסַפֵּר לְלָבָן אֵת כָּל־הַדְּבָרִים הָאֵלֶּה: וַיֹּאמֶר לוֹ
טו לָבָן אַךְ עַצְמִי וּבְשָׂרִי אָתָּה וַיֵּשֶׁב עִמּוֹ חֹדֶשׁ יָמִים: וַיֹּאמֶר לָבָן לְיַעֲקֹב
טז הֲכִי־אָחִי אַתָּה וַעֲבַדְתַּנִי חִנָּם הַגִּידָה לִּי מַה־מַּשְׂכֻּרְתֶּךָ: וּלְלָבָן שְׁתֵּי
יז בָנוֹת שֵׁם הַגְּדֹלָה לֵאָה וְשֵׁם הַקְּטַנָּה רָחֵל: וְעֵינֵי לֵאָה רַכּוֹת וְרָחֵל
יח הָיְתָה יְפַת־תֹּאַר וִיפַת מַרְאֶה: וַיֶּאֱהַב יַעֲקֹב אֶת־רָחֵל וַיֹּאמֶר אֶעֱבָדְךָ שלישי
יט שֶׁבַע שָׁנִים בְּרָחֵל בִּתְּךָ הַקְּטַנָּה: וַיֹּאמֶר לָבָן טוֹב תִּתִּי אֹתָהּ לָךְ
כ מִתִּתִּי אֹתָהּ לְאִישׁ אַחֵר שְׁבָה עִמָּדִי: וַיַּעֲבֹד יַעֲקֹב בְּרָחֵל שֶׁבַע שָׁנִים
כא וַיִּהְיוּ בְעֵינָיו כְּיָמִים אֲחָדִים בְּאַהֲבָתוֹ אֹתָהּ: וַיֹּאמֶר יַעֲקֹב אֶל־לָבָן
כב הָבָה אֶת־אִשְׁתִּי כִּי מָלְאוּ יָמָי וְאָבוֹאָה אֵלֶיהָ: וַיֶּאֱסֹף לָבָן אֶת־כָּל־
כג אַנְשֵׁי הַמָּקוֹם וַיַּעַשׂ מִשְׁתֶּה: וַיְהִי בָעֶרֶב וַיִּקַּח אֶת־לֵאָה בִתּוֹ וַיָּבֵא
כד אֹתָהּ אֵלָיו וַיָּבֹא אֵלֶיהָ: וַיִּתֵּן לָבָן לָהּ אֶת־זִלְפָּה שִׁפְחָתוֹ לְלֵאָה בִתּוֹ
כה שִׁפְחָה: וַיְהִי בַבֹּקֶר וְהִנֵּה־הִוא לֵאָה וַיֹּאמֶר אֶל־לָבָן מַה־זֹּאת עָשִׂיתָ

אונקלוס

וְאַעֲלֵיהּ לְבֵיתֵיהּ, וְאִשְׁתְּעִי לְלָבָן, יָת כָּל פִּתְגָּמַיָּא הָאִלֵּין: יד וַאֲמַר לֵיהּ לָבָן, בְּרַם, קָרִיבִי וּבִסְרִי אַתְּ, וִיתֵיב עִמֵּיהּ יְרַח יוֹמִין: טו וַאֲמַר לָבָן לְיַעֲקֹב, הֲמִדַּאֲחִי אַתְּ, וְתִפְלְחִנַּנִי מַגָּן, חַוִּי לִי מָא אַגְרָךְ: טז וּלְלָבָן תַּרְתֵּין בְּנָן, שׁוּם רַבְּתָא לֵאָה, וְשׁוּם זְעֵירְתָא רָחֵל: יז וְעֵינֵי לֵאָה יָאָיָן, וְרָחֵל הֲוָת, שַׁפִּירָא בְרֵיוָא וְיָאָיָא בְחֶזְוָא: יח וּרְחֵים יַעֲקֹב יָת רָחֵל, וַאֲמַר, אֶפְלְחִנָּךְ שְׁבַע שְׁנִין, בְּרָחֵל בְּרַתָּךְ זְעֵירְתָא: יט וַאֲמַר לָבָן, טַב דְּאֶתֵּין יָתַהּ לָךְ, מִדְּאֶתֵּין יָתַהּ לִגְבַר אָחֳרָן, תִּיב עִמִּי:

כ וּפְלַח יַעֲקֹב, בְּרָחֵל שְׁבַע שְׁנִין, וַהֲווֹ בְעֵינוֹהִי כְּיוֹמִין זְעִירִין, בִּדְרָחֵים יָתַהּ: כא וַאֲמַר יַעֲקֹב לְלָבָן הַב יָת אִתְּתִי, אֲרֵי שְׁלִימוּ יוֹמֵי פֻלְחָנִי, וְאֵיעוֹל לְוָתַהּ: כב וּכְנַשׁ לָבָן, יָת כָּל אֱנָשֵׁי אַתְרָא וַעֲבַד מִשְׁתְּיָא: כג וַהֲוָה בְרַמְשָׁא, וּדְבַר יָת לֵאָה בְרַתֵּיהּ, וְאַעֵיל יָתַהּ לְוָתֵיהּ, וְעָאל לְוָתַהּ: כד וִיהַב לָבָן לַהּ, יָת זִלְפָּה אַמְתֵיהּ, לְלֵאָה בְרַתֵּיהּ לְאַמְהוּ: כה וַהֲוָה בְצַפְרָא, וְהָא הִיא לֵאָה, וַאֲמַר לְלָבָן, מָא דָא עֲבַדְתְּ

29:17 וְעֵינֵי לֵאָה רַכּוֹת *Leah had sensitive eyes* – The word *rakot* could mean many things: beautiful (Onkelos and Rashbam), weak (Ramban and Radak), or sensitive. Rabbi Naftali Tzvi Yehuda Berlin suggests that Leah is unable to go out with the flocks because the bright sunlight hurts her eyes (*Haamek Davar*). But the word is more significant than that. It means – as Rashi, Radak, and midrashic tradition explain – "Leah is easily moved to tears." Sensitive, easily hurt, she will know that she is Yaakov's lesser love, and it will cause her pain. In a few deft strokes, which we only notice if we are listening carefully, the text has sketched Leah's situation and character.

29:20 וַיִּהְיוּ בְעֵינָיו כְּיָמִים אֲחָדִים *Seemed to him but a few days* – For several verses we have been kept in suspense. After a month, when Lavan asks Yaakov what he would like his wages to be in return for the work he expects from him, the text makes clear what we suspected at the outset. Yaakov has fallen in love with Raḥel. Yaakov is following his eyes, not generally considered a good thing in Tanakh. Ḥava followed

26 done to me? I served you for Raḥel, did I not? Why did you deceive me?" Lavan
said, "This is not done in our country – to marry off the younger before the
27 firstborn. Wait until the bridal week of this one is over and then we will give
you the other one also, in return for your serving me another seven years."
28 Yaakov did so. He completed Leah's bridal week; then Lavan gave him his
29 daughter Raḥel as a wife. Lavan gave his servant Bilha to his daughter Raḥel as
30 her maid. And Yaakov came also to Raḥel; and he loved Raḥel more than Leah.
31 And he served him for another seven years. When the Lord saw that Leah was
32 unloved, He opened her womb, but Raḥel was barren. Leah became pregnant
and had a son. She named him Reuven, saying, "The Lord has seen my affliction.

רש״י

כז **מַלֵּא שְׁבֻעַ זֹאת.** דָּבוּק הוּא, שֶׁהֲרֵי נָקוּד בַּחֲטַף, שְׁבוּעַ שֶׁל זֹאת, וְהֵן שִׁבְעַת יְמֵי הַמִּשְׁתֶּה. בְּתַלְמוּד יְרוּשַׁלְמִי בְּמוֹעֵד קָטָן (א, ז): **וְנִתְּנָה לְךָ.** לְשׁוֹן רַבִּים, כְּמוֹ: "נֵרְדָה וְנָבְלָה" (לעיל יא, ז), "וְנִשְׂרְפָה" (שם פסוק ג), אַף זֶה לְשׁוֹן 'וְנִתֵּן': **גַּם אֶת זֹאת.** מִיָּד לְאַחַר שִׁבְעַת יְמֵי הַמִּשְׁתֶּה, וְתַעֲבֹד לְאַחַר נִשּׂוּאֶיהָ:

ל **שֶׁבַע שָׁנִים אֲחֵרוֹת.** אֲחֵרוֹת הִקִּישָׁן לָרִאשׁוֹנוֹת, מָה רִאשׁוֹנוֹת בֶּאֱמוּנָה אַף הָאַחֲרוֹנוֹת בֶּאֱמוּנָה, וְאַף עַל פִּי שֶׁבְּרַמָּאוּת בָּא עָלָיו:

we know that Yaakov loves Raḥel, and has been married to Leah against his will. Then we read: "Yaakov came also [*gam*] to Raḥel; and he [also, *gam*] loved Raḥel..." (Gen. 29:30).

The implication at this point is clear. The repeated *gam*, "also," leads us to believe that the two sisters are equal in Yaakov's eyes. The story of the deception has – or so we must suppose on the basis of what we have so far heard – a happy ending after all. Yaakov has married both. He loves them both. The sibling rivalry that is so pronounced a theme of Genesis seems to finally be reaching a positive resolution.

The next word sends our expectation crashing to the ground: "...more than Leah" (29:30).

This is an ungrammatical construction. The words "also" and "more than" do not belong together in the same sentence. The effect – like a sudden discord in the middle of a Mozart symphony – is strident and shocking. Yaakov does not love the two sisters equally. He may love them both, but his passion is for Raḥel.

Immediately after, in verse 31, we read that Leah is *senua* – "hated." This is a phrase that cannot be understood literally. The previous verse has just said that Leah was not *senua*, but loved. The commentators and translators wrestled with this difficulty. Ramban (in his second interpretation) and Radak both read the word *senua* not as "hated" but as "[relatively] unloved" (commentaries on Gen. 29:31; we reflect this reading in our translation).

Yet though the text is semantically strange, is it psychologically lucid. Leah knows that Yaakov's heart is elsewhere. She may be loved but she feels the lesser love as a rejection. The words "the Lord saw" mean that God feels her sense of humiliation. Lavan's deception has human consequences, and they are tragic. Leah weeps inwardly for the husband she has acquired as a result of her father's wiles, the husband whose love is for someone else.

Judaism is supremely a religion of love: three loves. "Love the Lord your God with all your heart, with all your soul, and with all your might" (Deut. 6:5); "Love your neighbor as your own self" (Lev. 19:18); and "Love the stranger, for you yourselves were strangers" (Deut. 10:19).

But without justice, love alone is insufficient to sustain the world, insufficient even to maintain peace within a family. Yaakov's love for Raḥel, and later Yosef, is the cause of conflict between his two wives and their sons, and Yaakov pays heavily for it. Love is not enough, for it leaves the less loved feeling unloved, and the result is conflict and sometimes tragedy.

כו לִּי הֲלֹא בְרָחֵל עָבַדְתִּי עִמָּךְ וְלָמָּה רִמִּיתָנִי: וַיֹּאמֶר לָבָן לֹא־יֵעָשֶׂה
כז כֵן בִּמְקוֹמֵנוּ לָתֵת הַצְּעִירָה לִפְנֵי הַבְּכִירָה: מַלֵּא שְׁבֻעַ זֹאת וְנִתְּנָה
לְךָ גַּם־אֶת־זֹאת בַּעֲבֹדָה אֲשֶׁר תַּעֲבֹד עִמָּדִי עוֹד שֶׁבַע־שָׁנִים אֲחֵרוֹת:
כח וַיַּעַשׂ יַעֲקֹב כֵּן וַיְמַלֵּא שְׁבֻעַ זֹאת וַיִּתֶּן־לוֹ אֶת־רָחֵל בִּתּוֹ לוֹ לְאִשָּׁה:
כט ל וַיִּתֵּן לָבָן לְרָחֵל בִּתּוֹ אֶת־בִּלְהָה שִׁפְחָתוֹ לָהּ לְשִׁפְחָה: וַיָּבֹא גַּם אֶל־
רָחֵל וַיֶּאֱהַב גַּם־אֶת־רָחֵל מִלֵּאָה וַיַּעֲבֹד עִמּוֹ עוֹד שֶׁבַע־שָׁנִים אֲחֵרוֹת:
לא לב וַיַּרְא יהוה כִּי־שְׂנוּאָה לֵאָה וַיִּפְתַּח אֶת־רַחְמָהּ וְרָחֵל עֲקָרָה: וַתַּהַר כז
לֵאָה וַתֵּלֶד בֵּן וַתִּקְרָא שְׁמוֹ רְאוּבֵן כִּי אָמְרָה כִּי־רָאָה יהוה בְּעָנְיִי כִּי

אונקלוס

לִי, הֲלָא בְרָחֵל פְּלָחִית עִמָּךְ, וּלְמָא שַׁקַּרְתְּ בִּי: כו וַאֲמַר לָבָן, לָא מִתְעֲבֵיד כֵּן בְּאַתְרָנָא, לְמִתַּן זְעֵירְתָא קֳדָם רַבְּתָא: כז אַשְׁלֵים שְׁבוּעֲתָא דְדָא, וְנִתֵּין לָךְ אַף יָת דָּא, בְּפֻלְחָנָא דְתִפְלַח עִמִּי, עוֹד שְׁבַע שְׁנִין אָחֳרָנִין: כח וַעֲבַד יַעֲקֹב כֵּן, וְאַשְׁלֵים שְׁבוּעֲתָא דְדָא, וִיהַב לֵיהּ, יָת רָחֵל בְּרַתֵּיהּ לֵיהּ לְאִתּוּ: כט וִיהַב לָבָן לְרָחֵל בְּרַתֵּיהּ, יָת בִּלְהָה אַמְתֵיהּ, לַהּ לְאַמְהוּ: ל וְעָאל אַף לְוָת רָחֵל, וּרְחֵים אַף יָת רָחֵל מִלֵּאָה, וּפְלַח עִמֵּיהּ, עוֹד שְׁבַע שְׁנִין אָחֳרָנִין: לא וַחֲזָא יי אֲרֵי סְנִיאֲתָא לֵאָה, וִיהַב לַהּ עִדּוּי, וְרָחֵל עַקְרָא: לב וְעַדִּיאַת לֵאָה וִילֵידַת בַּר, וּקְרָת שְׁמֵיהּ רְאוּבֵן, אֲרֵי אֲמַרַת, אֲרֵי גְּלֵי קֳדָם יי עֻלְבָּנִי, אֲרֵי

Even the sentence Lavan uses to justify the deception – "This is not done in our country – to marry off the younger before the firstborn" – is deeply ironic. Does Lavan know that this, in effect, is what Yaakov once did in another place? The irony may be unintentional. Lavan may not know, but we, the readers, do. And so surely does Yaakov himself.

If these hints are signaling how the passage should be read, then the narrative is an example, unparalleled in its drama, of the single most fundamental moral axiom of the Torah, *midda keneged midda*, measure for measure (Shabbat 105b). Those who deceive will be deceived.

THE RIVALRY OF LEAH AND RAḤEL

Torah is written to be read aloud, and several of its literary devices are based on the timed sequence of the audial. Time and again, the Torah makes use of the fact that a later word has the power to confound expectations that have been formed based on what has been heard thus far. In our story

local people" to be witnesses to the marriage celebration. They could not know that he had promised that the bride would be Raḥel. They will have assumed, Lavan implies, that it would be Leah, since the local custom is that the elder is married first. Besides which, has Lavan in fact promised Raḥel? His answer, seven years earlier, when Yaakov first asked for Raḥel, was curiously evasive and oblique: "Better that I give her to you than to some other man. Stay on with me" (Gen. 29:19). It may be that he had already then formed the intention to deceive.

29:25 וְלָמָּה רִמִּיתָנִי *Why did you deceive me?* – Listen carefully to the text. The word Yaakov uses with Lavan, "Why did you deceive me [*rimitani*]?" is the very word Yitzḥak used to describe Yaakov's behavior in taking Esav's blessing: "Your brother came in deceit [*mirma*]" (Gen. 27:35). The word Lavan uses to describe the younger sibling is *tze'ira*, the word that appears in Rikva's oracle about Yaakov and Esav: "The greater shall the younger [*tza'ir*] serve" (25:23).

33 Now my husband will love me." She became pregnant again and had a son. She
said, "The LORD has heard that I am unloved, so He has given me this son also,"
34 and she named him Shimon. She became pregnant again and had a son and
said, "Now that I have borne him three sons, my husband will walk with me."
35 That is why he was named Levi. She became pregnant again and had a son. She
said, "This time I will praise the LORD," so she named him Yehuda. Then she
30 1 ceased having children. Aware that she had borne Yaakov no children, Raḥel
became envious of her sister. To Yaakov she said, "Give me children! If not, let
2 me die!" Yaakov grew angry with Raḥel, and said, "Am I in place of God, who

רש״י

לד **הַפַּעַם יִלָּוֶה אִישִׁי.** לְפִי שֶׁהָאִמָּהוֹת נְבִיאוֹת הָיוּ וְיוֹדְעוֹת שֶׁשְּׁנֵים עָשָׂר שְׁבָטִים יוֹצְאִים מִיַּעֲקֹב וְאַרְבַּע נָשִׁים יִשָּׂא, אָמְרָה: מֵעַתָּה אֵין לוֹ פִּתְחוֹן פֶּה עָלַי, שֶׁהֲרֵי נָטַלְתִּי כָּל חֶלְקִי בַּבָּנִים: **עַל כֵּן.** כָּל מִי שֶׁנֶּאֱמַר בּוֹ "עַל כֵּן" מְרֻבֶּה בְּאֻכְלוּסִין, חוּץ מִלֵּוִי, שֶׁהָאַחֲרוֹן הָיָה מְכַלֶּה בָּהֶם: **קָרָא שְׁמוֹ לֵוִי.** תָּמַהְתִּי, שֶׁבְּכֻלָּן כְּתִיב: "וַתִּקְרָא", וְזֶה כָּתַב בּוֹ: "קָרָא"! וְיֵשׁ מִדְרַשׁ אַגָּדָה בְּאֵלֶּה הַדְּבָרִים רַבָּה, שֶׁשָּׁלַח הַקָּדוֹשׁ בָּרוּךְ הוּא גַּבְרִיאֵל וֶהֱבִיאוֹ לְפָנָיו וְקָרָא לוֹ שֵׁם זֶה, וְנָתַן לוֹ עֶשְׂרִים וְאַרְבַּע מַתְּנוֹת כְּהֻנָּה, וְעַל שֵׁם שֶׁלִּוָּהוּ בְּמַתָּנוֹת קְרָאוֹ לֵוִי:

לה **הַפַּעַם אוֹדֶה.** שֶׁנָּטַלְתִּי יוֹתֵר מֵחֶלְקִי, מֵעַתָּה יֵשׁ לִי לְהוֹדוֹת:

ל א **וַתְּקַנֵּא רָחֵל בַּאֲחוֹתָהּ.** קִנְּאָה בְּמַעֲשֶׂיהָ, אָמְרָה: אִלּוּלֵי שֶׁצָּדְקָה מִמֶּנִּי לֹא זָכְתָה לְבָנִים: **הָבָה לִּי.** וְכִי כָּךְ עָשָׂה אָבִיךְ לְאִמֵּךְ? וַהֲלֹא הִתְפַּלֵּל עָלֶיהָ: **מֵתָה אָנֹכִי.** מִכָּאן לְמִי שֶׁאֵין לוֹ בָּנִים שֶׁחָשׁוּב כַּמֵּת:

ב **הֲתַחַת.** וְכִי בִּמְקוֹמוֹ אֲנִי?

29:32 **כִּי רָאָה יהוה** *The LORD has seen* – Reuven is Yaakov's firstborn. Yaakov is to say of him on his deathbed, "Reuven, you are my firstborn, my strength, first fruit of my manhood, excelling in rank, excelling in power" (Gen. 49:3). This is an impressive tribute, suggesting physical presence and commanding demeanor. But at his birth, his father's attention is elsewhere; he does not care for either Leah or her sons. (The text itself says, "The LORD saw that Leah was unloved.") Reuven is to know this and to feel his mother's shame and his father's apparent indifference intensely. Later, we will see the contrast between the hesitant Reuven and the confident – even overconfident – Yosef, loved and favored by his father. If we want our children to have the confidence to act when action is needed, then we need, from the beginning, to empower, encourage, and praise them.

29:35 **הַפַּעַם אוֹדֶה אֶת יהוה** *This time I will praise the LORD* – After three children have been born and brought Leah no closer to gaining the love she longs for, she seems to let her expectation go. *Hodaya,* appreciation, the acknowledgment that what we have is a gift, is one of the most profound religious emotions. To thank God is to know that I am not less worthwhile because someone else is more successful. Through prayer I know that I am valued for what I am. I learn to cherish what I have, rather than be diminished by what I do not have. To be a Jew – *Yehudi,* the name we acquired from Yehuda – is to offer thanks and praise.

30:2 **הֲתַחַת אֱלֹהִים אָנֹכִי...** *Am I in place of God...* – We are not all destined to have children. The rabbis said that the good we do constitutes our *toledot,* our posterity (Rashi on Gen. 6:9). But the Torah recognizes the agony of infertility: to wait in hope and wait again.

Lacking a solution to Raḥel's problem, Yaakov reacts in anger to her pain. His harsh words prompt her to suggest her own solution. He cannot stand in for God. Let a concubine stand in for her. When Yaakov fell in love he followed his eyes. The world of appearances is a false world of masks, disguises, and concealments. Yaakov must learn to listen.

Listen deeply to those you love and who love you. Listening is not easy. I confess I find it formidably hard. But listening alone bridges the abyss between soul and soul, self and other, I and the Divine. Jewish spirituality is the art of listening.

לג עַתָּה יֶאֱהָבַנִי אִישִׁי׃ וַתַּהַר עוֹד וַתֵּלֶד בֵּן וַתֹּאמֶר כִּי־שָׁמַע יהוה כִּי־
לד שְׂנוּאָה אָנֹכִי וַיִּתֶּן־לִי גַּם־אֶת־זֶה וַתִּקְרָא שְׁמוֹ שִׁמְעוֹן׃ וַתַּהַר עוֹד
וַתֵּלֶד בֵּן וַתֹּאמֶר עַתָּה הַפַּעַם יִלָּוֶה אִישִׁי אֵלַי כִּי־יָלַדְתִּי לוֹ שְׁלֹשָׁה
לה בָנִים עַל־כֵּן קָרָא־שְׁמוֹ לֵוִי׃ וַתַּהַר עוֹד וַתֵּלֶד בֵּן וַתֹּאמֶר הַפַּעַם אוֹדֶה
ל א אֶת־יהוה עַל־כֵּן קָרְאָה שְׁמוֹ יְהוּדָה וַתַּעֲמֹד מִלֶּדֶת׃ וַתֵּרֶא רָחֵל כִּי
לֹא יָלְדָה לְיַעֲקֹב וַתְּקַנֵּא רָחֵל בַּאֲחֹתָהּ וַתֹּאמֶר אֶל־יַעֲקֹב הָבָה־לִּי
ב בָנִים וְאִם־אַיִן מֵתָה אָנֹכִי׃ וַיִּחַר־אַף יַעֲקֹב בְּרָחֵל וַיֹּאמֶר הֲתַחַת

אונקלוס

כְּעַן יְרַחֲמִנַּנִי בַעְלִי׃ לג וְעַדִּיאַת עוֹד וִילֵידַת בַּר, וַאֲמַרַת, אֲרֵי שְׁמִיעַ
קֳדָם יי אֲרֵי סְנוּאֲתָא אֲנָא, וִיהַב לִי אַף יָת דֵּין, וּקְרָת שְׁמֵיהּ שִׁמְעוֹן׃
לד וְעַדִּיאַת עוֹד וִילֵידַת בַּר, וַאֲמַרַת, הָדָא זִמְנָא יִתְחַבַּר לִי בַּעְלִי,
אֲרֵי יְלֵידִית לֵיהּ תְּלָתָא בְנִין, עַל כֵּן קְרָא שְׁמֵיהּ לֵוִי׃ לה וְעַדִּיאַת עוֹד
וִילֵידַת בַּר, וַאֲמַרַת הָדָא זִמְנָא אוֹדֵי קֳדָם יי, עַל כֵּן, קְרָת שְׁמֵיהּ
יְהוּדָה, וְקָמַת מִלְּמֵילַד׃ ל א וַחֲזָת רָחֵל, אֲרֵי לָא יְלֵידַת לְיַעֲקֹב, וְקַנִּיאַת
רָחֵל בַּאֲחָתַהּ, וַאֲמַרַת לְיַעֲקֹב הַב לִי בְנִין, וְאִם לָא מָיְתָא אֲנָא׃
ב וּתְקֵיף רְגָזָא דְיַעֲקֹב בְּרָחֵל, וַאֲמַר, הֲמִנִּי אַתְּ בָּעְיָא הֲלָא מִן קֳדָם

Much of the moral life is generated by this tension between love and justice. It is no accident that this is the theme of many of the narratives of Genesis. Genesis is about people and their relationships while the rest of the Torah is predominantly about society.

At the heart of the moral life is a conflict with no simple resolution. Weaving together these two strands of love (Yaakov's intense feelings for Raḥel) and justice (the deceiver deceived), the story of Yaakov, Raḥel, and Leah turns out to be an essential prelude to the book of Exodus and the covenant between God and Israel, based on love and justice. For without justice, love is blind; and without love, justice is impersonal and cold. Yaakov's family needs both – and so do we.

29:32 וַתִּקְרָא שְׁמוֹ *She named him* – Read superficially, these verses are no more than a genealogy, a list of births, of the kind of which there are many in Genesis. Heard while attuned to Leah's plight, however, what we hear is heartbreaking. Leah is pleading for attention. Each of the names of her first three children is a cry to her husband Yaakov – to see, to listen, to be attached, to notice, to love her. Sadly, the lack of relationship between Yaakov and Leah at the birth of her children is carried through in the years to come. Yaakov's relationship with Reuven, Shimon, and Levi breaks down completely, with Reuven after the episode of Bilha's couch, with Shimon and Levi after the incident with Shekhem. On his deathbed he curses instead of blessing them (see ch. 49). Yet it is from Levi that Israel's spiritual leaders will come – Moshe, Aharon, Miriam, and eventually the *kohanim* and *levi'im* (priests and Levites); it is from Yehuda that will come its kings, David and his descendants.

Through painful experience, Yaakov must learn a truth about love: It not only unites, it also divides. It did so in his childhood, when Yitzḥak loved Esav and Rivka loved Yaakov. It does so again when he marries two sisters. It will do so a third time when he loves Raḥel's child Yosef more than his other sons. What Yaakov learns – and what we learn, hearing his story – is that love is not enough. We must also heed those who feel unloved. Without that, there will be conflict and tragedy. But to heed the unloved requires a specific capacity: the ability to listen – in Yaakov's case, to the unspoken tears of Leah and her feeling of rejection, made explicit in the names she gives her sons.

▶

3 has kept you from having children?" "Here is Bilha my slave," she said. "Come
to her. Let her give birth on my knees so that I too can build a family through
4 5 her." So she gave him her maid Bilha as a wife. Yaakov came to her, and she
6 became pregnant and bore Yaakov a son. Then Raḥel said, "God has vindicated
me. He has listened to my voice and given me a son." So she named him Dan.
7 Bilha, Raḥel's maid, became pregnant again and bore Yaakov a second son.
8 And Raḥel said, "I have struggled hard with my sister and I have won." So she
9 named him Naftali. Leah realized that she was no longer having children, so
10 she took her maid Zilpa and gave her to Yaakov as a wife. And Leah's maid
11 Zilpa bore Yaakov a son. Leah said, "Good fortune has come!" So she named
12 13 him Gad. Then Zilpa, Leah's maid, bore Yaakov a second son. Leah said, "How
14 blessed I am; young girls will call me blessed." So she named him Asher. During REVI'I
the wheat harvest, Reuven went for a walk and found mandrakes in the field.
He brought them to his mother Leah. Raḥel said to Leah, "Please give me some
15 of your son's mandrakes." She replied, "Is it not enough that you have taken
away my husband? Now you want to take my son's mandrakes too!" "Very

רש"י

אשר מנע ממך. את אומרת שאעשה כאבא, אני איני כאבא, אבא לא היו לו בנים, אני יש לי בנים, ממך מנע ולא ממני:

ג **על ברכי.** כתרגומו: "ואנא ארבי": **ואבנה גם אנכי.** מהו 'גם'? אמרה לו: זקנך אברהם היו לו בנים מהגר וחגר מתניו כנגד שרה. אמר לה: זקנתי הכניסה צרתה לביתה. אמרה לו: אם הדבר הזה מעכב "הנה אמתי": **ואבנה גם אנכי ממנה.** כשרה:

ו **דנני אלהים.** דנני וזכני:

ח **נפתולי אלהים.** מנחם בן סרוק פירשו במחברת 'צמיד פתיל' (במדבר יט, טו), חבורים מאת המקום נתחברתי עם אחותי לזכות לבנים. ואני מפרשו לשון 'עקש ופתלתל' (דברים לב, ה), נתעקשתי והפצרתי פצירות ונפתולים למקום להיות שוה לאחותי. "גם יכלתי" – הסכים על ידי. ואונקלוס תרגם לשון תפלה, כמו נפולי אלהים נפתלתי – בקשות החביבות לפניו נתקבלתי ונעתרתי כאחותי. "נפתלתי" – נתקבלה תפלתי. ומדרשי אגדה יש רבים בלשון נוטריקון:

י **ותלד זלפה.** בכלן נאמר הריון חוץ מזלפה, לפי שהיתה בחורה מכלן ותינוקת בשנים ואין הריון נכר בה, וכדי לרמות את יעקב נתנה לבן ללאה, שלא יבין שמכניסין לו את לאה, שכך מנהג לתן שפחה הגדולה לגדולה והקטנה לקטנה:

יא **בא גד.** בא מזל טוב לי, כמו: "גד גדי וסנוק לא" (שבת סז ע"ב). ומדרש אגדה שנולד מהול, כמו: "גדו אילנא" (דניאל ד, יח), ולא ידעתי על מה נכתב תבה אחת.

יד **בימי קציר חטים.** להגיד שבחן של שבטים, שעת הקציר היה, ולא פשט ידו בגזל להביא חטים ושעורים, אלא דבר ההפקר שאין אדם מקפיד בו: **דודאים.** סיגלי, עשב הוא, ובלשון ישמעאל יסמין:

טו **ולקחת גם את דודאי בני.** בתמיה, ולעשות עוד זאת לקח גם

negative consequences. It provokes a bitter row between the two sisters, Leah and Raḥel. Raḥel sees the mandrakes and wants them for herself. This is the only time that angry words are reported between the two sisters. Reuven, seeking to help Leah, ends up creating a scene in which her bitterness rises to the surface. Returning with the mandrakes, he might have bided his time until Leah was alone, but he does not. Reuven carries with him a lack of confidence, an uncertainty that at critical moments robs him of his capacity to carry through a course of action that he knows to be right. As we shall see later on with more consequence (see ch. 37, "Reuven's Good Intentions), he begins well but fails to drive the deed to closure.

ג אֱלֹהִים אָנֹכִי אֲשֶׁר־מָנַע מִמֵּךְ פְּרִי־בָטֶן: וַתֹּאמֶר הִנֵּה אֲמָתִי בִלְהָה
ד בֹּא אֵלֶיהָ וְתֵלֵד עַל־בִּרְכַּי וְאִבָּנֶה גַם־אָנֹכִי מִמֶּנָּה: וַתִּתֶּן־לוֹ אֶת־
ה בִּלְהָה שִׁפְחָתָהּ לְאִשָּׁה וַיָּבֹא אֵלֶיהָ יַעֲקֹב: וַתַּהַר בִּלְהָה וַתֵּלֶד לְיַעֲקֹב
ו בֵּן: וַתֹּאמֶר רָחֵל דָּנַנִּי אֱלֹהִים וְגַם שָׁמַע בְּקֹלִי וַיִּתֶּן־לִי בֵּן עַל־כֵּן
ז קָרְאָה שְׁמוֹ דָּן: וַתַּהַר עוֹד וַתֵּלֶד בִּלְהָה שִׁפְחַת רָחֵל בֵּן שֵׁנִי לְיַעֲקֹב:
ח וַתֹּאמֶר רָחֵל נַפְתּוּלֵי אֱלֹהִים ׀ נִפְתַּלְתִּי עִם־אֲחֹתִי גַּם־יָכֹלְתִּי וַתִּקְרָא
ט שְׁמוֹ נַפְתָּלִי: וַתֵּרֶא לֵאָה כִּי עָמְדָה מִלֶּדֶת וַתִּקַּח אֶת־זִלְפָּה שִׁפְחָתָהּ
י וַתִּתֵּן אֹתָהּ לְיַעֲקֹב לְאִשָּׁה: וַתֵּלֶד זִלְפָּה שִׁפְחַת לֵאָה לְיַעֲקֹב בֵּן:
יא יב וַתֹּאמֶר לֵאָה בגד וַתִּקְרָא אֶת־שְׁמוֹ גָּד: וַתֵּלֶד זִלְפָּה שִׁפְחַת לֵאָה בֵּן בָּא גָד
יג שֵׁנִי לְיַעֲקֹב: וַתֹּאמֶר לֵאָה בְּאָשְׁרִי כִּי אִשְּׁרוּנִי בָּנוֹת וַתִּקְרָא אֶת־שְׁמוֹ
יד אָשֵׁר: וַיֵּלֶךְ רְאוּבֵן בִּימֵי קְצִיר־חִטִּים וַיִּמְצָא דוּדָאִים בַּשָּׂדֶה וַיָּבֵא רביעי
אֹתָם אֶל־לֵאָה אִמּוֹ וַתֹּאמֶר רָחֵל אֶל־לֵאָה תְּנִי־נָא לִי מִדּוּדָאֵי בְּנֵךְ:
טו וַתֹּאמֶר לָהּ הַמְעַט קַחְתֵּךְ אֶת־אִישִׁי וְלָקַחַת גַּם אֶת־דּוּדָאֵי בְּנִי

אונקלוס

יְיָ תִּבְעֵן, דִּמְנַע מִנִּיךְ וַלְדָּא דִּמְעֵי: ג וַאֲמַרַת, הָא, אַמְתִי בִּלְהָה עוּל לְוָתַהּ, תְּלִיד וַאֲנָא אֲרַבֵּי, וְאֶתְבְּנֵי אַף אֲנָא מִנַּהּ: ד וִיהַבַת לֵיהּ, יָת בִּלְהָה אַמְתַהּ לְאִתּוּ, וְעָאל לְוָתַהּ יַעֲקֹב: ה וְעַדִּיאַת בִּלְהָה, וִילֵידַת לְיַעֲקֹב בַּר: ו וַאֲמַרַת רָחֵל דָּנַנִּי יְיָ, וְאַף קַבֵּיל צְלוֹתִי, וִיהַב לִי בַּר, עַל כֵּן, קְרָת שְׁמֵיהּ דָּן: ז וְעַדִּיאַת עוֹד, וִילֵידַת, בִּלְהָה אַמְתַהּ דְּרָחֵל, בַּר תִּנְיָן לְיַעֲקֹב: ח וַאֲמַרַת רָחֵל, קַבֵּיל בָּעוּתִי יְיָ בְּאִתְחַנָּנוּתִי בִּצְלוֹתִי, חַמֵּידִית דִּיהֵי לִי וְלַד כַּאֲחָתִי אַף אִתְיְהֵיב לִי, וּקְרָת שְׁמֵיהּ נַפְתָּלִי: ט וַחֲזָת לֵאָה, אֲרֵי קָמַת מִלְּמֵילַד, וּדְבַרַת יָת זִלְפָּה אַמְתַהּ, וִיהַבַת יָתַהּ, לְיַעֲקֹב לְאִתּוּ: י וִילֵידַת, זִלְפָּה, אַמְתַהּ דְּלֵאָה לְיַעֲקֹב בַּר: יא וַאֲמַרַת לֵאָה אֲתָא גָד, וּקְרָת יָת שְׁמֵיהּ גָּד: יב וִילֵידַת, זִלְפָּה, אַמְתַהּ דְּלֵאָה, בַּר תִּנְיָן לְיַעֲקֹב: יג וַאֲמַרַת לֵאָה, תֻּשְׁבַּחְתָּא הֲוָת לִי, אֲרֵי בְּכֵן יְשַׁבְּחֻנַּנִי נְשַׁיָּא, וּקְרָת יָת שְׁמֵיהּ אָשֵׁר: יד וַאֲזַל רְאוּבֵן בְּיוֹמֵי חֲצַד חִטִּין, וְאַשְׁכַּח יַבְרוּחִין בְּחַקְלָא, וְאַיְתִי יָתְהוֹן, לְלֵאָה אִמֵּיהּ, וַאֲמַרַת רָחֵל לְלֵאָה, הַבִי כְעַן לִי, מִיַּבְרוּחֵי דִּבְרִיךְ: טו וַאֲמַרַת לַהּ, הַזְעֵיר דִּדְבַרְתְּ יָת בַּעְלִי, וּלְמִסַּב, אַף יָת יַבְרוּחֵי

30:14 וַיָּבֵא אֹתָם אֶל־לֵאָה אִמּוֹ *He brought them to his mother Leah* – From the context it appears that mandrakes were believed to be both an aphrodisiac and a fertility drug. Reuven's first thought is to give them to his mother Leah. This tells us something about Reuven. He is not thinking about himself, but about her. He knows she feels unloved and identifies with her anguish with all the sensitivity of an eldest child. He hopes that, with the aid of the mandrakes, Leah will be able to win Yaakov's attention, perhaps even his love.

It is a strikingly mature and thoughtful act. Yet it has

▶

well," said Raḥel. "Let him sleep with you tonight in exchange for your son's
16 mandrakes." When Yaakov came back from the field that evening, Leah went
out to meet him and said, "You are to come to me, for I have hired you with my
17 son's mandrakes." So that night he slept with her. God listened to Leah, and she
18 became pregnant and bore Yaakov a fifth son. Leah said, "God has rewarded
19 me for giving my maid to my husband," so she named him Yissakhar. Leah
20 became pregnant again and bore Yaakov a sixth son. "God has given me a
precious gift," said Leah. "This time my husband will honor me, for I have
21 borne him six sons," so she named him Zevulun. Later she gave birth to a
22 daughter and named her Dina. Then God remembered Raḥel and listened to
23 her and enabled her to conceive. She became pregnant and gave birth to a son.
24 She said, "God has taken away my shame," and she named him Yosef, saying,
25 "May the Lord grant me another son also." After Raḥel had given birth to
26 Yosef, Yaakov said to Lavan, "Release me to go home to my own land. Give me
my wives and my children for whom I have worked for you, and let me go. You
27 know very well how much work I have done for you." But Lavan said to him, "If

רש״י

אֶת דּוּדָאֵי בְּנִי? וְתַרְגּוּמוֹ: "וּלְמִסַּב": **לָכֵן יִשְׁכַּב עִמָּךְ הַלַּיְלָה.** שֶׁלִּי הָיְתָה שְׁכִיבַת לַיְלָה זוֹ, וַאֲנִי נוֹתְנָה לָךְ תַּחַת דּוּדָאֵי בְנֵךְ. וּלְפִי שֶׁזִּלְזְלָה בְּמִשְׁכַּב הַצַּדִּיק לֹא זָכְתָה לִקָּבֵר עִמּוֹ:

טז **שָׂכֹר שְׂכַרְתִּיךָ.** נָתַתִּי לְרָחֵל שְׂכָרָהּ: **בַּלַּיְלָה הוּא.** הַקָּדוֹשׁ בָּרוּךְ הוּא סִיַּע בּוֹ שֶׁיָּצָא מִשָּׁם יִשָּׂשכָר:

יז **וַיִּשְׁמַע אֱלֹהִים אֶל לֵאָה.** שֶׁהָיְתָה מִתְאַוָּה וּמְחַזֶּרֶת לְהַרְבּוֹת שְׁבָטִים:

כ **זֶבֶד טוֹב.** כְּתַרְגּוּמוֹ: **יִזְבְּלֵנִי.** לְשׁוֹן 'בֵּית זְבֻל' (מלכים א׳ ח, יג), אברבירייר"א בְּלַעַז, בֵּית מָדוֹר. מֵעַתָּה לֹא תְהֵא עִקַּר דִּירָתוֹ אֶלָּא עִמִּי, שֶׁיֵּשׁ לִי בָּנִים כְּנֶגֶד כָּל נָשָׁיו:

כא **דִּינָה.** פֵּרְשׁוּ רַבּוֹתֵינוּ שֶׁדָּנָה לֵאָה דִּין בְּעַצְמָהּ: אִם זֶה זָכָר לֹא תְהֵא רָחֵל אֲחוֹתִי כְּאַחַת הַשְּׁפָחוֹת, וְנִתְפַּלְּלָה עָלָיו וְנֶהְפַּךְ לִנְקֵבָה:

כב **וַיִּזְכֹּר אֱלֹהִים אֶת רָחֵל.** זָכַר לָהּ שֶׁמָּסְרָה סִימָנֶיהָ לַאֲחוֹתָהּ, וְשֶׁהָיְתָה מְצֵרָה שֶׁמָּא תַּעֲלֶה בְּגוֹרָלוֹ שֶׁל עֵשָׂו, שֶׁמָּא יְגָרְשֶׁנָּה יַעֲקֹב לְפִי שֶׁאֵין לָהּ בָּנִים; וְאַף עֵשָׂו הָרָשָׁע כָּךְ עָלָה בְּלִבּוֹ כְּשֶׁשָּׁמַע שֶׁאֵין לָהּ בָּנִים. הוּא שֶׁיִּסֵּד הַפַּיָּט: "הָאַדְמוֹן כְּבָט שֶׁלֹּא אָלָה, נָבָה לְקַחְתָּהּ לוֹ וְנִתְבַּהֲלָה" (בפיוט "אתן חוג" בקרובות ליום א׳ דר"ה שחרית):

כג **אָסַף.** הִכְנִיסָהּ בִּמְקוֹם שֶׁלֹּא תֵרָאֶה. וְכֵן: "אֱסֹף חֶרְפָּתֵנוּ" (ישעיה ד, א), "וְלֹא יֵאָסֵף הַבַּיְתָה" (שמות ט, יט), "אָסְפוּ נָגְהָם" (יואל ד, טו), "וִירֵחֵךְ לֹא יֵאָסֵף" (ישעיה ס, כ), לֹא יִטָּמֵן: **חֶרְפָּתִי.** שֶׁהָיִיתִי לְחֶרְפָּה עַל שֶׁאֲנִי עֲקָרָה, וְהָיוּ אוֹמְרִים עָלַי שֶׁאֶעֱלֶה לְחֶלְקוֹ שֶׁל עֵשָׂו הָרָשָׁע. וְאַגָּדָה, כָּל זְמַן שֶׁאֵין לָאִשָּׁה בֵּן אֵין לָהּ בְּמִי לִתְלוֹת סִרְחוֹנָהּ, מִשֶּׁיֵּשׁ לָהּ בֵּן תּוֹלָה בּוֹ: מִי שָׁבַר כְּלִי זֶה? בִּנְךָ! מִי אָכַל תְּאֵנִים אֵלּוּ? בִּנְךָ!:

כד **יֹסֵף ה׳ לִי בֵּן אַחֵר.** יוֹדַעַת הָיְתָה בִּנְבוּאָה שֶׁאֵין יַעֲקֹב עָתִיד לְהַעֲמִיד אֶלָּא שְׁנֵים עָשָׂר שְׁבָטִים; אָמְרָה: יְהִי רָצוֹן שֶׁאוֹתוֹ שֶׁהוּא עָתִיד לְהַעֲמִיד יְהֵא מִמֶּנִּי, לְכָךְ לֹא נִתְפַּלְּלָה אֶלָּא עַל "בֵּן אַחֵר":

כה **כַּאֲשֶׁר יָלְדָה רָחֵל אֶת יוֹסֵף.** מִשֶּׁנּוֹלַד שִׂטְנוֹ שֶׁל עֵשָׂו, שֶׁנֶּאֱמַר: "וְהָיָה בֵית יַעֲקֹב אֵשׁ וּבֵית יוֹסֵף לֶהָבָה וּבֵית עֵשָׂו לְקַשׁ" (עובדיה א, יח), אֵשׁ בְּלֹא לֶהָבָה אֵינוֹ שׁוֹלֵט לְמֵרָחוֹק; מִשֶּׁנּוֹלַד יוֹסֵף בָּטַח יַעֲקֹב בְּהַקָּדוֹשׁ בָּרוּךְ הוּא וְרָצָה לָשׁוּב:

כו **תְּנָה אֶת נָשַׁי.** אֵינִי רוֹצֶה לָצֵאת כִּי אִם בִּרְשׁוּת:

כז **נִחַשְׁתִּי.** מְנַחֵשׁ הָיָה; נִסִּיתִי בְּנִחוּשׁ שֶׁלִּי שֶׁעַל יָדְךָ בָּאָה לִי בְרָכָה;

the Aramean sought to do to our father Yaakov: Pharaoh condemned only the boys to death, but Lavan sought to uproot everything.

"[Lavan] an Aramean [tried to] destroy my father" cannot be the plain sense of the verse from Deuteronomy, because, as Ibn Ezra points out, *oved* is an intransitive verb

טז וַתֹּאמֶר רָחֵל לָכֵן יִשְׁכַּב עִמָּךְ הַלַּיְלָה תַּחַת דּוּדָאֵי בְנֵךְ: וַיָּבֹא
יַעֲקֹב מִן־הַשָּׂדֶה בָּעֶרֶב וַתֵּצֵא לֵאָה לִקְרָאתוֹ וַתֹּאמֶר אֵלַי תָּבוֹא כִּי
יז שָׂכֹר שְׂכַרְתִּיךָ בְּדוּדָאֵי בְּנִי וַיִּשְׁכַּב עִמָּהּ בַּלַּיְלָה הוּא: וַיִּשְׁמַע אֱלֹהִים
יח אֶל־לֵאָה וַתַּהַר וַתֵּלֶד לְיַעֲקֹב בֵּן חֲמִישִׁי: וַתֹּאמֶר לֵאָה נָתַן אֱלֹהִים
יט שְׂכָרִי אֲשֶׁר־נָתַתִּי שִׁפְחָתִי לְאִישִׁי וַתִּקְרָא שְׁמוֹ יִשָּׂשכָר: וַתַּהַר עוֹד
כ לֵאָה וַתֵּלֶד בֵּן־שִׁשִּׁי לְיַעֲקֹב: וַתֹּאמֶר לֵאָה זְבָדַנִי אֱלֹהִים ׀ אֹתִי זֵבֶד
טוֹב הַפַּעַם יִזְבְּלֵנִי אִישִׁי כִּי־יָלַדְתִּי לוֹ שִׁשָּׁה בָנִים וַתִּקְרָא אֶת־
כא כב שְׁמוֹ זְבֻלוּן: וְאַחַר יָלְדָה בַּת וַתִּקְרָא אֶת־שְׁמָהּ דִּינָה: וַיִּזְכֹּר אֱלֹהִים כח
כג אֶת־רָחֵל וַיִּשְׁמַע אֵלֶיהָ אֱלֹהִים וַיִּפְתַּח אֶת־רַחְמָהּ: וַתַּהַר וַתֵּלֶד בֵּן
כד וַתֹּאמֶר אָסַף אֱלֹהִים אֶת־חֶרְפָּתִי: וַתִּקְרָא אֶת־שְׁמוֹ יוֹסֵף לֵאמֹר יֹסֵף
כה יְהוָה לִי בֵּן אַחֵר: וַיְהִי כַּאֲשֶׁר יָלְדָה רָחֵל אֶת־יוֹסֵף וַיֹּאמֶר יַעֲקֹב
כו אֶל־לָבָן שַׁלְּחֵנִי וְאֵלְכָה אֶל־מְקוֹמִי וּלְאַרְצִי: תְּנָה אֶת־נָשַׁי וְאֶת־יְלָדַי
אֲשֶׁר עָבַדְתִּי אֹתְךָ בָּהֵן וְאֵלֵכָה כִּי אַתָּה יָדַעְתָּ אֶת־עֲבֹדָתִי אֲשֶׁר
כז עֲבַדְתִּיךָ: וַיֹּאמֶר אֵלָיו לָבָן אִם־נָא מָצָאתִי חֵן בְּעֵינֶיךָ נִחַשְׁתִּי וַיְבָרְכֵנִי

אונקלוס

דִּבְרִי, וַאֲמַרַת רָחֵל, בְּכֵן יִשְׁכּוּב עִמִּיךְ בְּלֵילְיָא, חֲלַף יַבְרוּחֵי דִּבְרִיךְ: טז וְעָאל יַעֲקֹב מִן חַקְלָא בְּרַמְשָׁא, וּנְפַקַת לֵאָה לְקַדָּמוּתֵיהּ, וַאֲמַרַת לְוָתִי תֵּיעוֹל, אֲרֵי מֵיגָר אֲגַרְתָּךְ, בְּיַבְרוּחֵי דִּבְרִי, וּשְׁכֵיב עִמַּהּ בְּלֵילְיָא הוּא: יז וְקַבֵּיל יי צְלוֹתַהּ דְּלֵאָה, וְעַדִּיאַת, וִילֵידַת לְיַעֲקֹב בַּר חֲמִישָׁי: יח וַאֲמַרַת לֵאָה, יְהַב יי אַגְרִי, דִּיהַבִית אַמְתִּי לְבַעְלִי, וּקְרָת שְׁמֵיהּ יִשָּׂשכָר: יט וְעַדִּיאַת עוֹד לֵאָה, וִילֵידַת בַּר שְׁתִיתַאי לְיַעֲקֹב: כ וַאֲמַרַת לֵאָה, יְהַב יי יָתֵיהּ לִי חוּלָק טָב, הָדָא זִמְנָא יְהֵי מְדוֹרֵיהּ דְּבַעְלִי לְוָתִי, אֲרֵי יְלֵידִית לֵיהּ שִׁתָּא בְנִין, וּקְרָת יָת שְׁמֵיהּ זְבוּלוּן: כא וּבָתַר כֵּן יְלֵידַת בְּרַתָּא, וּקְרָת יָת שְׁמַהּ דִּינָה: כב וְעָאל דְּכְרָנַהּ דְּרָחֵל קֳדָם יי, וְקַבֵּיל צְלוֹתַהּ יי, וִיהַב לַהּ עִדּוּי: כג וְעַדִּיאַת וִילֵידַת בַּר, וַאֲמַרַת, כְּנַשׁ יי יָת חִסּוּדָי: כד וּקְרָת יָת שְׁמֵיהּ, יוֹסֵף לְמֵימַר, יוֹסֵיף יי, לִי בַּר אָחֳרָן: כה וַהֲוָה, כַּד יְלֵידַת רָחֵל יָת יוֹסֵף, וַאֲמַר יַעֲקֹב לְלָבָן, שַׁלְּחַנִי וַאֲהָךְ, לְאַתְרִי וּלְאַרְעִי: כו הַב יָת נְשַׁי וְיָת בְּנַי, דִּפְלַחִית יָתָךְ, בְּהוֹן וְאֵיזֵיל, אֲרֵי אַתְּ יְדַעְתְּ, יָת פָּלְחָנִי דִּפְלַחְתָּךְ: כז וַאֲמַר לֵיהּ לָבָן, אִם כְּעַן אַשְׁכַּחִית רַחֲמִין בְּעֵינָךְ, נַסִּיתִי, וּבָרְכַנִי

AN ARAMEAN SOUGHT MY FATHER'S DEATH

The narrative of Yaakov in Lavan's house gives rise to the strangest passage in the Haggada. Commenting on Deuteronomy 26:5, the passage we expound on Seder night, it says as follows:

Arami oved avi – Go [to the verse] and learn what Lavan

you will allow me to say so, I have learned by divination that it is because of you
28 that the LORD has blessed me." He added, "Name your hire and I will pay it." ḤAMISHI
29 Yaakov said, "You know well how I have worked for you and how your livestock
30 have fared under my care. You had little before I came, but it has swelled into
much. The LORD has blessed you wherever I have been. Now, when can I do
31 likewise for my own household?" Lavan asked, "What shall I give you?" Yaakov
replied, "Do not give me anything. If you do this one thing for me, I will
32 continue to shepherd and guard your flocks. Let me go through all your flocks
today and remove every speckled or spotted sheep, every dark-colored lamb,
33 and every spotted or speckled goat. They shall be my hire. Let my honesty

רש״י

כְּשֶׁבָּאתָ לְכָאן לֹא הָיוּ לִי בָּנִים, שֶׁנֶּאֱמַר: "וְהִנֵּה רָחֵל בִּתּוֹ בָּאָה עִם הַצֹּאן" (לעיל כט, ו), אֶפְשָׁר יֵשׁ לוֹ בָּנִים וְהוּא שׁוֹלֵחַ בִּתּוֹ אֵצֶל הָרוֹעִים? עַכְשָׁיו הָיוּ לוֹ בָּנִים, שֶׁנֶּאֱמַר: "וַיִּשְׁמַע אֶת דִּבְרֵי בְנֵי לָבָן" (להלן לא, א):

כח נָקְבָה שְׂכָרְךָ. כְּתַרְגּוּמוֹ: "פָּרֵשׁ אַגְרָךְ":

כט וְאֵת אֲשֶׁר הָיָה מִקְנְךָ אִתִּי. אֶת חֶשְׁבּוֹן מִעוּט מִקְנְךָ שֶׁבָּא לְיָדִי מִתְּחִלָּה, כַּמָּה הָיוּ:

ל לְרַגְלִי. עִם רַגְלִי, בִּשְׁבִיל בִּיאַת רַגְלִי בָּאת אֶצְלְךָ הַבְּרָכָה, כְּמוֹ: "הָעָם אֲשֶׁר בְּרַגְלֶיךָ" (שמות יא, ח), "לָעָם אֲשֶׁר בְּרַגְלָי" (שופטים ח, ה) – הַבָּאִים עִמִּי: גַּם אָנֹכִי לְבֵיתִי. לְצֹרֶךְ בֵּיתִי; עַכְשָׁיו אֵין עוֹשִׂין לְצָרְכִּי אֶלָּא בָּנַי, וְצָרִיךְ אֲנִי לִהְיוֹת עוֹשֶׂה גַּם אֲנִי עִמָּהֶם וְסוֹמְכָן, וְזֶהוּ 'גַּם':

לב נָקֹד. מְנֻמָּר בַּחֲבַרְבּוּרוֹת דַּקּוֹת כְּמוֹ נְקֻדָּה, פוּנְטוּר״א בְּלַעַז:

וְטָלוּא. לְשׁוֹן טְלָאִי, חֲבַרְבּוּרוֹת רְחָבוֹת: חוּם. "שָׁחוֹם", דּוֹמֶה לְאָדֹם, רו״ש בְּלַעַז, לְשׁוֹן מִשְׁנָה: "שְׁחַמְתִּית וְנִמְצֵאת לְבָנָה" (בבא בתרא פג ע״ב) לְעִנְיַן הַתְּבוּאָה: וְהָיָה שְׂכָרִי. אוֹתָן שֶׁיִּוָּלְדוּ מִכָּאן וּלְהַבָּא נְקֻדִּים וּטְלוּאִים בָּעִזִּים וּשְׁחוּמִים בַּכְּשָׂבִים יִהְיוּ שֶׁלִּי, וְאוֹתָן שֶׁיֶּשְׁנָן עַכְשָׁיו הַפְרֵשׁ מֵהֶם וְהַפְקִידֵם בְּיַד בָּנֶיךָ, שֶׁלֹּא תֹּאמַר לִי עַל הַנּוֹלָדִים מֵעַתָּה: אֵלּוּ הָיוּ שָׁם מִתְּחִלָּה; וְעוֹד, שֶׁלֹּא תֹּאמַר לִי: עַל יְדֵי הַזְּכָרִים שֶׁהֵם נְקֻדִּים וּטְלוּאִים תֵּלַדְנָה הַנְּקֵבוֹת דֻּגְמָתָן מִכָּאן וְאֵילָךְ:

לג וְעָנְתָה בִּי וְגוֹ'. אִם תַּחְשְׁדֵנִי שֶׁאֲנִי נוֹטֵל מִשֶּׁלְּךָ כְּלוּם, תַּעֲנֶה בִּי צִדְקָתִי, "כִּי תָבוֹא" צִדְקָתִי וְתָעִיד "עַל שְׂכָרִי לְפָנֶיךָ", שֶׁלֹּא תִמְצָא בַּעֲדָרַי כִּי אִם נְקֻדִּים וּטְלוּאִים, וְכֹל שֶׁתִּמְצָא בָּהֶן שֶׁאֵינוֹ נָקֹד אוֹ טָלוּא אוֹ חוּם, בְּיָדוּעַ שֶׁגְּנַבְתִּיו לְךָ וּבִגְנֵבָה הוּא שָׁרוּי אֶצְלִי:

the bringing of the first fruits an interpretation that connects it with Passover. And though it gives a far-fetched reading of the phrase, it gives a compelling interpretation to the narrative of Yaakov in Lavan's house. It tells us that the third patriarch, whose descent to Egypt will actually begin the story of the exodus, himself undergoes an exodus experience in his youth. *Maasei avot siman lebanim*, "the acts of the fathers are a sign for their children." Our ancestors experienced exile and exodus as if to say to their descendants: This is not unknown territory. And God was with us then; He will be with you now.

30:31 לֹא תִתֶּן לִי מְאוּמָה *Do not give me anything* – The thing that arouses Lavan's anger, his rage, is that Yaakov maintains his dignity and independence. Faced with a near-impossible existence as his father-in-law's slave, Yaakov always finds a way of carrying on. Yes, he has been cheated of his beloved Raḥel, but he works so that he can marry her too. Yes, he has been forced to work for nothing, but he uses his superior knowledge of animal husbandry to propose a deal which will allow him to build flocks of his own that will allow him to maintain what is now a large family. Hemmed in on all sides, he finds a way out. His methods are not those he would have chosen in other circumstances. He has to outwit an extremely cunning adversary. Yet in a seemingly impossible situation Yaakov retains his dignity, independence, and freedom. Yaakov is no man's slave.

כח כט יְהוָה בִּגְלָלֶךָ: וַיֹּאמַר נָקְבָה שְׂכָרְךָ עָלַי וְאֶתֵּנָה: וַיֹּאמֶר אֵלָיו אַתָּה חמישי
ל יָדַעְתָּ אֵת אֲשֶׁר עֲבַדְתִּיךָ וְאֵת אֲשֶׁר־הָיָה מִקְנְךָ אִתִּי: כִּי מְעַט אֲשֶׁר־
הָיָה לְךָ לְפָנַי וַיִּפְרֹץ לָרֹב וַיְבָרֶךְ יְהוָה אֹתְךָ לְרַגְלִי וְעַתָּה מָתַי אֶעֱשֶׂה
לא גַם־אָנֹכִי לְבֵיתִי: וַיֹּאמֶר מָה אֶתֶּן־לָךְ וַיֹּאמֶר יַעֲקֹב לֹא־תִתֶּן־לִי
מְאוּמָה אִם־תַּעֲשֶׂה־לִּי הַדָּבָר הַזֶּה אָשׁוּבָה אֶרְעֶה צֹאנְךָ אֶשְׁמֹר:
לב אֶעֱבֹר בְּכָל־צֹאנְךָ הַיּוֹם הָסֵר מִשָּׁם כָּל־שֶׂה ׀ נָקֹד וְטָלוּא וְכָל־שֶׂה־
לג חוּם בַּכְּשָׂבִים וְטָלוּא וְנָקֹד בָּעִזִּים וְהָיָה שְׂכָרִי: וְעָנְתָה־בִּי צִדְקָתִי

אונקלוס

יי בְּדִילָךְ: כח וַאֲמַר, פָּרֵישׁ אַגְרָךְ, עֲלַי וְאֶתֵּין: כט וַאֲמַר לֵיהּ, אַתְּ יְדַעְתְּ, יָת דִּפְלַחְתָּךְ, וְיָת, דַּהֲוָה בְעִירָךְ עִמִּי: ל אֲרֵי, זְעֵיר דַּהֲוָה לָךְ קֳדָמַי וּתְקֵיף לְסַגִּי, וּבָרֵיךְ יי, יָתָךְ בְּדִילִי, וּכְעַן, אִמָּתַי, אַעֲבֵיד אַף אֲנָא לְבֵיתִי: לא וַאֲמַר מָא אֶתֵּין לָךְ, וַאֲמַר יַעֲקֹב לָא תִתֵּין לִי מִדָּעַם, אִם תַּעֲבֵיד לִי פִּתְגָמָא הָדֵין, אֲתוּב, אֶרְעֵי עָנָךְ אֶטַּר: לב אֶעְבַּר בְּכָל עָנָךְ יוֹמָא דֵין, אַעְדִּי מִתַּמָּן, כָּל אִמַּר נְמוֹר וּרְקוֹע, וְכָל אִמַּר שְׁחוּם בְּאִמְּרַיָּא, וּרְקוֹע וּנְמוֹר בְּעִזַּיָּא, וִיהֵי אַגְרִי: לג וְתַסְהֵיד עֲלַי זָכוּתִי

meaning "lost," "wandering," or "on the brink of perishing." The text of *arami oved avi,* originally, had nothing to do with Passover. It appears in the Torah as the text of the declaration to be said on bringing first fruits to the Temple on Shavuot. In that context, the literal translation, "My ancestor was a wandering Aramean," makes eminent sense. The text is contrasting the past, when the patriarchs were forced to wander from place to place, with the present, when, thanks to God, the Israelites have a land of their own.

At some stage, however, the passage was placed in another context: the Mishna specifies that it be read and expounded on Seder night (Pesaḥim 4:10). What could be the connection between "My ancestor was a wandering Aramean" and the exodus?

Let me suggest an explanation. We have here a phrase with two quite different meanings, depending on the context in which we read it. The Sages formulated the principle that *maasei avot siman lebanim,* "the acts of the fathers are a sign for their children." The classic example, as we have seen, occurs in Genesis 12 when, almost immediately after arriving in the land of Canaan, Avraham and Sara are forced into exile in Egypt. Avraham's life is at risk. Sara is taken into Pharaoh's harem. God then strikes Pharaoh's household with plagues, and Pharaoh sends them away. The parallels between this and the story of the exodus are obvious. The event appears to recur both in Avraham's life and in Yitzḥak's.

Living with Lavan, however, Yaakov loses his freedom. He becomes, in effect, his father-in-law's slave. Eventually he has to escape, without letting Lavan know he is going. In this respect, Yaakov's experience is closer to the exodus than that of Avraham or Yitzḥak. No one stopped them from leaving. No one pursued them. It is Yaakov's experience in the house of Lavan that becomes the sharpest prefiguration of the exodus.

What then are we to make of the Haggada's comment "Pharaoh condemned only the boys to death, but Lavan sought to uproot everything"? The answer is not that Lavan sought to kill all the members of Yaakov's family. Quite the opposite. Yaakov works for some twenty years to earn his family and flocks. Yet Lavan still claims they are his. Were God not to intervene, he would keep Yaakov's entire family as prisoners. He seeks "to uproot everything" by denying them all the chance to go free.

It was the genius of the Sages to give a verse related to

testify for me in the future, whenever you come to check the wages you have
paid me. Any goat not speckled or spotted or any lamb not dark colored in my
34 possession shall be considered stolen." Lavan said, "Agreed. Let it be as you
35 have said." That day Lavan removed the streaked or spotted goats, all the
speckled or spotted female goats – every one that had a trace of white – and
36 every dark-colored lamb. These he placed in the care of his sons. Then he put a
three-day-journey's distance between him and Yaakov. Yaakov tended the rest
37 of Lavan's flock. Yaakov took fresh shoots of poplar, almond, and plane trees
38 and peeled white strips in them, exposing the white of the shoots. Then he set
the peeled shoots in all the water troughs so that they would be in front of the
flocks when they came to drink. They would mate when they came to drink,
39 and since they mated by the shoots, they bore streaked, speckled, and spotted
40 young. Yaakov set apart the young of the flock, and he made the others
belonging to Lavan face the streaked and dark-colored animals. Thus he bred
separate flocks for himself, and he did not let them breed with Lavan's flocks.
41 Whenever the stronger animals were mating, Yaakov would place the shoots in

רש״י

לד **הן.** לשון הין, קבלת דברים: **לו יהי כדברך.** הלואי שתחפץ בכך:

לה **ויסר.** לבן "ביום ההוא" וגו׳: **התישים.** עזים זכרים: **כל אשר לבן בו.** כל אשר היתה בו חברבורת לבנה: **ויתן.** לבן "ביד בניו":

לו **הנותרת.** הרעועות שבהן, החולות והעקרות שאינן אלא שירים, אותן מסר לו:

לז **מקל לבנה.** עץ הוא ושמו ׳לבנה׳, כמה דאת אמר: "תחת אלון ולבנה" (הושע ד, יג). ואומר אני, הוא שקורין טרינבל״א שהוא לבן: **לח.** כשהוא רטב: **ולוז.** ועוד לקח מקל לוז, עץ שגדלין בו אגוזים דקים, קולדר״י בלעז: **וערמון.** קשטניי״ר בלעז: **פצלות.** קלופים קלופים, שהיה עושהו מנמר: **מחשף הלבן.** גלוי לבן של מקל, כשהיה קולפו היה נראה ונגלה לבן שלו במקום הקלוף:

לח **ויצג.** "ודעיץ", לשון תחיבה ונעיצה הוא בלשון ארמי, והרבה יש בתלמוד: "דצה ושלפה" (שבת נ ע״ב), "דץ ביה מידי" (חולין נג ע״ב), ׳דצה׳ כמו ׳דעצה׳, אלא שמקצר את לשונו: **ברהטים.** במרוצות המים, בברכות העשויות בארץ להשקות שם הצאן: **אשר תבאן** וגו׳. ברהטים אשר תבאן הצאן לשתות, שם הציג המקלות "לנכח הצאן": **ויחמנה.** הבהמה רואה את המקלות והיא נרתעת לאחוריה, והזכר רובעה ויולדת כיוצא בו. רבי הושעיא אומר: המים נעשין זרע במעיהן ולא היו צריכות לזכר, וזהו "ויחמנה" וגו׳:

לט **אל המקלות.** אל מראית המקלות: **עקדים.** משנים במקום עקדתם, הם קרסלי ידיהם ורגליהם:

מ **והכשבים הפריד יעקב.** הנולדים עקדים ונקדים הבדיל והפריש לעצמן ועשה אותן עדר עדר לבדו, והוליך אותו העדר העקד לפני הצאן, ופני הצאן ההולכות אחריהם צופות אליהם, וזהו שאמר: "ויתן פני הצאן אל עקד", שהיו פני הצאן אל העקדים ואל "כל חום" שמצא "בצאן לבן": **וישת לו עדרים.** כמו שפרשתי:

מא **המקשרות.** כתרגומו, הבכירות, ואין לי עד במקרא. ומנחם חברו עם "אחיתפל בקשרים" (שמואל ב׳ טו, לא), "ויהי הקשר אמץ" (שם פסוק יב) – אותן המתקשרות יחד למהר עבורן:

an epigenetic effect – that is, it can cause a certain gene to be expressed which might not have been otherwise. If the peeled branches of poplar, almond, and plane trees are added to the water the sheep drank, they might affect the agouti gene that determines the color of fur in sheep and mice. However it happens, the result is evidently dramatic.

בְּיוֹם מָחָר כִּי־תָבוֹא עַל־שְׂכָרִי לְפָנֶיךָ כֹּל אֲשֶׁר־אֵינֶנּוּ נָקֹד וְטָלוּא
לד בָּעִזִּים וְחוּם בַּכְּשָׂבִים גָּנוּב הוּא אִתִּי׃ וַיֹּאמֶר לָבָן הֵן לוּ יְהִי כִדְבָרֶךָ׃
לה וַיָּסַר בַּיּוֹם הַהוּא אֶת־הַתְּיָשִׁים הָעֲקֻדִּים וְהַטְּלֻאִים וְאֵת כָּל־הָעִזִּים
הַנְּקֻדּוֹת וְהַטְּלֻאֹת כֹּל אֲשֶׁר־לָבָן בּוֹ וְכָל־חוּם בַּכְּשָׂבִים וַיִּתֵּן בְּיַד־בָּנָיו׃
לו וַיָּשֶׂם דֶּרֶךְ שְׁלֹשֶׁת יָמִים בֵּינוֹ וּבֵין יַעֲקֹב וְיַעֲקֹב רֹעֶה אֶת־צֹאן לָבָן
לז הַנּוֹתָרֹת׃ וַיִּקַּח־לוֹ יַעֲקֹב מַקַּל לִבְנֶה לַח וְלוּז וְעַרְמוֹן וַיְפַצֵּל בָּהֵן
לח פְּצָלוֹת לְבָנוֹת מַחְשֹׂף הַלָּבָן אֲשֶׁר עַל־הַמַּקְלוֹת׃ וַיַּצֵּג אֶת־הַמַּקְלוֹת
אֲשֶׁר פִּצֵּל בָּרְהָטִים בְּשִׁקְתוֹת הַמָּיִם אֲשֶׁר תָּבֹאןָ הַצֹּאן לִשְׁתּוֹת
לט לְנֹכַח הַצֹּאן וַיֵּחַמְנָה בְּבֹאָן לִשְׁתּוֹת׃ וַיֶּחֱמוּ הַצֹּאן אֶל־הַמַּקְלוֹת
מ וַתֵּלַדְןָ הַצֹּאן עֲקֻדִּים נְקֻדִּים וּטְלֻאִים׃ וְהַכְּשָׂבִים הִפְרִיד יַעֲקֹב וַיִּתֵּן
פְּנֵי הַצֹּאן אֶל־עָקֹד וְכָל־חוּם בְּצֹאן לָבָן וַיָּשֶׁת לוֹ עֲדָרִים לְבַדּוֹ וְלֹא
מא שָׁתָם עַל־צֹאן לָבָן׃ וְהָיָה בְּכָל־יַחֵם הַצֹּאן הַמְקֻשָּׁרוֹת וְשָׂם יַעֲקֹב

אונקלוס

ביום מחר, ארי תיעול על אגרי קדמך, כל דליתוהי נמור ורקוע
בעזיא, ושחום באמריא, גנובא הוא עמי: לד ואמר לבן ברם, לוי יהי
כפתגמך: לה ואעדי ביומא ההוא ית תישיא רגוליא ורקועיא, וית כל
עזיא נמורתא ורקועתא, כל דחיור ביה, וכל דשחום באמריא, ויהב
ביד בנוהי: לו ושוי, מהלך תלתא יומין, בינוהי ובין יעקב, ויעקב, רעי,
ית ענא דלבן דאשתארא: לז ונסיב ליה יעקב, חטרין דלבן, רטיבן
ודלוז ודדלוב, וקליף בהון קלפין חיורין, קלוף חיור, דעל חטריא:
לח ודעיץ, ית חטריא דקליף, ברטיא אתר בית שקיא דמיא, אתר
דאתין ענא למשתי לקבלהון דענא, ומתיחמן במיתיהון למשתי:
לט ואתיחמא ענא בחטריא, וילידן ענא, רגולין נמורין ורקועין:
מ ואמריא אפריש יעקב, ויהב, בריש ענא כל דרגול, וכל דשחום
בענא דלבן, ושוי ליה עדרין בלחודוהי, ולא עריבנון עם ענא
דלבן: מא והוי, בכל עדן דמתיחמן ענא מבכרתא, ומשוי יעקב

30:37 וַיִּקַּח־לוֹ יַעֲקֹב מַקַּל לִבְנֶה *Yaakov took fresh shoots*– Yaakov embarks on an extraordinary course of action. In charge of the flocks, he goes through an elaborate procedure involving peeled branches of poplar, almond, and plane trees, which he places with their drinking water. The result is that, though Lavan has removed all the streaked animals from the flock, those that remain do in fact produce streaked and spotted offspring.

How this happens has intrigued not only the commentators (who mostly assume that it was a miracle, God's way of assuring Yaakov's welfare) but also scientists. Some argue that Yaakov must have had an understanding of genetics. Two unspotted sheep can produce spotted offspring. Yaakov has doubtless noticed this in his many years of tending Lavan's flocks.

Others have suggested that prenatal nutrition can have

42 the troughs facing them so that they mated facing the shoots. But the weaker
animals he did not put there, so the weaker went to Lavan and the stronger to
43 Yaakov. Thus the man's wealth swelled into a fortune. He had large flocks,
31 1 female and male servants, camels and donkeys. Yaakov heard that Lavan's sons
were saying, "Yaakov has taken everything our father owned; of what belonged
2 to our father, he has made all these riches." And Yaakov saw that Lavan's manner
3 toward him was not what it had been. The LORD said to Yaakov, "Go back to
4 the land of your fathers where you were born; I will be with you." So Yaakov
5 sent word to Raḥel and Leah to come out to the field where his flock was. He
said to them, "I see that your father's manner toward me is not what it used to
6 be. But the God of my father has been with me. You well know how I have
7 worked for your father with all my strength. Your father cheated me, changing
8 my wages ten times, but God has not let him harm me. If he said, 'The speckled
animals shall be your hire,' then all the flock would give birth to speckled young.
If he said, 'The streaked animals shall be your hire,' then all the flock would give
9 birth to streaked young. God has taken your father's livestock and given it to
10 me. Once, during the breeding season, I had a dream: I saw that the rams

רש״י

מב **וּבְהַעֲטִיף.** לְשׁוֹן אִחוּר, כְּתַרְגּוּמוֹ "וּבְלַקִּישׁוּת". וּמְנַחֵם חִבְּרוֹ עִם "הַמַּחֲלָצוֹת וְהַמַּעֲטָפוֹת" (ישעיה ג, כב), לְשׁוֹן עֲטִיפַת כְּסוּת, כְּלוֹמַר, מִתְעַטְּפוֹת בְּעוֹרָן וְצַמְרָן וְאֵינָן מִתְאַוּוֹת לְהִתְיַחֵם עַל יְדֵי הַזְּכָרִים:

מג **צֹאן רַבּוֹת.** פָּרוֹת וְרָבוֹת מִשְּׁאָר צֹאן: **וּשְׁפָחוֹת וַעֲבָדִים.** מוֹכֵר צֹאנוֹ בְּדָמִים יְקָרִים וְלוֹקֵחַ לוֹ כָּל אֵלֶּה:

לא א **עָשָׂה.** כָּנַס, כְּמוֹ: "וַיַּעַשׂ חַיִל וַיַּךְ אֶת עֲמָלֵק" (שמואל א' יד, מח):

ג **שׁוּב אֶל אֶרֶץ אֲבוֹתֶיךָ.** וְשָׁם "אֶהְיֶה עִמָּךְ", אֲבָל בְּעוֹדְךָ מְחֻבָּר לַטָּמֵא אִי אֶפְשָׁר לְהַשְׁרוֹת שְׁכִינָתִי עָלֶיךָ:

ד **וַיִּקְרָא לְרָחֵל וּלְלֵאָה.** לְרָחֵל תְּחִלָּה וְאַחַר כָּךְ לְלֵאָה, שֶׁהִיא הָיְתָה עִקַּר הַבַּיִת, שֶׁבִּשְׁבִילָהּ נִזְדַּוֵּג יַעֲקֹב עִם לָבָן. וְאַף בָּנֶיהָ שֶׁל לֵאָה מוֹדִים בַּדָּבָר, שֶׁהֲרֵי בֹּעַז וּבֵית דִּינוֹ מִשֵּׁבֶט יְהוּדָה אוֹמְרִים: "כְּרָחֵל וּכְלֵאָה אֲשֶׁר בָּנוּ שְׁתֵּיהֶם" וְגוֹ' (רות ד, יא), הִקְדִּימוּ רָחֵל לְלֵאָה:

ז **עֲשֶׂרֶת מֹנִים.** אֵין 'מוֹנִים' פָּחוֹת מֵעֲשָׂרָה: **מֹנִים.** לְשׁוֹן סְכוּם כְּלַל הַחֶשְׁבּוֹן, וְהֵן עֲשִׂירִיּוֹת, לָמַדְנוּ שֶׁהֶחֱלִיף תְּנָאוֹ מֵאָה פְעָמִים:

י **וְהִנֵּה הָעַתֻּדִים.** אַף עַל פִּי שֶׁהִבְדִּילָם לָבָן כֻּלָּם שֶׁלֹּא יִתְעַבְּרוּ הַצֹּאן דֻּגְמָתָן, הָיוּ הַמַּלְאָכִים מְבִיאִין אוֹתָן מֵעֵדֶר הַמָּסוּר בְּיַד בְּנֵי

see here, as in the story of Yitzḥak in Gerar, Amy Chua's three conditions for the persecution of a minority (see ch. 26, "Stopping up the Wells"). Yaakov is a minority, outnumbered by Lavan's family. He is successful, and it is conspicuous. You can see it by looking at his flocks.

As with Lavan, so through the ages, the host society would eventually turn against the Jews. They claimed that Jews were exploiting them rather than what was in fact the case, that they were exploiting the Jews. And when Jews succeeded, they accused them of theft: "The flocks are my flocks! All that you see is mine!" (Gen. 31:43). They forgot that Jews had contributed massively to national prosperity. The fact that Jews had salvaged some self-respect, some independence, that they too had prospered, made antisemites not just envious but angry. That was when it became dangerous to be a Jew.

מב אֶת־הַמַּקְלוֹת לְעֵינֵי הַצֹּאן בָּרְהָטִים לְיַחְמֵנָּה בַּמַּקְלוֹת: וּבְהַעֲטִיף
מג הַצֹּאן לֹא יָשִׂים וְהָיָה הָעֲטֻפִים לְלָבָן וְהַקְּשֻׁרִים לְיַעֲקֹב: וַיִּפְרֹץ הָאִישׁ
מְאֹד מְאֹד וַיְהִי־לוֹ צֹאן רַבּוֹת וּשְׁפָחוֹת וַעֲבָדִים וּגְמַלִּים וַחֲמֹרִים:
לא א וַיִּשְׁמַע אֶת־דִּבְרֵי בְנֵי־לָבָן לֵאמֹר לָקַח יַעֲקֹב אֵת כָּל־אֲשֶׁר לְאָבִינוּ
ב וּמֵאֲשֶׁר לְאָבִינוּ עָשָׂה אֵת כָּל־הַכָּבֹד הַזֶּה: וַיַּרְא יַעֲקֹב אֶת־פְּנֵי לָבָן
ג וְהִנֵּה אֵינֶנּוּ עִמּוֹ כִּתְמוֹל שִׁלְשׁוֹם: וַיֹּאמֶר יהוה אֶל־יַעֲקֹב שׁוּב אֶל־ כט
ד אֶרֶץ אֲבוֹתֶיךָ וּלְמוֹלַדְתֶּךָ וְאֶהְיֶה עִמָּךְ: וַיִּשְׁלַח יַעֲקֹב וַיִּקְרָא לְרָחֵל
ה וּלְלֵאָה הַשָּׂדֶה אֶל־צֹאנוֹ: וַיֹּאמֶר לָהֶן רֹאֶה אָנֹכִי אֶת־פְּנֵי אֲבִיכֶן
ו כִּי־אֵינֶנּוּ אֵלַי כִּתְמֹל שִׁלְשֹׁם וֵאלֹהֵי אָבִי הָיָה עִמָּדִי: וְאַתֵּנָה יְדַעְתֶּן
ז כִּי בְּכָל־כֹּחִי עָבַדְתִּי אֶת־אֲבִיכֶן: וַאֲבִיכֶן הֵתֶל בִּי וְהֶחֱלִף אֶת־
ח מַשְׂכֻּרְתִּי עֲשֶׂרֶת מֹנִים וְלֹא־נְתָנוֹ אֱלֹהִים לְהָרַע עִמָּדִי: אִם־כֹּה יֹאמַר
נְקֻדִּים יִהְיֶה שְׂכָרֶךָ וְיָלְדוּ כָל־הַצֹּאן נְקֻדִּים וְאִם־כֹּה יֹאמַר עֲקֻדִּים
ט יִהְיֶה שְׂכָרֶךָ וְיָלְדוּ כָל־הַצֹּאן עֲקֻדִּים: וַיַּצֵּל אֱלֹהִים אֶת־מִקְנֵה אֲבִיכֶם
י וַיִּתֶּן־לִי: וַיְהִי בְּעֵת יַחֵם הַצֹּאן וָאֶשָּׂא עֵינַי וָאֵרֶא בַּחֲלוֹם וְהִנֵּה הָעַתֻּדִים

אונקלוס

יָת חֻטְרַיָּא, לְעֵינֵי עָנָא בְּרַטַיָּא, לְיַחֲמוּתְהוֹן בְּחֻטְרַיָּא: מב וּבְלַקִּישׁוּת עָנָא לָא מְשַׁוֵּי, וְהָוַן לַקִּישַׁיָּא לְלָבָן, וּבַכִּירַיָּא לְיַעֲקֹב: מג וּתְקֵיף גֻּבְרָא לַחֲדָא לַחֲדָא, וַהֲווֹ לֵיהּ עָן סַגִּיאָן, וְאַמְהָן וְעַבְדִּין, וְגַמְלִין וַחֲמָרִין: לא א וּשְׁמַע, יָת פִּתְגָּמֵי בְּנֵי לָבָן דְּאָמְרִין, נְסֵיב יַעֲקֹב, יָת כָּל דִּלַאֲבוּנָא, וּמִדִּלַאֲבוּנָא, קְנָא, יָת כָּל נִכְסַיָּא הָאִלֵּין: ב וַחֲזָא יַעֲקֹב יָת סְבַר אַפֵּי לָבָן, וְהָא לֵיתְנוּן, עִמֵּיהּ כְּמֵאִתְמָלֵי וּמִדְּקַמּוֹהִי: ג וַאֲמַר יי לְיַעֲקֹב, תּוּב, לַאֲרַע אֲבָהָתָךְ וּלְיַלָּדוּתָךְ, וִיהֵי מֵימְרִי בְּסַעֲדָךְ: ד וּשְׁלַח יַעֲקֹב, וּקְרָא לְרָחֵל

וּלְלֵאָה, לְחַקְלָא לְוָת עָנֵיהּ: ה וַאֲמַר לְהוֹן, חָזֵי אֲנָא יָת סְבַר אַפֵּי אֲבוּכוֹן, אֲרֵי לֵיתְנוּן עִמִּי כְּמֵאִתְמָלֵי וּמִדְּקַמּוֹהִי, וֵאלָהֵיהּ דְּאַבָּא, הֲוָה בְּסַעֲדִי: ו וְאַתִּין יְדַעְתִּין, אֲרֵי בְּכָל חֵילִי, פְּלַחִית יָת אֲבוּכוֹן: ז וַאֲבוּכוֹן שַׁקַּר בִּי, וְאַשְׁנִי יָת אַגְרִי עֲסַר זִמְנִין, וְלָא שַׁבְקֵיהּ יי, לְאַבְאָשָׁא עִמִּי: ח אִם כְּדֵין הֲוָה אָמַר, נְמוֹרִין יְהֵי אַגְרָךְ, וִילִידָן כָּל עָנָא נְמוֹרִין, וְאִם כְּדֵין הֲוָה אָמַר, רְגוֹלִין יְהֵי אַגְרָךְ, וִילִידָן כָּל עָנָא רְגוֹלִין: ט וְאַפְרֵישׁ יי, מִן בְּעִירָא דַּאֲבוּכוֹן וִיהַב לִי: י וַהֲוָה, בְּעִדָּן דְּאִתְיַחֲמָא עָנָא, וּזְקַפִית עֵינַי, וַחֲזֵית בְּחֶלְמָא, וְהָא תֵּישַׁיָּא

31:2 אֵינֶנּוּ עִמּוֹ כִּתְמוֹל שִׁלְשׁוֹם *Not what it had been* – Throughout the ages, antisemites saw in Jews people who would make them rich. Wherever Jews went they brought prosperity to their hosts. Yet they refused to be mere chattels. They refused to be owned. They had their own identity and way of life; they insisted on the basic human right to be free. We

▶

11 mounting the flock were streaked, speckled, or spotted. And in the dream an
12 angel of God said to me, 'Yaakov.' I replied, 'Here I am.' He said, 'Look up and
see that all the rams mounting the flock are streaked, speckled, or spotted, for I
13 have seen all that Lavan is doing to you. I am the God of Beit El, where you
anointed a pillar and made a vow to Me. Now – leave this land at once and
14 return to the land where you were born.'" Raḥel and Leah answered him, "Do
15 we still have a share in the inheritance of our father's estate? He treats us like
16 strangers. He has sold us and spent the money. All the wealth that God has
taken from our father belongs to us and our children. So do whatever God has
17 18 told you." So Yaakov put his children and wives on camels and drove all the SHISHI
livestock and wealth he had accumulated – the livestock he had acquired in
19 Padan Aram – heading for his father Yitzḥak in the land of Canaan. Meanwhile,
when Lavan had gone to shear his sheep, Raḥel had stolen her father's household
20 gods. Yaakov deceived Lavan the Aramean by not telling him that he was

רש״י

לָבָן לָעֵדֶר שֶׁבְּיַד יַעֲקֹב: **וּבְרֻדִּים.** כְּתַרְגּוּמוֹ: ״וּפַצִּיחִין״, פייסי״ד בְּלַעַז, חוּט שֶׁל לָבָן מַקִּיף אֶת גּוּפוֹ סָבִיב, חֲבַרְבּוּרֶת שֶׁלּוֹ פְּתוּחָה וּמְפֻלֶּשֶׁת מִזַּן אֶל זַן, וְאֵין לִי לַהֲבִיא לוֹ עֵד מִן הַמִּקְרָא:

יג **הָאֵל בֵּית אֵל.** כְּמוֹ ׳אֵל בֵּית אֵל׳, הַהֵ״א יְתֵרָה, וְדֶרֶךְ מִקְרָאוֹת לְדַבֵּר כֵּן, כְּמוֹ: ״כִּי אַתֶּם בָּאִים אֶל הָאָרֶץ כְּנָעַן״ (במדבר לד, ב): **מָשַׁחְתָּ שָּׁם.** לְשׁוֹן רִבּוּי וּגְדֻלָּה כְּנִמְשָׁח לַמַּלְכוּת, כָּךְ ״וַיִּצֹק שֶׁמֶן עַל רֹאשָׁהּ״ (לעיל כח, יח) לִהְיוֹת מְשׁוּחָה לַמִּזְבֵּחַ: **אֲשֶׁר נָדַרְתָּ לִּי.** וְצָרִיךְ אַתָּה לְשַׁלְּמוֹ (שם), שֶׁאָמַרְתָּ: ״יִהְיֶה בֵּית אֱלֹהִים״ (לעיל כח, כב), שֶׁתַּקְרִיב שָׁם קָרְבָּנוֹת:

יד **הַעוֹד לָנוּ.** לָמָּה נְעַכֵּב עַל יָדְךָ מִלָּשׁוּב, כְּלוּם אָנוּ מְיַחֲלוֹת לִירַשׁ מִנִּכְסֵי אָבִינוּ כְּלוּם בֵּין הַזְּכָרִים?:

טו **הֲלוֹא נָכְרִיּוֹת נֶחְשַׁבְנוּ לוֹ.** אֲפִלּוּ בְּשָׁעָה שֶׁדֶּרֶךְ בְּנֵי אָדָם לָתֵת נְדוּנְיָא לִבְנוֹתָיו, בִּשְׁעַת נִשּׂוּאִין, נָהַג עִמָּנוּ כְּנָכְרִיּוֹת, ״כִּי מְכָרָנוּ״ לְךָ בִּשְׂכַר הַפְּעֻלָּה: **אֶת כַּסְפֵּנוּ.** שֶׁעִכֵּב דְּמֵי שְׂכַר פְּעֻלָּתְךָ:

טז **כִּי כָל הָעֹשֶׁר.** ׳כִּי׳ זֶה מְשַׁמֵּשׁ בִּלְשׁוֹן ׳אֶלָּא׳, כְּלוֹמַר, מִשֶּׁל אָבִינוּ אֵין לָנוּ כְּלוּם, אֶלָּא מַה שֶּׁהִצִּיל הַקָּדוֹשׁ בָּרוּךְ הוּא מֵאָבִינוּ שֶׁלָּנוּ הוּא: **הִצִּיל.** לְשׁוֹן הִפְרִישׁ, וְכֵן כָּל לְשׁוֹן הַצָּלָה שֶׁבַּמִּקְרָא לְשׁוֹן הַפְרָשָׁה, שֶׁמַּפְרִישׁוֹ מִן הָרָעָה וּמִן הָאוֹיֵב:

יז **אֶת בָּנָיו וְאֶת נָשָׁיו.** הִקְדִּים זְכָרִים לִנְקֵבוֹת, וְעֵשָׂו הִקְדִּים נְקֵבוֹת לִזְכָרִים, שֶׁנֶּאֱמַר: ״וַיִּקַּח עֵשָׂו אֶת נָשָׁיו וְאֶת בָּנָיו״ וְגוֹ׳ (להלן לו, ו):

יח **מִקְנֵה קִנְיָנוֹ.** מַה שֶּׁקָּנָה מִצֹּאנוֹ, עֲבָדִים וּשְׁפָחוֹת וּגְמַלִּים וַחֲמוֹרִים:

יט **לִגְזֹז אֶת צֹאנוֹ.** שֶׁנָּתַן בְּיַד בָּנָיו דֶּרֶךְ שְׁלֹשֶׁת יָמִים בֵּינוֹ וּבֵין יַעֲקֹב: **וַתִּגְנֹב רָחֵל אֶת הַתְּרָפִים.** לְהַפְרִישׁ אֶת אָבִיהָ מֵעֲבוֹדָה זָרָה נִתְכַּוְּנָה:

text says explicitly, "Yaakov did not know" (31:32). When Lavan pursues and catches up with them, he accuses Yaakov's party of having stolen them. Yaakov indignantly denies this and says, "If you find your gods with anyone here, they shall not live" (31:32). Several chapters later, we will read that Raḥel dies prematurely, on the way. The possibility hinted at by the text, articulated by a midrash and by Rashi (Bereshit Rabba; Zohar ad loc.) is that, unwittingly, Yaakov has condemned her to death.

As with Rivka and Yitzḥak a generation earlier, misunderstanding flows from a failure of communication. Had Rivka told Yitzḥak about the oracle, and had Raḥel told Yaakov about the *terafim*, tragedy might have been averted. Judaism is a religion of holy words, and one of the themes of Genesis as a whole is the power of speech to create, mislead, harm, or heal. Lavan is charged "not to say anything to Yaakov for good or for bad" (31:24). Raḥel's own silence and Yaakov's careless speech may cost them everything.

הָעֹלִים עַל־הַצֹּאן עֲקֻדִּים נְקֻדִּים וּבְרֻדִּים׃ יא וַיֹּאמֶר אֵלַי מַלְאַךְ הָאֱלֹהִים
יב בַּחֲלוֹם יַעֲקֹב וָאֹמַר הִנֵּנִי׃ וַיֹּאמֶר שָׂא־נָא עֵינֶיךָ וּרְאֵה כָּל־הָעַתֻּדִים
הָעֹלִים עַל־הַצֹּאן עֲקֻדִּים נְקֻדִּים וּבְרֻדִּים כִּי רָאִיתִי אֵת כָּל־אֲשֶׁר
יג לָבָן עֹשֶׂה לָּךְ׃ אָנֹכִי הָאֵל בֵּית־אֵל אֲשֶׁר מָשַׁחְתָּ שָּׁם מַצֵּבָה אֲשֶׁר
נָדַרְתָּ לִּי שָׁם נֶדֶר עַתָּה קוּם צֵא מִן־הָאָרֶץ הַזֹּאת וְשׁוּב אֶל־אֶרֶץ
יד מוֹלַדְתֶּךָ׃ וַתַּעַן רָחֵל וְלֵאָה וַתֹּאמַרְנָה לוֹ הַעוֹד לָנוּ חֵלֶק וְנַחֲלָה
טו בְּבֵית אָבִינוּ׃ הֲלוֹא נָכְרִיּוֹת נֶחְשַׁבְנוּ לוֹ כִּי מְכָרָנוּ וַיֹּאכַל גַּם־אָכוֹל
טז אֶת־כַּסְפֵּנוּ׃ כִּי כָל־הָעֹשֶׁר אֲשֶׁר הִצִּיל אֱלֹהִים מֵאָבִינוּ לָנוּ הוּא וּלְבָנֵינוּ
יז וְעַתָּה כֹּל אֲשֶׁר אָמַר אֱלֹהִים אֵלֶיךָ עֲשֵׂה׃ וַיָּקָם יַעֲקֹב וַיִּשָּׂא אֶת־בָּנָיו ששי
יח וְאֶת־נָשָׁיו עַל־הַגְּמַלִּים׃ וַיִּנְהַג אֶת־כָּל־מִקְנֵהוּ וְאֶת־כָּל־רְכֻשׁוֹ אֲשֶׁר
רָכָשׁ מִקְנֵה קִנְיָנוֹ אֲשֶׁר רָכַשׁ בְּפַדַּן אֲרָם לָבוֹא אֶל־יִצְחָק אָבִיו אַרְצָה
יט כְּנָעַן׃ וְלָבָן הָלַךְ לִגְזֹז אֶת־צֹאנוֹ וַתִּגְנֹב רָחֵל אֶת־הַתְּרָפִים אֲשֶׁר
כ לְאָבִיהָ׃ וַיִּגְנֹב יַעֲקֹב אֶת־לֵב לָבָן הָאֲרַמִּי עַל־בְּלִי הִגִּיד לוֹ כִּי בֹרֵחַ

אונקלוס

דְּסָלְקִין עַל עָנָא, רְגוֹלִין נְמוֹרִין וּפְצִיחִין: יא וַאֲמַר לִי, מַלְאֲכָא דַּייָ, בְּחֶלְמָא יַעֲקֹב, וַאֲמָרִית הָאֲנָא: יב וַאֲמַר, זְקוֹף כְּעַן עֵינָךְ וַחֲזִי כָּל תֵּישַׁיָּא דְּסָלְקִין עַל עָנָא, רְגוֹלִין נְמוֹרִין וּפְצִיחִין, אֲרֵי גְּלֵי קֳדָמַי, יָת, כָּל דְּלָבָן עָבֵיד לָךְ: יג אֲנָא אֱלָהָא דְּאִתְגְּלֵיתִי עֲלָךְ בְּבֵית אֵל, דִּמְשַׁחְתָּא תַמָּן קָמָא, דְּקַיֵּימְתָּא קֳדָמַי, תַּמָּן קְיָם, כְּעַן, קוּם פּוּק מִן אַרְעָא הָדָא, וְתוּב לַאֲרַע יַלָּדוּתָךְ: יד וַאֲתֵיבַת רָחֵל וְלֵאָה, וַאֲמַרָא לֵיהּ, הַעוֹד לַנָא, חוּלָק וְאַחְסָנָא בְּבֵית אֲבוּנָא: טו הֲלָא נֻכְרָאָן, אִתְחֲשֵׁיבְנָא לֵיהּ אֲרֵי זַבְּנַנָא, וַאֲכַל אַף מֵיכַל יָת כַּסְפַּנָא: טז אֲרֵי כָל עוּתְרָא, דְּאַפְרֵישׁ יְיָ מֵאֲבוּנָא, דִּילַנָא הוּא וְדִבְנַנָא, וּכְעַן, כָּל דַּאֲמַר יְיָ, לָךְ עֲבֵיד: יז וְקָם יַעֲקֹב, וּנְטַל, יָת בְּנוֹהִי וְיָת נְשׁוֹהִי עַל גַּמְלַיָּא: יח וְדַבַּר יָת כָּל גֵּיתוֹהִי, וְיָת כָּל קִנְיָנֵיהּ דִּקְנָא, גֵּיתוֹהִי וְקִנְיָנֵיהּ, דִּקְנָא בְּפַדַּן אֲרָם, לְמֵיתֵי, לְוָת יִצְחָק אֲבוּהִי לַאֲרְעָא דִּכְנָעַן: יט וְלָבָן אֲזַל, לְמִגַּז יָת עָנֵיהּ, וּנְסֵיבַת רָחֵל, יָת צַלְמַנַיָּא דִּלַאֲבוּהָא: כ וּכְסִי יַעֲקֹב, מִן לָבָן אֲרַמָּאָה, עַל דְּלָא חַוִּי לֵיהּ, אֲרֵי אָזֵיל

31:19 וַתִּגְנֹב רָחֵל *Raḥel had stolen* – We are reminded of an earlier episode (see comment on Gen. 25:22). Yitzḥak, we recall, loved Esav; Rivka loved Yaakov. At least one possible explanation, offered by Abrabanel (commentary on Gen. 25:28), is that Rivka had been told by God, before the twins were born, that "the greater shall the younger serve" (Gen. 25:23). Hence her attachment to Yaakov, the younger, and her determination that he, not Esav, should have Yitzḥak's blessing.

Here, Raḥel steals her father's *terafim*, "icons" or "household gods," when they leave Lavan to return to the land of Canaan. She does not tell Yaakov that she has done so. The

21 running away. He fled with all he had, crossed the Euphrates, and headed for
22 the hill country of Gilad. On the third day, Lavan was told that Yaakov had fled.
23 Taking his kinsmen with him, he pursued him for seven days, catching up with
24 him in the hill country of Gilad. That night God came to Lavan the Aramean in
a dream and said to him, "Take care not to say anything to Yaakov for good or
25 for bad." When Lavan overtook him, Yaakov had pitched his tent in the hill
country, and Lavan and his kinsmen too encamped in the hill country of Gilad.
26 Lavan said to Yaakov, "What have you done? You have deceived me, and carried
27 off my daughters like captives of the sword. Why did you leave secretly? Why
did you deceive me by not telling me? I would have sent you off with celebration
28 and song, with tambourines and harps. You did not even let me kiss my
29 grandchildren and daughters goodbye. You have behaved foolishly. I have the
power to harm you, but last night your father's God spoke to me and said, 'Take
30 care not to say anything to Yaakov for good or for bad.' I realize you left because
you longed so much for your father's house. But why did you steal my gods?"
31 Yaakov answered Lavan, saying, "I was afraid; I thought you would take your
32 daughters away from me by force. But if you find your gods with anyone here,
they shall not live. In the presence of our kinsmen, see if there is anything of
yours here, and take it." Yaakov did not know that Raḥel was the one who had
33 stolen them. So Lavan went into Yaakov's tent, Leah's tent, and the tents of the
two female slaves, but found nothing. Leaving Leah's tent, he entered Raḥel's.

רש״י

כב **בַּיּוֹם הַשְּׁלִישִׁי.** שֶׁהֲרֵי דֶּרֶךְ שְׁלֹשֶׁת יָמִים הָיָה בֵּינֵיהֶם:

כג **אֶת אֶחָיו.** קְרוֹבָיו: **דֶּרֶךְ שִׁבְעַת יָמִים.** כָּל אוֹתָן שְׁלֹשָׁה יָמִים שֶׁהָלַךְ הַמַּגִּיד לְהַגִּיד לְלָבָן הָלַךְ יַעֲקֹב לְדַרְכּוֹ, נִמְצָא יַעֲקֹב רָחוֹק מִלָּבָן שִׁשָּׁה יָמִים, וּבַשְּׁבִיעִי הִשִּׂיגוֹ לָבָן. לָמַדְנוּ שֶׁכָּל מַה שֶּׁהָלַךְ יַעֲקֹב בְּשִׁבְעָה יָמִים הָלַךְ לָבָן בְּיוֹם אֶחָד:

כד **מִטּוֹב עַד רָע.** כָּל טוֹבָתָן שֶׁל רְשָׁעִים רָעָה הִיא אֵצֶל הַצַּדִּיקִים:

כו **כִּשְׁבֻיוֹת חָרֶב.** כָּל חַיִל הַבָּא לַמִּלְחָמָה קָרוּי חֶרֶב:

כז **וַתִּגְנֹב אֹתִי.** גָּנַבְתָּ אֶת דַּעְתִּי:

כט **יֶשׁ לְאֵל יָדִי.** יֵשׁ לְחַיִל וּלְכֹחַ יָדִי "לַעֲשׂוֹת עִמָּכֶם רָע". וְכָל 'אֵל' שֶׁהוּא קֹדֶשׁ, עַל שֵׁם עִזּוּז וְרוֹב אוֹנִים הוּא:

ל **נִכְסַפְתָּה.** חָמַדְתָּ, וְהַרְבֵּה יֵשׁ בַּמִּקְרָא: "נִכְסְפָה וְגַם כָּלְתָה נַפְשִׁי" (תהלים פד, ג), "לְמַעֲשֵׂה יָדֶיךָ תִכְסֹף" (איוב יד, טו):

לא **כִּי יָרֵאתִי וְגוֹ׳.** הֵשִׁיבוֹ עַל רִאשׁוֹן רִאשׁוֹן, שֶׁאָמַר לוֹ: "וַתִּנְהַג אֶת בְּנֹתַי" וְגוֹ׳ (לעיל פסוק כו):

לב **לֹא יִחְיֶה.** וּמֵאוֹתָהּ קְלָלָה מֵתָה רָחֵל בַּדֶּרֶךְ: **מָה עִמָּדִי.** מִשֶּׁלְּךָ:

לג **בְּאֹהֶל יַעֲקֹב.** הוּא אֹהֶל רָחֵל שֶׁהָיָה יַעֲקֹב תָּדִיר אֶצְלָהּ, וְכֵן הוּא אוֹמֵר: "בְּנֵי רָחֵל אֵשֶׁת יַעֲקֹב" (להלן מו, יט), וּבְכֻלָּן לֹא נֶאֱמַר 'אֵשֶׁת יַעֲקֹב': **וַיָּבֹא בְּאֹהֶל רָחֵל.** כְּשֶׁיָּצָא מֵאֹהֶל לֵאָה חָזַר לוֹ לְאֹהֶל רָחֵל קֹדֶם שֶׁחִפֵּשׂ בְּאֹהֶל הָאֲמָהוֹת. וְכָל כָּךְ לָמָּה? לְפִי שֶׁהָיָה מַכִּיר בָּהּ שֶׁהִיא מְמַשְׁמֶשֶׁת:

כא הוּא׃ וַיִּבְרַח הוּא וְכָל־אֲשֶׁר־לוֹ וַיָּקָם וַיַּעֲבֹר אֶת־הַנָּהָר וַיָּשֶׂם אֶת־
כב כג פָּנָיו הַר הַגִּלְעָד׃ וַיֻּגַּד לְלָבָן בַּיּוֹם הַשְּׁלִישִׁי כִּי בָרַח יַעֲקֹב׃ וַיִּקַּח אֶת־
אֶחָיו עִמּוֹ וַיִּרְדֹּף אַחֲרָיו דֶּרֶךְ שִׁבְעַת יָמִים וַיַּדְבֵּק אֹתוֹ בְּהַר הַגִּלְעָד׃
כד וַיָּבֹא אֱלֹהִים אֶל־לָבָן הָאֲרַמִּי בַּחֲלֹם הַלָּיְלָה וַיֹּאמֶר לוֹ הִשָּׁמֶר לְךָ
כה פֶּן־תְּדַבֵּר עִם־יַעֲקֹב מִטּוֹב עַד־רָע׃ וַיַּשֵּׂג לָבָן אֶת־יַעֲקֹב וְיַעֲקֹב תָּקַע
כו אֶת־אָהֳלוֹ בָּהָר וְלָבָן תָּקַע אֶת־אֶחָיו בְּהַר הַגִּלְעָד׃ וַיֹּאמֶר לָבָן לְיַעֲקֹב
כז מֶה עָשִׂיתָ וַתִּגְנֹב אֶת־לְבָבִי וַתְּנַהֵג אֶת־בְּנֹתַי כִּשְׁבֻיוֹת חָרֶב׃ לָמָּה
נַחְבֵּאתָ לִבְרֹחַ וַתִּגְנֹב אֹתִי וְלֹא־הִגַּדְתָּ לִּי וָאֲשַׁלֵּחֲךָ בְּשִׂמְחָה וּבְשִׁרִים
כח בְּתֹף וּבְכִנּוֹר׃ וְלֹא נְטַשְׁתַּנִי לְנַשֵּׁק לְבָנַי וְלִבְנֹתָי עַתָּה הִסְכַּלְתָּ עֲשׂוֹ׃
כט יֶשׁ־לְאֵל יָדִי לַעֲשׂוֹת עִמָּכֶם רָע וֵאלֹהֵי אֲבִיכֶם אֶמֶשׁ ׀ אָמַר אֵלַי
ל לֵאמֹר הִשָּׁמֶר לְךָ מִדַּבֵּר עִם־יַעֲקֹב מִטּוֹב עַד־רָע׃ וְעַתָּה הָלֹךְ הָלַכְתָּ
לא כִּי־נִכְסֹף נִכְסַפְתָּה לְבֵית אָבִיךָ לָמָּה גָנַבְתָּ אֶת־אֱלֹהָי׃ וַיַּעַן יַעֲקֹב
לב וַיֹּאמֶר לְלָבָן כִּי יָרֵאתִי כִּי אָמַרְתִּי פֶּן־תִּגְזֹל אֶת־בְּנוֹתֶיךָ מֵעִמִּי׃ עִם
אֲשֶׁר תִּמְצָא אֶת־אֱלֹהֶיךָ לֹא יִחְיֶה נֶגֶד אַחֵינוּ הַכֶּר־לְךָ מָה עִמָּדִי
לג וְקַח־לָךְ וְלֹא־יָדַע יַעֲקֹב כִּי רָחֵל גְּנָבָתַם׃ וַיָּבֹא לָבָן בְּאֹהֶל יַעֲקֹב ׀
וּבְאֹהֶל לֵאָה וּבְאֹהֶל שְׁתֵּי הָאֲמָהֹת וְלֹא מָצָא וַיֵּצֵא מֵאֹהֶל לֵאָה וַיָּבֹא

אונקלוס

הוּא: כא וַאֲזַל הוּא וְכָל דִּלֵיהּ, וְקָם וַעֲבַר יָת פְּרָת, וְשַׁוִּי יָת אַפּוֹהִי לְטוּרָא דְּגִלְעָד: כב וְאִתְחַוַּא לְלָבָן בְּיוֹמָא תְּלִיתָאָה, אֲרֵי אֲזַל יַעֲקֹב: כג וּדְבַר יָת אֲחוֹהִי עִמֵּיהּ, וּרְדַף בָּתְרוֹהִי, מַהֲלַךְ שִׁבְעָא יוֹמִין, וְאַדְבֵּיק יָתֵיהּ בְּטוּרָא דְּגִלְעָד: כד וַאֲתָא מֵימַר מִן קֳדָם יְיָ, לְוָת לָבָן אֲרַמָּאָה בְּחֶלְמָא דְּלֵילְיָא, וַאֲמַר לֵיהּ, אִסְתְּמַר לָךְ, דִּלְמָא תְּמַלֵּיל עִם יַעֲקֹב מִטָּב עַד בִּישׁ: כה וְאַדְבֵּיק לָבָן יָת יַעֲקֹב, וְיַעֲקֹב, פְּרַס יָת מַשְׁכְּנֵיהּ בְּטוּרָא, וְלָבָן, אַשְׁרֵי יָת אֲחוֹהִי בְּטוּרָא דְּגִלְעָד: כו וַאֲמַר לָבָן לְיַעֲקֹב, מָא עֲבַדְתָּא, וְכַסִּיתָא מִנִּי, וְדַבַּרְתְּ יָת בְּנָתַי, כִּשְׁבִיַּת חָרֶב: כז לְמָא אִטְמַרְתָּא לְמֵיזַל, וְכַסִּיתָא מִנִּי, וְלָא חַוִּיתָ לִי, וְשַׁלַּחְתָּךְ פּוֹן, בְּחֶדְוָא וּבְתֻשְׁבְּחָן בְּתֻפִּין וּבְכִנָּרִין: כח וְלָא שְׁבַקְתַּנִי, לְנַשָּׁקָא לִבְנַי וְלִבְנָתַי,

כְּעַן אַסְכֵּילְתָּא לְמֶעְבַּד: כט אִית חֵילָא בִידִי, לְמֶעְבַּד עִמְּכוֹן בִּישָׁא, וֵאלָהָא דַּאֲבוּכוֹן, בְּרַמְשָׁא אֲמַר לִי לְמֵימַר, אִסְתְּמַר לָךְ, מִלְּמַלָּלָא עִם יַעֲקֹב מִטָּב עַד בִּישׁ: ל וּכְעַן מֵיזַל אֲזַלְתָּא, אֲרֵי חֲמָדָא חֲמֵידְתָּא לְבֵית אֲבוּךְ, לְמָא נְסֵיבְתָּא יָת דַּחַלְתִּי: לא וַאֲתֵיב יַעֲקֹב וַאֲמַר לְלָבָן, אֲרֵי דְּחֵילִית, אֲרֵי אֲמָרִית, דִּלְמָא תֵּינוּס יָת בְּנָתָךְ מִנִּי: לב אֲתַר, דְּתַשְׁכַּח יָת דַּחַלְתָּךְ לָא יִתְקַיַּם, קֳדָם אַחֲנָא אִשְׁתְּמוֹדַע לָךְ, מָא דְעִמִּי וְסַב לָךְ, וְלָא יְדַע יַעֲקֹב, אֲרֵי רָחֵל נְסֵיבַתְנוּן: לג וְעָאל לָבָן, בְּמַשְׁכְּנָא דְיַעֲקֹב וּבְמַשְׁכְּנָא דְלֵאָה, וּבְמַשְׁכְּנָא, דְּתַרְתֵּין לְחֵינָתָא וְלָא אַשְׁכַּח, וּנְפַק מִמַּשְׁכְּנָא דְלֵאָה, וְעָאל

34 But Raḥel had taken the household gods and put them inside a camel cushion,
and was sitting on them; and Lavan rummaged through the tent but found
35 nothing. She said to her father, "Do not be angry, my lord, but I cannot get up
for you, for the way of women is with me now." So he searched but did not find
36 his household gods. Yaakov became indignant and confronted Lavan. "What is
my crime?" he asked Lavan. "What wrong did I do that you come chasing after
37 me? You have rummaged through all my possessions. What have you found
that belongs to your house? Put it here in front of my kinsmen and yours and
38 let them decide between the two of us! For the twenty years I was with you,
your sheep and goats did not miscarry. Not once did I take a ram from your
39 flock as food. I never brought you an animal torn by wild beasts. I bore the loss
myself. Whether it was stolen by day or by night you demanded payment from
40 me. By day I was ravaged by the heat; at night by the freezing cold. Sleep fled
41 from my eyes. Twenty years I spent working in your household – fourteen for
your two daughters and six for your flock – and ten times you changed my
42 wages. Had the God of my father – the God of Avraham, the Fear of Yitzḥak –
not been with me, you would have sent me away empty-handed. But God saw
43 my plight and the toil of my hands, and He rebuked you last night." Then Lavan SHEVI'I

רש״י

לד **בְּכַר הַגָּמָל.** לְשׁוֹן כָּרִים וּכְסָתוֹת, כְּתַרְגּוּמוֹ: ״בַּעֲבִיטָא דְגַמְלָא״, וְהִיא מַרְדַּעַת הָעֲשׂוּיָה כְּמִין כַּר. וּבְעֵרוּבִין שָׁנִינוּ: ״הִקִּיפוּהָ בַּעֲבִיטִין״ (דף טו ע״א), וְהֵן עֲבִיטֵי גְמַלִּים, בשטי״ל בְּלַעַז:

לו **דָלַקְתָּ.** רָדַפְתָּ, כְּמוֹ: ״עַל הֶהָרִים דְּלָקֻנוּ״ (איכה ד, יט), וּכְמוֹ: ״מִדְּלֹק אַחֲרֵי פְלִשְׁתִּים״ (שמואל א׳ יז, נג):

לז **וְיוֹכִיחוּ.** וִיבָרְרוּ עִם מִי הַדִּין, אפרוב״ר בְּלַעַז:

לח **לֹא שִׁכֵּלוּ.** לֹא הִפִּילוּ עִבּוּרָם, כְּמוֹ: ״רֶחֶם מַשְׁכִּיל״ (הושע ט, יד), ״תְּפַלֵּט פָּרָתוֹ וְלֹא תְשַׁכֵּל״ (איוב כא, י): **וְאֵילֵי צֹאנְךָ.** מִכָּאן אָמְרוּ: אַיִל בֶּן יוֹמוֹ קָרוּי אַיִל, שֶׁאִם לֹא כֵן מַה שִּׁבְחוֹ? אֵילִים לֹא אָכַל אֲבָל כְּבָשִׂים אָכַל – אִם כֵּן גַּזְלָן הוּא!:

לט **טְרֵפָה.** עַל יְדֵי אֲרִי וּזְאֵב: **אָנֹכִי אֲחַטֶּנָּה.** לָשׁוֹן: ״אֶל הַשַּׂעֲרָה וְלֹא יַחֲטִא״ (שופטים כ, טז), ״אֲנִי וּבְנִי שְׁלֹמֹה חַטָּאִים״ (מלכים א׳ א, כא) – חֲסֵרִים. אָנֹכִי אֲחַסְּרֶנָּה, אִם חָסְרָה חָסְרָה לִי, שֶׁ״מִיָּדִי תְּבַקְשֶׁנָּה״: **גְּנֻבְתִי יוֹם וּגְנֻבְתִי לָיְלָה.** גְּנוּבַת יוֹם אוֹ גְּנוּבַת לַיְלָה, הַכֹּל שִׁלַּמְתִּי: **גְּנֻבְתִי.** כְּמוֹ: ״רַבָּתִי בַגּוֹיִם שָׂרָתִי בַּמְּדִינוֹת״ (איכה א, א), ״מְלֵאֲתִי מִשְׁפָּט״ (ישעיה א, כא), ״אֹהַבְתִּי לָדוּשׁ״ (הושע י, יא):

מ **אֲכָלַנִי חֹרֶב.** לָשׁוֹן ״אֵשׁ אֹכְלָה״ (דברים ד, כד): **וְקֶרַח.** כְּמוֹ: ״מַשְׁלִיךְ קַרְחוֹ״ (תהלים קמז, יז), תַּרְגּוּמוֹ: ״גְּלִידָא״: **שְׁנָתִי.** לְשׁוֹן שֵׁנָה:

מא **וַתַּחֲלֵף אֶת מַשְׂכֻּרְתִּי.** הָיִיתָ מְשַׁנֶּה תְּנַאי שֶׁבֵּינֵינוּ, מִנָּקֹד לְטָלוּא, לַעֲקֻדִּים, לִבְרֻדִּים:

מב **וּפַחַד יִצְחָק.** לֹא רָצָה לוֹמַר ׳אֱלֹהֵי יִצְחָק׳, שֶׁאֵין הַקָּדוֹשׁ בָּרוּךְ הוּא מְיַחֵד שְׁמוֹ עַל הַצַּדִּיקִים בְּחַיֵּיהֶם, וְאַף עַל פִּי שֶׁאָמַר לוֹ בְּצֵאתוֹ מִבְּאֵר שֶׁבַע: ״אֲנִי ה׳ אֱלֹהֵי אַבְרָהָם אָבִיךָ וֵאלֹהֵי יִצְחָק״ (לעיל כח, יג) בִּשְׁבִיל שֶׁכָּהוּ עֵינָיו וַהֲרֵי הוּא כְּמֵת, יַעֲקֹב נִתְיָרֵא לוֹמַר: **וַיּוֹכַח.** לְשׁוֹן תּוֹכָחָה הוּא וְלֹא לְשׁוֹן הוֹכָחָה:

falter at certain moments. But the legacy of Yaakov is always with us.

Yaakov becomes the father of the people who will have their closest encounter with God in what Moshe is later to describe as "a barren, howling waste" (Deut. 32:10). Uniquely, Jews have survived a whole series of exiles, and though at first they said, "How can we sing the LORD's song on foreign soil?" (Ps. 137:4) they discovered that the *Shekhina*, the Divine Presence, was still with them. Though they had lost everything else, they had not lost contact with God.

לד בְּאֹהֶל רָחֵל: וְרָחֵל לָקְחָה אֶת־הַתְּרָפִים וַתְּשִׂמֵם בְּכַר הַגָּמָל וַתֵּשֶׁב
לה עֲלֵיהֶם וַיְמַשֵּׁשׁ לָבָן אֶת־כָּל־הָאֹהֶל וְלֹא מָצָא: וַתֹּאמֶר אֶל־אָבִיהָ
אַל־יִחַר בְּעֵינֵי אֲדֹנִי כִּי לוֹא אוּכַל לָקוּם מִפָּנֶיךָ כִּי־דֶרֶךְ נָשִׁים לִי
לו וַיְחַפֵּשׂ וְלֹא מָצָא אֶת־הַתְּרָפִים: וַיִּחַר לְיַעֲקֹב וַיָּרֶב בְּלָבָן וַיַּעַן יַעֲקֹב
לז וַיֹּאמֶר לְלָבָן מַה־פִּשְׁעִי מַה חַטָּאתִי כִּי דָלַקְתָּ אַחֲרָי: כִּי־מִשַּׁשְׁתָּ
אֶת־כָּל־כֵּלַי מַה־מָּצָאתָ מִכֹּל כְּלֵי־בֵיתֶךָ שִׂים כֹּה נֶגֶד אַחַי וְאַחֶיךָ
לח וְיוֹכִיחוּ בֵּין שְׁנֵינוּ: זֶה עֶשְׂרִים שָׁנָה אָנֹכִי עִמָּךְ רְחֵלֶיךָ וְעִזֶּיךָ לֹא שִׁכֵּלוּ
לט וְאֵילֵי צֹאנְךָ לֹא אָכָלְתִּי: טְרֵפָה לֹא־הֵבֵאתִי אֵלֶיךָ אָנֹכִי אֲחַטֶּנָּה מִיָּדִי
מ תְּבַקְשֶׁנָּה גְּנֻבְתִי יוֹם וּגְנֻבְתִי לָיְלָה: הָיִיתִי בַיּוֹם אֲכָלַנִי חֹרֶב וְקֶרַח
מא בַּלָּיְלָה וַתִּדַּד שְׁנָתִי מֵעֵינָי: זֶה־לִּי עֶשְׂרִים שָׁנָה בְּבֵיתֶךָ עֲבַדְתִּיךָ
אַרְבַּע־עֶשְׂרֵה שָׁנָה בִּשְׁתֵּי בְנֹתֶיךָ וְשֵׁשׁ שָׁנִים בְּצֹאנֶךָ וַתַּחֲלֵף אֶת־
מב מַשְׂכֻּרְתִּי עֲשֶׂרֶת מֹנִים: לוּלֵי אֱלֹהֵי אָבִי אֱלֹהֵי אַבְרָהָם וּפַחַד יִצְחָק
הָיָה לִי כִּי עַתָּה רֵיקָם שִׁלַּחְתָּנִי אֶת־עָנְיִי וְאֶת־יְגִיעַ כַּפַּי רָאָה אֱלֹהִים
מג וַיּוֹכַח אָמֶשׁ: וַיַּעַן לָבָן וַיֹּאמֶר אֶל־יַעֲקֹב הַבָּנוֹת בְּנֹתַי וְהַבָּנִים בָּנַי שביעי

אונקלוס

בְּמַשְׁכְּנָא דְרָחֵל: לד וְרָחֵל נְסִיבַת יָת צַלְמָנַיָּא, וְשַׁוִּיאַתְנוּן, בַּעֲבִיטָא דְגַמְלָא וִיתֵיבַת עֲלֵיהוֹן, וּמַשֵּׁישׁ לָבָן, יָת כָּל מַשְׁכְּנָא וְלָא אַשְׁכַּח: לה וַאֲמַרַת לַאֲבוּהָא, לָא יִתְקַף בְּעֵינֵי רִבּוֹנִי, אֲרֵי לָא אִכּוֹל לִמְקָם מִן קֳדָמָךְ, אֲרֵי אוֹרַח נְשִׁין לִי, וּבְלַשׁ, וְלָא אַשְׁכַּח יָת צַלְמָנַיָּא: לו וּתְקֵיף לְיַעֲקֹב וּנְצָא עִם לָבָן, וַאֲתֵיב יַעֲקֹב וַאֲמַר לְלָבָן, מָא חוֹבִי מָא סָרְחָנִי, אֲרֵי רְדַפְתָּא בָּתְרָי: לז אֲרֵי מַשֵּׁישְׁתָּא יָת כָּל מָנַי, מָא אַשְׁכַּחְתָּא מִכֹּל מָנֵי בֵיתָךְ, שַׁוִּי הָכָא, קֳדָם אַחַי וַאֲחָךְ, וְיוֹכְחוּן בֵּין תַּרְוַנָא: לח דְּנַן עַסְרִין שְׁנִין אֲנָא עִמָּךְ, רַחְלָךְ וְעִזָּךְ לָא אַתְכִּילוּ, וּדְכְרֵי עָנָךְ לָא אֲכָלִית: לט דִּתְבִירָא לָא אַיְתֵיתִי לָךְ, דַּהֲוָת שָׁגְיָא מִמִּנְיָנָא מִנִּי אַתְּ בָּעֵי לַהּ, נַטְרִית בִּימָמָא, וּנְטָרִית בְּלֵילְיָא: מ הֲוֵיתִי בִּימָמָא, אֲכַלַנִי שַׁרְבָא וּגְלִידָא נְחַת עֲלַי בְּלֵילְיָא, וְנַדַּת שֵׁינְתִי מֵעֵינָי: מא דְּנַן לִי, עַסְרִין שְׁנִין בְּבֵיתָךְ, פְּלַחְתָּךְ, אַרְבַּע עַסְרֵי שְׁנִין בְּתַרְתֵּין בְּנָתָךְ, וְשִׁית שְׁנִין בְּעָנָךְ, וְאַשְׁנֵיתָא יָת אַגְרִי עֲסַר זִמְנִין: מב אִלּוּ לָא פוֹן, אֱלָהֵיהּ דְּאַבָּא אֱלָהֵיהּ דְּאַבְרָהָם, וּדְדָחֵיל לֵיהּ יִצְחָק הֲוָה בְּסַעְדִּי, אֲרֵי כְעַן רֵיקָן שַׁלַּחְתַּנִי, יָת עַמְלִי, וְיָת לֵיאוּת יְדַי, גְּלֵי קֳדָם יְיָ וְאוֹכַח בְּרַמְשָׁא: מג וַאֲתֵיב לָבָן וַאֲמַר לְיַעֲקֹב, בְּנָתָא בְּנָתַי, וּבְנַיָּא בְּנַי

31:42 לוּלֵי אֱלֹהֵי אָבִי... הָיָה לִי *Had the God of my father... not been with me* – Yaakov is not what Noaḥ was: "righteous... a person of integrity in his generation," one who "walked with God" (Gen. 6:9). He does not, like Avraham, leave his land, his birthplace, and his father's house in response to a divine call. He does not, like Yitzḥak, offer himself up as a sacrifice. Nor does he have the burning sense of justice and willingness to intervene that we see in the vignettes of Moshe's early life. Yet we are defined for all time as the descendants of Yaakov, the children of Israel. Faith and courage may

spoke up and said to Yaakov, "The daughters are my daughters. The children
are my children. The flocks are my flocks. All that you see is mine. But what can
44 I do now about my daughters or the children they have borne? Come now, let
45 us make a covenant, you and I, and let it be a witness between us." So Yaakov
46 took a stone and set it up as a pillar. Yaakov said to his kinsmen, "Gather stones."
47 They took stones and made a mound, and there by the mound they ate. Lavan
48 called it Yegar Sahaduta, while Yaakov called it Galed. Lavan said, "This mound
49 is a witness between me and you this day." That is why it is called Galed. It is
also called Mitzpa because he said, "May the Lord keep watch between me
50 and you when we are out of each other's sight. If you mistreat my daughters or
take other wives besides my daughters, even though no one else is present,
51 remember that God is the witness between me and you." Lavan said to Yaakov,
52 "Here is the mound and here is the pillar I have set up between us. This mound
is a witness, and the pillar is a witness, that I will not go past this mound on
your side and that you will not go past this mound and pillar on my side with
53 intent to do harm. May the God of Avraham, the god of Naḥor, and the god of

רש״י

מג **מָה אֶעֱשֶׂה לָאֵלֶּה.** אֵיךְ תַּעֲלֶה עַל לִבִּי לְהָרַע לָהֶן?:

מד **וְהָיָה לְעֵד.** הַקָּדוֹשׁ בָּרוּךְ הוּא:

מו **לְאֶחָיו.** הֵם בָּנָיו, שֶׁהָיוּ לוֹ אַחִים נִגָּשִׁים לְצָרָה וּלְמִלְחָמָה עָלָיו:

מז-מח **יְגַר.** תַּרְגּוּם שֶׁל גַּל: **גַּלְעֵד.** גַּל עֵד:

מט **וְהַמִּצְפָּה אֲשֶׁר אָמַר וְגוֹ׳.** וְהַמִּצְפָּה אֲשֶׁר בְּהַר הַגִּלְעָד, כְּמוֹ שֶׁכָּתוּב: "וַיַּעֲבֹר אֶת מִצְפֵּה גִלְעָד" (שופטים יא, כט), וְלָמָּה נִקְרֵאת שְׁמָהּ 'מִצְפָּה'? לְפִי שֶׁאָמַר כָּל אֶחָד מֵהֶם לַחֲבֵרוֹ: "יִצֶף ה׳ בֵּינִי וּבֵינֶךָ" אִם תַּעֲבֹר אֶת הַבְּרִית: **כִּי נִסָּתֵר.** וְלֹא נִרְאֶה אִישׁ אֶת רֵעֵהוּ:

נ **בְּנֹתַי... בְּנֹתַי.** שְׁתֵּי פְעָמִים, אַף בִּלְהָה וְזִלְפָּה בְּנוֹתָיו הָיוּ מִפִּילֶגֶשׁ: **אִם תְּעַנֶּה אֶת בְּנֹתַי.** לִמְנוֹעַ מֵהֶן עוֹנַת תַּשְׁמִישׁ:

נא **יָרִיתִי.** כְּמוֹ: "יָרָה בַיָּם" (שמות טו, ד), כָּזֶה שֶׁהוּא יוֹרֶה חֲנִית:

נב **אִם אָנִי.** הֲרֵי 'אִם' מְשַׁמֵּשׁ בִּלְשׁוֹן 'אֲשֶׁר', כְּמוֹ: "עַד אִם דִּבַּרְתִּי דְּבָרָי" (לעיל כד, לג): **לְרָעָה.** לְרָעָה אִי אַתָּה עוֹבֵר, אֲבָל אַתָּה עוֹבֵר לִפְרַקְמַטְיָא:

נג **אֱלֹהֵי אַבְרָהָם.** קֹדֶשׁ: **וֵאלֹהֵי נָחוֹר.** חֹל: **אֱלֹהֵי אֲבִיהֶם.** חֹל:

is the refusal to let large powers crush the few, the weak, the refugee. Yaakov refuses to define himself as a slave, someone else's property. He maintains his inner dignity and freedom. He contributes to other people's prosperity but he defeats every attempt to be exploited. Yaakov is the voice that says: I too am human. I too have rights. I too am free.

31:50 **רְאֵה אֱלֹהִים עֵד** *God is the witness* – The key word in biblical ethics is *brit*, or "covenant." In a covenant, parties come together to pledge themselves to a code of mutual loyalty and protection. Like a contract, a covenant is born in the recognition that no individual can achieve his or her ends in isolation. Because we are different, we each have strengths that others need, and weaknesses that others can remedy. Unlike a contract, however, a covenant is more than a narrow legal agreement bound by mutual interest. It involves a commitment to go beyond the letter of the law, and to sustain the relationship even at times when it seems to go against the interests of one of the parties. As Daniel Elazar puts it, "in its heart of hearts, a covenant is an agreement in which a higher moral force, traditionally God, is either a direct party to or guarantor of a particular relationship." Having cemented their peace agreement, Lavan invoking "the god of Naḥor," Yaakov "the Fear of Yitzḥak" (Gen. 31:53),

וְהַצֹּאן צֹאנִי וְכֹל אֲשֶׁר־אַתָּה רֹאֶה לִי־הוּא וְלִבְנֹתַי מָה־אֶעֱשֶׂה לָאֵלֶּה
מד הַיּוֹם אוֹ לִבְנֵיהֶן אֲשֶׁר יָלָדוּ: וְעַתָּה לְכָה נִכְרְתָה בְרִית אֲנִי וָאָתָּה
מה מו וְהָיָה לְעֵד בֵּינִי וּבֵינֶךָ: וַיִּקַּח יַעֲקֹב אָבֶן וַיְרִימֶהָ מַצֵּבָה: וַיֹּאמֶר יַעֲקֹב
לְאֶחָיו לִקְטוּ אֲבָנִים וַיִּקְחוּ אֲבָנִים וַיַּעֲשׂוּ־גָל וַיֹּאכְלוּ שָׁם עַל־הַגָּל:
מז מח וַיִּקְרָא־לוֹ לָבָן יְגַר שָׂהֲדוּתָא וְיַעֲקֹב קָרָא לוֹ גַּלְעֵד: וַיֹּאמֶר לָבָן הַגַּל
מט הַזֶּה עֵד בֵּינִי וּבֵינְךָ הַיּוֹם עַל־כֵּן קָרָא־שְׁמוֹ גַּלְעֵד: וְהַמִּצְפָּה אֲשֶׁר
נ אָמַר יִצֶף יהוה בֵּינִי וּבֵינֶךָ כִּי נִסָּתֵר אִישׁ מֵרֵעֵהוּ: אִם־תְּעַנֶּה אֶת־
בְּנֹתַי וְאִם־תִּקַּח נָשִׁים עַל־בְּנֹתַי אֵין אִישׁ עִמָּנוּ רְאֵה אֱלֹהִים עֵד
נא בֵּינִי וּבֵינֶךָ: וַיֹּאמֶר לָבָן לְיַעֲקֹב הִנֵּה ׀ הַגַּל הַזֶּה וְהִנֵּה הַמַּצֵּבָה אֲשֶׁר
נב יָרִיתִי בֵּינִי וּבֵינֶךָ: עֵד הַגַּל הַזֶּה וְעֵדָה הַמַּצֵּבָה אִם־אָנִי לֹא־אֶעֱבֹר
אֵלֶיךָ אֶת־הַגַּל הַזֶּה וְאִם־אַתָּה לֹא־תַעֲבֹר אֵלַי אֶת־הַגַּל הַזֶּה וְאֶת־
נג הַמַּצֵּבָה הַזֹּאת לְרָעָה: אֱלֹהֵי אַבְרָהָם וֵאלֹהֵי נָחוֹר יִשְׁפְּטוּ בֵינֵינוּ

אונקלוס

וענא ענִי, וכל, דאת חזי דילי הוא, ולבנתי, מא אעביד לאלין יומא דין, או לבניהון דילידא: מד וכען, איתא, נגזר קים אנא ואת, ויהי לסהיד בינא ובינך: מה ונסיב יעקב אבנא, וזקפה קמא: מו ואמר יעקב לאחוהי לקוטו אבנין, ונסיבו אבנין ועבדו דגורא, ואכלו תמן על דגורא: מז וקרא ליה לבן, יגר שהדותא, ויעקב, קרא ליה גלעד: מח ואמר לבן, דגורא הדין סהיד, בינא ובינך יומא דין, על כן קרא שמיה גלעד: מט וסכותא דאמר, ייסך מימרא דיי בינא ובינך, ארי נתכסי גבר מחבריה: נ אם תעני ית בנתי, ואם תסב נשין על בנתי, לית אנש עמנא, חזי, מימרא דיי סהיד בינא ובינך: נא ואמר לבן ליעקב, הא דגורא הדין, והא קמתא, דאקימית בינא ובינך: נב סהיד דגורא הדין, וסהדא קמתא, אם אנא, לא אעבר לותך ית דגורא הדין, ואם את, לא תעבר לותי, ית דגורא הדין, וית קמתא הדא לבישו: נג אלהיה דאברהם, ואלהיה דנחור ידינון בינא,

They could still discover that "the Lord is in this place – and I did not know it!" (Gen. 28:16).

Avraham gave Jews the courage to challenge the idols of the age. Yitzḥak gave them the capacity for self-sacrifice. Moshe taught them to be passionate fighters for justice. But Yaakov gives them this: the knowledge that precisely when you feel most alone, God is still with you, giving you the courage to hope and the strength to dream.

31:43 וְכֹל אֲשֶׁר־אַתָּה רֹאֶה לִי הוּא *All that you see is mine* – It turns out that everything Lavan has ostensibly given Yaakov, in his own mind he has not given at all. Lavan treats Yaakov as his property, his slave. He is a non-person. In his eyes Yaakov has no rights, no independent existence. He has given Yaakov his daughters in marriage but still claims that they and their children belong to him, not Yaakov. He has given Yaakov an agreement as to the animals that will be his as his wages, yet still he insists that "the flocks are my flocks." Put this way, we begin to see Yaakov in a new light. Yaakov stands for minorities and small nations everywhere. Yaakov

54 their father be our judge." Yaakov swore by the Fear of his father Yitzḥak. He
offered a sacrifice on the hill and invited his kinsmen to break bread. And they
55 ate and spent the night upon that hill. Lavan rose early the next morning. He MAFTIR
kissed his grandchildren and daughters goodbye and blessed them. Lavan then
32 1 left to return home. Yaakov continued on his way – and angels of God
2 encountered him. When he saw them, Yaakov said, "This is God's own camp,"
and he named the place Maḥanayim.

The haftara for Parashat Vayetze is on page 1512.

רש״י

נד **וַיִּזְבַּח יַעֲקֹב זֶבַח.** שָׁחַט בְּהֵמוֹת לְמִשְׁתֶּה: **לְאֶחָיו.** לְאוֹהֲבָיו שֶׁעִם לָבָן: **לֶאֱכָל לָחֶם.** כָּל דְּבַר מַאֲכָל קָרוּי לֶחֶם, כְּמוֹ: ״עֲבַד לְחֶם רַב״ (דניאל ה, א), ״נַשְׁחִיתָה עֵץ בְּלַחְמוֹ״ (ירמיה יא, יט):

לב א **וַיִּפְגְּעוּ בוֹ מַלְאֲכֵי אֱלֹהִים.** מַלְאָכִים שֶׁל אֶרֶץ יִשְׂרָאֵל בָּאוּ לִקְרָאתוֹ לְלַוּוֹתוֹ לָאָרֶץ:

ב **מַחֲנָיִם.** שְׁתֵּי מַחֲנוֹת, שֶׁל חוּצָה לָאָרֶץ שֶׁבָּאוּ עִמּוֹ עַד כָּאן, וְשֶׁל אֶרֶץ יִשְׂרָאֵל שֶׁבָּאוּ לִקְרָאתוֹ:

32:2 וַיִּקְרָא שֵׁם־הַמָּקוֹם הַהוּא מַחֲנָיִם *He named the place Maḥanayim* – Literally, "Two camps," a phrase that will gain new resonances in the coming days (Gen. 32:7–8, 11). At the start of this *parasha*, we saw Yaakov fleeing from Esav and about to meet Lavan; now he is fleeing in the opposite direction, from Lavan to Esav, a meeting that fills him with dread (32:7). This journey, like Yaakov's first, contains an encounter with angels and a place of God; in both, the same verb appears: *vayifga* (28:11) – *vayifgeu* (32:2). Our verses here are recited, in some traditions, after *Tefillat HaDerekh*, the Traveler's Prayer.

From Yaakov we know we can find God not only in the holy or familiar places but also in the midst of a journey, alone at night. The most profound of all spiritual experiences, the base of all others, is the knowledge that, even when we are far from all that is familiar, we are never alone.

נד אֱלֹהֵ֥י אֲבִיהֶ֑ם וַיִּשָּׁבַ֣ע יַעֲקֹ֔ב בְּפַ֖חַד אָבִ֥יו יִצְחָֽק׃ וַיִּזְבַּ֨ח יַעֲקֹ֥ב זֶ֨בַח֙
נה בָּהָ֔ר וַיִּקְרָ֥א לְאֶחָ֖יו לֶאֱכָל־לָ֑חֶם וַיֹּ֣אכְלוּ לֶ֔חֶם וַיָּלִ֖ינוּ בָּהָֽר׃ וַיַּשְׁכֵּ֨ם מפטיר
לָבָ֜ן בַּבֹּ֗קֶר וַיְנַשֵּׁ֛ק לְבָנָ֥יו וְלִבְנוֹתָ֖יו וַיְבָ֣רֶךְ אֶתְהֶ֑ם וַיֵּ֛לֶךְ וַיָּ֥שָׁב לָבָ֖ן
לב א ב לִמְקֹמֽוֹ׃ וְיַעֲקֹ֖ב הָלַ֣ךְ לְדַרְכּ֑וֹ וַיִּפְגְּעוּ־ב֖וֹ מַלְאֲכֵ֥י אֱלֹהִֽים׃ וַיֹּ֤אמֶר
יַעֲקֹב֙ כַּאֲשֶׁ֣ר רָאָ֔ם מַחֲנֵ֥ה אֱלֹהִ֖ים זֶ֑ה וַיִּקְרָ֛א שֵֽׁם־הַמָּק֥וֹם הַה֖וּא
מַחֲנָֽיִם׃

The הפטרה *for* פרשת ויצא *is on page 1513.*

אונקלוס

אֱלָהָא דַּאֲבוּהוֹן, וְקַיֵּים יַעֲקֹב, בִּדְדָחֵיל לֵיהּ אֲבוּהִי יִצְחָק: נד וּנְכַס יַעֲקֹב נִכְסְתָא בְּטוּרָא, וּקְרָא לַאֲחוֹהִי לְמֵיכַל לַחְמָא, וַאֲכַלוּ לַחְמָא, וּבָתוּ בְּטוּרָא: נה וְאַקְדֵּים לָבָן בְּצַפְרָא, וְנַשֵּׁיק לִבְנוֹהִי, וְלִבְנָתֵיהּ וּבָרֵיךְ יָתְהוֹן, וַאֲזַל, וְתָב לָבָן לְאַתְרֵיהּ: לב א וְיַעֲקֹב אֲזַל לְאוֹרְחֵיהּ, וְעָרַעוּ בֵיהּ מַלְאֲכַיָּא דַייָ: ב וַאֲמַר יַעֲקֹב כַּד חֲזָנוּן, מַשְׁרִי מִן קֳדָם יי דָּא, וּקְרָא, שְׁמֵיהּ דְּאַתְרָא הַהוּא מַחֲנָיִם:

Lavan is able to kiss his grandchildren, bless his daughters, before sending them on their way.

31:55 וַיְבָרֶךְ אֶתְהֶם *And blessed them* – The story ends, against all odds, with Lavan's blessing. If Lavan is the eternal paradigm of hatred of conspicuously successful minorities, then Yaakov is the eternal paradigm of the human capacity to survive the hatred of others. In this strange way Yaakov becomes the voice of hope in the conversation of humankind, the living proof that hate never wins the final victory; freedom does.

PARASHAT VAYISHLAḤ

32 3 Yaakov sent messengers ahead of him to his brother Esav in the land of Se'ir,
4 the country of Edom. He instructed them, "Say the following to my lord Esav:
'Your servant Yaakov says, "I have been staying with Lavan; until now I have
5 remained there. And I have acquired cattle, donkeys, sheep, and male and
female servants. I am sending this message to my lord to find favor in your
6 eyes."'" And when the messengers returned to Yaakov, they said, "We came to
your brother Esav. He is on his way to meet you, and with him, four hundred

רש״י

ג וַיִּשְׁלַח יַעֲקֹב מַלְאָכִים. מַלְאָכִים מַמָּשׁ: אַרְצָה שֵׂעִיר. לְאֶרֶץ שֵׂעִיר, כָּל תֵּבָה שֶׁצְּרִיכָה לָמֶ״ד בִּתְחִלָּתָהּ הִטִּיל לָהּ הֵ״א בְּסוֹפָהּ:

ד גַּרְתִּי. לֹא נַעֲשֵׂיתִי שַׂר וְחָשׁוּב אֶלָּא גֵּר, אֵינְךָ כְּדַאי לִשְׂנֹאתִי עַל בִּרְכוֹת אָבִיךָ, שֶׁאָמַר לִי ״הֱוֵה גְבִיר לְאַחֶיךָ״ (לעיל כז, כט) – לֹא נִתְקַיְּמָה בִּי. דָּבָר אַחֵר, ״גַּרְתִּי״ בְּגִימַטְרִיָּא תַּרְיַ״ג, כְּלוֹמַר, עִם לָבָן הָרָשָׁע גַּרְתִּי וְתַרְיַ״ג מִצְוֹת שָׁמַרְתִּי, וְלֹא לָמַדְתִּי מִמַּעֲשָׂיו הָרָעִים:

ה וַיְהִי לִי שׁוֹר וַחֲמוֹר. אַבָּא אָמַר לִי: ״מִטַּל הַשָּׁמַיִם וּמִשְׁמַנֵּי הָאָרֶץ״ (לעיל כז, כח); זוֹ אֵינָהּ לֹא מִן הַשָּׁמַיִם וְלֹא מִן הָאָרֶץ: שׁוֹר וַחֲמוֹר. דֶּרֶךְ אֶרֶץ לוֹמַר עַל שְׁוָרִים הַרְבֵּה ׳שׁוֹר׳; אָדָם אוֹמֵר לַחֲבֵרוֹ: בַּלַּיְלָה קָרָא הַתַּרְנְגוֹל, וְאֵינוֹ אוֹמֵר: קָרְאוּ הַתַּרְנְגוֹלִים: וָאֶשְׁלְחָה לְהַגִּיד לַאדֹנִי. לְהוֹדִיעַ שֶׁאֲנִי בָּא אֵלֶיךָ: לִמְצֹא חֵן בְּעֵינֶיךָ. שֶׁאֲנִי שָׁלֵם עִמְּךָ וּמְבַקֵּשׁ אַהֲבָתְךָ:

ו בָּאנוּ אֶל אָחִיךָ אֶל עֵשָׂו. שֶׁהָיִיתָ אוֹמֵר אָחִי הוּא, אֲבָל הוּא נוֹהֵג עִמְּךָ כְּעֵשָׂו, עוֹדֶנּוּ בְּשִׂנְאָתוֹ:

Yaakov is the paradigm of what the French literary theorist and anthropologist René Girard called *mimetic desire*, meaning, we want what someone else wants, because we want to *be* that someone else. Most of us have such feelings from time to time. Girard argues that this has been the main source of conflict throughout history. The tension between Yaakov and Esav rises to an unbearable intensity when Esav discovers that Yaakov has taken the blessing Yitzḥak has reserved for him, and vows to kill Yaakov when Yitzḥak is no longer alive.

Yaakov flees to Lavan, where he encounters more conflict; he is on his way home when he hears that Esav is coming to meet him. In an unusually strong description of emotion the Torah tells us that Yaakov is "acutely afraid and distressed" (32:7) – frightened, no doubt, that Esav will try to kill him, and perhaps distressed that his brother's animosity is not without cause.

As long as Yaakov seeks to be Esav there is tension, conflict, rivalry. Esav feels cheated; Yaakov feels fear. On this night, about to meet Esav again after an absence of twenty-two years, Yaakov, "left alone," wrestles with himself. Finally, he throws off the image of Esav, the person he wants to be, which he has carried with him all these years. This is the critical moment in Yaakov's life.

After his wrestling match, Yaakov undergoes a change of personality. He gives back to Esav the blessing he has taken from him. The previous day he has given him back the material blessing by sending him a wealth of livestock. Now he gives him back the blessing that said, "Be lord over your brothers, and may your mother's sons bow down to you" (27:29). He even uses the words "Please accept *my blessing*." The result is that the two brothers meet and part in peace.

Yaakov, more than anyone else in Genesis, is surrounded by conflict. We have to resolve the tension in ourselves before we can do so for others. This may involve great struggle, but the outcome is an immense strength. No one is stronger than the person who knows who and what he is.

פרשת וישלח

לב ג וַיִּשְׁלַח יַעֲקֹב מַלְאָכִים לְפָנָיו אֶל־עֵשָׂו אָחִיו אַרְצָה שֵׂעִיר שְׂדֵה אֱדוֹם׃ ל
ד וַיְצַו אֹתָם לֵאמֹר כֹּה תֹאמְרוּן לַאדֹנִי לְעֵשָׂו כֹּה אָמַר עַבְדְּךָ יַעֲקֹב
ה עִם־לָבָן גַּרְתִּי וָאֵחַר עַד־עָתָּה׃ וַיְהִי־לִי שׁוֹר וַחֲמוֹר צֹאן וְעֶבֶד וְשִׁפְחָה
ו וָאֶשְׁלְחָה לְהַגִּיד לַאדֹנִי לִמְצֹא־חֵן בְּעֵינֶיךָ׃ וַיָּשֻׁבוּ הַמַּלְאָכִים אֶל־
יַעֲקֹב לֵאמֹר בָּאנוּ אֶל־אָחִיךָ אֶל־עֵשָׂו וְגַם הֹלֵךְ לִקְרָאתְךָ וְאַרְבַּע־

אונקלוס

ג וּשְׁלַח יַעֲקֹב אִזגַּדִּין קֳדָמוֹהִי, לְוָת עֵשָׂו אֲחוּהִי, לַאֲרַע דְּשֵׂעִיר לְחַקְלֵי אֱדוֹם׃ ד וּפַקֵּיד יָתְהוֹן לְמֵימַר, כְּדֵין תֵּימְרוּן, לְרִבּוֹנִי לְעֵשָׂו, כִּדְנַן אֲמַר עַבְדָּךְ יַעֲקֹב, עִם לָבָן דָּרִית, וְאוֹחֲרִית עַד כְּעַן׃ ה וַהֲווֹ לִי תּוֹרִין וּחְמָרִין, עָן וְעַבְדִּין וְאַמְהָן, וּשְׁלַחִית לְחַוָּאָה לְרִבּוֹנִי, לְאַשְׁכָּחָא רַחֲמִין בְּעֵינָךְ׃ ו וְתָבוּ אִזגַּדַּיָּא, לְוָת יַעֲקֹב לְמֵימַר, אֲתֵינָא לְוָת אֲחוּךְ לְוָת עֵשָׂו, וְאַף אָתֵי לְקַדָּמוּתָךְ, וְאַרְבַּע

VAYISHLAḤ

Vayishlaḥ tells the story of the meeting, after an estrangement that lasted twenty-two years, between Yaakov and Esav. Hearing that his brother is coming to meet him with a force of four hundred men, Yaakov is "acutely afraid and distressed" (Gen. 32:7). That night he wrestles with a mysterious stranger, in an episode that ends with his being given a new name, Yisrael. The next day the two brothers meet, not in violence but in peace. They embrace and then go their separate ways.

Yaakov's safe return to the land is not to be a happy ending, however. Dina, Yaakov's daughter – the only Jewish daughter mentioned in the entire patriarchal narrative – leaves the safety of home to go out to "see the daughters of the land" (34:1). She is raped and abducted by a local prince, Shekhem. The aftermath of this event brings untold suffering and bloodshed, and an apparent end to Yaakov's chance of living peacefully with his neighbors.

Following the death of Yitzḥak, the *parasha* that gives Israel its name ends with a proud genealogy of the descendants of Esav. Yaakov does not emerge as the triumphant, dominant brother. His heroism lies in the image of him wrestling with the angel of destiny and inner conflict and saying, "I will not let you go until you bless me" (32:26). That is how he rescues hope from catastrophe – as Jews have always done. Our darkest nights have always been preludes to our most creative dawns.

YAAKOV FACES ESAV

Yaakov is about to meet his brother Esav after an estrangement of twenty-two years. In a way unparalleled anywhere else in Genesis, the narrative builds up suspense. Yaakov is afraid. He divides his camp into two, that at least one may survive. He prays. He sends emissaries with gifts. He takes his family and possessions across the river. He makes every possible preparation, takes every possible precaution. Yet still we sense his disquiet. It is then that one of the most haunting scenes in the Torah takes place.

To understand the mysterious episode of Yaakov's nocturnal struggle with the stranger, we must step back and observe Yaakov's life trajectory. Yaakov was born holding on to Esav's heel. He bought Esav's birthright. He stole Esav's blessing. When his blind father asked him who he was, he replied, "I am Esav your firstborn" (Gen. 27:19). Yaakov was the child who wanted to be Esav.

Esav was the elder. Esav was strong, physically mature, a hunter. Above all, Esav was his father's favorite (25:28).

7 men." Yaakov was acutely afraid and distressed. He divided the people with
8 him into two camps, along with the flocks, the cattle, and the camels. "If Esav
comes and attacks one camp," he thought, "the other camp may still survive."
9 Then Yaakov prayed, "God of my father Avraham and God of my father Yitzḥak,
Lord, You who said to me, 'Go back to the land where you were born and I will
10 deal well with you,' I am unworthy of all the kindnesses and the faithfulness
that You have bestowed upon Your servant. When I crossed the Jordan I had
11 only my staff, and now I have become two camps. Rescue me, I pray, from my
brother's hand, from the hand of Esav. I am afraid he will come and kill us all,
12 mothers and children alike. Yet You said, 'I will deal well with you and make
13 your descendants countless, like the sand of the sea.'" He spent the night there. SHENI
Then, from what he had at hand, he selected a gift for his brother Esav:

רש"י

ז **ויירא... ויצר.** "ויירא" שמא יהרג, "ויצר לו" אם יהרג הוא את אחרים:

ח **המחנה האחת והכהו.** 'מחנה' משמש לשון זכר ולשון נקבה, "אם תחנה עלי מחנה" (תהלים כז, ג) הרי נקבה, "המחנה הזה" (להלן לג, ח) הרי זכר. וכן יש אחר דברים משמשים לשון זכר ולשון נקבה: "השמש יצא על הארץ" (לעיל יט, כג), "מקצה השמים מוצאו" (תהלים יט, ז) הרי זכר, "והשמש זרחה על המים" (מלכים ב' ג, כב) הרי נקבה; וכן רוח, "והנה רוח גדולה באה" (איוב א, יט) הרי נקבה, "ויגע בארבע פנות הבית" (שם) הרי זכר, "ורוח גדולה וחזק מפרק הרים" (מלכים א' יט, יא) הרי זכר ונקבה: **והיה המחנה הנשאר לפליטה.** על כרחו, כי אלחם עמו. התקין עצמו לשלשה דברים: לדורון לתפלה ולמלחמה. לדורון, "ותעבר המנחה על פניו" (להלן פסוק כב). לתפלה, "אלהי אבי אברהם" (להלן פסוק ט). למלחמה, "והיה המחנה הנשאר לפליטה":

ט **ואלהי אבי יצחק.** ולהלן הוא אומר: "ופחד יצחק" (לעיל לא, מב)! ועוד, מהו שחזר והזכיר שם המיחד? היה לו לכתב: 'האומר אלי שוב לארצך' וגו'! אלא כך אמר יעקב לפני הקדוש ברוך הוא: שתי הבטחות הבטחתני, אחת בצאתי מבית אבא אמרת לי: "אני ה' אלהי אברהם אביך ואלהי יצחק" (לעיל כח, יג), ושם אמרת לי: "ושמרתיך בכל אשר תלך" (שם טו); ובבית לבן אמרת לי: "שוב אל ארץ אבותיך ולמולדתך ואהיה עמך" (לעיל לא, ג), ושם נגלית אלי בשם המיחד לבדו, שנאמר: "ויאמר ה' אל יעקב שוב אל ארץ אבותיך" וגו' – בשתי הבטחות הללו אני בא לפניך:

י **קטנתי מכל החסדים.** נתמעטו זכיותי על ידי החסדים והאמת שעשית עמי, לכך אני ירא, שמא משהבטחתני נתלכלכתי בחטא ויגרם לי להמסר ביד עשו: **ומכל האמת.** אמתת דבריך ששמרת לי כל ההבטחות שהבטחתני: **כי במקלי.** לא היה עמי לא כסף ולא זהב ולא מקנה אלא מקלי לבדו. ומדרש אגדה, נתן מקלו בירדן ונבקע הירדן:

יא **מיד אחי מיד עשו.** מיד אחי שאין נוהג עמי כאח אלא כעשו הרשע:

יב **היטב איטיב.** "היטב" בזכותך, "איטיב" בזכות אבותיך: **ושמתי את זרעך כחול הים.** והיכן אמר לו כן? והלא לא אמר לו אלא "והיה זרעך כעפר הארץ" (לעיל כח, יד)! אלא שאמר לו: "כי לא אעזבך עד אשר אם עשיתי את אשר דברתי לך" (שם פסוק טו), ולאברהם אמר: "והרבה ארבה את זרעך ככוכבי השמים וכחול אשר על שפת הים" (לעיל כב, יז):

יג **הבא בידו.** ברשותו, וכן "ויקח את כל ארצו מידו" (במדבר כא, כו). ומדרש אגדה, "מן הבא בידו", אבנים טובות ומרגליות שאדם צר בצרור ונושאם בידו:

lesser of two evils, or the greater of two goods – but this does not cancel out all emotional pain. These mixed feelings were born thousands of years ago, when Yaakov, father of the Jewish people, experienced not only the physical fear of defeat but the moral distress of victory. Only those who are capable of feeling both can defend their bodies without endangering their souls.

ז מֵאוֹת אִישׁ עִמּוֹ: וַיִּירָא יַעֲקֹב מְאֹד וַיֵּצֶר לוֹ וַיַּחַץ אֶת־הָעָם אֲשֶׁר־אִתּוֹ
ח וְאֶת־הַצֹּאן וְאֶת־הַבָּקָר וְהַגְּמַלִּים לִשְׁנֵי מַחֲנוֹת: וַיֹּאמֶר אִם־יָבוֹא
עֵשָׂו אֶל־הַמַּחֲנֶה הָאַחַת וְהִכָּהוּ וְהָיָה הַמַּחֲנֶה הַנִּשְׁאָר לִפְלֵיטָה:
ט וַיֹּאמֶר יַעֲקֹב אֱלֹהֵי אָבִי אַבְרָהָם וֵאלֹהֵי אָבִי יִצְחָק יהוה הָאֹמֵר אֵלַי
י שׁוּב לְאַרְצְךָ וּלְמוֹלַדְתְּךָ וְאֵיטִיבָה עִמָּךְ: קָטֹנְתִּי מִכֹּל הַחֲסָדִים
וּמִכָּל־הָאֱמֶת אֲשֶׁר עָשִׂיתָ אֶת־עַבְדֶּךָ כִּי בְמַקְלִי עָבַרְתִּי אֶת־הַיַּרְדֵּן
יא הַזֶּה וְעַתָּה הָיִיתִי לִשְׁנֵי מַחֲנוֹת: הַצִּילֵנִי נָא מִיַּד אָחִי מִיַּד עֵשָׂו
יב כִּי־יָרֵא אָנֹכִי אֹתוֹ פֶּן־יָבוֹא וְהִכַּנִי אֵם עַל־בָּנִים: וְאַתָּה אָמַרְתָּ
הֵיטֵב אֵיטִיב עִמָּךְ וְשַׂמְתִּי אֶת־זַרְעֲךָ כְּחוֹל הַיָּם אֲשֶׁר לֹא־יִסָּפֵר
יג מֵרֹב: וַיָּלֶן שָׁם בַּלַּיְלָה הַהוּא וַיִּקַּח מִן־הַבָּא בְיָדוֹ מִנְחָה לְעֵשָׂו אָחִיו: שני

אונקלוס

מְאָה גֻּבְרָא עִמֵּיהּ: ז וּדְחֵיל יַעֲקֹב, לַחְדָּא וְעָקַת לֵיהּ, וּפַלֵּיג יָת עַמָּא דְּעִמֵּיהּ, וְיָת עָנָא וְיָת תּוֹרֵי, וְגַמְלַיָּא לְתַרְתֵּין מַשְׁרְיָן: ח וַאֲמַר, אִם יֵיתֵי עֵשָׂו, לְמַשְׁרִיתָא חֲדָא וְיִמְחֵינַהּ, וּתְהֵי, מַשְׁרִיתָא דְּתִשְׁתְּאַר לְשֵׁיזָבָא: ט וַאֲמַר יַעֲקֹב, אֱלָהֵיהּ דְּאַבָּא אַבְרָהָם, וֵאלָהֵיהּ דְּאַבָּא יִצְחָק, יי דַּאֲמַר לִי, תּוּב לְאַרְעָךְ, וּלְיַלָּדוּתָךְ וְאוֹטֵיב עִמָּךְ: י זְעֵירָן זָכְוָתִי, מִכֹּל חִסְדִּין וּמִכָּל טָבְוָן, דַּעֲבַדְתְּ עִם עַבְדָּךְ, אֲרֵי יְחִידַאי, עֲבָרִית יָת יַרְדְּנָא הָדֵין, וּכְעַן הֲוֵיתִי לְתַרְתֵּין מַשְׁרְיָן: יא שֵׁיזֵיבְנִי כְעַן, מִיְּדָא דַּאֲחִי מִיְּדָא דְּעֵשָׂו, אֲרֵי דָּחֵיל אֲנָא מִנֵּיהּ, דִּלְמָא יֵיתֵי וְיִמְחֵינַנִי, אִמָּא עַל בְּנַיָּא: יב וְאַתְּ אֲמַרְתְּ, אוֹטָבָא אוֹטֵיב עִמָּךְ, וַאֲשַׁוֵּי יָת בְּנָךְ סַגִּיאִין כְּחָלָא דְיַמָּא, דְּלָא יִתְמְנוֹן מִסְּגֵי: יג וּבָת תַּמָּן בְּלֵילְיָא הַהוּא, וּנְסֵיב, מִן דְּאַיְתִי בִידֵיהּ, תִּקְרֻבְתָּא לְעֵשָׂו אֲחוּהִי:

32:7 וַיִּירָא יַעֲקֹב מְאֹד וַיֵּצֶר לוֹ *Yaakov was acutely afraid and distressed* – Why the duplication? What is the difference between fear and distress? According to Rashi (quoting Bereshit Rabba 76:2), the first is a physical anxiety, the second a moral one. It is one thing to fear one's own death, quite another to contemplate being the cause of someone else's. If Esav were to try to kill Yaakov, he would be justified in fighting back, if necessary at the cost of Esav's life. Yet Yaakov is distressed at the possibility of being forced to kill *even if it is entirely justified*.

What we are encountering here is the concept of a moral dilemma. This phrase is often used imprecisely, to mean a moral problem, a difficult ethical decision. In numerous situations, two duties conflict and we have meta-halakhic principles to tell us which takes priority. There is always a decision-procedure and thus a determinate answer to the question "What should I do?"

But a dilemma is not simply a conflict. It arises in cases of conflict between right and right, or between wrong and wrong. The fact that one principle (self-defense) overrides another (the prohibition against killing) does not mean that, faced with such a choice, Yaakov is without qualms. Sometimes being moral means that one experiences distress at having to make such a choice. Doing the right thing may mean that one does not feel remorse or guilt, but one still feels regret or grief about the action that needs to be taken.

A moral system which leaves room for the existence of dilemmas is one that does not attempt to eliminate the complexities of the moral life. In a conflict between two rights or two wrongs, there may be a proper way to act – the

14 two hundred female goats, twenty male goats, two hundred ewes, twenty rams,
15 thirty milk camels and their young, forty cows, ten bulls, twenty female
16 donkeys, and ten male donkeys. He put them in the care of his servants, each
herd by itself, and he told the servants, "Go on ahead of me. Keep a space
17 between the herds." He instructed the first, "When my brother Esav meets you
and asks, 'To whom do you belong? Where are you going? Who owns all these
18 animals ahead of you?' you must say, 'They belong to your servant Yaakov; they
19 are a gift sent to my lord Esav – and he is coming behind us.'" He likewise
instructed the second and third and all the others who followed the herds,
20 "You shall say the same thing to Esav when you meet him. Also say, 'Your
servant Yaakov is coming behind us.'" He thought, "I will pacify him with these
gifts I am sending on ahead. Then I will face him. Perhaps he will accept me."
21 So the gifts went on ahead of him, while he remained in the camp that night.
22 That night Yaakov got up and took his two wives, two maidservants, and eleven
23 sons and crossed the ford of the Yabok. He took them and crossed the stream
24 with them and then brought across all that he had. And Yaakov was left alone.

רש״י

יד **עזים מאתים ותישים עשרים.** מאתים עזים צריכות עשרים תישים, וכן כלם הזכרים כדי צרך הנקבות. ובבראשית רבה (עו, ז) דורש מכאן לעונה האמורה בתורה, הטילים בכל יום, הפועלים שתים בשבת, החמרים אחת בשבת, הגמלים אחת לשלשים יום, הספנים אחת לששה חדשים. ואיני יודע לכון המדרש הזה בכוון, אך נראה בעיני שלמדנו מכאן שאין העונה שוה בכל אדם אלא לפי טרח המטל עליו, שמצינו כאן שמסר לכל תיש עשר עזים, וכן לכל איל, לפי שהם פנויים ממלאכה דרכן להרבות תשמיש ולעבר עשר נקבות, ובהמה משנתעברה אינה מקבלת זכר; ופרים שעוסקין במלאכה לא מסר לזכר אלא ארבע נקבות; ולחמור שהולך בדרך רחוקה – שתי נקבות לזכר; ולגמלים שהולכים דרך יותר רחוקה – נקבה אחת לזכר:

טו **גמלים מיניקות... שלשים.** ובניהם עמהם. ומדרש אגדה, "ובניהם", בנאיהם, זכר כנגד נקבה, ולפי שצנוע בתשמיש לא פרסמו הכתוב: **ועירם.** חמורים זכרים:

טז **עדר עדר לבדו.** כל מין ומין לעצמו: **עברו לפני.** דרך יום או פחות, ואני אבוא אחריכם: **ורוח תשימו.** עדר לפני חברו מלא עין, כדי להשביע עינו של רשע ולתמהו על רבוי הדורון:

יז **למי אתה.** של מי אתה? מי שולחך? ותרגומו: "דמאן את": **ולמי אלה.** למי המנחה הזאת שלוחה? למ״ד משמשת בראש התבה במקום 'של', כמו: "וכל אשר אתה ראה לי הוא" (לעיל לא, מג), שלי הוא, "לה' הארץ ומלואה" (תהלים כד, א), של ה':

יח **ואמרת לעבדך ליעקב.** על ראשון ראשון ועל אחרון אחרון. ששאלת "למי אתה" – "לעבדך ליעקב" אני, ותרגומו: "דעבדך דיעקב". וששאלת "ולמי אלה לפניך" – "מנחה היא שלוחה" וגו': **והנה גם הוא.** יעקב:

כ **אכפרה פניו.** אבטל רגזו, וכן: "וכפר בריתכם את מות" (ישעיה כח, יח), "לא תוכלי כפרה" (שם מז, יא). ונראה בעיני שכל כפרה שאצל עון וחטא ואצל פנים, כלן לשון קנוח והעברה הן, ולשון ארמי הוא, והרבה בתלמוד: "וכפר ידיה" (בבא מציעא כד ע״א) "בעי לכפורי ידיה בההוא גברא" (גיטין נו ע״א). וגם בלשון המקרא נקראים המזרקים של קדש "כפורי זהב" (עזרא א, י), על שם שהכהן מקנח ידיו בהן בשפת המזרק:

כא **על פניו.** כמו לפניו, וכן: "חמס ושד ישמע בה על פני תמיד" (ירמיה ו, ז), וכן: "המכעסים אתי על פני" (ישעיה סה, ג). ומדרש אגדה, "על פניו", אף הוא שרוי בכעס שהיה צריך לכל זה:

כב **ואת אחד עשר ילדיו.** ודינה היכן היתה? נתנה בתבה ונעל בפניה, שלא יתן בה עשו עיניו, ולכך נענש יעקב שמנעה מאחיו, שמא תחזירנו למוטב, ונפלה ביד שכם: **יבק.** שם הנהר:

כג **את אשר לו.** הבהמה והמטלטלים, עשה עצמו כגשר, נוטל מכאן ומניח כאן:

כד **ויותר יעקב.** שכח פכים קטנים וחזר עליהם: **ויאבק איש.** מנחם פרש, ויתעפר איש, לשון אבק שהיו מעלים עפר ברגליהם על ידי

יד טו עִזִּים מָאתַיִם וּתְיָשִׁים עֶשְׂרִים רְחֵלִים מָאתַיִם וְאֵילִים עֶשְׂרִים: גְּמַלִּים
מֵינִיקוֹת וּבְנֵיהֶם שְׁלֹשִׁים פָּרוֹת אַרְבָּעִים וּפָרִים עֲשָׂרָה אֲתֹנֹת עֶשְׂרִים
טז וַעְיָרִם עֲשָׂרָה: וַיִּתֵּן בְּיַד־עֲבָדָיו עֵדֶר עֵדֶר לְבַדּוֹ וַיֹּאמֶר אֶל־עֲבָדָיו
יז עִבְרוּ לְפָנַי וְרֶוַח תָּשִׂימוּ בֵּין עֵדֶר וּבֵין עֵדֶר: וַיְצַו אֶת־הָרִאשׁוֹן לֵאמֹר
כִּי יִפְגָּשְׁךָ עֵשָׂו אָחִי וּשְׁאֵלְךָ לֵאמֹר לְמִי־אַתָּה וְאָנָה תֵלֵךְ וּלְמִי אֵלֶּה
יח לְפָנֶיךָ: וְאָמַרְתָּ לְעַבְדְּךָ לְיַעֲקֹב מִנְחָה הִוא שְׁלוּחָה לַאדֹנִי לְעֵשָׂו
יט וְהִנֵּה גַם־הוּא אַחֲרֵינוּ: וַיְצַו גַּם אֶת־הַשֵּׁנִי גַּם אֶת־הַשְּׁלִישִׁי גַּם אֶת־
כָּל־הַהֹלְכִים אַחֲרֵי הָעֲדָרִים לֵאמֹר כַּדָּבָר הַזֶּה תְּדַבְּרוּן אֶל־עֵשָׂו
כ בְּמֹצַאֲכֶם אֹתוֹ: וַאֲמַרְתֶּם גַּם הִנֵּה עַבְדְּךָ יַעֲקֹב אַחֲרֵינוּ כִּי־אָמַר
אֲכַפְּרָה פָנָיו בַּמִּנְחָה הַהֹלֶכֶת לְפָנָי וְאַחֲרֵי־כֵן אֶרְאֶה פָנָיו אוּלַי יִשָּׂא
כא כב פָנָי: וַתַּעֲבֹר הַמִּנְחָה עַל־פָּנָיו וְהוּא לָן בַּלַּיְלָה־הַהוּא בַּמַּחֲנֶה: וַיָּקָם ׀
בַּלַּיְלָה הוּא וַיִּקַּח אֶת־שְׁתֵּי נָשָׁיו וְאֶת־שְׁתֵּי שִׁפְחֹתָיו וְאֶת־אַחַד עָשָׂר
כג יְלָדָיו וַיַּעֲבֹר אֵת מַעֲבַר יַבֹּק: וַיִּקָּחֵם וַיַּעֲבִרֵם אֶת־הַנָּחַל וַיַּעֲבֵר אֶת־
כד אֲשֶׁר־לוֹ: וַיִּוָּתֵר יַעֲקֹב לְבַדּוֹ וַיֵּאָבֵק אִישׁ עִמּוֹ עַד עֲלוֹת הַשָּׁחַר:

אונקלוס

יד עִזֵּי מָאתַן, וְתֵישַׁיָּא עַסְרִין, רַחְלֵי מָאתַן וְדִכְרֵי עַסְרִין: טו גַּמְלֵי מֵינְקָתָא, וּבְנֵיהוֹן תְּלָתִין, תּוֹרָתָא אַרְבְּעִין וְתוֹרֵי עַסְרָא, אֲתָנָן עַסְרִין, וְעִלֵּי עַסְרָא: טז וִיהַב בְּיַד עַבְדּוֹהִי, עֶדְרָא עֶדְרָא בִּלְחוֹדוֹהִי, וַאֲמַר לְעַבְדּוֹהִי עִיבַרוּ קֳדָמַי, וּרְוָחָא תְּשַׁוּוֹן, בֵּין עֶדְרָא וּבֵין עֶדְרָא: יז וּפַקֵּיד יָת קַדְמָאָה לְמֵימַר, אֲרֵי יְעָרְעִנָּךְ עֵשָׂו אֲחִי, וִישַׁאֲלִנָּךְ לְמֵימַר, דְּמַאן אַתְּ וּלְאָן אַתְּ אָזֵיל, וּדְמַאן אִלֵּין דִּקְדָמָךְ: יח וְתֵימַר דְּעַבְדָּךְ דְּיַעֲקֹב, תִּקְרֻבְתָּא הִיא דִּמְשַׁלְחָא, לְרִבּוֹנִי לְעֵשָׂו, וְהָא אַף הוּא אָתֵי בָּתְרַנָא: יט וּפַקֵּיד אַף יָת תִּנְיָנָא, אַף יָת תְּלִיתָאָה, אַף יָת כָּל דְּאָזְלִין, בָּתַר עֶדְרַיָּא לְמֵימַר, כְּפִתְגָּמָא הָדֵין תְּמַלְּלוּן עִם עֵשָׂו, כַּד תַּשְׁכְּחוּן יָתֵיהּ: כ וְתֵימְרוּן, אַף, הָא, עַבְדָּךְ יַעֲקֹב אָתֵי בָּתְרַנָא, אֲרֵי אֲמַר אֲנִיחֵנֵּיהּ לְרֻגְזֵיהּ, בְּתִקְרֻבְתָּא דְּאָזְלָא קֳדָמַי, וּבָתַר כֵּן אֶחֱזֵי אַפּוֹהִי, מָאִם יִסַּב אַפָּי: כא וַעֲבַרַת תִּקְרֻבְתָּא עַל אַפּוֹהִי, וְהוּא, בָּת בְּלֵילְיָא הַהוּא בְּמַשְׁרִיתָא: כב וְקָם בְּלֵילְיָא הוּא, וּדְבַר, יָת תַּרְתֵּין נְשׁוֹהִי וְיָת תַּרְתֵּין לְחֵינָתֵיהּ, וְיָת חַד עֲסַר בְּנוֹהִי, וַעֲבַר, יָת מַעֲבַר יֻבְקָא: כג וּדְבַרְנוּן, וְאַעְבְּרִנּוּן יָת נַחְלָא, וְאַעְבַּר יָת דִּלֵיהּ: כד וְאִשְׁתְּאַר יַעֲקֹב בִּלְחוֹדוֹהִי, וְאִשְׁתַּדַּל גֻּבְרָא עִמֵּיהּ, עַד דִּסְלֵיק צַפְרָא:

32:24 וַיִּוָּתֵר יַעֲקֹב לְבַדּוֹ *And Yaakov was left alone* – Rashi's grandson, Rashbam, gives an extraordinary interpretation of Yaakov's wrestling match (commentary on Gen. 32). Fearing the confrontation with Esav, Yaakov wanted to run away. He was already apart from his family when God sent an angel to wrestle with him to prevent him from doing so. On this reading, God is teaching Yaakov how to wrestle with his fears and defeat them.

25 And a man wrestled with him until dawn. When he saw that he could not
overpower him, the man wrenched Yaakov's hip in its socket so that the socket
26 of Yaakov's hip was strained as he wrestled with the man. "Let me go," said the
man, "for dawn is breaking." But he replied, "I will not let you go unless you
27 28 bless me." "What is your name?" asked the man. "Yaakov," he replied. "No
longer will your name be Yaakov, but Yisrael," said the man, "for you have
29 struggled with God and with men and have prevailed." Yaakov asked, "Please
tell me your name." But he said, "Why do you ask my name?" and he blessed
30 him there. Yaakov named the place Peniel, "for I have seen God face-to-face SHELISHI
31 and yet my life has been spared." The sun was rising on him as he moved on

רש״י

נִעְנוּעָם. וְלִי נִרְאֶה שֶׁהוּא לְשׁוֹן ׳וַיִּתְקַשֵּׁר׳ (מלכים ב׳ ט, יד), וּלְשׁוֹן אֲרַמִּי הוּא: ״בָּתַר דַּאֲבִיקוּ בֵּיהּ״ (סנהדרין מג ע״א) ״וַאֲבֵיק לֵיהּ מֵיבַק״ (מנחות מב ע״א) – לְשׁוֹן עֲנִיבָה, שֶׁכֵּן דֶּרֶךְ שְׁנַיִם שֶׁמִּתְעַצְּמִים לְהַפִּיל אִישׁ אֶת רֵעֵהוּ שֶׁחוֹבְקוֹ וְאוֹבְקוֹ בִּזְרוֹעוֹתָיו. וּפֵרְשׁוּ רַבּוֹתֵינוּ שֶׁהוּא שָׂרוֹ שֶׁל עֵשָׂו:

כה) **וַתֵּקַע.** נִתְקַעְקְעָה מִמְּקוֹם מַחְבַּרְתָּהּ. וְדוֹמֶה לוֹ: ״פֶּן תֵּקַע נַפְשִׁי מִמֵּךְ״ (ירמיה ו, ח), לְשׁוֹן הֲסָרָה. וּבַמִּשְׁנָה: ״לְקַעֲקֵעַ בֵּיצָתָן״, לְשָׁרֵשׁ שָׁרְשֵׁיהֶן:

כו) **כִּי עָלָה הַשָּׁחַר.** וְצָרִיךְ אֲנִי לוֹמַר שִׁירָה: **בֵּרַכְתָּנִי.** הוֹדֵה לִי עַל הַבְּרָכוֹת שֶׁבֵּרְכַנִי אָבִי, שֶׁעֵשָׂו מְעַרְעֵר עֲלֵיהֶן:

כח) **לֹא יַעֲקֹב.** לֹא יֵאָמֵר עוֹד שֶׁהַבְּרָכוֹת בָּאוּ לְךָ בְּעָקְבָה וּרְמִיָּה, כִּי אִם בִּשְׂרָרָה וְגִלּוּי פָּנִים, וְסוֹפְךָ שֶׁהַקָּדוֹשׁ בָּרוּךְ הוּא נִגְלֶה עָלֶיךָ בְּבֵית אֵל וּמַחֲלִיף שִׁמְךָ וְשָׁם הוּא מְבָרֶכְךָ, וַאֲנִי שָׁם אֶהְיֶה וְאוֹדֶה לְךָ עֲלֵיהֶן, וְזֶה שֶׁכָּתוּב: ״וַיָּשַׂר אֶל מַלְאָךְ וַיֻּכָל בָּכָה וַיִּתְחַנֶּן לוֹ״ (הושע יב, ה) – בָּכָה הַמַּלְאָךְ וַיִּתְחַנֶּן לוֹ, וּמַה נִּתְחַנֵּן לוֹ? ״בֵּית אֵל יִמְצָאֶנּוּ וְשָׁם יְדַבֵּר עִמָּנוּ״ (שם) – הַמְתֵּן לִי עַד שֶׁיְּדַבֵּר עִמָּנוּ שָׁם. וְלֹא רָצָה יַעֲקֹב, וְעַל כָּרְחוֹ הוֹדָה לוֹ עֲלֵיהֶן, וְזֶהוּ ״וַיְבָרֶךְ אֹתוֹ שָׁם״, שֶׁהָיָה מִתְחַנֵּן לְהַמְתִּין לוֹ וְלֹא רָצָה: **וְעִם אֲנָשִׁים.** עֵשָׂו וְלָבָן: **וַתּוּכָל.** לָהֶם:

כט) **לָמָּה זֶּה תִּשְׁאַל.** אֵין לָנוּ שֵׁם קָבוּעַ, מִשְׁתַּנִּים הֵם שְׁמוֹתֵינוּ הַכֹּל לְפִי מִצְוַת עֲבוֹדַת הַשְּׁלִיחוּת שֶׁאָנוּ מִשְׁתַּלְּחִים:

לא-לב) **וַיִּזְרַח לוֹ.** לְצָרְכּוֹ, לְרַפּאוֹת אֶת צַלְעָתוֹ, כְּמָה דְּאַתְּ אָמַר: ״שֶׁמֶשׁ צְדָקָה וּמַרְפֵּא בִּכְנָפֶיהָ״ (מלאכי ג, כ). וְאוֹתָן שָׁעוֹת שֶׁמִּהֲרָה לִשְׁקֹעַ כְּשֶׁיָּצָא

the obstinacy and resilience that can face hard times and say of them: "I will not let you go until you bless me." I will not give up or move on until I have extracted something positive from this pain and turned it into blessing.

32:30 **כִּי רָאִיתִי אֱלֹהִים** *For I have seen God* – Throughout the episode we do not even know who the adversary is. The text itself calls him "a man"; according to the prophet Hoshe'a, it is an angel (Hos. 12:4); for the Sages, it is the guardian angel of Esav (Bereshit Rabba 77:3, cited in Rashi on Gen. 32:24). Yaakov himself has no doubt. It is God. The adversary himself implies as much when he gives Yaakov the name Yisrael: "for you have struggled with God and with men and have prevailed." Hitherto, we have seen Yaakov struggle with human beings, with Esav and Lavan. Now, the text seems to suggest, he has struggled with God Himself.

the workings of the human brain, there is one thing we do not know and never will: what tomorrow will bring.

32:26 **לֹא אֲשַׁלֵּחֲךָ כִּי אִם בֵּרַכְתָּנִי** *I will not let you go unless you bless me* – These words of Yaakov to the angel lie at the very core of surviving crisis. Each of us knows from personal experience that events that seemed disappointing, painful, even humiliating at the time can be the most important in our lives. Through them we learned how to try harder next time; or they taught us a truth about ourselves; or they shifted our life into a new and more fruitful direction. We learn, not from our successes but from our failures. We mature and grow strong and become more understanding and forgiving through the mistakes we make. A protected life is a fragile and superficial life. Strength comes from knowing the worst and refusing to give in. Yaakov/Yisrael has bequeathed us many gifts, but few more valuable than

כה וירא כי לא יכל לו ויגע בכף־ירכו ותקע כף־ירך יעקב בהאבקו
כו עמו: ויאמר שלחני כי עלה השחר ויאמר לא אשלחך כי אם־
כז כח ברכתני: ויאמר אליו מה־שמך ויאמר יעקב: ויאמר לא יעקב יאמר
עוד שמך כי אם־ישראל כי־שרית עם־אלהים ועם־אנשים ותוכל:
כט וישאל יעקב ויאמר הגידה־נא שמך ויאמר למה זה תשאל לשמי
ל ויברך אתו שם: ויקרא יעקב שם המקום פניאל כי־ראיתי אלהים שלישי
לא פנים אל־פנים ותנצל נפשי: ויזרח־לו השמש כאשר עבר את־פנואל

אונקלוס

כה וחזא, ארי לא יכיל ליה, וקריב בפתי ירכיה, וזע פתי ירכא דיעקב, באשתדלותיה עמיה: כו ואמר שלחני, ארי סליק צפרא, ואמר לא אשלחנך, אלהין בריכתני: כז ואמר ליה מאן שמך, ואמר יעקב: כח ואמר, לא יעקב יתאמר עוד שמך, אלהין ישראל, ארי רב את קדם יי, ועם גבריא ויכילתא: כט ושאיל יעקב, ואמר חוי כען שמך, ואמר, למא דנן את שאיל לשמי, ובריך יתיה תמן: ל וקרא יעקב, שמיה דאתרא פניאל, ארי חזיתי מלאכא דיי אפין באפין, ואשתיזבת נפשי: לא ודנח ליה שמשא, כד עבר ית פנואל,

What actually happens the next day, when Yaakov finally comes face-to-face with Esav? Instead of attacking him, Esav runs to meet him and embraces him (Gen. 32:1). There is no anger, no violence, no lingering trace of resentment. Everything Yaakov fears fails to happen. Is this mere coincidence, happenstance? Were Yaakov's fears simply misplaced? I believe the Torah is teaching a deeper truth, that once Yaakov has resolved the conflict within himself, he removes the source of tension between himself and Esav. Even animals sense fear. Predators chase those who run away. The way of safety is to stay calm and still.

An inner sense of self-confidence and trust does not mean that one will never have to fight battles. Economics and politics are intrinsically conflictual. Much of life is a zero-sum competition for scarce goods in which some win, some lose. But spiritual goods – love, trust, friendship, the pursuit of knowledge – are not zero-sum. The more we share, the more we have. So our deepest psychological and spiritual goods need never be bought at the cost of others. That knowledge alone – that Yaakov and Esav can each have their own blessings without envying one another – is enough to remove many, even most, of the conflicts by which people cause one another pain.

32:24 ויאבק איש עמו *And a man wrestled with him* – Everything about this story is mysterious. It takes place at a liminal time between night and dawn, at an unspecified location, with no explanation, after the most elaborately conceived and executed preparations for any event in Genesis. Yaakov has prepared himself for three things: diplomacy, war, and prayer. He has sent huge gifts of cattle to appease Esav's anger. He has divided his camp in two so that even if one is destroyed the other might survive. He has prayed to God. He has covered every eventuality, adopted every strategy, anticipated, seemingly, every outcome – but not the one that actually happens, the appearance of an unnamed adversary who fights with him.

There is no way we can make ourselves immune to crises. That is the human condition and we cannot escape it. Faith is not certainty; it is the courage to live with uncertainty. Indeed, that is why we need faith: because life is uncertain. Even in the twenty-first century when we know so much about the universe, cosmology, the human genome, and

32 from Penuel, limping on his thigh. That is why, to this day, the Israelites do
not eat the sciatic nerve by the hip socket: because he wrenched Yaakov's hip
33 1 socket at the sciatic nerve. Yaakov looked up – and saw Esav coming with his
four hundred men. So he divided the children among Leah, Raḥel, and the two
2 maidservants. He put the maidservants and their children first, Leah and her
3 children behind, and Raḥel and Yosef at the rear. And he went ahead of them,
bowing down to the ground seven times until he came close to his brother.
4 Esav ran to meet him and embraced him. He threw his arms around his neck
5 and kissed him, and they wept. Esav looked up and saw the women and
children. He asked, "Who are these with you?" Yaakov answered, "They are the
6 children God has graciously given your servant." Then the maidservants and REVI'I
7 their children came forward and bowed down. Leah and her children came

רש״י

מִפְּנֵי שֶׁטֶּבַע מְהֵרָה לִזְרֹחַ בִּשְׁבִילוֹ, וְהוּא הָיָה צוֹלֵעַ כְּשֶׁזָּרְחָה הַשֶּׁמֶשׁ:

לב| **גִּיד הַנָּשֶׁה.** לָמָּה נִקְרָא שְׁמוֹ ׳גִּיד הַנָּשֶׁה׳? שֶׁנָּשָׁה מִמְּקוֹמוֹ וְעָלָה, וְהוּא לְשׁוֹן קְפִיצָה, וְכֵן: ״נָשְׁתָה גְבוּרָתָם״ (ירמיה נא, ל), וְכֵן: ״כִּי נַשַּׁנִי אֱלֹהִים אֶת כָּל עֲמָלִי״ (להלן מא, נא):

לג ב| **וְאֶת לֵאָה וִילָדֶיהָ אַחֲרֹנִים.** אַחֲרוֹן אַחֲרוֹן חָבִיב:

ג| **עָבַר לִפְנֵיהֶם.** אָמַר, אִם יָבֹא אוֹתוֹ רָשָׁע לְהִלָּחֵם, יִלָּחֵם בִּי תְּחִלָּה:

ד| **וַיְחַבְּקֵהוּ.** נִתְגַּלְגְּלוּ רַחֲמָיו כְּשֶׁרָאָהוּ מִשְׁתַּחֲוֶה כָּל הִשְׁתַּחֲוָיוֹת הַלָּלוּ: **וַיִּשָּׁקֵהוּ.** נָקוּד עָלָיו. וְיֵשׁ חוֹלְקִין בַּדָּבָר הַזֶּה בְּבָרַיְתָא דְּסִפְרֵי (בהעלתך סט): יֵשׁ שֶׁדָּרְשׁוּ נְקֻדָּה זוֹ לוֹמַר שֶׁלֹּא נְשָׁקוֹ בְּכָל לִבּוֹ; אָמַר רַבִּי שִׁמְעוֹן בֶּן יוֹחַאי: הֲלָכָה הִיא בְּיָדוּעַ שֶׁעֵשָׂו שׂוֹנֵא לְיַעֲקֹב, אֶלָּא שֶׁנִּכְמְרוּ רַחֲמָיו בְּאוֹתָהּ שָׁעָה וּנְשָׁקוֹ בְּכָל לִבּוֹ:

ה| **מִי אֵלֶּה לָּךְ.** מִי אֵלֶּה לִהְיוֹת שֶׁלָּךְ?:

wilderness try to return to Egypt. Yona seeks to escape his prophetic mission. Yeḥezkel predicts a time when Israel will want to "be like the nations, like the families of the lands" (Ezek. 20:32). In the nineteenth century, Jews sought in normalization a release from the destiny of differentness. But in the Holocaust, their way was blocked by the angel of death. We will never fully understand those dark biblical passages in which God turns His people toward life by the threat of death. Why must Jews endure suffering to continue to exist as a people? That remains a mystery no prophet has ever fathomed. Like Yaakov after his struggle, the Jewish people limps, still scarred by that encounter. But those who remain have, like Yaakov, taken up the journey again, no longer seeking flight from fate but instead determined to survive as Jews. The State of Israel, Diaspora Jewish activism, and a renascent Orthodoxy all express this fundamental affirmation. The Jewish people has returned to its perennial vocation: to be Israel, the people of the covenant, though this means struggling with God and with man. Thus the earliest law given to Israel alone is a reminder of Yaakov's struggle and the mark it left on him. It is fundamental to who we are as Jews.

33:4 **וַיָּרָץ עֵשָׂו לִקְרָאתוֹ וַיְחַבְּקֵהוּ** *Esav ran... and embraced him* – When Esav finally appears, all Yaakov's fears of the previous day turn out to be unfounded. He "runs" to meet Yaakov, throws his arms around his neck, kisses him, and weeps. That is not to say that Yaakov's fears were irrational. They were not. After all, Esav had vowed revenge twenty-two years before ("The days of mourning for my father are approaching... and then I will kill my brother Yaakov" [Gen. 27:41]). Esav, however, turns out to be an impulsive man who lives in the mood of the moment. He has none of Cassius's "lean and hungry look" or Iago's cold calculation. He is quick to anger, quick to forget. The anticlimax when the brothers meet is consistent with Esav's character, if not with Yaakov's fears.

לב וְה֥וּא צֹלֵ֖עַ עַל־יְרֵכֽוֹ׃ עַל־כֵּ֞ן לֹֽא־יֹאכְל֨וּ בְנֵֽי־יִשְׂרָאֵ֜ל אֶת־גִּ֣יד הַנָּשֶׁ֗ה
אֲשֶׁר֙ עַל־כַּ֣ף הַיָּרֵ֔ךְ עַ֖ד הַיּ֣וֹם הַזֶּ֑ה כִּ֤י נָגַע֙ בְּכַף־יֶ֣רֶךְ יַעֲקֹ֔ב בְּגִ֖יד הַנָּשֶֽׁה׃
לג א וַיִּשָּׂ֨א יַעֲקֹ֜ב עֵינָ֗יו וַיַּרְא֙ וְהִנֵּ֣ה עֵשָׂ֣ו בָּ֔א וְעִמּ֕וֹ אַרְבַּ֥ע מֵא֖וֹת אִ֑ישׁ וַיַּ֣חַץ
ב אֶת־הַיְלָדִ֗ים עַל־לֵאָה֙ וְעַל־רָחֵ֔ל וְעַ֖ל שְׁתֵּ֥י הַשְּׁפָחֽוֹת׃ וַיָּ֧שֶׂם אֶת־
הַשְּׁפָח֛וֹת וְאֶת־יַלְדֵיהֶ֖ן רִֽאשֹׁנָ֑ה וְאֶת־לֵאָ֤ה וִֽילָדֶ֙יהָ֙ אַחֲרֹנִ֔ים וְאֶת־רָחֵ֥ל
ג וְאֶת־יוֹסֵ֖ף אַחֲרֹנִֽים׃ וְה֖וּא עָבַ֣ר לִפְנֵיהֶ֑ם וַיִּשְׁתַּ֤חוּ אַ֙רְצָה֙ שֶׁ֣בַע פְּעָמִ֔ים
ד עַד־גִּשְׁתּ֖וֹ עַד־אָחִֽיו׃ וַיָּ֨רָץ עֵשָׂ֤ו לִקְרָאתוֹ֙ וַֽיְחַבְּקֵ֔הוּ וַיִּפֹּ֥ל עַל־צַוָּארָ֖ו
ה וַיִּשָּׁקֵ֑הוּ וַיִּבְכּֽוּ׃ וַיִּשָּׂ֣א אֶת־עֵינָ֗יו וַיַּ֤רְא אֶת־הַנָּשִׁים֙ וְאֶת־הַיְלָדִ֔ים וַיֹּ֖אמֶר
ו מִי־אֵ֣לֶּה לָּ֑ךְ וַיֹּאמַ֕ר הַיְלָדִ֕ים אֲשֶׁר־חָנַ֥ן אֱלֹהִ֖ים אֶת־עַבְדֶּֽךָ׃ וַתִּגַּ֧שְׁןָ רביעי
ז הַשְּׁפָח֛וֹת הֵ֥נָּה וְיַלְדֵיהֶ֖ן וַתִּֽשְׁתַּחֲוֶֽיןָ׃ וַתִּגַּ֧שׁ גַּם־לֵאָ֛ה וִילָדֶ֖יהָ וַיִּֽשְׁתַּחֲו֑וּ

אונקלוס

והוא מטלע על ירכיה: לב על כן, לא אכלין בני ישראל ית גידא נשיא, דעל פתי ירכא, עד יומא הדין, ארי קריב בפתי ירכא דיעקב, בגידא נשיא: לג א וזקף יעקב עינוהי, וחזא והא עשו אתי, ועמיה, ארבע מאה גברא, ופליג ית בניא, על לאה ועל רחל, ועל תרתין לחינתא: ב ושוי ית לחינתא, וית בניהון קדמותא, וית לאה ובנהא בתראין, וית רחל וית יוסף בתראין: ג והוא עבר קדמיהון, וסגיד על ארעא שבע זמנין, עד מקרביה לות אחוהי: ד ורהט עשו לקדמותיה וגפפיה, ונפל על צוריה ונשקיה, ובכו: ה וזקף ית עינוהי, וחזא ית נשיא וית בניא, ואמר מאן אלין לך, ואמר, בניא, דחן יי ית עבדך: ו וקריבא לחינתא, אנין ובניהון וסגידא: ז וקריבת אף לאה, ובנהא וסגידו,

32:31 צֹלֵעַ עַל־יְרֵכוֹ *Limping on his thigh* – Whatever Yaakov's struggle represents, it leaves a lasting mark. Crisis is real; the suffering to which it gives rise can cut deep. Even when you survive, you limp; long afterward, perhaps for a lifetime, you bear the scars. But they are honorable scars. They tell that you fought and won, and greater is one who fought and won than one who, fearing confrontation, takes the path of least resistance and submits.

The heroes of our faith do not live charmed lives. They suffer exiles, know danger, have their hopes disappointed and their expectations delayed. They fight, they struggle, but they neither give in nor give up. They are not serene. Sometimes they laugh in disbelief; there are times when they fear, tremble, weep, and even give way to anger. For they are human beings, not angels; they are people with whom we can identify, not saints to be worshipped. Yaakov teaches us that we cannot preempt crisis, nor should we minimize it, but we can survive it, thus becoming worthy of bearing the name of one who has struggled with God and with men and prevailed.

32:32 עַד הַיּוֹם הַזֶּה *To this day* – This passage above all others has seemed, at times of trauma, to epitomize Jewish destiny. For the Sages of the second century CE, it described the confrontation between Jews and Rome. For Ramban in thirteenth-century Spain, it foreshadowed the persecution of Jews at the hands of medieval Christianity. It is no less evocative in the wake of the Jewish encounter with Enlightenment. It is a heavy burden to be singled out by God to be different.

Man tries to flee from chosenness. The Israelites in the

forward and bowed down. And last, Yosef and Raḥel approached and bowed
8 down. Esav asked, "What did you mean by all the procession that I met before?"
9 He said, "To find favor in your eyes, my lord." But Esav said, "I have plenty, my
10 brother. Let what is yours remain yours." "No, please," said Yaakov. "If I have
found favor in your eyes, accept this gift from me, for seeing your face is like
11 seeing the face of God, and you have shown me favor. Please accept my blessing
that was brought to you, for God has been gracious to me, and I have everything."

רש"י

ז **נגש יוסף ורחל.** בכלן האמהות נגשות לפני הבנים, אבל ברחל – יוסף נגש לפניה; אמר: אמי יפת תאר, שמא יתלה בה עיניו אותו רשע, אעמוד כנגדה ואעכבנו מלהסתכל בה. מכאן זכה יוסף לברכת "עלי עין" (להלן מט, כב):

ח **מי לך כל המחנה.** מי כל המחנה אשר פגשתי שהוא שלך? כלומר, למה הוא לך? פשוטו של מקרא על מוליכי המנחה; ומדרשו, כתות של מלאכים פגע שהיו דוחפין אותו ואת אנשיו ואומרים להם: של מי אתם? והם אומרים להם: של עשו, והם אומרים: הכו הכו. ואלו אומרים: בנו של יצחק הוא, ולא היו משגיחים; בן בנו של אברהם, ולא היו משגיחים; אחיו של יעקב הוא, ואלו אומרים להם: אם כן משלנו אתם:

ט **יהי לך אשר לך.** כאן הודה לו על הברכות:

י **אל נא.** אל נא תאמר לי כן: **אם נא מצאתי חן בעיניך ולקחת מנחתי מידי כי על כן ראיתי פניך וגו'.** כי כדאי והגון לך שתקבל מנחתי, על אשר ראיתי פניך והן חשובין לי כראיית פני המלאך, שראיתי שר שלך, ועוד, על שנתרצית לי למחול על סרחוני. ולמה הזכיר לו ראיית המלאך? כדי שיתירא הימנו ויאמר: ראה מלאכים ונצול, איני יכול לו מעתה: **ותרצני.** נתפייסת לי, וכן כל רצון שבמקרא לשון פיוס, אפיימנ"ט בלעז; "כי לא לרצון יהיה לכם" (ויקרא כב, כ) – הקרבנות באות לפייס ולרצות, "שפתי צדיק ידעון רצון" (משלי י, לב) – יודעים לפייס ולרצות:

יא **ברכתי.** מנחה זו הבאה על ראיית פנים ולפרקים, אינה באה אלא לשאילת שלום. וכל ברכה שהיא לראיית פנים, כגון: "ויברך יעקב את פרעה" (להלן מז, י), "עשו אתי ברכה" (מלכים ב' יח, לא) דסנחריב, וכן: "לשאל לו לשלום ולברכו" (שמואל ב' ח, י) דתועי מלך חמת, כלם לשון ברכת שלום הן, שקורין בלעז סלודי"ר, אף זו, "ברכתי" – מו"ן סלו"ד: **אשר הבאת לך.** לא טרחת בה ואני יגעתי להגיעה עד שבאה לידך: **חנני.** נו"ן ראשונה מדגשת לפי שהיא משמשת במקום שתי נוני"ן, שהיה לו לומר 'חננני', שאין 'חנן' בלא שתי נוני"ן, והשלישית לשמוש כמו 'עשני' (ישעיה כט, טז), 'זבדני' (לעיל ל, כ): **יש לי כל.** כל ספוקי. ועשו דבר בלשון גאוה: "יש לי רב" (לעיל פסוק ט), יותר ויותר מכדי צרכי:

33:11 **קח נא את ברכתי** *Please accept my blessing* – First, Yaakov "went ahead of them, bowing down to the ground seven times" (Gen. 33:3). "Then the maidservants and their children came forward and bowed down. Leah and her children came forward and bowed down. And last, Yosef and Raḥel approached and bowed down" (33:6–7). The threefold repetition is significant, as is Yaakov's cautious way of presenting his family.

No less striking is Yaakov's use of language. Five times he calls Esav *adoni*, "my lord." Twice he calls himself Esav's *eved*, "servant." As with his physical gesture of sevenfold prostration, so with his sevenfold use of the words *adon* and *eved*, this is the choreography of self-abasement.

How are we to connect this with the wrestling match of the previous night? Surely Yaakov won a victory over his adversary. At the very least he refused to let him go until he received a blessing. The new name implied that henceforth Yaakov should have no doubts about his ability to survive any conflict. A man who has "struggled with God and with men and prevailed" is not one who needs to bow down to anyone. We would have expected Yaakov to show confidence rather than servility.

Esav initially refuses Yaakov's gifts, saying, "I have plenty [*yesh li rav*], my brother." Yaakov's reply is enigmatic:

> "No, please … if I have found favor in your eyes, accept this gift [*minḥa*] from me …. Please accept my blessing

ח וְאַחַר נִגַּשׁ יוֹסֵף וְרָחֵל וַיִּשְׁתַּחֲוּוּ׃ וַיֹּאמֶר מִי לְךָ כָּל־הַמַּחֲנֶה הַזֶּה אֲשֶׁר
ט פָּגָשְׁתִּי וַיֹּאמֶר לִמְצֹא־חֵן בְּעֵינֵי אֲדֹנִי׃ וַיֹּאמֶר עֵשָׂו יֶשׁ־לִי רָב אָחִי
י יְהִי לְךָ אֲשֶׁר־לָךְ׃ וַיֹּאמֶר יַעֲקֹב אַל־נָא אִם־נָא מָצָאתִי חֵן בְּעֵינֶיךָ
וְלָקַחְתָּ מִנְחָתִי מִיָּדִי כִּי עַל־כֵּן רָאִיתִי פָנֶיךָ כִּרְאֹת פְּנֵי אֱלֹהִים וַתִּרְצֵנִי׃
יא קַח־נָא אֶת־בִּרְכָתִי אֲשֶׁר הֻבָאת לָךְ כִּי־חַנַּנִי אֱלֹהִים וְכִי יֶשׁ־לִי־כֹל

אונקלוס

וּבָתַר כֵּן, קְרֵיב יוֹסֵף, וְרָחֵל וּסְגִידוּ: ח וַאֲמַר, מָא לָךְ, כָּל מַשְׁרִיתָא
הָדָא דְּעַרְעִית, וַאֲמַר, לְאַשְׁכָּחָא רַחֲמִין בְּעֵינֵי רִבּוֹנִי: ט וַאֲמַר עֵשָׂו
אִית לִי סַגִּי, אֲחִי, אַצְלַח בְּדִילָךְ: י וַאֲמַר יַעֲקֹב, בְּבָעוּ אִם כְּעַן
אַשְׁכַּחִית רַחֲמִין בְּעֵינָךְ, וּתְקַבֵּיל תִּקְרֻבְתִּי מִן יְדִי, אֲרֵי עַל כֵּן
חֲזֵיתִנּוּן לְאַפָּךְ, כְּחֵיזוּ, אַפֵּי רַבְרְבַיָּא וְאִתְרְעִית לִי: יא קַבֵּיל כְּעַן יָת
תִּקְרֻבְתִּי דְּאִתֵּיתִיאַת לָךְ, אֲרֵי רַחֵים עֲלַי יְיָ וַאֲרֵי אִית לִי כּוֹלָא,

33:10 כִּרְאֹת פְּנֵי אֱלֹהִים *Like seeing the face of God* – These words of Yaakov's echo his remark after the wrestling match, "Yaakov named the place Peniel, 'for I have seen God *face*-to-*face* and yet my life has been spared'" (Gen. 32:30). Altogether, chapters 32 and 33 echo time and again with variants on the word *panim*. This is missed in translation, because *panim* has many forms in Hebrew not evident in English. To take one example, chapter 32, verse 20 contains the Hebrew word *four times* – the second half of the verse, translated hyper-literally, reads: "He thought, 'I will wipe [the anger from] his *face* with these gifts I am sending on ahead of my *face*. Then I will see his *face*. Perhaps he will lift up my *face*.'" There is a drama here and it has to do with faces: the face of Esav, of Yaakov, and of God Himself. We are reminded that when Yaakov received Esav's blessing, Yitzḥak was blind. Yitzḥak gave the blessing to Yaakov only because *he could not see Yaakov's face*.

The lives of the patriarchs are significant not only for what they tell us about the past but also for what they tell us about the present – for their challenges are ours. Avraham is the man who has the strength of conviction to stand apart from the culture of his time. What carries him through is love (*ḥesed*) – love of God and, yes, the love of humanity that shines through all his deeds and words. Yitzḥak is the man who knows the reality of sacrifice. He lives, he survives, but not without seeing the knife lifted against him. He knows to the core of his being that to be a child of the covenant is neither easy nor safe. What carries him through is courage (*gevura*) – and for whatever reason, the historical record is clear: to remain Jewish takes courage.

In connection with Yaakov, though, the prophet Mikha speaks of *truth* ("You will show truth to Yaakov" [Mic. 7:20]). This does not imply truth in a cognitive sense (what are the facts?) but rather truth in an existential sense: Who am I? To which story do I belong and what part am I called on to play? The search for cognitive truth is not specific to the Abrahamic covenant. It is the heritage of all mankind. The truth with which Yaakov spends much of his life wrestling is quite different. It is a truth about identity. Central to it are the words *face* (in which mirror do I look to see who I am?), *name* (by which term do I know myself?), and *blessing* (to what destiny am I called?).

It is as if the man with whom he wrestled in the night says to him, "In the past, you struggled to be Esav. In the future you will struggle to be yourself. In the past you held on to Esav's heel. In the future you will hold on to God. You will not let go of Him; He will not let go of you. Now let go of Esav so that you can be free to hold on to God." Ours is another face, an alternative destiny, an altogether different blessing from Esav's. The face that is truly ours is the one we see reflected back at us by God. That is the meaning of the priestly blessing "May the Lord *raise His face* toward you and grant you *peace*" (Num. 6:26). Peace comes when we let go of the desire to be someone else and see our reflection in the face of God.

12 Yaakov pressed him, and he accepted. Then Esav said, "Let us be on our way.
13 I will go beside you." But Yaakov said, "My lord knows that the children
are fragile, and I must care for the nursing sheep and cattle. If they are driven
14 hard even for one day, all the flocks will die. Let my lord go on ahead of his
servant, and I will go slowly at the pace of the livestock before me and the
15 pace of the children until I come to my lord in Se'ir." Esav said, "Let me leave
some of my people with you." "Why do that?" he said. "Just let me find favor in
16 17 the eyes of my lord." So that day Esav started back on his way to Se'ir, and
Yaakov journeyed on to Sukkot. There he built himself a house and made huts

רש״י

יב **נִסְעָה.** כְּמוֹ: "שִׁמְעָה" (תהלים לט, יג), "סְלָחָה" (להלן מג, ח) שֶׁהוּא כְּמוֹ 'שְׁמַע', 'סְלַח', אַף 'נִסְעָה' כְּמוֹ 'נְסַע', וְהַנּוּ"ן יְסוֹד בַּתֵּבָה. וְתַרְגּוּם שֶׁל אוּנְקְלוֹס: "טוּל וּנְהָךְ", עֵשָׂו אָמַר לְיַעֲקֹב, נְסַע מִכָּאן וְנֵלֵךְ: **וְאֵלְכָה לְנֶגְדֶּךָ.** בְּשָׁוֶה לְךָ, טוֹבָה זוֹ אֶעֱשֶׂה לְךָ שֶׁאַאֲרִיךְ יְמֵי מַהֲלָכִי לָלֶכֶת לְאַט כַּאֲשֶׁר אַתָּה צָרִיךְ, וְזֶהוּ "לְנֶגְדֶּךָ" – בְּשָׁוֶה לְךָ:

יג **עָלוֹת עָלָי.** הַצֹּאן וְהַבָּקָר שֶׁהֵן "עָלוֹת", מֻטָּלוֹת "עָלַי", לְנַהֲלָן לְאַט: **עָלוֹת.** מְגַדְּלוֹת עוֹלְלֵיהֶן, לְשׁוֹן "עוֹלֵל וְיוֹנֵק" (ירמיה מד, ז; איכה ב, יא), "עוּל יָמִים" (ישעיה סה, כ), "וּשְׁתֵּי פָרוֹת עָלוֹת" (שמואל א׳ ו, ז), וּבְלַעַז אנפנטי"ש: **וּדְפָקוּם יוֹם אֶחָד.** לְיַגְּעָם בַּדֶּרֶךְ בִּמְרוּצָה, "וָמֵתוּ כָּל הַצֹּאן": **וּדְפָקוּם.** כְּמוֹ: "קוֹל דּוֹדִי דוֹפֵק" (שיר השירים ה, ב), נוֹקֵשׁ בַּדֶּלֶת:

יד **יַעֲבָר נָא אֲדֹנִי.** אַל נָא תַּאֲרִיךְ יְמֵי הֲלִיכָתְךָ, עֲבֹר כְּפִי דַּרְכְּךָ וְאַף אִם תִּתְרַחֵק: **אֶתְנַהֲלָה.** אֶתְנַהֵל, הֵ"א יְתֵרָה, כְּמוֹ: 'אֵרְדָה' (לעיל יח, כא), 'אֶשְׁמְעָה' (ירמיה ד, כא; תהלים פה, ט): **לְאִטִּי.** לְאַט שֶׁלִּי, לְשׁוֹן נַחַת, "הַהוֹלְכִים לְאַט" (ישעיה ח, ו), "לְאַט לִי לַנַּעַר" (שמואל ב׳ יח, ה): **לְאִטִּי.** הַלָּמֶ"ד מִן הַיְסוֹד וְאֵינָהּ מְשַׁמֶּשֶׁת, אֶתְנַהֵל נַחַת שֶׁלִּי: **לְרֶגֶל הַמְּלָאכָה.** לְפִי צֹרֶךְ הֲלִיכַת רַגְלֵי הַמְּלָאכָה הַמֻּטֶּלֶת לְפָנַי לְהוֹלִיךְ: **וּלְרֶגֶל הַיְלָדִים.** לְפִי רַגְלֵיהֶם שֶׁהֵם יְכוֹלִים לֵילֵךְ: **עַד אֲשֶׁר אָבֹא אֶל אֲדֹנִי שֵׂעִירָה.** הִרְחִיב לוֹ הַדֶּרֶךְ, שֶׁלֹּא הָיָה דַּעְתּוֹ לָלֶכֶת אֶלָּא עַד סֻכּוֹת, אָמַר: אִם דַּעְתּוֹ לַעֲשׂוֹת לִי רָעָה יַמְתִּין עַד בּוֹאִי אֶצְלוֹ. וְהוּא לֹא הָלַךְ, וְאֵימָתַי יֵלֵךְ? בִּימֵי הַמָּשִׁיחַ, שֶׁנֶּאֱמַר: "וְעָלוּ מוֹשִׁעִים בְּהַר צִיּוֹן לִשְׁפֹּט אֶת הַר עֵשָׂו" (עובדיה א, כא). וּמִדְרְשֵׁי אַגָּדָה יֵשׁ לְפָרָשָׁה זוֹ רַבִּים:

טו **וַיֹּאמֶר לָמָּה זֶּה.** תַּעֲשֶׂה לִי טוֹבָה זוֹ שֶׁאֵינִי צָרִיךְ לָהּ; "אֶמְצָא חֵן בְּעֵינֶיךָ" וְלֹא תְּשַׁלֵּם לִי עַתָּה שׁוּם גְּמוּל:

טז **וַיָּשָׁב בַּיּוֹם הַהוּא עֵשָׂו לְדַרְכּוֹ.** עֵשָׂו לְבַדּוֹ, וְאַרְבַּע מֵאוֹת אִישׁ שֶׁהָלְכוּ עִמּוֹ נִשְׁמְטוּ מֵאֶצְלוֹ אֶחָד אֶחָד. וְהֵיכָן פָּרַע לָהֶם הַקָּדוֹשׁ בָּרוּךְ הוּא? בִּימֵי דָּוִד, שֶׁנֶּאֱמַר: "כִּי אִם אַרְבַּע מֵאוֹת אִישׁ נַעַר אֲשֶׁר רָכְבוּ עַל הַגְּמַלִּים" (שמואל א׳ ל, יז):

יז **וַיִּבֶן לוֹ בָּיִת.** שָׁהָה שָׁם שְׁמוֹנָה עָשָׂר חֹדֶשׁ, קַיִץ וְחֹרֶף וְקַיִץ; קַיִץ – 'סֻכּוֹת', חֹרֶף – 'בַּיִת', וְקַיִץ – 'סֻכּוֹת':

33:17 **עַל־כֵּן קָרָא שֵׁם־הַמָּקוֹם סֻכּוֹת** *He named the place Sukkot* – The point is linguistic, but the message is remarkable. *Yaakov has just become the first member of the covenantal family to build a house, yet he does not call the place "House"* (as in Beit El or Beit Leḥem). *He calls it Sukkot, "cattle sheds."* It is as if Yaakov, consciously or unconsciously, already knows that to live the life of the covenant means to be ready to move on, to travel, to journey, to grow.

We will learn from the laws of the Jubilee (Lev. 26:34–35) that if we live as if the land is permanently ours, our stay there will be temporary. If we live as if it is only temporarily so, we will live there permanently. In this world of time and change, growth and decay, only God and His word are permanent. One of the most poignant lines in the book of Psalms – a verse cherished by the French Jewish philosopher Emmanuel Levinas – says, "I am but a stranger on earth – do not hide Your commandments from me" (Ps. 119:19). To be a Jew is to stay light on your feet, ready to begin the next stage of the journey, literally or metaphorically. An Englishman's home is his castle, they used to say. But a Jew's home is a tent, a tabernacle, a sukka. We know that life on earth is a temporary dwelling. That is why we value each moment and its newness.

יב יג וַיִּפְצַר־בּוֹ וַיִּקָּח׃ וַיֹּאמֶר נִסְעָה וְנֵלֵכָה וְאֵלְכָה לְנֶגְדֶּךָ׃ וַיֹּאמֶר אֵלָיו
אֲדֹנִי יֹדֵעַ כִּי־הַיְלָדִים רַכִּים וְהַצֹּאן וְהַבָּקָר עָלוֹת עָלָי וּדְפָקוּם יוֹם
יד אֶחָד וָמֵתוּ כָּל־הַצֹּאן׃ יַעֲבָר־נָא אֲדֹנִי לִפְנֵי עַבְדּוֹ וַאֲנִי אֶתְנַהֲלָה
לְאִטִּי לְרֶגֶל הַמְּלָאכָה אֲשֶׁר־לְפָנַי וּלְרֶגֶל הַיְלָדִים עַד אֲשֶׁר־אָבֹא
טו אֶל־אֲדֹנִי שֵׂעִירָה׃ וַיֹּאמֶר עֵשָׂו אַצִּיגָה־נָּא עִמְּךָ מִן־הָעָם אֲשֶׁר אִתִּי
טז וַיֹּאמֶר לָמָּה זֶּה אֶמְצָא־חֵן בְּעֵינֵי אֲדֹנִי׃ וַיָּשָׁב בַּיּוֹם הַהוּא עֵשָׂו לְדַרְכּוֹ
יז שֵׂעִירָה׃ וְיַעֲקֹב נָסַע סֻכֹּתָה וַיִּבֶן לוֹ בָּיִת וּלְמִקְנֵהוּ עָשָׂה סֻכֹּת עַל־כֵּן

אונקלוס

וְאַתְקֵיף בֵּיהּ וְקַבֵּיל׃ יב וַאֲמַר טוּל וּנְהָךְ, וַאֲהָךְ לְקִבְלָךְ׃ יג וַאֲמַר לֵיהּ, רִבּוֹנִי יָדַע אֲרֵי יְנַקַיָּא רַכִּיכִין, וְעָנָא וְתוֹרֵי מֵינְקָתָא עֲלַי, אִם אַדְחוֹקִנּוּן יוֹמָא חַד, וִימוּתוּן כָּל עָנָא׃ יד יִעְבַּר כְּעַן רִבּוֹנִי קֳדָם עַבְדֵּיהּ, וַאֲנָא אֲדַבַּר בְּנִיחַ, לְרֶגֶל עֲבִידְתָּא דִּקְדָמַי וּלְרֶגֶל יְנַקַיָּא, עַד, דְּאֵיתֵי לְוָת רִבּוֹנִי לְשֵׂעִיר׃ טו וַאֲמַר עֵשָׂו, אֶשְׁבּוֹק כְּעַן עִמָּךְ, מִן עַמָּא דְּעִמִּי, וַאֲמַר לְמָא דְּנָן, אַשְׁכַּח רַחֲמִין בְּעֵינֵי רִבּוֹנִי׃ טז וְתָב בְּיוֹמָא הַהוּא עֵשָׂו, לְאוֹרְחֵיהּ לְשֵׂעִיר׃ יז וְיַעֲקֹב נְטַל לְסֻכּוֹת, וּבְנָא לֵיהּ בֵּיתָא, וְלִבְעִירֵיהּ עֲבַד מְטַלָּן, עַל כֵּן,

> that was brought to you, for God has been gracious to me, and I have everything [*yesh li khol*]." (33:10–11)

We noted above that Yaakov is symbolically giving back the blessing he took all those years before. "Please accept [not just 'my gift' but also] '*my blessing.*'" The herds and flocks he sends to Esav represent wealth ("dew of heaven, the cream of the land," 27:28). The sevenfold bowing and calling himself "your servant" and Esav "my lord" represent power ("Be lord over your brothers, and may your mother's sons bow down to you," 27:29). Yaakov's blessing (28:3–4) has nothing to do with wealth or power. It has to do with children and a land – children he will instruct in the ways of the covenant and a land in which his descendants would strive to construct a covenantal society based on justice and compassion, law and love. Yaakov alters Esav's words, "I have plenty," into his own "I have everything" – meaning, "I no longer need either wealth or power to be complete."

He has, instead, to be himself, a person whose ears are attuned to the call of the Author of all. He has to be true to that which cannot be bought by wealth or controlled by power, namely, the human spirit as the breath of God, human dignity as the image of God.

33:17 וְיַעֲקֹב נָסַע *Yaakov journeyed on* – At almost every significant juncture in our history we have wrestled with civilizations who worshipped the gods of nature: wealth or power. Israel never knew the power of great empires, their invincible armies and weapons of destruction. When it longed for those things, as in the days of Shlomo, it lost its way.

Israel's strength never lay in itself, but in that which was other and greater than itself: the power that transcends all earthly powers, and the wealth that is not physical but spiritual, a matter of mind and heart. Despite this, Jews have often wished to be someone else, the Esavs of the age.

That is a feeling we must ultimately reject. The Torah does not ask us to think badly of Esav. To the contrary, it commands us: "Do not despise an Edomite [i.e., a descendant of Esav], for he is your kin" (Deut. 23:8). It does, however, ask us to wrestle alone, at night, in the depths of our soul, and discover the face, the name, and the blessing that are ours.

18 for his livestock; that is why he named the place Sukkot. Thus Yaakov,
having come from Padan Aram, arrived safely at the town of Shekhem in
19 Canaan, and he set up camp within sight of the town. He bought the plot of
ground where he pitched his tent from the sons of Ḥamor, father of Shekhem,
20 for one hundred *kesita* of silver. There he erected an altar and named it El Elohei
34 1 Yisrael. Dina, the daughter whom Leah had borne to Yaakov, went out ḤAMISHI
2 to see the daughters of the land. When Shekhem son of Ḥamor the Hivite,
prince of the land, saw her, he took hold of her, lay with her, and violated her.
3 He became deeply drawn to Dina, Yaakov's daughter, and, in love with the
4 young woman, he spoke to her heart. Shekhem said to his father Ḥamor, "Take
5 this girl as a wife for me." When Yaakov heard that he had defiled his daughter

רש״י

יח **שלם.** שלם בגופו, שנתרפא מצלעתו; שלם בממונו, שלא חסר כלום מכל אותו דורון; שלם בתורתו, שלא שכח תלמודו בבית לבן: **עיר שכם.** כמו 'לעיר', וכמוהו: "עד בואנה בית לחם" (רות א, יט): **בבאו מפדן ארם.** כאדם האומר לחבירו, יצא פלוני מבין שני אריות ובא שלם, אף כאן: ויבא שלם מפדן ארם, מלבן ומעשו שנזדווגו לו בדרך:

יט **קשיטה.** מעה. אמר רבי עקיבא: כשהלכתי לכרכי הים היו קורין למעה 'קשיטה':

כ **ויקרא לו אל אלהי ישראל.** לא שהמזבח קרוי "אלהי ישראל", אלא על שם שהיה הקדוש ברוך הוא עמו והצילו קרא שם המזבח על שם הנס, להיות שבחו של מקום נזכר בקריאת השם, כלומר, מי שהוא אל, הוא הקדוש ברוך הוא, הוא לאלהים לי ששמי ישראל. וכן מצינו במשה: "ויקרא שמו ה' נסי" (שמות יז, טו), לא שהמזבח קרוי ה', אלא על שם הנס קרא שם המזבח להזכיר שבחו של הקדוש ברוך הוא, ה' הוא נסי. ורבותינו אמרו שהקדוש ברוך הוא קראו ליעקב 'אל'. ודברי תורה "כפטיש יפוצץ סלע" (ירמיה כג, כט), מתחלקים לכמה טעמים, ואני ליישב פשוטו של מקרא באתי:

לד א **בת לאה.** ולא בת יעקב? אלא על שם יציאתה נקראת 'בת לאה', שאף היא יצאנית – "ותצא לאה לקראתו" (לעיל ל, טז):

ב **וישכב אתה.** כדרכה: **ויענה.** שלא כדרכה:

ג **על לב הנערה.** דברים המתישבים על הלב: ראי אביך בחלקת שדה קטנה כמה ממון בזבז, אני אשאך ותקני כל העיר וכל שדותיה:

irony is that successful defense against a power-maximizing aggressor requires a society to become more like the society that threatens it. Power can be stopped only by power."

There are, in other words, four possible outcomes: (1) destruction, (2) subjugation, (3) withdrawal, and (4) imitation. "In every one of these outcomes," writes Schmookler, "*the ways of power are spread throughout the system.*" If you introduce a single violent tribe into the region, violence will eventually prevail, however the other tribes choose to respond. That is the tragedy of the human condition.

Shekhem's single act of violence against Dina forces two of Yaakov's sons into violent reprisal. In the end everyone involved is either contaminated or dead. It is indicative of the moral depth of the Torah that it does not hide this terrible truth from us by depicting one side as guilty, the other as innocent.

Violence defiles us all. It did then. It does now.

34:3 **ותדבק נפשו בדינה** *He became deeply drawn to Dina* – Compare this with the description of Amnon, son of King David, who rapes his half-sister Tamar. That story too is a tale of bloody revenge. But the text says about Amnon that after raping Tamar, he "hated her with a fierce hatred; his hatred for her was fiercer than the love he had felt toward her. And Amnon said to her, 'Get up! Be gone!'" (II Sam. 13:15). Shekhem is not like that at all. He falls in love with Dina and wants to marry her.

יח קָרָא שֵׁם־הַמָּקוֹם סֻכּוֹת׃ וַיָּבֹא יַעֲקֹב שָׁלֵם עִיר שְׁכֶם אֲשֶׁר לא
יט בְּאֶרֶץ כְּנַעַן בְּבֹאוֹ מִפַּדַּן אֲרָם וַיִּחַן אֶת־פְּנֵי הָעִיר׃ וַיִּקֶן אֶת־חֶלְקַת
הַשָּׂדֶה אֲשֶׁר נָטָה־שָׁם אָהֳלוֹ מִיַּד בְּנֵי־חֲמוֹר אֲבִי שְׁכֶם בְּמֵאָה
לד כ א קְשִׂיטָה׃ וַיַּצֶּב־שָׁם מִזְבֵּחַ וַיִּקְרָא־לוֹ אֵל אֱלֹהֵי יִשְׂרָאֵל׃ וַתֵּצֵא חמישי
ב דִינָה בַּת־לֵאָה אֲשֶׁר יָלְדָה לְיַעֲקֹב לִרְאוֹת בִּבְנוֹת הָאָרֶץ׃ וַיַּרְא אֹתָהּ
שְׁכֶם בֶּן־חֲמוֹר הַחִוִּי נְשִׂיא הָאָרֶץ וַיִּקַּח אֹתָהּ וַיִּשְׁכַּב אֹתָהּ וַיְעַנֶּהָ׃
ג וַתִּדְבַּק נַפְשׁוֹ בְּדִינָה בַּת־יַעֲקֹב וַיֶּאֱהַב אֶת־הַנַּעֲרָ וַיְדַבֵּר עַל־לֵב
ד הַנַּעֲרָ׃ וַיֹּאמֶר שְׁכֶם אֶל־חֲמוֹר אָבִיו לֵאמֹר קַח־לִי אֶת־הַיַּלְדָּה הַזֹּאת
ה לְאִשָּׁה׃ וְיַעֲקֹב שָׁמַע כִּי טִמֵּא אֶת־דִּינָה בִתּוֹ וּבָנָיו הָיוּ אֶת־מִקְנֵהוּ

אונקלוס

קְרָא שְׁמֵיהּ דְּאַתְרָא סֻכּוֹת: יח וַאֲתָא יַעֲקֹב שְׁלִים לְקַרְתָּא דִשְׁכֶם, דִּבְאַרְעָא דִכְנַעַן, בְּמֵיתוֹהִי מִפַּדַּן אֲרָם, וּשְׁרָא לָקֳבֵיל קַרְתָּא: יט וּזְבַן יָת אַחְסָנַת חַקְלָא, דִּפְרַסִיהּ תַּמָּן לְמַשְׁכְּנֵיהּ, מִיַּד בְּנֵי חֲמוֹר אֲבוּהִי דִּשְׁכֶם, בִּמְאָה חֻרְפָן: כ וַאֲקֵים תַּמָּן מַדְבְּחָא, וּפְלַח עֲלוֹהִי, קֳדָם אֵל אֱלָהָא דְיִשְׂרָאֵל: לד א וּנְפַקַת דִּינָה בַּת לֵאָה, דִּילֵידַת לְיַעֲקֹב, לְמִחְזֵי בִּבְנָת אַרְעָא: ב וַחֲזָא יָתַהּ, שְׁכֶם בַּר חֲמוֹר, חִוָּאָה רַבָּא דְאַרְעָא, וּדְבַר יָתַהּ, וּשְׁכֵיב יָתַהּ וְעַנְּיַהּ: ג וְאִתְרְעִיאַת נַפְשֵׁיהּ, בְּדִינָה בַּת יַעֲקֹב, וּרְחֵים יָת עוּלֵימְתָּא, וּמַלֵּיל עַל לִבַּהּ דְּעוּלֵימְתָּא: ד וַאֲמַר שְׁכֶם, לַחֲמוֹר אֲבוּהִי לְמֵימַר, סַב לִי, יָת עוּלֵימְתָּא הָדָא לְאִתּוּ: ה וְיַעֲקֹב שְׁמַע, אֲרֵי סַאֵיב יָת דִּינָה בְּרַתֵּיהּ, וּבְנוֹהִי, הֲווֹ עִם גֵּיתוֹהִי

DINA AND SHEKHEM

The story of Dina seems to lack any kind of moral message. No one comes out of it well. Shekhem, the prince, would seem to be the chief villain. It is he who abducts and rapes Dina in the first place. Ḥamor, his father, fails to reprimand him or order Dina's release. Shimon and Levi are guilty of a horrendous act of violence. The other brothers engage in looting the town. Yaakov seems passive throughout. He neither acts nor instructs his sons on how to act. Even Dina herself seems at best to have been guilty of carelessness in going out into what is clearly a dangerous neighborhood – recall that both Avraham and Yitzḥak, her great-grandfather and grandfather, feared for their own lives because of the lawlessness of the times, particularly with regard to the abduction of women.

Who is in the right and who in the wrong is left conspicuously undecided in the text. The overall effect is a story with no irredeemable villains and no stainless heroes. Why then is it told at all? Stories do not appear in the Torah merely because they happened. *Torah* means "teaching," "instruction," "guidance." What teaching does the Torah want us to draw from this narrative out of which no one emerges well?

There is an important thought experiment devised by Andrew Schmookler known as the parable of the tribes. Imagine a group of tribes living close to one another. All choose the way of peace except one that is willing to use violence to achieve its ends. What happens to the peace-seeking tribes? One is defeated and destroyed by the violent tribe. A second is conquered and subjugated. A third flees to some remote and inaccessible place. If the fourth seeks to defend itself, it too will need to have recourse to violence. "The

Dina, his sons were in the field with his livestock, and so he stayed silent until
6 they came home. Shekhem's father Ḥamor came to Yaakov to speak with him.
7 Meanwhile, Yaakov's sons, having heard what had happened, came back from
the field. They were shocked and furious, for Shekhem had committed an
outrage in Israel by sleeping with Yaakov's daughter. Such a thing cannot be
8 done! But Ḥamor spoke with them and said, "My son Shekhem has his heart
9 set upon your daughter. Please give her to him as his wife. Intermarry with us.
10 Give us your daughters and take our daughters for yourselves. Settle with us.
11 The land is open to you. Live here, trade here, acquire property here." Then
Shekhem said to Dina's father and brothers, "Let me but find favor in your eyes
12 and I will give whatever you ask. Set the bridal price and gifts as high as you
like. I will give whatever you ask of me; only give me the young woman as my
13 wife." Yaakov's sons responded to Shekhem and his father Ḥamor, and they
14 spoke deceptively: he had, after all, defiled their sister Dina. They told them,
"We cannot do this. To give our sister to an uncircumcised man would be a
15 disgrace to us. Only on one condition will we agree with you: If you become
16 like us, circumcising all your males, then we will give you our daughters and
take your daughters for ourselves. We will live with you and become one
17 people. If you do not agree to be circumcised, we will take our daughter and

רש"י

ז **וְכֵן לֹא יֵעָשֶׂה.** לְעַנּוֹת אֶת הַבְּתוּלוֹת, שֶׁהָאֻמּוֹת גָּדְרוּ עַצְמָן מִן הָעֲרָיוֹת עַל יְדֵי הַמַּבּוּל:

ח **חָשְׁקָה.** חָפְצָה:

יב **מֹהַר.** כְּתֻבָּה:

יג **בְּמִרְמָה.** בְּחָכְמָה: **אֲשֶׁר טִמֵּא.** הַכָּתוּב אוֹמֵר שֶׁלֹּא הָיְתָה רְמִיָּה, שֶׁהֲרֵי "טִמֵּא אֶת דִּינָה אֲחֹתָם":

יד **חֶרְפָּה הִוא.** שֶׁמֶץ הוּא אֶצְלֵנוּ; הַבָּא לְחָרֵף אֶת חֲבֵרוֹ אוֹמֵר לוֹ: עָרֵל אַתָּה, אוֹ בֶּן עָרֵל. 'חֶרְפָּה' בְּכָל מָקוֹם – גִּדּוּף:

טו **נֵאוֹת.** נִתְרַצֶּה, לְשׁוֹן "וַיֵּאֹתוּ" (מלכים ב' יב, ט): **לְהִמֹּל.** לִהְיוֹת נִמּוֹל. אֵינוֹ לְשׁוֹן 'לִפְעֹל' אֶלָּא לְשׁוֹן 'לְהִפָּעֵל':

טז **וְנָתַנּוּ.** נוּ"ן שְׁנִיָּה מְדֻגֶּשֶׁת לְפִי שֶׁהִיא מְשַׁמֶּשֶׁת בִּמְקוֹם שְׁתֵּי נוּנִי"ן, 'וְנָתַנְנוּ': **וְאֶת בְּנֹתֵיכֶם נִקַּח לָנוּ.** אַתָּה מוֹצֵא בַּתְּנַאי שֶׁאָמַר חֲמוֹר לְיַעֲקֹב וּבִתְשׁוּבַת בְּנֵי יַעֲקֹב לַחֲמוֹר, שֶׁתָּלוּ הַחֲשִׁיבוּת בִּבְנֵי יַעֲקֹב לִקַּח בְּנוֹת שְׁכֶם אֶת שֶׁיִּבְחֲרוּ לָהֶם וּבְנוֹתֵיהֶם יִתְּנוּ לָהֶם לְפִי דַּעְתָּם, דִּכְתִיב: "וְנָתַנּוּ אֶת בְּנֹתֵינוּ" – לְפִי דַּעְתֵּנוּ, "וְאֶת בְּנֹתֵיכֶם נִקַּח לָנוּ" – בְּכָל אֲשֶׁר נַחְפֹּץ. וּכְשֶׁדִּבְּרוּ חֲמוֹר וּשְׁכֶם בְּנוֹ אֶל יוֹשְׁבֵי עִירָם הָפְכוּ הַדְּבָרִים: "אֶת בְּנֹתָם נִקַּח לָנוּ לְנָשִׁים וְאֶת בְּנֹתֵינוּ נִתֵּן לָהֶם" (להלן פסוק כא), כְּדֵי לְרַצּוֹתָם שֶׁיֵּאוֹתוּ לְהִמּוֹל:

they would still be outnumbered. Shimon and Levi must resort to a ruse.

This appears to be the brothers' perception of their predicament. The text, however, does not demonize the people of Shekhem and does not paint any of Yaakov's family in a completely positive light. It uses the same word for "deceptively" that it has used previously about Yaakov taking Esav's blessing and Lavan substituting Leah for Raḥel. In its description of all the characters – from Dina herself to her excessively violent rescuers, to the plundering other brothers and the passive Yaakov – the text seems written deliberately to alienate our sympathies.

ו בַּשָּׂדֶה וְהֶחֱרִשׁ יַעֲקֹב עַד־בֹּאָם: וַיֵּצֵא חֲמוֹר אֲבִי־שְׁכֶם אֶל־יַעֲקֹב
ז לְדַבֵּר אִתּוֹ: וּבְנֵי יַעֲקֹב בָּאוּ מִן־הַשָּׂדֶה כְּשָׁמְעָם וַיִּתְעַצְּבוּ הָאֲנָשִׁים
וַיִּחַר לָהֶם מְאֹד כִּי נְבָלָה עָשָׂה בְיִשְׂרָאֵל לִשְׁכַּב אֶת־בַּת־יַעֲקֹב וְכֵן
ח לֹא יֵעָשֶׂה: וַיְדַבֵּר חֲמוֹר אִתָּם לֵאמֹר שְׁכֶם בְּנִי חָשְׁקָה נַפְשׁוֹ בְּבִתְּכֶם
ט תְּנוּ נָא אֹתָהּ לוֹ לְאִשָּׁה: וְהִתְחַתְּנוּ אֹתָנוּ בְּנֹתֵיכֶם תִּתְּנוּ־לָנוּ וְאֶת־
י בְּנֹתֵינוּ תִּקְחוּ לָכֶם: וְאִתָּנוּ תֵּשֵׁבוּ וְהָאָרֶץ תִּהְיֶה לִפְנֵיכֶם שְׁבוּ וּסְחָרוּהָ
יא וְהֵאָחֲזוּ בָּהּ: וַיֹּאמֶר שְׁכֶם אֶל־אָבִיהָ וְאֶל־אַחֶיהָ אֶמְצָא־חֵן בְּעֵינֵיכֶם
יב וַאֲשֶׁר תֹּאמְרוּ אֵלַי אֶתֵּן: הַרְבּוּ עָלַי מְאֹד מֹהַר וּמַתָּן וְאֶתְּנָה כַּאֲשֶׁר
יג תֹּאמְרוּ אֵלָי וּתְנוּ־לִי אֶת־הַנַּעֲרָ לְאִשָּׁה: וַיַּעֲנוּ בְנֵי־יַעֲקֹב אֶת־שְׁכֶם
וְאֶת־חֲמוֹר אָבִיו בְּמִרְמָה וַיְדַבֵּרוּ אֲשֶׁר טִמֵּא אֵת דִּינָה אֲחֹתָם:
יד וַיֹּאמְרוּ אֲלֵיהֶם לֹא נוּכַל לַעֲשׂוֹת הַדָּבָר הַזֶּה לָתֵת אֶת־אֲחֹתֵנוּ לְאִישׁ
טו אֲשֶׁר־לוֹ עָרְלָה כִּי־חֶרְפָּה הִוא לָנוּ: אַךְ־בְּזֹאת נֵאוֹת לָכֶם אִם תִּהְיוּ
טז כָמֹנוּ לְהִמֹּל לָכֶם כָּל־זָכָר: וְנָתַנּוּ אֶת־בְּנֹתֵינוּ לָכֶם וְאֶת־בְּנֹתֵיכֶם נִקַּח־
יז לָנוּ וְיָשַׁבְנוּ אִתְּכֶם וְהָיִינוּ לְעַם אֶחָד: וְאִם־לֹא תִשְׁמְעוּ אֵלֵינוּ לְהִמּוֹל

אונקלוס

בְּחַקְלָא, וּשְׁתֵיק יַעֲקֹב עַד מֵיתֵיהוֹן: ו וּנְפַק, חֲמוֹר אֲבוּהִי דִשְׁכֶם לְוָת יַעֲקֹב, לְמַלָּלָא עִמֵּיהּ: ז וּבְנֵי יַעֲקֹב, עָאלוּ מִן חַקְלָא כַּד שְׁמַעוּ, וְאִתְנְסִיסוּ גֻבְרַיָּא, וּתְקֵיף לְהוֹן לַחְדָא, אֲרֵי קְלָנָא עֲבַד בְּיִשְׂרָאֵל, לְמִשְׁכַּב עִם בַּת יַעֲקֹב, וְכֵן לָא כָשַׁר דְּיִתְעֲבֵיד: ח וּמַלֵּיל חֲמוֹר עִמְּהוֹן לְמֵימַר, שְׁכֶם בְּרִי, אִתְרְעִיאַת נַפְשֵׁיהּ בִּבְרַתְּכוֹן, הַבוּ כְעַן יָתַהּ, לֵיהּ לְאִתּוּ: ט וְאִתְחַתְּנוּ בַנָא, בְּנָתְכוֹן תִּתְּנוּן לַנָא, וְיָת בְּנָתַנָא תִּסְּבוּן לְכוֹן: י וְעִמַּנָא תִּתְּבוּן, וְאַרְעָא תְּהֵי קֳדָמֵיכוֹן, תִּיבוּ וַעֲבִידוּ בַהּ סְחוֹרְתָא, וְאַחְסִינוּ בַהּ: יא וַאֲמַר שְׁכֶם לַאֲבוּהָא וּלְאַחָהָא, אַשְׁכַּח רַחֲמִין בְּעֵינֵיכוֹן, וּדְתֵימְרוּן לִי אֶתֵּין: יב אַסְגוּ עֲלַי לַחְדָא מֹהֲרִין וּמַתְּנָן, וְאֶתֵּין, כְּמָא דְתֵימְרוּן לִי, וְהַבוּ לִי יָת עוּלֵימְתָא לְאִתּוּ: יג וַאֲתִיבוּ בְנֵי יַעֲקֹב, יָת שְׁכֶם וְיָת חֲמוֹר אֲבוּהִי, בְּחָכְמָא וּמַלִּילוּ, דְּסָאֵיב, יָת דִּינָה אֲחָתְהוֹן: יד וַאֲמַרוּ לְהוֹן, לָא נִכּוּל לְמֶעְבַּד פִּתְגָמָא הָדֵין, לְמִתַּן יָת אֲחָתַנָא, לִגְבַר דְּלֵיהּ עָרְלָה, אֲרֵי חִסּוּדָא הִיא לַנָא: טו בְּרַם בְּדָא נִתְפַּס לְכוֹן, אִם תְּהוֹן כְּוָתַנָא, לְמִגְזַר לְכוֹן כָּל דְּכוּרָא: טז וְנִתֵּין יָת בְּנָתַנָא לְכוֹן, וְיָת בְּנָתְכוֹן נִסַּב לַנָא, וְנִתֵּיב עִמְּכוֹן, וּנְהֵי לְעַמָּא חַד: יז וְאִם לָא תְקַבְּלוּן, מִנַּנָא לְמִגְזַר,

34:13 וַיַּעֲנוּ...אָבִיו בְּמִרְמָה *They spoke deceptively* – Shimon and Levi, Dina's brothers, realize that they must act to rescue her. It is an almost impossible assignment. The hostage-taker is no ordinary individual. As the son of the king, he cannot be confronted directly. The king is unlikely to order his son to release her. The other townspeople, if challenged, will come to the prince's defense. It is Shimon and Levi against the town, two against many. Even were all of Yaakov's sons to be enlisted,

18 19 go." Their words gratified Ḥamor and his son Shekhem. The young man, the
most honored of his father's family, lost no time in doing it, because he longed
20 for Yaakov's daughter. Ḥamor and his son Shekhem came to the town gate and
21 spoke to their fellow townsmen. "These people are friendly toward us," they
said. "Let them live in the land and trade in it. We have space enough for them.
22 We can marry their daughters and they can marry ours. But only on one
condition will they agree to dwell with us as one people. Every male among us
23 must be circumcised as they are. Will not their livestock, property, and all their
animals be ours? Let us, then, agree to their terms and let them settle among us."
24 All the people who went out by the town gate listened to Ḥamor and his son
Shekhem, and all the males who went out by the town gate were circumcised.
25 On the third day, when the people were weak from pain, two of Yaakov's sons,
Shimon and Levi, Dina's brothers, took their swords, entered the unsuspecting
26 town, and killed every single male. They killed Ḥamor and his son Shekhem by
27 the sword, took Dina from Shekhem's house and left. Yaakov's sons came upon
28 the dead and plundered the town that had defiled their sister. They took their
flocks, their cattle, their donkeys, and everything else of theirs in the town and
29 out in the field. Their wealth, their children, and their women they took captive
30 and looted, and all that was in the houses. Yaakov said to Shimon and Levi, "You
have brought trouble upon me – you have made me odious to the inhabitants of

אונקלוס

וְנִדְבַּר יָת בְּרַתָּנָא וְנֵיזֵיל: יח וּשְׁפַרוּ פִתְגָּמֵיהוֹן בְּעֵינֵי חֲמוֹר, וּבְעֵינֵי שְׁכֶם בַּר חֲמוֹר: יט וְלָא אוֹחַר עוּלֵימָא לְמֶעְבַּד פִּתְגָּמָא, אֲרֵי אִתְרְעִי בְּבַת יַעֲקֹב, וְהוּא יַקִּיר, מִכֹּל בֵּית אֲבוּהִי: כ וַאֲתָא חֲמוֹר, וּשְׁכֶם בְּרֵיהּ לִתְרַע קַרְתְּהוֹן, וּמַלִּילוּ, עִם אֱנָשֵׁי קַרְתְּהוֹן לְמֵימַר: כא גֻּבְרַיָּא הָאִלֵּין שְׁלָם אִנּוּן עִמַּנָא, וְיִתְּבוּן בְּאַרְעָא וְיַעְבְּדוּן בַּהּ סְחוֹרְתָא, וְאַרְעָא, הָא פַתְיוּת יְדִין קֳדָמֵיהוֹן, יָת בְּנָתְהוֹן נִסַּב לַנָא ◀

רש"י

כא **שְׁלֵמִים.** בְּשָׁלוֹם וּבְלֵב שָׁלֵם: **וְהָאָרֶץ הִנֵּה רַחֲבַת יָדַיִם.** כְּאָדָם שֶׁיָּדוֹ רְחָבָה וּוַתְּרָנִית; כְּלוֹמַר, לֹא תַפְסִידוּ כְּלוּם, פְּרַקְמַטְיָא הַרְבֵּה בָּאָה לְכָאן וְאֵין לָהּ קוֹנִים:

כב **בְּהִמּוֹל.** בִּהְיוֹת נִמּוֹל:

כג **אַךְ נֵאוֹתָה לָהֶם.** לְדָבָר זֶה, וְעַל יְדֵי כֵן יֵשְׁבוּ אִתָּנוּ:

כה **שְׁנֵי בְנֵי יַעֲקֹב.** בָּנָיו הָיוּ, וְאַף עַל פִּי כֵן נָהֲגוּ עַצְמָן "שִׁמְעוֹן וְלֵוִי" – כִּשְׁאָר אֲנָשִׁים שֶׁאֵינָם בָּנָיו, שֶׁלֹּא נָטְלוּ עֵצָה הֵימֶנּוּ: **אֲחֵי דִינָה.** לְפִי שֶׁמָּסְרוּ עַצְמָן עָלֶיהָ נִקְרְאוּ אַחֶיהָ: **בֶּטַח.** שֶׁהָיוּ כּוֹאֲבִים. וּמִדְרַשׁ אַגָּדָה, בְּטוּחִים עַל כֹּחוֹ שֶׁל זָקֵן:

כז **עַל הַחֲלָלִים.** לְפַשֵּׁט אֶת הַחֲלָלִים:

כט **חֵילָם.** מָמוֹנָם, וְכֵן: "עָשָׂה לִי אֶת הַחַיִל הַזֶּה" (דברים ח, יז), "וְיִשְׂרָאֵל עֹשֶׂה חָיִל" (במדבר כד, יח), "וְעָזְבוּ לַאֲחֵרִים חֵילָם" (תהלים מט, יא): **שָׁבוּ.** לְשׁוֹן שְׁבִיָּה, לְפִיכָךְ טַעְמוֹ מִלְרַע:

ל **עֲכַרְתֶּם.** לְשׁוֹן מַיִם עֲכוּרִים, אֵין דַּעְתִּי צְלוּלָה עַכְשָׁיו. וְאַגָּדָה, צְלוּלָה הָיְתָה הֶחָבִית וַעֲכַרְתֶּם אוֹתָהּ. מָסֹרֶת הָיְתָה בְּיַד כְּנַעֲנִים שֶׁיִּפְּלוּ בְּיַד בְּנֵי יַעֲקֹב, אֶלָּא שֶׁהָיוּ אוֹמְרִים: "עַד אֲשֶׁר תִּפְרֶה וְנָחַלְתָּ אֶת הָאָרֶץ" (שמות כג, ל), לְפִיכָךְ הָיוּ שׁוֹתְקִין:

יח וְלָקַחְנוּ אֶת־בִּתֵּנוּ וְהָלָכְנוּ׃ וַיִּיטְבוּ דִבְרֵיהֶם בְּעֵינֵי חֲמוֹר וּבְעֵינֵי שְׁכֶם
יט בֶּן־חֲמוֹר׃ וְלֹא־אֵחַר הַנַּעַר לַעֲשׂוֹת הַדָּבָר כִּי חָפֵץ בְּבַת־יַעֲקֹב וְהוּא
כ נִכְבָּד מִכֹּל בֵּית אָבִיו׃ וַיָּבֹא חֲמוֹר וּשְׁכֶם בְּנוֹ אֶל־שַׁעַר עִירָם וַיְדַבְּרוּ
כא אֶל־אַנְשֵׁי עִירָם לֵאמֹר׃ הָאֲנָשִׁים הָאֵלֶּה שְׁלֵמִים הֵם אִתָּנוּ וְיֵשְׁבוּ
בָאָרֶץ וְיִסְחֲרוּ אֹתָהּ וְהָאָרֶץ הִנֵּה רַחֲבַת־יָדַיִם לִפְנֵיהֶם אֶת־בְּנֹתָם
כב נִקַּח־לָנוּ לְנָשִׁים וְאֶת־בְּנֹתֵינוּ נִתֵּן לָהֶם׃ אַךְ־בְּזֹאת יֵאֹתוּ לָנוּ הָאֲנָשִׁים
לָשֶׁבֶת אִתָּנוּ לִהְיוֹת לְעַם אֶחָד בְּהִמּוֹל לָנוּ כָּל־זָכָר כַּאֲשֶׁר הֵם נִמֹּלִים׃
כג מִקְנֵהֶם וְקִנְיָנָם וְכָל־בְּהֶמְתָּם הֲלוֹא לָנוּ הֵם אַךְ נֵאוֹתָה לָהֶם וְיֵשְׁבוּ
כד אִתָּנוּ׃ וַיִּשְׁמְעוּ אֶל־חֲמוֹר וְאֶל־שְׁכֶם בְּנוֹ כָּל־יֹצְאֵי שַׁעַר עִירוֹ וַיִּמֹּלוּ
כה כָּל־זָכָר כָּל־יֹצְאֵי שַׁעַר עִירוֹ׃ וַיְהִי בַיּוֹם הַשְּׁלִישִׁי בִּהְיוֹתָם כֹּאֲבִים
וַיִּקְחוּ שְׁנֵי־בְנֵי־יַעֲקֹב שִׁמְעוֹן וְלֵוִי אֲחֵי דִינָה אִישׁ חַרְבּוֹ וַיָּבֹאוּ עַל־
כו הָעִיר בֶּטַח וַיַּהַרְגוּ כָּל־זָכָר׃ וְאֶת־חֲמוֹר וְאֶת־שְׁכֶם בְּנוֹ הָרְגוּ לְפִי־חָרֶב
כז וַיִּקְחוּ אֶת־דִּינָה מִבֵּית שְׁכֶם וַיֵּצֵאוּ׃ בְּנֵי יַעֲקֹב בָּאוּ עַל־הַחֲלָלִים
כח וַיָּבֹזּוּ הָעִיר אֲשֶׁר טִמְּאוּ אֲחוֹתָם׃ אֶת־צֹאנָם וְאֶת־בְּקָרָם וְאֶת־
כט חֲמֹרֵיהֶם וְאֵת אֲשֶׁר־בָּעִיר וְאֶת־אֲשֶׁר בַּשָּׂדֶה לָקָחוּ׃ וְאֶת־כָּל־חֵילָם
ל וְאֶת־כָּל־טַפָּם וְאֶת־נְשֵׁיהֶם שָׁבוּ וַיָּבֹזּוּ וְאֵת כָּל־אֲשֶׁר בַּבָּיִת׃ וַיֹּאמֶר
יַעֲקֹב אֶל־שִׁמְעוֹן וְאֶל־לֵוִי עֲכַרְתֶּם אֹתִי לְהַבְאִישֵׁנִי בְּיֹשֵׁב הָאָרֶץ

אונקלוס

לִנְשִׁין, וְיַת בְּנָתַנָא נִתֵּין לְהוֹן: כב בְּרַם בְּדָא, יִתְפַּסוּן לַנָא גֻבְרַיָּא לְמִתַּב עִמַּנָא, לְמִהְוֵי לְעַמָּא חַד, בְּמִגְזַר לַנָא כָּל דְּכוּרָא, כְּמָא דְאִנּוּן גְּזִירִין: כג גֵּיתֵיהוֹן וְקִנְיָנְהוֹן וְכָל בְּעִירְהוֹן, הֲלָא דִילַנָא אִנּוּן, בְּרַם נִתְפַּס לְהוֹן, וְיִתְּבוּן עִמַּנָא: כד וְקַבִּילוּ מִן חֲמוֹר וּמִן שְׁכֶם בְּרֵיהּ, כָּל נָפְקֵי תְּרַע קַרְתֵּיהּ, וּגְזַרוּ כָּל דְּכוּרָא, כָּל נָפְקֵי תְּרַע קַרְתֵּיהּ: כה וַהֲוָה בְּיוֹמָא תְלִיתָאָה כַּד תְּקִיפוּ עֲלֵיהוֹן כֵּיבֵיהוֹן, וּנְסִיבוּ תְּרֵין בְּנֵי יַעֲקֹב, שִׁמְעוֹן וְלֵוִי, אֲחֵי דִינָה גְּבַר חַרְבֵּיהּ, וְעָאלוּ עַל קַרְתָּא דְּיָתְבָא לִרְחָצַן, וְקַטַלוּ כָּל דְּכוּרָא: כו וְיַת חֲמוֹר וְיַת שְׁכֶם בְּרֵיהּ, קְטַלוּ לְפִתְגָם דְּחָרֶב, וּדְבַרוּ יַת דִּינָה, מִבֵּית שְׁכֶם וּנְפַקוּ: כז בְּנֵי יַעֲקֹב, עָאלוּ לְחַלָּצָא קְטִילַיָּא, וּבַזּוּ קַרְתָּא, דְּסָאִיבוּ אֲחָתְהוֹן: כח יַת עָנְהוֹן וְיַת תּוֹרֵיהוֹן וְיַת חֲמָרֵיהוֹן, וְיַת דִּבְקַרְתָּא, וְיַת דִּבְחַקְלָא בַּזּוּ: כט וְיַת כָּל נִכְסֵיהוֹן וְיַת כָּל טַפְלְהוֹן וְיַת נְשֵׁיהוֹן, שְׁבוֹ וּבַזּוּ, וְיַת כָּל דִּבְבֵיתָא: ל וַאֲמַר יַעֲקֹב, לְשִׁמְעוֹן וּלְלֵוִי עֲכַרְתּוּן יָתִי, לְמִתַּן דְּבָבוּ בֵּינָא וּבֵין יָתֵיב אַרְעָא,

the land, the Canaanites and Perizzites. I am few in number, and if they join
31 forces and attack me, I and my household will be destroyed." But they said,
"Should our sister be treated like a whore?"
35 1 God said to Yaakov, "Arise, go up to Beit El. Stay there, and there build an altar
2 to God, who appeared to you as you fled your brother Esav." Yaakov told his
household and everyone with him, "Be rid of the alien gods you have with you.
3 Purify yourselves and change your clothes. Then come, let us go up to Beit El,
and there I will make an altar to God, who answered me in my time of trouble
4 and who has been with me wherever I have gone." They gave Yaakov all the alien
gods they had, and even the rings in their ears, and Yaakov buried them under a
5 terebinth near Shekhem. As they set out, the terror of God fell on the surrounding
6 towns so that no one pursued Yaakov's sons. Yaakov and all the people with him
7 came to Luz – that is, Beit El – in the land of Canaan. There he built an altar and
called the place El Beit El, because it was there that God had revealed Himself to
8 him as he fled his brother. Devora, Rivka's nurse, died and was buried under the
oak outside Beit El. And so it was named Oak of Weeping.

רש"י

מְתֵי מִסְפָּר. אֲנָשִׁים מוּעָטִים:

לא הַכְזוֹנָה. הֶפְקֵר: אֶת אֲחוֹתֵנוּ. "יָת אֲחָתַנָא":

לה א קוּם עֲלֵה. לְפִי שֶׁאֵחַרְתָּ נִדְרְךָ נֶעֱנַשְׁתָּ וּבָאָה לְךָ זֹאת מִבִּתְּךָ:

ב הַנֵּכָר. שֶׁיֵּשׁ בְּיֶדְכֶם מִשְּׁלַל שֶׁל שְׁכֶם: וְהִטַּהֲרוּ. מֵעֲבוֹדָה זָרָה: וְהַחֲלִיפוּ שִׂמְלֹתֵיכֶם. שֶׁמָּא יֵשׁ בְּיֶדְכֶם כְּסוּת שֶׁל עֲבוֹדָה זָרָה:

ד הָאֵלָה. מִין אִילַן סְרָק: עִם שְׁכֶם. אֵצֶל שְׁכֶם:

ה חִתַּת. פַּחַד:

ז אֵל בֵּית אֵל. הַקָּדוֹשׁ בָּרוּךְ הוּא בְּבֵית אֵל, גִּלּוּי שְׁכִינָתוֹ בְּבֵית אֵל. יֵשׁ תֵּבָה חֲסֵרָה בֵּי"ת הַמְשַׁמֶּשֶׁת בְּרֹאשָׁהּ, כְּמוֹ: "הִנֵּה הוּא בֵּית מָכִיר בֶּן עַמִּיאֵל" (שמואל ב' ט, ד) כְּמוֹ: 'בְּבֵית מָכִיר', "בֵּית אָבִיךָ" (להלן לח, יא) כְּמוֹ 'בְּבֵית אָבִיךָ': נִגְלוּ אֵלָיו הָאֱלֹהִים. בִּמְקוֹמוֹת הַרְבֵּה יֵשׁ שֵׁם אֱלָהוּת וְאַדְנוּת בִּלְשׁוֹן רַבִּים, כְּמוֹ: "אֲדֹנֵי יוֹסֵף" (להלן לט, כ), "אִם בְּעָלָיו עִמּוֹ" (שמות כב, יד) וְלֹא נֶאֱמַר 'בַּעְלוֹ', וְכֵן אֱלָהוּת שֶׁהוּא לְשׁוֹן שׁוֹפֵט וּמָרוּת נִזְכָּר בִּלְשׁוֹן רַבִּים, אֲבָל אֶחָד מִכָּל שְׁאָר הַשֵּׁמוֹת לֹא תִמְצָא בִּלְשׁוֹן רַבִּים:

ח וַתָּמָת דְּבֹרָה. מָה עִנְיַן דְּבוֹרָה בְּבֵית יַעֲקֹב? אֶלָּא לְפִי שֶׁאָמְרָה רִבְקָה לְיַעֲקֹב: "וְשָׁלַחְתִּי וּלְקַחְתִּיךָ מִשָּׁם" (לעיל כז, מה) שָׁלְחָה דְּבוֹרָה אֶצְלוֹ לְפַדַּן אֲרָם לָצֵאת מִשָּׁם, וּמֵתָה בַּדֶּרֶךְ. מִדִּבְרֵי רַבִּי מֹשֶׁה הַדַּרְשָׁן לָמַדְתִּיהָ: מִתַּחַת לְבֵית אֵל. הָעִיר יוֹשֶׁבֶת בָּהָר וְנִקְבְּרָה בְּרַגְלֵי הָהָר: תַּחַת הָאַלּוֹן. "בְּשִׁפּוּלֵי מֵישְׁרָא", שֶׁהָיָה מִישׁוֹר מִלְמַעְלָה בְּשִׁפּוּעַ הָהָר

of a crime, and yet neither brought him to court nor rescued the girl. They were therefore accomplices in his guilt. What Shekhem had done was a capital crime, and by sheltering him the townspeople were implicated (*Hilkhot Melakhim* 9:14). This is, incidentally, a fascinating ruling since it suggests that for Rambam the rule that "all Israel are responsible for one another" (Shevuot 39a) is not restricted to Israel. It applies to all societies. As Isaac Arama would write in the fifteenth century, any crime known about and allowed to continue ceases to be an offense of individuals only and becomes a sin of the community as a whole (*Akedat Yitzḥak*, Bereshit, Vayera 20, s.v. *UVeMidrash*).

Ramban disagrees (in his commentary on Gen. 34:13). The principle of collective responsibility does not, in his view, apply to non-Jewish societies. The Noahide covenant requires every society to set up courts of law, but it does not imply that a failure to prosecute a wrongdoer involves all members of the society in a capital crime.

35:8 **אַלּוֹן בָּכוּת** *Oak of Weeping* – This is our only reference

בַּֽכְּנַעֲנִ֖י וּבַפְּרִזִּ֑י וַאֲנִי֙ מְתֵ֣י מִסְפָּ֔ר וְנֶאֶסְפ֤וּ עָלַי֙ וְהִכּ֔וּנִי וְנִשְׁמַדְתִּ֖י אֲנִ֥י
לא וּבֵיתִֽי׃ וַיֹּאמְר֑וּ הַֽכְזוֹנָ֔ה יַעֲשֶׂ֖ה אֶת־אֲחוֹתֵֽנוּ׃
לה א וַיֹּ֤אמֶר אֱלֹהִים֙ אֶֽל־יַעֲקֹ֔ב ק֛וּם עֲלֵ֥ה בֵֽית־אֵ֖ל וְשֶׁב־שָׁ֑ם וַעֲשֵׂה־שָׁ֣ם
ב מִזְבֵּ֔חַ לָאֵל֙ הַנִּרְאֶ֣ה אֵלֶ֔יךָ בְּבָרְחֲךָ֔ מִפְּנֵ֖י עֵשָׂ֥ו אָחִֽיךָ׃ וַיֹּ֤אמֶר יַעֲקֹב֙
אֶל־בֵּית֔וֹ וְאֶ֖ל כָּל־אֲשֶׁ֣ר עִמּ֑וֹ הָסִ֜רוּ אֶת־אֱלֹהֵ֤י הַנֵּכָר֙ אֲשֶׁ֣ר בְּתֹֽכְכֶ֔ם
ג וְהִֽטַּהֲר֔וּ וְהַחֲלִ֖יפוּ שִׂמְלֹתֵיכֶֽם׃ וְנָק֥וּמָה וְנַעֲלֶ֖ה בֵּֽית־אֵ֑ל וְאֶֽעֱשֶׂה־שָּׁ֣ם
מִזְבֵּ֗חַ לָאֵ֞ל הָעֹנֶ֤ה אֹתִי֙ בְּי֣וֹם צָֽרָתִ֔י וַֽיְהִי֙ עִמָּדִ֔י בַּדֶּ֖רֶךְ אֲשֶׁ֥ר הָלָֽכְתִּי׃
ד וַיִּתְּנ֣וּ אֶֽל־יַעֲקֹ֗ב אֵ֣ת כָּל־אֱלֹהֵ֤י הַנֵּכָר֙ אֲשֶׁ֣ר בְּיָדָ֔ם וְאֶת־הַנְּזָמִ֖ים אֲשֶׁ֣ר
ה בְּאָזְנֵיהֶ֑ם וַיִּטְמֹ֤ן אֹתָם֙ יַעֲקֹ֔ב תַּ֥חַת הָאֵלָ֖ה אֲשֶׁ֥ר עִם־שְׁכֶֽם׃ וַיִּסָּ֑עוּ
וַיְהִ֣י ׀ חִתַּ֣ת אֱלֹהִ֗ים עַל־הֶֽעָרִים֙ אֲשֶׁר֙ סְבִיב֣וֹתֵיהֶ֔ם וְלֹ֣א רָֽדְפ֔וּ אַחֲרֵ֖י בְּנֵ֥י
ו יַעֲקֹֽב׃ וַיָּבֹ֨א יַעֲקֹ֜ב ל֗וּזָה אֲשֶׁר֙ בְּאֶ֣רֶץ כְּנַ֔עַן הִ֖וא בֵּֽית־אֵ֑ל ה֖וּא וְכָל־הָעָ֥ם
ז אֲשֶׁר־עִמּֽוֹ׃ וַיִּ֤בֶן שָׁם֙ מִזְבֵּ֔חַ וַיִּקְרָא֙ לַמָּק֔וֹם אֵ֖ל בֵּֽית־אֵ֑ל כִּ֣י שָׁ֗ם נִגְל֤וּ
ח אֵלָיו֙ הָֽאֱלֹהִ֔ים בְּבָרְח֖וֹ מִפְּנֵ֥י אָחִֽיו׃ וַתָּ֤מָת דְּבֹרָה֙ מֵינֶ֣קֶת רִבְקָ֔ה וַתִּקָּבֵ֛ר
מִתַּ֥חַת לְבֵֽית־אֵ֖ל תַּ֣חַת הָֽאַלּ֑וֹן וַיִּקְרָ֥א שְׁמ֖וֹ אַלּ֥וֹן בָּכֽוּת׃

אונקלוס

בִּכְנַעֲנָאָה וּבִפְרִזָּאָה, וַאֲנָא עַם דְּמִנְיָן, וְיִתְכַּנְּשׁוּן עֲלַי וְיִמְחוֹנַנִי, וְאֶשְׁתֵּיצֵי אֲנָא וֶאֱנָשׁ בֵּיתִי: לא וַאֲמַרוּ, הַכְנָפְקַת בָּרָא, יַעֲבֵיד יָת אֲחָתַנָא: לה א וַאֲמַר יי לְיַעֲקֹב, קוּם, סַק לְבֵית אֵל וְתִיב תַּמָּן, וַעֲבֵיד תַּמָּן מַדְבַּח, לְאֵל דְּאִתְגְּלִי לָךְ, בְּמֶעְרְקָךְ, מִן קֳדָם עֵשָׂו אֲחוּךְ: ב וַאֲמַר יַעֲקֹב לֶאֱנָשׁ בֵּיתֵיהּ, וּלְכָל דְּעִמֵּיהּ, אַעְדּוֹ, יָת טַעֲוַת עַמְמַיָּא דְּבֵינֵיכוֹן, וְאִדַּכּוֹ, וְשַׁנּוֹ כְּסוּתְכוֹן: ג וּנְקוּם וְנִסַּק לְבֵית אֵל, וְאַעֲבֵיד תַּמָּן מַדְבַּח, לְאֵל, דְּקַבֵּיל צְלוֹתִי בְּיוֹמָא דְּעָקְתִי, וַהֲוָה מֵימְרֵיהּ בְּסַעֲדִי, בְּאוֹרְחָא דַּאֲזָלִית: ד וִיהַבוּ לְיַעֲקֹב, יָת כָּל טַעֲוָת עַמְמַיָּא דִּבְיְדֵיהוֹן, וְיָת קְדָשַׁיָּא דִּבְאֻדְנֵיהוֹן, וְטַמַּר יָתְהוֹן יַעֲקֹב, תְּחוֹת בُטְמָא דְּעִם שְׁכֶם: ה וּנְטַלוּ, וַהֲוַת דַּחְלָא מִן קֳדָם יי, עַל עַמְמַיָּא דִּבְקִרְוֵי סַחְרָנֵיהוֹן, וְלָא רְדַפוּ, בָּתַר בְּנֵי יַעֲקֹב: ו וַאֲתָא יַעֲקֹב לְלוּז, דִּבְאַרְעָא דִּכְנַעַן, הִיא בֵּית אֵל, הוּא וְכָל עַמָּא דְּעִמֵּיהּ: ז וּבְנָא תַמָּן מַדְבְּחָא, וּקְרָא לְאַתְרָא, אֵל בֵּית אֵל, אֲרֵי תַמָּן, אִתְגְּלִיאוּ לֵיהּ מַלְאֲכַיָּא דַּיי, בְּמֶעְרְקֵיהּ מִן קֳדָם אֲחוּהִי: ח וּמִיתַת דְּבוֹרָה מֵינִקְתַּהּ דְּרִבְקָה, וְאִתְקְבַרַת, מִלְּרַע לְבֵית אֵל בְּשִׁפּוֹלֵי מֵישְׁרָא, וּקְרָא שְׁמֵיהּ מֵישַׁר בְּכִיתָא:

34:31 הַכְזוֹנָה יַעֲשֶׂה אֶת־אֲחוֹתֵנוּ *Should our sister be treated like a whore?* – Yaakov condemns his sons. His sons reject the criticism. Who is in the right and who in the wrong are left conspicuously undecided in the text. The debate continued and was taken up by two of the greatest rabbis in the Middle Ages. Rambam takes the side of Shimon and Levi. They were justified in what they did, he says. The other members of the town saw what Shekhem had done, knew that he was guilty

9 After Yaakov had returned from Padan Aram God appeared to him again and
10 blessed him. God said to him, "Your name is Yaakov; no longer shall you be
11 called Yaakov; Yisrael shall be your name." Thus He named him Yisrael. God
said to him: "I am El Shaddai. Be fertile and multiply. A nation, a community
12 of nations will come to be from you. Of your loins, kings shall come forth. The SHISHI
land I gave to Avraham and Yitzḥak I surely give to you; to your descendants
13 after you I will give the land." God went up from him at the place where He had
14 spoken with him. Yaakov set up a stone pillar at the place where God had talked
15 with him, and on it he offered a libation and poured oil. And Yaakov named
16 the place where God had spoken to him Beit El. From Beit El they moved on.
While they were still some distance from Efrat, Raḥel began to give birth; her
17 labor pains were intense. When her labor was at its worst, the midwife said

רש״י

והקבורה מלמטה. ומישור של בית אל היו קורין לו 'אלון'. ואגדה, נתבשר שם באבל שני, שהגד לו על אמו שמתה, ו'אלון' בלשון יוני – 'אחר', ולפי שהעלימו את יום מותה, שלא יקללו הבריות כרס שיצא עשו ממנו, אף הכתוב לא פרסמה:

ט **עוד.** פעם שני במקום הזה, אחד בלכתו ואחד בשובו: **ויברך אתו.** ברכת אבלים:

י **לא יקרא שמך עוד יעקב.** לשון אדם הבא במארב ועקבה, אלא לשון שר ונגיד:

יא **אני אל שדי.** שאני כדאי לברך, שהברכות שלי: **פרה ורבה.** על שם שעדין לא נולד בנימין, ואף על פי שכבר נתעברה ממנו: **גוי.** בנימין: **גוים.** מנשה ואפרים שעתידים לצאת מיוסף והם במנין השבטים: **ומלכים.** שאול ואיש בשת שהיו משבט בנימין שעדין לא נולד:

יד **במקום אשר דבר אתו.** איני יודע מה מלמדנו:

טז **כברת הארץ.** מנחם פרש לשון כביר, רבוי, מהלך רב. ומדרש אגדה, בזמן שהארץ חלולה ככברה, שהניר מצוי, הסתו עבר והשרב עדין לא בא. ואין זה פשוטו של מקרא, שהרי בנעמן מצינו: "וילך מאתו כברת ארץ" (מלכים ב׳ ה, יט). ואומר אני שהוא שם מדת קרקע, כמו מהלך פרסה או יותר, כמו שאתה אומר: 'צמד כרם', 'חלקת שדה', כך במהלך אדם נותן שם מדה – כברת ארץ:

name no longer be Yaakov but Yisrael," meaning, "Act in such a way that this is what people call you." *Be a prince. Be royalty. Be upright. Be yourself. Do not long to be someone else.* This will turn out to be a challenge not just now but many times in the Jewish future.

Centuries later, the prophet Hoshe'a says, "But also with Yehuda the LORD has a dispute: He will visit upon Yaakov as he deserves, as befits his deeds – He will repay him. In the womb he grasped his brother by the heel, and with all his strength he struggled with God" (Hos. 12:3–4). The name Yaakov seems to connote a lack of truth, of uprightness. Yirmeyahu uses it to mean someone who practices deception: "Let each man be on guard against his fellow, and let no one trust his own brother, for every brother acts deceitfully [*akov yaakov*], and every friend spreads slander" (Jer. 9:3). *And the fact that the Torah and tradition still use the word Yaakov, not just Israel, tells us that this impulse has not disappeared.* Yaakov seems to have wrestled with this throughout his life, and we still do today. It takes courage to be different, a minority, countercultural. It is easy to live for the moment like Esav, or to "be like the peoples of the world" as Yeḥezkel says. It can be much harder to stand tall, and true to our principles.

I believe the challenge issued by the angel still echoes today. Are we Yaakov, evasive, embarrassed by who we are? Or are we Yisrael, with the courage to stand upright and walk tall in the path of faith?

ט וַיֵּרָא אֱלֹהִים אֶל־יַעֲקֹב עוֹד בְּבֹאוֹ מִפַּדַּן אֲרָם וַיְבָרֶךְ אֹתוֹ׃ וַיֹּאמֶר־לוֹ לב
אֱלֹהִים שִׁמְךָ יַעֲקֹב לֹא־יִקָּרֵא שִׁמְךָ עוֹד יַעֲקֹב כִּי אִם־יִשְׂרָאֵל יִהְיֶה
יא שְׁמֶךָ וַיִּקְרָא אֶת־שְׁמוֹ יִשְׂרָאֵל׃ וַיֹּאמֶר לוֹ אֱלֹהִים אֲנִי אֵל שַׁדַּי פְּרֵה
יב וּרְבֵה גּוֹי וּקְהַל גּוֹיִם יִהְיֶה מִמֶּךָּ וּמְלָכִים מֵחֲלָצֶיךָ יֵצֵאוּ׃ וְאֶת־הָאָרֶץ ששי
אֲשֶׁר נָתַתִּי לְאַבְרָהָם וּלְיִצְחָק לְךָ אֶתְּנֶנָּה וּלְזַרְעֲךָ אַחֲרֶיךָ אֶתֵּן אֶת־
יג יד הָאָרֶץ׃ וַיַּעַל מֵעָלָיו אֱלֹהִים בַּמָּקוֹם אֲשֶׁר־דִּבֶּר אִתּוֹ׃ וַיַּצֵּב יַעֲקֹב
מַצֵּבָה בַּמָּקוֹם אֲשֶׁר־דִּבֶּר אִתּוֹ מַצֶּבֶת אָבֶן וַיַּסֵּךְ עָלֶיהָ נֶסֶךְ וַיִּצֹק עָלֶיהָ
טו שָׁמֶן׃ וַיִּקְרָא יַעֲקֹב אֶת־שֵׁם הַמָּקוֹם אֲשֶׁר דִּבֶּר אִתּוֹ שָׁם אֱלֹהִים בֵּית־
טז אֵל׃ וַיִּסְעוּ מִבֵּית אֵל וַיְהִי־עוֹד כִּבְרַת־הָאָרֶץ לָבוֹא אֶפְרָתָה וַתֵּלֶד
יז רָחֵל וַתְּקַשׁ בְּלִדְתָּהּ׃ וַיְהִי בְהַקְשֹׁתָהּ בְּלִדְתָּהּ וַתֹּאמֶר לָהּ הַמְיַלֶּדֶת

אונקלוס

ט וְאִתְגְּלִי יְיָ לְיַעֲקֹב עוֹד, בְּמֵיתוֹהִי מִפַּדַּן אֲרָם, וּבָרֵיךְ יָתֵיהּ: י וַאֲמַר
לֵיהּ יְיָ שְׁמָךְ יַעֲקֹב, לָא יִתְקְרֵי שְׁמָךְ עוֹד יַעֲקֹב, אֱלָהֵין יִשְׂרָאֵל
יְהֵי שְׁמָךְ, וּקְרָא יָת שְׁמֵיהּ יִשְׂרָאֵל: יא וַאֲמַר לֵיהּ יְיָ, אֲנָא אֵל שַׁדַּי
פּוּשׁ וּסְגִי, עַם, וּכְנִשַׁת שִׁבְטִין יְהוֹן מִנָּךְ, וּמַלְכִין דְּשַׁלְטִין בְּעַמְמַיָּא
מִנָּךְ יִפְּקוּן: יב וְיָת אַרְעָא, דִּיהַבִית, לְאַבְרָהָם וּלְיִצְחָק לָךְ אֶתְּנִנַּהּ,
וְלִבְנָךְ בָּתְרָךְ אֶתֵּין יָת אַרְעָא: יג וְאִסְתַּלַּק מֵעִלָּווֹהִי יְקָרָא דַּיְיָ,
בְּאַתְרָא דְּמַלֵּיל עִמֵּיהּ: יד וַאֲקֵים יַעֲקֹב קָמְתָא, בְּאַתְרָא, דְּמַלֵּיל
עִמֵּיהּ קָמַת אַבְנָא, וְנַסֵּיךְ עֲלַהּ נִסְכִּין, וַאֲרֵיק עֲלַהּ מִשְׁחָא: טו וּקְרָא
יַעֲקֹב יָת שְׁמֵיהּ דְּאַתְרָא, דְּמַלֵּיל עִמֵּיהּ תַּמָּן, יְיָ בֵּית אֵל: טז וּנְטַלוּ
מִבֵּית אֵל, וַהֲוָה עוֹד כְּרוֹב אַרְעָא לְמֵיעַל לְאֶפְרָת, וִילֵידַת רָחֵל
וְקַשִּׁיאַת בְּמֵילְדַהּ: יז וַהֲוָה בְּקַשְׁיוּתַהּ בְּמֵילְדַהּ, וַאֲמַרַת לַהּ חָיְתָא

to Rivka's nurse Devora, who presumably took this same path with her charge many years ago. We are made conscious of the passage of time, and of the death and grief that are bound up with that. This is, as Rambam said, "the way of the world" (*Hilkhot Avel* 13:11). We are embodied souls. We are flesh and blood. We grow old. We lose those we love. Outwardly we struggle to maintain our composure but inwardly we weep. According to one tradition, cited by Rashi, our verse also hints at "another weeping": Rivka's own death.

35:10 וַיִּקְרָא אֶת שְׁמוֹ יִשְׂרָאֵל *Thus He named him Yisrael* – Note, first, that this is not an adjustment of an existing name by the change or addition of a letter, as when God changed Avram's name to Avraham, or Sarai's to Sara. It is an entirely new name, as if to signal that what it represents is a complete change of character. Second, the name change happens not once but twice. Third – and this is the puzzle of puzzles – *having said twice that his name will no longer be Yaakov, the Torah continues to call him Yaakov*. God Himself does so. So do we, every time we pray to the God of Avraham, Yitzḥak, and Yaakov.

How then are we to understand what, first the stranger, then God, said to Yaakov? *Not as a statement but as a request, a challenge, an invitation*. Read it not as "Your name *shall* no longer be Yaakov but Yisrael." Instead read it as "*Let* your

18 to her, "Don't be afraid. You have another son." But she was dying. With her
19 last breath, she named him Ben Oni; but his father called him Binyamin. So
20 Raḥel died and was buried on the road to Efrat – that is, Beit Leḥem. Yaakov
21 erected a pillar at her grave. To this day, that pillar marks Raḥel's grave. Yisrael
22 traveled on, pitching his tent beyond Migdal Eder. While Yisrael was staying in
that region, Reuven went and lay with his father's concubine Bilha. And Yisrael
heard –
23 Yaakov had twelve sons. The sons of Leah were Reuven, Yaakov's firstborn,

רש״י

יז **כִּי גַם זֶה.** נוֹסָף לְךָ עַל יוֹסֵף. וְרַבּוֹתֵינוּ דָּרְשׁוּ, עִם כָּל שֵׁבֶט נוֹלְדָה תְאוֹמָה, וְעִם בִּנְיָמִין נוֹלְדָה תְאוֹמָה יְתֵרָה:

יח **בֶּן אוֹנִי.** בֶּן צַעֲרִי: **בִּנְיָמִין.** נִרְאֶה בְּעֵינַי לְפִי שֶׁהוּא לְבַדּוֹ נוֹלַד בְּאֶרֶץ כְּנַעַן שֶׁהִיא בַּנֶּגֶב כְּשֶׁאָדָם בָּא מֵאֲרַם נַהֲרַיִם, כְּמוֹ שֶׁנֶּאֱמַר: "בַּנֶּגֶב בְּאֶרֶץ כְּנָעַן" (במדבר לג, מ), "הָלוֹךְ וְנָסוֹעַ הַנֶּגְבָּה" (לעיל יב, ט); 'בִּנְיָמִין' – בֵּן יָמִין, לְשׁוֹן "צָפוֹן וְיָמִין אַתָּה בְרָאתָם" (תהלים פט, יג), לְפִיכָךְ הוּא מָלֵא:

כב **בִּשְׁכֹּן יִשְׂרָאֵל בָּאָרֶץ הַהִוא.** עַד שֶׁלֹּא בָא לְחֶבְרוֹן אֵצֶל יִצְחָק אֵרְעוּהוּ כָּל אֵלֶּה: **וַיִּשְׁכַּב.** מִתּוֹךְ שֶׁבִּלְבֵּל מִשְׁכָּבוֹ מַעֲלֶה עָלָיו הַכָּתוּב כְּאִלּוּ שְׁכָבָהּ. וְלָמָּה בִּלְבֵּל וְחִלֵּל יְצוּעָיו? שֶׁכְּשֶׁמֵּתָה רָחֵל נָטַל יַעֲקֹב מִטָּתוֹ שֶׁהָיְתָה נְתוּנָה תָּדִיר בְּאֹהֶל רָחֵל וְלֹא בִשְׁאָר אֳהָלִים, וּנְתָנָהּ בְּאֹהֶל בִּלְהָה. בָּא רְאוּבֵן וְתָבַע עֶלְבּוֹן אִמּוֹ, אָמַר: אִם אֲחוֹת אִמִּי הָיְתָה צָרָתָהּ, שִׁפְחַת אֲחוֹת אִמִּי תְּהֵא צָרָה לְאִמִּי?: **וַיִּהְיוּ בְנֵי יַעֲקֹב שְׁנֵים עָשָׂר.** מַתְחִיל לְעִנְיָן רִאשׁוֹן: מִשֶּׁנּוֹלַד בִּנְיָמִין נִשְׁלְמָה הַמִּטָּה וּמֵעַתָּה רְאוּיִים לְהִמָּנוֹת, וּמְנָאָן. וְרַבּוֹתֵינוּ דָּרְשׁוּ, לְלַמְּדֵנוּ בָּא שֶׁכֻּלָּם שָׁוִים וְכֻלָּם צַדִּיקִים, שֶׁלֹּא חָטָא רְאוּבֵן:

כג **בְּכוֹר יַעֲקֹב.** אֲפִלּוּ בִּשְׁעַת הַקַּלְקָלָה קְרָאוֹ בְּכוֹר: **בְּכוֹר יַעֲקֹב.** בְּכוֹר לְנַחֲלָה, בְּכוֹר לַעֲבוֹדָה, בְּכוֹר לַמִּנְיָן. וְלֹא נִתְּנָה בְכוֹרָה לְיוֹסֵף אֶלָּא לְעִנְיַן הַשְּׁבָטִים, שֶׁנַּעֲשָׂה לִשְׁנֵי שְׁבָטִים:

your father's bed and defiled it – went up onto my couch" (Gen. 49:4).

Describing the event, the Torah uses an unusual stylistic device. After the words "And Yisrael heard," the masoretic text indicates a paragraph break in the middle of a sentence. The effect is to signal a silence, a complete breakdown in communication. Hence the pathos of the rabbinic interpretation of the passage, which certainly fits all we know about Reuven. He is not seeking to displace Yaakov but rather to draw his father's attention to the hurt and distress of Leah. Yet Yaakov says nothing, giving Reuven no opportunity to clear his name or explain why he did what he did. This is not the first or last time we will meet Reuven as a tragic figure, "seen" but not heard.

THE CHILDREN OF ISRAEL

As the narrative breaks off at a tense moment, we take stock again of a genealogy. On this occasion what we hear is a list of what will become the tribes of Israel. For we are "the children of Israel." Why is Yaakov named as the father of our people, the hero of our faith? We are "the congregation of Yaakov." Yet it is Avraham who began the Jewish journey, Yitzḥak who was willing to be sacrificed, Yosef who will save his family in the years of famine, Moshe who will lead the people out of Egypt and give it its laws. It is Yehoshua who will take the people into the Promised Land, David who will become its greatest king, Shlomo who will build the Temple, and the prophets through the ages who will become the voice of God.

Yaakov is different. What makes him unique is that he has his most intense encounters with God – they are the most dramatic in the whole book of Genesis – in the midst of the journey, alone, at night, far from home, fleeing from one danger to the next, from Esav to Lavan on the outward journey, from Lavan to Esav on his homecoming.

In the midst of the first journey he has the blazing epiphany of the ladder stretching from earth to heaven, with angels ascending and descending, moving him to say on waking, "Truly, the Lord is in this place – and I did not know it…. This is none other than the House of God, and

יח אַל־תִּירְאִי כִּי־גַם־זֶה לָךְ בֵּן: וַיְהִי בְּצֵאת נַפְשָׁהּ כִּי מֵתָה וַתִּקְרָא שְׁמוֹ
יט בֶּן־אוֹנִי וְאָבִיו קָרָא־לוֹ בִנְיָמִין: וַתָּמָת רָחֵל וַתִּקָּבֵר בְּדֶרֶךְ אֶפְרָתָה
כ הִוא בֵּית לָחֶם: וַיַּצֵּב יַעֲקֹב מַצֵּבָה עַל־קְבֻרָתָהּ הִוא מַצֶּבֶת קְבֻרַת־
כא כב רָחֵל עַד־הַיּוֹם: וַיִּסַּע יִשְׂרָאֵל וַיֵּט אָהֳלֹה מֵהָלְאָה לְמִגְדַּל־עֵדֶר: וַיְהִי
בִּשְׁכֹּן יִשְׂרָאֵל בָּאָרֶץ הַהִוא וַיֵּלֶךְ רְאוּבֵן וַיִּשְׁכַּב אֶת־בִּלְהָה פִּילֶגֶשׁ
אָבִיו וַיִּשְׁמַע יִשְׂרָאֵל
כג וַיִּהְיוּ בְנֵי־יַעֲקֹב שְׁנֵים עָשָׂר: בְּנֵי לֵאָה בְּכוֹר יַעֲקֹב רְאוּבֵן וְשִׁמְעוֹן וְלֵוִי

אונקלוס

לָא תִדְחֲלִין, אֲרֵי אַף דֵּין לִיךְ בַּר: יח וַהֲוָה, בְּמִפַּק נַפְשַׁהּ אֲרֵי
מִיתָא, וּקְרָת שְׁמֵיהּ בַּר דְּוַי, וַאֲבוּהִי קְרָא לֵיהּ בִּנְיָמִין: יט וּמִיתַת
רָחֵל, וְאִתְקְבַרַת בְּאוֹרַח אֶפְרָת, הִיא בֵּית לָחֶם: כ וַאֲקִים יַעֲקֹב,
קָמְתָא עַל קְבוּרְתַהּ, הִיא, קָמַת קְבוּרְתָא דְּרָחֵל עַד יוֹמָא דֵין:

כא וּנְטַל יִשְׂרָאֵל, וּפְרַסֵיהּ לְמַשְׁכְּנֵיהּ, מֵהָלְאָה לְמִגְדְּלָא דְעֵדֶר:
כב וַהֲוָה, כַּד שְׁרָא יִשְׂרָאֵל בְּאַרְעָא הַהִיא, וַאֲזַל רְאוּבֵן, וּשְׁכֵיב
יָת בִּלְהָה לְחֵינְתָא דַּאֲבוּהִי, וּשְׁמַע יִשְׂרָאֵל, וַהֲווֹ בְנֵי יַעֲקֹב
תְּרֵי עֲסַר: כג בְּנֵי לֵאָה, בְּכְרֵיהּ דְּיַעֲקֹב רְאוּבֵן, וְשִׁמְעוֹן וְלֵוִי

35:18 וְאָבִיו קָרָא־לוֹ בִנְיָמִין *But his father called him Binyamin* – Yaakov's youngest son, like him, is named twice – Ben Oni, "The son of my suffering," by Raḥel, and Binyamin, "The son of my strength, my right hand," by Yaakov.

To be a Jew is to carry the name Yisrael, meaning "one who struggles with God and men and [yet] prevails." Yisrael, who would not let the stranger go until he blessed him. His is the wrestling match each of us has to undergo when evil threatens or tragedy strikes. Faith is the refusal to let go until you have turned suffering into a blessing. Rabbi Naḥman of Breslov taught a parable:

> Sometimes when people are joyous and dancing, they grab a man from outside the dancing circle, one who is sad and melancholy, and force him to join them in their dance. Thus it is with joy: when a person is happy, his own sadness and suffering stand off on the side. But it is a higher achievement to struggle and pursue that sadness, bringing it too into the joy, until it is transformed…you grab hold of this suffering, and force it to join with you in the rejoicing, just as in the parable.

Yaakov's story in our *parasha* ends with a death and a birth. The loss of Raḥel is a wound that will remain with him always. And yet he is challenged again to transform suffering, making even the angel of death join, for a moment, the dance of life.

35:22 וַיִּשְׁכַּב אֶת בִּלְהָה *Lay with… Bilha* – Read literally, this suggests that Reuven took his father's place in Bilha's tent – an almost Oedipal act of displacement, as we discover later in the Bible when Avshalom does the same with his father David's concubine (II Sam. 16:21). Rashi, following midrashic tradition, prefers a gentler explanation. When Raḥel dies, Yaakov, who until now slept in her tent, moves his bed to the tent of Bilha, her handmaid. This, for Reuven, is an unbearable provocation. It is bad enough that Yaakov preferred Raḥel to her sister Leah, but intolerable to Reuven that he should prefer her handmaid to his mother. Reuven therefore moves Yaakov's bed from Bilha's tent to Leah's.

Even according to this interpretation, however, it is clear that Yaakov misunderstands the act and believes that his son has in fact usurped his place. He never forgets or forgives the incident and on his deathbed he reminds Reuven of it: "Unstable as water, you shall not excel, for you went up onto

24 Shimon, Levi, Yehuda, Yissakhar, and Zevulun. The sons of Raḥel were Yosef
25 26 and Binyamin. The sons of Raḥel's maid Bilha were Dan and Naftali. The sons
of Leah's maid Zilpa were Gad and Asher. These were the sons of Yaakov, born
27 to him in Padan Aram. Yaakov came home to his father Yitzḥak at Mamre,
near Kiryat Arba – that is, Ḥevron – where Avraham and Yitzḥak had lived as
28 29 strangers. Yitzḥak lived one hundred and eighty years. Then he breathed his
last, and died, and was gathered to his people, aged, satisfied with his years. His
sons Esav and Yaakov buried him.
36 1 2 These are the descendants of Esav – that is, Edom. Esav took wives from among
the daughters of Canaan: Ada daughter of Eilon the Hittite, and Oholivama
3 daughter of Ana, granddaughter of Tzivon the Hivite – and also Basmat,
4 daughter of Yishmael and sister of Nevayot. Ada bore Elifaz to Esav, and Basmat
5 bore Reuel. Oholivama bore Yeush, Yalam, and Koraḥ. These were the sons of

רש״י

כז| **מַמְרֵא.** שֵׁם הַמִּישׁוֹר: **קִרְיַת הָאַרְבַּע.** שֵׁם הָעִיר: **מַמְרֵא קִרְיַת הָאַרְבַּע.** אֶל מִישׁוֹר שֶׁל קִרְיַת אַרְבַּע. וְאִם תֹּאמַר, הָיָה לוֹ לִכְתֹּב 'מַמְרֵא הַקִּרְיַת אַרְבַּע'? כֵּן דֶּרֶךְ הַמִּקְרָא בְּכָל דָּבָר שֶׁשְּׁמוֹ כָּפוּל, כְּגוֹן זֶה, וּכְגוֹן: בֵּית לֶחֶם, אֲבִי עֶזֶר, בֵּית אֵל, אִם הֻצְרַךְ לְהַטִּיל בּוֹ הֵ"א נוֹתְנָהּ בְּרֹאשׁ תֵּבָה הַשְּׁנִיָּה: "בֵּית הַלַּחְמִי" (שמואל א' טז, א), "בְּעָפְרַת אֲבִי הָעֶזְרִי" (שופטים ו, כד), "בָּנָה חִיאֵל בֵּית הָאֱלִי" (מלכים א' טז, לד):

כט| **וַיִּגְוַע יִצְחָק.** אֵין מֻקְדָּם וּמְאֻחָר בַּתּוֹרָה; מְכִירָתוֹ שֶׁל יוֹסֵף קְדָמָה לְמִיתָתוֹ שֶׁל יִצְחָק שְׁתֵּים עֶשְׂרֵה שָׁנָה, שֶׁהֲרֵי יִצְחָק מֵת בִּשְׁנַת מֵאָה וְעֶשְׂרִים לְיַעֲקֹב, שֶׁנֶּאֱמַר: "וְיִצְחָק בֶּן שִׁשִּׁים שָׁנָה בְּלֶדֶת אֹתָם" (לעיל כה, כו), צֵא שִׁשִּׁים מִמֵּאָה וּשְׁמוֹנִים נִשְׁאֲרוּ מֵאָה וְעֶשְׂרִים; וְיוֹסֵף נִמְכַּר בֶּן שֶׁבַע עֶשְׂרֵה שָׁנָה, וְאוֹתָהּ שָׁנָה שְׁנַת מֵאָה וּשְׁמוֹנֶה לְיַעֲקֹב, כֵּיצַד? בֶּן שִׁשִּׁים וְשָׁלֹשׁ נִתְבָּרֵךְ, אַרְבַּע עֶשְׂרֵה שָׁנָה נִטְמַן בְּבֵית עֵבֶר, הֲרֵי שִׁבְעִים וָשֶׁבַע, וְאַרְבַּע עֶשְׂרֵה עָבַד בְּאִשָּׁה, וּבְסוֹף אַרְבַּע עֶשְׂרֵה נוֹלַד יוֹסֵף, שֶׁנֶּאֱמַר: "וַיְהִי כַּאֲשֶׁר יָלְדָה רָחֵל אֶת יוֹסֵף" וְגוֹ' (לעיל ל, כה), הֲרֵי תִּשְׁעִים וְאַחַת, וְשֶׁבַע עֶשְׂרֵה עַד שֶׁלֹּא נִמְכַּר, הֲרֵי מֵאָה וּשְׁמוֹנֶה:

לו ב| **עָדָה בַּת אֵילוֹן.** הִיא "בָּשְׂמַת בַּת אֵילֹן" (לעיל כו, לד), וְנִקְרֵאת בָּשְׂמַת עַל שֵׁם שֶׁהָיְתָה מְקַטֶּרֶת בְּשָׂמִים לַעֲבוֹדָה זָרָה: **אָהֳלִיבָמָה.** הִיא יְהוּדִית, וְאוֹתוֹ רָשָׁע כִּנָּהּ שְׁמָהּ יְהוּדִית לוֹמַר שֶׁהִיא כּוֹפֶרֶת בַּעֲבוֹדָה זָרָה כְּדֵי לְהַטְעוֹת אֶת אָבִיו: **בַּת עֲנָה בַּת צִבְעוֹן.** אִם בַּת עֲנָה לֹא בַּת צִבְעוֹן? עֲנָה בְּנוֹ שֶׁל צִבְעוֹן, שֶׁנֶּאֱמַר: "וְאֵלֶּה בְנֵי צִבְעוֹן וְאַיָּה וַעֲנָה" (להלן פסוק כד)! מְלַמֵּד שֶׁבָּא צִבְעוֹן עַל כַּלָּתוֹ אֵשֶׁת עֲנָה וְיָצְאָה אָהֳלִיבָמָה מִבֵּין שְׁנֵיהֶם, וְהוֹדִיעֲךָ הַכָּתוּב שֶׁכֻּלָּן בְּנֵי מַמְזֵרוּת הָיוּ:

ג| **בָּשְׂמַת בַּת יִשְׁמָעֵאל.** וּלְהַלָּן קוֹרֵא לָהּ 'מָחֲלַת' (לעיל כח, ט)? מָצָאתִי בְּאַגָּדַת מִדְרַשׁ סֵפֶר שְׁמוּאֵל (פרק יז), שְׁלֹשָׁה מוֹחֲלִים לָהֶן עֲוֹנוֹתֵיהֶן: גֵּר שֶׁנִּתְגַּיֵּר, וְהָעוֹלֶה לִגְדֻלָּה, וְהַנּוֹשֵׂא אִשָּׁה. וְלָמַד הַטַּעַם מִכָּאן, לְכָךְ נִקְרֵאת 'מָחֲלַת', שֶׁנִּמְחֲלוּ עֲוֹנוֹתָיו: **אֲחוֹת נְבָיוֹת.** עַל שֵׁם שֶׁהוּא הִשִּׂיאָהּ לוֹ מִשֶּׁמֵּת יִשְׁמָעֵאל:

ה| **וְאָהֳלִיבָמָה יָלְדָה וְגוֹ'.** קֹרַח זֶה מַמְזֵר הָיָה, וּבֶן אֱלִיפַז הָיָה שֶׁבָּא

is lifted to the greatest heights of spirituality. He is the man who encounters angels. He is the person surprised by God. He is the one who, at the very moments he feels most alone, discovers that he is not alone, that God is with him, that he is accompanied by angels.

The path chosen by Yaakov/Yisrael is not for the faint-hearted. *S'iz shver tzu zayn a Yid*, they used to say: "It's hard to be a Jew." In some ways, it still is. It is not easy to face our fears and wrestle with them, refusing to let go until we have turned them into renewed strength and blessing. But speaking personally, I would have it no other way. Judaism is not faith as illusion, seeing the world through rose-tinted lenses as we would wish it to be. It is faith as relentless honesty, seeing evil as evil and fighting it to our human, all-too-human utmost. That struggle is our vocation and what makes us the children of Yaakov.

כד כה ויהודה ויששכר וזבלון: בני רחל יוסף ובנימן: ובני בלהה שפחת
כו רחל דן ונפתלי: ובני זלפה שפחת לאה גד ואשר אלה בני יעקב
כז אשר ילד־לו בפדן ארם: ויבא יעקב אל־יצחק אביו ממרא קרית
כח הארבע הוא חברון אשר־גר־שם אברהם ויצחק: ויהיו ימי יצחק
כט מאת שנה ושמנים שנה: ויגוע יצחק וימת ויאסף אל־עמיו זקן
ושבע ימים ויקברו אתו עשו ויעקב בניו:
לו א ב ואלה תלדות עשו הוא אדום: עשו לקח את־נשיו מבנות כנען
את־עדה בת־אילון החתי ואת־אהליבמה בת־ענה בת־צבעון
ג ד החוי: ואת־בשמת בת־ישמעאל אחות נביות: ותלד עדה לעשו
ה את־אליפז ובשמת ילדה את־רעואל: ואהליבמה ילדה את־יעיש יעוש

אונקלוס

וִיהוּדָה, וְיִשָּׂשכָר וּזְבוּלוּן: כד בְּנֵי רָחֵל, יוֹסֵף וּבִנְיָמִין: כה וּבְנֵי בִלְהָה אַמְתַהּ דְּרָחֵל, דָּן וְנַפְתָּלִי: כו וּבְנֵי זִלְפָּה, אַמְתַהּ דְּלֵאָה גָּד וְאָשֵׁר, אִלֵּין בְּנֵי יַעֲקֹב, דְּאִתְיְלִידוּ לֵיהּ בְּפַדַּן אֲרָם: כז וַאֲתָא יַעֲקֹב לְוָת יִצְחָק אֲבוּהִי, לְמַמְרֵא קִרְיַת אַרְבַּע, הִיא חֶבְרוֹן, דְּדָר תַּמָּן אַבְרָהָם וְיִצְחָק: כח וַהֲווֹ יוֹמֵי יִצְחָק, מְאָה וּתְמָנַן שְׁנִין: כט וְאִתְנְגִיד יִצְחָק וּמִית וְאִתְכְּנִישׁ לְעַמֵּיהּ, סִיב וּסְבַע יוֹמִין, וּקְבַרוּ יָתֵיהּ, עֵשָׂו וְיַעֲקֹב בְּנוֹהִי: לו א וְאִלֵּין, תּוּלְדָת עֵשָׂו הוּא אֱדוֹם: ב עֵשָׂו, נְסִיב יָת נְשׁוֹהִי מִבְּנָת כְּנָעַן, יָת עָדָה, בַּת אֵילוֹן חִתָּאָה, וְיָת אָהֳלִיבָמָה בַּת עֲנָה, בַּת צִבְעוֹן חִוָּאָה: ג וְיָת בָּשְׂמַת בַּת יִשְׁמָעֵאל אֲחָתֵיהּ דִּנְבָיוֹת: ד וִילֵידַת עָדָה, לְעֵשָׂו יָת אֱלִיפָז, וּבָשְׂמַת, יְלֵידַת יָת רְעוּאֵל: ה וְאָהֳלִיבָמָה יְלֵידַת, יָת יְעוּשׁ

this the gate of the heavens" (Gen. 28:16–17). None of the other patriarchs, not even Moshe, has a vision quite like this.

On the second, in our *parasha*, he has the haunting, enigmatic wrestling match with the man/angel/God, which leaves him limping but permanently transformed – the only person in the Torah to receive from God an entirely new name, Yisrael, which may mean "one who has struggled with God and with men" or "one who has become a prince [*sar*] before God."

Yaakov's meetings with angels are described by the same verb *p-g-a* (28:11, 32:1), which means "a chance encounter," as if they took Yaakov by surprise, which clearly they did. Yaakov's most spiritual moments are ones he does not plan. He is thinking of other things, about what he is leaving behind and what lies ahead of him. He is, as it were, "surprised by God."

Not everyone can aspire to the loving faith and total trust of an Avraham, or to the seclusion of a Yitzḥak. But Yaakov is someone we understand. We can feel his fear, understand his pain at the tensions in his family, and sympathize with his deep longing for a life of quietude and peace (the Sages say about the opening words of the next *parasha* that "Yaakov longed to live in peace, but was immediately thrust into the troubles of Yosef" [Bereshit Rabba 84:3; Rashi on Gen. 37:2]).

The point is not just that Yaakov is the most human of the patriarchs, but rather that at the depths of his despair he

6 Esav, born in the land of Canaan. Esav took his wives, sons and daughters, and
all the members of his household, together with his livestock, his other animals,
and all the possessions he had acquired in Canaan, and he moved to another
7 region, away from his brother Yaakov, for their possessions were too great for
them to remain together; because of all their livestock, the land where they
8 were living could not support them both. So Esav settled in the hill country
9 of Se'ir. Esav is Edom. These, then, are the descendants of Esav, ancestor of
10 the Edomites, in the hill country of Se'ir. These are the names of Esav's sons:
11 Elifaz, son of Esav's wife Ada, and Reuel, son of Esav's wife Basmat. The sons
12 of Elifaz were Teiman, Omar, Tzefo, Gatam, and Kenaz. Timna, a concubine of
Esav's son Elifaz, bore him Amalek. These are the descendants of Esav's wife
13 Ada. The sons of Reuel were Naḥat, Zeraḥ, Shama, and Miza. These were the
14 descendants of Esav's wife Basmat. The sons of Oholivama, daughter of Ana
and granddaughter of Tzivon, Esav's wife, whom she bore to Esav, were Yeush,
15 Yalam, and Koraḥ. These were the tribal chiefs among Esav's descendants. The
sons of Elifaz, Esav's firstborn, were the chiefs Teiman, Omar, Tzefo, Kenaz,
16 Koraḥ, Gatam, and Amalek. These were the chiefs descended from Elifaz in
17 Edom; they were grandsons of Ada. The sons of Esav's son Reuel were the
chiefs Naḥat, Zeraḥ, Shama, and Miza. These were the chiefs descended from
18 Reuel in Edom; they were grandsons of Esav's wife Basmat. The sons of Esav's
wife Oholivama were the chiefs Yeush, Yalam, and Koraḥ. These were the

אונקלוס

וְיָת יַעְלָם וְיָת קֹרַח, אִלֵּין בְּנֵי עֵשָׂו, דְּאִתְיְלִידוּ לֵיהּ בְּאַרְעָא דִכְנָעַן: ו וּדְבַר עֵשָׂו, יָת נְשׁוֹהִי, וְיָת בְּנוֹהִי וְיָת בְּנָתֵיהּ וְיָת כָּל נַפְשָׁת בֵּיתֵיהּ, וְיָת גֵּיתוֹהִי וְיָת כָּל בְּעִירֵיהּ, וְיָת כָּל קִנְיָנֵיהּ, דִּקְנָא בְּאַרְעָא דִכְנָעַן, וַאֲזַל לַאֲרַע אָחֳרִי, מִן קֳדָם יַעֲקֹב אֲחוּהִי: ז אֲרֵי הֲוָה קִנְיָנְהוֹן, סַגִּי מִלְּמִתַּב כַּחֲדָא, וְלָא יְכֵילַת, אֲרַע תּוֹתָבוּתְהוֹן לְסוֹבָרָא יָתְהוֹן, מִן קֳדָם גֵּיתֵיהוֹן: ח וִיתֵיב עֵשָׂו בְּטוּרָא דְשֵׂעִיר, עֵשָׂו הוּא אֱדוֹם: ט וְאִלֵּין,

רש״י

עַל חֵטְא אָבִיו, שֶׁהֲרֵי הוּא מָנוּי עִם אַלּוּפֵי אֱלִיפַז בְּסוֹף הָעִנְיָן:

ו וַיֵּלֶךְ אֶל אֶרֶץ. לָגוּר בַּאֲשֶׁר יִמְצָא:

ז וְלֹא יָכְלָה אֶרֶץ מְגוּרֵיהֶם. לְהַסְפִּיק מִרְעֶה לַבְּהֵמוֹת שֶׁלָּהֶם. וּמִדְרַשׁ אַגָּדָה, "מִפְּנֵי יַעֲקֹב אָחִיו", מִפְּנֵי שְׁטָר חוֹב שֶׁל גְּזֵרַת "כִּי גֵר יִהְיֶה זַרְעֲךָ" (לעיל טו, יג) הַמֻּטָּל עַל זַרְעוֹ שֶׁל יִצְחָק, אָמַר: אֵלֵךְ לִי מִכָּאן, אֵין לִי חֵלֶק לֹא בַּמַּתָּנָה שֶׁנִּתְּנָה לוֹ הָאָרֶץ הַזֹּאת וְלֹא בְּפִרְעוֹן הַשְּׁטָר, וּמִפְּנֵי הַבּוּשָׁה שֶׁמָּכַר בְּכוֹרָתוֹ:

ט וְאֵלֶּה. הַתּוֹלָדוֹת שֶׁהוֹלִידוּ בָּנָיו מִשֶּׁהָלַךְ לְשֵׂעִיר:

יב וְתִמְנַע הָיְתָה פִילֶגֶשׁ. לְהוֹדִיעַ גְּדֻלָּתוֹ שֶׁל אַבְרָהָם כַּמָּה הָיוּ תְּאֵבִים לְדָבֵק בְּזַרְעוֹ. תִּמְנַע זוֹ בַּת אַלּוּפִים הָיְתָה, שֶׁנֶּאֱמַר: "וַאֲחוֹת לוֹטָן תִּמְנָע" (להלן פסוק כב), וְלוֹטָן מֵאַלּוּפֵי יוֹשְׁבֵי שֵׂעִיר הָיָה, מִן הַחוֹרִים שֶׁיָּשְׁבוּ בָהּ לְפָנִים; אָמְרָה: אֵינִי זוֹכָה לְהִנָּשֵׂא לְךָ, הַלְוַאי וְאֶהְיֶה פִילֶגֶשׁ. וּבְדִבְרֵי הַיָּמִים (א׳ א, לו) מוֹנֶה אוֹתָהּ בְּבָנָיו שֶׁל אֱלִיפַז! מְלַמֵּד שֶׁבָּא עַל אִשְׁתּוֹ שֶׁל שֵׂעִיר וְיָצְאָה תִמְנַע מִבֵּינֵיהֶם, וּכְשֶׁגָּדְלָה נַעֲשֵׂית פִּילַגְשׁוֹ; וְזֶהוּ "וַאֲחוֹת לוֹטָן תִּמְנָע" וְלֹא מְנָאָהּ עִם בְּנֵי שֵׂעִיר, שֶׁהָיְתָה אֲחוֹתוֹ מִן הָאֵם וְלֹא מִן הָאָב:

טו אֵלֶּה אַלּוּפֵי בְנֵי עֵשָׂו. רָאשֵׁי מִשְׁפָּחוֹת:

ו וְאֶת־יַעְלָם וְאֶת־קֹרַח אֵלֶּה בְּנֵי עֵשָׂו אֲשֶׁר יֻלְּדוּ־לוֹ בְּאֶרֶץ כְּנָעַן׃ וַיִּקַּח
עֵשָׂו אֶת־נָשָׁיו וְאֶת־בָּנָיו וְאֶת־בְּנֹתָיו וְאֶת־כָּל־נַפְשׁוֹת בֵּיתוֹ וְאֶת־
מִקְנֵהוּ וְאֶת־כָּל־בְּהֶמְתּוֹ וְאֵת כָּל־קִנְיָנוֹ אֲשֶׁר רָכַשׁ בְּאֶרֶץ כְּנָעַן וַיֵּלֶךְ
ז אֶל־אֶרֶץ מִפְּנֵי יַעֲקֹב אָחִיו׃ כִּי־הָיָה רְכוּשָׁם רָב מִשֶּׁבֶת יַחְדָּו וְלֹא
ח יָכְלָה אֶרֶץ מְגוּרֵיהֶם לָשֵׂאת אֹתָם מִפְּנֵי מִקְנֵיהֶם׃ וַיֵּשֶׁב עֵשָׂו בְּהַר
ט שֵׂעִיר עֵשָׂו הוּא אֱדוֹם׃ וְאֵלֶּה תֹּלְדוֹת עֵשָׂו אֲבִי אֱדוֹם בְּהַר שֵׂעִיר׃
י אֵלֶּה שְׁמוֹת בְּנֵי־עֵשָׂו אֱלִיפַז בֶּן־עָדָה אֵשֶׁת עֵשָׂו רְעוּאֵל בֶּן־בָּשְׂמַת
יא יב אֵשֶׁת עֵשָׂו׃ וַיִּהְיוּ בְּנֵי אֱלִיפָז תֵּימָן אוֹמָר צְפוֹ וְגַעְתָּם וּקְנַז׃ וְתִמְנַע ׀
הָיְתָה פִילֶגֶשׁ לֶאֱלִיפַז בֶּן־עֵשָׂו וַתֵּלֶד לֶאֱלִיפַז אֶת־עֲמָלֵק אֵלֶּה בְּנֵי
יג עָדָה אֵשֶׁת עֵשָׂו׃ וְאֵלֶּה בְּנֵי רְעוּאֵל נַחַת וָזֶרַח שַׁמָּה וּמִזָּה אֵלֶּה הָיוּ
יד בְּנֵי בָשְׂמַת אֵשֶׁת עֵשָׂו׃ וְאֵלֶּה הָיוּ בְּנֵי אָהֳלִיבָמָה בַת־עֲנָה בַּת־צִבְעוֹן
טו אֵשֶׁת עֵשָׂו וַתֵּלֶד לְעֵשָׂו אֶת־יעיש וְאֶת־יַעְלָם וְאֶת־קֹרַח׃ אֵלֶּה אַלּוּפֵי יְעוּשׁ
בְנֵי־עֵשָׂו בְּנֵי אֱלִיפַז בְּכוֹר עֵשָׂו אַלּוּף תֵּימָן אַלּוּף אוֹמָר אַלּוּף צְפוֹ
טז אַלּוּף קְנַז׃ אַלּוּף־קֹרַח אַלּוּף גַּעְתָּם אַלּוּף עֲמָלֵק אֵלֶּה אַלּוּפֵי אֱלִיפַז
יז בְּאֶרֶץ אֱדוֹם אֵלֶּה בְּנֵי עָדָה׃ וְאֵלֶּה בְּנֵי רְעוּאֵל בֶּן־עֵשָׂו אַלּוּף נַחַת
אַלּוּף זֶרַח אַלּוּף שַׁמָּה אַלּוּף מִזָּה אֵלֶּה אַלּוּפֵי רְעוּאֵל בְּאֶרֶץ אֱדוֹם
יח אֵלֶּה בְּנֵי בָשְׂמַת אֵשֶׁת עֵשָׂו׃ וְאֵלֶּה בְּנֵי אָהֳלִיבָמָה אֵשֶׁת עֵשָׂו אַלּוּף
יְעוּשׁ אַלּוּף יַעְלָם אַלּוּף קֹרַח אֵלֶּה אַלּוּפֵי אָהֳלִיבָמָה בַּת־עֲנָה אֵשֶׁת

אונקלוס

תּוֹלְדַת עֵשָׂו אֲבוּהוֹן דֶּאֱדוֹמָאֵי, בְּטוּרָא דְשֵׂעִיר: י אִלֵּין שְׁמָהָת בְּנֵי עֵשָׂו, אֱלִיפַז, בַּר עָדָה אִתַּת עֵשָׂו, רְעוּאֵל, בַּר בָּשְׂמַת אִתַּת עֵשָׂו: יא וַהֲווֹ בְּנֵי אֱלִיפַז, תֵּימָן אוֹמָר, צְפוֹ וְגַעְתָּם וּקְנַז: יב וְתִמְנַע הֲוָת לְחֵינְתָא, לֶאֱלִיפַז בַּר עֵשָׂו, וִילֵידַת לֶאֱלִיפַז יָת עֲמָלֵק, אִלֵּין, בְּנֵי עָדָה אִתַּת עֵשָׂו: יג וְאִלֵּין בְּנֵי רְעוּאֵל, נַחַת וָזֶרַח שַׁמָּה וּמִזָּה, אִלֵּין הֲווֹ, בְּנֵי בָשְׂמַת אִתַּת עֵשָׂו: יד וְאִלֵּין הֲווֹ, בְּנֵי אָהֳלִיבָמָה בַּת עֲנָה, בַּת צִבְעוֹן אִתַּת עֵשָׂו, וִילֵידַת לְעֵשָׂו, יָת יְעוּשׁ וְיָת יַעְלָם וְיָת קֹרַח: טו אִלֵּין רַבְרְבֵי בְנֵי עֵשָׂו, בְּנֵי אֱלִיפַז בֻּכְרֵיהּ דְּעֵשָׂו, רַבָּא תֵימָן רַבָּא אוֹמָר, רַבָּא צְפוֹ רַבָּא קְנַז: טז רַבָּא קֹרַח, רַבָּא גַעְתָּם רַבָּא עֲמָלֵק, אִלֵּין רַבְרְבֵי אֱלִיפַז בְּאַרְעָא דֶאֱדוֹם, אִלֵּין בְּנֵי עָדָה: יז וְאִלֵּין, בְּנֵי רְעוּאֵל בַּר עֵשָׂו, רַבָּא נַחַת רַבָּא זֶרַח, רַבָּא שַׁמָּה רַבָּא מִזָּה, אִלֵּין רַבְרְבֵי רְעוּאֵל בְּאַרְעָא דֶאֱדוֹם, אִלֵּין, בְּנֵי בָשְׂמַת אִתַּת עֵשָׂו: יח וְאִלֵּין, בְּנֵי אָהֳלִיבָמָה אִתַּת עֵשָׂו, רַבָּא יְעוּשׁ, רַבָּא יַעְלָם רַבָּא קֹרַח, אִלֵּין רַבְרְבֵי, אָהֳלִיבָמָה, בַּת עֲנָה אִתַּת

19 chiefs descended from Esav's wife Oholivama daughter of Ana. These were
20 the sons of Esav – that is, Edom – and these were their chiefs. These SHEVI'I
are the sons of Se'ir the Horite who were settled in the land: Lotan, Shoval,
21 Tzivon, Ana, Dishon, Etzer, and Dishan. These were the chiefs of the Horites,
22 descendants of Se'ir in the land of Edom. Lotan's sons were Ḥori and Heimam.
23 Timna was Lotan's sister. Shoval's sons were Alvan, Manaḥat, Eival, Shefo, and
24 Onam. Tzivon's sons were Aya and Ana. This is the Ana who discovered hot
25 springs in the desert while pasturing the donkeys of his father Tzivon. Ana's
26 children were Dishon and Oholivama daughter of Ana. Dishon's sons were
27 Ḥemdan, Eshban, Yitran, and Keran. Etzer's sons were Bilhan, Zaavan, and
28 29 Akan. Dishan's sons were Utz and Aran. These were the tribal chiefs of the
30 Horites: chiefs Lotan, Shoval, Tzivon, Ana, Dishon, Etzer, and Dishan. These
were the Horite chiefs by their divisions in the land of Se'ir.
31 These were the kings who reigned in Edom before any king reigned over the

רש״י

כ **יֹשְׁבֵי הָאָרֶץ.** שֶׁהָיוּ יוֹשְׁבֶיהָ קֹדֶם שֶׁבָּא עֵשָׂו לְשָׁם. וְרַבּוֹתֵינוּ דָּרְשׁוּ, שֶׁהָיוּ בְּקִיאִין בְּיִשּׁוּבָהּ שֶׁל אֶרֶץ – מְלֹא קָנֶה זֶה לְזֵיתִים מְלֹא קָנֶה זֶה לִגְפָנִים, שֶׁהָיוּ טוֹעֲמִין הֶעָפָר וְיוֹדְעִין אֵי זוֹ נְטִיעָה רְאוּיָה לוֹ:

כד **וְאַיָּה וַעֲנָה.** וָי״ו יְתֵרָה, וְהוּא כְּמוֹ אַיָּה וַעֲנָה. וְהַרְבֵּה יֵשׁ בַּמִּקְרָא: ״תֵּת וְקֹדֶשׁ וְצָבָא מִרְמָס״ (דניאל ח, יג), ״נִרְדָּם וְרֶכֶב וָסוּס״ (תהלים עו, ז): **הוּא עֲנָה.** הָאָמוּר לְמַעְלָה שֶׁהוּא אָחִיו שֶׁל צִבְעוֹן, וְכָאן הוּא קוֹרֵא אוֹתוֹ בְּנוֹ! מְלַמֵּד שֶׁבָּא צִבְעוֹן עַל אִמּוֹ וְהוֹלִיד אֶת עֲנָה: **אֶת הַיֵּמִם.** פְּרָדִים, הִרְבִּיעַ חֲמוֹר עַל סוּס נְקֵבָה וְיָלְדָה פֶּרֶד, וְהוּא הָיָה מַמְזֵר וְהֵבִיא פְּסוּלִין לָעוֹלָם. וְלָמָּה נִקְרָא שְׁמָם ׳יֵמִים׳? שֶׁאֵימָתָן מֻטֶּלֶת עַל הַבְּרִיּוֹת, דְּאָמַר רַבִּי חֲנִינָא: מִיָּמַי לֹא שְׁאָלַנִי אָדָם עַל מַכַּת פִּרְדָּה לְבָנָה וְחָיָה. לֹא נִזְקַק לִכְתֹּב לָנוּ מִשְׁפְּחוֹת הַחוֹרִי אֶלָּא מִפְּנֵי תִּמְנַע, וּלְהוֹדִיעַ גְּדֻלַּת אַבְרָהָם כְּמוֹ שֶׁפֵּרַשְׁתִּי לְמַעְלָה (לעיל פסוק יב):

לא **וְאֵלֶּה הַמְּלָכִים וְגוֹ׳.** שְׁמוֹנָה הָיוּ, וּכְנֶגְדָּן הֶעֱמִיד יַעֲקֹב וּבִטֵּל מַלְכוּת עֵשָׂו בִּימֵיהֶם, וְאֵלּוּ הֵן: שָׁאוּל וְאִישׁ בֹּשֶׁת, דָּוִד וּשְׁלֹמֹה, רְחַבְעָם, אֲבִיָּה, אָסָא, יְהוֹשָׁפָט; וּבִימֵי יוֹרָם בְּנוֹ כָּתוּב: ״בְּיָמָיו פָּשַׁע אֱדוֹם מִתַּחַת יַד יְהוּדָה וַיַּמְלִכוּ עֲלֵיהֶם מֶלֶךְ״ (מלכים ב׳ ח, כ). וּבִימֵי שָׁאוּל כְּתִיב: ״וּמֶלֶךְ אֵין בֶּאֱדוֹם נִצָּב מֶלֶךְ״ (מלכים א׳ כב, מח):

celebrating the Homeric virtues and the Nietzschean will to power.

To be chosen does not mean that others are unchosen. To be secure in one's relationship with God does not depend on negating the possibility that others too may have a (different) relationship with Him. Yaakov was loved by his mother, Esav by his father; but what of God who is neither father nor mother, but both and more than both? Love rejects comparisons. Yaakov is Yaakov, heir to the covenant. Esav is Esav, doing what he does, being what he is, enjoying his own heritage and blessing. What a simple truth and how beautifully, subtly, it is conveyed. It is one of the Torah's most profound messages to humanity – and how deeply (in an age of "the clash of civilizations") the world needs to hear it today.

Something of the deepest possible consequence, therefore, is being intimated here. The choice of one does not mean the rejection of the other. Esav too will have his blessing, his heritage, his land. He too will have children who become kings, who will rule and not be ruled. He too will have his virtues recognized, above all his love and respect for his father. Not all are chosen for the rigors, spiritual and existential, of the Abrahamic covenant, but each has his or her place in the scheme of things, each has his or her virtues, talents, gifts. Each is precious in the eyes of God.

יט כ עֵשָׂו: אֵלֶּה בְנֵי־עֵשָׂו וְאֵלֶּה אַלּוּפֵיהֶם הוּא אֱדוֹם: אֵלֶּה שביעי
כא בְנֵי־שֵׂעִיר הַחֹרִי יֹשְׁבֵי הָאָרֶץ לוֹטָן וְשׁוֹבָל וְצִבְעוֹן וַעֲנָה: וְדִשׁוֹן
כב וְאֵצֶר וְדִישָׁן אֵלֶּה אַלּוּפֵי הַחֹרִי בְּנֵי שֵׂעִיר בְּאֶרֶץ אֱדוֹם: וַיִּהְיוּ בְנֵי־
כג לוֹטָן חֹרִי וְהֵימָם וַאֲחוֹת לוֹטָן תִּמְנָע: וְאֵלֶּה בְּנֵי שׁוֹבָל עַלְוָן וּמָנַחַת
כד וְעֵיבָל שְׁפוֹ וְאוֹנָם: וְאֵלֶּה בְנֵי־צִבְעוֹן וְאַיָּה וַעֲנָה הוּא עֲנָה אֲשֶׁר
כה מָצָא אֶת־הַיֵּמִם בַּמִּדְבָּר בִּרְעֹתוֹ אֶת־הַחֲמֹרִים לְצִבְעוֹן אָבִיו: וְאֵלֶּה
כו בְנֵי־עֲנָה דִּשֹׁן וְאָהֳלִיבָמָה בַּת־עֲנָה: וְאֵלֶּה בְּנֵי דִישָׁן חֶמְדָּן וְאֶשְׁבָּן
כז כח וְיִתְרָן וּכְרָן: אֵלֶּה בְּנֵי־אֵצֶר בִּלְהָן וְזַעֲוָן וַעֲקָן: אֵלֶּה בְנֵי־דִישָׁן עוּץ
כט וַאֲרָן: אֵלֶּה אַלּוּפֵי הַחֹרִי אַלּוּף לוֹטָן אַלּוּף שׁוֹבָל אַלּוּף צִבְעוֹן אַלּוּף
ל עֲנָה: אַלּוּף דִּשֹׁן אַלּוּף אֵצֶר אַלּוּף דִּישָׁן אֵלֶּה אַלּוּפֵי הַחֹרִי לְאַלֻּפֵיהֶם
בְּאֶרֶץ שֵׂעִיר:
לא וְאֵלֶּה הַמְּלָכִים אֲשֶׁר מָלְכוּ בְּאֶרֶץ אֱדוֹם לִפְנֵי מְלָךְ־מֶלֶךְ לִבְנֵי יִשְׂרָאֵל:

אונקלוס

עֵשָׂו: יט אִלֵּין בְּנֵי עֵשָׂו, וְאִלֵּין רַבְרְבָנֵיהוֹן הוּא אֱדוֹם: כ אִלֵּין בְּנֵי שֵׂעִיר חוֹרָאֵי, יָתְבֵי אַרְעָא, לוֹטָן וְשׁוֹבָל וְצִבְעוֹן וַעֲנָה: כא וְדִישׁוֹן וְאֵצֶר וְדִישָׁן, אִלֵּין רַבְרְבֵי חוֹרָאֵי, בְּנֵי שֵׂעִיר בְּאַרְעָא דֶאֱדוֹם: כב וַהֲווֹ בְנֵי לוֹטָן חוֹרִי וְהֵימָם, וַאֲחָתֵיהּ דְּלוֹטָן תִּמְנָע: כג וְאִלֵּין בְּנֵי שׁוֹבָל, עַלְוָן וּמָנַחַת וְעֵיבָל, שְׁפוֹ וְאוֹנָם: כד וְאִלֵּין בְּנֵי צִבְעוֹן וְאַיָּה וַעֲנָה, הוּא עֲנָה, דְּאַשְׁכַּח יָת גִּבָּרַיָּא בְּמַדְבְּרָא, כַּד הֲוָה רָעֵי יָת חֲמָרַיָּא לְצִבְעוֹן אֲבוּהִי: כה וְאִלֵּין בְּנֵי עֲנָה דִּישׁוֹן, וְאָהֳלִיבָמָה בַּת עֲנָה: כו וְאִלֵּין בְּנֵי דִישָׁן, חֶמְדָּן וְאֶשְׁבָּן וְיִתְרָן וּכְרָן: כז אִלֵּין בְּנֵי אֵצֶר, בִּלְהָן וְזַעֲוָן וַעֲקָן: כח אִלֵּין בְּנֵי דִישָׁן עוּץ וַאֲרָן: כט אִלֵּין רַבְרְבֵי חוֹרָאֵי, רַבָּא לוֹטָן רַבָּא שׁוֹבָל, רַבָּא צִבְעוֹן רַבָּא עֲנָה: ל רַבָּא דִישׁוֹן, רַבָּא אֵצֶר רַבָּא דִישָׁן, אִלֵּין רַבְרְבֵי חוֹרָאֵי, לְרַבְרְבָנֵיהוֹן בְּאַרְעָא דְשֵׂעִיר: לא וְאִלֵּין מַלְכַיָּא, דִּמְלַכוּ בְּאַרְעָא דֶאֱדוֹם, קֳדָם דִּימְלוֹךְ מַלְכָּא לִבְנֵי יִשְׂרָאֵל:

36:31 אֲשֶׁר מָלְכוּ...לִפְנֵי מְלָךְ־מֶלֶךְ לִבְנֵי יִשְׂרָאֵל *Who reigned... before any king reigned over the Israelites* – It is not surprising that Yaakov's first desire was to be like Esav. Esav is *Homo naturalis*, a man of nature. He knows that *homo homini lupus est*, "man is wolf to man." He has the strength and skill to fight and win in the Darwinian struggle to survive and the Hobbesian war of "all against all." These are his natural battlegrounds, and he relishes the contest. Long "before any king reigned over the Israelites," the descendants of Esav can boast legendary rulers.

Esav is the archetypal hero of a hundred myths and legends of the ancient world (and of action movies today). He is not without dignity, nor does he lack human feelings. The Midrash, for sound educational reasons, turned Esav into a bad man. The Torah itself is altogether more subtle and profound. Esav is not a bad man; he is a natural man,

32 Israelites. Bela son of Beor became king in Edom. His city was named Dinhava.
33 When Bela died, Yovav son of Zeraḥ from Botzra succeeded him as king.
34 When Yovav died, Ḥusham from the land of the Temanites succeeded him
35 as king. When Ḥusham died, Hadad son of Bedad, who defeated Midyan in
36 the country of Moav, succeeded him as king. His city was named Avit. When
37 Hadad died, Samla from Masreka succeeded him as king. When Samla died,
38 Sha'ul from Reḥovot HaNahar succeeded him as king. When Sha'ul died, Baal
39 Ḥanan son of Akhbor succeeded him as king. When Baal Ḥanan son of Akhbor
died, Hadar succeeded him as king. His city was named Pa'u, and his wife's
40 name was Meheitavel, daughter of Matred, daughter of Mei Zahav. These were MAFTIR
the chiefs descended from Esav, by their clans, localities, and names: the chiefs
41 42 43 Timna, Alva, Yetet, Oholivama, Ela, Pinon, Kenaz, Teiman, Mivtzar, Magdiel,
and Iram. These were the chiefs of Edom – of Esav, ancestor of the Edomites –
each with their own settlements in the land that they held.

The haftara for Parashat Vayishlaḥ is on page 1516.

רש״י

לג **יוֹבָב בֶּן זֶרַח מִבָּצְרָה.** בָּצְרָה מֵעָרֵי מוֹאָב הִיא, שֶׁנֶּאֱמַר: "וְעַל קְרִיּוֹת וְעַל בָּצְרָה" וְגוֹ' (ירמיה מח, כד), וּלְפִי שֶׁהֶעֱמִידָה מֶלֶךְ לֶאֱדוֹם עֲתִידָה לִלְקוֹת עִמָּהֶם, שֶׁנֶּאֱמַר: "כִּי זֶבַח לַה' בְּבָצְרָה" (ישעיה לד, ו):

לה **הַמַּכֶּה אֶת מִדְיָן בִּשְׂדֵה מוֹאָב.** שֶׁבָּא מִדְיָן עַל מוֹאָב לַמִּלְחָמָה וְהָלַךְ מֶלֶךְ אֱדוֹם לַעֲזֹר אֶת מוֹאָב. וּמִכָּאן אָנוּ לְמֵדִים שֶׁהָיוּ מִדְיָן וּמוֹאָב מְרִיבִים זֶה עִם זֶה, וּבִימֵי בִלְעָם עָשׂוּ שָׁלוֹם לְהִתְקַשֵּׁר עַל יִשְׂרָאֵל:

לט **בַּת מֵי זָהָב.** מַהוּ זָהָב; עָשִׁיר הָיָה וְאֵין זָהָב חָשׁוּב בְּעֵינָיו לִכְלוּם:

מ **וְאֵלֶּה שְׁמוֹת אַלּוּפֵי עֵשָׂו.** שֶׁנִּקְרְאוּ עַל שֵׁם מְדִינוֹתֵיהֶם לְאַחַר שֶׁמֵּת הֲדַר וּפָסְקָה מֵהֶם מַלְכוּת, וְהָרִאשׁוֹנִים הַנִּזְכָּרִים לְמַעְלָה הֵם שְׁמוֹת תּוֹלְדוֹתָם, וְכֵן מְפֹרָשׁ בְּדִבְרֵי הַיָּמִים: "וַיָּמָת הֲדָד וַיִּהְיוּ אַלּוּפֵי אֱדוֹם אַלּוּף תִּמְנָע" וְגוֹ' (דברי הימים א' א, נא):

מג **מַגְדִּיאֵל.** הִיא רוֹמִי:

לב לג וַיִּמְלֹךְ בֶּאֱדוֹם בֶּלַע בֶּן־בְּעוֹר וְשֵׁם עִירוֹ דִּנְהָבָה׃ וַיָּמָת בָּלַע וַיִּמְלֹךְ
לד תַּחְתָּיו יוֹבָב בֶּן־זֶרַח מִבָּצְרָה׃ וַיָּמָת יוֹבָב וַיִּמְלֹךְ תַּחְתָּיו חֻשָׁם מֵאֶרֶץ
לה הַתֵּימָנִי׃ וַיָּמָת חֻשָׁם וַיִּמְלֹךְ תַּחְתָּיו הֲדַד בֶּן־בְּדַד הַמַּכֶּה אֶת־מִדְיָן
לו בִּשְׂדֵה מוֹאָב וְשֵׁם עִירוֹ עֲוִית׃ וַיָּמָת הֲדָד וַיִּמְלֹךְ תַּחְתָּיו שַׂמְלָה
לז לח מִמַּשְׂרֵקָה׃ וַיָּמָת שַׂמְלָה וַיִּמְלֹךְ תַּחְתָּיו שָׁאוּל מֵרְחֹבוֹת הַנָּהָר׃ וַיָּמָת
לט שָׁאוּל וַיִּמְלֹךְ תַּחְתָּיו בַּעַל חָנָן בֶּן־עַכְבּוֹר׃ וַיָּמָת בַּעַל חָנָן בֶּן־עַכְבּוֹר
וַיִּמְלֹךְ תַּחְתָּיו הֲדַר וְשֵׁם עִירוֹ פָּעוּ וְשֵׁם אִשְׁתּוֹ מְהֵיטַבְאֵל בַּת־מַטְרֵד
מ בַּת מֵי זָהָב׃ וְאֵלֶּה שְׁמוֹת אַלּוּפֵי עֵשָׂו לְמִשְׁפְּחֹתָם לִמְקֹמֹתָם בִּשְׁמֹתָם מפטיר
מא אַלּוּף תִּמְנָע אַלּוּף עַלְוָה אַלּוּף יְתֵת׃ אַלּוּף אָהֳלִיבָמָה אַלּוּף אֵלָה
מב מג אַלּוּף פִּינֹן׃ אַלּוּף קְנַז אַלּוּף תֵּימָן אַלּוּף מִבְצָר׃ אַלּוּף מַגְדִּיאֵל אַלּוּף
עִירָם אֵלֶּה ׀ אַלּוּפֵי אֱדוֹם לְמֹשְׁבֹתָם בְּאֶרֶץ אֲחֻזָּתָם הוּא עֵשָׂו אֲבִי
אֱדוֹם׃

The הפטרה *for* פרשת וישלח *is on page 1517.*

אונקלוס

לב וּמְלַךְ בֶּאֱדוֹם, בֶּלַע בַּר בְּעוֹר, וְשׁוּם קַרְתֵּיהּ דִּנְהָבָה: לג וּמִית בֶּלַע, וּמְלַךְ תְּחוֹתוֹהִי, יוֹבָב בַּר זֶרַח מִבָּצְרָה: לד וּמִית יוֹבָב, וּמְלַךְ תְּחוֹתוֹהִי, חוּשָׁם מֵאֲרַע דָּרוֹמָא: לה וּמִית חוּשָׁם, וּמְלַךְ תְּחוֹתוֹהִי הֲדַד בַּר בְּדַד, דְּקַטִּיל יָת מִדְיָנָאֵי בְּחַקְלֵי מוֹאָב, וְשׁוּם קַרְתֵּיהּ עֲוִית: לו וּמִית הֲדַד, וּמְלַךְ תְּחוֹתוֹהִי, שַׂמְלָה מִמַּשְׂרֵקָה: לז וּמִית שַׂמְלָה, וּמְלַךְ תְּחוֹתוֹהִי, שָׁאוּל מֵרְחוֹבוֹת דְּעַל פְּרָת: לח וּמִית שָׁאוּל, וּמְלַךְ תְּחוֹתוֹהִי, בַּעַל חָנָן בַּר עַכְבּוֹר: לט וּמִית בַּעַל חָנָן בַּר עַכְבּוֹר, וּמְלַךְ תְּחוֹתוֹהִי הֲדַר, וְשׁוּם קַרְתֵּיהּ פָּעוּ, וְשׁוּם אִתְּתֵיהּ מְהֵיטַבְאֵל בַּת מַטְרֵד, בַּת מְצָרֵף דַּהֲבָא: מ וְאִלֵּין, שְׁמָהַת, רַבְרְבֵי עֵשָׂו לְזַרְעֳיָתְהוֹן, לְאַתְרֵיהוֹן בִּשְׁמָהָתְהוֹן, רַבָּא תִמְנַע, רַבָּא עַלְוָה רַבָּא יְתֵת: מא רַבָּא אָהֳלִיבָמָה, רַבָּא אֵלָה רַבָּא פִינֹן: מב רַבָּא קְנַז, רַבָּא תֵימָן רַבָּא מִבְצָר: מג רַבָּא מַגְדִּיאֵל רַבָּא עִירָם, אִלֵּין רַבְרְבֵי אֱדוֹם, לְמוֹתְבָנֵיהוֹן בַּאֲרַע אַחְסָנַתְהוֹן, הוּא עֵשָׂו אֲבוּהוֹן דֶּאֱדוֹמָאֵי:

Parashat Vayeshev

37 1 Yaakov settled where his father had lived as a stranger, in the land of Canaan.
2 This is the story of Yaakov. Yosef, seventeen years old, was shepherding the
flock with his brothers, an assistant to the sons of his father's wives Bilha and
3 Zilpa. And Yosef brought his father bad reports of them. Now, Yisrael loved
Yosef more than all his other sons, for he was a child of his old age; he made
4 him an ornately colored robe. But when his brothers saw that their father loved
him more than any of them, they hated him and could not say a peaceful word
5 to him. Then Yosef had a dream, and when he told it to his brothers, they hated

רש״י

לז א] **וַיֵּשֶׁב יַעֲקֹב.** אַחַר שֶׁכָּתַב לְךָ יִשּׁוּבֵי עֵשָׂו וְתוֹלְדוֹתָיו בְּדֶרֶךְ קְצָרָה, שֶׁלֹּא הָיוּ סְפוּנִים וַחֲשׁוּבִים לְפָרֵשׁ הֵיאַךְ נִתְיַשְּׁבוּ וְסֵדֶר מִלְחֲמוֹתֵיהֶם אֵיךְ הוֹרִישׁוּ אֶת הַחוֹרִי, פֵּרֵשׁ לְךָ יִשּׁוּבֵי יַעֲקֹב וְתוֹלְדוֹתָיו בְּדֶרֶךְ אֲרֻכָּה, כָּל גִּלְגּוּלֵי סִבָּתָם, לְפִי שֶׁהֵם חֲשׁוּבִים לִפְנֵי הַמָּקוֹם לְהַאֲרִיךְ בָּהֶם. וְכֵן אַתָּה מוֹצֵא בַּעֲשָׂרָה דוֹרוֹת שֶׁמֵּאָדָם וְעַד נֹחַ, פְּלוֹנִי הוֹלִיד פְּלוֹנִי, וּכְשֶׁבָּא לְנֹחַ הֶאֱרִיךְ בּוֹ. וְכֵן בַּעֲשָׂרָה דוֹרוֹת שֶׁמִּנֹּחַ וְעַד אַבְרָהָם קִצֵּר בָּהֶם, וּמִשֶּׁהִגִּיעַ אֵצֶל אַבְרָהָם הֶאֱרִיךְ בּוֹ. מָשָׁל לְמַרְגָּלִית שֶׁנָּפְלָה בֵּין הַחוֹל, אָדָם מְמַשְׁמֵשׁ בַּחוֹל וְכוֹבְרוֹ בִּכְבָרָה עַד שֶׁמּוֹצֵא אֶת הַמַּרְגָּלִית, וּמִשֶּׁמְּצָאָהּ הוּא מַשְׁלִיךְ אֶת הַצְּרוֹרוֹת מִיָּדוֹ וְנוֹטֵל הַמַּרְגָּלִית:

ב] **אֵלֶּה תֹּלְדוֹת יַעֲקֹב.** וְאֵלֶּה שֶׁל תּוֹלְדוֹת יַעֲקֹב, אֵלֶּה יִשּׁוּבֵיהֶם וְגִלְגּוּלֵיהֶם עַד שֶׁבָּאוּ לִכְלַל יִשּׁוּב; סִבָּה רִאשׁוֹנָה: "יוֹסֵף בֶּן שְׁבַע עֶשְׂרֵה" וְגוֹ', עַל יְדֵי זֶה נִתְגַּלְגְּלוּ וְיָרְדוּ לְמִצְרַיִם. זֶהוּ אַחַר יִשּׁוּב פְּשׁוּטוֹ שֶׁל מִקְרָא לִהְיוֹת דָּבוּר עַל אָפְנָיו. וּמִדְרַשׁ אַגָּדָה דּוֹרֵשׁ, תָּלָה הַכָּתוּב תּוֹלְדוֹת יַעֲקֹב בְּיוֹסֵף מִפְּנֵי כַּמָּה דְּבָרִים: אַחַת, שֶׁכָּל עַצְמוֹ שֶׁל יַעֲקֹב לֹא עָבַד אֵצֶל לָבָן אֶלָּא בְּרָחֵל, וְשֶׁהָיָה זִיו אִיקוֹנִין שֶׁל יוֹסֵף דּוֹמֶה לוֹ, וְכָל מַה שֶּׁאֵרַע לְיַעֲקֹב אֵרַע לְיוֹסֵף: זֶה נִשְׂטַם וְזֶה נִשְׂטַם, זֶה אָחִיו מְבַקֵּשׁ לְהָרְגוֹ וְזֶה אֶחָיו מְבַקְּשִׁים לְהָרְגוֹ, וְכֵן הַרְבֵּה בִּבְרֵאשִׁית רַבָּה (פד, ו): **וְהוּא נַעַר.** שֶׁהָיָה עוֹשֶׂה מַעֲשֵׂה נַעֲרוּת, מְתַקֵּן בִּשְׂעָרוֹ, מְמַשְׁמֵשׁ בְּעֵינָיו, כְּדֵי שֶׁיִּהְיֶה נִרְאֶה יָפֶה: **אֶת בְּנֵי בִלְהָה.** כְּלוֹמַר, וְרָגִיל אֵצֶל בְּנֵי בִלְהָה, לְפִי שֶׁהָיוּ אֶחָיו מְבַזִּין אוֹתָן וְהוּא מְקָרְבָן: **אֶת דִּבָּתָם רָעָה.** כָּל רָעָה שֶׁהָיָה רוֹאֶה בְּאֶחָיו בְּנֵי לֵאָה הָיָה מַגִּיד לְאָבִיו, שֶׁהָיוּ אוֹכְלִין אֵבֶר מִן הַחַי, וּמְזַלְזְלִין בִּבְנֵי הַשְּׁפָחוֹת לִקְרוֹתָן עֲבָדִים, וַחֲשׁוּדִים עַל הָעֲרָיוֹת. וּבִשְׁלָשְׁתָּן לָקָה: "וַיִּשְׁחֲטוּ שְׂעִיר עִזִּים" (להלן פסוק לא) בִּמְכִירָתוֹ, וְלֹא אֲכָלוּהוּ חַי; וְעַל דִּבָּה שֶׁסִּפֵּר עֲלֵיהֶם שֶׁקּוֹרִין לַאֲחֵיהֶם עֲבָדִים – "לְעֶבֶד נִמְכַּר יוֹסֵף" (תהלים קה, יז); וְעַל הָעֲרָיוֹת שֶׁסִּפֵּר עֲלֵיהֶם – "וַתִּשָּׂא אֵשֶׁת אֲדֹנָיו" וְגוֹ' (להלן לט, ז): **דִּבָּתָם.** כָּל לְשׁוֹן דִּבָּה פרלדי"ן בְּלַעַז. כָּל מַה שֶּׁהָיָה יָכוֹל לְדַבֵּר בָּהֶם רָעָה הָיָה מְסַפֵּר. 'דִּבָּה' – לְשׁוֹן "דּוֹבֵב שִׂפְתֵי יְשֵׁנִים" (שיר השירים ז, י):

ג] **בֶּן זְקֻנִים.** שֶׁנּוֹלַד לוֹ לְעֵת זִקְנָתוֹ. וְאוּנְקְלוֹס תִּרְגֵּם: "בַּר חַכִּים הוּא לֵיהּ", כָּל מַה שֶּׁלָּמַד מִשֵּׁם וָעֵבֶר מָסַר לוֹ. דָּבָר אַחֵר, שֶׁהָיָה זִיו אִיקוֹנִין שֶׁלּוֹ דּוֹמֶה לוֹ: **פַּסִּים.** לְשׁוֹן כְּלֵי מֵילָת, כְּמוֹ: "כַּרְפַּס וּתְכֵלֶת" (אסתר א, ו), וּכְמוֹ: "כְּתֹנֶת הַפַּסִּים" (שמואל ב' יג, יח) דְּתָמָר וְאַמְנוֹן. וּמִדְרַשׁ אַגָּדָה, עַל שֵׁם צָרוֹתָיו, שֶׁנִּמְכַּר לְפוֹטִיפַר וְלַסּוֹחֲרִים וְלַיִּשְׁמְעֵאלִים וְלַמִּדְיָנִים:

ד] **וְלֹא יָכְלוּ דַּבְּרוֹ לְשָׁלֹם.** מִתּוֹךְ גְּנוּתָם לָמַדְנוּ שִׁבְחָם, שֶׁלֹּא דִּבְּרוּ אַחַת בַּפֶּה וְאַחַת בַּלֵּב. **דַּבְּרוֹ.** לְדַבֵּר עִמּוֹ:

point, the core of the problem Genesis is intent on exploring. To create a universe, Genesis implies, is easy. It takes up no more than a single chapter (1:1–2:3). To create a human relationship is difficult. Yaakov's love for Yosef – innocent, human, benign – generates envy and hate. It is this honest confrontation with complexity that makes Genesis so profound a religious text. It refuses to simplify the human condition.

37:4 **וְלֹא יָכְלוּ דַּבְּרוֹ לְשָׁלֹם** *Could not say a peaceful word to him* – What this means, says Rabbi Yonatan Eybeshutz, is that had the brothers spoken, they could have told Yosef of their resentments. Yosef would be aware of their feelings and might moderate his behavior in some way. Once real communication had taken place, the brothers might have spoken their way to peace. As it is, the brothers' inability to speak allows

פרשת וישב

לז א וַיֵּשֶׁב יַעֲקֹב בְּאֶרֶץ מְגוּרֵי אָבִיו בְּאֶרֶץ כְּנָעַן: אֵלֶּה ׀ תֹּלְדוֹת יַעֲקֹב לג
יוֹסֵף בֶּן־שְׁבַע־עֶשְׂרֵה שָׁנָה הָיָה רֹעֶה אֶת־אֶחָיו בַּצֹּאן וְהוּא נַעַר
אֶת־בְּנֵי בִלְהָה וְאֶת־בְּנֵי זִלְפָּה נְשֵׁי אָבִיו וַיָּבֵא יוֹסֵף אֶת־דִּבָּתָם רָעָה
ג אֶל־אֲבִיהֶם: וְיִשְׂרָאֵל אָהַב אֶת־יוֹסֵף מִכָּל־בָּנָיו כִּי־בֶן־זְקֻנִים הוּא לוֹ
ד וְעָשָׂה לוֹ כְּתֹנֶת פַּסִּים: וַיִּרְאוּ אֶחָיו כִּי־אֹתוֹ אָהַב אֲבִיהֶם מִכָּל־אֶחָיו
ה וַיִּשְׂנְאוּ אֹתוֹ וְלֹא יָכְלוּ דַּבְּרוֹ לְשָׁלֹם: וַיַּחֲלֹם יוֹסֵף חֲלוֹם וַיַּגֵּד לְאֶחָיו

אונקלוס

לז א וִיתֵיב יַעֲקֹב, בַּאֲרַע תּוֹתָבוּת אֲבוּהִי, בְּאַרְעָא דִּכְנָעַן: ב אִלֵּין תּוֹלְדָת יַעֲקֹב, יוֹסֵף, בַּר שְׁבַע עַסְרֵי שְׁנִין הֲוָה רָעֵי עִם אֲחוֹהִי בְּעָנָא, וְהוּא רָבֵי, עִם בְּנֵי בִלְהָה, וְעִם בְּנֵי זִלְפָּה נְשֵׁי אֲבוּהִי, וְאַיְתִי יוֹסֵף, יָת דִּבְהוֹן בִּישָׁא לַאֲבוּהוֹן: ג וְיִשְׂרָאֵל, רְחֵים יָת יוֹסֵף מִכָּל בְּנוֹהִי, אֲרֵי בַר חַכִּים הוּא לֵיהּ, וַעֲבַד לֵיהּ כִּתּוּנָא דְפַסֵּי: ד וַחֲזוֹ אֲחוֹהִי, אֲרֵי יָתֵיהּ, רְחֵים אֲבוּהוֹן מִכָּל אֲחוֹהִי, וּסְנוֹ יָתֵיהּ, וְלָא צְבַן לְמַלָּלָא עִמֵּיהּ שְׁלָם: ה וַחֲלַם יוֹסֵף חֶלְמָא, וְחַוִּי לַאֲחוֹהִי,

VAYESHEV

With Vayeshev, the story shifts from Yaakov to his children. The tension we have already sensed between Leah and Raḥel is transferred to the next generation in the form of the rivalry between Yosef and his brothers, the story whose twists and turns take us to the end of Genesis.

Yosef is Yaakov's favorite son, firstborn of his beloved Raḥel. The envy and antagonism of his brothers leads them to sell Yosef into slavery in Egypt, an act that will many years later result in the entire family, by then a nation, being enslaved.

The story of Yosef is full of fascinating vignettes, homing in on the characters of Reuven, Yehuda, Tamar, Yaakov, and others. Common to them all is the power of the narrative to confound our expectations. Reuven, the firstborn, seems to suffer self-doubt that robs him of the courage to take decisive action. Tamar turns out to be a paradigm of moral sensibility and courage. Part of the continuing power of these stories lies in their defiance of narrative convention. You can never predict in advance, the Torah seems to suggest, where virtue is to be found.

37:1 וַיֵּשֶׁב יַעֲקֹב *Yaakov settled* – The story of Yosef begins on an ominous note which tends to be lost in translation: "Yaakov settled [*vayeshev*] where his father had lived as a stranger [*be'eretz megurei aviv*]." The contrast between the two verbs, "to settle, dwell" and "to sojourn, live as a stranger" – to live securely and insecurely – suggests that Yaakov wants what Avraham and Yitzḥak did not have: tranquility. Having fled twice, once from his brother Esav, a second time from his father-in-law Lavan, he longs for a quiet life. He will not achieve it. The Sages said: "Yaakov sought to dwell in peace; immediately there broke upon him the storm of Yosef" (Rashi, commentary on Gen. 37:2, on the basis of Bereshit Rabba 84:3).

37:4 וַיִּשְׂנְאוּ אֹתוֹ *They hated him* – The text sets up a contrast between love and hate. Twice we read that Yaakov loves Yosef, twice that his brothers hate him. They hate him *because* their father loves him. The same pair of verbs, "to love" and "to hate," have already appeared in the story of Yaakov's wives, the sisters Raḥel and Leah (Gen. 29:30–31). This is a crucial

6 7 him still more. "Listen to this dream I had," he said. "We were binding sheaves
in the field when my sheaf rose and stood upright and your sheaves gathered
8 around mine and bowed down to it." His brothers said to him, "Do you mean
to be king over us? Do you mean to rule over us?" Then they hated him even
9 more for his dreams and for what he said. Then he had another dream and told
it to his brothers. "I had another dream," he said. "This time, the sun, moon,
10 and eleven stars were bowing down to me." When he told his father as well as
his brothers, his father rebuked him and said, "What kind of dream is this that
you have had? Shall we really come, I and your mother and your brothers, to
11 bow to the ground before you?" His brothers were jealous of him; but his father
12 kept the matter in mind. When his brothers had gone to pasture their father's SHENI
13 flock near Shekhem, Yisrael said to Yosef, "Come, your brothers are pasturing
14 the flocks near Shekhem; I will send you to them." Yosef said, "Here I am." He
said to him, "Go and see how your brothers and the flocks are doing, and bring
me back word," and he sent him from the Ḥevron Valley, from where he walked
15 to Shekhem. A man found him wandering lost among the fields and asked him,

רש״י

ז **מְאַלְּמִים אֲלֻמִּים.** כְּתַרְגּוּמוֹ: "מְאַסְּרִין אֱסָרָן", עֲמָרִין, וְכֵן: "נֹשֵׂא אֲלֻמֹּתָיו" (תהלים קכו, ו), וְכָמוֹהוּ בִּלְשׁוֹן מִשְׁנָה: "וְהָאֲלֻמּוֹת נוֹטֵל וּמַכְרִיז" (בבא מציעא כב ע״ב): **קָמָה אֲלֻמָּתִי.** נִזְקְפָה: **וְגַם נִצָּבָה.** לַעֲמֹד עַל עָמְדָהּ בִּזְקִיפָה:

ח **וְעַל דְּבָרָיו.** עַל דִּבָּתָם רָעָה שֶׁהָיָה מֵבִיא לַאֲבִיהֶם:

י **וַיְסַפֵּר אֶל אָבִיו וְאֶל אֶחָיו.** לְאַחַר שֶׁסִּפֵּר אוֹתוֹ לְאֶחָיו חָזַר וְסִפְּרוֹ לְאָבִיו בִּפְנֵיהֶם: **וַיִּגְעַר בּוֹ.** לְפִי שֶׁהָיָה מַטִּיל שִׂנְאָה עָלָיו: **הֲבוֹא נָבוֹא.** וַהֲלֹא אִמְּךָ כְּבָר מֵתָה! וְהוּא לֹא הָיָה יוֹדֵעַ שֶׁהַדְּבָרִים מַגִּיעִין לְבִלְהָה שֶׁגִּדְּלַתּוּ כְּאִמּוֹ. וְרַבּוֹתֵינוּ לָמְדוּ מִכָּאן שֶׁאֵין חֲלוֹם בְּלֹא דְּבָרִים בְּטֵלִים, וְיַעֲקֹב נִתְכַּוֵּן לְהוֹצִיא הַדָּבָר מִלֵּב בָּנָיו שֶׁלֹּא יְקַנְאוּהוּ, לְכָךְ אָמַר לוֹ: "הֲבוֹא נָבוֹא" וְגוֹ׳, כְּשֵׁם שֶׁאִי אֶפְשָׁר בְּאִמְּךָ כָּךְ הַשְּׁאָר בָּטֵל:

יא **שָׁמַר אֶת הַדָּבָר.** הָיָה מַמְתִּין וּמְצַפֶּה מָתַי יָבוֹא, וְכֵן: "שׁוֹמֵר אֱמוּנִים" (ישעיה כו, ב), וְכֵן: "לֹא תִשְׁמֹר עַל חַטָּאתִי" (איוב יד, טז) – לֹא תַמְתִּין:

יב **לִרְעוֹת אֶת צֹאן.** נָקוּד עַל 'אֶת', שֶׁלֹּא הָלְכוּ אֶלָּא לִרְעוֹת אֶת עַצְמָן:

יג **הִנֵּנִי.** לְשׁוֹן עֲנָוָה וּזְרִיזוּת; נִזְדָּרֵז לְמִצְוַת אָבִיו, וְאַף עַל פִּי שֶׁהָיָה יוֹדֵעַ בְּאֶחָיו שֶׁשּׂוֹנְאִין אוֹתוֹ:

יד **מֵעֵמֶק חֶבְרוֹן.** וַהֲלֹא חֶבְרוֹן בָּהָר, שֶׁנֶּאֱמַר: "וַיַּעֲלוּ בַנֶּגֶב וַיָּבֹא עַד חֶבְרוֹן" (במדבר יג, כב)? אֶלָּא מֵעֵצָה עֲמֻקָּה שֶׁל אוֹתוֹ צַדִּיק הַקָּבוּר בְּחֶבְרוֹן, לְקַיֵּם מַה שֶּׁנֶּאֱמַר לְאַבְרָהָם בֵּין הַבְּתָרִים: "כִּי גֵר יִהְיֶה זַרְעֲךָ": **וַיָּבֹא שְׁכֶמָה.** מָקוֹם מוּכָן לְפֻרְעָנוּת, שָׁם קִלְקְלוּ הַשְּׁבָטִים, שָׁם עִנּוּ אֶת דִּינָה, שָׁם נֶחְלְקָה מַלְכוּת בֵּית דָּוִד, שֶׁנֶּאֱמַר: "וַיֵּלֶךְ רְחַבְעָם שְׁכֶמָה" (דברי הימים ב׳ י, א):

טו **וַיִּמְצָאֵהוּ אִישׁ.** זֶה גַּבְרִיאֵל:

I am not sure whether Ramban meant without Yosef's knowledge or without the guide's knowledge. I prefer to think both. The anonymous man – so the Torah is intimating – represents an intrusion of providence to make sure that Yosef goes to where he is supposed to be, so that the rest of the drama can unfold. He may not know he has such a role. Yosef surely does not know. To put it as simply as I can: *He is an angel who does not know he is an angel.* He has a vital role in the story. Without him, none of the events that take up the rest of the Torah will happen: no Yosef the slave, no Yosef the viceroy, no storage of food during the years of plenty, no descent of Yosef's family to Egypt, no exile, no slavery, no

ו וַיּוֹסִפוּ עוֹד שְׂנֹא אֹתוֹ: וַיֹּאמֶר אֲלֵיהֶם שִׁמְעוּ־נָא הַחֲלוֹם הַזֶּה אֲשֶׁר
ז חָלָמְתִּי: וְהִנֵּה אֲנַחְנוּ מְאַלְּמִים אֲלֻמִּים בְּתוֹךְ הַשָּׂדֶה וְהִנֵּה קָמָה
אֲלֻמָּתִי וְגַם־נִצָּבָה וְהִנֵּה תְסֻבֶּינָה אֲלֻמֹּתֵיכֶם וַתִּשְׁתַּחֲוֶיןָ לַאֲלֻמָּתִי:
ח וַיֹּאמְרוּ לוֹ אֶחָיו הֲמָלֹךְ תִּמְלֹךְ עָלֵינוּ אִם־מָשׁוֹל תִּמְשֹׁל בָּנוּ וַיּוֹסִפוּ
ט עוֹד שְׂנֹא אֹתוֹ עַל־חֲלֹמֹתָיו וְעַל־דְּבָרָיו: וַיַּחֲלֹם עוֹד חֲלוֹם אַחֵר וַיְסַפֵּר
אֹתוֹ לְאֶחָיו וַיֹּאמֶר הִנֵּה חָלַמְתִּי חֲלוֹם עוֹד וְהִנֵּה הַשֶּׁמֶשׁ וְהַיָּרֵחַ וְאַחַד
י עָשָׂר כּוֹכָבִים מִשְׁתַּחֲוִים לִי: וַיְסַפֵּר אֶל־אָבִיו וְאֶל־אֶחָיו וַיִּגְעַר־בּוֹ
אָבִיו וַיֹּאמֶר לוֹ מָה הַחֲלוֹם הַזֶּה אֲשֶׁר חָלָמְתָּ הֲבוֹא נָבוֹא אֲנִי וְאִמְּךָ
יא וְאַחֶיךָ לְהִשְׁתַּחֲוֹת לְךָ אָרְצָה: וַיְקַנְאוּ־בוֹ אֶחָיו וְאָבִיו שָׁמַר אֶת־
יב יג הַדָּבָר: וַיֵּלְכוּ אֶחָיו לִרְעוֹת אֶת־צֹאן אֲבִיהֶם בִּשְׁכֶם: וַיֹּאמֶר יִשְׂרָאֵל שני
אֶל־יוֹסֵף הֲלוֹא אַחֶיךָ רֹעִים בִּשְׁכֶם לְכָה וְאֶשְׁלָחֲךָ אֲלֵיהֶם וַיֹּאמֶר
יד לוֹ הִנֵּנִי: וַיֹּאמֶר לוֹ לֶךְ־נָא רְאֵה אֶת־שְׁלוֹם אַחֶיךָ וְאֶת־שְׁלוֹם הַצֹּאן
טו וַהֲשִׁבֵנִי דָּבָר וַיִּשְׁלָחֵהוּ מֵעֵמֶק חֶבְרוֹן וַיָּבֹא שְׁכֶמָה: וַיִּמְצָאֵהוּ אִישׁ

אונקלוס

וְאוֹסִיפוּ עוֹד סְנוֹ יָתֵיהּ: ו וַאֲמַר לְהוֹן, שְׁמַעוּ כְעַן, חֶלְמָא הָדֵין דַּחֲלָמִית: ז וְהָא, אֲנַחְנָא, מְאַסְּרִין אֱסָרָן בְּגוֹ חַקְלָא, וְהָא, קָמַת אֱסָרְתִי וְאַף אִזְדְּקֵיפַת, וְהָא מִסְתַּחֲרָן אֱסָרָתְכוֹן, וְסָגְדָן לַאֱסָרְתִי: ח וַאֲמַרוּ לֵיהּ אֲחוֹהִי, הֲמַלְכוּ אַתְּ מְדַמֵּי לְמִמְלַךְ עֲלַנָא, אוֹ שֻׁלְטָן אַתְּ סְבִיר לְמִשְׁלַט בְּנָא, וְאוֹסִיפוּ עוֹד סְנוֹ יָתֵיהּ, עַל חֶלְמוֹהִי וְעַל פִּתְגָמוֹהִי: ט וַחֲלַם עוֹד חֶלְמָא אָחֳרָנָא, וְאִשְׁתַּעִי יָתֵיהּ לַאֲחוֹהִי, וַאֲמַר, הָא חֲלָמִית חֶלְמָא עוֹד, וְהָא שִׁמְשָׁא וְסִיהֲרָא, וְחַד עֲסַר כּוֹכְבַיָּא, סָגְדִין לִי: י וְאִשְׁתַּעִי לַאֲבוּהִי וּלְאֲחוֹהִי, וּנְזַף בֵּיהּ אֲבוּהִי, וַאֲמַר לֵיהּ, מָא, חֶלְמָא הָדֵין דַּחֲלַמְתָּא, הֲמֵיתָא נֵיתֵי, אֲנָא וְאִמָּךְ וְאַחָךְ, לְמִסְגַּד לָךְ עַל אַרְעָא: יא וְקַנִּיאוּ בֵיהּ אֲחוֹהִי, וַאֲבוּהִי נְטַר יָת פִּתְגָמָא: יב וַאֲזַלוּ אֲחוֹהִי, לְמִרְעֵי, יָת עָנָא דַאֲבוּהוֹן בִּשְׁכֶם: יג וַאֲמַר יִשְׂרָאֵל לְיוֹסֵף, הֲלָא אַחָךְ רָעַן בִּשְׁכֶם, אֵיתָא וְאֶשְׁלְחִנָּךְ לְוָתְהוֹן, וַאֲמַר לֵיהּ הָאֲנָא: יד וַאֲמַר לֵיהּ, אֵיזֵיל כְּעַן חֲזֵי, יָת שְׁלָם אַחָךְ וְיָת שְׁלָם עָנָא, וַאֲתֵיבְנִי פִּתְגָמָא, וְשַׁלְחֵיהּ מִמֵּישַׁר חֶבְרוֹן, וַאֲתָא לִשְׁכֶם: טו וְאַשְׁכְּחֵיהּ גֻּבְרָא,

hatred to fester until they plot to kill him, eventually deciding to sell him as a slave, fracturing the family and causing their father inconsolable grief. As we have already seen several times in Genesis, a failure of words again begets tragedy.

37:15 וַיִּמְצָאֵהוּ אִישׁ וְהִנֵּה תֹעֶה *A man found him wandering* – I know of no comparable passage in the Torah: three verses dedicated to an apparently trivial, eminently forgettable detail of someone having to ask directions from a stranger. Who is this unnamed man? And what conceivable message does the episode hold for future generations, for us? Rashi says he is the angel Gabriel. Ibn Ezra says he is a passerby. Ramban, however, says that "the Holy One, blessed be He, sent him a guide without his knowledge."

16 "What are you looking for?" He replied, "I'm looking for my brothers. Can you
17 tell me where they are pasturing the sheep?" "They have moved on from here,"
said the man. "I heard them say, 'Let us go to Dotan.'" So Yosef went after his
18 brothers and found them at Dotan. They saw him in the distance, and by the
19 time he reached them, they had plotted to kill him. "Here comes the dreamer!"
20 they said to one another. "Now let us kill him and throw him into one of the
pits – we can say that a wild animal ate him – then we shall see what will come
21 of his dreams!" When Reuven heard this, he tried to save him from them. "Let
22 us not kill him," he said. "Do not shed blood," said Reuven. "Throw him into
this pit in the desert, but do not lay hands on him." His plan was to rescue him
23 and bring him back to his father. So when Yosef came to his brothers, they SHELISHI

רש״י

יז **נָסְעוּ מִזֶּה.** הִסִּיעוּ עַצְמָן מִן הָאַחְוָה: **נֵלְכָה דֹּתָיְנָה.** לְבַקֵּשׁ לְךָ נִכְלֵי דָתוֹת שֶׁיְּמִיתוּךָ בָּהֶם. וּלְפִי פְשׁוּטוֹ שֵׁם מָקוֹם הוּא, וְאֵין מִקְרָא יוֹצֵא מִידֵי פְשׁוּטוֹ:

יח **וַיִּתְנַכְּלוּ.** נִתְמַלְּאוּ נְכָלִים וַעֲרְמוּמִיּוּת: **אֹתוֹ.** כְּמוֹ 'אִתּוֹ' 'עִמּוֹ', כְּלוֹמַר אֵלָיו:

כ **וְנִרְאֶה מַה יִּהְיוּ חֲלֹמֹתָיו.** אָמַר רַבִּי יִצְחָק: מִקְרָא זֶה אוֹמֵר דָּרְשֵׁנִי, רוּחַ הַקֹּדֶשׁ אוֹמֶרֶת כֵּן, הֵם אוֹמְרִים "נַהַרְגֵהוּ", וְהַכָּתוּב מְסַיֵּם "וְנִרְאֶה מַה יִּהְיוּ חֲלֹמֹתָיו" – נִרְאֶה דְּבַר מִי יָקוּם, אִם שֶׁלָּכֶם אוֹ שֶׁלִּי. וְאִי אֶפְשָׁר שֶׁיֹּאמְרוּ הֵם: "וְנִרְאֶה מַה יִּהְיוּ חֲלֹמֹתָיו", שֶׁמִּכֵּיוָן שֶׁיַּהַרְגוּהוּ בָּטְלוּ חֲלוֹמוֹתָיו:

כא **לֹא נַכֶּנּוּ נָפֶשׁ.** מַכַּת נֶפֶשׁ, זוֹ הִיא מִיתָה:

כב **לְמַעַן הַצִּיל אֹתוֹ.** רוּחַ הַקֹּדֶשׁ מְעִידָה עַל רְאוּבֵן שֶׁלֹּא אָמַר זֹאת אֶלָּא לְהַצִּיל אוֹתוֹ, שֶׁיָּבֹא הוּא וְיַעֲלֶנּוּ מִשָּׁם. אָמַר: אֲנִי בְּכוֹר וְגָדוֹל שֶׁבְּכֻלָּן, לֹא יִתָּלֶה הַסִּרְחוֹן אֶלָּא בִּי:

כג **אֶת כֻּתָּנְתּוֹ.** זֶה חָלוּק: **אֶת כְּתֹנֶת הַפַּסִּים.** הוּא שֶׁהוֹסִיף לוֹ אָבִיו יוֹתֵר עַל אֶחָיו:

is the beginning of a sequence of events that will make the dreams come true.

REUVEN'S GOOD INTENTIONS

The brothers realize that, alone with no one to see them, they can kill Yosef and concoct a tale that will be impossible to refute. Only Reuven protests. It is at this point the Torah does something it does nowhere else. It makes a statement that, construed literally, is obviously false. The text states, literally: "When Reuven heard this, he saved [Yosef] from them." He did not. The discrepancy is so obvious that most translations, ours included, simply do not translate the phrase literally. What Reuven actually does is to attempt to save him. The Hebrew phrase tells us what might have been, not what actually is.

Reuven's plan is simple. He tells the brothers, in verse 22, not to kill Yosef but to let him die. The text – unusually, for it is rare for the Torah to describe a person's thoughts – explains Reuven's intent: His plan is to persuade the brothers to leave Yosef in the pit so that, when their attention is elsewhere, he can come back to it, lift him out, and take him home.

While Reuven is somewhere else, however, Yosef is taken from the pit and sold to a passing caravan of merchants. Reuven, unaware of all this, returns to the pit to rescue Yosef but finds him gone. He is bereft. "He … went back to his brothers, and said, 'The boy is gone, and I – where can I turn?'" (Gen. 37:30).

Commenting on this episode, the Midrash (Vayikra Rabba 34:8) states that if Reuven had only known that the Holy One, blessed be He, would record his intentions to save Yosef, he would have picked Yosef up on his shoulders and carried him back to his father.

If Reuven had only known, says the Midrash. If only he had known that the Torah would write of him, "When

טז וְהִנֵּה תֹעֶה בַּשָּׂדֶה וַיִּשְׁאָלֵהוּ הָאִישׁ לֵאמֹר מַה־תְּבַקֵּשׁ׃ וַיֹּאמֶר אֶת־
יז אַחַי אָנֹכִי מְבַקֵּשׁ הַגִּידָה־נָּא לִי אֵיפֹה הֵם רֹעִים׃ וַיֹּאמֶר הָאִישׁ נָסְעוּ
מִזֶּה כִּי שָׁמַעְתִּי אֹמְרִים נֵלְכָה דֹּתָיְנָה וַיֵּלֶךְ יוֹסֵף אַחַר אֶחָיו וַיִּמְצָאֵם
יח בְּדֹתָן׃ וַיִּרְאוּ אֹתוֹ מֵרָחֹק וּבְטֶרֶם יִקְרַב אֲלֵיהֶם וַיִּתְנַכְּלוּ אֹתוֹ לַהֲמִיתוֹ׃
יט כ וַיֹּאמְרוּ אִישׁ אֶל־אָחִיו הִנֵּה בַּעַל הַחֲלֹמוֹת הַלָּזֶה בָּא׃ וְעַתָּה ׀ לְכוּ
וְנַהַרְגֵהוּ וְנַשְׁלִכֵהוּ בְּאַחַד הַבֹּרוֹת וְאָמַרְנוּ חַיָּה רָעָה אֲכָלָתְהוּ וְנִרְאֶה
כא מַה־יִּהְיוּ חֲלֹמֹתָיו׃ וַיִּשְׁמַע רְאוּבֵן וַיַּצִּלֵהוּ מִיָּדָם וַיֹּאמֶר לֹא נַכֶּנּוּ נָפֶשׁ׃
כב וַיֹּאמֶר אֲלֵהֶם ׀ רְאוּבֵן אַל־תִּשְׁפְּכוּ־דָם הַשְׁלִיכוּ אֹתוֹ אֶל־הַבּוֹר הַזֶּה
אֲשֶׁר בַּמִּדְבָּר וְיָד אַל־תִּשְׁלְחוּ־בוֹ לְמַעַן הַצִּיל אֹתוֹ מִיָּדָם לַהֲשִׁיבוֹ
כג אֶל־אָבִיו׃ וַיְהִי כַּאֲשֶׁר־בָּא יוֹסֵף אֶל־אֶחָיו וַיַּפְשִׁיטוּ אֶת־יוֹסֵף אֶת־ שלישי

אונקלוס

וְהָא טָעֵי בְחַקְלָא, וּשְׁאֵלֵיהּ גֻּבְרָא, לְמֵימַר מָא אַתְּ בָּעֵי: טז וַאֲמַר, יָת אַחַי אֲנָא בָעֵי, חֲוִי כְעַן לִי, אֵיכָא אִנּוּן רָעַן: יז וַאֲמַר גֻּבְרָא נְטַלוּ מִכָּא, אֲרֵי שְׁמַעִית דְּאָמְרִין, נֵיזֵיל לְדוֹתָן, וַאֲזַל יוֹסֵף בָּתַר אֲחוֹהִי, וְאַשְׁכְּחִנּוּן בְּדוֹתָן: יח וַחֲזוֹ יָתֵיהּ מֵרָחִיק, וְעַד לָא קְרֵיב לְוָתְהוֹן, וְחַשִׁיבוּ עֲלוֹהִי לְמִקְטְלֵיהּ: יט וַאֲמַרוּ גְּבַר לַאֲחוּהִי, הָא, מָרֵי, חֶלְמַיָּא דֵיכִי אָתֵי: כ וּכְעַן אִיתוֹ וְנִקְטְלִנֵּיהּ, וְנִרְמִינֵיהּ בְּחַד מִן גֻּבַיָּא, וְנֵימַר, חַיְתָא בִשְׁתָּא אֲכַלְתֵּיהּ, וְנֶחֱזֵי, מָא יְהֵי בְּסוֹף חֶלְמוֹהִי: כא וּשְׁמַע רְאוּבֵן, וְשֵׁיזְבֵיהּ מִידְּהוֹן, וַאֲמַר, לָא נִקְטְלִנֵּיהּ נְפַשׁ: כב וַאֲמַר לְהוֹן רְאוּבֵן לָא תֵישְׁדוּן דַּם, רְמוֹ יָתֵיהּ, לְגֻבָּא הָדֵין דִּבְמַדְבְּרָא, וְיַד לָא תֵישְׁטוּן בֵּיהּ, בְּדִיל, לְשֵׁיזָבָא יָתֵיהּ מִידְּהוֹן, לַאֲתָבוּתֵיהּ לְוָת אֲבוּהִי: כג וַהֲוָה, כַּד אֲתָא יוֹסֵף לְוָת אֲחוֹהִי, וְאַשְׁלַחוּ יָת יוֹסֵף יָת

exodus. The message could not be more significant. When Heaven intends something to happen, and it seems to be impossible, sometimes it sends an angel down to earth – an angel who does not know he or she is an angel – to move the story from here to there.

I believe that there are times when we feel lost, and then someone says or does something that lifts us or points the way to a new direction and destination. Years later, looking back, we see how important that intervention was, even though it seemed slight at the time. That is when we know that we too encountered an angel who didn't know he or she was an angel.

37:18 וַיִּרְאוּ אֹתוֹ מֵרָחֹק *In the distance* – Imagine the scene. They can't see his face. All they can see is the "ornately colored robe" that so upsets them because it constantly reminds them that it is he, not they, whom their father loves. From far away, we don't see people as human beings, and when we stop seeing people as human beings, and they become instead symbols, objects of envy or hate, people can do terrible things to one another.

37:20 וְנִרְאֶה מַה יִּהְיוּ חֲלֹמֹתָיו *What will come of his dreams* – Here, the irony could not be more explicit. The words mean one thing to the brothers, the opposite to us, the listeners. Once we have reached the end of the story and go back to read it a second time, we realize that the very act intended to frustrate the dreams by killing the dreamer

▶

24 stripped him of his robe, the ornately colored robe he was wearing, and they
took him and threw him into the pit. The pit was empty; there was no water
25 in it. And they sat down and ate their meal. Looking up, they saw a caravan
of Ishmaelites coming from Gilad, their camels laden with spices, balm, and
26 myrrh, to be taken to Egypt. Yehuda said to his brothers, "What do we gain
27 by killing our brother and covering his blood? Let's sell him to the Ishmaelites
and not harm him with our own hands. After all, he is our brother, our own
28 flesh and blood." His brothers agreed. Some Midianite traders passed by and
they pulled Yosef up out of the pit, and they sold him to the Ishmaelites for

רש״י

כד| **והבור רק אין בו מים.** ממשמע שנאמר: "והבור רק" איני יודע שאין בו מים? מה תלמוד לומר: "אין בו מים"? מים אין בו, אבל נחשים ועקרבים יש בו:

כה| **ארחת.** כתרגומו: "שיירת", על שם הולכי ארח: **וגמליהם נשאים וגו׳.** למה פרסם הכתוב את משאם? להודיע מתן שכרן של צדיקים, שאין דרכן של ערביים לשאת אלא נפט ועטרן שריחן רע, ולזה נזדמנו בשמים שלא יזוק מריח רע: **נכאת.** כל כנוסי בשמים הרבה קרוי ׳נכאת׳, וכן: "ויראם את כל בית נכתה" (מלכים ב׳ כ, יג) – מרקחת בשמיו. ואונקלוס תרגם לשון שעוה: **וצרי.** שרף הנוטף מעצי הקטף, והוא נטף (שמות ל, לד) הנמנה עם סמני הקטרת: **ולט.** ׳לוטס׳ שמו בלשון משנה (שביעית ז, ו), ורבותי פרשוהו לי: שרש עשב ושמו אסטורוזינ״ה במסכת נדה (דף ח ע״א):

כו| **מה בצע.** מה ממון, כתרגומו: **וכסינו את דמו.** ונעלים את מיתתו:

כז| **וישמעו.** "וקבילו מניה", וכל שמיעה שהיא קבלת דברים, כגון זה, וכגון: "וישמע יעקב אל אביו" (לעיל כח, ז), "נעשה ונשמע" (שמות כד, ז), מתרגמין: ׳וקביל׳. וכל שהיא שמיעת האזן, כגון: "וישמעו את קול ה׳ אלהים מתהלך בגן" (לעיל ג, ח), "ורבקה שמעת" (לעיל כז, ה), "וישמע ישראל" (לעיל לה, כב), "שמעתי את תלנות" (שמות טז, יב), כלן מתרגמין: ושמעו, ושמעת, ושמע, שמיע קדמי:

כח| **ויעברו אנשים מדינים.** זו היא שיירה אחרת, והודיעך הכתוב שנמכר פעמים הרבה: **וימשכו.** בני יעקב את יוסף מן הבור וימכרוהו לישמעאלים, והישמעאלים למדנים, "והמדנים מכרו אתו אל מצרים" (להלן פסוק לו):

In case we miss the point, the Torah is to put it explicitly in Yosef's mouth. "Do not be distressed or angry with yourselves that you sold me here, for God sent me ahead of you to save lives.... So then, it was not you who sent me here, but God" (Gen. 45:5–8).

The Bible is making, here and elsewhere, a philosophical point of some delicacy and power. It is rejecting the law of contradiction: either p or not-p. It is rejecting what William Blake called "single vision." It is telling us that there may be no unequivocal answer to the question "Was event X a chance event, or was it intended by divine design?" It may be both. From one perspective, the story of Yosef is a series of random events, mingled with a series of human decisions that might have been otherwise. From another perspective, it is the working out of a providential pattern whose end was announced (in Yosef's dreams) at the beginning.

37:26 **מה בצע כי נהרג את אחינו** *What do we gain by killing our brother?* – Note that he does not say, "It is wrong to kill our brother." He says, "What do we gain?" This is the language not of principle but of pragmatism. Note too that he proposes selling Yosef as a slave at the very moment he recognizes that "he is our brother, our own flesh and blood." It is as if Yehuda were echoing Kayin when he said, "Am I my brother's keeper?" (Gen. 4:9).

37:28 **וימכרו את יוסף** *And they sold him* – It is a confusing episode. *Who* sells Yosef to the Ishmaelites? Is it the brothers or the Midianites? The subject "they" is ambiguous.

The commentators offered many interpretations. Of these, the simplest is given by Rashbam, who reads it as follows: The brothers, having thrown Yosef into the pit, sit down some distance away to eat. Reuven sneaks back to

כד כֻּתָּנְתּוֹ אֶת־כְּתֹנֶת הַפַּסִּים אֲשֶׁר עָלָיו: וַיִּקָּחֻהוּ וַיַּשְׁלִכוּ אֹתוֹ הַבֹּרָה
כה וְהַבּוֹר רֵק אֵין בּוֹ מָיִם: וַיֵּשְׁבוּ לֶאֱכָל־לֶחֶם וַיִּשְׂאוּ עֵינֵיהֶם וַיִּרְאוּ וְהִנֵּה
אֹרְחַת יִשְׁמְעֵאלִים בָּאָה מִגִּלְעָד וּגְמַלֵּיהֶם נֹשְׂאִים נְכֹאת וּצְרִי וָלֹט
כו הוֹלְכִים לְהוֹרִיד מִצְרָיְמָה: וַיֹּאמֶר יְהוּדָה אֶל־אֶחָיו מַה־בֶּצַע כִּי
כז נַהֲרֹג אֶת־אָחִינוּ וְכִסִּינוּ אֶת־דָּמוֹ: לְכוּ וְנִמְכְּרֶנּוּ לַיִּשְׁמְעֵאלִים וְיָדֵנוּ
כח אַל־תְּהִי־בוֹ כִּי־אָחִינוּ בְשָׂרֵנוּ הוּא וַיִּשְׁמְעוּ אֶחָיו: וַיַּעַבְרוּ אֲנָשִׁים
מִדְיָנִים סֹחֲרִים וַיִּמְשְׁכוּ וַיַּעֲלוּ אֶת־יוֹסֵף מִן־הַבּוֹר וַיִּמְכְּרוּ אֶת־יוֹסֵף

אונקלוס

כִּתּוּנֵיהּ, יָת כִּתּוּנָא דְּפַסֵּי דַּעֲלוֹהִי: כד וְנַסְבוּהִי, וּרְמוֹ יָתֵיהּ לְגֻבָּא, וְגֻבָּא רֵיקָן, לֵית בֵּיהּ מַיָּא: כה וְאַסְחַרוּ לְמֵיכַל לַחְמָא, וּזְקַפוּ עֵינֵיהוֹן וַחֲזוֹ, וְהָא שְׁיָרַת עַרְבָאֵי, אָתְיָא מִגִּלְעָד, וְגַמְלֵיהוֹן טְעִינִין, שְׁעַף וּקְטוֹף וּלְטוֹם, אָזְלִין לְאַחָתָא לְמִצְרָיִם: כו וַאֲמַר יְהוּדָה לַאֲחוֹהִי, מָא מָמוֹן מִתְהֲנֵי לַנָא, אֲרֵי נִקְטוֹל יָת אֲחוּנָא, וּנְכַסֵּי עַל דְּמֵיהּ: כז אֵיתוֹ וּנְזַבְּנִנֵּיהּ לְעַרְבָאֵי, וִידַנָא לָא תְהֵי בֵיהּ, אֲרֵי אֲחוּנָא בִסְרַנָא הוּא, וְקַבִּילוּ מִנֵּיהּ אֲחוֹהִי: כח וַעֲבַרוּ גֻּבְרֵי מִדְיָנָאֵי תַּגָּרֵי, וּנְגַדוּ וְאַסִּיקוּ יָת יוֹסֵף מִן גֻּבָּא, וְזַבִּינוּ יָת יוֹסֵף,

37:25 וְהִנֵּה אֹרְחַת יִשְׁמְעֵאלִים *They saw a caravan of Ishmaelites* – Here is another apparently random encounter. The story of Yosef is carefully constructed to be read on at least two levels. On the one hand, it is a story of chance human interactions. It is a tale of parental favoritism and sibling rivalry. People speak, have emotions, and make decisions that have consequences. It might have been otherwise.

Read at another level, it is a story of divine providence in which the end is foretold at the beginning – one of the very few such stories in the Bible. The outcome is announced through the dreams. Yosef will become a leader. His brothers will bow down to him. As in a Greek tragedy, every act, whatever its intention, has the effect of leading toward the predestined end.

On the one hand, the story of Yosef can be read as pure chance. At the key moment, he might not have found his brothers. He might have wandered around looking for them and then returned home. The traders may not have passed by at the decisive moment, unknowingly averting his death. The entire drama of Yosef's fall and rise might never have happened.

On the other hand, divine providence is active at every stage.

Reuven heard this, he saved him from them" – known that his intention was recognized and valued by God as if it were the deed – he might have found the courage to carry it through into action. But Reuven cannot know. He has not read the story. None of us can read the story of our life – we can only live it. The result is that we live in and with uncertainty. Doubt can lead to delay until the moment is lost. In an instant of arrested intention, Reuven loses his chance of changing history.

Reuven cannot read his story, but we can. Observing Reuven, we can see that God loves each of us, and that this can be a source of formidable strength. God heeds those not heard. He loves those whom others do not love. Reuven, still a young man, does not yet know this. But we, reading his story and the rest of Tanakh, do.

We are here for a reason, conceived in love, brought into being by the One who brought the universe into being, who knows our innermost thoughts, values our good intentions, and has more faith in us than we have in ourselves. That, if only we meditate on it, gives us the strength to turn intention into deed, lifting us from the person we might have been into the person we become.

29 twenty pieces of silver. They then brought Yosef to Egypt. Reuven returned to
30 the pit – and Yosef was not there. He tore his clothes, went back to his brothers,
31 and said, "The boy is gone, and I – where can I turn?" They took Yosef's robe,
32 slaughtered a goat, and dipped the robe in the blood. They had the ornately
colored robe brought to their father, and they said, "We found this. Try to
33 identify it. Is it your son's robe or not?" He recognized it and said, "It is my
son's robe! A wild animal must have eaten him! Yosef has been torn limb from
34 limb!" Yaakov tore his clothes, put sackcloth on his loins, and mourned for
35 his son for many days. All his sons and daughters tried to comfort him, but he
refused to be comforted and said, "I will go down to Sheol mourning for my
36 son." His father wept for him. Meanwhile, the Medanites had sold him in Egypt
to Potifar, one of Pharaoh's officials, captain of the guard.

רש״י

כט **וַיָּשָׁב רְאוּבֵן.** וּבִמְכִירָתוֹ לֹא הָיָה שָׁם, שֶׁהִגִּיעַ יוֹמוֹ לֵילֵךְ וּלְשַׁמֵּשׁ אֶת אָבִיו. דָּבָר אַחֵר, עָסוּק הָיָה בְּשַׂקּוֹ וּבְתַעֲנִיתוֹ עַל בִּלְבּוּל יְצוּעֵי אָבִיו:

ל **אָנָה אֲנִי בָא.** אָנָה אֶבְרַח מִצַּעֲרוֹ שֶׁל אַבָּא:

לא **שְׂעִיר עִזִּים.** דָּמוֹ דּוֹמֶה לְשֶׁל אָדָם: **הַכְּתֹנֶת.** זֶה שְׁמָהּ, וּכְשֶׁהִיא דְּבוּקָה לְתֵבָה אַחֶרֶת, כְּגוֹן "כְּתֹנֶת יוֹסֵף", "כְּתֹנֶת פַּסִּים" (לעיל פסוק ג), "כְּתֹנֶת בַּד" (ויקרא טז, ד), נָקוּד 'כְּתֹנֶת':

לג **וַיֹּאמֶר כְּתֹנֶת בְּנִי.** הִיא זוֹ: **חַיָּה רָעָה אֲכָלָתְהוּ.** נִצְנְצָה בּוֹ רוּחַ הַקֹּדֶשׁ, סוֹפוֹ שֶׁתִּתְגָּרֶה בוֹ אֵשֶׁת פּוֹטִיפַר. וְלָמָּה לֹא גִּלָּה לוֹ הַקָּדוֹשׁ בָּרוּךְ הוּא? לְפִי שֶׁהֶחֱרִימוּ וְקִלְּלוּ אֶת כָּל מִי שֶׁיְּגַלֶּה, וְשִׁתְּפוּ לְהַקָּדוֹשׁ בָּרוּךְ הוּא עִמָּהֶם. אֲבָל יִצְחָק הָיָה יוֹדֵעַ שֶׁהוּא חַי, אָמַר: הֵיאַךְ אֲגַלֶּה וְהַקָּדוֹשׁ בָּרוּךְ הוּא אֵינוֹ רוֹצֶה לְגַלּוֹת לוֹ?:

לד **יָמִים רַבִּים.** עֶשְׂרִים וּשְׁתַּיִם שָׁנָה מִשֶּׁפֵּרַשׁ מִמֶּנּוּ עַד שֶׁיָּרַד יַעֲקֹב לְמִצְרַיִם, שֶׁנֶּאֱמַר: "יוֹסֵף בֶּן שְׁבַע עֶשְׂרֵה שָׁנָה" וְגוֹ' (לעיל פסוק ב), וּבֶן שְׁלֹשִׁים שָׁנָה הָיָה בְּעָמְדוֹ לִפְנֵי פַרְעֹה (להלן מא, מו), וְשֶׁבַע שְׁנֵי הַשָּׂבָע, וְ"כִי זֶה שְׁנָתַיִם הָרָעָב" (להלן מה, ו) כְּשֶׁבָּא יַעֲקֹב לְמִצְרַיִם, הֲרֵי עֶשְׂרִים וּשְׁתַּיִם, כְּנֶגֶד עֶשְׂרִים וּשְׁתַּיִם שֶׁלֹּא קִיֵּם יַעֲקֹב כִּבּוּד אָב וָאֵם: עֶשְׂרִים שָׁנָה שֶׁהָיָה בְּבֵית לָבָן, וּשְׁתֵּי שָׁנִים בַּדֶּרֶךְ בְּשׁוּבוֹ מִבֵּית לָבָן, שָׁנָה וָחֵצִי בְּסֻכּוֹת וְשִׁשָּׁה חֳדָשִׁים בְּבֵית אֵל. וְזֶהוּ שֶׁאָמַר לְלָבָן: "זֶה לִּי עֶשְׂרִים שָׁנָה בְּבֵיתֶךָ" (לעיל לא, מא) – לִי הֵן, עָלַי הֵן, סוֹפִי לִלְקוֹת כְּנֶגְדָּן:

לה **וְכָל בְּנֹתָיו.** רַבִּי יְהוּדָה אוֹמֵר: אֲחָיוֹת תְּאוֹמוֹת נוֹלְדוּ עִם כָּל שֵׁבֶט וְשֵׁבֶט וּנְשָׂאוּם. רַבִּי נְחֶמְיָה אוֹמֵר: כְּנַעֲנִיּוֹת הָיוּ, אֶלָּא מַהוּ "וְכָל בְּנֹתָיו"? כַּלּוֹתָיו, שֶׁאֵין אָדָם נִמְנָע מִלִּקְרוֹא לַחֲתָנוֹ בְּנוֹ וּלְכַלָּתוֹ בִּתּוֹ: **וַיְמָאֵן לְהִתְנַחֵם.** אֵין אָדָם יָכוֹל לְקַבֵּל תַּנְחוּמִין עַל הַחַי וְסָבוּר שֶׁמֵּת, שֶׁעַל הַמֵּת נִגְזְרָה גְּזֵרָה שֶׁיִּשְׁתַּכַּח מִן הַלֵּב וְלֹא עַל הַחַי: **אֵרֵד אֶל בְּנִי.** כְּמוֹ 'עַל בְּנִי', וְהַרְבֵּה 'אֶל' מְשַׁמְּשִׁין בִּלְשׁוֹן 'עַל', "אֶל שָׁאוּל וְאֶל בֵּית הַדָּמִים" (שמואל ב' כא, א), "אֶל הִלָּקַח אֲרוֹן הָאֱלֹהִים וְאֶל חָמִיהָ וְאִישָׁהּ" (שמואל א' ד, כא): **אָבֵל שְׁאֹלָה.** כִּפְשׁוּטוֹ לְשׁוֹן קֶבֶר הוּא, בְּאֶבְלִי אֶקָּבֵר וְלֹא אֶתְנַחֵם כָּל יָמַי. וּבְמִדְרָשׁוֹ: גֵּיהִנָּם; סִימָן זֶה הָיָה מָסוּר בְּיָדִי מִפִּי הַגְּבוּרָה, אִם לֹא יָמוּת אֶחָד מִבָּנַי בְּחַיַּי מֻבְטָח אֲנִי שֶׁאֵינִי רוֹאֶה גֵּיהִנָּם: **וַיֵּבְךְּ אֹתוֹ אָבִיו.** יִצְחָק בּוֹכֶה הָיָה מִפְּנֵי צָרָתוֹ שֶׁל יַעֲקֹב, אֲבָל לֹא הָיָה מִתְאַבֵּל, שֶׁהָיָה יוֹדֵעַ שֶׁהוּא חַי:

לו **הַטַּבָּחִים.** שׁוֹחֲטֵי בַּהֲמוֹת הַמֶּלֶךְ:

mourning is seen in Judaism as a rebellion against reality. We are mortal. No one and nothing lives forever. Why then does Yaakov refuse to be comforted?

The traditional answer is surely the right one. Yaakov refuses to be comforted because he refuses to give up hope that Yosef is still alive – as, indeed, he is (Bereshit Rabba 84:21).

Hope is not costless in the way that optimism is. It carries with it a considerable price. When the prophets saw evil in the world, they refused to be comforted; those who hope refuse to be comforted while the hoped-for outcome is not yet reached. Theodicy is a comfort bought too cheaply. Given their history of suffering, Jews were rarely optimists. But they never gave up hope.

כט לַֽיִּשְׁמְעֵאלִ֖ים בְּעֶשְׂרִ֣ים כָּ֑סֶף וַיָּבִ֥יאוּ אֶת־יוֹסֵ֖ף מִצְרָֽיְמָה׃ וַיָּ֤שָׁב רְאוּבֵן֙
ל אֶל־הַבּ֔וֹר וְהִנֵּ֥ה אֵין־יוֹסֵ֖ף בַּבּ֑וֹר וַיִּקְרַ֖ע אֶת־בְּגָדָֽיו׃ וַיָּ֥שָׁב אֶל־אֶחָ֖יו
לא וַיֹּאמַ֑ר הַיֶּ֣לֶד אֵינֶ֔נּוּ וַאֲנִ֖י אָ֥נָה אֲנִי־בָֽא׃ וַיִּקְח֖וּ אֶת־כְּתֹ֣נֶת יוֹסֵ֑ף וַֽיִּשְׁחֲטוּ֙
לב שְׂעִ֣יר עִזִּ֔ים וַיִּטְבְּל֥וּ אֶת־הַכֻּתֹּ֖נֶת בַּדָּֽם׃ וַֽיְשַׁלְּח֞וּ אֶת־כְּתֹ֣נֶת הַפַּסִּ֗ים
וַיָּבִ֙יאוּ֙ אֶל־אֲבִיהֶ֔ם וַיֹּאמְר֖וּ זֹ֣את מָצָ֑אנוּ הַכֶּר־נָ֗א הַכְּתֹ֧נֶת בִּנְךָ֛ הִ֖וא
לג אִם־לֹֽא׃ וַיַּכִּירָ֤הּ וַיֹּ֙אמֶר֙ כְּתֹ֣נֶת בְּנִ֔י חַיָּ֥ה רָעָ֖ה אֲכָלָ֑תְהוּ טָרֹ֥ף טֹרַ֖ף
לד יוֹסֵֽף׃ וַיִּקְרַ֤ע יַעֲקֹב֙ שִׂמְלֹתָ֔יו וַיָּ֥שֶׂם שַׂ֖ק בְּמָתְנָ֑יו וַיִּתְאַבֵּ֥ל עַל־בְּנ֖וֹ
לה יָמִ֥ים רַבִּֽים׃ וַיָּקֻ֩מוּ֩ כָל־בָּנָ֨יו וְכָל־בְּנֹתָ֜יו לְנַחֲמ֗וֹ וַיְמָאֵן֙ לְהִתְנַחֵ֔ם וַיֹּ֕אמֶר
לו כִּֽי־אֵרֵ֧ד אֶל־בְּנִ֛י אָבֵ֖ל שְׁאֹ֑לָה וַיֵּ֥בְךְּ אֹת֖וֹ אָבִֽיו׃ וְהַמְּדָנִ֗ים מָכְר֤וּ אֹתוֹ֙
אֶל־מִצְרָ֔יִם לְפֽוֹטִיפַר֙ סְרִ֣יס פַּרְעֹ֔ה שַׂ֖ר הַטַּבָּחִֽים׃

אונקלוס

לְעַרְבָאֵי בְּעֶסְרִין כְּסַף, וְאַיְתִיאוּ יָת יוֹסֵף לְמִצְרָיִם: כט וְתָב רְאוּבֵן לְגֻבָּא, וְהָא לֵית יוֹסֵף בְּגֻבָּא, וּבַזַּע יָת לְבוּשׁוֹהִי: ל וְתָב לְוָת אֲחוֹהִי וַאֲמַר, עוּלֵימָא לֵיתוֹהִי, וַאֲנָא לְאָן אֲנָא אָתֵי: לא וּנְסִיבוּ יָת כִּתּוּנָא דְיוֹסֵף, וּנְכַסוּ צְפִיר בַּר עִזֵּי, וּטְבַלוּ יָת כִּתּוּנָא בִּדְמָא: לב וְשַׁלַּחוּ יָת כִּתּוּנָא דְפַסֵּי, וְאַיְתִיאוּ לַאֲבוּהוֹן, וַאֲמַרוּ דָּא אַשְׁכַּחְנָא, אִשְׁתְּמוֹדַע כְּעַן, הֲכִתּוּנָא דִבְרָךְ, הִיא אִם לָא: לג וְאִשְׁתְּמוֹדְעַהּ וַאֲמַר כִּתּוּנָא דִבְרִי, חֵיוְתָא בִּשְׁתָא אֲכַלְתֵּיהּ, מִקְטַל קְטִיל יוֹסֵף: לד וּבַזַּע יַעֲקֹב לְבוּשׁוֹהִי, וַאֲסַר סַקָּא בְּחַרְצֵיהּ, וְאִתְאַבַּל עַל בְּרֵיהּ יוֹמִין סַגִּיאִין: לה וְקָמוּ כָל בְּנוֹהִי וְכָל בְּנָתֵיהּ לְנַחָמוּתֵיהּ, וְסָרֵיב לְקַבָּלָא תַּנְחוּמִין, וַאֲמַר, אֲרֵי אֵיחוֹת לְוָת בְּרִי, כַּד אֲבִילְנָא לִשְׁאוֹל, וּבְכָא יָתֵיהּ אֲבוּהִי: לו וּמִדְיָנָאֵי, זַבִּינוּ יָתֵיהּ לְמִצְרָיִם, לְפוֹטִיפַר רַבָּא דְפַרְעֹה, רַב קָטוֹלַיָּא:

rescue Yosef, but finds the pit empty and cries, "The boy is gone, and I – where can I turn?" Rashbam points out that the brothers do not calm him by telling him they have sold Yosef. They seem as surprised as he is. It follows that the brothers, having seen the Ishmaelites in the distance, decide to sell Yosef to them, but before they have the chance to do so, a second group of travelers, the Midianites, hear Yosef's cries, see the possibility of selling him to the Ishmaelites, and do so.

In other words, the brothers intend to sell Yosef, and Yosef is sold, but *not by the brothers*. They seek to do the deed, and the deed is done, but not by them.

Unusually, but of immense significance, the Torah is telling us something about divine providence. Between intention and outcome there was an intervention – the appearance of the Midianites. We are being given a rare glimpse of the workings of providence in history. Nothing in the Yosef story happens by chance – and where an event most looks like chance, that is where divine intervention is most evident in retrospect.

37:35 וַיְמָאֵן לְהִתְנַחֵם *He refused to be comforted* – The Sages asked: Why did Yaakov refuse to be comforted? There are laws of mourning in Judaism, and they go back to its earliest days. There is the week of mourning; there is the first month; in some cases it takes a year. But there is a limit. Excessive

38 1 Around that time, Yehuda left his brothers and camped near an Adulamite REVI'I
2 named Ḥira. There, Yehuda met the daughter of Shua, a Canaanite, and he
3 married her and came to her. She became pregnant and had a son, whom he
4 named Er. She became pregnant again and had another son, and she named
5 him Onan. She had yet another son and named him Shela; Yehuda was in Keziv
6 when she gave birth to him. Yehuda took a wife for his firstborn, Er; her name
7 was Tamar. But Er, Yehuda's firstborn, was wicked in the Lord's sight, and the
8 Lord took his life. Yehuda then said to Onan, "Go in to your brother's wife and
9 fulfill your duty as her brother-in-law. Provide children for your brother." But
Onan knew that the children would not be considered his. Whenever he came
to his brother's wife, he let his seed go to waste on the ground so as not to have
10 children in his brother's name. What he did was wicked in the Lord's sight,
11 and so He took his life also. Then Yehuda said to his daughter-in-law Tamar,
"Live as a widow in your father's house until my son Shela grows up" – for he
thought he too might die like his brothers. So Tamar went to live in her father's

רש״י

לח א **וַיְהִי בָּעֵת הַהִוא.** לָמָּה נִסְמְכָה פָּרָשָׁה זוֹ לְכָאן וְהִפְסִיק בְּפָרָשָׁתוֹ שֶׁל יוֹסֵף? לְלַמֵּד שֶׁהוֹרִידוּהוּ אֶחָיו מִגְּדֻלָּתוֹ כְּשֶׁרָאוּ בְּצָרַת אֲבִיהֶם, אָמְרוּ: אַתָּה אָמַרְתָּ לְמָכְרוֹ, אִלּוּ אָמַרְתָּ לַהֲשִׁיבוֹ הָיִינוּ שׁוֹמְעִים לְךָ: וַיֵּט. מֵאֵת אֶחָיו: **עַד אִישׁ עֲדֻלָּמִי.** נִשְׁתַּתֵּף עִמּוֹ:

ב **כְּנַעֲנִי.** תַּגָּרָא:

ה **וְהָיָה בִכְזִיב.** שֵׁם הַמָּקוֹם. וְאוֹמֵר אֲנִי, עַל שֵׁם שֶׁפָּסְקָה מִלֶּדֶת נִקְרָא 'כְּזִיב', לְשׁוֹן: "הָיוֹ תִהְיֶה לִי כְּמוֹ אַכְזָב" (ירמיה טו, יח), "אֲשֶׁר לֹא יְכַזְּבוּ מֵימָיו" (ישעיה נח, יא), וְאִם לֹא כֵן מַה בָּא לְהוֹדִיעֵנוּ? וּבִבְרֵאשִׁית רַבָּה (פה, ד) רָאִיתִי: "וַתִּקְרָא שְׁמוֹ שֵׁלָה" וְגוֹ' – פָּסְקַת:

ז **רַע בְּעֵינֵי ה'.** כְּרָעָתוֹ שֶׁל אוֹנָן, מַשְׁחִית זַרְעוֹ, שֶׁנֶּאֱמַר בְּאוֹנָן: "וַיָּמֶת גַּם אֹתוֹ" (להלן פסוק י), כְּמִיתָתוֹ שֶׁל עֵר מִיתָתוֹ שֶׁל אוֹנָן. וְלָמָּה הָיָה עֵר מַשְׁחִית זַרְעוֹ? כְּדֵי שֶׁלֹּא תִתְעַבֵּר וְיַכְחִישׁ יָפְיָהּ:

ח **וְהָקֵם זֶרַע.** הַבֵּן יִקָּרֵא עַל שֵׁם הַמֵּת:

ט **וְשִׁחֵת אַרְצָה.** דָּשׁ מִבִּפְנִים וְזוֹרֶה מִבַּחוּץ:

יא **כִּי אָמַר וְגוֹ'.** כְּלוֹמַר, דּוֹחֶה הָיָה אוֹתָהּ בְּקַשׁ, שֶׁלֹּא הָיָה בְּדַעְתּוֹ לְהַשִּׂיאָהּ לוֹ: **כִּי אָמַר פֶּן יָמוּת.** מֻחְזֶקֶת הִיא זוֹ שֶׁיָּמוּתוּ אֲנָשֶׁיהָ:

too, exhibits loyalty to their in-laws, Ruth in refusing to be parted from Naomi, and Tamar, I will argue, in ensuring that she will not put her father-in-law Yehuda to shame (see note on v. 25).

In both stories, an extended form of levirate marriage is involved, and in both cases, the man who becomes the father of the child or children – Yehuda and Boaz – is not the closest in line. For Tamar, this was Shela, Yehuda's third son; for Ruth it was the anonymous Peloni Almoni (this phrase has come, in Hebrew, to mean "Mr. So-and-so" or "Mr. What's-his-name").

Finally, in both cases, the men pay tribute to the exemplary virtues of the women. Yehuda says of Tamar, "She is more righteous than I" (Gen. 38:26). Boaz says of Ruth, "This last kindness is yet greater than your first, for you have not gone after the young men, poor or rich" (Ruth 3:10).

These similarities are surely too pronounced to be accidental, and it is the Book of Ruth itself, in its closing lines, that provides the connection. The beginning of David's family tree is the son, Peretz, born to Yehuda and Tamar. The seventh generation is the son, Oved, born to Ruth and Boaz. The family tree of Israel's great and future king includes both Tamar and Ruth, two women whose virtue and loyalty, kindness and discretion, surely contributed to David's greatness.

לח א וַיְהִי בָּעֵת הַהִוא וַיֵּרֶד יְהוּדָה מֵאֵת אֶחָיו וַיֵּט עַד־אִישׁ עֲדֻלָּמִי וּשְׁמוֹ לד רביעי
ב חִירָה: וַיַּרְא־שָׁם יְהוּדָה בַּת־אִישׁ כְּנַעֲנִי וּשְׁמוֹ שׁוּעַ וַיִּקָּחֶהָ וַיָּבֹא
ג ד אֵלֶיהָ: וַתַּהַר וַתֵּלֶד בֵּן וַיִּקְרָא אֶת־שְׁמוֹ עֵר: וַתַּהַר עוֹד וַתֵּלֶד בֵּן
ה וַתִּקְרָא אֶת־שְׁמוֹ אוֹנָן: וַתֹּסֶף עוֹד וַתֵּלֶד בֵּן וַתִּקְרָא אֶת־שְׁמוֹ שֵׁלָה
ו וְהָיָה בִכְזִיב בְּלִדְתָּהּ אֹתוֹ: וַיִּקַּח יְהוּדָה אִשָּׁה לְעֵר בְּכוֹרוֹ וּשְׁמָהּ
ז ח תָּמָר: וַיְהִי עֵר בְּכוֹר יְהוּדָה רַע בְּעֵינֵי יְהֹוָה וַיְמִתֵהוּ יְהֹוָה: וַיֹּאמֶר
יְהוּדָה לְאוֹנָן בֹּא אֶל־אֵשֶׁת אָחִיךָ וְיַבֵּם אֹתָהּ וְהָקֵם זֶרַע לְאָחִיךָ:
ט וַיֵּדַע אוֹנָן כִּי לֹּא לוֹ יִהְיֶה הַזָּרַע וְהָיָה אִם־בָּא אֶל־אֵשֶׁת אָחִיו וְשִׁחֵת
י אַרְצָה לְבִלְתִּי נְתָן־זֶרַע לְאָחִיו: וַיֵּרַע בְּעֵינֵי יְהֹוָה אֲשֶׁר עָשָׂה וַיָּמֶת
יא גַּם־אֹתוֹ: וַיֹּאמֶר יְהוּדָה לְתָמָר כַּלָּתוֹ שְׁבִי אַלְמָנָה בֵית־אָבִיךְ עַד־
יִגְדַּל שֵׁלָה בְנִי כִּי אָמַר פֶּן־יָמוּת גַּם־הוּא כְּאֶחָיו וַתֵּלֶךְ תָּמָר וַתֵּשֶׁב

אונקלוס

לח א וַהֲוָה בְּעִדָּנָא הַהוּא, וּנְחַת יְהוּדָה מִלְּוָת אֲחוֹהִי, וּסְטָא, לְוָת גַּבְרָא עֲדֻלָּמָאָה וּשְׁמֵיהּ חִירָה: ב וַחֲזָא תַמָּן יְהוּדָה, בַּת גְּבַר תַּגָּר וּשְׁמֵיהּ שׁוּעַ, וְנַסְבַהּ וְעָאל לְוָתַהּ: ג וְעַדִּיאַת וִילֵידַת בַּר, וּקְרָא יָת שְׁמֵיהּ עֵר: ד וְעַדִּיאַת עוֹד וִילֵידַת בַּר, וּקְרָת יָת שְׁמֵיהּ אוֹנָן: ה וְאוֹסֵיפַת עוֹד וִילֵידַת בַּר, וּקְרָת יָת שְׁמֵיהּ שֵׁלָה, וַהֲוָה בִכְזִיב כַּד יְלֵידַת יָתֵיהּ: ו וּנְסֵיב יְהוּדָה, אִתְּתָא לְעֵר בְּכְרֵיהּ, וּשְׁמַהּ תָּמָר: ז וַהֲוָה, עֵר בְּכְרֵיהּ דִּיהוּדָה, בִּישׁ קֳדָם יְיָ, וַאֲמִיתֵיהּ יְיָ: ח וַאֲמַר יְהוּדָה לְאוֹנָן, עוֹל, לְוָת אִתַּת אֲחוּךְ וְיַבֵּים יָתַהּ, וַאֲקֵים זַרְעָא לַאֲחוּךְ: ט וִידַע אוֹנָן, אֲרֵי, לָא עַל שְׁמֵיהּ מִתְקְרֵי זַרְעָא, וְהָוֵי, כַּד עָלֵיל לְוָת אִתַּת אֲחוּהִי וּמְחַבֵּיל אוֹרְחֵיהּ עַל אַרְעָא, בְּדִיל דְּלָא לְקַיָּמָא זַרְעָא לַאֲחוּהִי: י וּבְאֵישׁ, קֳדָם יְיָ דַּעֲבַד, וַאֲמִית אַף יָתֵיהּ: יא וַאֲמַר יְהוּדָה לְתָמָר כַּלְּתֵיהּ תִּיבִי אַרְמְלָא בֵית אֲבוּיךְ, עַד דְּיִרְבֵּי שֵׁלָה בְרִי, אֲרֵי אֲמַר, דִּלְמָא יְמוּת אַף הוּא כַּאֲחוּהִי, וַאֲזַלַת תָּמָר,

TAMAR

Spliced within the story of Yosef is the story of Yehuda and the death of his children. Into this dark scenario enters one of the more unexpected heroines of the Torah, Tamar. The text gives us no inclination as to who she is, but from her entry into the narrative, this fascinating and mysterious figure begins to dominate the story. Tamar bears an uncanny resemblance to one other figure in Tanakh: Ruth, daughter-in-law of Naomi, eponymous heroine of one of the gentlest and loveliest books of the Hebrew Bible. The resemblances between their respective stories are many and striking.

Both women are driven by a specific kind of loyalty: the loyalty that motivates the biblical law of *yibbum*, levirate marriage. The Torah says about the childless widow who marries her brother-in-law and then has a child, "The firstborn son whom she bears will perpetuate the name of the dead brother, so that his name is not erased from Israel" (Deut. 25:6). Likewise the Book of Ruth explains, in the context of her marriage to Boaz, that "the dead man's name will not be cut off from among his brothers" (Ruth 4:10). Both, in other words, keep faith with their dead husbands in seeking to have a child that will bear his name. Each,

12 house. A long time passed, and Yehuda's wife, Shua's daughter, died. When he
had completed his time of mourning, he and his neighbor Ḥira the Adulamite
13 went to join his sheepshearers in Timna. Tamar was told, "Your father-in-law
14 is going to Timna to shear his sheep." And she took off her widow's clothes
and covered herself with a veil. Disguised, she sat at the entrance to Einayim
on the road to Timna, for she had seen that Shela was now grown up and yet
15 she had not been given to him as a wife. Yehuda saw her and thought she was
16 a prostitute, because she had covered her face. Not realizing that she was his
daughter-in-law, he turned aside to her on the road and said, "Come, let me
17 sleep with you." She said, "What will you give me to sleep with you?" He said,
"I will send you a young goat from my flock." "Only if you give me something
18 as a pledge until you send it," she said. "What pledge should I give you?" he
asked. She answered, "Your seal and cord, and the staff in your hand." He gave
19 them to her and went in to her – and she became pregnant by him. She got up
20 and left, removed her veil, and put on her widow's clothes again. And Yehuda
sent the young goat by his neighbor the Adulamite, to recover the pledge from
21 the woman, but he could not find her. He asked the local men, "Where is
the cult prostitute, the one by the roadside at Einayim?" They said, "No cult
22 prostitute has been here." So he went back to Yehuda and said, "I could not
find her. Besides, the local men said that there was no cult prostitute there."

רש״י

יב **וַיַּעַל עַל גֹּזְזֵי צֹאנוֹ.** וַיַּעַל תִּמְנָתָה לַעֲמֹד עַל גּוֹזְזֵי צֹאנוֹ:

יג **עֹלֶה תִמְנָתָה.** וּבְשִׁמְשׁוֹן הוּא אוֹמֵר: "וַיֵּרֶד שִׁמְשׁוֹן תִּמְנָתָה" (שופטים יד, א)! בְּשִׁפּוּעַ הָהָר הָיְתָה יוֹשֶׁבֶת, עוֹלִין לָהּ מִכָּאן וְיוֹרְדִין לָהּ מִכָּאן:

יד **וַתִּתְעַלָּף.** כִּסְּתָה פָנֶיהָ, שֶׁלֹּא יַכִּיר בָּהּ: **וַתֵּשֶׁב בְּפֶתַח עֵינַיִם.** בִּפְתִיחַת עֵינַיִם, בְּפָרָשַׁת דְּרָכִים שֶׁעַל דֶּרֶךְ תִּמְנָתָה. וְרַבּוֹתֵינוּ דָּרְשׁוּ, בְּפִתְחוֹ שֶׁל אַבְרָהָם אָבִינוּ שֶׁכָּל עֵינַיִם מְצַפּוֹת לִרְאוֹתוֹ: **כִּי רָאֲתָה כִּי גָדַל שֵׁלָה וְגוֹ׳.** לְפִיכָךְ הִפְקִירָה עַצְמָהּ אֵצֶל יְהוּדָה, שֶׁהָיְתָה מִתְאַוָּה לְהַעֲמִיד מִמֶּנּוּ בָּנִים:

טו **וַיַּחְשְׁבֶהָ לְזוֹנָה.** לְפִי שֶׁיּוֹשֶׁבֶת בְּפָרָשַׁת דְּרָכִים: **כִּי כִסְּתָה פָּנֶיהָ.** וְלֹא יָכֹל לִרְאוֹתָהּ וּלְהַכִּירָהּ. וּמִדְרַשׁ רַבּוֹתֵינוּ, "כִּי כִסְּתָה פָנֶיהָ", כְּשֶׁהָיְתָה בְּבֵית חָמִיהָ הָיְתָה צְנוּעָה, לְפִיכָךְ לֹא חֲשָׁדָהּ:

טז **וַיֵּט אֵלֶיהָ אֶל הַדֶּרֶךְ.** מִדֶּרֶךְ שֶׁהָיָה בָּהּ נָטָה אֶל הַדֶּרֶךְ אֲשֶׁר הִיא בָּהּ. וּבִלְשׁוֹן לַעַז דישטורני״ר: **הָבָה נָּא.** הָכִינִי עַצְמֵךְ וְדַעְתֵּךְ לְכָךְ. כָּל לְשׁוֹן 'הָבָה' לְשׁוֹן הַזְמָנָה הוּא, חוּץ מִמָּקוֹם שֶׁיֵּשׁ לְתַרְגְּמוֹ בִּלְשׁוֹן נְתִינָה, וְאַף אוֹתָן שֶׁל הַזְמָנָה קְרוֹבִים לִלְשׁוֹן נְתִינָה הֵם:

יז **עֵרָבוֹן.** מַשְׁכּוֹן:

יח **חֹתָמְךָ וּפְתִילֶךָ.** "עִזְקָתָךְ וְשׁוֹשִׁפָּךְ", טַבַּעַת שֶׁאַתָּה חוֹתֵם בָּהּ וְשִׂמְלָתְךָ שֶׁאַתָּה מִתְכַּסֶּה בָּהּ: **וַתַּהַר לוֹ.** גִּבּוֹרִים כַּיּוֹצֵא בּוֹ, צַדִּיקִים כַּיּוֹצֵא בּוֹ:

כא **הַקְּדֵשָׁה.** מְקֻדֶּשֶׁת וּמְזֻמֶּנֶת לִזְנוּת:

their names into Jewish history as role models who gave birth to royalty – to remind us, in case we ever forget, that true royalty lies in love and faithfulness, and that greatness often exists where we expect it least.

יב בֵּית אָבִיהָ׃ וַיִּרְבּוּ הַיָּמִים וַתָּמָת בַּת־שׁוּעַ אֵשֶׁת־יְהוּדָה וַיִּנָּחֶם יְהוּדָה
יג וַיַּעַל עַל־גֹּזְזֵי צֹאנוֹ הוּא וְחִירָה רֵעֵהוּ הָעֲדֻלָּמִי תִּמְנָתָה׃ וַיֻּגַּד לְתָמָר
יד לֵאמֹר הִנֵּה חָמִיךְ עֹלֶה תִמְנָתָה לָגֹז צֹאנוֹ׃ וַתָּסַר בִּגְדֵי אַלְמְנוּתָהּ
מֵעָלֶיהָ וַתְּכַס בַּצָּעִיף וַתִּתְעַלָּף וַתֵּשֶׁב בְּפֶתַח עֵינַיִם אֲשֶׁר עַל־דֶּרֶךְ
טו תִּמְנָתָה כִּי רָאֲתָה כִּי־גָדַל שֵׁלָה וְהִוא לֹא־נִתְּנָה לוֹ לְאִשָּׁה׃ וַיִּרְאֶהָ
טז יְהוּדָה וַיַּחְשְׁבֶהָ לְזוֹנָה כִּי כִסְּתָה פָּנֶיהָ׃ וַיֵּט אֵלֶיהָ אֶל־הַדֶּרֶךְ וַיֹּאמֶר
הָבָה נָּא אָבוֹא אֵלַיִךְ כִּי לֹא יָדַע כִּי כַלָּתוֹ הִוא וַתֹּאמֶר מַה־תִּתֶּן־לִּי
יז כִּי תָבוֹא אֵלָי׃ וַיֹּאמֶר אָנֹכִי אֲשַׁלַּח גְּדִי־עִזִּים מִן־הַצֹּאן וַתֹּאמֶר אִם־
יח תִּתֵּן עֵרָבוֹן עַד שָׁלְחֶךָ׃ וַיֹּאמֶר מָה הָעֵרָבוֹן אֲשֶׁר אֶתֶּן־לָּךְ וַתֹּאמֶר
חֹתָמְךָ וּפְתִילֶךָ וּמַטְּךָ אֲשֶׁר בְּיָדֶךָ וַיִּתֶּן־לָהּ וַיָּבֹא אֵלֶיהָ וַתַּהַר לוֹ׃
יט כ וַתָּקָם וַתֵּלֶךְ וַתָּסַר צְעִיפָהּ מֵעָלֶיהָ וַתִּלְבַּשׁ בִּגְדֵי אַלְמְנוּתָהּ׃ וַיִּשְׁלַח
יְהוּדָה אֶת־גְּדִי הָעִזִּים בְּיַד רֵעֵהוּ הָעֲדֻלָּמִי לָקַחַת הָעֵרָבוֹן מִיַּד הָאִשָּׁה
כא וְלֹא מְצָאָהּ׃ וַיִּשְׁאַל אֶת־אַנְשֵׁי מְקֹמָהּ לֵאמֹר אַיֵּה הַקְּדֵשָׁה הִוא
כב בָעֵינַיִם עַל־הַדָּרֶךְ וַיֹּאמְרוּ לֹא־הָיְתָה בָזֶה קְדֵשָׁה׃ וַיָּשָׁב אֶל־יְהוּדָה
וַיֹּאמֶר לֹא מְצָאתִיהָ וְגַם אַנְשֵׁי הַמָּקוֹם אָמְרוּ לֹא־הָיְתָה בָזֶה קְדֵשָׁה׃

אונקלוס

וִיתֵיבַת בֵּית אֲבוּהָא: יב וּסְגִיאוּ יוֹמַיָּא, וּמִיתַת בַּת שׁוּעַ אִתַּת יְהוּדָה, וְאִתְנְחֵם יְהוּדָה, וּסְלֵיק, עַל גָּזְזֵי עָנֵיהּ הוּא, וְחִירָה, רַחֲמֵיהּ עֲדֻלָּמָאָה לְתִמְנָת: יג וְאִתְחַוַּא לְתָמָר לְמֵימַר, הָא חֲמוּיִךְ, סָלֵיק לְתִמְנַת לְמִגַּז עָנֵיהּ: יד וְאַעְדִּיאַת לְבוּשֵׁי אַרְמְלוּתַהּ מִנַּהּ, וְאִתְכַּסִּיאַת בְּעִיפָא וְאִתַּקְּנַת, וִיתֵיבַת בְּפָרָשׁוּת עֵינַיִם, דְּעַל אוֹרַח תִּמְנָת, אֲרֵי חֲזָת אֲרֵי רְבָא שֵׁלָה, וְהִיא, לָא אִתְיְהִיבַת לֵיהּ לְאִתּוּ: טו וַחֲזָהּ יְהוּדָה, וְחַשְׁבַהּ כִּנְפֶקַת בָּרָא, אֲרֵי כַסִּיאַת אַפַּהָא: טז וּסְטָא לְוָתַהּ לְאוֹרְחָא, וַאֲמַר הַבִי כְעַן אֵיעוֹל לְוָתִיךְ, אֲרֵי לָא יְדַע, אֲרֵי כַלְּתֵיהּ הִיא, וַאֲמַרַת מָא תִתֵּין לִי, אֲרֵי תֵיעוֹל לְוָתִי: יז וַאֲמַר, אֲנָא, אֲשַׁדַּר גַּדְיָא בַּר עִזֵּי מִן עָנָא, וַאֲמַרַת, אִם תִּתֵּין מַשְׁכּוֹנָא עַד דְּתִשְׁלַח: יח וַאֲמַר, מָא מַשְׁכּוֹנָא דְּאֶתֵּין לִיךְ, וַאֲמַרַת, עִזְקָתָךְ וְשׁוֹשִׁפָּךְ, וְחֻטְרָךְ דִּבְיָדָךְ, וִיהַב לַהּ, וְעָאל לְוָתַהּ וְעַדִּיאַת לֵיהּ: יט וְקָמַת וַאֲזָלַת, וְאַעְדִּיאַת עִיפַהּ מִנַּהּ, וּלְבֵישַׁת לְבוּשֵׁי אַרְמְלוּתַהּ: כ וְשַׁדַּר יְהוּדָה יָת גַּדְיָא בַּר עִזֵּי, בְּיַד רַחֲמֵיהּ עֲדֻלָּמָאָה, לְמִסַּב מַשְׁכּוֹנָא מִיְּדָא דְּאִתְּתָא, וְלָא אַשְׁכְּחַהּ: כא וּשְׁאֵיל, יָת אֱנָשֵׁי אַתְרַהּ לְמֵימַר, אָן מְקַדַּשְׁתָּא, דְּהִיא בְּעֵינַיִם עַל אוֹרְחָא, וַאֲמַרוּ, לֵית הָכָא מְקַדַּשְׁתָּא: כב וְתָב לְוָת יְהוּדָה, וַאֲמַר לָא אַשְׁכַּחְתַּהּ, וְאַף אֱנָשֵׁי אַתְרָא אֲמַרוּ, לֵית הָכָא מְקַדַּשְׁתָּא:

I find it exceptionally moving that the Bible should cast in these heroic roles two figures at the extreme margins of Israelite society: women, childless widows, outsiders. Tamar and Ruth, powerless except for their moral courage, write

23 Yehuda said, "Let her keep what she has or we will become a laughingstock.
24 I tried to send her this young goat, but you could not find her." About three
months later, Yehuda was told, "Your daughter-in-law Tamar has behaved as a
loose woman; in fact she has become pregnant by her harlotry." "Take her out
25 and let her be burned," Yehuda said. As she was being brought out, she sent her
father-in-law a message: "I am pregnant by the man to whom these belong." She
26 added, "Please identify to whom this seal and cord and staff belong." Yehuda
recognized them and said, "She is more righteous than I. It was because I did
27 not give her to Shela my son." He did not know her intimately again. When the
28 time came for her to give birth, there were twins in her womb. As she was in
labor one child put out a hand, so the midwife took a crimson thread and tied

רש״י

כג **תִּקַּח לָהּ.** יִהְיֶה שֶׁלָּהּ מַה שֶּׁבְּיָדָהּ: **פֶּן נִהְיֶה לָבוּז.** אִם תְּבַקְשֶׁנָּה עוֹד יִתְפַּרְסֵם הַדָּבָר וְיִהְיֶה גְּנַאי, כִּי מָה עָלַי עוֹד לַעֲשׂוֹת לְאַמֵּת דְּבָרַי? "הִנֵּה שָׁלַחְתִּי הַגְּדִי הַזֶּה" וְגוֹ׳! וּלְפִי שֶׁרִמָּה יְהוּדָה אֶת אָבִיו בִּגְדִי עִזִּים שֶׁהִטְבִּיל כְּתֹנֶת יוֹסֵף בְּדָמוֹ, רִמּוּהוּ גַּם הוּא בִּגְדִי עִזִּים:

כד **כְּמִשְׁלֹשׁ חֳדָשִׁים.** רֻבּוֹ שֶׁל רִאשׁוֹן וְרֻבּוֹ שֶׁל אַחֲרוֹן וְאֶמְצָעִי שָׁלֵם. וּלְשׁוֹן "כְּמִשְׁלֹשׁ חֳדָשִׁים" כְּהִשְׁתַּלֵּשׁ הֶחֳדָשִׁים, כְּמוֹ: "וּמִשְׁלֹחַ מָנוֹת" (אסתר ט, יט), "מִשְׁלוֹחַ יָדָם" (ישעיה יא, יד), וְכֵן תִּרְגֵּם אוּנְקְלוֹס: "כְּתַלְתוּת יַרְחַיָּא": **הָרָה לִזְנוּנִים.** שֵׁם דָּבָר, מְעֻבֶּרֶת, כְּמוֹ: "אִשָּׁה הָרָה" (שמות כא, כב), וּכְמוֹ: "בָּרָה כַּחַמָּה" (שיר השירים ו, י): **וְתִשָּׂרֵף.** אָמַר אֶפְרַיִם מִקְשָׁאָה מִשּׁוּם רַבִּי מֵאִיר: בִּתּוֹ שֶׁל שֵׁם הָיְתָה שֶׁהוּא כֹּהֵן, לְפִיכָךְ דָּנוּהָ בִּשְׂרֵפָה (ב״ר פה, י):

כה **הִוא מוּצֵאת.** לִשָּׂרֵף: **וְהִיא שָׁלְחָה אֶל חָמִיהָ.** לֹא רָצְתָה לְהַלְבִּין פָּנָיו וְלוֹמַר: מִמְּךָ אֲנִי מְעֻבֶּרֶת! אֶלָּא "לָאִישׁ אֲשֶׁר אֵלֶּה לּוֹ". אָמְרָה: אִם יוֹדֶה – יוֹדֶה מֵעַצְמוֹ, וְאִם לָאו – יִשְׂרְפוּנִי וְאַל אַלְבִּין פָּנָיו. מִכָּאן אָמְרוּ: נוֹחַ לוֹ לְאָדָם שֶׁיַּפִּילוּהוּ לְכִבְשַׁן הָאֵשׁ וְאַל יַלְבִּין פְּנֵי חֲבֵרוֹ בָּרַבִּים: **הַכֶּר נָא.** אֵין "נָא" אֶלָּא לְשׁוֹן בַּקָּשָׁה: הַכֶּר נָא בּוֹרַאֲךָ וְאַל תְּאַבֵּד שָׁלֹשׁ נְפָשׁוֹת:

כו **צָדְקָה.** בִּדְבָרֶיהָ: **מִמֶּנִּי.** הִיא מְעֻבֶּרֶת. וְרַבּוֹתֵינוּ זִכְרוֹנָם לִבְרָכָה דָּרְשׁוּ שֶׁיָּצְתָה בַּת קוֹל וְאָמְרָה: מִמֶּנִּי וּמֵאִתִּי יָצְאוּ הַדְּבָרִים, לְפִי שֶׁהָיְתָה צְנוּעָה בְּבֵית חָמִיהָ גָּזַרְתִּי שֶׁיֵּצְאוּ מִמֶּנָּה מְלָכִים, וּמִשֵּׁבֶט יְהוּדָה גָּזַרְתִּי לְהַעֲמִיד מְלָכִים בְּיִשְׂרָאֵל: **כִּי עַל כֵּן לֹא נְתַתִּיהָ.** כִּי כַּדִּין עָשְׂתָה עַל אֲשֶׁר לֹא נְתַתִּיהָ לְשֵׁלָה בְנִי: **וְלֹא יָסַף עוֹד.** יֵשׁ אוֹמְרִים לֹא הוֹסִיף, וְיֵשׁ אוֹמְרִים לֹא פָסַק:

כז **בְּעֵת לִדְתָּהּ.** וּבְרִבְקָה הוּא אוֹמֵר: "וַיִּמְלְאוּ יָמֶיהָ לָלֶדֶת" (לעיל כה, כד), לְהַלָּן לִמְלֵאִים וְכָאן לַחֲסֵרִים: **וְהִנֵּה תְאוֹמִים.** מָלֵא, וּלְהַלָּן (לעיל כה, כד) "תוֹמִם" חָסֵר, לְפִי שֶׁהָאֶחָד רָשָׁע, אֲבָל אֵלּוּ שְׁנֵיהֶם צַדִּיקִים:

כח **וַיִּתֶּן יָד.** הוֹצִיא הָאֶחָד יָדוֹ לַחוּץ, וּלְאַחַר שֶׁקָּשְׁרָה עַל יָדוֹ הַשָּׁנִי הֶחֱזִירָהּ:

Tamar takes her sense of shame and uses it to sensitize herself to avoiding shaming others. Can we, dare we, do less?

38:26 **צָדְקָה מִמֶּנִּי** *She is more righteous than I* – This moment is a turning point in history. Yehuda is the first person in the Torah to explicitly admit he is wrong. We do not realize it yet, but this seems to be the moment at which he acquires the depth of character necessary for him to become the first real *baal teshuva*, the first penitent. We see this years later, when he – the man who proposed selling Yosef as a slave – becomes the man who is willing to spend the rest of his life in slavery so that his brother Binyamin can go free (Gen. 44:33). I have argued elsewhere that it is from here that we learn the principle that a penitent stands higher than even a perfectly righteous individual (Berakhot 34b). While Yehuda the penitent becomes the ancestor of Israel's kings, Yosef the righteous is only a viceroy, *mishneh lemelekh*, second to the king.

כג וַיֹּ֤אמֶר יְהוּדָה֙ תִּֽקַּֽח־לָ֔הּ פֶּ֖ן נִהְיֶ֣ה לָב֑וּז הִנֵּ֤ה שָׁלַ֙חְתִּי֙ הַגְּדִ֣י הַזֶּ֔ה וְאַתָּ֖ה
כד לֹ֥א מְצָאתָֽהּ׃ וַיְהִ֣י ׀ כְּמִשְׁלֹ֣שׁ חֳדָשִׁ֗ים וַיֻּגַּ֨ד לִֽיהוּדָ֤ה לֵאמֹר֙ זָֽנְתָה֙ תָּמָ֣ר
כה כַּלָּתֶ֔ךָ וְגַ֛ם הִנֵּ֥ה הָרָ֖ה לִזְנוּנִ֑ים וַיֹּ֣אמֶר יְהוּדָ֔ה הוֹצִיא֖וּהָ וְתִשָּׂרֵֽף׃ הִ֣וא
מוּצֵ֗את וְהִ֨יא שָׁלְחָ֤ה אֶל־חָמִ֙יהָ֙ לֵאמֹ֔ר לְאִישׁ֙ אֲשֶׁר־אֵ֣לֶּה לּ֔וֹ אָנֹכִ֖י
כו הָרָ֑ה וַתֹּ֙אמֶר֙ הַכֶּר־נָ֔א לְמִ֞י הַחֹתֶ֧מֶת וְהַפְּתִילִ֛ים וְהַמַּטֶּ֖ה הָאֵֽלֶּה׃ וַיַּכֵּ֣ר
יְהוּדָ֗ה וַיֹּ֙אמֶר֙ צָֽדְקָ֣ה מִמֶּ֔נִּי כִּֽי־עַל־כֵּ֥ן לֹא־נְתַתִּ֖יהָ לְשֵׁלָ֣ה בְנִ֑י וְלֹֽא־יָסַ֥ף
כז כח ע֖וֹד לְדַעְתָּֽהּ׃ וַיְהִ֖י בְּעֵ֣ת לִדְתָּ֑הּ וְהִנֵּ֥ה תְאוֹמִ֖ים בְּבִטְנָֽהּ׃ וַיְהִ֥י בְלִדְתָּ֖הּ
וַיִּתֶּן־יָ֑ד וַתִּקַּ֣ח הַמְיַלֶּ֗דֶת וַתִּקְשֹׁ֨ר עַל־יָד֤וֹ שָׁנִי֙ לֵאמֹ֔ר זֶ֖ה יָצָ֥א רִאשֹׁנָֽה׃

אונקלוס

כג וַאֲמַר יְהוּדָה תִּסַּב לַהּ, דִּלְמָא נְהֵי חוּךְ, הָא שַׁדַּרִית גַּדְיָא הָדֵין, וְאַתְּ לָא אַשְׁכַּחְתַּהּ: כד וַהֲוָה כִּתְלָתוּת יַרְחַיָּא, וְאִתְחֲוַא לִיהוּדָה לְמֵימַר זַנִּיאַת תָּמָר כַּלְּתָךְ, וְאַף, הָא מְעַדְּיָא מִזְּנוּתַהּ, וַאֲמַר יְהוּדָה, אַפְּקוּהָא וְתִתּוֹקַד: כה הִיא מִתַּפְּקָא, וְהִיא שְׁלַחַת לַחֲמוּהָא לְמֵימַר, לִגְבַר דְּאִלֵּין דִּילֵיהּ, מִנֵּיהּ אֲנָא מְעַדְּיָא, וַאֲמַרַת אִשְׁתְּמוֹדַע כְּעַן, דְּמַאן עִזְקְתָא וְשׁוֹשִׁפָא, וְחֻטְרָא הָאִלֵּין: כו וְאִשְׁתְּמוֹדַע יְהוּדָה, וַאֲמַר זַכָּאָה מִנִּי מְעַדְּיָא, אֲרֵי עַל כֵּן לָא יְהַבְתַּהּ לְשֵׁלָה בְרִי, וְלָא אוֹסִיף עוֹד לְמִדְּעַהּ: כז וַהֲוָה בְּעִדָּן מֵילְדַהּ, וְהָא תְיוֹמִין בִּמְעַהָא: כח וַהֲוָה בְּמֵילְדַהּ וִיהַב יְדָא, וּנְסֵיבַת חָיְתָא, וּקְטַרַת עַל יְדֵיהּ זְהוֹרִיתָא לְמֵימַר, דֵּין נְפַק קַדְמֵיתָא:

Judaism is a religion of words. God created the natural world with words. We create – and sometimes destroy – the social world with words. That is one reason why Judaism has so strong an ethic of speech. The other reason, surely, is its concern to protect human dignity. Psychological injury may be no less harmful – is often even more so – than physical injury. Hence the rule: never humiliate, never put to shame, never take refuge in the excuse that they were only words, that no physical harm was done.

Tamar, a childless widow, unable to remarry, is a person without position or power. Is it this that gives her unusual insight into the fact that psychological pain can be as serious as physical pain, that loss of dignity is a kind of loss of life? It says something about the nature of Jewish spirituality that the Torah attributes this moral greatness to her and not to a direct member of the covenantal family – to one of Yaakov's sons – and that the Rabbis took her deed as a binding precedent for all of us.

38:25 לְמִי הַחֹתֶמֶת וְהַפְּתִילִים וְהַמַּטֶּה הָאֵלֶּה *To whom this seal and cord and staff belong* – With great ingenuity and boldness, Tamar has broken through the bind in which Yehuda placed her. She has fulfilled her duty to the dead. But no less significantly, at least in one classic interpretation, she has spared Yehuda shame. By sending him a coded message – the pledge – she has ensured that he will know that he himself is the father of the child, but that no one else will. To do this, she takes the enormous risk of being put to death for adultery.

Her behavior is to become a model; the Rabbis inferred from her conduct a strong moral rule: "It is better that a person throw himself into a fiery furnace rather than shame his neighbor in public" (Bava Metzia 59a). This acute sensitivity to humiliation displayed by Tamar permeates much of rabbinic thought. The Talmud even includes in the definition of *onaat devarim*, "verbal oppression," the act of reminding a person of a past they may find shameful.

▶

29 it to his wrist, saying, "This one came out first." But he pulled his hand back and
then his brother came out. She said, "How you have burst through!" So he was
30 named Peretz. Then his brother came out with the crimson thread on his wrist.
39 1 He was named Zeraḥ. Meanwhile, Yosef had been brought down to ḤAMISHI
Egypt. Potifar, an Egyptian, one of Pharaoh's officials and captain of the guard,
2 had bought him from the Ishmaelites who had brought him there. The LORD
was with Yosef, and he became a successful man. He lived in the house of his
3 Egyptian master. And his master saw that the LORD was with him and that
4 the LORD granted him success in all he did; Yosef found favor in his eyes and
became his personal attendant. Potifar put him in charge of his household,
5 giving him responsibility for all he owned. From the moment he put him in
charge of his household and all he owned, the LORD blessed the Egyptian's
household because of Yosef. The LORD's blessing was in all he owned, in house
6 and field. And so he left all he had in Yosef's hands and, with him there, he had
no concern for anything but the food he ate. Now, Yosef was well built and
7 handsome, and after a while, his master's wife cast her eyes on Yosef. "Lie with SHISHI
8 me," she said. But he refused. "With me here," he told her, "my master does not
concern himself with the running of the house; he has entrusted me with all

רש״י

כט **פָּרַצְתָּ.** חָזַקְתָּ, עָלֶיךָ חֹזֶק:

ל **אֲשֶׁר עַל יָדוֹ הַשָּׁנִי.** אַרְבַּע יָדוֹת כְּתוּבוֹת כָּאן, כְּנֶגֶד אַרְבָּעָה חֲרָמִים שֶׁמָּעַל עָכָן שֶׁיָּצָא מִמֶּנּוּ. וְיֵשׁ אוֹמְרִים: כְּנֶגֶד אַרְבָּעָה דְּבָרִים שֶׁלָּקַח: אַדֶּרֶת שִׁנְעָר, וּשְׁתֵּי חֲתִיכוֹת כֶּסֶף שֶׁל מָאתַיִם שְׁקָלִים, וּלְשׁוֹן זָהָב (יהושע ז, כא). בְּרֵאשִׁית רַבָּה (פה, יד): **וַיִּקְרָא שְׁמוֹ זָרַח.** עַל שֵׁם זְרִיחַת מַרְאִית הַשָּׁנִי:

לט א **וְיוֹסֵף הוּרַד.** חוֹזֵר לָעִנְיָן רִאשׁוֹן, אֶלָּא שֶׁהִפְסִיק בּוֹ כְּדֵי לִסְמֹךְ יְרִידָתוֹ שֶׁל יְהוּדָה לִמְכִירָתוֹ שֶׁל יוֹסֵף, לוֹמַר שֶׁבִּשְׁבִילוֹ הוֹרִידוּהוּ מִגְּדֻלָּתוֹ. וְעוֹד, כְּדֵי לִסְמֹךְ מַעֲשֵׂה אִשְׁתּוֹ שֶׁל פּוֹטִיפַר לְמַעֲשֵׂה תָמָר, לוֹמַר לְךָ, מָה זוֹ לְשֵׁם שָׁמַיִם אַף זוֹ לְשֵׁם שָׁמַיִם, שֶׁרָאֲתָה בָּאִצְטְרוֹלוֹגִין שֶׁלָּהּ שֶׁעֲתִידָה לְהַעֲמִיד בָּנִים מִמֶּנּוּ, וְאֵינָהּ יוֹדַעַת אִם מִמֶּנָּה אִם מִבִּתָּהּ:

ג **כִּי ה׳ אִתּוֹ.** שֵׁם שָׁמַיִם שָׁגוּר בְּפִיו:

ד **וְכָל יֶשׁ לוֹ.** הֲרֵי לָשׁוֹן קָצָר, חָסֵר ׳אֲשֶׁר׳:

ו-ז **וְלֹא יָדַע אִתּוֹ מְאוּמָה.** לֹא הָיָה נוֹתֵן לִבּוֹ לִכְלוּם: **כִּי אִם הַלֶּחֶם.** הִיא אִשְׁתּוֹ, אֶלָּא שֶׁדִּבֵּר בְּלָשׁוֹן נְקִיָּה: **וַיְהִי יוֹסֵף יְפֵה תֹאַר.** כֵּיוָן שֶׁרָאָה עַצְמוֹ מוֹשֵׁל, הִתְחִיל אוֹכֵל וְשׁוֹתֶה וּמְסַלְסֵל בִּשְׂעָרוֹ. אָמַר הַקָּדוֹשׁ בָּרוּךְ הוּא: אָבִיךָ מִתְאַבֵּל, וְאַתָּה מְסַלְסֵל בִּשְׂעָרְךָ?! אֲנִי מְגָרֶה בְךָ אֶת הַדֹּב! מִיָּד – ״וַתִּשָּׂא אֵשֶׁת אֲדֹנָיו״ וְגוֹ׳; כָּל מָקוֹם שֶׁנֶּאֱמַר ׳אַחַר׳ – סָמוּךְ:

wife must be flattering as well as seductive. It is a decisive moment. A slave, with no realistic hope of rescue – is he to become an Egyptian, with all the sexual laissez-faire that implies? Or will he remain faithful to his past, his conscience, his identity? The *shalshelet* is an elegant commentary on Yosef's *crise de conscience.*

The Talmud (Sota 36b) gives a graphic description of his inner torment: "The image of his father appeared to him in the window and said, 'Yosef, your brothers' names are destined to be inscribed on the stones of the [High Priest's] breastplate, and you will be among them. Do you want your name to be erased? Do you want to be called an adulterer?'"

We have seen above how Reuven was thwarted by not knowing what was "destined to be written" (see ch. 37,

כט וַיְהִי ׀ כְּמֵשִׁיב יָדוֹ וְהִנֵּה יָצָא אָחִיו וַתֹּאמֶר מַה־פָּרַצְתָּ עָלֶיךָ פָּרֶץ
ל וַיִּקְרָא שְׁמוֹ פָּרֶץ: וְאַחַר יָצָא אָחִיו אֲשֶׁר עַל־יָדוֹ הַשָּׁנִי וַיִּקְרָא שְׁמוֹ
לט א זָרַח: וְיוֹסֵף הוּרַד מִצְרָיְמָה וַיִּקְנֵהוּ פּוֹטִיפַר סְרִיס פַּרְעֹה לה חמישי
שַׂר הַטַּבָּחִים אִישׁ מִצְרִי מִיַּד הַיִּשְׁמְעֵאלִים אֲשֶׁר הוֹרִדֻהוּ שָׁמָּה:
ב וַיְהִי יהוה אֶת־יוֹסֵף וַיְהִי אִישׁ מַצְלִיחַ וַיְהִי בְּבֵית אֲדֹנָיו הַמִּצְרִי:
ג וַיַּרְא אֲדֹנָיו כִּי יהוה אִתּוֹ וְכֹל אֲשֶׁר־הוּא עֹשֶׂה יהוה מַצְלִיחַ בְּיָדוֹ:
ד וַיִּמְצָא יוֹסֵף חֵן בְּעֵינָיו וַיְשָׁרֶת אֹתוֹ וַיַּפְקִדֵהוּ עַל־בֵּיתוֹ וְכָל־יֶשׁ־לוֹ
ה נָתַן בְּיָדוֹ: וַיְהִי מֵאָז הִפְקִיד אֹתוֹ בְּבֵיתוֹ וְעַל כָּל־אֲשֶׁר יֶשׁ־לוֹ וַיְבָרֶךְ
יהוה אֶת־בֵּית הַמִּצְרִי בִּגְלַל יוֹסֵף וַיְהִי בִּרְכַּת יהוה בְּכָל־אֲשֶׁר יֶשׁ־לוֹ
ו בַּבַּיִת וּבַשָּׂדֶה: וַיַּעֲזֹב כָּל־אֲשֶׁר־לוֹ בְּיַד־יוֹסֵף וְלֹא־יָדַע אִתּוֹ מְאוּמָה
כִּי אִם־הַלֶּחֶם אֲשֶׁר־הוּא אוֹכֵל וַיְהִי יוֹסֵף יְפֵה־תֹאַר וִיפֵה מַרְאֶה:
ז וַיְהִי אַחַר הַדְּבָרִים הָאֵלֶּה וַתִּשָּׂא אֵשֶׁת־אֲדֹנָיו אֶת־עֵינֶיהָ אֶל־יוֹסֵף ששי
ח וַתֹּאמֶר שִׁכְבָה עִמִּי: וַיְמָאֵן ׀ וַיֹּאמֶר אֶל־אֵשֶׁת אֲדֹנָיו הֵן אֲדֹנִי לֹא־

אונקלוס

כט וַהֲוָה כַּד אֲתֵיב יְדֵיהּ, וְהָא נְפַק אֲחוּהִי, וַאֲמַרַת, מָא תְּקוֹף סַגִּי
עֲלָךְ לְמִתְקַף, וּקְרָא שְׁמֵיהּ פָּרֶץ: ל וּבָתַר כֵּן נְפַק אֲחוּהִי, דְּעַל יְדֵיהּ
זְהוֹרִיתָא, וּקְרָא שְׁמֵיהּ זָרַח: לט א וְיוֹסֵף אִתַּחַת לְמִצְרַיִם, וְזַבְנֵיהּ,
פּוֹטִיפַר רַבָּא דְּפַרְעֹה, רַב קָטוֹלַיָּא גֻּבְרָא מִצְרָאָה, מִיְּדָא דַּעֲרָבָאֵי,
דְּאַחֲתוּהִי לְתַמָּן: ב וַהֲוָה מֵימְרָא דַּיי בְּסַעְדֵּיהּ דְּיוֹסֵף, וַהֲוָה גְּבַר
מַצְלַח, וַהֲוָה, בְּבֵית רִבּוֹנֵיהּ מִצְרָאָה: ג וַחֲזָא רִבּוֹנֵיהּ, אֲרֵי מֵימְרָא דַּיי
בְּסַעְדֵּיהּ, וְכֹל דְּהוּא עָבֵיד, יי מַצְלַח בִּידֵיהּ: ד וְאַשְׁכַּח יוֹסֵף רַחֲמִין,
בְּעֵינוֹהִי וְשַׁמֵּישׁ יָתֵיהּ, וּמַנְּיֵיהּ עַל בֵּיתֵיהּ, וְכָל דְּאִית לֵיהּ מְסַר בִּידֵיהּ:
ה וַהֲוָה, מֵעִדָּן דְּמַנִּי יָתֵיהּ בְּבֵיתֵיהּ, וְעַל כָּל דְּאִית לֵיהּ, וּבָרֵיךְ יי, יָת
בֵּית מִצְרָאָה בְּדִיל יוֹסֵף, וַהֲוָה, בִּרְכְתָא דַּיי בְּכָל דְּאִית לֵיהּ, בְּבֵיתָא
וּבְחַקְלָא: ו וּשְׁבַק כָּל דְּלֵיהּ בִּידָא דְּיוֹסֵף, וְלָא יְדַע עִמֵּיהּ מִדַּעַם,
אֱלָהֵין לַחְמָא דְּהוּא אָכֵיל, וַהֲוָה יוֹסֵף, שַׁפִּיר בְּרֵיוָא וְיָאֵי בְּחֶזְוָא:
ז וַהֲוָה, בָּתַר פִּתְגָּמַיָּא הָאִלֵּין, וּזְקַפַת אִתַּת רִבּוֹנֵיהּ, יָת עֵינַהָא לְוָת
יוֹסֵף, וַאֲמַרַת שְׁכוֹב עִמִּי: ח וְסָרֵיב וַאֲמַר לְאִתַּת רִבּוֹנֵיהּ, הָא רִבּוֹנִי, לָא

39:8 וַיְמָאֵן *But he refused* – Over "he refused" tradition has placed a *shalshelet,* the musical note meant to convey a psychological state of uncertainty and indecision.

We can imagine the conflict in Yosef's mind at this moment. On the one hand, his entire moral sense says: "No." It would be a betrayal of everything his family stands for: their ethic of sexual propriety and their strong sense of identity as children of the covenant. It would also be, as Yosef himself says, a betrayal of Potifar.

And yet, the temptation must be intense. He is in an urban civilization of a kind he has not seen before. It is his first experience of "bright lights, big city." He is far from home. No one can see him. After all the hostility he has suffered in his childhood, being propositioned by Potifar's

23 jail. Everything done there was under his direction. The warden did not need
to pay attention to anything he had entrusted to him, because the LORD was
with him, giving him success in all he did.
40 1 Some time later, the Egyptian king's cupbearer and baker gave offense to their SHEVI'I
2 master, the king of Egypt. Pharaoh was angry with the two officials, his chief
3 cupbearer, and his chief baker, and he placed them in custody in the house of
4 the captain of the guard, in the very place where Yosef was confined. The captain
of the guard assigned them to Yosef and it was he who attended them. When
5 they had been in custody for some time, the two of them – the imprisoned
cupbearer and baker of the king of Egypt – each had a dream on the same night,
6 each dream seeming to carry its own meaning. When Yosef came to them
7 the next morning, he saw that they were both distressed. He asked Pharaoh's
officials who were in custody with him in his master's house, "Why are you
8 looking so troubled today?" "We both had dreams," they told him, "but there
is no one to interpret them." Yosef replied, "Interpretation belongs to God. Tell
9 me your dreams." So the chief cupbearer told his dream to Yosef and said to

רש״י

כג **בַּאֲשֶׁר ה׳ אִתּוֹ.** בִּשְׁבִיל שֶׁה׳ אִתּוֹ:

מ א **אַחַר הַדְּבָרִים הָאֵלֶּה.** לְפִי שֶׁהִרְגִּילָה אוֹתָהּ אֲרוּרָה אֶת הַצַּדִּיק בְּפִי כֻּלָּם לְדַבֵּר בּוֹ, הֵבִיא לָהֶם הַקָּדוֹשׁ בָּרוּךְ הוּא סָרְחָנָם שֶׁל אֵלּוּ, שֶׁיִּפְנוּ אֲלֵיהֶם וְלֹא אֵלָיו; וְעוֹד שֶׁתָּבוֹא הָרְוָחָה לַצַּדִּיק עַל יְדֵיהֶם: **חָטְאוּ.** זֶה נִמְצָא זְבוּב בְּפַיָלֵי פּוֹטִירִין שֶׁלּוֹ, וְזֶה נִמְצָא צְרוֹר בִּגְלוּסְקִין שֶׁלּוֹ: **וְהָאֹפֶה.** אֶת פַּת הַמֶּלֶךְ, וְאֵין לְשׁוֹן אֲפִיָּה אֶלָּא בְּפַת, וּבְלַעַ״ז פישטו״ר:

ד **וַיִּפְקֹד שַׂר הַטַּבָּחִים אֶת יוֹסֵף.** לִהְיוֹת ״אִתָּם״: **וַיִּהְיוּ יָמִים בְּמִשְׁמָר.** שְׁנֵים עָשָׂר חֹדֶשׁ:

ה **וַיַּחַלְמוּ חֲלוֹם שְׁנֵיהֶם.** וַיַּחַלְמוּ שְׁנֵיהֶם חֲלוֹם, זֶהוּ פְּשׁוּטוֹ. וּמִדְרָשׁוֹ, כָּל אֶחָד חָלַם ״חֲלוֹם שְׁנֵיהֶם״ – שֶׁחָלַם אֶת חֲלוֹמוֹ וּפִתְרוֹן חֲבֵרוֹ, וְזֶהוּ שֶׁנֶּאֱמַר: ״וַיַּרְא שַׂר הָאֹפִים כִּי טוֹב פָּתָר״: **אִישׁ כְּפִתְרוֹן חֲלֹמוֹ.** כָּל אֶחָד חָלַם חֲלוֹם הַדּוֹמֶה לַפִּתְרוֹן הֶעָתִיד לָבֹא עֲלֵיהֶם:

ו **זֹעֲפִים.** עֲצֵבִים, כְּמוֹ: ״סַר וְזָעֵף״ (מלכים א׳ כ, מג), ״זַעַף ה׳ אֶשָּׂא״ (מיכה ז, ט):

3:4). We can make a difference, and it is potentially immense. That should be our mindset, always.

Few statements are more at odds with the way the world seems to us most of the time. Each of us knows that there is only one of us, and that there are billions of others in the world. What conceivable difference can we make? We are no more than a wave in the ocean, a grain of sand on the seashore, dust on the surface of infinity. Is it conceivable that with one act we could change the trajectory of our life, let alone that of humanity as a whole? Our *parasha* tells us that yes, it is. A stranger's directions, a brother's hesitation, a chance encounter in the wilderness, all have so far changed the course of Yosef's story and, by extension, Jewish history. Now in prison, home to the most powerless, Yosef's attentiveness to his fellow inmates will ultimately – though indirectly – change the course of world events. If the opportunity to help a vulnerable other presents itself, advises Rambam, do not hesitate. Our next act might tilt the balance of someone else's life and our own. We are not inconsequential. We can make a difference to our world. When we do so, we become God's partners in the work of redemption.

אֵת כָּל־הָאֲסִירִם אֲשֶׁר בְּבֵית הַסֹּהַר וְאֵת כָּל־אֲשֶׁר עֹשִׂים שָׁם הוּא
כג הָיָה עֹשֶׂה׃ אֵין ׀ שַׂר בֵּית־הַסֹּהַר רֹאֶה אֶת־כָּל־מְאוּמָה בְּיָדוֹ בַּאֲשֶׁר
יְהוָה אִתּוֹ וַאֲשֶׁר־הוּא עֹשֶׂה יְהוָה מַצְלִיחַ׃
מ א וַיְהִי אַחַר הַדְּבָרִים הָאֵלֶּה חָטְאוּ מַשְׁקֵה מֶלֶךְ־מִצְרַיִם וְהָאֹפֶה שביעי
ב לַאֲדֹנֵיהֶם לְמֶלֶךְ מִצְרָיִם׃ וַיִּקְצֹף פַּרְעֹה עַל שְׁנֵי סָרִיסָיו עַל שַׂר
ג הַמַּשְׁקִים וְעַל שַׂר הָאוֹפִים׃ וַיִּתֵּן אֹתָם בְּמִשְׁמַר בֵּית שַׂר הַטַּבָּחִים
ד אֶל־בֵּית הַסֹּהַר מְקוֹם אֲשֶׁר יוֹסֵף אָסוּר שָׁם׃ וַיִּפְקֹד שַׂר הַטַּבָּחִים אֶת־
ה יוֹסֵף אִתָּם וַיְשָׁרֶת אֹתָם וַיִּהְיוּ יָמִים בְּמִשְׁמָר׃ וַיַּחַלְמוּ חֲלוֹם שְׁנֵיהֶם
אִישׁ חֲלֹמוֹ בְּלַיְלָה אֶחָד אִישׁ כְּפִתְרוֹן חֲלֹמוֹ הַמַּשְׁקֶה וְהָאֹפֶה אֲשֶׁר
ו לְמֶלֶךְ מִצְרַיִם אֲשֶׁר אֲסוּרִים בְּבֵית הַסֹּהַר׃ וַיָּבֹא אֲלֵיהֶם יוֹסֵף בַּבֹּקֶר
ז וַיַּרְא אֹתָם וְהִנָּם זֹעֲפִים׃ וַיִּשְׁאַל אֶת־סְרִיסֵי פַרְעֹה אֲשֶׁר אִתּוֹ בְמִשְׁמַר
ח בֵּית אֲדֹנָיו לֵאמֹר מַדּוּעַ פְּנֵיכֶם רָעִים הַיּוֹם׃ וַיֹּאמְרוּ אֵלָיו חֲלוֹם חָלַמְנוּ
וּפֹתֵר אֵין אֹתוֹ וַיֹּאמֶר אֲלֵהֶם יוֹסֵף הֲלוֹא לֵאלֹהִים פִּתְרֹנִים סַפְּרוּ־נָא
ט לִי׃ וַיְסַפֵּר שַׂר־הַמַּשְׁקִים אֶת־חֲלֹמוֹ לְיוֹסֵף וַיֹּאמֶר לוֹ בַּחֲלוֹמִי וְהִנֵּה־

אונקלוס

יָת כָּל אֲסִירַיָּא, דִּבְבֵית אֲסִירֵי, וְיָת כָּל דְּעָבְדִין תַּמָּן, מִמֵּימְרֵיהּ הֲוָה מִתְעֲבֵיד: כג לֵית רַב בֵּית אֲסִירֵי, חָזֵי יָת כָּל סָרְחָן בִּידֵיהּ, בִּדְמֵימְרָא דַּיי בְּסַעְדֵּיהּ, וּדְהוּא עָבֵיד יי מַצְלַח: מ א וַהֲוָה, בָּתַר פִּתְגָּמַיָּא הָאִלֵּין, סְרַחוּ, שָׁקְיָא דְּמַלְכָּא דְמִצְרַיִם וְנַחְתּוֹמָא, לְרִבּוֹנְהוֹן לְמַלְכָּא דְמִצְרָיִם: ב וּרְגִיז פַּרְעֹה, עַל תְּרֵין רַבְרְבָנוֹהִי, עַל רַב שָׁקֵי, וְעַל רַב נַחְתּוֹמֵי: ג וִיהַב יָתְהוֹן בְּמַטְּרַת, בֵּית, רַב קָטוֹלַיָּא בְּבֵית אֲסִירֵי, אַתְרָא, דְּיוֹסֵף אֲסִיר תַּמָּן: ד וּמַנִּי, רַב קָטוֹלַיָּא יָת יוֹסֵף, עִמְּהוֹן וְשַׁמֵּישׁ יָתְהוֹן, וַהֲווֹ יוֹמִין בְּמַטְּרָא: ה וַחֲלַמוּ חֶלְמָא תַּרְוֵיהוֹן, גְּבַר חֶלְמֵיהּ בְּלֵילְיָא חַד, גְּבַר כְּפֻשְׁרָן חֶלְמֵיהּ, שָׁקְיָא וְנַחְתּוֹמָא, דִּלְמַלְכָּא דְמִצְרַיִם, דַּאֲסִירִין בְּבֵית אֲסִירֵי: ו וַאֲתָא לְוָתְהוֹן, יוֹסֵף בְּצַפְרָא, וַחֲזָא יָתְהוֹן, וְהָא אִנּוּן נְסִיסִין: ז וּשְׁאֵיל יָת רַבְרְבֵי פַרְעֹה, דְּעִמֵּיהּ בְּמַטְּרַת, בֵּית רִבּוֹנֵיהּ לְמֵימַר, מָדֵין, אַפֵּיכוֹן בִּישִׁין יוֹמָא דֵין: ח וַאֲמַרוּ לֵיהּ, חֶלְמָא חֲלַמְנָא, וּפָשַׁר לֵית לֵיהּ, וַאֲמַר לְהוֹן יוֹסֵף, הֲלָא מִן קֳדָם יי פֻּשְׁרַן חֶלְמַיָּא, אִשְׁתַּעוֹ כְעַן לִי: ט וְאִשְׁתַּעִי רַב שָׁקֵי, יָת חֶלְמֵיהּ לְיוֹסֵף, וַאֲמַר לֵיהּ, בְּחֶלְמִי, וְהָא

40:8 סַפְּרוּ־נָא לִי *Tell me your dreams* – In his *Hilkhot Teshuva*, Rambam makes one of the most empowering statements in religious literature. Having explained that we and the world are judged by the majority of our deeds, he continues: "Therefore we should see ourselves throughout the year as if our deeds and those of the world are evenly poised between good and bad, so that our next act may change both the balance of our lives and that of the world" (*Hilkhot Teshuva*

10 him, "In my dream I saw a vine in front of me. The vine had three branches. As
11 soon as it budded, it blossomed, and its clusters ripened into grapes. Pharaoh's
cup was in my hand; I took the grapes and squeezed them into Pharaoh's cup,
12 and I placed the cup in his hand." "This is what it means," Yosef said. "The three
13 branches are three days. In three days Pharaoh will lift your head and restore
you to your position. You will place Pharaoh's cup in his hand again, as you did
14 when you were his cupbearer. When it goes well with you, remember me and
do me this kindness: mention me to Pharaoh so as to free me from this place.
15 The truth is that I was kidnapped from the land of the Hebrews. Here too, I
16 have done nothing to deserve being placed in this pit." The chief baker saw that
he had given a favorable interpretation, so he said to Yosef, "I too had a dream.
17 There were three baskets of white bread on my head. In the top basket were all
sorts of baked food that Pharaoh eats, but birds were eating them out of the
18 basket above my head." "This is what it means," Yosef said. "The three baskets
19 are three days. In three days Pharaoh will lift your head from your body; he will
20 hang you from a stake, and birds will eat your flesh." The third day was Pharaoh's MAFTIR
birthday. He made a feast for all his servants, and from among them he singled
21 out his chief cupbearer and chief baker. He restored the chief cupbearer to his
22 position so that, as before, he placed the cup in Pharaoh's hand. But he hung

אונקלוס

גֻּפְנָא קֳדָמָי: י וּבְגֻפְנָא תְּלָתָא שִׁבְשִׁין, וְהִיא כַּד אַפְרַחַת אַפֵּיקַת לַבְלְבִין אֲנִיצַת נַץ, בְּשִׁילוּ אֶתְכָּלַהָא הֲווֹ עִנְבִין: יא וְכָסָא דְפַרְעֹה בִּידִי, וּנְסֵיבִית יָת עִנְבַיָּא, וַעֲצָרִית יָתְהוֹן לְכָסָא דְּפַרְעֹה, וִיהַבִית יָת כָּסָא עַל יְדָא דְּפַרְעֹה: יב וַאֲמַר לֵיהּ יוֹסֵף, דֵּין פֻּשְׁרָנֵיהּ, תְּלָתָא שִׁבְשִׁין, תְּלָתָא

רש"י

י שָׂרִיגִם. זְמוֹרוֹת אֲרֻכּוֹת שֶׁקּוֹרִין וידי"ץ: וְהִוא כְפֹרַחַת. דּוֹמָה לְפוֹרַחַת. "וְהִיא כְפֹרַחַת" – נִדְמֵית לִי בַּחֲלוֹמִי כְּאִלּוּ הִיא פוֹרַחַת, וְאַחַר הַפֶּרַח "עָלְתָה נִצָּהּ" וְנַעֲשׂוּ סְמָדַר, אשפני"ר בְּלַעַז, וְאַחַר כָּךְ "הִבְשִׁילוּ". "וְהִיא כַּד אַפְרַחַת אַפֵּיקַת לַבְלְבִין", עַד כָּאן תַּרְגּוּם שֶׁל "פֹּרַחַת". נֵץ גָּדוֹל מִפֶּרַח, כְּדִכְתִיב: "וּבֹסֶר גֹּמֵל יִהְיֶה נִצָּה" (ישעיה יח, ה), וּכְתִיב: "וַיֹּצֵא פֶרַח" וַהֲדַר "וַיָּצֵץ צִיץ" (במדבר יז, כג):

יא וָאֶשְׂחַט. כְּתַרְגּוּמוֹ "וַעֲצָרִית", וְהַרְבֵּה יֵשׁ בִּלְשׁוֹן מִשְׁנָה:

יב שְׁלֹשֶׁת יָמִים הֵם. סִימָן הֵם לְךָ לִשְׁלֹשֶׁת יָמִים, וְיֵשׁ מִדְרְשֵׁי אַגָּדָה הַרְבֵּה:

יג יִשָּׂא פַרְעֹה אֶת רֹאשֶׁךָ. לְשׁוֹן חֶשְׁבּוֹן, כְּשֶׁיִּפְקֹד שְׁאָר עֲבָדָיו לְשָׁרֵת לְפָנָיו בַּסְּעוּדָה, יִמְנֶה אוֹתְךָ עִמָּהֶם: כַּנֶּךָ. בָּסִיס שֶׁלְּךָ וּמוֹשָׁבְךָ:

יד כִּי אִם זְכַרְתַּנִי אִתְּךָ. אַחַר אִם זְכַרְתַּנִי אִתְּךָ, מֵאַחַר שֶׁיִּיטַב לְךָ כְּפִתְרוֹנִי: וְעָשִׂיתָ נָּא עִמָּדִי חָסֶד. אֵין 'נָא' אֶלָּא לְשׁוֹן בַּקָּשָׁה [הֲרֵי אַתָּה עוֹשֶׂה עִמִּי חֶסֶד]:

טז סַלֵּי חֹרִי. סַלִּים שֶׁל נְצָרִים קְלוּפִים חוֹרִין חוֹרִין, וּבִמְקוֹמֵנוּ יֵשׁ הַרְבֵּה, וְדֶרֶךְ מוֹכְרֵי פַּת כִּיסָנִין שֶׁקּוֹרִין אובלי"ש לְתִתָּם בְּאוֹתָם סַלִּים:

כ יוֹם הֻלֶּדֶת אֶת פַּרְעֹה. יוֹם לֵדָתוֹ, וְקוֹרִין לוֹ יוֹם גְּנוּסְיָא. וּלְשׁוֹן 'הֻלֶּדֶת', לְפִי שֶׁאֵין הַוָּלָד נוֹלָד אֶלָּא עַל יְדֵי אֲחֵרִים, שֶׁהַחַיָּה מְיַלֶּדֶת אֶת הָאִשָּׁה, וְעַל כֵּן הִיא נִקְרֵאת 'מְיַלֶּדֶת'; וְכֵן: "וּמוֹלְדוֹתַיִךְ בְּיוֹם הוּלֶּדֶת אוֹתָךְ" (יחזקאל טז, ד), וְכֵן: "אַחֲרֵי הֻכַּבֵּס אֶת הַנֶּגַע" (ויקרא יג, נה), שֶׁכִּבּוּסוֹ עַל יְדֵי אֲחֵרִים: וַיִּשָּׂא אֶת רֹאשׁ וְגוֹ'. מְנָאָם עִם שְׁאָר עֲבָדָיו, שֶׁהָיָה מוֹנֶה הַמְשָׁרְתִים שֶׁיְּשָׁרְתוּ לוֹ בִּסְעֻדָּתוֹ וְזָכַר אֶת אֵלּוּ בְּתוֹכָם, כְּמוֹ: "שְׂאוּ אֶת רֹאשׁ" (במדבר א, ב), לְשׁוֹן מִנְיָן:

י גֶ֣פֶן לְפָנָֽי׃ וּבַגֶּ֖פֶן שְׁלֹשָׁ֣ה שָֽׂרִיגִ֑ם וְהִ֤וא כְפֹרַ֙חַת֙ עָלְתָ֣ה נִצָּ֔הּ הִבְשִׁ֥ילוּ
יא אַשְׁכְּלֹתֶ֖יהָ עֲנָבִֽים׃ וְכ֥וֹס פַּרְעֹ֖ה בְּיָדִ֑י וָאֶקַּ֣ח אֶת־הָעֲנָבִ֗ים וָאֶשְׂחַ֤ט
יב אֹתָם֙ אֶל־כּ֣וֹס פַּרְעֹ֔ה וָאֶתֵּ֥ן אֶת־הַכּ֖וֹס עַל־כַּ֥ף פַּרְעֹֽה׃ וַיֹּ֤אמֶר לוֹ֙ יוֹסֵ֔ף
יג זֶ֖ה פִּתְרֹנ֑וֹ שְׁלֹ֙שֶׁת֙ הַשָּׂ֣רִגִ֔ים שְׁלֹ֥שֶׁת יָמִ֖ים הֵֽם׃ בְּע֣וֹד ׀ שְׁלֹ֣שֶׁת יָמִ֗ים
יִשָּׂ֤א פַרְעֹה֙ אֶת־רֹאשֶׁ֔ךָ וַהֲשִֽׁיבְךָ֖ עַל־כַּנֶּ֑ךָ וְנָתַתָּ֤ כוֹס־פַּרְעֹה֙ בְּיָד֔וֹ
יד כַּמִּשְׁפָּט֙ הָֽרִאשׁ֔וֹן אֲשֶׁ֥ר הָיִ֖יתָ מַשְׁקֵֽהוּ׃ כִּ֤י אִם־זְכַרְתַּ֙נִי֙ אִתְּךָ֔ כַּאֲשֶׁר֙
יִ֣יטַב לָ֔ךְ וְעָשִֽׂיתָ־נָּ֥א עִמָּדִ֖י חָ֑סֶד וְהִזְכַּרְתַּ֙נִי֙ אֶל־פַּרְעֹ֔ה וְהוֹצֵאתַ֖נִי
טו מִן־הַבַּ֥יִת הַזֶּֽה׃ כִּֽי־גֻנֹּ֣ב גֻּנַּ֔בְתִּי מֵאֶ֖רֶץ הָעִבְרִ֑ים וְגַם־פֹּה֙ לֹא־עָשִׂ֣יתִי
טז מְא֔וּמָה כִּֽי־שָׂמ֥וּ אֹתִ֖י בַּבּֽוֹר׃ וַיַּ֥רְא שַׂר־הָאֹפִ֖ים כִּ֣י ט֣וֹב פָּתָ֑ר וַיֹּ֙אמֶר֙
יז אֶל־יוֹסֵ֔ף אַף־אֲנִי֙ בַּחֲלוֹמִ֔י וְהִנֵּ֗ה שְׁלֹשָׁ֛ה סַלֵּ֥י חֹרִ֖י עַל־רֹאשִֽׁי׃ וּבַסַּ֣ל
הָעֶלְי֔וֹן מִכֹּ֛ל מַאֲכַ֥ל פַּרְעֹ֖ה מַעֲשֵׂ֣ה אֹפֶ֑ה וְהָע֗וֹף אֹכֵ֥ל אֹתָ֛ם מִן־הַסַּ֖ל
יח מֵעַ֥ל רֹאשִֽׁי׃ וַיַּ֤עַן יוֹסֵף֙ וַיֹּ֔אמֶר זֶ֖ה פִּתְרֹנ֑וֹ שְׁלֹ֙שֶׁת֙ הַסַּלִּ֔ים שְׁלֹ֥שֶׁת
יט יָמִ֖ים הֵֽם׃ בְּע֣וֹד ׀ שְׁלֹ֣שֶׁת יָמִ֗ים יִשָּׂ֨א פַרְעֹ֤ה אֶת־רֹֽאשְׁךָ֙ מֵֽעָלֶ֔יךָ וְתָלָ֥ה
כ אוֹתְךָ֖ עַל־עֵ֑ץ וְאָכַ֥ל הָע֛וֹף אֶת־בְּשָׂרְךָ֖ מֵעָלֶֽיךָ׃ וַיְהִ֣י ׀ בַּיּ֣וֹם הַשְּׁלִישִׁ֗י מפטיר
י֚וֹם הֻלֶּ֣דֶת אֶת־פַּרְעֹ֔ה וַיַּ֥עַשׂ מִשְׁתֶּ֖ה לְכָל־עֲבָדָ֑יו וַיִּשָּׂ֞א אֶת־רֹ֣אשׁ ׀
כא שַׂ֣ר הַמַּשְׁקִ֗ים וְאֶת־רֹ֛אשׁ שַׂ֥ר הָאֹפִ֖ים בְּת֥וֹךְ עֲבָדָֽיו׃ וַיָּ֛שֶׁב אֶת־שַׂ֥ר
כב הַמַּשְׁקִ֖ים עַל־מַשְׁקֵ֑הוּ וַיִּתֵּ֥ן הַכּ֖וֹס עַל־כַּ֥ף פַּרְעֹֽה׃ וְאֵ֛ת שַׂ֥ר הָאֹפִ֖ים

אונקלוס

יוֹמִין אִנּוּן: יג בְּסוֹף תְּלָתָא יוֹמִין, יִדְכְּרִנָּךְ פַּרְעֹה, וִיתִיבִנָּךְ עַל שִׁמּוּשָׁךְ, וְתִתֵּין כָּסָא דְּפַרְעֹה בִּידֵיהּ, כְּהִלְכְּתָא קַדְמֵיתָא, דַּהֲוֵיתָא מַשְׁקֵי לֵיהּ: יד אֱלָהֵין תִּדְכְּרִנַּנִי עִמָּךְ, כַּד יֵיטַב לָךְ, וְתַעֲבֵיד כְּעַן עִמִּי טֵיבוּ, וְתִדְכַּר עֲלַי קֳדָם פַּרְעֹה, וְתַפְּקִנַּנִי מִן בֵּית אֲסִירֵי הָדֵין: טו אֲרֵי מִגְנַב גְּנִיבְנָא, מֵאַרְעָא עִבְרָאֵי, וְאַף הָכָא לָא עֲבָדִית מִדַּעַם, אֲרֵי מַנִּיאוּ יָתִי בְּבֵית אֲסִירֵי: טז וַחֲזָא רַב נַחְתּוֹמֵי אֲרֵי יָאוּת פְּשַׁר, וַאֲמַר לְיוֹסֵף, אַף אֲנָא בְּחֶלְמִי, וְהָא, תְּלָתָא, סַלִּין דְּחִירוּ עַל רֵישִׁי: יז וּבְסַלָּא עִלָּאָה, מִכֹּל מֵיכְלָא דְּפַרְעֹה עוֹבַד נַחְתּוֹם, וְעוֹפָא, אָכֵיל יָתְהוֹן, מִן סַלָּא מֵעִלָּוֵי רֵישִׁי: יח וַאֲתֵיב יוֹסֵף וַאֲמַר, דֵּין פֻּשְׁרָנֵיהּ, תְּלָתָא סַלִּין, תְּלָתָא יוֹמִין אִנּוּן: יט בְּסוֹף תְּלָתָא יוֹמִין, יַעְדֵּי פַּרְעֹה יָת רֵישָׁךְ מִנָּךְ, וְיִצְלוֹב יָתָךְ עַל צְלִיבָא, וְיֵיכוֹל עוֹפָא, יָת בִּסְרָךְ מִנָּךְ: כ וַהֲוָה בְּיוֹמָא תְּלִיתָאָה, יוֹם בֵּית וַלְדָּא דְּפַרְעֹה, וַעֲבַד מִשְׁתְּיָא לְכָל עַבְדוֹהִי, וְאִדְּכַר, יָת רֵישׁ רַב שָׁקֵי, וְיָת רֵישׁ, רַב נַחְתּוֹמֵי בְּגוֹ עַבְדוֹהִי: כא וַאֲתֵיב, יָת רַב שָׁקֵי עַל שַׁקְיוּתֵיהּ, וִיהַב כָּסָא עַל יְדָא דְּפַרְעֹה: כב וְיָת, רַב נַחְתּוֹמֵי

23 up the chief baker, as Yosef had predicted. Still, the chief cupbearer did not
remember Yosef; he forgot him.

The haftara for Parashat Vayeshev is on page 1518.
On Ḥanukka read the haftara on page 1638.

רש״י

כג) **וְלֹא זָכַר שַׂר הַמַּשְׁקִים.** בּוֹ בַּיּוֹם: **וַיִּשְׁכָּחֵהוּ.** לְאַחַר מִכָּאן. מִפְּנֵי שֶׁתָּלָה בּוֹ יוֹסֵף לְזָכְרוֹ הֻזְקַק לִהְיוֹת אָסוּר שְׁתֵּי שָׁנִים, שֶׁנֶּאֱמַר: "אַשְׁרֵי הַגֶּבֶר אֲשֶׁר שָׂם ה׳ מִבְטַחוֹ וְלֹא פָנָה אֶל רְהָבִים" (תהלים מ, ה), וְלֹא בָּטַח עַל מִצְרַיִם הַקְּרוּיִים רַהַב:

and starvation, the one Jewish tradition calls "the *tzaddik*" (Yoma 35b). The human condition is not inherently tragic. Heroes are not fated to fall.

Yosef's story is a precise reversal of the narrative structure of Sophocles's *Oedipus*. Everything Laius and his son Oedipus do to *avert* the tragic fate announced by the oracle in fact brings it closer to fulfillment, whereas in the story of Yosef, every episode that seems to be leading to tragedy turns out in retrospect to be a necessary step to saving lives and fulfilling Yosef's dreams.

Do not think you understand the story of your life at halftime. That is the lesson of Yosef. There is no way of predicting how the story will end on the basis of the events narrated in Parashat Vayeshev. The turning point in his life is a highly improbable event that could not be predicted but which changes all else, not just for him but for large numbers of people and for the eventual course of Jewish history. God's hand is at work, even when Yosef feels abandoned by every human being he has encountered.

Judaism is the opposite of tragedy. Every bad thing that has happened to you thus far may be the necessary prelude to the good things that are about to happen because you have been strengthened and given courage by your ability to survive. Seen through the eye of faith, today's curse may be the beginning of tomorrow's blessing.

כג תָּלָה כַּאֲשֶׁר פָּתַר לָהֶם יוֹסֵף: וְלֹא־זָכַר שַׂר־הַמַּשְׁקִים אֶת־יוֹסֵף
וַיִּשְׁכָּחֵהוּ:

The הפטרה *for* פרשת וישב *is on page 1519.*
On חנוכה *read the* הפטרה *on page 1639.*

אונקלוס

צְלַב, כְּמָא דְּפַשַּׁר לְהוֹן יוֹסֵף: כג וְלָא אִדְּכַר רַב שָׁקֵי, יָת יוֹסֵף וְאַנְשְׁיֵהּ:

40:23 וַיִּשְׁכָּחֵהוּ *He forgot him* – The last line of the *parasha* delivers one of the cruelest blows of fate in the Torah. Seemingly his one chance of escape to freedom is now lost. Yosef, the beloved son in his magnificent robe has become Yosef, the prisoner bereft of hope. This is as near the Torah gets to Greek tragedy. It is a tale of Yosef's hubris leading, step after step, to his nemesis. Every good thing that happens to him turns out to be only the prelude to some new and unforeseen misfortune.

Two years later, at the beginning of the next *parasha*, we discover that all this has been leading to Yosef's supreme elevation. From the lowest pit he has risen to dizzying heights.

What is stunning about the way this story is told in the Torah is that it is constructed to lead us, as readers, in precisely the wrong direction. Parashat Vayeshev has the form of a Greek tragedy. Yosef has flaws in his character. He is vain about his appearance; he brings his father evil reports about his brothers (Gen. 37:2; Rashi; and see Bereshit Rabba 84:7); his narcissism leads directly to the advances of Potifar's wife (*Tanḥuma*, Vayeshev 8).

But the story of which he is a part is not a Greek tragedy. By its end – the death of Yosef in the final chapter of Genesis – he has become a different human being entirely, one who forgives his brothers the crime they committed against him, the man who saves an entire region from famine

Parashat Miketz

41 1 Two years passed. Then Pharaoh had a dream: he was standing by the Nile
2 when seven handsome, healthy cows came up out of the river and grazed
3 among the reeds. Then seven other cows came up from the river after them,
4 ugly and gaunt, and stood beside them by the riverbank. The ugly, gaunt cows
5 ate up the seven handsome, healthy cows. Pharaoh awoke. Falling back to
sleep, he had a second dream: he saw seven ears of grain, ripe and robust,
6 growing on a single stalk. Suddenly, seven other ears sprouted after them, thin

רש״י

מא א| וַיְהִי מִקֵּץ. כְּתַרְגּוּמוֹ "מִסּוֹף", וְכָל לְשׁוֹן 'קֵץ' סוֹף הוּא: עַל הַיְאֹר. כָּל שְׁאָר נְהָרוֹת אֵינָם קְרוּיִין יְאוֹרִים חוּץ מִנִּילוּס, מִפְּנֵי שֶׁכָּל הָאָרֶץ עֲשׂוּיָה יְאוֹרִים יְאוֹרִים בִּידֵי אָדָם וְנִילוּס עוֹלֶה בְּתוֹכָם וּמַשְׁקֶה אוֹתָם, לְפִי שֶׁאֵין גְּשָׁמִים יוֹרְדִין בְּמִצְרַיִם תָּדִיר כִּשְׁאָר אֲרָצוֹת:

ב| יְפוֹת מַרְאֶה. סִימָן הוּא לִימֵי שֹׂבַע, שֶׁהַבְּרִיּוֹת נִרְאוֹת יָפוֹת זוֹ לָזוֹ, שֶׁאֵין עַיִן בְּרִיָּה צָרָה בַּחֲבֶרְתָּהּ: בָּאָחוּ. בָּאֲגַם, מריש"ק בְּלַעַז, כְּמוֹ: "יִשְׂגֶּא אָחוּ" (איוב ח, יא):

ג| וְדַקּוֹת בָּשָׂר. טינבי"ש בְּלַעַז, לְשׁוֹן דַּק:

ד| וַתֹּאכַלְנָה. סִימָן שֶׁתְּהֵא כָּל שִׂמְחַת הַשָּׂבָע נִשְׁכַּחַת בִּימֵי הָרָעָב:

ה| בְּקָנֶה אֶחָד. טודי"ל בְּלַעַז: בְּרִיאוֹת. שיינ"ש בְּלַעַז:

me from this place. The truth is that I was kidnapped from the land of the Hebrews. Here too, I have done nothing to deserve being placed in this pit" (Gen. 40:14–15).

A double injustice has been done, and Yosef sees this as his one chance of regaining his freedom. But the end of the *parasha* delivers a devastating blow: "Still, the chief cupbearer *did not remember* Yosef, he *forgot* him" (40:23). The anticlimax is intense, emphasized by the double verb, "did not remember" and "forgot." We sense Yosef waiting day after day for news. None comes. His last, best hope has gone. He will never go free. Or so it seems.

To understand the power of this anticlimax, we must remember that only since the invention of printing and the free availability of books have we been accustomed to tell what happens next merely by turning a page. For many centuries, there were no printed books. People knew the biblical story primarily by *listening* to it week by week. Someone hearing the story for the first time would have to wait a week to discover what Yosef's fate would be.

The *parasha* break is thus a kind of real-life equivalent to the delay Yosef experienced in jail, which, as we now read, took "two years." It is then that Pharaoh has two dreams that no one in the court can interpret, prompting the chief butler to remember the man he had met in prison. Yosef is now transformed within hours from a prisoner-without-hope to viceroy of the greatest empire of the ancient world.

God answers our prayers – but often not when we thought or how we thought. Yosef seeks to get out of prison, and he does get out of prison. But not immediately, and not because the butler keeps his promise. The story is telling us something fundamental about the relationship between our dreams and our achievements. Yosef is the great dreamer of the Torah, and he becomes a leader, as he dreamed he would. But first he has to hone his practical and administrative skills, first in Potifar's house, then in prison. Even when God assures us that something will happen, it will not happen without our effort. A divine promise is not a *substitute for* human responsibility. To the contrary, it is a *call to* responsibility.

But effort alone is not enough. We need *siyyata diShmaya*, "the help of Heaven." We need the humility to acknowledge that we are dependent on forces not under our control. No one in Genesis invokes God more often than Yosef. He credits God for each of his successes. He recognizes that without

פרשת מקץ

מא א וַיְהִי מִקֵּץ שְׁנָתַיִם יָמִים וּפַרְעֹה חֹלֵם וְהִנֵּה עֹמֵד עַל־הַיְאֹר׃ ב וְהִנֵּה לו
מִן־הַיְאֹר עֹלֹת שֶׁבַע פָּרוֹת יְפוֹת מַרְאֶה וּבְרִיאֹת בָּשָׂר וַתִּרְעֶינָה
ג בָּאָחוּ׃ וְהִנֵּה שֶׁבַע פָּרוֹת אֲחֵרוֹת עֹלוֹת אַחֲרֵיהֶן מִן־הַיְאֹר רָעוֹת
מַרְאֶה וְדַקּוֹת בָּשָׂר וַתַּעֲמֹדְנָה אֵצֶל הַפָּרוֹת עַל־שְׂפַת הַיְאֹר׃
ד וַתֹּאכַלְנָה הַפָּרוֹת רָעוֹת הַמַּרְאֶה וְדַקֹּת הַבָּשָׂר אֵת שֶׁבַע הַפָּרוֹת
ה יְפֹת הַמַּרְאֶה וְהַבְּרִיאֹת וַיִּיקַץ פַּרְעֹה׃ וַיִּישָׁן וַיַּחֲלֹם שֵׁנִית וְהִנֵּה ׀ שֶׁבַע
ו שִׁבֳּלִים עֹלוֹת בְּקָנֶה אֶחָד בְּרִיאוֹת וְטֹבוֹת׃ וְהִנֵּה שֶׁבַע שִׁבֳּלִים דַּקּוֹת

אונקלוס

מא א וַהֲוָה, מִסּוֹף תַּרְתֵּין שְׁנִין, וּפַרְעֹה חָלֵים, וְהָא קָאֵים עַל נַהֲרָא: ב וְהָא מִן נַהֲרָא, סָלְקָן שְׁבַע תּוֹרָן, שַׁפִּירָן לְמִחְזֵי וּפַטִּימָן בְּסַר, וְרָעְיָן בְּאַחֲוָא: ג וְהָא שְׁבַע תּוֹרָן אָחֳרָנְיָן, סָלְקָא בָּתְרֵיהוֹן מִן נַהֲרָא, בִּישָׁן לְמִחְזֵי וַחֲסִירָן בְּסַר, וְקָמָא, לְקִבְלְהוֹן דְּתוֹרָתָא עַל כֵּיף נַהֲרָא: ד וַאֲכַלָא תּוֹרָתָא, דְּבִישָׁן לְמִחְזֵי וַחֲסִירָן בְּסַר, יָת שְׁבַע תּוֹרָתָא, דְּשַׁפִּירָן לְמִחְזֵי וּפַטִּימָתָא, וְאִתְּעַר פַּרְעֹה: ה וּדְמוּךְ, וַחֲלַם תִּנְיָנוּת, וְהָא שְׁבַע שֻׁבְּלִין, סָלְקָן, בְּקַנְיָא חַד פַּטִּימָן וְטָבָן: ו וְהָא שְׁבַע שֻׁבְּלִין, לַקְיָן

MIKETZ

Miketz is dominated by two of the great encounters in the Torah. The first brings about the reversal in Yosef's fortunes. Forgotten and abandoned in prison, he is brought out to interpret Pharaoh's dreams, which he does with ease. Having told Pharaoh that the dreams portend eventual drought and famine, he then articulates a solution to the problem. Pharaoh, impressed, appoints Yosef to high office in Egypt, second only to himself.

The second occurs when Yosef's brothers, driven by famine in Canaan, come to Egypt to buy food. They come before Yosef, but fail to recognize him as their brother, though he recognizes them. Yosef, without disclosing his identity, sets in motion a complex scenario, designed to test his brothers, that reaches a climax in the next *parasha*.

Three tensions come to the fore in this *parasha*. First, the subtle interplay between human choice and divine intervention is traced more delicately here than anywhere else in Tanakh. Next, the conversation between Pharaoh and Yosef exemplifies the interplay of particularity and universality in Judaism. Third, the meeting between Yosef and his brothers takes place in the context of three other narratives of recognition and nonrecognition in Genesis. This turns out to be one of the book's major themes: appearance and reality in human interaction, the difference between who we seem to be and who we are. These three tensions lie at the heart of Judaism, and they reach their fullest exposition here, in the story of Yosef.

"TWO YEARS PASSED"

For the first time in the whole story, Yosef decided, at the end of last week's *parasha*, to take fate into his own hands. Knowing that the chief butler was about to be restored to his position, he asked him to bring his case to the attention of Pharaoh: "When it goes well with you, remember me and do me this kindness: mention me to Pharaoh so as to free

7 and scorched by the east wind. The thin ears swallowed up the seven ripe, full
8 ears. Pharaoh awoke – and realized it had been a dream. In the morning his
mind was troubled, so he sent for all the magicians and sages of Egypt. Pharaoh
told them his dream, but no one could offer an interpretation that satisfied
9 him. Then the chief cupbearer said to Pharaoh, "I must recall my sins today.
10 Once, Pharaoh was angry with his servants and placed me and the chief baker
11 in custody in the house of the captain of the guard. One night he and I each had
12 a dream, and each dream seemed to have its own meaning. With us was a young
Hebrew, a slave of the captain of the guard. We told him our dreams and he
13 interpreted them for us, telling each of us the meaning of his dream. Things
turned out exactly as he interpreted them to us. I was restored to my position,
14 and the baker was hung up." So Pharaoh sent for Yosef. He was rushed from the
dungeon, had his hair cut, changed his clothes, and came before Pharaoh.
15 Pharaoh said to Yosef, "I had a dream and no one can interpret it; I have heard SHENI
16 that when you hear a dream you can interpret it." "Not I," replied Yosef to
17 Pharaoh. "God will give Pharaoh the answer that he needs." Pharaoh told Yosef:
18 "In my dream, I was standing by the bank of the Nile when seven handsome,

רש״י

ו **וּשְׁדוּפֹת.** הַסלִיד״ש בְּלַעַז, ״שְׁקִיפָן קִדּוּם״, חֲבוּטוֹת, לְשׁוֹן מַשְׁקוֹף הֶחָבוּט תָּמִיד עַל יְדֵי הַדֶּלֶת הַמַּכָּה עָלָיו: **קָדִים.** רוּחַ מִזְרָחִית שֶׁקּוֹרִין בי״ש״א:

ז **הַבְּרִיאוֹת.** שיינ״ש בְּלַעַז: **וְהִנֵּה חֲלוֹם.** וְהִנֵּה נִשְׁלַם חֲלוֹם שָׁלֵם לְפָנָיו וְהֻצְרַךְ לְפוֹתְרִים:

ח **וַתִּפָּעֶם רוּחוֹ.** ״וּמִטָּרְפָא רוּחֵיהּ״, מְקַשְׁקֶשֶׁת בְּתוֹכוֹ כְּפַעֲמוֹן. וּבִנְבוּכַדְנֶצַּר אוֹמֵר: ״וַתִּתְפָּעֶם רוּחוֹ״ (דניאל ב, א), לְפִי שֶׁהָיוּ שָׁם שְׁתֵּי פְעִימוֹת: שִׁכְחַת הַחֲלוֹם וְהַעֲלָמַת פִּתְרוֹנוֹ: **חַרְטֻמֵּי.** הַנֵּחָרִים בְּטִימֵי מֵתִים, שֶׁשּׁוֹאֲלִים בַּעֲצָמוֹת. 'טִימֵי' הֵן עֲצָמוֹת בִּלְשׁוֹן אֲרַמִּי, וּבַמִּשְׁנָה: בַּיִת שֶׁהוּא מָלֵא טִימַיָא – מָלֵא עֲצָמוֹת: **וְאֵין פּוֹתֵר אוֹתָם לְפַרְעֹה.** פּוֹתְרִים הָיוּ אוֹתָם, אֲבָל לֹא לְפַרְעֹה, שֶׁלֹּא הָיָה קוֹלָן נִכְנָס בְּאָזְנָיו וְלֹא הָיָה לוֹ קוֹרַת רוּחַ בְּפִתְרוֹנָם, שֶׁהָיוּ אוֹמְרִים: שֶׁבַע בָּנוֹת אַתָּה מוֹלִיד, שֶׁבַע בָּנוֹת אַתָּה קוֹבֵר:

יא **אִישׁ כְּפִתְרוֹן חֲלֹמוֹ.** חֲלוֹם הָרָאוּי לַפִּתְרוֹן שֶׁנִּפְתַּר לָנוּ וְדוֹמֶה לוֹ:

יב **נַעַר עִבְרִי עֶבֶד.** אֲרוּרִים הָרְשָׁעִים שֶׁאֵין טוֹבָתָם שְׁלֵמָה, מַזְכִּירוֹ בִּלְשׁוֹן בִּזָּיוֹן: ״נַעַר״ – שׁוֹטֶה וְאֵין רָאוּי לִגְדֻלָּה. ״עִבְרִי״ – אֲפִלּוּ לְשׁוֹנֵנוּ אֵינוֹ מַכִּיר. ״עֶבֶד״ – וְכָתוּב בְּנִמּוּסֵי מִצְרַיִם שֶׁאֵין עֶבֶד מוֹלֵךְ וְלֹא לוֹבֵשׁ בִּגְדֵי שָׂרִים: **אִישׁ כַּחֲלֹמוֹ.** לְפִי הַחֲלוֹם וְקָרוֹב לְעִנְיָנוֹ:

יג **אֹתִי הֵשִׁיב עַל כַּנִּי.** פַּרְעֹה הַנִּזְכָּר לְמַעְלָה, כְּמוֹ שֶׁאָמַר: ״פַּרְעֹה קָצַף עַל עֲבָדָיו״ (לעיל פסוק י):

יד **מִן הַבּוֹר.** מִן בֵּית הַסֹּהַר שֶׁהוּא עָשׂוּי כְּמִין גֻּמָּא, וְכֵן כָּל בּוֹר שֶׁבַּמִּקְרָא לְשׁוֹן גֻּמָּא הוּא, וְאַף אִם אֵין בּוֹ מַיִם קָרוּי בּוֹר, פוס״א בְּלַעַז: **וַיְגַלַּח.** מִפְּנֵי כְּבוֹד הַמַּלְכוּת:

טו **תִּשְׁמַע חֲלוֹם לִפְתֹּר אֹתוֹ.** תַּאֲזִין וְתָבִין חֲלוֹם לִפְתֹּר אוֹתוֹ. ״תִּשְׁמַע״ – לְשׁוֹן הֲבָנָה וְהַאֲזָנָה, כְּמוֹ: ״שֹׁמֵעַ יוֹסֵף״ (להלן מב, כג), ״אֲשֶׁר לֹא תִשְׁמַע לְשֹׁנוֹ״ (דברים כח, מט), אנטנדר״א בְּלַעַז:

טז **בִּלְעָדָי.** אֵין הַחָכְמָה מִשֶּׁלִּי, אֶלָּא ״אֱלֹהִים יַעֲנֶה״ – יִתֵּן עֲנִיָּה בְּפִי לִשְׁלוֹם פַּרְעֹה:

them to God. As R. Akiva said: "All is foreseen yet freedom of choice is given" (Avot 3:15). We and God are co-authors of the human story. Judaism found a simple way of resolving the paradox. For the bad we do, we take responsibility. For the good we achieve, we thank God. In this, Yosef is our mentor.

ז וּשְׁדוּפֹת קָדִים צֹמְחוֹת אַחֲרֵיהֶן: וַתִּבְלַעְנָה הַשִּׁבֳּלִים הַדַּקּוֹת אֵת
ח שֶׁבַע הַשִּׁבֳּלִים הַבְּרִיאוֹת וְהַמְּלֵאוֹת וַיִּיקַץ פַּרְעֹה וְהִנֵּה חֲלוֹם: וַיְהִי
בַבֹּקֶר וַתִּפָּעֶם רוּחוֹ וַיִּשְׁלַח וַיִּקְרָא אֶת־כָּל־חַרְטֻמֵּי מִצְרַיִם וְאֶת־
כָּל־חֲכָמֶיהָ וַיְסַפֵּר פַּרְעֹה לָהֶם אֶת־חֲלֹמוֹ וְאֵין־פּוֹתֵר אוֹתָם לְפַרְעֹה:
ט וַיְדַבֵּר שַׂר הַמַּשְׁקִים אֶת־פַּרְעֹה לֵאמֹר אֶת־חֲטָאַי אֲנִי מַזְכִּיר הַיּוֹם:
י פַּרְעֹה קָצַף עַל־עֲבָדָיו וַיִּתֵּן אֹתִי בְּמִשְׁמַר בֵּית שַׂר הַטַּבָּחִים אֹתִי
יא וְאֵת שַׂר הָאֹפִים: וַנַּחַלְמָה חֲלוֹם בְּלַיְלָה אֶחָד אֲנִי וָהוּא אִישׁ כְּפִתְרוֹן
יב חֲלֹמוֹ חָלָמְנוּ: וְשָׁם אִתָּנוּ נַעַר עִבְרִי עֶבֶד לְשַׂר הַטַּבָּחִים וַנְּסַפֶּר־לוֹ
יג וַיִּפְתָּר־לָנוּ אֶת־חֲלֹמֹתֵינוּ אִישׁ כַּחֲלֹמוֹ פָּתָר: וַיְהִי כַּאֲשֶׁר פָּתַר־לָנוּ
יד כֵּן הָיָה אֹתִי הֵשִׁיב עַל־כַּנִּי וְאֹתוֹ תָלָה: וַיִּשְׁלַח פַּרְעֹה וַיִּקְרָא אֶת־
טו יוֹסֵף וַיְרִיצֻהוּ מִן־הַבּוֹר וַיְגַלַּח וַיְחַלֵּף שִׂמְלֹתָיו וַיָּבֹא אֶל־פַּרְעֹה: וַיֹּאמֶר שני
פַּרְעֹה אֶל־יוֹסֵף חֲלוֹם חָלַמְתִּי וּפֹתֵר אֵין אֹתוֹ וַאֲנִי שָׁמַעְתִּי עָלֶיךָ
טז לֵאמֹר תִּשְׁמַע חֲלוֹם לִפְתֹּר אֹתוֹ: וַיַּעַן יוֹסֵף אֶת־פַּרְעֹה לֵאמֹר בִּלְעָדָי
יז אֱלֹהִים יַעֲנֶה אֶת־שְׁלוֹם פַּרְעֹה: וַיְדַבֵּר פַּרְעֹה אֶל־יוֹסֵף בַּחֲלֹמִי הִנְנִי
יח עֹמֵד עַל־שְׂפַת הַיְאֹר: וְהִנֵּה מִן־הַיְאֹר עֹלֹת שֶׁבַע פָּרוֹת בְּרִיאוֹת

אונקלוס

וּשְׁקִיפָן קִדּוּם, צָמְחָן בָּתְרֵיהוֹן: ז וּבְלַעָא שֻׁבְּלַיָּא לַקְיָתָא, יָת שְׁבַע
שֻׁבְּלַיָּא, פַּטִּימָתָא וּמַלְיָתָא, וְאִתְּעַר פַּרְעֹה וְהָא חֶלְמָא: ח וַהֲוָה
בְּצַפְרָא וּמִטָּרְפָא רוּחֵיהּ, וּשְׁלַח, וּקְרָא, יָת כָּל חָרָשֵׁי מִצְרַיִם וְיָת
כָּל חַכִּימַהָא, וְאִשְׁתְּעִי פַּרְעֹה לְהוֹן יָת חֶלְמֵיהּ, וְלֵית דְּפָשַׁר יָתְהוֹן
לְפַרְעֹה: ט וּמַלֵּיל רַב שָׁקֵי, עִם פַּרְעֹה לְמֵימַר, יָת סָרְחָנַי, אֲנָא מַדְכַּר
יוֹמָא דֵין: י פַּרְעֹה רְגִיז עַל עַבְדּוֹהִי, וִיהַב יָתִי בְּמַטְּרַת, בֵּית רַב קָטוֹלַיָּא,
יָתִי, וְיָת רַב נַחְתּוֹמֵי: יא וַחֲלַמְנָא חֶלְמָא, בְּלֵילְיָא חַד אֲנָא וְהוּא, גְּבַר,
כְּפֻשְׁרַן חֶלְמֵיהּ חֲלַמְנָא: יב וְתַמָּן עִמַּנָא עוּלֵים עִבְרַאי, עַבְדָּא לְרַב
קָטוֹלַיָּא, וְאִשְׁתָּעֵינָא לֵיהּ, וּפְשַׁר לָנָא יָת חֶלְמַנָא, גְּבַר כְּחֶלְמֵיהּ פְּשַׁר:
יג וַהֲוָה, כְּמָא דִּפְשַׁר לָנָא כֵּן הֲוָה, יָתִי, אֲתֵיב עַל שִׁמּוּשִׁי וְיָתֵיהּ צְלַב:
יד וּשְׁלַח פַּרְעֹה וּקְרָא יָת יוֹסֵף, וְאַרְהֲטוּהִי מִן בֵּית אֲסִירֵי, וְסַפַּר וְשַׁנִּי
כְּסוּתֵיהּ, וְעָאל לְוָת פַּרְעֹה: טו וַאֲמַר פַּרְעֹה לְיוֹסֵף, חֶלְמָא חֲלָמִית,
וּפָשַׁר לֵית לֵיהּ, וַאֲנָא, שְׁמָעִית עֲלָךְ לְמֵימַר, דְּאַתְּ שָׁמַע חֶלְמָא
וּמְפַשַּׁר לֵיהּ: טז וַאֲתֵיב יוֹסֵף יָת פַּרְעֹה, לְמֵימַר לָא מִן חָכְמְתִי, אֱלָהֵין
מִן קֳדָם יְיָ, יִתְּתַב שְׁלָמָא דְפַרְעֹה: יז וּמַלֵּיל פַּרְעֹה עִם יוֹסֵף, בְּחֶלְמִי,
הָאֲנָא קָאֵים עַל כֵּיף נַהֲרָא: יח וְהָא מִן נַהֲרָא, סָלְקָן שְׁבַע תּוֹרָן, פַּטִּימָן

41:16 בִּלְעָדָי *Not I* –When Yosef is forced to act harshly, he weeps. But when he speaks of his successes, he attributes God he could not have done what he does. And out of that humility comes patience.

19 healthy cows came up out of the river and grazed among the reeds. Then after
them came seven other cows, scrawny, very sickly, and thin – I never saw such
20 sickly cows in all Egypt. Then the thin, sickly cows ate up the first seven healthy
21 cows. But when they had eaten them you could not tell that they had eaten
22 them, for they still looked as bad as before. Then I awoke. In my dream I then
23 saw seven ears of grain, ripe and full, growing on a single stalk. Suddenly, seven
other ears sprouted after them, shriveled, thin, and scorched by the east wind,
24 and the thin ears swallowed the seven good ears. I told this to the magicians,
25 but none could explain it to me." Yosef said to Pharaoh, "The two dreams of
Pharaoh are one and the same. God has told Pharaoh what He is about to do.
26 The seven good cows are seven years, and so too the seven good ears are seven
27 years. It is one and the same dream. The seven thin, sickly cows that came up
after them are seven years, as are the seven empty ears scorched by the east
28 wind. They are seven years of famine. It is as I have told Pharaoh: God has
29 shown Pharaoh what He is about to do. Seven years are coming when there will
30 be great abundance throughout the land of Egypt. But after them will come
seven years of famine, when all the abundance in Egypt will be forgotten.

רש״י

יט **דַּלּוֹת.** כְּחוּשׁוֹת, כְּמוֹ: "מַדּוּעַ אַתָּה כָּכָה דַּל" (שמואל ב׳ יג, ד) דְּאַמְנוֹן: **וְרַקּוֹת בָּשָׂר.** כָּל לְשׁוֹן 'רַקּוֹת' שֶׁבַּתּוֹרָה "חֲסֵירָן בְּשַׂר", וּבְלַעַז בלוש"ש:

כג **צְנֻמוֹת.** 'צוֹנְמָא' בִּלְשׁוֹן אֲרַמִּי סֶלַע, הֲרֵי הֵן כְּעֵץ בְּלִי לַחְלוּחַ, קָשׁוֹת כְּסֶלַע; וְתַרְגּוּמוֹ 'נָצַן לָקְיָן'; 'נָצַן' – אֵין בָּהֶן אֶלָּא הַנֵּץ לְפִי שֶׁנִּתְרוֹקְנוּ מִן הַזֶּרַע:

כה-לב **שֶׁבַע שָׁנִים וְשֶׁבַע שָׁנִים.** כֻּלָּן אֵינָן אֶלָּא שֶׁבַע, וַאֲשֶׁר נִשְׁנָה הַחֲלוֹם פַּעֲמַיִם לְפִי שֶׁהַדָּבָר מְזֻמָּן, כְּמוֹ שֶׁפֵּרֵשׁ לוֹ בַּסּוֹף: "וְעַל הִשָּׁנוֹת הַחֲלוֹם" וְגוֹ׳: **וְנִשְׁכַּח כָּל הַשָּׂבָע.** הוּא פִּתְרוֹן הַבְּלִיעָה: **וְלֹא יִוָּדַע הַשָּׂבָע.** הוּא פִּתְרוֹן "וְלֹא נוֹדַע כִּי בָאוּ אֶל קִרְבֶּנָה" (לעיל פסוק כא): **נָכוֹן.** מְזֻמָּן. כְּשֶׁבַע שָׁנִים הַטּוֹבוֹת נֶאֱמַר: "הִגִּיד לְפַרְעֹה" (פסוק כה), לְפִי שֶׁהָיָה סָמוּךְ, וּבְשֶׁבַע שְׁנֵי רָעָב נֶאֱמַר: "הֶרְאָה אֶת פַּרְעֹה" (פסוק כח), לְפִי שֶׁהָיָה הַדָּבָר מֻפְלָג וְרָחוֹק נוֹפֵל בּוֹ לְשׁוֹן מַרְאֶה:

41:27 **שֶׁבַע שְׁנֵי רָעָב** *Seven years of famine* – Yosef's interpretations are neither magical nor miraculous. In the case of the butler and baker, he remembers that in three days' time it will be Pharaoh's birthday (Gen. 40:20). It was the custom of rulers to make a feast on their birthday and decide the fate of certain individuals (in Britain, the monarch's birthday honors continue this tradition). It is reasonable therefore to assume that the butler's and baker's dreams relate to this event and their unconscious hopes and fears (Ibn Ezra 40:12 and *Bekhor Shor* 40:12 both make this suggestion).

In the case of Pharaoh's dreams, Yosef may know ancient Egyptian traditions about seven-year famines. Nahum Sarna quotes an Egyptian text from the reign of King Djoser (ca. twenty-eighth century BCE):

> I was in distress on the Great Throne, and those who are in the palace were in heart's affliction from a very great evil, since the Nile had not come in my time for a space of seven years. Grain was scant, fruits were dried up, and everything which they eat was short. (*Understanding Genesis*)

What Pharaoh terms "the spirit of God" (41:38) in Yosef might in this case be something that we would call "insight."

יט בָּשָׂר וִיפֹת תֹּאַר וַתִּרְעֶינָה בָּאָחוּ: וְהִנֵּה שֶׁבַע פָּרוֹת אֲחֵרוֹת עֹלוֹת
אַחֲרֵיהֶן דַּלּוֹת וְרָעוֹת תֹּאַר מְאֹד וְרַקּוֹת בָּשָׂר לֹא־רָאִיתִי כָהֵנָּה
כ בְּכָל־אֶרֶץ מִצְרַיִם לָרֹעַ: וַתֹּאכַלְנָה הַפָּרוֹת הָרַקּוֹת וְהָרָעוֹת אֵת שֶׁבַע
כא הַפָּרוֹת הָרִאשֹׁנוֹת הַבְּרִיאֹת: וַתָּבֹאנָה אֶל־קִרְבֶּנָה וְלֹא נוֹדַע כִּי־בָאוּ
כב אֶל־קִרְבֶּנָה וּמַרְאֵיהֶן רַע כַּאֲשֶׁר בַּתְּחִלָּה וָאִיקָץ: וָאֵרֶא בַּחֲלֹמִי
כג וְהִנֵּה ׀ שֶׁבַע שִׁבֳּלִים עֹלֹת בְּקָנֶה אֶחָד מְלֵאֹת וְטֹבוֹת: וְהִנֵּה שֶׁבַע
כד שִׁבֳּלִים צְנֻמוֹת דַּקּוֹת שְׁדֻפוֹת קָדִים צֹמְחוֹת אַחֲרֵיהֶם: וַתִּבְלַעְןָ
הַשִּׁבֳּלִים הַדַּקֹּת אֵת שֶׁבַע הַשִּׁבֳּלִים הַטֹּבוֹת וָאֹמַר אֶל־הַחַרְטֻמִּים
כה וְאֵין מַגִּיד לִי: וַיֹּאמֶר יוֹסֵף אֶל־פַּרְעֹה חֲלוֹם פַּרְעֹה אֶחָד הוּא אֵת
כו אֲשֶׁר הָאֱלֹהִים עֹשֶׂה הִגִּיד לְפַרְעֹה: שֶׁבַע פָּרֹת הַטֹּבֹת שֶׁבַע שָׁנִים
כז הֵנָּה וְשֶׁבַע הַשִּׁבֳּלִים הַטֹּבֹת שֶׁבַע שָׁנִים הֵנָּה חֲלוֹם אֶחָד הוּא: וְשֶׁבַע
הַפָּרוֹת הָרַקּוֹת וְהָרָעֹת הָעֹלֹת אַחֲרֵיהֶן שֶׁבַע שָׁנִים הֵנָּה וְשֶׁבַע
כח הַשִּׁבֳּלִים הָרֵקוֹת שְׁדֻפוֹת הַקָּדִים יִהְיוּ שֶׁבַע שְׁנֵי רָעָב: הוּא הַדָּבָר
אֲשֶׁר דִּבַּרְתִּי אֶל־פַּרְעֹה אֲשֶׁר הָאֱלֹהִים עֹשֶׂה הֶרְאָה אֶת־פַּרְעֹה:
כט ל הִנֵּה שֶׁבַע שָׁנִים בָּאוֹת שָׂבָע גָּדוֹל בְּכָל־אֶרֶץ מִצְרָיִם: וְקָמוּ שֶׁבַע
שְׁנֵי רָעָב אַחֲרֵיהֶן וְנִשְׁכַּח כָּל־הַשָּׂבָע בְּאֶרֶץ מִצְרָיִם וְכִלָּה הָרָעָב

אונקלוס

בְּסַר וְשַׁפִּירָן לְמֶחֱזֵי, וְרָעְיָן בְּאַחְוָא: יט וְהָא, שְׁבַע תּוֹרָן אָחֳרָנְיָן סָלְקָא בָּתְרֵיהוֹן, חֲסִיכָן וּבִישָׁן לְמֶחֱזֵי, לַחֲדָא וַחֲסִירָן בְּסַר, לָא חֲזֵיתִי דִּכְוָתְהוֹן, בְּכָל אַרְעָא דְּמִצְרַיִם לְבִישׁוּ: כ וַאֲכַלָא תּוֹרָתָא, חֲסִיכָתָא וּבִישָׁתָא, יָת שְׁבַע תּוֹרָתָא, קַדְמָיָתָא פַּטִּימָתָא: כא וְעָאלָא לִמְעֵיהוֹן, וְלָא אִתְיְדַע אֲרֵי עָאלָא לִמְעֵיהוֹן, וּמֶחֱזֵיהוֹן בִּישׁ, כַּד בְּקַדְמֵיתָא, וְאִתְּעָרִית: כב וַחֲזֵית בְּחֶלְמִי, וְהָא שְׁבַע שֻׁבְּלִין, סָלְקָן, בְּקַנְיָא חַד מַלְיָן וְטָבָן: כג וְהָא שְׁבַע שֻׁבְּלִין, נָצָן לָקְיָן שְׁקִיפָן קִדּוּם, צָמְחָן בָּתְרֵיהוֹן: כד וּבְלַעָא שֻׁבְּלַיָּא לָקְיָתָא, יָת שְׁבַע שֻׁבְּלַיָּא טָבָתָא, וַאֲמָרִית לְחָרָשַׁיָּא, וְלֵית דִּמְחַוֵּי לִי: כה וַאֲמַר יוֹסֵף לְפַרְעֹה,

חֶלְמָא דְּפַרְעֹה חַד הוּא, יָת דַּיְיָ, עָתִיד לְמֶעְבַּד חַוִּי לְפַרְעֹה: כו שְׁבַע תּוֹרָתָא טָבָתָא, שְׁבַע שְׁנַיָּא אִנּוּן, וּשְׁבַע שֻׁבְּלַיָּא טָבָתָא, שְׁבַע שְׁנַיָּא אִנּוּן, חֶלְמָא חַד הוּא: כז וּשְׁבַע תּוֹרָתָא, חֲסִיכָתָא וּבִישָׁתָא דִּסְלִיקָא בָּתְרֵיהוֹן, שְׁבַע שְׁנַיָּא אִנּוּן, וּשְׁבַע שֻׁבְּלַיָּא לָקְיָתָא, דִּשְׁקִיפָן קִדּוּם, יְהֶוְיָן, שְׁבַע שְׁנֵי כַפְנָא: כח הוּא פִּתְגָּמָא, דְּמַלֵּילִית עִם פַּרְעֹה, דַּיְיָ, עָתִיד לְמֶעְבַּד אַחְזֵי יָת פַּרְעֹה: כט הָא, שְׁבַע שְׁנַיָּא אָתְיָן, סִבְעָא רַבָּא בְּכָל אַרְעָא דְּמִצְרָיִם: ל וִיקוּמוּן, שְׁבַע שְׁנֵי כַפְנָא בָּתְרֵיהוֹן, וְיִתְנְשֵׁי כָּל סִבְעָא בְּאַרְעָא דְּמִצְרָיִם, וִישֵׁיצֵי כַפְנָא

31 Famine will ravage the land. So devastating will the famine be that no one in
32 the land will know anything of abundance anymore. As for Pharaoh having the
same dream twice, this means that the matter has already been decided by God,
33 and He is soon to bring it about. So now let Pharaoh seek out an astute, wise
34 man and set him over the land of Egypt. Let Pharaoh appoint overseers across
the land and take a fifth of Egypt's harvest during the seven years of abundance.
35 Let them gather all that food in these coming good years, storing the grain
36 under Pharaoh's aegis so that there is food under guard in all the cities. The
food should be held in reserve for the land when the seven years of famine
37 come to Egypt, so that the country is not ruined by the famine." The plan
38 seemed good to Pharaoh and all his officials. Pharaoh said to them, "Could we

רש״י

לד| **וְחִמֵּשׁ.** כְּתַרְגּוּמוֹ: "וִיזָרְזוּן", וְכֵן: "וַחֲמֻשִׁים" (שמות יג, יח):

לה| **אֶת כָּל אֹכֶל.** שֵׁם דָּבָר הוּא, לְפִיכָךְ טַעְמוֹ בָּחָלֶ"ף וְנָקוּד בְּפַתָּח קָטָן (סגול). וְ'אוֹכֵל' שֶׁהוּא פּוֹעֵל, כְּגוֹן: "כִּי כָּל אֹכֵל חֵלֶב" (ויקרא ז, כה), טַעְמוֹ לְמַטָּה בַּכָּ"ף וְנָקוּד קָמָץ (צירי): **תַּחַת יַד פַּרְעֹה.** בִּרְשׁוּתוֹ וּבְאוֹצְרוֹתָיו:

לו| **וְהָיָה הָאֹכֶל.** הַצָּבוּר כְּשְׁאָר פִּקָּדוֹן גָּנוּז לְקִיּוּם הָאָרֶץ:

betray people. Dreams are mere dreams. Hopes are destined to be dashed on the rocks of reality.

But as events unfold in Miketz, we realize that at a deeper level some other force has been at work all along. God has been monitoring the entire sequence of events, arranging the necessary strategic interventions to ensure that the outcome will be as planned. This is not obvious, as it is, for example, in the story of the exodus. Here it is concealed. It takes reflection and the ability to read beneath the surface to sense it at all. This is more than a story about Yosef. It is a story about each of us. In Shakespeare's words, "There's a divinity that shapes our ends, rough-hew them how we will." It is only in retrospect that we understand the story of our life.

41:37 **וַיִּיטַב הַדָּבָר** *The plan seemed good* – Yosef has three gifts that many people have in isolation but few have in combination. The first is that he dreams dreams. Dreaming is often thought to be impractical. Not so; it is one of the most practical things we can do. There are people who spend months planning a holiday but not even a day planning a life. They let themselves be carried by the winds of chance and circumstance. That is a mistake. It is our dreams that give us direction.

Second, Yosef can interpret the dreams of others. Leaders interpret other people's dreams. They articulate the inchoate. They find a way of expressing the hopes and fears of a generation. Martin Luther King Jr.'s "I have a dream" speech was about taking the hopes of African Americans and giving them wings. Similarly, it is not Yosef's dreams that made him a leader; it is Pharaoh's. Our own dreams give us direction; it is other people's dreams that give us opportunity.

Yosef's most impressive achievement, though, is his third gift, the ability to implement dreams, solving the problem for which they are an early warning. No sooner has he told of a seven-year famine than he continues, without pause, to provide a solution.

Good leaders either are, or surround themselves with, problem solvers. It is easy to see what is going wrong. What makes someone a leader is the ability to find a way of putting it right.

Dream dreams, understand and articulate the dreams of others, and find ways of turning a dream into a reality – these three gifts are Yosef's lessons in leadership.

לא אֶת־הָאָרֶץ׃ וְלֹא־יִוָּדַע הַשָּׂבָע בָּאָרֶץ מִפְּנֵי הָרָעָב הַהוּא אַחֲרֵי־כֵן
לב כִּי־כָבֵד הוּא מְאֹד׃ וְעַל הִשָּׁנוֹת הַחֲלוֹם אֶל־פַּרְעֹה פַּעֲמָיִם כִּי־נָכוֹן
לג הַדָּבָר מֵעִם הָאֱלֹהִים וּמְמַהֵר הָאֱלֹהִים לַעֲשֹׂתוֹ׃ וְעַתָּה יֵרֶא פַרְעֹה
לד אִישׁ נָבוֹן וְחָכָם וִישִׁיתֵהוּ עַל־אֶרֶץ מִצְרָיִם׃ יַעֲשֶׂה פַרְעֹה וְיַפְקֵד
פְּקִדִים עַל־הָאָרֶץ וְחִמֵּשׁ אֶת־אֶרֶץ מִצְרַיִם בְּשֶׁבַע שְׁנֵי הַשָּׂבָע׃
לה וְיִקְבְּצוּ אֶת־כָּל־אֹכֶל הַשָּׁנִים הַטֹּבֹת הַבָּאֹת הָאֵלֶּה וְיִצְבְּרוּ־בָר תַּחַת
לו יַד־פַּרְעֹה אֹכֶל בֶּעָרִים וְשָׁמָרוּ׃ וְהָיָה הָאֹכֶל לְפִקָּדוֹן לָאָרֶץ לְשֶׁבַע
שְׁנֵי הָרָעָב אֲשֶׁר תִּהְיֶיןָ בְּאֶרֶץ מִצְרָיִם וְלֹא־תִכָּרֵת הָאָרֶץ בָּרָעָב׃
לז לח וַיִּיטַב הַדָּבָר בְּעֵינֵי פַרְעֹה וּבְעֵינֵי כָּל־עֲבָדָיו׃ וַיֹּאמֶר פַּרְעֹה אֶל־עֲבָדָיו לז

אונקלוס

יָת עַמָּא דְאַרְעָא: לא וְלָא יִתְיְדַע סִבְעָא בְּאַרְעָא, מִן קֳדָם, כַּפְנָא
הַהוּא דִּיהֵי בָתַר כֵּן, אֲרֵי תַּקִּיף הוּא לַחֲדָא: לב וְעַל דְּאִתְּנִי חֶלְמָא,
לְפַרְעֹה תַּרְתֵּין זִמְנִין, אֲרֵי תָקִּין פִּתְגָמָא מִן קֳדָם יְיָ, וּמוֹחֵי יְיָ לְמֶעְבְּדֵיהּ:
לג וּכְעַן יֶחֱזֵי פַרְעֹה, גְּבַר סָכְלְתָן וְחַכִּים, וִימַנֵּינֵיהּ עַל אַרְעָא דְמִצְרָיִם:
לד יַעֲבֵיד פַּרְעֹה, וִימַנֵּי מְהֵימְנִין עַל אַרְעָא, וִיזָרְזוּן יָת אַרְעָא דְמִצְרַיִם,
בְּשַׁבַע שְׁנֵי סִבְעָא: לה וְיִכְנְשׁוּן, יָת כָּל עֲבוּר שְׁנַיָּא טָבָתָא, דְּאָתְיָן
אִלֵּין, וְיִצְבְּרוּן עֲבוּרָא, תְּחוֹת יַד מְהֵימְנֵי פַרְעֹה, עֲבוּרָא בְּקִרְוַיָּא
וְיִטְּרוּן: לו וִיהֵי עֲבוּרָא גְּנִיז לְעַמָּא דְאַרְעָא, לְשֶׁבַע שְׁנֵי כַפְנָא, דִּיהוֹיָן
בְּאַרְעָא דְמִצְרָיִם, וְלָא יִשְׁתֵּיצֵי עַמָּא דְאַרְעָא בְּכַפְנָא: לז וּשְׁפַר
פִּתְגָמָא בְּעֵינֵי פַרְעֹה, וּבְעֵינֵי כָּל עַבְדּוֹהִי: לח וַאֲמַר פַּרְעֹה לְעַבְדּוֹהִי,

41:32 וּמְמַהֵר הָאֱלֹהִים לַעֲשֹׂתוֹ *He is soon to bring it about* – Pharaoh has not one dream, but two: one about cows, the other about ears of grain. Yosef explains that they are, substantively, the same dream, conveying the same message through different images. In the immediate context, this is just another piece of information about Egypt and its future. Viewed within the full context of Yosef's life story, however, it changes our entire understanding of events. For it is not Pharaoh alone who has two dreams with a similar structure. Yosef does as well. At the very beginning of the story, he dreams, once of sheaves of wheat bowing down to his sheaf, and then about the sun, moon, and stars bowing down to him.

At that stage we had no idea what the dreams signified. Were they a prophecy, or the fruit of the fevered imagination of an overindulged, overambitious boy? The tension in Yosef's narrative depends on this ambiguity. Only now, chapters and years later, are we given the vital information: a dream, repeated in different images, is not just a dream. It is a message sent by God about a future that will soon come to pass. Only in retrospect do we realize that Yosef's double dream was a sign that this too was no mere imagining. Yosef really is destined to be a leader to whom his family will bow.

There are several possible reasons why we were not given this information earlier. It may be that Yosef has only now come to understand it. Or it may simply be a literary device to create and maintain tension in the unfolding plot. It is also possible, though, that it signals something altogether deeper about the human condition seen through the eyes of faith. On the surface, the story of Yosef is about human beings and their relationships. It is not a happy story. People

39 find another like him, a man who has within him the spirit of God?" So Pharaoh SHELISHI
said to Yosef, "Since God has made all this known to you, there can be no one
40 else as astute or as wise as you. You shall be in charge of my court, and by your
command shall all my people be directed. Only the throne itself will make me
41 greater than you." Then Pharaoh said to Yosef, "I hereby place you in charge of
42 all the land of Egypt." Pharaoh removed his signet ring from his hand and
placed it on Yosef's. He had him robed in garments of the finest linen, and
43 placed a gold chain around his neck. He had him ride in the chariot of his
second-in-command, and ahead of him people proclaimed, "*Avrekh*." Thus was
44 he given authority over all Egypt. Pharaoh told Yosef, "I am Pharaoh, but

רש"י

לח **הנמצא כזה.** "הנשכח כדין", אם נלך ונבקשנו הנמצא כמוהו? 'הנמצא' לשון תמיהה, וכן כל ה"א המשמשת בראש תבה ונקודה בחטף פתח:

לט **אין נבון וחכם כמוך.** לבקש "איש נבון וחכם" שאמרת (לעיל פסוק לג), לא נמצא כמוך:

מ **ישק.** "יתזן", יתפרנס; כל צרכי עמי יהיו נעשים על ידך, כמו: "ובן משק ביתי" (לעיל טו, ב), וכמו: "נשקו בר" (תהלים ב, יב), גרניסו"ן בלעז: **רק הכסא.** שיהיו קורין לי מלך: **כסא.** לשון שם המלוכה, כמו: "ויגדל את כסאו מכסא אדני המלך" (מלכים א' א, לז):

מא **נתתי אתך.** "מניתי יתך"; ואף על פי כן לשון נתינה הוא, כמו: "ולתתך עליון" (דברים כו, יט). בין לגדלה בין לשפלות נופל לשון נתינה עליו, כמו: "נתתי אתכם נבזים ושפלים" (מלאכי ב, ט):

מב **ויסר פרעה את טבעתו.** נתינת טבעת המלך היא אות למי שנותנה לו להיות שני לו לגדלה: **בגדי שש.** דבר חשיבות הוא במצרים: **רבד.** ענק, ועל שהוא רצוף בטבעות קרוי 'רביד'; וכן: "רבדתי ערשי" (משלי ז, טז), רצפתי ערשי מרצפות. ובלשון משנה: "מקף רובדין של אבן" (מדות א, ח), "על הרובד שבעזרה" (יומא מג ע"ב), והיא רצפה:

מג **במרכבת המשנה.** השניה למרכבתו, המהלכת אצל שלו: **אברך.** כתרגומו: "דין אבא למלכא", 'רך' בלשון ארמי מלך, ב'השותפין': "לא ריכא ולא בר ריכא" (בבא בתרא ד ע"א). ובדברי אגדה, דרש רבי יהודה: "אברך" זה יוסף, שהוא אב בחכמה ורך בשנים. אמר לו רבי יוסי בן דורמסקית: ברבי, עד מתי אתה מעוות עלינו את הכתובים? אין 'אברך' אלא לשון ברכים, שהכל יהו נכנסין ויוצאין תחת ידו, כענין שנאמר: "ונתון אתו" וגו':

מד **אני פרעה.** שיש יכלת בידי לגזר גזרות על מלכותי, ואני גוזר שלא ירים איש את ידו בלעדיך, שלא ברשותך. דבר אחר, "אני פרעה", אני אהיה מלך, "ובלעדיך" וגו', זו דגמת "רק הכסא אגדל ממך" (לעיל פסוק מ) אלא שהצרך לפרש לו בשעת נתינת הטבעת: **את ידו ואת רגלו.** כתרגומו:

to HaLevi, God's proper name. Just as "the first patriarch" (a generic description) was called Avraham (a name), so "the Author of being" (*Elokim*) has a proper name, *Hashem*.

The story of Yosef is one of those relatively rare narratives in Tanakh in which a Jew (Israelite/Hebrew) comes to play a prominent part in a gentile society. As we search in the twenty-first century for a way to avoid a "clash of civilizations," it seems to me that humanity can learn much from the ancient and still compelling way of understanding the human condition that arises from his story. We are all "the image and likeness" of God – the One God we call *Elokim*. But there are many ways, each distinct and unique, in which different cultures and civilizations define their relationship with the Author of all being. We do not presume to judge them, except insofar as they succeed or fail in honoring the basic, universal principles of human dignity. We as Jews are (or should be) secure in our relationship with *Hashem*, the God who has revealed Himself in the intimacy of love, whose expression is Torah. Today, as then, the challenge of faith is to be true to our particular heritage while being a blessing to others, whatever their heritage. That is a formula for peace and graciousness in an era badly in need of both.

לט הֲנִמְצָא כָזֶה אִישׁ אֲשֶׁר רוּחַ אֱלֹהִים בּוֹ: וַיֹּאמֶר פַּרְעֹה אֶל־יוֹסֵף אַחֲרֵי שלישי
מ הוֹדִיעַ אֱלֹהִים אוֹתְךָ אֶת־כָּל־זֹאת אֵין־נָבוֹן וְחָכָם כָּמוֹךָ: אַתָּה
מא תִּהְיֶה עַל־בֵּיתִי וְעַל־פִּיךָ יִשַּׁק כָּל־עַמִּי רַק הַכִּסֵּא אֶגְדַּל מִמֶּךָּ: וַיֹּאמֶר
מב פַּרְעֹה אֶל־יוֹסֵף רְאֵה נָתַתִּי אֹתְךָ עַל כָּל־אֶרֶץ מִצְרָיִם: וַיָּסַר פַּרְעֹה
אֶת־טַבַּעְתּוֹ מֵעַל יָדוֹ וַיִּתֵּן אֹתָהּ עַל־יַד יוֹסֵף וַיַּלְבֵּשׁ אֹתוֹ בִּגְדֵי־שֵׁשׁ
מג וַיָּשֶׂם רְבִד הַזָּהָב עַל־צַוָּארוֹ: וַיַּרְכֵּב אֹתוֹ בְּמִרְכֶּבֶת הַמִּשְׁנֶה אֲשֶׁר־לוֹ
מד וַיִּקְרְאוּ לְפָנָיו אַבְרֵךְ וְנָתוֹן אֹתוֹ עַל כָּל־אֶרֶץ מִצְרָיִם: וַיֹּאמֶר פַּרְעֹה
אֶל־יוֹסֵף אֲנִי פַרְעֹה וּבִלְעָדֶיךָ לֹא־יָרִים אִישׁ אֶת־יָדוֹ וְאֶת־רַגְלוֹ בְּכָל־

אונקלוס

הֲנִשְׁכַּח כְּדֵין, גְּבַר, דְּרוּחַ נְבוּאָה מִן קֳדָם יי בֵּיהּ: לט וַאֲמַר פַּרְעֹה
לְיוֹסֵף, בָּתַר דְּהוֹדַע יי, יָתָךְ יָת כָּל דָּא, לֵית סָכְלְתָן וְחַכִּים כְּוָתָךְ:
מ אַתְּ תְּהֵי מְמַנָּא עַל בֵּיתִי, וְעַל מֵימְרָךְ יִתְּזַן כָּל עַמִּי, לְחוֹד כֻּרְסֵי
מַלְכוּתָא הָדֵין אֵיהֵי יַקִּיר מִנָּךְ: מא וַאֲמַר פַּרְעֹה לְיוֹסֵף, חֲזִי דְּמַנֵּיתִי
יָתָךְ, עַל כָּל אַרְעָא דְּמִצְרָיִם: מב וְאַעְדִּי פַּרְעֹה יָת עִזְקְתֵיהּ מֵעַל
יְדֵיהּ, וִיהַב יָתַהּ עַל יְדָא דְּיוֹסֵף, וְאַלְבֵּישׁ יָתֵיהּ לְבוּשִׁין דְּבוּץ,
וְשַׁוִּי, מָנִיכָא דְּדַהֲבָא עַל צַוְרֵיהּ: מג וְאַרְכֵּיב יָתֵיהּ, בִּרְתִכָּא תִּנְיֵתָא
דִּילֵיהּ, וְאַכְרִיזוּ קֳדָמוֹהִי דֵּין אַבָּא לְמַלְכָּא, וּמַנִּי יָתֵיהּ, עַל כָּל אַרְעָא
דְּמִצְרָיִם: מד וַאֲמַר פַּרְעֹה, לְיוֹסֵף אֲנָא פַּרְעֹה, וּבַר מִמֵּימְרָךְ, לָא
יְרִים גְּבַר יָת יְדֵיהּ לְמֵיחַד זֵין, וְיָת רַגְלֵיהּ לְמִרְכַּב עַל סוּסְיָא בְּכָל

PHARAOH, YOSEF, AND *ELOKIM*

Pharaonic Egypt was not a monotheistic culture. To be sure, there was a brief period under Ikhnaton (Amenhotep IV), when the official religion was reformed in the direction of monolatry (worship of one god without disputing the existence of others). But this was short-lived, and certainly not at the time of Yosef. The entire biblical portrayal of Egypt is predicated on the people's belief in many gods, against whom God will "execute judgments" (Ex. 12:12) in the days of Moshe. Why then does Yosef take it for granted that Pharaoh will understand his reference to God – an assumption proved correct when Pharaoh twice uses the word himself? What is the significance of the word *Elokim*?

Tanakh generally and the Torah specifically have two primary ways of referring to God, the four-letter name we allude to as *Hashem* ("the name" par excellence, translated here as LORD) and the word *Elokim*.

The Sages understood the difference in terms of the distinction between God-as-justice (*Elokim*) and God-as-mercy (*Hashem*). However, the philosopher-poet of the eleventh century, Yehuda HaLevi, proposed a quite different distinction, based not on ethical attributes but on modes of relationship (*Kuzari* IV:1). HaLevi's view was this: The ancients worshipped forces of nature, which they personified as gods. Each was known as *El* or *Eloah*. The word *El* therefore generically means "a force, a power, an element of nature." The fundamental difference between those belief systems and Judaism was that Judaism believed that the forces of nature were not independent and autonomous. They represented a single totality, one creative will, the Author of being. The Torah therefore speaks of *Elokim* in the plural, meaning, "the sum of all forces, the totality of all powers." Moving from the ancient to the contemporary world, we might say that *Elokim* is God as He is disclosed by science: the Big Bang, the various forces that give the universe its configuration, and the genetic code that shapes life from the simplest bacterium to *Homo sapiens*.

Hashem is a word of different logical form. It is, according

45 without your consent no one will lift hand or foot in all Egypt." And Pharaoh
gave Yosef the name Tzafenat Paneaḥ and gave him Asnat, daughter of Potifera,
46 priest of On, as his wife. Thus Yosef went out to oversee Egypt. When he
entered the service of Pharaoh, king of Egypt, Yosef was thirty years old.
Leaving Pharaoh's presence, Yosef traveled throughout the land of Egypt.
47 48 During the seven years of plenty the land produced in profusion. He gathered
all the grain produced during the seven years of plenty in Egypt and stored it in
49 the cities. In each city he stored the grain grown in the surrounding fields. Yosef
stored so much grain that it was like the sand of the sea. They had to stop
50 keeping records because it was beyond measure. Before the years of famine
came, two sons were born to Yosef by Asnat daughter of Potifera, priest of On.
51 Yosef named his firstborn Menashe, saying, "God has made me forget all my
52 troubles and all my father's family." The second son he named Efrayim, saying,
53 "God has made me fruitful in the land of my affliction." The seven years of REVI'I

רש"י

מה | **צָפְנַת פַּעְנֵחַ.** מְפָרֵשׁ הַצְּפוּנוֹת, וְאֵין לְ'פַעְנֵחַ' דִּמְיוֹן בַּמִּקְרָא: **פּוֹטִי פֶרַע.** הוּא פּוֹטִיפַר, וְנִקְרָא פּוֹטִיפֶרַע עַל שֶׁנִּסְתָּרֵס מֵאֵלָיו, לְפִי שֶׁלָּקַח אֶת יוֹסֵף לְמִשְׁכַּב זָכוּר:

מז | **וַתַּעַשׂ הָאָרֶץ.** כְּתַרְגּוּמוֹ, וְאֵין הַלָּשׁוֹן נֶעֱקָר מִלְּשׁוֹן עֲשִׂיָּה: **לִקְמָצִים.** קֹמֶץ עַל קֹמֶץ, יָד עַל יָד הָיוּ אוֹצְרִין:

מח | **אֹכֶל שְׂדֵה הָעִיר... נָתַן בְּתוֹכָהּ.** שֶׁכָּל אֶרֶץ וָאֶרֶץ מַעֲמֶדֶת פֵּרוֹתֶיהָ, וְנוֹתְנִין בַּתְּבוּאָה מֵעֲפַר הַמָּקוֹם וּמַעֲמִיד אֶת הַתְּבוּאָה מִלֵּרָקֵב:

מט | **עַד כִּי חָדַל לִסְפֹּר.** עַד אֲשֶׁר חָדַל לוֹ הַסּוֹפֵר לִסְפֹּר, וַהֲרֵי זֶה מִקְרָא קָצָר: **כִּי אֵין מִסְפָּר.** לְפִי שֶׁאֵין מִסְפָּר, וַהֲרֵי 'כִּי' מְשַׁמֵּשׁ בִּלְשׁוֹן 'דְּהָא':

נ | **בְּטֶרֶם תָּבוֹא שְׁנַת הָרָעָב.** מִכָּאן שֶׁאָדָם אָסוּר לְשַׁמֵּשׁ מִטָּתוֹ בִּשְׁנֵי רְעָבוֹן:

suffering is not a fate to be borne, but a challenge to be overcome. This is Yosef's life-changing idea. What can be healed is not holy. God does not want us to accept poverty and pain, but to cure them.

41:52 **כִּי־הִפְרַנִי אֱלֹהִים בְּאֶרֶץ עָנְיִי** *Fruitful in the land of my affliction* – Yosef names his firstborn child Menashe, thanking God who "has *made me forget* (*nashani*) all my troubles and all my father's family" (Gen. 41:51). The pain of exile is numbed by forgetting his past and identity. By the time Efrayim is born, Yosef's feelings have changed.

In a later age, a man not otherwise known for his positive psychology will sit down to write a letter to his coreligionists in a foreign land. The man is Yirmeyahu. The people to whom he is writing are the Jews who have been taken captive to Babylon after their defeat at its hands, a defeat that included the destruction of the Temple, the central symbol of their nation and the sign that God was in their midst.

We know exactly what the feeling of those exiles was. A psalm has recorded it in the most powerful way: "By the rivers of Babylon, there we sat and wept as we remembered Zion.... How can we sing the LORD's song on foreign soil?" (Ps. 137:1, 4).

This is, of course, what Yirmeyahu predicted. But there is no air of triumphalism in his letter, no "I told you so." What he writes is massively counterintuitive. Yet it would be no exaggeration to say that it will change the course of Jewish history, perhaps even, in an indirect way, that of Western civilization as a whole. This is what he writes:

> Build houses and dwell in them; plant gardens and eat their fruit. Take wives, and beget sons and daughters. Take wives for your sons and give your daughters to husbands so that they may give birth to sons and daughters.

מה אֶרֶץ מִצְרָיִם: וַיִּקְרָא פַרְעֹה שֵׁם־יוֹסֵף צָפְנַת פַּעְנֵחַ וַיִּתֶּן־לוֹ אֶת־
אָסְנַת בַּת־פּוֹטִי פֶרַע כֹּהֵן אֹן לְאִשָּׁה וַיֵּצֵא יוֹסֵף עַל־אֶרֶץ מִצְרָיִם:
מו וְיוֹסֵף בֶּן־שְׁלֹשִׁים שָׁנָה בְּעָמְדוֹ לִפְנֵי פַּרְעֹה מֶלֶךְ־מִצְרָיִם וַיֵּצֵא יוֹסֵף
מז מִלִּפְנֵי פַרְעֹה וַיַּעֲבֹר בְּכָל־אֶרֶץ מִצְרָיִם: וַתַּעַשׂ הָאָרֶץ בְּשֶׁבַע שְׁנֵי
מח הַשָּׂבָע לִקְמָצִים: וַיִּקְבֹּץ אֶת־כָּל־אֹכֶל ׀ שֶׁבַע שָׁנִים אֲשֶׁר הָיוּ בְּאֶרֶץ
מִצְרַיִם וַיִּתֶּן־אֹכֶל בֶּעָרִים אֹכֶל שְׂדֵה־הָעִיר אֲשֶׁר סְבִיבֹתֶיהָ נָתַן
מט בְּתוֹכָהּ: וַיִּצְבֹּר יוֹסֵף בַּר כְּחוֹל הַיָּם הַרְבֵּה מְאֹד עַד כִּי־חָדַל לִסְפֹּר
נ כִּי־אֵין מִסְפָּר: וּלְיוֹסֵף יֻלַּד שְׁנֵי בָנִים בְּטֶרֶם תָּבוֹא שְׁנַת הָרָעָב אֲשֶׁר
נא יָלְדָה־לּוֹ אָסְנַת בַּת־פּוֹטִי פֶרַע כֹּהֵן אוֹן: וַיִּקְרָא יוֹסֵף אֶת־שֵׁם הַבְּכוֹר
נב מְנַשֶּׁה כִּי־נַשַּׁנִי אֱלֹהִים אֶת־כָּל־עֲמָלִי וְאֵת כָּל־בֵּית אָבִי: וְאֵת שֵׁם
נג הַשֵּׁנִי קָרָא אֶפְרָיִם כִּי־הִפְרַנִי אֱלֹהִים בְּאֶרֶץ עָנְיִי: וַתִּכְלֶינָה שֶׁבַע רביעי

אונקלוס

אַרְעָא דְמִצְרָיִם: מה וּקְרָא פַרְעֹה שׁוּם יוֹסֵף גַּבְרָא דְמִטַּמְרָן גַּלְיָן לֵיהּ, וִיהַב לֵיהּ יָת אָסְנַת, בַּת פּוֹטִיפֶרַע, רַבָּא דְאוֹן לְאִתּוּ, וּנְפַק יוֹסֵף שַׁלִּיט עַל אַרְעָא דְמִצְרָיִם: מו וְיוֹסֵף בַּר תְּלָתִין שְׁנִין, כַּד קָם, קֳדָם פַּרְעֹה מַלְכָּא דְמִצְרַיִם, וּנְפַק יוֹסֵף מִן קֳדָם פַּרְעֹה, וַעֲבַר בְּכָל אַרְעָא דְמִצְרָיִם: מז וּכְנַשׁוּ דָיְרֵי אַרְעָא, בִּשְׁבַע שְׁנֵי סִבְעָא, עֲבוּרָא לְאוֹצְרִין: מח וּכְנַשׁ, יָת כָּל עֲבוּר שְׁבַע שְׁנַיָּא, דַהֲוָאָה בְּאַרְעָא דְמִצְרַיִם, וִיהַב עֲבוּרָא בְּקִרְוַיָּא, עֲבוּר חֲקַל קַרְתָּא, דִּבְסַחְרָנַהָא יְהַב בְּגַוַּהּ: מט וּכְנַשׁ יוֹסֵף עֲבוּרָא, כְּחָלָא דְיַמָּא סַגִּי לַחֲדָא, עַד, דִּפְסַק מִלְּמִמְנֵי אֲרֵי לֵית מִנְיָן: נ וּלְיוֹסֵף אִתְיְלִידוּ תְּרֵין בְּנִין, עַד לָא עָאלַת שַׁתָּא דְכַפְנָא, דִּילֵידַת לֵיהּ אָסְנַת, בַּת פּוֹטִיפֶרַע רַבָּא דְאוֹן: נא וּקְרָא יוֹסֵף, יָת שׁוּם בֻּכְרָא מְנַשֶּׁה, אֲרֵי אַנְשְׁיַנִי יי יָת כָּל עַמְלִי, וְיָת כָּל בֵּית אַבָּא: נב וְיָת, שׁוּם תִּנְיָנָא קְרָא אֶפְרָיִם, אֲרֵי אַפְשַׁנִי יי בְּאֲרַע שִׁעְבּוּדִי: נג וּשְׁלִימָא, שְׁבַע

41:49 כִּי אֵין מִסְפָּר *It was beyond measure* – The great break of Judaism from the ancient world of magic, mystery, and myth was the deconsecration of nature that followed from the fact that God created nature by an act of will, and by making us in His image, gave us too the creative power of will. That meant that for Jews, holiness lies not in the way the world is, but in the way it ought to be. Poverty, disease, famine, injustice, and the exploitation of the powerless by the powerful are not the will of God. They may be part of human nature, but we have the power to rise above nature. God wants us not to accept but to heal, to cure, to prevent. So Jews have tended to become, out of all proportion to their numbers, lawyers fighting injustice, doctors fighting disease, teachers fighting ignorance, economists fighting poverty, and (especially in modern Israel) agricultural technologists finding new ways to grow food in environments where it has never grown before.

Thus, in our *parasha*, Yosef interprets the dream as asked, diagnosing the problem. There will be a famine lasting seven years. But it is what he does next that is world-changing. He sees this not as a fate to be endured but as a problem to be solved. Then, without fuss, he solves it, saving a whole region from death by starvation.

What can be changed need not be endured. Human

54 abundance in Egypt came to an end, and the seven years of famine began, just
as Yosef had said they would. There was famine in all the other lands, but
55 throughout Egypt there was food. When all Egypt began to feel the famine, the
people cried to Pharaoh for food. Pharaoh told all the Egyptians, "Go to Yosef.
56 Whatever he tells you – do." The famine spread over the entire country. Yosef
then opened all the storehouses and sold grain to the Egyptians, for the famine
57 was worsening throughout Egypt. People from all over the region came to
Egypt to buy grain from Yosef, because all across the land the famine was
42 1 devastating. Knowing that there was grain in Egypt, Yaakov said to his sons,
2 "Why do you keep looking at one another?" He said, "I have heard that there is
grain in Egypt. Go down there and buy some for us so that we may live and not
3 4 die." So ten of Yosef's brothers went down to buy grain in Egypt. But Yaakov
did not send Yosef's brother Binyamin with them, for he was afraid that harm
5 might come to him. So Yisrael's sons were among those who came to buy grain,
6 the famine having reached as far as the land of Canaan. Yosef was the governor
of the land; it was he who dispensed food to all its people. When Yosef's

רש״י

נה **וַתִּרְעַב כָּל אֶרֶץ מִצְרַיִם.** שֶׁהִרְקִיבָה תְּבוּאָתָם שֶׁאָצְרוּ, חוּץ מִשֶּׁל יוֹסֵף: **אֲשֶׁר יֹאמַר לָכֶם תַּעֲשׂוּ.** לְפִי שֶׁהָיָה יוֹסֵף אוֹמֵר לָהֶם שֶׁיִּמּוֹלוּ, וּכְשֶׁבָּאוּ אֵצֶל פַּרְעֹה וְאוֹמְרִים: כָּךְ הוּא אוֹמֵר לָנוּ, אָמַר לָהֶם: וְלָמָּה לֹא צְבַרְתֶּם בָּר, וַהֲלֹא הִכְרִיז לָכֶם שֶׁשְּׁנֵי הָרָעָב בָּאִים? אָמְרוּ לוֹ: אָסַפְנוּ הַרְבֵּה וְהִרְקִיבָה. אָמַר לָהֶם: אִם כֵּן, ״אֲשֶׁר יֹאמַר לָכֶם תַּעֲשׂוּ״! הֲרֵי גָּזַר עַל הַתְּבוּאָה וְהִרְקִיבָה, מָה אִם יִגְזֹר עָלֵינוּ וְנָמוּת?:

נו **עַל כָּל פְּנֵי הָאָרֶץ.** מִי הֵם ״פְּנֵי הָאָרֶץ״? אֵלּוּ הָעֲשִׁירִים: **אֶת כָּל אֲשֶׁר בָּהֶם.** כְּתַרְגּוּמוֹ: ״דִּי בְהוֹן עֲבוּרָא״: **וַיִּשְׁבֹּר לְמִצְרַיִם.** ׳שֶׁבֶר׳ לְשׁוֹן מֶכֶר וּלְשׁוֹן קִנְיָן הוּא, כָּאן מְשַׁמֵּשׁ לְשׁוֹן מֶכֶר; ״שִׁבְרוּ לָנוּ מְעַט אֹכֶל״ (להלן מג, ב) – לְשׁוֹן קִנְיָן. וְאַל תֹּאמַר, אֵינוֹ כִּי אִם בִּתְבוּאָה, שֶׁאַף בְּיַיִן וְחָלָב מָצִינוּ: ״וּלְכוּ שִׁבְרוּ בְּלוֹא כֶסֶף וּבְלוֹא מְחִיר יַיִן וְחָלָב״ (ישעיה נה, א):

נז **וְכָל הָאָרֶץ בָּאוּ מִצְרַיְמָה.** אֶל יוֹסֵף לִשְׁבֹּר. וְאִם תִּדְרְשֵׁהוּ כְּסִדְרוֹ, הָיָה צָרִיךְ לִכְתֹּב: ׳לִשְׁבֹּר מִן יוֹסֵף׳:

מב א **וַיַּרְא יַעֲקֹב כִּי יֶשׁ שֶׁבֶר בְּמִצְרָיִם.** וּמֵהֵיכָן רָאָה? וַהֲלֹא לֹא רָאָה אֶלָּא שָׁמַע, שֶׁנֶּאֱמַר ״הִנֵּה שָׁמַעְתִּי״ וְגוֹ׳ (להלן פסוק ב)! וּמַהוּ ״וַיַּרְא״? רָאָה בְּאַסְפַּקְלַרְיָא שֶׁל קֹדֶשׁ שֶׁיֵּשׁ לוֹ שֶׁבֶר עוֹד בְּמִצְרַיִם, וְלֹא הָיְתָה נְבוּאָה מַמָּשׁ לְהוֹדִיעוֹ בְּפֵרוּשׁ שֶׁזֶּה יוֹסֵף: **לָמָּה תִּתְרָאוּ.** אַל תַּרְאוּ עַצְמְכֶם בִּפְנֵי בְנֵי יִשְׁמָעֵאל וּבְנֵי עֵשָׂו כְּאִלּוּ אַתֶּם שְׂבֵעִים; בְּאוֹתָהּ שָׁעָה עֲדַיִן הָיָה לָהֶם תְּבוּאָה. וּמִפִּי אֲחֵרִים שָׁמַעְתִּי, שֶׁהוּא לְשׁוֹן כְּחִישָׁה: לָמָּה תִּהְיוּ כְּחוּשִׁים בָּרָעָב? וְדוֹמֶה לוֹ: ״וּמַרְוֶה גַּם הוּא יוֹרֶא״ (משלי יא, כה); וְאֵין הַדָּבָר נָכוֹן בְּעֵינַי:

ב **רְדוּ שָׁמָּה.** וְלֹא אָמַר ׳לְכוּ׳! רֶמֶז לְמָאתַיִם וָעֶשֶׂר שָׁנִים שֶׁנִּשְׁתַּעְבְּדוּ לְמִצְרַיִם, כְּמִנְיַן רד״ו:

ג **וַיֵּרְדוּ אֲחֵי יוֹסֵף.** וְלֹא כָתַב ׳בְּנֵי יַעֲקֹב׳! מְלַמֵּד שֶׁהָיוּ מִתְחָרְטִים בִּמְכִירָתוֹ, וְנָתְנוּ לִבָּם לְהִתְנַהֵג עִמּוֹ בְּאַחֲוָה וְלִפְדּוֹתוֹ בְּכָל מָמוֹן שֶׁיַּפְסִיקוּ עֲלֵיהֶם: **עֲשָׂרָה.** מַה תַּלְמוּד לוֹמַר? וַהֲלֹא כְתִיב: ״וְאֶת בִּנְיָמִין אֲחִי יוֹסֵף לֹא שָׁלַח״ (להלן פסוק ד)! אֶלָּא לְעִנְיַן הָאַחֲוָה הָיוּ חֲלוּקִין לַעֲשָׂרָה, שֶׁלֹּא הָיְתָה אַהֲבַת כֻּלָּם וְשִׂנְאַת כֻּלָּם שָׁוָה לוֹ, אֲבָל לְעִנְיַן ״לִשְׁבֹּר בָּר״ כֻּלָּם לֵב אֶחָד לָהֶם. בִּרְאשִׁית רַבָּה (צא, ב):

ד **פֶּן יִקְרָאֶנּוּ אָסוֹן.** וּבַבַּיִת לֹא יִקְרָאֶנּוּ?! אָמַר רַבִּי אֱלִיעֶזֶר בֶּן יַעֲקֹב: מִכָּאן שֶׁהַשָּׂטָן מְקַטְרֵג בִּשְׁעַת הַסַּכָּנָה:

ה **בְּתוֹךְ הַבָּאִים.** מַטְמִינִין עַצְמָן שֶׁלֹּא יַכִּירוּם, לְפִי שֶׁצִּוָּם אֲבִיהֶם שֶׁלֹּא יִתְרָאוּ שֶׁלֹּא תִּשְׁלֹט בָּהֶם עַיִן רָעָה, שֶׁכֻּלָּם נָאִים וְכֻלָּם גִּבּוֹרִים:

ו **וַיִּשְׁתַּחֲווּ לוֹ אַפַּיִם.** נִשְׁתַּטְּחוּ לוֹ עַל פְּנֵיהֶם, וְכֵן כָּל הִשְׁתַּחֲוָאָה פִּשּׁוּט יָדַיִם וְרַגְלַיִם הוּא:

have found relief in forgetting his heritage. When Efrayim is born, however, he stands fully in the presence of the God of his fathers, even in "the land of his affliction," bringing life to himself and those around him.

נד שְׁנֵי הַשָּׂבָע אֲשֶׁר הָיָה בְּאֶרֶץ מִצְרָיִם: וַתְּחִלֶּינָה שֶׁבַע שְׁנֵי הָרָעָב
לָבוֹא כַּאֲשֶׁר אָמַר יוֹסֵף וַיְהִי רָעָב בְּכָל־הָאֲרָצוֹת וּבְכָל־אֶרֶץ מִצְרַיִם
נה הָיָה לָחֶם: וַתִּרְעַב כָּל־אֶרֶץ מִצְרַיִם וַיִּצְעַק הָעָם אֶל־פַּרְעֹה לַלָּחֶם
וַיֹּאמֶר פַּרְעֹה לְכָל־מִצְרַיִם לְכוּ אֶל־יוֹסֵף אֲשֶׁר־יֹאמַר לָכֶם תַּעֲשׂוּ:
נו וְהָרָעָב הָיָה עַל כָּל־פְּנֵי הָאָרֶץ וַיִּפְתַּח יוֹסֵף אֶת־כָּל־אֲשֶׁר בָּהֶם
נז וַיִּשְׁבֹּר לְמִצְרַיִם וַיֶּחֱזַק הָרָעָב בְּאֶרֶץ מִצְרָיִם: וְכָל־הָאָרֶץ בָּאוּ מִצְרַיְמָה
מב א לִשְׁבֹּר אֶל־יוֹסֵף כִּי־חָזַק הָרָעָב בְּכָל־הָאָרֶץ: וַיַּרְא יַעֲקֹב כִּי יֶשׁ־
ב שֶׁבֶר בְּמִצְרָיִם וַיֹּאמֶר יַעֲקֹב לְבָנָיו לָמָּה תִּתְרָאוּ: וַיֹּאמֶר הִנֵּה שָׁמַעְתִּי
כִּי יֶשׁ־שֶׁבֶר בְּמִצְרָיִם רְדוּ־שָׁמָּה וְשִׁבְרוּ־לָנוּ מִשָּׁם וְנִחְיֶה וְלֹא נָמוּת:
ג ד וַיֵּרְדוּ אֲחֵי־יוֹסֵף עֲשָׂרָה לִשְׁבֹּר בָּר מִמִּצְרָיִם: וְאֶת־בִּנְיָמִין אֲחִי יוֹסֵף
ה לֹא־שָׁלַח יַעֲקֹב אֶת־אֶחָיו כִּי אָמַר פֶּן־יִקְרָאֶנּוּ אָסוֹן: וַיָּבֹאוּ בְּנֵי
ו יִשְׂרָאֵל לִשְׁבֹּר בְּתוֹךְ הַבָּאִים כִּי־הָיָה הָרָעָב בְּאֶרֶץ כְּנָעַן: וְיוֹסֵף הוּא
הַשַּׁלִּיט עַל־הָאָרֶץ הוּא הַמַּשְׁבִּיר לְכָל־עַם הָאָרֶץ וַיָּבֹאוּ אֲחֵי יוֹסֵף

אונקלוס

שְׁנֵי סִבְעָא, דַּהֲוָאָה בְּאַרְעָא דְּמִצְרָיִם: נד וְשָׁרִיאָה, שְׁבַע שְׁנֵי כַפְנָא לְמֵיתֵי, כְּמָא דַּאֲמַר יוֹסֵף, וַהֲוָה כַּפְנָא בְּכָל אַרְעָתָא, וּבְכָל אַרְעָא דְּמִצְרַיִם הֲוָה לַחְמָא: נה וּכְפֵינַת כָּל אַרְעָא דְּמִצְרַיִם, וּצְוַח עַמָּא, קֳדָם פַּרְעֹה עַל לַחְמָא, וַאֲמַר פַּרְעֹה לְכָל מִצְרָאֵי אֱזִילוּ לְוָת יוֹסֵף, דְּיֵימַר לְכוֹן תַּעְבְּדוּן: נו וְכַפְנָא הֲוָה, עַל כָּל אַפֵּי אַרְעָא, וּפְתַח יוֹסֵף, יָת כָּל אוֹצְרַיָּא דִּבְהוֹן עֲבוּרָא וְזַבִּין לְמִצְרָאֵי, וּתְקֵיף כַּפְנָא בְּאַרְעָא דְּמִצְרָיִם: נז וְכָל דַּיְרֵי אַרְעָא אֲתוֹ לְמִצְרַיִם, לְמִזְבַּן עֲבוּרָא מִן יוֹסֵף, אֲרֵי תְּקֵיף כַּפְנָא בְּכָל אַרְעָא: מב א וַחֲזָא יַעֲקֹב, אֲרֵי אִית עֲבוּר מִזְדַּבַּן בְּמִצְרַיִם, וַאֲמַר יַעֲקֹב לִבְנוֹהִי, לְמָא תִתַּחֲזוֹן: ב וַאֲמַר, הָא שְׁמַעִית, אֲרֵי אִית עֲבוּר מִזְדַּבַּן בְּמִצְרַיִם, חוּתוּ לְתַמָּן וּזְבוּנוּ לַנָא מִתַּמָּן, וְנֵיחֵי וְלָא נְמוּת: ג וּנְחַתוּ אֲחֵי יוֹסֵף עַסְרָא, לְמִזְבַּן עֲבוּרָא מִמִּצְרָיִם: ד וְיָת בִּנְיָמִין אֲחוּהִי דְּיוֹסֵף, לָא שְׁלַח יַעֲקֹב עִם אֲחוֹהִי, אֲרֵי אֲמַר, דִּלְמָא יְעָרְעִנֵּיהּ מוֹתָא: ה וַאֲתוֹ בְּנֵי יִשְׂרָאֵל, לְמִזְבַּן עֲבוּרָא בְּגוֹ עָאלַיָּא, אֲרֵי הֲוָה כַפְנָא בְּאַרְעָא דִּכְנָעַן: ו וְיוֹסֵף, הוּא דְּשַׁלִּיט עַל אַרְעָא, הוּא מְזַבֵּין עֲבוּרָא לְכָל עַמָּא דְּאַרְעָא, וַאֲתוֹ אֲחֵי יוֹסֵף,

> Multiply there; do not be diminished. Seek the welfare of the city to which I have exiled you, and pray on its behalf to the Lord, for in its peace there shall be peace for you. (Jer. 29:5–7)

What Yirmeyahu is saying is that it is possible to survive in exile with your identity intact, your appetite for life undiminished, while contributing to the wider society and praying to God on its behalf. Yirmeyahu is introducing into history a highly consequential idea: the idea of a creative minority.

This maps a new path for the Jewish people, but the wisdom Yirmeyahu applies is born here. In the past Yosef may

7 brothers arrived, they bowed down to him, their faces to the ground. Yosef
recognized his brothers as soon as he saw them, but he acted like a stranger and
spoke harshly to them. "Where have you come from?" he asked. They replied,
8 "From the land of Canaan – to buy food." Yosef recognized his brothers, but
9 they did not recognize him. Then Yosef remembered the dreams he had

רש״י

ז וַיִּתְנַכֵּר אֲלֵיהֶם. נַעֲשָׂה לָהֶם כְּנָכְרִי בִּדְבָרִים לְדַבֵּר קָשׁוֹת:
ח וַיַּכֵּר יוֹסֵף וְגוֹ׳. לְפִי שֶׁהִנִּיחָם חֲתוּמֵי זָקָן: וְהֵם לֹא הִכִּרֻהוּ. שֶׁיָּצָא מֵאֶצְלָם בְּלֹא חֲתִימַת זָקָן וְעַכְשָׁיו בָּא בַּחֲתִימַת זָקָן. וּמִדְרַשׁ אַגָּדָה, "וַיַּכֵּר יוֹסֵף אֶת אֶחָיו", כְּשֶׁנִּמְסְרוּ בְּיָדוֹ הִכִּיר שֶׁהֵם אֶחָיו וְרִחֵם עֲלֵיהֶם, "וְהֵם לֹא הִכִּרֻהוּ" כְּשֶׁנָּפַל בְּיָדָם לִנְהֹג בּוֹ אַחֲוָה:

it means what it says: they saw him approach, and they planned murder. At another level, however, it is a philosophical statement about love and hate. They were able to contemplate fratricide because "they saw him at a distance" (Rabbi Ḥayyim of Kossov, *Torat Ḥayyim* on Gen. 37:18). They refused to allow him to come close. They could see his cloak, but in Emmanuel Levinas's terminology, they could not yet see his "face," his reality as a person. Distant physically, they would not let him come close emotionally.

Soon after, Yehuda uttered the devastatingly ironic words "Let's sell him to the Ishmaelites and not harm him with our own hands. *After all, he is our brother*, our own flesh and blood" (37:27). Genesis is about recognition and nonrecognition in the deepest sense, about the willingness to accord dignity to the other rather than see the other as a threat.

The irony of Yosef is that his siblings do not recognize him, in Egypt, as their brother. *They recognize him only as a stranger*, an Egyptian ruler called Tzafenat Pane'aḥ, who wears Egyptian robes of office and whom they assume cannot even speak their language. Eventually Yosef forces them to recognize that just as a brother can be a stranger (when kept "at a distance"), so a stranger can turn out to be a brother.

The dual meaning of the verb *n-k-r* gathers into itself the whole force and dramatic conflict of Genesis as a sustained exploration of recognition and estrangement, closeness and distance. It tells us that if only we listen closely to the voice of the other, we will find that beneath the skin we *are* brothers and sisters, members of the human family under the parenthood of God. When others become brothers and conflict is transformed into conciliation, we have begun the journey to society-as-a-family, and the redemptive drama can begin.

42:8 **וְהֵם לֹא הִכִּרֻהוּ** *They did not recognize him* – The encounter between Yosef and his brothers is the fifth in a series of stories in which clothes play a key role. The first is Yaakov who dresses in Esav's clothes while bringing his father a meal so that he can take his brother's blessing. The second is Yosef's "ornately colored robe" which the brothers bring back to their father stained in blood, saying that a wild animal must have seized him. The third is the story of Tamar taking off her widow's dress, covering herself with a veil, and making herself look as if she were a prostitute. The fourth is the robe Yosef leaves in the hands of Potifar's wife while escaping her attempt to seduce him. The fifth is the one in our *parasha*, in which Pharaoh dresses Yosef as a high-ranking Egyptian, with clothes of linen, a gold chain, and the royal signet ring.

What all five cases have in common is that they facilitate deception. In each case, they bring about a situation in which things are not as they seem. Appearances deceive. It is therefore with a frisson of discovery that we realize that the Hebrew word for garment, *b-g-d*, is also the Hebrew word for "betrayal," as in the confession formula, *Ashamnu, bagadnu*, "We have been guilty, we have acted treacherously."

Is this a mere literary conceit, a way of linking a series of otherwise unconnected stories? Or is there something more fundamental at stake?

ז וַיִּשְׁתַּחֲווּ־לוֹ אַפַּיִם אָרְצָה: וַיַּרְא יוֹסֵף אֶת־אֶחָיו וַיַּכִּרֵם וַיִּתְנַכֵּר אֲלֵיהֶם
וַיְדַבֵּר אִתָּם קָשׁוֹת וַיֹּאמֶר אֲלֵהֶם מֵאַיִן בָּאתֶם וַיֹּאמְרוּ מֵאֶרֶץ כְּנַעַן
ח ט לִשְׁבָּר־אֹכֶל: וַיַּכֵּר יוֹסֵף אֶת־אֶחָיו וְהֵם לֹא הִכִּרֻהוּ: וַיִּזְכֹּר יוֹסֵף אֵת

אונקלוס

וּסְגִידוּ לֵיהּ עַל אַפֵּיהוֹן עַל אַרְעָא: ז וַחֲזָא יוֹסֵף, יָת אֲחוֹהִי
וְאִשְׁתְּמוֹדְעִנּוּן, וְחַשֵּׁיב מָא דִּימַלֵּיל עִמְּהוֹן וּמַלֵּיל עִמְּהוֹן קַשְׁיָן,
וַאֲמַר לְהוֹן מְנָן אֲתֵיתוֹן, וַאֲמַרוּ, מֵאַרְעָא דִּכְנַעַן לְמִזְבַּן עֲבוּרָא:
ח וְאִשְׁתְּמוֹדַע יוֹסֵף יָת אֲחוֹהִי, וְאִנּוּן לָא אִשְׁתְּמוֹדְעוּהִי: ט וְאִדְּכַר
יוֹסֵף, יָת

YOSEF AND HIS BROTHERS MEET AGAIN

What happens when the brothers arrive in Egypt is wholly counterintuitive. The story is nearing closure. Yosef has become a ruler. His brothers have bowed down to him. All that remains is for Yaakov and Yosef's younger brother Binyamin to be brought to Egypt. There they will make their obeisance, and the end foretold at the beginning, in Yosef's childhood dreams, will be complete. We cannot but expect this to happen, given the story thus far.

What is going on in this strange and apparently pointless diversion? Why Yosef's false accusation? Why the deception and intrigue? Why force the brothers to bring Binyamin? How does it advance the narrative or tell us something we need to know? In terms of the dreams, it delays their fulfilment rather than hastens it.

The first explanation that comes to mind is revenge. The text, however, explicitly rules this out. At every stage of the stratagem, Yosef weeps. He weeps at their first meeting (Gen. 42:24), again at the second (43:30), and a third time at the end of Yehuda's speech (45:2). People taking revenge do not weep. Yosef is doing something he finds personally painful yet morally necessary. He bears them – as he says when he reveals his identity – no malice. He has forgiven them. Why then does he put them through such fear and subject them to such a trial?

I have argued elsewhere (*Not in God's Name*, ch. 1) that the source of violence lies in our need to exist in groups, which leads to in-group altruism and out-group hostility. The pathological form of this is the dualism that divides humanity into children of light and children of darkness, the one all good, the other all evil. *It follows that the most profound moralizing experience, the only one capable of defeating dualism, is to undergo role reversal.* Imagine a Crusader in the Middle Ages, or a German in 1939, discovering that he is a Jew. There can be no more life-changing trial than finding yourself *on the other side.*

That, in essence, is what Yosef is forcing his brothers to do. He is putting them through the intensely painful yet morally transformative ordeal of role reversal. They suspected him of ambition. Now they learn what it is to be under suspicion. They planned to sell him as a slave. Now they know what it feels like to face enslavement. They made Yaakov go through the grief of losing a son. Now they must witness that grief again, this time through no fault of their own. Above all, they treated their brother as a stranger. *Now they must learn that the stranger,* Tzafenat Pane'aḥ, ruler of Egypt, *is actually their brother.*

42:7 וַיַּכִּרֵם *Yosef recognized* – In Hebrew the root *n-k-r* is a contranym – one word with two contradictory meanings. It can mean "to recognize" or the opposite, "to be a stranger," someone who is *not* recognized. The root appears four times in these two verses, three in the sense of recognition, one in the sense of estrangement. "Yosef *recognized* his brothers, but they did *not recognize* him," and Yosef "*recognized* his brothers… but he *acted like a stranger.*"

The power of this contranym is intense. The central question of Genesis is: Are human beings friends or strangers, brothers or others? That has been hammering at our consciousness since Kayin and Hevel, the first human children. All those years before, Yosef's brothers "*saw him in the distance,* and by the time he reached them, they had plotted to kill him" (Gen. 37:18). This sentence, like so many others in the story of Yosef, has two meanings. On the surface,

dreamed about them. "You are spies!" he said. "You have come to see where
10 our land is exposed." "No, my lord," they said. "Your servants have come to buy
11 food. We all are sons of the same man. We are honest men. Your servants are
12 not spies." "Lies," he said. "You have come to see where our land is exposed."
13 "We were once twelve brothers," they replied, "sons of one man in Canaan. The
14 youngest is now with our father, and one is gone." But Yosef said, "It is as I said
15 to you – you are spies. This is how you will be tested. By Pharaoh's life, you will
16 not leave this place unless your youngest brother comes here. Let one of you go
and fetch your brother. The rest of you will remain confined here. This will test
whether or not you are telling the truth. If not, by Pharaoh's life, you are spies."
17 18 He had them placed in custody for three days. On the third day, Yosef said to
19 them, "If you do this you will live, for I am a God-fearing man. If you are honest, ḤAMISHI
let one of your brothers stay here in prison while the rest of you go and take
20 back grain for your starving households. Then bring your youngest brother to

רש״י

ט **אֲשֶׁר חָלַם לָהֶם.** עֲלֵיהֶם, וְיָדַע שֶׁנִּתְקַיְּמוּ, שֶׁהֲרֵי הִשְׁתַּחֲווּ לוֹ: **עֶרְוַת הָאָרֶץ.** גִּלּוּי הָאָרֶץ, מֵהֵיכָן הִיא נוֹחָה לְכָבֵשׁ, כְּמוֹ: "אֶת מְקֹרָהּ הֶעֱרָה" (ויקרא כ, יח), וּכְמוֹ: "עֵרֹם וְעֶרְיָה" (יחזקאל טז, ז), וְכֵן כָּל עֶרְוָה שֶׁבַּמִּקְרָא לְשׁוֹן גִּלּוּי. וְאוּנְקְלוֹס תִּרְגֵּם: "בִּדְקָא דְּאַרְעָא", כְּמוֹ: "בֶּדֶק הַבַּיִת" (מלכים ב' יב, ו) – רְעוּעַ הַבַּיִת, אֲבָל לֹא דִּקְדֵּק לְפָרְשׁוֹ אַחַר לְשׁוֹן הַמִּקְרָא:

י **לֹא אֲדֹנִי.** לֹא תֹאמַר כֵּן, וַהֲרֵי "עֲבָדֶיךָ בָּאוּ לִשְׁבָּר אֹכֶל":

יא **כֻּלָּנוּ בְּנֵי אִישׁ אֶחָד נָחְנוּ.** נִצְנְצָה בָּהֶם רוּחַ הַקֹּדֶשׁ וְכָלְלוּהוּ עִמָּהֶם, שֶׁאַף הוּא בֶּן אֲבִיהֶם: **כֵּנִים.** אֲמִתִּיִּים, כְּמוֹ: "כֵּן דִּבַּרְתָּ" (שמות י, כט), "כֵּן בְּנוֹת צְלָפְחָד דֹּבְרֹת" (במדבר כז, ז), "וְעֶבְרָתוֹ לֹא כֵן בַּדָּיו" (ישעיה טז, ו):

יב **כִּי עֶרְוַת הָאָרֶץ בָּאתֶם לִרְאוֹת.** שֶׁהֲרֵי נִכְנַסְתֶּם בַּעֲשָׂרָה שַׁעֲרֵי הָעִיר, לָמָּה לֹא נִכְנַסְתֶּם בְּשַׁעַר אֶחָד?:

יג **וַיֹּאמְרוּ שְׁנֵים עָשָׂר עֲבָדֶיךָ וְגוֹ'.** וּבִשְׁבִיל אוֹתוֹ אֶחָד שֶׁאֵינֶנּוּ, נִתְפַּזַּרְנוּ בָּעִיר לְבַקְּשׁוֹ:

יד **הוּא אֲשֶׁר דִּבַּרְתִּי.** הַדָּבָר אֲשֶׁר דִּבַּרְתִּי שֶׁאַתֶּם מְרַגְּלִים הוּא הָאֱמֶת וְהַנָּכוֹן, זֶהוּ לְפִי פְּשׁוּטוֹ. וּמִדְרָשׁוֹ, אָמַר לָהֶם: וְאִלּוּ מְצָאתֶם אוֹתוֹ וְיִפְסְקוּ עֲלֵיכֶם מָמוֹן הַרְבֵּה, תִּפְדּוּהוּ? אָמְרוּ לוֹ: הֵן. אָמַר לָהֶם: וְאִם יֹאמְרוּ לָכֶם שֶׁלֹּא יַחֲזִירוּהוּ בְּשׁוּם מָמוֹן, מַה תַּעֲשׂוּ? אָמְרוּ: לְכָךְ בָּאנוּ, לַהֲרֹג אוֹ לֵהָרֵג! אָמַר לָהֶם: "הוּא אֲשֶׁר דִּבַּרְתִּי אֲלֵכֶם", לַהֲרֹג בְּנֵי הָעִיר בָּאתֶם, מְנַחֵשׁ אֲנִי בִּגְבִיעַ שֶׁלִּי שֶׁשְּׁנַיִם מִכֶּם הֶחֱרִיבוּ כְּרַךְ גָּדוֹל שֶׁל שְׁכֶם:

טו **חֵי פַרְעֹה.** אִם יִחְיֶה פַרְעֹה. כְּשֶׁהָיָה נִשְׁבָּע לַשֶּׁקֶר הָיָה נִשְׁבָּע בְּחַיֵּי פַרְעֹה: **אִם תֵּצְאוּ מִזֶּה.** מִן הַמָּקוֹם הַזֶּה:

טז **הַאֱמֶת אִתְּכֶם.** אִם אֱמֶת אִתְּכֶם, לְפִיכָךְ הֵ"א נָקוּד פַּתָּח, שֶׁהוּא כְּמוֹ בִּלְשׁוֹן תֵּמַהּ. "וְאִם לֹא" תְּבִיאוּהוּ – "חֵי פַרְעֹה כִּי מְרַגְּלִים אַתֶּם":

יז **מִשְׁמָר.** בֵּית הָאֲסוּרִים:

יט **בְּבֵית מִשְׁמַרְכֶם.** שֶׁאַתֶּם אֲסוּרִים בּוֹ עַכְשָׁיו: **וְאַתֶּם לְכוּ הָבִיאוּ.** לְבֵית אֲבִיכֶם: **שֶׁבֶר רַעֲבוֹן בָּתֵּיכֶם.** מַה שֶּׁקְּנִיתֶם לְרַעֲבוֹן אַנְשֵׁי בָּתֵּיכֶם:

כ **וְיֵאָמְנוּ דִבְרֵיכֶם.** יִתְאַמְּתוּ וְיִתְקַיְּמוּ, כְּמוֹ: "אָמֵן אָמֵן" (במדבר ה, כב), וּכְמוֹ: "יֵאָמֶן נָא דְּבָרְךָ" (מלכים א' ח, כו):

42:20 **וְיֵאָמְנוּ דִבְרֵיכֶם** *So that your words can be verified* – This is illogical. The existence of another brother has nothing to do with whether or not they are spies. Indeed, were they to bring a child, there would be no way an Egyptian ruler would be able to tell whether he was their brother or not. The strangeness of the request does not, however, raise doubts in the minds of the brothers. They know they are in trouble; that is all. When, on the journey back, they discover

הַחֲלֹמוֹת אֲשֶׁר חָלַם לָהֶם וַיֹּאמֶר אֲלֵהֶם מְרַגְּלִים אַתֶּם לִרְאוֹת אֶת־
י עֶרְוַת הָאָרֶץ בָּאתֶם: וַיֹּאמְרוּ אֵלָיו לֹא אֲדֹנִי וַעֲבָדֶיךָ בָּאוּ לִשְׁבָּר־
יא אֹכֶל: כֻּלָּנוּ בְּנֵי אִישׁ־אֶחָד נָחְנוּ כֵּנִים אֲנַחְנוּ לֹא־הָיוּ עֲבָדֶיךָ מְרַגְּלִים:
יב יג וַיֹּאמֶר אֲלֵהֶם לֹא כִּי־עֶרְוַת הָאָרֶץ בָּאתֶם לִרְאוֹת: וַיֹּאמְרוּ שְׁנֵים
עָשָׂר עֲבָדֶיךָ אַחִים ׀ אֲנַחְנוּ בְּנֵי אִישׁ־אֶחָד בְּאֶרֶץ כְּנָעַן וְהִנֵּה הַקָּטֹן
יד אֶת־אָבִינוּ הַיּוֹם וְהָאֶחָד אֵינֶנּוּ: וַיֹּאמֶר אֲלֵהֶם יוֹסֵף הוּא אֲשֶׁר דִּבַּרְתִּי
טו אֲלֵכֶם לֵאמֹר מְרַגְּלִים אַתֶּם: בְּזֹאת תִּבָּחֵנוּ חֵי פַרְעֹה אִם־תֵּצְאוּ מִזֶּה
טז כִּי אִם־בְּבוֹא אֲחִיכֶם הַקָּטֹן הֵנָּה: שִׁלְחוּ מִכֶּם אֶחָד וְיִקַּח אֶת־אֲחִיכֶם
וְאַתֶּם הֵאָסְרוּ וְיִבָּחֲנוּ דִּבְרֵיכֶם הַאֱמֶת אִתְּכֶם וְאִם־לֹא חֵי פַרְעֹה כִּי
יז יח מְרַגְּלִים אַתֶּם: וַיֶּאֱסֹף אֹתָם אֶל־מִשְׁמָר שְׁלֹשֶׁת יָמִים: וַיֹּאמֶר אֲלֵהֶם לח
יט יוֹסֵף בַּיּוֹם הַשְּׁלִישִׁי זֹאת עֲשׂוּ וִחְיוּ אֶת־הָאֱלֹהִים אֲנִי יָרֵא: אִם־כֵּנִים חמישי
אַתֶּם אֲחִיכֶם אֶחָד יֵאָסֵר בְּבֵית מִשְׁמַרְכֶם וְאַתֶּם לְכוּ הָבִיאוּ שֶׁבֶר
כ רַעֲבוֹן בָּתֵּיכֶם: וְאֶת־אֲחִיכֶם הַקָּטֹן תָּבִיאוּ אֵלַי וְיֵאָמְנוּ דִבְרֵיכֶם וְלֹא

אונקלוס

חֶלְמַיָּא, דַּהֲוָה חָלֵים לְהוֹן, וַאֲמַר לְהוֹן אַלִּילֵי אַתּוּן, לְמִחְזֵי, יָת בִּדְקַהּ דְּאַרְעָא אֲתֵיתוּן: י וַאֲמַרוּ לֵיהּ לָא רִבּוֹנִי, וְעַבְדָּךְ אֲתוֹ לְמִזְבַּן עֲבוּרָא: יא כֻּלַּנָא, בְּנֵי גַּבְרָא חַד נַחְנָא, כֵּיוָנֵי אֲנַחְנָא, לָא הֲווֹ עַבְדָּךְ אַלִּילֵי: יב וַאֲמַר לְהוֹן, לָא, אֱלָהֵין בִּדְקַהּ דְּאַרְעָא אֲתֵיתוּן לְמִחְזֵי: יג וַאֲמַרוּ, תְּרֵי עֲסַר עַבְדָּךְ אַחִין אֲנַחְנָא, בְּנֵי גַּבְרָא חַד בְּאַרְעָא דִּכְנָעַן, וְהָא זְעֵירָא עִם אֲבוּנָא יוֹמָא דֵין, וְחַד לֵיתוֹהִי: יד וַאֲמַר לְהוֹן יוֹסֵף, הוּא, דְּמַלֵּילִית עִמְּכוֹן, לְמֵימַר אַלִּילֵי אַתּוּן: טו בְּדָא תִּתְבַּחֲרוּן, חַיֵּי פַרְעֹה אִם תִּפְּקוּן מִכָּא, אֱלָהֵין בְּמֵיתֵי, אֲחוּכוֹן זְעֵירָא הָלְכָא: טז שְׁלַחוּ מִנְּכוֹן חַד וְיִדְבַּר יָת אֲחוּכוֹן, וְאַתּוּן תִּתְאַסְרוּן, וְיִתְבַּחֲרוּן פִּתְגָּמֵיכוֹן, הַקְשׁוֹט אַתּוּן אָמְרִין, וְאִם לָא, חַיֵּי פַרְעֹה, אֲרֵי אַלִּילֵי אַתּוּן: יז וּכְנַשׁ יָתְהוֹן, לְבֵית מַטְּרָא תְּלָתָא יוֹמִין: יח וַאֲמַר לְהוֹן יוֹסֵף בְּיוֹמָא תְּלִיתָאָה, דָּא עֲבִידוּ וְאִתְקַיַּמוּ, מִן קֳדָם יי אֲנָא דָּחֵיל: יט אִם כֵּיוָנֵי אַתּוּן, אֲחוּכוֹן חַד, יִתְאֲסַר בְּבֵית מַטַּרְתְּכוֹן, וְאַתּוּן אִיזִילוּ אוֹבִילוּ, עֲבוּרָא דַּחֲסִיר בְּבָתֵּיכוֹן: כ וְיָת אֲחוּכוֹן זְעֵירָא תַּיְתוֹן לְוָתִי, וְיִתְהֵימְנוּן פִּתְגָּמֵיכוֹן וְלָא

"Yosef recognized his brothers, but they did not recognize him." The reason they did not recognize him is that, from the start, they allowed their feelings to be guided by what they saw, the "ornately colored robe" that inflamed their envy of their younger brother. Judge by appearances and you will miss the deeper truth about situations and people. You will even miss God Himself, for God cannot be seen, only heard. That is why the primary imperative in Judaism is *Shema Yisrael*, "Listen, Israel" (Deut. 6:4), and it is why, when we say the first line of the *Shema*, we place our hand over our eyes so that we cannot see.

Appearances deceive. Clothes betray. Deep understanding, whether of God or of human beings, needs the ability to listen.

21 me so that your words can be verified and you will not die." They agreed. And
they said to one another, "We are guilty, guilty because of what we did to our
brother. We saw his suffering when he pleaded with us but we did not listen.
22 That is why this trouble has come upon us." Then Reuven spoke up: "Did I not
tell you not to sin against the boy? But you would not listen. Now comes the
23 reckoning for his blood." They did not realize that Yosef could understand
24 them, for a translator stood between them. And Yosef turned away from them
and wept. Then he turned back to them and spoke again. He had Shimon taken
25 from them and placed in chains before their eyes. Yosef gave orders to fill their
bags with grain and put each man's money back in his sack. They were to be
26 given provisions for the journey. After this was done for them, they loaded
27 their grain on their donkeys and left. As one of them was opening his sack to
feed his donkey at the place where they stopped for the night, he saw his money
28 right there at the top of his pack. "My money has been returned!" he told his
brothers. "There it is in my pack!" Their hearts sank. Trembling, they turned to
29 one another, saying, "What is this that God has done to us?" When they came
to their father Yaakov in the land of Canaan, they told him all that had happened

רש״י

כא| **אֲבָל.** כְּתַרְגּוּמוֹ: ״בְּקוּשְׁטָא״. וְרָאִיתִי בִּבְרֵאשִׁית רַבָּה (צא, ח): לִשָּׁנָא דָּרוֹמָאָה הוּא, ״אֲבָל״ – בְּרַם: **בָּאָה אֵלֵינוּ.** טַעְמוֹ בְּבֵי״ת לְפִי שֶׁהוּא בִּלְשׁוֹן עָבָר, שֶׁכְּבָר בָּאָה, וְתַרְגּוּמוֹ: ״אֲתָת לָנָא״:

כב| **וְגַם דָּמוֹ.** אָתִין וְגַמִּין רִבּוּיִין – דָּמוֹ וְגַם דַּם הַזָּקֵן:

כג| **וְהֵם לֹא יָדְעוּ כִּי שֹׁמֵעַ יוֹסֵף.** מֵבִין לְשׁוֹנָם, וּבְפָנָיו הָיוּ מְדַבְּרִים כֵּן: **כִּי הַמֵּלִיץ בֵּינֹתָם.** כִּי כְּשֶׁהָיוּ מְדַבְּרִים עִמּוֹ הָיָה הַמֵּלִיץ בֵּינֵיהֶם הַיּוֹדֵעַ לָשׁוֹן עִבְרִית וְלָשׁוֹן מִצְרִית, וְהָיָה מֵלִיץ דִּבְרֵיהֶם לְיוֹסֵף וְדִבְרֵי יוֹסֵף לָהֶם, לְכָךְ הָיוּ סְבוּרִים שֶׁאֵין יוֹסֵף מַכִּיר בְּלָשׁוֹן עִבְרִית: **הַמֵּלִיץ.** זֶה מְנַשֶּׁה:

כד| **וַיִּסֹּב מֵעֲלֵיהֶם.** נִתְרַחֵק מֵעֲלֵיהֶם שֶׁלֹּא יִרְאוּהוּ בּוֹכֶה: **וַיֵּבְךְּ.** לְפִי שֶׁשָּׁמַע שֶׁהָיוּ מִתְחָרְטִין: **אֶת שִׁמְעוֹן.** הוּא הִשְׁלִיכוֹ לַבּוֹר, הוּא שֶׁאָמַר לְלֵוִי: ״הִנֵּה בַּעַל הַחֲלֹמוֹת הַלָּזֶה בָּא״ (לעיל לז, יט). דָּבָר אַחֵר, נִתְכַּוֵּן יוֹסֵף לְהַפְרִידוֹ מִלֵּוִי, שֶׁמָּא יִתְיָעֲצוּ שְׁנֵיהֶם לַהֲרֹג אוֹתוֹ: **וַיֶּאֱסֹר אֹתוֹ לְעֵינֵיהֶם.** לֹא אֲסָרוֹ אֶלָּא לְעֵינֵיהֶם, וְכֵיוָן שֶׁיָּצְאוּ הוֹצִיאוֹ וְהֶאֱכִילוֹ וְהִשְׁקָהוּ:

כז| **וַיִּפְתַּח הָאֶחָד.** הוּא לֵוִי שֶׁנִּשְׁאַר יָחִיד מִשִּׁמְעוֹן בֶּן זוּגוֹ: **בַּמָּלוֹן.** בַּמָּקוֹם שֶׁלָּנוּ בַּלַּיְלָה: **אַמְתַּחְתּוֹ.** הוּא שַׂק:

כח| **וְגַם הִנֵּה בְאַמְתַּחְתִּי.** גַּם הַכֶּסֶף בּוֹ עִם הַתְּבוּאָה: **מַה זֹּאת עָשָׂה אֱלֹהִים לָנוּ.** לַהֲבִיאֵנוּ לִידֵי עֲלִילָה זוֹ, שֶׁלֹּא הוּשַׁב אֶלָּא לְהִתְעוֹלֵל עָלֵינוּ:

suffering is punishment. It means that suffering is a source of personal challenge and spiritual growth which we would never have experienced otherwise. The pain is not diminished by this realization. But through it we find a way of living through pain without endless, fruitless thoughts of what might have been.

Yosef's brothers do not know that in this case it is he who is designing a situation of unfolding horror that will feel like a cruel repayment of their earlier crimes. Their test will be to see whether they bow to this apparent punishment and allow history to repeat, or whether they translate guilt into responsibility, and turn their past around.

כא תְמוּתוּ וַיַּעֲשׂוּ־כֵן: וַיֹּאמְרוּ אִישׁ אֶל־אָחִיו אֲבָל אֲשֵׁמִים ׀ אֲנַחְנוּ עַל־
אָחִינוּ אֲשֶׁר רָאִינוּ צָרַת נַפְשׁוֹ בְּהִתְחַנְנוֹ אֵלֵינוּ וְלֹא שָׁמָעְנוּ עַל־כֵּן
כב בָּאָה אֵלֵינוּ הַצָּרָה הַזֹּאת: וַיַּעַן רְאוּבֵן אֹתָם לֵאמֹר הֲלוֹא אָמַרְתִּי
אֲלֵיכֶם ׀ לֵאמֹר אַל־תֶּחֶטְאוּ בַיֶּלֶד וְלֹא שְׁמַעְתֶּם וְגַם־דָּמוֹ הִנֵּה נִדְרָשׁ:
כג כד וְהֵם לֹא יָדְעוּ כִּי שֹׁמֵעַ יוֹסֵף כִּי הַמֵּלִיץ בֵּינֹתָם: וַיִּסֹּב מֵעֲלֵיהֶם וַיֵּבְךְּ
וַיָּשָׁב אֲלֵהֶם וַיְדַבֵּר אֲלֵהֶם וַיִּקַּח מֵאִתָּם אֶת־שִׁמְעוֹן וַיֶּאֱסֹר אֹתוֹ
כה לְעֵינֵיהֶם: וַיְצַו יוֹסֵף וַיְמַלְאוּ אֶת־כְּלֵיהֶם בָּר וּלְהָשִׁיב כַּסְפֵּיהֶם אִישׁ
כו אֶל־שַׂקּוֹ וְלָתֵת לָהֶם צֵדָה לַדָּרֶךְ וַיַּעַשׂ לָהֶם כֵּן: וַיִּשְׂאוּ אֶת־שִׁבְרָם
כז עַל־חֲמֹרֵיהֶם וַיֵּלְכוּ מִשָּׁם: וַיִּפְתַּח הָאֶחָד אֶת־שַׂקּוֹ לָתֵת מִסְפּוֹא
כח לַחֲמֹרוֹ בַּמָּלוֹן וַיַּרְא אֶת־כַּסְפּוֹ וְהִנֵּה־הוּא בְּפִי אַמְתַּחְתּוֹ: וַיֹּאמֶר
אֶל־אֶחָיו הוּשַׁב כַּסְפִּי וְגַם הִנֵּה בְאַמְתַּחְתִּי וַיֵּצֵא לִבָּם וַיֶּחֶרְדוּ אִישׁ
כט אֶל־אָחִיו לֵאמֹר מַה־זֹּאת עָשָׂה אֱלֹהִים לָנוּ: וַיָּבֹאוּ אֶל־יַעֲקֹב אֲבִיהֶם

אונקלוס

תְּמוּתוּן, וַעֲבַדוּ כֵן: כא וַאֲמַרוּ גְּבַר לַאֲחוּהִי, בְּקֻשְׁטָא חַיָּבִין אֲנַחְנָא עַל אֲחוּנָא, דַּחֲזֵינָא, בְּעָקַת נַפְשֵׁיהּ, כַּד הֲוָה מִתְחַנַּן לַנָא וְלָא קַבֵּילְנָא מִנֵּיהּ, עַל כֵּן אֲתָת לַנָא, עָקְתָא הָדָא: כב וַאֲתֵיב רְאוּבֵן יָתְהוֹן לְמֵימַר, הֲלָא אֲמָרִית לְכוֹן לְמֵימַר, לָא תֶחֶטְאוּן בְּעוּלֵימָא וְלָא קַבֵּילְתּוּן, וְאַף דְּמֵיהּ הָא מִתְבְּעֵי: כג וְאִנּוּן לָא יָדְעִין, אֲרֵי שָׁמַע יוֹסֵף, אֲרֵי מְתֻרְגְּמָן הֲוָה בֵּינֵיהוֹן: כד וְאִסְתְּחַר מִלְּוָתְהוֹן וּבְכָא, וְתָב לְוָתְהוֹן וּמַלֵּיל עִמְּהוֹן, וּדְבַר מִלְּוָתְהוֹן יָת שִׁמְעוֹן, וַאֲסַר יָתֵיהּ לְעֵינֵיהוֹן: כה וּפַקֵּיד יוֹסֵף, וּמְלוֹ יָת מָנֵיהוֹן עֲבוּרָא, וּלְאָתָבָא כַּסְפֵּיהוֹן גְּבַר לְסַקֵּיהּ, וּלְמִתַּן לְהוֹן, זְוָדִין לְאוֹרְחָא, וַעֲבַד לְהוֹן כֵּן: כו וּנְטַלוּ יָת עֲבוּרְהוֹן עַל חֲמָרֵיהוֹן, וַאֲזַלוּ מִתַּמָּן: כז וּפְתַח חַד יָת סַקֵּיהּ, לְמִתַּן כִּסְתָּא, לַחֲמָרֵיהּ בְּבֵית מְבָתָא, וַחֲזָא יָת כַּסְפֵּיהּ, וְהָא הוּא בְּפוּם טְעוּנֵיהּ: כח וַאֲמַר לַאֲחוּהִי אִתָּתַב כַּסְפִּי, וְאַף הָא בִטְעוּנִי, וּנְפַק מַדַּע לִבְּהוֹן, וּתְוַהוּ, גְּבַר בַּאֲחוּהִי לְמֵימַר, מָא דָא, עֲבַד יְיָ לַנָא: כט וַאֲתוֹ, לְוָת יַעֲקֹב אֲבוּהוֹן

that the silver they have paid for the grain has been returned to them in their sacks, they tremble: "What is this that God has done to us?" (Gen. 41:28).

42:21 אֲבָל אֲשֵׁמִים אֲנַחְנוּ *We are guilty* – The Talmud says that "when sufferings come upon a person, he should examine his deeds" (Berakhot 5a). This seems to suggest that suffering is a sign of our having done something wrong and that we are being punished. But that is not what the Talmud means.

Rabbi Joseph Soleveitchik, in his essay "*Kol Dodi Dofek*," writes that when the Talmud sets out the halakhic approach to suffering, it is not seeking to answer the question "Why did this happen?" but rather "*Given* that this has happened, what then shall I do?" When it instructs us to examine our lives and undergo repentance, it does not mean that

30 to them. They said, "The man who is the lord of the land spoke to us harshly.
31 He accused us of spying on the land. We said to him, 'We are honest men; we
32 are not spies. We were twelve brothers, sons of the same father. One is gone,
33 and the youngest is now with our father in Canaan.' Then the man who is lord
of the land said to us, 'This is how I will know that you are honest men. Leave
one of your brothers with me, take something for your starving households,
34 and go. Then bring your youngest brother to me. Then I will know that you are
not spies but honest men. And then I will give you back your brother, and you
35 can trade in the land.'" They began emptying their sacks, and there in each one's
sack was his money bag. When they and their father saw the money bags, they
36 were afraid. Their father Yaakov said to them, "You have taken my children
away from me. Yosef is gone. Shimon is gone. Now you want to take Binyamin?
37 All this I must suffer!" Reuven said to his father, "You may kill my two sons if I
do not bring him back to you; entrust him to my care and I will bring him back
38 to you." "My son will not go down with you," said Yaakov. "His brother is dead,
and he is all I have left. If any harm comes to him on the way, you will bring
43 1 down my gray head in grief to Sheol." The famine in the land continued to be
2 severe. When they had eaten all the grain they had brought from Egypt, their

רש״י

לד| **וְאֶת הָאָרֶץ תִּסְחָרוּ.** תְּסוֹבְבוּ, וְכָל לְשׁוֹן 'סוֹחֲרִים' וּ'סְחוֹרָה' עַל שֵׁם שֶׁמְּחַזְּרִים וְסוֹבְבִים אַחַר הַפְּרַקְמַטְיָא:

לה| **צְרוֹר כַּסְפּוֹ.** קֶשֶׁר כַּסְפּוֹ:

לו| **אֹתִי שִׁכַּלְתֶּם.** מְלַמֵּד שֶׁחֲשָׁדָן שֶׁמָּא הֲרָגוּהוּ אוֹ מְכָרוּהוּ כְּיוֹסֵף: **שִׁכַּלְתֶּם.** כָּל מִי שֶׁבָּנָיו אֲבוּדִים קָרוּי 'שַׁכּוּל':

לח| **לֹא יֵרֵד בְּנִי עִמָּכֶם.** לֹא קִבֵּל דְּבָרָיו שֶׁל רְאוּבֵן, אָמַר: בְּכוֹר שׁוֹטֶה הוּא זֶה! הוּא אוֹמֵר לְהָמִית בָּנָיו, וְכִי בָּנָיו הֵם וְלֹא בָּנַי?!:

מג ב| **כַּאֲשֶׁר כִּלּוּ לֶאֱכֹל.** יְהוּדָה אָמַר לָהֶם: הַמְתִּינוּ לַזָּקֵן עַד שֶׁתִּכְלֶה פַּת מִן הַבַּיִת: **כַּאֲשֶׁר כִּלּוּ.** "כַּד שֵׁיצִיאוּ", וְהַמְתַרְגֵּם 'כַּד סְפִיקוּ' טוֹעֶה. "כַּאֲשֶׁר כִּלּוּ הַגְּמַלִּים לִשְׁתּוֹת" (לעיל כד, כב) מְתֻרְגָּם "כַּד סְפִיקוּ", כְּשֶׁשָּׁתוּ דֵּי סִפּוּקָם הוּא גְּמַר שְׁתִיָּתָם; אֲבָל זֶה, "כַּאֲשֶׁר כִּלּוּ לֶאֱכֹל", כַּאֲשֶׁר תַּם הָאֹכֶל הוּא, וּמְתַרְגְּמִינַן: "כַּד שֵׁיצִיאוּ":

42:38 **בְּיָגוֹן שְׁאוֹלָה** *In grief to Sheol* – The Hebrew word *Sheol* means the underworld, the realm of the dead. In Song of Songs we will read, "For love is as powerful as death itself, and jealousy unyielding as Sheol" (8:6). Why the same forceful use of language here and there?

Song of Songs signals that lovers belong to one another at the deepest level of their being. Any kind of betrayal of such a relationship is an ultimate wound and causes existential pain. Love and death are both inexorable, irresistible forces. Death is the extinction of self into nothingness. Love is the extinction of self into the other. Giving myself to the other, I live in the other's life. Thus the love of God is the force that defeats mortality: If the Other I love is eternal, then I am made eternal by our love.

Yaakov has survived the loss of Raḥel, compounded by the loss of her beloved first son. To survive the loss of her second, Binyamin, would be inconceivable. It would be, in every meaningful sense, the end of Yaakov's life.

ל אַרְצָה כְּנָעַן וַיַּגִּידוּ לוֹ אֵת כָּל־הַקֹּרֹת אֹתָם לֵאמֹר: דִּבֶּר הָאִישׁ אֲדֹנֵי
לא הָאָרֶץ אִתָּנוּ קָשׁוֹת וַיִּתֵּן אֹתָנוּ כִּמְרַגְּלִים אֶת־הָאָרֶץ: וַנֹּאמֶר אֵלָיו
לב כֵּנִים אֲנָחְנוּ לֹא הָיִינוּ מְרַגְּלִים: שְׁנֵים־עָשָׂר אֲנַחְנוּ אַחִים בְּנֵי אָבִינוּ
לג הָאֶחָד אֵינֶנּוּ וְהַקָּטֹן הַיּוֹם אֶת־אָבִינוּ בְּאֶרֶץ כְּנָעַן: וַיֹּאמֶר אֵלֵינוּ
הָאִישׁ אֲדֹנֵי הָאָרֶץ בְּזֹאת אֵדַע כִּי כֵנִים אַתֶּם אֲחִיכֶם הָאֶחָד הַנִּיחוּ
לד אִתִּי וְאֶת־רַעֲבוֹן בָּתֵּיכֶם קְחוּ וָלֵכוּ: וְהָבִיאוּ אֶת־אֲחִיכֶם הַקָּטֹן אֵלַי
וְאֵדְעָה כִּי לֹא מְרַגְּלִים אַתֶּם כִּי כֵנִים אַתֶּם אֶת־אֲחִיכֶם אֶתֵּן לָכֶם
לה וְאֶת־הָאָרֶץ תִּסְחָרוּ: וַיְהִי הֵם מְרִיקִים שַׂקֵּיהֶם וְהִנֵּה־אִישׁ צְרוֹר־כַּסְפּוֹ
לו בְּשַׂקּוֹ וַיִּרְאוּ אֶת־צְרֹרוֹת כַּסְפֵּיהֶם הֵמָּה וַאֲבִיהֶם וַיִּירָאוּ: וַיֹּאמֶר
אֲלֵהֶם יַעֲקֹב אֲבִיהֶם אֹתִי שִׁכַּלְתֶּם יוֹסֵף אֵינֶנּוּ וְשִׁמְעוֹן אֵינֶנּוּ וְאֶת־
לז בִּנְיָמִן תִּקָּחוּ עָלַי הָיוּ כֻלָּנָה: וַיֹּאמֶר רְאוּבֵן אֶל־אָבִיו לֵאמֹר אֶת־שְׁנֵי
בָנַי תָּמִית אִם־לֹא אֲבִיאֶנּוּ אֵלֶיךָ תְּנָה אֹתוֹ עַל־יָדִי וַאֲנִי אֲשִׁיבֶנּוּ
לח אֵלֶיךָ: וַיֹּאמֶר לֹא־יֵרֵד בְּנִי עִמָּכֶם כִּי־אָחִיו מֵת וְהוּא לְבַדּוֹ נִשְׁאָר
וּקְרָאָהוּ אָסוֹן בַּדֶּרֶךְ אֲשֶׁר תֵּלְכוּ־בָהּ וְהוֹרַדְתֶּם אֶת־שֵׂיבָתִי בְּיָגוֹן
מג א ב שְׁאוֹלָה: וְהָרָעָב כָּבֵד בָּאָרֶץ: וַיְהִי כַּאֲשֶׁר כִּלּוּ לֶאֱכֹל אֶת־הַשֶּׁבֶר
אֲשֶׁר הֵבִיאוּ מִמִּצְרָיִם וַיֹּאמֶר אֲלֵיהֶם אֲבִיהֶם שֻׁבוּ שִׁבְרוּ־לָנוּ מְעַט־

אונקלוס

לְאַרְעָא דִכְנַעַן, וְחַוִּיאוּ לֵיהּ, יָת, כָּל דְּעָרַעָא יָתְהוֹן לְמֵימַר: ל מַלֵּיל, גֻּבְרָא רִבּוֹנַהּ דְּאַרְעָא, עִמַּנָא קַשְׁיָן, וִיהַב יָתַנָא, כִּמְאַלְלֵי אַרְעָא: לא וַאֲמַרְנָא לֵיהּ כֵּיוָנֵי אֲנַחְנָא, לָא הֲוֵינָא אַלָּלֵי: לב תְּרֵי עֲסַר אֲנַחְנָא, אַחִין בְּנֵי אֲבוּנָא, חַד לֵיתוֹהִי, וּזְעֵירָא יוֹמָא דֵין, עִם אֲבוּנָא בְּאַרְעָא דִכְנָעַן: לג וַאֲמַר לַנָא, גֻּבְרָא רִבּוֹנַהּ דְּאַרְעָא, בְּדָא אֵדַע, אֲרֵי כֵּיוָנֵי אַתּוּן, אֲחוּכוֹן חַד שְׁבוּקוּ לְוָתִי, וְיָת עֲבוּרָא דַּחְסִיר בְּבָתֵּיכוֹן סַבוּ וְאִיזִילוּ: לד וְאַיְתוֹ, יָת אֲחוּכוֹן זְעֵירָא לְוָתִי, וְאֵדַע, אֲרֵי לָא אַלָּלֵי אַתּוּן, אֲרֵי כֵּיוָנֵי אַתּוּן, יָת אֲחוּכוֹן אֶתֵּין לְכוֹן, וְיָת אַרְעָא תַּעְבְּדוּן בַּהּ סְחוֹרְתָא: לה וַהֲוָה, אִנּוּן מְרִיקִין סַקֵּיהוֹן, וְהָא גְּבַר צְרוֹר כַּסְפֵּיהּ בְּסַקֵּיהּ, וַחֲזוֹ, יָת צְרָרֵי כַּסְפֵּיהוֹן, אִנּוּן וַאֲבוּהוֹן וּדְחִילוּ: לו וַאֲמַר לְהוֹן יַעֲקֹב אֲבוּהוֹן, יָתִי אַתְכֵּילְתּוּן, יוֹסֵף לֵיתוֹהִי וְשִׁמְעוֹן לָא הֲוָה כָּא, וְיָת בִּנְיָמִין תִּדְבְּרוּן, עֲלַי הֲוָאָה כֻלְּהוֹן: לז וַאֲמַר רְאוּבֵן לַאֲבוּהִי לְמֵימַר, יָת תְּרֵין בְּנֵי תְּמִית, אִם לָא אַיְתֵינֵיהּ לָךְ, הַב יָתֵיהּ עַל יְדִי, וַאֲנָא אֲתִיבִנֵּיהּ לָךְ: לח וַאֲמַר, לָא יֵיחוֹת בְּרִי עִמְּכוֹן, אֲרֵי אֲחוּהִי מִית וְהוּא בִלְחוֹדוֹהִי אִשְׁתְּאַר, וִיעָרְעִנֵּיהּ מוֹתָא בְּאוֹרְחָא דִּתְהָכוּן בַּהּ, וְתַחֲתוּן יָת סֵיבָתִי, בִּדְווֹנָא לִשְׁאוֹל: מג א וְכַפְנָא תְּקֵיף בְּאַרְעָא: ב וַהֲוָה, כַּד שֵׁיצִיאוּ לְמֵיכַל יָת עֲבוּרָא, דְּאַיְתִיאוּ מִמִּצְרָיִם, וַאֲמַר לְהוֹן אֲבוּהוֹן, תּוּבוּ זְבוּנוּ לַנָא זְעֵיר

3 father said to them, "Go back and buy us some more food." But Yehuda said to
him, "The man warned us, 'Do not appear before me unless your brother is
4 with you.' If you agree to send our brother with us, we will go and buy you food.
5 But if you will not send him, we cannot go. The man told us, 'Do not appear
6 before me unless your brother is with you.'" Yisrael said, "Why did you bring
7 this trouble on me by telling the man you had another brother?" They replied,
"The man kept asking about us and our family: 'Is your father still alive?' he
asked. 'Do you have a brother?' We simply answered his questions. How could
8 we know that he would say, 'Bring your brother here'?" And Yehuda said to his
father Yisrael, "Send the boy with me. Let us be on our way so that we, you, and
9 our children may live and not die. I myself am the guarantee for his safety: you
may hold me personally responsible. If I do not bring him back and set him
10 before you, I will have sinned against you for all time. We could have been there
11 and back twice if we had not hesitated so long." And then their father Yisrael
said to them, "If that is how it must be, then do this. Take some of the best
produce of the land in your bags, and bring them to the man as a gift – a little
balm and a little honey, some spices and myrrh, pistachio nuts and almonds.
12 Take with you double the money. Return the money that was put back into

רש"י

ג **העד העד.** לשון התראה, שסתם התראה מתרה בו בפני עדים, וכן: "העדתי בהבותיכם" (ירמיה יא, ז), "רד העד בעם" (שמות יט, כא): **לא תראו פני בלתי אחיכם אתכם.** לא תראוני בלא אחיכם אתכם. ואונקלוס תרגם: "אלהן כד אחוכון עמכון", ישב הדבר על אפנו ולא דקדק לתרגם אחר לשון המקרא:

ז **לנו ולמולדתנו.** למשפחותינו. ומדרשו, אפילו עצי עריסותינו גלה לנו: **ונגד לו.** שיש לנו אב ואח: **על פי הדברים האלה.** על פי שאלותיו אשר שאל הזקקנו להגיד: **כי יאמר.** אשר יאמר; 'כי' משמש בלשון 'אם' ו'אם' משמש בלשון 'אשר', הרי זה שמוש אחד מארבע לשונותיו, 'אי', שהרי 'כי' זה כמו 'אם', כמו: "עד אם דברתי דברי" (לעיל כד, לג):

ח **ונחיה.** נתנבא בו רוח הקדש, על ידי הליכה זו תחי רוחך, שנאמר: "ותחי רוח יעקב אביהם" (להלן מה, כז): **ולא נמות.** ברעב; בנימין ספק יתפש ספק לא יתפש, ואנו כלנו מתים ברעב אם לא נלך, מוטב שתניח את הספק ותתפש את הודאי:

ט **והצגתיו לפניך.** שלא אביאנו אליך מת כי אם חי: **וחטאתי לך כל הימים.** לעולם הבא:

י **לולא התמהמהנו.** על ידך, כבר היינו שבים עם שמעון, ולא נצטערת כל הימים הללו:

יא **אפוא.** לשון יתר הוא לתקן מלה בלשון עברי: אם כן אזדקק לעשות שאשלחנו עמכם, צריך אני לחזור ולבקש איה פה תקנה ועצה להשיאכם, ואומר אני: "זאת עשו": **מזמרת הארץ.** כתרגומו "מדמשבח בארעא", שהכל מזמרים עליו כשהוא בא לעולם: **נכאת.** שעוה. בראשית רבה (צא, יא): **בטנים.** לא ידעתי מה הם. ובפרושי אלף בי"ת של רבי מכיר ראיתי פסטקיא"ס, ודומה לי שהן אפרסקים:

יב **וכסף משנה.** פי שנים כראשון: **קחו בידכם.** לשבר אכל, שמא הוקר השער:

another." The people of Israel are "a single body and a single soul," moved by one another's pain, sharing responsibility for their collective fate. More than any other factor, that attitude preserved the Jewish nation through the deepest crises of its history, and sustains us today.

ג אֹֽכֶל: וַיֹּ֧אמֶר אֵלָ֛יו יְהוּדָ֖ה לֵאמֹ֑ר הָעֵ֣ד הֵעִד֩ בָּ֨נוּ הָאִ֤ישׁ לֵאמֹר֙ לֹֽא־
ד תִרְא֣וּ פָנַ֔י בִּלְתִּ֖י אֲחִיכֶ֥ם אִתְּכֶֽם: אִם־יֶשְׁךָ֛ מְשַׁלֵּ֥חַ אֶת־אָחִ֖ינוּ אִתָּ֑נוּ
ה נֵֽרְדָ֕ה וְנִשְׁבְּרָ֥ה לְךָ֖ אֹֽכֶל: וְאִם־אֵֽינְךָ֥ מְשַׁלֵּ֖חַ לֹ֣א נֵרֵ֑ד כִּֽי־הָאִ֞ישׁ אָמַ֣ר
ו אֵלֵ֗ינוּ לֹֽא־תִרְא֣וּ פָנַ֔י בִּלְתִּ֖י אֲחִיכֶ֥ם אִתְּכֶֽם: וַיֹּ֙אמֶר֙ יִשְׂרָאֵ֔ל לָמָ֥ה
ז הֲרֵעֹתֶ֖ם לִ֑י לְהַגִּ֣יד לָאִ֔ישׁ הַע֥וֹד לָכֶ֖ם אָֽח: וַיֹּאמְר֡וּ שָׁא֣וֹל שָֽׁאַל־הָ֠אִישׁ
לָ֣נוּ וּלְמֽוֹלַדְתֵּ֜נוּ לֵאמֹ֗ר הַע֨וֹד אֲבִיכֶ֥ם חַי֙ הֲיֵ֣שׁ לָכֶ֣ם אָ֔ח וַנַּ֨גֶּד־ל֔וֹ עַל־פִּ֖י
ח הַדְּבָרִ֣ים הָאֵ֑לֶּה הֲיָד֣וֹעַ נֵדַ֔ע כִּ֣י יֹאמַ֔ר הוֹרִ֖ידוּ אֶת־אֲחִיכֶֽם: וַיֹּ֨אמֶר
יְהוּדָ֜ה אֶל־יִשְׂרָאֵ֣ל אָבִ֗יו שִׁלְחָ֥ה הַנַּ֛עַר אִתִּ֖י וְנָק֣וּמָה וְנֵלֵ֑כָה וְנִֽחְיֶה֙
ט וְלֹ֣א נָמ֔וּת גַּם־אֲנַ֥חְנוּ גַם־אַתָּ֖ה גַּם־טַפֵּֽנוּ: אָנֹכִי֙ אֶֽעֶרְבֶ֔נּוּ מִיָּדִ֖י תְּבַקְשֶׁ֑נּוּ
י אִם־לֹ֨א הֲבִיאֹתִ֤יו אֵלֶ֙יךָ֙ וְהִצַּגְתִּ֣יו לְפָנֶ֔יךָ וְחָטָ֥אתִי לְךָ֖ כָּל־הַיָּמִֽים: כִּ֖י
יא לוּלֵ֣א הִתְמַהְמָ֑הְנוּ כִּֽי־עַתָּ֥ה שַׁ֖בְנוּ זֶ֥ה פַעֲמָֽיִם: וַיֹּ֨אמֶר אֲלֵהֶ֜ם יִשְׂרָאֵ֣ל
אֲבִיהֶ֗ם אִם־כֵּ֣ן ׀ אֵפוֹא֮ זֹ֣את עֲשׂוּ֒ קְח֞וּ מִזִּמְרַ֤ת הָאָ֙רֶץ֙ בִּכְלֵיכֶ֔ם וְהוֹרִ֥ידוּ
לָאִ֖ישׁ מִנְחָ֑ה מְעַ֤ט צֳרִי֙ וּמְעַ֣ט דְּבַ֔שׁ נְכֹ֣את וָלֹ֔ט בָּטְנִ֖ים וּשְׁקֵדִֽים:
יב וְכֶ֥סֶף מִשְׁנֶ֖ה קְח֣וּ בְיֶדְכֶ֑ם וְאֶת־הַכֶּ֜סֶף הַמּוּשָׁ֨ב בְּפִ֤י אַמְתְּחֹֽתֵיכֶם֙ תָּשִׁ֣יבוּ

אונקלוס

עֲבוּרָא: ג וַאֲמַר לֵיהּ, יְהוּדָה לְמֵימַר, אַסְהָדָא אַסְהֵיד בַּנָא גֻבְרָא לְמֵימַר לָא תִחְזוֹן אַפַּי, אֱלָהֵין כַּד אֲחוּכוֹן עִמְּכוֹן: ד אִם אִיתָךְ, מְשַׁלַּח יָת אֲחוּנָא עִמַּנָא, נֵיחוֹת, וְנִזְבּוֹן לָךְ עֲבוּרָא: ה וְאִם לֵיתָךְ מְשַׁלַּח לָא נֵיחוֹת, אֲרֵי גֻבְרָא, אֲמַר לַנָא לָא תִחְזוֹן אַפַּי, אֱלָהֵין כַּד אֲחוּכוֹן עִמְּכוֹן: ו וַאֲמַר יִשְׂרָאֵל, לְמָא אַבְאֵישְׁתּוּן לִי, לְחַוָּאָה לְגֻבְרָא, הַעוֹד לְכוֹן אֲחָא: ז וַאֲמַרוּ, שְׁאָלָא שְׁאֵיל גֻּבְרָא, לַנָא וּלְיַלָּדוּתַנָא לְמֵימַר, הַעוֹד אֲבוּכוֹן קַיָּם הַאִית לְכוֹן אֲחָא, וְחַוֵּינָא לֵיהּ, עַל מֵימַר פִּתְגָּמַיָּא הָאִלֵּין, הֲמִידַע הֲוֵינָא יָדְעִין, אֲרֵי יֵימַר, אַחִיתוּ יָת אֲחוּכוֹן: ח וַאֲמַר יְהוּדָה לְיִשְׂרָאֵל אֲבוּהִי, שְׁלַח עוּלֵימָא, עִמִּי וּנְקוּם וְנֵיזִיל, וְנֵיחֵי וְלָא נְמוּת, אַף אֲנַחְנָא אַף אַתְּ אַף טַפְלַנָא: ט אֲנָא מְעָרַבְנָא בֵּיהּ, מִן יְדִי תִּבְעֵינֵיהּ, אִם לָא אַיְתֵינֵיהּ לָךְ וַאֲקִימִנֵּיהּ קֳדָמָךְ, וְאֵיהֵי חָטֵי לָךְ כָּל יוֹמַיָּא: י אֲרֵי אִלּוּ לָא פוֹן בְּדָא אִתְעַכַּבְנָא, אֲרֵי כְעַן תַּבְנָא דְנַן תַּרְתֵּין זִמְנִין: יא וַאֲמַר לְהוֹן יִשְׂרָאֵל אֲבוּהוֹן, אִם כֵּן הוּא דָא עֲבִידוּ, סַבוּ, מִדִּמְשַׁבַּח בְּאַרְעָא בְּמָנֵיכוֹן, וַאֲחִיתוּ לְגֻבְרָא תִּקְרֻבְתָּא, זְעֵיר קְטַף וּזְעֵיר דְּבַשׁ, שְׁעַף וּלְטוֹם, בֻּטְמִין וְשִׁגְדִּין: יב וְכַסְפָּא עַל חַד תְּרֵין סַבוּ בִּידְכוֹן, וְיָת כַּסְפָּא, דְּאִתָּתַב בְּפוּם טְעוּנֵיכוֹן תְּתִיבוּן

43:9 אָנֹכִי אֶעֶרְבֶנּוּ *I myself am the guarantee* – Yehuda pledges himself and his freedom against Yaakov's "loan" of Binyamin. Just as Yaakov's life is bound up in his son's, so are Yehuda's freedom and well-being now conditional on Binyamin's. The language will be echoed in the Sages' maxim *Kol Yisrael arevin zeh bazeh*, literally, "All Israel are guarantors for one

13 your sacks. Perhaps it was a mistake. And take your brother. Go back to the
14 man at once. May El Shaddai grant you mercy before the man, that he may
send your other brother forth to you, and Binyamin. And as for me, if I am to
15 be bereaved, I will be bereaved." So the men took the gift and double the money
and set out with Binyamin. They went to Egypt and presented themselves to
16 Yosef. When Yosef saw Binyamin with them, he said to his house steward, SHISHI
"Take these men to my house. Slaughter an animal and prepare a meal, for they
17 will dine with me at noon." The man did as Yosef said and brought them to
18 Yosef's house. The men were frightened that they were being brought to Yosef's
house. They said, "We have been brought here because of the money that was
put back in our sacks the first time. He wants to attack us, seize us as slaves, and
19 take our donkeys." So they went up to Yosef's steward and spoke to him at the
20 entrance to the house. "If you please, my lord," they said, "we came here once
21 before to buy food. But at the place where we stopped for the night, we opened
our bags and each of us found his money, in its exact weight, in the mouth of
22 his bag. So we have brought it back with us. We have also brought additional
23 money to buy food. We do not know who put our money in our bags." He
replied, "All is well. Do not be afraid. Your God, the God of your father, must
have placed a hidden gift in your bags. I received the money you paid." Then he

רש״י

אוּלַי מִשְׁגֶּה הוּא. שֶׁמָּא הַמְמֻנֶּה עַל הַבַּיִת שְׁכָחוֹ שׁוֹגֵג:

יד **וְאֵל שַׁדַּי.** מֵעַתָּה אֵינְכֶם חֲסֵרִים כְּלוּם אֶלָּא תְּפִלָּה, הֲרֵינִי מִתְפַּלֵּל עֲלֵיכֶם: אֵל שֶׁיֵּשׁ דַּי בִּנְתִינַת רַחֲמָיו וּכְדֵי הַיְכֹלֶת בְּיָדוֹ לִתֵּן, "יִתֵּן לָכֶם רַחֲמִים", זֶהוּ פְּשׁוּטוֹ. וּמִדְרָשׁוֹ, מִי שֶׁאָמַר לָעוֹלָם דַּי יֹאמַר דַּי לְצָרוֹתַי, שֶׁלֹּא שָׁקַטְתִּי מִנְּעוּרַי: צָרַת לָבָן, צָרַת עֵשָׂו, צָרַת רָחֵל, צָרַת דִּינָה, צָרַת יוֹסֵף, צָרַת שִׁמְעוֹן, צָרַת בִּנְיָמִין: **וְשִׁלַּח לָכֶם.** "וְיִפְטַר לְכוֹן", כְּתַרְגּוּמוֹ, יִפְטְרֶנּוּ מֵאֲסוּרָיו, לְשׁוֹן "לַחָפְשִׁי יְשַׁלְּחֶנּוּ" (שמות כא, כו). וְאֵין נוֹפֵל בְּתַרְגּוּמוֹ לְשׁוֹן 'וִישַׁלַּח', שֶׁהֲרֵי לְשָׁם הֵם הוֹלְכִים אֶצְלוֹ: **אֶת אֲחִיכֶם.** זֶה שִׁמְעוֹן: **אַחֵר.** רוּחַ הַקֹּדֶשׁ נִזְרְקָה בוֹ, לְרַבּוֹת יוֹסֵף: **וַאֲנִי.** עַד שׁוּבְכֶם אֶהְיֶה שָׁכוּל מִסָּפֵק: **כַּאֲשֶׁר שָׁכֹלְתִּי.** מִיּוֹסֵף וּמִשִּׁמְעוֹן: **שָׁכָלְתִּי.** מִבִּנְיָמִין:

טו **וְאֶת בִּנְיָמִן.** מְתַרְגְּמִינַן "וּדְבַרוּ יָת בִּנְיָמִין", לְפִי שֶׁאֵין לְקִיחַת הַכֶּסֶף וּלְקִיחַת הָאָדָם שָׁוָה בְּלָשׁוֹן אֲרַמִּי; בְּדָבָר הַנִּקָּח בַּיָּד מְתַרְגְּמִינַן: "וּנְסֵיב", וְדָבָר הַנִּקָּח בְּהַנְהָגַת דְּבָרִים מְתַרְגְּמִינַן: "וּדְבַר":

טז **וּטְבֹחַ טֶבַח וְהָכֵן.** כְּמוֹ: 'וְלִטְבֹּחַ טֶבַח וּלְהָכֵן'. וְאֵין 'וּטְבֹחַ' לְשׁוֹן צִוּוּי, שֶׁהָיָה לוֹ לוֹמַר 'וּטְבַח': **בַּצָּהֳרָיִם.** זֶה מְתֻרְגָּם "בְּשֵׁירוּתָא" שֶׁהוּא לְשׁוֹן סְעוּדָה רִאשׁוֹנָה בְּלָשׁוֹן אֲרַמִּי, וּבְלַעַז דשני"ר, וְיֵשׁ הַרְבֵּה בַּתַּלְמוּד: "שְׁדָא לְכַלְבָּא שֵׁירוּתֵיהּ" (תענית יא ע"ב), "בָּצַע אַכּוּלָּא שֵׁירוּתֵיהּ" (ברכות לט ע"ב). אֲבָל כָּל תַּרְגּוּם שֶׁל 'צָהֳרַיִם' – טֵיהֲרָא:

יח **וַיִּירְאוּ הָאֲנָשִׁים.** כָּתוּב הוּא בִּשְׁנֵי יוּדִי"ן, וְתַרְגּוּמוֹ: "וּדְחִילוּ": **כִּי הוּבְאוּ בֵּית יוֹסֵף.** וְאֵין דֶּרֶךְ שְׁאָר הַבָּאִים לִשְׁבֹּר בָּר לָלוּן בְּבֵית יוֹסֵף כִּי אִם בְּפֻנְדְּקָאוֹת שֶׁבָּעִיר. "וַיִּירְאוּ" שֶׁאֵין זֶה אֶלָּא לְאָסְפָם אֶל מִשְׁמָר: **אֲנַחְנוּ מוּבָאִים.** אֶל תּוֹךְ הַבַּיִת הַזֶּה: **לְהִתְגֹּלֵל.** לִהְיוֹת מִתְגַּלְגֶּלֶת עָלֵינוּ עֲלִילַת הַכֶּסֶף וְלִהְיוֹתָהּ נוֹפֶלֶת עָלֵינוּ. וְאוּנְקְלוֹס שֶׁתִּרְגֵּם: "וּלְאִסְתַּקָּפָא עֲלַנָא" הוּא לְשׁוֹן 'לְהִתְעוֹלֵל', כִּדְמְתַרְגְּמִינַן "עֲלִילֹת דְּבָרִים" (דברים כב, יד) – "תַּסְקוּפֵי מִלִּין", וְלֹא תִרְגְּמוֹ אַחַר לְשׁוֹן הַמִּקְרָא. וּ"לְהִתְגֹּלֵל" שֶׁתִּרְגֵּם "לְאִתְרַבְרָבָא" הוּא לְשׁוֹן: "גֻּלַּת הַזָּהָב" (קהלת יב, ו), "וְהֻצַּב גֻּלְּתָה הֹעֲלָתָה" (נחום ב, ח), שֶׁהוּא לְשׁוֹן מַלְכוּת:

כ **בִּי אֲדֹנִי.** לְשׁוֹן בְּעָיָה וְתַחֲנוּנִים הוּא, וּבְלָשׁוֹן אֲרַמִּי: "בָּיָא בָּיָא" (יומא סט ע"ב): **יָרֹד יָרַדְנוּ.** יְרִידָה הִיא לָנוּ, רְגִילִים הָיִינוּ לְפַרְנֵס אֲחֵרִים, עַכְשָׁיו אָנוּ צְרִיכִים לְךָ:

כג **אֱלֹהֵיכֶם.** בִּזְכוּתְכֶם; וְאִם אֵין זְכוּתְכֶם כְּדַאי, "אֱלֹהֵי אֲבִיכֶם" – בִּזְכוּת אֲבִיכֶם "נָתַן לָכֶם מַטְמוֹן":

יג בְיֶדְכֶם אוּלַי מִשְׁגֶּה הוּא: וְאֶת־אֲחִיכֶם קָחוּ וְקוּמוּ שׁוּבוּ אֶל־הָאִישׁ:
יד וְאֵל שַׁדַּי יִתֵּן לָכֶם רַחֲמִים לִפְנֵי הָאִישׁ וְשִׁלַּח לָכֶם אֶת־אֲחִיכֶם אַחֵר לט
טו וְאֶת־בִּנְיָמִין וַאֲנִי כַּאֲשֶׁר שָׁכֹלְתִּי שָׁכָלְתִּי: וַיִּקְחוּ הָאֲנָשִׁים אֶת־הַמִּנְחָה
הַזֹּאת וּמִשְׁנֶה־כֶּסֶף לָקְחוּ בְיָדָם וְאֶת־בִּנְיָמִן וַיָּקֻמוּ וַיֵּרְדוּ מִצְרַיִם
טז וַיַּעַמְדוּ לִפְנֵי יוֹסֵף: וַיַּרְא יוֹסֵף אִתָּם אֶת־בִּנְיָמִין וַיֹּאמֶר לַאֲשֶׁר עַל־ ששי
בֵּיתוֹ הָבֵא אֶת־הָאֲנָשִׁים הַבָּיְתָה וּטְבֹחַ טֶבַח וְהָכֵן כִּי אִתִּי יֹאכְלוּ
יז הָאֲנָשִׁים בַּצָּהֳרָיִם: וַיַּעַשׂ הָאִישׁ כַּאֲשֶׁר אָמַר יוֹסֵף וַיָּבֵא הָאִישׁ אֶת־
יח הָאֲנָשִׁים בֵּיתָה יוֹסֵף: וַיִּירְאוּ הָאֲנָשִׁים כִּי הוּבְאוּ בֵּית יוֹסֵף וַיֹּאמְרוּ
עַל־דְּבַר הַכֶּסֶף הַשָּׁב בְּאַמְתְּחֹתֵינוּ בַּתְּחִלָּה אֲנַחְנוּ מוּבָאִים לְהִתְגֹּלֵל
יט עָלֵינוּ וּלְהִתְנַפֵּל עָלֵינוּ וְלָקַחַת אֹתָנוּ לַעֲבָדִים וְאֶת־חֲמֹרֵינוּ: וַיִּגְּשׁוּ
כ אֶל־הָאִישׁ אֲשֶׁר עַל־בֵּית יוֹסֵף וַיְדַבְּרוּ אֵלָיו פֶּתַח הַבָּיִת: וַיֹּאמְרוּ בִּי
כא אֲדֹנִי יָרֹד יָרַדְנוּ בַּתְּחִלָּה לִשְׁבָּר־אֹכֶל: וַיְהִי כִּי־בָאנוּ אֶל־הַמָּלוֹן
וַנִּפְתְּחָה אֶת־אַמְתְּחֹתֵינוּ וְהִנֵּה כֶסֶף־אִישׁ בְּפִי אַמְתַּחְתּוֹ כַּסְפֵּנוּ
כב בְּמִשְׁקָלוֹ וַנָּשֶׁב אֹתוֹ בְּיָדֵנוּ: וְכֶסֶף אַחֵר הוֹרַדְנוּ בְיָדֵנוּ לִשְׁבָּר־אֹכֶל
כג לֹא יָדַעְנוּ מִי־שָׂם כַּסְפֵּנוּ בְּאַמְתְּחֹתֵינוּ: וַיֹּאמֶר שָׁלוֹם לָכֶם אַל־תִּירָאוּ
אֱלֹהֵיכֶם וֵאלֹהֵי אֲבִיכֶם נָתַן לָכֶם מַטְמוֹן בְּאַמְתְּחֹתֵיכֶם כַּסְפְּכֶם

אונקלוס

בִּידְכוֹן, דִּלְמָא שָׁלוּ הֲוָת: יג וְיָת אֲחוּכוֹן דְּבַרוּ, וְקוּמוּ תּוּבוּ לְוָת גַּבְרָא: יד וְאֵל שַׁדַּי, יִתֵּין לְכוֹן רַחֲמִין קֳדָם גַּבְרָא, וְיִפְטַר לְכוֹן, יָת אֲחוּכוֹן אָחֳרָנָא וְיָת בִּנְיָמִין, וַאֲנָא, כְּמָא דִּתְכֵילִית תְּכֵילִית: טו וּנְסִיבוּ גֻּבְרַיָּא יָת תִּקְרֻבְתָּא הָדָא, וְעַל חַד תְּרֵין כַּסְפָּא, נְסִיבוּ בִּידְהוֹן וּדְבַרוּ יָת בִּנְיָמִין, וְקָמוּ וּנְחַתוּ לְמִצְרַיִם, וְקָמוּ קֳדָם יוֹסֵף: טז וַחֲזָא יוֹסֵף עִמְּהוֹן יָת בִּנְיָמִין, וַאֲמַר לִדְמְמַנָּא עַל בֵּיתֵיהּ, אָעֵיל יָת גֻּבְרַיָּא לְבֵיתָא, וְכוֹס נִכְסְתָא וְאַתְקֵין, אֲרֵי עִמִּי, אָכְלִין גֻּבְרַיָּא בְּשֵׁירוּתָא: יז וַעֲבַד גַּבְרָא, כְּמָא דַּאֲמַר יוֹסֵף, וְאָעֵיל גַּבְרָא, יָת גֻּבְרַיָּא לְבֵית יוֹסֵף: יח וּדְחִילוּ גֻּבְרַיָּא, אֲרֵי אִתָּעֲלוּ לְבֵית יוֹסֵף, וַאֲמַרוּ, עַל עֵיסַק כַּסְפָּא דְּאִתָּתַב בְּטָעֳנַנָא בְּקַדְמֵיתָא, אֲנַחְנָא מִתָּעֲלִין, לְאִתְרַבְרָבָא עֲלַנָא וּלְאִסְתַּקָּפָא עֲלַנָא, וּלְמִקְנֵי יָתַנָא, לְעַבְדִּין וּלְמִדְבַּר יָת חֲמָרָנָא: יט וּקְרִיבוּ לְוָת גַּבְרָא, דִּמְמַנָּא עַל בֵּית יוֹסֵף, וּמַלִּילוּ עִמֵּיהּ בִּתְרַע בֵּיתָא: כ וַאֲמַרוּ בְּבָעוּ רִבּוֹנִי, מֵיחַת נְחַתְנָא, בְּקַדְמֵיתָא לְמִזְבַּן עֲבוּרָא: כא וַהֲוָה כַּד אֲתֵינָא לְבֵית מְבָתָא, וּפְתַחְנָא יָת טָעֳנַנָא, וְהָא כְּסַף גְּבַר בְּפוּם טְעוּנֵיהּ, כַּסְפַּנָא בְּמַתְקְלֵיהּ, וַאֲתֵיבְנָא יָתֵיהּ בִּידַנָא: כב וְכַסְפָּא אָחֳרָנָא, אֲחֵיתְנָא בִידַנָא לְמִזְבַּן עֲבוּרָא, לָא יְדַעְנָא, מַאן שַׁוִּי כַּסְפַּנָא בְּטָעֳנַנָא: כג וַאֲמַר שְׁלָם לְכוֹן לָא תִדְחֲלוּן, אֱלָהֲכוֹן, וֵאלָהָא דַּאֲבוּכוֹן יְהַב לְכוֹן סִימָן בְּטָעֳנֵיכוֹן, כַּסְפְּכוֹן

24 brought Shimon out to them. He brought the brothers into Yosef's house, gave
25 them water to bathe their feet, and had fodder brought for their donkeys. They
set out their gifts in preparation for Yosef's arrival at noon, because they had
26 heard that they were going to eat there. When Yosef entered the house, they
presented him with the gifts they had brought and bowed low to the ground
27 before him. He asked them how they were. Then he asked, "How is the elderly
28 father about whom you spoke? Is he still alive?" They said, "Your servant our
29 father is alive and well." They bowed down and prostrated themselves. Then he
looked up and saw his brother Binyamin, his mother's son, and asked, "Is this
your youngest brother, the one you mentioned to me?" And he said, "God be
30 gracious to you, my son." At that, he hurried out, for he was overcome with SHEVI'I
feeling toward his brother and was on the verge of tears. He went into a private
31 room and there he wept. He washed his face and came out, controlling himself.
32 "Serve the food," he said. They served him apart, them apart, and the Egyptians
who ate with him apart, for the Egyptians could not eat with Hebrews, since to
33 Egyptians that was considered abhorrent. Seated by his direction in order of

רש״י

כד| **וַיָּבֵא הָאִישׁ.** הֲבָאָה אַחַר הֲבָאָה, לְפִי שֶׁהָיוּ דּוֹחֲפִים אוֹתוֹ חוּץ עַד שֶׁדִּבְּרוּ אֵלָיו פֶּתַח הַבַּיִת, וּמִשֶּׁאָמַר לָהֶם "שָׁלוֹם לָכֶם" (לעיל פסוק כג) נִמְשְׁכוּ וּבָאוּ אַחֲרָיו:

כה| **וַיָּכִינוּ.** הִזְמִינוּ, עִטְּרוּהָ בְּכֵלִים נָאִים:

כו| **הַבַּיְתָה.** מִפְּרוֹזְדוֹר לִטְרַקְלִין:

כח| **וַיִּקְּדוּ וַיִּשְׁתַּחֲוֻ.** עַל שְׁאֵלַת שָׁלוֹם. קִדָּה – כְּפִיפַת קָדְקֹד, הִשְׁתַּחֲוָאָה – מִשְׁתַּטֵּחַ לָאָרֶץ:

כט| **אֱלֹהִים יָחְנְךָ בְּנִי.** בִּשְׁאָר שְׁבָטִים שָׁמַעְנוּ חֲנִינָה: "אֲשֶׁר חָנַן אֱלֹהִים אֶת עַבְדֶּךָ" (לעיל לג, ה), וּבִנְיָמִין עֲדַיִן לֹא נוֹלַד, לְכָךְ בֵּרְכוֹ יוֹסֵף בַּחֲנִינָה:

ל| **כִּי נִכְמְרוּ רַחֲמָיו.** שְׁאָלוֹ: יֵשׁ לְךָ אָח מֵאֵם? אָמַר לוֹ: אָח הָיָה לִי וְאֵינִי יוֹדֵעַ הֵיכָן הוּא. יֵשׁ לְךָ בָּנִים? אָמַר לוֹ: יֵשׁ לִי עֲשָׂרָה. אָמַר לוֹ: וּמַה שְּׁמָם? אָמַר לוֹ: בֶּלַע וָבֶכֶר וְגוֹ' (להלן מו, כא). אָמַר לוֹ: מַה טִּיבָן שֶׁל שֵׁמוֹת הַלָּלוּ? אָמַר לוֹ: כֻּלָּם עַל שֵׁם אָחִי וְהַצָּרוֹת שֶׁמְּצָאוּהוּ, כִּדְאִיתָא בְּמַסֶּכֶת סוֹטָה (דף לו ע״ב); מִיָּד נִכְמְרוּ רַחֲמָיו: **נִכְמְרוּ.** נִתְחַמְּמוּ, וּבִלְשׁוֹן מִשְׁנָה: "עַל הַכֹּמֶר שֶׁל זֵיתִים" (בבא מציעא עד ע״א), וּבִלְשׁוֹן אֲרַמִּי: "מִכְמַר בִּשְׂרָא" (פסחים נח ע״א), וּבַמִּקְרָא: "עוֹרֵנוּ כְּתַנּוּר נִכְמָרוּ" (איכה ה, י) – נִתְחַמְּמוּ וְנִקְמְטוּ קְמָטִים קְמָטִים, "מִפְּנֵי זַלְעֲפוֹת רָעָב". כֵּן דֶּרֶךְ כָּל עוֹר, כְּשֶׁמְּחַמְּמִין אוֹתוֹ מִתְּכַוֵּץ – נִקְמָט וְנִכְוָץ:

לא| **וַיִּתְאַפַּק.** נִתְאַמֵּץ, וְהוּא לְשׁוֹן "אֲפִיקֵי מָגִנִּים" (איוב מא, ז), חֹזֶק. וְכֵן: "וּמְזִיחַ אֲפִיקִים רִפָּה" (שם יב, כא):

לב| **כִּי תוֹעֵבָה הִוא.** דָּבָר שָׂנְאוּי הוּא לְמִצְרִים "לֶאֱכֹל אֶת הָעִבְרִים", וְאוּנְקְלוֹס נָתַן טַעַם לַדָּבָר:

of his dreams and his elevation to a position of power. Yosef does everything he can for his brothers and makes it as clear as he possibly can that he does not harbor a grudge against them for what they did to him all those many years before. Still, all those years later, his brothers will not trust him and will fear that he may still seek their harm. Rav Lichtenstein comments: "[Yosef] weeps over the weakness inherent in power, over the terrible price that he has paid for it. His dreams have indeed been realized, on some level, but the tragedy remains just as real. The torn shreds of the family have not been made completely whole."

The gap between public grandeur and private vulnerability is nowhere better illustrated than here. Yosef is surrounded by Egyptian admirers and supporters, and now his brothers are with him. None of these imagine that, in his private room, he weeps.

בָּא אֵלָי וַיּוֹצֵא אֲלֵהֶם אֶת־שִׁמְעוֹן׃ וַיָּבֵא הָאִישׁ אֶת־הָאֲנָשִׁים בֵּיתָה כד
יוֹסֵף וַיִּתֶּן־מַיִם וַיִּרְחֲצוּ רַגְלֵיהֶם וַיִּתֵּן מִסְפּוֹא לַחֲמֹרֵיהֶם׃ וַיָּכִינוּ אֶת־ כה
הַמִּנְחָה עַד־בּוֹא יוֹסֵף בַּצָּהֳרָיִם כִּי שָׁמְעוּ כִּי־שָׁם יֹאכְלוּ לָחֶם׃ וַיָּבֹא כו
יוֹסֵף הַבַּיְתָה וַיָּבִיאוּ לוֹ אֶת־הַמִּנְחָה אֲשֶׁר־בְּיָדָם הַבָּיְתָה וַיִּשְׁתַּחֲווּ־לוֹ
אָרְצָה׃ וַיִּשְׁאַל לָהֶם לְשָׁלוֹם וַיֹּאמֶר הֲשָׁלוֹם אֲבִיכֶם הַזָּקֵן אֲשֶׁר כז
אֲמַרְתֶּם הַעוֹדֶנּוּ חָי׃ וַיֹּאמְרוּ שָׁלוֹם לְעַבְדְּךָ לְאָבִינוּ עוֹדֶנּוּ חָי וַיִּקְּדוּ כח
וַיִּשְׁתַּחֲוּ׃ וַיִּשָּׂא עֵינָיו וַיַּרְא אֶת־בִּנְיָמִין אָחִיו בֶּן־אִמּוֹ וַיֹּאמֶר הֲזֶה כט
שביעי אֲחִיכֶם הַקָּטֹן אֲשֶׁר אֲמַרְתֶּם אֵלָי וַיֹּאמַר אֱלֹהִים יָחְנְךָ בְּנִי׃ וַיְמַהֵר ל
יוֹסֵף כִּי־נִכְמְרוּ רַחֲמָיו אֶל־אָחִיו וַיְבַקֵּשׁ לִבְכּוֹת וַיָּבֹא הַחַדְרָה וַיֵּבְךְּ
שָׁמָּה׃ וַיִּרְחַץ פָּנָיו וַיֵּצֵא וַיִּתְאַפַּק וַיֹּאמֶר שִׂימוּ לָחֶם׃ וַיָּשִׂימוּ לוֹ לְבַדּוֹ לא לב
וְלָהֶם לְבַדָּם וְלַמִּצְרִים הָאֹכְלִים אִתּוֹ לְבַדָּם כִּי לֹא יוּכְלוּן הַמִּצְרִים
לֶאֱכֹל אֶת־הָעִבְרִים לֶחֶם כִּי־תוֹעֵבָה הִוא לְמִצְרָיִם׃ וַיֵּשְׁבוּ לְפָנָיו לג

אונקלוס

אֲתָא לְוָתִי, וְאַפֵּיק לְוָתְהוֹן יָת שִׁמְעוֹן: כד וְאַעֵיל גֻּבְרָא, יָת גֻּבְרַיָּא לְבֵית יוֹסֵף, וִיהַב מַיָּא וְאַסְחוּ רַגְלֵיהוֹן, וִיהַב כִּסְּתָא לְחַמָרֵיהוֹן: כה וְאַתְקִינוּ יָת תִּקְרֻבְתָּא, עַד דְּעָאל יוֹסֵף בְּשֵׁירוּתָא, אֲרֵי שְׁמַעוּ, אֲרֵי תַּמָּן אָכְלִין לַחְמָא: כו וְעָאל יוֹסֵף לְבֵיתָא, וְאַעִילוּ לֵיהּ, יָת תִּקְרֻבְתָּא דִּבְיֵדֵיהוֹן לְבֵיתָא, וּסְגִידוּ לֵיהּ עַל אַרְעָא: כז וּשְׁאֵיל לְהוֹן לִשְׁלָם, וַאֲמַר, הַשְׁלָם, אֲבוּכוֹן סָבָא דַּאֲמַרְתּוּן, הַעוֹד כְּעַן קַיָּם: כח וַאֲמַרוּ, שְׁלָם, לְעַבְדָּךְ לַאֲבוּנָא עַד כְּעַן קַיָּם, וּכְרַעוּ וּסְגִידוּ: כט וּזְקַף עֵינוֹהִי, וַחֲזָא, יָת בִּנְיָמִין אֲחוּהִי בַּר אִמֵּיהּ, וַאֲמַר, הֲדֵין אֲחוּכוֹן זְעֵירָא, דַּאֲמַרְתּוּן לִי, וַאֲמַר, מִן קֳדָם יי יִתְרַחַם עֲלָךְ בְּרִי: ל וְאוֹחִי יוֹסֵף, אֲרֵי אִתְגּוֹלַלוּ רַחֲמוֹהִי עַל אֲחוּהִי, וּבְעָא לְמִבְכֵּי, וְעָאל לְאִדְּרוֹן בֵּית מִשְׁכְּבָא וּבְכָא תַמָּן: לא וְאַסְחִי אַפּוֹהִי וּנְפַק, וְאִתְחַסַּן, וַאֲמַר שַׁווּ לַחְמָא: לב וְשַׁוִּיאוּ לֵיהּ, בִּלְחוֹדוֹהִי וּלְהוֹן בִּלְחוֹדֵיהוֹן, וּלְמִצְרָאֵי, דְּאָכְלִין עִמֵּיהּ בִּלְחוֹדֵיהוֹן, אֲרֵי לָא יָכְלִין מִצְרָאֵי, לְמֵיכַל עִם עִבְרָאֵי לַחְמָא, אֲרֵי בְעִירָא דְּמִצְרָאֵי דָּחֲלִין לֵיהּ עִבְרָאֵי אָכְלִין: לג וְאַסְחָרוּ קֳדָמוֹהִי,

43:30 וַיֵּבְךְּ שָׁמָּה *And there he wept* – No one in the Tanakh weeps as much as Yosef. Esav wept when he discovered that Yaakov had taken his blessing (Gen. 27:38). Yaakov wept when he saw the love of his life, Raḥel, for the first time (29:11). Both brothers, Yaakov and Esav, wept when they met again after their long estrangement (33:4). Yaakov wept when told that his beloved son Yosef was dead (37:35).

But Yosef's seven acts of weeping have no parallel. They span the full spectrum of emotion, from painful memory to the complicated joy of being reunited, first here, with his brother Binyamin, then with his father Yaakov. There are the complex tears immediately before and after he discloses his identity to his brothers, and there are the tears of bereavement at Yaakov's deathbed. The most intriguing are the last, the tears he sheds when he hears that his brothers fear that he will take revenge on them now that their father is no longer alive.

In his essay "Yosef's Tears," Rav Aharon Lichtenstein suggests that that last act of weeping is an expression of the price Yosef pays, over the course of his life, for the realization

34 age, oldest to youngest, they looked at one another in amazement. He sent
them portions from his table, giving Binyamin five times as much as anyone
44 1 else. And they drank and grew merry with him. Then Yosef instructed his
steward, "Fill the men's bags with as much food as they can carry, and put each
2 one's money in the mouth of his bag. Then put my chalice – the silver chalice – in
the mouth of the youngest one's bag, along with the money for his grain." He
3 did as Yosef told him. As morning showed its first light, the men were sent on
4 their way with their donkeys. They had not gone far from the city when Yosef
said to his steward, "Go after the men at once. When you catch up with them,
5 say to them, 'Why have you repaid good with evil? Is it not from this that my
master drinks and that he uses for divination? It is a wicked thing you have
6 7 done.'" He caught up with them and repeated those words to them. But they
said to him, "How can my lord say such things? Heaven forbid that we should
8 do such a thing! Look, we brought back to you from Canaan the money we
found in the mouths of our bags. Why would we steal silver or gold from your
9 master's house? If any of your servants is found with it, he shall die, and the rest
10 of us will become my lord's slaves." "Let it be as you say," he replied, "but only

רש״י

לג **הַבְּכֹר כִּבְכֹרָתוֹ.** מַכֶּה בַּגָּבִיעַ וְקוֹרֵא: רְאוּבֵן שִׁמְעוֹן לֵוִי וִיהוּדָה יִשָּׂשכָר וּזְבוּלוּן בְּנֵי אֵם אַחַת, הָסֵבּוּ כַּסֵּדֶר הַזֶּה שֶׁהוּא תּוֹלְדוֹתֵיכֶם, וְכֵן כֻּלָּם. כֵּיוָן שֶׁהִגִּיעַ לְבִנְיָמִין, אָמַר: זֶה אֵין לוֹ אֵם וַאֲנִי אֵין לִי אֵם, יֵשֵׁב אֶצְלִי:

לד **מַשְׂאֹת.** מָנוֹת: **חָמֵשׁ יָדוֹת.** חֶלְקוֹ עִם אֶחָיו, וּמַשְּׂאַת יוֹסֵף וְאָסְנַת וּמְנַשֶּׁה וְאֶפְרַיִם: **וַיִּשְׁכְּרוּ עִמּוֹ.** וּמִיּוֹם שֶׁמְּכָרוּהוּ לֹא שָׁתוּ יַיִן וְלֹא הוּא שָׁתָה יַיִן, וְאוֹתוֹ הַיּוֹם שָׁתוּ:

מד ב **גְּבִיעִי.** כּוֹס אָרֹךְ וְקוֹרִין לוֹ מדירנ״ו:

ז **חָלִילָה לַעֲבָדֶיךָ.** חֻלִּין הוּא לָנוּ, לְשׁוֹן גְּנַאי. וְתַרְגּוּם: ״חַס לְעַבְדָּךְ״, חַס מֵאֵת הַקָּדוֹשׁ בָּרוּךְ הוּא יְהֵא עָלֵינוּ מֵעֲשׂוֹת זֹאת. וְהַרְבֵּה יֵשׁ בַּתַּלְמוּד ״חַס וְשָׁלוֹם״:

ח **הֵן כֶּסֶף אֲשֶׁר מָצָאנוּ.** זֶה אֶחָד מֵעֲשָׂרָה קַל וָחֹמֶר הָאֲמוּרִים בַּתּוֹרָה; וְכֻלָּן מְנוּיִין בִּבְרֵאשִׁית רַבָּה (צב, ז):

י **גַּם עַתָּה.** אַף זוֹ מִן הַדִּין אֱמֶת ״כְדִבְרֵיכֶם כֶּן הוּא״ שֶׁכֻּלְּכֶם חַיָּבִים בַּדָּבָר; עֲשָׂרָה שֶׁנִּמְצֵאת גְּנֵבָה בְּיַד אֶחָד מֵהֶם כֻּלָּם נִתְפָּשִׂים, אֲבָל אֲנִי אֶעֱשֶׂה לָכֶם לִפְנִים מִשּׁוּרַת הַדִּין: ״אֲשֶׁר יִמָּצֵא אִתּוֹ יִהְיֶה לִּי עָבֶד״ וְגוֹ׳:

and sit to eat their meal, "he sent them portions from his table, giving Binyamin *five times as much* as anyone else" (Gen. 43:34).

In effect, Yosef has constructed a controlled experiment in "perfect repentance." When the cup is found in Binyamin's sack and the brothers say, "We are now my lord's slaves" (44:16), Yosef replies, "Heaven forbid that I should do such a thing.... The man in whose possession the chalice was found will become my slave. As for the rest of you, go back to your

in which they can purchase their freedom by leaving one of their number as a slave. It cannot be one of the brothers chosen at random. It must be one of whom they are jealous, as they were of Yosef. That is why he chooses Binyamin, the other son of Raḥel, his father's favorite wife. He has to add one further element. What provoked them to rage many years earlier was the physical emblem of favoritism, the richly embroidered cloak. That is why, in an otherwise inexplicable detail, when the brothers return with Binyamin

הַבְּכֹר כִּבְכֹרָתוֹ וְהַצָּעִיר כִּצְעִרָתוֹ וַיִּתְמְהוּ הָאֲנָשִׁים אִישׁ אֶל־רֵעֵהוּ׃
לד וַיִּשָּׂא מַשְׂאֹת מֵאֵת פָּנָיו אֲלֵהֶם וַתֵּרֶב מַשְׂאַת בִּנְיָמִן מִמַּשְׂאֹת כֻּלָּם
מד א חָמֵשׁ יָדוֹת וַיִּשְׁתּוּ וַיִּשְׁכְּרוּ עִמּוֹ׃ וַיְצַו אֶת־אֲשֶׁר עַל־בֵּיתוֹ לֵאמֹר מַלֵּא
אֶת־אַמְתְּחֹת הָאֲנָשִׁים אֹכֶל כַּאֲשֶׁר יוּכְלוּן שְׂאֵת וְשִׂים כֶּסֶף־אִישׁ
ב בְּפִי אַמְתַּחְתּוֹ׃ וְאֶת־גְּבִיעִי גְּבִיעַ הַכֶּסֶף תָּשִׂים בְּפִי אַמְתַּחַת הַקָּטֹן
ג וְאֵת כֶּסֶף שִׁבְרוֹ וַיַּעַשׂ כִּדְבַר יוֹסֵף אֲשֶׁר דִּבֵּר׃ הַבֹּקֶר אוֹר וְהָאֲנָשִׁים
ד שֻׁלְּחוּ הֵמָּה וַחֲמֹרֵיהֶם׃ הֵם יָצְאוּ אֶת־הָעִיר לֹא הִרְחִיקוּ וְיוֹסֵף אָמַר
לַאֲשֶׁר עַל־בֵּיתוֹ קוּם רְדֹף אַחֲרֵי הָאֲנָשִׁים וְהִשַּׂגְתָּם וְאָמַרְתָּ אֲלֵהֶם
ה לָמָּה שִׁלַּמְתֶּם רָעָה תַּחַת טוֹבָה׃ הֲלוֹא זֶה אֲשֶׁר יִשְׁתֶּה אֲדֹנִי בּוֹ וְהוּא
ו נַחֵשׁ יְנַחֵשׁ בּוֹ הֲרֵעֹתֶם אֲשֶׁר עֲשִׂיתֶם׃ וַיַּשִּׂגֵם וַיְדַבֵּר אֲלֵהֶם אֶת־
ז הַדְּבָרִים הָאֵלֶּה׃ וַיֹּאמְרוּ אֵלָיו לָמָּה יְדַבֵּר אֲדֹנִי כַּדְּבָרִים הָאֵלֶּה חָלִילָה
ח לַעֲבָדֶיךָ מֵעֲשׂוֹת כַּדָּבָר הַזֶּה׃ הֵן כֶּסֶף אֲשֶׁר מָצָאנוּ בְּפִי אַמְתְּחֹתֵינוּ
הֱשִׁיבֹנוּ אֵלֶיךָ מֵאֶרֶץ כְּנָעַן וְאֵיךְ נִגְנֹב מִבֵּית אֲדֹנֶיךָ כֶּסֶף אוֹ זָהָב׃
ט אֲשֶׁר יִמָּצֵא אִתּוֹ מֵעֲבָדֶיךָ וָמֵת וְגַם־אֲנַחְנוּ נִהְיֶה לַאדֹנִי לַעֲבָדִים׃
י וַיֹּאמֶר גַּם־עַתָּה כְדִבְרֵיכֶם כֶּן־הוּא אֲשֶׁר יִמָּצֵא אִתּוֹ יִהְיֶה־לִּי עָבֶד

אונקלוס

רבא כרביותיה, וזעירא כזעירותיה, ותהו גבריא גבר בחבריה׃
לד ונטל חולקין, מן קדמוהי לקדמיהון, וסגי, חולקא דבנימין,
מחולקי כלהון חמשא חולקין, ושתיאו ורויאו עמיה׃ מד א ופקיד,
ית דממנא על ביתיה למימר, מלי, ית טעני גבריא עבורא,
כמא דיכלין למטען, ושוי כסף גבר בפום טעניה׃ ב וית כלידי
כלידא דכספא, תשוי בפום טענא דזעירא, וית כסף זבינוהי,
ועבד, כפתגמא דיוסף דמליל׃ ג צפרא נהר, וגבריא אתפטרו,
אנון וחמריהון׃ ד אנון, נפקו מן קרתא לא ארחיקו, ויוסף אמר
לדממנא על ביתיה, קום רדוף בתר גבריא, ותדביקנון ותימר
להון, למא, שלימתון בשתא חלף טבתא׃ ה הלא דין, דשתי
רבוני ביה, והוא, בדקא מבדיק ביה, אבאישתון דעבדתון׃
ו ואדביקנון, ומליל עמהון, ית פתגמיא האלין׃ ז ואמרו ליה, למא
ימליל רבוני, כפתגמיא האלין, חס לעבדך, מלמעבד כפתגמא
הדין׃ ח הא כספא, דאשכחנא בפום טעננא, אתיבנהי לך מארעא
דכנען, ואיכדין, נגנוב מבית רבונך, מנין דכסף או מנין דדהב׃
ט דישתכח עמיה, מעבדך יתקטיל, ואף אנחנא, נהי לרבוני לעבדין׃
י ואמר, אף כען כפתגמיכון כן הוא, דישתכח עמיה יהי לי עבדא,

44:10 הוּא אֲשֶׁר יִמָּצֵא אִתּוֹ יִהְיֶה־לִּי עָבֶד *The one… shall be my slave* – They had sold their brother into slavery. How would they act if placed in the same situation again? Yosef plans the scene with meticulous care. He must create a situation

the one with whom it is found shall be my slave. The rest of you can go free."
11 Each of them quickly lowered his bag to the ground, and each opened his bag.
12 He searched, beginning with the oldest and ending with the youngest. The
13 chalice was found in Binyamin's bag. The brothers tore their clothes. Each
14 loaded his donkey again, and they returned to the city. Yehuda and his brothers MAFTIR
came to Yosef's house – he was still there – and they threw themselves on the
15 ground before him. Yosef said to them, "What is this thing you have done? Do
16 you not know that a man like me can find out the truth by divination?" Yehuda
replied, "What can we say to my lord? What can we speak? How can we prove
our innocence? God has uncovered your servants' guilt! We are now my lord's
17 slaves – we and the one in whose possession the chalice was found." "Heaven
forbid that I should do such a thing," he said. "The man in whose possession
the chalice was found will become my slave. As for the rest of you, go back to
your father in peace."

The haftara for Parashat Miketz is on page 1520.
On Ḥanukka read the haftara on page 1638 (even on Rosh Ḥodesh or Erev Rosh Ḥodesh Tevet).
On the second Shabbat of Ḥanukka read the haftara on page 1640.

רש״י

יב| **בַּגָּדוֹל הֵחֵל.** שֶׁלֹּא יַרְגִּישׁוּ שֶׁהָיָה יוֹדֵעַ הֵיכָן הוּא:

יג| **וַיַּעֲמֹס אִישׁ עַל חֲמֹרוֹ.** בַּעֲלֵי זְרוֹעַ הָיוּ, וְלֹא הֻצְרְכוּ לְסַיֵּעַ זֶה אֶת זֶה לִטְעֹן: **וַיָּשֻׁבוּ הָעִירָה.** מֶטְרוֹפּוֹלִין הָיְתָה וְהוּא אוֹמֵר "הָעִירָה", הָעִיר כָּל שֶׁהִיא?! אֶלָּא שֶׁלֹּא הָיְתָה חֲשׁוּבָה בְּעֵינֵיהֶם אֶלָּא כְּעִיר בֵּינוֹנִית שֶׁל עֲשָׂרָה בְּנֵי אָדָם לְעִנְיַן הַמִּלְחָמָה:

יד| **עוֹדֶנּוּ שָׁם.** שֶׁהָיָה מַמְתִּין לָהֶם:

טז| **הָאֱלֹהִים מָצָא.** יוֹדְעִים אָנוּ שֶׁלֹּא סָרַחְנוּ, אֲבָל מֵאֵת הַמָּקוֹם נִהְיְתָה לְהָבִיא לָנוּ זֹאת, מָצָא בַּעַל חוֹב מָקוֹם לִגְבּוֹת שְׁטַר חוֹבוֹ: **וּמַה נִּצְטַדָּק.** לְשׁוֹן צֶדֶק, וְכֵן כָּל תֵּבָה שֶׁתְּחִלַּת יְסוֹדָהּ צָדִ״י וְהִיא בָּאָה לְדַבֵּר בִּלְשׁוֹן מִתְפַּעֵל אוֹ נִתְפַּעֵל, נוֹתֵן טֵי״ת בִּמְקוֹם תָּי״ו, וְאֵינוֹ נוֹתְנָהּ לִפְנֵי אוֹת רִאשׁוֹנָה שֶׁל יְסוֹד הַתֵּבָה אֶלָּא בְּאֶמְצַע אוֹתִיּוֹת הָעִקָּר, כְּגוֹן "נִצְטַדָּק", "יִצְטַבַּע" (דניאל ד, יב) מִגִּזְרַת 'צֶבַע', "וַיִּצְטַיָּרוּ" (יהושע ט, ד) מִגִּזְרַת "צִיר אֱמוּנִים מַרְפֵּא" (משלי יג, יז), "הִצְטַיַּדְנוּ אֹתוֹ מִבָּתֵּינוּ" (יהושע ט, יב) מִגִּזְרַת "צֵדָה לַדָּרֶךְ" (לעיל מב, כה). וְתֵבָה שֶׁתְּחִלָּתָהּ סָמֶ״ךְ, כְּשֶׁהִיא מִתְפַּעֶלֶת מַפְרִיד תָּי״ו אֶת אוֹתִיּוֹת הָעִקָּר, כְּגוֹן: "וְיִסְתַּבֵּל הֶחָגָב" (קהלת יב, ה), "מִשְׂתַּכַּל הֲוֵית בְּקַרְנַיָּא" (דניאל ז, ח), "וְיִשְׁתַּמֵּר חֻקּוֹת עָמְרִי" (מיכה ו, טז), "וְסָר מֵרָע מִשְׁתּוֹלֵל" (ישעיה נט, טו) מִגִּזְרַת "מוֹלִיךְ יוֹעֲצִים שׁוֹלָל" (איוב יב, יז), "עוֹדְךָ מִסְתּוֹלֵל בְּעַמִּי" (שמות ט, יז) מִגִּזְרַת "דֶּרֶךְ לֹא סְלוּלָה" (ירמיה יח, טו):

in Egypt, as slaves, so that they will know from the inside what it feels like to be on the other side.

That is what Yosef is forcing his brothers to do. They must undergo what he went through when he was sold as a slave to a strange land far from home. This is not revenge, for which Yosef has neither desire nor need. It is, rather, the only way they will understand what evil feels like from the other side, not as perpetrator but as victim. That is the necessary prelude to repentance, itself the most compelling proof that we are free. Kayin is able to commit murder because, he says, "Am I my brother's keeper?" (Gen. 4:9). He does not feel Hevel's pain. He feels only his own at having his offering rejected. *The way we learn not to commit evil is to experience an event from the perspective of the victim.* Yehuda's repentance – showing that he *is* his brother Binyamin's keeper – redeems not only his own earlier sin, but also Kayin's.

In learning what this ordeal teaches them, the brothers enact the greatest of biblical themes: the defeat of tragedy in the name of hope.

יא וְאַתֶּם תִּהְיוּ נְקִיִּם: וַיְמַהֲרוּ וַיּוֹרִדוּ אִישׁ אֶת־אַמְתַּחְתּוֹ אָרְצָה וַיִּפְתְּחוּ
יב אִישׁ אַמְתַּחְתּוֹ: וַיְחַפֵּשׂ בַּגָּדוֹל הֵחֵל וּבַקָּטֹן כִּלָּה וַיִּמָּצֵא הַגָּבִיעַ
יג בְּאַמְתַּחַת בִּנְיָמִן: וַיִּקְרְעוּ שִׂמְלֹתָם וַיַּעֲמֹס אִישׁ עַל־חֲמֹרוֹ וַיָּשֻׁבוּ
יד הָעִירָה: וַיָּבֹא יְהוּדָה וְאֶחָיו בֵּיתָה יוֹסֵף וְהוּא עוֹדֶנּוּ שָׁם וַיִּפְּלוּ לְפָנָיו מפטיר
טו אָרְצָה: וַיֹּאמֶר לָהֶם יוֹסֵף מָה־הַמַּעֲשֶׂה הַזֶּה אֲשֶׁר עֲשִׂיתֶם הֲלוֹא
טז יְדַעְתֶּם כִּי־נַחֵשׁ יְנַחֵשׁ אִישׁ אֲשֶׁר כָּמֹנִי: וַיֹּאמֶר יְהוּדָה מַה־נֹּאמַר
לַאדֹנִי מַה־נְּדַבֵּר וּמַה־נִּצְטַדָּק הָאֱלֹהִים מָצָא אֶת־עֲוֺן עֲבָדֶיךָ הִנֶּנּוּ
יז עֲבָדִים לַאדֹנִי גַּם־אֲנַחְנוּ גַּם אֲשֶׁר־נִמְצָא הַגָּבִיעַ בְּיָדוֹ: וַיֹּאמֶר חָלִילָה
לִּי מֵעֲשׂוֹת זֹאת הָאִישׁ אֲשֶׁר נִמְצָא הַגָּבִיעַ בְּיָדוֹ הוּא יִהְיֶה־לִּי עָבֶד
וְאַתֶּם עֲלוּ לְשָׁלוֹם אֶל־אֲבִיכֶם:

The הפטרה *for* פרשת מקץ *is on page 1521.*
On חנוכה *read the* הפטרה *on page 1639 (even on* ראש חודש טבת *or* ערב ראש חודש טבת*).*
On the second שבת *of* חנוכה *read the* הפטרה *on page 1641.*

אונקלוס

וְאַתּוּן תְּהוֹן זַכָּאִין: יא וְאוֹחִיאוּ, וְאַחִיתוּ, גְּבַר יָת טְעִנֵיהּ לְאַרְעָא, וּפְתַחוּ גְּבַר טְעִנֵיהּ: יב וּבַלַּשׁ, בְּרַבָּא שָׁרִי, וּבִזְעֵירָא שֵׁיצִי, וְאִשְׁתְּכַח כַּלִּידָא, בִּטְעַן דְּבִנְיָמִין: יג וּבַזַּעוּ לְבוּשֵׁיהוֹן, וּרְמוֹ גְּבַר עַל חֲמָרֵיהּ, וְתָבוּ לְקַרְתָּא: יד וְעָאל יְהוּדָה וַאֲחוֹהִי לְבֵית יוֹסֵף, וְהוּא עַד כְּעַן תַּמָּן, וּנְפַלוּ קֳדָמוֹהִי עַל אַרְעָא: טו וַאֲמַר לְהוֹן יוֹסֵף, מָא עוֹבָדָא הָדֵין דַּעֲבַדְתּוּן, הֲלָא יְדַעְתּוּן, אֲרֵי בְדָקָא מְבַדֵּיק, גַּבְרָא דִּכְוָתִי: טז וַאֲמַר יְהוּדָה, מָא נֵימַר לְרִבּוֹנִי, מָא נְמַלֵּיל וּמָא נִזְכֵּי, מִן קֳדָם יְיָ, אִשְׁתְּכַח חוֹבָא בְּעַבְדָּךְ, הָא אֲנַחְנָא עַבְדִּין לְרִבּוֹנִי, אַף אֲנַחְנָא, אַף, דְּאִשְׁתְּכַח כַּלִּידָא בִּידֵיהּ: יז וַאֲמַר, חַס לִי, מִלְּמֶעְבַּד דָּא, גַּבְרָא, דְּאִשְׁתְּכַח כַּלִּידָא בִּידֵיהּ, הוּא יְהֵי לִי עַבְדָּא, וְאַתּוּן, סַקוּ לִשְׁלָם לְוָת אֲבוּכוֹן:

father in peace" (44:17). He gives them the chance to walk away in freedom if they are willing to leave Binyamin as a slave. This is the moment of trial.

44:16 **הִנֶּנּוּ עֲבָדִים לַאדֹנִי** *We are now my lord's slaves* – The length and weight of Yosef's story testifies that, within the highly structured book of Genesis, it is resolving the tension not of that generation alone, but of all that went before. Genesis is about failure and learning from failure, discovering that we can change. Yaakov discovers this after a long night of wrestling with the angel. His sons discover it after a long period of suspense and fear.

Here, as we have seen, it happens through role reversal. The most fundamental fact about consciousness is that I cannot feel someone else's pain. I can only feel my own. This is the source of the human tendency to divide the world into brothers and others, kin and non-kin, friends and strangers, the "Us" to whom I belong, and the "Them," the Other, to whom I do not belong. That is why the covenantal family, the children of Israel, begin their collective life as a nation

Parashat Vayigash

44 18 But Yehuda stepped forward to him. "If you please, my lord," he said, "let your
servant speak a word in my lord's hearing. Do not be angry with me, you who
19 are the equal of Pharaoh. My lord asked his servants, 'Do you have a father or a
20 brother?' And we told my lord, 'We have an elderly father and there is a young
son, a child of his old age. When his brother died, he was the only one of his
21 mother's sons left, and his father loves him.' Then you said to your servants,
22 'Bring him to me that I may set eyes on him.' But we said to my lord, 'The boy
23 cannot leave his father. If he left him, his father would die.' Then you told your
servants, 'Unless your youngest brother comes with you, you shall not see my
24 face again.' When we went back to your servant my father, we told him what my
25 lord had said. Then our father said, 'Go back and buy a little more food.'

רש"י

יח **ויגש אליו. דבר באזני אדני.** יכנסו דברי באזניך: **ואל יחר אפך.** מכאן אתה למד שדבר אליו קשות: **כי כמוך כפרעה.** חשוב אתה בעיני כמלך, זהו פשוטו. ומדרשו, סופך ללקות עליו בצרעת כמו שלקה פרעה על ידי זקנתי שרה על לילה אחת שעכבה. דבר אחר, מה פרעה גוזר ואינו מקיים מבטיח ואינו עושה, אף אתה כן. וכי זו היא שימת עין שאמרת לשום עינך עליו?! דבר אחר, "כי כמוך כפרעה", אם תקניטני אהרג אותך ואת אדונך:

יט-כ **אדני שאל את עבדיו.** מתחלה בעלילה באת עלינו, למה היה לך לשאול כל אלה? בתך היינו מבקשים או אחותנו אתה מבקש? ואף על פי כן: "ונאמר אל אדני", לא כחדנו ממך דבר: **ואחיו מת.** מפני היראה היה מוציא דבר שקר מפיו, אמר: אם אומר לו שהוא קים, יאמר הביאוהו אצלי: **לבדו לאמו.** מאותה האם אין לו עוד אח:

כב **ועזב את אביו ומת.** אם יעזב את אביו דואגים אנו שמא ימות בדרך, שהרי אמו בדרך מתה:

reserve, all his defenses, and as if unable to stop himself, he finally discloses his identity.

This moment contrasts with another, many chapters, and many years, earlier: "They saw him in the distance, and by the time he reached them, they had plotted to kill him" (Gen. 37:18).

At the beginning of the story, when Yosef was sent by his father to see how the brothers were doing, tending the sheep, they saw him from far away, from a distance. They couldn't see his face. All they could see was the "ornately colored robe" (37:3) that so upsets them because it reminded them that it was he not they whom their father loved. From far away, we don't see people as human beings, and when we stop seeing people as human beings, they become instead objects of envy or hate. Yosef and his brothers were too far apart in every way. Which is why it was only when Yehuda came close to Yosef – *Vayigash* – that the coldness between them thawed, and they became brothers, not strangers to one another. Distance damaged the relationship. *Vayigash* – Yehuda's act of drawing close – restored it.

YEHUDA'S TEST

Yehuda's final confrontation can only be fully understood in the context of his initial behavior toward Yosef. It is Yehuda, in his first recorded words, who suggested selling Yosef into slavery:

> Yehuda said to his brothers, "What do we gain by killing our brother and covering his blood? Let's sell him to

פרשת ויגש

מד יח וַיִּגַּשׁ אֵלָיו יְהוּדָה וַיֹּאמֶר בִּי אֲדֹנִי יְדַבֶּר־נָא עַבְדְּךָ דָבָר בְּאָזְנֵי אֲדֹנִי מ
יט וְאַל־יִחַר אַפְּךָ בְּעַבְדֶּךָ כִּי כָמוֹךָ כְּפַרְעֹה׃ אֲדֹנִי שָׁאַל אֶת־עֲבָדָיו
כ לֵאמֹר הֲיֵשׁ־לָכֶם אָב אוֹ־אָח׃ וַנֹּאמֶר אֶל־אֲדֹנִי יֶשׁ־לָנוּ אָב זָקֵן וְיֶלֶד
כא זְקֻנִים קָטָן וְאָחִיו מֵת וַיִּוָּתֵר הוּא לְבַדּוֹ לְאִמּוֹ וְאָבִיו אֲהֵבוֹ׃ וַתֹּאמֶר
כב אֶל־עֲבָדֶיךָ הוֹרִדֻהוּ אֵלָי וְאָשִׂימָה עֵינִי עָלָיו׃ וַנֹּאמֶר אֶל־אֲדֹנִי לֹא־
כג יוּכַל הַנַּעַר לַעֲזֹב אֶת־אָבִיו וְעָזַב אֶת־אָבִיו וָמֵת׃ וַתֹּאמֶר אֶל־עֲבָדֶיךָ
כד אִם־לֹא יֵרֵד אֲחִיכֶם הַקָּטֹן אִתְּכֶם לֹא תֹסִפוּן לִרְאוֹת פָּנָי׃ וַיְהִי כִּי
כה עָלִינוּ אֶל־עַבְדְּךָ אָבִי וַנַּגֶּד־לוֹ אֵת דִּבְרֵי אֲדֹנִי׃ וַיֹּאמֶר אָבִינוּ שֻׁבוּ

אונקלוס

יח וּקְרֵיב לְוָתֵיהּ יְהוּדָה, וַאֲמַר בְּבָעוּ רִבּוֹנִי, יְמַלֵּיל כְּעַן עַבְדָּךְ פִּתְגָּמָא קֳדָם רִבּוֹנִי, וְלָא יִתְקַף רֻגְזָךְ בְּעַבְדָּךְ, אֲרֵי כְּפַרְעֹה כֵּן אַתְּ: יט רִבּוֹנִי שְׁאֵיל, יָת עַבְדּוֹהִי לְמֵימַר, הַאִית לְכוֹן אַבָּא אוֹ אֲחָא: כ וַאֲמַרְנָא לְרִבּוֹנִי, אִית לַנָא אַבָּא סָבָא, וּבַר סֵיבְתִין זְעֵיר, וַאֲחוּהִי מִית, וְאִשְׁתְּאַר הוּא בִּלְחוֹדוֹהִי, לְאִמֵּיהּ וַאֲבוּהִי רָחֵים לֵיהּ: כא וַאֲמַרְתְּ לְעַבְדָּךְ, אַחֲתוּהִי לְוָתִי, וַאֲשַׁוֵּי עֵינִי עֲלוֹהִי: כב וַאֲמַרְנָא לְרִבּוֹנִי, לָא יְכוֹל עוּלֵימָא לְמִשְׁבַּק יָת אֲבוּהִי, וְאִם יִשְׁבּוֹק יָת אֲבוּהִי יְמוּת: כג וַאֲמַרְתְּ לְעַבְדָּךְ, אִם לָא יֵיחוֹת, אֲחוּכוֹן זְעֵירָא עִמְּכוֹן, לָא תֵיסְפוּן לְמִחֱזֵי אַפָּי: כד וַהֲוָה כַּד סְלֵיקְנָא, לְוָת עַבְדָּךְ אַבָּא, וְחַוֵּינָא לֵיהּ, יָת פִּתְגָּמֵי רִבּוֹנִי: כה וַאֲמַר אֲבוּנָא, תּוּבוּ

VAYIGASH

Vayigash begins with the climactic scene in which Yosef finally reveals himself to his brothers. Moved by Yehuda's impassioned plea for Binyamin's freedom, in return for which he declares himself ready to take Binyamin's place as a slave, Yosef discloses his identity and the estrangement of the brothers comes to an end. On Yosef's instructions, they return to Yaakov with the news that his beloved son is still alive, and the family is reunited. Egypt, meanwhile, is spared from mass starvation under Yosef's direction, at the cost of major upheavals, the significance of which will only be fully apparent in Exodus.

Yosef's forgiveness is the bridge between Genesis and Exodus. The first is about the children of Israel as a family, the second is about them as a nation. Central to both is the experience of slavery, first Yosef's and finally the entire people's.

44:18 וַיִּגַּשׁ אֵלָיו יְהוּדָה *Yehuda stepped forward to him* – What do porcupines do in winter? asked Schopenhauer. If they come too close to one another, they injure each other. If they stay too far apart, they freeze. Life, for porcupines, is a delicate balance between closeness and distance. It is hard to get it right and dangerous to get it wrong. And so it is for us.

That is the force of the word that gives our *parasha* its name: *Vayigash*, literally, "And he came close." For perhaps the first time in his life, Yehuda comes close to his brother Yosef. The irony is, of course, that he does not know it is Yosef. But that one act of coming close melts all of Yosef's

26 We said, 'We cannot go. We can go only if our youngest brother is with us. If he
27 is not with us, we cannot see the man's face.' Then your servant, my father, said
28 to us, 'You know that my wife bore me two sons. One is gone from me, and I
29 said, "He must have been torn to pieces." I have not seen him since. If you take
this one from me and harm befalls him, you will bring down my gray head in
30 grief to Sheol.' So now, if the boy is not with us when I go back to your servant
31 my father, so bound together are their lives that when he sees that the boy is SHENI
not with us, he will die. Your servants will have brought down the gray head of
32 your servant, our father, in grief to Sheol. Your servant offered himself to my
father as a guarantee for the boy. I said, 'If I do not bring him back to you, I will

רש״י

כט) **וְקָרָהוּ אָסוֹן.** שֶׁהַשָּׂטָן מְקַטְרֵג בִּשְׁעַת הַסַּכָּנָה: **וְהוֹרַדְתֶּם אֶת שֵׂיבָתִי וְגוֹ׳.** עַכְשָׁיו כְּשֶׁהוּא אֶצְלִי אֲנִי מִתְנַחֵם בּוֹ עַל אִמּוֹ וְעַל אָחִיו, וְאִם יָמוּת זֶה, דּוֹמֶה עָלַי שֶׁשְּׁלָשְׁתָּן מֵתוּ בְּיוֹם אֶחָד:

לא) **וְהָיָה כִּרְאוֹתוֹ כִּי אֵין הַנַּעַר וָמֵת.** אָבִיו מִצָּרָתוֹ:

לב) **כִּי עַבְדְּךָ עָרַב אֶת הַנַּעַר.** וְאִם תֹּאמַר, לָמָּה אֲנִי נִכְנָס לְתִגָּר יוֹתֵר מִשְּׁאָר אַחַי? הֵם כֻּלָּם מִבַּחוּץ, וַאֲנִי נִתְקַשַּׁרְתִּי בְּקֶשֶׁר חָזָק לִהְיוֹת מְנֻדֶּה בִּשְׁנֵי עוֹלָמוֹת:

an individual may be in virtue of his or her natural character, greater still is one who is capable of growth and change. That is the power of penitence, and it begins with Yehuda.

44:28 **אַךְ טָרֹף טֹרָף** *"He must have been torn to pieces"* – It is one of the great questions we naturally ask each time we read the story of Yosef. Why does he not, at some time during their twenty-two-year separation, send word to his father that he is alive? Yosef knows how much his father loves him. He must know how much their separation grieves him. He does not know what Yaakov thinks has happened to him, but he knows that it is his duty to communicate with him when the opportunity arises, to tell his father that he is alive and well. Why then does he not?

The story of Yosef's descent into slavery and exile began when his father sent him, alone, to see how the brothers were faring. It was there, at that meeting far from home, that they plotted to kill him, lowered him into a pit, and eventually sold him as a slave. What else could he conclude, as he reflected on the events that led up to his sale as a slave, other than that Yaakov had deliberately placed him in this danger? Why? Because of the immediately prior event, when Yosef had told his father that the sun and moon – his father and mother – would bow down to him.

This angered Yaakov, and Yosef knew it. His father had "rebuked" him. It was outrageous to suggest that his parents would prostrate themselves before him. It was wrong to imagine it, all the more so to say it.

Yosef did not communicate with his father because he believed his father no longer wanted to see him or hear from him. His father had terminated the relationship. That was a reasonable inference from the facts as Yosef knew them. He could not have known that Yaakov still loved him, that his brothers had deceived their father by showing him Yosef's bloodstained cloak, and that his father mourned for him and "refused to be comforted." We know these facts because the Torah tells us. But Yosef, far away, in another land, serving as a slave, could not know. This places the story in a completely new and tragic light.

Yosef's first thought when the truth is revealed is not about Yehuda or Binyamin, but about Yaakov. A doubt he has harbored for twenty-two years has been shown to be unfounded. Hence his first question: "Is my father really still alive?" (Gen. 45:3).

כו שִׁבְרוּ־לָנוּ מְעַט־אֹכֶל׃ וַנֹּאמֶר לֹא נוּכַל לָרֶדֶת אִם־יֵשׁ אָחִינוּ הַקָּטֹן
אִתָּנוּ וְיָרַדְנוּ כִּי־לֹא נוּכַל לִרְאוֹת פְּנֵי הָאִישׁ וְאָחִינוּ הַקָּטֹן אֵינֶנּוּ
כז אִתָּנוּ׃ וַיֹּאמֶר עַבְדְּךָ אָבִי אֵלֵינוּ אַתֶּם יְדַעְתֶּם כִּי שְׁנַיִם יָלְדָה־לִּי
כח אִשְׁתִּי׃ וַיֵּצֵא הָאֶחָד מֵאִתִּי וָאֹמַר אַךְ טָרֹף טֹרָף וְלֹא רְאִיתִיו עַד־הֵנָּה׃
כט וּלְקַחְתֶּם גַּם־אֶת־זֶה מֵעִם פָּנַי וְקָרָהוּ אָסוֹן וְהוֹרַדְתֶּם אֶת־שֵׂיבָתִי
ל בְּרָעָה שְׁאֹלָה׃ וְעַתָּה כְּבֹאִי אֶל־עַבְדְּךָ אָבִי וְהַנַּעַר אֵינֶנּוּ אִתָּנוּ וְנַפְשׁוֹ
לא קְשׁוּרָה בְנַפְשׁוֹ׃ וְהָיָה כִּרְאוֹתוֹ כִּי־אֵין הַנַּעַר וָמֵת וְהוֹרִידוּ עֲבָדֶיךָ שני
לב אֶת־שֵׂיבַת עַבְדְּךָ אָבִינוּ בְּיָגוֹן שְׁאֹלָה׃ כִּי עַבְדְּךָ עָרַב אֶת־הַנַּעַר
מֵעִם אָבִי לֵאמֹר אִם־לֹא אֲבִיאֶנּוּ אֵלֶיךָ וְחָטָאתִי לְאָבִי כָּל־הַיָּמִים׃

אונקלוס

זְבוּנוּ לַנָא זְעֵיר עֲבוּרָא: כו וַאֲמַרְנָא, לָא נִכּוֹל לְמֵיחַת, אִם אִית אֲחוּנָא זְעֵירָא עִמַּנָא וְנֵיחוֹת, אֲרֵי לָא נִכּוֹל, לְמִחְזֵי אַפֵּי גַּבְרָא, וַאֲחוּנָא זְעֵירָא לֵיתוֹהִי עִמַּנָא: כז וַאֲמַר, עַבְדָּךְ אַבָּא לַנָא, אַתּוּן יְדַעְתּוּן, אֲרֵי תְרֵין יְלֵידַת לִי אִתְּתִי: כח וּנְפַק חַד מִלְּוָתִי, וַאֲמָרִית, בְּרַם מִקְטַל קְטִיל, וְלָא חֲזֵיתֵיהּ עַד כְּעַן: כט וְתִדְבְּרוּן אַף יָת דֵּין, מִן קֳדָמַי וִיעָרְעִנֵּיהּ מוֹתָא, וְתַחֲתוּן יָת סֵיבְתִי, בְּבִשְׁתָּא לִשְׁאוֹל: ל וּכְעַן, כְּמֵיתַא לְוָת עַבְדָּךְ אַבָּא, וְעוּלֵימָא לֵיתוֹהִי עִמַּנָא, וְנַפְשֵׁיהּ חֲבִיבָא לֵיהּ כְּנַפְשֵׁיהּ: לא וִיהֵי, כַּד יִחְזֵי, אֲרֵי לֵית עוּלֵימָא וִימוּת, וְיַחֲתוּן עַבְדָּךְ, יָת סֵיבַת עַבְדָּךְ אֲבוּנָא, בִּדְווֹנָא לִשְׁאוֹל: לב אֲרֵי עַבְדָּךְ מְעָרַב בְּעוּלֵימָא, מִן אַבָּא לְמֵימַר, אִם לָא אַיְתֵינֵיהּ לָךְ, וָאֱהֵי חָטֵי

> the Ishmaelites and not harm him with our own hands. After all, he is our brother, our own flesh and blood." His brothers agreed. (Gen. 37:26–27)

This is a speech of monstrous callousness. There is no mention of the evil of murder, merely a pragmatic calculation ("What do we gain?"). At the very moment he calls Yosef "our own flesh and blood," Yehuda is proposing to sell him as a slave. At this point, Yehuda is the last person from whom we expect great things.

However, Yehuda – more than anyone else in the Torah – changes. The man we see confronting Yosef all these years later is not the same personality as the one who spoke when Yosef was trapped in the pit. Then he was prepared to see his brother sold into slavery. Now he is prepared to suffer that fate himself rather than see Binyamin held as a slave.

It is a precise reversal of character. Callousness has been replaced with concern. Indifference to his brother's fate has been transformed into courage on his behalf. Yehuda is willing to suffer what he once inflicted on Yosef so that the same fate should not befall Binyamin. At this point Yosef reveals his identity. We know why. Yehuda has passed the test that Yosef has carefully constructed for him. Yosef wants to know if Yehuda has changed. He has.

This is a highly significant moment in the history of the human spirit. Yehuda is the first penitent – the first *baal teshuva* – in the Torah.

Yosef is consistently known to tradition as *hatzaddik*, "the righteous." He also becomes *mishneh lamelekh*, "second to the king." Yehuda, however, becomes the father of Israel's kings. Where the penitent Yehuda stands, even the perfectly righteous Yosef cannot stand. However great

33 have sinned against my father for all time.' So, please, let your servant stay as
my lord's slave in place of the boy, and let the boy go back with his brothers.
34 For how can I go back to my father if the boy is not with me? I could not bear
45 1 to see the misery that would overwhelm my father!" Yosef could no longer
control himself in the company of all his attendants. He cried out, "Have
everyone leave my presence!" So no one else was with Yosef when he revealed
2 himself to his brothers. He wept so loudly that the Egyptians could hear him,
3 and the news reached Pharaoh's palace. Yosef said to his brothers, "I am Yosef.
Is my father really still alive?" His brothers were so bewildered at his presence
4 that they could not answer him. "Come close to me, please," said Yosef to his
brothers. They came close, and he said, "I am your brother Yosef, whom you
5 sold into Egypt. And now, do not be distressed or angry with yourselves that
6 you sold me here, for God sent me ahead of you to save lives. For two years

רש״י

לג **יֵשֶׁב נָא עַבְדְּךָ וְגוֹ׳.** לְכָל דָּבָר אֲנִי מְעֻלֶּה מִמֶּנּוּ, לִגְבוּרָה וּלְמִלְחָמָה וּלְשַׁמֵּשׁ:

מה א **לְהִתְאַפֵּק לְכֹל הַנִּצָּבִים.** לֹא יָכוֹל לִסְבֹּל שֶׁיִּהְיוּ מִצְרִים נִצָּבִים עָלָיו וְשׁוֹמְעִין שֶׁאֶחָיו מִתְבַּיְּשִׁין בְּהִוָּדְעוֹ לָהֶם:

ב **וַיִּשְׁמַע בֵּית פַּרְעֹה.** בֵּיתוֹ שֶׁל פַּרְעֹה, כְּלוֹמַר עֲבָדָיו וּבְנֵי בֵּיתוֹ, וְאֵין זֶה לְשׁוֹן בַּיִת מַמָּשׁ, אֶלָּא כְּמוֹ "בֵּית יִשְׂרָאֵל", "בֵּית יְהוּדָה", מישנייד״א בְּלַעַז:

ג **כִּי נִבְהֲלוּ.** מִפְּנֵי הַבּוּשָׁה:

ד **גְּשׁוּ נָא אֵלַי.** רָאָה אוֹתָם נְסוֹגִים לְאָחוֹר, אָמַר, עַכְשָׁיו אַחַי נִכְלָמִים, קָרָא לָהֶם בְּלָשׁוֹן רַכָּה וְתַחֲנוּנִים וְהֶרְאָה לָהֶם שֶׁהוּא מָהוּל:

ה **לְמִחְיָה.** לִהְיוֹת לָכֶם לְמִחְיָה:

ו **כִּי זֶה שְׁנָתַיִם הָרָעָב.** עָבְרוּ מִשְּׁנֵי הָרָעָב:

a guilt-repentance-and-forgiveness culture, the first of its kind in the world.

Humanity changes the day Yosef forgives his brothers. When we forgive and are worthy of being forgiven, we are no longer prisoners of our past.

45:3 אֲנִי יוֹסֵף *I am Yosef* – One of the key concepts of Judaism is *teshuva*, a complex concept involving remorse, repentance, and return. If we understand the three necessary components of *teshuva*, the logic of Yosef's course of action becomes clear. The drama to which he subjects his brothers is leading them – for the first time in recorded history – through the three stages of *teshuva*: (1) admission of guilt, (2) confession, and (3) behavioral change.

Yehuda, the very brother who was responsible for selling Yosef into slavery (Gen. 37:27), now offers to sacrifice his own freedom rather than let Binyamin be held as a slave. The circumstances are similar to what they were years earlier, but Yehuda's behavior is now diametrically opposite to what it was then. He has the opportunity and ability to repeat the offense, but he does not do so. Yehuda has fulfilled the conditions set out by the Sages and Rambam for "perfect *teshuva*" (*Hilkhot Teshuva* 2:1). As soon as he does so, Yosef reveals his identity and the drama is at an end. Not dreams, not revenge, but *teshuva* is what has driven Yosef all along.

God does not demand perfection; by giving us free will He empowers us to make mistakes. All He asks is that we acknowledge our mistakes and commit ourselves not to make them again – in a word, that we be capable of *teshuva*. Yehuda, by undergoing Yosef's test, demonstrates that the children of Israel have become *baalei teshuva*, masters of repentance, capable of learning from, and growing through, their mistakes. Jewish history, starting with exile and exodus in Egypt, can now begin.

לג וְעַתָּה יֵשֶׁב־נָא עַבְדְּךָ תַּחַת הַנַּעַר עֶבֶד לַאדֹנִי וְהַנַּעַר יַעַל עִם־אֶחָיו׃
לד כִּי־אֵיךְ אֶעֱלֶה אֶל־אָבִי וְהַנַּעַר אֵינֶנּוּ אִתִּי פֶּן אֶרְאֶה בָרָע אֲשֶׁר יִמְצָא
מה א אֶת־אָבִי׃ וְלֹא־יָכֹל יוֹסֵף לְהִתְאַפֵּק לְכֹל הַנִּצָּבִים עָלָיו וַיִּקְרָא הוֹצִיאוּ
ב כָל־אִישׁ מֵעָלָי וְלֹא־עָמַד אִישׁ אִתּוֹ בְּהִתְוַדַּע יוֹסֵף אֶל־אֶחָיו׃ וַיִּתֵּן
ג אֶת־קֹלוֹ בִּבְכִי וַיִּשְׁמְעוּ מִצְרַיִם וַיִּשְׁמַע בֵּית פַּרְעֹה׃ וַיֹּאמֶר יוֹסֵף אֶל־
אֶחָיו אֲנִי יוֹסֵף הַעוֹד אָבִי חָי וְלֹא־יָכְלוּ אֶחָיו לַעֲנוֹת אֹתוֹ כִּי נִבְהֲלוּ
ד מִפָּנָיו׃ וַיֹּאמֶר יוֹסֵף אֶל־אֶחָיו גְּשׁוּ־נָא אֵלַי וַיִּגָּשׁוּ וַיֹּאמֶר אֲנִי יוֹסֵף
ה אֲחִיכֶם אֲשֶׁר־מְכַרְתֶּם אֹתִי מִצְרָיְמָה׃ וְעַתָּה ׀ אַל־תֵּעָצְבוּ וְאַל־יִחַר
בְּעֵינֵיכֶם כִּי־מְכַרְתֶּם אֹתִי הֵנָּה כִּי לְמִחְיָה שְׁלָחַנִי אֱלֹהִים לִפְנֵיכֶם׃
ו כִּי־זֶה שְׁנָתַיִם הָרָעָב בְּקֶרֶב הָאָרֶץ וְעוֹד חָמֵשׁ שָׁנִים אֲשֶׁר אֵין־חָרִישׁ

אונקלוס

לְאַבָּא כָּל יוֹמַיָּא: לג וּכְעַן, יְתִיב כְּעַן עַבְדָּךְ תְּחוֹת עוּלֵימָא, עַבְדָּא לְרִבּוֹנִי, וְעוּלֵימָא יִסַּק עִם אֲחוֹהִי: לד אֲרֵי אֵיכְדֵּין אֶסַּק לְוָת אַבָּא, וְעוּלֵימָא לֵיתוֹהִי עִמִּי, דִּלְמָא אֶחְזֵי בְּבִשְׁתָּא, דְּתַשְׁכַּח יָת אַבָּא: מה א וְלָא יְכֵיל יוֹסֵף לְאִתְחַסָּנָא, לְכָל דְּקָיְמִין עִלָּווֹהִי, וּקְרָא, אַפִּיקוּ כָּל אֱנָשׁ מֵעִלָּוַי, וְלָא קָם אֱנָשׁ עִמֵּיהּ, כַּד אִתְיְדַע יוֹסֵף לַאֲחוֹהִי: ב וִיהַב יָת קָלֵיהּ בִּבְכִיתָא, וּשְׁמַעוּ מִצְרָאֵי, וּשְׁמַע אֱנָשׁ בֵּית פַּרְעֹה: ג וַאֲמַר יוֹסֵף לַאֲחוֹהִי אֲנָא יוֹסֵף, הַעוֹד כְּעַן אַבָּא קַיָּם, וְלָא יְכִילוּ אֲחוֹהִי לְאָתָבָא יָתֵיהּ פִּתְגָם, אֲרֵי אִתְבְּהִילוּ מִן קֳדָמוֹהִי: ד וַאֲמַר יוֹסֵף לַאֲחוֹהִי, קְרוּבוּ כְעַן לְוָתִי וּקְרִיבוּ, וַאֲמַר, אֲנָא יוֹסֵף אֲחוּכוֹן, דְּזַבֵּינְתּוּן יָתִי לְמִצְרָיִם: ה וּכְעַן לָא תִתְנַסְסוּן, וְלָא יִתְקַף בְּעֵינֵיכוֹן, אֲרֵי זַבֵּינְתּוּן יָתִי הָלְכָא, אֲרֵי לְקַיָּמָא, שַׁלְחַנִי יי קֳדָמֵיכוֹן: ו אֲרֵי דְנָן, תַּרְתֵּין שְׁנִין כַּפְנָא בְּגוֹ אַרְעָא, וְעוֹד חֲמֵשׁ שְׁנִין, דְּלֵית זְרוּעָא

YOSEF FORGIVES HIS BROTHERS

This is the first recorded moment in history in which one human being forgives another. The first time God forgives is after the sin of the golden calf. God does not forgive Adam and Ḥava or Kayin. He mitigates their punishment, but mitigation is not forgiveness. God does not forgive the generation of the flood, or the builders of Bavel, or the sinners of Sedom.

God, in short, does not forgive human beings until human beings learn to forgive. It takes Yosef to bring forgiveness into the world. Had God forgiven first, He would have made the human situation worse, not better. People would have said, "Why shouldn't I harm others? After all, God forgives." This is what God has been waiting for.

Forgiveness transformed the human situation. For the first time it established the possibility that we are not condemned endlessly to repeat the past. Genuine forgiveness only exists in a culture in which repentance exists. Repentance presupposes that we are free and morally responsible agents who are capable of change, specifically the change that comes about when we recognize that something we have done is wrong and we are responsible and must never do it again. When I repent, I show I can change. The future is not predestined. I can make it different from what it might have been. And when I forgive, I show that my action is not mere reaction, as revenge would be. Forgiveness breaks the irreversibility of the past. The possibility of that kind of moral transformation simply did not exist in ancient Greece or any other pagan culture. To put it technically, Greece was a shame-and-honor culture. Judaism was

now there has been famine in the land, and for another five years there will be
7 no plowing or reaping. So God sent me ahead of you to ensure your survival in
8 the land, and to save your lives by a great deliverance. So then, it was not you SHELISHI
who sent me here, but God. He has made me a father to Pharaoh, lord of his
9 whole household and ruler of all Egypt. Hurry back to my father and tell him,
'This is what your son Yosef says: God has made me lord of all Egypt. Come
10 down to me without delay. You may live in the region of Goshen where you
will be close to me, you, your children, and your grandchildren, your flocks and
11 herds and all that is yours. I will provide for you there, for there are still five
years of famine to come. Otherwise you, your household, and all who belong
12 to you will be destitute.' You and my brother Binyamin can see with your own
13 eyes that it is I who am speaking to you. Tell my father about all the honor
accorded to me in Egypt and about everything you have seen. Hurry now –
14 bring my father here." Then he threw his arms around his brother Binyamin's
15 neck and wept, and Binyamin wept on his neck; he kissed all his brothers and
16 wept over them. Only after that could his brothers speak to him. When the
news reached Pharaoh's palace that Yosef's brothers had come, Pharaoh and his

רש״י

ח **לְאָב.** חָבֵר וּפַטְרוֹן:

ט **וַעֲלוּ אֶל אָבִי.** אֶרֶץ יִשְׂרָאֵל גְּבוֹהָה מִכָּל הָאֲרָצוֹת:

יא **פֶּן תִּוָּרֵשׁ.** "דִּלְמָא תִתְמַסְכַּן", לְשׁוֹן: "מוֹרִישׁ וּמַעֲשִׁיר" (שמואל א׳ ב, ז):

יב **וְהִנֵּה עֵינֵיכֶם רֹאוֹת.** בִּכְבוֹדִי, וְשֶׁאֲנִי אֲחִיכֶם שֶׁאֲנִי מָהוּל, וְעוֹד, "כִּי פִי הַמְדַבֵּר אֲלֵיכֶם" בִּלְשׁוֹן הַקֹּדֶשׁ: **וְעֵינֵי אָחִי בִנְיָמִין.** הִשְׁוָה אֶת כֻּלָּם יַחַד, לוֹמַר כְּשֵׁם שֶׁאֵין בְּלִבִּי שִׂנְאָה לְהַטִּיל בְּבִנְיָמִין אָחִי, שֶׁלֹּא הָיָה בִּמְכִירָתִי, כָּךְ אֵין בְּלִבִּי עֲלֵיכֶם:

יד **וַיִּפֹּל עַל צַוְּארֵי בִנְיָמִן אָחִיו וַיֵּבְךְּ.** עַל שְׁנֵי מִקְדָּשׁוֹת שֶׁעֲתִידִין לִהְיוֹת בְּחֶלְקוֹ שֶׁל בִּנְיָמִין וְסוֹפָן לֵחָרֵב: **וּבִנְיָמִן בָּכָה עַל צַוָּארָיו.** עַל מִשְׁכַּן שִׁילֹה שֶׁעָתִיד לִהְיוֹת בְּחֶלְקוֹ שֶׁל יוֹסֵף וְסוֹפוֹ לֵחָרֵב:

טו **וְאַחֲרֵי כֵן.** מֵאַחַר שֶׁרָאוּהוּ בּוֹכֶה וְלִבּוֹ שָׁלֵם עִמָּהֶם, "דִּבְּרוּ אֶחָיו אִתּוֹ", שֶׁמִּתְּחִלָּה הָיוּ בּוֹשִׁים מִמֶּנּוּ:

טז **וְהַקֹּל נִשְׁמַע בֵּית פַּרְעֹה.** כְּמוֹ בְּבֵית פַּרְעֹה, וְזֶהוּ לְשׁוֹן בַּיִת מַמָּשׁ:

terms with himself and his experiences. Forgiveness lifts the forgiver even more than the one who is forgiven.

45:15 וְאַחֲרֵי כֵן *Only after that* – Yosef has reframed his entire past. He no longer sees himself as a man wronged by his brothers. He has come to see himself as a man charged with a life-saving mission by God. Everything that has happened to him was necessary so that he could achieve his purpose in life: to save an entire region from starvation during a famine, and to provide a safe haven for his family.

This single act of reframing allows Yosef to live without a burning sense of anger and injustice. It transforms the negative energies of feelings about the past into focused attention on the future. It enables him to be reconciled with his brothers. Yosef, without knowing it, has become the precursor of one of the great movements in psychotherapy in the modern world. He has shown the power of reframing. We cannot change the past. But by changing the way we think about the past, we can change the future.

Whatever situation we are in, by reframing it we can change our entire response, giving us the strength to survive, the courage to persist, and the resilience to emerge, on the far side of darkness, into the light of a new and better day.

ז וְקָצִיר: וַיִּשְׁלָחֵנִי אֱלֹהִים לִפְנֵיכֶם לָשׂוּם לָכֶם שְׁאֵרִית בָּאָרֶץ וּלְהַחֲיוֹת
ח לָכֶם לִפְלֵיטָה גְּדֹלָה: וְעַתָּה לֹא־אַתֶּם שְׁלַחְתֶּם אֹתִי הֵנָּה כִּי הָאֱלֹהִים שלישי
וַיְשִׂימֵנִי לְאָב לְפַרְעֹה וּלְאָדוֹן לְכָל־בֵּיתוֹ וּמֹשֵׁל בְּכָל־אֶרֶץ מִצְרָיִם:
ט מַהֲרוּ וַעֲלוּ אֶל־אָבִי וַאֲמַרְתֶּם אֵלָיו כֹּה אָמַר בִּנְךָ יוֹסֵף שָׂמַנִי אֱלֹהִים
י לְאָדוֹן לְכָל־מִצְרָיִם רְדָה אֵלַי אַל־תַּעֲמֹד: וְיָשַׁבְתָּ בְאֶרֶץ־גֹּשֶׁן וְהָיִיתָ
קָרוֹב אֵלַי אַתָּה וּבָנֶיךָ וּבְנֵי בָנֶיךָ וְצֹאנְךָ וּבְקָרְךָ וְכָל־אֲשֶׁר־לָךְ:
יא וְכִלְכַּלְתִּי אֹתְךָ שָׁם כִּי־עוֹד חָמֵשׁ שָׁנִים רָעָב פֶּן־תִּוָּרֵשׁ אַתָּה וּבֵיתְךָ
יב וְכָל־אֲשֶׁר־לָךְ: וְהִנֵּה עֵינֵיכֶם רֹאוֹת וְעֵינֵי אָחִי בִנְיָמִין כִּי־פִי הַמְדַבֵּר
יג אֲלֵיכֶם: וְהִגַּדְתֶּם לְאָבִי אֶת־כָּל־כְּבוֹדִי בְּמִצְרַיִם וְאֵת כָּל־אֲשֶׁר רְאִיתֶם
יד וּמִהַרְתֶּם וְהוֹרַדְתֶּם אֶת־אָבִי הֵנָּה: וַיִּפֹּל עַל־צַוְּארֵי בִנְיָמִן־אָחִיו וַיֵּבְךְּ
טו וּבִנְיָמִן בָּכָה עַל־צַוָּארָיו: וַיְנַשֵּׁק לְכָל־אֶחָיו וַיֵּבְךְּ עֲלֵהֶם וְאַחֲרֵי כֵן
טז דִּבְּרוּ אֶחָיו אִתּוֹ: וְהַקֹּל נִשְׁמַע בֵּית פַּרְעֹה לֵאמֹר בָּאוּ אֲחֵי יוֹסֵף וַיִּיטַב

אונקלוס

וחצדא: ז ושלחני יי קדמיכון, לשואה לכון, שארא בארעא, ולקימא לכון, לשיזבא רבא: ח וכען, לא אתון, שלחתון יתי הלכא, אלהין מן קדם יי, ושויני אבא לפרעה, ולרבון לכל אנש ביתיה, ושליט בכל ארעא דמצרים: ט אוחו וסקו לות אבא, ותימרון ליה, כדנן אמר ברך יוסף, שויני יי, לרבון לכל מצראי, חות לותי לא תתעכב: י ותתיב בארעא דגשן, ותהי קריב לי, את, ובנך ובני בנך, וענך ותורך וכל דלך: יא ואזון יתך תמן, ארי עוד, חמש שנין כפנא, דלמא תתמסכן, את ואנש ביתך וכל דלך: יב והא עיניכון חזין, ועיני אחי בנימין, ארי בלישנכון אנא ממליל עמכון: יג ותחוון לאבא, ית כל יקרי דבמצרים, וית כל דחזיתון, ותוחון, ותחתון ית אבא הלכא: יד ונפל, על צורא דבנימין אחוהי ובכא, ובנימין, בכא על צוריה: טו ונשיק לכל אחוהי ובכא עליהון, ובתר כן, מלילו אחוהי עמיה: טז וקלא אשתמע, בית פרעה למימר, אתו אחי יוסף, ושפר

45:8 וְעַתָּה לֹא־אַתֶּם שְׁלַחְתֶּם אֹתִי הֵנָּה כִּי הָאֱלֹהִים *It was not you who sent me here, but God* – Yosef makes no reference to the brothers' plot to kill him or to the fact that they sold him into slavery. He makes no mention of the lost years he spent, first as Potifar's slave, then as a prisoner in jail. Not only does he forgive them, he does everything possible to relieve them from a sense of guilt. He tells them that they were not really responsible; that it had been God's plan all along; that it had been for the best, so that he could save lives during the years of famine, and so that he could act as their protector in the years to come. It is a moment of supreme generosity of spirit.

To achieve this, Yosef has had to rethink the entire sequence of events. He no longer sees it in terms of a wrong done against him by his brothers. He sees it as part of a providential plan to bring him to where God needs him to be ("So then, it was not you who sent me here, but God"). He thinks not only of the moment twenty-two years earlier when he was sold as a slave, but of its long-term consequences. Before he can come to terms with his brothers, Yosef has to come to

▶

17 officials were gratified. Pharaoh said to Yosef, "Tell your brothers, 'Do this:
18 Load your animals and go back to Canaan. Bring your father and your families
and come to me. I will give you the best of the land of Egypt; you shall live off
19 the cream of the land. You are also instructed to do this: Take wagons from REVI'I
20 Egypt for your children and wives. Bring your father and come. Do not trouble
yourselves about your belongings, for the best of all Egypt will be yours.'"
21 Yisrael's sons did so. Yosef gave them wagons as Pharaoh had ordered, and gave
22 them provisions for the journey. To each he gave new clothes, but to Binyamin
23 he gave three hundred pieces of silver and five sets of clothes. To his father he
sent the following: ten donkeys loaded with the best things of Egypt and ten
24 female donkeys loaded with grain, bread, and food for his father's journey. He
sent his brothers on their way; and as they were leaving, he said to them, "Do
25 not quarrel on the way." So they went up out of Egypt and came to their father
26 Yaakov in Canaan. They told him, "Yosef is still alive; in fact, he is ruler over all
27 Egypt." His heart stood still; he did not believe them. But when they told him
everything Yosef had said to them, and when he saw the wagons that Yosef
28 had sent to carry him back, Yaakov's spirit was filled with new life. Yisrael ḤAMISHI
said, "It is enough: Yosef my son is still alive. I must go and see him before I
46 1 die." So Yisrael set out with all he had. When he reached Be'er Sheva, he

אונקלוס

בְּעֵינֵי פַּרְעֹה, וּבְעֵינֵי עַבְדוֹהִי: יז וַאֲמַר פַּרְעֹה לְיוֹסֵף, אֵימַר לַאֲחָךְ דָּא עֲבִידוּ, טְעוּנוּ יָת בְּעִירְכוֹן, וְאִיזִילוּ אוֹבִילוּ לְאַרְעָא דִּכְנָעַן: יח וּדְבָרוּ יָת אֲבוּכוֹן, וְיָת אֱנָשׁ בָּתֵּיכוֹן וְאֵיתוֹ לְוָתִי, וְאֶתֵּין לְכוֹן, יָת טוּב אַרְעָא דְּמִצְרַיִם, וְתֵיכְלוּן יָת טוּבָא דְּאַרְעָא: יט וְאַתְּ מְפַקַּד ◀

רש״י

יז טַעֲנוּ אֶת בְּעִירְכֶם. תְּבוּאָה:

יח אֶת טוּב אֶרֶץ מִצְרַיִם. אֶרֶץ גֹּשֶׁן (להלן מז, ו). נִבָּא וְאֵינוֹ יוֹדֵעַ מַה נִּבָּא, סוֹפָם לַעֲשׂוֹתָהּ כִּמְצוּלָה שֶׁאֵין בָּהּ דָּגִים: חֵלֶב הָאָרֶץ. כָּל 'חֵלֶב' לְשׁוֹן מֵיטָב הוּא:

יט וְאַתָּה צֻוֵּיתָה. מִפִּי לוֹמַר לָהֶם: "זֹאת עֲשׂוּ", כָּךְ אֱמֹר לָהֶם שֶׁבִּרְשׁוּתִי הוּא:

כג שָׁלַח כְּזֹאת. כַּחֶשְׁבּוֹן הַזֶּה, וּמַהוּ הַחֶשְׁבּוֹן? "עֲשָׂרָה חֲמֹרִים" וְגוֹ': מִטּוּב מִצְרָיִם. מָצִינוּ בַּתַּלְמוּד (מגילה טז ע״ב) שֶׁשָּׁלַח לוֹ יַיִן יָשָׁן, שֶׁדַּעַת זְקֵנִים נוֹחָה הֵימֶנּוּ. וּמִדְרַשׁ אַגָּדָה, גְּרִיסִין שֶׁל פּוֹל: בָּר וָלֶחֶם. כְּתַרְגּוּמוֹ: וּמָזוֹן. לִפְתָּן:

כד אַל תִּרְגְּזוּ בַּדָּרֶךְ. אַל תִּתְעַסְּקוּ בִּדְבַר הֲלָכָה שֶׁלֹּא תִּרְגַּז עֲלֵיכֶם הַדֶּרֶךְ. דָּבָר אַחֵר, אַל תַּפְסִיעוּ פְּסִיעָה גַּסָּה, וְהַכְנִיסוּ חַמָּה לָעִיר. וּלְפִי פְּשׁוּטוֹ שֶׁל מִקְרָא יֵשׁ לוֹמַר, לְפִי שֶׁהָיוּ נִכְלָמִים הָיָה דוֹאֵג שֶׁמָּא יָרִיבוּ בַּדֶּרֶךְ עַל דְּבַר מְכִירָתוֹ לְהִתְוַכֵּחַ זֶה עִם זֶה וְלוֹמַר: עַל יָדְךָ נִמְכַּר, אַתָּה סִפַּרְתָּ לָשׁוֹן הָרָע עָלָיו וְגָרַמְתָּ לָנוּ לִשְׂנֹאתוֹ:

כו וְכִי הוּא מֹשֵׁל. וַאֲשֶׁר הוּא מוֹשֵׁל: וַיָּפָג לִבּוֹ. נֶחֱלַף לִבּוֹ וְהָלַךְ מִלְּהַאֲמִין, לֹא הָיָה לִבּוֹ פּוֹנֶה אֶל הַדְּבָרִים, לְשׁוֹן 'מְפִיגִין טַעֲמָן' בִּלְשׁוֹן מִשְׁנָה, וּכְמוֹ: "מֵאֵין הֲפֻגוֹת" (איכה ג, מט), "וְרֵיחוֹ לֹא נָמָר" (ירמיה מח, יא) מְתַרְגְּמִינַן: "וְרֵיחֵיהּ לָא פָג":

כז אֵת כָּל דִּבְרֵי יוֹסֵף. סִימָן מָסַר לָהֶם בַּמֶּה הָיָה עוֹסֵק כְּשֶׁפֵּרַשׁ מִמֶּנּוּ, בְּפָרָשַׁת עֶגְלָה עֲרוּפָה, וְזֶהוּ שֶׁאָמַר: "וַיַּרְא אֶת הָעֲגָלוֹת אֲשֶׁר שָׁלַח יוֹסֵף" וְלֹא נֶאֱמַר: 'אֲשֶׁר שָׁלַח פַּרְעֹה': וַתְּחִי רוּחַ יַעֲקֹב. שָׁרְתָה עָלָיו שְׁכִינָה שֶׁפֵּרְשָׁה מִמֶּנּוּ:

כח רַב. רַב לִי עוֹד שִׂמְחָה וְחֶדְוָה הוֹאִיל וְ"עוֹד יוֹסֵף בְּנִי חַי":

יז בְּעֵינֵי פַרְעֹה וּבְעֵינֵי עֲבָדָיו׃ וַיֹּאמֶר פַּרְעֹה אֶל־יוֹסֵף אֱמֹר אֶל־אַחֶיךָ
יח זֹאת עֲשׂוּ טַעֲנוּ אֶת־בְּעִירְכֶם וּלְכוּ־בֹאוּ אַרְצָה כְּנָעַן׃ וּקְחוּ אֶת־אֲבִיכֶם
וְאֶת־בָּתֵּיכֶם וּבֹאוּ אֵלָי וְאֶתְּנָה לָכֶם אֶת־טוּב אֶרֶץ מִצְרַיִם וְאִכְלוּ
יט אֶת־חֵלֶב הָאָרֶץ׃ וְאַתָּה צֻוֵּיתָה זֹאת עֲשׂוּ קְחוּ־לָכֶם מֵאֶרֶץ מִצְרַיִם רביעי
כ עֲגָלוֹת לְטַפְּכֶם וְלִנְשֵׁיכֶם וּנְשָׂאתֶם אֶת־אֲבִיכֶם וּבָאתֶם׃ וְעֵינְכֶם אַל־
כא תָּחֹס עַל־כְּלֵיכֶם כִּי־טוּב כָּל־אֶרֶץ מִצְרַיִם לָכֶם הוּא׃ וַיַּעֲשׂוּ־כֵן בְּנֵי
יִשְׂרָאֵל וַיִּתֵּן לָהֶם יוֹסֵף עֲגָלוֹת עַל־פִּי פַרְעֹה וַיִּתֵּן לָהֶם צֵדָה לַדָּרֶךְ׃
כב לְכֻלָּם נָתַן לָאִישׁ חֲלִפוֹת שְׂמָלֹת וּלְבִנְיָמִן נָתַן שְׁלֹשׁ מֵאוֹת כֶּסֶף וְחָמֵשׁ
כג חֲלִפֹת שְׂמָלֹת׃ וּלְאָבִיו שָׁלַח כְּזֹאת עֲשָׂרָה חֲמֹרִים נֹשְׂאִים מִטּוּב
כד מִצְרָיִם וְעֶשֶׂר אֲתֹנֹת נֹשְׂאֹת בָּר וָלֶחֶם וּמָזוֹן לְאָבִיו לַדָּרֶךְ׃ וַיְשַׁלַּח
כה אֶת־אֶחָיו וַיֵּלֵכוּ וַיֹּאמֶר אֲלֵהֶם אַל־תִּרְגְּזוּ בַּדָּרֶךְ׃ וַיַּעֲלוּ מִמִּצְרָיִם
כו וַיָּבֹאוּ אֶרֶץ כְּנַעַן אֶל־יַעֲקֹב אֲבִיהֶם׃ וַיַּגִּדוּ לוֹ לֵאמֹר עוֹד יוֹסֵף חַי
כז וְכִי־הוּא מֹשֵׁל בְּכָל־אֶרֶץ מִצְרָיִם וַיָּפָג לִבּוֹ כִּי לֹא־הֶאֱמִין לָהֶם׃ וַיְדַבְּרוּ
אֵלָיו אֵת כָּל־דִּבְרֵי יוֹסֵף אֲשֶׁר דִּבֶּר אֲלֵהֶם וַיַּרְא אֶת־הָעֲגָלוֹת אֲשֶׁר־
כח שָׁלַח יוֹסֵף לָשֵׂאת אֹתוֹ וַתְּחִי רוּחַ יַעֲקֹב אֲבִיהֶם׃ וַיֹּאמֶר יִשְׂרָאֵל רַב חמישי
מו א עוֹד־יוֹסֵף בְּנִי חָי אֵלְכָה וְאֶרְאֶנּוּ בְּטֶרֶם אָמוּת׃ וַיִּסַּע יִשְׂרָאֵל וְכָל־

אונקלוס

דָּא עֲבִידוּ, סַבוּ לְכוֹן מֵאַרְעָא דְמִצְרַיִם עֶגְלָן, לְטַפְלְכוֹן וּלְנְשֵׁיכוֹן, וְתִטְּלוּן יָת אֲבוּכוֹן וְתֵיתוֹן: כ וְעֵינְכוֹן, לָא תְחוּס עַל מָנֵיכוֹן, אֲרֵי טוּב, כָּל אַרְעָא דְמִצְרַיִם דִּילְכוֹן הוּא: כא וַעֲבַדוּ כֵן בְּנֵי יִשְׂרָאֵל, וִיהַב לְהוֹן יוֹסֵף, עֶגְלָן עַל מֵימְרָא דְפַרְעֹה, וִיהַב לְהוֹן, זְוָדִין לְאוֹרְחָא: כב לְכֻלְּהוֹן יְהַב, לִגְבַר אִצְטְלָן דִּלְבוּשָׁא, וּלְבִנְיָמִין יְהַב תְּלָת מְאָה סִלְעִין דִּכְסַף, וְחַמְשָׁא אִצְטְלָן דִּלְבוּשָׁא: כג וּלְאֲבוּהִי, שְׁלַח כְּדֵין עַסְרָא חֲמָרִין, טְעִינִין מִטּוּב מִצְרָיִם, וַעֲסַר אֲתָנָן, טְעִינָן, עֲבוּר וּלְחֵים וּזְוָדִין, לַאֲבוּהִי לְאוֹרְחָא: כד וְשַׁלַּח יָת אֲחוֹהִי וַאֲזַלוּ, וַאֲמַר לְהוֹן, לָא תִתְנַצוּן בְּאוֹרְחָא: כה וּסְלִיקוּ מִמִּצְרָיִם, וַאֲתוֹ לְאַרְעָא דִכְנַעַן, לְוָת יַעֲקֹב אֲבוּהוֹן: כו וְחַוִּיאוּ לֵיהּ לְמֵימַר, עַד כְּעַן יוֹסֵף קַיָּם, וַאֲרֵי הוּא שַׁלִּיט בְּכָל אַרְעָא דְמִצְרָיִם, וַהֲוָאָה מִלַּיָּא פָּיְגָן עַל לִבֵּיהּ, אֲרֵי לָא הֵימֵין לְהוֹן: כז וּמַלִּילוּ עִמֵּיהּ, יָת כָּל פִּתְגָמֵי יוֹסֵף דְּמַלֵּיל עִמְּהוֹן, וַחֲזָא יָת עֶגְלָתָא, דִּשְׁלַח יוֹסֵף לְמִטַּל יָתֵיהּ, וּשְׁרָת, רוּחַ קֻדְשָׁא עַל יַעֲקֹב אֲבוּהוֹן: כח וַאֲמַר יִשְׂרָאֵל, סַגִּי לִי חֶדְוָא, עַד כְּעַן יוֹסֵף בְּרִי קַיָּם, אֵיזֵיל וְאֶחֱזֵינֵּיהּ עַד לָא אֱמוּת: מו א וּנְטַל יִשְׂרָאֵל וְכָל

2 offered up sacrifices to the God of his father Yitzḥak. And God spoke to
3 Yisrael in a night vision: "Yaakov, Yaakov." He replied, "Here I am." "I am God,
the God of your father," He said. "Do not be afraid to go down to Egypt, for
4 there I will make of you a great nation. I Myself will go down to Egypt with
you, and I Myself will also bring you back; and Yosef's hand will close your
5 eyes." Then Yaakov left Be'er Sheva. Yisrael's sons took their father Yaakov and
their children and wives in the wagons that Pharaoh had sent to carry him.
6 They took their livestock and all the possessions they had acquired in Canaan.
7 So Yaakov and all his descendants came to Egypt. He brought with him to
Egypt his sons and grandsons, daughters and granddaughters, and all his
8 descendants. These are the names of the children of Israel – Yaakov
9 and his descendants – who came to Egypt: Reuven, Yaakov's firstborn, and
10 Reuven's sons, Ḥanokh, Palu, Ḥetzron, and Karmi. Shimon's sons were Yemuel,
11 Yamin, Ohad, Yakhin, Tzoḥar, and Sha'ul, son of the Canaanite woman. Levi's
12 sons were Gershon, Kehat, and Merari. Yehuda's sons were Er, Onan, Shela,
Peretz, and Zeraḥ – but Er and Onan had died in Canaan. Peretz's sons were
13 Ḥetzron and Ḥamul. Yissakhar's sons were Tola, Puva, Yov, and Shimron.
14 15 Zevulun's sons were Sered, Elon, and Yaḥliel. These were the sons whom Leah
bore to Yaakov in Padan Aram, besides his daughter Dina. In all, male and
16 female, they numbered thirty-three. Gad's sons were Tzifyon, Ḥagi, Shuni,
17 Etzbon, Eri, Arodi, and Areli. Asher's sons were Yimna, Yishva, Yishvi, and

רש״י

מו א **בְּאֵרָה שָׁבַע.** כְּמוֹ לִבְאֵר שָׁבַע, הֵ״א בְּסוֹף תֵּבָה בִּמְקוֹם לָמֶ״ד בִּתְחִלָּתָהּ: **לֵאלֹהֵי אָבִיו יִצְחָק.** חַיָּב אָדָם בִּכְבוֹד אָבִיו יוֹתֵר מִבִּכְבוֹד זְקֵנוֹ, לְפִיכָךְ תָּלָה בְּיִצְחָק וְלֹא בְּאַבְרָהָם:

ב **יַעֲקֹב יַעֲקֹב.** לְשׁוֹן חִבָּה:

ג **אַל תִּירָא מֵרְדָה מִצְרַיְמָה.** לְפִי שֶׁהָיָה מֵצֵר עַל שֶׁנִּזְקַק לָצֵאת לְחוּצָה לָאָרֶץ:

ד **וְאָנֹכִי אַעַלְךָ.** הִבְטִיחוֹ לִהְיוֹת נִקְבָּר בָּאָרֶץ:

ו **אֲשֶׁר רָכְשׁוּ בְּאֶרֶץ כְּנַעַן.** אֲבָל מַה שֶּׁרָכַשׁ בְּפַדַּן אֲרָם נָתַן הַכֹּל לְעֵשָׂו בִּשְׁבִיל חֶלְקוֹ בִּמְעָרַת הַמַּכְפֵּלָה, אָמַר: נִכְסֵי חוּצָה לָאָרֶץ אֵינָן כְּדַאי לִי, וְזֶהוּ ״אֲשֶׁר כָּרִיתִי לִי״ (להלן נ, ה), הֶעֱמִיד לוֹ צִבּוּרִין שֶׁל זָהָב וְכֶסֶף כְּמִין כְּרִי, וְאָמַר לוֹ: טֹל אֶת אֵלּוּ:

ז **וּבְנוֹת בָּנָיו.** שֶׂרַח בַּת אָשֵׁר וְיוֹכֶבֶד בַּת לֵוִי:

ח **הַבָּאִים מִצְרַיְמָה.** עַל שֵׁם הַשָּׁעָה קוֹרֵא לָהֶם הַכָּתוּב ׳בָּאִים׳, וְאֵין לִתְמֹהַּ עַל אֲשֶׁר לֹא כָתַב ׳אֲשֶׁר בָּאוּ׳:

י **בֶּן הַכְּנַעֲנִית.** בֶּן דִּינָה שֶׁנִּבְעֲלָה לִכְנַעֲנִי; כְּשֶׁהָרְגוּ אֶת שְׁכֶם לֹא הָיְתָה דִּינָה רוֹצָה לָצֵאת עַד שֶׁנִּשְׁבַּע לָהּ שִׁמְעוֹן שֶׁיִּשָּׂאֶנָּה. בִּבְרֵאשִׁית רַבָּה (פ, יא):

טו **אֵלֶּה בְּנֵי לֵאָה... וְאֵת דִּינָה בִתּוֹ.** הַזְּכָרִים תָּלָה בְּלֵאָה וְהַנְּקֵבוֹת תָּלָה בְּיַעֲקֹב, לְלַמֶּדְךָ, אִשָּׁה מַזְרַעַת תְּחִלָּה יוֹלֶדֶת זָכָר, אִישׁ מַזְרִיעַ תְּחִלָּה יוֹלֶדֶת נְקֵבָה: **שְׁלֹשִׁים וְשָׁלֹשׁ.** וּבִפְרָטָן אִי אַתָּה מוֹצֵא אֶלָּא שְׁלֹשִׁים וּשְׁנַיִם, אֶלָּא זוֹ יוֹכֶבֶד שֶׁנּוֹלְדָה בֵּין הַחוֹמוֹת בִּכְנִיסָתָן לָעִיר, שֶׁנֶּאֱמַר: ״אֲשֶׁר יָלְדָה אֹתָהּ לְלֵוִי בְּמִצְרָיִם״ (במדבר כו, נט) – לֵדָתָהּ בְּמִצְרַיִם וְאֵין הוֹרָתָהּ בְּמִצְרַיִם:

ב אֲשֶׁר־לוֹ וַיָּבֹא בְּאֵרָה שָּׁבַע וַיִּזְבַּח זְבָחִים לֵאלֹהֵי אָבִיו יִצְחָק: וַיֹּאמֶר
אֱלֹהִים ׀ לְיִשְׂרָאֵל בְּמַרְאֹת הַלַּיְלָה וַיֹּאמֶר יַעֲקֹב ׀ יַעֲקֹב וַיֹּאמֶר הִנֵּנִי:
ג וַיֹּאמֶר אָנֹכִי הָאֵל אֱלֹהֵי אָבִיךָ אַל־תִּירָא מֵרְדָה מִצְרַיְמָה כִּי־לְגוֹי
ד גָּדוֹל אֲשִׂימְךָ שָׁם: אָנֹכִי אֵרֵד עִמְּךָ מִצְרַיְמָה וְאָנֹכִי אַעַלְךָ גַם־עָלֹה
ה וְיוֹסֵף יָשִׁית יָדוֹ עַל־עֵינֶיךָ: וַיָּקָם יַעֲקֹב מִבְּאֵר שָׁבַע וַיִּשְׂאוּ בְנֵי־יִשְׂרָאֵל
אֶת־יַעֲקֹב אֲבִיהֶם וְאֶת־טַפָּם וְאֶת־נְשֵׁיהֶם בָּעֲגָלוֹת אֲשֶׁר־שָׁלַח פַּרְעֹה
ו לָשֵׂאת אֹתוֹ: וַיִּקְחוּ אֶת־מִקְנֵיהֶם וְאֶת־רְכוּשָׁם אֲשֶׁר רָכְשׁוּ בְּאֶרֶץ
ז כְּנַעַן וַיָּבֹאוּ מִצְרָיְמָה יַעֲקֹב וְכָל־זַרְעוֹ אִתּוֹ: בָּנָיו וּבְנֵי בָנָיו אִתּוֹ בְּנֹתָיו
ח וּבְנוֹת בָּנָיו וְכָל־זַרְעוֹ הֵבִיא אִתּוֹ מִצְרָיְמָה: וְאֵלֶּה שְׁמוֹת
ט בְּנֵי־יִשְׂרָאֵל הַבָּאִים מִצְרַיְמָה יַעֲקֹב וּבָנָיו בְּכֹר יַעֲקֹב רְאוּבֵן: וּבְנֵי
י רְאוּבֵן חֲנוֹךְ וּפַלּוּא וְחֶצְרֹן וְכַרְמִי: וּבְנֵי שִׁמְעוֹן יְמוּאֵל וְיָמִין וְאֹהַד
יא יב וְיָכִין וְצֹחַר וְשָׁאוּל בֶּן־הַכְּנַעֲנִית: וּבְנֵי לֵוִי גֵּרְשׁוֹן קְהָת וּמְרָרִי: וּבְנֵי
יְהוּדָה עֵר וְאוֹנָן וְשֵׁלָה וָפֶרֶץ וָזָרַח וַיָּמָת עֵר וְאוֹנָן בְּאֶרֶץ כְּנַעַן וַיִּהְיוּ
יג יד בְנֵי־פֶרֶץ חֶצְרֹן וְחָמוּל: וּבְנֵי יִשָּׂשכָר תּוֹלָע וּפֻוָּה וְיוֹב וְשִׁמְרֹן: וּבְנֵי
טו זְבֻלוּן סֶרֶד וְאֵלוֹן וְיַחְלְאֵל: אֵלֶּה ׀ בְּנֵי לֵאָה אֲשֶׁר יָלְדָה לְיַעֲקֹב בְּפַדַּן
טז אֲרָם וְאֵת דִּינָה בִתּוֹ כָּל־נֶפֶשׁ בָּנָיו וּבְנוֹתָיו שְׁלֹשִׁים וְשָׁלֹשׁ: וּבְנֵי גָד
יז צִפְיוֹן וְחַגִּי שׁוּנִי וְאֶצְבֹּן עֵרִי וַאֲרוֹדִי וְאַרְאֵלִי: וּבְנֵי אָשֵׁר יִמְנָה וְיִשְׁוָה

אונקלוס

דִּילֵיהּ, וַאֲתָא לִבְאֵר שָׁבַע, וְדַבַּח דִּבְחִין, לֶאֱלָהָא דַּאֲבוּהִי יִצְחָק: ב וַאֲמַר יי לְיִשְׂרָאֵל בְּחֶזְוָא דְלֵילְיָא, וַאֲמַר יַעֲקֹב יַעֲקֹב, וַאֲמַר הָאֲנָא: ג וַאֲמַר, אֲנָא אֵל אֱלָהָא דַּאֲבוּךְ, לָא תִדְחַל מִלְּמֵיחַת לְמִצְרַיִם, אֲרֵי לְעַם סַגִּי אֲשַׁוֵּינָךְ תַּמָּן: ד אֲנָא, אֵיחוֹת עִמָּךְ לְמִצְרַיִם, וַאֲנָא אַסֵּקִנָּךְ אַף אַסָּקָא, וְיוֹסֵף, יְשַׁוֵּי יְדוֹהִי עַל עֵינָךְ: ה וְקָם יַעֲקֹב מִבְּאֵר שָׁבַע, וּנְטַלוּ בְנֵי יִשְׂרָאֵל יָת יַעֲקֹב אֲבוּהוֹן, וְיָת טַפְלְהוֹן וְיָת נְשֵׁיהוֹן, בְּעֶגְלָתָא, דִּשְׁלַח פַּרְעֹה לְמִטַּל יָתֵיהּ: ו וּדְבָרוּ יָת גֵּיתֵיהוֹן, וְיָת קִנְיָנְהוֹן דִּקְנוֹ בְּאַרְעָא דִכְנַעַן, וַאֲתוֹ לְמִצְרָיִם, יַעֲקֹב וְכָל בְּנוֹהִי עִמֵּיהּ: ז בְּנוֹהִי, וּבְנֵי בְנוֹהִי עִמֵּיהּ, בְּנָתֵיהּ, וּבְנָת בְּנוֹהִי וְכָל בְּנוֹהִי, אַיְתִי עִמֵּיהּ לְמִצְרָיִם: ח וְאִלֵּין שְׁמָהַת בְּנֵי יִשְׂרָאֵל, דְּעָאלוּ לְמִצְרַיִם יַעֲקֹב וּבְנוֹהִי, בֻּכְרֵיהּ דְּיַעֲקֹב רְאוּבֵן: ט וּבְנֵי רְאוּבֵן, חֲנוֹךְ וּפַלּוּא וְחֶצְרוֹן וְכַרְמִי: י וּבְנֵי שִׁמְעוֹן, יְמוּאֵל וְיָמִין, וְאֹהַד וְיָכִין וְצוֹחַר, וְשָׁאוּל בַּר כְּנַעֲנֵיתָא: יא וּבְנֵי לֵוִי, גֵּרְשׁוֹן, קְהָת וּמְרָרִי: יב וּבְנֵי יְהוּדָה, עֵר וְאוֹנָן, וְשֵׁלָה וָפֶרֶץ וָזָרַח, וּמִית עֵר וְאוֹנָן בְּאַרְעָא דִכְנַעַן, וַהֲווֹ בְנֵי פֶרֶץ חֶצְרוֹן וְחָמוּל: יג וּבְנֵי יִשָּׂשכָר, תּוֹלָע וּפֻוָּה וְיוֹב וְשִׁמְרוֹן: יד וּבְנֵי זְבוּלוּן, סֶרֶד וְאֵלוֹן וְיַחְלְאֵל: טו אִלֵּין בְּנֵי לֵאָה, דִּילֵידַת לְיַעֲקֹב בְּפַדַּן אֲרָם, וְיָת דִּינָה בְרַתֵּיהּ, כָּל נְפַשׁ בְּנוֹהִי, וּבְנָתֵיהּ תְּלָתִין וּתְלָת: טז וּבְנֵי גָד, צִפְיוֹן וְחַגִּי שׁוּנִי וְאֶצְבּוֹן, עֵרִי וַאֲרוֹדִי וְאַרְאֵלִי: יז וּבְנֵי אָשֵׁר, יִמְנָה וְיִשְׁוָה,

18 Beria. Their sister was Seraḥ. Beria's sons were Ḥever and Malkiel. These were
the children of Zilpa, whom Lavan had given to his daughter Leah; these she
19 bore to Yaakov – sixteen in all.The sons of Yaakov's wife Raḥel were Yosef and
20 Binyamin. In Egypt Menashe and Efrayim were born to Yosef; Asnat, daughter
21 of Potifera priest of On, bore them to him. Binyamin's sons were Bela, Bekher,
22 Ashbel, Gera, Naaman, Eḥi, Rosh, Mupim, Ḥupim, and Ard. These are the
23 24 children Raḥel bore to Yaakov – fourteen in all. Dan's son was Ḥushim. Naftali's
25 sons were Yaḥtze'el, Guni, Yetzer, and Shilem. These were the sons born to
26 Yaakov by Bilha, whom Lavan had given to his daughter Raḥel – seven in all. So
the number of people who came to Egypt with Yaakov – his direct descendants,
27 not including his sons' wives – were sixty-six in all. Yosef's sons, born to him in
Egypt, were two in number. Thus the total number of Yaakov's family who
28 came to Egypt was seventy. He sent Yehuda ahead of him to Yosef SHISHI
to show him the way to Goshen. When they came to the region of Goshen,

רש"י

יט **בני רחל אשת יעקב.** ובכולן לא נאמר כן! אלא שהיתה עקרו של בית:

כו-כז **כל הנפש הבאה ליעקב.** שיצאו מארץ כנען לבא למצרים, ואין 'הבאה' זו לשון עבר אלא לשון הווה, כמו: "בערב היא באה" (אסתר ב, יד), וכמו: "והנה רחל בתו באה עם הצאן" (לעיל כט, ו), לפיכך טעמו למטה באל"ף, לפי שכשיצאו לבוא מארץ כנען לא היו אלא ששים ושש. והשני, "כל הנפש לבית יעקב הבאה מצרימה שבעים" הוא לשון עבר, לפיכך טעמו למעלה בבי"ת, לפי שמשבאו שם היו שבעים, שמצאו שם יוסף ושני בניו, ונתוספה להם יוכבד בין החומות. ולדברי האומר תאומות נולדו עם השבטים צריכים אנו לומר שמתו לפני ירידתן למצרים, שהרי לא נמנו כאן. מצאתי בויקרא רבה (ד, ו): עשו שש נפשות היו לו והכתוב קורא אותן 'נפשות ביתו' (לעיל לו, ו) לשון רבים, לפי שהיו עובדין לאלהות הרבה; יעקב שבעים היו לו והכתוב קורא אותן 'נפש', לפי שהיו עובדין לאל אחד:

כח **להורת לפניו.** כתרגומו, לפנות לו מקום ולהורות היאך יתישב בה: לפניו. קודם שיגיע לשם. ומדרש אגדה, "להורת לפניו", לתקן לו בית תלמוד שמשם תצא הוראה:

was unable to remember anything for more than a few seconds. Unable to thread experiences together, he was caught in an endless present that had no connection with anything that had gone before. He had no past at all.

Two things broke through his isolation. One was his love for his wife. The other was music. He could still sing, play the organ, and conduct a choir with all his old skill and verve.

What was it about music that enabled him, while playing or conducting, to overcome amnesia? Sacks quotes the philosopher of music, Victor Zuckerkandl, who wrote, "Hearing a melody is hearing, having heard, and being about to hear, all at once.... Every melody declares to us that the past can be there without being remembered, the future without being foreknown." Music is a form of sensed continuity that can sometimes break through the most overpowering disconnections in our experience of time. Seraḥ's song allows Yaakov to integrate new knowledge that completely disrupts his experience of his past and future. She is blessed in return to become a symbol and bearer of a people's continuity through the horrific alienation of slavery.

Faith is more like music than science. Science analyzes; music integrates. And as music connects note to note, so faith connects episode to episode, life to life, age to age in a timeless melody that breaks into time. Faith is the ability to hear the music beneath the noise.

יח וְיִשְׁוִי וּבְרִיעָה וְשֶׂרַח אֲחֹתָם וּבְנֵי בְרִיעָה חֶבֶר וּמַלְכִּיאֵל׃ אֵלֶּה בְּנֵי
זִלְפָּה אֲשֶׁר־נָתַן לָבָן לְלֵאָה בִתּוֹ וַתֵּלֶד אֶת־אֵלֶּה לְיַעֲקֹב שֵׁשׁ עֶשְׂרֵה
יט כ נָפֶשׁ׃ בְּנֵי רָחֵל אֵשֶׁת יַעֲקֹב יוֹסֵף וּבִנְיָמִן׃ וַיִּוָּלֵד לְיוֹסֵף בְּאֶרֶץ מִצְרַיִם
אֲשֶׁר יָלְדָה־לּוֹ אָסְנַת בַּת־פּוֹטִי פֶרַע כֹּהֵן אֹן אֶת־מְנַשֶּׁה וְאֶת־אֶפְרָיִם׃
כא וּבְנֵי בִנְיָמִן בֶּלַע וָבֶכֶר וְאַשְׁבֵּל גֵּרָא וְנַעֲמָן אֵחִי וָרֹאשׁ מֻפִּים וְחֻפִּים
כב כג וָאָרְדְּ׃ אֵלֶּה בְּנֵי רָחֵל אֲשֶׁר יֻלַּד לְיַעֲקֹב כָּל־נֶפֶשׁ אַרְבָּעָה עָשָׂר׃ וּבְנֵי־
כד כה דָן חֻשִׁים׃ וּבְנֵי נַפְתָּלִי יַחְצְאֵל וְגוּנִי וְיֵצֶר וְשִׁלֵּם׃ אֵלֶּה בְּנֵי בִלְהָה
אֲשֶׁר־נָתַן לָבָן לְרָחֵל בִּתּוֹ וַתֵּלֶד אֶת־אֵלֶּה לְיַעֲקֹב כָּל־נֶפֶשׁ שִׁבְעָה׃
כו כָּל־הַנֶּפֶשׁ הַבָּאָה לְיַעֲקֹב מִצְרַיְמָה יֹצְאֵי יְרֵכוֹ מִלְּבַד נְשֵׁי בְנֵי־יַעֲקֹב
כז כָּל־נֶפֶשׁ שִׁשִּׁים וָשֵׁשׁ׃ וּבְנֵי יוֹסֵף אֲשֶׁר־יֻלַּד־לוֹ בְמִצְרַיִם נֶפֶשׁ שְׁנָיִם
כח כָּל־הַנֶּפֶשׁ לְבֵית־יַעֲקֹב הַבָּאָה מִצְרַיְמָה שִׁבְעִים׃ וְאֶת־ מא ששי
יְהוּדָה שָׁלַח לְפָנָיו אֶל־יוֹסֵף לְהוֹרֹת לְפָנָיו גֹּשְׁנָה וַיָּבֹאוּ אַרְצָה גֹּשֶׁן׃

אונקלוס

וִישְׁוִי וּבְרִיעָה וְשֶׂרַח אֲחָתְהוֹן, וּבְנֵי בְרִיעָה, חֶבֶר וּמַלְכִּיאֵל: יח אִלֵּין בְּנֵי זִלְפָּה, דִּיהַב לָבָן לְלֵאָה בְרַתֵּיהּ, וִילֵידַת יָת אִלֵּין לְיַעֲקֹב, שִׁית עַסְרֵי נַפְשָׁן: יט בְּנֵי רָחֵל אִתַּת יַעֲקֹב, יוֹסֵף וּבִנְיָמִין: כ וְאִתְיְלִיד לְיוֹסֵף בְּאַרְעָא דְמִצְרַיִם, דִּילֵידַת לֵיהּ אָסְנַת, בַּת פּוֹטִיפֶרַע רַבָּא דְאוֹן, יָת מְנַשֶּׁה וְיָת אֶפְרָיִם: כא וּבְנֵי בִנְיָמִין, בֶּלַע וָבֶכֶר וְאַשְׁבֵּל, גֵּרָא וְנַעֲמָן אֵחִי וָרֹאשׁ, מֻפִּים וְחֻפִּים וָאָרְדְּ: כב אִלֵּין בְּנֵי רָחֵל, דְּאִתְיְלִידוּ לְיַעֲקֹב, כָּל נַפְשָׁתָא אַרְבְּעַת עֲסַר: כג וּבְנֵי דָן חֻשִׁים: כד וּבְנֵי נַפְתָּלִי, יַחְצְאֵל וְגוּנִי וְיֵצֶר וְשִׁלֵּם: כה אִלֵּין בְּנֵי בִלְהָה, דִּיהַב לָבָן לְרָחֵל בְּרַתֵּיהּ, וִילֵידַת יָת אִלֵּין, לְיַעֲקֹב כָּל נַפְשָׁתָא שַׁבְעָא: כו כָּל נַפְשָׁתָא, דְּעָאלָא עִם יַעֲקֹב לְמִצְרַיִם נָפְקֵי יַרְכֵּיהּ, בַּר מִנְּשֵׁי בְנֵי יַעֲקֹב, כָּל נַפְשָׁתָא שִׁתִּין וְשִׁית: כז וּבְנֵי יוֹסֵף, דְּאִתְיְלִידוּ לֵיהּ בְמִצְרַיִם נַפְשָׁתָא תַּרְתֵּין, כָּל נַפְשָׁתָא לְבֵית יַעֲקֹב, דְּעָאלָא לְמִצְרַיִם שַׁבְעִין: כח וְיָת יְהוּדָה, שְׁלַח קֳדָמוֹהִי לְוָת יוֹסֵף, לְפַנָּאָה קֳדָמוֹהִי לְגֹשֶׁן, וַאֲתוֹ לַאֲרַע דְּגֹשֶׁן:

46:17 וְשֶׂרַח אֲחֹתָם *Their sister was Seraḥ* – Seraḥ will be mentioned again in a list of the Israelites who left Egypt (Num. 26:46). This inspires midrashic traditions about her longevity and her role in carrying knowledge of the past through the time of slavery to younger generations. A medieval midrash in *Sefer HaYashar* tells that the brothers are afraid, when they come back from Egypt, that the sudden revelation that Yosef is still alive will come as too great a shock to Yaakov, and that he will not believe them. They ask Seraḥ, who is "good and wise and could play the harp" to bear the news for them. Seraḥ weaves their message into a beautiful song, which she sings to Yaakov, accompanying herself on the harp. After hearing the words sung several times, Yaakov understands that they are true, and blesses his granddaughter, "Daughter, let death have no hold on you forever, for you have filled my spirit with new life."

"It is our task," said Itzhak Perlman, "to make music with what remains." In his book, *Musicophilia*, the late Oliver Sacks (no relation, alas) told the poignant story of Clive Wearing, an eminent musicologist who was struck by acute amnesia. He

29 Yosef harnessed his chariot and rode to Goshen to greet his father Yisrael. He
presented himself to him, threw his arms around his neck, and wept on his
30 shoulder for a long time. “Now I can die,” said Yisrael to Yosef. “I have seen
31 your face! You are still alive!” Yosef said to his brothers and his father’s
household, “I will go and speak to Pharaoh. I will tell him, ‘My brothers and my
32 father’s household have come to me from Canaan. The men are shepherds.
They tend livestock. They have brought their sheep and cattle and all they have.’
33 34 When Pharaoh summons you and asks, ‘What is your occupation?’ you should
say, ‘We and our fathers have tended livestock all our lives.’ Then you will be
allowed to settle in the region of Goshen, because the Egyptians abominate all
47 1 who keep sheep.” So Yosef went and told Pharaoh. He said, “My father and
brothers, together with their flocks, herds, and all they have, have come from

רש״י

כט| **וַיֶּאְסֹר יוֹסֵף מֶרְכַּבְתּוֹ.** הוּא עַצְמוֹ אָסַר אֶת הַסּוּסִים לַמֶּרְכָּבָה לְהִזְדָּרֵז לִכְבוֹד אָבִיו: **וַיֵּרָא אֵלָיו.** יוֹסֵף נִרְאָה אֶל אָבִיו: **וַיֵּבְךְּ עַל צַוָּארָיו עוֹד.** לְשׁוֹן הַרְבּוֹת בְּכִיָּה, וְכֵן: ״כִּי לֹא עַל אִישׁ יָשִׂים עוֹד״ (איוב לד, כג) לְשׁוֹן רִבּוּי הוּא, אֵינוֹ שָׂם עָלָיו עֲלִילוֹת נוֹסָפוֹת עַל חֲטָאָיו, אַף כָּאן, הִרְבָּה וְהוֹסִיף בִּבְכִי יוֹתֵר עַל הָרָגִיל. אֲבָל יַעֲקֹב לֹא נָפַל עַל צַוְּארֵי יוֹסֵף וְלֹא נְשָׁקוֹ, וְאָמְרוּ רַבּוֹתֵינוּ שֶׁהָיָה קוֹרֵא אֶת שְׁמַע:

ל| **אָמוּתָה הַפָּעַם.** פְּשׁוּטוֹ כְּתַרְגּוּמוֹ. וּמִדְרָשׁוֹ, סָבוּר הָיִיתִי לָמוּת שְׁתֵּי מִיתוֹת, בָּעוֹלָם הַזֶּה וְלָעוֹלָם הַבָּא, שֶׁנִּסְתַּלְּקָה מִמֶּנִּי שְׁכִינָה, וְהָיִיתִי אוֹמֵר שֶׁיִּתְבָּעֵנִי הַקָּדוֹשׁ בָּרוּךְ הוּא מִיתָתְךָ. עַכְשָׁיו שֶׁעוֹדְךָ חַי, לֹא אָמוּת אֶלָּא פַּעַם אַחַת:

לא-לב| **וְאֹמְרָה אֵלָיו אַחַי וְגוֹ׳.** וְעוֹד אֹמַר לוֹ: ״וְהָאֲנָשִׁים רֹעֵי צֹאן״ וְגוֹ׳:

לד| **בַּעֲבוּר תֵּשְׁבוּ בְּאֶרֶץ גֹּשֶׁן.** וְהִיא צְרִיכָה לָכֶם, שֶׁהִיא אֶרֶץ מִרְעֶה, וּכְשֶׁתֹּאמְרוּ לוֹ שֶׁאֵין אַתֶּם בְּקִיאִין בִּמְלָאכָה אַחֶרֶת יַרְחִיקְכֶם מֵעָלָיו וְיוֹשִׁיבְכֶם שָׁם: **כִּי תוֹעֲבַת מִצְרַיִם כָּל רֹעֵה צֹאן.** לְפִי שֶׁהֵם לָהֶם אֱלָהוֹת:

alone, far from the noise of the city, where they could be in communion with God.

Their lifestyle reflected some of the values of an earlier time. Hunter-gatherer societies were relatively egalitarian. It was only with the birth of agriculture and the division of labor, of trade and trading centers and economic surplus and marked inequalities of wealth, concentrated in cities with their distinctive hierarchies of power, that a whole cluster of phenomena began to appear – not just the benefits of civilization but the downside also.

The city is a dehumanizing environment and potentially a place where people worship symbolic representations of themselves. To this day, the temples, colossi, and pyramids of Egypt are awe-inspiring. They were meant to be. But there is a question to be asked about monumental architecture through the ages, much of it religious: At whose cost was it built? Virtually none was produced without exploitation on a massive scale. In Genesis and Exodus we hear little about the idolatry and pagan rituals that were later to earn the scorn of the prophets. We hear much, however, about something else, namely the hierarchical society by which some presume to rule over others. This, to the Torah, is unforgivable.

The Israelites will be commanded to create *a society that is not Egypt*, that is different, opposite, counter-cultural. It will be a society in which even slaves rest every seventh day and breathe the wide air of freedom. And those at the margins of society – as the Israelites with their alien lifestyle were in Egypt – are to be treated with dignity and included in national celebrations. This is the drama of Exodus, but the seeds of it are already to be found here. In Genesis, the lives of shepherds, from Hevel to Yisrael’s children, are set in contrast with four cities: Ḥanokh, Bavel, Sedom, and finally, the urban capital of Egypt. What the Torah is telling us, implicitly, is how and why Abrahamic monotheism was born.

כט וַיֶּאְסֹר יוֹסֵף מֶרְכַּבְתּוֹ וַיַּעַל לִקְרַאת־יִשְׂרָאֵל אָבִיו גֹּשְׁנָה וַיֵּרָא אֵלָיו
ל וַיִּפֹּל עַל־צַוָּארָיו וַיֵּבְךְּ עַל־צַוָּארָיו עוֹד: וַיֹּאמֶר יִשְׂרָאֵל אֶל־יוֹסֵף
לא אָמוּתָה הַפָּעַם אַחֲרֵי רְאוֹתִי אֶת־פָּנֶיךָ כִּי עוֹדְךָ חָי: וַיֹּאמֶר יוֹסֵף אֶל־
אֶחָיו וְאֶל־בֵּית אָבִיו אֶעֱלֶה וְאַגִּידָה לְפַרְעֹה וְאֹמְרָה אֵלָיו אַחַי וּבֵית־
לב אָבִי אֲשֶׁר בְּאֶרֶץ־כְּנַעַן בָּאוּ אֵלָי: וְהָאֲנָשִׁים רֹעֵי צֹאן כִּי־אַנְשֵׁי מִקְנֶה
לג הָיוּ וְצֹאנָם וּבְקָרָם וְכָל־אֲשֶׁר לָהֶם הֵבִיאוּ: וְהָיָה כִּי־יִקְרָא לָכֶם פַּרְעֹה
לד וְאָמַר מַה־מַּעֲשֵׂיכֶם: וַאֲמַרְתֶּם אַנְשֵׁי מִקְנֶה הָיוּ עֲבָדֶיךָ מִנְּעוּרֵינוּ
וְעַד־עַתָּה גַּם־אֲנַחְנוּ גַּם־אֲבֹתֵינוּ בַּעֲבוּר תֵּשְׁבוּ בְּאֶרֶץ גֹּשֶׁן כִּי־תוֹעֲבַת
מז א מִצְרַיִם כָּל־רֹעֵה צֹאן: וַיָּבֹא יוֹסֵף וַיַּגֵּד לְפַרְעֹה וַיֹּאמֶר אָבִי וְאַחַי
וְצֹאנָם וּבְקָרָם וְכָל־אֲשֶׁר לָהֶם בָּאוּ מֵאֶרֶץ כְּנָעַן וְהִנָּם בְּאֶרֶץ גֹּשֶׁן:

אונקלוס

כט וְטַקֵּיס יוֹסֵף רְתִכּוֹהִי, וּסְלֵיק, לְקַדָּמוּת יִשְׂרָאֵל אֲבוּהִי לְגֹשֶׁן, וְאִתַּחְזִי לֵיהּ, וּנְפַל עַל צַוְרֵיהּ, וּבְכָא עַל צַוְרֵיהּ עוֹד: ל וַאֲמַר יִשְׂרָאֵל, לְיוֹסֵף אִלּוּ אֲנָא מָאֵית זִמְנָא הָדָא מְנַחַם אֲנָא, בָּתַר דַּחֲזֵיתִנּוּן לְאַפָּךְ, אֲרֵי עַד כְּעַן קַיָּם אַתְּ: לא וַאֲמַר יוֹסֵף לַאֲחוֹהִי וּלְבֵית אֲבוּהִי, אֶסַּק וַאֲחַוֵּי לְפַרְעֹה, וְאֵימַר לֵיהּ, אַחַי וּבֵית אַבָּא, דִּבְאַרְעָא דִּכְנַעַן אֲתוֹ לְוָתִי: לב וְגֻבְרַיָּא רָעַן עָנָא, אֲרֵי גֻּבְרֵי מָרֵי גֵיתֵי הֲווֹ, וְעָנְהוֹן וְתוֹרֵיהוֹן, וְכָל דִּילְהוֹן אַיְתִיאוּ: לג וִיהֵי, אֲרֵי יִקְרֵי לְכוֹן פַּרְעֹה, וְיֵימַר מָא עוֹבָדֵיכוֹן: לד וְתֵימְרוּן, גֻּבְרֵי מָרֵי גֵיתֵי, הֲווֹ עַבְדָּךְ מִזְּעוּרַנָא וְעַד כְּעַן, אַף אֲנַחְנָא אַף אֲבָהָתַנָא, בְּדִיל, דְּתִתְּבוּן בְּאַרְעָא דְגֹשֶׁן, אֲרֵי מְרַחֲקִין מִצְרָאֵי כָּל רָעֵי עָנָא: מז א וַאֲתָא יוֹסֵף וְחַוִּי לְפַרְעֹה, וַאֲמַר, אַבָּא וְאַחַי, וְעָנְהוֹן וְתוֹרֵיהוֹן וְכָל דִּילְהוֹן, אֲתוֹ מֵאַרְעָא דִּכְנָעַן, וְהָאִנּוּן בְּאַרְעָא דְגֹשֶׁן:

46:30 כִּי עוֹדְךָ חָי *You are still alive* – After years of grief without resolution, Yaakov is now satisfied.

Yaakov has "refused to be comforted" (Gen. 37:35) until he sees Yosef again. The Jewish people took after him. Yirmeyahu heard it in a later age: "A sound is heard in Ramah: wailing, bitter weeping. It is Raḥel, weeping for her children. *She refuses to be consoled* for her children, for they are gone. This is what the Lord said…There is a reward for your labor, declares the Lord, and they will return from the land of the enemy. There is hope for your future, declares the Lord" (Jer. 31:14–15).

And Raḥel's children did return to the land. Jerusalem is once again the Jewish home. All the evidence may suggest otherwise: it may seem to signify irretrievable loss, a decree of history that cannot be overturned, a fate that must be accepted. Jews never believed the evidence because they had something else to set against it – a faith, a trust, an unbreakable hope that proved stronger than historical inevitability. It is not too much to say that Jewish survival was sustained in that hope. And that hope came from a simple – or perhaps not so simple – phrase in the life of Yaakov. He refused to be comforted. And so – while we live in a world still scarred by violence, poverty, and injustice – must we.

46:34 תוֹעֲבַת מִצְרַיִם כָּל רֹעֵה צֹאן *The Egyptians abominate all who keep sheep* – Their objection, historically, was a religious one. But in our narrative we are receiving our first intimation that Israel, with its humble shepherd origins, is to form a counterculture in relation to the urban superpower of Egypt.

All the patriarchs were shepherds. They moved from place to place. They lived in tents. They spent much of their time

2 Canaan and are now in the region of Goshen." He chose five of his brothers and
3 presented them to Pharaoh. Pharaoh asked the brothers, "What is your
occupation?" They replied, "Your servants are shepherds, as our fathers were
4 before." And they said to Pharaoh, "We have come to stay for a while in your
land because the famine is severe in Canaan and there is no pasture for your
servants' flocks. Please, then, let your servants settle in the region of Goshen."
5 6 Pharaoh said to Yosef, "Your father and brothers have come to you. The land of
Egypt is open before you. Settle your father and brothers in the best part of the
land. Let them live in the region of Goshen, and if there are able men among
7 them, you may give them charge of my own livestock." Then Yosef brought his
8 father Yaakov and presented him before Pharaoh. Yaakov blessed Pharaoh, and
9 Pharaoh asked Yaakov, "How old are you?" Yaakov said to Pharaoh, "The years
of my wandering are one hundred and thirty. Few and hard have been the years
of my life, and I have not reached the age my fathers reached in their own
10 11 wanderings." Yaakov blessed Pharaoh and left his presence. Yosef settled his SHEVI'I
father and brothers, giving them holdings in the best part of Egypt, in the
12 region of Ramesses, as Pharaoh had instructed. And Yosef provided his father,
his brothers, and all his father's household with food, befitting the numbers of
13 their dependents. And there was no food across the land, because the famine

רש״י

מז ב **וּמִקְצֵה אֶחָיו.** מִן הַפְּחוּתִים שֶׁבָּהֶם לִגְבוּרָה שֶׁאֵין נִרְאִים גִּבּוֹרִים, שֶׁאִם יִרְאֶה אוֹתָם גִּבּוֹרִים יַעֲשֶׂה אוֹתָם אַנְשֵׁי מִלְחַמְתּוֹ. וְאֵלֶּה הֵם: רְאוּבֵן, שִׁמְעוֹן, לֵוִי, יִשָּׂשכָר וּבִנְיָמִין, אוֹתָן שֶׁלֹּא כָּפַל מֹשֶׁה שְׁמוֹתָם כְּשֶׁבֵּרְכָן. אֲבָל שְׁמוֹת הַגִּבּוֹרִים כָּפַל: "וְזֹאת לִיהוּדָה... שְׁמַע ה' קוֹל יְהוּדָה" (דברים לג, ז); "וּלְגָד אָמַר בָּרוּךְ מַרְחִיב גָּד" (שם פסוק כ); "וּלְנַפְתָּלִי אָמַר נַפְתָּלִי" (שם פסוק כג); "וּלְדָן אָמַר דָּן" (שם פסוק כב); וְכֵן לִזְבוּלֻן (שם פסוק יח) וְכֵן לְאָשֵׁר (שם פסוק כד), זֶהוּ לְשׁוֹן בְּרֵאשִׁית רַבָּה (צה, ד) שֶׁהִיא אַגָּדַת אֶרֶץ יִשְׂרָאֵל. אֲבָל בְּתַלְמוּד בַּבְלִי שֶׁלָּנוּ מָצִינוּ שֶׁאוֹתָן שֶׁכָּפַל מֹשֶׁה שְׁמוֹתָן הֵם הַחַלָּשִׁים וְאוֹתָן הֵבִיא לִפְנֵי פַרְעֹה, וִיהוּדָה שֶׁהִכְפִּיל שְׁמוֹ לֹא הִכְפִּיל מִשּׁוּם חַלָּשׁוּת, אֶלָּא טַעַם יֵשׁ בַּדָּבָר, כִּדְאִיתָא בְּבָבָא קַמָּא (דף צב ע״א). וּבְבָרַיְתָא דְּסִפְרֵי שָׁנִינוּ בָּהּ בִּ'וְזֹאת הַבְּרָכָה' (שנד) כְּמוֹ תַּלְמוּד שֶׁלָּנוּ:

ו **אַנְשֵׁי חַיִל.** בְּקִיאִין בְּאֻמָּנוּתָן לִרְעוֹת צֹאן: **עַל אֲשֶׁר לִי.** עַל צֹאן שֶׁלִּי:

ז **וַיְבָרֶךְ יַעֲקֹב.** הִיא שְׁאֵלַת שָׁלוֹם כְּדֶרֶךְ כָּל הַנִּרְאִים לִפְנֵי הַמְּלָכִים לִפְרָקִים, סלודי״ר בְּלַעַז:

ט **שְׁנֵי מְגוּרַי.** יְמֵי גֵרוּתִי, כָּל יָמַי הָיִיתִי גֵּר בָּאָרֶץ: **וְלֹא הִשִּׂיגוּ.** בַּטּוֹבָה:

י **וַיְבָרֶךְ יַעֲקֹב.** כְּדֶרֶךְ כָּל הַנִּפְטָרִים מִלִּפְנֵי שָׂרִים, מְבָרְכִים אוֹתָם וְנוֹטְלִים רְשׁוּת. וּמַה בְּרָכָה בֵּרְכוֹ? שֶׁיַּעֲלֶה נִילוּס לְרַגְלָיו, לְפִי שֶׁאֵין מִצְרַיִם שׁוֹתָה מֵי גְשָׁמִים, אֶלָּא נִילוּס עוֹלֶה וּמַשְׁקָהּ, וּמִבִּרְכָתוֹ שֶׁל יַעֲקֹב וְאֵילָךְ הָיָה פַרְעֹה בָּא עַל נִילוּס וְהוּא עוֹלֶה לִקְרָאתוֹ וּמַשְׁקֶה אֶת הָאָרֶץ. תַּנְחוּמָא (נשא כו):

יא **רַעְמְסֵס.** מֵאֶרֶץ גֹּשֶׁן הִיא:

יב **לְפִי הַטָּף.** לְפִי הַצָּרִיךְ לְכָל בְּנֵי בֵיתָם:

יג **וְלֶחֶם אֵין בְּכָל הָאָרֶץ.** חוֹזֵר לָעִנְיָן הָרִאשׁוֹן לִתְחִלַּת שְׁנֵי הָרָעָב: וַתֵּלַהּ. כְּמוֹ וַתִּלְאֶה, לְשׁוֹן עֲיֵפוּת כְּתַרְגּוּמוֹ, וְדוֹמֶה לוֹ: "כְּמִתְלַהְלֵהַּ הַיֹּרֶה זִקִּים" (משלי כו, יח):

ב ג וּמִקְצֵה אֶחָיו לָקַח חֲמִשָּׁה אֲנָשִׁים וַיַּצִּגֵם לִפְנֵי פַרְעֹה: וַיֹּאמֶר פַּרְעֹה
אֶל־אֶחָיו מַה־מַּעֲשֵׂיכֶם וַיֹּאמְרוּ אֶל־פַּרְעֹה רֹעֵה צֹאן עֲבָדֶיךָ גַּם־
ד אֲנַחְנוּ גַּם־אֲבוֹתֵינוּ: וַיֹּאמְרוּ אֶל־פַּרְעֹה לָגוּר בָּאָרֶץ בָּאנוּ כִּי־אֵין
מִרְעֶה לַצֹּאן אֲשֶׁר לַעֲבָדֶיךָ כִּי־כָבֵד הָרָעָב בְּאֶרֶץ כְּנָעַן וְעַתָּה יֵשְׁבוּ־
ה נָא עֲבָדֶיךָ בְּאֶרֶץ גֹּשֶׁן: וַיֹּאמֶר פַּרְעֹה אֶל־יוֹסֵף לֵאמֹר אָבִיךָ וְאַחֶיךָ
ו בָּאוּ אֵלֶיךָ: אֶרֶץ מִצְרַיִם לְפָנֶיךָ הִוא בְּמֵיטַב הָאָרֶץ הוֹשֵׁב אֶת־אָבִיךָ
וְאֶת־אַחֶיךָ יֵשְׁבוּ בְּאֶרֶץ גֹּשֶׁן וְאִם־יָדַעְתָּ וְיֶשׁ־בָּם אַנְשֵׁי־חַיִל וְשַׂמְתָּם
ז שָׂרֵי מִקְנֶה עַל־אֲשֶׁר־לִי: וַיָּבֵא יוֹסֵף אֶת־יַעֲקֹב אָבִיו וַיַּעֲמִדֵהוּ לִפְנֵי
ח פַרְעֹה וַיְבָרֶךְ יַעֲקֹב אֶת־פַּרְעֹה: וַיֹּאמֶר פַּרְעֹה אֶל־יַעֲקֹב כַּמָּה יְמֵי
ט שְׁנֵי חַיֶּיךָ: וַיֹּאמֶר יַעֲקֹב אֶל־פַּרְעֹה יְמֵי שְׁנֵי מְגוּרַי שְׁלֹשִׁים וּמְאַת
שָׁנָה מְעַט וְרָעִים הָיוּ יְמֵי שְׁנֵי חַיַּי וְלֹא הִשִּׂיגוּ אֶת־יְמֵי שְׁנֵי חַיֵּי אֲבֹתַי
יא בִּימֵי מְגוּרֵיהֶם: וַיְבָרֶךְ יַעֲקֹב אֶת־פַּרְעֹה וַיֵּצֵא מִלִּפְנֵי פַרְעֹה: וַיּוֹשֵׁב שביעי
יוֹסֵף אֶת־אָבִיו וְאֶת־אֶחָיו וַיִּתֵּן לָהֶם אֲחֻזָּה בְּאֶרֶץ מִצְרַיִם בְּמֵיטַב
יב הָאָרֶץ בְּאֶרֶץ רַעְמְסֵס כַּאֲשֶׁר צִוָּה פַרְעֹה: וַיְכַלְכֵּל יוֹסֵף אֶת־אָבִיו
יג וְאֶת־אֶחָיו וְאֵת כָּל־בֵּית אָבִיו לֶחֶם לְפִי הַטָּף: וְלֶחֶם אֵין בְּכָל־הָאָרֶץ
כִּי־כָבֵד הָרָעָב מְאֹד וַתֵּלַהּ אֶרֶץ מִצְרַיִם וְאֶרֶץ כְּנַעַן מִפְּנֵי הָרָעָב:

אונקלוס

ב וּמִקְצָת אֲחוֹהִי, דְּבַר חַמְשָׁא גֻּבְרִין, וַאֲקֵימִנּוּן קֳדָם פַּרְעֹה: ג וַאֲמַר פַּרְעֹה, לַאֲחוֹהִי מָא עוֹבָדֵיכוֹן, וַאֲמַרוּ לְפַרְעֹה, רָעַן עָנָא עַבְדָּךְ, אַף אֲנַחְנָא אַף אֲבָהָתַנָא: ד וַאֲמַרוּ לְפַרְעֹה, לְאִתּוֹתָבָא בְּאַרְעָא אֲתֵינָא, אֲרֵי לֵית רִעְיָא, לְעָנָא דִּלְעַבְדָּךְ, אֲרֵי תְקֵיף כַּפְנָא בְּאַרְעָא דִּכְנָעַן, וּכְעַן, יִתְבוּן כְּעַן עַבְדָּךְ בְּאַרְעָא דְגֹשֶׁן: ה וַאֲמַר פַּרְעֹה, לְיוֹסֵף לְמֵימַר, אֲבוּךְ וַאֲחָךְ אֲתוֹ לְוָתָךְ: ו אַרְעָא דְמִצְרַיִם קֳדָמָךְ הִיא, בִּדְשַׁפִּיר בְּאַרְעָא, אוֹתֵיב יָת אֲבוּךְ וְיָת אֲחָךְ, יִתְבוּן בְּאַרְעָא דְגֹשֶׁן, וְאִם יְדַעְתְּ, וְאִית בְּהוֹן גֻּבְרִין דְּחֵילָא, וּתְמַנֵּינוּן, רַבָּנֵי גֵיתֵי עַל דִּילִי: ז וְאַיְתִי יוֹסֵף יָת יַעֲקֹב אֲבוּהִי, וַאֲקִימֵיהּ קֳדָם פַּרְעֹה, וּבָרֵיךְ יַעֲקֹב יָת פַּרְעֹה: ח וַאֲמַר פַּרְעֹה לְיַעֲקֹב, כַּמָּה, יוֹמֵי שְׁנֵי חַיָּךְ: ט וַאֲמַר יַעֲקֹב לְפַרְעֹה, יוֹמֵי שְׁנֵי תוֹתָבוּתִי, מְאָה וּתְלָתִין שְׁנִין, זְעִירִין וּבִישִׁין, הֲווֹ יוֹמֵי שְׁנֵי חַיַּי, וְלָא אַדְבִּיקוּ, יָת יוֹמֵי שְׁנֵי חַיֵּי אֲבָהָתַי, בְּיוֹמֵי תוֹתָבוּתְהוֹן: י וּבָרֵיךְ יַעֲקֹב יָת פַּרְעֹה, וּנְפַק מִן קֳדָם פַּרְעֹה: יא וְאוֹתֵיב יוֹסֵף יָת אֲבוּהִי וְיָת אֲחוֹהִי, וִיהַב לְהוֹן אַחְסָנָא בְּאַרְעָא דְמִצְרַיִם, בִּדְשַׁפִּיר בְּאַרְעָא בַּאֲרַע רַעְמְסֵס, כְּמָא דְפַקֵּיד פַּרְעֹה: יב וְזָן יוֹסֵף יָת אֲבוּהִי וְיָת אֲחוֹהִי, וְיָת כָּל בֵּית אֲבוּהִי, לַחְמָא לְפוּם טַפְלָא: יג וְלַחְמָא לֵית בְּכָל אַרְעָא, אֲרֵי תְקֵיף כַּפְנָא לַחְדָא, וְאִשְׁתַּלְהִי, עַמָּא דְאַרְעָא דְמִצְרַיִם וְעַמָּא דְאַרְעָא דִכְנַעַן, מִן קֳדָם כַּפְנָא:

14 was so severe. Egypt and Canaan languished because of the famine. Yosef
collected all the money that was to be found in Egypt and Canaan in payment
for the grain the people were buying, and he brought it into Pharaoh's palace.
15 When the money in Egypt and Canaan was gone, all the Egyptians came to
Yosef, saying, "Give us food. Why should we die before your eyes just because
16 there is no more money left?" "Bring your livestock," said Yosef, "and I will sell
17 you food in exchange for your livestock since there is no more money left." So
they brought their livestock to Yosef, and he gave them food in exchange for
horses, sheep, cattle, and donkeys. He supplied them with food that year in
18 exchange for all their livestock. That year passed, and they came to him the
following year and said, "We cannot hide from my lord that the money is gone
and the livestock belongs to you. There is nothing left for my lord except our
19 bodies and our land. Why should we and our land die before your eyes? Acquire
us and our land in exchange for food, and we with our land will be slaves to
Pharaoh. Give us seed so that we can live and not die and so that the land does not

רש"י

יד **בשבר אשר הם שברים.** נותנין לו את הכסף:

טו **אפס.** כתרגומו, "שלים":

יז **וינהלם.** כמו וינהגם, ודומה לו: "אין מנהל לה" (ישעיה נא, יח); "על מי מנוחות ינהלני" (תהלים כג, ב):

יח **בשנה השנית.** לשני הרעב: **כי אם תם הכסף.** כי אשר תם הכסף והמקנה ובא הכל אל ידי אדוני: **בלתי אם גויתנו.** כמו אם לא גויתנו:

יט **ותן זרע.** לזרוע האדמה. ואף על פי שאמר יוסף: "ועוד חמש שנים אשר אין חריש וקציר" (לעיל מה, ו), מכיון שבא יעקב למצרים באה ברכה לרגליו והתחילו לזרוע, וכלה הרעב. וכן שנינו בתוספתא דסוטה (י, ג): **לא תשם.** לא תהא שממה, "לא תבור", לשון שדה בור, שאינו חרוש:

Certainly, this entire passage represents the first intrusion of politics into the life of the family of the covenant. From the beginning of Exodus to the end of Deuteronomy, politics will dominate the narrative. But Yosef's appointment to a key position in the Egyptian court is our first introduction to it. And what it is telling us about is the sheer ambiguity of power. On the one hand, you cannot create or sustain a society without it. On the other hand, it almost cries out to be abused. Power is dangerous, even when used with the best of intentions by the best of people.

Tradition called Yosef *hatzaddik*, "the righteous." At the same time, the Talmud says that he died before his brothers "because he assumed airs of authority" (Berakhot 55a). Even a *tzaddik* with the best of intentions, when he or she enters politics and assumes airs of authority, can make mistakes. The great challenge of politics – ongoing and ever-present – is to keep policies humane and ensure that politicians remain humble, so that power, always so dangerous, is not used for harm.

hand – power that will eventually be used against the Israelites. More seriously, twice we encounter the phrase *avadim lePharo*, "slaves to Pharaoh" (47:19, 25) – one of the key phrases in the exodus account and in the answer to the questions of the child in the Seder service (Deut. 6:21). With this difference: *that it was said, not by the Israelites, but by the Egyptians.*

This passage raises a most serious question. We tend to assume that the enslavement of the Israelites in Egypt was a consequence of, and punishment for, the brothers selling Yosef as a slave. But Yosef himself turns the Egyptians into a nation of slaves. What is more, he creates the highly centralized power that will eventually be used against his people.

It may be that the Torah intends no criticism of Yosef. He is acting loyally to Pharaoh and judiciously to Egypt as a whole. Or it may be that there is an implied criticism of his character. As a child, he dreamt of power; as an adult he exercises it – but Judaism is critical of power and those who seek it.

יד וַיְלַקֵּט יוֹסֵף אֶת־כׇּל־הַכֶּסֶף הַנִּמְצָא בְאֶרֶץ־מִצְרַיִם וּבְאֶרֶץ כְּנַעַן
טו בַּשֶּׁבֶר אֲשֶׁר־הֵם שֹׁבְרִים וַיָּבֵא יוֹסֵף אֶת־הַכֶּסֶף בֵּיתָה פַרְעֹה׃ וַיִּתֹּם
הַכֶּסֶף מֵאֶרֶץ מִצְרַיִם וּמֵאֶרֶץ כְּנַעַן וַיָּבֹאוּ כׇל־מִצְרַיִם אֶל־יוֹסֵף לֵאמֹר
טז הָבָה־לָּנוּ לֶחֶם וְלָמָּה נָמוּת נֶגְדֶּךָ כִּי אָפֵס כָּסֶף׃ וַיֹּאמֶר יוֹסֵף הָבוּ
יז מִקְנֵיכֶם וְאֶתְּנָה לָכֶם בְּמִקְנֵיכֶם אִם־אָפֵס כָּסֶף׃ וַיָּבִיאוּ אֶת־מִקְנֵיהֶם
אֶל־יוֹסֵף וַיִּתֵּן לָהֶם יוֹסֵף לֶחֶם בַּסּוּסִים וּבְמִקְנֵה הַצֹּאן וּבְמִקְנֵה הַבָּקָר
יח וּבַחֲמֹרִים וַיְנַהֲלֵם בַּלֶּחֶם בְּכׇל־מִקְנֵהֶם בַּשָּׁנָה הַהִוא׃ וַתִּתֹּם הַשָּׁנָה
הַהִוא וַיָּבֹאוּ אֵלָיו בַּשָּׁנָה הַשֵּׁנִית וַיֹּאמְרוּ לוֹ לֹא־נְכַחֵד מֵאֲדֹנִי כִּי
אִם־תַּם הַכֶּסֶף וּמִקְנֵה הַבְּהֵמָה אֶל־אֲדֹנִי לֹא נִשְׁאַר לִפְנֵי אֲדֹנִי בִּלְתִּי
יט אִם־גְּוִיָּתֵנוּ וְאַדְמָתֵנוּ׃ לָמָּה נָמוּת לְעֵינֶיךָ גַּם־אֲנַחְנוּ גַּם־אַדְמָתֵנוּ
קְנֵה־אֹתָנוּ וְאֶת־אַדְמָתֵנוּ בַּלָּחֶם וְנִהְיֶה אֲנַחְנוּ וְאַדְמָתֵנוּ עֲבָדִים
כ לְפַרְעֹה וְתֶן־זֶרַע וְנִחְיֶה וְלֹא נָמוּת וְהָאֲדָמָה לֹא תֵשָׁם׃ וַיִּקֶן יוֹסֵף

אונקלוס

יד וְלַקִּיט יוֹסֵף, יָת כׇּל כַּסְפָּא דְּאִשְׁתְּכַח בְּאַרְעָא דְמִצְרַיִם וּבְאַרְעָא דִכְנַעַן, בְּעִבוּרָא דְּאִנּוּן זָבְנִין, וְאַיְתִי יוֹסֵף, יָת כַּסְפָּא לְבֵית פַּרְעֹה׃ טו וּשְׁלִים כַּסְפָּא, מֵאַרְעָא דְמִצְרַיִם וּמֵאַרְעָא דִכְנַעַן, וַאֲתוֹ כׇל מִצְרָאֵי לְוָת יוֹסֵף לְמֵימַר הַב לַנָא לַחְמָא, וּלְמָא נְמוּת לְקִבְלָךְ, אֲרֵי שְׁלִים כַּסְפָּא׃ טז וַאֲמַר יוֹסֵף הַבוּ גֵּיתֵיכוֹן, וְאֶתֵּין לְכוֹן בְּגֵיתֵיכוֹן, אִם שְׁלִים כַּסְפָּא׃ יז וְאַיְתִיאוּ יָת גֵּיתֵיהוֹן לְוָת יוֹסֵף, וִיהַב לְהוֹן יוֹסֵף לַחְמָא בְּסוּסָוָתָא, וּבְגֵיתֵי עָנָא, וּבְגֵיתֵי תוֹרֵי וּבִחְמָרַיָּא, וְזָנְנוּן בְּלַחְמָא בְּכׇל גֵּיתֵיהוֹן, בְּשַׁתָּא הַהִיא׃ יח וּשְׁלֵימַת שַׁתָּא הַהִיא, וַאֲתוֹ לְוָתֵיהּ בְּשַׁתָּא תִּנְיֵתָא, וַאֲמַרוּ לֵיהּ לָא נְכַסֵּי מִן רִבּוֹנִי, אֱלָהֵין שְׁלִים כַּסְפָּא, וְגֵיתֵי בְעִירָא לְוָת רִבּוֹנִי, לָא אִשְׁתְּאַר קֳדָם רִבּוֹנִי, אֱלָהֵין גְּוִיָּתַנָא וְאַרְעֲנָא׃ יט לְמָא נְמוּת לְעֵינָךְ, אַף אֲנַחְנָא אַף אַרְעֲנָא, קְנֵי יָתַנָא וְיָת אַרְעֲנָא בְּלַחְמָא, וּנְהֵי, אֲנַחְנָא וְאַרְעֲנָא עַבְדִין לְפַרְעֹה, וְהַב בַּר זְרַע, וְנֵיחֵי וְלָא נְמוּת, וְאַרְעָא לָא תְבוּר׃ כ וּקְנָא יוֹסֵף,

THE EGYPTIANS BECOME SLAVES

By this stage in the famine, the Egyptians have used up all their money buying grain. They come to Yosef asking for food, telling him they will die without it, and he replies by telling them that he will sell it to them in exchange for ownership of their livestock. They willingly do so: they bring their horses, donkeys, sheep, and cattle. The next year he sells them grain in exchange for their land. The result of these transactions is that within a short period of time – seemingly a mere three years – he has transferred to Pharaoh's ownership all the money, livestock, and private land, with the exception of the land of the priests, which he allowed them to retain.

Not only this, but the Torah tells us that Yosef "transferred [the people] town by town from one end of Egypt to the other" (Gen. 47:21) – a policy of enforced resettlement that would eventually be used against Israel by the Assyrians.

The question is: Is Yosef right to do this? Seemingly, he does it of his own accord. He is not asked to do so by Pharaoh. The result, however, of all these policies is that unprecedented wealth and power are now concentrated in Pharaoh's

20 become desolate." Thus Yosef acquired all the land of Egypt for Pharaoh. Each
Egyptian sold his field, because the famine had become too much for them. So the
21 land became Pharaoh's. As for the people, he transferred them town by town from
22 one end of Egypt to the other. The only land he did not acquire was that of the
priests, because they received an allotment of food from Pharaoh; they were able
to live on the allotment that Pharaoh gave them, and so they did not sell their land.
23 Yosef said to the people, "Today I have acquired you and your land for Pharaoh.
24 Here is seed for you to sow the land. When the harvest comes, give one-fifth to
Pharaoh. Four-fifths shall be yours as seed for your fields and as food for you, your
25 households, and your children." "You have saved our lives," they said. "May we MAFTIR
26 find favor in the eyes of my lord – we shall be slaves to Pharaoh." So Yosef made it
a law, as it is to this day, governing land in Egypt, that one-fifth of all produce
27 belongs to Pharaoh. Only the land of the priests did not become Pharaoh's. Thus
Yisrael settled in the land of Egypt, in the region of Goshen. They acquired
holdings in it and were fertile and greatly increased in number.

The haftara for Parashat Vayigash is on page 1522.

רש״י

כ **וַתְּהִי הָאָרֶץ לְפַרְעֹה.** קְנוּיָה לוֹ:

כא **וְאֶת הָעָם הֶעֱבִיר.** יוֹסֵף מֵעִיר לְעִיר לְזִכָּרוֹן שֶׁאֵין לָהֶם עוֹד חֵלֶק בָּאָרֶץ, וְהוֹשִׁיב שֶׁל עִיר זוֹ בַּחֲבֶרְתָּהּ. וְלֹא הֻצְרַךְ הַכָּתוּב לִכְתֹּב זֹאת, אֶלָּא לְהוֹדִיעֲךָ שִׁבְחוֹ שֶׁל יוֹסֵף, שֶׁנִּתְכַּוֵּן לְהָסִיר חֶרְפָּה מֵעַל אֶחָיו, שֶׁלֹּא יִהְיוּ קוֹרִין אוֹתָם גּוֹלִים: **מִקְצֵה גְבוּל מִצְרַיִם וְגוֹ׳.** כֵּן עָשָׂה לְכָל הֶעָרִים אֲשֶׁר בְּמַלְכוּת מִצְרַיִם, מִקְצֵה גְּבוּלָהּ וְעַד קְצֵה גְּבוּלָהּ:

כב **הַכֹּהֲנִים.** כּוּמָרִים. כָּל לְשׁוֹן ׳כֹּהֵן׳ מְשָׁרֵת לֶאֱלָהוּת הוּא, חוּץ מֵאוֹתָן שֶׁהֵם לְשׁוֹן גְּדֻלָּה, כְּמוֹ: ״כֹּהֵן מִדְיָן״ (שמות ב, טז), ״כֹּהֵן אוֹן״ (לעיל מא, מה): **חֹק לַכֹּהֲנִים.** חֹק כָּךְ וְכָךְ לֶחֶם לַיּוֹם:

כג **הֵא.** כְּמוֹ הִנֵּה:

כד **לְזֶרַע הַשָּׂדֶה.** שֶׁבְּכָל שָׁנָה: **וְלַאֲשֶׁר בְּבָתֵּיכֶם.** וְלֶאֱכֹל הָעֲבָדִים וְהַשְּׁפָחוֹת אֲשֶׁר בְּבָתֵּיכֶם: **טַפְּכֶם.** בָּנִים קְטַנִּים:

כה **נִמְצָא חֵן.** לַעֲשׂוֹת לָנוּ זֹאת כְּמוֹ שֶׁאָמַרְתָּ: **וְהָיִינוּ עֲבָדִים לְפַרְעֹה.** לְהַעֲלוֹת לוֹ הַמַּס הַזֶּה בְּכָל שָׁנָה:

כו **לְחֹק.** שֶׁלֹּא יַעֲבֹר:

כז **וַיֵּשֶׁב יִשְׂרָאֵל בְּאֶרֶץ מִצְרַיִם.** וְהֵיכָן? ״בְּאֶרֶץ גֹּשֶׁן״, שֶׁהִיא מֵאֶרֶץ מִצְרַיִם:

a fundamental statement. If brothers cannot live together in peace, then they cannot form a stable society or a cohesive nation. Rambam explains that forgiveness and the associated command not to bear a grudge (Lev. 19:18) are essential to the survival of society: "For as long as one nurses a grievance and keeps it in mind, one may come to take vengeance. The Torah emphatically warns us not to bear a grudge, so that the impression of the wrong shall be quite obliterated and be no longer remembered. This is the right principle. It alone makes civilization and human relationships possible (*Hilkhot Deot* 7:8). Forgiveness is not merely personal; it is also political. It is essential to the life of any nation that seeks to maintain its independence for long. There is no greater proof of this than Jewish history itself. Twice Israel suffered defeat and exile. The first – the conquest of the Northern Kingdom, followed a century and a half later by the destruction of the First Temple and the Babylonian exile – was a direct consequence of the division of the kingdom into two after the death of Shlomo. The second – defeat at the hands of the Romans and the destruction of the Second Temple – was the result of intense factionalism and internal strife, *sinat ḥinam*.

When people lack the ability to forgive, they are unable to resolve conflict. The result is division, factionalism, and the fragmentation of a nation into competing groups and sects. What individuals practice in the family can determine the course of nations. Those who seek freedom must learn to forgive.

אֶת־כׇּל־אַדְמַת מִצְרַיִם לְפַרְעֹה כִּי־מָכְרוּ מִצְרַיִם אִישׁ שָׂדֵהוּ כִּי־חָזַק
כא עֲלֵהֶם הָרָעָב וַתְּהִי הָאָרֶץ לְפַרְעֹה׃ וְאֶת־הָעָם הֶעֱבִיר אֹתוֹ לֶעָרִים
כב מִקְצֵה גְבוּל־מִצְרַיִם וְעַד־קָצֵהוּ׃ רַק אַדְמַת הַכֹּהֲנִים לֹא קָנָה כִּי חֹק
לַכֹּהֲנִים מֵאֵת פַּרְעֹה וְאָכְלוּ אֶת־חֻקָּם אֲשֶׁר נָתַן לָהֶם פַּרְעֹה עַל־כֵּן
כג לֹא מָכְרוּ אֶת־אַדְמָתָם׃ וַיֹּאמֶר יוֹסֵף אֶל־הָעָם הֵן קָנִיתִי אֶתְכֶם הַיּוֹם
כד וְאֶת־אַדְמַתְכֶם לְפַרְעֹה הֵא־לָכֶם זֶרַע וּזְרַעְתֶּם אֶת־הָאֲדָמָה׃ וְהָיָה
בַּתְּבוּאֹת וּנְתַתֶּם חֲמִישִׁית לְפַרְעֹה וְאַרְבַּע הַיָּדֹת יִהְיֶה לָכֶם לְזֶרַע
כה הַשָּׂדֶה וּלְאׇכְלְכֶם וְלַאֲשֶׁר בְּבָתֵּיכֶם וְלֶאֱכֹל לְטַפְּכֶם׃ וַיֹּאמְרוּ הֶחֱיִתָנוּ מפטיר
כו נִמְצָא־חֵן בְּעֵינֵי אֲדֹנִי וְהָיִינוּ עֲבָדִים לְפַרְעֹה׃ וַיָּשֶׂם אֹתָהּ יוֹסֵף לְחֹק
עַד־הַיּוֹם הַזֶּה עַל־אַדְמַת מִצְרַיִם לְפַרְעֹה לַחֹמֶשׁ רַק אַדְמַת הַכֹּהֲנִים
כז לְבַדָּם לֹא הָיְתָה לְפַרְעֹה׃ וַיֵּשֶׁב יִשְׂרָאֵל בְּאֶרֶץ מִצְרַיִם בְּאֶרֶץ גֹּשֶׁן
וַיֵּאָחֲזוּ בָהּ וַיִּפְרוּ וַיִּרְבּוּ מְאֹד׃

The הפטרה *for* פרשת ויגש *is on page 1523.*

אונקלוס

יָת כׇּל אַרְעָא דְּמִצְרַיִם לְפַרְעֹה, אֲרֵי זַבִּינוּ מִצְרָאֵי גְּבַר חַקְלֵיהּ, אֲרֵי תְּקֵיף עֲלֵיהוֹן כַּפְנָא, וַהֲוָת אַרְעָא לְפַרְעֹה: כא וְיָת עַמָּא, אַעְבַּר יָתֵיהּ מִקְּרֵי לִקְרֵי, מִסּוֹף תְּחוּם מִצְרַיִם וְעַד סוֹפֵיהּ: כב לְחוֹד, אֲרַע כּוּמְרַיָּא לָא קְנָא, אֲרֵי חוּלָקָא לְכוּמְרַיָּא מִן קֳדָם פַּרְעֹה, וְאָכְלִין יָת חוּלָקְהוֹן דִּיהַב לְהוֹן פַּרְעֹה, עַל כֵּן, לָא זַבִּינוּ יָת אֲרַעְהוֹן: כג וַאֲמַר יוֹסֵף לְעַמָּא, הָא קְנֵיתִי יָתְכוֹן יוֹמָא דֵין, וְיָת אֲרַעְכוֹן לְפַרְעֹה, הָא לְכוֹן בַּר זַרְעָא, וְתִזְרְעוּן יָת אַרְעָא: כד וִיהֵי בְּאֵיעוֹלֵי עֲלַלְתָּא, וְתִתְּנוּן חַד מִן חַמְשָׁא לְפַרְעֹה, וְאַרְבְּעָא חוּלָקִין, יְהֵי לְכוֹן לְבַר זְרַע חַקְלָא וּלְמֵיכַלְכוֹן, וְלֶאֱנָשׁ בָּתֵּיכוֹן וּלְמֵיכַל לְטַפְלְכוֹן: כה וַאֲמַרוּ קַיֵּימְתָּנָא, נִשְׁכַּח רַחֲמִין בְּעֵינֵי רִבּוֹנִי, וּנְהֵי עַבְדִּין לְפַרְעֹה: כו וְשַׁוִּי יָתַהּ יוֹסֵף, לִגְזֵירָא עַד יוֹמָא הָדֵין, עַל אַרְעָא דְּמִצְרַיִם, דִּיהוֹן יָהֲבִין חַד מִן חַמְשָׁא לְפַרְעֹה, לְחוֹד, אֲרַע כּוּמְרַיָּא בִּלְחוֹדֵיהוֹן, לָא הֲוָת לְפַרְעֹה: כז וִיתֵיב יִשְׂרָאֵל, בְּאַרְעָא דְּמִצְרַיִם בְּאַרְעָא דְּגֹשֶׁן, וְאַחְסִינוּ בַהּ, וּנְפִישׁוּ וּסְגִיאוּ לַחֲדָא:

47:27 **וַיֵּשֶׁב יִשְׂרָאֵל בְּאֶרֶץ מִצְרַיִם** *Settled in the land of Egypt* – The real significance of this passage goes far beyond the story of Yosef and his brothers. It is the essential prelude to the book of Exodus and the birth of Israel as a nation. The book of Genesis is, among other things, a set of variations on the theme of sibling rivalry: Kayin and Hevel, Yitzḥak and Yishmael, Yaakov and Esav, Yosef and his brothers. The book begins with fratricide and ends with reconciliation. There is a clear pattern to the final scene of each of the four narratives:

1. Kayin/Hevel	Murder
2. Yitzḥak/Yishmael	The two stand together at Avraham's funeral
3. Yaakov/Esav	Meet, embrace, go their separate ways
4. Yosef/brothers	Forgiveness, reconciliation, coexistence

In the development of these four narratives, the Torah is making

▶

Parashat Vayeḥi

47 28 Yaakov lived in Egypt for seventeen years; the years of his life were one hundred
29 and forty-seven. As the time of his death drew near, he summoned his son Yosef
and said to him, "If I have found favor in your eyes, place your hand under my
thigh and promise to deal kindly and truly with me: do not bury me in Egypt.
30 Let me lie with my fathers. Carry me from Egypt and bury me where they are
31 buried." "I will do as you say," he replied. Yaakov said, "Swear to me," and Yosef
swore. Then, at the head of the bed, Yisrael bowed.
48 1 Some time later, Yosef was told, "Your father is ill." He brought with him his
2 two sons, Menashe and Efrayim. And when Yaakov was told, "Your son Yosef
has come to see you," Yisrael summoned his strength and sat up in the bed.
3 Yaakov said to Yosef, "El Shaddai appeared to me in Luz in the land of Canaan.
4 He blessed me and said to me, 'I will make you fruitful and increase your

רש״י

כח **וַיְחִי יַעֲקֹב.** לָמָּה פָּרָשָׁה זוֹ סְתוּמָה? לְפִי שֶׁכֵּיוָן שֶׁנִּפְטַר יַעֲקֹב אָבִינוּ, נִסְתְּמוּ עֵינֵיהֶם וְלִבָּם שֶׁל יִשְׂרָאֵל מִצָּרַת הַשִּׁעְבּוּד, שֶׁהִתְחִילוּ לְשַׁעְבְּדָם. דָּבָר אַחֵר, שֶׁבִּקֵּשׁ לְגַלּוֹת אֶת הַקֵּץ לְבָנָיו וְנִסְתַּם מִמֶּנּוּ. בְּרֵאשִׁית רַבָּה (צו, א):

כט **וַיִּקְרְבוּ יְמֵי יִשְׂרָאֵל לָמוּת.** כָּל מִי שֶׁנֶּאֶמְרָה בּוֹ קְרִיבָה לָמוּת לֹא הִגִּיעַ לִימֵי אֲבוֹתָיו: **וַיִּקְרָא לִבְנוֹ לְיוֹסֵף.** לְמִי שֶׁהָיָה יְכֹלֶת בְּיָדוֹ לַעֲשׂוֹת: **שִׂים נָא יָדְךָ.** וְהִשָּׁבַע: **חֶסֶד וֶאֱמֶת.** חֶסֶד שֶׁעוֹשִׂין עִם הַמֵּתִים הוּא חֶסֶד שֶׁל אֱמֶת, שֶׁאֵינוֹ מְצַפֶּה לְתַשְׁלוּם גְּמוּל: **אַל נָא תִקְבְּרֵנִי בְּמִצְרָיִם.** סוֹפָהּ לִהְיוֹת עֲפָרָהּ כִּנִּים, וְשֶׁאֵין מֵתֵי חוּצָה לָאָרֶץ חַיִּים אֶלָּא בְּצַעַר גִּלְגּוּל מְחִלּוֹת, וְשֶׁלֹּא יַעֲשׂוּנִי מִצְרִים עֲבוֹדָה זָרָה:

ל **וְשָׁכַבְתִּי עִם אֲבֹתַי.** וָי״ו זֶה מְחֻבָּר לְמַעְלָה לִתְחִלַּת הַמִּקְרָא: "שִׂים נָא יָדְךָ תַּחַת יְרֵכִי" וְהִשָּׁבַע לִי, וַאֲנִי סוֹפִי לִשְׁכַּב עִם אֲבוֹתַי וְאַתָּה תִּשָּׂאֵנִי מִמִּצְרַיִם. וְאֵין לוֹמַר "וְשָׁכַבְתִּי עִם אֲבֹתַי" – הַשְׁכִּיבֵנִי עִם אֲבוֹתַי בַּמְּעָרָה, שֶׁהֲרֵי כְּתִיב אַחֲרָיו: "וּנְשָׂאתַנִי מִמִּצְרַיִם וּקְבַרְתַּנִי בִּקְבֻרָתָם"; וְעוֹד, מָצִינוּ בְּכָל מָקוֹם לְשׁוֹן שְׁכִיבָה עִם אֲבוֹתָיו הִיא הַגְּוִיעָה וְלֹא הַקְּבוּרָה, "וַיִּשְׁכַּב דָּוִד עִם אֲבֹתָיו וַיִּקָּבֵר בְּעִיר דָּוִד" (מלכים א׳ ב, י):

לא **וַיִּשְׁתַּחוּ יִשְׂרָאֵל.** תַּעֲלָא בְּעִדָּנֵיהּ סְגִיד לֵיהּ: **עַל רֹאשׁ הַמִּטָּה.** הָפַךְ עַצְמוֹ לְצַד הַשְּׁכִינָה; מִכָּאן אָמְרוּ שֶׁהַשְּׁכִינָה לְמַעְלָה מְרַאֲשׁוֹתָיו שֶׁל חוֹלֶה. דָּבָר אַחֵר, "עַל רֹאשׁ הַמִּטָּה", עַל שֶׁהָיְתָה מִטָּתוֹ שְׁלֵמָה וְלֹא הָיָה בָהּ רָשָׁע, שֶׁהֲרֵי יוֹסֵף מֶלֶךְ הוּא, וְעוֹד שֶׁנִּשְׁבָּה לְבֵין הַגּוֹיִם, וַהֲרֵי הוּא עוֹמֵד בְּצִדְקוֹ:

מח א **וַיֹּאמֶר לְיוֹסֵף.** אֶחָד מִן הַמַּגִּידִים, וַהֲרֵי זֶה מִקְרָא קָצָר. וְיֵשׁ אוֹמְרִים, אֶפְרַיִם הָיָה רָגִיל לִפְנֵי יַעֲקֹב בַּתַּלְמוּד, וּכְשֶׁחָלָה יַעֲקֹב בְּאֶרֶץ גֹּשֶׁן הָלַךְ אֶפְרַיִם אֵצֶל אָבִיו לְמִצְרַיִם לְהַגִּיד לוֹ: **וַיִּקַּח אֶת שְׁנֵי בָנָיו עִמּוֹ.** כְּדֵי שֶׁיְּבָרְכֵם יַעֲקֹב לִפְנֵי מוֹתוֹ:

ב **וַיַּגֵּד.** הַמַּגִּיד "לְיַעֲקֹב" וְלֹא פֵּרַשׁ מִי, וְהַרְבֵּה מִקְרָאוֹת קְצָרֵי לָשׁוֹן: **וַיִּתְחַזֵּק יִשְׂרָאֵל.** אָמַר, אַף עַל פִּי שֶׁהוּא בְּנִי, מֶלֶךְ הוּא, אֶחְלֹק לוֹ כָּבוֹד; מִכָּאן שֶׁחוֹלְקִים כָּבוֹד לַמַּלְכוּת. וְכֵן מֹשֶׁה חָלַק כָּבוֹד לַמַּלְכוּת: "וְיָרְדוּ כָל עֲבָדֶיךָ אֵלֶּה אֵלַי" (שמות יא, ח). וְכֵן אֵלִיָּהוּ: "וַיְשַׁנֵּס מָתְנָיו" וְגוֹ׳ (מלכים א׳ יח, מו):

someone else to lift you from depression. That is why Judaism is so insistent on not leaving people alone at times of maximum vulnerability. Hence the principles of visiting the sick, comforting mourners, including the lonely ("the migrants, orphans, and widows") in festive celebrations, and offering hospitality. Yaakov is at the end of his strength, but when he hears his loved ones have come to visit him, he finds the strength to lift himself.

פרשת ויחי

מז כח וַיְחִי יַעֲקֹב בְּאֶרֶץ מִצְרַיִם שְׁבַע עֶשְׂרֵה שָׁנָה וַיְהִי יְמֵי־יַעֲקֹב שְׁנֵי
כט חַיָּיו שֶׁבַע שָׁנִים וְאַרְבָּעִים וּמְאַת שָׁנָה: וַיִּקְרְבוּ יְמֵי־יִשְׂרָאֵל לָמוּת
וַיִּקְרָא ׀ לִבְנוֹ לְיוֹסֵף וַיֹּאמֶר לוֹ אִם־נָא מָצָאתִי חֵן בְּעֵינֶיךָ שִׂים־נָא
יָדְךָ תַּחַת יְרֵכִי וְעָשִׂיתָ עִמָּדִי חֶסֶד וֶאֱמֶת אַל־נָא תִקְבְּרֵנִי בְּמִצְרָיִם:
ל וְשָׁכַבְתִּי עִם־אֲבֹתַי וּנְשָׂאתַנִי מִמִּצְרַיִם וּקְבַרְתַּנִי בִּקְבֻרָתָם וַיֹּאמַר
לא אָנֹכִי אֶעֱשֶׂה כִדְבָרֶךָ: וַיֹּאמֶר הִשָּׁבְעָה לִי וַיִּשָּׁבַע לוֹ וַיִּשְׁתַּחוּ יִשְׂרָאֵל
עַל־רֹאשׁ הַמִּטָּה:
מח א וַיְהִי אַחֲרֵי הַדְּבָרִים הָאֵלֶּה וַיֹּאמֶר לְיוֹסֵף הִנֵּה אָבִיךָ חֹלֶה וַיִּקַּח מב
ב אֶת־שְׁנֵי בָנָיו עִמּוֹ אֶת־מְנַשֶּׁה וְאֶת־אֶפְרָיִם: וַיַּגֵּד לְיַעֲקֹב וַיֹּאמֶר הִנֵּה
ג בִּנְךָ יוֹסֵף בָּא אֵלֶיךָ וַיִּתְחַזֵּק יִשְׂרָאֵל וַיֵּשֶׁב עַל־הַמִּטָּה: וַיֹּאמֶר יַעֲקֹב
ד אֶל־יוֹסֵף אֵל שַׁדַּי נִרְאָה־אֵלַי בְּלוּז בְּאֶרֶץ כְּנָעַן וַיְבָרֶךְ אֹתִי: וַיֹּאמֶר

אונקלוס

כח וַחֲיָא יַעֲקֹב בְּאַרְעָא דְמִצְרַיִם, שְׁבַע עַסְרֵי שְׁנִין, וַהֲוָה יוֹמֵי יַעֲקֹב שְׁנֵי חַיּוֹהִי, מְאָה וְאַרְבְּעִין וּשְׁבַע שְׁנִין: כט וּקְרִיבוּ יוֹמֵי יִשְׂרָאֵל לִמְמָת, וּקְרָא לִבְרֵיהּ לְיוֹסֵף, וַאֲמַר לֵיהּ אִם כְּעַן אַשְׁכַּחִית רַחֲמִין בְּעֵינָךְ, שַׁו כְּעַן יְדָךְ תְּחוֹת יִרְכִּי, וְתַעֲבֵיד עִמִּי טֵיבוּ וּקְשׁוֹט, לָא כְעַן תִּקְבְּרִנַּנִי בְּמִצְרָיִם: ל וְאֶשְׁכּוֹב עִם אֲבָהָתַי, וְתִטְּלִנַּנִי מִמִּצְרַיִם, וְתִקְבְּרִנַּנִי בִּקְבוּרַתְהוֹן, וַאֲמַר, אֲנָא אַעֲבֵיד כְּפִתְגָמָךְ: לא וַאֲמַר, קַיֵּים לִי, וְקַיֵּים לֵיהּ, וּסְגֵיד יִשְׂרָאֵל עַל רֵישׁ עַרְסָא: מח א וַהֲוָה, בָּתַר פִּתְגָמַיָּא הָאִלֵּין, וַאֲמַר לְיוֹסֵף, הָא אֲבוּךְ מְרַע, וּדְבַר, יָת תְּרֵין בְּנוֹהִי עִמֵּיהּ, יָת מְנַשֶּׁה וְיָת אֶפְרָיִם: ב וְחַוִּי לְיַעֲקֹב, וַאֲמַר, הָא, בְּרָךְ יוֹסֵף אָתֵי לְוָתָךְ, וְאִתַּקַּף יִשְׂרָאֵל, וִיתֵיב עַל עַרְסָא: ג וַאֲמַר יַעֲקֹב לְיוֹסֵף, אֵל שַׁדַּי, אִתְגְּלִי לִי בְּלוּז בְּאַרְעָא דִכְנַעַן, וּבָרֵיךְ יָתִי: ד וַאֲמַר

VAYEḤI

With Parashat Vayeḥi, the book of Genesis, full of conflicts within the family, comes to a serene end. Yaakov, reunited with his beloved Yosef, sees his grandsons, the only such scene in the Torah. He blesses them; then, on his deathbed, he blesses his twelve sons. He dies and is buried in the cave of Makhpela with his parents and grandparents. Yosef forgives his brothers a second time, and he himself dies, having assured his brothers that God will eventually bring the family back to the Promised Land. The long patriarchal narrative is at an end and a new period – the birth of Israel as a nation – is about to begin.

48:2 וַיִּתְחַזֵּק יִשְׂרָאֵל וַיֵּשֶׁב עַל־הַמִּטָּה *Yisrael summoned his strength and sat up* – The Sages said, "A prisoner cannot release himself from prison" (Berakhot 5b). It takes

numbers. I will make you a community of peoples, and I will give this land to
5 your descendants as an everlasting possession.' Now, the two sons who were
born to you in Egypt before I came here shall be considered mine: Efrayim
6 and Menashe will be like Reuven and Shimon to me. Any child born to you
after shall be yours; in any inheritance they will be reckoned under the names
7 of their brothers. For I – as I was returning from Padan, Raḥel died beside me
in Canaan while we were still on the way, a short distance from Efrat. And I
8 buried her there beside the road to Efrat – that is, Beit Leḥem." Then Yisrael
9 looked at Yosef's sons and said, "Who are these?" Yosef told his father, "They
are my sons God has given me here." "Please bring them to me," Yaakov said,
10 "so that I can bless them." Yisrael's eyes were heavy with age and he could not SHENI
see. So Yosef brought them close to him, and he kissed and embraced them.
11 Yisrael said to Yosef, "I never expected to see you again, and now God has
12 shown me your children as well." Yosef then took them from between his knees
13 and bowed low, his face to the ground. Yosef took both of them, Efrayim on

רש״י

ד **ונתתיך לקהל עמים.** בשרני שעתידים לצאת ממני עוד קהל ועמים. ואף על פי שאמר לי: "גוי וקהל גוים" (לעיל לה, יא)! 'גוי' אמר לי על בנימין, 'קהל גוים' הרי שנים לבד מבנימין, ושוב לא נולד לי בן; למדני שעתיד אחד משבטי לחלק, ועתה אותה מתנה אני נותן לך:

ה **הנולדים לך... עד באי אליך.** לפני בואי אליך, כלומר, שנולדו משפרשת ממני עד שבאתי אצלך: **לי הם.** בחשבון שאר בני הם, לטול חלק בארץ איש כנגדו:

ו **ומולדתך.** אם תוליד עוד לא יהיו במנין בני, אלא בתוך שבטי אפרים ומנשה יהיו נכללים, ולא יהא להם שם בשבטים לענין הנחלה. ואף על פי שנחלקה הארץ למנין גלגלותם, כדכתיב: "לרב תרבה נחלתו" (במדבר כו, נד), וכל איש ואיש נטל בשוה חוץ מן הבכורות, מכל מקום לא נקראו שבטים אלא אלו:

ז **ואני בבאי מפדן וגו'.** ואף על פי שאני מטריח עליך להוליכני לקבר בארץ כנען, לא כך עשיתי לאמך, שהרי מתה סמוך לבית לחם: **כברת ארץ.** מדת ארץ, והם אלפים אמה כמדת תחום שבת, כדברי רבי משה הדרשן. ולא תאמר שעכבו עלי גשמים מלהוליכה ולקברה בחברון, עת הגריד היה שהארץ חלולה ומנוקבת ככברה: **ואקברה שם.** ולא הולכתיה אפילו לבית לחם להכניסה לארץ, וידעתי שיש בלבך עלי; אבל דע לך שעל פי הדבור קברתיה שם, שתהא לעזרה לבניה, כשיגלם נבוזראדן והיו עוברים דרך שם, יצאת רחל על קברה ובוכה ומבקשת עליהם רחמים, שנאמר: "קול ברמה נשמע" וגו' (ירמיה לא, יד). ואונקלוס תרגם: "כרוב ארעא", כדי שעור חרישת יום; ואומר אני שהיה להם קצב שהיו קורין אותו כדי מחרשה אחת, קרואיד"א בלעז, כדאמרינן: "כרוב ותני" (בבא מציעא קז ע"א), "כמה דמסיק תעלא מבי כרבא" (יומא מג ע"ב):

ח **וירא ישראל את בני יוסף.** בקש לברכם ונסתלקה שכינה ממנו, לפי שעתיד ירבעם ואחאב לצאת מאפרים, ויהוא ובניו ממנשה: **ויאמר מי אלה.** מהיכן יצאו אלו שאינן ראויין לברכה?

ט **בזה.** הראה לו שטר אירוסין ושטר כתבה, ובקש יוסף רחמים על הדבר, ונחה עליו רוח הקדש: **ויאמר קחם נא אלי ואברכם.** זהו שאמר הכתוב: "ואנכי תרגלתי לאפרים קחם על זרועותיו" (הושע יא, ג), תרגלתי רוחי ביעקב בשביל אפרים עד שלקחם על זרועותיו:

יא **לא פללתי.** לא מלאני לבי לחשב מחשבה שאראה פניך עוד. 'פללתי' לשון מחשבה, כמו: "הביאי עצה עשו פלילה" (ישעיה טז, ג):

יב **ויוצא יוסף אתם.** לאחר שנשקם הוציאם יוסף מעם ברכיו, כדי ליישבם זה לימין וזה לשמאל לסמך ידיו עליהם ולברכם: **וישתחו לאפיו.** כשחזר לאחוריו מלפני אביו:

אֵלַי הִנְנִי מַפְרְךָ וְהִרְבִּיתִךָ וּנְתַתִּיךָ לִקְהַל עַמִּים וְנָתַתִּי אֶת־הָאָרֶץ
ה הַזֹּאת לְזַרְעֲךָ אַחֲרֶיךָ אֲחֻזַּת עוֹלָם׃ וְעַתָּה שְׁנֵי־בָנֶיךָ הַנּוֹלָדִים לְךָ
בְּאֶרֶץ מִצְרַיִם עַד־בֹּאִי אֵלֶיךָ מִצְרַיְמָה לִי־הֵם אֶפְרַיִם וּמְנַשֶּׁה כִּרְאוּבֵן
ו וְשִׁמְעוֹן יִהְיוּ־לִי׃ וּמוֹלַדְתְּךָ אֲשֶׁר־הוֹלַדְתָּ אַחֲרֵיהֶם לְךָ יִהְיוּ עַל שֵׁם
ז אֲחֵיהֶם יִקָּרְאוּ בְּנַחֲלָתָם׃ וַאֲנִי ׀ בְּבֹאִי מִפַּדָּן מֵתָה עָלַי רָחֵל בְּאֶרֶץ
כְּנַעַן בַּדֶּרֶךְ בְּעוֹד כִּבְרַת־אֶרֶץ לָבֹא אֶפְרָתָה וָאֶקְבְּרֶהָ שָּׁם בְּדֶרֶךְ
ח אֶפְרָת הִוא בֵּית לָחֶם׃ וַיַּרְא יִשְׂרָאֵל אֶת־בְּנֵי יוֹסֵף וַיֹּאמֶר מִי־אֵלֶּה׃
ט וַיֹּאמֶר יוֹסֵף אֶל־אָבִיו בָּנַי הֵם אֲשֶׁר־נָתַן־לִי אֱלֹהִים בָּזֶה וַיֹּאמַר
י קָחֶם־נָא אֵלַי וַאֲבָרְכֵם׃ וְעֵינֵי יִשְׂרָאֵל כָּבְדוּ מִזֹּקֶן לֹא יוּכַל לִרְאוֹת שני
יא וַיַּגֵּשׁ אֹתָם אֵלָיו וַיִּשַּׁק לָהֶם וַיְחַבֵּק לָהֶם׃ וַיֹּאמֶר יִשְׂרָאֵל אֶל־יוֹסֵף
יב רְאֹה פָנֶיךָ לֹא פִלָּלְתִּי וְהִנֵּה הֶרְאָה אֹתִי אֱלֹהִים גַּם אֶת־זַרְעֶךָ׃ וַיּוֹצֵא
יג יוֹסֵף אֹתָם מֵעִם בִּרְכָּיו וַיִּשְׁתַּחוּ לְאַפָּיו אָרְצָה׃ וַיִּקַּח יוֹסֵף אֶת־שְׁנֵיהֶם

אונקלוס

לִי, הָאֲנָא מַפֵּישׁ לָךְ וּמַסְגֵּי לָךְ, וְאֶתְּנִנָּךְ לִכְנִשַׁת שִׁבְטִין, וְאֶתֵּין, יָת אַרְעָא הָדָא, לִבְנָךְ בָּתְרָךְ אַחְסָנַת עָלַם: ה וּכְעַן, תְּרֵין בְּנָךְ דְּאִתְיְלִידוּ לָךְ בְּאַרְעָא דְּמִצְרַיִם, עַד מֵיתַאי לְוָתָךְ, לְמִצְרַיִם דִּילִי אִנּוּן, אֶפְרַיִם וּמְנַשֶּׁה, כִּרְאוּבֵן וְשִׁמְעוֹן יְהוֹן קֳדָמַי: ו וּבְנִין, דְּתוֹלֵיד בָּתְרֵיהוֹן דִּילָךְ יְהוֹן, עַל שׁוּם אֲחֵיהוֹן, יִתְקְרוֹן בְּאַחְסָנַתְהוֹן: ז וַאֲנָא בְּמֵיתַאי מִפַּדָּן, מִיתַת עֲלַי רָחֵל, בְּאַרְעָא דִּכְנַעַן בְּאוֹרְחָא, בְּעוֹד כְּרוּב אַרְעָא לְמֵיעַל לְאֶפְרָת, וּקְבַרְתַּהּ תַּמָּן בְּאוֹרַח אֶפְרָת, הִיא בֵּית לָחֶם: ח וַחֲזָא יִשְׂרָאֵל יָת בְּנֵי יוֹסֵף, וַאֲמַר מַאן אִלֵּין: ט וַאֲמַר יוֹסֵף לַאֲבוּהִי, בְּנַי אִנּוּן, דִּיהַב לִי יי הָכָא, וַאֲמַר, קָרֵיבִנּוּן כְּעַן לְוָתִי וַאֲבָרֵיכִנּוּן: י וְעֵינֵי יִשְׂרָאֵל יְקָרָא מִסֵּיבוּ, לָא יָכוֹל לְמִחְזֵי, וְקָרֵיב יָתְהוֹן לְוָתֵיהּ, וְנַשֵּׁיק לְהוֹן וְגַפֵּיף לְהוֹן: יא וַאֲמַר יִשְׂרָאֵל לְיוֹסֵף, מִחְזֵי אַפָּךְ לָא סַבָּרִית, וְהָא אַחְזִי יָתִי, יי אַף יָת בְּנָךְ: יב וְאַפֵּיק יוֹסֵף, יָתְהוֹן מִן קֳדָמוֹהִי, וּסְגֵיד עַל אַפּוֹהִי עַל אַרְעָא: יג וּדְבַר יוֹסֵף יָת תַּרְוֵיהוֹן,

48:11 וְהִנֵּה הֶרְאָה אֹתִי אֱלֹהִים גַּם אֶת־זַרְעֶךָ *And now God has shown me your children as well* – We begin the Sabbath, as Yaakov will tell us in verse 20, blessing our children as he did his grandchildren. With an exquisite sense of symmetry, just as we begin the Sabbath with a grandparent's blessing so we end it with the words "May you live to see your children's children. Peace be on Israel" (Ps. 128:6, part of the Maariv service at the conclusion of the Sabbath).

What is the connection between grandchildren and peace? Surely this: that those who think about grandchildren care about the future, and those who think about the future make peace. It is those who constantly think of the past, of slights and humiliations and revenge, who make war.

To bless grandchildren and be blessed by them, to teach them and to be taught by them – these are the highest Jewish privileges and the serene end of Yaakov's troubled life. He, who has known so much suffering, can now talk of "the angel who has delivered me from all harm" (Gen. 48:16).

his right to Yisrael's left, and Menashe on his left to Yisrael's right, and brought
14 them close. Yisrael reached out his right hand and put it on Efrayim's head,
even though he was the younger. And, crossing his hands, he put his left hand
15 on Menashe's head even though he was the firstborn. He blessed Yosef and
said, "God before whom my fathers walked – Avraham and Yitzḥak – God who
16 has been my shepherd all my life to now, the angel who has delivered me from
all harm, may He bless the boys. Through them may my name be recalled, and
the names of my fathers, Avraham and Yitzḥak. May they grow to a multitude
17 upon the land." When Yosef saw that his father had placed his right hand on SHELISHI
Efrayim's head, he was displeased. He took hold of his father's hand to move it
18 from Efrayim's head to Menashe's head. Yosef said to his father, "Not so, father.
19 This is the firstborn. Put your right hand on his head." But his father refused: "I
know, my son, I know. He too will be a people, and he too will become great,
but his younger brother will become even greater, and his descendants will

רש״י

יג **אֶת אֶפְרַיִם בִּימִינוֹ מִשְּׂמֹאל יִשְׂרָאֵל.** הַבָּא לִקְרַאת חֲבֵרוֹ יְמִינוֹ כְּנֶגֶד שְׂמֹאל חֲבֵרוֹ, וְכֵוָן שֶׁיְּהֵא הַבְּכוֹר מְיֻמָּן לִבְרָכָה:

יד **שִׂכֵּל אֶת יָדָיו.** כְּתַרְגּוּמוֹ "אַחְכֵּימִנּוּן", בְּהַשְׂכֵּל וְחָכְמָה הִשְׂכִּיל אֶת יָדָיו לְכָךְ וּמִדַּעַת, כִּי יוֹדֵעַ הָיָה כִּי מְנַשֶּׁה הַבְּכוֹר וְאַף עַל פִּי כֵן לֹא שָׁת יְמִינוֹ עָלָיו:

טז **הַמַּלְאָךְ הַגֹּאֵל אֹתִי.** מַלְאָךְ הָרָגִיל לְהִשְׁתַּלֵּחַ אֵלַי בְּצָרָתִי, כָּעִנְיָן שֶׁנֶּאֱמַר: "וַיֹּאמֶר אֵלַי מַלְאַךְ הָאֱלֹהִים בַּחֲלוֹם יַעֲקֹב וְגוֹ', אָנֹכִי הָאֵל בֵּית אֵל" (לעיל לא, יא-יג): **יְבָרֵךְ אֶת הַנְּעָרִים.** מְנַשֶּׁה וְאֶפְרַיִם: **וְיִדְגּוּ.** כַּדָּגִים הַלָּלוּ שֶׁפָּרִים וְרָבִים וְאֵין עַיִן הָרָע שׁוֹלֶטֶת בָּהֶם:

יז **וַיִּתְמֹךְ יַד אָבִיו.** הֱרִימָהּ מֵעַל רֹאשׁ בְּנוֹ וּתְמָכָהּ בְּיָדוֹ:

יט **יָדַעְתִּי בְנִי יָדַעְתִּי.** שֶׁהוּא הַבְּכוֹר, וְגַם הוּא יִהְיֶה לְעָם וְיִגְדַּל – עָתִיד גִּדְעוֹן לָצֵאת מִמֶּנּוּ, שֶׁהַקָּדוֹשׁ בָּרוּךְ הוּא עוֹשֶׂה נֵס עַל יָדוֹ: **וְאוּלָם אָחִיו הַקָּטֹן יִגְדַּל מִמֶּנּוּ.** שֶׁעָתִיד יְהוֹשֻׁעַ לָצֵאת מִמֶּנּוּ, שֶׁיַּנְחִיל אֶת הָאָרֶץ וִילַמֵּד תּוֹרָה לְיִשְׂרָאֵל:

centuries. At first, Yosef felt relief. The years as a slave, then a prisoner, were over. In Canaan, he had been the youngest of eleven brothers in a family of shepherds. Now, in Egypt, he was at the center of the greatest civilization of the ancient world, second only to Pharaoh in rank and power. No one reminded him of his background. With his royal robes and ring and chariot, he was an Egyptian prince (as Moshe was later to be). The past was a bitter memory he sought to remove from his mind. Menashe means "forgetting."

But as time passed, Yosef began to feel quite different emotions. Yes, he had arrived; he had achieved the power and greatness of which he had dreamed in his youth. But the Egyptian nation was not his, nor was its culture. To be sure, his family was, by any worldly terms, undistinguished, unsophisticated. Yet they remained his family. Though they were no more than shepherds (a class the Egyptians despised), they had been spoken to by God – not the gods of the sun, the river, and death, the Egyptian pantheon – but God, the Creator of heaven and earth, who did not make His home in temples and pyramids and panoplies of power, but who spoke in the human heart as a voice, lifting a simple family to moral greatness.

By the time his second son was born, Yosef had undergone a profound change of heart. To be sure, he had all the trappings of earthly success – "God has made me fruitful" – but Egypt had become "the land of my affliction." Why? Because it was exile. By calling this child Efrayim, he was remembering what, when Menashe was born, he was trying to forget: who he was, where he came from, where he belonged.

On this reading, Yaakov's blessing of Efrayim over Menashe has nothing to do with their ages and everything to do with their names.

אֶת־אֶפְרַיִם בִּימִינוֹ מִשְּׂמֹאל יִשְׂרָאֵל וְאֶת־מְנַשֶּׁה בִשְׂמֹאלוֹ מִימִין
יד יִשְׂרָאֵל וַיַּגֵּשׁ אֵלָיו: וַיִּשְׁלַח יִשְׂרָאֵל אֶת־יְמִינוֹ וַיָּשֶׁת עַל־רֹאשׁ אֶפְרַיִם
וְהוּא הַצָּעִיר וְאֶת־שְׂמֹאלוֹ עַל־רֹאשׁ מְנַשֶּׁה שִׂכֵּל אֶת־יָדָיו כִּי מְנַשֶּׁה
טו הַבְּכוֹר: וַיְבָרֶךְ אֶת־יוֹסֵף וַיֹּאמַר הָאֱלֹהִים אֲשֶׁר הִתְהַלְּכוּ אֲבֹתַי לְפָנָיו
טז אַבְרָהָם וְיִצְחָק הָאֱלֹהִים הָרֹעֶה אֹתִי מֵעוֹדִי עַד־הַיּוֹם הַזֶּה: הַמַּלְאָךְ
הַגֹּאֵל אֹתִי מִכָּל־רָע יְבָרֵךְ אֶת־הַנְּעָרִים וְיִקָּרֵא בָהֶם שְׁמִי וְשֵׁם אֲבֹתַי
יז אַבְרָהָם וְיִצְחָק וְיִדְגּוּ לָרֹב בְּקֶרֶב הָאָרֶץ: וַיַּרְא יוֹסֵף כִּי־יָשִׁית אָבִיו שלישי
יַד־יְמִינוֹ עַל־רֹאשׁ אֶפְרַיִם וַיֵּרַע בְּעֵינָיו וַיִּתְמֹךְ יַד־אָבִיו לְהָסִיר אֹתָהּ
יח מֵעַל רֹאשׁ־אֶפְרַיִם עַל־רֹאשׁ מְנַשֶּׁה: וַיֹּאמֶר יוֹסֵף אֶל־אָבִיו לֹא־כֵן
יט אָבִי כִּי־זֶה הַבְּכֹר שִׂים יְמִינְךָ עַל־רֹאשׁוֹ: וַיְמָאֵן אָבִיו וַיֹּאמֶר יָדַעְתִּי
בְנִי יָדַעְתִּי גַּם־הוּא יִהְיֶה־לְּעָם וְגַם־הוּא יִגְדָּל וְאוּלָם אָחִיו הַקָּטֹן יִגְדַּל

אונקלוס

יָת אֶפְרַיִם בִּימִינֵיהּ מִסְּמָאלָא דְּיִשְׂרָאֵל, וְיָת מְנַשֶּׁה בִּסְמָאלֵיהּ מִימִּינָא דְּיִשְׂרָאֵל, וְקָרֵיב לְוָתֵיהּ: יד וְאוֹשֵׁיט יִשְׂרָאֵל יָת יַמִּינֵיהּ, וְשַׁוִּי עַל רֵישָׁא דְּאֶפְרַיִם וְהוּא זְעֵירָא, וְיָת סְמָאלֵיהּ עַל רֵישָׁא דִּמְנַשֶּׁה, אַחְכֵּימִנּוּן לִידוֹהִי, אֲרֵי מְנַשֶּׁה בֻּכְרָא: טו וּבָרֵיךְ יָת יוֹסֵף וַאֲמַר, יְיָ, דִּפְלַחוּ אֲבָהָתִי קֳדָמוֹהִי אַבְרָהָם וְיִצְחָק, יְיָ דְּזָן יָתִי, מִדְּאִיתַנִי עַד יוֹמָא הָדֵין: טז מַלְאֲכָא דִּפְרַק יָתִי מִכָּל בִּישָׁא, יְבָרֵיךְ יָת עוּלֵימַיָּא, וְיִתְקְרֵי בְהוֹן שְׁמִי, וְשׁוּם אֲבָהָתִי אַבְרָהָם וְיִצְחָק, וּכְנוּנֵי יַמָּא יִסְגּוֹן בְּגוֹ בְּנֵי אֱנָשָׁא עַל אַרְעָא: יז וַחֲזָא יוֹסֵף, אֲרֵי שַׁוִּי אֲבוּהִי יַד יַמִּינֵיהּ, עַל רֵישָׁא דְּאֶפְרַיִם וּבְאֵישׁ בְּעֵינוֹהִי, וְסַעֲדַהּ לִידָא דַּאֲבוּהִי, לְאַעְדָּאָה יָתַהּ, מֵעַל רֵישָׁא דְּאֶפְרַיִם לְאַנְחוּתַהּ עַל רֵישָׁא דִּמְנַשֶּׁה: יח וַאֲמַר יוֹסֵף, לַאֲבוּהִי לָא כֵן אַבָּא, אֲרֵי דֵין בֻּכְרָא, שַׁו יַמִּינָךְ עַל רֵישֵׁיהּ: יט וְסָרֵיב אֲבוּהִי, וַאֲמַר יְדַעְנָא בְּרִי יְדַעְנָא, אַף הוּא יְהֵי לְעַם וְאַף הוּא יִסְגֵּי, וּבְרַם, אֲחוּהִי זְעֵירָא יִסְגֵּי

EFRAYIM AND MENASHE – THE FIRST CHILDREN OF EXILE

The drama of younger and older brothers, which haunts the book of Genesis from Kayin and Hevel onward, reaches a strange climax in the story of Yosef's children. In light of all the conflict in his life and in his family's past, it is not difficult to understand the care Yosef takes to ensure that Yaakov blesses the firstborn first. Why, then, has his father seemingly not learned? Besides which, what possible reason could he have for favoring the younger of his grandchildren over the elder? He has not seen them before. He knows nothing about them. Why does Yaakov favor Efrayim over Menashe?

The explanation lies in the two things Yaakov does know. He knows that the stay of his family in Egypt will not be a short one, for God has told him so (Gen. 46:3–4). And he knows his grandsons' names.

> Yosef named his firstborn Menashe, saying, "God has made me forget (*nashani*) all my troubles and all my father's family." The second son he named Efrayim, saying, "God has made me fruitful (*fara*) in the land of my affliction." (41:51–52)

With the utmost brevity, the Torah has intimated an experience of exile that is to be repeated many times across the

20 become an abundance of nations." On that day, he blessed them: "By you shall
Israel bless, saying: May God make you like Efrayim and Menashe." He put
21 Efrayim before Menashe. Then Yisrael said to Yosef, "I am about to die, but
22 God will be with you and will bring you back to the land of your fathers. And
to you I give one portion more than your brothers, which I took from the
Amorites by my sword and my bow."
49 1 Then Yaakov called for his sons and said, "Gather together so that I can tell you REVI'I
2 what will happen to you in the days to come. Assemble and listen, Yaakov's

רש"י

וְזַרְעוֹ יִהְיֶה מְלֹא הַגּוֹיִם. כָּל הָעוֹלָם יִתְמַלֵּא בְּצֵאת שָׁמְעוֹ וּשְׁמוֹ, כְּשֶׁיַּעֲמִיד חַמָּה בְּגִבְעוֹן וְיָרֵחַ בְּעֵמֶק אַיָּלוֹן:

כ **בְּךָ יְבָרֵךְ יִשְׂרָאֵל.** הַבָּא לְבָרֵךְ אֶת בָּנָיו יְבָרְכֵם בְּבִרְכָתָם, וְיֹאמַר אִישׁ לִבְנוֹ: "יְשִׂמְךָ אֱלֹהִים כְּאֶפְרַיִם וְכִמְנַשֶּׁה": **וַיָּשֶׂם אֶת אֶפְרַיִם.** בְּבִרְכָתוֹ "לִפְנֵי מְנַשֶּׁה", לְהַקְדִּימוֹ בַּדְּגָלִים וּבַחֲנֻכַּת הַנְּשִׂיאִים:

כב **וַאֲנִי נָתַתִּי לְךָ.** לְפִי שֶׁאַתָּה טוֹרֵחַ לְהִתְעַסֵּק בִּקְבוּרָתִי, וְגַם "אֲנִי נָתַתִּי לְךָ" נַחֲלָה שֶׁתִּקָּבֵר בָּהּ, וְאֵי זוֹ? זוֹ שְׁכֶם, שֶׁנֶּאֱמַר: "וְאֶת עַצְמוֹת יוֹסֵף אֲשֶׁר הֶעֱלוּ בְנֵי יִשְׂרָאֵל מִמִּצְרַיִם קָבְרוּ בִשְׁכֶם" (יהושע כד, לב): **שְׁכֶם אַחַד עַל אַחֶיךָ.** שְׁכֶם מַמָּשׁ, הִיא תִּהְיֶה לְךָ חֵלֶק אֶחָד יְתֵרָה עַל אַחֶיךָ: **בְּחַרְבִּי וּבְקַשְׁתִּי.** כְּשֶׁהָרְגוּ שִׁמְעוֹן וְלֵוִי אֶת אַנְשֵׁי שְׁכֶם נִתְכַּנְּסוּ כָּל סְבִיבוֹתֵיהֶם לְהִזְדַּוֵּג לָהֶם, וְחָגַר יַעֲקֹב כְּלֵי מִלְחָמָה כְּנֶגְדָּן. דָּבָר אַחֵר, "שְׁכֶם אַחַד", הִיא הַבְּכוֹרָה, שֶׁיִּטְּלוּ בָנָיו שְׁנֵי חֲלָקִים, וּ'שְׁכֶם' לְשׁוֹן חֵלֶק הוּא, וְהַרְבֵּה יֵשׁ לוֹ דוֹמִים בַּמִּקְרָא: "אֲחַלְּקָה שְׁכֶם" (תהלים ס, ח); "כִּי תְּשִׁיתֵמוֹ שֶׁכֶם" (שם כא, יג), תָּשִׁית שׂוֹנְאַי לְפָנַי לַחֲלָקִים; "דֶּרֶךְ יְרַצְּחוּ שֶׁכְמָה" (הושע ו, ט), אִישׁ חֶלְקוֹ; "לְעָבְדוֹ שְׁכֶם אֶחָד" (צפניה ג, ט). "אֲשֶׁר לָקַחְתִּי מִיַּד הָאֱמֹרִי" – מִיַּד עֵשָׂו שֶׁעוֹשֶׂה מַעֲשֵׂה אֱמוֹרִי. דָּבָר אַחֵר, שֶׁהָיָה צָד אָבִיו בְּאִמְרֵי פִיו. "בְּחַרְבִּי וּבְקַשְׁתִּי" – הִיא חָכְמָתוֹ וּתְפִלָּתוֹ:

מט א **וְאַגִּידָה לָכֶם.** בִּקֵּשׁ לְגַלּוֹת אֶת הַקֵּץ וְנִסְתַּלְּקָה מִמֶּנּוּ שְׁכִינָה, וְהִתְחִיל אוֹמֵר דְּבָרִים אֲחֵרִים:

This is no minor detail. It is a fundamental feature of Jewish spirituality. We believe that we cannot predict the future when it comes to human beings. We *make* the future by our choices. We cannot obtain the script. The future is radically open.

Do not believe that the future is written. There is no fate we cannot change, no prediction we cannot defy. We are not predestined to fail; neither are we preordained to succeed. We do not predict the future, because we make the future: by our choices, our willpower, our persistence, and our determination to survive.

The proof is the Jewish people itself. The first reference to Israel outside the Tanakh is engraved on the Merneptah Stele, inscribed around 1225 BCE by Pharaoh Merneptah IV, Ramses II's successor. It reads: "Israel is laid waste, her seed is no more." It is, in short, an obituary. The Jewish people have been written off many times by their enemies, but they remain, after almost four millennia, still young and strong.

That is why, when Yaakov wants to tell his children what will happen to them in the future, the Divine Spirit is taken away from him. Our children continue to surprise us, as we continue to surprise others. Made in the image of God, we are free. Sustained by the blessings of God, we can become greater than anyone, even ourselves, could foresee.

49:2 **הִקָּבְצוּ וְשִׁמְעוּ** *Assemble and listen* – Yaakov blesses his twelve sons. His blessings to the eldest three sons, Reuven, Shimon, and Levi, read more like curses than blessings. There is discernible tension here. Yet the fact is that he is blessing all twelve together in the same room at the same time. We have not seen this before. There is no record of Avraham blessing either Yishmael or Yitzḥak. Yitzḥak blesses Esav and Yaakov separately. The mere fact that Yaakov is able to gather his sons together is unprecedented, and important. In the next chapter – the first of Exodus – the Israelites are, for the first time, described as a people. It is hard to see how they could live together as a people if they could not live together as a family.

The Torah is giving us an unexpected message here: The

כ מִמֶּנּוּ וְזַרְעוֹ יִהְיֶה מְלֹא־הַגּוֹיִם׃ וַיְבָרְכֵם בַּיּוֹם הַהוּא לֵאמוֹר בְּךָ יְבָרֵךְ
יִשְׂרָאֵל לֵאמֹר יְשִׂמְךָ אֱלֹהִים כְּאֶפְרַיִם וְכִמְנַשֶּׁה וַיָּשֶׂם אֶת־אֶפְרַיִם
כא לִפְנֵי מְנַשֶּׁה׃ וַיֹּאמֶר יִשְׂרָאֵל אֶל־יוֹסֵף הִנֵּה אָנֹכִי מֵת וְהָיָה אֱלֹהִים
כב עִמָּכֶם וְהֵשִׁיב אֶתְכֶם אֶל־אֶרֶץ אֲבֹתֵיכֶם׃ וַאֲנִי נָתַתִּי לְךָ שְׁכֶם אַחַד
עַל־אַחֶיךָ אֲשֶׁר לָקַחְתִּי מִיַּד הָאֱמֹרִי בְּחַרְבִּי וּבְקַשְׁתִּי׃
מט א וַיִּקְרָא יַעֲקֹב אֶל־בָּנָיו וַיֹּאמֶר הֵאָסְפוּ וְאַגִּידָה לָכֶם אֵת אֲשֶׁר־יִקְרָא מג רביעי
ב אֶתְכֶם בְּאַחֲרִית הַיָּמִים׃ הִקָּבְצוּ וְשִׁמְעוּ בְּנֵי יַעֲקֹב וְשִׁמְעוּ אֶל־

אונקלוס

מִנֵּיה, וּבְנוֹהִי יְהוֹן שָׁלְטִין בְּעַמְמַיָּא: כ וּבָרֵיכִנּוּן, בְּיוֹמָא הַהוּא לְמֵימַר, בָּךְ, יְבָרֵיךְ יִשְׂרָאֵל לְמֵימַר, יְשַׁוֵּינָךְ יי, כְּאֶפְרַיִם וְכִמְנַשֶּׁה, וְשַׁוִּי יָת אֶפְרַיִם קֳדָם מְנַשֶּׁה: כא וַאֲמַר יִשְׂרָאֵל לְיוֹסֵף, הָא אֲנָא מָאֵית, וִיהֵי מֵימְרָא דַיי בְּסַעְדְּכוֹן, וְיָתִיב יָתְכוֹן, לַאֲרַע אֲבָהָתְכוֹן: כב וַאֲנָא, יְהָבִית לָךְ, חוּלָק חַד יַתִּיר עַל אֲחָךְ, דִּנְסֵיבִית מִיְּדָא דֶאֱמוֹרָאָה, בִּצְלוֹתִי וּבְבָעוּתִי: מט א וּקְרָא יַעֲקֹב לִבְנוֹהִי, וַאֲמַר, אִתְכַּנַּשׁוּ וַאֲחַוֵּי לְכוֹן, יָת, דִּיעָרַע יָתְכוֹן בְּסוֹף יוֹמַיָּא: ב אִתְכַּנַּשׁוּ וּשְׁמַעוּ בְּנֵי יַעֲקֹב, וְקַבִּילוּ אֻלְפָּן מִן

Knowing that these were the first two children of his family to be born in exile, knowing too that the exile will be prolonged and at times difficult and dark, Yaakov seeks to signal to all future generations that there will be a constant tension between the desire to forget (to assimilate, acculturate, anaesthetize the hope of a return) and the promptings of memory (the knowledge that this is exile, that we are part of another story, that our ultimate home is somewhere else).

The child of forgetting (Menashe) may have blessings. But greater are the blessings of a child (Efrayim) who remembers the past and future of which he is a part.

48:20 כְּאֶפְרַיִם וְכִמְנַשֶּׁה *Like Efrayim and Menashe* – This is the blessing that Jewish parents use on Friday night to bless their sons. Why this blessing of all the blessings in the Torah? My predecessor Lord Jakobovits gave a most lovely explanation. He said that though there are many instances in the Torah and Tanakh in which parents bless their children, this is the only example of a grandparent blessing grandchildren.

Between parents and children, he said, there are often tensions. Parents worry about their children. Children sometimes rebel against their parents. The relationship is not always smooth.

Not so with grandchildren. There the relationship is one of love untroubled by tension or anxiety. When a grandparent blesses a grandchild he or she does so with a full heart. That is why this blessing by Yaakov of his grandchildren is to become the model of blessing across the generations.

YAAKOV'S DEATHBED SPEECH

Yaakov summons his children, wishing to bless them before he dies. The text begins with a strange semi-repetition: "Gather together so that I can tell you what will happen to you in the days to come. Assemble and listen.... Listen to your father Yisrael" (Gen. 49:1–2). The two verses seem to be saying the same thing twice, with one difference. In the first, there is a reference to "what will happen to you in the days to come" (literally, "at the end of days"). This is missing from the second.

Rashi, following the Talmud, says that "Yaakov wished to reveal what would happen in the end, but the Divine Presence was removed from him" (Rashi on Gen. 49:1; Pesaḥim 56a; Bereshit Rabba 99:5). He tried to foresee the future but found he could not.

3 sons. Listen to your father Yisrael. Reuven, you are my firstborn, my strength,
4 first fruit of my manhood, excelling in rank, excelling in power. Unstable as
water, you shall not excel, for you went up onto your father's bed and defiled
it – went up onto my couch.
5
6 Shimon and Levi are brothers; weapons of violence their wares. Let me never
join their council, nor my honor be of their assembly. For in their anger they

רש״י

ג-ד **וראשית אוני.** היא טפה ראשונה לו, שלא ראה קרי מימיו: **אוני.** כחי, כמו: "מצאתי און לי" (הושע יב, ט), "מרב אונים" (ישעיה מ, כו), "ולאין אונים" (שם כט): **יתר שאת.** ראוי היית להיות יתר על אחיך בכהנה, לשון נשיאות כפים: **ויתר עז.** במלכות, כמו: "ויתן עז למלכו" (שמואל א' ב, י). ומי גרם לך להפסיד? "פחז כמים" – הפחז והבהלה אשר מהרת להראות כעסך כמים הללו הממהרים למרוצתם, לכך "אל תותר" – אל תרבה לטל כל היתרות הללו שהיו ראויות לך. ומהו הפחז אשר פחזת? "כי עלית משכבי אביך", אז חללת אותו שעלה על יצועי, שם שכינה שדרכו להיות עולה על יצועי: **פחז.** שם דבר הוא, לפיכך טעמו למעלה וכלו נקוד פתח. ואלו היה לשון עבר, היה נקוד חציו קמץ וחציו פתח וטעמו למטה: **יצועי.** לשון משכב, על שם שמציעים אותו על ידי לבדין וסדינין. והרבה דומים לו: "אם אעלה על ערש יצועי" (תהלים קלב, ג), "אם זכרתיך על יצועי" (שם סג, ז):

ה **שמעון ולוי אחים.** בעצה אחת על שכם ועל יוסף: "ויאמרו איש אל אחיו וגו' ועתה לכו ונהרגהו" (לעיל לז, יט-כ). מי הם? אם תאמר ראובן או יהודה, הרי לא הסכימו בהריגתו. אם תאמר בני השפחות, הרי לא היתה שנאתן שלמה, שנאמר: "והוא נער את בני בלהה ואת בני זלפה" (לעיל לז, ב). יששכר וזבולון לא היו מדברים בפני אחיהם הגדולים מהם. על כרחך שמעון ולוי הם שקראם אביהם 'אחים': **כלי חמס.** אמנות זו של רציחה חמס הוא בידיהם, מברכת עשו היא זו, אמנות שלו היא, ואתם חמסתם אותה הימנו: **מכרתיהם.** לשון כלי זין, הסיף בלשון יוני מכי"ר. תנחומא (שם ט). דבר אחר, "מכרתיהם", בארץ מגורתם נהגו עצמן בכלי חמס, כמו: "מכרתיך ומלדתיך" (יחזקאל טז, ג), וזה תרגום של אונקלוס:

ו **בסדם אל תבא נפשי.** זה מעשה זמרי, כשנתקבצו שבטו של שמעון להביא את המדינית לפני משה, ואמרו לו: זו אסורה או מתרת? אם תאמר אסורה, בת יתרו מי התירה לך? – אל יזכר שמי בדבר, "זמרי בן סלוא נשיא בית אב לשמעני" (במדבר כה, יד), ולא כתב 'בן יעקב': **בקהלם.** כשיקהיל קרח שהוא משבטו של לוי את כל העדה על משה ועל אהרן, "אל תחד כבדי" שם, אל יתיחד עמהם שמי, שנאמר: "קרח בן יצהר בן קהת בן לוי" (במדבר טז, א), ולא נאמר 'בן יעקב'. אבל בדברי הימים (א' ו, כב-כג) כשנתיחסו בני קרח על הדוכן, נאמר: "בן קרח בן יצהר בן קהת בן לוי בן ישראל": **אל תחד כבדי.** כבוד לשון זכר הוא, ועל כרחך אתה צריך לפרש כמדבר אל הכבוד ואומר: אתה כבודי, אל תתיחד עמהם. כמו: "לא תחד אתם בקבורה" (ישעיה יד, כ): **כי באפם הרגו איש.** אלו חמור ואנשי שכם, ואינן חשובין

Reuven, then, is the greatest "might-have-been" in the Torah. His story is of potential unfulfilled, virtue not quite realized, greatness so close yet unachieved. It is impossible not to recognize in Reuven a person of the highest ethical sensibilities. He is a person of good intentions. He cares. He thinks. He is not led by the crowd or by his darker instincts. He penetrates to the moral core of a situation. That is the first thing we notice about him. The second, however, is that somehow his interventions backfire. They fail to achieve their effect. Attempting to make things better, Reuven makes them worse. Though he has conscience, he lacks courage. He knows what is right, but lacks the resolve to do it boldly and decisively. The Torah clearly wants us to reflect on Reuven's character. Between the lines it tells us what stands between what might have been and what was.

49:5 **כְּלֵי חָמָס מְכֵרֹתֵיהֶם** *Weapons of violence their wares* – Yaakov's horror at the action of his sons in chapter 34 does not end there. He returns to it now, on his deathbed, and in effect curses them. We are reminded of Andrew Schmookler's point, that "power is like a contaminant, a disease, which once introduced will gradually but inexorably become universal" (see ch. 34, "Dina and Shekhem"). Because Shimon and Levi misused force in their youth, Yaakov feels he must "scatter them in Israel" and deny them further power. The two brothers' tribes are separated on the map of Israel, and never allowed territorial strength.

ג יִשְׂרָאֵל אֲבִיכֶם: רְאוּבֵן בְּכֹרִי אַתָּה כֹּחִי וְרֵאשִׁית אוֹנִי יֶתֶר שְׂאֵת וְיֶתֶר
ד עָז: פַּחַז כַּמַּיִם אַל־תּוֹתַר כִּי עָלִיתָ מִשְׁכְּבֵי אָבִיךָ אָז חִלַּלְתָּ יְצוּעִי
עָלָה:
ה ו שִׁמְעוֹן וְלֵוִי אַחִים כְּלֵי חָמָס מְכֵרֹתֵיהֶם: בְּסֹדָם אַל־תָּבֹא נַפְשִׁי
בִּקְהָלָם אַל־תֵּחַד כְּבֹדִי כִּי בְאַפָּם הָרְגוּ אִישׁ וּבִרְצֹנָם עִקְּרוּ־שׁוֹר:

אונקלוס

יִשְׂרָאֵל אֲבוּכוֹן: ג רְאוּבֵן בְּכְרִי אַתְּ, חֵילִי וְרֵישׁ תְּקְפִי, לָךְ הֲוָה חֲזֵי לְמִסַּב תְּלָתָא חוּלָקִין בְּכֵירוּתָא כְּהֻנְּתָא וּמַלְכוּתָא: ד עַל דַּאֲזַלְתְּ לְקֳבֵיל אַפָּךְ הָא כְמַיָּא בְּרַם לָא אַהֲנֵיתָא חוּלָק יַתִּיר לָא תִסַּב, אֲרֵי סְלֵיקְתָּא בֵּית מִשְׁכְּבֵי אֲבוּךְ, בְּכֵן אַחֵילְתָּא לְשִׁיוּיֵי בְּרִי סְלֵיקְתָּא: ה שִׁמְעוֹן וְלֵוִי אַחִין, גֻּבְרִין גִּבָּרִין בַּאֲרַע תּוֹתָבוּתְהוֹן עֲבַדוּ גְּבוּרָא: ו בְּרָזְהוֹן לָא הֲוָת נַפְשִׁי, בְּאִתְכַּנּוֹשֵׁיהוֹן לְמֶהֱךְ לָא נְחָתִית מִן יְקָרִי, אֲרֵי בְּרֻגְזְהוֹן קְטַלוּ קְטוֹל, וּבִרְעוּתְהוֹן תָּרַעוּ שׁוּר סָנְאָה:

family is prior to all else, to the land, the nation, politics, economics, the pursuit of power, and the accumulation of wealth. From an external point of view, the impressive story is that Yosef reaches the heights of power in Egypt. The Egyptians themselves mourn the death of his father Yaakov and accompany the family on their way to bury him, so that the Canaanites, seeing the entourage, say, "Egypt is in deep mourning here" (Gen. 50:11). But that is externality. When we turn the page and begin the book of Exodus, we discover that the position of the Israelites in Egypt is very vulnerable indeed, and all the power Yosef has centralized in the hands of Pharaoh will eventually be used against them. Genesis is not about power. It is about families. Because that is where life together begins.

The book, then, ends on these three important resolutions: First, that grandparents are part of the family, and their blessing is important. Second, Yaakov shows that it is possible to bless all your children, even if you have a fractured relationship with some of them. Third, Yosef shows that it is possible to forgive your siblings even if they have done you great harm.

That, surprisingly, is what Genesis is about. Not about the creation of the world, which can be described in a single chapter, but about how to handle family conflict. As soon as Avraham's descendants can create strong families, they can move from Genesis to Exodus and their birth as a nation.

49:3–4 יֶתֶר שְׂאֵת וְיֶתֶר עָז: פַּחַז כַּמַּיִם *Excelling in power. Unstable as water* – By now we have a rich, composite, and penetrating portrait of Reuven – and we now know that the psychological key to his character is already given at his birth (see comments on 29:32 and 30:14 and ch. 37, "Reuven's Good Intentions"). Yaakov is a hero of faith, the man who gave Israel its name. Yet the complexity of Yaakov's character is light-years away from the idealized heroes of other religious traditions. In Yaakov we discover that the life of faith is not simple. We also discover something else. Every virtue carries with it a corresponding danger. The person who is overgenerous may condemn his own family to poverty. The individual (like Aharon – see Mishna Avot 1:12) who chooses peace at any price can sometimes allow those around him to make a golden calf. There is no single authoritative role model in Judaism. Instead there are many: Avraham, Yitzḥak, and Yaakov; Moshe, Aharon, and Miriam; kings, prophets, and priests; masters of halakha and Aggada; Sages and saints, poets and philosophers. The reason is that no one can embody all the virtues all the time. A strength here is a weakness there.

Yaakov loved, passionately and deeply. That was his strength, but also his weakness. His love for Raḥel meant that he could not bestow equal favor on Leah. His longing for a child by Raḥel meant that there was something lacking in his relationship with Leah's firstborn, Reuven. Had he loved less, there might have been no problem. He might have divided his attention more equally. But had he loved less, he would not have been Yaakov.

7 killed men; at their whim they hamstrung oxen. Cursed be their anger, for it is
most fierce, and their fury, for it is most cruel. I will divide them up in Yaakov,
and scatter them in Israel.
8 Yehuda, your brothers shall praise you. Your hand will be on the neck of your
9 foes. To you will your father's sons bow. Yehuda is a lion's cub. From the prey,
my son, you have risen. Like a lion he crouches, lies down, like a lioness; who
10 dares to rouse him? The scepter shall not pass from Yehuda, nor the staff from
between his feet, so that tribute will come to him and the homage of nations
11 be his. He tethers his donkey to vines, to the vine bough his donkey's colt; he
12 washes his clothes in wine, his robe in the blood of grapes. His eyes are darker
than wine, and his teeth whiter than milk.

רש"י

כֻּלָּם אֶלָּא כְּאִישׁ אֶחָד. וְכֵן הוּא אוֹמֵר בְּגִדְעוֹן: "וְהִכִּיתָ אֶת מִדְיָן כְּאִישׁ אֶחָד" (שופטים ו, טז). וְכֵן בְּמִצְרַיִם: "סוּס וְרֹכְבוֹ רָמָה בַיָּם" (שמות טו, א). זֶהוּ מִדְרָשׁוֹ. וּפְשׁוּטוֹ: אֲנָשִׁים הַרְבֵּה קוֹרֵא 'אִישׁ', כָּל אֶחָד לְעַצְמוֹ, בְּאַפָּם הָרְגוּ כָּל אִישׁ שֶׁכָּעֲסוּ עָלָיו, וְכֵן: "וַיִּלְמַד לִטְרָף טֶרֶף אָדָם אָכָל" (יחזקאל יט, ג): **וּבִרְצֹנָם עִקְּרוּ שׁוֹר.** רָצוּ לַעֲקֹר אֶת יוֹסֵף שֶׁנִּקְרָא שׁוֹר, שֶׁנֶּאֱמַר: "בְּכוֹר שׁוֹרוֹ הָדָר לוֹ" (דברים לג, יז). "עִקְּרוּ" אשיירטי"ר בְּלַעַז, לְשׁוֹן: "אֶת סוּסֵיהֶם תְּעַקֵּר" (יהושע יא, ו):

ז **אָרוּר אַפָּם.** אֲפִלּוּ בִּשְׁעַת תּוֹכָחָה לֹא קִלֵּל אֶלָּא אַפָּם, וְזֶהוּ שֶׁאָמַר בִּלְעָם: "מָה אֶקֹּב לֹא קַבֹּה אֵל" (במדבר כג, ח): **אֲחַלְּקֵם בְּיַעֲקֹב.** אַפְרִידֵם זֶה מִזֶּה, שֶׁלֹּא יְהֵא לֵוִי בְּמִנְיַן הַשְּׁבָטִים, וַהֲרֵי הֵם חֲלוּקִים. דָּבָר אַחֵר, אֵין לְךָ עֲנִיִּים סוֹפְרִים וּמְלַמְּדֵי תִינוֹקוֹת אֶלָּא מִשִּׁמְעוֹן, כְּדֵי שֶׁיִּהְיוּ נְפוּצִים, וְשִׁבְטוֹ שֶׁל לֵוִי עֲשָׂאוֹ מְחַזֵּר עַל הַגְּרָנוֹת לִתְרוּמוֹת וְלַמַּעַשְׂרוֹת, נָתַן לוֹ תְּפוּצָתוֹ דֶּרֶךְ כָּבוֹד:

ח **יְהוּדָה אַתָּה יוֹדוּךָ אַחֶיךָ.** לְפִי שֶׁהוֹכִיחַ אֶת הָרִאשׁוֹנִים בְּקַנְטוּרִים, הִתְחִיל יְהוּדָה נָסוֹג לַאֲחוֹרָיו, וּקְרָאוֹ יַעֲקֹב בְּדִבְרֵי רִצּוּי: לֹא אַתָּה כְּמוֹתָם: **יָדְךָ בְּעֹרֶף אֹיְבֶיךָ.** בִּימֵי דָוִד, "וְאֹיְבַי תַּתָּה לִּי עֹרֶף" (שמואל ב' כב, מא): **בְּנֵי אָבִיךָ.** עַל שֵׁם שֶׁהָיוּ מִנָּשִׁים הַרְבֵּה לֹא אָמַר 'בְּנֵי אִמְּךָ' כְּדֶרֶךְ שֶׁאָמַר יִצְחָק (לעיל כז, כט):

ט **גּוּר אַרְיֵה.** עַל דָּוִד נִתְנַבֵּא. בַּתְּחִלָּה "גּוּר", "בִּהְיוֹת שָׁאוּל מֶלֶךְ עָלֵינוּ אַתָּה... הַמּוֹצִיא וְהַמֵּבִי אֶת יִשְׂרָאֵל" (שמואל ב' ה, ב), וּלְבַסּוֹף "אַרְיֵה" כְּשֶׁהִמְלִיכוּהוּ עֲלֵיהֶם. וְזֶהוּ שֶׁתִּרְגֵּם אוּנְקְלוֹס: "שִׁלְטוֹן יְהֵא בְּשֵׁירוּיֵהּ", בִּתְחִלָּתוֹ: **מִטֶּרֶף.** מִמַּה שֶּׁחֲשַׁדְתִּיךָ בְּ"טָרֹף טֹרַף יוֹסֵף", "חַיָּה רָעָה אֲכָלָתְהוּ" (לעיל לז, לג), וְזֶהוּ יְהוּדָה שֶׁנִּמְשַׁל לְאַרְיֵה – "בְּנִי עָלִיתָ", סִלַּקְתָּ אֶת עַצְמְךָ וְאָמַרְתָּ: "מַה בֶּצַע" וְגוֹ' (לעיל לז, כו), וְכֵן מֵהֲרִיגַת תָּמָר שֶׁהוֹדָה "צָדְקָה מִמֶּנִּי" (לעיל לח, כו), לְפִיכָךְ "כָּרַע רָבַץ" וְגוֹ', בִּימֵי שְׁלֹמֹה "אִישׁ תַּחַת גַּפְנוֹ" וְגוֹ' (מלכים א' ה, ה):

י **לֹא יָסוּר שֵׁבֶט מִיהוּדָה.** מִדָּוִד וְאֵילָךְ, אֵלּוּ רָאשֵׁי גָלֻיּוֹת שֶׁבְּבָבֶל שֶׁרוֹדִים אֶת הָעָם בַּשֵּׁבֶט, שֶׁמְּמֻנִּים עַל פִּי הַמַּלְכוּת: **וּמְחֹקֵק מִבֵּין רַגְלָיו.** תַּלְמִידִים, אֵלּוּ נְשִׂיאֵי אֶרֶץ יִשְׂרָאֵל: **עַד כִּי יָבֹא שִׁילֹה.** מֶלֶךְ הַמָּשִׁיחַ שֶׁהַמְּלוּכָה שֶׁלּוֹ. וְכֵן תִּרְגְּמוֹ אוּנְקְלוֹס. וּמִדְרַשׁ אַגָּדָה, "שִׁילֹה", שַׁי לוֹ, שֶׁנֶּאֱמַר: "יֹבִילוּ שַׁי לַמּוֹרָא" (תהלים עו, יב): **וְלוֹ יִקְּהַת עַמִּים.** אֲסֵפַת הָעַמִּים; שֶׁהַיּוּ"ד עִקָּר הִיא בַּיְסוֹד, כְּמוֹ "יִפְעָתֵךְ" (יחזקאל כח, ז; יז), וּפְעָמִים שֶׁנּוֹפֶלֶת מִמֶּנּוּ. וְכַמָּה אוֹתִיּוֹת מְשַׁמְּשׁוֹת בְּלָשׁוֹן זֶה וְהֵם נִקְרָאִים עִקָּר נוֹפֵל, כְּגוֹן נוּ"ן שֶׁל 'נוֹגֵף' וְשֶׁל 'נוֹשֵׁךְ', וְאָלֶ"ף שֶׁבְּ"אַחְוָתִי בְּאָזְנֵיכֶם" (איוב יג, יז) וְשֶׁבְּ"אִבְחַת חֶרֶב" (יחזקאל כא, כ) "אָסוּךְ שָׁמֶן" (מלכים ב' ד, ב); אַף זֶה, "יִקְּהַת עַמִּים", אֲסֵפַת עַמִּים, שֶׁנֶּאֱמַר: "אֵלָיו גּוֹיִם יִדְרֹשׁוּ" (ישעיה יא, י), וְדוֹמֶה לוֹ: "עַיִן תִּלְעַג לְאָב וְתָבוּז לִיקְּהַת אֵם" (משלי ל, יז), לְקִבּוּץ קְמָטִים שֶׁבְּפָנֶיהָ מִפְּנֵי זִקְנָתָהּ. וּבַתַּלְמוּד: "דְּיָתְבֵי וּמַקְהוּ אַקְהָתָא בְּשׁוּקֵי דִּנְהַרְדְּעָא" בְּמַסֶּכֶת יְבָמוֹת (דף קי ע"ב). וְיָכוֹל הָיָה לוֹמַר: 'קְהִיַּת עַמִּים':

יא **אֹסְרִי לַגֶּפֶן עִירֹה.** נִתְנַבֵּא עַל אֶרֶץ יְהוּדָה שֶׁתְּהֵא מוֹשֶׁכֶת יַיִן כְּמַעְיָן, אִישׁ יְהוּדָה יֶאֱסֹר לַגֶּפֶן עַיִר אֶחָד וְיִטְעָנֶנּוּ מִגֶּפֶן אַחַת, וּמִשֹּׂרֵק אֶחָד בֶּן אָתוֹן אֶחָד: **שֹׂרֵקָה.** זְמוֹרָה אֲרֻכָּה, קורייד"א בְּלַעַז: **כִּבֵּס בַּיַּיִן.** כָּל זֶה לְשׁוֹן רִבּוּי יַיִן: **סוּתֹה.** לְשׁוֹן מִין בֶּגֶד הוּא, וְאֵין לוֹ דִּמְיוֹן בַּמִּקְרָא: **אֹסְרִי.** כְּמוֹ אוֹסֵר, דֻּגְמַת: "מְקִימִי מֵעָפָר דָּל" (תהלים קיג, ז), "הַיֹּשְׁבִי בַּשָּׁמָיִם" (שם קכג, א), וְכֵן "בְּנִי אֲתֹנוֹ" כְּעִנְיָן זֶה. וְאוּנְקְלוֹס תִּרְגֵּם בְּמֶלֶךְ הַמָּשִׁיחַ: "גֶּפֶן" הֵם יִשְׂרָאֵל, "עִירֹה" זוֹ יְרוּשָׁלַיִם, "שֹׂרֵקָה" – יִשְׂרָאֵל, "וְאָנֹכִי נְטַעְתִּיךְ שׂוֹרֵק" (ירמיה ב, כא), "בְּנִי אֲתֹנוֹ" – "יִבְנוּן הֵיכְלֵיהּ", לְשׁוֹן "שַׁעַר הָאִיתוֹן" בְּסֵפֶר יְחֶזְקֵאל (מ, טו). וְעוֹד תִּרְגְּמוֹ בְּפָנִים אֲחֵרִים: "גֶּפֶן" אֵלּוּ צַדִּיקִים, "בְּנֵי אֲתֹנוֹ" – "עָבְדֵי אוֹרָיְתָא בְּאוּלְפַן", עַל שֵׁם "רֹכְבֵי אֲתֹנוֹת צְחֹרוֹת" (שופטים ה, י), "כִּבֵּס בַּיַּיִן" – "יְהֵא אַרְגְּוָן טָב לִבְוּשׁוֹהִי", שֶׁצִּבְעוֹ דּוֹמֶה לְיַיִן. "וּצְבִעוֹנִין" הוּא לְשׁוֹן "סוּתֹה", שֶׁהָאִשָּׁה לוֹבַשְׁתָּן וּמְסִיתָה בָּהֶן אֶת הַזָּכָר לָתֵת עֵינָיו בָּהּ. וְאַף רַבּוֹתֵינוּ פֵּרְשׁוּ בַּתַּלְמוּד לְשׁוֹן הֲסָתַת שִׁכְרוּת, בְּמַסֶּכֶת כְּתֻבּוֹת (דף קיא ע"ב). וְעַל הַיַּיִן שֶׁמָּא תֹּאמַר אֵינוֹ מַרְוֶה, תַּלְמוּד לוֹמַר: "סוּתֹה":

יב **חַכְלִילִי.** לְשׁוֹן אֹדֶם, כְּתַרְגּוּמוֹ. וְכֵן: "לְמִי חַכְלִלוּת עֵינָיִם" (משלי כג,

ז אָר֤וּר אַפָּם֙ כִּ֣י עָ֔ז וְעֶבְרָתָ֖ם כִּ֣י קָשָׁ֑תָה אֲחַלְּקֵ֣ם בְּיַעֲקֹ֔ב וַאֲפִיצֵ֖ם
בְּיִשְׂרָאֵֽל׃
ח יְהוּדָ֗ה אַתָּה֙ יוֹד֣וּךָ אַחֶ֔יךָ יָדְךָ֖ בְּעֹ֣רֶף אֹיְבֶ֑יךָ יִשְׁתַּחֲוּ֥וּ לְךָ֖ בְּנֵ֥י אָבִֽיךָ׃
ט גּ֤וּר אַרְיֵה֙ יְהוּדָ֔ה מִטֶּ֖רֶף בְּנִ֣י עָלִ֑יתָ כָּרַ֨ע רָבַ֧ץ כְּאַרְיֵ֛ה וּכְלָבִ֖יא מִ֥י
י יְקִימֶֽנּוּ׃ לֹֽא־יָס֥וּר שֵׁ֙בֶט֙ מִֽיהוּדָ֔ה וּמְחֹקֵ֖ק מִבֵּ֣ין רַגְלָ֑יו עַ֚ד כִּֽי־יָבֹ֣א
יא שִׁילֹ֔ה וְל֖וֹ יִקְּהַ֥ת עַמִּֽים׃ אֹסְרִ֤י לַגֶּ֙פֶן֙ עִירֹ֔ה וְלַשֹּׂרֵקָ֖ה בְּנִ֣י אֲתֹנ֑וֹ כִּבֵּ֤ס
יב בַּיַּ֙יִן֙ לְבֻשׁ֔וֹ וּבְדַם־עֲנָבִ֖ים סוּתֹֽה׃ חַכְלִילִ֥י עֵינַ֖יִם מִיָּ֑יִן וּלְבֶן־שִׁנַּ֖יִם
מֵחָלָֽב׃

אונקלוס

ז לֵיט רֻגְזְהוֹן אֲרֵי תַקִּיף, וְחֵימַתְהוֹן אֲרֵי קַשְׁיָא, אֲפַלֵּיגְנוּן בְּיַעֲקֹב, וַאֲבַדְּרִנּוּן בְּיִשְׂרָאֵל: ח יְהוּדָה, אַתְּ אוֹדִיתָא וְלָא בְהֵיתְתָא בָּךְ יוֹדוּן אַחָךְ, יְדָךְ תִּתְקַף עַל בַּעֲלֵי דְבָבָךְ יִתַּבְרוּן סָנְאָךְ, יְהוֹן מְחַזְרֵי קְדָל קֳדָמָךְ, יְהוֹן מַקְדְּמִין לְמִשְׁאַל בִּשְׁלָמָךְ בְּנֵי אֲבוּךְ: ט שִׁלְטוֹן יְהֵי בְשֵׁירוּיָא וּבְסוֹפָא יִתְרַבָּא מַלְכָּא מִדְּבֵית יְהוּדָה, אֲרֵי מִדִּין קַטְלָא בְּרִי נַפְשָׁךְ סַלֵּיקְתָּא, יְנוּחַ יִשְׁרֵי בִּתְקוֹף כְּאַרְיָא, וּכְלֵיתָא וְלֵית מַלְכוּ דִּתְזַעְזְעִנֵּיהּ: י לָא יִעְדֵּי עָבֵיד שֻׁלְטָן מִדְּבֵית יְהוּדָה, וְסָפְרָא מִבְּנֵי בְנוֹהִי עַד עָלְמָא, עַד דְּיֵיתֵי מְשִׁיחָא דְּדִילֵיהּ הִיא מַלְכוּתָא, וְלֵיהּ יִשְׁתַּמְעוּן עַמְמַיָּא: יא יַסְחַר יִשְׂרָאֵל לְקַרְתֵּיהּ עַמָּא יִבְנוּן הֵיכְלֵיהּ, יְהוֹן צַדִּיקַיָּא סְחוֹר סְחוֹר לֵיהּ וְעָבְדֵי אוֹרָיְתָא בְּאֻלְפַן עִמֵּיהּ, יְהֵי אַרְגְּוָן טָב לְבוּשֵׁיהּ, וּכְסוּתֵיהּ מֵילָא מֵילָא צְבַע זְהוֹרִי וְצִבְעֲנִין: יב יִסְמְקוּן טוּרוֹהִי בְּכַרְמוֹהִי יְטוּפוּן נַעֲווֹהִי בַּחֲמַר, יְחִוְרָן בִּקְעָתֵיהּ בַּעֲבוּר וּבְעֶדְרֵי עָנֵיהּ:

49:12 **חַכְלִילִי עֵינַיִם מִיָּיִן וּלְבֶן־שִׁנַּיִם מֵחָלָב** *His eyes are darker than wine, and his teeth whiter than milk* – As we have noted before with regard to Yehuda, "Where penitents stand even the perfectly righteous cannot stand" (Berakhot 34b; see comment on 38:26). The Talmud brings a prooftext from Isaiah for this principle: "Peace, peace, to those far away and near" (Is. 57:19), placing the far (the penitent sinner) before the near (the perfectly righteous). However, almost certainly the real source is here in the story of Yosef and Yehuda.

Perhaps Yehuda's future was already implicit in his name, for though the verb *lehodot* from which it is derived means "to thank," it is also related to the verb *lehitvadot*, which means "to admit" or "to confess" – and confession is, according to Rambam, the core of the command to repent.

Leaders make mistakes. That is an occupational hazard of the role. Managers follow the rules, but leaders find themselves in situations for which there are no rules. What is more, leaders are also human, and their mistakes often have nothing to do with leadership and everything to do with human weakness and temptation. Does the misconduct of leaders affect our judgment of them as leaders or not? Judaism suggests it should. The prophet Natan was unsparing in his criticism of King David for consorting with another man's wife. But Judaism also takes note of what happens next.

What matters, suggests the Torah, is that you repent – you recognize and admit your wrongdoings, and you change as a result. As Rabbi Joseph B. Soloveitchik pointed out, both Sha'ul and David, Israel's first two kings, sinned. Both were reprimanded by a prophet. Both said *ḥatati*, "I have sinned" (I Sam. 15:24; II Sam. 12:13). But their fates were radically different. Sha'ul lost the throne; David did not. The reason, said Rabbi Soloveitchik, was that David confessed immediately. Sha'ul prevaricated and made excuses before admitting his sin (*Kol Dodi Dofek*, 26). Yehuda takes ownership of his darker side. Ultimately this is what makes him "like a lion," full of strength that he can choose to harness for the good.

13 Zevulun will live by the seashore; he will be a haven for ships. To Sidon his
border will reach.
14 15 Yissakhar is a strong-boned donkey, lying down among the sheep pens. Seeing
how good is his resting place, and how pleasant is the land, he will bend his
16 shoulder to the load, and work like a slave in harness. Dan will seek
17 justice for his people as one of Israel's tribes. Dan: a snake by the roadside, a
viper upon the path that bites the horse's heel, so that its rider falls backward.
18 19 I wait for Your salvation, LORD. Gad will be raided by raiders, but he ḤAMISHI
20 then will raid at their heels. From Asher will come rich food, he will
21 proffer the king's delights. Naftali is a deer set free, bearing loveliest
22 fawns. Yosef is a fruitful vine, a fruitful vine by a spring, whose
23 branches spread over a wall. Archers attacked him with bitterness, shot at him,

רש״י

כט), שֶׁכֵּן דֶּרֶךְ שׁוֹתֵי יַיִן עֵינֵיהֶם מַאֲדִימִין: **מֵחָלָב.** מֵרֹב חָלָב, שֶׁיְּהֵא בְּאַרְצוֹ מִרְעֶה טוֹב לְעֶדְרֵי צֹאן, וְכֵן פֵּרוּשׁ הַמִּקְרָא: אָדֹם עֵינַיִם יְהֵא מֵרֹב יַיִן, וּלְבֶן שִׁנַּיִם יְהֵא מֵרֹב חָלָב. וּלְפִי תַּרְגּוּמוֹ: "עֵינַיִם" לְשׁוֹן הָרִים, שֶׁמִּשָּׁם צוֹפִים לְמֵרָחוֹק. וְעוֹד תִּרְגְּמוֹ בְּפָנִים אֲחֵרִים, לְשׁוֹן מַעְיָנוֹת וְקִלּוּחַ הַיְּקָבִים: "נַעֲווֹהִי", יְקָבִים שֶׁלּוֹ, וְלָשׁוֹן אֲרַמִּי הוּא בְּמַסֶּכֶת עֲבוֹדָה זָרָה (דף עד ע״ב): "נַעֲוָא חַרְתָּאוּ". "יַחְוְרָן בְּקִעְתֵיהּ" – תַּרְגּוּם "שִׁנַּיִם", לְשׁוֹן "שֵׁנֵי הַסְּלָעִים" (שמואל א׳ יד, ד):

יג) **לְחוֹף יַמִּים.** עַל חוֹף יַמִּים תִּהְיֶה אַרְצוֹ. "חוֹף" כְּתַרְגּוּמוֹ "סְפַר", מרק״א בְּלַעַז. וְהוּא יִהְיֶה מָצוּי תָּדִיר אֶל חוֹף אֳנִיּוֹת, בִּמְקוֹם הַנָּמֵל שֶׁאֳנִיּוֹת מְבִיאוֹת שָׁם פְּרַקְמַטְיָא, שֶׁהָיָה זְבוּלוּן עוֹסֵק בִּפְרַקְמַטְיָא וּמַמְצִיא מָזוֹן לְשֵׁבֶט יִשָּׂשכָר, וְהֵם עוֹסְקִים בַּתּוֹרָה. הוּא שֶׁאָמַר מֹשֶׁה: "שְׂמַח זְבוּלֻן בְּצֵאתֶךָ וְיִשָּׂשכָר בְּאֹהָלֶיךָ" (דברים לג, יח), זְבוּלוּן יוֹצֵא בִּפְרַקְמַטְיָא וְיִשָּׂשכָר עוֹסֵק בַּתּוֹרָה בְּאֹהָלִים: **וְיַרְכָתוֹ עַל צִידֹן.** סוֹף גְּבוּלוֹ יִהְיֶה סָמוּךְ לְצִידוֹן. "יַרְכָתוֹ" – סוֹפוֹ, כְּמוֹ: "וּלְיַרְכְּתֵי הַמִּשְׁכָּן" (שמות כו, כב):

יד) **יִשָּׂשכָר חֲמֹר גָּרֶם.** חֲמוֹר בַּעַל עֲצָמוֹת, סוֹבֵל עֹל תּוֹרָה כַּחֲמוֹר חָזָק שֶׁמַּטְעִינִין אוֹתוֹ מַשָּׂא כָּבֵד: **רֹבֵץ בֵּין הַמִּשְׁפְּתָיִם.** כַּחֲמוֹר הַמְהַלֵּךְ בַּיּוֹם וּבַלַּיְלָה וְאֵין לוֹ לִינָה בַּבַּיִת, וּכְשֶׁהוּא רוֹבֵץ לָנוּחַ רוֹבֵץ בֵּין הַתְּחוּמִין, בִּתְחוּמֵי הָעֲיָרוֹת שֶׁמּוֹלִיךְ שָׁם חֲבִילוֹת שֶׁל פְּרַקְמַטְיָא:

טו) **וַיַּרְא מְנֻחָה כִּי טוֹב.** רָאָה לְחֶלְקוֹ אֶרֶץ מְבֹרֶכֶת וְטוֹבָה לְהוֹצִיא פֵּרוֹת: **וַיֵּט שִׁכְמוֹ לִסְבֹּל.** עֹל תּוֹרָה: **וַיְהִי.** לְכָל אֶחָיו יִשְׂרָאֵל "לְמַס עֹבֵד" – לִסְפֹּק לָהֶם הוֹרָאוֹת שֶׁל תּוֹרָה וְסִדְרֵי עִבּוּרִין, שֶׁנֶּאֱמַר: "וּמִבְּנֵי יִשָּׂשכָר יוֹדְעֵי בִינָה לַעִתִּים לָדַעַת מַה יַּעֲשֶׂה יִשְׂרָאֵל, רָאשֵׁיהֶם מָאתַיִם", מָאתַיִם סַנְהֶדְרָאוֹת הֶעֱמִיד, "וְכָל אֲחֵיהֶם עַל פִּיהֶם" (דברי הימים א׳ יב, לג): **וַיֵּט שִׁכְמוֹ.** הִשְׁפִּיל שִׁכְמוֹ, כְּמוֹ: "וַיֵּט שָׁמַיִם" (שמואל ב׳ כב, י), "הַטּוּ אָזְנְכֶם" (תהלים עח, א). וְאוּנְקְלוֹס תִּרְגְּמוֹ בְּפָנִים אֲחֵרִים: וַיֵּט שִׁכְמוֹ לִסְבֹּל מִלְחָמוֹת וְלִכְבֹּשׁ מְחוֹזוֹת, שֶׁהֵם יוֹשְׁבִים עַל הַסְּפָר, וַיְהִי הָאוֹיֵב כָּבוּשׁ תַּחְתָּיו לְמַס עֹבֵד:

טז) **דָּן יָדִין עַמּוֹ.** יִנְקֹם נִקְמַת עַמּוֹ מִפְּלִשְׁתִּים, כְּמוֹ: "כִּי יָדִין ה׳ עַמּוֹ" (דברים לב, לו): **כְּאַחַד שִׁבְטֵי יִשְׂרָאֵל.** כָּל יִשְׂרָאֵל יִהְיוּ כְּאֶחָד עִמּוֹ וְאֶת כֻּלָּם יָדִין, וְעַל שִׁמְשׁוֹן נִבָּא נְבוּאָה זוֹ. וְעוֹד יֵשׁ לְפָרֵשׁ, "כְּאַחַד שִׁבְטֵי יִשְׂרָאֵל", כַּמְיֻחָד שֶׁבַּשְּׁבָטִים, הוּא דָּוִד שֶׁבָּא מִיהוּדָה:

יז) **שְׁפִיפֹן.** הוּא נָחָשׁ, וְאוֹמֵר אֲנִי שֶׁקָּרוּי כֵּן עַל שֵׁם שֶׁהוּא נוֹשֵׁף, "וְאַתָּה תְּשׁוּפֶנּוּ עָקֵב" (לעיל ג, טו): **הַנֹּשֵׁךְ עִקְּבֵי סוּס.** כָּךְ דַּרְכּוֹ שֶׁל נָחָשׁ. וְדִמָּהוּ לְנָחָשׁ "הַנֹּשֵׁךְ עִקְּבֵי סוּס וַיִּפֹּל רֹכְבוֹ אָחוֹר", שֶׁלֹּא נָגַע בּוֹ, וְדֻגְמָתוֹ מָצִינוּ בְּשִׁמְשׁוֹן: "וַיִּלְפֹּת וְגוֹ׳ אֶת שְׁנֵי עַמּוּדֵי הַתָּוֶךְ" וְגוֹ׳ (שופטים טז, כט), וְשֶׁעַל הַגַּג מֵתוּ. וְאוּנְקְלוֹס תִּרְגֵּם: "כְּחִוֵי חוּרְמָן", שֵׁם מִין נָחָשׁ שֶׁאֵין רְפוּאָה לִנְשִׁיכָתוֹ וְהוּא צִפְעוֹנִי, וְקָרוּי חוּרְמָן עַל שֵׁם שֶׁעוֹשֶׂה הַכֹּל חֵרֶם, "וּכְפִתְנָא" כְּמוֹ פֶּתֶן, "יִכְמוֹן" – יֶאֱרֹב:

יח) **לִישׁוּעָתְךָ קִוִּיתִי ה׳.** נִתְנַבֵּא שֶׁיְּנַקְּרוּ פְּלִשְׁתִּים אֶת עֵינָיו, וְסוֹפוֹ לוֹמַר: "זָכְרֵנִי נָא וְחַזְּקֵנִי נָא אַךְ הַפַּעַם" וְגוֹ׳ (שם טז, כח):

יט) **גָּד גְּדוּד יְגוּדֶנּוּ.** גְּדוּדִים יָגוּדוּ הֵימֶנּוּ, שֶׁיַּעַבְרוּ אֶת הַיַּרְדֵּן עִם אֲחֵיהֶם לַמִּלְחָמָה כָּל חָלוּץ עַד וְנִכְבְּשָׁה הָאָרֶץ (עיין במדבר פרק לב): **וְהוּא יָגֻד עָקֵב.** כָּל גְּדוּדָיו יָשׁוּבוּ עַל עֲקֵבָם לְנַחֲלָתָם שֶׁלָּקְחוּ בְּעֵבֶר הַיַּרְדֵּן, וְלֹא יִפָּקֵד מֵהֶם אִישׁ: **עָקֵב.** בִּדְרָכָם וּבִמְסִלּוֹתָם שֶׁהָלְכוּ יָשׁוּבוּ, כְּמוֹ: "וְעִקְּבוֹתֶיךָ לֹא נֹדָעוּ" (תהלים עז, כ), וְכֵן: "בְּעִקְבֵי הַצֹּאן" (שיר השירים א, ח), בִּלְשׁוֹן לַעַז טרא״צי״ש:

כ) **מֵאָשֵׁר שְׁמֵנָה לַחְמוֹ.** מַאֲכָל הַבָּא מֵחֶלְקוֹ שֶׁל אָשֵׁר יְהֵא שָׁמֵן, שֶׁיִּהְיוּ זֵיתִים מְרֻבִּים בְּחֶלְקוֹ וְהוּא מוֹשֵׁךְ שֶׁמֶן כְּמַעְיָן. וְכֵן בֵּרְכוֹ מֹשֶׁה: "וְטֹבֵל בַּשֶּׁמֶן רַגְלוֹ" (דברים לג, כד), כְּמוֹ שֶׁשָּׁנִינוּ בִּמְנָחוֹת: פַּעַם אַחַת נִצְטָרְכוּ אַנְשֵׁי לוּדְקִיָא לְשֶׁמֶן וְכוּ׳ (מנחות פה ע״ב):

כא) **אַיָּלָה שְׁלֻחָה.** זוֹ בִּקְעַת גִּנּוֹסַר, שֶׁהִיא קַלָּה לְבַשֵּׁל פֵּרוֹתֶיהָ כְּאַיָּלָה זוֹ שֶׁהִיא קַלָּה לָרוּץ. "אַיָּלָה שְׁלֻחָה" – אַיָּלָה מְשֻׁלַּחַת לָרוּץ: **הַנֹּתֵן אִמְרֵי שָׁפֶר.** כְּתַרְגּוּמוֹ. דָּבָר אַחֵר, עַל מִלְחֶמֶת סִיסְרָא נִתְנַבֵּא: "וְלָקַחְתָּ עִמְּךָ

יג זְבוּלֻן לְחוֹף יַמִּים יִשְׁכֹּן וְהוּא לְחוֹף אֳנִיֹּת וְיַרְכָתוֹ עַל־צִידֹן׃
יד טו יִשָּׂשכָר חֲמֹר גָּרֶם רֹבֵץ בֵּין הַמִּשְׁפְּתָיִם׃ וַיַּרְא מְנֻחָה כִּי טוֹב וְאֶת־הָאָרֶץ
טז כִּי נָעֵמָה וַיֵּט שִׁכְמוֹ לִסְבֹּל וַיְהִי לְמַס־עֹבֵד׃ דָּן
יז יָדִין עַמּוֹ כְּאַחַד שִׁבְטֵי יִשְׂרָאֵל׃ יְהִי־דָן נָחָשׁ עֲלֵי־דֶרֶךְ שְׁפִיפֹן
יח עֲלֵי־אֹרַח הַנֹּשֵׁךְ עִקְּבֵי־סוּס וַיִּפֹּל רֹכְבוֹ אָחוֹר׃ לִישׁוּעָתְךָ קִוִּיתִי
יט כ יְהוָה׃ גָּד גְּדוּד יְגוּדֶנּוּ וְהוּא יָגֻד עָקֵב׃ מֵאָשֵׁר חמישי
כא שְׁמֵנָה לַחְמוֹ וְהוּא יִתֵּן מַעֲדַנֵּי־מֶלֶךְ׃ נַפְתָּלִי אַיָּלָה
כב שְׁלֻחָה הַנֹּתֵן אִמְרֵי־שָׁפֶר׃ בֵּן פֹּרָת יוֹסֵף בֵּן פֹּרָת
כג עֲלֵי־עָיִן בָּנוֹת צָעֲדָה עֲלֵי־שׁוּר׃ וַיְמָרְרֻהוּ וָרֹבּוּ וַיִּשְׂטְמֻהוּ בַּעֲלֵי

אונקלוס

יג **זְבוּלוּן**, עַל סְפַר יַמְמַיָּא יִשְׁרֵי, וְהוּא יְכַבֵּישׁ מְחוֹזִין בִּסְפִינָן, וְטוּב יַמָּא יֵיכוֹל, וּתְחוּמֵיהּ יְהֵי מְטֵי עַד צִידוֹן: יד **יִשָּׂשכָר** עַתִּיר בְּנִכְסִין, אַחְסַנְתֵּיהּ בֵּין תְּחוּמַיָּא: טו **וַחֲזָא חוּלָקָא אֲרֵי טָב**, **וְיָת אַרְעָא אֲרֵי** מַעְבְּדָא פֵּירִין, וִיכַבֵּישׁ מָחוֹזֵי עַמְמַיָּא וִישֵׁיצֵי יָת דָּיְרֵיהוֹן, וּדְיִשְׁתַּאֲרוּן בְּהוֹן יְהוֹן לֵיהּ פָּלְחִין וּמַסְּקֵי מִסִּין: טז מִדְּבֵית **דָּן** יִתְבְּחַר וִיקוּם גֻּבְרָא, בְּיוֹמוֹהִי יִתְפְּרֵיק עַמֵּיהּ, וּבִשְׁנוֹהִי יְנוּחוּן כַּחֲדָא **שִׁבְטַיָּא דְיִשְׂרָאֵל**: יז **יְהֵי** גֻּבְרָא דְּיִתְבְּחַר וִיקוּם מִדְּבֵית **דָּן**, אֵימְתֵיהּ תִּתְרְמֵי עַל עַמְמַיָּא וּמַחְתֵּיהּ תִּתַּקַּף בִּפְלִשְׁתָּאֵי, כְּחִוֵי חֻרְמָן יִשְׁרֵי עַל אוֹרְחָא וּכְפִתְנָא יִכְמוֹן עַל שְׁבִילָא, יְקַטֵּיל גִּבָּרֵי מַשְׁרִיַת פְּלִשְׁתָּאֵי פָּרָשִׁין עִם רִגְלָאִין, יְעַקַּר סוּסָוָן וּרְתִכִּין, וְיִמְגַּר רָכְבֵיהוֹן לַאֲחֲרָא: יח **לְפֻרְקָנָךְ סַבָּרִית יי**: יט **דְּבֵית גָּד** מַשְׁרְיָת מְזָיְנִין, כַּד יְעִבְרוּן יָת יַרְדְּנָא קֳדָם אֲחֵיהוֹן לִקְרָבָא, וּבְנִכְסִין סַגִּיאִין יְתוּבוּן לְאַרְעֲהוֹן: כ **דְּאָשֵׁר טָבָא** אַרְעֵיהּ, **וְהִיא** מַרְבְּיָא תַּפְנְקֵי מַלְכִין: כא **נַפְתָּלִי** בַּאֲרַע טָבָא יִתְרְמֵי עַדְבֵיהּ, אַחְסַנְתֵּיהּ תְּהֵי מַעְבְּדָא פֵּירִין, יְהוֹן מוֹדַן וּמְבָרְכִין עֲלֵיהוֹן: כב **בְּרִי דְיִסְגֵּי יוֹסֵף בְּרִי** דְּיִתְבָּרַךְ, כְּגוּפַן דִּנְצִיב **עַל עֵינָא דְמַיָּא**, תְּרֵין שִׁבְטִין יִפְּקוּן מִבְּנוֹהִי, יְקַבְּלוּן חוּלָקָא וְאַחְסַנְתָּא: כג **וְאִתְמָרְרוּ** עִמֵּיהּ וְנַקְמוּהִי, וְאַעִיקוּ לֵיהּ גֻּבְרִין גִּבָּרִין **בַּעֲלֵי**

רש״י

עֲשֶׂרֶת אֲלָפִים אִישׁ מִבְּנֵי נַפְתָּלִי" וְגוֹ' (שופטים ד, ו) וְהָלְכוּ שָׁם בִּזְרִיזוּת. וְכֵן נֶאֱמַר שָׁם לְשׁוֹן שִׁלּוּחַ: "בָּעֵמֶק שֻׁלַּח בְּרַגְלָיו" (שם ה, טו). "הַנֹּתֵן אִמְרֵי שָׁפֶר" – עַל יָדָם שָׁרוּ דְּבוֹרָה וּבָרָק שִׁירָה. וְרַבּוֹתֵינוּ דְּרָשׁוּהוּ עַל יוֹם קְבוּרַת יַעֲקֹב, כְּשֶׁעִרְעֵר עֵשָׂו עַל הַמְּעָרָה, בְּמַסֶּכֶת סוֹטָה (דף יג ע"א). וְתַרְגּוּמוֹ: "יִתְרְמֵי עַדְבֵיהּ", יִפֹּל חֶבְלוֹ, וְהוּא יוֹדֶה עַל חֶלְקוֹ אֲמָרִים נָאִים וָשֶׁבַח:

כב **בֵּן פֹּרָת**. בֶּן חֵן. וְהוּא לְשׁוֹן אֲרַמִּי: "אַפְרִין נִמְטְיֵהּ לְרַבִּי שִׁמְעוֹן" בְּסוֹף בָּבָא מְצִיעָא (דף קיט ע"א): **בֵּן פֹּרָת עֲלֵי עָיִן**. חִנּוֹ נָטוּי עַל הָעַיִן הָרוֹאָה אוֹתוֹ: **בָּנוֹת צָעֲדָה עֲלֵי שׁוּר**. בְּנוֹת מִצְרַיִם הָיוּ צוֹעֲדוֹת עַל הַחוֹמָה לְהִסְתַּכֵּל בְּיָפְיוֹ. "בָּנוֹת" הַרְבֵּה "צָעֲדָה" כָּל אַחַת וְאַחַת בַּמָּקוֹם שֶׁתּוּכַל לִרְאוֹתוֹ מִשָּׁם. דָּבָר אַחֵר, "עֲלֵי שׁוּר", עַל רְאִיָּתוֹ, כְּמוֹ: "אֲשׁוּרֶנּוּ וְלֹא קָרוֹב" (במדבר כד, יז). וּמִדְרְשֵׁי אַגָּדָה יֵשׁ רַבִּים, וְזֶה נוֹטֶה לְיִשּׁוּב הַמִּקְרָא: **פֹּרָת**. תָּי"ו שֶׁבּוֹ הוּא תִּקּוּן הַלָּשׁוֹן, כְּמוֹ: "עַל דִּבְרַת בְּנֵי הָאָדָם" (קהלת ג, יח): **שׁוּר**. כְּמוֹ לָשׁוּר, "עֲלֵי שׁוּר" – בִּשְׁבִיל לָשׁוּר. וְתַרְגּוּם שֶׁל אוּנְקְלוֹס "בָּנוֹת צָעֲדָה עֲלֵי שׁוּר" – "תְּרֵין שִׁבְטִין יִפְּקוּן מִבְּנוֹהִי" וְכוּ', וְכָתַב 'בָּנוֹת' עַל שֵׁם בְּנוֹת מְנַשֶּׁה בְּנוֹת צְלָפְחָד שֶׁנָּטְלוּ חֵלֶק בִּשְׁנֵי עִבְרֵי הַיַּרְדֵּן. "בְּרִי דִּיסְגֵּי יוֹסֵף" – 'פֹּרָת' לְשׁוֹן פְּרִיָּה וּרְבִיָּה. וְיֵשׁ מִדְרְשֵׁי אַגָּדָה הַמִּתְיַשְּׁבִים עַל הַלָּשׁוֹן: בְּשָׁעָה שֶׁבָּא עֵשָׂו לִקְרַאת יַעֲקֹב, בְּכֻלָּן קָדְמוּ הָאִמָּהוֹת לָלֶכֶת לִפְנֵי בְּנֵיהֶן לְהִשְׁתַּחֲווֹת, וּבְרָחֵל כְּתִיב: "וְאַחַר נִגַּשׁ יוֹסֵף וְרָחֵל וַיִּשְׁתַּחֲווּ" (לעיל לג, ז). אָמַר יוֹסֵף: הָרָשָׁע הַזֶּה עֵינוֹ רָמָה, שֶׁמָּא יִתֵּן עֵינָיו בְּאִמִּי. יָצָא לְפָנֶיהָ וְשִׁרְבֵּב קוֹמָתוֹ לְכַסּוֹתָהּ. וְהוּא שֶׁבֵּרְכוֹ אָבִיו: "בֵּן פֹּרָת", הִגְדַּלְתָּ עַצְמְךָ "יוֹסֵף, עֲלֵי עָיִן" שֶׁל עֵשָׂו, לְפִיכָךְ זָכִיתָ לִגְדֻלָּה. "בָּנוֹת צָעֲדָה עֲלֵי שׁוּר", לְהִסְתַּכֵּל בְּךָ בְּצֵאתְךָ עַל מִצְרַיִם. וְעוֹד דְּרָשׁוּהוּ לְעִנְיַן שֶׁלֹּא יִשְׁלֹט בְּזַרְעוֹ עַיִן הָרָע. וְאַף כְּשֶׁבֵּרַךְ מְנַשֶּׁה וְאֶפְרַיִם בֵּרְכָם כַּדָּגִים שֶׁאֵין עַיִן הָרָע שׁוֹלֶטֶת בָּהֶם:

כג **וַיְמָרְרֻהוּ וָרֹבּוּ**. וַיְמָרְרוּהוּ אֶחָיו, וַיְמָרְרוּהוּ פּוֹטִיפַר וְאִשְׁתּוֹ לְאָסְרוֹ, לָשׁוֹן: "וַיְמָרְרוּ אֶת חַיֵּיהֶם" (שמות א, יד): **וָרֹבּוּ**. נַעֲשׂוּ לוֹ אֶחָיו אַנְשֵׁי רִיב.

24 harassed him. But his bow stopped steady, and his arms held firm because of
25 the hand of the Mighty One of Yaakov, the Shepherd, Yisrael's Rock, because
of the God of your father who will help you, because of Shaddai who will
bless you with blessings of heaven above, blessings of the deep that lies under,
26 blessings of breast and of womb. May your father's blessing surpass even the
blessings of my forebears – to the bounds of the everlasting hills. May they rest
on the head of Yosef, on the brow of the elect of his brothers.
27 Binyamin is a ravening wolf, devouring prey in the morning, and by evening SHISHI
28 dividing the plunder." All these are the twelve tribes of Israel, and this is what
their father said to them when he blessed them, giving each his particular

רש״י

וְאֵין הַלָּשׁוֹן הַזֶּה לְשׁוֹן פָּעֲלוּ, שֶׁאִם כֵּן הָיָה לוֹ לִנָּקֵד 'וָרָבוּ', כְּמוֹ: "הֵמָּה מֵי מְרִיבָה אֲשֶׁר רָבוּ" וְגוֹ' (במדבר כ, יג), וְאַף אִם לְשׁוֹן רְבִיַּת חִצִּים הוּא, כֵּן הָיָה לוֹ לִנָּקֵד; וְאֵינוֹ אֶלָּא לְשׁוֹן פֻּעֲלוּ, כְּמוֹ: "שֹׁמּוּ שָׁמַיִם" (ירמיה ב, יב) שֶׁהוּא לְשׁוֹן הוּשַׁמּוּ, וְכֵן: "רוֹמּוּ מְעַט" (איוב כד, כד) שֶׁהוּא לְשׁוֹן הוּרְמוּ, אֶלָּא שֶׁלְּשׁוֹן הוּרְמוּ וְהוּשַׁמּוּ עַל יְדֵי אֲחֵרִים, וּלְשׁוֹן שֹׁמּוּ, רֹמּוּ, רֹבּוּ – מֵאֲלֵיהֶם הוּא, מְשׁוֹמְמִים אֶת עַצְמָם, נִתְרוֹמְמוּ מֵעַצְמָם, נַעֲשׂוּ אַנְשֵׁי רִיב. וְכֵן: "דֹּמּוּ יֹשְׁבֵי אִי" (ישעיה כג, ב) כְּמוֹ נָדַמּוּ. וְכֵן תִּרְגֵּם אוּנְקְלוֹס: "וְנַקְמוּהִי": בַּעֲלֵי חִצִּים. שֶׁלְּשׁוֹנָם כַּחֵץ, וְתַרְגּוּמוֹ לְשׁוֹן "וַתְּהִי הַמֶּחֱצָה" (במדבר לא, לו), אוֹתָן שֶׁהָיוּ רְאוּיִים לַחֲלֹק עִמּוֹ נַחֲלָה:

כד **וַתֵּשֶׁב בְּאֵיתָן קַשְׁתּוֹ.** נִתְיַשְּׁבָה בְּחֹזֶק: קַשְׁתּוֹ. חָזְקוֹ: **וַיָּפֹזּוּ זְרֹעֵי יָדָיו.** זוֹ הִיא נְתִינַת טַבַּעַת עַל יָדוֹ, לְשׁוֹן: "זָהָב מוּפָז" (מלכים א׳ י, יח), זֹאת הָיְתָה לוֹ מִידֵי הַקָּדוֹשׁ בָּרוּךְ הוּא שֶׁהוּא "אֲבִיר יַעֲקֹב", וּמִשָּׁם עָלָה לִהְיוֹת "רֹעֶה אֶבֶן יִשְׂרָאֵל", עִקָּרָן שֶׁל יִשְׂרָאֵל, לְשׁוֹן: "הָאֶבֶן הָרֹאשָׁה" (זכריה ד, ז), לְשׁוֹן מַלְכוּת. וְאוּנְקְלוֹס אַף הוּא כָּךְ תִּרְגְּמוֹ: "וַתֵּשֶׁב" – "וְתָבַת בְּהוֹן נְבִיאוּתֵיהּ", הַחֲלוֹמוֹת אֲשֶׁר חָלַם לָהֶם. "עַל דְּקַיֵּם אוֹרָיְתָא בְּסִתְרָא" – תּוֹסֶפֶת הוּא וְלֹא מִלָּשׁוֹן עִבְרִי שֶׁבַּמִּקְרָא. "וְשַׁוִּי תֻּקְפָּא רוּחְצָנֵיהּ" – תַּרְגּוּם שֶׁל "בְּאֵיתָן קַשְׁתּוֹ". וְכָךְ לְשׁוֹן הַתַּרְגּוּם עַל הָעִבְרִי: וַתֵּשֶׁב נְבוּאָתוֹ בִּשְׁבִיל שֶׁאֵיתָנוֹ שֶׁל הַקָּדוֹשׁ בָּרוּךְ הוּא הָיְתָה לוֹ לְקֶשֶׁת וּלְמִבְטָח, "בְּכֵן אִתְרְמַא דְּהַב" – לְכָךְ "וַיָּפֹזּוּ זְרֹעֵי יָדָיו", לְשׁוֹן 'פָּז': **אֶבֶן יִשְׂרָאֵל.** לְשׁוֹן נוֹטָרִיקוֹן, אָב וּבֵן, "אֲבָהָן וּבְנִין", יַעֲקֹב וּבָנָיו:

כה **מֵאֵל אָבִיךָ.** הָיְתָה לְךָ זֹאת, וְהוּא יַעְזְרֶךָּ: **וְאֵת שַׁדַּי.** וְעִם הַקָּדוֹשׁ בָּרוּךְ הוּא הָיָה לִבְּךָ כְּשֶׁלֹּא שָׁמַעְתָּ לְדִבְרֵי אֲדוֹנָתְךָ, וְהוּא יְבָרְכֶךָּ: **בִּרְכֹת שָׁדַיִם וָרָחַם.** "בִּרְכָתָא דַּאֲבוּךְ וּדְאִמָּךְ", כְּלוֹמַר יִתְבָּרְכוּ הַמּוֹלִידִים וְהַיּוֹלְדוֹת, שֶׁיִּהְיוּ הַזְּכָרִים מַזְרִיעִים טִפָּה הָרְאוּיָה לְהֵרָיוֹן, וְהַנְּקֵבוֹת לֹא יְשַׁכְּלוּ אֶת רֶחֶם שֶׁלָּהֶן לְהַפִּיל עֻבְּרֵיהֶן: **שָׁדַיִם.** "יָרֹה יִיָּרֶה" (שמות יט, יג) מְתַרְגְּמִינַן: "אִשְׁתְּדָאָה יִשְׁתְּדֵי", אַף שָׁדַיִם כָּאן עַל שֵׁם שֶׁהַזֶּרַע יוֹרֶה כַּחֵץ:

כו **בִּרְכֹת אָבִיךָ גָּבְרוּ וְגוֹ'.** הַבְּרָכוֹת שֶׁבֵּרְכַנִי הַקָּדוֹשׁ בָּרוּךְ הוּא גָּבְרוּ עַל הַבְּרָכוֹת שֶׁבֵּרַךְ אֶת הוֹרַי: **עַד תַּאֲוַת גִּבְעֹת עוֹלָם.** לְפִי שֶׁהַבְּרָכוֹת שֶׁלִּי גָּבְרוּ וְהָלְכוּ עַד סוֹף גְּבוּלֵי גִּבְעוֹת עוֹלָם, שֶׁנָּתַן לִי בְּרָכָה פְּרוּצָה בְּלִי מְצָרִים מַגַּעַת עַד אַרְבַּע קְצוֹת הָעוֹלָם, שֶׁנֶּאֱמַר: "וּפָרַצְתָּ יָמָּה וָקֵדְמָה" וְגוֹ' (לעיל כח, יד), מַה שֶּׁלֹּא אָמַר לְאַבְרָהָם אָבִינוּ וּלְיִצְחָק. לְאַבְרָהָם אָמַר לוֹ: "שָׂא נָא עֵינֶיךָ וּרְאֵה... צָפֹנָה וְגוֹ' כִּי אֶת כָּל הָאָרֶץ אֲשֶׁר אַתָּה רֹאֶה לְךָ אֶתְּנֶנָּה" (לעיל יג, יד-טו), וְלֹא הֶרְאָהוּ אֶלָּא אֶרֶץ יִשְׂרָאֵל בִּלְבַד. לְיִצְחָק אָמַר לוֹ: "כִּי לְךָ וּלְזַרְעֲךָ אֶתֵּן אֶת כָּל הָאֲרָצֹת הָאֵל וַהֲקִמֹתִי אֶת הַשְּׁבֻעָה" וְגוֹ' (לעיל כו, ג). וְזֶהוּ שֶׁאָמַר יְשַׁעְיָה: "וְהַאֲכַלְתִּיךָ נַחֲלַת יַעֲקֹב אָבִיךָ" (ישעיה נח, יד) וְלֹא אָמַר 'נַחֲלַת אַבְרָהָם': **הוֹרַי.** לְשׁוֹן הֵרָיוֹן, שֶׁהוֹרוּנִי בִּמְעֵי אִמִּי, כְּמוֹ "הֹרָה גָבֶר" (איוב ג, ג): **תַּאֲוַת.** אַשְׁמוּל"ץ, כָּךְ חִבְּרוֹ מְנַחֵם בֶּן סָרוּק: **עַד תַּאֲוַת.** עַד קְצוֹת, כְּמוֹ: "וְהִתְאַוִּיתֶם לָכֶם לִגְבוּל קֵדְמָה" (במדבר לד, י), "תְּתָאוּ לְבֹא חֲמָת" (שם פסוק ח): **תִּהְיֶיןָ.** כֻּלָּם "לְרֹאשׁ יוֹסֵף": **נְזִיר אֶחָיו.** "פְּרִישָׁא דַּאֲחוֹהִי", שֶׁנִּבְדַּל מֵאֶחָיו, כְּמוֹ: "וְיִנָּזְרוּ מִקָּדְשֵׁי בְנֵי יִשְׂרָאֵל" (ויקרא כב, ב), "נָזֹרוּ אָחוֹר" (ישעיה א, ד). וְרַבּוֹתֵינוּ דָּרְשׁוּ "וַתֵּשֶׁב בְּאֵיתָן קַשְׁתּוֹ" עַל כְּבִישַׁת יִצְרוֹ בְּאֵשֶׁת אֲדֹנָיו, וְקוֹרֵהוּ 'קֶשֶׁת' עַל שֵׁם שֶׁהַזֶּרַע יוֹרֶה כַּחֵץ. "וַיָּפֹזּוּ זְרֹעֵי יָדָיו", כְּמוֹ וַיָּפֹצוּ, שֶׁיָּצָא הַזֶּרַע מִבֵּין אֶצְבְּעוֹת יָדָיו. "מִידֵי אֲבִיר יַעֲקֹב", שֶׁנִּרְאֲתָה לוֹ דְּמוּת דְּיוֹקְנוֹ שֶׁל אָבִיו בַּחַלּוֹן וְכוּ', כִּדְאִיתָא בְּמַסֶּכֶת סוֹטָה (דף לו ע״ב). וְאוּנְקְלוֹס תִּרְגֵּם "תַּאֲוַת גִּבְעֹת עוֹלָם" לְשׁוֹן תַּאֲוָה וְחֶמְדָּה, וְ'גִבְעוֹת' לְשׁוֹן "מְצֻקֵי אֶרֶץ" (שמואל א׳ ב, ח) שֶׁאֲהָבָתַן אִמּוֹ וְהִזְקִיקַתּוּ לְקַבְּלָם:

כז **בִּנְיָמִין זְאֵב יִטְרָף.** זְאֵב הוּא אֲשֶׁר יִטְרֹף, נִבָּא עַל שֶׁהָיוּ עֲתִידִין לִהְיוֹת חַטְפָנִין, "וַחֲטַפְתֶּם לָכֶם אִישׁ אִשְׁתּוֹ" בְּפִילֶגֶשׁ בְּגִבְעָה (שופטים כא, כא). וְנִבָּא עַל שָׁאוּל שֶׁהָיָה נוֹצֵחַ בְּאוֹיְבָיו סָבִיב, שֶׁנֶּאֱמַר: "וְשָׁאוּל לָכַד הַמְּלוּכָה... וַיִּלָּחֶם... בְּמוֹאָב... וּבֶאֱדוֹם וְגוֹ' וּבְכֹל אֲשֶׁר יִפְנֶה יַרְשִׁיעַ" (שמואל א׳ יד, מז): **בַּבֹּקֶר יֹאכַל עַד.** לְשׁוֹן בִּזָּה וְשָׁלָל הַמְתֻרְגָּם: 'עֲדָאָה'. וְעוֹד יֵשׁ לוֹ דּוֹמֶה בְּלָשׁוֹן עִבְרִית: "אָז חֻלַּק עַד שָׁלָל" (ישעיה לג, כג), וְעַל שָׁאוּל הוּא אוֹמֵר, שֶׁעָמַד בִּתְחִלַּת בָּקְרָן וּזְרִיחָתָן שֶׁל יִשְׂרָאֵל: **וְלָעֶרֶב**

כד חִצִּים: וַתֵּשֶׁב בְּאֵיתָן קַשְׁתּוֹ וַיָּפֹזּוּ זְרֹעֵי יָדָיו מִידֵי אֲבִיר יַעֲקֹב מִשָּׁם
כה רֹעֶה אֶבֶן יִשְׂרָאֵל: מֵאֵל אָבִיךָ וְיַעְזְרֶךָּ וְאֵת שַׁדַּי וִיבָרְכֶךָּ בִּרְכֹת
כו שָׁמַיִם מֵעָל בִּרְכֹת תְּהוֹם רֹבֶצֶת תָּחַת בִּרְכֹת שָׁדַיִם וָרָחַם: בִּרְכֹת
אָבִיךָ גָּבְרוּ עַל־בִּרְכֹת הוֹרַי עַד־תַּאֲוַת גִּבְעֹת עוֹלָם תִּהְיֶיןָ לְרֹאשׁ
יוֹסֵף וּלְקָדְקֹד נְזִיר אֶחָיו:
כז כח בִּנְיָמִין זְאֵב יִטְרָף בַּבֹּקֶר יֹאכַל עַד וְלָעֶרֶב יְחַלֵּק שָׁלָל: כָּל־אֵלֶּה שִׁבְטֵי ששי
יִשְׂרָאֵל שְׁנֵים עָשָׂר וְזֹאת אֲשֶׁר־דִּבֶּר לָהֶם אֲבִיהֶם וַיְבָרֶךְ אוֹתָם אִישׁ

אונקלוס

פַלְגּוּתֵיהּ: כד וְתָבַת בְּהוֹן נְבִיּוּתֵיהּ, עַל דְּקַיֵּים אוֹרָיְתָא בְּסִתְרָא וְשַׁוִּי תֻּקְפָּא רְחַצָנֵיהּ, בְּכֵן אִתְרְמָא דְּהַב עַל דְּרָעוֹהִי אַחְסִין מַלְכוּתָא וּתְקֵיף, דָּא הֲוָת לֵיהּ מִן קֳדָם אֵל תַּקִּיפָא דְּיַעֲקֹב, דִּבְמֵימְרֵיהּ זָן אֲבָהָן וּבְנִין זַרְעָא דְּיִשְׂרָאֵל: כה מֵימַר אֱלָהָא דַּאֲבוּךְ יְהֵי בְּסַעֲדָךְ, וְיָת שַׁדַּי וִיבָרְכִנָּךְ, בִּרְכָן דְּנָחֲתָן מִטַּלָּא דִּשְׁמַיָּא מִלְּעֵילָא, בִּרְכָן דְּנָגְדָן מִמַּעֲמַקֵּי אַרְעָא מִלְּרַע, בִּרְכָתָא דַּאֲבוּךְ וּדְאִמָּךְ: כו בִּרְכָתָא דַּאֲבוּךְ, יִתּוֹסְפָן לָךְ עַל בִּרְכָתָא דִּלִי בָּרִיכוּ אֲבָהָתַי, דְּחַמִּידוּ לְהוֹן רַבְרְבַיָּא דְּמִן עָלְמָא, יְהֶוְיָן כָּל אִלֵּין לְרֵישָׁא דְּיוֹסֵף, גְּבְרָא פְּרִישָׁא דַּאֲחוֹהִי: כז בִּנְיָמִין בְּאַרְעֵיהּ תִּשְׁרֵי שְׁכִינְתָא וּבְאַחְסַנְתֵּיהּ יִתְבְּנֵי מַקְדְּשָׁא, בְּצַפְרָא וּבְפַנְיָא יְהוֹן מְקָרְבִין כָּהֲנַיָּא קֻרְבָּנָא, וּלְעִדַּן רַמְשָׁא יְהוֹן מְפַלְּגִין מוֹתַר חוּלָקְהוֹן מִשְּׁאָר קֻדְשַׁיָּא: כח כָּל אִלֵּין, שִׁבְטַיָּא דְּיִשְׂרָאֵל תְּרֵי עֲסַר, וְדָא דְּמַלֵּיל לְהוֹן אֲבוּהוֹן וּבָרֵיךְ יָתְהוֹן, גְּבַר

רש״י

יְחַלֵּק שָׁלָל. אַף מִשֶּׁתִּשְׁקַע שִׁמְשָׁן שֶׁל יִשְׂרָאֵל עַל יְדֵי נְבוּכַדְנֶאצַּר שֶׁיַּגְלֵם לְבָבֶל, "יְחַלֵּק שָׁלָל" – מָרְדְּכַי וְאֶסְתֵּר שֶׁהֵם מִבִּנְיָמִין יְחַלְּקוּ אֶת שְׁלַל הָמָן, שֶׁנֶּאֱמַר: "הִנֵּה בֵית הָמָן נָתַתִּי לְאֶסְתֵּר" (אסתר ח, ז). וְאוּנְקְלוֹס תִּרְגְּמוֹ עַל חֵלֶק הַכֹּהֲנִים בְּקָדְשֵׁי הַמִּקְדָּשׁ:

כח) וְזֹאת אֲשֶׁר דִּבֶּר לָהֶם אֲבִיהֶם וַיְבָרֶךְ אוֹתָם. וַהֲלֹא יֵשׁ מֵהֶם שֶׁלֹּא בֵּרְכָם אֶלָּא קִנְטְרָן? אֶלָּא כָּךְ פֵּרוּשׁוֹ: "וְזֹאת אֲשֶׁר דִּבֶּר לָהֶם אֲבִיהֶם", מַה שֶּׁאָמוּר בָּעִנְיָן. יָכוֹל שֶׁלֹּא בֵּרַךְ לִרְאוּבֵן שִׁמְעוֹן וְלֵוִי? תַּלְמוּד לוֹמַר: "וַיְבָרֶךְ אוֹתָם", כֻּלָּם בַּמַּשְׁמָע:

49:28 **וַיְבָרֶךְ אוֹתָם אִישׁ אֲשֶׁר כְּבִרְכָתוֹ** *Giving each his particular blessing* – One of the most important tasks of a leader, a parent, or a friend is focused praise. We see this illustrated in Pirkei Avot (2:8), in which Rabban Yoḥanan ben Zakkai enumerates the praises of his five beloved students: Eliezer ben Hyrcanus: a plastered well that never loses a drop; Yehoshua ben Ḥananya: happy is the one who gave him birth; Yosei the Priest: a pious man; Shimon ben Netanel: a man who fears sin; and Elazar ben Arakh: an ever-flowing spring.

It is not difficult to create followers. But how does a teacher encourage these followers to become creative intellects in their own right? It is far harder to create leaders than to create followers. Rabban Yoḥanan ben Zakkai was a great teacher because five of his students became giants in their own right. The Mishna is telling us how he did it: with focused praise. He showed each of his pupils where their particular strength lay.

I discovered the transformative power of focused praise from one of the more remarkable people I ever met, the late Lena Rustin. Lena was a speech therapist, specializing in helping children who struggled with stammers. Lena believed that the young children she was treating – they were, on average, around five years old – had to be understood in the context of their families. Families tend to develop an equilibrium. If a child stammers, everyone in the family adjusts to it. Therefore, if the child is to lose their stammer, all the relationships within the family will have to be renegotiated. Not only must the child change. So must everyone else.

29 blessing. Then he gave them instruction, saying, "I am about to be gathered
to my people. Bury me with my fathers in the cave in the field of Efron the
30 Hittite, the cave in the field of Makhpela near Mamre in Canaan, which
Avraham bought, together with the field, from Efron the Hittite as a burial
31 place. There Avraham and his wife Sara are buried, there Yitzḥak and his wife
32 Rivka are buried, and there I buried Leah. The field and the cave in it were
33 bought from the Hittites." There Yaakov finished instructing his sons. And
he drew his feet back onto the bed, breathed his last, and was gathered to
50 1 his people. Yosef fell on his father's face and wept over him and kissed him.
2 Then Yosef instructed his servants the physicians to embalm his father. So
3 the physicians embalmed Yisrael. It took them forty days; that was the time
4 required for embalming. The Egyptians mourned him for seventy days. When
the period of mourning was over, Yosef spoke to Pharaoh's court: "If I have
5 found favor in your eyes, please speak to Pharaoh on my behalf. Tell him, 'My
father made me swear an oath, saying, "I am about to die. Bury me in the
grave I prepared for myself in the land of Canaan." Now let me go up and
6 bury my father; then I will return.'" Pharaoh said, "Go and bury your father

רש״י

אֲשֶׁר כְּבִרְכָתוֹ. בְּרָכָה הָעֲתִידָה לָבֹא עַל כָּל אֶחָד וְאֶחָד ״בֵּרַךְ אֹתָם״. לֹא הָיָה לוֹ לוֹמַר אֶלָּא ׳אִישׁ אֲשֶׁר כְּבִרְכָתוֹ בֵּרַךְ אֹתוֹ׳, מַה תַּלְמוּד לוֹמַר: ״בֵּרַךְ אֹתָם״? לְפִי שֶׁנָּתַן לִיהוּדָה גְּבוּרַת אֲרִי וּלְבִנְיָמִין חֲטִיפָתוֹ שֶׁל זְאֵב וּלְנַפְתָּלִי קַלּוּתוֹ שֶׁל אַיָּל, יָכוֹל שֶׁלֹּא כְּלָלָן כֻּלָּם בְּכָל הַבְּרָכוֹת? תַּלְמוּד לוֹמַר: ״בֵּרַךְ אֹתָם״:

כט **נֶאֱסָף אֶל עַמִּי.** עַל שֵׁם שֶׁמַּכְנִיסִין הַנְּפָשׁוֹת אֶל מְקוֹם גְּנִיזָתָן, שֶׁיֵּשׁ אֲסִיפוֹת בְּלָשׁוֹן עִבְרִית שֶׁהֵן לְשׁוֹן הַכְנָסָה, כְּגוֹן: ״וְאֵין אִישׁ מְאַסֵּף אוֹתִי הַבָּיְתָה״ (שופטים יט, יח), ״וַאֲסַפְתּוֹ אֶל תּוֹךְ בֵּיתֶךָ״ (דברים כב, ב), ״בְּאָסְפְּכֶם אֶת תְּבוּאַת הָאָרֶץ״ (ויקרא כג, לט) – הַכְנָסָתָהּ לַבַּיִת מִפְּנֵי הַגְּשָׁמִים, ״בְּאָסְפְּךָ אֶת מַעֲשֶׂיךָ״ (שמות כג, טז), וְכָל אֲסִיפָה הָאֲמוּרָה בְּמִיתָה אַף הִיא לְשׁוֹן הַכְנָסָה: **אֶל אֲבֹתָי.** עִם אֲבוֹתַי:

לג **וַיֶּאֱסֹף רַגְלָיו.** הִכְנִיס רַגְלָיו: **וַיִּגְוַע וַיֵּאָסֶף.** וּמִיתָה לֹא נֶאֶמְרָה בּוֹ, וְאָמְרוּ רַבּוֹתֵינוּ: יַעֲקֹב אָבִינוּ לֹא מֵת:

נ ב **לַחֲנֹט אֶת אָבִיו.** עִנְיַן מִרְקַחַת בְּשָׂמִים הוּא:

ג **וַיִּמְלְאוּ לוֹ.** הִשְׁלִימוּ לוֹ יְמֵי חֲנִיטָתוֹ עַד שֶׁמָּלְאוּ לוֹ אַרְבָּעִים יוֹם: **וַיִּבְכּוּ אֹתוֹ מִצְרַיִם שִׁבְעִים יוֹם.** אַרְבָּעִים לַחֲנִיטָה וּשְׁלֹשִׁים לַבֶּכִי, לְפִי שֶׁבָּאָה לָהֶם בְּרָכָה לְרַגְלוֹ, שֶׁכָּלָה הָרָעָב וְהָיוּ מֵי נִילוּס מִתְבָּרְכִין:

ה **אֲשֶׁר כָּרִיתִי לִי.** כִּפְשׁוּטוֹ, כְּמוֹ: ״כִּי יִכְרֶה אִישׁ״ (שמות כא, לג). וּמִדְרָשׁוֹ עוֹד מִתְיַשֵּׁב עַל הַלָּשׁוֹן, כְּמוֹ אֲשֶׁר קָנִיתִי. אָמַר רַבִּי עֲקִיבָא: כְּשֶׁהָלַכְתִּי לִכְרַכֵּי הַיָּם הָיוּ קוֹרִין לִמְכִירָה ׳כִּירָה׳. וְעוֹד מִדְרָשׁוֹ לְשׁוֹן כְּרִי, דְּגוּר; שֶׁנָּטַל יַעֲקֹב כָּל כֶּסֶף וְזָהָב שֶׁהֵבִיא מִבֵּית לָבָן וְעָשָׂה אוֹתוֹ כְּרִי, וְאָמַר לְעֵשָׂו: טֹל זֶה בִּשְׁבִיל חֶלְקְךָ בַּמְּעָרָה:

makes it unthreatening? The answer Lena discovered was praise. She told the families with whom she was working that every day they must notice each member of the family doing something right, and say so – specifically, positively, and thankfully. She was creating, within each home, an atmosphere of mutual regard and continuous positive reinforcement. She wanted the atmosphere of the home to be one in which people felt safe to change and help others to do so.

Yaakov's deathbed blessings are not without criticism. Nonetheless, he gives each child an emblem for his own particular strength, which even today suffuses Jewish iconography and art and inspires us with the potential he saw in his sons.

כט אֲשֶׁר כְּבִרְכָתוֹ בֵּרַךְ אֹתָם: וַיְצַו אוֹתָם וַיֹּאמֶר אֲלֵהֶם אֲנִי נֶאֱסָף אֶל־
עַמִּי קִבְרוּ אֹתִי אֶל־אֲבֹתָי אֶל־הַמְּעָרָה אֲשֶׁר בִּשְׂדֵה עֶפְרוֹן הַחִתִּי:
ל בַּמְּעָרָה אֲשֶׁר בִּשְׂדֵה הַמַּכְפֵּלָה אֲשֶׁר־עַל־פְּנֵי מַמְרֵא בְּאֶרֶץ כְּנָעַן
אֲשֶׁר קָנָה אַבְרָהָם אֶת־הַשָּׂדֶה מֵאֵת עֶפְרֹן הַחִתִּי לַאֲחֻזַּת־קָבֶר:
לא שָׁמָּה קָבְרוּ אֶת־אַבְרָהָם וְאֵת שָׂרָה אִשְׁתּוֹ שָׁמָּה קָבְרוּ אֶת־יִצְחָק
לב וְאֵת רִבְקָה אִשְׁתּוֹ וְשָׁמָּה קָבַרְתִּי אֶת־לֵאָה: מִקְנֵה הַשָּׂדֶה וְהַמְּעָרָה
לג אֲשֶׁר־בּוֹ מֵאֵת בְּנֵי־חֵת: וַיְכַל יַעֲקֹב לְצַוֺּת אֶת־בָּנָיו וַיֶּאֱסֹף רַגְלָיו
נ א אֶל־הַמִּטָּה וַיִּגְוַע וַיֵּאָסֶף אֶל־עַמָּיו: וַיִּפֹּל יוֹסֵף עַל־פְּנֵי אָבִיו וַיֵּבְךְּ
ב עָלָיו וַיִּשַּׁק־לוֹ: וַיְצַו יוֹסֵף אֶת־עֲבָדָיו אֶת־הָרֹפְאִים לַחֲנֹט אֶת־אָבִיו
ג וַיַּחַנְטוּ הָרֹפְאִים אֶת־יִשְׂרָאֵל: וַיִּמְלְאוּ־לוֹ אַרְבָּעִים יוֹם כִּי כֵּן יִמְלְאוּ
ד יְמֵי הַחֲנֻטִים וַיִּבְכּוּ אֹתוֹ מִצְרַיִם שִׁבְעִים יוֹם: וַיַּעַבְרוּ יְמֵי בְכִיתוֹ
וַיְדַבֵּר יוֹסֵף אֶל־בֵּית פַּרְעֹה לֵאמֹר אִם־נָא מָצָאתִי חֵן בְּעֵינֵיכֶם
ה דַּבְּרוּ־נָא בְּאָזְנֵי פַרְעֹה לֵאמֹר: אָבִי הִשְׁבִּיעַנִי לֵאמֹר הִנֵּה אָנֹכִי מֵת
בְּקִבְרִי אֲשֶׁר כָּרִיתִי לִי בְּאֶרֶץ כְּנַעַן שָׁמָּה תִּקְבְּרֵנִי וְעַתָּה אֶעֱלֶה־נָּא
ו וְאֶקְבְּרָה אֶת־אָבִי וְאָשׁוּבָה: וַיֹּאמֶר פַּרְעֹה עֲלֵה וּקְבֹר אֶת־אָבִיךָ

אונקלוס

כִּבְרִכְתֵיהּ בָּרֵיךְ יָתְהוֹן: כט וּפַקֵּיד יָתְהוֹן, וַאֲמַר לְהוֹן אֲנָא מִתְכְּנֵישׁ לְעַמִּי, קְבַרוּ יָתִי לְוָת אֲבָהָתִי, בִּמְעָרְתָא, דִּבַחֲקַל עֶפְרוֹן חִתָּאָה: ל בִּמְעָרְתָא, דִּבַחֲקַל כָּפֵילְתָא, דְּעַל אַפֵּי מַמְרֵא בְּאַרְעָא דִּכְנָעַן, דִּזְבַן אַבְרָהָם יָת חַקְלָא, מִן עֶפְרוֹן חִתָּאָה לְאַחְסָנַת קְבוּרָא: לא תַּמָּן קְבַרוּ יָת אַבְרָהָם, וְיָת שָׂרָה אִתְּתֵיהּ, תַּמָּן קְבַרוּ יָת יִצְחָק, וְיָת רִבְקָה אִתְּתֵיהּ, וְתַמָּן קְבָרִית יָת לֵאָה: לב זְבִינֵי חַקְלָא, וּמְעָרְתָא דְּבֵיהּ מִן בְּנֵי חִתָּאָה: לג וְשֵׁיצִי יַעֲקֹב לְפַקָּדָא יָת בְּנוֹהִי, וּכְנַשׁ רַגְלוֹהִי לְעַרְסָא, וְאִתְנְגִיד וְאִתְכְּנֵישׁ לְעַמֵּיהּ: נ א וּנְפַל יוֹסֵף עַל אַפֵּי אֲבוּהִי, וּבְכָא עֲלוֹהִי וְנַשֵּׁיק לֵיהּ: ב וּפַקֵּיד יוֹסֵף יָת עַבְדּוֹהִי יָת אָסְוָתָא, לְמִחְנַט יָת אֲבוּהִי, וַחֲנַטוּ אָסְוָתָא יָת יִשְׂרָאֵל: ג וּשְׁלִימוּ לֵיהּ אַרְבְּעִין יוֹמִין, אֲרֵי, כֵּן שָׁלְמִין יוֹמֵי חֲנִיטַיָּא, וּבְכוֹ יָתֵיהּ, מִצְרָאֵי שִׁבְעִין יוֹמִין: ד וַעֲבַרוּ יוֹמֵי בְכִיתֵיהּ, וּמַלֵּיל יוֹסֵף, עִם בֵּית פַּרְעֹה לְמֵימַר, אִם כְּעַן אַשְׁכַּחִית רַחֲמִין בְּעֵינֵיכוֹן, מַלִּילוּ כְעַן, קֳדָם פַּרְעֹה לְמֵימַר: ה אַבָּא קַיֵּים עֲלַי לְמֵימַר, הָא אֲנָא מָאִית, בְּקִבְרִי, דְּאַתְקֵינִית לִי בְּאַרְעָא דִּכְנַעַן, תַּמָּן תִּקְבְּרִנַּנִי, וּכְעַן, אֶסַּק כְּעַן, וְאֶקְבַּר יָת אַבָּא וַאֲתוּב: ו וַאֲמַר פַּרְעֹה, סַק, וּקְבַר יָת אֲבוּךְ

By and large, we tend to resist change. We settle into patterns of behavior as they become more and more comfortable, like a well-used armchair. How do you create an atmosphere within a family that encourages change and

▶

7 as he had you swear." So Yosef went up to bury his father. With him went all
Pharaoh's officials, the elders of his palace, and all the other elders of Egypt,
8 together with all Yosef's household, his brothers, and his father's household. They
9 left only their children and flocks and herds in Goshen. With them too went a
10 chariot brigade and horsemen; it was a very large retinue. When they reached
the threshing floor of Atad, beyond the Jordan, they held a great and solemn
lamentation, and Yosef observed a seven-day period of mourning for his father.
11 When the Canaanites who lived there saw the mourning at the threshing floor of
Atad they said, "Egypt is in deep mourning here"; that is why the place beyond
12 the Jordan was called Avel Mitzrayim. So his sons did as he had instructed them.
13 They carried him to Canaan and buried him in the cave of the field of Makhpela,
near Mamre, which Avraham had bought as a burial site from Efron the Hittite.
14 After burying his father, Yosef returned to Egypt together with his brothers and
15 all those who had accompanied him to his father's burial. When Yosef's brothers
knew that their father was dead, they said, "What if Yosef really hates us and
16 decides to pay us back for all the wrong we did to him?" So they sent word to
17 Yosef saying, "Your father gave these instructions before his death: 'This is

רש"י

ו **כַּאֲשֶׁר הִשְׁבִּיעֶךָ.** וְאִם לֹא בִּשְׁבִיל הַשְּׁבוּעָה לֹא הָיִיתִי מַנִּיחֲךָ. אֲבָל יָרֵא לוֹמַר: עֲבֹר עַל הַשְּׁבוּעָה, שֶׁלֹּא יֹאמַר: אִם כֵּן, אֶעֱבֹר עַל הַשְּׁבוּעָה שֶׁנִּשְׁבַּעְתִּי לְךָ שֶׁלֹּא אֲגַלֶּה עַל לְשׁוֹן הַקֹּדֶשׁ שֶׁאֲנִי מַכִּיר עוֹדֵף עַל שִׁבְעִים לָשׁוֹן וְאַתָּה אֵינְךָ מַכִּיר בּוֹ, כִּדְאִיתָא בְּמַסֶּכֶת סוֹטָה (דף לו ע"ב):

י **גֹּרֶן הָאָטָד.** מֻקָּף אֲטָדִין הָיָה. וְרַבּוֹתֵינוּ דָּרְשׁוּ עַל שֵׁם הַמְּאֹרָע, שֶׁבָּאוּ כָּל מַלְכֵי כְנַעַן וּנְשִׂיאֵי יִשְׁמָעֵאל לַמִּלְחָמָה, וְכֵיוָן שֶׁרָאוּ כִּתְרוֹ שֶׁל יוֹסֵף תָּלוּי בַּאֲרוֹנוֹ שֶׁל יַעֲקֹב, עָמְדוּ כֻּלָּן וְתָלוּ בוֹ כִּתְרֵיהֶם, וְהִקִּיפוּהוּ כְּתָרִים כְּגֹרֶן הַמֻּקָּף סְיָג שֶׁל קוֹצִים:

יב-יג **כַּאֲשֶׁר צִוָּם.** מַהוּ אֲשֶׁר צִוָּם? "וַיִּשְׂאוּ אֹתוֹ בָנָיו" וְלֹא בְּנֵי בָנָיו, שֶׁכָּךְ צִוָּם: אַל יִשְׂאוּ מִטָּתִי לֹא אִישׁ מִצְרִי וְלֹא אֶחָד מִבְּנֵיכֶם, שֶׁהֵם מִבְּנוֹת כְּנַעַן, אֶלָּא אַתֶּם. וְקָבַע לָהֶם מָקוֹם, שְׁלֹשָׁה לַמִּזְרָח, וְכֵן לְאַרְבַּע רוּחוֹת, וּכְסִדְרָן לְמַסַּע מַחֲנֶה שֶׁל דְּגָלִים נִקְבְּעוּ כָּאן; לֵוִי לֹא יִשָּׂא, שֶׁהוּא עָתִיד לָשֵׂאת אֶת הָאָרוֹן, וְיוֹסֵף לֹא יִשָּׂא, שֶׁהוּא מֶלֶךְ, מְנַשֶּׁה וְאֶפְרַיִם יִהְיוּ תַּחְתֵּיהֶם. וְזֶהוּ "אִישׁ עַל דִּגְלוֹ בְאֹתֹת" (במדבר ב, ב) – בָּאוֹת שֶׁמָּסַר לָהֶם אֲבִיהֶם לָשֵׂאת מִטָּתוֹ:

יד **הוּא וְאֶחָיו וְכָל הָעֹלִים אִתּוֹ.** בַּחֲזָרָתָן כָּאן הִקְדִּים אֶחָיו לַמִּצְרִים הָעוֹלִים אִתּוֹ, וּבַהֲלִיכָתָן הִקְדִּים מִצְרִים לְאֶחָיו, שֶׁנֶּאֱמַר: "וַיַּעֲלוּ אִתּוֹ כָּל עַבְדֵי פַרְעֹה" וְגוֹ' וְאַחַר כָּךְ: "וְכֹל בֵּית יוֹסֵף וְאֶחָיו" (לעיל פסוק ז-ח)! אֶלָּא לְפִי שֶׁרָאוּ כָבוֹד שֶׁעָשׂוּ מַלְכֵי כְנַעַן, שֶׁתָּלוּ כִּתְרֵיהֶם בַּאֲרוֹנוֹ שֶׁל יַעֲקֹב, נָהֲגוּ בָהֶם כָּבוֹד:

טו **וַיִּרְאוּ אֲחֵי יוֹסֵף כִּי מֵת אֲבִיהֶם.** מַהוּ "וַיִּרְאוּ"? הִכִּירוּ בְמִיתָתוֹ אֵצֶל יוֹסֵף, שֶׁהָיוּ רְגִילִים לִסְעֹד עַל שֻׁלְחָנוֹ שֶׁל יוֹסֵף וְהָיָה מְקָרְבָן בִּשְׁבִיל כְּבוֹד אָבִיו, וּמִשֶּׁמֵּת יַעֲקֹב לֹא קֵרְבָן: **לוּ יִשְׂטְמֵנוּ.** שֶׁמָּא יִשְׂטְמֵנוּ. 'לוּ' מִתְחַלֵּק לְעִנְיָנִים הַרְבֵּה: יֵשׁ 'לוּ' מְשַׁמֵּשׁ בִּלְשׁוֹן בַּקָּשָׁה וּלְשׁוֹן הַלְוַאי, כְּגוֹן: "לוּ יְהִי כִדְבָרֶךָ" (לעיל ל, לד), "לוּ שְׁמָעֵנִי" (לעיל כג, יג), "וְלוּ הוֹאַלְנוּ" (יהושע ז, ז), "לוּ מַתְנוּ" (במדבר יד, ב); וְיֵשׁ 'לוּ' מְשַׁמֵּשׁ בִּלְשׁוֹן אִם וְאוּלַי, כְּגוֹן: "לוּ חָכְמוּ" (דברים לב, כט), "לוּ הִקְשַׁבְתָּ לְמִצְוֹתָי" (ישעיה מח, יח), "וְלוּ אָנֹכִי שֹׁקֵל עַל כַּפַּי" (שמואל ב' יח, יב); וְיֵשׁ 'לוּ' מְשַׁמֵּשׁ בִּלְשׁוֹן שֶׁמָּא: "לוּ יִשְׂטְמֵנוּ" וְאֵין לוֹ עוֹד דּוֹמֶה בַּמִּקְרָא, וְהוּא לְשׁוֹן אוּלַי, כְּמוֹ: "אֻלַי לֹא תֵלֵךְ הָאִשָּׁה אַחֲרָי" (לעיל כד, לט), לְשׁוֹן שֶׁמָּא הוּא. וְיֵשׁ 'אוּלַי' לְשׁוֹן בַּקָּשָׁה, כְּגוֹן: "אוּלַי יִרְאֶה ה' בְּעֵינִי" (שמואל ב' טז, יב), "אוּלַי ה' אוֹתִי" (יהושע יד, יב), הֲרֵי הוּא כְּמוֹ: "לוּ יְהִי כִדְבָרֶךָ" (לעיל ל, לד); וְיֵשׁ 'אוּלַי' לְשׁוֹן אִם: "אוּלַי יֵשׁ חֲמִשִּׁים צַדִּיקִם" (לעיל יח, כד):

טז **וַיְצַוּוּ אֶל יוֹסֵף.** כְּמוֹ: "וַיְצַוֵּם אֶל בְּנֵי יִשְׂרָאֵל" (שמות ו, יג), צִוָּה לְמֹשֶׁה וּלְאַהֲרֹן לִהְיוֹת שְׁלוּחִים אֶל בְּנֵי יִשְׂרָאֵל, אַף זֶה, וַיְצַוּוּ אֶל שְׁלוּחָם לִהְיוֹת שָׁלִיחַ אֶל יוֹסֵף לוֹמַר לוֹ כֵּן. וְאֶת מִי צִוּוּ? אֶת בְּנֵי בִלְהָה שֶׁהָיוּ רְגִילִין אֶצְלוֹ, שֶׁנֶּאֱמַר: "וְהוּא נַעַר אֶת בְּנֵי בִלְהָה" (לעיל לז, ב): **אָבִיךָ צִוָּה.** שִׁנּוּ בַּדָּבָר מִפְּנֵי הַשָּׁלוֹם, כִּי לֹא צִוָּה יַעֲקֹב כֵּן, שֶׁלֹּא נֶחְשַׁד יוֹסֵף בְּעֵינָיו:

ז כַּאֲשֶׁר הִשְׁבִּיעֶךָ׃ וַיַּעַל יוֹסֵף לִקְבֹּר אֶת־אָבִיו וַיַּעֲלוּ אִתּוֹ כָּל־עַבְדֵי
ח פַרְעֹה זִקְנֵי בֵיתוֹ וְכֹל זִקְנֵי אֶרֶץ־מִצְרָיִם׃ וְכֹל בֵּית יוֹסֵף וְאֶחָיו וּבֵית
ט אָבִיו רַק טַפָּם וְצֹאנָם וּבְקָרָם עָזְבוּ בְּאֶרֶץ גֹּשֶׁן׃ וַיַּעַל עִמּוֹ גַּם־רֶכֶב
י גַּם־פָּרָשִׁים וַיְהִי הַמַּחֲנֶה כָּבֵד מְאֹד׃ וַיָּבֹאוּ עַד־גֹּרֶן הָאָטָד אֲשֶׁר בְּעֵבֶר
הַיַּרְדֵּן וַיִּסְפְּדוּ־שָׁם מִסְפֵּד גָּדוֹל וְכָבֵד מְאֹד וַיַּעַשׂ לְאָבִיו אֵבֶל שִׁבְעַת
יא יָמִים׃ וַיַּרְא יוֹשֵׁב הָאָרֶץ הַכְּנַעֲנִי אֶת־הָאֵבֶל בְּגֹרֶן הָאָטָד וַיֹּאמְרוּ
אֵבֶל־כָּבֵד זֶה לְמִצְרָיִם עַל־כֵּן קָרָא שְׁמָהּ אָבֵל מִצְרַיִם אֲשֶׁר בְּעֵבֶר
יב יג הַיַּרְדֵּן׃ וַיַּעֲשׂוּ בָנָיו לוֹ כֵּן כַּאֲשֶׁר צִוָּם׃ וַיִּשְׂאוּ אֹתוֹ בָנָיו אַרְצָה כְּנַעַן
וַיִּקְבְּרוּ אֹתוֹ בִּמְעָרַת שְׂדֵה הַמַּכְפֵּלָה אֲשֶׁר קָנָה אַבְרָהָם אֶת־הַשָּׂדֶה
יד לַאֲחֻזַּת־קֶבֶר מֵאֵת עֶפְרֹן הַחִתִּי עַל־פְּנֵי מַמְרֵא׃ וַיָּשָׁב יוֹסֵף מִצְרַיְמָה
הוּא וְאֶחָיו וְכָל־הָעֹלִים אִתּוֹ לִקְבֹּר אֶת־אָבִיו אַחֲרֵי קָבְרוֹ אֶת־אָבִיו׃
טו וַיִּרְאוּ אֲחֵי־יוֹסֵף כִּי־מֵת אֲבִיהֶם וַיֹּאמְרוּ לוּ יִשְׂטְמֵנוּ יוֹסֵף וְהָשֵׁב יָשִׁיב
טז לָנוּ אֵת כָּל־הָרָעָה אֲשֶׁר גָּמַלְנוּ אֹתוֹ׃ וַיְצַוּוּ אֶל־יוֹסֵף לֵאמֹר אָבִיךָ
יז צִוָּה לִפְנֵי מוֹתוֹ לֵאמֹר׃ כֹּה־תֹאמְרוּ לְיוֹסֵף אָנָּא שָׂא נָא פֶּשַׁע אַחֶיךָ

אונקלוס

כְּמָא דְקַיֵּים עֲלָךְ: ז וּסְלֵיק יוֹסֵף לְמִקְבַּר יָת אֲבוּהִי, וּסְלִיקוּ עִמֵּיהּ, כָּל עַבְדֵי פַרְעֹה סָבֵי בֵיתֵיהּ, וְכֹל סָבֵי אַרְעָא דְמִצְרָיִם: ח וְכֹל בֵּית יוֹסֵף, וַאֲחוֹהִי וּבֵית אֲבוּהִי, לְחוֹד, טַפְלְהוֹן וְעָנְהוֹן וְתוֹרֵיהוֹן, שְׁבַקוּ בְּאַרְעָא דְגֹשֶׁן: ט וּסְלֵיק עִמֵּיהּ, אַף רְתִכִּין אַף פָּרָשִׁין, וַהֲוַת מַשְׁרִיתָא סַגִּיאָה לַחֲדָא: י וַאֲתוֹ עַד בֵּית אִדְּרֵי דְאָטָד, דִּבְעִבְרָא דְיַרְדְּנָא, וּסְפַדוּ תַמָּן, מִסְפַּד, רַב וְתַקִּיף לַחֲדָא, וַעֲבַד לַאֲבוּהִי, אֶבְלָא שִׁבְעָא יוֹמִין: יא וַחֲזָא, יָתֵיב אֲרַע כְּנַעֲנָאָה יָת אֶבְלָא, בְּבֵית אִדְּרֵי דְאָטָד, וַאֲמַרוּ, אֵבֶל תַּקִּיף דֵּין לְמִצְרָאֵי, עַל כֵּן, קְרָא שְׁמַהּ אָבֵל מִצְרַיִם, דִּבְעִבְרָא דְיַרְדְּנָא: יב וַעֲבַדוּ בְנוֹהִי לֵיהּ, כֵּן כְּמָא דְפַקֵּידִנּוּן: יג וּנְטַלוּ יָתֵיהּ בְּנוֹהִי לְאַרְעָא דִכְנַעַן, וּקְבַרוּ יָתֵיהּ, בִּמְעָרַת חֲקַל כָּפֵילְתָּא, דִּזְבַן אַבְרָהָם יָת חַקְלָא לְאַחְסָנַת קְבוּרָא, מִן עֶפְרוֹן חִתָּאָה עַל אַפֵּי מַמְרֵא: יד וְתָב יוֹסֵף לְמִצְרַיִם הוּא וַאֲחוֹהִי, וְכָל דִּסְלִיקוּ עִמֵּיהּ לְמִקְבַּר יָת אֲבוּהִי, בָּתַר דִּקְבַר יָת אֲבוּהִי: טו וַחֲזוֹ אֲחֵי יוֹסֵף אֲרֵי מִית אֲבוּהוֹן, וַאֲמַרוּ, דִּלְמָא יְטַּר לַנָא דְּבָבוּ יוֹסֵף, וְאָתָבָא יְתִיב לַנָא, יָת כָּל בִּשְׁתָּא, דִּגְמַלְנָא יָתֵיהּ: טז וּפַקִּידוּ, לְוָת יוֹסֵף לְמֵימַר, אֲבוּךְ פַּקֵּיד, קֳדָם מוֹתֵיהּ

50:16 אָבִיךָ צִוָּה לִפְנֵי מוֹתוֹ לֵאמֹר *Your father gave these instructions* – Years earlier, when Yosef revealed his true identity to them, he appeared to have forgiven them for selling him as a slave. Yet the brothers are not wholly reassured. Maybe he did not mean what he said. Perhaps he still harbors resentment. Perhaps the only reason he has not yet taken revenge is respect for Yaakov. There was a convention that there is to be no settling of scores between siblings in the lifetime of the father.

what you are to say to Yosef: "Please forgive the crime and sin of your brothers
who inflicted such harm upon you."' That being so, please forgive the crime of
18 these servants of your father's God." Yosef wept as they spoke to him. Then his
brothers came and threw themselves down before him and said, "We are your
19 slaves." But Yosef said to them, "Do not be afraid. Am I in place of God? You
20 intended to harm me, but God intended it for good, to bring about what is now

רש״י

יז| **שָׂא נָא לְפֶשַׁע עַבְדֵי אֱלֹהֵי אָבִיךָ.** אִם אָבִיךָ מֵת, אֱלֹהָיו קַיָּם וְהֵם עֲבָדָיו:

יח| **וַיֵּלְכוּ גַּם אֶחָיו.** מוּסָף עַל הַשְּׁלִיחוּת:

יט| **כִּי הֲתַחַת אֱלֹהִים אָנִי.** שֶׁמָּא בִּמְקוֹמוֹ אֲנִי? בִּתְמִיָּה. אִם הָיִיתִי רוֹצֶה לְהָרַע לָכֶם, כְּלוּם אֲנִי יָכוֹל? וַהֲלֹא אַתֶּם כֻּלְּכֶם חֲשַׁבְתֶּם עָלַי רָעָה וְהַקָּדוֹשׁ בָּרוּךְ הוּא חֲשָׁבָהּ לְטוֹבָה, וְהֵיאַךְ אֲנִי לְבַדִּי יָכוֹל לְהָרַע לָכֶם?

Meanwhile, the slave, through his or her work, acquires his own dignity as a producer. Thus the slave has "inner freedom" while the master has "inner bondage." This tension creates a dialectic – a conflict worked out through history – reaching equilibrium only when there are neither masters nor slaves, but merely human beings who treat one another not as means to an end but as ends in themselves. Thus understood, Yosef's tears are a prelude to the master-slave drama about to be enacted in the book of Exodus between Pharaoh and the Israelites.

We are reminded that Torah, Tanakh, and Judaism as a whole are a sustained critique of power. Prior to the Messianic age we cannot do without it – consider the tragedies Jews suffered in the centuries in which they lacked it. But power alienates. It breeds suspicion and distrust. It diminishes those it is used against, and thus diminishes those who use it.

Power may be a necessary evil, but it is an evil, and the less we have need of it, the better. Even Yosef the righteous weeps when he sees the extent to which power has set him apart from his brothers. Judaism is about an alternative social order which depends not on power but on love, loyalty, and the mutual responsibility created by covenant.

50:19 הֲתַחַת אֱלֹהִים אָנִי *Am I in place of God?* – A book replete with tensions, hatred, and competition ends with forgiveness. This closing is essential to the biblical drama of redemption, for if brothers cannot live together, how can nations? And if nations cannot live together, how can the human world survive? Only now, with the reconciliation of Yosef and his brothers, can the story move on to the birth of Israel as a nation, passing from the crucible of slavery to the constitution of freedom as a people under the sovereignty of God.

We now see the profound overarching structure of the book of Genesis. It begins with God creating the universe in freedom. It ends with Yaakov's family on the brink of creating a new social universe of freedom which begins in slavery, but ends in the giving and receiving of the Torah, Israel's "constitution of liberty." Israel is charged with the task of changing the moral vision of mankind, but it can only do so if individual Jews, of whom the forerunners were Yaakov's children, are capable of changing themselves – that ultimate assertion of freedom we call *teshuva*. Time then becomes an arena of change in which the future redeems the past and a new concept is born – the idea of hope.

50:20 אֱלֹהִים חֲשָׁבָהּ לְטֹבָה *God intended it for good* – At the start of the book, Adam and Ḥava sin, but deny responsibility. Both instead define themselves as victims: "The woman You put here with me – she gave me fruit"; "the serpent beguiled me" (Gen. 3:12, 13). By the end of Genesis, however, Yosef, who really was a victim, refuses to define himself as such. He says to his brothers, "You intended to harm me, but God intended … to bring about what is now being done: the saving of many lives. So, do not be afraid. I myself will provide for you and your children." This is an immensely

וְחַטָּאתָם כִּי־רָעָה גְמָלוּךָ וְעַתָּה שָׂא נָא לְפֶשַׁע עַבְדֵי אֱלֹהֵי אָבִיךָ
יח וַיֵּבְךְּ יוֹסֵף בְּדַבְּרָם אֵלָיו: וַיֵּלְכוּ גַּם־אֶחָיו וַיִּפְּלוּ לְפָנָיו וַיֹּאמְרוּ הִנֶּנּוּ
יט לְךָ לַעֲבָדִים: וַיֹּאמֶר אֲלֵהֶם יוֹסֵף אַל־תִּירָאוּ כִּי הֲתַחַת אֱלֹהִים אָנִי:
כ וְאַתֶּם חֲשַׁבְתֶּם עָלַי רָעָה אֱלֹהִים חֲשָׁבָהּ לְטֹבָה לְמַעַן עֲשֹׂה כַּיּוֹם הַזֶּה

אונקלוס

לְמֵימַר: יז כְּדֵין תֵּימְרוּן לְיוֹסֵף, בְּבָעוּ, שְׁבוֹק כְּעַן, לְחוֹבֵי אֲחָךְ
וְלִחְטָאֵיהוֹן אֲרֵי בִּשְׁתָּא גַּמְלוּךְ, וּכְעַן שְׁבוֹק כְּעַן, לְחוֹבֵי עַבְדֵי
אֱלָהָא דַּאֲבוּךְ, וּבְכָא יוֹסֵף בְּמַלָּלוּתְהוֹן עִמֵּיהּ: יח וַאֲזַלוּ אַף אֲחוֹהִי,
וּנְפַלוּ קֳדָמוֹהִי, וַאֲמַרוּ, הָא אֲנַחְנָא לָךְ לְעַבְדִין: יט וַאֲמַר לְהוֹן,
יוֹסֵף לָא תִדְחֲלוּן, אֲרֵי, דָּחֲלָא דַּיי אֲנָא: כ וְאַתּוּן, חֲשַׁבְתּוּן עֲלַי
בִּישָׁא, מִן קֳדָם יי אִתְחֲשֵׁיבַת לְטָבָא, בְּדִיל, לְמֶעְבַּד, כְּיוֹמָא הָדֵין

We know this from an earlier episode. After Yaakov took his brother's blessing, Esav said, "The days of mourning for my father are approaching… and then I will kill my brother Yaakov" (Gen. 27:41). Now the brothers are afraid.

The text makes it as plain as possible that the story they tell Yosef is a lie. If Yaakov had really said those words, he would have said them to Yosef himself. The time to have done so was on his deathbed in the previous chapter. The brothers' tale is what we may call a "white lie." Its primary aim was not to deceive but to ease a potentially explosive situation. Perhaps that is why Yosef weeps, understanding that his brothers still think him capable of revenge.

The Sages derived a principle from this text. *Mutar leshanot mipnei hashalom*: "It is permitted to tell an untruth (literally, 'to change' the facts) for the sake of peace" (Yevamot 65b). A white lie can be permitted in Jewish law.

Our grasp of truth is partial, fragmentary, incomplete. That is the human condition. The way to peace is to realize this. Truth matters, but peace matters more. That is Judaism's considered judgment. Many of the greatest crimes in history were committed by those who believed they were in possession of the truth while their opponents were sunk in error. To make peace between brothers, the Torah sanctions a statement that is less than the whole truth. Dishonesty? No. Tact, sensitivity, discretion? Yes. That is an idea both eminently sensible and humane.

50:17 וַיֵּבְךְּ יוֹסֵף *Yosef wept* – On the surface, Yosef holds all the power. His family are entirely dependent on him. But at a deeper level it is the other way round. He still yearns for their acceptance, their recognition, their closeness. He weeps at almost every stage of the fraught encounter with his family in Egypt.

Yosef and Mordekhai/Esther are supreme examples of Jews who reached positions of influence and power in non-Jewish circles. In early modern times in Europe they were called *Hofjuden*, "Court Jews," and other Jews often held deeply ambivalent feelings about them. The last verse in the Book of Esther says that "Mordekhai the Jew was second in command to King Aḥashverosh and revered too among the Jews – beloved of all the multitudes of his brothers (*lerov eḥav*)" (Esther 10:3). Rabbinic Hebrew reads that last phrase differently – not "all the multitudes of" but "most" of his brothers. Most but not all. Rashi (quoting Megilla 16b) says that some members of the Sanhedrin were critical of him because his political involvement (his "closeness to the king") distracted from the time he spent studying Torah. Ibn Ezra says, simply, "It is impossible to satisfy everyone, because people are envious [of other people's success]."

At a deeper level, we can recall Hegel's famous master-slave dialectic, an idea that had huge influence on nineteenth-century, especially Marxist, thought. Hegel argued that the early history of humanity was marked by a struggle for power in which some became masters, others slaves. On the face of it, masters rule while slaves obey. But in fact, the master is dependent on his slaves – he has leisure only because they do the work, and he is the master only because he is recognized as such by his slaves.

▶

21 being done: the saving of many lives. So, do not be afraid. I myself will provide SHEVI'I
for you and your children." And he comforted them and spoke to their hearts.
22 Yosef remained in Egypt together with his father's family, and he lived one
23 hundred and ten years. Yosef saw the third generation of Efrayim's children, and MAFTIR
24 the children of Menashe's son Makhir were also born on Yosef's knees. Yosef
said to his brothers, "I am about to die. But God will surely take note of you
and bring you out of this land to the land He promised to Avraham, Yitzḥak,
25 and Yaakov." Then Yosef bound the children of Israel by an oath: "When God

רש״י

כא| **וַיְדַבֵּר עַל לִבָּם.** דְּבָרִים הַמִּתְקַבְּלִים עַל הַלֵּב: עַד שֶׁלֹּא יְרַדְתֶּם לְכָאן הָיוּ מְרַנְּנִים עָלַי שֶׁאֲנִי עֶבֶד, וְעַל יְדֵיכֶם נוֹדַע שֶׁאֲנִי בֶּן חוֹרִין, וַאֲנִי הוֹרֵג אֶתְכֶם?! מָה הַבְּרִיּוֹת אוֹמְרוֹת? כַּת שֶׁל בַּחוּרִים רָאָה וְנִשְׁתַּבַּח בָּהֶם וְאָמַר: אַחַי הֵם, וּלְבַסּוֹף הֲרָגָם. יֵשׁ לְךָ אָח שֶׁהוֹרֵג אֶת אֶחָיו? דָּבָר אַחֵר, עֲשָׂרָה נֵרוֹת לֹא יָכְלוּ לְכַבּוֹת נֵר אֶחָד וְכוּ׳ (מגילה טז ע״ב):

כג| **עַל בִּרְכֵּי יוֹסֵף.** כְּתַרְגּוּמוֹ, גִּדְּלָן בֵּין בִּרְכָּיו:

instruction to "seek the welfare of the city to which I have exiled you; and pray on its behalf to the LORD, for in its peace there shall be peace for you" (Jer. 29:7; see comment on Gen. 41:52). But they knew that, at some date in the future, the Jewish people would return home. They never mistook the immediate for the ultimate. It was this more than anything that preserved their identity as a distinctive people, and sustained hope during the long centuries of exile and expulsion. It preserved Jews against the internal decay that has beset every other civilization. Forgetfulness of the past, heedlessness of the long-term future, and a loss of moral purpose in the pursuit of the here and now has been the beginning of the decline of other cultures. The sense of *galut* was the Jewish immune system. It meant that the past and future were as real as the present. This consciousness, inherited perhaps from Yosef, has saved Jews from the ravages of time.

THE ENDING THAT IS NOT AN ENDING

The story of the people of the covenant begins with God's call to Avraham to leave his land and travel "to the land that I will show you" (Gen. 12:1). Yet no sooner does he arrive than he is forced by famine to go to Egypt. That is the fate repeated by Yaakov and his children. Genesis ends not with life in Israel but with a death in Egypt, and Yosef's last request: "I am about to die. But God will surely take note of you and bring you out of this land to the land He promised to Avraham, Yitzḥak, and Yaakov.... When God takes note of you, carry my bones up from this place" (Gen. 50:24–25). A hope not yet realized, a journey not yet ended, a destination just beyond the horizon.

Normally we expect a story to create a tension that is resolved on the final page. The Tanakh defies narrative convention. Time and again, never more so than here, it introduces us to the story without an ending which looks forward to an open future rather than reaching closure. Is there some connection between this narrative form and the theme with which Yosef's story ends, namely forgiveness?

Hannah Arendt in *The Human Condition* offers us a profound insight into the connection between forgiveness and time. Human action, she argues, is potentially tragic. We can never foresee the consequences of our acts, but once done, they cannot be undone. This is reason enough to turn away with despair from the realm of human affairs and to hold in contempt the human capacity for freedom.

What transforms the human situation from tragedy to hope, she argues, is the possibility of forgiveness. Forgiving is "the only reaction which does not merely re-act but acts anew and unexpectedly, unconditioned by the act which provoked it and therefore freeing from its consequences both the one who forgives and the one who is forgiven."

Atonement and forgiveness are the supreme expressions

כא לְהַחֲיֹת עַם־רָב: וְעַתָּה אַל־תִּירָאוּ אָנֹכִי אֲכַלְכֵּל אֶתְכֶם וְאֶת־טַפְּכֶם שביעי
כב וַיְנַחֵם אוֹתָם וַיְדַבֵּר עַל־לִבָּם: וַיֵּשֶׁב יוֹסֵף בְּמִצְרַיִם הוּא וּבֵית אָבִיו
כג וַיְחִי יוֹסֵף מֵאָה וָעֶשֶׂר שָׁנִים: וַיַּרְא יוֹסֵף לְאֶפְרַיִם בְּנֵי שִׁלֵּשִׁים גַּם בְּנֵי מפטיר
כד מָכִיר בֶּן־מְנַשֶּׁה יֻלְּדוּ עַל־בִּרְכֵּי יוֹסֵף: וַיֹּאמֶר יוֹסֵף אֶל־אֶחָיו אָנֹכִי
מֵת וֵאלֹהִים פָּקֹד יִפְקֹד אֶתְכֶם וְהֶעֱלָה אֶתְכֶם מִן־הָאָרֶץ הַזֹּאת אֶל־
כה הָאָרֶץ אֲשֶׁר נִשְׁבַּע לְאַבְרָהָם לְיִצְחָק וּלְיַעֲקֹב: וַיַּשְׁבַּע יוֹסֵף אֶת־בְּנֵי
יִשְׂרָאֵל לֵאמֹר פָּקֹד יִפְקֹד אֱלֹהִים אֶתְכֶם וְהַעֲלִתֶם אֶת־עַצְמֹתַי מִזֶּה:

אונקלוס

לְקַיָּמָא עַם סַגִּי: כא וּכְעַן לָא תִדְחֲלוּן, אֲנָא, אֲזוּן יָתְכוֹן וְיָת טַפְלְכוֹן, וְנַחֵים יָתְהוֹן, וּמַלֵּיל תַּנְחוּמִין עַל לִבְּהוֹן: כב וִיתֵיב יוֹסֵף בְּמִצְרַיִם, הוּא וּבֵית אֲבוּהִי, וַחֲיָא יוֹסֵף, מְאָה וַעֲסַר שְׁנִין: כג וַחֲזָא יוֹסֵף לְאֶפְרַיִם, בְּנִין תְּלִיתָאִין, אַף, בְּנֵי מָכִיר בַּר מְנַשֶּׁה, אִתְיְלִידוּ וְרַבִּי יוֹסֵף: כד וַאֲמַר יוֹסֵף לַאֲחוֹהִי, אֲנָא מָאִית, וַיי מִדְכַּר דְּכִיר יָתְכוֹן, וְיַסֵּיק יָתְכוֹן מִן אַרְעָא הָדָא, לְאַרְעָא, דְּקַיֵּים, לְאַבְרָהָם לְיִצְחָק וּלְיַעֲקֹב: כה וְאוֹמֵי יוֹסֵף, יָת בְּנֵי יִשְׂרָאֵל לְמֵימַר, מִדְכַּר דְּכִיר יי יָתְכוֹן, וְתַסְּקוּן יָת גַּרְמַי מִכָּא:

significant transformation. Instead of asking, "Who did this to me?" Yosef asks about his suffering, "What redemptive deed has this put me in a position to perform?" He looks forward, not back. Instead of blaming others, he exercises responsibility. Yosef represents the first great biblical rejection of the culture of victimhood, the reaction that caused the first humans to lose paradise.

50:21 וַיְנַחֵם אוֹתָם *And he comforted them* – The Yosef story brings Genesis to closure by showing that sibling rivalry is not written indelibly into the human script. We can change, repent, and grow. The brothers show that they have changed when they demonstrate that they are no longer willing to let Binyamin – the Yosef-substitute – be enslaved (Gen. 44:33). Yosef, by his act of reconciliation, shows that he is not captive to the past and its resentments. His statement to his brothers shows the power of a religious vision to reframe history, liberating ourselves from the otherwise violent dynamic of revenge and retaliation. In a real sense, then, freedom extends to more than our ability to choose between alternative futures. It includes the freedom to reshape our understanding of the past, healing some of its legacy of pain. The point could not be more significant in the context of the sibling rivalries among cultures today. The past does not dictate the future. To the contrary, a future of reconciliation can, in some measure at least, retroactively redeem the past.

50:25 וְהַעֲלִתֶם אֶת־עַצְמֹתַי מִזֶּה *Carry my bones up from this place* – Wherever Jews were scattered, they saw their condition as *galut*, "exile," rather than mere dispersion, *tefutzot*. There were places like Germany, where they had lived for a thousand years. There were others, like Babylonia, in which there was continuous Jewish settlement for two and a half thousand years. Yet Jews saw themselves, and were seen by others, as being *here* but belonging *elsewhere*. This did not mean, as their critics claimed, that they had dual loyalties. Few groups were as loyal to their societies and non-Jewish rulers as were the Jews. They made significant contributions to the nations in which they lived, and whenever possible, added vastly to the arts, sciences, medicine, and the economy.

Since the days of Yirmeyahu they remembered his

26 takes note of you, carry my bones up from this place." Yosef died at the age of
one hundred and ten. He was embalmed and placed in a coffin there, in Egypt.

The haftara for Parashat Vayeḥi is on page 1524.

its close cousin, progress. Judaism believes in covenantal time, well described by Harold Fisch: "The covenant is a condition of our existence in time.... We cooperate with its purposes never quite knowing where it will take us, for 'the readiness is all.'" In a lovely phrase, he speaks of the Jewish imagination as shaped by "the unappeased memory of a future still to be fulfilled."

Tragedy gives rise to pessimism. Cyclical time leads to acceptance. Linear time begets optimism. Covenantal time gives birth to hope. These are radically different ways of relating to life and the universe. They are expressed in the different kinds of stories people tell. Jewish time always faces an open future. The last chapter is not yet written. The Messiah has not yet come. Until then, the story continues – and we, together with God, are the co-authors of the next chapter.

כו וַיָּמָת יוֹסֵף בֶּן־מֵאָה וָעֶשֶׂר שָׁנִים וַיַּחַנְטוּ אֹתוֹ וַיִּישֶׂם בָּאָרוֹן בְּמִצְרָיִם:

The הפטרה *for* פרשת ויחי *is on page 1525.*

אונקלוס

כו וּמִית יוֹסֵף, בַּר מְאָה וַעֲסַר שְׁנִין, וַחֲנַטוּ יָתֵיהּ, וְשָׁמוּהִי בַאֲרוֹנָא בְּמִצְרָיִם:

It was this revolutionary concept of time – based on human freedom – that Judaism contributed to the world. Many ancient cultures believed in cyclical time, in which all things return to their beginning. The Greeks developed a sense of tragic time, in which the ship of dreams is destined to founder on the hard rocks of reality. Europe of the Enlightenment introduced the idea of linear time, with of human freedom – the freedom to act differently in the future than one did in the past, the freedom not to be trapped in a cycle of vengeance and retaliation. Only those who can forgive can be free. Only a civilization based on forgiveness can construct a future that is not an endless repetition of the past. That, surely, is why the golden age of Judaism is perpetually in the future.

שמות
EXODUS

THE BOOK OF EXODUS

The book of Exodus, second of the Mosaic books, is not only a key text in Jewish history. It is also one of the most influential in the history of the West, its metanarrative of hope. In 1776, in Philadelphia, preparing for the American Declaration of Independence, Benjamin Franklin and Thomas Jefferson offered their designs for a seal for the new United States. Franklin proposed that it should bear a picture of Moshe lifting his staff to divide the Sea of Reeds, with the motto "Rebellion to tyrants is obedience to God." Jefferson preferred a picture of the Israelites in the wilderness being "led by a cloud by day and a pillar of fire at night." The American story – its "civil religion"– is supremely the story of the exodus.

That story told of how a small group, fleeing persecution, escaped, undertook a journey through a wilderness, crossed a sea in search of the Promised Land, and there sought to create a "new birth of freedom." The way would be long and hard. There would be diversions and digressions, resistances and rebellions. Yet that is what the founders of America sought, and their inspiration was the story of the Israelites as set out in the book of Exodus. It said that people could escape, could survive, and could defy the mightiest of empires. It said that faith is more powerful than power. Hope lies just beyond the visible horizon of hopelessness.

The story, however, does not end at the exodus. A free society is a moral achievement. The Ten Commandments, with their emphasis on the sanctity of life, the integrity of the family, respect for truth and for the property of others, summarize the essentials of a decent society in so short and simple a way as to be memorized by – engraved on the hearts of – an entire people. They remain the world's most famous moral code. This is the culmination of what the Torah has been about all along. To have a free society, there must be rule of law. In Exodus, then, we find the inseparable interweaving of narrative and law that will become the hallmark of Judaism.

It is an extraordinary drama – theological, political, but also human. That is why it has never lost its hold on those who know it, and why it continues to inspire us with the belief that when we open ourselves to the force of the Divine, extraordinary things can happen.

Parashat Shemot

1 1 And these are the names of the sons of Yisrael who came to Egypt with Yaakov,
2 3 each with his household: Reuven, Shimon, Levi and Yehuda; Yissakhar,
4 5 Zevulun and Binyamin; Dan and Naftali; Gad and Asher. The descendants of
6 Yaakov were seventy in all, and Yosef was already in Egypt. Then Yosef died,
7 and all his brothers, and all that generation. But the Israelites were fruitful and
burgeoned; they multiplied and became exceptionally strong, until the land
was filled with them.

רש״י

א א׳ **וְאֵלֶּה שְׁמוֹת בְּנֵי יִשְׂרָאֵל.** אַף עַל פִּי שֶׁמְּנָאָן בְּחַיֵּיהֶם בִּשְׁמוֹתָם חָזַר וּמְנָאָן בְּמִיתָתָם, לְהוֹדִיעַ חִבָּתָם שֶׁנִּמְשְׁלוּ לַכּוֹכָבִים שֶׁמּוֹצִיאָם וּמַכְנִיסָם בְּמִסְפָּר וּבִשְׁמוֹתָם, שֶׁנֶּאֱמַר: ״הַמּוֹצִיא בְמִסְפָּר צְבָאָם לְכֻלָּם בְּשֵׁם יִקְרָא״ (ישעיה מ, כו):

ה **וְיוֹסֵף הָיָה בְמִצְרָיִם.** וַהֲלֹא הוּא וּבָנָיו הָיוּ בִּכְלַל שִׁבְעִים, וּמַה בָּא לְלַמְּדֵנוּ? וְכִי לֹא הָיִינוּ יוֹדְעִים שֶׁהוּא הָיָה בְמִצְרַיִם? אֶלָּא לְהוֹדִיעֲךָ צִדְקָתוֹ שֶׁל יוֹסֵף, הוּא יוֹסֵף הָרוֹעֶה אֶת צֹאן אָבִיו, הוּא יוֹסֵף שֶׁהָיָה בְמִצְרַיִם וְנַעֲשָׂה מֶלֶךְ, וְעוֹמֵד בְּצִדְקוֹ:

ז **וַיִּשְׁרְצוּ.** שֶׁהָיוּ יוֹלְדוֹת שִׁשָּׁה בְּכֶרֶס אֶחָד:

It was the number of Israelites that gave them fear. They forced the Israelites to produce a precise number of bricks each day. Nations that quantify human life, reducing populations to numbers, eventually lose their humanity.

THE PEOPLE OF ISRAEL

As we move from Genesis to Exodus, the entire biblical landscape changes. The Jewish project is about to take on substance and form. For the first time, politics enters the narrative, center stage. God is to intervene in history in a series of miracles and wonders that have no precedent and no real sequels. For the first time we will encounter law in all its nuances – Torah, mitzva, *ḥok*, and *mishpat* – as the substance of the divine will. And for the first time we will encounter a transformative leader, Moshe, who emerges from the shadows of a strange, improbable childhood to become, despite his many hesitations, the man who is to leave his mark on the Jewish people to this day.

The reason for all these changes is the appearance, early in the first chapter of Exodus, of one word we have not heard before in connection with the covenantal family: the word *am*, "people" (Ex. 1:9). Not accidentally, it is an outsider who uses it first, Pharaoh, for it is he who first realizes the change that has come about. What had been a family has become a nation. With that, the very terms of Israel's existence are transformed.

Genesis was about individuals and their relationships. One of its recurring themes was the difficulty the matriarchs – Sara, Rivka, and Raḥel – had in conceiving children. Despite grandiose promises – that they would have as many children as the stars of the sky, the sands of the seashore, and the dust of the earth – having even a single child turned out to be difficult, even miraculous. Yet as we turn the pages and begin the new book, all of that vanishes, and a family of seventy members becomes a nation with six hundred thousand adult males. The Israelites, we are told in a cascade of verbs, "were fruitful and burgeoned; they multiplied and became exceptionally strong, until the land was filled with them" (1:7). Even the attempt by Pharaoh to limit childbirth by subjecting the Israelites to hard labor fails completely: "The more they were oppressed, the more they increased" (1:12).

Exodus is about the birth of a nation, described variously as an *am*, "people," *goy*, "nation," *kahal*, "congregation,"

פרשת שמות

א א וְאֵ֗לֶּה שְׁמוֹת֙ בְּנֵ֣י יִשְׂרָאֵ֔ל הַבָּאִ֖ים מִצְרָ֑יְמָה אֵ֣ת יַעֲקֹ֔ב אִ֥ישׁ וּבֵית֖וֹ א
ב ג ד בָּֽאוּ׃ רְאוּבֵ֣ן שִׁמְע֔וֹן לֵוִ֖י וִיהוּדָֽה׃ יִשָּׂשכָ֥ר זְבוּלֻ֖ן וּבִנְיָמִֽן׃ דָּ֥ן וְנַפְתָּלִ֖י
ה גָּ֥ד וְאָשֵֽׁר׃ וַֽיְהִ֗י כָּל־נֶ֛פֶשׁ יֹצְאֵ֥י יֶֽרֶךְ־יַעֲקֹ֖ב שִׁבְעִ֣ים נָ֑פֶשׁ וְיוֹסֵ֖ף הָיָ֥ה
ו ז בְּמִצְרָֽיִם׃ וַיָּ֤מָת יוֹסֵף֙ וְכָל־אֶחָ֔יו וְכֹ֖ל הַדּ֥וֹר הַהֽוּא׃ וּבְנֵ֣י יִשְׂרָאֵ֗ל פָּר֧וּ
וַֽיִּשְׁרְצ֛וּ וַיִּרְבּ֥וּ וַיַּֽעַצְמ֖וּ בִּמְאֹ֣ד מְאֹ֑ד וַתִּמָּלֵ֥א הָאָ֖רֶץ אֹתָֽם׃

אונקלוס

א א וְאִלֵּין, שְׁמָהַת בְּנֵי יִשְׂרָאֵל, דְּעָאלוּ לְמִצְרָיִם, עִם יַעֲקֹב, גְּבַר
וֶאֱנָשׁ בֵּיתֵיהּ עָאלוּ: ב רְאוּבֵן שִׁמְעוֹן, לֵוִי וִיהוּדָה: ג יִשָּׂשכָר זְבוּלוּן
וּבִנְיָמִין: ד דָּן וְנַפְתָּלִי גָּד וְאָשֵׁר: ה וַהֲוָה, כָּל נַפְשָׁתָא, נָפְקֵי יִרְכָּא
דְּיַעֲקֹב שַׁבְעִין נַפְשָׁן, וְיוֹסֵף דַּהֲוָה בְמִצְרָיִם: ו וּמִית יוֹסֵף וְכָל אֲחוֹהִי,
וְכָל דָּרָא הַהוּא: ז וּבְנֵי יִשְׂרָאֵל, נְפִישׁוּ וְאִתְיַלַּדוּ, וּסְגִיאוּ וּתְקִיפוּ
לַחֲדָא לַחֲדָא, וְאִתְמְלִיאַת אַרְעָא מִנְּהוֹן:

SHEMOT

Here, the drama of Exodus begins. In exile, the Jewish people multiply, until they are no longer a family but a nation. Pharaoh, fearing that they pose a threat to Egypt, enslaves them and orders their male children killed. Moshe, an Israelite child adopted by Pharaoh's daughter, is chosen by God to confront Pharaoh and lead the people to freedom. Reluctantly, Moshe agrees, but his initial intervention only makes things worse, and on this tense note the *parasha* ends. On the surface, Exodus is about freedom, slavery, and the fate of nations, but it is also about the power of individuals, driven by justice or compassion, to defy tyrants and change the course of history.

What was promised or distantly foreseen in Genesis becomes real at the beginning of Exodus: the promise of many children, of becoming "a great nation" (Gen. 12:1), and the nocturnal vision, with its "deep, dark dread" in which Avraham was told that his descendants would become strangers in a land not their own, where they would be enslaved and mistreated (ch. 15).

Narrative continuity is not merely a literary feature of the Torah. It is also part of its theology. For the Torah, history is meaningful. It tells a story. This was a unique conception of time. For Jews, as historian J. H. Plumb put it, "The past was no longer static, a mere store of information, example and event, but dynamic, an unfolding story." Exodus is the unfolding of the themes set out in Genesis.

1:1 וְאֵלֶּה *And these* – The word "and" signals an unbroken continuity between Genesis and Exodus, as does the opening genealogy, a more detailed version of which has already appeared in Genesis 46:8–27 (Ramban). Genesis is about the birth of Israel as a family. Exodus is about the birth of Israel as a nation. The two are inseparable. Even as a nation, Israel will still feel a sense of shared fate and mutual responsibility as if it were a single extended family.

1:1 שְׁמוֹת *The names* – Proper names are a marker of individuality, difference, distinctiveness. This follows from Judaism's insistence on the sanctity of human life and the dignity of the individual as the image and likeness of God (Gen. 9:6). When the Nazis sought to dehumanize Jews in the concentration camps, they took away their names and gave them numbers. The Egyptians were obsessed with numbers.

▶

8 Then a new king arose over Egypt, who had not known Yosef. And he said
9 to his people, "You see that the Israelite people are many and more powerful
10 than we. Come, let us deal wisely with them in case they increase, and if war

רש״י

ח וַיָּקָם מֶלֶךְ חָדָשׁ. רַב וּשְׁמוּאֵל, חַד אָמַר חָדָשׁ מַמָּשׁ, וְחַד אָמַר שֶׁנִּתְחַדְּשׁוּ גְּזֵרוֹתָיו: אֲשֶׁר לֹא יָדַע. עָשָׂה עַצְמוֹ כְּאִלּוּ לֹא יְדָעוֹ:

י הָבָה נִתְחַכְּמָה לוֹ. כָּל ׳הָבָה׳ לְשׁוֹן הֲכָנָה וְהַזְמָנָה לְדָבָר הוּא, הָכִינוּ עַצְמְכֶם לְכָךְ: נִתְחַכְּמָה לוֹ. לָעָם, נִתְחַכֵּם מַה לַּעֲשׂוֹת לוֹ. וְרַבּוֹתֵינוּ

The story is engraved in our memory. We tell it every year, and in summary form in our prayers every day. It is part of what it is to be a Jew. Yet there is one phrase that shines out from the narrative: "But the more they were oppressed, the more they increased and spread" (v. 12). This, no less than oppression itself, is part of what it means to be a Jew. The worse things get, the stronger we become. Jews are the people who not only survive but thrive in adversity.

Jewish history is not merely a story of Jews enduring catastrophes that might have spelled the end to less tenacious groups. It is the fact that after every disaster, Jews renewed themselves. They discovered some hitherto hidden reservoir of spirit that fueled new forms of collective self-expression as the carriers of God's message to the world.

1:9 עַם בְּנֵי יִשְׂרָאֵל *The Israelite people* – Though we are a fractious people, crisis unites us. As the Rabbis said: when it comes to the history of Jewish suffering, "the latter troubles make us forget the earlier ones" (Berakhot 13a). The entire book of Genesis is taken up with arguments within the family, between husbands and wives, parents and children, and between siblings. But as soon as the book of Exodus begins, the Israelites are faced with exile and slavery, and for the first time we hear the phrase *am Benei Yisrael*, "the Israelite people." Earlier rivalries have been forgotten, and a divided family has become a united people.

1:9 רַב וְעָצוּם מִמֶּנּוּ *More powerful than we* – Thus Pharaoh says to his people, but he cannot have believed this, or he would not risk provoking the Israelites by ordering the murder of every male child. In the case of antisemitism there is always a discrepancy between what Israel's enemies say and what they believe. They say that Hebrews/Israelites/Jews are powerful in order to arouse fear that mutates into hate, but they know that in fact they are, in earthly terms, powerless. They would not seek a confrontation that they believed they would lose.

At the same time, Pharaoh is speaking to real anxieties on the part of the people. We mentioned above that before our narrative began, northern Egypt had come under the rule of the Hyksos, a Semitic-speaking group from the coastal Levant. Their culture was Asiatic, they worshipped Baal Tzefon, the Canaanite storm god, and they preserved their non-Egyptian names. They built a huge citadel on the Nile. This period was preserved as a trauma in Egyptian memories as a time when the created order itself was overturned. The Israelites, with their distinctive identity and faith, could easily be portrayed as a new danger akin to the Hyksos. This would have readily been believed by the population as a whole.

Note that in the history of antisemitism, hate usually emerges in the wake of an event, unrelated to Jews, that was perceived by the host culture as a humiliation. The French defeat in the Franco-Prussian War of 1870 led to the antisemitism that reached a climax in the Dreyfus affair. German defeat in the First World War and the punitive terms of the Treaty of Versailles led to Nazism. The deep humiliation felt by the Egyptians as they remembered the Hyksos may well be the background to the events of this and the following chapters.

1:10 נִתְחַכְּמָה לוֹ *Deal wisely with them* – According to the Midrash, the "wise dealing" of Pharaoh consisted of inflicting slavery slowly and by degrees, so the Israelites became accustomed to it rather than trying to flee. First Pharaoh issued a proclamation calling on all Egyptians and Israelites to work on his construction projects for pay. Pharaoh himself joined them (Sota 11a). After a month, the Egyptians gradually withdrew, leaving the Israelites working alone.

ח ט וַיָּקָם מֶלֶךְ־חָדָשׁ עַל־מִצְרָיִם אֲשֶׁר לֹא־יָדַע אֶת־יוֹסֵף׃ וַיֹּאמֶר אֶל־עַמּוֹ
י הִנֵּה עַם בְּנֵי יִשְׂרָאֵל רַב וְעָצוּם מִמֶּנּוּ׃ הָבָה נִתְחַכְּמָה לוֹ פֶּן־יִרְבֶּה וְהָיָה

אונקלוס

ח וְקָם מַלְכָּא חֲדַתָּא עַל מִצְרַיִם, דְּלָא מְקַיֵּים גְּזֵירַת יוֹסֵף׃ ט וַאֲמַר
לְעַמֵּיהּ, הָא, עַמָּא בְּנֵי יִשְׂרָאֵל, סַגַּן וְתַקְּפִין מִנַּנָא׃ י הַבוּ נִתְחַכַּם
לְהוֹן, דִּלְמָא יִסְגּוֹן,

and *eda,* "community." No sooner do we see this than we understand what the Jewish project was intended from the outset to be. It is about politics, society, and the principles on which a people can come together to form associations. It is about justice, freedom, and the rule of law. It is about the sanctity of life and human dignity. Ultimately it is about the use and misuse of power. Exodus places frankly before us the risks inherent in power. It can be used to oppress, enslave, and, in extremis, to kill. That is what Pharaoh proposes at the beginning of Exodus.

It is important to understand precisely what is being argued in these opening pages. Pharaoh is not portrayed as the embodiment of evil. He is not a Haman. His people are not the Amalekites. Pharaoh is driven by political motives, not hate: "Come, let us deal wisely with them in case they increase, and if war breaks out they may join our enemies and fight against us" (1:10).

This is not a simple story of good versus evil. It is a critique of the politics of power, empires, hierarchical societies, and the division of populations into free human beings and slaves. Lord Acton summed it up in his famous dictum that "all power tends to corrupt and absolute power corrupts absolutely." In its place, the Torah proposes a different kind of politics, based not on power but on covenant, the free agreement of a free people who accord absolute sovereignty to God alone. The idea could hardly be more radical, and it has shaped the history of the West.

1:8 מֶלֶךְ־חָדָשׁ *A new king* – The Torah nowhere identifies which particular Pharaoh this was. There may be a suggestion here that the person matters less than the role, that the conduct of Pharaoh as described here and later has less to do with his personality and more to do with the system he leads and embodies. Its entire structure – a highly hierarchical society, with absolute power held by rulers, while much of the rest of the population is used as a conscripted labor force to construct monumental buildings – has an inherent tendency to cruelty.

The "new king," however, may refer to one of the rulers of the "new kingdom" which wrested back power from the foreign Hyksos (*heqau-khasut* in ancient Egyptian, "rulers from foreign lands"), who ruled the northern part of the country during the Second Intermediate Period (c. 1650–c. 1550 BCE). The Hyksos were a Semitic people who were traders and were at first welcomed, settling at Avaris. They prospered, attracted other non-Egyptian groups to join them, and eventually built up economic, political, and military power. It seems that this period remained a vivid part of national memory. The fear was that now another non-native population would take over the rule of this proud and ancient empire. Not all evil is irrational, but neither does the rationality of fear justify evil.

1:8 אֲשֶׁר לֹא־יָדַע אֶת־יוֹסֵף *Who had not known Yosef* – Genesis ends on an almost serene note. Yaakov has found his long-lost son. The family has been reunited. Yosef has forgiven his brothers. Under his protection and influence the family has settled in Goshen, one of the most prosperous regions of Egypt. They now have homes, property, food, the protection of Yosef, and the favor of Pharaoh. It must have seemed one of the golden moments of Avraham's family's history.

Then, as has happened so often since, "a new king arose over Egypt, who had not known Yosef" (Ex. 1:8). There is a political climate change. The family falls out of favor. Pharaoh tells his advisors: "You see that the Israelite people are many and more powerful than we. Come, let us deal wisely with them in case they increase" (vv. 9–10). And so the whole mechanism of oppression moves into operation: forced labor that turns into slavery that becomes attempted genocide.

breaks out they may join our enemies and fight against us and escape from the
11 land." So they placed slave masters over the Israelites to oppress them with
12 forced labor; they built supply cities for Pharaoh: Pitom and Ramesses. But
the more they were oppressed, the more they increased and spread; and the
13 Egyptians came to dread the Israelites. The Egyptians imposed backbreaking
14 labor on the Israelites, embittering their lives with harsh work in mortar and
brick and all field labors; all the work they forced upon them was intended to
15 break them. Then the king of Egypt said to the midwives of the Hebrews – one

רש״י

דָּרְשׁוּ, נִתְחַכֵּם לְמוֹשִׁיעָן שֶׁל יִשְׂרָאֵל, נְדוּנֵם בַּמַּיִם, שֶׁכְּבָר נִשְׁבַּע שֶׁלֹּא יָבִיא מַבּוּל לָעוֹלָם: **וְעָלָה מִן הָאָרֶץ.** עַל כָּרְחֵנוּ. וְרַבּוֹתֵינוּ דָּרְשׁוּ, כְּאָדָם שֶׁמְּקַלֵּל עַצְמוֹ וְתוֹלֶה קִלְלָתוֹ בַּחֲבֵרוֹ, וַהֲרֵי הוּא כְּאִלּוּ כָּתַב: 'וְעָלִינוּ מִן הָאָרֶץ' וְהֵם יִירָשׁוּהָ:

יא **עָלָיו.** עַל הָעָם: **מִסִּים.** לְשׁוֹן מַס, שָׂרִים שֶׁגּוֹבִין מֵהֶם הַמַּס. וּמַהוּ הַמַּס? שֶׁיִּבְנוּ עָרֵי מִסְכְּנוֹת לְפַרְעֹה: **לְמַעַן עַנֹּתוֹ בְּסִבְלֹתָם.** שֶׁל מִצְרַיִם: **עָרֵי מִסְכְּנוֹת.** כְּתַרְגּוּמוֹ. וְכֵן: "לֶךְ בֹּא אֶל הַסֹּכֵן הַזֶּה" (ישעיה כב, טו) – גִּזְבָּר הַמְמֻנֶּה עַל הָאוֹצָרוֹת: **אֶת פִּתֹם וְאֶת רַעַמְסֵס.** שֶׁלֹּא הָיוּ רְאוּיוֹת מִתְּחִלָּה לְכָךְ וַעֲשָׂאוּם חֲזָקוֹת וּבְצוּרוֹת לְאוֹצָר:

יב **וְכַאֲשֶׁר יְעַנּוּ אֹתוֹ.** בְּכָל מַה שֶּׁהֵם נוֹתְנִין לֵב לְעַנּוֹת כֵּן לֵב הַקָּדוֹשׁ בָּרוּךְ הוּא לְהַרְבּוֹת וּלְהַפְרִיץ: **כֵּן יִרְבֶּה.** כֵּן רָבֶה וְכֵן פּוֹרֵץ. וּמִדְרָשׁוֹ, רוּחַ הַקֹּדֶשׁ אוֹמֶרֶת כֵּן: אַתֶּם אוֹמְרִים "פֶּן יִרְבֶּה" וַאֲנִי אוֹמֵר "כֵּן יִרְבֶּה": **וַיָּקֻצוּ.** קָצוּ בְּחַיֵּיהֶם. וְרַבּוֹתֵינוּ דָּרְשׁוּ, כְּקוֹצִים הָיוּ בְּעֵינֵיהֶם:

יג **בְּפָרֶךְ.** בַּעֲבוֹדָה קָשָׁה הַמְפָרֶכֶת וּמְשַׁבֶּרֶת אֶת הַגּוּף:

טו **לַמְיַלְּדֹת.** הוּא לְשׁוֹן מוֹלִידוֹת, אֶלָּא שֶׁיֵּשׁ לָשׁוֹן קַל וְיֵשׁ לָשׁוֹן כָּבֵד, כְּמוֹ: שׁוֹבֵר וּמְשַׁבֵּר, דּוֹבֵר וּמְדַבֵּר, כָּךְ מוֹלִיד וּמְיַלֵּד: **שִׁפְרָה.** יוֹכֶבֶד, עַל שֵׁם שֶׁמְּשַׁפֶּרֶת אֶת הַוָּלָד: **פּוּעָה.** מִרְיָם, שֶׁפּוֹעָה וּמְדַבֶּרֶת וְהוֹגָה לַוָּלָד כְּדֶרֶךְ הַנָּשִׁים הַמְפַיְּסוֹת תִּינוֹק הַבּוֹכֶה. "פּוֹעָה" – לְשׁוֹן צְעָקָה, כְּמוֹ: "כַּיּוֹלֵדָה אֶפְעֶה" (ישעיה מב, יד):

house of Ramesses," was constructed near the old Hyksos capital of Avaris, where Ramesses's father, Seti I, had built a summer palace. Construction continued for twenty years, and a series of mansions, administrative buildings, and barracks grew up around the palace until it became a city. Documents from the time attest to the rich abundance of food that grew in the area, and there were granaries well stocked with wheat, the "supplies" referred to in the verse. As Toby Wilkinson describes it: "The royal quarter, covering four square miles, was located in a natural stronghold on the banks of the Nile, protected by canals and sand promontories. Court poets penned eulogies on the splendor of Ramesses's palaces.... The steps leading to the throne dais were adorned with prostrate images of the king's enemies, so that he might tread them underfoot each time he ascended or descended." This was very close to the Israelites' region in the land of Goshen and explains why Moshe is able to visit the Pharaoh often during the events preceding the exodus.

1:14 וַיְמָרְרוּ אֶת־חַיֵּיהֶם *Embittering their lives* – Jewish tradition would relate this term to the bitter herbs at the Seder service (Ex. 12:8). Note the fourfold repetition in this verse of the Hebrew root *a-v-d*, "slave, forced labor," as if to emphasize the intensity and relentlessness of the oppression. Both the previous verse and this one end with the word *befarekh*, meaning backbreaking labor, inhuman and dehumanizing work, of a kind that would later be forbidden to be demanded by one Israelite of another (Lev. 25:43, 46). According to Egyptian documents of the period, recently discovered, brickmaking quotas issued by slave masters were only rarely reached. It seems, therefore, to have been a deliberate policy toward slaves and prisoners of war to set them work targets that were virtually impossible to achieve, a form of physical and mental torture that may be what the Torah is referring to here as cruel or "backbreaking."

MIDWIVES TO THE HEBREWS

Who were Shifra and Puah? The truth is, we do not know. One midrash identifies them with Moshe's mother Yokheved and sister Miriam, using a midrashic technique

כִּֽי־תִקְרֶ֤אנָה מִלְחָמָה֙ וְנוֹסַ֤ף גַּם־הוּא֙ עַל־שֹׂ֣נְאֵ֔ינוּ וְנִלְחַם־בָּ֖נוּ וְעָלָ֥ה
יא מִן־הָאָֽרֶץ׃ וַיָּשִׂ֤ימוּ עָלָיו֙ שָׂרֵ֣י מִסִּ֔ים לְמַ֥עַן עַנֹּת֖וֹ בְּסִבְלֹתָ֑ם וַיִּ֜בֶן עָרֵ֤י
יב מִסְכְּנוֹת֙ לְפַרְעֹ֔ה אֶת־פִּתֹ֖ם וְאֶת־רַעַמְסֵֽס׃ וְכַאֲשֶׁר֙ יְעַנּ֣וּ אֹת֔וֹ כֵּ֥ן יִרְבֶּ֖ה
יג וְכֵ֣ן יִפְרֹ֑ץ וַיָּקֻ֕צוּ מִפְּנֵ֖י בְּנֵ֥י יִשְׂרָאֵֽל׃ וַיַּעֲבִ֧דוּ מִצְרַ֛יִם אֶת־בְּנֵ֥י יִשְׂרָאֵ֖ל
יד בְּפָֽרֶךְ׃ וַיְמָרְר֨וּ אֶת־חַיֵּיהֶ֜ם בַּעֲבֹדָ֣ה קָשָׁ֗ה בְּחֹ֙מֶר֙ וּבִלְבֵנִ֔ים וּבְכָל־עֲבֹדָ֖ה
טו בַּשָּׂדֶ֑ה אֵ֚ת כָּל־עֲבֹ֣דָתָ֔ם אֲשֶׁר־עָבְד֥וּ בָהֶ֖ם בְּפָֽרֶךְ׃ וַיֹּ֙אמֶר֙ מֶ֣לֶךְ מִצְרַ֔יִם
לַֽמְיַלְּדֹ֖ת הָֽעִבְרִיֹּ֑ת אֲשֶׁ֨ר שֵׁ֤ם הָֽאַחַת֙ שִׁפְרָ֔ה וְשֵׁ֥ם הַשֵּׁנִ֖ית פּוּעָֽה׃

אונקלוס

וִיהֵי, אֲרֵי יְעָרְעִנָּנָא קְרָב וְיִתּוֹסְפוּן אַף אִנּוּן עַל סָנְאַנָא, וִיגִיחוּן בַּנָא קְרָב וְיִסְקוּן מִן אַרְעָא: יא וּמַנִּיאוּ עֲלֵיהוֹן שִׁלְטוֹנִין מַבְאֲשִׁין, בְּדִיל לְעַנּוֹאֵיהוֹן בְּפָלְחָנְהוֹן, וּבְנוֹ, קִרְוֵי בֵית אוֹצְרֵי לְפַרְעֹה, יָת פִּיתוֹם וְיָת רַעְמְסֵס: יב וּכְמָא דִּמְעַנַּן לְהוֹן, כֵּן סָגַן וְכֵן תָּקְפִין, וְעָקַת לְמִצְרָאֵי, מִן קֳדָם בְּנֵי יִשְׂרָאֵל: יג וְאַפְלַחוּ מִצְרָאֵי, יָת בְּנֵי יִשְׂרָאֵל בְּקַשְׁיוּ: יד וְאַמַּרוּ יָת חַיֵּיהוֹן בְּפָלְחָנָא קַשְׁיָא, בְּטִינָא וּבִלְבְנֵי, וּבְכָל פָּלְחָנָא בְּחַקְלָא, יָת כָּל פָּלְחָנְהוֹן, דְּאַפְלַחוּ בְהוֹן בְּקַשְׁיוּ: טו וַאֲמַר מַלְכָּא דְמִצְרַיִם, לְחָיָתָא יְהוּדָיָתָא, דְּשׁוּם חֲדָא שִׁפְרָה, וְשׁוּם תִּנְיֵיתָא פּוּעָה:

Then they stopped being paid. By then the Israelites had become slaves and the Egyptians their taskmasters. Gradualism later became part of the Nazi program of genocide.

1:10 וְנוֹסַף גַּם־הוּא עַל־שֹׂנְאֵינוּ *They may join our enemies* – We do not have other ancient descriptions of the events of the exodus. But we have enough background information to understand the context in which a pharaoh would say this. It makes eminent sense, given the conditions of the time. A great drama was to begin that would leave its mark ever afterward on the life of the group whose descendants are the Jews of today.

The contrast between the two peoples could not have been greater. Egypt at that time was an indomitable power. It held sway over the whole ancient Near East. Ramesses II conducted successful campaigns against the Hittites and the Libyans and launched punitive raids against Edom and Moav. He used the technical prowess and prosperity of Egypt to undertake a series of monumental building projects that have few rivals in the ancient world. He had colossal statues of himself erected throughout the country. The prefix "Ra" in his name tells us that he was seen as the sun god, a divine being whose rule was written in the heavens and whose word carried absolute command.

The Israelites, for their part, were a landless people, entirely at the mercy of the Egyptians. They had no power and, at first, no effective leadership. They were easily conscripted into forced labor. No group seemed less likely to become the people of eternity.

Had anyone suggested at the time that it would not be the Egypt of the pharaohs that would survive and change the moral landscape of the world, but instead a group of Hebrew slaves, it would have seemed an ultimate absurdity. The Egyptians believed that the Israelites were already on the verge of extinction. The earliest known reference to Israel outside the Bible is an inscription produced by Ramesses's successor, Merneptah, in the thirteenth century BCE. The Merneptah Stele, a giant slab of black granite that stands today in the Cairo Museum, contains these words: "Israel is laid waste. His seed is no more."

1:11 אֶת־פִּתֹם וְאֶת־רַעַמְסֵס *Pitom and Ramesses* – Pitom or Per-Atum is the modern Tell el-Mashkuta in the eastern delta, a day's journey from Ramesses. Ramesses or Per-Ramses, "the

16 named Shifra, the other Puah – "When you help a Hebrew woman give birth,
17 look on the birth stool. If it is a boy, kill him, and if it is a girl, let her live." But
the midwives feared God, and did not do as the king of Egypt ordered them.
18 They let the babies live. Then the king of Egypt summoned the midwives and SHENI
demanded, "Why have you done this; why have you let the children live?"
19 But "Hebrew women," the midwives replied, "are not like Egyptians. They
are full of vigor, and have already given birth by the time the midwife arrives."
20 God was good to the midwives; and the people multiplied and grew very
21 strong. And because the midwives feared God, He granted them households.
22 Then Pharaoh commanded his entire people, saying, "Throw every boy that is
born into the Nile, and let all the girls live."

רש"י

טז **בילדכן.** כמו בהולידכן: **על האבנים.** מושב האשה היולדת, ובמקום אחר קורהו 'משבר' (שם לז, ג), וכמוהו: "עשה מלאכה על האבנים" (ירמיה יח, ג) – מושב כלי אומנות יוצר חרש: **אם בן הוא וגו'.** לא היה מקפיד אלא על הזכרים, שאמרו לו אצטגניניו שעתידות לילד בן המושיע אותם: **וחיה.** ותחיה:

יז **ותחיין את הילדים.** מספקות להם מזון. תרגום הראשון "וקיימא" והשני (בפסוק הבא) "וקיימתין". לפי שלשון עבר לנקבות רבות, תבה זו וכיוצא בה משמשת לשון פעלו ולשון פעלתן, כגון: "ותאמרן איש מצרי" (להלן ב, יט) לשון עבר, כמו 'ויאמרו' לזכרים. "ותדברנה בפיכם" (ירמיה מד, כה) לשון דברתם כמו 'ותדברו' לזכרים. וכן: "ותחללנה אתי אל עמי" (יחזקאל יג, יט) לשון עבר, חללתן, כמו 'ותחללו' לזכרים:

יט **כי חיות הנה.** בקיאות כמילדות, תרגום מילדות 'חייתא'. ורבותינו דרשו, הרי הן משולות כחיות השדה שאינן צריכות מילדת: "גור אריה" (בראשית מט, ט), "זאב יטרף" (שם פסוק כז), "בכור שורו" (דברים לג, יז), "אילה שלחה" (בראשית מט, כא). ומי שלא נכתב בו, הרי הכתוב כוללן: "מה אמך לביא" (יחזקאל יט, ב):

כ-כא **וייטב.** היטיב להן. וזה חלוק בתבה שיסודה שתי אותיות ונתן לה וי"ו יו"ד בראשה, כשהיא באה לדבר לשון ויפעיל הוא נוקד את היו"ד בצירי שהוא קמץ קטן, כגון: "וייטב אלהים למילדת"; "וירב בבת יהודה" (איכה ב, ה), הרבה תאניה; וכן "ויגל השארית" (דברי הימים ב' לו, כ) דנבוזראדן, הגלה את השארית; "ויפן זנב אל זנב" (שופטים טו, ד) – הפנה הזנבות זו לזו. כל אלו לשון הפעיל את אחרים. וכשהוא מדבר בלשון ויפעל הוא נוקד היו"ד בחיריק, כגון: "וייטב בעיניו" (ויקרא י, כ) – לשון הוטב; וכן "וירב העם" (להלן פסוק כ) – רבה העם; "ויגל יהודה" (מלכים ב' כה, כא) גלה יהודה; "ויפן כה וכה" (להלן ב, יב) – פנה לכאן ולכאן. ואל תשיבני: וילך, וישב, וירד, ויצא, לפי שאינן מגזרתן של אלו, שהרי היו"ד יסוד בהן: ירד, יצא, ילך, ישב, היו"ד אות שלישית בו: **וייטב אלהים למילדת.** מהו הטובה? "ויעש להם בתים" – בתי כהנה ולויה ומלכות, שקרויין בתים: "לבנות את בית ה' ואת בית המלך" (מלכים א' ט, א); כהנה ולויה מיוכבד, ומלכות ממרים, כדאיתא במסכת סוטה (דף יא ע"ב):

כב **לכל עמו.** אף עליהם גזר. יום שנולד משה אמרו לו אצטגניניו:

It is notable that only two, Yokheved and Miriam, are clearly Israelite. Pharaoh's daughter and Tzipora are clearly not, and the identity of Shifra and Puah is uncertain. The entire Exodus narrative is a delicate counterpoint between the particularity of Israel – "My son, My firstborn" (4:22) – and the universality of the moral law. We will see this several times in the following chapters.

Not every nation is expected to be holy. But every nation is expected to be moral. Thus we are presented with role models, such as these non-Israelite women, whose principled stand against tyranny and persecution transcends all ethnic and cultural boundaries.

1:21 **ויעש להם בתים** *He granted them households* – The story of Shifra and Puah is not a tragedy. It ends with a curious phrase: God "granted them households." What does this mean? Luzzatto (see above, "Midwives to the Hebrews") offers an insightful interpretation. Sometimes women become midwives when they are unable to have children of their own. That, he suggests, was the case with

טז וַיֹּאמֶר בְּיַלֶּדְכֶן אֶת־הָעִבְרִיּוֹת וּרְאִיתֶן עַל־הָאׇבְנָיִם אִם־בֵּן הוּא
יז וַהֲמִתֶּן אֹתוֹ וְאִם־בַּת הִוא וָחָיָה: וַתִּירֶאןָ הַמְיַלְּדֹת אֶת־הָאֱלֹהִים וְלֹא
יח עָשׂוּ כַּאֲשֶׁר דִּבֶּר אֲלֵיהֶן מֶלֶךְ מִצְרָיִם וַתְּחַיֶּיןָ אֶת־הַיְלָדִים: וַיִּקְרָא שני
מֶלֶךְ־מִצְרַיִם לַמְיַלְּדֹת וַיֹּאמֶר לָהֶן מַדּוּעַ עֲשִׂיתֶן הַדָּבָר הַזֶּה וַתְּחַיֶּיןָ
יט אֶת־הַיְלָדִים: וַתֹּאמַרְןָ הַמְיַלְּדֹת אֶל־פַּרְעֹה כִּי לֹא כַנָּשִׁים הַמִּצְרִיֹּת
כ הָעִבְרִיֹּת כִּי־חָיוֹת הֵנָּה בְּטֶרֶם תָּבוֹא אֲלֵהֶן הַמְיַלֶּדֶת וְיָלָדוּ: וַיֵּיטֶב
כא אֱלֹהִים לַמְיַלְּדֹת וַיִּרֶב הָעָם וַיַּעַצְמוּ מְאֹד: וַיְהִי כִּי־יָרְאוּ הַמְיַלְּדֹת
כב אֶת־הָאֱלֹהִים וַיַּעַשׂ לָהֶם בָּתִּים: וַיְצַו פַּרְעֹה לְכׇל־עַמּוֹ לֵאמֹר כׇּל־הַבֵּן
הַיִּלּוֹד הַיְאֹרָה תַּשְׁלִיכֻהוּ וְכׇל־הַבַּת תְּחַיּוּן:

אונקלוס

טז וַאֲמַר, כַּד תְּהֶוְיָן מְיַלְּדָן יָת יְהוּדָיָתָא, וְתִחְזְיָן עַל מַתְבְּרָא, אִם בְּרָא הוּא וְתִקְטְלָן יָתֵיהּ, וְאִם בְּרַתָּא הִיא וּתְקַיְּמִנַּהּ: יז וּדְחִילָא חָיָתָא מִן קֳדָם יי, וְלָא עֲבַדָא, כְּמָא דְּמַלֵּיל עִמְּהוֹן מַלְכָּא דְּמִצְרָיִם, וְקַיָּמָא יָת בְּנַיָּא: יח וּקְרָא מַלְכָּא דְּמִצְרַיִם לְחָיָתָא, וַאֲמַר לְהוֹן, מָדֵין עֲבַדְתִּין פִּתְגָּמָא הָדֵין, וְקַיֵּמְתִּין יָת בְּנַיָּא: יט וַאֲמַרָא חָיָתָא לְפַרְעֹה, אֲרֵי לָא כִנְשַׁיָּא, מִצְרָיָתָא יְהוּדָיָתָא, אֲרֵי חַכִּימָן אִנִּין, עַד לָא עָאלַת לְוָתְהוֹן, חָיְתָא יָלְדָן: כ וְאוֹטֵיב יי לְחָיָתָא, וּסְגִי עַמָּא, וּתְקִיפוּ לַחְדָּא: כא וַהֲוָה, כַּד דְּחִילָא חָיָתָא מִן קֳדָם יי, וַעֲבַד לְהוֹן בָּתִּין: כב וּפַקֵּיד פַּרְעֹה, לְכָל עַמֵּיהּ לְמֵימַר, כָּל בְּרָא דְּיִתְיְלֵיד לִיהוּדָאֵי, בְּנַהְרָא תִּרְמוֹנֵיהּ, וְכָל בְּרַתָּא תְּקַיְּמוּן:

of identifying unknown characters with characters who are more elaborated (Sota 11b, Rashi there). However, in describing them the Torah uses an ambiguous phrase. It calls them *hameyaldot haIvriot*, which could mean either "the Hebrew midwives" or "the midwives to the Hebrews." On the second interpretation, they may not have been Hebrews at all, but Egyptians. This is the view taken, among others, by the scholar and statesman Abrabanel and the Italian commentator Shmuel David Luzzatto. Luzzatto's reasoning is simple: could Pharaoh realistically have expected Hebrew women to murder their own people's children? Rather than decide one way or the other, it seems clear that the Torah's ambiguity on this point is deliberate. We do not know who they are or which people they belong to because their particular form of moral courage transcends nationality and race. In essence, they are being asked to commit a "crime against humanity," and the fact that they refuse to do so tells us something about the ethical parameters of humanity as such. Though Shifra and Puah are seemingly minor figures in the narrative, they are giants in the story of humanity. All we know about them is that they "feared God and did not do as the king of Egypt ordered them" (Ex. 1:17). In those words, a precedent is set that will eventually become the basis of the United Nations Universal Declaration of Human Rights. Shifra and Puah, by refusing to obey an immoral order, redefine the moral imagination of the world.

Shifra and Puah are the first of six courageous women who will play a vital part in the story of Israel's redemption in this *parasha*. The others are Yokheved and Miriam, Pharaoh's daughter, and Moshe's wife Tzipora. Moshe may be the central character in the unfolding drama of Israel's redemption, but without these women, there would be no Moshe. Their moral courage is a vital element in the story.

2 1 2 A man of the house of Levi went and married a daughter of Levi. And she became
pregnant and gave birth to a son. She saw what a fine child he was, and for three
3 months she kept him hidden. And when she could no longer hide him, she took a
papyrus basket and coated it with tar and pitch. She laid the child in it and placed
4 it among the reeds by the bank of the Nile, and his sister stood by at a distance to

רש"י

הַיּוֹם נוֹלָד וְאֵין אָנוּ יוֹדְעִים אִם מִמִּצְרַיִם אִם מִיִּשְׂרָאֵל, וְרוֹאִין אָנוּ שֶׁסּוֹפוֹ לִלְקוֹת בַּמַּיִם, לְפִיכָךְ גָּזַר אוֹתוֹ הַיּוֹם אַף עַל הַמִּצְרִים, שֶׁנֶּאֱמַר: "כָּל הַבֵּן הַיִּלּוֹד" וְלֹא נֶאֱמַר 'הַיִּלּוֹד לָעִבְרִים'. וְהֵם לֹא הָיוּ יוֹדְעִים שֶׁסּוֹפוֹ לִלְקוֹת עַל מֵי מְרִיבָה:

ב א **וַיִּקַּח אֶת בַּת לֵוִי.** פָּרוּשׁ הָיָה מִמֶּנָּה מִפְּנֵי גְּזֵרַת פַּרְעֹה וְהֶחֱזִירָהּ וְעָשָׂה בָּהּ לִקּוּחִין שְׁנִיִּים. וְאַף הִיא נֶהֶפְכָה לִהְיוֹת נַעֲרָה. וּבַת מֵאָה וּשְׁלֹשִׁים שָׁנָה הָיְתָה; שֶׁנּוֹלְדָה בְּבוֹאָם לְמִצְרַיִם בֵּין הַחוֹמוֹת, וּמָאתַיִם וְעֶשֶׂר נִשְׁתַּהוּ שָׁם, וּכְשֶׁיָּצְאוּ הָיָה מֹשֶׁה בֶּן שְׁמוֹנִים שָׁנָה – כְּשֶׁנִּתְעַבְּרָה מִמֶּנּוּ הָיְתָה בַּת מֵאָה וּשְׁלֹשִׁים, וְקוֹרֵא אוֹתָהּ 'בַּת לֵוִי':

ב **כִּי טוֹב הוּא.** כְּשֶׁנּוֹלַד נִתְמַלֵּא הַבַּיִת כֻּלּוֹ אוֹרָה:

ג **וְלֹא יָכְלָה עוֹד הַצְּפִינוֹ.** שֶׁמָּנוּ לָהּ הַמִּצְרִים מִיּוֹם שֶׁהֶחֱזִירָהּ, וְהִיא יְלָדַתּוּ לְשִׁשָּׁה חֳדָשִׁים וְיוֹם אֶחָד, שֶׁהַיּוֹלֶדֶת לְשִׁבְעָה יוֹלֶדֶת לִמְקֻטָּעִין, וְהֵם בָּדְקוּ אַחֲרֶיהָ לְסוֹף תִּשְׁעָה: **גֹּמֶא.** גֶּמִי בִּלְשׁוֹן מִשְׁנָה, וּבְלַעַז יונ"ק, וְדָבָר רַךְ הוּא וְעוֹמֵד בִּפְנֵי רַךְ וּבִפְנֵי קָשֶׁה: **בַחֵמָר וּבַזָּפֶת.** זֶפֶת מִבַּחוּץ וְטִיט מִבִּפְנִים, כְּדֵי שֶׁלֹּא יָרִיחַ אוֹתוֹ צַדִּיק רֵיחַ רַע שֶׁל זֶפֶת: **וַתָּשֶׂם בַּסּוּף.** הוּא לְשׁוֹן אֲגַם, רוסי"ל בְּלַעַז, וְדוֹמֶה לוֹ: "קָנֶה וָסוּף קָמֵלוּ" (ישעיה יט, ו):

2:2 **וַתֵּרֶא אֹתוֹ כִּי־טוֹב** *She saw what a fine child he was* – Literally, "She saw him that he was good." This language is an echo of the creation narrative: "And God saw… it was good" (Gen. 1:4, 10, 12, 18, 21, 25, 31). This is one of a series of evocations of the early chapters of Genesis (compare, for instance, the language of Ex. 1:7 with that of Gen. 1:28), suggesting that what we are reading is the story of a new creation: a covenanted nation that will emerge from the crucible of suffering to carry the Divine Presence in its midst.

2:2 **וַתִּצְפְּנֵהוּ** *She kept him hidden* – In standard versions of mythology, a ruler receives a warning about a child about to be born to him. The ruler takes steps to kill the child or let him die. The child is saved, often by being placed in a basket and floated down a river, and raised by people of humble birth. Only later does he learn that he has royal blood.

The story of Moshe is the precise opposite. He is found and raised by royalty – an Egyptian princess, Pharaoh's daughter – and learns that he is in fact not royalty but a member of what has become, in Egyptian eyes, a pariah people. The Moshe story is a subtle and brilliant assault on the concept, central (though not exclusive) to polytheistic religions, of a human hierarchy, in which rulers are marked from the outset by royal blood. Moshe is the representative of a people every member of whom has been adopted by God, a point made in the first words Moshe is commanded to say to Pharaoh: "Israel is My son, My firstborn" (Ex. 4:22).

2:3 **וַתָּשֶׂם בַּסּוּף עַל־שְׂפַת הַיְאֹר** *Placed it among the reeds by the bank of the Nile* – I try to imagine the courage of a woman willing to have a child once the decree has been issued to "throw every boy that is born into the Nile" (Ex. 1:22). The scene is Germany, 1939. Anti-Jewish edicts are in force. There is a sense of impending tragedy. To have a child at that time is a supreme act of hope in the midst of despair. That is the bravery of Yokheved.

What do we know about her? Surprisingly little. We see Yokheved's resourcefulness. For three months she hides the child. When she can do so no longer, she makes a papyrus basket and sets him afloat on the Nile, hoping he will be noticed and saved. Like many biblical women, she is a person of action, determination, and courage.

She gives birth to three children destined for greatness: Miriam, the prophetess; Aharon, Israel's first High Priest; and Moshe, its greatest leader. She endows her children, genetically or by example, with the gift of leadership. She and her husband are both from the tribe of Levi. A few chapters earlier, the Torah has told us that on his deathbed

ב א ב וַיֵּלֶךְ אִישׁ מִבֵּית לֵוִי וַיִּקַּח אֶת־בַּת־לֵוִי׃ וַתַּהַר הָאִשָּׁה וַתֵּלֶד בֵּן וַתֵּרֶא
ג אֹתוֹ כִּי־טוֹב הוּא וַתִּצְפְּנֵהוּ שְׁלֹשָׁה יְרָחִים׃ וְלֹא־יָכְלָה עוֹד הַצְּפִינוֹ
וַתִּקַּח־לוֹ תֵּבַת גֹּמֶא וַתַּחְמְרָה בַחֵמָר וּבַזָּפֶת וַתָּשֶׂם בָּהּ אֶת־הַיֶּלֶד
ד וַתָּשֶׂם בַּסּוּף עַל־שְׂפַת הַיְאֹר׃ וַתֵּתַצַּב אֲחֹתוֹ מֵרָחֹק לְדֵעָה מַה־יֵּעָשֶׂה

אונקלוס

ב א וַאֲזַל גַּבְרָא מִדְּבֵית לֵוִי, וּנְסֵיב יָת בַּת לֵוִי: ב וְעַדִּיאַת אִתְּתָא
וִילֵידַת בַּר, וַחֲזַת יָתֵיהּ אֲרֵי טָב הוּא, וְאַטְמַרְתֵּיהּ תְּלָתָא יַרְחִין:
ג וְלָא יְכֵילַת עוֹד לְאַטְמָרוּתֵיהּ, וּנְסֵיבַת לֵיהּ תֵּיבְתָא דְּגוֹמֶא,
וַחֲפָתַהּ בְּחֵימָרָא וּבְזִפְתָּא, וְשַׁוִּיאַת בַּהּ יָת רַבְיָא, וְשַׁוִּיתַהּ בְּיַעְרָא
עַל כֵּיף נַהְרָא: ד וְאִתְעַתַּדַת אֲחָתֵיהּ מֵרַחִיק, לְמִדַּע, מָא יִתְעֲבֵיד

Shifra and Puah. Because they saved children's lives, God rewarded them – measure for measure – with children of their own ("households," meaning families). "In reward for the righteous women of that generation, our ancestors were redeemed from Egypt" (Sota 11b). Shifra and Puah were two of those women, heroines of the spirit, giants in the story of humankind.

1:22 וַיְצַו פַּרְעֹה לְכָל־עַמּוֹ *Then Pharaoh commanded his entire people* – This is the beginning of a terrible crime against humanity – the mass murder of children – that will eventually return to haunt Pharaoh and his people. This is the message of the first plague, the river that turned into blood, and the last plague, the death of the firstborn. A fundamental theme here, as it was after the flood, is the sanctity of life, every life, even that of the young child. The reference to the entire people is a further emphasis on the fact that what was happening was public: all the people were complicit in the slow genocide of the male Israelite newborns. One of the fundamental unanswered questions about the Holocaust is: how was it that so many knew but did not protest? Evil, when initiated at the top of the social-political structure, is often contagious. That is why the Torah emphasizes the counter-examples, the midwives here, and Pharaoh's daughter in the next chapter. It is possible to take a stand against evil.

2:1 וַיֵּלֶךְ אִישׁ מִבֵּית לֵוִי וַיִּקַּח אֶת־בַּת־לֵוִי *A man of the house of Levi went and married a daughter of Levi* – The Talmud records the existential dilemma faced by Jews in the second century CE, having experienced the destruction of the Temple, the brutal suppression of the Bar Kokhba rebellion, and the Hadrianic persecutions. A statement in the name of R. Yishmael reads: "From the day that a government has come to power which issues cruel decrees against us and forbids us to observe the Torah and its commands… we ought by rights to bind ourselves not to marry and beget children, with the result that the seed of Avraham our father would come to an end of its own accord" (Bava Batra 60b). This haunting passage tells us that there were profoundly religious Jews like R. Yishmael who believed that on rational grounds one should not bring Jewish children into a world which had experienced nightmare. But R. Yishmael added that were this to be issued as a ruling it would not be obeyed, for the faith of ordinary Jews transcends logic.

Does this mean an irrational faith? The Rabbis implicitly posed the question elsewhere in the form of a projected dialogue between Amram, "a man of the house of Levi," and his daughter Miriam, at the time of Pharaoh's decree (Sota 12a). In this interpretation, Amram and the other Israelite men, seeing that every male Israelite child was to be cast into the river and drowned, thereupon divorced their wives and refused to have children. Amram's daughter protested. The decision, she said, was worse than Pharaoh's decree. It condemned both boys and girls. It deprived them of both this world and the next. Amram relented and he and his wife had a son: Moshe. The implication is clear. From faith comes redemption. Trust in the future is not always rational, but neither is it irrational. Rather it is, in crisis, the critical test of religious courage.

5 see what would happen to him. Pharaoh's daughter came down to bathe in the
Nile, while her attendants walked by the riverbank. She saw the basket among
6 the reeds and sent her maid to fetch it. When she opened it she saw him there,
the child; the boy was crying, and she was moved to pity for him: "This must be
7 one of the Hebrew boys." Then his sister asked Pharaoh's daughter, "Shall I go and
8 fetch one of the Hebrew women to nurse the child for you?" "Go," said Pharaoh's
9 daughter. So the girl went away and called the child's mother. "Take this child,"
Pharaoh's daughter told her. "Nurse him for me, and I will pay you your wage." So

רש״י

ה **לִרְחֹץ עַל הַיְאֹר.** סָרֵס הַמִּקְרָא וּפָרְשֵׁהוּ, וַתֵּרֶד בַּת פַּרְעֹה עַל הַיְאוֹר לִרְחֹץ בּוֹ: **עַל יַד הַיְאֹר.** אֵצֶל הַיְאוֹר, כְּמוֹ: "רְאוּ חֶלְקַת יוֹאָב אֶל יָדִי" (שמואל ב׳ יד, ל), וְהוּא לְשׁוֹן יָד מַמָּשׁ, שֶׁיַּד הָאָדָם סְמוּכָה לוֹ. וְרַבּוֹתֵינוּ אָמְרוּ, "הֹלְכֹת" לְשׁוֹן מִיתָה, הוֹלְכוֹת לָמוּת לְפִי שֶׁמִּחוּ בָּהּ. וְהַכָּתוּב מְסַיְּעָן, כִּי לָמָּה לָנוּ לִכְתֹּב: "וְנַעֲרֹתֶיהָ הֹלְכֹת"?: **אֶת אֲמָתָהּ.** אֶת שִׁפְחָתָהּ. וְרַבּוֹתֵינוּ דָּרְשׁוּ לְשׁוֹן יָד, אֲבָל לְפִי דִּקְדּוּק לְשׁוֹן הַקֹּדֶשׁ הָיָה לוֹ לְהִנָּקֵד 'אַמָּתָהּ' מֵ"ם דְּגוּשָׁה, וְהֵם דָּרְשׁוּ "אֶת אֲמָתָהּ" – אֶת יָדָהּ, וְנִשְׁתַּרְבְּבָה אַמָּתָהּ אַמּוֹת הַרְבֵּה:

ו **וַתִּפְתַּח וַתִּרְאֵהוּ.** אֶת מִי רָאֲתָה? "אֶת הַיֶּלֶד", זֶהוּ פְּשׁוּטוֹ. וּמִדְרָשׁוֹ, שֶׁרָאֲתָה עִמּוֹ שְׁכִינָה: **וְהִנֵּה נַעַר בֹּכֶה.** קוֹלוֹ כְּנַעַר:

ז **מִן הָעִבְרִיֹּת.** שֶׁהֶחֱזִירַתּוּ עַל מִצְרִיּוֹת הַרְבֵּה לִינֹק וְלֹא יָנַק, לְפִי שֶׁהָיָה עָתִיד לְדַבֵּר עִם הַשְּׁכִינָה:

ח **וַתֵּלֶךְ הָעַלְמָה.** הָלְכָה בִּזְרִיזוּת וַעֲלָמוּת כְּעֶלֶם:

ט **הֵילִיכִי.** נִתְנַבְּאָה וְלֹא יָדְעָה מַה נִּתְנַבְּאָה, הֵי שֶׁלִּיכִי:

committed to the child's welfare, taking the riskiest of strategies. She will adopt him and bring him up as her own son. This is courage of a high order.

Who then is Pharaoh's daughter? Nowhere is she explicitly named. However, the first book of Chronicles (4:18) mentions a daughter of Pharaoh, named Bitya, and it was she the Sages identified as the woman who saved Moshe. The name Bitya (sometimes rendered as Batya) means "the daughter of God." From this, the Sages drew one of their most striking lessons: "The Holy One, blessed be He, said to her: 'Moshe was not your son, yet you called him your son. You are not My daughter, but I shall call you My daughter'" (Vayikra Rabba 1:3). They added that she was one of the few people (tradition enumerates nine) who were so righteous that they entered paradise in their lifetime (Derekh Eretz Zuta 1).

Moral courage can sometimes be found in the heart of darkness. That the Torah itself tells the story the way it does has enormous implications. It means that when it comes to people, we must never generalize, never stereotype. The Egyptians were not all evil: even from Pharaoh himself a heroine was born. Nothing could signal more powerfully that the Torah is not an ethnocentric text; that we must recognize virtue wherever we find it, even among our enemies; and that the basic core of human values – humanity, compassion, courage – is truly universal. Faith may not be; goodness is.

2:6 **וְהִנֵּה־נַעַר בֹּכֶה** *The boy was crying* – The verse begins by calling Moshe a baby (*yeled*) and ends by calling him a boy or youth (*naar*). Rashi explains that "he cried in an adult way." On this, Rabbi Meir Shapiro of Lublin commented: "There are two ways of crying. A child cries when it is in pain. An adult cries when it sees someone else in pain." Already the princess felt in Moshe a sensitivity to the suffering of others.

2:7 **וַתֹּאמֶר אֲחֹתוֹ אֶל־בַּת־פַּרְעֹה** *Then his sister asked Pharaoh's daughter* – This encounter on the banks of the Nile, between an Egyptian princess and a young Israelite child, Moshe's sister Miriam, is profoundly moving. The contrast between them – in terms of age, culture, status, and power – could not be greater. Yet their deep humanity bridges all the differences, all the distance. Two heroines. May they inspire us.

ה לוֹ: וַתֵּרֶד בַּת־פַּרְעֹה לִרְחֹץ עַל־הַיְאֹר וְנַעֲרֹתֶיהָ הֹלְכֹת עַל־יַד הַיְאֹר
ו וַתֵּרֶא אֶת־הַתֵּבָה בְּתוֹךְ הַסּוּף וַתִּשְׁלַח אֶת־אֲמָתָהּ וַתִּקָּחֶהָ: וַתִּפְתַּח
וַתִּרְאֵהוּ אֶת־הַיֶּלֶד וְהִנֵּה־נַעַר בֹּכֶה וַתַּחְמֹל עָלָיו וַתֹּאמֶר מִיַּלְדֵי
ז הָעִבְרִים זֶה: וַתֹּאמֶר אֲחֹתוֹ אֶל־בַּת־פַּרְעֹה הַאֵלֵךְ וְקָרָאתִי לָךְ אִשָּׁה
ח מֵינֶקֶת מִן הָעִבְרִיֹּת וְתֵינִק לָךְ אֶת־הַיָּלֶד: וַתֹּאמֶר־לָהּ בַּת־פַּרְעֹה לֵכִי
ט וַתֵּלֶךְ הָעַלְמָה וַתִּקְרָא אֶת־אֵם הַיָּלֶד: וַתֹּאמֶר לָהּ בַּת־פַּרְעֹה הֵילִיכִי
אֶת־הַיֶּלֶד הַזֶּה וְהֵינִקִהוּ לִי וַאֲנִי אֶתֵּן אֶת־שְׂכָרֵךְ וַתִּקַּח הָאִשָּׁה הַיֶּלֶד

אונקלוס

לֵיהּ: ה וּנְחָתַת בַּת פַּרְעֹה לְמִסְחֵי עַל נַהְרָא, וְעוּלֵימָתַהָא מְהַלְּכָן
עַל כֵּיף נַהְרָא, וַחֲזָת יָת תֵּיבְתָא בְּגוֹ יַעְרָא, וְאוֹשֵׁיטַת יָת אַמְתַהּ
וּנְסֵיבְתַהּ: ו וּפְתַחַת וַחֲזָת יָת רַבְיָא, וְהָא עוּלֵימָא בָּכֵי, וְחַסַת
עֲלוֹהִי, וַאֲמַרַת, מִבְּנֵי יְהוּדָאֵי הוּא דֵין: ז וַאֲמַרַת אֲחָתֵיהּ לְבַת
פַּרְעֹה, הַאֵיזֵיל, וְאֶקְרֵי לִיךְ אִתְּתָא מֵינִקְתָּא, מִן יְהוּדָיָתָא, וְתוֹנִיק
לִיךְ יָת רַבְיָא: ח וַאֲמַרַת לַהּ בַּת פַּרְעֹה אִיזִילִי, וַאֲזַלַת עוּלֵימְתָא,
וּקְרָת יָת אִמֵּיהּ דְּרַבְיָא: ט וַאֲמַרַת לַהּ בַּת פַּרְעֹה, הָלִיכִי, יָת רַבְיָא
הָדֵין וְאוֹנִיקִיהוּ לִי, וַאֲנָא אֶתֵּין יָת אַגְרִיךְ, וּנְסֵיבַת אִתְּתָא, רַבְיָא

Yaakov delivers both a prediction and a curse: "Shimon and Levi are brothers; weapons of violence their wares. Let me never join their council, nor my honor be of their assembly. For in their anger they killed men, at their whim they hamstrung oxen. Cursed be their anger, for it is most fierce, and their fury, for it is most cruel" (Gen. 49:5–7).

We hear little subsequently about Shimon. But the children of Levi defy Yaakov's low opinion. From their ranks will eventually come not only the three leaders of the exodus, but Israel's priests and Levites, its spiritual ministers, for all time. There is more than a hint that something in Yokheved – her capacity for hope or her faith in life – transforms, in her children, violence into courage, and aggression into an unshakable determination to rescue people and set them on the path to liberty. She has the subtle gift of transforming vice into virtue. She becomes the mother of Israel's leaders.

PHARAOH'S DAUGHTER

Pharaoh afflicts the children of Israel, but it is another member of his own family who saves the decisive vestige of hope. Pharaoh's daughter is one of the most unexpected heroes of the Hebrew Bible. Without her, Moshe might not have lived. The whole story of the exodus would have been different. Yet she is not an Israelite. She has nothing to gain, and everything to lose, by her courage. Yet she seems to have no doubt, experiences no misgivings, makes no hesitation.

Pharaoh's daughter goes to bathe in the Nile, while her maids walk along the Nile's edge. She sees the basket in the reeds and sends her slave girl to fetch it. First she sees that it is a child and has pity on it. This is a natural, human, compassionate reaction. Only then does it dawn on her who the child must be. Who else would abandon a child? She remembers her father's decree against the Hebrews. Instantly the situation has changed. To save the baby would mean disobeying the royal command. That would be serious enough for an ordinary Egyptian, doubly so for a member of the royal family.

Nor is she alone when the event happens. Her maids are with her; her slave girl is standing beside her. She must face the risk that one of them, in a fit of pique, or even mere gossip, will tell someone about it. Rumors flourish in royal courts. Yet she does not shift her ground. She does not tell one of her servants to take the baby and hide it with a family far away. She has the courage of her compassion. She does not flinch.

Nor is this simply a moment's pity. She remains

10 the woman took the child and nursed him. The child grew, and she brought him
to Pharaoh's daughter and he became her son. She named him Moshe, "because,"
11 she said, "I drew him out of the water." One day, when Moshe had grown up, he SHELISHI
went out to his people and saw their forced labor. And he noticed an Egyptian
12 striking a Hebrew: one of his brothers. Looking this way and that and seeing no
13 one, he struck down the Egyptian and hid his body in the sand. The next day
he went out and saw two Hebrews fighting. He asked the guilty one, "Why are
14 you striking your own neighbor?" The man said, "Who made you a ruler and
judge over us? Do you intend to kill me as you killed the Egyptian?" Then Moshe

רש״י

י **מְשִׁיתִהוּ.** "שְׁחַלְתֵּיהּ", הוּא לְשׁוֹן הוֹצָאָה בִּלְשׁוֹן אֲרַמִּי: "כְּמִשְׁחַל בִּינִיתָא מֵחֲלָבָא" (ברכות ח ע"א). וּבִלְשׁוֹן עִבְרִי "מְשִׁיתִהוּ" לְשׁוֹן הֲסִירוֹתִיו, כְּמוֹ: "לֹא יָמוּשׁ" (יהושע א, ח), "לֹא מָשׁוּ" (במדבר יד, מד); כָּךְ חִבְּרוֹ מְנַחֵם. וַאֲנִי אוֹמֵר שֶׁאֵינוֹ מִמַּחְבֶּרֶת מָשׁ וְיָמוּשׁ, אֶלָּא מִגִּזְרַת מָשָׁה, וּלְשׁוֹן הוֹצָאָה הוּא; וְכֵן: "יַמְשֵׁנִי מִמַּיִם רַבִּים" (שמואל ב' כב, יז). שֶׁאִלּוּ הָיָה מִמַּחְבֶּרֶת מָשׁ, לֹא יִתָּכֵן לוֹמַר 'מְשִׁיתִיהוּ', אֶלָּא 'הֲמִישׁוֹתִיהוּ', כַּאֲשֶׁר יֵאָמֵר מִן קָם 'הֲקִימוֹתִי', וּמִן שָׁב 'הֲשִׁיבוֹתִי', וּמִן בָּא 'הֲבִיאוֹתִי'; אוֹ 'מַשְׁתִּיהוּ', כְּמוֹ: "וּמַשְׁתִּי אֶת עֲוֹן הָאָרֶץ" (זכריה ג, ט). אֲבָל 'מָשִׁיתִי' אֵינוֹ אֶלָּא מִגִּזְרַת תֵּבָה שֶׁפָּעַל שֶׁלָּהּ מְיֻסָּד בְּהֵ"א בְּסוֹף הַתֵּבָה, כְּגוֹן: מָשָׁה, בָּנָה, עָשָׂה, צִוָּה, פָּנָה, כְּשֶׁיָּבוֹא לוֹמַר בָּהֶם פָּעַלְתִּי תָּבֹא הַיּוּ"ד בִּמְקוֹם הֵ"א, כְּמוֹ: עָשִׂיתִי, בָּנִיתִי, פָּנִיתִי, צִוִּיתִי:

יא **וַיִּגְדַּל מֹשֶׁה.** וַהֲלֹא כְּבָר כָּתַב (לעיל פסוק י) "וַיִּגְדַּל הַיֶּלֶד"? אָמַר רַבִּי יְהוּדָה בְּרַבִּי אִלְעַאי, הָרִאשׁוֹן לְקוֹמָה וְהַשֵּׁנִי לִגְדֻלָּה, שֶׁמִּנָּהוּ פַּרְעֹה עַל בֵּיתוֹ: **וַיַּרְא בְּסִבְלֹתָם.** נָתַן עֵינָיו וְלִבּוֹ לִהְיוֹת מֵצֵר עֲלֵיהֶם: **אִישׁ מִצְרִי.** נוֹגֵשׂ הָיָה, מְמֻנֶּה עַל שׁוֹטְרֵי יִשְׂרָאֵל, וְהָיָה מַעֲמִידָם מִקְּרוֹת הַגֶּבֶר לִמְלַאכְתָּם: **מַכֶּה אִישׁ עִבְרִי.** מַלְקֵהוּ וְרוֹדֵהוּ; וּבַעְלָהּ שֶׁל שְׁלוֹמִית בַּת דִּבְרִי הָיָה, וְנָתַן עֵינָיו בָּהּ, וּבַלַּיְלָה הֶעֱמִידוֹ וְהוֹצִיאוֹ מִבֵּיתוֹ וְהוּא חָזַר וְנִכְנַס לַבַּיִת וּבָא עַל אִשְׁתּוֹ, כִּסְבוּרָה שֶׁהוּא בַּעְלָהּ. וְחָזַר הָאִישׁ לְבֵיתוֹ וְהִרְגִּישׁ בַּדָּבָר, וּכְשֶׁרָאָה אוֹתוֹ מִצְרִי שֶׁהִרְגִּישׁ בַּדָּבָר הָיָה מַכֵּהוּ וְרוֹדֵהוּ כָּל הַיּוֹם:

יב **וַיִּפֶן כֹּה וָכֹה.** רָאָה מֶה עָשָׂה לוֹ בַּבַּיִת וּמֶה עָשָׂה לוֹ בַּשָּׂדֶה. וּלְפִי פְּשׁוּטוֹ כְּמַשְׁמָעוֹ: **וַיַּרְא כִּי אֵין אִישׁ.** עָתִיד לָצֵאת מִמֶּנּוּ שֶׁיִּתְגַּיֵּר:

יג **שְׁנֵי אֲנָשִׁים עִבְרִים.** דָּתָן וַאֲבִירָם, הֵם שֶׁהוֹתִירוּ מִן הַמָּן: **נִצִּים.** מְרִיבִים: **לָמָּה תַכֶּה.** אַף עַל פִּי שֶׁלֹּא הִכָּהוּ נִקְרָא רָשָׁע בַּהֲרָמַת יָד: **רֵעֶךָ.** רָשָׁע כְּמוֹתְךָ:

יד **מִי שָׂמְךָ לְאִישׁ.** וַהֲרֵי עוֹדְךָ נַעַר: **הַלְהָרְגֵנִי אַתָּה אֹמֵר.** מִכָּאן אָנוּ לְמֵדִים שֶׁהֲרָגוֹ בְּשֵׁם הַמְּפֹרָשׁ: **וַיִּירָא מֹשֶׁה.** כִּפְשׁוּטוֹ. וּמִדְרָשׁוֹ, דָּאַג לוֹ עַל שֶׁרָאָה בְיִשְׂרָאֵל רְשָׁעִים דֵּילָטוֹרִין, אָמַר: מֵעַתָּה שֶׁמָּא אֵינָם רְאוּיִין לְהִגָּאֵל: **אָכֵן נוֹדַע הַדָּבָר.** כְּמַשְׁמָעוֹ. וּמִדְרָשׁוֹ, נוֹדַע לִי הַדָּבָר שֶׁהָיִיתִי תָּמֵהַּ עָלָיו, מֶה חָטְאוּ יִשְׂרָאֵל מִכָּל שִׁבְעִים אֻמּוֹת לִהְיוֹת נִרְדִּים בַּעֲבוֹדַת פֶּרֶךְ, אֲבָל רוֹאֶה אֲנִי שֶׁהֵם רְאוּיִים לְכָךְ:

whole Torah is the one given to him by the daughter of Pharaoh. Even the Holy One, blessed be He, did not call him by any other name."

2:11 **וַיֵּצֵא אֶל־אֶחָיו** *He went out to his people* – Miriam's strategy has worked: having been nursed by his own mother during his early years, he knows that the slaves he sees are "his people," "his brothers." To be a Jew is to know that one cannot be indifferent when one's people are suffering. "Israel," said R. Shimon bar Yoḥai, "is like a single body with one soul. When one is injured, all feel the pain." Moshe identifies with the Israelites at considerable cost to himself.

The passage is a brief tutorial in leadership. First Moshe goes out to the people. Though he did not grow up with them, he identifies with them. Second, he sees their suffering. He sees what they need to be liberated from and cannot do by themselves. Third, "looking this way and that" and seeing no one else prepared to act, he acts. There will be many years before he will be summoned to lead the people, but he is already acting like a leader.

י וַתְּנִיקֵהוּ: וַיִּגְדַּל הַיֶּלֶד וַתְּבִאֵהוּ לְבַת־פַּרְעֹה וַיְהִי־לָהּ לְבֵן וַתִּקְרָא
יא שְׁמוֹ מֹשֶׁה וַתֹּאמֶר כִּי מִן־הַמַּיִם מְשִׁיתִהוּ: וַיְהִי | בַּיָּמִים הָהֵם וַיִּגְדַּל שלישי
מֹשֶׁה וַיֵּצֵא אֶל־אֶחָיו וַיַּרְא בְּסִבְלֹתָם וַיַּרְא אִישׁ מִצְרִי מַכֶּה אִישׁ־
יב עִבְרִי מֵאֶחָיו: וַיִּפֶן כֹּה וָכֹה וַיַּרְא כִּי אֵין אִישׁ וַיַּךְ אֶת־הַמִּצְרִי וַיִּטְמְנֵהוּ
יג בַּחוֹל: וַיֵּצֵא בַּיּוֹם הַשֵּׁנִי וְהִנֵּה שְׁנֵי־אֲנָשִׁים עִבְרִים נִצִּים וַיֹּאמֶר לָרָשָׁע
יד לָמָּה תַכֶּה רֵעֶךָ: וַיֹּאמֶר מִי שָׂמְךָ לְאִישׁ שַׂר וְשֹׁפֵט עָלֵינוּ הַלְהָרְגֵנִי
אַתָּה אֹמֵר כַּאֲשֶׁר הָרַגְתָּ אֶת־הַמִּצְרִי וַיִּירָא מֹשֶׁה וַיֹּאמַר אָכֵן נוֹדַע

אונקלוס

וְאוֹנִקְתֵּיהּ: י וּרְבָא רַבְיָא, וְאֵיתִיתֵיהּ לְבַת פַּרְעֹה, וַהֲוָה לַהּ לְבַר, וּקְרָת שְׁמֵיהּ מֹשֶׁה, וַאֲמַרַת, אֲרֵי מִן מַיָּא שְׁחַלְתֵּיהּ: יא וַהֲוָה בְּיוֹמַיָּא הָאִנּוּן, וּרְבָא מֹשֶׁה וּנְפַק לְוָת אֲחוֹהִי, וַחֲזָא בְּפֻלְחָנְהוֹן, וַחֲזָא גְּבַר מִצְרַאי, מָחֵי לִגְבַר יְהוּדַאי מֵאֲחוֹהִי: יב וְאִתְפְּנִי לְכָא וּלְכָא, וַחֲזָא אֲרֵי לֵית אֱנָשׁ, וּמְחָא יָת מִצְרָאָה, וְטַמְרֵיהּ בְּחָלָא: יג וּנְפַק בְּיוֹמָא תִנְיָנָא, וְהָא, תְּרֵין גֻּבְרִין יְהוּדָאִין נָצַן, וַאֲמַר לְחַיָּבָא, לְמָא אַתְּ מָחֵי לְחַבְרָךְ: יד וַאֲמַר, מַאן שַׁוְיָךְ, לִגְבַר רַב וְדַיָּן עֲלַנָא, הַלְמִקְטְלִי אַתְּ אָמַר, כְּמָא דִּקְטַלְתָּא יָת מִצְרָאָה, וּדְחֵיל מֹשֶׁה

2:10 וַתִּקְרָא שְׁמוֹ מֹשֶׁה *She named him Moshe* – It takes a while before we realize that there is something strange about this sentence. It presupposes that Pharaoh's daughter spoke Hebrew. It also makes the impossible assumption that not only would she adopt a Hebrew child in direct contravention to her father's decree that every male child be killed, but would advertise the fact by giving him a Hebrew name. In short, the Hebrew etymology of the name is only half of the story.

Moshe – in the form Mose, Mses or Messes – is in fact an Egyptian word. It figures in the names of several Pharaohs, including Thutmose, and most significantly Ramesses himself. The word means "child." Understanding this, we stand before one of the Torah's boldest and most revolutionary strokes. Years later, two men are to be involved in a monumental confrontation: Ramesses and Moshe. Their names tell us what is at stake. Ramesses means "child of the sun god Ra." Ramesses, as we have seen, saw himself as a god and erected a temple at Abu Simbel to that proposition. Moshe is simply, anonymously, "a child" – with no more identification than that, exactly as there is no name given to his parents when we first encounter them in the biblical text, other than the bare description, "A man of the house of Levi went and married a daughter of Levi" (Ex. 2:1).

In the Torah, it is parents who give a child its name, and in the case of a special individual, God Himself. It is God who gives the name Yitzḥak to the first Jewish child; God's angel who gives Yaakov the name Yisrael; God who changes the names of Avram and Sarai to Avraham and Sara. We have already encountered one adoptive name – Tzafenat Pane'aḥ – the name by which Yosef was known in Egypt; yet in the Torah, Yosef remains Yosef. How surpassingly strange that the hero of the exodus, greatest of all the prophets, should bear not the name Amram and Yokheved have undoubtedly used thus far, but the one given to him by his adoptive mother, an Egyptian princess. A midrash (Shemot Rabba 1:26) draws our attention to the fact: "This is the reward for those who do kindness. Although Moshe had many names, the only one by which he is known in the

15 was afraid. "Surely," he thought, "the thing has become known." Word reached
Pharaoh and he sought to kill Moshe. But Moshe fled his presence and went to
16 live in the land of Midyan. There he sat down beside a well. The priest of Midyan
had seven daughters; they came to draw water and filled the troughs to water
17 their father's flock. Then the shepherds arrived and started to drive the young
women away. But Moshe stood up to defend them, and then watered their flock.
18 When the sisters returned to Reuel their father, he asked them, "How is it that
19 you have come back so quickly today?" They said, "An Egyptian rescued us from
20 the shepherds. He even drew water for us and watered the flock." "Where is he?"
he asked his daughters. "Why did you leave him there? Invite him in to have
21 something to eat." Moshe accepted an invitation to stay with the man, and he
22 gave Moshe his daughter Tzipora in marriage. She gave birth to a son, and Moshe
named him Gershom, saying, "I have been a stranger in an alien land."
23 Years passed, and the king of Egypt died. The Israelites sighed in their enslavement and cried out, and from their servitude their plea for help rose up
24 to God. And God heard their groaning, and remembered His covenant with

רש״י

טו **וישמע פרעה.** הם הלשינו עליו: **ויבקש להרג את משה.** מסרו לקוסטינר להרגו, ולא שלטה בו החרב, הוא שאמר משה: ״ויצלני מחרב פרעה״ (להלן יח, ד): **וישב על הבאר.** למד מיעקב שנזדווג לו זווגו מן הבאר:

טז **ולכהן מדין.** רב שבהן, ופרש לו מעבודה זרה ונדוהו מאצלם: **את הרהטים.** את בריכות מרוצות המים העשויות בארץ:

יז **ויגרשום.** מפני הנדוי:

כ **למה זה עזבתן.** הכיר בו שהוא מזרעו של יעקב, שהמים עולים לקראתו: **ויאכל לחם.** שמא ישא אחת מכם; כמה דאת אמר: ״כי אם הלחם אשר הוא אוכל״ (בראשית לט, ו):

כא **ויואל.** כתרגומו. ודומה לו: ״הואל נא ולין״ (שופטים יט, ו), ״ולו הואלנו״ (יהושע ז, ז), ״הואלתי לדבר״ (בראשית יח, לא). ומדרשו, לשון אלה, נשבע לו שלא יזוז ממדין כי אם ברשותו:

כג **וימת מלך מצרים.** נצטרע, והיה שוחט תינוקות ישראל ורוחץ בדמם:

כד **נאקתם.** צעקתם, וכן: ״מעיר מתים ינאקו״ (איוב כד, יב): **את בריתו את אברהם.** עם אברהם:

At the heart of Judaism are three beliefs about leadership: We are free. We are responsible. And together we can change the world.

2:22 **גֵּר הָיִיתִי בְּאֶרֶץ נָכְרִיָּה** *I have been a stranger in an alien land* – A double estrangement: he is "a stranger" from Israel the people; strange too in Egypt the "alien" land. Charles Péguy said that "being elsewhere" was "the great and secret virtue, the great vocation of this people." Even in Israel, says the Torah, "you are merely migrants and visitors to Me" (Lev. 25:23). To be a Jew is to fully know the contingency of life, the lack of ultimate, this-worldly security and yet still to fight for justice and believe that the battle can be won because with us is a force greater than we are, greater than we can know.

2:24 **וַיִּשְׁמַע אֱלֹהִים** *And God heard* – In the Torah the word *shema* means more than "hear." It means "listen, pay attention, and act accordingly." This explains an unusual feature

טו הַדָּבָר: וַיִּשְׁמַע פַּרְעֹה אֶת־הַדָּבָר הַזֶּה וַיְבַקֵּשׁ לַהֲרֹג אֶת־מֹשֶׁה וַיִּבְרַח
טז מֹשֶׁה מִפְּנֵי פַרְעֹה וַיֵּשֶׁב בְּאֶרֶץ־מִדְיָן וַיֵּשֶׁב עַל־הַבְּאֵר: וּלְכֹהֵן מִדְיָן
שֶׁבַע בָּנוֹת וַתָּבֹאנָה וַתִּדְלֶנָה וַתְּמַלֶּאנָה אֶת־הָרְהָטִים לְהַשְׁקוֹת
יז צֹאן אֲבִיהֶן: וַיָּבֹאוּ הָרֹעִים וַיְגָרְשׁוּם וַיָּקָם מֹשֶׁה וַיּוֹשִׁעָן וַיַּשְׁקְ אֶת־
יח צֹאנָם: וַתָּבֹאנָה אֶל־רְעוּאֵל אֲבִיהֶן וַיֹּאמֶר מַדּוּעַ מִהַרְתֶּן בֹּא הַיּוֹם:
יט וַתֹּאמַרְןָ אִישׁ מִצְרִי הִצִּילָנוּ מִיַּד הָרֹעִים וְגַם־דָּלֹה דָלָה לָנוּ וַיַּשְׁקְ
כ אֶת־הַצֹּאן: וַיֹּאמֶר אֶל־בְּנֹתָיו וְאַיּוֹ לָמָּה זֶּה עֲזַבְתֶּן אֶת־הָאִישׁ קִרְאֶן
כא לוֹ וְיֹאכַל לָחֶם: וַיּוֹאֶל מֹשֶׁה לָשֶׁבֶת אֶת־הָאִישׁ וַיִּתֵּן אֶת־צִפֹּרָה בִתּוֹ
כב לְמֹשֶׁה: וַתֵּלֶד בֵּן וַיִּקְרָא אֶת־שְׁמוֹ גֵּרְשֹׁם כִּי אָמַר גֵּר הָיִיתִי בְּאֶרֶץ
נָכְרִיָּה:
כג וַיְהִי בַיָּמִים הָרַבִּים הָהֵם וַיָּמָת מֶלֶךְ מִצְרַיִם וַיֵּאָנְחוּ בְנֵי־יִשְׂרָאֵל
מִן־הָעֲבֹדָה וַיִּזְעָקוּ וַתַּעַל שַׁוְעָתָם אֶל־הָאֱלֹהִים מִן־הָעֲבֹדָה:
כד וַיִּשְׁמַע אֱלֹהִים אֶת־נַאֲקָתָם וַיִּזְכֹּר אֱלֹהִים אֶת־בְּרִיתוֹ אֶת־

אונקלוס

וַאֲמַר, בְּקֻשְׁטָא אִתְיְדַע פִּתְגָמָא: טו וּשְׁמַע פַּרְעֹה יָת פִּתְגָמָא הָדֵין, וּבְעָא לְמִקְטַל יָת מֹשֶׁה, וַעֲרַק מֹשֶׁה מִן קֳדָם פַּרְעֹה, וִיתֵיב בְּאַרְעָא דְמִדְיָן וִיתֵיב עַל בֵּירָא: טז וּלְרַבָּא דְמִדְיָן שְׁבַע בְּנָן, וַאֲתַאָה וּדְלָאָה, וּמְלָאָה יָת רָטַיָּא, לְאַשְׁקָאָה עָנָא דַאֲבוּהוֹן: יז וַאֲתוֹ רָעַיָּא וְטָרְדוּנִין, וְקָם מֹשֶׁה וּפָרְקִנִּין, וְאַשְׁקִי יָת עָנְהוֹן: יח וַאֲתַאָה, לְוָת רְעוּאֵל אֲבוּהוֹן, וַאֲמַר, מָדֵין, אוֹחִיתִין לְמֵיתֵי יוֹמָא דֵין: יט וַאֲמַרָא, גַּבְרָא מִצְרָאָה, שֵׁיזְבַנָא מִידָא דְרָעַיָּא, וְאַף מִדְלָא דְלָא לַנָא, וְאַשְׁקִי יָת עָנָא: כ וַאֲמַר לִבְנָתֵיהּ וְאָן הוּא, לְמָא דְנָן שְׁבַקְתִּין יָת גַּבְרָא, קְרָן לֵיהּ וְיֵיכוּל לַחְמָא: כא וּצְבִי מֹשֶׁה לְמִתַּב עִם גַּבְרָא, וִיהַב, יָת צִפּוֹרָה בְרַתֵּיהּ לְמֹשֶׁה: כב וִילֵידַת בַּר, וּקְרָא יָת שְׁמֵיהּ גֵּרְשׁוֹם, אֲרֵי אֲמַר, דַּיָּר הֲוֵיתִי, בַּאֲרַע נֻכְרָאָה: כג וַהֲוָה בְּיוֹמַיָּא סַגִּיאַיָּא הָאִנּוּן, וּמִית מַלְכָּא דְמִצְרַיִם, וְאִתְאֲנַחוּ בְנֵי יִשְׂרָאֵל, מִן פֻּלְחָנָא דַהֲוָה קְשֵׁי עֲלֵיהוֹן וּזְעִיקוּ, וּסְלֵיקַת קְבִילַתְהוֹן, לִקְדָם יי מִן פֻּלְחָנָא: כד וּשְׁמִיעַ קֳדָם יי יָת קְבִילַתְהוֹן, וּדְכִיר יי יָת קְיָמֵיהּ, דְּעִם

2:17 וַיָּקָם מֹשֶׁה וַיּוֹשִׁעָן *Moshe stood up to defend them* – Leadership begins with taking responsibility. Contrast the opening of Genesis with the opening of Exodus. The opening chapters of Genesis are about failures of responsibility. Confronted by God with their sin, Adam blames Ḥava; Ḥava blames the serpent. Kayin says, "Am I my brother's keeper?" (Gen. 4:9). Even Noaḥ, "righteous … in his generation" (6:9), has no effect on his contemporaries.

By contrast, at the beginning of Exodus, Moshe takes responsibility. When he sees an Egyptian beating an Israelite, he intervenes. When he sees two Israelites fighting, he intervenes. In Midyan, when he sees shepherds abusing the daughters of Yitro, he intervenes. Moshe, an Israelite brought up as an Egyptian, could have avoided each of these confrontations, yet he does not. He is the supreme case of one who says: when I see wrong, if no one else is prepared to act, I will.

25 Avraham, with Yitzhak, and with Yaakov. God saw the Israelites, and God
3 1 knew. One day Moshe was tending the flock of his father-in-law Yitro, REVI'I
priest of Midyan. He led the flock to the far side of the wilderness and came
2 to Ḥorev, the mountain of God. Then an angel of the LORD appeared to him
in flames of fire from the midst of a bush – and he saw – the bush was ablaze
3 with fire but was not consumed. Moshe said, "I must turn aside to see this
4 wonder. Why does the bush not burn up?" The LORD saw that he had turned
aside to look, and God called to him from within the bush: "Moshe, Moshe."

רש״י

כה) **וַיֵּדַע אֱלֹהִים.** נָתַן עֲלֵיהֶם לֵב וְלֹא הֶעֱלִים עֵינָיו:

ג א) **אַחַר הַמִּדְבָּר.** לְהִתְרַחֵק מִן הַגָּזֵל שֶׁלֹּא יִרְעוּ בִּשְׂדוֹת אֲחֵרִים: **אֶל הַר הָאֱלֹהִים.** עַל שֵׁם הֶעָתִיד:

ב) **בְּלַבַּת אֵשׁ.** בְּשַׁלְהֶבֶת אֵשׁ, לִבּוֹ שֶׁל אֵשׁ כְּמוֹ: "לֵב הַשָּׁמַיִם" (דברים ד, יא), "בְּלֵב הָאֵלָה" (שמואל ב׳ יח, יד). וְאַל תִּתְמַהּ עַל הַתָּי״ו, יֵשׁ לָנוּ כַּיּוֹצֵא בּוֹ: "מָה אֲמֻלָה לִבָּתֵךְ" (יחזקאל טז, ל): **מִתּוֹךְ הַסְּנֶה.** וְלֹא אִילָן אַחֵר, מִשּׁוּם "עִמּוֹ אָנֹכִי בְצָרָה" (תהלים צא, טו): **אֻכָּל.** נֶאֱכָל, כְּמוֹ "לֹא עֻבַּד בָּהּ" (דברים כא, ג), "אֲשֶׁר לֻקַּח מִשָּׁם" (בראשית ג, כג):

ג) **אָסֻרָה.** מִכָּאן לְהִתְקָרֵב שָׁם:

argue, unless we carry in our memories the thought of what it is to be without power. Social justice is born not so much of political theory as it is of the sharp pain of injustice and the decision, having felt it, never to inflict it. "I know their anguish" (Ex. 3:7), says God – and we too are commanded to keep it in mind.

3:2 **מִתּוֹךְ הַסְּנֶה** *From the midst of a bush* – In Hebrew, the word *sneh*, "bush," appears three times in this one verse for emphasis. This is not a grand epiphany. The flickering flames made their home in the lowliest of vegetation. The highest of the high can be present in the lowest of the low. Already there is a hint of the anti-hierarchical thrust of monotheism, even if it takes many centuries fully to emerge. That God would make His first appearance in the exodus story in so humble a setting stands in the strongest possible contrast to ancient Egypt, where an appearance of a god was supposed to take place at an auspicious and predictable time in a magnificent building permanently consecrated as sacred space.

3:4 **הִנֵּנִי** *Here I am* – This single word is the ultimate human response to the call of God. When God summons us, He calls our name, and the most profound reply is simply *Hineni*, "Here I am." So said Avraham at the beginning of the binding of Yitzhak (Gen. 22:1). So said Yaakov when God told him not to be afraid to go to Egypt (46:2). So Moshe says now, as God appears to him at the burning bush (Ex. 3:4). So the young Shmuel will say when God appears to him at night (I Sam. 3:4), and Yeshayahu in the mystical vision that will mark the beginning of his mission (Is. 6:8). At the beginning of the human story, God called to Adam and Ḥava in Eden, "Where are you?" (Gen. 3:9). So He has done ever since: He calls to each one of us, here where we are, this person, in this situation, at this time, saying: there is an act only you can do, a situation only you can address, a moment that, if not seized, may never come again. God commands in generalities but calls in particulars. He knows our gifts, and He knows the needs of the world. That is why we are here. There is an act only we can do, and only at this time, and that is our task. The sum of these tasks is the meaning of our life, the purpose of our existence, the story we are called on to write.

There is no life without a task, no person without a talent, no situation without its possibility of sanctification. When God calls, He whispers our name – and the greatest reply is simply *Hineni*, "Here I am," ready to heed Your call, to mend a fragment of Your all-too-broken world. Rabbi Ḥayyim of Volozhin enjoins us: "Let nobody in Israel, God forbid, ask himself: What am I, and what can my humble acts achieve in the world? Let him rather understand this, that he may know

כה אַבְרָהָם אֶת־יִצְחָק וְאֶת־יַעֲקֹב׃ וַיַּרְא אֱלֹהִים אֶת־בְּנֵי יִשְׂרָאֵל וַיֵּדַע
ג א אֱלֹהִים׃ וּמֹשֶׁה הָיָה רֹעֶה אֶת־צֹאן יִתְרוֹ חֹתְנוֹ כֹּהֵן מִדְיָן ב רביעי
ב וַיִּנְהַג אֶת־הַצֹּאן אַחַר הַמִּדְבָּר וַיָּבֹא אֶל־הַר הָאֱלֹהִים חֹרֵבָה׃ וַיֵּרָא
מַלְאַךְ יהוה אֵלָיו בְּלַבַּת־אֵשׁ מִתּוֹךְ הַסְּנֶה וַיַּרְא וְהִנֵּה הַסְּנֶה בֹּעֵר
ג בָּאֵשׁ וְהַסְּנֶה אֵינֶנּוּ אֻכָּל׃ וַיֹּאמֶר מֹשֶׁה אָסֻרָה־נָּא וְאֶרְאֶה אֶת־
ד הַמַּרְאֶה הַגָּדֹל הַזֶּה מַדּוּעַ לֹא־יִבְעַר הַסְּנֶה׃ וַיַּרְא יהוה כִּי סָר לִרְאוֹת
וַיִּקְרָא אֵלָיו אֱלֹהִים מִתּוֹךְ הַסְּנֶה וַיֹּאמֶר מֹשֶׁה מֹשֶׁה וַיֹּאמֶר הִנֵּנִי׃

אונקלוס

אַבְרָהָם דְּעִם יִצְחָק וּדְעִם יַעֲקֹב׃ כה וּגְלֵי קֳדָם יי שִׁעְבּוּדָא דִּבְנֵי
יִשְׂרָאֵל, וַאֲמַר בְּמֵימְרֵיהּ לְמִפְרְקְהוֹן יי׃ ג א וּמֹשֶׁה, הֲוָה רָעֵי, יָת עָנָא,
דְּיִתְרוֹ חֲמוּהִי רַבָּא דְּמִדְיָן, וּדְבַר יָת עָנָא לַאֲתַר שְׁפַר רַעְיָא לְמַדְבְּרָא,
וַאֲתָא, לְטוּרָא דְּאִתְגְּלִי עֲלוֹהִי יְקָרָא דַּייָ לְחוֹרֵב׃ ב וְאִתְגְּלִי, מַלְאֲכָא
דַּייָ לֵיהּ, בְּשַׁלְהוֹבִית אִישָּׁתָא מִגּוֹ אֲסַנָּא, וַחֲזָא, וְהָא אֲסַנָּא בָּעַר
בְּאִישָּׁתָא, וַאֲסַנָּא לַיְתוֹהִי מִתְאֲכִיל׃ ג וַאֲמַר מֹשֶׁה, אֶתְפְּנֵי כְעַן וְאֶחֱזֵי,
יָת חֶזְוָנָא רַבָּא הָדֵין, מָדֵין לָא מִתּוֹקַד אֲסַנָּא׃ ד וַחֲזָא יי אֲרֵי אִתְפְּנִי
לְמִחְזֵי, וּקְרָא לֵיהּ יי מִגּוֹ אֲסַנָּא, וַאֲמַר, מֹשֶׁה מֹשֶׁה וַאֲמַר הָאֲנָא׃

of Biblical Hebrew, namely that it has no word that means "obey." Judaism does not demand blind obedience. To the contrary, it asks us, as far as possible, to understand the reasons for the commandments, though their full wisdom will always be beyond our understanding. Obedience in Judaism is a form of active listening. Premodern English used the word "hearken" to convey this, but there is now no word in common usage that has this precise sense. By "God heard," our verse means "He attended to the cries of the Israelites and set it in the context of the promise He had given the patriarchs that He would bring their children safely out of slavery and back to the land of Israel."

2:25 וַיֵּדַע אֱלֹהִים *And God knew* – As we see throughout the Torah, the verb "know" in Hebrew means something quite different from its meaning in Greek and subsequent Western thought. Knowledge, for the Greeks, was a form of cognition, a detached appraisal of facts. In the Torah, knowledge is not simply an intellectual attribute. It also has consequences for emotion and action. In this case, "and God knew" means that He not only saw the suffering of the Israelites. He was pained by it, and determined to act to redeem them.

THE BURNING BUSH

In this singularly powerful event, which marks the beginning of the exodus from Egypt, God reveals three characteristics that have molded Jewish spirituality ever since.

First, He is a God of history, not the abstract God of philosophy, nor even the intimate God of personal salvation. He is concerned with the behaviour of mankind, with society, freedom, and the politics of suffering. The consolation He offers lies in historical and political change: the exodus of a people and the building of a new social order.

Secondly, He is a God who cherishes freedom. Often the Mosaic books return to the theme, and always with reference to the exodus. Free your slaves in the year of release. Do not let them work for you on the seventh day. Remember that you were once a slave in the land of Egypt. It is as if any loss of freedom is an assault on the image of God that is man.

Thirdly, He is a God who wants His people never to forget the experience of being a minority without power. Do not oppress a stranger, commands the Bible, because you understand the heart of a stranger – you were once strangers yourselves. Plead the cause of the widow and the orphan, the underprivileged. Power corrupts, the Bible seems to

5 He answered, "Here I am." Then God said, "Do not come close. Remove the
6 shoes from your feet, for the place where you stand is holy ground. I," He said,
"am the God of your father, the God of Avraham, the God of Yitzḥak, and the
7 God of Yaakov." Then Moshe hid his face, for he was afraid to look at God. The
Lord continued, "I have seen My people's suffering in Egypt; I have heard
8 them cry out amid their oppressors; I know their anguish. So I have come to
rescue them from the hand of the Egyptians and bring them up from that land
to one that is good, spacious, a land flowing with milk and honey, the place of
9 the Canaanites, Hittites, Amorites, Perizzites, Hivites, and Jebusites. Now the
cry of the Israelites has reached Me; I have seen the oppression the Egyptians
10 subject them to. So go: I am sending you to Pharaoh to bring My people, the
11 Israelites, out of Egypt." But "who am I," said Moshe to God, "to go to Pharaoh,
12 to bring the Israelites out of Egypt?" God replied, "I will be with you. Proof

רש״י

ה **שַׁל.** שְׁלֹף וְהוֹצֵא, כְּמוֹ: "וְנָשַׁל הַבַּרְזֶל" (דברים יט, ה), "כִּי יִשַּׁל זֵיתֶךָ" (דברים כח, מ): **אַדְמַת קֹדֶשׁ הוּא.** הַמָּקוֹם:

י **וְעַתָּה לְכָה וְאֶשְׁלָחֲךָ אֶל פַּרְעֹה.** וְאִם תֹּאמַר, מַה תּוֹעִיל? "וְהוֹצֵא אֶת עַמִּי", יוֹעִילוּ דְּבָרֶיךָ וְתוֹצִיאֵם:

יא **מִי אָנֹכִי.** מָה אֲנִי חָשׁוּב לְדַבֵּר עִם הַמְּלָכִים? **וְכִי אוֹצִיא אֶת בְּנֵי יִשְׂרָאֵל.** וְאַף אִם חָשׁוּב אֲנִי, מַה זָּכוּ יִשְׂרָאֵל שֶׁיֵּעָשֶׂה לָהֶם נֵס וְאוֹצִיאֵם מִמִּצְרָיִם?

יב **וַיֹּאמֶר כִּי אֶהְיֶה עִמָּךְ.** הֱשִׁיבוֹ עַל רִאשׁוֹן רִאשׁוֹן וְעַל אַחֲרוֹן אַחֲרוֹן: שֶׁאָמַרְתָּ "מִי אָנֹכִי כִּי אֵלֵךְ אֶל פַּרְעֹה" – לֹא שֶׁלְּךָ הִיא כִּי אִם מִשֶּׁלִּי, "כִּי אֶהְיֶה עִמָּךְ"; "וְזֶה" הַמַּרְאֶה אֲשֶׁר רָאִיתָ בַּסְּנֶה, "לְךָ הָאוֹת כִּי אָנֹכִי שְׁלַחְתִּיךָ" וּכְדַאי אֲנִי לְהַצִּיל, כַּאֲשֶׁר רָאִיתָ הַסְּנֶה עוֹשֶׂה שְׁלִיחוּתִי וְאֵינֶנּוּ אֻכָּל כָּךְ תֵּלֵךְ בִּשְׁלִיחוּתִי וְאֵינְךָ נִזּוֹק. וְשֶׁשָּׁאַלְתָּ: מַה זְּכוּת יֵשׁ לְיִשְׂרָאֵל שֶׁיֵּצְאוּ מִמִּצְרַיִם? דָּבָר גָּדוֹל יֵשׁ לִי עַל הוֹצָאָה זוֹ, שֶׁהֲרֵי עֲתִידִים לְקַבֵּל הַתּוֹרָה עַל הָהָר הַזֶּה לְסוֹף שְׁלֹשָׁה חֳדָשִׁים.

3:11 **מִי אָנֹכִי** *Who am I* – Moshe's second question at the burning bush is "Who are you?" His first question, though, is *mi anokhi* – "Who am I?"

Israel was to be summoned to create a new kind of society, one that would be the opposite of Egypt. In the dramatic scene that unfolds in this chapter, we encounter a new kind of leader, the opposite of the kind of leadership associated with the pharaohs of Egypt. Moshe has none of the splendor and pride associated with rule in the ancient Near East. He has doubts, trepidations, and a profound sense of his own inadequacy. He is not driven by ambition or a sense of destiny. To the contrary, he feels overwhelmed by the double challenge of an all-powerful Egypt unlikely to agree to let the Israelites go, and an Israelite people he knows from his youth to be not easily led. This deeply human portrayal of Moshe leads into a remarkable conversation with God, sometimes fraught, but also caring, supportive, and full of hope. The exchange signals what will come to be one of Israel's most distinctive features: the extended conversation between heaven and earth out of which are born world-transforming energies that will eventually triumph over seemingly insuperable obstacles. On one level the story of the exodus is about divine miracles in the face of which human beings are powerless. At another level, the present chapter tells us that God needs Moshe. Divine energy needs human vehicles to bring it down to earth.

The most moving moment in this encounter comes when Moshe utters his first words to God: "Who am I?" The greatest leader who ever lived said, "Who am I?" We may be small in our own eyes but there is greatness within us when we hear and heed the divine call.

ה וַיֹּאמֶר אַל־תִּקְרַב הֲלֹם שַׁל־נְעָלֶיךָ מֵעַל רַגְלֶיךָ כִּי הַמָּקוֹם אֲשֶׁר
ו אַתָּה עוֹמֵד עָלָיו אַדְמַת־קֹדֶשׁ הוּא: וַיֹּאמֶר אָנֹכִי אֱלֹהֵי אָבִיךָ אֱלֹהֵי
אַבְרָהָם אֱלֹהֵי יִצְחָק וֵאלֹהֵי יַעֲקֹב וַיַּסְתֵּר מֹשֶׁה פָּנָיו כִּי יָרֵא מֵהַבִּיט
ז אֶל־הָאֱלֹהִים: וַיֹּאמֶר יהוה רָאֹה רָאִיתִי אֶת־עֳנִי עַמִּי אֲשֶׁר בְּמִצְרָיִם
ח וְאֶת־צַעֲקָתָם שָׁמַעְתִּי מִפְּנֵי נֹגְשָׂיו כִּי יָדַעְתִּי אֶת־מַכְאֹבָיו: וָאֵרֵד
לְהַצִּילוֹ ׀ מִיַּד מִצְרַיִם וּלְהַעֲלֹתוֹ מִן־הָאָרֶץ הַהִוא אֶל־אֶרֶץ טוֹבָה
וּרְחָבָה אֶל־אֶרֶץ זָבַת חָלָב וּדְבָשׁ אֶל־מְקוֹם הַכְּנַעֲנִי וְהַחִתִּי וְהָאֱמֹרִי
ט וְהַפְּרִזִּי וְהַחִוִּי וְהַיְבוּסִי: וְעַתָּה הִנֵּה צַעֲקַת בְּנֵי־יִשְׂרָאֵל בָּאָה אֵלָי וְגַם־
י רָאִיתִי אֶת־הַלַּחַץ אֲשֶׁר מִצְרַיִם לֹחֲצִים אֹתָם: וְעַתָּה לְכָה וְאֶשְׁלָחֲךָ
יא אֶל־פַּרְעֹה וְהוֹצֵא אֶת־עַמִּי בְנֵי־יִשְׂרָאֵל מִמִּצְרָיִם: וַיֹּאמֶר מֹשֶׁה אֶל־
הָאֱלֹהִים מִי אָנֹכִי כִּי אֵלֵךְ אֶל־פַּרְעֹה וְכִי אוֹצִיא אֶת־בְּנֵי יִשְׂרָאֵל
יב מִמִּצְרָיִם: וַיֹּאמֶר כִּי־אֶהְיֶה עִמָּךְ וְזֶה־לְּךָ הָאוֹת כִּי אָנֹכִי שְׁלַחְתִּיךָ

אונקלוס

ה וַאֲמַר לָא תִקְרַב הַלְכָא, שְׁרִי סֵינָךְ מֵעַל רַגְלָךְ, אֲרֵי אַתְרָא, דְּאַתְּ קָאֵים עֲלוֹהִי, אֲתַר קַדִּישׁ הוּא: ו וַאֲמַר, אֲנָא אֱלָהָא דַּאֲבוּךְ, אֱלָהֵיהּ דְּאַבְרָהָם, אֱלָהֵיהּ דְּיִצְחָק וֵאלָהֵיהּ דְּיַעֲקֹב, וּכְבַשׁנוּן מֹשֶׁה לְאַפּוֹהִי, אֲרֵי דְּחֵיל, מִלְּאִסְתַּכָּלָא בְּצֵית יְקָרָא דַּיי: ז וַאֲמַר יי, מִגְלָא גְּלֵי קֳדָמַי, שִׁעְבּוּד עַמִּי דִּבְמִצְרָיִם, וְיָת קְבִילַתְהוֹן שְׁמִיעַ קֳדָמַי מִן קֳדָם מַפְלְחֵיהוֹן, אֲרֵי גְּלֵי קֳדָמַי כֵּיבֵיהוֹן: ח וְאִתְגְּלֵיתִי, לְשֵׁיזָבוּתְהוֹן מִיְּדָא דְּמִצְרָאֵי, וּלְאַסָּקוּתְהוֹן מִן אַרְעָא הַהִיא, לַאֲרַע טָבָא וּפַתְיָא, לַאֲרַע, עָבְדָא חֲלַב וּדְבַשׁ, לַאֲתַר כְּנַעֲנָאֵי וְחִתָּאֵי, וֶאֱמוֹרָאֵי וּפְרִזָּאֵי, וְחִוָּאֵי וִיבוּסָאֵי: ט וּכְעַן, הָא, קְבִילַת בְּנֵי יִשְׂרָאֵל עָאלַת לִקְדָמַי, וְאַף גְּלֵי קֳדָמַי דּוּחְקָא, דְּמִצְרָאֵי דָּחֲקִין לְהוֹן: י וּכְעַן אֵיתָא, וְאֶשְׁלְחִנָּךְ לְוָת פַּרְעֹה, וְאַפֵּיק, יָת עַמִּי בְּנֵי יִשְׂרָאֵל מִמִּצְרָיִם: יא וַאֲמַר מֹשֶׁה קֳדָם יי, מַאן אֲנָא, אֲרֵי אֵיזֵיל לְוָת פַּרְעֹה, וַאֲרֵי אַפֵּיק, יָת בְּנֵי יִשְׂרָאֵל מִמִּצְרָיִם: יב וַאֲמַר אֲרֵי יְהֵי מֵימְרִי בְּסַעְדָּךְ, וְדֵין לָךְ אָתָא, אֲרֵי אֲנָא שְׁלַחְתָּךְ,

it and fix it in his thoughts: Not one detail of his acts, his words, and his thoughts, is ever lost. Each one leads back to its origin, where it takes effect in the height of heights."

3:5 שַׁל־נְעָלֶיךָ מֵעַל רַגְלֶיךָ *Remove the shoes from your feet* – Shoes were not worn by the priests in their service at the Temple. Yehoshua was told by "the commander of the Lord's hosts" to "remove the shoes from your feet, for the place where you stand is holy" (Josh. 5:15). Since shoes were worn as protection from dirt, wearing them in a holy place or in the presence of royalty was considered disrespectful. Shoes are a human artefact, symbolizing our powers of rational creativity, raising us protectively above the rough terrain of nature. But this cannot bring us to the holy. For that we must make ourselves vulnerable to a dimension outside and beyond ourselves. That vulnerability is what was symbolized when Moshe, and later the priests, removed their shoes when entering holy ground.

that I have sent you will come when, having brought the people out of Egypt,
13 you come to serve God upon this mountain." Moshe said to God, "When I go
to the Israelites and tell them, 'Your fathers' God has sent me to you,' they will
14 ask me, 'What is His name?' What shall I say?" God replied to Moshe, "I will be
what I will be." He said, "This is what you shall tell the Israelites: I will be sent me
15 to you." Then God said to Moshe, "You shall say this to the Israelites: The Lord
God of your fathers, the God of Avraham, the God of Yitzḥak, and the God of
Yaakov, has sent me to you. This is My name forever, and this is how I will be

רש״י

דָּבָר אַחֵר, "כִּי אֶהְיֶה עִמָּךְ", "וְזֶה" שֶׁתַּצְלִיחַ בִּשְׁלִיחוּתְךָ, "לְךָ הָאוֹת" עַל הַבְטָחָה אַחֶרֶת שֶׁאֲנִי מַבְטִיחֲךָ, שֶׁכְּשֶׁתּוֹצִיאֵם מִמִּצְרַיִם תַּעַבְדוּן אוֹתִי עַל הָהָר הַזֶּה, שֶׁתְּקַבְּלוּ הַתּוֹרָה עָלָיו, וְהִיא הַזְּכוּת הָעוֹמֶדֶת לְיִשְׂרָאֵל. וְדֻגְמַת לָשׁוֹן זֶה מָצִינוּ בִּישַׁעְיָה (לז, ל): "וְזֶה לְּךָ הָאוֹת אָכוֹל הַשָּׁנָה סָפִיחַ" וְגוֹ', מַפֶּלֶת סַנְחֵרִיב תִּהְיֶה לְךָ אוֹת עַל הַבְטָחָה אַחֶרֶת, שֶׁאַרְצְכֶם חֲרֵבָה מִפֵּרוֹת וַאֲנִי אֲבָרֵךְ הַסְּפִיחִים:

יד-טו **אֶהְיֶה אֲשֶׁר אֶהְיֶה.** "אֶהְיֶה" עִמָּם בְּצָרָה זוֹ, "אֲשֶׁר אֶהְיֶה" עִמָּם בְּשִׁעְבּוּד שְׁאָר מַלְכֻיּוֹת. אָמַר לְפָנָיו: רִבּוֹנוֹ שֶׁל עוֹלָם, מָה אֲנִי מַזְכִּיר לָהֶם צָרָה אַחֶרֶת? דַּיָּם בְּצָרָה זוֹ! אָמַר לוֹ: יָפֶה אָמַרְתָּ, "כֹּה תֹאמַר" וְגוֹ': **זֶה שְּׁמִי לְעֹלָם.** חָסֵר וָי"ו, לוֹמַר הַעֲלִימֵהוּ שֶׁלֹּא יִקָּרֵא כִּכְתָבוֹ: **וְזֶה זִכְרִי.** לִמְּדוֹ הֵיאַךְ נִקְרָא. וְכֵן דָּוִד הוּא אוֹמֵר: "ה' שִׁמְךָ לְעוֹלָם ה' זִכְרְךָ לְדֹר וָדֹר" (תהלים קלה, יג):

chaos. Until Israel appeared on the scene, religion was a way of consecrating the status quo. That is what the story of Israel would overturn.

Far from being timeless and immutable, God in the Torah is active, engaged, in constant dialogue with His people, urging, warning, challenging, forgiving. When Malakhi says in the name of God, "I am the Lord. I have not changed" (Mal. 3:6), He is not speaking about His essence as pure being, the unmoved mover, but about His moral commitments. God keeps His promises even when His children break theirs. Time, however, becomes something understood as a narrative, a journey or a quest. Throughout the Torah, the Promised Land lies in the future. Avraham, Yitzḥak, and Yaakov do not acquire it. Even Moshe, who spends forty years leading the people there, does not get to enter it. It is always just beyond. Soon but not yet. All this is hinted at in those three Hebrew words that mean "I will be what I will be." I am the God of the future tense.

3:15 **יהוה אֱלֹהֵי אֲבֹתֵיכֶם** *The Lord God of your fathers* – This phrase suggests some fundamental propositions. First, identity runs through genealogy. It is a matter of who my parents were, who their parents were, and so on. This is not always true. There are adopted children. There are children who make a conscious break from their parents. But for most of us, identity lies in uncovering the story of our ancestors, which, in the case of Jews, given the unparalleled dislocations of Jewish life, is almost always a tale of journeys, courage, suffering or escapes from suffering, and sheer endurance.

Second, it is not simply that God was the God of their ancestors. He is also the God who makes certain promises: that He will bring them from slavery to freedom, from exile to the Promised Land. The Israelites are part of a narrative extended over time. They are part of an unfinished story, and God is about to write the next chapter.

What is more, when God tells Moshe that He is the God of the Israelites' ancestors, He adds, "This is My name forever, and this is how I will be remembered [*zikhri*] through the ages." God is saying here that He is beyond time – "This is My name forever" – but when it comes to human understanding, He lives within time, "through the ages." The way He does this is through the handing on of memory: "This is how I will be remembered." Identity is not just a matter of who my parents were. It is also a matter of what they remembered and handed on to me. Personal identity is shaped by individual memory. Group identity is formed by collective memory.

בְּהוֹצִיאֲךָ אֶת־הָעָם מִמִּצְרַיִם תַּעַבְדוּן אֶת־הָאֱלֹהִים עַל הָהָר הַזֶּה׃
יג וַיֹּאמֶר מֹשֶׁה אֶל־הָאֱלֹהִים הִנֵּה אָנֹכִי בָא אֶל־בְּנֵי יִשְׂרָאֵל וְאָמַרְתִּי
לָהֶם אֱלֹהֵי אֲבוֹתֵיכֶם שְׁלָחַנִי אֲלֵיכֶם וְאָמְרוּ־לִי מַה־שְּׁמוֹ מָה אֹמַר
יד אֲלֵהֶם׃ וַיֹּאמֶר אֱלֹהִים אֶל־מֹשֶׁה אֶהְיֶה אֲשֶׁר אֶהְיֶה וַיֹּאמֶר כֹּה תֹאמַר
טו לִבְנֵי יִשְׂרָאֵל אֶהְיֶה שְׁלָחַנִי אֲלֵיכֶם׃ וַיֹּאמֶר עוֹד אֱלֹהִים אֶל־מֹשֶׁה כֹּה
תֹאמַר אֶל־בְּנֵי יִשְׂרָאֵל יְהוָה אֱלֹהֵי אֲבֹתֵיכֶם אֱלֹהֵי אַבְרָהָם אֱלֹהֵי
יִצְחָק וֵאלֹהֵי יַעֲקֹב שְׁלָחַנִי אֲלֵיכֶם זֶה־שְּׁמִי לְעֹלָם וְזֶה זִכְרִי לְדֹר דֹּר׃

אונקלוס

בְּאַפָּקוּתָךְ יָת עַמָּא מִמִּצְרַיִם, תִּפְלְחוּן קֳדָם יי, עַל טוּרָא הָדֵין׃ יג וַאֲמַר
מֹשֶׁה קֳדָם יי, הָא אֲנָא אָתֵי לְוָת בְּנֵי יִשְׂרָאֵל, וְאֵימַר לְהוֹן, אֱלָהָא
דַּאֲבָהָתְכוֹן שַׁלְחַנִי לְוָתְכוֹן, וְיֵימְרוּן לִי מַאן שְׁמֵיהּ, מָא אֵימַר לְהוֹן׃
יד וַאֲמַר יי לְמֹשֶׁה, אֶהְיֶה אֲשֶׁר אֶהְיֶה, וַאֲמַר, כִּדְנַן תֵּימַר לִבְנֵי יִשְׂרָאֵל,
אֶהְיֶה שַׁלְחַנִי לְוָתְכוֹן׃ טו וַאֲמַר עוֹד יי לְמֹשֶׁה, כִּדְנַן תֵּימַר לִבְנֵי יִשְׂרָאֵל,
יי אֱלָהָא דַּאֲבָהָתְכוֹן, אֱלָהֵיהּ דְּאַבְרָהָם, אֱלָהֵיהּ דְּיִצְחָק, וֵאלָהֵיהּ
דְּיַעֲקֹב שַׁלְחַנִי לְוָתְכוֹן, דֵּין שְׁמִי לְעָלַם, וְדֵין דָּכְרָנִי לְכָל דָּר וְדָר׃

I WILL BE WHAT I WILL BE

God's enigmatic reply to Moshe was translated into Greek as *ego eimi ho on*, and into Latin as *ego sum qui sum*, meaning "I am who I am," or "I am He who is." The early and medieval Christian theologians all understood the phrase to be speaking about ontology, the metaphysical nature of God's existence. It meant that He was "Being-itself, timeless, immutable, incorporeal, understood as the subsisting act of all existing." Augustine defines God as that which does not change and cannot change. Aquinas, continuing the same tradition, reads the Exodus formula as saying that God is "true being, that is being that is eternal, immutable, simple, self-sufficient, and the cause and principle of every creature."

But this is the God of the philosophers, not the God of the prophets. *Ehyeh asher ehyeh* means none of these things. It means "I will be what, where, or how I will be." The essential element of the phrase is the dimension omitted by all the early Christian translations, namely the future tense. There is no way, God is telling Moshe, that he or anyone else can know in advance what God is about to do. He tells him in general terms that He is about to rescue the Israelites from the hands of the Egyptians – but as for specifics, Moshe and the people will know God not through His essence but through His acts. The future tense is key here. They cannot know Him until He acts.

He will be a God of surprises. He will do things never seen before, create signs and wonders that will be spoken about for thousands of years. They will set in motion wave after wave of repercussions. People will learn that slavery is not an inevitable condition, that might is not right, that empires are not impregnable, and that a tiny people like the Israelites can do great things if they attach their destiny to Heaven. None of this could be predicted in advance. God is saying to Moshe and to the people: You will have to trust Me. The destination to which I am calling you is just beyond the visible horizon.

It is very hard to understand how revolutionary this was. Ancient religions were deeply conservative, designed to show that the existing social hierarchy was inevitable, part of the deep structure of reality, timeless and unchangeable. Just as there was a hierarchy in the heavens, and another within the animal kingdom, so there was a hierarchy in human society. That was order. Anything that challenged it represented

16 remembered through the ages. Go, gather the elders of Israel and tell them: The HAMISHI
Lord God of your fathers appeared to me – the God of Avraham, Yitzhak, and
Yaakov – saying: I have taken note of you and I have seen what is being inflicted
17 upon you in Egypt. And I promise to bring you out of the misery of Egypt to the
land of the Canaanites and Hittites, the Amorites and Perizzites, the Hivites and
18 Jebusites, to a land flowing with milk and honey. They will listen to you. Then
you and the elders of Israel shall go to the king of Egypt and tell him, 'The Lord
God of the Hebrews has revealed Himself to us. Send us forth now for a three-
19 day journey into the wilderness to sacrifice to the Lord our God.' But I know
20 that even by a mighty hand the king of Egypt would not send you forth. So I
will stretch out My hand and strike Egypt with all the wonders I will do there.
21 After that, he will send you forth. And I will grant this people favor in the eyes of
22 the Egyptians, so that when you leave, you will not leave empty-handed. Every
woman shall ask her neighbor, ask any woman lodging with her, for objects of
silver and gold, and clothing, and you shall put these on your sons and daugh-
4 1 ters, and despoil the Egyptians." But Moshe replied, "They will not believe me.

רש״י

טז **את זקני ישראל.** מיוחדים לישיבה. ואם תאמר זקנים סתם, היאך אפשר לו לאסוף זקנים של ששים רבוא?:

יח **ושמעו לקלך.** מכיון שתאמר להם לשון זה ישמעו לקולך, שכבר סימן זה מסור בידם מיעקב ומיוסף שבלשון זה הם נגאלים; יעקב אמר להם: "ואלהים פקד יפקד אתכם" (בראשית נ, כד), יוסף אמר להם: "פקד יפקד אלהים אתכם" (שם פסוק כה): **נקרה עלינו.** לשון מקרה, וכן: "ויקר אלהים" (במדבר כג, ד); "ואנכי אקרה כה" (שם פסוק טו) – אהא נקרה מאתו הלם:

יט **לא יתן אתכם מלך מצרים להלך.** אם אין אני מראה לו ידי החזקה; כלומר, כל עוד שאין אני מודיעו ידי החזקה לא יתן אתכם להלך: **לא יתן.** "לא ישבוק", כמו: "על כן לא נתתיך" (בראשית כ, ו), "ולא נתנו אלהים להרע עמדי" (שם לא, ז), וכלן לשון נתינה הם. ויש מפרשים, "ולא ביד חזקה", ולא בשביל שידו חזקה, כי מאז אשלח את ידי "והכיתי את מצרים" וגו' (פסוק כ), ומתרגמין אותו: "ולא מן קדם דחיליה תקיף". משמו של רבי יעקב ברבי מנחם נאמר לי:

כב **ומגרת ביתה.** מאותה שהיא גרה אתה בבית: **ונצלתם.** כתרגומו: "ותרוקנון", וכן: "וינצלו את מצרים" (להלן יב, לו), "ויתנצלו בני ישראל את עדים" (להלן לג, ו), והנו"ן בו יסוד. ומנחם חברו במחברת צד"י עם "ויצל אלהים את מקנה אביכם" (בראשית לא, ט), "אשר הציל אלהים מאבינו" (שם טז), ולא יאמנו דבריו, כי אם לא היתה הנו"ן יסוד והיא נקודה בחירק, לא תהא משמשת בלשון ופעלתם אלא בלשון ונפעלתם, כמו: "ונסחתם מעל האדמה" (דברים כח, סג), "ונתתם ביד אויב" (ויקרא כו, כה), "ונגפתם לפני אויביכם" (שם פסוק יז), "ונתכתם בתוכה" (יחזקאל כב, כא), "ואמרתם נצלנו" (ירמיה ז, י), לשון נפעלנו. וכל נו"ן שהיא באה בתבה לפרקים ונופלת ממנה, כנו"ן של נוגף, נושא, נותן, נושך, כשהיא מדברת לשון ופעלתם תנקד בשבא בחטף, כגון: "ונשאתם את אביכם" (בראשית מה, יט), "ונתתם להם את ארץ הגלעד" (במדבר לב, כט), "ונמלתם את בשר ערלתכם" (בראשית יז, יא). לכך אני אומר שזאת, הנקודה בחירק, מן היסוד היא, ויסוד שם דבר 'נצול', והוא מן הלשונות הכבדים, כמו דבור, כפור, למוד, כשידבר בלשון ופעלתם ינקד בחירק, כמו: "ודברתם אל הסלע" (במדבר כ, ח), "וכפרתם את הבית" (יחזקאל מה, כ), "ולמדתם אתם את בניכם" (דברים יא, יט):

remains that according to this verse, Moshe is not satisfied by God's assurance. His own experience of the fickleness of the people (one of them, years earlier, has already said, "Who made you a ruler and judge over us?" [2:14]) makes him doubt that they will be easy to lead. Whereas Moshe's other refusals focus on his own sense of inadequacy, here

טז לֵךְ וְאָסַפְתָּ אֶת־זִקְנֵי יִשְׂרָאֵל וְאָמַרְתָּ אֲלֵהֶם יהוה אֱלֹהֵי אֲבֹתֵיכֶם חמישי
נִרְאָה אֵלַי אֱלֹהֵי אַבְרָהָם יִצְחָק וְיַעֲקֹב לֵאמֹר פָּקֹד פָּקַדְתִּי אֶתְכֶם
יז וְאֶת־הֶעָשׂוּי לָכֶם בְּמִצְרָיִם׃ וָאֹמַר אַעֲלֶה אֶתְכֶם מֵעֳנִי מִצְרַיִם אֶל־
אֶרֶץ הַכְּנַעֲנִי וְהַחִתִּי וְהָאֱמֹרִי וְהַפְּרִזִּי וְהַחִוִּי וְהַיְבוּסִי אֶל־אֶרֶץ זָבַת
יח חָלָב וּדְבָשׁ׃ וְשָׁמְעוּ לְקֹלֶךָ וּבָאתָ אַתָּה וְזִקְנֵי יִשְׂרָאֵל אֶל־מֶלֶךְ מִצְרַיִם
וַאֲמַרְתֶּם אֵלָיו יהוה אֱלֹהֵי הָעִבְרִיִּים נִקְרָה עָלֵינוּ וְעַתָּה נֵלֲכָה־נָּא
יט דֶּרֶךְ שְׁלֹשֶׁת יָמִים בַּמִּדְבָּר וְנִזְבְּחָה לַיהוה אֱלֹהֵינוּ׃ וַאֲנִי יָדַעְתִּי כִּי
כ לֹא־יִתֵּן אֶתְכֶם מֶלֶךְ מִצְרַיִם לַהֲלֹךְ וְלֹא בְּיָד חֲזָקָה׃ וְשָׁלַחְתִּי אֶת־
יָדִי וְהִכֵּיתִי אֶת־מִצְרַיִם בְּכֹל נִפְלְאֹתַי אֲשֶׁר אֶעֱשֶׂה בְּקִרְבּוֹ וְאַחֲרֵי־כֵן
כא יְשַׁלַּח אֶתְכֶם׃ וְנָתַתִּי אֶת־חֵן הָעָם־הַזֶּה בְּעֵינֵי מִצְרָיִם וְהָיָה כִּי תֵלֵכוּן
כב לֹא תֵלְכוּ רֵיקָם׃ וְשָׁאֲלָה אִשָּׁה מִשְּׁכֶנְתָּהּ וּמִגָּרַת בֵּיתָהּ כְּלֵי־כֶסֶף וּכְלֵי
זָהָב וּשְׂמָלֹת וְשַׂמְתֶּם עַל־בְּנֵיכֶם וְעַל־בְּנֹתֵיכֶם וְנִצַּלְתֶּם אֶת־מִצְרָיִם׃
ד א וַיַּעַן מֹשֶׁה וַיֹּאמֶר וְהֵן לֹא־יַאֲמִינוּ לִי וְלֹא יִשְׁמְעוּ בְּקֹלִי כִּי יֹאמְרוּ

אונקלוס

טו אֱיזִיל וְתִכְנוֹשׁ יָת סָבֵי יִשְׂרָאֵל, וְתֵימַר לְהוֹן יְיָ, אֱלָהָא דַאֲבָהָתְכוֹן
אִתְגְּלִי לִי, אֱלָהֵיהּ דְּאַבְרָהָם, יִצְחָק וְיַעֲקֹב לְמֵימַר, מִדְכַּר דְּכִירְנָא
יָתְכוֹן, וְיָת דְּאִתְעֲבֵיד לְכוֹן בְּמִצְרָיִם: יז וַאֲמָרִית, אַסֵּיק יָתְכוֹן
מִשִּׁעְבּוּד מִצְרָאֵי, לַאֲרַע כְּנַעֲנָאֵי וְחִתָּאֵי, וֶאֱמוֹרָאֵי וּפְרִזָּאֵי, וְחִוָּאֵי
וִיבוּסָאֵי, לַאֲרַע, עָבְדָא חֲלַב וּדְבָשׁ: יח וִיקַבְּלוּן מִנָּךְ, וְתֵיתֵי, אַתְּ
וְסָבֵי יִשְׂרָאֵל לְוָת מַלְכָּא דְּמִצְרַיִם, וְתֵימְרוּן לֵיהּ יְיָ, אֱלָהָא דִּיהוּדָאֵי
אִתְקְרִי עֲלַנָא, וּכְעַן, נֵיזִיל כְּעַן, מַהֲלַךְ תְּלָתָא יוֹמִין בְּמַדְבְּרָא,
וּנְדַבַּח קֳדָם יְיָ אֱלָהַנָא: יט וּקְדָמַי גְּלֵי, אֲרֵי, לָא יִשְׁבּוֹק יָתְכוֹן,
מַלְכָּא דְמִצְרַיִם לְמֵיזַל, וְלָא מִן קֳדָם דְּחֵילֵיהּ תַּקִּיף: כ וְאֶשְׁלַח יָת
מְחַת גְּבוּרְתִּי וְאֶמְחֵי יָת מִצְרָאֵי, בְּכֹל פְּרִישָׁתִי, דְּאַעְבֵּיד בֵּינֵיהוֹן,
וּבָתַר כֵּן יְשַׁלַּח יָתְכוֹן: כא וְאֶתֵּין, יָת עַמָּא הָדֵין לְרַחֲמִין בְּעֵינֵי
מִצְרָאֵי, וִיהֵי אֲרֵי תְהָכוּן, לָא תְהָכוּן רֵיקָנִין: כב וְתִשְׁאַל אִתְּתָא
מִשְּׁבַבְתַּהּ וּמִקָּרִיבַת בֵּיתַהּ, מָנִין דִּכְסַף, וּמָנִין דִּדְהַב וּלְבוּשִׁין,
וּתְשַׁווּן, עַל בְּנֵיכוֹן וְעַל בְּנָתְכוֹן, וּתְרוֹקְנוּן יָת מִצְרָאֵי: ד א וַאֲתֵיב
מֹשֶׁה וַאֲמַר, וְהָא לָא יְהֵימְנוּן לִי, וְלָא יְקַבְּלוּן מִנִּי, אֲרֵי יֵימְרוּן,

4:1 וְהֵן לֹא־יַאֲמִינוּ לִי *They will not believe me* – The sages, ultra-sensitive to nuances in the text, noticed two important features of this response. The first is that God has already told Moshe, "They will listen to you" (Ex. 3:18). Moshe's reply seems to contradict God's prior assurance. To be sure, the commentators offered various harmonizing interpretations. Ibn Ezra suggests that God had told Moshe that the elders would listen to him, whereas Moshe expressed doubts about the mass of the people. Ramban says that Moshe did not doubt that they would believe initially, but he thought that they would lose faith as soon as they saw that Pharaoh would not let them go. There are other explanations, but the fact

▶

They will not listen to me. They will say, 'The LORD has not appeared to you.'"
2 3 "What is that in your hand?" asked the LORD. "A staff," he replied. "Throw it
to the ground." He threw it, and it turned into a snake; and Moshe fled back
4 from it. The LORD told Moshe, "Reach out your hand and take hold of its tail."
He reached out his hand and grasped it, and in his hand it turned back into a
5 staff. "This is so that they will believe that the LORD God of their fathers, the
6 God of Avraham, Yitzḥak, and Yaakov, appeared to you." The LORD spoke to
him again: "Put your hand inside your cloak." He put his hand inside his cloak;
7 when he took it out it was as white as snow. "Put it back inside your cloak," He
said. Moshe put his hand back inside his cloak, and when he took it out the skin
8 color had returned. "If they do not believe you and are not persuaded by the
9 first sign, they will believe the evidence of the second sign. And if they do not
believe either of these signs, and will not listen to you, then take some water

רש״י

ד ב| **מַזֶּה בְיָדֶךָ.** לְכָךְ נִכְתַּב תֵּבָה אַחַת, לִדְרֹשׁ: מִזֶּה שֶׁבְּיָדְךָ אַתָּה חַיָּב לִלְקוֹת, שֶׁחָשַׁדְתָּ בִּכְשֵׁרִים. וּפְשׁוּטוֹ, כְּאָדָם שֶׁאוֹמֵר לַחֲבֵרוֹ: מוֹדֶה אַתָּה שֶׁזּוֹ שֶׁלְּפָנֶיךָ אֶבֶן הִיא? אָמַר לוֹ: הֵן. אָמַר לוֹ: הֲרֵינִי עוֹשֶׂה אוֹתָהּ עֵץ:

ג| **וַיְהִי לְנָחָשׁ.** רָמַז לוֹ שֶׁסִּפֵּר לָשׁוֹן הָרָע עַל יִשְׂרָאֵל וְתָפַשׂ אֻמָּנוּתוֹ שֶׁל נָחָשׁ:

ד| **וַיַּחֲזֶק בּוֹ.** לְשׁוֹן אֲחִיזָה הוּא, וְהַרְבֵּה יֵשׁ בַּמִּקְרָא: "וַיַּחֲזִיקוּ הָאֲנָשִׁים בְּיָדוֹ" (בראשית יט, טז), "וְהֶחֱזִיקָה בִּמְבֻשָׁיו" (דברים כה, יא), "וְהֶחֱזַקְתִּי בִּזְקָנוֹ" (שמואל א' יז, לה), כָּל לְשׁוֹן חִזּוּק הַדָּבוּק לְבֵי"ת לְשׁוֹן אֲחִיזָה הוּא:

ו| **מְצֹרַעַת כַּשָּׁלֶג.** דֶּרֶךְ צָרַעַת לִהְיוֹת לְבָנָה, "אִם בַּהֶרֶת לְבָנָה הִוא" (ויקרא יג, ד). אַף בְּאוֹת זֶה רָמַז לוֹ שֶׁלָּשׁוֹן הָרָע סִפֵּר בְּאָמְרוֹ: "לֹא יַאֲמִינוּ לִי" (לעיל פסוק א), לְפִיכָךְ הִלְקָהוּ בְּצָרַעַת, כְּמוֹ שֶׁלָּקְתָה מִרְיָם עַל לְשׁוֹן הָרָע:

ז| **וַיּוֹצִאָהּ מֵחֵיקוֹ וְהִנֵּה שָׁבָה כִּבְשָׂרוֹ.** מִכָּאן שֶׁמִּדָּה טוֹבָה מְמַהֶרֶת לָבֹא מִמִּדַּת פֻּרְעָנוּת, שֶׁהֲרֵי בָּרִאשׁוֹנָה לֹא נֶאֱמַר 'מֵחֵיקוֹ':

ח| **וְהֶאֱמִינוּ לְקֹל הָאֹת הָאַחֲרוֹן.** מִשֶּׁתֹּאמַר לָהֶם: בִּשְׁבִילְכֶם לָקִיתִי עַל שֶׁסִּפַּרְתִּי עֲלֵיכֶם לָשׁוֹן הָרָע, יַאֲמִינוּ לְךָ, שֶׁכְּבָר לָמְדוּ בְּכָךְ שֶׁהַמִּזְדַּוְּגִים לָהֶם לוֹקִים בִּנְגָעִים, כְּגוֹן פַּרְעֹה וַאֲבִימֶלֶךְ בִּשְׁבִיל שָׂרָה:

In general, this "blight" was understood as a punishment for *lashon hara*, derogatory speech. Moshe, perhaps, had been guilty of the same sin. The Sages arrived at the following comment (Shabbat 97a):

> Reish Lakish said: He who entertains a suspicion against the innocent will be bodily afflicted, as it is written, "Moshe replied: 'They will not believe me.'" However, it was known to the Holy One, blessed be He, that Israel would believe. He said to Moshe: "They are believers, the children of believers, but you will ultimately disbelieve… as it is said, '[But the LORD said to Moshe…] "Because you did not put your trust in Me"'" (Num. 20:12).

biblical disease *tzaraat* was mistakenly translated in the Septuagint as leprosy, the bacterial infection, untreatable until the twentieth century, now known as Hansen's disease. The two illnesses have vastly different symptoms, and the mistranslation has historically compounded the stigma attached to Hansen's disease, causing unnecessary shame to sufferers who were already ostracized. We have therefore avoided the traditional translation. *Tzaraat* is always presented as a set of visible symptoms inflicted by God, so we have chosen to translate it "an impure blight," or here, simply "whiteness."

What, then, is the significance of this particular sign? The Sages recalled that later, Miriam was punished with *tzaraat* for speaking negatively about Moshe (Num. 12:10).

ב לֹא־נִרְאָה אֵלֶיךָ יְהוָה: וַיֹּאמֶר אֵלָיו יְהוָה מזה בְיָדֶךָ וַיֹּאמֶר מַטֶּה: מַה־זֶּה
ג וַיֹּאמֶר הַשְׁלִיכֵהוּ אַרְצָה וַיַּשְׁלִכֵהוּ אַרְצָה וַיְהִי לְנָחָשׁ וַיָּנָס מֹשֶׁה מִפָּנָיו:
ד וַיֹּאמֶר יְהוָה אֶל־מֹשֶׁה שְׁלַח יָדְךָ וֶאֱחֹז בִּזְנָבוֹ וַיִּשְׁלַח יָדוֹ וַיַּחֲזֶק־בּוֹ
ה וַיְהִי לְמַטֶּה בְּכַפּוֹ: לְמַעַן יַאֲמִינוּ כִּי־נִרְאָה אֵלֶיךָ יְהוָה אֱלֹהֵי אֲבֹתָם
ו אֱלֹהֵי אַבְרָהָם אֱלֹהֵי יִצְחָק וֵאלֹהֵי יַעֲקֹב: וַיֹּאמֶר יְהוָה לוֹ עוֹד הָבֵא־נָא
ז יָדְךָ בְּחֵיקֶךָ וַיָּבֵא יָדוֹ בְּחֵיקוֹ וַיּוֹצִאָהּ וְהִנֵּה יָדוֹ מְצֹרַעַת כַּשָּׁלֶג: וַיֹּאמֶר
הָשֵׁב יָדְךָ אֶל־חֵיקֶךָ וַיָּשֶׁב יָדוֹ אֶל־חֵיקוֹ וַיּוֹצִאָהּ מֵחֵיקוֹ וְהִנֵּה־שָׁבָה
ח כִּבְשָׂרוֹ: וְהָיָה אִם־לֹא יַאֲמִינוּ לָךְ וְלֹא יִשְׁמְעוּ לְקֹל הָאֹת הָרִאשׁוֹן
ט וְהֶאֱמִינוּ לְקֹל הָאֹת הָאַחֲרוֹן: וְהָיָה אִם־לֹא יַאֲמִינוּ גַּם לִשְׁנֵי הָאֹתוֹת

אונקלוס

לָא אִתְגְּלִי לָךְ יְיָ: ב וַאֲמַר לֵיהּ, יְיָ מָא דֵין בִּידָךְ, וַאֲמַר חֻטְרָא: ג וַאֲמַר רְמוֹהִי לְאַרְעָא, וּרְמָהִי לְאַרְעָא וַהֲוָה לְחִוְיָא, וַעֲרַק מֹשֶׁה מִן קֳדָמוֹהִי: ד וַאֲמַר יְיָ לְמֹשֶׁה, אוֹשֵׁיט יְדָךְ, וְאֵיחוֹד בְּדֻנְבֵיהּ, וְאוֹשֵׁיט יְדֵיהּ וְאַתְקֵיף בֵּיהּ, וַהֲוָה לְחֻטְרָא בִּידֵיהּ: ה בְּדִיל דִּיהֵימְנוּן, אֲרֵי אִתְגְּלִי לָךְ, יְיָ אֱלָהָא דַּאֲבָהָתְהוֹן, אֱלָהֵיהּ דְּאַבְרָהָם, אֱלָהֵיהּ דְּיִצְחָק וֵאלָהֵיהּ דְּיַעֲקֹב: ו וַאֲמַר יְיָ לֵיהּ עוֹד, אַעֵיל כְּעַן יְדָךְ בְּעִטְפָּךְ, וְאַעֵיל יְדֵיהּ בְּעִטְפֵיהּ, וְאַפְּקַהּ, וְהָא יְדֵיהּ חִוָּרָא כְּתַלְגָּא: ז וַאֲמַר, אֲתֵיב יְדָךְ לְעִטְפָּךְ, וַאֲתֵיב יְדֵיהּ לְעִטְפֵיהּ, וְאַפְּקַהּ מֵעִטְפֵיהּ, וְהָא תָבַת הֲוָת כְּבִסְרֵיהּ: ח וִיהֵי אִם לָא יְהֵימְנוּן לָךְ, וְלָא יְקַבְּלוּן, לְקָל אָתָא קַדְמָאָה, וִיהֵימְנוּן, לְקָל אָתָא בָתְרָאָה: ט וִיהֵי, אִם לָא יְהֵימְנוּן, אַף לִתְרֵין אָתַיָּא

he speaks not about himself but about the people. They will not believe him.

The text implies that Moshe is entitled to have doubts about his own worthiness for the task. What he is not entitled to do is to have doubts about the people. His doubts, it will transpire, are amply justified. The people are fractious. Moshe calls them a "stiff-necked people" (Deut. 9:6). Time and again during the wilderness years they complain, sin, and want to return to Egypt. Moshe is not wrong in his estimate of their character. Yet God reprimands him, indeed punishes him, by whitening his hand with "an impure blight" (see comment on v. 6). A fundamental principle of Jewish leadership is intimated here for the first time: a leader does not need faith in himself, but he must have faith in the people he is to lead.

That, according to the Sages, is what God is teaching Moshe: What matters is not whether they believe in you, but whether you believe in them. Unless you believe in them, you cannot lead in the way a prophet must lead. You must identify with them and have faith in them, seeing not only their surface faults but also their underlying virtues. Otherwise, you will be no better than a detached intellectual – and that is the beginning of the end. You will think yourself superior to others, and that is a corruption of the soul. If you do not believe in the people, eventually you will not even believe in God.

Who is a leader? To this, the Jewish answer is one who identifies with his or her people, mindful of their faults, to be sure, but convinced also of their potential greatness and their preciousness in the sight of God. In effect, God is saying to Moshe: Those people of whom you have doubts are believers. They are My people, and they are your people. Just as you believe in Me, so you must believe in them.

4:6 מְצֹרַעַת כַּשָּׁלֶג *White as snow* – In Hebrew, *metzoraat*. The

from the Nile and spill it on the ground. The water you take from the Nile
10 will become blood on the ground." Then Moshe said to the LORD, "Please, my
LORD, I am not a man of words; I was not yesterday, nor the day before, and
still I am not since You spoke to Your servant. I am slow of speech and tongue."
11 "Who gives man speech?" said the LORD to him. "Who makes people dumb
12 or deaf? Who gives them sight or blindness? Is it not I, the LORD? Now go. I
13 will help you speak and I will teach you what to say." But "Please, my LORD," he
14 said, "send someone else." Then the LORD's anger blazed against Moshe. "Have
you not a brother, Aharon the Levite? He, I know, is able to speak. Even now he
15 is setting out to meet you, and when he sees you his heart will rejoice. You shall

רש״י

ט **וְהָיוּ הַמַּיִם וְגוֹ׳.** וְהָיוּ וְהָיוּ, שְׁתֵּי פְעָמִים. נִרְאֶה בְּעֵינַי, אִלּוּ נֶאֱמַר: ׳וְהָיוּ הַמַּיִם אֲשֶׁר תִּקַּח מִן הַיְאֹר לְדָם בַּיַּבָּשֶׁת׳ שׁוֹמֵעַ אֲנִי שֶׁבְּיָדוֹ הֵם נֶהְפָּכִים לְדָם, וְאַף כְּשֶׁיִּהְיוּ לָאָרֶץ יִהְיוּ בַּהֲוָיָתָן, אֲבָל עַכְשָׁיו מְלַמְּדֵנוּ שֶׁלֹּא יִהְיוּ דָם עַד שֶׁיִּהְיוּ בַּיַּבָּשֶׁת:

י **גַּם מִתְּמוֹל וְגוֹ׳.** לָמַדְנוּ שֶׁשִּׁבְעַת יָמִים הָיָה הַקָּדוֹשׁ בָּרוּךְ הוּא מְפַתֶּה אֶת מֹשֶׁה בִּסְנֶה לֵילֵךְ בִּשְׁלִיחוּתוֹ: מִתְּמוֹל, שִׁלְשֹׁם, מֵאָז דַּבֶּרְךָ – הֲרֵי שְׁלֹשָׁה, וּשְׁלֹשָׁה גַּמִּין רִבּוּיִין הֵם הֲרֵי שִׁשָּׁה, וְהוּא הָיָה עוֹמֵד בַּיּוֹם הַשְּׁבִיעִי כְּשֶׁאָמַר לוֹ זֹאת עַד ״שְׁלַח נָא בְּיַד תִּשְׁלָח״ (להלן פסוק יג), עַד שֶׁחָרָה בּוֹ וְקִבֵּל עָלָיו. וְכָל זֶה, שֶׁלֹּא הָיָה רוֹצֶה לִטֹּל גְּדֻלָּה עַל אַהֲרֹן אָחִיו שֶׁהָיָה גָּדוֹל הֵימֶנּוּ, וְנָבִיא הָיָה, שֶׁנֶּאֱמַר: ״הֲנִגְלֹה נִגְלֵיתִי אֶל בֵּית אָבִיךָ בִּהְיוֹתָם בְּמִצְרַיִם״ (שמואל א׳ ב, כז), הוּא אַהֲרֹן. וְכֵן בִּיחֶזְקֵאל: ״וָאִוָּדַע לָהֶם בְּאֶרֶץ מִצְרָיִם וְגוֹ׳ וָאֹמַר אֲלֵהֶם אִישׁ שִׁקּוּצֵי עֵינָיו הַשְׁלִיכוּ״ (יחזקאל כ, ה-ז), וְאוֹתָהּ נְבוּאָה לְאַהֲרֹן נֶאֶמְרָה: **כְּבַד פֶּה.** בִּכְבֵדוּת אֲנִי מְדַבֵּר, וּבִלְשׁוֹן לַעַז בלב״א:

יא **מִי שָׂם פֶּה וְגוֹ׳.** מִי לִמֶּדְךָ לְדַבֵּר כְּשֶׁהָיִיתָ נִדּוֹן לִפְנֵי פַרְעֹה עַל הַמִּצְרִי? **אוֹ מִי יָשׂוּם אִלֵּם.** מִי עָשָׂה פַרְעֹה אִלֵּם שֶׁלֹּא נִתְאַמֵּץ בְּמִצְוַת הֲרִיגָתְךָ, וְאֶת מְשָׁרְתָיו חֵרְשִׁים שֶׁלֹּא שָׁמְעוּ בְּצַוּוֹתוֹ עָלֶיךָ, וְלָאִסְפַּקְלָטוֹרִין הַהוֹרְגִים מִי עֲשָׂאָם עִוְרִים שֶׁלֹּא רָאוּ כְּשֶׁבָּרַחְתָּ מִן הַבִּימָה וְנִמְלַטְתָּ? **הֲלֹא אָנֹכִי.** שֶׁשְּׁמִי ״ה׳״, עָשִׂיתִי כָּל זֹאת:

יג **בְּיַד תִּשְׁלָח.** בְּיַד מִי שֶׁאַתָּה רָגִיל לִשְׁלֹחַ, וְהוּא אַהֲרֹן. דָּבָר אַחֵר, בְּיַד אַחֵר שֶׁתִּרְצֶה לִשְׁלֹחַ, אֵין סוֹפִי לְהַכְנִיסָם לָאָרֶץ וְלִהְיוֹת גּוֹאֲלָם לֶעָתִיד, יֵשׁ לְךָ שְׁלוּחִים הַרְבֵּה:

יד **וַיִּחַר אַף.** רַבִּי יְהוֹשֻׁעַ בֶּן קָרְחָה אוֹמֵר: כָּל חֲרוֹן אַף שֶׁבַּתּוֹרָה עוֹשֶׂה רֹשֶׁם, וְזֶה לֹא נֶאֱמַר בּוֹ רֹשֶׁם, וְלֹא מָצִינוּ שֶׁבָּא עֹנֶשׁ עַל יְדֵי אוֹתוֹ חָרוֹן. אָמַר לוֹ רַבִּי יוֹסֵי: אַף בְּזוֹ נֶאֱמַר בּוֹ רֹשֶׁם: ״הֲלֹא אַהֲרֹן אָחִיךָ הַלֵּוִי״, שֶׁהָיָה עָתִיד לִהְיוֹת לֵוִי וְלֹא כֹהֵן, וְהַכְּהֻנָּה הָיִיתִי אוֹמֵר לָצֵאת מִמְּךָ, מֵעַתָּה לֹא יִהְיֶה כֵן, אֶלָּא הוּא יִהְיֶה כֹּהֵן וְאַתָּה לֵוִי, שֶׁנֶּאֱמַר: ״וּמֹשֶׁה אִישׁ הָאֱלֹהִים בָּנָיו יִקָּרְאוּ עַל שֵׁבֶט הַלֵּוִי״ (דברי הימים א׳ כג, יד): **הִנֵּה הוּא יֹצֵא לִקְרָאתֶךָ.** כְּשֶׁתֵּלֵךְ לְמִצְרַיִם: **וְרָאֲךָ וְשָׂמַח בְּלִבּוֹ.** לֹא כְּשֶׁאַתָּה סָבוּר שֶׁיְּהֵא מַקְפִּיד עָלֶיךָ שֶׁאַתָּה עוֹלֶה לִגְדֻלָּה. וּמִשָּׁם זָכָה אַהֲרֹן לַעֲדִי הַחֹשֶׁן הַנָּתוּן עַל הַלֵּב:

provokes divine anger because God has answered all of Moshe's hesitations and doubts. All that is left is an overwhelming sense of inadequacy, as if Moshe believes that he cannot do this, he is not a leader, he is not known to the Israelites, he has not grown up with them or suffered with them. Note how profoundly human is the Torah's portrayal of Moshe: the greatest of men, yet fraught with doubts and hesitations. What Moshe does not understand, however, was that each of his weaknesses is a strength: his youth in Egypt, his long stay in Midyan, his speech defect, his anger at injustice will all prove to be invaluable to his role. Ultimately, though, what provokes divine anger is his lack of faith in God's faith in him. That is one doubt too far. When God calls, He knows whom He is calling and why. Often His faith in us is greater than our faith in ourselves.

4:14 **וְשָׂמַח בְּלִבּוֹ** *His heart will rejoice* – Aharon, we may have thought, might have many reasons not to rejoice on seeing Moshe return. The brothers did not grow up together. Moshe was adopted by Pharaoh's daughter and raised in an

הָאֵ֗לֶּה וְלֹ֤א יִשְׁמְעוּן֙ לְקֹלֶ֔ךָ וְלָקַחְתָּ֙ מִמֵּימֵ֣י הַיְאֹ֔ר וְשָׁפַכְתָּ֖ הַיַּבָּשָׁ֑ה
י וְהָי֤וּ הַמַּ֙יִם֙ אֲשֶׁ֣ר תִּקַּ֣ח מִן־הַיְאֹ֔ר וְהָי֥וּ לְדָ֖ם בַּיַּבָּֽשֶׁת׃ וַיֹּ֨אמֶר מֹשֶׁ֣ה
אֶל־יהוה֮ בִּ֣י אֲדֹנָי֒ לֹא֩ אִ֨ישׁ דְּבָרִ֜ים אָנֹ֗כִי גַּ֤ם מִתְּמוֹל֙ גַּ֣ם מִשִּׁלְשֹׁ֔ם
יא גַּ֛ם מֵאָ֥ז דַּבֶּרְךָ֖ אֶל־עַבְדֶּ֑ךָ כִּ֧י כְבַד־פֶּ֛ה וּכְבַ֥ד לָשׁ֖וֹן אָנֹֽכִי׃ וַיֹּ֨אמֶר יהוה
אֵלָ֗יו מִ֣י שָׂ֣ם פֶּה֮ לָֽאָדָם֒ א֚וֹ מִֽי־יָשׂ֣וּם אִלֵּ֔ם א֣וֹ חֵרֵ֔שׁ א֥וֹ פִקֵּ֖חַ א֣וֹ עִוֵּ֑ר
יב הֲלֹ֥א אָנֹכִ֖י יהוה׃ וְעַתָּ֖ה לֵ֑ךְ וְאָנֹכִי֙ אֶֽהְיֶ֣ה עִם־פִּ֔יךָ וְהוֹרֵיתִ֖יךָ אֲשֶׁ֥ר
יג יד תְּדַבֵּֽר׃ וַיֹּ֖אמֶר בִּ֣י אֲדֹנָ֑י שְֽׁלַֽח־נָ֖א בְּיַד־תִּשְׁלָֽח׃ וַיִּֽחַר־אַ֨ף יהוה בְּמֹשֶׁ֗ה
וַיֹּ֙אמֶר֙ הֲלֹ֨א אַהֲרֹ֤ן אָחִ֙יךָ֙ הַלֵּוִ֔י יָדַ֕עְתִּי כִּֽי־דַבֵּ֥ר יְדַבֵּ֖ר ה֑וּא וְגַ֤ם הִנֵּה־הוּא֙
טו יֹצֵ֣א לִקְרָאתֶ֔ךָ וְרָאֲךָ֖ וְשָׂמַ֥ח בְּלִבּֽוֹ׃ וְדִבַּרְתָּ֣ אֵלָ֔יו וְשַׂמְתָּ֥ אֶת־הַדְּבָרִ֖ים

אונקלוס

הָאִלֵּין, וְלָא יְקַבְּלוּן מִנָּךְ, וְתִסַּב מִמַּיָּא דִבְנַהְרָא, וְתֵישׁוֹד לְיַבֶּשְׁתָּא,
וִיהוֹן מַיָּא דְּתִסַּב מִן נַהְרָא, וִיהוֹן לִדְמָא בְּיַבֶּשְׁתָּא: וַאֲמַר מֹשֶׁה
קֳדָם יי בְּבָעוּ יי, לָא גְּבַר דְּמִלּוּל אֲנָא, אַף מֵאִתְמָלֵי אַף מִדְּקַמּוֹהִי,
אַף מֵעִדָּן דְּמַלֵּילְתָּא עִם עַבְדָּךְ, אֲרֵי יַקִּיר מַמְלַל, וְעַמִּיק לִישָּׁן אֲנָא:
יא וַאֲמַר יי לֵיהּ, מַאן שַׁוִּי פֻּמָּא לַאֲנָשָׁא, אוֹ מַאן שַׁוִּי אִלֵּימָא, אוֹ
חֵרְשָׁא, אוֹ פַתִּיחָא אוֹ עַוִּירָא, הֲלָא אֲנָא יי: יב וּכְעַן אִיזִיל, וּמֵימְרִי
יְהֵי עִם פֻּמָּךְ, וְאַלְּפִנָּךְ דִּתְמַלֵּיל: יג וַאֲמַר בְּבָעוּ יי, שְׁלַח כְּעַן בְּיַד
מַאן דְּכָשַׁר לְמִשְׁלַח: יד וּתְקֵיף רָגְזָא דַּיי בְּמֹשֶׁה, וַאֲמַר הֲלָא אַהֲרֹן
אָחוּךְ לֵיוָאָה, גְּלֵי קֳדָמַי, אֲרֵי מַלָּלָא יְמַלֵּיל הוּא, וְאַף הָא הוּא נָפֵיק
לְקַדָּמוּתָךְ, וְיֶחֱזִינָךְ וְיֶחְדֵּי בְּלִבֵּיהּ: טו וּתְמַלֵּיל עִמֵּיהּ, וּתְשַׁוֵּי יָת פִּתְגָּמַיָּא

4:10 לֹא אִישׁ דְּבָרִים אָנֹכִי *I am not a man of words* – Some suggest that Moshe had a speech defect, perhaps a stammer. It may be simply that, having spent much of his adult life as a solitary shepherd, he is unused to speaking, especially in public. It may be, however, that far from being a disqualification, this is an important qualification (see Malbim). God chose an infertile, aged couple to be the progenitors of a nation that would eventually become numerous. Three of the matriarchs ("mothers"), Sara, Rivka, and Raḥel, were unable to have children. God chooses a fractious, often rebellious people to be the bearers of His covenant. He chooses one who is not a man of words to be the bearer of His word. Those whom God chooses testify in themselves to something beyond themselves. *The man God chooses to deliver His word to the world is a man who cannot naturally deliver words.* What Moshe reasonably sees as a disqualification is in fact part of his qualification.

Those who hear Moshe know that his words come from a source beyond himself. Moshe does not yet understand this, partly because his mission has not yet begun, partly because there has never before in Israel been a prophet like him who addresses an entire nation and gives them instruction from Heaven, and whose words, written down, will become holy and canonical. Other prophets also expressed a sense of inadequacy in giving voice to the divine word. Yeshayahu said, "My mouth has been defiled" (Is. 6:5). Yirmeyahu said, "I am not capable of speaking, for I am still only a boy" (Jer. 1:6). Only the true prophet understands how difficult it is to translate the voice of heaven into the language of earth. The prophets spoke not because they could but because they must. "The Lord God speaks; who would not prophesy?" (Amos 3:8).

4:13 שְׁלַח־נָא בְּיַד־תִּשְׁלָח *Send someone else* – This response

speak to him and place words in his mouth. I will help you both to speak, and I
16 will teach you what to do. He will speak on your behalf to the people – he will
17 be your voice; and you will be his access to God. Take this staff in your hand.
With it, you shall perform the signs."
18 Moshe left and returned to Yeter his father-in-law. He said to him, "Let me go SHISHI
back to my brothers in Egypt, to see if they are still alive." Yitro said to him, "Go
19 in peace." While Moshe was still in Midyan, the Lord said to him, "Go, return
20 to Egypt. All those who sought your life have died." So Moshe took his wife

רש״י

טז **וְדִבֶּר הוּא לְךָ.** בִּשְׁבִילְךָ יְדַבֵּר אֶל הָעָם. וְזֶה יוֹכִיחַ עַל כָּל לְךָ וְלִי וְלוֹ וְלָכֶם וְלָהֶם הַסְּמוּכִים לְדִבּוּר, שֶׁכֻּלָּם לָשׁוֹן עָלֶיךָ הֵם: **יִהְיֶה לְּךָ לְפֶה.** לְמֵלִיץ, לְפִי שֶׁאַתָּה כְּבַד פֶּה: **לֵאלֹהִים.** לְרַב וּלְשַׂר:

יח **וַיֵּשֶׁב אֶל יֶתֶר חֹתְנוֹ.** לִטֹּל רְשׁוּת, שֶׁהֲרֵי נִשְׁבַּע לוֹ. וְשִׁבְעָה שֵׁמוֹת הָיוּ לוֹ: רְעוּאֵל, יֶתֶר, יִתְרוֹ, קֵינִי, חוֹבָב, חֶבֶר, פּוּטִיאֵל:

יט **כִּי מֵתוּ כָּל הָאֲנָשִׁים.** מִי הֵם? דָּתָן וַאֲבִירָם; חַיִּים הָיוּ, אֶלָּא שֶׁיָּרְדוּ מִנִּכְסֵיהֶם, וְהֶעָנִי חָשׁוּב כַּמֵּת:

what Robert Alter has classed as a type-scene, that is, a stylized episode that happens more than once in Tanakh. One obvious example is young-man-meets-future-wife-at-well, a scene enacted with variations three times in the Torah: in the case of Avraham's servant and Rivka, Yaakov and Raḥel, and of course Moshe and Tzipora. There are differences between them, but sufficient similarities to make us realize that we are dealing with a convention. Rashbam compares the encounter here to Yaakov's nocturnal struggle with an unknown man and to the story of the prophet Yona. It is the latter that provides the key to understanding both the earlier narratives. Yona seeks to escape from his mission to go to Nineveh to warn the people that the city is about to be destroyed if they do not repent. He flees in a boat to Tarshish, but God brings a storm that threatens to sink the ship. The prophet is then thrown into the sea and swallowed by a giant fish that later vomits him out alive. Yona thus realizes that flight is impossible.

The same, says Rashbam, applies to Moshe, who has repeatedly expressed his reluctance to undertake the task God has set him. Evidently, Moshe is still prevaricating even after beginning the journey. Some commentators suggest that he has agreed with his father-in-law that at least one of his children *will* be brought up not as an Israelite but as a Midianite. Tzipora's prompt and decisive action saves a life.

It is a unique interpretation, sobering in its implications. Here are three great men, Yaakov, Moshe, and Yona, yet all three, according to Rashbam, are afraid. Of what? None is a coward.

They are afraid, essentially, of their mission. This is not physical fear. It is the fear that comes from a feeling of personal inadequacy. "Who am I…to bring the Israelites out of Egypt?" (Ex. 3:11) asks Moshe at the burning bush. Sometimes the greatest have the least self-confidence, because they know how immense is the responsibility and how small they feel in relation to it.

I sometimes feel that, consciously or subconsciously, some take flight from Judaism for this very reason. Who are we to be God's witnesses to the world, a light to the nations, role models for others? If even spiritual giants like Moshe sought to flee, how much more so you and me? This fear of unworthiness is one that surely most of us have had at some time or other.

The reason it is wrong is not that it is untrue, but that it is irrelevant. Writers grow by writing. Teachers grow by teaching. It is only by overcoming our sense of inadequacy that we throw ourselves into the task and find ourselves lifted and enlarged by so doing.

In Shakespeare's words: "Be not afraid of greatness: some are born great, some achieve greatness, and some have greatness thrust upon 'em." That is why God wrestled with Yaakov, Moshe, and Yona and would not let them escape. We

בְּפִיו וְאָנֹכִי אֶהְיֶה עִם־פִּיךָ וְעִם־פִּיהוּ וְהוֹרֵיתִי אֶתְכֶם אֵת אֲשֶׁר
טז תַּעֲשׂוּן׃ וְדִבֶּר־הוּא לְךָ אֶל־הָעָם וְהָיָה הוּא יִהְיֶה־לְּךָ לְפֶה וְאַתָּה
יז תִּהְיֶה־לּוֹ לֵאלֹהִים׃ וְאֶת־הַמַּטֶּה הַזֶּה תִּקַּח בְּיָדֶךָ אֲשֶׁר תַּעֲשֶׂה־בּוֹ
אֶת־הָאֹתֹת׃
יח וַיֵּלֶךְ מֹשֶׁה וַיָּשָׁב ׀ אֶל־יֶתֶר חֹתְנוֹ וַיֹּאמֶר לוֹ אֵלְכָה־נָּא וְאָשׁוּבָה ג ששי
אֶל־אַחַי אֲשֶׁר־בְּמִצְרַיִם וְאֶרְאֶה הַעוֹדָם חַיִּים וַיֹּאמֶר יִתְרוֹ לְמֹשֶׁה
יט לֵךְ לְשָׁלוֹם׃ וַיֹּאמֶר יְהוָה אֶל־מֹשֶׁה בְּמִדְיָן לֵךְ שֻׁב מִצְרָיִם כִּי־מֵתוּ
כ כָּל־הָאֲנָשִׁים הַמְבַקְשִׁים אֶת־נַפְשֶׁךָ׃ וַיִּקַּח מֹשֶׁה אֶת־אִשְׁתּוֹ וְאֶת־

אונקלוס

בְּפֻמֵּיהּ, וּמֵימְרִי, יְהֵי עִם פֻּמָּךְ וְעִם פֻּמֵּיהּ, וְאַלֵּיף יָתְכוֹן, יָת דְּתַעְבְּדוּן: טז וִימַלֵּיל הוּא לָךְ עִם עַמָּא, וִיהֵי הוּא יְהֵי לָךְ לִמְתֻרְגְּמָן, וְאַתְּ תְּהֵי לֵיהּ לְרַב: יז וְיָת חֻטְרָא הָדֵין תִּסַּב בִּידָךְ, דְּתַעְבֵּיד בֵּיהּ יָת אָתַיָּא: יח וַאֲזַל מֹשֶׁה, וְתָב לְוָת יֶתֶר חֲמוּהִי, וַאֲמַר לֵיהּ אֵיזֵיל כְּעַן, וְאֵתוּב לְוָת אַחַי דִּבְמִצְרַיִם, וְאֶחֱזֵי הַעוֹד כְּעַן קַיָּמִין, וַאֲמַר יִתְרוֹ, לְמֹשֶׁה אֵיזֵיל לִשְׁלָם: יט וַאֲמַר יי לְמֹשֶׁה בְּמִדְיָן, אֵיזֵיל תּוּב לְמִצְרָיִם, אֲרֵי מִיתוּ כָּל גֻּבְרַיָּא, דִּבְעוֹ לְמִקְטְלָךְ: כ וּדְבַר מֹשֶׁה יָת אִתְּתֵיהּ וְיָת בְּנוֹהִי,

Egyptian palace, while Aharon remained with the Israelites. Nor have they been together during the Israelites' sufferings. Moshe, fearing for his life, fled to Midyan.

Besides this, Moshe is Aharon's younger brother, and yet it is Moshe who is about to become the leader of the people. Always in the past, when the younger has taken something the elder might have believed belonged naturally to him, there was jealousy, animosity; this story played out at every stage of the book of Genesis. Each generation there, however, improved upon the last. Kayin killed Hevel, but Yosef and his brothers were reconciled. All of this has prepared the way for the fifth story of siblings in the Torah, one that will gloriously transcend all the others. Among Yokheved's children there is no rivalry. It is Miriam who watches over the young Moshe and ensures he knows who his parents and his people are. It is Aharon who acts as Moshe's spokesman in Egypt, and who becomes the first priest to stand beside the greatest of the prophets. The implication is that *only when a people has overcome its internal rivalries is it ready for the journey from slavery to freedom.*

And so, against all expectations, God assures Moshe: "When Aharon sees you, his heart will rejoice." And so it does: "The Lord said to Aharon, 'Go and meet Moshe in the wilderness.' And he went and met him at God's mountain, and kissed him" (Ex. 4:27).

Moshe and Aharon are quite different in temperament and role. Moshe is the man of truth, Aharon of peace. Without truth, there can be no vision to inspire a nation. But without internal peace, there is no nation to inspire. Their roles are in creative tension. Yet they work side by side, each respecting the distinctive gift of the other. As the Midrash says, "And kissed him" [the brothers kissed when they met] – This means: each rejoiced at the other's greatness (Shemot Rabba 5:10).

THE ENCOUNTER ON THE WAY TO EGYPT

What follows is an obscure episode in the life of Moshe, as shocking as it is enigmatic. On his way back to Egypt, "The Lord confronted Moshe and was about to kill him" (Ex. 4:24). Tzipora then saves Moshe's life by giving their son a *brit mila*. How are we to understand this?

Rashbam (on Gen. 32:29) takes this as an instance of

and sons and put them on a donkey, and he set out to return to Egypt, taking
21 in his hand the staff of God. The Lord said to Moshe, "When you return to
Egypt, see that you perform for Pharaoh all the wonders I have placed in your
power. But still I will strengthen his heart and he will not send the people forth.
22 23 Tell Pharaoh: This is what the Lord says, 'Israel is My son, My firstborn. I have
told you: Send forth My son, so that he may serve Me. If you refuse to let him
24 go, I will kill your son, your firstborn.'" At a lodging place on the way, the Lord
25 confronted Moshe and was about to kill him. But Tzipora took a flint knife
and cut off her son's foreskin, throwing it down at his feet, and said, "You are a

רש״י

כ) **על החמר.** חמור המיחד. הוא החמור שחבש אברהם לעקדת יצחק, והוא שעתיד מלך המשיח להגלות עליו, שנאמר: "עני ורכב על חמור" (זכריה ט, ט): **וישב ארצה מצרים ויקח משה את מטה.** אין מקדם ומאחר מדקדקים במקרא:

כא) **בלכתך לשוב מצרימה וגו'.** דע שעל מנת כן תלך, שתהא גבור בשליחותי לעשות כל מופתי לפני פרעה ולא תירא ממנו: **אשר שמתי בידך.** לא על שלש אותות האמורות למעלה, שהרי לא לפני פרעה צוה לעשותם אלא לפני ישראל שיאמינו לו, ולא מצינו שעשאם לפניו, אלא מופתים שאני עתיד לשום בידך במצרים, כמו: "כי ידבר אלכם פרעה" וגו' (להלן ז, ט). ואל תתמה על אשר כתב: "אשר שמתי", שכן משמעו: כשתדבר עמו כבר שמתים בידך:

כב) **ואמרת אל פרעה.** כשתשמע שלבו חזק וימאן לשלח אמר לו כן: **בני בכרי.** לשון גדלה, כמו: "אף אני בכור אתנהו" (תהלים פט, כח) זהו פשוטו. ומדרשו, כאן חתם הקדוש ברוך הוא על מכירת הבכורה שלקח יעקב מעשו:

כג) **ואמר אליך.** בשליחותו של מקום: "שלח את בני": **הנה אנכי הרג וגו'.** היא מכה אחרונה, ובה התרהו תחלה מפני שהיא קשה. וזה הוא שאמר איוב: "הן אל ישגיב בכחו" (איוב לו, כב), לפיכך "מי כמוהו מורה" – בשר ודם המבקש להנקם מחברו מעלים את דבריו, שלא יבקש הצלה. אבל הקדוש ברוך הוא ישגיב בכחו ואין יכלת להמלט מידו כי אם בשובו אליו, לפיכך הוא מורהו ומתרה בו לשוב:

כד) **ויהי.** משה, "בדרך במלון": **ויבקש המיתו.** לפי שלא מל את אליעזר בנו, ועל שנתרשל נענש מיתה. תניא, אמר רבי יוסי: חס ושלום, לא נתרשל, אלא אמר: אמול ואצא לדרך – סכנה היא לתינוק עד שלשה ימים! אמול ואשהה שלשה ימים – הקדוש ברוך הוא צוני: "לך שב מצרים"! ומפני מה נענש? לפי שנתעסק במלון תחלה. במסכת נדרים (דף לא ע״ב). והיה המלאך נעשה כמין נחש ובולעו מראשו ועד יריכיו וחוזר ובולעו מרגליו ועד אותו מקום, הבינה צפורה שבשביל המילה הוא:

כה) **ותגע לרגליו.** השליכתו לפני רגליו של משה:

humanization of the relationship between earth and heaven, implying as it does that every human is the child, or the image, of God, and that He is about to take Israel, a small and currently enslaved people, as His firstborn.

4:25 **ותקח צפרה צר** *Tzipora took a flint knife* – Though Moshe is the central figure in the drama of the exodus, there is a striking emphasis on the roles of six women, without whom there would not have been a Moshe. There is Yokheved, his mother, who had the courage to have a child at a time when all male Israelite children faced death. There is Miriam, his sister, who followed his fate and ensured that he knew who his people were. There are Shifra and Puah, the two midwives, who defy Pharaoh's decree of genocide. There is Pharaoh's daughter, who rescues Moshe and adopts him, knowing that in doing so she is acting in contravention of her father's will. And there is Tzipora, Moshe's Midianite wife, who accompanies him on his mission and here saves his life.

These are six stories of outstanding moral courage and they are all about women, at least two of whom, Tzipora and Pharaoh's daughter, are not Israelites (the identity of the midwives is left uncertain, perhaps deliberately so, see ch. 1, "Midwives to the Hebrews"). It is the women who recognize the sanctity of life and refuse to obey orders that desecrate life. It is the women who, fearing God, are fearless in the face of danger and of human evil. It is the women who

בָּנָיו וַיַּרְכִּבֵם֙ עַל־הַחֲמֹ֔ר וַיָּ֖שָׁב אַ֣רְצָה מִצְרָ֑יִם וַיִּקַּ֥ח מֹשֶׁ֛ה אֶת־מַטֵּ֥ה
כא הָאֱלֹהִ֖ים בְּיָדֽוֹ׃ וַיֹּ֣אמֶר יְהוָ֗ה אֶל־מֹשֶׁה֒ בְּלֶכְתְּךָ֙ לָשׁ֣וּב מִצְרַ֔יְמָה
רְאֵ֗ה כָּל־הַמֹּֽפְתִים֙ אֲשֶׁר־שַׂ֣מְתִּי בְיָדֶ֔ךָ וַעֲשִׂיתָ֖ם לִפְנֵ֣י פַרְעֹ֑ה וַאֲנִי֙
כב אֲחַזֵּ֣ק אֶת־לִבּ֔וֹ וְלֹ֥א יְשַׁלַּ֖ח אֶת־הָעָֽם׃ וְאָמַרְתָּ֖ אֶל־פַּרְעֹ֑ה כֹּ֚ה אָמַ֣ר
כג יְהוָ֔ה בְּנִ֥י בְכֹרִ֖י יִשְׂרָאֵֽל׃ וָאֹמַ֣ר אֵלֶ֗יךָ שַׁלַּ֤ח אֶת־בְּנִי֙ וְיַֽעַבְדֵ֔נִי וַתְּמָאֵ֖ן
כד לְשַׁלְּח֑וֹ הִנֵּה֙ אָנֹכִ֣י הֹרֵ֔ג אֶת־בִּנְךָ֖ בְּכֹרֶֽךָ׃ וַיְהִ֥י בַדֶּ֖רֶךְ בַּמָּל֑וֹן וַיִּפְגְּשֵׁ֣הוּ
כה יְהוָ֔ה וַיְבַקֵּ֖שׁ הֲמִיתֽוֹ׃ וַתִּקַּ֨ח צִפֹּרָ֜ה צֹ֗ר וַתִּכְרֹת֙ אֶת־עָרְלַ֣ת בְּנָ֔הּ וַתַּגַּ֖ע

אונקלוס

וְאַרְכֵּיבִנּוּן עַל חֲמָרָא, וְתָב לְאַרְעָא דְמִצְרָיִם, וּנְסֵיב מֹשֶׁה, יָת חֻטְרָא דְּאִתְעֲבִידוּ בֵיהּ נִסִּין מִן קֳדָם יי בִּידֵיהּ: כא וַאֲמַר יי לְמֹשֶׁה, בְּמֵהָכָךְ לְמִתַּב לְמִצְרַיִם, חֲזִי, כָּל מוֹפְתַיָּא דְּשַׁוִּיתִי בִּידָךְ, וְתַעְבֵּידִנּוּן קֳדָם פַּרְעֹה, וַאֲנָא אֲתַקֵּיף יָת לִבֵּיהּ, וְלָא יְשַׁלַּח יָת עַמָּא: כב וְתֵימַר לְפַרְעֹה, כִּדְנָן אֲמַר יי, בְּרִי בֻכְרִי יִשְׂרָאֵל: כג וַאֲמָרִית לָךְ, שַׁלַּח יָת בְּרִי וְיִפְלַח קֳדָמַי, וּמְסָרֵיב אַתְּ לְשַׁלָּחוּתֵיהּ, הָא אֲנָא קָטֵיל, יָת בְּרָךְ בֻּכְרָךְ: כד וַהֲוָה בְאוֹרְחָא בְּבֵית מְבָתָא, וַעֲרַע בֵּיהּ מַלְאֲכָא דַּיי, וּבְעָא לְמִקְטְלֵיהּ: כה וּנְסֵיבַת צִפּוֹרָה טִנָּרָא, וּגְזָרַת יָת עָרְלַת בְּרַהּ, וְקָרֵיבַת

may not be born great, but we have greatness thrust upon us. For we are all children of the man who was given the name Yisrael: one who struggled with God and with men and prevailed.

4:20 וַיִּקַּח מֹשֶׁה אֶת־אִשְׁתּוֹ וְאֶת־בָּנָיו *Moshe took his wife and sons* – Thus far we have only heard of one son, Gershom. The reference to "sons" in the plural may be an indication that the second son has only recently been born. If so, this might explain Moshe's reluctance to give him a circumcision. Circumcision was considered dangerous in the course of a journey.

4:22 בְּנִי בְכֹרִי יִשְׂרָאֵל *Israel is My son, My firstborn* – Biblical monotheism was a revolution thousands of years in advance of the culture of the West. The exodus was more than the liberation of slaves. It was a redrawing of the moral and political landscape. If the image of God is to be found not only in kings but in the human person as such, then all power that dehumanizes is *ipso facto* an abuse of power. Slavery, seen by all ancient thinkers as part of the natural order, becomes morally wrong, an offense not only against man but against God. When God tells Moshe to talk to Pharaoh of "Israel [...] My son, My firstborn" (Ex. 4:22), He is announcing to the most powerful ruler of the ancient world that though these people may be your slaves, they are My children. The story of the plagues in Egypt is as much political as theological. Theologically it affirms that the Creator of nature is supreme over the forces of nature. Politically it declares that over every human power stands the sovereignty of God, defender and guarantor of the rights of mankind.

This formulation, "My son, My firstborn," is one of the most revolutionary in the entire history of religion. Throughout history, individuals were singled out for reverence or obedience as the child of (or chief intermediary with) God or the gods. One individual was seen as divine or semidivine. That was true of ancient Egypt but also of virtually every other religion since. In this one phrase, however, a new order altogether is announced, one in which every single individual can see him- or herself as the child of God, and correspondingly see God not only as the supreme deity, Creator of the universe, but also, and essentially, as a parent. There is between Him and the Israelites a relationship of kinship, responsibility, and love. This is an extraordinary

26 bridegroom of blood to me." So He let him go. Then "A bridegroom of blood,"
she said, "because of circumcision."
27 The LORD said to Aharon, "Go and meet Moshe in the wilderness." And he
28 went and met him at God's mountain, and kissed him. And Moshe told Aharon
all that the LORD had said about his mission, and all the miraculous signs He
29 had commanded him to perform. So Moshe and Aharon went and gathered all
30 the elders of Israel. Aharon told them everything the LORD had said to Moshe,
31 and he performed the signs before the people. And the people believed. When
they heard that the LORD was watching over the Israelites, and that He had
5 1 seen their misery, they bowed their heads and prostrated themselves. After SHEVI'I
this, Moshe and Aharon came to Pharaoh; they said, "Thus says the LORD, God
of Israel: Send My people forth so that they may hold a festival for Me in the
2 wilderness." But Pharaoh said, "Who is this LORD that I should obey Him and
send Israel forth? I do not know the LORD, and I will not send Israel forth."
3 "The God of the Hebrews has revealed Himself to us," they said. "Let us take
a three-day journey into the wilderness and sacrifice to the LORD our God, or

רש"י

ותאמר. על בנה: "כי חתן דמים חתה לי" – חתה היית גורם להיות החתן שלי נרצח עליך, הורג חישי חתה לי:

כו **וירף.** המלאך "ממנו", "אז" הבינה שעל המילה בא להרגו, "אמרה: חתן דמים למולת" – חתני היה נרצח על דבר המילה: **למולת.** על דבר המולות, שם דבר הוא, והלמ"ד משמשת בלשון 'על', כמו: "ואמר פרעה לבני ישראל" (להלן יד, ג). ואונקלוס תרגם 'דמים', על דם המילה:

ה א **ואחר באו משה ואהרן וגו'.** אבל הזקנים נשמטו אחד אחד מאחר משה ואהרן עד שנשמטו כלם קודם שהגיעו לפלטין, לפי שיראו ללכת. ובסיני נפרע להם: "ונגש משה לבדו והם לא יגשו" (להלן כד, ב), החזירם לאחוריהם:

of allowing people to fulfil their religious obligations, and the danger of divine anger if they do not. The point being made by the Torah here is that not only would Pharaoh not contemplate giving the Israelites the freedom to leave permanently. He would not even accede to the minimal request Moshe and Aharon make. Many episodes in Genesis showed that it was impossible for the covenantal family to live by their ideals in a Canaanite society ruled by peoples of a very different culture. We now see that it is impossible for the Israelite people to do so in Egypt. A minor religious request is met by blunt refusal.

5:2 **לא ידעתי את־יהוה** *I do not know the LORD* – The meaning is: Regardless of whether there is such a God, in this territory I am the sole authority. I recognize no other. Where I and the gods I represent have sovereignty, no other has legitimacy. Other peoples may have their gods, but at best their power is territorially limited. Already hinted at here is the radical implication of monotheism: that the God of Israel is the God of everywhere, and the God of the Hebrews is the God of everyone. This challenges the entire structure of territorially constituted national or local deities. Egypt may have known a brief period of proto-monotheism under Akhenaten, but it was decisively rejected after his death. Pharaoh's long battle against accepting the reality of the God of Israel is no accident, nor is it mere stubbornness of character. The religion of Israel challenges the very essence of the social structure and hierarchical worldview of Egypt and the pharaohs.

כו לְרַגְלָיו וַתֹּאמֶר כִּי חֲתַן־דָּמִים אַתָּה לִי׃ וַיִּרֶף מִמֶּנּוּ אָז אָמְרָה חֲתַן
דָּמִים לַמּוּלֹת׃
כז וַיֹּאמֶר יהוה אֶל־אַהֲרֹן לֵךְ לִקְרַאת מֹשֶׁה הַמִּדְבָּרָה וַיֵּלֶךְ וַיִּפְגְּשֵׁהוּ
כח בְּהַר הָאֱלֹהִים וַיִּשַּׁק־לוֹ׃ וַיַּגֵּד מֹשֶׁה לְאַהֲרֹן אֵת כָּל־דִּבְרֵי יהוה אֲשֶׁר
כט שְׁלָחוֹ וְאֵת כָּל־הָאֹתֹת אֲשֶׁר צִוָּהוּ׃ וַיֵּלֶךְ מֹשֶׁה וְאַהֲרֹן וַיַּאַסְפוּ אֶת־
ל כָּל־זִקְנֵי בְּנֵי יִשְׂרָאֵל׃ וַיְדַבֵּר אַהֲרֹן אֵת כָּל־הַדְּבָרִים אֲשֶׁר־דִּבֶּר יהוה
לא אֶל־מֹשֶׁה וַיַּעַשׂ הָאֹתֹת לְעֵינֵי הָעָם׃ וַיַּאֲמֵן הָעָם וַיִּשְׁמְעוּ כִּי־פָקַד
ה א יהוה אֶת־בְּנֵי יִשְׂרָאֵל וְכִי רָאָה אֶת־עָנְיָם וַיִּקְּדוּ וַיִּשְׁתַּחֲווּ׃ וְאַחַר שביעי
בָּאוּ מֹשֶׁה וְאַהֲרֹן וַיֹּאמְרוּ אֶל־פַּרְעֹה כֹּה־אָמַר יהוה אֱלֹהֵי יִשְׂרָאֵל
ב שַׁלַּח אֶת־עַמִּי וְיָחֹגּוּ לִי בַּמִּדְבָּר׃ וַיֹּאמֶר פַּרְעֹה מִי יהוה אֲשֶׁר אֶשְׁמַע
בְּקֹלוֹ לְשַׁלַּח אֶת־יִשְׂרָאֵל לֹא יָדַעְתִּי אֶת־יהוה וְגַם אֶת־יִשְׂרָאֵל לֹא
ג אֲשַׁלֵּחַ׃ וַיֹּאמְרוּ אֱלֹהֵי הָעִבְרִים נִקְרָא עָלֵינוּ נֵלְכָה־נָּא דֶּרֶךְ שְׁלֹשֶׁת

אונקלוס

לְקָדָמוֹהִי, וַאֲמַרַת, בִּדְמָא דִמְהֻלְתָּא הָדֵין אִתְיְהֵיב חַתְנָא לַנָא: כו וְנָח מִנֵּיהּ, בְּכֵן אֲמַרַת, אִלּוּלֵי דְמָא דִמְהֻלְתָּא הָדֵין אִתְחַיַּב חַתְנָא קְטוֹל: כז וַאֲמַר יי לְאַהֲרֹן, אִיזֵיל, לְקַדָּמוּת מֹשֶׁה לְמַדְבְּרָא, וַאֲזַל, וְעַרְעֵיהּ, בְּטוּרָא דְּאִתְגְּלִי עֲלוֹהִי יְקָרָא דַיי וְנַשֵּׁיק לֵיהּ: כח וְחַוִּי מֹשֶׁה לְאַהֲרֹן, יָת כָּל פִּתְגָמַיָּא דַיי דְּשַׁלְחֵיהּ, וְיָת כָּל אָתַיָּא דְּפַקְּדֵיהּ: כט וַאֲזַל מֹשֶׁה וְאַהֲרֹן, וּכְנַשׁוּ, יָת כָּל סָבֵי בְּנֵי יִשְׂרָאֵל: ל וּמַלֵּיל אַהֲרֹן, יָת כָּל פִּתְגָמַיָּא, דְּמַלֵּיל יי עִם מֹשֶׁה, וַעֲבַד אָתַיָּא לְעֵינֵי עַמָּא: לא וְהֵימִין עַמָּא, וּשְׁמַעוּ, אֲרֵי דְכִיר יי יָת בְּנֵי יִשְׂרָאֵל, וַאֲרֵי גְּלֵי קֳדָמוֹהִי שִׁעְבּוּדְהוֹן, וּכְרַעוּ וּסְגִידוּ: ה א וּבָתַר כֵּן, עָאלוּ מֹשֶׁה וְאַהֲרֹן, וַאֲמַרוּ לְפַרְעֹה, כִּדְנַן אֲמַר יי אֱלָהָא דְיִשְׂרָאֵל, שַׁלַּח יָת עַמִּי, וְיֵיחֲגוּן קֳדָמַי בְּמַדְבְּרָא: ב וַאֲמַר פַּרְעֹה, שְׁמָא דַיי לָא אִתְגְּלִי לִי דְּאֵקַבֵּיל לְמֵימְרֵיהּ, לְשַׁלָּחָא יָת יִשְׂרָאֵל, לָא אִתְגְּלִי לִי שְׁמָא דַיי, וְאַף יָת יִשְׂרָאֵל לָא אֲשַׁלַּח: ג וַאֲמַרוּ, אֱלָהָא דִּיהוּדָאֵי אִתְקְרִי עֲלַנָא, נֵיזֵיל כְּעַן, מַהֲלַךְ תְּלָתָא

embody compassion as well as courage – and justice without compassion is not justice.

5:1 שַׁלַּח אֶת־עַמִּי *Send My people forth* – As instructed by God (Ex. 3:18) they make a relatively minor demand, a mere three days' journey into the wilderness, and for a specifically religious reason. The point is to reveal the character of Pharaoh and the regime over which he presides. They have not asked for freedom or for the right permanently to leave. Their simple request, and the punitive response from Pharaoh, illustrate the kind of society Egypt has become. The Egyptians themselves had many religious festivals. A text from the time of Ramesses II itemizes forty-six of them, many of them involving large public ceremonies. Egyptian records also show that workmen were given time off to perform religious duties, so what Moshe and Aharon were asking for was no more than standard practice at the time. The Egyptians would certainly have understood the importance

4 He may strike us with the plague or with the sword." The king of Egypt said to
them, "Why, Moshe and Aharon, would you take the people from their work?
5 Get back to your labor! Look," said Pharaoh, "how numerous the people of
the land have become; and yet you would have them rest from their labors."
6 That day, Pharaoh gave orders to the people's taskmasters and foremen: "Do
not give the people straw for bricks as before. Let them go and gather their
8 own straw. But require them to make the same quota of bricks as before. Do
not reduce it. They are lazy. That is why they are crying out, 'Send us forth to
9 sacrifice to our God.' Make the work harder for the people; and make sure they
10 do it instead of listening to lies." So the taskmasters and foremen went out and
11 told the people, "This is what Pharaoh says: I will no longer give you straw. You
must go and get your own straw wherever you can find it. Your production must
12 not fall short of what it was." So the people spread out all over Egypt to collect
13 stubble for straw. The taskmasters kept pressuring them, saying, "Complete
14 your daily work quota just as when there was straw." And the Israelite foremen

רש"י

ג **פן יפגענו.** 'פן יפגעך' היה להם לומר, אלא שחלקו כבוד למלכות. פגיעה זו לשון מקרה מות הוא:

ד **תפריעו את העם ממעשיו.** תבדילו ותרחיקו אותם ממלאכתם, ששומעין לכם וסבורים לנוח מן המלאכה. וכן: "פרעהו אל תעבר בו" (משלי ד, טו) – רחקהו. וכן: "ותפרעו כל עצתי" (שם א, כה). "כי פרע הוא" (להלן לב, כה) – נרחק ונתעב: **לכו לסבלתיכם.** לכו למלאכתכם שיש לכם לעשות בבתיכם. אבל מלאכת שעבוד מצרים לא היתה על שבטו של לוי, ותדע לך, שהרי משה ואהרן יוצאים ובאים:

ה **הן רבים עתה עם הארץ.** שהעבודה מטלת עליהם, ואתם משביתים אותם מסבלותם, הפסד גדול הוא זה:

ו **הנגשים.** מצריים היו והשוטרים היו ישראל. הנוגש ממנה על כמה שוטרים, והשוטר ממנה לרדות בעושי המלאכה:

ז **תבן.** אשטובל"א, היו גובלין אותו עם הטיט: **לבנים.** טיוול"ש, שעושים מטיט ומיבשין אותן בחמה, ויש ששורפין אותן בכבשן: **כתמול שלשם.** כאשר הייתם עושים עד הנה: **וקששו.** ולקטו:

ח **ואת מתכנת הלבנים.** סכום חשבון הלבנים שהיה כל אחד עושה ליום כשהיה התבן נתן להם, אותו סכום "תשימו עליהם" גם עתה, למען תכבד העבודה עליהם: **כי נרפים.** מן העבודה הם, לכך לבם פונה אל הבטלה ו"צעקים לאמר נלכה" וגו': **מתכנת.** "ותכן לבנים" (להלן פסוק יח), "ולו נתכנו עללות" (שמואל א' ב, ג), ו"את הכסף המתכן" (מלכים ב' יב, יב), כלם לשון חשבון הם: **נרפים.** המלאכה רפויה בידם ועזובה מהם והם נרפים ממנה, רטריי"ש בלעז:

ט **ואל ישעו בדברי שקר.** ואל יהגו וידברו תמיד בדברי רוח לאמר: "נלכה נזבחה". ודומה לו: "ואשעה בחקיך תמיד" (תהלים קיט, קיז), "למשל ולשנינה" (דברים כח, לז) – "ולשועי", "ויספר" (להלן יח, ח) – "ואשתעי". ואי אפשר לומר 'ישעו' לשון "וישע ה' אל הבל... ואל קין ואל מנחתו לא שעה" (בראשית ד, ד-ה) ולפרש 'אל ישעו' – אל יפנו, שאם כן היה לו לכתב: 'ואל ישעו אל דברי שקר' או 'לדברי שקר' כי כן גזרת כלם: "ישעה האדם על עשהו" (ישעיה יז, ז), "ולא שעו על קדוש ישראל" (שם לא, א), "ולא ישעה אל המזבחות" (שם יז, ח), ולא מצאתי שמוש של בי"ת סמוכה לאחריהם. אבל אחר לשון דבור כמתעסק לדבר בדבר נופל לשון שמוש בי"ת, כגון: "הנדברים בך" (יחזקאל לג, ל), "ותדבר מרים ואהרן במשה" (במדבר יב, א), "המלאך הדבר בי" (זכריה ד, א), "לדבר בם" (דברים יא, יט), "ואדברה בעדתיך" (תהלים קיט, מו). אף כאן, "אל ישעו בדברי שקר" – אל יהיו נדברים בדברי שוא והבאי:

יא **אתם לכו קחו לכם תבן.** וצריכים אתם לילך בזריזות "כי אין נגרע" דבר מכל סכום לבנים שהייתם עושים ליום בהיות התבן נתן לכם מזמן מבית המלך:

יב **לקשש קש לתבן.** לאסף אסיפה, ללקט לקט לצרך תבן הטיט: **קש.** לשון לקוט, על שם שדבר המתפזר הוא וצריך לקוששו הוא קרוי 'קש' באשר מקומות:

יג **אצים.** דוחקים: **דבר יום ביומו.** חשבון של כל יום כלו ביומו, כאשר עשיתם בהיות התבן מוכן:

יד **ויכו שטרי בני ישראל.** השוטרים ישראל היו וחסים על

יָמִים בַּמִּדְבָּר וְנִזְבְּחָה לַיהוָה אֱלֹהֵינוּ פֶּן־יִפְגָּעֵנוּ בַּדֶּבֶר אוֹ בֶחָרֶב׃
ד וַיֹּאמֶר אֲלֵהֶם מֶלֶךְ מִצְרַיִם לָמָּה מֹשֶׁה וְאַהֲרֹן תַּפְרִיעוּ אֶת־הָעָם
ה מִמַּעֲשָׂיו לְכוּ לְסִבְלֹתֵיכֶם׃ וַיֹּאמֶר פַּרְעֹה הֵן־רַבִּים עַתָּה עַם־הָאָרֶץ
ו וְהִשְׁבַּתֶּם אֹתָם מִסִּבְלֹתָם׃ וַיְצַו פַּרְעֹה בַּיּוֹם הַהוּא אֶת־הַנֹּגְשִׂים בָּעָם
ז וְאֶת־שֹׁטְרָיו לֵאמֹר׃ לֹא תֹאסִפוּן לָתֵת תֶּבֶן לָעָם לִלְבֹּן הַלְּבֵנִים
ח כִּתְמוֹל שִׁלְשֹׁם הֵם יֵלְכוּ וְקֹשְׁשׁוּ לָהֶם תֶּבֶן׃ וְאֶת־מַתְכֹּנֶת הַלְּבֵנִים
אֲשֶׁר הֵם עֹשִׂים תְּמוֹל שִׁלְשֹׁם תָּשִׂימוּ עֲלֵיהֶם לֹא תִגְרְעוּ מִמֶּנּוּ כִּי־
ט נִרְפִּים הֵם עַל־כֵּן הֵם צֹעֲקִים לֵאמֹר נֵלְכָה נִזְבְּחָה לֵאלֹהֵינוּ׃ תִּכְבַּד
י הָעֲבֹדָה עַל־הָאֲנָשִׁים וְיַעֲשׂוּ־בָהּ וְאַל־יִשְׁעוּ בְּדִבְרֵי־שָׁקֶר׃ וַיֵּצְאוּ
נֹגְשֵׂי הָעָם וְשֹׁטְרָיו וַיֹּאמְרוּ אֶל־הָעָם לֵאמֹר כֹּה אָמַר פַּרְעֹה אֵינֶנִּי
יא נֹתֵן לָכֶם תֶּבֶן׃ אַתֶּם לְכוּ קְחוּ לָכֶם תֶּבֶן מֵאֲשֶׁר תִּמְצָאוּ כִּי אֵין נִגְרָע
יב מֵעֲבֹדַתְכֶם דָּבָר׃ וַיָּפֶץ הָעָם בְּכָל־אֶרֶץ מִצְרָיִם לְקֹשֵׁשׁ קַשׁ לַתֶּבֶן׃
יג וְהַנֹּגְשִׂים אָצִים לֵאמֹר כַּלּוּ מַעֲשֵׂיכֶם דְּבַר־יוֹם בְּיוֹמוֹ כַּאֲשֶׁר בִּהְיוֹת
יד הַתֶּבֶן׃ וַיֻּכּוּ שֹׁטְרֵי בְּנֵי יִשְׂרָאֵל אֲשֶׁר־שָׂמוּ עֲלֵהֶם נֹגְשֵׂי פַרְעֹה לֵאמֹר

אונקלוס

יוֹמִין בְּמַדְבְּרָא, וּנְדַבַּח קֳדָם יְיָ אֱלָהַנָא, דִּלְמָא יְעָרְעִנַּנָא, בְּמוֹתָא אוֹ בִקְטוֹל: ד וַאֲמַר לְהוֹן מַלְכָּא דְמִצְרַיִם, לְמָא מֹשֶׁה וְאַהֲרֹן, תְּבַטְּלוּן יָת עַמָּא מֵעֲבִידַתְהוֹן, אִיזִילוּ לְפָלְחָנְכוֹן: ה וַאֲמַר פַּרְעֹה, הָא מְדַסְגִּיאִין כְּעַן עַמָּא דְאַרְעָא, וּתְבַטְּלוּן יָתְהוֹן מִפָּלְחָנְהוֹן: ו וּפַקֵּיד פַּרְעֹה בְּיוֹמָא הַהוּא, יָת שִׁלְטוֹנֵי עַמָּא, וְיָת סָרְכוֹהִי לְמֵימַר: ז לָא תֵיסְפוּן, לְמִתַּן תִּבְנָא לְעַמָּא, לְמִרְמֵי לִבְנִין כְּמֵאֶתְמָלֵי וּמִדְּקַמּוֹהִי, אִנּוּן יֵיזְלוּן, וִיגָבְבוּן לְהוֹן תִּבְנָא: ח וְיָת סְכוּם לִבְנַיָּא, דְאִנּוּן עָבְדִין מֵאֶתְמָלֵי וּמִדְּקַמּוֹהִי תְּמַנּוּן עֲלֵיהוֹן, לָא תִמְנְעוּן מִנֵּיהּ, אֲרֵי בַטְלָנִין אִנּוּן, עַל כֵּן, אִנּוּן מְצַוְחִין לְמֵימַר, נֵיזֵיל נְדַבַּח קֳדָם אֱלָהַנָא: ט יִתְקַף פָּלְחָנָא, עַל גֻּבְרַיָּא וְיִתְעַסְּקוּן בַּהּ, וְלָא יִתְעַסְּקוּן בְּפִתְגָמִין בְּטֵילִין: י וּנְפַקוּ, שִׁלְטוֹנֵי עַמָּא וְסָרְכוֹהִי, וַאֲמַרוּ לְעַמָּא לְמֵימַר, כִּדְנַן אֲמַר פַּרְעֹה, לֵית אֲנָא, יָהֵיב לְכוֹן תִּבְנָא: יא אַתּוּן, אִיזִילוּ סַבוּ לְכוֹן תִּבְנָא, מֵאֲתַר דְּתַשְׁכְּחוּן, אֲרֵי לָא יִתְמְנַע, מִפָּלְחָנְכוֹן מִדָּעַם: יב וְאִתְבַּדַּר עַמָּא בְּכָל אַרְעָא דְמִצְרָיִם, לְגַבָּבָא גְלֵי לְתִבְנָא: יג וְשִׁלְטוֹנַיָּא דָּחֲקִין לְמֵימַר, אַשְׁלִימוּ עֲבִידַתְכוֹן פִּתְגָם יוֹם בְּיוֹמֵיהּ, כְּמָא דַהֲוֵיתוֹן עָבְדִין כַּד מִתְיְהֵיב לְכוֹן תִּבְנָא: יד וּלְקוֹ, סָרְכֵי בְנֵי יִשְׂרָאֵל, דְּמַנִּיאוּ עֲלֵיהוֹן, שִׁלְטוֹנֵי פַרְעֹה לְמֵימַר,

רש"י

חַבְרֵיהֶם מִלְּדָחֲקָם, וּכְשֶׁהָיוּ מַשְׁלִימִים הַלְּבֵנִים לַנּוֹגְשִׂים שֶׁהֵם מִצְרִיִּים וְהָיָה חָסֵר מִן הַסְּכוּם, הָיוּ מַלְקִין אוֹתָם עַל שֶׁלֹּא דָּחֲקוּ אֶת עוֹשֵׂי הַמְּלָאכָה. לְפִיכָךְ זָכוּ אוֹתָן שׁוֹטְרִים לִהְיוֹת סַנְהֶדְרִין וְנֶאֱצַל מִן הָרוּחַ אֲשֶׁר עַל מֹשֶׁה וְהוּשַׂם עֲלֵיהֶם, שֶׁנֶּאֱמַר "אֶסְפָה לִּי שִׁבְעִים אִישׁ מִזִּקְנֵי יִשְׂרָאֵל", מֵאוֹתָן שֶׁיָּדַעְתָּ הַטּוֹבָה שֶׁעָשׂוּ בְּמִצְרַיִם "כִּי הֵם זִקְנֵי הָעָם וְשֹׁטְרָיו" (במדבר יא, טז): **וַיֻּכּוּ שֹׁטְרֵי בְּנֵי יִשְׂרָאֵל.**

whom Pharaoh's slave drivers had appointed were flogged. "Why have you not
fulfilled your quota of bricks," they were asked, "either yesterday or today as
15 you did before?" The Israelite foremen came and protested to Pharaoh, "Why
16 are you treating your servants like this? Your servants are given no straw, yet
17 they tell us, 'Make bricks!' We are being flogged for your people's failing." But
he said, "Lazy, that is what you are – lazy! That is why you keep saying, 'Send
18 us forth to sacrifice to the Lord.' Now go. Get to work. Straw will not be given
19 you, and you must complete your count of bricks." When the Israelite foremen
saw that they were not to reduce each day's quota, they knew that harm was
20 coming to them. Leaving Pharaoh, they met Moshe and Aharon, who stood
21 awaiting them. They said to them, "May the Lord look on you and judge,
because you have made us repellent in the eyes of Pharaoh and his officials;
22 you have put a sword in their hands to kill us." Then Moshe returned to the MAFTIR
Lord and said, "Why, Lord, have You brought harm to this people? Is this
23 why You sent me? Ever since I came to Pharaoh to speak in Your name, he

רש״י

אֲשֶׁר שָׂמוּ נֹגְשֵׂי פַרְעֹה אוֹתָם לְשׁוֹטְרִים עֲלֵיהֶם: **לֵאמֹר מַדּוּעַ וְגוֹ׳.** לָמָּה ״וַיֻּכּוּ״? שֶׁהָיוּ אוֹמְרִים לָהֶם: מַדּוּעַ לֹא כִלִּיתֶם גַּם תְּמוֹל גַּם הַיּוֹם חֹק הַקָּצוּב עֲלֵיכֶם לִלְבֹּן כִּתְמוֹל הַשְּׁלִישִׁי, שֶׁהוּא יוֹם שֶׁלִּפְנֵי אֶתְמוֹל, וְהוּא הָיָה בִּהְיוֹת הַתֶּבֶן נִתָּן לָהֶם: **וַיֻּכּוּ.** לְשׁוֹן וַיִּפְעֲלוּ, הֻכּוּ מִיַּד אֲחֵרִים, הַנּוֹגְשִׂים הִכּוּם:

טו **וּלְבֵנִים אוֹמְרִים לָנוּ.** הַנּוֹגְשִׂים, ״עֲשׂוּ״ כַּמִּנְיָן הָרִאשׁוֹן: **וְחָטָאת עַמֶּךָ.** אִלּוּ הָיָה נָקוּד פַּתָּח הָיִיתִי אוֹמֵר שֶׁהוּא דָּבוּק – וְדָבָר זֶה חַטָּאת עַמְּךָ הוּא. עַכְשָׁיו שֶׁהוּא קָמַץ, שֵׁם דָּבָר הוּא, וְכָךְ פֵּרוּשׁוֹ, וְדָבָר זֶה מֵבִיא חַטָּאת עַל עַמֶּךָ, כְּאִלּוּ כָּתוּב: ׳וְחַטָּאת לְעַמֶּךָ׳, כְּמוֹ: ״כְּבוֹאֲנָה בֵּית לֶחֶם״ (רות א, יט) שֶׁהוּא כְּמוֹ לְבֵית לֶחֶם, וְכֵן הַרְבֵּה:

יח **וְתֹכֶן לְבֵנִים.** חֶשְׁבּוֹן הַלְּבֵנִים, וְכֵן: ״אֶת הַכֶּסֶף הַמְתֻכָּן״ (מלכים ב׳ יב, יב) הַמָּנוּי, כְּמוֹ שֶׁאָמוּר בָּעִנְיָן: ״וַיָּצֻרוּ וַיִּמְנוּ אֶת הַכֶּסֶף״ (שם פסוק יא):

יט **וַיִּרְאוּ שֹׁטְרֵי בְנֵי יִשְׂרָאֵל.** אֶת חַבְרֵיהֶם הַנִּרְדִּים עַל יָדָם, ״בְּרָע״ – רָאוּ אוֹתָם בְּרָעָה וְצָרָה הַמּוֹצֵאת אוֹתָם בְּהַכְבִּידָם הָעֲבוֹדָה עֲלֵיהֶם ״לֵאמֹר: לֹא תִגְרְעוּ״ וְגוֹ׳:

כ **וַיִּפְגְּעוּ.** אֲנָשִׁים מִיִּשְׂרָאֵל, ״אֶת מֹשֶׁה וְאֶת אַהֲרֹן״ וְגוֹ׳. וְרַבּוֹתֵינוּ אָמְרוּ, כָּל ׳נִצִּים׳ וְ׳נִצָּבִים׳ דָּתָן וַאֲבִירָם הָיוּ, שֶׁנֶּאֱמַר בָּהֶם: ״יָצְאוּ נִצָּבִים״ (במדבר טז, כז):

כב **לָמָה הֲרֵעֹתָה לָעָם הַזֶּה.** וְאִם תֹּאמַר, מָה אִכְפַּת לְךָ? קוֹבֵל אֲנִי עַל שֶׁשְּׁלַחְתַּנִי:

Judge, there would be no justice and no question. There *is* a Judge. When then will justice be done? Above all else, Jewish thought through the centuries has been a sustained meditation on this question, never finding a final answer, realizing that here was a sacred mystery no human mind could penetrate. All other requests Moshe made on behalf of the Jewish people, says the Talmud (Berakhot 7a), were granted except this: to understand why the righteous suffer.

As tenaciously as those questioners ask, so they hold firm to the faith without which there is no question: that there is a moral rule governing the universe and that what happens to us is in some way related to what we do. Good is rewarded and evil has no ultimate dominion. No Jewish belief is more central than this. It forms the core of the Hebrew Bible, the writings of the rabbis, and the speculation of the Jewish mystics. Reward and punishment may be individual or collective, immediate or deferred, in this world or the next, apparent or veiled behind a screen of mystery, but they are there. For without them, life is "a tale told by an idiot, full of sound and fury, signifying nothing" (*Macbeth*).

מַדּוּעַ לֹא כִלִּיתֶם חָקְכֶם לִלְבֹּן כִּתְמוֹל שִׁלְשֹׁם גַּם־תְּמוֹל גַּם־הַיּוֹם:
טו וַיָּבֹאוּ שֹׁטְרֵי בְּנֵי יִשְׂרָאֵל וַיִּצְעֲקוּ אֶל־פַּרְעֹה לֵאמֹר לָמָּה תַעֲשֶׂה
טז כֹה לַעֲבָדֶיךָ: תֶּבֶן אֵין נִתָּן לַעֲבָדֶיךָ וּלְבֵנִים אֹמְרִים לָנוּ עֲשׂוּ וְהִנֵּה
יז עֲבָדֶיךָ מֻכִּים וְחָטָאת עַמֶּךָ: וַיֹּאמֶר נִרְפִּים אַתֶּם נִרְפִּים עַל־כֵּן אַתֶּם
יח אֹמְרִים נֵלְכָה נִזְבְּחָה לַיהוָה: וְעַתָּה לְכוּ עִבְדוּ וְתֶבֶן לֹא־יִנָּתֵן לָכֶם
יט וְתֹכֶן לְבֵנִים תִּתֵּנוּ: וַיִּרְאוּ שֹׁטְרֵי בְנֵי־יִשְׂרָאֵל אֹתָם בְּרָע לֵאמֹר לֹא־
כ תִגְרְעוּ מִלִּבְנֵיכֶם דְּבַר־יוֹם בְּיוֹמוֹ: וַיִּפְגְּעוּ אֶת־מֹשֶׁה וְאֶת־אַהֲרֹן
כא נִצָּבִים לִקְרָאתָם בְּצֵאתָם מֵאֵת פַּרְעֹה: וַיֹּאמְרוּ אֲלֵהֶם יֵרֶא יְהוָה
עֲלֵיכֶם וְיִשְׁפֹּט אֲשֶׁר הִבְאַשְׁתֶּם אֶת־רֵיחֵנוּ בְּעֵינֵי פַרְעֹה וּבְעֵינֵי עֲבָדָיו
כב לָתֶת־חֶרֶב בְּיָדָם לְהָרְגֵנוּ: וַיָּשָׁב מֹשֶׁה אֶל־יְהוָה וַיֹּאמַר אֲדֹנָי לָמָה מפטיר
כג הֲרֵעֹתָה לָעָם הַזֶּה לָמָּה זֶּה שְׁלַחְתָּנִי: וּמֵאָז בָּאתִי אֶל־פַּרְעֹה לְדַבֵּר

אונקלוס

מָדֵין, לָא אַשְׁלֵימְתּוּן גְּזֵירַתְכוֹן לְמִרְמֵי לִבְנִין כְּמֵאֶתְמָלֵי וּמִדְּקַמּוֹהִי, אַף תְּמָלֵי אַף יוֹמָא דֵין: טו וַאֲתוֹ, סָרְכֵי בְּנֵי יִשְׂרָאֵל, וּצְוַחוּ קֳדָם פַּרְעֹה לְמֵימַר, לְמָא תַעֲבֵיד כְּדֵין לְעַבְדָּךְ: טז תִּבְנָא, לָא מִתְיְהֵיב לְעַבְדָּךְ, וּלְבְנַיָּא, אָמְרִין לַנָא עֲבִידוּ, וְהָא עַבְדָּךְ, לָקַן וְחָטַן עֲלֵיהוֹן עַמָּךְ: יז וַאֲמַר, בַּטְלָנִין אַתּוּן בַּטְלָנִין, עַל כֵּן אַתּוּן אָמְרִין, נֵיזֵיל נְדַבַּח קֳדָם יי: יח וּכְעַן אִיזִילוּ פְּלַחוּ, וְתִבְנָא לָא יִתְיְהֵיב לְכוֹן, וּסְכוֹם לִבְנַיָּא תִּתְּנוּן: יט וַחֲזוֹ, סָרְכֵי בְנֵי יִשְׂרָאֵל, יָתְהוֹן בְּבִישׁ לְמֵימַר, לָא תִמְנְעוּן מִלִּבְנֵיכוֹן פִּתְגָם יוֹם בְּיוֹמֵיהּ: כ וְעָרְעוּ יָת מֹשֶׁה וְיָת אַהֲרֹן, קָיְמִין לְקַדָּמוּתְהוֹן, בְּמִפַּקְהוֹן מִלְּוָת פַּרְעֹה: כא וַאֲמַרוּ לְהוֹן, יִתְגְּלֵי יי, עֲלֵיכוֹן וְיִתְפְּרַע, דְּאַבְאֵישְׁתּוּן יָת רֵיחַנָא, בְּעֵינֵי פַרְעֹה וּבְעֵינֵי עַבְדּוֹהִי, לְמִתַּן חַרְבָּא בִּידֵהוֹן לְמִקְטְלַנָא: כב וְתָב מֹשֶׁה, לִקְדָם יי וַאֲמַר, יי, לְמָא אַבְאֵישְׁתָּא

5:22 לָמָּה הֲרֵעֹתָה לָעָם הַזֶּה *Why, Lord, have You brought harm to this people?* – Moshe, like Avraham, feels empowered by Heaven to challenge God Himself in the name of ideals God espouses. This is his first great act of pleading with Heaven on behalf of the people, something he will do at other supreme moments of crisis.

Those who ask in the Tanakh about the apparent injustices of the world are not doubters or sceptics. They are Judaism's supreme prophets. They do not ask because they lack belief; they ask because they believe. If there were no

5:21 יֵרֶא יהוה עֲלֵיכֶם וְיִשְׁפֹּט *May the Lord look on you and judge* – This is an extremely sharp response to Moshe and Aharon, calling down divine judgment on them for making the situation of the Israelites, already bad, even more unbearable. This is a critical moment in the story of the exodus and in the life of Moshe. He has been charged by God with a message and mission of deliverance. Instead, conditions have become worse. That is a point that tests the faith of both the people and the leader. Hence Moshe's anguished cry to God.

has dealt worse with this people; and You have done nothing to deliver Your
6 1 people." But the LORD said to Moshe, "Now you are about to see what I will do
to Pharaoh. By a mighty hand he will send them forth, and by a mighty hand
he will drive them from his land."

The haftara for Parashat Shemot is on page 1524.

רש״י

כג| **הֵרַע.** לְשׁוֹן הִפְעִיל הוּא, הִרְבָּה רָעָה עֲלֵיהֶם. וְתַרְגּוּמוֹ "אַבְאֵישׁ":
ו א| **עַתָּה תִרְאֶה וְגוֹ'.** הִרְהַרְתָּ עַל מִדּוֹתַי, לֹא כְּאַבְרָהָם שֶׁאָמַרְתִּי לוֹ: "כִּי בְיִצְחָק יִקָּרֵא לְךָ זָרַע" (בראשית כא, יב) וְאַחַר כָּךְ אָמַרְתִּי לוֹ: "הַעֲלֵהוּ... לְעֹלָה" (שם כב, ב) וְלֹא הִרְהֵר אַחֲרַי. לְפִיכָךְ – "עַתָּה תִרְאֶה", הֶעָשׂוּי לְפַרְעֹה תִּרְאֶה, וְלֹא הֶעָשׂוּי לְמַלְכֵי שִׁבְעָה אֻמּוֹת כְּשֶׁאֲבִיאֵם לָאָרֶץ: **כִּי בְיָד חֲזָקָה יְשַׁלְּחֵם.** מִפְּנֵי יָדִי שֶׁתֶּחֱזַק עָלָיו יְשַׁלְּחֵם: **וּבְיָד חֲזָקָה יְגָרְשֵׁם מֵאַרְצוֹ.** עַל כָּרְחָם שֶׁל יִשְׂרָאֵל יְגָרְשֵׁם וְלֹא יַסְפִּיקוּ לַעֲשׂוֹת לָהֶם צֵידָה, וְכֵן הוּא אוֹמֵר: "וַתֶּחֱזַק מִצְרַיִם עַל הָעָם" וְגוֹ' (להלן יב, לג):

"The biggest miracle of all is that we, the survivors of the Holocaust, after all that we witnessed and lived through, still believe and have faith in the Almighty God, may His name be blessed. This, my friends, is the miracle of miracles, the greatest miracle ever to have taken place." As he said these words, he wept. But still he believed.

What we see in Exodus is that it is those who argue who may become the agents of change. It is as if God intervenes in history only in response to a human call. God calls to us, but we too must call to Him. When those two calls meet, transformation takes place.

ו א בִשְׁמֶךָ הֵרַע לָעָם הַזֶּה וְהַצֵּל לֹא־הִצַּלְתָּ אֶת־עַמֶּךָ: וַיֹּאמֶר יהוה
אֶל־מֹשֶׁה עַתָּה תִרְאֶה אֲשֶׁר אֶעֱשֶׂה לְפַרְעֹה כִּי בְיָד חֲזָקָה יְשַׁלְּחֵם
וּבְיָד חֲזָקָה יְגָרְשֵׁם מֵאַרְצוֹ:

The הפטרה *for* פרשת שמות *is on page 1525.*

אונקלוס

לְעַמָּא הָדֵין, לְמָא דְנָן שְׁלַחְתָּנִי: כג וּמֵעִדָּן, דְּעָאלִית לְוָת פַּרְעֹה
לְמַלָּלָא בִּשְׁמָךְ, אַבְאֵישׁ לְעַמָּא הָדֵין, וְשֵׁיזָבָא לָא שֵׁיזֵיבְתָּא יָת
עַמָּךְ: ו א וַאֲמַר יי לְמֹשֶׁה, כְּעַן תִּחְזֵי, דְּאַעְבֵּיד לְפַרְעֹה, אֲרֵי בְּיַד
תַּקִּיפָא יְשַׁלְּחִנּוּן, וּבְיַד תַּקִּיפָא, יְתָרֵיכִנּוּן מֵאַרְעֵיהּ:

The faith of the Bible is neither optimistic nor naive. It contains no theodicies, no systematic answers, no easy consolations. At times, in the books of Job and Ecclesiastes and Lamentations, it comes close to the abyss of pain and despair. "I turned again and saw," says Ecclesiastes, "…the victims' tears and none to console them" (4:1). "It was," says Lamentations, "as if [God] were the enemy" (2:5). But the people of the book refused to stop wrestling with the question. To believe was painful, but to disbelieve was too easy, too superficial, untrue. The rabbi of Klausenburg, Rabbi Yekutiel Yehuda Halberstam, who survived Auschwitz and lost his wife and eleven children in the Holocaust, once said:

Parashat Vaera

6 2/3 Then God spoke to Moshe. "I am the Lord," He said to him. "As El Shaddai I
appeared to Avraham, Yitzḥak, and Yaakov – but by My name the Lord I did
4 not make Myself known to them. And I made a covenant with them to give

רש"י

ב| **וַיְדַבֵּר אֱלֹהִים אֶל מֹשֶׁה.** דִּבֵּר אִתּוֹ מִשְׁפָּט עַל שֶׁהִקְשָׁה לְדַבֵּר וְלוֹמַר: "לָמָה הֲרֵעֹתָה לָעָם הַזֶּה" (לעיל ה, כב): **וַיֹּאמֶר אֵלָיו אֲנִי ה'.** נֶאֱמָן לְשַׁלֵּם שָׂכָר טוֹב לַמִּתְהַלְּכִים לְפָנַי. וְלֹא לְחִנָּם שְׁלַחְתִּיךָ כִּי אִם לְקַיֵּם דְּבָרַי לָאָבוֹת הָרִאשׁוֹנִים. וּבַלָּשׁוֹן הַזֶּה מָצִינוּ שֶׁהוּא נִדְרָשׁ בְּכַמָּה מְקוֹמוֹת: "אֲנִי ה'" נֶאֱמָן לְפָרַע, כְּשֶׁהוּא אָמוּר אֵצֶל עֹנֶשׁ כְּגוֹן: "וְחִלַּלְתָּ אֶת שֵׁם אֱלֹהֶיךָ אֲנִי ה'" (ויקרא יט, יב); וּכְשֶׁהוּא אָמוּר אֵצֶל קִיּוּם מִצְוֹת כְּגוֹן: "וּשְׁמַרְתֶּם מִצְוֹתַי וַעֲשִׂיתֶם אֹתָם אֲנִי ה'" (שם כב, לא) נֶאֱמָן לִתֵּן שָׂכָר:

ג| **וָאֵרָא.** אֶל הָאָבוֹת: **בְּאֵל שַׁדָּי.** הִבְטַחְתִּים הַבְטָחוֹת וּבְכֻלָּן אָמַרְתִּי לָהֶם: "אֲנִי אֵל שַׁדַּי": **וּשְׁמִי ה' לֹא נוֹדַעְתִּי לָהֶם.** 'לֹא הוֹדַעְתִּי' אֵין כְּתִיב כָּאן אֶלָּא "לֹא נוֹדַעְתִּי", לֹא נִכַּרְתִּי לָהֶם בְּמִדַּת אֲמִתּוּת שֶׁלִּי שֶׁעָלֶיהָ נִקְרָא שְׁמִי ה', נֶאֱמָן לְאַמֵּת דְּבָרַי, שֶׁהֲרֵי הִבְטַחְתִּים וְלֹא קִיַּמְתִּי:

Rashi's explanation (on Ex. 6:3) is the simplest and most elegant:

> It is not written here "[My name 'the Lord'] I did not make known to them" but rather "[By the name 'the Lord'] I did not make Myself known to them" – meaning, I was not recognized by them in My attribute of "keeping faith," by reason of which My name is "the Lord," namely that I am faithful to fulfil My word. For I made promises to them but I did not fulfil them [during their lifetime].

The patriarchs received the covenantal promise. They would become a nation. They would inherit a land. Yet as the book of Genesis reaches its close, the family numbers a mere seventy souls in exile in Egypt. Now, the fulfilment of those promises is about to begin. Already in the first chapter of Exodus, we hear, for the first time, the phrase "the Israelite *people*" (Ex. 1:9). Israel has at last become a nation. Moshe has been told, by God, that He will bring them to a good and spacious land, "a land flowing with milk and honey" (3:8). "The Lord" therefore means the God who acts in history to fulfil His promises. The significance of this act, we shall see, goes far beyond the Israelite story.

6:2 **אֲנִי יהוה** *I am the Lord* – This brief sentence contains two transitions, from "spoke" to "said," and from "God" to "the Lord." Although these nuances are untranslatable in English, they both represent a move from justice to compassion, from harsh to gentle, from detached to intimate and confiding. God responded sharply to Moshe's question at the end of last week's *parasha*, "Why, Lord, have You brought harm to this people?" (Ex. 5:22). Now He speaks again as the loving God who is about to redeem His people.

6:3 **וּשְׁמִי יהוה לֹא נוֹדַעְתִּי לָהֶם** *But by My name the Lord I did not make Myself known* – The patriarchs knew God by the four-letter name "the Lord." It occurs 165 times in Genesis. In an earlier comment ("I am the Lord") we discussed Rashi's decoding of the verse: The patriarchs knew the God of promise. The Israelites were now about to see the God who delivers on a national scale. Note that the root *y-d-a* in Hebrew does not mean "to know" in a purely cognitive sense. It means "to have direct and immediate experience" of something. The patriarchs knew that God would fulfil His promises, but they did not live to see the full realization of the covenant.

In the ancient world, the idea of a God who promises would not have made sense outside Israel. "The Lord" is not a natural force, as in polytheism, or even the totality of natural forces. For this we have the word "God." "The Lord" is the concept of a God who places Himself under moral obligations for the future, hence a God who acts in history, who says "I will be who I will be." God told Avraham, "I am

פרשת וארא

ו ב וַיְדַבֵּ֥ר אֱלֹהִ֖ים אֶל־מֹשֶׁ֑ה וַיֹּ֥אמֶר אֵלָ֖יו אֲנִ֥י יְהוָֽה׃ ג וָאֵרָ֗א אֶל־אַבְרָהָ֛ם ד
אֶל־יִצְחָ֥ק וְאֶל־יַעֲקֹ֖ב בְּאֵ֣ל שַׁדָּ֑י וּשְׁמִ֣י יְהוָ֔ה לֹ֥א נוֹדַ֖עְתִּי לָהֶֽם׃ ד וְגַ֨ם

אונקלוס

ב וּמַלֵּיל יי עִם מֹשֶׁה, וַאֲמַר לֵיהּ אֲנָא יי: ג וְאִתְגְּלֵיתִי, לְאַבְרָהָם, לְיִצְחָק וּלְיַעֲקֹב בְּאֵל שַׁדַּי, וּשְׁמִי יי, לָא הוֹדַעִית לְהוֹן: ד וְאַף

VAERA

In Vaera, the story of the exodus begins in earnest, with an unprecedented series of divine interventions into history. Time and again plagues hit the Egyptians. Moshe repeatedly asks Pharaoh to release the people. Repeatedly, Pharaoh refuses. All the power of imperial Egypt is powerless against the God of creation and redemption. The plagues are a lesson, to Pharaoh and to the world, that there is something higher than power. There is justice, liberty, human dignity, the sanctity of life.

I AM THE LORD

Having given Moshe a brief and forceful answer to his anxieties at the end of last week's *parasha*, God now, in a separate address, explains to him in detail the world-changing significance of what is about to transpire. Nehama Leibowitz and others point out that the speech is a chiasmus:

Then God spoke to Moshe:

A. I am the LORD.

B. As El Shaddai I appeared to Avraham, Yitzḥak, and Yaakov – but by My name the LORD I did not make Myself known to them.

C. And I made a covenant with them to give them the land of Canaan…

D. And now, I have heard the groaning of the Israelites, whom the Egyptians are holding as slaves, and I remember My covenant.

E. Therefore, say to the Israelites: I am the LORD,

D1. and I will free you from the forced labor of the Egyptians.…Then you will know that I am the LORD your God…

C1. And I will bring you to the land that I promised to give

B1. to Avraham, Yitzḥak, and Yaakov; to you I will give it as a possession.

A1. I am the LORD.

The first and second halves of the speech each contain exactly fifty words in the Hebrew text. B and B1 are about the patriarchs; C and C1 about the land; D and D1 about Egypt and slavery. The first half is about the past, the second about the future. The first half refers to the Israelites in the third person ("them"), the second in the second person ("you"). The entire speech turns on the threefold repetition of "I am the LORD" – at the beginning, end, and middle of the speech.

What is meant by the opening proposition? "As El Shaddai I appeared to Avraham, Yitzḥak, and Yaakov –" but not "by My name the LORD." The verse distinguishes between El Shaddai (often rendered "Almighty God") and the four-letter name which, because of its sanctity, Jewish tradition referred to simply as *Hashem* – "the name" par excellence. As the classic Jewish commentators point out, the verse must be read with great care. It does not say that God did not "make this name known" to the patriarchs. God uses the phrase "I am the LORD" to both Avraham (Gen. 15:7) and Yaakov (28:13). Yet a fundamental distinction is being made between the experience the patriarchs had of God, and the experience the Israelites are about to have. What is it?

5 them the land of Canaan, the land where they lived as strangers. And now, I
have heard the groaning of the Israelites whom the Egyptians are holding as
6 slaves, and I remember My covenant. Therefore, say to the Israelites: I am the
Lord, and I will free you from the forced labor of the Egyptians, I will rescue
you from slavery. I will liberate you with an arm stretched forth and with great
7 acts of judgment. I will take you as My people and I will be your God. Then
you will know that I am the Lord your God, freeing you from Egyptian forced
8 labor. And I will bring you to the land that I promised to give to Avraham,
Yitzhak, and Yaakov; to you I will give it as a possession. I am the Lord."
9 Moshe told this to the Israelites, but in the brokenness of their spirit and the
brutal labor they did not listen to him.

רש״י

ד **וְגַם הֲקִמֹתִי אֶת בְּרִיתִי וְגוֹ׳.** וְגַם כְּשֶׁנִּרְאֵיתִי לָהֶם בְּאֵל שַׁדַּי הֲקִמֹתִי וְהֶעֱמַדְתִּי בְּרִית בֵּינִי וּבֵינֵיהֶם "לָתֵת לָהֶם אֶת אֶרֶץ כְּנָעַן" – לְאַבְרָהָם בְּפָרָשַׁת מִילָה נֶאֱמַר: "אֲנִי אֵל שַׁדַּי וְגוֹ׳ וְנָתַתִּי לְךָ וּלְזַרְעֲךָ אַחֲרֶיךָ אֶת אֶרֶץ מְגֻרֶיךָ" (בראשית יז, א-ח); לְיִצְחָק: "כִּי לְךָ וּלְזַרְעֲךָ אֶתֵּן אֶת כָּל הָאֲרָצֹת הָאֵל וַהֲקִמֹתִי אֶת הַשְּׁבֻעָה אֲשֶׁר נִשְׁבַּעְתִּי לְאַבְרָהָם" (שם כו, ג), וְאוֹתָהּ שְׁבוּעָה שֶׁנִּשְׁבַּעְתִּי לְאַבְרָהָם בְּאֵל שַׁדַּי נֶאֶמְרָה; לְיַעֲקֹב: "אֲנִי אֵל שַׁדַּי פְּרֵה וּרְבֵה וְגוֹ׳ וְאֶת הָאָרֶץ אֲשֶׁר" וְגוֹ׳ (שם לה, יא-יב). הֲרֵי שֶׁנִּדַּרְתִּי לָהֶם וְלֹא קִיַּמְתִּי:

ה **וְגַם אֲנִי.** כְּמוֹ שֶׁהֲקִמֹתִי וְהֶעֱמַדְתִּי הַבְּרִית יֵשׁ עָלַי לְקַיֵּם, לְפִיכָךְ "שָׁמַעְתִּי אֶת נַאֲקַת בְּנֵי יִשְׂרָאֵל" הַנֶּאֱנָקִים, "אֲשֶׁר מִצְרַיִם מַעֲבִדִים אֹתָם, וָאֶזְכֹּר" אוֹתוֹ הַבְּרִית, כִּי בַּבְּרִית בֵּין הַבְּתָרִים אָמַרְתִּי לוֹ: "וְגַם אֶת הַגּוֹי אֲשֶׁר יַעֲבֹדוּ דָּן אָנֹכִי" (שם טו, יד):

ו **לָכֵן.** עַל פִּי אוֹתָהּ הַשְּׁבוּעָה: **אֱמֹר לִבְנֵי יִשְׂרָאֵל אֲנִי ה׳.** הַנֶּאֱמָן בְּהַבְטָחָתִי: **וְהוֹצֵאתִי אֶתְכֶם.** כִּי כֵן הִבְטַחְתִּי: "וְאַחֲרֵי כֵן יֵצְאוּ בִּרְכֻשׁ גָּדוֹל" (שם): **סִבְלֹת.** טֹרַח מַשָּׂא מִצְרַיִם:

ח **נָשָׂאתִי אֶת יָדִי.** הֲרִימוֹתִיהָ לִשָּׁבַע בְּכִסְאִי:

ט **וְלֹא שָׁמְעוּ אֶל מֹשֶׁה.** לֹא קִבְּלוּ תַּנְחוּמִין: **מִקֹּצֶר רוּחַ.** כָּל מִי שֶׁהוּא מֵצֵר, רוּחוֹ וּנְשִׁימָתוֹ קְצָרָה וְאֵינוֹ יָכוֹל לְהַאֲרִיךְ בִּנְשִׁימָתוֹ. קָרוֹב לְעִנְיָן זֶה שָׁמַעְתִּי בְּפָרָשָׁה זוֹ מֵרַבִּי בָּרוּךְ בְּרַבִּי אֱלִיעֶזֶר, וְהֵבִיא לִי רְאָיָה מִמִּקְרָא זֶה: "בַּפַּעַם הַזֹּאת אוֹדִיעֵם אֶת יָדִי וְאֶת גְּבוּרָתִי וְיָדְעוּ כִּי

6:8 **וְהֵבֵאתִי אֶתְכֶם** *I will bring you* – The Mishna in Pesahim (10:1) speaks of four cups of wine at the Passover Seder. Traditionally, the first cup corresponds to "I will free you," the second to "I will rescue you," the third to "I will liberate you," and the fourth to "I will take you." Geographically, God will take the Israelites out of Egypt, physically He will save them from oppression, legally He will liberate them from Pharaoh's rule, and spiritually He will take them under His own protection and tutelage. Each of the four cups is a stage on the way to freedom, a way of pausing and giving thanks. The rabbis of the Middle Ages debated whether a fifth cup, corresponding to this fifth promise: "I will bring you to the land that I promised," should be drunk during the time of exile. Out of respect for Rambam (*Hilkhot Ḥametz UMatza* 8:10), we pour this extra cup, because of the promise. Out of respect for Rashi (Pesaḥim 118a), we do not drink it, because the promise is not yet fulfilled.

In our times, the Jewish people have returned to the land. According to one sage (the late Rabbi Menahem Kasher), we should now drink the fifth cup. Be that as it may, according to the sages, unresolved halakhic disputes will one day be resolved by Eliyahu. (According to one popular understanding, the word *teiku,* "Let it stand [undecided]," refers to Eliyahu: "[Eliyahu] the Tishbite will come and answer questions and problems.") It is thus the untouched fifth cup that became known as the cup of Eliyahu. It represents the hope that kept the Jewish people alive through the darkest night of exile.

6:9 **וְלֹא שָׁמְעוּ אֶל־מֹשֶׁה** *They did not listen to him* – When Moshe first met God at the burning bush, God told him to lead, and Moshe demurred on the grounds that the people

הֲקִמֹ֤תִי אֶת־בְּרִיתִי֙ אִתָּ֔ם לָתֵ֥ת לָהֶ֖ם אֶת־אֶ֣רֶץ כְּנָ֑עַן אֵ֛ת אֶ֥רֶץ מְגֻרֵיהֶ֖ם
ה אֲשֶׁר־גָּ֥רוּ בָֽהּ׃ וְגַ֣ם ׀ אֲנִ֣י שָׁמַ֗עְתִּי אֶֽת־נַאֲקַת֙ בְּנֵ֣י יִשְׂרָאֵ֔ל אֲשֶׁ֥ר מִצְרַ֖יִם
ו מַעֲבִדִ֣ים אֹתָ֑ם וָאֶזְכֹּ֖ר אֶת־בְּרִיתִֽי׃ לָכֵ֞ן אֱמֹ֥ר לִבְנֵֽי־יִשְׂרָאֵל֮ אֲנִ֣י יהוה֒
וְהוֹצֵאתִ֣י אֶתְכֶ֗ם מִתַּ֙חַת֙ סִבְלֹ֣ת מִצְרַ֔יִם וְהִצַּלְתִּ֥י אֶתְכֶ֖ם מֵעֲבֹדָתָ֑ם
ז וְגָאַלְתִּ֤י אֶתְכֶם֙ בִּזְר֣וֹעַ נְטוּיָ֔ה וּבִשְׁפָטִ֖ים גְּדֹלִֽים׃ וְלָקַחְתִּ֨י אֶתְכֶ֥ם לִי֙
לְעָ֔ם וְהָיִ֥יתִי לָכֶ֖ם לֵֽאלֹהִ֑ים וִידַעְתֶּ֗ם כִּ֣י אֲנִ֤י יהוה֙ אֱלֹ֣הֵיכֶ֔ם הַמּוֹצִ֣יא
ח אֶתְכֶ֔ם מִתַּ֖חַת סִבְל֥וֹת מִצְרָֽיִם׃ וְהֵבֵאתִ֤י אֶתְכֶם֙ אֶל־הָאָ֔רֶץ אֲשֶׁ֤ר
נָשָׂ֙אתִי֙ אֶת־יָדִ֔י לָתֵ֣ת אֹתָ֔הּ לְאַבְרָהָ֥ם לְיִצְחָ֖ק וּֽלְיַעֲקֹ֑ב וְנָתַתִּ֨י אֹתָ֥הּ
ט לָכֶ֛ם מוֹרָשָׁ֖ה אֲנִ֥י יהוֽה׃ וַיְדַבֵּ֥ר מֹשֶׁ֛ה כֵּ֖ן אֶל־בְּנֵ֣י יִשְׂרָאֵ֑ל וְלֹ֤א שָֽׁמְעוּ֙
אֶל־מֹשֶׁ֔ה מִקֹּ֣צֶר ר֔וּחַ וּמֵעֲבֹדָ֖ה קָשָֽׁה׃

אונקלוס

אֲקֵימִית יָת קְיָמִי עִמְּהוֹן, לְמִתַּן לְהוֹן יָת אַרְעָא דִּכְנָעַן, יָת, אֲרַע תּוֹתָבוּתְהוֹן דְּאִתּוֹתַבוּ בַהּ: ה וְאַף קֳדָמַי שְׁמִיעַ, יָת קְבִילַת בְּנֵי יִשְׂרָאֵל, דְּמִצְרָאֵי מַפְלְחִין בְּהוֹן, וּדְכִירְנָא יָת קְיָמִי: ו בְּכֵן, אֵימַר לִבְנֵי יִשְׂרָאֵל אֲנָא יי, וְאַפֵּיק יָתְכוֹן, מִגּוֹ דְּחוֹק פֻּלְחַן מִצְרָאֵי, וַאֲשֵׁיזֵיב יָתְכוֹן מִפֻּלְחָנְהוֹן, וְאֶפְרוֹק יָתְכוֹן בִּדְרָע מְרַמַם, וּבְדִינִין רַבְרְבִין: ז וַאֲקָרֵיב יָתְכוֹן קֳדָמַי לְעַם, וְאֶהֱוֵי לְכוֹן לֶאֱלָהּ, וְתִדְּעוּן, אֲרֵי אֲנָא יי אֱלָהֲכוֹן, דְּאַפֵּיק יָתְכוֹן, מִגּוֹ דְּחוֹק פֻּלְחַן מִצְרָאֵי: ח וְאַעֵיל יָתְכוֹן לְאַרְעָא, דְּקַיֵּימִית בְּמֵימְרִי, לְמִתַּן יָתַהּ, לְאַבְרָהָם לְיִצְחָק וּלְיַעֲקֹב, וְאֶתֵּין יָתַהּ לְכוֹן, יְרֻתָּא אֲנָא יי: ט וּמַלֵּיל מֹשֶׁה, כֵּן עִם בְּנֵי יִשְׂרָאֵל, וְלָא קַבִּילוּ מִן מֹשֶׁה, מֵעָיַק רוּחַ, וּמִפֻּלְחָנָא דַּהֲוָה קְשֵׁי עֲלֵיהוֹן:

the Lord" (Gen. 15:7) in the vision in which He revealed to him that his descendants would be strangers in the land not their own, where they would be enslaved and mistreated. The repetition of these words to Moshe here creates a vast temporal arch between Avraham and Moshe, the first and last scenes of exile.

6:6 וְהוֹצֵאתִי אֶתְכֶם מִתַּחַת סִבְלֹת מִצְרַיִם *I will free you from the forced labor of the Egyptians* – What is revolutionary in Judaism is not simply the concept of monotheism – that the universe is not a blind clash of conflicting powers but the result of a single creative will. It is that God is *involved* in His creation. God is not simply the force that brought the universe into being, nor is He reached only in the private recesses of the soul. At a certain point He intervenes in history, to rescue His people from slavery and set them on the path to freedom. This is the revolution, at once political and intellectual.

Judaism is the escape into history, the unique attempt to endow events with meaning, and to see in the chronicles of mankind something more than a mere succession of happenings – to see history as nothing less than a drama of redemption in which the fate of a nation reflects its loyalty or otherwise to a covenant with God.

Some 3,300 years ago, God tells Moshe that He will intervene in the arena of time, not only (though primarily) to rescue the Israelites but also "to have My name known throughout the land" (Ex. 9:16). The script of history will bear the mark of a hand – not human, but divine. And it begins with these words: "Therefore, say to the Israelites: I am the Lord, and I will free you from the forced labor of the Egyptians."

10 11 Then the LORD said to Moshe, "Go, tell Pharaoh, king of Egypt, to send the
12 Israelites forth from his land." But Moshe said to the LORD, "The Israelites, You
see, have not listened to me. How then will Pharaoh listen? And I am a man of
uncircumcised lips."
13 The LORD spoke to Moshe and Aharon; and He charged them with regard to
the Israelites and to Pharaoh, king of Egypt, to bring the Israelites out of the
14 land of Egypt. These were the heads of their ancestral houses. The SHENI
sons of Reuven, Yisrael's firstborn, were Ḥanokh, Palu, Ḥetzron, and Karmi;

רש"י

"שמי ה'" (ירמיה טז, כא); למדנו כשהקדוש ברוך הוא מאמן את דבריו, אפלו לפרענות, מודיע ששמו ה', וכל שכן האמנה לטובה. ורבותינו דרשוהו לענין של מעלה שאמר משה: "למה הרעתה" (לעיל ה, כב), אמר לו הקדוש ברוך הוא: חבל על דאבדין ולא משתכחין! יש לי להתאונן על מיתת האבות, הרבה פעמים נגליתי עליהם באל שדי ולא אמרו לי מה שמך, ואתה אמרת: "מה שמו, מה אמר אליהם" (לעיל ג, יג). **וגם הקמתי וגו'**. וכשבקש אברהם לקבר את שרה לא מצא קבר עד שקנה בדמים מרבים; וכן יצחק – עוררו עליו על הבארות אשר חפר; וכן יעקב – "ויקן את חלקת השדה" (בראשית לג, יט) לנטות אהלו; ולא הרהרו אחר מדותי, ואתה אמרת: "למה הרעתה". ואין המדרש מתישב אחר המקרא מפני כמה דברים: אחת, שלא נאמר: 'ושמי ה' לא שאלו לי'. ואם תאמר, לא הודיעם שכך שמו; הרי תחלה כשנגלה לאברהם בין הבתרים נאמר: "אני ה' אשר הוצאתיך מאור כשדים" (שם טו, ז)! ועוד, היאך הסמיכה נמשכת בדברים שהוא סומך לכאן: "וגם אני שמעתי וגו', לכן אמר לבני ישראל"? לכך אני אומר יתישב המקרא על פשוטו דבור על אפניו והדרשה תדרש, שנאמר: "הלוא כה דברי כאש נאם ה' וכפטיש יפצץ סלע" (ירמיה כג, כט), מתחלק לכמה ניצוצות:

יב **ערל שפתים.** אטום שפתים. וכן כל לשון ערלה אני אומר שהוא אטם: "ערלה אזנם" (שם ו, י) – אטומה משמע; "ערלי לב" (שם ט, כה) – אטומים מהבין; "שתה גם אתה והערל" (חבקוק ב, טז) – והאטם משכרות כוס הקללה; "ערלת בשר", שהגיד אטום ומכסה בה; "וערלתם ערלתו" (ויקרא יט, כג) – עשו לו אטם וכסוי איסור שיבדיל בפני אכילתו; "שלש שנים יהיה לכם ערלים" (שם) – אטום ומכסה ומבדל מלאכלו: **ואיך ישמעני פרעה.** זה אחד מעשרה קל וחמר שבתורה:

יג **וידבר ה' אל משה ואל אהרן.** לפי שאמר משה: "ואני ערל שפתים" צרף הקדוש ברוך הוא את אהרן עמו להיות לו למליץ: **ויצום אל בני ישראל.** צום עליהם להנהיגם בנחת ולסבל אותם: **ואל פרעה מלך מצרים.** צום עליו לחלק לו כבוד בדבריהם, זה מדרשו. ופשוטו, צום על דבר ישראל ועל שליחותו אל פרעה. ודבר הצווי מהו, מפרש בפרשה שניה לאחר סדר הייחס (להלן פסוק כט), אלא מתוך שהזכיר משה ואהרן, הפסיק הענין ב"אלה ראשי בית אבתם" ללמדנו היאך נולדו משה ואהרן ובמי נתיחסו:

יד **אלה ראשי בית אבתם.** מתוך שהזקק ליחס שבטו של לוי עד משה ואהרן בשביל משה ואהרן, התחיל ליחסם דרך תולדותם מראובן. ובפסיקתא הגדולה (פסיקתא ז) ראיתי, לפי שקנתרם יעקב אביהם לשלשה שבטים הללו בשעת מותו, חזר הכתוב ליחסם כאן לבדם, לומר שחשובים הם:

to his speech defect, or perhaps to a sense on the part of Moshe that, being all too human, he lacks the inspirational quality that might be expected in a person who claims to be the voice of God. His broken speech makes it difficult for people to be in awe of him as a holy man. He is more likely to evoke laughter or contempt than fear and trembling.

Moshe has not yet internalized the fact that he is never destined to succeed by words alone. God has already told him at the burning bush, "But I know that even by a mighty hand the king of Egypt would not send you forth" (Ex. 3:19). He is part of a drama larger than even he, greatest of the prophets, can understand at the time. Pharaoh cannot accede to the request, however eloquently it is made, without demeaning his stature as an emperor and demigod.

6:14 **אֵלֶּה רָאשֵׁי** *These were the heads* – The genealogy at this point marks a pause in the narrative. We have reached the end of the first phase: Moshe's intercession, the reliance on human

יא וַיְדַבֵּר יְהוָה אֶל־מֹשֶׁה לֵּאמֹר: בֹּא דַבֵּר אֶל־פַּרְעֹה מֶלֶךְ מִצְרָיִם
יב וִישַׁלַּח אֶת־בְּנֵי־יִשְׂרָאֵל מֵאַרְצוֹ: וַיְדַבֵּר מֹשֶׁה לִפְנֵי יְהוָה לֵאמֹר
הֵן בְּנֵי־יִשְׂרָאֵל לֹא־שָׁמְעוּ אֵלַי וְאֵיךְ יִשְׁמָעֵנִי פַרְעֹה וַאֲנִי עֲרַל
שְׂפָתָיִם:
יג וַיְדַבֵּר יְהוָה אֶל־מֹשֶׁה וְאֶל־אַהֲרֹן וַיְצַוֵּם אֶל־בְּנֵי יִשְׂרָאֵל וְאֶל־פַּרְעֹה
יד מֶלֶךְ מִצְרָיִם לְהוֹצִיא אֶת־בְּנֵי־יִשְׂרָאֵל מֵאֶרֶץ מִצְרָיִם: אֵלֶּה שני
רָאשֵׁי בֵית־אֲבֹתָם בְּנֵי רְאוּבֵן בְּכֹר יִשְׂרָאֵל חֲנוֹךְ וּפַלּוּא חֶצְרֹן וְכַרְמִי

אונקלוס

י וּמַלֵּיל יי עִם מֹשֶׁה לְמֵימַר: יא עוֹל מַלֵּיל, עִם פַּרְעֹה מַלְכָּא דְמִצְרָיִם, וִישַׁלַּח יָת בְּנֵי יִשְׂרָאֵל מֵאַרְעֵיהּ: יב וּמַלֵּיל מֹשֶׁה, קֳדָם יי לְמֵימַר, הָא בְנֵי יִשְׂרָאֵל לָא קַבִּילוּ מִנִּי, וְאֵיכְדֵין יְקַבֵּיל מִנִּי פַּרְעֹה, וַאֲנָא יַקִּיר מַמְלַל: יג וּמַלֵּיל יי עִם מֹשֶׁה וּלְאַהֲרֹן, וּפַקֵּידִנּוּן לְוָת בְּנֵי יִשְׂרָאֵל, וּלְוָת פַּרְעֹה מַלְכָּא דְמִצְרָיִם, לְאַפָּקָא יָת בְּנֵי יִשְׂרָאֵל מֵאַרְעָא דְמִצְרָיִם: יד אִלֵּין רֵישֵׁי בֵית אֲבָהָתְהוֹן, בְּנֵי רְאוּבֵן בֻּכְרָא דְיִשְׂרָאֵל, חֲנוֹךְ וּפַלּוּא חֶצְרוֹן וְכַרְמִי,

would not listen to him. He was not a man of words. He lacked eloquence. He could not sway crowds. He was not an inspirational leader.

Now we find that Moshe was both right and wrong, right that they do not listen to him, but wrong about why. It has nothing to do with his failures as a leader or a public speaker. In fact, it has nothing to do with Moshe at all. They do not listen "in the brokenness of their spirit and the brutal labor." In other words: *if you want to improve people's spiritual situation, you must first improve their physical situation*. That is one of the most humanizing insights of Judaism.

Rambam emphasizes this in his *Guide for the Perplexed* (III:27). The Torah, he says, has two aims: the well-being of the soul and the well-being of the body. The well-being of the soul is something inward and spiritual, but the well-being of the body requires a strong society and economy, where there is the rule of law, division of labor, and the promotion of trade. We have bodily well-being when all our physical needs are supplied, but none of us can do this on our own. We specialize and exchange. That is why we need a good, strong, just society.

Most religions are cultures of acceptance. There is poverty, hunger, and disease on earth because that is the way the world is; that is how God made it and wants it. That isn't Judaism at all. When it comes to the poverty and pain of the world, ours is a religion of protest, not acceptance. God is to be found in this world, not just the next. But for us to climb to spiritual heights we must first have satisfied our material needs.

Alleviating poverty, curing disease, ensuring the rule of law, and respecting human rights: these are spiritual tasks no less than prayer and Torah study. To be sure, the latter are higher, but the former are prior. People cannot hear God's message if their spirit is broken and their labor harsh.

6:12 **וְאֵיךְ יִשְׁמָעֵנִי פַרְעֹה** *How then will Pharaoh listen?* – This is a mode of reasoning known as *kal vaḥomer*, or *a fortiori*. If the Israelites, who are the beneficiaries of my message, do not listen, how much less so is Pharaoh likely to listen. Moshe seems aware that the argument he mounts is not a strong one. The text has already told us that the Israelites do not listen because of "the brokenness of their spirit and the brutal labor," which does not apply to Pharaoh. So Moshe adds, "I am a man of uncircumcised lips." God tacitly acknowledges this by including Aharon, the more fluent speaker, in the instructions.

6:12 **עֲרַל שְׂפָתָיִם** *Uncircumcised lips* – This is another reference

15 these were the families of Reuven. Shimon's sons were Yemuel, Yamin, Ohad,
Yakhin, Tzoḥar, and Sha'ul, son of a Canaanite woman; these are the families of
16 Shimon. These are the names of Levi's sons by their lineage: Gershon, Kehat,
17 and Merari. Levi lived one hundred thirty-seven years. The sons of Gershon
18 were Livni and Shimi, by their families. The sons of Kehat were Amram, Yitzhar,
19 Ḥevron, and Uziel. Kehat lived one hundred thirty-three years. The sons of
Merari were Maḥli and Mushi. These are the families of the Levites by their
20 lineage. Amram married Yokheved, his father's sister, who bore him Aharon and
21 Moshe. Amram lived one hundred thirty-seven years. The sons of Yitzhar were
22 Koraḥ, Nefeg, and Zikhri. The sons of Uziel were Mishael, Eltzafan, and Sitri.
23 Aharon married Elisheva, daughter of Aminadav and sister of Naḥshon, and she
24 bore him Nadav and Avihu, Elazar and Itamar. The sons of Koraḥ were Asir,
25 Elkana, and Aviasaf; these are the families of the Korahites. Elazar, Aharon's son,
married one of the daughters of Putiel, and she bore him Pinḥas. These were the
26 heads of the Levite clans by their families. These were the Aharon and Moshe to

רש״י

טז **וּשְׁנֵי חַיֵּי לֵוִי וְגוֹ׳.** לָמָּה נִמְנוּ שְׁנוֹתָיו שֶׁל לֵוִי? לְהוֹדִיעַ כַּמָּה יְמֵי הַשִּׁעְבּוּד, שֶׁכָּל זְמַן שֶׁאֶחָד מִן הַשְּׁבָטִים קַיָּם לֹא הָיָה שִׁעְבּוּד, שֶׁנֶּאֱמַר: ״וַיָּמָת יוֹסֵף וְכָל אֶחָיו״ (לעיל א, ו) וְאַחַר כָּךְ: ״וַיָּקָם מֶלֶךְ חָדָשׁ״ (שם פסוק ח), וְלֵוִי הֶאֱרִיךְ יָמִים עַל כֻּלָּם:

יח **וּשְׁנֵי חַיֵּי קְהָת... וּשְׁנֵי חַיֵּי עַמְרָם וְגוֹ׳.** מֵחֶשְׁבּוֹן זֶה אָנוּ לְמֵדִים עַל מוֹשַׁב בְּנֵי יִשְׂרָאֵל אַרְבַּע מֵאוֹת שָׁנָה שֶׁאָמַר הַכָּתוּב (בראשית טו, יג; ועיין להלן יב, מ), שֶׁלֹּא בְּאֶרֶץ מִצְרַיִם לְבַדָּהּ הָיוּ, אֶלָּא מִיּוֹם שֶׁנּוֹלַד יִצְחָק. שֶׁהֲרֵי קְהָת מִיּוֹרְדֵי מִצְרַיִם הָיָה, חֲשֹׁב כָּל שְׁנוֹתָיו וּשְׁנוֹת עַמְרָם וּשְׁמוֹנִים שֶׁל מֹשֶׁה, לֹא תִמְצָאֵם אַרְבַּע מֵאוֹת שָׁנָה, וְהַרְבֵּה שָׁנִים נִבְלָעִים לַבָּנִים בִּשְׁנֵי הָאָבוֹת:

כ **יוֹכֶבֶד דֹּדָתוֹ.** ״אֲחָת אֲבוּהִי״, בַּת לֵוִי, אֲחוֹת קְהָת:

כה **מִבְּנוֹת פּוּטִיאֵל.** מִזֶּרַע יִתְרוֹ שֶׁפִּטֵּם עֲגָלִים לַעֲבוֹדָה זָרָה, וּמִזֶּרַע יוֹסֵף שֶׁפִּטְפֵּט בְּיִצְרוֹ:

כו **הוּא אַהֲרֹן וּמֹשֶׁה.** אֵלּוּ שֶׁהֻזְכְּרוּ לְמַעְלָה שֶׁיָּלְדָה יוֹכֶבֶד לְעַמְרָם, ״הוּא אַהֲרֹן וּמֹשֶׁה אֲשֶׁר אָמַר ה׳״ וְגוֹ׳. יֵשׁ מְקוֹמוֹת שֶׁמַּקְדִּים אַהֲרֹן לְמֹשֶׁה וְיֵשׁ מְקוֹמוֹת שֶׁמַּקְדִּים מֹשֶׁה לְאַהֲרֹן, לוֹמַר שֶׁשְּׁקוּלִים שְׁנֵיהֶם

We are given surprisingly detailed information about Koraḥ, and about Aharon's son Elazar and his grandson Pinḥas. The two sons of Moshe, Gershom and Eliezer, are not mentioned. This is not the usual genealogy of the kind the Torah inserts at various occasions, but rather an advance identification of leading figures, not only from earlier generations but also in the future. Moshe's sons will not inherit his office, unlike Aharon's who will. It will be Elazar who becomes Aharon's successor, because Nadav and Avihu die prematurely. Elazar's son Pinḥas will play a leading role in a key episode in Israel's history. Koraḥ will eventually challenge Moshe's leadership, as will two figures from the tribe of Reuven. All these future events are hinted at in this genealogy.

6:20 **וַיִּקַּח עַמְרָם אֶת־יוֹכֶבֶד דֹּדָתוֹ לוֹ לְאִשָּׁה** *Amram married Yokheved, his father's sister* – Marriages of this kind were forbidden in later Torah law (Lev. 18:12), but not at the time. It is striking that the Torah does not suppress this fact about the marriage that yielded Israel three great leaders, Moshe, Aharon, and Miriam.

6:26 **אַהֲרֹן וּמֹשֶׁה** *Aharon and Moshe* – The names are given here in their chronological order, as opposed to their leadership positions. Netziv suggests that in this verse, which speaks about the Israelites, Aharon takes priority since he is well known to and beloved by the people. Moshe, who has spent much of his life in an Egyptian palace and in Midyan,

טו אֵלֶּה מִשְׁפְּחֹת רְאוּבֵן: וּבְנֵי שִׁמְעוֹן יְמוּאֵל וְיָמִין וְאֹהַד וְיָכִין וְצֹחַר
טז וְשָׁאוּל בֶּן־הַכְּנַעֲנִית אֵלֶּה מִשְׁפְּחֹת שִׁמְעוֹן: וְאֵלֶּה שְׁמוֹת בְּנֵי־לֵוִי
לְתֹלְדֹתָם גֵּרְשׁוֹן וּקְהָת וּמְרָרִי וּשְׁנֵי חַיֵּי לֵוִי שֶׁבַע וּשְׁלֹשִׁים וּמְאַת
יז יח שָׁנָה: בְּנֵי גֵרְשׁוֹן לִבְנִי וְשִׁמְעִי לְמִשְׁפְּחֹתָם: וּבְנֵי קְהָת עַמְרָם וְיִצְהָר
יט וְחֶבְרוֹן וְעֻזִּיאֵל וּשְׁנֵי חַיֵּי קְהָת שָׁלֹשׁ וּשְׁלֹשִׁים וּמְאַת שָׁנָה: וּבְנֵי מְרָרִי
כ מַחְלִי וּמוּשִׁי אֵלֶּה מִשְׁפְּחֹת הַלֵּוִי לְתֹלְדֹתָם: וַיִּקַּח עַמְרָם אֶת־יוֹכֶבֶד
דֹּדָתוֹ לוֹ לְאִשָּׁה וַתֵּלֶד לוֹ אֶת־אַהֲרֹן וְאֶת־מֹשֶׁה וּשְׁנֵי חַיֵּי עַמְרָם שֶׁבַע
כא כב וּשְׁלֹשִׁים וּמְאַת שָׁנָה: וּבְנֵי יִצְהָר קֹרַח וָנֶפֶג וְזִכְרִי: וּבְנֵי עֻזִּיאֵל מִישָׁאֵל
כג וְאֶלְצָפָן וְסִתְרִי: וַיִּקַּח אַהֲרֹן אֶת־אֱלִישֶׁבַע בַּת־עַמִּינָדָב אֲחוֹת נַחְשׁוֹן
לוֹ לְאִשָּׁה וַתֵּלֶד לוֹ אֶת־נָדָב וְאֶת־אֲבִיהוּא אֶת־אֶלְעָזָר וְאֶת־אִיתָמָר:
כד כה וּבְנֵי קֹרַח אַסִּיר וְאֶלְקָנָה וַאֲבִיאָסָף אֵלֶּה מִשְׁפְּחֹת הַקָּרְחִי: וְאֶלְעָזָר
בֶּן־אַהֲרֹן לָקַח־לוֹ מִבְּנוֹת פּוּטִיאֵל לוֹ לְאִשָּׁה וַתֵּלֶד לוֹ אֶת־פִּינְחָס
כו אֵלֶּה רָאשֵׁי אֲבוֹת הַלְוִיִּם לְמִשְׁפְּחֹתָם: הוּא אַהֲרֹן וּמֹשֶׁה אֲשֶׁר אָמַר

אונקלוס

אִלֵּין זַרְעִית רְאוּבֵן: טו וּבְנֵי שִׁמְעוֹן, יְמוּאֵל וְיָמִין וְאוֹהַד וְיָכִין וְצוֹחַר, וְשָׁאוּל בַּר כְּנַעֲנֵיתָא, אִלֵּין זַרְעִית שִׁמְעוֹן: טז וְאִלֵּין שְׁמָהָת בְּנֵי לֵוִי לְתוּלְדָתְהוֹן, גֵּרְשׁוֹן, וּקְהָת וּמְרָרִי, וּשְׁנֵי חַיֵּי לֵוִי, מְאָה וּתְלָתִין וּשְׁבַע שְׁנִין: יז בְּנֵי גֵרְשׁוֹן, לִבְנִי וְשִׁמְעִי לְזַרְעְיָתְהוֹן: יח וּבְנֵי קְהָת, עַמְרָם וְיִצְהָר, וְחֶבְרוֹן וְעֻזִּיאֵל, וּשְׁנֵי חַיֵּי קְהָת, מְאָה וּתְלָתִין וּתְלָת שְׁנִין: יט וּבְנֵי מְרָרִי מַחְלִי וּמוּשִׁי, אִלֵּין, זַרְעִית לֵוִי לְתוּלְדָתְהוֹן: כ וּנְסֵיב עַמְרָם, יָת יוֹכֶבֶד אֲחָת אֲבוּהִי לֵיהּ לְאִתּוּ, וִילֵידַת לֵיהּ, יָת אַהֲרֹן וְיָת מֹשֶׁה, וּשְׁנֵי חַיֵּי עַמְרָם, מְאָה וּתְלָתִין וּשְׁבַע שְׁנִין: כא וּבְנֵי יִצְהָר, קֹרַח וָנֶפֶג וְזִכְרִי: כב וּבְנֵי עֻזִּיאֵל, מִישָׁאֵל וְאֶלְצָפָן וְסִתְרִי: כג וּנְסֵיב אַהֲרֹן, יָת אֱלִישֶׁבַע בַּת עַמִּינָדָב, אֲחָתֵיהּ דְּנַחְשׁוֹן לֵיהּ לְאִתּוּ, וִילֵידַת לֵיהּ, יָת נָדָב וְיָת אֲבִיהוּא, יָת אֶלְעָזָר וְיָת אִיתָמָר: כד וּבְנֵי קֹרַח, אַסִּיר וְאֶלְקָנָה וַאֲבִיאָסָף, אִלֵּין זַרְעִית קֹרַח: כה וְאֶלְעָזָר בַּר אַהֲרֹן, נְסֵיב לֵיהּ מִבְּנָת פּוּטִיאֵל לֵיהּ לְאִתּוּ, וִילֵידַת לֵיהּ יָת פִּינְחָס, אִלֵּין, רֵישֵׁי, אֲבָהָת לֵיוָאֵי לְזַרְעְיָתְהוֹן: כו הוּא אַהֲרֹן וּמֹשֶׁה, דַּאֲמַר

efforts, and Pharaoh's initial obduracy. The narrative is now about to move from natural to supernatural, from request to sign to plague. To root these wondrous events in human history the text gives us a genealogy, with special emphasis on the tribe of Levi and the leadership of Moshe, Aharon, Aharon's sons, and in one case, Pinḥas, Aharon's grandson. This foreshadows the family's future role as priests. Levi was Yaakov's third son. Out of respect to the two older sons, a brief genealogy is given also for Reuven and Shimon. The genealogy supplies the information conspicuously withheld in chapter 2, where with the exception of his sister Miriam, Moshe's family appears anonymously. Until now, the emphasis has been on Moshe the individual. Now we see him as fully part of his people. He and Aharon may have been chosen by God to perform signs and wonders but they remain resolutely part of the family of the covenant.

27 whom the LORD said, "Bring the Israelites out of Egypt, by their battalions." It
was they who spoke up to Pharaoh, king of Egypt, to bring the Israelites out of
28 Egypt – this same Moshe and Aharon. So it came to pass on the day the LORD
29 spoke to Moshe in Egypt. The LORD said to Moshe, "I am the LORD. SHELISHI
30 Tell Pharaoh, king of Egypt, all that I am telling you." But Moshe replied to the
LORD, "You know that I have uncircumcised lips. How then will Pharaoh listen
to me?"
7 1 Then the LORD said to Moshe, "I am making you now like a god to Pharaoh,
2 and your brother Aharon will be your prophet. All that I command you, you
are to speak, and your brother Aharon to convey to Pharaoh, that he send the
3 Israelites forth from his land. But I will harden Pharaoh's heart and multiply

רש"י

כְּאֶחָד: **עַל צִבְאֹתָם.** כְּצִבְאוֹתָם, כָּל צִבְאָם לְשִׁבְטֵיהֶם. יֵשׁ 'עַל' שֶׁאֵינוֹ אֶלָּא בִּמְקוֹם אוֹת אַחַת: "וְעַל חַרְבְּךָ תִחְיֶה" (בראשית כז, מ) כְּמוֹ בְּחַרְבְּךָ; "עֲמַדְתֶּם עַל חַרְבְּכֶם" (יחזקאל לג, כו) בְּחַרְבְּכֶם:

כז **הֵם הַמְדַבְּרִים וְגוֹ'.** הֵם שֶׁנִּצְטַוּוּ הֵם שֶׁקִּיְּמוּ: **הוּא מֹשֶׁה וְאַהֲרֹן.** הֵם בִּשְׁלִיחוּתָם וּבְצִדְקָתָם מִתְּחִלָּה וְעַד סוֹף:

כח **וַיְהִי בְּיוֹם דִּבֶּר וְגוֹ'.** מְחֻבָּר לַמִּקְרָא שֶׁל אַחֲרָיו:

כט **וַיְדַבֵּר ה'.** הוּא הַדִּבּוּר עַצְמוֹ הָאָמוּר לְמַעְלָה, אֶלָּא מִתּוֹךְ שֶׁהִפְסִיקוֹ הָעִנְיָן בִּשְׁבִיל לְיַחֲסָם, חָזַר עָלָיו לְהַתְחִיל בּוֹ: **אֲנִי ה'.** כְּדַאי אֲנִי לְשָׁלְחֲךָ וּלְקַיֵּם דִּבְרֵי שְׁלִיחוּתִי:

ז א **נְתַתִּיךָ אֱלֹהִים לְפַרְעֹה.** שׁוֹפֵט וְרוֹדֶה, לִרְדּוֹתוֹ בְּמַכּוֹת וְיִסּוּרִין: **יִהְיֶה נְבִיאֶךָ.** כְּתַרְגּוּמוֹ: "מְתֻרְגְּמָנָךְ". וְכֵן כָּל לְשׁוֹן נְבוּאָה, אָדָם הַמַּכְרִיז וּמַשְׁמִיעַ לָעָם דִּבְרֵי תוֹכָחוֹת, וְהוּא מִגִּזְרַת "נִיב שְׂפָתָיִם" (ישעיה נז, יט), "יָנוּב חָכְמָה" (משלי י, לא), "וַיְכַל מֵהִתְנַבּוֹת" דִּשְׁמוּאֵל (שמואל א' י, יג), וּבְלַעַז קוֹרִין לוֹ פרידיצ"ר:

ב **אַתָּה תְדַבֵּר.** פַּעַם אַחַת כָּל שְׁלִיחוּת וּשְׁלִיחוּת לְפִי שֶׁשְּׁמַעְתָּ מִפִּי, וְאַהֲרֹן אָחִיךָ יְמַלִּיצֶנּוּ וִיטְעִימֶנּוּ בְּאָזְנֵי פַרְעֹה:

ג **וַאֲנִי אַקְשֶׁה.** מֵאַחַר שֶׁהִרְשִׁיעַ וְהִתְרִיס כְּנֶגְדִּי, וְגָלוּי לְפָנַי שֶׁאֵין נַחַת רוּחַ בָּאֻמּוֹת לָתֵת לֵב שָׁלֵם לָשׁוּב, טוֹב לִי שֶׁיִּתְקַשֶּׁה לִבּוֹ לְמַעַן הַרְבּוֹת בּוֹ אוֹתוֹתַי וְתַכִּירוּ אַתֶּם גְּבוּרוֹתַי. וְכֵן מִדָּתוֹ שֶׁל הַקָּדוֹשׁ בָּרוּךְ הוּא, מֵבִיא פֻרְעָנוּת עַל הָאֻמּוֹת כְּדֵי שֶׁיִּשְׁמְעוּ יִשְׂרָאֵל וְיִירְאוּ, שֶׁנֶּאֱמַר: "הִכְרַתִּי גוֹיִם נָשַׁמּוּ פִּנּוֹתָם... אָמַרְתִּי אַךְ תִּירְאִי אוֹתִי תִּקְחִי מוּסָר" (צפניה ג, ו-ז). וְאַף עַל פִּי כֵן, בְּחָמֵשׁ מַכּוֹת הָרִאשׁוֹנוֹת לֹא נֶאֱמַר: 'וַיְחַזֵּק ה' אֶת לֵב פַּרְעֹה', אֶלָּא: "וַיֶּחֱזַק לֵב פַּרְעֹה":

THE HARDENING OF PHARAOH'S HEART

The Egyptians – pharaohs especially – were preoccupied by death. Their funerary practices were elaborate in the extreme and were meant to prepare the person for life after death. According to Egyptian myth, the deceased underwent a trial to establish their worthiness to enjoy life after death in Aaru, the Field of Reeds, where souls live on in pleasure for eternity. They believed that the soul resides in the heart, and the trial consisted of the ceremony of the Weighing of the Heart. Other organs were removed after death, but the heart was left because it was needed for the trial.

On one side of the scales was a feather. On the other was placed the heart. If the heart was as light as the feather, the dead could continue to Aaru. If it was heavier, it was devoured by the goddess Ammit, and its owner was condemned to live in Duat, the underworld. An illustration, on papyrus in *The Book of the Dead,* shows the ceremony, undertaken in the Hall of Two Truths, overseen by Anubis, the Egyptian god of the dead.

The root *k-v-d*, "to make heavy," would thus have had a highly specific meaning for the Egyptians of that time. It would imply that Pharaoh's heart had become heavier than a feather. He would fail the heart-weighing ceremony and be denied what was most important to him – the prospect of joining the gods in the afterlife.

No one would have been in doubt as to why this was so.

יְהוָה לָהֶם הוֹצִיאוּ אֶת־בְּנֵי יִשְׂרָאֵל מֵאֶרֶץ מִצְרַיִם עַל־צִבְאֹתָם׃
כז הֵם הַֽמְדַבְּרִים אֶל־פַּרְעֹה מֶֽלֶךְ־מִצְרַיִם לְהוֹצִיא אֶת־בְּנֵי־יִשְׂרָאֵל
כח מִמִּצְרָיִם הוּא מֹשֶׁה וְאַהֲרֹן׃ וַיְהִי בְּיוֹם דִּבֶּר יְהוָה אֶל־מֹשֶׁה בְּאֶרֶץ
כט מִצְרָיִם׃ וַיְדַבֵּר יְהוָה אֶל־מֹשֶׁה לֵּאמֹר אֲנִי יְהוָה דַּבֵּר אֶל־ שלישי
ל פַּרְעֹה מֶלֶךְ מִצְרַיִם אֵת כָּל־אֲשֶׁר אֲנִי דֹּבֵר אֵלֶיךָ׃ וַיֹּאמֶר מֹשֶׁה לִפְנֵי
יְהוָה הֵן אֲנִי עֲרַל שְׂפָתַיִם וְאֵיךְ יִשְׁמַע אֵלַי פַּרְעֹה׃
ז א וַיֹּאמֶר יְהוָה אֶל־מֹשֶׁה רְאֵה נְתַתִּיךָ אֱלֹהִים לְפַרְעֹה וְאַהֲרֹן אָחִיךָ
ב יִהְיֶה נְבִיאֶךָ׃ אַתָּה תְדַבֵּר אֵת כָּל־אֲשֶׁר אֲצַוֶּךָּ וְאַהֲרֹן אָחִיךָ יְדַבֵּר
ג אֶל־פַּרְעֹה וְשִׁלַּח אֶת־בְּנֵי־יִשְׂרָאֵל מֵאַרְצוֹ׃ וַאֲנִי אַקְשֶׁה אֶת־לֵב פַּרְעֹה

אונקלוס

יי לְהוֹן, אַפִּיקוּ, יָת בְּנֵי יִשְׂרָאֵל, מֵאַרְעָא דְמִצְרַיִם עַל חֵילֵיהוֹן: כז אִנּוּן, דִּמְמַלְּלִין עִם פַּרְעֹה מַלְכָּא דְמִצְרַיִם, לְאַפָּקָא יָת בְּנֵי יִשְׂרָאֵל מִמִּצְרָיִם, הוּא מֹשֶׁה וְאַהֲרֹן: כח וַהֲוָה, בְּיוֹמָא דְּמַלֵּיל יי, עִם מֹשֶׁה בְּאַרְעָא דְמִצְרָיִם: כט וּמַלֵּיל יי, עִם מֹשֶׁה לְמֵימַר אֲנָא יי, מַלֵּיל, עִם פַּרְעֹה מַלְכָּא דְמִצְרַיִם, יָת, כָּל דַּאֲנָא מְמַלֵּיל עִמָּךְ: ל וַאֲמַר מֹשֶׁה קֳדָם יי, הָא אֲנָא יַקִּיר מַמְלַל, וְאֵיכְדֵין, יְקַבֵּיל מִנִּי פַּרְעֹה: ז א וַאֲמַר יי לְמֹשֶׁה, חֲזִי, דְּמַנִּיתָךְ רַב לְפַרְעֹה, וְאַהֲרֹן אֲחוּךְ יְהֵי מְתֻרְגְּמָנָךְ: ב אַתְּ תְּמַלֵּיל, יָת כָּל דַּאֲפַקְדִנָּךְ, וְאַהֲרֹן אֲחוּךְ יְמַלֵּיל עִם פַּרְעֹה, וִישַׁלַּח יָת בְּנֵי יִשְׂרָאֵל מֵאַרְעֵיהּ: ג וַאֲנָא אַקְשֵׁי יָת לִבָּא דְפַרְעֹה,

is relatively unknown to them. The next verse, however, speaks of their address to Pharaoh. Here Moshe takes precedence, since he is well known to the court and respected for his Egyptian ways (*Haamek Davar*).

The Sages, cited by Rashi, comment that the Torah is emphasizing that both brothers were equal in their worthiness, in their stature, in their rank. This again signals the end of the sibling rivalry that preoccupied much of the book of Genesis.

7:1 אֱלֹהִים לְפַרְעֹה *Like a god to Pharaoh* – Until now, Moshe has been described as a god to Aharon, in the sense of instructing him what to say. Here, however, the phrase has a sharper import. Central to the biblical vision is the absolute distinction between God and human beings. Humans are in the image of God, but they are not God. Hence the astonishingly realistic portrayal of the heroes of the Bible, each of whom is finite, frail, and fallible. Moshe argues, doubts, loses heart, yet he is the greatest leader we have known. The pharaohs, on the other hand, saw themselves as children of the gods, destined to join them after death. Ramesses II went further, having himself portrayed as a god at the temple at Abu Simbel. Just as there was a confrontation between Moshe (a mere "child") and Ramesses ("child of the sun god Ra"), so there is between the pharaoh who considers himself a god and Moshe, who knows he is all too human. Yet, says God, you will be a "god" to Pharaoh because, in your humility, My presence will shine through you, and Pharaoh will see that there is a force in the universe that transcends all the powers of nature and of empire. Pharaoh, arrogant, will be humbled. You, humble, will be uplifted. The lowliest of all peoples will be set free while the greatest of all empires will meet its nemesis.

4 My signs and wonders in the land of Egypt. Still Pharaoh will not listen to you.
Then I will set My hand against Egypt and, with great acts of judgment, bring
5 My battalions, My people the Israelites, forth out of the land of Egypt. When
I stretch out My hand against Egypt and bring the Israelites out from among
6 them, the Egyptians will know that I am the Lord." Moshe and Aharon did so;
7 they did exactly as the Lord commanded them. Moshe was eighty years old,
and Aharon eighty-three, when they spoke to Pharaoh.
8 9 Then the Lord said to Moshe, and to Aharon, "When Pharaoh says to you, REVI'I
'Perform a miracle,' tell Aharon: Take your staff and throw it down before
10 Pharaoh and it will become a serpent." So Moshe and Aharon went to Pharaoh
and did just as the Lord had commanded. Aharon threw down his staff before
11 Pharaoh and his officials, and it became a serpent. Pharaoh then summoned
his sages and sorcerers, and the Egyptian magicians did the same thing by their
12 sorcery. Each threw down his staff, and they became serpents – but Aharon's

רש״י

ד| **אֶת יָדִי.** יָד מַמָּשׁ, לְהַכּוֹת בָּהֶם:

ט| **מוֹפֵת.** אוֹת, לְהוֹדִיעַ שֶׁיֵּשׁ צֹרֶךְ בְּמִי שֶׁשּׁוֹלֵחַ אֶתְכֶם: **לְתַנִּין.** נָחָשׁ:

יא| **בְּלַהֲטֵיהֶם.** ״בְּלַחֲשֵׁיהוֹן״, וְאֵין לוֹ דִּמְיוֹן בַּמִּקְרָא. וְיֵשׁ לְדַמּוֹת לוֹ: ״לַהַט הַחֶרֶב הַמִּתְהַפֶּכֶת״ (בראשית ג, כד), דּוֹמֶה שֶׁהִיא מִתְהַפֶּכֶת עַל יְדֵי לַחַשׁ:

יב| **וַיִּבְלַע מַטֵּה אַהֲרֹן.** מֵאַחַר שֶׁחָזַר וְנַעֲשָׂה מַטֶּה בָּלַע אֶת כֻּלָּן:

It is less about free will than about the universality of morality. Pharaoh's conduct toward the Israelites was not only an offense against them but also against his own people's values. The narrative is telling us that *certain things are wrong, whoever does them and whoever they are done against*. They are wrong by Egyptian standards too. That is true of Pharaoh's decision to kill all male Israelite children. It is an unforgivable sin; that is the beginning of the eventually unstoppable hardening and heavying of the heart.

Pharaoh, in his repeated refusal to let the people go, may justify his decision on the grounds that he is securing *Ma'at*, order, against the threat of a growing minority in the midst of Egypt. However, with each plague the country is reduced to ever greater chaos. Tyrannies often justify themselves on the grounds that they are securing order. God is showing Egypt and ultimately the world that right is sovereign over might, that political order may not be secured at the cost of murder and oppression. The order Pharaoh seeks to protect is built on a foundation of injustice: the enslavement of the many for the benefit of the few. The more he tries to defend it, the heavier his heart grows.

7:9 לְתַנִּין *A serpent* – Evidently this is not the same sign as the one given to Moshe at the burning bush. There the text uses the word *naḥash*. Here it uses the word *tanin*. This word appears in Genesis 1:21 meaning a sea monster. Here the reference is to a crocodile, the deadly animal of which there were many in the Nile. An ancient Egyptian story tells of a magician, Ubaaner, who made a model of a crocodile out of wax, which then came alive and ate its intended victim. Sobek, one of the gods of the Nile, was often portrayed as a crocodile. The sign produced by Moshe and Aharon would thus be meaningful to the Egyptians. Yeḥezkel (29:3) calls Pharaoh a great crocodile. Thus, the sign is intended to convey that Pharaoh is being confronted by a power greater than any he could summon.

ד וְהִרְבֵּיתִי אֶת־אֹתֹתַי וְאֶת־מוֹפְתַי בְּאֶרֶץ מִצְרָיִם׃ וְלֹא־יִשְׁמַע אֲלֵכֶם
פַּרְעֹה וְנָתַתִּי אֶת־יָדִי בְּמִצְרָיִם וְהוֹצֵאתִי אֶת־צִבְאֹתַי אֶת־עַמִּי בְנֵי־
ה יִשְׂרָאֵל מֵאֶרֶץ מִצְרַיִם בִּשְׁפָטִים גְּדֹלִים׃ וְיָדְעוּ מִצְרַיִם כִּי־אֲנִי יהוה
ו בִּנְטֹתִי אֶת־יָדִי עַל־מִצְרָיִם וְהוֹצֵאתִי אֶת־בְּנֵי־יִשְׂרָאֵל מִתּוֹכָם׃ וַיַּעַשׂ
ז מֹשֶׁה וְאַהֲרֹן כַּאֲשֶׁר צִוָּה יהוה אֹתָם כֵּן עָשׂוּ׃ וּמֹשֶׁה בֶּן־שְׁמֹנִים שָׁנָה
וְאַהֲרֹן בֶּן־שָׁלֹשׁ וּשְׁמֹנִים שָׁנָה בְּדַבְּרָם אֶל־פַּרְעֹה׃
ח ט וַיֹּאמֶר יהוה אֶל־מֹשֶׁה וְאֶל־אַהֲרֹן לֵאמֹר׃ כִּי יְדַבֵּר אֲלֵכֶם פַּרְעֹה ה רביעי
לֵאמֹר תְּנוּ לָכֶם מוֹפֵת וְאָמַרְתָּ אֶל־אַהֲרֹן קַח אֶת־מַטְּךָ וְהַשְׁלֵךְ
י לִפְנֵי־פַרְעֹה יְהִי לְתַנִּין׃ וַיָּבֹא מֹשֶׁה וְאַהֲרֹן אֶל־פַּרְעֹה וַיַּעֲשׂוּ־כֵן
כַּאֲשֶׁר צִוָּה יהוה וַיַּשְׁלֵךְ אַהֲרֹן אֶת־מַטֵּהוּ לִפְנֵי פַרְעֹה וְלִפְנֵי עֲבָדָיו
יא וַיְהִי לְתַנִּין׃ וַיִּקְרָא גַּם־פַּרְעֹה לַחֲכָמִים וְלַמְכַשְּׁפִים וַיַּעֲשׂוּ גַם־הֵם
יב חַרְטֻמֵּי מִצְרַיִם בְּלַהֲטֵיהֶם כֵּן׃ וַיַּשְׁלִיכוּ אִישׁ מַטֵּהוּ וַיִּהְיוּ לְתַנִּינִם

אונקלוס

ואסגי ית אתותי, וית מופתי בארעא דמצרים: ד ולא יקביל מנכון פרעה, ואתין ית מחת גבורתי במצרים, ואפיק ית חילי, ית עמי בני ישראל מארעא דמצרים, בדינין רברבין: ה וידעון מצראי ארי אנא יי, כד ארים ית מחת גבורתי על מצרים, ואפיק ית בני ישראל מביניהון: ו ועבד משה ואהרן, כמא דפקיד יי, יתהון כן עבדו: ז ומשה בר תמנן שנין, ואהרן, בר תמנן ותלת שנין, במללותהון עם פרעה: ח ואמר יי, למשה ולאהרן למימר: ט ארי ימליל עמכון פרעה למימר, הבו לכון אתא, ותימר לאהרן, סב ית חטרך, ורמי קדם פרעה יהי לתנינא: י ועאל משה ואהרן לות פרעה, ועבדו כן, כמא דפקיד יי, ורמא אהרן ית חטריה, קדם פרעה, וקדם עבדוהי והוה לתנינא: יא וקרא אף פרעה, לחכימיא ולחרשיא, ועבדו אף אנון, חרשי מצרים, בלחשיהון כן: יב ורמו גבר חטריה, והוו לתנינין,

The feather represented *Ma'at,* the central Egyptian value that included the concepts of truth, balance, order, harmony, justice, morality, and law. This was fundamental to Egyptian culture, and it was the task of the Pharaoh to ensure that it prevailed. *Ma'at* means cosmic order. Its absence invites chaos. A Pharaoh whose heart had become heavier than the *Ma'at* feather was not only endangering his own afterlife, but threatening the entire people over whom he ruled with turmoil and disarray.

One of the things the deceased was supposed to do as part of the trial was to make a series of forty-two negative confessions, declaring himself innocent of the kind of sin that would exclude him from Paradise. They included: "I have not done injury to men. I have not oppressed those beneath me. I have not murdered. I have not commanded murder. I have not caused suffering to men." Pharaoh had done these things. If the "heavying" of his heart is an allusion to the Weighing of the Heart ceremony, it allows us to read the story in a new way.

13 staff swallowed up theirs. Pharaoh, nonetheless, was obstinate, and he would not
14 listen to them, just as the LORD had predicted. Then the LORD said to
15 Moshe, "Pharaoh's heart is unyielding. He refuses to send the people forth. So
go to Pharaoh in the morning as he goes out to the water. Place yourself by the
bank of the Nile where you will encounter him, taking in your hand the staff that
16 turned into a snake. Say to him: The LORD, God of the Hebrews, has sent me to
tell you: Send My people forth, so that they may serve Me in the wilderness. So
17 far, you have not listened. This is what the LORD says: This will make it known
to you that I am the LORD. With the staff in my hand I will strike the water in
18 the Nile and it will become blood. The fish in the Nile will die; the Nile will
19 stink and the Egyptians will be unable to drink its water." Then the
LORD said to Moshe, "Tell Aharon: Take your staff and stretch out your hand

רש״י

יד **כָּבֵד.** תַּרְגּוּמוֹ "יַקִּיר" וְלֹא 'אִתְיַקַּר', מִפְּנֵי שֶׁהוּא שֵׁם דָּבָר, כְּמוֹ: "כִּי כָבֵד מִמְּךָ הַדָּבָר" (להלן יח, יח):

טו **הִנֵּה יֹצֵא הַמַּיְמָה.** לִנְקָבָיו, שֶׁהָיָה עוֹשֶׂה עַצְמוֹ אֱלוֹהַּ וְאוֹמֵר שֶׁאֵינוֹ צָרִיךְ לִנְקָבָיו, וּמַשְׁכִּים וְיוֹצֵא לַנִּילוּס וְעוֹשֶׂה שָׁם צְרָכָיו:

טז **עַד כֹּה.** עַד הֵנָּה. וּמִדְרָשׁוֹ, עַד שֶׁתִּשְׁמַע מִמֶּנִּי מַכַּת בְּכוֹרוֹת שֶׁאֶפְתַּח בָּהּ בְּ"כֹה אָמַר ה' כַּחֲצֹת הַלַּיְלָה" וְגוֹ' (להלן יא, ד):

יז **וְנֶהֶפְכוּ לְדָם.** לְפִי שֶׁאֵין גְּשָׁמִים יוֹרְדִים בְּמִצְרַיִם וְנִילוּס עוֹלֶה וּמַשְׁקֶה אֶת הָאָרֶץ וּמִצְרַיִם עוֹבְדִים לַנִּילוּס, לְפִיכָךְ הִלְקָה אֶת יִרְאָתָם וְאַחַר כָּךְ הִלְקָה אוֹתָם:

יח **וְנִלְאוּ מִצְרַיִם.** לְבַקֵּשׁ רְפוּאָה לְמֵי הַיְאוֹר שֶׁיִּהְיוּ רְאוּיִין לִשְׁתּוֹת:

יט **אֱמֹר אֶל אַהֲרֹן.** לְפִי שֶׁהֵגֵן הַיְאוֹר עַל מֹשֶׁה כְּשֶׁנִּשְׁלַךְ לְתוֹכוֹ, לְפִיכָךְ לֹא לָקָה עַל יָדוֹ לֹא בַּדָּם וְלֹא בַּצְפַרְדְּעִים, וְלָקָה עַל יְדֵי אַהֲרֹן:

as five groups of two. The first two, blood and frogs, both emerge from the Nile. The second pair, lice and swarms of insects, are irritants. The third, the deadly epidemic and boils, are bodily conditions, affecting animals then humans. The fourth, hail and locusts, destroy the produce of the field. The fifth pair, darkness and the death of the firstborn, blot out, first light, then life.

The plagues are intended to show Pharaoh and his people the powerlessness of the gods in which they believe. What is at stake in this confrontation is the difference between myth – in which the gods are mere powers, to be tamed, propitiated, or manipulated – and biblical monotheism, in which ethics (justice, compassion, human dignity) constitute the meeting point of God and mankind. The symbolism of these plagues, often lost on us, would have been immediately apparent to the Egyptians.

7:17 **וְנֶהֶפְכוּ לְדָם** *It will become blood* – Again, this may be a reference to Egyptian tradition. A text known as the Admonitions of Ipuwer contains the statement that "the river is blood," one of the symptoms of its vivid description of the collapse of order and the reign of chaos. The Nile was the supreme source of life for ancient Egypt. Its water turning to blood transforms it into a symbol of death. Hence this is not just a wonder but a sign, a symbol. The river that turns to blood is a dramatic enactment of the fact that the Nile, source of life, had become a source of death when male Israelite children were thrown into it to be drowned. That crime, intended to be hidden, is now proclaimed to all in the most graphic way.

The cosmic order is being overturned. Pharaoh, seen as sustainer of that order, is being challenged in his own terms and in his own domain. Pharaohs were known to be capable of rewriting their own history, obliterating the more shameful episodes and aggrandizing their achievements. The plagues are saying, in effect, that there are crimes that cannot be concealed. Nature itself bears witness to the guilt of those who commit crimes against humanity.

יג וַיִּבְלַע מַטֵּה־אַהֲרֹן אֶת־מַטֹּתָם: וַיֶּחֱזַק לֵב פַּרְעֹה וְלֹא שָׁמַע אֲלֵהֶם
יד כַּאֲשֶׁר דִּבֶּר יְהוָה: וַיֹּאמֶר יְהוָה אֶל־מֹשֶׁה כָּבֵד לֵב
טו פַּרְעֹה מֵאֵן לְשַׁלַּח הָעָם: לֵךְ אֶל־פַּרְעֹה בַּבֹּקֶר הִנֵּה יֹצֵא הַמַּיְמָה
וְנִצַּבְתָּ לִקְרָאתוֹ עַל־שְׂפַת הַיְאֹר וְהַמַּטֶּה אֲשֶׁר־נֶהְפַּךְ לְנָחָשׁ תִּקַּח
טז בְּיָדֶךָ: וְאָמַרְתָּ אֵלָיו יְהוָה אֱלֹהֵי הָעִבְרִים שְׁלָחַנִי אֵלֶיךָ לֵאמֹר שַׁלַּח
יז אֶת־עַמִּי וְיַעַבְדֻנִי בַּמִּדְבָּר וְהִנֵּה לֹא־שָׁמַעְתָּ עַד־כֹּה: כֹּה אָמַר יְהוָה
בְּזֹאת תֵּדַע כִּי אֲנִי יְהוָה הִנֵּה אָנֹכִי מַכֶּה ׀ בַּמַּטֶּה אֲשֶׁר־בְּיָדִי עַל־
יח הַמַּיִם אֲשֶׁר בַּיְאֹר וְנֶהֶפְכוּ לְדָם: וְהַדָּגָה אֲשֶׁר־בַּיְאֹר תָּמוּת וּבָאַשׁ
יט הַיְאֹר וְנִלְאוּ מִצְרַיִם לִשְׁתּוֹת מַיִם מִן־הַיְאֹר: וַיֹּאמֶר
יְהוָה אֶל־מֹשֶׁה אֱמֹר אֶל־אַהֲרֹן קַח מַטְּךָ וּנְטֵה־יָדְךָ עַל־מֵימֵי מִצְרַיִם

אונקלוס

וּבְלַע חֻטְרָא דְאַהֲרֹן יָת חֻטְרֵיהוֹן: יג וְאִתַּקַּף לִבָּא דְפַרְעֹה, וְלָא קַבֵּיל מִנְּהוֹן, כְּמָא דְמַלֵּיל יי: יד וַאֲמַר יי לְמֹשֶׁה, יַקִּיר לִבָּא דְפַרְעֹה, סָרֵיב לְשַׁלָּחָא עַמָּא: טו אֵיזִיל לְוָת פַּרְעֹה בְּצַפְרָא, הָא נָפֵיק לְמַיָּא, וְתִתְעַתַּד לְקַדָּמוּתֵיהּ עַל כֵּיף נַהְרָא, וְחֻטְרָא, דְאִתְהֲפֵיךְ לְחִוְיָא תִּסַּב בִּידָךְ: טז וְתֵימַר לֵיהּ, יי, אֱלָהָא דִיהוּדָאֵי שַׁלְחַנִי לְוָתָךְ לְמֵימַר, שַׁלַּח יָת עַמִּי, וְיִפְלְחוּן קֳדָמַי בְּמַדְבְּרָא, וְהָא לָא קַבֵּילְתָּא עַד כְּעַן: יז כִּדְנַן אֲמַר יי, בְּדָא תִדַּע, אֲרֵי אֲנָא יי, הָא אֲנָא מָחֵי בְּחֻטְרָא דִבְידִי, עַל מַיָּא דִבְנַהְרָא וְיִתְהַפְּכוּן לִדְמָא: יח וְנוּנֵי דִבְנַהְרָא, יְמוּתוּן וְיִסְרֵי נַהְרָא, וְיִלְאוֹן מִצְרָאֵי, לְמִשְׁתֵּי מַיָּא מִן נַהְרָא: יט וַאֲמַר יי לְמֹשֶׁה, אֵימַר לְאַהֲרֹן, סַב חֻטְרָךְ וַאֲרֵים יְדָךְ עַל מַיָּא דְמִצְרָאֵי,

THE PLAGUES

The plagues have three aims: to persuade Pharaoh to let the Israelites go, to punish him and his people for their wrongs, and to communicate to Pharaoh and Egypt that there is a supreme power above and beyond all the forces operative in the universe, a power dedicated to justice and human dignity. The demonstration of God's power that is about to follow is as much for the Egyptians as for the Israelites. The Egyptians worship nature, personified as a series of gods. During the plagues, they will see a power higher than nature, capable of overriding their own most powerful gods. This is important for moral and political reasons. Only if there is a power greater than that of the greatest empire can universal human values like the sanctity of life override the will of the ruler. The gods of the ancient world were deifications of power. Since you worship power, God is saying tacitly to the Egyptians, I will show you a greater power. In the plagues, I will be speaking a language you understand.

The basic requirements of morality are universal. They derive from the covenant with Noaḥ, they are written into human nature, and they apply to all nations. An unjust empire may achieve military and architectural greatness, but in the absence of goodness, it will not survive.

The plagues themselves have an underlying structure. The first nine are divided into three groups of three. For the first plague in each triad, Moshe is commanded to confront Pharaoh in the morning in the open, usually by the Nile. For the second, he is commanded to go to Pharaoh in the palace. The third in each group occurs without warning (Rashbam). Another way of categorizing them is to see them

over the waters of Egypt, their rivers, canals, ponds, and reservoirs, and they
will turn into blood. There will be blood throughout Egypt, even inside vessels
20 of wood and of stone." Moshe and Aharon did just as the LORD commanded.
Aharon raised his staff, in full view of Pharaoh and his officials, and struck the
21 water of the Nile, and all the Nile's water turned into blood. The Nile fish died,
and the river stank so that the Egyptians could not drink its water. Throughout
22 the land of Egypt, blood appeared. But the Egyptian magicians did the same
thing by their sorcery. So Pharaoh's heart remained adamant, and he would not
23 listen to them, just as the LORD had predicted. Pharaoh turned and went back
24 into his palace and did not take even this to heart. The Egyptians all dug along
25 the Nile to get drinking water, unable to drink of the waters of the Nile. And
seven days went by after the LORD's striking of the Nile.
26 Then the LORD said to Moshe, "Go to Pharaoh and say to him: This is what
27 the LORD says: Send My people forth, so that they may serve Me. And if you
should refuse to send them forth – I will scourge your land with frogs from
28 end to end. The Nile will teem with frogs. They will come up into your palace,
into your bedroom and up onto your bed, into the houses of your officials and

רש״י

נַהֲרֹתָם. הֵם נְהָרוֹת הַמּוֹשְׁכִים כְּעֵין נְהָרוֹת שֶׁלָּנוּ: **יְאֹרֵיהֶם.** הֵם נְגָרִים וּבְרֵכוֹת הָעֲשׂוּיִם בִּידֵי אָדָם מִשְּׂפַת הַנָּהָר לַשָּׂדוֹת, וְנִילוּס מֵימָיו מִתְבָּרְכִים וְעוֹלֶה דֶּרֶךְ הַיְאוֹרִים וּמַשְׁקֶה הַשָּׂדוֹת: **אַגְמֵיהֶם.** קְווּצַת מַיִם שֶׁאֵינָן נוֹבְעִין וְאֵין מוֹשְׁכִין אֶלָּא עוֹמְדִין בְּמָקוֹם אֶחָד, וְקוֹרִין לוֹ אשטנ״ק: **בְּכָל אֶרֶץ מִצְרַיִם.** אַף בַּמֶּרְחֲצָאוֹת וּבָאַמְבָּטָאוֹת שֶׁבַּבָּתִּים: **וּבָעֵצִים וּבָאֲבָנִים.** מַיִם שֶׁבִּכְלֵי עֵץ וּבִכְלֵי אֶבֶן:

כב **בְּלָטֵיהֶם.** לַחַשׁ שֶׁאוֹמְרִין אוֹתוֹ בַּלָּט וּבַחֲשַׁאי. רַבּוֹתֵינוּ אָמְרוּ: 'בְּלָטֵיהֶם' – מַעֲשֵׂה שֵׁדִים, 'בְּלַהֲטֵיהֶם' – מַעֲשֵׂה כְּשָׁפִים: **וַיֶּחֱזַק לֵב פַּרְעֹה.** לוֹמַר עַל יְדֵי מְכַשְּׁפוּת אַתֶּם עוֹשִׂים כֵּן; תֶּבֶן אַתֶּם מַכְנִיסִים לְעֲפְרַיִם, עִיר שֶׁכֻּלָּהּ תֶּבֶן?! אַף אַתֶּם מְבִיאִין מְכַשְּׁפוּת לְמִצְרַיִם שֶׁכֻּלָּהּ כְּשָׁפִים?!:

כג **גַּם לָזֹאת.** לְמוֹפֵת הַמַּטֶּה שֶׁנֶּהְפַּךְ לְתַנִּין, וְלֹא לָזֶה שֶׁל דָּם:

כה **וַיִּמָּלֵא.** מִנְיַן שִׁבְעַת יָמִים שֶׁלֹּא שָׁב הַיְאוֹר לְקַדְמוּתוֹ, שֶׁהָיְתָה הַמַּכָּה מְשַׁמֶּשֶׁת רְבִיעַ חֹדֶשׁ, וּשְׁלֹשָׁה חֲלָקִים הָיָה מֵעִיד וּמַתְרֶה בָּהֶם:

כז **וְאִם מָאֵן אַתָּה.** וְאִם סָרְבָן אַתָּה. 'מָאֵן' כְּמוֹ מְמָאֵן, מְסָרֵב, אֶלָּא כִּנּוּי הָאָדָם עַל שֵׁם הַמִּפְעָל, כְּמוֹ: "שָׁלֵו" (איוב טז, יב), "וְשֹׁקֵט" (ירמיה מח, יא), "סַר וְזָעֵף" (מלכים א׳ כ, מג): **נֹגֵף אֶת כָּל גְּבוּלְךָ.** מַכֶּה. וְכֵן כָּל לְשׁוֹן מַגֵּפָה אֵינוֹ לְשׁוֹן מִיתָה אֶלָּא לְשׁוֹן מַכָּה, וְכֵן: "וְנָגְפוּ אִשָּׁה הָרָה" (להלן כא, כב) אֵינוֹ מִיתָה, וְכֵן: "וּבְטֶרֶם יִתְנַגְּפוּ רַגְלֵיכֶם" (ירמיה יג, טז), "פֶּן תִּגֹּף בָּאֶבֶן רַגְלֶךָ" (תהלים צא, יב), "וּלְאֶבֶן נֶגֶף" (ישעיה ח, יד):

כח **וְעָלוּ.** מִן הַיְאוֹר: **בְּבֵיתֶךָ.** וְאַחַר כָּךְ "בְּבֵית עֲבָדֶיךָ", הוּא הִתְחִיל בָּעֵצָה תְּחִלָּה – "וַיֹּאמֶר אֶל עַמּוֹ" (לעיל א, ט) וּמִמֶּנּוּ הִתְחִילָה הַפֻּרְעָנוּת:

demonstrate power without asking whether its use improves or harms the human condition. "I can" prevails over "I should."

7:27 הִנֵּה אָנֹכִי נֹגֵף אֶת־כָּל־גְּבוּלְךָ בַּצְפַרְדְּעִים *I will scourge your land with frogs* – The reference is probably to the frog goddess Heqet, Egyptian goddess of life, birth, and fertility, also associated with midwives. There may be a suggestion here of Pharaoh's first instructions to the midwives, to kill the male Israelite children at birth. The frogs would not only have been a source of irritation; they would have been an extension of the guilt of the river turning into blood, the sign now moving inland and coming close to the people. Again, the Egyptian magicians, obsessed with demonstrating their own power, are portrayed ironically. Far from making the frogs go away, they deepen the curse and produce even more.

עַל־נַהֲרֹתָם ׀ עַל־יְאֹרֵיהֶם וְעַל־אַגְמֵיהֶם וְעַל כָּל־מִקְוֵה מֵימֵיהֶם
כ וְיִהְיוּ־דָם וְהָיָה דָם בְּכָל־אֶרֶץ מִצְרַיִם וּבָעֵצִים וּבָאֲבָנִים: וַיַּעֲשׂוּ־כֵן
מֹשֶׁה וְאַהֲרֹן כַּאֲשֶׁר ׀ צִוָּה יהוה וַיָּרֶם בַּמַּטֶּה וַיַּךְ אֶת־הַמַּיִם אֲשֶׁר
בַּיְאֹר לְעֵינֵי פַרְעֹה וּלְעֵינֵי עֲבָדָיו וַיֵּהָפְכוּ כָּל־הַמַּיִם אֲשֶׁר־בַּיְאֹר לְדָם:
כא וְהַדָּגָה אֲשֶׁר־בַּיְאֹר מֵתָה וַיִּבְאַשׁ הַיְאֹר וְלֹא־יָכְלוּ מִצְרַיִם לִשְׁתּוֹת
כב מַיִם מִן־הַיְאֹר וַיְהִי הַדָּם בְּכָל־אֶרֶץ מִצְרָיִם: וַיַּעֲשׂוּ־כֵן חַרְטֻמֵּי מִצְרַיִם
כג בְּלָטֵיהֶם וַיֶּחֱזַק לֵב־פַּרְעֹה וְלֹא־שָׁמַע אֲלֵהֶם כַּאֲשֶׁר דִּבֶּר יהוה: וַיִּפֶן
כד פַּרְעֹה וַיָּבֹא אֶל־בֵּיתוֹ וְלֹא־שָׁת לִבּוֹ גַּם־לָזֹאת: וַיַּחְפְּרוּ כָל־מִצְרַיִם
כה סְבִיבֹת הַיְאֹר מַיִם לִשְׁתּוֹת כִּי לֹא יָכְלוּ לִשְׁתֹּת מִמֵּימֵי הַיְאֹר: וַיִּמָּלֵא
שִׁבְעַת יָמִים אַחֲרֵי הַכּוֹת־יהוה אֶת־הַיְאֹר:
כו וַיֹּאמֶר יהוה אֶל־מֹשֶׁה בֹּא אֶל־פַּרְעֹה וְאָמַרְתָּ אֵלָיו כֹּה אָמַר יהוה
כז שַׁלַּח אֶת־עַמִּי וְיַעַבְדֻנִי: וְאִם־מָאֵן אַתָּה לְשַׁלֵּחַ הִנֵּה אָנֹכִי נֹגֵף אֶת־כָּל־
כח גְּבוּלְךָ בַּצְפַרְדְּעִים: וְשָׁרַץ הַיְאֹר צְפַרְדְּעִים וְעָלוּ וּבָאוּ בְּבֵיתֶךָ וּבַחֲדַר
מִשְׁכָּבְךָ וְעַל־מִטָּתֶךָ וּבְבֵית עֲבָדֶיךָ וּבְעַמֶּךָ וּבְתַנּוּרֶיךָ וּבְמִשְׁאֲרוֹתֶיךָ:

אונקלוס

עַל נַהֲרֵיהוֹן עַל אֲרִתֵּיהוֹן וְעַל אַגְמֵיהוֹן, וְעַל כָּל בֵּית כְּנִישַׁת מֵימֵיהוֹן וִיהוֹן דְּמָא, וִיהֵי דְמָא בְּכָל אַרְעָא דְּמִצְרַיִם, וּבְמָנֵי אָעָא וּבְמָנֵי אַבְנָא: כ וַעֲבַדוּ כֵן מֹשֶׁה וְאַהֲרֹן, כְּמָא דְּפַקֵּיד יי, וַאֲרֵים בְּחֻטְרָא וּמְחָא יָת מַיָּא דִּבְנַהֲרָא, לְעֵינֵי פַרְעֹה, וּלְעֵינֵי עַבְדּוֹהִי, וְאִתְהַפִיכוּ, כָּל מַיָּא דִּבְנַהֲרָא לִדְמָא: כא וְנוּנֵי דִּבְנַהֲרָא מִיתוּ וּסְרִי נַהֲרָא, וְלָא יְכִילוּ מִצְרָאֵי, לְמִשְׁתֵּי מַיָּא מִן נַהֲרָא, וַהֲוָה דְמָא בְּכָל אַרְעָא דְמִצְרָיִם: כב וַעֲבַדוּ כֵן, חָרָשֵׁי מִצְרַיִם בְּלַחֲשֵׁיהוֹן, וְאִתַּקַּף לִבָּא דְפַרְעֹה וְלָא קַבֵּיל מִנְּהוֹן, כְּמָא דְּמַלֵּיל יי: כג וְאִתְפְּנִי פַרְעֹה, וְעָאל לְבֵיתֵיהּ, וְלָא שַׁוִּי לִבֵּיהּ אַף לְדָא: כד וַחֲפַרוּ כָל מִצְרָאֵי, סַחְרָנוּת נַהֲרָא מַיָּא לְמִשְׁתֵּי, אֲרֵי לָא יְכִילוּ לְמִשְׁתֵּי, מִמַּיָּא דִּבְנַהֲרָא: כה וּשְׁלִימוּ שִׁבְעָא יוֹמִין, בָּתַר דִּמְחָא יי יָת נַהֲרָא: כו וַאֲמַר יי לְמֹשֶׁה, עוֹל לְוָת פַּרְעֹה, וְתֵימַר לֵיהּ, כִּדְנָן אֲמַר יי, שַׁלַּח יָת עַמִּי וְיִפְלְחוּן קֳדָמַי: כז וְאִם מְסָרֵיב אַתְּ לְשַׁלָּחָא, הָא אֲנָא, מָחֵי, יָת כָּל תְּחוּמָךְ בְּעֻרְדְּעָנַיָּא: כח וְיִרְבֵּי נַהֲרָא עֻרְדְּעָנַיָּא, וְיִסְקוּן וְיֵיעֲלוּן בְּבֵיתָךְ, וּבְאִדְּרוֹן בֵּית מִשְׁכְּבָךְ וְעַל עַרְסָךְ, וּבְבֵית עַבְדָּךְ וּבְעַמָּךְ, וּבְתַנּוּרָךְ וּבְאָצְוָתָךְ:

7:22 וַיַּעֲשׂוּ־כֵן חַרְטֻמֵּי מִצְרַיִם בְּלָטֵיהֶם *But the Egyptian magicians did the same thing by their sorcery* – Magic was integral to the culture of ancient Egypt, and magicians were an important class within its society, thought to be able to cure illness, remove bad luck, and curse enemies and opponents. A bitterly ironic note is being struck here. The magicians, intent on demonstrating their skills, are oblivious to the fact that they are making the situation worse, not better. Constructive magic would have been to turn the blood back into water.

This is a classic example of the human tendency to

29 of all your people, into your ovens and your kneading pans. The frogs shall
8 1 climb up onto you and your people and all your officials." The LORD said to
Moshe, "Speak to Aharon: Stretch out your hand that holds your staff over the
rivers, the canals, and the pools, and cause frogs to climb up and out onto the
2 land of Egypt." So Aharon stretched out his hand over the waters of Egypt,
3 and frogs climbed up and covered the Egyptian land. But the magicians used
their sorcery and did the same, making frogs climb up over the land of Egypt.
4 Then Pharaoh called for Moshe and Aharon and said, "Pray to the LORD to
take the frogs away from me and from my people, and I will send your people
5 forth to sacrifice to the LORD." Moshe said to Pharaoh, "Gloat over me: you
name the time when I should pray that the frogs be removed, for you and your
officials, and your people, from you and your homes, remaining only in the
6 Nile." "Tomorrow," he replied. Moshe said, "It will be as you say. Then you will
7 know that there is none like the LORD our God. The frogs will depart from you HAMISHI

רש"י

כט **וּבְכָה וּבְעַמְּךָ.** בְּתוֹךְ מֵעֵיהֶם נִכְנָסִין וּמְקַרְקְרִין:

ח ב **וַתַּעַל הַצְּפַרְדֵּעַ.** צְפַרְדֵּעַ אַחַת הָיְתָה וְהָיוּ מַכִּין אוֹתָהּ וְהִיא מַתֶּזֶת נְחִילִים נְחִילִים, זֶהוּ מִדְרָשׁוֹ. וּפְשׁוּטוֹ יֵשׁ לוֹמַר, שֶׁרוֹץ הַצְּפַרְדְּעִים קוֹרֵא לְשׁוֹן יְחִידוּת. וְכֵן: "וַתְּהִי הַכִּנָּם" (להלן פסוק יד) הָרְחִישָׁה, פדוליר"א בְּלַעַז, וְאַף "וַתַּעַל הַצְּפַרְדֵּעַ" גרינוליי"רא בְּלַעַז:

ה **הִתְפָּאֵר עָלַי.** כְּמוֹ: "הֲיִתְפָּאֵר הַגַּרְזֶן עַל הַחֹצֵב בּוֹ" (ישעיה י, טו), מִשְׁתַּבֵּחַ לוֹמַר: אֲנִי גָּדוֹל מִמְּךָ. ונטי"ר בְּלַעַז. וְכֵן "הִתְפָּאֵר עָלַי", הִשְׁתַּבַּח לְהִתְחַכֵּם וְלִשְׁאֹל דָּבָר גָּדוֹל וְלוֹמַר שֶׁלֹּא אוּכַל לַעֲשׂוֹתוֹ: **לְמָתַי אַעְתִּיר לְךָ.** אֶת אֲשֶׁר אַעְתִּיר לְךָ הַיּוֹם עַל הַכְרָתַת הַצְּפַרְדְּעִים, לְמָתַי תִּרְצֶה שֶׁיִּכָּרְתוּ, וְתִרְאֶה אִם אֲשַׁלֵּם דְּבָרַי לַמּוֹעֵד שֶׁתִּקְבַּע לִי. אִלּוּ נֶאֱמַר 'מָתַי אַעְתִּיר', הָיָה מַשְׁמָע: מָתַי אֶתְפַּלֵּל? עַכְשָׁיו שֶׁנֶּאֱמַר 'לְמָתַי', אֲנִי הַיּוֹם אֶתְפַּלֵּל עָלֶיךָ שֶׁיִּכָּרְתוּ הַצְּפַרְדְּעִים לַזְּמַן שֶׁתִּקְבַּע לִי, אֱמֹר לְאֵיזֶה יוֹם תִּרְצֶה שֶׁיִּכָּרְתוּ. "אַעְתִּיר", "הַעְתִּירוּ", "וְהַעְתַּרְתִּי", וְלֹא נֶאֱמַר: 'אֶעְתַּר', 'עִתְרוּ', 'וְעָתַרְתִּי', מִפְּנֵי שֶׁכָּל לְשׁוֹן 'עֶתֶר' הַרְבּוֹת פֶּלֶל הוּא, וְכַאֲשֶׁר יֵאָמֵר: הַרְבּוּ, אַרְבֶּה, וְהִרְבֵּיתִי, לְשׁוֹן מַפְעִיל, כֵּן יֵאָמֵר: הַעְתִּירוּ, אַעְתִּיר, אַעְתִּיר דְּבָרִים, וְאָב לְכֻלָּם: "וְהַעְתַּרְתֶּם עָלַי דִּבְרֵיכֶם" (יחזקאל לה, יג), הִרְבֵּיתֶם:

ו **וַיֹּאמֶר לְמָחָר.** הִתְפַּלֵּל הַיּוֹם שֶׁיִּכָּרְתוּ לְמָחָר:

8:6 **לְמַעַן תֵּדַע** *Then you will know* – Note again, as throughout the story, the emphasis is on the impression the plagues make on the Egyptians, not the Israelites. As far as the Israelites are concerned, the only significant plague is the last one, the death of the firstborn. That is how matters are framed at the very beginning of Moshe's mission, when God tells him to tell Pharaoh, "Israel is My son, My firstborn. I have told you: Send forth My son, so that he may serve Me. If you refuse to let him go, I will kill your son, your firstborn" (Ex. 4:22). That plague happens so that Pharaoh and the Egyptians will set the Israelites free. The other plagues happen so that the Egyptians should know that "there is none like the LORD our God."

offers Pharaoh the chance to say: "I ended the plague, specifying exactly when it would end." Sometimes a face-saving formula is part of conflict resolution.

In a slightly different reading, Moshe, apparently on his own initiative, "gives Pharaoh the honor" of naming a specific time when the plague will stop, precisely because the river turning red, and an attack of frogs, were not unknown in Egypt, albeit on a far lower scale. It is thus more than possible that Pharaoh, his court, and the Egyptians as a whole might regard these things as freak natural occurrences. Moshe wants to show Pharaoh a clear sign that they are nothing of the kind, that they have been sent by God, who is supremely powerful even in Egypt, where other gods are believed to rule.

כט וּבְכָה וּבְעַמְּךָ וּבְכָל־עֲבָדֶיךָ יַעֲלוּ הַצְפַרְדְּעִים: ח א וַיֹּאמֶר יהוה אֶל־מֹשֶׁה
אֱמֹר אֶל־אַהֲרֹן נְטֵה אֶת־יָדְךָ בְּמַטֶּךָ עַל־הַנְּהָרֹת עַל־הַיְאֹרִים וְעַל־
ב הָאֲגַמִּים וְהַעַל אֶת־הַצְפַרְדְּעִים עַל־אֶרֶץ מִצְרָיִם: וַיֵּט אַהֲרֹן אֶת־יָדוֹ
ג עַל מֵימֵי מִצְרָיִם וַתַּעַל הַצְפַרְדֵּעַ וַתְּכַס אֶת־אֶרֶץ מִצְרָיִם: וַיַּעֲשׂוּ־כֵן
ד הַחַרְטֻמִּים בְּלָטֵיהֶם וַיַּעֲלוּ אֶת־הַצְפַרְדְּעִים עַל־אֶרֶץ מִצְרָיִם: וַיִּקְרָא
פַרְעֹה לְמֹשֶׁה וּלְאַהֲרֹן וַיֹּאמֶר הַעְתִּירוּ אֶל־יהוה וְיָסֵר הַצְפַרְדְּעִים
ה מִמֶּנִּי וּמֵעַמִּי וַאֲשַׁלְּחָה אֶת־הָעָם וְיִזְבְּחוּ לַיהוה: וַיֹּאמֶר מֹשֶׁה לְפַרְעֹה
הִתְפָּאֵר עָלַי לְמָתַי ׀ אַעְתִּיר לְךָ וְלַעֲבָדֶיךָ וּלְעַמְּךָ לְהַכְרִית הַצְפַרְדְּעִים
ו מִמְּךָ וּמִבָּתֶּיךָ רַק בַּיְאֹר תִּשָּׁאַרְנָה: וַיֹּאמֶר לְמָחָר וַיֹּאמֶר כִּדְבָרְךָ
ז לְמַעַן תֵּדַע כִּי־אֵין כַּיהוה אֱלֹהֵינוּ: וְסָרוּ הַצְפַרְדְּעִים מִמְּךָ וּמִבָּתֶּיךָ חמישי

אונקלוס

כט וּבָךְ וּבְעַמָּךְ וּבְכָל עַבְדָּךְ, יִסְקוּן עֻרְדְּעָנַיָּא: ח א וַאֲמַר יי לְמשֶׁה, אֵימַר לְאַהֲרֹן, אֲרֵים יָת יְדָךְ בְּחֻטְרָךְ, עַל נַהֲרַיָּא, עַל אָרְתַיָּא וְעַל אַגְמַיָּא, וְאַסֵּיק יָת עֻרְדְּעָנַיָּא עַל אַרְעָא דְמִצְרָיִם: ב וַאֲרֵים אַהֲרֹן יָת יְדֵיהּ, עַל מַיָּא דְמִצְרָאֵי, וּסְלִיקוּ עֻרְדְּעָנַיָּא, וַחֲפוֹ יָת אַרְעָא דְמִצְרָיִם: ג וַעֲבַדוּ כֵן חָרָשַׁיָּא בְּלַחֲשֵׁיהוֹן, וְאַסִּיקוּ יָת עֻרְדְּעָנַיָּא עַל אַרְעָא דְמִצְרָיִם: ד וּקְרָא פַרְעֹה לְמשֶׁה וּלְאַהֲרֹן, וַאֲמַר צַלּוֹ קֳדָם יי, וְיַעְדֵּי עֻרְדְּעָנַיָּא, מִנִּי וּמֵעַמִּי, וַאֲשַׁלַּח יָת עַמָּא, וְיִדְבְּחוּן קֳדָם יי: ה וַאֲמַר משֶׁה לְפַרְעֹה שְׁאַל לָךְ גְּבוּרָא הַב לָךְ זְמָן, לְאֵמָתַי אֲצַלֵּי עֲלָךְ, וְעַל עַבְדָּךְ וְעַל עַמָּךְ, לְשֵׁיצָאָה עֻרְדְּעָנַיָּא, מִנָּךְ וּמִבָּתָּךְ, לְחוֹד דִּבְנַהֲרָא יִשְׁתְּאֲרוּן: ו וַאֲמַר לִמְחַר, וַאֲמַר כְּפִתְגָמָךְ, בְּדִיל דְּתִדַּע, אֲרֵי לֵית כַּיי אֱלָהַנָא: ז וְיַעְדּוּן עֻרְדְּעָנַיָּא, מִנָּךְ וּמִבָּתָּךְ,

8:4 הַעְתִּירוּ אֶל־יהוה *Pray to the Lord* – This is the first time Pharaoh asks Moshe and Aharon to intervene on his behalf with God. Note that Pharaoh now uses the four-letter name of God, when earlier he said, "Who is this Lord…? I do not know the Lord." He uses the name twice, as if to emphasize the point: he now knows the Lord. This seems to be a momentary act of contrition on his part, but it does not last for long.

8:4 וַאֲשַׁלְּחָה אֶת־הָעָם *And I will send your people forth* – This is the first of what will be many instances of Pharaoh making a promise and then failing to keep it. Recall that this entire episode began with God saying that He was going to reveal Himself in His attribute of fulfilling covenantal promises (see ch. 6, "I am the Lord"). God keeps His word and we must keep ours. That is the essence of covenant. In politics, power is secondary. Fidelity, honoring one's word, keeping one's commitments, is primary. Without fidelity, there is no trust. A society without trust can only be maintained by the use of force. In the case of Egypt of the nineteenth dynasty, it resulted in a society in which the most important single institution was the army. This is not freedom but oppression.

8:5 הִתְפָּאֵר עָלַי *Gloat over me* – Alternatively, "I give you the honor." Moshe is offering Pharaoh a face-saving formula. He recognizes that one of the difficulties Pharaoh would confront in conceding the Israelites' request is a loss of face before his councilors, court, and people. A mighty emperor finds it difficult to capitulate to slaves. Moshe therefore

and from your homes, your officials, all your people. They will only remain in
8 the Nile." Moshe and Aharon departed Pharaoh's presence, and Moshe cried
9 out to the LORD about the frogs He had brought upon Pharaoh. The LORD did
10 as Moshe said, and the frogs in the houses, courtyards, and fields died; they
11 gathered them up into heaping piles, and the stench filled the whole land. But
when Pharaoh saw that respite had come, he hardened his heart and would
12 not listen, just as the LORD had predicted. Then the LORD said to
Moshe, "Tell Aharon: Extend your staff and strike the dust of the earth; all
13 over Egypt it will be transformed into lice." They did so. Aharon extended the
hand that held his staff and struck the dust of the earth, and suddenly there
were lice on the people, on the animals. The dust of the earth was turned to
14 lice all across Egypt. The magicians tried to produce lice with their sorcery,
but they could not. Meanwhile the lice still infested people and animals alike.
15 "This," the magicians told Pharaoh, "is the finger of God." But Pharaoh's heart
was toughened, and – as the LORD had predicted – he would not listen to

רש"י

ח **וַיֵּצֵא... וַיִּצְעַק.** מִיָּד, שֶׁיִּכָּרְתוּ לְמָחָר:

י **חֳמָרִם חֳמָרִם.** צִבּוּרִים צִבּוּרִים, כְּתַרְגּוּמוֹ "דְּגוֹרִין", גַּלִּין:

יא **וְהַכְבֵּד אֶת לִבּוֹ.** לְשׁוֹן פָּעוֹל הוּא, "הָלֵךְ הָלֹךְ" (ירמיה מא, ו), וְכֵן: "וְהַכּוֹת אֶת מוֹאָב" (מלכים ב' ג, כד), "וְשָׁאוֹל לוֹ בֵּאלֹהִים" (שמואל א' כב, יג), "הַכֵּה וּפָצֹעַ" (מלכים א' כ, לז): **כַּאֲשֶׁר דִּבֶּר ה'.** וְהֵיכָן דִּבֶּר? "וְלֹא יִשְׁמַע אֲלֵכֶם פַּרְעֹה" (לעיל ז, ד):

יב **אֱמֹר אֶל אַהֲרֹן.** לֹא הֶעָפָר כְּדַי לִלְקוֹת עַל יְדֵי מֹשֶׁה, לְפִי שֶׁהֵגֵן עָלָיו כְּשֶׁהָרַג אֶת הַמִּצְרִי וַיִּטְמְנֵהוּ בַּחוֹל (לעיל ב, יב), וְלָקָה עַל יְדֵי אַהֲרֹן:

יג **וַתְּהִי הַכִּנָּם.** הָרְחִישָׁה, פדולייר"א בְּלַעַ"ז:

יד **לְהוֹצִיא אֶת הַכִּנִּים.** לְבָרְאתָם מִמָּקוֹם אַחֵר: **וְלֹא יָכֹלוּ.** שֶׁאֵין הַשֵּׁד שׁוֹלֵט עַל בְּרִיָּה פְּחוּתָה מִכַּשְּׂעוֹרָה:

טו **אֶצְבַּע אֱלֹהִים הִוא.** מַכָּה זוֹ אֵינָהּ עַל יְדֵי כְשָׁפִים, מֵאֵת הַמָּקוֹם הִיא:

8:10 **וַתִּבְאַשׁ הָאָרֶץ** *The stench filled the whole land* – This graphic description is intended to give us a sense of what Egypt looks and feels like at this moment. You can smell decay and death everywhere. The fish have died. Now the frogs have died. At least some of the people may be wondering: are we next?

THE FINGER OF GOD

In a sense, this is the first appearance in the Torah of an idea, surprisingly persistent in religious thinking even today, called "the god of the gaps." This holds that a miracle is something for which we cannot yet find a scientific explanation. Science is natural; religion is supernatural. In the magicians' terms – what magicians (or technocrats) cannot reproduce must be the result of divine intervention. This approach leads inevitably to the conclusion that religion and science are opposed. The more we can explain scientifically or control technologically, the less need we have for faith. As the scope of science expands, the place of God progressively diminishes to a vanishing point.

What the Torah is intimating here is that this is a pagan mode of thought, not a Jewish one. The Egyptians admit that Moshe and Aharon are genuine prophets when they perform wonders beyond the scope of their own magic. But this is not why we believe in Moshe and Aharon. On this, Rambam (*Hilkhot Yesodei HaTorah* 8:1) is unequivocal. The

ח וּמֵעֲבָדֶיךָ וּמֵעַמֶּךָ רַק בַּיְאֹר תִּשָּׁאַרְנָה׃ וַיֵּצֵא מֹשֶׁה וְאַהֲרֹן מֵעִם פַּרְעֹה
ט וַיִּצְעַק מֹשֶׁה אֶל־יְהוָה עַל־דְּבַר הַצְפַרְדְּעִים אֲשֶׁר־שָׂם לְפַרְעֹה׃ וַיַּעַשׂ
יְהוָה כִּדְבַר מֹשֶׁה וַיָּמֻתוּ הַצְפַרְדְּעִים מִן־הַבָּתִּים מִן־הַחֲצֵרֹת וּמִן־
יא הַשָּׂדֹת׃ וַיִּצְבְּרוּ אֹתָם חֳמָרִם חֳמָרִם וַתִּבְאַשׁ הָאָרֶץ׃ וַיַּרְא פַּרְעֹה
כִּי הָיְתָה הָרְוָחָה וְהַכְבֵּד אֶת־לִבּוֹ וְלֹא שָׁמַע אֲלֵהֶם כַּאֲשֶׁר דִּבֶּר
יב יְהוָה׃ וַיֹּאמֶר יְהוָה אֶל־מֹשֶׁה אֱמֹר אֶל־אַהֲרֹן נְטֵה אֶת־
יג מַטְּךָ וְהַךְ אֶת־עֲפַר הָאָרֶץ וְהָיָה לְכִנִּם בְּכָל־אֶרֶץ מִצְרָיִם׃ וַיַּעֲשׂוּ־כֵן
וַיֵּט אַהֲרֹן אֶת־יָדוֹ בְמַטֵּהוּ וַיַּךְ אֶת־עֲפַר הָאָרֶץ וַתְּהִי הַכִּנָּם בָּאָדָם
יד וּבַבְּהֵמָה כָּל־עֲפַר הָאָרֶץ הָיָה כִנִּים בְּכָל־אֶרֶץ מִצְרָיִם׃ וַיַּעֲשׂוּ־כֵן
הַחַרְטֻמִּים בְּלָטֵיהֶם לְהוֹצִיא אֶת־הַכִּנִּים וְלֹא יָכֹלוּ וַתְּהִי הַכִּנָּם בָּאָדָם
טו וּבַבְּהֵמָה׃ וַיֹּאמְרוּ הַחַרְטֻמִּם אֶל־פַּרְעֹה אֶצְבַּע אֱלֹהִים הִוא וַיֶּחֱזַק

אונקלוס

וּמֵעַבְדָּךְ וּמֵעַמָּךְ, לְחוֹד דִּבְנַהְרָא יִשְׁתְּאֲרָן: ח וּנְפַק מֹשֶׁה, וְאַהֲרֹן מִלְּוָת פַּרְעֹה, וְצַלִּי מֹשֶׁה קֳדָם יי, עַל עֵיסַק עֻרְדְּעָנַיָּא דְּשַׁוִּי לְפַרְעֹה: ט וַעֲבַד יי כְּפִתְגָּמָא דְּמֹשֶׁה, וּמִיתוּ עֻרְדְּעָנַיָּא, מִן בָּתַּיָּא מִן דָּרָתָא וּמִן חַקְלָתָא: י וּכְנַשׁוּ יָתְהוֹן דְּגוֹרִין דְּגוֹרִין, וּסְרִיאוּ עַל אַרְעָא: יא וַחֲזָא פַּרְעֹה, אֲרֵי הֲוָת רַוְחָתָא, וְיַקַּר יָת לִבֵּיהּ, וְלָא קַבֵּיל מִנְּהוֹן, כְּמָא דְּמַלֵּיל יי: יב וַאֲמַר יי לְמֹשֶׁה, אֵימַר לְאַהֲרֹן, אֲרֵים יָת חֻטְרָךְ, וּמְחִי יָת עַפְרָא דְּאַרְעָא, וִיהֵי לְקַלְמְתָא בְּכָל אַרְעָא דְּמִצְרָיִם: יג וַעֲבַדוּ כֵן, וַאֲרֵים אַהֲרֹן יָת יְדֵיהּ בְּחֻטְרֵיהּ וּמְחָא יָת עַפְרָא דְּאַרְעָא, וַהֲוָת קַלְמְתָא, בֶּאֱנָשָׁא וּבִבְעִירָא, כָּל עַפְרָא דְּאַרְעָא, הֲוָת קַלְמְתָא בְּכָל אַרְעָא דְּמִצְרָיִם: יד וַעֲבַדוּ כֵן חָרָשַׁיָּא בְּלַחֲשֵׁיהוֹן, לְאַפָּקָא יָת קַלְמְתָא וְלָא יְכִילוּ, וַהֲוָת קַלְמְתָא, בֶּאֱנָשָׁא וּבִבְעִירָא: טו וַאֲמַרוּ חָרָשַׁיָּא לְפַרְעֹה, מַחָא מִן קֳדָם יי הִיא, וְאִתַּקַּף

Israel does not need miracles to learn that slavery is wrong or that power corrupts. They have learned it by being a powerless minority in a land not theirs. Egypt, however, does. And indeed the story of the exodus is to become a source of inspiration to many powerless minorities in the course of the centuries, and to lead them to fight and often to win their freedom. It is important for the Egyptians to understand that their system of moral order is showing fatal signs of self-contradiction, and that what they have thought of as strength is in fact weakness. One of the consequences of monotheism is that if there is a single God who is sovereign everywhere, then there is a single moral domain whose fundamental principles hold everywhere. That is not necessarily true of all moral principles, but it is certainly true of justice.

8:10 וַיִּצְבְּרוּ אֹתָם *They gathered them up* – The same root is used in Genesis (*tz-b-r*) to describe how the Egyptians, under Yosef's tutelage, gathered up grain to store for use during the years of famine (Gen. 41:35). This fine use of intertextuality highlights the fact that Egypt availed itself of Yosef's wisdom to avoid catastrophe, but then forgot Yosef and persecuted his people, thus creating catastrophe.

16 them. Then the LORD said to Moshe, "Rise up early in the morning
and confront Pharaoh as he goes out to the water; tell him: This is what the
17 LORD says: Send My people forth, so that they may serve Me. If you refuse to
send them forth, I will send swarms of insects onto you, your officials, your
people, and your houses. The Egyptians' houses will be filled with swarms of
18 insects; the ground they stand upon will be covered by them. On that day, I
will set the land of Goshen, where My people live, apart – there, there will
be no swarms – and then you will know that I am the LORD, here on earth.
19 Between My people and yours I will mark out a separation; tomorrow, this sign SHISHI
20 will come to be." The LORD did so. Great swarms of insects infested Pharaoh's

רש״י

כַּאֲשֶׁר דִּבֶּר ה׳. ״וְלֹא יִשְׁמַע אֲלֵכֶם פַּרְעֹה״ (לעיל ז, ד):

יז **מַשְׁלִיחַ בְּךָ.** מְגָרֶה בְּךָ, וְכֵן: ״וְשֶׁן בְּהֵמֹת אֲשַׁלַּח בָּם״ (דברים לב, כד) לְשׁוֹן שִׁסּוּי, אינציטיי״ר בְּלַעַז: **אֶת הֶעָרֹב.** כָּל מִינֵי חַיּוֹת רָעוֹת וּנְחָשִׁים וְעַקְרַבִּים בְּעִרְבּוּבְיָא, וְהָיוּ מַשְׁחִיתִים בָּהֶם. וְיֵשׁ טַעַם בַּדָּבָר בָּאַגָּדָה בְּכָל מַכָּה וּמַכָּה לָמָּה זוֹ וְלָמָּה זוֹ: בְּטַכְסִיסֵי מִלְחֲמוֹת מְלָכִים בָּא עֲלֵיהֶם, כְּסֵדֶר מַלְכוּת כְּשֶׁצָּרָה עַל עִיר; בַּתְּחִלָּה מְקַלְקֵל מַעְיְנוֹתֶיהָ, וְאַחַר כָּךְ תּוֹקֵעַ עֲלֵיהֶם וּמְרִיעִים בַּשּׁוֹפָרוֹת לְיָרְאָם וּלְבַהֲלָם, וְכֵן הַצְּפַרְדְּעִים מְקַרְקְרִים וְהוֹמִים וְכוּ׳, כִּדְאִיתָא בְּמִדְרַשׁ רַבִּי תַּנְחוּמָא (כא ד):

יח **וְהִפְלֵיתִי.** וְהִפְרַשְׁתִּי, וְכֵן: ״וְהִפְלָה ה׳״ (להלן ט, ד), וְכֵן: ״לֹא נִפְלֵאת הִוא מִמְּךָ״ (דברים ל, יא), לֹא מֻבְדֶּלֶת וּמֻפְרֶשֶׁת הִיא מִמְּךָ: **לְמַעַן תֵּדַע כִּי אֲנִי ה׳ בְּקֶרֶב הָאָרֶץ.** אַף עַל פִּי שֶׁשְּׁכִינָתִי בַּשָּׁמַיִם גְּזֵרָתִי מִתְקַיֶּמֶת בַּתַּחְתּוֹנִים:

יט **וְשַׂמְתִּי פְדֻת.** שֶׁיַּבְדִּיל ״בֵּין עַמִּי וּבֵין עַמֶּךָ״:

the modern world, such as John Locke, was the difference between liberty and license. Letting the people go – escaping tyranny – was not in and of itself a prelude to freedom. The key distinction throughout the exodus narrative is not between slavery and freedom but between servitude to a human ruler and service to God, creator of all. It is the second way that honors humanity, because it involves acknowledging as our sovereign the One who created each of us in His image.

Thus ends the first cycle of three plagues. The effect has been to move from Egypt's central symbol, the Nile, to homes throughout the land in the form of frogs, to something as tiny and almost invisible as lice. The sense of some large assault on the people and the land has become more and more pervasive as if they were harbingers of some terrible judgment.

8:17 **הֶעָרֹב** *Swarms of insects* – Others read "wild animals." However, the reading of the plague as insects accords better with the parallelism of the plague of lice, and makes more sense in terms of the Torah's description of "houses being filled" with them.

8:18 **כִּי אֲנִי יהוה בְּקֶרֶב הָאָרֶץ** *That I am the LORD, here on earth* – Among the most serious enablers of evil is the idea that no one sees what we are doing, that there is no ultimate justice in the world, that God is distant. This plague is meant to bring home to the Egyptians that God is everywhere, sees everything, and calls us all into judgment.

8:19 **וְשַׂמְתִּי פְדֻת** *I will mark out a separation* – The phrase "I will mark out a separation" – "*Vehifleti*" – comes from the same root as "wonder." The wonder is that a blind phenomenon of nature could make such a distinction between different religious and ethnic groups. God must be directing events. Geographically the distinction is facilitated by the positioning of the Israelites at the northern end of the Nile Delta, in Lower Egypt. It is as if God were saying through Moshe to Pharaoh: You have singled out this people for oppression; I will single them out for protection.

טו לֵב־פַּרְעֹה וְלֹא־שָׁמַע אֲלֵהֶם כַּאֲשֶׁר דִּבֶּר יְהוָה׃ וַיֹּאמֶר ו
יְהוָה אֶל־מֹשֶׁה הַשְׁכֵּם בַּבֹּקֶר וְהִתְיַצֵּב לִפְנֵי פַרְעֹה הִנֵּה יוֹצֵא הַמָּיְמָה
יז וְאָמַרְתָּ אֵלָיו כֹּה אָמַר יְהוָה שַׁלַּח עַמִּי וְיַעַבְדֻנִי׃ כִּי אִם־אֵינְךָ מְשַׁלֵּחַ
אֶת־עַמִּי הִנְנִי מַשְׁלִיחַ בְּךָ וּבַעֲבָדֶיךָ וּבְעַמְּךָ וּבְבָתֶּיךָ אֶת־הֶעָרֹב וּמָלְאוּ
יח בָּתֵּי מִצְרַיִם אֶת־הֶעָרֹב וְגַם הָאֲדָמָה אֲשֶׁר־הֵם עָלֶיהָ׃ וְהִפְלֵיתִי בַיּוֹם
הַהוּא אֶת־אֶרֶץ גֹּשֶׁן אֲשֶׁר עַמִּי עֹמֵד עָלֶיהָ לְבִלְתִּי הֱיוֹת־שָׁם עָרֹב
יט לְמַעַן תֵּדַע כִּי אֲנִי יְהוָה בְּקֶרֶב הָאָרֶץ׃ וְשַׂמְתִּי פְדֻת בֵּין עַמִּי וּבֵין ששי
כ עַמֶּךָ לְמָחָר יִהְיֶה הָאֹת הַזֶּה׃ וַיַּעַשׂ יְהוָה כֵּן וַיָּבֹא עָרֹב כָּבֵד בֵּיתָה

אונקלוס

לְבָּא דְפַרְעֹה וְלָא קַבִּיל מִנְּהוֹן, כְּמָא דְמַלִּיל יְיָ: טז וַאֲמַר יְיָ לְמֹשֶׁה, אַקְדֵּים בְּצַפְרָא וְאִתְעַתַּד קֳדָם פַּרְעֹה, הָא נָפֵיק לְמַיָּא, וְתֵימַר לֵיהּ, כִּדְנַן אֲמַר יְיָ, שַׁלַּח עַמִּי וְיִפְלְחוּן קֳדָמָי: יז אֲרֵי אִם לֵיתָךְ מְשַׁלַּח יָת עַמִּי, הָאֲנָא מְשַׁלַּח בָּךְ, וּבְעַבְדָּךְ וּבְעַמָּךְ, וּבְבָתָּךְ יָת עָרוֹבָא, וְיִתְמְלוֹן, בָּתֵּי מִצְרָאֵי יָת עָרוֹבָא, וְאַף אַרְעָא דְאִנּוּן עֲלַהּ: יח וְאַפְרֵישׁ בְּיוֹמָא הַהוּא יָת אַרְעָא דְגֹשֶׁן, דְעַמִּי שָׁרֵי עֲלַהּ, בְּדִיל דְלָא לְמֶהֱוֵי תַמָּן עָרוֹבָא, בְּדִיל דְתִדַּע, אֲרֵי, אֲנָא יְיָ שַׁלִּיט בְּגוֹ אַרְעָא: יט וַאֲשַׁוֵּי פֻרְקָן לְעַמִּי, וְעַל עַמָּךְ אַיְתִי מַחָא, לִמְחַר יְהֵי אָתָא הָדֵין: כ וַעֲבַד יְיָ כֵּן, וַאֲתָא עָרוֹבָא תַּקִּיף, לְבֵית

primary way in which we encounter God is not through miracles but through His word – the revelation – Torah – which is the Jewish people's constitution as a nation under the sovereignty of God.

To be sure, God is in the events which, seeming to defy nature, we call miracles. But He is also in nature itself. Far from diminishing our religious sense, science (rightly understood) should enlarge it, teaching us to see "How many are Your works, LORD; You made them all in wisdom" (Ps. 104:24). Above all, God is to be found in the voice heard at Sinai, teaching us how to construct a society that will be the opposite of Egypt: in which the few do not enslave the many, nor are strangers mistreated.

The best argument against the world of ancient Egypt was divine irony. The cultic priests and magicians who think they can control the sun and the Nile discover that they cannot even produce a louse. What the Egyptian magicians (and their latter-day successors) do not understand is that power over nature is not an end in itself, but solely the means to *ethical* ends. The lice are God's joke at the expense of the magicians who believe that because they control the forces of nature, they are masters of human destiny. They are wrong.

Technological prowess has led human beings, time and again, to believe that they were like gods. They could scale the heavens, bend nature to their purposes, and construct vast edifices to their glory. Yet in their wake they left a trail of devastation, and the civilizations they built declined and died, to be remembered only in relics and ruins. Humility is the only antidote to hubris. However great we are, we are small in the scheme of things. That is what God showed the Egyptians in the plague of lice.

8:16 שַׁלַּח עַמִּי וְיַעַבְדֻנִי *Send My people forth, so that they may serve Me* – The Torah does not frame the move from slavery to freedom in terms of the ability to do what you like. Rather, it promotes the freedom to do what you ought. That, for the intellectual architects of freedom in

palace and the houses of his officials. All across Egypt, swarms of insects
21 devastated the land. Pharaoh called for Moshe and Aharon. "Go," he said, "and
22 sacrifice to your God here in the land." But Moshe replied, "That would not be
right for us to do; our sacrifice to the LORD our God is an abomination to the
Egyptians. If, before the Egyptians' eyes, we offer the sacrifice they consider an
23 abomination, will they not stone us to death? Send us forth, three days' journey
into the wilderness, to sacrifice there to the LORD our God, as He will instruct
24 us." Pharaoh said, "I will send you forth; you shall sacrifice to the LORD your
25 God in the wilderness. Just do not go far away. Pray for me." Moshe said, "I

רש״י

כ) **תִּשָּׁחֵת הָאָרֶץ.** נִשְׁחֶתֶת הָאָרֶץ, "אִתְחַבַּלַת אַרְעָא":

כא) **זִבְחוּ לֵאלֹהֵיכֶם בָּאָרֶץ.** בִּמְקוֹמְכֶם, וְלֹא תֵּלְכוּ בַּמִּדְבָּר:

כב) **תּוֹעֲבַת מִצְרַיִם.** יִרְאַת מִצְרַיִם, כְּמוֹ: "וּלְמִלְכֹּם תּוֹעֲבַת בְּנֵי עַמּוֹן" (מלכים ב' כג, יג), וְאֵצֶל יִשְׂרָאֵל קוֹרֵא אוֹתָהּ תּוֹעֵבָה. וְעוֹד יֵשׁ לוֹמַר בְּלָשׁוֹן אַחֵר, "תּוֹעֲבַת מִצְרַיִם", דָּבָר שֶׁנָּאוּי הוּא לְמִצְרַיִם זְבִיחָה שֶׁאָנוּ זוֹבְחִים, שֶׁהֲרֵי יִרְאָתָם אָנוּ זוֹבְחִים: **וְלֹא יִסְקְלֻנוּ.** בִּתְמִיָּה:

The terms of this encounter between Moshe and Pharaoh are part of a wider pattern that we have already observed in the Torah. When Yaakov leaves Lavan we read: "Yaakov deceived Lavan the Aramean by not telling him that he was running away" (Gen. 31:20). He has to tell at best a half-truth when Esav suggests that they travel together (33:13–14). When Yaakov's sons are trying to rescue their sister Dina, who has been raped and abducted by Shekhem the Hivite, they "spoke deceptively" (34:13) when Shekhem and his father propose that the entire family should come and settle with them.

Earlier still we find that three times Avraham and Yitzḥak, forced to leave home because of famine, have to pretend that they are their wives' brothers, not their husbands, because they fear that otherwise they will be killed so that Sara or Rivka can be taken into the king's harem (chs. 12, 20, 26).

These echoes cannot be entirely accidental or coincidental to the biblical narrative as a whole. The implication seems to be this: Without their own land, Jews in the biblical age are in danger if they tell the truth. They are at constant risk of being killed or at best enslaved.

Why must they deceive? Because they are powerless in an age of power. They are a small family, at best a small nation, in an age of empires. They have to use their wits to survive. By and large they do not tell lies, but they can create a false impression. This is not how things should be. But it is how they were before Jews had their own land, their one and only defensible space. It is how people in impossible situations are forced to be if they are to exist at all.

No one should be forced to live a lie. When your nation is being enslaved, however, and its male children murdered, you have to liberate them by whatever means are possible. Moshe, who has already seen that his first encounter with Pharaoh made things worse for his people – they still have to make the same quota of bricks but now also have to gather their own straw (Ex. 5:6–8) – does not want to risk making them worse still.

The Torah here is not condoning deceit. To the contrary, it is condemning a system in which telling the truth may put your life at risk, as it still does in many tyrannical or totalitarian societies today. Judaism – a religion of dissent, questioning, and "arguments for the sake of Heaven" – is a faith that values intellectual honesty and moral truthfulness above all things. Every *Amida* ends with the prayer "My God, guard my tongue from evil and my lips from deceitful speech." The Torah is showing us here the connection between freedom and truth. Where there is freedom there can be truth. Without it, there cannot. A society in which people are forced to be less than fully honest merely to survive and not provoke further oppression is anathema to God, whose seal is truth.

פַּרְעֹה וּבֵית עֲבָדָיו וּבְכָל־אֶרֶץ מִצְרַיִם תִּשָּׁחֵת הָאָרֶץ מִפְּנֵי הֶעָרֹב׃
כא וַיִּקְרָא פַרְעֹה אֶל־מֹשֶׁה וּֽלְאַהֲרֹן וַיֹּאמֶר לְכוּ זִבְחוּ לֵאלֹהֵיכֶם בָּאָרֶץ׃
כב וַיֹּאמֶר מֹשֶׁה לֹא נָכוֹן לַעֲשׂוֹת כֵּן כִּי תּוֹעֲבַת מִצְרַיִם נִזְבַּח לַיהוָה
כג אֱלֹהֵינוּ הֵן נִזְבַּח אֶת־תּוֹעֲבַת מִצְרַיִם לְעֵינֵיהֶם וְלֹא יִסְקְלֻנוּ׃ דֶּרֶךְ
שְׁלֹשֶׁת יָמִים נֵלֵךְ בַּמִּדְבָּר וְזָבַחְנוּ לַיהוָה אֱלֹהֵינוּ כַּאֲשֶׁר יֹאמַר אֵלֵינוּ׃
כד וַיֹּאמֶר פַּרְעֹה אָנֹכִי אֲשַׁלַּח אֶתְכֶם וּזְבַחְתֶּם לַיהוָה אֱלֹהֵיכֶם בַּמִּדְבָּר
כה רַק הַרְחֵק לֹא־תַרְחִיקוּ לָלֶכֶת הַעְתִּירוּ בַּעֲדִי׃ וַיֹּאמֶר מֹשֶׁה הִנֵּה

אונקלוס

פַּרְעֹה וּלְבֵית עַבְדּוֹהִי, וּבְכָל אַרְעָא דְּמִצְרַיִם, אִתְחַבַּלַת אַרְעָא מִן קֳדָם עָרוֹבָא: כא וּקְרָא פַרְעֹה, לְמֹשֶׁה וּלְאַהֲרֹן, וַאֲמַר, אִיזִילוּ, דַּבַּחוּ קֳדָם אֱלָהֲכוֹן בְּאַרְעָא: כב וַאֲמַר מֹשֶׁה, לָא תָקֵין לְמֶעְבַּד כֵּן, אֲרֵי בְעִירָא דְּמִצְרָאֵי דָּחֲלִין לֵיהּ, מִנֵּיהּ אֲנַחְנָא נָסְבִין, לְדַבָּחָא קֳדָם יי אֱלָהַנָא, הָא נְדַבַּח, יָת בְּעִירָא דְּמִצְרָאֵי דָּחֲלִין לֵיהּ, וְאִנּוּן יְהוֹן חָזַן הֲלָא יִמְרוּן לְמִרְגְּמַנָא: כג מַהְלַךְ תְּלָתָא יוֹמִין, נֵיזֵיל בְּמַדְבְּרָא, וּנְדַבַּח קֳדָם יי אֱלָהַנָא, כְּמָא דְּיֵימַר לַנָא: כד וַאֲמַר פַּרְעֹה, אֲנָא, אֲשַׁלַּח יָתְכוֹן וּתְדַבְּחוּן, קֳדָם יי אֱלָהֲכוֹן בְּמַדְבְּרָא, לְחוֹד, אַרְחָקָא לָא תְרַחֲקוּן לְמֵיזַל, צַלּוֹ עֲלָי: כה וַאֲמַר מֹשֶׁה, הָא

8:21 וַיִּקְרָא פַרְעֹה אֶל־מֹשֶׁה וּלְאַהֲרֹן *Pharaoh called for Moshe and Aharon* – Note that he no longer turns to his magicians. He knows the plagues are intensifying, that the force driving them is beyond their replication or control. He must therefore turn directly to Moshe. He proposes a compromise response to the request of the Israelites. Yes, they may worship their God. At this point it seems as if he has acceded to their request. With one word, however, the last in his utterance, he takes it back. They may worship but only "in the land." They may not leave Egypt. Pharaoh's deteriorating character is manifest in the fact that the offer he makes here is less than he made in the previous plague, where he promised to let the people go. He must know that it will be unacceptable to Moshe.

Moshe's reply is calm and intentionally uses language that Pharaoh will understand. Rather than insisting on nothing less than their complete freedom, he appeals to Pharaoh's understanding that for the Israelites to worship their God in a public manner in Egypt would be an invitation to violence.

8:22 תּוֹעֲבַת מִצְרַיִם *An abomination to the Egyptians* – Shadal (on this verse) quotes the Greek historian Plutarch on how an Egyptian king fostered different religions among his diverse population, to prevent them coming together to unite against his rule and possibly dethrone him. On one occasion, religious differences between two of these groups led to a war, which required the Roman army to suppress it. Moshe is therefore being realistic, as well as understanding Pharaoh's mindset, when he suspects that, in Pharaoh's concession, he and his people are being invited into a trap.

MOSHE'S REQUEST

At no stage does Moshe say explicitly that he is proposing that the people should be allowed to leave permanently, never to return. He talks of a three-day journey. There is an argument between him and Pharaoh as to who is to go. Moshe consistently asks for permission to worship God at some place that is not Egypt. But he does not speak about freedom. Why not? Why does he create, and not correct, a false impression?

am going to leave you and pray to the LORD. Tomorrow, the swarms of insects
will move on from Pharaoh, his officials, and his people. But let Pharaoh no
more deceive us, refusing to send the people forth to make their sacrifice to the
26 27 LORD." Moshe left Pharaoh and prayed to the LORD. And the LORD did what
Moshe asked. He diverted the swarms of insects from Pharaoh, his officials, his
28 people – not one was left behind. But this time too, Pharaoh hardened his heart
and did not send the people forth.

9 1 Then the LORD said to Moshe, "Go to Pharaoh. Tell him: This is what the LORD,
2 God of the Hebrews, says: Send My people forth to serve Me. If you refuse to
3 send them forth, if you continue to hold them back, the LORD's hand will turn
against your livestock in the field. A deadly epidemic will strike horses, donkeys,
4 and camels, cattle and flocks. But the LORD will set Israel's livestock apart from
5 Egypt's; none belonging to the Israelites will die. The LORD has set His appointed
6 time; tomorrow the LORD will bring this about in the land." And the next day,
the LORD brought it to be. All the livestock of the Egyptians perished, but of
7 the Israelites' livestock, not one creature died. Pharaoh investigated the matter
and discovered that not one among Israel's livestock had died. But still Pharaoh's
heart remained hard, and he would not send the people forth.

רש״י

כה **התל.** כמו להתל:

כו-כז **ויסר הערב.** ולא מתו כמו שמתו הצפרדעים, שאם מתו היה להם הנאה בעורות: **ויעתר אל ה׳.** נתאמץ בתפלה. וכן אם בא לומר ׳ויעתיר׳ היה יכול לומר, ומשמע ויַרבה תפלה. וכשהוא אומר בלשון ויפעל, משמע ויַרבה להתפלל:

כח **גם בפעם הזאת.** אף על פי שאמר "אנכי אשלח אתכם" (לעיל פסוק כד) לא קים הבטחתו:

ט ב **מחזיק בם.** אוחז בם, כמו: "והחזיקה במבשיו" (דברים כה, יא):

ג **הנה יד ה׳ הויה.** לשון הוה, כי כן יאמר בלשון נקבה על שעבר ׳היתה׳ ועל העתיד ׳תהיה׳ ועל העומד ׳הויה׳, כמו: עושה, רוצה, רועה:

ד **והפלה.** והבדיל:

9:3 **דֶּבֶר** *A deadly epidemic* – A cattle disease, this constitutes a devastating assault on the Egyptian economy. Naturalistically, this may be a disease conveyed by the rotting frogs. As a sign, it may be intended to show the vulnerability of the various animal gods in Egyptian culture. More simply, by harming the Egyptian economy and people's livelihoods, it shows again that the country is suffering by prolonging the suffering of the Israelites. The Egyptians, not the Israelites, repeatedly become the losers. The plagues are intensifying in seriousness. No longer about temporary discomfort, they are now about laying waste to the country and its natural resources.

There is a wordplay between *dever*, "epidemic," in this verse, and the threefold appearance of *davar*, "word" or "thing," in the subsequent three verses. Unheeded, the word can turn into a plague.

9:7 **וַיִּשְׁלַח פַּרְעֹה** *Pharaoh investigated the matter* – Unlike other natural disasters, plagues spread. There are no effective boundaries. Pharaoh is thus genuinely perplexed as to how the Israelites' cattle are unaffected. He sends officials to the Israelite territory in Goshen to see whether it is true that none of their cattle have died. They confirm that it is. By now,

אָנֹכִי יוֹצֵא מֵעִמָּךְ וְהַעְתַּרְתִּי אֶל־יְהוָה וְסָר הֶעָרֹב מִפַּרְעֹה מֵעֲבָדָיו
וּמֵעַמּוֹ מָחָר רַק אַל־יֹסֵף פַּרְעֹה הָתֵל לְבִלְתִּי שַׁלַּח אֶת־הָעָם לִזְבֹּחַ
כו כז לַיהוָה׃ וַיֵּצֵא מֹשֶׁה מֵעִם פַּרְעֹה וַיֶּעְתַּר אֶל־יְהוָה׃ וַיַּעַשׂ יְהוָה כִּדְבַר
כח מֹשֶׁה וַיָּסַר הֶעָרֹב מִפַּרְעֹה מֵעֲבָדָיו וּמֵעַמּוֹ לֹא נִשְׁאַר אֶחָד׃ וַיַּכְבֵּד
פַּרְעֹה אֶת־לִבּוֹ גַּם בַּפַּעַם הַזֹּאת וְלֹא שִׁלַּח אֶת־הָעָם׃

ט א וַיֹּאמֶר יְהוָה אֶל־מֹשֶׁה בֹּא אֶל־פַּרְעֹה וְדִבַּרְתָּ אֵלָיו כֹּה־אָמַר יְהוָה
ב אֱלֹהֵי הָעִבְרִים שַׁלַּח אֶת־עַמִּי וְיַעַבְדֻנִי׃ כִּי אִם־מָאֵן אַתָּה לְשַׁלֵּחַ
ג וְעוֹדְךָ מַחֲזִיק בָּם׃ הִנֵּה יַד־יְהוָה הוֹיָה בְּמִקְנְךָ אֲשֶׁר בַּשָּׂדֶה בַּסּוּסִים
ד בַּחֲמֹרִים בַּגְּמַלִּים בַּבָּקָר וּבַצֹּאן דֶּבֶר כָּבֵד מְאֹד׃ וְהִפְלָה יְהוָה בֵּין
מִקְנֵה יִשְׂרָאֵל וּבֵין מִקְנֵה מִצְרָיִם וְלֹא יָמוּת מִכָּל־לִבְנֵי יִשְׂרָאֵל דָּבָר׃
ה ו וַיָּשֶׂם יְהוָה מוֹעֵד לֵאמֹר מָחָר יַעֲשֶׂה יְהוָה הַדָּבָר הַזֶּה בָּאָרֶץ׃ וַיַּעַשׂ
יְהוָה אֶת־הַדָּבָר הַזֶּה מִמָּחֳרָת וַיָּמָת כֹּל מִקְנֵה מִצְרָיִם וּמִמִּקְנֵה בְנֵי־
ז יִשְׂרָאֵל לֹא־מֵת אֶחָד׃ וַיִּשְׁלַח פַּרְעֹה וְהִנֵּה לֹא־מֵת מִמִּקְנֵה יִשְׂרָאֵל
עַד־אֶחָד וַיִּכְבַּד לֵב פַּרְעֹה וְלֹא שִׁלַּח אֶת־הָעָם׃

אונקלוס

אנא, נפיק מעמך ואצלי קדם יי, ויעדי ערובא, מפרעה, מעבדוהי ומעמיה מחר, לחוד, לא יוסיף פרעה לשקרא, בדיל דלא לשלחא ית עמא, לדבחא קדם יי: כו ונפק משה מלות פרעה, וצלי קדם יי: כז ועבד יי כפתגמא דמשה, ואעדי ערובא, מפרעה מעבדוהי ומעמיה, לא אשתאר חד: כח ויקר פרעה ית לביה, אף בזמנא הדא, ולא שלח ית עמא: ט א ואמר יי למשה, עול לות פרעה, ותמליל עמיה, כדנן אמר יי אלהא דיהודאי, שלח ית עמי ויפלחון קדמי: ב ארי, אם מסריב את לשלחא, ועד כען את מתקיף בהון: ג הא מחא מן קדם יי הויא, בבעירך דבחקלא, בסוסותא בחמרי בגמלי, בתורי ובענא, מותא סגי לחדא: ד ויפריש יי, בין בעירא דישראל, ובין בעירא דמצראי, ולא ימות, מכלא לבני ישראל מדעם: ה ושוי יי זמנא למימר, מחר, יעביד יי, פתגמא הדין בארעא: ו ועבד יי, ית פתגמא הדין מיומא דבתרוהי, ומית, כל בעירא דמצראי, ומבעירא דבני ישראל לא מית חד: ז ושלח פרעה, והא, לא מית, מבעירא דישראל

9:3 יַד־יְהוָה *The Lord's hand* – The lice were "the finger of God." This plague is the hand of the Lord. The expression "the hand of the Lord" was familiar in the ancient Near East. It signified power, sometimes punitive, sometimes coercive. The change in terminology signals an intensification of the plagues from temporary discomfort to permanent and serious loss. God through Moshe is showing Pharaoh how self-destructive his behaviour is. Pharaoh intends to harm the Israelites, but they will not be harmed. They will not lose any of their cattle to the disease. It will be his own people who suffer. Those who seek to harm others end by harming themselves.

8 Then the Lord said to Moshe and Aharon, "Take a handful of soot from a
9 furnace and throw it up in the air before Pharaoh's eyes. It will become a cloud
of dust over all the land of Egypt, and on people and animals it will become
a rash, breaking out into boils on people and animals throughout the land of
10 Egypt." So they took soot from the furnace and stood before Pharaoh. Moshe
threw it up in the air, and it became a rash that broke into boils on people and
11 animals. The magicians could not stand before Moshe because of their boils;
12 for the boils had affected them as they had the rest of the Egyptians. But the
Lord strengthened Pharaoh's heart, and he would not listen to them, just as the
13 Lord had told Moshe. Then the Lord said to Moshe, "Rise up early
in the morning and confront Pharaoh. Tell him: This is what the Lord, God

רש״י

ח **מְלֹא חָפְנֵיכֶם.** ילוינ״ש בְּלַעַז: **פִּיחַ כִּבְשָׁן.** דָּבָר הַנִּפָּח מִן הַגֶּחָלִים עֲמוּמִים הַנִּשְׂרָפִים בַּכִּבְשָׁן, וּבְלַעַז חולב״ש. 'פִּיחַ' לְשׁוֹן הֲפָחָה, שֶׁהָרוּחַ מְפִיחָן וּמַפְרִיחָן: **וּזְרָקוֹ מֹשֶׁה.** וְכָל דָּבָר הַנִּזְרָק בְּכֹחַ אֵינוֹ נִזְרָק אֶלָּא בְּיָד אַחַת, הֲרֵי נִסִּים הַרְבֵּה: אֶחָד, שֶׁהֶחֱזִיק קֻמְצוֹ שֶׁל מֹשֶׁה מְלֹא חָפְנַיִם שֶׁלּוֹ וְשֶׁל אַהֲרֹן; וְאֶחָד, שֶׁהָלַךְ הָאָבָק עַל כָּל אֶרֶץ מִצְרַיִם:

ט **פֹּרֵחַ אֲבַעְבֻּעֹת.** כְּתַרְגּוּמוֹ: "לִשְׁחִין סָגֵי אֲבַעְבּוּעִין" שֶׁעַל יָדוֹ צוֹמְחִין בָּהֶן בּוּעוֹת: **שְׁחִין.** לְשׁוֹן חֲמִימוּת, וְהַרְבֵּה יֵשׁ בִּלְשׁוֹן מִשְׁנָה: "שָׁנָה שְׁחוּנָה" (יומא נג ע״ב):

י **בָּאָדָם וּבַבְּהֵמָה.** וְאִם תֹּאמַר, מֵאַיִן הָיוּ לָהֶם הַבְּהֵמוֹת, וַהֲלֹא כְּבָר נֶאֱמַר: "וַיָּמָת כֹּל מִקְנֵה מִצְרָיִם" (לעיל פסוק ו)? לֹא נִגְזְרָה גְּזֵרָה אֶלָּא עַל אוֹתָן שֶׁבַּשָּׂדוֹת בִּלְבַד, שֶׁנֶּאֱמַר: "בְּמִקְנְךָ אֲשֶׁר בַּשָּׂדֶה" (לעיל פסוק ג), וְהַיָּרֵא אֶת דְּבַר ה' הִכְנִיס אֶת מִקְנֵהוּ אֶל הַבָּתִּים. וְכֵן שְׁנוּיָה בַּמְּכִילְתָּא אֵצֶל "וַיִּקַּח שֵׁשׁ מֵאוֹת רֶכֶב בָּחוּר" (להלן יד, ז):

breaking out into boils – answers to symptoms of anthrax, a known disease in ancient Egypt (see Deut. 28:27). If this is indeed the nature of the plague, it again suggests an intertwined presence of both supernatural and natural. Moshe and Aharon's act in throwing the soot into the air signals that what is about to happen next should not be treated as a mere natural occurrence.

9:12 **וַיְחַזֵּק יהוה אֶת־לֵב פַּרְעֹה** *But the Lord strengthened Pharaoh's heart* – This is the first time that God is described as hardening or strengthening Pharaoh's heart. Significantly, it happens in the sixth plague. During the first five, Pharaoh's refusal to let the Israelites go was his own choice. Rashi (on Ex. 7:3) understands God's hardening of Pharaoh's heart in the last five plagues as a form of punishment for the first five. Rambam interprets it as meaning that "repentance was withheld from him, and the liberty to turn from his wickedness was not accorded to him" (*Hilkhot Teshuva* 6:3). Rabbi Yosef Albo and Sforno suggest the opposite. God hardens Pharaoh's heart precisely to restore his free will. After the succession of plagues that have devastated the land, Pharaoh is under overwhelming pressure to let the Israelites go. Were he to do so, it would not be out of free choice, but rather under force majeure. God therefore toughens – strengthens – Pharaoh's heart so that even after the first five plagues he is genuinely free to say yes or no (*Sefer HaIkarim* 4:25; Sforno on Ex. 7:3). Simplest and most profound are the words of the talmudic Sages about *yetzer hara*, the evil impulse: "R. Assi said: At first the evil impulse is as thin as a spider's gossamer, but in the end it is as thick as a cart rope. Rava said: At first the evil impulse is called a 'wayfarer,' then a 'guest,' then finally a 'master'" (Sukka 52a–b). Evil traps the evildoer in its mesh. Slowly but surely he or she loses freedom and becomes not evil's master but its slave.

Meanwhile, the plagues are deepening. Animal disease has affected the cattle. Boils have had such an impact that Pharaoh's own court magicians are unable to stand. Shortly, his court will beg him to let the Israelites go. Pharaoh is

ח וַיֹּאמֶר יְהוָה אֶל־מֹשֶׁה וְאֶל־אַהֲרֹן קְחוּ לָכֶם מְלֹא חָפְנֵיכֶם פִּיחַ
ט כִּבְשָׁן וּזְרָקוֹ מֹשֶׁה הַשָּׁמַיְמָה לְעֵינֵי פַרְעֹה: וְהָיָה לְאָבָק עַל כָּל־אֶרֶץ
מִצְרָיִם וְהָיָה עַל־הָאָדָם וְעַל־הַבְּהֵמָה לִשְׁחִין פֹּרֵחַ אֲבַעְבֻּעֹת בְּכָל־
י אֶרֶץ מִצְרָיִם: וַיִּקְחוּ אֶת־פִּיחַ הַכִּבְשָׁן וַיַּעַמְדוּ לִפְנֵי פַרְעֹה וַיִּזְרֹק
אֹתוֹ מֹשֶׁה הַשָּׁמָיְמָה וַיְהִי שְׁחִין אֲבַעְבֻּעֹת פֹּרֵחַ בָּאָדָם וּבַבְּהֵמָה:
יא וְלֹא־יָכְלוּ הַחַרְטֻמִּים לַעֲמֹד לִפְנֵי מֹשֶׁה מִפְּנֵי הַשְּׁחִין כִּי־הָיָה הַשְּׁחִין
יב בַּחַרְטֻמִּם וּבְכָל־מִצְרָיִם: וַיְחַזֵּק יְהוָה אֶת־לֵב פַּרְעֹה וְלֹא שָׁמַע אֲלֵהֶם
יג כַּאֲשֶׁר דִּבֶּר יְהוָה אֶל־מֹשֶׁה: וַיֹּאמֶר יְהוָה אֶל־מֹשֶׁה
הַשְׁכֵּם בַּבֹּקֶר וְהִתְיַצֵּב לִפְנֵי פַרְעֹה וְאָמַרְתָּ אֵלָיו כֹּה־אָמַר יְהוָה

אונקלוס

עַד חַד, וְאִתְיַקַּר לִבָּא דְפַרְעֹה, וְלָא שַׁלַּח יָת עַמָּא: ח וַאֲמַר יְיָ לְמֹשֶׁה וּלְאַהֲרֹן, סַבוּ לְכוֹן מְלֵי חָפְנֵיכוֹן, פִּיחַ דְּאַתּוּנָא, וְיִזְרְקִנֵּיהּ מֹשֶׁה, לְצֵית שְׁמַיָּא לְעֵינֵי פַרְעֹה: ט וִיהֵי לְאַבְקָא, עַל כָּל אַרְעָא דְמִצְרָיִם, וִיהֵי עַל אֱנָשָׁא וְעַל בְּעִירָא, לְשְׁחִין סְגֵי, אֲבַעְבּוּעִין בְּכָל אַרְעָא דְמִצְרָיִם: י וּנְסִיבוּ יָת פִּיחַ דְּאַתּוּנָא, וְקָמוּ קֳדָם פַּרְעֹה, וּזְרַק יָתֵיהּ, מֹשֶׁה לְצֵית שְׁמַיָּא, וַהֲוָה, שְׁחִין אֲבַעְבּוּעִין, סְגֵי, בֶּאֱנָשָׁא וּבִבְעִירָא: יא וְלָא יְכִילוּ חָרָשַׁיָּא, לְמֵקָם, קֳדָם מֹשֶׁה מִן קֳדָם שִׁחְנָא, אֲרֵי הֲוָה שִׁחְנָא, בְּחָרָשַׁיָּא וּבְכָל מִצְרָאֵי: יב וְתַקִּיף יְיָ יָת לִבָּא דְפַרְעֹה, וְלָא קַבֵּיל מִנְּהוֹן, כְּמָא דְמַלֵּיל יְיָ עִם מֹשֶׁה: יג וַאֲמַר יְיָ לְמֹשֶׁה, אַקְדֵּים בְּצַפְרָא, וְאִתְעַתַּד קֳדָם פַּרְעֹה, וְתֵימַר לֵיהּ, כִּדְנַן אֲמַר יְיָ

Pharaoh has unmistakable evidence that a vast power is arrayed against him, and that he can disarm it by the simple act of letting the Israelites leave his country. Yet he does not do so. This act of sending people to check whether the Israelites have been protected, and then ignoring the evidence that they bring back, represents, perhaps, an extreme case of the confirmation bias in which we take note of the evidence that supports our view, and ignore that which negates it. This is a high point in Pharaoh's obstinacy: from this point onward, for the last five plagues, the text will tell us that God hardens, strengthens, or makes heavy his heart.

9:8 מְלֹא חָפְנֵיכֶם פִּיחַ *A handful of soot* – The Egyptians used furnaces to fire bricks, in addition to the sun-dried method used by the Israelites. This sixth plague suggests that the resource that they use for building is now about to be used for destructive purposes. There may be a distant reminder here of the backbreaking labor of brick making that the Egyptians imposed on the Israelites.

Boils in the Bible seem to be a peculiarly difficult trial. In the book that bears his name, Iyov withstands many terrible tragedies and does not lose faith until his body is covered with boils, at which point he breaks down and curses his fate. Here, the Torah adds that not only can the magicians not replicate this plague – since their failure to replicate the third plague, their inability has been taken for granted – but they are so badly afflicted by it that they can no longer stand. Moshe and Aharon are standing before Pharaoh, but the magicians are no longer able to stand before them. Having tried to humiliate Moshe and Aharon, now the magicians themselves are humiliated. Magicians in the ancient world also had a role as physicians. Now they cannot heal themselves. Their magic has failed them.

The description of the effects of the plague – a rash

14 of the Hebrews, says: Send My people forth to serve Me, or this time I will set
the full force of My plagues upon you, your officials, and your people so that
15 you will know that there is none like Me in all the world. By now I could have
stretched out My hand and struck you and your people with an epidemic that
16 would have wiped you off the face of the earth. But I have let you survive for this
purpose – to show you My power, and to have My name known throughout the
17 land. You are still abusing your power over My people, refusing to let them go. SHEVI'I
18 And so this time tomorrow I will bring a hailstorm on Egypt heavier than any it
19 has suffered, from the day Egypt was established until now. Give an order now
to bring in your livestock and all else you have in the field. Anyone or any animal
in the open, any not brought under shelter, will die when the hail beats down."
20 Those of Pharaoh's officials who feared the LORD's word hurried to bring in their
21 slaves and livestock. And those who set no stock in the LORD's word kept their
slaves and livestock where they were in the fields.

רש״י

יד **אֶת כָּל מַגֵּפֹתַי.** לָמַדְנוּ מִכָּאן שֶׁמַּכַּת בְּכוֹרוֹת שְׁקוּלָה כְּנֶגֶד כָּל הַמַּכּוֹת:

טו **כִּי עַתָּה שָׁלַחְתִּי אֶת יָדִי וְגוֹ׳.** כִּי אִלּוּ רָצִיתִי כְּשֶׁהָיְתָה יָדִי בְּמִקְנְךָ שֶׁהִכֵּיתִים בַּדֶּבֶר, שְׁלַחְתִּיהָ וְהִכֵּיתִי אוֹתְךָ וְאֶת עַמְּךָ עִם הַבְּהֵמוֹת וְנִכְחַדְתֶּם מִן הָאָרֶץ, אֲבָל "בַּעֲבוּר זֹאת הֶעֱמַדְתִּיךָ" וְגוֹ׳:

יז **עוֹדְךָ מִסְתּוֹלֵל בְּעַמִּי.** כְּתַרְגּוּמוֹ: "כְּבֵישַׁתְּ בֵּיהּ בְּעַמִּי" וְהוּא מִגִּזְרַת 'מְסִלָּה' (במדבר כ, יט) דְּמִתַּרְגְּמִינַן: "אֹרַח כְּבִישָׁא", וּבְלַעַז קלקי"ר. וּכְבָר פֵּרַשְׁתִּי בְּסוֹף וַיְהִי מִקֵּץ (בראשית מד, טז), כָּל תֵּבָה שֶׁתְּחִלַּת יְסוֹדָהּ סָמֶ"ךְ וְהִיא בָּאָה לְדַבֵּר בִּלְשׁוֹן מִתְפַּעֵל נוֹתֵן הַתָּי"ו שֶׁל שִׁמּוּשׁ בְּאֶמְצַע אוֹתִיּוֹת שֶׁל עִקָּר, כְּגוֹן זוֹ, וּכְגוֹן: "וְיִסְתַּבֵּל הֶחָגָב" (קהלת יב, ה) מִגִּזְרַת 'סַבָּל' (מלכים א׳ ה, כט); "כִּי תִשְׂתָּרֵר עָלֵינוּ" (במדבר טז, יג) מִגִּזְרַת 'שַׂר וְנָגִיד' (דברי הימים ב׳ לב, כא); "מִשְׂתַּכַּל הֲוֵית" (דניאל ז, ח):

יח **כָּעֵת מָחָר.** כָּעֵת הַזֹּאת לְמָחָר. שָׂרַט לוֹ שְׂרִיטָה בַּכֹּתֶל, לְמָחָר כְּשֶׁתַּגִּיעַ חַמָּה לְכָאן יֵרֵד הַבָּרָד: **הִוָּסְדָה.** שֶׁנִּתְיַסְּדָה. וְכָל תֵּבָה שֶׁתְּחִלַּת יְסוֹדָהּ יוּ"ד כְּגוֹן: יָסַד, יָלַד, יָדַע, יָסַר, כְּשֶׁהִיא מִתְפַּעֶלֶת תָּבֹא הַוָּי"ו בִּמְקוֹם הַיּוּ"ד כְּמוֹ: "הִוָּסְדָה", "הִוָּלְדָהּ" (הושע ב, ה), "וַיִּוָּדַע" (אסתר ב, כב), "וַיִּוָּלֵד לְיוֹסֵף" (בראשית מו, כ), "בִּדְבָרִים לֹא יִוָּסֶר עָבֶד" (משלי כט, יט):

יט **שְׁלַח הָעֵז.** כְּתַרְגּוּמוֹ: "שְׁלַח כְּנוֹשׁ". וְכֵן: "יֹשְׁבֵי הַגֵּבִים הֵעִיזוּ" (ישעיה י, לא). "הָעִזוּ בְּנֵי בִנְיָמִן" (ירמיה ו, א): **וְלֹא יֵאָסֵף הַבַּיְתָה.** לְשׁוֹן הַכְנָסָה הוּא:

כ **הֵנִיס.** הִבְרִיחַ:

communicates. A wonder, by contrast, conveys no message. It produces awe. A sign exists within culture, a wonder within nature. To the Israelites, the plagues are wonders. To the Egyptians, they are signs. They embody a truth, that there is a God of all the earth and all humanity, who stands above all other powers and represents a universal ethic of respect for persons. Rarely does God intervene in history as intensely as He does in the course of the exodus. But this story is meant to be handed on across the generations, giving hope to the hopeless and dignity to those ground down. There is a moral shape to events. As Dr. Martin Luther King, Jr. said: "The arc of history is long, but it bends toward justice.."

9:16 **סַפֵּר שְׁמִי בְּכָל־הָאָרֶץ** *My name known throughout the land* – In the ancient world, each nation had its gods, and they were territorially limited. They were gods of this place, not that. This is the essential meaning of Pharaoh's remark to Moshe when he demands the Israelites' release in the name of God. Pharaoh replies: "Who is this LORD that I should obey Him and send Israel forth? I do not know the LORD, and I will not send Israel forth" (Ex. 5:2). This does not mean that he does not know who the God of the Israelites is. It means that within Egypt, the gods of Egypt rule. The book of Exodus presents the idea of a God not territorially bound, a God of anywhere and everywhere.

יד אֱלֹהֵי הָעִבְרִים שַׁלַּח אֶת־עַמִּי וְיַעַבְדֻנִי׃ כִּי ׀ בַּפַּעַם הַזֹּאת אֲנִי שֹׁלֵחַ
אֶת־כָּל־מַגֵּפֹתַי אֶל־לִבְּךָ וּבַעֲבָדֶיךָ וּבְעַמֶּךָ בַּעֲבוּר תֵּדַע כִּי אֵין כָּמֹנִי
טו בְּכָל־הָאָרֶץ׃ כִּי עַתָּה שָׁלַחְתִּי אֶת־יָדִי וָאַךְ אוֹתְךָ וְאֶת־עַמְּךָ בַּדָּבֶר
טז וַתִּכָּחֵד מִן־הָאָרֶץ׃ וְאוּלָם בַּעֲבוּר זֹאת הֶעֱמַדְתִּיךָ בַּעֲבוּר הַרְאֹתְךָ
יז אֶת־כֹּחִי וּלְמַעַן סַפֵּר שְׁמִי בְּכָל־הָאָרֶץ׃ עוֹדְךָ מִסְתּוֹלֵל בְּעַמִּי לְבִלְתִּי שביעי
יח שַׁלְּחָם׃ הִנְנִי מַמְטִיר כָּעֵת מָחָר בָּרָד כָּבֵד מְאֹד אֲשֶׁר לֹא־הָיָה
יט כָמֹהוּ בְּמִצְרַיִם לְמִן־הַיּוֹם הִוָּסְדָה וְעַד־עָתָּה׃ וְעַתָּה שְׁלַח הָעֵז אֶת־
מִקְנְךָ וְאֵת כָּל־אֲשֶׁר לְךָ בַּשָּׂדֶה כָּל־הָאָדָם וְהַבְּהֵמָה אֲשֶׁר־יִמָּצֵא
כ בַשָּׂדֶה וְלֹא יֵאָסֵף הַבַּיְתָה וְיָרַד עֲלֵהֶם הַבָּרָד וָמֵתוּ׃ הַיָּרֵא אֶת־דְּבַר
יהוה מֵעַבְדֵי פַּרְעֹה הֵנִיס אֶת־עֲבָדָיו וְאֶת־מִקְנֵהוּ אֶל־הַבָּתִּים׃
כא וַאֲשֶׁר לֹא־שָׂם לִבּוֹ אֶל־דְּבַר יהוה וַיַּעֲזֹב אֶת־עֲבָדָיו וְאֶת־מִקְנֵהוּ
בַּשָּׂדֶה׃

אונקלוס

אלהא דיהודאי, שלח ית עמי ויפלחון קדמי: יד ארי בזמנא הדא, אנא שלח, ית כל מחתי בלבך, ובעבדך ובעמך, בדיל דתדע, ארי, לית דכותי בכל ארעא: טו ארי כען קריב קדמי, דשלחית פון ית מחת גבורתי, ומחית יתך, וית עמך במותא, ואשתיציתא מן ארעא: טז וברם, בדיל דא קיימתך, בדיל לאחזיותך ית חילי, ובדיל, דיהון משתען גבורת שמי בכל ארעא: יז עד כען כבישת ביה בעמי, בדיל דלא לשלחותהון: יח האנא מחית כעדנא הדין מחר, ברדא תקיף לחדא, דלא הוה דכותיה במצרים, למן יומא דאשתכללת ועד כען: יט וכען, שלח כנוש ית בעירך, וית כל דלך בחקלא, כל אנשא ובעירא דישתכח בחקלא, ולא יתכניש לביתא, ויחות עליהון, ברדא וימותון: כ דדחיל מפתגמא דיי, מעבדי פרעה, כנש, ית עבדוהי וית בעיריה לבתיא: כא ודלא שוי, לביה לפתגמא דיי, שבק, ית עבדוהי וית בעיריה בחקלא:

turned free men into slaves, is now himself a slave of the system he has created.

9:14 אֲנִי שֹׁלֵחַ אֶת־כָּל־מַגֵּפֹתַי אֶל־לִבְּךָ *I will set the full force of My plagues upon you* – The Hebrew emphasizes that they will be sent (literally) "into your heart." The point of the plagues is not just the physical phenomena they constitute, but rather the effect they have on Pharaoh and his people. They are not just wonders; they are signs. A sign is an encoded message. It

becoming more and more isolated, as often happens to absolute rulers when they lose the support of those around them. Their acts appear to the outside as ever more irrational. And they are indeed self-destructive. But Pharaoh is now a prisoner within the cage he has made for himself. Having steadfastly refused, in the name of *Ma'at*, order, to grant the Israelites their freedom to leave, he cannot back down now without making himself a laughingstock. Hence the irony and pathos of these last plagues. Pharaoh, having

22 The Lord said to Moshe, "Reach your hand out to the sky, that hail may
fall on all the land of Egypt, on the people and the animals and everything
23 growing in Egypt's fields." Moshe raised his staff toward the sky; the Lord sent
thunderclaps and hail. Fire struck the ground, and the Lord rained down hail
24 on the land of Egypt. The hail, with fire blazing inside it, battered so hard that
there had been nothing like it anywhere in Egypt since it first became a nation.
25 The hail struck everything in the open field throughout all Egypt: people,
animals, and everything growing in the fields, and it smashed asunder every
26 27 tree. Only in Goshen, where the Israelites lived, no hail fell. Then Pharaoh sent
for Moshe and Aharon and said to them, "This time I have sinned. The Lord is
28 in the right, and I and my people are guilty. Pray to the Lord. Enough of God's
29 thunder and hail – I will send you forth. You need not wait any longer." Moshe

רש״י

כב| **עַל הַשָּׁמַיִם.** לְצַד הַשָּׁמַיִם. וּמִדְרַשׁ אַגָּדָה, הִגְבִּיהוֹ הַקָּדוֹשׁ בָּרוּךְ הוּא לְמֹשֶׁה לְמַעְלָה מִן הַשָּׁמַיִם:

כד| **מִתְלַקַּחַת בְּתוֹךְ הַבָּרָד.** נֵס בְּתוֹךְ נֵס, הָאֵשׁ וְהַבָּרָד מְעֹרָבִין, וְהַבָּרָד מַיִם הוּא, וְלַעֲשׂוֹת רְצוֹן קוֹנָם עָשׂוּ שָׁלוֹם בֵּינֵיהֶם:

כח| **וָרָב.** דַּי לוֹ בְּמַה שֶּׁהוֹרִיד כְּבָר:

have been fertile breeding grounds for the lice, the swarms of flies and the infections they carried with them affecting first cattle, then humans. Various accounts of the plagues analyzed on naturalistic lines of epidemiology link these first six plagues together as a closely related group in the months following the inundation of the Nile in September-October. The last cycle of three plagues are set later, however, nearer harvest time, culminating in the tenth plague in the month of Nisan, that is, spring.

9:24 **וְאֵשׁ מִתְלַקַּחַת בְּתוֹךְ הַבָּרָד** *The hail, with fire blazing inside it* – A miracle within a miracle: Fire and ice coexist as they would not naturally do (Rashi, Ibn Ezra). The same phrase appears in the mystical vision of Yeḥezkel, when he sees "a cloud with flashing lightning" (Ezek. 1:4). The hail might have borne traces of a volcanic eruption, the ash from such an eruption, borne by the wind, precipitating the hailstorm. The hailstorm is unlikely to have had a specific religious connotation for the Egyptians. There were various sky gods, but none that seems to correlate with this kind of weather. The general impression, though, would have been powerful. The heavens are communicating their anger.

Hailstorms were rare in Egypt but could happen with devastating force. The language here is emphatic and unusual, emphasizing that such a storm has never happened since "Egypt… first became a nation" – a phrase frequently found in ancient Egyptian literature, but not in Hebrew literature. God is thus speaking to Pharaoh in his own language and idiom. Now He gives advance warning to Pharaoh and his court that they should take shelter, and protect the animals that survived the fifth plague. This has the effect that those who believe are saved the effects of the plague and those who do not are not.

9:27 **חָטָאתִי הַפָּעַם** *This time I have sinned* – This is the first expression of remorse on the part of Pharaoh. But it seems too brief and pro forma. Pharaoh divides the guilt between himself and his people. He peremptorily orders Moshe to pray to the Lord. Moshe takes him at his word and assures him the hailstorm will end, but makes it clear that he does not believe that Pharaoh is sincere.

כב וַיֹּאמֶר יְהוָה אֶל־מֹשֶׁה נְטֵה אֶת־יָדְךָ עַל־הַשָּׁמַיִם וִיהִי בָרָד בְּכָל־
אֶרֶץ מִצְרָיִם עַל־הָאָדָם וְעַל־הַבְּהֵמָה וְעַל כָּל־עֵשֶׂב הַשָּׂדֶה בְּאֶרֶץ
כג מִצְרָיִם: וַיֵּט מֹשֶׁה אֶת־מַטֵּהוּ עַל־הַשָּׁמַיִם וַיהוָה נָתַן קֹלֹת וּבָרָד
כד וַתִּהֲלַךְ־אֵשׁ אָרְצָה וַיַּמְטֵר יְהוָה בָּרָד עַל־אֶרֶץ מִצְרָיִם: וַיְהִי בָרָד וְאֵשׁ
מִתְלַקַּחַת בְּתוֹךְ הַבָּרָד כָּבֵד מְאֹד אֲשֶׁר לֹא־הָיָה כָמֹהוּ בְּכָל־אֶרֶץ
כה מִצְרַיִם מֵאָז הָיְתָה לְגוֹי: וַיַּךְ הַבָּרָד בְּכָל־אֶרֶץ מִצְרַיִם אֵת כָּל־אֲשֶׁר
בַּשָּׂדֶה מֵאָדָם וְעַד־בְּהֵמָה וְאֵת כָּל־עֵשֶׂב הַשָּׂדֶה הִכָּה הַבָּרָד וְאֶת־
כו כָּל־עֵץ הַשָּׂדֶה שִׁבֵּר: רַק בְּאֶרֶץ גֹּשֶׁן אֲשֶׁר־שָׁם בְּנֵי יִשְׂרָאֵל לֹא הָיָה
כז בָּרָד: וַיִּשְׁלַח פַּרְעֹה וַיִּקְרָא לְמֹשֶׁה וּלְאַהֲרֹן וַיֹּאמֶר אֲלֵהֶם חָטָאתִי
כח הַפָּעַם יְהוָה הַצַּדִּיק וַאֲנִי וְעַמִּי הָרְשָׁעִים: הַעְתִּירוּ אֶל־יְהוָה וְרַב מִהְיֹת
כט קֹלֹת אֱלֹהִים וּבָרָד וַאֲשַׁלְּחָה אֶתְכֶם וְלֹא תֹסִפוּן לַעֲמֹד: וַיֹּאמֶר אֵלָיו

אונקלוס

כב וַאֲמַר יי לְמֹשֶׁה, אֲרֵים יָת יְדָךְ עַל צֵית שְׁמַיָּא, וִיהֵי בַרְדָּא בְּכָל אַרְעָא דְּמִצְרָיִם, עַל אֱנָשָׁא וְעַל בְּעִירָא, וְעַל כָּל עִסְבָּא דְּחַקְלָא בְּאַרְעָא דְּמִצְרָיִם: כג וַאֲרֵים מֹשֶׁה יָת חֻטְרֵיהּ עַל צֵית שְׁמַיָּא, וַיי, יְהַב קָלִין וּבְרַד, וּמְהַלְּכָא אִישָּׁתָא עַל אַרְעָא, וְאַמְטַר יי, בַּרְדָּא עַל אַרְעָא דְּמִצְרָיִם: כד וַהֲוָה בַרְדָּא, וְאִישָּׁתָא, מִשְׁתַּלְהֲבָא בְּגוֹ בַּרְדָּא, תַּקִּיף לַחֲדָא, דְּלָא הֲוָה דִּכְוָתֵיהּ בְּכָל אַרְעָא דְּמִצְרַיִם, מֵעִדָּן דַּהֲוָת לְעַם: כה וּמְחָא בַרְדָּא בְּכָל אַרְעָא דְּמִצְרַיִם, יָת כָּל דִּבְחַקְלָא, מֵאֱנָשָׁא וְעַד בְּעִירָא, וְיָת כָּל עִסְבָּא דְּחַקְלָא מְחָא בַרְדָּא, וְיָת כָּל אִילָנֵי חַקְלָא תַּבַּר: כו לְחוֹד בְּאַרְעָא דְּגֹשֶׁן, דְּתַמָּן בְּנֵי יִשְׂרָאֵל, לָא הֲוָה בַּרְדָּא: כז וּשְׁלַח פַּרְעֹה, וּקְרָא לְמֹשֶׁה וּלְאַהֲרֹן, וַאֲמַר לְהוֹן חֲבֵית זִמְנָא הָדָא, יי זַכָּאָה, וַאֲנָא וְעַמִּי חַיָּבִין: כח צַלּוֹ קֳדָם יי, וְסַגִּי קֳדָמוֹהִי רְוַח, דְּלָא יְהוֹן עֲלָנָא, קָלִין דִּלְוָט

9:22 נְטֵה אֶת־יָדְךָ *Reach your hand out* – Now begins the third cycle of plagues (see ch. 7, "The Plagues") and an intensification of the drama they represent. Not only will they be devastating. They will be an unmistakable sign to Egypt that "the time is out of joint," that order has been turned into chaos, that the very forces of nature are fighting against them, that there is a supreme power beyond all the powers that they have traditionally worshipped, and that their resistance to God is destined to fail. At this point, Aharon disappears from the scene and Moshe alone stands before Pharaoh.

As happens with the first of each of the three plague cycles, God sends a message to Pharaoh, telling him why these devastating events are about to befall him and his people. In this case, the speech is unprecedentedly long and emphatic. I could, He says, have destroyed you completely. But I have let you survive in order that you know who and what I am. You are still "abusing your power" (Ex. 9:17) over My people. What you have been doing to them will now be done to you.

There is a sense of progression in the plagues. The first six were set in motion by the inundation of the Nile. First came the plague of blood. The change in the water would have sent the frogs to land. Their decomposing bodies may

said to him, "As I leave the city, I will spread out my hands to the LORD. The
thunder will stop and there will be no more hail. You will then know that the
30 world belongs to the LORD. But I know that you and your officials still do not
31 hold the LORD God in awe." By then the flax and barley had been destroyed,
32 because the barley was ripe and the flax in bud. But the wheat and emmer had
33 not been destroyed, because they ripen later. Moshe left Pharaoh and the city MAFTIR
and spread out his hands to the LORD. The thunder and hail stopped; the rain
34 did not pound the earth anymore. But when Pharaoh saw that the rain, hail,
and thunder had stopped, he once more turned to sinfulness. He hardened
35 his heart; his officials likewise. Pharaoh's heart was strengthened and he
refused to send the Israelites forth, just as the LORD had predicted at Moshe's
hand.

The haftara for Parashat Vaera is on page 1530.
On Rosh Ḥodesh Shevat read the haftara on page 1634.

רש״י

כט] **כְּצֵאתִי אֶת הָעִיר.** מִן הָעִיר. אֲבָל בְּתוֹךְ הָעִיר לֹא הִתְפַּלֵּל, לְפִי שֶׁהָיְתָה מְלֵאָה גִּלּוּלִים:

ל] **טֶרֶם תִּירְאוּן.** עֲדַיִן לֹא תִירְאוּן. וְכֵן כָּל טֶרֶם שֶׁבַּמִּקְרָא 'עֲדַיִן לֹא' הוּא, וְאֵינוֹ לְשׁוֹן קֹדֶם. "טֶרֶם יִשְׁכָּבוּ" (בראשית יט, ד) – "עַד לָא שְׁכִיבוּ", "טֶרֶם יִצְמָח" (שם ב, ה) – "עַד לָא צְמַח". אַף זֶה כֵּן הוּא, יָדַעְתִּי כִּי עֲדַיִן אֵינְכֶם יְרֵאִים, וּמִשֶּׁתִּהְיֶה הָרְוָחָה תַּעַמְדוּ בְּקִלְקוּלְכֶם:

לא] **וְהַפִּשְׁתָּה וְהַשְּׂעֹרָה נֻכָּתָה.** נִשְׁבְּרָה, לְשׁוֹן: "פַּרְעֹה נְכֹה" (מלכים ב' כג, כט), "נְכָאִים" (ישעיה טז, ז), וְכֵן "לֹא נֻכּוּ" (להלן פסוק לב). וְלֹא יִתָּכֵן לְפָרְשָׁם לְשׁוֹן הַכָּאָה, שֶׁאֵין נוּ"ן בִּמְקוֹם הֵ"א לְפָרֵשׁ 'נֻכָּתָה' כְּמוֹ 'הֻכָּתָה', 'נֻכּוּ' כְּמוֹ 'הֻכּוּ', אֶלָּא הַנּוּ"ן שֹׁרֶשׁ בַּתֵּבָה, וַהֲרֵי הוּא מִגִּזְרַת "וְשֻׁפּוּ עַצְמוֹתָיו" (איוב לג, כא): **כִּי הַשְּׂעֹרָה אָבִיב.** כְּבָר בִּכְּרָה וְעוֹמֶדֶת בְּקַשֶּׁיהָ, וְנִשְׁתַּבְּרוּ וְנָפְלוּ. וְכֵן הַפִּשְׁתָּה גָּדְלָה כְּבָר וְהִקְשָׁה לַעֲמֹד בְּגִבְעוֹלֶיהָ: **הַשְּׂעֹרָה אָבִיב.** עָמְדָה בְּאִבֶּיהָ, לְשׁוֹן "בְּאִבֵּי הַנָּחַל" (שיר השירים ו, יא):

לב] **כִּי אֲפִילֹת הֵנָּה.** מְאֻחָרוֹת, וַעֲדַיִן הָיוּ רַכּוֹת וִיכוֹלוֹת לַעֲמֹד בִּפְנֵי קָשֶׁה. וְאַף עַל פִּי שֶׁנֶּאֱמַר: "וְאֶת כָּל עֵשֶׂב הַשָּׂדֶה הִכָּה הַבָּרָד" (לעיל פסוק כה), יֵשׁ לְיַשֵּׁב פְּשׁוּטוֹ שֶׁל מִקְרָא בָּעֲשָׂבִים הָעוֹמְדִים בְּקַלְחָם הָרְאוּיִם לִלְקוֹת בַּבָּרָד. וּבְמִדְרַשׁ רַבִּי תַּנְחוּמָא (ו) יֵשׁ מֵרַבּוֹתֵינוּ שֶׁנֶּחְלְקוּ עַל זֹאת, וְדָרְשׁוּ "כִּי אֲפִילֹת", פִּלְאֵי פְלָאוֹת נַעֲשׂוּ לָהֶם שֶׁלֹּא לָקוּ:

לג] **לֹא נִתַּךְ.** לֹא הִגִּיעַ, וְאַף אוֹתָן שֶׁהָיוּ בָּאֲוִיר לֹא הִגִּיעוּ לָאָרֶץ. וְדוֹמֶה לוֹ: "וַתִּתַּךְ עָלֵינוּ הָאָלָה וְהַשְּׁבֻעָה" דְּעֶזְרָא (דניאל ט, יא), וַתַּגִּיעַ עָלֵינוּ. וּמְנַחֵם בֶּן סָרוּק חִבְּרוֹ בְּחֵלֶק "כְּהִתּוּךְ כֶּסֶף" (יחזקאל כב, כב), לְשׁוֹן יְצִיקַת מַתֶּכֶת, וְרוֹאֶה אֲנִי אֶת דְּבָרָיו; כְּתַרְגּוּמוֹ "וַיִּצֹק" – "וְאַתֵּיךְ" (להלן לח, ה), "לָצֶקֶת" – "לְאַתָּכָא" (שם פסוק כז). אַף זֶה "לֹא נִתַּךְ", לֹא הוּצַק לָאָרֶץ:

call today an international intervention in defense of human rights.

Note that it is not the hail, but the stopping of the hail, that will teach Pharaoh that "the world belongs to the LORD." God's greatness lies not only in power, but in the limitation of power, not only in His ability to create but also in His ability to cease. All natural forces continue until their energy is no more. God alone can say "stop." That is why the Sabbath, when God stopped creating, is holy. God's ability to stop the hail is greater than His ability to bring it in the first place (Rabbi Samson Raphael Hirsch). At the end of the *parasha* we are left in suspense; as the story continues to unfold we will witness God conclusively saying to Pharaoh, as to the sea (Job 38:11), "Just this far and no more."

מֹשֶׁה כְּצֵאתִי אֶת־הָעִיר אֶפְרֹשׂ אֶת־כַּפַּי אֶל־יְהוָה הַקֹּלוֹת יֶחְדָּלוּן
ל וְהַבָּרָד לֹא יִהְיֶה־עוֹד לְמַעַן תֵּדַע כִּי לַיהוָה הָאָרֶץ׃ וְאַתָּה וַעֲבָדֶיךָ
לא יָדַעְתִּי כִּי טֶרֶם תִּירְאוּן מִפְּנֵי יְהוָה אֱלֹהִים׃ וְהַפִּשְׁתָּה וְהַשְּׂעֹרָה
לב נֻכָּתָה כִּי הַשְּׂעֹרָה אָבִיב וְהַפִּשְׁתָּה גִּבְעֹל׃ וְהַחִטָּה וְהַכֻּסֶּמֶת לֹא נֻכּוּ
לג כִּי אֲפִילֹת הֵנָּה׃ וַיֵּצֵא מֹשֶׁה מֵעִם פַּרְעֹה אֶת־הָעִיר וַיִּפְרֹשׂ כַּפָּיו אֶל־ מפטיר
לד יְהוָה וַיַּחְדְּלוּ הַקֹּלוֹת וְהַבָּרָד וּמָטָר לֹא־נִתַּךְ אָרְצָה׃ וַיַּרְא פַּרְעֹה
כִּי־חָדַל הַמָּטָר וְהַבָּרָד וְהַקֹּלֹת וַיֹּסֶף לַחֲטֹא וַיַּכְבֵּד לִבּוֹ הוּא וַעֲבָדָיו׃
לה וַיֶּחֱזַק לֵב פַּרְעֹה וְלֹא שִׁלַּח אֶת־בְּנֵי יִשְׂרָאֵל כַּאֲשֶׁר דִּבֶּר יְהוָה בְּיַד־
מֹשֶׁה׃

The הפטרה *for* פרשת וארא *is on page 1531.*
On ראש חודש שבט *read the* הפטרה *on page 1635.*

אונקלוס

כט כְּאִלֵּין מִן קֳדָם יְיָ וּבְרַד, וַאֲשַׁלַּח יָתְכוֹן, וְלָא תֵיסְפוּן לְאִתְעַכָּבָא: וַאֲמַר לֵיהּ מֹשֶׁה, כְּמִפְּקִי מִן קַרְתָּא, אֶפְרוֹס יָת יְדַי בִּצְלוֹ קֳדָם יְיָ, קָלַיָּא יִתְמַנְעוּן, וּבַרְדָּא לָא יְהֵי עוֹד, בְּדִיל דְּתִדַּע, אֲרֵי דַּייָ אַרְעָא: ל וְאַתְּ וְעַבְדָּךְ, יְדַעְנָא, אֲרֵי עַד כְּעַן לָא אִתְכְּנַעְתּוּן, מִן קֳדָם יְיָ אֱלֹהִים: לא וְכִתָּנָא וְסַעֲרֵי לְקוֹ, אֲרֵי סַעֲרַיָּא אֲבִיב, וְכִתָּנָא גַּבְעֳלִין: לב וְחִטַּיָּא וְכוּנָתַיָּא לָא לְקָאָה, אֲרֵי אַפְלָתָא אִנִּין: לג וּנְפַק מֹשֶׁה, מִלְּוָת פַּרְעֹה יָת קַרְתָּא, וּפְרַס יְדוֹהִי בִּצְלוֹ קֳדָם יְיָ, וְאִתְמְנַעוּ קָלַיָּא וּבַרְדָּא, וּמִטְרָא דַּהֲוָה נָחֵית לָא מְטָא עַל אַרְעָא: לד וַחֲזָא פַּרְעֹה, אֲרֵי אִתְמְנַע מִטְרָא וּבַרְדָּא, וְקָלַיָּא וְאוֹסֵיף לְמֶחְטֵי, וְיַקַּרֵיהּ לְלִבֵּיהּ הוּא וְעַבְדוֹהִי: לה וְאִתַּקַּף לִבָּא דְּפַרְעֹה, וְלָא שַׁלַּח יָת בְּנֵי יִשְׂרָאֵל, כְּמָא דְּמַלֵּיל יְיָ בִּידָא דְּמֹשֶׁה:

9:29 **כְּצֵאתִי אֶת־הָעִיר** *As I leave the city* – Moshe cannot pray within the city lest people think he is praying to its gods. No one in Egypt now doubts God's power, but they may well doubt His identity. The Mekhilta goes further: "If Moshe would only pray outside the city, how much more so would God only speak to him outside the city. Why would He not speak to him within the city? Because it was full of abominations and idols" (*Meḥilta d'Rabbi Yishmael* Tractate Pisḥa 1).

The seat of politics is not where we meet God. The secularization of politics is driven by a religious vision. It says that power is not to be sacralized. Rulers, kings, and emperors are not holy. They are there to serve, not to be served. All power is subject to the overarching imperatives of the right and the just. The moment it oversteps those limits, it is *ultra vires* and may rightly be opposed.

Furthermore, for the first time, God and religion are deterritorialized. God created everything. He is God of everywhere. There is no longer a god of this city and a god of that, of these people as opposed to those. God is intervening to deliver one nation out of another, what we would

▶

Parashat Bo

10 1 Then the Lord said to Moshe, "Go to Pharaoh. I have hardened his heart and
2 his officials', that I may display these My signs before him, and so that you may
tell your children and grandchildren how I made the Egyptians a laughingstock
3 by the signs I revealed among them; and know that I am the Lord." Moshe and
Aharon came to Pharaoh and said to him, "Thus says the Lord, God of the
Hebrews: How much longer will you refuse to submit to Me? Send My people
4 forth to serve Me. For if you refuse to send My people forth, tomorrow I bring

רש״י

י א| **וַיֹּאמֶר ה׳ אֶל מֹשֶׁה בֹּא אֶל פַּרְעֹה.** וְהַתְרֵה בוֹ: **שִׁתִי.** שׂוּמִי, שֶׁחָשִׁית חֲנִי:

ב| **הִתְעַלַּלְתִּי.** שִׂחַקְתִּי, כְּמוֹ: "כִּי הִתְעַלַּלְתְּ בִּי" (במדבר כב, כט), "הֲלוֹא כַּאֲשֶׁר הִתְעוֹלֵל בָּהֶם" (שמואל א׳ ו, ו) הָאָמוּר בְּמִצְרַיִם. וְאֵינוֹ לְשׁוֹן פֹּעַל וּמַעֲלָלִים, שֶׁאִם כֵּן הָיָה לוֹ לִכְתֹּב 'עוֹלַלְתִּי', כְּמוֹ: "וְעוֹלֵל לָמוֹ כַּאֲשֶׁר עוֹלַלְתָּ לִי" (איכה א, כב), "אֲשֶׁר עוֹלַל לִי" (שם פסוק יב):

ג| **לֵעָנֹת.** כְּתַרְגּוּמוֹ: "לְאִתְכְּנָעָא", וְהוּא מִגִּזְרַת 'עָנִי', מֵאַנְתָּ לִהְיוֹת עָנִי וְשָׁפָל מִפָּנַי:

10:2 **וּלְמַעַן תְּסַפֵּר בְּאָזְנֵי בִנְךָ וּבֶן־בִּנְךָ** *And so that you may tell your children and grandchildren* – For the first time, the full significance of the plagues is made clear. It is not limited to Egypt or to that time. That there exists a power greater than the mightiest empire in the ancient world is a proposition to have resonance far beyond the boundaries of Egypt. And in our verse, we learn that it will provide a lesson beyond its time. It would be a story to be handed on across the generations, as it has been from the days of Moshe until today. Those who forget how freedom was won eventually lose it. Those who lived through these events died long ago, but their story never will. That was part of the divine plan from the outset: to tell a story about the liberation of slaves that would lead eventually to a civilization based on freedom, justice, and human rights.

10:3 **עַד־מָתַי מֵאַנְתָּ לֵעָנֹת מִפָּנָי** *How much longer will you refuse to submit to Me?* – There is a new tone of assertiveness here. Patience has worn thin. The Israelites are suffering. The Egyptians are suffering. Only Pharaoh's obstinacy stands in the way of the relief of both nations. Moshe and Aharon are no longer the importuning representatives of the powerless nation of slaves. They occupy the higher moral ground and can speak with authority.

10:4 **אַרְבֶּה** *Locusts* – The desert locust is a devastating visitor to the Middle East, Africa, and Asia even today. A swarm can be 460 square miles in size and contain between forty and eighty million locusts in less than half a square mile. Each locust can eat its weight in plants each day, so a swarm of this size would eat 423 million pounds of plants every day.

Egypt was ravaged by them from time to time and whenever there was an attack of locusts, people would be reminded of the most massive attack of all (Bekhor Shor, and see Joel 1). The locusts completed the work of the hail by destroying the wheat and the spelt that had remained after the hailstorm. Once, Yosef provided the country with grain during the seven years of famine. Now, nature is doing the reverse: destroying all the crops in the field. There is an echo here of the first words of God to Avraham: "And I will bless those who bless you, and those who curse you I will curse" (Gen. 12:33).

פרשת בא

י א וַיֹּאמֶר יהוה אֶל־מֹשֶׁה בֹּא אֶל־פַּרְעֹה כִּי־אֲנִי הִכְבַּדְתִּי אֶת־לִבּוֹ וְאֶת־ ז
ב לֵב עֲבָדָיו לְמַעַן שִׁתִי אֹתֹתַי אֵלֶּה בְּקִרְבּוֹ: וּלְמַעַן תְּסַפֵּר בְּאָזְנֵי בִנְךָ
וּבֶן־בִּנְךָ אֵת אֲשֶׁר הִתְעַלַּלְתִּי בְּמִצְרַיִם וְאֶת־אֹתֹתַי אֲשֶׁר־שַׂמְתִּי בָם
ג וִידַעְתֶּם כִּי־אֲנִי יהוה: וַיָּבֹא מֹשֶׁה וְאַהֲרֹן אֶל־פַּרְעֹה וַיֹּאמְרוּ אֵלָיו
כֹּה־אָמַר יהוה אֱלֹהֵי הָעִבְרִים עַד־מָתַי מֵאַנְתָּ לֵעָנֹת מִפָּנָי שַׁלַּח עַמִּי
ד וְיַעַבְדֻנִי: כִּי אִם־מָאֵן אַתָּה לְשַׁלֵּחַ אֶת־עַמִּי הִנְנִי מֵבִיא מָחָר אַרְבֶּה

אונקלוס

י א וַאֲמַר יי לְמֹשֶׁה, עוֹל לְוָת פַּרְעֹה, אֲרֵי אֲנָא, יַקָּרִית יָת לִבֵּיהּ
וְיָת לִבָּא דְעַבְדוֹהִי, בְּדִיל, לְשַׁוָּאָה, אָתַי אִלֵּין בֵּינֵיהוֹן: ב וּבְדִיל,
דְּתִשְׁתַּעֵי קֳדָם בְּרָךְ וּבַר בְּרָךְ, יָת נִסִּין דַּעֲבַדִית בְּמִצְרַיִם, וְיָת
אָתְוָתַי דְּשַׁוִּיתִי בְהוֹן, וְתִדְעוּן אֲרֵי אֲנָא יי: ג וְעָאל מֹשֶׁה וְאַהֲרֹן
לְוָת פַּרְעֹה, וַאֲמַרוּ לֵיהּ, כִּדְנַן אֲמַר יי אֱלָהָא דִיהוּדָאֵי, עַד אִמַּתִי
מְסָרֵיב אַתְּ, לְאִתְכְּנָעָא מִן קֳדָמַי, שַׁלַּח עַמִּי וְיִפְלְחוּן קֳדָמָי:
ד אֲרֵי, אִם מְסָרֵיב אַתְּ לְשַׁלָּחָא יָת עַמִּי, הָאֲנָא מַיְתֵי מְחַר, גּוֹבָא

BO

Parashat Bo introduces the institution of storytelling as a fundamental religious duty, recalling and re-enacting the events of the exodus every year, and in particular, making children central to the story. If we are the story we tell about ourselves, then as long as we never lose the story, we will never lose our identity.

Cultures are shaped by the range of stories to which they give rise. Some of these have a special role in shaping the self-understanding of those who tell them. We call them master-narratives. They are about large, ongoing groups of people: the tribe, the nation, the civilization. They hold the group together horizontally across space and vertically across time, giving it a shared identity handed on across the generations.

None has been more powerful than the exodus story, whose frame and context is set out in our *parasha*. It gave Jews the most tenacious identity ever held by a nation. In the eras of oppression, it gave hope of freedom. At times of exile, it promised return. It told two hundred generations of Jewish children who they were and of what story they were a part. It became the world's master-narrative of liberty, adopted by an astonishing variety of groups, from Puritans in the seventeenth century to African-Americans in the nineteenth and to Tibetan Buddhists today.

I believe that I am a character in our people's story, with my own chapter to write, and so are we all. To be a Jew is to see yourself as part of that story, to make it live in our time, and to do your best to hand it on to those who will come after us. All of this begins in Parashat Bo.

10:1 אֶת־לִבּוֹ וְאֶת־לֵב עֲבָדָיו *His heart and his officials'* – In fact, though, as we read in verse 7, the officials do experience a change of heart, warning Pharaoh that he is making a mistake that will cost him and his country dearly. This is strong evidence that even when the Torah says that God hardens someone's heart, this does not mean that they forfeit their free will.

▶

5 locusts to your land. They will cover the landscape so that you will not be able
to see the ground. They will eat what little remains after the hail, including all
6 the trees that grow up from your soil. They will fill your palaces, your officials'
houses, and all the houses of Egypt. Your parents and grandparents never saw
anything like this, from the day they arrived upon this earth until today." Then
7 Moshe turned and left Pharaoh. Pharaoh's officials then said to him, "How long
must we leave this man to ensnare us? Send the people forth to serve the Lord
8 their God. Do you not yet know that Egypt is being destroyed?" Moshe and
Aharon were summoned back to Pharaoh, and he said to them, "Go and serve
9 the Lord your God. Who exactly will be going?" "With our youths and our
elderly folk we will go," said Moshe, "with our sons and our daughters, our
10 sheep and our cattle, we all must go, for it will be our festival of the Lord." He
replied, "The Lord be with you if I let you and your children go! Look – evil
11 is staring you in the face. No! Let the men go and serve the Lord. That is

רש"י

ה **אֶת עֵין הָאָרֶץ.** אֶת מַרְאֵה הָאָרֶץ: **וְלֹא יוּכַל.** הָרוֹאֶה "לִרְאוֹת אֶת הָאָרֶץ", וּלְשׁוֹן קְצָרָה דִּבֵּר:

ז **הֲטֶרֶם תֵּדַע.** הַעוֹד לֹא יָדַעְתָּ "כִּי אָבְדָה מִצְרָיִם":

ח **וַיּוּשַׁב.** הוּשְׁבוּ עַל יְדֵי שָׁלִיחַ, שֶׁשָּׁלְחוּ אַחֲרֵיהֶם וֶהֱשִׁיבוּם אֶל פַּרְעֹה:

י **כַּאֲשֶׁר אֲשַׁלַּח אֶתְכֶם וְאֶת טַפְּכֶם.** אַף כִּי אֲשַׁלַּח גַּם אֶת הַצֹּאן וְאֶת הַבָּקָר כַּאֲשֶׁר אֲמַרְתֶּם: **רְאוּ כִּי רָעָה נֶגֶד פְּנֵיכֶם.** כְּתַרְגּוּמוֹ. וּמִדְרַשׁ אַגָּדָה שָׁמַעְתִּי, כּוֹכָב אֶחָד יֵשׁ שֶׁשְּׁמוֹ רָעָה, אָמַר לָהֶם פַּרְעֹה: רוֹאֶה אֲנִי בְּאִיצְטַגְנִינוּת שֶׁלִּי אוֹתוֹ כּוֹכָב עוֹלֶה לִקְרַאתְכֶם בַּמִּדְבָּר וְהוּא סִימָן דָּם וַהֲרִיגָה. וּכְשֶׁחָטְאוּ יִשְׂרָאֵל בָּעֵגֶל וּבִקֵּשׁ הַקָּדוֹשׁ בָּרוּךְ הוּא לְהָרְגָם, אָמַר מֹשֶׁה בִּתְפִלָּתוֹ: "לָמָּה יֹאמְרוּ מִצְרַיִם לֵאמֹר בְּרָעָה הוֹצִיאָם" (להלן לב, יב), זוֹ הִיא שֶׁאָמַר לָהֶם: "רְאוּ כִּי רָעָה נֶגֶד פְּנֵיכֶם". מִיָּד – "וַיִּנָּחֶם ה' עַל הָרָעָה" (שם פסוק יד) וְהָפַךְ אֶת הַדָּם לְדַם מִילָה שֶׁמָּל יְהוֹשֻׁעַ אוֹתָם. וְזֶהוּ שֶׁנֶּאֱמַר: "הַיּוֹם גַּלּוֹתִי אֶת חֶרְפַּת מִצְרַיִם מֵעֲלֵיכֶם" (יהושע ה, ט) שֶׁהָיוּ אוֹמְרִים לָכֶם: דָּם אָנוּ רוֹאִין עֲלֵיכֶם בַּמִּדְבָּר:

יא **לֹא כֵן.** כַּאֲשֶׁר אֲמַרְתֶּם לְהוֹלִיךְ הַטַּף עִמָּכֶם, אֶלָּא לְכוּ הַגְּבָרִים וְעִבְדוּ אֶת ה' כִּי אֹתָהּ בִּקַּשְׁתֶּם עַד הֵנָּה, "נִזְבְּחָה לֵאלֹהֵינוּ" (לעיל ה,

chapter continues to hold true: hate destroys the hater. Evil has two faces. The first – turned to the outside world – is what it does to its victim. The second – turned within – is what it does to its perpetrator. Evil traps the evildoer in its mesh. Slowly but surely, he or she loses freedom and becomes not evil's master but its slave.

10:9 **בִּנְעָרֵינוּ וּבִזְקֵנֵינוּ** *With our youths and our elderly folk* – It was the very young and the old who were sent straight to the gas chambers during the Holocaust. They were deemed of no use. Likewise, to a civilization like ancient Egypt, able-bodied men represented the wealth of the nation. Moshe is signaling a different set of values. We care about our young and our old. Our young are our future, our old are our past, and both are precious to us and to God. We owe respect to those who brought us into being and care for those we have brought into being. The phrase "with our youths and our elderly folk" has become familiar as an expression of Jewish collective responsibility, as if to say: We will not abandon anyone. "All Jews are responsible for one another" (Shevuot 39a).

10:10 **רָעָה נֶגֶד פְּנֵיכֶם** *Evil is staring you in the face* – The Hebrew *raa* may be an allusion to the Egyptian sun god Ra, as if Pharaoh were saying, "Your God may have done wonders for you, but our god has evil in store" (cf. Rashi). This would make sense in terms of the next plague, darkness, which was an eclipse of the sun god of Egypt.

ה בִּגְבֻלֶךָ: וְכִסָּה אֶת־עֵין הָאָרֶץ וְלֹא יוּכַל לִרְאֹת אֶת־הָאָרֶץ וְאָכַל ׀ אֶת־
יֶתֶר הַפְּלֵטָה הַנִּשְׁאֶרֶת לָכֶם מִן־הַבָּרָד וְאָכַל אֶת־כָּל־הָעֵץ הַצֹּמֵחַ
ו לָכֶם מִן־הַשָּׂדֶה: וּמָלְאוּ בָתֶּיךָ וּבָתֵּי כָל־עֲבָדֶיךָ וּבָתֵּי כָל־מִצְרַיִם
אֲשֶׁר לֹא־רָאוּ אֲבֹתֶיךָ וַאֲבוֹת אֲבֹתֶיךָ מִיּוֹם הֱיוֹתָם עַל־הָאֲדָמָה
ז עַד הַיּוֹם הַזֶּה וַיִּפֶן וַיֵּצֵא מֵעִם פַּרְעֹה: וַיֹּאמְרוּ עַבְדֵי פַרְעֹה אֵלָיו
עַד־מָתַי יִהְיֶה זֶה לָנוּ לְמוֹקֵשׁ שַׁלַּח אֶת־הָאֲנָשִׁים וְיַעַבְדוּ אֶת־יהוה
ח אֱלֹהֵיהֶם הֲטֶרֶם תֵּדַע כִּי אָבְדָה מִצְרָיִם: וַיּוּשַׁב אֶת־מֹשֶׁה וְאֶת־
אַהֲרֹן אֶל־פַּרְעֹה וַיֹּאמֶר אֲלֵהֶם לְכוּ עִבְדוּ אֶת־יהוה אֱלֹהֵיכֶם מִי וָמִי
ט הַהֹלְכִים: וַיֹּאמֶר מֹשֶׁה בִּנְעָרֵינוּ וּבִזְקֵנֵינוּ נֵלֵךְ בְּבָנֵינוּ וּבִבְנוֹתֵנוּ בְּצֹאנֵנוּ
י וּבִבְקָרֵנוּ נֵלֵךְ כִּי חַג־יהוה לָנוּ: וַיֹּאמֶר אֲלֵהֶם יְהִי כֵן יהוה עִמָּכֶם
יא כַּאֲשֶׁר אֲשַׁלַּח אֶתְכֶם וְאֶת־טַפְּכֶם רְאוּ כִּי רָעָה נֶגֶד פְּנֵיכֶם: לֹא כֵן

אונקלוס

בִּתְחוּמָךְ: ה וִיחַפֵּי יָת עֵין שִׁמְשָׁא דְאַרְעָא, וְלָא יִכּוֹל לְמֶחֱזֵי יָת אַרְעָא, וְיֵיכוֹל יָת שְׁאָר שֵׁיזָבְתָא, דְּאִשְׁתְּאַרַת לְכוֹן מִן בַּרְדָּא, וְיֵיכוֹל יָת כָּל אִילָנָא, דְּאַצְמַח לְכוֹן מִן חַקְלָא: ו וְיִתְמְלוֹן בָּתָּךְ, וּבָתֵּי כָּל עַבְדָּךְ וּבָתֵּי כָּל מִצְרָאֵי, דְּלָא חֲזוֹ אֲבָהָתָךְ וַאֲבָהָת אֲבָהָתָךְ, מִיּוֹם, מִהְוֵיהוֹן עַל אַרְעָא, עַד יוֹמָא הָדֵין, וְאִתְפְּנִי וּנְפַק מִלְּוָת פַּרְעֹה: ז וַאֲמַרוּ עַבְדֵי פַרְעֹה לֵיהּ, עַד אֵמָתַי יְהֵי דֵין לָנָא לְתַקְלָא, שַׁלַּח יָת גֻּבְרַיָּא, וְיִפְלְחוּן קֳדָם יי אֱלָהֲהוֹן, הַעוֹד כְּעַן לָא יְדַעְתָּא, אֲרֵי אֲבַדַת מִצְרָיִם: ח וְאִתָּתַב, יָת מֹשֶׁה וְיָת אַהֲרֹן לְוָת פַּרְעֹה, וַאֲמַר לְהוֹן, אִיזִילוּ פְּלַחוּ קֳדָם יי אֱלָהֲכוֹן, מַאן וּמַאן אָזְלִין: ט וַאֲמַר מֹשֶׁה, בְּעוּלֵימָנָא וּבְסָבַנָא נֵיזִיל, בִּבְנַנָא וּבִבְנָתַנָא, בְּעָנַנָא וּבְתוֹרַנָא נֵיזִיל, אֲרֵי חַגָּא קֳדָם יי לַנָא: י וַאֲמַר לְהוֹן, יְהֵי כֵן מֵימְרָא דַּיי בְּסַעְדְּכוֹן, כַּד אֲשַׁלַּח יָתְכוֹן וְיָת טַפְלְכוֹן, חֲזוֹ, אֲרֵי בִּישָׁא אַתּוּן סְבִירִין לְמֶעְבַּד לֵית קֳבֵיל אַפֵּיכוֹן לְאִסְתְּחָרָא: יא לָא כֵן,

10:6 אֲבֹתֶיךָ וַאֲבוֹת אֲבֹתֶיךָ *Your parents and grandparents* – A contrast with the earlier phrase, "your children and grandchildren." The Israelites look, in hope, to future generations. The Egyptians, in fear, turn toward the past.

10:6 וַיִּפֶן *Then Moshe turned* – It is one of the customs of absolute rulers that one does not turn their back on them. You leave, still facing them, bowing, and walking backward. The fact that Moshe turned and exited meant that he was not obeying this protocol, and by implication showing that he believed that Pharaoh's authority no longer commanded in one respect. For the first time, in the next verse, Pharaoh's own officials will tell him his policy has failed. Egypt is being destroyed. Much better to let the people leave than to allow this succession of disasters to continue.

Tragically, tyrants are held captive by their hate, and they lead their own people to destruction. In the closing stages of the Second World War, Hitler diverted trains from the Russian front in order to accelerate the transportation of Jews to Auschwitz. He endangered his own war efforts for the sake of continuing his genocidal program against the Jews. This was evil for evil's sake. The law of history articulated in this

what you are asking for." Then Pharaoh had Moshe and Aharon expelled from
12 his presence. The LORD said to Moshe, "Reach out your hand over SHENI
Egypt so that locusts swarm over the land and eat everything growing there,
13 all that is left after the hail." So Moshe stretched out his staff over Egypt,
and the LORD caused an east wind to blow across the land all that day and
14 night. By morning, the east wind had brought the locusts. They invaded all
of Egypt and settled throughout its land in a dense swarm. Never before had
15 there been such a plague of locusts, nor will there ever be again. They covered
all the landscape until the ground was black. They ate all that was left after
the hail: all the plants and all the fruit. Nothing green remained on trees or
16 plants throughout all Egypt. In haste, Pharaoh summoned Moshe and Aharon
17 and said, "I have sinned against the LORD your God and you. Forgive my sin
now, one more time. Pray to the LORD your God to take this death away from
18 19 me." Moshe left Pharaoh's presence and prayed to the LORD. And the LORD
turned the wind, westerly and very strong, and lifted the locusts and swept
20 them into the Sea of Reeds. Not one locust remained anywhere in Egypt. But
the LORD strengthened Pharaoh's heart and he would not send the Israelites
forth.

רש״י

ח, וְאֵין דֶּרֶךְ הַטַּף לִזְבֹּחַ: וַיְגָרֶשׁ אֹתָם. הֲרֵי זֶה לָשׁוֹן קָצָר וְלֹא פֵּרַשׁ מִי הַמְגָרֵשׁ:

יב **בָּאַרְבֶּה.** בִּשְׁבִיל מַכַּת הָאַרְבֶּה:

יד **וְאַחֲרָיו לֹא יִהְיֶה כֵּן.** וְאוֹתוֹ שֶׁהָיָה בִּימֵי יוֹאֵל שֶׁנֶּאֱמַר: "כָּמֹהוּ לֹא נִהְיָה מִן הָעוֹלָם" (יואל ב, ב) לָמַדְנוּ שֶׁהָיָה כָּבֵד מִשֶּׁל מֹשֶׁה – עַל יְדֵי מִינִין הַרְבֵּה שֶׁהָיוּ יַחַד: אַרְבֶּה, יֶלֶק, חָסִיל, גָּזָם; אֲבָל שֶׁל מֹשֶׁה מִין אֶחָד, וְכָמוֹהוּ לֹא נִהְיָה וְלֹא יִהְיֶה:

טו **כָּל יֶרֶק.** עָלֶה יָרֹק, וירדור״א בְּלַעַז:

יט **לֹא נִשְׁאַר אַרְבֶּה אֶחָד.** אַף הַמְלוּחִים שֶׁמָּלְחוּ מֵהֶן:

10:13 וַיהוה נִהַג רוּחַ־קָדִים *The LORD caused an east wind* – The text does not say that God created the locusts out of nothing or brought them in defiance of the laws of nature. A sirocco from the southeast like the wind that blasted the ears of corn in an earlier pharaoh's dream (Gen. 41:21) is precisely what would have brought a dense swarm of locusts, given the damp earth left by the plague of hail, which is particularly conducive to the hatching of large numbers of locusts. The naturalistic explanation again focusses our attention on the moral dimension of the plague. In Egyptian mythology, Pharaoh and the entire structure of its society represented order against the ever-threatening forces of chaos. Sheer chaos has now been unleashed against the land and its inhabitants. It is as if creation itself were protesting the injustice being perpetrated against an afflicted people who only sought the opportunity to leave the land and worship their own God.

10:17 שָׂא נָא חַטָּאתִי *Forgive my sin* – This is Pharaoh's first request for forgiveness, a measure of how far, finally, the reality of the plagues is beginning to close in on the ruler of Egypt. His prayer "to take this death away from me" is his darkest utterance thus far.

לְכוּ־נָא הַגְּבָרִים וְעִבְדוּ אֶת־יְהוָה כִּי אֹתָהּ אַתֶּם מְבַקְשִׁים וַיְגָרֶשׁ
יב אֹתָם מֵאֵת פְּנֵי פַרְעֹה׃ וַיֹּאמֶר יְהוָה אֶל־מֹשֶׁה נְטֵה יָדְךָ שני
עַל־אֶרֶץ מִצְרַיִם בָּאַרְבֶּה וְיַעַל עַל־אֶרֶץ מִצְרָיִם וְיֹאכַל אֶת־כָּל־עֵשֶׂב
יג הָאָרֶץ אֵת כָּל־אֲשֶׁר הִשְׁאִיר הַבָּרָד׃ וַיֵּט מֹשֶׁה אֶת־מַטֵּהוּ עַל־אֶרֶץ
מִצְרַיִם וַיהוָה נִהַג רוּחַ־קָדִים בָּאָרֶץ כָּל־הַיּוֹם הַהוּא וְכָל־הַלָּיְלָה
יד הַבֹּקֶר הָיָה וְרוּחַ הַקָּדִים נָשָׂא אֶת־הָאַרְבֶּה׃ וַיַּעַל הָאַרְבֶּה עַל כָּל־
אֶרֶץ מִצְרַיִם וַיָּנַח בְּכֹל גְּבוּל מִצְרָיִם כָּבֵד מְאֹד לְפָנָיו לֹא־הָיָה כֵן
טו אַרְבֶּה כָּמֹהוּ וְאַחֲרָיו לֹא יִהְיֶה־כֵּן׃ וַיְכַס אֶת־עֵין כָּל־הָאָרֶץ וַתֶּחְשַׁךְ
הָאָרֶץ וַיֹּאכַל אֶת־כָּל־עֵשֶׂב הָאָרֶץ וְאֵת כָּל־פְּרִי הָעֵץ אֲשֶׁר הוֹתִיר
הַבָּרָד וְלֹא־נוֹתַר כָּל־יֶרֶק בָּעֵץ וּבְעֵשֶׂב הַשָּׂדֶה בְּכָל־אֶרֶץ מִצְרָיִם׃
טז וַיְמַהֵר פַּרְעֹה לִקְרֹא לְמֹשֶׁה וּלְאַהֲרֹן וַיֹּאמֶר חָטָאתִי לַיהוָה אֱלֹהֵיכֶם
יז וְלָכֶם׃ וְעַתָּה שָׂא נָא חַטָּאתִי אַךְ הַפַּעַם וְהַעְתִּירוּ לַיהוָה אֱלֹהֵיכֶם
יח וְיָסֵר מֵעָלַי רַק אֶת־הַמָּוֶת הַזֶּה׃ וַיֵּצֵא מֵעִם פַּרְעֹה וַיֶּעְתַּר אֶל־יְהוָה׃
יט וַיַּהֲפֹךְ יְהוָה רוּחַ־יָם חָזָק מְאֹד וַיִּשָּׂא אֶת־הָאַרְבֶּה וַיִּתְקָעֵהוּ יָמָּה סּוּף
כ לֹא נִשְׁאַר אַרְבֶּה אֶחָד בְּכֹל גְּבוּל מִצְרָיִם׃ וַיְחַזֵּק יְהוָה אֶת־לֵב פַּרְעֹה
וְלֹא שִׁלַּח אֶת־בְּנֵי יִשְׂרָאֵל׃

אונקלוס

אֵיזִילוּ כְעַן גֻּבְרַיָּא וּפְלַחוּ קֳדָם יְיָ, אֲרֵי יָתַהּ אַתּוּן בָּעַן, וְתָרֵיךְ יָתְהוֹן, מִן קֳדָם פַּרְעֹה: יב וַאֲמַר יְיָ לְמֹשֶׁה, אֲרֵים יְדָךְ, עַל אַרְעָא דְמִצְרַיִם בְּגוֹבָא, וְיִסַּק עַל אַרְעָא דְמִצְרָיִם, וְיֵיכוֹל יָת כָּל עִסְבָּא דְאַרְעָא, יָת כָּל דְּאַשְׁאַר בַּרְדָּא: יג וַאֲרֵים מֹשֶׁה יָת חֻטְרֵיהּ עַל אַרְעָא דְמִצְרַיִם, וַיְיָ דַּבַּר רוּחַ קִדּוּמָא בְּאַרְעָא, כָּל יוֹמָא הַהוּא וְכָל לֵילְיָא, צַפְרָא הֲוָה, וְרוּחַ קִדּוּמָא, נְטַל יָת גּוֹבָא: יד וּסְלֵיק גּוֹבָא, עַל כָּל אַרְעָא דְמִצְרַיִם, וּשְׁרָא, בְּכָל תְּחוּם מִצְרָיִם, תַּקִּיף לַחֲדָא, קֳדָמוֹהִי, לָא הֲוָה כֵן גּוֹבָא דִכְוָתֵיהּ, וּבָתְרוֹהִי לָא יְהֵי כֵן: טו וַחֲפָא, יָת עֵין שִׁמְשָׁא דְּכָל אַרְעָא וַחֲשׁוֹכַת אַרְעָא, וַאֲכַל יָת כָּל עִסְבָּא דְּאַרְעָא, וְיָת כָּל פֵּירֵי אִילָנָא, דְּאַשְׁאַר בַּרְדָּא, וְלָא אִשְׁתְּאַר כָּל יָרוֹק בְּאִילָנָא, וּבְעִסְבָּא דְּחַקְלָא בְּכָל אַרְעָא דְמִצְרָיִם: טז וְאוֹחִי פַרְעֹה, לְמִקְרֵי לְמֹשֶׁה וּלְאַהֲרֹן, וַאֲמַר, חָבֵית, קֳדָם יְיָ אֱלָהֲכוֹן וּלְכוֹן: יז וּכְעַן, שְׁבוֹק כְּעַן לְחוֹבִי בְּרַם זִמְנָא הָדָא, וְצַלּוֹ קֳדָם יְיָ אֱלָהֲכוֹן, וְיַעְדֵּי מִנִּי, לְחוֹד יָת מוֹתָא הָדֵין: יח וּנְפַק מִלְּוָת פַּרְעֹה, וְצַלִּי קֳדָם יְיָ: יט וַהֲפַךְ יְיָ רוּחַ מַעַרְבָא תַּקִּיף לַחֲדָא, וּנְטַל יָת גּוֹבָא, וּרְמָהִי לְיַמָּא דְסוּף, לָא אִשְׁתְּאַר גּוֹבָא חַד, בְּכָל תְּחוּם מִצְרָיִם: כ וְתַקִּיף יְיָ יָת לִבָּא דְפַרְעֹה, וְלָא שַׁלַּח יָת בְּנֵי יִשְׂרָאֵל: כא וַאֲמַר יְיָ לְמֹשֶׁה, אֲרֵים יְדָךְ עַל צֵית שְׁמַיָּא, וִיהֵי חֲשׁוֹכָא עַל אַרְעָא דְמִצְרָיִם, בָּתַר דְּיִעְדֵּי

21 Then the Lord said to Moshe, "Reach out your hand toward the sky to bring
22 darkness down over Egypt – darkness so deep it can be felt." Moshe reached
out his hand toward the sky, and all across Egypt it was pitch dark for three days.
23 For three days, no one could see anyone else or even move. But in the Israelites'
24 homes, they had light. Then Pharaoh summoned Moshe and said, "Go, serve SHELISHI
the Lord. Just leave your flocks and herds. Your children may go with you."
25 "Then give us sacrifices and burnt offerings to present to the Lord our God,"
26 said Moshe. "Our livestock must go with us. Not a hoof can be left behind.
We must take them to serve the Lord our God, for until we arrive, we will

רש״י

כא] **וַיָמֵשׁ חֹשֶׁךְ.** וְיַחְשִׁיךְ עֲלֵיהֶם חֹשֶׁךְ יוֹתֵר מֵחֶשְׁכּוֹ שֶׁל לַיְלָה, וְחֹשֶׁךְ שֶׁל לַיְלָה יַאֲמִישׁ וְיַחְשִׁיךְ עוֹד: **וְיָמֵשׁ.** כְּמוֹ 'וְיַאֲמֵשׁ'. יֵשׁ לָנוּ תֵּבוֹת הַרְבֵּה חֲסֵרוֹת אָלֶ"ף, לְפִי שֶׁאֵין הֲבָרַת הָאָלֶ"ף נִכֶּרֶת כָּל כָּךְ אֵין הַכָּתוּב מַקְפִּיד עַל חֶסְרוֹנָהּ, כְּגוֹן: "וְלֹא יַהֵל שָׁם עֲרָבִי" (ישעיה יג, כ) כְּמוֹ 'לֹא יַאֲהֵל', לֹא יַטֶּה אָהֳלוֹ. וְכֵן: "וַתַּזְרֵנִי חַיִל" (שמואל ב' כב, מ) כְּמוֹ 'וַתְּאַזְּרֵנִי'. וְאוּנְקְלוֹס תִּרְגֵּם לְשׁוֹן הֲסָרָה, כְּמוֹ: "לֹא יָמִישׁ" (להלן יג, כב) – "בָּתַר דְּיִעְדֵּי קְבַל לֵילְיָא", כְּשֶׁיַּגִּיעַ סָמוּךְ לְאוֹר הַיּוֹם. אֲבָל אֵין הַדִּבּוּר מְיֻשָּׁב עַל הַוָּי"ו שֶׁל 'וְיָמֵשׁ', לְפִי שֶׁהוּא כָּתוּב אַחַר "וַיְהִי חֹשֶׁךְ". וּמִדְרַשׁ אַגָּדָה פּוֹתְרוֹ לְשׁוֹן "מְמַשֵּׁשׁ בַּצָּהֳרַיִם" (דברים כח, כט), שֶׁהָיָה כָּפוּל וּמְכֻפָּל וְעָב עַד שֶׁהָיָה בּוֹ מַמָּשׁ:

כב] **שְׁלֹשֶׁת יָמִים.** שִׁלּוּשׁ שֶׁל יָמִים, טרציינ"א בְּלַעַז. וְכֵן 'שִׁבְעַת יָמִים' בְּכָל מָקוֹם, שטיינ"א שֶׁל יָמִים: **וַיְהִי חֹשֶׁךְ אֲפֵלָה... שְׁלֹשֶׁת יָמִים.** חֹשֶׁךְ שֶׁל אֹפֶל שֶׁ"לֹּא רָאוּ אִישׁ אֶת אָחִיו" אוֹתָן שְׁלֹשֶׁת יָמִים, וְעוֹד שְׁלֹשֶׁת יָמִים אֲחֵרִים חֹשֶׁךְ מֻכְפָּל עַל זֶה שֶׁ"לֹּא קָמוּ אִישׁ מִתַּחְתָּיו", יוֹשֵׁב אֵין יָכוֹל לַעֲמֹד וְעוֹמֵד אֵין יָכוֹל לֵישֵׁב. וְלָמָּה הֵבִיא עֲלֵיהֶם חֹשֶׁךְ? שֶׁהָיוּ בְּיִשְׂרָאֵל בְּאוֹתוֹ הַדּוֹר רְשָׁעִים וְלֹא הָיוּ רוֹצִים לָצֵאת, וּמֵתוּ בִּשְׁלֹשֶׁת יְמֵי אֲפֵלָה, כְּדֵי שֶׁלֹּא יִרְאוּ מִצְרִים בְּמַפַּלְתָּם וְיֹאמְרוּ: אַף הֵם לוֹקִים כָּמוֹנוּ. וְעוֹד, שֶׁחִפְּשׂוּ יִשְׂרָאֵל וְרָאוּ אֶת כְּלֵיהֶם, וּכְשֶׁיָּצְאוּ וְהָיוּ שׁוֹאֲלִים מֵהֶן וְהָיוּ אוֹמְרִים: אֵין בְּיָדֵינוּ כְּלוּם, אוֹמֵר לוֹ: אֲנִי רְאִיתִיו בְּבֵיתְךָ וּבְמָקוֹם פְּלוֹנִי הוּא:

כד] **יֻצָּג.** יְהֵא מֻצָּג בִּמְקוֹמוֹ:

כה] **גַּם אַתָּה תִּתֵּן.** לֹא דַּיְּךָ שֶׁמִּקְנֵנוּ יֵלֵךְ עִמָּנוּ, אֶלָּא אַף מִשֶּׁלְּךָ תִּתֵּן:

כו] **פַּרְסָה.** פַּרְסַת רֶגֶל, פלנט"א בְּלַעַז: **לֹא נֵדַע מַה נַּעֲבֹד.** כַּמָּה תִּכְבַּד הָעֲבוֹדָה, שֶׁמָּא יִשְׁאַל יוֹתֵר מִמַּה שֶּׁיֵּשׁ בְּיָדֵינוּ:

sun god. In the beginning of time, according to Egyptian myth, the sun god ruled together with Nun, the primeval waters. Eventually there were many deities. Ra then created human beings from his tears. Seeing, however, that they were deceitful, he sent the goddess Hathor to destroy them; only a few survived.

The obliteration of the sun in the ninth plague signals that there is a power greater than Ra. Yet this signified less the power of God over the sun than the rejection by God of a civilization that turned one man into an absolute ruler – and that could tolerate the murder of children because that is what Ra himself did.

When God tells Moshe to say to Pharaoh, "Israel is My son, My firstborn," He is saying: I am the God who cares for His children, not one who kills His children. The ninth plague is a divine act of communication that says: there is not only physical darkness but also moral darkness. The best test of a civilization is to see how it treats children, its own, and others'.

10:21 **וַיָמֵשׁ חֹשֶׁךְ** *Darkness so deep it can be felt* – The phrase suggests what happened: a *ḥamsin*, a sandstorm of a kind not unfamiliar in Egypt, which can last for several days, producing sand- and dust-filled air that obliterates the light of the sun: "darkness so deep it can be felt." A *ḥamsin* is usually produced by a southern wind that blows into Egypt from the Sahara Desert. The worst sandstorm is usually the first of the season, in March. This fits the dating of the plague, which happened shortly before the death of the firstborn, on Passover.

כא וַיֹּאמֶר יהוה אֶל־מֹשֶׁה נְטֵה יָדְךָ עַל־הַשָּׁמַיִם וִיהִי חֹשֶׁךְ עַל־אֶרֶץ
כב מִצְרָיִם וְיָמֵשׁ חֹשֶׁךְ: וַיֵּט מֹשֶׁה אֶת־יָדוֹ עַל־הַשָּׁמָיִם וַיְהִי חֹשֶׁךְ־אֲפֵלָה
כג בְּכָל־אֶרֶץ מִצְרַיִם שְׁלֹשֶׁת יָמִים: לֹא־רָאוּ אִישׁ אֶת־אָחִיו וְלֹא־קָמוּ
אִישׁ מִתַּחְתָּיו שְׁלֹשֶׁת יָמִים וּלְכָל־בְּנֵי יִשְׂרָאֵל הָיָה אוֹר בְּמוֹשְׁבֹתָם:
כד וַיִּקְרָא פַרְעֹה אֶל־מֹשֶׁה וַיֹּאמֶר לְכוּ עִבְדוּ אֶת־יהוה רַק צֹאנְכֶם שלישי
כה וּבְקַרְכֶם יֻצָּג גַּם־טַפְּכֶם יֵלֵךְ עִמָּכֶם: וַיֹּאמֶר מֹשֶׁה גַּם־אַתָּה תִּתֵּן
כו בְיָדֵנוּ זְבָחִים וְעֹלֹת וְעָשִׂינוּ לַיהוה אֱלֹהֵינוּ: וְגַם־מִקְנֵנוּ יֵלֵךְ עִמָּנוּ
לֹא תִשָּׁאֵר פַּרְסָה כִּי מִמֶּנּוּ נִקַּח לַעֲבֹד אֶת־יהוה אֱלֹהֵינוּ וַאֲנַחְנוּ

אונקלוס

קֳבֵל לֵילְיָא: כב וַאֲרִים מֹשֶׁה, יָת יְדֵיהּ עַל צֵית שְׁמַיָּא, וַהֲוָה חֲשׁוֹךְ קְבַל, בְּכָל אַרְעָא דְּמִצְרַיִם תְּלָתָא יוֹמִין: כג לָא חֲזוֹ גְּבַר יָת אֲחוּהִי, וְלָא קָמוּ, אֱנָשׁ מִתְּחוֹתוֹהִי תְּלָתָא יוֹמִין, וּלְכָל בְּנֵי יִשְׂרָאֵל, הֲוָה נְהוֹרָא בְּמוֹתְבָנֵיהוֹן: כד וּקְרָא פַרְעֹה לְמֹשֶׁה, וַאֲמַר אִיזִילוּ פְּלַחוּ קֳדָם יְיָ, לְחוֹד, עָנְכוֹן וְתוֹרֵיכוֹן שְׁבוּקוּ, אַף טַפְלְכוֹן יֵיזֵיל עִמְּכוֹן: כה וַאֲמַר מֹשֶׁה, אַף אַתְּ, תִּתֵּין בִּידַנָא נִכְסַת קֻדְשִׁין וַעֲלָוָן, וְנַעְבֵּיד קֳדָם יְיָ אֱלָהַנָא: כו וְאַף בְּעִירַנָא יֵיזֵיל עִמַּנָא, לָא נִשְׁאַר מִנֵּיהּ מִדְּעַם, אֲרֵי מִנֵּיהּ אֲנַחְנָא נָסְבִין, לְמִפְלַח קֳדָם יְיָ אֱלָהַנָא, וַאֲנַחְנָא לֵית

THE PLAGUE OF DARKNESS

The ninth plague seems out of sequence. Thus far there have been eight plagues, and they have become steadily more serious. The first two seemed more like omens than anything else. The third and fourth caused worry, not crisis. The fifth affected animals, not human beings.

The sixth, boils, was again a discomfort, but a serious one, no longer an external issue but a bodily affliction. The seventh and eighth destroyed the Egyptian grain. Now there is no food. Still to come is the tenth plague, the death of the firstborn, in retribution for Pharaoh's murder of Israelite children. It is this that will break Pharaoh's resolve.

So we would expect the ninth plague to be very serious indeed, something that threatens, even if it does not take, human life. Instead it seems like an anticlimax: Darkness is a nuisance, but no more. Why then does it happen now?

The answer lies in a line from *Dayeinu*, the song we sing as part of the Haggada: "If God had executed judgment against them [the Egyptians] but had not done so against their gods, it would have been sufficient."

Not all the plagues are directed, in the first instance, against the Egyptians. Some are intended to show them the powerlessness of the gods in which they believed – we saw this most clearly in the first two plagues, which were symbolic representations of the Egyptian murder of Israelite children. These had a quite different symbolism for the Israelites, and for us. To the Egyptians' victims, their meaning was moral. They represented the rule of retributive justice: As you do, so shall you be done to.

Unlike all the other plagues, the significance of the tenth is disclosed to Moshe even before he sets out on his mission: "Tell Pharaoh: This is what the LORD says, 'Israel is My son, My firstborn. I have told you: Send forth My son.... If you refuse to let him go, I will kill your son, your firstborn'" (Ex. 4:22–23). The tenth plague is to be the enactment of retributive justice; the first nine are a prelude.

We can now understand the significance of the ninth plague. The greatest god in the Egyptian pantheon was Ra or Re, the sun god. The name of the Pharaoh often associated with the exodus, Ramesses II, means, as we have seen, *messes*, "son of" Ra. Egypt – so its people believed – was ruled by the sun. Its human ruler was semidivine, the child of the

27 not know what we must use to serve the Lord." But the Lord strengthened
28 Pharaoh's heart, and he would not agree to send the people forth. "Leave my
presence," said Pharaoh. "Take care never to see my face again, because on the
29 day you do, that day you will die!" Moshe replied, "As you say: I will not see
your face again."
11 1 Then the Lord said to Moshe, "One last plague will I send against Pharaoh,
against Egypt. After that, he will send you forth from here, and when he does,
2 he will drive you out completely. Now tell the people, men and women, to
3 ask of their neighbors articles of silver and of gold." The Lord granted the
people favor in the eyes of the Egyptians. And the man Moshe, too, was held
in high regard in the land of Egypt, among both Pharaoh's officials and the
4 people. Moshe said, "This is what the Lord says: Around REVI'I
5 midnight I will move throughout Egypt, and every firstborn son in Egypt will
die, from Pharaoh's firstborn presiding on his throne to the firstborn of the
6 slave girl at her hand mill; the firstborn of the cattle as well. A scream will ring
out across Egypt, unlike any that has been before, or any that will be again.

רש״י

כט **כן דברת.** יפה דברת ובזמנו דברת, אמת ש״לא אסף עוד ראות פניך״:

יא א **כלה.** ״גמירא״, כליל, כלכם ישלח:

ב **דבר נא.** אין ׳נא׳ אלא לשון בקשה; בבקשה ממך הזהירם על כך, שלא יאמר אותו צדיק, אברהם, ״ועבדום וענו אתם״ (בראשית טו, יג) קים בהם, ״ואחרי כן יצאו ברכש גדול״ (שם פסוק יד) לא קים בהם:

ד **ויאמר משה כה אמר ה׳.** בעמדו לפני פרעה נאמרה לו, שהרי משיצא מלפניו לא הוסיף ראות פניו: **כחצת הלילה.** כהחלק הלילה, ׳כחצת׳ כמו: ״כעלות״ (יהושע ד, יח, ועוד), ״ככלת״ (דברים כ, ט, ועוד) ״בחרות אפם בנו״ (תהלים קכד, ג). זהו פשוטו ליישבו על אפניו, שאין ׳חצות׳ שם דבר של חצי. ורבותינו דרשוהו כמו ׳כחצי הלילה׳, ואמרו שאמר משה ׳כחצת׳ דמשמע סמוך לו או לפניו או לאחריו, ולא אמר ׳בחצות׳, שמא יטעו אצטגניני פרעה ויאמרו: משה בדאי הוא:

ה **עד בכור השבי** (להלן יב, כט). למה לקו השבויים? כדי שלא יאמרו, יראתם תבעה עלבונם והביאה פרענות על מצרים: **מבכור פרעה... עד בכור השפחה.** כל הפחותים מבכור פרעה וחשובים מבכור השפחה היו בכלל. ולמה לקו בני השפחות? שאף הם היו משתעבדים בהם ושמחים בצרתם: **וכל בכור בהמה.** לפי שהיו עובדין לה – כשהקדוש ברוך הוא נפרע מן האמה נפרע מאלהיה:

know within their own pantheon, they began to realize that the Israelites are not mere slaves. They are people in their own right. Their own religion, different though it is from that of Egypt, has undeniable force. There is something remarkable that they did not fully understand but for which they have increasing awe. Thus their attitude to the Israelites shifts from contempt to respect.

11:3 **האיש משה** *The man Moshe* – The Egyptians recognized that Moshe had given Pharaoh every opportunity to avoid the plagues, and that he had ended them when requested to do so. He had been consistent in his words and legitimate in his request, unlike Pharaoh who showed obstinacy, made promises and failed to keep them, and held his own people hostage to his failure to let the Israelites leave.

כז לֹא־נֵדַע מַה־נַּעֲבֹד אֶת־יְהוָה עַד־בֹּאֵנוּ שָׁמָּה: וַיְחַזֵּק יְהוָה אֶת־
כח לֵב פַּרְעֹה וְלֹא אָבָה לְשַׁלְּחָם: וַיֹּאמֶר־לוֹ פַרְעֹה לֵךְ מֵעָלָי הִשָּׁמֶר
כט לְךָ אַל־תֹּסֶף רְאוֹת פָּנַי כִּי בְּיוֹם רְאֹתְךָ פָנַי תָּמוּת: וַיֹּאמֶר מֹשֶׁה כֵּן
דִּבַּרְתָּ לֹא־אֹסִף עוֹד רְאוֹת פָּנֶיךָ:
יא א וַיֹּאמֶר יְהוָה אֶל־מֹשֶׁה עוֹד נֶגַע אֶחָד אָבִיא עַל־פַּרְעֹה וְעַל־מִצְרַיִם ח
אַחֲרֵי־כֵן יְשַׁלַּח אֶתְכֶם מִזֶּה כְּשַׁלְּחוֹ כָּלָה גָּרֵשׁ יְגָרֵשׁ אֶתְכֶם מִזֶּה:
ב דַּבֶּר־נָא בְּאָזְנֵי הָעָם וְיִשְׁאֲלוּ אִישׁ ׀ מֵאֵת רֵעֵהוּ וְאִשָּׁה מֵאֵת רְעוּתָהּ
ג כְּלֵי־כֶסֶף וּכְלֵי זָהָב: וַיִּתֵּן יְהוָה אֶת־חֵן הָעָם בְּעֵינֵי מִצְרָיִם גַּם ׀
הָאִישׁ מֹשֶׁה גָּדוֹל מְאֹד בְּאֶרֶץ מִצְרַיִם בְּעֵינֵי עַבְדֵי־פַרְעֹה וּבְעֵינֵי
ד הָעָם: וַיֹּאמֶר מֹשֶׁה כֹּה אָמַר יְהוָה כַּחֲצֹת הַלַּיְלָה רביעי
ה אֲנִי יוֹצֵא בְּתוֹךְ מִצְרָיִם: וּמֵת כָּל־בְּכוֹר בְּאֶרֶץ מִצְרַיִם מִבְּכוֹר פַּרְעֹה
הַיֹּשֵׁב עַל־כִּסְאוֹ עַד בְּכוֹר הַשִּׁפְחָה אֲשֶׁר אַחַר הָרֵחָיִם וְכֹל בְּכוֹר
ו בְּהֵמָה: וְהָיְתָה צְעָקָה גְדֹלָה בְּכָל־אֶרֶץ מִצְרָיִם אֲשֶׁר כָּמֹהוּ לֹא

אונקלוס

אֲנַחְנָא יָדְעִין, מָא נִפְלַח קֳדָם יי, עַד מֵיתַנָא לְתַמָּן: כז וְתַקִּיף יי יָת לִבָּא דְּפַרְעֹה, וְלָא אֲבָא לְשַׁלָּחוּתְהוֹן: כח וַאֲמַר לֵיהּ פַּרְעֹה אִיזֵיל מֵעִלָּוַי, אִסְתְּמַר לָךְ, לָא תוֹסֵיף לְמִחְזֵי אַפַּי, אֲרֵי, בְּיוֹמָא, דְּתִחְזֵי אַפַּי תְּמוּת: כט וַאֲמַר מֹשֶׁה יָאוּת מַלֵּילְתָּא, לָא אוֹסֵיף עוֹד לְמִחְזֵי אַפָּךְ: יא א וַאֲמַר יי לְמֹשֶׁה, עוֹד מַכְתָּשׁ חַד אַיְתֵי עַל פַּרְעֹה וְעַל מִצְרָאֵי, בָּתַר כֵּן, יְשַׁלַּח יָתְכוֹן מִכָּא, כְּשַׁלָּחוּתֵיהּ, גְּמִירָא, תָּרָכָא, יְתָרֵיךְ יָתְכוֹן מִכָּא: ב מַלֵּיל כְּעַן קֳדָם עַמָּא, וְיִשְׁאֲלוּן, גְּבַר מִן חַבְרֵיהּ, וְאִתְּתָא מִן חַבְרְתַהּ, מָנִין דִּכְסַף וּמָנִין דִּדְהַב: ג וִיהַב יי, יָת עַמָּא לְרַחֲמִין בְּעֵינֵי מִצְרָאֵי, אַף גֻּבְרָא מֹשֶׁה, רַב לַחֲדָא בְּאַרְעָא דְּמִצְרַיִם, בְּעֵינֵי עַבְדֵי פַרְעֹה וּבְעֵינֵי עַמָּא: ד וַאֲמַר מֹשֶׁה, כִּדְנַן אֲמַר יי, כְּפַלְגוּת לֵילְיָא, אֲנָא מִתְגְּלֵי בְּגוֹ מִצְרָיִם: ה וִימוּת כָּל בֻּכְרָא בְּאַרְעָא דְּמִצְרַיִם, מִבֻּכְרָא דְּפַרְעֹה דַּעֲתִיד לְמִתַּב עַל כֻּרְסֵי מַלְכוּתֵיהּ, עַד בֻּכְרָא דְּאַמְתָא, דְּבָתַר רֵחַיָּא, וְכָל בֻּכְרָא דִּבְעִירָא: ו וּתְהֵי, צְוָחְתָּא רַבְּתָא בְּכָל אַרְעָא דְּמִצְרַיִם, דִּכְוָתַהּ לָא הֲוָת,

11:3 וַיִּתֵּן יהוה אֶת־חֵן הָעָם בְּעֵינֵי מִצְרָיִם *The Lord granted the people favor in the eyes of the Egyptians* – In fulfilment of his promise to Moshe at the burning bush (Ex. 3:21). The Egyptians are generous in their release of the Israelites, as the Israelites will later be commanded to be on the release of any of their own slaves (see Deut. 15:14). They do not blame the Israelites for the plagues. They recognize the justice of their cause.

Once the Egyptians have seen the power that was working on behalf of the Israelites, greater than anything they

7 But among the Israelites not a dog will bare its tongue at man or beast. Then
8 you will know that the LORD is setting Israel apart from Egypt. And all these
officials of yours will come and bow down to me, saying, 'Leave, you and all the
people behind you.' After that, I will leave." He turned and left Pharaoh, blazing
9 with anger. The LORD said to Moshe, "Pharaoh will not listen to you,
10 that My wonders may be multiplied in Egypt." Moshe and Aharon had produced
all these wonders before Pharaoh, but the LORD strengthened Pharaoh's heart,
12 1 and he did not let the Israelites leave his land. Then the LORD spoke
2 to Moshe and Aharon in the land of Egypt. He said, "This month shall be to
you the beginning of months; the opening of the year, this month will be for

רש״י

ז **לֹא יֶחֱרַץ כֶּלֶב לְשֹׁנוֹ.** אוֹמֵר אֲנִי שֶׁהוּא לְשׁוֹן שִׁנּוּן, לֹא יְשַׁנֵּן. וְכֵן: "לֹא חָרַץ לִבְנֵי יִשְׂרָאֵל לְאִישׁ אֶת לְשֹׁנוֹ" (יהושע י, כא) – לֹא שִׁנֵּן; "אָז תֶּחֱרָץ" (שמואל ב׳ ה, כד) – תִּשְׁתַּנֵּן; "לְמוֹרַג חָרוּץ" (ישעיה מא, טו) – שָׁנוּן; "מַחְשְׁבוֹת חָרוּץ" (משלי כא, ה) – אָדָם חָרִיף וְשָׁנוּן; "וְיַד חָרוּצִים תַּעֲשִׁיר" (שם י, ד) – חֲרִיפִים, סוֹחֲרִים שְׁנוּנִים: **אֲשֶׁר יַפְלֶה.** יַבְדִּיל:

ח **וְיָרְדוּ כָל עֲבָדֶיךָ.** חָלַק כָּבוֹד לַמַּלְכוּת, שֶׁהֲרֵי סוֹף שֶׁיָּרַד פַּרְעֹה בְּעַצְמוֹ אֵלָיו בַּלַּיְלָה, "וַיֹּאמֶר קוּמוּ צְּאוּ מִתּוֹךְ עַמִּי" (להלן יב, לא), וְלֹא אָמַר לוֹ מֹשֶׁה מִתְּחִלָּה: 'וְיָרַדְתָּ אֵלַי וְהִשְׁתַּחֲוִיתָ לִי': **אֲשֶׁר בְּרַגְלֶיךָ.** הַהוֹלְכִים אַחַר עֲצָתְךָ וְהִלּוּכְךָ: **וְאַחֲרֵי כֵן אֵצֵא.** עִם כָּל הָעָם מֵאַרְצְךָ: **וַיֵּצֵא מֵעִם פַּרְעֹה.** כְּשֶׁגָּמַר דְּבָרָיו יָצָא מִלְּפָנָיו: **בָּחֳרִי אָף.** עַל שֶׁאָמַר לוֹ: "אַל תֹּסֶף רְאוֹת פָּנַי" (לעיל י, כח):

ט **לְמַעַן רְבוֹת מוֹפְתָי.** מַכַּת בְּכוֹרוֹת וּקְרִיעַת יַם סוּף וּלְנַעֵר אֶת מִצְרַיִם:

י **וּמֹשֶׁה וְאַהֲרֹן עָשׂוּ וְגוֹ׳.** כְּבָר כָּתַב לָנוּ זֹאת בְּכָל הַמּוֹפְתִים, וְלֹא שְׁנָאָהּ כָּאן אֶלָּא בִּשְׁבִיל לְסָמְכָהּ לַפָּרָשָׁה שֶׁל אַחֲרֶיהָ: "וַיֹּאמֶר ה׳ אֶל מֹשֶׁה וְאֶל אַהֲרֹן", שֶׁבִּשְׁבִיל שֶׁאַהֲרֹן עָשָׂה וְטָרַח בַּמּוֹפְתִים כְּמֹשֶׁה, חָלַק לוֹ כָּבוֹד זֶה בְּמִצְוָה רִאשׁוֹנָה שֶׁכְּלָלוֹ עִם מֹשֶׁה בַּדִּבּוּר:

יב א **בְּאֶרֶץ מִצְרַיִם.** חוּץ לַכְּרַךְ. אוֹ אֵינוֹ אֶלָּא בְּתוֹךְ הַכְּרַךְ? תַּלְמוּד לוֹמַר: "כְּצֵאתִי אֶת הָעִיר" וְגוֹ׳ (לעיל ט, כט). וּמַה תְּפִלָּה קַלָּה לֹא הִתְפַּלֵּל בְּתוֹךְ הַכְּרַךְ, דִּבּוּר חָמוּר לֹא כָּל שֶׁכֵּן? וּמִפְּנֵי מָה לֹא נִדְבַּר עִמּוֹ בְּתוֹךְ הַכְּרַךְ? לְפִי שֶׁהָיְתָה מְלֵאָה גִּלּוּלִים:

ב **הַחֹדֶשׁ הַזֶּה.** הֶרְאָהוּ לְבָנָה בְּחִדּוּשָׁהּ וְאָמַר לוֹ: כְּשֶׁהַיָּרֵחַ מִתְחַדֵּשׁ יִהְיֶה לְךָ רֹאשׁ חֹדֶשׁ. וְאֵין מִקְרָא יוֹצֵא מִידֵי פְשׁוּטוֹ, עַל חֹדֶשׁ נִיסָן אָמַר לוֹ, זֶה יִהְיֶה רֹאשׁ לְסֵדֶר מִנְיַן הֶחֳדָשִׁים, שֶׁיְּהֵא אִיָּר קָרוּי שֵׁנִי, סִיוָן שְׁלִישִׁי: **הַזֶּה.** נִתְקַשָּׁה מֹשֶׁה עַל מוֹלַד הַלְּבָנָה בְּאֵיזוֹ שִׁעוּר תֵּרָאֶה וְתִהְיֶה רְאוּיָה לְקַדֵּשׁ, וְהֶרְאָה לוֹ בְּאֶצְבַּע אֶת הַלְּבָנָה בָּרָקִיעַ וְאָמַר לוֹ: כָּזֶה רְאֵה וְקַדֵּשׁ. וְכֵיצַד הֶרְאָהוּ? וַהֲלֹא לֹא הָיָה נִדְבָּר עִמּוֹ אֶלָּא בַּיּוֹם, שֶׁנֶּאֱמַר: "וַיְהִי בְּיוֹם דִּבֶּר ה׳" (לעיל ו, כח), "בְּיוֹם צַוֹּתוֹ" (ויקרא ז, לח), "מִן הַיּוֹם אֲשֶׁר צִוָּה ה׳ וָהָלְאָה" (במדבר טו, כג)? אֶלָּא סָמוּךְ לִשְׁקִיעַת הַחַמָּה נֶאֶמְרָה לוֹ פָּרָשָׁה זוֹ וְהֶרְאָהוּ עִם חֲשֵׁכָה:

The difference between a slave and a free human being does not lie in how long or hard each works. Free people often work long hours doing arduous tasks. The difference lies in who controls time. A slave works until he or she is allowed to stop. A free person decides when to begin and end. Control over time is the essential difference between slavery and freedom. Control over the calendar gave the Israelites authority over time. The first command to the Israelites was thus an essential prelude to freedom. It is said: Learn how to value time and make *it* holy. "Teach us to count our days rightly, that our hearts may grow wise" (Ps. 90:12).

If you are to be free, then time is the first thing you must learn to master. Part of the beauty of Judaism, and surely this is so for other faiths also, is that it gently restores control over time. Three times a day we stop what we are doing and turn to God in prayer. We recover perspective. We inhale a deep breath of eternity. Nor do we rush our meals. Before eating, and afterward, we say a blessing. That too allows us to focus attention on simple pleasures, turning our daily bread into momentary epiphany.

Under pressure of time we tend to ignore the things that are important but not urgent. The Sabbath, unusual amid the stresses of modern life, is a time dedicated to the things that are important but not urgent, like eating together as a

ז נִהְיָתָה וְכָמֹהוּ לֹא תֹסִף: וּלְכֹל ׀ בְּנֵי יִשְׂרָאֵל לֹא יֶחֱרַץ־כֶּלֶב לְשֹׁנוֹ
לְמֵאִישׁ וְעַד־בְּהֵמָה לְמַעַן תֵּדְעוּן אֲשֶׁר יַפְלֶה יהוה בֵּין מִצְרַיִם וּבֵין
ח יִשְׂרָאֵל: וְיָרְדוּ כָל־עֲבָדֶיךָ אֵלֶּה אֵלַי וְהִשְׁתַּחֲווּ־לִי לֵאמֹר צֵא אַתָּה
וְכָל־הָעָם אֲשֶׁר־בְּרַגְלֶיךָ וְאַחֲרֵי־כֵן אֵצֵא וַיֵּצֵא מֵעִם־פַּרְעֹה בָּחֳרִי־
ט אָף: וַיֹּאמֶר יהוה אֶל־מֹשֶׁה לֹא־יִשְׁמַע אֲלֵיכֶם
י פַּרְעֹה לְמַעַן רְבוֹת מוֹפְתַי בְּאֶרֶץ מִצְרָיִם: וּמֹשֶׁה וְאַהֲרֹן עָשׂוּ אֶת־כָּל־
הַמֹּפְתִים הָאֵלֶּה לִפְנֵי פַרְעֹה וַיְחַזֵּק יהוה אֶת־לֵב פַּרְעֹה וְלֹא־שִׁלַּח
יב א אֶת־בְּנֵי־יִשְׂרָאֵל מֵאַרְצוֹ: וַיֹּאמֶר יהוה אֶל־מֹשֶׁה וְאֶל־
ב אַהֲרֹן בְּאֶרֶץ מִצְרַיִם לֵאמֹר: הַחֹדֶשׁ הַזֶּה לָכֶם רֹאשׁ חֳדָשִׁים רִאשׁוֹן

אונקלוס

וְדִכְוָתַהּ לָא תוֹסִיף: ז וּלְכָל בְּנֵי יִשְׂרָאֵל, לָא יְנַזֵּיק כַּלְבָּא בְּלִישָׁנֵיהּ לְמִנְבַּח, לְמֵאֱנָשָׁא וְעַד בְּעִירָא, בְּדִיל דְּתִדְּעוּן, דְּיַפְרֵישׁ יְיָ, בֵּין מִצְרָאֵי וּבֵין יִשְׂרָאֵל: ח וְיֵיחֲתוּן כָּל עַבְדָּךְ אִלֵּין לְוָתִי וְיִבְעוֹן מִנִּי לְמֵימַר, פּוֹק אַתְּ וְכָל עַמָּא דְּעִמָּךְ, וּבָתַר כֵּן אֶפּוֹק, וּנְפַק מִלְּוָת פַּרְעֹה בִּתְקוֹף רְגַז: ט וַאֲמַר יְיָ לְמֹשֶׁה, לָא יְקַבֵּיל מִנְּכוֹן פַּרְעֹה, בְּדִיל, לְאַסְגָּאָה מוֹפְתַי בְּאַרְעָא דְּמִצְרָיִם: י וּמֹשֶׁה וְאַהֲרֹן, עֲבַדוּ, יָת כָּל מוֹפְתַיָּא הָאִלֵּין קֳדָם פַּרְעֹה, וְתַקֵּיף יְיָ יָת לִבָּא דְּפַרְעֹה, וְלָא שַׁלַּח יָת בְּנֵי יִשְׂרָאֵל מֵאַרְעֵיהּ: יב א וַאֲמַר יְיָ לְמֹשֶׁה וּלְאַהֲרֹן, בְּאַרְעָא דְּמִצְרַיִם לְמֵימַר: ב יַרְחָא הָדֵין, לְכוֹן רֵישׁ יַרְחַיָּא, קַדְמַאי הוּא לְכוֹן, לְיַרְחֵי שַׁתָּא: ג מַלִּילוּ, עִם כָּל כְּנִשְׁתָּא דְיִשְׂרָאֵל לְמֵימַר, בְּעַסְרָא לְיַרְחָא הָדֵין, וְיִסְבוּן

11:8 בָּחֳרִי־אָף *Blazing with anger* – Moshe displays anger here for the first time in these confrontations, yet it was the capacity for righteous indignation that marked Moshe as a leader many years before. The Egyptians had lacked this capacity. The "scream" (Ex. 11:6) echoes the verb that was used of the Israelites when their cry was heard in Heaven (3:7, 9). The Egyptians were silent while the Israelites were persecuted for many years. Now that what they did to others is being done to them, they are no longer silent. Their anguished cries fill the night (Rabbi Samson Raphael Hirsch). Meanwhile, Pharaoh's personal authority has been eroded by his capricious behaviour. "Your own officials," says Moshe to Pharaoh, "will bow down to me rather than you."

"THIS MONTH SHALL BE TO YOU…"

The texture of the narrative changes here. At the very height of the drama, as the final plague has been announced but not yet happened, we move from Egypt to the Israelites. Before talking about preparations for the exodus, God commands Moshe and Aharon to instruct the people on what will become a new foundation of their faith: the calendar. Events in Egypt will not remain simply as a historical past. They will shape the way that the Israelites experience time. The month of the exodus will become, each year, a month of new beginnings. It will be a time of memory and reenactment, of reexperiencing the story and handing it on to future generations. It will become the basis of their identity.

According to Jewish tradition, this is the first command the Jewish people ever received: the command to establish a calendar. Why? The Israelites are still slaves in Egypt. They are longing for freedom. They are about to begin the long journey across the desert. Why do they need a command about calendars and holy days? What has a diary to do with liberty?

Rabbi Avraham Pam explained it in the following way:

3 you. Speak to the entire community of Israel and say: On the tenth of this
month each man must take a lamb for his family; one for every household.
4 If the household is too small for a lamb, let him and a close neighbor take a
lamb together, to suit the number of people involved; they shall be counted
5 for the lamb in proportion to their eating. A one-year-old male shall you take,
6 flawless, from among the sheep or goats. You shall guard it until the fourteenth
day of this month. And then, in the afternoon, all the community of Israel shall

רש״י

ג **דברו אל כל עדת.** וכי אהרן מדבר? והלא כבר נאמר: "אתה תדבר" (לעיל ז, ב)! אלא חולקין כבוד זה לזה ואומרים זה לזה: למדני, והדבור יוצא מבין שניהם כאלו שניהם מדברים: **דברו אל כל עדת ישראל לאמר בעשר לחדש.** דברו היום בראש חדש שיקחוהו בעשור לחדש: **הזה.** פסח מצרים מקחו בעשור ולא פסח דורות: **שה לבית אבת.** למשפחה אחת. הרי שהיו מרבין יכול שה אחד לכלן? תלמוד לומר: "שה לבית":

ד **ואם ימעט הבית מהיות משה.** ואם יהיו מועטין מהיות משה אחד, שאין יכולין לאכלו ויבא לידי נותר – "ולקח הוא ושכנו" וגו', זהו משמעו לפשוטו. ועוד יש בו מדרש, ללמד שאחר שנמנו עליו יכולין להתמעט ולמשך ידיהם הימנו ולהמנות על שה אחר, אך אם באו למשך ידיהם ולהתמעט – "מהיות משה" יתמעטו, בעוד השה קים, בהיותו בחיים, ולא משנשחט: **במכסת.** חשבון, וכן: "מכסת הערכך" (ויקרא כז, כג): **לפי אכלו.** הראוי לאכילה, פרט לחולה ולזקן שאינו יכול לאכל כזית: **תכסו.** "תתמנון":

ה **תמים.** בלא מום: **בן שנה.** כל שנתו קרוי 'בן שנה', כלומר שנולד בשנה זו: **מן הכבשים ומן העזים.** או מזה או מזה, שאף עז קרוי 'שה', שנאמר: "ושה עזים" (דברים יד, ד):

ו **והיה לכם למשמרת.** זהו לשון בקור, שטעון בקור ממום ארבעה ימים קדם שחיטה. ומפני מה הקדים לקיחתו לשחיטתו ארבעה ימים, מה שלא צוה כן בפסח דורות? היה רבי מתיא בן חרש אומר: הרי הוא אומר: "ואעבר עליך ואראך והנה עתך עת דדים" (יחזקאל טז, ח), הגיעה שבועה שנשבעתי לאברהם שאגאל את בניו, ולא היו בידם מצות להתעסק בהם כדי שיגאלו, שנאמר: "ואת ערם ועריה" (שם פסוק ז), ונתן להם שתי מצות, דם פסח ודם מילה, שמלו באותו הלילה, שנאמר: "מתבוססת בדמיך" (שם פסוק ו) בשני דמים, ואומר: "גם את בדם בריתך שלחתי אסיריך מבור אין מים בו" (זכריה ט, יא); ושהיו שטופים בעבודה זרה, אמר להם: "משכו וקחו לכם" (להלן פסוק כא), משכו ידיכם מעבודה זרה וקחו לכם צאן של מצוה: **ושחטו אתו וגו'.** וכי כלן שוחטין? אלא מכאן ששלוחו של אדם כמותו: **קהל עדת ישראל.** קהל ועדה וישראל. מכאן אמרו: פסחי צבור נשחטים בשלש כתות זו אחר זו. נכנסה כת ראשונה ננעלו דלתות העזרה וכו', כדאיתא בפסחים (דף סד ע"א): **בין הערבים.** משש שעות ולמעלה קרוי 'בין הערבים', שהשמש נוטה לבית מבואו לערב. ולשון 'בין הערבים' נראה בעיני, אותן שעות שבין עריבת היום לעריבת הלילה, עריבת היום בתחלת שבע שעות מכי ינטו

the service of God. This is an essential part of their journey to freedom. Serving God, they have begun their liberation from servitude to human principalities and powers.

12:4 **ולקח הוא ושכנו הקרב אל־ביתו** *Let him and a close neighbor take a lamb together* – The shared meal bonds people together. The sense of kinship, of family bonds, of eating together and caring for one another, will prove essential to the people in their journey to freedom. It contrasts with the ninth plague of darkness in which "no one could see anyone else" (Ex. 10:23).

The Seder service, in which we yearly reenact this meal, opens with a strange invitation: "This is the bread of oppression our fathers ate in the land of Egypt. Let all who are hungry come in and eat." What hospitality is it to offer the hungry this taste of suffering? In fact, this is a profound insight into the nature of slavery and freedom. Matza represents two things: the food of slaves, and the bread eaten by the Israelites as they leave Egypt in liberty. What transforms the bread of oppression into the bread of freedom is *the willingness to share it.* One who fears tomorrow does not offer his bread to others. One who is willing to divide his food with a stranger has already shown himself capable of fellowship and faith, the two things from which hope is born. The Seder returns us to the solidarity of that original moment on the cusp of freedom.

ג הוּא לָכֶם לְחׇדְשֵׁי הַשָּׁנָה׃ דַּבְּרוּ אֶל־כׇּל־עֲדַת יִשְׂרָאֵל לֵאמֹר בֶּעָשֹׂר
ד לַחֹדֶשׁ הַזֶּה וְיִקְחוּ לָהֶם אִישׁ שֶׂה לְבֵית־אָבֹת שֶׂה לַבָּיִת׃ וְאִם־יִמְעַט
הַבַּיִת מִהְיוֹת מִשֶּׂה וְלָקַח הוּא וּשְׁכֵנוֹ הַקָּרֹב אֶל־בֵּיתוֹ בְּמִכְסַת נְפָשֹׁת
ה אִישׁ לְפִי אׇכְלוֹ תָּכֹסּוּ עַל־הַשֶּׂה׃ שֶׂה תָמִים זָכָר בֶּן־שָׁנָה יִהְיֶה לָכֶם
ו מִן־הַכְּבָשִׂים וּמִן־הָעִזִּים תִּקָּחוּ׃ וְהָיָה לָכֶם לְמִשְׁמֶרֶת עַד אַרְבָּעָה
עָשָׂר יוֹם לַחֹדֶשׁ הַזֶּה וְשָׁחֲטוּ אֹתוֹ כֹּל קְהַל עֲדַת־יִשְׂרָאֵל בֵּין הָעַרְבָּיִם׃

אונקלוס

לְהוֹן, גְּבַר, אִמַּר לְבֵית אַבָּא אִמְּרָא לְבֵיתָא: ד וְאִם זְעֵיר בֵּיתָא
מִלְּאִתְמְנָאָה עַל אִמְּרָא, וְיִסַּב הוּא, וְשֵׁיבָבֵיהּ, דְּקָרִיב לְבֵיתֵיהּ
בְּמִנְיַן נַפְשָׁתָא, גְּבַר לְפוּם מֵיכְלֵיהּ, תִּתְמְנוּן עַל אִמְּרָא: ה אִמַּר
שְׁלִים, דְּכַר בַּר שַׁתֵּיהּ יְהֵי לְכוֹן, מִן אִמְּרַיָּא וּמִן בְּנֵי עִזַּיָּא תִּסְּבוּן:
ו וִיהֵי לְכוֹן לְמַטְּרָא, עַד אַרְבְּעַת עַסְרָא, יוֹמָא לְיַרְחָא הָדֵין, וְיִכְּסוּן
יָתֵיהּ, כֹּל, קְהָלָא כְּנִשְׁתָּא דְיִשְׂרָאֵל בֵּין שִׁמְשַׁיָּא:

family, or celebrating together as a community, or simply giving thanks. These are the things that flood a life with unexpected happiness. Religious ritual is a way of structuring time so that we, not employers, the market, or the media, are in control. Life needs its pauses, its chapter breaks, if the soul is to have space to breathe. Otherwise, we may not be in Egypt but we can still be slaves.

12:2 לָכֶם *To you* – The determination of the calendar, and with it the date of the festivals, was handed over to the human court, unlike the seventh day that was made holy by God at the beginning of creation.

The Jewish calendar is both lunar and solar. Months are determined by the moon, and last either twenty-nine or thirty days. In ancient times, the length depended on eyewitnesses coming to the *beit din* and saying, "We saw the new moon." The seasons, however, are determined by the sun. To ensure an alignment between the lunar and solar calendars, there is a system of seven leap years in every cycle of nineteen years – a leap year involving an extra month, Adar 2. This additional Adar would also be established by the court. Hence on the Sabbath we speak of God who "sanctifies the Sabbath" but on festivals we speak of God who "sanctifies Israel who sanctify the festive seasons."

12:2 רֹאשׁ חֳדָשִׁים *The beginning of months* – Hebrew months tended to be numbered rather than named, as were the days of the week. This may have been to avoid using names that could have had idolatrous associations. This first month was sometimes called Aviv, meaning the ripening of ears of barley. Later, after the Babylonian exile, it became known as Nisan.

The fixing of the calendar on the basis of the exodus for the first time brought into the calendar the concept of historical time, time as an arena of change, from slavery to freedom, from Egypt to the Promised Land.

12:3 עֲדַת יִשְׂרָאֵל *Community of Israel* – This is the first time the term has been applied to the Israelites. It refers specifically to the people as a religious entity, a congregation bearing witness together (*eda* from the word *ed*, "a witness") to the sovereignty of God. At the beginning of Exodus, the Israelites were called an *am*, a "people," for the first time (Ex. 1:9). The difference between *am* and *eda* is best expressed in Rabbi Joseph B. Soloveitchik's terminology as the difference between *brit goral*, a covenant of fate, and *brit ye'ud*, a covenant of faith or destiny. A community of fate is defined by what happens to it. The *brit goral* was born in the experience of slavery in Egypt. A community of faith is defined by what it seeks to do and build. The *brit ye'ud* was formed in the revelation at Sinai. The reason that *eda* appears here for the first time is that it is here that Israel receives its first commands, turning it into a religious community directed to

7 slaughter it. They shall then take some of the blood and put it on the two sides
8 and top of the doorframes of the houses where they are to eat the lamb. They
shall eat the meat that night, roasted over a fire; with unleavened bread and
9 bitter herbs they shall eat it. Do not eat it raw or boiled in water; it must be
10 roasted over fire with its head, its legs, and its inner parts. Do not leave any of it
11 until morning; any left over until morning you shall burn with fire. This is how
you shall eat it: your belt secured, the sandals on your feet, your staff in your
12 hand. Eat it in haste. It is the Lord's Passover. I will pass through the land of

רש"י

צִלְלֵי עֶרֶב, וַעֲרִיבַת הַלַּיְלָה בִּתְחִלַּת הַלַּיְלָה. 'עֶרֶב' לְשׁוֹן נֶשֶׁף וְחֹשֶׁךְ, כְּמוֹ: "עָרְבָה כָּל שִׂמְחָה" (ישעיה כד, יא):

ז וְלָקְחוּ מִן הַדָּם. זוֹ קַבָּלַת הַדָּם. יָכוֹל בַּיָּד? תַּלְמוּד לוֹמַר: "אֲשֶׁר בַּסַּף" (להלן פסוק כב): **הַמְּזוּזֹת.** הֵם הַזְּקוּפוֹת, אַחַת מִכָּאן לַפֶּתַח וְאַחַת מִכָּאן: **הַמַּשְׁקוֹף.** הוּא הָעֶלְיוֹן, שֶׁהַדֶּלֶת שׁוֹקֵף עָלָיו כְּשֶׁסּוֹגְרִין אוֹתוֹ, לינט"ל בְּלַעַז. וּלְשׁוֹן 'שְׁקִיפָה' – חֲבָטָה, כְּמוֹ: "קוֹל עָלֶה נִדָּף" (ויקרא כו, לו) – "דְּשָׁקֵיף". "חַבּוּרָה" (להלן כא, כה) – מַשְׁקוֹפֵי: **עַל הַבָּתִּים אֲשֶׁר יֹאכְלוּ אֹתוֹ בָּהֶם.** וְלֹא עַל מַשְׁקוֹף וּמְזוּזוֹת שֶׁבְּבֵית הַתֶּבֶן וּבֵית הַבָּקָר, שֶׁאֵין דָּרִין בְּתוֹכוֹ:

ח **אֶת הַבָּשָׂר.** וְלֹא גִּידִים וַעֲצָמוֹת: **עַל מְרֹרִים.** כָּל עֵשֶׂב מַר נִקְרָא 'מָרוֹר'. וְצִוָּם לֶאֱכֹל מַר זֵכֶר לְ"וַיְמָרְרוּ אֶת חַיֵּיהֶם" (לעיל א, יד):

ט **אַל תֹּאכְלוּ מִמֶּנּוּ נָא.** שֶׁאֵינוֹ צָלוּי כָּל צָרְכּוֹ קוֹרֵהוּ 'נָא' בְּלָשׁוֹן עֲרָבִי: **וּבָשֵׁל מְבֻשָּׁל.** כָּל זֶה בְּאַזְהָרַת "אַל תֹּאכְלוּ": **בַּמָּיִם.** מִנַּיִן לִשְׁאָר מַשְׁקִים? תַּלְמוּד לוֹמַר: "וּבָשֵׁל מְבֻשָּׁל" מִכָּל מָקוֹם: **כִּי אִם צְלִי אֵשׁ.** לְמַעְלָה גָּזַר עָלָיו בְּמִצְוַת עֲשֵׂה, וְכָאן הוֹסִיף עָלָיו לֹא תַעֲשֶׂה: "אַל תֹּאכְלוּ מִמֶּנּוּ... כִּי אִם צְלִי אֵשׁ": **רֹאשׁוֹ עַל כְּרָעָיו.** צוֹלֵהוּ כֻּלּוֹ כְּאֶחָד עִם רֹאשׁוֹ וְעִם כְּרָעָיו וְעִם קִרְבּוֹ, וּבְנֵי מֵעָיו נוֹתֵן לְתוֹכוֹ לְאַחַר הֲדָחָתָן. וּלְשׁוֹן: "עַל כְּרָעָיו וְעַל קִרְבּוֹ" כִּלְשׁוֹן "עַל צִבְאֹתָם" (לעיל ו, כו) כְּמוֹ בְּצִבְאֹתָם, כְּמוֹת שֶׁהֵן, אַף זֶה כְּמוֹת שֶׁהוּא, כָּל בְּשָׂרוֹ מֻשְׁלָם:

י **וְהַנֹּתָר מִמֶּנּוּ עַד בֹּקֶר.** מַה תַּלְמוּד לוֹמַר "עַד בֹּקֶר" פַּעַם שְׁנִיָּה? לִתֵּן בֹּקֶר עַל בֹּקֶר, שֶׁהַבֹּקֶר מַשְׁמָעוֹ הָנֵץ הַחַמָּה, וּבָא הַכָּתוּב לְהַקְדִּים שֶׁאָסוּר בַּאֲכִילָה מֵעֲלוֹת הַשַּׁחַר; זֶהוּ לְפִי מַשְׁמָעוֹ. וְעוֹד מִדְרָשׁ אַחֵר, לִמֵּד שֶׁאֵינוֹ נִשְׂרָף בְּיוֹם טוֹב אֶלָּא מִמָּחֳרָת, וְכָךְ תִּדְרְשֶׁנּוּ: "וְהַנּוֹתָר מִמֶּנּוּ" בַּבֹּקֶר רִאשׁוֹן "עַד בֹּקֶר" שֵׁנִי תַּעֲמֹד וְתִשְׂרְפֶנּוּ:

יא **מָתְנֵיכֶם חֲגֻרִים.** מְזֻמָּנִים לַדֶּרֶךְ: **בְּחִפָּזוֹן.** לְשׁוֹן בֶּהָלָה וּמְהִירוּת, כְּמוֹ: "וַיְהִי דָוִד נֶחְפָּז לָלֶכֶת" (שמואל א' כג, כו), "אֲשֶׁר הִשְׁלִיכוּ אֲרָם בְּחָפְזָם" (מלכים ב' ז, טו): **פֶּסַח הוּא לַה'.** הַקָּרְבָּן קָרוּי 'פֶּסַח' עַל שֵׁם הַפְּסִיחָה, וְאַתֶּם עֲשׂוּ כָּל עֲבוֹדוֹתָיו לְשֵׁם שָׁמַיִם:

יב **וְעָבַרְתִּי.** כְּמֶלֶךְ הָעוֹבֵר מִמָּקוֹם לְמָקוֹם וּבְהַעֲבָרָה אַחַת וּבְרֶגַע

would do this, all these centuries later. This seems incomprehensible. Can we have gone through all that suffering in Egypt just so that we would eat matza and bitter herbs? If so, God could have left out the whole episode of Egypt. We need not have endured slavery. He could just have told us, "For seven days, eat matza and bitter herbs."

In fact, Rashi's interpretation is profound. Why were our ancestors slaves? Why did God allow it to happen? God wanted us at the beginning of history, of our history, to lose our freedom so that we would never let it be lost again. He wanted us to know what it feels like to be a slave, so that we would become the world's most consistent fighters for freedom. Why have we walked as a people through the "valley of the shadow of death" so many times? So that we never forget the sanctity of life. What you once lose, you never take for granted. This is why, even as they celebrate their freedom, the people taste their bitterness, as we do to this day.

12:11 **פֶּסַח** *Passover* – The word means to "skip over." It is understood to refer to the Lord passing over the houses of the Israelites during the night of the last plague.

Throughout the biblical period, there were two quite different holy times. Passover referred specifically to the fourteenth of Nisan, while the festival that we nowadays call by that name began on the fifteenth and was known as *Ḥag HaMatzot*, the Festival of Unleavened Bread. Only in the postbiblical era did the two come to be known by the same name.

ז וְלָקְחוּ מִן־הַדָּם וְנָתְנוּ עַל־שְׁתֵּי הַמְּזוּזֹת וְעַל־הַמַּשְׁקוֹף עַל הַבָּתִּים
ח אֲשֶׁר־יֹאכְלוּ אֹתוֹ בָּהֶם׃ וְאָכְלוּ אֶת־הַבָּשָׂר בַּלַּיְלָה הַזֶּה צְלִי־אֵשׁ
ט וּמַצּוֹת עַל־מְרֹרִים יֹאכְלֻהוּ׃ אַל־תֹּאכְלוּ מִמֶּנּוּ נָא וּבָשֵׁל מְבֻשָּׁל
י בַּמָּיִם כִּי אִם־צְלִי־אֵשׁ רֹאשׁוֹ עַל־כְּרָעָיו וְעַל־קִרְבּוֹ׃ וְלֹא־תוֹתִירוּ
יא מִמֶּנּוּ עַד־בֹּקֶר וְהַנֹּתָר מִמֶּנּוּ עַד־בֹּקֶר בָּאֵשׁ תִּשְׂרֹפוּ׃ וְכָכָה תֹּאכְלוּ
אֹתוֹ מָתְנֵיכֶם חֲגֻרִים נַעֲלֵיכֶם בְּרַגְלֵיכֶם וּמַקֶּלְכֶם בְּיֶדְכֶם וַאֲכַלְתֶּם
יב אֹתוֹ בְּחִפָּזוֹן פֶּסַח הוּא לַיהוָה׃ וְעָבַרְתִּי בְאֶרֶץ־מִצְרַיִם בַּלַּיְלָה הַזֶּה

אונקלוס

ז וְיִסְּבוּן מִן דְּמָא, וְיִתְּנוּן, עַל תְּרֵין סִפַּיָּא וְעַל שָׁקְפָּא, עַל בָּתַּיָּא, דְּיֵיכְלוּן יָתֵיהּ בְּהוֹן: ח וְיֵיכְלוּן יָת בִּסְרָא בְּלֵילְיָא הָדֵין, טְוֵי נוּר וּפַטִּיר, עַל מְרָרִין יֵיכְלֻנֵּיהּ: ט לָא תֵיכְלוּן מִנֵּיהּ כַּד חַי, וְאַף לָא כַּד בַּשָּׁלָא מְבַשַּׁל בְּמַיָּא, אֱלָהֵין טְוֵי נוּר, רֵישֵׁיהּ עַל כְּרָעוֹהִי וְעַל גַּוֵּיהּ: י וְלָא תַשְׁאֲרוּן מִנֵּיהּ עַד צַפְרָא, וּדְיִשְׁתְּאַר מִנֵּיהּ, עַד צַפְרָא בְּנוּרָא תּוֹקְדוּן: יא וּכְדֵין תֵּיכְלוּן יָתֵיהּ, חַרְצֵיכוֹן יְהוֹן אֲסִירִין, מְסָנֵיכוֹן בְּרַגְלֵיכוֹן, וְחֻטְרֵיכוֹן בִּידֵיכוֹן, וְתֵיכְלוּן יָתֵיהּ בִּבְהִילוּ, פִּסְחָא הוּא קֳדָם יְיָ: יב וְאֶתְגְּלֵי בְּאַרְעָא דְמִצְרַיִם בְּלֵילְיָא הָדֵין,

12:7 עַל־שְׁתֵּי הַמְּזוּזֹת וְעַל־הַמַּשְׁקוֹף *Two sides and top of the doorframes* – The door is a symbol of a threshold, in this case between the interior – the inner lives of the Israelites – and the Egyptian exterior. The blood of the sacrifice is the sign that the Israelites are willing to practice their faith despite knowing that it constitutes an abomination to the Egyptians. Moshe has told Pharaoh that it would be dangerous for the Israelites to worship God in Egypt, implying that they would sacrifice animals held holy by the Egyptians. The offering is thus a mark of religious courage. It is this willingness to keep faith with God despite the risks that serves as a protection at a time of divine anger.

12:8 מַצּוֹת *Unleavened bread* – This was mentioned during the story of the two visitors to Lot in Sedom (Gen. 19:3), as bread that could be prepared speedily. Already in advance of the exodus, there is a hint that it would be undertaken in haste. The fact that the Israelites were to eat it with their loins girded and their sandals on their feet, ready to leave, suggests that urgency was associated with this particular kind of bread. The Torah does not directly associate it with slavery, but Ibn Ezra suggests that slaves were given unleavened bread because, being hard, it takes longer to digest. It removes hunger for longer than ordinary bread. In the Seder, therefore, it has two symbolisms. It is the bread of oppression which becomes the bread of freedom. The difference between freedom and slavery lies not in the quality of bread we eat, but in the state of mind in which we eat it.

12:8 מְרֹרִים *Bitter herbs* – In the first chapter of Exodus we read that the Egyptians "embittered" the lives of the Israelites through hard labor (Ex. 1:14), so the verbal connection makes it likely that the bitterness of the herbs was symbolic of the Israelites' experience that they were about to leave.

This is the interpretation preserved in the Haggada. On Seder night, each of us must see ourselves as if we had personally left Egypt. "As it says, on that day you must tell your child, *baavur zeh asa Hashem li betzeiti miMitzrayim* – 'This is because of what the LORD did for *me* [not "my ancestors"], when I left Egypt'" (13:8). As we shall see there, Rashi reads this verse counterintuitively: "Why did God take me out of Egypt? *Baavur 'zeh'*: In order that I should fulfil *these mitzvot* of eating matza and bitter herbs." In other words, I am not doing this because of the past. The past happened so that I

Egypt that night, and will kill every firstborn in Egypt, man and beast. Against
13 all the gods of Egypt I will execute judgments. I am the Lord. The blood will
be your sign on the houses where you are. I will see the blood and I will pass
14 over you. No deadly plague will touch you when I strike the land of Egypt. This
day will become a memorial for you; you will celebrate it as a festival to the
15 Lord for all generations, a celebration that will be an everlasting law. For seven
days you shall eat unleavened bread. By the first day you shall have removed
leaven from your houses, for the soul of anyone who eats leavened bread from

רש״י

אֶחָד כֻּלָּן לוֹקִין: **כָּל בְּכוֹר בְּאֶרֶץ מִצְרַיִם.** אַף בְּכוֹרוֹת אֲחֵרִים וְהֵם בְּמִצְרַיִם. וּמִנַּיִן אַף בְּכוֹרֵי מִצְרַיִם שֶׁבִּמְקוֹמוֹת אֲחֵרִים? תַּלְמוּד לוֹמַר: ״לְמַכֵּה מִצְרַיִם בִּבְכוֹרֵיהֶם״ (תהלים קלו, י): **מֵאָדָם וְעַד בְּהֵמָה.** מִי שֶׁהִתְחִיל בַּעֲבֵרָה תְּחִלָּה מִמֶּנּוּ מַתְחֶלֶת הַפֻּרְעָנוּת: **וּבְכָל אֱלֹהֵי מִצְרַיִם.** שֶׁל עֵץ נִרְקֶבֶת וְשֶׁל מַתֶּכֶת נִמֶּסֶת וְנִתֶּכֶת לָאָרֶץ: **אֶעֱשֶׂה שְׁפָטִים אֲנִי ה׳.** אֲנִי בְּעַצְמִי וְלֹא עַל יְדֵי שָׁלִיחַ:

יג **וְהָיָה הַדָּם לָכֶם לְאֹת.** לָכֶם לְאוֹת וְלֹא לַאֲחֵרִים לְאוֹת. מִכָּאן שֶׁלֹּא נָתְנוּ הַדָּם אֶלָּא מִבִּפְנִים: **וְרָאִיתִי אֶת הַדָּם.** הַכֹּל גָּלוּי לְפָנָיו, אֶלָּא אָמַר הַקָּדוֹשׁ בָּרוּךְ הוּא: נוֹתֵן אֲנִי אֶת עֵינַי לִרְאוֹת שֶׁאַתֶּם עֲסוּקִים בְּמִצְוֹתַי וּפוֹסֵחַ אֲנִי עֲלֵיכֶם: **וּפָסַחְתִּי.** וְחָמַלְתִּי, וְדוֹמֶה לוֹ: ״פָּסוֹחַ וְהִמְלִיט״ (ישעיה לא, ה). וַאֲנִי אוֹמֵר כָּל פְּסִיחָה לְשׁוֹן דִּלּוּג וּקְפִיצָה, ״וּפָסַחְתִּי״ – מְדַלֵּג הָיָה מִבָּתֵּי יִשְׂרָאֵל לְבָתֵּי מִצְרַיִם, שֶׁהָיוּ שְׁרוּיִם זֶה בְּתוֹךְ זֶה. וְכֵן: ״פֹּסְחִים עַל שְׁתֵּי הַסְּעִפִּים״ (מלכים א׳ יח, כא). וְכֵן כָּל הַפִּסְחִים הוֹלְכִים כְּקוֹפְצִים. וְכֵן: ״פָּסוֹחַ וְהִמְלִיט״, מְדַלְּגוֹ וּמְמַלְּטוֹ מִבֵּין הַמּוּמָתִים: **וְלֹא יִהְיֶה בָכֶם נֶגֶף.** אֲבָל הוֹוֶה הוּא בְּמִצְרַיִם. הֲרֵי שֶׁהָיָה מִצְרִי בְּבֵיתוֹ שֶׁל יִשְׂרָאֵל, יָכוֹל יִמָּלֵט? תַּלְמוּד לוֹמַר: ״וְלֹא יִהְיֶה בָכֶם נֶגֶף״, אֲבָל הוֹוֶה בַּמִּצְרִים שֶׁבְּבָתֵּיכֶם. הֲרֵי שֶׁהָיָה יִשְׂרָאֵל בְּבֵיתוֹ שֶׁל מִצְרִי, שׁוֹמֵעַ אֲנִי יִלְקֶה כְּמוֹתוֹ? תַּלְמוּד לוֹמַר: ״וְלֹא יִהְיֶה בָכֶם נֶגֶף״:

יד **לְזִכָּרוֹן.** לְדוֹרוֹת: **וְחַגֹּתֶם אֹתוֹ.** יוֹם שֶׁהוּא לְךָ לְזִכָּרוֹן אַתָּה חוֹגְגוֹ. וַעֲדַיִן לֹא שָׁמַעְנוּ אֵי זֶהוּ יוֹם הַזִּכָּרוֹן, תַּלְמוּד לוֹמַר: ״זָכוֹר אֶת הַיּוֹם הַזֶּה אֲשֶׁר יְצָאתֶם״ (להלן יג, ג), לָמַדְנוּ שֶׁיּוֹם הַיְצִיאָה הוּא יוֹם שֶׁל זִכָּרוֹן. וְאֵי זֶה יוֹם יָצְאוּ? תַּלְמוּד לוֹמַר: ״מִמָּחֳרַת הַפֶּסַח יָצְאוּ״ (במדבר לג, ג), הֱוֵי אוֹמֵר יוֹם חֲמִשָּׁה עָשָׂר בְּנִיסָן הוּא שֶׁל יוֹם טוֹב, שֶׁהֲרֵי לֵיל חֲמִשָּׁה עָשָׂר אָכְלוּ אֶת הַפֶּסַח וְלַבֹּקֶר יָצְאוּ: **לְדֹרֹתֵיכֶם.** שׁוֹמֵעַ אֲנִי מִעוּט דּוֹרוֹת שְׁנַיִם, תַּלְמוּד לוֹמַר: ״חֻקַּת עוֹלָם תְּחָגֻּהוּ״:

טו **שִׁבְעַת יָמִים.** סטיי״נא שֶׁל יָמִים: **שִׁבְעַת יָמִים מַצּוֹת תֹּאכֵלוּ.** וּבְמָקוֹם אַחֵר הוּא אוֹמֵר: ״שֵׁשֶׁת יָמִים תֹּאכַל מַצּוֹת״ (דברים טז, ח), לִמְּדָנוּ עַל שְׁבִיעִי שֶׁאֵינוֹ חוֹבָה לֶאֱכֹל מַצָּה, וּבִלְבַד שֶׁלֹּא יֹאכַל חָמֵץ. מִנַּיִן אַף שִׁשָּׁה רְשׁוּת? זוֹ מִדָּה בַּתּוֹרָה: דָּבָר שֶׁהָיָה בִּכְלָל וְיָצָא מִן הַכְּלָל לְלַמֵּד, לֹא לְלַמֵּד עַל עַצְמוֹ בִּלְבַד יָצָא אֶלָּא לְלַמֵּד עַל הַכְּלָל כֻּלּוֹ יָצָא, מַה שְּׁבִיעִי רְשׁוּת אַף שִׁשָּׁה רְשׁוּת. יָכוֹל אַף לַיְלָה הָרִאשׁוֹן רְשׁוּת? תַּלְמוּד לוֹמַר: ״בָּעֶרֶב תֹּאכְלוּ מַצֹּת״ (להלן פסוק יח), הַכָּתוּב קְבָעוֹ חוֹבָה: **אַךְ בַּיּוֹם הָרִאשׁוֹן תַּשְׁבִּיתוּ שְּׂאֹר.** מֵעֶרֶב יוֹם טוֹב, וְקָרוּי רִאשׁוֹן שֶׁהוּא לִפְנֵי הַשִּׁבְעָה, וּמָצִינוּ מֻקְדָּם קָרוּי רִאשׁוֹן, ״הֲרִאישׁוֹן אָדָם תִּוָּלֵד״ (איוב טו, ז), הֲלִפְנֵי אָדָם נוֹלַדְתָּ. אוֹ אֵינוֹ אֶלָּא רִאשׁוֹן שֶׁל שִׁבְעָה? תַּלְמוּד לוֹמַר: ״לֹא תִשְׁחַט עַל חָמֵץ״ (להלן לד, כה), לֹא תִשְׁחַט הַפֶּסַח וַעֲדַיִן חָמֵץ קַיָּם: **הַנֶּפֶשׁ הַהִוא.** כְּשֶׁהִיא בְּנַפְשָׁהּ וּבְדַעְתָּהּ, פְּרָט לְאָנוּס: **מִיִּשְׂרָאֵל.** שׁוֹמֵעַ אֲנִי תִּכָּרֵת מִיִּשְׂרָאֵל וְתֵלֵךְ לָהּ לְעַם אַחֵר? תַּלְמוּד לוֹמַר בְּמָקוֹם אַחֵר: ״מִלְּפָנַי״ (ויקרא כב, ג), בְּכָל מָקוֹם שֶׁהוּא רְשׁוּתִי:

These are unique commands. Not only must we (at least on Seder night) eat matza, not only must we refrain, throughout the festival, from eating leavened bread or any product that has even the slightest admixture of *ḥametz*, we must also ensure that no leaven or leaven-containing food is in our possession and we must take active steps to remove it, destroy it, and disown it. We do not find such extreme measures in the case of any other forbidden food. The halakhic logic is the temporary nature of the ban on leaven. During the rest of the year it is permitted. Therefore, were there any in the house or in our ownership during the festival we might come to eat it inadvertently; hence we must remove it completely (*Sefer Mitzvot Katan*, 222). The psychological logic is that Passover is a time of departure, the beginning of a journey, the transformation of a nation from slavery to freedom. Clearing the house of *ḥametz* is a symbolic jettisoning of the past, the preparation for a leave-taking.

וְהִכֵּיתִי כָל־בְּכוֹר בְּאֶרֶץ מִצְרַיִם מֵאָדָם וְעַד־בְּהֵמָה וּבְכָל־אֱלֹהֵי
יג מִצְרַיִם אֶעֱשֶׂה שְׁפָטִים אֲנִי יהוה: וְהָיָה הַדָּם לָכֶם לְאֹת עַל הַבָּתִּים
אֲשֶׁר אַתֶּם שָׁם וְרָאִיתִי אֶת־הַדָּם וּפָסַחְתִּי עֲלֵכֶם וְלֹא־יִהְיֶה בָכֶם
יד נֶגֶף לְמַשְׁחִית בְּהַכֹּתִי בְּאֶרֶץ מִצְרָיִם: וְהָיָה הַיּוֹם הַזֶּה לָכֶם לְזִכָּרוֹן
טו וְחַגֹּתֶם אֹתוֹ חַג לַיהוה לְדֹרֹתֵיכֶם חֻקַּת עוֹלָם תְּחָגֻּהוּ: שִׁבְעַת יָמִים
מַצּוֹת תֹּאכֵלוּ אַךְ בַּיּוֹם הָרִאשׁוֹן תַּשְׁבִּיתוּ שְּׂאֹר מִבָּתֵּיכֶם כִּי | כָּל־
אֹכֵל חָמֵץ וְנִכְרְתָה הַנֶּפֶשׁ הַהִוא מִיִּשְׂרָאֵל מִיּוֹם הָרִאשֹׁן עַד־יוֹם

אונקלוס

וְאֶקְטוֹל כָּל בְּכְרָא בְּאַרְעָא דְמִצְרַיִם, מֵאֱנָשָׁא וְעַד בְּעִירָא, וּבְכָל טַעֲוָת מִצְרָאֵי, אַעֲבֵיד דִּינִין אֲנָא יי: יג וִיהֵי דְמָא לְכוֹן לְאָת, עַל בָּתַּיָּא דְּאַתּוּן תַּמָּן, וְאֶחֱזֵי יָת דְּמָא, וְאֵחוֹס עֲלֵיכוֹן, וְלָא יְהֵי בְכוֹן מוֹתָא לְחַבָּלָא, בְּמִקְטְלִי בְּאַרְעָא דְמִצְרָיִם: יד וִיהֵי יוֹמָא הָדֵין לְכוֹן לְדֻכְרָנָא, וּתְחַגּוּן יָתֵיהּ חַגָּא קֳדָם יי, לְדָרֵיכוֹן, קְיָם עָלַם תְּחַגְּנֵיהּ: טו שִׁבְעָא יוֹמִין פַּטִּירָא תֵּיכְלוּן, בְּרַם בְּיוֹמָא קַדְמָאָה, תְּבַטְּלוּן חֲמִירָא מִבָּתֵּיכוֹן, אֲרֵי כָּל דְּיֵיכוֹל חֲמִיעַ, וְיִשְׁתֵּיצֵי, אֱנָשָׁא הַהוּא מִיִּשְׂרָאֵל, מִיּוֹמָא קַדְמָאָה עַד יוֹמָא

12:14 הַיּוֹם הַזֶּה לָכֶם לְזִכָּרוֹן *This day… a memorial for you* – In ancient Israel, a new concept of time was born. This did more than change the history of the West; in a sense, it created it. Until Tanakh, time was generally conceived as a series of eternal recurrences, endlessly repeating a pattern that belonged to the immutable structure of the universe. The seasons – spring, summer, autumn, winter – and the lifecycle – birth, growth, decline, and death – were a reiterated sequence in which nothing fundamentally changed. This is variously called cyclical, or cosmological, or mythic time.

A world of cyclical time is one in which nothing ultimately changes. All that lives, dies, but life itself lives on. Winds, storms, floods, and drought wreak devastation, but nature recovers, homes are rebuilt, fields are replanted, and the cycle begins again. Myth justifies the status quo. Inequalities are seen as written into the structure of the universe. All attempts to change society are destined to fail. People are what they are, and the world is what it has always been. At best this view leads to resignation, at worst to despair. There is no ultimate meaning in history.

The Jewish understanding of time that emerges from Tanakh, by contrast, was utterly revolutionary. For the first time people began to conceive that God had created the universe in freedom, and that by making man in His image, He endowed him too with freedom. That being so, he might be different tomorrow from what he was today, and if he could change himself, he could begin to change the world. Time became an arena of change. With this, the concept of history (as opposed to myth) was born.

12:15 תַּשְׁבִּיתוּ שְּׂאֹר מִבָּתֵּיכֶם *You shall have removed leaven from your houses* – The Torah not only commands us to eat matza on Passover and to avoid eating leaven or leavened products. It also contains three distinct commands about removing all leaven from our property and possession: (1) "By the first day you shall have removed leaven from your houses" (Ex. 12:15). This involves the physical removal of all leaven and is the source of the command of *biur ḥametz,* the burning or destruction of leavened products. (2) "No bread or leavening shall be seen in all your land" (13:7). (3) "During these seven days, leaven must not be found in your houses" (12:19). Whereas the first source enjoins a positive act to remove all *ḥametz,* the second and third are the negative corollaries, forbidding us to leave any leaven or leavened products in our possession.

16 the first day to the seventh will be severed from Israel. The first day shall be
a sacred assembly and the seventh day shall be a sacred assembly. On them
no work may be done but preparing the food for everyone to eat. That alone
17 may you do. Safeguard the unleavened bread, because on this very day I will
have brought your battalions out of Egypt. You shall observe this day for all
18 generations; it is an everlasting law. From the fourteenth day of the first month
in the evening until the twenty-first day of the month in the evening, you may
19 eat only unleavened bread. During these seven days, leaven must not be found
in your houses. Anyone, whether newcomer or native born, who eats leavened
20 food will have his soul severed from the community of Israel. Eat nothing
leavened. Wherever you may live, you shall eat unleavened bread."
21 Then Moshe called together all the elders of Israel and instructed them, HAMISHI
"Each select or acquire one of the flock for yourselves, for your families and
22 slaughter the Passover sacrifice. Take a bunch of hyssop, dip it in the blood in
the bowl, and put some of the blood on the top and two sides of the doorframe.
23 None of you shall leave by the doors of your houses until morning. When the
Lord passes through to strike Egypt and sees the blood on the top and sides
of a doorframe, He will pass over that doorway and will not let the destroyer
24 enter your houses to strike you down. Keep this as a law for you and for your

רש״י

טז **מִקְרָא קֹדֶשׁ.** ׳מִקְרָא׳ שֵׁם דָּבָר, קְרָא אוֹתוֹ קֹדֶשׁ לַאֲכִילָה וּשְׁתִיָּה וּכְסוּת: **לֹא יֵעָשֶׂה בָהֶם.** אֲפִלּוּ עַל יְדֵי אֲחֵרִים: **הוּא לְבַדּוֹ.** הוּא וְלֹא מַכְשִׁירָיו שֶׁאֶפְשָׁר לַעֲשׂוֹתָן מֵעֶרֶב יוֹם טוֹב: **לְכָל נֶפֶשׁ.** אַף לִבְהֵמָה. יָכוֹל אַף לַגּוֹיִם? תַּלְמוּד לוֹמַר: ״אַךְ״:

יז **וּשְׁמַרְתֶּם אֶת הַמַּצּוֹת.** שֶׁלֹּא יָבֹאוּ לִידֵי חִמּוּץ. מִכָּאן אָמְרוּ: תָּפַח, תִּלְטוֹשׁ בְּצוֹנֵן. רַבִּי יֹאשִׁיָּה אוֹמֵר: אַל תְּהִי קוֹרֵא ״אֶת הַמַּצּוֹת״ אֶלָּא ׳אֶת הַמִּצְוֹת׳, כְּדֶרֶךְ שֶׁאֵין מַחְמִיצִין אֶת הַמַּצָּה כָּךְ אֵין מַחְמִיצִין אֶת הַמִּצְוָה, אֶלָּא אִם בָּאָה לְיָדְךָ עֲשֵׂה אוֹתָהּ מִיָּד: **וּשְׁמַרְתֶּם אֶת הַיּוֹם הַזֶּה.** מִמְּלָאכָה: **לְדֹרֹתֵיכֶם חֻקַּת עוֹלָם.** לְפִי שֶׁלֹּא נֶאֱמַר ׳דּוֹרוֹת׳ וְ׳חֻקַּת עוֹלָם׳ עַל הַמְּלָאכָה אֶלָּא עַל הַחֲגִיגָה (לעיל פסוק יד), לְכָךְ חָזַר וּשְׁנָאוֹ כָּאן, שֶׁלֹּא תֹּאמַר: אַזְהָרַת ״כָּל מְלָאכָה לֹא יֵעָשֶׂה״ (לעיל פסוק טז) לֹא לְדוֹרוֹת נֶאֶמְרָה אֶלָּא לְאוֹתוֹ הַדּוֹר:

יח **עַד יוֹם הָאֶחָד וְעֶשְׂרִים.** לָמָּה נֶאֱמַר? וַהֲלֹא כְּבָר נֶאֱמַר: ״שִׁבְעַת יָמִים״ (לעיל פסוק טו)? לְפִי שֶׁנֶּאֱמַר ״יָמִים״, לֵילוֹת מִנַּיִן? תַּלְמוּד לוֹמַר: ״עַד יוֹם הָאֶחָד וְעֶשְׂרִים״ וְגוֹ׳:

יט **לֹא יִמָּצֵא בְּבָתֵּיכֶם.** מִנַּיִן לִגְבוּלִין? תַּלְמוּד לוֹמַר: ״בְּכָל גְּבֻלֶךָ״ (להלן יג, ז). מַה תַּלְמוּד לוֹמַר ״בָּתִּים״? מַה בֵּיתְךָ בִּרְשׁוּתְךָ אַף גְּבוּלְךָ שֶׁבִּרְשׁוּתְךָ, יָצָא חֲמֵצוֹ שֶׁל נָכְרִי שֶׁהוּא אֵצֶל יִשְׂרָאֵל וְלֹא קִבֵּל עָלָיו אַחֲרָיוּת: **כִּי כָּל אֹכֵל מַחְמֶצֶת.** לַעֲנֹשׁ כָּרֵת עַל הַשְּׂאוֹר. וַהֲלֹא כְּבָר עָנַשׁ עַל הֶחָמֵץ? אֶלָּא שֶׁלֹּא תֹּאמַר: חָמֵץ שֶׁרָאוּי לַאֲכִילָה עָנַשׁ עָלָיו, שְׂאוֹר שֶׁאֵינוֹ רָאוּי לַאֲכִילָה לֹא יֵעָנֵשׁ עָלָיו; וְאִם עָנַשׁ עַל הַשְּׂאוֹר וְלֹא עָנַשׁ עַל הֶחָמֵץ, הָיִיתִי אוֹמֵר: שְׂאוֹר שֶׁהוּא מְחַמֵּץ אֲחֵרִים עָנַשׁ עָלָיו, חָמֵץ שֶׁאֵינוֹ מְחַמֵּץ אֲחֵרִים לֹא יֵעָנֵשׁ עָלָיו – לְכָךְ נֶאֶמְרוּ שְׁנֵיהֶם: **בַּגֵּר וּבְאֶזְרַח הָאָרֶץ.** לְפִי שֶׁהַנֵּס נַעֲשָׂה לְיִשְׂרָאֵל הֻצְרַךְ לְרַבּוֹת אֶת הַגֵּרִים:

כ **מַחְמֶצֶת לֹא תֹאכֵלוּ.** אַזְהָרָה עַל אֲכִילַת שְׂאוֹר: **כָּל מַחְמֶצֶת.** לְהָבִיא אֶת תַּעֲרֻבְתּוֹ: **בְּכֹל מוֹשְׁבֹתֵיכֶם תֹּאכְלוּ מַצּוֹת.** זֶה בָּא לְלַמֵּד שֶׁתְּהֵא רְאוּיָה לְהֵאָכֵל בְּכָל מוֹשְׁבוֹתֵיכֶם, פְּרָט לְמַעֲשֵׂר שֵׁנִי וְחַלּוֹת תּוֹדָה:

כא **מִשְׁכוּ.** מִי שֶׁיֵּשׁ לוֹ צֹאן יִמְשֹׁךְ מִשֶּׁלּוֹ: **וּקְחוּ.** מִי שֶׁאֵין לוֹ יִקַּח מִן הַשּׁוּק: **לְמִשְׁפְּחֹתֵיכֶם.** ״שֶׂה לְבֵית אָבֹת״ (לעיל פסוק ג):

כב **אֵזוֹב.** מִין יָרָק שֶׁיֵּשׁ לוֹ גִּבְעוֹלִין: **אֲגֻדַּת אֵזוֹב.** שְׁלֹשָׁה קְלָחִין קְרוּיִין אֲגֻדָּה: **אֲשֶׁר בַּסַּף.** בַּכְּלִי, כְּמוֹ: ״סִפּוֹת כֶּסֶף״ (מלכים ב׳ יב, יד): **מִן הַדָּם אֲשֶׁר בַּסַּף.** לָמָּה חָזַר וּשְׁנָאוֹ? שֶׁלֹּא תֹּאמַר טְבִילָה אַחַת לְשָׁלֹשׁ הַמַּתָּנוֹת, לְכָךְ נֶאֱמַר עוֹד: ״אֲשֶׁר בַּסַּף״, שֶׁתְּהֵא כָּל נְתִינָה וּנְתִינָה ״מִן הַדָּם אֲשֶׁר בַּסַּף״, עַל כָּל הַגָּעָה טְבִילָה: **וְאַתֶּם לֹא תֵצְאוּ וְגוֹ׳.** מַגִּיד שֶׁמֵּאַחַר

טז השביעי: וביום הראשון מקרא-קדש וביום השביעי מקרא-קדש
יהיה לכם כל-מלאכה לא-יעשה בהם אך אשר יאכל לכל-נפש
יז הוא לבדו יעשה לכם: ושמרתם את-המצות כי בעצם היום הזה
הוצאתי את-צבאותיכם מארץ מצרים ושמרתם את-היום הזה
יח לדרתיכם חקת עולם: בראשן בארבעה עשר יום לחדש בערב
יט תאכלו מצת עד יום האחד ועשרים לחדש בערב: שבעת ימים
שאר לא ימצא בבתיכם כי | כל-אכל מחמצת ונכרתה הנפש ההוא
כ מעדת ישראל בגר ובאזרח הארץ: כל-מחמצת לא תאכלו בכל
מושבתיכם תאכלו מצות:
כא ויקרא משה לכל-זקני ישראל ויאמר אלהם משכו וקחו לכם צאן חמישי
כב למשפחתיכם ושחטו הפסח: ולקחתם אגדת אזוב וטבלתם בדם
אשר-בסף והגעתם אל-המשקוף ואל-שתי המזוזת מן-הדם אשר
כג בסף ואתם לא תצאו איש מפתח-ביתו עד-בקר: ועבר יהוה לנגף
את-מצרים וראה את-הדם על-המשקוף ועל שתי המזוזת ופסח
כד יהוה על-הפתח ולא יתן המשחית לבא אל-בתיכם לנגף: ושמרתם

אונקלוס

שביעאה: טז וביומא קדמאה מערע קדיש, וביומא שביעאה, מערע קדיש יהי לכון, כל עבידא לא יתעביד בהון, ברם מא דמתאכיל לכל נפש, הוא בלחודוהי יתעביד לכון: יז ותטרון ית פטירא, ארי, בכרן יומא הדין, אפיקית ית חיליכון מארעא דמצרים, ותטרון, ית יומא הדין, לדריכון קים עלם: יח בניסן, בארבעת עסרא יומא לירחא ברמשא, תיכלון פטירא, עד, יומא חד ועסרין, לירחא ברמשא: יט שבעא יומין, חמירא, לא ישתכח בבתיכון, ארי כל דייכול מחמעא, וישתיצי, אנשא ההוא

מכנשתא דישראל, בגיוריא וביציביא דארעא: כ כל מחמעא לא תיכלון, בכל מותבניכון, תיכלון פטירא: כא וקרא משה, לכל סבי ישראל ואמר להון, אתנגידו, וסבו לכון מן בני ענא, לזרעיתכון וכוסו פסחא: כב ותסבון אסרת איזובא, ותטבלון בדמא דבמנא, ותדון לשקפא ולתרין ספיא, מן דמא דבמנא, ואתון, לא תפקון, אנש מתרע ביתיה עד צפרא: כג ויתגלי יי למחמי ית מצראי, ויחזי ית דמא על שקפא, ועל תרין ספיא, וייחוס יי על תרעא, ולא ישבוק מחבלא, למיעל לבתיכון למחמי: כד ותטרון

רש"י

שנתנה רשות למשחית לחבל אינו מבחין בין צדיק לרשע. ולילה רשות למחבלים הוא, שנאמר: "בו תרמש כל חיתו יער" (תהלים קד, כ).

כג ופסח. וחמל, ויש לומר, ודלג: ולא יתן המשחית. ולא יתן לו יכלת לבא, כמו: "ולא נתנו אלהים להרע עמדי" (בראשית לא, ז).

25 children forever. When you enter the land the Lord will give you as He has
26 promised, you shall keep this ceremony. And when your children say to you,
27 'What does this ceremony mean to you?' you shall say, 'It is the Passover
sacrifice to the Lord who passed over the houses of the Israelites in Egypt,
for He struck the Egyptians; but our homes, He spared.'" Then the people
28 bowed down and prostrated themselves. The Israelites proceeded to do exactly
29 as the Lord had commanded Moshe and Aharon. It happened at SHISHI
midnight: the Lord struck down all the firstborn in Egypt, from the firstborn
of Pharaoh, presiding on his throne, to the firstborn of the prison captives,
30 and all the firstborn cattle. Pharaoh arose that night, he and all his officials and
all Egypt – for a great scream rang out across Egypt, for there was no house

רש"י

כה **כאשר דבר.** והיכן דבר? "והבאתי אתכם אל הארץ" וגו' (לעיל ו, ח):

כז **ויקד העם.** על בשורת הגאלה וביאת הארץ ובשורת הבנים שיהיו להם ויתחלום:

כח **וילכו ויעשו בני ישראל.** וכי כבר עשו? והלא מראש חדש נאמר להם! אלא מכיון שקבלו עליהם מעלה עליהם הכתוב כאלו עשו: **וילכו ויעשו.** אף ההליכה מנה הכתוב, לתן שכר להליכה ושכר לעשיה: **כאשר צוה ה' את משה ואהרן.** להגיד שבחן של ישראל שלא הפילו דבר מכל מצות משה ואהרן. ומהו "כן עשו"? אף משה ואהרן כן עשו:

כט **וה'.** כל מקום שנאמר "וה'" – הוא ובית דינו, שהוי"ו לשון תוספת הוא, כמו: פלוני ופלוני: **הכה כל בכור.** אף של אמה אחרת והוא במצרים: **מבכר פרעה.** אף פרעה בכור היה ונשתייר מן הבכורות, ועליו הוא אומר: "בעבור הראתך את כחי" (לעיל ט, טז) – בים סוף: **עד בכור השבי.** שהיו שמחין לאידם של ישראל. ועוד, שלא יאמרו: יראתנו הביאה הפרענות. ובכור השפחה בכלל היה, שהרי מנה מן החשוב שבכלן עד הפחות, ובכור השפחה חשוב מבכור השבי:

ל **ויקם פרעה.** ממטתו: **לילה.** ולא כדרך המלכים בשלש שעות ביום: **הוא.** תחלה ואחר כך "עבדיו", מלמד שהיה הוא מחזר על בתי עבדיו ומעמידן:

fact that Jews knew their texts even in ages of mass illiteracy; the record of Jewish scholarship and intellect; the astonishing overrepresentation of Jews among the shapers of the modern mind; the Jewish reputation, sometimes admired, sometimes feared, sometimes caricatured for mental agility, argument, debate, and the ability to see all sides of a disagreement.

Moshe wanted us to teach our children a story. He wanted us to help our children understand who they are, where they came from, what happened to their ancestors to make them the distinctive people they became, and what moments in their history shaped their lives and dreams. He wanted us to give our children an identity by turning history into memory, and memory itself into a sense of responsibility. Jews were not summoned to be a nation of intellectuals. They were called on to be actors in a drama of redemption, a people invited by God to bring blessings into the world by the way they lived and sanctified life.

The long walk to freedom is not just a matter of history and politics, let alone miracles. It has to do with the relationship between parents and children. It is about telling the story and passing it on across the generations. It is about a sense of God's presence in our lives. It is about making space for transcendence, wonder, gratitude, humility, empathy, love, forgiveness, and compassion, ornamented by ritual, song, and prayer. These help to give a child confidence, trust, and hope, along with a sense of identity, belonging, and at-home-ness in the universe.

כה אֶת־הַדָּבָר הַזֶּה לְחָק־לְךָ וּלְבָנֶיךָ עַד־עוֹלָם׃ וְהָיָה כִּי־תָבֹאוּ אֶל־
הָאָרֶץ אֲשֶׁר יִתֵּן יהוה לָכֶם כַּאֲשֶׁר דִּבֵּר וּשְׁמַרְתֶּם אֶת־הָעֲבֹדָה הַזֹּאת׃
כו וְהָיָה כִּי־יֹאמְרוּ אֲלֵיכֶם בְּנֵיכֶם מָה הָעֲבֹדָה הַזֹּאת לָכֶם׃ וַאֲמַרְתֶּם
זֶבַח־פֶּסַח הוּא לַיהוה אֲשֶׁר פָּסַח עַל־בָּתֵּי בְנֵי־יִשְׂרָאֵל בְּמִצְרַיִם בְּנָגְפּוֹ
כח אֶת־מִצְרַיִם וְאֶת־בָּתֵּינוּ הִצִּיל וַיִּקֹּד הָעָם וַיִּשְׁתַּחֲווּ׃ וַיֵּלְכוּ וַיַּעֲשׂוּ בְּנֵי
כט יִשְׂרָאֵל כַּאֲשֶׁר צִוָּה יהוה אֶת־מֹשֶׁה וְאַהֲרֹן כֵּן עָשׂוּ׃ ט וַיְהִי ׀ ששי
בַּחֲצִי הַלַּיְלָה וַיהוה הִכָּה כָל־בְּכוֹר בְּאֶרֶץ מִצְרַיִם מִבְּכֹר פַּרְעֹה הַיֹּשֵׁב
ל עַל־כִּסְאוֹ עַד בְּכוֹר הַשְּׁבִי אֲשֶׁר בְּבֵית הַבּוֹר וְכֹל בְּכוֹר בְּהֵמָה׃ וַיָּקָם
פַּרְעֹה לַיְלָה הוּא וְכָל־עֲבָדָיו וְכָל־מִצְרַיִם וַתְּהִי צְעָקָה גְדֹלָה בְּמִצְרָיִם

אונקלוס

יָת פִּתְגָּמָא הָדֵין, לִקְיָם לָךְ וְלִבְנָךְ עַד עָלְמָא: כה וִיהֵי אֲרֵי תֵיעֲלוּן לְאַרְעָא, דְּיִתֵּין יְיָ, לְכוֹן כְּמָא דְּמַלֵּיל, וְתִטְּרוּן יָת פָּלְחָנָא הָדֵין: כו וִיהֵי, אֲרֵי יֵימְרוּן לְכוֹן בְּנֵיכוֹן, מָא פָּלְחָנָא הָדָא לְכוֹן: כז וְתֵימְרוּן, דְּיבַח חֲיָס הוּא קֳדָם יְיָ, דְּחָס, עַל בָּתֵּי בְנֵי יִשְׂרָאֵל בְּמִצְרַיִם, כַּד מְחָא יָת מִצְרָאֵי וְיָת בָּתַּנָא שֵׁיזֵיב, וּכְרַע עַמָּא וּסְגִידוּ: כח וַאֲזַלוּ וַעֲבַדוּ בְּנֵי יִשְׂרָאֵל, כְּמָא דְּפַקֵּיד יְיָ, יָת מֹשֶׁה וְאַהֲרֹן כֵּן עֲבַדוּ: כט וַהֲוָה בְּפַלְגוּת לֵילְיָא, וַייָ קְטַל כָּל בֻּכְרָא בְּאַרְעָא דְּמִצְרַיִם, מִבֻּכְרָא דְּפַרְעֹה דַּעֲתִיד לְמִתַּב עַל כֻּרְסֵי מַלְכוּתֵיהּ, עַד בֻּכְרָא דְּשִׁבְיָא, דִּבְבֵית אֲסִירֵי, וְכָל בֻּכְרָא דִּבְעִירָא: ל וְקָם פַּרְעֹה בְּלֵילְיָא, הוּא וְכָל עַבְדּוֹהִי וְכָל מִצְרָאֵי, וַהֲוָת, צְוָחְתָּא רַבְּתָא בְּמִצְרַיִם,

EDUCATION

This is the first of four references to children and their instruction in connection with the exodus – three of them in Exodus 12 and 13. They became the "four children" of the Haggada. Already at the outset, one of the most distinctive features of Judaism is enshrined in Jewish law: the centrality of education as the conversation between the generations.

A study from Emory University shows that having a family narrative connects children to something larger than themselves. It helps them make sense of how they fit into the world that existed before they were born. It gives them the starting point of an identity. That in turn becomes the basis of confidence. It enables children to say: This is who I am. This is the story of which I am a part. These are the people who came before me and whose descendant I am. These are the roots of which I am the stem reaching upward toward the sun.

▷

Three times in the course of the *parasha* (Ex. 12:26–27; 13:8, 14), Moshe turns to the theme of responding to one's children's questions. He speaks not about tomorrow but about the distant future. He does not celebrate the moment of liberation. Instead he wants to ensure that it will form part of the people's memory until the end of time. He wants each generation to pass on the story to the next. He wants Jewish parents to become educators, and Jewish children to be guardians of the past for the sake of the future. Inspired by God, Moshe teaches the Israelites the lesson arrived at via a different route by the Chinese: *If you plan for a year, plant rice. If you plan for a decade, plant a tree. If you plan for a century, educate a child.*

Jews became famous throughout the ages for putting education first. Where others built castles and palaces, Jews built schools and houses of study. From this flowed all the familiar achievements in which we take collective pride: the

31 without its dead. That night, Pharaoh summoned Moshe and Aharon and said,
"Get up, get out from among my people, you and the Israelites. Go. Serve the
32 LORD exactly as you requested; take your sheep and cattle also, just as you said.
33 Just go. But bless me too." The Egyptians too urged the people to make haste
34 and leave the land. "All of us will die," they said. The people took their dough
before it could rise, carrying it on their shoulders in kneading pans wrapped
35 in their clothing. As Moshe had told them, the Israelites had requested items
36 of silver and gold, and clothing, of the Egyptians, and the LORD had given the
people favor in the eyes of the Egyptians and they had granted their request.
Thus they despoiled Egypt.
37 The Israelites traveled from Ramesses to Sukkot. There were about six hundred

רש"י

כי אין בית אשר אין שם מת. יש שם בכור – מת, אין שם בכור – גדול שבבית קרוי בכור, שנאמר "אף אני בכור אתנהו" (תהלים פט, כח). דבר אחר, מצריות מזנות תחת בעליהן ויולדות מרווקים פנויים והיו להם בכורות הרבה, פעמים הם חמשה לאשה אחת, כל אחד בכור לאביו:

לא-לב **ויקרא למשה ולאהרן לילה.** מגיד שהיה מחזר על פתחי העיר וצועק: היכן משה שרוי? היכן אהרן שרוי?: **גם אתם.** הגברים: **גם בני ישראל.** הטף: **ולכו עבדו את ה' כדברכם.** הכל כמו שאמרתם ולא כמו שאמרתי אני. בטל "לא אשלח" (לעיל ה, ב), בטל "מי ומי ההלכים" (לעיל י, ח), בטל "רק צאנכם ובקרכם יצג" (לעיל י, כד) – "גם צאנכם גם בקרכם קחו"; ומהו "כאשר דברתם"? "גם אתה תתן בידנו זבחים ועלת" (לעיל י, כה) – "קחו כאשר דברתם": **וברכתם גם אתי.** התפללו עלי שלא אמות, שאני בכור:

לג **כלנו מתים.** אמרו: לא כגזרת משה הוא, שהרי אמר: "ומת כל בכור" (לעיל יא, ה) וכאן אף הפשוטים מתים, חמשה או עשרה בבית אחד:

לד **טרם יחמץ.** המצרים לא הניחום לשהות כדי חמוץ: **משארתם.** שירי מצה ומרור: **על שכמם.** אף על פי שבהמות הרבה הוליכו עמהם, מחבבים היו את המצוה:

לה **כדבר משה.** שאמר להם במצרים: "וישאלו איש מאת רעהו" (לעיל יא, ב): **ושמלת.** אף הן היו חשובות להם מן הכסף ומן הזהב, והמאחר בפסוק חשוב:

לו **וישאלום.** אף מה שלא היו שואלים מהם היו נותנים להם, אתה אומר אחד, טול שנים ולך: **וינצלו.** "ורוקינו":

לז **מרעמסס סכתה.** מאה ועשרים מיל היו, ובאו שם לפי שעה, שנאמר: "ואשא אתכם על כנפי נשרים" (להלן יט, ד): **הגברים.** מבן עשרים ומעלה:

do so for the sake of the future, not the past. "Do not oppress a stranger," says the Torah, because "you know what it is to be a stranger" (Ex. 23:9). In other words: what you suffered, do not inflict. Memory is a moral tutorial. In Santayana's famous words: "Those who cannot remember the past are destined to repeat it." Israel remembers its past precisely in order *not* to repeat it. Moshe's message is: remember, but not in order to hate.

That means drawing a line over the resentments of the past. That is why, when a slave went free, his master had to give him gifts. This was not to compensate for the fact of slavery. There is no way of giving back the years spent in servitude. But there is a way of ensuring that the parting is done with goodwill, with some symbolic compensation. The gifts allow the former slave to reach emotional closure, to feel that a new chapter is beginning, to leave without anger and a sense of humiliation. One who has received gifts finds it hard to hate. That is the significance of the silver and gold taken from the Egyptians by the Israelites at the express command of God.

לא כִּי־אֵין בַּיִת אֲשֶׁר אֵין־שָׁם מֵת׃ וַיִּקְרָא לְמֹשֶׁה וּלְאַהֲרֹן לַיְלָה וַיֹּאמֶר
קוּמוּ צְּאוּ מִתּוֹךְ עַמִּי גַּם־אַתֶּם גַּם־בְּנֵי יִשְׂרָאֵל וּלְכוּ עִבְדוּ אֶת־יְהוָה
לב כְּדַבֶּרְכֶם׃ גַּם־צֹאנְכֶם גַּם־בְּקַרְכֶם קְחוּ כַּאֲשֶׁר דִּבַּרְתֶּם וָלֵכוּ וּבֵרַכְתֶּם
לג גַּם־אֹתִי׃ וַתֶּחֱזַק מִצְרַיִם עַל־הָעָם לְמַהֵר לְשַׁלְּחָם מִן־הָאָרֶץ כִּי
לד אָמְרוּ כֻּלָּנוּ מֵתִים׃ וַיִּשָּׂא הָעָם אֶת־בְּצֵקוֹ טֶרֶם יֶחְמָץ מִשְׁאֲרֹתָם
לה צְרֻרֹת בְּשִׂמְלֹתָם עַל־שִׁכְמָם׃ וּבְנֵי־יִשְׂרָאֵל עָשׂוּ כִּדְבַר מֹשֶׁה וַיִּשְׁאֲלוּ
לו מִמִּצְרַיִם כְּלֵי־כֶסֶף וּכְלֵי זָהָב וּשְׂמָלֹת׃ וַיהוָה נָתַן אֶת־חֵן הָעָם בְּעֵינֵי
מִצְרַיִם וַיַּשְׁאִלוּם וַיְנַצְּלוּ אֶת־מִצְרָיִם׃
לז וַיִּסְעוּ בְנֵי־יִשְׂרָאֵל מֵרַעְמְסֵס סֻכֹּתָה כְּשֵׁשׁ־מֵאוֹת אֶלֶף רַגְלִי הַגְּבָרִים

אונקלוס

אֲרֵי לֵית בֵּיתָא תַּמָּן, דְּלָא הֲוָה בֵּיהּ מִיתָא׃ לא וּקְרָא לְמֹשֶׁה וּלְאַהֲרֹן בְּלֵילְיָא, וַאֲמַר קוּמוּ פּוּקוּ מִגּוֹ עַמִּי, אַף אַתּוּן אַף בְּנֵי יִשְׂרָאֵל, וְאִיזִילוּ, פְּלַחוּ קֳדָם יי כְּמָא דַּהֲוֵיתוּן אָמְרִין׃ לב אַף עָנְכוֹן אַף תּוֹרֵיכוֹן דְּבָרוּ, כְּמָא דְּמַלֵּילְתּוּן וְאִיזִילוּ, וְצַלּוֹ אַף עֲלָי׃ לג וּתְקִיפוּ מִצְרָאֵי עַל עַמָּא, לְאוֹחָאָה לְשַׁלָּחוּתְהוֹן מִן אַרְעָא, אֲרֵי אֲמַרוּ כֻּלַּנָא מָיְתִין׃ לד וּנְטַל עַמָּא, יָת לֵישְׁהוֹן עַד לָא חֲמַע, מוֹתַר אָצְוָתְהוֹן, צְרִיר בִּלְבוּשֵׁיהוֹן עַל כַּתְפֵיהוֹן׃ לה וּבְנֵי יִשְׂרָאֵל עֲבַדוּ כְּפִתְגָּמָא דְּמֹשֶׁה, וּשְׁאִילוּ מִמִּצְרָאֵי, מָנִין דִּכְסַף, וּמָנִין דִּדְהַב וּלְבוּשִׁין׃ לו וַיְיָ, יְהַב יָת עַמָּא לְרַחֲמִין, בְּעֵינֵי מִצְרָאֵי וְאַשְׁאִילוּנוּן, וְרוֹקִינוּ יָת מִצְרָיִם׃ לז וּנְטַלוּ בְּנֵי יִשְׂרָאֵל, מֵרַעְמְסֵס לְסֻכּוֹת, כְּשִׁית מְאָה אַלְפִין גֻּבְרָא, רַגְלָאָה

This is remarkable. The Israelites were enslaved by the Egyptians. They owe them no debt of gratitude. On the contrary, they are entitled to feel a lingering resentment. Yet Moshe insists that they should not do so. They should bear the Egyptians no ill will. Why? In this brief command we have one of the most profound insights into the nature of a free society.

A people driven by hate cannot be free. Had the people carried with them a burden of hatred and a desire for revenge, Moshe would have taken the Israelites out of Egypt, but he would not have taken Egypt out of the Israelites. They would still be there, bound by chains of anger as restricting as any metal. To be free you have to let go of hate.

There is a fundamental difference between living *with* the past and living *in* the past. Judaism is a religion of memory. We remember the exodus annually, even daily. But we

12:32 **וּבֵרַכְתֶּם גַּם־אֹתִי** *But bless me too* – Finally, too late, in the midst of grief, Pharaoh poignantly acknowledges that there is a power in the universe greater than Egypt and its gods.

12:35 **כְּלֵי־כֶסֶף וּכְלֵי זָהָב** *Items of silver and gold* – Why the silver and gold? The Israelites are in such a hurry to leave, and the Egyptians so hasty in urging their departure, that they do not even have time for the dough to rise. Why then is God so insistent that they take the time to ask for these parting gifts? What conceivable use do they have for them in the long journey across the wilderness?

It is not until we reach the end of the Mosaic books that we can begin to understand it. Moshe insists: "Do not despise an Edomite, for he is your kin. Do not despise an Egyptian, for you lived as a stranger in his land" (Deut. 23:8).

►

38 thousand men on foot, quite apart from the children. And a great variety of
other people went up with them, as well as large droves of livestock, flocks
39 and cattle. With the dough they had brought from Egypt, they baked cakes of
unleavened bread, not risen. They had been driven out of Egypt and could not
40 delay, and had prepared no other provisions. The Israelites had lived in Egypt
41 for four hundred thirty years. At the end of four hundred thirty years, to the
42 very day, all the LORD's battalions left Egypt. All that night, the LORD watched
over them to bring them out of Egypt; and still this night is kept as one of
watchfulness for the LORD throughout the generations of Israel.
43 The LORD said to Moshe and Aharon, "This is the law of the Passover sacrifice.
44 No foreigner may eat of it. But any slave who has been acquired for money

רש״י

לח| **עֵרֶב רַב.** תַּעֲרֹבֶת אֻמּוֹת שֶׁל גֵּרִים:

לט| **עֻגֹת מַצּוֹת.** חֲרָרָה שֶׁל מַצָּה. בָּצֵק שֶׁלֹּא הֶחֱמִיץ קָרוּי מַצָּה: **וְגַם צֵדָה לֹא עָשׂוּ לָהֶם.** לַדֶּרֶךְ. מַגִּיד שִׁבְחָן שֶׁל יִשְׂרָאֵל, שֶׁלֹּא אָמְרוּ: הֵיאַךְ נֵצֵא לַמִּדְבָּר בְּלֹא צֵדָה? אֶלָּא הֶאֱמִינוּ וְהָלְכוּ. הוּא שֶׁמְּפֹרָשׁ בַּקַּבָּלָה: "זָכַרְתִּי לָךְ חֶסֶד נְעוּרַיִךְ אַהֲבַת כְּלוּלֹתָיִךְ לֶכְתֵּךְ אַחֲרַי בַּמִּדְבָּר בְּאֶרֶץ לֹא זְרוּעָה" (ירמיה ב, ב), מַה שָּׂכָר מְפֹרָשׁ אַחֲרָיו? "קֹדֶשׁ יִשְׂרָאֵל לַה׳" וְגוֹ׳ (שם פסוק ג):

מ| **אֲשֶׁר יָשְׁבוּ בְּמִצְרָיִם.** אַחַר שְׁאָר הַיְשִׁיבוֹת שֶׁיָּשְׁבוּ גֵּרִים בְּאֶרֶץ לֹא לָהֶם: **שְׁלֹשִׁים שָׁנָה וְאַרְבַּע מֵאוֹת שָׁנָה.** בֵּין הַכֹּל, מִשֶּׁנּוֹלַד יִצְחָק עַד עַכְשָׁיו הָיוּ אַרְבַּע מֵאוֹת שָׁנָה. מִשֶּׁהָיָה לוֹ זֶרַע לְאַבְרָהָם נִתְקַיֵּם: "כִּי גֵר יִהְיֶה זַרְעֲךָ" (בראשית טו, יג), וּשְׁלֹשִׁים שָׁנָה הָיוּ מִשֶּׁנִּגְזְרָה גְּזֵרַת בֵּין הַבְּתָרִים עַד שֶׁנּוֹלַד יִצְחָק. וְאִי אֶפְשָׁר לוֹמַר בְּאֶרֶץ מִצְרַיִם לְבַדָּהּ, שֶׁהֲרֵי קְהָת מִן הַבָּאִים עִם יַעֲקֹב הָיָה, צֵא וַחֲשֹׁב כָּל שְׁנוֹתָיו וְכָל שְׁנוֹת עַמְרָם בְּנוֹ וּשְׁמוֹנִים שֶׁל מֹשֶׁה, לֹא תִּמְצָאֵם כָּל כָּךְ. וְעַל כָּרְחֲךָ הַרְבֵּה שָׁנִים הָיוּ לִקְהָת עַד שֶׁלֹּא יָרַד לְמִצְרַיִם, וְהַרְבֵּה מִשְּׁנוֹת עַמְרָם נִבְלָעִים בִּשְׁנוֹת קְהָת, וְהַרְבֵּה מִשְּׁמוֹנִים שֶׁל מֹשֶׁה נִבְלָעִים בִּשְׁנוֹת עַמְרָם, הֲרֵי שֶׁלֹּא תִּמְצָא אַרְבַּע מֵאוֹת לְבִיאַת מִצְרַיִם; וְהֻזְקַקְתָּ לוֹמַר עַל כָּרְחֲךָ שֶׁאַף שְׁאָר הַיְשִׁיבוֹת נִקְרְאוּ גֵּרוּת, וַאֲפִלּוּ בְּחֶבְרוֹן, שֶׁנֶּאֱמַר: "אֲשֶׁר גָּר שָׁם אַבְרָהָם וְיִצְחָק" (בראשית לה, כז), וְאוֹמֵר: "אֵת אֶרֶץ מְגֻרֵיהֶם אֲשֶׁר גָּרוּ בָהּ" (לעיל ו, ד). לְפִיכָךְ אַתָּה צָרִיךְ לוֹמַר "כִּי גֵר יִהְיֶה זַרְעֲךָ" – מִשֶּׁהָיָה לוֹ זֶרַע. וּכְשֶׁתִּמְנֶה אַרְבַּע מֵאוֹת שָׁנָה מִשֶּׁנּוֹלַד יִצְחָק, תִּמְצָא מִבִּיאָתָן לְמִצְרַיִם עַד יְצִיאָתָן מָאתַיִם וָעֶשֶׂר שָׁנִים. וְזֶה אֶחָד מִן הַדְּבָרִים שֶׁשִּׁנּוּ לְתַלְמַי הַמֶּלֶךְ:

מא| **וַיְהִי מִקֵּץ שְׁלֹשִׁים שָׁנָה... וַיְהִי בְּעֶצֶם הַיּוֹם הַזֶּה.** מַגִּיד שֶׁכֵּיוָן שֶׁהִגִּיעַ הַקֵּץ לֹא עִכְּבָן הַמָּקוֹם כְּהֶרֶף עַיִן. בַּחֲמִשָּׁה עָשָׂר בְּנִיסָן בָּאוּ מַלְאֲכֵי הַשָּׁרֵת אֵצֶל אַבְרָהָם לְבַשְּׂרוֹ, בַּחֲמִשָּׁה עָשָׂר בְּנִיסָן נוֹלַד יִצְחָק, בַּחֲמִשָּׁה עָשָׂר בְּנִיסָן נִגְזְרָה גְּזֵרַת בֵּין הַבְּתָרִים:

מב| **לֵיל שִׁמֻּרִים.** שֶׁהָיָה הַקָּדוֹשׁ בָּרוּךְ הוּא שׁוֹמֵר וּמְצַפֶּה לוֹ לְקַיֵּם הַבְטָחָתוֹ "לְהוֹצִיאָם מֵאֶרֶץ מִצְרַיִם": **הוּא הַלַּיְלָה הַזֶּה לַה׳.** הוּא הַלַּיְלָה שֶׁאָמַר לְאַבְרָהָם: בַּלַּיְלָה הַזֶּה אֲנִי גוֹאֵל אֶת בָּנֶיךָ: **שִׁמֻּרִים לְכָל בְּנֵי יִשְׂרָאֵל לְדֹרֹתָם.** מְשֻׁמָּר וּבָא מִן הַמַּזִּיקִין, כְּעִנְיָן שֶׁנֶּאֱמַר: "וְלֹא יִתֵּן הַמַּשְׁחִית" וְגוֹ׳ (לעיל פסוק כג):

מג| **זֹאת חֻקַּת הַפָּסַח.** בְּאַרְבָּעָה עָשָׂר בְּנִיסָן נֶאֶמְרָה לָהֶם פָּרָשָׁה זוֹ: **כָּל בֶּן נֵכָר.** שֶׁנִּתְנַכְּרוּ מַעֲשָׂיו לְאָבִיו שֶׁבַּשָּׁמַיִם, וְאֶחָד הַגּוֹי וְאֶחָד יִשְׂרָאֵל מְשֻׁמָּד בַּמַּשְׁמָע:

מד| **וּמַלְתָּה אֹתוֹ אָז יֹאכַל בּוֹ.** רַבּוֹ; מַגִּיד שֶׁמִּילַת עֲבָדָיו מְעַכַּבְתּוֹ מִלֶּאֱכֹל בַּפֶּסַח, דִּבְרֵי רַבִּי יְהוֹשֻׁעַ. רַבִּי אֱלִיעֶזֶר אוֹמֵר: אֵין מִילַת עֲבָדָיו מְעַכַּבְתּוֹ מִלֶּאֱכֹל בַּפֶּסַח, אִם כֵּן מַה תַּלְמוּד לוֹמַר: "אָז יֹאכַל בּוֹ"? הָעֶבֶד:

loyalty, this sense of identity, without coercion? The answer will unfold through the rest of the Torah.

12:39 **וְלֹא יָכְלוּ לְהִתְמַהְמֵהַּ** *They… could not delay* – The Egyptians were pressing them to leave. The same verb appears in Genesis 19:16 when the angels urged Lot and his family to leave Sedom because the city was about to be destroyed. Lot delayed, and it was almost fatal. Here, God brings about a sequence of events that makes it impossible for the Israelites to delay in the event that they have second thoughts. Their frequently expressed longing to return to Egypt during their years in the desert shows how necessary this was. Had they delayed, they might never have left.

לח לְבַד מִטָּף׃ וְגַם־עֵרֶב רַב עָלָה אִתָּם וְצֹאן וּבָקָר מִקְנֶה כָּבֵד מְאֹד׃
לט וַיֹּאפוּ אֶת־הַבָּצֵק אֲשֶׁר הוֹצִיאוּ מִמִּצְרַיִם עֻגֹת מַצּוֹת כִּי לֹא חָמֵץ
כִּי־גֹרְשׁוּ מִמִּצְרַיִם וְלֹא יָכְלוּ לְהִתְמַהְמֵהַּ וְגַם־צֵדָה לֹא־עָשׂוּ לָהֶם׃
מ וּמוֹשַׁב בְּנֵי יִשְׂרָאֵל אֲשֶׁר יָשְׁבוּ בְּמִצְרָיִם שְׁלֹשִׁים שָׁנָה וְאַרְבַּע מֵאוֹת
מא שָׁנָה׃ וַיְהִי מִקֵּץ שְׁלֹשִׁים שָׁנָה וְאַרְבַּע מֵאוֹת שָׁנָה וַיְהִי בְּעֶצֶם הַיּוֹם
מב הַזֶּה יָצְאוּ כָּל־צִבְאוֹת יהוה מֵאֶרֶץ מִצְרָיִם׃ לֵיל שִׁמֻּרִים הוּא לַיהוה
לְהוֹצִיאָם מֵאֶרֶץ מִצְרָיִם הוּא־הַלַּיְלָה הַזֶּה לַיהוה שִׁמֻּרִים לְכָל־בְּנֵי
יִשְׂרָאֵל לְדֹרֹתָם׃
מג וַיֹּאמֶר יהוה אֶל־מֹשֶׁה וְאַהֲרֹן זֹאת חֻקַּת הַפָּסַח כָּל־בֶּן־נֵכָר לֹא־
מד יֹאכַל בּוֹ׃ וְכָל־עֶבֶד אִישׁ מִקְנַת־כָּסֶף וּמַלְתָּה אֹתוֹ אָז יֹאכַל בּוֹ׃

אונקלוס

בַּר מִטַּפְלָא׃ לח וְאַף נֻכְרָאִין סַגִּיאִין סְלִיקוּ עִמְּהוֹן, וְעָנָא וְתוֹרֵי, בְּעִירָא סַגִּי לַחֲדָא׃ לט וַאֲפוֹ יָת לֵישָׁא, דְּאַפִּיקוּ מִמִּצְרַיִם, גְּרִיצָן פַּטִּירָן אֲרֵי לָא חֲמַע, אֲרֵי אִתָּרַכוּ מִמִּצְרַיִם, וְלָא יְכִילוּ לְאִתְעַכָּבָא, וְאַף זְוָדִין לָא עֲבַדוּ לְהוֹן׃ מ וּמוֹתַב בְּנֵי יִשְׂרָאֵל, דִּיתִיבוּ בְּמִצְרָיִם, אַרְבַּע מְאָה וּתְלָתִין שְׁנִין׃ מא וַהֲוָה, מִסּוֹף אַרְבַּע מְאָה וּתְלָתִין שְׁנִין, וַהֲוָה, בִּכְרַן יוֹמָא הָדֵין, נְפַקוּ, כָּל חֵילַיָּא דַּיי מֵאַרְעָא דְּמִצְרָיִם׃ מב לֵילֵי נְטִיר הוּא קֳדָם יי, לְאַפָּקוּתְהוֹן מֵאַרְעָא דְּמִצְרָיִם, הוּא לֵילְיָא הָדֵין קֳדָם יי, נְטִיר, לְכָל בְּנֵי יִשְׂרָאֵל לְדָרֵיהוֹן׃ מג וַאֲמַר יי לְמֹשֶׁה וְאַהֲרֹן, דָּא גְּזֵירַת פִּסְחָא, כָּל בַּר יִשְׂרָאֵל דְּיִשְׁתְּמַד לָא יֵיכוֹל בֵּיהּ׃ מד וְכָל עֶבֶד גְּבַר זְבִין כַּסְפָּא, וְתִגְזַר יָתֵיהּ, בְּכֵן יֵיכוֹל בֵּיהּ׃

12:38 **עֶרֶב רַב** *A great variety of other people* – The Bible has a strange but unmistakable fascination with diversity. One of the oddest elements of the biblical narrative is the way it describes the Israelites, not as a unified nation but as a group of twelve tribes. As early as this verse, we hear of the *erev rav*, an unidentified "variety of others" or "mixed multitude" who leave Egypt as part of Israel. Biblical Israel is a nation whose unity is not ethnic but civic. That is why, for example, the twenty-fifth chapter of Leviticus will be about minority rights. The *ger* – a migrant or "resident alien" is one who does not share the religion of the majority, but does share its political culture.

We sometimes forget, because Judaism is quite old, that the Bible presents Judaism or Abrahamic faith as a latecomer, not as the original faith of humanity. By the time Moshe appears, Egypt is already old. The Judaic project is a critique of empires and imperialism. I can define imperialism in the same words that I define religious fundamentalism today. Imperialism, like fundamentalism, is the attempt to impose a single truth on a plural world.

The Tanakh does not gloss over the fact that biblical Israel was an ethnic mix; it seems to go out of its way to emphasize it. There are two ways of reading the story of the exodus. One is as a tale of divine intervention in history; this is how we have read the text so far. The other is about how Moshe turned a ragtag crowd of escaping slaves, fractious, fearful, and disputatious, into a cohesive nation with an identity so strong that it was able to survive devastating defeats, as well as a two-thousand-year exile. That nation continued to see itself as a nation even when scattered and dispersed across the world. How do you create that kind of identity out of diversity? How do you build this sort of

45 and circumcised may eat it. No gentile resident or hired laborer may eat of it.
46 It should be eaten in a single house; bring none of the meat outside the house.
47 Do not break any of its bones. All the community of Israel shall observe this.
48 If a stranger lives among you and wishes to offer a Passover sacrifice to the
LORD, every male in his household must be circumcised. Then he may join in
observing it and be like a native born. But no uncircumcised man may eat of it.
49 There shall be one and the same law for the native born and the stranger who
50 lives among you." All the Israelites did exactly as the LORD had commanded
51 Moshe and Aharon. And on that very day the LORD brought the
Israelites out of Egypt in their battalions.
13 1 2 The LORD said to Moshe, "Consecrate every firstborn to Me. Man and beast, SHEVI'I
3 the first to emerge from every womb among the Israelites is Mine." Moshe said
to the people, "Remember this day, the day you left Egypt, the house of slaves,
when with a mighty hand the LORD rescued you from here. No leaven may be
4 5 eaten. Today, in the month of Aviv, you are leaving. And when the LORD brings

רש"י

מה) **תושב.** זה גר תושב: **ושכיר.** זה הגוי. ומה תלמוד לומר? והלא ערלים הם, ונאמר: "וכל ערל לא יאכל בו" (להלן פסוק מח)! אלא כגון ערבי מהול וגבעוני מהול והוא תושב או שכיר:

מו) **בבית אחד יאכל.** בחבורה אחת, שלא יעשו הנמנין עליו שתי חבורות ויחלקוהו. אתה אומר בחבורה אחת, או אינו אלא "בבית אחד" כמשמעו, וללמד שאם התחילו והיו אוכלים בחצר וירדו גשמים שלא יכנסו לבית? תלמוד לומר: "על הבתים אשר יאכלו אתו בהם" (לעיל פסוק ז), מכאן שהאוכל אוכל בשני מקומות: **לא תוציא מן הבית.** מן החבורה: **ועצם לא תשברו בו.** הראוי לאכילה, כגון שיש עליו כזית בשר, יש בו משום שבירת עצם, אין עליו כזית בשר אין בו משום שבירת עצם:

מז) **כל עדת ישראל יעשו אתו.** למה נאמר? לפי שהוא אומר בפסח מצרים: "שה לבית אבת" (לעיל פסוק ג) שנמנו עליו למשפחות, יכול אף פסח דורות כן? תלמוד לומר: "כל עדת ישראל יעשו אתו":

מח) **ועשה פסח.** יכול כל המתגייר יעשה פסח מיד? תלמוד לומר: "והיה כאזרח הארץ", מה אזרח בארבעה עשר אף גר בארבעה עשר: **וכל ערל לא יאכל בו.** להביא את שמתו אחיו מחמת מילה, שאינו משמד לערלות ואינו למד מ"בן נכר לא יאכל בו" (לעיל פסוק מג):

מט) **תורה אחת וגו'.** להשוות גר לאזרח אף לשאר מצות שבתורה:

יג ב) **פטר כל רחם.** שפתח את הרחם תחלה, כמו: "פוטר מים ראשית מדון" (משלי יז, יד), וכן: "יפטירו בשפה" (תהלים כב, ח) – יפתחו שפתים: **לי הוא.** לעצמי קניתים על ידי שהכיתי בכורי מצרים:

ג) **זכור את היום הזה.** למד שמזכירין יציאת מצרים בכל יום:

ד) **בחדש האביב.** וכי לא היינו יודעין באי זה חדש? אלא כך אמר להם: ראו חסד שגמלכם, שהוציא אתכם בחדש שהוא כשר לצאת, לא חמה ולא צנה ולא גשמים. וכן הוא אומר: "מוציא אסירים בכושרות" (תהלים סח, ז), חדש שהוא כשר לצאת:

ה) **אל ארץ הכנעני וגו'.** אף על פי שלא מנה אלא חמשה עממים, כל שבעה גוים במשמע שכלן בכלל כנעני הם, ואחת ממשפחות כנען היתה שלא נקרא לה שם אלא 'כנעני':

When this service was later transferred to the tribe of Levi and to the priests, the father of a firstborn was to redeem his son for the sum of five shekels (Num. 18:16) in a ceremony known as *pidyon haben*. The substance of this ceremony has not changed since biblical times, though the wording we now use is more recent. Thus the exodus is to be recalled in perpetuity not only by the celebration of Passover but also by the dedication of firstborn animals to God, and by the redemption of firstborn males.

מה מו תּוֹשָׁב וְשָׂכִיר לֹא־יֹאכַל בּוֹ׃ בְּבַיִת אֶחָד יֵאָכֵל לֹא־תוֹצִיא מִן־הַבַּיִת
מז מִן־הַבָּשָׂר חוּצָה וְעֶצֶם לֹא תִשְׁבְּרוּ־בוֹ׃ כָּל־עֲדַת יִשְׂרָאֵל יַעֲשׂוּ אֹתוֹ׃
מח וְכִי־יָגוּר אִתְּךָ גֵּר וְעָשָׂה פֶסַח לַיהוה הִמּוֹל לוֹ כָל־זָכָר וְאָז יִקְרַב
מט לַעֲשֹׂתוֹ וְהָיָה כְּאֶזְרַח הָאָרֶץ וְכָל־עָרֵל לֹא־יֹאכַל בּוֹ׃ תּוֹרָה אַחַת יִהְיֶה
נ לָאֶזְרָח וְלַגֵּר הַגָּר בְּתוֹכְכֶם׃ וַיַּעֲשׂוּ כָּל־בְּנֵי יִשְׂרָאֵל כַּאֲשֶׁר צִוָּה יהוה
נא אֶת־מֹשֶׁה וְאֶת־אַהֲרֹן כֵּן עָשׂוּ׃ וַיְהִי בְּעֶצֶם הַיּוֹם הַזֶּה הוֹצִיא
יהוה אֶת־בְּנֵי יִשְׂרָאֵל מֵאֶרֶץ מִצְרַיִם עַל־צִבְאֹתָם׃
יג א ב וַיְדַבֵּר יהוה אֶל־מֹשֶׁה לֵּאמֹר׃ קַדֶּשׁ־לִי כָל־בְּכוֹר פֶּטֶר כָּל־רֶחֶם שביעי
ג בִּבְנֵי יִשְׂרָאֵל בָּאָדָם וּבַבְּהֵמָה לִי הוּא׃ וַיֹּאמֶר מֹשֶׁה אֶל־הָעָם זָכוֹר י
אֶת־הַיּוֹם הַזֶּה אֲשֶׁר יְצָאתֶם מִמִּצְרַיִם מִבֵּית עֲבָדִים כִּי בְּחֹזֶק יָד
ד הוֹצִיא יהוה אֶתְכֶם מִזֶּה וְלֹא יֵאָכֵל חָמֵץ׃ הַיּוֹם אַתֶּם יֹצְאִים בְּחֹדֶשׁ
ה הָאָבִיב׃ וְהָיָה כִי־יְבִיאֲךָ יהוה אֶל־אֶרֶץ הַכְּנַעֲנִי וְהַחִתִּי וְהָאֱמֹרִי

אונקלוס

מה תּוֹתָבָא וַאֲגִירָא לָא יֵיכוֹל בֵּיהּ: מו בַּחֲבוּרָא חֲדָא יִתְאֲכִיל, לָא תַפְּקוּן מִן בֵּיתָא, מִן בִּסְרָא לְבָרָא, וְגַרְמָא לָא תִתְבְּרוּן בֵּיהּ: מז כָּל כְּנִשְׁתָּא דְיִשְׂרָאֵל יַעְבְּדוּן יָתֵיהּ: מח וַאֲרֵי יִתְגַּיַּר עִמְּכוֹן גִּיּוֹרָא, וְיַעֲבֵיד פִּסְחָא קֳדָם יי, מִגְזַר לֵיהּ כָּל דְּכוּרָא, וּבְכֵן יִקְרַב לְמֶעְבְּדֵיהּ, וִיהֵי כְּיַצִּיבֵי אַרְעָא, וְכָל עַרְלָא לָא יֵיכוֹל בֵּיהּ: מט אוֹרָיְתָא חֲדָא, תְּהֵי לְיַצִּיבַיָּא, וּלְגִיּוֹרַיָּא דְּיִתְגַּיְּרוּן בֵּינֵיכוֹן: נ וַעֲבַדוּ כָּל בְּנֵי יִשְׂרָאֵל, כְּמָא דְפַקֵּיד יי, יָת מֹשֶׁה וְיָת אַהֲרֹן כֵּן עֲבַדוּ: נא וַהֲוָה, בִּכְרַן יוֹמָא הָדֵין, אַפֵּיק יי, יָת בְּנֵי יִשְׂרָאֵל, מֵאַרְעָא דְמִצְרַיִם עַל חֵילֵיהוֹן: יג א וּמַלֵּיל יי עִם מֹשֶׁה לְמֵימַר: ב אַקְדֵּישׁ קֳדָמַי כָּל בְּכְרָא, פָּתַח כָּל וַלְדָּא בִּבְנֵי יִשְׂרָאֵל, בַּאֲנָשָׁא וּבִבְעִירָא, דִּילִי הוּא: ג וַאֲמַר מֹשֶׁה לְעַמָּא, הֲווֹ דְכִירִין, יָת יוֹמָא הָדֵין דִּנְפַקְתּוּן מִמִּצְרַיִם מִבֵּית עַבְדוּתָא, אֲרֵי בִּתְקוֹף יַד, אַפֵּיק יי, יָתְכוֹן מִכָּא, וְלָא יִתְאֲכִיל חֲמִיעַ: ד יוֹמָא דֵין אַתּוּן נָפְקִין, בְּיַרְחָא דַאֲבִיבָא: ה וִיהֵי אֲרֵי יַעֲלִנָּךְ יי, לַאֲרַע כְּנַעֲנָאֵי, וְחִתָּאֵי וֶאֱמוֹרָאֵי וְחִוָּאֵי וִיבוּסָאֵי,

12:49 לַגֵּר הַגָּר בְּתוֹכְכֶם *The stranger who lives among you* – This is a *ger tzedek*, a convert to Judaism. This principle of "one and the same law" for the born Jew and the convert establishes the people of the covenant as a community of faith, not just an ethnic group defined by biological descent from Avraham and Sara. The covenant with Avraham was based on kinship. The covenant to be initiated between God and Israel is to be based on consent. Those who choose to become Jews are not to be discriminated against in any way. Racism is forbidden in Judaism, unlike fifteenth-century Spain where, by the law of *limpieza de sangre*, "purity of blood," prejudice against Jews continued even after they had converted – an anticipation of the Nuremberg Laws in Nazi Germany.

13:2 קַדֶּשׁ־לִי כָל־בְּכוֹר *Consecrate every firstborn* – Originally, until the sin of the golden calf, the firstborn of all tribes were consecrated to perform God's service, since it was their lives that had been protected by God during the last plague.

▶

you into the land of the Canaanites, Hittites, Amorites, Hivites, and Jebusites,
the land that He promised your ancestors He would give you – one flowing
6 with milk and with honey – you shall keep this ceremony in this month. For
seven days you shall eat unleavened bread; the seventh day shall be a festival to
7 the LORD. Unleavened bread shall be eaten for those seven days; no bread or
8 leavening shall be seen in all your land. On that day you must tell your child,
9 'This is because of what the LORD did for me when I left Egypt.' It shall be a
sign on your arm, a reminder between your eyes, so that the LORD's teaching
be on your tongue, for with a mighty hand the LORD brought you out of Egypt.
10 Celebrate this law each year at its set time.
11 When the LORD brings you to the land of the Canaanites, as He promised you
12 and your ancestors, and He gives it to you, you shall give over to the LORD the
first to emerge from every womb. Every male firstborn of your animals shall be
13 His. You shall redeem every firstborn donkey with a lamb; otherwise, you must
break the donkey's neck. You must redeem every firstborn among your sons.

רש"י

נשבע לאבתיך. באברהם הוא אומר: "ביום ההוא כרת ה' את אברם" וגו' (בראשית טו, יח), וביצחק הוא אומר: "גור בארץ הזאת" וגו' (שם כו, ג), וביעקב הוא אומר: "הארץ אשר אתה שכב עליה" וגו' (שם כח, יג): **זבת חלב ודבש.** חלב זב מן העזים, והדבש זב מן התמרים ומן התאנים: **את העבדה הזאת.** של פסח. והלא כבר נאמר למעלה: "והיה כי תבאו אל הארץ" וגו' (לעיל יב, כה), ולמה חזר ושנאה? בשביל דבר שנתחדש בה: בפרשה ראשונה נאמר: "והיה כי יאמרו אליכם בניכם מה העבדה הזאת לכם" (שם פסוק כו), בבן רשע הכתוב מדבר שהוציא עצמו מן הכלל; וכאן: "והגדת לבנך" (להלן פסוק ח), בבן שאינו יודע לשאל, והכתוב מלמדך שתפתח לו אתה בדברי אגדה המושכין את הלב:

ח **בעבור זה.** בעבור שאקיים מצותיו כגון פסח מצה ומרור הללו: **עשה ה' לי.** רמז תשובה לבן רשע, לומר: "עשה ה' לי", ולא לך, שאלו היית שם לא היית כדאי לגאל:

ט **והיה לך לאות.** יציאת מצרים תהיה לך לאות על ידך ובין עיניך, שתכתב פרשיות הללו ותקשרם בראש ובזרוע: **על ידך.** שמאל, לפיכך 'ידכה' מלא בפרשה שניה (להלן פסוק טז) לדרש בו, יד שהיא כהה:

י **מימים ימימה.** משנה לשנה:

יא **נשבע לך.** והיכן נשבע לך? "והבאתי אתכם אל הארץ אשר נשאתי" וגו' (לעיל ו, ח): **ונתנה לך.** תהא בעיניך כאלו נתנה לך בו ביום ואל תהי בעיניך כירשת אבות:

יב **והעברת.** אין "והעברת" אלא לשון הפרשה, וכן הוא אומר: "והעברתם את נחלתו לבתו" (במדבר כז, ח): **שגר בהמה.** נפל ששגרתו אמו ושלחתו בלא עתו, ולמדך הכתוב שהוא קדוש בבכורה לפטר את הבא אחריו. ואף שאינו נפל קרוי 'שגר', כמו: "שגר אלפיך" (דברים ז, יג), אבל זה לא בא אלא ללמד על הנפל, שהרי כבר כתב "כל פטר רחם". ואם תאמר, אף בכור בהמה טמאה במשמע, בא ופרש במקום אחר: "בבקרך ובצאנך" (שם טו, יט). לשון אחר יש לפרש, "והעברת כל פטר רחם" – בבכור אדם הכתוב מדבר:

יג **פטר חמר.** ולא פטר שאר בהמה טמאה, וגזרת הכתוב היא, לפי שנמשלו בכורי מצרים לחמורים. ועוד, שסיעו את ישראל ביציאתן ממצרים, שאין לך אחד מישראל שלא נשא עמו הרבה חמורים טעונים מכספם ומזהבם של מצרים: **תפדה בשה.** נותן שה לכהן

unity and sovereignty of God, commitment to the commandments, and – as in these two passages – the engagement of God *in history* and the deliverance of His people from slavery.

The texts contained in the tefillin embody what could have been abstract ideas. It is the genius of Judaism to turn such ideas into concrete actions and physical symbols. Tefillin, in particular, represent a daily engagement with the fundamentals of faith, worn as gestures of love and dedication.

וְהַחִוִּי וְהַיְבוּסִי אֲשֶׁר נִשְׁבַּע לַאֲבֹתֶיךָ לָתֶת לָךְ אֶרֶץ זָבַת חָלָב וּדְבָשׁ
ו וְעָבַדְתָּ אֶת־הָעֲבֹדָה הַזֹּאת בַּחֹדֶשׁ הַזֶּה׃ שִׁבְעַת יָמִים תֹּאכַל מַצֹּת
ז וּבַיּוֹם הַשְּׁבִיעִי חַג לַיהוה׃ מַצּוֹת יֵאָכֵל אֵת שִׁבְעַת הַיָּמִים וְלֹא־יֵרָאֶה
ח לְךָ חָמֵץ וְלֹא־יֵרָאֶה לְךָ שְׂאֹר בְּכָל־גְּבֻלֶךָ׃ וְהִגַּדְתָּ לְבִנְךָ בַּיּוֹם הַהוּא
ט לֵאמֹר בַּעֲבוּר זֶה עָשָׂה יהוה לִי בְּצֵאתִי מִמִּצְרָיִם׃ וְהָיָה לְךָ לְאוֹת
עַל־יָדְךָ וּלְזִכָּרוֹן בֵּין עֵינֶיךָ לְמַעַן תִּהְיֶה תּוֹרַת יהוה בְּפִיךָ כִּי בְּיָד חֲזָקָה
י הוֹצִאֲךָ יהוה מִמִּצְרָיִם׃ וְשָׁמַרְתָּ אֶת־הַחֻקָּה הַזֹּאת לְמוֹעֲדָהּ מִיָּמִים
יָמִימָה׃
יא וְהָיָה כִּי־יְבִאֲךָ יהוה אֶל־אֶרֶץ הַכְּנַעֲנִי כַּאֲשֶׁר נִשְׁבַּע לְךָ וְלַאֲבֹתֶיךָ
יב וּנְתָנָהּ לָךְ׃ וְהַעֲבַרְתָּ כָל־פֶּטֶר־רֶחֶם לַיהוה וְכָל־פֶּטֶר ׀ שֶׁגֶר בְּהֵמָה
יג אֲשֶׁר יִהְיֶה לְךָ הַזְּכָרִים לַיהוה׃ וְכָל־פֶּטֶר חֲמֹר תִּפְדֶּה בְשֶׂה וְאִם־לֹא

אונקלוס

דְקַיֵּים לַאֲבָהָתָךְ לְמִתַּן לָךְ, אֲרַע, עָבְדָא חֲלַב וּדְבַשׁ, וְתִפְלַח, יָת פֻּלְחָנָא הָדָא בְּיַרְחָא הָדֵין: ו שִׁבְעָא יוֹמִין תֵּיכוּל פַּטִּירָא, וּבְיוֹמָא שְׁבִיעָאָה, חַגָּא קֳדָם יי: ז פַּטִּירָא יִתְאֲכִיל, יָת שִׁבְעָא יוֹמִין, וְלָא יִתַּחְזֵי לָךְ חֲמִיעַ, וְלָא יִתַּחְזֵי לָךְ, חֲמִיר בְּכָל תְּחוּמָךְ: ח וּתְחַוֵּי לִבְרָךְ, בְּיוֹמָא הַהוּא לְמֵימַר, בְּדִיל דָּא, עֲבַד יי לִי, בְּמִפְּקִי מִמִּצְרָיִם: ט וִיהֵי לָךְ לְאָת עַל יְדָךְ, וּלְדָכְרָן בֵּין עֵינָךְ, בְּדִיל, דִּתְהֵי, אוֹרַיְתָא דַּיי בְּפֻמָּךְ, אֲרֵי בְּיַד תַּקִּיפָא, אַפְּקָךְ יי מִמִּצְרָיִם: י וְתִטַּר, יָת קְיָמָא הָדֵין בְּזִמְנֵיהּ, מִזְּמַן לִזְמַן: יא וִיהֵי, אֲרֵי יַעֲלִנָּךְ יי לַאֲרַע כְּנַעֲנָאֵי, כְּמָא דְקַיֵּים לָךְ וְלַאֲבָהָתָךְ, וְיִתְּנַהּ לָךְ: יב וְתַעְבַּר כָּל פָּתַח וַלְדָּא קֳדָם יי, וְכָל פָּתַח וְלַד בְּעִירָא, דִּיהוֹן לָךְ, דִּכְרִין תַּקְדֵּישׁ קֳדָם יי: יג וְכָל בְּכְרָא דִּחְמָרָא תִּפְרוֹק בְּאִמְּרָא, וְאִם לָא

13:8 וְהִגַּדְתָּ לְבִנְךָ *You must tell your child* – This is taken in the Haggada as a commandment to instruct a child even if he or she does not ask a question. The task of education, of inducting a child into the history of its people, begins very young, even before the child has questions. The verb used in this verse is the source of the name of the Haggada, for the recounting of the story of the exodus on the night of Passover. This response has traditionally had two radically different interpretations. According to Rashbam it means: I am doing what I am doing now because of what God did for me (and my ancestors) in Egypt. I am expressing gratitude for what happened then. However, according to Rashi and Ibn Ezra, as we saw earlier, it means: God acted in Egypt so that I would do what I am doing now, *so that* I would serve Him and strive to do His will. On the first interpretation, the present is a commemoration of the past. On the second, the past was a preparation for the present and future.

13:9 וְהָיָה לְךָ לְאוֹת *It shall be a sign* – The texts, contained in leather boxes, known as tefillin – related to *tefilla*, meaning "prayer" – are worn as a sign on the arm, symbolic of action, and a reminder between the eyes, signifying thought. The tefillin contain four sections from the Torah (Ex. 13:1–10, 11–16; Deut. 6:4–9, 11:13–21). They thus combine passages declaring the

14 And in the future, when your children ask, 'What is this?' you shall answer, MAFTIR
'With a mighty hand the LORD brought us out of Egypt, the house of slaves.
15 And when Pharaoh was obstinate and refused to set us free, the LORD killed all
the firstborn sons in Egypt, man and beast alike. That is why I sacrifice every
16 male firstborn animal to the LORD, and redeem all my firstborn sons.' It shall
be a sign on your arm and an emblem between your eyes – with a mighty hand
the LORD rescued us from Egypt."

The haftara for Parashat Bo is on page 1532.

רש״י

וּפֶטֶר חֲמוֹר מֻתָּר בַּהֲנָאָה, וְהַשֶּׂה חֻלִּין בְּיַד כֹּהֵן: **וַעֲרַפְתּוֹ.** עוֹרְפוֹ בְּקוֹפִיץ מֵאֲחוֹרָיו וְהוֹרְגוֹ. הוּא הִפְסִיד מָמוֹנוֹ שֶׁל כֹּהֵן לְפִיכָךְ יֻפְסַד מָמוֹנוֹ: **וְכֹל בְּכוֹר אָדָם בְּבָנֶיךָ תִּפְדֶּה.** חָמֵשׁ סְלָעִים פִּדְיוֹנוֹ קָצוּב בְּמָקוֹם אַחֵר (במדבר יח, טז):

יד **כִּי יִשְׁאָלְךָ בִנְךָ מָחָר.** יֵשׁ 'מָחָר' שֶׁהוּא עַכְשָׁיו וְיֵשׁ 'מָחָר' שֶׁהוּא לְאַחַר זְמַן, כְּגוֹן זֶה וּכְגוֹן: "מָחָר יֹאמְרוּ בְנֵיכֶם לְבָנֵינוּ" (יהושע כב, כד) דִּבְנֵי גָד וּבְנֵי רְאוּבֵן: **מַה זֹּאת.** זֶה תִּינוֹק טִפֵּשׁ שֶׁאֵינוֹ יוֹדֵעַ לְהַעֲמִיק שְׁאֵלָתוֹ וְסוֹתֵם וְשׁוֹאֵל: "מַה זֹּאת". וּבְמָקוֹם אַחֵר הוּא אוֹמֵר: "מָה הָעֵדֹת וְהַחֻקִּים וְהַמִּשְׁפָּטִים" וְגוֹ' (דברים ו, כ), הֲרֵי זוֹ שְׁאֵלַת בֵּן חָכָם. דִּבְּרָה תּוֹרָה כְּנֶגֶד אַרְבָּעָה בָנִים: רָשָׁע, וְשֶׁאֵינוֹ מֵבִין לִשְׁאֹל, וְהַשּׁוֹאֵל דֶּרֶךְ סְתוּמָה, וְהַשּׁוֹאֵל דֶּרֶךְ חָכְמָה:

טז **וּלְטוֹטָפֹת.** תְּפִלִּין, וְעַל שֵׁם שֶׁהֵם אַרְבָּעָה בָּתִּים קְרוּיִים 'טוֹטָפֹת', 'טָט' בְּכַתְפֵּי שְׁתַּיִם 'פַּת' בְּאַפְרִיקֵי שְׁתַּיִם. וּמְנַחֵם חִבְּרוֹ עִם "וְהַטֵּף אֶל דָּרוֹם" (יחזקאל כא, ב), "אַל תַּטִּפוּ" (מיכה ב, ו), לְשׁוֹן דִּבּוּר, כְּמוֹ: "וּלְזִכָּרוֹן בֵּין עֵינֶיךָ" (לעיל פסוק ט), שֶׁהָרוֹאֶה אוֹתָם קְשׁוּרִים בֵּין הָעֵינַיִם יִזְכֹּר הַנֵּס וִידַבֵּר בּוֹ:

questions of God, and in which the Rabbis of the Mishna and Midrash constantly disagree.

You cannot build a healthy society out of emotionally unhealthy families and angry and conflicted children. Faith begins in families. Hope is born in the home.

13:14 **וְאָמַרְתָּ אֵלָיו** *You shall answer* – About to gain their freedom, the Israelites are told that they have to become a nation of educators. That is what makes Moshe a great leader. What the Torah is teaching is that freedom is won, not on the battlefield, nor in the political arena, nor in the courts, national or international, but in the human imagination and will. To defend a country you need an army. But to defend a free society you need schools. You need families and an educational system in which ideals are passed on from one generation to the next, and never lost, or despaired of, or obscured. There has never been a more profound understanding of freedom. It is not difficult, Moshe was saying, to gain liberty, but to sustain it is the work of a hundred generations. Forget it and you lose it.

Freedom needs three institutions: parenthood, education, and memory. You must tell your children about slavery and the long journey to liberation. They must annually taste the bread of affliction and the bitter herbs of slave labor. They must know what oppression feels like if they are to fight against it in every age. So Jews became the people whose passion was education, whose citadels were schools, and whose heroes were teachers. The result was that by the time the Second Temple was destroyed, Jews had constructed the world's first system of universal compulsory education, paid for by public funds. None has given education a higher position in the scale of communal priorities. From the very outset, Israel knew that freedom cannot be created by legislation, nor can it be sustained by political structures alone. This basic principle is so crucial to Judaism that it is established here in Parashat Bo – before the Torah has even been given.

יד תִפְדֶּ֖ה וַעֲרַפְתּ֑וֹ וְכֹ֨ל בְּכ֥וֹר אָדָ֛ם בְּבָנֶ֖יךָ תִּפְדֶּֽה׃ וְהָיָ֞ה כִּֽי־יִשְׁאָלְךָ֥ בִנְךָ֛ מפטיר
מָחָ֖ר לֵאמֹ֣ר מַה־זֹּ֑את וְאָמַרְתָּ֣ אֵלָ֔יו בְּחֹ֣זֶק יָ֔ד הוֹצִיאָ֧נוּ יהו֛ה מִמִּצְרַ֖יִם
טו מִבֵּ֥ית עֲבָדִֽים׃ וַיְהִ֗י כִּֽי־הִקְשָׁ֣ה פַרְעֹה֮ לְשַׁלְּחֵנוּ֒ וַיַּהֲרֹ֨ג יהו֤ה כָּל־בְּכוֹר֙
בְּאֶ֣רֶץ מִצְרַ֔יִם מִבְּכֹ֥ר אָדָ֖ם וְעַד־בְּכ֣וֹר בְּהֵמָ֑ה עַל־כֵּן֩ אֲנִ֨י זֹבֵ֜חַ לַֽיהו֗ה
טז כָּל־פֶּ֤טֶר רֶ֙חֶם֙ הַזְּכָרִ֔ים וְכָל־בְּכ֥וֹר בָּנַ֖י אֶפְדֶּֽה׃ וְהָיָ֤ה לְאוֹת֙ עַל־יָ֣דְכָ֔ה
וּלְטוֹטָפֹ֖ת בֵּ֣ין עֵינֶ֑יךָ כִּ֚י בְּחֹ֣זֶק יָ֔ד הוֹצִיאָ֥נוּ יהו֖ה מִמִּצְרָֽיִם׃

The הפטרה *for* פרשת בא *is on page 1533.*

אונקלוס

תִפְרוֹק וְתִקְפֵיהּ, וְכָל בְּכְרָא דַּאֲנָשָׁא, בִּבְנָךְ תִּפְרוֹק: יד וִיהֵי, אֲרֵי
יִשְׁאֲלִנָּךְ בְּרָךְ, מְחַר לְמֵימַר מָא דָא, וְתֵימַר לֵיהּ, בִּתְקוֹף יַד, אַפְּקַנָא
יי, מִמִּצְרַיִם מִבֵּית עַבְדוּתָא: טו וַהֲוָה, כַּד אַקְשִׁי פַרְעֹה לְשַׁלָּחוּתַנָא,
וּקְטַל יי כָּל בְּכְרָא בְּאַרְעָא דְמִצְרַיִם, מִבְּכְרָא דַּאֲנָשָׁא וְעַד בְּכְרָא
דִּבְעִירָא, עַל כֵּן אֲנָא דָּבַח קֳדָם יי, כָּל פָּתַח וְלַד דִּכְרַיָּא, וְכָל בְּכְרָא
דִּבְנַי אֶפְרוֹק: טז וִיהֵי לְאָת עַל יְדָךְ, וּלְתְפִלִּין בֵּין עֵינָךְ, אֲרֵי בִּתְקוֹף
יַד, אַפְּקַנָא יי מִמִּצְרָיִם:

13:14 מַה־זֹּאת *What is this?* – In context, the child is asking about the law of the firstborn. In the Haggada, however, this is the question attributed to the simple child, and it is asked in the context of the Passover ritual. Note how concerned the Torah is that a parent should take the questions of a child seriously. In fact, according to the Haggada, parents should encourage their children to ask questions. It is part of the logic of the Torah that we understand its commands and practices, that we question what we do not understand, and that we internalize what we do understand.

Children are naturally spiritual. They are fascinated by the vastness of the universe and our place in it. They have the same sense of wonder that we find in some of the greatest of the psalms. They love stories, songs, and rituals. They like the shape and structure they give to time, and relationships, and the moral life. To be sure, skeptics and atheists have often derided religion as a child's view of reality, but that only serves to strengthen the corollary, that a child's view of reality is instinctively, intuitively religious. Deprive a child of that by ridiculing faith, abandoning ritual, and focussing instead on academic achievement and other forms of success, and you starve him or her of some of the most important elements of emotional and psychological well-being.

Spirituality plays a part in a child's resilience, physical and mental health, and healing. It is a key dimension of adolescence and its intense search for identity and purpose. The teenage years often take the form of a spiritual quest. And when there is a cross-generational bond through which children and parents come to share a sense of connection to something larger, an enormous inner strength is born. Indeed, the parent-child relationship, especially in Judaism, mirrors the relationship between God and us.

That is why Moshe so often emphasizes the role of the *question* in the process of education: "When your child asks you…" (Deut. 6:20) – a feature ritualized at the Seder table in the form of the *Ma Nishtana*. Judaism is a questioning and argumentative faith, in which even the greatest ask

▶

Parashat Beshalaḥ

13 17 When Pharaoh let the people go, God did not lead them through the land of
the Philistines, though it was the shorter way. "If the people face war," thought
18 God, "they will change their minds and go back to Egypt." So He led them
on a roundabout course, by way of the wilderness, to the Sea of Reeds. The
19 Israelites left Egypt armed for battle. And Moshe took with him the remains of
Yosef, who had bound the Israelites by oath: "When God comes to your aid,
20 bring my remains with you out of here." They set out from Sukkot and camped
21 at Etam, at the edge of the desert. The LORD went ahead of them by day in a

רש״י

יז **וַיְהִי בְּשַׁלַּח פַּרְעֹה. וְלֹא נָחָם.** נְהָגָם, כְּמוֹ: "לֵךְ נְחֵה אֶת הָעָם" (להלן לב, לד), "בְּהִתְהַלֶּכְךָ תַּנְחֶה אֹתָךְ" (משלי ו, כב): **כִּי קָרוֹב הוּא.** וְנוֹחַ לָשׁוּב בְּאוֹתוֹ הַדֶּרֶךְ לְמִצְרַיִם. וּמִדְרְשֵׁי אַגָּדָה יֵשׁ הַרְבֵּה: **בִּרְאֹתָם מִלְחָמָה.** כְּגוֹן מִלְחֶמֶת "וַיֵּרֶד הָעֲמָלֵקִי וְהַכְּנַעֲנִי" וְגוֹ' (במדבר יד, מה), אִם הָלְכוּ דֶּרֶךְ יָשָׁר הָיוּ חוֹזְרִים. מָה אִם כְּשֶׁהִקִּיפָם דֶּרֶךְ מְעֻקָּם אָמְרוּ: "נִתְּנָה רֹאשׁ וְנָשׁוּבָה מִצְרָיְמָה" (שם פסוק ד), אִם הוֹלִיכָם בִּפְשׁוּטָה עַל אַחַת כַּמָּה וְכַמָּה: **פֶּן יִנָּחֵם.** יַחְשְׁבוּ מַחֲשָׁבָה עַל שֶׁיָּצְאוּ וְיִתְּנוּ לֵב לָשׁוּב:

יח **וַיַּסֵּב.** הֱסִבָּם מִן הַדֶּרֶךְ הַפְּשׁוּטָה לַדֶּרֶךְ הָעֲקֻמָּה: **יַם סוּף.** כְּמוֹ לְיַם סוּף. וְ'סוּף' הוּא לְשׁוֹן אֲגַם שֶׁמְּגַדְּלִים בּוֹ קָנִים, וְכֵן: "וַתָּשֶׂם בַּסּוּף" (לעיל ב, ג), "קָנֶה וָסוּף קָמֵלוּ" (ישעיה יט, ו): **וַחֲמֻשִׁים.** אֵין 'חֲמֻשִׁים' אֶלָּא מְזֻיָּנִים, וְכֵן הוּא אוֹמֵר: "וְאַתֶּם תַּעַבְרוּ חֲמֻשִׁים" (יהושע א, יד). וְכֵן תִּרְגֵּם אוֹנְקְלוֹס "מְזָרְזִין", כְּמוֹ: "וַיָּרֶק אֶת חֲנִיכָיו" (בראשית יד, יד), "וְזָרֵיז". דָּבָר אַחֵר, "וַחֲמֻשִׁים", מְחֻמָּשִׁים, אֶחָד מֵחֲמִשָּׁה יָצְאוּ וְאַרְבָּעָה חֲלָקִים מֵתוּ בִּשְׁלֹשֶׁת יְמֵי אֲפֵלָה:

יט **הַשְׁבֵּעַ הִשְׁבִּיעַ.** הִשְׁבִּיעָם שֶׁיַּשְׁבִּיעוּ לִבְנֵיהֶם. וְלָמָּה לֹא הִשְׁבִּיעַ לְבָנָיו שֶׁיִּשָּׂאוּהוּ לְאֶרֶץ כְּנַעַן מִיָּד כְּמוֹ שֶׁהִשְׁבִּיעַ יַעֲקֹב? אָמַר יוֹסֵף: אֲנִי שַׁלִּיט הָיִיתִי בְּמִצְרַיִם וְהָיָה סִפֵּק בְּיָדִי לַעֲשׂוֹת, אֲבָל בָּנַי לֹא יַנִּיחוּם מִצְרִים לַעֲשׂוֹת, לְכָךְ הִשְׁבִּיעָם לִכְשֶׁיִּגָּאֲלוּ וְיֵצְאוּ מִשָּׁם שֶׁיִּשָּׂאוּהוּ: **וְהַעֲלִיתֶם אֶת עַצְמֹתַי מִזֶּה אִתְּכֶם.** לְאֶחָיו הִשְׁבִּיעַ כֵּן, לָמַדְנוּ שֶׁאַף עַצְמוֹת כָּל הַשְּׁבָטִים הֶעֱלוּ עִמָּהֶם, שֶׁנֶּאֱמַר "אִתְּכֶם":

כ **וַיִּסְעוּ מִסֻּכֹּת.** בַּיּוֹם הַשֵּׁנִי, שֶׁהֲרֵי בָּרִאשׁוֹן בָּאוּ מֵרַעְמְסֵס לְסֻכּוֹת (לעיל יב, לז):

כא **לַנְחֹתָם הַדֶּרֶךְ.** נָקוּד פַּתָּח, שֶׁהוּא כְּמוֹ לְהַנְחוֹתָם, כְּמוֹ: "לַרְאֹתְכֶם בַּדֶּרֶךְ אֲשֶׁר תֵּלְכוּ בָהּ" (דברים א, לג) שֶׁהוּא כְּמוֹ לְהַרְאוֹתְכֶם, אַף כָּאן

> It was the result of God's wisdom that the Israelites were led about in the wilderness until they acquired courage. For it is a well-known fact that traveling in the wilderness, deprived of bodily enjoyments like bathing, produces courage.... Besides, another generation arose during the wanderings, which had not been accustomed to degradation and slavery. (*Guide for the Perplexed* III:32)

In other words: it takes a generation born in freedom to build a society of freedom. It is hard to overemphasize the importance of this insight. Change takes time. Even God Himself does not force the pace. He led the Israelites on a *circuitous* route, knowing that they could not face the full challenge of liberty immediately. There are no shortcuts on the long walk to freedom. The rest of the Torah is the story of this extended detour.

13:19 **אֶת־עַצְמוֹת יוֹסֵף** *The remains of Yosef* – A moving fulfillment of Yosef's last request, shortly before he died (Gen. 50:25). It was a mark of honor that the remains were carried by Moshe himself. There are cultures that forget the past and there are cultures that are held captive by the past. Jews do neither. We carry the past with us.

13:21 **בְּעַמּוּד עָנָן לַנְחֹתָם הַדֶּרֶךְ** *A column of cloud to guide them* – One of the most beautiful sentences in the whole of Judaism occurs early in the book of Yirmeya (2:2). Speaking

פרשת בשלח

יג יז וַיְהִי בְּשַׁלַּח פַּרְעֹה אֶת־הָעָם וְלֹא־נָחָם אֱלֹהִים דֶּרֶךְ אֶרֶץ פְּלִשְׁתִּים
כִּי קָרוֹב הוּא כִּי ׀ אָמַר אֱלֹהִים פֶּן־יִנָּחֵם הָעָם בִּרְאֹתָם מִלְחָמָה וְשָׁבוּ
יח מִצְרָיְמָה׃ וַיַּסֵּב אֱלֹהִים ׀ אֶת־הָעָם דֶּרֶךְ הַמִּדְבָּר יַם־סוּף וַחֲמֻשִׁים
יט עָלוּ בְנֵי־יִשְׂרָאֵל מֵאֶרֶץ מִצְרָיִם׃ וַיִּקַּח מֹשֶׁה אֶת־עַצְמוֹת יוֹסֵף עִמּוֹ
כִּי הַשְׁבֵּעַ הִשְׁבִּיעַ אֶת־בְּנֵי יִשְׂרָאֵל לֵאמֹר פָּקֹד יִפְקֹד אֱלֹהִים אֶתְכֶם
כ וְהַעֲלִיתֶם אֶת־עַצְמֹתַי מִזֶּה אִתְּכֶם׃ וַיִּסְעוּ מִסֻּכֹּת וַיַּחֲנוּ בְאֵתָם בִּקְצֵה
כא הַמִּדְבָּר׃ וַיהוָה הֹלֵךְ לִפְנֵיהֶם יוֹמָם בְּעַמּוּד עָנָן לַנְחֹתָם הַדֶּרֶךְ וְלַיְלָה

אונקלוס

יז וַהֲוָה, כַּד שַׁלַּח פַּרְעֹה יָת עַמָּא, וְלָא דַבַּרְנוּן יי, אוֹרַח אֲרַע
פְּלִשְׁתָּאֵי, אֲרֵי קְרִיבָא הִיא, אֲרֵי אֲמַר יי, דִּלְמָא יְזוּעוּן עַמָּא,
בְּמִחְזֵיהוֹן קְרָבָא וִיתוּבוּן לְמִצְרָיִם: יח וְאַסְחַר יי יָת עַמָּא, אוֹרַח
מַדְבְּרָא לְיַמָּא דְסוּף, וּמְזָרְזִין, סְלִיקוּ בְנֵי יִשְׂרָאֵל מֵאַרְעָא דְמִצְרָיִם:

יט וְאַסֵּיק מֹשֶׁה, יָת גַּרְמֵי יוֹסֵף עִמֵּיהּ, אֲרֵי אוֹמָאָה אוֹמֵי, יָת בְּנֵי
יִשְׂרָאֵל לְמֵימַר, מִדְכַּר דְּכִיר יי יָתְכוֹן, וְתַסְקוּן יָת גַּרְמַי, מִכָּא עִמְּכוֹן:
כ וּנְטַלוּ מִסֻּכּוֹת, וּשְׁרוֹ בְאֵיתָם, בִּסְטַר מַדְבְּרָא: כא וַיי, מְדַבַּר קֳדָמֵיהוֹן
בִּימָמָא, בְּעַמּוּדָא דַעֲנָנָא לְדַבָּרוּתְהוֹן בְּאוֹרְחָא, וּבְלֵילְיָא,

BESHALAḤ

Parashat Beshalaḥ begins with a battle, it ends with a battle, and in the middle is the great miracle, the turning point – the crossing of the Reed Sea. As so often in the Mosaic books, we are presented with a chiasmus, a literary structure of the form ABCBA, in which the end is a mirror image of the beginning, and the climax is at the center.

Occupying the central role in Parashat Beshalaḥ is the episode of the Reed Sea, which turns out to be a division in more than one sense. Literally, the waters are divided. But metaphorically, the fate of the Israelites is also divided: into a before and after. Before, they are still in Egyptian territory, still – that is to say – under the sway of Pharaoh. It is no accident that Pharaoh and his chariots pursue the Israelites to the very edge of their territory. Anywhere within Egypt, Pharaoh rules – or at least, he believes he does.

Once across the sea, however, the Israelites have traversed a boundary. They are now in no-man's-land, the desert. Again it is no accident that here, where no king rules, they can experience with pristine clarity the sovereignty of God. Israel becomes the first – historically, the only – people to be ruled directly by God. The Reed Sea was a boundary between two domains – in this case the boundary between human and divine rule. Once crossed, there is no going back.

THE JOURNEY BEGINS

The journey from Egypt begins with a detour: "God did not lead them through the land of the Philistines.…'If the people face war,' thought God, 'they will change their minds and go back to Egypt.'" For Rambam, this minor detail in the larger story is a key text. Why did God not simply put courage into their hearts? Because God does not intervene in human nature. It is no accident that the generation that left Egypt was not the generation to cross the Jordan and enter the Promised Land. That privilege will belong to their children:

column of cloud to guide them, and at night in a column of fire to give them
22 light, so that they might travel day and night. Neither the column of cloud by
day nor that of fire by night once departed from the people.
14 1 2 Then the LORD said to Moshe, "Speak to the Israelites and tell them to turn
back and camp in front of Pi HaḤirot, between Migdol and the sea, before Baal
3 Tzefon. Encamp facing it, by the sea. Pharaoh will think that the Israelites are
4 lost across the land, that they are trapped in the desert. I will toughen Pharaoh's
heart, and he will pursue them. I will be glorified over Pharaoh and all his force,
5 and the Egyptians will know that I am the LORD." And so they did. When
the king of Egypt was told that the Israelites had escaped, he and his officials
changed their minds about the people: "What have we done, releasing the
6 Israelites from serving us?" So the king harnessed his chariot and brought out
7 his army. He took six hundred elite chariots and all the other chariots of Egypt,

רש"י

להנחותם על ידי שליח. ומי הוא השליח? עמוד הענן, והקדוש ברוך הוא בכבודו מוליכו לפניהם, ומכל מקום את עמוד הענן הכין להנחותם על ידו, שהרי על ידי עמוד הענן הם הולכים. עמוד הענן אינו לאורה אלא להורותם הדרך:

כב **לא ימיש.** הקדוש ברוך הוא את "עמוד הענן יומם ועמוד האש לילה", מגיד שעמוד הענן משלים לעמוד האש ועמוד האש משלים לעמוד הענן, שעד שלא ישקע זה עולה זה:

יד ב **וישבו.** לאחוריהם, לצד מצרים היו מקרבין כל יום השלישי, כדי להטעות את פרעה שיאמר תועים הם בדרך, כמו שנאמר: "ואמר פרעה לבני ישראל" וגו' (להלן פסוק ג): **ויחנו לפני פי החירת.** היא פיתום, ועכשיו נקראת 'פי החירות' על שם שנעשו שם בני חורין. והם שני סלעים גבוהים זקופים, והגיא שביניהם קרוי פי הסלעים: **לפני בעל צפן.** הוא נשאר מכל אלהי מצרים כדי להטעותן שיאמרו: קשה יראתן. ועליו פרש איוב: "משגיא לגוים ויאבדם" (איוב יב, כג):

ג **ואמר פרעה.** כשישמע שהם שבים לאחוריהם: **לבני ישראל.** על בני ישראל. וכן: "ה' ילחם לכם" (להלן פסוק יד) – עליכם; "אמרי לי אחי הוא" (בראשית כ, יג) – אמרי עלי: **נבכים הם.** כלואים ומשוקעים, ובלעז שירי"ר. כמו: "נבכי ים" (איוב לח, טז), "בעמק הבכא" (תהלים פד, ז), "מבכי נהרות" (איוב כח, יא). "נבכים הם" – כלואים הם במדבר, שאינן יודעין לצאת ממנו ולהיכן ילכו:

ד **ואכבדה בפרעה.** כשהקדוש ברוך הוא מתנקם ברשעים שמו מתגדל ומתכבד. וכן הוא אומר: "ונשפטתי אתו" וגו' ואחר כך: "והתגדלתי והתקדשתי ונודעתי" וגו' (יחזקאל לח, כב-כג), ואומר: "שמה שבר רשפי קשת" ואחר כך: "נודע ביהודה אלהים" (תהלים עו, ב-ד), ואומר: "נודע ה' משפט עשה" (שם ט, יז): **בפרעה ובכל חילו.** הוא התחיל בעבירה וממנו התחילה הפורענות: **ויעשו כן.** להגיד שבחן ששמעו לקול משה, ולא אמרו: היאך נתקרב אל רודפינו? אנו צריכים לברוח! אלא אמרו: אין לנו אלא דברי בן עמרם:

ה **ויגד למלך מצרים.** איקטורין שלח עמהם, וכיון שהגיעו לשלשת ימים שקבעו לילך ולשוב וראו שאינן חוזרין למצרים, באו והגידו לפרעה ביום הרביעי. ובחמישי ובששי רדפו אחריהם, ליל שביעי ירדו לים, בשחרית אמרו שירה, והוא יום שביעי של פסח. לכך אנו קורין השירה ביום השביעי: **ויהפך.** נהפך ממה שהיה, שהרי אמר להם: "קומו צאו מתוך עמי" (לעיל יב, לא), ונהפך לב עבדיו, שהרי לשעבר היו אומרים לו: "עד מתי יהיה זה לנו למוקש" (לעיל י, ז) ועכשיו נהפכו לרדוף אחריהם בשביל ממונם שהשאילום: **מעבדנו.** מעבד אותנו:

ו **ויאסר את רכבו.** הוא בעצמו: **ואת עמו לקח עמו.** משכם בדברים: לקינו ונטלו ממוננו ושלחנום; בואו עמי ואני לא אתנהג כשאר מלכים, דרך מלכים עבדיו קודמין לו במלחמה, ואני אקדים לפניכם, שנאמר: "ופרעה הקריב" (להלן פסוק י), הקריב עצמו ומהר לפני חילותיו; דרך מלכים ליטול ביזה בראש כמו שיבחר, אני אשוה עמכם בחלק, שנאמר: "אחלק שלל" (להלן טו, ט):

ז **בחור.** נבחרים. 'בחור' לשון יחיד, כל רכב ורכב שבמנין זה היה בחור: **וכל רכב מצרים.** ועמהם כל שאר הרכב. ומהיכן היו הבהמות הללו? אם תאמר משל מצרים, הרי נאמר: "וימת כל מקנה מצרים" (לעיל ט, ו)! ואם משל ישראל, והלא נאמר: "וגם מקננו ילך עמנו" (לעיל י, כו)! משל מי היו? מ"הירא את דבר ה'" (לעיל ט, כ). מכאן היה

כב בְּעַמּוּד אֵשׁ לְהָאִיר לָהֶם לָלֶכֶת יוֹמָם וָלָיְלָה׃ לֹא־יָמִישׁ עַמּוּד הֶעָנָן
יוֹמָם וְעַמּוּד הָאֵשׁ לָיְלָה לִפְנֵי הָעָם׃
יד א ב וַיְדַבֵּר יְהוָה אֶל־מֹשֶׁה לֵּאמֹר׃ דַּבֵּר אֶל־בְּנֵי יִשְׂרָאֵל וְיָשֻׁבוּ וְיַחֲנוּ לִפְנֵי
פִּי הַחִירֹת בֵּין מִגְדֹּל וּבֵין הַיָּם לִפְנֵי בַּעַל צְפֹן נִכְחוֹ תַחֲנוּ עַל־הַיָּם׃
ג וְאָמַר פַּרְעֹה לִבְנֵי יִשְׂרָאֵל נְבֻכִים הֵם בָּאָרֶץ סָגַר עֲלֵיהֶם הַמִּדְבָּר׃
ד וְחִזַּקְתִּי אֶת־לֵב־פַּרְעֹה וְרָדַף אַחֲרֵיהֶם וְאִכָּבְדָה בְּפַרְעֹה וּבְכָל־חֵילוֹ
ה וְיָדְעוּ מִצְרַיִם כִּי־אֲנִי יְהוָה וַיַּעֲשׂוּ־כֵן׃ וַיֻּגַּד לְמֶלֶךְ מִצְרַיִם כִּי בָרַח
הָעָם וַיֵּהָפֵךְ לְבַב פַּרְעֹה וַעֲבָדָיו אֶל־הָעָם וַיֹּאמְרוּ מַה־זֹּאת עָשִׂינוּ
ו כִּי־שִׁלַּחְנוּ אֶת־יִשְׂרָאֵל מֵעָבְדֵנוּ׃ וַיֶּאְסֹר אֶת־רִכְבּוֹ וְאֶת־עַמּוֹ לָקַח
ז עִמּוֹ׃ וַיִּקַּח שֵׁשׁ־מֵאוֹת רֶכֶב בָּחוּר וְכֹל רֶכֶב מִצְרָיִם וְשָׁלִשִׁם עַל־כֻּלּוֹ׃

אונקלוס

בְּעַמּוּדָא דְּאִישָּׁתָא לְאַנְהָרָא לְהוֹן, לְמֵיזַל בִּימָמָא וּבְלֵילְיָא׃ כב לָא עֲדֵי, עַמּוּדָא דַּעֲנָנָא בִּימָמָא, וְאַף לָא עַמּוּדָא דְּאִישָּׁתָא בְּלֵילְיָא, מִן קֳדָם עַמָּא׃ יד א וּמַלֵּיל יי עִם מֹשֶׁה לְמֵימָר׃ ב מַלֵּיל עִם בְּנֵי יִשְׂרָאֵל, וִיתוּבוּן, וְיִשְׁרוֹן קֳדָם פּוּם חִירָתָא, בֵּין מִגְדּוֹל וּבֵין יַמָּא, קֳדָם בְּעֵיל צְפוֹן, לְקִבְלֵיהּ תִּשְׁרוֹן עַל יַמָּא׃ ג וְיֵימַר פַּרְעֹה עַל בְּנֵי יִשְׂרָאֵל, מְעַרְבְלִין אִנּוּן בְּאַרְעָא, אֲחַד עֲלֵיהוֹן מַדְבְּרָא׃ ד וַאֲתַקֵּיף יָת לִבָּא דְּפַרְעֹה וְיִרְדּוֹף בָּתְרֵיהוֹן, וְאֶתְיַקַּר בְּפַרְעֹה וּבְכָל מַשִׁרְיָתֵיהּ, וְיִדְּעוּן מִצְרָאֵי אֲרֵי אֲנָא יי, וַעֲבַדוּ כֵן׃ ה וְאִתְחַוַּא לְמַלְכָּא דְּמִצְרַיִם, אֲרֵי אֲזַל עַמָּא, וְאִתְהֲפֵיךְ, לִבָּא דְּפַרְעֹה וְעַבְדּוֹהִי בְּעַמָּא, וַאֲמַרוּ מָא דָא עֲבַדְנָא, אֲרֵי שַׁלַּחְנָא יָת יִשְׂרָאֵל מִלְּמִפְלְחַנָא׃ ו וְטַקֵּיס יָת רְתִכֵּיהּ, וְיָת עַמֵּיהּ דְּבַר עִמֵּיהּ׃ ז וּדְבַר, שֵׁית מְאָה רְתִכִּין בְּחִירָן, וְכָל רְתִכֵּי מִצְרָאֵי, וְגִבָּרִין מְמַנַּן עַל כֻּלְּהוֹן׃

to the Israelites, who have hitherto been seen as a fractious and rebellious people, God says, "I recall on your behalf the devotion of your youth, your bridal love, when you followed Me into the wilderness, a land unseeded," an unknown land. Yirmeyahu is telling us that God loves the Jewish people because they had the courage to take a risk, to go into a place they had never seen before, with no map and no roads, just the column of cloud and the column of fire.

We all face an unknown and unknowable future. Every single course of action we take, every commitment, has its underside of doubt. That is what faith is. Not the absence of doubt, but the ability to recognize doubt, live with it, and still take the risk of commitment.

Judaism is not described as a state of being. It is about walking, about the way, about following the call of God. The road is long, the work is hard, and there will be many setbacks and false turnings. We need grit, resilience, stamina, and persistence. In place of a column of cloud leading the way, we need the advice of mentors and the encouragement of friends. But the journey is exhilarating, and there is no other way.

8 with officers over them all. The LORD strengthened the heart of Pharaoh, king
of Egypt, and he pursued the Israelites, who were leaving in defiance of them.
9 The Egyptians, with all the king's horses and chariots, cavalry and infantry, SHENI
chased and caught up with them as they were encamped by the sea near Pi
10 HaḤirot, before Baal Tzefon. Pharaoh drew near – the Israelites looked up:
there were the Egyptians thundering after them. They were terrified and cried
11 to the LORD for help. "Were there no graves in Egypt?" they asked Moshe. "Is
that why you brought us here to die in the desert? What have you done to us,
12 bringing us out of Egypt? Did we not tell you in Egypt: Leave us alone – let us
serve the Egyptians. Better a life in servitude to Egypt than death in the desert."
13 But Moshe told the people, "Fear not. Stand firm and see the deliverance the
LORD will bring you today. The Egyptians you see today, you shall never see
14 again. The LORD will fight for you. You stay silent."

רש"י

רבי שמעון אומר: כשר שבגוים הרג, טוב שבנחשים רצץ את מוחו. **ושלשם על כלו.** שרי צבאות, כתרגומו:

ח **ויחזק ה' את לב פרעה.** שהיה תולה אם לרדף אם לאו, וחזק את לבו לרדף: **ביד רמה.** בגבורה גבוהה ומפרסמת:

י **ופרעה הקריב.** היה לו לכתב: 'ופרעה קרב', מהו "הקריב"? הקריב עצמו ונתאמץ לקדם לפניהם כמו שהתנה עמהם: **נסע אחריהם.** בלב אחד כאיש אחד. דבר אחר, "והנה מצרים נסע אחריהם", ראו שר של מצרים נוסע מן השמים לעזר למצרים. תנחומא (יג): **ויצעקו.** תפשו אמנות אבותם; באברהם הוא אומר: "אל המקום אשר עמד שם" (בראשית יט, כז), ביצחק: "לשוח בשדה" (שם כד, סג), ביעקב: "ויפגע במקום" (שם כח, יא):

יא **המבלי אין קברים.** וכי מחמת חסרון קברים, שאין קברים במצרים לקבר שם, לקחתנו משם? שיפו"ר פלינג"א דינו"ן פוסי"ש בלעז:

יב **אשר דברנו אליך במצרים.** והיכן דברו? "ירא ה' עליכם וישפט" (לעיל ה, כא): **ממתנו.** מאשר נמות. ואם היה נקוד מלאפום היה נראה 'ממיתתנו', עכשיו שנקוד בשורק נראה 'מאשר נמות'. וכן: "מי יתן מותנו" (להלן טז, ג), שנמות, וכן: "מי יתן מותי" דאבשלום (שמואל ב' יט, א), שאמות, כמו: "ליום קומי לעד" (צפניה ג, ח), "עד שובי בשלום" (דברי הימים ב' יח, כו), שאקום, שאשוב:

יג **כי אשר ראיתם את מצרים וגו'.** מה שראיתם אותם אינו אלא היום, היום הוא שראיתם אותם ולא תוסיפו עוד:

יד **ילחם לכם.** בשבילכם. וכן: "כי ה' נלחם להם" (להלן פסוק כה), וכן: "אם לאל תריבון" (איוב יג, ח), וכן: "ואשר דבר לי" (בראשית כד, ז), וכן: "האתם תריבון לבעל" (שופטים ו, לא):

act, not a human one. The point is stressed by the enigmatic scene that unfolds in the night. The cloud between the camps appears "as cloud and darkness for one, but lighting the night for the other." This may mean that, as in the ninth plague, there was light for the Israelites, darkness for the Egyptians (Rashi on Ex. 20:14) – a suspension of the laws of nature. This allowed the Israelites to journey onward through the parted sea while the Egyptians were forced to encamp in the darkness. It is also symbolic of good and evil, characterized throughout Tanakh as forms, respectively, of light and darkness. When God then "looked down at the Egyptian army" (14:24), a metaphorical expression of intense divine involvement, the verb "looked down" (*sh-k-f*) recalls the narrative of the destruction of Sedom (Gen. 19:28). Here as there, it is intended to convey the idea that God is high above those who hold themselves to be above God. The people are passive at this point; they are witnesses to a drama playing out between God and Egypt.

ח וַיְחַזֵּק יהוה אֶת־לֵב פַּרְעֹה מֶלֶךְ מִצְרַיִם וַיִּרְדֹּף אַחֲרֵי בְּנֵי יִשְׂרָאֵל וּבְנֵי
ט יִשְׂרָאֵל יֹצְאִים בְּיָד רָמָה: וַיִּרְדְּפוּ מִצְרַיִם אַחֲרֵיהֶם וַיַּשִּׂיגוּ אוֹתָם חֹנִים שני
עַל־הַיָּם כָּל־סוּס רֶכֶב פַּרְעֹה וּפָרָשָׁיו וְחֵילוֹ עַל־פִּי הַחִירֹת לִפְנֵי בַּעַל
י צְפֹן: וּפַרְעֹה הִקְרִיב וַיִּשְׂאוּ בְנֵי־יִשְׂרָאֵל אֶת־עֵינֵיהֶם וְהִנֵּה מִצְרַיִם ׀
יא נֹסֵעַ אַחֲרֵיהֶם וַיִּירְאוּ מְאֹד וַיִּצְעֲקוּ בְנֵי־יִשְׂרָאֵל אֶל־יהוה: וַיֹּאמְרוּ
אֶל־מֹשֶׁה הֲמִבְּלִי אֵין־קְבָרִים בְּמִצְרַיִם לְקַחְתָּנוּ לָמוּת בַּמִּדְבָּר מַה־
יב זֹּאת עָשִׂיתָ לָּנוּ לְהוֹצִיאָנוּ מִמִּצְרָיִם: הֲלֹא־זֶה הַדָּבָר אֲשֶׁר דִּבַּרְנוּ
אֵלֶיךָ בְמִצְרַיִם לֵאמֹר חֲדַל מִמֶּנּוּ וְנַעַבְדָה אֶת־מִצְרָיִם כִּי טוֹב לָנוּ
יג עֲבֹד אֶת־מִצְרַיִם מִמֻּתֵנוּ בַּמִּדְבָּר: וַיֹּאמֶר מֹשֶׁה אֶל־הָעָם אַל־תִּירָאוּ
הִתְיַצְּבוּ וּרְאוּ אֶת־יְשׁוּעַת יהוה אֲשֶׁר־יַעֲשֶׂה לָכֶם הַיּוֹם כִּי אֲשֶׁר
יד רְאִיתֶם אֶת־מִצְרַיִם הַיּוֹם לֹא תֹסִפוּ לִרְאֹתָם עוֹד עַד־עוֹלָם: יהוה
יִלָּחֵם לָכֶם וְאַתֶּם תַּחֲרִשׁוּן:

אונקלוס

ח וְתַקֵּיף יְיָ יָת לִבָּא דְּפַרְעֹה מַלְכָּא דְמִצְרַיִם, וּרְדַף, בָּתַר בְּנֵי יִשְׂרָאֵל, וּבְנֵי יִשְׂרָאֵל, נָפְקִין בְּרֵישׁ גְּלֵי: ט וּרְדַפוּ מִצְרָאֵי בָּתְרֵיהוֹן, וְאַדְבִּיקוּ יָתְהוֹן כַּד שָׁרַן עַל יַמָּא, כָּל סוּסָוַת רְתִכֵּי פַרְעֹה, וּפָרָשׁוֹהִי וּמַשִּׁרְיָתֵיהּ, עַל פּוּם חִירָתָא, קֳדָם בְּעֵיל צְפוֹן: י וּפַרְעֹה קָרִיב, וּזְקַפוּ בְנֵי יִשְׂרָאֵל יָת עֵינֵיהוֹן, וְהָא מִצְרָאֵי נָטְלִין בָּתְרֵיהוֹן, וּדְחִילוּ לַחֲדָא, וּזְעִיקוּ בְנֵי יִשְׂרָאֵל קֳדָם יְיָ: יא וַאֲמַרוּ לְמֹשֶׁה, הֲמִדְּלֵית קִבְרִין בְּמִצְרַיִם, דְּבַרְתַּנָא לִמְמָת בְּמַדְבְּרָא, מָא דָא עֲבַדְתְּ לַנָא, לְאַפָּקוּתַנָא מִמִּצְרָיִם: יב הֲלָא דֵין פִּתְגָמָא, דְּמַלֵּילְנָא עִמָּךְ בְּמִצְרַיִם לְמֵימַר, שְׁבוֹק מִנַּנָא וְנִפְלַח יָת מִצְרָאֵי, אֲרֵי טָב לַנָא דְּנִפְלַח יָת מִצְרָאֵי, מִדִּנְמוּת בְּמַדְבְּרָא: יג וַאֲמַר מֹשֶׁה לְעַמָּא לָא תִדְחֲלוּן, אִתְעַתַּדוּ, וַחֲזוֹ יָת פֻּרְקָנָא דַייָ, דְּיַעֲבֵיד לְכוֹן יוֹמָא דֵין, אֲרֵי, דַּחֲזֵיתוֹן יָת מִצְרָאֵי יוֹמָא דֵין, לָא תֵיסְפוּן, לְמִחְזֵיהוֹן עוֹד עַד עָלְמָא: יד יְיָ יְגִיחַ לְכוֹן קְרָב, וְאַתּוּן תִּשְׁתְּקוּן:

14:13 אַל־תִּירָאוּ *Fear not* – The Sages, their ears ever attuned to nuance, detected four responses in Moshe's words:

> Our ancestors were divided into four groups at the sea. One group said, "Let us throw ourselves into the sea." Another said, "Let us go back to Egypt." A third said, "Let us wage war against them." A fourth said, "Let us cry out against them." To the first, who said, "Let us throw ourselves into the sea," Moshe said, "Stand firm and see the deliverance the LORD will bring." To the second, who said, "Let us go back to Egypt," he said, "The Egyptians you see today, you shall never see again." To the third, who said, "Let us wage war against them," he said, "The LORD will fight for you." To the fourth, who said, "Let us cry out against them," he said, "You stay silent." (Yerushalmi, Taanit 2:5.)

The battle against the Egyptians, we are assured, was a divine

15 The LORD said to Moshe, "Why are you crying out to Me? Speak to the SHELISHI
16 Israelites; have them move forward. Raise your staff, stretch out your hand
over the sea and divide it, and the Israelites will walk through the sea on dry
17 land. I will strengthen the Egyptians' hearts and they will go after them. Then
will My glory bear down hard upon Pharaoh and his entire army, his chariots
18 and cavalry. And when My glory bears down upon Pharaoh, his chariots and
19 cavalry, the Egyptians will know that I am the LORD." Then the angel of God
who had been traveling ahead of the Israelite camp moved and went behind
20 them, and the column of cloud moved from in front of them to their rear. It
came between the Egyptian and Israelite camps, as cloud and darkness for
21 one, but lighting the night for the other, keeping the two apart all night. Then
Moshe stretched out his hand over the sea, and the LORD drove the sea back

רש״י

טו **מַה תִּצְעַק אֵלָי.** לִמְּדָנוּ שֶׁהָיָה מֹשֶׁה עוֹמֵד וּמִתְפַּלֵּל, אָמַר לוֹ הַקָּדוֹשׁ בָּרוּךְ הוּא: לֹא עֵת עַתָּה לְהַאֲרִיךְ שֶׁיִּשְׂרָאֵל נְתוּנִין בְּצָרָה. דָּבָר אַחֵר, "מַה תִּצְעַק אֵלָי", עָלַי הַדָּבָר וְלֹא עָלֶיךָ, כְּמוֹ שֶׁנֶּאֱמַר לְהַלָּן: "עַל בָּנַי וְעַל פֹּעַל יָדַי תְּצַוֻּנִי" (ישעיה מה, יא): **דַּבֵּר אֶל בְּנֵי יִשְׂרָאֵל וְיִסָּעוּ.** אֵין לָהֶם אֶלָּא לִסַּע, שֶׁאֵין הַיָּם עוֹמֵד בִּפְנֵיהֶם, כְּדַאי זְכוּת אֲבוֹתֵיהֶם וְהָאֱמוּנָה שֶׁהֶאֱמִינוּ בִּי וְיָצְאוּ, לִקְרֹעַ לָהֶם אֶת הַיָּם:

יט-כ **וַיֵּלֶךְ מֵאַחֲרֵיהֶם.** לְהַבְדִּיל בֵּין מַחֲנֵה מִצְרַיִם וּבֵין מַחֲנֵה יִשְׂרָאֵל וּלְקַבֵּל חִצִּים וּבַלִּיסְטְרָאוֹת שֶׁל מִצְרַיִם. בְּכָל מָקוֹם הוּא אוֹמֵר: "מַלְאַךְ ה'" וְכָאן: "מַלְאַךְ הָאֱלֹהִים", אֵין 'אֱלֹהִים' בְּכָל מָקוֹם אֶלָּא דִּין, מְלַמֵּד שֶׁהָיוּ יִשְׂרָאֵל נְתוּנִין בַּדִּין בְּאוֹתָהּ שָׁעָה אִם לְהִנָּצֵל אִם לְהֵאָבֵד עִם מִצְרַיִם: **וַיָּבֹא בֵּין מַחֲנֵה מִצְרַיִם.** מָשָׁל לִמְהַלֵּךְ בַּדֶּרֶךְ וּבְנוֹ מְהַלֵּךְ לְפָנָיו. בָּאוּ לִסְטִים לִשְׁבּוֹתוֹ, נְטָלוֹ מִלְּפָנָיו נְתָנוֹ לְאַחֲרָיו. בָּא זְאֵב מֵאַחֲרָיו, נְתָנוֹ לְפָנָיו. בָּאוּ לִסְטִים לְפָנָיו וּזְאֵבִים מֵאַחֲרָיו, נְתָנוֹ עַל זְרוֹעוֹ וְנִלְחַם בָּהֶם. כָּךְ: "וְאָנֹכִי תִרְגַּלְתִּי לְאֶפְרַיִם קָחָם עַל זְרוֹעֹתָיו" (הושע יא, ג): **וַיִּסַּע עַמּוּד הֶעָנָן.** כְּשֶׁחָשְׁכָה וְהִשְׁלִים עַמּוּד הֶעָנָן אֶת הַמַּחֲנֶה לְעַמּוּד הָאֵשׁ, לֹא נִסְתַּלֵּק הֶעָנָן כְּמוֹ שֶׁהָיָה רָגִיל לְהִסְתַּלֵּק עַרְבִית לְגַמְרֵי, אֶלָּא נָסַע וְהָלַךְ לוֹ מֵאַחֲרֵיהֶם לְהַחֲשִׁיךְ לְמִצְרַיִם: **וַיְהִי הֶעָנָן וְהַחֹשֶׁךְ.** לְמִצְרַיִם: **וַיָּאֶר.** עַמּוּד הָאֵשׁ "אֶת הַלַּיְלָה" לְיִשְׂרָאֵל, וְהוֹלֵךְ לִפְנֵיהֶם כְּדַרְכּוֹ לָלֶכֶת כָּל הַלַּיְלָה. וְהַחֹשֶׁךְ שֶׁל עֲרָפֶל לְצַד מִצְרַיִם: **וְלֹא קָרַב זֶה אֶל זֶה.** מַחֲנֶה אֶל מַחֲנֶה:

כא **בְּרוּחַ קָדִים עַזָּה.** בְּרוּחַ קָדִים שֶׁהִיא עַזָּה שֶׁבָּרוּחוֹת, הִיא הָרוּחַ שֶׁהַקָּדוֹשׁ בָּרוּךְ הוּא נִפְרָע בָּהּ מִן הָרְשָׁעִים, שֶׁנֶּאֱמַר: "כְּרוּחַ קָדִים אֲפִיצֵם" (ירמיה יח, יז), "יָבוֹא קָדִים רוּחַ ה'" (הושע יג, טו), "רוּחַ הַקָּדִים שְׁבָרֵךְ בְּלֵב יַמִּים" (יחזקאל כז, כו), "הָגָה בְּרוּחוֹ הַקָּשָׁה בְּיוֹם קָדִים" (ישעיה כז, ח):

is that it happened just there, just then, when the Israelites seemed trapped, unable to go forward because of the sea, unable to turn back because of the Egyptian army pursuing them.

There is a significant difference between these two interpretations. The first appeals to our sense of wonder. How extraordinary that the laws of nature should be suspended to allow an escaping people to go free. It is a story to appeal to the imagination.

But the naturalistic explanation is wondrous at another level entirely. Here the Torah is using the device of irony. What made the Egyptians of the time of Ramesses so formidable was the fact that they possessed the latest and most powerful form of military technology, the horse-drawn chariot. It made them unbeatable in battle, and fearsome.

What happens at the sea is poetic justice of the most exquisite kind. There is only one circumstance in which a group of people traveling by foot can escape a highly trained army of charioteers, namely, when the route passes through a muddy seabed. The people can walk across, but the chariot wheels get stuck in the mud. The Egyptian army can neither advance nor retreat. The wind drops. The water returns. The powerful are now powerless, while the powerless have made their way to freedom.

טו וַיֹּאמֶר יהוה אֶל־מֹשֶׁה מַה־תִּצְעַק אֵלָי דַּבֵּר אֶל־בְּנֵי־יִשְׂרָאֵל וְיִסָּעוּ׃ יא שלישי
טז וְאַתָּה הָרֵם אֶת־מַטְּךָ וּנְטֵה אֶת־יָדְךָ עַל־הַיָּם וּבְקָעֵהוּ וְיָבֹאוּ בְנֵי־
יז יִשְׂרָאֵל בְּתוֹךְ הַיָּם בַּיַּבָּשָׁה׃ וַאֲנִי הִנְנִי מְחַזֵּק אֶת־לֵב מִצְרַיִם וְיָבֹאוּ
יח אַחֲרֵיהֶם וְאִכָּבְדָה בְּפַרְעֹה וּבְכָל־חֵילוֹ בְּרִכְבּוֹ וּבְפָרָשָׁיו׃ וְיָדְעוּ מִצְרַיִם
יט כִּי־אֲנִי יהוה בְּהִכָּבְדִי בְּפַרְעֹה בְּרִכְבּוֹ וּבְפָרָשָׁיו׃ וַיִּסַּע מַלְאַךְ הָאֱלֹהִים
הַהֹלֵךְ לִפְנֵי מַחֲנֵה יִשְׂרָאֵל וַיֵּלֶךְ מֵאַחֲרֵיהֶם וַיִּסַּע עַמּוּד הֶעָנָן מִפְּנֵיהֶם
כ וַיַּעֲמֹד מֵאַחֲרֵיהֶם׃ וַיָּבֹא בֵּין ׀ מַחֲנֵה מִצְרַיִם וּבֵין מַחֲנֵה יִשְׂרָאֵל וַיְהִי
הֶעָנָן וְהַחֹשֶׁךְ וַיָּאֶר אֶת־הַלָּיְלָה וְלֹא־קָרַב זֶה אֶל־זֶה כָּל־הַלָּיְלָה׃
כא וַיֵּט מֹשֶׁה אֶת־יָדוֹ עַל־הַיָּם וַיּוֹלֶךְ יהוה ׀ אֶת־הַיָּם בְּרוּחַ קָדִים עַזָּה

אונקלוס

טו וַאֲמַר יי לְמֹשֶׁה, קַבֵּילִית צְלוֹתָךְ, מַלֵּיל עִם בְּנֵי יִשְׂרָאֵל וְיִטְּלוּן׃
טז וְאַתְּ טוֹל יָת חֻטְרָךְ, וַאֲרֵים יָת יְדָךְ, עַל יַמָּא וּבְזַעְהִי, וְיֵיעֲלוּן
בְּנֵי יִשְׂרָאֵל, בְּגוֹ יַמָּא בְּיַבֶּשְׁתָּא׃ יז וַאֲנָא, הָאֲנָא מְתַקֵּיף יָת לִבָּא
דְּמִצְרָאֵי, וְיֵיעֲלוּן בָּתְרֵיהוֹן, וְאֶתְיַקַּר בְּפַרְעֹה וּבְכָל מַשִּׁרְיָתֵיהּ,
בִּרְתִכּוֹהִי וּבְפָרָשׁוֹהִי׃ יח וְיִדְּעוּן מִצְרָאֵי אֲרֵי אֲנָא יי, בְּאִתְיְקָרוּתִי
בְּפַרְעֹה, בִּרְתִכּוֹהִי וּבְפָרָשׁוֹהִי׃ יט וּנְטַל מַלְאֲכָא דַּיי, דִּמְדַבַּר קֳדָם
מַשִּׁרְיָתָא דְּיִשְׂרָאֵל, וַאֲתָא מִבָּתְרֵיהוֹן, וּנְטַל, עַמּוּדָא דַּעֲנָנָא
מִן קֳדָמֵיהוֹן, וּשְׁרָא מִבָּתְרֵיהוֹן׃ כ וְעָאל, בֵּין מַשִּׁרְיָתָא דְּמִצְרָאֵי,
וּבֵין מַשִּׁרְיָתָא דְּיִשְׂרָאֵל, וַהֲוָה עֲנָנָא וְקַבְלָא לְמִצְרָאֵי, וּלְיִשְׂרָאֵל
נְהַר כָּל לֵילְיָא, וְלָא אִתְקְרִיבוּ דֵּין, לְוָת דֵּין כָּל לֵילְיָא׃ כא וַאֲרֵים
מֹשֶׁה יָת יְדֵיהּ עַל יַמָּא, וְדַבַּר יי יָת יַמָּא, בְּרוּחַ קִדּוּמָא תַּקִּיף

14:20 וְלֹא־קָרַב זֶה אֶל־זֶה כָּל־הַלָּיְלָה *Keeping the two apart all night* – Literally, "They did not draw near one to another all night." The only other appearance of the phrase *zeh el zeh*, "one to another," in Tanakh is the basis for the *Kedusha* section of each *Amida* prayer: "And they [the angels] called out *one to another*, 'Holy, holy, holy – the Lord of Hosts'" (Is. 6:3). This verbal echo inspired a midrash with halakhic implications. According to the Talmud (Megilla 10b; Sanhedrin 39b), when the angels wished to sing the Song of the Sea, God silenced them: "Shall you sing a song while My creatures are drowning?" God does not rejoice in the downfall of the wicked. Sympathy should know no religious or national borders. The division of the Sea of Reeds, at which the Egyptians died, took place on the seventh day of Passover, and this, according to the *Beit Yosef* (*siman* 490), is the reason why full Hallel is not said on that day as it is on other festivals.

THE SPLITTING OF THE SEA

The splitting of the Reed Sea is engraved in Jewish memory. We recite it daily during the morning service, at the transition from the *Pesukei DeZimra* to the beginning of communal prayer. We speak of it again after the *Shema*, just before the *Amida*. It was the supreme miracle of the exodus. But in what sense?

The passage can be read in two ways. The first is that what happened was a suspension of the laws of nature. It was a supernatural event. The waters stood, literally, like a wall.

The second is that what happened was miraculous not because the laws of nature were suspended. To the contrary, as computer simulation has shown, the exposure of dry land at a particular point in the Reed Sea can be a natural outcome of the strong east wind. What made it miraculous

by a strong east wind all night, turning it to dry land and dividing the waters.
22 So the Israelites walked through the sea on dry land. To their right and left, the
23 water was like a wall. The Egyptians chased after them. All Pharaoh's horses,
24 chariots, and cavalry followed them into the sea. During the last watch of the
night, the LORD looked down at the Egyptian army from a column of fire and
25 cloud and threw them into a panic, clogging their chariot wheels so that it was
hard for them to move. The Egyptians said, "Let us flee from the Israelites. The
LORD is fighting for them against Egypt."
26 Then the LORD said to Moshe, "Stretch out your hand over the sea. The waters REVI'I

רש"י

ויבקעו המים. כל מים שבעולם:

כג **כל סוס פרעה.** וכי סוס אחד היה?! מגיד שאין כלם חשובין לפני המקום אלא כסוס אחד:

כד **באשמרת הבקר.** שלשת חלקי הלילה קרויין אשמרת, ואותה שלפני היום קורא "אשמרת הבקר". ואומר אני, שהוא חלוק למשמרות שיר מלאכי השרת כת אחר כת לשלשה חלקים, לכך קרוי אשמרת, וזהו שתרגם אונקלוס: "מטרת": **וישקף.** ויבט, כלומר פנה אליהם להשחיתם. ותרגומו: "ואסתכי" אף הוא לשון הבטה, כמו: "שדה צפים" (במדבר כג, יד), "חקל סכותא": **בעמוד אש וענן.** עמוד ענן יורד ועושה אותו כטיט, ועמוד אש מרתיחו, וטלפי סוסיהם משתמטות: **ויהם.** לשון מהומה, אשטורדי"שון בלעז. ערבבם, נטל סגניות שלהם. ושנינו בפרקי רבי אליעזר בנו של רבי יוסי הגלילי, כל מקום שנאמר 'מהומה' הרעשת קול הוא, וזה אב לכלן: "וירעם ה' בקול גדול... על פלשתים ויהמם" (שמואל א' ז, י):

כה **ויסר את אפן מרכבתיו.** מכח האש נשרפו הגלגלים, והמרכבות נגררות, והיושבים בהם נעים ואבריהן מתפרקים: **וינהגהו בכבדת.** בהנהגה שהיא כבדה וקשה להם. במדה שמדדו, "ויכבד לבו הוא ועבדיו" (לעיל ט, לד), אף כאן, "וינהגהו בכבדת": **נלחם להם במצרים.** במצריים. דבר אחר "במצרים", בארץ מצרים; שכשם שאלו לוקים על הים כך לוקים אותם שנשארו במצרים:

כו **וישבו המים.** שזקופים ועומדים כחומה, ישובו למקומם ויכסו "על מצרים":

14:14). The scene resonates with the message of the book of Psalms:

> He does not take delight in the strength of horses,
> or pleasure in the fleetness of man.
> The LORD takes pleasure in those who fear Him,
> who put their hope in His loyalty. (Ps. 147:10–11)

While the Israelites watch, the chariots become bogged down in the mud. By the time the Egyptians realize what is happening, they are trapped. The mightiest army of the ancient world is defeated, and its warriors drowned, not by a superior army, not by human opposition at all, but by their own folly in being so focused on capturing the Israelites that they ignored the fact that they were driving into mud where their chariots could not go. Strength has turned to weakness, and what gave the Egyptian army its speed now mires them in immobility.

out of the land of Egypt. I am the LORD your God" (Lev. 25:55).

14:25 **וַיָּסַר אֵת אֹפַן מַרְכְּבֹתָיו וַיְנַהֲגֵהוּ בִּכְבֵדֻת** *Clogging their chariot wheels* – As we saw earlier, in the time of the Torah, Egypt was famous for its horses. They still were, in the time of Shlomo, five centuries later (I Kings 10:26–29). No other nation could rival them. This meant that they could outmaneuver any rival military force. Horses gave them speed, and chariots gave them protection. They were impregnable, and the sight of six hundred of them approaching would have been terrifying to a well-drilled army, let alone an unruly, disorganized group of slaves.

When the Israelites lost heart and blamed Moshe for bringing them out of Egypt, Moshe's reply was short and sharp: "The LORD will fight for you. You stay silent" (Ex.

כב כׇּל־הַלָּיְלָה וַיָּשֶׂם אֶת־הַיָּם לֶחָרָבָה וַיִּבָּקְעוּ הַמָּיִם׃ וַיָּבֹאוּ בְנֵי־יִשְׂרָאֵל
כג בְּתוֹךְ הַיָּם בַּיַּבָּשָׁה וְהַמַּיִם לָהֶם חוֹמָה מִימִינָם וּמִשְּׂמֹאלָם׃ וַיִּרְדְּפוּ
מִצְרַיִם וַיָּבֹאוּ אַחֲרֵיהֶם כֹּל סוּס פַּרְעֹה רִכְבּוֹ וּפָרָשָׁיו אֶל־תּוֹךְ הַיָּם׃
כד וַיְהִי בְּאַשְׁמֹרֶת הַבֹּקֶר וַיַּשְׁקֵף יהוה אֶל־מַחֲנֵה מִצְרַיִם בְּעַמּוּד
כה אֵשׁ וְעָנָן וַיָּהׇם אֵת מַחֲנֵה מִצְרָיִם׃ וַיָּסַר אֵת אֹפַן מַרְכְּבֹתָיו וַיְנַהֲגֵהוּ
בִּכְבֵדֻת וַיֹּאמֶר מִצְרַיִם אָנוּסָה מִפְּנֵי יִשְׂרָאֵל כִּי יהוה נִלְחָם לָהֶם
בְּמִצְרָיִם׃
כו וַיֹּאמֶר יהוה אֶל־מֹשֶׁה נְטֵה אֶת־יָדְךָ עַל־הַיָּם וְיָשֻׁבוּ הַמַּיִם עַל־מִצְרַיִם רביעי

אונקלוס

כָּל לֵילְיָא, וְשַׁוִּי יָת יַמָּא לְיַבֶּשְׁתָּא, וְאִתְבְּזַעוּ מַיָּא: כב וְעָאלוּ בְנֵי
יִשְׂרָאֵל, בְּגוֹ יַמָּא בְּיַבֶּשְׁתָּא, וּמַיָּא לְהוֹן שׁוּרִין, מִיַּמִּינְהוֹן וּמִסְּמָאלְהוֹן:
כג וּרְדַפוּ מִצְרָאֵי וְעָאלוּ בָתְרֵיהוֹן, כָּל סוּסָוַת פַּרְעֹה, רְתִכּוֹהִי וּפָרָשׁוֹהִי,
לְגוֹ יַמָּא: כד וַהֲוָה בְּמַטְּרַת צַפְרָא, וְאִסְתְּכֵי יְיָ לְמַשְׁרִיתָא דְּמִצְרָאֵי,
בְּעַמּוּדָא דְאִישָׁתָא וַעֲנָנָא, וְשַׁגֵּישׁ, יָת מַשְׁרִיתָא דְּמִצְרָאֵי: כה וְאַעְדִּי,
יָת גִּלְגְּלֵי רְתִכֵּיהוֹן, וּמְדַבְּרִין לְהוֹן בִּתְקוֹף, וַאֲמַרוּ מִצְרָאֵי, נְעָרוֹק מִן
קֳדָם יִשְׂרָאֵל, אֲרֵי דָא הִיא גְּבוּרְתָא דַייָ, דַּעֲבַד לְהוֹן קְרָבִין בְּמִצְרָיִם:
כו וַאֲמַר יְיָ לְמֹשֶׁה, אֲרֵים יָת יְדָךְ עַל יַמָּא, וִיתוּבוּן מַיָּא עַל מִצְרָאֵי,

There are, then, two possible perspectives on the crossing of the Reed Sea, two ways of reading the biblical narrative. To some, the miracle was the suspension of the laws of nature. To others, the fact that there was a naturalistic explanation did not make the event any less miraculous. That the Israelites should arrive at the sea precisely where the waters were unexpectedly shallow, that a strong east wind should blow when and how it did, and that the Egyptians' greatest military asset should have proved their undoing – all these things were wonders, and we have never forgotten them.

14:22 מִימִינָם וּמִשְּׂמֹאלָם *To their right and left* – The symbolism of the sea reminds us of the ancient ceremony of covenant making. The key verb of covenant is "to cut." An animal, or several animals, were divided, and the parties to the covenant stood or sat between them. The division of things normally united or whole stood as a symbol of the unification of entities (persons, tribes, nations) previously divided. In this context, a key passage is the covenant "cut" between God and Avraham in Genesis 15. God tells Avraham to cut various animals in half and arrange the halves opposite each other. "On that day the Lord made [literally, 'cut'] a covenant with Avram" (Gen. 15:18).

So at the Reed Sea, the Israelites passed "between the pieces" (the waters, rather than the halves of animals) in a ratification of the covenant with Avraham. They passed from one domain to another, from being slaves – *avadim* – to Pharaoh to becoming servants – *avadim* – to God. This surely is the meaning of the phrase in the Song of the Sea: "until Your people crossed, Lord, until the people You acquired crossed over" (Ex. 15:16).

The crossing of the sea is both an act of covenant making and a transfer of possession. The Israelites are now God's possession rather than Pharaoh's. They have entered new territory, not just geographically but also existentially.

Geula, redemption, is a legal as well as religious term. It means "to buy back." Thus God, redeeming the Israelites, became in legal terms their owner. "For it is to Me that *the Israelites are servants*. They are My servants, whom I brought

27 will flow back over the Egyptians and their chariots and cavalry." Moshe
stretched out his hand over the sea, and at daybreak the water came back in
full force. The Egyptians fled at its approach but the LORD swept them into
28 the sea. The waters returned, covering the chariots, the cavalry, and the whole
Egyptian army that had followed the Israelites into the sea. Not one of them
29 remained. But the Israelites had walked through the sea on dry land, with a
30 wall of water to their right and left. That day, the LORD saved the Israelites
from the Egyptians. And when the Israelites saw the Egyptians dead on the
31 seashore, and witnessed the wondrous power the LORD had unleashed against
the Egyptians, the people were in awe of the LORD, and they believed in Him
and in Moshe His servant.

15 1 And then, Moshe and the Israelites sang this song to the LORD: I will sing to

רש"י

כז| **לפנות בקר.** לעת שהבקר פונה לבא: **לאיתנו.** לתקפו הראשון: **נסים לקראתו.** שהיו מהוממים ומטורפים ורצין לקראת המים: **וינער ה'.** כאדם שמנער את הקדרה והופך העליון למטה והתחתון למעלה, כך היו עולין ויורדין ומשתברין בים. ונתן הקדוש ברוך הוא בהם חיות לקבל היסורין. "ושניק", הוא לשון טרוף בלשון ארמי, והרבה יש במדרשי אגדה:

כח| **ויכסו את הרכב... לכל חיל פרעה.** כן דרך המקראות לכתב למ"ד יתרה, כמו: "לכל כליו תעשה נחשת" (להלן כז, ג), וכן: "לכל כלי המשכן בכל עבדתו" (שם פסוק יט), "ויתדתם ומיתריהם לכל כליהם" (במדבר ד, לב), ואינה אלא תקון לשון:

ל| **וירא ישראל את מצרים מת.** שפלטן הים על שפתו, כדי שלא יאמרו ישראל: כשם שאנו עולים מצד זה כך הם עולין מצד אחר רחוק ממנו וירדפו אחרינו:

לא| **את היד הגדלה.** את הגבורה הגדולה שעשתה ידו של הקדוש ברוך הוא. והרבה לשונות נופלין על לשון "יד" וכלן לשון יד ממש הן, והמפרש יתקן הלשון אחר ענין הדבור:

טו א| **אז ישיר משה.** אז כשראה הנס עלה בלבו שישיר שירה. וכן: "אז ידבר יהושע" (יהושע י, יב), וכן: "ובית יעשה לבת פרעה" (מלכים א' ז, ח), חשב בלבו שיעשה לה, אף כאן, "ישיר", אמר לו לבו שישיר, וכן עשה: "ויאמרו לאמר אשירה לה'". וכן ביהושע כשראה הנס אמר

prophets" (Num. 11:29). There are times when it is important to show that "there is only one leader for the generation, not two" (Sanhedrin 8a), and others when the highest mark of leadership is inviting others to share in it (Sanhedrin ad loc.).

We are each called on to fill a number of leadership roles: as parents, teachers, friends, team members, and team leaders. And there is no one Torah model of leadership. There is no doubt, however, that Judaism favors as an ideal the role of parent, encouraging those we lead to continue the journey we have begun, and go further than we did. A good leader creates followers. A great leader creates leaders. That was Moshe's greatest achievement – that he left behind him a people willing, in each generation, to accept responsibility for taking further the great task he had begun.

THE SONG OF THE SEA

For the first time since their departure from Egypt, the Israelites do something together. They sing. In recollection of that moment, tradition has named the week when we read this passage *Shabbat Shira*, the Sabbath of Song. The first of the great celebratory songs in Israel's history, it subsequently became known as "the song" par excellence. The song has three strophes: the first (vv. 1–6) celebrating the victory at the sea, the second (7–11) restating it in more vivid imagery, and the third (12–18) looking toward the future. The concluding verse of each strophe (vv. 6, 11, and 18) is a majestic statement of God's sovereignty and might. There are several views in the Mishna, Tosefta, and Talmud (Sota 30b) as to how it was sung. Some say that the Israelites repeated "I will

כז עַל־רִכְבּוֹ וְעַל־פָּרָשָׁיו: וַיֵּט מֹשֶׁה אֶת־יָדוֹ עַל־הַיָּם וַיָּשָׁב הַיָּם לִפְנוֹת
בֹּקֶר לְאֵיתָנוֹ וּמִצְרַיִם נָסִים לִקְרָאתוֹ וַיְנַעֵר יהוה אֶת־מִצְרַיִם בְּתוֹךְ
כח הַיָּם: וַיָּשֻׁבוּ הַמַּיִם וַיְכַסּוּ אֶת־הָרֶכֶב וְאֶת־הַפָּרָשִׁים לְכֹל חֵיל פַּרְעֹה
כט הַבָּאִים אַחֲרֵיהֶם בַּיָּם לֹא־נִשְׁאַר בָּהֶם עַד־אֶחָד: וּבְנֵי יִשְׂרָאֵל הָלְכוּ
ל בַיַּבָּשָׁה בְּתוֹךְ הַיָּם וְהַמַּיִם לָהֶם חֹמָה מִימִינָם וּמִשְּׂמֹאלָם: וַיּוֹשַׁע
יהוה בַּיּוֹם הַהוּא אֶת־יִשְׂרָאֵל מִיַּד מִצְרָיִם וַיַּרְא יִשְׂרָאֵל אֶת־מִצְרַיִם
לא מֵת עַל־שְׂפַת הַיָּם: וַיַּרְא יִשְׂרָאֵל אֶת־הַיָּד הַגְּדֹלָה אֲשֶׁר עָשָׂה יהוה
בְּמִצְרַיִם וַיִּירְאוּ הָעָם אֶת־יהוה וַיַּאֲמִינוּ בַּיהוה וּבְמֹשֶׁה עַבְדּוֹ:

טו א אָז יָשִׁיר־מֹשֶׁה וּבְנֵי יִשְׂרָאֵל אֶת־הַשִּׁירָה הַזֹּאת לַיהוה וַיֹּאמְרוּ

אונקלוס

עַל רְתִכֵּיהוֹן וְעַל פָּרָשֵׁיהוֹן: כז וַאֲרֵים מֹשֶׁה יָת יְדֵיהּ עַל יַמָּא, וְתָב יַמָּא, לְעִדָּן צַפְרָא לְתֻקְפֵּיהּ, וּמִצְרָאֵי עָרְקִין לָקֳדָמוּתֵיהּ, וְשַׁנִּיק יְיָ, יָת מִצְרָאֵי בְּגוֹ יַמָּא: כח וְתָבוּ מַיָּא, וַחֲפוֹ יָת רְתִכַּיָּא וְיָת פָּרָשַׁיָּא, לְכָל מַשִּׁרְיַת פַּרְעֹה, דְּעָאלוּ בָּתְרֵיהוֹן בְּיַמָּא, לָא אִשְׁתְּאַר בְּהוֹן עַד חַד: כט וּבְנֵי יִשְׂרָאֵל, הַלִּיכוּ בְּיַבֶּשְׁתָּא בְּגוֹ יַמָּא, וּמַיָּא לְהוֹן שׁוּרִין, מִיַּמִּינְהוֹן וּמִסְּמָאלְהוֹן: ל וּפְרַק יְיָ, בְּיוֹמָא הַהוּא, יָת יִשְׂרָאֵל מִיְּדָא דְמִצְרָאֵי, וַחֲזָא יִשְׂרָאֵל יָת מִצְרָאֵי, מָיְתִין עַל כֵּיף יַמָּא: לא וַחֲזָא יִשְׂרָאֵל יָת גְּבוּרַת יְדָא רַבְּתָא, דַּעֲבַד יְיָ בְּמִצְרָאֵי, וּדְחִילוּ עַמָּא מִן קֳדָם יְיָ, וְהֵימִינוּ בְּמֵימְרָא דַּייָ, וּבִנְבִיאוּת מֹשֶׁה עַבְדֵּיהּ: טו א בְּכֵן שַׁבַּח מֹשֶׁה וּבְנֵי יִשְׂרָאֵל, יָת תֻּשְׁבַּחְתָּא הָדָא קֳדָם יְיָ, וַאֲמַרוּ

14:28 לֹא־נִשְׁאַר בָּהֶם עַד־אֶחָד *Not one of them remained* – This is the moral climax of the episode. Pharaoh had decreed that every male Israelite child be drowned. The first plague, in which the river turned into blood, was intended to remind the Egyptians that they were being punished for this crime, but the plague made no impression on Pharaoh. He merely instructed his magicians to show that they could do likewise. Now the punishment comes, measure for measure: those who drowned innocent children were themselves drowned. According to Targum Onkelos this is the meaning of Yitro's later statement, "He brought upon them what they schemed against others" (Ex. 18:11). The miracle at the sea was intended to demonstrate the moral truth that evil eventually turns against its perpetrator.

14:31 וַיַּאֲמִינוּ בַּיהוה וּבְמֹשֶׁה עַבְדּוֹ *They believed in Him and in Moshe His servant* – This is the first time the people are described as believing in Moshe's leadership. The phrase "His servant" is pointed in this context. The rulers of the ancient world saw themselves as demigods who commanded obedience. The Torah insists that the truth is the opposite: greatness is humility, and to be a leader is to be a servant. On this, the Sages asked: What is it to be a leader of the Jewish people? Is it to hold official authority, of which the supreme example is a king? Is it to have the kind of personal relationship with one's followers that rests not on honor and deference but on encouraging people to grow, accept responsibility, and continue the journey you have begun? Or is it something in between?

There is no single answer. At times, Moshe asserted his authority (for example, during the Koraḥ rebellion). At another, he said, "Would that all the LORD's people were

the Lord, for He has triumphed in glory; / horse and horseman He hurled
2 into the sea. / The Lord is my strength and song – / and now my salvation. /
3 This is my God, I will glorify Him, / my father's God, I will exalt Him. / The
4 Lord is a Master of war; / the Lord is His name. / Pharaoh's chariots and

רש"י

לו לבו שידבר, וכן עשה: "ויאמר לעיני ישראל" (יהושע שם). וכן שירת הבאר שפתח בה: "אז ישיר ישראל", פירש אחריו: "עלי באר ענו לה" (במדבר כא, יז); "אז יבנה שלמה במה" (מלכים א' יא, ז) פירשו בו חכמי ישראל שבקש לבנות ולא בנה. למדנו שהיו"ד על שם המחשבה נאמרה. זהו ליישב פשוטו. אבל מדרשו, אמרו רבותינו זכרונם לברכה, מכאן רמז לתחיית המתים מן התורה, וכן בכלן, חוץ משל שלמה שפירשוהו בקש לבנות ולא בנה. ואין לומר וליישב לשון הזה כשאר דברים הנכתבים בלשון עתיד והן מיד, כגון: "ככה יעשה איוב" (איוב א, ה), "על פי ה' יחנו" (במדבר ט, כ), "ויש אשר יהיה הענן" (שם), לפי שהן דבר ההוה תמיד ונופל בו בין לשון עתיד בין לשון עבר, אבל זה שלא היה אלא לשעה אינו יכול ליישבו בלשון הזה: **כי גאה גאה.** כתרגומו. דבר אחר, "כי גאה גאה", על כל השירות וכל מה שאקלס בו עוד יש נוספות, ולא כמדת מלך בשר ודם שמקלסין אותו ואין בו: **סוס ורכבו.** שניהם קשורים זה בזה, והמים מעלין אותן לרום ויורדין לעמק ואינן נפרדין: **רמה.** השליך, וכן: "ורמיו לגוא אתון נורא" (דניאל ג, כא). ומדרש אגדה, כתוב אחד אומר "רמה" וכתוב אחד אומר "ירה", מלמד שהיו עולין לרום ויורדין לתהום, כמו: "מי ירה אבן פנתה" (איוב לח, ו) מלמעלה למטה:

ב **עזי וזמרת יה.** אונקלוס תרגם "עזי" כמו 'עזי', "וזמרת" כמו 'וזמרתי'. ואני תמה על לשון המקרא, שאין לך כמוהו בנקדתו במקרא אלא בשלשה מקומות שהוא סמוך אצל "וזמרת", וכל שאר מקומות נקוד שורק, "ה' עזי ומעזי" (ירמיה טז, יט), "עזו אליך אשמרה" (תהלים נט, י). וכן כל תבה בת שתי אותיות הנקודה מלאפום, כשהיא מארכת באות שלישית ואין השנית בשבא בחטף, הראשונה נקודה בשורק, כגון: עז עזי, רק רקי, חק חקי, על עלו, "יסור... עלו" (ישעיה יד, כה), כל כלו, "ושלשם על כלו" (לעיל יד, ז). ואלו שלשה "עזי וזמרת" של כאן ושל ישעיה (יב, ב) ושל תהלים (קיח, יד) נקודים בחטף קמץ; ועוד, אין באחד מהם כתוב 'וזמרתי' אלא "וזמרת", וכלם סמוך להם: "ויהי לי לישועה". לכך אני אומר ליישב לשון המקרא, שאין "עזי" כמו 'עזי' ולא "וזמרת" כמו 'וזמרתי', אלא "עזי" שם דבר הוא, כמו: "היושבי בשמים" (שם קכג, א), "שכני בחגוי סלע" (עובדיה א, ג), "שכני סנה" (דברים לג, טז). וזהו השבח: עז וזמרת יה הוא היה לי לישועה. ו"זמרת" דבוק הוא לתבת ה', כמו "לעזרת ה'" (שופטים ה, כג), "בעברת ה'" (ישעיה ט, יח), "על דברת בני האדם" (קהלת ג, יח). ולשון "וזמרת" לשון "לא תזמר" (ויקרא כה, ד), "זמיר עריצים" (ישעיה כה, ה), כסוח וכריתה, עזו ונקמתו של אלהינו היה לנו לישועה. ואל תתמה על לשון "ויהי" שלא נאמר 'היה', שיש לנו מקראות מדברים בלשון זה, וזה דגמתו: "את קירות הבית סביב להיכל ולדביר ויעש צלעות סביב" (מלכים א' ו, ה), היה לו לומר: 'עשה צלעות סביב'; וכן בדברי הימים (ב' י, יז): "ובני ישראל הישבים בערי יהודה וימלך עליהם רחבעם", היה לו לומר: 'מלך עליהם רחבעם'; "מבלתי יכלת ה' וגו' וישחטם" (במדבר יד, טז), היה לו לומר: 'שחטם'; "והאנשים אשר שלח משה... וימתו" (שם פסוקים לו-לז), 'מתו' היה לו לומר; "ואשר לא שם לבו אל דבר ה' ויעזב" (לעיל ט, כא), היה לו לומר: 'עזב': **זה אלי.** בכבודו נגלה עליהם והיו מראין אותו באצבע, ראתה שפחה על הים מה שלא ראו נביאים: **ואנוהו.** אונקלוס תרגם לשון נוה, "נוה שאנן" (ישעיה לג, כ), "לנוה צאן" (שם סה, י). דבר אחר, "ואנוהו", לשון נוי, אספר נויו ושבחו לבאי עולם, כגון: "מה דודך מדוד" (שיר השירים ה, ט), "דודי צח ואדום" (שם פסוק י) וכל הענין: **אלהי אבי.** הוא זה, "וארממנהו": **אלהי אבי.** לא אני תחלת הקדשה, מחזקת ועומדת לי הקדשה ואלהותו עלי מימי אבותי:

ג **ה' איש מלחמה.** בעל מלחמות, כמו: "איש נעמי" (רות א, ג), וכל 'איש' ו'אישך' מתרגמין בעל. וכן: "וחזקת והיית לאיש" (מלכים א' ב, ב), לגבור: **ה' שמו.** מלחמותיו לא בכלי זין אלא בשמו הוא נלחם, "ואנכי בא אליך בשם ה' צבאות" (שמואל א' יז, מה). דבר אחר, "ה' שמו", אף בשעה שהוא נלחם ונוקם מאויביו, אוחז הוא במדתו לרחם על קראיו ולזון את כל באי עולם, ולא כמדת מלכי אדמה כשהוא עסוק במלחמה פונה עצמו מכל עסקים ואין בו כח לעשות זו וזו:

ד **ירה בים.** "שדי בימא", "שדי" לשון ירייה. וכן הוא אומר: "או ירה יירה" (להלן יט, יג), "או אשתדאה ישתדי", והתי"ו משמשת באלו במקום יתפעל: **ומבחר.** שם דבר, כמו: "מרכב" (ויקרא טו, ט), "משכב" (שם פסוק ד),

our children absorb and, hopefully, make their own. Or, as the English poet William Wordsworth wrote in his great poem, "The Prelude": "What we love others will love, and we will show them how."

לֵאמֹר אָשִׁירָה לַיהוָה כִּי־גָאֹה גָּאָה סוּס
ב וְרֹכְבוֹ רָמָה בַיָּם: עָזִּי וְזִמְרָת יָהּ וַיְהִי־לִי
לִישׁוּעָה זֶה אֵלִי וְאַנְוֵהוּ אֱלֹהֵי
ג אָבִי וַאֲרֹמְמֶנְהוּ: יְהוָה אִישׁ מִלְחָמָה יְהוָה
ד שְׁמוֹ: מַרְכְּבֹת פַּרְעֹה וְחֵילוֹ יָרָה בַיָּם וּמִבְחַר

אונקלוס

לְמֵימַר, נְשַׁבַּח וְנוֹדֵי קֳדָם יְיָ, אֲרֵי אִתְגְּאִי עַל גֵּיוְתָנַיָּא וְגֵיאוּתָא דִּילֵיהּ הִיא, סוּסְיָא וְרָכְבֵיהּ רְמָא בְיַמָּא: ב תֻּקְפִּי וְתֻשְׁבַּחְתִּי דְּחִילָא יְיָ, אֲמַר בְּמֵימְרֵיהּ וַהֲוָה לִי לְפָרִיק, דֵּין אֱלָהִי וְאֶבְנֵי לֵיהּ מַקְדַּשׁ, אֱלָהָא דַּאֲבָהָתִי וְאֶפְלַח קֳדָמוֹהִי: ג יְיָ מָרֵי נִצְחָן קְרָבַיָּא, יְיָ שְׁמֵיהּ: ד רְתִכֵּי פַרְעֹה, וּמַשִׁרְיָתֵיהּ שְׁדִי בְיַמָּא, וּמִבְחַר

sing to the Lord" after each verse; others that they sang it line by line after Moshe; others that Moshe began each line and the Israelites completed it; yet others (a view adopted by Rashi) that the entire people were divinely inspired to sing it in unison. It was a moment of collective epiphany, and it expressed itself as song.

When language aspires to the transcendent and the soul longs to break free of the gravitational pull of the earth, it modulates into song. Goethe said, "Religious worship cannot do without music. It is one of the foremost means to work upon man with an effect of marvel." Mystics go further and speak of the song of the universe, what Pythagoras called "the music of the spheres." This is what Psalm 19 means when it says, "The heavens tell of God's glory; the skies proclaim His handiwork. . . . There is no speech, there are no words, their voice is not heard, yet their music carries across the land, their words to the end of the earth." Beneath the silence, audible only to the inner ear, creation sings to its Creator. Words are the language of the mind. Music is the language of the soul.

15:2 עָזִּי וְזִמְרָת יָהּ *The Lord is my strength and song* – This verse is echoed in Isaiah 12:2, which is part of the Havdala service, encouraging us as we begin the new week. It could also be translated "my strength and might." The root *z-m-r* means both "to sing" and "to prune," and thus by extension "to cut off" an enemy.

Our faith is expressed in our music. When we pray, we do not read; we sing. When we engage with sacred texts, we do not recite; we chant. Every text and every time has, in Judaism, its own specific melody. There are different tunes for Shaḥarit, Minḥa, and Maariv, the morning, afternoon, and evening prayers. There are different melodies and moods for the prayers for a weekday, the Sabbath, the three pilgrimage festivals, Passover, Shavuot, and Sukkot (which have much musically in common but also tunes distinctive to each), and for the *Yamim Nora'im*, Rosh HaShana and Yom Kippur.

There are different tunes for different texts. There is one kind of cantillation for Torah, another for the *haftara* from the prophetic books, and yet another for *Ketuvim*, the Writings, especially the five Megillot. There is a particular chant for studying the texts of the written Torah, for studying Mishna and Gemara. So by music alone we can tell what kind of day it is and what kind of text is being used. There is a map of holy words and it is written in melodies and songs. Perhaps that's what prayer, faith, spirituality really are: more like poetry than prose, more like music than speech.

15:2 אֱלֹהֵי אָבִי וַאֲרֹמְמֶנְהוּ *My father's God, I will exalt Him* – What you love, your children will learn to love. And there is no other way to teach your children. It is not only what you say to them. It is not even what you do to them. It is the way your life reflects your loves. Those are the things

army / He hurled into the sea; / the best of his officers / drowned in the Sea of
5 Reeds. / The deep waters covered them; / they sank to the depths like a stone. /
6 Your right hand, LORD, majestic in power, / Your right hand, LORD, shatters
7 the enemy. / In the greatness of Your majesty, You overthrew those who rose
8 against You. / You sent forth Your rage; it consumed them like stubble. / By the
blast of Your nostrils the waters heaped; / the surge stood upright as a wall; /
9 the deeps congealed at the heart of the sea. / The enemy said, "I will give chase,
will overtake, / I will divide the spoils. / My desire shall gorge its fill of them. /
10 I will draw my sword, / and my hand destroy them." /You blew with Your
wind; the sea covered over them. / They sank like lead in mighty waters. /
11 Who is like You, LORD, among the mighty? / Who is like You – majestic in

רש"י

"מִקְרָא קֹדֶשׁ" (לעיל יב, טז): **טֻבְּעוּ.** אֵין טְבִיעָה אֶלָּא בִּמְקוֹם טִיט, כְּמוֹ: "טָבַעְתִּי בִּיוֵן מְצוּלָה" (תהלים סט, ג), "וַיִּטְבַּע יִרְמְיָהוּ בַּטִּיט" (ירמיה לח, ו), מְלַמֵּד שֶׁנַּעֲשָׂה הַיָּם טִיט, לִגְמֹל לָהֶם כְּמִדָּתָם שֶׁשִּׁעְבְּדוּ אֶת יִשְׂרָאֵל בְּחֹמֶר וּבִלְבֵנִים:

ה **יְכַסְיֻמוּ.** כְּמוֹ 'יְכַסּוּם'. וְהַיּוּ"ד הָאֶמְצָעִית יְתֵרָה בּוֹ וְדֶרֶךְ מִקְרָאוֹת בְּכָךְ, כְּמוֹ: "וּבְקָרְךָ וְצֹאנְךָ יִרְבְּיֻן" (דברים ח, יג), "יִרְוְיֻן מִדֶּשֶׁן בֵּיתֶךָ" (תהלים לו, ט), וְהַיּוּ"ד רִאשׁוֹנָה שֶׁמַּשְׁמָעָהּ לְשׁוֹן עָתִיד, כָּךְ פָּרְשֵׁהוּ: טֻבְּעוּ בְּיַם סוּף כְּדֵי שֶׁיַּחְזְרוּ הַמַּיִם וִיכַסּוּ אוֹתָן. "יְכַסְיֻמוּ" אֵין דּוֹמֶה לוֹ בַּמִּקְרָא בִּנְקֻדָּתוֹ, וְדַרְכּוֹ לִהְיוֹת נָקוּד 'יְכַסְיוּמוֹ' מְלָאפוּם: **כְּמוֹ אָבֶן.** וּבְמָקוֹם אַחֵר "צָלְלוּ כַּעוֹפֶרֶת" (להלן פסוק י), וּבְמָקוֹם אַחֵר "יֹאכְלֵמוֹ כַּקַּשׁ" (להלן פסוק ז). הָרְשָׁעִים כַּקַּשׁ הוֹלְכִים וּמִטָּרְפִין עוֹלִין וְיוֹרְדִין, בֵּינוֹנִים כָּאֶבֶן, וְהַכְּשֵׁרִים כַּעוֹפֶרֶת שֶׁנָּחוּ מִיָּד:

ו **יְמִינְךָ יְמִינְךָ.** שְׁתֵּי פְעָמִים, כְּשֶׁיִּשְׂרָאֵל עוֹשִׂין רְצוֹנוֹ שֶׁל מָקוֹם הַשְּׂמֹאל נַעֲשֵׂית יָמִין: **יְמִינְךָ ה' נֶאְדָּרִי בַּכֹּחַ.** לְהַצִּיל אֶת יִשְׂרָאֵל, וִימִינְךָ הַשֵּׁנִית "תִּרְעַץ אוֹיֵב": **נֶאְדָּרִי.** כְּמוֹ: "רַבָּתִי עָם" (איכה א, א), "שָׂרָתִי בַּמְּדִינוֹת" (שם), "גְּנֻבְתִי יוֹם" (בראשית לא, לט): **תִּרְעַץ אוֹיֵב.** תָּמִיד הִיא רוֹעֶצֶת וּמְשַׁבֶּרֶת הָאוֹיֵב, וְדוֹמֶה לוֹ: "וַיִּרְעֲצוּ וַיְרֹצְצוּ אֶת בְּנֵי יִשְׂרָאֵל", בְּשׁוֹפְטִים (י, ח):

ז **תַּהֲרֹס קָמֶיךָ.** תָּמִיד אַתָּה הוֹרֵס קָמֶיךָ הַקָּמִים נֶגְדְּךָ. וּמִי הֵם הַקָּמִים כְּנֶגְדּוֹ? אֵלּוּ הַקָּמִים עַל יִשְׂרָאֵל. וְכֵן הוּא אוֹמֵר: "כִּי הִנֵּה אוֹיְבֶיךָ יֶהֱמָיוּן" (תהלים פג, ג), וּמַה הִיא הַהֶמְיָה? "עַל עַמְּךָ יַעֲרִימוּ סוֹד" (שם פסוק ד), וְעַל זֶה קוֹרֵא אוֹתָם אוֹיְבָיו:

ח **וּבְרוּחַ אַפֶּיךָ.** הַיּוֹצֵא מִשְּׁנֵי נְחִירַיִם שֶׁל אַף. דִּבֶּר הַכָּתוּב כִּבְיָכוֹל בַּשְּׁכִינָה דֻּגְמַת מֶלֶךְ בָּשָׂר וָדָם, כְּדֵי לְהַשְׁמִיעַ אֹזֶן הַבְּרִיּוֹת כְּפִי הַהֹוֶה שֶׁיּוּכְלוּ לְהָבִין דָּבָר. כְּשֶׁאָדָם כּוֹעֵס יוֹצֵא רוּחַ מִנְּחִירָיו, וְכֵן: "עָלָה עָשָׁן בְּאַפּוֹ" (שם יח, ט), וְכֵן: "וּמֵרוּחַ אַפּוֹ יִכְלוּ" (איוב ד, ט). וְזֶהוּ שֶׁאָמַר: "לְמַעַן שְׁמִי אַאֲרִיךְ אַפִּי" (ישעיה מח, ט), כְּשֶׁזַּעְפּוֹ נָחָה נְשִׁימָתוֹ אֲרֻכָּה וּכְשֶׁהוּא כּוֹעֵס נְשִׁימָתוֹ קְצָרָה, "וּתְהִלָּתִי אֶחֱטָם לָךְ" (שם), וּלְמַעַן תְּהִלָּתִי אָשִׂים חֲטָם בְּאַפִּי לִסְתֹּם נְחִירַי בִּפְנֵי הָאַף וְהָרוּחַ שֶׁלֹּא יֵצְאוּ "לָךְ", בִּשְׁבִילְךָ. "אֶחֱטָם" כְּמוֹ 'נָאקָה בַּחֲטָם' בְּמַסֶּכֶת שַׁבָּת (דף נא ע"ב), כָּךְ נִרְאֶה בְּעֵינַי. וְכָל אַף וְחָרוֹן שֶׁבַּמִּקְרָא אֲנִי אוֹמֵר כֵּן: "חָרָה אַף" (ישעיה ה, כה) כְּמוֹ: "וְעַצְמִי חָרָה מִנִּי חֹרֶב" (איוב ל, ל) לְשׁוֹן שְׂרֵפָה וּמוֹקֵד, שֶׁהַנְּחִירַיִם מִתְחַמְּמִים וְנֶחֱרִים בְּעֵת הַקֶּצֶף, וְחָרוֹן מִגִּזְרַת חָרָה כְּמוֹ רָצוֹן מִגִּזְרַת רָצָה, וְכֵן חֵמָה לְשׁוֹן חֲמִימוּת, עַל כֵּן הוּא אוֹמֵר: "וַחֲמָתוֹ בָּעֲרָה בוֹ" (אסתר א, יב), וּבְנוֹחַ הַחֵמָה אוֹמֵר: "נִתְקָרְרָה דַּעְתּוֹ" (יבמות סג ע"א): **נֶעֶרְמוּ מַיִם.** אוּנְקְלוֹס תִּרְגֵּם לְשׁוֹן עַרְמִימוּת. וּלְשׁוֹן צַחוּת הַמִּקְרָא כְּמוֹ: "עֲרֵמַת חִטִּים" (שיר השירים ז, ג), וְ"נִצְּבוּ כְמוֹ נֵד" יוֹכִיחַ: **נֶעֶרְמוּ.** מִמּוֹקֵד רוּחַ שֶׁיָּצָא מֵאַפְּךָ יָבְשׁוּ הַמַּיִם וְהֵם נַעֲשׂוּ כְּמִין גַּלִּים וּכְרִיּוֹת שֶׁל עֲרֵמָה שֶׁהֵם גְּבוֹהִים: **כְמוֹ נֵד.** כְּתַרְגּוּמוֹ, "כְּשׁוּר", כְּחוֹמָה: **נֵד.** לְשׁוֹן צִבּוּר וְכִנּוּס, כְּמוֹ: "נֵד קָצִיר בְּיוֹם נַחֲלָה" (ישעיה יז, יא), "כֹּנֵס כַּנֵּד" (תהלים לג, ז), לֹא כָתַב 'כֹּנֵס כַּנֹּאד' אֶלָּא "כַּנֵּד", וְאִלּוּ הָיָה "כַּנֵּד" כְּמוֹ 'כַּנֹּאד' וְ'כֹנֵס' לְשׁוֹן הַכְנָסָה, הָיָה לוֹ לִכְתֹּב 'מַכְנִיס כְּבַנֹּאד מֵי הַיָּם'. אֶלָּא 'כֹּנֵס' לְשׁוֹן אוֹסֵף וְצוֹבֵר הוּא, וְכֵן: "קָמוּ נֵד אֶחָד" (יהושע ג, טז), "וַיַּעַמְדוּ נֵד אֶחָד" (שם פסוק יג), וְאֵין לְשׁוֹן קִימָה וַעֲמִידָה בְּנֹאדוֹת אֶלָּא בְּחוֹמוֹת וְצִבּוּרִים. וְלֹא מָצִינוּ 'נֹאד' נָקוּד אֶלָּא בִּמְלָאפוּם, כְּמוֹ: "שִׂימָה דִמְעָתִי בְנֹאדֶךָ" (תהלים נו, ט), "אֶת נֹאד הֶחָלָב" (שופטים ד, יט): **קָפְאוּ.** כְּמוֹ: "וְכַגְּבִנָּה תַּקְפִּיאֵנִי" (איוב י, י), שֶׁהִקְשׁוּ וְנַעֲשׂוּ כָּאֲבָנִים, וְהַמַּיִם זוֹרְקִים אֶת הַמִּצְרִים עַל הָאֶבֶן בְּכֹחַ וְנִלְחָמִים בָּם בְּכָל מִינֵי קֹשִׁי: **בְּלֶב יָם.** בְּחֹזֶק הַיָּם. וְדֶרֶךְ הַמִּקְרָאוֹת לְדַבֵּר כֵּן: "עַד לֵב הַשָּׁמַיִם" (דברים ד, יא), "בְּלֵב הָאֵלָה" (שמואל ב' יח, יד), לְשׁוֹן עִקָּרוֹ וְתָקְפּוֹ שֶׁל דָּבָר:

ט **אָמַר אוֹיֵב.** לְעַמּוֹ כְּשֶׁפִּתָּם בִּדְבָרִים, אֶרְדֹּף וְאַשִּׂיגֵם וַאֲחַלֵּק שָׁלָל עִם שָׂרַי וַעֲבָדַי: **תִּמְלָאֵמוֹ.** תִּמָּלֵא מֵהֶם: **נַפְשִׁי.** רוּחִי וּרְצוֹנִי. וְאַל תִּתְמַהּ עַל תֵּבָה הַמְדַבֶּרֶת בִּשְׁתַּיִם, "תִּמְלָאֵמוֹ" תִּמָּלֵא מֵהֶם, יֵשׁ הַרְבֵּה

ה שָׁלִשָׁיו טֻבְּעוּ בְיַם־סוּף: תְּהֹמֹת יְכַסְיֻמוּ יָרְדוּ בִמְצוֹלֹת
ו כְּמוֹ־אָבֶן: יְמִינְךָ יהוה נֶאְדָּרִי בַּכֹּחַ יְמִינְךָ
ז יהוה תִּרְעַץ אוֹיֵב: וּבְרֹב גְּאוֹנְךָ תַּהֲרֹס
ח קָמֶיךָ תְּשַׁלַּח חֲרֹנְךָ יֹאכְלֵמוֹ כַּקַּשׁ: וּבְרוּחַ
אַפֶּיךָ נֶעֶרְמוּ מַיִם נִצְּבוּ כְמוֹ־נֵד
ט נֹזְלִים קָפְאוּ תְהֹמֹת בְּלֶב־יָם: אָמַר
אוֹיֵב אֶרְדֹּף אַשִּׂיג אֲחַלֵּק שָׁלָל תִּמְלָאֵמוֹ
י נַפְשִׁי אָרִיק חַרְבִּי תּוֹרִישֵׁמוֹ יָדִי: נָשַׁפְתָּ
בְרוּחֲךָ כִּסָּמוֹ יָם צָלְלוּ כַּעוֹפֶרֶת בְּמַיִם
יא אַדִּירִים: מִי־כָמֹכָה בָּאֵלִם יהוה מִי
כָּמֹכָה נֶאְדָּר בַּקֹּדֶשׁ נוֹרָא תְהִלֹּת עֹשֵׂה

אונקלוס

גִּבָּרוֹהִי אִטְּבַעוּ בְּיַמָּא דְסוּף: ה תְּהוֹמַיָּא חֲפוֹ עֲלֵיהוֹן, נְחַתוּ לְעִמְקַיָּא כְּאַבְנָא: ו יַמִּינָךְ יְיָ, אַדִּירָא בְּחֵילָא, יַמִּינָךְ יְיָ תְּבַרַת סָנְאָה: ז וּבִסְגֵי תְקָפָךְ תַּבַּרְתָּנוּן לִדְקָמוּ עַל עַמָּךְ, שַׁלַּחְתְּ רֻגְזָךְ, שֵׁיצֵינוּן כְּנוּרָא לְקַשָּׁא: ח וּבְמֵימַר פֻּמָּךְ חֲכִימוּ מַיָּא, קָמוּ כְשׁוּר אָזְלַיָּא, קְפוֹ תְהוֹמֵי בְּלִבָּא דְיַמָּא: ט דַּהֲוָה אָמַר סָנְאָה, אֶרְדּוֹף אַדְבֵּיק אֲפַלֵּיג בִּזְתָּא, תִּסְבַּע מִנְּהוֹן נַפְשִׁי, אֶשְׁלוֹף חַרְבִּי, תְּשֵׁיצֵינוּן יְדִי: י אֲמַרְתְּ בְּמֵימְרָךְ חֲפָא עֲלֵיהוֹן יַמָּא, אִשְׁתְּקַעוּ כַּאֲבָרָא, בְּמַיִּין תַּקִּיפִין: יא לֵית בָּר מִנָּךְ אַתְּ הוּא אֱלָהָא יְיָ, לֵית אֱלָהּ אֶלָּא אַתְּ אַדִּיר בְּקֻדְשָׁא, דְּחִיל תֻּשְׁבְּחָן עָבֵיד

רש״י

כַּלָּשׁוֹן הַזֶּה: "כִּי אֶרֶץ הַנֶּגֶב נְתַתָּנִי" (שופטים א, טו) כְּמוֹ נָתַתָּ לִי; "וְלֹא יָכְלוּ דַּבְּרוֹ לְשָׁלֹם" (בראשית לז, ד) כְּמוֹ דַּבֵּר עִמּוֹ; "בָּנַי יְצָאֻנִי" (ירמיה י, כ) כְּמוֹ יָצְאוּ מִמֶּנִּי; "מִסְפַּר צְעָדַי אַגִּידֶנּוּ" (איוב לא, לז) כְּמוֹ אַגִּיד לוֹ; אַף כָּאן "תִּמְלָאֵמוֹ" תִּמָּלֵא נַפְשִׁי מֵהֶם: **אָרִיק חַרְבִּי.** אֶשְׁלֹף. וְעַל שֵׁם שֶׁהוּא מֵרִיק אֶת הַתַּעַר בִּשְׁלִיפָתוֹ וְנִשְׁאָר רֵיק נוֹפֵל בּוֹ לְשׁוֹן הֲרָקָה, כְּמוֹ: "מְרִיקִים שַׂקֵּיהֶם" (בראשית מב, לה), "וְכֵלָיו יָרִיקוּ" (ירמיה מח, יב). וְאַל תֹּאמַר, אֵין לְשׁוֹן רֵיקוּת נוֹפֵל עַל הַיּוֹצֵא אֶלָּא עַל הַתִּיק וְעַל הַשַּׂק וְעַל הַכְּלִי שֶׁיָּצָא מִמֶּנּוּ, אֲבָל לֹא עַל הַחֶרֶב וְעַל הַיַּיִן, וְלִדְחֹק וּלְפָרֵשׁ "אָרִיק חַרְבִּי" כִּלְשׁוֹן "וַיָּרֶק אֶת חֲנִיכָיו" (בראשית יד, יד), אֶזְדַּיֵּן בְּחַרְבִּי – מָצִינוּ הַלָּשׁוֹן מוּסָב אַף עַל הַיּוֹצֵא, "שֶׁמֶן תּוּרַק" (שיר השירים א, ג), "וְלֹא הוּרַק מִכְּלִי אֶל כֶּלִי" (ירמיה מח, יא), 'לֹא הוּרַק הַכְּלִי' אֵין כָּתוּב כָּאן אֶלָּא "לֹא הוּרַק הַיַּיִן מִכְּלִי אֶל כְּלִי", מָצִינוּ הַלָּשׁוֹן מוּסָב עַל הַיַּיִן, וְכֵן: "וְהֵרִיקוּ חַרְבוֹתָם עַל יְפִי חָכְמָתֶךָ" (יחזקאל כח, ז) דְּחִירָם: **תּוֹרִישֵׁמוֹ.** לְשׁוֹן רִישׁוּת וְדַלּוּת, כְּמוֹ: "מוֹרִישׁ וּמַעֲשִׁיר" (שמואל א׳ ב, ז):

י **נָשַׁפְתָּ.** לְשׁוֹן הֲפָחָה, וְכֵן "וְגַם נָשַׁף בָּהֶם" (ישעיה מ, כד): **צָלְלוּ.** שָׁקְעוּ, עָמְקוּ, לְשׁוֹן "מְצוּלָה": **כַּעוֹפֶרֶת.** אֲבָר, פלו"ס בְּלַעַז:

יא **בָּאֵלִם.** בַּחֲזָקִים, כְּמוֹ: "וְאֶת אֵילֵי הָאָרֶץ לָקָח" (יחזקאל יז, יג), "אֱיָלוּתִי לְעֶזְרָתִי חוּשָׁה" (תהלים כב, כ): **נוֹרָא תְהִלֹּת.** יָרֵאוּי מִלְּהַגִּיד תְּהִלּוֹתֶיךָ פֶּן יִמְעֲטוּ, עַל כֵּן: "לְךָ דֻמִיָּה תְהִלָּה" (שם סה, ב):

15:11 נוֹרָא תְהִלֹּת *Awesome in glory* – One of the many, many Hebrew words for praise. In one sentence alone, the Siddur mentions *lehodot, lehallel, leshabe'aḥ, lefa'er, leromem, lehader, levarekh, le'aleh, ulekales*. To be a Jew is to live amidst the praise

12 holiness, / awesome in glory, working wonders? / You reached out Your right
13 hand – / the earth swallowed them up. / In Your love, You guided out the
people You redeemed. / In Your strength, You led them to Your holy abode. /
14 15 Nations heard and they trembled; / terror seized the Philistines. / The chiefs
of Edom were dismayed, then, / Moav's leaders were seized with trembling, /
16 the people of Canaan melted away. / Dread, terror fell upon them; / by Your
arm's power they were stilled as stone – / until Your people crossed, Lord, /
17 until the people You acquired crossed over. / You will bring them, You will
plant them on the mountain, Your heritage – / the place, Lord, that You made

רש"י

יב| **נָטִיתָ יְמִינְךָ.** כשהקדוש ברוך הוא נוטה ידו הרשעים כלים ונופלים, לפי שהכל נתון בידו ונופלים בהטייתה, וכן הוא אומר: "וה' יטה ידו וכשל עוזר ונפל עזר" (ישעיה לא, ג). משל לכלי זכוכית הנתונים ביד אדם, מטה ידו מעט והם נופלים ומשתברים: **תִּבְלָעֵמוֹ אָרֶץ.** מכאן שזכו לקבורה, בשכר שאמרו: "ה' הצדיק" (לעיל ט, כז):

יג| **נֵהַלְתָּ.** לשון מנהל. ואונקלוס תרגם לשון נושא וסובל, ולא דקדק לפרש אחר לשון העברית:

יד| **יִרְגָּזוּן.** מתרגזין: **יֹשְׁבֵי פְּלָשֶׁת.** מפני שהרגו את בני אפרים שמהרו את הקץ ויצאו בחזקה, כמפורש בדברי הימים (א' ז, כא): "והרגום אנשי גת":

טו| **אַלּוּפֵי אֱדוֹם אֵילֵי מוֹאָב.** והלא לא היה להם לירא כלום, שהרי לא עליהם הולכים? אלא מפני אנינות שהיו מתאוננים ומצטערים על כבודם של ישראל: **נָמֹגוּ.** נמסו, כמו: "ברביבים תמוגגנה" (תהלים סה, יח), אמרו: עלינו הם באים לכלותינו ולירש את ארצנו:

טז| **תִּפֹּל עֲלֵיהֶם אֵימָתָה.** על הרחוקים: **וָפַחַד.** על הקרובים, כענין שנאמר: "כי שמענו את אשר הוביש" וגו' (יהושע ב, י): **עַד יַעֲבֹר... עַד יַעֲבֹר.** כתרגומו: **קָנִיתָ.** חבבת משאר אומות, כחפץ הקנוי בדמים יקרים שחביב על האדם:

יז-יח| **תְּבִאֵמוֹ.** נתנבא משה שלא יכנס לארץ, לכך לא נאמר 'תביאנו': **מָכוֹן לְשִׁבְתְּךָ.** מקדש של מטה מכוון כנגד כסא של מעלה אשר "פעלת": **מִקְּדָשׁ.** הטעם עליו זקף גדול להפרידו מתבת השם שלאחריו, המקדש אשר כוננו ידיך ה'. חביב בית המקדש, שהעולם נברא ביד אחת, שנאמר "אף ידי יסדה ארץ" (ישעיה מח, יג), ומקדש בשתי ידים. ואימתי יבנה בשתי ידים? בזמן שה' ימלך לעלם ועד, לעתיד לבא שכל המלוכה שלו, ו"לעלם ועד" לשון עולמית הוא והוי"ו בו יסוד, לפיכך היא פתוחה, אבל "ואנכי היודע ועד" (ירמיה כט, כג) שהוי"ו בו שמוש, קמוצה היא:

In the prison of his days
Teach the free man how to praise.

15:13 **נָחִיתָ בְחַסְדְּךָ... נֵהַלְתָּ בְעָזְּךָ** *In Your love, You guided.... In Your strength, You led* – Both phrases are suggestive of a shepherd leading his sheep, and indeed, both are echoed in Psalm 23, "The Lord is my Shepherd." The contrast is striking between the military images of God acting against the enemies of His people, and the pastoral imagery here of God's tender concern for His people, His flock. The assertion that immediately follows, that the people of the land would be terrified when they heard of the miracle at the Reed Sea, was confirmed by later reports in the days of Yehoshua (Josh. 2:9–11).

15:17 **מִקְּדָשׁ אֲדֹנָי כּוֹנְנוּ יָדֶיךָ** *The Sanctuary... that Your hands established* – The building of the Temple by Shlomo, begun "in the four hundred and eightieth year after the Israelites left Egypt" (I Kings 6:1), is the only event in the history of Israel to be dated by reference to the exodus. And here, as the Israelites cross the Reed Sea, they end their song by looking forward to the building of the Temple.

The Temple was the symbol of the presence of God among a people that had established itself as a sovereign power in its own land. The building of the Temple was thus the final act in the drama begun by the exodus, and brought it to closure.

יב יג פֶלֶא: נָטִיתָ יְמִינְךָ תִּבְלָעֵמוֹ אָרֶץ: נָחִיתָ
בְחַסְדְּךָ עַם־זוּ גָּאָלְתָּ נֵהַלְתָּ בְעָזְּךָ אֶל־נְוֵה
יד קָדְשֶׁךָ: שָׁמְעוּ עַמִּים יִרְגָּזוּן חִיל
טו אָחַז יֹשְׁבֵי פְּלָשֶׁת: אָז נִבְהֲלוּ אַלּוּפֵי
אֱדוֹם אֵילֵי מוֹאָב יֹאחֲזֵמוֹ רָעַד נָמֹגוּ
טז כֹּל יֹשְׁבֵי כְנָעַן: תִּפֹּל עֲלֵיהֶם אֵימָתָה
וָפַחַד בִּגְדֹל זְרוֹעֲךָ יִדְּמוּ כָּאָבֶן עַד־
יַעֲבֹר עַמְּךָ יהוה עַד־יַעֲבֹר עַם־זוּ
יז קָנִיתָ: תְּבִאֵמוֹ וְתִטָּעֵמוֹ בְּהַר נַחֲלָתְךָ מָכוֹן
לְשִׁבְתְּךָ פָּעַלְתָּ יהוה מִקְּדָשׁ אֲדֹנָי כּוֹנְנוּ

אונקלוס

פְּרִישָׁן: יב אֲרֵימְתְּ יְמִינָךְ, בְּלַעְתְּנוּן אַרְעָא: יג דַּבַּרְהִי בְּטָבְוָתָךְ לְעַמָּא
דְּנָן דִּפְרַקְתָּא, סוֹבַרְהִי בְּתֻקְפָּךְ לְדֵירָא דְקֻדְשָׁךְ: יד שְׁמַעוּ עַמְמַיָּא
וְזָעוּ, דַּחְלָא אֲחַדְתִּנּוּן, לְדָהֲווֹ יָתְבִין בִּפְלָשֶׁת: טו בְּכֵן אִתְבְּהִילוּ
רַבְרְבֵי אֱדוֹם, תַּקִּיפֵי מוֹאָב, אֲחַדְנוּן רְתֵיתָא, אִתְּבָרוּ, כֹּל דַּהֲווֹ
יָתְבִין בִּכְנָעַן: טז תִּפֵּיל עֲלֵיהוֹן אֵימְתָא וְדַחְלְתָא, בִּסְגֵי תְקָפָךְ
יִשְׁתְּקוּן כְּאַבְנָא, עַד דְּיִעְבַּר עַמָּךְ יי יָת אַרְנוֹנָא, עַד דְּיִעְבַּר, עַמָּא
דְּנָן דִּפְרַקְתָּא יָת יַרְדְּנָא: יז תַּעֵילִנּוּן, וְתַשְׁרֵינוּן בְּטוּרָא דְאַחְסָנְתָךְ,
אֲתַר לְבֵית שְׁכִינְתָךְ, אַתְקֵינְתָּא יי, מַקְדְּשָׁא, יי אַתְקְנָהִי

of God. It is the air our spirit breathes, the music the Jewish soul sings. We gave the English language the word *halleluya*, "praise be to God," and the book of Psalms remains the most beautiful poetry of praise ever written.

Jewish prayer always starts with praise. It takes different forms in different services, but it is always there before anything else. Why? Because on the bad days we can be distracted by worry, depressed by anxiety, clouded by fear. We turn in on ourselves, as if we were shut in a small, airless room, unable to see the sunlight or breathe the free air.

Which is why prayer as praise is so important. It says: Don't look in; look out. Don't look down; look up. The world is full of light, said the Jewish mystics, if we only know how to open our eyes. The Psalms are a symphony of praise. They say: See the glory of creation. Look at all the beauty that surrounds you. Listen to the song of a bird. Look carefully at the beauty of a tree, its leaves shimmering in the breeze. Pause and inhale the sheer miracle of being. Remind yourself, slowly, gently: I am here. The universe is here. I am alive. I am free. I am capable of love and I am loved. And I will praise the force that made all this and allowed me to be here and see it.

Then feel the restlessness subside, the striving cease, the pulse slow, and know for a moment the sheer blessedness of being. It is there, waiting to be uncovered, in the secret places of the soul. Praise is where the journey into happiness begins.

Among my favorite lines of poetry are the words of W. H. Auden about the power of the imagination to liberate us from negative emotion:

In the desert of the heart
Let the healing fountain start.

18 for Your dwelling, / the Sanctuary, Lord, that Your hands established. / The
19 Lord will reign for ever and all time. // This they sang when Pharaoh's horses,
chariots, and cavalry had gone into the sea / and the Lord had brought the
waters of the sea back over them / while the Israelites had walked on dry land
through the sea.

20 Then Miriam, the prophetess, sister of Aharon, took a tambourine in her hand,
21 and all the women followed her with tambourines and dance. And Miriam led
them in song: Sing to the Lord, for He has triumphed in glory; / horse and
22 horseman He hurled into the sea. Moshe then led the Israelites from
the Sea of Reeds out into the desert of Shur. For three days, they journeyed
23 across the desert without finding water. Eventually they came to Mara, but
they could not drink the water there because it was bitter; because of this it

רש״י

יט **כִּי בָא סוּס פַּרְעֹה.** כַּאֲשֶׁר בָּא סוּס פַּרְעֹה וְגוֹ׳:

כ **וַתִּקַּח מִרְיָם הַנְּבִיאָה.** הֵיכָן נִתְנַבְּאָה? כְּשֶׁהָיְתָה ״אֲחוֹת אַהֲרֹן״ קֹדֶם שֶׁנּוֹלַד מֹשֶׁה. אָמְרָה: עֲתִידָה אִמִּי שֶׁתֵּלֵד בֵּן וְכוּ׳ כִּדְאִיתָא בְּסוֹטָה (דף יב ע״ב). דָּבָר אַחֵר, ״אֲחוֹת אַהֲרֹן״, לְפִי שֶׁמָּסַר נַפְשׁוֹ עָלֶיהָ כְּשֶׁנִּצְטָרְעָה נִקְרֵאת עַל שְׁמוֹ: **אֶת הַתֹּף.** כְּלִי שֶׁל מִינֵי זֶמֶר: **בְּתֻפִּים וּבִמְחֹלֹת.** מֻבְטָחוֹת הָיוּ צַדְקָנִיּוֹת שֶׁבַּדּוֹר שֶׁהַקָּדוֹשׁ בָּרוּךְ הוּא עוֹשֶׂה לָהֶם נִסִּים, וְהוֹצִיאוּ תֻּפִּים מִמִּצְרַיִם:

כא **וַתַּעַן לָהֶם מִרְיָם.** מֹשֶׁה אָמַר שִׁירָה לָאֲנָשִׁים, הוּא אוֹמֵר וְהֵם עוֹנִין אַחֲרָיו, וּמִרְיָם אָמְרָה שִׁירָה לַנָּשִׁים:

כב **וַיַּסַּע מֹשֶׁה.** הִסִּיעָן בְּעַל כָּרְחָם, שֶׁעִטְּרוּ מִצְרַיִם אֶת סוּסֵיהֶם בְּתַכְשִׁיטֵי זָהָב וָכֶסֶף וַאֲבָנִים טוֹבוֹת, וְהָיוּ יִשְׂרָאֵל מוֹצְאִין אוֹתָן בַּיָּם. וּגְדוֹלָה הָיְתָה בִּזַּת הַיָּם מִבִּזַּת מִצְרַיִם, שֶׁנֶּאֱמַר: ״תּוֹרֵי זָהָב נַעֲשֶׂה לָּךְ עִם נְקֻדּוֹת הַכָּסֶף״ (שיר השירים א, יא), לְפִיכָךְ הֻצְרַךְ לְהַסִּיעָן בְּעַל כָּרְחָם:

כג **וַיָּבֹאוּ מָרָתָה.** כְּמוֹ ׳לְמָרָה׳, הֵ״א בְּסוֹף תֵּבָה בִּמְקוֹם לָמֶ״ד בִּתְחִלָּתָהּ, וְהַתָּי״ו הִיא בִּמְקוֹם הֵ״א הַנִּשְׁרֶשֶׁת בְּתֵבַת מָרָה, וּבִסְמִיכָתָהּ, כְּשֶׁהִיא נִדְבֶּקֶת לַהֵ״א שֶׁהוּא מוֹסִיף בִּמְקוֹם הַלָּמֶ״ד, תֵּהָפֵךְ הֵ״א שֶׁל שֹׁרֶשׁ לְתָי״ו. וְכֵן כָּל הֵ״א שֶׁהִיא שֹׁרֶשׁ בִּנְקֵבָה תֵּהָפֵךְ לְתָי״ו בִּסְמִיכָתָהּ,

through the plagues, but at the same time gives him the "strength" or "hardness" of heart to disbelieve. And in our *parasha*, God demonstrates His presence to the Israelites at the division of the Reed Sea: they "see" and therefore "believe," yet here in the very next passage they are rebellious again. The faith that requires this kind of confirmation is not faith.

A fundamental axiom of Torah is that God is not seen but heard. He is not to be found in "objective" history (events as they are grasped by the senses) but in covenantal history (events as they are perceived through the "word" of faith). Genesis is a set of variations on the dissonance between the divine word (the promise of children and a land) and empirical reality (the childlessness of the matriarchs and the landlessness of the patriarchs).

The only empirical claim the Torah makes about itself is that the people who live by its covenant will, obscurely but unmistakably, testify to the presence of God in history. This I believe to be true.

One of the great Enlightenment ideas is that texts (religious texts especially) are a veil covering a pristine core of historical truth, which must be removed if objectivity is to be arrived at. This is a way not of reading the Bible but of misreading it, to which the most eloquent commentary is the Bible itself. God is not seen with the senses but heard with the ear of faith. He is, to use Buber's terms, not in the "It" of empiricism but the "Thou" of relationship: the relationship of loyalty, fidelity, and trust whose formal expression is covenant.

יח יט יְדִיד: יהוה ׀ יִמְלֹךְ לְעֹלָם וָעֶד: כִּי
בָא סוּס פַּרְעֹה בְּרִכְבּוֹ וּבְפָרָשָׁיו בַּיָּם וַיָּשֶׁב יהוה עֲלֵהֶם אֶת־מֵי
הַיָּם וּבְנֵי יִשְׂרָאֵל הָלְכוּ בַיַּבָּשָׁה בְּתוֹךְ הַיָּם:

כ וַתִּקַּח מִרְיָם הַנְּבִיאָה אֲחוֹת אַהֲרֹן אֶת־הַתֹּף בְּיָדָהּ וַתֵּצֶאןָ כָל־הַנָּשִׁים
כא אַחֲרֶיהָ בְּתֻפִּים וּבִמְחֹלֹת: וַתַּעַן לָהֶם מִרְיָם שִׁירוּ לַיהוה כִּי־גָאֹה
כב גָּאָה סוּס וְרֹכְבוֹ רָמָה בַיָּם: וַיַּסַּע מֹשֶׁה אֶת־יִשְׂרָאֵל מִיַּם־
סוּף וַיֵּצְאוּ אֶל־מִדְבַּר־שׁוּר וַיֵּלְכוּ שְׁלֹשֶׁת־יָמִים בַּמִּדְבָּר וְלֹא־מָצְאוּ
כג מָיִם: וַיָּבֹאוּ מָרָתָה וְלֹא יָכְלוּ לִשְׁתֹּת מַיִם מִמָּרָה כִּי מָרִים הֵם עַל־כֵּן

אונקלוס

יְדָךְ: יח יי מַלְכוּתֵיהּ קָאֵים לְעָלַם וּלְעָלְמֵי עָלְמַיָּא: יט אֲרֵי עָאלוּ סוּסָוָת פַּרְעֹה, בִּרְתִכּוֹהִי וּבְפָרָשׁוֹהִי בְּיַמָּא, וַאֲתֵיב יי, עֲלֵיהוֹן יָת מֵי יַמָּא, וּבְנֵי יִשְׂרָאֵל, הַלִּיכוּ בְּיַבֶּשְׁתָּא בְּגוֹ יַמָּא: כ וּנְסֵיבַת מִרְיָם נְבִיאֲתָא, אֲחָתֵיהּ דְּאַהֲרֹן, יָת תֻּפָּא בִּידַהּ, וּנְפַקָא כָל נְשַׁיָּא בַּתְרַהָא, בְּתֻפִּין וּבְחִנְגִּין: כא וּמְעַנְיָא לְהוֹן מִרְיָם, שַׁבַּחוּ וְאוֹדוּ קֳדָם יי אֲרֵי אִתְגָּאִי עַל גֵּיוְתָנַיָּא וְגֵיאוּתָא דִּילֵיהּ הִיא, סוּסְיָא וְרָכְבֵיהּ רְמָא בְיַמָּא: כב וְאַטֵּיל מֹשֶׁה יָת יִשְׂרָאֵל מִיַּמָּא דְסוּף, וּנְפַקוּ לְמַדְבְּרָא דְחַגְרָא, וַאֲזַלוּ תְּלָתָא יוֹמִין, בְּמַדְבְּרָא וְלָא אַשְׁכַּחוּ מַיָּא: כג וַאֲתוֹ לְמָרָה, וְלָא יְכִילוּ, לְמִשְׁתֵּי מַיָּא מִמָּרָה, אֲרֵי מְרִירִין אִנּוּן, עַל כֵּן

15:18 יהוה יִמְלֹךְ לְעֹלָם וָעֶד *The Lord will reign for ever* – A key verse, marking the first time in the Torah that God has been described as a king. Crossing the sea has been for the Israelites not just a miraculous experience, nor merely an escape from defeat and death, but also a fundamental rite of passage: Israel has become the nation whose sovereign is God Himself.

15:19 וּבְנֵי יִשְׂרָאֵל הָלְכוּ בַיַּבָּשָׁה בְּתוֹךְ הַיָּם *The Israelites had walked on dry land through the sea* – Emil Fackenheim has spoken of "epoch-making events" that transform the course of history. The French philosopher Alain Badiou has similarly proposed the concept of an "event" as a "rupture in ontology" through which individuals are brought face to face with a truth that changes them and their world. It is as if all normal perception fades away and we know that we are in the presence of something momentous, to which we sense we must remain faithful for the rest of our lives. It is through transformative events that we feel ourselves addressed, summoned, by something beyond history, breaking through into history. In this sense, the division of the Reed Sea was something other and deeper than a suspension of the laws of nature. It was the transformative moment at which the people "were in awe of the Lord, and they believed in Him and in Moshe His servant" (Ex. 14:31) and called themselves "the people You acquired" (15:16).

15:22 שְׁלֹשֶׁת־יָמִים *Three days* – This is how long it takes, from the euphoric moment when the people "witnessed the wondrous power the Lord had unleashed against the Egyptians … and they believed in Him and in Moshe His servant" (Ex. 14:31) for their doubts to spill out into protest.

Two of the most powerful parodies of the "scientific" approach to faith (what is believable is only that which is empirically confirmed) are contained in the book of Exodus. God "empirically" confirms His existence to Pharaoh

24 was named Mara. The people railed against Moshe – "What are we to drink?"
25 Moshe cried out to the LORD. And the LORD showed him a piece of wood,
which he threw into the water – and the water became sweet. It was there that
the LORD gave His people decree and law; it was there that He put them to the
26 test. He said, "If you listen faithfully to the voice of the LORD your God, doing
what is right in His eyes, heeding His commands and keeping His decrees, I
will not bring on you any of the sicknesses I brought on the Egyptians, for I
27 am the LORD – your Healer." And then they arrived at Eilim, where HAMISHI
there were twelve springs and seventy date palms. They encamped there by
16 1 the water. They set out from Eilim, and on the fifteenth day of the second
month after leaving Egypt, the congregation of Israel all arrived at the desert of

רש"י

כמו: "חמה אין לי" (ישעיה כז, ד), "וחמתו בערה בו" (אסתר א, יב), הרי ה"א של שרש נהפכה לתי"ו מפני שנסמכה על הוי"ו הנוספת. וכן: "עבד ואמה" (ויקרא כה, מד), "הנה אמתי בלהה" (בראשית ל, ג); "לנפש חיה" (שם ב, ז), "וזהמתו חיתו לחם" (איוב לג, כ); "בין הרמה" (שופטים ד, ה), "ותשבתו הרמתה" (שמואל א' ז, יז):

כד **וילנו.** לשון נפעלו הוא. וכן התרגום לשון נפעלו הוא, "ואתרעמו". וכן דרך לשון תלונה להסב הדבור אל האדם: מתלונן, מתרועם, ולא יאמר: לונן, רועם. וכן יאמר הלועז דקומפלינ"ט ש"יי, מסב הדבור אליו באמרו ש"יי:

כה **שם שם לו.** במרה נתן להם מקצת פרשיות של תורה שיתעסקו בהם: שבת ופרה אדמה ודינין: **ושם נסהו.** לעם, וראה קשי ערפו שלא נמלכו במשה בלשון יפה: בקש עלינו שיהיו לנו מים לשתות, אלא נתלוננו:

כו **אם שמוע תשמע.** זו קבלה שיקבלו עליהם: **תעשה.** היא עשיה:

והאזנת. תטה אזנים לדקדק בהם: **כל חקיו.** דברים שאינן אלא גזרת מלך בלא שום טעם, ויצר הרע מקנטר עליהם, מה איסור באלו? למה נאסרו? כגון לבישת כלאים ואכילת חזיר ופרה אדמה וכיוצא בהם: **לא אשים עליך.** ואם אשים הרי היא כלא הושמה, "כי אני ה' רפאך". ולפי פשוטו, "כי אני ה' רפאך" המלמדך תורה ומצות למען תנצל מהם, כרופא הזה האומר לאדם: אל תאכל דבר זה פן יביאך לידי חלי זה. וכן הוא אומר: "רפאות תהי לשרך" (משלי ג, ח):

כז **שתים עשרה עינת מים.** כנגד שנים עשר שבטים נזדמנו להם: **ושבעים תמרים.** כנגד שבעים זקנים:

טז א **בחמשה עשר יום.** נתפרש היום של חניה זו לפי שבו ביום כלתה החררה שהוציאו ממצרים והצרכו למן, ללמדנו שאכלו משירי הבצק ששים ואחת סעודות, וירד להם מן בששה עשר באייר, ויום אחד בשבת היה, כדאיתא במסכת שבת (דף פז ע"ב):

23:15), meaning Sunday. To them, it celebrated the freedom of being in the wilderness and receiving sustenance from heaven by a miracle.

The Pharisees, however, link the counting of the Omer not to the beginning, but to the end of the period of the manna (Josh. 5:11–12, "On the day after the Passover sacrifice, they ate of the yield of the land.... The manna stopped *falling the day after they had eaten from the yield of the* land"). To them, freedom means building a society, creating farms, plowing the land, producing our own food. The Zohar, indeed, calls manna *nahama dekisufa*, the bread of shame. Why? Because we did not work for it.

We should not need miracles, nor should we rely on them. Judaism is a religion that celebrates law: the natural law that governs the physical universe, and the moral law that governs the human universe. God is found in order, not in the miraculous suspension of that order. Faith is about seeing the miraculous in the everyday, not about waiting every day for the miraculous.

כד כה קָרָא־שְׁמָהּ מָרָה: וַיִּלֹּנוּ הָעָם עַל־מֹשֶׁה לֵּאמֹר מַה־נִּשְׁתֶּה: וַיִּצְעַק
אֶל־יהוה וַיּוֹרֵהוּ יהוה עֵץ וַיַּשְׁלֵךְ אֶל־הַמַּיִם וַיִּמְתְּקוּ הַמָּיִם שָׁם שָׂם
כו לוֹ חֹק וּמִשְׁפָּט וְשָׁם נִסָּהוּ: וַיֹּאמֶר אִם־שָׁמוֹעַ תִּשְׁמַע לְקוֹל ׀ יהוה
אֱלֹהֶיךָ וְהַיָּשָׁר בְּעֵינָיו תַּעֲשֶׂה וְהַאֲזַנְתָּ לְמִצְוֺתָיו וְשָׁמַרְתָּ כָּל־חֻקָּיו
כָּל־הַמַּחֲלָה אֲשֶׁר־שַׂמְתִּי בְמִצְרַיִם לֹא־אָשִׂים עָלֶיךָ כִּי אֲנִי יהוה
כז רֹפְאֶךָ: וַיָּבֹאוּ אֵילִמָה וְשָׁם שְׁתֵּים עֶשְׂרֵה עֵינֹת מַיִם וְשִׁבְעִים חמישי
טז א תְּמָרִים וַיַּחֲנוּ־שָׁם עַל־הַמָּיִם: וַיִּסְעוּ מֵאֵילִם וַיָּבֹאוּ כָּל־עֲדַת בְּנֵי־
יִשְׂרָאֵל אֶל־מִדְבַּר־סִין אֲשֶׁר בֵּין־אֵילִם וּבֵין סִינָי בַּחֲמִשָּׁה עָשָׂר יוֹם

אונקלוס

קְרָא שְׁמַהּ מָרָה: כד וְאִתְרָעַמוּ עַמָּא, עַל מֹשֶׁה לְמֵימַר מָא נִשְׁתֵּי: כה וְצַלִּי קֳדָם יי, וְאַלְפֵיהּ יי אָעָא, וּרְמָא לְמַיָּא, וּבְסִימוּ מַיָּא, תַּמָּן גְּזַר לֵיהּ, קְיָם וְדִין וְתַמָּן נַסְּיֵיהּ: כו וַאֲמַר אִם קַבָּלָא תְקַבֵּיל, לְמֵימְרָא דַּיי אֱלָהָךְ, וּדְכָשַׁר קֳדָמוֹהִי תַּעְבֵּיד, וּתְצִית לְפִקּוֹדוֹהִי, וְתִטַּר כָּל קְיָמוֹהִי, כָּל מַרְעִין, דְּשַׁוִּיתִי בְּמִצְרַיִם לָא אֲשַׁוֵּינוּן עֲלָךְ, אֲרֵי, אֲנָא יי אָסְךְ: כז וַאֲתוֹ לְאֵילִים, וְתַמָּן, תְּרֵי עֲסַר, מַבּוּעִין דְּמַיִין וְשִׁבְעִין דִּקְלִין, וּשְׁרוֹ תַמָּן עַל מַיָּא: טז א וּנְטַלוּ מֵאֵילִים, וַאֲתוֹ, כָּל כְּנִשְׁתָּא דִּבְנֵי יִשְׂרָאֵל לְמַדְבְּרָא דְסִין, דְּבֵין אֵילִים וּבֵין סִינָי, בַּחֲמֵישַׁת עַסְרָא יוֹמָא

15:25 וַיּוֹרֵהוּ יהוה עֵץ וַיַּשְׁלֵךְ אֶל־הַמַּיִם *The LORD showed him a piece of wood, which he threw into the water* – One would not expect that further "polluting" the water would make it fit for drinking. A beautiful midrash explores the symbolism of this event: "See how different are the ways of God from the ways of flesh and blood. Flesh and blood seek to use sweetness to heal bitterness. But the One at whose word the world became – He is not so. Rather, He uses bitterness to heal bitterness. How so? He places the thing that harms into the thing that is harmed – and uses it to perform a miracle" (Mekhilta). We often seek to "cure" suffering through distraction and denial. That is not God's way. Pain and loneliness are forms of energy that can be transformed if we turn them outward, using them to recognize and redeem someone else's pain and loneliness. To heal where others harm, mend where others destroy, to redeem evil by turning its negative energies to good: these are the mark of the ethics of responsibility, born in the radical faith that God calls on us to exercise our freedom by becoming His partners in the work of creation. "Good represents the reality of which God is the dream," wrote Iris Murdoch. And in the words of W. B. Yeats, "In dreams begin responsibilities." Among many survivors of unspeakable tragedy I sense an extraordinary gesture of *tikkun*, mending. When we face up to evil courageously, as free people, we find that though it can never be justified as the will of God, it can in some ways be redeemed. Perhaps this is the message the Sages heard in this brief story, just days after the end of the people's centuries-long slavery.

16:1 בַּחֲמִשָּׁה עָשָׂר יוֹם לַחֹדֶשׁ הַשֵּׁנִי *The fifteenth day of the second month* – This was one month after leaving Egypt. Rashi explains: "Because that was the day the supply of matza ran out and they needed food… and the manna fell on the sixteenth [of Iyar], and that was Sunday."

The timing mentioned here, as we shall later see, appears to be the reason behind the Sadducee ruling that we begin the counting of the Omer "the day after the Sabbath" (Lev.

2 Sin, between Eilim and Sinai. In the desert, all the community started railing
3 against Moshe and Aharon. The Israelites said to them, "If only we had died by
the LORD's hand in Egypt, when we sat by the fleshpots and ate our fill of bread.
Instead, you have brought us out into this desert to kill the entire assembly
4 by starvation." Then the LORD said to Moshe, "I am going to rain
down bread from heaven. Let the people go out and gather enough for each
5 day; I will test them to see whether they will follow My law or not. On the
sixth day, they will have to prepare what they bring in. It will be twice as much
6 as they gather on all other days." So Moshe and Aharon told all the Israelites,
"At evening you will know that it was the LORD who brought you out of Egypt,
7 and by morning you shall see the LORD's glory, for He has heard you railing
8 against Him. As for us, what are we that you rail against us?" Then Moshe said,
"In the evening, the LORD will give you meat to eat, and in the morning bread
to fill you, for He has heard you railing against Him. We – what are we? It is
9 not us you rail against, but the LORD." Then Moshe said to Aharon, "Tell all
the community of Israel to come before the LORD, because He has heard your
10 railing." As soon as Aharon had spoken to the whole community of Israel, they
looked toward the desert – and the glory of the LORD appeared in the midst of
cloud.

רש״י

ב **וַיִּלּוֹנוּ.** לְפִי שֶׁכָּלָה הַלֶּחֶם:

ג **מִי יִתֵּן מוּתֵנוּ.** שֶׁנָּמוּת. וְאֵינוֹ שֵׁם דָּבָר כְּמוֹ ׳מוֹתֵנוּ׳, אֶלָּא כְּמוֹ: עֲשׂוֹתֵנוּ, חֲנוֹתֵנוּ, שׁוּבֵנוּ – לַעֲשׂוֹת אֲנַחְנוּ, לַחֲנוֹת אֲנַחְנוּ, לָמוּת אֲנַחְנוּ. ״לְוַי דְּמִיתְנָא״ – לוּ מַתְנוּ, הַלְוַאי וְהָיִינוּ מֵתִים:

ד **דְּבַר יוֹם בְּיוֹמוֹ.** צֹרֶךְ אֲכִילַת יוֹם יִלְקְטוּ בְּיוֹמוֹ, וְלֹא יִלְקְטוּ הַיּוֹם לְצֹרֶךְ מָחָר: **לְמַעַן אֲנַסֶּנּוּ.** כִּי אֲנַסֶּנּוּ ״הֲיֵלֵךְ בְּתוֹרָתִי״, אִם יִשְׁמְרוּ מִצְוֹת הַתְּלוּיוֹת בּוֹ, שֶׁלֹּא יוֹתִירוּ מִמֶּנּוּ וְלֹא יֵצְאוּ בְּשַׁבָּת לִלְקֹט:

ה **וְהָיָה מִשְׁנֶה.** לַיּוֹם וְלַמָּחֳרָת: **מִשְׁנֶה.** עַל שֶׁהָיוּ רְגִילִים לִלְקֹט יוֹם יוֹם שֶׁל שְׁאָר יְמוֹת הַשָּׁבוּעַ:

ו **עֶרֶב.** כְּמוֹ לָעֶרֶב: **וִידַעְתֶּם כִּי ה׳ הוֹצִיא אֶתְכֶם מֵאֶרֶץ מִצְרָיִם.** לְפִי שֶׁאֲמַרְתֶּם לָנוּ: ״כִּי הוֹצֵאתֶם אֹתָנוּ״ (לעיל פסוק ג), תֵּדְעוּ כִּי לֹא אֲנַחְנוּ הַמּוֹצִיאִים אֶלָּא ה׳ הוֹצִיא אֶתְכֶם, שֶׁיָּגִיז לָכֶם אֶת הַשְּׂלָו:

ז **וּבֹקֶר וּרְאִיתֶם.** לֹא עַל הַכָּבוֹד שֶׁנֶּאֱמַר: ״וְהִנֵּה כְּבוֹד ה׳ נִרְאָה בֶּעָנָן״ (להלן פסוק י) נֶאֱמַר, אֶלָּא כָּךְ אָמַר לָהֶם: עֶרֶב וִידַעְתֶּם כִּי הַיְּכֹלֶת בְּיָדוֹ לִתֵּן תַּאֲוַתְכֶם, וּבָשָׂר יִתֵּן, אַךְ לֹא בְּפָנִים מְאִירוֹת יִתְּנֶנּוּ לָכֶם, כִּי שֶׁלֹּא כַּהֹגֶן שְׁאַלְתֶּם אוֹתוֹ, וּמִכָּרֵס מְלֵאָה. וְהַלֶּחֶם שֶׁשְּׁאַלְתֶּם לְצֹרֶךְ, בִּירִידָתוֹ לַבֹּקֶר תִּרְאוּ אֶת כְּבוֹד אוֹר פָּנָיו, שֶׁיּוֹרִידֵהוּ לָכֶם דֶּרֶךְ חִבָּה בַּבֹּקֶר שֶׁיֵּשׁ שָׁהוּת לַהֲכִינוֹ, וְטַל מִלְמַעְלָה וְטַל מִלְמַטָּה כְּמֻנָּח בְּקֻפְסָא: **אֶת תְּלֻנֹּתֵיכֶם עַל ה׳.** כְּמוֹ אֲשֶׁר עַל ה׳: **וְנַחְנוּ מָה.** מָה אֲנַחְנוּ חֲשׁוּבִין: **כִּי תַלִּינוּ עָלֵינוּ.** שֶׁתַּרְעִימוּ עָלֵינוּ אֶת הַכֹּל, אֶת בְּנֵיכֶם וּנְשֵׁיכֶם וּבְנוֹתֵיכֶם וְעֵרֶב רַב. וְעַל כָּרְחִי אֲנִי זָקוּק לְפָרֵשׁ ״תַּלִּינוּ״ בִּלְשׁוֹן תַּפְעִילוּ, מִפְּנֵי דָּגֵשׁוּתוֹ וּקְרִיָּתוֹ. שֶׁאִלּוּ הָיָה רָפֶה הָיִיתִי מְפָרְשׁוֹ בִּלְשׁוֹן תִּפְעֲלוּ, כְּמוֹ: ״וַיָּלֶן הָעָם עַל מֹשֶׁה״ (להלן יז, ג), אוֹ אִם הָיָה דָּגוּשׁ וְאֵין בּוֹ יוּ״ד וְנִקְרָא ׳תִּלּוֹנוּ׳, הָיִיתִי מְפָרְשׁוֹ לְשׁוֹן תִּתְלוֹנְנוּ. עַכְשָׁיו הוּא מַשְׁמָע תַּלִּינוּ אֶת אֲחֵרִים, כְּמוֹ בַּמְרַגְּלִים: ״וַיַּלִּינוּ עָלָיו אֶת כָּל הָעֵדָה״ (במדבר יד, לו):

ח **בָּשָׂר לֶאֱכֹל.** וְלֹא לִשְׂבֹּעַ, לִמְּדָה תוֹרָה דֶּרֶךְ אֶרֶץ שֶׁאֵין אוֹכְלִין בָּשָׂר לָשׂבַע. וּמָה רָאָה לְהוֹרִיד לֶחֶם בַּבֹּקֶר וּבָשָׂר בָּעֶרֶב? לְפִי שֶׁהַלֶּחֶם שָׁאֲלוּ כַּהֹגֶן, שֶׁאִי אֶפְשָׁר לוֹ לָאָדָם בְּלֹא לֶחֶם, אֲבָל בָּשָׂר שָׁאֲלוּ שֶׁלֹּא כַּהֹגֶן, שֶׁהַרְבֵּה בְּהֵמוֹת הָיוּ לָהֶם, וְעוֹד שֶׁהָיָה אֶפְשָׁר לָהֶם בְּלֹא בָּשָׂר, לְפִיכָךְ נָתַן לָהֶם בִּשְׁעַת טֹרַח שֶׁלֹּא כַּהֹגֶן: **אֲשֶׁר אַתֶּם מַלִּינִם עָלָיו.** אֶת הָאֲחֵרִים הַשּׁוֹמְעִים אֶתְכֶם מִתְלוֹנְנִים:

ט **קִרְבוּ.** לַמָּקוֹם שֶׁהֶעָנָן יָרַד:

ב לַחֹדֶשׁ הַשֵּׁנִי לְצֵאתָם מֵאֶרֶץ מִצְרָיִם: וילינו כָּל־עֲדַת בְּנֵי־יִשְׂרָאֵל וַיִּלּוֹנוּ
ג עַל־מֹשֶׁה וְעַל־אַהֲרֹן בַּמִּדְבָּר: וַיֹּאמְרוּ אֲלֵהֶם בְּנֵי יִשְׂרָאֵל מִי־יִתֵּן
מוּתֵנוּ בְיַד־יהוה בְּאֶרֶץ מִצְרַיִם בְּשִׁבְתֵּנוּ עַל־סִיר הַבָּשָׂר בְּאָכְלֵנוּ
לֶחֶם לָשֹׂבַע כִּי־הוֹצֵאתֶם אֹתָנוּ אֶל־הַמִּדְבָּר הַזֶּה לְהָמִית אֶת־כָּל־
ד הַקָּהָל הַזֶּה בָּרָעָב: וַיֹּאמֶר יהוה אֶל־מֹשֶׁה הִנְנִי מַמְטִיר יב
לָכֶם לֶחֶם מִן־הַשָּׁמָיִם וְיָצָא הָעָם וְלָקְטוּ דְּבַר־יוֹם בְּיוֹמוֹ לְמַעַן אֲנַסֶּנּוּ
ה הֲיֵלֵךְ בְּתוֹרָתִי אִם־לֹא: וְהָיָה בַּיּוֹם הַשִּׁשִּׁי וְהֵכִינוּ אֵת אֲשֶׁר־יָבִיאוּ
ו וְהָיָה מִשְׁנֶה עַל אֲשֶׁר־יִלְקְטוּ יוֹם ׀ יוֹם: וַיֹּאמֶר מֹשֶׁה וְאַהֲרֹן אֶל־
כָּל־בְּנֵי יִשְׂרָאֵל עֶרֶב וִידַעְתֶּם כִּי יהוה הוֹצִיא אֶתְכֶם מֵאֶרֶץ מִצְרָיִם:
ז וּבֹקֶר וּרְאִיתֶם אֶת־כְּבוֹד יהוה בְּשָׁמְעוֹ אֶת־תְּלֻנֹּתֵיכֶם עַל־יהוה
ח וְנַחְנוּ מָה כִּי תלונו עָלֵינוּ: וַיֹּאמֶר מֹשֶׁה בְּתֵת יהוה לָכֶם בָּעֶרֶב בָּשָׂר תַּלִּינוּ
לֶאֱכֹל וְלֶחֶם בַּבֹּקֶר לִשְׂבֹּעַ בִּשְׁמֹעַ יהוה אֶת־תְּלֻנֹּתֵיכֶם אֲשֶׁר־אַתֶּם
ט מַלִּינִם עָלָיו וְנַחְנוּ מָה לֹא־עָלֵינוּ תְלֻנֹּתֵיכֶם כִּי עַל־יהוה: וַיֹּאמֶר
מֹשֶׁה אֶל־אַהֲרֹן אֱמֹר אֶל־כָּל־עֲדַת בְּנֵי יִשְׂרָאֵל קִרְבוּ לִפְנֵי יהוה
י כִּי שָׁמַע אֵת תְּלֻנֹּתֵיכֶם: וַיְהִי כְּדַבֵּר אַהֲרֹן אֶל־כָּל־עֲדַת בְּנֵי־יִשְׂרָאֵל
וַיִּפְנוּ אֶל־הַמִּדְבָּר וְהִנֵּה כְּבוֹד יהוה נִרְאָה בֶּעָנָן:

אונקלוס

לְיַרְחָא תִּנְיָנָא, לְמִפַּקְהוֹן מֵאַרְעָא דְּמִצְרָיִם: ב וְאִתְרְעַמוּ, כָּל כְּנִשְׁתָּא דִּבְנֵי יִשְׂרָאֵל, עַל מֹשֶׁה וְעַל אַהֲרֹן בְּמַדְבְּרָא: ג וַאֲמַרוּ לְהוֹן בְּנֵי יִשְׂרָאֵל, לְוַי דְּמִיתְנָא קֳדָם יי בְּאַרְעָא דְּמִצְרַיִם, כַּד הֲוֵינָא יָתְבִין עַל דּוּדֵי בִסְרָא, כַּד הֲוֵינָא אָכְלִין לַחְמָא וְסָבְעִין, אֲרֵי אַפֵּיקְתּוּן יָתַנָא לְמַדְבְּרָא הָדֵין, לְקַטָּלָא, יָת כָּל קְהָלָא הָדֵין בְּכַפְנָא: ד וַאֲמַר יי לְמֹשֶׁה, הָאֲנָא מַחֵית לְכוֹן, לַחְמָא מִן שְׁמַיָּא, וְיִפְּקוּן עַמָּא וְיִלְקְטוּן פִּתְגָם יוֹם בְּיוֹמֵיהּ, בְּדִיל דַּאֲנַסֵּינּוּן, הַיְהָכוּן בְּאוֹרָיְתִי אִם לָא: ה וִיהֵי בְּיוֹמָא שְׁתִיתָאָה, וִיתַקְּנוּן יָת דְּיַיְתוּן, וִיהֵי עַל חַד תְּרֵין, עַל דְּיִלְקְטוּן יוֹם יוֹם: ו וַאֲמַר מֹשֶׁה וְאַהֲרֹן, לְכָל בְּנֵי יִשְׂרָאֵל, בְּרַמְשָׁא, וְתִדְּעוּן, אֲרֵי יי, אַפֵּיק יָתְכוֹן מֵאַרְעָא דְּמִצְרָיִם: ז וּבְצַפְרָא, וְתֶחֱזוֹן יָת יְקָרָא דַּיי, בְּדִשְׁמִיעַן קֳדָמוֹהִי תֻּרְעֲמָתְכוֹן עַל יי, וְנַחְנָא מָא, אֲרֵי מִתְרַעַמְתּוּן עֲלַנָא: ח וַאֲמַר מֹשֶׁה, בְּדְיִתֵּן יי לְכוֹן בְּרַמְשָׁא בִּסְרָא לְמֵיכַל, וְלַחְמָא בְּצַפְרָא לְמִסְבַּע, בְּדִשְׁמִיעַן קֳדָם יי תֻּרְעֲמָתְכוֹן, דְּאַתּוּן מִתְרַעֲמִין עֲלוֹהִי, וְנַחְנָא מָא, לָא עֲלַנָא תֻּרְעֲמָתְכוֹן אֱלָהֵין עַל מֵימְרָא דַּיי: ט וַאֲמַר מֹשֶׁה לְאַהֲרֹן, אֵימַר, לְכָל כְּנִשְׁתָּא דִּבְנֵי יִשְׂרָאֵל, קְרוּבוּ קֳדָם יי, אֲרֵי שְׁמִיעָן קֳדָמוֹהִי תֻּרְעֲמָתְכוֹן: י וַהֲוָה, כַּד מַלֵּיל אַהֲרֹן עִם כָּל כְּנִשְׁתָּא דִּבְנֵי יִשְׂרָאֵל, וְאִתְפְּנִיאוּ לְמַדְבְּרָא, וְהָא יְקָרָא דַּיי, אִתְגְּלִי בַּעֲנָנָא:

11 12 The LORD spoke to Moshe and said, "I have heard the Israelites' railing. Tell SHISHI
them: At twilight you shall eat meat, and in the morning your fill of bread.
13 Then you will know that I am the LORD your God." That evening a flock of
quail flew in and covered the camp; next morning a layer of dew surrounded
14 the camp. When the dew covering lifted, fine flakes covered the floor of the
15 desert like fine frost on the ground. When the Israelites saw it, they asked one
another, "What is it?" for they did not recognize it. Moshe said to them, "This is
16 the bread the LORD has given you to eat. This is what the LORD has instructed:
Each of you gather as much as you need, an omer for every person; each take
17 enough for all the people in your tent." The people of Israel did so. Some
18 gathered more, others less. But when they measured it with an omer measure,
those who had gathered much had none left over, and those who gathered but
19 little did not fall short. All had gathered as much as they could eat. "Let no
20 one leave any over for the morning," said Moshe; but they did not listen to
Moshe. Some of them left part of it till morning, and it became worm infested
21 and stank. Moshe was enraged with them. Every morning they gathered it, all
22 as much as they could eat, and when the sun grew hot, it melted away. When
the sixth day came, they gathered a double portion, two omer each. All the

רש"י

יג **השלו.** מין עוף, ושמן מאד: **היתה שכבת הטל.** הטל שוכב על המן, ובמקום אחר הוא אומר: "וברדת הטל" וגו' (במדבר יא, ט), הטל יורד על הארץ והמן יורד עליו וחוזר ויורד טל עליו, והרי הוא כמונח בקופסא:

יד **ותעל שכבת הטל.** כשהחמה זורחת עולה טל שעל המן לקראת החמה כדרך טל עולה לקראת חמה, אף אם תמלא שפופרת של ביצה טל ותסתום את פיה ותניחה בחמה, היא עולה מאליה באויר. ורבותינו דרשו שהטל עולה מן הארץ. וכעלות שכבת הטל נתגלה המן, וראו והנה על פני המדבר דבר דק, מחספס – מגלה, ואין דומה לו במקרא. ויש לומר "מחספס" לשון "חפיסה ודלוסקמא" שבלשון משנה; כשנתגלה משכבת הטל ראו שהיה דבר דק מחספס בתוכו בין שתי שכבות הטל. ואונקלוס תרגם: "מקלף", לשון "מחשף הלבן" (בראשית ל, לז): **ככפר.** כפור – גליד"א בלעז. "דעדק כגיר", "כאבני גר" (ישעיה כז, ט), והוא מין צבע שחור כדאמרינן גבי כסוי הדם: "הגיר והזרניך" (חולין פח ע"ב). "דעדק כגיר כגלידא על ארעא", דק היה כגיר ושוכב מגלד כקרח על הארץ. וכן פירושו, "דק ככפר", שטוח קלוש ומחבר כגליד. "דק" טינבי"ש בלעז, שהיה מגליד גלד דק מלמעלה. ו'כגיר' שתרגם אונקלוס, תוספת הוא על לשון העברית ואין לו תבה בפסוק:

טו **מן הוא.** הכנת מזון הוא, כמו: "וימן להם המלך" (דניאל א, ה): **כי לא ידעו מה הוא.** שיקראוהו בשמו:

טז **עמר.** שם מדה: **מספר נפשתיכם.** כפי מנין נפשות שיש לאיש באהלו תקחו, עמר לכל גלגלת:

יז **המרבה והממעיט.** יש שלקטו הרבה ויש שלקטו מעט, וכשבאו לביתם מדדו בעמר איש איש מה שלקטו, ומצאו שהמרבה ללקט לא העדיף על עמר לגלגלת אשר באהלו, והממעיט ללקט לא מצא חסר מעמר לגלגלת, וזהו נס גדול שנעשה בו:

כ **ויותרו אנשים.** דתן ואבירם: **וירם תולעים.** לשון רמה: **ויבאש.** הרי זה מקרא הפוך, שבתחלה הבאיש ולבסוף התליע, כענין שנאמר: "ולא הבאיש ורמה לא היתה בו" (להלן פסוק כד), וכן דרך כל המתליעים:

כא **וחם השמש ונמס.** הנשאר בשדה נעשה נחלים ושותין ממנו אילים וצבאים, ואמות העולם צדין מהם וטועמים בהם טעם מן ויודעים מה שבחן של ישראל. "פשר" (אונקלוס), לשון פושרין, על ידי השמש מתחמם ומפשיר: **ונמס.** דישטמפרי"ר. ודגמתו בסנהדרין בסוף 'ארבע מיתות' (דף סז ע"ב):

כב **לקטו לחם משנה.** כשמדדו את לקיטתם באהליהם מצאו כפלים, "שני העמר לאחד". ומדרש אגדה, "לחם משנה" משנה, אותו

יא יב וַיְדַבֵּר יְהוָה אֶל־מֹשֶׁה לֵּאמֹר׃ שָׁמַעְתִּי אֶת־תְּלוּנֹּת בְּנֵי יִשְׂרָאֵל דַּבֵּר ששי
אֲלֵהֶם לֵאמֹר בֵּין הָעַרְבַּיִם תֹּאכְלוּ בָשָׂר וּבַבֹּקֶר תִּשְׂבְּעוּ־לָחֶם וִידַעְתֶּם
יג כִּי אֲנִי יְהוָה אֱלֹהֵיכֶם׃ וַיְהִי בָעֶרֶב וַתַּעַל הַשְּׂלָו וַתְּכַס אֶת־הַמַּחֲנֶה
יד וּבַבֹּקֶר הָיְתָה שִׁכְבַת הַטַּל סָבִיב לַמַּחֲנֶה׃ וַתַּעַל שִׁכְבַת הַטָּל וְהִנֵּה
טו עַל־פְּנֵי הַמִּדְבָּר דַּק מְחֻסְפָּס דַּק כַּכְּפֹר עַל־הָאָרֶץ׃ וַיִּרְאוּ בְנֵי־יִשְׂרָאֵל
וַיֹּאמְרוּ אִישׁ אֶל־אָחִיו מָן הוּא כִּי לֹא יָדְעוּ מַה־הוּא וַיֹּאמֶר מֹשֶׁה
טז אֲלֵהֶם הוּא הַלֶּחֶם אֲשֶׁר נָתַן יְהוָה לָכֶם לְאָכְלָה׃ זֶה הַדָּבָר אֲשֶׁר צִוָּה
יְהוָה לִקְטוּ מִמֶּנּוּ אִישׁ לְפִי אָכְלוֹ עֹמֶר לַגֻּלְגֹּלֶת מִסְפַּר נַפְשֹׁתֵיכֶם
יז אִישׁ לַאֲשֶׁר בְּאָהֳלוֹ תִּקָּחוּ׃ וַיַּעֲשׂוּ־כֵן בְּנֵי יִשְׂרָאֵל וַיִּלְקְטוּ הַמַּרְבֶּה
יח וְהַמַּמְעִיט׃ וַיָּמֹדּוּ בָעֹמֶר וְלֹא הֶעְדִּיף הַמַּרְבֶּה וְהַמַּמְעִיט לֹא הֶחְסִיר
יט אִישׁ לְפִי־אָכְלוֹ לָקָטוּ׃ וַיֹּאמֶר מֹשֶׁה אֲלֵהֶם אִישׁ אַל־יוֹתֵר מִמֶּנּוּ
כ עַד־בֹּקֶר׃ וְלֹא־שָׁמְעוּ אֶל־מֹשֶׁה וַיּוֹתִרוּ אֲנָשִׁים מִמֶּנּוּ עַד־בֹּקֶר וַיָּרֻם
כא תּוֹלָעִים וַיִּבְאַשׁ וַיִּקְצֹף עֲלֵהֶם מֹשֶׁה׃ וַיִּלְקְטוּ אֹתוֹ בַּבֹּקֶר בַּבֹּקֶר אִישׁ
כב כְּפִי אָכְלוֹ וְחַם הַשֶּׁמֶשׁ וְנָמָס׃ וַיְהִי ׀ בַּיּוֹם הַשִּׁשִּׁי לָקְטוּ לֶחֶם מִשְׁנֶה

אונקלוס

יא ומליל יי עם משה למימר: יב שמיע קדמי, ית תרעמת בני ישראל, מליל עמהון למימר, בין שמשיא תיכלון בסרא, ובצפרא תסבעון לחמא, ותדעון, ארי, אנא יי אלהכון: יג והוה ברמשא, וסליקת שליו, וחפת ית משריתא, ובצפרא, הות נחתת טלא, סחור סחור למשריתא: יד וסליקת נחתת טלא, והא, על אפי מדברא דעדק מקלף, דעדק כגיר כגלידא על ארעא: טו וחזו בני ישראל, ואמרו, גבר לאחוהי מנא הוא, ארי, לא ידעין מא הוא, ואמר משה להון, הוא לחמא, דיהב יי, לכון למיכל: טז דין פתגמא דפקיד יי, לקוטו מניה, גבר לפום מיכליה, עמרא לגלגלתא, מנין נפשתכון, גבר לדבמשכניה תסבון: יז ועבדו כן בני ישראל, ולקטו, דאסגי ודאזער: יח וכלו בעמרא, ולא אותר דאסגי, ודאזער לא חסר, גבר לפום מיכליה לקטו: יט ואמר משה להון, אנש, לא ישאר מניה עד צפרא: כ ולא קבילו מן משה, ואשארו גבריא מניה עד צפרא, ורחיש רחשא וסרי, ורגיז עליהון משה: כא ולקטו יתיה בצפר בצפר, גבר כפום מיכליה, ומא דמשתאר מניה על אפי חקלא כד חמא עלוהי שמשא פשר: כב והוה ביומא שתיתאה, לקטו לחמא על חד תרין,

רש״י

היום נשתנה לשבח בריחו וטעמו: ויגידו למשה. שאלוהו מה היום מימים? ומכאן יש ללמוד שעדיין לא הגיד להם משה פרשת שבת שנצטוה לומר להם: "והיה ביום הששי והכינו" וגו' (לעיל פסוק ה), עד ששאלו את זאת. אמר להם: "הוא אשר דבר ה'" (בפסוק הבא), שנצטויתי לומר לכם. ולכך ענשו הכתוב, שאמר לו: "עד אנה מאנתם" (להלן פסוק כח) ולא הוציאו מן הכלל:

23 leaders of the community came and reported this to Moshe. "This," he told
them, "is what the LORD has said: Tomorrow is a day of rest, a holy Sabbath
to the LORD. Bake now what you need to bake and cook what you need to
24 cook. Whatever is left, keep carefully aside for the morning." So they put it
aside until the morning, as Moshe had instructed them, and it did not stink,
25 nor did worms infest it. And Moshe said, "Today, eat this, for today is a Sabbath
26 to the LORD; today you will not find it on the ground. Six days shall you gather
27 it, but on the seventh day, the Sabbath, it will not be there." Some people did
28 go out to gather it on the seventh day; but they found none. Then the
LORD said to Moshe, "How long will you refuse to keep My commandments
29 and laws? Understand that the LORD has given you a Sabbath – that is why He
gave you two days' bread on the sixth day. You shall each rest where you are:
30 let no man depart from where he is on the seventh day." So the people rested
31 on the seventh day. The House of Israel named it manna. It looked like white

רש״י

כג| **אֵת אֲשֶׁר תֹּאפוּ אֵפוּ.** מַה שֶּׁאַתֶּם רוֹצִים לֶאֱפוֹת בַּתַּנּוּר, ״אֱפוּ״ הַיּוֹם הַכֹּל לִשְׁנֵי יָמִים. וּמַה שֶּׁאַתֶּם צְרִיכִים לְבַשֵּׁל מִמֶּנּוּ בַּמַּיִם, ״בַּשְּׁלוּ״ הַיּוֹם. לְשׁוֹן אֲפִיָּה נוֹפֵל בְּלֶחֶם וּלְשׁוֹן בִּשּׁוּל בְּתַבְשִׁיל: **לְמִשְׁמֶרֶת.** לִגְנִיזָה:

כה| **וַיֹּאמֶר מֹשֶׁה אִכְלֻהוּ הַיּוֹם.** שַׁחֲרִית שֶׁהָיוּ רְגִילִים לָצֵאת וְלִלְקֹט, בָּאוּ לִשְׁאֹל אִם נֵצֵא אִם לָאו, אָמַר לָהֶם: אֶת שֶׁבִּיָדְכֶם אִכְלוּ. לָעֶרֶב חָזְרוּ לְפָנָיו: מַהוּ לָצֵאת? אָמַר לָהֶם: ״שַׁבָּת הַיּוֹם״. רָאָה אוֹתָם דּוֹאֲגִים שֶׁמָּא פָּסַק הַמָּן וְלֹא יֵרֵד עוֹד, אָמַר לָהֶם: ״הַיּוֹם לֹא תִמְצָאֻהוּ״, מַה תַּלְמוּד לוֹמַר ״הַיּוֹם״? הַיּוֹם לֹא תִמְצָאוּהוּ אֲבָל מָחָר תִּמְצָאוּהוּ:

כו| **וּבַיּוֹם הַשְּׁבִיעִי שַׁבָּת.** ״שַׁבָּת״ הוּא, הַמָּן ״לֹא יִהְיֶה בּוֹ״. וְלֹא בָא הַכָּתוּב אֶלָּא לְרַבּוֹת יוֹם הַכִּפּוּרִים וְיָמִים טוֹבִים:

כח| **עַד אָנָה מֵאַנְתֶּם.** מָשָׁל הֶדְיוֹט הוּא, בַּהֲדֵי הוּצָא לָקֵי כְּרָבָא, עַל יְדֵי הָרְשָׁעִים מִתְגַּנִּין הַכְּשֵׁרִים:

כט| **רְאוּ.** בְּעֵינֵיכֶם כִּי ה׳ בִּכְבוֹדוֹ מַזְהִיר אֶתְכֶם עַל הַשַּׁבָּת, שֶׁהֲרֵי נֵס נַעֲשֶׂה בְּכָל עֶרֶב שַׁבָּת לָתֵת לָכֶם לֶחֶם יוֹמָיִם: **שְׁבוּ אִישׁ תַּחְתָּיו.** מִכָּאן סָמְכוּ חֲכָמִים אַרְבַּע אַמּוֹת לַיּוֹצֵא חוּץ לַתְּחוּם: **אַל יֵצֵא אִישׁ מִמְּקֹמוֹ.** אֵלּוּ אַלְפַּיִם אַמָּה, וְלֹא בִּמְפֹרָשׁ, שֶׁאֵין תְּחוּמִין אֶלָּא מִדִּבְרֵי סוֹפְרִים, וְעִקָּרוֹ שֶׁל מִקְרָא עַל לוֹקְטֵי הַמָּן נֶאֱמַר:

לא| **וְהוּא כְּזֶרַע גַּד.** עֵשֶׂב שֶׁשְּׁמוֹ אליי״נדרי, וְזֶרַע שֶׁלּוֹ עָגֹל וְאֵינוֹ לָבָן, וְהַמָּן הָיָה לָבָן, וְאֵינוֹ נִמְשָׁל לְזֶרַע גַּד אֶלָּא לְעִנְיַן הָעִגּוּל, ״כְּזֶרַע גַּד״ הָיָה וְהוּא ״לָבָן״: **כְּצַפִּיחִת.** בָּצֵק שֶׁמְּטַגְּנִין אוֹתוֹ בִּדְבַשׁ, וְקוֹרִין לוֹ ׳אֶסְקְרִיטִין׳ בִּלְשׁוֹן מִשְׁנָה (חלה א, ד; פסחים לז ע״א), וְהוּא תַּרְגּוּם שֶׁל אוּנְקְלוֹס:

a consumer society urging us to spend our way to happiness, free to be ourselves in the company of those we love. Somehow this one day has renewed its meaning in generation after generation, despite the most profound economic and industrial change. In Moshe's day it meant freedom from slavery to Pharaoh. In the nineteenth and early twentieth century it meant freedom from sweatshop working conditions of long hours for little pay. In ours, it means freedom from emails, smartphones, and the demands of 24/7 availability.

God wants the Israelites to begin their one-day-in-seven rehearsal of freedom almost as soon as they leave Egypt, because real freedom, of the seven-days-in-seven kind, takes time, centuries, millennia. The Torah regards slavery as wrong, but it does not abolish it immediately because people are not yet ready. Neither Britain nor America abolished it until the nineteenth century, and even then not without a struggle. Yet the outcome is inevitable once the Sabbath has been set in motion. Slaves who know freedom one day in seven will eventually rise against their chains.

כג שְׁנֵי הָעֹמֶר לָאֶחָד וַיָּבֹאוּ כָּל־נְשִׂיאֵי הָעֵדָה וַיַּגִּידוּ לְמֹשֶׁה: וַיֹּאמֶר
אֲלֵהֶם הוּא אֲשֶׁר דִּבֶּר יהוה שַׁבָּתוֹן שַׁבַּת־קֹדֶשׁ לַיהוה מָחָר אֵת
אֲשֶׁר־תֹּאפוּ אֵפוּ וְאֵת אֲשֶׁר־תְּבַשְּׁלוּ בַּשֵּׁלוּ וְאֵת כָּל־הָעֹדֵף הַנִּיחוּ
כד לָכֶם לְמִשְׁמֶרֶת עַד־הַבֹּקֶר: וַיַּנִּיחוּ אֹתוֹ עַד־הַבֹּקֶר כַּאֲשֶׁר צִוָּה מֹשֶׁה
כה וְלֹא הִבְאִישׁ וְרִמָּה לֹא־הָיְתָה־בּוֹ: וַיֹּאמֶר מֹשֶׁה אִכְלֻהוּ הַיּוֹם כִּי־שַׁבָּת
כו הַיּוֹם לַיהוה הַיּוֹם לֹא תִמְצָאֻהוּ בַּשָּׂדֶה: שֵׁשֶׁת יָמִים תִּלְקְטֻהוּ וּבַיּוֹם
כז הַשְּׁבִיעִי שַׁבָּת לֹא יִהְיֶה־בּוֹ: וַיְהִי בַּיּוֹם הַשְּׁבִיעִי יָצְאוּ מִן־הָעָם לִלְקֹט
כח וְלֹא מָצָאוּ: וַיֹּאמֶר יהוה אֶל־מֹשֶׁה עַד־אָנָה מֵאַנְתֶּם לִשְׁמֹר יג
כט מִצְוֺתַי וְתוֹרֹתָי: רְאוּ כִּי־יהוה נָתַן לָכֶם הַשַּׁבָּת עַל־כֵּן הוּא נֹתֵן לָכֶם
בַּיּוֹם הַשִּׁשִּׁי לֶחֶם יוֹמָיִם שְׁבוּ ׀ אִישׁ תַּחְתָּיו אַל־יֵצֵא אִישׁ מִמְּקֹמוֹ בַּיּוֹם
ל לא הַשְּׁבִיעִי: וַיִּשְׁבְּתוּ הָעָם בַּיּוֹם הַשְּׁבִעִי: וַיִּקְרְאוּ בֵית־יִשְׂרָאֵל אֶת־שְׁמוֹ

אונקלוס

תְּרֵין עֻמְרִין לְחַד, וַאֲתוֹ כָּל רַבְרְבֵי כְנִשְׁתָּא, וְחַוִּיאוּ לְמֹשֶׁה: כג וַאֲמַר לְהוֹן, הוּא דְּמַלֵּיל יי, שְׁבָא שַׁבְּתָא קַדִּשָׁא, קֳדָם יי מְחַר, יָת דְּאַתּוּן עֲתִידִין לְמֵיפָא אֵיפוֹ, וְיָת דְּאַתּוּן עֲתִידִין לְבַשָּׁלָא בַּשִּׁילוּ, וְיָת כָּל מוֹתָרָא, אַצְנַעוּ לְכוֹן, לְמַטְּרָא עַד צַפְרָא: כד וְאַצְנַעוּ יָתֵיהּ עַד צַפְרָא, כְּמָא דְּפַקֵּיד מֹשֶׁה, וְלָא סְרִי, וְרִחְשָׁא לָא הֲוָת בֵּיהּ: כה וַאֲמַר מֹשֶׁה אִכְלוּהִי יוֹמָא דֵין, אֲרֵי שַׁבְּתָא יוֹמָא דֵין קֳדָם יי, יוֹמָא דֵין, לָא תַשְׁכְּחֻנֵּיהּ בְּחַקְלָא: כו שִׁתָּא יוֹמִין תִּלְקְטֻנֵּיהּ, וּבְיוֹמָא שְׁבִיעָאָה, שַׁבְּתָא לָא יְהֵי בֵיהּ: כז וַהֲוָה בְּיוֹמָא שְׁבִיעָאָה, נְפַקוּ מִן עַמָּא לְמִלְקַט, וְלָא אַשְׁכַּחוּ: כח וַאֲמַר יי לְמֹשֶׁה, עַד אֵמָתַי אַתּוּן מְסָרְבִין, לְמִטַּר פִּקּוֹדַי וְאוֹרָיְתָי: כט חֲזוֹ, אֲרֵי יי יְהַב לְכוֹן שַׁבְּתָא, עַל כֵּן, הוּא יָהֵיב לְכוֹן, בְּיוֹמָא שְׁתִיתָאָה לְחֵים תְּרֵין יוֹמִין, תִּיבוּ אֱנָשׁ תְּחוֹתוֹהִי, לָא יִפּוֹק אֱנָשׁ, מֵאַתְרֵיהּ בְּיוֹמָא שְׁבִיעָאָה: ל וּשְׁבַתוּ עַמָּא בְּיוֹמָא שְׁבִיעָאָה: לא וּקְרוֹ בֵית יִשְׂרָאֵל, יָת שְׁמֵיהּ

THE SABBATH

The Sabbath is among the first commands the Israelites receive on leaving Egypt. They are not to gather manna on the seventh day. Instead, a double portion will fall on the sixth. To this day we have two challot on the Sabbath, in memory of that time. On this day, we do not live from hand to mouth.

The Sabbath changed the way the world thought about time. Prior to Judaism, people measured time either by the sun – the solar calendar of 365 days aligning us with the seasons – or by the moon, that is, by months of roughly thirty days. The idea of the seven-day week – which has no counterpart in nature – was born in the Torah and spread throughout the world via Christianity and Islam. We have years because of the sun, months because of the moon, and weeks because of the Jews.

What the Sabbath did and still does is to create space within our lives and within society as a whole in which we are truly free. Free from the pressures of work, free from the demands of ruthless employers, free from the siren calls of

▶

32 coriander seeds, and tasted like wafers made with honey. Moshe said, "This is
what the LORD commands: Let an omer of it be kept carefully aside for your
descendants, that they may see the bread I fed you in the desert when I brought
33 you out of Egypt." Moshe said to Aharon, "Take an urn, put an omer of manna
34 in it, and place it before the LORD to be kept for future generations." As the
LORD commanded Moshe, so Aharon placed it before the Ark of Testimony to
35 be kept with care. The Israelites ate manna for forty years, until they came to
the land where they could settle down. They ate the manna until they came to
36 the border of Canaan. An omer is a tenth of an ephah.

17 1 All the community of Israel moved on after that from the desert of Sin, traveling SHEVI'I
from place to place as the LORD guided them, and they camped at Refidim, but
2 there was no water there for the people to drink. The people started to wrangle
with Moshe. "Give us water to drink," they raged. "Why do you wrangle with
3 me?" asked Moshe. "Why are you testing the LORD?" But the people were
thirsty for water. They railed against Moshe, "Why did you bring us out of

רש״י

לב| **לְמִשְׁמֶרֶת.** לִגְנִיזָה: **לְדֹרֹתֵיכֶם.** בִּימֵי יִרְמְיָהוּ, כְּשֶׁהָיָה יִרְמְיָהוּ מוֹכִיחָם: לָמָּה אֵין אַתֶּם עוֹסְקִים בַּתּוֹרָה? וְהֵם אוֹמְרִים: נַנִּיחַ מְלַאכְתֵּנוּ וְנַעֲסֹק בַּתּוֹרָה, מֵהֵיכָן נִתְפַּרְנֵס? הוֹצִיא לָהֶם צִנְצֶנֶת הַמָּן, אָמַר לָהֶם: "הַדּוֹר אַתֶּם רְאוּ דְבַר ה'" (ירמיה ב, לא), 'שִׁמְעוּ' לֹא נֶאֱמַר אֶלָּא "רְאוּ", בָּזֶה נִתְפַּרְנְסוּ אֲבוֹתֵיכֶם, הַרְבֵּה שְׁלוּחִין יֵשׁ לוֹ לַמָּקוֹם לְהָכִין מָזוֹן לִירֵאָיו:

לג| **צִנְצֶנֶת.** צְלוֹחִית שֶׁל חֶרֶס, כְּתַרְגּוּמוֹ: **וְהַנַּח אוֹתוֹ לִפְנֵי ה'.** לִפְנֵי הָאָרוֹן. וְלֹא נֶאֱמַר מִקְרָא זֶה עַד שֶׁנִּבְנָה אֹהֶל מוֹעֵד, אֶלָּא שֶׁנִּכְתַּב כָּאן בְּפָרָשַׁת הַמָּן:

לה| **אַרְבָּעִים שָׁנָה.** וַהֲלֹא חָסֵר שְׁלֹשִׁים יוֹם, שֶׁהֲרֵי בַּחֲמִשָּׁה עָשָׂר בְּאִיָּר יָרַד לָהֶם הַמָּן תְּחִלָּה וּבַחֲמִשָּׁה עָשָׂר בְּנִיסָן פָּסַק, שֶׁנֶּאֱמַר: "וַיִּשְׁבֹּת הַמָּן מִמָּחֳרָת" (יהושע ה, יב)? אֶלָּא מַגִּיד שֶׁהָעוּגוֹת שֶׁהוֹצִיאוּ יִשְׂרָאֵל מִמִּצְרַיִם טָעֲמוּ בָּהֶם טַעַם מָן: **אֶל אֶרֶץ נוֹשָׁבֶת.** לְאַחַר שֶׁעָבְרוּ אֶת הַיַּרְדֵּן: **אֶל קְצֵה אֶרֶץ כְּנָעַן.** בִּתְחִלַּת הַגְּבוּל קֹדֶם שֶׁעָבְרוּ אֶת הַיַּרְדֵּן, וְהֵם עַרְבוֹת מוֹאָב. נִמְצְאוּ מַכְחִישִׁין זֶה אֶת זֶה! אֶלָּא בְּעַרְבוֹת מוֹאָב כְּשֶׁמֵּת מֹשֶׁה בְּשִׁבְעָה בַּאֲדָר פָּסַק הַמָּן מִלֵּרֵד, וְנִסְתַּפְּקוּ מִמָּן שֶׁלָּקְטוּ בּוֹ בַּיּוֹם עַד שֶׁהִקְרִיבוּ הָעֹמֶר בְּשִׁשָּׁה עָשָׂר בְּנִיסָן, שֶׁנֶּאֱמַר: "וַיֹּאכְלוּ מֵעֲבוּר הָאָרֶץ מִמָּחֳרַת הַפֶּסַח" (יהושע ה, יא):

לו| **עֲשִׂרִית הָאֵיפָה.** הָאֵיפָה שָׁלֹשׁ סְאִין, וְהַסְּאָה שֵׁשֶׁת קַבִּין, וְהַקַּב אַרְבָּעָה לֻגִּין, וְהַלֹּג שֵׁשׁ בֵּיצִים; נִמְצָא עֲשִׂירִית הָאֵיפָה אַרְבָּעִים וְשָׁלֹשׁ בֵּיצִים וְחֹמֶשׁ בֵּיצָה, וְהוּא שִׁעוּר לַחַלָּה וְלַמְּנָחוֹת:

יז ב| **מַה תְּנַסּוּן.** לוֹמַר, הֲיוּכַל לָתֵת מַיִם בְּאֶרֶץ צִיָּה:

remember the battle with Amalek. In between, the everyday miracle of the manna is archived too for future memory. Even as they live it, the national story is being inscribed.

17:3 **וַיָּלֶן הָעָם עַל־מֹשֶׁה** *They railed against Moshe* – Note that as early as their first complaint (Ex. 14:11), the people have blamed Moshe, as if the decision were his, not God's – an ominous precursor of many complaints that were to follow during their time in the wilderness. His successes have been celebrated, but in times of difficulty the people turn against him.

In every field, leaders are tested not by their successes but by their response to failure. It can sometimes be easy to succeed. The conditions may be favorable. The economic, political, or personal climate is good. When there is an economic boom, most businesses flourish. In the first months

לב מָן וְהוּא כְּזֶרַע גַּד לָבָן וְטַעְמוֹ כְּצַפִּיחִת בִּדְבָשׁ: וַיֹּאמֶר מֹשֶׁה זֶה הַדָּבָר
אֲשֶׁר צִוָּה יהוה מְלֹא הָעֹמֶר מִמֶּנּוּ לְמִשְׁמֶרֶת לְדֹרֹתֵיכֶם לְמַעַן ׀ יִרְאוּ
אֶת־הַלֶּחֶם אֲשֶׁר הֶאֱכַלְתִּי אֶתְכֶם בַּמִּדְבָּר בְּהוֹצִיאִי אֶתְכֶם מֵאֶרֶץ
לג מִצְרָיִם: וַיֹּאמֶר מֹשֶׁה אֶל־אַהֲרֹן קַח צִנְצֶנֶת אַחַת וְתֶן־שָׁמָּה מְלֹא־
לד הָעֹמֶר מָן וְהַנַּח אֹתוֹ לִפְנֵי יהוה לְמִשְׁמֶרֶת לְדֹרֹתֵיכֶם: כַּאֲשֶׁר צִוָּה
לה יהוה אֶל־מֹשֶׁה וַיַּנִּיחֵהוּ אַהֲרֹן לִפְנֵי הָעֵדֻת לְמִשְׁמָרֶת: וּבְנֵי יִשְׂרָאֵל
אָכְלוּ אֶת־הַמָּן אַרְבָּעִים שָׁנָה עַד־בֹּאָם אֶל־אֶרֶץ נוֹשָׁבֶת אֶת־
לו הַמָּן אָכְלוּ עַד־בֹּאָם אֶל־קְצֵה אֶרֶץ כְּנָעַן: וְהָעֹמֶר עֲשִׂרִית הָאֵיפָה
הוּא:
יז א וַיִּסְעוּ כָּל־עֲדַת בְּנֵי־יִשְׂרָאֵל מִמִּדְבַּר־סִין לְמַסְעֵיהֶם עַל־פִּי יהוה שביעי
ב וַיַּחֲנוּ בִּרְפִידִים וְאֵין מַיִם לִשְׁתֹּת הָעָם: וַיָּרֶב הָעָם עִם־מֹשֶׁה וַיֹּאמְרוּ
תְּנוּ־לָנוּ מַיִם וְנִשְׁתֶּה וַיֹּאמֶר לָהֶם מֹשֶׁה מַה־תְּרִיבוּן עִמָּדִי מַה־תְּנַסּוּן
ג אֶת־יהוה: וַיִּצְמָא שָׁם הָעָם לַמַּיִם וַיָּלֶן הָעָם עַל־מֹשֶׁה וַיֹּאמֶר לָמָּה

אונקלוס

מַנָּא, וְהוּא, כְּבַר זְרַע גִּדָּא חִיוָּר, וְטַעְמֵיהּ כְּאִסְקְרִיטָן בִּדְבַשׁ: לב וַאֲמַר מֹשֶׁה, דֵּין פִּתְגָמָא דְּפַקֵּיד יי, מְלֵי עֻמְרָא מִנֵּיהּ, לְמַטְּרָא לְדָרֵיכוֹן, בְּדִיל דְּיִחְזוֹן יָת לַחְמָא, דְּאוֹכֵילִית יָתְכוֹן בְּמַדְבְּרָא, בְּאַפָּקוּתִי יָתְכוֹן מֵאַרְעָא דְּמִצְרָיִם: לג וַאֲמַר מֹשֶׁה לְאַהֲרֹן, סַב צְלוֹחִית חֲדָא, וְהַב תַּמָּן מְלֵי עֻמְרָא מַנָּא, וְאַצְנַע יָתֵיהּ קֳדָם יי, לְמַטְּרָא לְדָרֵיכוֹן: לד כְּמָא דְּפַקֵּיד יי לְמֹשֶׁה, וְאַצְנְעֵיהּ אַהֲרֹן, קֳדָם סָהֲדוּתָא לְמַטְּרָא: לה וּבְנֵי יִשְׂרָאֵל, אֲכַלוּ יָת מַנָּא אַרְבְּעִין שְׁנִין, עַד דְּעָאלוּ לַאֲרַע יָתֵיבְתָּא, יָת מַנָּא אֲכַלוּ, עַד דַּאֲתוֹ, לִסְיָפֵי אַרְעָא דִּכְנָעַן: לו וְעֻמְרָא, חַד מִן עַסְרָא בִּתְלָת סְאִין הוּא: יז א וּנְטַלוּ, כָּל כְּנִשְׁתָּא דִּבְנֵי יִשְׂרָאֵל מִמַּדְבְּרָא דְסִין, לְמַטְלָנֵיהוֹן עַל מֵימְרָא דַּיי, וּשְׁרוֹ בִּרְפִידִים, וְלֵית מַיָּא לְמִשְׁתֵּי עַמָּא: ב וּנְצָא עַמָּא עִם מֹשֶׁה, וַאֲמַרוּ, הַבוּ לַנָא מַיָּא וְנִשְׁתֵּי, אֲמַר לְהוֹן מֹשֶׁה, מָא נָצַן אַתּוּן עִמִּי, מָא מְנַסַּן אַתּוּן קֳדָם יי: ג וּצְחִי תַמָּן עַמָּא לְמַיָּא, וְאִתְרַעַם עַמָּא עַל מֹשֶׁה, וַאֲמַר, לְמָא

16:33 לְדֹרֹתֵיכֶם *For future generations* – Religions are guardians of memory. Much of Judaism is timeless – our beliefs, our values, our way of life. The days, the years, the centuries pass, but Judaism and the Jewish people remain. But there is something else in Jewish existence that renders us acutely sensitive to time. In one of the classics of modern Jewish scholarship, *Zakhor,* Professor Yosef Hayim Yerushalmi writes: "It was ancient Israel that first assigned a decisive significance to history and thus forged a new world-view.... 'The heavens,' in the words of the psalmist, might still 'tell of God's glory' (Ps. 19:2), but it was human history that revealed His will and purpose.... Far from attempting a flight from history, biblical religion allows itself to be saturated by it and is inconceivable apart from it." Jews are a people of memory.

As the Israelites left Egypt, they were taught to reenact the story for their children. In but a few verses, they will be told to

4 Egypt? Was it to kill me, my children, and all my livestock by thirst?" "What
shall I do with this people?" Moshe cried to the LORD. "Another moment and
5 they will stone me." The LORD answered Moshe, "Walk out to face the people
taking some of the elders of Israel with you. Take the staff with which you
6 struck the Nile in your hand, and go. I will be there before you by the rock at
Ḥorev. Strike the rock; water will come out of it and the people will drink."
7 And that is what Moshe did, before the eyes of the elders of Israel. He named
the place Masa and Meriva, because the people had quarreled and had tested
the LORD, demanding, "Is the LORD among us or not?"
8
9 Then, at Refidim, Amalek came and attacked Israel. Moshe said to Yehoshua,

רש״י

ד **עוֹד מְעַט.** אִם אַמְתִּין ״עוֹד מְעַט, וּסְקָלֻנִי״:

ה **עֲבֹר לִפְנֵי הָעָם.** וּרְאֵה אִם יִסְקְלוּךָ, לָמָּה הוֹצֵאתָ לַעַז עַל בָּנַי?: **וְקַח אִתְּךָ מִזִּקְנֵי יִשְׂרָאֵל.** לְעֵדוּת, שֶׁיִּרְאוּ שֶׁעַל יָדְךָ הַמַּיִם יוֹצְאִים מִן הַצּוּר, וְלֹא יֹאמְרוּ: מַעְיָנוֹת הָיוּ שָׁם מִימֵי קֶדֶם: **וּמַטְּךָ אֲשֶׁר הִכִּיתָ בּוֹ אֶת הַיְאֹר.** מַה תַּלְמוּד לוֹמַר: ״אֲשֶׁר הִכִּיתָ בּוֹ אֶת הַיְאֹר״? אֶלָּא שֶׁהָיוּ יִשְׂרָאֵל אוֹמְרִים עַל הַמַּטֶּה שֶׁאֵינוֹ מוּכָן אֶלָּא לְפֻרְעָנוּת, בּוֹ לָקָה פַּרְעֹה וּמִצְרַיִם כַּמָּה מַכּוֹת בְּמִצְרַיִם וְעַל הַיָּם, לְכָךְ נֶאֱמַר: ״אֲשֶׁר הִכִּיתָ בּוֹ אֶת הַיְאֹר״ וְהֵם אוֹמְרִים עָלָיו שֶׁאֵינוֹ אֶלָּא לְפֻרְעָנוּת, יִרְאוּ עַתָּה שֶׁאַף לְטוֹבָה הוּא מוּכָן:

ו **וְהִכִּיתָ בַצּוּר.** ׳עַל הַצּוּר׳ לֹא נֶאֱמַר אֶלָּא ״בַצּוּר״, מִכָּאן שֶׁהַמַּטֶּה הָיָה שֶׁל מִין דָּבָר חָזָק וּשְׁמוֹ סַנְפִּירִינוֹן, וְהַצּוּר נִבְקַע מִפָּנָיו:

ח **וַיָּבֹא עֲמָלֵק.** סָמַךְ פָּרָשָׁה זוֹ לְמִקְרָא זֶה, לוֹמַר, תָּמִיד אֲנִי בֵּינֵיכֶם וּמְזֻמָּן לְכָל צָרְכֵיכֶם, וְאַתֶּם אוֹמְרִים: ״הֲיֵשׁ ה׳ בְּקִרְבֵּנוּ אִם אָיִן״ (לעיל פסוק ז)?! חַיֵּיכֶם שֶׁהַכֶּלֶב בָּא וְנוֹשֵׁךְ אֶתְכֶם וְאַתֶּם צוֹעֲקִים לִי וְתֵדְעוּ הֵיכָן אֲנִי. מָשָׁל לְאָדָם שֶׁהִרְכִּיב בְּנוֹ עַל כְּתֵפוֹ וְיָצָא לַדֶּרֶךְ, הָיָה אוֹתוֹ הַבֵּן רוֹאֶה חֵפֶץ וְאוֹמֵר: אַבָּא, טֹל חֵפֶץ זֶה וְתֵן לִי! וְהוּא נוֹתֵן לוֹ, וְכֵן שְׁנִיָּה וְכֵן שְׁלִישִׁית. פָּגְעוּ בְּאָדָם אֶחָד, אָמַר לוֹ אוֹתוֹ הַבֵּן: רָאִיתָ אֶת אַבָּא? אָמַר לוֹ אָבִיו: אֵינְךָ יוֹדֵעַ הֵיכָן אֲנִי?! הִשְׁלִיכוֹ מֵעָלָיו, וּבָא הַכֶּלֶב וּנְשָׁכוֹ:

leader empowers the people to do it for themselves.

The Torah focuses our attention on one detail as the battle with Amalek begins: Moshe climbs to the top of a hill overlooking the battlefield, with a staff in his hand:

> Whenever Moshe held his hand high, the Israelites prevailed, but whenever he let his hand drop, the Amalekites prevailed. But Moshe's hands grew heavy. So they took a stone and placed it under him and he sat, while Aharon and Ḥur held up his hands, one on each side, so that his hands held true until sunset. (17:11–12)

What is going on here? The passage could be read in two ways. The staff in Moshe's hand – with which he performed miracles in Egypt and at the sea – might be a sign that the Israelites' victory was a miraculous one. Alternatively, it might simply be a reminder to the Israelites that God was with them, giving them strength.

A mishna resolves the question, which is very unusual, since the Mishna in general is a book of law rather than biblical commentary: "Did the hands of Moshe make or break [the course of the] war? Rather, the text implies that whenever the Israelites looked up and dedicated their hearts to their Father in heaven, they prevailed, but otherwise they fell" (Mishna Rosh HaShana 3:8). Neither the staff nor Moshe's upraised hands were performing a miracle. They were simply reminding the Israelites to look up to heaven and remember that God was with them. This gave them the confidence and courage to win.

A leader, we learn, must empower the team. He cannot do the work for them; they must do it for themselves. But he must, at the same time, give them the absolute confidence that they can succeed. During the battle, he must betray no sign of weakness or doubt.

Yet all leaders have their moments of exhaustion.

זֶה הֶעֱלִיתָנוּ מִמִּצְרַיִם לְהָמִית אֹתִי וְאֶת־בָּנַי וְאֶת־מִקְנַי בַּצָּמָא׃
ד וַיִּצְעַק מֹשֶׁה אֶל־יְהוָה לֵאמֹר מָה אֶעֱשֶׂה לָעָם הַזֶּה עוֹד מְעַט
ה וּסְקָלֻנִי׃ וַיֹּאמֶר יְהוָה אֶל־מֹשֶׁה עֲבֹר לִפְנֵי הָעָם וְקַח אִתְּךָ מִזִּקְנֵי
ו יִשְׂרָאֵל וּמַטְּךָ אֲשֶׁר הִכִּיתָ בּוֹ אֶת־הַיְאֹר קַח בְּיָדְךָ וְהָלָכְתָּ׃ הִנְנִי עֹמֵד
לְפָנֶיךָ שָּׁם ׀ עַל־הַצּוּר בְּחֹרֵב וְהִכִּיתָ בַצּוּר וְיָצְאוּ מִמֶּנּוּ מַיִם וְשָׁתָה הָעָם
ז וַיַּעַשׂ כֵּן מֹשֶׁה לְעֵינֵי זִקְנֵי יִשְׂרָאֵל׃ וַיִּקְרָא שֵׁם הַמָּקוֹם מַסָּה וּמְרִיבָה
עַל־רִיב ׀ בְּנֵי יִשְׂרָאֵל וְעַל נַסֹּתָם אֶת־יְהוָה לֵאמֹר הֲיֵשׁ יְהוָה בְּקִרְבֵּנוּ
אִם־אָיִן׃
ח וַיָּבֹא עֲמָלֵק וַיִּלָּחֶם עִם־יִשְׂרָאֵל בִּרְפִידִם׃ וַיֹּאמֶר מֹשֶׁה אֶל־יְהוֹשֻׁעַ

אונקלוס

דנן אסיקתנא ממצרים, לקטלא יתי, וית בני וית בעירי בצהותא: ד וצלי משה קדם יי למימר, מא אעביד לעמא הדין, עוד זעיר פון ורגמוני: ה ואמר יי למשה, עבר קדם עמא, ודבר עמך מסבי ישראל, וחטרך, דמחיתא ביה ית נהרא, סב בידך ותיזיל: ו האנא קאים קדמך תמן על טנרא בחורב, ותמחי בטנרא, ויפקון מניה, מיא וישתי עמא, ועבד כן משה, לעיני סבי ישראל: ז וקרא שמיה דאתרא, נסיתא ומצותא, על דנצו בני ישראל, ועל דנסיאו קדם יי למימר, האית שכינתא דיי, ביננא אם לא: ח ואתא עמלק, ואגיח קרבא עם ישראל ברפידים: ט ואמר משה ליהושע

it is important to remember that even the greatest people failed; what made them great is that they kept going.

AMALEK

The contrast between God's expectations from Israel before and after the crossing of the Reed Sea could not be more complete. Before, facing the approaching Egyptians, Moshe said to the people: "Stand firm and see the deliverance the LORD will bring you today.... The LORD will fight for you; you stay silent" (Ex. 14:13). In other words: Do nothing. God will do it for you. And He did.

In the case of the Amalekites, however, Moshe says to Yehoshua, "Choose men for us, and go out and do battle against Amalek" (17:9). Yehoshua does so and the people wage war. This is the great transition: the Israelites are moving from a situation in which the leader (with the help of God) does everything for the people, to one in which the

after a general election, the successful leader carries the charisma of victory. In the first year, most marriages are happy. It takes no special skill to succeed in good times.

But then the climate changes. Eventually, it always does. That is when many businesses and politicians and marriages fail. There are times when even the greatest people stumble. At such moments, character is tested. The great human beings are not those who never fail. They are those who survive failure, who never give up or give in. They keep trying. They treat failure as a learning experience. And from every refusal to be defeated, they become stronger, wiser, and more determined.

That is the story of Moshe's life. Eventually he will become the man of whom it was said that he was "a hundred and twenty years old when he died," a man whose "eyes had not grown dim, nor his vitality fled" (Deut. 34:7). If there are times when we too feel discouraged and demoralized,

"Choose men for us, and go out and do battle against Amalek. Tomorrow I will
10 stand on top of the hill with the staff of God in my hand." Yehoshua fought the
Amalekites as Moshe had directed him, while Moshe, Aharon, and Ḥur climbed
11 to the top of the hill. Whenever Moshe held his hand high, the Israelites prevailed,
12 but whenever he let his hand drop, the Amalekites prevailed. But Moshe's hands
grew heavy. So they took a stone and placed it under him and he sat, while Aharon
and Ḥur held up his hands, one on each side, so that his hands held true until
13 sunset. And Yehoshua overcame Amalek and his people by the sword.
14 Then the LORD said to Moshe, "Write this as a memorial on a scroll, and commit MAFTIR
it to Yehoshua's ears: I will erase the memory of Amalek, utterly, from under
15 the heavens." Moshe built an altar and named it "The LORD Is My Banner,"

רש"י

ט **בחר לנו.** לי ולך, השוהו לו. מכאן אמרו: "יהי כבוד תלמידך חביב עליך כשלך" (אבות ד, טו). כבוד חברך כמורא רבך, מנין? "ויאמר אהרן אל משה בי אדני" (במדבר יב, יא), והלא גדול האחין היה, ועשה את חברו כרבו. ו"מורא רבך כמורא שמים", שנאמר: "אדני משה כלאם" (שם יא, כח), כלם מן העולם, חייבין הם כליה המורדים בך כאלו פשעו בהקדוש ברוך הוא: **וצא הלחם.** צא מן הענן והלחם בו: **מחר.** בעת המלחמה "אנכי נצב": **בחר לנו אנשים.** גבורים ויראי חטא, שתהא זכותן מסייעתן. דבר אחר, בחר לנו אנשים שיודעין לבטל כשפים, לפי שבני עמלק מכשפים היו:

י **ומשה אהרן וחור.** מכאן לתענית שצריכים שלשה לעבר לפני התבה, שבתענית היו שרויים: **חור.** בנה של מרים היה:

יא **כאשר ירים משה ידו.** וכי ידיו של משה נוצחות היו המלחמה? וכו', כדאיתא בראש השנה (דף כט ע"א):

יב **וידי משה כבדים.** בשביל שנתעצל במצוה ומנה אחר תחתיו, נתיקרו ידיו: **ויקחו.** אהרן וחור "אבן, וישימו תחתיו", ולא ישב לו על כר וכסת, אמר: ישראל שרויין בצער, אף אני אהיה עמהם בצער: **ויהי ידיו אמונה.** ויהי משה ידיו באמונה פרושות השמים בתפלה נאמנה ונכונה: **עד בא השמש.** שהיו עמלקים מחשבין את השעות באצטרולוגיאה באיזו שעה הם נוצחים, והעמיד להם משה חמה וערבב את השעות:

יג **ויחלש יהושע.** חתך ראשי גבוריו ולא השאיר אלא חלשים שבהם, ולא הרגם כלם. מכאן אנו למדים שעשו על פי הדבור של שכינה:

יד **כתב זאת זכרון.** שבא עמלק להזדווג לישראל קדם לכל האמות: **ושים באזני יהושע.** המכניס את ישראל לארץ, שיצוה את ישראל לשלם לו את גמולו. כאן נרמז לו למשה שיהושע מכניס את ישראל לארץ: **כי מחה אמחה.** לכך אני מזהירך כן, כי חפץ אני למחותו:

טו **ויקרא שמו.** של מזבח "ה' נסי" – הקדוש ברוך הוא עשה לנו כאן נס. לא שהמזבח קרוי ה', אלא המזכיר שמו של מזבח זוכר את הנס שעשה המקום, ה' הוא נס שלנו:

overcome by fear at the danger or difficulty that confronted them, and each wanted to escape. Yaakov's angel, Moshe's encounter, and the tempest that threatened to sink Yona's ship were all ways in which Heaven cut off the line of retreat.

Any great undertaking comes with fear. Often we fear failure. Sometimes we even fear success. We long for the security of the familiar, the life we have known. We are afraid of uncharted territory, and the journey itself exposes our vulnerability. Rashbam is telling us that if we have these feelings we should not feel ashamed. Even the greatest people have felt fear. Courage is not fearlessness. It is, in the words of a well-known book title, feeling the fear but doing it anyway.

Sometimes the only way to do this is to know that there is no way back. That is what crossing the Reed Sea meant for the Israelites, and why it was essential that they experienced it at an early stage in their journey. It marked the point of no return, the line of no retreat, the critical point at which they could only move forward.

בְּחַר־לָנוּ אֲנָשִׁים וְצֵא הִלָּחֵם בַּעֲמָלֵק מָחָר אָנֹכִי נִצָּב עַל־רֹאשׁ
י הַגִּבְעָה וּמַטֵּה הָאֱלֹהִים בְּיָדִי׃ וַיַּעַשׂ יְהוֹשֻׁעַ כַּאֲשֶׁר אָמַר־לוֹ מֹשֶׁה
יא לְהִלָּחֵם בַּעֲמָלֵק וּמֹשֶׁה אַהֲרֹן וְחוּר עָלוּ רֹאשׁ הַגִּבְעָה׃ וְהָיָה כַּאֲשֶׁר
יב יָרִים מֹשֶׁה יָדוֹ וְגָבַר יִשְׂרָאֵל וְכַאֲשֶׁר יָנִיחַ יָדוֹ וְגָבַר עֲמָלֵק׃ וִידֵי מֹשֶׁה
כְּבֵדִים וַיִּקְחוּ־אֶבֶן וַיָּשִׂימוּ תַחְתָּיו וַיֵּשֶׁב עָלֶיהָ וְאַהֲרֹן וְחוּר תָּמְכוּ
יג בְיָדָיו מִזֶּה אֶחָד וּמִזֶּה אֶחָד וַיְהִי יָדָיו אֱמוּנָה עַד־בֹּא הַשָּׁמֶשׁ׃ וַיַּחֲלֹשׁ
יְהוֹשֻׁעַ אֶת־עֲמָלֵק וְאֶת־עַמּוֹ לְפִי־חָרֶב׃
יד וַיֹּאמֶר יְהוָה אֶל־מֹשֶׁה כְּתֹב זֹאת זִכָּרוֹן בַּסֵּפֶר וְשִׂים בְּאָזְנֵי יְהוֹשֻׁעַ כִּי־ מפטיר
טו מָחֹה אֶמְחֶה אֶת־זֵכֶר עֲמָלֵק מִתַּחַת הַשָּׁמָיִם׃ וַיִּבֶן מֹשֶׁה מִזְבֵּחַ וַיִּקְרָא

אונקלוס

בְּחַר לַנָא גֻּבְרִין, וּפוֹק אֲגִיחַ קְרָבָא בַּעֲמָלֵק, מְחַר, אֲנָא קָאֵים עַל רֵישׁ רָמְתָא, וְחֻטְרָא דְּאִתְעֲבִידוּ בֵיהּ נִסִּין מִן קֳדָם יי בִּידִי: י וַעֲבַד יְהוֹשֻׁעַ, כְּמָא דַּאֲמַר לֵיהּ מֹשֶׁה, לְאַגָּחָא קְרָבָא בַּעֲמָלֵק, וּמֹשֶׁה אַהֲרֹן וְחוּר, סְלִיקוּ לְרֵישׁ רָמְתָא: יא וַהֲוֵי, כַּד מָרֵים מֹשֶׁה, יְדוֹהִי מִתְגַּבְּרִין דְּבֵית יִשְׂרָאֵל, וְכַד מַנַּח, יְדוֹהִי מִתַּבְּרִין דְּבֵית עֲמָלֵק: יב וִידֵי מֹשֶׁה יְקַרָא, וּנְסִיבוּ אַבְנָא, וְשַׁוִּיאוּ תְּחוֹתוֹהִי וִיתֵיב עֲלַהּ, וְאַהֲרֹן וְחוּר סְעִידִין בִּידוֹהִי, מִכָּא חַד וּמִכָּא חַד, וַהֲוָאָה יְדוֹהִי, פְּרִיסָן בִּצְלוֹ עַד דְּעָאל שִׁמְשָׁא: יג וְתַבַּר יְהוֹשֻׁעַ, יָת עֲמָלֵק וְיָת עַמֵּיהּ לְפִתְגַּם דְּחָרֶב: יד וַאֲמַר יי לְמֹשֶׁה, כְּתוֹב דָּא דָּכְרָנָא בְּסִפְרָא, וְשַׁוִּי קֳדָם יְהוֹשֻׁעַ, אֲרֵי מִמְחָא אֶמְחֵי יָת דָּכְרָנֵיהּ דַּעֲמָלֵק, מִתְּחוֹת שְׁמַיָּא: טו וּבְנָא מֹשֶׁה מַדְבְּחָא, וּפְלַח

Moshe's hands "grew heavy." At such times the leader needs support – even Moshe needs the help of Aharon and Ḥur. In the end, though, his upraised hands were the sign the Israelites needed that God was giving them the strength to prevail, and they did.

"Not with valor and not with strength, but with My spirit," said the prophet (Zech. 4:6). Jewish history is a sustained set of variations on this theme. A small people that, in the face of difficulty, continues to look up will win great victories and achieve great things.

17:9 **וְצֵא הִלָּחֵם בַּעֲמָלֵק** *Do battle against Amalek* – Our *parasha* began with God's concern that "if the people face war… they will change their minds and go back to Egypt." (Ex. 13:17). Yet it ends with another battle, against the Amalekites. And here, *there is no complaint on the part of the people*, no fear, no trauma, no despair. Faced by the Amalekites, the Israelites do not say they want to return to Egypt. Their sheer silence stands in the strongest possible contrast to their earlier complaints about water and food. The Israelites turn out to be good warriors. Having crossed the sea, the people have no way back. They have crossed the Rubicon. Their boats and bridges are burned. They look only forward, for there is no return.

Rashbam connects Yaakov's wrestling match with the angel to the episode in which Moshe, returning to Egypt, is attacked by God (4:24), and also links this to Yona on the stormy ship (commentary on Gen. 32:21–29). All three, he says, were

16 saying, "There is a hand on the LORD's throne. The LORD will be at war with
Amalek throughout the ages."

The haftara for Parashat Beshalaḥ is on page 1534.

רש״י

טז] וַיֹּאמֶר. מֹשֶׁה "כִּי יָד עַל כֵּס יָהּ" – יָדוֹ שֶׁל הַקָּדוֹשׁ בָּרוּךְ הוּא הוּרְמָה לִשָּׁבַע בְּכִסְאוֹ לִהְיוֹת לוֹ מִלְחָמָה וְאֵיבָה בַּעֲמָלֵק עוֹלָמִית. וּמַהוּ "כֵּס" וְלֹא נֶאֱמַר 'כִּסֵּא', וְאַף הַשֵּׁם נֶחֱלַק לְחֶצְיוֹ? נִשְׁבַּע הַקָּדוֹשׁ בָּרוּךְ הוּא שֶׁאֵין שְׁמוֹ שָׁלֵם וְאֵין כִּסְאוֹ שָׁלֵם עַד שֶׁיִּמָּחֶה שְׁמוֹ שֶׁל עֵשָׂו כֻּלּוֹ, וּכְשֶׁיִּמָּחֶה שְׁמוֹ יִהְיֶה הַשֵּׁם שָׁלֵם וְהַכִּסֵּא שָׁלֵם, שֶׁנֶּאֱמַר: "הָאוֹיֵב תַּמּוּ חֳרָבוֹת לָנֶצַח" (תהלים ט, ז) זֶהוּ עֵשָׂו שֶׁכָּתוּב בּוֹ: "וְעֶבְרָתוֹ שְׁמָרָה נֶצַח" (עמוס א, יא), "וְעָרִים נָתַשְׁתָּ אָבַד זִכְרָם הֵמָּה" (תהלים שם), מַהוּ אוֹמֵר אַחֲרָיו? "וַה' לְעוֹלָם יֵשֵׁב" (שם פסוק ח), הֲרֵי הַשֵּׁם שָׁלֵם, "כּוֹנֵן לַמִּשְׁפָּט כִּסְאוֹ" (שם), הֲרֵי הַכִּסֵּא שָׁלֵם:

But the war we fight changes us – and that is something God cannot do for us. We can only do it for ourselves. As long as the Israelites were totally dependent on God, they remained querulous and quarrelsome, in a state of arrested development. Only when they fought their own battles did they eventually – and painfully slowly – begin to acknowledge God. This battle – the one that requires our courage, our eyes turned to heaven – is the one that continues as the journey starts in earnest, and onward to this day.

טז שְׁמ֖וֹ יְהֹוָ֥ה ׀ נִסִּֽי׃ וַיֹּ֗אמֶר כִּֽי־יָד֙ עַל־כֵּ֣ס יָ֔הּ מִלְחָמָ֥ה לַיהֹוָ֖ה בַּעֲמָלֵ֑ק
מִדֹּ֖ר דֹּֽר׃

The הפטרה *for* פרשת בשלח *is on page 1535.*

אונקלוס

עֲלוֹהִי קֳדָם יי דַּעֲבַד לֵיהּ נִסִּין: טז וַאֲמַר, בִּשְׁבוּעָה אֲמִירָא דָּא מִן קֳדָם דְּחִילָא דִּשְׁכִינְתֵּיהּ עַל כֻּרְסֵי יְקָרָא, דַּעֲתִיד דְּיִתְּגַח קְרָבָא קֳדָם יי בִּדְבֵית עֲמָלֵק, לְשֵׁיצָיוּתְהוֹן מִדָּרֵי עָלְמָא:

17:16 **מדר דר** *Throughout the ages* – The opening and closing verses of Beshalaḥ both contain as their key word *milḥama*, "war." The opening verse states: "When Pharaoh let the people go, God did not lead them through the land of the Philistines, though it was the shorter way. 'If the people face war,' thought God, 'they will change their minds and go back to Egypt'" (Ex. 13:17). The closing verse says: "The Lord will be at war with Amalek throughout the ages" (17:16).

The difference between them is between the war God fights for us, and the war we fight for God. The first is miraculous, the second only metaphorically so. The war God fights changes nature, even to the point of dividing a sea.

Parashat Yitro

18 1 Moshe's father-in-law Yitro, priest of Midyan, heard about all that God had done
for Moshe and for His people Israel when the Lord brought Israel out of Egypt.
2 3 Yitro had received Moshe's wife Tzipora after he had sent her home, together
with her two sons. One was named Gershom, for Moshe had said, "I have been
4 a stranger in a foreign land," and the other, Eliezer, for he had said, "My father's
5 God has helped me, saving me from Pharaoh's sword." And now Moshe's father-
in-law Yitro came to Moshe in the desert, bringing his sons and his wife, to
6 where he was encamped by the mountain of God. Yitro sent word to Moshe, "I
am coming to you – your father-in-law Yitro – together with your wife and both
7 of your sons." Moshe went out to greet his father-in-law and bowed down and
kissed him. Each asked after the other's welfare, and they went inside the tent.
8 And Moshe told his father-in-law all that the Lord had done to Pharaoh and
the Egyptians, for Israel's sake, all the hardship they had encountered along the
9 way, and how the Lord had rescued them. Yitro delighted in all the good that

רש״י

יח א **וישמע יתרו.** מה שמועה שמע? קריעת ים סוף ומלחמת עמלק: **יתרו.** שבעה שמות נקראו לו: רעואל, יתר, יתרו, חובב, חבר, קיני, פוטיאל. יתר, על שם שיתר פרשה אחת בתורה: "ואתה תחזה" (להלן פסוק כא); יתרו, לכשנתגייר וקיים המצוות הוסיפו לו אות; חובב, שחבב את התורה, חובב הוא יתרו, שנאמר: "מבני חבב חתן משה" (שופטים ד, יא). ויש אומרים: רעואל אביו של יתרו היה, ומהו אומר: "ותבאנה אל רעואל אביהן" (לעיל ב, יח)? שהתינוקות קורין לאבי אביהן אבא. בספרי (בהעלותך עח): **חתן משה.** כאן היה יתרו מתכבד במשה: אני חותן המלך, ולשעבר היה משה תולה הגדולה בחמיו, שנאמר: "וישב אל יתר חתנו" (לעיל ד, יח): **למשה ולישראל.** שקול משה כנגד כל ישראל: **את כל אשר עשה.** להם בירידת המן ובבאר ובעמלק: **כי הוציא ה' וגו'.** זו גדולה על כלם:

ב **אחר שלוחיה.** כשאמר לו הקדוש ברוך הוא במדין: "לך שב מצרים", "ויקח משה את אשתו ואת בניו" וגו' (לעיל ד, יט-כ), ויצא אהרן לקראתו "ויפגשהו בהר האלהים" (שם פסוק כז); אמר לו: מי הם הללו? אמר לו: זו אשתי שנשאתי במדין ואלו בני. אמר לו: והיכן אתה מוליכן? אמר לו: למצרים. אמר לו: על הראשונים אנו מצטערים ואתה בא להוסיף עליהם? אמר לה: לכי לבית אביך. נטלה שני בניה והלכה לה:

ד **ויצלני מחרב פרעה.** כשגלו דתן ואבירם על דבר המצרי ובקש להרג את משה, נעשה צוארו כעמוד של שיש:

ה **אל המדבר.** אף אנו יודעים שבמדבר היו, אלא בשבחו של יתרו דבר הכתוב, שהיה יושב בכבודו של עולם, ונדבו לבו לצאת אל המדבר מקום תהו לשמע דברי תורה:

ו **ויאמר אל משה.** על ידי שליח: **אני חתנך יתרו וגו'.** אם אין אתה יוצא בגיני צא בגין אשתך, ואם אין אתה יוצא בגין אשתך צא בגין שני בניה:

ז **ויצא משה.** כבוד גדול נתכבד יתרו באותה שעה; כיון שיצא משה יצא אהרן נדב ואביהוא, ומי הוא שראה את אלו יוצאין ולא יצא?: **וישתחו וישק לו.** איני יודע מי השתחוה למי, כשהוא אומר: "איש לרעהו", מי הקרוי "איש"? זה משה (ראה במדבר יב, ג):

ח **ויספר משה לחתנו.** למשך את לבו לקרבו לתורה: **את כל התלאה.** שעל הים ושל עמלק: **התלאה.** למ"ד אל"ף מן היסוד של תבה, והתי"ו הוא תקון ויסוד הנופל ממנו לפרקים. וכן: תרומה, תנופה, תקומה, תנואה:

ט **ויחד יתרו.** וישמח יתרו, זהו פשוטו. ומדרשו, נעשה בשרו חדודין חדודין, מצר על אבוד מצרים. "היינו דאמרי אנשי: גיורא, עד עשרה

פרשת יתרו

יח א וַיִּשְׁמַע יִתְרוֹ כֹהֵן מִדְיָן חֹתֵן מֹשֶׁה אֵת כָּל־אֲשֶׁר עָשָׂה אֱלֹהִים לְמֹשֶׁה יד
ב וּלְיִשְׂרָאֵל עַמּוֹ כִּי־הוֹצִיא יהוה אֶת־יִשְׂרָאֵל מִמִּצְרָיִם: וַיִּקַּח יִתְרוֹ חֹתֵן
ג מֹשֶׁה אֶת־צִפֹּרָה אֵשֶׁת מֹשֶׁה אַחַר שִׁלּוּחֶיהָ: וְאֵת שְׁנֵי בָנֶיהָ אֲשֶׁר שֵׁם
ד הָאֶחָד גֵּרְשֹׁם כִּי אָמַר גֵּר הָיִיתִי בְּאֶרֶץ נָכְרִיָּה: וְשֵׁם הָאֶחָד אֱלִיעֶזֶר
ה כִּי־אֱלֹהֵי אָבִי בְּעֶזְרִי וַיַּצִּלֵנִי מֵחֶרֶב פַּרְעֹה: וַיָּבֹא יִתְרוֹ חֹתֵן מֹשֶׁה וּבָנָיו
וְאִשְׁתּוֹ אֶל־מֹשֶׁה אֶל־הַמִּדְבָּר אֲשֶׁר־הוּא חֹנֶה שָׁם הַר הָאֱלֹהִים:
ו וַיֹּאמֶר אֶל־מֹשֶׁה אֲנִי חֹתֶנְךָ יִתְרוֹ בָּא אֵלֶיךָ וְאִשְׁתְּךָ וּשְׁנֵי בָנֶיהָ עִמָּהּ:
ז וַיֵּצֵא מֹשֶׁה לִקְרַאת חֹתְנוֹ וַיִּשְׁתַּחוּ וַיִּשַּׁק־לוֹ וַיִּשְׁאֲלוּ אִישׁ־לְרֵעֵהוּ
ח לְשָׁלוֹם וַיָּבֹאוּ הָאֹהֱלָה: וַיְסַפֵּר מֹשֶׁה לְחֹתְנוֹ אֵת כָּל־אֲשֶׁר עָשָׂה יהוה
לְפַרְעֹה וּלְמִצְרַיִם עַל אוֹדֹת יִשְׂרָאֵל אֵת כָּל־הַתְּלָאָה אֲשֶׁר מְצָאָתַם
ט בַּדֶּרֶךְ וַיַּצִּלֵם יהוה: וַיִּחַדְּ יִתְרוֹ עַל כָּל־הַטּוֹבָה אֲשֶׁר־עָשָׂה יהוה

אונקלוס

יח א וּשְׁמַע, יִתְרוֹ רַבָּא דְמִדְיָן חֲמוּהִי דְמֹשֶׁה, יָת כָּל דַּעֲבַד יי לְמֹשֶׁה, וּלְיִשְׂרָאֵל עַמֵּיהּ, אֲרֵי אַפֵּיק יי, יָת יִשְׂרָאֵל מִמִּצְרָיִם: ב וּדְבַר, יִתְרוֹ חֲמוּהִי דְמֹשֶׁה, יָת צִפּוֹרָה אִתַּת מֹשֶׁה, בָּתַר דְּשַׁלְּחַהּ: ג וְיָת תְּרֵין בְּנַהָא, דְשׁוּם חַד גֵּרְשׁוֹם, אֲרֵי אֲמַר, דַּיָּר הֲוֵיתִי, בַּאֲרַע נֻכְרָאָה: ד וְשׁוּם חַד אֱלִיעֶזֶר, אֲרֵי אֱלָהֵיהּ דְּאַבָּא הֲוָה בְּסַעֲדִי, וְשֵׁיזְבַנִי מֵחַרְבָּא דְּפַרְעֹה: ה וַאֲתָא, יִתְרוֹ חֲמוּהִי דְמֹשֶׁה, וּבְנוֹהִי וְאִתְּתֵיהּ לְוָת מֹשֶׁה, לְמַדְבְּרָא, דְּהוּא, שָׁרֵי תַמָּן לְטוּרָא דְּאִתְגְּלִי עֲלוֹהִי יְקָרָא דַיי: ו וַאֲמַר לְמֹשֶׁה, אֲנָא, חֲמוּךְ יִתְרוֹ אָתֵי לְוָתָךְ, וְאִתְּתָךְ, וּתְרֵין בְּנַהָא עִמַּהּ: ז וּנְפַק מֹשֶׁה לְקַדָּמוּת חֲמוּהִי, וּסְגֵיד וְנַשֵּׁיק לֵיהּ, וּשְׁאִילוּ גְּבַר לְחַבְרֵיהּ לִשְׁלָם, וְעָאלוּ לְמַשְׁכְּנָא: ח וְאִשְׁתָּעִי מֹשֶׁה לַחֲמוּהִי, יָת כָּל דַּעֲבַד יי לְפַרְעֹה וּלְמִצְרָאֵי, עַל עֵיסַק יִשְׂרָאֵל, יָת כָּל עָקְתָא דְּאַשְׁכַּחְתְּנוּן בְּאוֹרְחָא, וְשֵׁיזֵיבִנּוּן יי: ט וַחֲדִי יִתְרוֹ, עַל כָּל טָבְתָא, דַּעֲבַד יי

YITRO

Parashat Yitro is divided into two episodes. In the first (ch. 18), Israel receives its first system of governance – devolved to leaders of thousands, hundreds, fifties, and tens – at the advice of Yitro, Moshe's father-in-law, whose name the *parasha* bears. In the second (chs. 19–20), it receives its eternal constitution by way of a covenant with God, making the entire nation into "a kingdom of priests." A brief summation of its key elements is given by the voice of God Himself in the form of the Ten Commandments (or Utterances). The twin tablets with their ten commands are the enduring symbol of eternal law under the sovereignty of God.

Both episodes, Yitro and the revelation at Sinai, have one theme in common, namely the *delegation, distribution, and democratization* of human leadership. Only God can rule alone.

10 the LORD had done for Israel, in His liberating them from the Egyptians, and
said, "Blessed be the LORD who has rescued you from Egypt and Pharaoh
11 and liberated the people from the Egyptians' hands. Now I know that the
LORD is greater than all gods – for He brought upon them what they schemed
12 against others." Then Yitro brought a burnt offering and sacrifices to God. And
Aharon and all the elders of Israel came to break bread with Moshe's father-
13 in-law before God. The next day Moshe sat to serve the people as judge. From SHENI
14 morning to evening the people stood before him. When Moshe's father-in-law
saw everything Moshe did for the people, he asked, "What is this that you do
for the people? Why do you sit alone while all the people stand over you from
15 morning to evening?" "The people come to me to inquire of God," Moshe

רש״י

דָּרֵי לָא תְּבַזֵּי אֲרַמָּאָה בְּאַפֵּיהּ" (סנהדרין צד ע"א): **עַל כָּל הַטּוֹבָה.** טוֹבַת הַמָּן וְהַבְּאֵר וְהַתּוֹרָה. וְעַל כֻּלָּן "אֲשֶׁר הִצִּילוֹ מִיַּד מִצְרָיִם", עַד עַכְשָׁיו לֹא הָיָה עֶבֶד יָכוֹל לִבְרֹחַ מִמִּצְרַיִם, שֶׁהָיְתָה הָאָרֶץ מְסֻגֶּרֶת, וְאֵלּוּ יָצְאוּ שִׁשִּׁים רִבּוֹא:

י **אֲשֶׁר הִצִּיל אֶתְכֶם מִיַּד מִצְרַיִם.** אֻמָּה קָשָׁה: **וּמִיַּד פַּרְעֹה.** מֶלֶךְ קָשֶׁה: **מִתַּחַת יַד מִצְרָיִם.** כְּתַרְגּוּמוֹ, לְשׁוֹן רִדּוּי וּמָרוּת הַיָּד שֶׁהָיוּ מַכְבִּידִים עֲלֵיהֶם, הִיא הָעֲבוֹדָה:

יא **עַתָּה יָדַעְתִּי.** מַכִּירוֹ הָיִיתִי לְשֶׁעָבַר, וְעַכְשָׁיו בְּיוֹתֵר: **מִכָּל הָאֱלֹהִים.** מְלַמֵּד שֶׁהָיָה מַכִּיר בְּכָל עֲבוֹדָה זָרָה שֶׁבָּעוֹלָם, שֶׁלֹּא הִנִּיחַ עֲבוֹדָה זָרָה שֶׁלֹּא עֲבָדָהּ: **כִּי בַדָּבָר אֲשֶׁר זָדוּ עֲלֵיהֶם.** כְּתַרְגּוּמוֹ, בַּמַּיִם דִּמּוּ לְאַבְּדָם וְהֵם נֶאֶבְדוּ בַּמַּיִם: **אֲשֶׁר זָדוּ.** אֲשֶׁר הִרְשִׁיעוּ. וְרַבּוֹתֵינוּ דְּרָשׁוּהוּ לְשׁוֹן: "וַיָּזֶד יַעֲקֹב נָזִיד" (בראשית כה, כט), בַּקְּדֵרָה שֶׁבִּשְּׁלוּ בָּהּ נִתְבַּשְּׁלוּ:

יב **עֹלָה.** כְּמַשְׁמָעָהּ, שֶׁהִיא כֻּלָּהּ כָּלִיל: **וּזְבָחִים.** שְׁלָמִים: **וַיָּבֹא אַהֲרֹן וְגוֹ׳.** וּמֹשֶׁה הֵיכָן הָלַךְ? וַהֲלֹא הוּא שֶׁיָּצָא לִקְרָאתוֹ וְגָרַם לוֹ אֶת כָּל הַכָּבוֹד? אֶלָּא שֶׁהָיָה עוֹמֵד וּמְשַׁמֵּשׁ לִפְנֵיהֶם: **לִפְנֵי הָאֱלֹהִים.** מִכָּאן שֶׁהַנֶּהֱנֶה מִסְּעוּדָה שֶׁתַּלְמִידֵי חֲכָמִים מְסֻבִּין בָּהּ כְּאִלּוּ נֶהֱנֶה מִזִּיו הַשְּׁכִינָה:

יג **וַיְהִי מִמָּחֳרָת.** מוֹצָאֵי יוֹם הַכִּפּוּרִים הָיָה, כָּךְ שָׁנִינוּ בְּסִפְרֵי (ראה מכילתא יתרו, עמלק א). וּמַהוּ "מִמָּחֳרָת"? לְמָחֳרַת רִדְתּוֹ מִן הָהָר. וְעַל כָּרְחֲךָ אִי אֶפְשָׁר לוֹמַר אֶלָּא מִמָּחֳרַת יוֹם הַכִּפּוּרִים, שֶׁהֲרֵי קֹדֶם מַתַּן תּוֹרָה אִי אֶפְשָׁר לוֹמַר "וְהוֹדַעְתִּי אֶת חֻקֵּי" וְגוֹ׳ (להלן פסוק טז), וּמִשֶּׁנִּתְּנָה תּוֹרָה עַד יוֹם הַכִּפּוּרִים לֹא יָשַׁב מֹשֶׁה לִשְׁפֹּט אֶת הָעָם, שֶׁהֲרֵי בְּשִׁבְעָה עָשָׂר בְּתַמּוּז יָרַד וְשִׁבֵּר אֶת הַלּוּחוֹת, וּלְמָחָר עָלָה בְּהַשְׁכָּמָה וְשָׁהָה שְׁמוֹנִים יוֹם וְיָרַד בְּיוֹם הַכִּפּוּרִים. וְאֵין פָּרָשָׁה זוֹ כְּתוּבָה כַּסֵּדֶר, שֶׁלֹּא נֶאֱמַר: "וַיְהִי מִמָּחֳרָת" עַד שָׁנָה שְׁנִיָּה. אַף לְדִבְרֵי הָאוֹמֵר יִתְרוֹ קֹדֶם מַתַּן תּוֹרָה בָּא, שִׁלּוּחוֹ אֶל אַרְצוֹ לֹא הָיָה אֶלָּא עַד שָׁנָה שְׁנִיָּה, שֶׁהֲרֵי נֶאֱמַר כָּאן: "וַיְשַׁלַּח מֹשֶׁה אֶת חֹתְנוֹ" (להלן פסוק כז), וּמָצִינוּ בְּמַסַּע הַדְּגָלִים שֶׁאָמַר לוֹ מֹשֶׁה: "נֹסְעִים אֲנַחְנוּ אֶל הַמָּקוֹם וְגוֹ׳ אַל נָא תַּעֲזֹב אוֹתָנוּ" (במדבר י, כט-לא), וְאִם זֶה קֹדֶם מַתַּן תּוֹרָה, מִשֶּׁשִּׁלְּחוֹ וְהָלַךְ הֵיכָן מָצִינוּ שֶׁחָזַר? וְאִם תֹּאמַר, שָׁם לֹא נֶאֱמַר יִתְרוֹ אֶלָּא חוֹבָב, וּבְנוֹ שֶׁל יִתְרוֹ הָיָה – הוּא חוֹבָב הוּא יִתְרוֹ, שֶׁהֲרֵי כָּתוּב: "מִבְּנֵי חֹבָב חֹתֵן מֹשֶׁה" (שופטים ד, יא): **וַיֵּשֶׁב מֹשֶׁה... וַיַּעֲמֹד הָעָם.** יוֹשֵׁב כְּמֶלֶךְ וְכֻלָּן עוֹמְדִים, וְהֻקְשָׁה הַדָּבָר לְיִתְרוֹ שֶׁהָיָה מְזַלְזֵל בִּכְבוֹדָן שֶׁל יִשְׂרָאֵל וְהוֹכִיחוֹ עַל כָּךְ, שֶׁנֶּאֱמַר: "מַדּוּעַ אַתָּה יוֹשֵׁב לְבַדֶּךָ" וְכֻלָּם נִצָּבִים: **מִן הַבֹּקֶר עַד הָעָרֶב.** אֶפְשָׁר לוֹמַר כֵּן?! אֶלָּא כָּל דַּיָּן שֶׁדָּן דִּין אֱמֶת לַאֲמִתּוֹ אֲפִלּוּ שָׁעָה אַחַת מַעֲלֶה עָלָיו הַכָּתוּב כְּאִלּוּ עוֹסֵק בַּתּוֹרָה כָּל הַיּוֹם, וּכְאִלּוּ נַעֲשָׂה שֻׁתָּף לְהַקָּדוֹשׁ בָּרוּךְ הוּא בְּמַעֲשֵׂה בְרֵאשִׁית שֶׁנֶּאֱמַר בּוֹ: "וַיְהִי עֶרֶב וַיְהִי בֹקֶר יוֹם אֶחָד" (בראשית א, ה):

טו **כִּי יָבֹא.** כִּי בָא, לְשׁוֹן הֹוֶה, "לְמִתְבַּע אֻלְפָן", לִשְׁאֹל תַּלְמוּד מִפִּי הַגְּבוּרָה:

advice, coming, as it were, from the outside, gives Israel its first system of governance. The religion of Israel is not the religion of everyone, but the God of Israel is the God of everyone. You do not have to be Jewish to be good, wise, or beloved of God.

י לְיִשְׂרָאֵל אֲשֶׁר הִצִּילוֹ מִיַּד מִצְרָיִם׃ וַיֹּאמֶר יִתְרוֹ בָּרוּךְ יְהוָה אֲשֶׁר
הִצִּיל אֶתְכֶם מִיַּד מִצְרַיִם וּמִיַּד פַּרְעֹה אֲשֶׁר הִצִּיל אֶת־הָעָם מִתַּחַת
יא יַד־מִצְרָיִם׃ עַתָּה יָדַעְתִּי כִּי־גָדוֹל יְהוָה מִכָּל־הָאֱלֹהִים כִּי בַדָּבָר
יב אֲשֶׁר זָדוּ עֲלֵיהֶם׃ וַיִּקַּח יִתְרוֹ חֹתֵן מֹשֶׁה עֹלָה וּזְבָחִים לֵאלֹהִים וַיָּבֹא
אַהֲרֹן וְכֹל ׀ זִקְנֵי יִשְׂרָאֵל לֶאֱכָל־לֶחֶם עִם־חֹתֵן מֹשֶׁה לִפְנֵי הָאֱלֹהִים׃
יג וַיְהִי מִמָּחֳרָת וַיֵּשֶׁב מֹשֶׁה לִשְׁפֹּט אֶת־הָעָם וַיַּעֲמֹד הָעָם עַל־מֹשֶׁה שני
יד מִן־הַבֹּקֶר עַד־הָעָרֶב׃ וַיַּרְא חֹתֵן מֹשֶׁה אֵת כָּל־אֲשֶׁר־הוּא עֹשֶׂה לָעָם
וַיֹּאמֶר מָה־הַדָּבָר הַזֶּה אֲשֶׁר אַתָּה עֹשֶׂה לָעָם מַדּוּעַ אַתָּה יוֹשֵׁב לְבַדֶּךָ
טו וְכָל־הָעָם נִצָּב עָלֶיךָ מִן־בֹּקֶר עַד־עָרֶב׃ וַיֹּאמֶר מֹשֶׁה לְחֹתְנוֹ כִּי־יָבֹא

אונקלוס

לְיִשְׂרָאֵל, דְּשֵׁיזֵיבְנוּן מִידָא דְּמִצְרָאֵי: י וַאֲמַר יִתְרוֹ, בְּרִיךְ יְיָ, דְּשֵׁיזֵיב יָתְכוֹן, מִידָא דְמִצְרָאֵי וּמִידָא דְּפַרְעֹה, דְּשֵׁיזֵיב יָת עַמָּא, מִתְּחוֹת מָרוּת מִצְרָאֵי: יא כְּעַן יְדַעְנָא, אֲרֵי רַב יְיָ וְלֵית אֱלָהּ בַּר מִנֵּיהּ, אֲרֵי בְּפִתְגָּמָא, דְּחַשִׁיבוּ מִצְרָאֵי לְמִדַּן יָת יִשְׂרָאֵל בֵּיהּ דָּנִנּוּן: יב וְקָרֵיב, יִתְרוֹ חֲמוּהִי דְּמֹשֶׁה, עֲלָוָן וְנִכְסַת קֻדְשִׁין קֳדָם יְיָ, וַאֲתָא אַהֲרֹן, וְכֹל סָבֵי יִשְׂרָאֵל,

לְמֵיכַל לַחְמָא, עִם חֲמוּהִי דְּמֹשֶׁה קֳדָם יְיָ: יג וַהֲוָה בְּיוֹמָא דְּבָתְרוֹהִי, וִיתֵיב מֹשֶׁה לְמִדַּן יָת עַמָּא, וְקָם עַמָּא עִלָּוֹהִי דְּמֹשֶׁה, מִן צַפְרָא עַד רַמְשָׁא: יד וַחֲזָא חֲמוּהִי דְּמֹשֶׁה, יָת, כָּל דְּהוּא עָבֵיד לְעַמָּא, וַאֲמַר, מָא פִתְגָּמָא הָדֵין דְּאַתְּ עָבֵיד לְעַמָּא, מָדֵין, אַתְּ יָתֵיב בִּלְחוֹדָךְ, וְכָל עַמָּא, קָיְמִין עִלָּוָךְ מִן צַפְרָא עַד רַמְשָׁא: טו וַאֲמַר מֹשֶׁה לַחֲמוּהִי, אֲרֵי אָתַן

18:10 בָּרוּךְ יהוה *Blessed be the* Lord – The quintessential Jewish expression of thanks, gratitude, and acknowledgment is *barukh Hashem*, meaning "thank God" or "praise be to the Lord."

Hasidim say of the Baal Shem Tov that he would travel around the little towns and villages of Eastern Europe, asking Jews how they were. However poor or troubled they were, invariably they would reply, "*Barukh Hashem*." It was an instinctive expression of faith, and every Jew knew it. They might have lacked the learning of the great talmudic scholar, or the wealth of the successful, but they believed they had much to thank God for, and they did so. When asked what he was doing and why, the Baal Shem Tov would reply by quoting the verse "But You are the Holy One, enthroned on Israel's praises" (Ps. 22:4). Every time a Jew says *Barukh Hashem*, he or she is helping to make a throne for the *Shekhina*, the Divine Presence.

Three people in the Torah use this expression – but all of them are non-Jews, people outside the Abrahamic covenant. The first is Noaḥ: "Blessed be the Lord, God of Shem" (Gen. 9:26). The second is Avraham's servant, presumed to be Eliezer, whom Avraham sends to find a wife for Yitzḥak: "Blessed be the Lord, God of my master Avraham, who has not withheld His kindness and faithfulness from my master" (24:27). The third is Yitro here. You do not need to be Jewish to have a sense of reverence for the Creator or to recognize, as Yitro did, His hand in miraculous events.

God is universal. Therefore humanity, created in His image, is universal. This is an essential reminder. The great problems humanity faces are global, while our most effective political agencies are at most national. We need to find a way of combining our universal humanity with our cultural and religious particularity.

No one demonstrates this better than Yitro. His wise

16 replied. "When they have a dispute, they come to me and I judge between one
17 neighbor and another, and I make God's laws and teachings known." Moshe's
18 father-in-law said to him, "What you are doing is not good. You will be worn
away, and this people along with you. It is too heavy a burden for you. You
19 cannot carry it alone. Now listen to me, let me advise you; and may God be with
you. You speak for the people before God, and bring their concerns to Him.
20 And you must acquaint them with His precepts and laws, and make known to
21 them the path they are to walk and the way they must act. You, as well, must
seek out among the people capable men – God-fearing, trustworthy men, who

רש״י

טז **כִּי יִהְיֶה לָהֶם דָּבָר.** מִי שֶׁיִּהְיֶה לוֹ דָּבָר בָּא אֵלַי:

יז **וַיֹּאמֶר חֹתֵן מֹשֶׁה.** דֶּרֶךְ כָּבוֹד קוֹרְאוֹ הַכָּתוּב, חוֹתְנוֹ שֶׁל מֶלֶךְ:

יח **נָבֹל תִּבֹּל.** כְּתַרְגּוּמוֹ. וּלְשׁוֹנוֹ לְשׁוֹן כְּמִישָׁה, פלייסטר״א בְּלַעַז, כְּמוֹ: "וְהֶעָלֶה נָבֵל" (ירמיה ח, יג), "כִּנְבֹל עָלֶה מִגֶּפֶן" (ישעיה לד, ד), שֶׁהוּא כָּמוּשׁ עַל יְדֵי חַמָּה וְעַל יְדֵי קֶרַח וְכֹחוֹ תָּשׁ וְנִלְאֶה: **גַּם אַתָּה.** לְרַבּוֹת אַהֲרֹן וְחוּר וְשִׁבְעִים זְקֵנִים: **כִּי כָבֵד מִמְּךָ.** כָּבְדּוֹ רַב יוֹתֵר מִכֹּחֲךָ:

יט **אִיעָצְךָ וִיהִי אֱלֹהִים עִמָּךְ.** בְּעֵצָה, אָמַר לוֹ: צֵא הִמָּלֵךְ בַּגְּבוּרָה: **הֱיֵה אַתָּה לָעָם מוּל הָאֱלֹהִים.** שָׁלִיחַ וּמֵלִיץ בֵּינוֹתָם לַמָּקוֹם וְשׁוֹאֵל מִשְׁפָּטִים מֵאִתּוֹ: **אֶת הַדְּבָרִים.** דִּבְרֵי רִיבוֹתָם:

כא **וְאַתָּה תֶחֱזֶה.** בְּרוּחַ הַקֹּדֶשׁ שֶׁעָלֶיךָ: **אַנְשֵׁי חַיִל.** עֲשִׁירִים, שֶׁאֵין צְרִיכִין לְהַחֲנִיף וּלְהַכִּיר פָּנִים: **אַנְשֵׁי אֱמֶת.** אֵלּוּ בַּעֲלֵי הַבְטָחָה שֶׁהֵם כְּדַאי לִסְמֹךְ עַל דִּבְרֵיהֶם, שֶׁעַל יְדֵי כָּךְ יִהְיוּ דִּבְרֵיהֶם נִשְׁמָעִין: **שֹׂנְאֵי בָצַע.** שֶׁשּׂוֹנְאִים אֶת מָמוֹנָם בַּדִּין, כְּהַהִיא דְּאָמְרִינַן: כָּל דַּיָּנָא דְּמַפְּקִין מָמוֹנָא מִנֵּיהּ בְּדִינָא לָאו דַּיָּנָא הוּא: **שָׂרֵי אֲלָפִים.** הֵם הָיוּ שֵׁשׁ מֵאוֹת

The idea that humanity is created in the image of God is a subtle one, because central to the Tanakh is the idea that God has no image. His very name, God tells Moshe, is *Ehye asher Ehye*, "I will be what I will be" (Ex. 3:14). God is Being in its infinite, open-ended unpredictability. What is divine about humanity is its diversity, not its uniformity.

But the individual is not self-sufficient. Each of us lacks some gift that someone else has. To achieve anything we must form associations, and this gives rise to the political process. Rambam puts it thus:

> This great variety [among humans] and the necessity of social life are essential elements in man's nature. But the well-being of society demands that there should be a leader able to regulate the actions of man; he must complete every shortcoming, remove every excess, and prescribe for the conduct of all, so that the natural variety should be counterbalanced by the uniformity of legislation, and the order of society be well established. I therefore maintain that the Law, though not a product of nature, is nonetheless not entirely foreign to nature. (*Guide for the Perplexed* II:40)

People are different, but they must be able to form societies. This requires laws, a legislator, and a source of legislative authority. Humanity needs political structures. In the narrative of our *parasha*, a legal system exists and must be honed before the laws are even given. We need *ḥokhma* to support Torah, and in this case it comes from Yitro.

18:17 **לֹא־טוֹב** *Not good* – Moshe must learn to delegate and share the burden of leadership. Interestingly, the sentence "What you are doing is not good (*lo tov*)" is one of only two places in the Torah where the phrase "not good" occurs. The other (Gen. 2:18) is "It is not good for man to be alone." We cannot live alone; we cannot lead alone. That is one of the axioms of biblical anthropology. The Hebrew word for life, *ḥayyim*, is in the plural, as if to signify that life is essentially shared.

18:21 **וְאַתָּה תֶחֱזֶה... אַנְשֵׁי־חַיִל** *Seek out… capable men* – The Kotzker Rebbe once drew attention to a difficulty in Rashi's writing. In the opening verse of our *parasha* (Ex. 18:1), Rashi says that Yitro was given the name Yeter ("he added")

טז אֵלַי הָעָם לִדְרֹשׁ אֱלֹהִים: כִּי־יִהְיֶה לָהֶם דָּבָר בָּא אֵלַי וְשָׁפַטְתִּי בֵּין
יז אִישׁ וּבֵין רֵעֵהוּ וְהוֹדַעְתִּי אֶת־חֻקֵּי הָאֱלֹהִים וְאֶת־תּוֹרֹתָיו: וַיֹּאמֶר
יח חֹתֵן מֹשֶׁה אֵלָיו לֹא־טוֹב הַדָּבָר אֲשֶׁר אַתָּה עֹשֶׂה: נָבֹל תִּבֹּל גַּם־
אַתָּה גַּם־הָעָם הַזֶּה אֲשֶׁר עִמָּךְ כִּי־כָבֵד מִמְּךָ הַדָּבָר לֹא־תוּכַל עֲשֹׂהוּ
יט לְבַדֶּךָ: עַתָּה שְׁמַע בְּקֹלִי אִיעָצְךָ וִיהִי אֱלֹהִים עִמָּךְ הֱיֵה אַתָּה לָעָם
כ מוּל הָאֱלֹהִים וְהֵבֵאתָ אַתָּה אֶת־הַדְּבָרִים אֶל־הָאֱלֹהִים: וְהִזְהַרְתָּה
אֶתְהֶם אֶת־הַחֻקִּים וְאֶת־הַתּוֹרֹת וְהוֹדַעְתָּ לָהֶם אֶת־הַדֶּרֶךְ יֵלְכוּ
כא בָהּ וְאֶת־הַמַּעֲשֶׂה אֲשֶׁר יַעֲשׂוּן: וְאַתָּה תֶחֱזֶה מִכָּל־הָעָם אַנְשֵׁי־חַיִל
יִרְאֵי אֱלֹהִים אַנְשֵׁי אֱמֶת שֹׂנְאֵי בָצַע וְשַׂמְתָּ עֲלֵהֶם שָׂרֵי אֲלָפִים שָׂרֵי

אונקלוס

לְוָתִי, עַמָּא לְמִתְבַּע אֻלְפַן מִן קֳדָם יְיָ: טז כַּד הָוֵי לְהוֹן דִּינָא אָתַן לְוָתִי, וְדָאֵינְנָא, בֵּין גַּבְרָא וּבֵין חַבְרֵיהּ, וּמְהוֹדַעְנָא לְהוֹן, יָת קְיָמַיָּא דַּיְיָ וְיָת אוֹרָיָתֵיהּ: יז וַאֲמַר, חֲמוּהִי דְּמֹשֶׁה לֵיהּ, לָא תָקִין פִּתְגָּמָא, דְּאַתְּ עָבֵיד: יח מִלְאָה תִלְאֵי, אַף אַתְּ, אַף עַמָּא הָדֵין דְּעִמָּךְ, אֲרֵי יַקִּיר מִנָּךְ פִּתְגָּמָא, לָא תִכּוֹל לְמֶעְבְּדֵיהּ בִּלְחוֹדָךְ: יט כְּעַן, קַבֵּיל מִנִּי אַמְלְכִנָּךְ, וִיהֵי מֵימְרָא דַּיְיָ בְּסַעְדָּךְ, הֱוִי אַתְּ לְעַמָּא, תָּבַע אֻלְפַן מִן קֳדָם יְיָ, וּתְהֵי מַיְתֵי אַתְּ, יָת פִּתְגָּמַיָּא לִקְדָם יְיָ: כ וְתַזְהַר יָתְהוֹן, יָת קְיָמַיָּא וְיָת אוֹרָיָתָא, וּתְהוֹדַע לְהוֹן, יָת אוֹרְחָא דִּיְהָכוּן בַּהּ, וְיָת עוֹבָדָא דְּיַעְבְּדוּן: כא וְאַתְּ תִּחְזֵי מִכָּל עַמָּא, גֻּבְרִין דְּחֵילָא דַּחֲלַיָּא דַּיְיָ, גֻּבְרִין דִּקְשׁוֹט דְּסָנַן לְקַבָּלָא מָמוֹן, וּתְמַנֵּי עֲלֵיהוֹן, רַבָּנֵי אַלְפֵי רַבָּנֵי

YITRO ADVISES MOSHE

One of the classic commentaries, *Ohr HaḤayyim* (authored by Rabbi Ḥayyim ibn Attar of Morocco, later of Israel, 1696–1743) made a striking observation on Yitro's lesson to Moshe:

> It seems to me that the reason [that this teaching came from Yitro] is that God wanted to show the Israelites of that generation – and of all generations – that there are among the nations of the world great masters of understanding and intellect (*gedolim behavana u'vehaskala*). The example of this was Yitro: his advice and the way he chose to organize a society. For there are indeed among the nations people who recognize well-authenticated propositions (*devarim me'usharim*).

The forms and structures of governance are not specifically Jewish. They are part of *ḥokhma*, the wisdom of humankind. Jews have known many forms of leadership. In fact, the Torah says about monarchy that a time will come when the people say, "I will set a king over me, like all the surrounding nations" (Deut. 17:14) – the only case in the entire Torah in which the people of Israel are commanded – or permitted – to imitate other nations. There is nothing uniquely Jewish about political structures.

Religion does not specify an ideal form of government, but it does provide us with a set of values or principles against which a system can be judged. What are they? The first is the epic statement of the opening chapter of the Tanakh, that the human individual is created "in the image of God" (Gen. 1:27). This is a religious and ethical proposition. But it is also a political one. The person is prior to the collective. The starting point of political theory must lie in the rights, freedom, and dignity of the individual, not in those of the state. It is this that forms the biblical basis of modern political theory, and an eternal protest against totalitarianism.

despise corruption; and appoint them over the people as leaders of thousands,
22 hundreds, fifties, and tens. Have them serve as daily judges for the people; let
them bring the major cases to you, but judge the minor ones themselves. In
23 this way they will lighten your load, and bear it together with you. If you do
this, and God so commands, then you will endure, and all these people will be
24 able to go home in peace." Moshe listened to his father-in-law and did all that SHELISHI
25 he said. Moshe chose capable men from all Israel and made them chiefs over
26 the people, leaders of thousands, hundreds, fifties, and tens. They judged the
people every day. Any major case they brought to Moshe, but they decided
27 every minor matter themselves. Then Moshe parted from his father-in-law, and
the latter went forth, back to his own land.
19 1 On the first day of the third month after the Israelites had left Egypt they REVI'I
2 came to the Sinai Desert. Setting out from Refidim they had arrived at the

רש״י

שָׂרִים לְשֵׁשׁ מֵאוֹת אֶלֶף: שָׂרֵי מֵאוֹת. שֵׁשֶׁת אֲלָפִים הָיוּ: שָׂרֵי חֲמִשִּׁים. שְׁנֵים עָשָׂר אֶלֶף: וְשָׂרֵי עֲשָׂרֹת. שִׁשִּׁים אֶלֶף:

כב וְשָׁפְטוּ. "וִידוּנוּן", לְשׁוֹן צִוּוּי: וְהָקֵל מֵעָלֶיךָ. דָּבָר זֶה לְהָקֵל מֵעָלֶיךָ. "וְהָקֵל" כְּמוֹ: "וְהַכְבֵּד אֶת לִבּוֹ" (לעיל ח, יא), "וְהַכּוֹת אֶת מוֹאָב" (מלכים ב׳ ג, כד), לְשׁוֹן הֹוֶה:

כג וְצִוְּךָ אֱלֹהִים וְיָכָלְתָּ עֲמֹד. הַמֶּלֶךְ בַּגְּבוּרָה, אִם מְצַוֶּה אוֹתְךָ לַעֲשׂוֹת כֵּן – תּוּכַל לַעֲמֹד, וְאִם יְעַכֵּב עַל יָדְךָ – לֹא תוּכַל לַעֲמֹד: וְגַם כָּל הָעָם הַזֶּה. אַהֲרֹן נָדָב וַאֲבִיהוּא וְשִׁבְעִים זְקֵנִים הַנִּלְוִים עַתָּה עִמָּךְ:

כו וְשָׁפְטוּ. "וְדָיְנִין יָת עַמָּא": יְבִיאוּן. "מֵיתַן": יִשְׁפּוּטוּ הֵם. כְּמוֹ יִשְׁפְּטוּ. וְכֵן: "לֹא תַעֲבוּרִי" (רות ב, ח) כְּמוֹ לֹא תַעַבְרִי. וְתַרְגּוּמוֹ: "דָּיְנִין אִנּוּן". מִקְרָאוֹת הָעֶלְיוֹנִים (לעיל פסוק כב) הָיוּ לְשׁוֹן צִוּוּי, לְכָךְ מְתַרְגְּמִין: וִידוּנוּן, יַיְתוֹן, יְדוּנוּן, וּמִקְרָאוֹת הַלָּלוּ לְשׁוֹן עֲשִׂיָּה:

כז וַיֵּלֶךְ לוֹ אֶל אַרְצוֹ. לְגַיֵּר בְּנֵי מִשְׁפַּחְתּוֹ:

יט א בַּיּוֹם הַזֶּה. בְּרֹאשׁ חֹדֶשׁ. לֹא הָיָה צָרִיךְ לִכְתֹּב אֶלָּא 'בַּיּוֹם הַהוּא', מַהוּ "בַּיּוֹם הַזֶּה"? שֶׁיִּהְיוּ דִּבְרֵי תוֹרָה חֲדָשִׁים עָלֶיךָ כְּאִלּוּ הַיּוֹם נִתְּנוּ:

ב וַיִּסְעוּ מֵרְפִידִים. מַה תַּלְמוּד לוֹמַר לַחֲזֹר וּלְפָרֵשׁ מֵהֵיכָן נָסְעוּ? וַהֲלֹא כְּבָר כָּתַב שֶׁבִּרְפִידִים הָיוּ חוֹנִים (לעיל יז, א), בְּיָדוּעַ שֶׁמִּשָּׁם נָסְעוּ! אֶלָּא לְהַקִּישׁ נְסִיעָתָן מֵרְפִידִים לְבִיאָתָן לְמִדְבַּר סִינַי; מַה בִּיאָתָן לְמִדְבַּר סִינַי בִּתְשׁוּבָה אַף נְסִיעָתָן מֵרְפִידִים בִּתְשׁוּבָה: וַיִּחַן שָׁם יִשְׂרָאֵל. כְּאִישׁ אֶחָד בְּלֵב אֶחָד, אֲבָל שְׁאָר כָּל הַחֲנִיּוֹת בְּתַרְעֹמֶת

would bring ordinary people – with no special prophetic or legal gifts – into the seats of judgment. Precisely because they *lacked* Moshe's intuitive knowledge of law and justice, they were able to propose equitable solutions, and an equitable solution is one in which both sides feel they have been heard. Both gain; both believe the result is fair.

Moshe was the *ish haElokim* (Ps. 90:1), the supreme "man of God." Yet there was, Netziv implies, one thing he could not do, which others – less great in every other respect – could achieve. They could bring peace between contending parties. They could create nonviolent, noncoercive forms of conflict resolution. Not knowing the law with the depth that Moshe did, not having his intuitive sense of truth, they had instead to exercise patience. They had to listen to both sides. They had to arrive at an equitable verdict that both parties could see as fair. A mediator has different gifts from a prophet, a liberator, a lawgiver – more modest perhaps, but sometimes no less necessary. That is why the delegation of judgment would not only help Moshe avoid total exhaustion; it would also help "all these people" to "go home in peace."

Judaism is a social faith. It is about networks of relationship. It is about families, communities, and ultimately a nation, in which each of us, great or small, has a role to play. There is something ordinary individuals (heads of thousands, hundreds, tens) can achieve that even Moshe in all his glory cannot achieve. That is why a nation is greater than any individual, and why each of us has something to give.

כב מֵאוֹת שָׂרֵי חֲמִשִּׁים וְשָׂרֵי עֲשָׂרֹת: וְשָׁפְטוּ אֶת־הָעָם בְּכָל־עֵת וְהָיָה
כָּל־הַדָּבָר הַגָּדֹל יָבִיאוּ אֵלֶיךָ וְכָל־הַדָּבָר הַקָּטֹן יִשְׁפְּטוּ־הֵם וְהָקֵל
כג מֵעָלֶיךָ וְנָשְׂאוּ אִתָּךְ: אִם אֶת־הַדָּבָר הַזֶּה תַּעֲשֶׂה וְצִוְּךָ אֱלֹהִים וְיָכָלְתָּ
כד עֲמֹד וְגַם כָּל־הָעָם הַזֶּה עַל־מְקֹמוֹ יָבֹא בְשָׁלוֹם: וַיִּשְׁמַע מֹשֶׁה לְקוֹל שלישי
כה חֹתְנוֹ וַיַּעַשׂ כֹּל אֲשֶׁר אָמָר: וַיִּבְחַר מֹשֶׁה אַנְשֵׁי־חַיִל מִכָּל־יִשְׂרָאֵל
וַיִּתֵּן אֹתָם רָאשִׁים עַל־הָעָם שָׂרֵי אֲלָפִים שָׂרֵי מֵאוֹת שָׂרֵי חֲמִשִּׁים
כו וְשָׂרֵי עֲשָׂרֹת: וְשָׁפְטוּ אֶת־הָעָם בְּכָל־עֵת אֶת־הַדָּבָר הַקָּשֶׁה יְבִיאוּן
כז אֶל־מֹשֶׁה וְכָל־הַדָּבָר הַקָּטֹן יִשְׁפּוּטוּ הֵם: וַיְשַׁלַּח מֹשֶׁה אֶת־חֹתְנוֹ
וַיֵּלֶךְ לוֹ אֶל־אַרְצוֹ:

יט א בַּחֹדֶשׁ הַשְּׁלִישִׁי לְצֵאת בְּנֵי־יִשְׂרָאֵל מֵאֶרֶץ מִצְרָיִם בַּיּוֹם הַזֶּה בָּאוּ רביעי
ב מִדְבַּר סִינָי: וַיִּסְעוּ מֵרְפִידִים וַיָּבֹאוּ מִדְבַּר סִינַי וַיַּחֲנוּ בַּמִּדְבָּר וַיִּחַן־שָׁם

אונקלוס

מָאוָתָא, רַבָּנֵי חַמְשִׁין וְרַבָּנֵי עֲסוֹרְיָתָא: כב וִידִינוּן יָת עַמָּא בְּכָל עִדָּן, וִיהֵי, כָּל פִּתְגָם רַב יַיְתוּן לְוָתָךְ, וְכָל פִּתְגָם זְעֵיר יְדִינוּן אִנּוּן, וְיֵיקְלוּן מִנָּךְ, וִיסוֹבְרוּן עִמָּךְ: כג אִם יָת פִּתְגָמָא הָדֵין תַּעְבֵּיד, וִיפַקְּדִנָּךְ יְיָ, וְתִכּוּל לְמִקָּם, וְאַף כָּל עַמָּא הָדֵין, עַל אַתְרֵיהּ יְהָךְ בִּשְׁלָם: כד וְקַבֵּיל מֹשֶׁה לְמֵימַר חֲמוּהִי, וַעֲבַד, כֹּל דַּאֲמַר: כה וּבְחַר מֹשֶׁה גֻּבְרִין דְּחֵילָא מִכָּל יִשְׂרָאֵל, וּמַנִּי יָתְהוֹן, רֵישִׁין עַל עַמָּא, רַבָּנֵי אַלְפֵי רַבָּנֵי מָאוָתָא, רַבָּנֵי חַמְשִׁין וְרַבָּנֵי עֲסוֹרְיָתָא: כו וְדָיְנִין יָת עַמָּא בְּכָל עִדָּן, יָת פִּתְגָם קְשֵׁי מַיְתַן לְוָת מֹשֶׁה, וְכָל פִּתְגָם זְעֵיר דָּיְנִין אִנּוּן: כז וְשַׁלַּח מֹשֶׁה יָת חֲמוּהִי, וַאֲזַל לֵיהּ לְאַרְעֵיהּ: יט א בְּיַרְחָא תְּלִיתָאָה, לְמִפַּק בְּנֵי יִשְׂרָאֵל מֵאַרְעָא דְּמִצְרָיִם, בְּיוֹמָא הָדֵין, אֲתוֹ לְמַדְבְּרָא דְּסִינָי: ב וּנְטַלוּ מֵרְפִידִים, וַאֲתוֹ לְמַדְבְּרָא דְּסִינַי, וּשְׁרוֹ בְּמַדְבְּרָא, וּשְׁרָא תַמָּן

because "he added a passage to the Torah beginning [here with the words] 'You, as well, must seek out'" (18:21).

The Kotzker pointed out that the passage that Yitro added to the Torah does not begin, "Seek out." It begins several verses earlier when he says, "What you are doing is not good" (18:17). The answer the Kotzker gives is simple. Saying "What you are doing is not good" is not an addition to the Torah – it is merely stating a problem. The addition consists of the solution: delegate. It is easy to see what is going wrong. What makes someone a leader is the ability to find a way of putting it right.

18:21 שָׂרֵי אֲלָפִים שָׂרֵי מֵאוֹת שָׂרֵי חֲמִשִּׁים וְשָׂרֵי עֲשָׂרֹת *Leaders of thousands, hundreds, fifties, and tens* – The great nineteenth-century scholar Netziv (Rabbi Naftali Tzvi Yehuda Berlin) made an unexpected, counterintuitive observation on this point (*Harḥev Davar* on Ex. 18:23). The Talmud (Sanhedrin 6b) teaches that Moshe preferred strict justice to peace. He was not a man to compromise or mediate. In addition, as the greatest of the prophets, he knew almost instantly which of the parties before him was innocent and which guilty, who had right on his side and who did not. It was therefore impossible for him to mediate, since this is only permitted before the judge has reached a verdict, which in Moshe's case was almost immediately.

By delegating the judicial function downward, Moshe

Sinai Desert, encamping in the wilderness, and there Israel camped, facing the
3 mountain, while Moshe went up to God. And the LORD called to him from the
mountain: "This is what you shall say to the House of Yaakov, what you shall tell
4 the people of Israel: You yourselves have seen what I did to the Egyptians: how
5 I lifted you up on eagles' wings and brought you to Me. Now, if you faithfully
heed My voice and keep My covenant, you will be My treasure among all the
6 peoples, although the whole earth is Mine. A kingdom of priests and a holy

רש"י

וּבְמַחֲלֹקֶת: **נֶגֶד הָהָר.** לְמִזְרָחוֹ, וְכָל מָקוֹם שֶׁאַתָּה מוֹצֵא 'נֶגֶד' – פָּנִים לַמִּזְרָח:

ג **וּמֹשֶׁה עָלָה.** בַּיּוֹם הַשֵּׁנִי, וְכָל עֲלִיּוֹתָיו בְּהַשְׁכָּמָה הָיוּ, שֶׁנֶּאֱמַר: "וַיַּשְׁכֵּם מֹשֶׁה בַבֹּקֶר" (להלן לד, ד): **כֹּה תֹאמַר.** בַּלָּשׁוֹן הַזֶּה וְכַסֵּדֶר הַזֶּה: **לְבֵית יַעֲקֹב.** אֵלּוּ הַנָּשִׁים, תֹּאמַר לָהֶן בְּלָשׁוֹן רַכָּה: **וְתַגֵּיד לִבְנֵי יִשְׂרָאֵל.** עֳנָשִׁין וְדִקְדּוּקִין פָּרֵשׁ לַזְּכָרִים, דְּבָרִים הַקָּשִׁין כְּגִידִין:

ד **אַתֶּם רְאִיתֶם.** וְלֹא מָסֹרֶת הִיא בְּיֶדְכֶם, בַּדְּבָרִים אֲשֶׁר עָשִׂיתִי בְּמִצְרַיִם, עַל כַּמָּה עֲבֵרוֹת הָיוּ חַיָּבִין לִי קֹדֶם שֶׁנִּזְדַּוְּגוּ לָכֶם, וְלֹא נִפְרַעְתִּי מֵהֶם אֶלָּא עַל יֶדְכֶם: **וָאֶשָּׂא אֶתְכֶם.** זֶה יוֹם שֶׁבָּאוּ יִשְׂרָאֵל לְרַעְמְסֵס, שֶׁהָיוּ יִשְׂרָאֵל מְפֻזָּרִין בְּכָל אֶרֶץ גֹּשֶׁן, וּלְשָׁעָה קַלָּה כְּשֶׁבָּאוּ לִסַּע וְלָצֵאת נִקְבְּצוּ כֻּלָּם לְרַעְמְסֵס. וְאוּנְקְלוֹס תִּרְגֵּם "וָאֶשָּׂא" כְּמוֹ וָאַסִּיעַ אֶתְכֶם: "וְאַטֵּלִית יָתְכוֹן", תִּקֵּן אֶת הַדִּבּוּר דֶּרֶךְ כָּבוֹד לְמַעְלָה: **עַל כַּנְפֵי נְשָׁרִים.** כַּנֶּשֶׁר הַנּוֹשֵׂא גּוֹזָלָיו עַל כְּנָפָיו, שֶׁכָּל שְׁאָר הָעוֹפוֹת נוֹתְנִים אֶת בְּנֵיהֶם בֵּין רַגְלֵיהֶם, לְפִי שֶׁמִּתְיָרְאִין מֵעוֹף אַחֵר שֶׁפּוֹרֵחַ עַל גַּבֵּיהֶם, אֲבָל הַנֶּשֶׁר הַזֶּה אֵינוֹ מִתְיָרֵא אֶלָּא מִן הָאָדָם שֶׁמָּא יִזְרֹק בּוֹ חֵץ, לְפִי שֶׁאֵין עוֹף פּוֹרֵחַ עַל גַּבָּיו, לְכָךְ נוֹתְנוֹ עַל כְּנָפָיו, אוֹמֵר: מוּטָב יִכָּנֵס הַחֵץ בִּי וְלֹא בְּבָנַי. אַף אֲנִי עָשִׂיתִי כֵן: "וַיִּסַּע מַלְאַךְ הָאֱלֹהִים וְגוֹ' וַיָּבֹא בֵּין מַחֲנֵה מִצְרַיִם" וְגוֹ' (לעיל יד, יט-כ), וְהָיוּ מִצְרַיִם זוֹרְקִים חִצִּים וְאַבְנֵי בַלִּיסְטְרָאוֹת וְהֶעָנָן מְקַבְּלָם: **וָאָבִא אֶתְכֶם אֵלָי.** כְּתַרְגּוּמוֹ:

ה **וְעַתָּה.** אִם עַתָּה תְּקַבְּלוּ עֲלֵיכֶם יֶעֱרַב לָכֶם מִכָּאן וְאֵילַךְ, שֶׁכָּל הַתְחָלוֹת קָשׁוֹת: **וּשְׁמַרְתֶּם אֶת בְּרִיתִי.** שֶׁאֶכְרֹת עִמָּכֶם עַל שְׁמִירַת הַתּוֹרָה: **סְגֻלָּה.** אוֹצָר חָבִיב, כְּמוֹ: "וּסְגֻלַּת מְלָכִים" (קהלת ב, ח), כְּלֵי יְקָר וַאֲבָנִים טוֹבוֹת שֶׁהַמְּלָכִים גּוֹנְזִים אוֹתָם, כָּךְ אַתֶּם לִי סְגֻלָּה מִשְּׁאָר אֻמּוֹת. וְלֹא תֹאמְרוּ, אַתֶּם לְבַדְּכֶם שֶׁלִּי וְאֵין לִי אֲחֵרִים עִמָּכֶם, וּמַה יֵּשׁ לִי עוֹד שֶׁתְּהֵא חִבַּתְכֶם נִכֶּרֶת? – "כִּי לִי כָּל הָאָרֶץ", וְהֵם בְּעֵינַי וּלְפָנַי לִכְלוּם:

ו **וְאַתֶּם תִּהְיוּ לִי מַמְלֶכֶת כֹּהֲנִים.** שָׂרִים, כְּמָה דְאַתְּ אָמַר: "וּבְנֵי דָוִד כֹּהֲנִים הָיוּ" (שמואל ב' ח, יח):

special closeness to Him. In "heeding My voice and keeping My covenant," they undertake to be His emissaries and exemplars, His ambassadors to humanity, probably the most challenging vocation anyone has ever been given. It does not mean that we are better than anyone else. It does not mean that we are worse. It means that the task to which we have been summoned is different. A chosen people is not a master race but its opposite: a servant community. Some nations in the history of humanity have given the world the idea of beauty, or of science, or of philosophy, or of music. It has been our task always to be God's witnesses in the world. In Jewish history we see time and time again, in multiple and variegated ways, that Jews have always been a people who testify in themselves to something greater than themselves. Jews have always done extraordinary things because they were challenged by God to perform this daunting task – the task of acting to bring humanity to see the universe as God's work and the Bible as God's will. God wants us to be the people who are true to our faith, while being a blessing to others regardless of their faith. Jews are the voice of hope in the conversation of humankind. That is what we were chosen for, and I can think of no higher vocation.

A KINGDOM OF PRIESTS AND A HOLY NATION

This phrase was to become the mission statement of the Jewish people. Indeed, with the possible exception of the United States, the Jewish people is the only nation ever to have had a mission statement. Most are defined in terms of language, geography, political structure, long association, and the like. Jews became a nation by adopting a task, by covenanting with God. Absent that, it is hard to say what it is to be a Jew.

ג יִשְׂרָאֵל נֶגֶד הָהָר: וּמֹשֶׁה עָלָה אֶל־הָאֱלֹהִים וַיִּקְרָא אֵלָיו יהוה מִן־הָהָר
ד לֵאמֹר כֹּה תֹאמַר לְבֵית יַעֲקֹב וְתַגֵּיד לִבְנֵי יִשְׂרָאֵל: אַתֶּם רְאִיתֶם אֲשֶׁר
עָשִׂיתִי לְמִצְרָיִם וָאֶשָּׂא אֶתְכֶם עַל־כַּנְפֵי נְשָׁרִים וָאָבִא אֶתְכֶם אֵלָי:
ה וְעַתָּה אִם־שָׁמוֹעַ תִּשְׁמְעוּ בְּקֹלִי וּשְׁמַרְתֶּם אֶת־בְּרִיתִי וִהְיִיתֶם לִי סְגֻלָּה
ו מִכָּל־הָעַמִּים כִּי־לִי כָּל־הָאָרֶץ: וְאַתֶּם תִּהְיוּ־לִי מַמְלֶכֶת כֹּהֲנִים וְגוֹי טו

אונקלוס

יִשְׂרָאֵל לָקֳבֵיל טוּרָא: ג וּמֹשֶׁה סְלֵיק לְקֳדָם יְיָ, וּקְרָא לֵיהּ יְיָ מִן טוּרָא לְמֵימַר, כְּדֵין תֵּימַר לְבֵית יַעֲקֹב, וּתְחַוֵּי לִבְנֵי יִשְׂרָאֵל: ד אַתּוּן חֲזֵיתוּן, דַּעֲבַדִית לְמִצְרָאֵי, וְאַטֵּילִית יָתְכוֹן כִּד עַל גַּדְפֵּי נִשְׁרִין, וְקָרֵיבִית יָתְכוֹן לְפֻלְחָנִי: ה וּכְעַן, אִם קַבָּלָא תְקַבְּלוּן לְמֵימְרִי, וְתִטְּרוּן יָת קְיָמִי, וּתְהוֹן קֳדָמַי חַבִּיבִין מִכָּל עַמְמַיָּא, אֲרֵי דִילִי כָּל אַרְעָא: ו וְאַתּוּן תְּהוֹן קֳדָמַי, מַלְכִין כָּהֲנִין

19:2 וַיִּחַן־שָׁם יִשְׂרָאֵל *There Israel camped* – Rashi notes that when the Israelites arrive in the wilderness of Sinai prior to receiving the Ten Commandments, the Torah's description shifts from the plural to the singular: *Vayiḥan sham Yisrael*, "There Israel [singular] camped." Rashi, always sensitive to the nuances of the biblical text, spells out the implication. At this moment, he writes, the people of Israel are "like one person with one heart." They have been transformed from the plural to the singular. Within sight of Mount Sinai, within reach of revelation, about to receive their call and consummation as a people, they are united.

19:3 בֵּית יַעֲקֹב *The House of Yaakov* – According to the Sages, when God was about to give the Torah at Sinai, He told Moshe to consult first with the women and only then with the men. This is the meaning of the verse "This is what you shall say to the House of Yaakov, what you shall tell the people of Israel." The House of Yaakov, our Sages tell us, refers to the women (Mekhilta DeRabbi Yishmael 19:3:1). Shemot Rabba gives various explanations for this idea, never questioning the fact that women received the Torah first.

In 1917, Sarah Schenirer founded the first Bais Yaakov school for women, naming it after our verse. Since then, women have risen in the ranks of Torah scholars. The Belzer Rebbe, a great hasidic leader, and the Chofetz Chaim, the major Torah scholar of his generation, both blessed this endeavor. After World War II, in America, Rabbi Joseph B. Soloveitchik and the Lubavitcher Rebbe promoted the role of women as students of Torah and teachers of Torah. From this revolution came thousands of new Torah teachers and hundreds of thousands of new Torah learners, drawing support in part from this midrashic tradition.

The call to "the House of Yaakov" and "the people of Israel" – the Torah's "constitution of liberty" – includes everyone: men, women, and children. It is the first moment, by thousands of years, that citizenship is conceived as being universal. With this, something unprecedented enters the human horizon, though it will take centuries, millennia, before its full implications will be understood. At Sinai, the politics of freedom are born.

19:4 אַתֶּם רְאִיתֶם *You yourselves have seen* – The emphasis is on the immediacy of the experience. The people have witnessed a divine intervention into history. They have been redeemed from slavery under Pharaoh. God is now proposing that they become a nation under His own direct sovereignty in fulfillment of what He had earlier told Moshe: "I will take you as My people and I will be your God" (Ex. 6:7). This will mark the culmination of their seven-week journey from servitude to law-governed liberty.

19:5 וִהְיִיתֶם לִי סְגֻלָּה מִכָּל־הָעַמִּים *My treasure among all the peoples* – God is the creator of the universe and the God of all humanity, but through the covenant, Israel is to have a

nation you shall be to Me. These are the words you must speak to the Israelites."
7 So Moshe came and summoned the elders of the people, and set before them ḤAMISHI
8 all that the LORD had commanded him. And the people answered as one – "All
that the LORD has spoken we will do." Moshe brought their answer back to the

רש״י

אֵלֶּה הַדְּבָרִים. לֹא פָּחוֹת וְלֹא יוֹתֵר:

ח| וַיָּשֶׁב מֹשֶׁה אֶת דִּבְרֵי הָעָם וְגוֹ׳. בְּיוֹם הַמָּחֳרָת שֶׁהוּא שְׁלִישִׁי, שֶׁהֲרֵי בְּהַשְׁכָּמָה עָלָה. וְכִי צָרִיךְ הָיָה מֹשֶׁה לְהָשִׁיב? אֶלָּא בָּא הַכָּתוּב

Judaism knows the faith of individuals: that is what Genesis is about, and the book of Psalms, the lexicon of the soul in dialogue with God. Judaism also knows the faith of humanity as a whole: that is the meaning of the first eleven chapters of Genesis and their culmination in the Noahide covenant, the covenant God makes with all mankind. But Judaism's great concerns are with the life we construct together and the terms on which we do so: justice, compassion, human dignity, peace, the limited and proper conduct of war, care for the dependent, welfare for the poor, concern for the long-term viability of the environment, and above all, the rule of law, in which strong and weak, powerful and powerless, are subject to the same code of conduct applied equally to all. These institutions and ideals are essentially political; hence they require the constitution of a nation as a political entity. That is the meaning of the phrase *goy kadosh*, "a holy nation." At Sinai, the Jewish people, until then mainly an aggregate of individuals linked by family, memory, and the experience of exodus, fully became a body politic, with the Torah as its written constitution. The Vilna Gaon notes the connection between the words *goy*, "nation," and *geviya*, "body." A nation is a group of individuals whose relationship to one another is as of limbs to a body. Sinai creates the terms of collective existence. Henceforth the Israelites are implicated in one another's fate.

What does it mean to be a holy nation? Holiness is the space we make for God. Holiness is that bounded emptiness filled by the Divine Presence. In addition to the holiness of empty time (the Sabbath) and the holiness of empty space (the Tabernacle), the phrase "holy nation" designates a third emptiness: the empty throne (cathedra, seat of authority). The place occupied in other nations by the monarch, ruler, or pharaoh is in the case of Israel to be left empty for God. Israel is to become a republic of faith under His direct sovereignty. He is the author of its constitution, the framer of its rules, the one who guides it through its long journeys, sustains it in hours of need, and gives it hope in times of crisis. The essence of the Sinai revelation is that the Israelites become the first – indeed the only – nation formed on the basis of a covenant with God.

19:8 **וַיַּעֲנוּ כָל־הָעָם יַחְדָּו** *And the people answered as one* – Only when the people have signaled their consent does God proceed with the covenant and the accompanying revelation. The fact of choice is fundamental, for the Tanakh portrays God not as an overwhelming force, but as a constitutional sovereign. The supreme power, God, grants His people the freedom to decide whether or not to enter into the covenant. Thus is born the first principle of a free society: there is no justified government without the consent of the governed, even if the governor is Creator of heaven and earth.

No less essential is the participation of the whole people, for each must give his or her consent. It is a point the Tanakh emphasizes twice: "And *all the people* answered as one" (Ex. 19:8, literally translated); "*The people all* responded with one voice" (24:3). This is not democracy in the modern or even the Greek sense, but it is a corollary of the idea that the human person as such is in the image of God. In covenant as the Tanakh understands it, each individual has significance, dignity, moral worth, the right to be heard, a voice.

Despite the abyss between the infinite power of God and the finitude of humankind, at the heart of the Sinai covenant is the idea of reciprocity and mutuality. It is God's call to human responsibility.

ז קָדוֹשׁ אֵלֶּה הַדְּבָרִים אֲשֶׁר תְּדַבֵּר אֶל־בְּנֵי יִשְׂרָאֵל: וַיָּבֹא מֹשֶׁה וַיִּקְרָא חמישי
לְזִקְנֵי הָעָם וַיָּשֶׂם לִפְנֵיהֶם אֵת כָּל־הַדְּבָרִים הָאֵלֶּה אֲשֶׁר צִוָּהוּ יְהוָה:
ח וַיַּעֲנוּ כָל־הָעָם יַחְדָּו וַיֹּאמְרוּ כֹּל אֲשֶׁר־דִּבֶּר יְהוָה נַעֲשֶׂה וַיָּשֶׁב מֹשֶׁה

אונקלוס

וְעַם קַדִּישׁ, אִלֵּין פִּתְגָּמַיָּא, דִּתְמַלֵּיל עִם בְּנֵי יִשְׂרָאֵל: ז וַאֲתָא מֹשֶׁה,
וּקְרָא לְסָבֵי עַמָּא, וְסַדַּר קֳדָמֵיהוֹן, יָת כָּל פִּתְגָּמַיָּא הָאִלֵּין, דְּפַקְדֵיהּ יְיָ:
ח וַאֲתִיבוּ כָל עַמָּא כַּחֲדָא וַאֲמַרוּ, כֹּל, דְּמַלֵּיל יְיָ נַעֲבֵיד, וַאֲתֵיב מֹשֶׁה,

What is a kingdom of priests? Jews never were literally a kingdom of priests. Priesthood fell to Aharon and his sons. What is more, priesthood is not seen by the Torah as a distinctively Jewish phenomenon. Yitro, for instance, is described as a Midianite priest.

Ibn Ezra and Ramban interpret the word to mean "servants." A priest is one consecrated to the service of God. This is now to be the task of all Israelites. Others – Saadia Gaon, Rashi, Rashbam – understand it to mean princes, based on II Samuel 18:1. There, David's sons are described as *kohanim*, which cannot mean priests and must mean royalty, princes. The Israelites are called on to be *a nation of servant leaders*.

I want to suggest a different interpretation, by looking at the wider context against which the biblical narrative is set. The earliest writing systems involved a huge number of hieroglyphic or pictographic symbols. The result was that in each society where there was writing, there was a literate elite, a knowledge class, often involved in administration. Only the few had access to knowledge, and so to power. The invention of the alphabet reduced the number of symbols needed to be learned to less than thirty. We cannot give a precise date for the first alphabet – sometime between 1800 and 2000 BCE seems likely. But unlike the pre-alphabetical scripts, the alphabet seems to have been invented only once. All the hundreds of scripts that exist are direct or indirect descendants of the proto-Semitic writing from the Sinai Desert.

Was it divine providence that led to this invention becoming available at exactly the right time and place to be used by the Israelites for the holiest of purposes, namely, recording the divine word? Or was it this new development that allowed the Israelites to develop the consciousness – the high levels of abstraction, essential to monotheism, made possible by literacy – that allowed them to decipher the word of the One God? One way or another, the alphabet created a possibility that never existed before, namely of a society of mass, even universal, literacy.

Functionally, a priest in the ancient world was one who could read and write. A kingdom of priests is therefore *a nation of universal literacy*. The law God was about to reveal at Mount Sinai would become the possession of every member of the nation. He or she could know it, read it, study it, internalize it, and make it their own.

Torah was not a code written by a distant king, imposed by force. Nor was it an esoteric mystery understood by only a scholarly elite. It was to be available to, and intelligible by, everyone. God was to become a teacher, Israel His pupils, and the Torah the text that bound them to one another. Every Jew was expected to be both a prince and a servant, a student and a teacher; that is to say, every one of them was called on to be a leader.

Never was leadership more profoundly democratized.

19:6 גּוֹי קָדוֹשׁ *A holy nation* – The concept of a nation is fundamental to Judaism, because the nation is a basic unit of culture. As a sociopolitical entity, it constructs its own form of order through law, ritual, and custom. It is where many smaller groupings, families and communities, come together to create the basic terms of their common life. And God wants His presence to inform public life – otherwise He would have limited His concerns to the individual and the soul.

▶

9 Lord. Then the Lord said to Moshe, "I will come to you in a dense cloud, that
the people may hear Me speaking to you. They will then believe you forever."
10 When Moshe reported the words of the people to the Lord, the Lord said to
Moshe, "Go to the people and consecrate them today and tomorrow; let them
11 wash their clothes and be ready for the third day, for on that third day the Lord
12 will descend on Mount Sinai before all the peoples' eyes. Set a boundary for
the people around the mountain; tell them to take care not to ascend to it, nor
even touch its edge. Anyone who touches the mountain must be put to death.
13 No hand shall touch him: he shall be stoned or shot with arrows; beast or man,
he shall not live. When the ram's horn sounds a long blast – only then may
14 they go up on the mountain." So Moshe came down from the mountain to the
15 people; he consecrated them and they cleansed their clothes. "Be ready for the
16 third day," he told them, "and do not draw close to your wives." The third day
came; and that morning there was thunder and lightning and a dense cloud on
the mountain and the sound of a ram's horn, intensely loud, and all the people
17 in the camp shook. Then Moshe led the people out of the camp to meet God,
18 and they stood at the foot of the mountain. Mount Sinai was enveloped in
smoke because the Lord had descended on it in fire. Smoke billowed up from

רש"י

לְלַמֶּדְךָ דֶּרֶךְ אֶרֶץ מִמֹּשֶׁה, שֶׁלֹּא אָמַר: הוֹאִיל וְיוֹדֵעַ מִי שֶׁשְּׁלָחַנִי, אֵינִי צָרִיךְ לְהָשִׁיב:

ט **בְּעַב הֶעָנָן.** בְּמַעֲבֵה הֶעָנָן, וְזֶהוּ עֲרָפֶל: **וְגַם בְּךָ.** גַּם בַּנְּבִיאִים הַבָּאִים אַחֲרֶיךָ: **וַיַּגֵּד מֹשֶׁה אֶת דִּבְרֵי וְגוֹ'.** בַּיּוֹם הַמָּחֳרָת שֶׁהוּא רְבִיעִי לַחֹדֶשׁ: **אֶת דִּבְרֵי הָעָם וְגוֹ'.** תְּשׁוּבָה עַל דָּבָר זֶה שָׁמַעְתִּי מֵהֶם, שֶׁרְצוֹנָם לִשְׁמֹעַ מִמְּךָ, אֵינוֹ דּוֹמֶה הַשּׁוֹמֵעַ מִפִּי שָׁלִיחַ לַשּׁוֹמֵעַ מִפִּי הַמֶּלֶךְ, רְצוֹנֵנוּ לִרְאוֹת אֶת מַלְכֵּנוּ:

י **וְקִדַּשְׁתָּם.** וְזִמַּנְתָּם, שֶׁיָּכִינוּ עַצְמָם "הַיּוֹם וּמָחָר":

יא **וְהָיוּ נְכֹנִים.** מֵאִשָּׁה: **לַיּוֹם הַשְּׁלִישִׁי.** שֶׁהוּא שִׁשָּׁה בַּחֹדֶשׁ, וּבַחֲמִישִׁי בָּנָה מֹשֶׁה אֶת הַמִּזְבֵּחַ תַּחַת הָהָר וּשְׁתֵּים עֶשְׂרֵה מַצֵּבָה, כָּל הָעִנְיָן הָאָמוּר בְּפָרָשַׁת וְאֵלֶּה הַמִּשְׁפָּטִים (להלן פרק כד), וְאֵין מֻקְדָּם וּמְאֻחָר בַּתּוֹרָה: **לְעֵינֵי כָל הָעָם.** מְלַמֵּד שֶׁלֹּא הָיָה בָּהֶם סוּמָא, שֶׁנִּתְרַפְּאוּ כֻּלָּם:

יב **וְהִגְבַּלְתָּ.** קְבַע לָהֶם תְּחוּמִין לְסִימָן, שֶׁלֹּא יִקְרְבוּ מִן הַגְּבוּל וָהָלְאָה: **לֵאמֹר.** הַגְּבוּל אוֹמֵר לָהֶם: הִשָּׁמְרוּ מֵעֲלוֹת מִכָּאן וּלְהַלָּן, וְאַתָּה הַזְהִירֵם עַל כָּךְ: **וּנְגֹעַ בְּקָצֵהוּ.** אֲפִלּוּ בְּקָצֵהוּ:

יג **יָרֹה יִיָּרֶה.** מִכָּאן לְנִסְקָלִין שֶׁהֵם נִדְחִין לְמַטָּה מִבֵּית הַסְּקִילָה, שֶׁהָיָה גָּבוֹהַּ שְׁתֵּי קוֹמוֹת: **יִיָּרֶה.** יֻשְׁלַךְ לְמַטָּה לָאָרֶץ, כְּמוֹ: "יָרָה בַיָּם" (לעיל טו, ד): **בִּמְשֹׁךְ הַיֹּבֵל.** כְּשֶׁיִּמְשֹׁךְ הַיּוֹבֵל קוֹל אָרֹךְ, הוּא סִימָן סִלּוּק שְׁכִינָה וְהַפְסָקַת הַקּוֹל, וְכֵיוָן שֶׁאֶסְתַּלֵּק הֵם רַשָּׁאִין לַעֲלוֹת: **הַיֹּבֵל.** הוּא שׁוֹפָר שֶׁל אַיִל, שֶׁכֵּן בַּעֲרַבְיָא קוֹרִין לְדִכְרָא 'יוּבְלָא'. וְשׁוֹפָר שֶׁל אֵילוֹ שֶׁל יִצְחָק הָיָה:

יד **מִן הָהָר אֶל הָעָם.** מְלַמֵּד שֶׁלֹּא הָיָה מֹשֶׁה פּוֹנֶה לַעֲסָקָיו, אֶלָּא מִן הָהָר אֶל הָעָם:

טו **הֱיוּ נְכֹנִים לִשְׁלֹשֶׁת יָמִים.** לְסוֹף שְׁלֹשֶׁת יָמִים, הוּא יוֹם רְבִיעִי, שֶׁהוֹסִיף מֹשֶׁה יוֹם אֶחָד מִדַּעְתּוֹ, כְּדִבְרֵי רַבִּי יוֹסֵי. וּלְדִבְרֵי הָאוֹמֵר בְּשִׁשָּׁה בַּחֹדֶשׁ נִתְּנוּ עֲשֶׂרֶת הַדִּבְּרוֹת, לֹא הוֹסִיף מֹשֶׁה כְּלוּם, וְ"לִשְׁלֹשֶׁת יָמִים" כְּמוֹ 'לַיּוֹם הַשְּׁלִישִׁי': **אַל תִּגְּשׁוּ אֶל אִשָּׁה.** כָּל שְׁלֹשֶׁת יָמִים הַלָּלוּ, כְּדֵי שֶׁיִּהְיוּ הַנָּשִׁים טוֹבְלוֹת לַיּוֹם הַשְּׁלִישִׁי וְיִהְיוּ טְהוֹרוֹת לְקַבֵּל תּוֹרָה, שֶׁאִם יְשַׁמְּשׁוּ תּוֹךְ שְׁלֹשָׁה שֶׁמָּא תִּפְלֹט הָאִשָּׁה שִׁכְבַת זֶרַע לְאַחַר טְבִילָתָהּ וְתַחֲזֹר וְתִטְמָא, אֲבָל מִשֶּׁשָּׁהֲתָה שְׁלֹשָׁה יָמִים כְּבָר הַזֶּרַע מַסְרִיחַ וְאֵינוֹ רָאוּי לְהַזְרִיעַ, וְטָהוֹר מִלְּטַמֵּא אֶת הַפּוֹלֶטֶת:

טז **בִּהְיֹת הַבֹּקֶר.** מְלַמֵּד שֶׁהִקְדִּים עַל יָדָם, מַה שֶּׁאֵין דֶּרֶךְ בָּשָׂר וָדָם לַעֲשׂוֹת כֵּן שֶׁיְּהֵא הָרַב מַמְתִּין לְתַלְמִיד. וְכֵן מָצִינוּ בִּיחֶזְקֵאל: "קוּם צֵא אֶל הַבִּקְעָה... וָאָקוּם וָאֵצֵא אֶל הַבִּקְעָה וְהִנֵּה שָׁם כְּבוֹד ה' עֹמֵד" (יחזקאל ג, כב-כג):

יז **לִקְרַאת הָאֱלֹהִים.** מַגִּיד שֶׁהָיְתָה שְׁכִינָה יוֹצְאָה לִקְרָאתָם כְּחָתָן

ט אֶת־דִּבְרֵ֥י הָעָ֖ם אֶל־יְהֹוָֽה׃ וַיֹּ֨אמֶר יְהֹוָ֜ה אֶל־מֹשֶׁ֗ה הִנֵּ֨ה אָנֹכִ֜י בָּ֣א
אֵלֶ֘יךָ֮ בְּעַ֣ב הֶֽעָנָן֒ בַּעֲב֞וּר יִשְׁמַ֤ע הָעָם֙ בְּדַבְּרִ֣י עִמָּ֔ךְ וְגַם־בְּךָ֖ יַאֲמִ֣ינוּ
י לְעוֹלָ֑ם וַיַּגֵּ֥ד מֹשֶׁ֛ה אֶת־דִּבְרֵ֥י הָעָ֖ם אֶל־יְהֹוָֽה׃ וַיֹּ֨אמֶר יְהֹוָ֤ה אֶל־מֹשֶׁה֙
יא לֵ֣ךְ אֶל־הָעָ֔ם וְקִדַּשְׁתָּ֥ם הַיּ֖וֹם וּמָחָ֑ר וְכִבְּס֖וּ שִׂמְלֹתָֽם׃ וְהָי֥וּ נְכֹנִ֖ים לַיּ֣וֹם
הַשְּׁלִישִׁ֑י כִּ֣י ׀ בַּיּ֣וֹם הַשְּׁלִשִׁ֗י יֵרֵ֧ד יְהֹוָ֛ה לְעֵינֵ֥י כׇל־הָעָ֖ם עַל־הַ֥ר סִינָֽי׃
יב וְהִגְבַּלְתָּ֤ אֶת־הָעָם֙ סָבִ֣יב לֵאמֹ֔ר הִשָּׁמְר֥וּ לָכֶ֛ם עֲל֥וֹת בָּהָ֖ר וּנְגֹ֣עַ בְּקָצֵ֑הוּ
יג כׇּל־הַנֹּגֵ֥עַ בָּהָ֖ר מ֥וֹת יוּמָֽת׃ לֹא־תִגַּ֨ע בּ֜וֹ יָ֗ד כִּֽי־סָק֤וֹל יִסָּקֵל֙ אוֹ־יָרֹ֣ה יִיָּרֶ֔ה
יד אִם־בְּהֵמָ֥ה אִם־אִ֖ישׁ לֹ֣א יִֽחְיֶ֑ה בִּמְשֹׁךְ֙ הַיֹּבֵ֔ל הֵ֖מָּה יַעֲל֥וּ בָהָֽר׃ וַיֵּ֧רֶד
טו מֹשֶׁ֛ה מִן־הָהָ֖ר אֶל־הָעָ֑ם וַיְקַדֵּשׁ֙ אֶת־הָעָ֔ם וַֽיְכַבְּס֖וּ שִׂמְלֹתָֽם׃ וַיֹּ֨אמֶר֙
טז אֶל־הָעָ֔ם הֱי֥וּ נְכֹנִ֖ים לִשְׁלֹ֣שֶׁת יָמִ֑ים אַֽל־תִּגְּשׁ֖וּ אֶל־אִשָּֽׁה׃ וַיְהִ֡י בַיּוֹם֩
הַשְּׁלִישִׁ֜י בִּֽהְיֹ֣ת הַבֹּ֗קֶר וַיְהִי֩ קֹלֹ֨ת וּבְרָקִ֜ים וְעָנָ֤ן כָּבֵד֙ עַל־הָהָ֔ר וְקֹ֥ל
יז שֹׁפָ֖ר חָזָ֣ק מְאֹ֑ד וַיֶּחֱרַ֥ד כׇּל־הָעָ֖ם אֲשֶׁ֥ר בַּֽמַּחֲנֶֽה׃ וַיּוֹצֵ֨א מֹשֶׁ֧ה אֶת־הָעָ֛ם
יח לִקְרַ֥את הָֽאֱלֹהִ֖ים מִן־הַֽמַּחֲנֶ֑ה וַיִּֽתְיַצְּב֖וּ בְּתַחְתִּ֥ית הָהָֽר׃ וְהַ֤ר סִינַי֙
עָשַׁ֣ן כֻּלּ֔וֹ מִ֠פְּנֵי אֲשֶׁ֨ר יָרַ֥ד עָלָ֛יו יְהֹוָ֖ה בָּאֵ֑שׁ וַיַּ֤עַל עֲשָׁנוֹ֙ כְּעֶ֣שֶׁן הַכִּבְשָׁ֔ן

אונקלוס

יָת פִּתְגָמֵי עַמָּא לִקְדָם יְיָ: ט וַאֲמַר יְיָ לְמֹשֶׁה, הָא אֲנָא, מִתְגְּלֵי לָךְ בְּעֵיבָא דַעֲנָנָא, בְּדִיל, דְּיִשְׁמַע עַמָּא בְּמַלָּלוּתִי עִמָּךְ, וְאַף בָּךְ יְהֵימְנוּן לְעָלַם, וְחַוִּי מֹשֶׁה, יָת פִּתְגָמֵי עַמָּא לִקְדָם יְיָ: י וַאֲמַר יְיָ לְמֹשֶׁה אִיזֵיל לְוָת עַמָּא, וּתְזַמֵּינִנּוּן יוֹמָא דֵין וּמְחַר, וִיחַוְּרוּן לְבוּשֵׁיהוֹן: יא וִיהוֹן זְמִינִין לְיוֹמָא תְלִיתָאָה, אֲרֵי בְּיוֹמָא תְלִיתָאָה, יִתְגְּלֵי יְיָ, לְעֵינֵי כָּל עַמָּא עַל טוּרָא דְסִינָי: יב וְתַתְחֵים יָת עַמָּא סְחוֹר סְחוֹר לְמֵימַר, אִסְתַּמַּרוּ לְכוֹן, מִלְּמִסַּק בְּטוּרָא וּלְמִקְרַב בְּסוֹפֵיהּ, כָּל דְּיִקְרַב בְּטוּרָא אִתְקְטָלָא יִתְקְטִיל: יג לָא תִקְרַב בֵּיהּ יַד, אֲרֵי אִתְרְגָמָא יִתְרְגֵים אוֹ אִשְׁתְּדָאָה יִשְׁתְּדֵי, אִם בְּעִירָא אִם אֱנָשָׁא לָא יִתְקַיַּם, בְּמִיגַּד שׁוֹפָרָא, אִנּוּן מָרְשַׁן לְמִסַּק בְּטוּרָא: יד וּנְחַת מֹשֶׁה, מִן טוּרָא לְוָת עַמָּא, וְזַמֵּין יָת עַמָּא, וְחַוַּרוּ לְבוּשֵׁיהוֹן: טו וַאֲמַר לְעַמָּא, הֲווֹ זְמִינִין לִתְלָתָא יוֹמִין, לָא תִקְרְבוּן לְצַד אִתְּתָא: טז וַהֲוָה בְּיוֹמָא תְלִיתָאָה בְּמִהְוֵי צַפְרָא, וַהֲווֹ קָלִין וּבַרְקִין, וַעֲנָנָא תַקִּיף עַל טוּרָא, וְקָל שׁוֹפָרָא תַּקִּיף לַחֲדָא, וְזָע כָּל עַמָּא דִּבְמַשְׁרִיתָא: יז וְאַפֵּיק מֹשֶׁה יָת עַמָּא, לְקַדָּמוּת מֵימְרָא דַּייָ מִן מַשְׁרִיתָא, וְאִתְעַתַּדוּ בְּשִׁפּוֹלֵי טוּרָא: יח וְטוּרָא דְסִינַי תְּנַן כֻּלֵּיהּ, מִן קֳדָם, דְּאִתְגְּלִי עֲלוֹהִי, יְיָ בְּאֶשָּׁתָא, וּסְלֵיק תְּנָנֵיהּ כִּתְנַנָא דְאַתּוּנָא, וְזָע כָּל טוּרָא לַחֲדָא: יט וַהֲוָה קָל שׁוֹפָרָא, אָזֵיל וְתָקֵיף לַחֲדָא, מֹשֶׁה

רש״י

הַיּוֹצֵא לִקְרַאת כַּלָּה, וְזֶהוּ שֶׁנֶּאֱמַר: ״ה׳ מִסִּינַי בָּא״ (דברים לג, ב) וְלֹא נֶאֱמַר: ״לְסִינַי בָּא״: בְּתַחְתִּית הָהָר. לְפִי פְשׁוּטוֹ בְּרַגְלֵי הָהָר. וּמִדְרָשׁוֹ, שֶׁנִּתְלַשׁ הָהָר מִמְּקוֹמוֹ וְנִכְפָּה עֲלֵיהֶם כְּגִיגִית:

יח עָשַׁן כֻּלּוֹ. אֵין ׳עָשַׁן׳ זֶה שֵׁם דָּבָר, שֶׁהֲרֵי נָקוּד הַשִּׁי״ן פַּתָּח, אֶלָּא לְשׁוֹן פָּעַל, כְּמוֹ חָמַר, שָׁמַר, שָׁמַע. לְכָךְ תַּרְגּוּמוֹ: ״תְּנַן כֻּלֵּיהּ״ וְלֹא תִרְגֵּם ׳תְּנָנָא׳. וְכָל ׳עָשָׁן׳ שֶׁבַּמִּקְרָא נְקוּדִים קָמָץ, מִפְּנֵי שֶׁהֵם שֵׁם דָּבָר:

19 it as if from a furnace, and the mountain shook violently as one. As the sound
of the ram's horn grew louder and louder, Moshe spoke and God answered him
20 aloud. And the LORD descended on Mount Sinai, to the top of the mountain, SHISHI
21 and called Moshe to the mountaintop, and Moshe ascended. The LORD told
Moshe, "Go back down – warn the people not to force their way through to
22 look at the LORD, or many will die. Even priests who come near to the LORD
must first consecrate themselves, or the LORD will break out against them."
23 Moshe replied to the LORD, "The people cannot climb Mount Sinai. You
Yourself warned us to set a boundary around the mountain and consecrate
24 it." The LORD said to him, "Go down, and come back together with Aharon.
But do not let the priests or people force their way through to come up to the
25 LORD, or He will break out against them." So Moshe went down to the people
20 1 2 and told them. Then God spoke all these words: "I am the

רש"י

הַכִּבְשָׁן. שֶׁל סִיד. יָכוֹל כְּכִבְשָׁן זֶה וְלֹא יוֹתֵר? תַּלְמוּד לוֹמַר: "בֹּעֵר בָּאֵשׁ עַד לֵב הַשָּׁמַיִם" (דברים ד, יא). וּמַה תַּלְמוּד לוֹמַר: "כִּבְשָׁן"? לְשַׁבֵּר אֶת הָאֹזֶן מַה שֶּׁהִיא יְכוֹלָה לִשְׁמֹעַ, נוֹתֵן לַבְּרִיּוֹת סִימָן הַנִּכָּר לָהֶם. כַּיּוֹצֵא בוֹ: "כְּאַרְיֵה יִשְׁאָג" (הושע יא, י), וְכִי מִי נָתַן כֹּחַ בָּאֲרִי אֶלָּא הוּא, וְהַכָּתוּב מוֹשְׁלוֹ כְּאַרְיֵה? אֶלָּא אָנוּ מְכַנִּין וּמְדַמִּין אוֹתוֹ לִבְרִיּוֹתָיו כְּדֵי לְשַׁבֵּר אֶת הָאֹזֶן מַה שֶּׁיְּכוֹלָה לִשְׁמֹעַ. כַּיּוֹצֵא בוֹ: "וְקוֹלוֹ כְּקוֹל מַיִם רַבִּים" (יחזקאל מג, ב), וְכִי מִי נָתַן קוֹל לַמַּיִם אֶלָּא הוּא, וְאַתָּה מְכַנֶּה אוֹתוֹ לְדַמּוֹתוֹ לִבְרִיּוֹתָיו, כְּדֵי לְשַׁבֵּר אֶת הָאֹזֶן:

יט **הוֹלֵךְ וְחָזֵק מְאֹד.** מִנְהַג הֶדְיוֹט כָּל זְמַן שֶׁהוּא מַאֲרִיךְ לִתְקֹעַ קוֹלוֹ מַחֲלִישׁ וְכוֹהֶה, אֲבָל כָּאן "הוֹלֵךְ וְחָזֵק מְאֹד". וְלָמָּה כָּךְ מִתְּחִלָּה? לְשַׁבֵּר אָזְנֵיהֶם מַה שֶּׁיְּכוֹלִין לִשְׁמֹעַ: **מֹשֶׁה יְדַבֵּר.** כְּשֶׁהָיָה מֹשֶׁה מְדַבֵּר וּמַשְׁמִיעַ הַדִּבְּרוֹת לְיִשְׂרָאֵל, שֶׁהֲרֵי לֹא שָׁמְעוּ מִפִּי הַגְּבוּרָה אֶלָּא "אָנֹכִי" וְ"לֹא יִהְיֶה לְךָ", וְהַקָּדוֹשׁ בָּרוּךְ הוּא מְסַיְּעוֹ לָתֵת בּוֹ כֹּחַ לִהְיוֹת קוֹלוֹ מַגְבִּיר וְנִשְׁמָע: **יַעֲנֶנּוּ בְקוֹל.** יַעֲנֶנּוּ עַל דְּבַר הַקּוֹל, כְּמוֹ: "אֲשֶׁר יַעֲנֶה בָאֵשׁ" (מלכים א' יח, כד), עַל דְּבַר הָאֵשׁ לְהוֹרִידוֹ:

כ **וַיֵּרֶד ה' עַל הַר סִינַי.** יָכוֹל יָרַד עָלָיו מַמָּשׁ? תַּלְמוּד לוֹמַר: "כִּי מִן הַשָּׁמַיִם דִּבַּרְתִּי עִמָּכֶם" (להלן כ, יט)! מְלַמֵּד שֶׁהִרְכִּין שָׁמַיִם הַתַּחְתּוֹנִים וְהָעֶלְיוֹנִים וְהִצִּיעָן עַל גַּבֵּי הָהָר כְּמַצָּע עַל הַמִּטָּה, וְיָרַד כִּסֵּא הַכָּבוֹד עֲלֵיהֶם:

כא **הָעֵד בָּעָם.** הַתְרֵה בָהֶם שֶׁלֹּא לַעֲלוֹת בָּהָר: **פֶּן יֶהֶרְסוּ וְגוֹ'.** שֶׁלֹּא יֶהֶרְסוּ אֶת מַצָּבָם עַל יְדֵי שֶׁתַּאֲוָתָם "אֶל ה' לִרְאוֹת" וְיִקְרְבוּ לְצַד הָהָר: **וְנָפַל מִמֶּנּוּ רָב.** כָּל מַה שֶּׁיִּפֹּל מֵהֶם, וַאֲפִלּוּ הוּא יְחִידִי, חָשׁוּב לְפָנַי רָב: **פֶּן יֶהֶרְסוּ.** כָּל הֲרִיסָה מְפָרֶדֶת אֲסִיפַת הַבִּנְיָן, אַף הַנִּפְרָדִין מִמַּצַּב אֲנָשִׁים הוֹרְסִים אֶת הַמַּצָּב:

כב **וְגַם הַכֹּהֲנִים.** אַף הַבְּכוֹרוֹת שֶׁהָעֲבוֹדָה בָּהֶם: **הַנִּגָּשִׁים אֶל ה'.** לְהַקְרִיב קָרְבָּנוֹת, אַף הֵם אַל יִסְמְכוּ עַל חֲשִׁיבוּתָם לַעֲלוֹת: **יִתְקַדָּשׁוּ.** יִהְיוּ מְזֻמָּנִים לְהִתְיַצֵּב עַל עָמְדָן: **פֶּן יִפְרֹץ.** לְשׁוֹן פִּרְצָה, יַהֲרֹג בָּהֶם וְיַעֲשֶׂה בָהֶם פִּרְצָה:

כג **לֹא יוּכַל הָעָם.** אֵינִי צָרִיךְ לְהָעִיד בָּהֶם, שֶׁהֲרֵי מֻתְרִין וְעוֹמְדִין הֵם הַיּוֹם שְׁלֹשָׁה יָמִים, וְלֹא יוּכְלוּ לַעֲלוֹת, שֶׁאֵין לָהֶם רְשׁוּת:

כד **לֶךְ רֵד.** וְהָעֵד בָּהֶם שֵׁנִית, שֶׁמְּזָרְזִין אֶת הָאָדָם קֹדֶם מַעֲשֶׂה וְחוֹזְרִין וּמְזָרְזִין אוֹתוֹ בִּשְׁעַת מַעֲשֶׂה: **וְעָלִיתָ אַתָּה וְאַהֲרֹן עִמָּךְ וְהַכֹּהֲנִים.** יָכוֹל אַף הֵם "עִמָּךְ"? תַּלְמוּד לוֹמַר: "וְעָלִיתָ אַתָּה". אֱמֹר מֵעַתָּה, אַתָּה מְחִצָּה לְעַצְמְךָ, וְאַהֲרֹן מְחִצָּה לְעַצְמוֹ; מֹשֶׁה נִגַּשׁ יוֹתֵר מֵאַהֲרֹן וְאַהֲרֹן יוֹתֵר מִן הַכֹּהֲנִים, "וְהָעָם" כָּל עִקָּר "אַל יֶהֶרְסוּ" אֶת מַצָּבָם "לַעֲלֹת אֶל ה'": **פֶּן יִפְרָץ בָּם.** אַף עַל פִּי שֶׁהוּא נָקוּד חֲטַף קָמַץ אֵינוֹ זָז מִגִּזְרָתוֹ. כָּךְ דֶּרֶךְ כָּל תֵּבָה שֶׁנְּקֻדָּתָהּ מְלָאפוּם, כְּשֶׁהִיא סְמוּכָה בְּמַקָּף מִשְׁתַּנֶּה הַנִּקּוּד לַחֲטַף קָמַץ:

כה **וַיֹּאמֶר אֲלֵהֶם.** הַתְרָאָה זוֹ:

כ א **וַיְדַבֵּר אֱלֹהִים.** אֵין "אֱלֹהִים" אֶלָּא דַּיָּן, לְפִי שֶׁיֵּשׁ פָּרָשִׁיּוֹת בַּתּוֹרָה שֶׁאִם עֲשָׂאָן אָדָם מְקַבֵּל שָׂכָר וְאִם לָאו אֵינוֹ מְקַבֵּל עֲלֵיהֶם פֻּרְעָנוּת,

first three commands, through which the people declare their obedience and loyalty to God above all else, establish the single most important principle of a free society, namely the *moral limits of power.*

יט וַיֶּחֱרַ֥ד כָּל־הָהָ֖ר מְאֹֽד׃ וַיְהִי֙ ק֣וֹל הַשֹּׁפָ֔ר הוֹלֵ֖ךְ וְחָזֵ֣ק מְאֹ֑ד מֹשֶׁ֣ה יְדַבֵּ֔ר
כ וְהָאֱלֹהִ֖ים יַעֲנֶ֥נּוּ בְקֽוֹל׃ וַיֵּ֧רֶד יהוה עַל־הַ֥ר סִינַ֖י אֶל־רֹ֣אשׁ הָהָ֑ר וַיִּקְרָ֨א ששי
כא יהוה לְמֹשֶׁ֛ה אֶל־רֹ֥אשׁ הָהָ֖ר וַיַּ֥עַל מֹשֶֽׁה׃ וַיֹּ֤אמֶר יהוה֙ אֶל־מֹשֶׁ֔ה רֵ֖ד
כב הָעֵ֣ד בָּעָ֑ם פֶּן־יֶהֶרְס֤וּ אֶל־יהוה֙ לִרְא֔וֹת וְנָפַ֥ל מִמֶּ֖נּוּ רָֽב׃ וְגַ֧ם הַכֹּהֲנִ֛ים
כג הַנִּגָּשִׁ֥ים אֶל־יהוה יִתְקַדָּ֑שׁוּ פֶּן־יִפְרֹ֥ץ בָּהֶ֖ם יהוה׃ וַיֹּ֤אמֶר מֹשֶׁה֙ אֶל־
יהוה לֹא־יוּכַ֣ל הָעָ֔ם לַעֲלֹ֖ת אֶל־הַ֣ר סִינָ֑י כִּֽי־אַתָּ֞ה הַעֵדֹ֤תָה בָּ֙נוּ֙ לֵאמֹ֔ר
כד הַגְבֵּ֥ל אֶת־הָהָ֖ר וְקִדַּשְׁתּֽוֹ׃ וַיֹּ֨אמֶר אֵלָ֤יו יהוה֙ לֶךְ־רֵ֔ד וְעָלִ֥יתָ אַתָּ֖ה
וְאַהֲרֹ֣ן עִמָּ֑ךְ וְהַכֹּהֲנִ֣ים וְהָעָ֗ם אַל־יֶֽהֶרְס֛וּ לַעֲלֹ֥ת אֶל־יהוה פֶּן־יִפְרָץ־
כ כה א בָּֽם׃ וַיֵּ֥רֶד מֹשֶׁ֖ה אֶל־הָעָ֑ם וַיֹּ֖אמֶר אֲלֵהֶֽם׃ וַיְדַבֵּ֣ר אֱלֹהִ֔ים
ב אֵ֛ת כָּל־הַדְּבָרִ֥ים הָאֵ֖לֶּה לֵאמֹֽר׃ אָנֹכִ֖י יהוה אֱלֹהֶ֑יךָ

אונקלוס

מְמַלֵּיל, וּמִן קֳדָם יי מִתְעֲנֵי לֵיהּ בְּקָל: כ וְאִתְגְּלִי יי, עַל טוּרָא דְּסִינַי
לְרֵישׁ טוּרָא, וּקְרָא יי לְמֹשֶׁה, לְרֵישׁ טוּרָא וּסְלֵיק מֹשֶׁה: כא וַאֲמַר יי
לְמֹשֶׁה, חוֹת אַסְהֵיד בְּעַמָּא, דִּלְמָא יִפַּגְּרוּן קֳדָם יי לְמִחְזֵי, וְיִפּוֹל מִנְּהוֹן
סַגִּי: כב וְאַף כָּהֲנַיָּא, דְּקָרִיבִין לְשַׁמָּשָׁא קֳדָם יי יִתְקַדְּשׁוּן, דִּלְמָא יִקְטוֹל
בְּהוֹן יי: כג וַאֲמַר מֹשֶׁה קֳדָם יי, לָא יִכּוֹל עַמָּא, לְמִסַּק לְטוּרָא דְּסִינַי,
אֲרֵי אַתְּ, אַסְהֵידְתְּ בַּנָא לְמֵימַר, תַּחֵים יָת טוּרָא וְקַדֵּישְׁהִי: כד וַאֲמַר
לֵיהּ יי אִיזֵיל חוֹת, וְתִסַּק אַתְּ וְאַהֲרֹן עִמָּךְ, וְכָהֲנַיָּא וְעַמָּא, לָא יִפַּגְּרוּן,
לְמִסַּק לִקֳדָם יי דִּלְמָא יִקְטוֹל בְּהוֹן: כה וּנְחַת מֹשֶׁה לְוָת עַמָּא, וַאֲמַר
לְהוֹן: כ א וּמַלֵּיל יי, יָת, כָּל פִּתְגָמַיָּא הָאִלֵּין לְמֵימַר: ב אֲנָא יי אֱלָהָךְ,

19:20 וַיֵּרֶד יהוה *And the Lord descended* – Rambam explains that this is a figurative expression. God, beyond space, does not literally ascend or descend. The word "descend" in this context refers to revelation (*Guide for the Perplexed* I:10). There was thunder, lightning, smoke, and fire, and the mountain itself trembled. The Israelites felt a terrifying, palpable sense of the closeness of God. It was a unique moment: heaven and earth seemed almost to touch.

THE TEN COMMANDMENTS

The Ten Commandments that appear in Parashat Yitro have long held a special place not only in Judaism but also within the broader configuration of values we call the Judeo-Christian ethic. They remain the supreme expression of the higher law to which all human law is bound. Most depictions of the Ten Commandments divide them into two, because of the "two tablets of stone" (Deut. 4:13) on which they were engraved. The first five, roughly speaking, are about the relationship between humans and God, the second five about the relationship between humans and other humans. However, it seems to me that the commandments are also structured, like the ten plagues, in three groups of three, with a tenth that is set apart from the rest.

The first three – no other gods besides Me, no graven images, and no taking of God's name in vain – define the Jewish people as "one nation under God." God is our ultimate sovereign. Therefore all other earthly rule is subject to the overarching imperatives linking Israel to God. God is a living force: make no graven images. And sovereignty presupposes reverence: do not take My name in vain. These

Lord your God who brought you out of the land of Egypt, out of the house
3 4 of slaves. Have no other gods than Me. Do not make for yourself any carved
image or likeness of any creature in the heavens above or the earth beneath
5 or the water beneath the earth. Do not bow down to them or worship them,
for I the Lord your God demand absolute loyalty. For those who hate Me,
I hold the descendants to account for the sins of the fathers to the third and
6 fourth generation, but to those who love Me and keep My commands – I shall

רש״י

יָכוֹל אַף עֲשֶׂרֶת הַדִּבְּרוֹת כֵּן? תַּלְמוּד לוֹמַר: ״וַיְדַבֵּר אֱלֹהִים״, דַּיָּן לִפָּרַע: **אֵת כָּל הַדְּבָרִים הָאֵלֶּה.** מְלַמֵּד שֶׁאָמַר הַקָּדוֹשׁ בָּרוּךְ הוּא עֲשֶׂרֶת הַדִּבְּרוֹת בְּדִבּוּר אֶחָד, מַה שֶּׁאִי אֶפְשָׁר לְאָדָם לוֹמַר כֵּן. אִם כֵּן מַה תַּלְמוּד לוֹמַר עוֹד ״אָנֹכִי״ וְ״לֹא יִהְיֶה לְךָ״? שֶׁחָזַר וּפֵרַשׁ עַל כָּל דִּבּוּר וְדִבּוּר בִּפְנֵי עַצְמוֹ: **לֵאמֹר.** מְלַמֵּד שֶׁהָיוּ עוֹנִין עַל הֵן – הֵן, וְעַל לָאו – לָאו:

ב] **אֲשֶׁר הוֹצֵאתִיךָ מֵאֶרֶץ מִצְרַיִם.** כְּדַאי הִיא הַהוֹצָאָה שֶׁתִּהְיוּ מְשֻׁעְבָּדִים לִי. דָּבָר אַחֵר, לְפִי שֶׁנִּגְלָה בַּיָּם כְּגִבּוֹר מִלְחָמָה וְנִגְלָה כָּאן כְּזָקֵן מָלֵא רַחֲמִים, שֶׁנֶּאֱמַר: ״וְתַחַת רַגְלָיו כְּמַעֲשֵׂה לִבְנַת הַסַּפִּיר״ (להלן כד, י), זוֹ הָיְתָה לְפָנָיו בִּשְׁעַת הַשִּׁעְבּוּד, ״וּכְעֶצֶם הַשָּׁמַיִם״ (שם) מִשֶּׁנִּגְאֲלוּ, הוֹאִיל וַאֲנִי מִשְׁתַּנֶּה בְּמַרְאוֹת, אַל תֹּאמְרוּ שְׁתֵּי רְשֻׁיּוֹת הֵן! אָנֹכִי הוּא אֲשֶׁר הוֹצֵאתִיךָ מִמִּצְרַיִם וְעַל הַיָּם. דָּבָר אַחֵר, לְפִי שֶׁהָיוּ שׁוֹמְעִין קוֹלוֹת הַרְבֵּה, שֶׁנֶּאֱמַר ״אֶת הַקּוֹלֹת״ (להלן פסוק טו), קוֹלוֹת בָּאִין מֵאַרְבַּע רוּחוֹת וּמִן הַשָּׁמַיִם וּמִן הָאָרֶץ, אַל תֹּאמְרוּ רְשֻׁיּוֹת הַרְבֵּה הֵן! וְלָמָּה אָמַר לְשׁוֹן יָחִיד, ״אֱלֹהֶיךָ״? לִתֵּן פִּתְחוֹן פֶּה לְמֹשֶׁה לְלַמֵּד סַנֵּגוֹרְיָא בְּמַעֲשֵׂה הָעֵגֶל, וְזֶה הוּא שֶׁאָמַר: ״לָמָה ה׳ יֶחֱרֶה אַפְּךָ בְּעַמֶּךָ״ (להלן לב, יא), לֹא לָהֶם צִוִּיתָ ״לֹא יִהְיֶה לָכֶם אֱלֹהִים אֲחֵרִים״, אֶלָּא לִי לְבַדִּי:

מִבֵּית עֲבָדִים. מִבֵּית פַּרְעֹה שֶׁהֱיִיתֶם עֲבָדִים לוֹ. אוֹ אֵינוֹ אוֹמֵר אֶלָּא ״מִבֵּית עֲבָדִים״ שֶׁהָיוּ עֲבָדִים לַעֲבָדִים? תַּלְמוּד לוֹמַר: ״וַיִּפְדְּךָ מִבֵּית עֲבָדִים מִיַּד פַּרְעֹה מֶלֶךְ מִצְרַיִם״ (דברים ז, ח), אֱמוֹר מֵעַתָּה, עֲבָדִים לַמֶּלֶךְ הָיוּ וְלֹא עֲבָדִים לַעֲבָדִים:

ג] **לֹא יִהְיֶה לְךָ.** לָמָּה נֶאֱמַר? לְפִי שֶׁנֶּאֱמַר: ״לֹא תַעֲשֶׂה לְךָ״, אֵין לִי אֶלָּא שֶׁלֹּא יַעֲשֶׂה, הֶעָשׂוּי כְּבָר מִנַּיִן שֶׁלֹּא יְקַיֵּם? תַּלְמוּד לוֹמַר: ״לֹא יִהְיֶה לְךָ״: **אֱלֹהִים אֲחֵרִים.** שֶׁאֵינָן אֱלֹהוּת, אֶלָּא אֲחֵרִים עֲשָׂאוּם אֱלֹהִים עֲלֵיהֶם. וְלֹא יִתָּכֵן לְפָרֵשׁ ״אֱלֹהִים אֲחֵרִים״ זוּלָתִי, שֶׁגְּנַאי הוּא כְּלַפֵּי מַעְלָה לְקָרוֹתָם אֱלֹהוּת אֶצְלוֹ. דָּבָר אַחֵר, ״אֱלֹהִים אֲחֵרִים״, שֶׁהֵם אֲחֵרִים לְעוֹבְדֵיהֶם, צוֹעֲקִים אֲלֵיהֶם וְאֵינָן עוֹנִין אוֹתָם, וְדוֹמֶה כְּאִלּוּ הוּא אַחֵר שֶׁאֵינוֹ מַכִּירוֹ מֵעוֹלָם: **עַל פָּנָי.** כָּל זְמַן שֶׁאֲנִי קַיָּם, שֶׁלֹּא תֹּאמַר, לֹא נִצְטַוּוּ עַל עֲבוֹדָה זָרָה אֶלָּא אוֹתוֹ הַדּוֹר:

ד] **פֶּסֶל.** עַל שֵׁם שֶׁנִּפְסָל כָּל תְּמוּנַת דָּבָר ״אֲשֶׁר בַּשָּׁמַיִם״ וְגוֹ׳:

ה-ו] **אֵל קַנָּא.** מְקַנֵּא לִפָּרַע וְאֵינוֹ עוֹבֵר עַל מִדָּתוֹ לִמְחֹל עַל עֲבוֹדָה זָרָה. כָּל לְשׁוֹן ׳קַנָּא׳ אנפרינמנ״ט בְּלַעַז, נוֹתֵן לֵב לִפָּרַע: **לְשֹׂנְאָי.** כְּתַרְגּוּמוֹ, כְּשֶׁאוֹחֲזִין מַעֲשֵׂה אֲבוֹתֵיהֶם בִּידֵיהֶם. **וְנֹצֵר חֶסֶד** שֶׁאָדָם עוֹשֶׂה, לְשַׁלֵּם שָׂכָר עַד לְאַלְפַּיִם דּוֹר. נִמְצֵאת מִדָּה טוֹבָה יְתֵרָה עַל מִדַּת

create a kind of silence of the soul. We need to learn to listen – and listening is an art, one of the greatest there is.

There is a listening beyond words, a silence that gives meaning to speech. In that silence, we know and are known by God. God is the personal dimension of existence, the "Thou" beneath the "It," the "Ought" beyond the "Is," the Self that speaks to self in moments of total disclosure. Opening ourselves to the universe, we find God reaching out to us. At that moment we make the life-changing discovery that though we seem utterly insignificant, we are utterly significant, a fragment of God's presence in the world. Eternity preceded us; infinity will come after us. Yet we know that this day, this moment, this place, this circumstance, is full of the light of infinite radiance, whose proof is the mere fact that we are here to experience it. Faith is where God and human beings touch across the abyss of infinity. Feeling, we are felt. Acting, we are acted upon. Living, we are lived. And if we make ourselves transparent to existence, then our lives too radiate that Divine Presence which, celebrating life, gives life to those whose lives we touch.

20:5 **עַל־שִׁלֵּשִׁים וְעַל־רִבֵּעִים** *To the third and fourth generation* – Deuteronomy 24:16 tells us, "A person shall be put to death only for his own sin." Yirmeya 31:28–29 and Yeḥezkel 18:2–4 both reinforce the point that there is no intergenerational transfer of guilt. So what then is the meaning of "I

ג אֲשֶׁר הוֹצֵאתִיךָ מֵאֶרֶץ מִצְרַיִם מִבֵּית עֲבָדִים: לֹא־יִהְיֶה לְךָ אֱלֹהִים
ד אֲחֵרִים עַל־פָּנָי: לֹא־תַעֲשֶׂה לְךָ פֶסֶל וְכָל־תְּמוּנָה אֲשֶׁר בַּשָּׁמַיִם מִמַּעַל
ה וַאֲשֶׁר בָּאָרֶץ מִתָּחַת וַאֲשֶׁר בַּמַּיִם מִתַּחַת לָאָרֶץ: לֹא־תִשְׁתַּחֲוֶה
לָהֶם וְלֹא תָעָבְדֵם כִּי אָנֹכִי יהוה אֱלֹהֶיךָ אֵל קַנָּא פֹּקֵד עֲוֺן אָבֹת עַל־
ו בָּנִים עַל־שִׁלֵּשִׁים וְעַל־רִבֵּעִים לְשֹׂנְאָי: וְעֹשֶׂה חֶסֶד לַאֲלָפִים לְאֹהֲבַי

אונקלוס

דְּאַפֵּיקְתָּךְ, מֵאַרְעָא דְמִצְרַיִם מִבֵּית עַבְדוּתָא: ג לָא יְהֵי לָךְ אֱלָהּ אָחֳרָן בַּר מִנִּי: ד לָא תַעֲבֵיד לָךְ צֵילַם וְכָל דְּמוּ, דְּבִשְׁמַיָּא מִלְּעֵילָּא וְדִבְאַרְעָא מִלְּרַע, וְדִבְמַיָּא מִלְּרַע לְאַרְעָא: ה לָא תִסְגּוֹד לְהוֹן וְלָא תִפְלְחִנּוּן, אֲרֵי אֲנָא, יי אֱלָהָךְ אֵל קַנָּא, מַסְעַר, חוֹבֵי אֲבָהָן עַל בְּנִין מָרָדִין, עַל דָּר תְּלִיתַאי וְעַל דָּר רְבִיעַאי לְסָנְאַי, כַּד מַשְׁלְמִין בְּנַיָּא לְמִחְטֵי בָּתַר אֲבָהָתְהוֹן: ו וְעָבֵיד טֵיבוּ לְאַלְפֵי דָרִין, לְרָחֲמַי

The second three commands – the Sabbath, honoring parents, and the prohibition of murder – are all about the principle of *the createdness of life*. They establish limits to the idea of autonomy, namely, that we are free to do whatever we like so long as it does not harm others. The Sabbath is the day dedicated to seeing God as Creator and the universe as His creation. Hence, one day in seven, human hierarchies are suspended and everyone is free. Honoring parents acknowledges our human createdness. It tells us that not everything that matters is the result of our choice, chief of which is the fact that we exist at all. "Do not murder" restates the central principle of the universal Noahide covenant that murder is not just a crime against man but a sin against God in whose image we are created. Thus, commands four to six tell us to remember where we came from if we are to be mindful of how to live.

The third three – against adultery, theft, and bearing false witness – establish the basic institutions on which society depends. Marriage is sacred because it is the human bond closest in approximation to the covenant between us and God. It is the human institution par excellence that depends on loyalty and fidelity, and it is the matrix of a free society. The prohibition against theft establishes the integrity of property. The prohibition of false testimony is the precondition of justice.

Finally comes the stand-alone prohibition against envying your neighbor's house, wife, slave, maid, ox, donkey, or anything else belonging to him or her. This seems odd if we think of the Ten Commandments as statutes, but not if we think of them as the basic principles of a free society. Envy is the failure to understand the principle of creation as set out in Genesis 1, that everything has its place in the scheme of things. Each of us has our own task and our own blessings, and we are each loved and cherished by God. Live by these truths and there is order. Abandon them and there is chaos. Nothing is more pointless and destructive than to let someone else's happiness diminish your own.

So the prohibition of envy counters the most basic force undermining the social harmony and order that are the aim of the Ten Commandments as a whole. Not only do they forbid it; they also help us rise above it. Thirty-three centuries after they were first given, the Ten Commandments remain the simplest, shortest guide to the creation and maintenance of a good society.

20:2 אָנֹכִי יהוה אֱלֹהֶיךָ *I am the* L*ORD your God* – As the Midrash narrates this moment:

> When the Holy One, blessed be He, gave the Torah, no bird called, no fowl took flight, no ox lowed, the *ofanim* did not fly, the *seraphim* did not utter "Holy, holy," the ocean did not stir, created man did not speak: the whole world was silent and still – and the voice emerged: "I am the LORD your God." (Shemot Rabba 29)

"Judaism is full of silences," said Elie Wiesel, "but we don't talk about them." Undergirding all human speech is that sense of "something far more deeply interfused," as Wordsworth called it. Beneath the noise there is the music, the hymn of creation to its Creator, but to hear it we need to

7 act with faithful love for thousands. Do not speak the name of the
Lord your God in vain, for the Lord will not hold guiltless those who speak
His name in vain.
8 9 Remember the Sabbath to keep it holy. Six days you shall work, and carry
10 out all your labors, but the seventh is a Sabbath to the Lord your God.
On it, do no work – neither you, nor your son or daughter, your male or
11 female servant, your livestock, or the migrant within your gates. For in six
days the Lord made heaven and earth, the sea, and all that they contain,
and He rested on the seventh day. And so the Lord blessed the Sabbath
12 day and made it holy. Honor your father

רש״י

פֻּרְעָנוּת אַחַת עַל חֲמֵשׁ מֵאוֹת, שֶׁזּוֹ לְאַרְבָּעָה דוֹרוֹת וְזוֹ לַאֲלָפִים:

ז **לַשָּׁוְא.** חִנָּם, לַהֶבֶל. וְאֵי זֶהוּ שְׁבוּעַת שָׁוְא? נִשְׁבַּע לְשַׁנּוֹת אֶת הַיָּדוּעַ, עַל עַמּוּד שֶׁל אֶבֶן שֶׁהוּא שֶׁל זָהָב:

ח ״זָכוֹר״ וְ״שָׁמוֹר״ בְּדִבּוּר אֶחָד נֶאֶמְרוּ. וְכֵן: ״מְחַלְלֶיהָ מוֹת יוּמָת״ (להלן לא, יד), ״וּבְיוֹם הַשַּׁבָּת שְׁנֵי כְבָשִׂים״ (במדבר כח, ט); וְכֵן: ״לֹא תִלְבַּשׁ שַׁעַטְנֵז״, ״גְּדִלִים תַּעֲשֶׂה לָּךְ״ (דברים כב, יא-יב); וְכֵן: ״עֶרְוַת אֵשֶׁת אָחִיךָ״ (ויקרא יח, טז), ״יְבָמָהּ יָבֹא עָלֶיהָ״ (דברים כה, ה); הוּא שֶׁנֶּאֱמַר: ״אַחַת דִּבֶּר אֱלֹהִים שְׁתַּיִם זוּ שָׁמָעְתִּי״ (תהלים סב, יב). ״זָכוֹר״ לְשׁוֹן פָּעוֹל הוּא, כְּמוֹ: ״אָכוֹל וְשָׁתוֹ״ (ישעיה כב, יג), ״הָלוֹךְ וּבָכֹה״ (שמואל ב׳ ג, טז), וְכֵן פִּתְרוֹנוֹ: תְּנוּ לֵב לִזְכֹּר תָּמִיד אֶת יוֹם הַשַּׁבָּת, שֶׁאִם נִזְדַּמֵּן לְךָ חֵפֶץ יָפֶה תְּהֵא מַזְמִינוֹ לַשַּׁבָּת:

ט **וְעָשִׂיתָ כָּל מְלַאכְתֶּךָ.** כְּשֶׁתָּבֹא שַׁבָּת יְהֵא בְעֵינֶיךָ כְּאִלּוּ כָּל מְלַאכְתְּךָ עֲשׂוּיָה, שֶׁלֹּא תְּהַרְהֵר אַחַר מְלָאכָה:

י **אַתָּה וּבִנְךָ וּבִתֶּךָ.** אֵלּוּ קְטַנִּים. אוֹ אֵינוֹ אֶלָּא גְּדוֹלִים? אָמַרְתָּ, הֲרֵי כְּבָר מֻזְהָרִין הֵם, אֶלָּא לֹא בָא אֶלָּא לְהַזְהִיר הַגְּדוֹלִים עַל שְׁבִיתַת הַקְּטַנִּים, וְזֶהוּ שֶׁשָּׁנִינוּ: קָטָן שֶׁבָּא לְכַבּוֹת אֵין שׁוֹמְעִין לוֹ, מִפְּנֵי שֶׁשְּׁבִיתָתוֹ עָלֶיךָ:

יא **וַיָּנַח בַּיּוֹם הַשְּׁבִיעִי.** כִּבְיָכוֹל הִכְתִּיב בְּעַצְמוֹ מְנוּחָה, לִלְמֹד הֵימֶנּוּ קַל וָחֹמֶר לָאָדָם שֶׁמְּלַאכְתּוֹ בְּעָמָל וּבִיגִיעָה שֶׁיְּהֵא נָח בַּשַּׁבָּת: **בֵּרַךְ... וַיְקַדְּשֵׁהוּ.** בֵּרְכוֹ בַּמָּן, לְכָפְלוֹ בַּשִּׁשִּׁי לֶחֶם מִשְׁנֶה, וְקִדְּשׁוֹ בַּמָּן, שֶׁלֹּא הָיָה יוֹרֵד בּוֹ:

of the Sabbath is not an experience of unfreedom. The overwhelming sense conveyed in Jewish literature, secular as well as religious, is that the day was eagerly looked forward to and joyfully welcomed – precisely as a day of release, a day of expansiveness and leisure." It is expansive the way a public park is expansive: by not being private property. The Sabbath is time we, not I, own. It is essential that on the Sabbath no one – not slaves, servants, employees, even farm animals – can be made to work against their will.

20:11 **וַיְקַדְּשֵׁהוּ** *Made it holy* – The universe was created in six days, yet creation itself involved seven days. The seventh day is declared by God Himself to be holy. The holy is where human beings renounce their independence and self-sufficiency, the very things that are the mark of their humanity, and for a moment acknowledge their utter dependence on He who spoke and brought the universe into being. The essence of the Sabbath is that it is a day of not doing, a cessation, a stopping point, a pause, an absence of activity.

The Sabbath is the time when humans cease, for a day, to be creators and become conscious of themselves as creations. Just as God had to make space for the finite, so human beings have to make space for the infinite. One way to understand the holy, then, is that it is a time or space that in itself testifies to the existence of something beyond itself. The Sabbath points to a time beyond time: to creation.

The Sabbath is one of those phenomena which you have to live in order to understand. For countless generations of Jews, it was the moment at which we renew our attachment to family and community, during which we live the truth that the world is not wholly ours to bend to our will but something given to us in trust to conserve for future generations, and in which the inequalities of a market economy are

ז וּלְשֹׁמְרֵי מִצְוֺתָי׃ לֹא תִשָּׂא אֶת־שֵׁם־יהוה אֱלֹהֶיךָ לַשָּׁוְא
כִּי לֹא יְנַקֶּה יהוה אֵת אֲשֶׁר־יִשָּׂא אֶת־שְׁמוֹ לַשָּׁוְא׃
ח ט זָכוֹר אֶת־יוֹם הַשַּׁבָּת לְקַדְּשׁוֹ׃ שֵׁשֶׁת יָמִים תַּעֲבֹד וְעָשִׂיתָ כָּל־
י מְלַאכְתֶּךָ׃ וְיוֹם הַשְּׁבִיעִי שַׁבָּת לַיהוה אֱלֹהֶיךָ לֹא־תַעֲשֶׂה כָל־
מְלָאכָה אַתָּה ׀ וּבִנְךָ וּבִתֶּךָ עַבְדְּךָ וַאֲמָתְךָ וּבְהֶמְתֶּךָ וְגֵרְךָ אֲשֶׁר
יא בִּשְׁעָרֶיךָ׃ כִּי שֵׁשֶׁת־יָמִים עָשָׂה יהוה אֶת־הַשָּׁמַיִם וְאֶת־הָאָרֶץ
אֶת־הַיָּם וְאֶת־כָּל־אֲשֶׁר־בָּם וַיָּנַח בַּיּוֹם הַשְּׁבִיעִי עַל־כֵּן בֵּרַךְ
יב יהוה אֶת־יוֹם הַשַּׁבָּת וַיְקַדְּשֵׁהוּ׃ כַּבֵּד אֶת־

אונקלוס

וּלְנָטְרֵי פִקּוֹדָי׃ ז לָא תֵימֵי, בִּשְׁמָא דַּייָ אֱלָהָךְ לְמַגָּנָא, אֲרֵי לָא יְזַכֵּי יי, יָת, דְּיֵימֵי בִשְׁמֵיהּ לְשִׁקְרָא׃ ח הֲוִי דְּכִיר יָת יוֹמָא דְשַׁבְּתָא לְקַדָּשׁוּתֵיהּ׃ ט שִׁתָּא יוֹמִין תִּפְלַח וְתַעֲבֵיד כָּל עֲבִידְתָךְ׃ י וְיוֹמָא שְׁבִיעָאָה, שַׁבְּתָא קֳדָם יי אֱלָהָךְ, לָא תַעֲבֵיד כָּל עֲבִידָא, אַתְּ וּבְרָךְ וּבְרַתָּךְ, עַבְדָּךְ וְאַמְתָךְ וּבְעִירָךְ, וְגִיּוֹרָךְ דִּבְקִרְוָךְ׃ יא אֲרֵי שִׁתָּא יוֹמִין עֲבַד יי יָת שְׁמַיָּא וְיָת אַרְעָא, יָת יַמָּא וְיָת כָּל דִּבְהוֹן, וְנָח בְּיוֹמָא שְׁבִיעָאָה, עַל כֵּן, בָּרֵיךְ יי, יָת יוֹמָא דְשַׁבְּתָא וְקַדְּשֵׁיהּ׃ יב יַקַּר יָת

blasphemy front-page news throughout the world, and it has led to the shedding of blood. Are we fated to live between these two extremes?

A free society is a moral achievement, and it is made by us and our habits of thought, speech, and deed. Even as we revere God's name, it is not our task to conquer or convert the world or enforce uniformity of belief. It is our task to be a blessing to the world. To invoke God to justify violence is not an act of sanctity but of sacrilege. It is in itself a kind of blasphemy. It is to take God's name in vain.

20:10 אַתָּה וּבִנְךָ וּבִתֶּךָ עַבְדְּךָ וַאֲמָתְךָ וּבְהֶמְתֶּךָ וְגֵרְךָ *You, nor your son or daughter… servant… livestock… migrant* – The difference between a holiday and a holy day is that a holiday is private; a holy day is public. We take a vacation as individuals choosing to do so for our own enjoyment. The biblical Sabbath, by contrast, is a collective good. Michael Walzer writes that it is "enjoined for everyone, enjoyed by everyone." He also notes the paradox of holy days. They are an abridgment of liberty – a holy day is not one on which we are free to do what we like. Nonetheless, "the historical experience

hold the descendants to account for the sins of the fathers"? According to Sanhedrin 27b, children are only punished for the sins of their parents if they themselves commit those sins. The phrase is therefore a warning to parents not to have a negative influence on their children, not a statement of vicarious guilt or punishment. "To the third and fourth generation" – if they also reject Me.

The other side of this equation follows in the next verse. Jewish identity, historically, has constantly been learned and relearned, enacted and reinforced, and passed on as a precious gift to the next generation. The secret of Jewish continuity is that Jews cared about it. They created continuity by making the transmission of tradition their first duty and greatest joy.

20:7 לֹא תִשָּׂא אֶת־שֵׁם־יהוה אֱלֹהֶיךָ לַשָּׁוְא *Do not speak the name… in vain* – T. S. Eliot believed that blasphemy was no longer possible. He thought that you could blaspheme only if you profoundly believed in the reality of that which you profaned. No one, according to Eliot, believed that strongly anymore. Yet in our day, other religions have made

and mother. Then you will live long in the land that the Lord your God is
13 giving you. Do not murder. Do not
commit adultery. Do not steal. Do not
14 bear false witness against your neighbor. Do not
crave your neighbor's house. Do not
crave your neighbor's wife, his male or female servant, his ox, his donkey, or
anything else that is your neighbor's."

רש״י

יב| **לְמַעַן יַאֲרִכוּן יָמֶיךָ.** אִם תְּכַבֵּד – יַאֲרִיכוּן, וְאִם לָאו – יִקְצְרוּן, שֶׁדִּבְרֵי תוֹרָה נוֹטָרִיקוֹן הֵם נִדְרָשִׁים, מִכְּלָל הֵן לָאו וּמִכְּלָל לָאו הֵן:

יג| **לֹא תִנְאָף.** אֵין נִאוּף אֶלָּא בְּאֵשֶׁת אִישׁ, שֶׁנֶּאֱמַר: "מוֹת יוּמַת הַנֹּאֵף וְהַנֹּאָפֶת" (ויקרא כ, י), וְאוֹמֵר: "הָאִשָּׁה הַמְּנָאֶפֶת תַּחַת אִישָׁהּ תִּקַּח אֶת זָרִים" (יחזקאל טז, לב): **לֹא תִגְנֹב.** בְּגוֹנֵב נְפָשׁוֹת הַכָּתוּב מְדַבֵּר. "לֹא תִגְנֹבוּ" (ויקרא יט, יא) בְּגוֹנֵב מָמוֹן. אוֹ אֵינוֹ אֶלָּא זֶה בְּגוֹנֵב מָמוֹן וּלְהַלָּן בְּגוֹנֵב נְפָשׁוֹת? אָמַרְתָּ, דָּבָר לָמֵד מֵעִנְיָנוֹ, "לֹא תִרְצַח, לֹא תִנְאָף" מִיתַת בֵּית דִּין, אַף "לֹא תִגְנֹב" דָּבָר שֶׁחַיָּבִין עָלָיו מִיתַת בֵּית דִּין:

A world of safe distances, of reservations and precautions, can never hope to recapture that state. We, individually and collectively, are the guardians of the world of trust, and the family is its birthplace.

20:13 **לֹא תִגְנֹב** *Do not steal* – Whereas Jefferson defined as inalienable rights those of "life, liberty, and the pursuit of happiness," John Locke, closer in spirit to the Tanakh, saw them as "life, liberty, or possession." The biblical respect for property rights is a revolution against the ancient world and the power it gave rulers to regard the property of the tribe or the people as their own. By contrast, when Moshe finds his leadership challenged by the Israelites during the Koraḥ rebellion, he says about his relation to the people, "I have not taken a single donkey from them, nor have I wronged any one of them" (Num. 16:15). For a ruler to abuse property rights is, for the Tanakh, one of the great corruptions of power. Judaism is the religion of a people born in slavery and longing for redemption. The great assault of slavery against human dignity is that it deprives me of the ownership of the wealth I create.

20:13 **לֹא תַעֲנֶה בְרֵעֲךָ עֵד שָׁקֶר** *Do not bear false witness* – A just society needs more than a structure of laws, courts, and enforcement agencies. There is no freedom without justice, but there is no justice without each of us accepting individual and collective responsibility for "telling the truth, the whole truth, and nothing but the truth."

20:14 **לֹא תַחְמֹד** *Do not crave* – Envy, desiring what someone else has, is an emotion, not a thought, a word, or a deed. Surely, one would think, we cannot help our emotions. They used to be called the "passions," precisely because we are passive in relation to them. So how can envy be forbidden at all? Surely it only makes sense to command or forbid matters that are within our control. In any case, why should the occasional spasm of envy matter if it does not lead to anything harmful to other people?

It matters because envy is one of the prime drivers of violence in society. It is what led Kayin to murder Hevel. Most poignantly, envy lay at the heart of the hatred of the brothers for Yosef. They resented his special treatment at the hands of their father, the richly embroidered cloak he wore, and his dreams of becoming the ruler of them all. That is what led them to contemplate killing him and eventually to sell him as a slave.

The antidote to envy is gratitude. "Who is rich?" asked Ben Zoma, and replied, "One who rejoices in what he has" (Mishna Avot 4:1). Through gratitude we learn to celebrate what we have instead of thinking about what other people have, and to be what we are instead of wanting to be what we are not.

אָבִיךָ וְאֶת־אִמֶּךָ לְמַעַן יַאֲרִכוּן יָמֶיךָ עַל הָאֲדָמָה אֲשֶׁר־יהוה אֱלֹהֶיךָ
יג נֹתֵן לָךְ׃ לֹא תִרְצָח לֹא־
תִנְאָף לֹא תִגְנֹב לֹא
יד תַעֲנֶה בְרֵעֲךָ עֵד שָׁקֶר׃ לֹא
תַחְמֹד בֵּית רֵעֶךָ לֹא־
תַחְמֹד אֵשֶׁת רֵעֶךָ וְעַבְדּוֹ וַאֲמָתוֹ וְשׁוֹרוֹ וַחֲמֹרוֹ וְכֹל אֲשֶׁר
לְרֵעֶךָ׃

אונקלוס

אֲבוּךְ וְיָת אִמָּךְ, בְּדִיל דְּיֵירְכוּן יוֹמָךְ, עַל אַרְעָא, דַּיְיָ אֱלָהָךְ יָהֵיב לָךְ: יג לָא תִקְטוֹל נְפַשׁ, לָא תְגוּף, לָא תִגְנוּב, לָא תַסְהֵיד בְּחַבְרָךְ סָהֲדוּתָא דְשִׁקְרָא: יד לָא תַחְמֵיד בֵּית חַבְרָךְ, לָא תַחְמֵיד אִתַּת חַבְרָךְ, וְעַבְדֵּיהּ וְאַמְתֵּיהּ וְתוֹרֵיהּ וּחְמָרֵיהּ, וְכֹל דִּלְחַבְרָךְ:

counterbalanced by a world in which money does not count, in which we are all equal citizens. The Jewish writer Ahad Ha'am was surely correct when he said that more than the Jews have kept the Sabbath, the Sabbath has kept the Jews. It was and is the one day in seven in which we live out all those values which are in danger of being obscured in the daily rush of events, the day in which we stop making a living and learn instead simply how to live.

20:12 כַּבֵּד אֶת־אָבִיךָ וְאֶת־אִמֶּךָ *Honor your father and mother* – As we have seen, the first five commands are generally considered to be about our relationship with God, the second five about our relationships with our fellow humans. The command to honor parents, the fifth command, belongs to the first group because it is about the duties we owe to those who brought us into being. Collectively, they represent ontological gratitude, an attitude of thankfulness and respect to those to whom we owe the gift of life itself.

20:13 לֹא תִנְאָף *Do not commit adultery* – In marriage we ask for and offer a commitment to share not this or that aspect of life but life itself. Marriage is the supreme example of a moral bond. Like all things seriously worthwhile, it involves the realization of a possibility at the price of excluding others. Every relationship has its rows, its tensions, its disappointments, its languid passages, but marriage is where we live through these things in the knowledge – given by commitment, renewed by love's rituals – that they will not drive us apart. Marriage is surrounded by a wall (the Rabbis called it a "hedge of roses") that we may not cross. On the other side is adultery.

Adultery involves putting short-term pleasure ahead of lifelong happiness. It sets my desires above my feeling for, and obligation to, others. It devalues the currency of commitment: the word spoken, the pledge given, the promise undertaken. And like so many ostensibly unpublic acts, it affects the world around us. What we do today others may do in the future, affected, consciously or unconsciously, by our example. We tacitly teach our partners, friends, and above all our children, that despite our most serious undertakings, the word of another person cannot be trusted. When that happens, we are all diminished.

When marriage is betrayed, something of our world has been lost – and it is not something small. Love freely given and freely received, the sharing of a life, is the most profound redemption ever experienced from loneliness, the point at which the political and moral enterprise begin.

15 Every one of the people witnessed the thunder and lightning and the sound of SHEVI'I
the ram's horn and the smoke-covered mountain; they saw and they shook – and
16 they stood at a distance, and said to Moshe, "Speak to us yourself and we will
17 listen, but let not God say any more to us, or we will die." "Do not be afraid," said
Moshe to the people, "God has come to lift you up, so that the awe of Him will
18 be with you always, keeping you from sin." But the people remained at a distance
19 while Moshe approached the thick darkness where God was. Then the MAFTIR
Lord said to Moshe, "This is what you shall tell the Israelites: You yourselves
20 have seen that I, from the heavens, have spoken to you. Have no others alongside
21 Me; make yourselves no silver gods, no golden gods. Make for Me an altar of
earth and on that sacrifice your burnt offerings and peace offerings, your sheep
and your cattle. Wherever I cause My name to be invoked, I will come to you and
22 I will bless you. If you make Me an altar of stones, do not build it of hewn stone,

רש״י

טו **וְכָל הָעָם רֹאִים.** מְלַמֵּד שֶׁלֹּא הָיָה בָהֶם אֶחָד סוּמָא. וּמִנַּיִן שֶׁלֹּא הָיָה בָהֶם אִלֵּם? תַּלְמוּד לוֹמַר: "וַיַּעֲנוּ כָּל הָעָם" (לעיל יט, ח). וּמִנַּיִן שֶׁלֹּא הָיָה בָהֶם חֵרֵשׁ? תַּלְמוּד לוֹמַר: "נַעֲשֶׂה וְנִשְׁמָע" (להלן כד, ז): **רֹאִים אֶת הַקּוֹלֹת.** רוֹאִים אֶת הַנִּשְׁמָע, שֶׁאִי אֶפְשָׁר לִרְאוֹת בְּמָקוֹם אַחֵר: **אֶת הַקּוֹלֹת.** הַיּוֹצְאִין מִפִּי הַגְּבוּרָה: **וַיָּנֻעוּ.** אֵין 'נוֹעַ' אֶלָּא זִיעַ: **וַיַּעַמְדוּ מֵרָחֹק.** הָיוּ נִרְתָּעִין לַאֲחוֹרֵיהֶם שְׁנֵים עָשָׂר מִיל כְּאֹרֶךְ מַחֲנֵיהֶם, וּמַלְאֲכֵי הַשָּׁרֵת בָּאִין וּמְסַיְּעִין אוֹתָן לְהַחֲזִירָם, שֶׁנֶּאֱמַר: "מַלְכֵי צְבָאוֹת יִדֹּדוּן יִדֹּדוּן" (תהלים סח, יג):

יז **לְבַעֲבוּר נַסּוֹת אֶתְכֶם.** לְגַדֵּל אֶתְכֶם בָּעוֹלָם, שֶׁיֵּצֵא לָכֶם שֵׁם בָּאֻמּוֹת שֶׁהוּא בִּכְבוֹדוֹ נִגְלָה עֲלֵיכֶם: **נַסּוֹת.** לְשׁוֹן הֲרָמָה וּגְדֻלָּה, כְּמוֹ: "הָרִימוּ נֵס" (ישעיה סב, י), "אָרִים נִסִּי" (שם מט, כב), "וְכַנֵּס עַל הַגִּבְעָה" (שם ל, יז) שֶׁהוּא זָקוּף: **וּבַעֲבוּר תִּהְיֶה יִרְאָתוֹ.** עַל יְדֵי שֶׁרְאִיתֶם אוֹתוֹ יָרוּי וּמְאֻיָּם, תֵּדְעוּ כִּי אֵין זוּלָתוֹ וְתִירְאוּ מִפָּנָיו:

יח **נִגַּשׁ אֶל הָעֲרָפֶל.** לִפְנִים מִשָּׁלֹשׁ מְחִיצוֹת: חֹשֶׁךְ, עָנָן וַעֲרָפֶל, שֶׁנֶּאֱמַר: "וְהָהָר בֹּעֵר בָּאֵשׁ עַד לֵב הַשָּׁמַיִם חֹשֶׁךְ עָנָן וַעֲרָפֶל" (דברים ד, יא). עֲרָפֶל הוּא עַב הֶעָנָן, שֶׁאָמַר לוֹ: "הִנֵּה אָנֹכִי בָּא אֵלֶיךָ בְּעַב הֶעָנָן" (לעיל יט, ט):

יט **כֹּה תֹאמַר.** בַּלָּשׁוֹן הַזֶּה: **אַתֶּם רְאִיתֶם.** יֵשׁ הֶפְרֵשׁ בֵּין מַה שֶּׁאָדָם רוֹאֶה לְמַה שֶּׁאֲחֵרִים מְסִיחִין לוֹ, שֶׁמַּה שֶּׁאֲחֵרִים מְסִיחִין לוֹ פְּעָמִים שֶׁלִּבּוֹ חָלוּק מִלְּהַאֲמִין: **כִּי מִן הַשָּׁמַיִם דִּבַּרְתִּי.** וְכָתוּב אַחֵר אוֹמֵר: "וַיֵּרֶד ה' עַל הַר סִינַי" (לעיל יט, כ)! בָּא הַכָּתוּב הַשְּׁלִישִׁי וְהִכְרִיעַ בֵּינֵיהֶם: "מִן הַשָּׁמַיִם הִשְׁמִיעֲךָ אֶת קֹלוֹ לְיַסְּרֶךָּ וְעַל הָאָרֶץ הֶרְאֲךָ אֶת אִשּׁוֹ הַגְּדוֹלָה" (דברים ד, לו), כְּבוֹדוֹ בַּשָּׁמַיִם וְאִשּׁוֹ וּגְבוּרָתוֹ עַל הָאָרֶץ. דָּבָר אַחֵר, הִרְכִּין שָׁמַיִם וּשְׁמֵי שָׁמַיִם וְהִצִּיעָן עַל הָהָר, וְכֵן הוּא אוֹמֵר: "וַיֵּט שָׁמַיִם וַיֵּרַד" (שמואל ב' כב, י):

כ **לֹא תַעֲשׂוּן אִתִּי.** לֹא תַעֲשׂוּן דְּמוּת שַׁמָּשַׁי הַמְשַׁמְּשִׁים לְפָנַי בַּמָּרוֹם: **אֱלֹהֵי כֶסֶף.** בָּא לְהַזְהִיר עַל הַכְּרוּבִים שֶׁאַתָּה עוֹשֶׂה לַעֲמֹד אִתִּי שֶׁלֹּא יִהְיוּ שֶׁל כֶּסֶף, שֶׁאִם שִׁנִּיתָם לַעֲשׂוֹתָם שֶׁל כֶּסֶף הֲרֵי הֵן לְפָנַי כֶּאֱלֹהוֹת: **וֵאלֹהֵי זָהָב.** בָּא לְהַזְהִיר שֶׁלֹּא יוֹסִיף עַל שְׁנַיִם, שֶׁאִם עָשִׂיתָ אַרְבָּעָה הֲרֵי הֵן לְפָנַי כֵּאלֹהֵי זָהָב: **לֹא תַעֲשׂוּ לָכֶם.** שֶׁלֹּא תֹאמַר, הֲרֵינִי עוֹשֶׂה כְּרוּבִים בְּבָתֵּי כְנֵסִיּוֹת וּבְבָתֵּי מִדְרָשׁוֹת כְּדֶרֶךְ שֶׁאֲנִי עוֹשֶׂה בְּבֵית עוֹלָמִים, לְכָךְ נֶאֱמַר: "לֹא תַעֲשׂוּ לָכֶם":

כא **מִזְבַּח אֲדָמָה.** מְחֻבָּר בָּאֲדָמָה, שֶׁלֹּא יִבְנֶנּוּ עַל גַּבֵּי עַמּוּדִים אוֹ עַל גַּבֵּי כִּפִּים. דָּבָר אַחֵר, שֶׁהָיָה מְמַלֵּא אֶת חֲלַל מִזְבַּח הַנְּחֹשֶׁת אֲדָמָה בִּשְׁעַת חֲנָיָתָן: **תַּעֲשֶׂה לִּי.** שֶׁתְּהֵא תְחִלַּת עֲשִׂיָּתוֹ לִשְׁמִי: **וְזָבַחְתָּ עָלָיו.** אֶצְלוֹ, כְּמוֹ: "וְעָלָיו מַטֵּה מְנַשֶּׁה" (במדבר ב, כ). אוֹ אֵינוֹ אֶלָּא עָלָיו מַמָּשׁ? תַּלְמוּד לוֹמַר: "הַבָּשָׂר וְהַדָּם עַל מִזְבַּח ה' אֱלֹהֶיךָ" (דברים יב, כז), וְאֵין שְׁחִיטָה בְּרֹאשׁ הַמִּזְבֵּחַ: **אֶת עֹלֹתֶיךָ וְאֶת שְׁלָמֶיךָ.** אֲשֶׁר מִצֹּאנְךָ וּמִבְּקָרֶךָ. "אֶת צֹאנְךָ וְאֶת בְּקָרֶךָ" פֵּרוּשׁ לְ"אֶת עֹלֹתֶיךָ וְאֶת שְׁלָמֶיךָ": **בְּכָל הַמָּקוֹם אֲשֶׁר אַזְכִּיר אֶת שְׁמִי.** אֲשֶׁר אֶתֵּן לְךָ רְשׁוּת לְהַזְכִּיר שֵׁם הַמְפֹרָשׁ שֶׁלִּי, שָׁם "אָבוֹא אֵלֶיךָ", אַשְׁרֶה אֶת שְׁכִינָתִי, "וּבֵרַכְתִּיךָ". מִכָּאן אַתָּה לָמֵד שֶׁלֹּא נִתַּן רְשׁוּת לְהַזְכִּיר שֵׁם הַמְפֹרָשׁ אֶלָּא בַּמָּקוֹם שֶׁהַשְּׁכִינָה בָּאָה שָׁם, וְזֶהוּ בֵּית הַבְּחִירָה, שָׁם נִתַּן רְשׁוּת לַכֹּהֲנִים לְהַזְכִּיר שֵׁם הַמְפֹרָשׁ בִּנְשִׂיאוּת כַּפַּיִם וּלְבָרֵךְ אֶת הָעָם:

כב **וְאִם מִזְבַּח אֲבָנִים.** רַבִּי יִשְׁמָעֵאל אוֹמֵר: כָּל אִם וְאִם שֶׁבַּתּוֹרָה רְשׁוּת חוּץ מִשְּׁלֹשָׁה: "וְאִם מִזְבַּח אֲבָנִים תַּעֲשֶׂה לִּי", הֲרֵי 'אִם' זֶה

טו וְכָל־הָעָם רֹאִים אֶת־הַקּוֹלֹת וְאֶת־הַלַּפִּידִם וְאֵת קוֹל הַשֹּׁפָר וְאֶת־ שביעי
טז הָהָר עָשֵׁן וַיַּרְא הָעָם וַיָּנֻעוּ וַיַּעַמְדוּ מֵרָחֹק: וַיֹּאמְרוּ אֶל־מֹשֶׁה דַּבֵּר־
יז אַתָּה עִמָּנוּ וְנִשְׁמָעָה וְאַל־יְדַבֵּר עִמָּנוּ אֱלֹהִים פֶּן־נָמוּת: וַיֹּאמֶר מֹשֶׁה
אֶל־הָעָם אַל־תִּירָאוּ כִּי לְבַעֲבוּר נַסּוֹת אֶתְכֶם בָּא הָאֱלֹהִים וּבַעֲבוּר
יח תִּהְיֶה יִרְאָתוֹ עַל־פְּנֵיכֶם לְבִלְתִּי תֶחֱטָאוּ: וַיַּעֲמֹד הָעָם מֵרָחֹק וּמֹשֶׁה
יט נִגַּשׁ אֶל־הָעֲרָפֶל אֲשֶׁר־שָׁם הָאֱלֹהִים: וַיֹּאמֶר יהוה מפטיר
אֶל־מֹשֶׁה כֹּה תֹאמַר אֶל־בְּנֵי יִשְׂרָאֵל אַתֶּם רְאִיתֶם כִּי מִן־הַשָּׁמַיִם
כ דִּבַּרְתִּי עִמָּכֶם: לֹא תַעֲשׂוּן אִתִּי אֱלֹהֵי כֶסֶף וֵאלֹהֵי זָהָב לֹא תַעֲשׂוּ לָכֶם:
כא מִזְבַּח אֲדָמָה תַּעֲשֶׂה־לִּי וְזָבַחְתָּ עָלָיו אֶת־עֹלֹתֶיךָ וְאֶת־שְׁלָמֶיךָ אֶת־
צֹאנְךָ וְאֶת־בְּקָרֶךָ בְּכָל־הַמָּקוֹם אֲשֶׁר אַזְכִּיר אֶת־שְׁמִי אָבוֹא אֵלֶיךָ
כב וּבֵרַכְתִּיךָ: וְאִם־מִזְבַּח אֲבָנִים תַּעֲשֶׂה־לִּי לֹא־תִבְנֶה אֶתְהֶן גָּזִית כִּי

אונקלוס

טו וְכָל עַמָּא חָזַן יָת קָלַיָּא וְיָת בְּעוֹרַיָּא, וְיָת קָל שׁוֹפָרָא, וְיָת טוּרָא דְּתָנַן, וַחֲזָא עַמָּא וְזָעוּ, וְקָמוּ מֵרַחִיק: טז וַאֲמַרוּ לְמֹשֶׁה, מַלֵּיל אַתְּ עִמַּנָא וּנְקַבֵּיל, וְלָא יִתְמַלַּל עִמַּנָא, מִן קֳדָם יי דִּלְמָא נְמוּת: יז וַאֲמַר מֹשֶׁה לְעַמָּא לָא תִדְחֲלוּן, אֲרֵי, בְּדִיל לְנַסָּאָה יָתְכוֹן, אִתְגְּלִי לְכוֹן יְקָרָא דַיי, וּבְדִיל, דִּתְהֵי דַּחַלְתֵיהּ, עַל אַפֵּיכוֹן בְּדִיל דְּלָא תְחוּבוּן: יח וְקָם עַמָּא מֵרַחִיק, וּמֹשֶׁה קְרֵיב לְצַד אֲמִטְתָא, דְּתַמָּן יְקָרָא דַיי:

יט וַאֲמַר יי לְמֹשֶׁה, כִּדְנַן תֵּימַר לִבְנֵי יִשְׂרָאֵל, אַתּוּן חֲזֵיתוּן, אֲרֵי מִן שְׁמַיָּא, מַלֵּילִית עִמְּכוֹן: כ לָא תַעְבְּדוּן קֳדָמַי, דַּחֲלָן דִּכְסַף וְדַחֲלָן דִּדְהַב, לָא תַעְבְּדוּן לְכוֹן: כא מַדְבַּח אַדְמְתָא תַּעֲבֵיד קֳדָמַי, וּתְהֵי דָּבַח עֲלוֹהִי, יָת עֲלָוָתָךְ וְיָת נִכְסַת קֻדְשָׁךְ, מִן עָנָךְ וּמִן תּוֹרָךְ, בְּכָל אֲתַר דְּאַשְׁרֵי שְׁכִינְתִי, לְתַמָּן אֶשְׁלַח בִּרְכָתִי לָךְ וַאֲבָרְכִנָּךְ: כב וְאִם מַדְבַּח אַבְנִין תַּעֲבֵיד קֳדָמַי, לָא תִבְנֵי יָתְהוֹן פְּסִילָן, דִּלְמָא

20:22 כִּי חַרְבְּךָ הֵנַפְתָּ עָלֶיהָ וַתְּחַלְלֶהָ *In wielding a sword upon it, you profane it* – Despite the apparent militarism of the early texts of Judaism, their underlying value was always peace. In the book of Samuel, when David wishes to build the Ark a permanent home, God tells him not to build the Temple, assuring him that the work would be done by his son, Shlomo. David explains this in his own words in Chronicles: "The word of the Lord came to me, saying, 'You have shed much blood and waged mighty wars – you will not build a House for My name, for you have shed too much blood upon the earth before Me'" (I Chr. 22:8).

By the eighth century BCE the prophets of Israel became the first people in history to envisage a world at peace. The classic instance is Yeshayahu, who foresaw a time when the nations "shall beat their swords into plowshares, their spears into pruning hooks. Nation shall not raise sword against nation; no more will they learn to make war" (Is. 2:4). His vision of a world in which "there will be no wrong or violence on all My holy mountain, for the knowledge of the Lord will fill the earth as waters cover the ocean" (11:9) is part of the Tanakh's decisive break with the ethic of militarism that dominated the ancient world. The vision

23 for in wielding a sword upon it, you profane it. Do not ascend to My altar with
steps, for your nakedness must not be exposed on it.

The haftara for Parashat Yitro is on page 1540.

רש״י

מְשַׁמֵּשׁ בִּלְשׁוֹן 'כַּאֲשֶׁר', וְכַאֲשֶׁר תַּעֲשֶׂה לִּי מִזְבַּח אֲבָנִים "לֹא תִבְנֶה אֶתְהֶן גָּזִית", שֶׁהֲרֵי חוֹבָה עָלֶיךָ לִבְנוֹת מִזְבַּח אֲבָנִים, שֶׁנֶּאֱמַר: "אֲבָנִים שְׁלֵמוֹת תִּבְנֶה" (דברים כז, ו). וְכֵן: "אִם כֶּסֶף תַּלְוֶה" (להלן כב, כד) חוֹבָה הוּא, שֶׁנֶּאֱמַר: "וְהַעֲבֵט תַּעֲבִיטֶנּוּ" (דברים טו, ח), וְאַף זֶה מְשַׁמֵּשׁ בִּלְשׁוֹן 'כַּאֲשֶׁר'. וְכֵן: "וְאִם תַּקְרִיב מִנְחַת בִּכּוּרִים" (ויקרא ב, יד), זוֹ מִנְחַת הָעֹמֶר שֶׁהִיא חוֹבָה. וְעַל כָּרְחֲךָ אֵין 'אִם' הַלָּלוּ תְּלוּיִין אֶלָּא וַדַּאי, וּבִלְשׁוֹן 'כַּאֲשֶׁר' הֵם מְשַׁמְּשִׁים: **גָּזִית.** לְשׁוֹן גְּזִיזָה, שֶׁפּוֹסְלָן וּמְכַתְּתָן בְּבַרְזֶל: **כִּי חַרְבְּךָ הֵנַפְתָּ עָלֶיהָ.** הֲרֵי "כִּי" זֶה מְשַׁמֵּשׁ בִּלְשׁוֹן 'פֶּן' שֶׁהוּא 'דִּלְמָא', פֶּן תָּנִיף חַרְבְּךָ עָלֶיהָ: **וַתְּחַלְלֶהָ.** הָא לָמַדְתָּ שֶׁאִם הֵנַפְתָּ עָלֶיהָ בַּרְזֶל – חִלַּלְתָּ, שֶׁהַמִּזְבֵּחַ נִבְרָא לְהַאֲרִיךְ יָמָיו שֶׁל אָדָם וְהַבַּרְזֶל נִבְרָא לְקַצֵּר יָמָיו שֶׁל אָדָם, אֵין זֶה בְּדִין שֶׁיּוּנַף הַמְקַצֵּר עַל הַמַּאֲרִיךְ. וְעוֹד, שֶׁהַמִּזְבֵּחַ מֵטִיל שָׁלוֹם בֵּין יִשְׂרָאֵל לַאֲבִיהֶם שֶׁבַּשָּׁמַיִם, לְפִיכָךְ לֹא יָבֹא עָלָיו כּוֹרֵת וּמְחַבֵּל. וַהֲרֵי דְּבָרִים קַל וָחֹמֶר: וּמָה אֲבָנִים שֶׁאֵינָן רוֹאוֹת וְלֹא שׁוֹמְעוֹת וְלֹא מְדַבְּרוֹת, עַל יְדֵי שֶׁמַּטִּילוֹת שָׁלוֹם אָמְרָה תוֹרָה: "לֹא תָנִיף עֲלֵיהֶם בַּרְזֶל" (דברים כז, ה), הַמֵּטִיל שָׁלוֹם בֵּין אִישׁ לְאִשְׁתּוֹ, בֵּין מִשְׁפָּחָה לְמִשְׁפָּחָה, בֵּין אָדָם לַחֲבֵרוֹ, עַל אַחַת כַּמָּה וְכַמָּה שֶׁלֹּא תְבוֹאֵהוּ פֻּרְעָנוּת:

כג **וְלֹא תַעֲלֶה בְמַעֲלֹת.** כְּשֶׁאַתָּה בּוֹנֶה כֶּבֶשׁ לַמִּזְבֵּחַ לֹא תַעֲשֵׂהוּ מַעֲלוֹת מַעֲלוֹת, אשקלונ״ש בְּלַעַז, אֶלָּא חָלָק יְהֵא וּמְשֻׁפָּע: **אֲשֶׁר לֹא תִגָּלֶה עֶרְוָתְךָ.** שֶׁעַל יְדֵי הַמַּעֲלוֹת אַתָּה צָרִיךְ לְהַרְחִיב פְּסִיעוֹתֶיךָ. וְאַף עַל פִּי שֶׁאֵינוֹ גִּלּוּי עֶרְוָה מַמָּשׁ, שֶׁהֲרֵי כְּתִיב: "וַעֲשֵׂה לָהֶם מִכְנְסֵי בָד" (להלן כח, מב), מִכָּל מָקוֹם הַרְחָבַת הַפְּסִיעוֹת קָרוֹב לְגִלּוּי עֶרְוָה הוּא, וְאַתָּה נוֹהֵג בָּם מִנְהַג בִּזָּיוֹן. וַהֲרֵי דְּבָרִים קַל וָחֹמֶר: וּמָה אֲבָנִים הַלָּלוּ שֶׁאֵין בָּהֶם דַּעַת לְהַקְפִּיד עַל בִּזְיוֹנָן, אָמְרָה תוֹרָה: הוֹאִיל וְיֵשׁ בָּהֶם צֹרֶךְ לֹא תִנְהַג בָּהֶם מִנְהַג בִּזָּיוֹן, חֲבֵרְךָ שֶׁהוּא בִּדְמוּת יוֹצֶרְךָ וּמַקְפִּיד עַל בִּזְיוֹנוֹ, עַל אַחַת כַּמָּה וְכַמָּה:

כג חרבך הנפת עליה ותחללה: ולא־תעלה במעלת על־מזבחי אשר
לא־תגלה ערותך עליו:

The הפטרה *for* פרשת יתרו *is on page 1541.*

אונקלוס

תְרִים חַרְבָּךְ, עֲלַהּ וְתַחֲלְנַהּ: כג וְלָא תִסַּק בְּדַרְגִּין עַל מַדְבְּחִי, דְּלָא תִתְגַּלֵּי עֶרְיְתָךְ עֲלוֹהִי:

of peace would not be revived, outside the Judeo-Christian tradition, until Kant's secular essay on "perpetual peace" in 1795. No soul was ever saved by hate. No truth was ever proved by violence. No redemption was ever brought by holy war. The sword, though sometimes necessary, cannot build the altar, only profane it. It is with this hint that we conclude the *parasha*, and the narrative of our founding and greatest revelation.

▶

PARASHAT MISHPATIM

21 1 And these are the laws that you shall set before them. If you buy a Hebrew slave,
2 he shall serve for six years, but in the seventh he shall go forth free, without

רש״י

כא א **וְאֵלֶּה הַמִּשְׁפָּטִים.** כָּל מָקוֹם שֶׁנֶּאֱמַר ׳אֵלֶּה׳ – פָּסַל אֶת הָרִאשׁוֹנִים, ׳וְאֵלֶּה׳ – מוֹסִיף עַל הָרִאשׁוֹנִים, מָה הָרִאשׁוֹנִים מִסִּינַי, אַף אֵלּוּ מִסִּינַי. וְלָמָּה נִסְמְכָה פָּרָשַׁת דִּינִין לְפָרָשַׁת מִזְבֵּחַ? לוֹמַר לְךָ שֶׁתָּשִׂים סַנְהֶדְרִין אֵצֶל הַמִּקְדָּשׁ: **אֲשֶׁר תָּשִׂים לִפְנֵיהֶם.** אָמַר לוֹ הַקָּדוֹשׁ בָּרוּךְ הוּא לְמֹשֶׁה: לֹא תַעֲלֶה עַל דַּעְתְּךָ לוֹמַר אֶשְׁנֶה לָהֶם הַפֶּרֶק וְהַהֲלָכָה שְׁנַיִם אוֹ שְׁלֹשָׁה פְּעָמִים עַד שֶׁתְּהֵא סְדוּרָה בְּפִיהֶם כְּמִשְׁנָתָהּ, וְאֵינִי מַטְרִיחַ עַצְמִי לַהֲבִינָם טַעֲמֵי הַדָּבָר וּפֵרוּשׁוֹ, לְכָךְ נֶאֱמַר: "אֲשֶׁר תָּשִׂים לִפְנֵיהֶם", כְּשֻׁלְחָן הֶעָרוּךְ וּמוּכָן לֶאֱכֹל לִפְנֵי הָאָדָם: **לִפְנֵיהֶם.** וְלֹא לִפְנֵי גוֹיִם, וַאֲפִלּוּ יָדַעְתָּ בְּדִין אֶחָד שֶׁהַגּוֹיִם דָּנִין אוֹתוֹ כְּדִינֵי יִשְׂרָאֵל אַל תְּבִיאֵהוּ בְּעַרְכָּאוֹת שֶׁלָּהֶם, שֶׁהַמֵּבִיא דִּינֵי יִשְׂרָאֵל לִפְנֵי גוֹיִם מְחַלֵּל אֶת הַשֵּׁם וּמְיַקֵּר שֵׁם עֲבוֹדָה זָרָה לְהַחֲשִׁיבָהּ, שֶׁנֶּאֱמַר: "כִּי לֹא כְצוּרֵנוּ צוּרָם וְאֹיְבֵינוּ פְּלִילִים" (דברים לב, לא), כְּשֶׁאוֹיְבֵינוּ פְּלִילִים זֶהוּ עֵדוּת לְעִלּוּי יִרְאָתָם:

ב **כִּי תִקְנֶה עֶבֶד עִבְרִי.** עֶבֶד שֶׁהוּא עִבְרִי. אוֹ אֵינוֹ אֶלָּא עַבְדּוֹ שֶׁל עִבְרִי, עֶבֶד כְּנַעֲנִי שֶׁלְּקַחְתּוֹ מִיִּשְׂרָאֵל, וְעָלָיו הוּא אוֹמֵר: "שֵׁשׁ שָׁנִים יַעֲבֹד", וּמָה אֲנִי מְקַיֵּם "וְהִתְנַחַלְתֶּם אֹתָם" (ויקרא כה, מו) – בְּלָקוּחַ מִן הַגּוֹי, אֲבָל בְּלָקוּחַ מִיִּשְׂרָאֵל יֵצֵא בְּשֵׁשׁ? תַּלְמוּד לוֹמַר: "כִּי יִמָּכֵר לְךָ אָחִיךָ הָעִבְרִי" (דברים טו, יב), לֹא אָמַרְתִּי אֶלָּא בְּאָחִיךָ: **כִּי תִקְנֶה.** מִיַּד בֵּית דִּין שֶׁמְּכָרוּהוּ בִּגְנֵבָתוֹ, כְּמוֹ שֶׁנֶּאֱמַר: "אִם אֵין לוֹ וְנִמְכַּר בִּגְנֵבָתוֹ" (להלן כב, ב). אוֹ אֵינוֹ אֶלָּא בְּמוֹכֵר עַצְמוֹ מִפְּנֵי דָחְקוֹ, אֲבָל מְכָרוּהוּ בֵּית דִּין לֹא יֵצֵא בְּשֵׁשׁ? כְּשֶׁהוּא אוֹמֵר:

SLAVERY

We have read in the first part of Exodus about the Israelites' historic experience of slavery. So, understandably, the social legislation of Mishpatim begins with slavery. What is fascinating is not only what it says but what it doesn't say.

It doesn't say: abolish slavery. Surely it should have done that. Is that not the whole point of the story thus far? Yosef's brothers sell him into slavery. Generations later, when a pharaoh arises who "had not known Yosef" (Ex. 1:8), the entire Israelite people become Egypt's slaves. Slavery, like vengeance, is a vicious circle that has no natural end. Why not, then, give it a supernatural end? Why did God not say, "There shall be no more slavery"?

The Torah has already given us an implicit answer. Change is possible in human nature but it takes time: time on a vast scale, centuries, even millennia. There is little doubt that in terms of the Torah's value system, the exercise of power by one person over another, without their consent, is a fundamental assault against human dignity. This is not just true of the relationship between master and slave. It is even true, according to many classic Jewish commentators, of the relationship between king and subjects, rulers and ruled.

So slavery is to be abolished, but it is a fundamental principle of God's relationship with us that He does not force us to change faster than we are able to do of our own free will. Mishpatim does not abolish slavery, but it sets in motion a series of fundamental laws that will lead people, albeit at their own pace, to abolish it of their own accord.

In these laws, a fundamental change is taking place in the nature of slavery. No longer is it a permanent status; it is a temporary condition. A Hebrew slave goes free after seven years. He or she knows this. Liberty awaits the slave not at the whim of the master but by divine command. When you know that within a fixed time you are going to be free, you may be a slave in body, but in your own mind you are a free human being who has temporarily lost his or her liberty.

A slave may stay a slave, but not without being reminded that this is not what God wants for His people. The result of these laws was to create a dynamic that would in the end lead to an abolition of slavery, at a time of free human choosing.

God has patience, though it is often sorely tried. He wants slavery abolished but He wants it to be done by free human beings coming to see of their own accord the evil it is and the evil it does. The God of history, who taught us to study history, has faith that eventually we will learn the

פרשת משפטים

כא א וְאֵ֙לֶּה֙ הַמִּשְׁפָּטִ֔ים אֲשֶׁ֥ר תָּשִׂ֖ים לִפְנֵיהֶֽם׃ ב כִּ֤י תִקְנֶה֙ עֶ֣בֶד עִבְרִ֔י שֵׁ֥שׁ שָׁנִ֖ים טז

אונקלוס

כא א וְאִלֵּין דִּינַיָּא, דְּתַסְדַּר קֳדָמֵיהוֹן: ב אֲרֵי תִזְבּוֹן עַבְדָּא בַר יִשְׂרָאֵל, שֵׁית שְׁנִין

MISHPATIM

Following the revelation at Mount Sinai, Parashat Mishpatim fleshes out the details of the law that was to govern the Israelites: laws relating to slaves and their release; personal injuries and property laws; laws of social responsibility, justice, and compassion; and laws relating to the Sabbath and the festivals. It ends with a ratification of the covenant, and Moshe ascending the mountain for forty days.

The contrast between the *parasha* of Yitro and that of Mishpatim is immense. In the former, the Torah takes us to the greatest encounter ever between human beings and God, the revelation at Mount Sinai, with its broad statement of principles, the Ten Commandments. In the latter, we are plunged into a plethora of detail. We seem to move from the sublime to the prosaic, from an all-encompassing moral and spiritual vision to the small print of a legal code.

Mishpatim, with its detailed rules and regulations, can sometimes seem an anticlimax after the breathtaking grandeur of the revelation at Sinai. It should not be. Parashat Yitro contains the vision, but God is in the details. God is in heaven, but we honor Him here on earth: that is what Torah – the word that means "law, teaching, ethical instruction" – is about. It is precisely through law that we enact spiritual truths in physical circumstances, creating fragments of heaven in our interactions on earth.

21:1 **וְאֵלֶּה הַמִּשְׁפָּטִים** *And these are the laws* – Rashi comments on this verse:

> *And these are the laws* – Wherever [the Torah] uses the word "these" it signals a discontinuity with what has been stated previously. Wherever it uses the term "and these" it signals a continuity. Just as the former commands were given at Sinai, so these were given at Sinai. Why then are the civil laws placed in juxtaposition with the laws concerning the altar? To tell you to place the Sanhedrin near the Temple.
>
> *That you shall set before them* – You should not think, "I will teach them a section of law two or three times until they know the words verbatim but I will not take the trouble to make them understand the reason and its significance." Therefore the Torah states, "That you shall set before them," like a fully laid table with everything ready for eating.

Three remarkable propositions are being set out here. The first is that just as the general principles of Judaism (*Aseret HaDibrot* means not "Ten Commandments" but "Ten Utterances" or overarching principles) are divine, so are the details. There are those who believe that what is holy in Judaism is its broad vision, never so compellingly expressed as in the Decalogue at Sinai. The truth, however, is that "just as the former were given at Sinai, so these were given at Sinai." The greatness of Judaism is not simply in its noble vision, but in the way it brings this vision down to earth in detailed legislation.

The second principle, no less fundamental, is that civil law is not secular law. We do not believe in the idea "render to Caesar what is Caesar's and to God what belongs to God." We believe in the separation of powers but not in the secularization of law or the spiritualization of faith. The Sanhedrin or Supreme Court must be placed near the Temple to teach that law itself must be driven by a religious vision.

The third principle is the idea that law does not belong to lawyers. It is the heritage of every Jew. Legal knowledge is not the closely guarded property of an elite. It is – in the famous phrase – the "heritage of Yaakov's assembly" (Deut. 33:4). Judaism expected everyone to know and understand the law.

3 paying anything. If he came alone, he shall leave alone. But if he was a married
4 man, his wife shall leave with him. If his master gave him a wife and she bore
him sons or daughters, the woman and her children shall remain her master's,
5 while he shall leave alone. But if the slave declares, 'I love my master, my wife,
6 and my children; I do not want to go free,' then his master shall bring him
before the judges. He shall take him to the door or to the doorpost and pierce
7 his ear with an awl; after that he shall then remain his slave forever. If
a man sells his daughter as a maidservant, she does not go free in the usual way
8 of slaves. If her master, who intended to wed her, finds that he dislikes her, he

רש״י

"וְכִי יָמוּךְ אָחִיךָ עִמָּךְ וְנִמְכַּר לָךְ" (ויקרא כה, לט) הֲרֵי מוֹכֵר עַצְמוֹ מִפְּנֵי דָּחְקוֹ אָמוּר, וּמָה אֲנִי מְקַיֵּם "כִּי תִקְנֶה"? בְּנִמְכָּר בְּבֵית דִּין: **לַחָפְשִׁי.** לַחֵרוּת:

ג **אִם בְּגַפּוֹ יָבֹא.** שֶׁלֹּא הָיָה נָשׂוּי אִשָּׁה, כְּתַרְגּוּמוֹ: "אִם בִּלְחוֹדוֹהִי". וּלְשׁוֹן 'בְּגַפּוֹ', בִּכְנָפוֹ, שֶׁלֹּא בָּא אֶלָּא כְּמוֹת שֶׁהוּא יְחִידִי בְּתוֹךְ לְבוּשׁוֹ, בִּכְנַף בִּגְדוֹ: **בְּגַפּוֹ יֵצֵא.** מַגִּיד שֶׁאִם לֹא הָיָה נָשׂוּי מִתְּחִלָּה, אֵין רַבּוֹ מוֹסֵר לוֹ שִׁפְחָה כְּנַעֲנִית לְהוֹלִיד מִמֶּנָּה עֲבָדִים: **אִם בַּעַל אִשָּׁה הוּא.** יִשְׂרְאֵלִית: **וְיָצְאָה אִשְׁתּוֹ עִמּוֹ.** וְכִי מִי הִכְנִיסָהּ שֶׁתֵּצֵא? אֶלָּא מַגִּיד הַכָּתוּב שֶׁהַקּוֹנֶה עֶבֶד עִבְרִי חַיָּב בִּמְזוֹנוֹת אִשְׁתּוֹ וּבָנָיו:

ד **אִם אֲדֹנָיו יִתֶּן לוֹ אִשָּׁה.** מִכָּאן שֶׁהָרְשׁוּת בְּיַד רַבּוֹ לִמְסֹר לוֹ שִׁפְחָה כְּנַעֲנִית לְהוֹלִיד מִמֶּנָּה עֲבָדִים. אוֹ אֵינוֹ אֶלָּא בְּיִשְׂרְאֵלִית? תַּלְמוּד לוֹמַר: "הָאִשָּׁה וִילָדֶיהָ תִּהְיֶה לַאדֹנֶיהָ", הָא אֵינוֹ מְדַבֵּר אֶלָּא בִּכְנַעֲנִית, שֶׁהֲרֵי הָעִבְרִיָּה אַף הִיא יוֹצְאָה בְּשֵׁשׁ, וַאֲפִלּוּ לִפְנֵי שֵׁשׁ אִם הֵבִיאָה סִימָנִין יוֹצְאָה, שֶׁנֶּאֱמַר: "אָחִיךָ הָעִבְרִי אוֹ הָעִבְרִיָּה" (דברים טו, יב), מְלַמֵּד שֶׁאַף הָעִבְרִיָּה יוֹצְאָה בְּשֵׁשׁ:

ה **אֶת אִשְׁתִּי.** הַשִּׁפְחָה:

ו **אֶל הָאֱלֹהִים.** לְבֵית דִּין, צָרִיךְ שֶׁיִּמָּלֵךְ בְּמוֹכְרָיו שֶׁמְּכָרוּהוּ לוֹ: **אֶל הַדֶּלֶת אוֹ אֶל הַמְּזוּזָה.** יָכוֹל שֶׁתְּהֵא הַמְּזוּזָה כְּשֵׁרָה לִרְצֹעַ עָלֶיהָ? תַּלְמוּד לוֹמַר: "וְנָתַתָּה בְאָזְנוֹ וּבַדֶּלֶת" (דברים טו, יז), בַּדֶּלֶת וְלֹא בַּמְּזוּזָה, הָא מַה תַּלְמוּד לוֹמַר: "אוֹ אֶל הַמְּזוּזָה"? הִקִּישׁ דֶּלֶת לִמְזוּזָה, מַה מְּזוּזָה מְעוֹמָד אַף דֶּלֶת מְעוֹמָד. רַבִּי שִׁמְעוֹן הָיָה דּוֹרֵשׁ מִקְרָא זֶה כְּמִין חֹמֶר: מַה נִּשְׁתַּנּוּ דֶּלֶת וּמְזוּזָה מִכָּל כֵּלִים שֶׁבַּבַּיִת? אָמַר הַקָּדוֹשׁ בָּרוּךְ הוּא: דֶּלֶת וּמְזוּזָה שֶׁהָיוּ עֵדִי בְּמִצְרַיִם כְּשֶׁפָּסַחְתִּי עַל הַמַּשְׁקוֹף וְעַל שְׁתֵּי הַמְּזוּזוֹת, וְאָמַרְתִּי: "כִּי לִי בְנֵי יִשְׂרָאֵל עֲבָדִים" (ויקרא כה, נה), וְלֹא עֲבָדִים לַעֲבָדִים, וְהָלַךְ זֶה וְקָנָה אָדוֹן לְעַצְמוֹ, יֵרָצַע בִּפְנֵיהֶם: **וְרָצַע אֲדֹנָיו אֶת אָזְנוֹ.** הַיְמָנִית. אוֹ אֵינוֹ אֶלָּא שֶׁל שְׂמֹאל? תַּלְמוּד לוֹמַר: 'אֹזֶן' 'אֹזֶן' לִגְזֵרָה שָׁוָה, שֶׁנֶּאֱמַר בִּמְצֹרָע: "תְּנוּךְ אֹזֶן הַמִּטַּהֵר הַיְמָנִית" (ויקרא יד, יד). וּמָה רָאָה אֹזֶן לֵרָצַע מִכָּל הָאֵבָרִים? אָמַר רַבָּן יוֹחָנָן בֶּן זַכַּאי: אֹזֶן שֶׁשָּׁמְעָה בְּסִינַי: "לֹא תִגְנֹב" (לעיל כ, יג) וְהָלַךְ וְגָנַב, תֵּרָצַע. וְאִם מוֹכֵר עַצְמוֹ הוּא, אֹזֶן שֶׁשָּׁמְעָה "כִּי לִי בְנֵי יִשְׂרָאֵל עֲבָדִים" (ויקרא כה, נה) וְהָלַךְ וְקָנָה אָדוֹן לְעַצְמוֹ, תֵּרָצֵעַ: **וַעֲבָדוֹ לְעֹלָם.** עַד הַיּוֹבֵל. אוֹ אֵינוֹ אֶלָּא 'לְעוֹלָם' כְּמַשְׁמָעוֹ? תַּלְמוּד לוֹמַר: "וְאִישׁ אֶל מִשְׁפַּחְתּוֹ תָּשֻׁבוּ" (ויקרא כה, י), מַגִּיד שֶׁחֲמִשִּׁים שָׁנָה קְרוּיִם 'עוֹלָם'. וְלֹא שֶׁיְּהֵא עוֹבְדוֹ כָּל חֲמִשִּׁים שָׁנָה, אֶלָּא עוֹבְדוֹ עַד הַיּוֹבֵל, בֵּין סָמוּךְ בֵּין מֻפְלָג:

ז **וְכִי יִמְכֹּר אִישׁ אֶת בִּתּוֹ לְאָמָה.** בִּקְטַנָּה הַכָּתוּב מְדַבֵּר. יָכוֹל אֲפִלּוּ הֵבִיאָה סִימָנִים? אָמַרְתָּ, קַל וָחֹמֶר: וּמַה מְּכוּרָה קֹדֶם לָכֵן יוֹצְאָה בְּסִימָנִין, כְּמוֹ שֶׁכָּתוּב: "וְיָצְאָה חִנָּם אֵין כָּסֶף" (להלן פסוק יא) שֶׁאָנוּ דּוֹרְשִׁים אוֹתוֹ לְסִימָנֵי נַעֲרוּת, שֶׁאֵינָהּ מְכוּרָה אֵינוֹ דִּין שֶׁלֹּא תִּמָּכֵר?: **לֹא תֵצֵא כְּצֵאת הָעֲבָדִים.** כִּיצִיאַת עֲבָדִים כְּנַעֲנִים שֶׁיּוֹצְאִים בְּשֵׁן וָעַיִן, אֲבָל זוֹ לֹא תֵצֵא בְּשֵׁן וָעַיִן אֶלָּא עוֹבֶדֶת שֵׁשׁ, אוֹ עַד הַיּוֹבֵל, אוֹ עַד שֶׁתָּבִיא סִימָנִין, וְכָל הַקּוֹדֵם קוֹדֵם לְחֵרוּתָהּ, וְנוֹתֵן לָהּ דְּמֵי עֵינָהּ אוֹ דְּמֵי שִׁנָּהּ. אוֹ אֵינוֹ אֶלָּא "לֹא תֵצֵא כְּצֵאת הָעֲבָדִים" בְּשֵׁשׁ וּבַיּוֹבֵל? תַּלְמוּד לוֹמַר: "כִּי יִמָּכֵר לְךָ אָחִיךָ הָעִבְרִי אוֹ הָעִבְרִיָּה" (דברים טו, יב), מַקִּישׁ עִבְרִיָּה לְעִבְרִי לְכָל יְצִיאוֹתָיו: מָה עִבְרִי יוֹצֵא בְּשֵׁשׁ וּבַיּוֹבֵל, אַף עִבְרִיָּה יוֹצְאָה בְּשֵׁשׁ וּבַיּוֹבֵל. וּמַהוּ "לֹא תֵצֵא כְּצֵאת הָעֲבָדִים"? לֹא תֵצֵא בְּרָאשֵׁי אֵבָרִים כַּעֲבָדִים כְּנַעֲנִים. יָכוֹל הָעִבְרִי יוֹצֵא בְּרָאשֵׁי אֵבָרִים? תַּלְמוּד לוֹמַר: "הָעִבְרִי אוֹ הָעִבְרִיָּה", מַקִּישׁ עִבְרִי לְעִבְרִיָּה, מָה הָעִבְרִיָּה אֵינָהּ יוֹצְאָה בְּרָאשֵׁי אֵבָרִים, אַף הוּא אֵינוֹ יוֹצֵא בְּרָאשֵׁי אֵבָרִים:

ח **אִם רָעָה בְּעֵינֵי אֲדֹנֶיהָ.** שֶׁלֹּא נָשְׂאָה חֵן בְּעֵינָיו לְכָנְסָהּ: **אֲשֶׁר לֹא יְעָדָהּ.** שֶׁהָיָה לוֹ לְיַעֲדָהּ וּלְהַכְנִיסָהּ לוֹ לְאִשָּׁה, וְכֶסֶף קְנִיָּתָהּ הוּא כֶּסֶף קִדּוּשֶׁיהָ. וְכָאן רָמַז לְךָ הַכָּתוּב שֶׁמִּצְוָה בְּיִעוּד, וְרָמַז לְךָ שֶׁאֵינָהּ צְרִיכָה קִדּוּשִׁין אֲחֵרִים: **וְהֶפְדָּהּ.** יִתֵּן לָהּ מָקוֹם לְהִפָּדוֹת וְלָצֵאת, שֶׁאַף הוּא מְסַיֵּעַ בְּפִדְיוֹנָהּ. וּמַה הוּא מָקוֹם שֶׁנּוֹתֵן לָהּ? שֶׁמְּגָרֵעַ מִפִּדְיוֹנָהּ בְּמִסְפַּר הַשָּׁנִים שֶׁעָשְׂתָה אֶצְלוֹ, כְּאִלּוּ הִיא שְׂכוּרָה אֶצְלוֹ. כֵּיצַד? הֲרֵי שֶׁקְּנָאָהּ בְּמָנֶה וְעָשְׂתָה אֶצְלוֹ שְׁתֵּי שָׁנִים, אוֹמְרִים לוֹ, יוֹדֵעַ הָיִיתָ שֶׁעֲתִידָה לָצֵאת לְסוֹף שֵׁשׁ, נִמְצָא שֶׁקָּנִיתָ עֲבוֹדַת כָּל שָׁנָה וְשָׁנָה בִּשְׁתוּת הַמָּנֶה, וְעָשְׂתָה אֶצְלְךָ שְׁתֵּי שָׁנִים, הֲרֵי שְׁלִישִׁית הַמָּנֶה. טֹל שְׁנֵי שְׁלִישֵׁי מָנֶה וְתֵצֵא מֵאֶצְלְךָ: **לְעַם נָכְרִי לֹא יִמְשֹׁל לְמָכְרָהּ.** אֵינוֹ רַשַּׁאי לְמָכְרָהּ לְאַחֵר,

ג יַעֲבֹד וּבַשְּׁבִעִת יֵצֵא לַחָפְשִׁי חִנָּם׃ אִם־בְּגַפּוֹ יָבֹא בְּגַפּוֹ יֵצֵא אִם־בַּעַל
ד אִשָּׁה הוּא וְיָצְאָה אִשְׁתּוֹ עִמּוֹ׃ אִם־אֲדֹנָיו יִתֶּן־לוֹ אִשָּׁה וְיָלְדָה־
לוֹ בָנִים אוֹ בָנוֹת הָאִשָּׁה וִילָדֶיהָ תִּהְיֶה לַאדֹנֶיהָ וְהוּא יֵצֵא בְגַפּוֹ׃
ה וְאִם־אָמֹר יֹאמַר הָעֶבֶד אָהַבְתִּי אֶת־אֲדֹנִי אֶת־אִשְׁתִּי וְאֶת־בָּנָי לֹא
ו אֵצֵא חָפְשִׁי׃ וְהִגִּישׁוֹ אֲדֹנָיו אֶל־הָאֱלֹהִים וְהִגִּישׁוֹ אֶל־הַדֶּלֶת אוֹ אֶל־
ז הַמְּזוּזָה וְרָצַע אֲדֹנָיו אֶת־אָזְנוֹ בַּמַּרְצֵעַ וַעֲבָדוֹ לְעֹלָם׃ וְכִי־
ח יִמְכֹּר אִישׁ אֶת־בִּתּוֹ לְאָמָה לֹא תֵצֵא כְּצֵאת הָעֲבָדִים׃ אִם־רָעָה
בְּעֵינֵי אֲדֹנֶיהָ אֲשֶׁר־לֹא יְעָדָהּ וְהֶפְדָּהּ לְעַם נָכְרִי לֹא־יִמְשֹׁל לְמָכְרָהּ לוֹ

אונקלוס

יִפְלַח, וּבִשְׁבִיעֵיתָא, יִפּוֹק לְבַר חוֹרִין מַגָּן׃ ג אִם בִּלְחוֹדוֹהִי יֵיעוֹל בִּלְחוֹדוֹהִי יִפּוֹק, אִם בְּעֵיל אִתְּתָא הוּא, וְתִפּוֹק אִתְּתֵיהּ עִמֵּיהּ׃ ד אִם רִבּוֹנֵיהּ יִתֵּין לֵיהּ אִתְּתָא, וּתְלִיד לֵיהּ בְּנִין אוֹ בְנָן, אִתְּתָא וּבְנַהָא, תְּהֵי לְרִבּוֹנַהּ, וְהוּא יִפּוֹק בִּלְחוֹדוֹהִי׃ ה וְאִם מֵימַר יֵימַר עַבְדָּא, רְחֵימְנָא יָת רִבּוֹנִי, יָת אִתְּתִי וְיָת בְּנַי, לָא אֶפּוֹק בַּר חוֹרִין׃ ו וִיקָרְבִנֵּיהּ רִבּוֹנֵיהּ לִקְדָם דַּיָּנַיָּא, וִיקָרְבִנֵּיהּ לְוָת דַּשָּׁא, אוֹ דִּלְוָת מְזוּזְתָא, וְיִרְצַע רִבּוֹנֵיהּ יָת אֻדְנֵיהּ בְּמַרְצְעָא, וִיהֵי לֵיהּ עֶבֶד פָּלַח לְעָלַם׃ ז וַאֲרֵי יְזַבֵּין גְּבַר, יָת בְּרַתֵּיהּ לְאַמְהוּ, לָא תִפּוֹק כְּמַפְּקָנוּת עַבְדַּיָּא׃ ח אִם בִּישַׁת, בְּעֵינֵי רִבּוֹנַהּ, דִּיקַיְּמַהּ לֵיהּ וְיִפְרְקִנַּהּ, לִגְבַר אָחֳרָן, לֵית לֵיהּ רְשׁוּ לְזַבּוֹנַהּ בְּמִשְׁלְטֵיהּ בַהּ׃ ט וְאִם לִבְרֵיהּ יְקַיְּמִנַּהּ,

lesson of history: that freedom is indivisible. We must grant freedom to others if we truly seek it for ourselves.

21:6 וְרָצַע אֲדֹנָיו אֶת־אָזְנוֹ בַּמַּרְצֵעַ *Pierce his ear with an awl* – Rashi explains:

> Why was the ear chosen to be pierced rather than all the other limbs of the body? Said R. Yoḥanan b. Zakkai: The ear that heard on Mount Sinai: "For it is to Me that the Israelites are servants," and he nevertheless went ahead and acquired a master for himself, should [have his ear] pierced.

A Hebrew slave is to go free after six years. If the slave has grown so used to his condition that he wishes not to go free, then he undergoes a stigmatizing ceremony, having his ear pierced, which thereafter remains as a visible sign of shame. These stipulations have the effect of turning slavery from a lifelong fate into a temporary condition, and one that is perceived to be a humiliation rather than something written indelibly into the human script.

21:7 וְכִי־יִמְכֹּר אִישׁ אֶת־בִּתּוֹ לְאָמָה *If a man sells his daughter as a maidservant* – The Rabbis refused to rationalize poverty. It is not a blessed condition. It is, they said, "a kind of death," and "worse than fifty plagues." They said: "Nothing is harder to bear than poverty, for he who is crushed by poverty is like one to whom all the troubles of the world cling and upon whom all the curses of Deuteronomy have descended. If all other troubles were placed on one side and poverty on the other, poverty would outweigh them all."

Poverty in the ancient world, as in too many places today, can lead directly to slavery. The Torah does not gloss this fact over, but it does demand that we recognize the humanity of the person caught in this net. The Rabbis had the sanest view of poverty I know, and they did so because most of them were poor. They neither valued poverty, nor did they see in the distribution of wealth a divinely ordained social order. I know of nothing in the literature of Judaism that speaks of submissively accepting one's "station in life"; neither may the needy be exploited without restraint. We are a community, sharing a collective fate and responsibility.

must let her be redeemed. He has no right to sell her to foreigners, because he
9 has broken faith with her. If he intends her for his son, he shall grant her all the
10 rights of a daughter. If he marries another woman alongside her, he shall not
11 reduce her food, her clothing, or marital rights. If he fails her in any of these
12 three things, she shall go forth free without paying anything. One
13 person who strikes another so that he dies shall be put to death. If he did not
lie in wait to harm him, but it came about by an act of God – I am setting apart
14 a place where he may find refuge. But if someone schemes against
another and kills him by stealth, you shall take him even from My altar and
15 he shall die. One who wounds his father or mother shall be put to
16 death. One who kidnaps a person shall be put to death, whether the
17 victim has been sold or found in his possession. One who curses his
18 father or mother shall be put to death. If two people fight and one

רש"י

לא האדון ולא האב: **בבגדו בה.** אם בא לבגד בה שלא לקיים בה מצות יעוד. וכן אביה, מאחר שבגד בה ומכרה לזה:

ט **ואם לבנו ייעדנה.** האדון, מלמד שאף בנו קם תחתיו ליעדה אם ירצה אביו, ואינו צריך לקדשה קדושין אחרים, אלא אומר לה: הרי את מיועדת לי בכסף שקבל אביך בדמיך: **כמשפט הבנות.** שאר כסות ועונה:

י **אם אחרת יקח לו.** עליה: **שארה כסותה ועונתה לא יגרע.** מן האמה שיעד לו כבר: **שארה.** מזונות: **כסותה.** כמשמעו: **ענתה.** תשמיש:

יא **ואם שלש אלה לא יעשה לה.** אם אחת משלש אלה לא יעשה לה. ומה הן השלש? ייעדנה לו, או לבנו, או יגרע מפדיונה ותצא, וזה לא יעדה לא לו ולא לבנו, והיא לא היה בידה לפדות את עצמה: **ויצאה חנם.** רבה לה יציאה לזו יותר ממה שרבה לעבדים. ומה היא היציאה? למדך שתצא בסימנים – תשהא עמו עד שתצא בסימנים. ואם הגיעו שש שנים קודם סימנים, כבר למדנו שתצא, שנאמר: "העברי או העבריה ועבדך שש שנים" (דברים טו, יב), ומהו האמור כאן: "ויצאה חנם"? שאם קדמו סימנים לשש שנים תצא בהן. או אינו אומר שתצא אלא בבגרות? תלמוד לומר: "אין כסף" לרבות יציאת בגרות. ואם לא נאמרו שניהם, הייתי אומר: "ויצאה חנם" זו בגרות, לכך נאמרו שניהם, שלא לתן פתחון פה לבעל הדין לחלק:

יב **מכה איש ומת.** כמה כתובים נאמרו בפרשת רוצחין, ומה שבידי לפרש למה באו כלם אפרש: **מכה איש ומת.** למה נאמר? לפי שנאמר: "ואיש כי יכה כל נפש אדם מות יומת" (ויקרא כד, יז), שומע אני הכאה בלא מיתה? תלמוד לומר: "מכה איש ומת", אינו חייב אלא בהכאה של מיתה. ואם נאמר "מכה איש" ולא נאמר "ואיש כי יכה", הייתי אומר אינו חייב עד שיכה איש, הכה את האשה ואת הקטן מנין? תלמוד לומר: "כי יכה כל נפש אדם", אפלו קטן ואפלו אשה. ועוד, אלו נאמר "מכה איש" שומע אני אפלו קטן שהכה והרג יהא חייב? תלמוד לומר: "ואיש כי יכה", ולא קטן שהכה. ועוד, "כי יכה כל נפש אדם" אפלו נפלים במשמע, תלמוד לומר: "מכה איש", עד שיכה בן קיימא הראוי להיות איש:

יג **ואשר לא צדה.** לא ארב לו ולא נתכון. 'צדה' לשון ארב, וכן הוא אומר: "ואתה צדה את נפשי לקחתה" (שמואל א' כד, יא). ולא יתכן לומר 'צדה' לשון "הצד ציד" (בראשית כז, לג), שצידת חיות אין נופל ה"א בפעל שלה, ושם דבר בה 'ציד', וזה שם דבר בו 'צדיה', ופעל שלו 'צודה', וזה פעל שלו 'צד'. ואומר אני, פתרונו כתרגומו: "ודלא כמן ליה". ומנחם חברו בחלק 'צד ציד', ואין אני מודה לו. ואם יש לחברו באחת ממחלקת של 'צד', נחברנו בחלק "על צד תנשאו" (ישעיה סו, יב), "צדה אורה" (שמואל א' כ, כ), "ומלין לצד עלאה ימלל" (דניאל ז, כה), אף כאן "אשר לא צדה" לא צדד למצא לו שום צד מיתה. ואף זה יש להרהר עליו, מכל מקום לשון אורב הוא: **והאלהים אנה לידו.** זמן לידו. לשון: "לא תאנה אליך רעה" (תהלים צא, י), "לא יאנה לצדיק כל און" (משלי יב, כא), "מתאנה הוא לי" (מלכים ב' ה, ז) – מזדמן למצא לי עלה: **והאלהים אנה לידו.** ולמה תצא זאת מלפניו? הוא שאמר דוד: "כאשר יאמר משל הקדמני מרשעים יצא רשע"

ט י בְּבִגְדוֹ־בָהּ׃ וְאִם־לִבְנוֹ יִיעָדֶנָּה כְּמִשְׁפַּט הַבָּנוֹת יַעֲשֶׂה־לָּהּ׃ אִם־
יא אַחֶרֶת יִקַּח־לוֹ שְׁאֵרָהּ כְּסוּתָהּ וְעֹנָתָהּ לֹא יִגְרָע׃ וְאִם־שְׁלָשׁ־
יב אֵלֶּה לֹא יַעֲשֶׂה לָהּ וְיָצְאָה חִנָּם אֵין כָּסֶף׃ מַכֵּה אִישׁ
יג וָמֵת מוֹת יוּמָת׃ וַאֲשֶׁר לֹא צָדָה וְהָאֱלֹהִים אִנָּה לְיָדוֹ וְשַׂמְתִּי לְךָ
יד מָקוֹם אֲשֶׁר יָנוּס שָׁמָּה׃ וְכִי־יָזִד אִישׁ עַל־רֵעֵהוּ
טו לְהָרְגוֹ בְעָרְמָה מֵעִם מִזְבְּחִי תִּקָּחֶנּוּ לָמוּת׃ וּמַכֵּה אָבִיו
טז וְאִמּוֹ מוֹת יוּמָת׃ וְגֹנֵב אִישׁ וּמְכָרוֹ וְנִמְצָא בְיָדוֹ מוֹת
יז יח יוּמָת׃ וּמְקַלֵּל אָבִיו וְאִמּוֹ מוֹת יוּמָת׃ וְכִי־

אונקלוס

כְּהִלְכַת בְּנָת יִשְׂרָאֵל יַעֲבֵיד לַהּ׃ י אִם אֻחֲרַנְתָּא יִסַּב לֵיהּ, זִיוּנַהּ, כְּסוּתַהּ וְעָנְתַהּ לָא יִמְנַע׃ יא וְאִם תְּלָת אִלֵּין, לָא יַעֲבֵיד לַהּ, וְתִפּוֹק מַגָּן דְּלָא כְסַף׃ יב דְּיִמְחֵי לֶאֱנָשׁ, וְיִקְטְלִנֵּיהּ אִתְקְטָלָא יִתְקְטִיל׃ יג וּדְלָא כְמַן לֵיהּ, וּמִן קֳדָם יי אִתְמְסַר לִידֵיהּ, וַאֲשַׁוֵּי לָךְ אֲתַר, דְּיֵעְרוֹק לְתַמָּן׃ יד וַאֲרֵי יַרְשַׁע גְּבַר, עַל חַבְרֵיהּ לְמִקְטְלֵיהּ בִּנְכִילוּ, מִן מַדְבְּחִי, תְּדַבְּרִנֵּיהּ לְמִקְטַל׃ טו וּדְיִמְחֵי אֲבוּהִי, וְאִמֵּיהּ אִתְקְטָלָא יִתְקְטִיל׃ טז וּדְיִגְנוֹב נַפְשָׁא מִבְּנֵי יִשְׂרָאֵל וִיזַבְּנִנֵּיהּ, וְיִשְׁתְּכַח בִּידֵיהּ אִתְקְטָלָא יִתְקְטִיל׃ יז וּדְילוּט אֲבוּהִי, וְאִמֵּיהּ אִתְקְטָלָא יִתְקְטִיל׃ יח וַאֲרֵי

רש״י

(שמואל א׳ כד, יג) וּמָשָׁל הַקַּדְמֹנִי הִיא הַתּוֹרָה שֶׁהִיא מְשַׁל הַקָּדוֹשׁ בָּרוּךְ הוּא שֶׁהוּא קַדְמוֹנוֹ שֶׁל עוֹלָם. וְהֵיכָן אָמְרָה תוֹרָה: ״מֵרְשָׁעִים יֵצֵא רֶשַׁע״? – ״וְהָאֱלֹהִים אִנָּה לְיָדוֹ״. בַּמֶּה הַכָּתוּב מְדַבֵּר? בִּשְׁנֵי בְנֵי אָדָם, אֶחָד הָרַג שׁוֹגֵג וְאֶחָד הָרַג מֵזִיד, וְלֹא הָיוּ עֵדִים בַּדָּבָר שֶׁיָּעִידוּ, זֶה לֹא נֶהֱרַג וְזֶה לֹא גָלָה. הַקָּדוֹשׁ בָּרוּךְ הוּא מְזַמְּנָן לְפֻנְדָּק אֶחָד, זֶה שֶׁהָרַג שׁוֹגֵג עוֹלֶה בַּסֻּלָּם וְנוֹפֵל עַל זֶה שֶׁהָרַג מֵזִיד וְהוֹרְגוֹ, וְעֵדִים מְעִידִים עָלָיו וּמְחַיְּבִים אוֹתוֹ לִגְלוֹת. נִמְצָא זֶה שֶׁהָרַג שׁוֹגֵג גּוֹלֶה וְזֶה שֶׁהָרַג מֵזִיד נֶהֱרָג: **וְשַׂמְתִּי לְךָ מָקוֹם.** אַף בַּמִּדְבָּר, שֶׁיָּנוּס שָׁמָּה. וְאֵי זֶה מָקוֹם קוֹלְטוֹ? זֶה מַחֲנֵה לְוִיָּה:

יד] **וְכִי יָזִד.** לָמָּה נֶאֱמַר? לְפִי שֶׁנֶּאֱמַר: ״מַכֵּה אִישׁ״ וְגוֹ׳ (לעיל פסוק יב), שׁוֹמֵעַ אֲנִי אֲפִלּוּ גּוֹי, וְהָרוֹפֵא שֶׁהֵמִית, וּשְׁלִיחַ בֵּית דִּין שֶׁהֵמִית בְּמַלְקוּת אַרְבָּעִים, וְהָאָב הַמַּכֶּה אֶת בְּנוֹ, וְהָרַב הָרוֹדֶה אֶת תַּלְמִידוֹ, וְהַשּׁוֹגֵג? תַּלְמוּד לוֹמַר: ״וְכִי יָזִד״ וְלֹא שׁוֹגֵג, ״עַל רֵעֵהוּ״ וְלֹא עַל גּוֹי, ״לְהָרְגוֹ בְעָרְמָה״ וְלֹא שְׁלִיחַ בֵּית דִּין וְהָרוֹפֵא וְהָרוֹדֶה בְּנוֹ וְתַלְמִידוֹ, שֶׁאַף עַל פִּי שֶׁהֵם מְזִידִין אֵין מַעֲרִימִין: **מֵעִם מִזְבְּחִי.** אִם הָיָה כֹּהֵן וְרוֹצֶה לַעֲבֹד עֲבוֹדָה, ״תִּקָּחֶנּוּ לָמוּת״:

טו] **וּמַכֵּה אָבִיו וְאִמּוֹ.** לְפִי שֶׁלָּמַדְנוּ עַל הַחוֹבֵל בַּחֲבֵרוֹ שֶׁהוּא בְּתַשְׁלוּמִין וְלֹא בְּמִיתָה, הֻצְרַךְ לוֹמַר עַל הַחוֹבֵל בְּאָבִיו שֶׁהוּא בְּמִיתָה. וְאֵינוֹ חַיָּב אֶלָּא בְּהַכָּאָה שֶׁיֵּשׁ בָּהּ חַבּוּרָה: **אָבִיו וְאִמּוֹ.** אוֹ זֶה אוֹ זֶה: **מוֹת יוּמָת.** בְּחֶנֶק:

טז] **וְגֹנֵב אִישׁ וּמְכָרוֹ.** לָמָּה נֶאֱמַר? לְפִי שֶׁנֶּאֱמַר: ״כִּי יִמָּצֵא אִישׁ גֹּנֵב נֶפֶשׁ מֵאֶחָיו״ (דברים כד, ז), אֵין לִי אֶלָּא אִישׁ שֶׁגָּנַב נֶפֶשׁ, אִשָּׁה אוֹ טֻמְטוּם אוֹ אַנְדְּרוֹגִינוֹס שֶׁגָּנְבוּ מִנַּיִן? תַּלְמוּד לוֹמַר: ״וְגֹנֵב אִישׁ וּמְכָרוֹ״. וּלְפִי שֶׁנֶּאֱמַר כָּאן: ״וְגֹנֵב אִישׁ״, אֵין לִי אֶלָּא גּוֹנֵב אִישׁ, גּוֹנֵב אִשָּׁה מִנַּיִן? תַּלְמוּד לוֹמַר: ״גֹּנֵב נֶפֶשׁ״. לְכָךְ הֻצְרְכוּ שְׁנֵיהֶם, מַה שֶּׁחִסֵּר זֶה גִּלָּה זֶה: **וְנִמְצָא בְיָדוֹ.** שֶׁרָאוּהוּ עֵדִים שֶׁגְּנָבוֹ וּמְכָרוֹ, ״וְנִמְצָא״ כְּבָר קֹדֶם הַמְּכִירָה: **מוֹת יוּמָת.** בְּחֶנֶק. כָּל מִיתָה הָאֲמוּרָה בַּתּוֹרָה סְתָם חֶנֶק הִיא:

יז] **וּמְקַלֵּל אָבִיו וְאִמּוֹ.** לָמָּה נֶאֱמַר? לְפִי שֶׁהוּא אוֹמֵר: ״אִישׁ אִישׁ אֲשֶׁר יְקַלֵּל אֶת אָבִיו״ (ויקרא כ, ט), אֵין לִי אֶלָּא אִישׁ שֶׁקִּלֵּל אֶת אָבִיו, אִשָּׁה שֶׁקִּלְּלָה אֶת אָבִיהָ מִנַּיִן? תַּלְמוּד לוֹמַר: ״וּמְקַלֵּל אָבִיו וְאִמּוֹ״, סְתָם, בֵּין אִישׁ וּבֵין אִשָּׁה. אִם כֵּן לָמָּה נֶאֱמַר: ״אִישׁ אֲשֶׁר יְקַלֵּל״? לְהוֹצִיא אֶת הַקָּטָן: **מוֹת יוּמָת.** בִּסְקִילָה, וְכָל מָקוֹם שֶׁנֶּאֱמַר ׳דָּמָיו בּוֹ׳, בִּסְקִילָה, וּבִנְיַן אָב לְכֻלָּם: ״בָּאֶבֶן יִרְגְּמוּ אֹתָם דְּמֵיהֶם בָּם״ (ויקרא כ, כז), וּבִמְקַלֵּל אָבִיו נֶאֱמַר: ״דָּמָיו בּוֹ״ (שם פסוק ט):

strikes another with a stone or with his fist – if the victim does not die but is
19 confined to bed, and afterward he gets up and walks outdoors even leaning on
a cane, the assailant is absolved, but he must pay for the victim's loss of time
20 and provide for his cure. If a man strikes his slave, male or female, SHENI
21 with a rod and the slave dies there and then, the death shall be avenged. But
if the slave survives a day, two days – since the money lost is the master's, the
22 death shall not be avenged. If two men fight and one of them hits a
pregnant woman, and she miscarries but suffers no irreparable injury herself,
the offender must be fined, as the woman's husband demands and as the judges

רש״י

יח **וְכִי יְרִיבֻן אֲנָשִׁים.** לָמָּה נֶאֱמַר? לְפִי שֶׁנֶּאֱמַר: "עַיִן תַּחַת עַיִן" (להלן פסוק כד), לֹא לָמַדְנוּ אֶלָּא דְּמֵי אֵבָרָיו, אֲבָל שֶׁבֶת וְרִפּוּי לֹא לָמַדְנוּ, לְכָךְ נֶאֶמְרָה פָּרָשָׁה זוֹ: **וְנָפַל לְמִשְׁכָּב.** כְּתַרְגּוּמוֹ: "וְיִפּוֹל לְבוּטְלָן", לְחֹלִי שֶׁמְּבַטְּלוֹ מִמְּלַאכְתּוֹ:

יט **עַל מִשְׁעַנְתּוֹ.** עַל בֻּרְיוֹ וְכֹחוֹ: **וְנִקָּה הַמַּכֶּה.** וְכִי תַּעֲלֶה עַל דַּעְתְּךָ שֶׁיֵּהָרֵג זֶה שֶׁלֹּא הָרַג?! אֶלָּא לִמֶּדְךָ כָּאן שֶׁחוֹבְשִׁים אוֹתוֹ עַד שֶׁנִּרְאֶה אִם יִתְרַפֵּא זֶה. וְכֵן מַשְׁמָעוֹ: כְּשֶׁקָּם זֶה וְהוֹלֵךְ עַל מִשְׁעַנְתּוֹ אָז נִקָּה הַמַּכֶּה, אֲבָל עַד שֶׁלֹּא יָקוּם זֶה לֹא נִקָּה הַמַּכֶּה: **רַק שִׁבְתּוֹ.** בִּטּוּל מְלַאכְתּוֹ מֵחֲמַת הַחֹלִי. אִם קָטַע יָדוֹ אוֹ רַגְלוֹ רוֹאִין בִּטּוּל מְלַאכְתּוֹ מֵחֲמַת הַחֹלִי כְּאִלּוּ הוּא שׁוֹמֵר קִשּׁוּאִין, שֶׁהֲרֵי אַף לְאַחַר הַחֹלִי אֵינוֹ רָאוּי לִמְלֶאכֶת יָד וָרֶגֶל, וְהוּא כְּבָר נָתַן לוֹ מֵחֲמַת נִזְקוֹ דְּמֵי יָדוֹ וְרַגְלוֹ, שֶׁנֶּאֱמַר: "יָד תַּחַת יָד רֶגֶל תַּחַת רָגֶל" (להלן פסוק כד): **וְרַפֹּא יְרַפֵּא.** כְּתַרְגּוּמוֹ, יְשַׁלֵּם שְׂכַר הָרוֹפֵא:

כ **וְכִי יַכֶּה אִישׁ אֶת עַבְדּוֹ אוֹ אֶת אֲמָתוֹ.** בְּעֶבֶד כְּנַעֲנִי הַכָּתוּב מְדַבֵּר. אוֹ אֵינוֹ אֶלָּא בְּעִבְרִי? תַּלְמוּד לוֹמַר: "כִּי כַסְפּוֹ הוּא", מַה כַּסְפּוֹ קָנוּי לוֹ עוֹלָמִית, אַף עֶבֶד הַקָּנוּי לוֹ עוֹלָמִית. וַהֲרֵי הָיָה בִּכְלַל "מַכֵּה אִישׁ וָמֵת" (לעיל פסוק יב), אֶלָּא בָּא הַכָּתוּב וְהוֹצִיאוֹ מִן הַכְּלָל לִהְיוֹת נִדּוֹן בְּדִין יוֹם אוֹ יוֹמַיִם, שֶׁאִם לֹא מֵת תַּחַת יָדוֹ וְשָׁהָה מֵעֵת לְעֵת – פָּטוּר: **בַּשֵּׁבֶט.** כְּשֶׁיֵּשׁ בּוֹ כְּדֵי לְהָמִית הַכָּתוּב מְדַבֵּר. אוֹ אֲפִלּוּ אֵין בּוֹ כְּדֵי לְהָמִית? תַּלְמוּד לוֹמַר בְּיִשְׂרָאֵל: "וְאִם בְּאֶבֶן יָד אֲשֶׁר יָמוּת בָּהּ הִכָּהוּ" (במדבר לה, יז), וַהֲלֹא דְּבָרִים קַל וָחֹמֶר: וּמַה יִּשְׂרָאֵל חָמוּר, אֵין חַיָּב עָלָיו אֶלָּא אִם כֵּן הִכָּהוּ בְּדָבָר שֶׁיֵּשׁ בּוֹ כְּדֵי לְהָמִית וְעַל אֵבֶר שֶׁהוּא כְּדֵי לָמוּת בְּהַכָּאָה זוֹ, עֶבֶד הַקַּל לֹא כָּל שֶׁכֵּן?: **נָקֹם יִנָּקֵם.** מִיתַת סַיִף. וְכֵן הוּא אוֹמֵר: "חֶרֶב נֹקֶמֶת נְקַם בְּרִית" (ויקרא כו, כה):

כא **אַךְ אִם יוֹם אוֹ יוֹמַיִם יַעֲמֹד לֹא יֻקַּם.** אִם עַל יוֹם אֶחָד הוּא פָּטוּר עַל יוֹמַיִם לֹא כָּל שֶׁכֵּן?! אֶלָּא יוֹם שֶׁהוּא כְּיוֹמַיִם, וְאֵי זֶה זֶהוּ? זֶה מֵעֵת לְעֵת: **לֹא יֻקַּם כִּי כַסְפּוֹ הוּא.** הָא אַחֵר שֶׁהִכָּהוּ, אַף עַל פִּי שֶׁשָּׁהָה מֵעֵת לְעֵת קֹדֶם שֶׁמֵּת, חַיָּב:

כב **וְכִי יִנָּצוּ אֲנָשִׁים.** זֶה עִם זֶה, וְנִתְכַּוֵּן לְהַכּוֹת אֶת חֲבֵרוֹ וְהִכָּה אֶת הָאִשָּׁה: **וְנָגְפוּ.** אֵין נְגִיפָה אֶלָּא לְשׁוֹן דְּחִיפָה וְהַכָּאָה, כְּמוֹ: "פֶּן תִּגֹּף בָּאֶבֶן רַגְלֶךָ" (תהלים צא, יב), "וּבְטֶרֶם יִתְנַגְּפוּ רַגְלֵיכֶם" (ירמיה יג, טז), "וּלְאֶבֶן נֶגֶף" (ישעיה ח, יד): **וְלֹא יִהְיֶה אָסוֹן.** בָּאִשָּׁה: **עָנוֹשׁ יֵעָנֵשׁ.** לְשַׁלֵּם דְּמֵי וְלָדוֹת לַבַּעַל. שָׁמִין אוֹתָהּ כַּמָּה הָיְתָה רְאוּיָה לִמָּכֵר בַּשּׁוּק לְהַעֲלוֹת בְּדָמֶיהָ בִּשְׁבִיל הֶרְיוֹנָהּ: **עָנוֹשׁ יֵעָנֵשׁ.** יִגְבּוּ מָמוֹן מִמֶּנּוּ, כְּמוֹ: "וְעָנְשׁוּ אֹתוֹ מֵאָה כֶסֶף" (דברים כב, יט): **כַּאֲשֶׁר יָשִׁית עָלָיו וְגוֹ׳.** כְּשֶׁיִּתְבָּעֶנּוּ הַבַּעַל בְּבֵית דִּין לְהָשִׁית עָלָיו עֹנֶשׁ עַל כָּךְ: **וְנָתַן.** הַמַּכֶּה דְּמֵי וְלָדוֹת: **בִּפְלִלִים.** עַל פִּי הַדַּיָּנִים:

It is fascinating to see how this difference arose – over a difference in understanding of a single word, *ason*. This is the fundamental truth behind the Jewish belief in *Torah Shebe'al Peh*, the "Oral Law": The meaning of a text is not given by the text itself. Between a text and its meaning stands the act of interpretation. Rules of interpretation handed down across the generations guide our reading. There have been sectarian groups within Judaism – Sadducees, Karaites, and others – who accepted the Written Torah but not the Oral Law, but in reality such a doctrine is untenable. We need an authoritative tradition of interpretation – in Judaism, the Oral Law – to give us a basis not only to understand the text, but also to apply it to new circumstances without departing from its fundamental truths.

יְרִיבֻ֣ן אֲנָשִׁ֔ים וְהִכָּה־אִישׁ֙ אֶת־רֵעֵ֔הוּ בְּאֶ֖בֶן א֣וֹ בְאֶגְרֹ֑ף וְלֹ֥א יָמ֖וּת
יט וְנָפַ֥ל לְמִשְׁכָּֽב׃ אִם־יָק֞וּם וְהִתְהַלֵּ֥ךְ בַּח֛וּץ עַל־מִשְׁעַנְתּ֖וֹ וְנִקָּ֣ה הַמַּכֶּ֑ה
כ רַ֥ק שִׁבְתּ֛וֹ יִתֵּ֖ן וְרַפֹּ֥א יְרַפֵּֽא׃ וְכִֽי־יַכֶּה֩ אִ֨ישׁ אֶת־עַבְדּ֜וֹ א֤וֹ שני
כא אֶת־אֲמָתוֹ֙ בַּשֵּׁ֔בֶט וּמֵ֖ת תַּ֣חַת יָד֑וֹ נָקֹ֖ם יִנָּקֵֽם׃ אַ֥ךְ אִם־י֛וֹם א֥וֹ יוֹמַ֖יִם
כב יַעֲמֹ֑ד לֹ֣א יֻקַּ֔ם כִּ֥י כַסְפּ֖וֹ הֽוּא׃ וְכִֽי־יִנָּצ֣וּ אֲנָשִׁ֗ים וְנָ֨גְפ֜וּ
אִשָּׁ֤ה הָרָה֙ וְיָצְא֣וּ יְלָדֶ֔יהָ וְלֹ֥א יִהְיֶ֖ה אָס֑וֹן עָנ֣וֹשׁ יֵעָנֵ֗שׁ כַּאֲשֶׁ֨ר יָשִׁ֤ית

אונקלוס

יִנְצוּן גֻּבְרִין, וְיִמְחֵי גְּבַר יָת חַבְרֵיהּ, בְּאַבְנָא אוֹ בִּכְרֻמֵיזָא, וְלָא
יְמוּת וְיִפּוֹל לְבִטְלָן: יט אִם יְקוּם, וִיהַלֵּיךְ בְּבָרָא, עַל בֻּרְיֵיהּ וִיהֵי זַכָּא
מָחְיָא, לְחוֹד בְּטְלָנֵיהּ, יִתֵּין וַאֲגַר אַסְיָא יְשַׁלֵּים: כ וַאֲרֵי יִמְחֵי גְּבַר
יָת עַבְדֵּיהּ, אוֹ יָת אַמְתֵיהּ בְּשָׁלְטָן, וִימוּת תְּחוֹת יְדֵיהּ, אִתְדָּנָא
יִתְדָּן: כא בְּרַם אִם יוֹמָא, אוֹ תְּרֵין יוֹמִין יִתְקַיַּם, לָא יִתְדָּן, אֲרֵי
כַסְפֵּיהּ הוּא: כב וַאֲרֵי יִנְצוּן גֻּבְרִין, וְיִמְחוֹן, אִתְּתָא מְעַדְּיָא וְיִפְּקוּן
וַלְדַּהָא, וְלָא יְהֵי מוֹתָא, אִתְגְּבָאָה יִתְגְּבֵי, כְּמָא דִּישַׁוֵּי עֲלוֹהִי בַּעְלַהּ

TEXT AND INTERPRETATION: THE CASE OF ACCIDENTAL MISCARRIAGE

The word *ason*, irreparable injury, apparently means a fatal accident. The law under consideration is about harm to an innocent third party when people are engaged in a public and potentially murderous fight. If the third party is a pregnant woman, and as a result of being hit she miscarries but suffers no other injury, the person responsible must pay compensation for the loss of the unborn child, but suffers no other penalty. If, however, the woman dies, he is guilty of a much more serious offence (the Sages disagreed as to whether this means that he is liable to capital punishment or not [Sanhedrin 79a]).

On this interpretation, causing a woman to miscarry – being responsible for the death of a fetus – is not a capital offense. Until birth, the fetus does not have the legal status of a person. Such was the view of the Sages in the land of Israel.

However, the Alexandrian Jewish community during the late Second Temple period developed its own traditions, at times quite different from those of the rabbinic mainstream. In one of his works, its most famous member, the philosopher Philo, turns to this passage.

Philo follows the Septuagint, the Greek translation of the Tanakh made in the third century BCE during the reign of Ptolemy II. There are numerous divergences between the Septuagint and the Hebrew text, and this is one of them.

The Greek version translates *ason* not as "calamity," but rather as "form." Now, according to Philo, the verses are talking about damage to the fetus. In the first case, "there is no *ason*" means the fetus was "unformed" – i.e., the woman miscarries, but the fetus was at an early stage of development. The next verse speaks of a fetus "that has form," i.e., the woman was at a later stage of pregnancy. In this view, feticide – and hence abortion – can be a capital crime, an act of murder.

Judaism followed the opinion of the Sages of the land of Israel. In Judaism, abortion is not murder. Still, while a fetus may not be a person in Jewish law, it is a potential person, and must therefore be protected. We permit abortion to save the life of the mother or to protect her from life-threatening illness.

However, Philo's reading had an impact on the development of Christian teaching. The first Christian texts were written in Greek rather than Hebrew. The early Christian teachings on abortion thus followed Philo rather than the Sages. If the fetus was formed, then causing its death was murder. So taught Tertullian in the second century.

23 rule. But if she suffers an irreparable injury, he must compensate life for life, eye
24
25 for eye, tooth for tooth, hand for hand, foot for foot, burn for burn, wound for
26 wound, bruise for bruise. If a man should strike the eye of his slave,
male or female, and maim it, he must send the slave out free on account of his
27 eye. If he knocks out the tooth of his slave, male or female, he must send the
slave out free on account of his tooth.
28 If an ox gores a man or a woman to death, the ox shall be stoned, and its flesh
29 not eaten, but the owner of the ox shall not be liable. But if the ox has already
gored in the past, and its owner was warned but failed to guard it, and it kills
a man or a woman, the ox shall be stoned, and its owner also shall be put to

רש״י

כג **וְאִם אָסוֹן יִהְיֶה.** בָּאִשָּׁה: **וְנָתַתָּה נֶפֶשׁ תַּחַת נָפֶשׁ.** רַבּוֹתֵינוּ חוֹלְקִים בַּדָּבָר: יֵשׁ אוֹמְרִים נֶפֶשׁ מַמָּשׁ, וְיֵשׁ אוֹמְרִים מָמוֹן, אֲבָל לֹא נֶפֶשׁ מַמָּשׁ, שֶׁהַמִּתְכַּוֵּן לַהֲרֹג אֶת זֶה וְהָרַג אֶת זֶה פָּטוּר מִמִּיתָה, וּמְשַׁלֵּם לְיוֹרְשָׁיו דָּמָיו כְּמוֹ שֶׁהָיָה נִמְכָּר בַּשּׁוּק:

כד **עַיִן תַּחַת עַיִן.** סִמֵּא עֵין חֲבֵרוֹ נוֹתֵן לוֹ דְּמֵי עֵינוֹ כַּמָּה שֶׁפָּחֲתוּ דָּמָיו לְמָכְרוֹ בַּשּׁוּק, וְכֵן כֻּלָּם, וְלֹא נְטִילַת אֵבֶר מַמָּשׁ, כְּמוֹ שֶׁדָּרְשׁוּ רַבּוֹתֵינוּ בְּפֶרֶק ׳הַחוֹבֵל׳ (בבא קמא פג ע״ב – פד ע״א):

כה **כְּוִיָּה תַּחַת כְּוִיָּה.** מִכְוַת אֵשׁ. וְעַד עַכְשָׁיו דִּבֵּר בַּחֲבָלָה שֶׁיֵּשׁ בָּהּ פְּחַת דָּמִים, וְעַכְשָׁיו בְּשֶׁאֵין בָּהּ פְּחַת דָּמִים אֶלָּא צַעַר, כְּגוֹן כְּוָאוֹ בִּשְׁפוּד עַל צִפָּרְנוֹ, אוֹמְדִים כַּמָּה אָדָם כַּיּוֹצֵא בָּזֶה רוֹצֶה לִטֹּל לִהְיוֹת מִצְטַעֵר כָּךְ: **פֶּצַע.** הִיא מַכָּה הַמּוֹצִיאָה דָּם, שֶׁפָּצַע אֶת בְּשָׂרוֹ, נברדור״א בְּלַעַ״ז. הַכֹּל לְפִי מַה שֶּׁהוּא, אִם יֵשׁ בּוֹ פְּחַת דָּמִים נוֹתֵן נֶזֶק, וְאִם נָפַל לְמִשְׁכָּב נוֹתֵן שֶׁבֶת וְרִפּוּי וּבֹשֶׁת וָצַעַר. וּמִקְרָא זֶה יָתֵר הוּא, וּבְ׳הַחוֹבֵל׳ דְּרָשׁוּהוּ רַבּוֹתֵינוּ לְחַיֵּב עַל הַצַּעַר אֲפִלּוּ בִּמְקוֹם נֶזֶק, שֶׁאַף עַל פִּי שֶׁנּוֹתֵן לוֹ דְּמֵי יָדוֹ אֵין פּוֹטְרִין אוֹתוֹ מִן הַצַּעַר, לוֹמַר הוֹאִיל וְקָנָה יָדוֹ יֵשׁ עָלָיו לְחָתְכָהּ בְּכָל מַה שֶּׁיִּרְצֶה, אֶלָּא אוֹמְרִים יֵשׁ לוֹ לְחָתְכָהּ בְּסַם שֶׁאֵינוֹ מִצְטַעֵר כָּל כָּךְ, וְזֶה חֲתָכָהּ בְּבַרְזֶל וְצִעֲרוֹ: **חַבּוּרָה.** הִיא מַכָּה שֶׁהַדָּם נִצְרָר בָּהּ וְאֵינוֹ יוֹצֵא אֶלָּא שֶׁמַּאֲדִים הַבָּשָׂר כְּנֶגְדּוֹ. וּלְשׁוֹן חַבּוּרָה טק״א בְּלַעַז, כְּמוֹ: ״וְנָמֵר חֲבַרְבֻּרֹתָיו״ (ירמיה יג, כג), וְתַרְגּוּמוֹ ״מַשְׁקוֹפִי״, לְשׁוֹן חֲבָטָה, בטדור״א בְּלַעַז, וְכֵן: ״שְׁדֻפוֹת קָדִים״ (בראשית מא, כג), ״שְׁקִיפָן קִדּוּם״, חֲבוּטוֹת בָּרוּחַ. וְכֵן: ״עַל הַמַּשְׁקוֹף״ (לעיל יב, ז), עַל שֵׁם שֶׁהַדֶּלֶת נוֹקֵשׁ עָלָיו:

כו **אֶת עֵין עַבְדּוֹ.** כְּנַעֲנִי, אֲבָל עִבְרִי אֵינוֹ יוֹצֵא בְּשֵׁן וָעַיִן, כְּמוֹ שֶׁאָמַרְנוּ אֵצֶל ״לֹא תֵצֵא כְּצֵאת הָעֲבָדִים״ (לעיל פסוק ז): **תַּחַת עֵינוֹ.** וְכֵן בְּעֶשְׂרִים וְאַרְבָּעָה רָאשֵׁי אֵבָרִים: אֶצְבְּעוֹת הַיָּדַיִם וְהָרַגְלַיִם וּשְׁתֵּי אָזְנַיִם וְהַחֹטֶם וְרֹאשׁ הַגְּוִיָּה שֶׁהוּא גִּיד הָאַמָּה. וְלָמָּה נֶאֶמְרוּ שֵׁן וָעַיִן? שֶׁאִם נֶאֱמַר עַיִן וְלֹא נֶאֱמַר שֵׁן, הָיִיתִי אוֹמֵר, מָה עַיִן שֶׁנִּבְרָא עִמּוֹ אַף כָּל שֶׁנִּבְרָא עִמּוֹ, וַהֲרֵי שֵׁן לֹא נִבְרָא עִמּוֹ. וְאִם נֶאֱמַר שֵׁן וְלֹא נֶאֱמַר עַיִן, הָיִיתִי אוֹמֵר, אֲפִלּוּ שֵׁן תִּינוֹק שֶׁיֵּשׁ לָהּ חֲלִיפִין, לְכָךְ נֶאֱמַר עַיִן:

כח **וְכִי יִגַּח שׁוֹר.** אֶחָד שׁוֹר וְאֶחָד כָּל בְּהֵמָה וְחַיָּה וָעוֹף, אֶלָּא שֶׁדִּבֵּר הַכָּתוּב בַּהוֹוֶה: **וְלֹא יֵאָכֵל אֶת בְּשָׂרוֹ.** מִמַּשְׁמָע שֶׁנֶּאֱמַר: ״סָקוֹל יִסָּקֵל הַשּׁוֹר״ אֵינִי יוֹדֵעַ שֶׁהוּא נְבֵלָה וּנְבֵלָה אֲסוּרָה בַּאֲכִילָה? אֶלָּא מַה תַּלְמוּד לוֹמַר: ״וְלֹא יֵאָכֵל אֶת בְּשָׂרוֹ״? שֶׁאֲפִלּוּ שְׁחָטוֹ לְאַחַר שֶׁנִּגְמַר דִּינוֹ אָסוּר בַּאֲכִילָה. בַּהֲנָאָה מִנַּיִן? תַּלְמוּד לוֹמַר: ״וּבַעַל הַשּׁוֹר נָקִי״, כְּאָדָם הָאוֹמֵר לַחֲבֵרוֹ: יָצָא פְלוֹנִי נָקִי מִנְּכָסָיו וְאֵין לוֹ בָּהֶם הֲנָאָה שֶׁל כְּלוּם. זֶהוּ מִדְרָשׁוֹ. וּפְשׁוּטוֹ כְּמַשְׁמָעוֹ, לְפִי שֶׁנֶּאֱמַר בְּמוּעָד: ״וְגַם בְּעָלָיו יוּמָת״, הֻצְרַךְ לוֹמַר בְּתָם: ״וּבַעַל הַשּׁוֹר נָקִי״:

כט **מִתְּמֹל שִׁלְשֹׁם.** הֲרֵי שָׁלֹשׁ נְגִיחוֹת: **וְהוּעַד בִּבְעָלָיו.** לְשׁוֹן הַתְרָאָה בְּעֵדִים, כְּמוֹ: ״הָעֵד הֵעִד בָּנוּ הָאִישׁ״ (בראשית מג, ג): **וְהֵמִית אִישׁ וְגוֹ׳.** לְפִי שֶׁנֶּאֱמַר: ״וְכִי יִגַּח״ (לעיל פסוק כח), אֵין לִי אֶלָּא שֶׁהֱמִיתוֹ בִּנְגִיחָה,

something else. It means, among other things, that my freedom is not bought at the price of yours. The theology and the legal details of *tzedaka* will be expanded upon in Leviticus and Deuteronomy, but the basic principles are laid out in our *parasha*. Freedom means responsibility as *mishpat*, delineated in the cases here, and also responsibility as *tzedaka*.

ability to lead responsible lives, which are contingent on having certain basic freedoms. Responsibility requires freedom.

Individual freedom may be best described, as Isaiah Berlin argued, in terms of "negative liberty," namely the absence of constraints (*ḥofesh*). But *collective* freedom (*ḥerut*) is

כג עָלָיו בַּעַל הָאִשָּׁה וְנָתַן בִּפְלִלִים: וְאִם־אָסוֹן יִהְיֶה וְנָתַתָּה נֶפֶשׁ תַּחַת
כד כה נָפֶשׁ: עַיִן תַּחַת עַיִן שֵׁן תַּחַת שֵׁן יָד תַּחַת יָד רֶגֶל תַּחַת רָגֶל: כְּוִיָּה
כו תַּחַת כְּוִיָּה פֶּצַע תַּחַת פָּצַע חַבּוּרָה תַּחַת חַבּוּרָה: וְכִי־יַכֶּה
אִישׁ אֶת־עֵין עַבְדּוֹ אוֹ־אֶת־עֵין אֲמָתוֹ וְשִׁחֲתָהּ לַחָפְשִׁי יְשַׁלְּחֶנּוּ
כז תַּחַת עֵינוֹ: וְאִם־שֵׁן עַבְדּוֹ אוֹ־שֵׁן אֲמָתוֹ יַפִּיל לַחָפְשִׁי יְשַׁלְּחֶנּוּ תַּחַת
שִׁנּוֹ:
כח וְכִי־יִגַּח שׁוֹר אֶת־אִישׁ אוֹ אֶת־אִשָּׁה וָמֵת סָקוֹל יִסָּקֵל הַשּׁוֹר וְלֹא
כט יֵאָכֵל אֶת־בְּשָׂרוֹ וּבַעַל הַשּׁוֹר נָקִי: וְאִם שׁוֹר נַגָּח הוּא מִתְּמֹל שִׁלְשֹׁם
וְהוּעַד בִּבְעָלָיו וְלֹא יִשְׁמְרֶנּוּ וְהֵמִית אִישׁ אוֹ אִשָּׁה הַשּׁוֹר יִסָּקֵל

אונקלוס

דְאִתְּתָא, וְיִתֵּין מְמֵימַר דַּיָּנַיָּא: כג וְאִם מוֹתָא יְהֵי, וְתִתֵּין נַפְשָׁא חֲלָף נַפְשָׁא: כד עֵינָא חֲלָף עֵינָא, שִׁנָּא חֲלָף שִׁנָּא, יְדָא חֲלָף יְדָא, רִגְלָא חֲלָף רִגְלָא: כה כְּוָאָה חֲלָף כְּוָאָה, פִּדְעָא חֲלָף פִּדְעָא, מַשְׁקוֹפִי, חֲלָף מַשְׁקוֹפִי: כו וַאֲרֵי יִמְחֵי גְבַר, יָת עֵינָא דְעַבְדֵּיהּ, אוֹ יָת עֵינָא דְאַמְתֵּיהּ וִיחַבְּלִנַּהּ, לְבַר חוֹרִין יִפְטְרִנֵּיהּ חֲלָף עֵינֵיהּ: כז וְאִם שִׁנָּא דְעַבְדֵּיהּ, אוֹ שִׁנָּא דְאַמְתֵּיהּ יַפֵּיל, לְבַר חוֹרִין יִפְטְרִנֵּיהּ חֲלָף שִׁנֵּיהּ: כח וַאֲרֵי יִגַּח תּוֹרָא יָת גֻּבְרָא, אוֹ יָת אִתְּתָא וִימוּת, אִתְרְגָמָא יִתְרְגֵים תּוֹרָא, וְלָא יִתְאֲכִיל יָת בִּסְרֵיהּ, וּמָרֵיהּ דְתוֹרָא יְהֵי זַכָּאִי: כט וְאִם, תּוֹר נַגָּח הוּא מֵאִתְמָלֵי וּמִדְּקַמּוֹהִי, וְאִתַּסְהַד בְּמָרֵיהּ וְלָא נַטְרֵיהּ, וְיִקְטוֹל גְּבַר אוֹ אִתָּא, תּוֹרָא יִתְרְגֵים,

21:29 וְהוּעַד בִּבְעָלָיו *Its owner was warned* – The *parasha* entitled Mishpatim begins, as we might expect, with *mishpat*, meaning retributive justice or the rule of law, and specifically with cases delineating a person's responsibility to compensate for harm he or she causes others. A free society must be governed by law, impartially administered, through which the guilty are punished, the innocent acquitted, the injured compensated, and human rights secured. *Tzedaka*, by contrast, refers to distributive justice, a less procedural and more substantive idea, which becomes the focus from 22:21. God, for the Israelites, is actively concerned with the economic and political order, especially with those who, because they lack power, or even a "voice," became the victims of injustice and inequity.

The society the Israelites are to construct, we are told, will stand as a living contrast to what they have experienced in Egypt: poverty, persecution, and enslavement. Their release from bondage was only the first stage on their journey to freedom. The second – their covenant with God – involves collective responsibility to ensure that no one will be excluded from the shared graciousness of the community and its life. This requires both *mishpat*, the rule of law, and *tzedaka*, a just distribution of resources, a fair chance at a dignified livelihood. This view has close affinities with Amartya Sen's concept of "development as freedom":

> The adult who lacks the means of having medical treatment for an ailment from which she suffers is not only prey to preventable morbidity and possibly escapable mortality, but may also be denied the freedom to do various things – for herself and for others – that she may wish to do as a responsible human being. The bonded laborer born into semi-slavery, the subjugated girl child stifled by a repressive society, the helpless landless laborer without substantial means of earning an income are all deprived not only in terms of well-being, but also in terms of the

30 death. If a ransom is imposed on his life, then he shall pay whatever is imposed
31 on him and redeem his life. This rule also applies if the ox gores a minor son or
32 daughter, but if the ox gores a slave, male or female, the owner shall give thirty
33 shekels of silver to the master, and the ox must be stoned. If a man
uncovers a hole or digs one and fails to cover it, and an ox or a donkey falls into
34 it, the one responsible for the pit shall make restitution. He shall give its owner
35 its full value, and the dead animal shall be his. If one man's ox injures
another's so that it dies, they shall sell the live ox and share the money. The
36 dead animal they shall also share. If, however, it is known that the ox had gored
in the past, and still the owner failed to guard it, he shall pay an ox for an ox, and
37 the dead animal shall be his. If a man steals an ox or a sheep and kills
22 1 it or sells it, he shall pay five oxen for an ox, four sheep for a sheep. If a burglar
is caught tunneling in, and is struck and killed, there is no bloodguilt on his

רש״י

הֱמִיתוֹ בִּנְשִׁיכָה דְּחִיפָה בְּעִיטָה מִנַּיִן? תַּלְמוּד לוֹמַר: ״וְהֵמִית״: **וְגַם בְּעָלָיו יוּמָת.** בִּידֵי שָׁמַיִם. יָכוֹל בִּידֵי אָדָם? תַּלְמוּד לוֹמַר: ״מוֹת יוּמַת הַמַּכֶּה רֹצֵחַ הוּא״ (במדבר לה, כא), עַל רְצִיחָתוֹ אַתָּה הוֹרְגוֹ וְאִי אַתָּה הוֹרְגוֹ עַל רְצִיחַת שׁוֹרוֹ:

ל) **אִם כֹּפֶר יוּשַׁת עָלָיו.** ׳אִם׳ זֶה אֵינוֹ תָּלוּי, וַהֲרֵי הוּא כְּמוֹ: ״אִם כֶּסֶף תַּלְוֶה״ (להלן כב, כד), לְשׁוֹן ׳אֲשֶׁר׳, זֶה מִשְׁפָּטוֹ שֶׁיָּשִׁיתוּ עָלָיו בֵּית דִּין כֹּפֶר: **וְנָתַן פִּדְיֹן נַפְשׁוֹ.** דְּמֵי נִזָּק, דִּבְרֵי רַבִּי יִשְׁמָעֵאל. רַבִּי עֲקִיבָא אוֹמֵר: דְּמֵי מַזִּיק:

לא) **אוֹ בֵן יִגָּח.** בֵּן שֶׁהוּא קָטָן: **אוֹ בַת.** שֶׁהִיא קְטַנָּה. לְפִי שֶׁנֶּאֱמַר: ״וְהֵמִית אִישׁ אוֹ אִשָּׁה״ (לעיל פסוק כט), יָכוֹל אֵינוֹ חַיָּב אֶלָּא עַל הַגְּדוֹלִים? תַּלְמוּד לוֹמַר: ״אוֹ בֵן יִגָּח״ וְגוֹ׳, לְחַיֵּב עַל הַקְּטַנִּים כַּגְּדוֹלִים:

לב) **אִם עֶבֶד אוֹ אָמָה.** כְּנַעֲנִיִּים: **שְׁלֹשִׁים שְׁקָלִים יִתֵּן.** גְּזֵרַת הַכָּתוּב הוּא, בֵּין שֶׁהוּא שָׁוֶה אֶלֶף זוּז בֵּין שֶׁאֵינוֹ שָׁוֶה אֶלָּא דִּינָר. וְהַשֶּׁקֶל מִשְׁקָלוֹ אַרְבָּעָה זְהוּבִים שֶׁהֵם חֲצִי אוּנְקִיָּא לְמִשְׁקַל הַיָּשָׁר שֶׁל קוֹלוֹנְיָא:

לג) **וְכִי יִפְתַּח אִישׁ בּוֹר.** שֶׁהָיָה מְכֻסֶּה וְגִלָּהוּ: **אוֹ כִּי יִכְרֶה.** לָמָּה נֶאֱמַר? אִם עַל הַפְּתִיחָה חַיָּב עַל הַכְּרִיָּה לֹא כָּל שֶׁכֵּן?! אֶלָּא לְהָבִיא כּוֹרֶה אַחַר כּוֹרֶה שֶׁהוּא חַיָּב: **וְלֹא יְכַסֶּנּוּ.** הָא אִם כִּסָּהוּ פָּטוּר, וּבְחוֹפֵר בִּרְשׁוּת הָרַבִּים דִּבֶּר הַכָּתוּב: **שׁוֹר אוֹ חֲמוֹר.** הוּא הַדִּין לְכָל בְּהֵמָה וְחַיָּה, שֶׁבְּכָל מָקוֹם שֶׁנֶּאֱמַר שׁוֹר וַחֲמוֹר אָנוּ לְמֵדִין אוֹתוֹ ׳שׁוֹר׳ ׳שׁוֹר׳ מִשַּׁבָּת, שֶׁנֶּאֱמַר: ״לְמַעַן יָנוּחַ שׁוֹרְךָ וַחֲמֹרֶךָ״ (להלן כג, יב), מַה לְּהַלָּן כָּל בְּהֵמָה וְחַיָּה כְּשׁוֹר, שֶׁהֲרֵי נֶאֱמַר בְּמָקוֹם אַחֵר: ״וְכָל בְּהֶמְתֶּךָ״ (דברים ה, יד), אַף כָּאן כָּל בְּהֵמָה וְחַיָּה כְּשׁוֹר, וְלֹא נֶאֱמַר שׁוֹר וַחֲמוֹר אֶלָּא ׳שׁוֹר׳ וְלֹא אָדָם, ׳חֲמוֹר׳ וְלֹא כֵּלִים:

לד) **בַּעַל הַבּוֹר.** בַּעַל הַתַּקָּלָה, אַף עַל פִּי שֶׁאֵין הַבּוֹר שֶׁלּוֹ, שֶׁעֲשָׂאוֹ בִּרְשׁוּת הָרַבִּים, עֲשָׂאוֹ הַכָּתוּב בְּעָלָיו לְהִתְחַיֵּב בְּנִזְקָיו: **כֶּסֶף יָשִׁיב לִבְעָלָיו.** ״יָשִׁיב״ לְרַבּוֹת שָׁוֶה כֶּסֶף וַאֲפִלּוּ סֻבִּין: **וְהַמֵּת יִהְיֶה לוֹ.** לַנִּזָּק. שָׁמִין אֶת הַנְּבֵלָה וְנוֹטְלָהּ בְּדָמִים, וּמְשַׁלֵּם לוֹ הַמַּזִּיק עָלֶיהָ תַּשְׁלוּמֵי נִזְקוֹ:

לה) **וְכִי יִגֹּף.** יִדְחֹף, בֵּין בְּקַרְנָיו בֵּין בְּגוּפוֹ בֵּין בְּרַגְלָיו בֵּין שֶׁנְּשָׁכוֹ בְּשִׁנָּיו כֻּלָּן בִּכְלַל נְגִיפָה הֵם, שֶׁאֵין נְגִיפָה אֶלָּא לְשׁוֹן מַכָּה: **שׁוֹר אִישׁ.** שׁוֹר שֶׁל אִישׁ: **וּמָכְרוּ אֶת הַשּׁוֹר וְגוֹ׳.** בְּשָׁוִים הַכָּתוּב מְדַבֵּר, שׁוֹר שָׁוֶה מָאתַיִם שֶׁהֵמִית שׁוֹר שָׁוֶה מָאתַיִם, בֵּין שֶׁהַנְּבֵלָה שָׁוָה הַרְבֵּה בֵּין שֶׁהִיא שָׁוָה מְעַט, כְּשֶׁנּוֹטֵל זֶה חֲצִי הַחַי וַחֲצִי הַמֵּת וְזֶה חֲצִי הַחַי וַחֲצִי הַמֵּת נִמְצָא כָּל אֶחָד מַפְסִיד חֲצִי נֶזֶק שֶׁהִזִּיקָה הַמִּיתָה. לָמַדְנוּ שֶׁהַתָּם מְשַׁלֵּם חֲצִי נֶזֶק, שֶׁמִּן הַשָּׁוִין אַתָּה לָמֵד לְשֶׁאֵינָן שָׁוִין כִּי דִין הַתָּם לְשַׁלֵּם חֲצִי נֶזֶק, לֹא פָּחוֹת וְלֹא יוֹתֵר. אוֹ יָכוֹל אַף בְּשֶׁאֵינָן שָׁוִין בִּדְמֵיהֶן כְּשֶׁהֵן חַיִּים אָמַר הַכָּתוּב: וְחָצוּ אֶת שְׁנֵיהֶם? אִם אָמַרְתָּ כֵּן, פְּעָמִים שֶׁהַמַּזִּיק מִשְׂתַּכֵּר הַרְבֵּה, כְּשֶׁהַנְּבֵלָה שָׁוָה לִמָּכֵר לְגוֹיִם הַרְבֵּה יוֹתֵר מִדְּמֵי שׁוֹר הַמַּזִּיק, וְאִי אֶפְשָׁר שֶׁיֹּאמַר הַכָּתוּב שֶׁיְּהֵא הַמַּזִּיק נִשְׂכָּר. אוֹ פְּעָמִים שֶׁהַנִּזָּק נוֹטֵל הַרְבֵּה יוֹתֵר מִדְּמֵי נֶזֶק שָׁלֵם, שֶׁחֲצִי דְּמֵי שׁוֹר הַמַּזִּיק שָׁוִין יוֹתֵר מִכָּל דְּמֵי שׁוֹר הַנִּזָּק, וְאִם אָמַרְתָּ כֵּן, הֲרֵי תָּם חָמוּר מִמּוּעָד. עַל כָּרְחֲךָ לֹא דִּבֵּר הַכָּתוּב אֶלָּא בְּשָׁוִין, וְלִמֶּדְךָ שֶׁהַתָּם מְשַׁלֵּם חֲצִי נֶזֶק, וּמִן הַשָּׁוִין תִּלְמַד לְשֶׁאֵינָן שָׁוִין, שֶׁהַמִּשְׁתַּלֵּם חֲצִי נִזְקוֹ שָׁמִין לוֹ אֶת הַנְּבֵלָה, וּמַה שֶּׁפָּחֲתוּ דָּמָיו בִּשְׁבִיל הַמִּיתָה, נוֹטֵל חֲצִי הַפְּחָת וְהוֹלֵךְ. וְלָמָּה אָמַר הַכָּתוּב בַּלָּשׁוֹן הַזֶּה, וְלֹא אָמַר: ׳יְשַׁלֵּם חֶצְיוֹ׳? לְלַמֵּד שֶׁאֵין הַתָּם מְשַׁלֵּם אֶלָּא מִגּוּפוֹ, וְאִם נָגַח וּמֵת אֵין הַנִּזָּק נוֹטֵל אֶלָּא הַנְּבֵלָה, וְאִם אֵינָהּ מַגַּעַת לַחֲצִי נִזְקוֹ יַפְסִיד. אוֹ שׁוֹר שָׁוֶה מָנֶה שֶׁנָּגַח שׁוֹר שָׁוֶה חָמֵשׁ מֵאוֹת זוּז אֵינוֹ נוֹטֵל אֶלָּא

ל וְגַם־בְּעָלָיו יוּמָת: אִם־כֹּפֶר יוּשַׁת עָלָיו וְנָתַן פִּדְיֹן נַפְשׁוֹ כְּכֹל אֲשֶׁר־
לא יוּשַׁת עָלָיו: אוֹ־בֵן יִגָּח אוֹ־בַת יִגָּח כַּמִּשְׁפָּט הַזֶּה יֵעָשֶׂה לּוֹ: אִם־
לב עֶבֶד יִגַּח הַשּׁוֹר אוֹ אָמָה כֶּסֶף ׀ שְׁלֹשִׁים שְׁקָלִים יִתֵּן לַאדֹנָיו וְהַשּׁוֹר
לג יִסָּקֵל: וְכִי־יִפְתַּח אִישׁ בּוֹר אוֹ כִּי־יִכְרֶה אִישׁ בֹּר וְלֹא
לד יְכַסֶּנּוּ וְנָפַל־שָׁמָּה שּׁוֹר אוֹ חֲמוֹר: בַּעַל הַבּוֹר יְשַׁלֵּם כֶּסֶף יָשִׁיב לִבְעָלָיו
לה וְהַמֵּת יִהְיֶה־לּוֹ: וְכִי־יִגֹּף שׁוֹר־אִישׁ אֶת־שׁוֹר רֵעֵהוּ
וָמֵת וּמָכְרוּ אֶת־הַשּׁוֹר הַחַי וְחָצוּ אֶת־כַּסְפּוֹ וְגַם אֶת־הַמֵּת יֶחֱצוּן:
לו אוֹ נוֹדַע כִּי שׁוֹר נַגָּח הוּא מִתְּמוֹל שִׁלְשֹׁם וְלֹא יִשְׁמְרֶנּוּ בְּעָלָיו שַׁלֵּם
לז יְשַׁלֵּם שׁוֹר תַּחַת הַשּׁוֹר וְהַמֵּת יִהְיֶה־לּוֹ: כִּי יִגְנֹב־
אִישׁ שׁוֹר אוֹ־שֶׂה וּטְבָחוֹ אוֹ מְכָרוֹ חֲמִשָּׁה בָקָר יְשַׁלֵּם תַּחַת הַשּׁוֹר
כב א וְאַרְבַּע־צֹאן תַּחַת הַשֶּׂה: אִם־בַּמַּחְתֶּרֶת יִמָּצֵא הַגַּנָּב וְהֻכָּה וָמֵת

אונקלוס

וְאַף מָרֵיהּ יִתְקְטִיל: ל אִם מָמוֹן יְשַׁוּוֹן עֲלוֹהִי, וְיִתֵּין פֻּרְקַן נַפְשֵׁיהּ, כְּכֹל דִּישַׁוּוֹן עֲלוֹהִי: לא אוֹ לְבַר יִשְׂרָאֵל יִגַּח תּוֹרָא אוֹ לְבַת יִשְׂרָאֵל יִגַּח, כְּדִינָא הָדֵין יִתְעֲבֵיד לֵיהּ: לב אִם לְעַבְדָּא, יִגַּח תּוֹרָא אוֹ לְאַמְתָא, כַּסְפָּא תְּלָתִין סִלְעִין, יִתֵּין לְרִבּוֹנֵיהּ, וְתוֹרָא יִתְרְגֵים: לג וַאֲרֵי יִפְתַּח גְּבַר גּוּב, אוֹ, אֲרֵי יִכְרֵי גְּבַר, גּוּב וְלָא יְכַסֵּינֵיהּ, וְיִפּוֹל תַּמָּן תּוֹרָא אוֹ חֲמָרָא: לד מָרֵיהּ דְּגֻבָּא יְשַׁלֵּים, כַּסְפָּא יָתֵיב לְמָרוֹהִי, וּמִיתָא יְהֵי דִּילֵיהּ: לה וַאֲרֵי יִגּוֹף תּוֹר דִּגְבַר, יָת תּוֹרָא דְּחַבְרֵיהּ וִימוּת, וְיִזַבְּנוּן, יָת תּוֹרָא חַיָּא וְיִפְלְגוּן יָת כַּסְפֵּיהּ, וְאַף יָת דְּמֵי מִיתָא יִפְלְגוּן: לו אוֹ אִתְיְדַע, אֲרֵי, תּוֹר נַגָּח הוּא מֵאִתְמָלֵי וּמִדְּקַמּוֹהִי, וְלָא נַטְרֵיהּ מָרֵיהּ, שַׁלָּמָא יְשַׁלֵּים תּוֹרָא חֲלַף תּוֹרָא, וּמִיתָא יְהֵי דִּילֵיהּ: לז אֲרֵי יִגְנוֹב גְּבַר תּוֹר אוֹ אִמַּר, וְיִכְסְנֵיהּ אוֹ יְזַבְּנִנֵּיהּ, חַמְשָׁא תוֹרִין, יְשַׁלֵּים חֲלַף תּוֹרָא, וְאַרְבַּע עָנָא חֲלַף אִמְּרָא: כב א אִם בְּמַחְתַּרְתָּא, יִשְׁתְּכַח גַּנָּבָא וְיִתְמְחֵי וִימוּת,

רש"י

אֶת הַשּׁוֹר, שֶׁלֹּא נִתְחַיֵּב הַתָּם לְחַיֵּב אֶת בְּעָלָיו לְשַׁלֵּם מִן הָעֲלִיָּה: לו אוֹ נוֹדַע. אוֹ לֹא הָיָה תָּם, אֶלָּא "נוֹדַע כִּי שׁוֹר נַגָּח הוּא" הַיּוֹם וּמִתְּמוֹל שִׁלְשֹׁם, הֲרֵי שָׁלֹשׁ נְגִיחוֹת: שַׁלֵּם יְשַׁלֵּם שׁוֹר. נֶזֶק שָׁלֵם: וְהַמֵּת יִהְיֶה לּוֹ. לַנִּזָּק, וְעָלָיו יַשְׁלִים הַמַּזִּיק עַד שֶׁיִּשְׁתַּלֵּם נִזָּק כָּל נִזְקוֹ: לז חֲמִשָּׁה בָקָר וגו'. אָמַר רַבָּן יוֹחָנָן בֶּן זַכַּאי: חָס הַמָּקוֹם עַל כְּבוֹדָן שֶׁל בְּרִיּוֹת, שׁוֹר שֶׁהוֹלֵךְ בְּרַגְלָיו וְלֹא נִתְבַּזָּה בּוֹ הַגַּנָּב לְנָשְׂאוֹ עַל כְּתֵפוֹ – מְשַׁלֵּם חֲמִשָּׁה; שֶׂה שֶׁנּוֹשְׂאוֹ עַל כְּתֵפוֹ – מְשַׁלֵּם אַרְבָּעָה הוֹאִיל וְנִתְבַּזָּה בּוֹ. אָמַר רַבִּי מֵאִיר: בֹּא וּרְאֵה כַּמָּה גְּדוֹלָה כֹּחָהּ שֶׁל מְלָאכָה, שׁוֹר שֶׁבִּטְּלוֹ מִמְּלַאכְתּוֹ – חֲמִשָּׁה, שֶׂה שֶׁלֹּא בִּטְּלוֹ מִמְּלַאכְתּוֹ – אַרְבָּעָה: תַּחַת הַשּׁוֹר... תַּחַת הַשֶּׂה. שָׁנָה הַכָּתוּב, לוֹמַר שֶׁאֵין מִדַּת תַּשְׁלוּמֵי אַרְבָּעָה וַחֲמִשָּׁה נוֹהֶגֶת אֶלָּא בְּשׁוֹר וָשֶׂה בִּלְבַד:
כב א אִם בַּמַּחְתֶּרֶת. כְּשֶׁהָיָה חוֹתֵר אֶת הַבַּיִת:

22:1 **אִם־בַּמַּחְתֶּרֶת יִמָּצֵא הַגַּנָּב** *If a burglar is caught tunneling in* – Where the Ten Commandments presented us with moral absolutes: "Do not murder," we now begin to deal with situations of moral complexity. Self-defense, we see here, is permitted in Jewish law (Sanhedrin 72a). Yet the rules of defense and self-defense are not an open-ended permission to kill. We recall Yaakov's emotional state as he prepared for the possibility of a fight with his brother Esav in Parashat

2 account. But if the sun has risen on him, there is bloodguilt on his account. A
thief must make restitution; if he lacks the means, he shall be sold as a slave
3 to repay his debt. If what he stole – an ox, ass, or sheep – is found alive in
4 his possession, he shall pay double. If a person lets a field or vineyard SHISHI
be damaged, either by letting his livestock loose or by letting them graze in
5 someone else's field, he must repay the best of his field or vineyard. If
a fire is started and spreads to thorns, so that grain is destroyed, stacked or
standing or growing in the field, the person who started the fire must redress
6 the damage. If one person entrusts another with money or goods, and
they are stolen from his house, then if the thief is found he must pay double.
7 If the thief is not found, then the owner of the house must swear before the
8 court that he has not laid hands on his neighbor's goods himself. In every case
of betrayal of trust, whether concerning an ox, donkey or sheep, clothing, or
any loss that one can point to and say, 'This is it,' – both parties' claims shall
be brought to the court. The one the court finds guilty shall pay the other

רש״י

אֵין לוֹ דָּמִים. אֵין זוֹ רְצִיחָה, הֲרֵי הוּא כְּמֵת מֵעִקָּרוֹ. כָּאן לִמְּדַתְךָ תּוֹרָה: אִם בָּא לְהָרְגְךָ הַשְׁכֵּם לְהָרְגוֹ, וְזֶה לַהֲרָגְךָ בָּא, שֶׁהֲרֵי יוֹדֵעַ הוּא שֶׁאֵין אָדָם מַעֲמִיד עַצְמוֹ וְרוֹאֶה שֶׁנּוֹטְלִין מָמוֹנוֹ בְּפָנָיו וְשׁוֹתֵק, לְפִיכָךְ עַל מְנָת כֵּן בָּא שֶׁאִם יַעֲמֹד בַּעַל הַמָּמוֹן כְּנֶגְדּוֹ יַהַרְגֶנּוּ:

ב **אִם זָרְחָה הַשֶּׁמֶשׁ עָלָיו.** אֵין זֶה אֶלָּא כְּמִין מָשָׁל, אִם בָּרוּר לְךָ הַדָּבָר שֶׁיֵּשׁ לוֹ שָׁלוֹם עִמְּךָ, כַּשֶּׁמֶשׁ הַזֶּה שֶׁהוּא שָׁלוֹם בָּעוֹלָם כָּךְ פָּשׁוּט לְךָ שֶׁאֵינוֹ בָּא לַהֲרֹג אֲפִלּוּ יַעֲמֹד בַּעַל הַמָּמוֹן כְּנֶגְדּוֹ, כְּגוֹן אָב הַחוֹתֵר לִגְנֹב מָמוֹן הַבֵּן, בְּיָדוּעַ שֶׁרַחֲמֵי הָאָב עַל הַבֵּן וְאֵינוֹ בָּא עַל עִסְקֵי נְפָשׁוֹת: **דָּמִים לוֹ.** כְּחַי הוּא חָשׁוּב, וּרְצִיחָה הִיא אִם יַהַרְגֶנּוּ בַּעַל הַבַּיִת: **שַׁלֵּם יְשַׁלֵּם.** הַגַּנָּב מָמוֹן שֶׁגָּנַב וְאֵינוֹ חַיָּב מִיתָה. וְאוּנְקְלוֹס שֶׁתִּרְגֵּם: "אִם עֵינָא דְסָהֲדַיָּא נְפַלַת עֲלוֹהִי" לָקַח לוֹ שִׁטָּה אַחֶרֶת, לוֹמַר שֶׁאִם מְצָאוּהוּ עֵדִים קֹדֶם שֶׁבָּא בַּעַל הַבַּיִת וּכְשֶׁבָּא בַּעַל הַבַּיִת נֶגְדּוֹ הִתְרוּ בוֹ שֶׁלֹּא יַהַרְגֵהוּ, "דָּמִים לוֹ", חַיָּב עָלָיו אִם הֲרָגוֹ, שֶׁמֵּאַחַר שֶׁיֵּשׁ רוֹאִים לָהֶם אֵין הַגַּנָּב הַזֶּה בָּא עַל עִסְקֵי נְפָשׁוֹת, וְלֹא יַהֲרֹג אֶת בַּעַל הַמָּמוֹן:

ג **אִם הִמָּצֵא תִמָּצֵא בְיָדוֹ.** בִּרְשׁוּתוֹ, שֶׁלֹּא טָבַח וְלֹא מָכַר: **מִשּׁוֹר עַד חֲמוֹר.** כָּל דָּבָר בִּכְלַל תַּשְׁלוּמֵי כֶפֶל, בֵּין שֶׁיֵּשׁ בּוֹ רוּחַ חַיִּים בֵּין שֶׁאֵין בּוֹ רוּחַ חַיִּים, שֶׁהֲרֵי נֶאֱמַר מִקְרָא אַחֵר: "עַל שֶׂה עַל שַׂלְמָה עַל כָּל אֲבֵדָה וְגוֹ' יְשַׁלֵּם שְׁנַיִם לְרֵעֵהוּ" (להלן פסוק ח): **חַיִּים שְׁנַיִם יְשַׁלֵּם.** וְלֹא יְשַׁלֵּם לוֹ מֵתִים, אֶלָּא חַיִּים אוֹ דְּמֵי חַיִּים:

ד **כִּי יַבְעֶר... אֶת בְּעִירֹה וּבִעֵר.** כֻּלָּם לְשׁוֹן בְּהֵמָה, כְּמוֹ: "אֲנַחְנוּ וּבְעִירֵנוּ" (במדבר כ, ד): **כִּי יַבְעֶר.** יוֹלִיךְ בְּהֵמוֹתָיו בְּשָׂדֶה וְכֶרֶם שֶׁל חֲבֵרוֹ וְיַזִּיק אוֹתָהּ בְּאַחַת מִשְּׁתֵּי אֵלּוּ: אוֹ בְּשִׁלּוּחַ בְּעִירֹה אוֹ בְּבִעוּר. וּפֵרְשׁוּ רַבּוֹתֵינוּ: 'שִׁלּוּחַ' הוּא נִזְקֵי מִדְרַךְ כַּף רֶגֶל, "וּבִעֵר" הוּא נִזְקֵי הַשֵּׁן הָאוֹכֶלֶת וּמְבַעֶרֶת: **בִּשְׂדֵה אַחֵר.** בְּשָׂדֶה שֶׁל אִישׁ אַחֵר: **מֵיטַב שָׂדֵהוּ... יְשַׁלֵּם.** שָׁמִין אֶת הַנֶּזֶק, וְאִם בָּא לְשַׁלֵּם לוֹ קַרְקַע דְּמֵי נִזְקוֹ יְשַׁלֵּם לוֹ מִמֵּיטַב שְׂדוֹתָיו, אִם הָיָה נִזְקוֹ סֶלַע יִתֵּן לוֹ שָׁוֶה סֶלַע מֵעִדִּית שֶׁיֵּשׁ לוֹ. לִמֶּדְךָ הַכָּתוּב שֶׁהַנִּזָּקִין שָׁמִין לָהֶם בְּעִדִּית:

ה **כִּי תֵצֵא אֵשׁ.** אֲפִלּוּ מֵעַצְמָהּ: **וּמָצְאָה קֹצִים.** קרדונ"ש בְּלַעַז: **וְנֶאֱכַל גָּדִישׁ.** שֶׁלִּחֲכָה בַּקּוֹצִים עַד שֶׁהִגִּיעָה לַגָּדִישׁ אוֹ לַקָּמָה הַמְחֻבֶּרֶת לַקַּרְקַע: **אוֹ הַשָּׂדֶה.** שֶׁלִּחֲכָה אֶת נִירוֹ וְצָרִיךְ לָנִיר אוֹתָהּ פַּעַם שְׁנִיָּה: **שַׁלֵּם יְשַׁלֵּם הַמַּבְעִר.** אַף עַל פִּי שֶׁהִדְלִיק בְּתוֹךְ שֶׁלּוֹ וְהִיא יָצְאָה מֵעַצְמָהּ עַל יְדֵי קוֹצִים שֶׁמָּצְאָה, חַיָּב לְשַׁלֵּם, לְפִי שֶׁלֹּא שָׁמַר אֶת גַּחַלְתּוֹ שֶׁלֹּא תֵצֵא וְתַזִּיק:

ו **וְגֻנַּב מִבֵּית הָאִישׁ.** לְפִי דְבָרָיו: **אִם יִמָּצֵא הַגַּנָּב.** יְשַׁלֵּם הַגַּנָּב שְׁנַיִם לַבְּעָלִים:

ז **אִם לֹא יִמָּצֵא הַגַּנָּב.** וּבָא הַשּׁוֹמֵר הַזֶּה שֶׁהוּא בַּעַל הַבַּיִת: **וְנִקְרַב.** אֶל הַדַּיָּנִין לָדוּן עִם זֶה וּלְהִשָּׁבַע לוֹ שֶׁלֹּא שָׁלַח יָדוֹ בְּשֶׁלּוֹ:

ח **עַל כָּל דְּבַר פֶּשַׁע.** שֶׁיִּמָּצֵא שַׁקְרָן בִּשְׁבוּעָתוֹ, שֶׁיָּעִידוּ עֵדִים שֶׁהוּא עַצְמוֹ גְּנָבוֹ, וְיַרְשִׁיעוּהוּ אֱלֹהִים עַל פִּי הָעֵדִים: **יְשַׁלֵּם שְׁנַיִם לְרֵעֵהוּ.** לִמֶּדְךָ הַכָּתוּב שֶׁהַטּוֹעֵן בְּפִקָּדוֹן לוֹמַר נִגְנַב הֵימֶנּוּ, וְנִמְצָא שֶׁהוּא עַצְמוֹ גְּנָבוֹ, מְשַׁלֵּם תַּשְׁלוּמֵי כֶפֶל. וְאֵימָתַי? בִּזְמַן שֶׁנִּשְׁבַּע וְאַחַר כָּךְ

ב אֵין לוֹ דָּמִים: אִם־זָרְחָה הַשֶּׁמֶשׁ עָלָיו דָּמִים לוֹ שַׁלֵּם יְשַׁלֵּם אִם־אֵין
ג לוֹ וְנִמְכַּר בִּגְנֵבָתוֹ: אִם־הִמָּצֵא תִמָּצֵא בְיָדוֹ הַגְּנֵבָה מִשּׁוֹר עַד־חֲמוֹר
ד עַד־שֶׂה חַיִּים שְׁנַיִם יְשַׁלֵּם: כִּי יַבְעֶר־אִישׁ שָׂדֶה אוֹ־כֶרֶם שלישי
וְשִׁלַּח אֶת־בְּעִירֹה וּבִעֵר בִּשְׂדֵה אַחֵר מֵיטַב שָׂדֵהוּ וּמֵיטַב כַּרְמוֹ
ה יְשַׁלֵּם: כִּי־תֵצֵא אֵשׁ וּמָצְאָה קֹצִים וְנֶאֱכַל גָּדִישׁ אוֹ הַקָּמָה
ו אוֹ הַשָּׂדֶה שַׁלֵּם יְשַׁלֵּם הַמַּבְעִר אֶת־הַבְּעֵרָה: כִּי־יִתֵּן אִישׁ
אֶל־רֵעֵהוּ כֶּסֶף אוֹ־כֵלִים לִשְׁמֹר וְגֻנַּב מִבֵּית הָאִישׁ אִם־יִמָּצֵא הַגַּנָּב
ז יְשַׁלֵּם שְׁנָיִם: אִם־לֹא יִמָּצֵא הַגַּנָּב וְנִקְרַב בַּעַל־הַבַּיִת אֶל־הָאֱלֹהִים
ח אִם־לֹא שָׁלַח יָדוֹ בִּמְלֶאכֶת רֵעֵהוּ: עַל־כָּל־דְּבַר־פֶּשַׁע עַל־שׁוֹר עַל־
חֲמוֹר עַל־שֶׂה עַל־שַׂלְמָה עַל־כָּל־אֲבֵדָה אֲשֶׁר יֹאמַר כִּי־הוּא זֶה

אונקלוס

לֵית לֵיהּ דַּם: ב אִם עֵינָא דְסָהֲדַיָּא, נְפַלַת עֲלוֹהִי דְּמָא לֵיהּ, שַׁלָּמָא יְשַׁלֵּים, אִם לֵית לֵיהּ, וְיִזְדַּבַּן בִּגְנֻבְתֵּיהּ: ג אִם אִשְׁתְּכָחָא תִשְׁתְּכַח בִּידֵיהּ גְּנֻבְתָּא, מִתּוֹר עַד חֲמָר, עַד אִמַּר אִנּוּן חַיִּין, עַל חַד תְּרֵין יְשַׁלֵּים: ד אֲרֵי יוֹכֵיל גְּבַר חֲקַל אוֹ כְרַם, וִישַׁלַּח יָת בְּעִירֵיהּ, וְיֵיכוֹל בַּחֲקַל אָחֳרָן, שְׁפַר חַקְלֵיהּ, וּשְׁפַר כַּרְמֵיהּ יְשַׁלֵּים: ה אֲרֵי יִתַּפַּק נוּר, וְיַשְׁכַּח כֻּבִּין וְיֵיכוֹל גְּדִישִׁין, אוֹ קָמָא אוֹ חֲקַל, שַׁלָּמָא יְשַׁלֵּים, דְּאַדְלֵיק יָת דְּלֵיקְתָא: ו אֲרֵי יִתֵּין גְּבַר לְחַבְרֵיהּ, כְּסַף אוֹ מָנִין לְמִטַּר, וְיִתְגַּנְבוּן מִבֵּית גַּבְרָא, אִם יִשְׁתְּכַח גַּנָּבָא יְשַׁלֵּים עַל חַד תְּרֵין: ז אִם לָא יִשְׁתְּכַח גַּנָּבָא, וְיִתְקָרַב מָרֵיהּ דְּבֵיתָא לִקֳדָם דַּיָּנַיָּא, אִם לָא אוֹשֵׁיט, יְדֵיהּ בְּמָא דִּמְסַר לֵיהּ חַבְרֵיהּ: ח עַל כָּל פִּתְגָּם דְּחוֹב, עַל תּוֹר, עַל חֲמָר, עַל אִמַּר עַל כְּסוּ עַל כָּל אֲבֵידְתָא, דְּיֵימַר אֲרֵי הוּא דֵין,

רש״י

אֵלּוּ עֵדִים, שֶׁכָּךְ דָּרְשׁוּ רַבּוֹתֵינוּ: "וְנִקְרַב בַּעַל הַבַּיִת אֶל הָאֱלֹהִים", קְרִיבָה זוֹ שְׁבוּעָה הִיא. אַתָּה אוֹמֵר לִשְׁבוּעָה אוֹ אֵינוֹ אֶלָּא לְדִין, שֶׁכֵּיוָן שֶׁבָּא לַדִּין וְכָפַר לוֹמַר נִגְנְבָה, מִיָּד יִתְחַיֵּב כֶּפֶל אִם בָּאוּ עֵדִים שֶׁהוּא בְיָדוֹ? נֶאֱמַר כָּאן שְׁלִיחוּת יָד וְנֶאֱמַר לְמַטָּה שְׁלִיחוּת יָד: "שְׁבֻעַת ה' תִּהְיֶה בֵּין שְׁנֵיהֶם אִם לֹא שָׁלַח יָדוֹ" (להלן פסוק י), מַה לְּהַלָּן שְׁבוּעָה אַף כָּאן שְׁבוּעָה: **אֲשֶׁר יֹאמַר כִּי הוּא זֶה.** לְפִי פְשׁוּטוֹ, אֲשֶׁר יֹאמַר הָעֵד: "כִּי הוּא זֶה" שֶׁנִּשְׁבַּעְתָּ עָלָיו הֲרֵי הוּא אֶצְלְךָ, עַד הַדַּיָּנִין "יָבֹא דְּבַר שְׁנֵיהֶם" וְיַחְקְרוּ אֶת הָעֵדוּת, וְאִם כְּשֵׁרִים הֵם וְהִרְשִׁיעוּהוּ לְשׁוֹמֵר

Vayishlaḥ (Gen. 32:7): In the words of the Midrash, "He was 'acutely afraid' that he might be killed; he was 'distressed' that he might kill" (Rashi on Bereshit Rabba 76:2).

If Esav were to try to kill Yaakov, Yaakov would be justified in fighting back, if necessary at the cost of Esav's life. Why then should this possibility raise moral qualms? The principle at stake, according to the *Siftei Ḥakhamim*, is the minimum use of force. Yaakov was distressed at the possibility that in the heat of conflict he might kill some of the combatants when injury alone might have been all that was necessary to defend the lives of those – including himself – who were under attack. Even the heroes of the Tanakh struggle with situations of moral uncertainty. But halakha is here beginning to give us a framework through which to examine and refine our moral choices.

9 double. If one person entrusts another with a donkey, ox, sheep, or
any animal, for safekeeping, and it dies or is injured or is carried away unseen,
10 an oath before the LORD shall settle between them; if the second man swears
that he did not lay his hands on his charge, then the owner must accept this,
11 and no restitution need be made. But if the charge was stolen from him, he
12 must make restitution to the owner. If it was torn by a wild animal and the
second man brings the remains as evidence, he need not make good the loss.
13 If one person borrows a creature from his neighbor, and it is injured or dies
14 while the owner is not there, he must make restitution. But if the owner was
present, he need not make restitution; if the animal was hired, only the hiring
15 fee is due. If a man seduces a virgin who is not betrothed, and lies with
16 her, he must pay her bride price and marry her. If her father refuses to let him
17 marry her, he must still pay out the full bride price for virgins. Do not
18 allow a witch to live. And any person who lies with an animal shall be put to
19 death. Whoever sacrifices to any other deity shall be utterly destroyed.

רש״י

זה – "ישלם שנים", ואם ירשיעו את העדים שנמצאו זוממין, ישלמו הם שנים לשומר. ורבותינו זכרונם לברכה דרשו: "כי הוא זה" ללמד שאין מחייבין אותו שבועה אלא אם כן הודה במקצת, לומר: כך וכך אני חייב לך והמותר נגנב ממני:

ט–י **כי יתן איש אל רעהו חמור או שור.** פרשה ראשונה נאמרה בשומר חנם, לפיכך פטר בו את הגנבה, כמו שכתוב: "וגנב מבית האיש... אם לא ימצא הגנב ונקרב בעל הבית" (לעיל פסוקים ו–ז) לשבועה, למדת שפוטר עצמו בשבועה זו; ופרשה זו אמורה בשומר שכר, לפיכך אינו פטור אם נגנבה, כמו שכתוב: "אם גנב יגנב מעמו ישלם" (להלן פסוק יא). אבל על האנס, כמו "מת" מעצמו "או נשבר או נשבה" בחזקה על ידי לסטים, ו"אין ראה" שיעיד בדבר – "שבעת ה' תהיה", ישבע שכן הוא כדבריו, והוא לא שלח בה יד להשתמש בה לעצמו, שאם שלח בה יד ואחר כך נאנסה חייב באנסיה: **ולקח בעליו.** השבועה: **ולא ישלם.** לו השומר כלום:

יב **אם טרף יטרף.** על ידי חיה רעה: **יבאהו עד.** יביא עדים שנטרפה באנס ופטור: **הטרפה לא ישלם.** אינו אומר 'טרפה לא ישלם' אלא "הטרפה", יש טרפה שהוא משלם ויש טרפה שאינו משלם: טרפת חתול ושועל ונמיה משלם; טרפת זאב ארי ודב ונחש אינו משלם. ומי לחשך לדון כן? שהרי כתוב: "ומת או נשבר או נשבה", מה מיתה שאין יכול להציל, אף שבר ושביה שאין יכול להציל:

יג **וכי ישאל.** בא ללמד על השואל שחייב באנסין: **בעליו אין עמו.** אם בעליו של שור אינו עם השואל במלאכתו:

יד **אם בעליו עמו.** בין שהוא באותה מלאכה בין שהוא במלאכה אחרת. היה עמו בשעת שאלה אינו צריך להיות עמו בשעת שבירה ומיתה: **אם שכיר הוא.** אם השור אינו שאול אלא שכור, "בא בשכרו" ליד השוכר הזה ולא בשאלה, ואין כל הנאה שלו שהרי על ידי שכרו נשתמש, ואין לו משפט שואל להתחייב באנסין. ולא פרש מה דינו אם כשומר חנם או כשומר שכר, לפיכך נחלקו בו חכמי ישראל: שוכר כיצד משלם? רבי מאיר אומר: כשומר חנם, רבי יהודה אומר: כשומר שכר:

טו **וכי יפתה.** מדבר על לבה עד ששומעת לו, וכן תרגומו: "וארי ישדל". שדול בלשון ארמי כפתוי בלשון עברי: **מהר ימהרנה.** יפסק לה מהר כמשפט איש לאשתו, שכותב לה כתבה וישאנה:

טז **כמהר הבתולות.** שהוא קצוב חמשים כסף אצל התופס את הבתולה ושוכב עמה באנס, שנאמר: "ונתן האיש השכב עמה לאבי הנער חמשים כסף" (דברים כב, כט):

יז **מכשפה לא תחיה.** אלא תומת בבית דין. ואחד זכרים ואחד נקבות, אלא שדבר הכתוב בהוה, שהנשים מצויות בכשפים:

יח **כל שכב עם בהמה מות יומת.** בסקילה, רובע כנרבעת, שכתוב בהם: "דמיהם בם" (ויקרא כ, טז):

יט **לאלהים.** לעבודה זרה. אלו היה נקוד 'לאלהים', היה צריך לפרש ולכתב 'אחרים', עכשיו שאמר: "לאלהים" אין צריך לפרש 'אחרים'; שכל למ"ד ובי"ת המשמשת בראש התבה, אם נקודה

עַד הָאֱלֹהִים יָבֹא דְּבַר־שְׁנֵיהֶם אֲשֶׁר יַרְשִׁיעֻן אֱלֹהִים יְשַׁלֵּם שְׁנַיִם
ט לְרֵעֵהוּ׃ כִּי־יִתֵּן אִישׁ אֶל־רֵעֵהוּ חֲמוֹר אוֹ־שׁוֹר אוֹ־שֶׂה
י וְכָל־בְּהֵמָה לִשְׁמֹר וּמֵת אוֹ־נִשְׁבַּר אוֹ־נִשְׁבָּה אֵין רֹאֶה׃ שְׁבֻעַת יהוה
תִּהְיֶה בֵּין שְׁנֵיהֶם אִם־לֹא שָׁלַח יָדוֹ בִּמְלֶאכֶת רֵעֵהוּ וְלָקַח בְּעָלָיו וְלֹא
יא יב יְשַׁלֵּם׃ וְאִם־גָּנֹב יִגָּנֵב מֵעִמּוֹ יְשַׁלֵּם לִבְעָלָיו׃ אִם־טָרֹף יִטָּרֵף יְבִאֵהוּ
עֵד הַטְּרֵפָה לֹא יְשַׁלֵּם׃
יג וְכִי־יִשְׁאַל אִישׁ מֵעִם רֵעֵהוּ וְנִשְׁבַּר אוֹ־מֵת בְּעָלָיו אֵין־עִמּוֹ שַׁלֵּם יְשַׁלֵּם׃
יד טו אִם־בְּעָלָיו עִמּוֹ לֹא יְשַׁלֵּם אִם־שָׂכִיר הוּא בָּא בִּשְׂכָרוֹ׃ וְכִי־
יְפַתֶּה אִישׁ בְּתוּלָה אֲשֶׁר לֹא־אֹרָשָׂה וְשָׁכַב עִמָּהּ מָהֹר יִמְהָרֶנָּה
טז לּוֹ לְאִשָּׁה׃ אִם־מָאֵן יְמָאֵן אָבִיהָ לְתִתָּהּ לוֹ כֶּסֶף יִשְׁקֹל כְּמֹהַר
יז יח הַבְּתוּלֹת׃ מְכַשֵּׁפָה לֹא תְחַיֶּה׃ כָּל־שֹׁכֵב עִם־בְּהֵמָה
יט מוֹת יוּמָת׃ זֹבֵחַ לָאֱלֹהִים יָחֳרָם בִּלְתִּי לַיהוה לְבַדּוֹ׃

אונקלוס

לְקֳדָם דַּיָּנַיָּא, יֵיעוֹל דִּין תַּרְוֵיהוֹן, דִּיחַיְּבוּן דַּיָּנַיָּא, יְשַׁלֵּים עַל חַד תְּרֵין לְחַבְרֵיהּ: ט אֲרֵי יִתֵּין גְּבַר לְחַבְרֵיהּ, חֲמָר אוֹ תוֹר אוֹ אִמַּר, וְכָל בְּעִירָא לְמִטַּר, וּמִית, אוֹ אִתְּבַר אוֹ אִשְׁתְּבִי לֵית דְּחָזֵי: י מוֹמָתָא דַּיְיָ, תְּהֵי בֵּין תַּרְוֵיהוֹן, אִם לָא אוֹשֵׁיט, יְדֵיהּ בְּמָא דִּמְסַר לֵיהּ חַבְרֵיהּ, וִיקַבֵּיל מָרֵיהּ מִנֵּיהּ מוֹמָתָא וְלָא יְשַׁלֵּים: יא וְאִם אִתְגְּנָבָא יִתְגְּנֵיב מֵעִמֵּיהּ, יְשַׁלֵּים לְמָרוֹהִי: יב אִם אִתְבְּרָא יִתְבַּר יַיְתֵי סָהֲדִין, דִּתְבִיר לָא יְשַׁלֵּים: יג וַאֲרֵי יִשְׁאַל גְּבַר, מִן חַבְרֵיהּ וְיִתְּבַר אוֹ יְמוּת, מָרֵיהּ לֵית עִמֵּיהּ שַׁלָּמָא יְשַׁלֵּים: יד אִם מָרֵיהּ עִמֵּיהּ לָא יְשַׁלֵּים, אִם אֲגִירָא הוּא, עָאל בַּאֲגָרֵיהּ: טו וַאֲרֵי יְשַׁדֵּיל גְּבַר, בְּתוּלְתָא, דְּלָא מְאָרְסָא וְיִשְׁכּוֹב עִמַּהּ, קַיָּמָא, יְקַיְּמִנַּהּ לֵיהּ לְאִתּוּ: טז אִם מִצְבָּא לָא יִצְבֵּי, אֲבוּהָא לְמִתְּנַהּ לֵיהּ, כַּסְפָּא יִתְקוֹל, כְּמֹהַר בְּתוּלָתָא: יז חָרָשָׁא לָא תַחֵי: יח כָּל דְּיִשְׁכּוֹב עִם בְּעִירָא אִתְקְטָלָא יִתְקְטִיל: יט דִּידַבַּח לְטָעֲוַת עַמְמַיָּא יִתְקְטִיל, אֱלָהֵין לִשְׁמָא דַּיְיָ בִּלְחוֹדוֹהִי:

רש"י

כַּחֲטַף, כְּגוֹן: לְמֶלֶךְ, לְמִדְבָּר, לְעִיר, צָרִיךְ לְפָרֵשׁ לְאֵיזֶה מֶלֶךְ, לְאֵיזֶה מִדְבָּר, לְאֵיזֶה עִיר. וְכֵן: לִמְלָכִים, לִרְגָלִים צָרִיךְ לְפָרֵשׁ לְאֵיזֶה, וְאִם אֵינוֹ מְפָרֵשׁ, כָּל מְלָכִים בַּמַּשְׁמָע. וְכֵן 'לֵאלֹהִים' כָּל אֱלֹהִים בַּמַּשְׁמָע, אֲפִלּוּ קֹדֶשׁ. אֲבָל כְּשֶׁהִיא נְקוּדָה פַּתָּח, כְּמוֹ: לַמֶּלֶךְ, לַמִּדְבָּר, לָעִיר, נוֹדַע בְּאֵיזֶה מֶלֶךְ מְדַבֵּר, וְכֵן 'לָעִיר' נוֹדַע בְּאֵיזֶה עִיר מְדַבֵּר, וְכֵן "לָאֱלֹהִים", לְאוֹתָן שֶׁהִזְהַרְתִּים עֲלֵיהֶם בְּמָקוֹם אַחֵר. כַּיּוֹצֵא בוֹ: "אֵין כָּמוֹךָ בָאֱלֹהִים" (תהלים פו, ח), לְפִי שֶׁלֹּא פֵּרֵשׁ הֶעָרֵךְ לִנָּקֵד פַּתָּח: יָחֳרָם. יוּמָת. וְלָמָּה נֶאֱמַר "יָחֳרָם"? וַהֲלֹא כְּבָר נֶאֶמְרָה בוֹ מִיתָה בְּמָקוֹם אַחֵר: "וְהוֹצֵאתָ אֶת הָאִישׁ הַהוּא אוֹ אֶת הָאִשָּׁה הַהִוא" וְגוֹ' (דברים יז, ה), אֶלָּא לְפִי שֶׁלֹּא פֵּרֵשׁ עַל אֵיזוֹ עֲבוֹדָה חַיָּב מִיתָה, שֶׁלֹּא תֹּאמַר כָּל עֲבוֹדוֹת בְּמִיתָה, בָּא וּפֵרֵשׁ לְךָ כָּאן: "זֹבֵחַ לָאֱלֹהִים", מַה זְּבִיחָה עֲבוֹדָה הַנַּעֲשֵׂית בִּפְנִים לַשָּׁמַיִם, אַף אֲנִי מַרְבֶּה הַמְקַטֵּר וְהַמְנַסֵּךְ שֶׁהֵן עֲבוֹדָה בִּפְנִים, וְחַיָּבִים עֲלֵיהֶם לְכָל עֲבוֹדָה זָרָה, בֵּין שֶׁדַּרְכָּהּ לְעָבְדָהּ בְּכָךְ בֵּין שֶׁאֵין דַּרְכָּהּ לְעָבְדָהּ בְּכָךְ. אֲבָל שְׁאָר עֲבוֹדוֹת, כְּגוֹן: הַמְכַבֵּד וְהַמְרַבֵּץ וְהַמְגַפֵּף וְהַמְנַשֵּׁק, אֵינָן בְּמִיתָה:

20 Do not oppress a stranger or exploit him, for you yourselves were strangers in
21 22 the land of Egypt. Do not abuse a widow or an orphan. For if you do abuse
23 them, if they cry out to Me, I will unquestionably heed their cry. My anger will
flare and I will kill you by the sword – and then your wives will be widows and
your children orphans.
24 If you lend money to one of My people who is poor, do not act with him as
25 a harsh creditor, and do not charge him interest. If you take your neighbor's
26 garment as collateral, return it to him before the sun sets, because it is his only
clothing, the sole covering for his skin. What else does he have in which to

רש"י

כ) **וגר לא תונה.** אונאת דברים, קונטרליאי"ר בלעז, כמו: "והאכלתי את מוניך את בשרם" (ישעיה מט, כו): **ולא תלחצנו.** בגזלת ממון: **כי גרים הייתם.** אם הוניתו אף הוא יכול להונותך ולומר לך: אף אתה מגרים באת. מום שבך אל תאמר לחברך. כל לשון 'גר' אדם שלא נולד באותה מדינה, אלא בא ממדינה אחרת לגור שם:

כא) **כל אלמנה ויתום לא תענון.** הוא הדין לכל אדם, אלא שדבר הכתוב בהוה, לפי שהם תשושי כח ודבר מצוי לענותם:

כב) **אם ענה תענה אתו.** הרי זה מקרא קצר. גזם ולא פירש ענשו, כמו: "לכן כל הרג קין" (בראשית ד, טו), ולא פירש ענשו. אף כאן: "אם ענה תענה אתו" לשון גזום, כלומר, סופך לטול את שלך, למה? "כי אם צעק יצעק אלי" וגו':

כג) **והיו נשיכם אלמנות.** ממשמע שנאמר: "והרגתי אתכם" איני יודע ש"נשיכם אלמנות ובניכם יתומים"? אלא הרי זו קללה אחרת, שיהיו הנשים צרורות כאלמנות חיות, שלא יהיו עדים למיתת בעליהן ותהיינה אסורות להנשא, והבנים יהיו יתומים, שלא יניחום בית דין לירד לנכסי אביהם, לפי שאין יודעים אם מתו אם נשבו:

כד) **אם כסף תלוה את עמי.** רבי ישמעאל אומר: כל אם ואם שבתורה רשות חוץ משלשה, וזה אחד מהן: **את עמי.** עמי וגוי, עמי קודם. עני ועשיר, עני קודם. עניי עירך ועניי עיר אחרת, עניי עירך קודמין. וזה משמעו: "אם כסף תלוה, את עמי" תלוהו, ולא לגוי. ולאיזה מעמי? "את העני". ולאיזה עני? לאותו ש"עמך". דבר אחר "את עמי", שלא תנהג בו מנהג בזיון בהלואה, שהוא עמי: **את העני עמך.** הוי מסתכל בעצמך כאלו אתה עני: **לא תהיה לו כנשה.** לא תתבענו בחזקה. אם אתה יודע שאין לו, אל תהי דומה עליו כאלו הלויתו אלא כאלו לא הלויתו, כלומר לא תכלימהו: **נשך.** רבית, שהוא כנשיכת נחש, שנושך חבורה קטנה ברגלו ואינו מרגיש, ופתאם הוא מבצבץ ונופח עד קדקדו, כך רבית אינו מרגיש ואינו נכר, עד שהרבית עולה ומחסרו ממון הרבה:

כה) **אם חבל תחבל.** כל לשון חבלה אינו משכון בשעת הלואה, אלא שממשכנין את הלוה כשמגיע הזמן ואינו פורע. "חבל תחבל", כפל לך בחבלה עד כמה פעמים, אמר הקדוש ברוך הוא, כמה אתה חיב לי, והרי נפשך עולה אצלי בכל לילה ולילה נותנת דין וחשבון ומתחיבת לפני ואני מחזירה לך, אף אתה טול והשב טול והשב: **עד בא השמש תשיבנו לו.** כל היום תשיבנו לו עד בא השמש, וכבוא השמש תחזור ותטלנו עד שיבא בקר של מחר. ובכסות יום הכתוב מדבר, שאין צריך לה בלילה:

כו) **כי הוא כסותה.** זו טלית: **שמלתו.** זו חלוק: **במה ישכב.** לרבות את המצע:

is presented as the basis of both justice and compassion in the great social legislation of these verses.

In Judaism, we believe we connect to God in three different ways: creation, revelation, redemption. To see the beauty of creation is one way God speaks to us. When we sit and learn Torah, especially when we sit and learn Torah together, we are hearing God's word. When we look at how Rashi refracted that word – and Ramban, and Rashbam, and Ibn Ezra – we are hearing that several-thousand-year-old conversation between heaven and earth that we call the Written Torah and the Oral Torah. And when we become part of that conversation we see God in revelation.

But there is a third way: redemption. When we hear the cry of a child or the cry of a person dying of hunger, we are hearing God calling to us to be His partner in the work of redemption. This is encountering God in a different way, one that is much more active than in creation and revelation, but one where we feel we are partners with God in making

כ כא וְגֵר לֹא־תוֹנֶה וְלֹא תִלְחָצֶנּוּ כִּי־גֵרִים הֱיִיתֶם בְּאֶרֶץ מִצְרָיִם: כָּל־
כב אַלְמָנָה וְיָתוֹם לֹא תְעַנּוּן: אִם־עַנֵּה תְעַנֶּה אֹתוֹ כִּי אִם־צָעֹק יִצְעַק
כג אֵלַי שָׁמֹעַ אֶשְׁמַע צַעֲקָתוֹ: וְחָרָה אַפִּי וְהָרַגְתִּי אֶתְכֶם בֶּחָרֶב וְהָיוּ
נְשֵׁיכֶם אַלְמָנוֹת וּבְנֵיכֶם יְתֹמִים:
כד אִם־כֶּסֶף ׀ תַּלְוֶה אֶת־עַמִּי אֶת־הֶעָנִי עִמָּךְ לֹא־תִהְיֶה לוֹ כְּנֹשֶׁה לֹא־ יז
כה תְשִׂימוּן עָלָיו נֶשֶׁךְ: אִם־חָבֹל תַּחְבֹּל שַׂלְמַת רֵעֶךָ עַד־בֹּא הַשֶּׁמֶשׁ
כו תְּשִׁיבֶנּוּ לוֹ: כִּי הִוא כְסוּתֹה לְבַדָּהּ הִוא שִׂמְלָתוֹ לְעֹרוֹ בַּמֶּה יִשְׁכָּב

אונקלוס

כ וּלְגִיּוֹרָא לָא תוֹנוֹן וְלָא תְעִיקוּן, אֲרֵי דַיָּרִין הֲוֵיתוֹן בְּאַרְעָא דְמִצְרָיִם: כא כָּל אַרְמְלָא וְיִיתַם לָא תְעַנּוֹן: כב אִם עַנָּאָה תְעַנֵּי יָתֵיהּ, אֲרֵי אִם מִקְבַּל יִקְבַּל קֳדָמַי, קַבָּלָא אֲקַבֵּיל קְבִילְתֵיהּ: כג וְיִתְקַף רֻגְזִי, וְאֶקְטוֹל יָתְכוֹן בְּחַרְבָּא, וִיהֹוְיָן נְשֵׁיכוֹן אַרְמְלָן, וּבְנֵיכוֹן יַתְמִין: כד אִם כַּסְפָּא תוֹזֵיף בְּעַמִּי, לְעַנְיָא דְעִמָּךְ, לָא תְהֵי לֵיהּ כְּרָשְׁיָא, לָא תְשַׁווֹן עֲלוֹהִי חִיבְּלְיָא: כה אִם מִשְׁכּוֹנָא תִסַּב כְּסוּתָא דְחַבְרָךְ, עַד מֵיעַל שִׁמְשָׁא תְתִיבִנֵּיהּ לֵיהּ: כו אֲרֵי הִיא כְסוּתֵיהּ בִּלְחוֹדַהּ, הִיא תְּתֵבֵיהּ לְמַשְׁכְּבֵיהּ, בְּמָא יִשְׁכּוּב,

22:20 כִּי־גֵרִים הֱיִיתֶם בְּאֶרֶץ מִצְרָיִם *For you yourselves were strangers in the land of Egypt* – Mishpatim contains many laws of social justice – against taking advantage of a widow or orphan, for example, or taking interest on a loan to a fellow member of the covenantal community. The first and last of these laws, however, is the much-repeated command against harming a *ger*, a "stranger" or "migrant." Clearly something fundamental is at stake here.

According to R. Eliezer, the Torah "warns against the wronging of a *ger* in thirty-six places; others say, in forty-six places" (Bava Metzia 59b). Whatever the precise number, the repetition throughout the Mosaic books is remarkable. Sometimes the stranger is mentioned along with the poor; other times, with the widow and orphan. On several occasions the Torah specifies: "There shall be one law for you, for migrant and for native born alike" (Lev. 24:22; see also Ex. 12:49; Num. 15:16, 29). Not only must the stranger not be wronged; he or she must be included in the positive welfare provisions of Jewish society.

The Torah asks: why should you not hate the stranger? Because you once stood where he stands now. You know the heart of the stranger because you were once a stranger in the land of Egypt. If you are human, so is he. If he is less than human, so are you. You must fight the hatred in your heart, says God, as I once fought the greatest ruler and the strongest empire in the ancient world on your behalf. I made you into the world's archetypal strangers so that you would fight for the rights of strangers.

There is only one reply strong enough to answer the question "Why should I not hate the stranger?": Because the stranger is me.

22:24 אִם־כֶּסֶף תַּלְוֶה אֶת־עַמִּי אֶת־הֶעָנִי *If you lend money to one of My people who is poor* – According to Rashi, the Hebrew word *im*, which often means "if," should here be understood as "when." Helping the poor is not an option but an obligation. Society needs morality, a concern for the welfare of others, an active commitment to justice and compassion, a willingness to ask not just what is good for me, but what is good for all of us together.

22:26 וְשָׁמַעְתִּי *I will be listening* – The emphasis on listening lies at the heart of the unique intimacy Jews feel with God. In terms of power, there is no possible relationship between an infinite Creator and His finite creations. In terms of speech, there is. God's greatness is that He hears the unheard. Hearing

27 sleep? And if he cries out to Me, I will be listening: I am gracious. Do REVI'I
28 not curse a judge, and do not deride a leader of your people. Do not delay
offerings from your harvest of grain or wine. The firstborn of your sons you
29 must give to Me. Likewise with your oxen and sheep; let them stay with their
30 mothers for seven days, and on the eighth, give them over to Me. You are to
be My holy people. Do not eat flesh torn by beasts in the wild. Throw it to the
23 1 dogs. Do not accept a false report. Do not join with an unscrupulous
2 person to bear corrupt witness. Do not follow the crowd to do evil. When you
give testimony in a lawsuit, do not pervert justice by siding with the crowd.
3 4 Do not show favoritism even to a poor man in a dispute. If you come

רש״י

כז **אֱלֹהִים לֹא תְקַלֵּל.** הֲרֵי זוֹ אַזְהָרָה לְבִרְכַּת הַשֵּׁם, וְאַזְהָרָה לְקִלְלַת דַּיָּן:

כח **מְלֵאָתְךָ.** חוֹבָה הַמּוּטֶלֶת עָלֶיךָ כְּשֶׁתִּתְמַלֵּא תְּבוּאָתְךָ לְהִתְבַּשֵּׁל, וְהֵם בִּכּוּרִים: **וְדִמְעֲךָ.** הִיא תְרוּמָה, וְאֵינִי יוֹדֵעַ מַהוּ לְשׁוֹן דֶּמַע: **לֹא תְאַחֵר.** לֹא תְשַׁנֶּה סֵדֶר הַפְרָשָׁתָן לְאַחֵר אֶת הַמֻּקְדָּם וּלְהַקְדִּים אֶת הַמְאֻחָר, שֶׁלֹּא יַקְדִּים תְּרוּמָה לְבִכּוּרִים וּמַעֲשֵׂר לִתְרוּמָה: **בְּכוֹר בָּנֶיךָ תִּתֶּן לִי.** לִפְדּוֹתוֹ חָמֵשׁ סְלָעִים מִן הַכֹּהֵן. וַהֲלֹא כְּבָר צִוָּה עָלָיו בְּמָקוֹם אַחֵר (במדבר יח, טז)? אֶלָּא כְּדֵי לִסְמֹךְ לוֹ: "כֵּן תַּעֲשֶׂה לְשֹׁרְךָ", מַה בְּכוֹר אָדָם לְאַחַר שְׁלֹשִׁים יוֹם פּוֹדֵהוּ, שֶׁנֶּאֱמַר: "וּפְדוּיָו מִבֶּן חֹדֶשׁ תִּפְדֶּה" (שם), אַף בְּכוֹר בְּהֵמָה גַּסָּה מִטַּפֵּל בּוֹ שְׁלֹשִׁים יוֹם וְאַחַר כָּךְ נוֹתְנוֹ לַכֹּהֵן:

כט **שִׁבְעַת יָמִים יִהְיֶה עִם אִמּוֹ.** זוֹ אַזְהָרָה לַכֹּהֵן, שֶׁאִם בָּא לְמַהֵר הַקְרָבָתוֹ לֹא יְמַהֵר קֹדֶם שְׁמוֹנָה, לְפִי שֶׁהוּא מְחֻסַּר זְמַן: **בַּיּוֹם הַשְּׁמִינִי תִּתְּנוֹ לִי.** יָכוֹל יְהֵא חוֹבָה לְבוֹ בַּיּוֹם? נֶאֱמַר כָּאן: "שְׁמִינִי" וְנֶאֱמַר לְהַלָּן: "וּמִיּוֹם הַשְּׁמִינִי וָהָלְאָה יֵרָצֶה" (ויקרא כב, כז), מַה שְּׁמִינִי הָאָמוּר לְהַלָּן לְהַכְשִׁיר מִשְּׁמִינִי וּלְהַלָּן, אַף שְׁמִינִי הָאָמוּר כָּאן לְהַכְשִׁיר מִשְּׁמִינִי וּלְהַלָּן. וְכֵן מַשְׁמָעוֹ: וּבַיּוֹם הַשְּׁמִינִי אַתָּה רַשַּׁאי לְתִתּוֹ לִי:

ל **וְאַנְשֵׁי קֹדֶשׁ תִּהְיוּן לִי.** אִם אַתֶּם קְדוֹשִׁים וּפְרוּשִׁים מִשִּׁקּוּצֵי נְבֵלוֹת וּטְרֵפוֹת הֲרֵי אַתֶּם שֶׁלִּי, וְאִם לָאו אֵינְכֶם שֶׁלִּי: **וּבָשָׂר בַּשָּׂדֶה טְרֵפָה.** אַף בַּבַּיִת כֵּן, אֶלָּא שֶׁדִּבֶּר הַכָּתוּב בַּהֹוֶה, מָקוֹם שֶׁדֶּרֶךְ בְּהֵמוֹת לְטָּרֵף. וְכֵן: "כִּי בַשָּׂדֶה מְצָאָהּ" (דברים כב, כז). וְכֵן: "אֲשֶׁר לֹא יִהְיֶה טָהוֹר מִקְּרֵה לָיְלָה" (שם כג, יא), הוּא הַדִּין לְמִקְרֵה יוֹם, אֶלָּא שֶׁדִּבֶּר הַכָּתוּב בַּהֹוֶה. "וּבְשַׂר תְּלִישׁ מִן חֵיוַת חַיָּא", בָּשָׂר שֶׁנִּתְלַשׁ עַל יְדֵי טְרֵפַת זְאֵב אוֹ אֲרִי מִן חַיָּה כְּשֵׁרָה אוֹ בְּהֵמָה כְּשֵׁרָה בְּחַיֶּיהָ: **לַכֶּלֶב תַּשְׁלִכוּן אֹתוֹ.** אַף הַגּוֹי כַּכֶּלֶב. אוֹ אֵינוֹ אֶלָּא כֶּלֶב כְּמַשְׁמָעוֹ, תַּלְמוּד לוֹמַר בִּנְבֵלָה: "אוֹ מָכֹר לְנָכְרִי" (שם יד, כא), קַל וָחֹמֶר לִטְרֵפָה שֶׁמֻּתֶּרֶת בְּכָל הֲנָאוֹת. אִם כֵּן מַה תַּלְמוּד לוֹמַר: "לַכֶּלֶב"? לְמֶדְךָ שֶׁהַכֶּלֶב מְכֻבָּד מִן הַגּוֹי שֶׁהַנְּבֵלָה לַגּוֹי וְהַטְּרֵפָה לַכֶּלֶב. וּלְלַמֶּדְךָ שֶׁאֵין הַקָּדוֹשׁ בָּרוּךְ הוּא מְקַפֵּחַ שְׂכַר כָּל בְּרִיָּה, שֶׁנֶּאֱמַר: "וּלְכֹל בְּנֵי יִשְׂרָאֵל לֹא יֶחֱרַץ כֶּלֶב לְשֹׁנוֹ" (לעיל יא, ז), אָמַר הַקָּדוֹשׁ בָּרוּךְ הוּא: תְּנוּ לוֹ שְׂכָרוֹ:

כג א **לֹא תִשָּׂא שֵׁמַע שָׁוְא.** כְּתַרְגּוּמוֹ, "לָא תְקַבֵּל שְׁמַע דִּשְׁקַר", אַזְהָרָה לִמְקַבֵּל לָשׁוֹן הָרָע וְלַדַּיָּן שֶׁלֹּא יִשְׁמַע דִּבְרֵי בַּעַל דִּין עַד שֶׁיָּבוֹא בַּעַל דִּין חֲבֵרוֹ: **אַל תָּשֶׁת יָדְךָ עִם רָשָׁע.** הַטּוֹעֵן אֶת חֲבֵרוֹ תְּבִיעַת שֶׁקֶר, שֶׁתַּבְטִיחֵהוּ לִהְיוֹת לוֹ עֵד חָמָס:

ב **לֹא תִהְיֶה אַחֲרֵי רַבִּים לְרָעֹת.** יֵשׁ בְּמִקְרָא זֶה מִדְרְשֵׁי חַכְמֵי יִשְׂרָאֵל, אֲבָל אֵין לְשׁוֹן הַמִּקְרָא מְיֻשָּׁב בָּהֶן עַל אָפְנָיו. מִכָּאן דָּרְשׁוּ שֶׁאֵין מַטִּין לְחוֹבָה בְּהַכְרָעַת דַּיָּן אֶחָד. וְסוֹף הַמִּקְרָא דָּרְשׁוּ: "אַחֲרֵי רַבִּים לְהַטֹּת", שֶׁאִם יֵשׁ שְׁנַיִם הַמְחַיְּבִין יוֹתֵר עַל הַמְזַכִּין, הַטֵּה הַדִּין עַל פִּיהֶם לְחוֹבָה, וּבְדִינֵי נְפָשׁוֹת הַכָּתוּב מְדַבֵּר. וְאֶמְצַע הַמִּקְרָא דָּרְשׁוּ: "וְלֹא תַעֲנֶה עַל רִב", עַל רַב, שֶׁאֵין חוֹלְקִין עַל מֻפְלָא שֶׁבְּבֵית דִּין, לְפִיכָךְ מַתְחִילִין בְּדִינֵי נְפָשׁוֹת מִן הַצַּד, לַקְּטַנִּים שֶׁבָּהֶם שׁוֹאֲלִין תְּחִלָּה שֶׁיֹּאמְרוּ אֶת דַּעְתָּם. וּלְפִי דִּבְרֵי רַבּוֹתֵינוּ כָּךְ פִּתְרוֹן הַמִּקְרָא: "לֹא תִהְיֶה אַחֲרֵי רַבִּים לְרָעֹת", לְחַיֵּב מִיתָה בִּשְׁבִיל דַּיָּן אֶחָד שֶׁיִּרְבּוּ מְחַיְּבִין עַל הַמְזַכִּין; וְלֹא תַעֲנֶה עַל הָרַב לִנְטוֹת מִדְּבָרָיו, וּלְפִי שֶׁהוּא חָסֵר יוּ"ד דָּרְשׁוּ בּוֹ כֵּן; "אַחֲרֵי רַבִּים לְהַטֹּת", וְיֵשׁ רַבִּים שֶׁאַתָּה נוֹטֶה אַחֲרֵיהֶם, וְאֵימָתַי? בִּזְמַן שֶׁהֵן שְׁנַיִם הַמַּכְרִיעִין בִּמְחַיְּבִין יוֹתֵר מִן הַמְזַכִּין, וּמִמַּשְׁמָע שֶׁנֶּאֱמַר: "לֹא תִהְיֶה אַחֲרֵי רַבִּים לְרָעֹת" שׁוֹמֵעַ אֲנִי: אֲבָל הֱיֵה עִמָּהֶם לְטוֹבָה, מִכָּאן אָמְרוּ: דִּינֵי נְפָשׁוֹת מַטִּין עַל פִּי אֶחָד לִזְכוּת וְעַל פִּי שְׁנַיִם לְחוֹבָה. וְאוּנְקְלוֹס תִּרְגֵּם: "לָא תִתְמְנַע מִלְּאַלָּפָא מָא דִבְעֵינָךְ עַל דִּינָא", וּלְשׁוֹן הָעִבְרִי לְפִי הַתַּרְגּוּם כָּךְ הוּא נִדְרָשׁ: "לֹא תַעֲנֶה עַל רִב לִנְטֹת", אִם יִשְׁאָלְךָ דָּבָר לַמִּשְׁפָּט לֹא תַעֲנֶה לִנְטוֹת לְצַד אֶחָד וּלְסַלֵּק עַצְמְךָ מִן הָרִיב, אֶלָּא הֱוֵי דָּן אוֹתוֹ לַאֲמִתּוֹ. וַאֲנִי אוֹמֵר לְיַשְּׁבוֹ עַל אָפְנָיו כִּפְשׁוּטוֹ כָּךְ פִּתְרוֹנוֹ: "לֹא תִהְיֶה אַחֲרֵי רַבִּים לְרָעֹת" – אִם רָאִיתָ רְשָׁעִים מַטִּין מִשְׁפָּט, לֹא תֹאמַר: הוֹאִיל וְרַבִּים הֵם הִנְנִי נוֹטֶה אַחֲרֵיהֶם. "וְלֹא תַעֲנֶה עַל רִב לִנְטֹת" וְגוֹ' – וְאִם יִשְׁאָלְךָ הַנִּדּוֹן עַל אוֹתוֹ הַמִּשְׁפָּט, אַל תַּעֲנֶנּוּ עַל הָרִיב דָּבָר הַנּוֹטֶה אַחֲרֵי אוֹתָן רַבִּים לְהַטּוֹת אֶת הַמִּשְׁפָּט מֵאֲמִתּוֹ, אֶלָּא אֱמֹר אֶת הַמִּשְׁפָּט כַּאֲשֶׁר הוּא, וְקוֹלָר יְהֵא תָּלוּי בְּצַוַּאר הָרַבִּים:

ג **לֹא תֶהְדַּר.** לֹא תַחְלֹק לוֹ כָּבוֹד לְזַכּוֹתוֹ בַּדִּין, וְלוֹמַר: דַּל הוּא, אֲזַכֶּנּוּ וַאֲכַבְּדֶנּוּ:

כז וְהָיָה כִּי־יִצְעַק אֵלַי וְשָׁמַעְתִּי כִּי־חַנּוּן אָנִי׃ אֱלֹהִים לֹא רביעי
כח תְקַלֵּל וְנָשִׂיא בְעַמְּךָ לֹא תָאֹר׃ מְלֵאָתְךָ וְדִמְעֲךָ לֹא תְאַחֵר בְּכוֹר
כט בָּנֶיךָ תִּתֶּן־לִי׃ כֵּן־תַּעֲשֶׂה לְשֹׁרְךָ לְצֹאנֶךָ שִׁבְעַת יָמִים יִהְיֶה עִם־
ל אִמּוֹ בַּיּוֹם הַשְּׁמִינִי תִּתְּנוֹ־לִי׃ וְאַנְשֵׁי־קֹדֶשׁ תִּהְיוּן לִי וּבָשָׂר בַּשָּׂדֶה
כג א טְרֵפָה לֹא תֹאכֵלוּ לַכֶּלֶב תַּשְׁלִכוּן אֹתוֹ׃ לֹא תִשָּׂא שֵׁמַע
ב שָׁוְא אַל־תָּשֶׁת יָדְךָ עִם־רָשָׁע לִהְיֹת עֵד חָמָס׃ לֹא־תִהְיֶה אַחֲרֵי־
ג רַבִּים לְרָעֹת וְלֹא־תַעֲנֶה עַל־רִב לִנְטֹת אַחֲרֵי רַבִּים לְהַטֹּת׃ וְדָל לֹא
ד תֶהְדַּר בְּרִיבוֹ׃ כִּי תִפְגַּע שׁוֹר אֹיִבְךָ אוֹ חֲמֹרוֹ תֹּעֶה הָשֵׁב

אונקלוס

וִיהֵי אֲרֵי יִקְבֵּל קֳדָמַי, וַאֲקַבֵּיל קְבִילְתֵיהּ אֲרֵי חַנָּנָא אֲנָא׃ כז דַּיָּנָא לָא תְקִיל, וְרַבָּא בְעַמָּךְ לָא תְלוּט׃ כח בְּכוּרָךְ וְדִמְעָךְ לָא תְאַחַר, בּוּכְרָא דִבְנָךְ תַּפְרֵישׁ קֳדָמַי׃ כט כֵּן תַּעֲבֵיד לְתוֹרָךְ לְעָנָךְ, שִׁבְעָא יוֹמִין יְהֵי עִם אִמֵּיהּ, בְּיוֹמָא תְמִינָאָה תַּפְרְשִׁנֵּיהּ קֳדָמָי׃ ל וֶאֱנָשִׁין קַדִּישִׁין תְּהוֹן קֳדָמַי, וּבְסַר תְּלִישׁ מִן חֵיוָא חַיָּא לָא תֵיכְלוּן, לְכַלְבָּא תִּרְמוֹן יָתֵיהּ׃

כג א לָא תְקַבֵּיל שֵׁימַע דִּשְׁקַר, לָא תְשַׁוֵּי יְדָךְ עִם חַיָּבָא, לְמֶהֱוֵי לֵיהּ סָהִיד שְׁקָר׃ ב לָא תְהֵי בָּתַר סַגִּיאֵי לְאַבְאָשָׁא, וְלָא תִתְמְנַע מִלְּאַלָּפָא מָא דִבְעֵינָךְ עַל דִּינָא, בָּתַר סַגִּיאֵי שַׁלֵּים דִּינָא׃ ג וְעַל מִסְכֵּינָא, לָא תְרַחֵים בְּדִינֵיהּ׃ ד אֲרֵי תְעָרַע, תּוֹרָא דְסָנְאָךְ, אוֹ חֲמָרֵיהּ

the world a little better. This is what is being modeled in our verse. God hears and holds us to account for the suffering of others; God hears and demonstrates the attention we must pay in order to bring that suffering to an end.

22:26 כִּי־חַנּוּן אָנִי *I am gracious* – This is law with a human face. Superficially, we are dealing with a simple economic transaction. Someone borrows money and gives the lender an item of clothing as security for the repayment of the loan, an everyday occurrence in ancient times. Yet the Torah insists that we must not forget the existential human situation. The borrower may be poor. The cloak may be the only one he has. The lender must not forget this fact. In strict, legal terms, he may be within his rights simply to hold on to the pledge, but a decent society depends on more than legal rights.

God Himself says about the poor borrower's cries, "I will be listening: I am gracious." God, the lawgiver, is not a remote abstraction. He is a direct personal presence in the lives of those who keep His law. And just as God tempers justice with compassion, so must His people do likewise.

23:2 וְלֹא־תַעֲנֶה עַל־רִב לִנְטֹת *Do not pervert justice* – God may be found in the innermost depths of the human soul, but God is equally to be found in the public square and in the structures of society: the marketplace, the corridors of power, and the courts of law. There must be no gap, no dissociation of sensibilities, between the court of justice (the meeting place of man and man) and the Temple (the meeting place of man and God).

23:2 אַחֲרֵי רַבִּים לְהַטֹּת *Siding with the crowd* – Do not assume that a majority is always right. The herd instinct is to be avoided. Popular sentiment often conflicts with truth and justice. We must not sacrifice individual judgment to conform to the crowd when we suspect they may be wrong.

23:3 וְדָל לֹא תֶהְדַּר בְּרִיבוֹ *Do not show favoritism even to a poor man* – In Judaism, God is our lawgiver. This is foreshadowed in the first chapter of the Torah, with its statement of the equal and absolute dignity of the human person as the image of God (Gen. 1:27). Law and justice are primary vehicles of

5 across your enemy's ox or donkey going astray – bring it back to him. If
you see the donkey of someone who hates you, fallen under its load, resist the
6 impulse to leave it there. Help him to release it. Do not subvert the ḤAMISHI
7 rights of the needy when they come to court. Keep far from a false charge.
Do not bring death on the innocent and righteous, for I will not acquit the
8 wrongdoer. Take no bribe, for bribes blind the sighted and subvert the cause
9 of the just. Do not oppress a stranger. You know what it is to be a stranger, for

רש״י

ה **כִּי תִרְאֶה חֲמוֹר שֹׂנַאֲךָ וְגוֹ׳.** הֲרֵי "כִּי" מְשַׁמֵּשׁ לְשׁוֹן 'דִּלְמָא', שֶׁהוּא מֵאַרְבַּע לְשׁוֹנוֹת שֶׁל שִׁמּוּשֵׁי 'כִּי'. וְכָךְ פִּתְרוֹנוֹ: שֶׁמָּא תִרְאֶה חֲמוֹרוֹ "רֹבֵץ תַּחַת מַשָּׂאוֹ, וְחָדַלְתָּ מֵעֲזֹב לוֹ", בִּתְמִיָּה; "עָזֹב תַּעֲזֹב עִמּוֹ" – עֲזִיבָה זוֹ לְשׁוֹן עֶזְרָה, וְכֵן: "עָצוּר וְעָזוּב" (דברים לב, לו), וְכֵן: "וַיַּעַזְבוּ יְרוּשָׁלַםִ עַד הַחוֹמָה" (נחמיה ג, ח), מִלְאוּהָ עָפָר לַעֲזֹר וּלְסַיֵּעַ אֶת חֹזֶק הַחוֹמָה. כַּיּוֹצֵא בוֹ: "כִּי תֹאמַר בִּלְבָבְךָ רַבִּים הַגּוֹיִם הָאֵלֶּה מִמֶּנִּי" וְגוֹ׳ (דברים ז, יז), שֶׁמָּא תֹאמַר כֵּן, בִּתְמִיָּה – "לֹא תִירָא מֵהֶם" (שם פסוק יח). וּמִדְרָשׁוֹ, כָּךְ דָּרְשׁוּ רַבּוֹתֵינוּ: "כִּי תִרְאֶה וְחָדַלְתָּ", פְּעָמִים שֶׁאַתָּה חוֹדֵל וּפְעָמִים שֶׁאַתָּה עוֹזֵר. הָא כֵּיצַד? זָקֵן וְאֵינָהּ לְפִי כְבוֹדוֹ – "וְחָדַלְתָּ", אוֹ בֶּהֱמַת גּוֹי וּמַשָּׂאוֹ שֶׁל יִשְׂרָאֵל – "וְחָדַלְתָּ": **עָזֹב תַּעֲזֹב עִמּוֹ.** לְפָרֵק הַמַּשָּׂא. "מִלְמִשְׁקַל לֵיהּ", מִלִּטֹּל מַשָּׂאוֹ מִמֶּנּוּ:

ו **אֶבְיֹנְךָ.** לְשׁוֹן אוֹבֶה, שֶׁהוּא מְדֻלְדָּל וְתָאֵב לְכָל טוֹבָה:

ז **וְנָקִי וְצַדִּיק אַל תַּהֲרֹג.** מִנַּיִן לַיּוֹצֵא מִבֵּית דִּין חַיָּב, וְאָמַר אֶחָד: יֵשׁ לִי לְלַמֵּד עָלָיו זְכוּת, שֶׁמַּחֲזִירִין אוֹתוֹ? תַּלְמוּד לוֹמַר: "וְנָקִי אַל תַּהֲרֹג", וְאַף עַל פִּי שֶׁאֵינוֹ "צַדִּיק", שֶׁלֹּא נִצְטַדֵּק בְּבֵית דִּין, מִכָּל מָקוֹם "נָקִי" הוּא מִדִּין מִיתָה, שֶׁהֲרֵי יֵשׁ לְךָ לְזַכּוֹתוֹ. וּמִנַּיִן לַיּוֹצֵא מִבֵּית דִּין זַכַּאי, וְאָמַר אֶחָד: יֵשׁ לִי לְלַמֵּד עָלָיו חוֹבָה, שֶׁאֵין מַחֲזִירִין אוֹתוֹ לְבֵית דִּין? תַּלְמוּד לוֹמַר: "וְצַדִּיק אַל תַּהֲרֹג", וְזֶה צַדִּיק הוּא שֶׁנִּצְטַדֵּק בְּבֵית דִּין: **כִּי לֹא אַצְדִּיק רָשָׁע.** אֵין עָלֶיךָ לְהַחֲזִירוֹ, כִּי אֲנִי לֹא אַצְדִּיקֶנּוּ בְּדִינִי, אִם יָצָא מִיָּדְךָ זַכַּאי יֵשׁ לִי שְׁלוּחִים הַרְבֵּה לַהֲמִיתוֹ בַּמִּיתָה שֶׁנִּתְחַיֵּב בָּהּ:

ח **וְשֹׁחַד לֹא תִקָּח.** אֲפִלּוּ לִשְׁפֹּט אֱמֶת, וְכָל שֶׁכֵּן כְּדֵי לְהַטּוֹת הַדִּין, שֶׁהֲרֵי כְּדֵי לְהַטּוֹת אֶת הַדִּין כְּבָר נֶאֱמַר: "לֹא תַטֶּה מִשְׁפָּט" (לעיל פסוק ו): **יְעַוֵּר פִּקְחִים.** אֲפִלּוּ חָכָם בַּתּוֹרָה וְנוֹטֵל שֹׁחַד, סוֹף שֶׁתִּטָּרֵף דַּעְתּוֹ עָלָיו, וְיִשְׁתַּכַּח תַּלְמוּדוֹ וְיִכְהֶה מְאוֹר עֵינָיו: **וִיסַלֵּף.** כְּתַרְגּוּמוֹ: "וּמְקַלְקֵל": **דִּבְרֵי צַדִּיקִים.** דְּבָרִים הַמְצֻדָּקִים, מִשְׁפְּטֵי אֱמֶת. וְכֵן תַּרְגּוּמוֹ: "פִּתְגָּמִין תְּרִיצִין", יְשָׁרִים:

ט **וְגֵר לֹא תִלְחָץ.** בְּהַרְבֵּה מְקוֹמוֹת הִזְהִירָה תוֹרָה עַל הַגֵּר, מִפְּנֵי שֶׁסּוּרוֹ רָע: **אֶת נֶפֶשׁ הַגֵּר.** כַּמָּה קָשֶׁה לוֹ כְּשֶׁלּוֹחֲצִין אוֹתוֹ:

in the land of Egypt – According to Ramban (on Ex. 22:22), this command has two dimensions. The first is the relative powerlessness of the stranger. He or she is not surrounded by family, friends, neighbors, a community of those ready to come to their defense. Therefore, the Torah warns against wronging them because God has made Himself protector of those who have no one else to defend them. This is the political dimension of the command.

The second reason is the psychological vulnerability of the stranger. Moshe himself, while living among the Midianites, said: "I have been a stranger in an alien land" (2:22). The stranger is one who lives outside the normal securities of home and belonging. He or she is, or feels, alone – and throughout the Torah, God is especially sensitive to the sigh of the oppressed, the feelings of the rejected, the cry of the unheard. That is the emotional dimension of the command.

Rabbi Ḥayyim ibn Attar (*Ohr HaḤayyim* on 22:20) adds a further fascinating insight. It may be, he says, that the very sanctity that Israelites feel as children of the covenant may lead them to look down on those who lack a similar lineage. Therefore they are commanded not to feel superior to the *ger*, but instead to remember the degradation their ancestors experienced in Egypt. This becomes a command of humility in the face of strangers.

Whichever way we look at it, there is something striking about this almost endlessly iterated concern for the stranger – together with the historical reminder that "you yourselves were slaves in the land of Egypt." It is as if, in this series of laws, we are nearing the core of the mystery of Jewish existence itself. What is the Torah implying?

To be a Jew is to be a stranger. It seems that this was why Avraham was commanded to leave his land, home, and father's house; why, long before Yosef was born, Avraham was already told that his descendants would be strangers in a land

ה תְּשִׁיבֶ֥נּוּ לֽוֹ׃ כִּֽי־תִרְאֶ֞ה חֲמ֣וֹר שֹׂנַאֲךָ֗ רֹבֵץ֙ תַּ֣חַת מַשָּׂא֔וֹ
ו וְחָדַלְתָּ֖ מֵעֲזֹ֣ב ל֑וֹ עָזֹ֥ב תַּעֲזֹ֖ב עִמּֽוֹ׃ לֹ֥א תַטֶּ֛ה מִשְׁפַּ֥ט חמישי
ז אֶבְיֹנְךָ֖ בְּרִיבֽוֹ׃ מִדְּבַר־שֶׁ֖קֶר תִּרְחָ֑ק וְנָקִ֤י וְצַדִּיק֙ אַֽל־תַּהֲרֹ֔ג כִּ֥י לֹֽא־
ח אַצְדִּ֖יק רָשָֽׁע׃ וְשֹׁ֖חַד לֹ֣א תִקָּ֑ח כִּ֤י הַשֹּׁ֙חַד֙ יְעַוֵּ֣ר פִּקְחִ֔ים וִֽיסַלֵּ֖ף דִּבְרֵ֥י
ט צַדִּיקִֽים׃ וְגֵ֖ר לֹ֣א תִלְחָ֑ץ וְאַתֶּ֗ם יְדַעְתֶּם֙ אֶת־נֶ֣פֶשׁ הַגֵּ֔ר כִּֽי־גֵרִ֥ים הֱיִיתֶ֖ם

אונקלוס

דְטָעֵי, אָתָבָא תְּתִיבִנֵּיהּ לֵיהּ: ה אֲרֵי תֶחֱזֵי חֲמָרָא דְּסָנְאָךְ, רְבִיעַ תְּחוֹת טְעוּנֵיהּ, וְתִתְמְנַע מִלְּמִשְׁקַל לֵיהּ, מִשְׁבָּק תִּשְׁבּוֹק מָא דִבְלִבָּךְ עֲלוֹהִי וּתְפָרֵיק עִמֵּיהּ: ו לָא תַצְלֵי, דִּין מִסְכֵּינָךְ בְּדִינֵיהּ:
ז מִפִּתְגָמָא דְשִׁקְרָא הֱוֵי רַחִיק, וּדְזַכֵּי וּדְנָפַק זַכַּי מִן דִּינָא לָא תִקְטוֹל, אֲרֵי לָא אֲזַכֵּי חַיָּבָא: ח וְשׁחְדָּא לָא תְקַבֵּיל, אֲרֵי שׁחְדָּא מְעַוַּר עֵינֵי חַכִּימִין, וּמְקַלְקֵיל פִּתְגָמִין תְּרִיצִין: ט וּלְגִיּוֹרָא לָא תָעִיקוּן, וְאַתּוּן, יְדַעְתּוּן יָת נַפְשָׁא דְגִיּוֹרָא, אֲרֵי דַיָּרִין הֲוֵיתוּן

equality. That is why society must be based on the rule of law, impartially administered, treating all alike. Charity is one thing, justice another. We must never pervert the latter for the sake of the former. Each has its specific place in the moral life and they must not be confused.

23:4 שׁוֹר אֹיִבְךָ *Your enemy's ox* – There are two principles at stake in these laws. One is concern for the animal. Jewish law forbids *tzaar baalei ḥayim*, the needless infliction of pain on animals. (Other examples in the Torah include sending the mother bird away [Deut. 22:6] and not muzzling an ox when it is treading grain [Deut. 25:4].) It is as if the Torah is saying: A conflict between two human beings should not lead either of them to ignore the fact that the donkey is laboring under its load. It is innocent. Why should it suffer?

The second principle is stronger still. It says, in effect: Your enemy is also a human being. Hostility may divide you, but there is something deeper that connects you: the covenant of human solidarity. Distress, difficulty – these things transcend the language of difference. A decent society will be one in which enemies do not allow their rancor or animosity to prevent them from coming to one another's assistance when they need help. If someone is in trouble, help. Don't stop to ask if they are friend or foe. Get involved.

There is more at stake than merely helping someone in distress. There is also the challenge of overcoming estrangement, distance, and ill feeling. The phrase "resist the impulse to leave it there" (Ex. 23:5) seems superfluous, but it is not. What it highlights is that when we see our enemy suffering, our first instinct is to pass by. Hence part of the logic of the command is to suppress the evil inclination.

There is something distinctive about the Torah's approach to hatred and enemies. It is realistic rather than utopian. It does not say, "Love your enemy." It says to help him. Saints apart, we cannot love our enemies, and if we try to, we may pay a high psychological price. Instead the Torah says: When your enemy is in trouble, come to his assistance. That way, part of the hatred will be dissipated. The fault lines between people can be redrawn so that erstwhile enemies are on the same side, not opposite sides, of the table. Sometimes, all it takes is a shared task that both can achieve together but neither can do alone. Who knows whether help given may not turn hostility to gratitude and from there to friendship? That is a practical way of moving beyond hate. At the heart of the law of the overladen donkey is one of Judaism's most beautiful axioms: "Who is a hero? One who turns an enemy into a friend" (Avot DeRabbi Natan 23).

23:7 נָקִי וְצַדִּיק *The innocent and righteous* – This is the basis of the ruling that if fresh evidence comes to light after an individual has been deemed guilty, the case may be reopened. The reverse is not the case. If the accused has been acquitted, no retrial is ordered.

23:9 כִּי־גֵרִים הֱיִיתֶם בְּאֶרֶץ מִצְרָיִם *For you yourselves were strangers*

10 you yourselves were strangers in the land of Egypt. For six years, sow your land
11 and gather its crops, but in the seventh let it rest and lie fallow. Let the needy
of your people eat from it, and what they leave, let the wild animals eat. Do the
12 same with your vineyards and olive groves. For six days carry out your work,
but on the seventh you must cease, so that your ox and donkey may rest, and
13 even the children of maidservants and strangers be revived. Take care in all
that I have said to you. Never invoke the names of other gods; let them never
14 15 pass your lips. Three times a year, celebrate a festival for Me. Keep the Festival
of Unleavened Bread. For seven days, eat unleavened bread as I commanded
you, at the time appointed, in the month of Aviv, for at that time you left Egypt.
16 Do not appear before Me empty-handed. Likewise, keep the Festival of the
Harvest, of the first fruits of the produce that you sowed in the field. Keep the
Festival of Ingathering at the end of the year, when you gather in the fruit of your

רש״י

י **וְאָסַפְתָּ אֶת תְּבוּאָתָהּ.** לְשׁוֹן הַכְנָסָה לַבַּיִת, כְּמוֹ: ״וַאֲסַפְתּוֹ אֶל תּוֹךְ בֵּיתֶךָ״ (דברים כב, ב):

יא **תִּשְׁמְטֶנָּה.** מֵעֲבוֹדָה: **וּנְטַשְׁתָּהּ.** מֵאֲכִילָה אַחַר זְמַן הַבִּעוּר. דָּבָר אַחֵר, ״תִּשְׁמְטֶנָּה״ מֵעֲבוֹדָה גְמוּרָה, כְּגוֹן חֲרִישָׁה וּזְרִיעָה. ״וּנְטַשְׁתָּהּ״ מִלְּזַבֵּל וּמִלְּקַשְׁקֵשׁ: **וְיִתְרָם תֹּאכַל חַיַּת הַשָּׂדֶה.** לְהַקִּישׁ מַאֲכַל אֶבְיוֹן לְמַאֲכַל חַיָּה, מַה חַיָּה אוֹכֶלֶת בְּלֹא מַעֲשֵׂר אַף אֶבְיוֹנִים אוֹכְלִים בְּלֹא מַעֲשֵׂר, מִכָּאן אָמְרוּ: אֵין מַעֲשֵׂר בַּשְּׁבִיעִית: **כֵּן תַּעֲשֶׂה לְכַרְמְךָ.** וּתְחִלַּת הַמִּקְרָא מְדַבֵּר בִּשְׂדֵה הַלָּבָן, כְּמוֹ שֶׁאָמוּר לְמַעְלָה הֵימֶנּוּ: ״תִּזְרַע אֶת אַרְצֶךָ״ (בפסוק הקודם):

יב **וּבַיּוֹם הַשְּׁבִיעִי תִּשְׁבֹּת.** אַף בַּשָּׁנָה הַשְּׁבִיעִית לֹא תַעֲקֹר שַׁבַּת בְּרֵאשִׁית מִמְּקוֹמָהּ, שֶׁלֹּא תֹאמַר: הוֹאִיל וְכָל הַשָּׁנָה קְרוּיָה שַׁבָּת לֹא תִנְהַג בָּהּ שַׁבַּת בְּרֵאשִׁית: **לְמַעַן יָנוּחַ שׁוֹרְךָ וַחֲמֹרֶךָ.** תֵּן לוֹ נַיְחָא, לְהַתִּיר שֶׁיְּהֵא תוֹלֵשׁ וְאוֹכֵל עֲשָׂבִים מִן הַקַּרְקַע. אוֹ אֵינוֹ אֶלָּא יַחְבְּשֶׁנּוּ בְּתוֹךְ הַבַּיִת? אָמַרְתָּ, אֵין זֶה נַיְחָא אֶלָּא צַעַר: **בֶּן אֲמָתְךָ.** בְּעֶבֶד עָרֵל הַכָּתוּב מְדַבֵּר: **וְהַגֵּר.** זֶה גֵּר תּוֹשָׁב:

יג **וּבְכֹל אֲשֶׁר אָמַרְתִּי אֲלֵיכֶם תִּשָּׁמֵרוּ.** לַעֲשׂוֹת כָּל מִצְוֹת עֲשֵׂה בְּאַזְהָרָה, שֶׁכָּל שְׁמִירָה שֶׁבַּתּוֹרָה אַזְהָרָה הִיא בִּמְקוֹם לָאו: **לֹא תַזְכִּירוּ.** שֶׁלֹּא יֹאמַר לוֹ: שְׁמֹר לִי בְּצַד עֲבוֹדָה זָרָה פְּלוֹנִית, אוֹ תַּעֲמֹד עִמִּי בְּיוֹם עֲבוֹדָה זָרָה פְּלוֹנִית. דָּבָר אַחֵר, ״וּבְכֹל אֲשֶׁר אָמַרְתִּי אֲלֵיכֶם תִּשָּׁמֵרוּ וְשֵׁם אֱלֹהִים אֲחֵרִים לֹא תַזְכִּירוּ״, לְלַמֶּדְךָ שֶׁשְּׁקוּלָה עֲבוֹדָה זָרָה כְּנֶגֶד כָּל הַמִּצְוֹת כֻּלָּן, וְהַנִּזְהָר בָּהּ כְּשׁוֹמֵר אֶת כֻּלָּן: **לֹא יִשָּׁמַע.** מִן הַגּוֹי ״עַל פִּיךָ״ – שֶׁלֹּא תַעֲשֶׂה שֻׁתָּפוּת עִם הַגּוֹי וְיִשָּׁבַע לְךָ בַּעֲבוֹדָה זָרָה שֶׁלּוֹ, נִמְצֵאתָ שֶׁאַתָּה גּוֹרֵם שֶׁיִּזָּכֵר עַל יָדְךָ:

יד **רְגָלִים.** פְּעָמִים, וְכֵן: ״כִּי הִכִּיתַנִי זֶה שָׁלֹשׁ רְגָלִים״ (במדבר כב, כח):

טו **חֹדֶשׁ הָאָבִיב.** שֶׁהַתְּבוּאָה מִתְמַלֵּאת בּוֹ בְּאִבֶּיהָ. לָשׁוֹן אַחֵר, ״אָבִיב״, לְשׁוֹן אָב, בְּכוֹר וְרִאשׁוֹן לְבַשֵּׁל פֵּרוֹת: **וְלֹא יֵרָאוּ פָנַי רֵיקָם.** כְּשֶׁתָּבֹאוּ לֵרָאוֹת פָּנַי בָּרְגָלִים, הָבִיאוּ לִי עוֹלוֹת:

טז **וְחַג הַקָּצִיר.** הוּא חַג שָׁבוּעוֹת: **בִּכּוּרֵי מַעֲשֶׂיךָ.** שֶׁהוּא זְמַן הֲבָאַת בִּכּוּרִים, שֶׁשְּׁתֵּי הַלֶּחֶם הַבָּאִין בָּעֲצֶרֶת הָיוּ מַתִּירִין הֶחָדָשׁ לַמְּנָחוֹת וּלְהָבִיא בִּכּוּרִים לַמִּקְדָּשׁ, שֶׁנֶּאֱמַר: ״וּבְיוֹם הַבִּכּוּרִים״ וְגוֹ׳ (שם כח, כו): **וְחַג הָאָסִף.** הוּא חַג הַסֻּכּוֹת: **בְּאָסְפְּךָ אֶת מַעֲשֶׂיךָ.** שֶׁכָּל יְמוֹת הַחַמָּה הַתְּבוּאָה מִתְיַבֶּשֶׁת בַּשָּׂדוֹת, וּבֶחָג אוֹסְפִים אוֹתָהּ אֶל הַבַּיִת מִפְּנֵי הַגְּשָׁמִים:

Behind this are two concerns. One is environmental. As Rambam points out (*Guide for the Perplexed* III:39), land which is overexploited eventually erodes and loses its fertility. The Israelites were therefore commanded to conserve the soil by giving it periodic fallow years, not pursuing short-term gain at the cost of long-term desolation. The second, no less significant, is theological. "The land," says God, "is Mine; you are merely migrants and visitors to Me" (Lev. 25:23). We are guests on earth. What we possess, we do not own, we merely hold in trust. There are conditions to that trust, the most fundamental of which is that we must show concern for the good of all.

י בְּאֶרֶץ מִצְרָיִם: וְשֵׁשׁ שָׁנִים תִּזְרַע אֶת־אַרְצֶךָ וְאָסַפְתָּ אֶת־תְּבוּאָתָהּ:
יא וְהַשְּׁבִיעִת תִּשְׁמְטֶנָּה וּנְטַשְׁתָּהּ וְאָכְלוּ אֶבְיֹנֵי עַמֶּךָ וְיִתְרָם תֹּאכַל חַיַּת
יב הַשָּׂדֶה כֵּן־תַּעֲשֶׂה לְכַרְמְךָ לְזֵיתֶךָ: שֵׁשֶׁת יָמִים תַּעֲשֶׂה מַעֲשֶׂיךָ וּבַיּוֹם
הַשְּׁבִיעִי תִּשְׁבֹּת לְמַעַן יָנוּחַ שׁוֹרְךָ וַחֲמֹרֶךָ וְיִנָּפֵשׁ בֶּן־אֲמָתְךָ וְהַגֵּר:
יג וּבְכֹל אֲשֶׁר־אָמַרְתִּי אֲלֵיכֶם תִּשָּׁמֵרוּ וְשֵׁם אֱלֹהִים אֲחֵרִים לֹא תַזְכִּירוּ
יד טו לֹא יִשָּׁמַע עַל־פִּיךָ: שָׁלֹשׁ רְגָלִים תָּחֹג לִי בַּשָּׁנָה: אֶת־חַג הַמַּצּוֹת
תִּשְׁמֹר שִׁבְעַת יָמִים תֹּאכַל מַצּוֹת כַּאֲשֶׁר צִוִּיתִךָ לְמוֹעֵד חֹדֶשׁ הָאָבִיב
טז כִּי־בוֹ יָצָאתָ מִמִּצְרָיִם וְלֹא־יֵרָאוּ פָנַי רֵיקָם: וְחַג הַקָּצִיר בִּכּוּרֵי מַעֲשֶׂיךָ
אֲשֶׁר תִּזְרַע בַּשָּׂדֶה וְחַג הָאָסִף בְּצֵאת הַשָּׁנָה בְּאָסְפְּךָ אֶת־מַעֲשֶׂיךָ

אונקלוס

בְּאַרְעָא דְמִצְרָיִם: י וְשִׁית שְׁנִין תִּזְרַע יָת אַרְעָךְ, וְתִכְנוֹשׁ יָת עֲלַלְתַּהּ: יא וּשְׁבִיעֵיתָא תַּשְׁמְטִנַּהּ וְתִרְטְשִׁנַּהּ, וְיֵיכְלוּן מִסְכֵּינֵי עַמָּךְ, וּשְׁאָרְהוֹן, תֵּיכוֹל חֵיוַת בָּרָא, כֵּן תַּעְבֵּיד לְכַרְמָךְ לְזֵיתָךְ: יב שִׁתָּא יוֹמִין תַּעְבֵּיד עוֹבָדָךְ, וּבְיוֹמָא שְׁבִיעָאָה תְּנוּחַ, בְּדִיל דִּינוּחַ, תּוֹרָךְ וּחֲמָרָךְ, וְיִשְׁקוֹט בַּר אַמְתָךְ וְגִיּוֹרָא: יג וּבְכֹל, דַּאֲמָרִית לְכוֹן תִּסְתַּמְרוּן, וְשׁוּם טַעֲוַת עַמְמַיָּא לָא תִדְכְּרוּן, לָא יִשְׁתְּמַע עַל פֻּמְכוֹן: יד תְּלָת זִמְנִין, תֵּיחֲגוּן קֳדָמַי בְּשַׁתָּא: טו יָת חַגָּא דְּפַטִּירַיָּא תִּטַּר, שִׁבְעָא יוֹמִין תֵּיכוֹל פַּטִּירָא כְּמָא דְּפַקֵּידְתָּךְ, לִזְמַן יַרְחָא דַּאֲבִיבָא, אֲרֵי בֵיהּ נְפַקְתָּא מִמִּצְרָיִם, וְלָא יִתַּחְזוֹן קֳדָמַי רֵיקָנִין: טז וְחַגָּא דַּחֲצָדָא בִּכּוּרֵי עוֹבָדָךְ, דְּתִזְרַע בַּחֲקְלָא, וְחַגָּא דִּכְנָשָׁא בְּמִפְּקֵהּ דְּשַׁתָּא, בְּמִכְנְשָׁךְ יָת עוֹבָדָךְ

not their own; why Moshe had to suffer personal exile before assuming leadership of the people; why the Israelites underwent persecution before inheriting their own land; and why the Torah is so insistent that this experience should become a permanent part of their collective memory. The Israelites in Egypt knew what it was to be marginal and isolated, to suffer and be treated like pariahs. You will not succeed in caring for the stranger, implies God, until you yourselves know in your very bones and sinews what it feels like to be a stranger.

SHEMITTA AND THE SABBATH

The Torah here juxtaposes two commands enjoining periodic rest. On the Sabbath all agricultural work is forbidden "so that your ox and donkey may rest" (Ex. 23:12). The Sabbath sets a limit to our intervention in nature and the pursuit of economic growth. We become conscious that we are creations, not just creators. The earth is not ours, but God's. For six days it is handed over to us, but on the seventh we symbolically abdicate that power. We may perform no "work," which is to say, an act that alters the state of something for human purposes. The Sabbath is a weekly reminder of the integrity of nature and the boundaries of human striving.

The seventh year, like the seventh day, must also be a time of rest – in this case for the land. The law, with its stipulation that the produce of the field should be available to all, appears here because of its association with other commands to have care for the poor. We see here a convergence of the interests of people and land, what we call today an ethic of sustainability. What the Sabbath does for humans and animals, the Sabbatical Year does for the people as a whole and for the land. The earth, too, is entitled to its periodic rest. The Torah warns that if the Israelites do not respect this, they will suffer exile: "Then shall the land make appeasement for its Sabbaths, for as long as it lies desolate and you are in your enemies' lands. Then the land will rest and make appeasement for its Sabbaths" (Lev. 26:34).

17 labor from the field. Three times a year, all the males among you shall appear
18 before the Master, the Lord. Do not offer the blood of My sacrifice together
with anything leavened. Do not let the fat of My festive offering remain until
19 morning. Bring the best first fruits of your land to the House of the Lord your
God. Do not boil a kid in the milk of its mother.
20 I am sending a messenger ahead of you to guard you on the way and to bring SHISHI
21 you to the place that I have prepared. Heed his presence and listen to his voice.
Do not rebel against him, for he will not let your transgression pass, because
22 My name is with him. But if you listen carefully to him and do all that I tell
23 you, then I will be an enemy to your enemies, a foe to your foes. When My
messenger goes ahead of you and brings you to the Amorites, Hittites, Perizzites,
24 Canaanites, Hivites, and Jebusites, and I wipe them out, do not bow down to

רש״י

יז **שָׁלֹשׁ פְּעָמִים וְגוֹ׳.** לְפִי שֶׁהָעִנְיָן מְדַבֵּר בַּשְּׁבִיעִית, הֻצְרַךְ לוֹמַר שֶׁלֹּא יִסְתָּרְסוּ רְגָלִים מִמְּקוֹמָן: **כָּל זְכוּרְךָ.** הַזְּכָרִים שֶׁבְּךָ:

יח **לֹא תִזְבַּח עַל חָמֵץ וְגוֹ׳.** לֹא תִשְׁחַט אֶת הַפֶּסַח בְּאַרְבָּעָה עָשָׂר בְּנִיסָן עַד שֶׁתְּבַעֵר הֶחָמֵץ: **וְלֹא יָלִין חֵלֶב חַגִּי וְגוֹ׳.** חוּץ לַמִּזְבֵּחַ: **עַד בֹּקֶר.** יָכוֹל אַף עַל הַמַּעֲרָכָה יִפָּסֵל בְּלִינָה? תַּלְמוּד לוֹמַר: "עַל מוֹקְדָה עַל הַמִּזְבֵּחַ כָּל הַלַּיְלָה" (ויקרא ו, ב): **וְלֹא יָלִין.** אֵין לִינָה אֶלָּא בְּעַמּוּד הַשַּׁחַר, שֶׁנֶּאֱמַר: "עַד בֹּקֶר", אֲבָל כָּל הַלַּיְלָה יָכוֹל לְהַעֲלוֹתוֹ מִן הָרִצְפָּה לַמִּזְבֵּחַ:

יט **רֵאשִׁית בִּכּוּרֵי אַדְמָתְךָ.** אַף הַשְּׁבִיעִית חַיֶּבֶת בַּבִּכּוּרִים, לְכָךְ נֶאֶמְרָה אַף כָּאן: **בִּכּוּרֵי אַדְמָתְךָ.** כֵּיצַד? אָדָם נִכְנָס לְתוֹךְ שָׂדֵהוּ, רוֹאֶה תְּאֵנָה שֶׁבִּכְּרָה, כּוֹרֵךְ עָלֶיהָ גֶּמִי לְסִימָן וּמַקְדִּישָׁהּ (ביכורים ג, א). וְאֵין בִּכּוּרִים אֶלָּא מִשִּׁבְעַת הַמִּינִין הָאֲמוּרִים בַּמִּקְרָא: "אֶרֶץ חִטָּה וּשְׂעֹרָה" וְגוֹ׳ (דברים ח, ח): **לֹא תְבַשֵּׁל גְּדִי.** אַף עֵגֶל וָכֶבֶשׂ בִּכְלַל 'גְּדִי', שֶׁאֵין גְּדִי אֶלָּא לְשׁוֹן וָלָד רַךְ, מִמַּה שֶּׁאַתָּה מוֹצֵא בְּכַמָּה מְקוֹמוֹת בַּתּוֹרָה שֶׁכָּתוּב 'גְּדִי' וְהֻצְרַךְ לְפָרֵשׁ אַחֲרָיו 'עִזִּים', כְּגוֹן: "אָנֹכִי אֲשַׁלַּח גְּדִי עִזִּים" (בראשית לח, יז), "אֶת גְּדִי הָעִזִּים" (שם פסוק כ; שופטים יג, יט), "שְׁנֵי גְּדָיֵי עִזִּים" (בראשית כז, ט), לְלַמֶּדְךָ שֶׁכָּל מָקוֹם שֶׁנֶּאֱמַר 'גְּדִי' סְתָם אַף עֵגֶל וָכֶבֶשׂ בְּמַשְׁמָע. וּבִשְׁלֹשָׁה מְקוֹמוֹת נִכְתַּב בַּתּוֹרָה: אֶחָד לְאִסּוּר אֲכִילָה וְאֶחָד לְאִסּוּר הֲנָאָה וְאֶחָד לְאִסּוּר בִּשּׁוּל:

כ **הִנֵּה אָנֹכִי שֹׁלֵחַ מַלְאָךְ.** כָּאן נִתְבַּשְּׂרוּ שֶׁעֲתִידִין לַחֲטֹא וּשְׁכִינָה אוֹמֶרֶת לָהֶם: "כִּי לֹא אֶעֱלֶה בְּקִרְבְּךָ" (להלן לג, ג): **אֲשֶׁר הֲכִנֹתִי.** אֲשֶׁר זִמַּנְתִּי לָתֵת לָכֶם, זֶהוּ פְּשׁוּטוֹ. וּמִדְרָשׁוֹ, "אֶל הַמָּקוֹם אֲשֶׁר הֲכִנֹתִי", כְּבָר מְקוֹמִי נִכָּר כְּנֶגְדּוֹ. וְזֶה אֶחָד מִן הַמִּקְרָאוֹת שֶׁאוֹמְרִים שֶׁבֵּית הַמִּקְדָּשׁ שֶׁל מַעְלָה מְכֻוָּן כְּנֶגֶד בֵּית הַמִּקְדָּשׁ שֶׁל מַטָּה:

כא **אַל תַּמֵּר בּוֹ.** לְשׁוֹן הַמְרָאָה, "אֲשֶׁר יַמְרֶה אֶת פִּיךָ" (יהושע א, יח), "וַיַּמְרוּ בִי" (יחזקאל כ, ח): **כִּי לֹא יִשָּׂא לְפִשְׁעֲכֶם.** אֵינוֹ מְלֻמָּד בְּכָךְ, שֶׁהוּא מִן הַכַּת שֶׁאֵין חוֹטְאִין. וְעוֹד, שֶׁהוּא שָׁלִיחַ וְאֵינוֹ עוֹשֶׂה אֶלָּא שְׁלִיחוּתוֹ: **כִּי שְׁמִי בְּקִרְבּוֹ.** מְחֻבָּר לְרֹאשׁ הַמִּקְרָא, "הִשָּׁמֶר מִפָּנָיו" כִּי שְׁמִי מְשֻׁתָּף בּוֹ; וְרַבּוֹתֵינוּ אָמְרוּ, זֶה מֶטַטְרוֹן שֶׁשְּׁמוֹ כְּשֵׁם רַבּוֹ. מֶטַטְרוֹן בְּגִימַטְרִיָּא שַׁדַּי:

כב **וְצַרְתִּי.** כְּתַרְגּוּמוֹ: "וְאָעִיק":

revelation is both necessary and possible, and takes place not through a show of power but through the communication of meaning, namely words, promises, commands, and prayers. Language becomes invested with holiness. In the Torah, God speaks to us. In prayer, we speak to God. Because God is God, man can become man. This was an utterly new form of religious consciousness, and remains only incompletely understood today.

Moshe was not a Jewish equivalent of Pharaoh, a man-god, a doer of mighty deeds with the forces of nature at his command. Rather, he and his successors are "messengers." The prophets (as Ralbag understands the work *malakh* here), or the angels who inspire them (as others interpret), are God's messengers, able to ensure our safe passage only if we "listen carefully to him and do all that I" – God – "tell you."

יז מִן־הַשָּׂדֶה: שָׁלֹשׁ פְּעָמִים בַּשָּׁנָה יֵרָאֶה כָּל־זְכוּרְךָ אֶל־פְּנֵי הָאָדֹן ׀
יח יהוה: לֹא־תִזְבַּח עַל־חָמֵץ דַּם־זִבְחִי וְלֹא־יָלִין חֵלֶב־חַגִּי עַד־בֹּקֶר:
יט רֵאשִׁית בִּכּוּרֵי אַדְמָתְךָ תָּבִיא בֵּית יהוה אֱלֹהֶיךָ לֹא־תְבַשֵּׁל גְּדִי
בַּחֲלֵב אִמּוֹ:
כ הִנֵּה אָנֹכִי שֹׁלֵחַ מַלְאָךְ לְפָנֶיךָ לִשְׁמָרְךָ בַּדָּרֶךְ וְלַהֲבִיאֲךָ אֶל־הַמָּקוֹם ששי
כא אֲשֶׁר הֲכִנֹתִי: הִשָּׁמֶר מִפָּנָיו וּשְׁמַע בְּקֹלוֹ אַל־תַּמֵּר בּוֹ כִּי לֹא יִשָּׂא
כב לְפִשְׁעֲכֶם כִּי שְׁמִי בְּקִרְבּוֹ: כִּי אִם־שָׁמוֹעַ תִּשְׁמַע בְּקֹלוֹ וְעָשִׂיתָ כֹּל
כג אֲשֶׁר אֲדַבֵּר וְאָיַבְתִּי אֶת־אֹיְבֶיךָ וְצַרְתִּי אֶת־צֹרְרֶיךָ: כִּי־יֵלֵךְ מַלְאָכִי
לְפָנֶיךָ וֶהֱבִיאֲךָ אֶל־הָאֱמֹרִי וְהַחִתִּי וְהַפְּרִזִּי וְהַכְּנַעֲנִי הַחִוִּי וְהַיְבוּסִי
כד וְהִכְחַדְתִּיו: לֹא־תִשְׁתַּחֲוֶה לֵאלֹהֵיהֶם וְלֹא תָעָבְדֵם וְלֹא תַעֲשֶׂה

אונקלוס

מִן חַקְלָא: יז תְּלָת זִמְנִין בְּשַׁתָּא, יִתַּחְזוֹן כָּל דְּכוּרָךְ, קֳדָם רִבּוֹן עָלְמָא יְיָ: יח לָא תִכּוֹס עַל חֲמִיעַ דַּם פִּסְחִי, וְלָא יְבִיתוּן בַּר מִמַּדְבְּחָא, תַּרְבֵּי נִכְסַת חַגָּא עַד צַפְרָא: יט רֵישׁ, בִּכּוּרֵי אַרְעָךְ, תַּיְתֵי, לְבֵית מַקְדְּשָׁא דַּייָ אֱלָהָךְ, לָא תֵיכְלוּן בְּסַר בַּחֲלַב: כ הָא אֲנָא, שָׁלַח מַלְאֲכָא קֳדָמָךְ, לְמִטְּרָךְ בְּאוֹרְחָא, וּלְאַעָלוּתָךְ, לְאַתְרָא דְּאַתְקֵינִית: כא אִסְתְּמַר מִן קֳדָמוֹהִי, וְקַבֵּיל לְמֵימְרֵיהּ לָא תְסָרֵיב לְקִבְלֵיהּ, אֲרֵי לָא יִשְׁבּוֹק לְחוֹבֵיכוֹן, אֲרֵי בִשְׁמִי מֵימְרֵיהּ: כב אֲרֵי אִם קַבָּלָא תְקַבֵּיל לְמֵימְרֵיהּ, וְתַעֲבֵיד, כֹּל דַּאֲמַלֵּיל, וְאַסְנֵי יָת סָנְאָךְ, וְאָעִיק לִדְמְעִיקִין לָךְ: כג אֲרֵי יְהָךְ מַלְאֲכִי קֳדָמָךְ, וְיַעֲלִנָּךְ, לְוָת אֱמוֹרָאֵי וְחִתָּאֵי, וּפְרִזָּאֵי וּכְנַעֲנָאֵי, חִוָּאֵי וִיבוּסָאֵי, וַאֲשֵׁיצֵינוּן: כד לָא תִסְגּוֹד לְטָעֲוָתְהוֹן וְלָא תִפְלְחִנִּין, וְלָא תַעֲבֵיד

23:19 לֹא־תְבַשֵּׁל גְּדִי בַּחֲלֵב אִמּוֹ *Do not boil a kid in the milk of its mother* – This is an instance of the general prohibition of mixing meat and milk, which is stated three times in the Torah to forbid (1) the cooking itself, (2) eating, and (3) deriving benefit from the mixture. Judaism sees the human situation in terms of integration and balance. We are body and soul. Hence the Judaic imperative is neither hedonistic nor ascetic, but rather transformative. We are commanded not to indulge in the act of eating nor to abhor it, but rather to *sanctify* it. From this flow the dietary laws, a key element of *kedusha*, the life of holiness.

23:20 הִנֵּה אָנֹכִי שֹׁלֵחַ מַלְאָךְ *I am sending a messenger* – The Haggada, with its insistence that God brought us out of Egypt "not through an angel, not through a seraph, not through any emissary," is striking for its almost complete omission of any reference to Moshe and his part in the redemption. The emphasis throughout is on the saving acts of God. The pharaohs, by contrast, were regarded as incarnate gods, usually of the sun. The Torah was the first document in history to insist that God cannot be identified either with a phenomenon of nature or with a human being, however exalted.

This separation nonetheless allows a possibility of communication. God speaks to mankind. Mankind speaks to God. Between them lies the bond of language.

In the world of myth there was no need for revelation. The gods constantly revealed themselves, in the rising and setting sun, the rain that fell, the wind that blew. In Judaism,

their gods or worship them, and do not do as they do. Demolish their gods
25 and shatter their worship pillars. Serve the LORD your God, and He will bless
26 your bread, your water. I will banish all sickness from your midst. No SHEVI'I
woman in your land will suffer miscarriage or barrenness. I will fill out the full
27 measure of your years. I will send My terror before you, throwing into panic
all the people you come upon. All you will see of your enemies will be their
28 fleeing backs. I will send hornets ahead of you, and they will drive the Hivites,
29 Canaanites, and Hittites out before you. I will not drive them out in a single
year, lest the land become desolate and the wild animals too numerous for you.
30 No – little by little I will drive them out before you, as you burgeon and come
31 to take possession of the land. I will set your borders from the Sea of Reeds to
the Sea of the Philistines, and from the wilderness to the Euphrates, for I will
deliver the inhabitants of the land into your hands: you will drive them out
32 33 before you. Make no covenant with them and their gods. They must not stay in
your land, for they would make you sin against Me. If you worship their gods,
it will be a trap for you."
24 1 Then He said to Moshe, "Ascend to the LORD, you and Aharon, Nadav and
2 Avihu, and seventy of Israel's elders and bow down from afar. Moshe alone
shall approach the LORD. The others must not come close, nor shall the people

רש"י

כד] **הָרֵס תְּהָרְסֵם.** לְאוֹתָם אֱלֹהוֹת: **מַצֵּבֹתֵיהֶם.** אֲבָנִים שֶׁהֵם מַצִּיבִין לְהִשְׁתַּחֲווֹת לָהֶם:

כו] **לֹא תִהְיֶה מְשַׁכֵּלָה.** אִם תַּעֲשֶׂה רְצוֹנִי: **מְשַׁכֵּלָה.** מַפֶּלֶת נְפָלִים אוֹ קוֹבֶרֶת אֶת בָּנֶיהָ קְרוּיָה מְשַׁכֵּלָה:

כז] **וְהַמֹּתִי.** כְּמוֹ וְהֵמַמְתִּי, וְתַרְגּוּמוֹ: "וַאֲשַׁגֵּשׁ". וְכֵן כָּל תֵּבָה שֶׁפַּעַל שֶׁלָּהּ בְּכֶפֶל אוֹת אַחֲרוֹנָה, כְּשֶׁתֵּהָפֵךְ לְדַבֵּר בִּלְשׁוֹן פָּעַלְתִּי יֵשׁ מְקוֹמוֹת שֶׁנּוֹטֵל אוֹת הַכְּפוּלָה וּמַדְגִּישׁ אֶת הָאוֹת וְנוֹקְדוֹ בְּמַלְאָפוּם, כְּגוֹן: "וְהַמֹּתִי" מִגִּזְרַת "וְהָמַם גַּלְגַּל עֶגְלָתוֹ" (ישעיה כח, כח); "וְסַבּוֹתִי" (קהלת ב, כ) מִגִּזְרַת "וְסָבַב בֵּית אֵל" (שמואל א' ז, טז); "דַּלּוֹתִי" (תהלים קטז, ו) מִגִּזְרַת "דָּלְלוּ וְחָרְבוּ" (ישעיה יט, ו); "עַל כַּפַּיִם חַקֹּתִיךְ" (שם מט, טז) מִגִּזְרַת "חִקְקֵי לֵב" (שופטים ה, טו); "אֶת מִי רַצּוֹתִי" (שמואל א' יב, ג) מִגִּזְרַת "רִצַּץ עָזַב דַּלִּים" (איוב כ, יט). וְהַמְתַרְגֵּם "וְהַמֹּתִי" - 'וְאֲקַטֵּיל' טוֹעֶה הוּא, שֶׁאִלּוּ מִגִּזְרַת מִיתָה הָיָה, אֵין הֵ"א שֶׁלָּהּ בְּפַתָּח וְלֹא מֵ"ם שֶׁלָּהּ מְדֻגֶּשֶׁת וְלֹא נְקוּדָה מַלְאָפוּם, אֶלָּא 'וְהֵמַתִּי', כְּגוֹן: "וְהֵמַתָּה אֶת הָעָם הַזֶּה" (במדבר יד, טו), וְהַתָּי"ו מְדֻגֶּשֶׁת לְפִי שֶׁתָּבֹא בִּמְקוֹם שְׁתֵּי תָוִי"ן, הָאַחַת נִשְׁרֶשֶׁת, לְפִי שֶׁאֵין 'מִיתָה' בְּלֹא תָי"ו, וְהָאַחֶרֶת מְשַׁמֶּשֶׁת, כְּמוֹ: אָמַרְתִּי, חָטָאתִי, עָשִׂיתִי. וְכֵן 'וְנָתַתִּי' הַתָּי"ו מְדֻגֶּשֶׁת, שֶׁהִיא בָּאָה בִּמְקוֹם שְׁתַּיִם, לְפִי שֶׁהָיָה צָרִיךְ שָׁלֹשׁ תָּוִי"ן, שְׁתַּיִם לַיְסוֹד כְּמוֹ: "בְּיוֹם תֵּת ה'" (יהושע י, יב), "מַתַּת אֱלֹהִים הִיא" (קהלת ג, יג), וְהַשְּׁלִישִׁית לְשִׁמּוּשׁ: **עֹרֶף.** שֶׁיָּנוּסוּ לְפָנֶיךָ וְיַהַפְכוּ לְךָ עָרְפָּם:

כח] **הַצִּרְעָה.** מִין שֶׁרֶץ הָעוֹף, וְהָיְתָה מַכָּה אוֹתָם בְּעֵינֵיהֶם וּמַטִּילָה בָּם אֶרֶס וְהֵם מֵתִים. וְהַצִּרְעָה לֹא עָבְרָה אֶת הַיַּרְדֵּן. וְחִתִּי וּכְנַעֲנִי הֵם אֶרֶץ סִיחוֹן וְעוֹג, לְפִיכָךְ מִכָּל שֶׁבַע אֻמּוֹת לֹא מָנָה כָּאן אֶלָּא אֵלּוּ. וְחִוִּי, אַף עַל פִּי שֶׁהוּא מֵעֵבֶר הַיַּרְדֵּן וָהָלְאָה, שָׁנוּ רַבּוֹתֵינוּ בְּמַסֶּכֶת סוֹטָה (דף לו ע"א): עַל שְׂפַת הַיַּרְדֵּן עָמְדָה וְזָרְקָה בָּהֶם מָרָה:

כט] **שְׁמָמָה.** רֵיקָנִית מִבְּנֵי אָדָם, לְפִי שֶׁאַתֶּם מְעַט וְאֵין בָּכֶם כְּדֵי לְמַלְּאוֹת אוֹתָהּ: **וְרַבָּה עָלֶיךָ.** וְתִרְבֶּה עָלֶיךָ:

ל] **עַד אֲשֶׁר תִּפְרֶה.** תִּרְבֶּה, לְשׁוֹן פְּרִי, כְּמוֹ: "פְּרוּ וּרְבוּ" (בראשית א, כב):

לא] **וְשַׁתִּי.** לְשׁוֹן הֲשָׁתָה, וְהַתָּי"ו מְדֻגֶּשֶׁת מִפְּנֵי שֶׁבָּאָה תַּחַת שְׁתַּיִם, שֶׁאֵין שִׁיתָה בְּלֹא תָי"ו, וְהָאַחַת לְשִׁמּוּשׁ: **עַד הַנָּהָר.** פְּרָת: **וְגֵרַשְׁתָּמוֹ.** וּתְגָרְשֵׁם:

לג] **כִּי תַעֲבֹד וְגוֹ'.** הֲרֵי אֵלּוּ "כִּי" מְשַׁמְּשִׁין בִּמְקוֹם 'אֲשֶׁר', וְכֵן בְּכַמָּה

כה כְּמַעֲשֵׂיהֶם כִּי הָרֵס תְּהָרְסֵם וְשַׁבֵּר תְּשַׁבֵּר מַצֵּבֹתֵיהֶם: וַעֲבַדְתֶּם
אֵת יהוה אֱלֹהֵיכֶם וּבֵרַךְ אֶת־לַחְמְךָ וְאֶת־מֵימֶיךָ וַהֲסִרֹתִי מַחֲלָה
כו מִקִּרְבֶּךָ: לֹא תִהְיֶה מְשַׁכֵּלָה וַעֲקָרָה בְּאַרְצֶךָ אֶת־מִסְפַּר שביעי
כז יָמֶיךָ אֲמַלֵּא: אֶת־אֵימָתִי אֲשַׁלַּח לְפָנֶיךָ וְהַמֹּתִי אֶת־כָּל־הָעָם אֲשֶׁר
כח תָּבֹא בָּהֶם וְנָתַתִּי אֶת־כָּל־אֹיְבֶיךָ אֵלֶיךָ עֹרֶף: וְשָׁלַחְתִּי אֶת־הַצִּרְעָה
כט לְפָנֶיךָ וְגֵרְשָׁה אֶת־הַחִוִּי אֶת־הַכְּנַעֲנִי וְאֶת־הַחִתִּי מִלְּפָנֶיךָ: לֹא
אֲגָרְשֶׁנּוּ מִפָּנֶיךָ בְּשָׁנָה אֶחָת פֶּן־תִּהְיֶה הָאָרֶץ שְׁמָמָה וְרַבָּה עָלֶיךָ
ל חַיַּת הַשָּׂדֶה: מְעַט מְעַט אֲגָרְשֶׁנּוּ מִפָּנֶיךָ עַד אֲשֶׁר תִּפְרֶה וְנָחַלְתָּ
לא אֶת־הָאָרֶץ: וְשַׁתִּי אֶת־גְּבֻלְךָ מִיַּם־סוּף וְעַד־יָם פְּלִשְׁתִּים וּמִמִּדְבָּר
לב עַד־הַנָּהָר כִּי ׀ אֶתֵּן בְּיֶדְכֶם אֵת יֹשְׁבֵי הָאָרֶץ וְגֵרַשְׁתָּמוֹ מִפָּנֶיךָ: לֹא־
לג תִכְרֹת לָהֶם וְלֵאלֹהֵיהֶם בְּרִית: לֹא יֵשְׁבוּ בְּאַרְצְךָ פֶּן־יַחֲטִיאוּ אֹתְךָ
לִי כִּי תַעֲבֹד אֶת־אֱלֹהֵיהֶם כִּי־יִהְיֶה לְךָ לְמוֹקֵשׁ:
כד א וְאֶל־מֹשֶׁה אָמַר עֲלֵה אֶל־יהוה אַתָּה וְאַהֲרֹן נָדָב וַאֲבִיהוּא וְשִׁבְעִים
ב מִזִּקְנֵי יִשְׂרָאֵל וְהִשְׁתַּחֲוִיתֶם מֵרָחֹק: וְנִגַּשׁ מֹשֶׁה לְבַדּוֹ אֶל־יהוה וְהֵם

אונקלוס

כְּעוּבָדֵיהוֹן, אֲרֵי פַגָּרָא תְּפַגְּרִנּוּן, וְתַבָּרָא תְּתַבַּר קָמָתְהוֹן: כה וְתִפְלְחוּן, קֳדָם יי אֱלָהֲכוֹן, וִיבָרֵךְ יָת מֵיכְלָךְ וְיָת מִשְׁתְּיָךְ, וְאַעְדֵּי מַרְעִין בִּישִׁין מִבֵּינָךְ: כו לָא תְהֵי, תַּכְלָא וְעַקָרָא בְּאַרְעָךְ, יָת מִנְיַן יוֹמָךְ אַשְׁלֵים: כז יָת אֵימְתִי אֲשַׁלַּח קֳדָמָךְ, וַאֲשַׁגֵּישׁ יָת כָּל עַמָּא, דְּאַתְּ אָתֵי לְאַגָּחָא קְרָבָא בְּהוֹן, וְאֶמְסַר יָת כָּל בַּעֲלֵי דְּבָבָךְ, קֳדָמָךְ מַחְזְרֵי קְדָל: כח וְאֶשְׁלַח יָת עֲרָעִיתָא קֳדָמָךְ, וּתְתָרֵיךְ, יָת חִוָּאֵי יָת כְּנַעֲנָאֵי, וְיָת חִתָּאֵי מִן קֳדָמָךְ: כט לָא אֲתָרֵיכִנּוּן, מִן קֳדָמָךְ בְּשַׁתָּא חֲדָא, דִּלְמָא תְהֵי אַרְעָא צָדְיָא, וְתִסְגֵּי עֲלָךְ חֵיוַת בָּרָא: ל זְעֵיר זְעֵיר, אֲתָרֵיכִנּוּן מִן קֳדָמָךְ, עַד דְּתִסְגֵּי, וְתַחְסֵין יָת אַרְעָא: לא וַאֲשַׁוֵּי יָת תְּחוּמָךְ, מִיַּמָּא דְסוּף וְעַד יַמָּא דִפְלִשְׁתָּאֵי, וּמִמַּדְבְּרָא עַד פְּרָת, אֲרֵי אֶמְסַר בִּידְכוֹן, יָת יָתְבֵי אַרְעָא, וּתְתָרֵיכִנּוּן מִן קֳדָמָךְ: לב לָא תִגְזַר לְהוֹן, וּלְטָעֲוָתְהוֹן קְיָם: לג לָא יִתְּבוּן בְּאַרְעָךְ, דִּלְמָא יְחַיְּבוּן יָתָךְ קֳדָמָי, אֲרֵי תִפְלַח יָת טָעֲוָתְהוֹן, אֲרֵי יְהוֹן לָךְ לְתַקְלָא: כד א וּלְמֹשֶׁה אֲמַר סַק לִקְדָם יי, אַתְּ וְאַהֲרֹן נָדָב וַאֲבִיהוּא, וְשַׁבְעִין מִסָּבֵי יִשְׂרָאֵל, וְתִסְגְּדוּן מֵרַחִיק: ב וְיִתְקָרַב מֹשֶׁה בִּלְחוֹדוֹהִי לִקְדָם יי, וְאִנּוּן

רש"י

מְקוֹמוֹת. וְזֶהוּ לְשׁוֹן 'חִי', שֶׁהוּא אֶחָד מֵאַרְבָּעָה לְשׁוֹנוֹת שֶׁהַ'כִּי' מְשַׁמֵּשׁ. וְגַם מָצִינוּ בְּהַרְבֵּה מְקוֹמוֹת 'אִם' מְשַׁמֵּשׁ בִּלְשׁוֹן 'אֲשֶׁר', כְּמוֹ: "וְאִם תַּקְרִיב מִנְחַת בִּכּוּרִים" (ויקרא ב, יד) שֶׁהוּא חוֹבָה:

כד א וְאֶל מֹשֶׁה אָמַר. פָּרָשָׁה זוֹ נֶאֶמְרָה קֹדֶם עֲשֶׂרֶת הַדִּבְּרוֹת, בְּאַרְבָּעָה בְּסִיוָן נֶאֱמַר לוֹ: "עֲלֵה":

ב וְנִגַּשׁ מֹשֶׁה לְבַדּוֹ. אֶל הָעֲרָפֶל:

3 come up with him." Moshe came and told the people all the LORD's words
and laws, and the people all responded with one voice, "All that the LORD has
4 spoken we shall do." Then Moshe wrote down all the LORD's words. Early the
next morning he rose and built an altar at the base of the mountain, and also
5 twelve pillars for the twelve tribes of Israel. Then he sent young men of Israel,
and they sacrificed bulls as burnt offerings and peace offerings to the LORD.
6 Moshe took half the blood and put it in bowls. The other half he sprinkled
7 on the altar. Then he took the book of the covenant and read it aloud to the
people. They replied, "All that the LORD has spoken we shall do and we shall
8 heed." Then Moshe took the blood, sprinkled it on the people, and said, "This

רש"י

ג **וַיָּבֹא מֹשֶׁה וַיְסַפֵּר לָעָם.** בּוֹ בַּיּוֹם: **אֵת כָּל דִּבְרֵי ה׳.** מִצְוַת פְּרִישָׁה וְהַגְבָּלָה: **וְאֵת כָּל הַמִּשְׁפָּטִים.** שֶׁבַע מִצְוֹת שֶׁנִּצְטַוּוּ בְּנֵי נֹחַ, וְשַׁבָּת וְכִבּוּד אָב וָאֵם וּפָרָה אֲדֻמָּה וְדִינִין שֶׁנִּתְּנוּ לָהֶם בְּמָרָה:

ד **וַיִּכְתֹּב מֹשֶׁה.** מִבְּרֵאשִׁית וְעַד מַתַּן תּוֹרָה, וְכָתַב מִצְוֹת שֶׁנִּצְטַוּוּ בְּמָרָה: **וַיַּשְׁכֵּם בַּבֹּקֶר.** בַּחֲמִשָּׁה בְּסִיוָן:

ה **אֶת נַעֲרֵי.** הַבְּכוֹרוֹת:

ו **וַיִּקַּח מֹשֶׁה חֲצִי הַדָּם.** מִי חִלְּקוֹ? מַלְאָךְ בָּא וְחִלְּקוֹ: **בָּאַגָּנֹת.** שְׁתֵּי אַגָּנוֹת, אֶחָד לַחֲצִי דַּם עוֹלָה וְאֶחָד לַחֲצִי דַּם שְׁלָמִים לְהַזּוֹת אוֹתָם עַל הָעָם. וּמִכָּאן לָמְדוּ רַבּוֹתֵינוּ שֶׁנִּכְנְסוּ אֲבוֹתֵינוּ לַבְּרִית בְּמִילָה וּטְבִילָה וְהַרְצָאַת דָּמִים; שֶׁאֵין הַזָּאָה בְּלֹא טְבִילָה:

ז **סֵפֶר הַבְּרִית.** מִבְּרֵאשִׁית וְעַד מַתַּן תּוֹרָה, וּמִצְוֹת שֶׁנִּצְטַוּוּ בְּמָרָה:

Torah as ratifying the covenant three times: once before they heard the commandments and twice afterward. There is a fascinating difference between the way the Torah describes the first two of these responses and the third:

> And the people *answered as one* – "All that the LORD has spoken we will do (*naaseh*)." (Ex. 19:8)
>
> Moshe came and told the people all the LORD's words and laws, and the people *all responded with one voice*, "All that the LORD has spoken we shall do (*naaseh*)." (24:3)
>
> Then he took the book of the covenant and read it aloud to the people. They *replied*, "All that the LORD has spoken we shall do and we shall heed (*naaseh venishma*)." (24:7)

The first two responses, which refer only to action (*naaseh*), are given unanimously. The people respond "as one." They do so "with one voice." The third, which refers not only to doing but also to listening or understanding (*nishma*), involves no unanimity. *Nishma* here means many things, as

books about these things is not enough. So it is with faith. We only truly understand Judaism by living in accordance with its commands. You cannot comprehend a faith from the outside. Doing leads to understanding.

The modern Western mind tends to put things in the opposite order. We seek to understand what we are committing ourselves to before making the commitment. That is fine when what is at stake is signing a contract, buying a new mobile phone, or purchasing a subscription, but not when making a deep existential commitment. The only way to understand marriage is to get married. The only way to understand whether a certain career path is right for you is to actually try it for an extended period. Those who hover on the edge of a commitment, reluctant to make a decision until all the facts are in, will eventually find that life has passed them by. The only way to understand a way of life is to take the risk of living it. So, *naaseh venishma* – we shall do, and eventually, through extended practice and long exposure, we shall understand.

24:7 **נַעֲשֶׂה** *We shall do* – The Israelites are described by the

ג לֹא יִגָּשׁוּ וְהָעָם לֹא יַעֲלוּ עִמּוֹ: וַיָּבֹא מֹשֶׁה וַיְסַפֵּר לָעָם אֵת כָּל־דִּבְרֵי
יהוה וְאֵת כָּל־הַמִּשְׁפָּטִים וַיַּעַן כָּל־הָעָם קוֹל אֶחָד וַיֹּאמְרוּ כָּל־
ד הַדְּבָרִים אֲשֶׁר־דִּבֶּר יהוה נַעֲשֶׂה: וַיִּכְתֹּב מֹשֶׁה אֵת כָּל־דִּבְרֵי יהוה
וַיַּשְׁכֵּם בַּבֹּקֶר וַיִּבֶן מִזְבֵּחַ תַּחַת הָהָר וּשְׁתֵּים עֶשְׂרֵה מַצֵּבָה לִשְׁנֵים
ה עָשָׂר שִׁבְטֵי יִשְׂרָאֵל: וַיִּשְׁלַח אֶת־נַעֲרֵי בְּנֵי יִשְׂרָאֵל וַיַּעֲלוּ עֹלֹת וַיִּזְבְּחוּ
ו זְבָחִים שְׁלָמִים לַיהוה פָּרִים: וַיִּקַּח מֹשֶׁה חֲצִי הַדָּם וַיָּשֶׂם בָּאַגָּנֹת
ז וַחֲצִי הַדָּם זָרַק עַל־הַמִּזְבֵּחַ: וַיִּקַּח סֵפֶר הַבְּרִית וַיִּקְרָא בְּאָזְנֵי הָעָם
ח וַיֹּאמְרוּ כֹּל אֲשֶׁר־דִּבֶּר יהוה נַעֲשֶׂה וְנִשְׁמָע: וַיִּקַּח מֹשֶׁה אֶת־הַדָּם

אונקלוס

לָא יִתְקָרְבוּן, וְעַמָּא, לָא יִסְּקוּן עִמֵּיהּ: ג וַאֲתָא מֹשֶׁה, וְאִשְׁתָּעִי לְעַמָּא יָת כָּל פִּתְגָּמַיָּא דַּיְיָ, וְיָת כָּל דִּינַיָּא, וַאֲתֵיב כָּל עַמָּא, קָלָא חַד וַאֲמַרוּ, כָּל פִּתְגָּמַיָּא, דְּמַלִּיל יי נַעֲבֵיד: ד וּכְתַב מֹשֶׁה, יָת כָּל פִּתְגָּמַיָּא דַּיְיָ, וְאַקְדֵּים בְּצַפְרָא, וּבְנָא מַדְבְּחָא בְּשִׁפּוֹלֵי טוּרָא, וְתַרְתָּא עַסְרֵי קָמָא, לִתְרֵי עֲסַר שִׁבְטַיָּא דְּיִשְׂרָאֵל: ה וּשְׁלַח, יָת בְּכוֹרֵי בְּנֵי יִשְׂרָאֵל, וְאַסִּיקוּ עֲלָוָן, וְנַכִּיסוּ, נִכְסַת קֻדְשִׁין, קֳדָם יי תּוֹרִין: ו וּנְסֵיב מֹשֶׁה פַּלְגוּת דְּמָא, וְשַׁוִּי בְּמִזְרְקַיָּא, וּפַלְגוּת דְּמָא, זְרַק עַל מַדְבְּחָא: ז וּנְסֵיב סִפְרָא דִקְיָמָא, וּקְרָא קֳדָם עַמָּא, וַאֲמַרוּ, כֹּל, דְּמַלִּיל יי נַעֲבֵיד וּנְקַבֵּיל: ח וּנְסֵיב מֹשֶׁה יָת דְּמָא,

WE SHALL DO AND WE SHALL HEED

Two words that we read toward the end of our *parasha* – *naaseh venishma*, "we shall do and we shall heed" – are among the most famous in Judaism. They are what our ancestors said when they accepted the covenant at Sinai.

What, though, do the words actually mean? *Naaseh* is straightforward. It means "we shall do." It is about action, behavior, deed. But *nishma* is unclear. It could mean "we shall hear." But it could also mean "we shall obey" or "we shall heed." Or it could mean "we shall understand." Here are some of the classic ways of interpreting *naaseh venishma*:

1. "We shall do and then we shall hear." This is the view of the Talmud (Shabbat 88a) and Rashi. The people expressed their total faith in God. They accepted the covenant even before they heard its terms. They said "we shall do" before they knew what it was that God wanted them to do.
2. "We shall do [what we have already been commanded until now] and we shall obey [all future commands]." This is the view of Rashbam. The Israelites' statement thus looked both back and forward. The people understood that they were on a spiritual as well as a physical journey and they might not know all the details of the law at once. *Nishma* here means not "to hear" but "to heed, hearken, obey; to respond faithfully in deed."
3. "We shall do and we shall understand" (Rabbi Yitzḥak Arama in *Akedat Yitzḥak*). The word *shema* can have the sense of understanding, as in God's statement about the Tower of Bavel: "Let us go down and confuse their language so that one will not understand (*yishme'u*) the speech of another" (Gen. 11:7).

According to this last explanation, when the Israelites put "doing" before "understanding," they were giving expression to a profound philosophical truth. There are certain things we only understand by doing. We only understand leadership by leading. We only understand authorship by writing. We only understand music by listening. Reading

is the blood of the covenant that the Lord is making with you regarding all
9 these words." Then Moshe went up with Aharon, Nadav, Avihu, and seventy
10 of Israel's elders. They saw a vision of the God of Israel, and beneath His feet
11 what looked like a lapis lazuli pavement as clear as the sky itself. And He
did the leaders of Israel no harm – and they looked upon God and they ate
12 and they drank. The Lord said to Moshe, "Ascend to Me on the

רש״י

ח **ויזרק.** ענין הזאה, ותרגומו: "וזרק על מדבחא לכפרא על עמא":

י **ויראו את אלהי ישראל.** נסתכלו והציצו ונתחייבו מיתה, אלא שלא רצה הקדוש ברוך הוא לערבב שמחת התורה, והמתין לנדב ואביהוא עד יום חנכת המשכן, ולזקנים עד "ויהי העם כמתאננים... ותבער בם אש ה' ותאכל בקצה המחנה" (במדבר יא, א), בקצינים שבמחנה: **כמעשה לבנת הספיר.** היא היתה לפניו בשעת השעבוד, לזכר צרתן של ישראל שהיו משעבדים במעשה לבנים: **וכעצם השמים לטהר.** משנגאלו היה אור וחדוה לפניו: **וכעצם.** כתרגומו, לשון מראה: **לטהר.** לשון ברור וצלול:

יא **ואל אצילי.** הם נדב ואביהוא והזקנים: **לא שלח ידו.** מכלל שהיו ראויים להשלחת יד: **ויחזו את האלהים.** היו מסתכלין בו בלב גס מתוך אכילה ושתיה, כך מדרש תנחומא. ואונקלוס לא תרגם כן; "אצילי" לשון גדולים, כמו: "ומאציליה קראתיך" (ישעיה מא, ט), "ויאצל מן הרוח" (במדבר יא, כה), "שש אמות אצילה" (יחזקאל מא, ח):

יב **ויאמר ה' אל משה.** לאחר מתן תורה:

24:10 **ויראו** *They saw a vision* – This mystical, visual experience of God is striking – perhaps shocking – in the context of the earthbound legal passages that surround it. Why is it here?

As we have discussed, law and narrative are intimately bound up in the Torah. Ideas do not appear from nowhere, nor are all thoughts possible within every configuration of culture. The world of myth was profoundly conservative. Indeed, throughout most of history, religions and civilizations have tended to reinforce, rather than challenge, the status quo. They have taught acceptance, not protest; continuity, not revolution. Their governing assumption has been that the world is as it is because that is the nature of things. In the struggle for survival, the strong win, the weak die, power rules, and fate is blind. From where, then, do the thoughts arise that we can change the world and humanize it, making it less random and cruel and creating within its deserts oases of justice and gardens of grace?

The key idea is *transcendence*, that God is to be found not within nature but beyond it. "The heavens are My throne; the world, My footstool" (Is. 66:1). At a stroke, this idea relativized all human institutions. Nothing in society is as it is because it could not be otherwise. God is free: therefore the human person, created in His image, is also free. Hierarchy, inequality, the corruptions of power, the exploitation of the weak, imperial conquest, and the enslavement of peoples are not justified merely because they exist. For the first time a gap is opened up between "is" and "ought." Not everything that is, is good. Not all that is done is right. We can imagine a world different from the way it is now and has been in the past, and because we can imagine it, we can decide to act in such a way as to begin to bring it about. When God is conceived of as both beyond the natural universe *and* endowing humanity with His most distinctive attribute, creativity, a momentous human freedom is born. For the first time, religion becomes a world-transforming rather than world-accepting force. When the elders experience God enthroned above a paving "as clear as the sky itself," when the people of Israel sense His presence over the mountaintop "like consuming fire" (Ex. 24:17), they know that they are accountable to something and someone beyond their own realm. The moral and the mystical are intertwined. It is with this knowledge that we enter the *parashot* of the *Mishkan* (Tabernacle).

וַיִּזְרֹק עַל־הָעָם וַיֹּאמֶר הִנֵּה דַם־הַבְּרִית אֲשֶׁר כָּרַת יהוה עִמָּכֶם עַל
ט כָּל־הַדְּבָרִים הָאֵלֶּה: וַיַּעַל מֹשֶׁה וְאַהֲרֹן נָדָב וַאֲבִיהוּא וְשִׁבְעִים מִזִּקְנֵי
י יִשְׂרָאֵל: וַיִּרְאוּ אֵת אֱלֹהֵי יִשְׂרָאֵל וְתַחַת רַגְלָיו כְּמַעֲשֵׂה לִבְנַת הַסַּפִּיר
יא וּכְעֶצֶם הַשָּׁמַיִם לָטֹהַר: וְאֶל־אֲצִילֵי בְּנֵי יִשְׂרָאֵל לֹא שָׁלַח יָדוֹ וַיֶּחֱזוּ
יב אֶת־הָאֱלֹהִים וַיֹּאכְלוּ וַיִּשְׁתּוּ: וַיֹּאמֶר יהוה אֶל־מֹשֶׁה

אונקלוס

וּזְרַק עַל מַדְבְּחָא לְכַפָּרָא עַל עַמָּא, וַאֲמַר, הָא דֵין דַּם קְיָמָא דִּגְזַר יי
עִמְּכוֹן, עַל כָּל פִּתְגָּמַיָּא הָאִלֵּין: ט וּסְלֵיק מֹשֶׁה וְאַהֲרֹן, נָדָב
וַאֲבִיהוּא, וְשִׁבְעִין מִסָּבֵי יִשְׂרָאֵל: י וַחֲזוֹ, יָת יְקָר אֱלָהָא דְּיִשְׂרָאֵל,
וּתְחוֹת כֻּרְסֵי יְקָרֵיהּ, כְּעוֹבַד אֶבֶן טָבָא, וּכְמֶחֱזֵי שְׁמַיָּא לְבָרִירוּ:
יא וּלְרַבְרְבֵי בְּנֵי יִשְׂרָאֵל, לָא הֲוָה נִזְקָא, וַחֲזוֹ יָת יְקָרָא דַּיי, וַהֲווֹ חָדַן
בְּקֻרְבָּנֵיהוֹן דְּאִתְקַבַּלוּ בְּרַעֲוָא כְּאִלּוּ אָכְלִין וְשָׁתַן: יב וַאֲמַר יי לְמֹשֶׁה,

we have seen: listening, paying attention, understanding, absorbing, internalizing, and obeying. It refers, in other words, *to the spiritual, inward dimension of Judaism.*

From this, an important consequence follows. Judaism is a *community of doing* rather than of "hearing." There is an authoritative code of Jewish law. When it comes to halakha, the way of Jewish doing, we seek consensus.

By contrast, though there are undoubtedly principles of Jewish faith, *when it comes to spirituality there is no single normative Jewish approach.* Judaism has had its priests and prophets, its rationalists and mystics, its philosophers and poets. Tanakh speaks in a multiplicity of voices. The Torah contains law and narrative, history and mystic vision, ritual and prayer. There are norms about how to act as Jews. But there are few about how to think and feel as Jews. We do the godly deed "together." We respond to His commands "with one voice." But we hear God's presence in many ways, for though God is one, we are all different, and we encounter Him each in our own way.

24:8 עַל כָּל־הַדְּבָרִים הָאֵלֶּה *Regarding all these words* – The word "Torah" is untranslatable because it means several different things that appear together only in the book that bears that name. Torah means "law." But it also means "teaching," "instruction," "guidance," or more generally, "direction." It is also the generic name for the five books, from Genesis to Deuteronomy, that comprise both narrative and law.

In general, law and narrative are two distinct literary genres that have very little overlap. Most books of law do not contain narratives, and most narratives do not contain law. Even if people in Britain or America today know the history behind a given law, there is no canonical text that brings the two together. In any case, in most societies there are many different ways of telling the story. Moreover, most laws are enacted without a statement of why they came to be, what they were intended to achieve, and what historical experience led to their enactment.

So the Torah is a unique combination of *nomos* and narrative, history and law, the formative experiences of a nation and the way that nation sought to live its collective life so as never to forget the lessons it learned along the way. It brings together vision and detail in a way that has never been surpassed.

That is how we must lead if we want people to come with us, giving of their best. There must be a vision to inspire us, telling us why we should do what we are asked to do. There must be a narrative: this is what happened, this is who we are, and this is why the vision is so important to us. Then there must be the law, the code, the fastidious attention to detail, that allow us to translate vision into reality and turn the pain of the past into the blessings of the future. That extraordinary combination, to be found in almost no other law code, is what gives Torah its enduring power – hence "the covenant that the Lord is making with you regarding *all* these words."

mountain, and as you stand there I will give you the stone tablets with the
13 teaching and commandments that I have written to instruct the people." So
Moshe set out with Yehoshua, his disciple, and ascended the mountain of God.
14 He told the elders, "Wait for us here until we return to you. Aharon and Ḥur
15 will stay here with you; whoever has a dispute shall go to them." As Moshe MAFTIR
16 climbed the mountain, it was covered in a cloud. The glory of the LORD rested
on Mount Sinai, and the cloud covered it for six days. On the seventh, He
17 called to Moshe from within the cloud. To the Israelites the appearance of the
18 LORD's glory on the mountaintop was like consuming fire. Moshe entered the
cloud and climbed the mountain, and he stayed there for forty days and forty
nights.

The haftara for Parashat Mishpatim is on page 1543.
On Rosh Ḥodesh Adar I read the haftara on page 1635.
On Erev Rosh Ḥodesh Adar I read the haftara on page 1637.
However, on the Shabbat of Parashat Shekalim, even if it is also Rosh Ḥodesh or Erev Rosh Ḥodesh Adar, read the haftara on page 1643.

רש"י

עֲלֵה אֵלַי הָהָרָה וֶהְיֵה שָׁם. אַרְבָּעִים יוֹם: **אֶת לֻחֹת הָאֶבֶן וְהַתּוֹרָה וְהַמִּצְוָה אֲשֶׁר כָּתַבְתִּי לְהוֹרֹתָם.** כָּל שֵׁשׁ מֵאוֹת וּשְׁלֹשׁ עֶשְׂרֵה מִצְוֹת בִּכְלַל עֲשֶׂרֶת הַדִּבְּרוֹת הֵן. וְרַבֵּנוּ סְעַדְיָה פֵּרֵשׁ בָּאַזְהָרוֹת שֶׁיִּסַּד לְכָל דִּבּוּר וְדִבּוּר מִצְוֹת הַתְּלוּיוֹת בּוֹ:

יג **וַיָּקָם מֹשֶׁה וִיהוֹשֻׁעַ מְשָׁרְתוֹ.** לֹא יָדַעְתִּי מַה טִּיבוֹ שֶׁל יְהוֹשֻׁעַ כָּאן. וְאוֹמֵר אֲנִי, שֶׁהָיָה הַתַּלְמִיד מְלַוֶּה לָרַב עַד מְקוֹם הַגְבָּלַת תְּחוּמֵי הָהָר, שֶׁאֵינוֹ רַשַּׁאי לֵילֵךְ מִשָּׁם וָהָלְאָה, וּמִשָּׁם "וַיַּעַל מֹשֶׁה" לְבַדּוֹ "אֶל הַר הָאֱלֹהִים", וִיהוֹשֻׁעַ נָטָה שָׁם אָהֳלוֹ וְנִתְעַכֵּב שָׁם כָּל אַרְבָּעִים יוֹם, שֶׁכֵּן מָצִינוּ כְּשֶׁיָּרַד מֹשֶׁה: "וַיִּשְׁמַע יְהוֹשֻׁעַ אֶת קוֹל הָעָם בְּרֵעֹה" (להלן לב, יז), לָמַדְנוּ שֶׁלֹּא הָיָה יְהוֹשֻׁעַ עִמָּהֶם:

יד **וְאֶל הַזְּקֵנִים אָמַר.** בְּצֵאתוֹ מִן הַמַּחֲנֶה: **שְׁבוּ לָנוּ בָזֶה.** וְהִתְעַכְּבוּ כָּאן עִם שְׁאָר הָעָם בַּמַּחֲנֶה לִהְיוֹת נְכוֹנִים לִשְׁפֹּט לְכָל אִישׁ רִיבוֹ: **חוּר.** בְּנָהּ שֶׁל מִרְיָם הָיָה, וְאָבִיו כָּלֵב בֶּן יְפֻנֶּה, שֶׁנֶּאֱמַר: "וַיִּקַּח לוֹ כָלֵב אֶת אֶפְרָת וַתֵּלֶד לוֹ אֶת חוּר" (דברי הימים א' ב, יט), אֶפְרָת זוֹ מִרְיָם, כִּדְאִיתָא בְּסוֹטָה (דף יא ע"ב): **מִי בַעַל דְּבָרִים.** מִי שֶׁיֵּשׁ לוֹ דִּין:

טז **וַיְכַסֵּהוּ הֶעָנָן.** רַבּוֹתֵינוּ חוֹלְקִים בַּדָּבָר: יֵשׁ מֵהֶם אוֹמְרִים, אֵלּוּ שִׁשָּׁה יָמִים שֶׁמֵּרֹאשׁ חֹדֶשׁ; "וַיְכַסֵּהוּ הֶעָנָן" לָהָר; "וַיִּקְרָא אֶל מֹשֶׁה בַּיּוֹם הַשְּׁבִיעִי" לוֹמַר עֲשֶׂרֶת הַדִּבְּרוֹת, וּמֹשֶׁה וְכָל בְּנֵי יִשְׂרָאֵל עוֹמְדִים, אֶלָּא שֶׁחָלַק הַכָּתוּב כָּבוֹד לְמֹשֶׁה. וְיֵשׁ אוֹמְרִים, "וַיְכַסֵּהוּ הֶעָנָן" לְמֹשֶׁה "שֵׁשֶׁת יָמִים" לְאַחַר עֲשֶׂרֶת הַדִּבְּרוֹת, וְהֵם הָיוּ בִּתְחִלַּת אַרְבָּעִים יוֹם שֶׁעָלָה מֹשֶׁה לְקַבֵּל הַלּוּחוֹת, וְלִמֶּדְךָ שֶׁכָּל הַנִּכְנָס לְמַחֲנֵה שְׁכִינָה טָעוּן פְּרִישָׁה שִׁשָּׁה יָמִים:

יח **בְּתוֹךְ הֶעָנָן.** עָנָן זֶה כְּמִין עָשָׁן הוּא, וְעָשָׂה לוֹ הַקָּדוֹשׁ בָּרוּךְ הוּא לְמֹשֶׁה שְׁבִיל בְּתוֹכוֹ:

עלה אלי ההרה והיה־שם ואתנה לך את־לחת האבן והתורה
יג והמצוה אשר כתבתי להורתם: ויקם משה ויהושע משרתו ויעל
יד משה אל־הר האלהים: ואל־הזקנים אמר שבו־לנו בזה עד אשר־
נשוב אליכם והנה אהרן וחור עמכם מי־בעל דברים יגש אלהם:
טו טז ויעל משה אל־ההר ויכס הענן את־ההר: וישכן כבוד־יהוה על־ מפטיר
הר סיני ויכסהו הענן ששת ימים ויקרא אל־משה ביום השביעי
יז מתוך הענן: ומראה כבוד יהוה כאש אכלת בראש ההר לעיני
יח בני ישראל: ויבא משה בתוך הענן ויעל אל־ההר ויהי משה בהר
ארבעים יום וארבעים לילה:

The הפטרה *for* פרשת משפטים *is on page 1543.*
On ראש חודש אדר א' *read the* הפטרה *on page 1635.*
On ערב ראש חודש אדר א' *read the haftara on page 1637.*
However, on the שבת *of* פרשת שקלים*, even if it also* ראש חודש
or ערב ראש חודש אדר א'*, read the* הפטרה *on page 1643.*

אונקלוס

סק לקדמי, לטורא והוי תמן, ואתין לך ית לוחי אבנא, ואוריתא
ותפקידתא, דכתבית לאלופיהון: יג וקם משה, ויהושע משמשניה,
וסליק משה לטורא דאתגלי עלוהי יקרא דיי: יד ולסביא אמר
אוריכו לנא הכא, עד דנתוב לותכון, והא אהרן וחור עמכון,
מאן דאית ליה דינא יתקרב לקדמיהון: טו וסליק משה לטורא,
וחפא עננא ית טורא: טז ושרא יקרא דיי על טורא דסיני, וחפהי
עננא שתא יומין, וקרא למשה, ביומא שביעאה מגו עננא:
יז וחיזו יקרא דיי, כאישא אכלא בריש טורא, לעיני בני ישראל:
יח ועאל משה, בגו עננא וסליק לטורא, והוה משה בטורא,
ארבעין יממין, וארבעין לילון:

Parashat Teruma

25 1 2 The Lord spoke to Moshe, saying, "Tell the Israelites to take an offering for
3 Me; take My offering from all whose heart moves them to give. These are the

רש״י

כה ב ויקחו לי תרומה. "לי" – לשמי: תרומה. הפרשה, יפרישו לי ממונם נדבה: ידבנו לבו. לשון נדבה, והוא לשון רצון טוב, פיישנ"ט בלעז: תקחו את תרומתי. אמרו רבותינו, שלש תרומות אמורות כאן: אחת תרומת בקע לגלגלת שנעשו מהם האדנים, כמו שמפרש באלה פקודי (להלן לח, כו-כז); ואחת תרומת המזבח בקע לגלגלת, לקופות לקנות מהן קרבנות צבור; ואחת תרומת המשכן נדבת כל אחד ואחד שהתנדבו. שלשה עשר דברים האמורים בענין כלם הוצרכו למלאכת המשכן או לבגדי כהונה כשתדקדק בהם:

in Exodus 32–34, in the middle of the account of the making of the Tabernacle, so clearly there is some connection between them.

Putting all this together we arrive at the boldest of all Exodus's political statements. A nation – at least, the kind of nation the Israelites are called on to become – is *created through the act of creation itself.* Not all the miracles of Exodus combined, not even the revelation at Sinai itself, turn the Israelites into a nation. In commanding Moshe to get the people to make the Tabernacle, God is in effect saying: *To turn a group of individuals into a covenantal nation, they must build something together.*

Freedom cannot be conferred by an outside force, not even by God Himself. It can be achieved only by collective, collaborative effort on the part of the people. Hence the construction of the Tabernacle. A people is made by making. A nation is built by building. What they built was a "home" for the Divine Presence. The Tabernacle, placed at the center of the camp with the tribes arrayed around it, symbolized the public square, the common good, the voice that had summoned them to collective freedom. It was a visible emblem of community. Within the Tabernacle was the Ark, within the Ark were the tablets of stone, and on the tablets of stone were written the details of the covenant. It was the home of their constitution of liberty. What was true for the Israelites holds true in each generation. Society, like the Tabernacle, is the home we must build together.

25:2 כָּל־אִישׁ אֲשֶׁר יִדְּבֶנּוּ לִבּוֹ *All whose heart moves them to give* – The emphasis is on the voluntary nature of the gifts. Yet the Sanctuary and its service were overwhelmingly compulsory, not voluntary. The regular offerings were minutely prescribed. So too were the contributions. During the initial construction of the Sanctuary, everyone had to give a half shekel for the silver sockets. In addition, there was an annual mandatory half shekel for the sacrifices. Why then was the Sanctuary specifically to be built through voluntary donations?

The Sanctuary was intended to stand at the heart, geographical and spiritual, of a nation that had been taken by God from slavery to freedom. The faith of Israel therefore had to be an expression of liberty. Faith, coerced, is not faith. Worship, forced, is not true worship. A Sanctuary built by conscripted labor conflicts with the very nature of God to whom it is dedicated.

It was thus not accidental, but of the essence, that the first House of God – small and portable – was built through free, uncoerced, voluntary contributions. For God lives not in houses of wood and stone, but in the minds and souls of free human beings. He is to be found not in monumental architecture, but in the willing heart.

25:3 וְזֹאת הַתְּרוּמָה אֲשֶׁר תִּקְחוּ מֵאִתָּם *The offerings you shall receive from them* – How do you feel the presence of God in the midst of everyday life? The answer, I believe, is in the name of this *parasha*, Teruma. It means "an offering." God said to Moshe: "Tell the Israelites to take an offering for Me; take My offering from all whose heart moves them to give"

פרשת תרומה

כה א וַיְדַבֵּ֥ר יְהוָ֖ה אֶל־מֹשֶׁ֥ה לֵּאמֹֽר׃ ב דַּבֵּר֙ אֶל־בְּנֵ֣י יִשְׂרָאֵ֔ל וְיִקְחוּ־לִ֖י תְּרוּמָ֑ה יח
ג מֵאֵ֤ת כׇּל־אִישׁ֙ אֲשֶׁ֣ר יִדְּבֶ֣נּוּ לִבּ֔וֹ תִּקְח֖וּ אֶת־תְּרוּמָתִֽי׃ וְזֹאת֙ הַתְּרוּמָ֔ה

אונקלוס

כה א וּמַלֵּיל יי עִם מֹשֶׁה לְמֵימַר: ב מַלֵּיל עִם בְּנֵי יִשְׂרָאֵל, וְיַפְרְשׁוּן קֳדָמַי אַפְרָשׁוּתָא, מִן כָּל גְּבַר דְּיִתְרְעֵי לִבֵּיהּ, תִּסְּבוּן יָת אַפְרָשׁוּתִי: ג וְדָא אַפְרָשׁוּתָא,

TERUMA

Parashat Teruma begins the longest single passage in the book of Exodus, continuing to the end of the book and interrupted only by the episode of the golden calf. Its subject is the *Mishkan*, the Tabernacle or Sanctuary that the Israelites were commanded to make as a center of worship and as a visible sign of the presence of God in their midst. The length and painstaking detail of the narrative indicate that the Divine Presence is not brought fully to earth in sudden moments of inspiration but through the long and collaborative process through which the people Israel fashions its life in accordance with the divine command. Israel is a people at whose center is the space we make for God. In the desert it was in the Tabernacle in the middle of the camp, in Israel it was in the Temple in Jerusalem, elsewhere it was in the synagogue at the core of the community. Jews wrestled with the paradox of the encounter between the infinity of God and the finitude of man. When Solomon dedicated the Temple he said, "For will God truly dwell on earth? If the heavens – the highest heavens – cannot contain You, how will this House that I have built?" (I Kings 8:27). The answer the Torah gave is that God exists in the space we make for Him, and the purpose of the Sanctuary is to open such a space at the heart of our collective life.

CALLING FOR CONTRIBUTIONS

The early chapters of Exodus are all about the politics of freedom. But the last section, beginning here and covering roughly a third of the book, is taken up with an apparently minor and irrelevant episode told and retold in exhaustive detail: the construction of the Tabernacle.

This was the first house of worship built by the Israelites. It was a modest affair, made of poles, beams, skins, and drapes, all of which could be taken apart, carried on their journeys, and reassembled at their next encampment. It had, or so it seems, no lasting significance. Once the Israelites had entered the land, the Tabernacle was left in Shilo for several centuries until King David established Jerusalem as the capital of the newly united kingdom, and his son Shlomo built the Temple. So why is the story of the Tabernacle told at such length?

The Torah is a political as well as a spiritual text, and it tells a political story. Despite the miracles, the essential narrative is remarkably human. The Israelites are portrayed as a querulous, almost ungovernable group. Moshe, their deliverer, comes to them with the news that they are about to go free. His first intervention, however, only makes things worse, and the people complain. Eventually the people leave, but Pharaoh and his army pursue them. Trapped between the approaching Egyptian chariots and the Sea of Reeds, again the Israelites complain. Moshe performs a miracle. The sea divides. But three days later, they are complaining again, this time about the lack of water.

Some six weeks later, at Mount Sinai, they receive the great revelation. God speaks directly to the people and they forge a covenant. Moshe ascends the mountain to receive the tablets on which the covenant provisions are engraved. While he is away, the Israelites commit their greatest sin: the worshipping of the golden calf. The episode will be told

4 offerings you shall receive from them: gold, silver and bronze; sky-blue, purple,
5 and scarlet wool; linen and goats' hair; rams' hides dyed red and fine leather;
6 acacia wood; oil for the lamps; spices for the anointing oil and the fragrant
7 incense; and rock crystal together with other precious stones for the ephod and
8 breast piece. They shall make Me a Sanctuary and I will dwell in their midst.
9 Form the Tabernacle and form all of its furnishings following the patterns that

רש״י

ג **זָהָב וָכֶסֶף וּנְחֹשֶׁת וְגוֹ׳.** כֻּלָּם בָּאוּ בִּנְדָבָה אִישׁ אִישׁ מַה שֶּׁנְּדָבוֹ לִבּוֹ, חוּץ מִן הַכֶּסֶף שֶׁבָּא בְּשָׁוֶה, מַחֲצִית הַשֶּׁקֶל לְכָל אֶחָד. וְלֹא מָצִינוּ בְּכָל מְלֶאכֶת הַמִּשְׁכָּן שֶׁהֻצְרַךְ שָׁם כֶּסֶף יוֹתֵר, שֶׁנֶּאֱמַר: ״וְכֶסֶף פְּקוּדֵי הָעֵדָה וְגוֹ׳ בֶּקַע לַגֻּלְגֹּלֶת״ וְגוֹ׳ (להלן לח, כה-כו). וּשְׁאָר הַכֶּסֶף הַבָּא שָׁם בִּנְדָבָה (להלן לה, כד) עֲשָׂאוּהוּ לִכְלֵי שָׁרֵת:

ד **וּתְכֵלֶת.** צֶמֶר צָבוּעַ בְּדַם חִלָּזוֹן, וְצִבְעוֹ יָרֹק: **וְאַרְגָּמָן.** צֶמֶר צָבוּעַ מִמִּין צֶבַע שֶׁשְּׁמוֹ אַרְגָּמָן: **וְשֵׁשׁ.** הוּא פִּשְׁתָּן: **וְעִזִּים.** נוֹצָה שֶׁל עִזִּים, לְכָךְ תִּרְגֵּם אוּנְקְלוֹס: ״וּמַעְזֵי״, דָּבָר הַבָּא מִן הָעִזִּים וְלֹא עִזִּים עַצְמָן, שֶׁתַּרְגּוּם שֶׁל עִזִּים ׳עִזַּיָּא׳:

ה **מְאָדָּמִים.** צְבוּעוֹת הָיוּ אָדֹם לְאַחַר עִבּוּדָן: **תְּחָשִׁים.** מִין חַיָּה, וְלֹא הָיְתָה אֶלָּא לְשָׁעָה, וְהַרְבֵּה גְּוָנִים הָיוּ לָהּ, לְכָךְ מְתֻרְגָּם ״סַסְגוֹנָא״, שֶׁשָּׂשׂ וּמִתְפָּאֵר בִּגְוָנִין שֶׁלּוֹ: **וַעֲצֵי שִׁטִּים.** וּמֵאַיִן הָיוּ לָהֶם בַּמִּדְבָּר? פֵּרֵשׁ רַבִּי תַּנְחוּמָא, יַעֲקֹב אָבִינוּ צָפָה בְּרוּחַ הַקֹּדֶשׁ שֶׁעֲתִידִין יִשְׂרָאֵל לִבְנוֹת מִשְׁכָּן בַּמִּדְבָּר, וְהֵבִיא אֲרָזִים לְמִצְרַיִם וּנְטָעָם, וְצִוָּה לְבָנָיו לִטְּלָם עִמָּהֶם כְּשֶׁיֵּצְאוּ מִמִּצְרַיִם:

ו **שֶׁמֶן לַמָּאֹר.** שֶׁמֶן זַיִת זָךְ לְהַעֲלוֹת נֵר תָּמִיד: **בְּשָׂמִים לְשֶׁמֶן הַמִּשְׁחָה.** שֶׁנַּעֲשָׂה לִמְשֹׁחַ כְּלֵי הַמִּשְׁכָּן וְהַמִּשְׁכָּן לְקַדְּשׁוֹ, וְהֻצְרְכוּ לוֹ בְּשָׂמִים, כְּמוֹ שֶׁמְּפֹרָשׁ בְּ׳כִי תִשָּׂא׳ (להלן ל, כג-כה): **וְלִקְטֹרֶת הַסַּמִּים.** שֶׁהָיוּ מַקְטִירִין בְּכָל בֹּקֶר וָעֶרֶב, כְּמוֹ שֶׁמְּפֹרָשׁ בְּ׳וְאַתָּה תְּצַוֶּה׳ (להלן ל, ז-ח). וּלְשׁוֹן קְטֹרֶת, הַעֲלָאַת קִיטוֹר וְתִימְרוֹת עָשָׁן:

ז **אַבְנֵי שֹׁהַם.** שְׁתַּיִם הֻצְרְכוּ שָׁם לְצֹרֶךְ הָאֵפוֹד הָאָמוּר בְּ׳וְאַתָּה תְּצַוֶּה׳ (שם כח, ט-יב): **מִלֻּאִים.** עַל שֵׁם שֶׁעוֹשִׂין לָהֶם בַּזָּהָב מוֹשָׁב כְּמִין גּוּמָא וְנוֹתְנִין הָאֶבֶן שָׁם לְמַלֹּאות הַגּוּמָא, קְרוּיִים ״אַבְנֵי מִלּוּאִים״, וּמְקוֹם הַמּוֹשָׁב קָרוּי מִשְׁבֶּצֶת: **לָאֵפֹד וְלַחֹשֶׁן.** הַשֹּׁהַם לָאֵפוֹד וְאַבְנֵי הַמִּלּוּאִים לַחֹשֶׁן. וְחֹשֶׁן וְאֵפוֹד מְפֹרָשִׁים בְּ׳וְאַתָּה תְּצַוֶּה׳ (שם כח, ו-ל), וְהֵם מִינֵי תַּכְשִׁיט:

ח **וְעָשׂוּ לִי מִקְדָּשׁ.** וְעָשׂוּ לִשְׁמִי בֵּית קְדֻשָּׁה:

ט **כְּכֹל אֲשֶׁר אֲנִי מַרְאֶה אוֹתְךָ.** כָּאן ״אֵת תַּבְנִית הַמִּשְׁכָּן״. הַמִּקְרָא הַזֶּה מְחֻבָּר לַמִּקְרָא שֶׁלְּמַעְלָה הֵימֶנּוּ: ״וְעָשׂוּ לִי מִקְדָּשׁ... כְּכֹל אֲשֶׁר אֲנִי מַרְאֶה אוֹתְךָ... וְכֵן תַּעֲשׂוּ״ לְדוֹרוֹת, אִם יֹאבַד אֶחָד מִן הַכֵּלִים, אוֹ כְּשֶׁתַּעֲשׂוּ לִי כְּלֵי בֵּית עוֹלָמִים כְּגוֹן שֻׁלְחָנוֹת וּמְנוֹרוֹת וְכִיּוֹרוֹת וּמְכוֹנוֹת שֶׁעָשָׂה שְׁלֹמֹה, כְּתַבְנִית אֵלּוּ תַּעֲשׂוּ אוֹתָם. וְאִם לֹא הָיָה הַמִּקְרָא מְחֻבָּר לְמַעְלָה הֵימֶנּוּ, לֹא הָיָה לוֹ לִכְתֹּב: ״וְכֵן תַּעֲשׂוּ״ אֶלָּא ״כֵּן תַּעֲשׂוּ״, וְהָיָה מְדַבֵּר עַל עֲשִׂיַּת אֹהֶל מוֹעֵד וְכֵלָיו:

of the Jewish heart. It is the ultimate expression of monotheism – that wherever we gather to turn our hearts toward Heaven, there the Divine Presence can be found.

THE DETAILS OF THE TABERNACLE

Moshe is shown a pattern image of what the Tabernacle is to look like: "the patterns that I show you" (see Ibn Ezra). What is the eternal significance of the dimensions of this modest, portable, temporary construction? To put the question more sharply still: Is not the very idea of a specific size for the home of the *Shekhina*, the Divine Presence, liable to mislead? A transcendent God cannot be contained in space. What difference could it make whether the Tabernacle was large or small? Either way, it was a symbol, a focus, of the Divine Presence that is everywhere, wherever human beings open their heart to God. Its exact dimensions should not matter.

Torah commentators, especially Nehama Leibowitz, have drawn attention to the way the terminology of the construction of the Tabernacle is the same as that used to describe God's creation of the universe. The key Hebrew words – for *make, see, complete, bless, sanctify, work, behold* – appear in both texts. The latter creation mirrors the former. As God made the universe, so He instructed the Israelites to make the *Mishkan*. The Tabernacle was, in other words, a microcosmos, a symbolic reminder of the world God made. The fact that the Divine Presence rested within it was not meant to suggest that God is here not there, in this place not that. It was meant to signal, powerfully and palpably, that just as God exists within its walls, so too does

ד אֲשֶׁר תִּקְחוּ מֵאִתָּם זָהָב וָכֶסֶף וּנְחֹשֶׁת׃ וּתְכֵלֶת וְאַרְגָּמָן וְתוֹלַעַת
ה שָׁנִי וְשֵׁשׁ וְעִזִּים׃ וְעֹרֹת אֵילִם מְאָדָּמִים וְעֹרֹת תְּחָשִׁים וַעֲצֵי שִׁטִּים׃
ו שֶׁמֶן לַמָּאֹר בְּשָׂמִים לְשֶׁמֶן הַמִּשְׁחָה וְלִקְטֹרֶת הַסַּמִּים׃ אַבְנֵי־שֹׁהַם
ח ט וְאַבְנֵי מִלֻּאִים לָאֵפֹד וְלַחֹשֶׁן׃ וְעָשׂוּ לִי מִקְדָּשׁ וְשָׁכַנְתִּי בְּתוֹכָם׃ כְּכֹל
אֲשֶׁר אֲנִי מַרְאֶה אוֹתְךָ אֵת תַּבְנִית הַמִּשְׁכָּן וְאֵת תַּבְנִית כָּל־כֵּלָיו

אונקלוס

דְּתִסְּבוּן מִנְּהוֹן, דַּהְבָא וְכַסְפָּא וּנְחָשָׁא: ד וְתַכְלָא וְאַרְגְּוָנָא, וּצְבַע זְהוֹרִי וּבוּץ וּמַעְזֵי: ה וּמַשְׁכֵי דִּדְכְרֵי מְסַמְּקֵי, וּמַשְׁכֵי סַסְגּוֹנָא וְאָעֵי שִׁטִּין: ו מִשְׁחָא לְאַנְהָרוּתָא, בֻּסְמַיָּא לִמְשַׁח רְבוּתָא, וְלִקְטֹרֶת בֻּסְמַיָּא: ז אַבְנֵי בֻרְלָא, וְאַבְנֵי אַשְׁלָמוּתָא, לְשַׁקָּעָא בְּאֵיפוֹדָא וּבְחֻשְׁנָא: ח וְיַעְבְּדוּן קֳדָמַי מַקְדַּשׁ, וְאַשְׁרֵי שְׁכִינְתִי בֵּינֵיהוֹן: ט כְּכֹל, דַּאֲנָא מַחְזֵי יָתָךְ, יָת דְּמוּת מַשְׁכְּנָא, וְיָת דְּמוּת כָּל מָנוֹהִי,

Hence the resonant word that gives its name to this *parasha*: Teruma. I've translated it as "an offering," but it actually has a subtly different meaning for which there is no simple English equivalent. It means "something you lift up" by dedicating it to a sacred cause. You lift it up, and then it lifts you up.

25:8 בְּתוֹכָם *In their midst* – The Jewish mystics pointed out the linguistic strangeness of this verse. It should have said, "They shall make Me a Sanctuary and I will dwell in it," the Sanctuary, not "and I will dwell in their midst." The reason for this wording is that the Divine Presence lives not in a building, but in its builders, not in a physical place but in the human heart. The Sanctuary was not a place in which the objective existence of God was somehow more concentrated than elsewhere. Rather, it was a place whose holiness had the effect of opening hearts to the One worshipped there. God exists everywhere, but not everywhere do we feel the presence of God in the same way. The essence of "the holy" is that it is a place where we set aside all human devices and desires and enter a domain wholly set aside for God.

If the concept of the *Mishkan*, the Tabernacle, is that God lives in the human heart whenever it opens itself unreservedly to Heaven, then the way is open to the synagogue: the supreme statement of the idea that if God is everywhere, He can be reached anywhere. After the destruction of the Temple, the synagogue became Jerusalem in exile, the home

(Ex. 25:2). In other words, the best way of encountering God is to give.

The very act of giving flows from, or leads to, the understanding that what we give is part of what we were given. It is a way of giving thanks, an act of gratitude. That is the difference in the human mind between the presence of God and the absence of God.

If God is present, it means that what we have is His. He created the universe. He made us. He gave us life. He breathed into us the very air we breathe. All around us is the majesty, the plenitude, of God's generosity: the light of the sun, the green of the leaves, the song of the birds.

When life is something given, you acknowledge this by giving back. But *if life is not a given because there is no giver*, if the universe came into existence only because of a random fluctuation in the quantum field, if our moral convictions are self-serving means of self-preservation, and our spiritual aspirations mere delusions, then it is difficult to feel gratitude for the gift of life. There is no gift if there is no giver. There is only a series of meaningless accidents, and it is difficult to feel gratitude for an accident.

The Torah therefore tells us something simple and practical. Give, and you will come to see life as a gift. *You don't need to be able to prove God exists. All you need is to be thankful that you exist – and the rest will follow.* That is how God came to be close to the Israelites through the building of the Sanctuary. *Where people give voluntarily to one another and to holy causes, that is where the Divine Presence rests.*

10 I show you. Make an Ark of acacia wood, two and a half cubits long,
11 a cubit and a half wide, and a cubit and a half high. Overlay it with pure gold,
12 inside and out, and around it make a gold rim. Cast four gold rings for it and
place them on its four corners, two rings on one side and two on the other.
13 14 Make staves of acacia wood and overlay them with gold; place these staves in
15 the rings on the sides of the Ark so that the Ark may be carried. The staves must
16 stay in the rings of the Ark; they must not be removed. Inside the Ark, place the
17 tablets of the Covenant that I will give you. Make an Ark cover of pure gold, SHENI
18 two and a half cubits long and a cubit and a half wide. Make two cherubim of

רש״י

י **ועשו ארון.** כמין ארונות שעושים בלא רגלים עשוים כמין ארגז שקורין אשקרי״ן, יושב על שוליו:

יא **מבית ומחוץ תצפנו.** שלשה ארונות עשה בצלאל, שנים של זהב ואחד של עץ, ארבעה כתלים ושולים לכל אחד, ופתוחים מלמעלה. נתן של עץ בתוך של זהב, ושל זהב בתוך של עץ, וחפה שפתו העליונה בזהב, נמצא מצפה מבית ומחוץ: **זר זהב.** כמין כתר מקיף לו סביב למעלה משפתו, שעשה הארון החיצון גבוה מן הפנימי עד שעלה למול עבי הכפרת ולמעלה הימנו משהו, וכשהכפרת שוכב על עבי הכתלים עולה הזר למעלה מכל עבי הכפרת כל שהוא, והוא סימן לכתר תורה:

יב **ויצקת.** לשון התכה, כתרגומו: **פעמתיו.** כתרגומו: "זויתיה". ובזויות העליונות סמוך לכפרת היו נתונות, שתים מכאן ושתים מכאן לרחבו של ארון, והבדים נתונים בהם, וארכו של ארון מפסיק בין הבדים אמתים וחצי בין בד לבד, שיהיו שני בני אדם הנושאים את הארון מהלכין ביניהם, וכן מפורש במנחות בפרק 'שתי הלחם' (דף צח ע״ב): **ושתי טבעת על צלעו האחת.** הן הן ארבע טבעות שבתחלת המקרא, ופרש לך היכן היו. והוי״ו זו יתרה היא, ופתרונו כמו שתי טבעת. ויש לך לישבה כן: ושתים מן הטבעות האלו על צלעו האחת: **צלעו.** צדו:

יג **בדי.** מוטות:

טו **לא יסרו ממנו.** לעולם:

טז **ונתת אל הארן.** כמו בארון: **העדת.** התורה שהיא לעדות ביני וביניכם שצויתי אתכם מצוות הכתובות בה:

יז **כפרת.** כסוי על הארון, שהיה פתוח מלמעלה ומניחו עליו כמין דף: **אמתים וחצי ארכה.** כארכו של ארון, ורחבה כרחבו של ארון, ומנחת על עבי הכתלים ארבעתם. ואף על פי שלא נתן שעור לעביה, פרשו רבותינו שהיה עביה טפח:

יח **כרבים.** דמות פרצוף תינוק להם: **מקשה תעשה אתם.** שלא תעשם בפני עצמם ותחברם בראשי הכפרת לאחר עשייתם כמעשה צורפים שקורין שולדדי״ן, אלא הטל זהב הרבה בתחלת עשיית הכפרת, והכה בפטיש ובקרנס באמצע וראשין בולטין למעלה,

Why "they shall make," not "you"? Why the shift from the singular to the plural?

The Ark was made to hold the tablets of stone given to Moshe by God at Mount Sinai. The Torah calls the tablets "the testimony" since they were the physical symbol of the Sinai covenant. According to the Sages, "both the [complete second set of] tablets and the fragments of the [first] tablets [which Moshe broke after the golden calf] were in the Ark" (Berakhot 8b; Bava Batra 14b; Menaḥot 99a). The Ark, in short, symbolized and represented Torah.

The reason, therefore, that the construction of the Ark is commanded in the plural is that everyone is to have a share in it (see Ramban on this verse). Unlike other aspects of service in the Sanctuary or Temple, Torah is the heritage of everyone. All Israel were parties to the covenant. All were expected to know and study its terms. Judaism might know other hierarchies, but when it came to knowledge, study, and the dignity conferred by scholarship, everyone stood on equal footing. That is why, here alone in its list of the component parts of the Sanctuary, the Torah shifts from the second-person singular to the third-person plural. When it comes to the Ark, home and symbol of the most significant form of knowledge, everyone must have an equal share.

י וְכֵן תַּעֲשׂוּ׃ וְעָשׂוּ אֲרוֹן עֲצֵי שִׁטִּים אַמָּתַיִם וָחֵצִי אָרְכּוֹ
יא וְאַמָּה וָחֵצִי רָחְבּוֹ וְאַמָּה וָחֵצִי קֹמָתוֹ׃ וְצִפִּיתָ אֹתוֹ זָהָב טָהוֹר מִבַּיִת
יב וּמִחוּץ תְּצַפֶּנּוּ וְעָשִׂיתָ עָלָיו זֵר זָהָב סָבִיב׃ וְיָצַקְתָּ לּוֹ אַרְבַּע טַבְּעֹת
זָהָב וְנָתַתָּה עַל אַרְבַּע פַּעֲמֹתָיו וּשְׁתֵּי טַבָּעֹת עַל־צַלְעוֹ הָאֶחָת וּשְׁתֵּי
יג טַבָּעֹת עַל־צַלְעוֹ הַשֵּׁנִית׃ וְעָשִׂיתָ בַדֵּי עֲצֵי שִׁטִּים וְצִפִּיתָ אֹתָם זָהָב׃
יד וְהֵבֵאתָ אֶת־הַבַּדִּים בַּטַּבָּעֹת עַל צַלְעֹת הָאָרֹן לָשֵׂאת אֶת־הָאָרֹן
טו טז בָּהֶם׃ בְּטַבְּעֹת הָאָרֹן יִהְיוּ הַבַּדִּים לֹא יָסֻרוּ מִמֶּנּוּ׃ וְנָתַתָּ אֶל־הָאָרֹן
יז אֵת הָעֵדֻת אֲשֶׁר אֶתֵּן אֵלֶיךָ׃ וְעָשִׂיתָ כַפֹּרֶת זָהָב טָהוֹר אַמָּתַיִם וָחֵצִי שני
יח אָרְכָּהּ וְאַמָּה וָחֵצִי רָחְבָּהּ׃ וְעָשִׂיתָ שְׁנַיִם כְּרֻבִים זָהָב מִקְשָׁה תַּעֲשֶׂה

אונקלוס

וְכֵן תַּעְבְּדוּן: י וְיַעְבְּדוּן אֲרוֹנָא דְּאָעֵי שִׁטִּין, תַּרְתֵּין אַמִּין וּפַלְגָא אֻרְכֵּיהּ, וְאַמְּתָא וּפַלְגָא פְּתָיֵהּ, וְאַמְּתָא וּפַלְגָא רוּמֵיהּ: יא וְתַחְפֵּי יָתֵיהּ דְּהַב דְּכֵי, מִגָּיו וּמִבָּרָא תַּחְפֵינֵיהּ, וְתַעְבֵּיד עֲלוֹהִי, זִיר דִּדְהַב סְחוֹר סְחוֹר: יב וְתַתֵּיךְ לֵיהּ, אַרְבַּע עִזְקָן דִּדְהַב, וְתִתֵּין, עַל אַרְבַּע זָוְיָתֵיהּ, וְתַרְתֵּין עִזְקָן, עַל סִטְרֵיהּ חַד, וְתַרְתֵּין עִזְקָן, עַל סִטְרֵיהּ תִּנְיָנָא: יג וְתַעְבֵּיד אֲרִיחֵי דְּאָעֵי שִׁטִּין, וְתַחְפֵּי יָתְהוֹן דַּהֲבָא: יד וְתַעֵיל יָת אֲרִיחַיָּא בְּעִזְקָתָא, עַל סִטְרֵי אֲרוֹנָא, לְמִטַּל יָת אֲרוֹנָא בְּהוֹן: טו בְּעִזְקָת אֲרוֹנָא, יְהוֹן אֲרִיחַיָּא, לָא יַעְדּוֹן מִנֵּיהּ: טז וְתִתֵּין בַּאֲרוֹנָא, יָת סָהֲדוּתָא, דְּאֶתֵּין לָךְ: יז וְתַעְבֵּיד כַּפֻּרְתָּא דִּדְהַב דְּכֵי, תַּרְתֵּין אַמִּין וּפַלְגָא אֻרְכַּהּ, וְאַמְּתָא וּפַלְגָא פְּתָיַהּ: יח וְתַעְבֵּיד, תְּרֵין כְּרוּבִין דִּדְהַב, נְגִיד תַּעְבֵּיד

He exist throughout the macrocosmos. It was a man-made structure to focus attention on the divinely created universe. It was in space what the Sabbath is in time: a reminder of creation.

The dimensions of the universe are precise, mathematically exact. Had they differed in even the slightest degree, the universe, or life, would not exist. The misplacement of even a few of the 3.1 billion letters in the human genome can lead to devastating genetic conditions. The famous "butterfly effect" – the beating of a butterfly's wing somewhere may cause a tsunami elsewhere, thousands of miles away – tells us that small actions can have large consequences. Precision matters. Order matters. That is the message the Tabernacle was intended to convey.

God creates order in the natural universe. We are charged with creating order in the human universe. That means painstaking care in what we say, what we do, and what we must restrain ourselves from doing. There is a precise choreography to the moral and spiritual life as there is a precise architecture to the Tabernacle. Being good, specifically being holy, is not a matter of acting as the spirit moves us. It is a matter of aligning ourselves to the Will that made the world. Law, structure, precision: of these things the cosmos is made and without them it would cease to be. The fact the Torah records the precise dimensions of the Tabernacle signals that the same applies to human behavior.

25:10 **וְעָשׂוּ אֲרוֹן עֲצֵי שִׁטִּים** *Make an Ark of acacia wood – Ve'asu* – literally, "they shall make." God instructs Moshe in the making of the Sanctuary and its appurtenances, detail by detail. In each case the verb is in the second-person singular: *vetzipita, ve'asita, veyatzakta, venatata, veheveta,* "you shall cover…you shall make…you shall pour…you shall place…you shall bring." However, there is one exception to this rule: the Ark. There the verb is in the third-person plural.

19 beaten gold and place them at the two ends of the cover: one cherub at one end
and one at the other; the cherubim shall be made of one piece with the cover.
20 These cherubim should have wings spread upward, sheltering the cover. They
21 should face one another, and look toward the cover. Place the cover on top of
the Ark, and inside the Ark place the tablets of the Covenant that I will give
22 you. There, from above the cover, between the two cherubim, above the Ark
of the Testimony, I will meet with you and speak with you, and give you all My
commands to the Israelites.
23 Make a table of acacia wood, two cubits long, a cubit wide, and a cubit and
24 25 a half high. Overlay it with pure gold and around it make a gold rim. Make a
frame a handbreadth wide all around, and around the frame also make a gold

רש״י

וַעֲיֵיר הַכְּרוּבִים בִּבְלִיטַת קְצוֹתָיו: **מִקְשָׁה.** בטדי״ץ בְּלַעַז, כְּמוֹ: ״דָּא לְדָא נָקְשָׁן״ (דניאל ה, ו): **קְצוֹת הַכַּפֹּרֶת.** רָאשֵׁי הַכַּפֹּרֶת:

יט **וַעֲשֵׂה כְּרוּב אֶחָד מִקָּצָה.** שֶׁלֹּא תֹּאמַר, שְׁנַיִם כְּרוּבִים לְכָל קָצֶה וְקָצֶה, לְכָךְ הֻצְרַךְ לְפָרֵשׁ: ״כְּרוּב אֶחָד מִקָּצָה מִזֶּה״: **מִן הַכַּפֹּרֶת.** עַצְמָהּ, ״תַּעֲשׂוּ אֶת הַכְּרֻבִים״. זֶהוּ פֵּרוּשׁוֹ שֶׁל ״מִקְשָׁה תַּעֲשֶׂה אֹתָם״, שֶׁלֹּא תַּעֲשֵׂם בִּפְנֵי עַצְמָם וּתְחַבְּרֵם לַכַּפֹּרֶת:

כ **פֹּרְשֵׂי כְנָפַיִם.** שֶׁלֹּא תַּעֲשֶׂה כַּנְפֵיהֶם שׁוֹכְבִים, אֶלָּא פְּרוּשִׂים וּגְבוֹהִים לְמַעְלָה אֵצֶל רָאשֵׁיהֶם, שֶׁיְּהֵא עֲשָׂרָה טְפָחִים בֶּחָלָל שֶׁבֵּין הַכְּנָפַיִם לַכַּפֹּרֶת, כִּדְאִיתָא בְּסֻכָּה (דף ה ע״ב):

כא **וְאֶל הָאָרֹן תִּתֵּן אֶת הָעֵדֻת.** לֹא יָדַעְתִּי לָמָּה נִכְפַּל, שֶׁהֲרֵי כְּבָר נֶאֱמַר: ״וְנָתַתָּ אֶל הָאָרֹן אֵת הָעֵדֻת״ (לעיל פסוק טז)! וְיֵשׁ לוֹמַר, שֶׁבָּא לְלַמֵּד שֶׁבְּעוֹדוֹ אָרוֹן לְבַדּוֹ בְּלֹא כַּפֹּרֶת יִתֵּן תְּחִלָּה הָעֵדוּת לְתוֹכוֹ, וְאַחַר כָּךְ יִתֵּן אֶת הַכַּפֹּרֶת עָלָיו, וְכֵן מָצִינוּ כְּשֶׁהֵקִים אֶת הַמִּשְׁכָּן, נֶאֱמַר: ״וַיִּתֵּן אֶת הָעֵדֻת אֶל הָאָרֹן״ וְאַחַר כָּךְ: ״וַיִּתֵּן אֶת הַכַּפֹּרֶת עַל הָאָרֹן מִלְמָעְלָה״ (להלן מ, כ):

כב **וְנוֹעַדְתִּי.** כְּשֶׁאֶקְבַּע מוֹעֵד לְךָ לְדַבֵּר עִמְּךָ, אוֹתוֹ מָקוֹם אֶקְבַּע לַמּוֹעֵד, שֶׁאָבֹא שָׁם לְדַבֵּר אֵלֶיךָ: **וְדִבַּרְתִּי אִתְּךָ מֵעַל הַכַּפֹּרֶת.** וּבְמָקוֹם אַחֵר הוּא אוֹמֵר: ״וַיְדַבֵּר ה׳ אֵלָיו מֵאֹהֶל מוֹעֵד לֵאמֹר״ (ויקרא א, א), זֶה הַמִּשְׁכָּן מִחוּץ לַפָּרֹכֶת, נִמְצְאוּ שְׁנֵי כְתוּבִים מַכְחִישִׁים זֶה אֶת זֶה! בָּא הַכָּתוּב הַשְּׁלִישִׁי וְהִכְרִיעַ בֵּינֵיהֶם: ״וּבְבֹא מֹשֶׁה אֶל אֹהֶל מוֹעֵד... וַיִּשְׁמַע אֶת הַקּוֹל מִדַּבֵּר אֵלָיו מֵעַל הַכַּפֹּרֶת״ וְגוֹ׳ (במדבר ז, פט), מֹשֶׁה הָיָה נִכְנָס לַמִּשְׁכָּן, וְכֵיוָן שֶׁבָּא בְּתוֹךְ הַפֶּתַח קוֹל יוֹרֵד מִן הַשָּׁמַיִם לְבֵין הַכְּרוּבִים, וּמִשָּׁם יוֹצֵא וְנִשְׁמַע לְמֹשֶׁה בְּאֹהֶל מוֹעֵד: **וְאֵת כָּל אֲשֶׁר אֲצַוֶּה אוֹתְךָ אֶל בְּנֵי יִשְׂרָאֵל.** הֲרֵי וָי״ו זוֹ יְתֵרָה וּטְפֵלָה. וְכָמוֹהָ הַרְבֵּה בַּמִּקְרָא, וְכֹה תִּפְתָּר: וַאֲשֶׁר אֲדַבֵּר עִמְּךָ שָׁם ״אֵת כָּל אֲשֶׁר אֲצַוֶּה אוֹתְךָ אֶל בְּנֵי יִשְׂרָאֵל״ הוּא:

כג **קֹמָתוֹ.** גֹּבַהּ רַגְלָיו עִם עֳבִי הַשֻּׁלְחָן:

כד **זֵר זָהָב.** סִימָן לְכֶתֶר מַלְכוּת, שֶׁהַשֻּׁלְחָן שֵׁם עֹשֶׁר וּגְדֻלָּה, כְּמוֹ שֶׁאוֹמְרִים: שֻׁלְחַן מְלָכִים:

25:22 **מֵעַל הַכַּפֹּרֶת** *There, from above the cover* – At the heart of the Tabernacle, framed between the two cherubim, where in a different shrine one might expect to find the graven image of a god, God will reveal Himself from an empty space.

The holy, in the Tanakh, simply means *God's domain* – those points in time and space at which His presence is peculiarly visible. That is what Yeshayahu means when he says of Israel: "'You are My witnesses,' so says the Lord… 'that I am He'" (Is. 43:10). Holiness is the space vacated by us so that God's presence can be felt in our midst. Every time we set aside our desires in order to act on the basis of God's will, not our own, we engage in self-limitation – we take up a little less space ourselves, creating the space in which God can be felt. The everyday world is the space God makes for us. *Kedusha*, holiness, is the space we make for God.

יט אֹתָם מִשְּׁנֵי קְצוֹת הַכַּפֹּרֶת: וַעֲשֵׂה כְּרוּב אֶחָד מִקָּצָה מִזֶּה וּכְרוּב־
אֶחָד מִקָּצָה מִזֶּה מִן־הַכַּפֹּרֶת תַּעֲשׂוּ אֶת־הַכְּרֻבִים עַל־שְׁנֵי קְצוֹתָיו:
כ וְהָיוּ הַכְּרֻבִים פֹּרְשֵׂי כְנָפַיִם לְמַעְלָה סֹכְכִים בְּכַנְפֵיהֶם עַל־הַכַּפֹּרֶת
כא וּפְנֵיהֶם אִישׁ אֶל־אָחִיו אֶל־הַכַּפֹּרֶת יִהְיוּ פְּנֵי הַכְּרֻבִים: וְנָתַתָּ אֶת־
הַכַּפֹּרֶת עַל־הָאָרֹן מִלְמָעְלָה וְאֶל־הָאָרֹן תִּתֵּן אֶת־הָעֵדֻת אֲשֶׁר
כב אֶתֵּן אֵלֶיךָ: וְנוֹעַדְתִּי לְךָ שָׁם וְדִבַּרְתִּי אִתְּךָ מֵעַל הַכַּפֹּרֶת מִבֵּין שְׁנֵי
הַכְּרֻבִים אֲשֶׁר עַל־אֲרוֹן הָעֵדֻת אֵת כָּל־אֲשֶׁר אֲצַוֶּה אוֹתְךָ אֶל־בְּנֵי
יִשְׂרָאֵל:
כג וְעָשִׂיתָ שֻׁלְחָן עֲצֵי שִׁטִּים אַמָּתַיִם אָרְכּוֹ וְאַמָּה רָחְבּוֹ וְאַמָּה וָחֵצִי
כד כה קֹמָתוֹ: וְצִפִּיתָ אֹתוֹ זָהָב טָהוֹר וְעָשִׂיתָ לּוֹ זֵר זָהָב סָבִיב: וְעָשִׂיתָ לּוֹ

אונקלוס

יָתְהוֹן, מִתְּרֵין סִטְרֵי כָּפֻרְתָּא: יט וַעֲבֵיד, כְּרוּבָא חַד מִסִּטְרָא מִכָּא, וּכְרוּבָא חַד מִסִּטְרָא מִכָּא, מִן כָּפֻרְתָּא, תַּעְבְּדוּן יָת כְּרוּבַיָּא עַל תְּרֵין סִטְרוֹהִי: כ וִיהוֹן כְּרוּבַיָּא פְּרִיסִין גַּדְפֵיהוֹן לְעֵילָא, מְטַלְּן בְּגַדְפֵיהוֹן עַל כָּפֻרְתָּא, וְאַפֵּיהוֹן חַד לָקֳבֵיל חַד, לָקֳבֵיל כָּפֻרְתָּא, יְהוֹן אַפֵּי כְרוּבַיָּא: כא וְתִתֵּין יָת כָּפֻרְתָּא, עַל אֲרוֹנָא מִלְעֵילָא, וּבַאֲרוֹנָא, תִּתֵּין יָת סָהֲדוּתָא, דְּאֶתֵּין לָךְ: כב וַאֲזַמֵּין מֵימְרִי לָךְ תַּמָּן, וַאֲמַלֵּיל עִמָּךְ מֵעִלָּוֵי כָּפֻרְתָּא, מִבֵּין תְּרֵין כְּרוּבַיָּא, דְּעַל אֲרוֹנָא דְסָהֲדוּתָא, יָת כָּל דַּאֲפַקֵּיד, יָתָךְ לְוָת בְּנֵי יִשְׂרָאֵל: כג וְתַעְבֵּיד פָּתוֹרָא דְּאָעֵי שִׁטִּין, תַּרְתֵּין אַמִּין אָרְכֵּיהּ וְאַמְּתָא פְּתָיֵיהּ, וְאַמְּתָא וּפַלְגָּא רוּמֵיהּ: כד וְתַחְפֵּי יָתֵיהּ דְּהַב דְּכֵי, וְתַעְבֵּיד לֵיהּ, זֵיר דִּדְהַב סְחוֹר סְחוֹר: כה וְתַעְבֵּיד לֵיהּ

25:20 וּפְנֵיהֶם אִישׁ אֶל־אָחִיו *They should face one another* - This strange and lovely detail begs for explanation. Above the Ark are to be two figures, cherubim, their faces turned to one another. Ostensibly this was a great risk. The Israelites had been told not to make any likeness that might be worshipped as a god, an idol. Why then were the figures introduced into the Holy of Holies?

The Sages say the cherubim were like children (Rashi, based on Sukka 5b), or, in another interpretation, that they were intertwined like lovers (Yoma 54a). It was *between the two cherubim* that God spoke to Moshe. The message of this symbol is so significant that it is deemed by God Himself to be sufficient to outweigh the risk of misunderstanding. *God speaks where two persons turn their faces to one another* in love, embrace, generosity, and care. God's presence is everywhere. But not everywhere are we ready to receive it. When we open our "I" to another's "Thou" – that is where God lives. We discover God's image in ourself by discerning it in another. God lives in *the between* that joins self to self through acts of covenantal kindness, *ḥesed*.

Emmanuel Levinas was right to see the concept of "face" as fundamental to our humanity. Society is faceless; *ḥesed* is a relationship of face-to-face. The Torah repeatedly emphasizes that we cannot see God face-to-face. It follows that we can only see God in the face of another.

26 rim. Make for it four gold rings, and place the rings on the four corners where
27 the four legs are. The rings should be attached next to the frame as holders
28 for staves to carry the table. Make the staves of acacia wood and overlay them
29 with gold; by these the table shall be carried. You must also make, out of pure
30 gold, its bowls, spoons, pitchers, and jars for pouring libations. On this table
the showbread must be placed before Me at all times.
31 Make a candelabrum of pure gold. Its base and shaft, cups, knobs, and flowers

רש״י

כה **מִסְגֶּרֶת.** כְּתַרְגּוּמוֹ: ״גְּדָנְפָא״. וְנֶחְלְקוּ חַכְמֵי יִשְׂרָאֵל בַּדָּבָר: יֵשׁ אוֹמְרִים לְמַעְלָה הָיְתָה סָבִיב לַשֻּׁלְחָן, כְּמוֹ לְבַזְבְּזִין שֶׁבִּשְׂפַת שֻׁלְחַן שָׂרִים, וְיֵשׁ אוֹמְרִים לְמַטָּה הָיְתָה תְּקוּעָה מֵרֶגֶל לְרֶגֶל בְּאַרְבַּע רוּחוֹת הַשֻּׁלְחָן, וְדַף הַשֻּׁלְחָן שׁוֹכֵב עַל אוֹתָהּ מִסְגֶּרֶת: **וְעָשִׂיתָ זֵר זָהָב לְמִסְגַּרְתּוֹ.** הוּא זֵר הָאָמוּר לְמַעְלָה, וּפֵרֵשׁ לְךָ כָּאן שֶׁעַל הַמִּסְגֶּרֶת הָיָה:

כז **לְעֻמַּת הַמִּסְגֶּרֶת תִּהְיֶיןָ הַטַּבָּעֹת.** בָּרַגְלַיִם תְּקוּעוֹת כְּנֶגֶד רָאשֵׁי הַמִּסְגֶּרֶת: **לְבָתִּים לְבַדִּים.** אוֹתָן הַטַּבָּעוֹת יִהְיוּ בָּתִּים לְהַכְנִיס בָּהֶן הַבַּדִּים: **לְבָתִּים.** לְצֹרֶךְ בָּתִּים: **לְבַדִּים.** כְּתַרְגּוּמוֹ: ״לְאַתְרָא לַאֲרִיחַיָּא״:

כח **וְנִשָּׂא בָם.** לְשׁוֹן נִפְעַל, יִהְיֶה נִשָּׂא בָּם אֶת הַשֻּׁלְחָן:

כט **וְעָשִׂיתָ קְעָרֹתָיו וְכַפֹּתָיו.** קְעָרֹתָיו זֶה דְּפוּס, שֶׁהָיָה עָשׂוּי כִּדְפוּס הַלֶּחֶם. וְהַלֶּחֶם הָיָה עָשׂוּי כְּמִין תֵּבָה פְּרוּצָה מִשְּׁתֵּי רוּחוֹתֶיהָ, שׁוּלַיִם לוֹ לְמַטָּה, וְזוֹקֵף מִכָּאן וּמִכָּאן כְּלַפֵּי מַעְלָה כְּמִין כְּתָלִים. וּלְכָךְ קָרוּי לֶחֶם הַפָּנִים, שֶׁיֵּשׁ לוֹ פָּנִים רוֹאִים לְכָאן וּלְכָאן לְצִדֵּי הַבַּיִת מִזֶּה וּמִזֶּה. וְנוֹתֵן אָרְכּוֹ לְרָחְבּוֹ שֶׁל שֻׁלְחָן, וּכְתָלָיו זְקוּפִים כְּנֶגֶד שְׂפַת הַשֻּׁלְחָן. וְהָיָה עָשׂוּי לוֹ דְּפוּס זָהָב וּדְפוּס בַּרְזֶל, בְּשֶׁל בַּרְזֶל הוּא נֶאֱפֶה, וּכְשֶׁמּוֹצִיאוֹ מִן הַתַּנּוּר נוֹתְנוֹ בְּשֶׁל זָהָב עַד לְמָחָר, בְּשַׁבָּת, שֶׁמְּסַדְּרוֹ עַל הַשֻּׁלְחָן, וְאוֹתוֹ דְּפוּס קָרוּי קְעָרָה: **וְכַפֹּתָיו.** בָּזִיכִין שֶׁנּוֹתְנִין בָּהֶם לְבוֹנָה, שְׁתַּיִם הָיוּ לִשְׁנֵי קָמְצֵי לְבוֹנָה שֶׁנּוֹתְנִין עַל שְׁתֵּי הַמַּעֲרָכוֹת, שֶׁנֶּאֱמַר: ״וְנָתַתָּ עַל הַמַּעֲרֶכֶת לְבֹנָה זַכָּה״ (ויקרא כד, ז): **וּקְשׂוֹתָיו.** הֵן כְּמִין חֲצָאֵי קָנִים חֲלוּלִים הַנִּסְדָּקִין לְאָרְכָּן, דֻּגְמָתָן עוֹשֶׂה שֶׁל זָהָב וּמְסַדֵּר שְׁלֹשָׁה עַל רֹאשׁ כָּל לֶחֶם, שֶׁיֵּשֵׁב לֶחֶם הָאֶחָד עַל גַּבֵּי אוֹתָן הַקָּנִים, וּמַבְדִּילִין בֵּין לֶחֶם לְלֶחֶם כְּדֵי שֶׁתִּכָּנֵס הָרוּחַ בֵּינֵיהֶם וְלֹא יִתְעַפְּשׁוּ. וּבִלְשׁוֹן עֲרָבִי כָּל דָּבָר חָלוּל קָרוּי קסו״א: **וּמְנַקִּיֹּתָיו.** תַּרְגּוּמוֹ: ״וּמְכִילָתֵיהּ״, הֵן סְנִיפִין כְּמִין יְתֵדוֹת זָהָב עוֹמְדִין בָּאָרֶץ וּגְבוֹהִין עַד לְמַעְלָה מִן הַשֻּׁלְחָן הַרְבֵּה כְּנֶגֶד גֹּבַהּ מַעֲרֶכֶת הַלֶּחֶם, וּמְפֻצָּלִים שִׁשָּׁה פִּצּוּלִים, זֶה לְמַעְלָה מִזֶּה, וְרָאשֵׁי הַקָּנִים שֶׁבֵּין לֶחֶם לְלֶחֶם סְמוּכִין עַל אוֹתָן פִּצּוּלִין, כְּדֵי שֶׁלֹּא יִכְבַּד מַשָּׂא הַלֶּחֶם הָעֶלְיוֹנִים עַל הַתַּחְתּוֹנִים וְיִשָּׁבְרוּ. וּלְשׁוֹן ״מְכִילָתֵיהּ״ סוֹבְלוֹתָיו, כְּמוֹ: ״נִלְאֵיתִי הָכִיל״ (ירמיה ו, יא). אֲבָל לְשׁוֹן 'מְנַקִּיֹּת' אֵינִי יוֹדֵעַ אֵיךְ נוֹפֵל עַל סְנִיפִין. וְיֵשׁ מֵחַכְמֵי יִשְׂרָאֵל אוֹמְרִים, ״קְשׂוֹתָיו״ אֵלּוּ סְנִיפִין, שֶׁמַּקְשִׁין אוֹתוֹ וּמַחֲזִיקִים אוֹתוֹ שֶׁלֹּא יִשָּׁבֵר, ״וּמְנַקִּיֹּתָיו״ אֵלּוּ הַקָּנִים, שֶׁמְּנַקִּין אוֹתוֹ שֶׁלֹּא יִתְעַפֵּשׁ. אֲבָל אוּנְקְלוֹס שֶׁתִּרְגֵּם: ״וּמְכִילָתֵיהּ״ הָיָה שׁוֹנֶה כְּדִבְרֵי הָאוֹמֵר מְנַקִּיּוֹת הֵן סְנִיפִין: **אֲשֶׁר יֻסַּךְ בָּהֵן.** אֲשֶׁר יְכֻסֶּה בָּהֶן. וְעַל קְשׂוֹתָיו הוּא אוֹמֵר: ״אֲשֶׁר יֻסַּךְ״, שֶׁהָיוּ עָלָיו כְּמִין סְכָךְ וְכִסּוּי, וְכֵן בְּמָקוֹם אַחֵר הוּא אוֹמֵר: ״וְאֵת קְשׂוֹת הַנָּסֶךְ״ (במדבר ד, ז). וְזֶה וָזֶה, 'יֻסַּךְ' וְ'הַנָּסֶךְ', לְשׁוֹן סְכָךְ וְכִסּוּי הֵם:

ל **לֶחֶם פָּנִים.** שֶׁהָיוּ לוֹ פָּנִים כְּמוֹ שֶׁפֵּרַשְׁתִּי. וּמִנְיַן הַלֶּחֶם וְסֵדֶר מַעַרְכוֹתָיו מְפֹרָשִׁים בְּ'אֱמֹר אֶל הַכֹּהֲנִים' (ויקרא כד, ה-ט):

לא **מִקְשָׁה תֵּיעָשֶׂה הַמְּנוֹרָה.** שֶׁלֹּא יַעֲשֶׂנָּה חֻלְיוֹת, וְלֹא יַעֲשֶׂה קָנֶיהָ וְנֵרוֹתֶיהָ אֵבָרִים אֵבָרִים וְאַחַר כָּךְ יַדְבִּיקֵם כְּדֶרֶךְ הַצּוֹרְפִים שֶׁקּוֹרִין שולדרי״ן, אֶלָּא כֻּלָּהּ בָּאָה מֵחֲתִיכָה אַחַת, וּמַקִּישׁ בַּקֻּרְנָס וְחוֹתֵךְ בִּכְלֵי הָאֻמָּנוּת וּמַפְרִיד הַקָּנִים אֵילָךְ וְאֵילָךְ. תַּרְגּוּמוֹ שֶׁל ״מִקְשָׁה״: ״נְגִיד״, לְשׁוֹן הַמְשָׁכָה, שֶׁמַּמְשִׁיךְ הָאֵבָרִים מִן הָעֶשֶׁת לְכָאן וּלְכָאן בְּהַקָּשַׁת הַקֻּרְנָס. וּלְשׁוֹן ״מִקְשָׁה״ מַכַּת קֻרְנָס, בטדי״ץ בְּלַעַז: **תֵּיעָשֶׂה הַמְּנוֹרָה.** מֵאֵלֶיהָ, לְפִי שֶׁהָיָה מֹשֶׁה מִתְקַשֶּׁה בָּהּ, אָמַר לוֹ הַקָּדוֹשׁ בָּרוּךְ הוּא: הַשְׁלֵךְ אֶת הַכִּכָּר לָאוּר וְהִיא נַעֲשֵׂית מֵאֵלֶיהָ. לְכָךְ לֹא נִכְתַּב 'תַּעֲשֶׂה': **יְרֵכָהּ.** הוּא הָרֶגֶל שֶׁלְּמַטָּה הֶעָשׂוּי כְּמִין תֵּבָה, וּשְׁלֹשֶׁת הָרַגְלַיִם יוֹצְאִין הֵימֶנָּה מַטָּה: **וְקָנָהּ.** הַקָּנֶה הָאֶמְצָעִי שֶׁלָּהּ הָעוֹלֶה בְּאֶמְצַע הַיָּרֵךְ זָקוּף כְּלַפֵּי מַעְלָה, וְעָלָיו נֵר הָאֶמְצָעִי עָשׂוּי כְּמִין בָּזֵךְ לָצוּק הַשֶּׁמֶן לְתוֹכוֹ וְלָתֵת הַפְּתִילָה: **גְּבִיעֶיהָ.** הֵן כְּמִין כּוֹסוֹת שֶׁעוֹשִׂין מִזְּכוּכִית אֲרֻכִּים וּקְצָרִים, וְקוֹרִין לָהֶם מדרינ״ש, וְאֵלּוּ עֲשׂוּיִין שֶׁל זָהָב וּבוֹלְטִין וְיוֹצְאִין מִכָּל קָנֶה וְקָנֶה כַּמִּנְיָן שֶׁנָּתַן בָּהֶם הַכָּתוּב, וְלֹא הָיוּ בָּהּ אֶלָּא לְנוֹי: **כַּפְתֹּרֶיהָ.** כְּמִין תַּפּוּחִים הָיוּ עֲגֻלִּין סָבִיב, בּוֹלְטִין סְבִיבוֹת הַקָּנֶה הָאֶמְצָעִי, כְּדֶרֶךְ שֶׁעוֹשִׂין לַמְּנוֹרוֹת שֶׁלִּפְנֵי הַשָּׂרִים וְקוֹרִין לָהֶם פומיל״ש, וּמִנְיָן שֶׁלָּהֶם כָּתוּב בַּפָּרָשָׁה, כַּמָּה כַּפְתּוֹרִים בּוֹלְטִין מִמֶּנָּה וְכַמָּה חָלָק בֵּין כַּפְתּוֹר לְכַפְתּוֹר: **וּפְרָחֶיהָ.** צִיּוּרִין עֲשׂוּיִין בָּהּ כְּמִין פְּרָחִים: **מִמֶּנָּה יִהְיוּ.** הַכֹּל מִקְשָׁה יוֹצֵא מִתּוֹךְ חֲתִיכַת הָעֶשֶׁת, וְלֹא יַעֲשֵׂם לְבַדָּם וְיַדְבִּיקֵם:

מִסְגֶּרֶת טֹפַח סָבִיב וְעָשִׂיתָ זֵר־זָהָב לְמִסְגַּרְתּוֹ סָבִיב׃ כו וְעָשִׂיתָ לּוֹ אַרְבַּע
טַבְּעֹת זָהָב וְנָתַתָּ אֶת־הַטַּבָּעֹת עַל אַרְבַּע הַפֵּאֹת אֲשֶׁר לְאַרְבַּע
כז רַגְלָיו׃ לְעֻמַּת הַמִּסְגֶּרֶת תִּהְיֶיןָ הַטַּבָּעֹת לְבָתִּים לְבַדִּים לָשֵׂאת אֶת־
כח הַשֻּׁלְחָן׃ וְעָשִׂיתָ אֶת־הַבַּדִּים עֲצֵי שִׁטִּים וְצִפִּיתָ אֹתָם זָהָב וְנִשָּׂא־בָם
כט אֶת־הַשֻּׁלְחָן׃ וְעָשִׂיתָ קְּעָרֹתָיו וְכַפֹּתָיו וּקְשׂוֹתָיו וּמְנַקִּיֹּתָיו אֲשֶׁר יֻסַּךְ
ל בָּהֵן זָהָב טָהוֹר תַּעֲשֶׂה אֹתָם׃ וְנָתַתָּ עַל־הַשֻּׁלְחָן לֶחֶם פָּנִים לְפָנַי
תָּמִיד׃
לא וְעָשִׂיתָ מְנֹרַת זָהָב טָהוֹר מִקְשָׁה תֵּיעָשֶׂה הַמְּנוֹרָה יְרֵכָהּ וְקָנָהּ גְּבִיעֶיהָ

אונקלוס

גְּדַנְפָא, רוּמֵיהּ פְּשָׁכָא סְחוֹר סְחוֹר, וְתַעֲבֵיד זִיר דִּדְהַב, לִגְדַנְפֵיהּ סְחוֹר
סְחוֹר: כו וְתַעֲבֵיד לֵיהּ, אַרְבַּע עִזְקָן דִּדְהַב, וְתִתֵּין יָת עִזְקָתָא, עַל אַרְבַּע
זָוְיָתָא, דִּלְאַרְבַּע רַגְלוֹהִי: כז לָקֳבֵיל גְּדַנְפָא, יְהֶוְיָן עִזְקָתָא, לְאַתְרָא
לַאֲרִיחַיָּא, לְמִטַּל יָת פָּתוֹרָא: כח וְתַעֲבֵיד יָת אֲרִיחַיָּא דְּאָעֵי שִׁטִּין,
וְתַחְפֵי יָתְהוֹן דַּהֲבָא, וִיהוֹן נָטְלִין בְּהוֹן יָת פָּתוֹרָא: כט וְתַעֲבֵיד מְגִסּוֹהִי
וּבָזִכּוֹהִי, וְקַסְוָתֵיהּ וּמְכִילָתֵיהּ, דְּיִתְנְסַךְ בְּהוֹן, דִּהַב דְּכֵי תַּעֲבֵיד
יָתְהוֹן: ל וְתִתֵּין עַל פָּתוֹרָא, לְחֵים אַפַּיָּא קֳדָמַי תְּדִירָא: לא וְתַעֲבֵיד
מְנָרְתָא דִּדְהַב דְּכֵי, נְגִיד, תִּתְעֲבֵיד מְנָרְתָא שִׁדַּהּ וּקְנַהּ, כַּלִּידַהָא,

25:31 **מְנֹרַת זָהָב טָהוֹר** *A candelabrum of pure gold* – In the Tabernacle we meet the aesthetic side of Judaism – art that points to something beyond itself. The Tabernacle itself was a kind of microcosm of the universe, with one overriding particularity: that in it you felt the presence of something beyond – what the Torah calls "the glory of the LORD," which "filled the Tabernacle" (Ex. 40:35).

The strongest positive Jewish statement on art of which I am aware was made by Rabbi Avraham HaKohen Kook, the first Ashkenazic chief rabbi of (pre-state) Israel, describing his time in London during the First World War:

"I used to visit the National Gallery, and my favorite pictures were those of Rembrandt. I really think that Rembrandt was a *tzaddik*. Do you know that when I first saw Rembrandt's works, they reminded me of the rabbinic statement about the creation of light?

"We are told that when God created light [on the first day of creation, as opposed to the natural light of the sun on the fourth day], it was so strong and pellucid that one could see from one end of the world to the other, but God was afraid that the wicked might abuse it. What did He do? He reserved that light for the righteous in the World to Come. But now and then there are great men who are blessed and privileged to see it. I think that Rembrandt was one of them, and the light in his pictures is the very light that God created on Genesis day."

I suspect that what Rabbi Kook saw in those paintings was Rembrandt's ability to convey the beauty of ordinary people. He makes no attempt to beautify or idealize his subjects. The light that shines from them is, simply, their humanity.

How fitting that one of the most iconic symbols in Jewish art was to be the Menora, the seven-branched candelabrum. In Rome, the Arch of Titus was erected by Titus's brother Domitian to commemorate the victorious Roman siege of Jerusalem in the year 70. It shows Roman soldiers carrying away the spoils of war, most famously the Menora. Rome won that military conflict. Yet its civilization declined and fell, while Jews and Judaism survived. We survive "not with valor and not with strength" but by the quality of our light.

32 shall be hammered from a single piece. Six branches shall extend from its sides,
33 three on one side, three on the other. On each branch there shall be three finely
crafted cups, each with a knob and a flower. All six branches extending from
34 the candelabrum shall be like this. The shaft of the candelabrum shall have
35 four finely crafted cups, each with a knob and a flower. For the six branches
that extend from the candelabrum, there must be a knob at the base of each
36 pair of branches. The knobs and their branches shall be of one piece with it,
37 the whole of it a single, hammered piece of pure gold. Make its seven lamps
38 and mount them so that they light the space in front of it. Make its tongs and
39 pans of pure gold. All these items shall be made from a talent of pure gold.
40 Take care to make them according to that design that is shown to you on
26 1 the mountain. As for the Tabernacle itself, make it with ten sheets SHELISHI
of finely spun linen and sky-blue, purple, and scarlet wool, with a design of

רש״י

לב **יֹצְאִים מִצִּדֶּיהָ.** לְכָאן וּלְכָאן בַּאֲלַכְסוֹן, נִמְשָׁכִים וְעוֹלִין עַד כְּנֶגֶד גָּבְהָהּ שֶׁל מְנוֹרָה שֶׁהוּא קָנֶה הָאֶמְצָעִי, וְיוֹצְאִים מִתּוֹךְ קָנֶה הָאֶמְצָעִי זֶה לְמַעְלָה מִזֶּה, הַתַּחְתּוֹן אָרֹךְ וְשֶׁל מַעְלָה קָצָר הֵימֶנּוּ וְהָעֶלְיוֹן קָצָר הֵימֶנּוּ, לְפִי שֶׁהָיָה גֹּבַהּ רָאשֵׁיהֶן שָׁוֶה לְגָבְהוֹ שֶׁל קָנֶה הָאֶמְצָעִי הַשְּׁבִיעִי שֶׁמִּמֶּנּוּ יוֹצְאִים הַשִּׁשָּׁה:

לג **מְשֻׁקָּדִים.** כְּתַרְגּוּמוֹ, מְצֻיָּרִים הָיוּ כְּדֶרֶךְ שֶׁעוֹשִׂין לִכְלֵי כֶּסֶף וְזָהָב שֶׁקּוֹרִין נייל״ר: **שְׁלֹשָׁה גְבִעִים.** בּוֹלְטִין מִכָּל קָנֶה וְקָנֶה: **כַּפְתֹּר וָפֶרַח.** הָיָה לְכָל קָנֶה וְקָנֶה:

לד **וּבַמְּנֹרָה אַרְבָּעָה גְבִעִים.** בְּגוּפָהּ שֶׁל מְנוֹרָה הָיוּ אַרְבָּעָה גְּבִיעִים, אֶחָד בּוֹלֵט בָּהּ לְמַטָּה מִן הַקָּנִים, וְהַשְּׁלֹשָׁה לְמַעְלָה מִן יְצִיאַת הַקָּנִים הַיּוֹצְאִים מִצִּדֶּיהָ: **מְשֻׁקָּדִים כַּפְתֹּרֶיהָ וּפְרָחֶיהָ.** זֶה אֶחָד מֵחֲמִשָּׁה מִקְרָאוֹת שֶׁאֵין לָהֶם הֶכְרֵעַ, אֵין יָדוּעַ אִם ״גְּבִעִים מְשֻׁקָּדִים״ אוֹ ״מְשֻׁקָּדִים כַּפְתֹּרֶיהָ וּפְרָחֶיהָ״:

לה **וְכַפְתֹּר תַּחַת שְׁנֵי הַקָּנִים.** מִתּוֹךְ הַכַּפְתּוֹר הָיוּ הַקָּנִים נִמְשָׁכִים מִשְּׁנֵי צִדֶּיהָ אֵילָךְ וְאֵילָךְ. כָּךְ שָׁנִינוּ בִּמְלֶאכֶת הַמִּשְׁכָּן: גָּבְהָהּ שֶׁל מְנוֹרָה שְׁמוֹנָה עָשָׂר טְפָחִים. הָרַגְלַיִם וְהַפֶּרַח שְׁלֹשָׁה טְפָחִים, הוּא הַפֶּרַח הָאָמוּר בַּיָּרֵךְ שֶׁנֶּאֱמַר: ״עַד יְרֵכָהּ עַד פִּרְחָהּ״ (במדבר ח, ד), וּטְפָחַיִם חָלָק, וְטֶפַח שֶׁבּוֹ גָּבִיעַ מֵהָאַרְבָּעָה גְּבִיעִים וְכַפְתּוֹר וָפֶרַח מִשְּׁנֵי כַּפְתּוֹרִים וּשְׁנֵי פְרָחִים הָאֲמוּרִים בַּמְּנוֹרָה עַצְמָהּ, שֶׁנֶּאֱמַר: ״מְשֻׁקָּדִים כַּפְתֹּרֶיהָ וּפְרָחֶיהָ״ (בפסוק הקודם), לָמַדְנוּ שֶׁהָיוּ בַּקָּנֶה שְׁנֵי כַפְתּוֹרִים וּשְׁנֵי פְרָחִים לְבַד מִן הַשְּׁלֹשָׁה כַּפְתּוֹרִים שֶׁהַקָּנִים נִמְשָׁכִין מִתּוֹכָן, שֶׁנֶּאֱמַר: ״וְכַפְתֹּר תַּחַת שְׁנֵי הַקָּנִים״ וְגוֹ׳, וּטְפָחַיִם חָלָק, וְטֶפַח כַּפְתּוֹר, וּשְׁנֵי קָנִים יוֹצְאִים מִמֶּנּוּ אֵילָךְ וְאֵילָךְ נִמְשָׁכִים וְעוֹלִים כְּנֶגֶד גָּבְהָהּ שֶׁל מְנוֹרָה, וְטֶפַח חָלָק, וְטֶפַח כַּפְתּוֹר, וּשְׁנֵי קָנִים יוֹצְאִים מִמֶּנּוּ, וְטֶפַח חָלָק, וְטֶפַח כַּפְתּוֹר, וּשְׁנֵי קָנִים יוֹצְאִים מִמֶּנּוּ, וּטְפָחַיִם חָלָק, נִשְׁתַּיְּרוּ שָׁם שְׁלֹשָׁה טְפָחִים, שֶׁבָּהֶם שְׁלֹשָׁה גְּבִיעִים וְכַפְתּוֹר וָפֶרַח. נִמְצְאוּ גְּבִיעִים שְׁנַיִם וְעֶשְׂרִים, שְׁמוֹנָה עֶשְׂרֵה לְשִׁשָּׁה קָנִים שְׁלֹשָׁה לְכָל אֶחָד וְאֶחָד, וְאַרְבָּעָה בְּגוּפָהּ שֶׁל מְנוֹרָה; וְאַחַד עָשָׂר כַּפְתּוֹרִים, שִׁשָּׁה בְּשֵׁשֶׁת הַקָּנִים, וּשְׁלֹשָׁה בְּגוּפָהּ שֶׁל מְנוֹרָה שֶׁהַקָּנִים יוֹצְאִים מֵהֶם, וּשְׁנַיִם עוֹד בַּמְּנוֹרָה שֶׁנֶּאֱמַר: ״מְשֻׁקָּדִים כַּפְתֹּרֶיהָ״ וּמִעוּט כַּפְתּוֹרִים שְׁנַיִם, הָאֶחָד לְמַטָּה אֵצֶל הַיָּרֵךְ וְהָאֶחָד בִּשְׁלֹשָׁה טְפָחִים הָעֶלְיוֹנִים עִם הַשְּׁלֹשָׁה גְּבִיעִים. וְתִשְׁעָה פְרָחִים הָיוּ לָהּ, שִׁשָּׁה לְשֵׁשֶׁת הַקָּנִים, שֶׁנֶּאֱמַר: ״בַּקָּנֶה הָאֶחָד כַּפְתֹּר וָפֶרַח״ (לעיל פסוק לג), וּשְׁלֹשָׁה לַמְּנוֹרָה, שֶׁנֶּאֱמַר: ״מְשֻׁקָּדִים כַּפְתֹּרֶיהָ וּפְרָחֶיהָ״ (בפסוק הקודם) וּמִעוּט פְּרָחִים שְׁנַיִם, וְאֶחָד הָאָמוּר בְּפָרָשַׁת ׳בְּהַעֲלֹתְךָ׳ (במדבר ח, ד) ״עַד יְרֵכָהּ עַד פִּרְחָהּ״. וְאִם תְּדַקְדֵּק בְּמִשְׁנָה זוֹ הַכְּתוּבָה לְמַעְלָה תִּמְצָאֵם כְּמִנְיָנָם אִישׁ אִישׁ בִּמְקוֹמוֹ:

לז **אֶת נֵרֹתֶיהָ.** כְּמִין בָּזִיכִין שֶׁנּוֹתְנִין בְּתוֹכָם הַשֶּׁמֶן וְהַפְּתִילוֹת: **וְהֵאִיר עַל עֵבֶר פָּנֶיהָ.** עֲשֵׂה פִּי שֵׁשֶׁת הַנֵּרוֹת שֶׁבְּרָאשֵׁי הַקָּנִים הַיּוֹצְאִים מִצִּדֶּיהָ מֻסַבִּים כְּלַפֵּי הָאֶמְצָעִי, כְּדֵי שֶׁיִּהְיוּ הַנֵּרוֹת כְּשֶׁתַּדְלִיקֵם מְאִירִים ״אֶל עֵבֶר פָּנֶיהָ״, מוּסָב אוֹרָם אֶל צַד פְּנֵי הַקָּנֶה הָאֶמְצָעִי שֶׁהוּא גּוּף הַמְּנוֹרָה:

לח **וּמַלְקָחֶיהָ.** הֵם הַצְּבָתִים הָעֲשׂוּיִין לִקַּח בָּהֶם הַפְּתִילוֹת מִתּוֹךְ הַשֶּׁמֶן לְיַשְּׁבָן וּלְמָשְׁכָן בְּפִי הַנֵּרוֹת, וְעַל שֵׁם שֶׁלּוֹקְחִים בָּהֶם קְרוּיִים מֶלְקָחַיִם, וְ״צֵיבְתָהָא״ שֶׁתִּרְגֵּם אוּנְקְלוֹס, לְשׁוֹן צְבַת, טנייל״ש בְּלַעַז: **וּמַחְתֹּתֶיהָ.** הֵם כְּמִין בָּזִיכִין קְטַנִּים שֶׁחוֹתֶה בָּהֶן אֶת הָאֵפֶר שֶׁבַּנֵּר בַּבֹּקֶר בַּבֹּקֶר, כְּשֶׁהוּא מֵטִיב אֶת הַנֵּרוֹת מֵאֵפֶר הַפְּתִילוֹת שֶׁדָּלְקוּ הַלַּיְלָה וְכָבוּ. וּלְשׁוֹן מַחְתָּה פושיידור״א בְּלַעַז, כְּמוֹ: ״לַחְתּוֹת אֵשׁ מִיָּקוּד״ (ישעיה ל, יד):

לב כַּפְתֹּרֶיהָ וּפְרָחֶיהָ מִמֶּנָּה יִהְיוּ: וְשִׁשָּׁה קָנִים יֹצְאִים מִצִּדֶּיהָ שְׁלֹשָׁה ׀
לג קְנֵי מְנֹרָה מִצִּדָּהּ הָאֶחָד וּשְׁלֹשָׁה קְנֵי מְנֹרָה מִצִּדָּהּ הַשֵּׁנִי: שְׁלֹשָׁה
גְבִעִים מְשֻׁקָּדִים בַּקָּנֶה הָאֶחָד כַּפְתֹּר וָפֶרַח וּשְׁלֹשָׁה גְבִעִים מְשֻׁקָּדִים
בַּקָּנֶה הָאֶחָד כַּפְתֹּר וָפָרַח כֵּן לְשֵׁשֶׁת הַקָּנִים הַיֹּצְאִים מִן־הַמְּנֹרָה:
לד לה וּבַמְּנֹרָה אַרְבָּעָה גְבִעִים מְשֻׁקָּדִים כַּפְתֹּרֶיהָ וּפְרָחֶיהָ: וְכַפְתֹּר תַּחַת
שְׁנֵי הַקָּנִים מִמֶּנָּה וְכַפְתֹּר תַּחַת שְׁנֵי הַקָּנִים מִמֶּנָּה וְכַפְתֹּר תַּחַת־שְׁנֵי
לו הַקָּנִים מִמֶּנָּה לְשֵׁשֶׁת הַקָּנִים הַיֹּצְאִים מִן־הַמְּנֹרָה: כַּפְתֹּרֵיהֶם וּקְנֹתָם
לז מִמֶּנָּה יִהְיוּ כֻּלָּהּ מִקְשָׁה אַחַת זָהָב טָהוֹר: וְעָשִׂיתָ אֶת־נֵרֹתֶיהָ שִׁבְעָה
לח וְהֶעֱלָה אֶת־נֵרֹתֶיהָ וְהֵאִיר עַל־עֵבֶר פָּנֶיהָ: וּמַלְקָחֶיהָ וּמַחְתֹּתֶיהָ זָהָב
לט מ טָהוֹר: כִּכַּר זָהָב טָהוֹר יַעֲשֶׂה אֹתָהּ אֵת כָּל־הַכֵּלִים הָאֵלֶּה: וּרְאֵה
כו א וַעֲשֵׂה בְּתַבְנִיתָם אֲשֶׁר־אַתָּה מָרְאֶה בָּהָר: וְאֶת־הַמִּשְׁכָּן יט שלישי
תַּעֲשֶׂה עֶשֶׂר יְרִיעֹת שֵׁשׁ מָשְׁזָר וּתְכֵלֶת וְאַרְגָּמָן וְתֹלַעַת שָׁנִי כְּרֻבִים

אונקלוס

חַזּוּרַהָא וְשׁוֹשַׁנַּהָא מִנַּהּ יְהוֹן: לב וְשִׁתָּא קְנִין, נָפְקִין מִסִּטְרַהָא, תְּלָתָא קְנֵי מְנָרְתָא, מִסִּטְרַהּ חַד, וּתְלָתָא קְנֵי מְנָרְתָא, מִסִּטְרַהּ תִּנְיָנָא: לג תְּלָתָא כַלִּידִין, מְצַיְּרִין, בְּקַנְיָא חַד חַזּוּר וְשׁוֹשָׁן, וּתְלָתָא כַלִּידִין, מְצַיְּרִין, בְּקַנְיָא חַד חַזּוּר וְשׁוֹשָׁן, כֵּן לְשִׁתָּא קְנִין, דְּנָפְקִין מִן מְנָרְתָא: לד וּבִמְנָרְתָא אַרְבְּעָא כַלִּידִין, מְצַיְּרִין, חַזּוּרַהָא וְשׁוֹשַׁנַּהָא: לה וְחַזּוּר, תְּחוֹת תְּרֵין קְנִין דְּמִנַּהּ, וְחַזּוּר תְּחוֹת תְּרֵין קְנִין דְּמִנַּהּ, וְחַזּוּר, תְּחוֹת תְּרֵין קְנִין דְּמִנַּהּ, לְשִׁתָּא קְנִין, דְּנָפְקִין מִן מְנָרְתָא: לו חַזּוּרֵיהוֹן וּקְנֵיהוֹן מִנַּהּ יְהוֹן, כֻּלַּהּ, נְגִידָא חֲדָא דִּדְהַב דְּכֵי: לז וְתַעְבֵּיד יָת בּוֹצִינַהָא שִׁבְעָא, וְתַדְלֵיק יָת בּוֹצִינַהָא, וִיהוֹן מְנַהֲרִין לָקֳבֵיל אַפַּהָא: לח וְצֵיבְתַהָא וּמַחְתְּיָתַהָא דִּדְהַב דְּכֵי: לט כַּכְּרָא, דִּדְהַבָא דָּכְיָא יַעְבֵּיד יָתַהּ, יָת כָּל מָנַיָּא הָאִלֵּין: מ וַחְזִי וַעְבֵיד, בִּדְמוּתְהוֹן, דְּאַתְּ מִתַּחְזֵי בְּטוּרָא: כו א וְיָת מַשְׁכְּנָא תַּעְבֵּיד עֲסַר יְרִיעָן, דְּבוּץ שְׁזִיר, וְתַכְלָא וְאַרְגְּוָנָא וּצְבַע זְהוֹרִי, צוּרַת כְּרוּבִין,

רש״י

לט כִּכַּר זָהָב טָהוֹר. שֶׁלֹּא יִהְיֶה מִשְׁקָלָהּ עִם כָּל כֵּלֶיהָ אֶלָּא כִּכָּר, לֹא פָּחוֹת וְלֹא יוֹתֵר. וְהַכִּכָּר שֶׁל חוֹל שִׁשִּׁים מָנֶה, וְשֶׁל קֹדֶשׁ הָיָה כָּפוּל, מֵאָה וְעֶשְׂרִים מָנֶה, וְהַמָּנֶה הוּא לִיטְרָא שֶׁשּׁוֹקְלִין בָּהּ כֶּסֶף לְמִשְׁקַל קוֹלוֹנְיָא, וְהֵם מֵאָה זְהוּבִים, עֶשְׂרִים וַחֲמִשָּׁה סְלָעִים, וְהַסֶּלַע אַרְבָּעָה זְהוּבִים:

מ וּרְאֵה וַעֲשֵׂה. רְאֵה כָּאן בָּהָר תַּבְנִית שֶׁאֲנִי מַרְאֶה אוֹתְךָ, מַגִּיד שֶׁנִּתְקַשָּׁה מֹשֶׁה בְּמַעֲשֵׂה הַמְּנוֹרָה עַד שֶׁהֶרְאָה לוֹ הַקָּדוֹשׁ בָּרוּךְ הוּא מְנוֹרָה שֶׁל אֵשׁ: אֲשֶׁר אַתָּה מָרְאֶה. כְּתַרְגּוּמוֹ: ״דְּאַתְּ מִתַּחְזֵי בְּטוּרָא״. אִלּוּ הָיָה נָקוּד ׳מַרְאֶה׳ בְּפַתָּח, הָיָה פִּתְרוֹנוֹ, אַתָּה מַרְאֶה לַאֲחֵרִים, עַכְשָׁיו שֶׁנָּקוּד חֲטַף קָמָץ, פִּתְרוֹנוֹ ׳דְּאַתְּ מִתַּחְזֵי׳, שֶׁאֲחֵרִים מַרְאִים לְךָ:

כו א וְאֶת הַמִּשְׁכָּן תַּעֲשֶׂה עֶשֶׂר יְרִיעֹת. לִהְיוֹת לוֹ לְגַג וּלְמְחִצּוֹת מִחוּץ לַקְּרָשִׁים, שֶׁהַיְרִיעוֹת תְּלוּיוֹת מֵאֲחוֹרֵיהֶן לְכַסּוֹתָן: שֵׁשׁ מָשְׁזָר וּתְכֵלֶת וְאַרְגָּמָן וְתֹלַעַת שָׁנִי. הֲרֵי אַרְבָּעָה מִינִין בְּכָל חוּט וְחוּט, אֶחָד שֶׁל פִּשְׁתִּים וּשְׁלֹשָׁה שֶׁל צֶמֶר, וְכָל מִין וּמִין חוּטוֹ כָּפוּל שִׁשָּׁה, הֲרֵי אַרְבָּעָה מִינִין כְּשֶׁהֵן שְׁזוּרִין יַחַד עֶשְׂרִים וְאַרְבָּעָה כְּפָלִים לַחוּט: כְּרֻבִים מַעֲשֵׂה חֹשֵׁב. כְּרוּבִים הָיוּ מְצֻיָּרִין בָּהֶם בַּאֲרִיגָתָן, וְלֹא בִּרְקִימָה שֶׁהוּא מַעֲשֵׂה

2 cherubim worked into them. Each sheet shall be twenty-eight cubits long
3 and four cubits wide; all the sheets should be the same size. Five of the sheets
4 should be sewn together; the other five likewise. Make loops of sky-blue wool
on the upper edge of the end sheet in the first set, and likewise on the upper
5 edge of the outermost sheet in the second set. Make fifty loops on each sheet
on one side and fifty on the upper edge of the corresponding sheets in the
6 other set, with the loops opposite one another. And make fifty gold clasps.
With the clasps, join the sheets together so that the Tabernacle becomes one
7 whole. Make sheets of goats' hair as a tent over the Tabernacle; make eleven
8 of these sheets. Each sheet shall be thirty cubits long and four cubits wide,

רש״י

מַחַט, אֶלָּא בַּאֲרִיגָה בִּשְׁנֵי כְתָלִים, פַּרְצוּף אֶחָד מִכָּאן וּפַרְצוּף אֶחָד מִכָּאן, אֲרִי מִצַּד זֶה וְנֶשֶׁר מִצַּד זֶה, כְּמוֹ שֶׁאוֹרְגִין חֲגוֹרוֹת שֶׁל מֶשִׁי שֶׁקּוֹרִין בְּלַעַז פייסי״ש:

ג **תִּהְיֶיןָ חֹבְרֹת.** תּוֹפְרָן בְּמַחַט זוֹ בְּצַד זוֹ, חָמֵשׁ לְבַד וְחָמֵשׁ לְבַד: **אִשָּׁה אֶל אֲחֹתָהּ.** כָּךְ דֶּרֶךְ הַמִּקְרָא לְדַבֵּר בְּדָבָר שֶׁהוּא לְשׁוֹן נְקֵבָה; וּבְדָבָר שֶׁהוּא לְשׁוֹן זָכָר אוֹמֵר: 'אִישׁ אֶל אָחִיו', כְּמוֹ שֶׁנֶּאֱמַר בַּכְּרוּבִים: "וּפְנֵיהֶם אִישׁ אֶל אָחִיו" (לעיל כה, כ):

ד **לֻלְאֹת.** לנזול״ש בְּלַעַז, וְכֵן תִּרְגֵּם אוּנְקְלוֹס: "עֲנֻבִין", לְשׁוֹן עֲנִיבָה: **מִקָּצָה בַּחֹבָרֶת.** בְּאוֹתָהּ יְרִיעָה שֶׁבְּסוֹף הַחִבּוּר, קְבוּצַת חֲמֵשֶׁת הַיְרִיעוֹת קְרוּיָה חֹבֶרֶת: **וְכֵן תַּעֲשֶׂה בִּשְׂפַת הַיְרִיעָה הַקִּיצוֹנָה בַּמַּחְבֶּרֶת הַשֵּׁנִית.** בְּאוֹתָהּ יְרִיעָה שֶׁהִיא קִיצוֹנָה, לְשׁוֹן קָצֶה, כְּלוֹמַר לְסוֹף הַחוֹבֶרֶת:

ה **מַקְבִּילֹת הַלֻּלָאֹת אִשָּׁה אֶל אֲחֹתָהּ.** שְׁמֹר שֶׁתַּעֲשֶׂה הַלּוּלָאוֹת מְכֻוָּנוֹת בְּמִדָּה אַחַת הַבְדָּלָתָן זוֹ מִזּוֹ, וּכְמִדָּתָן בִּירִיעָה זוֹ כֵּן יְהֵא בַּחֲבֶרְתָּהּ, כְּשֶׁתִּפְרֹשׂ חוֹבֶרֶת אֵצֶל חוֹבֶרֶת יִהְיוּ הַלּוּלָאוֹת שֶׁל יְרִיעָה זוֹ מְכֻוָּנוֹת כְּנֶגֶד לוּלָאוֹת שֶׁל זוֹ. וְזֶהוּ לְשׁוֹן 'מַקְבִּילֹת', זוֹ כְּנֶגֶד זוֹ, תַּרְגּוּמוֹ שֶׁל 'נֶגֶד' (לעיל י, י) – 'לָקֳבֵל'. הַיְרִיעוֹת אָרְכָּן עֶשְׂרִים וּשְׁמוֹנֶה וְרָחְבָּן אַרְבַּע, וּכְשֶׁחִבֵּר חָמֵשׁ יְרִיעוֹת יַחַד נִמְצָא רָחְבָּן עֶשְׂרִים, וְכֵן הַחוֹבֶרֶת הַשֵּׁנִית. וְהַמִּשְׁכָּן אָרְכּוֹ שְׁלֹשִׁים מִן הַמִּזְרָח לַמַּעֲרָב, שֶׁנֶּאֱמַר: "עֶשְׂרִים קְרָשִׁים לִפְאַת נֶגְבָּה תֵימָנָה" (להלן לו, כג; כעין זה להלן פסוק יח), וְכֵן לַצָּפוֹן (להלן פסוק כ), וְכָל קֶרֶשׁ אַמָּה וַחֲצִי הָאַמָּה (להלן פסוק טז), הֲרֵי שְׁלֹשִׁים מִן הַמִּזְרָח לַמַּעֲרָב. רֹחַב הַמִּשְׁכָּן מִן הַצָּפוֹן לַדָּרוֹם עֶשֶׂר אַמּוֹת, שֶׁנֶּאֱמַר: "וּלְיַרְכְּתֵי הַמִּשְׁכָּן יָמָּה וְגוֹ' וּשְׁנֵי קְרָשִׁים... לִמְקֻצְעֹת" (להלן פסוקים כב-כג) הֲרֵי עֶשֶׂר, וּבִמְקוֹמָם אֲפָרְשֵׁם לַמִּקְרָאוֹת הַלָּלוּ. נוֹתֵן הַיְרִיעוֹת אָרְכָּן לְרָחְבּוֹ שֶׁל מִשְׁכָּן, עֶשֶׂר אַמּוֹת הָאֶמְצָעִיּוֹת לְגַג חֲלַל רֹחַב הַמִּשְׁכָּן, וְאַמָּה מִכָּאן וְאַמָּה מִכָּאן לָעֳבִי רָאשֵׁי הַקְּרָשִׁים, שֶׁעָבְיָן אַמָּה, נִשְׁתַּיְּרוּ שֵׁשׁ עֶשְׂרֵה אַמָּה, שְׁמוֹנֶה לַצָּפוֹן וּשְׁמוֹנֶה לַדָּרוֹם, מְכַסּוֹת קוֹמַת הַקְּרָשִׁים שֶׁגָּבְהָן עֶשֶׂר, נִמְצְאוּ שְׁתֵּי אַמּוֹת הַתַּחְתּוֹנוֹת מְגֻלּוֹת. רָחְבָּן שֶׁל יְרִיעוֹת אַרְבָּעִים אַמָּה כְּשֶׁהֵן מְחֻבָּרוֹת, עֶשְׂרִים אַמָּה לְחוֹבֶרֶת. שְׁלֹשִׁים מֵהֶן לְגַג חֲלַל הַמִּשְׁכָּן לְאָרְכּוֹ, וְאַמָּה כְּנֶגֶד עֳבִי רָאשֵׁי הַקְּרָשִׁים שֶׁבַּמַּעֲרָב, וְאַמָּה לְכַסּוֹת עֳבִי הָעַמּוּדִים שֶׁבַּמִּזְרָח, שֶׁלֹּא הָיוּ קְרָשִׁים בַּמִּזְרָח אֶלָּא אַרְבָּעָה עַמּוּדִים שֶׁהַמָּסָךְ פָּרוּשׂ וְתָלוּי בָּוָוִין שֶׁבָּהֶן כְּמִין וִילוֹן, נִשְׁתַּיְּרוּ שְׁמוֹנֶה אַמּוֹת הַתְּלוּיִין עַל אֲחוֹרֵי הַמִּשְׁכָּן שֶׁבַּמַּעֲרָב, וּשְׁתֵּי אַמּוֹת הַתַּחְתּוֹנוֹת מְגֻלּוֹת. זוֹ מָצָאתִי בַּבָּרַיְתָא דְאַרְבָּעִים וָתֵשַׁע מִדּוֹת. אֲבָל בְּמַסֶּכֶת שַׁבָּת (דף צח ע״ב) אֵין הַיְרִיעוֹת מְכַסּוֹת אֶת עַמּוּדֵי הַמִּזְרָח, וְתֵשַׁע אַמּוֹת תְּלוּיוֹת אֲחוֹרֵי הַמִּשְׁכָּן, וְהַכָּתוּב מְסַיְּעֵנוּ: "וְנָתַתָּה אֶת הַפָּרֹכֶת תַּחַת הַקְּרָסִים" (להלן פסוק לג), וְאִם כְּדִבְרֵי הַבָּרַיְתָא הַזֹּאת, נִמְצֵאת פָּרֹכֶת מְשׁוּכָה מִן הַקְּרָסִים וְלַמַּעֲרָב אַמָּה:

ו **קַרְסֵי זָהָב.** פירמיל״ש בְּלַעַז, וּמַכְנִיסִין רֹאשָׁן אֶחָד בַּלּוּלָאוֹת שֶׁבְּחוֹבֶרֶת זוֹ וְרֹאשָׁן אֶחָד בַּלּוּלָאוֹת שֶׁבְּחוֹבֶרֶת זוֹ וּמְחַבְּרָן בָּהֶן:

ז **יְרִיעֹת עִזִּים.** מִנּוֹצָה שֶׁל עִזִּים: **לְאֹהֶל עַל הַמִּשְׁכָּן.** לִפְרֹשׂ אוֹתָן עַל הַיְרִיעוֹת הַתַּחְתּוֹנוֹת:

roamed in tent and tabernacle. But wherever I roamed, among all the Israelites, have I ever spoken a word to any of the tribes of Israel whom I charged to shepherd my people Israel, saying, "Why have you not built Me a cedarwood palace?" (II Sam. 7:5–7)

This reply contains a tantalizing suggestion: that God does not seek the glory of great buildings. It is only the barest hint, but it lingers in the mind.

What was the result of this monumental building project? After Shlomo's death, the people came to his son and

ב מַעֲשֵׂה חֹשֵׁב תַּעֲשֶׂה אֹתָם: אֹרֶךְ ׀ הַיְרִיעָה הָאַחַת שְׁמֹנֶה וְעֶשְׂרִים
בָּאַמָּה וְרֹחַב אַרְבַּע בָּאַמָּה הַיְרִיעָה הָאֶחָת מִדָּה אַחַת לְכָל־הַיְרִיעֹת:
ג חֲמֵשׁ הַיְרִיעֹת תִּהְיֶיןָ חֹבְרֹת אִשָּׁה אֶל־אֲחֹתָהּ וְחָמֵשׁ יְרִיעֹת חֹבְרֹת
ד אִשָּׁה אֶל־אֲחֹתָהּ: וְעָשִׂיתָ לֻלְאֹת תְּכֵלֶת עַל שְׂפַת הַיְרִיעָה הָאֶחָת
מִקָּצָה בַּחֹבָרֶת וְכֵן תַּעֲשֶׂה בִּשְׂפַת הַיְרִיעָה הַקִּיצוֹנָה בַּמַּחְבֶּרֶת
ה הַשֵּׁנִית: חֲמִשִּׁים לֻלָאֹת תַּעֲשֶׂה בַּיְרִיעָה הָאֶחָת וַחֲמִשִּׁים לֻלָאֹת
תַּעֲשֶׂה בִּקְצֵה הַיְרִיעָה אֲשֶׁר בַּמַּחְבֶּרֶת הַשֵּׁנִית מַקְבִּילֹת הַלֻּלָאֹת
ו אִשָּׁה אֶל־אֲחֹתָהּ: וְעָשִׂיתָ חֲמִשִּׁים קַרְסֵי זָהָב וְחִבַּרְתָּ אֶת־הַיְרִיעֹת
ז אִשָּׁה אֶל־אֲחֹתָהּ בַּקְּרָסִים וְהָיָה הַמִּשְׁכָּן אֶחָד: וְעָשִׂיתָ יְרִיעֹת עִזִּים
ח לְאֹהֶל עַל־הַמִּשְׁכָּן עַשְׁתֵּי־עֶשְׂרֵה יְרִיעֹת תַּעֲשֶׂה אֹתָם: אֹרֶךְ ׀ הַיְרִיעָה

אונקלוס

עוֹבַד אֻמָּן תַּעֲבֵיד יָתְהוֹן: ב אָרְכָּא דִירִיעֲתָא חֲדָא, עֶסְרִין וְתַמְנֵי אַמִּין, וּפְתָיָא אַרְבַּע אַמִּין, דִּירִיעֲתָא חֲדָא, מִשְׁחֲתָא חֲדָא לְכָל יְרִיעָתָא: ג חֲמֵשׁ יְרִיעָן, יְהוֹיָן מְלָפְפָן, חֲדָא עִם חֲדָא, וַחֲמֵשׁ יְרִיעָן מְלָפְפָן, חֲדָא עִם חֲדָא: ד וְתַעֲבֵיד עֲנוּבִין דִּתְכִלְתָּא, עַל סִפְתָּא דִירִיעֲתָא חֲדָא, מִסִּטְרָא בֵּית לוֹפֵי, וְכֵן תַּעֲבֵיד בְּסִפְתָּא דִירִיעֲתָא, בְּסִטְרָא, בֵּית לוֹפֵי תִנְיָנָא: ה חַמְשִׁין עֲנוּבִין, תַּעֲבֵיד בִּירִיעֲתָא חֲדָא, וְחַמְשִׁין עֲנוּבִין, תַּעֲבֵיד בְּסִטְרָא דִירִיעֲתָא, דְּבֵית לוֹפֵי תִנְיָנָא, מְכַוְּנָן עֲנוּבַיָּא, חֲדָא לָקֳבֵיל חֲדָא: ו וְתַעֲבֵיד, חַמְשִׁין פּוּרְפִין דִּדְהַב, וּתְלָפֵיף יָת יְרִיעָתָא, חֲדָא עִם חֲדָא בְּפוּרְפַיָּא, וִיהֵי מַשְׁכְּנָא חַד: ז וְתַעֲבֵיד יְרִיעָן דִּמְעַזֵּי, לִפְרָסָא עַל מַשְׁכְּנָא, חֲדָא עֶסְרֵי יְרִיעָן תַּעֲבֵיד יָתְהוֹן: ח אָרְכָּא דִירִיעֲתָא

A TENT

In one sense the Temple and the Tabernacle were similar things. They were both places of worship, at the symbolic center of society. Both involved the contributions of many kinds of people. Both were projects of society as a whole.

There was, however, a difference. The Tabernacle, a simple tent, was made out of voluntary contributions. The Temple, a palatial stone building, was not. To build it, Shlomo had to turn the Israelites into a vast labor-force: "King Shlomo began to levy forced labor upon all of Israel; the levy was thirty thousand men. He had ten thousand men sent to Lebanon every month, in shifts; they would spend a month in Lebanon and two months at home.... At the king's command, they quarried enormous blocks of prime stone so that the foundations of the House would be laid with hewn stone" (I Kings 5:27–31).

Is this not precisely what the Israelites left Egypt to avoid, becoming a mere labor force for a ruler engaged in a grand project, even if it is the holiest of holies? Is this not, albeit temporarily and for a sacred cause, a new form of slavery?

No less fascinating is the explanation given in the second book of Samuel for why God, when David first mooted the idea of a Temple, said no:

> Shall you be the one to build a house for Me, for My abode? For I have not dwelt in a house from the day I brought the Israelites out of Egypt to this day; I have

9 all eleven sheets the same size. Join five of the sheets by themselves, and the
10 other six by themselves. Fold the sixth sheet over the front of the Tent. Make
fifty loops on the edge of the end sheet of one set, and fifty on the edge of the
11 end sheet of the other. Make, also, fifty bronze clasps. Put the clasps through
12 the loops, joining the tent together so that it becomes one whole. As for the
additional length of the tent sheets, the extra half sheet is to hang down at the
13 rear of the Tabernacle. The extra cubit at either end of each of the tent sheets
14 should hang over the sides of the Tabernacle to cover it on both sides. Make a
covering for the tent from rams' hides dyed red. Above it make a covering of fine
leather.
15 16 Make the upright boards for the Tabernacle of acacia wood. Each board shall REVI'I

רש״י

ח **שְׁלֹשִׁים בָּאַמָּה.** שֶׁכְּשֶׁנּוֹתְנָן אָרְכָּן לְרֹחַב הַמִּשְׁכָּן כְּמוֹ שֶׁנָּתַן אֶת הָרִאשׁוֹנוֹת, נִמְצְאוּ אֵלּוּ עוֹדְפוֹת אַמָּה מִכָּאן וְאַמָּה מִכָּאן, לְכַסּוֹת אַחַת מֵהַשְּׁתַּיִם אַמּוֹת שֶׁנִּשְׁאֲרוּ מְגֻלּוֹת בַּקְּרָשִׁים. וְהָאַמָּה הַתַּחְתּוֹנָה שֶׁל קֶרֶשׁ שֶׁאֵין הַיְרִיעָה מְכַסָּה אוֹתוֹ, הִיא הָאַמָּה הַתְּחוּבָה בְּנֶקֶב הָאֶדֶן, שֶׁהָאֲדָנִים גָּבְהָן אַמָּה:

ט **וְכָפַלְתָּ אֶת הַיְרִיעָה הַשִּׁשִּׁית.** שֶׁעוֹדֶפֶת בְּאֵלּוּ הָעֶלְיוֹנוֹת יוֹתֵר מִן הַתַּחְתּוֹנוֹת: **אֶל מוּל פְּנֵי הָאֹהֶל.** חֲצִי רָחְבָּהּ הָיָה תָּלוּי וְכָפוּל עַל הַמָּסָךְ שֶׁבַּמִּזְרָח כְּנֶגֶד הַפֶּתַח, דּוֹמֶה לְכַלָּה צְנוּעָה הַמְּכֻסָּה בְּצָעִיף עַל פָּנֶיהָ:

יב-יג **וְסֶרַח הָעֹדֵף בִּירִיעֹת הָאֹהֶל.** עַל יְרִיעוֹת הַמִּשְׁכָּן. 'יְרִיעֹת הָאֹהֶל' הֵן הָעֶלְיוֹנוֹת שֶׁל עִזִּים שֶׁקְּרוּיִם אֹהֶל, כְּמוֹ שֶׁאָמוּר בָּהֶן: "לְאֹהֶל עַל הַמִּשְׁכָּן" (לעיל פסוק ז), וְכָל אֹהֶל הָאָמוּר בָּהֶן אֵינוֹ אֶלָּא לְשׁוֹן גַּג, שֶׁמַּאֲהִילוֹת וּמְסַכְּכוֹת עַל הַתַּחְתּוֹנוֹת. וְהֵן הָיוּ עוֹדְפוֹת עַל הַתַּחְתּוֹנוֹת חֲצִי הַיְרִיעָה לַמַּעֲרָב, שֶׁהַחֲצִי שֶׁל יְרִיעָה אַחַת עֶשְׂרֵה הַיְתֵרָה הָיָה נִכְפָּל אֶל מוּל פְּנֵי הָאֹהֶל, נִשְׁאֲרוּ שְׁתֵּי אַמּוֹת רֹחַב חֶצְיָהּ עוֹדֵף עַל רֹחַב הַתַּחְתּוֹנוֹת: **תִּסְרַח עַל אֲחֹרֵי הַמִּשְׁכָּן.** לְכַסּוֹת שְׁתֵּי אַמּוֹת שֶׁהָיוּ מְגֻלּוֹת בַּקְּרָשִׁים: **וְהָאַמָּה מִזֶּה וְהָאַמָּה מִזֶּה.** לַצָּפוֹן וְלַדָּרוֹם: **בָּעֹדֵף בְּאֹרֶךְ יְרִיעֹת הָאֹהֶל.** שֶׁהֵן עוֹדְפוֹת עַל אֹרֶךְ יְרִיעוֹת הַמִּשְׁכָּן שְׁתֵּי אַמּוֹת: **יִהְיֶה סָרוּחַ עַל צִדֵּי הַמִּשְׁכָּן.** לַצָּפוֹן וְלַדָּרוֹם, כְּמוֹ שֶׁפֵּרַשְׁתִּי לְמַעְלָה. לִמְּדָה תּוֹרָה דֶּרֶךְ אֶרֶץ, שֶׁיְּהֵא אָדָם חָס עַל הַיָּפֶה: **אֲחֹרֵי הַמִּשְׁכָּן.** הוּא צַד הַמַּעֲרָב, לְפִי שֶׁהַפֶּתַח בַּמִּזְרָח שֶׁהֵן פָּנָיו, וְצָפוֹן וְדָרוֹם קְרוּיִין צְדָדִין לַיָּמִין וְלַשְּׂמֹאל:

יד **מִכְסֶה לָאֹהֶל.** לְאוֹתוֹ גַּג שֶׁל יְרִיעוֹת עִזִּים, עֲשֵׂה עוֹד מִכְסֶה אֶחָד שֶׁל "עֹרֹת אֵילִם מְאָדָּמִים", וְעוֹד לְמַעְלָה מִמֶּנּוּ "מִכְסֵה עֹרֹת תְּחָשִׁים", וְאוֹתָן מִכְסָאוֹת לֹא הָיוּ מְכַסִּין אֶלָּא אֶת הַגַּג, אָרְכָּן שְׁלֹשִׁים וְרָחְבָּן עֶשֶׂר, אֵלּוּ דִּבְרֵי רַבִּי נְחֶמְיָה. וּלְדִבְרֵי רַבִּי יְהוּדָה מִכְסֶה אֶחָד הָיָה, חֶצְיוֹ שֶׁל עוֹרוֹת אֵילִים מְאָדָּמִים וְחֶצְיוֹ שֶׁל עוֹרוֹת תְּחָשִׁים:

טו **וְעָשִׂיתָ אֶת הַקְּרָשִׁים.** הָיָה לוֹ לוֹמַר: 'וְעָשִׂיתָ קְרָשִׁים', כְּמוֹ שֶׁנֶּאֱמַר בְּכָל דָּבָר וְדָבָר. מַהוּ "הַקְּרָשִׁים"? מֵאוֹתָן הָעוֹמְדִין וּמְיֻחָדִין לְכָךְ; יַעֲקֹב אָבִינוּ נָטַע אֲרָזִים בְּמִצְרַיִם, וּכְשֶׁמֵּת צִוָּה לְבָנָיו לְהַעֲלוֹתָם עִמָּהֶם כְּשֶׁיֵּצְאוּ מִמִּצְרַיִם, וְאָמַר לָהֶם שֶׁעָתִיד הַקָּדוֹשׁ בָּרוּךְ הוּא לְצַוּוֹת אוֹתָן לַעֲשׂוֹת מִשְׁכָּן בַּמִּדְבָּר מֵעֲצֵי שִׁטִּים, רְאוּ שֶׁיִּהְיוּ מְזֻמָּנִים בְּיֶדְכֶם. הוּא שֶׁיִּסֵּד הַבַּבְלִי בַּפִּיּוּט שֶׁלּוֹ: "טָס מַטַּע מְזֻרָזִים, קוֹרוֹת בָּתֵּינוּ אֲרָזִים" (יוצר ליום ראשון של פסח), שֶׁנִּזְדָּרְזוּ לִהְיוֹת מוּכָנִים בְּיָדָם מִקֹּדֶם לָכֵן: **עֲצֵי שִׁטִּים עֹמְדִים.** אשטנטי״ש בְּלַעַז, שֶׁיְּהֵא אֹרֶךְ הַקְּרָשִׁים זָקוּף לְמַעְלָה בְּקִירוֹת הַמִּשְׁכָּן, וְלֹא תַּעֲשֶׂה הַכְּתָלִים בִּקְרָשִׁים שׁוֹכְבִים לִהְיוֹת רֹחַב הַקְּרָשִׁים לְגֹבַהּ הַכְּתָלִים קֶרֶשׁ עַל קֶרֶשׁ:

טז **עֶשֶׂר אַמּוֹת אֹרֶךְ הַקָּרֶשׁ.** לָמַדְנוּ גָּבְהוֹ שֶׁל מִשְׁכָּן עֶשֶׂר אַמּוֹת:

together, all of us, without delegating away responsibility to others. Governments administer states. We, the people, build societies.

What can be done voluntarily cannot necessarily be done coercively. The Tabernacle, a fragile tent built of voluntary contributions, united the nation. The Temple, built by conscripted labor, divided it.

הָאַחַת שְׁלֹשִׁים בָּאַמָּה וְרֹחַב אַרְבַּע בָּאַמָּה הַיְרִיעָה הָאֶחָת מִדָּה
ט אַחַת לְעַשְׁתֵּי עֶשְׂרֵה יְרִיעֹת: וְחִבַּרְתָּ אֶת־חֲמֵשׁ הַיְרִיעֹת לְבָד וְאֶת־
שֵׁשׁ הַיְרִיעֹת לְבָד וְכָפַלְתָּ אֶת־הַיְרִיעָה הַשִּׁשִּׁית אֶל־מוּל פְּנֵי הָאֹהֶל:
י וְעָשִׂיתָ חֲמִשִּׁים לֻלָאֹת עַל שְׂפַת הַיְרִיעָה הָאֶחָת הַקִּיצֹנָה בַּחֹבָרֶת
יא וַחֲמִשִּׁים לֻלָאֹת עַל שְׂפַת הַיְרִיעָה הַחֹבֶרֶת הַשֵּׁנִית: וְעָשִׂיתָ קַרְסֵי
נְחֹשֶׁת חֲמִשִּׁים וְהֵבֵאתָ אֶת־הַקְּרָסִים בַּלֻּלָאֹת וְחִבַּרְתָּ אֶת־הָאֹהֶל
יב וְהָיָה אֶחָד: וְסֶרַח הָעֹדֵף בִּירִיעֹת הָאֹהֶל חֲצִי הַיְרִיעָה הָעֹדֶפֶת
יג תִּסְרַח עַל אֲחֹרֵי הַמִּשְׁכָּן: וְהָאַמָּה מִזֶּה וְהָאַמָּה מִזֶּה בָּעֹדֵף בְּאֹרֶךְ
יְרִיעֹת הָאֹהֶל יִהְיֶה סָרוּחַ עַל־צִדֵּי הַמִּשְׁכָּן מִזֶּה וּמִזֶּה לְכַסֹּתוֹ:
יד וְעָשִׂיתָ מִכְסֶה לָאֹהֶל עֹרֹת אֵילִם מְאָדָּמִים וּמִכְסֵה עֹרֹת תְּחָשִׁים
מִלְמָעְלָה:
טו טז וְעָשִׂיתָ אֶת־הַקְּרָשִׁים לַמִּשְׁכָּן עֲצֵי שִׁטִּים עֹמְדִים: עֶשֶׂר אַמּוֹת אֹרֶךְ רביעי

אונקלוס

חֲדָא, תְּלָתִין אַמִּין, וּפְתָיָא אַרְבַּע אַמִּין, דִּירִיעֲתָא חֲדָא, מִשְׁחֲתָא חֲדָא, לְחַדָא עֶסְרֵי יְרִיעָן: ט וּתְלָפֵיף, יָת חֲמֵשׁ יְרִיעָן לְחוֹד, וְיָת שִׁית יְרִיעָן לְחוֹד, וְתֵעִיף יָת יְרִיעֲתָא שְׁתִיתֵיתָא, לָקֳבֵיל אַפֵּי מַשְׁכְּנָא: י וְתַעְבֵּיד חַמְשִׁין עֲנוּבִין, עַל סִפְתָא דִּירִיעֲתָא חֲדָא, בְּסִטְרָא בֵּית לוֹפֵי, וְחַמְשִׁין עֲנוּבִין, עַל סִפְתָא דִּירִיעֲתָא, דְּבֵית לוֹפֵי תִנְיָנָא: יא וְתַעְבֵּיד, פּוּרְפִין דִּנְחָשׁ חַמְשִׁין, וְתַעֵיל יָת פּוּרְפַיָּא בַּעֲנוּבַיָּא, וּתְלַפֵּיף יָת מַשְׁכְּנָא וִיהֵי חַד: יב וְסִרְחָא דְּיָתִיר, בִּירִיעַת מַשְׁכְּנָא, פַּלְגוּת יְרִיעֲתָא דְּיַתְרָא, תִּסְרַח, עַל אֲחוֹרֵי מַשְׁכְּנָא: יג וְאַמְּתָא מִכָּא, וְאַמְּתָא מִכָּא בִּדְיָתִיר, בְּאוֹרֶךְ יְרִיעַת מַשְׁכְּנָא, יְהֵי סְרִיחַ, עַל סִטְרֵי מַשְׁכְּנָא, מִכָּא וּמִכָּא לְכַסָּיוּתֵיהּ: יד וְתַעְבֵּיד חוּפָאָה לְמַשְׁכְּנָא, דְּמַשְׁכֵּי דִּכְרֵי מְסַמְּקֵי, וְחוּפָאָה, דְּמַשְׁכֵּי סָסְגוֹנָא מִלְעֵילָא: טו וְתַעְבֵּיד יָת דַּפַּיָּא לְמַשְׁכְּנָא, דְּאָעֵי שִׁטִּין קָיְמִין: טז עֲסַר אַמִּין אָרְכָּא

successor, Reḥavam, and staged a protest. "Your father made our yoke heavy – now, relieve the heavy workload and the harsh yoke your father placed upon us, and we will serve you" (I Kings 12:4). The elders who had counseled Shlomo told Reḥavam to grant their request. Reḥavam's young friends, however, told him to refuse. Reḥavam did refuse. The nation split in two, the ten northerly tribes declaring an independent kingdom under Yorovam. It was the end of the united kingdom. No subsequent ruler was able to reunite the tribes.

The Tabernacle and Temple, in contemporary language, mark the difference between society and state. Civil society, where the covenantal virtues are exercised, is made up of voluntary associations. When the state takes over the work of civil institutions, it is not the same thing under a different name: it is a different thing entirely. That is the difference between contract and covenant, between what people do because the government decides, and what they do out of a sense of shared commitment. Society is what we make

17 be ten cubits long and one and a half cubits wide. Each board should have
two matching tenons; all the Tabernacle's boards should be made in this way.
18 19 Make twenty boards for the southern side of the Tabernacle, and forty silver
sockets under the twenty boards, two sockets under the first board for its two
20 tenons, and two under the next. For the second side of the Tabernacle, the
21 northern side, there should be twenty boards, along with their forty silver
22 sockets, two under the first board and two under each of the others. Make six
23 boards for the west side of the Tabernacle, and two additional boards for the
24 Tabernacle's rear corners. These should adjoin each other at the bottom, and
be joined together at the top by a ring. So it should be for both sides; they
25 shall form the two corners. So there should be eight boards and sixteen silver
26 sockets, two sockets under each board. Make crossbars, too, of acacia wood,

רש״י

וְאַמָּה וַחֲצִי הָאַמָּה רֹחַב. לָמַדְנוּ אָרְכּוֹ שֶׁל מִשְׁכָּן לְעֶשְׂרִים קְרָשִׁים שֶׁהָיוּ בַּצָּפוֹן וּבַדָּרוֹם מִן הַמִּזְרָח לַמַּעֲרָב, שְׁלֹשִׁים אַמָּה:

יז **שְׁתֵּי יָדוֹת לַקֶּרֶשׁ הָאֶחָד.** הָיָה חוֹרֵץ אֶת הַקֶּרֶשׁ מִלְּמַטָּה בְּאֶמְצָעוֹ בְּגֹבַהּ אַמָּה, מַנִּיחַ רְבִיעַ רָחְבּוֹ מִכָּאן וּרְבִיעַ רָחְבּוֹ מִכָּאן וְהֵן הֵן הַיָּדוֹת, וְהֶחָרִיץ חֲצִי רֹחַב הַקֶּרֶשׁ בָּאֶמְצַע. וְאוֹתָן הַיָּדוֹת מַכְנִיס בָּאֲדָנִים שֶׁהָיוּ חֲלוּלִים, וְהָאֲדָנִים גָּבְהָן אַמָּה וְיוֹשְׁבִים רְצוּפִים אַרְבָּעִים זֶה אֵצֶל זֶה. וִידוֹת הַקֶּרֶשׁ הַנִּכְנָסוֹת בַּחֲלַל הָאֲדָנִים חֲרוּצוֹת מִשָּׁלֹשׁ צִדֵּיהֶן, רֹחַב הֶחָרִיץ כְּעֳבִי שְׂפַת הָאֶדֶן, שֶׁיְּכַסֶּה הַקֶּרֶשׁ אֶת כָּל רֹאשׁ הָאֶדֶן, שֶׁאִם לֹא כֵן נִמְצָא רֶוַח בֵּין קֶרֶשׁ לְקֶרֶשׁ כְּעֳבִי שְׂפַת שְׁנֵי הָאֲדָנִים שֶׁיַּפְסִיקוּ בֵּינֵיהֶם, וְזֶהוּ שֶׁנֶּאֱמַר: "וְיִהְיוּ תֹאֲמִם מִלְּמַטָּה" (להלן פסוק כד), שֶׁיַּחֲרֹץ אֶת צִדֵּי הַיָּדוֹת כְּדֵי שֶׁיִּתְחַבְּרוּ הַקְּרָשִׁים זֶה אֵצֶל זֶה: **מְשֻׁלָּבֹת.** עֲשׂוּיוֹת כְּמִין שְׁלִיבוֹת סֻלָּם מֻבְדָּלוֹת זוֹ מִזּוֹ, וּמְשֻׁפִּין רָאשֵׁיהֶם לִכָּנֵס בְּתוֹךְ חֲלַל הָאֶדֶן כִּשְׁלִיבָה הַנִּכְנֶסֶת בְּנֶקֶב עַמּוּדֵי הַסֻּלָּם: **אִשָּׁה אֶל אֲחֹתָהּ.** מְכֻוָּנוֹת זוֹ כְּנֶגֶד זוֹ, שֶׁיִּהְיוּ חֲרִיצֵיהֶם שָׁוִים זוֹ כְּמִדַּת זוֹ, כְּדֵי שֶׁלֹּא יִהְיוּ שְׁתֵּי יָדוֹת זוֹ מְשׁוּכָה לְצַד פְּנִים וְזוֹ מְשׁוּכָה לְצַד חוּץ בְּעֳבִי הַקֶּרֶשׁ שֶׁהוּא אַמָּה. וְתַרְגּוּם שֶׁל "יָדוֹת" - "צִירִין", לְפִי שֶׁדּוֹמוֹת לְצִירֵי הַדֶּלֶת הַנִּכְנָסִים בְּחוֹרֵי הַמִּפְתָּן:

יח **לִפְאַת נֶגְבָּה תֵימָנָה.** אֵין 'פֵּאָה' זוֹ לְשׁוֹן מִקְצוֹעַ, אֶלָּא כָּל הָרוּחַ קְרוּיָה פֵּאָה. כְּתַרְגּוּמוֹ: "לְרוּחַ עֵבֶר דָּרוֹמָא":

כב **וּלְיַרְכְּתֵי.** לְשׁוֹן סוֹף, כְּתַרְגּוּמוֹ: "וְלִסְיָפֵי". וּלְפִי שֶׁהַפֶּתַח בַּמִּזְרָח, קָרוּי מִזְרָח פָּנִים וְהַמַּעֲרָב אֲחוֹרַיִם, וְזֶהוּ סוֹף, שֶׁהַפָּנִים הֵן הָרֹאשׁ: **תַּעֲשֶׂה שִׁשָּׁה קְרָשִׁים.** הֲרֵי תֵּשַׁע אַמּוֹת רֹחַב:

כג **וּשְׁנֵי קְרָשִׁים תַּעֲשֶׂה לִמְקֻצְעֹת.** אֶחָד לְמִקְצוֹעַ צְפוֹנִית מַעֲרָבִית וְאֶחָד לְמַעֲרָבִית דְּרוֹמִית. כָּל שְׁמוֹנָה קְרָשִׁים בְּסֵדֶר אֶחָד הֵן, אֶלָּא שֶׁאֵלּוּ הַשְּׁתַּיִם אֵינָן בַּחֲלַל הַמִּשְׁכָּן, אֶלָּא חֲצִי אַמָּה מִזּוֹ וַחֲצִי אַמָּה מִזּוֹ נִרְאוֹת בֶּחָלָל, לְהַשְׁלִים רָחְבּוֹ לְעֶשֶׂר, וְהָאַמָּה מִזֶּה וְהָאַמָּה מִזֶּה בָּאוֹת כְּנֶגֶד אַמַּת עֳבִי קַרְשֵׁי הַמִּשְׁכָּן הַצָּפוֹן וְהַדָּרוֹם, כְּדֵי שֶׁיְּהֵא הַמִּקְצוֹעַ מִבַּחוּץ שָׁוֶה:

כד **וְיִהְיוּ.** כָּל הַקְּרָשִׁים "תֹאֲמִם" זֶה לָזֶה "מִלְּמַטָּה", שֶׁלֹּא יַפְסִיק עֳבִי שְׂפַת שְׁנֵי הָאֲדָנִים בֵּינֵיהֶם לְהַרְחִיקָם זוֹ מִזּוֹ. זֶהוּ שֶׁפֵּרַשְׁתִּי שֶׁיִּהְיוּ צִירֵי הַיָּדוֹת חֲרוּצִים מִצִּדֵּיהֶן, שֶׁיְּהֵא רֹחַב הַקֶּרֶשׁ בּוֹלֵט לְצִדָּיו חוּץ לַיָּדוֹת הַקֶּרֶשׁ לְכַסּוֹת אֶת שְׂפַת הָאֶדֶן, וְכֵן הַקֶּרֶשׁ שֶׁאֶצְלוֹ, וְנִמְצְאוּ תוֹאֲמִים זֶה לָזֶה. וְקֶרֶשׁ הַמִּקְצוֹעַ שֶׁבְּסֵדֶר הַמַּעֲרָב חָרוּץ לְרָחְבּוֹ בְּעָבְיוֹ, כְּנֶגֶד חָרִיץ שֶׁל צַד קֶרֶשׁ הַצְּפוֹנִי וְהַדְּרוֹמִי, כְּדֵי שֶׁלֹּא יַפְרִידוּ הָאֲדָנִים בֵּינֵיהֶם: **וְיַחְדָּו יִהְיוּ תַמִּים.** כְּמוֹ "תֹאֲמִם": **עַל רֹאשׁוֹ.** שֶׁל קֶרֶשׁ: **אֶל הַטַּבַּעַת הָאֶחָת.** כָּל קֶרֶשׁ וְקֶרֶשׁ הָיָה חָרוּץ לְמַעְלָה בְּרָחְבּוֹ שְׁנֵי חֲרִיצִין בִּשְׁנֵי צִדָּיו כְּדֵי עֳבִי טַבַּעַת, וּמַכְנִיסוֹ בְּטַבַּעַת אַחַת, נִמְצָא מַתְאִים לַקֶּרֶשׁ שֶׁאֶצְלוֹ. אֲבָל אוֹתָן טַבָּעוֹת לֹא יָדַעְתִּי אִם קְבוּעוֹת הֵן אִם מְטֻלְטָלוֹת. וּבַקֶּרֶשׁ שֶׁבַּמִּקְצוֹעַ הָיָה טַבַּעַת בְּעֳבִי הַקֶּרֶשׁ הַדְּרוֹמִי וְהַצְּפוֹנִי וְרֹאשׁ קֶרֶשׁ הַמִּקְצוֹעַ שֶׁבְּסֵדֶר מַעֲרָב נִכְנָס לְתוֹכוֹ, נִמְצְאוּ שְׁנֵי הַכְּתָלִים מְחֻבָּרִים: **כֵּן יִהְיֶה לִשְׁנֵיהֶם.** הַקְּרָשִׁים שֶׁבַּמִּקְצוֹעַ, לַקֶּרֶשׁ שֶׁבְּסוֹף צָפוֹן וְלַקֶּרֶשׁ הַמַּעֲרָבִי. וְכֵן "לִשְׁנֵי הַמִּקְצֹעֹת":

כה **וְהָיוּ שְׁמֹנָה קְרָשִׁים.** הֵן הָאֲמוּרוֹת לְמַעְלָה: "תַּעֲשֶׂה שִׁשָּׁה קְרָשִׁים וּשְׁנֵי קְרָשִׁים תַּעֲשֶׂה לִמְקֻצְעֹת" (לעיל פסוקים כב-כג), נִמְצְאוּ שְׁמֹנָה קְרָשִׁים בְּסֵדֶר מַעֲרָבִי. כָּךְ שְׁנוּיָה בְּמִשְׁנַת מַעֲשֵׂה סֵדֶר הַקְּרָשִׁים בִּמְלֶאכֶת הַמִּשְׁכָּן (ברייתא דמלאכת המשכן, פרק א): הָיָה עוֹשֶׂה אֶת הָאֲדָנִים חֲלוּלִים, וְחוֹרֵץ אֶת הַקֶּרֶשׁ מִלְּמַטָּה רְבִיעַ מִכָּאן וּרְבִיעַ מִכָּאן וְהֶחָרִיץ חֶצְיוֹ בָּאֶמְצַע, וְעָשָׂה לוֹ שְׁתֵּי יָדוֹת כְּמִין שְׁנֵי חַמּוּקִין, וְלִי נִרְאֶה שֶׁהַגִּרְסָא: כְּמִין שְׁנֵי חֲוָקִין, כְּמִין שְׁתֵּי שְׁלִיבוֹת סֻלָּם הַמֻּבְדָּלוֹת זוֹ מִזּוֹ, וּמְשֻׁפּוֹת לִכָּנֵס בַּחֲלַל הָאֶדֶן כִּשְׁלִיבָה הַנִּכְנֶסֶת בְּנֶקֶב עַמּוּד הַסֻּלָּם, וְהוּא לְשׁוֹן ◄

יז הַקָּרֶשׁ וְאַמָּה וַחֲצִי הָאַמָּה רֹחַב הַקָּרֶשׁ הָאֶחָד׃ שְׁתֵּי יָדוֹת לַקֶּרֶשׁ
הָאֶחָד מְשֻׁלָּבֹת אִשָּׁה אֶל־אֲחֹתָהּ כֵּן תַּעֲשֶׂה לְכֹל קַרְשֵׁי הַמִּשְׁכָּן׃
יח וְעָשִׂיתָ אֶת־הַקְּרָשִׁים לַמִּשְׁכָּן עֶשְׂרִים קֶרֶשׁ לִפְאַת נֶגְבָּה תֵימָנָה׃
יט וְאַרְבָּעִים אַדְנֵי־כֶסֶף תַּעֲשֶׂה תַּחַת עֶשְׂרִים הַקָּרֶשׁ שְׁנֵי אֲדָנִים תַּחַת־
הַקֶּרֶשׁ הָאֶחָד לִשְׁתֵּי יְדֹתָיו וּשְׁנֵי אֲדָנִים תַּחַת־הַקֶּרֶשׁ הָאֶחָד לִשְׁתֵּי
כ כא יְדֹתָיו׃ וּלְצֶלַע הַמִּשְׁכָּן הַשֵּׁנִית לִפְאַת צָפוֹן עֶשְׂרִים קָרֶשׁ׃ וְאַרְבָּעִים
אַדְנֵיהֶם כָּסֶף שְׁנֵי אֲדָנִים תַּחַת הַקֶּרֶשׁ הָאֶחָד וּשְׁנֵי אֲדָנִים תַּחַת הַקֶּרֶשׁ
כב כג הָאֶחָד׃ וּלְיַרְכְּתֵי הַמִּשְׁכָּן יָמָּה תַּעֲשֶׂה שִׁשָּׁה קְרָשִׁים׃ וּשְׁנֵי קְרָשִׁים
כד תַּעֲשֶׂה לִמְקֻצְעֹת הַמִּשְׁכָּן בַּיַּרְכָתָיִם׃ וְיִהְיוּ תֹאֲמִם מִלְּמַטָּה וְיַחְדָּו
יִהְיוּ תַמִּים עַל־רֹאשׁוֹ אֶל־הַטַּבַּעַת הָאֶחָת כֵּן יִהְיֶה לִשְׁנֵיהֶם לִשְׁנֵי
כה הַמִּקְצֹעֹת יִהְיוּ׃ וְהָיוּ שְׁמֹנָה קְרָשִׁים וְאַדְנֵיהֶם כֶּסֶף שִׁשָּׁה עָשָׂר אֲדָנִים
שְׁנֵי אֲדָנִים תַּחַת הַקֶּרֶשׁ הָאֶחָד וּשְׁנֵי אֲדָנִים תַּחַת הַקֶּרֶשׁ הָאֶחָד׃
כו וְעָשִׂיתָ בְרִיחִם עֲצֵי שִׁטִּים חֲמִשָּׁה לְקַרְשֵׁי צֶלַע־הַמִּשְׁכָּן הָאֶחָד׃

אונקלוס

דדפא, ואמתא ופלגות אמתא, פתיא דדפא חד: יז תרין צירין, לדפא חד, משלבין, חד לקביל חד, כן תעביד, לכל דפי משכנא: יח ותעביד ית דפיא למשכנא, עסרין דפין, לרוח עיבר דרומא: יט וארבעין סמכין דכסף, תעביד, תחות עסרין דפין, תרין סמכין, תחות דפא חד לתרין צירוהי, ותרין סמכין, תחות דפא חד לתרין צירוהי: כ ולסטר משכנא, תנינא לרוח צפונא, עסרין דפין: כא וארבעין סמכיהון דכסף, תרין סמכין, תחות דפא חד, ותרין סמכין, תחות דפא חד: כב ולסיפי משכנא מערבא, תעביד שתא דפין: כג ותרין דפין תעביד, לזוית משכנא, בסופהון: כד ויהון מכונין מלרע, וכחדא, יהון מכונין על רישיהון, לעזקתא חדא, כן יהי לתרויהון, לתרתין זוין יהון: כה ויהון תמניא דפין, וסמכיהון דכסף, שתת עסר סמכין, תרין סמכין, תחות דפא חד, ותרין סמכין, תחות דפא חד: כו ותעביד עברי דאעי שטין, חמשא, לדפי סטר משכנא חד:

רש״י

״משלבת״, עשויות כמין שליבה. ומכניסן לתוך שני אדנים, שנאמר: ״שני אדנים... ושני אדנים״ (לעיל פסוק יט). וחורץ את הקרש מלמעלה אצבע מכאן ואצבע מכאן ונותן לתוך טבעת אחת של זהב, כדי שלא יהיו נפרדים זה מזה, שנאמר: ״ויהיו תאמם מלמטה״ וגו׳ (לעיל פסוק כד). כך היא המשנה, והפרוש שלה הצעתי למעלה בסדר המקראות:

כו בריחם. כתרגומו ״עברין״, ובלעז אשפר״ש: חמשה לקרשי צלע המשכן. אלו חמשה שלשה הן, אלא שהבריח העליון והתחתון עשוי משתי חתיכות, זה מבריח עד חצי הכתל וזה מבריח עד חצי הכתל, זה נכנס בטבעת מכאן זה וזה נכנס בטבעת מכאן זה עד שמגיעין זה לזה, נמצאו העליון והתחתון שנים שהן ארבעה. אבל האמצעי ארכו כנגד כל הכתל, ומבריח מקצה הכתל ועד קצהו, שנאמר: ״והבריח התיכן וגו׳ מברח מן הקצה אל הקצה״ (להלן פסוק כח). שהעליונים והתחתונים היו להן טבעות בקרשים לכנס לתוכן, שתי טבעות לכל קרש, משלבים בתוך עשר אמות של גבה

27 five for the boards of the first side of the Tabernacle, five for the boards of the
second side of the Tabernacle, and five for the boards of the western side of the
28 Tabernacle at the rear. The central crossbar should go through the middle of
29 the boards from one end to the other. Overlay the boards with gold, and make
gold rings for the crossbars. The crossbars too should be overlaid with gold.
30 So shall you set up the Tabernacle, according to the plan you were shown on
31 the mountain. Make a curtain of sky-blue, purple, and scarlet wool, HAMISHI
32 and finely spun linen with a design of cherubim worked into it. Hang it on
four gold-covered posts of acacia wood with gold hooks, set on four sockets of
33 silver. Hang the curtain under the clasps and bring the Ark of the Testimony
behind it, so that the curtain separates the holy place from the Holy of Holies.
34 35 Put the cover on the Ark of the Testimony in the Holy of Holies. The table
shall be placed on the north side of the Tabernacle outside the curtain, and the
36 candelabrum on the south side, opposite the table. Make a screen for the entrance
to the Tent, embroidered with sky-blue, purple, and scarlet wool and finely
37 spun linen. Make five posts of acacia wood for the screen and overlay them
with gold; their hooks, also, shall be of gold. Cast for them, too, five sockets

רש״י

הַקֶּרֶשׁ, חֵלֶק אֶחָד מִן הַטַּבַּעַת הָעֶלְיוֹנָה וּלְמַעְלָה וְחֵלֶק אֶחָד מִן הַתַּחְתּוֹנָה וּלְמַטָּה, וְכָל חֵלֶק הוּא רְבִיעַ אֹרֶךְ הַקֶּרֶשׁ, וּשְׁנֵי חֲלָקִים בֵּין טַבַּעַת לְטַבַּעַת, כְּדֵי שֶׁיִּהְיוּ כָּל הַטַּבָּעוֹת מְכֻוָּנִין זֶה כְּנֶגֶד זֶה. אֲבָל לַבְּרִיחַ הַתִּיכוֹן אֵין טַבָּעוֹת, אֶלָּא הַקְּרָשִׁים נְקוּבִין בְּעָבְיָן, וְהוּא נִכְנָס בָּהֶם דֶּרֶךְ הַנְּקָבִים שֶׁהֵם מְכֻוָּנִין זֶה מוּל זֶה, וְזֶהוּ שֶׁנֶּאֱמַר: "בְּתוֹךְ הַקְּרָשִׁים" (שם). הַבְּרִיחִים הָעֶלְיוֹנִים וְהַתַּחְתּוֹנִים שֶׁבַּצָּפוֹן וְשֶׁבַּדָּרוֹם אֹרֶךְ כָּל אֶחָד חֲמֵשׁ עֶשְׂרֵה אַמָּה, וְהַתִּיכוֹן אָרְכּוֹ שְׁלֹשִׁים אַמָּה, וְזֶהוּ "מִן הַקָּצֶה אֶל הַקָּצֶה" (שם), מִן הַמִּזְרָח וְעַד הַמַּעֲרָב. וַחֲמִשָּׁה בְרִיחִים שֶׁבַּמַּעֲרָב, אֹרֶךְ הָעֶלְיוֹנִים וְהַתַּחְתּוֹנִים שֵׁשׁ אַמּוֹת, וְהַתִּיכוֹן אָרְכּוֹ שְׁתֵּים עֶשְׂרֵה, כְּנֶגֶד רֹחַב שְׁמוֹנָה קְרָשִׁים. כָּךְ הִיא מְפֹרֶשֶׁת בִּמְלֶאכֶת הַמִּשְׁכָּן:

כט **בָּתִּים לַבְּרִיחִם.** הַטַּבָּעוֹת שֶׁתַּעֲשֶׂה בָּהֶן יִהְיוּ בָּתִּים לְהִכָּנֵס בָּהֶן הַבְּרִיחִים: **וְצִפִּיתָ אֶת הַבְּרִיחִם זָהָב.** לֹא שֶׁהָיָה הַזָּהָב מְדֻבָּק עַל הַבְּרִיחִים, שֶׁאֵין עֲלֵיהֶם שׁוּם צִפּוּי, אֶלָּא בַּקֶּרֶשׁ הָיָה קוֹבֵעַ כְּמִין שְׁנֵי פִּיפִיּוֹת שֶׁל זָהָב כְּמִין שְׁנֵי סִדְקֵי קָנֶה חָלוּק, וְקוֹבְעָן אֵצֶל הַטַּבָּעוֹת לְכָאן וּלְכָאן, אָרְכָּן מְמַלֵּא אֶת רֹחַב הַקֶּרֶשׁ מִן הַטַּבַּעַת לְכָאן וּמִמֶּנָּה לְכָאן, וְהַבְּרִיחַ נִכְנָס לְתוֹכוֹ וּמִמֶּנּוּ לַטַּבַּעַת וּמִן הַטַּבַּעַת לַפֶּה הַשֵּׁנִי, נִמְצְאוּ הַבְּרִיחִים מְצֻפִּים זָהָב כְּשֶׁהֵן תְּחוּבִין בַּקְּרָשִׁים. וְהַבְּרִיחִים הַלָּלוּ מִבַּחוּץ הָיוּ; בְּלִיטַת הַטַּבָּעוֹת וְהַפִּיפִיּוֹת לֹא הָיְתָה נִרְאֵית בְּתוֹךְ הַמִּשְׁכָּן, אֶלָּא כָּל הַכֹּתֶל חָלָק מִבִּפְנִים:

ל **וַהֲקֵמֹתָ אֶת הַמִּשְׁכָּן.** לְאַחַר שֶׁיִּגָּמֵר הֲקִימֵהוּ: **הָרְאֵיתָ בָּהָר.** קֹדֶם לָכֵן, שֶׁאֲנִי עָתִיד לְלַמֶּדְךָ וּלְהַרְאוֹתְךָ סֵדֶר הֲקָמָתוֹ:

לא **פָּרֹכֶת.** לְשׁוֹן מְחִצָּה הוּא, וּבִלְשׁוֹן חֲכָמִים: פַּרְגּוֹד, דָּבָר הַמַּבְדִּיל בֵּין הַמֶּלֶךְ וּבֵין הָעָם: **תְּכֵלֶת וְאַרְגָּמָן.** כָּל מִין וּמִין הָיָה כָּפוּל, בְּכָל חוּט וָחוּט שִׁשָּׁה חוּטִין: **מַעֲשֵׂה חֹשֵׁב.** כְּבָר פֵּרַשְׁתִּי שֶׁזּוֹ הִיא אֲרִיגָה שֶׁל שְׁתֵּי קִירוֹת, וְהַצִּיּוּרִין שֶׁמִּשְּׁנֵי עֲבָרֶיהָ אֵינָן דּוֹמִין זֶה לָזֶה: **כְּרֻבִים.** צִיּוּרִין שֶׁל בְּרִיּוֹת יַעֲשֶׂה בָּהּ:

לב אַרְבָּעָה עַמּוּדִים תְּקוּעִים בְּתוֹךְ אַרְבָּעָה אֲדָנִים, וְאֻנְקְלִיּוֹת קְבוּעִין בָּהֶן עֲקֻמִּין לְמַעְלָה, לְהוֹשִׁיב עֲלֵיהֶן כְּלוֹנָס שֶׁרֹאשׁ הַפָּרֹכֶת כָּרוּךְ בָּהּ; וְהָאֻנְקְלִיּוֹת הֵן הַוָּוִין, שֶׁהֲרֵי כְּמִין וָוִין הֵן עֲשׂוּיִים. וְהַפָּרֹכֶת אָרְכָּהּ עֶשֶׂר אַמּוֹת לְרָחְבּוֹ שֶׁל מִשְׁכָּן, וְרָחְבָּהּ עֶשֶׂר אַמּוֹת כְּגָבְהָן שֶׁל קְרָשִׁים, פְּרוּסָה בִּשְׁלִישׁוֹ שֶׁל מִשְׁכָּן, שֶׁיְּהֵא הֵימֶנָּה וְלִפְנִים עֶשֶׂר אַמּוֹת וְהֵימֶנָּה וְלַחוּץ עֶשְׂרִים אַמָּה. נִמְצָא בֵּית קָדְשֵׁי הַקֳּדָשִׁים עֶשֶׂר עַל עֶשֶׂר, שֶׁנֶּאֱמַר: "וְנָתַתָּה אֶת הַפָּרֹכֶת תַּחַת הַקְּרָסִים" (להלן פסוק לג) הַמְחַבְּרִים אֶת שְׁתֵּי חוֹבְרוֹת שֶׁל יְרִיעוֹת הַמִּשְׁכָּן; רֹחַב הַחוֹבֶרֶת עֶשְׂרִים אַמָּה, וּכְשֶׁפְּרָסָהּ עַל גַּג הַמִּשְׁכָּן מִן הַפֶּתַח לַמַּעֲרָב, כָּלְתָה בִּשְׁנֵי שְׁלִישֵׁי הַמִּשְׁכָּן, וְהַחוֹבֶרֶת הַשֵּׁנִית כִּסְּתָה שְׁלִישׁוֹ שֶׁל מִשְׁכָּן, וְהַמּוֹתָר תָּלוּי לַאֲחוֹרָיו לְכַסּוֹת אֶת הַקְּרָשִׁים:

לה **וְשַׂמְתָּ אֶת הַשֻּׁלְחָן.** שֻׁלְחָן בַּצָּפוֹן מָשׁוּךְ מִן הַכֹּתֶל הַצְּפוֹנִי שְׁתֵּי אַמּוֹת וּמֶחֱצָה, וּמְנוֹרָה בַּדָּרוֹם מְשׁוּכָה מִן הַכֹּתֶל הַדְּרוֹמִי שְׁתֵּי אַמּוֹת וּמֶחֱצָה, וּמִזְבַּח הַזָּהָב נָתוּן כְּנֶגֶד אֲוִיר שֶׁבֵּין שֻׁלְחָן לַמְּנוֹרָה מָשׁוּךְ

כז וַחֲמִשָּׁה בְרִיחִם לְקַרְשֵׁי צֶלַע־הַמִּשְׁכָּן הַשֵּׁנִית וַחֲמִשָּׁה בְרִיחִם לְקַרְשֵׁי
כח צֶלַע הַמִּשְׁכָּן לַיַּרְכָתַיִם יָמָּה: וְהַבְּרִיחַ הַתִּיכֹן בְּתוֹךְ הַקְּרָשִׁים מַבְרִחַ
כט מִן־הַקָּצֶה אֶל־הַקָּצֶה: וְאֶת־הַקְּרָשִׁים תְּצַפֶּה זָהָב וְאֶת־טַבְּעֹתֵיהֶם
ל תַּעֲשֶׂה זָהָב בָּתִּים לַבְּרִיחִם וְצִפִּיתָ אֶת־הַבְּרִיחִם זָהָב: וַהֲקֵמֹתָ אֶת־
לא הַמִּשְׁכָּן כְּמִשְׁפָּטוֹ אֲשֶׁר הָרְאֵיתָ בָּהָר: וְעָשִׂיתָ פָרֹכֶת כ חמישי
תְּכֵלֶת וְאַרְגָּמָן וְתוֹלַעַת שָׁנִי וְשֵׁשׁ מָשְׁזָר מַעֲשֵׂה חֹשֵׁב יַעֲשֶׂה אֹתָהּ
לב כְּרֻבִים: וְנָתַתָּה אֹתָהּ עַל־אַרְבָּעָה עַמּוּדֵי שִׁטִּים מְצֻפִּים זָהָב וָוֵיהֶם
לג זָהָב עַל־אַרְבָּעָה אַדְנֵי־כָסֶף: וְנָתַתָּה אֶת־הַפָּרֹכֶת תַּחַת הַקְּרָסִים
וְהֵבֵאתָ שָׁמָּה מִבֵּית לַפָּרֹכֶת אֵת אֲרוֹן הָעֵדוּת וְהִבְדִּילָה הַפָּרֹכֶת
לד לָכֶם בֵּין הַקֹּדֶשׁ וּבֵין קֹדֶשׁ הַקֳּדָשִׁים: וְנָתַתָּ אֶת־הַכַּפֹּרֶת עַל אֲרוֹן
לה הָעֵדֻת בְּקֹדֶשׁ הַקֳּדָשִׁים: וְשַׂמְתָּ אֶת־הַשֻּׁלְחָן מִחוּץ לַפָּרֹכֶת וְאֶת־
הַמְּנֹרָה נֹכַח הַשֻּׁלְחָן עַל צֶלַע הַמִּשְׁכָּן תֵּימָנָה וְהַשֻּׁלְחָן תִּתֵּן עַל־צֶלַע
לו צָפוֹן: וְעָשִׂיתָ מָסָךְ לְפֶתַח הָאֹהֶל תְּכֵלֶת וְאַרְגָּמָן וְתוֹלַעַת שָׁנִי וְשֵׁשׁ
לז מָשְׁזָר מַעֲשֵׂה רֹקֵם: וְעָשִׂיתָ לַמָּסָךְ חֲמִשָּׁה עַמּוּדֵי שִׁטִּים וְצִפִּיתָ אֹתָם

אונקלוס

כז וַחֲמְשָׁא עַבְרִין, לְדַפֵּי סְטַר מַשְׁכְּנָא תִּנְיָנָא, וַחֲמְשָׁא עַבְרִין, לְדַפֵּי סְטַר מַשְׁכְּנָא, לְסוֹפֵיהוֹן מַעַרְבָא: כח וְעַבְרָא מְצִיעָאָה בְּגוֹ דַּפַּיָּא, מְעַבַּר, מִן סְיָפֵי לִסְיָפֵי: כט וְיָת דַּפַּיָּא תַּחְפֵּי דַּהֲבָא, וְיָת עִזְקָתְהוֹן תַּעֲבֵיד דַּהֲבָא, אַתְרָא לְעַבְרַיָּא, וְתַחְפֵּי יָת עַבְרַיָּא דַּהֲבָא: ל וּתְקִים יָת מַשְׁכְּנָא, כְּהִלְכְתֵיהּ, דְּאִתַּחְזֵיתָא בְּטוּרָא: לא וְתַעֲבֵיד פָּרֻכְתָּא, תַּכְלָא וְאַרְגְּוָנָא, וּצְבַע זְהוֹרִי וּבוּץ שְׁזִיר, עוֹבַד אֻמָּן, יַעֲבֵיד יָתַהּ צוּרַת כְּרוּבִין: לב וְתִתֵּין יָתַהּ, עַל אַרְבְּעָא עַמּוּדֵי שִׁטִּין, מְחַפַּן דַּהֲבָא, וָוֵיהוֹן דַּהֲבָא, עַל אַרְבְּעָא סַמְכִין דִּכְסַף: לג וְתִתֵּין יָת פָּרֻכְתָּא תְּחוֹת פּוּרְפַיָּא, וְתַעֵיל לְתַמָּן מִגָּיו לְפָרֻכְתָּא, יָת אֲרוֹנָא דְּסָהֲדוּתָא, וְתַפְרֵישׁ פָּרֻכְתָּא לְכוֹן, בֵּין קֻדְשָׁא, וּבֵין קֹדֶשׁ קֻדְשַׁיָּא: לד וְתִתֵּין יָת כַּפֻּרְתָּא, עַל אֲרוֹנָא דְּסָהֲדוּתָא, בְּקֹדֶשׁ קֻדְשַׁיָּא: לה וּתְשַׁוֵּי יָת פָּתוֹרָא מִבָּרָא לְפָרֻכְתָּא, וְיָת מְנָרְתָא לָקֳבֵיל פָּתוֹרָא, עַל סְטַר מַשְׁכְּנָא דָּרוֹמָא, וּפָתוֹרָא, תִּתֵּין עַל סְטַר צִפּוּנָא: לו וְתַעֲבֵיד פְּרָסָא לִתְרַע מַשְׁכְּנָא, תַּכְלָא וְאַרְגְּוָנָא, וּצְבַע זְהוֹרִי וּבוּץ שְׁזִיר, עוֹבַד צַיָּר: לז וְתַעֲבֵיד לִפְרָסָא, חַמְשָׁא עַמּוּדֵי שִׁטִּין, וְתַחְפֵּי יָתְהוֹן

רש״י

קָמְעָה כְּלַפֵּי הַמִּזְרָח, וְכֻלָּם נְתוּנִים מִן חֲצִי הַמִּשְׁכָּן וְלִפְנִים. כֵּיצַד? אֹרֶךְ הַמִּשְׁכָּן מִן הַפֶּתַח לַפָּרֹכֶת עֶשְׂרִים אַמָּה, הַמִּזְבֵּחַ וְהַשֻּׁלְחָן וְהַמְּנוֹרָה מְשׁוּכִים מִן הַפֶּתַח לְצַד מַעֲרָב עֶשֶׂר אַמּוֹת:

לו **וְעָשִׂיתָ מָסָךְ.** וִילוֹן שֶׁהוּא מֵסֵךְ כְּנֶגֶד הַפֶּתַח, כְּמוֹ: "שַׂכְתָּ בַעֲדוֹ" (איוב א, י), לְשׁוֹן מָגֵן: **מַעֲשֵׂה רֹקֵם.** הַצּוּרוֹת עֲשׂוּיוֹת בּוֹ מַעֲשֵׂה מַחַט, כְּפַרְצוּף שֶׁל עֵבֶר זֶה כָּךְ פַּרְצוּף שֶׁל עֵבֶר זֶה: **רֹקֵם.** שֵׁם הָאֻמָּן וְלֹא שֵׁם הָאֻמָּנוּת, וְתַרְגּוּמוֹ: "עוֹבַד צַיָּר" וְלֹא 'עוֹבַד צִיּוּר'. מִדַּת הַמָּסָךְ כְּמִדַּת הַפָּרֹכֶת, עֶשֶׂר אַמּוֹת עַל עֶשֶׂר אַמּוֹת:

27 1 of bronze. Make the altar from acacia wood. It should be square, five SHISHI
2 cubits long, five cubits wide, and three cubits high. Make horns for it on its four
3 corners, the horns being of one piece with it, and overlay it with bronze. Make
pots for removing its ashes, together with shovels, basins, forks, and pans.
4 Make all of these of bronze. Make a grate of bronze mesh for it, and on the
5 mesh make four bronze rings at its four corners. The grate should be set below,
under the ledge of the altar, so that the mesh reaches the middle of the altar.

רש״י

כז א **וְעָשִׂיתָ אֶת הַמִּזְבֵּחַ וְגוֹ׳ וְשָׁלֹשׁ אַמּוֹת קֹמָתוֹ.** דְּבָרִים כִּכְתָבָן, דִּבְרֵי רַבִּי יְהוּדָה. רַבִּי יוֹסֵי אוֹמֵר: נֶאֱמַר כָּאן "רָבוּעַ" וְנֶאֱמַר בַּפְּנִימִי "רָבוּעַ" (להלן ל, א), מַה לְּהַלָּן גָּבְהוֹ פִּי שְׁנַיִם כְּאָרְכּוֹ, אַף כָּאן גָּבְהוֹ פִּי שְׁנַיִם כְּאָרְכּוֹ; וּמָה אֲנִי מְקַיֵּם "וְשָׁלֹשׁ אַמּוֹת קֹמָתוֹ"? מִשְּׂפַת סוֹבֵב וּלְמַעְלָה:

ב **מִמֶּנּוּ תִּהְיֶיןָ קַרְנֹתָיו.** שֶׁלֹּא יַעֲשֵׂם לְבַדָּם וִיחַבְּרֵם בּוֹ: **וְצִפִּיתָ אֹתוֹ נְחֹשֶׁת.** לְכַפֵּר עַל עַזּוּת מֵצַח, שֶׁנֶּאֱמַר: "וּמִצְחֲךָ נְחוּשָׁה" (ישעיה מח, ד):

ג **סִירֹתָיו.** כְּמִין יוֹרוֹת: **לְדַשְּׁנוֹ.** לְהָסִיר דִּשְׁנוֹ לְתוֹכָם; וְהוּא שֶׁתִּרְגֵּם אוּנְקְלוֹס: "לְמִסְפֵּי קִטְמֵיהּ", לִסְפּוֹת הַדֶּשֶׁן לְתוֹכָם. כִּי יֵשׁ מִלּוֹת בִּלְשׁוֹן עִבְרִית מִלָּה אַחַת מִתְחַלֶּפֶת בַּפִּתְרוֹן לְשַׁמֵּשׁ בִּנְיָן וּסְתִירָה, כְּמוֹ "וַתַּשְׁרֵשׁ שָׁרָשֶׁיהָ" (תהלים פ, י), "אֱוִיל מַשְׁרִישׁ" (איוב ה, ג), וְחִלּוּפוֹ: "וּבְכָל תְּבוּאָתִי תְשָׁרֵשׁ" (שם לא, יב). וְכָמוֹהוּ: "בִּסְעִפֶיהָ פֹּרִיָּה" (ישעיה יז, ו), וְחִלּוּפוֹ: "מְסָעֵף פֻּארָה" (שם י, לג), מְפַסֵּחַ סְעִיפֶיהָ. וְכָמוֹהוּ: "וְזֶה הָאַחֲרוֹן עִצְּמוֹ" (ירמיה נ, יז), שִׁבֵּר עַצְמוֹתָיו. וְכָמוֹהוּ: "וַיִּסְקְלֻהוּ בָאֲבָנִים" (מלכים א׳ כא, יג), וְחִלּוּפוֹ: "סַקְּלוּ מֵאֶבֶן" (ישעיה סב, י), הָסִירוּ אֲבָנֶיהָ, וְכֵן: "וַיְעַזְּקֵהוּ וַיְסַקְּלֵהוּ" (שם ה, ב). אַף כָּאן "לְדַשְּׁנוֹ" לְהָסִיר דִּשְׁנוֹ, וּבְלַעַז אדשנדרי"ר: **וְיָעָיו.** כְּתַרְגּוּמוֹ, מַגְרֵפוֹת שֶׁנּוֹטֵל בָּהֶם הַדֶּשֶׁן, וְהֵן כְּמִין כִּסּוּי קְדֵרָה, וְהוּא שֶׁל מַתֶּכֶת דַּק וְלוֹ בֵּית יָד, וּבְלַעַז וודי"ל: **וּמִזְרְקֹתָיו.** לְקַבֵּל בָּהֶם דַּם הַזְּבָחִים: **וּמִזְלְגֹתָיו.** כְּמִין אֻנְקְלִיּוֹת כְּפוּפִין, וּמַכֶּה בָּהֶן בַּבָּשָׂר וְנִתְחָבִין בּוֹ, וּמְהַפְּכִין בָּהֶן עַל גַּחֲלֵי הַמַּעֲרָכָה שֶׁיְּהֵא מְמַהֵר שְׂרֵפָתָן, וּבְלַעַז קרוצי"ש, וּבִלְשׁוֹן חֲכָמִים: צִנּוֹרִיּוֹת: **וּמַחְתֹּתָיו.** בֵּית קִבּוּל יֵשׁ לָהֶם לִטֹּל בָּהֶן גֶּחָלִים מִן הַמִּזְבֵּחַ לְשֵׂאתָם עַל מִזְבַּח הַפְּנִימִי לַקְטֹרֶת. וְעַל שֵׁם חֲתִיָּתָן קְרוּיִים מַחְתּוֹת, כְּמוֹ: "לַחְתּוֹת אֵשׁ מִיָּקוּד" (ישעיה ל, יד), לְשׁוֹן שְׁאִיבַת אֵשׁ מִמְּקוֹמָהּ, וְכֵן: "הֲיַחְתֶּה אִישׁ אֵשׁ בְּחֵיקוֹ" (משלי ו, כז): **לְכָל כֵּלָיו.** כְּמוֹ כָּל כֵּלָיו:

ד **מִכְבָּר.** לְשׁוֹן כְּבָרָה שֶׁקּוֹרִין קריב"ל, כְּמִין לְבוּשׁ עָשׂוּ לוֹ לַמִּזְבֵּחַ, עָשׂוּי חוֹרִין חוֹרִין כְּמִין רֶשֶׁת. וּמִקְרָא זֶה מְסֹרָס וְכָךְ פִּתְרוֹנוֹ: וְעָשִׂיתָ לוֹ מִכְבָּר נְחֹשֶׁת מַעֲשֵׂה רֶשֶׁת:

ה **כַּרְכֹּב הַמִּזְבֵּחַ.** סוֹבֵב. כָּל דָּבָר הַמַּקִּיף סָבִיב בְּעִגּוּל קָרוּי כַּרְכֹּב, כְּמוֹ שֶׁשָּׁנִינוּ בְּ'הַכֹּל שׁוֹחֲטִין': "אֵלּוּ הֵן גָּלְמֵי כְּלֵי עֵץ, כָּל שֶׁעָתִיד לָשׁוּף וּלְכַרְכֵּב" (חולין כה ע"א), וְהוּא שֶׁעוֹשִׂין חֲרִיצִין עֲגֻלִּין בְּקַרְשֵׁי דַּפְנֵי הַתֵּבוֹת וְסַפְסְלֵי הָעֵץ, אַף לַמִּזְבֵּחַ עָשָׂה חָרִיץ סְבִיבוֹ בְּדָפְנוֹ לְנוֹי, וְהוּא לְסוֹף שֵׁשׁ אַמּוֹת שֶׁל גָּבְהוֹ כְּדִבְרֵי הָאוֹמֵר (זבחים נט ע"ב – ס ע"א) מָה אֲנִי מְקַיֵּם "וְשָׁלֹשׁ אַמּוֹת קֹמָתוֹ"? מִשְּׂפַת סוֹבֵב וּלְמַעְלָה. אֲבָל סוֹבֵב לְהִלּוּךְ הַכֹּהֲנִים לֹא הָיָה לְמִזְבַּח הַנְּחֹשֶׁת אֶלָּא עַל רֹאשׁוֹ לִפְנִים מִקַּרְנוֹתָיו. וְכֵן שָׁנִינוּ בִּזְבָחִים (דף סב ע"א): אֵיזֶהוּ כַּרְכֹּב? בֵּין קֶרֶן לְקֶרֶן, וְלִפְנִים מֵהֶן אַמָּה שֶׁל הִלּוּךְ רַגְלֵי הַכֹּהֲנִים, שְׁתֵּי אַמּוֹת הַלָּלוּ קְרוּיִים כַּרְכֹּב. וְדִקְדַּקְנוּ שָׁם: וְהָכְתִיב: "תַּחַת כַּרְכֻּבּוֹ מִלְמָטָּה" (להלן לח, ד), לָמַדְנוּ שֶׁהַכַּרְכֹּב בְּדָפְנוֹ הוּא וּלְבוּשׁ הַמִּכְבָּר תַּחְתָּיו! וְתֵרֵץ הַמְתָרֵץ: תְּרֵי הֲווּ, אַחַד לְנוֹי וְאַחַד לַכֹּהֲנִים דְּלֹא נִשְׁתַּרְקוּ; זֶה שֶׁבַּדֹּפֶן לְנוֹי הָיָה, וּמִתַּחְתָּיו הִלְבִּישׁוּ הַמִּכְבָּר, וְהִגִּיעַ רָחְבּוֹ עַד חֲצִי הַמִּזְבֵּחַ, וְהוּא הָיָה סִימָן לַחֲצִי גָּבְהוֹ לְהַבְדִּיל בֵּין דָּמִים הָעֶלְיוֹנִים לְדָמִים הַתַּחְתּוֹנִים, וּכְנֶגְדּוֹ עָשׂוּ לְמִזְבַּח בֵּית עוֹלָמִים חֲגוֹרַת חוּט הַסִּקְרָא בְּאֶמְצָעוֹ (מדות ג, א). וְכֶבֶשׁ שֶׁהָיוּ עוֹלִין בּוֹ, אַף עַל פִּי שֶׁלֹּא פֵּרְשׁוֹ בְּעִנְיָן זֶה, כְּבָר שָׁמַעְנוּ בְּפָרָשַׁת 'מִזְבַּח אֲדָמָה תַּעֲשֶׂה לִּי': "וְלֹא תַעֲלֶה בְמַעֲלֹת" (לעיל כ, כב), לֹא תַּעֲשֶׂה לוֹ מַעֲלוֹת בַּכֶּבֶשׁ שֶׁלּוֹ, אֶלָּא כֶּבֶשׁ חָלָק, לָמַדְנוּ שֶׁהָיָה לוֹ כֶּבֶשׁ. כָּךְ שָׁנִינוּ בַּמְּכִילְתָּא (בחדש פרשה יא). וּ'מִזְבַּח אֲדָמָה' הוּא מִזְבַּח הַנְּחֹשֶׁת, שֶׁהָיוּ מְמַלְּאִין חֲלָלוֹ אֲדָמָה בִּמְקוֹם חֲנִיָּתָן. וְהַכֶּבֶשׁ הָיָה בִּדְרוֹם הַמִּזְבֵּחַ מֻבְדָּל מִן הַמִּזְבֵּחַ מְלֹא חוּט הַשַּׂעֲרָה, וְרַגְלָיו מַגִּיעִין עַד אַמָּה סָמוּךְ לְקַלְעֵי הֶחָצֵר שֶׁבַּדָּרוֹם, כְּדִבְרֵי הָאוֹמֵר עֶשֶׂר אַמּוֹת קוֹמָתוֹ; וּלְדִבְרֵי הָאוֹמֵר דְּבָרִים כִּכְתָבָן "שָׁלֹשׁ אַמּוֹת קֹמָתוֹ" (זבחים נט ע"ב), לֹא הָיָה אֹרֶךְ הַכֶּבֶשׁ אֶלָּא עֶשֶׂר אַמּוֹת. כָּךְ מָצָאתִי בְּמִשְׁנַת אַרְבָּעִים וְתֵשַׁע מִדּוֹת. וְזֶה שֶׁהוּא מֻבְדָּל מִן הַמִּזְבֵּחַ מְלֹא הַחוּט, בְּמַסֶּכֶת זְבָחִים (דף סב ע"ב) לְמַדְנוּהָ מִן הַמִּקְרָא:

כז א זָהָב וָוֵיהֶם זָהָב וְיָצַקְתָּ לָהֶם חֲמִשָּׁה אַדְנֵי נְחֹשֶׁת׃ וְעָשִׂיתָ ששי
אֶת־הַמִּזְבֵּחַ עֲצֵי שִׁטִּים חָמֵשׁ אַמּוֹת אֹרֶךְ וְחָמֵשׁ אַמּוֹת רֹחַב רָבוּעַ
ב יִהְיֶה הַמִּזְבֵּחַ וְשָׁלֹשׁ אַמּוֹת קֹמָתוֹ׃ וְעָשִׂיתָ קַרְנֹתָיו עַל אַרְבַּע פִּנֹּתָיו
ג מִמֶּנּוּ תִּהְיֶיןָ קַרְנֹתָיו וְצִפִּיתָ אֹתוֹ נְחֹשֶׁת׃ וְעָשִׂיתָ סִּירֹתָיו לְדַשְּׁנוֹ וְיָעָיו
ד וּמִזְרְקֹתָיו וּמִזְלְגֹתָיו וּמַחְתֹּתָיו לְכָל־כֵּלָיו תַּעֲשֶׂה נְחֹשֶׁת׃ וְעָשִׂיתָ לּוֹ
מִכְבָּר מַעֲשֵׂה רֶשֶׁת נְחֹשֶׁת וְעָשִׂיתָ עַל־הָרֶשֶׁת אַרְבַּע טַבְּעֹת נְחֹשֶׁת
ה עַל אַרְבַּע קְצוֹתָיו׃ וְנָתַתָּה אֹתָהּ תַּחַת כַּרְכֹּב הַמִּזְבֵּחַ מִלְּמָטָּה וְהָיְתָה

אונקלוס

דַּהֲבָא, וָוֵיהוֹן דַּהֲבָא, וְתַתֵּיךְ לְהוֹן, חַמְשָׁא סַמְכִין דִּנְחָשָׁא:
כז א וְתַעְבֵּיד יָת מַדְבְּחָא דְּאָעֵי שִׁטִּין, חֲמֵשׁ אַמִּין אֻרְכָּא וַחֲמֵשׁ אַמִּין
פֻּתְיָא, מְרַבַּע יְהֵי מַדְבְּחָא, וּתְלָת אַמִּין רוּמֵיהּ: ב וְתַעְבֵּיד קַרְנוֹהִי,
עַל אַרְבַּע זָוְיָתֵיהּ, מִנֵּיהּ יְהֶוְיָן קַרְנוֹהִי, וְתַחְפֵּי יָתֵיהּ נְחָשָׁא: ג וְתַעְבֵּיד
פְּסַכְתֵּירְוָתֵיהּ לְמִסְפֵּי קִטְמֵיהּ, וּמַגְרוֹפְיָתֵיהּ וּמִזְרְקוֹהִי, וְצִנּוֹרְיָתֵיהּ
וּמַחְתְּיָתֵיהּ, לְכָל מָנוֹהִי תַּעְבֵּיד נְחָשָׁא: ד וְתַעְבֵּיד לֵיהּ סְרָדָא, עוֹבַד
מְצָדְתָּא דִּנְחָשָׁא, וְתַעְבֵּיד עַל מְצָדְתָּא, אַרְבַּע עִזְקָן דִּנְחָשָׁא, עַל
אַרְבְּעָא סִטְרוֹהִי: ה וְתִתֵּין יָתַהּ, תְּחוֹת, סוֹבֵיבָא דְּמַדְבְּחָא מִלְּרַע, וּתְהֵי

27:1 **וְעָשִׂיתָ אֶת־הַמִּזְבֵּחַ** *Make the altar* – The building of the Tabernacle is a preparation for an activity central to the Torah, yet in many ways foreign to us: sacrifice. The major institutions of the modern world were predicated on the model of the *rational actor*, that is, one who acts to maximize the benefits to him- or herself. Hobbes's account of the social contract was that it is in the interests of each of us to hand over some of our rights to a central power charged with ensuring the rule of law and the defense of the realm. Adam Smith's insight into the market economy was that if we each act to maximize our own advantage, the result is the growth of the commonwealth. Modern politics and economics were built on the foundation of the rational pursuit of self-interest.

There was nothing wrong with this. It was an attempt to create peace in a Europe that had for centuries been ravaged by war. The democratic state and the market economy were serious attempts to harness the power of self-interest to combat the destructive passions that led to violence. The fact that politics and economics were based on self-interest did not negate the possibility that families and communities were sustained by altruism. It was a good system, not a bad one.

Now, however, after several centuries, the idea of love-as-sacrifice has grown thin in many areas of life. We see this specifically in relationships. *Lose the concept of sacrifice within a society, and sooner or later marriage falters, parenthood declines, and the society slowly ages and dies.* My predecessor, Lord Jakobovits, had a lovely way of putting this. The Talmud says that when a man divorces his first wife, "the altar sheds tears" (Gittin 90b). What is the connection between the altar and a marriage? Both, he said, are about sacrifices. Marriages fail when the partners are unwilling to make sacrifices for one another.

In the eleventh century, Rabbi Yehuda HaLevi expressed something close to awe at the fact that Jews stayed Jewish despite the fact that "with a word lightly spoken" they could have converted to the majority faith and lived a life of relative ease (*Kuzari* IV:23). Jews and Judaism survived despite the many sacrifices people had to make for it. Equally possible, though, is that Judaism survived *because* of those sacrifices. Where people make sacrifices for their ideals, the ideals stay strong. Not all sacrifice is holy. But the principle of sacrifice remains. It is the gift we bring to what and whom we love.

6 And make staves of acacia wood for the altar, and overlay them with bronze.
7 Place the poles in the rings, so that the poles will be on the two sides of the altar
8 when it is carried. Make it hollow, with planks; make it as it was shown to you
9 on the mountain. Make the courtyard of the Tabernacle thus: on the SHEVI'I
south side there should be hangings a hundred cubits long of finely spun linen,
10 all the length of the courtyard on that side, with twenty posts and their twenty
11 bronze sockets. The hooks and bands of the posts shall be of silver. Likewise
on the north side; the hangings shall be a hundred cubits long, with twenty
posts and their twenty corresponding bronze sockets, with hooks and bands
12 of silver. The width of the hangings at the western end of the courtyard shall be
fifty cubits, and it should have ten posts and their ten corresponding sockets.
13 14 The width of the courtyard at the front, facing east, shall be fifty cubits: fifteen
15 cubits of hangings with three posts and three sockets on one side, and fifteen
16 cubits of hangings with three posts and three sockets on the other, and for the
gate of the courtyard there shall be an embroidered screen of twenty cubits of
sky-blue, purple, and scarlet wool and finely spun linen, with four posts and
17 four sockets. All the posts around the courtyard should be banded with silver. MAFTIR

רש״י

ז| **בַּטַּבָּעֹת.** בְּאַרְבַּע טַבָּעוֹת שֶׁנַּעֲשׂוּ לַמִּכְבָּר:

ח| **נְבוּב לֻחֹת.** כְּתַרְגּוּמוֹ: ״חֲלִיל לוּחִין״, לוּחוֹת עֲצֵי שִׁטִּים מִכָּל צַד וְהֶחָלָל בָּאֶמְצַע, וְלֹא יְהֵא כֻּלּוֹ עֵץ אֶחָד שֶׁיְּהֵא עָבְיוֹ חָמֵשׁ אַמּוֹת עַל חָמֵשׁ אַמּוֹת כְּמִין סַדָּן:

ט| **קְלָעִים.** עֲשׂוּיִין כְּמִין קַלְעֵי סְפִינָה נְקָבִים נְקָבִים, מַעֲשֵׂה קְלִיעָה וְלֹא מַעֲשֵׂה אוֹרֵג. וְתַרְגּוּמוֹ: ״סְרָדִין״, כְּתַרְגּוּמוֹ שֶׁל ״מִכְבָּר״ (לעיל פסוק ד) הַמְּתֻרְגָּם: ״סְרָדָא״, לְפִי שֶׁהֵן מְנֻקָּבִין כִּכְבָרָה: **לַפֵּאָה הָאֶחָת.** כָּל הָרוּחַ קָרוּי פֵּאָה:

י| **וְעַמֻּדָיו עֶשְׂרִים.** חָמֵשׁ אַמּוֹת בֵּין עַמּוּד לְעַמּוּד: **וְאַדְנֵיהֶם.** שֶׁל הָעַמּוּדִים ״נְחֹשֶׁת״. הָאֲדָנִים יוֹשְׁבִין עַל הָאָרֶץ וְהָעַמּוּדִים תְּקוּעִים לְתוֹכָן. וְהָיָה עוֹשֶׂה כְּמִין קֻנְדָּסִין שֶׁקּוֹרִין פלא״ש אָרְכָּן שִׁשָּׁה טְפָחִים וְרָחְבָּן שְׁלֹשָׁה, וְטַבַּעַת נְחֹשֶׁת קְבוּעָה בּוֹ בְּאֶמְצָעוֹ, וְכוֹרֵךְ שְׂפַת הַקֶּלַע סְבִיבָיו בְּמֵיתָרִים כְּנֶגֶד כָּל עַמּוּד וְעַמּוּד, וְתוֹלֶה הַקֻּנְדָּס דֶּרֶךְ טַבַּעְתּוֹ בָּאַנְקְלִי שֶׁבָּעַמּוּד, הֶעָשׂוּי כְּמִין וָי״ו, רֹאשׁוֹ זָקוּף לְמַעְלָה וְרֹאשׁוֹ אֶחָד תָּקוּעַ בָּעַמּוּד, כְּאוֹתָן שֶׁעוֹשִׂין לְהַצִּיב דְּלָתוֹת שֶׁקּוֹרִין גונזי״ש, וְרֹחַב הַקֶּלַע תָּלוּי מִלְּמַטָּה וְהִיא קוֹמַת מְחִצּוֹת הֶחָצֵר: **וָוֵי הָעַמֻּדִים.** הֵם הָאַנְקְלִיּוֹת: **וַחֲשֻׁקֵיהֶם.** מֻקָּפִין הָיוּ הָעַמּוּדִים בְּחוּטֵי כֶּסֶף סָבִיב. וְאֵינִי יוֹדֵעַ אִם עַל פְּנֵי כֻלָּם אִם בְּרָאשָׁם אִם בְּאֶמְצָעָם, אַךְ יוֹדֵעַ אֲנִי שֶׁ׳חִשּׁוּק׳ לְשׁוֹן חֲגוֹרָה, שֶׁכָּךְ מָצִינוּ בְּפִילֶגֶשׁ בַּגִּבְעָה: ״וְעִמּוֹ צֶמֶד חֲמוֹרִים חֲבוּשִׁים״ (שופטים יט, י), תַּרְגּוּמוֹ: ׳חֲשִׁיקִין׳:

יג| **לִפְאַת קֵדְמָה מִזְרָחָה.** פְּנֵי הַמִּזְרָח קָרוּי ׳קֶדֶם׳, לְשׁוֹן פָּנִים, ׳אָחוֹר׳ לְשׁוֹן אֲחוֹרַיִם. לְפִיכָךְ מִזְרָח קָרוּי קֶדֶם שֶׁהוּא פָּנִים, וּמַעֲרָב קָרוּי אָחוֹר, כְּמָה דְאַתְּ אָמַר: ״הַיָּם הָאַחֲרוֹן״ (דברים יא, כד) – ״יַמָּא מַעַרְבָאָה״ (אונקלוס שם): **חֲמִשִּׁים אַמָּה.** אוֹתָן חֲמִשִּׁים אַמָּה לֹא הָיוּ סְתוּמִים כֻּלָּם בִּקְלָעִים, לְפִי שֶׁשָּׁם הַפֶּתַח, אֶלָּא חֲמֵשׁ עֶשְׂרֵה אַמָּה קְלָעִים לְכֶתֶף הַפֶּתַח מִכָּאן וְכֵן לַכָּתֵף הַשֵּׁנִית, נִשְׁאַר רֹחַב חֲלַל הַפֶּתַח בֵּינְתַיִם עֶשְׂרִים אַמָּה, וְזֶהוּ שֶׁנֶּאֱמַר: ״וּלְשַׁעַר הֶחָצֵר מָסָךְ עֶשְׂרִים אַמָּה״ (להלן פסוק טז), וִילוֹן לְהָסֵךְ כְּנֶגֶד הַפֶּתַח עֶשְׂרִים אַמָּה אֹרֶךְ, כְּרֹחַב הַפֶּתַח:

יד| **עַמֻּדֵיהֶם שְׁלֹשָׁה.** חָמֵשׁ אַמּוֹת בֵּין עַמּוּד לְעַמּוּד, בֵּין עַמּוּד שֶׁבְּרֹאשׁ הַדָּרוֹם הָעוֹמֵד בְּמִקְצוֹעַ דְּרוֹמִית מִזְרָחִית עַד עַמּוּד שֶׁהוּא מִן הַשְּׁלֹשָׁה שֶׁבַּמִּזְרָח חָמֵשׁ אַמּוֹת, וּמִמֶּנּוּ לַשֵּׁנִי חָמֵשׁ אַמּוֹת, וּמִן הַשֵּׁנִי לַשְּׁלִישִׁי חָמֵשׁ אַמּוֹת, וְכֵן לַכָּתֵף הַשֵּׁנִית, וְאַרְבָּעָה עַמּוּדִים לַמָּסָךְ. הֲרֵי עֲשָׂרָה עַמּוּדִים לַמִּזְרָח כְּנֶגֶד עֲשָׂרָה לַמַּעֲרָב:

יז| **כָּל עַמּוּדֵי הֶחָצֵר סָבִיב וְגוֹ׳.** לְפִי שֶׁלֹּא פֵּרֵשׁ וָוִין וַחֲשׁוּקִים וְאַדְנֵי נְחֹשֶׁת אֶלָּא לַצָּפוֹן וְלַדָּרוֹם, אֲבָל לַמִּזְרָח וְלַמַּעֲרָב לֹא נֶאֱמַר וָוִין וַחֲשׁוּקִים וְאַדְנֵי נְחֹשֶׁת, לְכָךְ בָּא וְלִמֵּד כָּאן:

ו הָרֶשֶׁת עַד חֲצִי הַמִּזְבֵּחַ: וְעָשִׂיתָ בַדִּים לַמִּזְבֵּחַ בַּדֵּי עֲצֵי שִׁטִּים וְצִפִּיתָ
ז אֹתָם נְחֹשֶׁת: וְהוּבָא אֶת־בַּדָּיו בַּטַּבָּעֹת וְהָיוּ הַבַּדִּים עַל־שְׁתֵּי צַלְעֹת
ח הַמִּזְבֵּחַ בִּשְׂאֵת אֹתוֹ: נְבוּב לֻחֹת תַּעֲשֶׂה אֹתוֹ כַּאֲשֶׁר הֶרְאָה אֹתְךָ
ט בָּהָר כֵּן יַעֲשׂוּ: וְעָשִׂיתָ אֵת חֲצַר הַמִּשְׁכָּן לִפְאַת נֶגֶב־ שביעי
תֵּימָנָה קְלָעִים לֶחָצֵר שֵׁשׁ מָשְׁזָר מֵאָה בָאַמָּה אֹרֶךְ לַפֵּאָה הָאֶחָת:
י וְעַמֻּדָיו עֶשְׂרִים וְאַדְנֵיהֶם עֶשְׂרִים נְחֹשֶׁת וָוֵי הָעַמֻּדִים וַחֲשֻׁקֵיהֶם כָּסֶף:
יא וְכֵן לִפְאַת צָפוֹן בָּאֹרֶךְ קְלָעִים מֵאָה אֹרֶךְ וְעַמֻּדָו עֶשְׂרִים וְאַדְנֵיהֶם
יב עֶשְׂרִים נְחֹשֶׁת וָוֵי הָעַמֻּדִים וַחֲשֻׁקֵיהֶם כָּסֶף: וְרֹחַב הֶחָצֵר לִפְאַת־
יג יָם קְלָעִים חֲמִשִּׁים אַמָּה עַמֻּדֵיהֶם עֲשָׂרָה וְאַדְנֵיהֶם עֲשָׂרָה: וְרֹחַב
יד הֶחָצֵר לִפְאַת קֵדְמָה מִזְרָחָה חֲמִשִּׁים אַמָּה: וַחֲמֵשׁ עֶשְׂרֵה אַמָּה
טו קְלָעִים לַכָּתֵף עַמֻּדֵיהֶם שְׁלֹשָׁה וְאַדְנֵיהֶם שְׁלֹשָׁה: וְלַכָּתֵף הַשֵּׁנִית
טז חֲמֵשׁ עֶשְׂרֵה קְלָעִים עַמֻּדֵיהֶם שְׁלֹשָׁה וְאַדְנֵיהֶם שְׁלֹשָׁה: וּלְשַׁעַר
הֶחָצֵר מָסָךְ ׀ עֶשְׂרִים אַמָּה תְּכֵלֶת וְאַרְגָּמָן וְתוֹלַעַת שָׁנִי וְשֵׁשׁ מָשְׁזָר
יז מַעֲשֵׂה רֹקֵם עַמֻּדֵיהֶם אַרְבָּעָה וְאַדְנֵיהֶם אַרְבָּעָה: כָּל־עַמּוּדֵי הֶחָצֵר מפטיר

אונקלוס

מְצַדְתָא, עַד פַּלְגוּת מַדְבְּחָא: ו וְתַעֲבֵיד אֲרִיחַיָא לְמַדְבְּחָא, אֲרִיחֵי דְאָעֵי שִׁטִּין, וְתַחְפֵּי יָתְהוֹן נְחָשָׁא: ז וְיֵעִיל יָת אֲרִיחוֹהִי בְּעִזְקָתָא, וִיהוֹן אֲרִיחַיָא, עַל תְּרֵין, סִטְרֵי מַדְבְּחָא בְּמִטַּל יָתֵיהּ: ח חֲלִיל לוּחִין תַּעֲבֵיד יָתֵיהּ, כְּמָא דְאַחְזִי יָתָךְ, בְּטוּרָא כֵּן יַעְבְּדוּן: ט וְתַעֲבֵיד, יָת דָּרַת מַשְׁכְּנָא, לְרוּחַ עֵיבַר דָּרוֹמָא, סְרָדֵי לְדָרְתָא דְּבוּץ שְׁזִיר, מְאָה אַמִּין אָרְכָּא, לְרוּחָא חֲדָא: י וְעַמּוּדוֹהִי עֶסְרִין, וְסָמְכֵיהוֹן עֶסְרִין דִּנְחָשָׁא, וָוֵי עַמּוּדַיָא, וְכִבּוּשֵׁיהוֹן כְּסַף: יא וְכֵן לְרוּחַ צִפּוּנָא בְּאָרְכָּא, סְרָדֵי מְאָה אָרְכָּא, וְעַמּוּדוֹהִי עֶסְרִין, וְסָמְכֵיהוֹן עֶסְרִין דִּנְחָשָׁא, וָוֵי עַמּוּדַיָא, וְכִבּוּשֵׁיהוֹן כְּסַף: יב וּפְתָיָא דְדָרְתָא לְרוּחַ מַעַרְבָא, סְרָדֵי חַמְשִׁין אַמִּין, עַמּוּדֵיהוֹן עַסְרָא, וְסָמְכֵיהוֹן עַסְרָא: יג וּפְתָיָא דְדָרְתָא, לְרוּחַ, קִדּוּמָא מַדִּנְחָא חַמְשִׁין אַמִּין: יד וַחֲמֵשׁ עֶסְרֵי אַמִּין, סְרָדֵי לְעִבְרָא, עַמּוּדֵיהוֹן תְּלָתָא, וְסָמְכֵיהוֹן תְּלָתָא: טו וּלְעִבְרָא תִּנְיָנָא, חֲמֵשׁ עֶסְרֵי סְרָדִין, עַמּוּדֵיהוֹן תְּלָתָא, וְסָמְכֵיהוֹן תְּלָתָא: טז וְלִתְרַע דָּרְתָא, פְּרָסָא עֶסְרִין אַמִּין, תִּכְלָא וְאַרְגְּוָנָא, וּצְבַע זְהוֹרִי, וּבוּץ שְׁזִיר עוֹבַד צַיָּר, עַמּוּדֵיהוֹן אַרְבְּעָא, וְסָמְכֵיהוֹן אַרְבְּעָא: יז כָּל עַמּוּדֵי דָרְתָא

18 Their hooks shall be of silver, and their sockets of bronze. The courtyard shall
be a hundred cubits long, fifty cubits wide, and five cubits high, with hangings
19 of finely spun linen and sockets of bronze. All the Tabernacle utensils, for every
use, as well as all its tent pegs and the tent pegs of the courtyard, shall be of
bronze.

The haftara for Parashat Teruma is on page 1546.
On Rosh Ḥodesh Adar I read the haftara on page 1634.
However, on the Shabbat of Parashat Shekalim, even if it also Rosh Ḥodesh or Erev Rosh Ḥodesh Adar, read the haftara on page 1642.

רש״י

יח **אֹרֶךְ הֶחָצֵר.** הַצָּפוֹן וְהַדָּרוֹם שֶׁמִּן הַמִּזְרָח לַמַּעֲרָב ״מֵאָה בָּאַמָּה״: **וְרֹחַב חֲמִשִּׁים בַּחֲמִשִּׁים.** חָצֵר שֶׁבַּמִּזְרָח הָיְתָה מְרֻבַּעַת חֲמִשִּׁים עַל חֲמִשִּׁים, שֶׁהַמִּשְׁכָּן אָרְכּוֹ שְׁלֹשִׁים וְרָחְבּוֹ עֶשֶׂר, הֶעֱמִיד מִזְרַח פִּתְחוֹ בִּשְׂפַת חֲמִשִּׁים הַחִיצוֹנִים שֶׁל אֹרֶךְ הֶחָצֵר, נִמְצָא כֻּלּוֹ בַּחֲמִשִּׁים הַפְּנִימִיִּים, וְכָלָה אָרְכּוֹ לְסוֹף שְׁלֹשִׁים, נִמְצְאוּ עֶשְׂרִים אַמָּה רֶוַח לַאֲחוֹרָיו בֵּין הַקְּלָעִים שֶׁבַּמַּעֲרָב לַיְרִיעוֹת שֶׁל אֲחוֹרֵי הַמִּשְׁכָּן. וְרֹחַב הַמִּשְׁכָּן עֶשֶׂר אַמּוֹת בְּאֶמְצַע רֹחַב הֶחָצֵר, נִמְצְאוּ לוֹ עֶשְׂרִים אַמָּה רֶוַח לַצָּפוֹן וְלַדָּרוֹם מִן קַלְעֵי הֶחָצֵר לִירִיעוֹת הַמִּשְׁכָּן, וְכֵן לַמַּעֲרָב, וַחֲמִשִּׁים עַל חֲמִשִּׁים חָצֵר לְפָנָיו: **וְקֹמָה חָמֵשׁ אַמּוֹת.** גֹּבַהּ מְחִיצוֹת הֶחָצֵר, וְהוּא רֹחַב הַקְּלָעִים: **וְאַדְנֵיהֶם נְחֹשֶׁת.** לְהָבִיא אַדְנֵי הַמָּסָךְ, שֶׁלֹּא תֹּאמַר, לֹא נֶאֶמְרוּ אַדְנֵי נְחֹשֶׁת אֶלָּא לְעַמּוּדֵי הַקְּלָעִים, אֲבָל אַדְנֵי הַמָּסָךְ שֶׁל מִין אַחֵר. כָּךְ נִרְאֶה בְּעֵינַי שֶׁלְּכָךְ חָזַר וּשְׁנָאָן:

יט **לְכֹל כְּלֵי הַמִּשְׁכָּן.** שֶׁהָיוּ צְרִיכִין לַהֲקָמָתוֹ וּלְהוֹרָדָתוֹ, כְּגוֹן מַקָּבוֹת לִתְקֹעַ יְתֵדוֹת וְעַמּוּדִים: **יְתֵדֹת.** כְּמִין נִגְרֵי נְחֹשֶׁת עֲשׂוּיִין לִירִיעוֹת הָאֹהֶל וּלְקַלְעֵי הֶחָצֵר קְשׁוּרִים בְּמֵיתָרִים סָבִיב בִּשְׁפּוּלֵיהֶן כְּדֵי שֶׁלֹּא תְּהֵא הָרוּחַ מַגְבִּיהָתָן. וְאֵינִי יוֹדֵעַ אִם תְּחוּבִין בָּאָרֶץ, אוֹ קְשׁוּרִין וּתְלוּיִין וְכָבְדָּן מַכְבִּיד שִׁפּוּלֵי הַיְרִיעוֹת שֶׁלֹּא יָנוּעוּ בָּרוּחַ. וְאוֹמֵר אֲנִי שֶׁשְּׁמָן מוֹכִיחַ עֲלֵיהֶם שֶׁהֵם תְּקוּעִים בָּאָרֶץ, לְכָךְ נִקְרְאוּ יְתֵדוֹת, וּמִקְרָא זֶה מְסַיְּעֵנִי: ״אֹהֶל בַּל יִצְעָן בַּל יִסַּע יְתֵדֹתָיו לָנֶצַח״ (ישעיה לג, כ):

יח סָבִיב֙ מְחֻשָּׁקִ֣ים כֶּ֔סֶף וָוֵיהֶ֖ם כָּ֑סֶף וְאַדְנֵיהֶ֖ם נְחֹֽשֶׁת׃ אֹ֤רֶךְ הֶֽחָצֵר֙ מֵאָ֣ה
בָֽאַמָּ֔ה וְרֹ֣חַב ׀ חֲמִשִּׁ֣ים בַּחֲמִשִּׁ֗ים וְקֹמָ֛ה חָמֵ֥שׁ אַמּ֖וֹת שֵׁ֣שׁ מָשְׁזָ֑ר
יט וְאַדְנֵיהֶ֖ם נְחֹֽשֶׁת׃ לְכֹל֙ כְּלֵ֣י הַמִּשְׁכָּ֔ן בְּכֹ֖ל עֲבֹדָת֑וֹ וְכָל־יְתֵדֹתָ֛יו וְכָל־
יִתְדֹ֥ת הֶחָצֵ֖ר נְחֹֽשֶׁת׃

The הפטרה *for* פרשת תרומה *is on page 1547.*
On ראש חודש אדר א' *read the* הפטרה *on page 1635.*
However, on the שבת *of* פרשת שקלים*, even if it also* ראש חודש
or ערב ראש חודש אדר א'*, read the* הפטרה *on page 1643.*

אונקלוס

סְחוֹר סְחוֹר מְכַבְּשִׁין כְּסַף, וָוֵיהוֹן כְּסַף, וְסָמְכֵיהוֹן דִּנְחָשָׁא: יח אֻרְכָּא דְּדָרְתָא מְאָה אַמִּין, וּפֻתְיָא חַמְשִׁין בְּחַמְשִׁין, וְרוּמָא, חֲמֵשׁ אַמִּין דְּבוּץ שְׁזִיר, וְסָמְכֵיהוֹן דִּנְחָשָׁא: יט לְכָל מָנֵי מַשְׁכְּנָא, בְּכָל פָּלְחָנֵיהּ, וְכָל סִכּוֹהִי, וְכָל סִכֵּי דָּרְתָא דִּנְחָשָׁא:

PARASHAT TETZAVEH

27 20 Command the Israelites to bring you pure oil from crushed olives for light,
21 to kindle the lamp, every night. From evening to morning, before the LORD,
Aharon and his sons shall set it up to burn in the Tent of Meeting, outside
the curtain that veils the Ark of the Testimony. This shall be a rule for all time
28 1 for the Israelites, throughout their generations. From among the
Israelites, draw your brother Aharon and his sons close to you to serve Me

רש״י

כ וְאַתָּה תְּצַוֶּה. זָךְ. בְּלִי שְׁמָרִים, כְּמוֹ שֶׁשָּׁנִינוּ בִּמְנָחוֹת (דף פו ע״א), מְגַרְגְּרוֹ בְּרֹאשׁ הַזַּיִת וְכוּ׳: כָּתִית. הַזֵּיתִים, כּוֹתֵשׁ בְּמַכְתֶּשֶׁת וְאֵינוֹ טוֹחֲנָן בָּרֵחַיִם, כְּדֵי שֶׁלֹּא יְהוּ בּוֹ שְׁמָרִים, וְאַחַר שֶׁהוֹצִיא טִפָּה רִאשׁוֹנָה מַכְנִיסָן לָרֵחַיִם וְטוֹחֲנָן. וְהַשֶּׁמֶן הַשֵּׁנִי פָּסוּל לַמְּנוֹרָה וְכָשֵׁר לַמְּנָחוֹת, שֶׁנֶּאֱמַר: ״כָּתִית לַמָּאוֹר״, וְלֹא כָּתִית לַמְּנָחוֹת (שם): לְהַעֲלֹת נֵר תָּמִיד. מַדְלִיק עַד שֶׁתְּהֵא שַׁלְהֶבֶת עוֹלָה מֵאֵלֶיהָ: תָּמִיד. כָּל לַיְלָה וְלַיְלָה קָרוּי ׳תָּמִיד׳, כְּמוֹ שֶׁאַתָּה אוֹמֵר: ״עֹלַת תָּמִיד״ (להלן כט, מב; במדבר כח, ו) וְאֵינָהּ אֶלָּא מִיּוֹם לְיוֹם, וְכֵן בְּמִנְחַת חֲבִתִּין: ״תָּמִיד״ (ויקרא ו, יג) וְאֵינָהּ אֶלָּא מַחֲצִיתָהּ בַּבֹּקֶר וּמַחֲצִיתָהּ בָּעֶרֶב. אֲבָל ״תָּמִיד״ הָאָמוּר בְּלֶחֶם הַפָּנִים (לעיל כה, ל) מִשַּׁבָּת לְשַׁבָּת הוּא:

כא מֵעֶרֶב עַד בֹּקֶר. תֵּן לָהּ מִדָּתָהּ שֶׁתְּהֵא דוֹלֶקֶת מֵעֶרֶב וְעַד בֹּקֶר. וְשִׁעֲרוּ חֲכָמִים חֲצִי לֹג לְלֵילֵי טֵבֵת הָאֲרֻכִּין, וְכֵן לְכָל הַלֵּילוֹת, וְאִם יִוָּתֵר אֵין בְּכָךְ כְּלוּם:

כח א וְאַתָּה הַקְרֵב אֵלֶיךָ. לְאַחַר שֶׁתִּגָּמֵר מְלֶאכֶת הַמִּשְׁכָּן:

Whatever the reason, in Parashat Tetzaveh, for once, it is Aharon, the first of the priests, who holds center stage, undiminished by the rival presence of his brother. For whereas Moshe lit the fire in the souls of the Jewish people, it was Aharon who tended the flame and turned it into a *ner tamid*, literally, "an eternal light."

28:1 לְכַהֲנוֹ־לִי *To serve Me as priests* – At its heart, Judaism is a priestly religion. We can see this through the very organization of the Mosaic books. They are organized as a chiastic or mirror-image structure, of the form ABCBA. Here is the simplest way of describing it:

- A. Genesis: prehistory of Israel
  - B. Exodus: the journey to Sinai
    - C. Leviticus: priesthood, sacrifice, and holiness
  - B1. Numbers: the journey from Sinai
- A1. Deuteronomy: the future of Israel

In a chiasmus, the key term is the middle one. The middle book of the Pentateuch, Leviticus, is about priests and the service of the Sanctuary. So too is the last third of Exodus

love. We can become like the olive which, when crushed, produces the pure oil that fuels the light of holiness.

27:21 אַהֲרֹן וּבָנָיו *Aharon and his sons* – Moshe the prophet dominates four of the five books of the Torah. Tetzaveh, as commentators have noted, is the only *parasha* from the birth of Moshe at the beginning of the book of Exodus to the end of Deuteronomy that does not contain his name. For most of the narrative he is front and center. Here, he is in the background. Several interpretations have been offered.

The Vilna Gaon suggests that it is related to the fact that in most years Parashat Tetzaveh is read during the week in which the seventh of Adar falls: the day of Moshe's death. During this week we sense the loss of the greatest leader in Jewish history – and his absence from Tetzaveh expresses that loss.

The Baal HaTurim (on Ex. 27:20) relates it to Moshe's plea, in next week's *parasha*, for God to forgive Israel. "If not," says Moshe, "please blot me out of the book You have written" (32:32). There is a principle that "the curse of a sage comes true, even if it was conditional" (Makkot 11a). Thus for one week his name was "blotted out" from the Torah.

פרשת תצוה

כז כ וְאַתָּה תְּצַוֶּה ׀ אֶת־בְּנֵי יִשְׂרָאֵל וְיִקְחוּ אֵלֶיךָ שֶׁמֶן זַיִת זָךְ כָּתִית לַמָּאוֹר כא
כא לְהַעֲלֹת נֵר תָּמִיד: בְּאֹהֶל מוֹעֵד מִחוּץ לַפָּרֹכֶת אֲשֶׁר עַל־הָעֵדֻת
יַעֲרֹךְ אֹתוֹ אַהֲרֹן וּבָנָיו מֵעֶרֶב עַד־בֹּקֶר לִפְנֵי יְהוָה חֻקַּת עוֹלָם לְדֹרֹתָם
כח א מֵאֵת בְּנֵי יִשְׂרָאֵל: וְאַתָּה הַקְרֵב אֵלֶיךָ אֶת־אַהֲרֹן אָחִיךָ
וְאֶת־בָּנָיו אִתּוֹ מִתּוֹךְ בְּנֵי יִשְׂרָאֵל לְכַהֲנוֹ־לִי אַהֲרֹן נָדָב וַאֲבִיהוּא

אונקלוס

כ וְאַתְּ, תְּפַקֵּיד יָת בְּנֵי יִשְׂרָאֵל, וְיִסְּבוּן לָךְ, מְשַׁח זֵיתָא דָּכְיָא, כְּתִישָׁא לְאַנְהָרָא, לְאַדְלָקָא בּוֹצִינַיָּא תְּדִירָא: כא בְּמַשְׁכַּן זִמְנָא מִבָּרָא לְפָרֻכְתָּא דְּעַל סָהֲדוּתָא, יְסַדַּר יָתֵיהּ אַהֲרֹן וּבְנוֹהִי, מֵרַמְשָׁא עַד צַפְרָא קֳדָם יְיָ, קְיָם עָלַם לְדָרֵיהוֹן, מִן בְּנֵי יִשְׂרָאֵל: כח א וְאַתְּ, קָרֵיב לְוָתָךְ יָת אַהֲרֹן אֲחוּךְ וְיָת בְּנוֹהִי עִמֵּיהּ, מִגּוֹ, בְּנֵי יִשְׂרָאֵל לְשַׁמָּשָׁא קֳדָמַי, אַהֲרֹן, נָדָב וַאֲבִיהוּא,

TETZAVEH

In Parashat Tetzaveh, the role of the priests in the service of the Tabernacle takes center stage. For once the limelight is no longer on Moshe, but on his brother Aharon, the High Priest. We read about the task of the priesthood, their robes of office and their consecration, as well as further details about the Tabernacle itself.

For the first time we find the Torah speaking about *sacred vestments*, those of the priests and the High Priest worn while officiating in the sacred place. For the first time too we encounter this phrase, used about the vestments: *lekhavod uletiferet*, "for glory and for splendor" (Ex. 28:2). Until this point, *kavod* in the sense of glory or honor was attributed only to God. As for *tiferet*, this is the first time it appears in the Torah.

With Parashat Tetzaveh, something new enters Judaism: *Torat Kohanim*, the world and mindset of the priest. Rapidly it became a central dimension of Judaism. It dominates the next book of the Torah, Leviticus.

27:20 לְהַעֲלֹת נֵר תָּמִיד *To kindle the lamp, every night* – Our *parasha* begins with the words "Command the Israelites to bring you pure oil from crushed olives for light, to kindle the lamp, every night" (Ex. 27:20). The Sages drew a comparison between the olive and the Jewish people:

> R. Yehoshua b. Levi asked: Why is Israel compared to an olive? Just as an olive is first bitter, then sweet, so Israel suffers in the present but great good is stored up for them in the time to come. And just as the olive only yields its oil by being crushed – as it is written, "pure oil from crushed olives for light" – so Israel fulfills [its full potential in] the Torah only when it is pressed by suffering. (*Midrash Pitron Torah* on Num. 13:2)

The oil was, of course, for the candelabrum, whose perpetual light symbolizes the divine light that floods the universe for those who see it through the eyes of faith. To produce this light, the olives must be crushed.

The Talmud gives an account of various Sages who fell ill. When asked, "Are your sufferings precious to you?" they replied, "Neither they nor their reward" (Berakhot 5b). There is no glorification of hardships here. When they befall us or someone close to us, they can lead us to despair. Alternatively, we can respond stoically. We can practice the attribute of *gevura*, strength in adversity. But there is a third possibility. We can respond with compassion, kindness, and

▶

2 as priests – Aharon and his sons Nadav and Avihu, Elazar and Itamar. Make
3 sacred vestments for your brother Aharon, for glory and for splendor. Speak
to all the skilled craftsmen whom I have endowed with a spirit of wisdom, and
have them make Aharon's vestments; these will consecrate him to serve Me as
4 priest. These are the garments they shall make: a breast piece, an ephod, a robe,
a quilted tunic, a miter, and a sash; sacred vestments shall they make, for your

רש"י

ג **לקדשו לכהנו לי.** לקדשו להכניסו בכהנה על ידי הבגדים, שיהא כהן לי. ולשון 'כהנה' שרות הוא, סירוינטריא"ה בלעז:

ד **חשן.** תכשיט כנגד הלב: **ואפוד.** לא שמעתי ולא מצאתי בברייתא פרוש תבניתו. ולבי אומר לי שהוא חגורה לו מאחוריו, רחבו כרחב גב איש כמין סינר שקורין רינ"ט שחוגרות השרות כשרוכבות על הסוסים, כך מעשהו מלמטה, שנאמר: "ודוד חגור אפוד בד" (שמואל ב' ו, יד), למדנו שהאפוד חגורה היא. ואי אפשר לומר אין בו אלא החגורה לבדה, שהרי נאמר: "ויתן עליו את האפד" (ויקרא ח, ז) ואחר כך: "ויחגר אותו בחשב האפד" ותרגם אונקלוס: "בהמין אפודא", למדנו שהחשב הוא החגור, והאפוד שם תכשיט לבדו. ואי אפשר לומר שעל שם שתי הכתפות שבו הוא קרוי אפוד, שהרי נאמר: "שתי כתפות האפוד" (להלן פסוק כז), למדנו שהאפוד שם לבד, והכתפות שם לבד, והחשב שם לבד. לכך אני אומר שעל שם הסינר של מטה קרוי אפוד, על שם שאופדו ומקשטו בו, כמו שנאמר: "ויאפד לו בו" (ויקרא ח, ז). והחשב הוא חגור שלמעלה הימנו, והכתפות קבועות בו. ועוד אומר לי לבי שיש ראיה שהוא מין לבוש, שתרגם יונתן: "ודוד חגור אפוד בד" (שמואל ב' ו, יד) – "כרדוט דבוץ", ותרגם כמו כן "מעילים" – "כרדוטין" במעשה תמר אחות אבשלום, "כי כן תלבשן בנות המלך הבתולת מעילים" (שם יג, יח): **ומעיל.** הוא כמין חלוק, וכן הכתנת, אלא שהכתנת סמוך לבשרו, ומעיל קרוי חלוק העליון: **תשבץ.** עשויין משבצות לנוי. והמשבצות הם כמין גומות העשויות בתכשיטי זהב למושב קביעת אבנים טובות ומרגליות, כמו שנאמר באבני האפוד: "מסבת משבצות זהב" (להלן פסוק יא), ובלעז קורין אותן קשטונ"ש: **מצנפת.** כמין כפת כובע שקורין קופי"א, שהרי במקום אחר קורא להם "מגבעת" (להלן כט, ט) ומתרגמינן: "כובעין": **ואבנט.** היא חגורה על הכתנת, והאפוד חגורה על המעיל, כמו שמצינו בסדר לבישתן: "ויתן עליו את הכתנת ויחגר אתו באבנט, וילבש אתו את המעיל ויתן עליו את האפד" (ויקרא ח, ז): **בגדי קדש.** מתרומה המקדשת לשמי יעשו אותם:

office. Their work is holy. Their domain is the Tabernacle, the physical embodiment of sacred space. They are charged with mediating between the people and God. Their clothes mark their office and role.

In a famous phrase, the book of Psalms proclaims, "Your priests are robed in righteousness" (Ps. 132:9). It is clear then that the phrase in Tetzaveh, "for glory and for splendor," does not mean "for the glory and splendor of the priest." It means "for the glory of God and the splendor of His presence" (Sforno on Ex. 28:2). The task of the priest – and the message of his clothes – was to be a "signal of transcendence," to point *in* himself to something *beyond* himself, to be a living symbol of the Divine Presence in the midst of the nation.

28:3 **וְאַתָּה תְּדַבֵּר** *Speak* – Three times the word *ve'ata*, "And you," appears in the Hebrew: "[*And you*] command the Israelites" (about the oil for the candelabrum that Aharon and his sons would keep alight) (Ex. 27:20); "[*And you*] draw your brother Aharon and his sons close to you. . ." (28:1); "[*And you*] speak to all the skilled craftsmen" (and command them to make the vestments Aharon and the other priests would wear) (28:3). The Torah emphasizes God's insistence that it be Moshe who bestows this honor on Aharon.

Moshe must show the people – and Aharon himself – that he has the humility, the power of self-effacement, needed to make space for someone else to share in the leadership of the people, someone whose strengths are not his, whose role is different, someone who may be more popular, closer to the people, than Moshe – as in fact Aharon turns out to be.

It takes a special kind of character to make space for those whom one is entitled to see as rivals. Early on, when they met after the revelation at the burning bush, Aharon showed that character in relation to Moshe, and now Moshe is called on to show it in relation to Aharon. True leadership involves humility and magnanimity. The smaller the ego, the greater the leader.

אֶלְעָזָר וְאִיתָמָר בְּנֵי אַהֲרֹן׃ וְעָשִׂיתָ בִגְדֵי־קֹדֶשׁ לְאַהֲרֹן אָחִיךָ לְכָבוֹד ב
וּלְתִפְאָרֶת׃ וְאַתָּה תְּדַבֵּר אֶל־כָּל־חַכְמֵי־לֵב אֲשֶׁר מִלֵּאתִיו רוּחַ חָכְמָה ג
וְעָשׂוּ אֶת־בִּגְדֵי אַהֲרֹן לְקַדְּשׁוֹ לְכַהֲנוֹ־לִי׃ וְאֵלֶּה הַבְּגָדִים אֲשֶׁר יַעֲשׂוּ ד
חֹשֶׁן וְאֵפוֹד וּמְעִיל וּכְתֹנֶת תַּשְׁבֵּץ מִצְנֶפֶת וְאַבְנֵט וְעָשׂוּ בִגְדֵי־קֹדֶשׁ

אונקלוס

אֶלְעָזָר וְאִיתָמָר בְּנֵי אַהֲרֹן׃ ב וְתַעְבֵּיד לְבוּשֵׁי קֻדְשָׁא לְאַהֲרֹן אֲחוּךְ, לִיקָר וּלְתֻשְׁבְּחָא׃ ג וְאַתְּ, תְּמַלֵּיל עִם כָּל חַכִּימֵי לִבָּא, דְּאַשְׁלֵימִית עִמְּהוֹן רוּחַ חָכְמָא, וְיַעְבְּדוּן, יָת לְבוּשֵׁי אַהֲרֹן, לְקַדָּשׁוּתֵיהּ לְשַׁמָּשָׁא קֳדָמָי׃ ד וְאִלֵּין לְבוּשַׁיָּא דְּיַעְבְּדוּן, חֻשְׁנָא וְאֵיפוֹדָא וּמְעִילָא, וְכִתּוּנִין מְרַמְּצָן מִצְנְפָן וְהִמְיָנִין, וְיַעְבְּדוּן לְבוּשֵׁי קֻדְשָׁא,

(25–40) and the first third of Numbers (1–10). We tend to forget this, because the narrative drama lies elsewhere, and besides, we have not had a Temple and sacrifices for almost two thousand years.

Judaism is a religion of ritual, of repeated daily deeds. It is a religion of holiness whose focus is both on the home and on the house of worship, the successor institution to the Tabernacle. It is a religion of education, and the priests were the first educators (Deut. 30:10; Mal. 2:4–7). All the great achievements of Israel's kings and the incandescent moral passion of Israel's prophets would not have been possible without the continuity and devotion of the priests. This constancy and dedication of the priesthood is beautifully summed up by the opening verses of Tetzaveh. *Kindle the lamp every night... throughout their generations* (Ex. 27:20–21).

PRIESTLY VESTMENTS

With the words "for glory and for splendor," something new enters Jewish life. Never before have we encountered clothes marking off their wearers as holy people charged with a particular function in religious life.

This whole section of the biblical narrative strikes us as strange, given all we know of what has come before. Avraham, Yitzḥak, and Yaakov did not wear special clothes. Nor did Moshe. They were shepherds. They dressed simply. In any event, what they wore is utterly irrelevant to the biblical message. As Erich Auerbach noted in his classic study, "Odysseus' Scar," the great difference between Homer and the Torah is that Homer constantly describes appearances; the Torah rarely does. Throughout Genesis, whenever a garment is a key element in the story, it involves some deception or betrayal.

Why then did God command Moshe to set in motion the making of special garments for the priests, "for glory and for splendor"? The answer, I suggest, lies in the analysis given by the nineteenth-century sociologist Max Weber. Weber was fascinated by the question of leadership. What is it that gives some individuals authority over others? His most famous insight – it has become part of the language of everyday speech – is that certain rare figures have what he called charisma. Charismatic leaders, by the force of their personality, are able to exercise influence over others.

Yet charisma begins to die almost as soon as it is born. Charismatic authority is personal. It is unique to the individual who wields it, and it cannot be replicated over time. But a group, in order to survive, needs a form of leadership that is resistant to change. That is why, after the appearance in its midst of a charismatic leader, the group must undergo what Weber called the routinization of charisma. This is the process whereby a certain form of authority is vested, not in an individual-as-individual but in an individual (or group) as bearers-of-an-office. Thus charisma is handed down from generation to generation in an orderly and predictable way.

Parashat Tetzaveh describes exactly this in the process through which Moshe invests priestly authority in Aharon and his sons. The *bigdei kehuna*, the "priestly vestments," are its visible symbol. The priests are – by virtue of birth and descent, not personal qualities – the carriers of sacred

5 brother Aharon and his sons to serve Me in. They should use gold, and sky-
blue, purple, and scarlet wool, and fine linen.
6 They are to make the ephod of finely spun linen embroidered with gold, and
7 sky-blue, purple, and scarlet wool. It should have two shoulder pieces attached
8 to its two edges so that it can be joined together. The decorated waistband on
it shall be like it and of one piece with it, made of gold, of sky-blue, purple, and
9 scarlet wool, and finely spun linen. Take two rock crystal stones and engrave on
10 them the names of Yisrael's sons: six names on one stone and the remaining six

רש״י

ה **וְהֵם יִקְחוּ.** אוֹתָם חַכְמֵי לֵב שֶׁיַּעֲשׂוּ הַבְּגָדִים יְקַבְּלוּ מִן הַמִּתְנַדְּבִים "אֶת הַזָּהָב וְאֶת הַתְּכֵלֶת" לַעֲשׂוֹת מֵהֶן אֶת הַבְּגָדִים:

ו **וְעָשׂוּ אֶת הָאֵפֹד.** אִם בָּאתִי לְפָרֵשׁ מַעֲשֵׂה הָאֵפוֹד וְהַחֹשֶׁן עַל סֵדֶר הַמִּקְרָאוֹת, הֲרֵי פֵּרוּשָׁן פְּרָקִים, וְיִשְׁגֶּה הַקּוֹרֵא בְּצֵרוּפָן. לְכָךְ אֲנִי כּוֹתֵב מַעֲשֵׂיהֶם כְּמוֹת שֶׁהוּא לְמַעַן יָרוּץ קוֹרֵא בוֹ, וְאַחַר כָּךְ אֲפָרֵשׁ עַל סֵדֶר הַמִּקְרָאוֹת. הָאֵפוֹד עָשׂוּי כְּמִין סִינָר שֶׁל נָשִׁים רוֹכְבוֹת סוּסִים, וְחוֹגֵר אוֹתוֹ מֵאֲחוֹרָיו כְּנֶגֶד לִבּוֹ לְמַטָּה מֵאַצִּילָיו, רָחְבּוֹ כְּמִדַּת רֹחַב גַּבּוֹ שֶׁל אָדָם וְיוֹתֵר, וּמַגִּיעַ עַד עֲקֵבָיו. וְהַחֵשֶׁב מְחֻבָּר בְּרֹאשׁוֹ עַל פְּנֵי רָחְבּוֹ מַעֲשֵׂה אוֹרֵג, וּמַאֲרִיךְ לְכָאן וּלְכָאן כְּדֵי לְהַקִּיף וְלַחֲגֹר בּוֹ. וְהַכְּתֵפוֹת מְחֻבָּרוֹת בַּחֵשֶׁב, אֶחָד לְיָמִין וְאֶחָד לִשְׂמֹאל, מֵאֲחוֹרֵי הַכֹּהֵן לִשְׁנֵי קְצוֹת רָחְבּוֹ שֶׁל סִינָר, וּכְשֶׁזּוֹקְפָן עוֹמְדוֹת לוֹ עַל שְׁנֵי כְּתֵפָיו. וְהֵן כְּמִין שְׁתֵּי רְצוּעוֹת עֲשׂוּיוֹת מִמִּין הָאֵפוֹד, אֲרֻכּוֹת כְּדֵי שִׁעוּר לְזָקְפָן אֵצֶל צַוָּארוֹ מִכָּאן וּמִכָּאן, וְנִקְפָּלוֹת לְפָנָיו לְמַטָּה מִכְּתֵפָיו מְעַט. וְאַבְנֵי הַשֹּׁהַם קְבוּעוֹת בָּהֶם, אַחַת עַל כֶּתֶף יָמִין וְאַחַת עַל כֶּתֶף שְׂמֹאל, וְהַמִּשְׁבְּצוֹת נְתוּנוֹת בְּרָאשֵׁיהֶם לִפְנֵי כְּתֵפָיו, וּשְׁתֵּי עֲבוֹתֹת הַזָּהָב תְּחוּבוֹת בִּשְׁתֵּי טַבָּעוֹת שֶׁבַּחֹשֶׁן בִּשְׁנֵי קְצוֹת רָחְבּוֹ הָעֶלְיוֹן, אַחַת לְיָמִין וְאַחַת לִשְׂמֹאל, וּשְׁנֵי רָאשֵׁי הַשַּׁרְשֶׁרֶת תְּקוּעִין בַּמִּשְׁבְּצוֹת לְיָמִין, וְכֵן שְׁנֵי רָאשֵׁי הַשַּׁרְשֶׁרֶת הַשְּׂמָאלִית תְּקוּעִין בַּמִּשְׁבֶּצֶת שֶׁבְּכֶתֶף שְׂמֹאל, נִמְצָא הַחֹשֶׁן תָּלוּי בְּמִשְׁבְּצוֹת הָאֵפוֹד עַל לִבּוֹ מִלְּפָנָיו. וְעוֹד שְׁתֵּי טַבָּעוֹת בִּשְׁנֵי קְצוֹת הַחֹשֶׁן בְּתַחְתִּיתוֹ, וּכְנֶגְדָּם שְׁתֵּי טַבָּעוֹת בִּשְׁתֵּי כִּתְפוֹת הָאֵפוֹד מִלְּמַטָּה בְּרֹאשׁוֹ הַתַּחְתּוֹן הַמְחֻבָּר בַּחֵשֶׁב, טַבְּעוֹת הַחֹשֶׁן אֶל מוּל טַבְּעוֹת הָאֵפוֹד שׁוֹכְבִים זֶה עַל זֶה, וּמְרַכְּסָן בִּפְתִיל תְּכֵלֶת תָּחוּב בְּטַבְּעוֹת הָאֵפוֹד וְהַחֹשֶׁן, שֶׁיְּהֵא תַּחְתִּית הַחֹשֶׁן דָּבוּק לְחֵשֶׁב הָאֵפוֹד, וְלֹא יְהֵא נָד וְנִבְדָּל הוֹלֵךְ וְחוֹזֵר: **זָהָב תְּכֵלֶת וְאַרְגָּמָן תּוֹלַעַת שָׁנִי וְשֵׁשׁ מָשְׁזָר.** חֲמֵשֶׁת מִינִים הַלָּלוּ שְׁזוּרִין בְּכָל חוּט וָחוּט. הָיוּ מְרַדְּדִין אֶת הַזָּהָב כְּמִין טַסִּים דַּקִּים וְקוֹצְצִין פְּתִילִים מֵהֶם, וְטוֹוִין אוֹתָן חוּט שֶׁל זָהָב עִם שִׁשָּׁה חוּטִין שֶׁל תְּכֵלֶת, וְחוּט שֶׁל זָהָב עִם שִׁשָּׁה חוּטִין שֶׁל אַרְגָּמָן, וְכֵן בְּתוֹלַעַת שָׁנִי וְכֵן בַּשֵּׁשׁ, שֶׁכָּל הַמִּינִין חוּטָן כָּפוּל שִׁשָּׁה וְחוּט שֶׁל זָהָב עִם כָּל אֶחָד וְאֶחָד. וְאַחַר כָּךְ שׁוֹזֵר אֶת כֻּלָּם כְּאֶחָד, נִמְצָא חוּטָן כָּפוּל עֶשְׂרִים וּשְׁמוֹנָה. וְכֵן מְפֹרָשׁ בְּמַסֶּכֶת יוֹמָא (דף עב ע״א), וְלָמֵד מִן הַמִּקְרָא הַזֶּה: "וַיְרַקְּעוּ אֶת פַּחֵי הַזָּהָב וְקִצֵּץ פְּתִילִם לַעֲשׂוֹת" אֶת פְּתִילֵי הַזָּהָב "בְּתוֹךְ הַתְּכֵלֶת וּבְתוֹךְ הָאַרְגָּמָן" וְגוֹ' (להלן לט, ג). לָמַדְנוּ שֶׁחוּט שֶׁל זָהָב שָׁזוּר עִם כָּל מִין וּמִין: **מַעֲשֵׂה חֹשֵׁב.** כְּבָר פֵּרַשְׁתִּי (רש״י לעיל כו, א) שֶׁהִיא אֲרִיגַת שְׁתֵּי קִירוֹת, שֶׁאֵין צוּרַת שְׁנֵי עֲבָרֶיהָ דּוֹמוֹת זוֹ לָזוֹ:

ז **שְׁתֵּי כְתֵפֹת וְגוֹ'.** הַסִּינָר מִלְּמַטָּה, וְחֵשֶׁב הָאֵפוֹד הִיא הַחֲגוֹרָה, וּמְעוּדָה לוֹ מִלְמַעְלָה דֻּגְמַת סִינַר הַנָּשִׁים. וּמִגַּבּוֹ שֶׁל כֹּהֵן הָיוּ מְחֻבָּרוֹת בַּחֵשֶׁב שְׁתֵּי חֲתִיכוֹת כְּמִין שְׁתֵּי רְצוּעוֹת רְחָבוֹת, אַחַת כְּנֶגֶד כָּל כָּתֵף וְכָתֵף, וְזוֹקְפָן עַל שְׁתֵּי כִּתְפוֹתָיו עַד שֶׁנִּקְפָּלוֹת לְפָנָיו כְּנֶגֶד הֶחָזֶה, וְעַל יְדֵי חִבּוּרָן לְטַבְּעוֹת הַחֹשֶׁן נֶאֱחָזִין מִלְּפָנָיו כְּנֶגֶד לִבּוֹ שֶׁאֵין נוֹפְלוֹת, כְּמוֹ שֶׁמְּפֹרָשׁ בָּעִנְיָן, וְהָיוּ זְקוּפוֹת וְהוֹלְכוֹת כְּנֶגֶד כְּתֵפָיו, וּשְׁתֵּי אַבְנֵי שֹׁהַם קְבוּעוֹת בָּהֶן, אַחַת בְּכָל אַחַת: **אֶל שְׁנֵי קְצוֹתָיו.** אֶל רָחְבּוֹ שֶׁל אֵפוֹד, שֶׁלֹּא הָיָה רָחְבּוֹ אֶלָּא כְּנֶגֶד גַּבּוֹ שֶׁל כֹּהֵן, וְגָבְהוֹ עַד כְּנֶגֶד הָאַצִּילִים שֶׁקּוֹרִין קודי״ש, שֶׁנֶּאֱמַר: "לֹא יַחְגְּרוּ בַּיָּזַע" (יחזקאל מד, יח), אֵין חוֹגְרִין בִּמְקוֹם זֵיעָה, לֹא לְמַעְלָה מֵאַצִּילֵיהֶם וְלֹא לְמַטָּה מִמָּתְנֵיהֶם, אֶלָּא כְּנֶגֶד אַצִּילֵיהֶם: **וְחֻבָּר.** הָאֵפוֹד עִם אוֹתָן שְׁתֵּי כִּתְפוֹת הָאֵפוֹד, יְחַבֵּר אוֹתָם בְּמַחַט לְמַטָּה בַּחֵשֶׁב, וְלֹא יַאַרְגֵם עִמּוֹ, אֶלָּא אוֹרְגָם לְבַד וְאַחַר כָּךְ מְחַבְּרָם:

ח **וְחֵשֶׁב אֲפֻדָּתוֹ.** חֲגוֹר שֶׁעַל יָדוֹ הוּא מְאַפְּדוֹ וּמְתַקְּנוֹ לַכֹּהֵן וּמְקַשְּׁטוֹ: **אֲשֶׁר עָלָיו.** לְמַעְלָה בִּשְׂפַת הַסִּינָר, וְהִיא הַחֲגוֹרָה: **כְּמַעֲשֵׂהוּ.** כַּאֲרִיגַת הַסִּינָר מַעֲשֵׂה חוֹשֵׁב וּמֵחֲמֵשֶׁת מִינִים, כָּךְ אֲרִיגַת הַחֵשֶׁב מַעֲשֵׂה חוֹשֵׁב וּמֵחֲמֵשֶׁת מִינִים: **מִמֶּנּוּ יִהְיֶה.** עִמּוֹ יִהְיֶה אָרוּג, וְלֹא יַאַרְגֶנּוּ לְבַד וִיחַבְּרֶנּוּ:

Judaism does not believe in art for art's sake, but in art in the service of God. Art gives back as a votive offering to God a little of the beauty He has made in this created world.

ה לְאַהֲרֹן אָחִיךָ וּלְבָנָיו לְכַהֲנוֹ־לִי׃ וְהֵם יִקְחוּ אֶת־הַזָּהָב וְאֶת־הַתְּכֵלֶת
וְאֶת־הָאַרְגָּמָן וְאֶת־תּוֹלַעַת הַשָּׁנִי וְאֶת־הַשֵּׁשׁ׃
ו וְעָשׂוּ אֶת־הָאֵפֹד זָהָב תְּכֵלֶת וְאַרְגָּמָן תּוֹלַעַת שָׁנִי וְשֵׁשׁ מָשְׁזָר מַעֲשֵׂה
ז ח חֹשֵׁב׃ שְׁתֵּי כְתֵפֹת חֹבְרֹת יִהְיֶה־לּוֹ אֶל־שְׁנֵי קְצוֹתָיו וְחֻבָּר׃ וְחֵשֶׁב
אֲפֻדָּתוֹ אֲשֶׁר עָלָיו כְּמַעֲשֵׂהוּ מִמֶּנּוּ יִהְיֶה זָהָב תְּכֵלֶת וְאַרְגָּמָן וְתוֹלַעַת
ט שְׁנִי וְשֵׁשׁ מָשְׁזָר׃ וְלָקַחְתָּ אֶת־שְׁתֵּי אַבְנֵי־שֹׁהַם וּפִתַּחְתָּ עֲלֵיהֶם שְׁמוֹת
י בְּנֵי יִשְׂרָאֵל׃ שִׁשָּׁה מִשְּׁמֹתָם עַל הָאֶבֶן הָאֶחָת וְאֶת־שְׁמוֹת הַשִּׁשָּׁה

אונקלוס

לְאַהֲרֹן אֲחוּךְ, וְלִבְנוֹהִי לְשַׁמָּשָׁא קֳדָמָי: ה וְאִנּוּן יִסְּבוּן יָת דַּהֲבָא, וְיָת תַּכְלָא וְיָת אַרְגְּוָנָא, וְיָת צְבַע זְהוֹרִי וְיָת בּוּצָא: ו וְיַעְבְּדוּן יָת אֵיפוֹדָא, דַּהֲבָא, תַּכְלָא וְאַרְגְּוָנָא, צְבַע זְהוֹרִי, וּבוּץ שְׁזִיר עוֹבַד אֻמָּן: ז תַּרְתֵּין כִּתְפִין מְלָפְפָן, יְהוֹן לֵיהּ, עַל תְּרֵין סִטְרוֹהִי וְיִתְלָפַף: ח וְהִמְיַן תִּקּוּנֵיהּ דַּעֲלוֹהִי, כְּעוֹבָדֵיהּ מִנֵּיהּ יְהֵי, דַּהֲבָא, תַּכְלָא וְאַרְגְּוָנָא, וּצְבַע זְהוֹרִי וּבוּץ שְׁזִיר: ט וְתִסַּב, יָת תַּרְתֵּין אַבְנֵי בֻרְלָא, וְתִגְלוֹף עֲלֵיהוֹן, שְׁמָהָת בְּנֵי יִשְׂרָאֵל: י שִׁתָּא מִשְּׁמָהָתְהוֹן, עַל אַבְנָא חֲדָא, וְיָת שְׁמָהָת, שִׁתָּא

THE AESTHETIC IN JUDAISM

The aesthetic dimension does not always figure prominently in Judaism. The great empires – Mesopotamia, Egypt, Assyria, Babylon, Greece, and Rome – built monumental palaces and temples. Their royal courts were marked by magnificent robes, cloaks, crowns, and regalia. Judaism, by contrast, often seems almost puritanical in its avoidance of pomp and display. Worshipping the invisible God, Judaism tended to devalue the visual in favor of the oral and aural: words heard, rather than appearances seen.

Yet the service of the Tabernacle and Temple were different. Here appearances – dignity, beauty – made a difference. Why? Rambam gives this explanation:

> In order to exalt the Temple, those who ministered there received great honor, and the priests and Levites were therefore distinguished from the rest. It was commanded that the priest should be clothed properly with the most splendid and fine clothes, "sacred vestments for glory and for splendor"... for the multitude does not estimate man by his true form but by... the beauty of his garments, and the Temple was to be held in great reverence by all. (*Guide for the Perplexed* III:45)

Rambam suggests that to those who really understand the religious life, appearances should not matter, but "the multitude," the masses, are not like that. They are impressed by spectacle, the glitter of gold, the jewels of the breast piece, and the pristine purity of white linen robes.

Taking Rambam a step further, we may note that this chimes with an immense body of recent research into neuroscience, evolutionary psychology, and behavioral economics which has established beyond doubt that we are not, for the most part, rational animals. It is not that we are incapable of reason, but that reason alone does not move us to action. For that, we need emotion – and emotion goes deeper than the prefrontal cortex, the brain's center of conscious reflection. Art speaks to emotion. It moves us in ways that go deeper than words.

That is why great art has a spirituality that applies to the visual beauty and pageantry of the service of Tabernacle and Temple. We can define now the nature of the aesthetic in Judaism. It is art devoted to the greater glory of God. That is the implication of the fact that the word *kavod*, "glory," is attributed in the Torah only to God – and to the priest officiating in the House of God.

11 names on the other, in the order of their birth. Engrave the two stones with the
names of Yisrael's sons as a gem cutter engraves a seal, then mount them in gold
12 filigree settings. Place the two stones on the shoulder pieces of the ephod as
remembrance stones for the sons of Yisrael. Thus will Aharon carry their names
13 on his shoulders as a remembrance before the LORD. Make SHENI
14 gold filigree settings and two sets of pure gold chains braided into cords, and
15 attach the cords of chains to the settings. Make a breast piece for
judgment. Make it with the same skilled craftsmanship as the ephod: of gold,
16 of sky-blue, purple, and scarlet wool, and of finely spun linen. It shall be square
17 and folded double, a span long and a span wide. Mount four rows of precious
18 stones onto it: the first row a carnelian, an olivine, and a garnet; the second row
19 an emerald, a lapis lazuli, and a green quartz; the third row an amber, a jet, and
20 a sardonyx; and the fourth an aquamarine, a rock crystal, and an opal. Mount

רש״י

י **כְּתוֹלְדֹתָם.** כְּסֵדֶר שֶׁנּוֹלְדוּ: רְאוּבֵן, שִׁמְעוֹן, לֵוִי, יְהוּדָה, דָּן, נַפְתָּלִי עַל הָאַחַת; וְעַל הַשֵּׁנִית: גָּד, אָשֵׁר, יִשָּׂשכָר, זְבוּלֻן, יוֹסֵף, בִּנְיָמִין מָלֵא, שֶׁכֵּן הוּא כָּתוּב בִּמְקוֹם תּוֹלַדְתּוֹ (בראשית לה, יח), עֶשְׂרִים וְחָמֵשׁ אוֹתִיּוֹת בְּכָל אַחַת וְאַחַת:

יא **מַעֲשֵׂה חָרַשׁ אֶבֶן.** מַעֲשֵׂה אֻמָּן שֶׁל אֲבָנִים. ׳חָרַשׁ׳ זֶה, דָּבוּק הוּא לַתֵּבָה שֶׁלְּאַחֲרָיו וּלְפִיכָךְ הוּא נָקוּד פַּתָּח בְּסוֹפוֹ, וְכֵן: ״חָרַשׁ עֵצִים נָטָה קָו״ (ישעיה מד, יג), חָרָשׁ שֶׁל עֵצִים, וְכֵן: ״חָרַשׁ בַּרְזֶל מַעֲצָד״ (שם פסוק יב), כָּל אֵלֶּה דְּבוּקִים וּפְתוּחִים: **פִּתּוּחֵי חֹתָם.** כְּתַרְגּוּמוֹ: ״כְּתַב מְפָרַשׁ כִּגְלַף דְּעִזְקָא״, חֲרוּצוֹת הָאוֹתִיּוֹת בְּתוֹכָן כְּמוֹ שֶׁחוֹרְצִין חוֹתְמֵי טַבָּעוֹת שֶׁהֵם לַחְתֹּם אִגְּרוֹת, כְּתָב נִכָּר וּמְפֹרָשׁ: **עַל שְׁמֹת.** כְּמוֹ בִּשְׁמוֹת: **מֻסַבֹּת מִשְׁבְּצוֹת.** מֻקָּפוֹת הָאֲבָנִים בְּמִשְׁבְּצוֹת זָהָב, שֶׁעוֹשֶׂה מוֹשַׁב הָאֶבֶן בְּזָהָב כְּמִין גּוּמָא לְמִדַּת הָאֶבֶן וּמְשַׁקְּעָהּ בַּמִּשְׁבֶּצֶת, נִמְצֵאת הַמִּשְׁבֶּצֶת סוֹבֶבֶת אֶת הָאֶבֶן סָבִיב, וּמְחַבֵּר הַמִּשְׁבֶּצֶת בָּאֵפוֹד:

יב **לְזִכָּרֹן.** שֶׁיִּרְאֶה הַקָּדוֹשׁ בָּרוּךְ הוּא שְׁבָטִים כְּתוּבִים לְפָנָיו וְיִזְכֹּר צִדְקָתָם:

יג **וְעָשִׂיתָ מִשְׁבְּצֹת.** מִעוּט ״מִשְׁבְּצוֹת״ שְׁתַּיִם, וְלֹא פֵּרַשׁ לְךָ עַתָּה בְּפָרָשָׁה זוֹ אֶלָּא מִקְצָת צָרְכָּן, וּבְפָרָשַׁת הַחֹשֶׁן גּוֹמֵר לְךָ פֵּרוּשָׁן:

יד **שַׁרְשְׁרֹת זָהָב.** שַׁלְשְׁלָאוֹת: **מִגְבָּלֹת.** לְסוֹף גְּבוּל הַחֹשֶׁן ״תַּעֲשֶׂה אֹתָם״: **מַעֲשֵׂה עֲבֹת.** מַעֲשֵׂה קְלִיעַת חוּטִין, וְלֹא מַעֲשֵׂה נְקָבִים וּכְפָלִים כְּאוֹתָן שֶׁעוֹשִׂין לְבוֹרוֹת, אֶלָּא כְּאוֹתָן שֶׁעוֹשִׂין לְעַרְדַּסְקָאוֹת שֶׁקּוֹרִין אנצינסייר״ש: **וְנָתַתָּה אֶת שַׁרְשְׁרֹת.** שֶׁל עֲבוֹתוֹת הָעֲשׂוּיוֹת מַעֲשֵׂה עֲבוֹת, עַל מִשְׁבְּצוֹת הַלָּלוּ. וְלֹא זֶה הוּא מְקוֹם צַוָּאַת עֲשִׂיָּתָן שֶׁל שַׁרְשְׁרוֹת וְלֹא צַוָּאַת קְבִיעָתָן, וְאֵין ״תַּעֲשֶׂה״ הָאָמוּר כָּאן לְשׁוֹן צִוּוּי, וְאֵין ״וְנָתַתָּה״ הָאָמוּר כָּאן לְשׁוֹן צִוּוּי, אֶלָּא לְשׁוֹן עָתִיד, כִּי בְּפָרָשַׁת הַחֹשֶׁן חוֹזֵר וּמְצַוֶּה עַל עֲשִׂיָּתָן וְעַל קְבִיעָתָן, וְלֹא נִכְתַּב כָּאן אֶלָּא לְהוֹדִיעַ מִקְצָת צֹרֶךְ הַמִּשְׁבְּצוֹת שֶׁצִּוָּה לַעֲשׂוֹת עִם הָאֵפוֹד, וְכָתַב לְךָ זֹאת לוֹמַר לְךָ, הַמִּשְׁבְּצוֹת הַלָּלוּ יִזְקְקוּ לָךְ, לִכְשֶׁתַּעֲשֶׂה שַׁרְשְׁרוֹת מִגְבָּלוֹת עַל הַחֹשֶׁן, תִּתְּנֵם עַל הַמִּשְׁבְּצוֹת הַלָּלוּ:

טו **חֹשֶׁן מִשְׁפָּט.** שֶׁמְּכַפֵּר עַל קִלְקוּל הַדִּין. דָּבָר אַחֵר, ״מִשְׁפָּט״, שֶׁמְּבָרֵר דְּבָרָיו וְהַבְטָחָתוֹ אֱמֶת, דריסנמנ״ט בְּלַעַז. שֶׁהַמִּשְׁפָּט מְשַׁמֵּשׁ שָׁלֹשׁ לְשׁוֹנוֹת: דִּבְרֵי בַּעֲלֵי הַדִּין, וּגְמַר הַדִּין, וְעֹנֶשׁ הַדִּין, אִם עֹנֶשׁ מִיתָה אִם עֹנֶשׁ מַכּוֹת אִם עֹנֶשׁ מָמוֹן. וְזֶה מְשַׁמֵּשׁ לְשׁוֹן בֵּרוּר דְּבָרִים, שֶׁמְּפָרֵשׁ וּמְבָרֵר דְּבָרָיו: **כְּמַעֲשֵׂה אֵפֹד.** מַעֲשֵׂה חוֹשֵׁב וּמֵחֲמֵשֶׁת מִינִין:

טז **זֶרֶת אָרְכּוֹ וְזֶרֶת רָחְבּוֹ.** כָּפוּל וּמֻטָּל לוֹ לְפָנָיו כְּנֶגֶד לִבּוֹ, שֶׁנֶּאֱמַר: ״וְהָיוּ עַל לֵב אַהֲרֹן״ (להלן פסוק ל), תָּלוּי בְּכִתְפוֹת הָאֵפוֹד הַבָּאוֹת מֵאֲחוֹרָיו עַל כְּתֵפָיו וְנִקְפָּלוֹת וְיוֹרְדוֹת לְפָנָיו מְעַט, וְהַחֹשֶׁן תָּלוּי בָּהֶן בְּשַׁרְשְׁרוֹת וְטַבָּעוֹת, כְּמוֹ שֶׁמְּפֹרָשׁ בָּעִנְיָן:

יז **וּמִלֵּאתָ בוֹ.** עַל שֵׁם שֶׁהָאֲבָנִים מְמַלְּאוֹת גּוּמוֹת הַמִּשְׁבְּצוֹת הַמְּתֻקָּנוֹת לָהֶן, קוֹרֵא אוֹתָן בִּלְשׁוֹן מִלּוּאִים:

כ **מְשֻׁבָּצִים זָהָב יִהְיוּ.** הַטּוּרִים ״בְּמִלּוּאֹתָם״, מֻקָּפִים מִשְׁבְּצוֹת זָהָב בְּעֹמֶק שִׁעוּר שֶׁיִּתְמַלֵּא בָּעֳבִי הָאֶבֶן. זֶהוּ לְשׁוֹן ״בְּמִלּוּאֹתָם״, כְּשִׁעוּר מִלּוּי עָבְיָן שֶׁל אֲבָנִים יִהְיֶה עֹמֶק הַמִּשְׁבְּצוֹת, לֹא פָּחוֹת וְלֹא יוֹתֵר:

יא הַנּוֹתָרִים עַל־הָאֶבֶן הַשֵּׁנִית כְּתוֹלְדֹתָם: מַעֲשֵׂה חָרַשׁ אֶבֶן פִּתּוּחֵי
חֹתָם תְּפַתַּח אֶת־שְׁתֵּי הָאֲבָנִים עַל־שְׁמֹת בְּנֵי יִשְׂרָאֵל מֻסַבֹּת
יב מִשְׁבְּצוֹת זָהָב תַּעֲשֶׂה אֹתָם: וְשַׂמְתָּ אֶת־שְׁתֵּי הָאֲבָנִים עַל כִּתְפֹת
הָאֵפֹד אַבְנֵי זִכָּרֹן לִבְנֵי יִשְׂרָאֵל וְנָשָׂא אַהֲרֹן אֶת־שְׁמוֹתָם לִפְנֵי יְהוָה
יג יד עַל־שְׁתֵּי כְתֵפָיו לְזִכָּרֹן: וְעָשִׂיתָ מִשְׁבְּצֹת זָהָב: וּשְׁתֵּי שני
שַׁרְשְׁרֹת זָהָב טָהוֹר מִגְבָּלֹת תַּעֲשֶׂה אֹתָם מַעֲשֵׂה עֲבֹת וְנָתַתָּה אֶת־
טו שַׁרְשְׁרֹת הָעֲבֹתֹת עַל־הַמִּשְׁבְּצֹת: וְעָשִׂיתָ חֹשֶׁן מִשְׁפָּט
מַעֲשֵׂה חֹשֵׁב כְּמַעֲשֵׂה אֵפֹד תַּעֲשֶׂנּוּ זָהָב תְּכֵלֶת וְאַרְגָּמָן וְתוֹלַעַת שָׁנִי
טז וְשֵׁשׁ מָשְׁזָר תַּעֲשֶׂה אֹתוֹ: רָבוּעַ יִהְיֶה כָּפוּל זֶרֶת אָרְכּוֹ וְזֶרֶת רָחְבּוֹ:
יז וּמִלֵּאתָ בוֹ מִלֻּאַת אֶבֶן אַרְבָּעָה טוּרִים אָבֶן טוּר אֹדֶם פִּטְדָה וּבָרֶקֶת
יח יט הַטּוּר הָאֶחָד: וְהַטּוּר הַשֵּׁנִי נֹפֶךְ סַפִּיר וְיָהֲלֹם: וְהַטּוּר הַשְּׁלִישִׁי לֶשֶׁם
כ שְׁבוֹ וְאַחְלָמָה: וְהַטּוּר הָרְבִיעִי תַּרְשִׁישׁ וְשֹׁהַם וְיָשְׁפֵה מְשֻׁבָּצִים זָהָב

אונקלוס

דְּאִשְׁתְּאַרוּ, עַל אַבְנָא תִּנְיֵיתָא כְּתוֹלְדָתְהוֹן: יא עוֹבַד אֻמָּן אֶבֶן טָבָא, כְּתַב מְפָרַשׁ כִּגְלַף דְּעִזְקָא, תִּגְלוֹף יָת תַּרְתֵּין אַבְנַיָּא, עַל שְׁמָהָת בְּנֵי יִשְׂרָאֵל, מְשַׁקְּעָן, מְרַמְּצָן דִּדְהַב תַּעֲבֵיד יָתְהוֹן: יב וּתְשַׁוֵּי יָת תַּרְתֵּין אַבְנַיָּא, עַל כִּתְפֵי אֵיפוֹדָא, אַבְנֵי דָּכְרָנָא לִבְנֵי יִשְׂרָאֵל, וְיִטּוֹל אַהֲרֹן יָת שְׁמָהָתְהוֹן, קֳדָם יְיָ, עַל תַּרְתֵּין כַּתְפוֹהִי לְדָכְרָנָא: יג וְתַעֲבֵיד מְרַמְּצָן דִּדְהַב: יד וְתַרְתֵּין תִּכִּין דִּדְהַב דְּכֵי, מְתַחְמָן, תַּעֲבֵיד יָתְהוֹן עוֹבַד גְּדִילוּ, וְתִתֵּין, יָת תִּכַּיָּא גְּדִילָתָא עַל מְרַמְּצָתָא:

טו וְתַעֲבֵיד, חֹשֶׁן דִּינָא עוֹבַד אֻמָּן, כְּעוֹבַד אֵיפוֹדָא תַּעְבְּדִנֵּיהּ, דַּהֲבָא, תַּכְלָא וְאַרְגְּוָנָא, וּצְבַע זְהוֹרִי, וּבוּץ שְׁזִיר תַּעֲבֵיד יָתֵיהּ: טז מְרַבַּע יְהֵי עִיף, זַרְתָּא אֻרְכֵּיהּ וְזַרְתָּא פְּתָיֵיהּ: יז וְתַשְׁלֵים בֵּיהּ אַשְׁלָמוּת אַבְנָא, אַרְבְּעָא סִדְרִין דְּאֶבֶן טָבָא, סִדְרָא קַדְמָאָה, סָמְקָן יָרְקָן וּבָרְקָן, סִדְרָא חַד: יח וְסִדְרָא תִּנְיָנָא, אִזְמַרַגְדִּין שַׁבְזִיז וְסַבְהֲלוֹם: יט וְסִדְרָא תְּלִיתָאָה, קַנְכֵּירֵי טַרְקְיָא וְעֵין עִגְלָא: כ וְסִדְרָא רְבִיעָאָה, כְּרוּם יַמָּא וּבֻרְלָא וּפַנְתֵּירֵי, מְרַמְּצָן בִּדְהַב,

28:15 וְעָשִׂיתָ חֹשֶׁן *Make a breast piece* – The Torah instructs Moshe to use five different fibers for the priestly vestments (Ex. 28:5): gold thread; finely twisted linen (see Rashi on Ex. 25:4); and wool dyed in three different colors – sky-blue, purple, and scarlet. Six threads of each of the four fibers were spun together with a single gold thread to create one yarn. This composite yarn was then further spun to produce a yarn of twenty-eight threads from which the ephod and breast piece were then woven (Yoma 72a). The *ḥoshen* – the breast piece – is a piece of fabric woven of this yarn and then folded over with the Urim and Tumim placed inside. On its front, twelve precious stones bearing the names of the twelve tribes are attached in a golden setting.

The detailed descriptions of these beautiful objects confirm what we noted above: that there is a place for the aesthetic in *avoda*, divine service. In the words of the Song of the Sea: *Zeh Keli ve'anvehu*, "This is my God, I will glorify Him" (Ex. 15:3). For beauty inspires love, and from love flows the service of the heart.

21 them in gold filigree settings. The stones shall correspond to the names of
Yisrael's sons. Each stone should be engraved like a seal, with one of the names
22 of the twelve tribes. Make chains of pure gold, braided into cords, for the breast
23 piece. Make the breast piece two gold rings and attach them to its two corners.
24 Then fasten the two gold chains to the two gold rings at the corners of the
25 breast piece. Attach the other ends of the chains to the two settings. They will
26 thus be joined to the ephod's shoulder pieces at the front. Make two gold rings
and place them at the two other corners of the breast piece on the edge, inside,
27 next to the ephod. Make two more gold rings and attach them to the bottom of
the ephod's two shoulder pieces facing its front, close to its seam and above the
28 ephod's woven waistband. The breast piece shall be held in place by a cord of

רש"י

כא **אִישׁ עַל שְׁמוֹ.** כְּסֵדֶר תּוֹלְדוֹתָם סֵדֶר הָאֲבָנִים: אֹדֶם לִרְאוּבֵן, פִּטְדָה לְשִׁמְעוֹן, וְכֵן כֻּלָּם:

כב **עַל הַחֹשֶׁן.** בִּשְׁבִיל הַחֹשֶׁן, לְקָבְעָם בְּטַבְּעוֹתָיו, כְּמוֹ שֶׁמְּפֹרָשׁ לְמַטָּה בָּעִנְיָן: **שַׁרְשֹׁת.** לְשׁוֹן שָׁרָשֵׁי אִילָן שֶׁהֵן מַאֲחִזִין לָאִילָן לְהֵאָחֵז וּלְהִתָּקַע בָּאָרֶץ, אַף אֵלּוּ יִהְיוּ מַאֲחִזִין לַחֹשֶׁן, שֶׁבָּהֶם יִהְיֶה תָּלוּי בָּאֵפוֹד, וְהֵן שְׁתֵּי שַׁרְשְׁרוֹת הָאֲמוּרוֹת לְמַעְלָה בְּעִנְיַן הַמִּשְׁבְּצוֹת (לעיל פסוק יד). וְאַף 'שַׁרְשְׁרוֹת' פָּתַר מְנַחֵם בֶּן סָרוּק לְשׁוֹן שָׁרָשִׁים, וְאָמַר שֶׁהָרֵי"שׁ יְתֵרָה כְּמוֹ מֵ"ם שֶׁבְּ'שִׁלְשׁוֹם' (בראשית לא, ב) וּמֵ"ם שֶׁבְּ'רֵיקָם' (שם פסוק מב). וְאֵינִי רוֹאֶה אֶת דְּבָרָיו, אֶלָּא 'שַׁרְשֶׁרֶת' בִּלְשׁוֹן עִבְרִית כְּ'שַׁלְשֶׁלֶת' בִּלְשׁוֹן מִשְׁנָה (כלים יד, ג): **גַּבְלֻת.** הוּא "מִגְבָּלֹת" הָאָמוּר לְמַעְלָה (לעיל פסוק יד), שֶׁתִּתְקָעֵם בְּטַבָּעוֹת שֶׁיִּהְיוּ בִּגְבוּל הַחֹשֶׁן. וְכָל 'גְּבוּל' לְשׁוֹן קָצֶה, אשומי"ל בְּלַעַז: **מַעֲשֵׂה עֲבֹת.** מַעֲשֵׂה קְלִיעָה:

כג **עַל הַחֹשֶׁן.** לְצֹרֶךְ הַחֹשֶׁן, כְּדֵי לְקָבְעָם בּוֹ. וְלֹא יִתָּכֵן לוֹמַר שֶׁתְּהֵא תְּחִלַּת עֲשִׂיָּתָן עָלָיו, שֶׁאִם כֵּן מַה הוּא שֶׁחוֹזֵר וְאוֹמֵר: "וְנָתַתָּ אֶת שְׁתֵּי הַטַּבָּעוֹת", וַהֲלֹא כְּבָר נְתוּנִים בּוֹ! הָיָה לוֹ לִכְתֹּב בִּתְחִלַּת הַמִּקְרָא: 'וְעָשִׂיתָ עַל קְצוֹת הַחֹשֶׁן שְׁתֵּי טַבְּעוֹת זָהָב'! וְאַף בְּשַׁרְשְׁרוֹת צָרִיךְ אַתָּה לִפְתֹּר כֵּן: **עַל שְׁנֵי קְצוֹת הַחֹשֶׁן.** לִשְׁתֵּי פֵּאוֹת שֶׁכְּנֶגֶד הַצַּוָּאר, לַיְּמָנִית וְלַשְּׂמָאלִית, הַבָּאִים מוּל כִּתְפוֹת הָאֵפוֹד:

כד **וְנָתַתָּה אֶת שְׁתֵּי עֲבֹתֹת הַזָּהָב.** הֵן הֵן "שַׁרְשֹׁת גַּבְלֻת" הַכְּתוּבוֹת לְמַעְלָה (לעיל פסוק כב), וְלֹא פֵּרַשׁ מְקוֹם קִבּוּעָן בַּחֹשֶׁן, עַכְשָׁיו מְפָרֵשׁ לְךָ שֶׁיְּהֵא תּוֹחֵב אוֹתָן בַּטַּבָּעוֹת. וְתֵדַע לְךָ שֶׁהֵן הֵן הָרִאשׁוֹנוֹת, שֶׁהֲרֵי בְּפָרָשַׁת 'אֵלֶּה פְקוּדֵי' לֹא הֻכְפְּלוּ:

כה **וְאֵת שְׁתֵּי קְצוֹת.** שֶׁל "שְׁתֵּי הָעֲבֹתֹת", שְׁנֵי רָאשֵׁיהֶם שֶׁל כָּל אַחַת וְאַחַת: **תִּתֵּן עַל שְׁתֵּי הַמִּשְׁבְּצוֹת.** הֵן הֵן הַכְּתוּבוֹת לְמַעְלָה בֵּין פָּרָשַׁת הַחֹשֶׁן וּפָרָשַׁת הָאֵפוֹד, וְלֹא פֵּרַשׁ אֶת צָרְכָּן וְאֶת מְקוֹמָן, עַכְשָׁיו מְפָרֵשׁ שֶׁיִּתָּקַע בָּהֶן רָאשֵׁי הָעֲבוֹתוֹת הַתְּחוּבוֹת בְּטַבְּעוֹת הַחֹשֶׁן לְיָמִין וְלִשְׂמֹאל אֵצֶל הַצַּוָּאר, שְׁנֵי רָאשֵׁי שַׁרְשֶׁרֶת הַיְמָנִית תּוֹקֵעַ בְּמִשְׁבֶּצֶת שֶׁל יָמִין, וְכֵן בְּשֶׁל שְׂמֹאל שְׁנֵי רָאשֵׁי שַׁרְשֶׁרֶת הַשְּׂמָאלִית: **וְנָתַתָּה.** הַמִּשְׁבְּצוֹת "עַל כִּתְפוֹת הָאֵפוֹד". אַחַת בְּזוֹ וְאַחַת בְּזוֹ, נִמְצְאוּ כִּתְפוֹת הָאֵפוֹד מַחֲזִיקִין אֶת הַחֹשֶׁן שֶׁלֹּא יִפֹּל, וּבָהֶן הוּא תָּלוּי. וַעֲדַיִן שְׂפַת הַחֹשֶׁן הַתַּחְתּוֹנָה הוֹלֶכֶת וּבָאָה וְנוֹקֶשֶׁת עַל כְּרֵסוֹ וְאֵינָהּ דְּבוּקָה לוֹ יָפֶה, לְכָךְ הִצְרַךְ עוֹד שְׁתֵּי טַבָּעוֹת לְתַחְתִּיתוֹ כְּמוֹ שֶׁמְּפָרֵשׁ וְהוֹלֵךְ: **אֶל מוּל פָּנָיו.** שֶׁל אֵפוֹד, שֶׁלֹּא יִתֵּן הַמִּשְׁבְּצוֹת בְּעֵבֶר הַכְּתֵפוֹת שֶׁכְּלַפֵּי הַמְּעִיל, אֶלָּא בָּעֵבֶר הָעֶלְיוֹן שֶׁכְּלַפֵּי הַחוּץ, וְהוּא קָרוּי 'מוּל פָּנָיו' שֶׁל אֵפוֹד, כִּי אוֹתוֹ עֵבֶר שֶׁאֵינוֹ נִרְאֶה אֵינוֹ קָרוּי פָּנִים:

כו **עַל שְׁנֵי קְצוֹת הַחֹשֶׁן.** הֵן שְׁתֵּי פֵּאוֹתָיו הַתַּחְתּוֹנוֹת לְיָמִין וְלִשְׂמֹאל: **עַל שְׂפָתוֹ אֲשֶׁר אֶל עֵבֶר הָאֵפוֹד בָּיְתָה.** הֲרֵי לְךָ שְׁנֵי סִימָנִין: הָאֶחָד שֶׁיִּתְּנֵם בִּשְׁנֵי קְצוֹת שֶׁל תַּחְתִּיתוֹ שֶׁהוּא כְּנֶגֶד הָאֵפוֹד, שֶׁעֶלְיוֹנוֹ אֵינוֹ כְּנֶגֶד הָאֵפוֹד, שֶׁהֲרֵי סָמוּךְ לַצַּוָּאר הוּא וְהָאֵפוֹד נָתוּן עַל מָתְנָיו. וְעוֹד נָתַן סִימָן, שֶׁלֹּא יִקְבָּעֵם בְּעֵבֶר הַחֹשֶׁן שֶׁכְּלַפֵּי הַחוּץ אֶלָּא בָּעֵבֶר שֶׁכְּלַפֵּי פְּנִים, שֶׁנֶּאֱמַר "בָּיְתָה", וְאוֹתוֹ הָעֵבֶר הוּא לְצַד הָאֵפוֹד, שֶׁחֵשֶׁב הָאֵפוֹד חוֹגְרוֹ לַכֹּהֵן וְנִקְפָּל הַסִּינָר לִפְנֵי הַכֹּהֵן עַל מָתְנָיו וּקְצָת כְּרֵסוֹ מִכָּאן וּמִכָּאן עַד כְּנֶגֶד קְצוֹת הַחֹשֶׁן, וּקְצוֹתָיו שׁוֹכְבִין עָלָיו:

כז **עַל שְׁתֵּי כִתְפוֹת הָאֵפוֹד מִלְמַטָּה.** שֶׁהַמִּשְׁבְּצוֹת נִתְּנוּ בְּרָאשֵׁי כִּתְפוֹת הָאֵפוֹד הָעֶלְיוֹנִים הַבָּאִים עַל כְּתֵפָיו כְּנֶגֶד גְּרוֹנוֹ וְנִקְפָּלוֹת וְיוֹרְדוֹת לְפָנָיו, וְהַטַּבָּעוֹת צִוָּה לִתֵּן בְּרֹאשָׁן הַשֵּׁנִי שֶׁהוּא מְחֻבָּר לָאֵפוֹד, וְהוּא שֶׁנֶּאֱמַר: "לְעֻמַּת מַחְבַּרְתּוֹ", סָמוּךְ לִמְקוֹם חִבּוּרָן בָּאֵפוֹד לְמַעְלָה מִן הַחֲגוֹרָה מְעַט, שֶׁהַמַּחְבֶּרֶת לְעֻמַּת הַחֲגוֹרָה, וְאֵלּוּ נְתוּנִים מְעַט בְּגֹבַהּ זְקִיפַת הַכְּתֵפוֹת, הוּא שֶׁנֶּאֱמַר: "מִמַּעַל לְחֵשֶׁב הָאֵפוֹד", וְהֵן כְּנֶגֶד סוֹף הַחֹשֶׁן. וְנוֹתֵן פְּתִיל תְּכֵלֶת בְּאוֹתָן הַטַּבָּעוֹת וּבְטַבְּעוֹת הַחֹשֶׁן, וְרוֹכְסָן בְּאוֹתוֹ פְּתִיל לְיָמִין וְלִשְׂמֹאל, שֶׁלֹּא יְהֵא תַּחְתִּית הַחֹשֶׁן הוֹלֵךְ לְפָנִים וְחוֹזֵר לְאָחוֹר וְנוֹקֵשׁ עַל כְּרֵסוֹ, וְנִמְצָא מְיֻשָּׁב עַל הַמְּעִיל יָפֶה: **מִמּוּל פָּנָיו.** בָּעֵבֶר הַחִיצוֹן:

כא יִהְיוּ בְּמִלּוּאֹתָם׃ וְהָאֲבָנִים תִּהְיֶיןָ עַל־שְׁמֹת בְּנֵי־יִשְׂרָאֵל שְׁתֵּים עֶשְׂרֵה
עַל־שְׁמֹתָם פִּתּוּחֵי חוֹתָם אִישׁ עַל־שְׁמוֹ תִּהְיֶיןָ לִשְׁנֵי עָשָׂר שָׁבֶט׃
כב כג וְעָשִׂיתָ עַל־הַחֹשֶׁן שַׁרְשֹׁת גַּבְלֻת מַעֲשֵׂה עֲבֹת זָהָב טָהוֹר׃ וְעָשִׂיתָ
עַל־הַחֹשֶׁן שְׁתֵּי טַבְּעוֹת זָהָב וְנָתַתָּ אֶת־שְׁתֵּי הַטַּבָּעוֹת עַל־שְׁנֵי קְצוֹת
כד הַחֹשֶׁן׃ וְנָתַתָּה אֶת־שְׁתֵּי עֲבֹתֹת הַזָּהָב עַל־שְׁתֵּי הַטַּבָּעֹת אֶל־קְצוֹת
כה הַחֹשֶׁן׃ וְאֵת שְׁתֵּי קְצוֹת שְׁתֵּי הָעֲבֹתֹת תִּתֵּן עַל־שְׁתֵּי הַמִּשְׁבְּצוֹת
כו וְנָתַתָּה עַל־כִּתְפוֹת הָאֵפֹד אֶל־מוּל פָּנָיו׃ וְעָשִׂיתָ שְׁתֵּי טַבְּעוֹת זָהָב
וְשַׂמְתָּ אֹתָם עַל־שְׁנֵי קְצוֹת הַחֹשֶׁן עַל־שְׂפָתוֹ אֲשֶׁר אֶל־עֵבֶר הָאֵפוֹד
כז בָּיְתָה׃ וְעָשִׂיתָ שְׁתֵּי טַבְּעוֹת זָהָב וְנָתַתָּה אֹתָם עַל־שְׁתֵּי כִתְפוֹת
הָאֵפוֹד מִלְּמַטָּה מִמּוּל פָּנָיו לְעֻמַּת מַחְבַּרְתּוֹ מִמַּעַל לְחֵשֶׁב הָאֵפוֹד׃
כח וְיִרְכְּסוּ אֶת־הַחֹשֶׁן מִטַּבְּעֹתָו אֶל־טַבְּעֹת הָאֵפוֹד בִּפְתִיל תְּכֵלֶת

אונקלוס

יְהוֹן בְּאַשְׁלָמוּתְהוֹן: כא וְאַבְנַיָּא, יְהוֹיָן, עַל שְׁמָהַת בְּנֵי יִשְׂרָאֵל, תַּרְתָּא עַסְרֵי עַל שְׁמָהָתְהוֹן, כְּתַב מְפָרַשׁ כִּגְלָף דְּעִזְקָא גְּבַר עַל שְׁמֵיהּ, יְהוֹיָן, לִתְרֵי עֲסַר שִׁבְטִין: כב וְתַעֲבֵיד עַל חֻשְׁנָא, תִּכִּין מְתַחְמָן עוֹבָד גְּדִילוּ, דִּדְהַב דְּכֵי: כג וְתַעֲבֵיד עַל חֻשְׁנָא, תַּרְתֵּין עִזְקָן דִּדְהַב, וְתִתֵּין, יָת תַּרְתֵּין עִזְקָתָא, עַל תְּרֵין סִטְרֵי חֻשְׁנָא: כד וְתִתֵּין, יָת תַּרְתֵּין גְּדִילָן דִּדְהַב, עַל תַּרְתֵּין עִזְקָתָא, בְּסִטְרֵי חֻשְׁנָא: כה וְיָת תַּרְתֵּין גְּדִילָן דְּעַל תְּרֵין סִטְרוֹהִי, תִּתֵּין עַל תַּרְתֵּין מְרַמְּצָתָא, וְתִתֵּין, עַל כִּתְפֵי אֵיפוֹדָא לָקֳבֵיל אַפּוֹהִי: כו וְתַעֲבֵיד, תַּרְתֵּין עִזְקָן דִּדְהַב, וּתְשַׁוֵּי יָתְהוֹן, עַל תְּרֵין סִטְרֵי חֻשְׁנָא, עַל סִפְתֵיהּ, דִּלְעִבְרָא דְּאֵיפוֹדָא לְגָיו: כז וְתַעֲבֵיד תַּרְתֵּין עִזְקָן דִּדְהַב, וְתִתֵּין יָתְהוֹן, עַל תַּרְתֵּין כִּתְפֵי אֵיפוֹדָא מִלְּרַע מִלָּקֳבֵיל אַפּוֹהִי, לָקֳבֵיל בֵּית לוֹפֵי, מֵעִלָּוֵי, לְהֶמְיַן אֵיפוֹדָא: כח וְיַחֲדוּן יָת חֻשְׁנָא, מֵעִזְקָתֵיהּ, לְעִזְקַת אֵיפוֹדָא בְּחוּטָא דִּתְכִילְתָא,

רש״י

כח) וְיִרְכְּסוּ. לְשׁוֹן חִבּוּר, וְכֵן: "מֵרֻכְסֵי אִישׁ" (תהלים לא, כא), חִבּוּרֵי חֶבְלֵי רְשָׁעִים, וְכֵן: "וְהָרְכָסִים לְבִקְעָה" (ישעיה מ, ד), הָרִים הַסְּמוּכִים זֶה לָזֶה שֶׁאִי אֶפְשָׁר לֵירֵד לַגַּיְא שֶׁבֵּינֵיהֶם אֶלָּא בְּקֹשִׁי גָּדוֹל, שֶׁמִּתּוֹךְ סְמִיכָתָן הַגַּיְא זְקוּפָה וַעֲמֻקָּה, יִהְיוּ לְבִקְעַת מִישׁוֹר וְנוֹחָה לֵילֵךְ:

28:21 בְּנֵי־יִשְׂרָאֵל... לִשְׁנֵי עָשָׂר שָׁבֶט *Yisrael's sons.... the twelve tribes* – The families descended from Yaakov were clans when the book began. Now they are tribes. For the next several centuries, Israel will remain an amphictyony: a federation of tribes.

The central insight of monotheism is that if God is the parent of humanity, then we are all members of a single family. The Enlightenment gave us the concept of universal rights, but this remains a "thin" morality, stronger in abstract ideas than in its grip on the moral imagination. Far more powerful is the biblical idea that those in need are our brothers and sisters. Early Israelite religion was the attempt to create a heterogenous, classless, decentralized association of tribes conceived as a brotherhood – and at least in larger measure than in Canaanite society, as a sisterhood – of social, economic and political equals. When the High Priest carries the people's "remembrance before the Lord" (Ex. 28:29), then it is not in the form of one name, one symbol, but of twelve: twelve brothers, twelve stones, all different, all precious.

sky blue from its rings to the rings of the ephod, so that the breast piece remains
secured above the ephod's waistband, and does not come loose from the ephod.
29 Thus will Aharon carry the names of Yisrael's sons on the breast piece of
judgment at his heart whenever he enters the Sanctuary, as a remembrance
30 before the Lord at all times. Place the Urim and Tumim in the breast piece of
judgment so that they too will be at Aharon's heart when he comes before the
Lord. Aharon will then always be carrying at his heart Israel's means of
31 judgment, before the Lord. SHELISHI Make the robe of the ephod entirely of
32 sky-blue wool. It should have an opening for the head in the middle with a
woven border around it like the neck of a coat of mail, so that it does not tear.
33 Around the hem of the robe make pomegranates of sky-blue, purple, and scarlet
34 wool, and between them put gold bells, so that gold bells and pomegranates

רש״י

לִהְיוֹת עַל חֵשֶׁב הָאֵפוֹד. לִהְיוֹת הַחֹשֶׁן דָּבוּק אֶל חֵשֶׁב הָאֵפוֹד: **וְלֹא יִזַּח.** לְשׁוֹן נִתּוּק, וְלָשׁוֹן עֲרָבִי הוּא, כְּדִבְרֵי דוּנַשׁ בֶּן לַבְרַט:

ל **אֶת הָאוּרִים וְאֶת הַתֻּמִּים.** הוּא כְּתָב שֵׁם הַמְּפֹרָשׁ שֶׁהָיָה נוֹתְנוֹ בְּתוֹךְ כִּפְלֵי הַחֹשֶׁן, שֶׁעַל יָדוֹ הוּא מֵאִיר דְּבָרָיו וּמְתַמֵּם אֶת דְּבָרָיו. וּבְמִקְדָּשׁ שֵׁנִי הָיָה הַחֹשֶׁן, שֶׁאִי אֶפְשָׁר לְכֹהֵן גָּדוֹל לִהְיוֹת מְחֻסַּר בְּגָדִים, אֲבָל אוֹתוֹ הַשֵּׁם לֹא הָיָה בְּתוֹכוֹ. וְעַל שֵׁם אוֹתוֹ הַכְּתָב הוּא קָרוּי 'מִשְׁפָּט', שֶׁנֶּאֱמַר: "וְשָׁאַל לוֹ בְּמִשְׁפַּט הָאוּרִים" (במדבר כז, כא): **אֶת מִשְׁפַּט בְּנֵי יִשְׂרָאֵל.** דָּבָר שֶׁהֵם נִשְׁפָּטִים וְנוֹכָחִים עַל יָדוֹ אִם לַעֲשׂוֹת דָּבָר אוֹ לֹא לַעֲשׂוֹת. וּלְפִי מִדְרַשׁ אַגָּדָה שֶׁהַחֹשֶׁן מְכַפֵּר עַל מְעֻוְּתֵי הַדִּין, נִקְרָא "מִשְׁפָּט" עַל שֵׁם סְלִיחַת הַמִּשְׁפָּט:

לא **אֶת מְעִיל הָאֵפוֹד.** שֶׁהָאֵפוֹד נָתוּן עָלָיו לַחֲגוֹרָה: **כְּלִיל תְּכֵלֶת.** כֻּלּוֹ תְּכֵלֶת, שֶׁאֵין מִין אַחֵר מְעֹרָב בּוֹ:

לב **וְהָיָה פִי רֹאשׁוֹ.** פִּי הַמְּעִיל שֶׁבְּגָבְהוֹ, הוּא פְּתִיחַת בֵּית הַצַּוָּאר: **בְּתוֹכוֹ.** כְּתַרְגּוּמוֹ: "כְּפִיל לְגַוֵּהּ", כָּפוּל לְתוֹכוֹ לִהְיוֹת לוֹ לְשָׂפָה כְּפִילָתוֹ. וְהָיָה מַעֲשֵׂה אוֹרֵג וְלֹא בְּמַחַט: **כְּפִי תַחְרָא.** לָמַדְנוּ שֶׁהַשִּׁרְיוֹנִים שֶׁלָּהֶם פִּיהֶם כָּפוּל: **לֹא יִקָּרֵעַ.** כְּדֵי שֶׁלֹּא יִקָּרֵעַ. וְהַקּוֹרְעוֹ עוֹבֵר בְּלָאו, שֶׁזֶּה מִמִּנְיַן לָאוִין שֶׁבַּתּוֹרָה. וְכֵן: "וְלֹא יִזַּח הַחֹשֶׁן" (לעיל פסוק כח), וְכֵן: "לֹא יָסֻרוּ מִמֶּנּוּ" (לעיל כה, טו) הַנֶּאֱמָר בְּבַדֵּי הָאָרוֹן:

לג **רִמֹּנֵי.** עֲגֻלִּים וַחֲלוּלִים הָיוּ, כְּמִין רִמּוֹנִים הָעֲשׂוּיִים כְּבֵיצַת תַּרְנְגֹלֶת: **וּפַעֲמֹנֵי זָהָב.** זָגִים עִם עִנְבָּלִים שֶׁבְּתוֹכָם: **בְּתוֹכָם סָבִיב.** בֵּינֵיהֶם סָבִיב, בֵּין שְׁנֵי רִמּוֹנִים פַּעֲמוֹן אֶחָד דָּבוּק וְתָלוּי בְּשׁוּלֵי הַמְּעִיל:

לד **פַּעֲמֹן זָהָב וְרִמּוֹן.** אֶצְלוֹ: **פַּעֲמֹן זָהָב וְרִמּוֹן.** אֶצְלוֹ:

Quite different was the service of the priests. Here, what was primary was the sacrifice, not the words – in fact, for the most part the priestly worship took place in silence. The actions of the priests were precisely regulated; moreover, any deviation, such as the spontaneous offering of Aharon's two sons, Nadav and Avihu, was fraught with danger. The priests did the same thing, in the same place, at the same time, following a daily, weekly, monthly, and yearly cycle.

The patriarchs spoke to God because they felt moved to do so, not because there was an obligation to pray. Throughout the biblical era, the primary form of organized worship was the sacrifices offered by the priests, first in the Tabernacle, later in the Temple, on behalf of the whole people. Only when the Temple was destroyed did prayer replace sacrifice. For Rambam, at the heart of prayer is the prophetic experience of the individual in conversation with God. For Ramban, by contrast, prayer is the collective worship of the Jewish people, a continuation of the pattern set by the Temple service.

Jewish prayer as it has existed for almost two thousand years is a synthesis of two modes of biblical spirituality, supremely exemplified by two brothers: Moshe the prophet and Aharon the High Priest. Without the prophetic tradition, we would have no spontaneity. Without the priestly tradition, we would have no continuity. The Rabbis brought together what, for more than a thousand years, had existed

כט לִהְיוֹת עַל־חֵשֶׁב הָאֵפוֹד וְלֹא־יִזַּח הַחֹשֶׁן מֵעַל הָאֵפוֹד׃ וְנָשָׂא אַהֲרֹן
אֶת־שְׁמוֹת בְּנֵי־יִשְׂרָאֵל בְּחֹשֶׁן הַמִּשְׁפָּט עַל־לִבּוֹ בְּבֹאוֹ אֶל־הַקֹּדֶשׁ
ל לְזִכָּרֹן לִפְנֵי־יהוה תָּמִיד׃ וְנָתַתָּ אֶל־חֹשֶׁן הַמִּשְׁפָּט אֶת־הָאוּרִים וְאֶת־
הַתֻּמִּים וְהָיוּ עַל־לֵב אַהֲרֹן בְּבֹאוֹ לִפְנֵי יהוה וְנָשָׂא אַהֲרֹן אֶת־מִשְׁפַּט
לא בְּנֵי־יִשְׂרָאֵל עַל־לִבּוֹ לִפְנֵי יהוה תָּמִיד׃ וְעָשִׂיתָ אֶת־מְעִיל שלישי
לב הָאֵפוֹד כְּלִיל תְּכֵלֶת׃ וְהָיָה פִי־רֹאשׁוֹ בְּתוֹכוֹ שָׂפָה יִהְיֶה לְפִיו סָבִיב
לג מַעֲשֵׂה אֹרֵג כְּפִי תַחְרָא יִהְיֶה־לּוֹ לֹא יִקָּרֵעַ׃ וְעָשִׂיתָ עַל־שׁוּלָיו רִמֹּנֵי
תְּכֵלֶת וְאַרְגָּמָן וְתוֹלַעַת שָׁנִי עַל־שׁוּלָיו סָבִיב וּפַעֲמֹנֵי זָהָב בְּתוֹכָם
לד סָבִיב׃ פַּעֲמֹן זָהָב וְרִמּוֹן פַּעֲמֹן זָהָב וְרִמּוֹן עַל־שׁוּלֵי הַמְּעִיל סָבִיב׃

אונקלוס

לְמֶהֱוֵי עַל הֶמְיַן אֵיפוֹדָא, וְלָא יִתְפָּרַק חֻשְׁנָא, מֵעִלָּוֵי אֵיפוֹדָא: כט וְיִטּוֹל אַהֲרֹן, יָת שְׁמָהָת בְּנֵי יִשְׂרָאֵל, בְּחֻשֶׁן דִּינָא, עַל לִבֵּיהּ בְּמֵיעֲלֵיהּ לְקֻדְשָׁא, לְדֻכְרָנָא קֳדָם יי תְּדִירָא: ל וְתִתֵּין בְּחֻשֶׁן דִּינָא, יָת אוּרַיָּא וְיָת תֻּמַּיָּא, וִיהוֹן עַל לִבָּא דְאַהֲרֹן, בְּמֵיעֲלֵיהּ לִקְדָם יי, וְיִטּוֹל אַהֲרֹן, יָת דִּין בְּנֵי יִשְׂרָאֵל עַל לִבֵּיהּ, קֳדָם יי תְּדִירָא: לא וְתַעֲבֵיד, יָת מְעִיל אֵיפוֹדָא גְּמִיר תַּכְלָא: לב וִיהֵי פֻמֵּיהּ כְּפִיל לְגַוֵּיהּ, תּוֹרָא, יְהֵי מַקַּף לְפֻמֵּיהּ סְחוֹר סְחוֹר עוֹבַד מָחֵי, כְּפוּם שִׁרְיָן, יְהֵי לֵיהּ דְּלָא יִתְבְּזַע: לג וְתַעֲבֵיד עַל שִׁפּוֹלוֹהִי, רִמּוֹנֵי תַכְלָא וְאַרְגְּוָנָא וּצְבַע זְהוֹרִי, עַל שִׁפּוֹלוֹהִי סְחוֹר סְחוֹר, וְזוֹגִין דִּדְהַב, בֵּינֵיהוֹן סְחוֹר סְחוֹר: לד זוֹגָא דִדְהַבָא וְרִמּוֹנָא, זוֹגָא דִדְהַבָא וְרִמּוֹנָא, עַל שִׁפּוֹלֵי מְעִילָא סְחוֹר סְחוֹר:

PROPHETIC AND PRIESTLY PRAYER

The breast piece with its Urim and Tumim will perform the function of an oracle, something through which the High Priest can discern God's instructions. The prophets, too, convey God's will. What then is the difference between them? Priests and prophets represent not just two different roles, but two different ways of being, two distinct modes of consciousness. This is reflected in a talmudic debate on the nature of prayer:

> It has been stated: R. Yosei son of R. Ḥanina said: The [morning, afternoon, and evening] prayers were instituted by the patriarchs. R. Yehoshua b. Levi said: The prayers were instituted to replace the daily sacrifices. (Berakhot 26b)

According to R. Yosei son of R. Ḥanina, the patriarchs set the precedent for prayer. Avraham established the morning prayer, as it is said, "Avraham rose early the next morning and returned to the place where he had stood before the Lord" (Gen. 19:27). Yitzḥak instituted the afternoon prayer, as it is said, "He had gone out in the field toward evening to meditate" (24:63). Yaakov instituted the evening prayer when he received his vision, at night, of a ladder stretching from earth to heaven (28:12–15). The Sages cited prooftexts to show that each of these was an occasion of prayer.

According to R. Yehoshua b. Levi, however, the prayers correspond to the daily sacrifices: The morning and afternoon prayers represent the morning and afternoon offerings. The evening prayer mirrors the completion of the sacrificial process (the burning of the limbs), which was done at night.

When prophets prayed, they used words. They addressed God directly in speech. Prophetic prayer in the Bible is spontaneous. We think of Avraham's prayer on behalf of Sedom and Amora, Yaakov's prayer before his encounter with Esav, Moshe's prayer to God to forgive the Israelites after the golden calf. No two such prayers are alike.

35 alternate around the hem of the robe. Aharon shall wear this robe whenever he
ministers, and its sound will be heard when he enters the Sanctuary before the
36 Lord and when he leaves, so that he will not die. Make a headplate
37 of pure gold and engrave on it, as on a seal: Holy to the Lord. Attach a cord of
38 sky blue to it, so that it can be fixed to the miter, affixed to the miter's front. It
shall remain on Aharon's forehead, that Aharon may bear away all guilt that
arises from the holy offerings the Israelites consecrate, from all their sacred
gifts; it shall be on his forehead always, that they may find favor in the Lord's
39 sight. Quilt the tunic of fine linen. Make a miter out of fine linen, and an
40 embroidered sash. Make tunics, sashes, and caps for Aharon's sons, for glory
41 and for splendor. Put these on your brother Aharon and his sons; then anoint,

רש"י

לה **ולא ימות.** מכלל לאו אתה שומע הן: אם יהיו לו לא יתחייב מיתה, הא אם יכנס מחסר אחד מן הבגדים הללו חייב מיתה בידי שמים:

לו **ציץ.** כמין טס של זהב היה, רחב שתי אצבעות, מקיף על המצח מאזן לאזן:

לז **על פתיל תכלת.** ובמקום אחר הוא אומר: "ויתנו עליו פתיל תכלת" (להלן לט, לא), ועוד, כתיב כאן: "והיה על המצנפת", ולמטה הוא אומר: "והיה על מצח אהרן" (בפסוק הבא), ובשחיטת קדשים שנינו: "שערו היה נראה בין ציץ למצנפת ששם מניח תפלין" (זבחים יט ע"א), למדנו שהמצנפת למעלה בגבה הראש ואינה עמוקה לכנס בה כל הראש עד המצח, והציץ מלמטה, והפתילים היו נוקבין ותלויין בו בשני ראשים ובאמצעיתו, ששה בשלשה מקומות הללו, פתיל מלמעלה – אחד מבחוץ ואחד מבפנים כנגדו, וקושר ראשי הפתילים מאחורי העורף שלשתן, ונמצאו בין אורך הטס ופתילי ראשיו מקיפין את הקדקד; והפתיל האמצעי, כשראשו קשור עם ראשי השנים, הולך על פני רחב הראש מלמעלה, ונמצא עשוי כמין כובע. ועל פתיל האמצעי הוא אומר: "והיה על המצנפת", והיה נותן הציץ על ראשו כמין כובע על המצנפת, והפתיל האמצעי מחזיקו שאינו נופל, והטס תלוי כנגד מצחו. ונתקיימו כל המקראות: פתיל על הציץ, וציץ על הפתיל, ופתיל על המצנפת מלמעלה:

לח **ונשא אהרן.** לשון סליחה, ואף על פי כן אינו זז ממשמעו, אהרן נושא את המשא של עון, נמצא מסלק העון מן הקדשים: **את עון הקדשים.** לרצות על הדם ועל החלב שקרבו בטמאה, כמו ששנינו: אי זה עון הוא נושא? אם עון פגול, הרי כבר נאמר וכו'. ואין לומר שיכפר על הכהן שהקריבם טמאים, שהרי "עון הקדשים" נאמר ולא עון המקריב! אינו מרצה אלא להכשיר הקרבן: **והיה על מצחו תמיד.** אי אפשר לומר שיהא על מצחו תמיד, שהרי אינו עליו אלא בשעת העבודה! אלא "תמיד לרצון להם", אפילו אינו על מצחו, שלא היה כהן גדול עובד באותה שעה. ולדברי האומר עודהו על מצחו מכפר ומרצה ואם לאו אינו מרצה, נדרש "על מצחו תמיד" ללמד שימשמש בו בעודו על מצחו, שלא יסיח דעתו ממנו:

לט **ושבצת.** עשה אותה משבצות משבצות, וכלה של שש:

מ **ולבני אהרן תעשה.** ארבעה בגדים הללו ולא יותר: כתנת, ואבנט, ומגבעות היא מצנפת, ומכנסים כתובים למטה בפרשה (להלן פסוק מב):

מא **והלבשת אתם את אהרן.** אותם האמורים באהרן: "חשן ואפוד ומעיל וכתנת תשבץ מצנפת ואבנט" (לעיל פסוק ד), וציץ, ומכנסים כתובים למטה בכלם: **ואת בניו אתו.** אותם הכתובים בהם:

individuals into a collectively responsible group. You cannot sustain a national identity or even a marriage without loyalty. You cannot socialize successive generations without respect for figures of authority. You cannot defend the nonnegotiable value of human dignity without a sense of the sacred. That is why the prophetic ethic of justice and compassion had to be supplemented with the priestly ethic of holiness.

לה וְהָיָה עַל־אַהֲרֹן לְשָׁרֵת וְנִשְׁמַע קוֹלוֹ בְּבֹאוֹ אֶל־הַקֹּדֶשׁ לִפְנֵי יְהוָה
לו וּבְצֵאתוֹ וְלֹא יָמוּת׃ וְעָשִׂיתָ צִּיץ זָהָב טָהוֹר וּפִתַּחְתָּ עָלָיו
לז פִּתּוּחֵי חֹתָם קֹדֶשׁ לַיהוָה׃ וְשַׂמְתָּ אֹתוֹ עַל־פְּתִיל תְּכֵלֶת וְהָיָה עַל־
לח הַמִּצְנָפֶת אֶל־מוּל פְּנֵי־הַמִּצְנֶפֶת יִהְיֶה׃ וְהָיָה עַל־מֵצַח אַהֲרֹן וְנָשָׂא
אַהֲרֹן אֶת־עֲוֺן הַקֳּדָשִׁים אֲשֶׁר יַקְדִּישׁוּ בְּנֵי יִשְׂרָאֵל לְכָל־מַתְּנֹת
לט קָדְשֵׁיהֶם וְהָיָה עַל־מִצְחוֹ תָּמִיד לְרָצוֹן לָהֶם לִפְנֵי יְהוָה׃ וְשִׁבַּצְתָּ
מ הַכְּתֹנֶת שֵׁשׁ וְעָשִׂיתָ מִצְנֶפֶת שֵׁשׁ וְאַבְנֵט תַּעֲשֶׂה מַעֲשֵׂה רֹקֵם׃ וְלִבְנֵי
אַהֲרֹן תַּעֲשֶׂה כֻתֳּנֹת וְעָשִׂיתָ לָהֶם אַבְנֵטִים וּמִגְבָּעוֹת תַּעֲשֶׂה לָהֶם
מא לְכָבוֹד וּלְתִפְאָרֶת׃ וְהִלְבַּשְׁתָּ אֹתָם אֶת־אַהֲרֹן אָחִיךָ וְאֶת־בָּנָיו אִתּוֹ

אונקלוס

לה וִיהֵי עַל אַהֲרֹן לְשַׁמָּשָׁא, וְיִשְׁתְּמַע קָלֵיהּ, בְּמֵיעֲלֵיהּ לְקֻדְשָׁא, לִקְדָם
יְיָ, וּבְמִפְּקֵיהּ וְלָא יְמוּת: לו וְתַעֲבֵיד צִיצָא דִּדְהַב דְּכֵי, וְתִגְלוֹף עֲלוֹהִי
כְּתָב מְפָרַשׁ, קֹדֶשׁ לַייָ: לז וּתְשַׁוֵּי יָתֵיהּ עַל חוּטָא דִּתְכִילְתָּא, וִיהֵי עַל
מַצְנַפְתָּא, לָקֳבֵיל אַפֵּי מַצְנַפְתָּא יְהֵי: לח וִיהֵי עַל בֵּית עֵינוֹהִי דְּאַהֲרֹן,
וְיִטּוֹל אַהֲרֹן יָת עֲוָיַת קֻדְשַׁיָּא, דִּיקַדְּשׁוּן בְּנֵי יִשְׂרָאֵל, לְכָל מַתְּנַת
קֻדְשֵׁיהוֹן, וִיהֵי עַל בֵּית עֵינוֹהִי תְּדִירָא, לְרַעֲוָא לְהוֹן קֳדָם יְיָ: לט וּתְרַמֵּיץ
כִּתּוּנָא דְּבוּצָא, וְתַעֲבֵיד מַצְנַפְתָּא דְּבוּצָא, וְהִמְיָן תַּעֲבֵיד עוֹבַד צַיָּר:
מ וְלִבְנֵי אַהֲרֹן תַּעֲבֵיד כִּתּוּנִין, וְתַעֲבֵיד לְהוֹן הִמְיָנִין, וְקוֹבְעִין תַּעֲבֵיד לְהוֹן,
לִיקָר וּלְתֻשְׁבְּחָא: מא וְתַלְבֵּישׁ יָתְהוֹן יָת אַהֲרֹן אֲחוּךְ, וְיָת בְּנוֹהִי עִמֵּיהּ,

There were choirs of Levites singing psalms. Beauty speaks to emotion and emotion to the soul, lifting us in ways reason cannot do to heights of love and awe, taking us above the narrow confines of the self into the circle at whose center is God.

The Sanctuary and priesthood introduced into Jewish life the ethic of *kedusha*, holiness, which strengthened the values of loyalty, respect, and the sacred by creating an environment of reverence, the humility felt by the people once they had these symbols of the Divine Presence in their midst. As Rambam wrote in a famous passage in *Guide for the Perplexed* (III:51), we do not act when in the presence of a king as we do when we are merely in the company of friends or family. In the Sanctuary people sensed they were in the presence of the King.

Reverence gives power to ritual, ceremony, social conventions, and civilities. It helps transform autonomous

apart: the prophetic and priestly traditions, one with its emphasis on the heart, the other with its fixed forms.

Moshe was the lonely man of faith, wrestling with God. Aharon was closer to the community, ministering to God on their behalf. Our heritage derives from both. The priestly dimension of worship – collective, structured, never changing – is the other hemisphere of the Jewish mind, the voice of eternity in the midst of time.

28:35 **וְלֹא יָמוּת** *So that he will not die* – Transgression of this dress code would condemn the priest to death. A deep solemnity surrounds the beauty. The service of the Sanctuary performed by the priests in their vestments worn *lekhavod*, "for glory," established the principle of respect. That explains, as we have noted, the presence of the aesthetic dimension of the service of the Sanctuary. It had beauty, gravitas, and majesty. In the time of the Temple it had music.

42 ordain, and consecrate them to serve Me as priests. Make them linen trousers
43 to cover their nakedness, reaching from waist to thigh. They must be worn by
Aharon and his sons whenever they enter the Tent of Meeting or approach the
altar to minister in the Sanctuary so that they do not incur guilt and die. This
29 1 shall be a law for Aharon and his descendants for all time. This is what REVI'I
you must do to consecrate them to serve Me as priests. Take a young bull, two
2 unblemished rams, and unleavened bread, unleavened loaves mixed with oil,
3 and unleavened wafers brushed with oil – all made of fine wheat flour. Place
these in a basket and bring them in the basket together with the young bull and
4 two rams. Bring Aharon and his sons to the entrance of the Tent of Meeting,
5 and you shall wash them with water. Then take the vestments and dress Aharon
in the tunic, the robe of the ephod, the ephod itself, and the breast piece. Fasten

רש״י

וּמָשַׁחְתָּ אֹתָם. אֶת אַהֲרֹן וְאֶת בָּנָיו בְּשֶׁמֶן הַמִּשְׁחָה: **וּמִלֵּאתָ אֶת יָדָם.** כָּל מִלּוּי יָדַיִם לְשׁוֹן חִנּוּךְ, כְּשֶׁהוּא נִכְנָס לְדָבָר לִהְיוֹת מֻחְזָק בּוֹ מֵאוֹתוֹ יוֹם וָהָלְאָה הוּא, וּבִלְשׁוֹן לַעַז כְּשֶׁמְּמַנִּין אָדָם עַל פְּקֻדַּת דָּבָר, נוֹתֵן הַשַּׁלִּיט בְּיָדוֹ בֵּית יָד שֶׁל עוֹר שֶׁקּוֹרִין גואנ״ט, וְעַל יָדוֹ הוּא מַחֲזִיקוֹ בַּדָּבָר, וְקוֹרִין לְאוֹתָהּ מְסִירָה רוויסטי״ר, וְהוּא מִלּוּי יָדַיִם:

מב **וַעֲשֵׂה לָהֶם.** לְאַהֲרֹן וּלְבָנָיו: **מִכְנְסֵי בָד.** הֲרֵי שְׁמוֹנָה בְגָדִים לְכֹהֵן גָּדוֹל וְאַרְבָּעָה לְכֹהֵן הֶדְיוֹט:

מג **וְהָיוּ.** כָּל הַבְּגָדִים הָאֵלֶּה, ״עַל אַהֲרֹן״ הָרְאוּיִים לוֹ, ״וְעַל בָּנָיו״ הָאֲמוּרִים בָּהֶם: **בְּבֹאָם אֶל אֹהֶל מוֹעֵד.** לַהֵיכָל, וְכֵן לַמִּשְׁכָּן: **וָמֵתוּ.** הָא לָמַדְתָּ שֶׁהַמְשַׁמֵּשׁ מְחֻסַּר בְּגָדִים – בְּמִיתָה: **חֻקַּת עוֹלָם לוֹ.** כָּל מָקוֹם שֶׁנֶּאֱמַר: ׳חֻקָּה׳ לְעַכֵּב:

כט א **לְקַח.** כְּמוֹ קַח. וּשְׁתֵּי גְזָרוֹת הֵן, אַחַת שֶׁל קִיחָה וְאַחַת שֶׁל לְקִיחָה, וְלָהֶן פִּתְרוֹן אֶחָד: **פַּר אֶחָד.** לְכַפֵּר עַל מַעֲשֵׂה הָעֵגֶל שֶׁהוּא פָּר:

ב **וְלֶחֶם מַצּוֹת וְחַלֹּת מַצֹּת... וּרְקִיקֵי מַצּוֹת.** הֲרֵי אֵלּוּ שְׁלֹשָׁה מִינִין: רְבוּכָה וְחַלּוֹת וּרְקִיקִין. ״לֶחֶם מַצּוֹת״ הִיא הַקְּרוּיָה לְמַטָּה בָּעִנְיָן: ״חַלַּת לֶחֶם שֶׁמֶן״ (להלן פסוק כג), עַל שֵׁם שֶׁנּוֹתֵן שֶׁמֶן בָּרְבוּכָה כְּנֶגֶד הַחַלּוֹת וְהָרְקִיקִין. וְכָל הַמִּינִין בָּאִים עֶשֶׂר עֶשֶׂר חַלּוֹת: **בְּלוּלֹת בַּשֶּׁמֶן.** כְּשֶׁהֵן קֶמַח יוֹצֵק בָּהֶן שֶׁמֶן וּבוֹלְלָן: **מְשֻׁחִים בַּשָּׁמֶן.** אַחַר אֲפִיָּתָן מוֹשְׁחָן כְּמִין כ״י, כָּ״ף יְוָנִית, שֶׁהִיא עֲשׂוּיָה כְּנוּ״ן שֶׁלָּנוּ:

ג **וְהִקְרַבְתָּ אֹתָם.** אֶל חֲצַר הַמִּשְׁכָּן בְּיוֹם הֲקָמָתוֹ:

ד **וְרָחַצְתָּ.** טְבִילַת כָּל הַגּוּף:

ה **וְאָפַדְתָּ.** קַשֵּׁט וְתַקֵּן הַחֲגוֹרָה וְהַסִּינָר סְבִיבוֹתָיו:

The story of Aharon and Moshe, the fifth chapter in the biblical story of brotherhood, is where, finally, fraternity reaches the heights. And that surely is the meaning of Psalm 133, with its explicit reference to Aharon and his sacred garments: "How good and pleasant it is when brothers dwell together – like fragrant oil on the head flowing down onto the beard, Aharon's beard that flows down over the collar of his robes" (Ps. 133:1–2). It was thanks to Aharon, and the honor he showed Moshe, that at last brothers learned to live together in unity.

the relationship between Moshe and Aharon. Here, for the first time, there is no hint of sibling rivalry (some develops later in Numbers 12, but is resolved by Moshe's humility). The brothers work together from the very outset of the mission to lead the Israelites to freedom. They address the people together. They stand together when confronting Pharaoh. They perform signs and wonders together. They share leadership in the wilderness together. For the first time, brothers *function* as a team, with different gifts, different talents, different roles, but without hostility, each complementing the other.

מב וּמָשַׁחְתָּ אֹתָם וּמִלֵּאתָ אֶת־יָדָם וְקִדַּשְׁתָּ אֹתָם וְכִהֲנוּ־לִי׃ וַעֲשֵׂה לָהֶם
מג מִכְנְסֵי־בָד לְכַסּוֹת בְּשַׂר עֶרְוָה מִמָּתְנַיִם וְעַד־יְרֵכַיִם יִהְיוּ׃ וְהָיוּ עַל־
אַהֲרֹן וְעַל־בָּנָיו בְּבֹאָם ׀ אֶל־אֹהֶל מוֹעֵד אוֹ בְגִשְׁתָּם אֶל־הַמִּזְבֵּחַ
לְשָׁרֵת בַּקֹּדֶשׁ וְלֹא־יִשְׂאוּ עָוֹן וָמֵתוּ חֻקַּת עוֹלָם לוֹ וּלְזַרְעוֹ
כט א אַחֲרָיו׃ וְזֶה הַדָּבָר אֲשֶׁר תַּעֲשֶׂה לָהֶם לְקַדֵּשׁ אֹתָם לְכַהֵן כב רביעי
ב לִי לְקַח פַּר אֶחָד בֶּן־בָּקָר וְאֵילִם שְׁנַיִם תְּמִימִם׃ וְלֶחֶם מַצּוֹת וְחַלֹּת
מַצֹּת בְּלוּלֹת בַּשֶּׁמֶן וּרְקִיקֵי מַצּוֹת מְשֻׁחִים בַּשָּׁמֶן סֹלֶת חִטִּים תַּעֲשֶׂה
ג אֹתָם׃ וְנָתַתָּ אוֹתָם עַל־סַל אֶחָד וְהִקְרַבְתָּ אֹתָם בַּסָּל וְאֶת־הַפָּר
ד וְאֵת שְׁנֵי הָאֵילִם׃ וְאֶת־אַהֲרֹן וְאֶת־בָּנָיו תַּקְרִיב אֶל־פֶּתַח אֹהֶל מוֹעֵד
ה וְרָחַצְתָּ אֹתָם בַּמָּיִם׃ וְלָקַחְתָּ אֶת־הַבְּגָדִים וְהִלְבַּשְׁתָּ אֶת־אַהֲרֹן אֶת־
הַכֻּתֹּנֶת וְאֵת מְעִיל הָאֵפֹד וְאֶת־הָאֵפֹד וְאֶת־הַחֹשֶׁן וְאָפַדְתָּ לוֹ בְּחֵשֶׁב

אונקלוס

ותרבי יתהון, ותקריב ית קורבנהון, ותקדיש יתהון וישמשון קדמי: מב ועביד להון מכנסין דבוץ, לכסאה בסר עריא, מחרצין ועד ירכן יהון: מג ויהון על אהרן ועל בנוהי, במיעלהון למשכן זמנא, או במקרבהון למדבחא לשמשא בקודשא, ולא יקבלון חובא ולא ימותון, קים עלם, ליה ולבנוהי בתרוהי: כט א ודין פתגמא, דתעביד להון, לקדשא יתהון לשמשא קדמי, סב, תור חד בר תורי, ודכרין תרין שלמין: ב ולחים פטיר, וגריצן פטירן דפילן במשח, ואספוגין פטירין דמשיחין במשח, סולת דחטין תעביד יתהון: ג ותתין יתהון על סלא חד, ותקריב יתהון בסלא, וית תורא, וית תרין דכרין: ד וית אהרן וית בנוהי תקריב, לתרע משכן זמנא, ותסחי יתהון במיא: ה ותסב ית לבושיא, ותלביש ית אהרן ית כתונא, וית מעיל איפודא, וית איפודא וית חושנא, ותתקין ליה, בהמין

28:43 חֻקַּת עוֹלָם לוֹ וּלְזַרְעוֹ אַחֲרָיו *A law for Aharon and his descendants for all time* – One of the recurring themes of Genesis is sibling rivalry. This story is told, at ever-increasing length, four times: between Kayin and Hevel, Yitzḥak and Yishmael, Yaakov and Esav, and Yosef and his brothers.

There is an identifiable pattern to this set of narratives, best seen in the way each ends. The story of Kayin and Hevel ends with murder, fratricide. Yitzḥak and Yishmael – though they grow up apart – are seen together at Avraham's funeral. Evidently there had been a reconciliation, though this is told between the lines (and spelled out in Midrash), not directly in the text. Yaakov and Esav meet, embrace, and go their separate ways. Yosef and his brothers are reconciled and live together in peace, Yosef providing them with food, land, and protection. Genesis is telling us a story of great consequence. Fraternity – one of the key words of the French Revolution – is not simple or straightforward. It is often fraught with conflict and contention. Yet slowly, brothers can learn that there is another way.

But it is not the end of the story. There is a fifth chapter,

6 the ephod on him by its woven waistband. Put the miter on his head and on the
7 miter place the sacred diadem. Take the anointing oil, pour it on his head, and
8 anoint him. Then bring his sons forward and dress them with the tunics. Gird
9 Aharon and his sons with the sashes and fasten their headdresses. The priesthood
shall be theirs as a law for all time. Thus you shall ordain Aharon and his sons.
10 Then bring the young bull in front of the Tent of Meeting, and have Aharon and
11 his sons lay their hands on its head. Slaughter the bull before the LORD at the
12 entrance of the Tent of Meeting. Take some of the bull's blood and put it on the
horns of the altar with your finger. Pour out the rest of the blood at the base of the
13 altar. Take all the fat that covers the entrails, the diaphragm of the liver, and the
14 two kidneys with the fat around them, and burn them on the altar. Burn the bull's
15 flesh, its hide, and its waste outside the camp; it is a purification offering. Then
take one of the rams and have Aharon and his sons lay their hands upon its head,
16 then slaughter it; let them take its blood and sprinkle it on all the sides of the altar.
17 Cut the ram into pieces, wash its entrails and legs, and put them with its pieces
18 and its head. Burn the entire ram on the altar. It is a burnt offering to the LORD, a
19 pleasing aroma, a fire offering to the LORD. Then take the second ram, and have HAMISHI
20 Aharon and his sons lay their hands on its head. Slaughter the ram, take some of

אונקלוס

אֵיפוֹדָא: ו וּתְשַׁוֵּי מַצְנַפְתָּא עַל רֵישֵׁיהּ, וְתִתֵּין, יָת כְּלִילָא דְקֻדְשָׁא עַל מַצְנַפְתָּא: ז וְתִסַּב יָת מִשְׁחָא דִרְבוּתָא, וּתְרִיק עַל רֵישֵׁיהּ, וּתְרַבֵּי יָתֵיהּ: ח וְיָת בְּנוֹהִי תְּקָרֵיב, וְתַלְבֵּישִׁנּוּן כִּתּוּנִין: ט וּתְזָרֵיז יָתְהוֹן הֶמְיָנִין אַהֲרֹן וּבְנוֹהִי, וְתַתְקֵין לְהוֹן קוֹבְעִין, וּתְהֵי לְהוֹן, כְּהֻנְּתָא

רש״י

ו נֵזֶר הַקֹּדֶשׁ. זֶה הַצִּיץ: עַל הַמִּצְנֶפֶת. כְּמוֹ שֶׁפֵּרַשְׁתִּי לְמַעְלָה (לעיל כח, לז), עַל יְדֵי הַפְּתִיל הָאֶמְצָעִי וּשְׁנֵי פְתִילִין שֶׁבְּרֹאשׁוֹ הַקְּשׁוּרִין שְׁלָשְׁתָּן מֵאֲחוֹרֵי הָעֹרֶף, הוּא נוֹתְנוֹ עַל הַמִּצְנֶפֶת כְּמִין כּוֹבַע:

ז וּמָשַׁחְתָּ אֹתוֹ. אַף מְשִׁיחָה זוֹ כְּמִין כ״י, נוֹתֵן שֶׁמֶן עַל רֹאשׁוֹ וּבֵין רִיסֵי עֵינָיו וּמְחַבְּרָן בְּאֶצְבָּעוֹ:

ט וְהָיְתָה לָהֶם. מִלּוּי יָדַיִם זֶה לִכְהֻנַּת עוֹלָם: וּמִלֵּאתָ. עַל יְדֵי הַדְּבָרִים הָאֵלֶּה: יַד אַהֲרֹן וְיַד בָּנָיו. בְּמִלּוּי וּפְקֻדַּת הַכְּהֻנָּה:

יא פֶּתַח אֹהֶל מוֹעֵד. בַּחֲצַר הַמִּשְׁכָּן שֶׁלִּפְנֵי הַפֶּתַח:

יב עַל קַרְנֹת. לְמַעְלָה בַּקְּרָנוֹת מַמָּשׁ: וְאֶת כָּל הַדָּם. שְׁיָרֵי הַדָּם: אֶל יְסוֹד הַמִּזְבֵּחַ. כְּמִין בְּלִיטַת בֵּית קִבּוּל עָשׂוּי לוֹ סָבִיב סָבִיב לְאַחַר שֶׁעָלָה חַמָּה מִן הָאָרֶץ:

יג הַחֵלֶב הַמְכַסֶּה אֶת הַקֶּרֶב. הוּא הַקְּרוּם שֶׁעַל הַכָּרֵס שֶׁקּוֹרִין טיל״א: וְאֵת הַיֹּתֶרֶת. הוּא טַרְפְּשָׁא דְּכַבְדָּא שֶׁקּוֹרִין איבל״ש: עַל הַכָּבֵד. אַף מִן הַכָּבֵד יִטֹּל עִמָּהּ:

יד תִּשְׂרֹף בָּאֵשׁ. לֹא מָצִינוּ חַטָּאת חִיצוֹנָה נִשְׂרֶפֶת אֶלָּא זוֹ:

טז וְזָרַקְתָּ. בִּכְלִי, אוֹחֵז בַּמִּזְרָק וְזוֹרֵק כְּנֶגֶד הַקֶּרֶן, כְּדֵי שֶׁיֵּרָאֶה לְכָאן וּלְכָאן. וְאֵין קָרְבָּן טָעוּן מַתָּנָה בְּאֶצְבַּע אֶלָּא חַטָּאת בִּלְבַד, אֲבָל שְׁאָר זְבָחִים אֵינָן טְעוּנִין קֶרֶן וְלֹא אֶצְבַּע, שֶׁמַּתַּן דָּמָם מֵחֲצִי הַמִּזְבֵּחַ וּלְמַטָּה, וְאֵינוֹ עוֹלֶה בַּכֶּבֶשׁ אֶלָּא עוֹמֵד בָּאָרֶץ וְזוֹרֵק: סָבִיב. כָּךְ מְפֹרָשׁ בִּשְׁחִיטַת קָדָשִׁים (זבחים נג ע״ב), שֶׁאֵין ״סָבִיב״ אֶלָּא שְׁתֵּי מַתָּנוֹת שֶׁהֵן אַרְבַּע, הָאַחַת בְּקֶרֶן זָוִית זוֹ וְהָאַחַת בְּשֶׁכְּנֶגְדָּהּ בַּאֲלַכְסוֹן, וְכָל מַתָּנָה נִרְאֵית בִּשְׁנֵי צִדֵּי הַקֶּרֶן אֵילָךְ וְאֵילָךְ, נִמְצָא הַדָּם נָתוּן בְּאַרְבַּע רוּחוֹת סָבִיב, לְכָךְ קָרוּי סָבִיב:

יז עַל נְתָחָיו. עִם נְתָחָיו, מוּסָף עַל שְׁאָר הַנְּתָחִים:

יח רֵיחַ נִיחוֹחַ. נַחַת רוּחַ לְפָנַי שֶׁאָמַרְתִּי וְנַעֲשָׂה רְצוֹנִי: אִשֶּׁה. לְשׁוֹן אֵשׁ, וְהִיא הַקְטָרַת אֵבָרִים שֶׁעַל הָאֵשׁ:

כ תְּנוּךְ. הוּא הַסְּחוּס הָאֶמְצָעִי שֶׁבְּתוֹךְ הָאֹזֶן שֶׁקּוֹרִין טנררו״ס:

ו הָאֵפֹד: וְשַׂמְתָּ הַמִּצְנֶפֶת עַל־רֹאשׁוֹ וְנָתַתָּ אֶת־נֵזֶר הַקֹּדֶשׁ עַל־
ז הַמִּצְנָפֶת: וְלָקַחְתָּ אֶת־שֶׁמֶן הַמִּשְׁחָה וְיָצַקְתָּ עַל־רֹאשׁוֹ וּמָשַׁחְתָּ
ח ט אֹתוֹ: וְאֶת־בָּנָיו תַּקְרִיב וְהִלְבַּשְׁתָּם כֻּתֳּנֹת: וְחָגַרְתָּ אֹתָם אַבְנֵט אַהֲרֹן
וּבָנָיו וְחָבַשְׁתָּ לָהֶם מִגְבָּעֹת וְהָיְתָה לָהֶם כְּהֻנָּה לְחֻקַּת עוֹלָם וּמִלֵּאתָ
י יַד־אַהֲרֹן וְיַד־בָּנָיו: וְהִקְרַבְתָּ אֶת־הַפָּר לִפְנֵי אֹהֶל מוֹעֵד וְסָמַךְ אַהֲרֹן
יא וּבָנָיו אֶת־יְדֵיהֶם עַל־רֹאשׁ הַפָּר: וְשָׁחַטְתָּ אֶת־הַפָּר לִפְנֵי יְהוָה פֶּתַח
יב אֹהֶל מוֹעֵד: וְלָקַחְתָּ מִדַּם הַפָּר וְנָתַתָּה עַל־קַרְנֹת הַמִּזְבֵּחַ בְּאֶצְבָּעֶךָ
יג וְאֶת־כָּל־הַדָּם תִּשְׁפֹּךְ אֶל־יְסוֹד הַמִּזְבֵּחַ: וְלָקַחְתָּ אֶת־כָּל־הַחֵלֶב
הַמְכַסֶּה אֶת־הַקֶּרֶב וְאֵת הַיֹּתֶרֶת עַל־הַכָּבֵד וְאֵת שְׁתֵּי הַכְּלָיֹת וְאֶת־
יד הַחֵלֶב אֲשֶׁר עֲלֵיהֶן וְהִקְטַרְתָּ הַמִּזְבֵּחָה: וְאֶת־בְּשַׂר הַפָּר וְאֶת־עֹרוֹ
טו וְאֶת־פִּרְשׁוֹ תִּשְׂרֹף בָּאֵשׁ מִחוּץ לַמַּחֲנֶה חַטָּאת הוּא: וְאֶת־הָאַיִל
טז הָאֶחָד תִּקָּח וְסָמְכוּ אַהֲרֹן וּבָנָיו אֶת־יְדֵיהֶם עַל־רֹאשׁ הָאָיִל: וְשָׁחַטְתָּ
יז אֶת־הָאָיִל וְלָקַחְתָּ אֶת־דָּמוֹ וְזָרַקְתָּ עַל־הַמִּזְבֵּחַ סָבִיב: וְאֶת־הָאַיִל
תְּנַתֵּחַ לִנְתָחָיו וְרָחַצְתָּ קִרְבּוֹ וּכְרָעָיו וְנָתַתָּ עַל־נְתָחָיו וְעַל־רֹאשׁוֹ:
יח וְהִקְטַרְתָּ אֶת־כָּל־הָאַיִל הַמִּזְבֵּחָה עֹלָה הוּא לַיהוָה רֵיחַ נִיחוֹחַ אִשֶּׁה
יט לַיהוָה הוּא: וְלָקַחְתָּ אֵת הָאַיִל הַשֵּׁנִי וְסָמַךְ אַהֲרֹן וּבָנָיו אֶת־יְדֵיהֶם חמישי
כ עַל־רֹאשׁ הָאָיִל: וְשָׁחַטְתָּ אֶת־הָאַיִל וְלָקַחְתָּ מִדָּמוֹ וְנָתַתָּה עַל־תְּנוּךְ

אונקלוס

לִקְיָם עָלַם, וּתְקָרֵיב קֻרְבָּנָא דְּאַהֲרֹן וְקֻרְבָּנָא דִּבְנוֹהִי: י וּתְקָרֵיב יָת תּוֹרָא, לִקְדָם מַשְׁכַּן זִמְנָא, וְיִסְמוֹךְ אַהֲרֹן וּבְנוֹהִי, יָת יְדֵיהוֹן עַל רֵישׁ תּוֹרָא: יא וְתִכּוֹס יָת תּוֹרָא קֳדָם יְיָ, בִּתְרַע מַשְׁכַּן זִמְנָא: יב וְתִסַּב מִדְּמָא דְתוֹרָא, וְתִתֵּין, עַל קַרְנַת מַדְבְּחָא בְּאֶצְבְּעָךְ, וְיָת כָּל דְּמָא תִּשְׁפּוֹךְ, לִיסוֹדָא דְמַדְבְּחָא: יג וְתִסַּב, יָת כָּל תַּרְבָּא דְּחָפֵי יָת גַּוָּא, וְיָת חֲצַרָא דְּעַל כַּבְדָּא, וְיָת תַּרְתֵּין כּוּלְיָן, וְיָת תַּרְבָּא דַּעֲלֵיהוֹן, וְתַסֵּיק לְמַדְבְּחָא: יד וְיָת בְּסַר תּוֹרָא וְיָת מַשְׁכֵּיהּ וְיָת אֻכְלֵיהּ, תּוֹקֵיד בְּנוּרָא, מִבָּרָא לְמַשְׁרִיתָא, חַטָּתָא הוּא: טו וְיָת דִּכְרָא חַד תִּסַּב, וְיִסְמְכוּן, אַהֲרֹן וּבְנוֹהִי, יָת יְדֵיהוֹן עַל רֵישׁ דִּכְרָא: טז וְתִכּוֹס יָת דִּכְרָא, וְתִסַּב יָת דְּמֵיהּ, וְתִזְרוֹק עַל מַדְבְּחָא סְחוֹר סְחוֹר: יז וְיָת דִּכְרָא, תְּפַלֵּיג לְאֶבְרוֹהִי, וּתְחַלֵּיל גַּוֵּיהּ וּכְרָעוֹהִי, וְתִתֵּין עַל אֶבְרוֹהִי וְעַל רֵישֵׁיהּ: יח וְתַסֵּיק יָת כָּל דִּכְרָא לְמַדְבְּחָא, עֲלָתָא הוּא קֳדָם יְיָ, לְאִתְקַבָּלָא בְרַעֲוָא, קֻרְבָּנָא קֳדָם יְיָ הוּא: יט וְתִסַּב, יָת דִּכְרָא תִּנְיָנָא, וְיִסְמוֹךְ אַהֲרֹן וּבְנוֹהִי, יָת יְדֵיהוֹן עַל רֵישׁ דִּכְרָא: כ וְתִכּוֹס יָת דִּכְרָא, וְתִסַּב מִדְּמֵיהּ וְתִתֵּין, עַל רוּם

its blood and put it on the ridges of the right ears of Aharon and his sons, and on
the thumbs of their right hands and on the big toes of their right feet. Sprinkle
21 the rest of the blood on the sides of the altar. Collect some of the blood on the
altar and some of the anointing oil and sprinkle it on Aharon and his vestments,
and on his sons and his sons' vestments. Then he, and his sons with him, and
22 their vestments, will be consecrated. From the ram take its fat parts – the broad
tail, the fat that covers the entrails, the diaphragm of the liver, and the two
kidneys with the fat on them – and the right thigh, for this is the ram of
23 ordination. From the basket of unleavened bread before the Lord, take one
24 loaf of bread, one loaf of oil bread, and one wafer. Place all of these on the
palms of Aharon and his sons, and have them wave them as a wave offering
25 before the Lord. Then take them from their hands and burn them on the altar
with the burnt offering, for a pleasing aroma before the Lord. It is a fire offering
26 to the Lord. Take the breast of Aharon's ram of ordination and wave it as a
27 wave offering before the Lord; it shall be your portion. From Aharon and his

רש"י

בֹּהֶן יָדָם. הַגּוּדָל, וּבַפֶּרֶק הָאֶמְצָעִי:

כב **הַחֵלֶב.** זֶה חֵלֶב הַדַּקִּים אוֹ הַקֵּבָה: **וְהָאַלְיָה.** מִן הַכְּלָיוֹת וּלְמַטָּה, כְּמוֹ שֶׁמְּפֹרָשׁ בְּ'וַיִּקְרָא' (ג, ט), שֶׁנֶּאֱמַר: "לְעֻמַּת הֶעָצֶה יְסִירֶנָּה", מָקוֹם שֶׁהַכְּלָיוֹת יוֹעֲצוֹת. וּבְאֵמוּרֵי הַפָּר לֹא נֶאֱמַר אַלְיָה, שֶׁאֵין אַלְיָה קְרֵבָה אֶלָּא בְּכֶבֶשׂ וְכִבְשָׂה וְאַיִל, אֲבָל שׁוֹר וָעֵז אֵין טְעוּנִים אַלְיָה: **וְאֵת שׁוֹק הַיָּמִין.** לֹא מָצִינוּ הַקְטָרָה בְּשׁוֹק הַיָּמִין עִם הָאֵמוּרִים אֶלָּא זוֹ בִּלְבַד: **כִּי אֵיל מִלֻּאִים הוּא.** שְׁלָמִים, לְשׁוֹן שְׁלֵמוּת, שֶׁמַּשְׁלִים בַּכֹּל. מַגִּיד הַכָּתוּב שֶׁהַמִּלּוּאִים שְׁלָמִים, שָׁלוֹם לַמִּזְבֵּחַ וּלְעוֹבֵד הָעֲבוֹדָה וְלַבְּעָלִים, לְכָךְ אֲנִי מַצְרִיכוֹ הֶחָזֶה לִהְיוֹת לְעוֹבֵד הָעֲבוֹדָה לְמָנָה, וְזֶהוּ מֹשֶׁה שֶׁשִּׁמֵּשׁ בַּמִּלּוּאִים, וְהַשְּׁאָר אָכְלוּ אַהֲרֹן וּבָנָיו שֶׁהֵם בְּעָלִים כַּמְפֹרָשׁ בָּעִנְיָן:

כג **וְכִכַּר לֶחֶם.** מִן הַחַלּוֹת: **וְחַלַּת לֶחֶם שֶׁמֶן.** מִמִּין הָרְבוּכָה: **וְרָקִיק.** מִן הָרְקִיקִין, אֶחָד מֵעֲשָׂרָה שֶׁבְּכָל מִין וָמִין. וְלֹא מָצִינוּ תְּרוּמַת לֶחֶם הַבָּא עִם זֶבַח נִקְטֶרֶת אֶלָּא זוֹ בִּלְבַד, שֶׁתְּרוּמַת לַחְמֵי תוֹדָה וְאֵיל נָזִיר נְתוּנָה לַכֹּהֲנִים עִם חָזֶה וָשׁוֹק, וּמִזֶּה לֹא הָיָה לְמֹשֶׁה לְמָנָה אֶלָּא חָזֶה בִּלְבַד:

כד **עַל כַּפֵּי אַהֲרֹן... וְהֵנַפְתָּ.** שְׁנֵיהֶם עֲסוּקִין בַּתְּנוּפָה, הַבְּעָלִים וְהַכֹּהֵן; הָא כֵּיצַד? כֹּהֵן מַנִּיחַ יָדוֹ תַּחַת יַד הַבְּעָלִים וּמֵנִיף, וּבָזֶה הָיוּ אַהֲרֹן וּבָנָיו בְּעָלִים וּמֹשֶׁה כֹּהֵן: **תְּנוּפָה.** מוֹלִיךְ וּמֵבִיא, לְמִי שֶׁאַרְבַּע רוּחוֹת הָעוֹלָם שֶׁלּוֹ, וּתְנוּפָה מְעַכֶּבֶת וּמְבַטֶּלֶת פֻּרְעָנוּת רוּחוֹת רָעוֹת. וּמַעֲלֶה וּמוֹרִיד, לְמִי שֶׁהַשָּׁמַיִם וְהָאָרֶץ שֶׁלּוֹ, וּמְעַכֶּבֶת טְלָלִים רָעִים:

כה **עַל הָעֹלָה.** עַל הָאַיִל הָרִאשׁוֹן שֶׁהֶעֱלֵיתָ עוֹלָה: **לְרֵיחַ נִיחוֹחַ.** לְנַחַת רוּחַ לְמִי שֶׁאָמַר וְנַעֲשָׂה רְצוֹנוֹ: **אִשֶּׁה.** לָאֵשׁ נִתָּן: **לַה'.** לִשְׁמוֹ שֶׁל מָקוֹם:

כז-כח **וְקִדַּשְׁתָּ אֵת חֲזֵה הַתְּנוּפָה וְאֵת שׁוֹק הַתְּרוּמָה וְגוֹ'.** קַדְּשֵׁם לְדוֹרוֹת לִהְיוֹת נוֹהֶגֶת תְּרוּמָתָם וַהֲנָפָתָם בְּחָזֶה וָשׁוֹק שֶׁל שְׁלָמִים, אֲבָל

In this respect, religion is like being married to the Divine Presence. A person may experience long stretches of loyalty between the moments of high passion. Spirituality is the poetry of the soul. Religion is the prose. If they come together, however, as they did in the choreography of the wave offering, we may touch upon something of the priests' experience of a life "upraised" and consecrated to God.

Religion is the behavior we adopt when we express our sense of belonging to a group who, at key points in its history, encountered the Divine. You can be spiritual without being religious. You can be religious without being spiritual. It is almost like the distinction between love and marriage. Love is an emotion. Marriage is an institution. They are linked, but they are not the same.

אֹזֶן אַהֲרֹן וְעַל־תְּנוּךְ אֹזֶן בָּנָיו הַיְמָנִית וְעַל־בֹּהֶן יָדָם הַיְמָנִית וְעַל־
כא בֹּהֶן רַגְלָם הַיְמָנִית וְזָרַקְתָּ אֶת־הַדָּם עַל־הַמִּזְבֵּחַ סָבִיב: וְלָקַחְתָּ מִן־
הַדָּם אֲשֶׁר עַל־הַמִּזְבֵּחַ וּמִשֶּׁמֶן הַמִּשְׁחָה וְהִזֵּיתָ עַל־אַהֲרֹן וְעַל־בְּגָדָיו
וְעַל־בָּנָיו וְעַל־בִּגְדֵי בָנָיו אִתּוֹ וְקָדַשׁ הוּא וּבְגָדָיו וּבָנָיו וּבִגְדֵי בָנָיו
כב אִתּוֹ: וְלָקַחְתָּ מִן־הָאַיִל הַחֵלֶב וְהָאַלְיָה וְאֶת־הַחֵלֶב ׀ הַמְכַסֶּה אֶת־
הַקֶּרֶב וְאֵת יֹתֶרֶת הַכָּבֵד וְאֵת ׀ שְׁתֵּי הַכְּלָיֹת וְאֶת־הַחֵלֶב אֲשֶׁר עֲלֵיהֶן
כג וְאֵת שׁוֹק הַיָּמִין כִּי אֵיל מִלֻּאִים הוּא: וְכִכַּר לֶחֶם אַחַת וְחַלַּת לֶחֶם
כד שֶׁמֶן אַחַת וְרָקִיק אֶחָד מִסַּל הַמַּצּוֹת אֲשֶׁר לִפְנֵי יְהוָה: וְשַׂמְתָּ הַכֹּל
כה עַל כַּפֵּי אַהֲרֹן וְעַל כַּפֵּי בָנָיו וְהֵנַפְתָּ אֹתָם תְּנוּפָה לִפְנֵי יְהוָה: וְלָקַחְתָּ
אֹתָם מִיָּדָם וְהִקְטַרְתָּ הַמִּזְבֵּחָה עַל־הָעֹלָה לְרֵיחַ נִיחוֹחַ לִפְנֵי יְהוָה
כו אִשֶּׁה הוּא לַיהוָה: וְלָקַחְתָּ אֶת־הֶחָזֶה מֵאֵיל הַמִּלֻּאִים אֲשֶׁר לְאַהֲרֹן
כז וְהֵנַפְתָּ אֹתוֹ תְּנוּפָה לִפְנֵי יְהוָה וְהָיָה לְךָ לְמָנָה: וְקִדַּשְׁתָּ אֵת ׀ חֲזֵה

אונקלוס

אֻדְנָא דְאַהֲרֹן, וְעַל רוּם אֻדְנָא דִבְנוֹהִי דְיַמִּינָא, וְעַל אִלְיוֹן יַדְהוֹן דְיַמִּינָא, וְעַל אִלְיוֹן רַגְלְהוֹן דְיַמִּינָא, וְתִזְרוֹק יָת דְמָא, עַל מַדְבְּחָא סְחוֹר סְחוֹר: כא וְתִסַּב, מִן דְמָא דְעַל מַדְבְּחָא וּמִמִּשְׁחָא דִרְבוּתָא, וְתַדֵּי עַל אַהֲרֹן וְעַל לְבוּשׁוֹהִי, וְעַל בְּנוֹהִי, וְעַל לְבוּשֵׁי בְנוֹהִי עִמֵּיהּ, וְיִתְקַדַּשׁ הוּא וּלְבוּשׁוֹהִי, וּבְנוֹהִי, וּלְבוּשֵׁי בְנוֹהִי עִמֵּיהּ: כב וְתִסַּב מִן דִּכְרָא, תַּרְבָּא וְאַלִּיתָא, וְיָת תַּרְבָּא דְחָפֵי יָת גַּוָּא, וְיָת חֲצַר כַּבְדָא וְיָת תַּרְתֵּין כּוֹלְיָן, וְיָת תַּרְבָּא דַעֲלֵיהוֹן, וְיָת שָׁקָא דְיַמִּינָא, אֲרֵי, דְּכַר קֻרְבָּנַיָּא הוּא: כג וּפִתָּא דִלְחֵים חֲדָא, וּגְרִיצְתָא דִלְחֵים מְשַׁח, חֲדָא וְאֶסְפּוֹג חַד, מִסַּלָּא דְפַטִּירַיָּא, דִּקְדָם יְיָ: כד וּתְשַׁוֵּי כוֹלָּא, עַל יְדֵי אַהֲרֹן, וְעַל יְדֵי בְנוֹהִי, וּתְרִים יָתְהוֹן, אֲרָמָא קֳדָם יְיָ: כה וְתִסַּב יָתְהוֹן מִיַּדְהוֹן, וְתַסֵּיק לְמַדְבְּחָא עַל עֲלָתָא, לְאִתְקַבָּלָא בְרַעֲוָא קֳדָם יְיָ, קֻרְבָּנָא הוּא קֳדָם יְיָ: כו וְתִסַּב יָת חֶדְיָא, מִדְּכַר קֻרְבָּנַיָּא דִלְאַהֲרֹן, וּתְרִים יָתֵיהּ, אֲרָמָא קֳדָם יְיָ, וִיהֵי לָךְ לְחֻלָק: כז וּתְקַדֵּישׁ, יָת חֶדְיָא

29:24 תְּנוּפָה לִפְנֵי יהוה *A wave offering before the Lord* – The ritual is described in more detail in the Talmud: "He extends [the offering to each of the four directions] and brings them back, then raises and lowers them. R. Ḥiyya bar Abba says in the name of R. Yoḥanan: He extends it and brings it back in order to dedicate it to Him to whom the four directions belong. He raises and lowers it in order to dedicate it to Him to whom the heavens and earth belong" (Menaḥot 62a). We recognize these gestures from the Sukkot ritual of the four species. The priests enact the ritual side of religion, the side that is perhaps hardest to relate to looking in from the outside.

The Baal Shem Tov, champion of the worship of the heart, compared those atheists who mock religion to a deaf man who for the first time comes upon a violinist playing in the town square while the townspeople, moved by the lilt and rhythm of his playing, dance in joy. Unable to hear the music, he concludes that they are all mad.

Religious ritual and spirituality are two quite different things. Spirituality is the direct encounter with God.

▶

sons' ram of ordination, consecrate the breast, the wave offering and the thigh,
28 the upraised gift. These parts shall be the Israelites' due to Aharon and his sons
for all time. They are the Israelites' gift from their peace offerings, their gift to
29 the LORD. Aharon's sacred vestments shall pass on to his sons after him. In
30 them they shall be anointed and ordained. The son who succeeds him as priest,
entering the Tent of Meeting to minister in the Sanctuary, shall wear them for
31 seven days. Take the ram of ordination and, in the sacred precinct, cook its
32 flesh. Aharon and his sons shall eat the meat of the ram, and the bread in the
33 basket, near the entrance of the Tent of Meeting. They shall eat these things,
through which atonement will be made, to be ordained and consecrated.
34 Because they are consecrated no layman may eat of them. If any of the meat of
the ordination ram or any of the bread is left over until morning, you shall burn
35 what remains with fire. It must not be eaten, for it is consecrated. This is what
you must do for Aharon and his sons, just as I have commanded you. Their
36 ordination shall take seven days. Each day, offer a bull as a purification offering
for atonement. Purify the altar by making atonement for it, and consecrate it

רש״י

לא להקטרה, אלא "והיה לאהרן ולבניו" לאכול: **לחק עולם מאת בני ישראל.** שהשלמים לבעלים, ואת החזה והשוק יתנו לכהן: **תנופה.** לשון הולכה והבאה, ונטלי״ר בלעז: **הורם.** לשון מעלה ומוריד: **כי תרומה הוא.** החזה והשוק הזה:

כט **יהיו לבניו אחריו.** למי שבא בגדלה אחריו: **למשחה.** להתגדל בהם, שיש משיחה שהיא לשון שררה, כמו: "לך נתתים למשחה" (במדבר יח, ח), "אל תגעו במשיחי" (תהלים קה, טו): **ולמלא בם את ידם.** על ידי הבגדים הוא מתלבש בכהנה גדולה:

ל **שבעת ימים.** רצופין: **ילבשם הכהן.** אשר יקום מבניו תחתיו לכהנה גדולה, כשימנוהו להיות כהן גדול: **אשר יבא אל אהל מועד.** אותו כהן המוכן לכנס לפני ולפנים ביום הכפורים, וזהו כהן גדול, שאין עבודת יום הכפורים כשרה אלא בו: **תחתיו מבניו.** מלמד שאם יש לו לכהן גדול בן ממלא את מקומו, ימנוהו כהן גדול תחתיו:

לא **במקם קדש.** בחצר אהל מועד, שהשלמים הללו קדשי קדשים היו:

לב **פתח אהל מועד.** כל החצר קרוי כן:

לג **ואכלו אתם.** אהרן ובניו, לפי שהם בעליהם: **אשר כפר בהם.** להם כל זרות ותעוב: **למלא את ידם.** באיל ולחם הללו: **לקדש אתם.** שעל ידי המלואים הללו נתמלאו ידיהם ונתקדשו לכהנה: **כי קדש הם.** קדשי קדשים. ומכאן למדנו אזהרה לזר האוכל קדשי קדשים (מכות יח ע״א), שנתן המקרא טעם לדבר משום ד"קדש הם":

לה **ועשית לאהרן ולבניו ככה.** שנה הכתוב וכפל לעכב, שאם חסר דבר אחד מכל האמור בענין, לא נתמלאו ידיהם להיות כהנים ועבודתם פסולה: **אתכה.** כמו אותך: **שבעת ימים תמלא.** בענין הזה ובקרבנות הללו בכל יום:

לו **על הכפרים.** בשביל הכפורים, לכפר על המזבח מכל זרות ותעוב. ולפי שנאמר: "שבעת ימים תמלא ידם" (בפסוק הקודם), אין לי אלא דבר הבא בשבילם, כגון האילים והלחם, אבל הבא בשביל המזבח, כגון פר שהוא לחטוי המזבח, לא שמענו, לכך הצרך מקרא

to do is confess the sin, express remorse, and resolve not to repeat it in the future. Atonement is no longer mediated by a third party. It needs no priest, no sacrifice and no Temple ritual. It is a direct relationship between the individual and God. This is one of rabbinic Judaism's most magnificent ideas – the concept, long prefigured in the Torah but never explicitly set out as such, of *teshuva*, the "return" of the sinner to God. This, then, is where our rituals of *teshuva* begin. For now, atonement is enacted publicly. The priests enter their new office in a state of moral and spiritual cleanliness, unburdened by the past.

הַתְּנוּפָ֗ה וְאֵת֙ שׁ֣וֹק הַתְּרוּמָ֔ה אֲשֶׁ֥ר הוּנַ֖ף וַאֲשֶׁ֣ר הוּרָ֑ם מֵאֵיל֙ הַמִּלֻּאִ֔ים
כח מֵאֲשֶׁ֥ר לְאַהֲרֹ֖ן וּמֵאֲשֶׁ֥ר לְבָנָֽיו׃ וְהָיָה֩ לְאַהֲרֹ֨ן וּלְבָנָ֜יו לְחָק־עוֹלָ֗ם מֵאֵת֙
בְּנֵ֣י יִשְׂרָאֵ֔ל כִּ֥י תְרוּמָ֖ה ה֑וּא וּתְרוּמָ֞ה יִהְיֶ֨ה מֵאֵ֤ת בְּנֵֽי־יִשְׂרָאֵל֙ מִזִּבְחֵ֣י
כט שַׁלְמֵיהֶ֔ם תְּרוּמָתָ֖ם לַיהוָֽה׃ וּבִגְדֵ֤י הַקֹּ֙דֶשׁ֙ אֲשֶׁ֣ר לְאַהֲרֹ֔ן יִהְי֥וּ לְבָנָ֖יו
ל אַחֲרָ֑יו לְמָשְׁחָ֣ה בָהֶ֔ם וּלְמַלֵּא־בָ֖ם אֶת־יָדָֽם׃ שִׁבְעַ֣ת יָמִ֗ים יִלְבָּשָׁ֛ם
לא הַכֹּהֵ֥ן תַּחְתָּ֖יו מִבָּנָ֑יו אֲשֶׁ֨ר יָבֹ֛א אֶל־אֹ֥הֶל מוֹעֵ֖ד לְשָׁרֵ֥ת בַּקֹּֽדֶשׁ׃ וְאֵ֛ת
לב אֵ֥יל הַמִּלֻּאִ֖ים תִּקָּ֑ח וּבִשַּׁלְתָּ֥ אֶת־בְּשָׂר֖וֹ בְּמָקֹ֥ם קָדֹֽשׁ׃ וְאָכַ֨ל אַהֲרֹ֤ן
לג וּבָנָיו֙ אֶת־בְּשַׂ֣ר הָאַ֔יִל וְאֶת־הַלֶּ֖חֶם אֲשֶׁ֣ר בַּסָּ֑ל פֶּ֖תַח אֹ֥הֶל מוֹעֵֽד׃ וְאָכְל֤וּ
אֹתָם֙ אֲשֶׁ֣ר כֻּפַּ֣ר בָּהֶ֔ם לְמַלֵּ֥א אֶת־יָדָ֖ם לְקַדֵּ֣שׁ אֹתָ֑ם וְזָ֥ר לֹא־יֹאכַ֖ל
לד כִּי־קֹ֥דֶשׁ הֵֽם׃ וְאִם־יִוָּתֵ֞ר מִבְּשַׂ֧ר הַמִּלֻּאִ֛ים וּמִן־הַלֶּ֖חֶם עַד־הַבֹּ֑קֶר
לה וְשָׂרַפְתָּ֤ אֶת־הַנּוֹתָר֙ בָּאֵ֔שׁ לֹ֥א יֵאָכֵ֖ל כִּי־קֹ֥דֶשׁ הֽוּא׃ וְעָשִׂ֜יתָ לְאַהֲרֹ֤ן
לו וּלְבָנָיו֙ כָּ֔כָה כְּכֹ֖ל אֲשֶׁר־צִוִּ֣יתִי אֹתָ֑כָה שִׁבְעַ֥ת יָמִ֖ים תְּמַלֵּ֥א יָדָֽם׃ וּפַ֨ר
חַטָּ֜את תַּעֲשֶׂ֤ה לַיּוֹם֙ עַל־הַכִּפֻּרִ֔ים וְחִטֵּאתָ֙ עַל־הַמִּזְבֵּ֔חַ בְּכַפֶּרְךָ֖ עָלָ֑יו

אונקלוס

דַּאֲרָמוּתָא, וְיָת שָׁקָא דְּאַפְרָשׁוּתָא, דְּאִתָּרַם וּדְאִתַּפְרַשׁ, מִדְּכַר קֻרְבָּנַיָּא, מִדִּלְאַהֲרֹן וּמִדִּלִבְנוֹהִי: כח וִיהֵי לְאַהֲרֹן וְלִבְנוֹהִי לִקְיָם עָלַם, מִן בְּנֵי יִשְׂרָאֵל, אֲרֵי אַפְרָשׁוּתָא הוּא, וְאַפְרָשׁוּתָא, יְהֵי מִן בְּנֵי יִשְׂרָאֵל מִנִּכְסַת קֻדְשֵׁיהוֹן, אַפְרָשׁוּתְהוֹן קֳדָם יְיָ: כט וּלְבוּשֵׁי קֻדְשָׁא דִּלְאַהֲרֹן, יְהוֹן לִבְנוֹהִי בָּתְרוֹהִי, לְרַבָּאָה בְהוֹן, וּלְקָרָבָא בְהוֹן יָת קֻרְבָּנְהוֹן: ל שִׁבְעָא יוֹמִין, יִלְבְּשִׁנּוּן כַּהֲנָא, תְּחוֹתוֹהִי מִבְּנוֹהִי, דְּיֵיעוֹל, לְמַשְׁכַּן זִמְנָא לְשַׁמָּשָׁא בְקֻדְשָׁא: לא וְיָת, דְּכַר קֻרְבָּנַיָּא תִּסַּב, וּתְבַשֵּׁיל יָת בִּסְרֵיהּ בַּאֲתַר קַדִּישׁ: לב וְיֵיכוֹל אַהֲרֹן וּבְנוֹהִי יָת בְּסַר דִּכְרָא, וְיָת לַחְמָא דִּבְסַלָּא, בִּתְרַע מַשְׁכַּן זִמְנָא: לג וְיֵיכְלוּן יָתְהוֹן דְּאִתְכַּפַּר בְּהוֹן, לְקָרָבָא יָת קֻרְבָּנְהוֹן לְקַדָּשָׁא יָתְהוֹן, וְחִילוֹנַי לָא יֵיכוֹל אֲרֵי קֻדְשָׁא אִנּוּן: לד וְאִם יִשְׁתְּאַר, מִבְּסַר קֻרְבָּנַיָּא, וּמִן לַחְמָא עַד צַפְרָא, וְתוֹקֵיד יָת דְּאִשְׁתְּאַר בְּנוּרָא, לָא יִתְאֲכֵיל אֲרֵי קֻדְשָׁא הוּא: לה וְתַעְבֵּיד, לְאַהֲרֹן וְלִבְנוֹהִי כְּדֵין, כְּכֹל דְּפַקֵּידִית יָתָךְ, שִׁבְעָא יוֹמִין תְּקָרֵיב קֻרְבָּנְהוֹן: לו וְתוֹרָא דְּחַטָּתָא, תַּעְבֵּיד לְיוֹמָא עַל כִּפּוּרַיָּא, וּתְדַכֵּי עַל מַדְבְּחָא, בְּכַפָּרוּתָךְ עֲלוֹהִי,

29:33 אֲשֶׁר כֻּפַּר בָּהֶם *Through which atonement will be made* – Rituals of atonement are to form a large part of the Tabernacle's, later the Temple's, function. Interestingly, R. Akiva's response to the end of the Temple and its atonement rites is not to be one of mourning, but a paradoxical sense of uplift. Tragedy will not defeat hope. Indeed, it will bring about a spiritual advance. Far from being separated from God, the sinner will now be able to become closer to the Divine Presence. His words are these: "Happy are you, O Israel. Before whom are you being purified and who purifies you? Your Father who is in heaven" (Yoma 85b).

He meant this: Now that there is no Temple and no High Priest, atonement need no longer be vicarious. The sinner can obtain forgiveness directly. All he or she needs

37 by anointing it. For seven days, make atonement for the altar and consecrate it,
so that the altar becomes holy of holies – and anything that touches it will
38 become holy. This is what you shall offer on the altar: two yearling SHISHI
39 lambs each day, with constancy. Offer one lamb in the morning, and the other
40 in the afternoon. With the first lamb offer a tenth measure of fine flour mixed
with a quarter of a hin of beaten oil, and a quarter of a hin of wine as a libation.
41 Offer the other lamb in the afternoon together with a grain offering and libation
42 as in the morning, as a pleasing aroma, a fire offering to the LORD. This shall be
the regular burnt offering throughout your generations at the entrance of the
Tent of Meeting before the LORD. There I will meet with you, there I will speak
43 to you, and there I will meet with the Israelites. It will be sanctified by My

רש״י

זֶה. וּמִדְרַשׁ תּוֹרַת כֹּהֲנִים (ויקרא ח, יד מלואים טו) אוֹמֵר: כַּפָּרַת הַמִּזְבֵּחַ הֶעָרְכָה שֶׁמָּא הִתְנַדֵּב אִישׁ מִיִּשְׂרָאֵל דָּבָר גָּזֵל בִּמְלֶאכֶת הַמִּשְׁכָּן וְהַמִּזְבֵּחַ: וְחִטֵּאתָ. ״וּתְדַכֵּי״, לְשׁוֹן מַתְּנַת דָּמִים הַנְּתוּנִים בְּאֶצְבַּע קָרוּי חִטּוּי: וּמָשַׁחְתָּ אֹתוֹ. בְּשֶׁמֶן הַמִּשְׁחָה. וְכָל הַמְּשִׁיחוֹת כְּמִין כ״י:

לז | וְהָיָה הַמִּזְבֵּחַ קֹדֶשׁ. וּמַה הִיא קְדֻשָּׁתוֹ? ״כָּל הַנֹּגֵעַ בַּמִּזְבֵּחַ יִקְדָּשׁ״, אֲפִלּוּ קָרְבָּן פָּסוּל שֶׁעָלָה עָלָיו, קִדְּשׁוֹ הַמִּזְבֵּחַ לְהַכְשִׁירוֹ שֶׁלֹּא יֵרֵד. מִתּוֹךְ שֶׁנֶּאֱמַר: ״כָּל הַנֹּגֵעַ... יִקְדָּשׁ״, שׁוֹמֵעַ אֲנִי בֵּין רָאוּי בֵּין שֶׁאֵינוֹ רָאוּי, כְּגוֹן דָּבָר שֶׁלֹּא הָיָה פְּסוּלוֹ בַּקֹּדֶשׁ, כְּגוֹן הָרוֹבֵעַ וְהַנִּרְבָּע וּמֻקְצֶה וְנֶעֱבָד וְהַטְּרֵפָה וְכַיּוֹצֵא בָּהֶן, תַּלְמוּד לוֹמַר: ״וְזֶה אֲשֶׁר תַּעֲשֶׂה״ הַסָּמוּךְ אַחֲרָיו, מָה עוֹלָה רְאוּיָה אַף כָּל רָאוּי, שֶׁנִּרְאָה לוֹ כְּבָר וְנִפְסַל מִשֶּׁבָּא לָעֲזָרָה, כְּגוֹן הַלָּן וְהַיּוֹצֵא וְהַטָּמֵא וְשֶׁנִּשְׁחַט בְּמַחֲשֶׁבֶת חוּץ לִזְמַנּוֹ וְחוּץ לִמְקוֹמוֹ וְכַיּוֹצֵא בָּהֶן:

מ | וְעִשָּׂרֹן סֹלֶת. עֲשִׂירִית הָאֵיפָה, אַרְבָּעִים וְשָׁלֹשׁ בֵּיצִים וְחֹמֶשׁ בֵּיצָה: בְּשֶׁמֶן כָּתִית. לֹא לְחוֹבָה נֶאֱמַר ׳כָּתִית׳ אֶלָּא לְהַכְשִׁיר, לְפִי שֶׁנֶּאֱמַר: ״כָּתִית לַמָּאוֹר״ (לעיל כז, כ) וּמַשְׁמַע לַמָּאוֹר וְלֹא לַמְּנָחוֹת, יָכוֹל לְפָסְלוֹ לַמְּנָחוֹת? תַּלְמוּד לוֹמַר כָּאן: ״כָּתִית״, וְלֹא נֶאֱמַר: ״כָּתִית לַמָּאוֹר״ אֶלָּא לְמַעֵט מְנָחוֹת שֶׁאֵין צָרִיךְ כָּתִית, שֶׁאַף הַטָּחוּן בָּרֵיחַיִם כָּשֵׁר בָּהֶן: רֶבַע הַהִין. שְׁלֹשָׁה לֻגִּין: וְנֵסֶךְ. לַסְּפָלִים, כְּמוֹ שֶׁשָּׁנִינוּ בְּמַסֶּכֶת סֻכָּה (דף מח ע״ב): שְׁנֵי סְפָלִים שֶׁל כֶּסֶף הָיוּ בְּרֹאשׁ הַמִּזְבֵּחַ וּמְנֻקָּבִים כְּמִין שְׁנֵי חֳטָמִין דַּקִּים, נוֹתֵן הַיַּיִן לְתוֹכוֹ וְהוּא מְקַלֵּחַ וְיוֹצֵא דֶּרֶךְ הַחֹטֶם וְנוֹפֵל עַל גַּג הַמִּזְבֵּחַ, וּמִשָּׁם יוֹרֵד לַשִּׁיתִין בְּמִזְבֵּחַ בֵּית עוֹלָמִים, וּבְמִזְבֵּחַ הַנְּחֹשֶׁת יוֹרֵד מִן הַמִּזְבֵּחַ לָאָרֶץ:

מא | לְרֵיחַ נִיחֹחַ. עַל הַמִּנְחָה נֶאֱמַר, שֶׁמִּנְחַת נְסָכִים כֻּלָּהּ כָּלִיל. וְסֵדֶר הַקְרָבָתָם, הָאֵבָרִים בַּתְּחִלָּה וְאַחַר כָּךְ הַמִּנְחָה, שֶׁנֶּאֱמַר: ״עֹלָה וּמִנְחָה״ (ויקרא כג, לז):

מב | תָּמִיד. מִיּוֹם אֶל יוֹם, לֹא יַפְסִיק יוֹם בֵּינְתַיִם: אֲשֶׁר אִוָּעֵד לָכֶם. כְּשֶׁאֶקְבַּע מוֹעֵד לְדַבֵּר אֵלֶיךָ, שָׁם אֶקְבָּעֶנּוּ לָבֹא. וְיֵשׁ מֵרַבּוֹתֵינוּ לְמֵדִים מִכָּאן שֶׁמֵּעַל מִזְבַּח הַנְּחֹשֶׁת הָיָה הַקָּדוֹשׁ בָּרוּךְ הוּא מְדַבֵּר עִם מֹשֶׁה מִשֶּׁהוּקַם הַמִּשְׁכָּן. וְיֵשׁ אוֹמְרִים מֵעַל הַכַּפֹּרֶת, כְּמוֹ שֶׁנֶּאֱמַר: ״וְדִבַּרְתִּי אִתְּךָ מֵעַל הַכַּפֹּרֶת״ (לעיל כה, כב), וַ״אֲשֶׁר אִוָּעֵד לָכֶם״ הָאָמוּר כָּאן אֵינוֹ אָמוּר עַל הַמִּזְבֵּחַ, אֶלָּא עַל ״אֹהֶל מוֹעֵד״ הַנִּזְכָּר בַּמִּקְרָא:

מג | וְנֹעַדְתִּי שָׁמָּה. אֶתְוַעֵד עִמָּם בְּדִבּוּר, כְּמֶלֶךְ הַקּוֹבֵעַ מְקוֹם מוֹעֵד לְדַבֵּר עִם עֲבָדָיו שָׁם: וְנִקְדַּשׁ. הַמִּשְׁכָּן ״בִּכְבֹדִי״, שֶׁתִּשְׁרֶה שְׁכִינָתִי בּוֹ. וּמִדְרַשׁ אַגָּדָה, אַל תִּקְרֵי ׳בִּכְבֹדִי׳ אֶלָּא ׳בִּכְבוּדַי׳, בַּמְכֻבָּדִים שֶׁלִּי, כָּאן רָמַז לוֹ מִיתַת בְּנֵי אַהֲרֹן בְּיוֹם הֲקָמָתוֹ, וְזֶהוּ שֶׁאָמַר מֹשֶׁה: ״הוּא אֲשֶׁר דִּבֶּר ה׳ לֵאמֹר בִּקְרֹבַי אֶקָּדֵשׁ״ (ויקרא י, ג), וְהֵיכָן דִּבֵּר? ״וְנִקְדַּשׁ בִּכְבֹדִי״:

discipline to our lives and change the way we feel, think, and act.

Judaism is about changing us so that we become creative artists whose greatest creation is our own life. And that needs daily rituals: the Shaḥarit, Minḥa, and Maariv prayers, the food we eat, the way we behave at work or in the home, the choreography of holiness which is the special contribution of the priestly dimension of Judaism, set out in this *parasha* and throughout the book of Leviticus. These rituals have an effect. We now know through PET and fMRI scans that repeated spiritual exercise reconfigures the brain. It gives us inner resilience. It makes us more grateful. It gives us a sense of basic trust in the source of our being. It shapes our identity, the way we act and talk and think.

The more you seek spiritual heights, the more you need the ritual and routine of halakha, the Jewish "way" to God.

לז וּמְשַׁחְתָּ אֹתוֹ לְקַדְּשׁוֹ׃ שִׁבְעַת יָמִים תְּכַפֵּר עַל־הַמִּזְבֵּחַ וְקִדַּשְׁתָּ אֹתוֹ
לח וְהָיָה הַמִּזְבֵּחַ קֹדֶשׁ קָדָשִׁים כָּל־הַנֹּגֵעַ בַּמִּזְבֵּחַ יִקְדָּשׁ׃ וְזֶה ששי
אֲשֶׁר תַּעֲשֶׂה עַל־הַמִּזְבֵּחַ כְּבָשִׂים בְּנֵי־שָׁנָה שְׁנַיִם לַיּוֹם תָּמִיד׃
לט אֶת־הַכֶּבֶשׂ הָאֶחָד תַּעֲשֶׂה בַבֹּקֶר וְאֵת הַכֶּבֶשׂ הַשֵּׁנִי תַּעֲשֶׂה בֵּין
מ הָעַרְבָּיִם׃ וְעִשָּׂרֹן סֹלֶת בָּלוּל בְּשֶׁמֶן כָּתִית רֶבַע הַהִין וְנֵסֶךְ רְבִיעִת
מא הַהִין יָיִן לַכֶּבֶשׂ הָאֶחָד׃ וְאֵת הַכֶּבֶשׂ הַשֵּׁנִי תַּעֲשֶׂה בֵּין הָעַרְבַּיִם כְּמִנְחַת
מב הַבֹּקֶר וּכְנִסְכָּהּ תַּעֲשֶׂה־לָּהּ לְרֵיחַ נִיחֹחַ אִשֶּׁה לַיהוָה׃ עֹלַת תָּמִיד
לְדֹרֹתֵיכֶם פֶּתַח אֹהֶל־מוֹעֵד לִפְנֵי יְהוָה אֲשֶׁר אִוָּעֵד לָכֶם שָׁמָּה
מג לְדַבֵּר אֵלֶיךָ שָׁם׃ וְנֹעַדְתִּי שָׁמָּה לִבְנֵי יִשְׂרָאֵל וְנִקְדַּשׁ בִּכְבֹדִי׃

אונקלוס

וּתְרַבֵּי יָתֵיהּ לְקַדָּשׁוּתֵיהּ: לז שִׁבְעָא יוֹמִין, תְּכַפַּר עַל מַדְבְּחָא, וּתְקַדֵּישׁ יָתֵיהּ, וִיהֵי מַדְבְּחָא קֹדֶשׁ קֻדְשִׁין, כָּל דְּיִקְרַב בְּמַדְבְּחָא יִתְקַדַּשׁ: לח וְדֵין, דְּתַעֲבֵיד עַל מַדְבְּחָא, אִמְּרִין בְּנֵי שְׁנָא, תְּרֵין לְיוֹמָא תְּדִירָא: לט יָת אִמְּרָא חַד תַּעֲבֵיד בְּצַפְרָא, וְיָת אִמְּרָא תִנְיָנָא, תַּעֲבֵיד בֵּין שִׁמְשַׁיָּא: מ וְעֶסְרוֹנָא סֻלְתָּא, דְּפִיל בִּמְשַׁח כָּתִישָׁא רַבְעוּת הִינָא, וְנִסְכָּא, רַבְעוּת הִינָא חַמְרָא, לְאִמְּרָא חַד: מא וְיָת אִמְּרָא תִנְיָנָא, תַּעֲבֵיד בֵּין שִׁמְשַׁיָּא, כְּמִנְחַת צַפְרָא וּכְנִסְכַּהּ תַּעֲבֵיד לַהּ, לְאִתְקַבָּלָא בְרַעֲוָא, קֻרְבָּנָא קֳדָם יְיָ: מב עֲלַת תְּדִירָא לְדָרֵיכוֹן, בִּתְרַע מַשְׁכַּן זִמְנָא קֳדָם יְיָ, דַּאֲזַמֵּין מֵימְרִי לְכוֹן תַּמָּן, לְמַלָּלָא עִמָּךְ תַּמָּן: מג וַאֲזַמֵּין מֵימְרִי תַּמָּן לִבְנֵי יִשְׂרָאֵל, וְאֶתְקַדַּשׁ בִּיקָרִי:

THE REGULAR BURNT OFFERING

Any form of sustained spiritual growth requires daily effort and regular rituals. Hence the remarkable aggadic passage (brought in the preface of *Ein Yaakov*) in which various Sages put forward their idea of *klal gadol baTorah*, "the great principle of the Torah." Ben Azzai says it is the verse "This is the book of Adam's descendants: On the day God created humankind, He made them in the likeness of God" (Gen. 5:1). Ben Zoma says that there is a more embracing principle: "Listen, Israel: the LORD our God – the LORD is one" (Deut. 6:4). Ben Nannas says there is a yet more embracing principle: "Love your neighbor as your own self" (Lev. 19:18). Ben Pazi says we find a more embracing principle still. He quotes a verse from this *parasha*: "Offer one lamb in the morning, and the other in the afternoon" (Ex. 29:39). In a word: "routine." The passage concludes: "The law follows Ben Pazi."

The meaning of Ben Pazi's statement is clear: all the high ideals in the world count for little until they are turned into habits of action that become habits of the heart. We can all recall moments of insight when we had a great idea, a transformative thought, the glimpse of a project that could change our lives. A day, a week, or a year later the thought has been forgotten or become a distant memory, at best a might-have-been.

The people who change the world, whether in small or epic ways, are those who turn peak experiences into daily routines, who know that the details matter, and who have developed the discipline of hard work, sustained over time.

Judaism's greatness is that it takes high ideals and exalted visions – the human person as God's image, belief in God's unity, and the love of neighbor – and turns them into patterns of behavior. Halakha, Jewish law, involves a set of routines that, like those of the great creative minds, give

44 glory. I will consecrate the Tent of Meeting and the altar. I will also consecrate
45 Aharon and his sons to serve Me as priests. I will have My presence dwell
46 among the Israelites and I shall be their God. Then they will know that I am the
Lord their God, who brought them out of Egypt to dwell among them. I am
the Lord their God.

30 1 2 Make an altar on which to burn incense; make it of acacia wood. It shall be SHEVI'I
square, a cubit long, a cubit wide, and two cubits high, its horns of one piece
3 with it. Overlay it with pure gold on its top, all around its sides, and on its horns,
4 and around it make a gold molding. Make two gold rings for it under its molding
5 on both sides to hold the staves used to carry it. Make the staves of acacia wood
6 and overlay them with gold. Put it in front of the screen that veils the Ark of
the Testimony, in front of the cover above the Ark, where I will meet with you.
7 Aharon should burn incense on it every morning when he tends the lamps,
8 and before evening when he lights the lamps. It shall be a perpetual incense MAFTIR
9 offering before the Lord throughout your generations. Offer no unauthorized
10 incense on it, or any burnt offering, grain offering, or libation. Once a year
Aharon shall make atonement on its horns; once a year, with the blood of the
purification offering of atonement, he shall make atonement on it, throughout
your generations. It is holy of holies to the Lord."

The haftara for Parashat Tetzaveh is on page 1548.
On the Shabbat of Parashat Zakhor or on Purim Meshulash in Jerusalem read the haftara on page 1644.

אונקלוס

מד **וַאֲקַדֵּישׁ, יָת מַשְׁכַּן זִמְנָא וְיָת מַדְבְּחָא, וְיָת אַהֲרֹן וְיָת בְּנוֹהִי, אֲקַדֵּישׁ לְשַׁמָּשָׁא קֳדָמָי: מה וְאַשְׁרֵי שְׁכִינְתִּי, בְּגוֹ בְּנֵי יִשְׂרָאֵל, וְאֶהֱוֵי לְהוֹן לֶאֱלָהּ: מו וְיִדְּעוּן, אֲרֵי אֲנָא יי אֱלָהֲהוֹן, דְּאַפֵּיקִית יָתְהוֹן, מֵאַרְעָא דְמִצְרַיִם לְאַשְׁרָאָה שְׁכִינְתִּי בֵּינֵיהוֹן, אֲנָא יי אֱלָהֲהוֹן: ל א וְתַעְבֵּיד**

◀

רש״י

מו **לְשָׁכְנִי בְתוֹכָם.** עַל מְנָת לִשְׁכֹּן אֲנִי בְּתוֹכָם:

ל א **מִקְטַר קְטֹרֶת.** לְהַעֲלוֹת עָלָיו קִטּוּר עֲשַׁן סַמִּים:

ג **אֶת גַּגּוֹ.** זֶה הָיָה לוֹ גַּג, אֲבָל מִזְבַּח הָעוֹלָה לֹא הָיָה לוֹ גַּג, אֶלָּא מְמַלְּאִים חֲלָלוֹ אֲדָמָה בְּכָל חֲנִיָּתָן: **זֵר זָהָב.** סִימָן לְכֶתֶר כְּהֻנָּה:

ד **צַלְעֹתָיו.** כָּאן הוּא לְשׁוֹן זָוִיּוֹת, כְּתַרְגּוּמוֹ, לְפִי שֶׁנֶּאֱמַר: "עַל שְׁנֵי צִדָּיו", שְׁתֵּי זָוִיּוֹתָיו שֶׁבִּשְׁנֵי צִדָּיו: **וְהָיָה.** מַעֲשֵׂה הַטַּבָּעוֹת הָאֵלֶּה "לְבָתִּים לְבַדִּים", בַּיִת תִּהְיֶה הַטַּבַּעַת לַבַּד:

ו **לִפְנֵי הַפָּרֹכֶת.** שֶׁמָּא תֹּאמַר מָשׁוּךְ מִכְּנֶגֶד הָאָרוֹן לַצָּפוֹן אוֹ לַדָּרוֹם? תַּלְמוּד לוֹמַר: "לִפְנֵי הַכַּפֹּרֶת", מְכֻוָּן כְּנֶגֶד הָאָרוֹן מִבַּחוּץ:

ז-ח **בְּהֵיטִיבוֹ.** לְשׁוֹן נִקּוּי הַבָּזִיכִין שֶׁל הַמְּנוֹרָה מִדֶּשֶׁן הַפְּתִילוֹת שֶׁנִּשְׂרְפוּ בַּלַּיְלָה, וְהָיָה מְטִיבָן בְּכָל בֹּקֶר וָבֹקֶר: **הַנֵּרֹת.** לוּצִי"שׁ בְּלַעַז, וְכֵן כָּל נֵרוֹת הָאֲמוּרוֹת בַּמְּנוֹרָה, חוּץ מִמָּקוֹם שֶׁנֶּאֱמַר שָׁם הַעֲלָאָה, שֶׁהוּא לְשׁוֹן הַדְלָקָה: **וּבְהַעֲלֹת.** כְּשֶׁיַּדְלִיקֵם לְהַעֲלוֹת לַהַבְתָּן "יַקְטִירֶנָּה". בְּכָל יוֹם מַקְטִיר פְּרָס שַׁחֲרִית וּפְרָס בֵּין הָעַרְבַּיִם:

ט **לֹא תַעֲלוּ עָלָיו.** עַל מִזְבֵּחַ זֶה: **קְטֹרֶת זָרָה.** שׁוּם קְטֹרֶת שֶׁל נְדָבָה, כֻּלָּן זָרוֹת לוֹ חוּץ מִזּוֹ: **וְעֹלָה וּמִנְחָה.** וְלֹא עוֹלָה וּמִנְחָה. עוֹלָה שֶׁל בְּהֵמָה וָעוֹף, מִנְחָה הִיא שֶׁל מִין לֶחֶם:

י **וְכִפֶּר אַהֲרֹן.** מַתַּן דָּמִים "עַל קַרְנֹתָיו": **אַחַת בַּשָּׁנָה.** בְּיוֹם הַכִּפּוּרִים, הוּא שֶׁנֶּאֱמַר בְּ'אַחֲרֵי מוֹת': "וְיָצָא אֶל הַמִּזְבֵּחַ אֲשֶׁר לִפְנֵי ה' וְכִפֶּר עָלָיו" (ויקרא טז, יח): **חַטַּאת הַכִּפֻּרִים.** הֵם פַּר וְשָׂעִיר שֶׁל יוֹם הַכִּפּוּרִים הַמְכַפְּרִים עַל טֻמְאַת מִקְדָּשׁ וְקָדָשָׁיו: **קֹדֶשׁ קָדָשִׁים הוּא.** הַמִּזְבֵּחַ מְקֻדָּשׁ לַדְּבָרִים הַלָּלוּ בִּלְבַד וְלֹא לַעֲבוֹדָה אַחֶרֶת:

מד וְקִדַּשְׁתִּי אֶת־אֹהֶל מוֹעֵד וְאֶת־הַמִּזְבֵּחַ וְאֶת־אַהֲרֹן וְאֶת־בָּנָיו אֲקַדֵּשׁ
מה מו לְכַהֵן לִי: וְשָׁכַנְתִּי בְּתוֹךְ בְּנֵי יִשְׂרָאֵל וְהָיִיתִי לָהֶם לֵאלֹהִים: וְיָדְעוּ כִּי
אֲנִי יְהוָה אֱלֹהֵיהֶם אֲשֶׁר הוֹצֵאתִי אֹתָם מֵאֶרֶץ מִצְרַיִם לְשָׁכְנִי בְתוֹכָם
אֲנִי יְהוָה אֱלֹהֵיהֶם:

ל א ב וְעָשִׂיתָ מִזְבֵּחַ מִקְטַר קְטֹרֶת עֲצֵי שִׁטִּים תַּעֲשֶׂה אֹתוֹ: אַמָּה אָרְכּוֹ כג שביעי
ג וְאַמָּה רָחְבּוֹ רָבוּעַ יִהְיֶה וְאַמָּתַיִם קֹמָתוֹ מִמֶּנּוּ קַרְנֹתָיו: וְצִפִּיתָ אֹתוֹ
זָהָב טָהוֹר אֶת־גַּגּוֹ וְאֶת־קִירֹתָיו סָבִיב וְאֶת־קַרְנֹתָיו וְעָשִׂיתָ לּוֹ זֵר זָהָב
ד סָבִיב: וּשְׁתֵּי טַבְּעֹת זָהָב תַּעֲשֶׂה־לּוֹ ׀ מִתַּחַת לְזֵרוֹ עַל שְׁתֵּי צַלְעֹתָיו
ה תַּעֲשֶׂה עַל־שְׁנֵי צִדָּיו וְהָיָה לְבָתִּים לְבַדִּים לָשֵׂאת אֹתוֹ בָּהֵמָּה: וְעָשִׂיתָ
ו אֶת־הַבַּדִּים עֲצֵי שִׁטִּים וְצִפִּיתָ אֹתָם זָהָב: וְנָתַתָּה אֹתוֹ לִפְנֵי הַפָּרֹכֶת
אֲשֶׁר עַל־אֲרֹן הָעֵדֻת לִפְנֵי הַכַּפֹּרֶת אֲשֶׁר עַל־הָעֵדֻת אֲשֶׁר אִוָּעֵד לְךָ
ז שָׁמָּה: וְהִקְטִיר עָלָיו אַהֲרֹן קְטֹרֶת סַמִּים בַּבֹּקֶר בַּבֹּקֶר בְּהֵיטִיבוֹ אֶת־
ח הַנֵּרֹת יַקְטִירֶנָּה: וּבְהַעֲלֹת אַהֲרֹן אֶת־הַנֵּרֹת בֵּין הָעַרְבַּיִם יַקְטִירֶנָּה מפטיר
ט קְטֹרֶת תָּמִיד לִפְנֵי יְהוָה לְדֹרֹתֵיכֶם: לֹא־תַעֲלוּ עָלָיו קְטֹרֶת זָרָה וְעֹלָה
י וּמִנְחָה וְנֵסֶךְ לֹא תִסְּכוּ עָלָיו: וְכִפֶּר אַהֲרֹן עַל־קַרְנֹתָיו אַחַת בַּשָּׁנָה
מִדַּם חַטַּאת הַכִּפֻּרִים אַחַת בַּשָּׁנָה יְכַפֵּר עָלָיו לְדֹרֹתֵיכֶם קֹדֶשׁ־קָדָשִׁים
הוּא לַיהוָה:

The הפטרה *for* פרשת תצוה *is on page 1549.*
On the שבת *of* פרשת זכור *or on* פורים משולש *in Jerusalem read the* הפטרה *on page 1645.*

אונקלוס

מַדְבְּחָא לְאַקְטָרָא עֲלוֹהִי קְטֹרֶת בֻּסְמִין, דְּאָעֵי שִׁטִּין תַּעֲבֵיד יָתֵיהּ: ב אַמְּתָא אֻרְכֵּיהּ, וְאַמְּתָא פֻּתְיֵיהּ מְרַבַּע יְהֵי, וְתַרְתֵּין אַמִּין רוּמֵיהּ, מִנֵּיהּ קַרְנוֹהִי: ג וְתַחְפֵי יָתֵיהּ דְּהַב דְּכֵי, יָת אִגָּרֵיהּ וְיָת כָּתְלוֹהִי, סְחוֹר סְחוֹר וְיָת קַרְנוֹהִי, וְתַעֲבֵיד לֵיהּ, זֵיר דִּדְהַב סְחוֹר סְחוֹר: ד וְתַרְתֵּין עִזְקָן דִּדְהַב, תַּעֲבֵיד לֵיהּ מִלְּרַע לְזֵירֵיהּ, עַל תַּרְתֵּין זָוְיָתֵיהּ, תַּעֲבֵיד עַל תְּרֵין סִטְרוֹהִי, וִיהֵי לְאַתְרָא לַאֲרִיחַיָּא, לְמִטַּל יָתֵיהּ בְּהוֹן: ה וְתַעֲבֵיד יָת אֲרִיחַיָּא דְּאָעֵי שִׁטִּין, וְתַחְפֵי יָתְהוֹן דַּהֲבָא: ו וְתִתֵּין יָתֵיהּ קֳדָם פָּרֻכְתָּא, דְּעַל אֲרוֹנָא דְסָהֲדוּתָא, קֳדָם כָּפֻּרְתָּא, דְּעַל סָהֲדוּתָא, דַּאֲזַמֵּן מֵימְרִי לָךְ תַּמָּן: ז וְיַקְטַר עֲלוֹהִי, אַהֲרֹן קְטֹרֶת בֻּסְמִין, בִּצְפַר בִּצְפַר, בְּאַתְקָנוּתֵיהּ יָת בּוֹצִינַיָּא יַקְטְרִנַּהּ: ח וּבְאַדְלָקוּת אַהֲרֹן יָת בּוֹצִינַיָּא, בֵּין שִׁמְשַׁיָּא יַקְטְרִנַּהּ, קְטֹרֶת בֻּסְמִין תְּדִירָא, קֳדָם יי לְדָרֵיכוֹן: ט לָא תַסְּקוּן עֲלוֹהִי, קְטֹרֶת בֻּסְמִין נֻכְרָאִין וַעֲלָתָא וּמִנְחָתָא, וְנִסְכָּא, לָא תְנַסְּכוּן עֲלוֹהִי: י וִיכַפַּר אַהֲרֹן עַל קַרְנָתֵיהּ, חֲדָא בְּשַׁתָּא, מִדַּם חַטַּאת כִּפּוּרַיָּא, חֲדָא בְּשַׁתָּא יְכַפַּר עֲלוֹהִי לְדָרֵיכוֹן, קֹדֶשׁ קֻדְשִׁין הוּא קֳדָם יי:

Parashat Ki Tisa

30 11 12 The Lord said to Moshe, "When you take the census of the Israelites, as you
count, each must give ransom for his life to the Lord, so that no plague strikes
13 them when you count them. Everyone numbered in the census shall give
half a shekel according to the Sanctuary weight, where the shekel is twenty
14 gerah. This half shekel is an offering to the Lord. Every male over twenty is

רש״י

יב) **כי תשא.** לשון קבלה, כתרגומו. כשתחפץ לקבל סכום מנינם לדעת כמה הם, אל תמנם לגלגלת, אלא יתנו כל אחד מחצית השקל, ותמנה את השקלים ותדע מנינם: **ולא יהיה בהם נגף.** שהמנין שולט בו עין הרע והדבר בא עליהם, כמו שמצינו בימי דוד (שמואל ב׳ כד, א-י):

יג) **זה יתנו.** הראה לו כמין מטבע של אש ומשקלה מחצית השקל, ואמר לו: כזה יתנו: **העבר על הפקדים.** דרך המונין מעבירין את הנמנין זה אחר זה, וכן: "כל אשר יעבר תחת השבט" (ויקרא כז, לב), וכן: "תעברנה הצאן על ידי מונה" (ירמיה לג, יג): **מחצית השקל בשקל הקדש.** במשקל השקל שקצבתי לך לשקול בו שקלי הקדש, כגון שקלים האמורין בפרשת ערכין (ויקרא כז, א-ח) ושדה אחזה (שם פסוק טז-יט): **עשרים גרה השקל.** עכשיו פירש לך כמה הוא: **גרה.** לשון מעה, וכן בשמואל: "יבוא להשתחוות לו לאגורת כסף וככר לחם" (שמואל א׳ ב, לו): **עשרים גרה השקל.** השלם, שהשקל ארבעה זוזים, והזוז מתחלתו חמש מעות, אלא באו והוסיפו עליו שתות והעלוהו לשש מעה כסף, ומחצית השקל הזה שאמרתי לך יתנו תרומה לה׳:

יד) **מבן עשרים שנה ומעלה.** למדך כאן שאין פחות מבן עשרים יוצא לצבא ונמנה בכלל אנשים:

that there is strength in numbers we would, God forbid, give way to despair. For four thousand years the strength of the Jewish people has never lain in numbers.

Where then did it lie? To this the Torah gives an answer of great beauty. In effect, God tells Moshe, "Do not count Jews. *Ask them to give, and then count the contributions.* That is how you measure the strength of the Jewish people." In terms of numbers we are small. But in terms of our contributions, we are vast. In almost every age, Jews have given something special to the world. In one era it was the Tanakh, the most influential document in the history of the world. In later centuries Jews produced a never-ending stream of scholars, saints, poets, and philosophers.

It is not that Jews are brighter, cleverer, more energetic or talented than others. That is a racist doctrine and I reject it. Nor is it that Jews, more than others, are driven to succeed. That is at the heart of much antisemitic propaganda, and it is false. The simple answer, given in the Torah and engraved in Jewish sensibility, is that *to be a Jew is to be asked to give*, to contribute, to make a difference, to help in the monumental task that has engaged Jews since the dawn of our history, to make the world a home for the Divine Presence, a place of justice, compassion, human dignity, and the sanctity of life. Though our ancestors cherished their relationship with God, they never saw it as a privilege. Instead they saw it as a responsibility. God challenged them to give. In that familiar yet astonishing phrase, he invited them to be His "partners in the work of creation" (Shabbat 119b).

30:13 מַחֲצִית הַשֶּׁקֶל *Half a shekel* – Why should each person give specifically *half* a shekel? Moshe is saying: Never think that you need to do it all. Each of us must be conscious that we can't complete the task; we need someone else to make the shekel whole. But neither is our contribution insignificant. We contribute our half, confident that others will join us, perhaps inspired by what we do. We can change the world, but we need partners, and the best way of finding them is to lead by personal example. Virtue is contagious. One good deed begets another. What is important is that we begin.

פרשת כי תשא

ל יא יב וַיְדַבֵּר יְהֹוָה אֶל־מֹשֶׁה לֵּאמֹר: כִּי תִשָּׂא אֶת־רֹאשׁ בְּנֵי־יִשְׂרָאֵל
לִפְקֻדֵיהֶם וְנָתְנוּ אִישׁ כֹּפֶר נַפְשׁוֹ לַיהֹוָה בִּפְקֹד אֹתָם וְלֹא־יִהְיֶה בָהֶם
יג נֶגֶף בִּפְקֹד אֹתָם: זֶה ׀ יִתְּנוּ כָּל־הָעֹבֵר עַל־הַפְּקֻדִים מַחֲצִית הַשֶּׁקֶל
בְּשֶׁקֶל הַקֹּדֶשׁ עֶשְׂרִים גֵּרָה הַשֶּׁקֶל מַחֲצִית הַשֶּׁקֶל תְּרוּמָה לַיהֹוָה:
יד כֹּל הָעֹבֵר עַל־הַפְּקֻדִים מִבֶּן עֶשְׂרִים שָׁנָה וָמָעְלָה יִתֵּן תְּרוּמַת יְהֹוָה:

אונקלוס

יא וּמַלֵּיל יי עִם מֹשֶׁה לְמֵימַר: יב אֲרֵי תְקַבֵּיל, יָת חֻשְׁבַּן בְּנֵי יִשְׂרָאֵל לְמִנְיָנֵיהוֹן, וְיִתְּנוּן, גְּבַר פֻּרְקַן נַפְשֵׁיהּ, קֳדָם יי כַּד תִּמְנֵי יָתְהוֹן, וְלָא יְהֵי בְהוֹן, מוֹתָא כַּד תִּמְנֵי יָתְהוֹן: יג דֵּין יִתְּנוּן, כָּל דְּעָבַר עַל מִנְיָנַיָּא, פַּלְגּוּת סִלְעָא בְּסִלְעֵי קֻדְשָׁא, עֶסְרִין מָעִין סִלְעָא, פַּלְגּוּת סִלְעָא, אַפְרָשׁוּתָא קֳדָם יי: יד כֹּל, דְּעָבַר עַל מִנְיָנַיָּא, מִבַּר עֶסְרִין שְׁנִין וּלְעֵילָא, יִתֵּין אַפְרָשׁוּתָא קֳדָם יי:

KI TISA

Ki Tisa begins with the final details about the Tabernacle, including a collection of money from the people that is to serve as a census. The *parasha* then moves into high drama with one of the most gripping narratives in Jewish history. The people, panicking in the absence of Moshe (who is up the mountain, receiving the tablets from God), make a golden calf and dance before it. God tells Moshe to go down. Coming down the mountain, and facing Israel, he smashes the tablets, symbol of the covenant. He censures the people, then reascends the mountain in a prolonged attempt to reestablish the shattered relationship. God forgives and proclaims His attributes of mercy, which are part of our liturgy today. Moshe returns, with a second set of tablets, unaware that his face is now radiant.

THE CENSUS

The *parasha* begins with God's command to Moshe to take a census of the people. But it is phrased in a curious manner. Moshe is told not to count the people directly, but obliquely. Each is to give half a shekel and only thus was their number to be calculated.

The verse warns Moshe to do it this way, "so that no plague strikes them when you count them." Evidently, it is dangerous to count Jews. Many centuries later, ignoring this warning, King David took a census of the people, and disaster struck the nation (II Sam. 24). To this day, we do not needlessly count Jews, even to calculate whether there is a minyan (a quorum of ten men) in the synagogue. Our custom is to take a verse with ten words and use that instead. But why is it dangerous to count Jews?

The classic commentators on Exodus 30:12 give several answers. Rashi says that counting is fraught with the danger of the "evil eye." Rabbeinu Baḥya suggests that when people are counted, they are numbered as individuals, separated from the community. There is a danger that an individual's merit may be insufficient to save him from adverse judgment.

I want to suggest another explanation. Why do nations count their numbers? To estimate their strength – military, political, or economic. Behind the ancient practice of counting populations is the assumption that there is strength in numbers. The larger the people, the stronger it is. That is why it is dangerous to count Jews. If we ever came to believe

15 to be included in the census and must give the LORD's offering. The rich shall
not give more, and the poor shall not give less, than this half shekel. It is an
16 offering to the LORD to redeem your lives. Take this redemption money from
the Israelites and assign it for the service of the Tent of Meeting. It shall be a
remembrance for the Israelites before the LORD, to redeem your lives."
17 18 The LORD said to Moshe, "Make a bronze laver with a bronze base for washing.
19 Place it between the Tent of Meeting and the altar, and put water in it, for
20 Aharon and his sons to wash their hands and feet. When they enter the Tent
of Meeting or approach the altar to minister by presenting a food offering to
21 the LORD, they must wash with water, so that they do not die. They must wash
their hands and feet so that they do not die; it shall be an eternal law for them,
for Aharon and his offspring, throughout the generations."
22 23 Then the LORD said to Moshe, "Take the finest spices: five hundred shekel of
liquid myrrh, and half as much, two hundred fifty, of fragrant cinnamon, as well

רש"י

טו **לְכַפֵּר עַל נַפְשֹׁתֵיכֶם.** שֶׁלֹּא תִנָּגְפוּ עַל יְדֵי מִנְיָן. דָּבָר אַחֵר, "לְכַפֵּר עַל נַפְשֹׁתֵיכֶם", לְפִי שֶׁרָמַז לָהֶם כָּאן שָׁלֹשׁ תְּרוּמוֹת, שֶׁנִּכְתַּב כָּאן "תְּרוּמַת ה'" שָׁלֹשׁ פְּעָמִים: אַחַת תְּרוּמַת אֲדָנִים, שֶׁמְּנָאָן כְּשֶׁהִתְחִילוּ בִּנְדְבַת הַמִּשְׁכָּן, שֶׁנָּתְנוּ כָּל אֶחָד וְאֶחָד מַחֲצִית הַשֶּׁקֶל וְעָלָה לִמְאַת הַכִּכָּר, שֶׁנֶּאֱמַר: "וְכֶסֶף פְּקוּדֵי הָעֵדָה מְאַת כִּכָּר" (להלן לח, כה), וּמֵהֶם נַעֲשׂוּ הָאֲדָנִים, שֶׁנֶּאֱמַר: "וַיְהִי מְאַת כִּכַּר הַכֶּסֶף" וְגוֹ' (שם פסוק כז); וְהַשֵּׁנִית אַף הִיא עַל יְדֵי מִנְיָן שֶׁמְּנָאָן מִשֶּׁהוּקַם הַמִּשְׁכָּן, הוּא הַמִּנְיָן הָאָמוּר בִּתְחִלַּת חוּמַשׁ הַפְּקוּדִים "בְּאֶחָד לַחֹדֶשׁ הַשֵּׁנִי בַּשָּׁנָה הַשֵּׁנִית" (במדבר א, א), וְנָתְנוּ כָּל אֶחָד מַחֲצִית הַשֶּׁקֶל, וְהֵן לִקְנוֹת מֵהֶן קָרְבְּנוֹת צִבּוּר שֶׁל כָּל שָׁנָה וְשָׁנָה, וְהֻשְׁווּ בָּהֶם עֲנִיִּים וַעֲשִׁירִים, וְעַל אוֹתָהּ תְּרוּמָה נֶאֱמַר: "לְכַפֵּר עַל נַפְשֹׁתֵיכֶם", שֶׁהַקָּרְבָּנוֹת לְכַפָּרָה הֵם בָּאִים; וְהַשְּׁלִישִׁית הִיא תְּרוּמַת הַמִּשְׁכָּן, כְּמוֹ שֶׁנֶּאֱמַר: "כָּל מֵרִים תְּרוּמַת כֶּסֶף וּנְחֹשֶׁת" (להלן לה, כד), וְלֹא הָיְתָה יַד כֻּלָּם שָׁוָה בָּהּ, אֶלָּא אִישׁ מַה שֶּׁנְּדָבוֹ לִבּוֹ:

טז **וְנָתַתָּ אֹתוֹ עַל עֲבֹדַת אֹהֶל מוֹעֵד.** לָמַדְתָּ שֶׁנִּצְטַוּוּ לִמְנוֹתָם בִּתְחִלַּת נִדְבַת הַמִּשְׁכָּן אַחַר מַעֲשֵׂה הָעֵגֶל, מִפְּנֵי שֶׁנִּתְּנָה בָּהֶם מַגֵּפָה, כְּמוֹ שֶׁנֶּאֱמַר: "וַיִּגֹּף ה' אֶת הָעָם" (להלן לב, לה). מָשָׁל לְצֹאן הַחֲבִיבָה עַל בְּעָלֶיהָ שֶׁנָּפַל בָּהּ דֶּבֶר, וּמִשֶּׁפָּסַק אָמַר לוֹ לָרוֹעֶה: בְּבַקָּשָׁה מִמְּךָ, מְנֵה אֶת צֹאנִי וְדַע כַּמָּה נוֹתְרוּ בָּהּ, לְהוֹדִיעוֹ שֶׁהִיא חֲבִיבָה עָלָיו. וְאִי אֶפְשָׁר לוֹמַר שֶׁהַמִּנְיָן הַזֶּה הוּא הָאָמוּר בְּחוּמַשׁ הַפְּקוּדִים, שֶׁהֲרֵי נֶאֱמַר בּוֹ: "בְּאֶחָד לַחֹדֶשׁ הַשֵּׁנִי" (במדבר א, א), וְהַמִּשְׁכָּן הוּקַם בְּאֶחָד לַחֹדֶשׁ הָרִאשׁוֹן, שֶׁנֶּאֱמַר: "בְּיוֹם הַחֹדֶשׁ הָרִאשׁוֹן בְּאֶחָד לַחֹדֶשׁ תָּקִים" וְגוֹ' (להלן מ, ב), וּמֵהַמִּנְיָן הַזֶּה נַעֲשׂוּ הָאֲדָנִים מִשְּׁקָלִים שֶׁלּוֹ, שֶׁנֶּאֱמַר: "וַיְהִי מְאַת כִּכַּר הַכֶּסֶף לָצֶקֶת" וְגוֹ' (להלן לח, כז), הָא לָמַדְתָּ שְׁנַיִם הָיוּ: אֶחָד בִּתְחִלַּת נִדְבָתָן אַחַר יוֹם הַכִּפּוּרִים בְּשָׁנָה רִאשׁוֹנָה, וְאֶחָד בְּשָׁנָה שְׁנִיָּה בְּאִיָּר מִשֶּׁהוּקַם הַמִּשְׁכָּן. וְאִם תֹּאמַר, וְכִי אֶפְשָׁר שֶׁבִּשְׁנֵיהֶם הָיוּ יִשְׂרָאֵל שָׁוִים שֵׁשׁ מֵאוֹת אֶלֶף וּשְׁלֹשֶׁת אֲלָפִים וַחֲמֵשׁ מֵאוֹת וַחֲמִשִּׁים? שֶׁהֲרֵי בְּכֶסֶף פְּקוּדֵי הָעֵדָה נֶאֱמַר כֵּן (להלן לח, כו), וּבְחוּמַשׁ הַפְּקוּדִים אַף בּוֹ נֶאֱמַר כֵּן: "וַיִּהְיוּ כָּל הַפְּקֻדִים שֵׁשׁ מֵאוֹת אֶלֶף וּשְׁלֹשֶׁת אֲלָפִים וַחֲמֵשׁ מֵאוֹת וַחֲמִשִּׁים" (במדבר א, מו), וַהֲלֹא בִּשְׁתֵּי שָׁנִים הָיוּ, וְאִי אֶפְשָׁר שֶׁלֹּא הָיוּ בִּשְׁעַת מִנְיָן הָרִאשׁוֹן בְּנֵי תְּשַׁע עֶשְׂרֵה שָׁנָה שֶׁלֹּא נִמְנוּ וּבַשְּׁנִיָּה נַעֲשׂוּ בְּנֵי עֶשְׂרִים! תְּשׁוּבָה לַדָּבָר, אֵצֶל שְׁנוֹת הָאֲנָשִׁים בְּשָׁנָה אַחַת נִמְנוּ, אֲבָל לְמִנְיַן יְצִיאַת מִצְרַיִם הָיוּ שְׁתֵּי שָׁנִים, לְפִי שֶׁלִּיצִיאַת מִצְרַיִם מוֹנִין מִנִּיסָן, כְּמוֹ שֶׁשָּׁנִינוּ בְּמַסֶּכֶת רֹאשׁ הַשָּׁנָה (דף ב ע"ב), וְנִבְנָה הַמִּשְׁכָּן בָּרִאשׁוֹנָה וְהוּקַם בַּשְּׁנִיָּה, שֶׁנִּתְחַדְּשָׁה שָׁנָה בְּאֶחָד בְּנִיסָן, אֲבָל שְׁנוֹת הָאֲנָשִׁים מְנוּיִין לְמִנְיַן שְׁנוֹת עוֹלָם הַמַּתְחִילִין מִתִּשְׁרֵי, נִמְצְאוּ שְׁנֵיהֶם הַמִּנְיָנִים בְּשָׁנָה אַחַת, הַמִּנְיָן הָאֶחָד הָיָה בְּתִשְׁרֵי לְאַחַר יוֹם הַכִּפּוּרִים, שֶׁנִּתְרַצָּה הַמָּקוֹם לְיִשְׂרָאֵל לִסְלֹחַ לָהֶם וְנִצְטַוּוּ עַל הַמִּשְׁכָּן, וְהַשֵּׁנִי בְּאֶחָד בְּאִיָּר: **עַל עֲבֹדַת אֹהֶל מוֹעֵד.** הֵן הָאֲדָנִים שֶׁנַּעֲשׂוּ בוֹ:

יח **כִּיּוֹר.** כְּמִין דּוּד גְּדוֹלָה וְלָהּ דַּדִּים הַמְרִיקִים בְּפִיהֶם מַיִם: **וְכַנּוֹ.** כְּתַרְגּוּמוֹ: "בְּסִיסֵיהּ", מוֹשָׁב מְתֻקָּן לַכִּיּוֹר: **לְרָחְצָה.** מוּסָב עַל הַכִּיּוֹר: **וּבֵין הַמִּזְבֵּחַ.** מִזְבַּח הָעוֹלָה, שֶׁכָּתוּב בּוֹ שֶׁהוּא לִפְנֵי פֶּתַח מִשְׁכַּן אֹהֶל מוֹעֵד (להלן מ, כט), וְהָיָה הַכִּיּוֹר מָשׁוּךְ קִמְעָא וְעוֹמֵד כְּנֶגֶד אֲוִיר שֶׁבֵּין הַמִּזְבֵּחַ וְהַמִּשְׁכָּן וְאֵינוֹ מַפְסִיק כְּלָל בֵּינְתַיִם, מִשּׁוּם שֶׁנֶּאֱמַר: "וְאֵת מִזְבַּח הָעֹלָה שָׂם פֶּתַח מִשְׁכַּן אֹהֶל מוֹעֵד" (שם), כְּלוֹמַר, מִזְבֵּחַ לִפְנֵי אֹהֶל מוֹעֵד וְאֵין כִּיּוֹר לִפְנֵי אֹהֶל מוֹעֵד, הָא כֵּיצַד? מָשׁוּךְ קִמְעָא כְּלַפֵּי הַדָּרוֹם. כָּךְ שְׁנוּיָה בִּזְבָחִים (דף נט ע"א):

טו הֶֽעָשִׁ֣יר לֹֽא־יַרְבֶּ֗ה וְהַדַּל֙ לֹ֣א יַמְעִ֔יט מִֽמַּחֲצִ֖ית הַשָּׁ֑קֶל לָתֵת֙ אֶת־
טז תְּרוּמַ֣ת יְהוָ֔ה לְכַפֵּ֖ר עַל־נַפְשֹׁתֵיכֶֽם׃ וְלָקַחְתָּ֞ אֶת־כֶּ֣סֶף הַכִּפֻּרִ֗ים מֵאֵת֙
בְּנֵ֣י יִשְׂרָאֵ֔ל וְנָתַתָּ֣ אֹת֔וֹ עַל־עֲבֹדַ֖ת אֹ֣הֶל מוֹעֵ֑ד וְהָיָה֩ לִבְנֵ֨י יִשְׂרָאֵ֤ל
לְזִכָּרוֹן֙ לִפְנֵ֣י יְהוָ֔ה לְכַפֵּ֖ר עַל־נַפְשֹׁתֵיכֶֽם׃
יז יח וַיְדַבֵּ֥ר יְהוָ֖ה אֶל־מֹשֶׁ֥ה לֵּאמֹֽר׃ וְעָשִׂ֜יתָ כִּיּ֥וֹר נְחֹ֛שֶׁת וְכַנּ֥וֹ נְחֹ֖שֶׁת לְרָחְצָ֑ה
יט וְנָתַתָּ֣ אֹת֗וֹ בֵּֽין־אֹ֤הֶל מוֹעֵד֙ וּבֵ֣ין הַמִּזְבֵּ֔חַ וְנָתַתָּ֥ שָׁ֖מָּה מָֽיִם׃ וְרָחֲצ֛וּ
כ אַהֲרֹ֥ן וּבָנָ֖יו מִמֶּ֑נּוּ אֶת־יְדֵיהֶ֖ם וְאֶת־רַגְלֵיהֶֽם׃ בְּבֹאָ֞ם אֶל־אֹ֧הֶל מוֹעֵ֛ד
יִרְחֲצוּ־מַ֖יִם וְלֹ֣א יָמֻ֑תוּ א֣וֹ בְגִשְׁתָּ֤ם אֶל־הַמִּזְבֵּחַ֙ לְשָׁרֵ֔ת לְהַקְטִ֥יר אִשֶּׁ֖ה
כא לַֽיהוָֽה׃ וְרָחֲצ֛וּ יְדֵיהֶ֥ם וְרַגְלֵיהֶ֖ם וְלֹ֣א יָמֻ֑תוּ וְהָיְתָ֨ה לָהֶ֧ם חָק־עוֹלָ֛ם ל֥וֹ
וּלְזַרְע֖וֹ לְדֹרֹתָֽם׃
כב כג וַיְדַבֵּ֥ר יְהוָ֖ה אֶל־מֹשֶׁ֥ה לֵּאמֹֽר׃ וְאַתָּ֣ה קַח־לְךָ֮ בְּשָׂמִ֣ים רֹאשׁ֒ מָר־דְּרוֹר֙
חֲמֵ֣שׁ מֵא֔וֹת וְקִנְּמָן־בֶּ֥שֶׂם מַחֲצִית֖וֹ חֲמִשִּׁ֣ים וּמָאתָ֑יִם וּקְנֵה־בֹ֖שֶׂם

אונקלוס

טו דְּעַתִּיר לָא יַסְגֵּי, וּדְמִסְכֵּין לָא יַזְעַר, מִפַּלְגוּת סִלְעָא, לְמִתַּן יָת אַפְרָשׁוּתָא קֳדָם יְיָ, לְכַפָּרָא עַל נַפְשָׁתְכוֹן: טז וְתִסַּב יָת כְּסַף כִּפּוּרַיָּא, מִן בְּנֵי יִשְׂרָאֵל, וְתִתֵּין יָתֵיהּ, עַל פָּלְחַן מַשְׁכַּן זִמְנָא, וִיהֵי לִבְנֵי יִשְׂרָאֵל לְדָכְרָנָא קֳדָם יְיָ, לְכַפָּרָא עַל נַפְשָׁתְכוֹן: יז וּמַלֵּיל יְיָ עִם מֹשֶׁה לְמֵימַר: יח וְתַעְבֵּיד, כִּיּוֹרָא דִנְחָשָׁא, וּבְסִיסֵיהּ דִּנְחָשָׁא לְקִדּוּשׁ, וְתִתֵּין יָתֵיהּ, בֵּין מַשְׁכַּן זִמְנָא וּבֵין מַדְבְּחָא, וְתִתֵּין תַּמָּן מַיָּא: יט וִיקַדְּשׁוּן, אַהֲרֹן וּבְנוֹהִי מִנֵּיהּ, יָת יְדֵיהוֹן וְיָת רַגְלֵיהוֹן: כ בְּמֵיעַלְהוֹן, לְמַשְׁכַּן זִמְנָא, יְקַדְּשׁוּן מַיָּא וְלָא יְמוּתוּן, אוֹ בְּמִקְרַבְהוֹן לְמַדְבְּחָא לְשַׁמָּשָׁא, לְאַסָּקָא קֻרְבָּנָא קֳדָם יְיָ: כא וִיקַדְּשׁוּן, יְדֵיהוֹן וְרַגְלֵיהוֹן וְלָא יְמוּתוּן, וּתְהֵי לְהוֹן קְיָם עָלַם, לֵיהּ וְלִבְנוֹהִי לְדָרֵיהוֹן: כב וּמַלֵּיל יְיָ עִם מֹשֶׁה לְמֵימַר: כג וְאַתְּ סַב לָךְ בֻּסְמִין רֵישָׁא, מֵירָא דָכְיָא מַתְקַל חֲמֵשׁ מְאָה, וְקִנְּמָן בְּסַם פַּלְגוּתֵיהּ מַתְקַל מָאתַן וְחַמְשִׁין, וּקְנֵי בֻסְמָא

רש״י

יט **אֶת יְדֵיהֶם וְאֶת רַגְלֵיהֶם.** בְּבַת אַחַת הָיָה מְקַדֵּשׁ יָדָיו וְרַגְלָיו. וְכָךְ שָׁנִינוּ בִּזְבָחִים (דף יט ע״ב): כֵּיצַד קִדּוּשׁ יָדַיִם וְרַגְלַיִם? מַנִּיחַ יָדוֹ הַיְמָנִית עַל גַּבֵּי רַגְלוֹ הַיְמָנִית, וְיָדוֹ הַשְּׂמָאלִית עַל גַּבֵּי רַגְלוֹ הַשְּׂמָאלִית, וּמְקַדֵּשׁ:

כ **בְּבֹאָם אֶל אֹהֶל מוֹעֵד.** לְהַקְטִיר שַׁחֲרִית וּבֵין הָעַרְבַּיִם קְטֹרֶת, אוֹ לְהַזּוֹת מִדַּם פַּר כֹּהֵן הַמָּשִׁיחַ וּשְׂעִירֵי עֲבוֹדָה זָרָה:

וְלֹא יָמֻתוּ. הָא אִם לֹא יִרְחֲצוּ – יָמוּתוּ, שֶׁבַּתּוֹרָה נֶאֶמְרוּ כְּלָלוֹת, וּמִכְּלָל לָאו אַתָּה שׁוֹמֵעַ הֵן: **אֶל הַמִּזְבֵּחַ.** הַחִיצוֹן, שֶׁאֵין כָּאן בִּיאַת אֹהֶל מוֹעֵד אֶלָּא בֶּחָצֵר:

כא **וְלֹא יָמֻתוּ.** לְחַיֵּב מִיתָה עַל הַמְשַׁמֵּשׁ בַּמִּזְבֵּחַ וְאֵינוֹ רְחוּץ יָדַיִם וְרַגְלַיִם, שֶׁהַמִּיתָה הָרִאשׁוֹנָה לֹא שָׁמַעְנוּ אֶלָּא עַל הַנִּכְנָס לַהֵיכָל:

כג **בְּשָׂמִים רֹאשׁ.** חֲשׁוּבִים: **וְקִנְּמָן בֶּשֶׂם.** לְפִי שֶׁהַקִּנָּמוֹן קְלִפַּת עֵץ הוּא, יֵשׁ שֶׁהוּא טוֹב וְיֵשׁ בּוֹ רֵיחַ טוֹב וְטַעַם, וְיֵשׁ שֶׁאֵינוֹ אֶלָּא כְּעֵץ, לְכָךְ הֻצְרַךְ לוֹמַר "קִנְּמָן בֶּשֶׂם", מִן הַטּוֹב: **מַחֲצִיתוֹ חֲמִשִּׁים וּמָאתָיִם.** מַחֲצִית הֲבָאָתוֹ תְּהֵא "חֲמִשִּׁים וּמָאתָיִם", נִמְצָא כֻּלּוֹ חֲמֵשׁ מֵאוֹת, כְּמוֹ שִׁעוּר מָר דְּרוֹר. אִם כֵּן לָמָּה נֶאֱמַר בּוֹ חֲצָאִין? גְּזֵרַת הַכָּתוּב הָיְתָה לַהֲבִיאוֹ לַחֲצָאִין, לְהַרְבּוֹת בּוֹ שְׁנֵי הֶכְרֵעוֹת, שֶׁאֵין שׁוֹקְלִין עַיִן בְּעַיִן. וְכָךְ שְׁנוּיָה בִּכְרֵתוֹת (דף ה ע״א): **וּקְנֵה בֹשֶׂם.** קָנֶה שֶׁל בֹּשֶׂם, לְפִי שֶׁיֵּשׁ קָנִים שֶׁאֵינָן

24 as two hundred fifty of aromatic cane, and five hundred shekel of cassia – all
25 according to the Sanctuary weight – and a hin of olive oil. Make from these a
sacred anointing oil, blended as by a perfumer; it shall be a sacred anointing oil.
26 27 With it, anoint the Tent of Meeting and the Ark of the Testimony, the table and
28 all its utensils, the candelabrum and its utensils, the incense altar, the sacrificial
29 altar with all its utensils, and the laver and its base. You shall consecrate them
and they will become holy of holies, and whatever touches them will become
30 holy. You shall anoint Aharon and his sons and consecrate them to serve Me as
31 priests. And you shall tell the Israelites: This shall be My sacred anointing oil
32 throughout the generations. Do not pour it on anyone else's body, and do not
make any other oil with the same formula. It is sacred, and shall remain sacred to
33 you. Whoever makes perfume like it or applies it to a layperson shall be severed
34 from his people." The LORD said to Moshe, "Take sweet spices, equal
35 parts of stacte, onycha, galbanum, and pure frankincense and make them into

רש״י

שֶׁל בֹּשֶׂם הָעֵרֶךְ לוֹמַר: "בֹּשֶׂם": **חֲמִשִּׁים וּמָאתָיִם.** סַךְ מִשְׁקַל כֻּלּוֹ:

כד **וְקִדָּה.** שֵׁם שֹׁרֶשׁ עֵשֶׂב, וּבִלְשׁוֹן חֲכָמִים 'קְצִיעָה': **הִין.** שְׁנֵים עָשָׂר לֹג. וְנֶחְלְקוּ בּוֹ חַכְמֵי יִשְׂרָאֵל: רַבִּי מֵאִיר אוֹמֵר: בּוֹ שָׁלְקוּ אֶת הָעִקָּרִין. אָמַר לוֹ רַבִּי יְהוּדָה: וַהֲלֹא לָסוּךְ אֶת הָעִקָּרִין אֵינוֹ סִפֵּק, אֶלָּא שְׁרָאוּם בְּמַיִם שֶׁלֹּא יִבְלְעוּ אֶת הַשֶּׁמֶן, וְאַחַר כָּךְ הֵצִיף עֲלֵיהֶם הַשֶּׁמֶן עַד שֶׁקָּלַט הָרֵיחַ, וְקִפְּחוֹ לַשֶּׁמֶן מֵעַל הָעִקָּרִין:

כה **רֹקַח מִרְקַחַת.** 'רֹקַח' שֵׁם דָּבָר הוּא, וְהַטַּעַם מוֹכִיחַ, שֶׁהוּא לְמַעְלָה. וַהֲרֵי הוּא כְּמוֹ 'רֶקַח' (שיר השירים ח, ב), 'רֶגַע' (להלן לג, ה), וְאֵינוֹ כְּמוֹ "רֹגַע הַיָּם" (ישעיה נא, טו) וּכְמוֹ "רֹקַע הָאָרֶץ" (שם מב, ה) שֶׁהַטַּעַם לְמַטָּה. וְכָל דָּבָר הַמְעֹרָב בַּחֲבֵרוֹ עַד שֶׁזֶּה קוֹפֵחַ מִזֶּה אוֹ רֵיחַ אוֹ טַעַם, קָרוּי 'מִרְקַחַת': **רֹקַח מִרְקַחַת.** רֹקַח הֶעָשׂוּי עַל יְדֵי אֻמָּנוּת וְתַעֲרֹבֶת: **מַעֲשֵׂה רֹקֵחַ.** שֵׁם הָאֻמָּן בַּדָּבָר:

כו **וּמָשַׁחְתָּ בוֹ.** כָּל הַמְּשִׁיחוֹת כְּמִין כ"י, חוּץ מִשֶּׁל מְלָכִים שֶׁהֵן כְּמִין נֵזֶר:

כט **וְקִדַּשְׁתָּ אֹתָם.** מְשִׁיחָה זוֹ מְקַדַּשְׁתָּם לִהְיוֹת קֹדֶשׁ קָדָשִׁים. וּמָה הִיא קְדֻשָּׁתָם? "כָּל הַנֹּגֵעַ" וְגוֹ' – כָּל הָרָאוּי לִכְלִי שָׁרֵת מִשֶּׁנִּכְנַס לְתוֹכוֹ, קָדוֹשׁ קְדֻשַּׁת הַגּוּף לִפָּסֵל בְּיוֹצֵא וּלְינָה וּטְבוּל יוֹם, וְאֵינוֹ נִפְדֶּה לָצֵאת לְחֻלִּין, אֲבָל דָּבָר שֶׁאֵינוֹ רָאוּי לָהֶם אֵין מְקַדְּשִׁין. וּשְׁנוּיָה הִיא מִשְׁנָה שְׁלֵמָה אֵצֶל מִזְבֵּחַ: מִתּוֹךְ שֶׁנֶּאֱמַר: "כָּל הַנֹּגֵעַ בַּמִּזְבֵּחַ יִקְדָּשׁ" (לעיל כט, לז), שׁוֹמֵעַ אֲנִי בֵּין רָאוּי בֵּין שֶׁאֵינוֹ רָאוּי, תַּלְמוּד לוֹמַר: "כְּבָשִׂים", מַה כְּבָשִׂים רְאוּיִים אַף כָּל רָאוּי (זבחים פג ע"ב). כָּל מְשִׁיחַת מִשְׁכָּן וְכֹהֲנִים וּמְלָכִים מְתֻרְגָּם לְשׁוֹן 'רִבּוּי', לְפִי שֶׁאֵין דֶּרֶךְ מְשִׁיחָתָן אֶלָּא לִגְדֻלָּה, כִּי כֵּן יִסַּד הַמֶּלֶךְ שֶׁזֶּה חִנּוּךְ גְּדֻלָּתָן. וּשְׁאָר מְשִׁיחוֹת, כְּגוֹן 'רְקִיקִין מְשׁוּחִין', "וְרֵאשִׁית שְׁמָנִים יִמְשָׁחוּ" (עמוס ו, ו) לְשׁוֹן אֲרַמִּית בָּהֶן כִּלְשׁוֹן עִבְרִית:

לא **לְדֹרֹתֵיכֶם.** מִכָּאן לָמְדוּ רַבּוֹתֵינוּ לוֹמַר שֶׁכֻּלּוֹ קַיָּם לֶעָתִיד לָבֹא, "זֶה" בְּגִימַטְרִיָּא תְּרֵיסַר לֻגִּין הֲווֹ:

לב **לֹא יִיסָךְ.** בִּשְׁנֵי יוּדִי"ן, לְשׁוֹן לֹא יִפָּעֵל, כְּמוֹ: "לְמַעַן יִיטַב לָךְ" (דברים ו, יח): **עַל בְּשַׂר אָדָם לֹא יִיסָךְ.** מִן הַשֶּׁמֶן הַזֶּה עַצְמוֹ: **וּבְמַתְכֻּנְתּוֹ לֹא תַעֲשׂוּ כָּמֹהוּ.** בְּסִכּוּם סַמָּנָיו לֹא תַעֲשׂוּ אַחֵר כָּמֹהוּ בְּמִשְׁקַל סַמָּנִין הַלָּלוּ לְפִי מִדַּת הִין שֶׁמֶן, אֲבָל אִם פִּחֵת אוֹ רִבָּה סַמָּנִין לְפִי מִדַּת הִין שֶׁמֶן – מֻתָּר. וְאַף הֶעָשׂוּי בְּמַתְכֻּנְתּוֹ שֶׁל זֶה, אֵין הַסָּךְ מִמֶּנּוּ חַיָּב, אֶלָּא הָרוֹקְחוֹ: **וּבְמַתְכֻּנְתּוֹ.** לְשׁוֹן חֶשְׁבּוֹן, כְּמוֹ "מַתְכֹּנֶת הַלְּבֵנִים" (לעיל ה, ח), וְכֵן "בְּמַתְכֻּנְתָּהּ" (להלן פסוק לז) שֶׁל קְטֹרֶת:

לג **וַאֲשֶׁר יִתֵּן מִמֶּנּוּ.** מֵאוֹתוֹ שֶׁל מֹשֶׁה: **עַל זָר.** שֶׁאֵינוֹ צֹרֶךְ כְּהֻנָּה וּמַלְכוּת:

לד **נָטָף.** הוּא צֳרִי. וְעַל שֶׁאֵינוֹ אֶלָּא שְׂרָף הַנּוֹטֵף מֵעֲצֵי הַקְּטָף קָרוּי 'נָטָף', וּבְלַעַז גוֹמ"א, וְהַצֳּרִי קוֹרִין לוֹ טריאק"ה: **וּשְׁחֵלֶת.** שֹׁרֶשׁ בֹּשֶׂם חָלָק וּמַצְהִיר כְּצִפֹּרֶן, וּבִלְשׁוֹן הַמִּשְׁנָה קָרוּי צִפֹּרֶן, וְזֶהוּ שֶׁתִּרְגֵּם אוֹנְקְלוֹס: "וְטוּפְרָא": **וְחֶלְבְּנָה.** בֹּשֶׂם שֶׁרֵיחוֹ רַע וְקוֹרִין לוֹ גלבנ"א. וּמְנָאָהּ הַכָּתוּב בֵּין סַמְמֵי הַקְּטֹרֶת, לְלַמְּדֵנוּ שֶׁלֹּא יֵקַל בְּעֵינֵינוּ לְצָרֵף עִמָּנוּ בַּאֲגֻדַּת תַּעֲנִיּוֹתֵינוּ וּתְפִלּוֹתֵינוּ אֶת פּוֹשְׁעֵי יִשְׂרָאֵל שֶׁיִּהְיוּ נִמְנִין עִמָּנוּ: **סַמִּים.** אֲחֵרִים: **וּלְבֹנָה זַכָּה.** מִכָּאן לָמְדוּ רַבּוֹתֵינוּ אַחַד עָשָׂר סַמָּנִין נֶאֶמְרוּ לוֹ לְמֹשֶׁה בְּסִינַי: מִעוּט "סַמִּים" שְׁנַיִם, "נָטָף וּשְׁחֵלֶת וְחֶלְבְּנָה" שְׁלֹשָׁה, הֲרֵי חֲמִשָּׁה. "סַמִּים", לְרַבּוֹת עוֹד כְּמוֹ אֵלּוּ, הֲרֵי

כד חֲמִשִּׁים וּמָאתָיִם: וְקִדָּה חֲמֵשׁ מֵאוֹת בְּשֶׁקֶל הַקֹּדֶשׁ וְשֶׁמֶן זַיִת הִין:
כה וְעָשִׂיתָ אֹתוֹ שֶׁמֶן מִשְׁחַת־קֹדֶשׁ רֹקַח מִרְקַחַת מַעֲשֵׂה רֹקֵחַ שֶׁמֶן
כו מִשְׁחַת־קֹדֶשׁ יִהְיֶה: וּמָשַׁחְתָּ בוֹ אֶת־אֹהֶל מוֹעֵד וְאֵת אֲרוֹן הָעֵדֻת:
כז וְאֶת־הַשֻּׁלְחָן וְאֶת־כָּל־כֵּלָיו וְאֶת־הַמְּנֹרָה וְאֶת־כֵּלֶיהָ וְאֵת מִזְבַּח
כח הַקְּטֹרֶת: וְאֶת־מִזְבַּח הָעֹלָה וְאֶת־כָּל־כֵּלָיו וְאֶת־הַכִּיֹּר וְאֶת־כַּנּוֹ:
כט ל וְקִדַּשְׁתָּ אֹתָם וְהָיוּ קֹדֶשׁ קָדָשִׁים כָּל־הַנֹּגֵעַ בָּהֶם יִקְדָּשׁ: וְאֶת־אַהֲרֹן
לא וְאֶת־בָּנָיו תִּמְשָׁח וְקִדַּשְׁתָּ אֹתָם לְכַהֵן לִי: וְאֶל־בְּנֵי יִשְׂרָאֵל תְּדַבֵּר
לב לֵאמֹר שֶׁמֶן מִשְׁחַת־קֹדֶשׁ יִהְיֶה זֶה לִי לְדֹרֹתֵיכֶם: עַל־בְּשַׂר אָדָם לֹא
לג יִיסָךְ וּבְמַתְכֻּנְתּוֹ לֹא תַעֲשׂוּ כָּמֹהוּ קֹדֶשׁ הוּא קֹדֶשׁ יִהְיֶה לָכֶם: אִישׁ אֲשֶׁר
לד יִרְקַח כָּמֹהוּ וַאֲשֶׁר יִתֵּן מִמֶּנּוּ עַל־זָר וְנִכְרַת מֵעַמָּיו: וַיֹּאמֶר
יְהוָה אֶל־מֹשֶׁה קַח־לְךָ סַמִּים נָטָף ׀ וּשְׁחֵלֶת וְחֶלְבְּנָה סַמִּים וּלְבֹנָה
לה זַכָּה בַּד בְּבַד יִהְיֶה: וְעָשִׂיתָ אֹתָהּ קְטֹרֶת רֹקַח מַעֲשֵׂה רוֹקֵחַ מְמֻלָּח

אונקלוס

מתקל מאתן וחמשין: כד וקציעתא, מתקל חמש מאה בסלעי קודשא, ומשח זיתא מלי הינא: כה ותעביד יתיה, משח רבות קודשא, בוסם מבסם עובד בסמנו, משח רבות קודשא יהי: כו ותרבי ביה ית משכן זמנא, וית ארונא דסהדותא: כז וית פתורא וית כל מנוהי, וית מנרתא וית מנהא, וית מדבחא דקטרת בסמיא: כח וית מדבחא דעלתא וית כל מנוהי, וית כיורא וית בסיסיה: כט ותקדיש יתהון, ויהון קודש קודשין, כל דיקרב בהון יתקדש: ל וית אהרן וית בנוהי תרבי, ותקדיש יתהון לשמשא קדמי: לא ועם בני ישראל תמליל למימר, משח, רבות קודשא יהי דין, לי לדריכון: לב על בסרא דאנשא לא יתסך, ובדמותיה, לא תעבדון כותיה, קודשא הוא, קודשא יהי לכון: לג גבר דיבסים דכותיה, ודיתין מניה על חילוני, וישתיצי מעמיה: לד ואמר יי למשה סב לך בסמין, נטופא וטפרא וחלבונתא, בסמין ולבונתא דכיתא, מתקל במתקל יהי: לה ותעביד יתה קטרת בסמין, בוסם עובד בסמנו, מערב

רש״י

עשרה. "ולבנה", הרי אחד עשר. ואלו הן: הצרי והצפרן, החלבנה והלבונה, מור וקציעה, שבלת נרד וכרכם, הרי שמונה, שהשבלת ונרד אחד, שהנרד דומה לשבלת; הקשט והקלופה והקנמון, הרי אחד עשר. בורית כרשינה אינו נקטר, אלא בו שפין את הצפרן ללבנה שתהא נאה: **בד בבד יהיה.** אלו הארבעה הנזכרים כאן יהיו שוין משקל במשקל, כמשקלו של זה כך משקלו של זה, וכן שנינו: "הצרי והצפרן החלבנה והלבונה משקל שבעים שבעים מנה" (כריתות ו ע"א), ולשון "בד" נראה בעיני שהוא לשון 'יחיד', אחד כאחד יהיו, זה כמות זה:

לה **ממלח.** כתרגומו, "מערב", שיערב שחיקתן יפה יפה זה עם זה. ואומר אני שדומה לו: "וייראו המלחים" (יונה א, ה), "מלחיך וחבליך" (יחזקאל כז, כז), על שם שמהפכין את המים במשוטות כשמנהיגים את הספינה, כאדם המהפך בכף ביצים טרופות לערבן עם המים, וכל דבר שאדם רוצה לערב יפה יפה מהפכו באצבע או בכף:

36 incense, blended as by a perfumer, salted, pure and sacred. Beat some of it into
powder and put part of it before the covenant in the Tent of Meeting where I
37 will meet with you. It shall be holy of holies to you. Do not make any incense
with this formula for yourselves. It must, for you, remain sacred to the LORD.
38 The person who makes any incense like it to use as perfume shall be severed
31 1 2 from his people." The LORD said to Moshe, "See, I have called by
3 name Betzalel, son of Uri, son of Ḥur from the tribe of Yehuda, and I have filled
him with a divine spirit, with wisdom, understanding, and knowledge in every
4 5 craft. He will fashion works of art in gold, silver, and bronze. He will cut stones
6 for setting, carve wood, and work in every craft. I have assigned to him Oholiav,
son of Aḥisamakh from the tribe of Dan. I have also put wisdom into the heart
of all the wise-hearted, so that they will be able to make all I have commanded
7 you: the Tent of Meeting, the Ark of the Testimony and its cover, and all other
8 furnishings of the Tent; the table and its utensils, the pure candelabrum and all
9 its utensils, the incense altar, the sacrificial altar with all its utensils, the laver

רש״י

מְמֻלָּח טָהוֹר קֹדֶשׁ. מְמֻלָּח יִהְיֶה, וְטָהוֹר יִהְיֶה, וְקֹדֶשׁ יִהְיֶה:

לו **וְנָתַתָּה מִמֶּנָּה וְגוֹ׳.** הִיא קְטֹרֶת שֶׁבְּכָל יוֹם וָיוֹם שֶׁעַל מִזְבַּח הַפְּנִימִי, שֶׁהוּא ״בְּאֹהֶל מוֹעֵד״: **אֲשֶׁר אִוָּעֵד לְךָ שָׁמָּה.** כָּל מוֹעֲדֵי דִּבּוּר שֶׁאֶקְבַּע לְךָ, אֲנִי קוֹבְעָם לְאוֹתוֹ מָקוֹם:

לז **בְּמַתְכֻּנְתָּהּ.** בְּמִנְיַן סַמָּנֶיהָ: **קֹדֶשׁ תִּהְיֶה לְךָ לַה׳.** שֶׁלֹּא תַּעֲשֶׂנָּה אֶלָּא לִשְׁמִי:

לח **לְהָרִיחַ בָּהּ.** אֲבָל עוֹשֶׂה אַתָּה בְּמַתְכֻּנְתָּהּ מִשֶּׁלְּךָ כְּדֵי לְמָסְרָהּ לַצִּבּוּר:

לא ב **קָרָאתִי בְשֵׁם.** לַעֲשׂוֹת מְלַאכְתִּי, אֶת בְּצַלְאֵל:

ג **בְּחָכְמָה.** מַה שֶּׁאָדָם שׁוֹמֵעַ מֵאֲחֵרִים וְלָמֵד: **וּבִתְבוּנָה.** מֵבִין דָּבָר מִלִּבּוֹ מִתּוֹךְ דְּבָרִים שֶׁלָּמַד: **וּבְדַעַת.** רוּחַ הַקֹּדֶשׁ:

ד **לַחְשֹׁב מַחֲשָׁבֹת.** אֲרִיגַת מַעֲשֵׂה חוֹשֵׁב:

ה **וּבַחֲרֹשֶׁת.** לְשׁוֹן אָמָּנוּת, כְּמוֹ: ״חָרָשׁ חָכָם״ (ישעיה מ, כ). וְאוּנְקְלוֹס פֵּרֵשׁ וְשִׁנָּה בְּפֵרוּשָׁן, שֶׁאֻמַּן אֲבָנִים קָרוּי ״אֻמָּן״ וְחָרַשׁ עֵץ קָרוּי ״נַגָּר״: **לְמַלֹּאת.** לְהוֹשִׁיבָהּ בַּמִּשְׁבֶּצֶת שֶׁלָּהּ בִּמְלוּאָהּ, לַעֲשׂוֹת הַמִּשְׁבֶּצֶת לְמִדַּת מוֹשַׁב הָאֶבֶן וְעָבְיָהּ:

ו **וּבְלֵב כָּל חֲכַם לֵב וְגוֹ׳.** וְעוֹד שְׁאָר חַכְמֵי לֵב יֵשׁ בָּכֶם, וְכָל אֲשֶׁר נָתַתִּי בּוֹ חָכְמָה, ״וְעָשׂוּ אֵת כָּל אֲשֶׁר צִוִּיתִךָ״:

ז **וְאֶת הָאָרֹן לָעֵדֻת.** לְצֹרֶךְ לוּחוֹת הָעֵדוּת:

ח **הַטְּהֹרָה.** עַל שֵׁם זָהָב טָהוֹר:

The stem of Yefet reached its fullest blossoming in the Greeks; that of Shem in the Hebrews, Israel, who bore and bear the name (Shem) of God through the world of nations.... Yefet has ennobled the world aesthetically. Shem has enlightened it spiritually and morally.

Yet as we see from the case of Betzalel, Judaism is not indifferent to aesthetics. The key to Betzalel lies in his name. It means "in the shadow of God." Betzalel's gift lay in his ability to communicate, through his work, that art is the shadow cast by God. Religious art is never "art for art's sake." It points to something beyond itself. The Tabernacle is to be a kind of microcosm of the universe, with one overriding particularity: that in it you felt the presence of something beyond – what the Torah calls "the glory of the LORD" which "filled the Tabernacle" (Ex. 40:35).

לו טָהוֹר קֹדֶשׁ: וְשָׁחַקְתָּ מִמֶּנָּה הָדֵק וְנָתַתָּה מִמֶּנָּה לִפְנֵי הָעֵדֻת בְּאֹהֶל
לז מוֹעֵד אֲשֶׁר אִוָּעֵד לְךָ שָׁמָּה קֹדֶשׁ קָדָשִׁים תִּהְיֶה לָכֶם: וְהַקְּטֹרֶת
אֲשֶׁר תַּעֲשֶׂה בְּמַתְכֻּנְתָּהּ לֹא תַעֲשׂוּ לָכֶם קֹדֶשׁ תִּהְיֶה לְךָ לַיהוָה:
לח אִישׁ אֲשֶׁר־יַעֲשֶׂה כָמוֹהָ לְהָרִיחַ בָּהּ וְנִכְרַת מֵעַמָּיו:
לא א וַיְדַבֵּר כד
ב יְהוָה אֶל־מֹשֶׁה לֵּאמֹר: רְאֵה קָרָאתִי בְשֵׁם בְּצַלְאֵל בֶּן־אוּרִי בֶן־חוּר
ג לְמַטֵּה יְהוּדָה: וָאֲמַלֵּא אֹתוֹ רוּחַ אֱלֹהִים בְּחָכְמָה וּבִתְבוּנָה וּבְדַעַת
ד וּבְכָל־מְלָאכָה: לַחְשֹׁב מַחֲשָׁבֹת לַעֲשׂוֹת בַּזָּהָב וּבַכֶּסֶף וּבַנְּחֹשֶׁת:
ה ו וּבַחֲרֹשֶׁת אֶבֶן לְמַלֹּאת וּבַחֲרֹשֶׁת עֵץ לַעֲשׂוֹת בְּכָל־מְלָאכָה: וַאֲנִי
הִנֵּה נָתַתִּי אִתּוֹ אֵת אָהֳלִיאָב בֶּן־אֲחִיסָמָךְ לְמַטֵּה־דָן וּבְלֵב כָּל־
ז חֲכַם־לֵב נָתַתִּי חָכְמָה וְעָשׂוּ אֵת כָּל־אֲשֶׁר צִוִּיתִךָ: אֵת ׀ אֹהֶל מוֹעֵד
ח וְאֶת־הָאָרֹן לָעֵדֻת וְאֶת־הַכַּפֹּרֶת אֲשֶׁר עָלָיו וְאֵת כָּל־כְּלֵי הָאֹהֶל: וְאֶת־
הַשֻּׁלְחָן וְאֶת־כֵּלָיו וְאֶת־הַמְּנֹרָה הַטְּהֹרָה וְאֶת־כָּל־כֵּלֶיהָ וְאֵת מִזְבַּח
ט הַקְּטֹרֶת: וְאֶת־מִזְבַּח הָעֹלָה וְאֶת־כָּל־כֵּלָיו וְאֶת־הַכִּיּוֹר וְאֶת־כַּנּוֹ:

אונקלוס

דְּכֵי לְקֻדְשָׁא: לו וְתִשְׁחוֹק מִנַּהּ וְתַדִּיק, וְתִתֵּין מִנַּהּ, קֳדָם סָהֲדוּתָא בְּמַשְׁכַּן זִמְנָא, דַּאֲזָמֵין מֵימְרִי לָךְ תַּמָּן, קֹדֶשׁ קֻדְשִׁין תְּהֵי לְכוֹן: לז וּקְטֹרֶת בֻּסְמִין דְּתַעֲבֵיד, בִּדְמוּתַהּ, לָא תַעְבְּדוּן לְכוֹן, קֻדְשָׁא, תְּהֵי לָךְ קֳדָם יְיָ: לח גְּבַר, דְּיַעֲבֵיד דִּכְוָתַהּ לְאָרָחָא בַהּ, וְיִשְׁתֵּיצֵי מֵעַמֵּיהּ: לא א וּמַלֵּיל יְיָ עִם מֹשֶׁה לְמֵימַר: ב חֲזִי דְּרַבֵּיתִי בְשׁוּם, בְּצַלְאֵל, בַּר אוּרִי בַּר חוּר לְשִׁבְטָא דִיהוּדָה: ג וְאַשְׁלֵימִית עִמֵּיהּ רוּחַ מִן קֳדָם יְיָ, בְּחָכְמָא, וּבְסֻכְלְתָנוּ וּבְמַדַּע וּבְכָל עֲבִידָא: ד לְאַלָּפָא אֻמָּנָן, לְמֶעֱבַד, בְּדַהֲבָא וּבְכַסְפָּא וּבִנְחָשָׁא: ה וּבְאֻמָּנוּת אֶבֶן טָבָא, לְאַשְׁלָמָא וּבְנַגָּרוּת אָעָא, לְמֶעֱבַד בְּכָל עֲבִידָא: ו וַאֲנָא הָא יְהַבִית עִמֵּיהּ, יָת אָהֳלִיאָב, בַּר אֲחִיסָמָךְ לְשִׁבְטָא דְדָן, וּבְלֵב כָּל חַכִּימֵי לִבָּא יְהַבִית חָכְמְתָא, וְיַעְבְּדוּן, יָת כָּל דְּפַקֵּידְתָּךְ: ז יָת מַשְׁכַּן זִמְנָא, וְיָת אֲרוֹנָא לְסָהֲדוּתָא, וְיָת כָּפֻרְתָּא דַּעֲלוֹהִי, וְיָת כָּל מָנֵי מַשְׁכְּנָא: ח וְיָת פָּתוּרָא וְיָת מָנוֹהִי, וְיָת מְנָרְתָא דָכִיתָא וְיָת כָּל מָנַהָא, וְיָת מַדְבְּחָא דִקְטֹרֶת בֻּסְמַיָּא: ט וְיָת מַדְבְּחָא דַעֲלָתָא וְיָת כָּל מָנוֹהִי, וְיָת כִּיּוֹרָא וְיָת בְּסִיסֵיהּ: י וְיָת לְבוּשֵׁי שִׁמּוּשָׁא,

31:2 בְּצַלְאֵל *Betzalel* – Betzalel is a rare type in the Tanakh – the artist, the craftsman, the shaper of beauty in the service of God, the man who, together with Oholiav, fashioned the articles associated with the Tabernacle. Judaism – in contrast to ancient Greece – did not cherish the visual arts.

It was Rabbi Samson Raphael Hirsch who distinguished ancient Greece from ancient Israel in terms of the contrast between aesthetics and ethics. In his comment on the verse "May God enlarge Yefet, and let him dwell in the tents of Shem" (Gen. 9:27), he observes:

▶

10 and its base, the service vestments, the sacred vestments for Aharon the priest
11 and the vestments for his sons for when they serve as priests, the anointing oil,
and the fragrant incense for the Sanctuary; they shall make them exactly as I
have commanded you."
12 13 Then the LORD said to Moshe, "Speak to the Israelites and say: Nevertheless,
you shall keep My Sabbaths. It is a sign between Me and you throughout
14 the generations, that you may know that I, the LORD, make you holy. Keep
the Sabbath, for it is holy to you. Whoever profanes it shall be put to death.
15 Whoever does work on it shall be severed from his people. Six days shall work
be done, but the seventh day is a Sabbath of complete rest, sacred to the LORD.
16 Whoever does any work on the Sabbath shall be put to death. The Israelites
shall keep the Sabbath, making it a day of rest throughout their generations
17 as a covenant forever. It is an eternal sign between Me and the Israelites that
in six days the LORD made heaven and earth, and on the seventh day He
18 ceased and was revived." When He had finished speaking to Moshe SHENI
on Mount Sinai, He gave him the two tablets of the Covenant, stone tablets,

רש״י

י **וְאֵת בִּגְדֵי הַשְּׂרָד.** אוֹמֵר אֲנִי לְפִי פְּשׁוּטוֹ שֶׁל מִקְרָא שֶׁאִי אֶפְשָׁר לוֹמַר שֶׁבְּבִגְדֵי כְהֻנָּה מְדַבֵּר, לְפִי שֶׁנֶּאֱמַר אֶצְלָם: "וְאֶת בִּגְדֵי הַקֹּדֶשׁ לְאַהֲרֹן הַכֹּהֵן וְאֶת בִּגְדֵי בָנָיו לְכַהֵן", אֶלָּא אֵלּוּ בִּגְדֵי הַשְּׂרָד הֵם בִּגְדֵי הַתְּכֵלֶת וְהָאַרְגָּמָן וְתוֹלַעַת שָׁנִי הָאֲמוּרִים בְּפָרָשַׁת מַסָּעוֹת: וְנָתְנוּ עָלָיו בֶּגֶד תְּכֵלֶת (עיין במדבר ד, ז), וְנָתְנוּ עָלָיו בֶּגֶד אַרְגָּמָן (שם פסוק יג-יד), וְנָתְנוּ עֲלֵיהֶם בֶּגֶד תּוֹלַעַת שָׁנִי (שם פסוק ח). וְנִרְאִין דְּבָרַי, שֶׁנֶּאֱמַר: "וּמִן הַתְּכֵלֶת וְהָאַרְגָּמָן וְתוֹלַעַת הַשָּׁנִי עָשׂוּ בִגְדֵי שְׂרָד לְשָׁרֵת בַּקֹּדֶשׁ" (להלן לט, א), וְלֹא הֻזְכַּר שֵׁשׁ עִמָּהֶם, וְאִם בְּבִגְדֵי כְהֻנָּה מְדַבֵּר, לֹא מָצִינוּ בְּאֶחָד מֵהֶם אַרְגָּמָן אוֹ תּוֹלַעַת שָׁנִי בְּלֹא שֵׁשׁ: **בִּגְדֵי הַשְּׂרָד.** יֵשׁ מְפָרְשִׁים לְשׁוֹן עֲבוֹדָה וְשֵׁרוּת, כְּתַרְגּוּמוֹ: "לְבוּשֵׁי שִׁמּוּשָׁא", וְאֵין לוֹ דִּמְיוֹן בַּמִּקְרָא. וַאֲנִי אוֹמֵר שֶׁהוּא לָשׁוֹן אֲרַמִּי כְּתַרְגּוּמוֹ שֶׁל "קְלָעִים" (לעיל כז, ט) וְתַרְגּוּם שֶׁל "מִכְבָּר" (שם פסוק ד), שֶׁהָיוּ אֲרוּגִים בְּמַחַט, עֲשׂוּיִים נְקָבִים נְקָבִים, לעזי"ץ בְּלַעַז:

יא **וְאֵת קְטֹרֶת הַסַּמִּים לַקֹּדֶשׁ.** לְצֹרֶךְ הַקְטָרַת הֵיכָל שֶׁהוּא קֹדֶשׁ:

יג **וְאַתָּה דַּבֵּר אֶל בְּנֵי יִשְׂרָאֵל.** וְאַתָּה, אַף עַל פִּי שֶׁהִפְקַדְתִּיךָ לְצַוּוֹתָם עַל מְלֶאכֶת הַמִּשְׁכָּן, אַל יֵקַל בְּעֵינֶיךָ לִדְחוֹת אֶת הַשַּׁבָּת מִפְּנֵי אוֹתָהּ מְלָאכָה: **אַךְ אֶת שַׁבְּתֹתַי תִּשְׁמֹרוּ.** אַף עַל פִּי שֶׁתִּהְיוּ רְדוּפִין וּזְרִיזִין בִּזְרִיזוּת הַמְּלָאכָה, שַׁבָּת אַל תִּדָּחֶה מִפָּנֶיהָ. כָּל אַכִין וְרַקִּין מִעוּטִין, לְמַעֵט שַׁבָּת מִמְּלֶאכֶת הַמִּשְׁכָּן: **כִּי אוֹת הִוא בֵּינִי וּבֵינֵיכֶם.** אוֹת גְּדוֹלָה הִיא בֵּינֵינוּ שֶׁבָּחַרְתִּי בָכֶם, בְּהַנְחִילִי לָכֶם אֶת יוֹם מְנוּחָתִי לִמְנוּחָה: **לָדַעַת.** הָאֻמּוֹת בָּהּ "כִּי אֲנִי ה' מְקַדִּשְׁכֶם":

יד **מוֹת יוּמָת.** אִם יֵשׁ עֵדִים וְהַתְרָאָה: **וְנִכְרְתָה.** בְּלֹא הַתְרָאָה: **מְחַלְלֶיהָ.** הַנּוֹהֵג בָּהּ חֹל בִּקְדֻשָּׁתָהּ:

טו **שַׁבַּת שַׁבָּתוֹן.** מְנוּחַת מַרְגּוֹעַ וְלֹא מְנוּחַת עֲרַאי: **קֹדֶשׁ לַה'.** שְׁמִירַת קְדֻשָּׁתָהּ לִשְׁמִי וּבְמִצְוָתִי:

יז **וַיִּנָּפַשׁ.** כְּתַרְגּוּמוֹ "וְנָח". וְכָל לְשׁוֹן 'נֹפֶשׁ' הוּא לְשׁוֹן נֶפֶשׁ, שֶׁמֵּשִׁיב נַפְשׁוֹ וּנְשִׁימָתוֹ בְּהַרְגִּיעוֹ מִטֹּרַח הַמְּלָאכָה. וּמִי שֶׁכָּתוּב בּוֹ: "לֹא יִיעַף וְלֹא יִיגָע" (ישעיה מ, כח) וְכָל פָּעֳלוֹ בְּמַאֲמָר, הִכְתִּיב מְנוּחָה בְּעַצְמוֹ, לְשַׁבֵּר הָאֹזֶן מַה שֶּׁהִיא יְכוֹלָה לִשְׁמֹעַ:

יח **וַיִּתֵּן אֶל מֹשֶׁה וְגוֹ'.** אֵין מֻקְדָּם וּמְאֻחָר בַּתּוֹרָה. מַעֲשֵׂה הָעֵגֶל קֹדֶם לְצִוּוּי מְלֶאכֶת הַמִּשְׁכָּן יָמִים רַבִּים הָיָה, שֶׁהֲרֵי בְּשִׁבְעָה עָשָׂר בְּתַמּוּז נִשְׁתַּבְּרוּ הַלּוּחוֹת וּבְיוֹם הַכִּפּוּרִים נִתְרַצָּה הַקָּדוֹשׁ בָּרוּךְ הוּא לְיִשְׂרָאֵל, וּלְמָחֳרָת הִתְחִילוּ בְּנִדְבַת הַמִּשְׁכָּן וְהוּקַם בְּאֶחָד בְּנִיסָן: **כְּכַלֹּתוֹ.** 'כְּכַלֹּתוֹ' כְּתִיב חָסֵר, שֶׁנִּמְסְרָה לוֹ תּוֹרָה בְּמַתָּנָה כְּכַלָּה לֶחָתָן, שֶׁלֹּא הָיָה יָכוֹל לִלְמֹד כֻּלָּהּ בִּזְמַן מוּעָט כָּזֶה. דָּבָר אַחֵר, מָה כַּלָּה מִתְקַשֶּׁטֶת בְּעֶשְׂרִים וְאַרְבָּעָה קִשּׁוּטִין, הֵן הָאֲמוּרִים בְּסֵפֶר יְשַׁעְיָה (ג,

We need time for *thinking* as well as for doing. So the Sabbath is a holy time, meaning time set apart, time out from the relentless pressures of activity: a day dedicated to thinking about the purpose of what we do.

י וְאֵת בִּגְדֵי הַשְּׂרָד וְאֶת־בִּגְדֵי הַקֹּדֶשׁ לְאַהֲרֹן הַכֹּהֵן וְאֶת־בִּגְדֵי בָנָיו לְכַהֵן׃
יא וְאֵת שֶׁמֶן הַמִּשְׁחָה וְאֶת־קְטֹרֶת הַסַּמִּים לַקֹּדֶשׁ כְּכֹל אֲשֶׁר־צִוִּיתִךָ
יַעֲשׂוּ׃
יב יג וַיֹּאמֶר יהוה אֶל־מֹשֶׁה לֵּאמֹר׃ וְאַתָּה דַּבֵּר אֶל־בְּנֵי יִשְׂרָאֵל לֵאמֹר
אַךְ אֶת־שַׁבְּתֹתַי תִּשְׁמֹרוּ כִּי אוֹת הִוא בֵּינִי וּבֵינֵיכֶם לְדֹרֹתֵיכֶם לָדַעַת
יד כִּי אֲנִי יהוה מְקַדִּשְׁכֶם׃ וּשְׁמַרְתֶּם אֶת־הַשַּׁבָּת כִּי קֹדֶשׁ הִוא לָכֶם
מְחַלְלֶיהָ מוֹת יוּמָת כִּי כָּל־הָעֹשֶׂה בָהּ מְלָאכָה וְנִכְרְתָה הַנֶּפֶשׁ הַהִוא
טו מִקֶּרֶב עַמֶּיהָ׃ שֵׁשֶׁת יָמִים יֵעָשֶׂה מְלָאכָה וּבַיּוֹם הַשְּׁבִיעִי שַׁבַּת שַׁבָּתוֹן
טז קֹדֶשׁ לַיהוה כָּל־הָעֹשֶׂה מְלָאכָה בְּיוֹם הַשַּׁבָּת מוֹת יוּמָת׃ וְשָׁמְרוּ
בְנֵי־יִשְׂרָאֵל אֶת־הַשַּׁבָּת לַעֲשׂוֹת אֶת־הַשַּׁבָּת לְדֹרֹתָם בְּרִית עוֹלָם׃
יז בֵּינִי וּבֵין בְּנֵי יִשְׂרָאֵל אוֹת הִוא לְעֹלָם כִּי־שֵׁשֶׁת יָמִים עָשָׂה יהוה
יח אֶת־הַשָּׁמַיִם וְאֶת־הָאָרֶץ וּבַיּוֹם הַשְּׁבִיעִי שָׁבַת וַיִּנָּפַשׁ׃ וַיִּתֵּן שני
אֶל־מֹשֶׁה כְּכַלֹּתוֹ לְדַבֵּר אִתּוֹ בְּהַר סִינַי שְׁנֵי לֻחֹת הָעֵדֻת לֻחֹת אֶבֶן

אונקלוס

וְיָת לְבוּשֵׁי קֻדְשָׁא לְאַהֲרֹן כָּהֲנָא, וְיָת לְבוּשֵׁי בְנוֹהִי לְשַׁמָּשָׁא: יא וְיָת מִשְׁחָא דִּרְבוּתָא, וְיָת קְטֹרֶת בֻּסְמַיָּא לְקֻדְשָׁא, כְּכֹל דְּפַקֵּידְתָּךְ יַעְבְּדוּן: יב וַאֲמַר יי לְמֹשֶׁה לְמֵימַר: יג וְאַתְּ, מַלֵּיל עִם בְּנֵי יִשְׂרָאֵל לְמֵימַר, בְּרַם יָת יוֹמֵי שַׁבַּיָּא דִּילִי תִּטְּרוּן, אֲרֵי אָת הִיא, בֵּין מֵימְרִי וּבֵינֵיכוֹן לְדָרֵיכוֹן, לְמִדַּע, אֲרֵי, אֲנָא יי מְקַדֵּשְׁכוֹן: יד וְתִטְּרוּן יָת שַׁבְּתָא, אֲרֵי, קֻדְשָׁא הִיא לְכוֹן, דִּיחַלְּלִנַּהּ אִתְקְטָלָא יִתְקְטִיל, אֲרֵי, כָּל דְּיַעֲבֵיד בַּהּ עֲבִידְתָּא, וְיִשְׁתֵּיצֵי, אֲנָשָׁא הַהוּא מִגּוֹ עַמֵּיהּ: טו שִׁתָּא יוֹמִין יִתְעֲבֵיד עֲבִידְתָּא, וּבְיוֹמָא שְׁבִיעָאָה, שַׁבָּא שַׁבְּתָא, קֻדְשָׁא קֳדָם יי, כָּל דְּיַעֲבֵיד עֲבִידְתָּא, בְּיוֹמָא דְשַׁבְּתָא אִתְקְטָלָא יִתְקְטִיל: טז וְיִטְּרוּן בְּנֵי יִשְׂרָאֵל יָת שַׁבְּתָא, לְמֶעְבַּד יָת שַׁבְּתָא, לְדָרֵיהוֹן קְיָם עָלַם: יז בֵּין מֵימְרִי, וּבֵין בְּנֵי יִשְׂרָאֵל, אָת הִיא לְעָלַם, אֲרֵי שִׁתָּא יוֹמִין, עֲבַד יי יָת שְׁמַיָּא וְיָת אַרְעָא, וּבְיוֹמָא שְׁבִיעָאָה, שְׁבַת וְנָח: יח וִיהַב לְמֹשֶׁה, כַּד שֵׁיצִי לְמַלָּלָא עִמֵּיהּ בְּטוּרָא דְסִינַי, תְּרֵין לוּחֵי סַהֲדוּתָא, לוּחֵי אַבְנָא,

31:17 וּבַיּוֹם הַשְּׁבִיעִי שָׁבַת וַיִּנָּפַשׁ *And on the seventh day He ceased and was revived* – The creation of the Tabernacle, we have seen, reflects the creation of the world. For six days God created the world and on the seventh day He rested (see Gen. 2:2). So we are instructed that for six days we too should labor to create, and on the seventh day we should rest. Why? Does an all-powerful God *need* to rest? And if we sometimes need to relax, can we be said to be imitating God?

Perhaps the simplest answer is this. All of nature is creative, but only God and humanity create consciously for a purpose. For us, unlike the plant or animal kingdoms, creation is not a process of ceaseless activity. It involves moments of contemplation when we reflect on *why* we act.

32 1 inscribed by the finger of God. When the people saw that Moshe was long
delayed in coming down the mountain, they gathered around Aharon and said
to him, "Get up, make us gods to go before us. This man Moshe who brought
2 us out of Egypt – we have no idea what has become of him." So Aharon said
to them, "Remove the gold rings from the ears of your wives, your sons, and
3 your daughters and bring them to me." So all the people took the gold rings

רש"י

(יח-כד), אף תלמיד חכם צריך להיות בקי בעשרים וארבעה ספרים: **לדבר אתו.** החקים והמשפטים שב'ואלה המשפטים': **לדבר אתו.** מלמד שהיה משה שומע מפי הגבורה וחוזרין ושונין את ההלכה שניהם יחד: **לחת.** 'לחת' כתיב, שהיו שתיהן שוות:

לב א **כי בשש משה.** כתרגומו לשון איחור, וכן: "בשש רכבו" (שופטים ה, כח), "ויחילו עד בוש" (שם ג, כה). כי כשעלה משה להר אמר להם: לסוף ארבעים יום אני בא בתוך שש שעות. כסבורים הם שאותו יום שעלה מן המנין הוא, והוא אמר להם שלמים, ארבעים יום ולילו עמו, ויום עלייתו אין לילו עמו. בשבעה בסיון עלה, נמצא יום ארבעים בשבעה עשר בתמוז. בששה עשר בא שטן וערבב את העולם והראה דמות חשך ואפלה וערבוביא, לומר ודאי מת משה לכך בא ערבוביא לעולם. אמר להם: מת משה, שכבר באו שש שעות ולא בא וכו', כדאיתא במסכת שבת (דף פט ע"א). ואי אפשר לומר שלא טעו אלא ביום המעונן בין קודם חצות בין לאחר חצות, שהרי לא ירד משה עד יום המחרת, שנאמר: "וישכימו ממחרת ויעלו עלת" (להלן פסוק ו): **אשר ילכו לפנינו.** אלהות הרבה אוו להם: **כי זה משה האיש.** כמין דמות משה הראה להם השטן שנושאים אותו באויר רקיע השמים: **אשר העלנו מארץ מצרים.** והיה מורה לנו דרך אשר נעלה בה, עתה צריכין אנו לאלהות "אשר ילכו לפנינו":

ב **באזני נשיכם.** אמר אהרן בלבו: הנשים והילדים חסים על תכשיטיהן, שמא יתעכב הדבר ובתוך כך יבא משה. והם לא המתינו ופרקו מעל עצמן: **פרקו.** לשון צווי מגזרת 'פרק' ליחיד, כמו 'ברכו' מגזרת 'ברך':

ג **ויתפרקו.** לשון פריקת משא, כשנטלום מאזניהם נמצאו הם מפורקים מנזמיהם, דישקריי"ר בלע"ז:

order in the life of the spirit. There must be a structure of leadership that does not depend on chance."

This is one of the decisive moments in Judaism. The long digression between Exodus 23 and Leviticus 25 is, as Ramban saw (commentary on Lev. 25:1), entirely taken up with the consequences of the golden calf and the new relationship it inaugurated between God and the people. All of it – the appointment of the priests and Levites, the construction of the Sanctuary, the offerings to be made there, the special demands of purity for all who entered its precincts, the holiness demanded of a people with God in its midst – is about *bringing God close*, living safely in the constant presence of the Divine. This is God's answer to Moshe: "They shall make Me a Sanctuary and I will dwell (*veshakhanti*) in their midst" (Ex. 25:8).

32:2 **וְהָבִיאוּ אֵלָי** *Bring them to me* – Aharon is the de facto leader of the people in the absence of Moshe. Surely, Aharon should have seen the danger unfolding, and told them to wait, have patience and trust. What is going on in his mind?

Essentially there are three lines of defense among the commentators. According to the first, Aharon is playing for time. He tells the people to take the gold rings from the ears of their wives, sons, and daughters, reasoning to himself, "While they are quarreling with their children and wives about the gold, there will be a delay and Moshe will come" (Zohar).

The second defense is in the Talmud and is based on the fact that when Moshe departed to ascend the mountain, he left not just Aharon but also Ḥur in charge of the people (Ex. 24:14). Yet Ḥur does not figure in the narrative of the golden calf. According to the Talmud, Ḥur opposed the people, and was then killed by them. Aharon saw this and decided that proceeding with the making of the calf was the lesser of two evils: "'Can priest [Aharon] and prophet [Ḥur] be murdered in the Temple of the Lord?' (Lam. 2:20). If that

לב א כְּתֻבִ֖ים בְּאֶצְבַּ֥ע אֱלֹהִֽים׃ וַיַּ֣רְא הָעָ֔ם כִּֽי־בֹשֵׁ֥שׁ מֹשֶׁ֖ה לָרֶ֣דֶת מִן־הָהָ֑ר
וַיִּקָּהֵ֨ל הָעָ֜ם עַֽל־אַהֲרֹ֗ן וַיֹּאמְר֤וּ אֵלָיו֙ ק֣וּם ׀ עֲשֵׂה־לָ֣נוּ אֱלֹהִ֗ים אֲשֶׁ֤ר
יֵֽלְכוּ֙ לְפָנֵ֔ינוּ כִּי־זֶ֣ה ׀ מֹשֶׁ֣ה הָאִ֗ישׁ אֲשֶׁ֤ר הֶֽעֱלָ֙נוּ֙ מֵאֶ֣רֶץ מִצְרַ֔יִם לֹ֥א
ב יָדַ֖עְנוּ מֶה־הָ֥יָה לֽוֹ׃ וַיֹּ֤אמֶר אֲלֵהֶם֙ אַהֲרֹ֔ן פָּֽרְקוּ֙ נִזְמֵ֣י הַזָּהָ֔ב אֲשֶׁר֙
ג בְּאׇזְנֵ֣י נְשֵׁיכֶ֔ם בְּנֵיכֶ֖ם וּבְנֹתֵיכֶ֑ם וְהָבִ֖יאוּ אֵלָֽי׃ וַיִּתְפָּֽרְקוּ֙ כׇּל־הָעָ֔ם אֶת־

אונקלוס

כְּתִיבִין בְּאֶצְבְּעָא דַייָ: לב א וַחֲזָא עַמָּא, אֲרֵי אוֹחַר מֹשֶׁה לְמֵיחַת מִן
טוּרָא, וְאִתְכְּנִישׁ עַמָּא עַל אַהֲרֹן, וַאֲמַרוּ לֵיהּ קוּם עֲבֵיד לַנָא דַחְלָן,
דִּיהָכוּן קֳדָמַנָא, אֲרֵי דֵין מֹשֶׁה גֻּבְרָא, דְּאַסְּקַנָא מֵאַרְעָא דְמִצְרַיִם,
לָא יְדַעְנָא מָא הֲוָה לֵיהּ: ב וַאֲמַר לְהוֹן אַהֲרֹן, פָּרִיקוּ קְדָשֵׁי דְדַהֲבָא,
דִּבְאֻדְנֵי נְשֵׁיכוֹן, בְּנֵיכוֹן וּבְנָתְכוֹן, וְאֵיתוֹ לְוָתִי: ג וּפָרִיקוּ כָּל עַמָּא, יָת

THE GOLDEN CALF

The classical commentators, notably Ibn Ezra and Ramban, observed that the Sinai revelation does not end where it appears to. It will resume in Leviticus 25: "The Lord spoke to Moshe on Mount Sinai." That chapter is about principles of social justice: the Jubilee year, the release of debts, and the liberation of slaves, precisely the subjects we associate with Exodus. The obvious place for these laws is in Parashat Mishpatim.

What we have, then, between Exodus 24 and Leviticus 25 is a massive parenthesis, some forty chapters long. What caused it?

There is only one plausible candidate: the episode of the golden calf. Moshe ascends Mount Sinai after the great revelation. Eventually the people panic. Without Moshe how can they receive the will and word of God? They become a mob. Unused to such pressure, Aharon makes what turns out to be a disastrous decision and builds the calf.

Moshe is told by God, "Quick – go down. Your people… are acting ruinously" (Ex. 32:7). He prays to God to forgive them. He then goes down, smashes the tablets, burns the calf, has everyone drink its ashes, and has the Levites execute punishment against the main wrongdoers. Then he returns to God, asking again for forgiveness. God agrees, but only partially. The guilty will suffer but the people as a whole will survive.

Thus far, the story is clear. What happens next is not. First God says that the people must move on and continue their journey to the Promised Land. They do so only fifty chapters later, in Numbers 10. God then says that He will not be "among you" (Ex. 33:3). It would be too dangerous for God to be close to the people, given their tendency to provoke Him to anger. Moshe urges God to reconsider His decision. Then the subject changes to what seem to be metaphysical inquiries about the nature of God. In chapter 34 comes the famous scene in which God places Moshe in a crevice in a rock and passes before him, reciting the words that became known as God's Thirteen Attributes of Mercy.

Moshe, in this bewildering series of conversations, is exploring the fundamental parameters of the relationship between God and humanity. Can an infinite God be close to finite human beings? If not, what hope is there for humanity? So far the people have experienced God only as a terrifying, overwhelming force. In His apparent absence, however, they are lost. When they made the calf, wrongheaded though they were, they were seeking a way of encountering God without terror.

Predictability too has become problematic. It is as if Moshe says to God, "Sometimes You are angry, and sometimes You are moved by compassion. Precisely because You are free, we cannot predict which will prevail: punishment or forgiveness. But we have staked our entire existence on You. How can we live, not knowing when You will next be angry, and whether our prayers for forgiveness will succeed? What will happen in the future if the people sin and there is no Moshe to pray for them? There must be some sustainable

4 from their ears and brought them to Aharon. He took the gold from them and,
fashioning it with a chisel, made a molten calf. And they said, "These, Israel,
5 are your gods who brought you out of Egypt!" Seeing this, Aharon built an
altar in front of it and announced, "Tomorrow will be a festival to the LORD."
6 The next day, they rose early and sacrificed burnt offerings and brought peace
offerings. The people sat down to eat and drink and then stood up to engage in
revelry.
7 The LORD said to Moshe, "Quick – go down. Your people, whom you brought
8 out of Egypt, are acting ruinously. They have deviated swiftly from the way I
commanded them; they have made themselves a molten calf and are bowing
down and sacrificing to it, saying, 'These, Israel, are your gods who brought
9 you out of Egypt!'" Then the LORD said to Moshe, "I have seen this people;

רש״י

אֶת נִזְמֵי. כְּמוֹ מִנִּזְמֵי. כְּמוֹ: "כְּצֵאתִי אֶת הָעִיר" (לעיל ט, כט) – מִן הָעִיר:

ד **וַיָּצַר אֹתוֹ בַּחֶרֶט.** יֵשׁ לְתַרְגְּמוֹ בִּשְׁנֵי פָּנִים: הָאֶחָד – "וַיָּצַר" לְשׁוֹן קְשִׁירָה, "בַּחֶרֶט" לְשׁוֹן סוּדָר, כְּמוֹ "וְהַמִּטְפָּחוֹת וְהָחֲרִיטִים" (ישעיה ג, כב), "וַיָּצַר כִּכְּרַיִם כֶּסֶף בִּשְׁנֵי חֲרִטִים" (מלכים ב׳ ה, כג). וְהַשֵּׁנִי – "וַיָּצַר" לְשׁוֹן צוּרָה, "בַּחֶרֶט" כְּלִי אֻמָּנוּת הַצּוֹרְפִין שֶׁחוֹרְצִין וְחוֹרְתִין בּוֹ צוּרוֹת בַּזָּהָב כְּעֵט סוֹפֵר הַחוֹרֵט אוֹתִיּוֹת בְּלוּחוֹת וּפִנְקָסִין, כְּמוֹ: "וּכְתֹב עָלָיו בְּחֶרֶט אֱנוֹשׁ" (ישעיה ח, א), וְזֶהוּ שֶׁתִּרְגֵּם אוּנְקְלוֹס: "וְצַר יָתֵיהּ בְּזִיפָא" לְשׁוֹן זִיּוּף, הוּא כְּלִי אֻמָּנוּת שֶׁחוֹרְצִין בּוֹ בַּזָּהָב אוֹתִיּוֹת וּשְׁקוּדִים שֶׁקּוֹרִין בְּלַעַז נייי״ל, וּמְזַיְּפִין עַל יָדוֹ חוֹתָמוֹת: **עֵגֶל מַסֵּכָה.** כֵּיוָן שֶׁהִשְׁלִיכוֹ לָאוּר בַּכּוּר, בָּאוּ מְכַשְּׁפֵי עֵרֶב רַב שֶׁעָלוּ עִמָּהֶם מִמִּצְרַיִם וַעֲשָׂאוּהוּ בִּכְשָׁפִים. וְיֵשׁ אוֹמְרִים: מִיכָה הָיָה שָׁם, שֶׁיָּצָא מִתּוֹךְ דְּמוּסֵי בִנְיָן שֶׁנִּתְמַכְמֵךְ בּוֹ בְּמִצְרַיִם, וְהָיָה בְּיָדוֹ שֵׁם וְטַס שֶׁכָּתַב בּוֹ מֹשֶׁה: "עֲלֵה שׁוֹר עֲלֵה שׁוֹר" לְהַעֲלוֹת אֲרוֹנוֹ שֶׁל יוֹסֵף מִתּוֹךְ נִילוּס, וְהִשְׁלִיכוֹ לְתוֹךְ הַכּוּר וְיָצָא הָעֵגֶל: **מַסֵּכָה.** לְשׁוֹן מַתֶּכֶת. דָּבָר אַחֵר, מֵאָה וְעֶשְׂרִים וַחֲמִשָּׁה קַנְטְרִין זָהָב הָיוּ בּוֹ כְּגִימַטְרִיָּא שֶׁל מַסֵּכָה: **אֵלֶּה אֱלֹהֶיךָ.** וְלֹא נֶאֱמַר 'אֵלֶּה אֱלֹהֵינוּ', מִכָּאן שֶׁעֵרֶב רַב שֶׁעָלוּ מִמִּצְרַיִם הֵם שֶׁנִּקְהֲלוּ עַל אַהֲרֹן וְהֵם שֶׁעֲשָׂאוּהוּ, וְאַחַר כָּךְ הִטְעוּ אֶת יִשְׂרָאֵל אַחֲרָיו:

ה **וַיַּרְא אַהֲרֹן.** שֶׁהָיָה בּוֹ רוּחַ חַיִּים, שֶׁנֶּאֱמַר: "בְּתַבְנִית שׁוֹר אֹכֵל עֵשֶׂב" (תהלים קו, כ), וְרָאָה שֶׁהִצְלִיחַ מַעֲשֵׂה שָׂטָן, וְלֹא הָיָה לוֹ פֶּה לִדְחוֹתָם לְגַמְרֵי: **וַיִּבֶן מִזְבֵּחַ.** לִדְחוֹתָם: **וַיִּקְרָא... חַג לַה׳ מָחָר.** וְלֹא הַיּוֹם, שֶׁמָּא יָבֹא מֹשֶׁה קֹדֶם שֶׁיַּעַבְדוּהוּ, זֶהוּ פְּשׁוּטוֹ. וּמִדְרָשׁוֹ בְּוַיִּקְרָא רַבָּה (י, ג): דְּבָרִים הַרְבֵּה רָאָה אַהֲרֹן; רָאָה חוּר בֶּן אֲחוֹתוֹ שֶׁהָיָה מוֹכִיחָם וַהֲרָגוּהוּ, וְזֶהוּ "וַיִּבֶן מִזְבֵּחַ לְפָנָיו", וַיָּבֶן מִזָּבוּחַ לְפָנָיו; וְעוֹד רָאָה וְאָמַר, מוּטָב שֶׁיִּתָּלֶה בִּי הַסִּרְחוֹן וְלֹא בָּהֶם; וְעוֹד רָאָה וְאָמַר, אִם הֵם בּוֹנִים אוֹתוֹ הַמִּזְבֵּחַ, זֶה מֵבִיא צְרוֹר וְזֶה מֵבִיא אֶבֶן וְנִמְצֵאת מְלַאכְתָּן בְּבַת אַחַת, מִתּוֹךְ שֶׁאֲנִי בּוֹנֶה אוֹתוֹ אֲנִי מִתְעַצֵּל בִּמְלַאכְתִּי, וּבֵין כָּךְ וּבֵין כָּךְ מֹשֶׁה בָּא. **חַג לַה׳.** בְּלִבּוֹ הָיָה לַשָּׁמַיִם, בָּטוּחַ הָיָה שֶׁיָּבֹא מֹשֶׁה וְיַעַבְדוּ אֶת הַמָּקוֹם:

ו **וַיַּשְׁכִּימוּ.** הַשָּׂטָן זֵרְזָם כְּדֵי שֶׁיֶּחֶטְאוּ: **לְצַחֵק.** יֵשׁ בְּמַשְׁמָע הַזֶּה גִּלּוּי עֲרָיוֹת, כְּמוֹ שֶׁנֶּאֱמַר: "לְצַחֶק בִּי" (בראשית לט, יז), וּשְׁפִיכוּת דָּמִים, כְּמוֹ שֶׁנֶּאֱמַר: "יָקוּמוּ נָא הַנְּעָרִים וִישַׂחֲקוּ לְפָנֵינוּ" (שמואל ב׳ ב, יד), אַף כָּאן נֶהֱרַג חוּר:

ז **וַיְדַבֵּר.** לְשׁוֹן קֹשִׁי הוּא, כְּמוֹ: "וַיְדַבֵּר אִתָּם קָשׁוֹת" (בראשית מב, ז): **לֶךְ רֵד.** מִגְּדֻלָּתְךָ, לֹא נָתַתִּי לְךָ גְּדֻלָּה אֶלָּא בִּשְׁבִילָם. בְּאוֹתָהּ שָׁעָה נִתְנַדָּה מֹשֶׁה מִפִּי בֵּית דִּין שֶׁלְּמַעְלָה: **שִׁחֵת עַמְּךָ.** שִׁחֵת הָעָם לֹא נֶאֱמַר, אֶלָּא "עַמְּךָ", עֵרֶב רַב שֶׁקִּבַּלְתָּ מֵעַצְמְךָ וְגִיַּרְתָּם וְלֹא נִמְלַכְתָּ בִּי, וְאָמַרְתָּ: טוֹב שֶׁיִּדָּבְקוּ גֵּרִים בַּשְּׁכִינָה – הֵם שִׁחֲתוּ וְהִשְׁחִיתוּ:

do likewise. The golden calf is an idol. The Sanctuary is the home of the Divine Presence. There is nothing in common between them except this, that they both come into being through voluntary donations. The Talmud Yerushalmi (Shekalim 1:1) expresses amazement: "One cannot understand the nature of this people: if appealed to for the calf they give; if appealed to for the Sanctuary they give." Jewishly, to live is to give.

ד נִזְמֵי הַזָּהָב אֲשֶׁר בְּאָזְנֵיהֶם וַיָּבִיאוּ אֶל־אַהֲרֹן: וַיִּקַּח מִיָּדָם וַיָּצַר אֹתוֹ
בַּחֶרֶט וַיַּעֲשֵׂהוּ עֵגֶל מַסֵּכָה וַיֹּאמְרוּ אֵלֶּה אֱלֹהֶיךָ יִשְׂרָאֵל אֲשֶׁר הֶעֱלוּךָ
ה מֵאֶרֶץ מִצְרָיִם: וַיַּרְא אַהֲרֹן וַיִּבֶן מִזְבֵּחַ לְפָנָיו וַיִּקְרָא אַהֲרֹן וַיֹּאמַר חַג
ו לַיהוָה מָחָר: וַיַּשְׁכִּימוּ מִמָּחֳרָת וַיַּעֲלוּ עֹלֹת וַיַּגִּשׁוּ שְׁלָמִים וַיֵּשֶׁב הָעָם
לֶאֱכֹל וְשָׁתוֹ וַיָּקֻמוּ לְצַחֵק:
ז וַיְדַבֵּר יְהוָה אֶל־מֹשֶׁה לֶךְ־רֵד כִּי שִׁחֵת עַמְּךָ אֲשֶׁר הֶעֱלֵיתָ מֵאֶרֶץ
ח מִצְרָיִם: סָרוּ מַהֵר מִן־הַדֶּרֶךְ אֲשֶׁר צִוִּיתִם עָשׂוּ לָהֶם עֵגֶל מַסֵּכָה
וַיִּשְׁתַּחֲווּ־לוֹ וַיִּזְבְּחוּ־לוֹ וַיֹּאמְרוּ אֵלֶּה אֱלֹהֶיךָ יִשְׂרָאֵל אֲשֶׁר הֶעֱלוּךָ
ט מֵאֶרֶץ מִצְרָיִם: וַיֹּאמֶר יְהוָה אֶל־מֹשֶׁה רָאִיתִי אֶת־הָעָם הַזֶּה וְהִנֵּה

אונקלוס

קָדָשֵׁי דְדַהֲבָא דִּבְאֻדְנֵיהוֹן, וְאֵיתִיאוּ לְוָת אַהֲרֹן: ד וּנְסֵיב מִידֵיהוֹן, וְצַר יָתֵיהּ בְּזִיפָא, וַעֲבַדֵיהּ עֵיגַל מַתְּכָא, וַאֲמַרוּ, אִלֵּין דַּחְלָתָךְ יִשְׂרָאֵל, דְּאַסְּקוּךְ מֵאַרְעָא דְּמִצְרָיִם: ה וַחֲזָא אַהֲרֹן, וּבְנָא מַדְבְּחָא קֳדָמוֹהִי, וּקְרָא אַהֲרֹן וַאֲמַר, חַגָּא קֳדָם יי מְחַר: ו וְאַקְדִּימוּ בְּיוֹמָא דְּבָתְרוֹהִי, וְאַסִּיקוּ עֲלָוָן, וְקָרִיבוּ נִכְסַן, וְאַסְחַר עַמָּא לְמֵיכַל וּלְמִשְׁתֵּי, וְקָמוּ לְחַיָּכָא: ז וּמַלֵּיל יי עִם מֹשֶׁה, אִיזֵיל חוּת, אֲרֵי חַבִּיל עַמָּךְ, דְּאַסֵּיקְתָּא מֵאַרְעָא דְּמִצְרָיִם: ח סְטוֹ בִּפְרִיעַ, מִן אוֹרְחָא דְּפַקֵּידְתִּנּוּן, עֲבַדוּ לְהוֹן, עֵיגֶל מַתְּכָא, וּסְגִידוּ לֵיהּ וְדַבַּחוּ לֵיהּ, וַאֲמַרוּ, אִלֵּין דַּחְלָתָךְ יִשְׂרָאֵל, דְּאַסְּקוּךְ מֵאַרְעָא דְּמִצְרָיִם: ט וַאֲמַר יי לְמֹשֶׁה, גְּלֵי קֳדָמַי עַמָּא הָדֵין, וְהָא

happens, the people will never be forgiven. Better let them worship the golden calf, for which they may yet find forgiveness through repentance" (Sanhedrin 7a).

The third, argued by Ibn Ezra, is that the calf is not an idol at all, and what the Israelites are doing is, in Aharon's view, permissible. After all, their initial complaint is: "This man Moshe … we have no idea what has become of him" (Ex. 32:1). They do not want a god-substitute but a Moshe-substitute, an oracle, something through which they can discern God's instructions.

So there is a systematic attempt in the history of interpretation to mitigate or minimize Aharon's culpability, even to reveal heroic aspects of his actions. Recall the famous words of Hillel: "Be like the disciples of Aharon, loving peace, pursuing peace, loving people, and drawing them close to the Torah" (Avot 1:12). There are well-known aggadic traditions about how Aharon was able to turn enemies into friends and sinners into observers of the law. Sifra says that Aharon never said to anyone, "You have sinned" – all the more remarkable since one of the tasks of the High Priest was, once a year on Yom Kippur, to atone for the sins of the nation.

Peacemaking is not the only task of leadership. When Aharon is left to lead, the people make a golden calf. But neither is a passion for truth and justice sufficient. Moshe needs an Aharon to hold the people together. Every leadership team needs both a voice of truth and a force for peace – both a Moshe and an Aharon.

32:3 וַיָּבִיאוּ אֶל־אַהֲרֹן *Brought them to Aharon* – One of the most striking characteristics of the children of Israel is that, whenever they are asked, they give. When asked to make a donation to the building of the Sanctuary, they give without demur. When asked to contribute to the golden calf, they

10 it is a stiff-necked people. So do not try to stop Me when My anger burns
11 against them. I will put an end to them and make of you a great nation." Moshe
implored the Lord his God, "Why, O Lord, unleash Your anger against Your
people, whom You brought out of Egypt with such vast power and mighty
12 force? Why should the Egyptians be able to say that You brought them out
with evil intent, to kill them in the mountains and purge them from the face
of the earth? Turn from Your fierce anger and relent from doing evil to Your
13 people. Remember Avraham, Yitzḥak, and Yisrael, Your servants, to whom
You swore by Your very Self, telling them, 'I will make your descendants as
many as the stars of the heavens, and give them this land of which I spoke,
14 to inherit forever.'" Then the Lord relented from the evil He had spoken of
doing to His people.
15 Then Moshe turned and came down the mountain with the two tablets of
16 testimony in his hand, inscribed on both sides, front and back. The tablets were
the work of God, and the writing was God's writing, engraved on the tablets.

רש״י

ט **קְשֵׁה עֹרֶף.** מַחֲזִירִין קְשִׁי עָרְפָּם לְנֶגֶד מוֹכִיחֵיהֶם וּמְמָאֲנִים לִשְׁמֹעַ:

י **הַנִּיחָה לִּי.** עֲדַיִן לֹא שָׁמַעְנוּ שֶׁהִתְפַּלֵּל מֹשֶׁה עֲלֵיהֶם, וְהוּא אוֹמֵר "הַנִּיחָה לִי"? אֶלָּא כָּאן פָּתַח לוֹ פֶּתַח וְהוֹדִיעוֹ שֶׁהַדָּבָר תָּלוּי בּוֹ, שֶׁאִם יִתְפַּלֵּל עֲלֵיהֶם לֹא יְכַלֵּם:

יא **לָמָה ה׳ יֶחֱרֶה אַפְּךָ.** כְּלוּם מִתְקַנֵּא אֶלָּא חָכָם בְּחָכָם גִּבּוֹר בְּגִבּוֹר:

יב **וְהִנָּחֵם.** הִתְעַשֵּׁת לָהֶם מַחֲשָׁבָה אַחֶרֶת לְהֵיטִיב: **עַל הָרָעָה.** אֲשֶׁר חָשַׁבְתָּ לָהֶם:

יג **זְכֹר לְאַבְרָהָם.** אִם עָבְרוּ עַל עֲשֶׂרֶת הַדִּבְּרוֹת, אַבְרָהָם אֲבִיהֶם נִתְנַסָּה בְּעֶשֶׂר נִסְיוֹנוֹת וַעֲדַיִן לֹא קִבֵּל שְׂכָרוֹ, תְּנֵהוּ לוֹ, וְיֵצְאוּ עֶשֶׂר בְּעֶשֶׂר: **לְאַבְרָהָם לְיִצְחָק וּלְיִשְׂרָאֵל.** וְאִם אֵינָן נִצּוֹלִין בִּזְכוּתָן, מָה אַתָּה אוֹמֵר לִי: "וְאֶעֱשֶׂה אוֹתְךָ לְגוֹי גָּדוֹל"? אִם כִּסֵּא שֶׁל שָׁלֹשׁ רַגְלַיִם אֵינוֹ עוֹמֵד לְפָנֶיךָ, קַל וָחֹמֶר לְכִסֵּא שֶׁל רֶגֶל אֶחָד: **אֲשֶׁר נִשְׁבַּעְתָּ לָהֶם בָּךְ.** לֹא נִשְׁבַּעְתָּ לָהֶם בְּדָבָר שֶׁהוּא כָּלֶה, לֹא בַּשָּׁמַיִם וְלֹא בָּאָרֶץ, לֹא בֶּהָרִים וְלֹא בַּגְּבָעוֹת, אֶלָּא בְּךָ שֶׁאַתָּה קַיָּם וְכֵן שְׁבוּעָתְךָ תִּתְקַיֵּם, שֶׁנֶּאֱמַר: "בִּי נִשְׁבַּעְתִּי נְאֻם ה׳" (בראשית כב, טז), וּלְיִצְחָק נֶאֱמַר: "וַהֲקִמֹתִי אֶת הַשְּׁבֻעָה אֲשֶׁר נִשְׁבַּעְתִּי לְאַבְרָהָם אָבִיךָ" (שם כו, ג), וּלְיַעֲקֹב נֶאֱמַר: "אֲנִי אֵל שַׁדַּי פְּרֵה וּרְבֵה" (שם לה, יא), נִשְׁבַּע לוֹ בְּאֵל שַׁדַּי:

טו **מִשְּׁנֵי עֶבְרֵיהֶם.** הָיוּ הָאוֹתִיּוֹת נִקְרָאוֹת, וּמַעֲשֵׂה נִסִּים הוּא:

טז **מַעֲשֵׂה אֱלֹהִים הֵמָּה.** כְּמַשְׁמָעוֹ, הוּא בִּכְבוֹדוֹ עֲשָׂאָן. דָּבָר אַחֵר, כְּאָדָם הָאוֹמֵר לַחֲבֵרוֹ: כָּל עֲסָקָיו שֶׁל פְּלוֹנִי בִּמְלָאכָה פְּלוֹנִית, כָּךְ כָּל שַׁעֲשׁוּעָיו שֶׁל הַקָּדוֹשׁ בָּרוּךְ הוּא בַּתּוֹרָה: **חָרוּת.** לְשׁוֹן 'חֶרֶט' וְ'חָרוּת' אֶחָד הוּא, שְׁנֵיהֶם לְשׁוֹן חִקּוּק, אנטליי״ר בְּלַעַ״ז:

the annulment of a vow, when Moshe annulled the vow of God. The Sages understood the verse "Then the Lord *relented* from the evil He had spoken of doing to His people" (Ex. 32:14) to mean that God expressed regret for the vow He had taken – a precondition for a vow to be annulled.

This is why *Kol Nidrei*, the prayer with which we begin Yom Kippur, is a formula for the annulment of vows. We must always strive to fulfill our promises. But given the choice between justice and forgiveness, forgiveness is generally to be preferred. Invoking this principle, *Kol Nidrei* recalls the first Yom Kippur, when the Almighty let His compassion override His justice, the basis of all divine forgiveness.

י עַם־קְשֵׁה־עֹרֶף הוּא׃ וְעַתָּה הַנִּיחָה לִּי וְיִחַר־אַפִּי בָהֶם וַאֲכַלֵּם וְאֶעֱשֶׂה
יא אוֹתְךָ לְגוֹי גָּדוֹל׃ וַיְחַל מֹשֶׁה אֶת־פְּנֵי יהוה אֱלֹהָיו וַיֹּאמֶר לָמָה יהוה
יֶחֱרֶה אַפְּךָ בְּעַמֶּךָ אֲשֶׁר הוֹצֵאתָ מֵאֶרֶץ מִצְרַיִם בְּכֹחַ גָּדוֹל וּבְיָד
יב חֲזָקָה׃ לָמָּה יֹאמְרוּ מִצְרַיִם לֵאמֹר בְּרָעָה הוֹצִיאָם לַהֲרֹג אֹתָם בֶּהָרִים
וּלְכַלֹּתָם מֵעַל פְּנֵי הָאֲדָמָה שׁוּב מֵחֲרוֹן אַפֶּךָ וְהִנָּחֵם עַל־הָרָעָה
יג לְעַמֶּךָ׃ זְכֹר לְאַבְרָהָם לְיִצְחָק וּלְיִשְׂרָאֵל עֲבָדֶיךָ אֲשֶׁר נִשְׁבַּעְתָּ לָהֶם
בָּךְ וַתְּדַבֵּר אֲלֵהֶם אַרְבֶּה אֶת־זַרְעֲכֶם כְּכוֹכְבֵי הַשָּׁמָיִם וְכָל־הָאָרֶץ
יד הַזֹּאת אֲשֶׁר אָמַרְתִּי אֶתֵּן לְזַרְעֲכֶם וְנָחֲלוּ לְעֹלָם׃ וַיִּנָּחֶם יהוה עַל־
הָרָעָה אֲשֶׁר דִּבֶּר לַעֲשׂוֹת לְעַמּוֹ׃
טו וַיִּפֶן וַיֵּרֶד מֹשֶׁה מִן־הָהָר וּשְׁנֵי לֻחֹת הָעֵדֻת בְּיָדוֹ לֻחֹת כְּתֻבִים מִשְּׁנֵי כה
טז עֶבְרֵיהֶם מִזֶּה וּמִזֶּה הֵם כְּתֻבִים׃ וְהַלֻּחֹת מַעֲשֵׂה אֱלֹהִים הֵמָּה וְהַמִּכְתָּב

אונקלוס

עִם קְשֵׁי קְדָל הוּא׃ י וּכְעַן אַנַּח בָּעוּתָךְ מִן קֳדָמַי, וְיִתְקַף רֻגְזִי בְּהוֹן וַאֲשֵׁיצֵינוּן, וְאַעֲבֵיד יָתָךְ לְעַם סַגִּי׃ יא וְצַלִּי מֹשֶׁה, קֳדָם יי אֱלָהֵיהּ, וַאֲמַר, לְמָא יי יִתְקַף רֻגְזָךְ בְּעַמָּךְ, דְּאַפֵּיקְתָּא מֵאַרְעָא דְּמִצְרַיִם, בְּחֵיל רַב וּבְיַד תַּקִּיפָא׃ יב לְמָא יֵימְרוּן מִצְרָאֵי לְמֵימַר, בְּבִישָׁא אַפֵּיקִנּוּן לְקַטָּלָא יָתְהוֹן בֵּינֵי טוּרַיָּא, וּלְשֵׁיצָיוּתְהוֹן, מֵעַל אַפֵּי אַרְעָא, תּוּב מִתְּקוֹף רֻגְזָךְ, וְתוּב מִן בִּשְׁתָּא דְּמַלֵּילְתָּא לְמֶעְבַּד לְעַמָּךְ׃ יג אִדְּכַר, לְאַבְרָהָם לְיִצְחָק וּלְיִשְׂרָאֵל עַבְדָּךְ, דְּקַיֵּימְתָּא לְהוֹן בְּמֵימְרָךְ, וּמַלֵּילְתָּא עִמְּהוֹן, אַסְגֵּי יָת בְּנֵיכוֹן, כְּכוֹכְבֵי שְׁמַיָּא, וְכָל אַרְעָא הָדָא דַּאֲמַרִית, אֶתֵּין לִבְנֵיכוֹן, וְיַחְסְנוּן לְעָלַם׃ יד וְתָב יי, מִן בִּשְׁתָּא, דְּמַלֵּיל לְמֶעְבַּד לְעַמֵּיהּ׃ טו וְאִתְפְּנִי, וּנְחַת מֹשֶׁה מִן טוּרָא, וּתְרֵין לוּחֵי סָהֲדוּתָא בִּידֵיהּ, לוּחֵי, כְּתִיבִין מִתְּרֵין עִבְרֵיהוֹן, מִכָּא וּמִכָּא אִנּוּן כְּתִיבִין׃ טז וְלוּחַיָּא, עוֹבָדָא דַּייָ אִנּוּן, וּכְתָבָא,

32:11 וַיְחַל מֹשֶׁה *Moshe implored* – Moshe's prayers, as recorded in the Torah, are daring. But the Midrash makes them more audacious still. The text introducing Moshe's prayer begins with the Hebrew words "*Vayeḥal Moshe*" (Ex. 32:11). Normally these are translated as "Moshe besought, implored, entreated, pleaded, or attempted to pacify" God. However, *the same verb is used in the context of annulling or breaking a vow* (Num. 30:3). On this basis the Sages advanced a remarkable interpretation:

> [*Vayeḥal Moshe* means] "Moshe *absolved God of His vow*." When the Israelites made the golden calf, Moshe sought to persuade God to forgive them, but God said, "I have already taken an oath that '*whoever sacrifices to any other deity shall be utterly destroyed*' (Ex. 22:19). I cannot retract what I have said." Moshe replied, "Lord of the universe, You have given me the power to annul oaths, for You taught me that one who takes an oath cannot break their word but a scholar can absolve them. I hereby absolve You of Your vow." (Abridged from Shemot Rabba 43:4)

According to the Sages this original act of divine forgiveness, the one on which Yom Kippur is based, came about through

17 When Yehoshua heard the noise of the people shouting, he said to Moshe,
18 "The sound of war is coming from the camp." But Moshe said, "It is neither
the sound of triumph nor the wailing of defeat. What I hear is the sound of
19 revelry." As he approached the camp and saw the calf and the dancing, Moshe's
anger blazed, and he flung the tablets from his hands and smashed them at the
20 foot of the mountain. Then he took the calf that they had made, burned it with
fire, ground it to fine powder, scattered it on the water, and made the Israelites
21 drink it. "What did this people do to you," said Moshe to Aharon, "that you
22 should have brought so great a sin upon it?" Aharon replied, "Do not be angry
23 with me. You know that the people are set on evil. They said to me, 'Make us
gods to go before us. This man Moshe who brought us out of Egypt – we have
24 no idea what has become of him.' So I told them, 'Who has gold? Take it off.'

רש"י

יז **בְּרֵעֹה.** כַּהֲרִיעוֹ, שֶׁהָיוּ מְרִיעִים וּשְׂמֵחִים וְצוֹחֲקִים:

יח **אֵין קוֹל עֲנוֹת גְּבוּרָה.** אֵין קוֹל הַזֶּה נִרְאֶה קוֹל עֲנִיַּת גִּבּוֹרִים הַצּוֹעֲקִים 'נִצָּחוֹן', וְלֹא קוֹל חַלָּשִׁים הַצּוֹעֲקִים 'וַי' אוֹ 'נִיסָה': **קוֹל עַנּוֹת.** קוֹל חֵרוּפִין וְגִדּוּפִין הַמְעַנִּין אֶת נֶפֶשׁ שׁוֹמְעָן כְּשֶׁנֶּאֱמָרִין לוֹ:

יט **וַיַּשְׁלֵךְ מִיָּדָו וְגוֹ'.** אָמַר: מַה פֶּסַח שֶׁהוּא אַחַת מִן הַמִּצְוֹת, אָמְרָה תּוֹרָה: "כָּל בֶּן נֵכָר לֹא יֹאכַל בּוֹ" (לעיל יב, מג), הַתּוֹרָה כֻּלָּהּ כָּאן וְכֻלָּם מְשֻׁמָּדִים, וְאֶתְּנֶנָּה לָהֶם?!: **תַּחַת הָהָר.** לְרַגְלֵי הָהָר:

כ **וַיִּזֶר.** לְשׁוֹן נִפּוּץ, וְכֵן: "יְזֹרֶה עַל נָוֵהוּ גָּפְרִית" (איוב יח, טו), וְכֵן: "כִּי חִנָּם מְזֹרָה הָרָשֶׁת" (משלי א, יז) שֶׁזּוֹרִין בָּהּ דָּגָן וְקִטְנִית: **וַיַּשְׁקְ אֶת בְּנֵי יִשְׂרָאֵל.** נִתְכַּוֵּן לְבָדְקָן כְּסוֹטוֹת. שָׁלֹשׁ מִיתוֹת נִדּוֹנוּ שָׁם: אִם יֵשׁ עֵדִים וְהַתְרָאָה, בְּסַיִף, כְּמִשְׁפַּט אַנְשֵׁי עִיר הַנִּדַּחַת שֶׁהֵן מְרֻבִּין; עֵדִים בְּלֹא הַתְרָאָה, בְּמַגֵּפָה, שֶׁנֶּאֱמַר: "וַיִּגֹּף ה' אֶת הָעָם" (להלן פסוק לה); לֹא עֵדִים וְלֹא הַתְרָאָה, בְּהַדְרוֹקָן, שֶׁבְּדָקוּם הַמַּיִם וְצָבוּ בִטְנֵיהֶם:

כא **מֶה עָשָׂה לְךָ הָעָם הַזֶּה.** כַּמָּה יִסּוּרִים סָבַלְתָּ שֶׁיִּסְּרוּךָ עַד שֶׁלֹּא תָבִיא עֲלֵיהֶם חֵטְא זֶה:

כב **כִּי בְרָע הוּא.** בְּדֶרֶךְ רַע הֵם הוֹלְכִין תָּמִיד וּבְנִסְיוֹנוֹת לִפְנֵי הַמָּקוֹם:

כד **וָאֹמַר לָהֶם.** דָּבָר אֶחָד, וְהֵם מִהֲרוּ וְ"הִתְפָּרָקוּ": **וָאַשְׁלִכֵהוּ בָאֵשׁ.** וְלֹא יָדַעְתִּי שֶׁיֵּצֵא הָעֵגֶל הַזֶּה, "וַיֵּצֵא":

trial, and punishment, but because of their love of God, their concern for their neighbors, and their shared sense of past and future. With this, we can appreciate the strangest fact of all in Jewish history – that without sovereignty and a land, without police or an army, without any of the normal accoutrements of nationhood, the Jewish people kept Jewish law voluntarily in exile for two thousand years.

32:24 וַיִּתְּנוּ־לִי *They gave it to me* – Aharon blames the people. He denies responsibility for making the calf. "I threw it into the fire, and out came this calf!" This is the same kind of denial of responsibility we recall from the story of Adam and Ḥava (Gen. 3). The man says, "It was the woman." The woman says, "It was the serpent." It wasn't me. I was the victim, not the perpetrator. In anyone, such evasion is a moral failure; in a leader, all the more so.

It is easy to be critical of people who fail the leadership test when it involves defying the crowd, but it is hard to oppose a mob. They can ignore you, remove you, even assassinate you. Even Moshe was helpless in the face of the people during the later episode of the spies (Num. 14:5). Nor is it easy for Moshe to restore order now. He does so only by the most dramatic action: smashing the tablets and grinding the calf to dust. The Israelites at the foot of the mountain know nothing of how close they had come to being utterly destroyed.

יז מִכְתַּב אֱלֹהִים הוּא חָרוּת עַל־הַלֻּחֹת: וַיִּשְׁמַע יְהוֹשֻׁעַ אֶת־קוֹל הָעָם
יח בְּרֵעֹה וַיֹּאמֶר אֶל־מֹשֶׁה קוֹל מִלְחָמָה בַּמַּחֲנֶה: וַיֹּאמֶר אֵין קוֹל עֲנוֹת
יט גְּבוּרָה וְאֵין קוֹל עֲנוֹת חֲלוּשָׁה קוֹל עַנּוֹת אָנֹכִי שֹׁמֵעַ: וַיְהִי כַּאֲשֶׁר
קָרַב אֶל־הַמַּחֲנֶה וַיַּרְא אֶת־הָעֵגֶל וּמְחֹלֹת וַיִּחַר־אַף מֹשֶׁה וַיַּשְׁלֵךְ
כ מִיָּדָו אֶת־הַלֻּחֹת וַיְשַׁבֵּר אֹתָם תַּחַת הָהָר: וַיִּקַּח אֶת־הָעֵגֶל אֲשֶׁר
עָשׂוּ וַיִּשְׂרֹף בָּאֵשׁ וַיִּטְחַן עַד אֲשֶׁר־דָּק וַיִּזֶר עַל־פְּנֵי הַמַּיִם וַיַּשְׁקְ
כא אֶת־בְּנֵי יִשְׂרָאֵל: וַיֹּאמֶר מֹשֶׁה אֶל־אַהֲרֹן מֶה־עָשָׂה לְךָ הָעָם הַזֶּה
כב כִּי־הֵבֵאתָ עָלָיו חֲטָאָה גְדֹלָה: וַיֹּאמֶר אַהֲרֹן אַל־יִחַר אַף אֲדֹנִי אַתָּה
כג יָדַעְתָּ אֶת־הָעָם כִּי בְרָע הוּא: וַיֹּאמְרוּ לִי עֲשֵׂה־לָנוּ אֱלֹהִים אֲשֶׁר יֵלְכוּ
לְפָנֵינוּ כִּי־זֶה ׀ מֹשֶׁה הָאִישׁ אֲשֶׁר הֶעֱלָנוּ מֵאֶרֶץ מִצְרַיִם לֹא יָדַעְנוּ
כד מֶה־הָיָה לוֹ: וָאֹמַר לָהֶם לְמִי זָהָב הִתְפָּרָקוּ וַיִּתְּנוּ־לִי וָאַשְׁלִכֵהוּ בָאֵשׁ

אונקלוס

כְּתָבָא דַּיְיָ הוּא, מְפָרַשׁ עַל לוּחַיָּא: יז וּשְׁמַע יְהוֹשֻׁעַ, יָת קָל עַמָּא
כַּד מְיַבְּבִין, וַאֲמַר לְמֹשֶׁה, קָל קְרָבָא בְּמַשְׁרִיתָא: יח וַאֲמַר, לָא קָל
גִּבָּרִין דְּנָצְחִין בִּקְרָבָא, וְאַף לָא קָל חַלָּשִׁין דְּמִתַּבְּרִין, קָל דִּמְחַיְּכִין,
אֲנָא שָׁמַע: יט וַהֲוָה, כַּד קְרֵיב לְמַשְׁרִיתָא, וַחֲזָא יָת עֶגְלָא וְחִנְגִּין,
וּתְקֵיף רָגְזָא דְּמֹשֶׁה, וּרְמָא מִידוֹהִי יָת לוּחַיָּא, וְתַבַּר יָתְהוֹן בְּשִׁפּוֹלֵי
טוּרָא: כ וּנְסֵיב, יָת עֶגְלָא דַּעֲבַדוּ וְאוֹקֵיד בְּנוּרָא, וְשָׁף עַד דַּהֲוָה
דַּקִּיק, וּדְרָא עַל אַפֵּי מַיָּא, וְאַשְׁקִי יָת בְּנֵי יִשְׂרָאֵל: כא וַאֲמַר מֹשֶׁה
לְאַהֲרֹן, מָא עֲבַד לָךְ עַמָּא הָדֵין, אֲרֵי אֵיתֵיתָא עֲלוֹהִי חוֹבָא רַבָּא:
כב וַאֲמַר אַהֲרֹן, לָא יִתְקַף רָגְזָא דְּרִבּוֹנִי, אַתְּ יְדַעְתְּ יָת עַמָּא, אֲרֵי
בְּבִישׁ הוּא: כג וַאֲמַרוּ לִי, עֲבֵיד לָנָא דַּחְלָן, דִּיהָכוּן קֳדָמָנָא, אֲרֵי דֵין
מֹשֶׁה גַּבְרָא, דְּאַסְּקָנָא מֵאַרְעָא דְּמִצְרַיִם, לָא יְדַעְנָא מָא הֲוָה לֵיהּ:
כד וַאֲמָרִית לְהוֹן לְמָאן דִּדְהַבָּא, פָּרִיקוּ וִיהַבוּ לִי, וּרְמֵיתֵיהּ בְּנוּרָא,

32:16 חָרוּת עַל־הַלֻּחֹת *Engraved on the tablets* – In Pirkei Avot (6:2), the Sages saw in this verse a brilliant play on words. Noting the similarity between *ḥerut*, "freedom," and *ḥarut*, "engraved," they reread "engraved on the tablets" as "freedom on the tablets." The Rabbis said, "Read not *ḥarut* but *ḥerut* [not 'engraved' but 'freedom'], for the only person who is truly free is one who occupies himself with Torah study." What they meant was that if the law is engraved on the hearts of its citizens, it does not need to be enforced by police. True freedom – *ḥerut* – is the ability to control oneself without having to be controlled by others, accepting voluntarily the moral restraints without which liberty becomes license and society itself a battleground of warring instincts and desires.

This idea of freedom depends, for its success, not on power, but on moral obligation. It places a greater burden on the educated conscience, requires unique institutions, and needs constant education. The people must know the law; they must hand it on to their children; they must speak of it constantly until it becomes part of their innermost being. But the gain is immense. It means that Israel, if it is loyal to the covenant, will keep the law, not because of fear of arrest,

25 They gave it to me, I threw it into the fire – and out came this calf." Moshe
saw that the people were running wild, for Aharon had let them run beyond
26 control and become a laughingstock to their enemies. So Moshe stood at the
gate of the camp and said, "Who is for the LORD? Come to me." All the Levites
27 rallied round him. He said to them, "This is what the LORD God of Israel says:
Let each of you put sword on thigh and go back and forth from gate to gate
28 throughout the camp – slaying brother, neighbor, kinsman." The Levites did
29 as Moshe had ordered. Some three thousand people fell that day. Moshe said,
"Dedicate yourselves to the LORD today. You have been willing to act even
30 against your son or brother. May He bestow a blessing on you this day." On the
following day, Moshe said to the people, "You have committed a grievous sin.
Now I must go back up to the LORD. Perhaps I can secure atonement for your
31 sin." So Moshe went back to the LORD and said, "I beg of You. This people has
32 committed a grievous sin. They made gods of gold for themselves. But now, if
only You would forgive their sin – but if not, please blot me out of the book
33 You have written." The LORD said to Moshe, "I will blot out of My book those
34 who have sinned against Me. Now go and lead the people to the place about
which I have spoken to you. My messenger shall go before you. But when the
35 time comes for Me to punish, I will punish them for their sin." Thus the LORD
struck the people with a plague for what they had done with the calf Aharon

רש״י

כה **פָּרֻעַ.** מְגֻלֶּה, נִתְגַּלָּה שִׁמְצוֹ וּקְלוֹנוֹ, כְּמוֹ: "וּפָרַע אֶת רֹאשׁ הָאִשָּׁה" (במדבר ה, יח): **לְשִׁמְצָה בְּקָמֵיהֶם.** לִהְיוֹת לָהֶם הַדָּבָר הַזֶּה לִגְנוּת בְּפִי כָּל הַקָּמִים עֲלֵיהֶם:

כו **מִי לַה׳ אֵלָי.** יָבֹא אֵלַי: **כָּל בְּנֵי לֵוִי.** מִכָּאן שֶׁכָּל הַשֵּׁבֶט כָּשֵׁר:

כז **כֹּה אָמַר וְגוֹ׳.** וְהֵיכָן אָמַר? "זֹבֵחַ לָאֱלֹהִים יָחֳרָם" (לעיל כב, יט), כָּךְ שְׁנוּיָה בַּמְּכִילְתָּא: **אָחִיו.** מֵאִמּוֹ, וְהוּא יִשְׂרָאֵל:

כט **מִלְאוּ יֶדְכֶם.** אַתֶּם הַהוֹרְגִים אוֹתָם, בְּדָבָר זֶה תִּתְחַנְּכוּ לִהְיוֹת כֹּהֲנִים לַמָּקוֹם: **כִּי אִישׁ.** מִכֶּם, יְמַלֵּא יָדוֹ "בִּבְנוֹ וּבְאָחִיו":

ל **אֲכַפְּרָה בְּעַד חַטַּאתְכֶם.** אָשִׂים כֹּפֶר וְקִנּוּחַ וּסְתִימָה לְנֶגֶד חַטָּאתְכֶם, לְהַבְדִּיל בֵּינֵיכֶם וּבֵין הַחֵטְא:

לא **אֱלֹהֵי זָהָב.** אַתָּה הוּא שֶׁגָּרַמְתָּ לָהֶם, שֶׁהִשְׁפַּעְתָּ לָהֶם זָהָב וְכָל חֶפְצָם, מַה יַּעֲשׂוּ שֶׁלֹּא יֶחֶטְאוּ? מָשָׁל לְמֶלֶךְ שֶׁהָיָה מַאֲכִיל וּמַשְׁקֶה אֶת בְּנוֹ וּמְקַשְּׁטוֹ, וְתוֹלֶה לוֹ כִּיס בְּצַוָּארוֹ, וּמַעֲמִידוֹ בְּפֶתַח בֵּית זוֹנוֹת, מַה יַּעֲשֶׂה הַבֵּן שֶׁלֹּא יֶחֱטָא?:

לב **וְעַתָּה אִם תִּשָּׂא חַטָּאתָם.** הֲרֵי טוֹב, אֵינִי אוֹמֵר לְךָ מְחֵנִי, "וְאִם אַיִן – מְחֵנִי", וְזֶה מִקְרָא קָצָר, וְכֵן הַרְבֵּה: **מִסִּפְרְךָ.** מִכָּל הַתּוֹרָה כֻּלָּהּ, שֶׁלֹּא יֹאמְרוּ עָלַי שֶׁלֹּא הָיִיתִי כְּדַאי לְבַקֵּשׁ עֲלֵיהֶם רַחֲמִים:

לד **אֶל אֲשֶׁר דִּבַּרְתִּי לָךְ.** יֵשׁ כָּאן "לָךְ" אֵצֶל דִּבּוּר בִּמְקוֹם 'אֵלֶיךָ', וְכֵן: "לְדַבֶּר לוֹ עַל אֲדֹנִיָּהוּ" (מלכים א׳ ב, יט): **הִנֵּה מַלְאָכִי.** וְלֹא אֲנִי: **וּבְיוֹם פָּקְדִי וְגוֹ׳.** עַתָּה שָׁמַעְתִּי אֵלֶיךָ מִלְּכַלּוֹתָם יַחַד, וְתָמִיד תָּמִיד כְּשֶׁאֶפְקֹד עֲלֵיהֶם עֲוֹנוֹתֵיהֶם, "וּפָקַדְתִּי עֲלֵיהֶם" מְעַט מִן הֶעָוֹן הַזֶּה עִם שְׁאָר הָעֲוֹנוֹת. וְאֵין פֻּרְעָנוּת בָּאָה עַל יִשְׂרָאֵל שֶׁאֵין בָּהּ קְצָת מִפִּרְעוֹן עֲוֹן הָעֵגֶל:

לה **וַיִּגֹּף ה׳ אֶת הָעָם.** מִיתָה בִּידֵי שָׁמַיִם לְעֵדִים בְּלֹא הַתְרָאָה:

Moshe presents to God here: forgive their sin or blot me out of the book you have written. When Jews – the people of the book – think of life, they think of a book. Our lives are each a chapter in the book of Jewish life, of which we, with God, are the co-authors.

כה וַיֵּצֵא הָעֵגֶל הַזֶּה׃ וַיַּרְא מֹשֶׁה אֶת־הָעָם כִּי פָרֻעַ הוּא כִּי־פְרָעֹה אַהֲרֹן
כו לְשִׁמְצָה בְּקָמֵיהֶם׃ וַיַּעֲמֹד מֹשֶׁה בְּשַׁעַר הַמַּחֲנֶה וַיֹּאמֶר מִי לַיהוָה אֵלָי
כז וַיֵּאָסְפוּ אֵלָיו כׇּל־בְּנֵי לֵוִי׃ וַיֹּאמֶר לָהֶם כֹּה־אָמַר יהוה אֱלֹהֵי יִשְׂרָאֵל
שִׂימוּ אִישׁ־חַרְבּוֹ עַל־יְרֵכוֹ עִבְרוּ וָשׁוּבוּ מִשַּׁעַר לָשַׁעַר בַּמַּחֲנֶה וְהִרְגוּ
כח אִישׁ־אֶת־אָחִיו וְאִישׁ אֶת־רֵעֵהוּ וְאִישׁ אֶת־קְרֹבוֹ׃ וַיַּעֲשׂוּ בְנֵי־לֵוִי כִּדְבַר
כט מֹשֶׁה וַיִּפֹּל מִן־הָעָם בַּיּוֹם הַהוּא כִּשְׁלֹשֶׁת אַלְפֵי אִישׁ׃ וַיֹּאמֶר מֹשֶׁה
מִלְאוּ יֶדְכֶם הַיּוֹם לַיהוָה כִּי אִישׁ בִּבְנוֹ וּבְאָחִיו וְלָתֵת עֲלֵיכֶם הַיּוֹם
ל בְּרָכָה׃ וַיְהִי מִמָּחֳרָת וַיֹּאמֶר מֹשֶׁה אֶל־הָעָם אַתֶּם חֲטָאתֶם חֲטָאָה
לא גְדֹלָה וְעַתָּה אֶעֱלֶה אֶל־יהוה אוּלַי אֲכַפְּרָה בְּעַד חַטַּאתְכֶם׃ וַיָּשׇׁב
מֹשֶׁה אֶל־יהוָה וַיֹּאמַר אָנָּא חָטָא הָעָם הַזֶּה חֲטָאָה גְדֹלָה וַיַּעֲשׂוּ לָהֶם
לב אֱלֹהֵי זָהָב׃ וְעַתָּה אִם־תִּשָּׂא חַטָּאתָם וְאִם־אַיִן מְחֵנִי נָא מִסִּפְרְךָ אֲשֶׁר
לג כָּתָבְתָּ׃ וַיֹּאמֶר יהוָה אֶל־מֹשֶׁה מִי אֲשֶׁר חָטָא־לִי אֶמְחֶנּוּ מִסִּפְרִי׃
לד וְעַתָּה לֵךְ ׀ נְחֵה אֶת־הָעָם אֶל אֲשֶׁר־דִּבַּרְתִּי לָךְ הִנֵּה מַלְאָכִי יֵלֵךְ
לה לְפָנֶיךָ וּבְיוֹם פׇּקְדִי וּפָקַדְתִּי עֲלֵיהֶם חַטָּאתָם׃ וַיִּגֹּף יהוָה אֶת־הָעָם

אונקלוס

וּנְפַק עִגְלָא הָדֵין: כה וַחֲזָא מֹשֶׁה יָת עַמָּא, אֲרֵי בְטִיל הוּא, אֲרֵי בַטֵּילִנּוּן אַהֲרֹן, לְאַסָּבוּתְהוֹן שׁוּם בִּישׁ לְדָרֵיהוֹן: כו וְקָם מֹשֶׁה בִּתְרַע מַשְׁרִיתָא, וַאֲמַר, מַאן דַּחֲלַיָּא דַּיְיָ יֵיתוֹן לְוָתִי, וְאִתְכְּנִישׁוּ לְוָתֵיהּ כָּל בְּנֵי לֵוִי: כז וַאֲמַר לְהוֹן, כִּדְנָן אֲמַר יְיָ אֱלָהָא דְיִשְׂרָאֵל, שַׁווֹ גְּבַר חַרְבֵּיהּ עַל יִרְכֵּיהּ, עִיבַרוּ וְתוּבוּ, מִתְּרַע לִתְרַע בְּמַשְׁרִיתָא, וּקְטוּלוּ גְּבַר יָת אֲחוּהִי, וּגְבַר יָת חַבְרֵיהּ וֶאֱנָשׁ יָת קָרִיבֵיהּ: כח וַעֲבַדוּ בְנֵי לֵוִי כְּפִתְגָּמָא דְמֹשֶׁה, וּנְפַל מִן עַמָּא בְּיוֹמָא הַהוּא, כִּתְלָתָא אַלְפִין גַּבְרָא: כט וַאֲמַר מֹשֶׁה, קָרִיבוּ יַדְכוֹן יוֹמָא דֵין קֻרְבָּנָא קֳדָם יְיָ, אֲרֵי, גְּבַר בִּבְרֵיהּ וּבַאֲחוּהִי, וּלְאַיְתָאָה עֲלֵיכוֹן, יוֹמָא דֵין בִּרְכָן: ל וַהֲוָה בְּיוֹמָא דְבָתְרוֹהִי, וַאֲמַר מֹשֶׁה לְעַמָּא, אַתּוּן חַבְתּוּן חוֹבָא רַבָּא, וּכְעַן אֶסַּק לִקְדָם יְיָ, מָאִם אֲכַפַּר עַל חוֹבֵיכוֹן: לא וְתָב מֹשֶׁה, לִקְדָם יְיָ וַאֲמַר, בְּבָעוּ, חָב, עַמָּא הָדֵין חוֹבָא רַבָּא, וַעֲבַדוּ לְהוֹן דַּחְלָן דִּדְהַב: לב וּכְעַן אִם שְׁבַקְתְּ לְחוֹבֵיהוֹן, וְאִם לָא, מְחֵינִי כְעַן, מִסִּפְרָךְ דִּכְתַבְתָּא: לג וַאֲמַר יְיָ לְמֹשֶׁה, מַאן דְּחָב קֳדָמַי, אֶמְחֵינֵיהּ מִסִּפְרִי: לד וּכְעַן, אִיזֵיל דַּבַּר יָת עַמָּא, לַאֲתַר דְּמַלֵּילִית לָךְ, הָא מַלְאֲכִי יְהָךְ קֳדָמָךְ, וּבְיוֹם אַסְעָרוּתִי, וְאַסְעַר עֲלֵיהוֹן חוֹבֵיהוֹן: לה וּמְחָא יְיָ יָת עַמָּא,

32:32 מִסִּפְרְךָ אֲשֶׁר כָּתָבְתָּ *The book You have written* – On Rosh HaShana and Yom Kippur, we ask God to inscribe us in the book of life. The idea that our lives are written in a book by God goes back to the daring ultimatum that

▶

33 1 had made. The LORD said to Moshe, "Go. Set out from here – you
and the people you brought out of Egypt – to the land I promised to Avraham,
2 Yitzḥak, and Yaakov, saying, 'I will give this to your descendants.' I will send
a messenger ahead of you and drive out the Canaanites and Amorites, the
3 Hittites and the Perizzites, the Hivites, and the Jebusites. You will come to a
land flowing with milk and honey, but I will not go among you, because you are
4 a stiff-necked people; I might destroy you on the way." When the people heard
5 this distressing news, they were grief-stricken. None put on their finery; for the
LORD had said to Moshe, "Tell the Israelites: You are a stiff-necked people. If
for one moment I were to go among you, I might destroy you. So now take off
6 your finery; and I will consider what to do with you." So the Israelites stripped
7 themselves of their finery from Mount Ḥorev onward. Moshe took the tent
and pitched it at a distance outside the camp, calling it the Tent of Meeting.
Whoever sought the LORD would go to the Tent of Meeting, outside the camp.

רש״י

לג א **לֵךְ עֲלֵה מִזֶּה.** אֶרֶץ יִשְׂרָאֵל גְּבוֹהָה מִכָּל הָאֲרָצוֹת, לְכָךְ נֶאֱמַר "עֲלֵה". דָּבָר אַחֵר, כְּלַפֵּי שֶׁאָמַר לוֹ בִּשְׁעַת הַכַּעַס: "לֶךְ רֵד" (לעיל לב, ז), אָמַר לוֹ בִּשְׁעַת רָצוֹן: "לֵךְ עֲלֵה": **אַתָּה וְהָעָם.** כָּאן לֹא נֶאֱמַר 'וְעַמְּךָ':

ב **וְגֵרַשְׁתִּי אֶת הַכְּנַעֲנִי וְגוֹ׳.** שֵׁשׁ אֻמּוֹת הֵן, וְהַגִּרְגָּשִׁי עָמַד וּפִנָּה מִפְּנֵיהֶם מֵאֵלָיו:

ג **אֶל אֶרֶץ זָבַת חָלָב וּדְבָשׁ.** אֲנִי אוֹמֵר לְךָ לְהַעֲלוֹתָם: **כִּי לֹא אֶעֱלֶה בְּקִרְבְּךָ.** לְכָךְ אֲנִי אוֹמֵר לָךְ: "וְשָׁלַחְתִּי לְפָנֶיךָ מַלְאָךְ": **כִּי עַם קְשֵׁה עֹרֶף אַתָּה.** וּכְשֶׁשְּׁכִינָתִי בְּקִרְבְּכֶם וְאַתֶּם מַמְרִים בִּי מַרְבֶּה אֲנִי עֲלֵיכֶם זַעַם: **אֲכֶלְךָ.** לְשׁוֹן כִּלָּיוֹן:

ד **הַדָּבָר הָרָע.** שֶׁאֵין הַשְּׁכִינָה שׁוֹרָה וּמְהַלֶּכֶת עִמָּם: **אִישׁ עֶדְיוֹ.** כְּתָרִים שֶׁנִּתְּנוּ לָהֶם בְּחוֹרֵב כְּשֶׁאָמְרוּ: "נַעֲשֶׂה וְנִשְׁמָע" (לעיל כד, ז):

ה **רֶגַע אֶחָד אֶעֱלֶה בְקִרְבְּךָ וְכִלִּיתִיךָ.** אִם אֶעֱלֶה בְּקִרְבְּךָ וְאַתֶּם מַמְרִים בִּי בְּקַשְׁיוּת עָרְפְּכֶם, אֶזְעֹם עֲלֵיכֶם רֶגַע אֶחָד – שֶׁהוּא שִׁעוּר זַעְמוֹ, שֶׁנֶּאֱמַר: "חֲבִי כִמְעַט רֶגַע עַד יַעֲבָר זָעַם" (ישעיה כו, כ) – וַאֲכַלֶּה אֶתְכֶם, לְפִיכָךְ טוֹב לָכֶם שֶׁאֶשְׁלַח מַלְאָךְ: **וְעַתָּה.** פֻּרְעָנוּת זוֹ תִּלְקוּ מִיָּד, שֶׁתּוֹרִידוּ עֶדְיְכֶם מֵעֲלֵיכֶם: **וְאֵדְעָה מָה אֶעֱשֶׂה לָּךְ.** בִּפְקֻדַּת שְׁאָר הֶעָוֹן אֲנִי יוֹדֵעַ מַה בְּלִבִּי לַעֲשׂוֹת:

ו **אֶת עֶדְיָם מֵהַר חוֹרֵב.** אֶת הָעֲדִי שֶׁהָיָה בְּיָדָם מֵהַר חוֹרֵב:

ז **וּמֹשֶׁה.** מֵאוֹתוֹ עָוֹן וָהָלְאָה "יִקַּח אֶת הָאֹהֶל", לְשׁוֹן הֹוֶה הוּא, לוֹקֵחַ אָהֳלוֹ וְנוֹטֵהוּ מִחוּץ לַמַּחֲנֶה, אָמַר: מְנֻדֶּה לָרַב מְנֻדֶּה לַתַּלְמִיד: **הַרְחֵק.** אַלְפַּיִם אַמָּה, כְּעִנְיָן שֶׁנֶּאֱמַר: "אַךְ רָחוֹק יִהְיֶה בֵּינֵיכֶם וּבֵינָו כְּאַלְפַּיִם אַמָּה בַּמִּדָּה" (יהושע ג, ד): **וְקָרָא לוֹ.** וְהָיָה קוֹרֵא לוֹ "אֹהֶל מוֹעֵד", הוּא בֵּית וַעַד לִמְבַקְשֵׁי תוֹרָה: **כָּל מְבַקֵּשׁ ה׳.** מִכָּאן לִמְבַקֵּשׁ פְּנֵי זָקֵן כִּמְקַבֵּל פְּנֵי שְׁכִינָה: **יֵצֵא אֶל אֹהֶל מוֹעֵד.** כְּמוֹ 'יוֹצֵא'. דָּבָר אַחֵר, "וְהָיָה כָּל מְבַקֵּשׁ ה׳", אֲפִלּוּ מַלְאֲכֵי הַשָּׁרֵת כְּשֶׁהָיוּ שׁוֹאֲלִים מְקוֹם שְׁכִינָה, חַבְרֵיהֶם אוֹמְרִים לָהֶם הֲרֵי הוּא בְּאָהֳלוֹ שֶׁל מֹשֶׁה:

tomorrow. But You are eternal. You are their God. They need *You* to be close to them.

It is as if Moshe is saying: Until now, they have experienced You delivering plague after plague to the Egyptians, bringing the world's greatest empire to its knees, dividing the sea, overturning the very order of nature itself. At Mount Sinai, merely hearing Your voice, they were so overwhelmed that they said: If we continue to hear the voice, "we will die" (Ex. 20:16). The people need, says Moshe, to experience not only the *greatness* of God but the *closeness* of God, not just God heard in thunder and lightning at the top of the mountain, not just prophetic revelation such as mine, but as a perpetual presence in the valley below. That is why Moshe removes the tent and pitches it outside the camp, as if to say to God: It is not my presence the people need in their midst, but Yours.

לג א עַל אֲשֶׁר עָשׂוּ אֶת־הָעֵגֶל אֲשֶׁר עָשָׂה אַהֲרֹן׃ וַיְדַבֵּר יהוה
אֶל־מֹשֶׁה לֵךְ עֲלֵה מִזֶּה אַתָּה וְהָעָם אֲשֶׁר הֶעֱלִיתָ מֵאֶרֶץ מִצְרָיִם
אֶל־הָאָרֶץ אֲשֶׁר נִשְׁבַּעְתִּי לְאַבְרָהָם לְיִצְחָק וּלְיַעֲקֹב לֵאמֹר לְזַרְעֲךָ
ב אֶתְּנֶנָּה׃ וְשָׁלַחְתִּי לְפָנֶיךָ מַלְאָךְ וְגֵרַשְׁתִּי אֶת־הַכְּנַעֲנִי הָאֱמֹרִי וְהַחִתִּי
ג וְהַפְּרִזִּי הַחִוִּי וְהַיְבוּסִי׃ אֶל־אֶרֶץ זָבַת חָלָב וּדְבָשׁ כִּי לֹא אֶעֱלֶה
ד בְּקִרְבְּךָ כִּי עַם־קְשֵׁה־עֹרֶף אַתָּה פֶּן־אֲכֶלְךָ בַּדָּרֶךְ׃ וַיִּשְׁמַע הָעָם
ה אֶת־הַדָּבָר הָרָע הַזֶּה וַיִּתְאַבָּלוּ וְלֹא־שָׁתוּ אִישׁ עֶדְיוֹ עָלָיו׃ וַיֹּאמֶר
יהוה אֶל־מֹשֶׁה אֱמֹר אֶל־בְּנֵי־יִשְׂרָאֵל אַתֶּם עַם־קְשֵׁה־עֹרֶף רֶגַע
אֶחָד אֶעֱלֶה בְקִרְבְּךָ וְכִלִּיתִיךָ וְעַתָּה הוֹרֵד עֶדְיְךָ מֵעָלֶיךָ וְאֵדְעָה מָה
ו ז אֶעֱשֶׂה־לָּךְ׃ וַיִּתְנַצְּלוּ בְנֵי־יִשְׂרָאֵל אֶת־עֶדְיָם מֵהַר חוֹרֵב׃ וּמֹשֶׁה יִקַּח
אֶת־הָאֹהֶל וְנָטָה־לוֹ ׀ מִחוּץ לַמַּחֲנֶה הַרְחֵק מִן־הַמַּחֲנֶה וְקָרָא לוֹ
אֹהֶל מוֹעֵד וְהָיָה כָּל־מְבַקֵּשׁ יהוה יֵצֵא אֶל־אֹהֶל מוֹעֵד אֲשֶׁר מִחוּץ

אונקלוס

עַל דְּאִשְׁתַּעְבַּדוּ לְעִגְלָא, דַּעֲבַד אַהֲרֹן׃ לג א וּמַלֵּיל יי עִם מֹשֶׁה
אִיזִיל סַק מִכָּא, אַתְּ וְעַמָּא, דְּאַסֵּיקְתָּא מֵאַרְעָא דְּמִצְרָיִם, לְאַרְעָא,
דְּקַיֵּימִית, לְאַבְרָהָם לְיִצְחָק וּלְיַעֲקֹב לְמֵימַר, לִבְנָךְ אֶתְּנִנַּהּ׃ ב וְאֶשְׁלַח
קֳדָמָךְ מַלְאֲכָא, וַאֲתָרֵיךְ, יָת כְּנַעֲנָאֵי אֱמוֹרָאֵי, וְחִתָּאֵי וּפְרִזָּאֵי, חִוָּאֵי
וִיבוּסָאֵי׃ ג לַאֲרַע, עָבְדָא חֲלַב וּדְבַשׁ, אֲרֵי לָא אֲסַלֵּיק שְׁכִינְתִּי
מִבֵּינָךְ, אֲרֵי עַם קְשֵׁי קְדָל אַתְּ, דִּלְמָא אֲשֵׁיצֵינָךְ בְּאוֹרְחָא׃ ד וּשְׁמַע
עַמָּא, יָת פִּתְגָמָא בִּישָׁא, הָדֵין וְאִתְאַבַּלוּ, וְלָא שַׁווֹ, גְּבַר תִּקּוּן זֵינֵיהּ
עֲלוֹהִי׃ ה וַאֲמַר יי לְמֹשֶׁה, אֵימַר לִבְנֵי יִשְׂרָאֵל אַתּוּן עַם קְשֵׁי קְדָל,
שָׁעָה חֲדָא, אֲסַלֵּיק שְׁכִינְתִּי מִבֵּינָךְ וַאֲשֵׁיצֵינָךְ, וּכְעַן, אַעְדִּ תִּקּוּן
זֵינָךְ מִנָּךְ, גְּלֵי קֳדָמַי מָא אַעְבֵּיד לָךְ׃ ו וְאַעְדִּיוּ בְּנֵי יִשְׂרָאֵל, יָת תִּקּוּן
זֵינְהוֹן מִטּוּרָא דְּחוֹרֵב׃ ז וּמֹשֶׁה נְסֵיב יָת מַשְׁכְּנָא, וּפַרְסֵיהּ לֵיהּ מִבָּרָא
לְמַשְׁרִיתָא, אַרְחֵיק מִן מַשְׁרִיתָא, וְקָרֵי לֵיהּ מַשְׁכַּן בֵּית אֻלְפָנָא, וְהָוֵי
כָּל דְּתָבַע אֻלְפָן מִן קֳדָם יי, נָפֵיק לְמַשְׁכַּן בֵּית אֻלְפָנָא, דְּמִבָּרָא

33:8 וְהָיָה כְּצֵאת מֹשֶׁה *When Moshe went out* – At times of distress, a leader has to be close to the people, not distant. For Moshe, then, to leave the camp must be demoralizing. This is a cryptic text, but it seems to me that the most powerful interpretation is this: Moshe is making an audacious prayer, so audacious that the Torah does not state it directly and explicitly. We have to reconstruct it from clues within the text.

The previous chapter implies that the people panic because of the absence of Moshe, their leader. God Himself implies as much when He says to Moshe, "Go down. *Your* people, whom *you* brought up out of Egypt, are acting ruinously" (Ex. 32:7). The suggestion is that Moshe's absence or distance was the cause of the sin. He should have stayed closer to the people. Moshe takes the point. He does go down. He does punish the guilty. He does pray for God to forgive the people. Having restored order to the people, Moshe now introduces an entirely new approach. He is, in effect, saying to God: What the people need is not for *me* to be close to them. I am just a human, here today, gone

8 And when Moshe went out to the Tent, all the people would rise, standing at
the openings of their tents, and watch Moshe until he had entered the Tent.
9 When Moshe entered the Tent, the pillar of cloud would descend and stand
10 at the Tent's opening while He spoke with Moshe. When the people saw the
pillar of cloud standing at the Tent's opening, all the people would rise and
11 bow down, each at the opening of his own tent. The LORD would speak to
Moshe face-to-face, as one person speaks to his friend. And then Moshe would
return to the camp, but his young disciple, Yehoshua son of Nun, did not leave
the Tent.
12 Moshe said to the LORD, "You told me to lead this people forth, but You have SHELISHI
not let me know whom You will send with me. And You said, 'I have known you
13 by name, and you have found favor in My sight.' So now, if I have found favor
in Your sight, please show me Your ways, so that I may know You and continue
14 to find favor in Your sight. And look upon this nation: it is Your people." "My
15 presence," He replied, "will go with you, and I will grant you rest." Then Moshe

רש"י

ח **והיה.** לשון הוה: **כצאת משה מן המחנה.** ללכת אל האהל: **יקומו כל העם.** עומדים מפניו, ואין יושבין עד שנתכסה מהם: **והביטו אחרי משה.** לשבח: אשרי ילוד אשה שככך מובטח שהשכינה תכנס אחריו לפתח אהלו:

ט **ודבר עם משה.** כמו ומדבר עם משה, ותרגומו: "ומתמלל עם משה" שהוא כבוד שכינה, כמו: "וישמע את הקול מדבר אליו" (במדבר ז, פט), ואינו קורא 'מדבר' אליו; כשהוא קורא 'מדבר' פתרונו, הקול מדבר בינו לבין עצמו וההדיוט שומע מאליו, וכשהוא קורא 'מדבר' משמע שהמלך מדבר עם ההדיוט:

י **והשתחוו.** לשכינה:

יא **ודבר ה' אל משה פנים אל פנים.** ומתמלל עם משה: **ושב אל המחנה.** לאחר שנדבר עמו היה משה שב אל המחנה ומלמד לזקנים מה שלמד. והדבר הזה נהג משה מיום הכפורים עד שהוקם המשכן ולא יותר, שהרי בשבעה עשר בתמוז נשתברו הלוחות, ובשמונה עשר שרף את העגל ודן את החוטאים, ובתשעה עשר עלה, שנאמר: "ויהי ממחרת ויאמר משה אל העם" וגו' (לעיל לב, ל), עשה שם ארבעים יום ובקש רחמים, שנאמר: "ואתנפל לפני ה'" וגו' (דברים ט, יח), ובראש חדש אלול נאמר לו: "ועלית בבקר אל הר סיני" (להלן לד, ב) לקבל לוחות האחרונות, ועשה שם ארבעים יום, שנאמר בהם: "ואנכי עמדתי בהר כימים הראשנים" וגו' (דברים י, י), מה הראשונים ברצון אף האחרונים ברצון, אמור מעתה אמצעיים היו בכעס. בעשרה בתשרי נתרצה הקדוש ברוך הוא לישראל בשמחה ובלב שלם, ואמר לו למשה: סלחתי כדברך, ומסר לו לוחות אחרונות, וירד, והתחיל לצוותם על מלאכת המשכן, ועשאוהו עד אחד בניסן, ומשהוקם לא נדבר עמו עוד אלא מאהל מועד: **ושב אל המחנה.** תרגומו: "ותאיב למשריתא" לפי שהוא לשון הוה, וכן כל הענין: "וראה כל העם" (לעיל פסוק י) – "וחזן", "ונצבו" (לעיל פסוק ח) – "וקימין", "והביטו" (שם) – "ומסתכלין", "והשתחוו" (לעיל פסוק י) – "וסגדין". ומדרשו: "ודבר ה' אל משה" שישוב אל המחנה, אמר לו: אני בכעס ואתה בכעס, אם כן מי יקרבם?

יב **ראה אתה אמר אלי.** ראה, תן עיניך ולבך על דבריך: אתה אמר אלי וגו' ואתה לא הודעתני וגו'. שאמרת לי: "הנה אנכי שלח מלאך" (לעיל כג, כ), אין זו הודעה, שאיני חפץ בו: **ואתה אמרת.** הכרתיך משאר בני אדם בשם חשיבות, שהרי אמרת לי: "הנה אנכי בא אליך בעב הענן וגו' וגם בך יאמינו לעולם" (לעיל יט, ט):

יג **ועתה.** אם אמת שמצאתי חן בעיניך: **הודעני נא את דרכך.** מה שכר אתה נותן למוצאי חן בעיניך: **ואדעך למען אמצא חן בעיניך.** ואדע בזו מדת תגמולך, מה היא מציאת חן שמצאתי בעיניך. ופתרון "למען אמצא חן" – למען אכיר כמה שכר מציאת החן: **וראה כי עמך הגוי הזה.** שלא תאמר: "ואעשה אותך לגוי גדול" (לעיל לב, י) ואת אלה תעזב, ראה כי עמך הם מקדם, ואם בהם תמאס, איני סומך על היוצאים מחלצי שיתקימו; ואת תשלום השכר שלי בעם הזה תודיעני. ורבותינו דרשוהו במסכת ברכות (דף ז ע"א), ואני ליישב המקראות על אפניהם ועל סדרם באתי:

ח לַמַּחֲנֶה: וְהָיָה כְּצֵאת מֹשֶׁה אֶל־הָאֹהֶל יָקוּמוּ כָּל־הָעָם וְנִצְּבוּ אִישׁ
ט פֶּתַח אָהֳלוֹ וְהִבִּיטוּ אַחֲרֵי מֹשֶׁה עַד־בֹּאוֹ הָאֹהֱלָה: וְהָיָה כְּבֹא מֹשֶׁה
י הָאֹהֱלָה יֵרֵד עַמּוּד הֶעָנָן וְעָמַד פֶּתַח הָאֹהֶל וְדִבֶּר עִם־מֹשֶׁה: וְרָאָה
כָל־הָעָם אֶת־עַמּוּד הֶעָנָן עֹמֵד פֶּתַח הָאֹהֶל וְקָם כָּל־הָעָם וְהִשְׁתַּחֲווּ
יא אִישׁ פֶּתַח אָהֳלוֹ: וְדִבֶּר יהוה אֶל־מֹשֶׁה פָּנִים אֶל־פָּנִים כַּאֲשֶׁר יְדַבֵּר
אִישׁ אֶל־רֵעֵהוּ וְשָׁב אֶל־הַמַּחֲנֶה וּמְשָׁרְתוֹ יְהוֹשֻׁעַ בִּן־נוּן נַעַר לֹא
יָמִישׁ מִתּוֹךְ הָאֹהֶל:
יב וַיֹּאמֶר מֹשֶׁה אֶל־יהוה רְאֵה אַתָּה אֹמֵר אֵלַי הַעַל אֶת־הָעָם הַזֶּה שלישי
וְאַתָּה לֹא הוֹדַעְתַּנִי אֵת אֲשֶׁר־תִּשְׁלַח עִמִּי וְאַתָּה אָמַרְתָּ יְדַעְתִּיךָ
יג בְשֵׁם וְגַם־מָצָאתָ חֵן בְּעֵינָי: וְעַתָּה אִם־נָא מָצָאתִי חֵן בְּעֵינֶיךָ הוֹדִעֵנִי
נָא אֶת־דְּרָכֶךָ וְאֵדָעֲךָ לְמַעַן אֶמְצָא־חֵן בְּעֵינֶיךָ וּרְאֵה כִּי עַמְּךָ הַגּוֹי
יד טו הַזֶּה: וַיֹּאמַר פָּנַי יֵלֵכוּ וַהֲנִחֹתִי לָךְ: וַיֹּאמֶר אֵלָיו אִם־אֵין פָּנֶיךָ הֹלְכִים

אונקלוס

לְמַשְׁרִיתָא: ח וַהֲוֵי, כַּד נָפֵיק מֹשֶׁה לְמַשְׁכְּנָא, קָיְמִין כָּל עַמָּא, וּמִתְעַתְּדִין, גְּבַר בִּתְרַע מַשְׁכְּנֵיהּ, וּמִסְתַּכְּלִין אֲחוֹרֵי מֹשֶׁה, עַד דְּעָלֵיל לְמַשְׁכְּנָא: ט וַהֲוֵי, כַּד עָלֵיל מֹשֶׁה לְמַשְׁכְּנָא, נָחֵית עַמּוּדָא דַעֲנָנָא, וְקָאֵים בִּתְרַע מַשְׁכְּנָא, וּמִתְמַלַּל עִם מֹשֶׁה: י וְחָזַן כָּל עַמָּא יָת עַמּוּדָא דַעֲנָנָא, קָאֵים בִּתְרַע מַשְׁכְּנָא, וְקָיְמִין כָּל עַמָּא וְסָגְדִין, גְּבַר בִּתְרַע מַשְׁכְּנֵיהּ: יא וּמְמַלֵּיל יי עִם מֹשֶׁה מְמַלַּל עִם מְמַלַּל, כְּמָא דִּמְמַלֵּיל גֻּבְרָא עִם חַבְרֵיהּ, וְתָאֵיב לְמַשְׁרִיתָא, וּמְשֻׁמְשָׁנֵיהּ, יְהוֹשֻׁעַ בַּר נוּן עוּלֵימָא, לָא עָדֵי מִגּוֹ מַשְׁכְּנָא: יב וַאֲמַר מֹשֶׁה קֳדָם יי, חֲזִי, דְּאַתְּ, אָמַר לִי אַסֵּיק יָת עַמָּא הָדֵין, וְאַתְּ לָא הוֹדַעְתַּנִי, יָת דְּתִשְׁלַח עִמִּי, וְאַתְּ אֲמַרְתְּ רַבִּיתָךְ בְּשׁוּם, וְאַף אַשְׁכַּחְתָּא רַחֲמִין קֳדָמָי: יג וּכְעַן, אִם כְּעַן אַשְׁכָּחִית רַחֲמִין קֳדָמָךְ, הוֹדַעְנִי כְעַן יָת אוֹרַח טוּבָךְ, וְאֵדַּע רַחֲמָךְ, בְּדִיל דְּאַשְׁכַּח רַחֲמִין קֳדָמָךְ, וּגְלֵי קֳדָמָךְ, אֲרֵי עַמָּךְ עַמָּא הָדֵין: יד וַאֲמַר, שְׁכִינְתִּי תְּהָךְ וַאֲנִיחַ לָךְ: טו וַאֲמַר קֳדָמוֹהִי, אִם לֵית שְׁכִינְתָךְ מְהַלְּכָא

רש״י

יד וַיֹּאמַר פָּנַי יֵלֵכוּ. כְּתַרְגּוּמוֹ. לֹא אֶשְׁלַח עוֹד מַלְאָךְ, אֲנִי בְּעַצְמִי אֵלֵךְ, כְּמוֹ: "וּפָנֶיךָ הֹלְכִים בַּקְרָב" (שמואל ב' יז, יא).

טו וַיֹּאמֶר אֵלָיו. בְּזוֹ אֲנִי חָפֵץ, כִּי עַל יְדֵי מַלְאָךְ "אַל תַּעֲלֵנוּ מִזֶּה".

33:13 הוֹדִעֵנִי נָא אֶת־דְּרָכֶךָ *Please show me Your ways* – As noted earlier, Moshe seeks here to understand the very nature of God Himself. Is it possible for God to be close to where people are? Can transcendence become immanence? Can the God who is vaster than the universe live within the universe in a predictable, comprehensible way, not just in the form of miraculous intervention?

said to Him, "If Your presence does not go with us, do not make us leave this
16 place. For unless You go with us, how shall it be known that I and Your people
have found favor in Your sight? That is how I and Your people are distinguished
from every other people on the face of the earth."
17 Then the Lord said to Moshe, "In this too I will do what you ask, for you REVI'I
18 have found favor in My sight; for I know you by name." Then Moshe said,
19 "Show me, please, Your glory." And He said, "I will cause all My goodness to
pass before you and in your presence I will proclaim My name: The Lord.
But I will be gracious to whom I choose to be gracious, and will show mercy
20 to whom I decide to show mercy. Nor," He said, "can you see My face. For no
21 one can see Me and live." Then the Lord said, "Look, there is a place by Me
22 where you may stand on the rock, and while My glory passes by I will put you
in a cleft of the rock, and I will shield you with My hand until I have passed.
23 Then I will take My hand away, and you will see My back, but My face may
not be seen."
34 1 The Lord said to Moshe, "Carve two tablets of stone like the first, and I will ḤAMISHI

רש״י

טז **וּבַמֶּה יִוָּדַע אֵפוֹא.** יִוָּדַע מְצִיאַת הַחֵן, "הֲלוֹא בְּלֶכְתְּךָ עִמָּנוּ". וְעוֹד דָּבָר אַחֵר אֲנִי שׁוֹאֵל מִמְּךָ, שֶׁלֹּא תַשְׁרֶה שְׁכִינָתְךָ עוֹד עַל אֻמּוֹת הָעוֹלָם: **וְנִפְלִינוּ אֲנִי וְעַמְּךָ.** וְנִהְיֶה מֻבְדָּלִים בַּדָּבָר הַזֶּה "מִכָּל הָעָם", כְּמוֹ: "וְהִפְלָה ה׳ בֵּין מִקְנֵה יִשְׂרָאֵל" וְגוֹ׳ (לעיל ט, ז):

יז **גַּם אֶת הַדָּבָר הַזֶּה.** שֶׁלֹּא תִשְׁרֶה שְׁכִינָתִי עוֹד עַל אֻמּוֹת הָעוֹלָם, "אֶעֱשֶׂה". וְאֵין דְּבָרָיו שֶׁל בִּלְעָם עַל יְדֵי שְׁרִיַּת שְׁכִינָה, אֶלָּא "נֹפֵל וּגְלוּי עֵינָיִם" (במדבר כד, ד), כְּגוֹן: "וְאֵלַי דָּבָר יְגֻנָּב" (איוב ד, יב), שׁוֹמְעִין עַל יְדֵי שָׁלִיחַ:

יח **וַיֹּאמַר הַרְאֵנִי נָא אֶת כְּבֹדֶךָ.** רָאָה מֹשֶׁה שֶׁהָיָה עֵת רָצוֹן וּדְבָרָיו מְקֻבָּלִים, וְהוֹסִיף לִשְׁאֹל לְהַרְאוֹתוֹ מַרְאִית כְּבוֹדוֹ:

יט **וַיֹּאמֶר אֲנִי אַעֲבִיר וְגוֹ׳.** הִגִּיעָה שָׁעָה שֶׁתִּרְאֶה בִּכְבוֹדִי מַה שֶּׁאַרְשֶׁה אוֹתְךָ לִרְאוֹת, לְפִי שֶׁאֲנִי רוֹצֶה וְצָרִיךְ לְלַמֶּדְךָ סֵדֶר תְּפִלָּה, שֶׁכְּשֶׁנִּצְרַכְתָּ לְבַקֵּשׁ רַחֲמִים עַל יִשְׂרָאֵל הִזְכַּרְתָּ לִי זְכוּת אָבוֹת, כִּסְבוּר אַתָּה שֶׁאִם תַּמָּה זְכוּת אָבוֹת אֵין עוֹד תִּקְוָה, אֲנִי אַעֲבִיר כָּל מִדַּת טוּבִי לְפָנֶיךָ עַל הַצּוּר וְאַתָּה נָתוּן בַּמְּעָרָה: **וְקָרָאתִי בְשֵׁם ה׳ לְפָנֶיךָ.** לְלַמֶּדְךָ סֵדֶר בַּקָּשַׁת רַחֲמִים אַף אִם תִּכְלֶה זְכוּת אָבוֹת, וּכְסֵדֶר שֶׁאַתָּה רוֹאֶה אוֹתִי מְעֻטָּף וְקוֹרֵא שְׁלֹשׁ עֶשְׂרֵה מִדּוֹת הֱוֵי מְלַמֵּד אֶת יִשְׂרָאֵל לַעֲשׂוֹת כֵּן, וְעַל יְדֵי שֶׁיַּזְכִּירוּ לְפָנַי 'רַחוּם וְחַנּוּן', כִּי רַחֲמַי לֹא כָלִים: **וְחַנֹּתִי אֶת אֲשֶׁר אָחֹן.** אוֹתָן פְּעָמִים שֶׁאֶרְצֶה לָחֹן: **וְרִחַמְתִּי.** עֵת שֶׁאֶחְפֹּץ לְרַחֵם. עַד כָּאן לֹא הִבְטִיחוֹ אֶלָּא עִתִּים אֶעֱנֶה עִתִּים לֹא אֶעֱנֶה, אֲבָל בִּשְׁעַת מַעֲשֵׂה אָמַר לוֹ: "הִנֵּה אָנֹכִי כֹּרֵת בְּרִית" (להלן לד, י), הִבְטִיחוֹ שֶׁאֵינָן חוֹזְרוֹת רֵיקָם:

כ **וַיֹּאמֶר לֹא תוּכַל וְגוֹ׳.** אַף כְּשֶׁאַעֲבִיר כָּל טוּבִי עַל פָּנֶיךָ, אֵינִי נוֹתֵן לְךָ רְשׁוּת לִרְאוֹת אֶת פָּנַי:

כא **הִנֵּה מָקוֹם אִתִּי.** בָּהָר אֲשֶׁר אֲנִי מְדַבֵּר עִמְּךָ תָּמִיד, יֵשׁ מָקוֹם מוּכָן לִי לְצָרְכְּךָ שֶׁאַטְמִינְךָ שָׁם שֶׁלֹּא תִזּוֹק, וּמִשָּׁם תִּרְאֶה מַה שֶּׁתִּרְאֶה, זֶהוּ פְּשׁוּטוֹ. וּמִדְרָשׁוֹ, עַל מָקוֹם שֶׁהַשְּׁכִינָה שָׁם מְדַבֵּר, וְאוֹמֵר 'הַמָּקוֹם אִתִּי' וְאֵינוֹ אוֹמֵר 'אֲנִי בַּמָּקוֹם', שֶׁהַקָּדוֹשׁ בָּרוּךְ הוּא מְקוֹמוֹ שֶׁל עוֹלָם וְאֵין עוֹלָמוֹ מְקוֹמוֹ:

כב **בַּעֲבֹר כְּבֹדִי.** כְּשֶׁאֶעֱבֹר לְפָנֶיךָ: **בְּנִקְרַת הַצּוּר.** כְּמוֹ: "הַעֵינֵי הָאֲנָשִׁים הָהֵם תְּנַקֵּר" (במדבר טז, יד), "יִקְּרוּהָ עֹרְבֵי נַחַל" (משלי ל, יז), "אֲנִי קַרְתִּי וְשָׁתִיתִי מַיִם" (ישעיה לז, כה), גִּזְרָה אַחַת לָהֶם: **נִקְרַת הַצּוּר.** כְּרִיַּת הַצּוּר: **וְשַׂכֹּתִי כַפִּי.** מִכָּאן שֶׁנִּתְּנָה רְשׁוּת לַמְחַבְּלִים לְחַבֵּל, וְתַרְגּוּמוֹ: "וְאַגֵּין בְּמֵימְרִי", כִּנּוּי הוּא לְדֶרֶךְ כָּבוֹד שֶׁל מַעְלָה, שֶׁאֵינוֹ צָרִיךְ לְסוֹכֵךְ עָלָיו בְּכַף מַמָּשׁ:

כג **וַהֲסִרֹתִי אֶת כַּפִּי.** "וְאַעְדֵּי יָת דִּבְרַת יְקָרִי", כְּשֶׁאֲסַלֵּק הַנְהָגַת כְּבוֹדִי מִכְּנֶגֶד פָּנֶיךָ לָלֶכֶת מִשָּׁם וּלְהַלָּן: **וְרָאִיתָ אֶת אֲחֹרָי.** הֶרְאָהוּ קֶשֶׁר שֶׁל תְּפִלִּין:

לד א **פְּסָל לְךָ.** הֶרְאָהוּ מַחְצַב סַנְפִּרִינוֹן מִתּוֹךְ אָהֳלוֹ, וְאָמַר לוֹ: הַפְּסֹלֶת יִהְיֶה שֶׁלְּךָ, וּמִשָּׁם נִתְעַשֵּׁר מֹשֶׁה הַרְבֵּה: **פְּסָל לְךָ.** אַתָּה שִׁבַּרְתָּ הָרִאשׁוֹנוֹת, אַתָּה "פְּסָל לְךָ" אֲחֵרוֹת. מָשָׁל לְמֶלֶךְ שֶׁהָלַךְ לִמְדִינַת הַיָּם

טז אַל־תַּעֲלֵנוּ מִזֶּה׃ וּבַמֶּה ׀ יִוָּדַע אֵפוֹא כִּי־מָצָאתִי חֵן בְּעֵינֶיךָ אֲנִי וְעַמֶּךָ
הֲלוֹא בְּלֶכְתְּךָ עִמָּנוּ וְנִפְלֵינוּ אֲנִי וְעַמְּךָ מִכָּל־הָעָם אֲשֶׁר עַל־פְּנֵי
הָאֲדָמָה׃
יז וַיֹּאמֶר יהוה אֶל־מֹשֶׁה גַּם אֶת־הַדָּבָר הַזֶּה אֲשֶׁר דִּבַּרְתָּ אֶעֱשֶׂה כִּי־ רביעי
יח יט מָצָאתָ חֵן בְּעֵינַי וָאֵדָעֲךָ בְּשֵׁם׃ וַיֹּאמַר הַרְאֵנִי נָא אֶת־כְּבֹדֶךָ׃ וַיֹּאמֶר
אֲנִי אַעֲבִיר כָּל־טוּבִי עַל־פָּנֶיךָ וְקָרָאתִי בְשֵׁם יהוה לְפָנֶיךָ וְחַנֹּתִי
כ אֶת־אֲשֶׁר אָחֹן וְרִחַמְתִּי אֶת־אֲשֶׁר אֲרַחֵם׃ וַיֹּאמֶר לֹא תוּכַל לִרְאֹת
כא אֶת־פָּנָי כִּי לֹא־יִרְאַנִי הָאָדָם וָחָי׃ וַיֹּאמֶר יהוה הִנֵּה מָקוֹם אִתִּי
כב וְנִצַּבְתָּ עַל־הַצּוּר׃ וְהָיָה בַּעֲבֹר כְּבֹדִי וְשַׂמְתִּיךָ בְּנִקְרַת הַצּוּר וְשַׂכֹּתִי
כג כַפִּי עָלֶיךָ עַד־עָבְרִי׃ וַהֲסִרֹתִי אֶת־כַּפִּי וְרָאִיתָ אֶת־אֲחֹרָי וּפָנַי לֹא
יֵרָאוּ׃
לד א וַיֹּאמֶר יהוה אֶל־מֹשֶׁה פְּסָל־לְךָ שְׁנֵי־לֻחֹת אֲבָנִים כָּרִאשֹׁנִים וְכָתַבְתִּי חמישי

אונקלוס

בֵּינַנָא, לָא תַסְּקִנַּנָא מִכָּא: טז וּבְמָא יִתְיְדַע הָכָא, אֲרֵי אַשְׁכַּחִית רַחֲמִין קֳדָמָךְ אֲנָא וְעַמָּךְ, הֲלָא בִּמְהָךְ שְׁכִינְתָךְ עִמַּנָא, וְיִתְעַבְדָן לַנָא פְּרִישָׁן לִי וּלְעַמָּךְ, מִשְּׁנֵי מִכָּל עַמָּא, דְּעַל אַפֵּי אַרְעָא: יז וַאֲמַר יי לְמֹשֶׁה, אַף יָת פִּתְגָמָא הָדֵין, דְּמַלֵּילְתָּא אַעֲבֵיד, אֲרֵי אַשְׁכַּחְתָּא רַחֲמִין קֳדָמַי, וְרַבִּיתָךְ בְּשׁוֹם: יח וַאֲמַר, אַחְזֵינִי כְעַן יָת יְקָרָךְ: יט וַאֲמַר, אֲנָא אַעְבַר כָּל טוּבִי עַל אַפָּךְ, וְאֶקְרֵי בִשְׁמָא דַּיי קֳדָמָךְ, וַאֲחוֹן לְמַאן דַּאֲחוֹן, וַאֲרַחֵים עַל מַאן דַּאֲרַחֵים: כ וַאֲמַר, לָא תִכּוֹל לְמִחְזֵי יָת אַפֵּי שְׁכִינְתִי, אֲרֵי, לָא יִחְזֵינַנִי אֱנָשָׁא וְיִתְקַיַּם: כא וַאֲמַר יי, הָא אֲתַר מְתַקַּן קֳדָמַי, וְתִתְעַתַּד עַל טִנָּרָא: כב וִיהֵי בְּמִעְבַּר יְקָרִי, וַאֲשַׁוֵּינָךְ בִּמְעָרַת טִנָּרָא, וְאַגֵּין בְּמֵימְרִי, עֲלָךְ עַד דְּאֶעְבַּר: כג וְאַעְדֵּי יָת דִּבְרַת יְקָרִי, וְתִחְזֵי יָת דִּבַתְרַי, וּדְקֳדָמַי לָא יִתַּחֲזוֹן: לד א וַאֲמַר יי לְמֹשֶׁה, פְּסָל לָךְ, תְּרֵין לוּחֵי

34:1 פְּסָל־לְךָ שְׁנֵי־לֻחֹת אֲבָנִים כָּרִאשֹׁנִים *Carve two tablets of stone like the first* – The first tablets made by God are smashed. The second tablets, the joint work of God and Moshe, remain intact. Surely the opposite should be true: the greater the holiness, the more eternal the object. Why was the more holy object broken while the less holy stayed whole?

This question leads us to a fundamental principle in Jewish spirituality. The Zohar distinguishes between two types of Divine-human encounter, calling them *itaruta dele'eyla* and *itaruta deletata*, respectively "an awakening from above" and "an awakening from below." The first is initiated by God, the second by mankind. An "awakening from above" is a supernatural event that bursts through the chains of causality that at other times bind the natural world. An "awakening from below" originates in human beings.

An "awakening from above" may change nature, but it does not necessarily change human nature. Those to whom it happens are passive. While it lasts, it is overwhelming – but only while it lasts. Thereafter, people revert to what they were. An "awakening from below," by contrast, leaves a permanent mark. Because human beings have taken the initiative, something in them changes. They now know they are capable of

2 inscribe on them the words that were on the first tablets that you broke. Be
ready in the morning. Climb Mount Sinai in the morning and present yourself
3 to Me there on the mountaintop. Let no one come up with you. No one else
should be seen anywhere on the mountain, nor may flocks or herds graze
4 near the mountain." So Moshe carved two stone tablets like the first. He rose
early in the morning and climbed Mount Sinai, as the LORD had commanded
5 him. In his hand he took the two tablets of stone. The LORD descended in a
6 cloud and stood with him there, and proclaimed the name: The LORD. And
the LORD passed before him, and proclaimed, "The LORD, the LORD, God
compassionate and gracious, slow to anger, abounding in kindness and truth,
7 extending kindness for thousands of generations, forgiving sin, rebellion, and

רש״י

וְהִנִּיחַ אֲרוּסָתוֹ עִם הַשְּׁפָחוֹת. מִתּוֹךְ קִלְקוּל הַשְּׁפָחוֹת יָצָא עָלֶיהָ שֵׁם רָע. עָמַד שׁוֹשְׁבִינָהּ וְקָרַע כְּתֻבָּתָהּ, אָמַר: אִם יֹאמַר הַמֶּלֶךְ לְהָרְגָהּ, אֹמַר לוֹ: עֲדַיִן אֵינָהּ אִשְׁתְּךָ. בָּדַק הַמֶּלֶךְ וּמָצָא שֶׁלֹּא הָיָה הַקִּלְקוּל אֶלָּא מִן הַשְּׁפָחוֹת, נִתְרַצָּה לָהּ. אָמַר לוֹ שׁוֹשְׁבִינָהּ: כְּתֹב לָהּ כְּתֻבָּה אַחֶרֶת, שֶׁנִּקְרְעָה הָרִאשׁוֹנָה. אָמַר לוֹ הַמֶּלֶךְ: אַתָּה קָרַעְתָּ אוֹתָהּ, אַתָּה קְנֵה לָךְ נְיָר אַחֵר וַאֲנִי אֶכְתֹּב לָהּ בִּכְתַב יָדִי. כָּךְ הַמֶּלֶךְ זֶה הַקָּדוֹשׁ בָּרוּךְ הוּא, הַשְּׁפָחוֹת אֵלּוּ עֵרֶב רַב, וְהַשּׁוֹשְׁבִין זֶה מֹשֶׁה. לְכָךְ נֶאֱמַר: "פְּסָל לְךָ":

ב| **נָכוֹן.** מְזֻמָּן:

ג| **וְאִישׁ לֹא יַעֲלֶה עִמָּךְ.** הָרִאשׁוֹנוֹת עַל יְדֵי שֶׁהָיוּ בִּתְשׁוּאוֹת וְקוֹלוֹת וְקוֹלוֹת, שָׁלְטָה בָּהֶן עַיִן רָעָה, אֵין לְךָ יָפֶה מִן הַצְּנִיעוּת:

ה| **וַיִּקְרָא בְשֵׁם ה׳.** מְתַרְגְּמִינַן: "וּקְרָא בִשְׁמָא דַה'":

ו| **ה׳ ה׳.** הוּא מִדַּת רַחֲמִים, אַחַת קֹדֶם שֶׁיֶּחֱטָא וְאַחַת לְאַחַר שֶׁיֶּחֱטָא וְיָשׁוּב: **אֵל.** אַף זוֹ מִדַּת רַחֲמִים, וְכֵן הוּא אוֹמֵר: "אֵלִי אֵלִי לָמָה עֲזַבְתָּנִי" (תהלים כב, ב), וְאֵין לוֹמַר לְמִדַּת הַדִּין: "לָמָה עֲזַבְתָּנִי". כָּךְ מָצָאתִי בַּמְּכִילְתָּא (שירה ג, טו, ב): **אֶרֶךְ אַפַּיִם.** מַאֲרִיךְ אַפּוֹ וְאֵינוֹ מְמַהֵר לִפָּרַע, שֶׁמָּא יַעֲשֶׂה תְּשׁוּבָה: **וְרַב חֶסֶד.** לִצְרִיכֵי חֶסֶד, שֶׁאֵין לָהֶם זְכֻיּוֹת כָּל כָּךְ: **וֶאֱמֶת.** לְשַׁלֵּם שָׂכָר טוֹב לְעוֹשֵׂי רְצוֹנוֹ:

ז| **נֹצֵר חֶסֶד.** שֶׁהָאָדָם עוֹשֶׂה לְפָנָיו: **לָאֲלָפִים.** לִשְׁנֵי אֲלָפִים דּוֹרוֹת. 'עֲוֹנוֹת' אֵלּוּ הַזְּדוֹנוֹת, 'פְּשָׁעִים' אֵלּוּ הַמְּרָדִים שֶׁאָדָם עוֹשֶׂה לְהַכְעִיס: **וְנַקֵּה לֹא יְנַקֶּה.** לְפִי פְּשׁוּטוֹ מַשְׁמָע שֶׁאֵינוֹ מְוַתֵּר עַל הֶעָוֹן לְגַמְרֵי, אֶלָּא נִפְרָע מִמֶּנּוּ מְעַט מְעַט. וְרַבּוֹתֵינוּ דָּרְשׁוּ, "מְנַקֶּה" הוּא לַשָּׁבִים "וְלֹא יְנַקֶּה" לְשֶׁאֵינָן שָׁבִים: **פֹּקֵד עֲוֹן אָבוֹת עַל בָּנִים.** כְּשֶׁאוֹחֲזִים מַעֲשֵׂה

as "womb." Hence, it means the kind of compassion a mother has for a child.

5. *Gracious*: The root *ḥ-n-n* (from the Hebrew word *ḥanun*, meaning "gracious") refers to behavior that comes from the generosity of the one who does it, not the merits of the one to whom, or for whom, it is done.
6. *Slow to anger*: Thus giving time for wrongdoers to repent.
7. *Abounding in kindness*: According to a person's needs, not their deserts.
8. *And truth*: Giving a just reward to those who do His will.
9. *Extending kindness for thousands of generations*: God remembers through the ages the kindness of the patriarchs and the merits of our ancestors.
10. *Forgiving sin*: Sins committed knowingly.
11. *Rebellion*: Sins committed in a spirit of defiance.
12. *And error*: Sins committed unwittingly, either because we did not know what we were doing or did not know that it was forbidden.
13. *And acquitting*: Literally, "cleansing" those who repent.

Note that this last attribute was derived by deliberately cutting the verse off before the end – the emphatic negative in the Hebrew is *venakeh lo yenakeh*, literally, "and acquitting He will not acquit." (This very different conclusion is discussed in the next comment.)

עַל־הַלֻּחֹת אֶת־הַדְּבָרִים אֲשֶׁר הָיוּ עַל־הַלֻּחֹת הָרִאשֹׁנִים אֲשֶׁר
ב שִׁבַּרְתָּ׃ וֶהְיֵה נָכוֹן לַבֹּקֶר וְעָלִיתָ בַבֹּקֶר אֶל־הַר סִינַי וְנִצַּבְתָּ לִי שָׁם
ג עַל־רֹאשׁ הָהָר׃ וְאִישׁ לֹא־יַעֲלֶה עִמָּךְ וְגַם־אִישׁ אַל־יֵרָא בְּכָל־הָהָר
ד גַּם־הַצֹּאן וְהַבָּקָר אַל־יִרְעוּ אֶל־מוּל הָהָר הַהוּא׃ וַיִּפְסֹל שְׁנֵי־לֻחֹת
אֲבָנִים כָּרִאשֹׁנִים וַיַּשְׁכֵּם מֹשֶׁה בַבֹּקֶר וַיַּעַל אֶל־הַר סִינַי כַּאֲשֶׁר צִוָּה
ה יְהוָה אֹתוֹ וַיִּקַּח בְּיָדוֹ שְׁנֵי לֻחֹת אֲבָנִים׃ וַיֵּרֶד יְהוָה בֶּעָנָן וַיִּתְיַצֵּב עִמּוֹ
ו שָׁם וַיִּקְרָא בְשֵׁם יְהוָה׃ וַיַּעֲבֹר יְהוָה ׀ עַל־פָּנָיו וַיִּקְרָא יְהוָה ׀ יְהוָה אֵל
ז רַחוּם וְחַנּוּן אֶרֶךְ אַפַּיִם וְרַב־חֶסֶד וֶאֱמֶת׃ נֹצֵר חֶסֶד לָאֲלָפִים נֹשֵׂא
עָוֹן וָפֶשַׁע וְחַטָּאָה וְנַקֵּה לֹא יְנַקֶּה פֹּקֵד ׀ עֲוֹן אָבוֹת עַל־בָּנִים וְעַל־בְּנֵי

אונקלוס

אַבְנַיָּא כְּקַדְמָאֵי, וְאֶכְתּוֹב עַל לוּחַיָּא, יָת פִּתְגָמַיָּא, דַּהֲווֹ, עַל לוּחַיָּא קַדְמָאֵי דְּתַבַּרְתָּא: ב וֶהֱוֵי זְמִין לְצַפְרָא, וְתִסַּק בְּצַפְרָא לְטוּרָא דְסִינַי, וְתִתְעַתַּד קֳדָמַי, תַּמָּן עַל רֵישׁ טוּרָא: ג וֶאֱנָשׁ לָא יִסַּק עִמָּךְ, וְאַף אֱנָשׁ לָא יִתַּחְזֵי בְּכָל טוּרָא, אַף עָנָא וְתוֹרֵי לָא יִרְעוֹן, לָקֳבֵיל טוּרָא הַהוּא: ד וּפְסַל, תְּרֵין לוּחֵי אַבְנַיָּא כְּקַדְמָאֵי, וְאַקְדֵּים מֹשֶׁה בְּצַפְרָא וּסְלֵיק לְטוּרָא דְסִינַי, כְּמָא דְּפַקֵּיד יי יָתֵיהּ, וּנְסֵיב בִּידֵיהּ, תְּרֵין לוּחֵי אַבְנַיָּא: ה וְאִתְגְּלִי יי בַּעֲנָנָא, וְאִתְעַתַּד עִמֵּיהּ תַּמָּן, וּקְרָא בִּשְׁמָא דַיי: ו וְאַעְבַּר יי שְׁכִינְתֵיהּ עַל אַפּוֹהִי וּקְרָא, יי יי, אֱלָהָא רַחֲמָנָא וְחַנָּנָא, מַרְחִיק רְגַז וּמַסְגֵּי לְמֶעְבַּד טָבְוָן וְקוּשְׁט: ז נָטֵיר טֵיבוּ לְאַלְפֵי דָרִין, שָׁבֵיק לַעֲוָיָן, וְלִמְרוֹד וּלְחוֹבִין, סָלַח לִדְתָיְבִין לְאוֹרָיְתֵיהּ וּלְדְלָא תָּיְבִין לָא מְזַכֵּי, מַסְעַר חוֹבֵי אֲבָהָן, עַל בְּנִין וְעַל בְּנֵי בְנִין מָרָדִין, עַל דָּר תְּלִיתָאֵי וְעַל דָּר רְבִיעָאֵי:

great things, and because they did so once, they are aware that they can do so again. An awakening from above temporarily transforms the external world; an awakening from below permanently transforms our internal world.

In Judaism, the natural is greater than the supernatural in the sense that an "awakening from below" is more powerful in transforming us, and longer lasting in its effects, than is an "awakening from above." That was why the second tablets survived intact while the first did not. Divine intervention changes nature, but it is human initiative – our approach to God – that changes us.

THE THIRTEEN ATTRIBUTES OF MERCY

The Thirteen Attributes of Mercy, the name given by the Sages to God's declaration here, are the basis of all *Seliḥot*, prayers for forgiveness, for they are God's self-definition as the source of compassion and pardon that frames the moral life. They tell us that God "do[es] not desire the death of the wicked one, but that he should turn from his course and live" (Ezek. 33:11). When we repent and make good the harm we have done, God forgives. It is as if God is binding Himself to forgive the penitent in each generation by this description of Himself. The Thirteen Attributes derived by the Sages are as follows:

1. *The Lord:* The name that signifies God's attribute of compassion as opposed to strict justice.
2. *The Lord:* God retains the same compassion even after we have sinned, thus making repentance possible.
3. *God*: The power and force through which God sustains the universe and all that lives.
4. *Compassionate*: The root *r-ḥ-m* (from the Hebrew word *raḥum*, meaning "compassionate") is the same

▶

error, but who does not acquit the guilty, holding descendants to account
for the sins of the fathers, children and grandchildren to the third and fourth
8 9 generation." Moshe quickly bowed and prostrated himself, and he said, "If now
I have found favor in Your sight, O Lord, please, let my Lord go among us.
Though this is a stiff-necked people, pardon our sins and errors, and keep us
10 as Your own." The LORD said, "Now am I hereby making a covenant. Before SHISHI
your entire people I will perform such wonders as never have been performed
anywhere on earth, for any nation. All the peoples you live among shall see:
11 how awe-inspiring are the deeds that I the LORD will do for you. Be vigilant
in what I am commanding you this day. I am going to drive out before you the

רש״י

אֲבוֹתֵיהֶם בִּידֵיהֶם, שֶׁכְּבָר פֵּרֵשׁ בְּמִקְרָא אַחֵר "לְשֹׂנְאָי" (לעיל כ, ה): **וְעַל רִבֵּעִים.** דּוֹר רְבִיעִי. נִמְצֵאת מִדָּה טוֹבָה מְרֻבָּה עַל מִדַּת פֻּרְעָנוּת אַחַת לַחֲמֵשׁ מֵאוֹת, שֶׁבְּמִדָּה טוֹבָה הוּא אוֹמֵר: "נֹצֵר חֶסֶד לָאֲלָפִים":

ח **וַיְמַהֵר מֹשֶׁה.** כְּשֶׁרָאָה מֹשֶׁה שְׁכִינָה עוֹבֶרֶת וְשָׁמַע קוֹל הַקְּרִיאָה, מִיָּד "וַיִּשְׁתָּחוּ":

ט **יֵלֶךְ נָא ה׳ בְּקִרְבֵּנוּ.** כְּמוֹ שֶׁהִבְטַחְתָּ, מֵאַחַר שֶׁאַתָּה נוֹשֵׂא עָוֹן, וְאִם "עַם קְשֵׁה עֹרֶף הוּא" וְיַמְרוּ בְּךָ וְאָמַרְתָּ עַל זֹאת: "פֶּן אֲכֶלְךָ בַּדָּרֶךְ" (לעיל לג, ג) – אַתָּה תִּסְלַח "לַעֲוֹנֵנוּ" וְגוֹ׳. יֵשׁ 'כִּי' בִּמְקוֹם 'אִם': **וּנְחַלְתָּנוּ.** וּתְנֵנוּ לְךָ לְנַחֲלָה מְיֻחֶדֶת. זוֹ הִיא בַּקָּשַׁת "וְנִפְלֵינוּ אֲנִי וְעַמְּךָ" (שם פסוק טז), שֶׁלֹּא תַּשְׁרֶה שְׁכִינָתְךָ עַל הָאֻמּוֹת:

י **כֹּרֵת בְּרִית.** עַל זֹאת: **אֶעֱשֶׂה נִפְלָאֹת.** לְשׁוֹן "וְנִפְלֵינוּ", שֶׁתִּהְיוּ מֻבְדָּלִים בָּזוֹ מִכָּל הָאֻמּוֹת, שֶׁלֹּא תִּשְׁרֶה שְׁכִינָתִי עֲלֵיהֶם:

יא **אֶת הָאֱמֹרִי וְגוֹ׳.** שֵׁשׁ אֻמּוֹת יֵשׁ כָּאן, כִּי הַגִּרְגָּשִׁי עָמַד וּפִנָּה מִפְּנֵיהֶם:

How can Moshe invoke the people's obstinacy as the very reason for God to maintain His presence among them? The commentators offer a variety of interpretations. Rashi reads the word *ki* as "if": "If they are stiff-necked, then forgive them." Ibn Ezra and *Ḥizkuni*, reflected in our translation, read it as "although" or "despite the fact that" (*af al pi*). Alternatively, suggests Ibn Ezra, the verse might be read, "[I admit that] it is a stiff-necked people – therefore forgive our wickedness and our sin, and take us as Your inheritance."

There is a striking line of interpretation that can be traced across the centuries. In the twentieth century it was given expression by Rabbi Yitzchak Nissenbaum. The fact that Rabbi Nissenbaum lived and died in the Warsaw Ghetto gives added poignancy to his words. The argument he attributed to Moshe is this:

> Almighty God, look upon this people with favor, because what is now their greatest vice will one day be their most heroic virtue. They are indeed an obstinate people. When they have everything to thank You for, they complain. Mere weeks after hearing Your voice they make a golden calf. But just as now they are stiff-necked in their disobedience, so one day they will be equally stiff-necked in their loyalty. Nations will call on them to assimilate, but they will refuse. Mightier religions will urge them to convert, but they will resist. They will suffer humiliation, persecution, even torture and death because of the name they bear and the faith they profess, but they will stay true to the covenant their ancestors made with You. They will go to their deaths saying *Ani maamin*, "I believe." This is a people awesome in its obstinacy – and though now it is their failing, there will be times far into the future when it will be their noblest strength. (Cited in Aaron Yaakov Greenberg, ed., *Itturei Torah*)

ח בָּנִים עַל־שִׁלֵּשִׁים וְעַל־רִבֵּעִים: וַיְמַהֵר מֹשֶׁה וַיִּקֹּד אַרְצָה וַיִּשְׁתָּחוּ:
ט וַיֹּאמֶר אִם־נָא מָצָאתִי חֵן בְּעֵינֶיךָ אֲדֹנָי יֵלֶךְ־נָא אֲדֹנָי בְּקִרְבֵּנוּ כִּי עַם־
י קְשֵׁה־עֹרֶף הוּא וְסָלַחְתָּ לַעֲוֺנֵנוּ וּלְחַטָּאתֵנוּ וּנְחַלְתָּנוּ: וַיֹּאמֶר הִנֵּה ששי
אָנֹכִי כֹּרֵת בְּרִית נֶגֶד כָּל־עַמְּךָ אֶעֱשֶׂה נִפְלָאֹת אֲשֶׁר לֹא־נִבְרְאוּ בְכָל־
הָאָרֶץ וּבְכָל־הַגּוֹיִם וְרָאָה כָל־הָעָם אֲשֶׁר־אַתָּה בְקִרְבּוֹ אֶת־מַעֲשֵׂה
יא יהוה כִּי־נוֹרָא הוּא אֲשֶׁר אֲנִי עֹשֶׂה עִמָּךְ: שְׁמָר־לְךָ אֵת אֲשֶׁר אָנֹכִי
מְצַוְּךָ הַיּוֹם הִנְנִי גֹרֵשׁ מִפָּנֶיךָ אֶת־הָאֱמֹרִי וְהַכְּנַעֲנִי וְהַחִתִּי וְהַפְּרִזִּי

אונקלוס

ח וְאוֹחִי מֹשֶׁה, וּכְרַע עַל אַרְעָא וּסְגִיד: ט וַאֲמַר, אִם כְּעַן אַשְׁכַּחִית רַחֲמִין קֳדָמָךְ יי, תְּהָךְ כְּעַן שְׁכִינְתָא דַּיי בֵּינָנָא, אֲרֵי עַם קְשֵׁי קְדָל הוּא, וְתִשְׁבּוֹק, לְחוֹבַנָא וּלְחֲטָאֲנָא וְתַחְסְנִנָּנָא: י וַאֲמַר, הָא אֲנָא גָּזַר קְיָם, קֳדָם כָּל עַמָּךְ אַעֲבֵיד פְּרִישָׁן, דְּלָא אִתְבְּרִיאוּ בְּכָל אַרְעָא וּבְכָל עַמְמַיָּא, וְיִחֱזֵי כָל עַמָּא, דְּאַתְּ בֵּינֵיהוֹן, יָת עוֹבָדָא דַּיי אֲרֵי דְּחִיל הוּא, דַּאֲנָא עָבֵיד עִמָּךְ: יא טַר לָךְ, יָת דַּאֲנָא מְפַקֵּיד לָךְ יוֹמָא דֵין, הָאֲנָא מְתָרֵיךְ מִן קֳדָמָךְ, יָת אֱמוֹרָאֵי וּכְנַעֲנָאֵי, וְחִתָּאֵי וּפְרִזָּאֵי,

34:7 לֹא יְנַקֶּה *Who does not acquit the guilty* – God is compassionate and lives in love and forgiveness. This is an essential element of Jewish faith. But the Torah includes a caveat. There is compassion but there is also justice.

Why so? Why must there be punishment as well as forgiveness? The Sages said that "when God created the universe He did so under the attribute of justice, but then saw it could not survive. What did He do? He added compassion to justice and created the world" (Rashi on Gen. 1:1). This statement prompts the same question: Why did God not abandon justice altogether? Why is forgiveness alone not enough?

Some fascinating recent research provides us with an extraordinary and unexpected answer. Studies show that those who believe in a punitive God cheat and steal less than those who believe in a forgiving God. What is more, however, people who believe in a punitive God also punish people less than others who believe in a forgiving God. Subjects who believe that, as the Torah says, God "does not acquit the guilty" are more willing to leave punishment to God. Those who focus on divine forgiveness are more likely to practice human retribution or revenge.

A world without divine justice would be one where there is more resentment, punishment, and crime – and less public-spiritedness and forgiveness, even among religious believers. The more we believe that God punishes the guilty, the more forgiving we can become. The less we believe that God punishes the guilty, the more resentful and punitive we become. This is a counterintuitive truth, yet one that allows us to see the profound wisdom of the Torah in helping us create a humane and compassionate society. This is why, at the very moment He is declaring His compassion, grace, and forgiveness, God insists that He does not leave the guilty unpunished.

34:9 כִּי עַם־קְשֵׁה־עֹרֶף הוּא *Though this is a stiff-necked people* – The Hebrew word *ki*, most often meaning "because," reads as though Moshe is in fact citing a reason for God remaining with the Israelites. Yet this is the very attribute that God had previously given for wishing to abandon them: "Then the Lord said to Moshe, 'I have seen this people; it is a stiff-necked people. So do not try to stop Me when My anger burns against them. I will put an end to them'" (Ex. 32:9–10).

12 Amorites, Canaanites, Hittites, Perizzites, Hivites, and Jebusites. Take care not
to make a treaty with the inhabitants of the land you are going to; for they would
13 become a dangerous trap to you. Tear down their altars, smash their worship
14 pillars, and cut down their sacred trees, for you must worship no other god. The
Lord, known to demand absolute loyalty, is your God who demands it indeed.
15 You must not make a treaty with the inhabitants of the land, for they will lust
after their gods and sacrifice to them; they will invite you to join them and you
16 will eat of their sacrifice, and you will take their daughters as wives for your
sons, and their daughters will lust after their gods and cause your sons to do as
17 18 they do. Make for yourselves no molten gods. Keep the Festival of Unleavened
Bread. For seven days, eat unleavened bread as I commanded you, at the time
19 appointed, in the month of Aviv, because in that month you left Egypt. The first
to emerge from every womb is Mine; among all your livestock, firstborn cattle,
20 and sheep. Redeem each firstborn donkey with a sheep; if you do not redeem
it, you must break its neck. Also redeem all your firstborn sons. Do not appear
21 before Me empty-handed. Six days you shall work, but on the seventh day you
22 shall rest, ceasing from labor even at plowing time and harvest time. Observe

רש״י

יג| **אֲשֵׁרָיו.** הוּא אִילָן שֶׁעוֹבְדִים אוֹתוֹ:

יד| **קַנָּא שְׁמוֹ.** מְקַנֵּא לִפָּרַע וְאֵינוֹ מוֹחֵל, וְזֶהוּ כָּל לְשׁוֹן קִנְאָה, אוֹחֵז בְּנִצְחוֹנוֹ וּפוֹרֵעַ מֵעוֹזְבָיו:

טו-טז| **וְאָכַלְתָּ מִזִּבְחוֹ.** כְּסָבוּר אַתָּה שֶׁאֵין עֹנֶשׁ בַּאֲכִילָתוֹ, וַאֲנִי מַעֲלֶה עָלֶיךָ כְּמוֹדֶה בַּעֲבוֹדָתָם, שֶׁמִּתּוֹךְ כָּךְ אַתָּה בָא וְלוֹקֵחַ "מִבְּנֹתָיו לְבָנֶיךָ":

יח| **חֹדֶשׁ הָאָבִיב.** חֹדֶשׁ הַבַּכִּיר, שֶׁהַתְּבוּאָה מְבַכֶּרֶת בְּבִשּׁוּלָהּ:

יט| **כָּל פֶּטֶר רֶחֶם לִי.** בָּאָדָם: **וְכָל מִקְנְךָ תִּזָּכָר וְגוֹ׳.** וְכָל מִקְנְךָ אֲשֶׁר תִּזָּכָר בְּפֶטֶר שׁוֹר וָשֶׂה, אֲשֶׁר יִפְטֹר זָכָר אֶת רַחְמָהּ. 'פֶּטֶר' לְשׁוֹן פְּתִיחָה, וְכֵן: "פּוֹטֵר מַיִם רֵאשִׁית מָדוֹן" (משלי יז, יד). תָּי"ו שֶׁל "תִּזָּכָר" לְשׁוֹן נְקֵבָה הִיא, מוּסָב עַל הַיּוֹלֶדֶת:

כ| **וּפֶטֶר חֲמוֹר.** וְלֹא שְׁאָר בְּהֵמָה טְמֵאָה: **תִּפְדֶּה בְשֶׂה.** נוֹתֵן שֶׂה לַכֹּהֵן וְהוּא חֻלִּין בְּיַד כֹּהֵן, וּפֶטֶר חֲמוֹר מֻתָּר בַּעֲבוֹדָה לַבְּעָלִים: **וַעֲרַפְתּוֹ.** עוֹרְפוֹ בְּקוֹפִיץ. הוּא הִפְסִיד מָמוֹן כֹּהֵן, לְפִיכָךְ יִפְסַד מָמוֹנוֹ: **כֹּל בְּכוֹר בָּנֶיךָ תִּפְדֶּה.** חֲמִשָּׁה סְלָעִים פִּדְיוֹנוֹ קָצוּב, שֶׁנֶּאֱמַר: "וּפְדוּיָו מִבֶּן חֹדֶשׁ תִּפְדֶּה" וְגוֹ׳ (במדבר יח, טז): **וְלֹא יֵרָאוּ פָנַי רֵיקָם.** לְפִי פְּשׁוּטוֹ שֶׁל מִקְרָא דָּבָר בִּפְנֵי עַצְמוֹ הוּא וְאֵינוֹ מוּסָב עַל הַבְּכוֹר, שֶׁאֵין בְּמִצְוַת בְּכוֹר רְאִיַּת פָּנִים, אֶלָּא אַזְהָרָה אַחֶרֶת הִיא: וּכְשֶׁתַּעֲלוּ לָרֶגֶל לֵרָאוֹת "לֹא יֵרָאוּ פָנַי רֵיקָם", מִצְוָה עֲלֵיכֶם לְהָבִיא עוֹלַת רְאִיַּת פָּנִים. וּלְפִי מִדְרַשׁ בָּרַיְתָא, מִקְרָא יָתֵר הוּא וּמֻפְנֶה לִגְזֵרָה שָׁוָה, לְלַמֵּד עַל הַעֲנָקָתוֹ שֶׁל עֶבֶד עִבְרִי שֶׁהוּא חֲמִשָּׁה סְלָעִים מִכָּל מִין וָמִין כְּפִדְיוֹן בְּכוֹר. בְּמַסֶּכֶת קִדּוּשִׁין (דף יז ע"א):

כא| **בֶּחָרִישׁ וּבַקָּצִיר תִּשְׁבֹּת.** לָמָּה נִזְכַּר חָרִישׁ וְקָצִיר? יֵשׁ מֵרַבּוֹתֵינוּ אוֹמְרִים: עַל חָרִישׁ שֶׁל עֶרֶב שְׁבִיעִית הַנִּכְנָס לִשְׁבִיעִית וְקָצִיר שֶׁל שְׁבִיעִית הַיּוֹצֵא לְמוֹצָאֵי שְׁבִיעִית, לְלַמֶּדְךָ שֶׁמּוֹסִיפִין מֵחֹל עַל הַקֹּדֶשׁ. וְכָךְ מַשְׁמָעוֹ: "שֵׁשֶׁת יָמִים תַּעֲבֹד וּבַיּוֹם הַשְּׁבִיעִי תִּשְׁבֹּת", וַעֲבוֹדַת שֵׁשֶׁת הַיָּמִים שֶׁהִתַּרְתִּי לְךָ, יֵשׁ שָׁנָה שֶׁהֶחָרִישׁ וְהַקָּצִיר אָסוּר. וְאֵין צָרִיךְ

The Sabbath is our refuge from what has become, by now, a consumer culture. There are limits to our striving, our labors, our consumption of the earth's finite resources. Any culture that loses its sense of limits eventually self-destructs. The Sabbath tells us that happiness lies not in what we buy, but in what we are; that true contentment is to be found not by seeking what we lack but by giving thanks for what we have; and that we should never allow ourselves to be so busy making a living that we have all too little time to live. Above all, we should never be led by the crowd when it stampedes in pursuit of gain, for that is how gold becomes a golden calf.

יב וְהַחִוִּי וְהַיְבוּסִי: הִשָּׁמֶר לְךָ פֶּן־תִּכְרֹת בְּרִית לְיוֹשֵׁב הָאָרֶץ אֲשֶׁר
יג אַתָּה בָּא עָלֶיהָ פֶּן־יִהְיֶה לְמוֹקֵשׁ בְּקִרְבֶּךָ: כִּי אֶת־מִזְבְּחֹתָם תִּתֹּצוּן
יד וְאֶת־מַצֵּבֹתָם תְּשַׁבֵּרוּן וְאֶת־אֲשֵׁרָיו תִּכְרֹתוּן: כִּי לֹא תִשְׁתַּחֲוֶה
טו לְאֵל אַחֵר כִּי יהוה קַנָּא שְׁמוֹ אֵל קַנָּא הוּא: פֶּן־תִּכְרֹת בְּרִית לְיוֹשֵׁב
הָאָרֶץ וְזָנוּ ׀ אַחֲרֵי אֱלֹהֵיהֶם וְזָבְחוּ לֵאלֹהֵיהֶם וְקָרָא לְךָ וְאָכַלְתָּ
טז מִזִּבְחוֹ: וְלָקַחְתָּ מִבְּנֹתָיו לְבָנֶיךָ וְזָנוּ בְנֹתָיו אַחֲרֵי אֱלֹהֵיהֶן וְהִזְנוּ אֶת־
יז יח בָּנֶיךָ אַחֲרֵי אֱלֹהֵיהֶן: אֱלֹהֵי מַסֵּכָה לֹא תַעֲשֶׂה־לָּךְ: אֶת־חַג הַמַּצּוֹת
תִּשְׁמֹר שִׁבְעַת יָמִים תֹּאכַל מַצּוֹת אֲשֶׁר צִוִּיתִךָ לְמוֹעֵד חֹדֶשׁ הָאָבִיב
יט כִּי בְּחֹדֶשׁ הָאָבִיב יָצָאתָ מִמִּצְרָיִם: כָּל־פֶּטֶר רֶחֶם לִי וְכָל־מִקְנְךָ תִּזָּכָר
כ פֶּטֶר שׁוֹר וָשֶׂה: וּפֶטֶר חֲמוֹר תִּפְדֶּה בְשֶׂה וְאִם־לֹא תִפְדֶּה וַעֲרַפְתּוֹ
כא כֹּל בְּכוֹר בָּנֶיךָ תִּפְדֶּה וְלֹא־יֵרָאוּ פָנַי רֵיקָם: שֵׁשֶׁת יָמִים תַּעֲבֹד וּבַיּוֹם
כב הַשְּׁבִיעִי תִּשְׁבֹּת בֶּחָרִישׁ וּבַקָּצִיר תִּשְׁבֹּת: וְחַג שָׁבֻעֹת תַּעֲשֶׂה לְךָ

אונקלוס

וְחִוָּאֵי וִיבוּסָאֵי: יב אִסְתְּמַר לָךְ, דִּלְמָא תִגְזַר קְיָם לְיָתֵיב אַרְעָא, דְּאַתְּ עָלֵיל עֲלַהּ, דִּלְמָא יְהֵי לְתַקְלָא בֵּינָךְ: יג אֲרֵי יָת אֵיגוֹרֵיהוֹן תְּתָרְעוּן, וְיָת קָמָתְהוֹן תְּתַבְּרוּן, וְיָת אֲשֵׁירֵיהוֹן תְּקַצְּצוּן: יד אֲרֵי, לָא תִסְגּוֹד לְטַעֲוַת עַמְמַיָּא, אֲרֵי יי קַנָּא שְׁמֵיהּ, אֵל קַנָּא הוּא: טו דִּלְמָא תִגְזַר קְיָם לְיָתֵיב אַרְעָא, וְיִטְעוֹן בָּתַר טַעֲוָתְהוֹן, וִידַבְּחוּן לְטַעֲוָתְהוֹן, וְיִקְרוֹן לָךְ, וְתֵיכוֹל מִדִּבְחֵיהוֹן: טז וְתִסַּב מִבְּנָתְהוֹן לִבְנָךְ, וְיִטְעוֹן בְּנָתְהוֹן, בָּתַר טַעֲוָתְהוֹן, וְיַטְעְיָן יָת בְּנָךְ, בָּתַר טַעֲוָתְהוֹן: יז דַּחְלָן דְּמַתְּכָא לָא תַעֲבֵיד לָךְ: יח יָת חַגָּא דְּפַטִּירַיָּא תִּטַּר, שִׁבְעָא יוֹמִין, תֵּיכוֹל פַּטִּירָא דְּפַקֵּידְתָּךְ, לִזְמַן יַרְחָא דַּאֲבִיבָא, אֲרֵי בְּיַרְחָא דַּאֲבִיבָא, נְפַקְתָּא מִמִּצְרָיִם: יט כָּל פָּתַח וַלְדָּא דִּילִי הוּא, וְכָל בְּעִירָךְ דִּכְרִין תַּקְדֵּישׁ, בְּכוֹר תּוֹר וְאִמַּר: כ וּבְכָרָא דִּחְמָרָא תִּפְרוֹק בְּאִמְּרָא, וְאִם לָא תִפְרוֹק וְתִקְפֵיהּ, כָּל בְּכְרָא דִּבְנָךְ תִּפְרוֹק, וְלָא יִתַּחְזוֹן קֳדָמַי רֵיקָנִין: כא שִׁתָּא יוֹמִין תִּפְלַח, וּבְיוֹמָא שְׁבִיעָאָה תְּנוּחַ, בִּזְרוּעָא וּבַחְצָדָא תְּנוּחַ: כב וְחַגָּא דְּשָׁבוּעַיָּא תַּעֲבֵיד לָךְ,

34:21 וּבַיּוֹם הַשְּׁבִיעִי תִּשְׁבֹּת *On the seventh day you shall rest* – Immediately before and after the golden calf event, Moshe gives the Israelites the same command, namely the Sabbath. The Sabbath is the antidote to the golden calf.

The golden calf is a symbol of what can happen when people turn gold, a medium of exchange, into an object of worship. The Sabbath, on the other hand, is the day when we stop thinking of the *price* of things and focus instead on the *value* of things. On the Sabbath we can't sell or buy. We can't work or pay others to work for us. It is the day dedicated to the celebration of the things that have value but no price. Husbands sing a song of praise to their wives. Parents bless their children. We take time to have a meal together with family and friends. In the synagogue we renew our sense of community. People share their joys with others and find comfort for their grief. We listen to Torah together, reminding ourselves of the story of which we are a part. We pray together, thanking God for our blessings.

▶

the Festival of Weeks, of the first fruits of the wheat harvest, as well as the
23 Festival of Ingathering at the close of the year. Three times a year all the males
24 among you shall appear before the Master, the LORD, God of Israel. For I will
banish nations before you and enlarge your territory. No one will covet your
land when you go up, three times a year, to appear before the LORD your God.
25 Do not offer the blood of My sacrifice with anything leavened. Do not let any
26 of the Passover festival sacrifice remain until morning. Bring the best first fruits
of your land to the House of the LORD your God. Do not cook a kid in the milk
of its mother."
27 Then the LORD said to Moshe, "Write down these words, for in accordance SHEVI'I
28 with these words I have made a covenant with you and with Israel." He stayed
there with the LORD for forty days and forty nights, eating no bread and
drinking no water. And on the tablets, He wrote the words of the covenant, the
29 Ten Commandments. When Moshe came down from Mount Sinai with the
two tablets of testimony in his hand, he was unaware that the skin of his face

רש״י

לוֹמַר חָרִישׁ וְקָצִיר שֶׁל שְׁבִיעִית, שֶׁהֲרֵי כְּבָר נֶאֱמַר: "שָׂדְךָ לֹא תִזְרָע" וְגוֹ' (ויקרא כה, ד). וְיֵשׁ מֵהֶם אוֹמְרִים: אֵינוֹ מְדַבֵּר אֶלָּא בְּשַׁבָּת, וְחָרִישׁ וְקָצִיר שֶׁהֻזְכַּר בּוֹ לוֹמַר לְךָ, מַה חָרִישׁ רְשׁוּת אַף קָצִיר רְשׁוּת, יָצָא קְצִיר הָעֹמֶר שֶׁהוּא מִצְוָה וְדוֹחֶה אֶת הַשַּׁבָּת:

כב] **בִּכּוּרֵי קְצִיר חִטִּים.** שֶׁאַתָּה מֵבִיא בּוֹ שְׁתֵּי הַלֶּחֶם מִן הַחִטִּים בִּכּוּרִים, שֶׁהִיא מִנְחָה רִאשׁוֹנָה הַבָּאָה מִן הֶחָדָשׁ חִטִּים לַמִּקְדָּשׁ, כִּי מִנְחַת הָעֹמֶר הַבָּאָה בַּפֶּסַח, מִן הַשְּׂעוֹרִים הִיא: **וְחַג הָאָסִיף.** בִּזְמַן שֶׁאַתָּה אוֹסֵף תְּבוּאָתְךָ מִן הַשָּׂדֶה לַבַּיִת. אֲסִיפָה זוֹ לְשׁוֹן הַכְנָסָה לַבַּיִת, כְּמוֹ: "וַאֲסַפְתּוֹ אֶל תּוֹךְ בֵּיתֶךָ" (דברים כב, ב): **תְּקוּפַת הַשָּׁנָה.** שֶׁהִיא בַּחֲזֶרֶת הַשָּׁנָה, בִּתְחִלַּת הַשָּׁנָה הַבָּאָה: **תְּקוּפַת.** לְשׁוֹן מְסִבָּה וְהַקָּפָה:

כג] **כָּל זְכוּרְךָ.** כָּל הַזְּכָרִים שֶׁבְּךָ. הַרְבֵּה מִצְוֹת בַּתּוֹרָה נֶאֶמְרוּ וְנִכְפְּלוּ, וְיֵשׁ מֵהֶם שָׁלֹשׁ פְּעָמִים וְאַרְבַּע, לְחַיֵּב וְלַעֲנֹשׁ עַל מִנְיַן לָאוִין שֶׁבָּהֶם וְעַל מִנְיַן עֲשֵׂה שֶׁבָּהֶם:

כד] **אוֹרִישׁ.** כְּתַרְגּוּמוֹ: "אֲתָרֵיךְ", וְכֵן: "הָחֵל רָשׁ" (דברים ב, לא), וְכֵן: "וַיּוֹרֶשׁ אֶת הָאֱמֹרִי" (במדבר כא, לב), לְשׁוֹן גֵּרוּשִׁין: **וְהִרְחַבְתִּי אֶת גְּבֻלֶךָ.** וְאַתָּה רָחוֹק מִבֵּית הַבְּחִירָה וְאֵינְךָ יָכוֹל לֵרָאוֹת לְפָנַי תָּמִיד, לְכָךְ אֲנִי קוֹבֵעַ לְךָ שָׁלֹשׁ רְגָלִים הַלָּלוּ:

כה] **לֹא תִשְׁחַט וְגוֹ'.** לֹא תִשְׁחַט אֶת הַפֶּסַח וַעֲדַיִן חָמֵץ קַיָּם, אַזְהָרָה לַשּׁוֹחֵט אוֹ לַזּוֹרֵק אוֹ לְאֶחָד מִבְּנֵי חֲבוּרָה: **וְלֹא יָלִין.** כְּתַרְגּוּמוֹ. אֵין לִינָה מוֹעֶלֶת בְּרֹאשׁ הַמִּזְבֵּחַ, וְאֵין לִינָה אֶלָּא בְּעַמּוּד הַשַּׁחַר: **זֶבַח חַג הַפָּסַח.** אֵמוּרָיו, וּמִכָּאן אַתָּה לָמֵד לְכָל הֶקְטֵר חֲלָבִים וְאֵבָרִים:

כו] **רֵאשִׁית בִּכּוּרֵי אַדְמָתְךָ.** מִשִּׁבְעַת הַמִּינִין הָאֲמוּרִים בְּשֶׁבַח אַרְצְךָ: "אֶרֶץ חִטָּה וּשְׂעֹרָה וְגֶפֶן" וְגוֹ' (דברים ח, ח) "וּדְבָשׁ" – הֵן תְּמָרִים: **לֹא תְבַשֵּׁל גְּדִי.** אַזְהָרָה לְבָשָׂר בְּחָלָב. וּשְׁלֹשָׁה פְּעָמִים כָּתוּב בַּתּוֹרָה: אֶחָד לַאֲכִילָה, וְאֶחָד לַהֲנָאָה, וְאֶחָד לְאִסּוּר בִּשּׁוּל: **גְּדִי.** כָּל וָלָד רַךְ בַּמַּשְׁמָע וְאַף עֵגֶל וָכֶבֶשׂ, מִמָּה שֶׁהֻצְרַךְ לְפָרֵשׁ בְּכַמָּה מְקוֹמוֹת: 'גְּדִי עִזִּים' (בראשית לח, יז, ועוד) לָמַדְתָּ שֶׁ'גְּדִי' סְתָם כָּל יוֹנְקִים בַּמַּשְׁמָע: **בַּחֲלֵב אִמּוֹ.** פְּרָט לָעוֹף, שֶׁאֵין לוֹ חֲלֵב אֵם, שֶׁאֵין אִסּוּרוֹ מִן הַתּוֹרָה אֶלָּא מִדִּבְרֵי סוֹפְרִים:

כז] **אֶת הַדְּבָרִים הָאֵלֶּה.** וְלֹא אַתָּה רַשַּׁאי לִכְתֹּב תּוֹרָה שֶׁבְּעַל פֶּה:

כט] **וַיְהִי בְּרֶדֶת מֹשֶׁה.** כְּשֶׁהֵבִיא לוּחוֹת אַחֲרוֹנוֹת בְּיוֹם הַכִּפּוּרִים: **כִּי קָרַן.** לְשׁוֹן קַרְנַיִם, שֶׁהָאוֹר מַבְהִיק וּבוֹלֵט כְּמִין קֶרֶן. וּמֵהֵיכָן זָכָה מֹשֶׁה לְקַרְנֵי הַהוֹד? רַבּוֹתֵינוּ אָמְרוּ: מִן הַמְּעָרָה, שֶׁנָּתַן הַקָּדוֹשׁ בָּרוּךְ הוּא יָדוֹ עַל פָּנָיו, שֶׁנֶּאֱמַר: "וְשַׂכֹּתִי כַפִּי" (לעיל לג, כב):

of this phrase. One reads it as "a loud voice that was never heard again," the other as "a loud voice that did not cease," i.e., a voice that was always heard again. Both are true. The first refers to the Written Torah, given once and never to be repeated. The second applies to the Oral Torah, whose study has never ceased.

It also helps us understand why it is only after the second tablets, not the first, that "when Moshe came down

כג בִּכּוּרֵי קְצִיר חִטִּים וְחַג הָאָסִיף תְּקוּפַת הַשָּׁנָה: שָׁלֹשׁ פְּעָמִים בַּשָּׁנָה
כד יֵרָאֶה כָּל־זְכוּרְךָ אֶת־פְּנֵי הָאָדֹן ׀ יהוה אֱלֹהֵי יִשְׂרָאֵל: כִּי־אוֹרִישׁ
גּוֹיִם מִפָּנֶיךָ וְהִרְחַבְתִּי אֶת־גְּבֻלֶךָ וְלֹא־יַחְמֹד אִישׁ אֶת־אַרְצְךָ בַּעֲלֹתְךָ
כה לֵרָאוֹת אֶת־פְּנֵי יהוה אֱלֹהֶיךָ שָׁלֹשׁ פְּעָמִים בַּשָּׁנָה: לֹא־תִשְׁחַט עַל־
כו חָמֵץ דַּם־זִבְחִי וְלֹא־יָלִין לַבֹּקֶר זֶבַח חַג הַפָּסַח: רֵאשִׁית בִּכּוּרֵי אַדְמָתְךָ
תָּבִיא בֵּית יהוה אֱלֹהֶיךָ לֹא־תְבַשֵּׁל גְּדִי בַּחֲלֵב אִמּוֹ:
כז וַיֹּאמֶר יהוה אֶל־מֹשֶׁה כְּתָב־לְךָ אֶת־הַדְּבָרִים הָאֵלֶּה כִּי עַל־פִּי ׀ כו שביעי
כח הַדְּבָרִים הָאֵלֶּה כָּרַתִּי אִתְּךָ בְּרִית וְאֶת־יִשְׂרָאֵל: וַיְהִי־שָׁם עִם־יהוה
אַרְבָּעִים יוֹם וְאַרְבָּעִים לַיְלָה לֶחֶם לֹא אָכַל וּמַיִם לֹא שָׁתָה וַיִּכְתֹּב
כט עַל־הַלֻּחֹת אֵת דִּבְרֵי הַבְּרִית עֲשֶׂרֶת הַדְּבָרִים: וַיְהִי בְּרֶדֶת מֹשֶׁה מֵהַר

אונקלוס

בִּכּוּרֵי חֲצַד חִטִּין, וְחַגָּא דִּכְנָשָׁא, בְּמִפְּקַהּ דְּשַׁתָּא: כג תְּלָת זִמְנִין בְּשַׁתָּא, יִתַּחֲזוֹן כָּל דְּכוּרָךְ, קֳדָם רִבּוֹן עָלְמָא יי אֱלָהָא דְּיִשְׂרָאֵל: כד אֲרֵי אֲתָרֵיךְ עַמְמִין מִן קֳדָמָךְ, וְאַפְתֵּי יָת תְּחוּמָךְ, וְלָא יַחְמֵיד אֱנָשׁ יָת אַרְעָךְ, בְּמִסְּקָךְ, לְאִתַּחֲזָאָה קֳדָם יי אֱלָהָךְ, תְּלָת זִמְנִין בְּשַׁתָּא: כה לָא תִכּוֹס עַל חֲמִיעַ דַּם פִּסְחִי, וְלָא יְבִיתוּן לְצַפְרָא בַּר מִמַּדְבְּחָא, תַּרְבֵּי נִכְסַת חַגָּא דְּפִסְחָא: כו רֵישׁ, בִּכּוּרֵי אַרְעָךְ, תַּיְתֵי, לְבֵית מַקְדְּשָׁא דַּיי אֱלָהָךְ, לָא תֵיכְלוּן בְּסַר בַּחֲלַב: כז וַאֲמַר יי לְמֹשֶׁה, כְּתוֹב לָךְ יָת פִּתְגָּמַיָּא הָאִלֵּין, אֲרֵי, עַל מֵימַר פִּתְגָּמַיָּא הָאִלֵּין, גְּזָרִית עִמָּךְ, קְיָם וְעִם יִשְׂרָאֵל: כח וַהֲוָה תַמָּן קֳדָם יי, אַרְבְּעִין יְמָמִין וְאַרְבְּעִין לֵילָוָן, לַחְמָא לָא אֲכַל, וּמַיָּא לָא שְׁתִי, וּכְתַב עַל לוּחַיָּא, יָת פִּתְגָּמֵי קְיָמָא, עַסְרָא פִּתְגָּמִין: כט וַהֲוָה, כַּד נְחַת מֹשֶׁה מִטּוּרָא

34:26 לֹא־תְבַשֵּׁל גְּדִי בַּחֲלֵב אִמּוֹ *Do not cook a kid in the milk of its mother* – This is the origin of the prohibition against mixing meat and milk. Rambam infers from its association with the festivals that this was an idolatrous practice associated with pagan festivities (*Guide for the Perplexed* III:48). The pagan imagination often celebrated the blurring of boundaries: man-god, man-beast, androgyny, and other hybrids. The biblical imagination, on the other hand, is predicated on clear boundaries.

34:29 קָרַן עוֹר פָּנָיו *The skin of his face shone with light* – According to tradition, when Moshe was given the first tablets, he was given only *Torah Shebikhtav*, the Written Torah. At the time of the second tablets, he was given *Torah Shebe'al Peh*, the Oral Torah as well. The difference between the Written and Oral Torah is profound. The first is the word of God, with no human contribution. The second is a partnership – the word of God as interpreted by the mind of man. Any attempt to reduce the Oral Torah to the Written – by relying on prophecy or divine communication – mistakes its essential nature as the collaborative partnership between God and man, where revelation meets interpretation. Thus, the difference between the two precisely mirrors that between the first and second tablets. The first were divine, the second the result of Divine-human collaboration. This helps us understand a glorious ambiguity. The Torah says that at Sinai the Israelites heard a "loud voice *velo yasaf*" (Deut. 5:19). Two contradictory interpretations are given

▶

30 shone with light, because he had been speaking with God. When Aharon and
all the Israelites saw the light that shone from the skin of Moshe's face, they
31 were afraid to come close to him. But Moshe called them, and Aharon and all
32 the community leaders came back to him, and Moshe spoke. After that, all the
Israelites approached, and he instructed them in all that the Lord had spoken
33 to him on Mount Sinai. And when Moshe had finished speaking to them, he MAFTIR
34 veiled his face. Whenever Moshe came before the Lord to speak with Him,
he would remove the veil until he came out. When he came out and told the
35 Israelites what he had been commanded, the Israelites would see how the skin
of Moshe's face shone with light, and he would veil his face again until he went
back in to speak with Him.

The haftara for Parashat Ki Tisa is on page 1550.
On Purim Meshulash in Jerusalem read the haftara on page 1644.
On the Shabbat of Parashat Para read the haftara on page 1648.

רש״י

ל| **וַיִּירְאוּ מִגֶּשֶׁת אֵלָיו.** בֹּא וּרְאֵה כַּמָּה גָּדוֹל כֹּחָהּ שֶׁל עֲבֵרָה, שֶׁעַד שֶׁלֹּא פָּשְׁטוּ יְדֵיהֶם בַּעֲבֵרָה מַהוּ אוֹמֵר? "וּמַרְאֵה כְּבוֹד ה' כְּאֵשׁ אֹכֶלֶת בְּרֹאשׁ הָהָר לְעֵינֵי בְּנֵי יִשְׂרָאֵל" (לעיל כד, יז), וְלֹא יְרֵאִים וְלֹא מִזְדַּעְזְעִים; וּמִשֶּׁעָשׂוּ אֶת הָעֵגֶל, אַף מִקַּרְנֵי הוֹדוֹ שֶׁל מֹשֶׁה הָיוּ מַרְתִּיעִים וּמִזְדַּעְזְעִים:

לא| **הַנְּשִׂאִים בָּעֵדָה.** כְּמוֹ נְשִׂיאֵי הָעֵדָה: **וַיְדַבֵּר מֹשֶׁה אֲלֵהֶם.** שְׁלִיחוּתוֹ שֶׁל מָקוֹם. וּלְשׁוֹן הוֶֹה הוּא כָּל הָעִנְיָן הַזֶּה:

לב| **וְאַחֲרֵי כֵן נִגְּשׁוּ.** אַחַר שֶׁלִּמֵּד לַזְּקֵנִים חוֹזֵר וּמְלַמֵּד הַפָּרָשָׁה אוֹ הַהֲלָכָה לְיִשְׂרָאֵל. תָּנוּ רַבָּנָן: כֵּיצַד סֵדֶר הַמִּשְׁנָה? מֹשֶׁה הָיָה לָמֵד מִפִּי הַגְּבוּרָה. נִכְנַס אַהֲרֹן, שָׁנָה לוֹ מֹשֶׁה פִּרְקוֹ, נִסְתַּלֵּק אַהֲרֹן וְיָשַׁב לוֹ לִשְׂמֹאל מֹשֶׁה. נִכְנְסוּ בָנָיו, שָׁנָה לָהֶם מֹשֶׁה פִּרְקָם, נִסְתַּלְּקוּ הֵם, יָשַׁב אֶלְעָזָר לִימִין מֹשֶׁה וְאִיתָמָר לִשְׂמֹאל אַהֲרֹן. נִכְנְסוּ זְקֵנִים, שָׁנָה לָהֶם מֹשֶׁה פִּרְקָם, נִסְתַּלְּקוּ זְקֵנִים, יָשְׁבוּ לַצְּדָדִין. נִכְנְסוּ כָּל הָעָם, שָׁנָה לָהֶם מֹשֶׁה פִּרְקָם. נִמְצָא בְּיַד כָּל הָעָם אֶחָד, בְּיַד הַזְּקֵנִים שְׁנַיִם, בְּיַד בְּנֵי אַהֲרֹן שְׁלֹשָׁה, בְּיַד אַהֲרֹן אַרְבָּעָה וְכוּ', כִּדְאִיתָא בְּעֵרוּבִין (דף נד ע״ב):

לג-לה| **וַיִּתֵּן עַל פָּנָיו מַסְוֶה.** כְּתַרְגּוּמוֹ: "בֵּית אַפֵּי", לְשׁוֹן אֲרַמִּי הוּא בַּתַּלְמוּד (כתובות סב ע״ב): "סְוִי לִבַּהּ", וְעוֹד בִּכְתֻבּוֹת (דף ס ע״א): "הֲוָה קָא מַסְוֵי לְאַפַּהּ", לְשׁוֹן הַבָּטָה, הָיָה מִסְתַּכֵּל בָּהּ. אַף כָּאן "מַסְוֶה", בֶּגֶד הַנִּתָּן כְּנֶגֶד הַפַּרְצוּף וּבֵית הָעֵינַיִם. וְלִכְבוֹד קַרְנֵי הַהוֹד שֶׁלֹּא יָזוּנוּ הַכֹּל מֵהֶם הָיָה נוֹתֵן הַמַּסְוֶה כְּנֶגְדָּן, וְנוֹטְלוֹ בְּשָׁעָה שֶׁהָיָה מְדַבֵּר עִם יִשְׂרָאֵל, וּבְשָׁעָה שֶׁהַמָּקוֹם נִדְבַּר עִמּוֹ "עַד צֵאתוֹ", וּבְצֵאתוֹ – "וְיָצָא" בְּלֹא מַסְוֶה "וְדִבֶּר אֶל בְּנֵי יִשְׂרָאֵל" וְרָאוּ קַרְנֵי הַהוֹד בְּפָנָיו. וּכְשֶׁהוּא מִסְתַּלֵּק מֵהֶם, "וְהֵשִׁיב... אֶת הַמַּסְוֶה עַל פָּנָיו עַד בֹּאוֹ לְדַבֵּר אִתּוֹ", וּכְשֶׁבָּא לְדַבֵּר אִתּוֹ – נוֹטְלוֹ מֵעַל פָּנָיו:

סִינַ֔י וּשְׁנֵ֨י לֻחֹ֤ת הָֽעֵדֻת֙ בְּיַד־מֹשֶׁ֔ה בְּרִדְתּ֖וֹ מִן־הָהָ֑ר וּמֹשֶׁ֣ה לֹֽא־יָדַ֗ע
ל כִּ֥י קָרַ֛ן ע֥וֹר פָּנָ֖יו בְּדַבְּר֥וֹ אִתּֽוֹ׃ וַיַּ֨רְא אַהֲרֹ֜ן וְכָל־בְּנֵ֤י יִשְׂרָאֵל֙ אֶת־מֹשֶׁ֔ה
לא וְהִנֵּ֥ה קָרַ֖ן ע֣וֹר פָּנָ֑יו וַיִּֽירְא֖וּ מִגֶּ֥שֶׁת אֵלָֽיו׃ וַיִּקְרָ֤א אֲלֵהֶם֙ מֹשֶׁ֔ה וַיָּשֻׁ֣בוּ
לב אֵלָ֔יו אַהֲרֹ֥ן וְכָל־הַנְּשִׂאִ֖ים בָּעֵדָ֑ה וַיְדַבֵּ֥ר מֹשֶׁ֖ה אֲלֵהֶֽם׃ וְאַחֲרֵי־כֵ֥ן נִגְּשׁ֖וּ
לג כָּל־בְּנֵ֣י יִשְׂרָאֵ֑ל וַיְצַוֵּ֗ם אֵת֩ כָּל־אֲשֶׁ֨ר דִּבֶּ֧ר יְהוָ֛ה אִתּ֖וֹ בְּהַ֥ר סִינָֽי׃ וַיְכַ֣ל מפטיר
לד מֹשֶׁ֔ה מִדַּבֵּ֖ר אִתָּ֑ם וַיִּתֵּ֥ן עַל־פָּנָ֖יו מַסְוֶֽה׃ וּבְבֹ֨א מֹשֶׁ֜ה לִפְנֵ֤י יְהוָה֙ לְדַבֵּ֣ר
אִתּ֔וֹ יָסִ֥יר אֶת־הַמַּסְוֶ֖ה עַד־צֵאת֑וֹ וְיָצָ֗א וְדִבֶּר֙ אֶל־בְּנֵ֣י יִשְׂרָאֵ֔ל אֵ֖ת
לה אֲשֶׁ֥ר יְצֻוֶּֽה׃ וְרָא֤וּ בְנֵֽי־יִשְׂרָאֵל֙ אֶת־פְּנֵ֣י מֹשֶׁ֔ה כִּ֣י קָרַ֔ן ע֖וֹר פְּנֵ֣י מֹשֶׁ֑ה
וְהֵשִׁ֨יב מֹשֶׁ֤ה אֶת־הַמַּסְוֶה֙ עַל־פָּנָ֔יו עַד־בֹּא֖וֹ לְדַבֵּ֥ר אִתּֽוֹ׃

The הפטרה *for* פרשת כי תשא *is on page 1551.*
On פורים משולש *in Jerusalem read the* הפטרה *on page 1645.*
On the שבת *of* פרשת פרה *read the* הפטרה *on page 1649.*

אונקלוס

דְּסִינַי, וּתְרֵין לוּחֵי סָהֲדוּתָא בִּידָא דְמֹשֶׁה, בְּמֵיחֲתֵיהּ מִן טוּרָא, וּמֹשֶׁה לָא יְדַע, אֲרֵי סְגִי, זִיו יְקָרָא דְּאַפּוֹהִי בְּמַלָּלוּתֵיהּ עִמֵּיהּ: ל וַחֲזָא אַהֲרֹן, וְכָל בְּנֵי יִשְׂרָאֵל יָת מֹשֶׁה, וְהָא סְגִי זִיו יְקָרָא דְּאַפּוֹהִי, וּדְחִילוּ מִלְּאִתְקָרָבָא לְוָתֵיהּ: לא וּקְרָא לְהוֹן מֹשֶׁה, וְתָבוּ לְוָתֵיהּ, אַהֲרֹן וְכָל רַבְרְבַיָּא בִּכְנִשְׁתָּא, וּמַלֵּיל מֹשֶׁה עִמְּהוֹן: לב וּבָתַר כֵּן אִתְקָרַבוּ כָּל בְּנֵי יִשְׂרָאֵל, וּפַקֵּידִנּוּן, יָת כָּל דְּמַלֵּיל יְיָ, עִמֵּיהּ בְּטוּרָא דְּסִינָי: לג וְשֵׁיצִי מֹשֶׁה, מִלְּמַלָּלָא עִמְּהוֹן, וִיהַב עַל אַפּוֹהִי בֵּית אַפֵּי: לד וְכַד עָלֵיל מֹשֶׁה, קֳדָם יְיָ לְמַלָּלָא עִמֵּיהּ, מַעְדֵּי יָת בֵּית אַפֵּי עַד מִפְּקֵיהּ, וְנָפֵיק, וּמְמַלֵּיל עִם בְּנֵי יִשְׂרָאֵל, יָת דְּמִתְפַּקַּד: לה וְחָזַן בְּנֵי יִשְׂרָאֵל יָת אַפֵּי מֹשֶׁה, אֲרֵי סְגִי, זִיו יְקָרָא דְּאַפֵּי מֹשֶׁה, וּמְתִיב מֹשֶׁה יָת בֵּית אַפֵּי עַל אַפּוֹהִי, עַד דְּעָלֵיל לְמַלָּלָא עִמֵּיהּ:

from Mount Sinai with the two tablets of testimony in his hand, he was unaware that the skin of his face shone with light, because he had been speaking with God" (Ex. 34:29). Receiving the first tablets, Moshe is passive. Therefore, nothing in him changes. For the second, he is active. He has a share in the making. He carves the stone on which the words are to be engraved. That is why he becomes a different person. His face shines.

Parashat Vayak'hel

35 1 Moshe assembled all the community of Israel and said to them, "These are the
2 things the Lord has commanded you to do. For six days, let work be done, but
the seventh must be sacred to you. It is a Sabbath of complete rest dedicated to
3 the Lord. Whoever does work on it shall be put to death. Do not light a fire in
any of your dwellings on the Sabbath day."

רש״י

לד א **וַיַּקְהֵל מֹשֶׁה.** לְמָחֳרַת יוֹם הַכִּפּוּרִים כְּשֶׁיָּרַד מִן הָהָר. וְהוּא לְשׁוֹן הִפְעִיל, שֶׁאֵינוֹ אוֹסֵף אֲנָשִׁים בַּיָּדַיִם, אֶלָּא הֵן נֶאֱסָפִים עַל פִּי דִּבּוּרוֹ, וְתַרְגּוּמוֹ: "וְאַכְנֵישׁ":

ב **שֵׁשֶׁת יָמִים.** הִקְדִּים לָהֶם אַזְהָרַת שַׁבָּת לְצִוּוּי מְלֶאכֶת הַמִּשְׁכָּן, לוֹמַר שֶׁאֵינוֹ דּוֹחֶה אֶת הַשַּׁבָּת:

ג **לֹא תְבַעֲרוּ אֵשׁ.** יֵשׁ מֵרַבּוֹתֵינוּ אוֹמְרִים הַבְעָרָה לְלָאו יָצָאת, וְיֵשׁ אוֹמְרִים לְחַלֵּק יָצָאת:

time]. As R. Yoḥanan said in the name of R. Shimon b. Yoḥai: …"But as for me, may my prayer come to You, Lord, in a moment of favor" (Ps. 69:14). When is a time of favor? The time when the congregation is praying. (Berakhot 7b–8a)

In other words, even if one is unable to go to the synagogue, one should try to pray at the same time as the community. Rabbi Joseph B. Soloveitchik explains that if one does so, one's prayer is joined to that of the community.

Rabbi Shneur Zalman of Liadi once said to his disciples, "One must live with the times." The disciples were puzzled; surely Judaism is timeless. Eventually the Rebbe's brother, Rabbi Yehuda Leib, explained, "He meant one must live with the weekly *parasha*." Somehow or other, that must be the time zone in which Jews live.

We live in the intersection between the timely and the timeless, between what is happening now and what God said to us over three thousand years ago. By praying at the same time as the rest of the community, we become "like one person with one heart" (Rashi on Ex. 19:2). There is such a thing as a community in time. This is why the narrative of the Tabernacle is inseparable from the law of the Sabbath.

35:3 **בְּיוֹם הַשַּׁבָּת** *On the Sabbath day* – The Talmud raises the following question: What happens if you are far away from human habitation and you forget what day it is? How do you observe the Sabbath? Two answers are offered:

> R. Huna said: "If one is traveling on a road or in the wilderness and does not know when the Sabbath falls, he must count six days [from the day he realizes he has forgotten] and observe one." R. Ḥiyya b. Rav said: "He must observe one, and then count six [week]days." On what do they differ? One master holds that it is like the world's creation. The other holds that it is like [the case of] Adam. (Shabbat 69b)

From God's point of view, the Sabbath was the seventh day. From the point of view of the first human beings – created on the sixth day – the Sabbath was the first. We now have an insight into why, in God's instruction to Moshe in Parashat Ki Tisa, the command of the Sabbath appears after the details of the construction of the Tabernacle, while here, in Moshe's instruction to the people, it appears before. For God, the Sabbath was the last day of creation; for human beings it was the first.

In divine creation, there is no gap between intention and execution. God spoke, and the world came into existence. With human beings, it is otherwise. Creativity is fraught with risk. The law of unintended consequences tells us that revolutions rarely turn out as planned. Policies designed to

פרשת ויקהל

לה א וַיַּקְהֵ֣ל מֹשֶׁ֗ה אֶֽת־כָּל־עֲדַ֛ת בְּנֵ֥י יִשְׂרָאֵ֖ל וַיֹּ֣אמֶר אֲלֵהֶ֑ם אֵ֚לֶּה הַדְּבָרִ֔ים
ב אֲשֶׁר־צִוָּ֥ה יְהֹוָ֖ה לַעֲשֹׂ֥ת אֹתָֽם׃ שֵׁ֣שֶׁת יָמִים֮ תֵּעָשֶׂ֣ה מְלָאכָה֒ וּבַיּ֣וֹם
הַשְּׁבִיעִ֗י יִהְיֶ֨ה לָכֶ֥ם קֹ֛דֶשׁ שַׁבַּ֥ת שַׁבָּת֖וֹן לַיהֹוָ֑ה כָּל־הָעֹשֶׂ֥ה ב֛וֹ מְלָאכָ֖ה
ג יוּמָֽת׃ לֹא־תְבַעֲר֣וּ אֵ֔שׁ בְּכֹ֖ל מֹשְׁבֹתֵיכֶ֑ם בְּי֖וֹם הַשַּׁבָּֽת׃

אונקלוס

לה א וְאַכְנֵישׁ מֹשֶׁה, יָת כָּל כְּנִשְׁתָּא, דִּבְנֵי יִשְׂרָאֵל וַאֲמַר לְהוֹן,
אִלֵּין פִּתְגָּמַיָּא, דְּפַקֵּיד יי לְמֶעֱבַד יָתְהוֹן: ב שִׁתָּא יוֹמִין תִּתְעֲבֵיד
עֲבִידְתָּא, וּבְיוֹמָא שְׁבִיעָאָה, יְהֵי לְכוֹן קֻדְשָׁא, שַׁבָּא שַׁבְּתָא קֳדָם
יי, כָּל דְּיַעֲבֵיד בֵּיהּ, עֲבִידְתָּא יִתְקְטִיל: ג לָא תְבַעֲרוּן אִישָׁתָא, בְּכָל
מוֹתְבָנֵיכוֹן, בְּיוֹמָא דְשַׁבְּתָא:

VAYAK'HEL

Immediately after his return from the mountaintop, having secured forgiveness for the people for the sin of the golden calf, Moshe assembles them and commands them first, about the Sabbath and then about the making of the Tabernacle. The *parasha* repeats much of what was said earlier in Parashat Teruma, with this difference: there, we read the instructions; here, the Torah reports on their execution. The people give willingly, and Betzalel and Oholiav, the craftsmen, fashion the various structures. Our *parasha* raises questions about why the long account of the Tabernacle appears in Exodus, a book concerned with nation-building, the Torah's understanding of community, and the place of aesthetics in Judaism.

THE SABBATH AND THE SANCTUARY

Why here does Moshe repeat the commandment of keeping the Sabbath? The conventional and authoritative explanation is that this passage shows us that the Sabbath takes priority over the building of the Tabernacle. But the passage also has another meaning. God is saying, "I am going to give the Jewish people two sanctuaries, not one. The first is the Tabernacle, a sanctuary in space, in place. The second is the Sabbath, a sanctuary in time."

Why do we need both? Because we have a principle in Judaism: "Before God brings a sickness to the world, He brings the cure" (Megilla 13b). God knew that the day would come when Jews would suffer exile and dispersion. They would no longer have a Temple in Jerusalem; they would no longer have a land; they would no longer have a home. "Even so," says God, "however dispersed you are, you will still have a sanctuary. It will exist not in space, but in time. That sanctuary is called the Sabbath. It will happen not because you are together physically in one place, but because spiritually you will be together at the same time."

And so it happened. Jews lost all the attributes of a people. They weren't living in the same place, under the same conditions, or within the same culture. What forged them as one people was that they said the same prayers, at the same time, all facing the same spot, Jerusalem. They observed the same festivals, honored the same days. They were a community in time, not in space.

This idea has halachic implications:

> R. Yitzḥak said to R. Naḥman: Why did the master not come to the synagogue to pray? R. Naḥman said to him: I was [weak and] unable to come.… R. Yitzḥak said: The master should tell the congregation to send a messenger when the congregation is praying to come and inform the master [so that you may pray at the same

4 Then Moshe said to all the community of Israel, "This is what the Lord has
5 commanded. Bring of what is yours an offering to the Lord. Let everyone
whose heart moves him bring an offering to the Lord: gold, silver, and bronze;
6 7 sky-blue, purple, and scarlet wool; linen and goats' hair; rams' hides dyed red
8 and fine leather; acacia wood; oil for the lamp; spices for the anointing oil and
9 the fragrant incense; and rock crystal together with other precious stones for
10 the ephod and breast piece. And let all among you who are skilled come and
11 make the things that the Lord has commanded: the Tabernacle, its tent and
12 covering, its hooks and frames, its bars, posts, and sockets; the Ark and its staves,
13 the cover and the curtain for the screen; the table, its staves and all its utensils,
14 and the showbread; the candelabrum for light, together with its utensils,
15 lamps, and the oil for lighting; the incense altar with its staves, the anointing
oil and the fragrant incense, and the entrance screen for the entrance of the
16 Tabernacle; the sacrificial altar, its bronze grate, its staves and all its utensils,
17 the laver and its base; the hangings of the courtyard, its posts and its sockets,

רש״י

ד **זֶה הַדָּבָר אֲשֶׁר צִוָּה ה׳.** לִי ״לֵאמֹר״ לָכֶם:

ה **נְדִיב לִבּוֹ.** עַל שֵׁם שֶׁלִּבּוֹ נְדָבוֹ קָרוּי ׳נְדִיב לֵב׳. כְּבָר פֵּרַשְׁתִּי נִדְבַת הַמִּשְׁכָּן וּמְלַאכְתּוֹ בִּמְקוֹם צַוָּאָתָם:

יא **אֶת הַמִּשְׁכָּן.** יְרִיעוֹת הַתַּחְתּוֹנוֹת הַנִּרְאוֹת בְּתוֹכוֹ קָרוּי ׳מִשְׁכָּן׳: **אֶת אָהֳלוֹ.** הוּא אֹהֶל יְרִיעוֹת עִזִּים הֶעָשׂוּי לְגַג: **וְאֶת מִכְסֵהוּ.** מִכְסֵה עוֹרוֹת אֵילִים וְהַתְּחָשִׁים:

יב **וְאֵת פָּרֹכֶת הַמָּסָךְ.** פָּרֹכֶת הַמְּחִצָּה. כָּל דָּבָר הַמֵּגֵן בֵּין מִלְמַעְלָה בֵּין מִכְּנֶגֶד קָרוּי ׳מָסָךְ׳ וּ׳סְכָךְ׳, וְכֵן: ״שַׂכְתָּ בַעֲדוֹ״ (איוב א, י), ״הִנְנִי שָׂךְ אֶת דַּרְכֵּךְ״ (הושע ב, ח):

יג **לֶחֶם הַפָּנִים.** כְּבָר פֵּרַשְׁתִּי (לעיל כה, כט) עַל שֵׁם שֶׁהָיוּ לוֹ פָּנִים לְכָאן וּלְכָאן, שֶׁהָיָה עָשׂוּי כְּמִין תֵּבָה פְרוּצָה:

יד **וְאֶת כֵּלֶיהָ.** מֶלְקָחַיִם וּמַחְתּוֹת: **נֵרֹתֶיהָ.** לוּצִינ״שׂ בְּלַעַז, בָּזִיכִים שֶׁהַשֶּׁמֶן וְהַפְּתִילוֹת נְתוּנִין בָּהֶן: **וְאֵת שֶׁמֶן הַמָּאוֹר.** אַף הוּא צָרִיךְ חַכְמֵי לֵב, שֶׁהוּא מְשֻׁנֶּה מִשְּׁאָר שְׁמָנִים, כְּמוֹ שֶׁמְּפֹרָשׁ בִּמְנָחוֹת (דף פו ע״א): מְגַרְגְּרוֹ בְּרֹאשׁ הַזַּיִת, וְהוּא כָּתִית וָזָךְ:

טו **מָסַךְ הַפֶּתַח.** וִילוֹן שֶׁלִּפְנֵי הַמִּזְרָח, שֶׁלֹּא הָיוּ שָׁם קְרָשִׁים וְלֹא יְרִיעוֹת:

יז **אֶת עַמֻּדָיו וְאֶת אֲדָנֶיהָ.** הֲרֵי ׳חָצֵר׳ קָרוּי כָּאן לָשׁוֹן זָכָר וּלְשׁוֹן נְקֵבָה, וְכֵן דְּבָרִים הַרְבֵּה: **וְאֵת מָסַךְ שַׁעַר הֶחָצֵר.** וִילוֹן פָּרוּשׂ לְצַד הַמִּזְרָח, עֶשְׂרִים אַמָּה אֶמְצָעִיּוֹת שֶׁל רֹחַב הֶחָצֵר, שֶׁהָיָה חֲמִשִּׁים רֹחַב, וּסְתוּמִין הַיְמֶנּוּ לְצַד צָפוֹן חֲמֵשׁ עֶשְׂרֵה אַמָּה וְכֵן לַדָּרוֹם, שֶׁנֶּאֱמַר: ״וַחֲמֵשׁ עֶשְׂרֵה אַמָּה קְלָעִים לַכָּתֵף״ (לעיל כז, יד):

rest. It is an anticipation of "the end of history," the Messianic age. On it, we recover the lost harmonies of the Garden of Eden. We do not strive to do; we are content to be. We are not allowed to exercise power or dominance over other human beings, nor even domestic animals. Rich and poor inhabit the Sabbath alike, with equal dignity and freedom. The Sabbath is a dress rehearsal for an ideal society that has not yet come to pass.

God wanted us to know what we were aiming for, so that we would not lose our way in the wilderness of time. That is why, when it came to the human execution of the building, the Sabbath came first, even though the Messianic age, the "Sabbath of history," will come last. God is "telling of the end from the beginning" (Is. 46:10) – the fulfilled rest that follows creative labor, the peace that will one day take the place of strife – so that, before beginning the journey, we catch a glimpse of the destination.

ד וַיֹּאמֶר מֹשֶׁה אֶל־כָּל־עֲדַת בְּנֵי־יִשְׂרָאֵל לֵאמֹר זֶה הַדָּבָר אֲשֶׁר־צִוָּה
ה יְהוָה לֵאמֹר: קְחוּ מֵאִתְּכֶם תְּרוּמָה לַיהוָה כֹּל נְדִיב לִבּוֹ יְבִיאֶהָ אֵת
ו תְּרוּמַת יְהוָה זָהָב וָכֶסֶף וּנְחֹשֶׁת: וּתְכֵלֶת וְאַרְגָּמָן וְתוֹלַעַת שָׁנִי וְשֵׁשׁ
ז ח וְעִזִּים: וְעֹרֹת אֵילִם מְאָדָּמִים וְעֹרֹת תְּחָשִׁים וַעֲצֵי שִׁטִּים: וְשֶׁמֶן
ט לַמָּאוֹר וּבְשָׂמִים לְשֶׁמֶן הַמִּשְׁחָה וְלִקְטֹרֶת הַסַּמִּים: וְאַבְנֵי־שֹׁהַם וְאַבְנֵי
י מִלֻּאִים לָאֵפוֹד וְלַחֹשֶׁן: וְכָל־חֲכַם־לֵב בָּכֶם יָבֹאוּ וְיַעֲשׂוּ אֵת כָּל־אֲשֶׁר
יא צִוָּה יְהוָה: אֶת־הַמִּשְׁכָּן אֶת־אָהֳלוֹ וְאֶת־מִכְסֵהוּ אֶת־קְרָסָיו וְאֶת־
יב קְרָשָׁיו אֶת־בְּרִיחָו אֶת־עַמֻּדָיו וְאֶת־אֲדָנָיו: אֶת־הָאָרֹן וְאֶת־בַּדָּיו אֶת־
יג הַכַּפֹּרֶת וְאֵת פָּרֹכֶת הַמָּסָךְ: אֶת־הַשֻּׁלְחָן וְאֶת־בַּדָּיו וְאֶת־כָּל־כֵּלָיו
יד וְאֵת לֶחֶם הַפָּנִים: וְאֶת־מְנֹרַת הַמָּאוֹר וְאֶת־כֵּלֶיהָ וְאֶת־נֵרֹתֶיהָ וְאֵת
טו שֶׁמֶן הַמָּאוֹר: וְאֶת־מִזְבַּח הַקְּטֹרֶת וְאֶת־בַּדָּיו וְאֵת שֶׁמֶן הַמִּשְׁחָה וְאֵת
טז קְטֹרֶת הַסַּמִּים וְאֶת־מָסַךְ הַפֶּתַח לְפֶתַח הַמִּשְׁכָּן: אֵת | מִזְבַּח הָעֹלָה
וְאֶת־מִכְבַּר הַנְּחֹשֶׁת אֲשֶׁר־לוֹ אֶת־בַּדָּיו וְאֶת־כָּל־כֵּלָיו אֶת־הַכִּיֹּר וְאֶת־
יז כַּנּוֹ: אֵת קַלְעֵי הֶחָצֵר אֶת־עַמֻּדָיו וְאֶת־אֲדָנֶיהָ וְאֵת מָסַךְ שַׁעַר הֶחָצֵר:

אונקלוס

ד וַאֲמַר מֹשֶׁה, לְכָל כְּנִשְׁתָּא דִּבְנֵי יִשְׂרָאֵל לְמֵימַר, דֵּין פִּתְגָּמָא, דְּפַקֵּיד יי לְמֵימַר: ה סַבוּ מִנְּכוֹן אַפְרָשׁוּתָא קֳדָם יי, כָּל דְּיִתְרְעֵי לִבֵּיהּ, יַיְתֵי, יָת אַפְרָשׁוּתָא קֳדָם יי, דַּהֲבָא וְכַסְפָּא וּנְחָשָׁא: ו וְתַכְלָא וְאַרְגְּוָנָא, וּצְבַע זְהוֹרִי וּבוּץ וּמַעֲזֵי: ז וּמַשְׁכֵי דְדִכְרֵי מְסַמְּקֵי, וּמַשְׁכֵי סָסְגוֹנָא וְאָעֵי שִׁטִּין: ח וּמִשְׁחָא לְאַנְהָרוּתָא, וּבֻסְמַיָּא לִמְשַׁח רְבוּתָא, וְלִקְטֹרֶת בֻּסְמַיָּא: ט וְאַבְנֵי בֵרְלָא, וְאַבְנֵי אַשְׁלָמוּתָא, לְשַׁקָּעָא בְּאֵיפוֹדָא וּבְחֻשְׁנָא: י וְכָל חַכִּימֵי לִבָּא דִּבְכוֹן, יֵיתוֹן וְיַעְבְּדוּן, יָת כָּל דְּפַקֵּיד יי: יא יָת מַשְׁכְּנָא, יָת פְּרָסֵיהּ וְיָת חוּפָאֵיהּ, פֻּרְפּוֹהִי דַּפּוֹהִי, עַבְרוֹהִי, עַמּוּדוֹהִי וְסָמְכוֹהִי: יב יָת אֲרוֹנָא וְיָת אֲרִיחוֹהִי יָת כַּפֻּרְתָּא, וְיָת פָּרֻכְתָּא דִּפְרָסָא: יג יָת פָּתוֹרָא וְיָת אֲרִיחוֹהִי וְיָת כָּל מָנוֹהִי, וְיָת לְחֵים אַפַּיָּא: יד וְיָת מְנָרְתָא דְּאַנְהוֹרֵי, וְיָת מָנַהָא וְיָת בּוֹצִינַהָא, וְיָת מִשְׁחָא דְּאַנְהָרוּתָא: טו וְיָת מַדְבְּחָא דִּקְטֹרֶת בֻּסְמַיָּא וְיָת אֲרִיחוֹהִי, וְיָת מִשְׁחָא דִּרְבוּתָא, וְיָת קְטֹרֶת בֻּסְמַיָּא, וְיָת פְּרָסָא דְּתַרְעָא לִתְרַע מַשְׁכְּנָא: טז יָת מַדְבְּחָא דַּעֲלָתָא, וְיָת סְרָדָא דִּנְחָשָׁא דִּילֵיהּ, יָת אֲרִיחוֹהִי וְיָת כָּל מָנוֹהִי, יָת כִּיּוֹרָא וְיָת בְּסִיסֵיהּ: יז יָת סְרָדֵי דָּרְתָא, יָת עַמּוּדוֹהִי וְיָת סָמְכַהָא, וְיָת, פְּרָסָא דִּתְרַע דָּרְתָא:

happen as they will. This kind of resignation, however, is wholly out of keeping with the Judaic view of history. The other solution, then, is to reveal the end at the beginning. That is the meaning of the Sabbath. It is not simply a day of

help the poor may have the opposite effect. Even a novelist may not know how the story will turn out until he has written it.

One possible response to this is simply to let things

18 and the screen for the gate of the court; the tent pegs of the Tabernacle and of
19 the courtyard and their ropes; the vestments for ministering in the Sanctuary,
and the sacred vestments for Aharon the priest and for his sons for their priestly
20 21 service." So all the community of Israel left Moshe's presence. And they came, SHENI
everyone whose heart inspired him and whose spirit moved him, and brought
an offering for the LORD, to be used for the Tent of Meeting and all its service,
22 and for the sacred vestments. All whose hearts moved them – the men with
the women – brought brooches, earrings, signet rings and pendants, all kinds
of gold ornaments, together with all those who gave gold as a wave offering to
23 the LORD. Everyone who had sky-blue, purple, or scarlet wool, linen or goats'
24 hair, rams' hides dyed red or fine leather brought them. Whoever could make
an offering of silver or bronze brought it as an offering to the LORD, as did
25 everyone who had acacia wood that could be used for the work. Every skilled
woman spun with her own hands, and brought what she had spun: sky-blue,
26 purple, and scarlet wool and fine linen. All the women whose hearts inspired
27 them used their skill to spin the goats' hair. The leaders brought rock crystal
stones and other precious stones for setting in the ephod and the breast piece,
28 together with spices and oil for the light, the anointing oil and the fragrant
29 incense. So the Israelites – all the men and women whose hearts moved them to

רש״י

יח| **יִתְדֹת.** לִתְקֹעַ וְלִקְשֹׁר בָּהֶם סוֹפֵי הַיְרִיעוֹת בָּאָרֶץ שֶׁלֹּא יָנוּעוּ בָּרוּחַ: **מֵיתְרֵיהֶם.** חֲבָלִים לִקְשֹׁר:

יט| **בִּגְדֵי הַשְּׂרָד.** לְכַסּוֹת הָאָרוֹן וְהַשֻּׁלְחָן וְהַמְּנוֹרָה וְהַמִּזְבְּחוֹת בִּשְׁעַת סִלּוּק הַמַּסָּעוֹת:

כב| **עַל הַנָּשִׁים.** עִם הַנָּשִׁים וּסְמוּכִין אֲלֵיהֶם: **חָח.** הוּא תַּכְשִׁיט שֶׁל זָהָב עָגֹל נָתוּן עַל הַזְּרוֹעַ וְהוּא הַצָּמִיד: **וְכוּמָז.** כְּלִי זָהָב הוּא נָתוּן כְּנֶגֶד אוֹתוֹ מָקוֹם לָאִשָּׁה. וְרַבּוֹתֵינוּ פֵּרְשׁוּ שֵׁם 'כּוּמָז': כָּאן מְקוֹם זִמָּה:

כג| **וְכָל אִישׁ אֲשֶׁר נִמְצָא אִתּוֹ.** תְּכֵלֶת אוֹ אַרְגָּמָן אוֹ תּוֹלַעַת שָׁנִי אוֹ עוֹרוֹת אֵילִים אוֹ תְּחָשִׁים, כֻּלָּם "הֵבִיאוּ":

כו| **טָווּ אֶת הָעִזִּים.** הִיא הָיְתָה אֻמָּנוּת יְתֵרָה, שֶׁמֵּעַל גַּבֵּי הָעִזִּים טָווִין אוֹתָם:

כז| **וְהַנְּשִׂאִם הֵבִיאוּ.** אָמַר רַבִּי נָתָן: מָה רָאוּ נְשִׂיאִים לְהִתְנַדֵּב בַּחֲנֻכַּת הַמִּזְבֵּחַ בַּתְּחִלָּה, וּבִמְלֶאכֶת הַמִּשְׁכָּן לֹא הִתְנַדְּבוּ בַּתְּחִלָּה? אֶלָּא כָּךְ אָמְרוּ נְשִׂיאִים: יִתְנַדְּבוּ צִבּוּר מַה שֶּׁמִּתְנַדְּבִין, וּמַה שֶּׁמְּחַסְּרִין – אָנוּ מַשְׁלִימִין אוֹתוֹ. כֵּיוָן שֶׁהִשְׁלִימוּ צִבּוּר אֶת הַכֹּל, שֶׁנֶּאֱמַר: "וְהַמְּלָאכָה הָיְתָה דַיָּם" (להלן לו, ז), אָמְרוּ נְשִׂיאִים: מָה עָלֵינוּ לַעֲשׂוֹת? "הֵבִיאוּ אֵת אַבְנֵי הַשֹּׁהַם" וְגוֹ׳, לְכָךְ הִתְנַדְּבוּ בַּחֲנֻכַּת הַמִּזְבֵּחַ תְּחִלָּה. וּלְפִי שֶׁנִּתְעַצְּלוּ מִתְּחִלָּה נֶחְסְרָה אוֹת מִשְּׁמָם, "וְהַנְּשִׂאִם" כְּתִיב:

what is yours an offering to the LORD. Let everyone whose heart moves him bring an offering to the LORD: gold, silver and bronze.... And let all among you who are skilled come and make the things that the LORD has commanded..." (Ex. 35:5, 10). The beauty of a *kehilla* – a community – is that when it is driven by a constructive purpose, it gathers together the distinct and separate contributions of many individuals. Moshe turned the *kehilla* with its diversity into a community with a singleness of purpose, while preserving the range of the gifts they each brought to God.

Society is what we build together. A nation is made by contributions, not claims; active citizenship, not rights; what we give, not what we demand. Every member of the group must be able to make a unique contribution and then

יח יט אֶת־יִתְדֹת הַמִּשְׁכָּן וְאֶת־יִתְדֹת הֶחָצֵר וְאֶת־מֵיתְרֵיהֶם: אֶת־בִּגְדֵי
הַשְּׂרָד לְשָׁרֵת בַּקֹּדֶשׁ אֶת־בִּגְדֵי הַקֹּדֶשׁ לְאַהֲרֹן הַכֹּהֵן וְאֶת־בִּגְדֵי בָנָיו
כ כא לְכַהֵן: וַיֵּצְאוּ כָּל־עֲדַת בְּנֵי־יִשְׂרָאֵל מִלִּפְנֵי מֹשֶׁה: וַיָּבֹאוּ כָּל־אִישׁ שני
אֲשֶׁר־נְשָׂאוֹ לִבּוֹ וְכֹל אֲשֶׁר נָדְבָה רוּחוֹ אֹתוֹ הֵבִיאוּ אֶת־תְּרוּמַת יהוה
כב לִמְלֶאכֶת אֹהֶל מוֹעֵד וּלְכָל־עֲבֹדָתוֹ וּלְבִגְדֵי הַקֹּדֶשׁ: וַיָּבֹאוּ הָאֲנָשִׁים
עַל־הַנָּשִׁים כֹּל ׀ נְדִיב לֵב הֵבִיאוּ חָח וָנֶזֶם וְטַבַּעַת וְכוּמָז כָּל־כְּלִי זָהָב
כג וְכָל־אִישׁ אֲשֶׁר הֵנִיף תְּנוּפַת זָהָב לַיהוה: וְכָל־אִישׁ אֲשֶׁר־נִמְצָא אִתּוֹ
תְּכֵלֶת וְאַרְגָּמָן וְתוֹלַעַת שָׁנִי וְשֵׁשׁ וְעִזִּים וְעֹרֹת אֵילִם מְאָדָּמִים וְעֹרֹת
כד תְּחָשִׁים הֵבִיאוּ: כָּל־מֵרִים תְּרוּמַת כֶּסֶף וּנְחֹשֶׁת הֵבִיאוּ אֵת תְּרוּמַת
יהוה וְכֹל אֲשֶׁר נִמְצָא אִתּוֹ עֲצֵי שִׁטִּים לְכָל־מְלֶאכֶת הָעֲבֹדָה הֵבִיאוּ:
כה וְכָל־אִשָּׁה חַכְמַת־לֵב בְּיָדֶיהָ טָווּ וַיָּבִיאוּ מַטְוֶה אֶת־הַתְּכֵלֶת וְאֶת־
כו הָאַרְגָּמָן אֶת־תּוֹלַעַת הַשָּׁנִי וְאֶת־הַשֵּׁשׁ: וְכָל־הַנָּשִׁים אֲשֶׁר נָשָׂא לִבָּן
כז אֹתָנָה בְּחָכְמָה טָווּ אֶת־הָעִזִּים: וְהַנְּשִׂאִם הֵבִיאוּ אֵת אַבְנֵי הַשֹּׁהַם
כח וְאֵת אַבְנֵי הַמִּלֻּאִים לָאֵפוֹד וְלַחֹשֶׁן: וְאֶת־הַבֹּשֶׂם וְאֶת־הַשָּׁמֶן לְמָאוֹר
כט וּלְשֶׁמֶן הַמִּשְׁחָה וְלִקְטֹרֶת הַסַּמִּים: כָּל־אִישׁ וְאִשָּׁה אֲשֶׁר נָדַב לִבָּם

אונקלוס

יח ית סכי משכנא, וית סכי דרתא וית אטוניהון: יט ית לבושי שמושא לשמשא בקדשא, ית לבושי קדשא לאהרן כהנא, וית לבושי בנוהי לשמשא: כ ונפקו, כל כנשתא דבני ישראל מן קדם משה: כא ואתו, כל גבר דאתרעי לביה, וכל, דאשלימת רוחיה עמיה, איתיאו, ית אפרשותא קדם יי, לעבידת משכן זמנא ולכל פלחניה, וללבושי קדשא: כב ומיתן גבריא על נשיא, כל דאתרעי לביה, איתיאו, שירין ושבין, ועזקן ומחוך כל מן דדהב, וכל גבר, דארים, ארמות דדהבא קדם יי: כג וכל גבר דאשתכח עמיה, תכלא וארגונא, וצבע זהורי ובוץ ומעזי, ומשכי דדכרי מסמקי, ומשכי ססגונא איתיאו: כד כל דארים, ארמות כסף ונחש, איתיאו, ית אפרשותא קדם יי, וכל, דאשתכח עמיה, אעי שטין, לכל עבידת פלחנא איתיאו: כה וכל אתתא חכימת לבא בידהא עזלא, ומיתן כד עזיל, ית תכלא וית ארגונא, ית צבע זהורי וית בוצא: כו וכל נשיא, דאתרעי לבהון, עמהון בחכמא, עזלן ית מעזיא: כז ורברביא איתיאו, ית אבני בורלא, וית אבני אשלמותא, לשקעא באיפודא ובחשנא: כח וית בסמא וית משחא, לאנהרותא, ולמשח רבותא, ולקטרת בסמיא: כט כל גבר ואתא, דאתרעי לבהון

35:29 כָּל־אִישׁ וְאִשָּׁה אֲשֶׁר נָדַב לִבָּם אֹתָם לְהָבִיא... נְדָבָה לַיהוה *All the men and women whose hearts moved them to bring anything… as a freewill offering to the LORD* – Moshe emphasizes that each has something different to give: "Bring of

▶

bring anything for the work that the LORD, through Moshe, had commanded –
brought it as a freewill offering to the LORD.
30 Then Moshe said to the Israelites, "Know that the LORD has summoned by SHELISHI /SHENI/
31 name Betzalel, son of Uri, son of Ḥur, of the tribe of Yehuda, and has filled him
32 with a divine spirit of wisdom, understanding, and knowledge in every craft, to
33 devise designs, working in gold, silver, and bronze, as well as cutting stones for
34 setting, carving wood, and working in every other craft. He has also given him
the ability to teach others, together with Oholiav, son of Aḥisamakh of the tribe
35 of Dan. He has filled them with the skill to do all kinds of work, as engravers,
designers, embroiderers in sky-blue, purple, or scarlet wool or fine linen, and as
36 1 weavers. They will be able to carry out all the necessary work and design. And
so Betzalel and Oholiav shall carry out everything the LORD has commanded,
together with all the skilled people to whom the LORD has granted expertise
2 and acumen to do all the work necessary for the service of the Sanctuary." Then
Moshe summoned Betzalel and Oholiav and all the skilled craftsmen to whom
God had given expertise and who were inspired to dedicate themselves and

רש"י

ל) **חור.** בְּנָהּ שֶׁל מִרְיָם הָיָה:

לד) **וְאָהֳלִיאָב.** מִשֵּׁבֶט דָּן, מִן הַיְּרוּדִין שֶׁבַּשְּׁבָטִים, מִבְּנֵי הַשְּׁפָחוֹת, וְהִשְׁוָהוּ הַמָּקוֹם לִבְצַלְאֵל לִמְלֶאכֶת הַמִּשְׁכָּן וְהוּא מִגְּדוֹלֵי הַשְּׁבָטִים, לְקַיֵּם מַה שֶּׁנֶּאֱמַר: "וְלֹא נִכַּר שׁוֹעַ לִפְנֵי דָל" (איוב לד, יט):

intense connection – until around the eighteenth century – between art and religion, image-making was seen as potentially idolatrous. Hence the second of the Ten Commandments: "Do not make for yourself any carved image or likeness of any creature in the heavens above or the earth beneath or the waters beneath the earth" (Ex. 20:4). This concern continued long after the biblical era. The Greeks, who achieved unrivaled excellence in the visual arts, were, in the religious sphere, still a pagan people of myth and mystery, while the Romans had a disturbing tendency to turn caesars into gods and erect statues to them.

Yet as we see from the case of Betzalel, Judaism is not indifferent to aesthetics. The concept of *hiddur mitzva*, "beautifying the commandment," meant, for the Sages, that we should strive to fulfill the commands in the most aesthetically pleasing way. The priestly garments were meant to be "for glory and for splendor" (28:2). The very terms applied to Betzalel – wisdom, understanding, and knowledge – are applied by the book of Proverbs to God Himself as Creator of the universe:

> The LORD founded the earth with wisdom;
> He established the heavens with discernment;
> With His knowledge were the depths carved out,
> And the sky dropped dew. (Prov. 3:19–20)

The Greeks, and many in the Western world who inherited their tradition, believed in the holiness of beauty. Keats gave succinct expression to this creed in the last lines of his "Ode to a Grecian Urn": "Beauty is Truth, truth is beauty, that is all/Ye know on earth and all ye need to know." Jews believe in the opposite: *hadrat kodesh*, the beauty of holiness: "Render to the LORD the glory due His name; bow to the LORD in the splendor of holiness" (Ps. 29:2). Art in Judaism always has a spiritual purpose: to make us aware of the universe as a work of art, testifying to the supreme Artist, God Himself.

אֹתָם לְהָבִיא לְכָל־הַמְּלָאכָה אֲשֶׁר צִוָּה יְהוָה לַעֲשׂוֹת בְּיַד־מֹשֶׁה
הֵבִיאוּ בְנֵי־יִשְׂרָאֵל נְדָבָה לַיהוָה׃
ל וַיֹּאמֶר מֹשֶׁה אֶל־בְּנֵי יִשְׂרָאֵל רְאוּ קָרָא יְהוָה בְּשֵׁם בְּצַלְאֵל בֶּן־ שלישי /שני/
לא אוּרִי בֶן־חוּר לְמַטֵּה יְהוּדָה׃ וַיְמַלֵּא אֹתוֹ רוּחַ אֱלֹהִים בְּחָכְמָה
לב בִּתְבוּנָה וּבְדַעַת וּבְכָל־מְלָאכָה׃ וְלַחְשֹׁב מַחֲשָׁבֹת לַעֲשֹׂת בַּזָּהָב
לג וּבַכֶּסֶף וּבַנְּחֹשֶׁת׃ וּבַחֲרֹשֶׁת אֶבֶן לְמַלֹּאת וּבַחֲרֹשֶׁת עֵץ לַעֲשׂוֹת
לד בְּכָל־מְלֶאכֶת מַחֲשָׁבֶת׃ וּלְהוֹרֹת נָתַן בְּלִבּוֹ הוּא וְאָהֳלִיאָב בֶּן־
לה אֲחִיסָמָךְ לְמַטֵּה־דָן׃ מִלֵּא אֹתָם חָכְמַת־לֵב לַעֲשׂוֹת כָּל־מְלֶאכֶת
חָרָשׁ ׀ וְחֹשֵׁב וְרֹקֵם בַּתְּכֵלֶת וּבָאַרְגָּמָן בְּתוֹלַעַת הַשָּׁנִי וּבַשֵּׁשׁ וְאֹרֵג
לו א עֹשֵׂי כָּל־מְלָאכָה וְחֹשְׁבֵי מַחֲשָׁבֹת׃ וְעָשָׂה בְצַלְאֵל וְאָהֳלִיאָב וְכֹל ׀
אִישׁ חֲכַם־לֵב אֲשֶׁר נָתַן יְהוָה חָכְמָה וּתְבוּנָה בָּהֵמָּה לָדַעַת לַעֲשֹׂת
ב אֶת־כָּל־מְלֶאכֶת עֲבֹדַת הַקֹּדֶשׁ לְכֹל אֲשֶׁר־צִוָּה יְהוָה׃ וַיִּקְרָא מֹשֶׁה
אֶל־בְּצַלְאֵל וְאֶל־אָהֳלִיאָב וְאֶל כָּל־אִישׁ חֲכַם־לֵב אֲשֶׁר נָתַן יְהוָה
חָכְמָה בְּלִבּוֹ כֹּל אֲשֶׁר נְשָׂאוֹ לִבּוֹ לְקָרְבָה אֶל־הַמְּלָאכָה לַעֲשֹׂת

אונקלוס

עִמְּהוֹן, לְאֵיתָאָה לְכָל עֲבִידְתָּא, דְּפַקֵּיד יי, לְמֶעְבַּד בִּידָא דְמֹשֶׁה, אֵיתִיאוּ בְנֵי יִשְׂרָאֵל, נְדַבְתָּא קֳדָם יי: ל וַאֲמַר מֹשֶׁה לִבְנֵי יִשְׂרָאֵל, חֲזוֹ, דְּרַבִּי יי בְּשׁוּם, בְּצַלְאֵל, בַּר אוּרִי בַר חוּר לְשִׁבְטָא דִיהוּדָה: לא וְאַשְׁלֵים עִמֵּיהּ רוּחַ מִן קֳדָם יי, בְּחָכְמְתָא, בְּסֻכְלְתָנוּ וּבְמַדַּע וּבְכָל עֲבִידָא: לב וּלְאַלָּפָא אֻמָּנְוָן, לְמֶעְבַּד, בְּדַהֲבָא וּבְכַסְפָּא וּבִנְחָשָׁא: לג וּבְאֻמָּנוּת אֶבֶן טָבָא, לְאַשְׁלָמָא וּבְנַגָּרוּת אָעָא, לְמֶעְבַּד בְּכָל עֲבִידַת אֻמָּנָן: לד וּלְאַלָּפָא יְהַב בְּלִבֵּיהּ, הוּא, וְאָהֳלִיאָב בַּר אֲחִיסָמָךְ לְשִׁבְטָא דְדָן: לה אַשְׁלֵים עִמְּהוֹן חַכִּימוּת לִבָּא, לְמֶעְבַּד כָּל עֲבִידַת נַגָּר וְאֻמָּן, וְצַיָּר בְּתַכְלָא וּבְאַרְגְּוָנָא, בִּצְבַע זְהוֹרִי, וּבְבוּצָא וּמָחֵי, עָבְדֵי כָּל עֲבִידָא, וּמַלְפֵי אֻמָּנְוָן: לו א וְיַעֲבֵיד בְּצַלְאֵל וְאָהֳלִיאָב, וְכָל גְּבַר חַכִּים לִבָּא, דִּיהַב יי, חָכְמְתָא וְסֻכְלְתָנוּתָא בְּהוֹן, לְמִדַּע לְמֶעְבַּד, יָת כָּל עֲבִידַת פָּלְחַן קֻדְשָׁא, לְכָל דְּפַקֵּיד יי: ב וּקְרָא מֹשֶׁה, לִבְצַלְאֵל וּלְאָהֳלִיאָב, וּלְכָל גְּבַר חַכִּים לִבָּא, דִּיהַב יי, חָכְמְתָא בְּלִבֵּיהּ, כָּל דְּאִתְרְעֵי לִבֵּיהּ, לְמִקְרַב לַעֲבִידְתָּא לְמֶעְבַּד

feel that it has been valued. What matters is that together we build something none of us could make alone. Each must be able to say with pride: I helped make this.

35:33 לַעֲשׂוֹת בְּכָל־מְלֶאכֶת מַחֲשָׁבֶת *Working in every other craft* – The Israelites worshipped the invisible God who transcended the universe. Other than the human person, God has no image. Even when He revealed Himself to the people at Sinai, "you heard the sound of words but saw no image; there was only a voice" (Deut. 4:12). Given the

▶

3 come to carry out the work. From Moshe they received all the offerings the
Israelites had brought for the work of the Sanctuary. And the people kept
4 bringing him additional gifts every morning. So all the craftsmen engaged in the
5 work of the Sanctuary left what they were doing, and said to Moshe, "The people
are bringing more than is necessary for the work the LORD has commanded
6 us to do." Moshe ordered an announcement to be made throughout the camp:
"Let no man or woman make anything more as an offering for the Sanctuary." So
7 the people brought no more; for what they already had was more than enough
8 for all the work that was to be done. All the skilled craftsmen among REVI'I
those engaged in the work made the Tabernacle with ten sheets of fine linen
9 and sky-blue, purple, and scarlet wool, with a woven design of cherubim. All
the sheets were of the same size: twenty-eight cubits long and four cubits wide.
10 11 Five sheets were sewn together, and likewise the second five. He made loops of
sky-blue wool on the edge of the outermost sheet of the first set and likewise on
12 the outermost sheet of the second set: fifty loops on the first sheet and fifty on
the edge of the end sheet of the other set, so that the loops were opposite one
13 another. He made fifty gold clasps and used them to fasten the two sets of sheets
together so that the Tabernacle was all of one piece.
14 He made sheets of goats' hair for a tent over the Tabernacle. There were eleven
15 such sheets. All eleven were the same size: thirty cubits long and four cubits
16 17 wide. He joined five of the sheets into one set and six into another. He made

אונקלוס

יָתַהּ: ג וּנְסִיבוּ מִן קֳדָם מֹשֶׁה, יָת כָּל אַפְרָשׁוּתָא דְּאֵיתִיאוּ בְּנֵי יִשְׂרָאֵל, לַעֲבִידַת, פָּלְחַן קֻדְשָׁא לְמֶעְבַּד יָתַהּ, וְאִנּוּן, מֵיתַן לֵיהּ עוֹד, נְדַבְתָּא בִּצְפַר בִּצְפַר: ד וַאֲתוֹ כָּל חַכִּימַיָּא, דְּעָבְדִין, יָת כָּל עֲבִידַת קֻדְשָׁא, גְּבַר גְּבַר מֵעֲבִידְתֵיהּ דְּאִנּוּן עָבְדִין: ה וַאֲמַרוּ לְמֹשֶׁה לְמֵימַר, מַסְגַּן עַמָּא לְאֵיתָאָה, מִסַּת פָּלְחָנָא לַעֲבִידְתָא, דְּפַקֵּיד יי לְמֶעְבַּד יָתַהּ: ו וּפַקֵּיד מֹשֶׁה, וְאַעְבַּרוּ כָּרוֹז בְּמַשְׁרִיתָא לְמֵימַר, גְּבַר וְאִתָּא, לָא יַעְבְּדוּן עוֹד, עֲבִידְתָא לְאַפְרָשׁוּת קֻדְשָׁא, וּפְסַק עַמָּא מִלְּאֵיתָאָה: ז וַעֲבִידְתָא, הֲוָת מִסַּת, לְכָל עֲבִידְתָא לְמֶעְבַּד יָתַהּ, וְיַתְרַת: ח וַעֲבַדוּ כָּל חַכִּימֵי לִבָּא, בְּעָבְדֵי עֲבִידְתָא, יָת מַשְׁכְּנָא עֲסַר יְרִיעָן, דְּבוּץ שְׁזִיר, וְתַכְלָא וְאַרְגְּוָנָא וּצְבַע זְהוֹרִי, צוּרַת כְּרוּבִין, עוֹבָד אֻמָּן עֲבַד יָתְהוֹן: ט אֻרְכָּא דִּירִיעֲתָא חֲדָא, עֶסְרִין וְתַמְנֵי אַמִּין, וּפֻתְיָא אַרְבַּע אַמִּין, דִּירִיעֲתָא חֲדָא, מִשְׁחֲתָא חֲדָא לְכָל יְרִיעָתָא: י וְלָפֵיף יָת חֲמֵשׁ יְרִיעָן, חֲדָא עִם חֲדָא, וַחֲמֵשׁ יְרִיעָן לָפֵיף, חֲדָא עִם חֲדָא: יא וַעֲבַד עֲנוּבִין דְּתַכְלָא, עַל סִפְתָּא דִּירִיעֲתָא חֲדָא, מִסִּטְרָא בֵּית לוֹפֵי, כֵּן עֲבַד בְּסִפְתָּא דִּירִיעֲתָא, בְּסִטְרָא, בֵּית לוֹפֵי תִּנְיָנָא: יב חַמְשִׁין עֲנוּבִין, עֲבַד בִּירִיעֲתָא חֲדָא, וְחַמְשִׁין עֲנוּבִין, עֲבַד בְּסִטְרָא דִּירִיעֲתָא, דְּבֵית לוֹפֵי תִּנְיָנָא, מְכַוְּנָן עֲנוּבַיָּא, חֲדָא לְקֳבֵיל חֲדָא: יג וַעֲבַד, חַמְשִׁין פֻּרְפִּין דִּדְהַב, וְלָפֵיף יָת

רש״י

ה מִדֵּי הָעֲבֹדָה. יוֹתֵר מִכְּדֵי צֹרֶךְ הָעֲבוֹדָה:

ו וַיִּכָּלֵא. לְשׁוֹן מְנִיעָה:

ז וְהַמְּלָאכָה הָיְתָה דַיָּם לְכָל הַמְּלָאכָה. וּמְלֶאכֶת הַהֲבָאָה "הָיְתָה דַיָּם" שֶׁל עוֹשֵׂי הַמִּשְׁכָּן, "לְכָל הַמְּלָאכָה" שֶׁל מִשְׁכָּן "לַעֲשׂוֹת אוֹתָהּ" וּלְהוֹתֵר: וְהוֹתֵר. כְּמוֹ: "וְהַכְבֵּד אֶת לִבּוֹ" (לעיל ח, יח), "וְהַכּוֹת אֶת מוֹאָב" (מלכים ב׳ ג, כד):

ג אֹתָהּ: וַיִּקְחוּ מִלִּפְנֵי מֹשֶׁה אֵת כָּל־הַתְּרוּמָה אֲשֶׁר הֵבִיאוּ בְּנֵי יִשְׂרָאֵל
לִמְלֶאכֶת עֲבֹדַת הַקֹּדֶשׁ לַעֲשֹׂת אֹתָהּ וְהֵם הֵבִיאוּ אֵלָיו עוֹד נְדָבָה
ד בַּבֹּקֶר בַּבֹּקֶר: וַיָּבֹאוּ כָּל־הַחֲכָמִים הָעֹשִׂים אֵת כָּל־מְלֶאכֶת הַקֹּדֶשׁ
ה אִישׁ אִישׁ מִמְּלַאכְתּוֹ אֲשֶׁר־הֵמָּה עֹשִׂים: וַיֹּאמְרוּ אֶל־מֹשֶׁה לֵּאמֹר
מַרְבִּים הָעָם לְהָבִיא מִדֵּי הָעֲבֹדָה לַמְּלָאכָה אֲשֶׁר־צִוָּה יְהוָה לַעֲשֹׂת
ו אֹתָהּ: וַיְצַו מֹשֶׁה וַיַּעֲבִירוּ קוֹל בַּמַּחֲנֶה לֵאמֹר אִישׁ וְאִשָּׁה אַל־יַעֲשׂוּ־
ז עוֹד מְלָאכָה לִתְרוּמַת הַקֹּדֶשׁ וַיִּכָּלֵא הָעָם מֵהָבִיא: וְהַמְּלָאכָה הָיְתָה
ח דַיָּם לְכָל־הַמְּלָאכָה לַעֲשׂוֹת אֹתָהּ וְהוֹתֵר: וַיַּעֲשׂוּ רביעי
כָל־חֲכַם־לֵב בְּעֹשֵׂי הַמְּלָאכָה אֶת־הַמִּשְׁכָּן עֶשֶׂר יְרִיעֹת שֵׁשׁ מָשְׁזָר
וּתְכֵלֶת וְאַרְגָּמָן וְתוֹלַעַת שָׁנִי כְּרֻבִים מַעֲשֵׂה חֹשֵׁב עָשָׂה אֹתָם:
ט אֹרֶךְ הַיְרִיעָה הָאַחַת שְׁמֹנֶה וְעֶשְׂרִים בָּאַמָּה וְרֹחַב אַרְבַּע בָּאַמָּה
י הַיְרִיעָה הָאֶחָת מִדָּה אַחַת לְכָל־הַיְרִיעֹת: וַיְחַבֵּר אֶת־חֲמֵשׁ הַיְרִיעֹת
יא אַחַת אֶל־אֶחָת וְחָמֵשׁ יְרִיעֹת חִבַּר אַחַת אֶל־אֶחָת: וַיַּעַשׂ לֻלְאֹת
תְּכֵלֶת עַל שְׂפַת הַיְרִיעָה הָאֶחָת מִקָּצָה בַּמַּחְבָּרֶת כֵּן עָשָׂה בִּשְׂפַת
יב הַיְרִיעָה הַקִּיצוֹנָה בַּמַּחְבֶּרֶת הַשֵּׁנִית: חֲמִשִּׁים לֻלָאֹת עָשָׂה בַּיְרִיעָה
הָאֶחָת וַחֲמִשִּׁים לֻלָאֹת עָשָׂה בִּקְצֵה הַיְרִיעָה אֲשֶׁר בַּמַּחְבֶּרֶת הַשֵּׁנִית
יג מַקְבִּילֹת הַלֻּלָאֹת אַחַת אֶל־אֶחָת: וַיַּעַשׂ חֲמִשִּׁים קַרְסֵי זָהָב וַיְחַבֵּר
אֶת־הַיְרִיעֹת אַחַת אֶל־אַחַת בַּקְּרָסִים וַיְהִי הַמִּשְׁכָּן אֶחָד:
יד וַיַּעַשׂ יְרִיעֹת עִזִּים לְאֹהֶל עַל־הַמִּשְׁכָּן עַשְׁתֵּי־עֶשְׂרֵה יְרִיעֹת עָשָׂה
טו אֹתָם: אֹרֶךְ הַיְרִיעָה הָאַחַת שְׁלֹשִׁים בָּאַמָּה וְאַרְבַּע אַמּוֹת רֹחַב
טז הַיְרִיעָה הָאֶחָת מִדָּה אַחַת לְעַשְׁתֵּי עֶשְׂרֵה יְרִיעֹת: וַיְחַבֵּר אֶת־חֲמֵשׁ

אונקלוס

יְרִיעָתָא, חֲדָא עִם חֲדָא בְּפוּרְפַיָּא, וַהֲוָה מַשְׁכְּנָא חַד: יד וַעֲבַד יְרִיעָן
דִּמְעִזֵּי, לִפְרָסָא עַל מַשְׁכְּנָא, חֲדָא עַסְרֵי יְרִיעָן עֲבַד יָתְהוֹן: טו אֻרְכָּא
דִּירִיעֲתָא חֲדָא, תְּלָתִין אַמִּין, וְאַרְבַּע אַמִּין, פְּתָיָא דִּירִיעֲתָא
חֲדָא, מְשַׁחְתָּא חֲדָא, לַחֲדָא עַסְרֵי יְרִיעָן: טז וְלַפֵּיף, יָת חֲמֵשׁ

fifty loops on the edge of the outermost sheet of the first set, and fifty loops on
18 the edge of the second set. He made fifty bronze clasps to join the tent together
19 into a single piece. And for the tent he made a covering of rams' skins dyed red,
20 with a covering of fine leather above. Then he made the upright boards HAMISHI
21 for the Tabernacle from acacia wood. Each was ten cubits long and a cubit and
22 a half wide. Each board had two matching tenons; all the Tabernacle's boards
23 24 were made in this way. He made twenty boards for the south side, and forty
silver sockets to go under them, two sockets under each board, one under each
25 tenon. For the second side of the Tabernacle, the north side, he made twenty
26 27 boards and their forty silver sockets, two under each board. For the rear of the
28 Tabernacle on the west side he made six boards, along with two boards for each
29 of the rear corners of the Tabernacle. They were even at the bottom, and joined
30 at the top by a ring. This was so for the other corner also. So there were eight
31 boards and sixteen silver sockets, two under each board. He made crossbars of
32 acacia wood, five for the boards of the first side of the Tabernacle, five for the
boards of the second, and five for those of the rear of the Tabernacle on the west
33 side. He made the central crossbar to go across the middles of the boards from
34 one end to the other. He overlaid the boards with gold, and made gold rings to
35 hold the crossbars; he overlaid the crossbars themselves with gold. He made
the curtain of sky-blue, purple, and scarlet wool and finely spun linen, with a

אונקלוס

יריען לחוד, וית שית יריען לחוד: יז ועבד ענבין חמשין, על ספתא דיריעתא, בסטרא בית לופי, וחמשין ענבין, עבד על ספתא דיריעתא, דבית לופי תנינא: יח ועבד, פרפין דנחש חמשין, ללפפא ית משכנא למהוי חד: יט ועבד חופאה למשכנא, דמשכי דכרי מסמקי, וחופאה, דמשכי ססגונא מלעילא: כ ועבד ית דפיא למשכנא, דאעי שטין קימין: כא עסר אמין ארכא דדפא, ואמתא ופלגות אמתא, פתיא דדפא חד: כב תרין צירין, לדפא חד, משלבין, חד לקביל חד, כן עבד, לכל דפי משכנא: כג ועבד ית דפיא למשכנא, עסרין דפין, לרוח עיבר דרומא: כד וארבעין סמכין דכסף, עבד, תחות עסרין דפין, תרין סמכין, תחות דפא חד לתרין צירוהי, ותרין סמכין, תחות דפא חד לתרין צירוהי: כה ולסטר משכנא, תנינא לרוח צפונא, עבד עסרין דפין: כו וארבעין סמכיהון דכסף, תרין סמכין, תחות דפא חד, ותרין סמכין, תחות דפא חד: כז ולסיפי משכנא מערבא, עבד שתא דפין: כח ותרין דפין עבד, לזוית משכנא, בסופהון: כט והוו מכונין מלרע, וכחדא, הוו מכונין ברישיהון, לעזקתא חדא, כן עבד לתרויהון, לתרתין זוין: ל והוו תמניא דפין, וסמכיהון דכסף, שתת עסר סמכין, תרין סמכין תרין סמכין, תחות דפא חד: לא ועבד עברי דאעי שטין, חמשא, לדפי סטר משכנא חד: לב וחמשא עברין, לדפי סטר משכנא תנינא, וחמשא עברין לדפי משכנא, לסופהון מערבא: לג ועבד ית עברא מציעאה, לאעברא בגו דפיא, מן סיפי לסיפי: לד וית דפיא חפא דהבא, וית עזקתהון עבד דהבא, אתרא לעבריא, וחפא ית עבריא דהבא: לה ועבד ית פרכתא, תכלא וארגונא, וצבע זהורי ובוץ שזיר, עובד אמן, עבד יתה צורת כרובין:

הַיְרִיעֹ֖ת לְבָ֑ד וְאֶת־שֵׁ֥שׁ הַיְרִיעֹ֖ת לְבָֽד׃ יז וַיַּ֤עַשׂ לֻֽלָאֹת֙ חֲמִשִּׁ֔ים עַ֚ל
שְׂפַ֣ת הַיְרִיעָ֔ה הַקִּיצֹנָ֖ה בַּמַּחְבָּ֑רֶת וַחֲמִשִּׁ֣ים לֻלָאֹ֗ת עָשָׂה֙ עַל־שְׂפַ֣ת
יח הַיְרִיעָ֔ה הַחֹבֶ֖רֶת הַשֵּׁנִֽית׃ וַיַּ֛עַשׂ קַרְסֵ֥י נְח֖שֶׁת חֲמִשִּׁ֑ים לְחַבֵּ֥ר אֶת־
יט הָאֹ֖הֶל לִהְיֹ֥ת אֶחָֽד׃ וַיַּ֤עַשׂ מִכְסֶה֙ לָאֹ֔הֶל עֹרֹ֥ת אֵילִ֖ם מְאָדָּמִ֑ים וּמִכְסֵ֛ה
כ עֹרֹ֥ת תְּחָשִׁ֖ים מִלְמָֽעְלָה׃ וַיַּ֥עַשׂ אֶת־הַקְּרָשִׁ֖ים לַמִּשְׁכָּ֑ן חמישי
כא עֲצֵ֥י שִׁטִּ֖ים עֹמְדִֽים׃ עֶ֥שֶׂר אַמֹּ֖ת אֹ֣רֶךְ הַקָּ֑רֶשׁ וְאַמָּה֙ וַחֲצִ֣י הָֽאַמָּ֔ה רֹ֖חַב
כב הַקֶּ֥רֶשׁ הָאֶחָֽד׃ שְׁתֵּ֣י יָדֹ֗ת לַקֶּ֙רֶשׁ֙ הָֽאֶחָ֔ד מְשֻׁלָּבֹ֔ת אַחַ֖ת אֶל־אֶחָ֑ת כֵּ֣ן
כג עָשָׂ֔ה לְכֹ֖ל קַרְשֵׁ֥י הַמִּשְׁכָּֽן׃ וַיַּ֥עַשׂ אֶת־הַקְּרָשִׁ֖ים לַמִּשְׁכָּ֑ן עֶשְׂרִ֣ים קְרָשִׁ֔ים
כד לִפְאַ֖ת נֶ֥גֶב תֵּימָֽנָה׃ וְאַרְבָּעִים֙ אַדְנֵי־כֶ֔סֶף עָשָׂ֕ה תַּ֖חַת עֶשְׂרִ֣ים הַקְּרָשִׁ֑ים
שְׁנֵ֨י אֲדָנִ֜ים תַּֽחַת־הַקֶּ֤רֶשׁ הָֽאֶחָד֙ לִשְׁתֵּ֣י יְדֹתָ֔יו וּשְׁנֵ֧י אֲדָנִ֛ים תַּֽחַת־
כה הַקֶּ֥רֶשׁ הָאֶחָ֖ד לִשְׁתֵּ֥י יְדֹתָֽיו׃ וּלְצֶ֧לַע הַמִּשְׁכָּ֛ן הַשֵּׁנִ֖ית לִפְאַ֣ת צָפ֑וֹן עָשָׂ֖ה
כו עֶשְׂרִ֥ים קְרָשִֽׁים׃ וְאַרְבָּעִ֥ים אַדְנֵיהֶ֖ם כָּ֑סֶף שְׁנֵ֣י אֲדָנִ֗ים תַּ֚חַת הַקֶּ֣רֶשׁ
כז הָאֶחָ֔ד וּשְׁנֵ֣י אֲדָנִ֔ים תַּ֖חַת הַקֶּ֥רֶשׁ הָאֶחָֽד׃ וּֽלְיַרְכְּתֵ֥י הַמִּשְׁכָּ֖ן יָ֑מָּה עָשָׂ֖ה
כח כט שִׁשָּׁ֥ה קְרָשִֽׁים׃ וּשְׁנֵ֤י קְרָשִׁים֙ עָשָׂ֔ה לִמְקֻצְעֹ֖ת הַמִּשְׁכָּ֑ן בַּיַּרְכָתָֽיִם׃ וְהָי֣וּ
תוֹאֲמִם֮ מִלְּמַ֒טָּה֒ וְיַחְדָּ֗ו יִהְי֤וּ תַמִּים֙ אֶל־רֹאשׁ֔וֹ אֶל־הַטַּבַּ֖עַת הָאֶחָ֑ת
ל כֵּ֚ן עָשָׂ֣ה לִשְׁנֵיהֶ֔ם לִשְׁנֵ֖י הַמִּקְצֹעֹֽת׃ וְהָיוּ֙ שְׁמֹנָ֣ה קְרָשִׁ֔ים וְאַדְנֵיהֶ֣ם כֶּ֔סֶף
לא שִׁשָּׁ֥ה עָשָׂ֖ר אֲדָנִ֑ים שְׁנֵ֣י אֲדָנִ֔ים שְׁנֵ֣י אֲדָנִ֔ים תַּ֖חַת הַקֶּ֥רֶשׁ הָאֶחָֽד׃ וַיַּ֥עַשׂ
לב בְּרִיחֵ֖י עֲצֵ֣י שִׁטִּ֑ים חֲמִשָּׁ֕ה לְקַרְשֵׁ֥י צֶֽלַע־הַמִּשְׁכָּ֖ן הָאֶחָֽת׃ וַחֲמִשָּׁ֣ה
בְרִיחִ֔ם לְקַרְשֵׁ֥י צֶֽלַע־הַמִּשְׁכָּ֖ן הַשֵּׁנִ֑ית וַחֲמִשָּׁ֤ה בְרִיחִם֙ לְקַרְשֵׁ֣י הַמִּשְׁכָּ֔ן
לג לַיַּרְכָתַ֖יִם יָֽמָּה׃ וַיַּ֖עַשׂ אֶת־הַבְּרִ֣יחַ הַתִּיכֹ֑ן לִבְרֹ֙חַ֙ בְּת֣וֹךְ הַקְּרָשִׁ֔ים מִן־
לד הַקָּצֶ֖ה אֶל־הַקָּצֶֽה׃ וְֽאֶת־הַקְּרָשִׁ֞ים צִפָּ֣ה זָהָ֗ב וְאֶת־טַבְּעֹתָם֙ עָשָׂ֣ה זָהָ֔ב
לה בָּתִּ֖ים לַבְּרִיחִ֑ם וַיְצַ֥ף אֶת־הַבְּרִיחִ֖ם זָהָֽב׃ וַיַּ֙עַשׂ֙ אֶת־הַפָּרֹ֔כֶת תְּכֵ֥לֶת
וְאַרְגָּמָ֖ן וְתוֹלַ֣עַת שָׁנִ֑י וְשֵׁ֣שׁ מָשְׁזָ֔ר מַעֲשֵׂ֥ה חֹשֵׁ֖ב עָשָׂ֥ה אֹתָ֖הּ כְּרֻבִֽים׃

36 design of cherubim worked into it. He also made four posts of acacia wood for
it and overlaid them with gold. Their hooks were of gold, and he cast for them
37 four sockets of silver. He made an embroidered screen for the entrance of the
38 Tent, of sky-blue, purple, and scarlet wool and finely spun linen, as well as five
posts with their hooks. He overlaid their tops and bands with gold, but their
five sockets were of bronze.

37 1 Betzalel made the Ark of acacia wood, two and a half cubits long, a cubit and a
2 half wide, and a cubit and a half high. He overlaid it with pure gold inside and
3 out, and encircled it around with a gold rim. He cast four gold rings for its four
4 corners, two rings on one side and two on the other. He made staves of acacia
5 wood and overlaid them with gold. He then placed the staves in the rings on
6 the Ark's sides so that it could be carried. He made a cover of pure gold, two
7 and a half cubits long and a cubit and a half wide. He made two cherubim of
8 beaten gold for the two ends of the cover, one cherub at one end and one at
9 the other. He made them of one piece with the cover, and the wings of the
cherubim were spread upward, sheltering the cover. They faced each other,
their faces toward the cover.

10 He made a table of acacia wood, two cubits long, a cubit wide, and a cubit and a

אונקלוס

לו ועבד לה, ארבעא עמודי שטין, וחפנון דהבא, וויהון דהבא, ואתיך להון, ארבעא סמכין דכסף: לז ועבד פרסא לתרע משכנא, תכלא וארגונא, וצבע זהורי ובוץ שזיר, עובד צייר: לח וית עמודוהי חמשא וית וויהון, וחפי רישיהון, וכבושיהון דהבא, וסמכיהון חמשא דנחשא: לז א ועבד בצלאל, ית ארונא דאעי שטין, תרתין אמין ופלגא ארכיה, ואמתא ופלגא פתייה, ואמתא ופלגא רומיה: ב וחפהי, דהב דכי מגיו ומברא, ועבד ליה, זיר דדהב סחור סחור: ג ואתיך ליה, ארבע עזקן דדהב, על ארבע זויתיה, ותרתין עזקן, על סטריה חד, ותרתין עזקן, על סטריה תנינא: ד ועבד אריחי דאעי שטין, וחפא יתהון דהבא: ה ואעיל ◀

רש״י

לז א ויעש בצלאל. לפי שנתן נפשו על המלאכה יותר משאר חכמים, נקראת על שמו:

Someone afflicted with melancholy may dispel it by listening to music and various kinds of song, by strolling in gardens, by experiencing beautiful buildings, by associating with beautiful pictures, and similar sorts of things that broaden the soul. (Ch. 5)

Art, in short, is balm to the soul.

This is true of the products of human artistry, but also of the process. God, taught R. Akiva, deliberately left the world unfinished so that it could be completed by the work of human beings (Tanḥuma, Tazria 5). The creative God seeks creativity from mankind. Work gives human beings two things. First it gives a person independence, one of the essentials of a free society. The second, no less significant, however, is creativity. Work is more than mere labor. Biblical Hebrew has two words to express the difference: *melakha* is work as creation; *avoda* is work as service or servitude. Both are central to the Tabernacle, a labor of love.

לו ויעש לה ארבעה עמודי שטים ויצפם זהב וויהם זהב ויצק להם
לז ארבעה אדני־כסף: ויעש מסך לפתח האהל תכלת וארגמן ותולעת
לח שני ושש משזר מעשה רקם: ואת־עמודיו חמשה ואת־וויהם וצפה
ראשיהם וחשקיהם זהב ואדניהם חמשה נחשת:

לז א ויעש בצלאל את־הארן עצי שטים אמתים וחצי ארכו ואמה וחצי כז
ב רחבו ואמה וחצי קמתו: ויצפהו זהב טהור מבית ומחוץ ויעש לו
ג זר זהב סביב: ויצק לו ארבע טבעת זהב על ארבע פעמתיו ושתי
ד טבעת על־צלעו האחת ושתי טבעת על־צלעו השנית: ויעש בדי
ה עצי שטים ויצף אתם זהב: ויבא את־הבדים בטבעת על צלעת
ו הארן לשאת את־הארן: ויעש כפרת זהב טהור אמתים וחצי ארכה
ז ואמה וחצי רחבה: ויעש שני כרבים זהב מקשה עשה אתם משני
ח קצות הכפרת: כרוב־אחד מקצה מזה וכרוב־אחד מקצה מזה
ט מן־הכפרת עשה את־הכרבים משני קצוותו: ויהיו הכרבים פרשי קצותיו
כנפים למעלה סככים בכנפיהם על־הכפרת ופניהם איש אל־אחיו
אל־הכפרת היו פני הכרבים:

י ויעש את־השלחן עצי שטים אמתים ארכו ואמה רחבו ואמה
יא יב וחצי קמתו: ויצף אתו זהב טהור ויעש לו זר זהב סביב: ויעש לו

אונקלוס

ית אריחיא בעזקתא, על סטרי ארונא, למטל ית ארונא: ו ועבד כפרתא דדהב דכי, תרתין אמין ופלגא ארכה, ואמתא ופלגא פתיה: ז ועבד, תרין כרובין דדהב, נגיד עבד יתהון, מתרין סטרי כפרתא: ח כרובא חד מסטרא מכא, וכרובא חד מסטרא מכא, מן כפרתא, עבד ית כרוביא מתרין סטרוהי: ט והוו כרוביא פריסין גדפיהון לעילא, מטלן בגדפיהון על כפרתא, ואפיהון חד לקביל חד, לקביל כפרתא, הוו אפי כרוביא: י ועבד ית פתורא דאעי שטין, תרתין אמין ארכיה ואמתא פתייה, ואמתא

36:35 עשה אתה כרבים *With a design of cherubim worked into it* – The makers of the Tabernacle are not only craftsmen following the measurements and materials prescribed. Artistic creativity is required too. In the work known as the Eight Chapters (*Shemoneh Perakim*) – the introduction to Rambam's commentary on Mishna Avot – he speaks about the therapeutic power of beauty and its importance:

11 12 half high. He overlaid it with pure gold and around it made a gold rim. He also
made a frame a handbreadth wide around it and made a gold rim for the frame.
13 14 He cast four gold rings and placed the rings on the corners of its four legs. The
15 rings were close to the frame to hold the staves used to carry the table. He made
16 the staves for carrying the table of acacia wood overlaid with gold. The articles
for the table – the bowls, spoons, jars, and pitchers for pouring libations – he
made of pure gold.

17 He made the candelabrum of pure beaten gold. Its base and shaft, cups, knobs, SHISHI /SHELISHI/
18 and flowers were hammered from a single piece. Six branches extended from
19 its sides, three on one side, three on the other. On each of the six branches
extending from the candelabrum were three finely crafted cups, each with a
20 knob and a flower. On the candelabrum itself there were four finely crafted
21 cups, each with a knob and a flower. At the base of each of the three pairs
of branches extending from the candelabrum there was a knob of one piece
22 with it; their knobs and branches were of one piece with it, so that the whole
23 of it was a single piece of pure beaten gold. Its seven lamps and its tongs and
24 pans were of pure gold; it and all its utensils were made from a talent of pure
gold.

25 He made the incense altar of acacia wood, square, a cubit long, a cubit wide,
26 and two cubits high, with horns of one piece with it. He overlaid its top, its
sides all around, and its horns with pure gold and around it he made a gold
27 molding. Under the molding he made two gold rings on the two sides, to
28 hold the staves by which it was carried. The staves themselves were made of

אונקלוס

ופלגא רומיה: יא וחפא יתיה דהב דכי, ועבד ליה, זיר דדהב סחור
סחור: יב ועבד ליה גדנפא, רומיה פשכא סחור סחור, ועבד זיר
דדהב, לגדנפיה סחור סחור: יג ואתיך ליה, ארבע עזקן דדהב,
ויהב ית עזקתא, על ארבע זויתא, דלארבע רגלוהי: יד לקביל
גדנפא, הואה עזקתא, אתרא לאריחיא, למטל ית פתורא: טו ועבד
ית אריחיא דאעי שטין, וחפא יתהון דהבא, למטל ית פתורא: טז
ועבד, ית מניא דעל פתורא, ית מגסוהי וית בזכוהי וית מכילתיה,
וית קסותא, דיתנסך בהון, דהב דכי: יז ועבד ית מנרתא דדהב דכי,
נגיד, עבד ית מנרתא שדה וקנה, כלידהא, חזורהא ושושנהא מנה
הוו: יח ושתא קנין, נפקין מסטרהא, תלתא קני מנרתא, מסטרה חד,
ותלתא קני מנרתא, מסטרה תנינא: יט תלתא כלידין, מצירין, בקניא
חד חזור ושושן, ותלתא כלידין, מצירין, בקניא חד חזור ושושן, כן

לשתא קנין, דנפקין מן מנרתא: כ ובמנרתא ארבעא כלידין, מצירין,
חזורהא ושושנהא: כא וחזור, תחות תרין קנין דמנה, וחזור תחות
תרין קנין דמנה, וחזור, תחות תרין קנין דמנה, לשתא קנין, דנפקין
מנה: כב חזוריהון וקניהון מנה הוו, כלה, נגידא חדא דדהב דכי: כג
ועבד ית בוצינהא שבעא, וציבתהא ומחתיתהא דדהב דכי: כד
ככרא, דדהבא דכיא עבד יתה, וית כל מנהא: כה ועבד, ית מדבחא
דקטרת בסמיא דאעי שטין, אמתא ארכיה ואמתא פתייה מרבע,
ותרתין אמין רומיה, מניה הואה קרנוהי: כו וחפא יתיה דהב דכי,
ית אגריה וית כתלוהי, סחור סחור וית קרנוהי, ועבד ליה, זיר
דדהב סחור סחור: כז ותרתין עזקן דדהב, עבד ליה מלרע לזיריה,
על תרתין זויתיה, על תרין סטרוהי, לאתרא לאריחיא, למטל
יתיה בהון: כח ועבד ית אריחיא דאעי שטין, וחפא יתהון דהבא:

יג מִסְגֶּרֶת טֹפַח סָבִיב וַיַּעַשׂ זֵר־זָהָב לְמִסְגַּרְתּוֹ סָבִיב׃ וַיִּצֹק לוֹ אַרְבַּע
טַבְּעֹת זָהָב וַיִּתֵּן אֶת־הַטַּבָּעֹת עַל אַרְבַּע הַפֵּאֹת אֲשֶׁר לְאַרְבַּע רַגְלָיו׃
יד לְעֻמַּת הַמִּסְגֶּרֶת הָיוּ הַטַּבָּעֹת בָּתִּים לַבַּדִּים לָשֵׂאת אֶת־הַשֻּׁלְחָן׃
טו וַיַּעַשׂ אֶת־הַבַּדִּים עֲצֵי שִׁטִּים וַיְצַף אֹתָם זָהָב לָשֵׂאת אֶת־הַשֻּׁלְחָן׃
טז וַיַּעַשׂ אֶת־הַכֵּלִים ׀ אֲשֶׁר עַל־הַשֻּׁלְחָן אֶת־קְעָרֹתָיו וְאֶת־כַּפֹּתָיו וְאֵת
מְנַקִּיֹּתָיו וְאֶת־הַקְּשָׂוֹת אֲשֶׁר יֻסַּךְ בָּהֵן זָהָב טָהוֹר׃
יז וַיַּעַשׂ אֶת־הַמְּנֹרָה זָהָב טָהוֹר מִקְשָׁה עָשָׂה אֶת־הַמְּנֹרָה יְרֵכָהּ וְקָנָהּ ששי/שלישי/
יח גְּבִיעֶיהָ כַּפְתֹּרֶיהָ וּפְרָחֶיהָ מִמֶּנָּה הָיוּ׃ וְשִׁשָּׁה קָנִים יֹצְאִים מִצִּדֶּיהָ
שְׁלֹשָׁה ׀ קְנֵי מְנֹרָה מִצִּדָּהּ הָאֶחָד וּשְׁלֹשָׁה קְנֵי מְנֹרָה מִצִּדָּהּ הַשֵּׁנִי׃
יט שְׁלֹשָׁה גְבִעִים מְשֻׁקָּדִים בַּקָּנֶה הָאֶחָד כַּפְתֹּר וָפֶרַח וּשְׁלֹשָׁה גְבִעִים
מְשֻׁקָּדִים בְּקָנֶה אֶחָד כַּפְתֹּר וָפָרַח כֵּן לְשֵׁשֶׁת הַקָּנִים הַיֹּצְאִים מִן־
כ כא הַמְּנֹרָה׃ וּבַמְּנֹרָה אַרְבָּעָה גְבִעִים מְשֻׁקָּדִים כַּפְתֹּרֶיהָ וּפְרָחֶיהָ׃ וְכַפְתֹּר
תַּחַת שְׁנֵי הַקָּנִים מִמֶּנָּה וְכַפְתֹּר תַּחַת שְׁנֵי הַקָּנִים מִמֶּנָּה וְכַפְתֹּר
כב תַּחַת־שְׁנֵי הַקָּנִים מִמֶּנָּה לְשֵׁשֶׁת הַקָּנִים הַיֹּצְאִים מִמֶּנָּה׃ כַּפְתֹּרֵיהֶם
כג וּקְנֹתָם מִמֶּנָּה הָיוּ כֻּלָּהּ מִקְשָׁה אַחַת זָהָב טָהוֹר׃ וַיַּעַשׂ אֶת־נֵרֹתֶיהָ
כד שִׁבְעָה וּמַלְקָחֶיהָ וּמַחְתֹּתֶיהָ זָהָב טָהוֹר׃ כִּכָּר זָהָב טָהוֹר עָשָׂה אֹתָהּ
וְאֵת כָּל־כֵּלֶיהָ׃
כה וַיַּעַשׂ אֶת־מִזְבַּח הַקְּטֹרֶת עֲצֵי שִׁטִּים אַמָּה אָרְכּוֹ וְאַמָּה רָחְבּוֹ רָבוּעַ
כו וְאַמָּתַיִם קֹמָתוֹ מִמֶּנּוּ הָיוּ קַרְנֹתָיו׃ וַיְצַף אֹתוֹ זָהָב טָהוֹר אֶת־גַּגּוֹ וְאֶת־
כז קִירֹתָיו סָבִיב וְאֶת־קַרְנֹתָיו וַיַּעַשׂ לוֹ זֵר זָהָב סָבִיב׃ וּשְׁתֵּי טַבְּעֹת זָהָב
עָשָׂה־לוֹ ׀ מִתַּחַת לְזֵרוֹ עַל שְׁתֵּי צַלְעֹתָיו עַל שְׁנֵי צִדָּיו לְבָתִּים לְבַדִּים
כח לָשֵׂאת אֹתוֹ בָּהֶם׃ וַיַּעַשׂ אֶת־הַבַּדִּים עֲצֵי שִׁטִּים וַיְצַף אֹתָם זָהָב׃
כט וַיַּעַשׂ אֶת־שֶׁמֶן הַמִּשְׁחָה קֹדֶשׁ וְאֶת־קְטֹרֶת הַסַּמִּים טָהוֹר מַעֲשֵׂה

29 acacia wood, overlaid with gold. As well as this, with the skill of a perfumer, he
38 1 prepared the sacred anointing oil and the fragrant incense. He made SHEVI'I /REVI'I/
the sacrificial altar of acacia wood, square, five cubits long, five cubits wide,
2 and three cubits high. He made horns on its four corners, of one piece with it,
3 and then overlaid it with bronze. He made all the altar's utensils: pots, shovels,
4 basins, forks, and pans, out of bronze. He made a grate of bronze mesh beneath
5 the ledge, extending downward to the middle of the altar. Four rings were cast
6 for the four corners of the bronze mesh, to hold the staves, which were made of
7 acacia wood and overlaid with bronze. He placed the staves in the rings on the
sides of the altar so that it could be carried. The altar itself was hollow, made of
8 planks. He made the bronze laver and its bronze base from the mirrors

רש״י

לח ז **נְבוּב לֻחֹת.** ׳נָבוּב׳ הוּא חָלוּל, וְכֵן: ״וְעָבְיוֹ אַרְבַּע אֶצְבָּעוֹת נָבוּב״ (ירמיה נב, כא): **נְבוּב לֻחֹת.** הַלּוּחוֹת שֶׁל עֲצֵי שִׁטִּים לְכָל רוּחַ, וְהֶחָלָל בָּאֶמְצַע:

ח **בְּמַרְאֹת הַצֹּבְאֹת.** בְּנוֹת יִשְׂרָאֵל הָיוּ בְּיָדָן מַרְאוֹת שֶׁרוֹאוֹת בָּהֶן כְּשֶׁהֵן מִתְקַשְּׁטוֹת, וְאַף אוֹתָן לֹא עִכְּבוּ מִלְּהָבִיא לְנִדְבַת הַמִּשְׁכָּן, וְהָיָה מוֹאֵס מֹשֶׁה בָּהֶן מִפְּנֵי שֶׁעֲשׂוּיִים לְיֵצֶר הָרָע. אָמַר לוֹ הַקָּדוֹשׁ בָּרוּךְ הוּא: קַבֵּל, כִּי אֵלּוּ חֲבִיבִין עָלַי מִן הַכֹּל, שֶׁעַל יְדֵיהֶם הֶעֱמִידוּ הַנָּשִׁים צְבָאוֹת רַבּוֹת בְּמִצְרַיִם. כְּשֶׁהָיוּ בַּעְלֵיהֶן יְגֵעִים בַּעֲבוֹדַת פֶּרֶךְ בַּשָּׂדֶה, הָיוּ הוֹלְכוֹת וּמוֹלִיכוֹת לָהֶם מַאֲכָל וּמִשְׁתֶּה וּמַאֲכִילוֹת אוֹתָם, וְנוֹטְלוֹת הַמַּרְאוֹת, וְכָל אַחַת רוֹאָה עַצְמָהּ עִם בַּעְלָהּ בַּמַּרְאָה, וּמְשַׁדַּלְתּוֹ בִּדְבָרִים: ׳אֲנִי נָאָה מִמְּךָ׳, וּמִתּוֹךְ כָּךְ מְבִיאוֹת אוֹתָם לִידֵי תַאֲוָה וְנִזְקָקוֹת לָהֶם וּמִתְעַבְּרוֹת וְיוֹלְדוֹת שָׁם, שֶׁנֶּאֱמַר: ״תַּחַת הַתַּפּוּחַ עוֹרַרְתִּיךָ״ (שיר השירים ח, ה), וְזֶהוּ שֶׁנֶּאֱמַר: ״בְּמַרְאֹת הַצֹּבְאֹת״. וְנַעֲשָׂה הַכִּיּוֹר מֵהֶם שֶׁהוּא לָשׂוּם שָׁלוֹם בֵּין אִישׁ לְאִשְׁתּוֹ, לְהַשְׁקוֹת מִמַּיִם שֶׁבְּתוֹכוֹ אֶת שֶׁקִּנֵּא לָהּ בַּעְלָהּ. וְתֵדַע לְךָ שֶׁהֵן מַרְאוֹת מַמָּשׁ, שֶׁהֲרֵי נֶאֱמַר: ״וּנְחֹשֶׁת הַתְּנוּפָה שִׁבְעִים כִּכָּר וְגוֹ׳ וַיַּעַשׂ בָּהּ״ וְגוֹ׳ (להלן פסוקים כט–ל), וְכִיּוֹר וְכַנּוֹ לֹא הֻזְכְּרוּ שָׁם, לָמַדְתָּ שֶׁלֹּא הָיָה נְחֹשֶׁת שֶׁל כִּיּוֹר מִנְּחֹשֶׁת הַתְּנוּפָה. כָּךְ דָּרַשׁ רַבִּי תַּנְחוּמָא (פקודי ט). וְכֵן תִּרְגֵּם אוּנְקְלוֹס: ״בְּמַחְזְיַת נְשַׁיָּא״, וְהוּא תַּרְגּוּם שֶׁל ׳מַרְאוֹת׳, מירואו״ר בְּלַעַז. וְכֵן מָצִינוּ בִּישַׁעְיָה: ״וְהַגִּלְיֹנִים״ (ג, כג) מְתַרְגְּמִינַן: ״וּמַחְזְיָתָא״: **אֲשֶׁר צָבְאוּ.** לְהָבִיא נִדְבָתָן:

So it is with faith. When all the science is in – when we know exactly when and how the universe came into being – the question will still be open. Does life have a meaning, a higher purpose? Are all our prayers in vain? Is there nothing beyond the physical universe? Are all our hopes illusions and our aspirations no more than self-deluding dreams?

Faith and faithlessness are framing beliefs. But which we choose makes all the difference. You can live without optimism and trust, just as you can live without music or a sense of humor. But it is a limited life. And in the same way, you can live without faith. But you will miss out on all that comes from the belief that life has a meaning, that God created the universe in love and forgiveness and asks us to love and forgive others. Like the smell of the incense enveloping Jerusalem, the mystery that is faith can pervade our lives and fill them, unmistakably, with a scent of holiness.

WOMEN AND THE MAKING OF THE TABERNACLE

The Torah goes out of its way to emphasize the role women played in making the Tabernacle. Indeed, an unusual locution in Ex. 35:22, *haanashim al hanashim*, "the men with the women," implies that the women came to make their donations first, and the men merely followed their lead (Ibn Ezra, Ramban, Rabbeinu Baḥya).

This cryptic verse hints at a further perspective. The Sages (Tanḥuma, Pekudei 9) told a story about it, retold here by Rashi:

> The Israelite women were in possession of mirrors that they used when adorning themselves. And yet, they did

שביעי /רביעי/

לח א רֹקֵחַ׃ וַיַּעַשׂ אֶת־מִזְבַּח הָעֹלָה עֲצֵי שִׁטִּים חָמֵשׁ אַמּוֹת
ב אָרְכּוֹ וְחָמֵשׁ־אַמּוֹת רָחְבּוֹ רָבוּעַ וְשָׁלֹשׁ אַמּוֹת קֹמָתוֹ׃ וַיַּעַשׂ קַרְנֹתָיו
ג עַל אַרְבַּע פִּנֹּתָיו מִמֶּנּוּ הָיוּ קַרְנֹתָיו וַיְצַף אֹתוֹ נְחֹשֶׁת׃ וַיַּעַשׂ אֶת־כָּל־
כְּלֵי הַמִּזְבֵּחַ אֶת־הַסִּירֹת וְאֶת־הַיָּעִים וְאֶת־הַמִּזְרָקֹת אֶת־הַמִּזְלָגֹת
ד וְאֶת־הַמַּחְתֹּת כָּל־כֵּלָיו עָשָׂה נְחֹשֶׁת׃ וַיַּעַשׂ לַמִּזְבֵּחַ מִכְבָּר מַעֲשֵׂה
ה רֶשֶׁת נְחֹשֶׁת תַּחַת כַּרְכֻּבּוֹ מִלְּמַטָּה עַד־חֶצְיוֹ׃ וַיִּצֹק אַרְבַּע טַבָּעֹת
ו בְּאַרְבַּע הַקְּצָוֹת לְמִכְבַּר הַנְּחֹשֶׁת בָּתִּים לַבַּדִּים׃ וַיַּעַשׂ אֶת־הַבַּדִּים
ז עֲצֵי שִׁטִּים וַיְצַף אֹתָם נְחֹשֶׁת׃ וַיָּבֵא אֶת־הַבַּדִּים בַּטַּבָּעֹת עַל צַלְעֹת
ח הַמִּזְבֵּחַ לָשֵׂאת אֹתוֹ בָּהֶם נְבוּב לֻחֹת עָשָׂה אֹתוֹ׃ וַיַּעַשׂ אֵת
הַכִּיּוֹר נְחֹשֶׁת וְאֵת כַּנּוֹ נְחֹשֶׁת בְּמַרְאֹת הַצֹּבְאֹת אֲשֶׁר צָבְאוּ פֶּתַח
ט אֹהֶל מוֹעֵד׃ וַיַּעַשׂ אֶת־הֶחָצֵר לִפְאַת ׀ נֶגֶב תֵּימָנָה קַלְעֵי

אונקלוס

כט וַעֲבַד, יָת מִשְׁחָא דִרְבוּתָא קֻדְשָׁא, וְיָת קְטֹרֶת בֻּסְמַיָּא דְּכֵי, עוֹבַד בָּסְמָנוּ׃ לח א וַעֲבַד, יָת מַדְבְּחָא דַעֲלָתָא דְּאָעֵי שִׁטִּין, חֲמֵשׁ אַמִּין אֻרְכֵּיהּ, וַחֲמֵשׁ אַמִּין פְּתָיֵהּ מְרַבַּע, וּתְלָת אַמִּין רוּמֵיהּ׃ ב וַעֲבַד קַרְנוֹהִי, עַל אַרְבַּע זָוְיָתֵיהּ, מִנֵּיהּ הֲוָאָה קַרְנוֹהִי, וַחֲפָא יָתֵיהּ נְחָשָׁא׃ ג וַעֲבַד יָת כָּל מָנֵי מַדְבְּחָא, יָת פְּסַכְתֵּירְוָתָא וְיָת מַגְרוֹפְיָתָא וְיָת מִזְרְקַיָּא, יָת צִנּוֹרְיָתָא וְיָת מַחְתְּיָתָא, כָּל מָנוֹהִי עֲבַד נְחָשָׁא׃ ד וַעֲבַד לְמַדְבְּחָא סְרָדָא, עוֹבַד מְצָדְתָא דִּנְחָשָׁא, תְּחוֹת סוֹבֵיבֵיהּ, מִלְּרַע עַד פַּלְגֵּיהּ׃ ה וְאַתֵּיךְ, אַרְבַּע עִזְקָן, בְּאַרְבַּע זָוְיָתָא לִסְרָדָא דִּנְחָשָׁא, אַתְרָא לַאֲרִיחַיָּא׃ ו וַעֲבַד יָת אֲרִיחַיָּא דְּאָעֵי שִׁטִּין, וַחֲפָא יָתְהוֹן נְחָשָׁא׃ ז וְאַעֵיל יָת אֲרִיחַיָּא בְּעִזְקָתָא, עַל סִטְרֵי מַדְבְּחָא, לְמִטַּל יָתֵיהּ בְּהוֹן, חֲלִיל לוּחִין עֲבַד יָתֵיהּ׃ ח וַעֲבַד, יָת כִּיּוֹרָא דִּנְחָשָׁא, וְיָת בְּסִיסֵיהּ דִּנְחָשָׁא, בְּמַחְזְיָת נְשַׁיָּא, דְּאָתְיָן לְצַלָּאָה, בִּתְרַע מַשְׁכַּן

37:29 וְאֶת־קְטֹרֶת הַסַּמִּים טָהוֹר מַעֲשֵׂה רֹקֵחַ *With the skill of a perfumer… the fragrant incense* – While sacrifices were offered only in the Tabernacle and later the Temple, the Mishna tells us that the scent of the incense spread out so far from Jerusalem that "goats … on Mount Mikhvar [beyond the River Jordan] would sneeze" (Tamid 3:8). As with worship, so with knowledge; there are things that are limited and measurable, and things, equally real, that cannot be pinned down and yet color everything else. What we call "faith" falls in the latter category.

Does faith make a difference? And is it possible to have faith, even in the twenty-first century, after all we have learned from science? The answer to both questions is yes. Jewish faith isn't irrational or naive or prescientific. Faith is what I call a framing belief.

Compare trust. Is it right or wrong to go through life trusting people? Some do. Some don't. If you trust people, some of them will take advantage of you, and it will hurt. If you go through life cynical and suspicious, you will protect yourself against betrayal, but never know love or friendship, the deep communion of souls. There are some things you cannot achieve without trust. So which is the rational option: trust or suspicion? There is no rational option. These are framing beliefs.

9 of the women who served at the entrance of the Tent of Meeting. He
made the courtyard thus: on the south side, the hangings were of finely spun
10 linen, a hundred cubits long, with twenty posts and their twenty bronze
11 sockets. The posts' hooks and bands were of silver. Likewise on the north side:
the hangings were a hundred cubits long, with twenty pillars and their bronze
12 sockets, and hooks and bands of silver. On the west side the hangings were
fifty cubits long, with ten posts and ten sockets, and hooks and bands of silver.
13 14 The east side was also fifty cubits long: fifteen cubits of hangings with three
15 posts and three sockets on one side, and fifteen cubits of hangings with three
16 posts and three sockets on the other. All the hangings of the courtyard were
17 of finely spun linen. The sockets for the posts were of bronze, the posts' hooks
and bands were of silver, and their tops were overlaid with silver; all the posts
18 had silver bands. At the entrance of the courtyard there was an embroidered MAFTIR

---

and sexual desire, so that the Israelites would have no more children.

The women realized this, and decided to frustrate Pharaoh's plan. As Rashi writes,

> As they visited with their men, the women would invite them to gaze at their reflections in the mirrors. Flirting with her husband, a wife would say: "You know I'm more beautiful than you are!" This sort of talk had the effect of arousing the men who would sleep with their wives, who would then conceive and give birth there as the verse states: "Beneath the apple tree I roused you where your mother bore you" (Song. 8:5). This is why the mirrors are referred to as *mar'ot hatzove'ot* ["mirrors of the women who served," but also: "mirrors of the hosts," that is, the mirrors of the multitudes of Israelite children who were born thanks to their use]. And this is why the mirrors were repurposed to make the laver.

Intimate relations resumed. The women conceived. Because of this was there a new generation of Jewish children. The women, by their faith, courage, and ingenuity, secured Jewish survival.

The story tells us that without the faith of women, Jews and Judaism would never have survived. But it also tells us something fundamental to the Jewish understanding of love in the religious life. Where classical Greece drew a distinction between *eros* (love as intense physical desire) and *agape* (a calm, detached love of humanity in general and things in general), Judaism sees love as supremely both physical *and* spiritual. This is the love we find in passages like Psalms 63:2: "My soul thirsts for You, my flesh longs for You in a parched and weary land that has no water." This is not the language of meditation or contemplation, philosophical or mystical. It is the language of passion.

Moshe, in Rashi's account of our verse, believes that closeness to God is about celibacy and purity. God teaches him otherwise, that passionate love, when offered as a gift to God, is the most precious love of all. The women, who offered to God the mirrors through which they aroused their husbands' love in the dark days of Egypt, understand what it means to love God "with all your heart, with all your soul, and with all your might" (Deut. 6:5).

THE COMPLETION OF THE BUILDING WORK

From the Ark of the Covenant to the bronze pegs, the Tabernacle and its furnishings are now complete. But this is not enough: After the making of the golden calf in Parashat Ki Tisa, life needed to begin again. A shattered people had to be rebuilt. This is the other story of our *parasha*. The verb *vayak'hel*, "[Moshe] assembled," is crucial to an understanding of his task. For the use of this word at the start of the *parasha* reminds us of an earlier occasion on which it appeared:

י הֶחָצֵר שֵׁשׁ מָשְׁזָר מֵאָה בָּאַמָּה׃ עַמּוּדֵיהֶם עֶשְׂרִים וְאַדְנֵיהֶם עֶשְׂרִים
יא נְחֹשֶׁת וָוֵי הָעַמּוּדִים וַחֲשֻׁקֵיהֶם כָּסֶף׃ וְלִפְאַת צָפוֹן מֵאָה בָאַמָּה
עַמּוּדֵיהֶם עֶשְׂרִים וְאַדְנֵיהֶם עֶשְׂרִים נְחֹשֶׁת וָוֵי הָעַמּוּדִים וַחֲשֻׁקֵיהֶם
יב כָּסֶף׃ וְלִפְאַת־יָם קְלָעִים חֲמִשִּׁים בָּאַמָּה עַמּוּדֵיהֶם עֲשָׂרָה וְאַדְנֵיהֶם
יג עֲשָׂרָה וָוֵי הָעַמֻּדִים וַחֲשׁוּקֵיהֶם כָּסֶף׃ וְלִפְאַת קֵדְמָה מִזְרָחָה חֲמִשִּׁים
יד אַמָּה׃ קְלָעִים חֲמֵשׁ־עֶשְׂרֵה אַמָּה אֶל־הַכָּתֵף עַמּוּדֵיהֶם שְׁלֹשָׁה
טו וְאַדְנֵיהֶם שְׁלֹשָׁה׃ וְלַכָּתֵף הַשֵּׁנִית מִזֶּה וּמִזֶּה לְשַׁעַר הֶחָצֵר קְלָעִים
טז חֲמֵשׁ עֶשְׂרֵה אַמָּה עַמֻּדֵיהֶם שְׁלֹשָׁה וְאַדְנֵיהֶם שְׁלֹשָׁה׃ כָּל־קַלְעֵי
יז הֶחָצֵר סָבִיב שֵׁשׁ מָשְׁזָר׃ וְהָאֲדָנִים לָעַמֻּדִים נְחֹשֶׁת וָוֵי הָעַמּוּדִים
וַחֲשׁוּקֵיהֶם כֶּסֶף וְצִפּוּי רָאשֵׁיהֶם כָּסֶף וְהֵם מְחֻשָּׁקִים כֶּסֶף כֹּל עַמֻּדֵי
יח הֶחָצֵר׃ וּמָסַךְ שַׁעַר הֶחָצֵר מַעֲשֵׂה רֹקֵם תְּכֵלֶת וְאַרְגָּמָן וְתוֹלַעַת שָׁנִי מפטיר
וְשֵׁשׁ מָשְׁזָר וְעֶשְׂרִים אַמָּה אֹרֶךְ וְקוֹמָה בְרֹחַב חָמֵשׁ אַמּוֹת לְעֻמַּת

אונקלוס

זִמְנָא: ט וַעֲבַד יָת דָּרְתָא, לְרוּחַ עֵיבַר דָּרוֹמָא, סְרָדֵי דָרְתָא דְּבוּץ שְׁזִיר, מְאָה אַמִּין: י עַמּוּדֵיהוֹן עַסְרִין, וְסָמְכֵיהוֹן עַסְרִין דִּנְחָשָׁא, וָוֵי עַמּוּדַיָּא, וְכִבּוּשֵׁיהוֹן כְּסַף: יא וּלְרוּחַ צִפּוּנָא מְאָה אַמִּין, עַמּוּדֵיהוֹן עַסְרִין, וְסָמְכֵיהוֹן עַסְרִין דִּנְחָשָׁא, וָוֵי עַמּוּדַיָּא, וְכִבּוּשֵׁיהוֹן כְּסַף: יב וּלְרוּחַ מַעַרְבָא, סְרָדֵי חַמְשִׁין אַמִּין, עַמּוּדֵיהוֹן עַסְרָא, וְסָמְכֵיהוֹן עַסְרָא, וָוֵי עַמּוּדַיָּא, וְכִבּוּשֵׁיהוֹן כְּסַף: יג וּלְרוּחַ קִדּוּמָא מַדִּנְחָא חַמְשִׁין אַמִּין: יד סְרָדֵי, חֲמֵשׁ עַסְרֵי אַמִּין לְעִבְרָא, עַמּוּדֵיהוֹן תְּלָתָא, וְסָמְכֵיהוֹן תְּלָתָא: טו וּלְעִבְרָא תִנְיָנָא, מִכָּא וּמִכָּא לִתְרַע דָּרְתָא, סְרָדֵי, חֲמֵשׁ עַסְרֵי אַמִּין, עַמּוּדֵיהוֹן תְּלָתָא, וְסָמְכֵיהוֹן תְּלָתָא: טז כָּל סְרָדֵי דָרְתָא, סְחוֹר סְחוֹר דְּבוּץ שְׁזִיר: יז וְסָמְכַיָּא לְעַמּוּדַיָּא דִּנְחָשָׁא, וָוֵי עַמּוּדַיָּא, וְכִבּוּשֵׁיהוֹן כְּסַף, וְחִפּוּי רֵישֵׁיהוֹן כְּסַף, וְאִנּוּן מְכַבְּשִׁין כְּסַף, כָּל עַמּוּדֵי דָּרְתָא: יח וּפְרָסָא, דִּתְרַע דָּרְתָא עוֹבַד צַיָּר, תַּכְלָא וְאַרְגְּוָנָא, וּצְבַע זְהוֹרִי וּבוּץ שְׁזִיר, וְעַסְרִין אַמִּין אֻרְכָּא, וְרוּמָא בִּפְתָיָא חֲמֵשׁ אַמִּין,

not hesitate to donate them to the Tabernacle project. Now at first Moshe considered the mirrors distasteful and inappropriate, because these objects indulged the evil inclination. But the Holy One, blessed be He, said: You should accept these mirrors, for they are dearer to Me than any of the other donations the people have brought. For it was these mirrors that assisted Israel to burgeon to huge numbers in Egypt. While the women's husbands were exhausting themselves with oppressive labor in the fields, their wives would bring them food and drink to sustain them.

The Egyptians sought not merely to enslave but also to put an end to the people of Israel. One way of doing so was to kill all male children. Another was to interrupt normal family life. The people, both men and women, were laboring all day. At night, says the Midrash, they were forbidden to return home. The intention was to destroy both privacy

screen of sky-blue, purple, and scarlet wool and finely spun linen, twenty cubits
19 long and five cubits wide, like the hangings of the courtyard. It had four posts
with four bronze sockets and with hooks and bands of silver; their tops were
20 overlaid with silver. All the tent pegs for the Tabernacle and the surrounding
courtyard were of bronze.

The haftara for Parashat Vayak'hel is on page 1554.
When Vayak'hel and Pekudei are read together read the haftara on page 1556.

On the Shabbat of Parashat Shekalim read the haftara on page 1642.
On the Shabbat of Parashat Para read the haftara on page 1648.
On the Shabbat of Parashat HaḤodesh read the haftara on page 1650.

רש״י

יח | לְעֻמַּת קַלְעֵי הֶחָצֵר. כְּמִדַּת קַלְעֵי הֶחָצֵר:

(Berakhot 64a). People have to become builders if they are to grow from childhood to adulthood.

The building of the Tabernacle was the first great project the Israelites undertook together. It involved their generosity and skill. It gave them the chance to give back to God a little of what He had given them. It conferred on them the dignity of labor and creative endeavor. It brought to closure their birth as a nation and it symbolized the challenge of the future. The society they were summoned to create in the land of Israel would be one in which everyone would play their part. As John Ruskin wrote, "The highest reward for a man's toil is not what he gets from it, but what he becomes by it." Or as the early Zionist settlers said, they came to the land "*livnot u'lehibanot,* to build and to be built."

Hence the principle of Judaism that we are called on to become co-creators with God. And hence, too, the corollary: that leaders do not do the work on behalf of the people. They teach people how to do the work. It is not what God does for us but what we do for God that allows us to reach dignity and responsibility. A community is a group of people who build something together. "All your children will be students of the LORD, and great will be your children's peace": How do you lay the groundwork for peace? asked the Rabbis. By turning children into builders.

יט קַלְעֵ֥י הֶחָצֵֽר׃ וְעַמֻּֽדֵיהֶם֙ אַרְבָּעָ֔ה וְאַדְנֵיהֶ֥ם אַרְבָּעָ֖ה נְחֹ֑שֶׁת וָוֵיהֶ֣ם
כ כֶּ֔סֶף וְצִפּ֧וּי רָאשֵׁיהֶ֛ם וַחֲשֻׁקֵיהֶ֖ם כָּֽסֶף׃ וְֽכָל־הַיְתֵדֹ֗ת לַמִּשְׁכָּ֛ן וְלֶחָצֵ֖ר
סָבִ֑יב נְחֹֽשֶׁת׃

The הפטרה *for* פרשת ויקהל *is on page 1555.*
When ויקהל *and* פקודי *are read together read the* הפטרה *on page 1557.*

On the שבת *of* פרשת שקלים *read the* הפטרה *on page 1643.*
On the שבת *of* פרשת פרה *read the* הפטרה *on page 1649.*
On the שבת *of* פרשת החודש *read the* הפטרה *on 1651.*

אונקלוס

לָקֳבֵיל סְרָדֵי דָּרְתָּא: יט וְעַמּוּדֵיהוֹן אַרְבְּעָא, וְסָמְכֵיהוֹן אַרְבְּעָא
דִּנְחָשָׁא, וָוֵיהוֹן כְּסַף, וְחִפּוּי רֵישֵׁיהוֹן, וְכִבּוּשֵׁיהוֹן כְּסַף: כ וְכָל
סִכַּיָּא, לְמַשְׁכְּנָא וּלְדָרְתָא, סְחוֹר סְחוֹר דִּנְחָשָׁא:

> When the people saw that Moshe was long delayed in coming down the mountain, they gathered (*vayikahel*) around Aharon and said to him, "Get up, make us gods to go before us." (Ex. 32:1)

Vayak'hel is the redemption of a past misdemeanor. Just as the sin of the calf was committed by the people acting as a community (a *kahal* or *kehilla*), so atonement is to be achieved by their again acting as a *kehilla*, this time by making a home for the Divine Presence as they earlier sought to make a substitute for it. Just as the people were assembled for bad, so they have now been gathered for good.

This simple action has transformed the Israelites. During the whole time the Tabernacle was being constructed, there were no complaints, no rebellions, no dissension. The people contributed – some gold or silver or bronze, some brought skins and drapes, others gave their time and skill. They gave so much that Moshe had to order them to stop.

The people had to become God's "partners in the work of creation" (Shabbat 10a). That, I believe, is what the Sages meant when they reinterpreted a verse in the book of Isaiah: "All your children will be students of the LORD, and great will be your children's peace" (54:13). To this the Rabbis added a comment, based on a Hebrew wordplay: "Call them not 'your children' (*banayikh*) but 'your builders' (*bonayikh*)"

Parashat Pekudei

38 21 These are the accounts of the Tabernacle, the Tabernacle of testimony, recorded
at Moshe's command by the Levites under Itamar, son of Aharon the priest.
22 Betzalel, son of Uri, son of Ḥur, from the tribe of Yehuda, made everything
23 that the LORD had commanded Moshe. He was assisted by Oholiav, son of
Aḥisamakh, from the tribe of Dan, an engraver, designer, and embroiderer in
24 sky-blue, purple, and scarlet wool and fine linen. All the gold used in all
the sacred work, donated as wave offerings, came to twenty-nine talents and 730
25 shekels according to the Sanctuary weight. The silver of those recorded in the

רש״י

כא| **אֵלֶּה פְקוּדֵי.** בְּפָרָשָׁה זוֹ נִמְנוּ כָּל מִשְׁקְלֵי נִדְבַת הַמִּשְׁכָּן לַכֶּסֶף, לַזָּהָב וְלַנְּחֹשֶׁת, וְנִמְנוּ כָּל כֵּלָיו לְכָל עֲבוֹדָתוֹ: **הַמִּשְׁכָּן מִשְׁכַּן.** שְׁנֵי פְעָמִים, רֶמֶז לַמִּקְדָּשׁ שֶׁנִּתְמַשְׁכֵּן בִּשְׁנֵי חֻרְבָּנִין עַל עֲוֹנוֹתֵיהֶן שֶׁל יִשְׂרָאֵל: **מִשְׁכַּן הָעֵדֻת.** עֵדוּת לְיִשְׂרָאֵל שֶׁוִּתֵּר לָהֶם הַקָּדוֹשׁ בָּרוּךְ הוּא עַל מַעֲשֵׂה הָעֵגֶל, שֶׁהֲרֵי הִשְׁרָה שְׁכִינָתוֹ בֵּינֵיהֶם: **עֲבֹדַת הַלְוִיִּם.** פְּקוּדֵי הַמִּשְׁכָּן וְכֵלָיו הִיא עֲבוֹדָה הַמְּסוּרָה לַלְוִיִּם בַּמִּדְבָּר, לָשֵׂאת וּלְהוֹרִיד וּלְהָקִים אִישׁ אִישׁ לְמַשָּׂאוֹ הַמֻּפְקָד עָלָיו, כְּמוֹ שֶׁאָמוּר בְּפָרָשַׁת נָשֹׂא (במדבר ד): **בְּיַד אִיתָמָר.** הוּא הָיָה פָּקִיד עֲלֵיהֶם, לִמְסֹר לְכָל בֵּית אָב עֲבוֹדָה שֶׁעָלָיו:

כב| **וּבְצַלְאֵל בֶּן אוּרִי... עָשָׂה.** ״אֵת כָּל אֲשֶׁר צִוָּה אוֹתוֹ מֹשֶׁה״ אֵין כְּתִיב כָּאן אֶלָּא ״אֵת כָּל אֲשֶׁר צִוָּה ה׳ אֶת מֹשֶׁה״, אֲפִלּוּ דְּבָרִים שֶׁלֹּא אָמַר לוֹ רַבּוֹ הִסְכִּימָה דַּעְתּוֹ לְמַה שֶּׁנֶּאֱמַר לְמֹשֶׁה בְּסִינַי:

כד| **כִּכָּר.** שִׁשִּׁים מָנֶה. וּמָנֶה שֶׁל קֹדֶשׁ כָּפוּל הָיָה, הֲרֵי הַכִּכָּר מֵאָה וְעֶשְׂרִים מָנֶה, וְהַמָּנֶה עֶשְׂרִים וַחֲמִשָּׁה סְלָעִים, הֲרֵי כִּכָּר שֶׁל קֹדֶשׁ שְׁלֹשֶׁת אֲלָפִים שְׁקָלִים, לְפִיכָךְ מָנָה בִּפְרוֹטְרוֹט כָּל הַשְּׁקָלִים שֶׁפְּחוּתִין בְּמִנְיָנָם מִשְּׁלֹשֶׁת אֲלָפִים שֶׁאֵין מַגִּיעִין לְכִכָּר:

Moshe, a man of complete honesty, may thus have acted "beyond the strict requirement of the law" (Berakhot 45b). It is precisely the fact that Moshe did not need to do what he did that gives the passage its force. Trust is of the essence in public life. There must be transparency and accountability when it comes to public funds even if the people involved have impeccable reputations. A nation that suspects its leaders of corruption cannot function effectively as a free, just, and open society.

It is the mark of a good society that public leadership is seen as a form of service rather than a means to power, which is all too easily abused. A free society is built on moral foundations, and those must be unshakable. Moshe's personal example, in giving an accounting of the funds that had been collected for the first collective project of the Jewish people, sets a vital precedent for all time.

Levites under Itamar," in other words, by independent auditors.

Accusations of corruption and personal enrichment have often been leveled against leaders, both with and without justification. We might think that since God sees all we do, this is enough to safeguard against wrongdoing. Yet Judaism never says this. When humans commit a sin they worry that other people might see them. They forget that God certainly sees them. Temptation befuddles the brain, and no one should believe they are immune to it.

Interestingly, a later passage in Tanakh seems to indicate that Moshe's accounting was not strictly necessary. The book of Kings relates an episode in which, during the reign of King Yehoash, money was raised for the restoration of the Temple: "They did not need to keep track of the men who received the money to pay out to the workers, for they dealt honestly" (II Kings 12:16).

פרשת פקודי

לח כא אֵלֶּה פְקוּדֵי הַמִּשְׁכָּן מִשְׁכַּן הָעֵדֻת אֲשֶׁר פֻּקַּד עַל־פִּי מֹשֶׁה עֲבֹדַת כח
כב הַלְוִיִּם בְּיַד אִיתָמָר בֶּן־אַהֲרֹן הַכֹּהֵן׃ וּבְצַלְאֵל בֶּן־אוּרִי בֶן־חוּר לְמַטֵּה
כג יְהוּדָה עָשָׂה אֵת כָּל־אֲשֶׁר־צִוָּה יְהוָה אֶת־מֹשֶׁה׃ וְאִתּוֹ אָהֳלִיאָב בֶּן־
אֲחִיסָמָךְ לְמַטֵּה־דָן חָרָשׁ וְחֹשֵׁב וְרֹקֵם בַּתְּכֵלֶת וּבָאַרְגָּמָן וּבְתוֹלַעַת
כד הַשָּׁנִי וּבַשֵּׁשׁ׃ כָּל־הַזָּהָב הֶעָשׂוּי לַמְּלָאכָה בְּכֹל מְלֶאכֶת
הַקֹּדֶשׁ וַיְהִי ׀ זְהַב הַתְּנוּפָה תֵּשַׁע וְעֶשְׂרִים כִּכָּר וּשְׁבַע מֵאוֹת וּשְׁלֹשִׁים
כה שֶׁקֶל בְּשֶׁקֶל הַקֹּדֶשׁ׃ וְכֶסֶף פְּקוּדֵי הָעֵדָה מְאַת כִּכָּר וְאֶלֶף וּשְׁבַע

אונקלוס

כא אִלֵּין מִנְיָנֵי מַשְׁכְּנָא מַשְׁכְּנָא דְסָהֲדוּתָא, דְּאִתְמְנִיאוּ עַל מֵימְרָא דְּמֹשֶׁה, פָּלְחַן לֵיוָאֵי, בִּידָא דְּאִיתָמָר, בַּר אַהֲרֹן כָּהֲנָא: כב וּבְצַלְאֵל, בַּר אוּרִי בַר חוּר לְשִׁבְטָא דִּיהוּדָה, עֲבַד, יָת כָּל דְּפַקֵּיד יי יָת מֹשֶׁה: כג וְעִמֵּיהּ, אָהֳלִיאָב, בַּר אֲחִיסָמָךְ, לְשִׁבְטָא דְּדָן נַגַּר וְאֻמָּן, וְצַיָּר, בְּתַכְלָא וּבְאַרְגְּוָנָא, וּבִצְבַע זְהוֹרִי וּבְבוּצָא: כד כָּל דַּהֲבָא, דְּאִתְעֲבֵיד לַעֲבִידְתָא, בְּכֹל עֲבִידַת קֻדְשָׁא, וַהֲוָה דְּהַב אֲרָמוּתָא, עֶסְרִין וּתְשַׁע כַּכְּרִין, וּשְׁבַע מְאָה וּתְלָתִין, סִלְעִין בְּסִלְעֵי קֻדְשָׁא: כה וּכְסַף, מִנְיָנֵי כְּנִשְׁתָּא מְאָה כַּכְּרִין, וְאֶלֶף וּשְׁבַע

PEKUDEI

With Pekudei, the book of Exodus reaches its end, if not its closure. Moshe orders an account to be made of all the donations given for the construction of the Tabernacle and how they were used. The priestly garments are sewn. No sooner has Moshe finally erected the Tabernacle than there is an epiphany, a majestic disclosure of the Divine Presence. After a tale full of setbacks, the Israelites have made a home for God, and His presence is now constantly in their midst.

Concluding the book of Exodus will enable us to look back at its remarkable narrative structure, the pattern beneath the surface, showing how tightly it, together with Genesis, forms a literary unity of immense coherence and power, in which, through a series of dramas both personal and political, the meaning of the universe and our place within it are explored.

THE ACCOUNTS OF THE TABERNACLE

Parashat Pekudei derives its name from the detailed account, or reckoning, of the contributions made toward the construction of the Tabernacle. Its opening passage lists the exact amounts of gold, silver, and bronze collected, and the purposes to which they were put. Why did Moshe give this precise accounting? A midrash suggests an answer:

> "And watch Moshe" (Ex. 33:8) – People criticized Moshe. They used to say to one another, "… Moshe is eating and drinking what belongs to us. All that he has belongs to us." The other would reply: "A man who is in charge of the work of the Sanctuary – what do you expect? That he should not get rich?" As soon as he heard this, Moshe replied, "By your life, as soon as the Sanctuary is complete, I will make a full reckoning with you." (Tanḥuma, Buber, Pekudei 4)

Moshe issued a detailed reckoning to avoid coming under suspicion that he had personally appropriated some of the donated money. Note the emphasis that the accounting was undertaken not by Moshe himself but "by the

▶

census came to a hundred talents and 1,775 shekels, according to the Sanctuary
26 weight. One beka – half a shekel according to the Sanctuary weight – was given
27 by each of the 603,550 men aged twenty or over included in the census. A
hundred talents of silver were used for casting the sockets of the Sanctuary
and the curtain, one talent for each socket: a hundred talents for the hundred
28 sockets. Of 1,775 shekels he made the hooks and bands of the posts and their
29 silver-plated tops. The bronze given as an offering came to seventy talents and
30 2,400 shekels. With this were made the sockets for the entrance of the Tent
of Meeting, the bronze altar with its bronze mesh, and all the utensils of the
31 altar, the sockets around the courtyard, the sockets at the courtyard gate, and
39 1 all the tent pegs for the Tabernacle and the surrounding courtyard. From the
sky-blue, purple, and scarlet wool they made woven garments for ministering
in the Sanctuary. They also made sacred vestments for Aharon, as the LORD
commanded Moshe.

רש״י

כו **בֶּקַע.** הוּא שֵׁם מִשְׁקָל שֶׁל מַחֲצִית הַשֶּׁקֶל: **לְשֵׁשׁ מֵאוֹת אֶלֶף וְגוֹ׳.** כָּךְ הָיוּ יִשְׂרָאֵל, וְכָךְ עָלָה מִנְיָנָם אַחַר שֶׁהוּקַם הַמִּשְׁכָּן בְּסֵפֶר וַיְדַבֵּר (במדבר ב, לב), וְאַף עַתָּה בְּנִדְבַת הַמִּשְׁכָּן כָּךְ הָיוּ. וּמִנְיַן חֲצָאֵי הַשְּׁקָלִים שֶׁל שֵׁשׁ מֵאוֹת אֶלֶף עוֹלֶה מְאַת כִּכָּר, כָּל אֶחָד שֶׁל שְׁלֹשֶׁת אֲלָפִים שְׁקָלִים. כֵּיצַד? שֵׁשׁ מֵאוֹת אֶלֶף חֲצָאִין, הֲרֵי הֵן שְׁלֹשׁ מֵאוֹת אֶלֶף שְׁלֵמִים, הֲרֵי מְאַת כִּכָּר. וְהַשְּׁלֹשֶׁת אֲלָפִים וַחֲמֵשׁ מֵאוֹת וַחֲמִשִּׁים חֲצָאִין, עוֹלִין אֶלֶף וּשְׁבַע מֵאוֹת וַחֲמִשָּׁה וְשִׁבְעִים שְׁקָלִים:

כז **לָצֶקֶת.** ״לְהַתִּיךְ״: **אֵת אַדְנֵי הַקֹּדֶשׁ.** שֶׁל קַרְשֵׁי הַמִּשְׁכָּן, שֶׁהֵם אַרְבָּעִים וּשְׁמוֹנָה קְרָשִׁים וְלָהֶן תִּשְׁעִים וְשִׁשָּׁה אֲדָנִים, וְאַדְנֵי הַפָּרֹכֶת אַרְבָּעָה, הֲרֵי מֵאָה. וְכָל שְׁאָר הָאֲדָנִים ״נְחֹשֶׁת״ כָּתוּב בָּהֶם:

כח **וְצִפָּה רָאשֵׁיהֶם.** שֶׁל עַמּוּדִים מֵהֶם, שֶׁבְּכֻלָּן כָּתוּב וְצִפָּה רָאשֵׁיהֶם וַחֲשֻׁקֵיהֶם כָּסֶף (עיין לעיל לח, י-כ):

לט א **וּמִן הַתְּכֵלֶת וְהָאַרְגָּמָן וְגוֹ׳.** שֵׁשׁ לֹא נֶאֱמַר כָּאן; מִכָּאן אֲנִי אוֹמֵר שֶׁאֵין בִּגְדֵי שְׂרָד הַלָּלוּ בִּגְדֵי כְהֻנָּה, שֶׁבְּבִגְדֵי כְהֻנָּה הָיָה שֵׁשׁ, אֶלָּא הֵם בְּגָדִים שֶׁמְּכַסִּים בָּהֶם כְּלֵי הַקֹּדֶשׁ בִּשְׁעַת סִלּוּק מַסָּעוֹת, שֶׁלֹּא הָיָה בָהֶם שֵׁשׁ:

Noaḥ did so: all that *God commanded him, he fulfilled.* (Gen. 6:22)

Noaḥ did *all that the LORD commanded him.* (7:5)

They came, male and female of all flesh, *as God had commanded him.* (7:16)

Do these two passages, taken together, tell us something larger about the biblical vision? The first eleven chapters of Genesis and the book of Exodus as a whole tell a story of human failure – a failure to observe the moral order by which life, liberty, and human dignity are sacred. The result in both cases was catastrophe: in the first, a world ruined by the flood, in the second, an Egypt devastated by the plagues. Both stories involve a physical construction, an ark and a Tabernacle, and in both, the Torah's emphasis is on precise dimensions ordained by God and faithfully carried out by human beings.

There is, to be sure, a great difference between these two structures. Noaḥ needed the ark only until the floodwaters subsided. The Israelites need the Tabernacle, or some equivalent of it (the Temple, later the synagogue), forever. Yet both were symbols of order in a disordered world. The Tabernacle will be the symbolic focus of Israel's collective life. It tells them that they are a nation at whose center is the Divine Presence. It bears witness to the sovereignty of right over might, the rule of justice over the rule of power. It is their ark in the wilderness. Without sacred order, there is no social order.

There is deep symbolism here: God creates order.

כו מֵאוֹת וַחֲמִשָּׁה וְשִׁבְעִים שֶׁקֶל בְּשֶׁקֶל הַקֹּדֶשׁ׃ בֶּקַע לַגֻּלְגֹּלֶת מַחֲצִית
הַשֶּׁקֶל בְּשֶׁקֶל הַקֹּדֶשׁ לְכֹל הָעֹבֵר עַל־הַפְּקֻדִים מִבֶּן עֶשְׂרִים שָׁנָה
וָמַעְלָה לְשֵׁשׁ־מֵאוֹת אֶלֶף וּשְׁלֹשֶׁת אֲלָפִים וַחֲמֵשׁ מֵאוֹת וַחֲמִשִּׁים׃
כז וַיְהִי מְאַת כִּכַּר הַכֶּסֶף לָצֶקֶת אֵת אַדְנֵי הַקֹּדֶשׁ וְאֵת אַדְנֵי הַפָּרֹכֶת
כח מְאַת אֲדָנִים לִמְאַת הַכִּכָּר כִּכָּר לָאָדֶן׃ וְאֶת־הָאֶלֶף וּשְׁבַע הַמֵּאוֹת
וַחֲמִשָּׁה וְשִׁבְעִים עָשָׂה וָוִים לָעַמּוּדִים וְצִפָּה רָאשֵׁיהֶם וְחִשַּׁק אֹתָם׃
כט ל וּנְחֹשֶׁת הַתְּנוּפָה שִׁבְעִים כִּכָּר וְאַלְפַּיִם וְאַרְבַּע־מֵאוֹת שָׁקֶל׃ וַיַּעַשׂ
בָּהּ אֶת־אַדְנֵי פֶּתַח אֹהֶל מוֹעֵד וְאֵת מִזְבַּח הַנְּחֹשֶׁת וְאֶת־מִכְבַּר
לא הַנְּחֹשֶׁת אֲשֶׁר־לוֹ וְאֵת כָּל־כְּלֵי הַמִּזְבֵּחַ׃ וְאֶת־אַדְנֵי הֶחָצֵר סָבִיב
וְאֶת־אַדְנֵי שַׁעַר הֶחָצֵר וְאֵת כָּל־יִתְדֹת הַמִּשְׁכָּן וְאֶת־כָּל־יִתְדֹת
לט א הֶחָצֵר סָבִיב׃ וּמִן־הַתְּכֵלֶת וְהָאַרְגָּמָן וְתוֹלַעַת הַשָּׁנִי עָשׂוּ בִגְדֵי־שְׂרָד
לְשָׁרֵת בַּקֹּדֶשׁ וַיַּעֲשׂוּ אֶת־בִּגְדֵי הַקֹּדֶשׁ אֲשֶׁר לְאַהֲרֹן כַּאֲשֶׁר צִוָּה יהוה
אֶת־מֹשֶׁה׃

אונקלוס

מאה, ושבעין וחמש, סלעין בסלעי קודשא: כו תקלא לגלגלתא, פלגות סלעא בסלעי קודשא, לכל דעבר על מניניא, מבר עסרין שנין ולעילא, לשית מאה ותלתא אלפין, וחמש מאה וחמשין: כז והואה, מאה ככרי כספא, לאתכא, ית סמכי קודשא, וית סמכי פרכתא, מאה סמכין, למאה ככרין ככרא לסמכא: כח וית אלף, ושבע מאה ושבעין וחמש, עבד ווין לעמודיא, וחפי רישיהון וכביש יתהון: כט ונחש ארמותא שבעין ככרין, ותרין אלפין וארבע מאה סלעין: ל ועבד בה, ית סמכי תרע משכן זמנא, וית מדבחא דנחשא, וית סרדא דנחשא דיליה, וית כל מני מדבחא: לא וית סמכי דרתא סחור סחור, וית סמכי תרע דרתא, וית כל סכי משכנא, וית כל סכי דרתא סחור סחור: לט א ומן תכלא וארגונא וצבע זהורי, עבדו לבושי שמושא לשמשא בקודשא, ועבדו, ית לבושי קודשא דלאהרן, כמא דפקיד יי ית משה:

39:1 כַּאֲשֶׁר צִוָּה יהוה אֶת־מֹשֶׁה *As the LORD commanded Moshe* – Parashat Pekudei, and with it the book of Exodus as a whole, draws to a conclusion with an extraordinary emphasis on obedience. This phrase, "as the LORD commanded Moshe," appears seven times in the passage describing how the Israelites constructed the Tabernacle, and the formula "as the LORD commanded" appears three additional times in the summarizing verses, 39:32–43. In the next chapter, narrating how Moshe set up the Tabernacle, seven times we hear the phrase "as the LORD commanded him." Where have we heard this language before?

The answer takes us back to another construction project, the first in the Torah: Noaḥ's ark. Three times we hear virtually the same phrase:

SHENI /HAMISHI/

2 He made the ephod of gold, with sky-blue, purple, and scarlet wool and finely
3 spun linen. They hammered out thin sheets of gold and cut strands to be worked
into the sky-blue, purple, and scarlet wool and fine linen – highly skilled work.
4 They made fixed shoulder pieces for the ephod; these were affixed to its two
5 ends. Its decorated waistband was like it and of one piece with the ephod, made
with gold, with sky-blue, purple, and scarlet wool and finely spun linen, as the
6 LORD commanded Moshe. They mounted the rock crystal stones in
gold filigree settings and engraved them as a seal with the names of Yisrael's
7 sons. He fastened them on the shoulder pieces of the ephod as remembrance
stones for Yisrael's sons, as the LORD commanded Moshe.
8 He made the breast piece with the same skilled craftsmanship as the ephod:
9 of gold, of sky-blue, purple, and scarlet wool, and of finely spun linen. It was
10 square and folded double, a span long and a span wide. Then they mounted
four rows of precious stones on it. The first row was a carnelian, an olivine,
11 and a garnet; the second row was an emerald, a lapis lazuli, and a green quartz;
12 13 the third row was an amber, a jet, and a sardonyx; and the fourth was an
aquamarine, a rock crystal, and an opal. They were mounted in gold filigree
14 settings. There were twelve stones, one for each of the names of Yisrael's sons.
15 Each was engraved like a seal with the name of one of the twelve tribes. For the
16 breast piece they made chains of pure gold, braided like cords. They made two
gold filigree settings and two gold rings, and attached the rings to two of the
17 corners of the breast piece. They fastened the two gold chains to the rings at the

ב ועבד ית איפודא, דהבא, תכלא וארגונא, וצבע זהורי ובוץ שזיר: ג ורדידו, ית טסי דדהבא וקציצו חוטין, למעבד, בגו תכלא ובגו ארגונא, ובגו, צבע זהורי ובגו בוצא, עובד אמן: ד כתפין עבדו ליה מלפפן, על תרין סטרוהי מלפף: ה והמין תקוניה דעלוהי, מניה הוא כעובדיה, דהבא, תכלא וארגונא, וצבע זהורי ובוץ שזיר, כמא דפקיד יי ית משה: ו ועבדו ית אבני ברלא, משקען מרמצן דדהב, גליפן כתב מפרש, על שמהת בני ישראל: ז ושוי יתהון, על כתפי איפודא, אבני דכרנא לבני ישראל, כמא דפקיד יי ית משה: ח ועבד ית חשנא, עובד אמן כעובד איפודא, דהבא, תכלא וארגונא, וצבע זהורי ובוץ שזיר: ט מרבע הוה, עיף עבדו ית חשנא, זרתא ארכיה, וזרתא פתייה עיף: י ואשלימו ביה, ארבעא סדרין דאבן טבא, סדרא קדמאה, סמקן ירקן וברקן, סדרא חד: יא וסדרא תנינא, אזמרגדין שבזיז וסבהלום: יב וסדרא תליתאה, קנכירי טרקיא ועין עגלא: יג וסדרא רביעאה, כרום ימא וברלא ופנתירי, משקען, מרמצן דדהב באשלמותהון: יד ואבניא, על שמהת בני ישראל אנין, תרתא עסרי על שמהתהון, כתב

רש״י

ג וירקעו. כמו: "לרקע הארץ" (תהלים קלו, ו), כתרגומו "ורדידו". טסין היו מרדדין מן הזהב, אשטנדר״א בלעז, טסין דקות. כאן הוא מלמדך היאך היו טווין את הזהב עם החוטין: מרדדין הטסין דקין, וקוצצין מהן פתילים לאורך הטס, לעשות אותן פתילים תערבת עם כל מין ומין בחשן ואפוד, שנאמר בהן "זהב" (לעיל כח, ו; טו), חוט אחד של זהב עם ששה חוטין של תכלת, וכן עם כל מין ומין, שכל המינים חוטן כפול ששה, והזהב חוט שביעי עם כל אחד ואחד:

ב וַיַּעַשׂ אֶת־הָאֵפֹד זָהָב תְּכֵלֶת וְאַרְגָּמָן וְתוֹלַעַת שָׁנִי וְשֵׁשׁ מָשְׁזָר׃ שני /חמישי/
ג וַיְרַקְּעוּ אֶת־פַּחֵי הַזָּהָב וְקִצֵּץ פְּתִילִם לַעֲשׂוֹת בְּתוֹךְ הַתְּכֵלֶת וּבְתוֹךְ
ד הָאַרְגָּמָן וּבְתוֹךְ תּוֹלַעַת הַשָּׁנִי וּבְתוֹךְ הַשֵּׁשׁ מַעֲשֵׂה חֹשֵׁב׃ כְּתֵפֹת
ה עָשׂוּ־לוֹ חֹבְרֹת עַל־שְׁנֵי קְצוֹתָו חֻבָּר׃ וְחֵשֶׁב אֲפֻדָּתוֹ אֲשֶׁר עָלָיו קְצוֹתָיו
מִמֶּנּוּ הוּא כְּמַעֲשֵׂהוּ זָהָב תְּכֵלֶת וְאַרְגָּמָן וְתוֹלַעַת שָׁנִי וְשֵׁשׁ מָשְׁזָר
ו כַּאֲשֶׁר צִוָּה יְהוָה אֶת־מֹשֶׁה׃ וַיַּעֲשׂוּ אֶת־אַבְנֵי הַשֹּׁהַם
מֻסַבֹּת מִשְׁבְּצֹת זָהָב מְפֻתָּחֹת פִּתּוּחֵי חוֹתָם עַל־שְׁמוֹת בְּנֵי יִשְׂרָאֵל׃
ז וַיָּשֶׂם אֹתָם עַל כִּתְפֹת הָאֵפֹד אַבְנֵי זִכָּרוֹן לִבְנֵי יִשְׂרָאֵל כַּאֲשֶׁר צִוָּה
יְהוָה אֶת־מֹשֶׁה׃
ח וַיַּעַשׂ אֶת־הַחֹשֶׁן מַעֲשֵׂה חֹשֵׁב כְּמַעֲשֵׂה אֵפֹד זָהָב תְּכֵלֶת וְאַרְגָּמָן
ט וְתוֹלַעַת שָׁנִי וְשֵׁשׁ מָשְׁזָר׃ רָבוּעַ הָיָה כָּפוּל עָשׂוּ אֶת־הַחֹשֶׁן זֶרֶת
י אָרְכּוֹ וְזֶרֶת רָחְבּוֹ כָּפוּל׃ וַיְמַלְאוּ־בוֹ אַרְבָּעָה טוּרֵי אָבֶן טוּר אֹדֶם
יא יב פִּטְדָה וּבָרֶקֶת הַטּוּר הָאֶחָד׃ וְהַטּוּר הַשֵּׁנִי נֹפֶךְ סַפִּיר וְיָהֲלֹם׃ וְהַטּוּר
יג הַשְּׁלִישִׁי לֶשֶׁם שְׁבוֹ וְאַחְלָמָה׃ וְהַטּוּר הָרְבִיעִי תַּרְשִׁישׁ שֹׁהַם וְיָשְׁפֵה
יד מוּסַבֹּת מִשְׁבְּצֹת זָהָב בְּמִלֻּאֹתָם׃ וְהָאֲבָנִים עַל־שְׁמֹת בְּנֵי־יִשְׂרָאֵל
הֵנָּה שְׁתֵּים עֶשְׂרֵה עַל־שְׁמֹתָם פִּתּוּחֵי חֹתָם אִישׁ עַל־שְׁמוֹ לִשְׁנֵים
טו עָשָׂר שָׁבֶט׃ וַיַּעֲשׂוּ עַל־הַחֹשֶׁן שַׁרְשְׁרֹת גַּבְלֻת מַעֲשֵׂה עֲבֹת זָהָב
טז טָהוֹר׃ וַיַּעֲשׂוּ שְׁתֵּי מִשְׁבְּצֹת זָהָב וּשְׁתֵּי טַבְּעֹת זָהָב וַיִּתְּנוּ אֶת־שְׁתֵּי
יז הַטַּבָּעֹת עַל־שְׁנֵי קְצוֹת הַחֹשֶׁן׃ וַיִּתְּנוּ שְׁתֵּי הָעֲבֹתֹת הַזָּהָב עַל־שְׁתֵּי

אונקלוס

מְפָרַשׁ כִּגְלָף דְּעִזְקָא גְּבַר עַל שְׁמֵיהּ, לִתְרֵי עֲסַר שִׁבְטִין: טו וַעֲבַדוּ עַל חֻשְׁנָא, תִּכִּין מְתַחֲמָן עוֹבַד גְּדִילוּ, דִּדְהַב דְּכֵי: טז וַעֲבַדוּ, תַּרְתֵּין מְרַמְּצָן דִּדְהַב, וְתַרְתֵּין עִזְקָן דִּדְהַב, וִיהַבוּ, יָת תַּרְתֵּין עִזְקָתָא, עַל תְּרֵין סִטְרֵי חֻשְׁנָא: יז וִיהַבוּ, תַּרְתֵּין גְּדִילָן דִּדְהַב, עַל תַּרְתֵּין

Human beings create chaos. Yet when human beings create their own symbolic order – the ark, the Tabernacle – by precise and exacting obedience to God's command, there is a chance for humanity to survive.

18 corners of the breast piece, and the other ends of the chains to the two settings,
19 attaching them to the ephod's shoulder pieces at the front. They made two gold
rings and placed them at the two other corners of the breast piece on the edge,
20 inside, next to the ephod. Then they made two more gold rings and attached
them to the bottom of the ephod's two shoulder pieces facing the priest's front,
21 close to the seam and above the ephod's woven waistband. They tied the rings
of the breast piece to the rings of the ephod with a sky-blue cord, connecting it
to the waistband so that the breast piece would remain secured to the ephod,
as the LORD had commanded Moshe.
22 23 They made the robe of the ephod woven entirely of sky-blue wool, with an SHELISHI /SHISHI/
opening in the center like the neck of a coat of mail, with a woven border
24 around it so that it would not tear. They made pomegranates of finely spun sky-
25 blue, purple, and scarlet wool around the hem of the robe. And they made bells
of pure gold and attached them around the hem between the pomegranates.
26 The bells and pomegranates alternated around the hem of the robe worn for
27 ministering, as the LORD commanded Moshe. For Aharon and his
28 sons, they made tunics woven from fine linen, together with a linen miter,
29 linen headdresses, and trousers of finely spun linen. The sash was embroidered
out of finely spun linen and sky-blue, purple, and scarlet wool, as the LORD
30 commanded Moshe. They made the headplate, the holy diadem, of
31 pure gold and engraved on it, as on a seal: Holy to the LORD. Then they attached
a sky-blue cord to it to affix it to the miter, as the LORD had commanded

אונקלוס

עִזְקָתָא, עַל סִטְרֵי חָשְׁנָא: יח וְיָת תַּרְתֵּין גְּדִילָן דְּעַל תְּרֵין סִטְרוֹהִי, יְהַבוּ עַל תַּרְתֵּין מְרַמְּצָתָא, וִיהַבוּנִין, עַל כִּתְפֵי אֵיפוֹדָא לָקֳבֵיל אַפּוֹהִי: יט וַעֲבַדוּ, תַּרְתֵּין עִזְקָן דִּדְהַב, וְשַׁוִּיאוּ, עַל תְּרֵין סִטְרֵי חָשְׁנָא, עַל סִפְתֵיהּ, דִּלְעִבְרָא דְּאֵיפוֹדָא לְגָיו: כ וַעֲבַדוּ תַּרְתֵּין עִזְקָן דִּדְהַב, וִיהַבוּנִין, עַל תַּרְתֵּין כִּתְפֵי אֵיפוֹדָא מִלְּרַע מִלָּקֳבֵיל אַפּוֹהִי, לָקֳבֵיל בֵּית לוֹפֵי, מֵעִלָּוֵי, לְהֶמְיַן אֵיפוֹדָא: כא וְאַחֲדוּ יָת חָשְׁנָא, מֵעִזְקָתֵיהּ לְעִזְקַת אֵיפוֹדָא בְּחוּטָא דִּתְכִילְתָא, לְמֶהֱוֵי עַל הֶמְיַן אֵיפוֹדָא, וְלָא יִתְפָּרַק חָשְׁנָא, מֵעִלָּוֵי אֵיפוֹדָא, כְּמָא דְּפַקֵּיד יי יָת מֹשֶׁה: כב וַעֲבַד, יָת מְעִיל אֵיפוֹדָא עוֹבַד מָחֵי, גְּמִיר תִּכְלָא: כג וּפוּמֵּיהּ דִּמְעִילָא כְּפִיל לְגַוֵּיהּ כְּפוּם שִׁרְיָן, תּוֹרָא מַקַּף לְפוּמֵּיהּ, סְחוֹר סְחוֹר דְּלָא יִתְבְּזַע:

רש״י

כח וְאֶת פַּאֲרֵי הַמִּגְבָּעֹת. תִּפְאֶרֶת הַמִּגְבָּעוֹת, הַמִּגְבָּעוֹת הַמְפֹאָרִין:

לא לָתֵת עַל הַמִּצְנֶפֶת מִלְמָעְלָה. שֶׁעַל יְדֵי הַפְּתִילִים הָיָה מוֹשִׁיבוֹ עַל הַמִּצְנֶפֶת כְּמִין כֶּתֶר. וְאִי אֶפְשָׁר לוֹמַר הַצִּיץ עַל הַמִּצְנֶפֶת, שֶׁהֲרֵי בִּשְׁחִיטַת קָדָשִׁים שָׁנִינוּ: שְׂעָרוֹ הָיָה נִרְאֶה בֵּין צִיץ לְמִצְנֶפֶת שֶׁשָּׁם מַנִּיחַ תְּפִלִּין (זבחים יט ע״א), וְהַצִּיץ הָיָה נָתוּן עַל הַמֵּצַח, הֲרֵי הַמִּצְנֶפֶת לְמַעְלָה וְהַצִּיץ לְמַטָּה. כָּאן הוּא אוֹמֵר: ״וַיִּתְּנוּ עָלָיו פְּתִיל תְּכֵלֶת״, וּבְעִנְיַן הַצַּוָּאָה הוּא אוֹמֵר: ״וְשַׂמְתָּ אֹתוֹ עַל פְּתִיל תְּכֵלֶת״ (לעיל כח, לז)? שְׁנֵי חוּטִין הָיוּ בְּכָל קָצֶה וְקָצֶה, אֶחָד מִמַּעַל וְאֶחָד מִתַּחַת לְנֶגֶד מִצְחוֹ, וְכֵן בָּאֶמְצַע, וְקוֹשֵׁר רָאשֵׁיהֶם הַשְּׁנַיִם כֻּלָּם יַחַד מֵאֲחוֹרָיו לְמוּל עָרְפּוֹ, וּמוֹשִׁיבוֹ עַל הַמִּצְנֶפֶת. וְאַל תִּתְמַהּ שֶׁלֹּא נֶאֱמַר ׳פְּתִילֵי תְכֵלֶת׳ הוֹאִיל וּמְרֻבִּין הֵן, שֶׁהֲרֵי מָצִינוּ בַּחֹשֶׁן וְאֵפוֹד: ״וַיִּרְכְּסוּ אֶת הַחֹשֶׁן״ וְגוֹ׳ (לעיל פסוק כא), וְעַל כָּרְחֲךָ פָּחוֹת מִשְּׁנַיִם לֹא הָיוּ, שֶׁהֲרֵי בִּשְׁנֵי קְצוֹת הַחֹשֶׁן הָיוּ שְׁתֵּי טַבְּעוֹת הַחֹשֶׁן וּבִשְׁתֵּי כִּתְפוֹת הָאֵפוֹד הָיוּ טַבְּעוֹת הָאֵפוֹד שֶׁכְּנֶגְדָּן, וּלְפִי דֶּרֶךְ קְשִׁירָה אַרְבָּעָה חוּטִין הָיוּ, וּמִכָּל מָקוֹם פָּחוֹת מִשְּׁנַיִם אִי אֶפְשָׁר:

יח הַטַּבָּעֹת עַל־קְצוֹת הַחֹשֶׁן׃ וְאֵת שְׁתֵּי קְצוֹת שְׁתֵּי הָעֲבֹתֹת נָתְנוּ
יט עַל־שְׁתֵּי הַמִּשְׁבְּצֹת וַיִּתְּנֻם עַל־כִּתְפֹת הָאֵפֹד אֶל־מוּל פָּנָיו׃ וַיַּעֲשׂוּ
שְׁתֵּי טַבְּעֹת זָהָב וַיָּשִׂימוּ עַל־שְׁנֵי קְצוֹת הַחֹשֶׁן עַל־שְׂפָתוֹ אֲשֶׁר אֶל־
כ עֵבֶר הָאֵפֹד בָּיְתָה׃ וַיַּעֲשׂוּ שְׁתֵּי טַבְּעֹת זָהָב וַיִּתְּנֻם עַל־שְׁתֵּי כִתְפֹת
הָאֵפֹד מִלְּמַטָּה מִמּוּל פָּנָיו לְעֻמַּת מֶחְבַּרְתּוֹ מִמַּעַל לְחֵשֶׁב הָאֵפֹד׃
כא וַיִּרְכְּסוּ אֶת־הַחֹשֶׁן מִטַּבְּעֹתָיו אֶל־טַבְּעֹת הָאֵפֹד בִּפְתִיל תְּכֵלֶת
לִהְיֹת עַל־חֵשֶׁב הָאֵפֹד וְלֹא־יִזַּח הַחֹשֶׁן מֵעַל הָאֵפֹד כַּאֲשֶׁר צִוָּה יְהוָה
אֶת־מֹשֶׁה׃
כב כג וַיַּעַשׂ אֶת־מְעִיל הָאֵפֹד מַעֲשֵׂה אֹרֵג כְּלִיל תְּכֵלֶת׃ וּפִי־הַמְּעִיל בְּתוֹכוֹ שלישי /ששי/
כד כְּפִי תַחְרָא שָׂפָה לְפִיו סָבִיב לֹא יִקָּרֵעַ׃ וַיַּעֲשׂוּ עַל־שׁוּלֵי הַמְּעִיל רִמּוֹנֵי
כה תְּכֵלֶת וְאַרְגָּמָן וְתוֹלַעַת שָׁנִי מָשְׁזָר׃ וַיַּעֲשׂוּ פַעֲמֹנֵי זָהָב טָהוֹר וַיִּתְּנוּ
אֶת־הַפַּעֲמֹנִים בְּתוֹךְ הָרִמֹּנִים עַל־שׁוּלֵי הַמְּעִיל סָבִיב בְּתוֹךְ הָרִמֹּנִים׃
כו פַּעֲמֹן וְרִמֹּן פַּעֲמֹן וְרִמֹּן עַל־שׁוּלֵי הַמְּעִיל סָבִיב לְשָׁרֵת כַּאֲשֶׁר צִוָּה יְהוָה
כז אֶת־מֹשֶׁה׃ וַיַּעֲשׂוּ אֶת־הַכָּתְנֹת שֵׁשׁ מַעֲשֵׂה אֹרֵג לְאַהֲרֹן
כח וּלְבָנָיו׃ וְאֵת הַמִּצְנֶפֶת שֵׁשׁ וְאֶת־פַּאֲרֵי הַמִּגְבָּעֹת שֵׁשׁ וְאֶת־מִכְנְסֵי
כט הַבָּד שֵׁשׁ מָשְׁזָר׃ וְאֶת־הָאַבְנֵט שֵׁשׁ מָשְׁזָר וּתְכֵלֶת וְאַרְגָּמָן וְתוֹלַעַת
ל שָׁנִי מַעֲשֵׂה רֹקֵם כַּאֲשֶׁר צִוָּה יְהוָה אֶת־מֹשֶׁה׃ וַיַּעֲשׂוּ
אֶת־צִיץ נֵזֶר־הַקֹּדֶשׁ זָהָב טָהוֹר וַיִּכְתְּבוּ עָלָיו מִכְתַּב פִּתּוּחֵי חוֹתָם
לא קֹדֶשׁ לַיהוָה׃ וַיִּתְּנוּ עָלָיו פְּתִיל תְּכֵלֶת לָתֵת עַל־הַמִּצְנֶפֶת מִלְמָעְלָה

אונקלוס

כד וַעֲבַדוּ עַל שִׁפּוֹלֵי מְעִילָא, רִמּוֹנֵי, תִּכְלָא וְאַרְגְּוָנָא וּצְבַע זְהוֹרִי, שְׁזִיר: כה וַעֲבַדוּ זוֹגִין דִּדְהַב דְּכֵי, וִיהַבוּ יָת זוֹגַיָּא בְּגוֹ רִמּוֹנַיָּא, עַל שִׁפּוֹלֵי מְעִילָא סְחוֹר סְחוֹר, בְּגוֹ רִמּוֹנַיָּא: כו זוֹגָא וְרִמּוֹנָא זוֹגָא וְרִמּוֹנָא, עַל שִׁפּוֹלֵי מְעִילָא סְחוֹר סְחוֹר, לְשַׁמָּשָׁא, כְּמָא דְּפַקֵּיד יי יָת מֹשֶׁה: כז וַעֲבַדוּ, יָת כִּתּוּנִין דְּבוּצָא עוֹבַד מָחֵי, לְאַהֲרֹן וְלִבְנוֹהִי: כח וְיָת מִצְנַפְתָּא דְבוּצָא, וְיָת שְׁבַח קוֹבְעַיָּא דְבוּצָא, וְיָת מִכְנְסֵי בוּצָא דְבוּץ שְׁזִיר: כט וְיָת הֶמְיָנָא דְבוּץ שְׁזִיר, וְתִכְלָא וְאַרְגְּוָנָא, וּצְבַע זְהוֹרִי עוֹבַד צַיָּר, כְּמָא דְּפַקֵּיד יי יָת מֹשֶׁה: ל וַעֲבַדוּ, יָת צִיצָא כְּלִילָא דְקֻדְשָׁא דִּדְהַב דְּכֵי, וּכְתַבוּ עֲלוֹהִי, כְּתָב מְפָרַשׁ כִּגְלַף דְּעִזְקָא, קֹדֶשׁ לַיי: לא וִיהַבוּ עֲלוֹהִי חוּטָא דְתִכְלְתָא, לְמִתַּן עַל מִצְנַפְתָּא מִלְּעֵילָא,

32 Moshe. Thus all the work on the Tabernacle, the Tent of Meeting, was
completed. The Israelites did everything exactly as the LORD had commanded
Moshe.
33 They brought the Tabernacle to Moshe: the Tent and all its furnishings, its REVI'I
34 clasps, frames, crossbars, posts, and sockets; the covering of reddened rams'
hides and the covering of fine leather and the curtain that covered the screen;
35 36 the Ark of the Testimony and its carrying staves; the Ark cover; the table with
37 all its utensils; the showbread; the pure gold candelabrum with its row of
38 lamps and all its accessories, together with the oil for lighting; the gold altar,
the anointing oil, the fragrant incense, and the curtain for the entrance to the
39 Tent; the bronze altar with its bronze mesh, its staves, and all its utensils; the
40 laver with its base; the hangings for the courtyard, its posts and sockets, and

רש"י

לב| **וַיַּעֲשׂוּ בְּנֵי יִשְׂרָאֵל.** אֶת הַמְּלָאכָה, "כְּכֹל אֲשֶׁר צִוָּה ה'" וְגוֹ':

לג| **וַיָּבִיאוּ אֶת הַמִּשְׁכָּן וְגוֹ'.** שֶׁלֹּא הָיוּ יְכוֹלִין לַהֲקִימוֹ, וּלְפִי שֶׁלֹּא עָשָׂה מֹשֶׁה שׁוּם מְלָאכָה בַּמִּשְׁכָּן הִנִּיחַ לוֹ הַקָּדוֹשׁ בָּרוּךְ הוּא הֲקָמָתוֹ, שֶׁלֹּא הָיָה יָכוֹל לַהֲקִימוֹ שׁוּם אָדָם מֵחֲמַת כֹּבֶד הַקְּרָשִׁים שֶׁאֵין כֹּחַ בְּאָדָם לְזָקְפָן, וּמֹשֶׁה הֶעֱמִידוֹ. אָמַר מֹשֶׁה לִפְנֵי הַקָּדוֹשׁ בָּרוּךְ הוּא: אֵיךְ אֶפְשָׁר הֲקָמָתוֹ עַל יְדֵי אָדָם? אָמַר לוֹ: עֲסֹק אַתָּה בְּיָדְךָ, נִרְאֶה כִּמְקִימוֹ, וְהוּא נִזְקָף וְקָם מֵאֵלָיו. וְזֶהוּ שֶׁנֶּאֱמַר: "הוּקַם הַמִּשְׁכָּן" (להלן מ, יז), הוּקַם מֵאֵלָיו. מִדְרַשׁ רַבִּי תַּנְחוּמָא (פקודי יא):

And so it came to be. Throughout history Jews found themselves scattered and dispersed among the nations, never knowing when they would be forced to leave and find a new home. In the fifteenth century alone, Jews were expelled from Vienna and Linz in 1421, from Cologne in 1424, Augsburg in 1439, Bavaria in 1442, Moravia in 1454, Perugia in 1485, Vicenza in 1486, Parma in 1488, Milan and Lucca in 1489, Spain in 1492, and Portugal in 1497.

How did they survive, their identity intact, their faith, though sorely challenged, still strong? Because they believed that God was with them, even in exile. Because they were sustained by the line from Psalms (23:4), "Though I walk through the valley of the shadow of death, I fear no evil, for You are with me." Because they still had the Torah, God's unbreakable covenant, with its promise that "yet even then, when they are in the land of their enemies, I will not reject them nor despise them and annihilate them, will not break My covenant with them, for I am the LORD their God" (Lev. 26:44). The Torah became, in the famous phrase of Heinrich Heine, "the portable homeland of the Jew."

masse the way we do alone. That is why societies of people not themselves wicked can perform collective acts of great evil. Without the Divine Presence symbolized at the heart of the camp, human beings will do what they have always done: oppress one another, fight with one another, and exploit one another. There can be no just society without some collective form of *yirat Shamayim*, some "reverence for Heaven." This moment, then – the completion and placement of the Tabernacle, in full view of all, at the center of the camp – is the culmination of Exodus.

39:35 אֶת־אֲרוֹן הָעֵדֻת וְאֶת־בַּדָּיו *The Ark...its carrying staves* – The Torah has already stipulated that "the staves must stay in the rings of the Ark; they must not be removed" (Ex. 25:15). Rabbi Samson Raphael Hirsch explained that the ark is to be permanently ready when the need arises for the Israelites to travel. Why is the same not true about the other objects in the Tabernacle, such as the altar and the candelabrum? To show supremely, said Rabbi Hirsch, that the Torah is not limited to any one place.

לב כַּאֲשֶׁר צִוָּה יְהוָה אֶת־מֹשֶׁה׃ וַתֵּכֶל כָּל־עֲבֹדַת מִשְׁכַּן
אֹהֶל מוֹעֵד וַיַּעֲשׂוּ בְּנֵי יִשְׂרָאֵל כְּכֹל אֲשֶׁר צִוָּה יְהוָה אֶת־מֹשֶׁה כֵּן
עָשׂוּ׃
לג וַיָּבִיאוּ אֶת־הַמִּשְׁכָּן אֶל־מֹשֶׁה אֶת־הָאֹהֶל וְאֶת־כָּל־כֵּלָיו קְרָסָיו כט רביעי
לד קְרָשָׁיו בְּרִיחָו וְעַמֻּדָיו וַאֲדָנָיו׃ וְאֶת־מִכְסֵה עוֹרֹת הָאֵילִם הַמְאָדָּמִים
לה וְאֶת־מִכְסֵה עֹרֹת הַתְּחָשִׁים וְאֵת פָּרֹכֶת הַמָּסָךְ׃ אֶת־אֲרוֹן הָעֵדֻת
לו וְאֶת־בַּדָּיו וְאֵת הַכַּפֹּרֶת׃ אֶת־הַשֻּׁלְחָן אֶת־כָּל־כֵּלָיו וְאֵת לֶחֶם הַפָּנִים׃
לז אֶת־הַמְּנֹרָה הַטְּהֹרָה אֶת־נֵרֹתֶיהָ נֵרֹת הַמַּעֲרָכָה וְאֶת־כָּל־כֵּלֶיהָ וְאֵת
לח שֶׁמֶן הַמָּאוֹר׃ וְאֵת מִזְבַּח הַזָּהָב וְאֵת שֶׁמֶן הַמִּשְׁחָה וְאֵת קְטֹרֶת
לט הַסַּמִּים וְאֵת מָסַךְ פֶּתַח הָאֹהֶל׃ אֵת ׀ מִזְבַּח הַנְּחֹשֶׁת וְאֶת־מִכְבַּר
מ הַנְּחֹשֶׁת אֲשֶׁר־לוֹ אֶת־בַּדָּיו וְאֶת־כָּל־כֵּלָיו אֶת־הַכִּיֹּר וְאֶת־כַּנּוֹ׃ אֵת
קַלְעֵי הֶחָצֵר אֶת־עַמֻּדֶיהָ וְאֶת־אֲדָנֶיהָ וְאֶת־הַמָּסָךְ לְשַׁעַר הֶחָצֵר

אונקלוס

כְּמָא דְּפַקֵּיד יי יָת מֹשֶׁה: לב וּשְׁלֵימַת, כָּל עֲבִידַת, מַשְׁכְּנָא מַשְׁכַּן זִמְנָא, וַעֲבַדוּ בְּנֵי יִשְׂרָאֵל, כְּכֹל, דְּפַקֵּיד יי, יָת מֹשֶׁה כֵּן עֲבַדוּ: לג וְאֵיתִיאוּ יָת מַשְׁכְּנָא לְוָת מֹשֶׁה, יָת מַשְׁכְּנָא וְיָת כָּל מָנוֹהִי, פֻּרְפוֹהִי דַּפּוֹהִי, עָבְרוֹהִי וְעַמּוּדוֹהִי וְסָמְכוֹהִי: לד וְיָת חוּפָאָה, דְּמַשְׁכֵּי דִּכְרֵי מְסֻמְּקֵי, וְיָת חוּפָאָה דְּמַשְׁכֵּי סָסְגוֹנָא, וְיָת פָּרֻכְתָּא דִּפְרָסָא: לה יָת אֲרוֹנָא דְּסָהֲדוּתָא וְיָת אֲרִיחוֹהִי, וְיָת כַּפֻּרְתָּא: לו יָת פָּתוּרָא יָת כָּל מָנוֹהִי, וְיָת לְחֵים אַפַּיָּא: לז יָת מְנָרְתָּא דָּכִיתָא יָת בּוֹצִינַהָא, בּוֹצִינֵי, סִדְרָא וְיָת כָּל מָנַהָא, וְיָת מִשְׁחָא דְּאַנְהָרוּתָא: לח וְיָת מַדְבְּחָא דְּדַהֲבָא, וְיָת מִשְׁחָא דִּרְבוּתָא, וְיָת קְטֹרֶת בֻּסְמַיָּא, וְיָת פְּרָסָא דִּתְרַע מַשְׁכְּנָא: לט יָת מַדְבְּחָא דִּנְחָשָׁא, וְיָת סְרָדָא דִּנְחָשָׁא דִּילֵיהּ, יָת אֲרִיחוֹהִי וְיָת כָּל מָנוֹהִי, יָת כִּיּוֹרָא וְיָת בְּסִיסֵיהּ: מ יָת סְרָדֵי דָּרְתָּא יָת עַמּוּדַהָא וְיָת סָמְכַהָא, וְיָת פְּרָסָא לִתְרַע דָּרְתָּא,

39:32 וַתֵּכֶל כָּל־עֲבֹדַת מִשְׁכַּן אֹהֶל מוֹעֵד *Thus all the work on the Tabernacle, the Tent of Meeting, was completed* – The placement of the Tabernacle at the heart of the camp suggests that societies need, in the public domain, a constant reminder of the presence of God. That, after all, is why the Tabernacle appears in Exodus, not Genesis. Genesis is about individuals, Exodus about societies. Individuals can be moral without being conventionally religious. You do not need to believe in God to rescue a drowning child, give food to the hungry or shelter to the homeless. The Torah describes the courage, for example, of Pharaoh's daughter without implying that she was in receipt of a divine revelation. The Torah seems to use the phrase "fear of God" in roughly the same way as we speak about the moral sense (see Gen. 20:11). Rav Nissim Gaon (990–1062) in his introduction to the Talmud says that humans have been bound by the commands of morality since man first walked on earth. Individually, we can and should be moral, regardless of our specific religious commitments.

But man is a social animal. We form societies. And societies beat to a different pulse than do individuals. Reinhold Niebuhr made this distinction famous in the title of his book, *Moral Man and Immoral Society*. We do not act *en*

the screen for the courtyard gate; the ropes and tent pegs for the courtyard; all
41 the furnishings for the service of the Tabernacle, the Tent of Meeting; and the
woven garments for ministering in the Sanctuary, both the sacred vestments
for Aharon the priest and the vestments for his sons to wear when serving
42 as priests. The Israelites had completed all the work exactly as the LORD
43 commanded Moshe. Moshe saw that all the work had been done just as the
LORD had commanded – and Moshe blessed them.
40 1 2 Then the LORD spoke to Moshe, saying, "On the first day of the first month HAMISHI /SHEVI'I/
3 you shall set up the Tabernacle of the Tent of Meeting. Put in it the Ark of the
4 Testimony, and screen the Ark with the curtain. Bring in the table and set it.
5 Bring in the candelabrum and light its lamps. Put the golden incense altar in
front of the Ark of the Testimony, and hang the screen for the Tabernacle's
6 entrance. Put the sacrificial altar in front of the entrance of the Tabernacle of
7 the Tent of Meeting. Place the laver between the Tent of Meeting and the altar,
8 and put water in it. Arrange the courtyard all around, and put in place the screen
9 for the courtyard gate. Take the anointing oil and anoint the Tabernacle and
everything in it. Consecrate it and all its furnishings so that it becomes holy.
10 Anoint the sacrificial altar and all its utensils, consecrating it so that it becomes
11 12 holy of holies. Anoint the laver with its base, making it holy. Then bring Aharon
and his sons to the entrance of the Tent of Meeting, and cleanse them with

רש״י

מג | **וַיְבָרֶךְ אֹתָם מֹשֶׁה.** אָמַר לָהֶם: יְהִי רָצוֹן שֶׁתִּשְׁרֶה שְׁכִינָה בְּמַעֲשֵׂה יְדֵיכֶם, "וִיהִי נֹעַם ה' אֱלֹהֵינוּ עָלֵינוּ" וְגוֹ' (תהלים צ, יז), וְהוּא אֶחָד מֵאַחַד עָשָׂר מִזְמוֹרִים שֶׁבִּ'תְפִלָּה לְמֹשֶׁה' (תהלים צ-ק):

מ ג | **וְסַכֹּתָ עַל הָאָרֹן.** לְשׁוֹן הֲגָנָה, שֶׁהֲרֵי מְחִצָּה הָיְתָה:
ד | **וְעָרַכְתָּ אֶת עֶרְכּוֹ.** שְׁתֵּי מַעַרְכוֹת שֶׁל לֶחֶם הַפָּנִים:

39:43 **וַיְבָרֶךְ אֹתָם מֹשֶׁה** *And Moshe blessed them* – As Israel's first creative achievement reaches its culmination, Moshe blesses them, saying, according to the Sages (Sifrei Bemidbar, Pinhas 143), "May it be God's will that His presence rests in the work of your hands." Our potential greatness is that we can create structures, relationships, and lives that become homes for the Divine Presence. Blessing them and celebrating their achievement, Moshe shows them what they could be. That is potentially a life-changing experience.

Not all of us can paint like Monet or compose like Mozart. But we each have gifts, capacities that can lie dormant throughout life until someone awakens them. We can achieve heights of which we never thought ourselves capable. All it takes is for us to meet someone who believes in us, challenges us, and then, when we have responded to the challenge, blesses and celebrates our achievements. That is what Moshe does for the Israelites after the sin of the golden calf. First he gets them to create, and then he blesses them and their creation with one of the simplest and most moving of all blessings, that the *Shekhina* should dwell in the work of their hands.

אֶת־מֵיתָרָיו וִיתֵדֹתֶיהָ וְאֵת כָּל־כְּלֵי עֲבֹדַת הַמִּשְׁכָּן לְאֹהֶל מוֹעֵד׃
מא אֶת־בִּגְדֵי הַשְּׂרָד לְשָׁרֵת בַּקֹּדֶשׁ אֶת־בִּגְדֵי הַקֹּדֶשׁ לְאַהֲרֹן הַכֹּהֵן
מב וְאֶת־בִּגְדֵי בָנָיו לְכַהֵן׃ כְּכֹל אֲשֶׁר־צִוָּה יְהוָה אֶת־מֹשֶׁה כֵּן עָשׂוּ בְּנֵי
מג יִשְׂרָאֵל אֵת כָּל־הָעֲבֹדָה׃ וַיַּרְא מֹשֶׁה אֶת־כָּל־הַמְּלָאכָה וְהִנֵּה עָשׂוּ
אֹתָהּ כַּאֲשֶׁר צִוָּה יְהוָה כֵּן עָשׂוּ וַיְבָרֶךְ אֹתָם מֹשֶׁה׃
מ א ב וַיְדַבֵּר יְהוָה אֶל־מֹשֶׁה לֵּאמֹר׃ בְּיוֹם־הַחֹדֶשׁ הָרִאשׁוֹן בְּאֶחָד לַחֹדֶשׁ חמישי /שביעי/
ג תָּקִים אֶת־מִשְׁכַּן אֹהֶל מוֹעֵד׃ וְשַׂמְתָּ שָׁם אֵת אֲרוֹן הָעֵדוּת וְסַכֹּתָ עַל־
ד הָאָרֹן אֶת־הַפָּרֹכֶת׃ וְהֵבֵאתָ אֶת־הַשֻּׁלְחָן וְעָרַכְתָּ אֶת־עֶרְכּוֹ וְהֵבֵאתָ
ה אֶת־הַמְּנֹרָה וְהַעֲלֵיתָ אֶת־נֵרֹתֶיהָ׃ וְנָתַתָּה אֶת־מִזְבַּח הַזָּהָב לִקְטֹרֶת
ו לִפְנֵי אֲרוֹן הָעֵדֻת וְשַׂמְתָּ אֶת־מָסַךְ הַפֶּתַח לַמִּשְׁכָּן׃ וְנָתַתָּה אֵת מִזְבַּח
ז הָעֹלָה לִפְנֵי פֶּתַח מִשְׁכַּן אֹהֶל־מוֹעֵד׃ וְנָתַתָּ אֶת־הַכִּיֹּר בֵּין־אֹהֶל
ח מוֹעֵד וּבֵין הַמִּזְבֵּחַ וְנָתַתָּ שָׁם מָיִם׃ וְשַׂמְתָּ אֶת־הֶחָצֵר סָבִיב וְנָתַתָּ
ט אֶת־מָסַךְ שַׁעַר הֶחָצֵר׃ וְלָקַחְתָּ אֶת־שֶׁמֶן הַמִּשְׁחָה וּמָשַׁחְתָּ אֶת־
הַמִּשְׁכָּן וְאֶת־כָּל־אֲשֶׁר־בּוֹ וְקִדַּשְׁתָּ אֹתוֹ וְאֶת־כָּל־כֵּלָיו וְהָיָה קֹדֶשׁ׃
י וּמָשַׁחְתָּ אֶת־מִזְבַּח הָעֹלָה וְאֶת־כָּל־כֵּלָיו וְקִדַּשְׁתָּ אֶת־הַמִּזְבֵּחַ וְהָיָה
יא הַמִּזְבֵּחַ קֹדֶשׁ קָדָשִׁים׃ וּמָשַׁחְתָּ אֶת־הַכִּיֹּר וְאֶת־כַּנּוֹ וְקִדַּשְׁתָּ אֹתוֹ׃
יב וְהִקְרַבְתָּ אֶת־אַהֲרֹן וְאֶת־בָּנָיו אֶל־פֶּתַח אֹהֶל מוֹעֵד וְרָחַצְתָּ אֹתָם

אונקלוס

יָת אֲטוּנוֹהִי וְסִכַּהָא, וְיָת, כָּל מָנֵי, פָּלְחַן מַשְׁכְּנָא לְמַשְׁכַּן זִמְנָא: מא יָת לְבוּשֵׁי שִׁמּוּשָׁא לְשַׁמָּשָׁא בְקֻדְשָׁא, יָת לְבוּשֵׁי קֻדְשָׁא לְאַהֲרֹן כָּהֲנָא, וְיָת לְבוּשֵׁי בְנוֹהִי לְשַׁמָּשָׁא: מב כְּכֹל, דְּפַקֵּיד יי יָת מֹשֶׁה, כֵּן עֲבַדוּ בְנֵי יִשְׂרָאֵל, יָת כָּל פֻּלְחָנָא: מג וַחֲזָא מֹשֶׁה יָת כָּל עֲבִידְתָא, וְהָא עֲבַדוּ יָתַהּ, כְּמָא דְּפַקֵּיד יי כֵּן עֲבַדוּ, וּבָרֵיךְ יָתְהוֹן מֹשֶׁה: מ א וּמַלֵּיל יי עִם מֹשֶׁה לְמֵימַר: ב בְּיוֹם יַרְחָא קַדְמָאָה בְּחַד לְיַרְחָא, תְּקִים, יָת מַשְׁכְּנָא מַשְׁכַּן זִמְנָא: ג וּתְשַׁוֵּי תַמָּן, יָת אֲרוֹנָא דְסָהֲדוּתָא, וְתַטֵּיל עַל אֲרוֹנָא יָת פָּרֻכְתָּא: ד וְתָעֵיל יָת פָּתוּרָא, וְתַסְדַּר יָת סִדְרֵיהּ, וְתָעֵיל יָת מְנָרְתָא, וְתַדְלֵיק יָת בּוֹצִינַהָא: ה וְתִתֵּין, יָת מַדְבְּחָא דְדַהֲבָא לִקְטֹרֶת בֻּסְמַיָּא, קֳדָם אֲרוֹנָא דְסָהֲדוּתָא, וּתְשַׁוֵּי, יָת פְּרָסָא דְתַרְעָא לְמַשְׁכְּנָא: ו וְתִתֵּין, יָת מַדְבְּחָא דַעֲלָתָא, קֳדָם, תְּרַע מַשְׁכְּנָא מַשְׁכַּן זִמְנָא: ז וְתִתֵּין יָת כִּיּוֹרָא, בֵּין מַשְׁכַּן זִמְנָא וּבֵין מַדְבְּחָא, וְתִתֵּין תַּמָּן מַיָּא: ח וּתְשַׁוֵּי יָת דָּרְתָא סְחוֹר סְחוֹר, וְתִתֵּין, יָת פְּרָסָא דִתְרַע דָּרְתָא: ט וְתִסַּב יָת מִשְׁחָא דִרְבוּתָא, וּתְרַבֵּי יָת מַשְׁכְּנָא וְיָת כָּל דְּבֵיהּ, וּתְקַדֵּישׁ יָתֵיהּ, וְיָת כָּל מָנוֹהִי וִיהֵי קֻדְשָׁא: י וּתְרַבֵּי, יָת מַדְבְּחָא דַעֲלָתָא וְיָת כָּל מָנוֹהִי, וּתְקַדֵּישׁ יָת מַדְבְּחָא, וִיהֵי מַדְבְּחָא קֹדֶשׁ קֻדְשִׁין: יא וּתְרַבֵּי יָת כִּיּוֹרָא וְיָת בְּסִיסֵיהּ, וּתְקַדֵּישׁ יָתֵיהּ: יב וּתְקָרֵיב יָת אַהֲרֹן וְיָת בְּנוֹהִי, לִתְרַע

13 water. Robe Aharon with the sacred vestments and anoint him and consecrate
14 him, that he may serve Me as priest. Then bring his sons forward, robe them
15 with tunics, and anoint them as you anointed their father, that they may
serve Me as priests. Through this anointing, theirs will become an everlasting
16 priesthood throughout the generations." Moshe did exactly as the LORD had
17 commanded him. On the first day of the first month of the second SHISHI
18 year the Tabernacle was set up. Moshe set up the Tabernacle, placed its sockets,
19 erected its frames, inserted its bars, and put up its posts. He spread the tent
over the Tabernacle and placed the covering over the tent, as the LORD had
20 commanded him. He took the covenant and put it in the Ark. He
21 inserted the carrying staves into the Ark and placed the cover on top of it. He
brought the Ark into the Tabernacle and hung the cloth curtain, screening off
22 the Ark of the Testimony, as the LORD had commanded him. He put
the table in the Tent of Meeting, outside the curtain on the north side of the

רש״י

יט וַיִּפְרֹשׂ אֶת הָאֹהֶל. הֵן יְרִיעוֹת הָעִזִּים:

כ אֶת הָעֵדֻת. הַלּוּחוֹת:

The world had but a single Creator, but the Tabernacle constructed by man was built out of difference and diversity. Each of the Israelites brought his or her own distinctive contribution. Each was valued equally. The Tabernacle was built out of the differential contributions of the various groups and tribes. It represented *orchestrated diversity*, or in social terms, integration without assimilation. Because we are not the same, we each have something unique to contribute, something only we can give.

In an age of religious conformity, John Milton argued that God wants difference, for it is only through the clash of opinions that truth is honed and refined. "Where there is much desire to learn, there of necessity will be much arguing, much writing, many opinions; for *opinion in men is but knowledge in the making*." The path to truth passes through the city of many voices. The strength and vigor of argument within a culture is a measure of its spiritual health.

His refutation of those who believed that society requires us all to hold the same faith is based on the building of the Temple. It is absurd to insist on uniformity, as if:

> While the temple of the Lord was building, some cutting, some squaring the marble, others hewing the cedars, there should be a sort of irrational men who could not consider there must be many schisms and many dissections made in the quarry and in the timber, ere the house of God can be built. And when every stone is laid artfully together, it cannot be united into a continuity, it can but be contiguous in this world; neither can every piece of the building be of one form; nay rather the perfection consists in this, that, out of many moderate varieties and brotherly dissimilitudes that are not vastly disproportional, arises the goodly and the graceful symmetry that commends the whole pile and structure. (*Areopagitica*, 1644)

Society, for Milton, is the arena in which all sorts of groups, different yet linked in a collective task, each have a contribution to make to "the whole pile and structure." It is precisely this integrated diversity that gives society its complex beauty, its "goodly and gracious symmetry." Just as God creates the natural universe, so we are called on to create the social universe – a universe, like that of the planets and stars, that is ordered, rule-governed, a space of integrated diversity, a world we can see and say, as God saw and said, that it is good.

יג בַּמָּֽיִם׃ וְהִלְבַּשְׁתָּ֙ אֶת־אַהֲרֹ֔ן אֵ֖ת בִּגְדֵ֣י הַקֹּ֑דֶשׁ וּמָשַׁחְתָּ֥ אֹת֛וֹ וְקִדַּשְׁתָּ֥
יד טו אֹת֖וֹ וְכִהֵ֥ן לִֽי׃ וְאֶת־בָּנָ֖יו תַּקְרִ֑יב וְהִלְבַּשְׁתָּ֥ אֹתָ֖ם כֻּתֳּנֹֽת׃ וּמָשַׁחְתָּ֣ אֹתָ֗ם
כַּאֲשֶׁ֤ר מָשַׁ֙חְתָּ֙ אֶת־אֲבִיהֶ֔ם וְכִהֲנ֖וּ לִ֑י וְהָ֨יְתָ֜ה לִהְיֹ֨ת לָהֶ֧ם מָשְׁחָתָ֛ם
טז לִכְהֻנַּ֥ת עוֹלָ֖ם לְדֹרֹתָֽם׃ וַיַּ֖עַשׂ מֹשֶׁ֑ה כְּ֠כֹל אֲשֶׁ֨ר צִוָּ֧ה יהוה אֹת֖וֹ כֵּ֥ן
יז עָשָֽׂה׃ וַיְהִ֞י בַּחֹ֧דֶשׁ הָרִאשׁ֛וֹן בַּשָּׁנָ֥ה הַשֵּׁנִ֖ית בְּאֶחָ֣ד ששי
יח לַחֹ֑דֶשׁ הוּקַ֖ם הַמִּשְׁכָּֽן׃ וַיָּ֨קֶם מֹשֶׁ֜ה אֶת־הַמִּשְׁכָּ֗ן וַיִּתֵּן֙ אֶת־אֲדָנָ֔יו וַיָּ֙שֶׂם֙
יט אֶת־קְרָשָׁ֔יו וַיִּתֵּ֖ן אֶת־בְּרִיחָ֑יו וַיָּ֖קֶם אֶת־עַמּוּדָֽיו׃ וַיִּפְרֹ֤שׂ אֶת־הָאֹ֙הֶל֙
עַל־הַמִּשְׁכָּ֔ן וַיָּ֜שֶׂם אֶת־מִכְסֵ֥ה הָאֹ֛הֶל עָלָ֖יו מִלְמָ֑עְלָה כַּאֲשֶׁ֛ר צִוָּ֥ה
כ יהוה אֶת־מֹשֶֽׁה׃ וַיִּקַּ֞ח וַיִּתֵּ֤ן אֶת־הָעֵדֻת֙ אֶל־הָ֣אָרֹ֔ן וַיָּ֥שֶׂם
כא אֶת־הַבַּדִּ֖ים עַל־הָאָרֹ֑ן וַיִּתֵּ֧ן אֶת־הַכַּפֹּ֛רֶת עַל־הָאָרֹ֖ן מִלְמָֽעְלָה׃ וַיָּבֵ֣א
אֶת־הָאָרֹן֮ אֶל־הַמִּשְׁכָּן֒ וַיָּ֗שֶׂם אֵ֚ת פָּרֹ֣כֶת הַמָּסָ֔ךְ וַיָּ֖סֶךְ עַ֖ל אֲר֣וֹן הָעֵד֑וּת
כב כַּאֲשֶׁ֛ר צִוָּ֥ה יהוה אֶת־מֹשֶֽׁה׃ וַיִּתֵּ֤ן אֶת־הַשֻּׁלְחָן֙ בְּאֹ֣הֶל

אונקלוס

מַשְׁכַּן זִמְנָא, וְתַסְחֵי יָתְהוֹן בְּמַיָּא: יג וְתַלְבֵּישׁ יָת אַהֲרֹן, יָת לְבוּשֵׁי קֻדְשָׁא, וּתְרַבֵּי יָתֵיהּ, וּתְקַדֵּישׁ יָתֵיהּ וִישַׁמֵּישׁ קֳדָמָי: יד וְיָת בְּנוֹהִי תְּקָרֵיב, וְתַלְבֵּישׁ יָתְהוֹן כִּתּוּנִין: טו וּתְרַבֵּי יָתְהוֹן, כְּמָא דְּרַבֵּיתָא יָת אֲבוּהוֹן, וִישַׁמְּשׁוּן קֳדָמָי, וּתְהֵי, לְמִהְוֵי לְהוֹן רְבוּתְהוֹן, לִכְהֻנַּת עָלַם לְדָרֵיהוֹן: טז וַעֲבַד מֹשֶׁה, כְּכֹל, דְּפַקֵּיד יי, יָתֵיהּ כֵּן עֲבַד: יז וַהֲוָה, בְּיַרְחָא קַדְמָאָה, בְּשַׁתָּא תִנְיֵיתָא בְּחַד לְיַרְחָא, אִתָּקַם מַשְׁכְּנָא: יח וַאֲקֵים מֹשֶׁה יָת מַשְׁכְּנָא, וִיהַב יָת סָמְכוֹהִי, וְשַׁוִּי יָת דַּפּוֹהִי, וִיהַב יָת עָבְרוֹהִי, וַאֲקֵים יָת עַמּוּדוֹהִי: יט וּפְרַס יָת פְּרָסָא עַל מַשְׁכְּנָא, וְשַׁוִּי, יָת חוֹפָאָה דְּמַשְׁכְּנָא, עֲלוֹהִי מִלְּעֵילָא, כְּמָא דְּפַקֵּיד יי יָת מֹשֶׁה: כ וּנְסֵיב, וִיהַב יָת סָהֲדוּתָא בַּאֲרוֹנָא, וְשַׁוִּי יָת אֲרִיחַיָּא עַל אֲרוֹנָא, וִיהַב יָת כַּפֻּרְתָּא, עַל אֲרוֹנָא מִלְּעֵילָא: כא וְאַעֵיל יָת אֲרוֹנָא לְמַשְׁכְּנָא, וְשַׁוִּי, יָת פָּרֻכְתָּא דִּפְרָסָא, וְאַטֵּיל, עַל אֲרוֹנָא דְסָהֲדוּתָא, כְּמָא דְּפַקֵּיד יי יָת מֹשֶׁה: כב וִיהַב יָת פָּתוּרָא בְּמַשְׁכַּן

THE COMPLETION AND CONSTRUCTION OF THE TABERNACLE

The date of the completion of the Tabernacle – the first day of the first month (Ex. 40:17) – is the anniversary of creation, as well as the day on which dry land appeared after the flood (Gen. 8:13), the start of the recreated universe after the great destruction. A set of linguistic parallels between the Israelites' construction of the Tabernacle and God's creation of the universe culminates at its end: "Moshe saw that all the work had been done … and Moshe blessed them"; "And so Moshe completed the work" (Ex. 39:43, 40:33; compare Gen. 1:31–2:3). The effect is to suggest that the Tabernacle was the human counterpart of the divine creation of the universe. Though the creation of the universe takes a mere thirty-four verses (Gen. 1:1–2:3), the making of the Tabernacle takes several hundred. Although the Torah is interested in the natural universe, the home God makes for man, it is even more interested in the social universe, the home man makes for God.

23 Tabernacle, and arranged the bread on it before the LORD, as the LORD had
24 commanded him. He placed the candelabrum in the Tent of Meeting,
25 opposite the table, on the Tabernacle's south side, and lit the lamps before the
26 LORD, as the LORD had commanded him. He placed the golden altar
27 in the Tent of Meeting, in front of the curtain, and on it he burned fragrant
28 incense, as the LORD had commanded him. He hung the curtain at SHEVI'I
29 the entrance of the Tabernacle. He put the sacrificial altar at the entrance of
the Tabernacle of the Tent of Meeting, and on it sacrificed a burnt offering
30 and a grain offering, as the LORD had commanded him. He placed
the laver between the Tent of Meeting and the altar, and in it he put water for
31 washing. Moshe, Aharon, and his sons would wash their hands and feet there,
32 for they washed themselves whenever they went into the Tent of Meeting or
33 approached the altar, as the LORD had commanded Moshe. Then he
set up the courtyard around the Tabernacle and the altar, and hung the curtain
for the courtyard gate. And so Moshe completed the work.
34 Then the cloud covered the Tent of Meeting, and the glory of the LORD filled MAFTIR
35 the Tabernacle. Moshe could not now enter the Tent of Meeting, because the

רש״י

כב| **עַל יֶרֶךְ הַמִּשְׁכָּן צָפֹנָה.** בַּחֲצִי הַצְּפוֹנִי שֶׁל רֹחַב הַבַּיִת: **יֶרֶךְ.** כְּתַרְגּוּמוֹ: ״צִדָּא״, כַּיָּרֵךְ הַזֶּה שֶׁהוּא בְּצִדּוֹ שֶׁל אָדָם:

כז| **וַיַּקְטֵר עָלָיו קְטֹרֶת.** שַׁחֲרִית וְעַרְבִית, כְּמוֹ שֶׁנֶּאֱמַר: ״בַּבֹּקֶר בַּבֹּקֶר בְּהֵיטִיבוֹ אֶת הַנֵּרֹת וְגוֹ׳ וּבְהַעֲלֹת אַהֲרֹן״ וְגוֹ׳ (לעיל ל, ז-ח):

כט| **אַף בַּיּוֹם הַשְּׁמִינִי לַמִּלּוּאִים** שֶׁהוּא יוֹם הֲקָמַת הַמִּשְׁכָּן, שִׁמֵּשׁ מֹשֶׁה וְהִקְרִיב קָרְבְּנוֹת צִבּוּר, חוּץ מֵאוֹתָן שֶׁנִּצְטַוּוּ לְבוֹ בַּיּוֹם, שֶׁנֶּאֱמַר: ״קְרַב אֶל הַמִּזְבֵּחַ״ וְגוֹ׳ (ויקרא ט, ז): **אֶת הָעֹלָה.** עוֹלַת הַתָּמִיד: **וְאֶת הַמִּנְחָה.** מִנְחַת נְסָכִים שֶׁל תָּמִיד, כְּמוֹ שֶׁנֶּאֱמַר: ״וְעִשָּׂרֹן סֹלֶת בָּלוּל בְּשֶׁמֶן״ וְגוֹ׳ (לעיל כט, מ):

לא| **וְרָחֲצוּ מִמֶּנּוּ מֹשֶׁה וְאַהֲרֹן וּבָנָיו.** יוֹם שְׁמִינִי לַמִּלּוּאִים הֻשְׁווּ כֻּלָּם לַכְּהֻנָּה, וְתַרְגּוּמוֹ: ״וּמְקַדְּשִׁין מִנֵּיהּ״, בּוֹ בַּיּוֹם קִדֵּשׁ מֹשֶׁה עִמָּהֶם:

לב| **וּבְקָרְבָתָם.** כְּמוֹ וּבְקָרְבָם, כְּשֶׁיִּקְרְבוּ:

לה| **וְלֹא יָכֹל מֹשֶׁה לָבוֹא אֶל אֹהֶל מוֹעֵד.** וְכָתוּב אֶחָד אוֹמֵר: ״וּבְבֹא מֹשֶׁה אֶל אֹהֶל מוֹעֵד״ (במדבר ז, פט), בָּא הַכָּתוּב הַשְּׁלִישִׁי וְהִכְרִיעַ בֵּינֵיהֶם: ״כִּי שָׁכַן עָלָיו הֶעָנָן״, אֱמוֹר מֵעַתָּה, כָּל זְמַן שֶׁהָיָה הֶעָנָן עָלָיו לֹא הָיָה יָכוֹל לָבֹא, נִסְתַּלֵּק הֶעָנָן, נִכְנָס וּמְדַבֵּר עִמּוֹ:

Mount Sinai: "The glory of the LORD rested on Mount Sinai, and the cloud covered it for six days. On the seventh, He called to Moshe from within the cloud." (Ex. 24:16)

The Tabernacle: "Then the cloud covered the Tent of Meeting, and the glory of the LORD filled the Tabernacle." (40:34)

The difference between them is that the sanctity of Mount Sinai was momentary, while that of the Tabernacle (later transferred to the Temple) is permanent. The revelation at Sinai was conducted by God. So overwhelming was it that the people say to Moshe, "Let not God say any more to us or we will die" (20:16). By contrast, the Tabernacle involves human labor. The Israelites made it; they prepared the structured space the Divine Presence would fill. Forty days after the revelation at Sinai, the Israelites made a golden calf. But after constructing the Sanctuary, that generation will make no more idols. That is the difference between the things that are done for us and the things we have a share in doing ourselves. The former change us for a moment, the latter for a lifetime.

כג מוֹעֵד עַל יֶרֶךְ הַמִּשְׁכָּן צָפֹנָה מִחוּץ לַפָּרֹכֶת: וַיַּעֲרֹךְ עָלָיו עֵרֶךְ לֶחֶם
כד לִפְנֵי יהוה כַּאֲשֶׁר צִוָּה יהוה אֶת־מֹשֶׁה: וַיָּשֶׂם אֶת־
כה הַמְּנֹרָה בְּאֹהֶל מוֹעֵד נֹכַח הַשֻּׁלְחָן עַל יֶרֶךְ הַמִּשְׁכָּן נֶגְבָּה: וַיַּעַל הַנֵּרֹת
כו לִפְנֵי יהוה כַּאֲשֶׁר צִוָּה יהוה אֶת־מֹשֶׁה: וַיָּשֶׂם אֶת־מִזְבַּח
כז הַזָּהָב בְּאֹהֶל מוֹעֵד לִפְנֵי הַפָּרֹכֶת: וַיַּקְטֵר עָלָיו קְטֹרֶת סַמִּים כַּאֲשֶׁר
כח צִוָּה יהוה אֶת־מֹשֶׁה: וַיָּשֶׂם אֶת־מָסַךְ הַפֶּתַח לַמִּשְׁכָּן: שביעי
כט וְאֵת מִזְבַּח הָעֹלָה שָׂם פֶּתַח מִשְׁכַּן אֹהֶל־מוֹעֵד וַיַּעַל עָלָיו אֶת־הָעֹלָה
ל וְאֶת־הַמִּנְחָה כַּאֲשֶׁר צִוָּה יהוה אֶת־מֹשֶׁה: וַיָּשֶׂם
אֶת־הַכִּיֹּר בֵּין־אֹהֶל מוֹעֵד וּבֵין הַמִּזְבֵּחַ וַיִּתֵּן שָׁמָּה מַיִם לְרָחְצָה:
לא לב וְרָחֲצוּ מִמֶּנּוּ מֹשֶׁה וְאַהֲרֹן וּבָנָיו אֶת־יְדֵיהֶם וְאֶת־רַגְלֵיהֶם: בְּבֹאָם
אֶל־אֹהֶל מוֹעֵד וּבְקָרְבָתָם אֶל־הַמִּזְבֵּחַ יִרְחָצוּ כַּאֲשֶׁר צִוָּה יהוה
לג אֶת־מֹשֶׁה: וַיָּקֶם אֶת־הֶחָצֵר סָבִיב לַמִּשְׁכָּן וְלַמִּזְבֵּחַ וַיִּתֵּן
אֶת־מָסַךְ שַׁעַר הֶחָצֵר וַיְכַל מֹשֶׁה אֶת־הַמְּלָאכָה:
לד לה וַיְכַס הֶעָנָן אֶת־אֹהֶל מוֹעֵד וּכְבוֹד יהוה מָלֵא אֶת־הַמִּשְׁכָּן: וְלֹא־יָכֹל מפטיר
מֹשֶׁה לָבוֹא אֶל־אֹהֶל מוֹעֵד כִּי־שָׁכַן עָלָיו הֶעָנָן וּכְבוֹד יהוה מָלֵא

אונקלוס

זִמְנָא, עַל שִׁדָּא דְּמַשְׁכְּנָא צִפּוּנָא, מִבָּרָא לְפָרֻכְתָּא: כג וְסַדַּר עֲלוֹהִי, סִדְרִין דִּלְחֵים קֳדָם יי, כְּמָא דְּפַקֵּיד יי יָת מֹשֶׁה: כד וְשַׁוִּי יָת מְנָרְתָא בְּמַשְׁכַּן זִמְנָא, לָקֳבֵיל פָּתוּרָא, עַל שִׁדָּא דְּמַשְׁכְּנָא דָּרוֹמָא: כה וְאַדְלֵיק בּוֹצִינַיָּא קֳדָם יי, כְּמָא דְּפַקֵּיד יי יָת מֹשֶׁה: כו וְשַׁוִּי, יָת מַדְבְּחָא דְּדַהֲבָא בְּמַשְׁכַּן זִמְנָא, קֳדָם פָּרֻכְתָּא: כז וְאַקְטַר עֲלוֹהִי קְטֹרֶת בֻּסְמִין, כְּמָא דְּפַקֵּיד יי יָת מֹשֶׁה: כח וְשַׁוִּי, יָת פְּרָסָא דִּתְרַעָא לְמַשְׁכְּנָא: כט וְיָת מַדְבְּחָא דַּעֲלָתָא, שַׁוִּי, בִּתְרַע מַשְׁכְּנָא מַשְׁכַּן זִמְנָא, וְאַסֵּיק עֲלוֹהִי, יָת עֲלָתָא וְיָת מִנְחָתָא, כְּמָא דְּפַקֵּיד יי יָת מֹשֶׁה: ל וְשַׁוִּי יָת כִּיּוֹרָא, בֵּין מַשְׁכַּן זִמְנָא וּבֵין מַדְבְּחָא, וִיהַב תַּמָּן, מַיָּא לְקִדּוּשׁ: לא וּמְקַדְּשִׁין מִנֵּיהּ, מֹשֶׁה וְאַהֲרֹן וּבְנוֹהִי, יָת יְדֵיהוֹן וְיָת רַגְלֵיהוֹן: לב בְּמֵיעַלְהוֹן לְמַשְׁכַּן זִמְנָא, וּבְמִקְרַבְהוֹן, לְמַדְבְּחָא מְקַדְּשִׁין, כְּמָא דְּפַקֵּיד יי יָת מֹשֶׁה: לג וַאֲקֵים יָת דָּרְתָא, סְחוֹר סְחוֹר לְמַשְׁכְּנָא וּלְמַדְבְּחָא, וִיהַב, יָת פְּרָסָא דִּתְרַע דָּרְתָא, וְשֵׁיצִי מֹשֶׁה יָת עֲבִידְתָּא: לד וַחֲפָא עֲנָנָא יָת מַשְׁכַּן זִמְנָא, וִיקָרָא דַּיי, אִתְמְלִי יָת מַשְׁכְּנָא: לה וְלָא יָכֵיל מֹשֶׁה, לְמֵיעַל לְמַשְׁכַּן זִמְנָא, אֲרֵי שְׁרָא עֲלוֹהִי עֲנָנָא, וִיקָרָא דַּיי, אִתְמְלִי

40:34 וּכְבוֹד יהוה מָלֵא אֶת־הַמִּשְׁכָּן *The glory of the Lord filled the Tabernacle* – The Torah speaks about the revelations of "the Lord's glory" at Mount Sinai and the Tabernacle in almost identical terms:

36 cloud had settled on it, and the glory of the LORD filled the Tabernacle. In all
the journeys of the Israelites, when the cloud rose from the Tabernacle, they
37 would set out. But if the cloud did not lift, they did not move on; they waited
38 until it had lifted. The LORD's cloud was over the Tabernacle by day, and fire
was in it at night, in view of all the House of Israel through all their journeys.

The haftara for Parashat Pekudei is on page 1556.
On the Shabbat of Parashat Shekalim read the haftara on page 1642.
On the Shabbat of Parashat Para read the haftara on page 1648.
On the Shabbat of Parashat HaḤodesh read the haftara on page 16510

רש״י

לח) **לְעֵינֵי כָל בֵּית יִשְׂרָאֵל בְּכָל מַסְעֵיהֶם.** בְּכָל מַסָּע שֶׁהָיוּ נוֹסְעִים, הָיָה הֶעָנָן שׁוֹכֵן בִּמְקוֹם אֲשֶׁר יַחֲנוּ שָׁם. מְקוֹם חֲנִיָּתָן אַף הוּא קָרוּי מַסָּע, וְכֵן: ״וַיֵּלֶךְ לְמַסָּעָיו״ (בראשית יג, ג), וְכֵן: ״אֵלֶּה מַסְעֵי״ (במדבר לג, א), לְפִי שֶׁמִּמְּקוֹם הַחֲנִיָּה חָזְרוּ וְנָסְעוּ, לְכָךְ נִקְרְאוּ כֻּלָּן מַסָּעוֹת:

political, yet adding up to a momentous proposition: that just as God created order in the universe, so we are called on to create order in our personal lives and in society as a whole. We are God's image; we are God's children; we are God's partners.

40:38 **בְּכָל־מַסְעֵיהֶם** *Through all their journeys* – The Tabernacle is constructed in such a way as to be portable. It will be dismantled and its parts carried as the Israelites make their way to the next stage of their journey. When the time comes for the Israelites to move on, the cloud moves from its resting place above the Tent of Meeting to a position outside the camp, signaling the direction they must now take.

However, there is a small but significant difference between the two instances of the phrase "in all their journeys," one in verse 36 and one in verse 38. In the first instance the words are to be taken literally. When the cloud lifted and moved on ahead, the Israelites knew they were about to travel. In the second instance, the words cannot be taken literally, as the cloud was not "over the Tabernacle" in all their journeys. On the contrary: It was there only when they stopped traveling and instead pitched camp. During the journeys the cloud went on ahead.

Noting this, Rashi (on Ex. 40:38) makes the following comment:

> The word *masa* can denote a destination…. The desert locations are referred to as such because they served as resting places prior to the nation setting out again.

The point is linguistic, yet Rashi has encapsulated in a few brief words the existential truth at the heart of Judaism. In Jewish history, even an encampment is called a journey. So long as we have not yet reached our destination, even a place of rest is merely temporary.

To be a Jew is to travel, and to know that here where we are is a mere resting place, not yet a home. It is defined not by the fact that we are here, but by the knowledge that eventually – after a day, a week, a year, a century, sometimes even a millennium – we will have to move on. Thus, the portable Tabernacle, even more than the Temple in Jerusalem, became the symbol of Jewish life.

How and why it happened is contained in those simple words of Rashi at the end of Exodus. Even when at rest, Jews knew that they would one day have to uproot their tents, dismantle the Tabernacle, and move on. Even an encampment is called a journey. A people that never stops traveling is one that never grows old or stale or complacent. It may live in the here and now, but it is always conscious of the distant past and the still-beckoning future. It is with this word, with its two entwined meanings, that the book of Exodus comes to a close. The journey through the wilderness has begun.

לו אֶת־הַמִּשְׁכָּֽן׃ וּבְהֵעָל֤וֹת הֶֽעָנָן֙ מֵעַ֣ל הַמִּשְׁכָּ֔ן יִסְע֖וּ בְּנֵ֣י יִשְׂרָאֵ֑ל בְּכֹ֖ל
לז לח מַסְעֵיהֶֽם׃ וְאִם־לֹ֥א יֵעָלֶ֖ה הֶֽעָנָ֑ן וְלֹ֣א יִסְע֔וּ עַד־י֖וֹם הֵעָלֹתֽוֹ׃ כִּ֣י עֲנַ֨ן
יהוה עַל־הַמִּשְׁכָּן֙ יוֹמָ֔ם וְאֵ֕שׁ תִּהְיֶ֥ה לַ֖יְלָה בּ֑וֹ לְעֵינֵ֥י כָל־בֵּֽית־יִשְׂרָאֵ֖ל
בְּכָל־מַסְעֵיהֶֽם׃

The הפטרה *for* פרשת פקודי *is on page 1557.*
On the שבת *of* פרשת שקלים *read the* הפטרה *on page 1643.*
On the שבת *of* פרשת פרה *read the* הפטרה *on page 1649.*
On the שבת *of* פרשת החודש *read the* הפטרה *on page 1651.*

אונקלוס

יָת מַשְׁכְּנָא: לו וּבְאִסְתַּלָּקוּת עֲנָנָא מֵעִלָּוֵי מַשְׁכְּנָא, נָטְלִין בְּנֵי יִשְׂרָאֵל, בְּכָל מַטְלָנֵיהוֹן: לז וְאִם לָא מִסְתַּלַּק עֲנָנָא, וְלָא נָטְלִין, עַד יוֹם אִסְתַּלָּקוּתֵיהּ: לח אֲרֵי עֲנַן יְקָרָא דַּיי עַל מַשְׁכְּנָא בִּימָמָא, וְחֵיזוּ אִישָׁתָא, הֲוֵי בְּלֵילְיָא בֵיהּ, לְעֵינֵי כָל בֵּית יִשְׂרָאֵל בְּכָל מַטְלָנֵיהוֹן:

EXODUS: THE NARRATIVE STRUCTURE

Human creation mirrors divine creation. Thus, the end of Exodus brings us back to the beginning of Genesis. On close examination, we see that Genesis and Exodus are joined as a single mirror-image symmetry, whose structure is this:

Creation of the universe (Genesis 1–3)
Humanity and its failings (3–6)
Flood (7–10)
Hubris: The Tower of Bavel (11)
The family of the covenant (12–50)
The people of the covenant (Exodus 1–4)
Hubris: Pharaoh (5–6)
Plagues (7–11)
The people and their failings (12–18; 32–33)
Creation of the Sanctuary (25–31; 34–40)

The difference between Genesis and Exodus is that the *family* of the covenant has become the *people* of the covenant. Framing the narrative as a whole are the creation of the universe and the creation of the Tabernacle.

At the heart of Genesis and Exodus are journeys: Avraham's from the east in Genesis, Moshe's from the west in Exodus. There is, the narrative implies, a way back from sin to harmony, exile to return. Seen from this perspective, the Sanctuary is more than an atonement for the sin of the golden calf. It is also a kind of atonement for the sin of Adam and Ḥava in Eden. After the flood, God accepts the fact of human sinfulness. After the golden calf, He accepts the fact of Israel's collective sinfulness. When people sacrifice – when they offer something of themselves to God – God will grant atonement. The second tablets that rested in the Ark as a permanent sign of divine forgiveness are thus, for Israel, the counterpart of the rainbow in the days of Noaḥ, with its promise that God would never again destroy all life. God is just, but God forgives. Human beings are sinful, but humans can be forgiven.

The ideal society, according to the Torah, is one of *ordered liberty*, brought about by the rule of law. So the presence of the Sanctuary with its precisely ordered spaces at the heart of the camp is not just a symbol of God's presence, but also of God's order, which characterizes both creation (natural order, science) and redemption (social order, justice). The ordered society the Israelites are commanded to create brings to a kind of closure the story with which the Torah began, God's creation of an ordered universe.

Genesis-Exodus, then, is a single literary unit, in which the meaning of the universe and our place within it is explored through a series of dramas, some personal, others

ויקרא
LEVITICUS

THE BOOK OF VAYIKRA

The third book of the Torah is markedly different from the others. It contains no journey. It is set entirely at Sinai. It occupies only a brief section of time: a single month. There is almost no narrative. Yet set at the center of the Mosaic books, it is the key to understanding Israel's vocation as "a kingdom of priests and a holy nation" (Ex. 19:6), the first collective mission statement in history. Vayikra was not the first name the Sages gave the book. They called it *Torat Kohanim*, "The Law of the Priests," because much of it is about the Sanctuary and its service, the world of the priests. Hence its English name, Leviticus, from the Greek and Latin meaning "matters concerning the Levites," the tribe from which the priests came.

Much of the book is indeed about the work of the priests and the Sanctuary. But the book is larger than that. It opens out into broad vistas of personal morality and social justice. The great code in Leviticus 19 tells us that every Jew, not just a priestly elite, is called on to be holy. So tradition eventually settled on the name Vayikra, "He called."

Vayikra is a – perhaps even *the* – key text of Judaism. It is here that we read for the first time the command to "love your neighbor as your own self" (Lev. 19:18). It is the source of the even greater moral principle "The stranger... love him as your own self, for you yourselves were strangers in the land of Egypt" (19:34). It is Leviticus that forbids us to exact vengeance or bear a grudge, taking a stand against the psychopathology of hatred and violence. It contains one of the most remarkable of religious ideas, that we are summoned to be holy because God is holy. Not only are we created in God's image, we are called on to act in God's ways.

At a more practical but no less profound level, Vayikra sets out an entire infrastructure for justice and equity in political and economic life. It humanizes slavery and sets in motion a process that must end in its abolition. It speaks about debt relief and the return of ancestral land in the Jubilee year.

Vayikra is a precisely structured book, divided into three parts. The first (chs. 1–10) is about the holy. Specifically, it is about sacrifices and how to come close to God in the House of God. The second part (chs. 11–16) is set at the boundary between the holy and the world. It is about the things that prevent us from entering sacred space. The third (chs. 17–27) is about taking the holy into the world. The book begins with an elite, the priests, sons of Aharon, a minority within a minority, one specific family within the tribe of Levi. It culminates in a call from God to the entire nation. It begins in the Sanctuary, but ends in society. It democratizes *kedusha*, holiness, the sign of God's presence, so that it becomes part of the life of the whole people.

Parashat Vayikra

1 1 The Lord called to Moshe. From the Tent of Meeting He spoke to him and said,
2 "Speak to the Israelites. Say: When one of you brings an animal offering to the

רש״י

א א וַיִּקְרָא אֶל מֹשֶׁה. לְכָל דִּבְּרוֹת וּלְכָל אֲמִירוֹת וּלְכָל צִוּוּיִים קָדְמָה קְרִיאָה, לְשׁוֹן חִבָּה, לָשׁוֹן שֶׁמַּלְאֲכֵי הַשָּׁרֵת מִשְׁתַּמְּשִׁין בּוֹ, שֶׁנֶּאֱמַר: "וְקָרָא זֶה אֶל זֶה" (ישעיה ו, ג). אֲבָל לִנְבִיאֵי אֻמּוֹת הָעוֹלָם נִגְלָה עֲלֵיהֶן בִּלְשׁוֹן עֲרַאי, בִּלְשׁוֹן טֻמְאָה, שֶׁנֶּאֱמַר: "וַיִּקָּר אֱלֹהִים אֶל בִּלְעָם" (במדבר כג, ד): וַיִּקְרָא אֶל מֹשֶׁה. הַקּוֹל הוֹלֵךְ וּמַגִּיעַ לְאָזְנָיו וְכָל יִשְׂרָאֵל לֹא שׁוֹמְעִין. יָכוֹל אַף לַהַפְסָקוֹת הָיְתָה קְרִיאָה? תַּלְמוּד לוֹמַר: "וַיְדַבֵּר", לְדִבּוּר הָיְתָה קְרִיאָה וְלֹא לַהַפְסָקוֹת. וּמֶה הָיוּ הַפְסָקוֹת מְשַׁמְּשׁוֹת? לִתֵּן רֶוַח לְמֹשֶׁה לְהִתְבּוֹנֵן בֵּין פָּרָשָׁה לְפָרָשָׁה וּבֵין עִנְיָן לְעִנְיָן, קַל וָחֹמֶר לְהֶדְיוֹט הַלָּמֵד מִן הַהֶדְיוֹט: אֵלָיו. לְמַעֵט אֶת אַהֲרֹן. רַבִּי יְהוּדָה בֶּן בְּתֵירָה אוֹמֵר: שְׁלֹשָׁה עָשָׂר דִּבְּרוֹת נֶאֶמְרוּ בַּתּוֹרָה לְמֹשֶׁה וּלְאַהֲרֹן, וּכְנֶגְדָּן נֶאֶמְרוּ שְׁלֹשָׁה עָשָׂר מִעוּטִין, לְלַמֶּדְךָ, שֶׁלֹּא לְאַהֲרֹן נֶאֶמְרוּ, אֶלָּא לְמֹשֶׁה שֶׁיֹּאמַר לְאַהֲרֹן. וְאֵלּוּ הֵן שְׁלֹשָׁה עָשָׂר מִעוּטִין: "לְדַבֵּר אִתּוֹ" (במדבר ז, פט), "מִדַּבֵּר אֵלָיו" (שם), "וַיְדַבֵּר אֵלָיו" (שם), "וְנוֹעַדְתִּי לְךָ" (שמות כה, כב), כֻּלָּן בְּתוֹרַת כֹּהֲנִים (פרק ב, ב). יָכוֹל יִשְׁמְעוּ אֶת קוֹל הַקְּרִיאָה? תַּלְמוּד לוֹמַר, קוֹל לוֹ, קוֹל אֵלָיו, מֹשֶׁה שָׁמַע וְכָל יִשְׂרָאֵל לֹא שָׁמְעוּ: מֵאֹהֶל מוֹעֵד. מְלַמֵּד שֶׁהָיָה הַקּוֹל נִפְסָק וְלֹא הָיָה יוֹצֵא חוּץ לָאֹהֶל. יָכוֹל מִפְּנֵי שֶׁהַקּוֹל נָמוּךְ? תַּלְמוּד לוֹמַר: "אֶת הַקּוֹל" (במדבר ז, פט), מַהוּ "הַקּוֹל"? הוּא הַקּוֹל הַמִּתְפָּרֵשׁ בַּכְּתוּבִים: "קוֹל ה' בַּכֹּחַ, קוֹל ה' בֶּהָדָר, קוֹל ה' שֹׁבֵר אֲרָזִים" (תהלים כט, ד-ה). אִם כֵּן, לָמָּה נֶאֱמַר: "מֵאֹהֶל מוֹעֵד"? מְלַמֵּד שֶׁהָיָה הַקּוֹל נִפְסָק. כַּיּוֹצֵא בּוֹ: "וְקוֹל כַּנְפֵי הַכְּרוּבִים נִשְׁמַע עַד הֶחָצֵר הַחִיצֹנָה" (יחזקאל י, ה). יָכוֹל מִפְּנֵי שֶׁהַקּוֹל נָמוּךְ? תַּלְמוּד לוֹמַר: "כְּקוֹל אֵל שַׁדַּי בְּדַבְּרוֹ" (שם), אִם כֵּן, לָמָּה נֶאֱמַר: "עַד הֶחָצֵר הַחִיצֹנָה"? שֶׁכֵּיוָן שֶׁמַּגִּיעַ שָׁם הָיָה נִפְסָק: מֵאֹהֶל מוֹעֵד לֵאמֹר. יָכוֹל מִכָּל הַבַּיִת? תַּלְמוּד לוֹמַר: "מֵעַל הַכַּפֹּרֶת" (במדבר ז, פט). יָכוֹל מֵעַל הַכַּפֹּרֶת כֻּלָּהּ? תַּלְמוּד לוֹמַר: "מִבֵּין שְׁנֵי הַכְּרֻבִים" (שם): לֵאמֹר. צֵא וֶאֱמֹר לָהֶם דִּבְרֵי כִבּוּשִׁין: בִּשְׁבִילְכֶם הוּא נִדְבָּר עִמִּי. שֶׁכֵּן מָצִינוּ, שֶׁכָּל שְׁמוֹנֶה וּשְׁלֹשִׁים שָׁנָה שֶׁהָיוּ יִשְׂרָאֵל בַּמִּדְבָּר כִּמְנֻדִּים, מִן הַמְרַגְּלִים וְאֵילָךְ, לֹא נִתְיַחֵד הַדִּבּוּר עִם מֹשֶׁה, שֶׁנֶּאֱמַר: "וַיְהִי כַאֲשֶׁר תַּמּוּ כָּל אַנְשֵׁי הַמִּלְחָמָה לָמוּת... וַיְדַבֵּר ה' אֵלַי לֵאמֹר" (דברים ב, טז-יז). דָּבָר אַחֵר, צֵא וֶאֱמֹר לָהֶם דְּבָרַי וַהֲשִׁיבֵנִי אִם יְקַבְּלוּם, כְּמוֹ שֶׁנֶּאֱמַר: "וַיָּשֶׁב מֹשֶׁה אֶת דִּבְרֵי הָעָם" וְגוֹ' (שמות יט, ח):

ב אָדָם כִּי יַקְרִיב מִכֶּם. כְּשֶׁיַּקְרִיב, בְּקָרְבְּנוֹת נְדָבָה דִּבֵּר הָעִנְיָן: אָדָם. לָמָּה נֶאֱמַר? מָה אָדָם הָרִאשׁוֹן לֹא הִקְרִיב מִן הַגָּזֵל, שֶׁהַכֹּל הָיָה

however, understands *keri*, like *vayikar*, to be related to *mikre*, "chance," the way of the world. To regard something as *mikre* means to see it as if it had no larger significance. That, he says, is not how we as Jews should view our fate (*Hilkhot Taanit* 1:1–3).

The difference between *vayikra* and *vayikar* lies in the small *alef*. An *alef* is almost inaudible. The small *alef* in the Torah scroll at the beginning of the word *Vayikra* is almost invisible. It is as if the Torah were intimating that the presence of God in history will not always be as clear as it was during the exodus or the division of the Sea of Reeds. Often, it will depend on our own sensitivity. For those who look, it will be visible. For those who listen, it will be audible. But we will need to look and listen. God does not force His presence on us against our will. We have to search Him out.

If we choose *not* to see or hear, then *Vayikra* will become *Vayikar*. God's call will be inaudible. History will seem no more than "a tale / Told by an idiot, full of sound and fury, / Signifying nothing" (*Macbeth*). It is a self-fulfilling expectation. *If you believe that history is chance, then it will become so.*

But if you believe otherwise, it will be otherwise. The word *vayikra* at the beginning and the sevenfold *keri* at the end enfold the priestly book in prophetic time. Israel's timeless encounters with God allow it to negotiate safely the currents and rapids of history. We must all choose: will we live the life of *vayikra*, calling, or *keri* – vocation or accident, destiny or chance?

1:2 קָרְבָּן לַיהוה מִן־הַבְּהֵמָה *An animal offering* – Rabbi Shneur Zalman of Liadi, the first Rebbe of Lubavitch, noticed a grammatical oddity in our verse. In Hebrew,

פרשת ויקרא

א א ב וַיִּקְרָא אֶל־מֹשֶׁה וַיְדַבֵּר יהוה אֵלָיו מֵאֹהֶל מוֹעֵד לֵאמֹר: דַּבֵּר אֶל־בְּנֵי א
יִשְׂרָאֵל וְאָמַרְתָּ אֲלֵהֶם אָדָם כִּי־יַקְרִיב מִכֶּם קָרְבָּן לַיהוה מִן־הַבְּהֵמָה

אונקלוס

א א וּקְרָא לְמֹשֶׁה, וּמַלֵּיל יי עִמֵּיהּ, מִמַּשְׁכַּן זִמְנָא לְמֵימַר: ב מַלֵּיל, עִם בְּנֵי יִשְׂרָאֵל וְתֵימַר לְהוֹן, אֱנָשׁ, אֲרֵי יְקָרֵיב מִנְּכוֹן, קֻרְבָּנָא קֳדָם יי, מִן בְּעִירָא,

VAYIKRA

This *parasha*, with which the book opens, details the various kinds of sacrifices the Israelites brought to the Tabernacle. There were five: the burnt offering (*ola*), the grain offering (*minḥa*), the peace offering (*shelamim*), the purification offering (*ḥatat*), and the guilt offering (*asham*).

Sacrifice, in the broadest sense, is the fundamental activity in relation to the holy. God sacrifices something of Himself to make space for us. We sacrifice something of ourselves to make space for Him. Sacrifice is what God allows us to give Him, to show our love and gratitude for what He has given us.

The discussion of sacrifices in Parashat Vayikra raises many fascinating questions. Among them, as we shall see, are the issue of how the sacrificial service relates to prophetic ethics, the symbolic meaning of sacrifice, how sacrifices can teach us about the nature of sin itself, and what the description of the sacrifice brought by an elder or judge can tell us about the nature and challenges of leadership.

THE LORD CALLED

The phrase "The Lord called to Moshe" is clearly a prelude. Once we get to "He spoke to him and said," we know we are about to hear substantive details. The redundancy of using three verbs for God's speech ("called," "spoke," and "said") cries out for attention. What is more, there is something strangely conspicuous about the way the first of these three verbs is written in a Torah scroll. Its last letter, an *alef*, is written small – almost to the point of invisibility. The standard-size letters spell out the word *vayikar*, meaning "he encountered" or "he chanced upon." Unlike *vayikra*, which refers to a call, a meeting by request, *vayikar* suggests the opposite: an accidental meeting, a mere happenstance.

The Sages, always alert to the way a word in one place chimes with one in another, recall that *vayikar* is the verb the Torah uses for God's encounter with the pagan prophet Bilam (Num. 23:16). Rashi comments: "All [God's] communications [to Moshe], whether they use the words 'speak' or 'say' or 'command,' were preceded by a call [*keria*], which is a term of endearment, used by the angels when they address one another, as it is said, 'And they called out one to another' [*vekara zeh el zeh*, Is. 6:3]. However, to the prophets of the nations of the world, His appearance is described by an expression signifying a casual encounter and uncleanness, as it says, 'The Lord met Bilam' (Num. 23:16)." For Rashi, the verb "to call" denotes something more than mere speech. It implies affection, intimacy, a relationship of love.

In the final *parasha* of the book of Leviticus, Parashat Beḥukotai, we encounter an echo of *vayikar*, the meeting of happenstance. There, the passage known as the *tokheḥa*, the "warning" or "rebuke," tells of the curses that will befall the Israelites if they fail to keep their covenant with God. These curses contain a recurring motif: the word *keri*, an unusual word which by the mishnaic period will denote "uncleanness," as hinted by Rashi above. It appears seven times in the *tokheḥa* – always a sign of significance – and nowhere else in the whole Torah.

The commentators disagree as to what the word *keri* means there. Saadia Gaon understands it as "if you are rebellious," and Ibn Ezra as "if you are overconfident." Rambam,

3 Lord, you may bring it either from the herd or from the flock. If the offering is
a burnt offering from the herd, one must offer a male animal without blemish.
The one making the offering shall bring it to the entrance to the Tent of Meeting
4 to be accepted on his behalf before the Lord; and, that it be accepted on his
behalf, to make his atonement, he shall lay his hand on the head of the burnt
5 offering and shall have the bull slaughtered before the Lord. And Aharon's
sons the priests shall present the blood, dashing it against each side of the altar

רש"י

שלו, אף אתם לא תקריבו מן הגזל: **הבהמה.** יכול אף חיה בכלל? תלמוד לומר: "בקר וצאן": **מן הבהמה.** ולא כלה, להוציא את הרובע ואת הנרבע: **מן הבקר.** להוציא את הנעבד: **מן הצאן.** להוציא את המקצה: **ומן הצאן.** להוציא את הנוגח שהמית. כשהוא אומר למטה מן הענין: "מן הבקר" (פסוק ג), שאין תלמוד לומר – להוציא את הטרפה: **תקריבו.** מלמד ששנים מתנדבים עולה בשתפות: **קרבנכם.** מלמד שהיא באה נדבת צבור, היא עולת קיץ המזבח, הבאה מן המותרות:

ג **זכר.** ולא נקבה. כשהוא אומר: "זכר" למטה (פסוק י), שאין תלמוד לומר – זכר ולא טמטום ואנדרוגינוס: **תמים.** בלא מום: **אל פתח אהל מועד.** מטפל בהבאתו עד העזרה. מהו אומר "יקריב יקריב"? אפלו נתערבה עולת ראובן בעולת שמעון, יקריב כל אחת לשם מי שהוא. וכן עולה בחלין, ימכרו החלין לצרכי עולות, והרי הן כלן עולות, ותקרב כל אחת לשם מי שהוא. יכול אפלו נתערבה בפסולין, או בשאינו מינו? תלמוד לומר: "יקריבנו": **יקריב אתו.** מלמד שכופין אותו. יכול בעל כרחו? תלמוד לומר: "לרצנו", הא כיצד? כופין אותו עד שיאמר: 'רוצה אני': **לפני ה' וסמך.** אין סמיכה בבמה:

ד **על ראש העלה.** להביא עולת חובה לסמיכה, ולהביא עולת הצאן: **העלה.** פרט לעולת העוף: **ונרצה לו.** על מה הוא מרצה לו? אם תאמר על כריתות ומיתות בית דין או מיתה בידי שמים או מלקות – הרי ענשן אמור, הא אינו מרצה אלא על עשה ועל לאו שנתק לעשה:

ה **ושחט... והקריבו... הכהנים.** מקבלה ואילך מצות כהנה, למד על השחיטה שכשרה בזר: **לפני ה'.** בעזרה: **והקריבו.** זו קבלה שהיא הראשונה, ומשמעה לשון הולכה, למדנו שתיהן: **בני אהרן.** יכול חללים? תלמוד לומר: "הכהנים": **את הדם וזרקו את הדם.** מה תלמוד לומר: 'דם' 'דם' שתי פעמים? להביא את שנתערב במינו או בשאינו מינו. יכול אף בפסולים, או בחטאות הפנימיות או בחטאות החיצוניות, שאלו למעלה והיא למטה? תלמוד לומר במקום אחר: "דמו" (להלן פסוק יח): **וזרקו.** עומד למטה וזורק מן הכלי לכתל המזבח למטה מחוט הסקרא כנגד הזויות, לכך נאמר: "סביב", שיהא הדם נתון בארבע רוחות המזבח. או יכול יקיפנו כחוט? תלמוד לומר: "וזרקו", ואי אפשר להקיף בזריקה. אי "וזרקו", יכול בזריקה אחת? תלמוד לומר: "סביב". הא כיצד? נותן שתי מתנות שהן ארבע: **אשר פתח אהל מועד.** ולא בזמן שהוא מפרק:

ו **והפשיט את העלה.** מה תלמוד לומר "העלה"? לרבות את כל העולות להפשט ונתוח:

word *boker*, "dawn," literally, "to break through," as the first rays of sunlight break through the darkness of night. Cattle, stampeding, break through barriers. Unless constrained by fences, cattle are no respecters of boundaries. To sacrifice the *bakar* is to learn to recognize and respect boundaries – between holy and profane, pure and impure, permitted and forbidden. Barriers of the mind can sometimes be stronger than walls.

Finally, the word *tzon*, "flock," represents the herd instinct – the powerful drive to move in a given direction because others are doing likewise. The great figures of Judaism – Avraham, Moshe, the prophets – were distinguished precisely by their ability to stand apart from the herd, to be different, to challenge the idols of the age, to refuse to capitulate to the intellectual fashions of the moment. That, ultimately, is the meaning of holiness in Judaism.

We can transcend the *behema*, the *bakar*, and the *tzon*. By bringing that which is animal within us close to God, we allow the material to be suffused with the spiritual. We become no longer slaves of nature but servants of the living God.

ג מִן־הַבָּקָר וּמִן־הַצֹּאן תַּקְרִיבוּ אֶת־קׇרְבַּנְכֶם׃ אִם־עֹלָה קׇרְבָּנוֹ מִן־
הַבָּקָר זָכָר תָּמִים יַקְרִיבֶנּוּ אֶל־פֶּתַח אֹהֶל מוֹעֵד יַקְרִיב אֹתוֹ לִרְצֹנוֹ
ד ה לִפְנֵי יְהוָה׃ וְסָמַךְ יָדוֹ עַל רֹאשׁ הָעֹלָה וְנִרְצָה לוֹ לְכַפֵּר עָלָיו׃ וְשָׁחַט
אֶת־בֶּן הַבָּקָר לִפְנֵי יְהוָה וְהִקְרִיבוּ בְּנֵי אַהֲרֹן הַכֹּהֲנִים אֶת־הַדָּם וְזָרְקוּ
ו אֶת־הַדָּם עַל־הַמִּזְבֵּחַ סָבִיב אֲשֶׁר־פֶּתַח אֹהֶל מוֹעֵד׃ וְהִפְשִׁיט אֶת־

אונקלוס

מִן תּוֹרֵי וּמִן עָנָא, תְּקָרְבוּן יָת קֻרְבָּנְכוֹן: ג אִם עֲלָתָא קֻרְבָּנֵיהּ מִן תּוֹרֵי, דְּכַר שְׁלִים יְקָרְבִנֵּיהּ, לִתְרַע, מַשְׁכַּן זִמְנָא יְקָרֵיב יָתֵיהּ, לְרַעֲוָא לֵיהּ קֳדָם יי: ד וְיִסְמוֹךְ יְדֵיהּ, עַל רֵישׁ עֲלָתָא, וְיִתְרְעֵי לֵיהּ לְכַפָּרָא עֲלוֹהִי: ה וְיִכּוֹס, יָת בַּר תּוֹרֵי קֳדָם יי, וִיקָרְבוּן, בְּנֵי אַהֲרֹן כָּהֲנַיָּא יָת דְּמָא, וְיִזְרְקוּן יָת דְּמָא עַל מַדְבְּחָא סְחוֹר סְחוֹר, דִּבִתְרַע מַשְׁכַּן זִמְנָא: ו וְיַשְׁלַח יָת

The noun *korban,* "sacrifice," and the verb *lehakriv,* "to offer something as a sacrifice," actually mean "that which is brought close" and "the act of bringing close." The key element is not only giving something up (the usual meaning of sacrifice), but rather bringing something close to God. *Lehakriv* is to bring the animal element within us to be transformed through the divine fire that once burned on the altar, and still burns at the heart of prayer if we truly seek closeness to God.

1:2 מִן־הַבָּקָר וּמִן־הַצֹּאן *From the herd or from the flock* – In the allegorical interpretation of Rabbi Shneur Zalman of Liadi (see previous comment), each of the three types of animal mentioned in the verse – *behema,* "animal," *bakar,* "cattle," and *tzon,* "flock" – represents a separate animal-like feature of the human personality.

Behema represents the animal instinct itself. The word refers to domesticated animals. It does not imply the savage instincts of the predator. It means something more tame. Animals spend their time searching for food. Their lives are bounded by the struggle to survive. To sacrifice the animal within us is to be moved by something more than mere survival. The godly soul within us is the force that makes us look up, beyond the physical world, beyond mere survival, in search of meaning, purpose, goal.

The Hebrew word *bakar,* "cattle," reminds us of the

the word order of the sentence is unexpected. We would expect to read: *Adam mikem ki yakriv,* "When one of you offers a sacrifice." Instead, it says *Adam ki yakriv mikem,* literally, "When one offers a sacrifice *of you.*" The essence of sacrifice, said Rabbi Shneur Zalman (*Likkutei Torah,* Vayikra 2a ff.), is that we offer ourselves. We bring to God our faculties, our energies, our thoughts and emotions. The physical form of sacrifice – an animal offered on the altar – is an external manifestation of an inner act. The real sacrifice is *mikem,* "of you." We give God something of ourselves.

What exactly is it that we give God when we offer a sacrifice? The Jewish mystics, among them Rabbi Shneur Zalman, spoke about two souls that each of us has – the animal soul (*nefesh habahamit*) and the godly soul. On the one hand we are physical beings. We are part of nature. We have physical needs: food, drink, shelter. We are born, we live, we die.

Yet we are not simply animals. We have immortal longings. We can think, speak, and communicate. We can reach out to others. We are the one life-form known to us in the universe that can ask the question "why?" We can formulate ideas and be moved by high ideals. Physically, we are almost nothing; spiritually, we are brushed by the wings of eternity. We have a godly soul. What we offer God is not just an animal, but also the *nefesh habahamit,* the animal soul within us.

6 at the entrance to the Tent of Meeting. The burnt offering shall then be skinned
7 and cut into pieces. The sons of Aharon the priest shall arrange wood on the
8 fire they will have placed upon the altar. Then Aharon's sons the priests shall
arrange the pieces of the sacrifice, with the head and the fat, upon the wood
9 on the altar fire; the inner organs and legs shall first be washed with water. The
priest shall then burn it all on the altar as a burnt offering, an offering of fire,
10 a pleasing aroma to the LORD. If the offering is a burnt offering from
the flock, whether a sheep or a goat, one must offer a male without blemish.
11 The one making the sacrifice shall have it slaughtered on the north side of the
altar before the LORD, and Aharon's sons the priests shall dash its blood against
12 each side of the altar. The sacrifice shall be cut into pieces, including the head
and the fat, and the priest shall arrange these upon the wood on the altar fire,
13 the inner organs and legs having been washed with water. The priest shall then
offer it all, sending it up in smoke upon the altar as a burnt offering, an offering
of fire, a pleasing aroma to the LORD.
14 If the offering for the LORD is to be a burnt offering of fowl, one may offer SHENI

רש"י

אֹתָהּ לִנְתָחֶיהָ. וְלֹא נְתָחֶיהָ לִנְתָחִים:

ז **וְנָתְנוּ אֵשׁ.** אַף עַל פִּי שֶׁהָאֵשׁ יוֹרֶדֶת מִן הַשָּׁמַיִם, מִצְוָה לְהָבִיא מִן הַהֶדְיוֹט: **בְּנֵי אַהֲרֹן הַכֹּהֵן.** כְּשֶׁהוּא בִּכְהוּנּוֹ, הָא אִם עָבַד בְּבִגְדֵי כֹּהֵן הֶדְיוֹט עֲבוֹדָתוֹ פְּסוּלָה:

ח **בְּנֵי אַהֲרֹן הַכֹּהֲנִים.** כְּשֶׁהֵם בִּכְהוּנָּם, הָא כֹּהֵן הֶדְיוֹט שֶׁעָבַד בִּשְׁמוֹנָה בְּגָדִים עֲבוֹדָתוֹ פְּסוּלָה: **אֵת הַנְּתָחִים אֶת הָרֹאשׁ.** לְפִי שֶׁאֵין הָרֹאשׁ בִּכְלַל הֶפְשֵׁט, שֶׁכְּבָר הֻתַּז בִּשְׁחִיטָה, לְפִיכָךְ הֻצְרַךְ לִמְנוֹתוֹ לְעַצְמוֹ: **וְאֶת הַפָּדֶר.** לָמָּה נֶאֱמַר? לְלַמֶּדְךָ שֶׁמַּעֲלֵהוּ עִם הָרֹאשׁ וּמְכַסֶּה בּוֹ אֶת בֵּית הַשְּׁחִיטָה, וְזֶהוּ דֶּרֶךְ כָּבוֹד שֶׁל מַעְלָה: **אֲשֶׁר עַל הַמִּזְבֵּחַ.** שֶׁלֹּא יִהְיוּ הַגְּזִירִין יוֹצְאִין חוּץ לַמַּעֲרָכָה:

ט **עֹלָה.** לְשֵׁם עוֹלָה יַקְטִירֶנּוּ: **אִשֵּׁה.** כְּשֶׁיִּשְׁחָטֶנּוּ יְהֵא שׁוֹחֲטוֹ לְשֵׁם הָאֵשׁ. וְכָל 'אִשֶּׁה' לְשׁוֹן אֵשׁ, פוּאִידְ"א בְּלַעַז: **נִיחוֹחַ.** נַחַת רוּחַ לְפָנַי שֶׁאָמַרְתִּי וְנַעֲשָׂה רְצוֹנִי:

י **וְאִם מִן הַצֹּאן.** וָי"ו מוֹסִיף עַל עִנְיָן רִאשׁוֹן. וְלָמָּה הֶפְסֵק? לִתֵּן רֶוַח לְמֹשֶׁה לְהִתְבּוֹנֵן בֵּין פָּרָשָׁה לְפָרָשָׁה: **מִן הַצֹּאן מִן הַכְּשָׂבִים מִן הָעִזִּים.** הֲרֵי אֵלּוּ שְׁלֹשָׁה מִעוּטִין: פְּרָט לְזָקֵן וּלְחוֹלֶה וְלִמְזֹהָם:

יא **עַל יֶרֶךְ הַמִּזְבֵּחַ.** עַל צַד הַמִּזְבֵּחַ: **צָפֹנָה לִפְנֵי ה'.** וְאֵין צָפוֹן בְּבָמָה:

יד **מִן הָעוֹף.** וְלֹא כָל הָעוֹף, לְפִי שֶׁנֶּאֱמַר: "תָּמִים זָכָר בַּבָּקָר בַּכְּשָׂבִים וּבָעִזִּים" (להלן כב, יט), תַּמּוּת וְזַכְרוּת בִּבְהֵמָה וְאֵין תַּמּוּת וְזַכְרוּת בְּעוֹפוֹת, יָכוֹל אַף מְחֻסַּר אֵבֶר? תַּלְמוּד לוֹמַר: "מִן הָעוֹף": **תֹּרִים.** גְּדוֹלִים וְלֹא

God is king – maker and sovereign of the vast universe. Yet even before God is our king, He is our father, our parent, the one who brought us into being in love, who nurtured and sustained us, who taught us His ways, and who tenderly watches over our destiny. Sacrifice – the gift we bring to God – is the gift of the made to its Maker, the owned to its Owner, the child to its Parent. If creation is an act of love, sacrifice is an acknowledgment of that love.

grown to maturity, brings a parent a gift to express his or her thanks. This too may seem absurd. What can a child give a parent that remotely approximates what a parent gives a child, namely, life itself? Yet it is so, and the reverse is also true. The cruelest thing a child can do is *not* to acknowledge his or her parents. The Talmud attributes to R. Akiva the phrase *Avinu Malkenu*, "Our Father, our King" (Taanit 25b). Those two words encapsulate the essence of Jewish worship.

ז הָעֹלָה וְנִתַּח אֹתָהּ לִנְתָחֶיהָ: וְנָתְנוּ בְּנֵי אַהֲרֹן הַכֹּהֵן אֵשׁ עַל־הַמִּזְבֵּחַ
ח וְעָרְכוּ עֵצִים עַל־הָאֵשׁ: וְעָרְכוּ בְּנֵי אַהֲרֹן הַכֹּהֲנִים אֵת הַנְּתָחִים אֶת־
הָרֹאשׁ וְאֶת־הַפָּדֶר עַל־הָעֵצִים אֲשֶׁר עַל־הָאֵשׁ אֲשֶׁר עַל־הַמִּזְבֵּחַ:
ט וְקִרְבּוֹ וּכְרָעָיו יִרְחַץ בַּמָּיִם וְהִקְטִיר הַכֹּהֵן אֶת־הַכֹּל הַמִּזְבֵּחָה עֹלָה
י אִשֵּׁה רֵיחַ־נִיחוֹחַ לַיהוה: וְאִם־מִן־הַצֹּאן קָרְבָּנוֹ מִן־
יא הַכְּשָׂבִים אוֹ מִן־הָעִזִּים לְעֹלָה זָכָר תָּמִים יַקְרִיבֶנּוּ: וְשָׁחַט אֹתוֹ עַל
יֶרֶךְ הַמִּזְבֵּחַ צָפֹנָה לִפְנֵי יהוה וְזָרְקוּ בְּנֵי אַהֲרֹן הַכֹּהֲנִים אֶת־דָּמוֹ
יב עַל־הַמִּזְבֵּחַ סָבִיב: וְנִתַּח אֹתוֹ לִנְתָחָיו וְאֶת־רֹאשׁוֹ וְאֶת־פִּדְרוֹ וְעָרַךְ
יג הַכֹּהֵן אֹתָם עַל־הָעֵצִים אֲשֶׁר עַל־הָאֵשׁ אֲשֶׁר עַל־הַמִּזְבֵּחַ: וְהַקֶּרֶב
וְהַכְּרָעַיִם יִרְחַץ בַּמָּיִם וְהִקְרִיב הַכֹּהֵן אֶת־הַכֹּל וְהִקְטִיר הַמִּזְבֵּחָה
עֹלָה הוּא אִשֵּׁה רֵיחַ נִיחֹחַ לַיהוה:
יד וְאִם מִן־הָעוֹף עֹלָה קָרְבָּנוֹ לַיהוה וְהִקְרִיב מִן־הַתֹּרִים אוֹ מִן־בְּנֵי שני

אונקלוס

עֲלָתָא, וִיפַלֵּיג יָתַהּ לְאֶבְרַהָא: ז וְיִתְּנוּן, בְּנֵי אַהֲרֹן כָּהֲנָא, אִישָׁתָא עַל מַדְבְּחָא, וִיסַדְּרוּן אָעַיָּא עַל אִישָׁתָא: ח וִיסַדְּרוּן, בְּנֵי אַהֲרֹן כָּהֲנַיָּא, יָת אֶבְרַיָּא, יָת רֵישָׁא וְיָת תַּרְבָּא, עַל אָעַיָּא דְּעַל אִישָׁתָא, דְּעַל מַדְבְּחָא: ט וְגַוֵּיהּ וּכְרָעוֹהִי יְחַלֵּיל בְּמַיָּא, וְיַסֵּיק כָּהֲנָא יָת כּוֹלָּא לְמַדְבְּחָא, עֲלָתָא, קֻרְבַּן דְּמִתְקַבַּל בְּרַעֲוָא קֳדָם יְיָ: י וְאִם מִן עָנָא קֻרְבָּנֵיהּ מִן אִמְּרַיָּא, אוֹ מִן בְּנֵי עִזַּיָּא לַעֲלָתָא, דְּכַר שְׁלִים יְקָרְבִנֵּיהּ:

יא וְיִכּוֹס יָתֵיהּ, עַל שִׁדָּא דְמַדְבְּחָא, צִפּוּנָא קֳדָם יְיָ, וְיִזְרְקוּן, בְּנֵי אַהֲרֹן כָּהֲנַיָּא יָת דְּמֵיהּ, עַל מַדְבְּחָא סְחוֹר סְחוֹר: יב וִיפַלֵּיג יָתֵיהּ לְאֶבְרוֹהִי, וְיָת רֵישֵׁיהּ וְיָת תַּרְבֵּיהּ, וִיסַדַּר כָּהֲנָא יָתְהוֹן, עַל אָעַיָּא דְּעַל אִישָׁתָא, דְּעַל מַדְבְּחָא: יג וְגַוָּא וּכְרָעַיָּא יְחַלֵּיל בְּמַיָּא, וִיקָרֵיב כָּהֲנָא יָת כּוֹלָּא וְיַסֵּיק לְמַדְבְּחָא, עֲלָתָא הוּא, קֻרְבַּן דְּמִתְקַבַּל בְּרַעֲוָא קֳדָם יְיָ: יד וְאִם מִן עוֹפָא, עֲלָתָא קֻרְבָּנֵיהּ קֳדָם יְיָ, וִיקָרֵיב מִן שַׁפְנִינַיָּא, אוֹ, מִן בְּנֵי

1:9 רֵיחַ־נִיחוֹחַ לַיהוה *A pleasing aroma to the LORD* – The sacrifices of the biblical age were ways in which the individual or the nation said, in effect: What we have, God, is really Yours. The world exists because of You. *We* exist because of You. Nothing we have is ultimately ours. The gesture of sacrifice is, on the face of it, absurd. What we give to God is something that already belongs to Him. As King David said: "Who am I and who are my people that we should have the power to offer so freely? For all is from You, and we have given You only what is Yours" (1 Chr. 29:14). Yet to *give back* to God is a profound instinct of the soul. Doing so, we acknowledge our dependency. We cast off the carapace of self-absorption. That is why, in one of its most striking phrases, the Torah speaks of sacrifice as being *rei'aḥ niḥo'aḥ*, "a pleasing aroma," to God.

One of the sweetest savors of parenthood is when a child,

15 doves or pigeons. The priest shall bring the offering to the altar, sever its neck,
16 and burn it on the altar; its blood shall be drained against the altar wall: the
priest shall remove the crop with its feathers and throw that to the east side
17 of the altar, to the place where the ashes are gathered. Then he shall tear the
bird open by its wings, without dividing it completely. The priest shall then
send it up in smoke upon the altar, on the wood of the altar fire. It is a burnt
2 1 offering, an offering of fire, a pleasing aroma to the LORD. When one
brings a grain offering to the LORD, it shall be of fine flour. The one who brings
2 the sacrifice shall pour oil over it, then place incense upon it, and bring it to
Aharon's sons, the priests. From this, the priest shall scoop out a handful of its
fine flour and oil, together with all its incense, and send this remembrance up in
3 smoke upon the altar as an offering of fire, a pleasing aroma to the LORD. What
remains of the grain offering shall belong to Aharon and his sons; it is holy of

רש״י

קְטַנִּים: **בְּנֵי יוֹנָה**. קְטַנִּים וְלֹא גְּדוֹלִים: **מִן הַתֹּרִים אוֹ מִן בְּנֵי הַיּוֹנָה**. פְּרָט לִתְחִלַּת הַצִּהוּב שֶׁבָּזֶה וְשֶׁבָּזֶה שֶׁהוּא פָּסוּל, שֶׁגָּדוֹל הוּא אֵצֶל בְּנֵי יוֹנָה וְקָטָן אֵצֶל תּוֹרִים:

טו **וְהִקְרִיבוֹ**. אֲפִילוּ פְּרִידָה אַחַת יָבִיא: **הַכֹּהֵן וּמָלַק**. אֵין מְלִיקָה בִּכְלִי אֶלָּא בְּעַצְמוֹ שֶׁל כֹּהֵן, קוֹצֵץ בְּצִפָּרְנוֹ מִמּוּל הָעֹרֶף, וְחוֹתֵךְ הַמַּפְרֶקֶת עַד שֶׁמַּגִּיעַ לַסִּימָנִין וְקוֹצְצָן: **וְנִמְצָה דָמוֹ**. לְשׁוֹן "וּמִיץ אַפַּיִם" (משלי ל, לג), "כִּי אָפֵס הַמֵּץ" (ישעיה טז, ד). כּוֹבֵשׁ בֵּית הַשְּׁחִיטָה עַל קִיר הַמִּזְבֵּחַ וְהַדָּם מִתְמַצֶּה וְיוֹרֵד: **וּמָלַק וְהִקְטִיר וְנִמְצָה**. אֶפְשָׁר לוֹמַר כֵּן, מֵאַחַר שֶׁהוּא מַקְטִיר הוּא מוֹצֶה?! אֶלָּא, מַה הַקְטָרָה הָרֹאשׁ בְּעַצְמוֹ וְהַגּוּף בְּעַצְמוֹ אַף מְלִיקָה כֵּן. וּפְשׁוּטוֹ שֶׁל מִקְרָא, מְסֹרָס הוּא: "וּמָלַק וְהִקְטִיר", וְקֹדֶם הַקְטָרָה "וְנִמְצָה דָמוֹ" כְּבָר:

טז **מֻרְאָתוֹ**. מְקוֹם הָרְאִי, זֶה הַזֶּפֶק: **בְּנֹצָתָהּ**. עִם בְּנֵי מֵעֶיהָ. וְ'נוֹצָה' לְשׁוֹן דָּבָר הַמָּאוּס, כְּמוֹ: "כִּי נָצוּ גַּם נָעוּ" (איכה ד, טו), וְזֶהוּ שֶׁתִּרְגֵּם אוּנְקְלוֹס: "בְּאוּכְלֵיהּ", וְזֶהוּ מִדְרָשׁוֹ שֶׁל אַבָּא יוֹסֵי בֶּן חָנָן, שֶׁאָמַר: נוֹטֵל אֶת הַקֻּרְקְבָן עִמָּהּ. וְרַבּוֹתֵינוּ זִכְרוֹנָם לִבְרָכָה אָמְרוּ: קוֹדֵר סָבִיב הַזֶּפֶק בְּסַכִּין כְּעֵין אֲרֻבָּה, וְנוֹטְלוֹ עִם הַנּוֹצָה שֶׁעַל הָעוֹר. בְּעוֹלַת בְּהֵמָה שֶׁאֵינָהּ אוֹכֶלֶת אֶלָּא בְּאֵבוּס בְּעָלֶיהָ, נֶאֱמַר: "וְהַקֶּרֶב וְהַכְּרָעַיִם יִרְחַץ בַּמַּיִם וְגוֹ' וְהִקְטִיר" (לעיל פסוק יג), וּבָעוֹף, שֶׁנִּזּוֹן מִן הַגָּזֵל, נֶאֱמַר: "וְהִשְׁלִיךְ" אֶת הַמֵּעַיִם שֶׁאָכְלוּ מִן הַגָּזֵל: **אֵצֶל הַמִּזְבֵּחַ קֵדְמָה**. בְּמִזְרָחוֹ שֶׁל כֶּבֶשׁ: **אֶל מְקוֹם הַדָּשֶׁן**. מָקוֹם שֶׁנּוֹתְנִין שָׁם תְּרוּמַת הַדֶּשֶׁן בְּכָל בֹּקֶר וְדִשּׁוּן מִזְבֵּחַ הַפְּנִימִי וְהַמְּנוֹרָה, וְכֻלָּם נִבְלָעִים שָׁם בִּמְקוֹמָן:

יז **וְשִׁסַּע**. אֵין שִׁסּוּעַ אֶלָּא בְּיָד, וְכֵן הוּא אוֹמֵר בְּשִׁמְשׁוֹן: "וַיְשַׁסְּעֵהוּ כְּשַׁסַּע הַגְּדִי" (שופטים יד, ו): **בִּכְנָפָיו**. עִם כְּנָפָיו, אֵינוֹ צָרִיךְ לִמְרֹט כַּנְפֵי נוֹצָתוֹ: **בִּכְנָפָיו**. נוֹצָה מַמָּשׁ. וַהֲלֹא אֵין לְךָ הֶדְיוֹט שֶׁמֵּרִיחַ רֵיחַ כְּנָפַיִם נִשְׂרָפִים וְאֵין נַפְשׁוֹ קָצָה עָלָיו, וְלָמָּה אָמַר הַכָּתוּב יַקְרִיב? כְּדֵי שֶׁיְּהֵא הַמִּזְבֵּחַ שָׂבֵעַ וּמְהֻדָּר בְּקָרְבָּנוֹ שֶׁל עָנִי: **לֹא יַבְדִּיל**. אֵינוֹ מַפְרִיקוֹ לִגְמָרֵי לִשְׁתֵּי חֲתִיכוֹת, אֶלָּא קוֹרְעוֹ מִגַּבּוֹ. נֶאֱמַר בָּעוֹף 'רֵיחַ נִיחֹחַ' וְנֶאֱמַר בַּבְּהֵמָה 'רֵיחַ נִיחֹחַ' (לעיל פסוקים ט; יג), לוֹמַר לְךָ, אֶחָד הַמַּרְבֶּה וְאֶחָד הַמַּמְעִיט, וּבִלְבַד שֶׁיְּכַוֵּן אֶת לִבּוֹ לַשָּׁמַיִם:

ב א **וְנֶפֶשׁ כִּי תַקְרִיב**. לֹא נֶאֱמַר 'נֶפֶשׁ' בְּכָל קָרְבְּנוֹת נְדָבָה אֶלָּא בְּמִנְחָה. מִי דַּרְכּוֹ לְהִתְנַדֵּב מִנְחָה? עָנִי. אָמַר הַקָּדוֹשׁ בָּרוּךְ הוּא: מַעֲלֶה אֲנִי עָלָיו כְּאִלּוּ הִקְרִיב נַפְשׁוֹ: **סֹלֶת יִהְיֶה קָרְבָּנוֹ**. הָאוֹמֵר: 'הֲרֵי עָלַי מִנְחָה' סְתָם, מֵבִיא מִנְחַת סֹלֶת שֶׁהִיא הָרִאשׁוֹנָה שֶׁבַּמְּנָחוֹת, וְנִקְמֶצֶת כְּשֶׁהִיא סֹלֶת כְּמוֹ שֶׁמְּפֹרָשׁ בָּעִנְיָן. לְפִי שֶׁנֶּאֶמְרוּ כָּאן חֲמִשָּׁה מִינֵי מְנָחוֹת וְכֻלָּן בָּאוֹת אֲפוּיוֹת קֹדֶם קְמִיצָה חוּץ מִזּוֹ, לְכָךְ קְרוּיָה מִנְחַת סֹלֶת: **סֹלֶת**. אֵין 'סֹלֶת' אֶלָּא מִן הַחִטִּין, שֶׁנֶּאֱמַר: "סֹלֶת חִטִּים" (שמות כט, ב), וְאֵין מִנְחָה פְּחוּתָה מֵעִשָּׂרוֹן, שֶׁנֶּאֱמַר: "וְעִשָּׂרוֹן סֹלֶת... לְמִנְחָה" (ויקרא יד, כא), עִשָּׂרוֹן לְכָל מִנְחָה: **וְיָצַק עָלֶיהָ שֶׁמֶן**. עַל כֻּלָּהּ: **וְנָתַן עָלֶיהָ לְבֹנָה**. עַל מִקְצָתָהּ, מֵנִיחַ קֹמֶץ לְבוֹנָה עָלֶיהָ לְצַד אֶחָד. וּמָה רָאִיתָ לוֹמַר כֵּן? שֶׁאֵין רִבּוּי אַחַר רִבּוּי בַּתּוֹרָה אֶלָּא לְמַעֵט. דָּבָר אַחֵר, שֶׁמֶן עַל כֻּלָּהּ מִפְּנֵי שֶׁהוּא נִבְלָל עִמָּהּ וְנִקְמָץ עִמָּהּ, כְּמוֹ שֶׁנֶּאֱמַר: "מִסָּלְתָּהּ וּמִשַּׁמְנָהּ" (פסוק ב), וּלְבוֹנָה עַל מִקְצָתָהּ, שֶׁאֵינָהּ נִבְלֶלֶת עִמָּהּ וְלֹא נִקְמֶצֶת עִמָּהּ, שֶׁנֶּאֱמַר: "עַל כָּל לְבֹנָתָהּ", שֶׁלְּאַחַר שֶׁקָּמַץ מְלַקֵּט אֶת הַלְּבוֹנָה כֻּלָּהּ מֵעָלֶיהָ וּמַקְטִירָהּ: **וְיָצַק, וְנָתַן, וֶהֱבִיאָהּ**. מְלַמֵּד שֶׁיְּצִיקָה וּבְלִילָה כְּשֵׁרִים בְּזָר:

ב **הַכֹּהֲנִים וְקָמַץ**. מִקְּמִיצָה וְאֵילָךְ מִצְוַת כְּהֻנָּה: **וְקָמַץ מִשָּׁם**. מִמָּקוֹם שֶׁרַגְלֵי הַזָּר עוֹמְדוֹת, לְלַמֶּדְךָ שֶׁהַקְּמִיצָה כְּשֵׁרָה בְּכָל מָקוֹם בָּעֲזָרָה, אַף בְּאַחַת עֶשְׂרֵה אַמָּה שֶׁל מְקוֹם דְּרִיסַת רַגְלֵי

טו הַיּוֹנָה אֶת־קָרְבָּנוֹ: וְהִקְרִיבוֹ הַכֹּהֵן אֶל־הַמִּזְבֵּחַ וּמָלַק אֶת־רֹאשׁוֹ
טז וְהִקְטִיר הַמִּזְבֵּחָה וְנִמְצָה דָמוֹ עַל קִיר הַמִּזְבֵּחַ: וְהֵסִיר אֶת־מֻרְאָתוֹ
יז בְּנֹצָתָהּ וְהִשְׁלִיךְ אֹתָהּ אֵצֶל הַמִּזְבֵּחַ קֵדְמָה אֶל־מְקוֹם הַדָּשֶׁן: וְשִׁסַּע
אֹתוֹ בִכְנָפָיו לֹא יַבְדִּיל וְהִקְטִיר אֹתוֹ הַכֹּהֵן הַמִּזְבֵּחָה עַל־הָעֵצִים
ב א אֲשֶׁר עַל־הָאֵשׁ עֹלָה הוּא אִשֵּׁה רֵיחַ נִיחֹחַ לַיהוָה: וְנֶפֶשׁ
כִּי־תַקְרִיב קָרְבַּן מִנְחָה לַיהוָה סֹלֶת יִהְיֶה קָרְבָּנוֹ וְיָצַק עָלֶיהָ שֶׁמֶן
ב וְנָתַן עָלֶיהָ לְבֹנָה: וֶהֱבִיאָהּ אֶל־בְּנֵי אַהֲרֹן הַכֹּהֲנִים וְקָמַץ מִשָּׁם מְלֹא
קֻמְצוֹ מִסָּלְתָּהּ וּמִשַּׁמְנָהּ עַל כָּל־לְבֹנָתָהּ וְהִקְטִיר הַכֹּהֵן אֶת־אַזְכָּרָתָהּ
ג הַמִּזְבֵּחָה אִשֵּׁה רֵיחַ נִיחֹחַ לַיהוָה: וְהַנּוֹתֶרֶת מִן־הַמִּנְחָה לְאַהֲרֹן

אונקלוס

יוֹנָה יָת קֻרְבָּנֵיהּ: טו וִיקָרְבִנֵּיהּ כָּהֲנָא לְמַדְבְּחָא, וְיִמְלוֹק יָת רֵישֵׁיהּ, וְיַסֵּיק לְמַדְבְּחָא, וְיִתְמְצֵי דְמֵיהּ, עַל כּוֹתֶל מַדְבְּחָא: טז וְיַעְדֵּי יָת זָפְקֵיהּ בְּאֻכְלֵיהּ, וְיִרְמֵי יָתַהּ, בִּסְטַר מַדְבְּחָא קִדּוּמָא, בַּאֲתַר דְּמַקְּרִין קִטְמָא: יז וִיפָרֵיק יָתֵיהּ בְּכַנְפוֹהִי לָא יַפְרֵישׁ, וְיַסֵּיק יָתֵיהּ כָּהֲנָא לְמַדְבְּחָא, עַל אָעַיָּא דְּעַל אִישָּׁתָא, עֲלָתָא הוּא, קֻרְבַּן דְּמִתְקַבַּל בְּרַעֲוָא קֳדָם יי: ב א וֶאֱנָשׁ, אֲרֵי יְקָרֵיב, קֻרְבַּן מִנְחָתָא קֳדָם יי, סֻלְתָּא יְהֵי קֻרְבָּנֵיהּ, וְיָרִיק עֲלַהּ מִשְׁחָא, וְיִתֵּין עֲלַהּ לְבוֹנְתָא: ב וְיַיְתֵינַהּ, לְוָת בְּנֵי אַהֲרֹן כָּהֲנַיָּא, וְיִקְמוֹץ מִתַּמָּן מְלֵי קֻמְצֵיהּ, מִסֻּלְתַּהּ וּמִמִּשְׁחַהּ, עַל כָּל לְבוֹנְתַהּ, וְיַסֵּיק כָּהֲנָא יָת אַדְכָּרְתַהּ לְמַדְבְּחָא, קֻרְבַּן דְּמִתְקַבַּל בְּרַעֲוָא קֳדָם יי: ג וּדְיִשְׁתְּאַר מִן מִנְחָתָא, לְאַהֲרֹן

רש״י

יִשְׂרָאֵל: מְלֹא קֻמְצוֹ. יָכוֹל מְבֹרָץ, מְבֹצְבָּץ וְיוֹצֵא לְכָל צַד? תַּלְמוּד לוֹמַר בְּמָקוֹם אַחֵר: "וְהֵרִים מִמֶּנּוּ בְּקֻמְצוֹ" (להלן ו, ח), לֹא יְהֵא כָּשֵׁר אֶלָּא מַה שֶּׁבְּתוֹךְ הַקֹּמֶץ. אִי "בְּקֻמְצוֹ", יָכוֹל חָסֵר? תַּלְמוּד לוֹמַר: "מְלֹא". הָא כֵּיצַד? חוֹפֶה שָׁלֹשׁ אֶצְבְּעוֹתָיו עַל פַּס יָדוֹ, וְזֶהוּ "קֹמֶץ" בְּמַשְׁמַע לְשׁוֹן הָעִבְרִית: עַל כָּל לְבֹנָתָהּ. לְבַד כָּל הַלְּבוֹנָה יְהֵא הַקֹּמֶץ מָלֵא: לְבֹנָתָהּ וְהִקְטִיר. אַף הַלְּבוֹנָה בְּהַקְטָרָה: מְלֹא קֻמְצוֹ מִסָּלְתָּהּ וּמִשַּׁמְנָהּ. הָא אִם קָמַץ וְעָלָה בְּיָדוֹ גַּרְגִּיר מֶלַח אוֹ קֹרֶט לְבוֹנָה, פְּסוּלָה: אַזְכָּרָתָהּ. הַקֹּמֶץ הָעוֹלֶה לַגָּבוֹהַּ הוּא זִכְרוֹן הַמִּנְחָה, שֶׁבּוֹ נִזְכָּר בְּעָלֶיהָ לְטוֹבָה וּלְנַחַת רוּחַ:

ג לְאַהֲרֹן וּלְבָנָיו. כֹּהֵן גָּדוֹל נוֹטֵל חֵלֶק בָּרֹאשׁ שֶׁלֹּא בְמַחֲלֹקֶת,

2:1 סלת *Fine flour* – Flour was milled painstakingly with hand mills, and fine white wheat flour was the most labor intensive and desirable kind. Its preparation evoked the devotion of the priest, the endlessly repeated, precisely prescribed rites, the humble, unspectacular acts of devotion that translate faith into the lives of its followers.

Torat Kohanim sees the religious life as built on the foundations of its rituals that, barring catastrophe, never change. Even though we no longer have a Temple or sacrifices or a functioning priesthood, Judaism continues to be a religion of rituals, and it is this that sustains its continuity through time, etching its days with the charisma of grace, more like a marriage than a romance but no less moving for the quietness of its beauty.

4 holies among the fire offerings to the LORD. When you bring a grain
offering baked in an oven, it shall be of fine flour: unleavened loaves mixed
5 with oil or unleavened wafers spread with oil. If your offering is grain
prepared on a griddle, it shall be of fine flour mixed with oil, and unleavened.
6
7 Crumble it into pieces and pour oil over it; this is a grain offering. If SHELISHI
8 your offering is grain prepared in a pan, it shall be of fine flour in oil. You shall
bring the grain offering made in one of these ways to the LORD, presenting it
9 to the priest, who will bring it to the altar. The priest shall lift a remembrance
from the grain offering and send it up in smoke upon the altar as an offering
10 of fire, a pleasing aroma to the LORD. What is left of this grain offering shall
belong to Aharon and his sons; it is holy of holies among the fire offerings to
11 the LORD. No grain offering that you bring to the LORD shall be made with
leaven, for no leaven or honey may be used in a fire offering to the LORD, sent
12 up in smoke. You may bring them as offerings of first produce to the LORD, but
13 they may not be offered on the altar as a pleasing aroma. You shall season all
your grain offerings with salt; do not omit from your grain offering the salt of
14 your covenant with God. You shall offer salt with all your offerings. If
you bring a grain offering of first produce to the LORD, it shall be brought as
soon as it ripens on the stalk. Roasted in fire, crushed from fresh kernels; thus

רש״י

וְהַהֶדְיוֹט בְּמַחֲלֹקֶת: **קֹדֶשׁ קָדָשִׁים.** הִיא לָהֶם ״מֵאִשֵּׁי ה׳״ – אֵין לָהֶם חֵלֶק בָּהּ אֶלָּא לְאַחַר מַתְּנוֹת הָאִשִּׁים:

ד **וְכִי תַקְרִב וגו׳.** שֶׁאָמַר: ׳הֲרֵי עָלַי מִנְחַת מַאֲפֵה תַנּוּר׳, וְלִמֵּד הַכָּתוּב שֶׁיָּבִיא אוֹ חַלּוֹת אוֹ רְקִיקִין, הַחַלּוֹת בְּלוּלוֹת וְהָרְקִיקִין מְשׁוּחִין. וְנֶחְלְקוּ רַבּוֹתֵינוּ בִּמְשִׁיחָתָן, יֵשׁ אוֹמְרִים: מוֹשְׁחָן וְחוֹזֵר וּמוֹשְׁחָן עַד שֶׁכָּלֶה כָּל הַשֶּׁמֶן שֶׁבַּלֹּג, שֶׁכָּל הַמְּנָחוֹת טְעוּנוֹת לֹג שֶׁמֶן. וְיֵשׁ אוֹמְרִים: מוֹשְׁחָן כְּמִין כ״י וּשְׁאָר הַשֶּׁמֶן נֶאֱכָל בִּפְנֵי עַצְמוֹ לַכֹּהֲנִים. מַה תַּלְמוּד לוֹמַר ״בַּשֶּׁמֶן״ ״בַּשֶּׁמֶן״ שְׁתֵּי פְעָמִים? לְהַכְשִׁיר שֶׁמֶן שֵׁנִי וּשְׁלִישִׁי הַיּוֹצֵא מִן הַזֵּיתִים, וְאֵין צָרִיךְ שֶׁמֶן רִאשׁוֹן אֶלָּא לַמְּנוֹרָה, שֶׁנֶּאֱמַר בּוֹ: ״זָךְ״ (שמות כז, כ). וְשָׁנִינוּ בִּמְנָחוֹת (דף עו ע״א): כָּל הַמְּנָחוֹת הָאֲפוּיוֹת לִפְנֵי קְמִיצָתָן וְנִקְמָצוֹת עַל יְדֵי פְתִיתָה, כֻּלָּן בָּאוֹת עֶשֶׂר עֶשֶׂר חַלּוֹת, וְהָאוֹמֵר בָּהּ ׳רְקִיקִין׳ בָּאָה עֶשֶׂר רְקִיקִין:

ה **וְאִם מִנְחָה עַל הַמַּחֲבַת.** שֶׁאָמַר: ׳הֲרֵי עָלַי מִנְחַת מַחֲבַת׳. וּכְלִי הוּא שֶׁהָיָה בַּמִּקְדָּשׁ שֶׁאוֹפִין בּוֹ מִנְחָה עַל הָאוּר בַּשֶּׁמֶן, וְהַכְּלִי אֵינוֹ עָמֹק אֶלָּא צָף, וּמַעֲשֵׂי הַמִּנְחָה שֶׁבְּתוֹכוֹ קָשִׁין, שֶׁמִּתּוֹךְ שֶׁהִיא צָפָה הָאוּר שׂוֹרֵף אֶת הַשֶּׁמֶן. וְכֻלָּן טְעוּנוֹת מַתְּנוֹת שֶׁמֶן: יְצִיקָה וּבְלִילָה וּמַתַּן שֶׁמֶן בַּכְּלִי קֹדֶם לַעֲשִׂיָּתָן: **סֹלֶת בְּלוּלָה בַשֶּׁמֶן.** מְלַמֵּד שֶׁבּוֹלְלָן בְּעוֹדָן סֹלֶת:

ו **פָּתוֹת אֹתָהּ פִּתִּים.** לְרַבּוֹת כָּל הַמְּנָחוֹת הַנֶּאֱפוֹת קֹדֶם קְמִיצָה – לִפְתִיתָה: **וְיָצַקְתָּ עָלֶיהָ שֶׁמֶן מִנְחָה הִוא.** לְרַבּוֹת כָּל הַמְּנָחוֹת לִיצִיקָה. יָכוֹל אַף מִנְחַת מַאֲפֵה תַנּוּר כֵּן? תַּלְמוּד לוֹמַר: ״עָלֶיהָ״. אוֹצִיא אֶת הַחַלּוֹת וְלֹא אוֹצִיא אֶת הָרְקִיקִין? תַּלְמוּד לוֹמַר: ״הִוא״:

ז **מַרְחֶשֶׁת.** כְּלִי הוּא שֶׁהָיָה בַּמִּקְדָּשׁ, עָמֹק, וּמִתּוֹךְ שֶׁהִיא עֲמֻקָּה, שַׁמְנָהּ צָבוּר וְאֵין הָאוּר שׂוֹרְפוֹ, לְפִיכָךְ מַעֲשֵׂי מִנְחָה הָעֲשׂוּיִין לְתוֹכָהּ רוֹחֲשִׁין. כָּל דָּבָר רַךְ עַל יְדֵי מַשְׁקֶה נִרְאֶה כְּרוֹחֵשׁ וּמְנַעֲנֵעַ:

ח **אֲשֶׁר יֵעָשֶׂה מֵאֵלֶּה.** מֵאֶחָד מִן הַמִּינִים הַלָּלוּ: **וְהִקְרִיבָהּ.** בְּעָלֶיהָ ״אֶל הַכֹּהֵן״: **וְהִגִּישָׁהּ.** הַכֹּהֵן: **אֶל הַמִּזְבֵּחַ.** מַגִּיעָהּ לְקֶרֶן דְּרוֹמִית מַעֲרָבִית שֶׁל מִזְבֵּחַ:

ט **אֶת אַזְכָּרָתָהּ.** הִיא הַקֹּמֶץ:

יא **וְכָל דְּבַשׁ.** כָּל מְתִיקַת פְּרִי קְרוּיָה דְּבַשׁ:

יב **קָרְבַּן רֵאשִׁית תַּקְרִיבוּ אֹתָם.** מַה יֵּשׁ לְךָ לְהָבִיא מִן הַשְּׂאוֹר וּמִן הַדְּבַשׁ? ״קָרְבַּן רֵאשִׁית״, שְׁתֵּי הַלֶּחֶם שֶׁל עֲצֶרֶת הַבָּאִים מִן הַשְּׂאוֹר, שֶׁנֶּאֱמַר: ״חָמֵץ תֵּאָפֶינָה״ (ויקרא כג, יז), וּבִכּוּרִים מִן הַדְּבַשׁ, כְּמוֹ בִּכּוּרֵי תְאֵנִים וּתְמָרִים:

ד וּלְבָנָיו קֹדֶשׁ קׇדָשִׁים מֵאִשֵּׁי יְהֹוָה: וְכִי תַקְרִב קׇרְבַּן
מִנְחָה מַאֲפֵה תַנּוּר סֹלֶת חַלּוֹת מַצֹּת בְּלוּלֹת בַּשֶּׁמֶן וּרְקִיקֵי מַצּוֹת
ה מְשֻׁחִים בַּשָּׁמֶן: וְאִם־מִנְחָה עַל־הַמַּחֲבַת קׇרְבָּנֶךָ
ו סֹלֶת בְּלוּלָה בַשֶּׁמֶן מַצָּה תִהְיֶה: פָּתוֹת אֹתָהּ פִּתִּים וְיָצַקְתָּ עָלֶיהָ
ז שָׁמֶן מִנְחָה הִוא: וְאִם־מִנְחַת מַרְחֶשֶׁת קׇרְבָּנֶךָ שלישי
ח סֹלֶת בַּשֶּׁמֶן תֵּעָשֶׂה: וְהֵבֵאתָ אֶת־הַמִּנְחָה אֲשֶׁר יֵעָשֶׂה מֵאֵלֶּה לַיהֹוָה
ט וְהִקְרִיבָהּ אֶל־הַכֹּהֵן וְהִגִּישָׁהּ אֶל־הַמִּזְבֵּחַ: וְהֵרִים הַכֹּהֵן מִן־הַמִּנְחָה
י אֶת־אַזְכָּרָתָהּ וְהִקְטִיר הַמִּזְבֵּחָה אִשֵּׁה רֵיחַ נִיחֹחַ לַיהֹוָה: וְהַנּוֹתֶרֶת
יא מִן־הַמִּנְחָה לְאַהֲרֹן וּלְבָנָיו קֹדֶשׁ קׇדָשִׁים מֵאִשֵּׁי יְהֹוָה: כׇּל־הַמִּנְחָה
אֲשֶׁר תַּקְרִיבוּ לַיהֹוָה לֹא תֵעָשֶׂה חָמֵץ כִּי כׇל־שְׂאֹר וְכׇל־דְּבַשׁ לֹא־
יב תַקְטִירוּ מִמֶּנּוּ אִשֶּׁה לַיהֹוָה: קׇרְבַּן רֵאשִׁית תַּקְרִיבוּ אֹתָם לַיהֹוָה
יג וְאֶל־הַמִּזְבֵּחַ לֹא־יַעֲלוּ לְרֵיחַ נִיחֹחַ: וְכׇל־קׇרְבַּן מִנְחָתְךָ בַּמֶּלַח תִּמְלָח
וְלֹא תַשְׁבִּית מֶלַח בְּרִית אֱלֹהֶיךָ מֵעַל מִנְחָתֶךָ עַל כׇּל־קׇרְבָּנְךָ תַּקְרִיב
יד מֶלַח: וְאִם־תַּקְרִיב מִנְחַת בִּכּוּרִים לַיהֹוָה אָבִיב

אונקלוס

וְלִבְנוֹהִי, קֹדֶשׁ קֻדְשִׁין מִקֻּרְבָּנַיָּא דַּייָ: ד וַאֲרֵי תְקָרֵיב, קֻרְבַּן מִנְחָתָא מַאֲפֵה תַנּוּר, סוֹלֶת גְּרִיצָן פַּטִּירָן דְּפִילָן בִּמְשַׁח, וְאֶסְפּוֹגִין פַּטִּירִין דִּמְשִׁיחִין בִּמְשַׁח: ה וְאִם מִנְחָתָא עַל מַסְרֵיתָא קֻרְבָּנָךְ, סֻלְתָּא, דְּפִילָא בִּמְשַׁח פַּטִּיר תְּהֵי: ו בַּצַּע יָתַהּ בִּצּוּעִין, וּתְרִיק עֲלַהּ מִשְׁחָא, מִנְחָתָא הִיא: ז וְאִם מִנְחָתָא רְדָתָא קֻרְבָּנָךְ, סוֹלֶת בִּמְשַׁח תִּתְעֲבֵיד: ח וְתַיְתֵי יָת מִנְחָתָא, דְּיִתְעֲבֵיד, מֵאִלֵּין קֳדָם יי, וִיקָרְבִנַּהּ לְכָהֲנָא, וִיקָרְבִנַּהּ לְמַדְבְּחָא: ט וְיַפְרֵישׁ כָּהֲנָא מִן מִנְחָתָא יָת אַדְכָּרְתַהּ, וְיַסֵּיק לְמַדְבְּחָא, קֻרְבַּן דְּמִתְקַבַּל בְּרַעֲוָא קֳדָם יי: י וּדְיִשְׁתְּאַר מִן מִנְחָתָא, לְאַהֲרֹן וְלִבְנוֹהִי, קֹדֶשׁ קֻדְשִׁין מִקֻּרְבָּנַיָּא דַּייָ: יא כָּל מִנְחָתָא, דִּתְקָרְבוּן קֳדָם יי, לָא תִתְעֲבֵיד חֲמִיעַ, אֲרֵי כָל חֲמִיר וְכָל דְּבַשׁ, לָא תַסְּקוּן מִנֵּיהּ, קֻרְבָּנָא קֳדָם יי: יב קֻרְבַּן קַדְמַאי, תְּקָרְבוּן יָתְהוֹן קֳדָם יי, וּלְמַדְבְּחָא לָא יִתַּסְקוּן לְאִתְקַבָּלָא בְּרַעֲוָא: יג וְכָל קֻרְבַּן מִנְחָתָךְ בְּמִלְחָא תִּמְלַח, וְלָא תְבַטֵּיל, מְלַח קְיָם אֱלָהָךְ, מֵעַל מִנְחָתָךְ, עַל כָּל קֻרְבָּנָךְ תְּקָרֵיב מִלְחָא: יד וְאִם תְּקָרֵיב, מִנְחַת בִּכּוּרִין קֳדָם יי, אֲבִיב,

רש״י

יג מֶלַח בְּרִית. שֶׁהַבְּרִית כְּרוּתָה לַמֶּלַח מִשֵּׁשֶׁת יְמֵי בְרֵאשִׁית, שֶׁהֻבְטְחוּ הַמַּיִם הַתַּחְתּוֹנִים לִקָּרֵב בַּמִּזְבֵּחַ בַּמֶּלַח, וְנִסּוּךְ הַמַּיִם בֶּחָג: עַל כׇּל קׇרְבָּנְךָ. עַל עוֹלַת בְּהֵמָה וָעוֹף וְאֵמוּרֵי כׇל הַקֳּדָשִׁים כֻּלָּן:

יד וְאִם תַּקְרִיב. הֲרֵי "אִם" מְשַׁמֵּשׁ בִּלְשׁוֹן 'כִּי', שֶׁהֲרֵי אֵין זֶה רְשׁוּת, שֶׁהֲרֵי בְּמִנְחַת הָעֹמֶר הַכָּתוּב מְדַבֵּר, שֶׁהִיא חוֹבָה. וְכֵן: "וְאִם יִהְיֶה הַיֹּבֵל" וְגוֹ' (במדבר לו, ד): מִנְחַת בִּכּוּרִים. בְּמִנְחַת הָעֹמֶר הַכָּתוּב מְדַבֵּר,

15 shall you bring the grain offering of first produce. You shall put oil and incense
16 on it; it is a grain offering. The priest shall send its remembrance up in smoke –
some of the crushed new grain and oil together with all of the incense – as a fire
offering to the LORD.

3 1 If one's sacrifice is a peace offering, and brought from the herd, whether male or REVI'I
2 female, the animal one offers before the LORD must be without blemish. The one
bringing the offering shall lay his hand on its head and have it slaughtered at the
entrance to the Tent of Meeting. Aharon's sons the priests shall dash the blood
3 against each side of the altar. A priest shall present of the peace offering a fire
offering to the LORD: the fat that covers the entrails and all the fat surrounding
4 them; the two kidneys and the fat that is on them at the loins; and the diaphragm
5 of the liver, which should be removed with the kidneys. Aharon's sons shall send
all these up in smoke upon the altar, along with the burnt offering on the wood
on the altar fire – a fire offering, a pleasing aroma to the LORD.

רש"י

שֶׁהִיא בָּאָה אָבִיב, בִּשְׁעַת בִּשּׁוּל הַתְּבוּאָה, וּמִן הַשְּׂעוֹרִים הִיא בָּאָה, נֶאֱמַר כָּאן: "אָבִיב" וְנֶאֱמַר לְהַלָּן: "כִּי הַשְּׂעֹרָה אָבִיב" (שמות ט, לא): **קָלוּי בָּאֵשׁ.** שֶׁמְּיַבְּשִׁין אוֹתָהּ עַל הָאוּר בְּאַבּוּב שֶׁל קַלָּאִים, שֶׁאִלּוּלֵי כֵן אֵינָהּ נִטְחֶנֶת בָּרֵיחַיִם, לְפִי שֶׁהִיא לַחָה: **גֶּרֶשׂ כַּרְמֶל.** גְּרוּסָה בְּעוֹדָהּ לַחָה: **גֶּרֶשׂ.** לְשׁוֹן שְׁבִירָה וּטְחִינָה גַּסָּה בְּרֵיחַיִם שֶׁל גְּרוֹסוֹת, כְּמוֹ: "וַיַּגְרֵס בֶּחָצָץ" (איכה ג, טז), וְכֵן: "גָּרְסָה נַפְשִׁי" (תהלים קיט, כ): **כַּרְמֶל.** בְּעוֹד הַכַּר מָלֵא, שֶׁהַתְּבוּאָה לַחָה וּמְלֵאָה בַּקַּשִּׁין שֶׁלָּהּ, וְעַל כֵּן נִקְרָאִים הַמְּלִילוֹת 'כַּרְמֶל', וְכֵן: "וְכַרְמֶל בְּצִקְלֹנוֹ" (מלכים ב' ד, מב):

ג א **שְׁלָמִים.** שֶׁמַּטִּילִים שָׁלוֹם בָּעוֹלָם. "שְׁלָמִים" – שֶׁיֵּשׁ בָּהֶם שָׁלוֹם לַמִּזְבֵּחַ וְלַכֹּהֲנִים וְלַבְּעָלִים:

ג **וְאֵת כָּל הַחֵלֶב וְגוֹ'.** לְהָבִיא חֵלֶב שֶׁעַל הַקֵּבָה, דִּבְרֵי רַבִּי יִשְׁמָעֵאל. רַבִּי עֲקִיבָא אוֹמֵר: לְהָבִיא חֵלֶב שֶׁעַל הַדַּקִּין:

ד **הַכְּסָלִים.** פלנק"ש בְּלַעַז, שֶׁהַחֵלֶב שֶׁעַל הַכְּלָיוֹת כְּשֶׁהַבְּהֵמָה חַיָּה הוּא בְּגֹבַהּ הַכְּסָלִים וְהֵם לְמַטָּה, וְזֶהוּ הַחֵלֶב שֶׁתַּחַת הַמָּתְנַיִם שֶׁקּוֹרִין בְּלַעַז לונביל"ש, לְבֶן הַנִּרְאֶה לְמַעְלָה בְּגֹבַהּ הַכְּסָלִים, וּבְתַחְתִּיתוֹ הַבָּשָׂר חוֹפֵהוּ: **הַיֹּתֶרֶת.** הוּא דֹּפֶן הַמָּסָךְ שֶׁקּוֹרִין איבלי"ש, וּבִלְשׁוֹן אֲרַמִּי "חַצְרָא": **עַל הַכָּבֵד.** שֶׁיִּטֹּל מִן הַכָּבֵד עִמָּהּ מְעַט, וּבְמָקוֹם אַחֵר הוּא אוֹמֵר: "וְאֶת הַיֹּתֶרֶת מִן הַכָּבֵד" (ויקרא ט, י): **עַל הַכָּבֵד עַל הַכְּלָיוֹת.** לְבַד מִן הַכָּבֵד וּלְבַד מִן הַכְּלָיוֹת "יְסִירֶנָּה" לְזוֹ:

ה **עַל הָעֹלָה.** מִלְּבַד הָעוֹלָה, לָמַדְנוּ שֶׁתִּקְדֹּם עוֹלַת תָּמִיד לְכָל קָרְבָּן עַל הַמַּעֲרָכָה:

that it can lead people to think that there are two domains, the Temple and the world, serving God and caring for one's fellow humans, and they are disconnected. Judaism rejects the concept of two disconnected domains. Psychologically, ethically, and spiritually, they are part of a single indivisible system. To serve God is to serve humanity.

That was the point made memorably by Mikha: "Man, God has told you what is good and what the LORD seeks from you: only to do justice, love goodness, and walk modestly with your God" (Mic. 6:8). Yirmeyahu said of King Yoshiyahu: "He took up the cause of the poor and the destitute with good results. 'That is the way to know Me,' declares the LORD" (Jer. 22:16). Knowing God, said Yirmeyahu, means caring for those in need.

Rambam said essentially the same at the end of *Guide for the Perplexed* (III:54). He quotes Yirmeyahu: "'Someone may boast only of his conscious devotion to Me, for I the LORD act with loving-kindness, justice, and righteousness in the world. For it is these things that I desire,' declares the LORD" (Jer. 9:23). To know God is to know what it is to act with kindness, justice, and righteousness.

טו קָלוּי בָּאֵשׁ גֶּרֶשׂ כַּרְמֶל תַּקְרִיב אֵת מִנְחַת בִּכּוּרֶיךָ: וְנָתַתָּ עָלֶיהָ
טז שֶׁמֶן וְשַׂמְתָּ עָלֶיהָ לְבֹנָה מִנְחָה הִוא: וְהִקְטִיר הַכֹּהֵן אֶת־אַזְכָּרָתָהּ
מִגִּרְשָׂהּ וּמִשַּׁמְנָהּ עַל כָּל־לְבֹנָתָהּ אִשֶּׁה לַיהוָה:
ג א וְאִם־זֶבַח שְׁלָמִים קָרְבָּנוֹ אִם מִן־הַבָּקָר הוּא מַקְרִיב אִם־זָכָר אִם־ רביעי
ב נְקֵבָה תָּמִים יַקְרִיבֶנּוּ לִפְנֵי יהוה: וְסָמַךְ יָדוֹ עַל־רֹאשׁ קָרְבָּנוֹ וּשְׁחָטוֹ
פֶּתַח אֹהֶל מוֹעֵד וְזָרְקוּ בְּנֵי אַהֲרֹן הַכֹּהֲנִים אֶת־הַדָּם עַל־הַמִּזְבֵּחַ
ג סָבִיב: וְהִקְרִיב מִזֶּבַח הַשְּׁלָמִים אִשֶּׁה לַיהוָה אֶת־הַחֵלֶב הַמְכַסֶּה
ד אֶת־הַקֶּרֶב וְאֵת כָּל־הַחֵלֶב אֲשֶׁר עַל־הַקֶּרֶב: וְאֵת שְׁתֵּי הַכְּלָיֹת
וְאֶת־הַחֵלֶב אֲשֶׁר עֲלֵהֶן אֲשֶׁר עַל־הַכְּסָלִים וְאֶת־הַיֹּתֶרֶת עַל־הַכָּבֵד
ה עַל־הַכְּלָיוֹת יְסִירֶנָּה: וְהִקְטִירוּ אֹתוֹ בְנֵי־אַהֲרֹן הַמִּזְבֵּחָה עַל־הָעֹלָה
אֲשֶׁר עַל־הָעֵצִים אֲשֶׁר עַל־הָאֵשׁ אִשֵּׁה רֵיחַ נִיחֹחַ לַיהוָה:

אונקלוס

קְלֵי בְנוּר פֵּירוּכַן רַכִּיכַן, תְּקָרֵיב, יָת מִנְחַת בִּכּוּרָךְ: טו וְתִתֵּין עֲלַהּ מִשְׁחָא, וּתְשַׁוֵּי עֲלַהּ לְבוֹנְתָא, מִנְחֲתָא הִיא: טז וְיַסֵּיק כָּהֲנָא יָת אַדְכַּרְתַהּ, מִגּוּרְסַהּ וּמִמִּשְׁחַהּ, עַל כָּל לְבוֹנְתַהּ, קֻרְבָּנָא קֳדָם יְיָ: ג א וְאִם נִכְסַת קֻדְשַׁיָּא קֻרְבָּנֵיהּ, אִם מִן תּוֹרֵי הוּא מְקָרֵיב, אִם דְּכַר אִם נֻקְבָא, שְׁלִים יְקָרְבִנֵּיהּ קֳדָם יְיָ: ב וְיִסְמוֹךְ יְדֵיהּ עַל רֵישׁ קֻרְבָּנֵיהּ, וְיִכְּסִנֵּיהּ, בִּתְרַע מַשְׁכַּן זִמְנָא, וְיִזְרְקוּן, בְּנֵי אַהֲרֹן כָּהֲנַיָּא יָת דְּמָא, עַל מַדְבְּחָא סְחוֹר סְחוֹר: ג וִיקָרֵיב מִנִּכְסַת קֻדְשַׁיָּא, קֻרְבָּנָא קֳדָם יְיָ, יָת תַּרְבָּא דְּחָפֵי יָת גַּוָּא, וְיָת כָּל תַּרְבָּא, דְּעַל גַּוָּא: ד וְיָת תַּרְתֵּין כּוֹלְיָן, וְיָת תַּרְבָּא דַּעֲלֵיהוֹן, דְּעַל גִּסְסַיָּא, וְיָת חִצְרָא דְּעַל כַּבְדָּא, עַל כּוֹלְיָתָא יַעְדֵּינַהּ: ה וְיַסְּקוּן יָתֵיהּ בְּנֵי אַהֲרֹן לְמַדְבְּחָא, עַל עֲלָתָא, דְּעַל אָעַיָּא דְּעַל אִישָּׁתָא, קֻרְבַּן דְּמִתְקַבַּל בְּרַעֲוָא קֳדָם יְיָ:

PEACE OFFERING

The act of bringing a sacrifice was fraught with ambiguity. Jews were not the only people in ancient times to have temples, priests, and sacrifices. Almost everyone did. It was precisely here that the religion of ancient Israel came closest, outwardly, to the practices of their pagan neighbors. But the sacrificial systems of other cultures were based on totally different beliefs. In many religions sacrifices were seen as a way of placating or appeasing the gods. The Aztecs believed that sacrificial offerings fed the gods who sustained the universe. Walter Burkert speculated that the ancient Greeks experienced guilt when they killed animals for food, so they offered sacrifices as a way of appeasing their consciences.

All these ideas are alien to Judaism. God cannot be bribed or appeased. Nor can we bring Him anything that is not His. God sustains the universe; the universe does not sustain Him. And wrongs righted by sacrifice do not excuse other wrongs. So intention and mindset were essential in the sacrificial system. The thought that "if I bring a sacrifice to God, He will overlook my other faults" – in effect, the idea that I can bribe the Judge of all the earth – turns a sacred act into a pagan one, and produces precisely the opposite result than the one intended by the Torah. It turns religious worship from a way to the right and the good into a way of easing the conscience of those who practice the wrong and the bad.

The danger of the sacrificial system, said the prophets, is

6 If one's offering is a peace offering from the flock, whether male or female, it
7 must be without blemish. If one brings a sheep as his offering, he shall present
8 it before the LORD. He shall lay his hand on the head of the offering and have
it slaughtered at the entrance to the Tent of Meeting. Aharon's sons the priests
9 shall dash the blood against each side of the altar. The priest shall present the
fat from the peace offering as a fire offering to the LORD: the whole broad tail,
removed close to the backbone; the fat that covers the entrails and all the fat
10 surrounding them; the two kidneys and the fat that is on them at the loins; and
11 the diaphragm of the liver, which should be removed with the kidneys. The
priest shall send these up in smoke upon the altar: foodstuffs – a fire offering
to the LORD.
12 If the sacrifice is a goat, the one bringing it shall present it before the LORD.
13 He shall lay his hand on the head of the offering and have it slaughtered at
the entrance to the Tent of Meeting. Aharon's sons the priests shall dash the
14 blood against each side of the altar. The priest shall present of the offering
a fire offering to the LORD: the fat that covers the entrails and all the fat
15 surrounding them; the two kidneys and the fat that is on them at the loins; and
16 the diaphragm of the liver, which should be removed with the kidneys. The
priest shall send these up in smoke upon the altar: foodstuffs – a fire offering
17 to the LORD. All the fatty parts belong to the LORD: this is an everlasting
statute throughout your generations in all your dwellings: you shall not eat
either that fat or blood."
4 1 2 The LORD spoke to Moshe: "Tell the Israelites: If a person sins unintentionally ḤAMISHI

אונקלוס

ו וְאִם מִן עָנָא קֻרְבָּנֵיהּ, לְנִכְסַת קֻדְשַׁיָּא קֳדָם יְיָ, דְּכַר אוֹ נֻקְבָּא, שְׁלִים יְקָרְבִנֵּיהּ: ז אִם אִמַּר הוּא מְקָרֵיב יָת קֻרְבָּנֵיהּ, וִיקָרֵיב יָתֵיהּ קֳדָם יְיָ: ח וְיִסְמוֹךְ יָת יְדֵיהּ עַל רֵישׁ קֻרְבָּנֵיהּ, וְיִכּוֹס יָתֵיהּ, קֳדָם מַשְׁכַּן זִמְנָא, וְיִזְרְקוּן, בְּנֵי אַהֲרֹן יָת דְּמֵיהּ, עַל מַדְבְּחָא סְחוֹר סְחוֹר:

רש"י

ז אִם כֶּשֶׂב. לְפִי שֶׁיֵּשׁ בְּאֵמוּרֵי הַכֶּשֶׂב מַה שֶּׁאֵין בְּאֵמוּרֵי הָעֵז, שֶׁהַכֶּשֶׂב חֶלְיָתוֹ קְרֵבָה, לְכָךְ נֶחְלְקוּ לִשְׁתֵּי פָּרָשִׁיּוֹת:

ח וְזָרְקוּ. שְׁתֵּי מַתָּנוֹת שֶׁהֵן אַרְבַּע, וְעַל יְדֵי הַכְּלִי הוּא זוֹרֵק, וְאֵינוֹ נוֹתֵן בָּאֶצְבַּע אֶלָּא חַטָּאת:

ט חֶלְבּוֹ. הַמֻּבְחָר שֶׁבּוֹ, וּמַהוּ זֶה? "הָאַלְיָה תְמִימָה": לְעֻמַּת הֶעָצֶה. לְמַעְלָה מִן הַכְּלָיוֹת הַיּוֹעֲצוֹת:

יא לֶחֶם אִשֶּׁה לַה'. לַחְמוֹ שֶׁל אֵשׁ לְשֵׁם גָּבוֹהַּ: לֶחֶם. לְשׁוֹן מַאֲכָל, וְכֵן: "נַשְׁחִיתָה עֵץ בְּלַחְמוֹ" (ירמיה יא, יט), "עֲבַד לְחֶם רַב" (דניאל ה, א), "לִשְׂחוֹק עֹשִׂים לֶחֶם" (קהלת י, יט):

4:2 נֶפֶשׁ כִּי־תֶחֱטָא בִשְׁגָגָה *If a person sins unintentionally* – The *ḥatat* is often translated as "sin offering"; from the same Hebrew root are derived the words both for "sin" and "purification." The sins for which a purification offering had to be

ו וְאִם־מִן־הַצֹּאן קׇרְבָּנוֹ לְזֶבַח שְׁלָמִים לַיהוָה זָכָר אוֹ נְקֵבָה תָּמִים
ז יַקְרִיבֶנּוּ: אִם־כֶּשֶׂב הוּא־מַקְרִיב אֶת־קׇרְבָּנוֹ וְהִקְרִיב אֹתוֹ לִפְנֵי יהוה:
ח וְסָמַךְ אֶת־יָדוֹ עַל־רֹאשׁ קׇרְבָּנוֹ וְשָׁחַט אֹתוֹ לִפְנֵי אֹהֶל מוֹעֵד וְזָרְקוּ
ט בְּנֵי אַהֲרֹן אֶת־דָּמוֹ עַל־הַמִּזְבֵּחַ סָבִיב: וְהִקְרִיב מִזֶּבַח הַשְּׁלָמִים אִשֶּׁה
לַיהוה חֶלְבּוֹ הָאַלְיָה תְמִימָה לְעֻמַּת הֶעָצֶה יְסִירֶנָּה וְאֶת־הַחֵלֶב
י הַמְכַסֶּה אֶת־הַקֶּרֶב וְאֵת כׇּל־הַחֵלֶב אֲשֶׁר עַל־הַקֶּרֶב: וְאֵת שְׁתֵּי
הַכְּלָיֹת וְאֶת־הַחֵלֶב אֲשֶׁר עֲלֵהֶן אֲשֶׁר עַל־הַכְּסָלִים וְאֶת־הַיֹּתֶרֶת
יא עַל־הַכָּבֵד עַל־הַכְּלָיֹת יְסִירֶנָּה: וְהִקְטִירוֹ הַכֹּהֵן הַמִּזְבֵּחָה לֶחֶם אִשֶּׁה
לַיהוָה:
יב יג וְאִם־עֵז קׇרְבָּנוֹ וְהִקְרִיבוֹ לִפְנֵי יהוה: וְסָמַךְ אֶת־יָדוֹ עַל־רֹאשׁוֹ וְשָׁחַט
אֹתוֹ לִפְנֵי אֹהֶל מוֹעֵד וְזָרְקוּ בְּנֵי אַהֲרֹן אֶת־דָּמוֹ עַל־הַמִּזְבֵּחַ סָבִיב:
יד וְהִקְרִיב מִמֶּנּוּ קׇרְבָּנוֹ אִשֶּׁה לַיהוָה אֶת־הַחֵלֶב הַמְכַסֶּה אֶת־הַקֶּרֶב
טו וְאֵת כׇּל־הַחֵלֶב אֲשֶׁר עַל־הַקֶּרֶב: וְאֵת שְׁתֵּי הַכְּלָיֹת וְאֶת־הַחֵלֶב
אֲשֶׁר עֲלֵהֶן אֲשֶׁר עַל־הַכְּסָלִים וְאֶת־הַיֹּתֶרֶת עַל־הַכָּבֵד עַל־הַכְּלָיֹת
טז יְסִירֶנָּה: וְהִקְטִירָם הַכֹּהֵן הַמִּזְבֵּחָה לֶחֶם אִשֶּׁה לְרֵיחַ נִיחֹחַ כׇּל־חֵלֶב
יז לַיהוָה: חֻקַּת עוֹלָם לְדֹרֹתֵיכֶם בְּכֹל מוֹשְׁבֹתֵיכֶם כׇּל־חֵלֶב וְכׇל־דָּם לֹא
תֹאכֵלוּ:
ד א ב וַיְדַבֵּר יהוה אֶל־מֹשֶׁה לֵּאמֹר: דַּבֵּר אֶל־בְּנֵי יִשְׂרָאֵל לֵאמֹר נֶפֶשׁ כִּי־ ב חמישי

אונקלוס

ט וִיקָרֵיב מִנִּכְסַת קֻדְשַׁיָּא קֻרְבָּנָא קֳדָם יְיָ, תַּרְבֵּיהּ אַלְיְתָא שַׁלְמְתָא, לָקֳבֵיל שַׁזְרְתָא יַעְדֵּינַהּ, וְיָת תַּרְבָּא דְּחָפֵי יָת גַּוָּא, וְיָת כָּל תַּרְבָּא, דְּעַל גַּוָּא: י וְיָת תַּרְתֵּין כּוֹלְיָן, וְיָת תַּרְבָּא דַּעֲלֵיהוֹן, דְּעַל גִּסְסַיָּא, וְיָת חַצְרָא דְּעַל כַּבְדָּא, עַל כּוֹלְיָתָא יַעְדֵּינַהּ: יא וְיַסְּקִנֵּיהּ כָּהֲנָא לְמַדְבְּחָא, לְחֵים קֻרְבָּנָא קֳדָם יְיָ: יב וְאִם מִן בְּנֵי עִזַּיָּא קֻרְבָּנֵיהּ, וִיקָרְבִנֵּיהּ קֳדָם יְיָ: יג וְיִסְמוֹךְ יָת יְדֵיהּ עַל רֵישֵׁיהּ, וְיִכּוֹס יָתֵיהּ, קֳדָם מַשְׁכַּן זִמְנָא, וְיִזְרְקוּן, בְּנֵי אַהֲרֹן יָת דְּמֵיהּ, עַל מַדְבְּחָא סְחוֹר סְחוֹר: יד וִיקָרֵיב מִנֵּיהּ קֻרְבָּנֵיהּ, קֻרְבָּנָא קֳדָם יְיָ, יָת תַּרְבָּא דְּחָפֵי יָת גַּוָּא, וְיָת כָּל תַּרְבָּא, דְּעַל גַּוָּא: טו וְיָת תַּרְתֵּין כּוֹלְיָן, וְיָת תַּרְבָּא דַּעֲלֵיהוֹן, דְּעַל גִּסְסַיָּא, וְיָת חַצְרָא דְּעַל כַּבְדָּא, עַל כּוֹלְיָתָא יַעְדֵּינַהּ: טז וְיַסֵּיקִנּוּן כָּהֲנָא לְמַדְבְּחָא, לְחֵים קֻרְבָּנָא לְאִתְקַבָּלָא בְרַעֲוָא, כָּל תַּרְבָּא קֳדָם יְיָ: יז קְיָם עָלַם לְדָרֵיכוֹן, בְּכָל מוֹתְבָנֵיכוֹן, כָּל תַּרְבָּא וְכָל דְּמָא לָא תֵיכְלוּן: ד א וּמַלֵּיל יְיָ עִם מֹשֶׁה לְמֵימַר: ב מַלֵּיל, עִם בְּנֵי יִשְׂרָאֵל לְמֵימַר, אֱנָשׁ, אֲרֵי

with regard to any of the LORD's commands, doing what should not be done;
3 any transgression – if it is the anointed priest who sins, bringing guilt upon his
people, he shall bring an unblemished young bull to the LORD as a purification
4 offering for the sin he has committed. He shall bring the bull before the LORD
at the entrance to the Tent of Meeting, lay his hand upon the bull's head, and
5 slaughter the bull before the LORD. The anointed priest shall take some of the
6 bull's blood and bring it into the Tent of Meeting. The priest shall dip his finger
into the blood and sprinkle of it seven times before the LORD in front of the
7 Sanctuary's inner curtain. Then the priest shall apply some of the blood to the
horns of the altar of fragrant incense, which is in the Tent of Meeting before
the LORD. The rest of the bull's blood he shall pour out at the base of the altar
8 of burnt offerings, at the entrance to the Tent of Meeting. He shall remove all
the fat from the bull of the purification offering: the fat that covers the entrails
9 and all the fat surrounding them; the two kidneys and the fat that is on them
at the loins; and the diaphragm of the liver, which should be removed with the

רש״י

ד ב **מִכֹּל מִצְוֹת ה׳.** פֵּרְשׁוּ רַבּוֹתֵינוּ: אֵין חַטָּאת בָּאָה אֶלָּא עַל דָּבָר שֶׁזְּדוֹנוֹ לָאו וְכָרֵת: **מֵאַחַת מֵהֵנָּה.** מִמִּקְצָת אַחַת מֵהֶן, כְּגוֹן הַכּוֹתֵב בְּשַׁבָּת ׳שֵׁם׳ מִ׳שִּׁמְעוֹן׳, ׳נֹחַ׳ מִ׳נָּחוֹר׳, ׳דָּן׳ מִ׳דָּנִיֵּאל׳:

ג **אִם הַכֹּהֵן הַמָּשִׁיחַ יֶחֱטָא לְאַשְׁמַת הָעָם.** מִדְרָשׁוֹ, אֵינוֹ חַיָּב אֶלָּא בְּהֶעְלֵם דָּבָר עִם שִׁגְגַת מַעֲשֶׂה, כְּמוֹ שֶׁנֶּאֱמַר בְּאַשְׁמַת הָעָם: ״וְנֶעְלַם דָּבָר מֵעֵינֵי הַקָּהָל וְעָשׂוּ״ (להלן פסוק יג). וּפְשׁוּטוֹ לְפִי הָאַגָּדָה, כְּשֶׁכֹּהֵן גָּדוֹל חוֹטֵא ״אַשְׁמַת הָעָם״ הִיא, שֶׁזֶּה שֶׁהֵן תְּלוּיִין בּוֹ לְכַפֵּר עֲלֵיהֶם וּלְהִתְפַּלֵּל בַּעֲדָם נַעֲשָׂה מְקֻלְקָל: **פַּר.** יָכוֹל זָקֵן? תַּלְמוּד לוֹמַר: ״בֶּן״. אִי ״בֶּן״, יָכוֹל קָטָן? תַּלְמוּד לוֹמַר: ״פַּר״, הָא כֵּיצַד? זֶה פַּר בֶּן שָׁלֹשׁ:

ה **אֶל אֹהֶל מוֹעֵד.** לַמִּשְׁכָּן, וּבְבֵית עוֹלָמִים – לַהֵיכָל:

ו **אֶת פְּנֵי פָּרֹכֶת הַקֹּדֶשׁ.** כְּנֶגֶד מְקוֹם קְדֻשָּׁתָהּ, מְכֻוָּן כְּנֶגֶד בֵּין הַבַּדִּים, וְלֹא הָיוּ נוֹגְעִים דָּמִים בַּפָּרֹכֶת, וְאִם נָגְעוּ נָגְעוּ:

ז **וְאֵת כָּל דַּם.** שְׁיָרֵי הַדָּם:

ח **וְאֶת כָּל חֵלֶב פַּר.** ׳חֶלְבּוֹ׳ הָיָה לוֹ לוֹמַר, מַה תַּלְמוּד לוֹמַר: ״פַּר״? לְרַבּוֹת פַּר שֶׁל יוֹם הַכִּפּוּרִים לִכְלָיוֹת וְלַחֲלָבִים וְיוֹתֶרֶת: **הַחַטָּאת.** לְהָבִיא שְׂעִירֵי עֲבוֹדָה זָרָה לִכְלָיוֹת וְלַחֲלָבִים וְיוֹתֶרֶת: **יָרִים מִמֶּנּוּ.** מִן הַמְחֻבָּר, שֶׁלֹּא יְנַתְּחֶנּוּ קֹדֶם הֲסָרַת חֶלְבּוֹ. תּוֹרַת כֹּהֲנִים:

The prophet said so long ago: "For it is goodness I yearn for, not sacrifice" (Hos. 6:6). Charity and kindness are our substitutes for sacrifice, and like the sin offering of old, they help mend what is broken in the world and in our soul.

The sin offering tells us that the wrong we do, or let happen, even if we did not intend it, still requires atonement. Unfashionable though this is, a morality that speaks about action, not just intention – about what happens through us even if we did not mean to do it – is more compelling, more true to the human situation, than one that speaks of intention alone.

saying, "I didn't mean to do it." Wrong was done – and it was done by us. Therefore we must perform an act that signals our contrition. We cannot just walk away as if the act had nothing to do with us.

The law of the sin offering reminds us that we can do harm unintentionally, and this can have consequences, both physical and psychological. The best way of putting things right, of achieving purification, is to make a sacrifice: to do something that costs us something. In ancient times, that took the form of a sacrifice offered on the altar at the Temple. Nowadays, the best way of doing so is to give money to charity (*tzedaka*) or perform an act of kindness to others (*ḥesed*).

תֶחֱטָא בִשְׁגָגָה מִכֹּל מִצְוֺת יְהוָה אֲשֶׁר לֹא תֵעָשֶׂינָה וְעָשָׂה מֵאַחַת
ג מֵהֵנָּה: אִם הַכֹּהֵן הַמָּשִׁיחַ יֶחֱטָא לְאַשְׁמַת הָעָם וְהִקְרִיב עַל חַטָּאתוֹ
ד אֲשֶׁר חָטָא פַּר בֶּן־בָּקָר תָּמִים לַיהוָה לְחַטָּאת: וְהֵבִיא אֶת־הַפָּר אֶל־
פֶּתַח אֹהֶל מוֹעֵד לִפְנֵי יְהוָה וְסָמַךְ אֶת־יָדוֹ עַל־רֹאשׁ הַפָּר וְשָׁחַט אֶת־
ה הַפָּר לִפְנֵי יְהוָה: וְלָקַח הַכֹּהֵן הַמָּשִׁיחַ מִדַּם הַפָּר וְהֵבִיא אֹתוֹ אֶל־אֹהֶל
ו מוֹעֵד: וְטָבַל הַכֹּהֵן אֶת־אֶצְבָּעוֹ בַּדָּם וְהִזָּה מִן־הַדָּם שֶׁבַע פְּעָמִים לִפְנֵי
ז יְהוָה אֶת־פְּנֵי פָּרֹכֶת הַקֹּדֶשׁ: וְנָתַן הַכֹּהֵן מִן־הַדָּם עַל־קַרְנוֹת מִזְבַּח
קְטֹרֶת הַסַּמִּים לִפְנֵי יְהוָה אֲשֶׁר בְּאֹהֶל מוֹעֵד וְאֵת ׀ כָּל־דַּם הַפָּר יִשְׁפֹּךְ
ח אֶל־יְסוֹד מִזְבַּח הָעֹלָה אֲשֶׁר־פֶּתַח אֹהֶל מוֹעֵד: וְאֶת־כָּל־חֵלֶב פַּר
הַחַטָּאת יָרִים מִמֶּנּוּ אֶת־הַחֵלֶב הַמְכַסֶּה עַל־הַקֶּרֶב וְאֵת כָּל־הַחֵלֶב
ט אֲשֶׁר עַל־הַקֶּרֶב: וְאֵת שְׁתֵּי הַכְּלָיֹת וְאֶת־הַחֵלֶב אֲשֶׁר עֲלֵיהֶן אֲשֶׁר

אונקלוס

יחוב בשלו מכל פקודיא דיי, דלא כשרין לאתעבדא, ויעביד, מן
חד מנהון: ג אם כהנא רבא, יחוב לחובת עמא, ויקריב, על חובתיה
דחב, תור בר תורי שלים, קדם יי לחטתא: ד וייתי ית תורא, לתרע,
משכן זמנא לקדם יי, ויסמוך ית ידיה על ריש תורא, ויכוס ית תורא
קדם יי: ה ויסב, כהנא רבא מדמא דתורא, ויעיל יתיה למשכן זמנא:
ו ויטבול כהנא, ית אצבעיה בדמא, וידי מן דמא, שבע זמנין קדם
יי, קדם פרכתא דקדשא: ז ויתין כהנא מן דמא, על קרנת, מדבחא
דקטורת בסמיא דקדם יי, דבמשכן זמנא, וית כל דמא דתורא,
ישפוך ליסודא דמדבחא דעלתא, דבתרע משכן זמנא: ח וית
כל תרב, תורא דחטתא יפריש מניה, ית תרבא דחפי על גוא,
וית כל תרבא, דעל גוא: ט וית תרתין כולין, וית תרבא דעליהון,

you have broken the Sabbath, you are more likely to feel regret than remorse. You feel sorry but not guilty.

We think of a sin as something we did intentionally, yielding to temptation perhaps, or in a moment of rebellion. That is what Jewish law calls *bezadon* in Biblical Hebrew or *bemezid* in Rabbinic Hebrew. That is the kind of act we would have thought calls for a sin offering. In Jewish law, though, such an act cannot be atoned for by an offering at all. So how are we to make sense of the sin offering?

The answer is that our acts leave traces in the world. The very fact that unintentional sins require atonement tells us that we cannot dissociate ourselves from our actions by

brought were those committed inadvertently, *beshogeg*. The sinner had forgotten either the law or some relevant fact. To give a contemporary example: Suppose the phone rings on the Sabbath and you answer it. Assuming this is a biblical-level prohibition, you would only be liable for a purification offering if either you forgot the law that you may not answer a phone on the Sabbath, or you forgot the fact that that day was the Sabbath. For a moment you thought it was Friday or Sunday.

It is just this kind of act that we do not tend to see as a sin at all. It was a mistake. You forgot. You did not mean to do anything wrong. And when you realize that inadvertently

10 kidneys, just as it is removed from the ox of the peace offering. The priest shall
11 send these up in smoke upon the altar of burnt offerings. But the bull's skin and
12 all its flesh, together with its head, legs, entrails, and dung – all the rest of the
bull – he shall take to a ritually pure place outside the camp, to the ash heap,
and burn upon a wood fire; at the ash heap it shall be burned.
13 If it is the entire community of Israel that commits an unintentional sin, the
congregation unwittingly violating one of the LORD's commands, doing what
14 must not be done, when the sin that they committed becomes known, the
community shall bring a young bull as a purification offering, presenting it
15 before the Tent of Meeting. The community elders shall lay their hands on the
bull's head before the LORD and, before the LORD, the bull shall be slaughtered.
16 The anointed priest shall take some of the bull's blood into the Tent of Meeting.
17 The priest shall dip his finger into the blood and sprinkle it seven times before
18 the LORD in front of the curtain. Then he shall apply some of the blood to
the horns of the altar before the LORD in the Tent of Meeting, and pour out
all the rest at the base of the altar of burnt offerings, at the entrance to the
19 Tent of Meeting. Then he shall remove all its fat and send it up in smoke upon
20 the altar. He shall do the same with this bull as he does with the bull of his
purification offering; he shall do the same with this. So shall the priest make

רש״י

ט-יא **כאשר יורם.** כאותן אמורין המפרשין בשור זבח השלמים. וכי מה פירש בזבח השלמים שלא פירש כאן? אלא להקישו לשלמים: מה שלמים לשמן, אף זה לשמו; ומה שלמים שלום לעולם, אף זה שלום לעולם. ובשחיטת קדשים מצריכו ללמוד הימנו שאין למדין למד מן הלמד בקדשים, בפרק 'איזהו מקומן' (זבחים מט ע״ב): **על הכבד, על הכליות, על ראשו, ועל כרעיו.** כלן לשון תוספת הן, כמו: 'מלבד':

יב **אל מקום טהור.** לפי שיש מחוץ לעיר מקום מוכן לטמאה, להשליך אבנים מנגעות ולבית הקברות, הצרך לומר ב״מחוץ למחנה״ זה, שהוא חוץ לעיר, שיהא המקום טהור: **מחוץ למחנה.** חוץ לשלש מחנות, ובבית עולמים – חוץ לעיר, כמו שפרשוהו רבותינו במסכת יומא (דף סח ע״א) ובסנהדרין (דף מב ע״ב): **אל שפך הדשן.** מקום ששופכין בו הדשן המסלק מן המזבח, כמו שנאמר: ״והוציא את הדשן אל מחוץ למחנה״ (להלן ו, ד): **על שפך הדשן ישרף.** שאין תלמוד לומר, אלא ללמד שאפלו אין שם דשן:

יג **עדת ישראל.** אלו סנהדרין: **ונעלם דבר.** טעו להורות באחת מכל כריתות שבתורה שהוא מתר: **הקהל ועשו.** שעשו הצבור על פיהם:

יז **את פני הפרכת.** ולמעלה הוא אומר: ״את פני פרכת הקדש״ (לעיל פסוק ו)! משל למלך שסרחה עליו מדינה, אם מעוטה סרחה – פמליא שלו מתקימת, ואם כלה סרחה – אין פמליא שלו מתקימת. אף כאן, כשחטא כהן משיח עדין שם קדשת המקום על המקדש, משחטאו כלם אם ושלום נסתלקה הקדשה:

יח **יסוד מזבח העלה אשר פתח אהל מועד.** זה יסוד מערבי שהוא כנגד הפתח:

יט-כ **ואת כל חלבו ירים.** אף על פי שלא פירש כאן יותרת ושתי כליות, למדין הם מ״ועשה לפר כאשר עשה״ וגו׳. ומפני מה לא נתפרשו בו? תנא דבי רבי ישמעאל: משל למלך שזעם על אוהבו, ומעט בסרחונו מפני חבתו: **ועשה לפר.** זה, ״כאשר עשה לפר החטאת״, כמו שמפרש בפר כהן משיח, להביא יותרת ושתי כליות שפירש שם (לעיל פסוק ט), שלא פירש כאן, ולכפל במצות העבודות, ללמד שאם חסר אחת מכל המתנות – פסל, לפי שמצינו בנתנין על המזבח החיצון שנתנן במתנה אחת – כפר, הצרך לומר כאן שמתנה אחת מהן מעכבת:

י עַל־הַכְּסָלִים וְאֶת־הַיֹּתֶרֶת עַל־הַכָּבֵד עַל־הַכְּלָיוֹת יְסִירֶנָּה׃ כַּאֲשֶׁר
יא יוּרָם מִשּׁוֹר זֶבַח הַשְּׁלָמִים וְהִקְטִירָם הַכֹּהֵן עַל מִזְבַּח הָעֹלָה׃ וְאֶת־
יב עוֹר הַפָּר וְאֶת־כָּל־בְּשָׂרוֹ עַל־רֹאשׁוֹ וְעַל־כְּרָעָיו וְקִרְבּוֹ וּפִרְשׁוֹ׃ וְהוֹצִיא
אֶת־כָּל־הַפָּר אֶל־מִחוּץ לַמַּחֲנֶה אֶל־מָקוֹם טָהוֹר אֶל־שֶׁפֶךְ הַדֶּשֶׁן
וְשָׂרַף אֹתוֹ עַל־עֵצִים בָּאֵשׁ עַל־שֶׁפֶךְ הַדֶּשֶׁן יִשָּׂרֵף׃
יג וְאִם כָּל־עֲדַת יִשְׂרָאֵל יִשְׁגּוּ וְנֶעְלַם דָּבָר מֵעֵינֵי הַקָּהָל וְעָשׂוּ אַחַת
יד מִכָּל־מִצְוֺת יְהוָה אֲשֶׁר לֹא־תֵעָשֶׂינָה וְאָשֵׁמוּ׃ וְנוֹדְעָה הַחַטָּאת אֲשֶׁר
חָטְאוּ עָלֶיהָ וְהִקְרִיבוּ הַקָּהָל פַּר בֶּן־בָּקָר לְחַטָּאת וְהֵבִיאוּ אֹתוֹ לִפְנֵי
טו אֹהֶל מוֹעֵד׃ וְסָמְכוּ זִקְנֵי הָעֵדָה אֶת־יְדֵיהֶם עַל־רֹאשׁ הַפָּר לִפְנֵי יְהוָה
טז וְשָׁחַט אֶת־הַפָּר לִפְנֵי יְהוָה׃ וְהֵבִיא הַכֹּהֵן הַמָּשִׁיחַ מִדַּם הַפָּר אֶל־
יז אֹהֶל מוֹעֵד׃ וְטָבַל הַכֹּהֵן אֶצְבָּעוֹ מִן־הַדָּם וְהִזָּה שֶׁבַע פְּעָמִים לִפְנֵי
יח יְהוָה אֶת־פְּנֵי הַפָּרֹכֶת׃ וּמִן־הַדָּם יִתֵּן ׀ עַל־קַרְנֹת הַמִּזְבֵּחַ אֲשֶׁר לִפְנֵי
יְהוָה אֲשֶׁר בְּאֹהֶל מוֹעֵד וְאֵת כָּל־הַדָּם יִשְׁפֹּךְ אֶל־יְסוֹד מִזְבַּח הָעֹלָה
יט אֲשֶׁר־פֶּתַח אֹהֶל מוֹעֵד׃ וְאֵת כָּל־חֶלְבּוֹ יָרִים מִמֶּנּוּ וְהִקְטִיר הַמִּזְבֵּחָה׃
כ וְעָשָׂה לַפָּר כַּאֲשֶׁר עָשָׂה לְפַר הַחַטָּאת כֵּן יַעֲשֶׂה־לּוֹ וְכִפֶּר עֲלֵהֶם

אונקלוס

דְּעַל גִּסְסַיָּא, וְיָת חַצְרָא דְּעַל כַּבְדָּא, עַל כּוֹלְיָתָא יַעְדֵּינַהּ׃ י כְּמָא
דְּמִתַּפְרַשׁ, מִתּוֹר נִכְסַת קֻדְשַׁיָּא, וְיַסֵּיקִנּוּן כַּהֲנָא, עַל מַדְבְּחָא
דַּעֲלָתָא׃ יא וְיָת מְשַׁךְ תּוֹרָא וְיָת כָּל בִּסְרֵיהּ, עַל רֵישֵׁיהּ וְעַל כְּרָעוֹהִי,
וְגַוֵּיהּ וְאֻכְלֵיהּ׃ יב וְיַפֵּיק יָת כָּל תּוֹרָא, לְמִבָּרָא לְמַשְׁרִיתָא, לַאֲתַר דְּכֵי
לַאֲתַר בֵּית מֵישַׁד קִטְמָא, וְיוֹקֵיד יָתֵיהּ, עַל אָעַיָּא בְּאֶשָּׁתָא, עַל
אֲתַר בֵּית מֵישַׁד קִטְמָא יִתּוֹקַד׃ יג וְאִם כָּל כְּנִשְׁתָּא דְּיִשְׂרָאֵל יִשְׁתְּלוּן,
וִיהֵי מְכַסָּא פִּתְגָּמָא, מֵעֵינֵי קְהָלָא, וְיַעְבְּדוּן, חַד מִכָּל פִּקּוֹדַיָּא דַּייָ,
דְּלָא כָשְׁרִין לְאִתְעֲבָדָא וִיחוּבוּן׃ יד וְתִתְיְדַע חוֹבְתָא, דְּחָבוּ עֲלַהּ,

וִיקָרְבוּן קְהָלָא, תּוֹר בַּר תּוֹרֵי לְחַטָּאתָא, וְיַיְתוּן יָתֵיהּ, לִקְדָם מַשְׁכַּן
זִמְנָא׃ טו וְיִסְמְכוּן, סָבֵי כְּנִשְׁתָּא יָת יְדֵיהוֹן, עַל רֵישׁ תּוֹרָא קֳדָם
יְיָ, וְיִכּוֹס יָת תּוֹרָא קֳדָם יְיָ׃ טז וְיַעֵיל, כַּהֲנָא רַבָּא מִדְּמָא דְּתוֹרָא,
לְמַשְׁכַּן זִמְנָא׃ יז וְיִטְבּוֹל כַּהֲנָא, אֶצְבְּעֵיהּ מִן דְּמָא, וְיַדֵּי, שְׁבַע זִמְנִין
קֳדָם יְיָ, קֳדָם פָּרֻכְתָּא׃ יח וּמִן דְּמָא, יִתֵּין עַל קַרְנַת מַדְבְּחָא, דִּקְדָם
יְיָ, דִּבְמַשְׁכַּן זִמְנָא, וְיָת כָּל דְּמָא, יִשְׁפּוֹךְ לִיסוֹדָא דְּמַדְבְּחָא דַּעֲלָתָא,
דִּבְתְרַע מַשְׁכַּן זִמְנָא׃ יט וְיָת כָּל תַּרְבֵּיהּ יַפְרֵישׁ מִנֵּיהּ, וְיַסֵּיק לְמַדְבְּחָא׃
כ וְיַעְבֵּיד לְתוֹרָא, כְּמָא דַּעֲבַד לְתוֹרָא דְּחַטָּאתָא, כֵּן יַעֲבֵיד לֵיהּ, וִיכַפַּר

21 atonement for the people, and they shall be forgiven. The priest shall then take
the bull outside the camp and burn it just as he burns the first bull. This is the
community's purification offering.
22 When a leader sins unintentionally with regard to any of the LORD's commands,
23 doing what must not be done and thus incurring guilt, when the sin that he
has committed is made known to him, he shall bring an unblemished male
24 goat as his offering. He shall lay his hand upon the goat's head, and it shall
be slaughtered in the place where burnt offerings are slaughtered before the
25 LORD. It is a purification offering. The priest shall take some of the blood from
the purification offering with his finger, and apply it to the horns of the altar of
burnt offerings. The rest of the blood he shall pour out at the base of the altar
26 of burnt offerings. He shall send up all its fat in smoke upon the altar, like the
fat of the peace offerings. So shall the priest make atonement for that leader for
his sin, and he will be forgiven.

רש"י

כב **אֲשֶׁר נָשִׂיא יֶחֱטָא.** לְשׁוֹן 'אַשְׁרֵי', אַשְׁרֵי הַדּוֹר שֶׁהַנָּשִׂיא שֶׁלּוֹ נוֹתֵן לֵב לְהָבִיא כַּפָּרָה עַל שִׁגְגָתוֹ, קַל וָחֹמֶר שֶׁמִּתְחָרֵט עַל זְדוֹנוֹתָיו:

כג **אוֹ הוֹדַע.** כְּמוֹ: אִם הוֹדַע הַדָּבָר, הַרְבֵּה 'אוֹ' יֵשׁ מְשַׁמְּשִׁין בִּלְשׁוֹן 'אִם' וְ'אִם' בִּמְקוֹם 'אוֹ', וְכֵן: "אוֹ נוֹדַע כִּי שׁוֹר נַגָּח הוּא" (שמות כא, לו): **הוֹדַע אֵלָיו.** כְּשֶׁחָטָא הָיָה סָבוּר שֶׁהוּא הֶתֵּר, וּלְאַחַר מִכָּאן נוֹדַע לוֹ שֶׁאִסּוּר הָיָה:

כד **בִּמְקוֹם אֲשֶׁר יִשְׁחַט אֶת הָעֹלָה.** בַּצָּפוֹן, שֶׁהוּא מְפֹרָשׁ בָּעוֹלָה (לעיל א, יא): **חַטָּאת הוּא.** לִשְׁמוֹ כָּשֵׁר, שֶׁלֹּא לִשְׁמוֹ פָּסוּל:

כה **וְאֶת דָּמוֹ.** שְׁיָרֵי הַדָּם:

כו **כְּחֵלֶב זֶבַח הַשְּׁלָמִים.** כְּאוֹתָן אֵמוּרִין הַמְפֹרָשִׁים בְּעֵז הָאָמוּר אֵצֶל שְׁלָמִים (לעיל ג, יד-טו):

It deals in matters – specifically the pursuit of wealth or power – that are, in the short term, zero-sum games. The more I have, the less you have. Politics is the mediation of conflict by justice backed with power. Whatever course a politician takes, it will please some and anger others. From this, there is no escape.

Politics also involves difficult judgments. A leader must balance competing claims and will sometimes get it wrong.

There are no universal rules when it comes to leadership. It is an art, not a science. A ruler sometimes has to make decisions that a conscientious individual would shrink from in private life. He may have to wage a war, knowing that some will die. In many cases, only after the event will the leader know whether the decision was justified. Leaders make mistakes. As the Torah signals, it is only a matter of "when," not "if."

The Jewish approach to leadership is thus an unusual combination of realism and idealism – realistic in its acknowledgment that leaders inevitably make mistakes, idealistic in its constant subjection of politics to ethics, power to responsibility, pragmatism to conscience. What matters is not that leaders never get it wrong, but that they are always exposed to prophetic critique and that they constantly engage in Torah study to remind themselves of transcendent standards and ultimate aims. The most important thing from a Torah perspective is that a leader is sufficiently honest to admit his mistakes. Hence the significance of the purification offering.

Leadership, then, demands two kinds of courage: the strength to take a risk, and the humility to admit when a risk fails.

כא הַכֹּהֵ֖ן וְנִסְלַ֥ח לָהֶֽם׃ וְהוֹצִ֣יא אֶת־הַפָּ֗ר אֶל־מִחוּץ֙ לַֽמַּחֲנֶ֔ה וְשָׂרַ֣ף אֹת֔וֹ
כַּאֲשֶׁ֣ר שָׂרַ֔ף אֵ֖ת הַפָּ֣ר הָרִאשׁ֑וֹן חַטַּ֥את הַקָּהָ֖ל הֽוּא׃
כב אֲשֶׁ֥ר נָשִׂ֖יא יֶחֱטָ֑א וְעָשָׂ֡ה אַחַ֣ת מִכָּל־מִצְוֺת֩ יְהוָ֨ה אֱלֹהָ֜יו אֲשֶׁ֧ר לֹא־
כג תֵעָשֶׂ֛ינָה בִּשְׁגָגָ֖ה וְאָשֵֽׁם׃ אֽוֹ־הוֹדַ֤ע אֵלָיו֙ חַטָּאת֔וֹ אֲשֶׁ֥ר חָטָ֖א בָּ֑הּ וְהֵבִ֨יא
כד אֶת־קָרְבָּנ֜וֹ שְׂעִ֥יר עִזִּ֛ים זָכָ֖ר תָּמִֽים׃ וְסָמַ֤ךְ יָדוֹ֙ עַל־רֹ֣אשׁ הַשָּׂעִ֔יר וְשָׁחַ֣ט
כה אֹת֔וֹ בִּמְק֛וֹם אֲשֶׁר־יִשְׁחַ֥ט אֶת־הָעֹלָ֖ה לִפְנֵ֣י יְהוָ֑ה חַטָּ֖את הֽוּא׃ וְלָקַ֨ח
הַכֹּהֵ֜ן מִדַּ֤ם הַחַטָּאת֙ בְּאֶצְבָּע֔וֹ וְנָתַ֕ן עַל־קַרְנֹ֖ת מִזְבַּ֣ח הָעֹלָ֑ה וְאֶת־דָּמ֣וֹ
כו יִשְׁפֹּ֔ךְ אֶל־יְס֖וֹד מִזְבַּ֥ח הָעֹלָֽה׃ וְאֶת־כָּל־חֶלְבּוֹ֙ יַקְטִ֣יר הַמִּזְבֵּ֔חָה כְּחֵ֖לֶב
זֶ֣בַח הַשְּׁלָמִ֑ים וְכִפֶּ֨ר עָלָ֧יו הַכֹּהֵ֛ן מֵחַטָּאת֖וֹ וְנִסְלַ֥ח לֽוֹ׃

אונקלוס

עֲלֵיהוֹן, כָּהֲנָא וְיִשְׁתְּבֵיק לְהוֹן: כא וְיַפֵּיק יָת תּוֹרָא, לְמִבָּרָא לְמַשְׁרִיתָא, וְיוֹקֵיד יָתֵיהּ, כְּמָא דְּאוֹקֵיד, יָת תּוֹרָא קַדְמָאָה, חַטַּאת קְהָלָא הוּא: כב אִם רַבָּא יְחוּב, וְיַעֲבֵיד, חַד מִכָּל פִּקּוֹדַיָּא דַּיי אֱלָהֵיהּ, דְּלָא כָשְׁרִין לְאִתְעֲבָדָא, בְּשָׁלוּ וִיחוּב: כג אוֹ אִתְיְדַע לֵיהּ חוֹבְתֵיהּ, דַּחֲב בַּהּ, וְיַיְתֵי יָת קֻרְבָּנֵיהּ, צְפִיר בַּר עִזִּין דְּכַר שְׁלִים: כד וְיִסְמוֹךְ יְדֵיהּ עַל רֵישׁ צְפִירָא, וְיִכּוֹס יָתֵיהּ, בְּאַתְרָא, דְּיִכּוֹס יָת עֲלָתָא קֳדָם יי, חַטָּתָא הוּא: כה וְיִסַּב כָּהֲנָא, מִדְּמָא דְחַטָּתָא בְּאֶצְבְּעֵיהּ, וְיִתֵּין, עַל קַרְנַת מַדְבְּחָא דַעֲלָתָא, וְיָת דְּמֵיהּ יִשְׁפּוֹךְ, לִיסוֹדָא דְּמַדְבְּחָא דַעֲלָתָא: כו וְיָת כָּל תַּרְבֵּיהּ יַסֵּיק לְמַדְבְּחָא, כִּתְרַב נִכְסַת קֻדְשַׁיָּא, וִיכַפַּר עֲלוֹהִי כָּהֲנָא, מֵחוֹבְתֵיהּ וְיִשְׁתְּבֵיק לֵיהּ:

THE SINS OF LEADERS

The Torah prescribes four different kinds of offerings, depending on the offender. One is the High Priest, a second is "the entire community" (understood by the Sages to mean the great Sanhedrin, the Supreme Court), a third is "a leader" (*nasi*), and the fourth is an ordinary individual. In three of the four cases, the law is introduced by the word *im*, "if" – if such a person commits a sin. In the case of the leader, however, the law is prefaced by the word *asher*, "when." It is *possible* that a High Priest, the Supreme Court, or an individual may err. But in the case of a leader, the *nasi*, it is probable or even certain.

Nasi is the generic word for a leader: a ruler, king, judge, elder, or prince. Usually it refers to the holder of political power. Why does the Torah consider this type of leadership particularly prone to error? Sforno (on Lev. 4:21–22) cites the phrase "Yeshurun grew fat, and kicked" (Deut. 32:15). Those who have advantages over others, whether of wealth or power, can lose their moral sense.

Rabbi Elie Munk, citing the Zohar, explains that the High Priest and the Sanhedrin were in constant contact with that which was holy. They lived in a world of ideals. The king or political ruler, by contrast, was involved in secular affairs: war and peace, the administration of government, and international relations. They were more likely to sin because their day-to-day concerns were not religious but pragmatic.

Rabbi Meir Simḥa of Dvinsk (*Meshekh Ḥokhma* on Lev. 4:21–22) points out that a king was especially vulnerable to being led astray by popular sentiment. Neither a priest nor a judge in the Sanhedrin was answerable to the people. The king, however, relied on popular support. Thus, for a whole series of reasons, a political leader is more exposed to temptation and error than a priest or judge.

I would also add that politics is an arena of conflict.

27 If an individual among the people sins unintentionally with regard to any of SHISHI
the LORD's commands, doing what should not be done and thus incurring
28 guilt, when the sin he has committed is made known to him, he shall bring an
unblemished female goat as his offering to atone for the sin that he committed.
29 He shall lay his hand on the head of the purification offering, and it shall be
30 slaughtered in the same place as the burnt offerings. The priest shall take
some of its blood with his finger, and apply it to the horns of the altar of burnt
31 offerings. The rest of the blood he shall pour out at the base of the altar. The
priest shall remove all its fat, just as the fat is removed from a peace offering,
and send it up in smoke upon the altar as a pleasing aroma to the LORD. So
shall the priest make atonement for that person, and he will be forgiven.
32 If one brings a sheep as a purification offering, it shall be an unblemished
33 female. One shall lay one's hand upon the head of the purification offering, and
34 it shall be slaughtered in the place where burnt offerings are slaughtered. The
priest shall take some of its blood with his finger, and apply it to the horns of
the altar of burnt offerings. The rest of the blood he shall pour out at the base of
35 the altar. He shall remove all its fat, as the fat of a sheep is removed from a peace
offering. The priest shall send it up in smoke upon the altar with the other fire
offerings to the LORD. So shall the priest make atonement for that person for
the sin that he committed, and he will be forgiven.
5 1 If a person sins by failing to testify after hearing a public adjuration to do so:
if he knows or has seen something, yet does not speak up, and thus bears his
2 guilt; or sins through touching an impure thing – the carcass of an impure
beast, or a carcass of impure livestock, or the carcass of an impure creeping

אונקלוס

כז וְאִם אֱנָשׁ חַד, יְחוּב בְּשָׁלוּ מֵעַמָּא דְּאַרְעָא, בְּמֶעְבְּדֵיהּ, חַד מִפִּקּוֹדַיָּא דַּייָ, דְּלָא כָשְׁרִין לְאִתְעֲבָדָא וִיחוּב: כח אוֹ אִתְיְדַע לֵיהּ, חוֹבְתֵיהּ דְּחָב, וְיֵיתֵי קֻרְבָּנֵיהּ, צְפִירַת עִזֵּי שַׁלְמָא נֻקְבָּא, עַל חוֹבְתֵיהּ דְּחָב: כט וְיִסְמוֹךְ יָת יְדֵיהּ, עַל רֵישׁ חַטָּתָא, וְיִכּוֹס יָת חַטָּתָא, בְּאַתְרָא דַּעֲלָתָא: ל וְיִסַּב כָּהֲנָא מִדְּמַהּ בְּאֶצְבְּעֵיהּ, וְיִתֵּין, עַל קַרְנַת מַדְבְּחָא דַּעֲלָתָא, וְיָת כָּל דְּמַהּ יִשְׁפּוֹךְ, לִיסוֹדָא דְּמַדְבְּחָא: לא וְיָת כָּל

רש״י

לא כַּאֲשֶׁר הוּסַר חֵלֶב מֵעַל זֶבַח הַשְּׁלָמִים. כָּאֵמוּרֵי עֵז הָאֲמוּרִים בִּשְׁלָמִים (לעיל ס״ס):

לג וְשָׁחַט אֹתָהּ לְחַטָּאת. שֶׁתְּהֵא שְׁחִיטָתָהּ לְשֵׁם חַטָּאת:

לה כַּאֲשֶׁר יוּסַר חֵלֶב הַכֶּשֶׂב. שֶׁנִּתְרַבּוּ אֵמוּרִין בָּאַלְיָה, אַף חַטָּאת כְּשֶׁהִיא בָּאָה כִּבְשָׂה טְעוּנָה אַלְיָה עִם הָאֵמוּרִין: עַל אִשֵּׁי ה׳. עַל מְדוּרוֹת הָאֵשׁ הָעֲשׂוּיוֹת לַשֵּׁם, פוּאיילי״ש בְּלַעַז:

ה א וְשָׁמְעָה קוֹל אָלָה. בְּדָבָר שֶׁהוּא עֵד בּוֹ, שֶׁהִשְׁבִּיעוּהוּ שְׁבוּעָה שֶׁאִם יוֹדֵעַ לוֹ בְּעֵדוּת שֶׁיָּעִיד לוֹ:

ב אוֹ נֶפֶשׁ אֲשֶׁר תִּגַּע וְגוֹ׳. וּלְאַחַר הַטֻּמְאָה הַזּוֹ יֹאכַל קָדָשִׁים אוֹ יִכָּנֵס לַמִּקְדָּשׁ, שֶׁהוּא דָּבָר שֶׁזְּדוֹנוֹ כָּרֵת. בְּמַסֶּכֶת שְׁבוּעוֹת (דף ו ע״ב – ז ע״ב; יד ע״ב) נִדְרַשׁ כֵּן: וְנֶעְלַם מִמֶּנּוּ. הַטֻּמְאָה:

כז וְאִם־נֶפֶשׁ אַחַת תֶּחֱטָא בִשְׁגָגָה מֵעַם הָאָרֶץ בַּעֲשֹׂתָהּ אַחַת מִמִּצְוֺת ששי
כח יְהוָה אֲשֶׁר לֹא־תֵעָשֶׂינָה וְאָשֵׁם׃ אוֹ הוֹדַע אֵלָיו חַטָּאתוֹ אֲשֶׁר חָטָא
וְהֵבִיא קָרְבָּנוֹ שְׂעִירַת עִזִּים תְּמִימָה נְקֵבָה עַל־חַטָּאתוֹ אֲשֶׁר חָטָא׃
כט וְסָמַךְ אֶת־יָדוֹ עַל רֹאשׁ הַחַטָּאת וְשָׁחַט אֶת־הַחַטָּאת בִּמְקוֹם
ל הָעֹלָה׃ וְלָקַח הַכֹּהֵן מִדָּמָהּ בְּאֶצְבָּעוֹ וְנָתַן עַל־קַרְנֹת מִזְבַּח הָעֹלָה
לא וְאֶת־כָּל־דָּמָהּ יִשְׁפֹּךְ אֶל־יְסוֹד הַמִּזְבֵּחַ׃ וְאֶת־כָּל־חֶלְבָּהּ יָסִיר כַּאֲשֶׁר
הוּסַר חֵלֶב מֵעַל זֶבַח הַשְּׁלָמִים וְהִקְטִיר הַכֹּהֵן הַמִּזְבֵּחָה לְרֵיחַ נִיחֹחַ
לַיהוָה וְכִפֶּר עָלָיו הַכֹּהֵן וְנִסְלַח לוֹ׃
לב לג וְאִם־כֶּבֶשׂ יָבִיא קָרְבָּנוֹ לְחַטָּאת נְקֵבָה תְמִימָה יְבִיאֶנָּה׃ וְסָמַךְ אֶת־
יָדוֹ עַל רֹאשׁ הַחַטָּאת וְשָׁחַט אֹתָהּ לְחַטָּאת בִּמְקוֹם אֲשֶׁר יִשְׁחַט
לד אֶת־הָעֹלָה׃ וְלָקַח הַכֹּהֵן מִדַּם הַחַטָּאת בְּאֶצְבָּעוֹ וְנָתַן עַל־קַרְנֹת
לה מִזְבַּח הָעֹלָה וְאֶת־כָּל־דָּמָהּ יִשְׁפֹּךְ אֶל־יְסוֹד הַמִּזְבֵּחַ׃ וְאֶת־כָּל־חֶלְבָּהּ
יָסִיר כַּאֲשֶׁר יוּסַר חֵלֶב־הַכֶּשֶׂב מִזֶּבַח הַשְּׁלָמִים וְהִקְטִיר הַכֹּהֵן אֹתָם
הַמִּזְבֵּחָה עַל אִשֵּׁי יְהוָה וְכִפֶּר עָלָיו הַכֹּהֵן עַל־חַטָּאתוֹ אֲשֶׁר־חָטָא
וְנִסְלַח לוֹ׃
ה א וְנֶפֶשׁ כִּי־תֶחֱטָא וְשָׁמְעָה קוֹל אָלָה וְהוּא עֵד אוֹ רָאָה אוֹ יָדָע אִם־
ב לוֹא יַגִּיד וְנָשָׂא עֲוֺנוֹ׃ אוֹ נֶפֶשׁ אֲשֶׁר תִּגַּע בְּכָל־דָּבָר טָמֵא אוֹ בְנִבְלַת
חַיָּה טְמֵאָה אוֹ בְּנִבְלַת בְּהֵמָה טְמֵאָה אוֹ בְּנִבְלַת שֶׁרֶץ טָמֵא וְנֶעְלַם

אונקלוס

תַּרְבַּהּ יַעְדֵּי, כְּמָא דְּאִתְעֲדָּא תְּרַב מֵעַל נִכְסַת קֻדְשַׁיָּא, וְיַסֵּיק כָּהֲנָא לְמַדְבְּחָא, לְאִתְקַבָּלָא בְרַעֲוָא קֳדָם יְיָ, וִיכַפַּר עֲלוֹהִי, כָּהֲנָא וְיִשְׁתְּבֵיק לֵיהּ׃ לב וְאִם אִמַּר, יַיְתֵי קֻרְבָּנֵיהּ לְחַטָּתָא, נֻקְבָּא שַׁלְמְתָא יַיְתֵינַהּ׃ לג וְיִסְמוֹךְ יָת יְדֵיהּ, עַל רֵישׁ חַטָּתָא, וְיִכּוֹס יָתַהּ לְחַטָּתָא, בְּאַתְרָא, דְּיִכּוֹס יָת עֲלָתָא׃ לד וְיִסַּב כָּהֲנָא, מִדְּמָא דְּחַטָּתָא בְּאֶצְבְּעֵיהּ, וְיִתֵּין, עַל קַרְנָת מַדְבְּחָא דַּעֲלָתָא, וְיָת כָּל דְּמַהּ יִשְׁפּוֹךְ, לִיסוֹדָא דְּמַדְבְּחָא׃ לה וְיָת כָּל תַּרְבַּהּ יַעְדֵּי, כְּמָא דְּמִתְעֲדָּא תְּרַב אִמַּר מִנִּכְסַת קֻדְשַׁיָּא, וְיַסֵּיק כָּהֲנָא יָתְהוֹן לְמַדְבְּחָא, עַל קֻרְבָּנַיָּא דַּייָ, וִיכַפַּר עֲלוֹהִי כָּהֲנָא, עַל חוֹבְתֵיהּ דְּחָב וְיִשְׁתְּבֵיק לֵיהּ׃ ה א וֶאֱנָשׁ אֲרֵי יְחוּב, וְיִשְׁמַע קָל מוֹמֵי, וְהוּא סָהִיד, אוֹ חֲזָא אוֹ יְדַע, אִם לָא יְחַוֵּי וִיקַבֵּיל חוֹבֵיהּ׃ ב אוֹ אֱנָשׁ, דְּיִקְרַב בְּכָל מִדַּעַם מְסָאַב, אוֹ בְנִבְלַת חַיְתָא מְסָאַבְתָּא, אוֹ בְּנִבְלַת בְּעִירָא מְסָאֲבָא, אוֹ, בְּנִבְלַת רְחֵישׁ מְסָאַב, וִיהֵי מְכַסֵּא

3 creature – and it escapes his notice, and while impure, he incurs guilt; or sins
by touching human impurity of any kind that makes him impure, and it escapes
4 his notice, but later he realizes his guilt; or sins by making a verbal oath to do
something, bad or good – whatever one might carelessly swear – and it escapes
5 his attention, but later he realizes his guilt; in any one of these ways – when he
realizes the guilt he has incurred in any of these ways, he shall confess the sin
6 he has committed, and bring the amends of his guilt to the LORD for the sin he
has committed: a female sheep or goat as a purification offering. So shall the
7 priest make atonement for that person for his sin. If he cannot afford a sheep,
he shall bring two doves or two pigeons as his guilt offering to the LORD, one
8 as a purification offering and the other as a burnt offering. He shall bring them
to the priest, who will offer the first as a purification offering, severing its neck
9 at the back without detaching the head. Then he shall sprinkle some of the
blood of the purification offering against the side of the altar; the rest of the
10 blood shall be drained out at its base. This is the purification offering. He shall
then offer the second bird as a burnt offering in the prescribed way. So shall

רש״י

וְאָשֵׁם. בַּאֲכִילַת קֹדֶשׁ אוֹ בְּבִיאַת מִקְדָּשׁ:

ג **בְּטֻמְאַת אָדָם.** זוֹ טֻמְאַת מֵת: **לְכֹל טֻמְאָתוֹ.** לְרַבּוֹת טֻמְאַת מַגַּע זָבִין וְזָבוֹת: **אֲשֶׁר יִטְמָא.** לְרַבּוֹת הַנּוֹגֵעַ בְּבוֹעֵל נִדָּה: **בָּהּ.** לְרַבּוֹת בּוֹלֵעַ נִבְלַת עוֹף טָהוֹר, וְלֹא יָדַע, שֶׁשָּׁכַח הַטֻּמְאָה: **וְאָשֵׁם.** בַּאֲכִילַת קֹדֶשׁ אוֹ בְּבִיאַת מִקְדָּשׁ:

ד **בִשְׂפָתַיִם.** וְלֹא בַּלֵּב: **לְהָרַע.** לְעַצְמוֹ: **אוֹ לְהֵיטִיב.** לְעַצְמוֹ, כְּגוֹן אֹכַל וְלֹא אֹכַל, אִישַׁן וְלֹא אִישַׁן: **לְכֹל אֲשֶׁר יְבַטֵּא.** לְרַבּוֹת לְשֶׁעָבַר: **וְנֶעְלַם מִמֶּנּוּ.** וְעָבַר עַל שְׁבוּעָתוֹ. כָּל אֵלֶּה בְּקָרְבָּן עוֹלֶה וְיוֹרֵד כַּמְפֹרָשׁ כָּאן, אֲבָל שְׁבוּעָה שֶׁיֵּשׁ בָּהּ כְּפִירַת מָמוֹן אֵינָהּ בְּקָרְבָּן זֶה אֶלָּא בְּאָשָׁם (להלן פסוקים כ-כו):

ח **וְהִקְרִיב אֶת אֲשֶׁר לַחַטָּאת רִאשׁוֹנָה.** חַטָּאת קוֹדֶמֶת לְעוֹלָה. לְמָה הַדָּבָר דּוֹמֶה? לִפְרַקְלִיט שֶׁנִּכְנַס לְרַצּוֹת, רִצָּה פְּרַקְלִיט, נִכְנַס דּוֹרוֹן אַחֲרָיו: **וְלֹא יַבְדִּיל.** אֵינוֹ מוֹלֵק אֶלָּא סִימָן אֶחָד: **עָרְפּוֹ.** הוּא גֹּבַהּ הָרֹאשׁ הַמְשֻׁפָּע לְצַד הַצַּוָּאר. 'מוּל עֹרֶף' – מוּל הָרוֹאֶה אֶת הָעֹרֶף, וְהוּא אֹרֶךְ כָּל אֲחוֹרֵי הַצַּוָּאר:

ט **וְהִזָּה מִדַּם הַחַטָּאת.** בָּעוֹלָה לֹא הִטְעִין אֶלָּא מִצּוּי (לעיל א, טו) וּבַחַטָּאת הַזָּאָה וּמִצּוּי, אוֹחֵז בָּעוֹף וּמַתִּיז וְהַדָּם נִתָּז וְהוֹלֵךְ לַמִּזְבֵּחַ: **חַטָּאת הוּא.** לִשְׁמָהּ כְּשֵׁרָה, שֶׁלֹּא לִשְׁמָהּ פְּסוּלָה:

י **כַּמִּשְׁפָּט.** כַּדָּת הָאֲמוּרָה בְּעוֹלַת הָעוֹף שֶׁל נְדָבָה בְּרֹאשׁ הַפָּרָשָׁה:

bring or come close to God. Yet the very ideas of *closeness* and *distance* seem inappropriate when speaking of God, who does not occupy physical space.

The barrier between us and God is not physical; it is metaphysical, psychological. It comes from our sense that we are self-sufficient. We overcome this tragic loneliness by giving something of ourselves away – and here the two senses of the word *korban*, sacrificing and coming close, come together. This is one reason why, under the wedding canopy, the groom gives the bride a ring. A gift bespeaks love, and love – the space we make for the other – is the redemption of our solitude. In ancient times, when flocks and herds were the measure of a person's wealth, our ancestors brought sacrificial animals as their gift of love.

Even then, though, they were no more than the outer form of the essential act, which is *coming close in love through giving up something of ourselves to the Beloved*. Those who cannot sacrifice cannot love. Love, loyalty, sacrifice: these are what bind us to the other, defeating the solipsism and narcissism that leave us small and alone.

ג מִמֶּנּוּ וְהוּא טָמֵא וְאָשֵׁם׃ אוֹ כִי יִגַּע בְּטֻמְאַת אָדָם לְכֹל טֻמְאָתוֹ אֲשֶׁר
ד יִטְמָא בָּהּ וְנֶעְלַם מִמֶּנּוּ וְהוּא יָדַע וְאָשֵׁם׃ אוֹ נֶפֶשׁ כִּי תִשָּׁבַע לְבַטֵּא
בִשְׂפָתַיִם לְהָרַע ׀ אוֹ לְהֵיטִיב לְכֹל אֲשֶׁר יְבַטֵּא הָאָדָם בִּשְׁבֻעָה וְנֶעְלַם
ה מִמֶּנּוּ וְהוּא־יָדַע וְאָשֵׁם לְאַחַת מֵאֵלֶּה׃ וְהָיָה כִי־יֶאְשַׁם לְאַחַת מֵאֵלֶּה
ו וְהִתְוַדָּה אֲשֶׁר חָטָא עָלֶיהָ׃ וְהֵבִיא אֶת־אֲשָׁמוֹ לַיהוָה עַל חַטָּאתוֹ
אֲשֶׁר חָטָא נְקֵבָה מִן־הַצֹּאן כִּשְׂבָּה אוֹ־שְׂעִירַת עִזִּים לְחַטָּאת וְכִפֶּר
ז עָלָיו הַכֹּהֵן מֵחַטָּאתוֹ׃ וְאִם־לֹא תַגִּיעַ יָדוֹ דֵּי שֶׂה וְהֵבִיא אֶת־אֲשָׁמוֹ
אֲשֶׁר חָטָא שְׁתֵּי תֹרִים אוֹ־שְׁנֵי בְנֵי־יוֹנָה לַיהוָה אֶחָד לְחַטָּאת וְאֶחָד
ח לְעֹלָה׃ וְהֵבִיא אֹתָם אֶל־הַכֹּהֵן וְהִקְרִיב אֶת־אֲשֶׁר לַחַטָּאת רִאשׁוֹנָה
ט וּמָלַק אֶת־רֹאשׁוֹ מִמּוּל עָרְפּוֹ וְלֹא יַבְדִּיל׃ וְהִזָּה מִדַּם הַחַטָּאת עַל־
קִיר הַמִּזְבֵּחַ וְהַנִּשְׁאָר בַּדָּם יִמָּצֵה אֶל־יְסוֹד הַמִּזְבֵּחַ חַטָּאת הוּא׃
י וְאֶת־הַשֵּׁנִי יַעֲשֶׂה עֹלָה כַּמִּשְׁפָּט וְכִפֶּר עָלָיו הַכֹּהֵן מֵחַטָּאתוֹ אֲשֶׁר־

אונקלוס

מניה, והוא מסאב וחב: ג או ארי יקרב בסואבת אנשא, לכל סאובתיה, דיסתאב בה, ויהי מכסא מניה, והוא ידע וחב: ד או אנש, ארי יקיים לפרשא בספון, לאבאשא או לאיטבא, לכל, דיפריש אנשא, בקיום ויהי מכסא מניה, והוא ידע וחב לחדא מאלין: ה ויהי ארי יחוב לחדא מאלין, ויודי, דחב עלה: ו וייתי ית אשמיה לקדם יי, על חובתיה דחב, נקבא מן ענא אמרתא, או צפירת עזי לחטתא, ויכפר עלוהי, כהנא מחובתיה: ז ואם לא תמטי

ידיה כמסת אמרא, וייתי ית חובתיה דחב, תרתין שפנינין, או תרין בני יונה לקדם יי, חד לחטתא וחד לעלתא: ח וייתי יתהון לות כהנא, ויקריב, ית דלחטתא קדמותא, וימלוק ית רישיה, מקביל קדליה ולא יפריש: ט וידי, מדמא דחטתא על כותל מדבחא, ודישתאר בדמא, יתמצי ליסודא דמדבחא, חטתא הוא: י וית תנינא, יעביד עלתא כדחזי, ויכפר עלוהי כהנא, מחובתיה דחב

5:5 וְהִתְוַדָּה *He shall confess* – Leviticus establishes Judaism's culture of repentance. In our daily and annual prayers for forgiveness, God asks us: What have you done with your life thus far? Have you thought about others or only about yourself? Have you brought healing to a place of human pain or hope where you found despair? You may have avoided malicious actions, but have you sinned by inattention? You may have been a success, but have you also been a blessing?

To ask these questions in the company of others publicly willing to confess their faults, knowing that God forgives every failure we acknowledge as a failure, and that He has faith in us even when we lose faith in ourselves, can be a life-changing experience. That is when we discover that, even in a secular age, God is still there, open to us whenever we are willing to open ourselves to Him.

5:7 אֲשָׁמוֹ *Offering* – As we have seen, the Hebrew word for sacrifice, *korban*, comes from the root *k-r-v*, which means to

the priest make atonement for that person for the sin he has committed, and
11 he will be forgiven. If he cannot afford two doves or two pigeons, he SHEVI'I
shall bring the purification offering of a tenth of an ephah of fine flour as the
sacrifice for his sin. He shall not put any oil on it, nor place on it any incense,
12 for it is a purification offering. He shall bring it to the priest, and the priest
shall lift a handful from it – its remembrance – and send it up in smoke upon
13 the altar with the LORD's fire offerings. It is a purification offering. Thus shall
the priest make atonement for that person for whichever one of these sins he
has committed, and he will be forgiven. The rest of the offering, as in the case
14 of a grain offering, shall belong to the priest." And the LORD spoke to
15 Moshe: "If a person commits a trespass, sinning unintentionally with respect
to any of the LORD's sacred objects, he shall bring an unblemished ram from
the flock, valued in silver shekel by the Sanctuary weight, as his guilt offering to
16 the LORD; it is a guilt offering. He shall make restitution for his trespass against
the sacred object, adding one-fifth to its value and giving it to the priest. The
priest shall make his atonement with the ram of the guilt offering, and he will
be forgiven.
17 If a person sins without realizing it, doing any of the things that the LORD
18 commanded not to be done, he incurs guilt and is subject to punishment. He
shall bring an unblemished ram from the flock, of the appropriate value, as a

רש״י

יא| **כִּי חַטָּאת הִוא.** וְאֵין בַּדִּין שֶׁיְּהֵא קָרְבָּנָהּ מְהֻדָּר:

יב| **חַטָּאת הִוא.** נִקְמְצָה וְנִקְטְרָה לִשְׁמָהּ כְּשֵׁרָה, שֶׁלֹּא לִשְׁמָהּ פְּסוּלָה:

יג| **עַל חַטָּאתוֹ אֲשֶׁר חָטָא.** כָּאן שִׁנָּה הַכָּתוּב, שֶׁהֲרֵי בַּעֲשִׁירוּת וּבְדַלּוּת נֶאֱמַר: ״מֵחַטָּאתוֹ״ (לעיל פסוק ו ופסוק י), וְכָאן בְּדַלֵּי דַלּוּת נֶאֱמַר: ״עַל חַטָּאתוֹ״, דִּקְדְּקוּ רַבּוֹתֵינוּ מִכָּאן, שֶׁאִם חָטָא כְּשֶׁהוּא עָשִׁיר וְהִפְרִישׁ מָעוֹת לְכִשְׂבָּה אוֹ שְׂעִירָה וְהֶעֱנִי, יָבִיא מִמִּקְצָתָן שְׁתֵּי תוֹרִים. הִפְרִישׁ מָעוֹת לִשְׁתֵּי תוֹרִים וְהֶעֱנִי, יָבִיא מִמִּקְצָתָן עֲשִׂירִית הָאֵיפָה. הִפְרִישׁ מָעוֹת לַעֲשִׂירִית הָאֵיפָה וְהֶעֱשִׁיר, יוֹסִיף עֲלֵיהֶן וְיָבִיא קָרְבַּן עָשִׁיר, לְכָךְ נֶאֱמַר כָּאן: ״עַל חַטָּאתוֹ״: **מֵאַחַת מֵאֵלֶּה.** מֵאַחַת מִשָּׁלֹשׁ כַּפָּרוֹת הָאֲמוּרוֹת בָּעִנְיָן: אוֹ בַּעֲשִׁירוּת, אוֹ בְּדַלּוּת, אוֹ בְּדַלֵּי דַלּוּת. וּמַה תַּלְמוּד לוֹמַר? שֶׁיָּכוֹל הַחֲמוּרִים שֶׁבָּהֶם יִהְיוּ בְּכִשְׂבָּה אוֹ שְׂעִירָה, וְהַקַּלִּין יִהְיוּ בָּעוֹף, וְהַקַּלִּין שֶׁבַּקַּלִּין יִהְיוּ בַּעֲשִׂירִית הָאֵיפָה? תַּלְמוּד לוֹמַר: ״מֵאַחַת מֵאֵלֶּה״, לְהַשְׁווֹת קַלִּין לַחֲמוּרִין לְכִשְׂבָּה וּשְׂעִירָה אִם הִשִּׂיגָה יָדָם, וְאֶת הַחֲמוּרִין לְקַלִּין לַעֲשִׂירִית הָאֵיפָה בְּדַלֵּי דַלּוּת: **וְהָיְתָה לַכֹּהֵן כַּמִּנְחָה.** לְלַמֵּד עַל מִנְחַת חוֹטֵא שֶׁיִּהְיוּ שְׁיָרֶיהָ נֶאֱכָלִין, זֶהוּ לְפִי פְּשׁוּטוֹ. וְרַבּוֹתֵינוּ דָּרְשׁוּ, ״וְהָיְתָה לַכֹּהֵן״, וְאִם חוֹטֵא זֶה כֹּהֵן הוּא, תְּהֵא כִּשְׁאָר מִנְחַת נִדְבַת כֹּהֵן, שֶׁהִיא ״כָּלִיל תִּהְיֶה לֹא תֵאָכֵל״ (להלן ו, טז):

טו| **כִּי תִמְעֹל מַעַל.** אֵין מְעִילָה בְּכָל מָקוֹם אֶלָּא שִׁנּוּי, וְכֵן הוּא אוֹמֵר: ״וַיִּמְעֲלוּ בֵּאלֹהֵי אֲבוֹתֵיהֶם וַיִּזְנוּ אַחֲרֵי אֱלֹהֵי עַמֵּי הָאָרֶץ״ (דברי הימים א׳ ה, כה), וְכֵן הוּא אוֹמֵר בְּסוֹטָה: ״וּמָעֲלָה בוֹ מָעַל״ (במדבר ה, יב): **וְחָטְאָה בִּשְׁגָגָה מִקָּדְשֵׁי ה׳.** שֶׁנֶּהֱנָה מִן הַהֶקְדֵּשׁ. וְהֵיכָן הֻזְהַר? נֶאֱמַר כָּאן ׳חֵטְא׳ וְנֶאֱמַר לְהַלָּן ׳חֵטְא׳ בִּתְרוּמָה: ״וְלֹא יִשְׂאוּ עָלָיו חֵטְא״ (להלן כב, ט), מַה לְּהַלָּן הִזְהִיר, אַף כָּאן הִזְהִיר. אִי מַה לְּהַלָּן לֹא הִזְהִיר אֶלָּא עַל הָאוֹכֵל אַף כָּאן לֹא הִזְהִיר אֶלָּא עַל הָאוֹכֵל? תַּלְמוּד לוֹמַר: ״תִמְעֹל מַעַל״, רִבָּה: **מִקָּדְשֵׁי ה׳.** הַמְיֻחָדִים לַשֵּׁם, יָצְאוּ קָדָשִׁים קַלִּים: **אַיִל.** לְשׁוֹן ׳קָשֶׁה׳, כְּמוֹ: ״וְאֶת אֵילֵי הָאָרֶץ לָקָח״ (יחזקאל יז, יג), אַף כָּאן קָשֶׁה, בֶּן שְׁתֵּי שָׁנִים: **בְּעֶרְכְּךָ כֶּסֶף שְׁקָלִים.** שֶׁיְּהֵא שָׁוֶה שְׁתֵּי סְלָעִים:

טז| **וְאֵת אֲשֶׁר חָטָא מִן הַקֹּדֶשׁ יְשַׁלֵּם.** קֶרֶן וָחֹמֶשׁ לַהֶקְדֵּשׁ:

יז| **וְלֹא יָדַע וְאָשֵׁם וְהֵבִיא.** הָעִנְיָן הַזֶּה מְדַבֵּר בְּמִי שֶׁבָּא סְפֵק כָּרֵת לְיָדוֹ וְלֹא יָדַע אִם עָבַר עָלָיו אִם לָאו, כְּגוֹן חֵלֶב וְשֻׁמָּן לְפָנָיו וּכְסָבוּר שֶׁשְּׁתֵּיהֶן הֶתֵּר וְאָכַל אֶת הָאַחַת. אָמְרוּ לוֹ: אַחַת שֶׁל חֵלֶב הָיְתָה,

יא חָטָא וְנִסְלַח לוֹ׃ וְאִם־לֹא תַשִּׂיג יָדוֹ לִשְׁתֵּי תֹרִים אוֹ שביעי
לִשְׁנֵי בְנֵי־יוֹנָה וְהֵבִיא אֶת־קָרְבָּנוֹ אֲשֶׁר חָטָא עֲשִׂירִת הָאֵפָה סֹלֶת
לְחַטָּאת לֹא־יָשִׂים עָלֶיהָ שֶׁמֶן וְלֹא־יִתֵּן עָלֶיהָ לְבֹנָה כִּי חַטָּאת הִוא׃
יב וֶהֱבִיאָהּ אֶל־הַכֹּהֵן וְקָמַץ הַכֹּהֵן ׀ מִמֶּנָּה מְלוֹא קֻמְצוֹ אֶת־אַזְכָּרָתָהּ
יג וְהִקְטִיר הַמִּזְבֵּחָה עַל אִשֵּׁי יְהוָה חַטָּאת הִוא׃ וְכִפֶּר עָלָיו הַכֹּהֵן
עַל־חַטָּאתוֹ אֲשֶׁר־חָטָא מֵאַחַת מֵאֵלֶּה וְנִסְלַח לוֹ וְהָיְתָה לַכֹּהֵן
יד טו כַּמִּנְחָה׃ וַיְדַבֵּר יְהוָה אֶל־מֹשֶׁה לֵּאמֹר׃ נֶפֶשׁ כִּי־תִמְעֹל
מַעַל וְחָטְאָה בִּשְׁגָגָה מִקָּדְשֵׁי יְהוָה וְהֵבִיא אֶת־אֲשָׁמוֹ לַיהוָה אַיִל
טז תָּמִים מִן־הַצֹּאן בְּעֶרְכְּךָ כֶּסֶף־שְׁקָלִים בְּשֶׁקֶל־הַקֹּדֶשׁ לְאָשָׁם׃ וְאֵת
אֲשֶׁר חָטָא מִן־הַקֹּדֶשׁ יְשַׁלֵּם וְאֶת־חֲמִישִׁתוֹ יוֹסֵף עָלָיו וְנָתַן אֹתוֹ
לַכֹּהֵן וְהַכֹּהֵן יְכַפֵּר עָלָיו בְּאֵיל הָאָשָׁם וְנִסְלַח לוֹ׃
יז וְאִם־נֶפֶשׁ כִּי תֶחֱטָא וְעָשְׂתָה אַחַת מִכָּל־מִצְוֹת יְהוָה אֲשֶׁר לֹא
יח תֵעָשֶׂינָה וְלֹא־יָדַע וְאָשֵׁם וְנָשָׂא עֲוֹנוֹ׃ וְהֵבִיא אַיִל תָּמִים מִן־הַצֹּאן

אונקלוס

וְיִשְׁתְּבֵיק לֵיהּ: יא וְאִם לָא תַדְבֵּיק יְדֵיהּ לְתַרְתֵּין שַׁפְנִינִין, אוֹ לִתְרֵין בְּנֵי יוֹנָה, וְיַיְתֵי יָת קֻרְבָּנֵיהּ דְּחָב, חַד מִן עַסְרָא בִּתְלָת סְאִין, סֻלְתָּא לְחַטָּתָא, לָא יְשַׁוֵּי עֲלַהּ מִשְׁחָא, וְלָא יִתֵּין עֲלַהּ לְבוֹנְתָא, אֲרֵי חַטָּתָא הִיא: יב וְיַיְתֵינַהּ לְוָת כָּהֲנָא, וְיִקְמוֹץ כָּהֲנָא מִנַּהּ, מְלֵי קֻמְצֵיהּ, יָת אַדְכָּרְתַהּ וְיַסֵּיק לְמַדְבְּחָא, עַל קֻרְבָּנַיָּא דַּייָ, חַטָּתָא הִיא: יג וִיכַפַּר עֲלוֹהִי כָּהֲנָא, עַל חוֹבְתֵיהּ דְּחָב, מֵחֲדָא מֵאִלֵּין וְיִשְׁתְּבֵיק לֵיהּ, וּתְהֵי לְכָהֲנָא כְּמִנְחָתָא: יד וּמַלֵּיל יי עִם מֹשֶׁה לְמֵימַר: טו אֱנָשׁ אֲרֵי יְשַׁקַּר שְׁקַר, וְיֵחוֹב בְּשָׁלוּ, מִקֻּדְשַׁיָּא דַּייָ, וְיַיְתֵי יָת אֲשָׁמֵיהּ לִקְדָם יי דְּכַר שְׁלִים מִן עָנָא, בְּפֻרְסָנֵיהּ, כְּסַף סִלְעִין בְּסִלְעֵי קֻדְשָׁא לַאֲשָׁמָא: טז וְיָת דְּחָב מִן קֻדְשָׁא יְשַׁלֵּים, וְיָת חֻמְשֵׁיהּ יוֹסֵיף עֲלוֹהִי, וְיִתֵּין יָתֵיהּ לְכָהֲנָא, וְכָהֲנָא, יְכַפַּר עֲלוֹהִי, בִּדְכְרָא דַּאֲשָׁמָא וְיִשְׁתְּבֵיק לֵיהּ: יז וְאִם אֱנָשׁ אֲרֵי יֵחוֹב, וְיַעֲבֵיד, חַד מִכָּל פִּקּוֹדַיָּא דַּייָ, דְּלָא כָשְׁרִין לְאִתְעֲבָדָא, וְלָא יְדַע וְחָב וִיקַבֵּיל חוֹבֵיהּ: יח וְיַיְתֵי, דְּכַר שְׁלִים מִן עָנָא,

רש״י

וְלֹא יָדַע אִם זוֹ שֶׁל חֵלֶב אָכַל – הֲרֵי זֶה מֵבִיא אָשָׁם תָּלוּי, וּמֵגֵן עָלָיו כָּל זְמַן שֶׁלֹּא נוֹדַע לוֹ שֶׁוַּדַּאי חָטָא, וְאִם יִוָּדַע לוֹ לְאַחַר זְמַן, יָבִיא חַטָּאת: וְלֹא יָדַע וְאָשֵׁם וְנָשָׂא עֲוֹנוֹ. רַבִּי יוֹסֵי הַגְּלִילִי אוֹמֵר: הֲרֵי הַכָּתוּב עָנַשׁ אֶת מִי שֶׁלֹּא יָדַע, עַל אַחַת כַּמָּה וְכַמָּה שֶׁיֵּעָנֵשׁ אֶת מִי שֶׁיָּדַע. רַבִּי יוֹסֵי אוֹמֵר: אִם נַפְשְׁךָ לֵידַע מַתַּן שְׂכָרָן שֶׁל צַדִּיקִים, צֵא וּלְמַד מֵאָדָם הָרִאשׁוֹן, שֶׁלֹּא נִצְטַוָּה אֶלָּא עַל מִצְוַת לֹא תַעֲשֶׂה וְעָבַר עָלֶיהָ, רְאֵה כַּמָּה מִיתוֹת נִקְנְסוּ עָלָיו וּלְדוֹרוֹתָיו. וְכִי אֵיזוֹ מִדָּה מְרֻבָּה, שֶׁל טוֹבָה אוֹ שֶׁל פֻּרְעָנוּת? הֱוֵי אוֹמֵר מִדָּה טוֹבָה. אִם מִדַּת פֻּרְעָנוּת מְעֻטָּה, רְאֵה כַּמָּה מִיתוֹת נִקְנְסוּ לוֹ וּלְדוֹרוֹתָיו, מִדָּה טוֹבָה הַמְרֻבָּה, הַיּוֹשֵׁב לוֹ מִן הַפִּגּוּלִין וְהַנּוֹתָרוֹת וְהַמִּתְעַנֶּה בְּיוֹם הַכִּפּוּרִים, עַל אַחַת כַּמָּה וְכַמָּה שֶׁיִּזְכֶּה לוֹ וּלְדוֹרוֹתָיו וּלְדוֹרוֹת דּוֹרוֹתָיו עַד סוֹף כָּל הַדּוֹרוֹת. רַבִּי עֲקִיבָא אוֹמֵר: הֲרֵי הוּא אוֹמֵר: "עַל פִּי שְׁנַיִם עֵדִים

guilt offering to the priest. The priest shall atone for him for that unintentional
19 sin, committed unknowingly, and he will be forgiven. This is a guilt offering,
for he had incurred guilt before the Lord."
20 21 The Lord spoke to Moshe: "If a person sins, committing a trespass against the
Lord by lying to his neighbor about a deposit or pledge, or by robbery, or by
22 defrauding his neighbor, or by finding lost property and lying about it; if he
23 swears falsely about anything he does in any of the ways a person sins, afterward
acknowledging guilt for the sin, he shall return what he took by robbery or
fraud, or the deposit left with him for safekeeping, or the lost property that he
24 found, or anything else about which he swore falsely. He shall repay its value MAFTIR
and add to that a fifth; he shall pay this to its owner on the day he presents his
25 guilt offering. And as his guilt offering to the Lord he shall bring the priest an

רש״י

אוֹ שְׁלֹשָׁה" וְגוֹ' (דברים יז, ו), אִם מִתְקַיֶּמֶת הָעֵדוּת בִּשְׁנַיִם, לָמָּה פֵּרַט לְךָ הַכָּתוּב שְׁלֹשָׁה, אֶלָּא לְהָבִיא שְׁלִישִׁי לְהַחֲמִיר עָלָיו כְּאִלּוּ הוֹעִיל וְלַעֲשׂוֹת דִּינוֹ כַּיּוֹצֵא בְּאֵלּוּ לְעִנְיַן עֹנֶשׁ וַהֲזָמָּה; אִם כָּךְ עָנַשׁ הַכָּתוּב לַנִּטְפָּל לְעוֹבְרֵי עֲבֵרָה כְּעוֹבְרֵי עֲבֵרָה, עַל אַחַת כַּמָּה וְכַמָּה שֶׁיְּשַׁלֵּם שָׂכָר טוֹב לַנִּטְפָּל לְעוֹשֵׂי מִצְוָה כְּעוֹשֵׂי מִצְוָה. רַבִּי אֶלְעָזָר בֶּן עֲזַרְיָה אוֹמֵר: "כִּי תִקְצֹר קְצִירְךָ בְשָׂדֶךָ וְשָׁכַחְתָּ עֹמֶר בַּשָּׂדֶה" (דברים כד, יט), הֲרֵי הוּא אוֹמֵר: "לְמַעַן יְבָרֶכְךָ" וְגוֹ' (שם), קָבַע הַכָּתוּב בְּרָכָה לְמִי שֶׁבָּאת עַל יָדוֹ מִצְוָה בְּלֹא יָדַע, אֱמֹר מֵעַתָּה: הָיְתָה סֶלַע צְרוּרָה בִּכְנָפָיו וְנָפְלָה הֵימֶנּוּ וּמְצָאָהּ הֶעָנִי וְנִתְפַּרְנֵס בָּהּ, הֲרֵי הַקָּדוֹשׁ בָּרוּךְ הוּא קוֹבֵעַ לוֹ בְּרָכָה:

יח **בְּעֶרְכְּךָ לְאָשָׁם.** בָּעֵרֶךְ הָאָמוּר לְמַעְלָה (פסוק טו): **אֲשֶׁר שָׁגָג וְהוּא לֹא יָדַע.** הָא אִם יָדַע לְאַחַר זְמַן, לֹא נִתְכַּפֵּר לוֹ בְּאָשָׁם זֶה, עַד שֶׁיָּבִיא חַטָּאת. הָא לְמָה זֶה דּוֹמֶה? לְעֶגְלָה עֲרוּפָה שֶׁנִּתְעָרְפָה וְאַחַר כָּךְ נִמְצָא הַהוֹרֵג – הֲרֵי זֶה יֵהָרֵג:

יט **אָשָׁם הוּא אָשֹׁם אָשַׁם.** הָרִאשׁוֹן כֻּלּוֹ קָמוּץ, שֶׁהוּא שֵׁם דָּבָר, וְהָאַחֲרוֹן חֶצְיוֹ קָמַץ וְחֶצְיוֹ פַּתָּח, שֶׁהוּא לְשׁוֹן פָּעַל. וְאִם תֹּאמַר, מִקְרָא שֶׁלֹּא לְצֹרֶךְ הוּא! כְּבָר דָּרוּשׁ הוּא בְּתוֹרַת כֹּהֲנִים (ג, ו): "אָשֹׁם אָשַׁם", לְהָבִיא אֲשַׁם שִׁפְחָה חֲרוּפָה שֶׁיְּהֵא אַיִל בֶּן שְׁתֵּי שָׁנִים. יָכוֹל שֶׁאֲנִי מְרַבֶּה אֲשַׁם נָזִיר וַאֲשַׁם מְצֹרָע? תַּלְמוּד לוֹמַר: "הוּא":

כא **נֶפֶשׁ כִּי תֶחֱטָא.** אָמַר רַבִּי עֲקִיבָא: מַה תַּלְמוּד לוֹמַר: "וּמָעֲלָה מַעַל בַּה'"? לְפִי שֶׁכָּל הַמַּלְוֶה וְהַלֹּוֶה וְהַנּוֹשֵׂא וְהַנּוֹתֵן אֵינוֹ עוֹשֶׂה אֶלָּא בְּעֵדִים וּבִשְׁטָר, לְפִיכָךְ בִּזְמַן שֶׁהוּא מְכַחֵשׁ, מְכַחֵשׁ בָּעֵדִים וּבַשְּׁטָר; אֲבָל הַמַּפְקִיד אֵצֶל חֲבֵרוֹ וְאֵינוֹ רוֹצֶה שֶׁתֵּדַע בּוֹ נְשָׁמָה אֶלָּא שְׁלִישִׁי שֶׁבֵּינֵיהֶם, לְפִיכָךְ בִּזְמַן שֶׁהוּא מְכַחֵשׁ מְכַחֵשׁ בַּשְּׁלִישִׁי שֶׁבֵּינֵיהֶם: **בִתְשׂוּמֶת יָד.** שֶׂשָּׂם בְּיָדוֹ מָמוֹן לְהִתְעַסֵּק אוֹ בְּמִלְוֶה: **אוֹ בְגָזֵל.** שֶׁגָּזַל מִיָּדוֹ כְּלוּם: **אוֹ עָשַׁק.** הוּא שְׂכַר שָׂכִיר:

כב **וְכִחֶשׁ בָּהּ.** שֶׁכָּפַר עַל אַחַת מִכָּל אֵלֶּה "אֲשֶׁר יַעֲשֶׂה הָאָדָם", לַחֲטֹא וּלְהִשָּׁבַע עַל שֶׁקֶר לִכְפִירַת מָמוֹן:

כג **כִּי יֶחֱטָא וְאָשֵׁם.** כְּשֶׁיַּכִּיר בְּעַצְמוֹ לָשׁוּב בִּתְשׁוּבָה וְלָדַעַת וּלְהוֹדוֹת כִּי חָטָא וְאָשֵׁם:

כד **בְּרֹאשׁוֹ.** הוּא הַקֶּרֶן, רֹאשׁ הַמָּמוֹן: **לַאֲשֶׁר הוּא לוֹ.** לְמִי שֶׁהַמָּמוֹן שֶׁלּוֹ:

circumstances, Jews have felt called on to bring the presence of God into the public places of our shared life. We must resist the flight into solitude, for we are called on neither to forsake nor to accept the world but to change it, creating in its midst a society of justice and compassion, equity and moral integrity, never yielding to despair even after a succession of failures. God is not in another world but in this, the world of deceit and desire, collision and collusion. He is here, less as a presence than as a challenge, a call, a summons, a command. And so, when we betray the trust on which society is built, it is God we trespass against.

בְּעֶרְכְּךָ לְאָשָׁם אֶל־הַכֹּהֵן וְכִפֶּר עָלָיו הַכֹּהֵן עַל שִׁגְגָתוֹ אֲשֶׁר־שָׁגָג
יט וְהוּא לֹא־יָדַע וְנִסְלַח לוֹ: אָשָׁם הוּא אָשֹׁם אָשַׁם לַיהוָה:
כ כא וַיְדַבֵּר יְהוָה אֶל־מֹשֶׁה לֵּאמֹר: נֶפֶשׁ כִּי תֶחֱטָא וּמָעֲלָה מַעַל בַּיהוָה
וְכִחֵשׁ בַּעֲמִיתוֹ בְּפִקָּדוֹן אוֹ־בִתְשׂוּמֶת יָד אוֹ בְגָזֵל אוֹ עָשַׁק אֶת־
כב עֲמִיתוֹ: אוֹ־מָצָא אֲבֵדָה וְכִחֶשׁ בָּהּ וְנִשְׁבַּע עַל־שָׁקֶר עַל־אַחַת מִכֹּל
כג אֲשֶׁר־יַעֲשֶׂה הָאָדָם לַחֲטֹא בָהֵנָּה: וְהָיָה כִּי־יֶחֱטָא וְאָשֵׁם וְהֵשִׁיב
אֶת־הַגְּזֵלָה אֲשֶׁר גָּזָל אוֹ אֶת־הָעֹשֶׁק אֲשֶׁר עָשָׁק אוֹ אֶת־הַפִּקָּדוֹן
כד אֲשֶׁר הָפְקַד אִתּוֹ אוֹ אֶת־הָאֲבֵדָה אֲשֶׁר מָצָא: אוֹ מִכֹּל אֲשֶׁר־יִשָּׁבַע מפטיר
עָלָיו לַשֶּׁקֶר וְשִׁלַּם אֹתוֹ בְּרֹאשׁוֹ וַחֲמִשִׁתָיו יֹסֵף עָלָיו לַאֲשֶׁר הוּא לוֹ
כה יִתְּנֶנּוּ בְּיוֹם אַשְׁמָתוֹ: וְאֶת־אֲשָׁמוֹ יָבִיא לַיהוָה אַיִל תָּמִים מִן־הַצֹּאן

אונקלוס

בְּפֻרְסָנֵיהּ לַאֲשָׁמָא לְוָת כָּהֲנָא, וִיכַפַּר עֲלוֹהִי כָּהֲנָא, עַל שָׁלוּתֵיהּ דְּאִשְׁתְּלִי, וְהוּא לָא יְדַע וְיִשְׁתְּבֵיק לֵיהּ: יט אֲשָׁמָא הוּא, עַל חוֹבְתֵיהּ דְּחָב אֲשָׁמָא יְקָרֵיב קֳדָם יְיָ: כ וּמַלֵּיל יְיָ עִם מֹשֶׁה לְמֵימַר: כא אֱנָשׁ אֲרֵי יְחוֹב, וִישַׁקַּר שְׁקַר קֳדָם יְיָ, וִיכַדֵּיב בְּחַבְרֵיהּ בְּפִקְדוֹנָא, אוֹ בְשׁוּתָּפוּת יְדָא אוֹ בִגְזֵילָא, אוֹ עֲשַׁק יָת חַבְרֵיהּ: כב אוֹ אַשְׁכַּח אֲבֵידְתָא, וְכַדֵּיב בַּהּ וְאִשְׁתְּבַע עַל שִׁקְרָא, עַל חֲדָא, מִכֹּל, דְּיַעְבֵּיד אֱנָשָׁא לְמֶחֱב בְּהוֹן: כג וִיהֵי אֲרֵי יֶחְטֵי וִיחוֹב, וְיָתֵיב יָת גְּזֵילָא דִּגְזַל, אוֹ יָת עִשְׁקָא דַּעֲשַׁק, אוֹ יָת פִּקְדוֹנָא, דְּאִתַּפְקַד לְוָתֵיהּ, אוֹ יָת אֲבֵידְתָא דְּאַשְׁכַּח: כד אוֹ, מִכּוֹלָא, דְּיִשְׁתְּבַע עֲלוֹהִי לְשִׁקְרָא, וִישַׁלֵּים יָתֵיהּ בְּרֵישֵׁיהּ, וְחֻמְשׁוֹהִי יוֹסֵיף עֲלוֹהִי, לִדְהוּא דִּילֵיהּ, יִתְּנִנֵּיהּ בְּיוֹמָא דְּחוֹבְתֵיהּ: כה וְיָת אֲשָׁמֵיהּ יַיְתֵי לִקְדָם יְיָ, דְּכַר שְׁלִים מִן עָנָא,

5:21 וּמָעֲלָה מַעַל בַּיהוה *A trespass against the Lord* – Faith, for many Western thinkers, was something encountered in the privacy of the soul. There are religious traditions built around the private experiences of the individual. But they are not Judaism. Solitude, for the Torah, is not humanity's highest state, nor is it the condition in which we come most fully into the presence of God. The individual must share his life with others.

The Torah's narratives about persons-in-relation are often painful. They tell a story of conflicts, rivalries, jealousies, antagonisms, rifts, murmurings, and rebellions. In our collective life we seldom if ever reach the serenity that sometimes comes upon an individual when, alone, he or she contemplates the universe. Nonetheless it is here that we must struggle to make a space for God.

Religion has often been humanity's most profound source of consolation. It is hard to live long in the company of society without deep disillusionment. Faced with the apparent arbitrariness of the world, the individual driven by a glimpse of perfection can come to find it in an alternative reality, the world within the soul in whose quietude can be heard the mystic reverberations of infinity.

Judaism's most revolutionary gesture is to have declined this consolation. With unusual courage, often in dire

26 unblemished ram from the flock of the appropriate value. The priest shall make
his atonement before the LORD, and he will be forgiven for whatever he did to
incur this guilt."

The haftara for Parashat Vayikra is on page 1558.
On the Shabbat of Parashat HaḤodesh read the haftara on page 1650.

---

behave that way again. In guilt cultures there is repentance and forgiveness. Shame is not like that. It is a stain on the sinner that cannot be fully removed. A shame culture does not provide forgiveness; it offers something similar but different, namely appeasement, usually accompanied by an act of self-abasement. In a guilt culture it makes sense to confess your sins. In a shame culture it makes no sense at all – instead it becomes all-important to cover up your wrongdoing by any means possible.

Ultimately, guilt cultures produce strong individuals precisely because they force us to accept responsibility. When things go wrong we don't waste time blaming others. We don't luxuriate in that most addictive, destructive drug, victimhood. We say, honestly and seriously, "I'm sorry. Forgive me. Now let me do what I can to put it right." That way, we and the people we offend can move on. Through our mistakes we discover the strength to heal, learn, and grow. Shame cultures produce people who conform. Guilt cultures produce people with the courage to be free.

כו בְּעֶרְכְּךָ֛ לְאָשָׁ֖ם אֶל־הַכֹּהֵֽן׃ וְכִפֶּ֨ר עָלָ֧יו הַכֹּהֵ֛ן לִפְנֵ֥י יְהוָ֖ה וְנִסְלַ֣ח ל֑וֹ
עַל־אַחַ֛ת מִכֹּ֥ל אֲשֶׁר־יַעֲשֶׂ֖ה לְאַשְׁמָ֥ה בָֽהּ׃

The הפטרה *for* פרשת ויקרא *is on page 1559.*
On the שבת *of* פרשת החודש *read the* הפטרה *on page 1651.*

אונקלוס

בְּפֻרְסָנֵיהּ לַאֲשָׁמָא לְוָת כָּהֲנָא: כו וִיכַפַּר עֲלוֹהִי כָּהֲנָא, קֳדָם יי וְיִשְׁתְּבֵיק לֵיהּ, עַל חֲדָא, מִכָּל דְּיַעֲבֵיד לְמֶחֱב בַּהּ:

5:26 לְאַשְׁמָה בָהּ *This guilt* – After repaying and compensating the victim of a crime, the criminal brings a guilt offering. There is a key distinction between guilt cultures and shame cultures. Guilt cultures conceive of morality as a voice within – the voice of conscience that tells us whether or not we have done wrong. Shame cultures think of morality as an external demand – what other people expect of us. To feel shame is to experience or imagine what one looks like in the sight of others who pass judgment on us. Shame cultures are other-directed. Guilt cultures are inner-directed. Guilt cultures make a sharp distinction between the sinner and the sin. The act may be wrong, but the agent's integrity as a person remains intact. That is why guilt can be relieved by remorse, confession, restitution, and the resolve never to

PARASHAT TZAV

6 1 2 The LORD spoke to Moshe: "Instruct Aharon and his sons: This is the law of
the burnt offering. The burnt offering shall remain on the altar hearth all night
3 until the morning, and the altar fire shall be kept alight upon it. The priest shall
dress in his linen vestments, with linen undergarments against his skin. He
shall lift the ashes of the burnt offering that the fire consumed on the altar,

רש"י

ו ב **צו את אהרן.** אין 'צו' אלא לשון זרוז, מיד ולדורות. אמר רבי שמעון: ביותר צריך הכתוב לזרז מקום שיש בו חסרון כיס: **זאת תורת העלה וגו'.** הרי הענין הזה בא ללמד על הקטר חלבים ואברים, שיהא כשר כל הלילה, וללמד על הפסולין, איזה אם עלה ירד ואיזה אם עלה לא ירד, שכל 'תורת' לרבות הוא בא, לומר, תורה אחת לכל העולים ואפלו פסולין, שאם עלו לא ירדו: **הוא העלה.** מעט את הרובע ואת הנרבע וכיוצא בהן, שלא היה פסולן בקדש, שנפסלו קדם שבאו לעזרה:

ג **מדו בד.** היא הכתנת, ומה תלמוד לומר "מדו"? שתהא כמדתו: **על בשרו.** שלא יהא דבר חוצץ בינתים: **והרים את הדשן.** היה חותה מלא המחתה מן המאכלות הפנימיות, ונותנן במזרחו של כבש: **הדשן אשר תאכל האש את העלה.** ועשאתה דשן, מאותו דשן ירים תרומה "ושמו אצל המזבח":

to worship Him. But they, accustomed to religious practices in the ancient world, could not yet conceive of *avoda shebalev*, the "service of the heart," namely prayer. They were accustomed to the way things were done in Egypt (and virtually everywhere else at that time), where worship meant sacrifice. On this reading, Yirmeyahu in the *haftara* meant that from a divine perspective sacrifices were *bediavad,* not *lekhatḥila*, an after-the-fact concession, not something desired at the outset.

A third interpretation is that the entire sequence of events from Exodus 25 to Leviticus 25 was a response to the episode of the golden calf. This, I argued in Parashat Ki Tisa, represented a passionate need on the part of the people to have God close, not distant; in the camp, not at the top of the mountain; accessible to everyone, not just Moshe; and on a daily basis, not just at rare moments of miracle. Though central to the Judaism we know now, this was not part of God's original intention for the Israelites.

This debate aside, Yirmeyahu's message in the *haftara* is clear: his insistence on the moral dimension of Judaism: "I the LORD act with loving-kindness, justice, and righteousness in the world, for it is these things that I desire" (Jer. 9:23). What is genuinely unexpected is that the Sages joined sections of the Torah and passages from the prophetic literature so different from one another that they sound as if they are coming from different universes with different laws of gravity.

Judaism is a choral symphony scored for many voices. It is an ongoing argument between different points of view. Without detailed laws, no sacrifices. Without sacrifices in the biblical age, no coming close to God. But if there are only sacrifices with no prophetic voice, then people may serve God while abusing their fellow humans. They may think themselves righteous while they are, in fact, merely self-righteous.

I believe that this fugue between Torah and haftara, priestly and prophetic voices, is one of Judaism's great glories. We hear in both voices how to act and why. Without the how, action is lame; without the why, behavior is blind. Combine priestly detail and prophetic vision and you have spiritual greatness.

פרשת צו

ו א וַיְדַבֵּר יְהוָה אֶל־מֹשֶׁה לֵּאמֹר׃ ב צַו אֶת־אַהֲרֹן וְאֶת־בָּנָיו לֵאמֹר זֹאת
תּוֹרַת הָעֹלָה הִוא הָעֹלָה עַל מוֹקְדָה עַל־הַמִּזְבֵּחַ כָּל־הַלַּיְלָה עַד־
ג הַבֹּקֶר וְאֵשׁ הַמִּזְבֵּחַ תּוּקַד בּוֹ׃ וְלָבַשׁ הַכֹּהֵן מִדּוֹ בַד וּמִכְנְסֵי־בַד יִלְבַּשׁ
עַל־בְּשָׂרוֹ וְהֵרִים אֶת־הַדֶּשֶׁן אֲשֶׁר תֹּאכַל הָאֵשׁ אֶת־הָעֹלָה עַל־

אונקלוס

ו א וּמַלֵּיל יי עִם מֹשֶׁה לְמֵימַר: ב פַּקֵּיד יָת אַהֲרֹן וְיָת בְּנוֹהִי
לְמֵימַר, דָּא אוֹרָיְתָא דַּעֲלָתָא, הִיא עֲלָתָא, דְּמִתּוֹקְדָא עַל
מַדְבְּחָא כָּל לֵילְיָא עַד צַפְרָא, וְאִישָּׁתָא דְּמַדְבְּחָא תְּהֵי יָקְדָא
בֵיהּ: ג וְיִלְבַּשׁ כָּהֲנָא לְבוּשִׁין דְּבוּץ, וּמִכְנְסִין דְּבוּץ יִלְבַּשׁ עַל
בִּסְרֵיהּ, וְיַפְרֵישׁ יָת דִּשְׁנָא, דְּתֵיכוֹל אִישָּׁתָא, יָת עֲלָתָא עַל

TZAV

Parashat Tzav continues the laws of sacrifices begun in the previous *parasha*, this time from the perspective of the priests performing the ritual. Rules are set out for burnt and grain offerings, sin and guilt offerings, and peace offerings, each with its own specific procedures. Details are then set out for the induction of Aharon and his sons into office, prior to the inauguration of the service of the Sanctuary.

A rigorous set of laws is now established for those who enter the Sanctuary's sacred space. They are differential: some for the High Priest, others for ordinary priests, yet others for the people as a whole. The result is to be a form of Divine Presence, known in Rabbinic Hebrew as the *Shekhina*, very different from the God of creation who makes universes and the God of redemption who overthrows empires. This is the God who is close, who can be met in fixed places at predictable times, who travels with the people in the desert and will later be with them even in exile. This is God as *shakhen*, as "neighbor," and also as *kavod*, "glory." This is God as He gives a specific kind of dignity to man.

6:2 צו את־אהרן ואת־בניו לאמר זאת תורת העלה *Instruct Aharon and his sons: This is the law of the burnt offering* – Fascinatingly, while the *parasha* presents the sacrificial service as a key element of Jewish worship, the *haftara*, the reading from the Prophets, that the Sages selected for Parashat Tzav appears immediately to negate the very substance of the *parasha*:

> For when I brought your forefathers out of Egypt, I did not speak to them, nor did I command them about matters of burnt offerings and sacrifices. Rather, this is what I commanded them: Heed My voice so that I will be your God and you will be My people. Walk in all the ways as I will command you so that it will be good for you. (Jer. 7:22–23)

What does this mean? The simplest interpretation is that it means "I did not *only* give them commands about burnt offerings and sacrifices." I commanded them but they were not the whole of the law, nor were they even its primary purpose.

A second interpretation is the famously controversial view of Rambam (*Guide for the Perplexed* III:32) that the sacrifices were not what God would have wanted in an ideal world. What He wanted was *avoda*: He wanted the Israelites

4 and place them by the altar's side. Then he shall take off his vestments, put on
other garments, and take the ashes to a ritually pure place outside the camp.
5 The altar fire shall be kept alight; it shall not go out. Every morning the priest
shall add wood to it, lay out the burnt offering upon it, and send the fat parts of
6 the peace offering up in smoke upon it. A daily fire shall be kept alight on the
7 altar; it shall not go out. This is the law of the grain offering. Aharon's
8 sons shall bring these before the LORD in front of the altar. The priest shall lift
a handful of the fine flour and oil from the grain offering, and all the incense on
it, and send this remembrance up in smoke upon the altar as a pleasing aroma
9 to the LORD. Aharon and his sons shall eat what is left of it. It shall be eaten as
unleavened bread in a holy place; in the courtyard of the Tent of Meeting shall
10 they eat it. It shall not be baked with any leaven. I have given it as their portion
of My fire offerings; it is holy of holies, like the purification offering and the

רש״י

ד **וּפָשַׁט אֶת בְּגָדָיו.** אֵין זוֹ חוֹבָה אֶלָּא דֶּרֶךְ אֶרֶץ, שֶׁלֹּא יְלַכְלֵךְ בְּהוֹצָאַת הַדֶּשֶׁן בְּגָדִים שֶׁהוּא מְשַׁמֵּשׁ בָּהֶן תָּמִיד; בְּגָדִים שֶׁבִּשֵּׁל בָּהֶן קְדֵרָה לְרַבּוֹ אַל יִמְזֹג בָּהֶן כּוֹס לְרַבּוֹ, לְכָךְ: ״וְלָבַשׁ בְּגָדִים אֲחֵרִים״, פְּחוּתִין מֵהֶן: **וְהוֹצִיא אֶת הַדֶּשֶׁן.** הַצָּבוּר בַּתַּפּוּחַ, כְּשֶׁהוּא רַבָּה וְאֵין מָקוֹם לַמַּעֲרָכָה מוֹצִיאוֹ מִשָּׁם. וְאֵין זֶה חוֹבָה בְּכָל יוֹם, אֲבָל הַתְּרוּמָה חוֹבָה בְּכָל יוֹם:

ה **וְהָאֵשׁ עַל הַמִּזְבֵּחַ תּוּקַד בּוֹ.** רִבָּה כָּאן יְקִידוֹת הַרְבֵּה: ״עַל מוֹקְדָה״ (לעיל פסוק ב), ״וְאֵשׁ הַמִּזְבֵּחַ תּוּקַד בּוֹ״ (שם), ״וְהָאֵשׁ עַל הַמִּזְבֵּחַ תּוּקַד בּוֹ״, ״אֵשׁ תָּמִיד תּוּקַד עַל הַמִּזְבֵּחַ״ (להלן פסוק ו). כֻּלָּן נִדְרְשׁוּ בְּמַסֶּכֶת יוֹמָא (דף מה ע״א) שֶׁנֶּחְלְקוּ רַבּוֹתֵינוּ בְּמִנְיַן הַמַּעֲרָכוֹת שֶׁהָיוּ שָׁם: **וְעָרַךְ עָלֶיהָ הָעֹלָה.** עוֹלַת תָּמִיד הִיא תִּקְדֹּם: **חֶלְבֵי הַשְּׁלָמִים.** אִם יָבִיאוּ שָׁם שְׁלָמִים. וְרַבּוֹתֵינוּ לָמְדוּ מִכָּאן: ״עָלֶיהָ״, עַל עוֹלַת הַבֹּקֶר, הַשְׁלֵם כָּל הַקָּרְבָּנוֹת כֻּלָּם, מִכָּאן שֶׁלֹּא יְהֵא דָּבָר מְאֻחָר לְתָמִיד שֶׁל בֵּין הָעַרְבַּיִם:

ו **אֵשׁ תָּמִיד.** אֵשׁ שֶׁנֶּאֱמַר בָּהּ ״תָּמִיד״, הִיא שֶׁמַּדְלִיקִין בָּהּ אֶת הַנֵּרוֹת, שֶׁנֶּאֱמַר בָּהּ: ״לְהַעֲלֹת נֵר תָּמִיד״ (שמות כז, כ), אַף הִיא מֵעַל הַמִּזְבֵּחַ הַחִיצוֹן תּוּקָד: **לֹא תִכְבֶּה.** הַמְכַבֶּה אֵשׁ עַל הַמִּזְבֵּחַ עוֹבֵר בִּשְׁנֵי לָאוִין:

ז **וְזֹאת תּוֹרַת הַמִּנְחָה.** תּוֹרָה אַחַת לְכֻלָּן, לְהַטְעִינָן שֶׁמֶן וּלְבוֹנָה הָאֲמוּרִין בָּעִנְיָן, שֶׁיָּכוֹל אֵין לִי טְעוּנוֹת שֶׁמֶן וּלְבוֹנָה אֶלָּא מִנְחַת יִשְׂרָאֵל שֶׁהִיא נִקְמֶצֶת, מִנְחַת כֹּהֲנִים שֶׁהִיא כָּלִיל מִנַּיִן? תַּלְמוּד לוֹמַר: ״תּוֹרַת״: **הַקְרֵב אֹתָהּ.** הִיא הַגָּשָׁה בְּקֶרֶן דְּרוֹמִית מַעֲרָבִית: **לִפְנֵי ה׳.** הוּא מַעֲרָב, שֶׁהוּא לְצַד אֹהֶל מוֹעֵד: **אֶל פְּנֵי הַמִּזְבֵּחַ.** הוּא הַדָּרוֹם שֶׁהוּא פָּנָיו שֶׁל מִזְבֵּחַ, שֶׁהַכֶּבֶשׁ נָתוּן לְאוֹתוֹ הָרוּחַ:

ח **בְּקֻמְצוֹ.** שֶׁלֹּא יַעֲשֶׂה מִדָּה לַקֹּמֶץ: **מִסֹּלֶת הַמִּנְחָה וּמִשַּׁמְנָהּ.** מִכָּאן שֶׁקּוֹמֵץ מִמָּקוֹם שֶׁנִּתְרַבָּה שַׁמְנָהּ: **וְאֵת כָּל הַלְּבֹנָה אֲשֶׁר עַל הַמִּנְחָה וְהִקְטִיר.** שֶׁמְּלַקֵּט אֶת לְבוֹנָתָהּ לְאַחַר קְמִיצָה וּמַקְטִירוֹ. וּלְפִי שֶׁלֹּא פֵּרַשׁ כֵּן אֶלָּא בְּאַחַת מִן הַמְּנָחוֹת בְּ׳וַיִּקְרָא׳ (לעיל ב, ב), הֻצְרַךְ לִשְׁנוֹת פָּרָשָׁה זוֹ, לִכְלֹל כָּל הַמְּנָחוֹת כְּמִשְׁפָּטָן:

ט **בְּמָקוֹם קָדֹשׁ.** וְאֵיזֶהוּ? ״בַּחֲצַר אֹהֶל מוֹעֵד״:

י **לֹא תֵאָפֶה חָמֵץ חֶלְקָם.** אַף הַשְּׁיָרִים אֲסוּרִים בְּחָמֵץ: **כַּחַטָּאת וְכָאָשָׁם.** מִנְחַת חוֹטֵא הֲרֵי הִיא כְּחַטָּאת, לְפִיכָךְ קְמָצָהּ שֶׁלֹּא לִשְׁמָהּ

the verbs *h-v-h*, *h-v-v*, and *y-h-v*, all of which have the sense of giving, bringing, or offering.

That is why, when they were a nation of farmers and shepherds, the Israelites demonstrated their love of God by bringing Him a symbolic gift of their flocks and herds, their grain and fruit, that is, their livelihood. To love is to want to bring an offering to the Beloved. To love is to give. This is true in many aspects of life. A happily married couple is constantly making sacrifices for one another. Parents make huge sacrifices for their children. People drawn to a calling often sacrifice remunerative careers for the sake of their ideals. In ages of patriotism, people make sacrifices for their country. In strong communities people make sacrifices for one another when someone is in distress or needs help. Sacrifice is the superglue of relationship. It bonds us to one another. Sacrifice is the choreography of love.

ד הַמִּזְבֵּחַ וְשָׂמוֹ אֵצֶל הַמִּזְבֵּחַ: וּפָשַׁט אֶת־בְּגָדָיו וְלָבַשׁ בְּגָדִים אֲחֵרִים
ה וְהוֹצִיא אֶת־הַדֶּשֶׁן אֶל־מִחוּץ לַמַּחֲנֶה אֶל־מָקוֹם טָהוֹר: וְהָאֵשׁ עַל־
הַמִּזְבֵּחַ תּוּקַד־בּוֹ לֹא תִכְבֶּה וּבִעֵר עָלֶיהָ הַכֹּהֵן עֵצִים בַּבֹּקֶר בַּבֹּקֶר
ו וְעָרַךְ עָלֶיהָ הָעֹלָה וְהִקְטִיר עָלֶיהָ חֶלְבֵי הַשְּׁלָמִים: אֵשׁ תָּמִיד תּוּקַד
ז עַל־הַמִּזְבֵּחַ לֹא תִכְבֶּה: וְזֹאת תּוֹרַת הַמִּנְחָה הַקְרֵב אֹתָהּ
ח בְּנֵי־אַהֲרֹן לִפְנֵי יהוה אֶל־פְּנֵי הַמִּזְבֵּחַ: וְהֵרִים מִמֶּנּוּ בְּקֻמְצוֹ מִסֹּלֶת
הַמִּנְחָה וּמִשַּׁמְנָהּ וְאֵת כָּל־הַלְּבֹנָה אֲשֶׁר עַל־הַמִּנְחָה וְהִקְטִיר הַמִּזְבֵּחַ
ט רֵיחַ נִיחֹחַ אַזְכָּרָתָהּ לַיהוה: וְהַנּוֹתֶרֶת מִמֶּנָּה יֹאכְלוּ אַהֲרֹן וּבָנָיו
י מַצּוֹת תֵּאָכֵל בְּמָקוֹם קָדֹשׁ בַּחֲצַר אֹהֶל־מוֹעֵד יֹאכְלוּהָ: לֹא תֵאָפֶה
חָמֵץ חֶלְקָם נָתַתִּי אֹתָהּ מֵאִשָּׁי קֹדֶשׁ קָדָשִׁים הִוא כַּחַטָּאת וְכָאָשָׁם:

אונקלוס

מַדְבְּחָא, וִישַׁוֵּינֵיהּ, בִּסְטַר מַדְבְּחָא: ד וְיִשְׁלַח יָת לְבוּשׁוֹהִי, וְיִלְבַּשׁ לְבוּשִׁין אָחֳרָנִין, וְיַפֵּיק יָת דִּשְׁנָא לְמִבָּרָא לְמַשְׁרִיתָא, לַאֲתַר דְּכֵי: ה וְאִישָׁתָא עַל מַדְבְּחָא תְּהֵי יָקְדָא בֵיהּ לָא תִטְפֵּי, וִיבָעַר עֲלַהּ כָּהֲנָא, אָעִין בִּצְפַר בִּצְפַר, וְיַסְדַּר עֲלַהּ עֲלָתָא, וְיַסֵּיק עֲלַהּ תַּרְבֵּי נִכְסַת קֻדְשַׁיָּא: ו אִישָׁתָא, תְּדִירָא, תְּהֵי יָקְדָא עַל מַדְבְּחָא לָא תִטְפֵּי: ז וְדָא אוֹרָיְתָא דְּמִנְחָתָא, דִּיקָרְבוּן יָתַהּ בְּנֵי אַהֲרֹן קֳדָם יְיָ, לִקְדָם מַדְבְּחָא: ח וְיַפְרֵישׁ מִנֵּיהּ בִּקְמְצֵיהּ, מִסֻּלְתָּא דְּמִנְחָתָא וּמִמִּשְׁחַהּ, וְיָת כָּל לְבוֹנְתָא, דְּעַל מִנְחָתָא, וְיַסֵּיק לְמַדְבְּחָא, לְאִתְקַבָּלָא בְּרַעֲוָא, אַדְכָּרְתַהּ קֳדָם יְיָ: ט וּדְיִשְׁתְּאַר מִנַּהּ, יֵיכְלוּן אַהֲרֹן וּבְנוֹהִי, פַּטִּיר תִּתְאֲכִיל בַּאֲתַר קַדִּישׁ, בְּדָרַת מַשְׁכַּן זִמְנָא יֵיכְלֻנַּהּ: י לָא תִתְאֲפֵי חֲמִיעַ, חוּלָקְהוֹן, יְהַבִית יָתַהּ מִקֻּרְבָּנָי, קֹדֶשׁ קֻדְשִׁין הִיא, כְּחַטָּתָא וְכַאֲשָׁמָא:

6:6 אֵשׁ תָּמִיד תּוּקַד עַל־הַמִּזְבֵּחַ *A daily fire shall be kept alight on the altar* – One of our most potent symbols is the *ner tamid*, the everlasting light that, like the bush Moshe saw in the desert, "was ablaze with fire but was not consumed." We are an eternal people bound to the eternal God. The days, the years, the centuries pass, but Judaism and the Jewish people remain. This fire must be tended from morning to morning. The Jewish people have always translated identity into action. "No people," wrote Matthew Arnold, "ever felt so strongly as the people of the Old Testament, the Hebrew people, that conduct is three-fourths of our life and its largest concern." In the thirteenth century the *Sefer HaḤinukh* expressed the same truth in slightly different words: "The heart is drawn after the deed" (mitzva 16). That is one of the central truths of Torah and halakha. To be a Jew requires an ongoing program of Jewish learning and Jewish doing. We are what we do; our everyday rituals tend the flame.

6:7 תּוֹרַת הַמִּנְחָה *The law of the grain offering* – *Minḥa*, the grain offering brought alongside all other sacrifices, literally means "gift" or "tribute." Sacrifice is not the same act across cultures. One must seek to understand a practice in terms of the distinctive beliefs of the culture in which it takes place. What then could sacrifice possibly mean in a religion in which God is the creator and owner of all?

The simplest answer is this: *We love what we are willing to make sacrifices for*. The verb "to love," *a-h-v*, is related to

11 guilt offering. Any male among Aharon's descendants may eat it as their eternal
share of the Lord's fire offerings throughout their generations; anything that
touches it is sanctified."
12 13 The Lord spoke to Moshe: "This is the offering of Aharon and his sons that SHENI
each shall present to the Lord on the day when he is anointed: one-tenth of an
ephah of fine flour as a continual grain offering, half in the morning and half in
14 the evening. It shall be made on a griddle with oil. You shall bring it well mixed,
and offer it in pieces like a crumbled grain offering, as a pleasing aroma to the
15 Lord. The priest among Aharon's sons who is anointed to succeed him shall
prepare it; it is the Lord's perpetual share, to be sent up in smoke in its entirety.
16 Any grain offering from a priest shall be wholly burned; it shall not be eaten."
17 18 The Lord spoke to Moshe: "Tell Aharon and his sons: This is the law of the
purification offering. The purification offering shall be slaughtered before the
19 Lord at the place where burnt offerings are slaughtered; it is holy of holies. The
priest who offers it as a purification offering shall eat of it. It shall be eaten in a holy

רש״י

פְּסוּלָה. מִנְחַת נְדָבָה הֲרֵי הִיא כְּאָשָׁם, לְפִיכָךְ קְמָצָהּ שֶׁלֹּא לִשְׁמָהּ כְּשֵׁרָה:

יא **כָּל זָכָר.** אֲפִלּוּ בַּעַל מוּם. לָמָּה נֶאֱמַר? אִם לַאֲכִילָה, הֲרֵי כְּבָר אָמוּר: "לֶחֶם אֱלֹהָיו מִקָּדְשֵׁי הַקֳּדָשִׁים" וְגוֹ' (להלן כא, כב), אֶלָּא לְרַבּוֹת בַּעֲלֵי מוּמִין לְמַחֲלֹקֶת: **כֹּל אֲשֶׁר יִגַּע וְגוֹ'.** קָדָשִׁים קַלִּים אוֹ חֻלִּין שֶׁיִּגְּעוּ בָּהּ וְיִבְלְעוּ מִמֶּנָּה: **יִקְדָּשׁ.** לִהְיוֹת כָּמוֹהָ, שֶׁאִם פְּסוּלָה יִפָּסְלוּ, וְאִם כְּשֵׁרָה יֵאָכְלוּ כְּחֹמֶר הַמִּנְחָה:

יג **זֶה קָרְבַּן אַהֲרֹן וּבָנָיו.** אַף הַהֶדְיוֹטוֹת מַקְרִיבִין עֲשִׂירִית הָאֵיפָה בַּיּוֹם שֶׁהֵן מִתְחַנְּכִין לַעֲבוֹדָה, אֲבָל כֹּהֵן גָּדוֹל בְּכָל יוֹם, שֶׁנֶּאֱמַר: "מִנְחָה תָּמִיד... וְהַכֹּהֵן הַמָּשִׁיחַ תַּחְתָּיו מִבָּנָיו... חָק עוֹלָם":

יד **מֻרְבֶּכֶת.** חֲלוּטָה בְּרוֹתְחִין כָּל צָרְכָּהּ: **תֻּפִינֵי.** אֲפוּיָה אֲפִיּוֹת הַרְבֵּה: אַחַר חֲלִיטָתָהּ אוֹפָהּ בַּתַּנּוּר וְחוֹזֵר וּמְטַגְּנָהּ בַּמַּחֲבַת: **מִנְחַת פִּתִּים.** מְלַמֵּד שֶׁטְּעוּנָה פְּתִיתָה:

טו-טז **הַמָּשִׁיחַ תַּחְתָּיו מִבָּנָיו.** הַמָּשִׁיחַ מִבָּנָיו תַּחְתָּיו: **כָּלִיל תָּקְטָר.** אֵין נִקְמֶצֶת לִהְיוֹת שְׁיָרֶיהָ נֶאֱכָלִין, אֶלָּא כֻּלָּהּ כָּלִיל, וְכֵן "כָּל מִנְחַת כֹּהֵן" שֶׁל נְדָבָה, "כָּלִיל תִּהְיֶה": **כָּלִיל.** כֻּלָּהּ שָׁוָה לַגָּבוֹהַּ:

יט **הַמְחַטֵּא אֹתָהּ.** הָעוֹבֵד עֲבוֹדוֹתֶיהָ, שֶׁהִיא נַעֲשֵׂית חַטָּאת עַל יָדוֹ: **הַמְחַטֵּא אֹתָהּ יֹאכְלֶנָּה.** הָרָאוּי לַעֲבוֹדָה, יָצָא טָמֵא בִּשְׁעַת זְרִיקַת דָּמִים, שֶׁאֵינוֹ חוֹלֵק בַּבָּשָׂר. וְאִי אֶפְשָׁר לוֹמַר שֶׁאוֹסֵר שְׁאָר כֹּהֲנִים בַּאֲכִילָתָהּ חוּץ מִן הַזּוֹרֵק דָּמָהּ, שֶׁהֲרֵי נֶאֱמַר לְמַטָּה: "כָּל זָכָר בַּכֹּהֲנִים יֹאכַל אֹתָהּ" (להלן פסוק כב):

dispersion. Ritual turns us from lonely individuals into members of the covenant.

The American anthropologist Roy A. Rappaport argues that ritual is the enactment of meaning. Human beings are meaning-seeking animals, and one way of achieving meaning is through language. But language also allows us to tell lies. Ritual does not speak, it enacts. Ritual inducts us into a world of shared values. We may sometimes betray those values, but by taking part in the ritual we enter the world they define. Without ritual, there is no community, no continuity, and no shared structure of meanings. The priest is inducted then, with a sacrifice that is "wholly burned; it shall not be eaten" (Lev. 6:16). He is leaving the everyday world of functionality and entering one of ritual, meaning, and holiness.

יא כָּל־זָכָר בִּבְנֵי אַהֲרֹן יֹאכְלֶנָּה חָק־עוֹלָם לְדֹרֹתֵיכֶם מֵאִשֵּׁי יהוה כֹּל
אֲשֶׁר־יִגַּע בָּהֶם יִקְדָּשׁ׃
יב יג וַיְדַבֵּר יהוה אֶל־מֹשֶׁה לֵּאמֹר׃ זֶה קָרְבַּן אַהֲרֹן וּבָנָיו אֲשֶׁר־יַקְרִיבוּ ג שני
לַיהוה בְּיוֹם הִמָּשַׁח אֹתוֹ עֲשִׂירִת הָאֵפָה סֹלֶת מִנְחָה תָּמִיד מַחֲצִיתָהּ
יד בַּבֹּקֶר וּמַחֲצִיתָהּ בָּעָרֶב׃ עַל־מַחֲבַת בַּשֶּׁמֶן תֵּעָשֶׂה מֻרְבֶּכֶת תְּבִיאֶנָּה
טו תֻּפִינֵי מִנְחַת פִּתִּים תַּקְרִיב רֵיחַ־נִיחֹחַ לַיהוה׃ וְהַכֹּהֵן הַמָּשִׁיחַ תַּחְתָּיו
טז מִבָּנָיו יַעֲשֶׂה אֹתָהּ חָק־עוֹלָם לַיהוה כָּלִיל תָּקְטָר׃ וְכָל־מִנְחַת כֹּהֵן
כָּלִיל תִּהְיֶה לֹא תֵאָכֵל׃
יז יח וַיְדַבֵּר יהוה אֶל־מֹשֶׁה לֵּאמֹר׃ דַּבֵּר אֶל־אַהֲרֹן וְאֶל־בָּנָיו לֵאמֹר זֹאת
תּוֹרַת הַחַטָּאת בִּמְקוֹם אֲשֶׁר תִּשָּׁחֵט הָעֹלָה תִּשָּׁחֵט הַחַטָּאת לִפְנֵי
יט יהוה קֹדֶשׁ קָדָשִׁים הִוא׃ הַכֹּהֵן הַמְחַטֵּא אֹתָהּ יֹאכְלֶנָּה בְּמָקוֹם קָדֹשׁ

אונקלוס

יא כָּל דְּכוּרָא, בִּבְנֵי אַהֲרֹן יֵיכְלִנַּהּ, קְיָם עֲלַם לְדָרֵיכוֹן, מִקֻּרְבָּנַיָּא דַּיי, כֹּל, דְּיִקְרַב בְּהוֹן יִתְקַדַּשׁ: יב וּמַלֵּיל יי עִם מֹשֶׁה לְמֵימַר: יג דֵּין, קֻרְבָּנָא דְּאַהֲרֹן וְדִבְנוֹהִי דִּיקָרְבוּן קֳדָם יי, בְּיוֹמָא דִּירַבּוֹן יָתֵיהּ, חַד מִן עַסְרָא בִּתְלָת סְאִין סֻלְתָּא, מִנְחֲתָא תְּדִירָא, פַּלְגוּתַהּ בְּצַפְרָא, וּפַלְגוּתַהּ בְּרַמְשָׁא: יד עַל מַסְרֵיתָא, בִּמְשַׁח, תִּתְעֲבֵיד רְבִיכָא תַּיְתֵינַהּ, תּוּפִינֵי מִנְחַת בִּצּוּעִין, תְּקָרֵיב לְאִתְקַבָּלָא בְּרַעֲוָא קֳדָם יי: טו וְכָהֲנָא דְּיִתְרַבֵּא תְּחוֹתוֹהִי, מִבְּנוֹהִי יַעֲבֵיד יָתַהּ, קְיָם עֲלַם, קֳדָם יי גְּמִיר תִּתַּסַּק: טז וְכָל מִנְחֲתָא דְּכָהֲנָא, גְּמִיר תְּהֵי לָא תִתְאֲכִיל: יז וּמַלֵּיל יי עִם מֹשֶׁה לְמֵימַר: יח מַלֵּיל עִם אַהֲרֹן וְעִם בְּנוֹהִי לְמֵימַר, דָּא אוֹרָיְתָא דְּחַטָּתָא, בְּאַתְרָא, דְּתִתְנְכֵיס עֲלָתָא, תִּתְנְכֵיס חַטָּתָא קֳדָם יי, קֹדֶשׁ קֻדְשִׁין הִיא: יט כָּהֲנָא, דִּמְכַפַּר בִּדְמַהּ יֵיכְלִנַּהּ, בַּאֲתַר קַדִּישׁ תִּתְאֲכִיל, בְּדָרַת מַשְׁכַּן זִמְנָא: כ כֹּל,

6:13 בְּיוֹם הִמָּשַׁח אֹתוֹ *On the day when he is anointed* – Moshe took up his mantle with no great ceremony; not so Aharon, who assumes office in a carefully ordered ceremony. This feature of Aharon's initiation befits his distinctive role. Unlike prophets and kings, the priest does not live in the world of everyday. He is the guardian of sacred space and time, the points at which we withdraw from the world to remind ourselves how small we are and how brief are our lives, yet how great they can be when we allow ourselves to be brushed by the wings of eternity. In a word, the priest inhabits the world of *ritual,* where each human act coincides with divine will, and order is safeguarded against the threat of chaos.

Ritual has fared badly in the West. Many see ritual as part of the mindset of myth and magic. But ritual in Leviticus is not magic or primitive technology. We serve God not to bring success, but to be close to Him because He is clarity in a world of confusion, life in a world too often obsessed with death, the enduring presence in the midst of change.

As such, ritual binds us to Jews in other times and places. More than anything else, the shared life of ritual sustained Jews as a nation through two thousand years of exile and

20 place, in the courtyard of the Tent of Meeting. Anything that touches its flesh is
sanctified; if any of its blood splashes on a garment, you shall wash that part in a
21 holy place. An earthen vessel in which it was cooked shall be broken, but if it was
22 cooked in a bronze vessel, that shall be scoured and rinsed with water. Any male
23 among the priests may eat of it; it is holy of holies. But no purification offering
shall be eaten from which blood is brought inside the Tent of Meeting to make
atonement within the Sanctuary; that shall be burned with fire.
7 1 2 And this is the law of the guilt offering; it is holy of holies. The guilt offering shall
be slaughtered at the place where burnt offerings are slaughtered, and its blood
3 dashed against each side of the altar. All its fat shall be offered: the broad tail, the
4 fat covering the entrails, the two kidneys and the fat around them at the loins, and
5 the diaphragm of the liver, which shall be removed with the kidneys. The priest
shall turn these into smoke on the altar as a fire offering for the LORD; it is a guilt
6 offering. Any male priest may eat of it and it shall be eaten in a holy place; it is
7 holy of holies. The guilt offering follows the same law as the purification offering:
8 it belongs to the priest who makes atonement with it. The priest who offers any
person's burnt offering shall keep the skin of the burnt offering that he has offered.
9 Any grain offering baked in an oven or prepared in a pan or griddle also belongs
10 to the priest who offers it, while every other grain offering, whether mixed with
oil or dry, shall belong equally to all of Aharon's sons.

רש״י

כ **כֹּל אֲשֶׁר יִגַּע בִּבְשָׂרָהּ.** כָּל דָּבָר אֹכֶל אֲשֶׁר יִגַּע וְיִבְלַע מִמֶּנָּה: **יִקְדָּשׁ.** לִהְיוֹת כָּמוֹהָ, אִם פְּסוּלָה תִּפָּסֵל, וְאִם הִיא כְּשֵׁרָה תֵּאָכֵל כַּחֹמֶר שֶׁבָּהּ: **וַאֲשֶׁר יִזֶּה מִדָּמָהּ עַל הַבֶּגֶד.** וְאִם הֻזָּה מִדָּמָהּ עַל הַבֶּגֶד, אוֹתוֹ הַבֶּגֶד מְקוֹם הַדָּם ״אֲשֶׁר יִזֶּה עָלֶיהָ תְּכַבֵּס״ בְּתוֹךְ הָעֲזָרָה: **אֲשֶׁר יִזֶּה.** יְהֵא נִזֶּה, כְּמוֹ: ״וְלֹא יִטֶּה לָאָרֶץ מִנְלָם״ (איוב טו, כט), יְהֵא נָטוּי:

כא **יִשָּׁבֵר.** לְפִי שֶׁהַבְּלִיעָה שֶׁנִּבְלַעַת בּוֹ נַעֲשֵׂית נוֹתָר, וְהוּא הַדִּין לְכָל הַקֳּדָשִׁים: **וּמֹרַק.** לְשׁוֹן ״תַּמְרוּקֵי הַנָּשִׁים״ (אסתר ב, יב), אישקור״מנט בְּלַעַ״ז: **וּמֹרַק וְשֻׁטַּף.** לִפְלֹט אֶת בְּלִיעָתוֹ. אֲבָל כְּלִי חֶרֶס לִמֶּדְךָ הַכָּתוּב כָּאן שֶׁאֵינוֹ יוֹצֵא מִידֵי דָּפְיוֹ לְעוֹלָם:

כב **כָּל זָכָר בַּכֹּהֲנִים יֹאכַל אֹתָהּ.** הָא לָמַדְתָּ שֶׁ״הַמְחַטֵּא אֹתָהּ״ הָאָמוּר לְמַעְלָה (פסוק יט) לֹא לְהוֹצִיא שְׁאָר הַכֹּהֲנִים, אֶלָּא לְהוֹצִיא אֶת שֶׁאֵינוֹ רָאוּי לְחִטּוּי:

כג **וְכָל חַטָּאת וְגוֹ׳.** שֶׁאִם הִכְנִיס מִדַּם חַטָּאת הַחִיצוֹנָה לִפְנִים פְּסוּלָה:

ז א **קֹדֶשׁ קָדָשִׁים הוּא.** הוּא קָרֵב וְאֵין תְּמוּרָתוֹ קְרֵבָה:

ג **וְאֵת כָּל חֶלְבּוֹ וְגוֹ׳.** עַד כָּאן לֹא נִתְפָּרְשׁוּ אֵמוּרִין בָּאָשָׁם, לְכָךְ הֻצְרַךְ לְפָרְשָׁם כָּאן, אֲבָל חַטָּאת כְּבָר נִתְפָּרֵשׁ בָּהּ בְּפָרָשַׁת וַיִּקְרָא (לעיל פרק ד): **אֵת הָאַלְיָה.** לְפִי שֶׁאָשָׁם אֵינוֹ בָּא אֶלָּא אַיִל אוֹ כֶּבֶשׂ, וְאַיִל וְכֶבֶשׂ נִתְרַבּוּ בְּאַלְיָה (לעיל ג, ט):

ה **אָשָׁם הוּא.** עַד שֶׁיִּנָּתֵק שְׁמוֹ מִמֶּנּוּ, לִמֵּד עַל אָשָׁם שֶׁמֵּתוּ בְּעָלָיו אוֹ שֶׁנִּתְכַּפְּרוּ בְעָלָיו, אַף עַל פִּי שֶׁעוֹמֵד לִהְיוֹת דָּמָיו עוֹלָה לְקַיִץ הַמִּזְבֵּחַ, אִם שְׁחָטוֹ סְתָם אֵינוֹ כָּשֵׁר לְעוֹלָה קֹדֶם שֶׁנִּתַּק לִרְעִיָּה. וְאֵינוֹ בָּא לְלַמֵּד עַל הָאָשָׁם שֶׁיְּהֵא פָּסוּל שֶׁלֹּא לִשְׁמוֹ, כְּמוֹ שֶׁדָּרְשׁוּ ״הוּא״ הַכָּתוּב בַּחַטָּאת (לעיל ד, כד), לְפִי שֶׁאָשָׁם לֹא נֶאֱמַר בּוֹ ״אָשָׁם הוּא״ אֶלָּא לְאַחַר הַקְטָרַת אֵמוּרִין, וְהוּא עַצְמוֹ שֶׁלֹּא הֻקְטְרוּ אֵמוּרָיו כָּשֵׁר:

ו **קֹדֶשׁ קָדָשִׁים הוּא.** בְּתוֹרַת כֹּהֲנִים הוּא נִדְרָשׁ:

ז **תּוֹרָה אַחַת לָהֶם.** בְּדָבָר זֶה: **הַכֹּהֵן אֲשֶׁר יְכַפֶּר בּוֹ.** הָרָאוּי לְכַפָּרָה חוֹלֵק בּוֹ, פְּרָט לִטְבוּל יוֹם וּמְחֻסַּר כִּפּוּרִים וְאוֹנֵן:

ח **עוֹר הָעֹלָה אֲשֶׁר הִקְרִיב לַכֹּהֵן לוֹ יִהְיֶה.** פְּרָט לִטְבוּל יוֹם וּמְחֻסַּר כִּפּוּרִים וְאוֹנֵן, שֶׁאֵינָן חוֹלְקִים בָּעוֹרוֹת:

ט **לַכֹּהֵן הַמַּקְרִיב אֹתָהּ וְגוֹ׳.** יָכוֹל לוֹ לְבַדּוֹ? תַּלְמוּד לוֹמַר: ״לְכָל בְּנֵי אַהֲרֹן תִּהְיֶה״ (להלן פסוק י). יָכוֹל לְכֻלָּן? תַּלְמוּד לוֹמַר: ״לַכֹּהֵן הַמַּקְרִיב״, הָא כֵּיצַד? לְבֵית אָב שֶׁל יוֹם שֶׁמַּקְרִיבִין אוֹתָהּ:

כ תֵּאָכֵ֔ל בַּחֲצַ֖ר אֹ֥הֶל מוֹעֵֽד׃ כֹּ֛ל אֲשֶׁר־יִגַּ֥ע בִּבְשָׂרָ֖הּ יִקְדָּ֑שׁ וַאֲשֶׁ֨ר יִזֶּ֤ה
כא מִדָּמָהּ֙ עַל־הַבֶּ֔גֶד אֲשֶׁר֙ יִזֶּ֣ה עָלֶ֔יהָ תְּכַבֵּ֖ס בְּמָק֥וֹם קָדֹֽשׁ׃ וּכְלִי־חֶ֛רֶשׂ אֲשֶׁ֥ר
כב תְּבֻשַּׁל־בּ֖וֹ יִשָּׁבֵ֑ר וְאִם־בִּכְלִ֤י נְחֹ֨שֶׁת֙ בֻּשָּׁ֔לָה וּמֹרַ֥ק וְשֻׁטַּ֖ף בַּמָּֽיִם׃ כָּל־זָכָ֥ר
כג בַּכֹּהֲנִ֖ים יֹאכַ֣ל אֹתָ֑הּ קֹ֥דֶשׁ קָֽדָשִׁ֖ים הִֽוא׃ וְכָל־חַ֠טָּאת אֲשֶׁ֨ר יוּבָ֤א מִדָּמָהּ֙
אֶל־אֹ֥הֶל מוֹעֵ֛ד לְכַפֵּ֥ר בַּקֹּ֖דֶשׁ לֹ֣א תֵאָכֵ֑ל בָּאֵ֖שׁ תִּשָּׂרֵֽף׃
ז א ב וְזֹ֥את תּוֹרַ֖ת הָאָשָׁ֑ם קֹ֥דֶשׁ קָֽדָשִׁ֖ים הֽוּא׃ בִּמְק֗וֹם אֲשֶׁ֤ר יִשְׁחֲטוּ֙ אֶת־
ג הָֽעֹלָ֔ה יִשְׁחֲט֖וּ אֶת־הָאָשָׁ֑ם וְאֶת־דָּמ֛וֹ יִזְרֹ֥ק עַל־הַמִּזְבֵּ֖חַ סָבִֽיב׃ וְאֶת־כָּל־
ד חֶלְבּ֖וֹ יַקְרִ֣יב מִמֶּ֑נּוּ אֵ֚ת הָֽאַלְיָ֔ה וְאֶת־הַחֵ֖לֶב הַֽמְכַסֶּ֥ה אֶת־הַקֶּֽרֶב׃ וְאֵת֙
שְׁתֵּ֣י הַכְּלָיֹ֔ת וְאֶת־הַחֵ֙לֶב֙ אֲשֶׁ֣ר עֲלֵיהֶ֔ן אֲשֶׁ֖ר עַל־הַכְּסָלִ֑ים וְאֶת־הַיֹּתֶ֙רֶת֙
ה עַל־הַכָּבֵ֔ד עַל־הַכְּלָיֹ֖ת יְסִירֶֽנָּה׃ וְהִקְטִ֨יר אֹתָ֤ם הַכֹּהֵן֙ הַמִּזְבֵּ֔חָה אִשֶּׁ֖ה
ו לַֽיהוָ֑ה אָשָׁ֖ם הֽוּא׃ כָּל־זָכָ֥ר בַּכֹּהֲנִ֖ים יֹאכְלֶ֑נּוּ בְּמָק֤וֹם קָדוֹשׁ֙ יֵאָכֵ֔ל קֹ֥דֶשׁ
ז קָֽדָשִׁ֖ים הֽוּא׃ כַּֽחַטָּאת֙ כָּֽאָשָׁ֔ם תּוֹרָ֥ה אַחַ֖ת לָהֶ֑ם הַכֹּהֵ֛ן אֲשֶׁ֥ר יְכַפֶּר־בּ֖וֹ
ח ל֥וֹ יִהְיֶֽה׃ וְהַ֨כֹּהֵ֔ן הַמַּקְרִ֖יב אֶת־עֹ֣לַת אִ֑ישׁ ע֤וֹר הָֽעֹלָה֙ אֲשֶׁ֣ר הִקְרִ֔יב
ט לַכֹּהֵ֖ן ל֥וֹ יִהְיֶֽה׃ וְכָל־מִנְחָ֗ה אֲשֶׁ֤ר תֵּאָפֶה֙ בַּתַּנּ֔וּר וְכָל־נַעֲשָׂ֥ה בַמַּרְחֶ֖שֶׁת
י וְעַֽל־מַחֲבַ֑ת לַכֹּהֵ֛ן הַמַּקְרִ֥יב אֹתָ֖הּ ל֥וֹ תִהְיֶֽה׃ וְכָל־מִנְחָ֥ה בְלוּלָֽה־בַשֶּׁ֖מֶן
וַחֲרֵבָ֑ה לְכָל־בְּנֵ֧י אַהֲרֹ֛ן תִּהְיֶ֖ה אִ֥ישׁ כְּאָחִֽיו׃

אונקלוס

דְיִקְרַב בְּבִסְרַהּ יִתְקַדַּשׁ, וּדְיִדֵּי מִדְּמַהּ עַל לְבוּשָׁא, דְּיִדֵּי עֲלַהּ, תְּחַוַּר בַּאֲתַר קַדִּישׁ: כא וּמָן דַּחֲסַף, דְּתִתְבַּשַּׁל בֵּיהּ יִתְּבַר, וְאִם בְּמָנָא דִנְחָשָׁא תִּתְבַּשַּׁל, וְיִתְמְרֵיק וְיִשְׁתְּטֵיף בְּמַיָּא: כב כָּל דְּכוּרָא בְּכָהֲנַיָּא יֵיכוּל יָתַהּ, קֹדֶשׁ קֻדְשִׁין הִיא: כג וְכָל חַטָּתָא, דְּיִתָּעַל מִדְּמַהּ, לְמַשְׁכַּן זִמְנָא, לְכַפָּרָא בְּקֻדְשָׁא לָא תִתְאֲכִיל, בְּנוּרָא תִּתּוֹקַד: ז א וְדָא אוֹרָיְתָא דַּאֲשָׁמָא, קֹדֶשׁ קֻדְשִׁין הוּא: ב בְּאַתְרָא, דְּיִכְּסוּן יָת עֲלָתָא, יִכְּסוּן יָת אֲשָׁמָא, וְיָת דְּמֵיהּ, יִזְרוֹק עַל מַדְבְּחָא סְחוֹר סְחוֹר: ג וְיָת כָּל תַּרְבֵּיהּ יְקָרֵיב מִנֵּיהּ, יָת אַלְיְתָא, וְיָת תַּרְבָּא דְּחָפֵי יָת גַּוָּא: ד וְיָת תַּרְתֵּין כּוֹלְיָן, וְיָת תַּרְבָּא דַּעֲלֵיהוֹן, דְּעַל גִּסְסַיָּא, וְיָת חַצְרָא דְּעַל כַּבְדָּא, עַל כּוֹלְיָתָא יַעְדֵּינַהּ: ה וְיַסֵּיק יָתְהוֹן כָּהֲנָא לְמַדְבְּחָא, קֻרְבָּנָא קֳדָם יְיָ, אֲשָׁמָא הוּא: ו כָּל דְּכוּרָא בְּכָהֲנַיָּא יֵיכְלִנֵּיהּ, בַּאֲתַר קַדִּישׁ יִתְאֲכִיל, קֹדֶשׁ קֻדְשִׁין הוּא: ז כְּחַטָּתָא כֵּן אֲשָׁמָא, אוֹרָיְתָא חֲדָא לְהוֹן, כָּהֲנָא, דִּיכַפַּר בֵּיהּ דִּילֵיהּ יְהֵי: ח וְכָהֲנָא, דִּמְקָרֵיב יָת עֲלַת גְּבַר, מְשַׁךְ עֲלָתָא דִּיקָרֵיב, לְכָהֲנָא דִּילֵיהּ יְהֵי: ט וְכָל מִנְחָתָא, דְּתִתְאֲפֵי בְּתַנּוּרָא, וְכָל דְּתִתְעֲבֵיד בְּרָדְתָא וְעַל מַסְרֵיתָא, לְכָהֲנָא, דִּמְקָרֵיב יָתַהּ דִּילֵיהּ תְּהֵי: י וְכָל מִנְחָתָא דְּפִילָא בִמְשַׁח וּדְלָא פִילָא, לְכָל בְּנֵי אַהֲרֹן, תְּהֵי גְּבַר כַּאֲחוּהִי:

רש״י

י בְּלוּלָה בַשֶּׁמֶן. זוֹ מִנְחַת נְדָבָה: וַחֲרֵבָה. זוֹ מִנְחַת חוֹטֵא וּמִנְחַת קְנָאוֹת שֶׁאֵין בָּהֶן שֶׁמֶן:

11 12 This is the law of the peace sacrifice that one may offer to the Lord: If it is SHELISHI
offered for thanksgiving, one offers unleavened loaves mixed with oil with the
thanksgiving sacrifice, and unleavened wafers spread with oil, and loaves of
13 fine flour mixed with oil. This offering, together with loaves of leavened bread,
14 he shall present with the peace sacrifice of thanksgiving. Of these he shall offer
one of each kind as a gift raised up to the Lord. This shall belong to the priest
15 who dashed the blood of the peace offering. The flesh of the peace sacrifice
of thanksgiving shall be eaten on the day it is offered; you may not leave any
16 of it to the morning. If the sacrifice is to fulfill a vow, however, or is a freewill
offering, it shall be eaten on the day when one offers the sacrifice, while what
17 is left over may be eaten the next day. Whatever of the flesh of the sacrifice is

רש״י

יב **אִם עַל תּוֹדָה יַקְרִיבֶנּוּ.** אִם עַל דְּבַר הוֹדָאָה עַל נֵס שֶׁנַּעֲשָׂה לוֹ, כְּגוֹן יוֹרְדֵי הַיָּם וְהוֹלְכֵי מִדְבָּרוֹת וַחֲבוּשֵׁי בֵּית הָאֲסוּרִים וְחוֹלֶה שֶׁנִּתְרַפֵּא שֶׁהֵן צְרִיכִין לְהוֹדוֹת, שֶׁכָּתוּב בָּהֶן: "יוֹדוּ לַה' חַסְדּוֹ וְנִפְלְאוֹתָיו לִבְנֵי אָדָם" (תהלים קז, ח ועוד), "וְיִזְבְּחוּ זִבְחֵי תוֹדָה" (שם פסוק כב). אִם עַל אַחַת מֵאֵלֶּה נָדַר שְׁלָמִים הַלָּלוּ, שַׁלְמֵי תוֹדָה הֵן, וּטְעוּנוֹת לֶחֶם הָאָמוּר בָּעִנְיָן, וְאֵינָן נֶאֱכָלִין אֶלָּא לְיוֹם וָלַיְלָה כְּמוֹ שֶׁמְּפֹרָשׁ כָּאן (להלן פסוק טו): **וְהִקְרִיב עַל זֶבַח הַתּוֹדָה.** אַרְבָּעָה מִינֵי לֶחֶם: חַלּוֹת וּרְקִיקִין וּרְבוּכָה – שְׁלֹשָׁה מִינֵי מַצָּה, וּכְתִיב: "עַל חַלֹּת לֶחֶם חָמֵץ" וְגוֹ' (להלן פסוק יג). וְכָל מִין וָמִין עֶשֶׂר חַלּוֹת, כָּךְ מְפֹרָשׁ בִּמְנָחוֹת (דף עז ע״א), וְשִׁעוּרָן חָמֵשׁ סְאִין יְרוּשַׁלְמִיּוֹת שֶׁהֵן שֵׁשׁ מִדְבָּרִיּוֹת, עֶשְׂרִים עִשָּׂרוֹן: **מֻרְבֶּכֶת.** לֶחֶם חָלוּט בְּרוֹתְחִין כָּל צָרְכּוֹ:

יג **יַקְרִיב קָרְבָּנוֹ עַל זֶבַח.** מַגִּיד שֶׁאֵין הַלֶּחֶם קָדוֹשׁ קְדֻשַּׁת הַגּוּף לִפָּסֵל בְּיוֹצֵא וּטְבוּל יוֹם וּמִלָּצֵאת לְחֻלִּין בְּפִדְיוֹן, עַד שֶׁיִּשָּׁחֵט הַזֶּבַח:

יד **אֶחָד מִכָּל קָרְבָּן.** לֶחֶם אֶחָד מִכָּל מִין וָמִין יִטֹּל תְּרוּמָה לַכֹּהֵן הָעוֹבֵד עֲבוֹדָתָהּ, וְהַשְּׁאָר נֶאֱכָל לַבְּעָלִים. וּבְשָׂרָהּ לַבְּעָלִים חוּץ מֵחָזֶה וָשׁוֹק שֶׁבָּהּ, כְּמוֹ שֶׁמְּפֹרָשׁ לְמַטָּה תְּנוּפַת חָזֶה וָשׁוֹק בִּשְׁלָמִים (להלן פסוקים כט-לד), וְהַתּוֹדָה קְרוּיָה שְׁלָמִים:

טו **וּבְשַׂר זֶבַח תּוֹדַת שְׁלָמָיו.** יֵשׁ כָּאן רִבּוּיִין הַרְבֵּה, לְרַבּוֹת חַטָּאת וְאָשָׁם וְאֵיל נָזִיר וַחֲגִיגַת אַרְבָּעָה עָשָׂר שֶׁיִּהְיוּ נֶאֱכָלִין לְיוֹם וָלַיְלָה: **בְּיוֹם קָרְבָּנוֹ יֵאָכֵל.** וְכִזְמַן בְּשָׂרָהּ זְמַן לַחְמָהּ: **לֹא יַנִּיחַ מִמֶּנּוּ עַד בֹּקֶר.** אוֹכֵל הוּא כָּל הַלַּיְלָה. אִם כֵּן, לָמָּה אָמְרוּ עַד חֲצוֹת? כְּדֵי לְהַרְחִיק אָדָם מִן הָעֲבֵרָה:

טז **וְאִם נֶדֶר אוֹ נְדָבָה.** שֶׁלֹּא הֱבִיאָהּ עַל הוֹדָאָה שֶׁל נֵס, אֵינָהּ טְעוּנָה לֶחֶם, וְנֶאֱכֶלֶת לִשְׁנֵי יָמִים, כְּמוֹ שֶׁמְּפֹרָשׁ בָּעִנְיָן: **וּמִמָּחֳרָת וְהַנּוֹתָר מִמֶּנּוּ.** בָּרִאשׁוֹן, יֵאָכֵל. וָי״ו זוֹ יְתֵרָה הִיא, וְיֵשׁ כָּמוֹהָ הַרְבֵּה בַּמִּקְרָא, כְּגוֹן: "וְאֵלֶּה בְנֵי צִבְעוֹן וְאַיָּה וַעֲנָה" (בראשית לו, כד), "תֵּת וְקֹדֶשׁ וְצָבָא מִרְמָס" (דניאל ח, יג):

of thanks. What this does is to *foreground the background*, focusing our attention on the things we normally take for granted. It is a cognitive shift designed to make us attentive to the myriad blessings with which we are surrounded.

This is neither easy nor natural. For sound biological reasons, we are hyperalert to potential threats and dangers. It takes focused attention to become aware, day to day, of how much we have to be grateful for. That, in different ways, is the logic of prayer, of making blessings, of the Sabbath, and many other elements of Jewish life. And learning to offer up thanks is a way to bring *shalom* – well-being, peace – into the world.

likely. It helps people avoid overreacting to negative experiences by seeking revenge. It enhances self-respect, making it less likely that you will envy others for their achievements or success. Saying "thank you" enhances friendships and elicits better performance from employees. Grateful people tend to have better relationships.

Jewish prayer is an ongoing seminar in gratitude. Our morning prayers open with the *Birkot HaShaḥar*, the morning blessings, in which we give thanks to God for giving us back our consciousness after sleep, for the human body and our restored soul, the earth we stand on and the freedom with which we rise, and so on through a repeated refrain

יא יב וְזֹאת תּוֹרַת זֶבַח הַשְּׁלָמִים אֲשֶׁר יַקְרִיב לַיהוָה: אִם עַל־תּוֹדָה יַקְרִיבֶנּוּ שלישי
וְהִקְרִיב ׀ עַל־זֶבַח הַתּוֹדָה חַלּוֹת מַצּוֹת בְּלוּלֹת בַּשֶּׁמֶן וּרְקִיקֵי מַצּוֹת
יג מְשֻׁחִים בַּשָּׁמֶן וְסֹלֶת מֻרְבֶּכֶת חַלֹּת בְּלוּלֹת בַּשָּׁמֶן: עַל־חַלֹּת לֶחֶם
יד חָמֵץ יַקְרִיב קָרְבָּנוֹ עַל־זֶבַח תּוֹדַת שְׁלָמָיו: וְהִקְרִיב מִמֶּנּוּ אֶחָד מִכָּל־
טו קָרְבָּן תְּרוּמָה לַיהוָה לַכֹּהֵן הַזֹּרֵק אֶת־דַּם הַשְּׁלָמִים לוֹ יִהְיֶה: וּבְשַׂר
טז זֶבַח תּוֹדַת שְׁלָמָיו בְּיוֹם קָרְבָּנוֹ יֵאָכֵל לֹא־יַנִּיחַ מִמֶּנּוּ עַד־בֹּקֶר: וְאִם־
נֶדֶר ׀ אוֹ נְדָבָה זֶבַח קָרְבָּנוֹ בְּיוֹם הַקְרִיבוֹ אֶת־זִבְחוֹ יֵאָכֵל וּמִמָּחֳרָת
יז וְהַנּוֹתָר מִמֶּנּוּ יֵאָכֵל: וְהַנּוֹתָר מִבְּשַׂר הַזָּבַח בַּיּוֹם הַשְּׁלִישִׁי בָּאֵשׁ יִשָּׂרֵף:

אונקלוס

יא וְדָא אוֹרָיְתָא דְּנִכְסַת קֻדְשַׁיָּא, דִּיקָרֵיב קֳדָם יְיָ: יב אִם עַל
תּוֹדְתָא יְקָרְבִנֵּיהּ, וִיקָרֵיב עַל נִכְסַת תּוֹדְתָא, גְּרִיצָן פַּטִּירָן דְּפִילָן
בִּמְשַׁח, וְאֶסְפּוֹגִין פַּטִּירִין דִּמְשִׁיחִין בִּמְשַׁח, וְסוֹלֶת רְבִיכָא, גְּרִיצָן
דְּפִילָן בִּמְשַׁח: יג עַל גְּרִיצָן דִּלְחֵים חֲמִיעַ, יְקָרֵיב קֻרְבָּנֵיהּ, עַל נִכְסַת
תּוֹדַת קֻדְשׁוֹהִי: יד וִיקָרֵיב מִנֵּיהּ חַד מִכָּל קֻרְבָּנָא, אַפְרָשׁוּתָא קֳדָם
יְיָ, לְכָהֲנָא, דְּיִזְרוֹק, יָת דַּם נִכְסַת קֻדְשַׁיָּא דִּילֵיהּ יְהֵי: טו וּבְסַר,
נִכְסַת תּוֹדַת קֻדְשׁוֹהִי, בְּיוֹם קֻרְבָּנֵיהּ יִתְאֲכֵיל, לָא יַצְנַע מִנֵּיהּ עַד
צַפְרָא: טז וְאִם נִדְרָא אוֹ נְדַבְתָּא, נִכְסַת קֻרְבָּנֵיהּ, בְּיוֹמָא, דִּיקָרֵיב
יָת נִכְסְתֵיהּ יִתְאֲכֵיל, וּבְיוֹמָא דְבָתְרוֹהִי, וּדְיִשְׁתְּאַר מִנֵּיהּ יִתְאֲכֵיל:
יז וּדְיִשְׁתְּאַר מִבְּסַר נִכְסְתָא, בְּיוֹמָא תְּלִיתָאָה, בְּנוּרָא יִתּוֹקַד:

THANKSGIVING

The first words we are taught to say each morning, immediately on waking, are *Modeh/Moda ani*, "I give thanks." We thank before we think. The source of the command to give thanks is the *korban toda*, the thanksgiving offering.

Though we have been without sacrifices for almost two thousand years, a trace of this command survives in the form of the *HaGomel* blessing, "Who bestows good things on the unworthy," said in the synagogue, at the time of the reading of the Torah, by one who has survived a hazardous situation. This is defined by the Sages (on the basis of Psalm 107) as one who has survived a sea crossing, traveled across a desert, recovered from serious illness, or been released from captivity (Berakhot 54b).

Insurance companies sometimes describe natural catastrophes as "acts of God." Human emotion tends to do the opposite. God is in the good news, the miraculous deliverance, the escape from catastrophe. That instinct – to offer thanks to a force, a presence, over and above natural circumstances and human intervention – is itself a signal of transcendence. Though not a proof of the existence of God, it is nonetheless an intimation of something deeply spiritual in the human heart. It tells us that we are not random concatenations of selfish genes, blindly reproducing themselves. Our bodies may be products of nature ("You are dust, and you will return to dust" [Gen. 3:19]), but there is something within us that reaches out to Someone beyond us: the soul of the universe, the divine "You" to whom we offer our thanks. That is what was once expressed in the thanksgiving offering, and still is, in the *HaGomel* prayer and many others.

7:13 זֶבַח תּוֹדַת שְׁלָמָיו *Peace sacrifice of thanksgiving* – The thanksgiving offering is one of several kinds of "peace sacrifices," so named, according to one interpretation in the Sifra, because "one who brings one brings peace (*shalom*) to the world." We now know of the multiple effects of developing gratitude. It improves physical health and immunity against disease. Thankfulness reduces toxic emotions such as resentment, frustration, and regret, and makes depression less

18 left over on the third day shall be burned with fire. If any of the flesh of the
peace sacrifice is eaten on the third day, it shall not be accepted, nor shall it be
credited to the one who offered it. It is offensive, and anyone who eats of it is
19 liable to punishment. Flesh that touches any impure thing shall not be eaten; it
shall be burned with fire. As for other flesh, any ritually pure person may eat it,
20 but one who eats the flesh of a peace sacrifice to the LORD in a state of impurity
21 shall be severed from his people. When anyone touches any impure thing –
human impurity, or an impure animal, or any impure, detested creature – and
then eats flesh from the LORD's peace sacrifice, that person shall be severed
22 23 from his people." The LORD spoke to Moshe: "Tell the Israelites: Do not eat
24 the fat of an ox, sheep, or goat. The fat of one of these that died naturally or was
25 killed by another animal may be put to other use, but you may not eat it. For
anyone who eats the fat of an animal of which a fire offering could be offered to
26 the LORD – he is severed from his people. Do not eat any blood, whether that

רש״י

יח) **ואם האכל יאכל וגו׳.** במחשב בשחיטה לאכלו בשלישי הכתוב מדבר. יכול אם אכל ממנו בשלישי יפסל למפרע? תלמוד לומר: ״המקריב אתו לא יחשב״, בשעת הקרבה הוא נפסל, ואינו נפסל בשלישי. וכן פרושו: בשעת הקרבתו לא תעלה זאת במחשבה, ואם חשב – ״פגול יהיה״: **והנפש האכלת ממנו.** אפלו בתוך הזמן, ״עונה תשא״:

יט) **והבשר.** של קדש שלמים ״אשר יגע בכל טמא לא יאכל״: **והבשר.** לרבות אבר שיצא מקצתו, שהפנימי מתר: **כל טהור יאכל בשר.** מה תלמוד לומר? לפי שנאמר: ״ודם זבחיך ישפך... והבשר תאכל״ (דברים יב, כז), יכול לא יאכלו שלמים אלא הבעלים? לכך נאמר: ״כל טהור יאכל בשר״:

כ) **וטמאתו עליו.** בטמאת הגוף הכתוב מדבר, אבל טהור שאכל את הטמא אינו ענוש כרת אלא באזהרה: ״והבשר אשר יגע בכל טמא״ וגו׳ (לעיל פסוק יט). ואזהרת טמא שאכל את הטהור אינה מפרשת בתורה, אלא חכמים למדוה בגזרה שוה: שלש כריתות אמורות באוכלי קדשים בטמאת הגוף, ודרשום רבותינו בשבועות (דף ז ע״א) אחת לכלל, ואחת לפרט, ואחת ללמד על קרבן עולה ויורד שלא נאמר אלא על טמאת מקדש וקדשיו:

כד) **יעשה לכל מלאכה.** בא ולמד על החלב שאינו מטמא טמאת נבלות: **ואכל לא תאכלהו.** אמרה תורה: יבוא אסור נבלה וטרפה ויחול על אסור חלב, שאם אכלו יתחיב אף על לאו של נבלה, ולא תאמר אין אסור חל על אסור:

of rules: *regulatory* and *constitutive*. Regulatory rules, as their name implies, regulate something that exists independently of the rules. There were employers and employees before there was employment law. A practice exists and then come the laws to ensure fairness, justice, and so on. In Judaism, *mishpatim*, social legislation, are of this kind.

Constitutive laws *create* a practice. The laws of chess create the game called chess. Without the laws, there is no game. Rabban Yoḥanan was saying that the laws of purity are like this. They are not like medicine, because impurity is not like a disease. Before there were laws of purity, death did not defile and the waters did not purify. The laws created a new reality, but that does not mean that they are irrational or incomprehensible. Chapters 11–16 will give us a broad mapping of the Torah's rules of purity and impurity. Here we see them introduced in their natural context – the Tabernacle with its sacrifices.

THE PROHIBITION AGAINST EATING BLOOD

The ban on eating blood is not just one prohibition among others; it is fundamental to the Torah. It occupies a central place in the covenant God makes with Noaḥ – and through

יח וְאִם הֵאָכֹל יֵאָכֵל מִבְּשַׂר־זֶבַח שְׁלָמָיו בַּיּוֹם הַשְּׁלִישִׁי לֹא יֵרָצֶה
הַמַּקְרִיב אֹתוֹ לֹא יֵחָשֵׁב לוֹ פִּגּוּל יִהְיֶה וְהַנֶּפֶשׁ הָאֹכֶלֶת מִמֶּנּוּ עֲוֺנָהּ
יט תִּשָּׂא: וְהַבָּשָׂר אֲשֶׁר־יִגַּע בְּכָל־טָמֵא לֹא יֵאָכֵל בָּאֵשׁ יִשָּׂרֵף וְהַבָּשָׂר
כ כָּל־טָהוֹר יֹאכַל בָּשָׂר: וְהַנֶּפֶשׁ אֲשֶׁר־תֹּאכַל בָּשָׂר מִזֶּבַח הַשְּׁלָמִים
כא אֲשֶׁר לַיהוה וְטֻמְאָתוֹ עָלָיו וְנִכְרְתָה הַנֶּפֶשׁ הַהִוא מֵעַמֶּיהָ: וְנֶפֶשׁ כִּי־
תִגַּע בְּכָל־טָמֵא בְּטֻמְאַת אָדָם אוֹ | בִּבְהֵמָה טְמֵאָה אוֹ בְּכָל־שֶׁקֶץ
טָמֵא וְאָכַל מִבְּשַׂר־זֶבַח הַשְּׁלָמִים אֲשֶׁר לַיהוה וְנִכְרְתָה הַנֶּפֶשׁ הַהִוא
כב כג מֵעַמֶּיהָ: וַיְדַבֵּר יהוה אֶל־מֹשֶׁה לֵּאמֹר: דַּבֵּר אֶל־בְּנֵי יִשְׂרָאֵל לֵאמֹר
כד כָּל־חֵלֶב שׁוֹר וְכֶשֶׂב וָעֵז לֹא תֹאכֵלוּ: וְחֵלֶב נְבֵלָה וְחֵלֶב טְרֵפָה יֵעָשֶׂה
כה לְכָל־מְלָאכָה וְאָכֹל לֹא תֹאכְלֻהוּ: כִּי כָּל־אֹכֵל חֵלֶב מִן־הַבְּהֵמָה אֲשֶׁר
כו יַקְרִיב מִמֶּנָּה אִשֶּׁה לַיהוה וְנִכְרְתָה הַנֶּפֶשׁ הָאֹכֶלֶת מֵעַמֶּיהָ: וְכָל־דָּם

אונקלוס

יח ואם אתאכלא יתאכיל, מבסר נכסת קודשוהי, ביומא תליתאה לא יהי לרעוא, דמקריב יתיה, לא יתחשיב, ליה מרחק יהי, ואנש, דייכול מניה חוביה יקביל: יט ובסר קודשא, דיקרב בכל מסאב לא יתאכיל, בנורא יתוקד, ובסר קודשא, כל דידכי לקודשא ייכול בסר קודשא: כ ואנש דייכול בסרא, מנכסת קודשיא דקדם יי, וסאובתיה עלוהי, וישתיצי, אנשא ההוא מעמיה: כא ואנש ארי יקרב בכל מסאב, בסואבת אנשא או בבעירא מסאבא, או בכל שקיץ מסאב, וייכול, מבסר נכסת קודשיא דקדם יי, וישתיצי, אנשא ההוא מעמיה: כב ומליל יי עם משה למימר: כג מליל, עם בני ישראל למימר, כל תרב, תור ואמר, ועז לא תיכלון: כד ותרב נבילא ותרב תבירא, יתעביד לכל עבידא, ומיכל לא תיכלוניה: כה ארי כל דייכול תרבא, מן בעירא, דיקריב מנה, קורבנא קדם יי, וישתיצי, אנשא דייכול מעמיה: כו וכל דמא

7:19 וְהַבָּשָׂר אֲשֶׁר־יִגַּע בְּכָל־טָמֵא *Flesh that touches any impure thing* – There is a famous midrash in which a Roman challenges Rabban Yoḥanan b. Zakkai on the ritual of the red heifer. The Roman finds the law incomprehensible, irrational, and superstitious. Yoḥanan b. Zakkai asks the Roman whether he believes in exorcism. The Roman says he does. Well then, says Yoḥanan, that is what the rite of the red heifer is, a kind of exorcism. It expels unclean spirits. The Roman, satisfied, leaves.

There then follows a remarkable scene. The students turn to Rabban Yoḥanan and say, "You gave him an answer to satisfy a Roman, but what will you answer us?" Yoḥanan then says, "Know that it is not death that defiles or the ritual that purifies. Rather, God is saying: 'I have established a statute and instituted a decree, and you have no permission to transgress them'" (Bemidbar Rabba, Ḥukat 19).

The passage is telling us that not only do we find the laws of purity hard to understand. So do the Sages, or at least the disciples of the Sages. However, we should not misunderstand Rabban Yoḥanan's reply to his students. It has often been taken to mean that the laws we call *ḥukim*, "statutes," have no reason, or at least none we can understand. What I believe Rabban Yoḥanan was doing was making a sharp distinction – made in our time by philosopher John Rawls – between two kinds

27 of a bird or of an animal, in any of your dwellings. Anyone who eats any blood
shall be cut off from his people."
28 29 And the LORD spoke to Moshe: "Tell the Israelites: One who brings a peace
sacrifice to the LORD is to bring the offering of his peace sacrifice before the
30 LORD himself; with his own hands he shall present the LORD's fire offerings.
He shall bring the animal's fat and breast so that the breast can be displayed,
31 this way and that, as a wave offering before the LORD. The priest shall send the
fat up in smoke upon the altar, but the breast shall go to Aharon and his sons.
32 The right thigh of your peace offering you shall give as an upraised gift to the
33 priest. The one among the sons of Aharon who offers the blood and fat of the
34 peace offering shall receive the right thigh as his portion. For I have taken from

רש״י

כו **לָעוֹף וְלַבְּהֵמָה.** פְּרָט לְדַם דָּגִים וַחֲגָבִים: **בְּכֹל מוֹשְׁבֹתֵיכֶם.** לְפִי שֶׁהִיא חוֹבַת הַגּוּף וְאֵינָהּ חוֹבַת קַרְקַע, נוֹהֶגֶת בְּכָל מוֹשָׁבוֹת, וּבְמַסֶּכֶת קִדּוּשִׁין בְּפֶרֶק רִאשׁוֹן (דף לז ע״ב) מְפֹרָשׁ לָמָּה הֻצְרַךְ לוֹמַר:

ל **יָדָיו תְּבִיאֶינָה וְגוֹ׳.** שֶׁתְּהֵא יַד הַבְּעָלִים מִלְמַעְלָה וְהַחֵלֶב וְהֶחָזוֹת נְתוּנִין בָּהּ, וְיַד כֹּהֵן מִלְּמַטָּה וּמְנִיפָן: **אֵת אִשֵּׁי ה׳.** וּמַה הֵן הָאִשִּׁים? ״אֶת הַחֵלֶב עַל הֶחָזֶה יְבִיאֶנּוּ״, כְּשֶׁמְּבִיאוֹ מִבֵּית הַמִּטְבָּחַיִם נוֹתֵן חֵלֶב עַל הֶחָזֶה, וּכְשֶׁנּוֹתְנוֹ לְיַד הַמֵּנִיף נִמְצָא הֶחָזֶה לְמַעְלָה וְהַחֵלֶב לְמַטָּה, וְזֶהוּ הָאָמוּר בְּמָקוֹם אַחֵר: ״שׁוֹק הַתְּרוּמָה וַחֲזֵה הַתְּנוּפָה עַל אִשֵּׁי הַחֲלָבִים יָבִיאוּ לְהָנִיף״ וְגוֹ׳ (להלן י, טו), וּלְאַחַר הַתְּנוּפָה נוֹתְנוֹ לַכֹּהֵן הַמַּקְטִיר, וְנִמְצָא הֶחָזֶה לְמַטָּה, וְזֶהוּ שֶׁנֶּאֱמַר: ״וַיָּשִׂימוּ אֶת הַחֲלָבִים עַל הֶחָזוֹת וַיַּקְטֵר הַחֲלָבִים הַמִּזְבֵּחָה״ (להלן ט, כ). לָמַדְנוּ שֶׁשְּׁלֹשָׁה כֹּהֲנִים זְקוּקִין לָהּ, כָּךְ מְפֹרָשׁ בִּמְנָחוֹת (דף סב ע״א): **אֶת הַחֵלֶב עַל הֶחָזֶה יְבִיאֶנּוּ.** וְ״אֶת הֶחָזֶה״ לָמָּה מְבִיאוֹ? ״לְהָנִיף אֹתוֹ״ הוּא מְבִיאוֹ, וְלֹא שֶׁיְּהֵא הוּא מִן הָאִשִּׁים. לְפִי שֶׁנֶּאֱמַר: ״אֵת אִשֵּׁי ה׳ אֶת הַחֵלֶב עַל הֶחָזֶה״, יָכוֹל שֶׁיְּהֵא אַף הֶחָזֶה לָאִשִּׁים? לְכָךְ נֶאֱמַר: ״אֶת הֶחָזֶה לְהָנִיף״ וְגוֹ׳:

לא **וְהִקְטִיר הַכֹּהֵן אֶת הַחֵלֶב.** וְאַחַר כָּךְ ״וְהָיָה הֶחָזֶה לְאַהֲרֹן״, לָמַדְנוּ שֶׁאֵין הַבָּשָׂר נֶאֱכָל בְּעוֹד הָאֵמוּרִים לְמַטָּה מִן הַמִּזְבֵּחַ:

לב **שׁוֹק.** מִן הַפֶּרֶק שֶׁל אַרְכֻּבָּה הַנִּמְכֶּרֶת עִם הָרֹאשׁ עַד הַפֶּרֶק הָאֶמְצָעִי שֶׁהוּא סֹבֶךְ שֶׁל רֶגֶל:

לג **הַמַּקְרִיב אֶת דַּם הַשְּׁלָמִים וְגוֹ׳.** מִי שֶׁהוּא רָאוּי לִזְרִיקָתוֹ וּלְהַקְטִיר חֲלָבָיו, יָצָא טָמֵא בִּשְׁעַת זְרִיקַת דָּמִים אוֹ בִּשְׁעַת הֶקְטֵר חֲלָבִים שֶׁאֵינוֹ חוֹלֵק בַּבָּשָׂר:

לד **תְּנוּפָה, תְּרוּמָה.** מוֹלִיךְ וּמֵבִיא, מַעֲלֶה וּמוֹרִיד:

endowment from earlier times. It leaves two legacies: one, the human tendency to band together in the face of an external threat; the other, the willingness to risk self-sacrifice for the sake of the group. These emotions appear at times of war. They are not the *cause* of war, but they invest it with "the profound feelings – dread, awe, and the willingness to sacrifice – that make it 'sacred' to us." They help explain why it is so easy to mobilize people by conjuring up the specter of an external enemy.

Evolutionary psychology has taught us about these genetic residues from earlier times which – because they are not rational – cannot be cured by reason alone, but only by ritual, strict prohibition, and habituation. The contemporary world continues to be scarred by violence and terror. Sadly, the ban against blood sacrifice is still relevant.

In this perspective, we can see that Rambam and Ramban were both correct. Rambam was right to see in blood sacrifice a central idolatrous practice. Ramban was equally correct to see it as a symptom of human cruelty. The instinct against which it is a protest – sacrificing life to exorcise fear – still lives on.

We now sense the profound wisdom of the law forbidding the eating of blood. Only thus could human beings be gradually cured of a deeply ingrained instinct, deriving from a world of predators and prey, in which the key choice is to kill or be killed.

כז לֹא תֹאכְלוּ בְּכֹל מוֹשְׁבֹתֵיכֶם לָעוֹף וְלַבְּהֵמָה: כָּל־נֶפֶשׁ אֲשֶׁר־תֹּאכַל
כָּל־דָּם וְנִכְרְתָה הַנֶּפֶשׁ הַהִוא מֵעַמֶּיהָ:
כח כט וַיְדַבֵּר יְהוָה אֶל־מֹשֶׁה לֵּאמֹר: דַּבֵּר אֶל־בְּנֵי יִשְׂרָאֵל לֵאמֹר הַמַּקְרִיב
ל אֶת־זֶבַח שְׁלָמָיו לַיהוָה יָבִיא אֶת־קָרְבָּנוֹ לַיהוָה מִזֶּבַח שְׁלָמָיו: יָדָיו
תְּבִיאֶינָה אֵת אִשֵּׁי יְהוָה אֶת־הַחֵלֶב עַל־הֶחָזֶה יְבִיאֶנּוּ אֵת הֶחָזֶה
לא לְהָנִיף אֹתוֹ תְּנוּפָה לִפְנֵי יְהוָה: וְהִקְטִיר הַכֹּהֵן אֶת־הַחֵלֶב הַמִּזְבֵּחָה
לב וְהָיָה הֶחָזֶה לְאַהֲרֹן וּלְבָנָיו: וְאֵת שׁוֹק הַיָּמִין תִּתְּנוּ תְרוּמָה לַכֹּהֵן
לג מִזִּבְחֵי שַׁלְמֵיכֶם: הַמַּקְרִיב אֶת־דַּם הַשְּׁלָמִים וְאֶת־הַחֵלֶב מִבְּנֵי אַהֲרֹן
לד לוֹ תִהְיֶה שׁוֹק הַיָּמִין לְמָנָה: כִּי אֶת־חֲזֵה הַתְּנוּפָה וְאֵת ׀ שׁוֹק הַתְּרוּמָה

אונקלוס

לָא תֵיכְלוּן, בְּכֹל מוֹתְבָנֵיכוֹן, דְּעוֹפָא וְדִבְעִירָא: כז כָּל אֱנָשׁ דְּיֵיכוֹל כָּל דַּם, וְיִשְׁתֵּיצֵי, אֱנָשָׁא הַהוּא מֵעַמֵּיהּ: כח וּמַלֵּיל יי עִם מֹשֶׁה לְמֵימַר: כט מַלֵּיל, עִם בְּנֵי יִשְׂרָאֵל לְמֵימַר, דִּמְקָרֵיב, יָת נִכְסַת קֻדְשׁוֹהִי קֳדָם יי, יַיְתֵי יָת קֻרְבָּנֵיהּ, לִקְדָם יי מִנִּכְסַת קֻדְשׁוֹהִי: ל יְדוֹהִי יַיְתְיָן, יָת קֻרְבָּנַיָּא דַּיי, יָת תַּרְבָּא עַל חַדְיָא יַיְתֵינֵיהּ, יָת חַדְיָא, לַאֲרָמָא יָתֵיהּ, אֲרָמָא קֳדָם יי: לא וְיַסֵּיק כָּהֲנָא, יָת תַּרְבָּא לְמַדְבְּחָא, וִיהֵי חַדְיָא, לְאַהֲרֹן וְלִבְנוֹהִי: לב וְיָת שָׁקָא דְיַמִּינָא, תִּתְּנוּן אַפְרָשׁוּתָא לְכָהֲנָא, מִנִּכְסַת קֻדְשֵׁיכוֹן: לג דִּמְקָרֵיב, יָת דַּם נִכְסַת קֻדְשַׁיָּא, וְיָת תַּרְבָּא מִבְּנֵי אַהֲרֹן, דִּילֵיהּ תְּהֵי, שָׁקָא דְיַמִּינָא לַחֲלָק: לד אֲרֵי יָת חַדְיָא דַּאֲרָמוּתָא, וְיָת שָׁקָא דְאַפְרָשׁוּתָא, יָת

Barbara Ehrenreich, in her book *Blood Rites: Origins and History of the Passions of War*, argues that one of the most formative experiences of the first human beings must have been the terror of being attacked by an animal predator. They knew that the likely outcome was that one of the group, usually an outsider, an invalid, a child, or perhaps an animal, would fall as prey, giving the others a chance to escape. It was this embedded memory that became the basis of subsequent sacrificial rites. As she puts it, "The sacrificial ritual in many ways mimics the crisis of a predator's attack. An animal or perhaps a human member of the group is singled out for slaughter, often in a spectacularly bloody manner." The eating of the victim and his or its blood temporarily occupies the predator, allowing the rest of the group to escape in safety. That is why blood is offered to the gods.

Ehrenreich's view is that the sacrificial response – fear and guilt – survives to the present as part of our genetic

him, all humanity – after the flood: "But flesh with its lifeblood still in it you may not eat" (Gen. 9:4). So too, Moshe returns to the subject in his great closing addresses in the book of Deuteronomy: "But make sure that you do not eat the blood, for blood is life, and you must not eat the life with the meat" (Deut. 12:23).

What is so wrong about eating blood? Rambam and Ramban offer apparently conflicting interpretations. For Rambam (*Guide for the Perplexed* III:46), it is part of the Torah's extended battle against idolatry. Idolators believed that blood was the food of the spirits, and that by eating it they would have "something in common with the spirits." Eating blood is forbidden because of its association with idolatry.

Ramban (on Lev. 17:13) says, contrariwise, that the ban has to do with human nature. We are affected by what we eat. Eating blood, implies Ramban, makes us cruel, bestial, animal-like.

the peace sacrifices of the Israelites the breast of the wave offering and the thigh
of the upraised gift, and given them to Aharon the priest and to his sons as their
35 perpetual share from the Israelites. This is the anointed right of Aharon and his
sons from the LORD's fire offerings from the day they are presented to serve
36 the LORD as priests; when the LORD anointed them as priests He commanded
that these be given them by the Israelites as their perpetual share throughout
37 the generations." This, then, is the law for the burnt offering, the grain offering,
the purification offering, the guilt offering, the ordination offering, and the
38 peace offering, which the LORD commanded Moshe at Mount Sinai when
he commanded the Israelites to bring their offerings to the LORD, in the
Wilderness of Sinai.
8 1 2 The LORD said to Moshe: "Take Aharon, and his sons with him, the vestments, REVI'I
the anointing oil, a bull for the purification offering, two rams, and a basket of
3 unleavened bread, and assemble the whole community at the entrance to the
4 Tent of Meeting." Moshe did as the LORD commanded him; and the community
5 was assembled at the entrance to the Tent of Meeting. And Moshe told the
6 community, "This is what the LORD has commanded us to do." Then Moshe
7 brought Aharon and his sons close, and he washed them with water. He put the

רש״י

לז **ולמלואים.** ליום חנוך הכהונה:

ח ב **קח את אהרן.** פרשה זו נאמרה שבעת ימים קדם הקמת המשכן, שאין מקדם ומאחר בתורה: **קח את אהרן.** קחנו בדברים ומשכהו: **ואת פר החטאת וגו׳.** אלו האמורים בענין צואת המלואים ב״ואתה תצוה״ (שמות כט), ועכשיו ביום ראשון למלואים חזר וזרזו בשעת מעשה:

ג **הקהל אל פתח אהל מועד.** זה אחד מן המקומות שהחזיק מועט את המרבה:

ה **זה הדבר.** דברים שתראו שאני עושה לפניכם צוני הקדוש ברוך הוא לעשות, ואל תאמרו לכבודי ולכבוד אחי אני עושה. כל הענין הזה פרשתי ב״ואתה תצוה״ (שמות כט, א-לז):

Moshe and then recorded, structured, and ordered as the priestly code, *Torat Kohanim*.

8:3 **וְאֵת כָּל־הָעֵדָה הַקְהֵל** *Assemble the whole community* – Why must the whole people come to the initiation of the priesthood? I suggest that it is because the priesthood plays an essential part in protecting a society's integrity. Religions help safeguard governments against corruption. They can do this in two distinct ways corresponding to the biblical realms of prophecy and priesthood. Prophecy has a critical function. Yeḥezkel defined his role as "watchman" to the House of Israel, giving warnings of impending catastrophe (Ezek. 3:17, 33:7). But priesthood is about constructing communities where the life of faith is given tangible expression. Without prophecy, a society can become corrupt at the top. But without priesthood, it can erode from below. It can lose its structures of family and community life, within which the civic virtues are learned and enacted. Prophecy is dramatic; priesthood is not. Prophecy makes headlines; priesthood rarely does. But both are necessary to the civil order. Without the matrix of institutions within which individual responsibility and the moral sentiments are nurtured, no freedoms are secure for long. Here, the entire nation is called to witness the inauguration of the first priests. While their work will be contained in the Tabernacle, it will be of the utmost significance to the community as a whole.

לָקַחְתִּי מֵאֵת בְּנֵי־יִשְׂרָאֵל מִזִּבְחֵי שַׁלְמֵיהֶם וָאֶתֵּן אֹתָם לְאַהֲרֹן הַכֹּהֵן
לה וּלְבָנָיו לְחָק־עוֹלָם מֵאֵת בְּנֵי יִשְׂרָאֵל׃ זֹאת מִשְׁחַת אַהֲרֹן וּמִשְׁחַת
לו בָּנָיו מֵאִשֵּׁי יהוה בְּיוֹם הִקְרִיב אֹתָם לְכַהֵן לַיהוה׃ אֲשֶׁר צִוָּה יהוה
לָתֵת לָהֶם בְּיוֹם מָשְׁחוֹ אֹתָם מֵאֵת בְּנֵי יִשְׂרָאֵל חֻקַּת עוֹלָם לְדֹרֹתָם׃
לז זֹאת הַתּוֹרָה לָעֹלָה לַמִּנְחָה וְלַחַטָּאת וְלָאָשָׁם וְלַמִּלּוּאִים וּלְזֶבַח
לח הַשְּׁלָמִים׃ אֲשֶׁר צִוָּה יהוה אֶת־מֹשֶׁה בְּהַר סִינָי בְּיוֹם צַוֹּתוֹ אֶת־בְּנֵי
יִשְׂרָאֵל לְהַקְרִיב אֶת־קָרְבְּנֵיהֶם לַיהוה בְּמִדְבַּר סִינָי׃
ח א ב וַיְדַבֵּר יהוה אֶל־מֹשֶׁה לֵּאמֹר׃ קַח אֶת־אַהֲרֹן וְאֶת־בָּנָיו אִתּוֹ וְאֵת ד רביעי
הַבְּגָדִים וְאֵת שֶׁמֶן הַמִּשְׁחָה וְאֵת ׀ פַּר הַחַטָּאת וְאֵת שְׁנֵי הָאֵילִים
ג ד וְאֵת סַל הַמַּצּוֹת׃ וְאֵת כָּל־הָעֵדָה הַקְהֵל אֶל־פֶּתַח אֹהֶל מוֹעֵד׃ וַיַּעַשׂ
מֹשֶׁה כַּאֲשֶׁר צִוָּה יהוה אֹתוֹ וַתִּקָּהֵל הָעֵדָה אֶל־פֶּתַח אֹהֶל מוֹעֵד׃
ה ו וַיֹּאמֶר מֹשֶׁה אֶל־הָעֵדָה זֶה הַדָּבָר אֲשֶׁר־צִוָּה יהוה לַעֲשׂוֹת׃ וַיַּקְרֵב
ז מֹשֶׁה אֶת־אַהֲרֹן וְאֶת־בָּנָיו וַיִּרְחַץ אֹתָם בַּמָּיִם׃ וַיִּתֵּן עָלָיו אֶת־הַכֻּתֹּנֶת

אונקלוס

נסיבית מן בני ישראל, מנכסת קודשיהון, ויהבית יתהון, לאהרן כהנא ולבנוהי לקים עלם, מן בני ישראל: לה דא רבות אהרן ורבות בנוהי, מקרבניא דיי, ביומא דיקריב יתהון, לשמשא קדם יי: לו דפקיד יי למתן להון, ביומא דירבון יתהון, מן בני ישראל, קים עלם לדריהון: לז דא אוריתא, לעלתא למנחתא, ולחטתא ולאשמא, ולקרבניא, ולנכסת קדשיא: לח דפקיד יי, ית משה בטורא דסיני, ביומא דפקיד ית בני ישראל,

לקרבא ית קרבנהון, קדם יי במדברא דסיני: ח א ומליל יי עם משה למימר: ב קריב ית אהרן וית בנוהי עמיה, וית לבושיא, וית משחא דרבותא, וית תורא דחטאתא, וית תרין דכרין, וית סלא דפטיריא: ג וית כל כנשתא כנוש, לתרע משכן זמנא: ד ועבד משה, כמא דפקיד יי יתיה, ואתכנישת כנשתא, לתרע משכן זמנא: ה ואמר משה לכנשתא, דין פתגמא, דפקיד יי למעבד: ו וקריב משה, ית אהרן וית בנוהי, ואסחי יתהון במיא: ז ויהב עלוהי ית כתונא,

7:37 זֹאת הַתּוֹרָה לָעֹלָה *This, then, is the law for the burnt offering* – The major part of Leviticus is a series of God's direct speeches to Moshe. The formulation in this verse, part of the book's frame, concludes the series of speeches concerning the sacrifices, and will continue on to different areas of ritual law.

Judaism's fundamental solution to the distance between God and man is *language*. Words alone have the power to cross the abyss between finite humans and the infinite God. God spoke to Adam, Kayin, Noaḥ, the patriarchs and matriarchs, and, of course, "The Lord spoke to Moshe."

Direct divine communication is a solution that worked for individuals. What happens when the Israelites become a nation? The answer comes in the form of this forty-chapter digression in the story of the Israelites' journey from Egypt to the Promised Land: a series of revelations spoken to

tunic on Aharon, tied the sash around him, clothed him in the robe, and placed
the ephod on him. He bound the ephod's decorated belt about him, securing
8 the ephod to him. Then he put the breast piece on him, and inside the breast
9 piece he placed the Urim and Tumim. On his head he placed the miter, and
on the miter in front, he placed the golden head plate, the holy diadem, as the
10 LORD had commanded him. Then Moshe took the anointing oil and anointed
11 the Tabernacle and everything in it; thus he consecrated them. He sprinkled
some of the oil on the altar seven times. He anointed the altar and all its vessels,
12 and the laver and its base, thus consecrating them. Some of the anointing oil
13 he poured on Aharon's head, anointing him, consecrating him. Then Moshe
brought close Aharon's sons, dressed them in their tunics, bound sashes about
them, and placed their headdresses on them, just as the LORD had commanded
14 him. Moshe drew close the bull for the purification offering, and Aharon and his HAMISHI
15 sons laid their hands on its head. It was slaughtered, and Moshe took the blood
and applied it with his finger to all the altar's horns, purifying the altar. The rest of
the blood he poured out at the altar's base. Thus he consecrated it so that, upon
16 it, atonement could be made. Moshe removed all the fat around the entrails, the
diaphragm of the liver, the two kidneys and their fat, and sent them up in smoke
17 upon the altar. But the rest of the bull, its skin, its flesh, and its dung, he burned
18 with fire outside the camp as the LORD had commanded him. Then Moshe drew
close the ram for the burnt offering, and Aharon and his sons laid their hands
19 on its head. Moshe slaughtered it and dashed the blood against each side of the
20 altar. He cut the ram into pieces and sent the head, pieces, and suet up in smoke.

אונקלוס

וְזָרֵיז יָתֵיהּ בְּהִמְיָנָא, וְאַלְבֵּישׁ יָתֵיהּ יָת מְעִילָא, וִיהַב עֲלוֹהִי יָת אֵיפוֹדָא, וְזָרֵיז יָתֵיהּ, בְּהִמְיַן אֵיפוֹדָא, וְאַתְקֵין לֵיהּ בֵּיהּ: ח וְשַׁוִּי עֲלוֹהִי יָת חֻשְׁנָא, וִיהַב בְּחֻשְׁנָא, יָת אוּרַיָּא וְיָת תֻּמַּיָּא: ט וְשַׁוִּי יָת מַצְנַפְתָּא עַל רֵישֵׁיהּ, וְשַׁוִּי עַל מַצְנַפְתָּא לָקֳבֵיל אַפּוֹהִי, יָת צִיצָא דְדַהֲבָא כְּלִילָא דְקֻדְשָׁא, כְּמָא דְפַקֵּיד יי יָת מֹשֶׁה: י וּנְסֵיב מֹשֶׁה יָת מִשְׁחָא דִרְבוּתָא, וְרַבִּי יָת מַשְׁכְּנָא וְיָת כָּל דְּבֵיהּ, וְקַדֵּישׁ יָתְהוֹן: יא וְאַדִּי מִנֵּיהּ, עַל מַדְבְּחָא שְׁבַע זִמְנִין, וְרַבִּי יָת מַדְבְּחָא וְיָת כָּל מָנוֹהִי, וְיָת כִּיּוֹרָא, וְיָת בְּסִיסֵיהּ לְקַדָּשׁוּתְהוֹן: יב וַאֲרֵיק מִמִּשְׁחָא דִרְבוּתָא, עַל רֵישָׁא דְאַהֲרֹן,

רש״י

ח | אֶת הָאוּרִים. כְּתָב שֶׁל שֵׁם הַמְפֹרָשׁ:

ט | וַיָּשֶׂם עַל הַמִּצְנֶפֶת. פְּתִילֵי תְכֵלֶת הַקְּבוּעִים בַּצִּיץ נוֹתֵן עַל הַמִּצְנֶפֶת, נִמְצָא הַצִּיץ תָּלוּי בַּמִּצְנֶפֶת:

יא | וַיַּז מִמֶּנּוּ עַל הַמִּזְבֵּחַ. לֹא יָדַעְתִּי הֵיכָן נִצְטַוָּה בַּהַזָּאוֹת הַלָּלוּ:

יב | וַיִּצֹק, וַיִּמְשַׁח. בַּתְּחִלָּה יוֹצֵק עַל רֹאשׁוֹ, וְאַחַר כָּךְ נוֹתֵן בֵּין רִיסֵי עֵינָיו וּמוֹשֵׁךְ בְּאֶצְבָּעוֹ מִזֶּה לָזֶה:

יג | וַיַּחֲבֹשׁ. לְשׁוֹן קְשִׁירָה:

טו | וַיְחַטֵּא אֶת הַמִּזְבֵּחַ. חִטְּאוֹ וְטִהֲרוֹ מִזָּרוּת לִכָּנֵס לִקְדֻשָּׁה: וַיְקַדְּשֵׁהוּ. בַּעֲבוֹדָה זוֹ, "לְכַפֵּר עָלָיו" מֵעַתָּה כָּל הַכַּפָּרוֹת:

טז | "עַל הַכָּבֵד" (שמות כט, יג), לְבַד הַכָּבֵד, שֶׁהָיָה נוֹטֵל מְעַט מִן הַכָּבֵד עִמָּהּ:

וַיַּחְגֹּר אֹתוֹ בָּאַבְנֵט וַיַּלְבֵּשׁ אֹתוֹ אֶת־הַמְּעִיל וַיִּתֵּן עָלָיו אֶת־הָאֵפֹד
ח וַיַּחְגֹּר אֹתוֹ בְּחֵשֶׁב הָאֵפֹד וַיֶּאְפֹּד לוֹ בּוֹ׃ וַיָּשֶׂם עָלָיו אֶת־הַחֹשֶׁן וַיִּתֵּן
ט אֶל־הַחֹשֶׁן אֶת־הָאוּרִים וְאֶת־הַתֻּמִּים׃ וַיָּשֶׂם אֶת־הַמִּצְנֶפֶת עַל־
רֹאשׁוֹ וַיָּשֶׂם עַל־הַמִּצְנֶפֶת אֶל־מוּל פָּנָיו אֵת צִיץ הַזָּהָב נֵזֶר הַקֹּדֶשׁ
י כַּאֲשֶׁר צִוָּה יהוה אֶת־מֹשֶׁה׃ וַיִּקַּח מֹשֶׁה אֶת־שֶׁמֶן הַמִּשְׁחָה וַיִּמְשַׁח
יא אֶת־הַמִּשְׁכָּן וְאֶת־כָּל־אֲשֶׁר־בּוֹ וַיְקַדֵּשׁ אֹתָם׃ וַיַּז מִמֶּנּוּ עַל־הַמִּזְבֵּחַ
שֶׁבַע פְּעָמִים וַיִּמְשַׁח אֶת־הַמִּזְבֵּחַ וְאֶת־כָּל־כֵּלָיו וְאֶת־הַכִּיֹּר וְאֶת־כַּנּוֹ
יב לְקַדְּשָׁם׃ וַיִּצֹק מִשֶּׁמֶן הַמִּשְׁחָה עַל רֹאשׁ אַהֲרֹן וַיִּמְשַׁח אֹתוֹ לְקַדְּשׁוֹ׃
יג וַיַּקְרֵב מֹשֶׁה אֶת־בְּנֵי אַהֲרֹן וַיַּלְבִּשֵׁם כֻּתֳּנֹת וַיַּחְגֹּר אֹתָם אַבְנֵט וַיַּחֲבֹשׁ
יד לָהֶם מִגְבָּעוֹת כַּאֲשֶׁר צִוָּה יהוה אֶת־מֹשֶׁה׃ וַיַּגֵּשׁ אֵת פַּר הַחַטָּאת חמישי
טו וַיִּסְמֹךְ אַהֲרֹן וּבָנָיו אֶת־יְדֵיהֶם עַל־רֹאשׁ פַּר הַחַטָּאת׃ וַיִּשְׁחָט וַיִּקַּח
מֹשֶׁה אֶת־הַדָּם וַיִּתֵּן עַל־קַרְנוֹת הַמִּזְבֵּחַ סָבִיב בְּאֶצְבָּעוֹ וַיְחַטֵּא אֶת־
טז הַמִּזְבֵּחַ וְאֶת־הַדָּם יָצַק אֶל־יְסוֹד הַמִּזְבֵּחַ וַיְקַדְּשֵׁהוּ לְכַפֵּר עָלָיו׃ וַיִּקַּח
אֶת־כָּל־הַחֵלֶב אֲשֶׁר עַל־הַקֶּרֶב וְאֵת יֹתֶרֶת הַכָּבֵד וְאֶת־שְׁתֵּי הַכְּלָיֹת
יז וְאֶת־חֶלְבְּהֶן וַיַּקְטֵר מֹשֶׁה הַמִּזְבֵּחָה׃ וְאֶת־הַפָּר וְאֶת־עֹרוֹ וְאֶת־בְּשָׂרוֹ
וְאֶת־פִּרְשׁוֹ שָׂרַף בָּאֵשׁ מִחוּץ לַמַּחֲנֶה כַּאֲשֶׁר צִוָּה יהוה אֶת־מֹשֶׁה׃
יח וַיַּקְרֵב אֵת אֵיל הָעֹלָה וַיִּסְמְכוּ אַהֲרֹן וּבָנָיו אֶת־יְדֵיהֶם עַל־רֹאשׁ
יט כ הָאָיִל׃ וַיִּשְׁחָט וַיִּזְרֹק מֹשֶׁה אֶת־הַדָּם עַל־הַמִּזְבֵּחַ סָבִיב׃ וְאֶת־הָאַיִל
נִתַּח לִנְתָחָיו וַיַּקְטֵר מֹשֶׁה אֶת־הָרֹאשׁ וְאֶת־הַנְּתָחִים וְאֶת־הַפָּדֶר׃

אונקלוס

וְרַבִּי יָתֵיהּ לְקַדָּשׁוּתֵיהּ: יג וְקָרֵיב מֹשֶׁה יָת בְּנֵי אַהֲרֹן, וְאַלְבֵּישִׁנּוּן כִּתּוּנִין
וְזָרֵיז יָתְהוֹן הִמְיָנִין, וְאַתְקֵין לְהוֹן קוֹבָעִין, כְּמָא דְּפַקֵּיד יי יָת מֹשֶׁה:
יד וְקָרֵיב, יָת תּוֹרָא דְּחַטָּתָא, וּסְמַךְ אַהֲרֹן וּבְנוֹהִי יָת יְדֵיהוֹן, עַל
רֵישׁ תּוֹרָא דְּחַטָּתָא: טו וּנְכַס, וּנְסֵיב מֹשֶׁה יָת דְּמָא וִיהַב, עַל קַרְנָת
מַדְבְּחָא סְחוֹר סְחוֹר בְּאֶצְבְּעֵיהּ, וְדַכֵּי יָת מַדְבְּחָא, וְיָת דְּמָא, אֲרֵיק
לִיסוֹדָא דְּמַדְבְּחָא, וְקַדְּשֵׁיהּ לְכַפָּרָא עֲלוֹהִי: טז וּנְסֵיב, יָת כָּל תַּרְבָּא
דְּעַל גַּוָּא, וְיָת חֲצַר כַּבְדָּא, וְיָת תַּרְתֵּין כּוֹלְיָן וְיָת תַּרְבְּהוֹן, וְאַסֵּיק
מֹשֶׁה לְמַדְבְּחָא: יז וְיָת תּוֹרָא וְיָת מַשְׁכֵּיהּ וְיָת בִּסְרֵיהּ וְיָת אֻכְלֵיהּ,
אוֹקֵיד בְּנוּרָא, מִבָּרָא לְמַשְׁרִיתָא, כְּמָא דְּפַקֵּיד יי יָת מֹשֶׁה: יח וְקָרֵיב,
יָת דִּכְרָא דַּעֲלָתָא, וּסְמַכוּ, אַהֲרֹן וּבְנוֹהִי, יָת יְדֵיהוֹן עַל רֵישׁ דִּכְרָא:
יט וּנְכַס, וּזְרַק מֹשֶׁה יָת דְּמָא, עַל מַדְבְּחָא סְחוֹר סְחוֹר: כ וְיָת דִּכְרָא,
פַּלֵּיג לְאֶבְרוֹהִי, וְאַסֵּיק מֹשֶׁה יָת רֵישָׁא, וְיָת אֶבְרַיָּא וְיָת תַּרְבָּא:

21 After washing the entrails and legs with water, Moshe sent the entire ram up in
smoke upon the altar. It was a burnt offering for a pleasing aroma: a fire offering
22 to the LORD, as the LORD had commanded Moshe. Moshe then drew close the SHISHI
second ram, the ram of ordination. Aharon and his sons laid their hands upon its
23 head. It was slaughtered; and Moshe took some of its blood and applied it to the
24 ridge of Aharon's right ear, to his right thumb, and to his right big toe. He drew
Aharon's sons close and put some of the blood on the ridges of their right ears,
on their right thumbs, and on their right big toes. Moshe dashed the rest of the
25 blood against each of the altar's sides. Then he took the fat, the broad tail, all the
fat around the entrails, the diaphragm of the liver, and the two kidneys with their
26 fat, as well as the right thigh. He took a loaf of unleavened bread from the basket,
before the LORD, and also one loaf of oil bread, and one wafer, and placed them
27 on the fat and on the right thigh. All of this he placed on the palms of Aharon
and of his sons, and displayed them this way and that as a wave offering before
28 the LORD. Then Moshe took them from their hands and burnt them upon the
altar with the burnt offering. This was the ordination offering, a pleasing aroma,
29 a fire offering to the LORD. Moshe then took the breast and waved it as a wave

רש״י

כב) **איל המלאים.** איל השלמים, שמלואים לשון שלמים, שממלאין ומשלימין את הכהנים בכהונתם:

כו) **וחלת לחם שמן.** היא רבוכה, שהיה מרבה בה שמן כנגד החלות והרקיקין, כך מפרש במנחות (דף עח ע״א):

כח) **ויקטר המזבחה.** משה שמש כל שבעת ימי המלואים בחלוק לבן: **על העלה.** אחר העלה, ולא מצינו שוק של שלמים קרב בכל מקום חוץ מזה:

offerings in the Tabernacle. He will mediate the *avoda*, the Israelites' sacred service to God. Once a year on Yom Kippur he will perform the service that will secure atonement for the people from its sins. Aharon is about to become the one kind of leader Moshe is not destined to be: a High Priest.

The Talmud adds a further dimension to the poignancy of the moment. At the burning bush, Moshe had repeatedly resisted God's call to lead the people. Eventually God told him that Aharon would go with him, helping him speak (Ex. 4:14–16). The Talmud says that at that moment Moshe lost the chance to be a priest. "Originally [said God] I had intended that you would be the priest and Aharon your brother would be a Levite. Now he will be the priest and you will be a Levite" (Zevaḥim 102a).

That is Moshe's inner struggle, conveyed by the *shalshelet*. He is about to induct his brother into an office he himself will never hold. He surely feels joy for his brother, but he cannot altogether avoid a sense of loss. Perhaps he already senses that though he is the prophet and liberator, Aharon will have a privilege Moshe is denied, namely, seeing his children and their descendants inherit his role. The son of a priest is a priest. The son of a prophet is rarely a prophet. To say yes to who we are, we have to have the courage to say no to who we are not. Pain and internal conflict are involved. But we emerge less conflicted than we were before. That is the meaning of the *shalshelet*.

This applies especially to leaders. There are things Moshe is not destined to do. He will not become a priest. That task falls to Aharon. He will not lead the people across the Jordan. That will be Yehoshua's role. Moshe has to accept both facts if he is to be honest with himself. And great leaders, if they are to be honest with those they lead, must be honest with themselves.

כא וְאֶת־הַקֶּרֶב וְאֶת־הַכְּרָעַיִם רָחַץ בַּמָּיִם וַיַּקְטֵר מֹשֶׁה אֶת־כָּל־הָאַיִל
הַמִּזְבֵּחָה עֹלָה הוּא לְרֵיחַ־נִיחֹחַ אִשֶּׁה הוּא לַיהוָה כַּאֲשֶׁר צִוָּה יהוה
כב אֶת־מֹשֶׁה: וַיַּקְרֵב אֶת־הָאַיִל הַשֵּׁנִי אֵיל הַמִּלֻּאִים וַיִּסְמְכוּ אַהֲרֹן וּבָנָיו ששי
כג אֶת־יְדֵיהֶם עַל־רֹאשׁ הָאָיִל: וַיִּשְׁחָט ׀ וַיִּקַּח מֹשֶׁה מִדָּמוֹ וַיִּתֵּן עַל־תְּנוּךְ
אֹזֶן־אַהֲרֹן הַיְמָנִית וְעַל־בֹּהֶן יָדוֹ הַיְמָנִית וְעַל־בֹּהֶן רַגְלוֹ הַיְמָנִית:
כד וַיַּקְרֵב אֶת־בְּנֵי אַהֲרֹן וַיִּתֵּן מֹשֶׁה מִן־הַדָּם עַל־תְּנוּךְ אָזְנָם הַיְמָנִית
וְעַל־בֹּהֶן יָדָם הַיְמָנִית וְעַל־בֹּהֶן רַגְלָם הַיְמָנִית וַיִּזְרֹק מֹשֶׁה אֶת־הַדָּם
כה עַל־הַמִּזְבֵּחַ סָבִיב: וַיִּקַּח אֶת־הַחֵלֶב וְאֶת־הָאַלְיָה וְאֶת־כָּל־הַחֵלֶב
אֲשֶׁר עַל־הַקֶּרֶב וְאֵת יֹתֶרֶת הַכָּבֵד וְאֶת־שְׁתֵּי הַכְּלָיֹת וְאֶת־חֶלְבְּהֶן
כו וְאֵת שׁוֹק הַיָּמִין: וּמִסַּל הַמַּצּוֹת אֲשֶׁר ׀ לִפְנֵי יהוה לָקַח חַלַּת מַצָּה
אַחַת וְחַלַּת לֶחֶם שֶׁמֶן אַחַת וְרָקִיק אֶחָד וַיָּשֶׂם עַל־הַחֲלָבִים וְעַל שׁוֹק
כז הַיָּמִין: וַיִּתֵּן אֶת־הַכֹּל עַל כַּפֵּי אַהֲרֹן וְעַל כַּפֵּי בָנָיו וַיָּנֶף אֹתָם תְּנוּפָה
כח לִפְנֵי יהוה: וַיִּקַּח מֹשֶׁה אֹתָם מֵעַל כַּפֵּיהֶם וַיַּקְטֵר הַמִּזְבֵּחָה עַל־הָעֹלָה
כט מִלֻּאִים הֵם לְרֵיחַ נִיחֹחַ אִשֶּׁה הוּא לַיהוָה: וַיִּקַּח מֹשֶׁה אֶת־הֶחָזֶה

אונקלוס

כא וְיָת גַּוָּא וְיָת כְּרָעַיָּא חֲלִיל בְּמַיָּא, וְאַסֵּיק מֹשֶׁה יָת כָּל דִּכְרָא
לְמַדְבְּחָא, עֲלָתָא הוּא לְאִתְקַבָּלָא בְרַעֲוָא קֻרְבָּנָא הוּא קֳדָם יי,
כְּמָא דְפַקֵּיד יי יָת מֹשֶׁה: כב וְקָרֵיב יָת דִּכְרָא תִּנְיָנָא, דְּכַר קֻרְבָּנַיָּא,
וּסְמַכוּ, אַהֲרֹן וּבְנוֹהִי, יָת יְדֵיהוֹן עַל רֵישׁ דִּכְרָא: כג וּנְכַס וּנְסֵיב
מֹשֶׁה מִדְּמֵיהּ, וִיהַב, עַל רוּם אֻדְנָא דְאַהֲרֹן דְּיַמִּינָא, וְעַל אִלְיוֹן יְדֵיהּ
דְּיַמִּינָא, וְעַל אִלְיוֹן רַגְלֵיהּ דְּיַמִּינָא: כד וְקָרֵיב יָת בְּנֵי אַהֲרֹן, וִיהַב מֹשֶׁה
מִן דְּמָא עַל רוּם אֻדְנְהוֹן דְּיַמִּינָא, וְעַל אִלְיוֹן יְדֵיהוֹן דְּיַמִּינָא, וְעַל
אִלְיוֹן רַגְלֵיהוֹן דְּיַמִּינָא, וּזְרַק מֹשֶׁה יָת דְּמָא, עַל מַדְבְּחָא סְחוֹר סְחוֹר:
כה וּנְסֵיב יָת תַּרְבָּא וְיָת אַלְיְתָא, וְיָת כָּל תַּרְבָּא דְּעַל גַּוָּא, וְיָת חֲצַר
כַּבְדָּא, וְיָת תַּרְתֵּין כּוּלְיָן וְיָת תַּרְבְּהוֹן, וְיָת שָׁקָא דְּיַמִּינָא: כו וּמִסַּלָּא
דְּפַטִּירַיָּא, דִּקְדָם יי, נְסֵיב, גְּרִיצְתָא פַטִּירְתָא חֲדָא וּגְרִיצְתָא דִּלְחֵים
מְשַׁח, חֲדָא וְאֶסְפּוֹג חַד, וְשַׁוִּי עַל תַּרְבַּיָּא, וְעַל שָׁקָא דְּיַמִּינָא: כז וִיהַב
יָת כּוֹלָא, עַל יְדֵי אַהֲרֹן, וְעַל יְדֵי בְנוֹהִי, וַאֲרֵים יָתְהוֹן, אֲרָמָא קֳדָם יי:
כח וּנְסֵיב מֹשֶׁה יָתְהוֹן מֵעַל יְדֵיהוֹן, וְאַסֵּיק לְמַדְבְּחָא עַל עֲלָתָא, קֻרְבָּנַיָּא

8:23 וַיִּשְׁחָט *It was slaughtered* – Over the word *vayishḥat*, "slaughtered," there is a *shalshelet* (chain). This rare note appears in the Torah four times only. Each time it is a sign of an inner crisis. There is not the slightest sign in the text that suggests that Moshe is undergoing a crisis here, yet we may intuit what Moshe's inner turmoil is about. Until now he has led the Jewish people. Aharon, his older brother, assisted him, accompanying him on his missions to Pharaoh, acting as his spokesman, aide, and second-in-command. Now, however, Aharon is about to undertake a new leadership role in his own right. No longer will he be a shadow of Moshe. He will do what Moshe himself cannot. He will preside over the daily

offering before the LORD. This was Moshe's portion of the ordination ram, as the
30 LORD had commanded him. Moshe took some of the anointing oil and some of SHEVI'I
the blood from the altar and sprinkled it on Aharon and on his vestments, and
on his sons and theirs. Thus Moshe consecrated Aharon and his vestments, and
31 his sons and their vestments. Then Moshe said to Aharon and his sons: "Cook
the meat at the entrance to the Tent of Meeting and eat it there together with the
bread in the basket of the ordination offering, as I have charged you: Aharon and
32 his sons shall eat it. Whatever is left over of the meat and the bread, burn with
33 fire. Do not leave the entrance to the Tent of Meeting for seven days, until the MAFTIR
days of your ordination are complete, for your ordination will take seven days,
34 each like today. This is what the LORD has commanded to be done to make your
35 atonement. Stay, then, at the entrance to the Tent of Meeting for seven days, day
and night, keeping the LORD's charge – and you will not die. This is what I have
36 been commanded." And Aharon and his sons did everything that the LORD had
commanded through Moshe.

The haftara for Parashat Tzav is on page 1560.
On the Shabbat of Parashat Para read the haftara on page 1648. On Shabbat HaGadol read the haftara on page 1652.

רש״י

לד **צִוָּה ה׳ לַעֲשֹׂת.** כָּל שִׁבְעַת הַיָּמִים. וְרַבּוֹתֵינוּ דָּרְשׁוּ: "לַעֲשֹׂת" – זֶה מַעֲשֵׂה פָרָה, "לְכַפֵּר" – זֶה מַעֲשֵׂה יוֹם הַכִּפּוּרִים, וּלְלַמֵּד שֶׁכֹּהֵן גָּדוֹל טָעוּן פְּרִישָׁה קֹדֶם יוֹם הַכִּפּוּרִים שִׁבְעַת יָמִים, וְכֵן הַכֹּהֵן הַשּׂוֹרֵף אֶת הַפָּרָה:

לה **וְלֹא תָמוּתוּ.** הָא אִם לֹא תַּעֲשׂוּ כֵן הֲרֵי אַתֶּם חַיָּבִים מִיתָה:

לו **וַיַּעַשׂ אַהֲרֹן וּבָנָיו.** לְהַגִּיד שִׁבְחָן, שֶׁלֹּא הִטּוּ יָמִין וּשְׂמֹאל:

is extraordinary. The people were being criticized not for disobeying God's law but for obeying it. What distressed the prophets to the core of their being was the idea that you could serve God and at the same time act disdainfully, cruelly, unjustly, insensitively, or callously toward other people. "So long as I am in God's good graces, that is all that matters." If you think that, they seem to say, then you haven't understood either God or Torah.

The first thing the Torah tells us about humanity is that we are each in the image and likeness of God Himself. Therefore, if you wrong a human being, you are abusing the only creation in the universe on which God has set His image. A sin against any person is a sin against God.

It is specifically in the book of sacrifices, Leviticus, that we find the twin commands to love your neighbor as yourself, and love the stranger (Lev. 19:18, 33–34). The sacrifices that express our love and awe of God should lead to love of the neighbor and the stranger. There should be a seamless transition from commands between us and God to commands between us and our fellow humans.

Amos, Hoshea, Yeshayahu, Mikha, and Yirmeyahu all witnessed societies in which people were punctilious in bringing their offerings to the Temple, but in which there was bribery, corruption, perversion of justice, abuse of power, and the exploitation of the powerless by the powerful. The prophets saw in this a profound and dangerous contradiction.

To love God is to love our fellow humans. To honor God is to honor our fellow humans. We may not ask God to listen to us if we are unwilling to listen to others. We may not ask God to forgive us if we are unwilling to forgive others. To know God is to seek to imitate Him, which means, said Yirmeyahu (Jer. 9:23) and Rambam (*Guide for the Perplexed* III:54), to exercise kindness, justice, and righteousness. This requires true obedience paired with an inner moral compass; in the prophet Mikha's summary, "only to do justice, love goodness, and walk modestly with your God" (Mic. 6:8).

וַיְנִיפֵהוּ תְנוּפָה לִפְנֵי יְהוָה מֵאֵיל הַמִּלֻּאִים לְמֹשֶׁה הָיָה לְמָנָה כַּאֲשֶׁר
ל צִוָּה יְהוָה אֶת־מֹשֶׁה׃ וַיִּקַּח מֹשֶׁה מִשֶּׁמֶן הַמִּשְׁחָה וּמִן־הַדָּם אֲשֶׁר שביעי
עַל־הַמִּזְבֵּחַ וַיַּז עַל־אַהֲרֹן עַל־בְּגָדָיו וְעַל־בָּנָיו וְעַל־בִּגְדֵי בָנָיו אִתּוֹ
לא וַיְקַדֵּשׁ אֶת־אַהֲרֹן אֶת־בְּגָדָיו וְאֶת־בָּנָיו וְאֶת־בִּגְדֵי בָנָיו אִתּוֹ׃ וַיֹּאמֶר
מֹשֶׁה אֶל־אַהֲרֹן וְאֶל־בָּנָיו בַּשְּׁלוּ אֶת־הַבָּשָׂר פֶּתַח אֹהֶל מוֹעֵד וְשָׁם
תֹּאכְלוּ אֹתוֹ וְאֶת־הַלֶּחֶם אֲשֶׁר בְּסַל הַמִּלֻּאִים כַּאֲשֶׁר צִוֵּיתִי לֵאמֹר
לב לג אַהֲרֹן וּבָנָיו יֹאכְלֻהוּ׃ וְהַנּוֹתָר בַּבָּשָׂר וּבַלָּחֶם בָּאֵשׁ תִּשְׂרֹפוּ׃ וּמִפֶּתַח מפטיר
אֹהֶל מוֹעֵד לֹא תֵצְאוּ שִׁבְעַת יָמִים עַד יוֹם מְלֹאת יְמֵי מִלֻּאֵיכֶם כִּי
לד שִׁבְעַת יָמִים יְמַלֵּא אֶת־יֶדְכֶם׃ כַּאֲשֶׁר עָשָׂה בַּיּוֹם הַזֶּה צִוָּה יְהוָה
לה לַעֲשֹׂת לְכַפֵּר עֲלֵיכֶם׃ וּפֶתַח אֹהֶל מוֹעֵד תֵּשְׁבוּ יוֹמָם וָלַיְלָה שִׁבְעַת
לו יָמִים וּשְׁמַרְתֶּם אֶת־מִשְׁמֶרֶת יְהוָה וְלֹא תָמוּתוּ כִּי־כֵן צֻוֵּיתִי׃ וַיַּעַשׂ
אַהֲרֹן וּבָנָיו אֵת כָּל־הַדְּבָרִים אֲשֶׁר־צִוָּה יְהוָה בְּיַד־מֹשֶׁה׃

The הפטרה *for* פרשת צו *is on page 1561.*
On the שבת *of* פרשת פרה *read the* הפטרה *on page 1649. On* שבת הגדול *read the* הפטרה *on page 1653.*

אונקלוס

אִנּוּן לְאִתְקַבָּלָא בְּרַעֲוָא, קֻרְבָּנָא הוּא קֳדָם יְיָ: כט וּנְסֵיב מֹשֶׁה יָת חַדְיָא, וַאֲרִימֵיהּ אֲרָמָא קֳדָם יְיָ, מִדְּכַר קֻרְבָּנַיָּא, לְמֹשֶׁה הֲוָה לְחוּלָק, כְּמָא דְּפַקֵּיד יְיָ יָת מֹשֶׁה: ל וּנְסֵיב מֹשֶׁה מִמִּשְׁחָא דִּרְבוּתָא, וּמִן דְּמָא דְּעַל מַדְבְּחָא, וְאַדִּי עַל אַהֲרֹן עַל לְבוּשׁוֹהִי, וְעַל בְּנוֹהִי, וְעַל לְבוּשֵׁי בְנוֹהִי עִמֵּיהּ, וְקַדֵּישׁ יָת אַהֲרֹן יָת לְבוּשׁוֹהִי, וְיָת בְּנוֹהִי, וְיָת לְבוּשֵׁי בְנוֹהִי עִמֵּיהּ: לא וַאֲמַר מֹשֶׁה לְאַהֲרֹן וְלִבְנוֹהִי, בַּשִּׁילוּ יָת בִּסְרָא בִּתְרַע מַשְׁכַּן זִמְנָא, וְתַמָּן תֵּיכְלוּן יָתֵיהּ, וְיָת לַחְמָא, דִּבְסַל קֻרְבָּנַיָּא, כְּמָא דְּפַקֵּידִית לְמֵימַר, אַהֲרֹן וּבְנוֹהִי יֵיכְלֻנֵּיהּ: לב וּדְיִשְׁתְּאַר בְּבִסְרָא וּבְלַחְמָא, בְּנוּרָא תּוֹקְדוּן: לג וּמִתְּרַע מַשְׁכַּן זִמְנָא, לָא תִפְּקוּן שִׁבְעָא יוֹמִין, עַד יוֹם מִשְׁלַם, יוֹמֵי קֻרְבָּנְכוֹן, אֲרֵי שִׁבְעָא יוֹמִין, יִתְקָרַב קֻרְבַּנְכוֹן: לד כְּמָא דַּעֲבַד בְּיוֹמָא הָדֵין, פַּקֵּיד יְיָ, לְמֶעְבַּד לְכַפָּרָא עֲלֵיכוֹן: לה וּבִתְרַע מַשְׁכַּן זִמְנָא, תִּתְּבוּן יֵימָם וְלֵילֵי שִׁבְעָא יוֹמִין, וְתִטְּרוּן, יָת מַטְּרַת מֵימְרָא דַּייָ וְלָא תְמוּתוּן, אֲרֵי כֵן אִתְפַּקֵּדִית: לו וַעֲבַד אַהֲרֹן וּבְנוֹהִי, יָת כָּל פִּתְגָּמַיָּא, דְּפַקֵּיד יְיָ בִּידָא דְמֹשֶׁה:

JUSTICE AND OBEDIENCE

We have not had the sacrificial service since the destruction of the Second Temple almost two thousand years ago. What is deeply relevant today, however, is the *critique* of sacrifices we find among the prophets of the First Temple. That critique was sharp and deep and formed many of their most powerful addresses including the *haftara* for Parashat Tzav.

Strongest of all is the beginning of the book of Isaiah, read on *Shabbat Ḥazon* (before the Ninth of Av): "'Why,' says the Lord, 'would I want all these offerings? I am sated with burnt offerings, with rams and fleshy creatures' fat, the blood of bulls and sheep and goats – I do not want them. You come, appear before Me. Who asked all this of you, who asked you for all this: trampling My courtyards? Bring no more your empty gifts – they are foul incense to Me'" (Is. 1:11–13).

This entire line of thought, sustained across centuries,

PARASHAT SHEMINI

9 1 On the eighth day, Moshe called to Aharon and his sons, and to the elders of
2 Israel. "Take a bull calf for yourself as a purification offering," he told Aharon,
"and a ram for a burnt offering, both without blemish, and offer them up before
3 the LORD. Then tell the Israelites: Take a goat for a purification offering, and
4 a calf and a lamb, both yearlings without blemish, for a burnt offering, a bull
and a ram for a peace offering to offer up before the LORD, and a grain offering
5 mixed with oil – for on this day the LORD will be revealed to you." They brought
what Moshe had commanded to the space before the Tent of Meeting, and all
6 the community drew near and stood before the LORD. Moshe said, "This is
what the LORD has commanded you to do so that the LORD's glory be revealed

רש״י

ט א| וַיְהִי בַּיּוֹם הַשְּׁמִינִי. לַמִּלּוּאִים, הוּא רֹאשׁ חֹדֶשׁ נִיסָן, שֶׁהוּקַם הַמִּשְׁכָּן בּוֹ בַּיּוֹם, וְנָטַל עֶשֶׂר עֲטָרוֹת הַשְּׁנוּיוֹת בְּסֵדֶר עוֹלָם: וּלְזִקְנֵי יִשְׂרָאֵל. לְהַשְׁמִיעָם שֶׁעַל פִּי הַדִּבּוּר אַהֲרֹן נִכְנָס וּמְשַׁמֵּשׁ בִּכְהֻנָּה גְּדוֹלָה, וְלֹא יֹאמְרוּ: מֵאֵלָיו נִכְנָס:

ב| קַח לְךָ עֵגֶל. לְהוֹדִיעַ שֶׁמְּכַפֵּר לוֹ הַקָּדוֹשׁ בָּרוּךְ הוּא עַל יְדֵי עֵגֶל זֶה עַל מַעֲשֵׂה הָעֵגֶל שֶׁעָשָׂה:

ד| כִּי הַיּוֹם ה׳ נִרְאָה אֲלֵיכֶם. לְהַשְׁרוֹת שְׁכִינָתוֹ בְּמַעֲשֵׂה יְדֵיכֶם, לְכָךְ קָרְבָּנוֹת הַלָּלוּ בָּאִין חוֹבָה לְיוֹם זֶה:

each other and produce light for his needs. (Bereshit Rabba 12:6)

There is a fundamental difference between the light of the first day ("God said, 'Let there be light'" [Gen. 1:3]) and that of the eighth day. The light of the first day was created by God. The light of the eighth day is what God taught us to create. It symbolizes our "partnership with God in the work of creation" (Shabbat 10a, 119b). On the Sabbath we remember God's creation. On the eighth day (Motza'ei Shabbat) we celebrate our creativity as the image and partner of God. (This, according to the Sages, is the reason we light a *Havdala* candle at the end of the Sabbath to inaugurate the new week (Pesikta Rabbati 23).

We believe that God wants human beings to exercise power responsibly, creatively, and within limits set by the integrity of nature. The rabbinic account of how God taught Adam and Ḥava the secret of making fire is the precise opposite of the Greek myth of Prometheus, who stole the spark of fire that Zeus wanted to keep as a divine secret. God seeks to confer dignity on the beings He made in His image as an act of love. He does not hide the secrets of the universe from us. The creative God empowers us to be creative and begins by teaching us how. That is the symbolism of the eighth day.

We now understand the symbolic significance of the eighth day in relation to the Tabernacle. As we have noted elsewhere, the linguistic parallels in the Torah show that the construction of the Tabernacle in the wilderness mirrors the divine creation of the world. The Tabernacle was intended to be a miniature universe, constructed by human beings. Just as God made the earth as a home for mankind, so the Israelites in the wilderness built the Tabernacle as a symbolic home for God.

Thus the day it begins is, figuratively as well as literally, the eighth day. If the first day represents divine creation, the eighth day signifies human creation under the tutelage and sovereignty of God.

פרשת שמיני

ט א ב וַיְהִי בַּיּוֹם הַשְּׁמִינִי קָרָא מֹשֶׁה לְאַהֲרֹן וּלְבָנָיו וּלְזִקְנֵי יִשְׂרָאֵל: וַיֹּאמֶר
אֶל־אַהֲרֹן קַח־לְךָ עֵגֶל בֶּן־בָּקָר לְחַטָּאת וְאַיִל לְעֹלָה תְּמִימִם וְהַקְרֵב
ג לִפְנֵי יהוה: וְאֶל־בְּנֵי יִשְׂרָאֵל תְּדַבֵּר לֵאמֹר קְחוּ שְׂעִיר־עִזִּים לְחַטָּאת
ד וְעֵגֶל וָכֶבֶשׂ בְּנֵי־שָׁנָה תְּמִימִם לְעֹלָה: וְשׁוֹר וָאַיִל לִשְׁלָמִים לִזְבֹּחַ לִפְנֵי
ה יהוה וּמִנְחָה בְּלוּלָה בַשָּׁמֶן כִּי הַיּוֹם יהוה נִרְאָה אֲלֵיכֶם: וַיִּקְחוּ אֵת
אֲשֶׁר צִוָּה מֹשֶׁה אֶל־פְּנֵי אֹהֶל מוֹעֵד וַיִּקְרְבוּ כָּל־הָעֵדָה וַיַּעַמְדוּ לִפְנֵי
ו יהוה: וַיֹּאמֶר מֹשֶׁה זֶה הַדָּבָר אֲשֶׁר־צִוָּה יהוה תַּעֲשׂוּ וְיֵרָא אֲלֵיכֶם

אונקלוס

ט א והוה ביומא תמינאה, קרא משה, לאהרן ולבנוהי, ולסבי ישראל: ב ואמר לאהרן, סב לך, עיגל בר תורי לחטתא, ודכר לעלתא שלמין, וקריב קדם יי: ג ועם בני ישראל תמליל למימר, סבו צפיר בר עזין לחטתא, ועיגל ואמר בני שנא, שלמין לעלתא: ד ותור ודכר לנכסת קודשיא, לדבחא קדם יי, ומנחתא דפילא במשח, ארי יומא דין, יקרא דיי מתגלי לכון: ה וקריבו, ית דפקיד משה, לקדם משכן זמנא, וקריבו כל כנשתא, וקמו קדם יי: ו ואמר משה, דין פתגמא, דפקיד יי תעבדון, ויתגלי לכון יקרא דיי: ו ואמר משה

SHEMINI

Parashat Shemini tells the story of the inauguration of the Tabernacle. For many chapters we have read of the preparations for the moment at which God would bring His presence to rest in the midst of the people. Five *parashot* (Teruma, Tetzaveh, Ki Tisa, Vayak'hel, and Pekudei) describe the instructions for building the Sanctuary. Two (Vayikra, Tzav) detail the sacrificial offerings to be brought there. All is now ready. For seven days, beginning on the twenty-third of Adar, Moshe consecrated Aharon and the priests. Now, on Rosh Ḥodesh Nisan, the eighth day, the time has come for Aharon to begin his service, ministering to the people on behalf of God. This is the day about which the Sages say that God rejoiced as much as He had at the creation of the universe (Megilla 10b). Yet the celebration is overshadowed by the shocking deaths of two of Aharon's sons, Nadav and Avihu, who offered an "unauthorized fire" (Lev. 10:1) at the inauguration ceremony.

The second half of the *parasha* details the dietary laws, a list of permitted and forbidden species, animals, fish, and birds. Why are these laws placed here? We shall see that in fact they have a deep connection to the Sanctuary.

THE EIGHTH DAY

To understand the symbolism of the "eighth day," the phrase that gives this *parasha* its name, let us go back to creation itself, more specifically to the conclusion of the first Sabbath. The Midrash tells us:

> With the going out of the Sabbath, the celestial light began to fade. Adam was afraid that the serpent would attack him in the dark. Therefore, God illuminated his understanding, and he learned to rub two stones against

7 to you." Moshe said to Aharon, "Approach the altar, prepare your purification
offering and burnt offering, and make atonement for you and for the people.
Then prepare the people's offering to make atonement for them, as the LORD
8 has commanded." Aharon drew close to the altar and slaughtered the calf of
9 his purification offering. Aharon's sons presented him with the blood, and he
dipped his finger into it and applied the blood to the horns of the altar; the
10 rest of the blood he poured out at the altar's base. Then he sent the fat, the
kidneys, and the diaphragm of the liver from the purification offering up in
11 smoke upon the altar as the LORD had commanded Moshe, and he burned
12 the flesh and skin with fire outside the camp. Then he slaughtered the burnt
offering. Aharon's sons presented him with the blood, and he dashed it on each
13 side of the altar. Then they presented him with the burnt offering in its pieces,
14 with its head, and he sent them up in smoke upon the altar. Having washed
the entrails and legs, he sent them up in smoke upon the altar with the burnt
15 offering. Then he brought close the people's offering. He took the goat of the
people's purification offering, slaughtered it, and prepared it as a purification
16 offering like the first. He presented the burnt offering and sacrificed it in the
17 prescribed way. He then presented the grain offering, took a handful from it, SHENI
and sent this portion up in smoke upon the altar, with the morning's burnt

רש״י

ז | קְרַב אֶל הַמִּזְבֵּחַ. שֶׁהָיָה אַהֲרֹן בּוֹשׁ וְיָרֵא לָגֶשֶׁת, אָמַר לוֹ מֹשֶׁה: לָמָּה אַתָּה בּוֹשׁ? לְכָךְ נִבְחַרְתָּ: אֶת חַטָּאתְךָ. עֵגֶל בֶּן בָּקָר: וְאֶת עֹלָתֶךָ. אַיִל: קָרְבַּן הָעָם. שְׂעִיר עִזִּים וְעֵגֶל וָכֶבֶשׂ. כָּל מָקוֹם שֶׁנֶּאֱמַר 'עֵגֶל' בֶּן שָׁנָה הוּא, וּמִכָּאן אַתָּה לָמֵד:

יא | וְאֶת הַבָּשָׂר וְאֶת הָעוֹר וְגוֹ׳. לֹא מָצִינוּ חַטָּאת חִיצוֹנָה נִשְׂרֶפֶת אֶלָּא זוֹ וְשֶׁל מִלּוּאִים (שמות כט, יד), וְכֻלָּן עַל פִּי הַדִּבֵּר:

יב | וַיַּמְצִאוּ. לְשׁוֹן הוֹשָׁטָה וְהַזְמָנָה:

טו | וַיְחַטְּאֵהוּ. עָשָׂהוּ כְּמִשְׁפַּט חַטָּאת: כָּרִאשׁוֹן. כָּעֵגֶל שֶׁלּוֹ:

טז | וַיַּעֲשֶׂהָ כַּמִּשְׁפָּט. הַמְפֹרָשׁ בְּעוֹלַת נְדָבָה בְּ׳וַיִּקְרָא׳ (לעיל פרק א):

יז | וַיְמַלֵּא כַפּוֹ. הִיא קְמִיצָה: מִלְּבַד עֹלַת הַבֹּקֶר. כָּל אֵלֶּה עָשָׂה אַחַר עוֹלַת הַתָּמִיד:

to the Divine Presence. The second is that Aharon, seeing the "horns" of the altar, is reminded of the golden calf, his great sin. How could he, who played a key role in that terrible event, now take on the role of atoning for the people's sins? Moshe has to remind him that it is precisely to atone for sins that the altar was made; the fact that he had been chosen by God to be High Priest is an unequivocal sign that he has been forgiven.

There is perhaps a third explanation. Until now Aharon has been in all respects second to Moshe. Yes, he had been at his side throughout, helping him speak and lead. But there is a vast psychological difference between being second-in-command and being a leader in your own right. We probably all know of examples of people who quite readily serve in an assisting capacity but who are terrified at the prospect of leading on their own.

Whichever explanation is true – and perhaps they all are – Aharon is reticent at taking on his new role, and Moshe has to give him the confidence to step forward. "This," he therefore tells him, "is what you have been chosen to do."

ז כְּבוֹד יְהוָה: וַיֹּאמֶר מֹשֶׁה אֶל־אַהֲרֹן קְרַב אֶל־הַמִּזְבֵּחַ וַעֲשֵׂה אֶת־
חַטָּאתְךָ וְאֶת־עֹלָתֶךָ וְכַפֵּר בַּעַדְךָ וּבְעַד הָעָם וַעֲשֵׂה אֶת־קָרְבַּן הָעָם
ח וְכַפֵּר בַּעֲדָם כַּאֲשֶׁר צִוָּה יְהוָה: וַיִּקְרַב אַהֲרֹן אֶל־הַמִּזְבֵּחַ וַיִּשְׁחַט
ט אֶת־עֵגֶל הַחַטָּאת אֲשֶׁר־לוֹ: וַיַּקְרִבוּ בְּנֵי אַהֲרֹן אֶת־הַדָּם אֵלָיו וַיִּטְבֹּל
אֶצְבָּעוֹ בַּדָּם וַיִּתֵּן עַל־קַרְנוֹת הַמִּזְבֵּחַ וְאֶת־הַדָּם יָצַק אֶל־יְסוֹד
י הַמִּזְבֵּחַ: וְאֶת־הַחֵלֶב וְאֶת־הַכְּלָיֹת וְאֶת־הַיֹּתֶרֶת מִן־הַכָּבֵד מִן־
יא הַחַטָּאת הִקְטִיר הַמִּזְבֵּחָה כַּאֲשֶׁר צִוָּה יְהוָה אֶת־מֹשֶׁה: וְאֶת־הַבָּשָׂר
יב וְאֶת־הָעוֹר שָׂרַף בָּאֵשׁ מִחוּץ לַמַּחֲנֶה: וַיִּשְׁחַט אֶת־הָעֹלָה וַיַּמְצִאוּ בְּנֵי
יג אַהֲרֹן אֵלָיו אֶת־הַדָּם וַיִּזְרְקֵהוּ עַל־הַמִּזְבֵּחַ סָבִיב: וְאֶת־הָעֹלָה הִמְצִיאוּ
יד אֵלָיו לִנְתָחֶיהָ וְאֶת־הָרֹאשׁ וַיַּקְטֵר עַל־הַמִּזְבֵּחַ: וַיִּרְחַץ אֶת־הַקֶּרֶב
טו וְאֶת־הַכְּרָעָיִם וַיַּקְטֵר עַל־הָעֹלָה הַמִּזְבֵּחָה: וַיַּקְרֵב אֵת קָרְבַּן הָעָם
וַיִּקַּח אֶת־שְׂעִיר הַחַטָּאת אֲשֶׁר לָעָם וַיִּשְׁחָטֵהוּ וַיְחַטְּאֵהוּ כָּרִאשׁוֹן:
טז יז וַיַּקְרֵב אֶת־הָעֹלָה וַיַּעֲשֶׂהָ כַּמִּשְׁפָּט: וַיַּקְרֵב אֶת־הַמִּנְחָה וַיְמַלֵּא כַפּוֹ שני

אונקלוס

לְאַהֲרֹן, קְרַב לְמַדְבְּחָא וַעֲבֵיד, יָת חַטָּתָךְ וְיָת עֲלָתָךְ, וְכַפַּר עֲלָךְ וְעַל עַמָּא, וַעֲבֵיד, יָת קֻרְבַּן עַמָּא וְכַפַּר עֲלֵיהוֹן, כְּמָא דְּפַקֵּיד יי: ח וּקְרֵב אַהֲרֹן לְמַדְבְּחָא, וּנְכַס, יָת עִגְלָא דְּחַטָּתָא דִּילֵיהּ: ט וְקָרִיבוּ, בְּנֵי אַהֲרֹן יָת דְּמָא לֵיהּ, וּטְבַל אֶצְבְּעֵיהּ בִּדְמָא, וִיהַב עַל קַרְנָת מַדְבְּחָא, וְיָת דְּמָא אֲרֵיק, לִיסוֹדָא דְּמַדְבְּחָא: י וְיָת תַּרְבָּא וְיָת כּוֹלְיָתָא, וְיָת חַצְרָא מִן כַּבְדָּא מִן חַטָּתָא, אַסֵּיק לְמַדְבְּחָא, כְּמָא דְּפַקֵּיד יי יָת מֹשֶׁה: יא וְיָת בִּסְרָא וְיָת מַשְׁכָּא, אוֹקֵיד בְּנוּרָא, מִבַּרָא לְמַשְׁרִיתָא: יב וּנְכַס יָת עֲלָתָא, וְאַמְטִיאוּ, בְּנֵי אַהֲרֹן לֵיהּ יָת דְּמָא, וּזְרָקֵיהּ עַל מַדְבְּחָא סְחוֹר סְחוֹר: יג וְיָת עֲלָתָא, אַמְטִיאוּ לֵיהּ, לְאֶבְרָהָא וְיָת רֵישָׁא, וְאַסֵּיק עַל מַדְבְּחָא: יד וְחַלִּיל יָת גַּוָּא וְיָת כְּרָעַיָּא, וְאַסֵּיק עַל עֲלָתָא לְמַדְבְּחָא: טו וְקָרֵיב, יָת קֻרְבַּן עַמָּא, וּנְסֵיב, יָת צְפִירָא דְּחַטָּתָא דִּלְעַמָּא, וּנְכַסֵיהּ וְכַפַּר בִּדְמֵיהּ כְּקַדְמָאָה: טז וְקָרֵיב יָת עֲלָתָא, וַעֲבַדַהּ כִּדְחָזֵי: יז וְקָרֵיב יָת מִנְחָתָא, וּמְלָא יְדֵיהּ

9:7 קְרַב אֶל־הַמִּזְבֵּחַ *Approach the altar* – The Sages sense a nuance in the words "Approach the altar," as if Aharon were standing at a distance from it, reluctant to come near. They said: "Initially Aharon was ashamed to come close. Moshe said to him, 'Do not be ashamed. This is what you have been chosen to do'" (Rashi on Lev. 9:7, quoting Sifra, Shemini 9:8).

Why is Aharon ashamed? Tradition gives two explanations, both brought by Ramban (on Lev. 9:7). The first is that Aharon is overwhelmed by trepidation at coming so close

18 offering. He slaughtered the ox and the ram: the people's peace sacrifice.
Aharon's sons presented him with the blood, and he dashed it against each side
19 of the altar, and the fat parts of the ox and ram: the broad tail, the covering
20 fat, the kidneys, and the diaphragm of the liver. They laid the fat parts over
21 the breasts, and he sent them up in smoke upon the altar. But the breasts and
right thigh Aharon displayed, this way and that, as a wave offering before the
22 LORD, as Moshe had commanded. Then Aharon raised his hands to the people
and blessed them. And, having presented the purification offering, the burnt
23 offering, and the peace sacrifice, he stepped down. Moshe and Aharon entered
the Tent of Meeting; when they came out, they blessed the people, and the
24 glory of the LORD was revealed to all the people. And from before the LORD, SHELISHI
fire came forth. It consumed the burnt offering and the fat pieces on the altar;
and all the people saw it, and cried out for joy, and threw themselves facedown
10 1 upon the ground. Aharon's sons Nadav and Avihu took their fire pans, put fire
in them, and placed incense upon it, and they offered unauthorized fire before

רש״י

יט| **וְהַמְכַסֶּה.** חֵלֶב הַמְכַסֶּה אֶת הַקֶּרֶב:

כ| **וַיָּשִׂימוּ אֶת הַחֲלָבִים עַל הֶחָזוֹת.** לְאַחַר הַתְּנוּפָה נְתָנָן כֹּהֵן הַמֵּנִיף לְכֹהֵן אַחֵר לְהַקְטִירָם, נִמְצְאוּ הָעֶלְיוֹנִים לְמַטָּה:

כב| **וַיְבָרְכֵם.** בִּרְכַּת כֹּהֲנִים: יְבָרֶכְךָ, יָאֵר, יִשָּׂא: **וַיֵּרֶד.** מֵעַל הַמִּזְבֵּחַ:

כג| **וַיָּבֹא מֹשֶׁה וְאַהֲרֹן.** לָמָּה נִכְנְסוּ? מָצָאתִי בְּפָרָשַׁת מִלּוּאִים בַּבָּרַיְתָא הַנּוֹסֶפֶת עַל תּוֹרַת כֹּהֲנִים שֶׁלָּנוּ (מכילתא דמלואים, פרשתא א, ל): לָמָּה נִכְנַס מֹשֶׁה עִם אַהֲרֹן? לְלַמְּדוֹ עַל מַעֲשֵׂה הַקְּטֹרֶת. אוֹ לֹא נִכְנַס אֶלָּא לְדָבָר אַחֵר? הֲרֵינִי דָּן: יְרִידָה וּבִיאָה טְעוּנוֹת בְּרָכָה, מַה יְּרִידָה מֵעֵין עֲבוֹדָה, אַף בִּיאָה מֵעֵין עֲבוֹדָה, הָא לָמַדְתָּ, לָמָּה נִכְנַס מֹשֶׁה עִם אַהֲרֹן – לְלַמְּדוֹ עַל מַעֲשֵׂה הַקְּטֹרֶת. דָּבָר אַחֵר, כֵּיוָן שֶׁרָאָה אַהֲרֹן שֶׁקָּרְבוּ כָּל הַקָּרְבָּנוֹת וְנַעֲשׂוּ כָּל הַמַּעֲשִׂים וְלֹא יָרְדָה שְׁכִינָה לְיִשְׂרָאֵל, הָיָה מִצְטַעֵר וְאוֹמֵר: יוֹדֵעַ אֲנִי שֶׁכָּעַס הַקָּדוֹשׁ בָּרוּךְ הוּא עָלַי וּבִשְׁבִילִי לֹא יָרְדָה שְׁכִינָה לְיִשְׂרָאֵל. אָמַר לוֹ לְמֹשֶׁה: מֹשֶׁה אָחִי, כָּךְ עָשִׂיתָ לִי, שֶׁנִּכְנַסְתִּי וְנִתְבַּיַּשְׁתִּי; מִיָּד נִכְנַס מֹשֶׁה עִמּוֹ וּבִקְּשׁוּ רַחֲמִים וְיָרְדָה שְׁכִינָה לְיִשְׂרָאֵל: **וַיֵּצְאוּ וַיְבָרְכוּ אֶת הָעָם.** אָמְרוּ: ״וִיהִי נֹעַם ה׳ אֱלֹהֵינוּ עָלֵינוּ״ (תהלים צ, יז), יְהִי רָצוֹן שֶׁתִּשְׁרֶה שְׁכִינָה בְּמַעֲשֵׂה יְדֵיכֶם; לְפִי שֶׁכָּל שִׁבְעַת יְמֵי הַמִּלּוּאִים שֶׁהֶעֱמִידוֹ מֹשֶׁה לַמִּשְׁכָּן וְשִׁמֵּשׁ בּוֹ וּפֵרְקוֹ בְּכָל יוֹם, לֹא שָׁרְתָה בּוֹ שְׁכִינָה, וְהָיוּ יִשְׂרָאֵל נִכְלָמִים וְאוֹמְרִים לְמֹשֶׁה: מֹשֶׁה רַבֵּנוּ, כָּל הַטֹּרַח שֶׁטָּרַחְנוּ שֶׁתִּשְׁרֶה שְׁכִינָה בֵּינֵינוּ וְנֵדַע שֶׁנִּתְכַּפֵּר לָנוּ עֲוֹן הָעֵגֶל, לְכָךְ אָמַר לָהֶם: ״זֶה הַדָּבָר אֲשֶׁר צִוָּה ה׳ תַּעֲשׂוּ וְיֵרָא אֲלֵיכֶם כְּבוֹד ה׳״ (לעיל פסוק ו), אַהֲרֹן אָחִי כְּדַאי וְחָשׁוּב מִמֶּנִּי, שֶׁעַל יְדֵי קָרְבְּנוֹתָיו וַעֲבוֹדָתוֹ תִּשְׁרֶה שְׁכִינָה בָּכֶם, וְתֵדְעוּ שֶׁהַמָּקוֹם בָּחַר בּוֹ:

כד| **וַיָּרֹנּוּ.** כְּתַרְגּוּמוֹ:

The word *olam*, "universe," is semantically linked to the word *ne'elam*, "hidden." *Creation involves concealment*. To give mankind some of his own creative powers – the use of language to think, communicate, understand, imagine alternative futures, and choose between them – God must do more than create *Homo sapiens*. He must efface Himself (what the kabbalists called *tzimtzum*) to create space for human action. No other act more profoundly indicates the love and generosity implicit in creation. God as we encounter Him in the Torah is like a parent who knows He must hold back, let go, refrain from intervening, if His children are to become responsible and mature.

However, to be true to God's purposes, there must be times and places at which humanity experiences the reality of the Divine. The holy is that segment of time and space God has reserved for His presence. Those times and

יח מִמֶּנָּה וַיַּקְטֵר עַל־הַמִּזְבֵּחַ מִלְּבַד עֹלַת הַבֹּקֶר: וַיִּשְׁחַט אֶת־הַשּׁוֹר
וְאֶת־הָאַיִל זֶבַח הַשְּׁלָמִים אֲשֶׁר לָעָם וַיַּמְצִאוּ בְּנֵי אַהֲרֹן אֶת־הַדָּם
יט אֵלָיו וַיִּזְרְקֵהוּ עַל־הַמִּזְבֵּחַ סָבִיב: וְאֶת־הַחֲלָבִים מִן־הַשּׁוֹר וּמִן־הָאַיִל
כ הָאַלְיָה וְהַמְכַסֶּה וְהַכְּלָיֹת וְיֹתֶרֶת הַכָּבֵד: וַיָּשִׂימוּ אֶת־הַחֲלָבִים עַל־
כא הֶחָזוֹת וַיַּקְטֵר הַחֲלָבִים הַמִּזְבֵּחָה: וְאֵת הֶחָזוֹת וְאֵת שׁוֹק הַיָּמִין הֵנִיף
כב אַהֲרֹן תְּנוּפָה לִפְנֵי יהוה כַּאֲשֶׁר צִוָּה מֹשֶׁה: וַיִּשָּׂא אַהֲרֹן אֶת־יָדָו אֶל־
כג הָעָם וַיְבָרְכֵם וַיֵּרֶד מֵעֲשֹׂת הַחַטָּאת וְהָעֹלָה וְהַשְּׁלָמִים: וַיָּבֹא מֹשֶׁה
וְאַהֲרֹן אֶל־אֹהֶל מוֹעֵד וַיֵּצְאוּ וַיְבָרְכוּ אֶת־הָעָם וַיֵּרָא כְבוֹד־יהוה
כד אֶל־כָּל־הָעָם: וַתֵּצֵא אֵשׁ מִלִּפְנֵי יהוה וַתֹּאכַל עַל־הַמִּזְבֵּחַ אֶת־הָעֹלָה שלישי
י א וְאֶת־הַחֲלָבִים וַיַּרְא כָּל־הָעָם וַיָּרֹנּוּ וַיִּפְּלוּ עַל־פְּנֵיהֶם: וַיִּקְחוּ בְנֵי־אַהֲרֹן
נָדָב וַאֲבִיהוּא אִישׁ מַחְתָּתוֹ וַיִּתְּנוּ בָהֵן אֵשׁ וַיָּשִׂימוּ עָלֶיהָ קְטֹרֶת

אונקלוס

מִנַּהּ, וְאַסֵּיק עַל מַדְבְּחָא, בַּר מֵעֲלַת צַפְרָא: יח וּנְכַס יָת תּוֹרָא וְיָת דִּכְרָא, נִכְסַת קֻדְשַׁיָּא דִּלְעַמָּא, וְאַמְטִיאוּ, בְּנֵי אַהֲרֹן יָת דְּמָא לֵיהּ, וּזְרָקֵיהּ עַל מַדְבְּחָא סְחוֹר סְחוֹר: יט וְיָת תַּרְבַּיָּא מִן תּוֹרָא, וּמִן דִּכְרָא, אַלִּיְתָא וְחָפֵי גַוָּא וְכוֹלְיָתָא, וַחֲצַר כַּבְדָּא: כ וְשַׁוִּיאוּ יָת תַּרְבַּיָּא עַל חַדְוָתָא, וְאַסֵּיק תַּרְבַּיָּא לְמַדְבְּחָא: כא וְיָת חַדְוָתָא, וְיָת שָׁקָא דְּיַמִּינָא, אֲרֵים אַהֲרֹן, אֲרָמָא קֳדָם יי, כְּמָא דְּפַקֵּיד מֹשֶׁה: כב וַאֲרֵים אַהֲרֹן יָת יְדוֹהִי, לְעַמָּא וּבָרֵיכִנּוּן, וּנְחַת, מִלְּמֶעְבַּד חַטָּתָא, וַעֲלָתָא וְנִכְסַת קֻדְשַׁיָּא: כג וְעָאל מֹשֶׁה וְאַהֲרֹן לְמַשְׁכַּן זִמְנָא, וּנְפַקוּ, וּבָרִיכוּ יָת עַמָּא, וְאִתְגְּלִי יְקָרָא דַּיי לְכָל עַמָּא: כד וּנְפַקַת אִישָׁתָא מִן קֳדָם יי, וַאֲכַלַת עַל מַדְבְּחָא, יָת עֲלָתָא וְיָת תַּרְבַּיָּא, וַחֲזָא כָּל עַמָּא וְשַׁבַּחוּ, וּנְפַלוּ עַל אַפֵּיהוֹן: י א וּנְסִיבוּ בְנֵי אַהֲרֹן, נָדָב וַאֲבִיהוּא גְּבַר מַחְתִּיתֵיהּ, וִיהַבוּ בְהוֹן אִישָׁתָא, וְשַׁוִּיאוּ עֲלַהּ קְטֹרֶת בֻּסְמִין,

NADAV AND AVIHU

Celebration turns to tragedy when the two eldest sons of Aharon die. The shock is immense. The Sages and commentators offer many explanations. Nadav and Avihu die because: they enter the Holy of Holies (Tanḥuma, Buber, Aḥarei Mot 7); they are not wearing the requisite clothes (Vayikra Rabba 20:9); they take fire from the kitchen, not the altar (Tanḥuma ad loc.); they do not consult Moshe and Aharon (*Yalkut Shimoni* 1:524); nor do they consult one another (Tanḥuma ad loc.). According to some they are guilty of hubris. They are impatient to assume leadership roles themselves (Aggada, Buber, Vayikra 10); and they have not married, considering themselves above such things (Vayikra Rabba 20:10). Yet others see their deaths as delayed punishment for an earlier sin, when at Mount Sinai "they ate and they drank" in the presence of God (Ex. 24:9–11).

The explanation explicit in the Torah itself is that Nadav and Avihu died because they offered unauthorized – literally, "strange" – fire, meaning "fire He had not commanded" (Lev. 10:1). To understand the significance of this, we must remind ourselves of the meaning of *kadosh*, "holy," and thus of *mikdash* as the home of the holy, and of its place in the world.

▶

2 the LORD: fire He had not commanded. And fire came forth from before the
3 LORD and consumed them. They died before the LORD. Moshe said to Aharon,
"Of this the LORD spoke when He said: I will be sanctified through those close
to Me, and before all the people I will be honored." And Aharon was silent.
4 Moshe called to Mishael and Eltzafan, sons of Uziel, Aharon's uncle; "Draw
near," he said, "carry your kinsmen from the Sanctuary and take them outside
5 the camp." They approached and, as Moshe had instructed them, they carried

רש״י

י ב **וַתֵּצֵא אֵשׁ.** רַבִּי אֱלִיעֶזֶר אוֹמֵר: לֹא מֵתוּ בְּנֵי אַהֲרֹן אֶלָּא עַל יְדֵי שֶׁהוֹרוּ הֲלָכָה בִּפְנֵי מֹשֶׁה רַבָּן. רַבִּי יִשְׁמָעֵאל אוֹמֵר: שְׁתוּיֵי יַיִן נִכְנְסוּ לַמִּקְדָּשׁ; תֵּדַע, שֶׁאַחַר מִיתָתָן הִזְהִיר הַנּוֹתָרִים שֶׁלֹּא יִכָּנְסוּ שְׁתוּיֵי יַיִן לַמִּקְדָּשׁ. מָשָׁל לְמֶלֶךְ שֶׁהָיָה לוֹ בֶּן בַּיִת וְכוּ׳ [נאמן, מצאו עומד על פתח חנויות והתיז את ראשו בשתיקה, ומינה בן בית אחר תחתיו, ואין אנו יודעים מפני מה הרג את הראשון, אלא ממה שמצוה את השני ואמר לא תכנס בפתח חנויות, אנו יודעין שמתוך כך הרג הראשון], כִּדְאִיתָא בְּוַיִּקְרָא רַבָּה (יב, א):

ג **הוּא אֲשֶׁר דִּבֶּר וְגוֹ׳.** הֵיכָן דִּבֵּר? "וְנֹעַדְתִּי שָׁמָּה לִבְנֵי יִשְׂרָאֵל וְנִקְדַּשׁ בִּכְבֹדִי" (שמות כט, מג), אַל תִּקְרֵי ׳בִּכְבֹדִי׳ אֶלָּא ׳בִּמְכֻבָּדַי׳. אָמַר לוֹ מֹשֶׁה לְאַהֲרֹן: אַהֲרֹן אָחִי, יוֹדֵעַ הָיִיתִי שֶׁיִּתְקַדֵּשׁ הַבַּיִת בִּמְיֻדָּעָיו שֶׁל מָקוֹם, וְהָיִיתִי סָבוּר אוֹ בִּי אוֹ בְּךָ, עַכְשָׁיו רוֹאֶה אֲנִי שֶׁהֵם גְּדוֹלִים מִמֶּנִּי וּמִמְּךָ:

וַיִּדֹּם אַהֲרֹן. וְקִבֵּל שָׂכָר עַל שְׁתִיקָתוֹ, וּמַה שָּׂכָר קִבֵּל? שֶׁנִּתְיַחֵד עִמּוֹ הַדִּבּוּר, שֶׁנֶּאֶמְרָה לוֹ לְבַדּוֹ פָּרָשַׁת שְׁתוּיֵי יַיִן: **בִּקְרֹבַי.** בִּבְחִירַי: **וְעַל פְּנֵי כָל הָעָם אֶכָּבֵד.** כְּשֶׁהַקָּדוֹשׁ בָּרוּךְ הוּא עוֹשֶׂה דִּין בַּצַּדִּיקִים, מִתְיָרֵא וּמִתְעַלֶּה וּמִתְקַלֵּס; אִם כֵּן בְּאֵלּוּ, כָּל שֶׁכֵּן בָּרְשָׁעִים. וְכֵן הוּא אוֹמֵר: "נוֹרָא אֱלֹהִים מִמִּקְדָּשֶׁיךָ" (תהלים סח, לו), אַל תִּקְרֵי ׳מִמִּקְדָּשֶׁיךָ׳, אֶלָּא ׳מִמְּקֻדָּשֶׁיךָ׳:

ד **דֹּד אַהֲרֹן.** עֻזִּיאֵל אֲחִי עַמְרָם הָיָה, שֶׁנֶּאֱמַר: "וּבְנֵי קְהָת" וְגוֹ׳ (שמות ו, יח): **שְׂאוּ אֶת אֲחֵיכֶם וְגוֹ׳.** כְּאָדָם הָאוֹמֵר לַחֲבֵרוֹ: הַעֲבֵר אֶת הַמֵּת מִלִּפְנֵי הַכַּלָּה, שֶׁלֹּא לְעַרְבֵּב אֶת הַשִּׂמְחָה:

ה **בְּכֻתֳּנֹתָם.** שֶׁל מֵתִים, מְלַמֵּד שֶׁלֹּא נִשְׂרְפוּ בִּגְדֵיהֶם אֶלָּא נִשְׁמָתָם, כְּמִין שְׁנֵי חוּטִין שֶׁל אֵשׁ נִכְנְסוּ לְתוֹךְ חָטְמֵיהֶם:

Why then is spontaneity wrong for Nadav and Avihu, but right for Moshe? Prophecy and priesthood involve different tasks, different sensibilities. The priest serves God in a way that never changes over time (except of course when the Temple was destroyed and its service, presided over by the priests, came to an end). The prophet serves God in a way that is constantly changing. When people are at ease, the prophet warns of forthcoming catastrophe. When they suffer and are in the depths of despair, the prophets bring consolation and hope.

The words said by the priest are always the same. The priestly blessing uses the same words today as it did in the days of Moshe and Aharon. But the words used by the prophet are never the same. "No two prophets use the same style" (Sanhedrin 89a). For a prophet, spontaneity is of the essence. But for the priest engaged in divine service, it is out of place.

10:3 **וַיִּדֹּם אַהֲרֹן** *Aharon was silent* – Moshe tries to comfort his brother, who has lost two of his sons. He tells him that God has said, "I will be sanctified through those close to Me" (Lev. 10:3). According to Rashi, he is saying, "Now I see that they [Nadav and Avihu] were greater than you and me." The holier the person, the more demanding is God with them.

It is as if Moshe were saying to Aharon: "My brother, do not give up now. We have come so far. I know your heart is broken. So is mine. Did we not think – you and I – that our troubles were behind us, that after all we suffered in Egypt, and at the Sea of Reeds, and in the battle against Amalek, and in the sin of the golden calf, we were finally safe and free? And now this has happened. Aharon, don't give up, don't lose faith, don't despair. Your children died not because they were evil but because they were holy. Though their act was wrong, their intentions were good. They merely tried too hard." But despite Moshe's words of consolation, "Aharon was silent," lost in a grief too deep for words.

ב וַיַּקְרִיבוּ לִפְנֵי יהוה אֵשׁ זָרָה אֲשֶׁר לֹא צִוָּה אֹתָם׃ וַתֵּצֵא אֵשׁ מִלִּפְנֵי
ג יהוה וַתֹּאכַל אוֹתָם וַיָּמֻתוּ לִפְנֵי יהוה׃ וַיֹּאמֶר מֹשֶׁה אֶל־אַהֲרֹן הוּא
אֲשֶׁר־דִּבֶּר יהוה ׀ לֵאמֹר בִּקְרֹבַי אֶקָּדֵשׁ וְעַל־פְּנֵי כָל־הָעָם אֶכָּבֵד וַיִּדֹּם
ד אַהֲרֹן׃ וַיִּקְרָא מֹשֶׁה אֶל־מִישָׁאֵל וְאֶל אֶלְצָפָן בְּנֵי עֻזִּיאֵל דֹּד אַהֲרֹן
וַיֹּאמֶר אֲלֵהֶם קִרְבוּ שְׂאוּ אֶת־אֲחֵיכֶם מֵאֵת פְּנֵי־הַקֹּדֶשׁ אֶל־מִחוּץ
ה לַמַּחֲנֶה׃ וַיִּקְרְבוּ וַיִּשָּׂאֻם בְּכֻתֳּנֹתָם אֶל־מִחוּץ לַמַּחֲנֶה כַּאֲשֶׁר דִּבֶּר

אונקלוס

וְקָרִיבוּ, קֳדָם יי אִישָּׁתָא נֻכְרֵיתָא, דְּלָא פַּקֵּיד יָתְהוֹן: ב וּנְפַקַת אִישָּׁתָא, מִן קֳדָם יי וַאֲכַלַת יָתְהוֹן, וּמִיתוּ קֳדָם יי: ג וַאֲמַר מֹשֶׁה לְאַהֲרֹן, הוּא דְּמַלֵּיל יי לְמֵימַר בְּקָרִיבַי אֶתְקַדַּשׁ, וְעַל אַפֵּי כָל עַמָּא אֶתְיַקַּר, וּשְׁתֵיק אַהֲרֹן: ד וּקְרָא מֹשֶׁה, לְמִישָׁאֵל וּלְאֶלְצָפָן, בְּנֵי עֻזִּיאֵל אַחְבּוּהִי דְּאַהֲרֹן, וַאֲמַר לְהוֹן, קְרֻבוּ, טוּלוּ יָת אֲחֵיכוֹן מִן קֳדָם אַפֵּי קֻדְשָׁא, לְמִבָּרָא לְמַשְׁרִיתָא: ה וּקְרִיבוּ, וּנְטַלוּנִין בְּכִתּוּנֵיהוֹן, לְמִבָּרָא לְמַשְׁרִיתָא, כְּמָא דְּמַלֵּיל

places require absolute obedience. The most fundamental mistake – the mistake of Nadav and Avihu – is to take the powers that belong to man's encounter with the world, and apply them to man's encounter with the Divine. Had Nadav and Avihu used their own initiative to fight evil and injustice, the human domain, they would have been heroes. Because they used their own initiative in the arena of the holy, they erred. They asserted their own presence in the absolute presence of God.

That is the function of the holy – it is the point at which "I am" is silent in the overwhelming presence of "there is." That is what Nadav and Avihu forget – that to enter holy space or time requires ontological humility, the total renunciation of human initiative and desire. When we confuse God's will with our will, we turn the holy – the source of life – into something unholy and a source of death.

10:2 וַתֵּצֵא אֵשׁ *And fire came forth* – The story of Nadav and Avihu reminds us yet again of the warning first spelled out in the days of Kayin and Hevel. *The first act of worship led to the first murder* (Gen. 4). Worship generates power, which can be benign but can also be profoundly dangerous.

The episode of Nadav and Avihu is written in three kinds of fire. First there is the fire from heaven:

> And from before the Lord, fire came forth. It consumed the burnt offering. (Lev. 9:24)

This was the fire of favor, consummating the service of the Sanctuary. Then came the "unauthorized fire" offered by the two sons.

> Aharon's sons Nadav and Avihu took their fire pans, put fire in them, and placed incense upon it; and they offered unauthorized fire before the Lord, fire He had not commanded. (10:1)

Then there was the counterfire from heaven:

> And fire came forth from before the Lord and consumed them. They died before the Lord. (10:2)

The message is simple and intensely serious: Religion is not what the European Enlightenment thought it would become: mute, marginal, and mild. It is fire – and like fire, it warms but it also burns.

10:2 וַיָּמֻתוּ לִפְנֵי יהוה *They died before the Lord* – The highest virtue for the priest is obedience: doing as God told us to do. Prophets, by contrast, often acted on the spur of the moment. That is what Moshe does when he smashes the tablets on seeing the golden calf.

6 Nadav and Avihu out by their tunics to a place outside the camp. Moshe said
to Aharon and to Elazar and Itamar his sons, "Do not dishevel your hair or tear
your clothes or you will die and bring fury down upon the whole community.
Your brothers, the whole House of Israel, may mourn the burning that the
7 Lord has brought about. But you must not leave the entrance to the Tent of
Meeting or you will die, for the Lord's anointing oil is upon you." They did as
Moshe had told them.
8 9 And the Lord spoke to Aharon: "You and your sons must not drink wine
or strong drink when you enter the Tent of Meeting, so that you do not die.
10 This is an everlasting statute throughout your generations, to enable you to
11 distinguish between sacred and profane, and between impure and pure, and to
teach the Israelites all the statutes that the Lord has spoken to them through
Moshe."

רש״י

ו **אַל תִּפְרָעוּ.** אַל תְּגַדְּלוּ שֵׂעָר, מִכָּאן שֶׁאָבֵל אָסוּר בְּתִסְפֹּרֶת, אֲבָל אַתֶּם אַל תְּעַרְבְּבוּ שִׂמְחָתוֹ שֶׁל מָקוֹם: **וְלֹא תָמֻתוּ.** הָא אִם תַּעֲשׂוּ – תָּמוּתוּ: **וַאֲחֵיכֶם כָּל בֵּית יִשְׂרָאֵל.** מִכָּאן שֶׁצָּרָתָן שֶׁל תַּלְמִידֵי חֲכָמִים מֻטֶּלֶת עַל הַכֹּל לְהִתְאַבֵּל בָּהּ:

ט **יַיִן וְשֵׁכָר.** יַיִן דֶּרֶךְ שִׁכְרוּתוֹ: **בְּבֹאֲכֶם אֶל אֹהֶל מוֹעֵד.** אֵין לִי אֶלָּא בְּבוֹאֲכֶם לַהֵיכָל. בְּגִשְׁתָּם לַמִּזְבֵּחַ מִנַּיִן? נֶאֱמַר כָּאן בִּיאַת אֹהֶל מוֹעֵד וְנֶאֱמַר בְּקִדּוּשׁ יָדַיִם וְרַגְלַיִם בִּיאַת אֹהֶל מוֹעֵד (שמות ל, כ), מַה לְּהַלָּן עָשָׂה גִּישַׁת מִזְבֵּחַ כְּבִיאַת אֹהֶל מוֹעֵד, אַף כָּאן עָשָׂה גִּישַׁת מִזְבֵּחַ כְּבִיאַת אֹהֶל מוֹעֵד:

י **וּלְהַבְדִּיל.** כְּדֵי שֶׁתַּבְדִּילוּ בֵּין עֲבוֹדָה קְדוֹשָׁה לִמְחֻלֶּלֶת. הָא לָמַדְתָּ שֶׁאִם עָבַד – עֲבוֹדָתוֹ פְּסוּלָה:

יא **וּלְהוֹרֹת.** לִמֵּד שֶׁאָסוּר שִׁכּוֹר בְּהוֹרָאָה. יָכוֹל יְהֵא חַיָּב מִיתָה? תַּלְמוּד לוֹמַר: "אַתָּה וּבָנֶיךָ אִתָּךְ... וְלֹא תָמֻתוּ" (לעיל פסוק ט), כֹּהֲנִים בַּעֲבוֹדָתָם בְּמִיתָה וְאֵין חֲכָמִים בְּהוֹרָאָתָם בְּמִיתָה:

of faith is contained, giving light and a glimpse of the glory of God. Otherwise it can eventually become a raging inferno, spreading destruction and claiming lives. Intoxication in the arena of the sacred is dangerous. That is why Judaism contains so many laws and so much attention to detail – and the closer we come to God, the more details we need.

10:10 **וּבֵין הַטָּמֵא וּבֵין הַטָּהוֹר** *Between impure and pure* – The sequence of passages beginning with chapter 11 of Leviticus (toward the end of Parashat Shemini), occupying the whole of Parashot Tazria and Metzora and culminating in chapter 16 (the opening of Parashat Aḥarei Mot), is a tightly organized sequence of laws revolving around the keywords *tameh* and *tahor*, "impure" and "pure." The purity sequence is preceded by a general statement about the role of the priests: "to distinguish between sacred (*kodesh*) and profane (*ḥol*), and between impure (*tameh*) and pure (*tahor*)." That was one of the fundamental priestly duties, to "distinguish," differentiate, and maintain the boundaries between different states and conditions, especially those that had to do with the strict demands of holy space, the Tabernacle, and later, the Temple.

The story of creation tells us that nature is not a blind struggle between contending forces in which the strongest wins and power is the most important gift. To the contrary: The universe is fundamentally good. It is a place of ordered harmony, the intelligible design of a single Creator. That harmony is constantly threatened by mankind. In the covenant with Noaḥ, God establishes a minimum threshold of order for human civilization. In the covenant with Israel, He establishes a higher code of holiness. The principle of holiness, as of creation itself, is the maintenance of boundaries, within which every form of life receives its due.

ו מֹשֶׁה: וַיֹּאמֶר מֹשֶׁה אֶל־אַהֲרֹן וּלְאֶלְעָזָר וּלְאִיתָמָר ׀ בָּנָיו רָאשֵׁיכֶם
אַל־תִּפְרָעוּ ׀ וּבִגְדֵיכֶם לֹא־תִפְרֹמוּ וְלֹא תָמֻתוּ וְעַל כָּל־הָעֵדָה יִקְצֹף
ז וַאֲחֵיכֶם כָּל־בֵּית יִשְׂרָאֵל יִבְכּוּ אֶת־הַשְּׂרֵפָה אֲשֶׁר שָׂרַף יְהוָה: וּמִפֶּתַח
אֹהֶל מוֹעֵד לֹא תֵצְאוּ פֶּן־תָּמֻתוּ כִּי־שֶׁמֶן מִשְׁחַת יְהוָה עֲלֵיכֶם וַיַּעֲשׂוּ
כִּדְבַר מֹשֶׁה:
ח ט וַיְדַבֵּר יְהוָה אֶל־אַהֲרֹן לֵאמֹר: יַיִן וְשֵׁכָר אַל־תֵּשְׁתְּ ׀ אַתָּה ׀ וּבָנֶיךָ אִתָּךְ ה
י בְּבֹאֲכֶם אֶל־אֹהֶל מוֹעֵד וְלֹא תָמֻתוּ חֻקַּת עוֹלָם לְדֹרֹתֵיכֶם: וּלֲהַבְדִּיל
יא בֵּין הַקֹּדֶשׁ וּבֵין הַחֹל וּבֵין הַטָּמֵא וּבֵין הַטָּהוֹר: וּלְהוֹרֹת אֶת־בְּנֵי יִשְׂרָאֵל
אֵת כָּל־הַחֻקִּים אֲשֶׁר דִּבֶּר יְהוָה אֲלֵיהֶם בְּיַד־מֹשֶׁה:

אונקלוס

מֹשֶׁה: ו וַאֲמַר מֹשֶׁה לְאַהֲרֹן, וּלְאֶלְעָזָר וּלְאִיתָמָר בְּנוֹהִי, רֵישֵׁיכוֹן לָא תְרַבּוֹן פֵּרוּעַ וּלְבוּשֵׁיכוֹן לָא תְבַזְּעוּן וְלָא תְמוּתוּן, וְעַל כָּל כְּנִשְׁתָּא יְהֵי רֻגְזָא, וַאֲחֵיכוֹן כָּל בֵּית יִשְׂרָאֵל, יִבְכּוֹן יָת יְקֵידְתָא, דְּאוֹקֵיד יי: ז וּמִתְּרַע מַשְׁכַּן זִמְנָא, לָא תִפְּקוּן דִּלְמָא תְמוּתוּן, אֲרֵי מְשַׁח, רְבוּתָא דַּיי עֲלֵיכוֹן, וַעֲבַדוּ כְּפִתְגָמָא דְּמֹשֶׁה: ח וּמַלֵּיל יי, עִם אַהֲרֹן לְמֵימַר: ט חֲמַר וּמְרַוֵי, לָא תִשְׁתֵּי אַתְּ וּבְנָךְ עִמָּךְ, בְּמֵיעַלְכוֹן, לְמַשְׁכַּן זִמְנָא וְלָא תְמוּתוּן, קְיָם עָלַם לְדָרֵיכוֹן: י וּלְאַפְרָשָׁא, בֵּין קֻדְשָׁא וּבֵין חֻלָּא, וּבֵין מְסָאֲבָא וּבֵין דָּכְיָא: יא וּלְאַלָּפָא יָת בְּנֵי יִשְׂרָאֵל, יָת כָּל קְיָמַיָּא, דְּמַלֵּיל יי, לְהוֹן בִּידָא דְמֹשֶׁה:

10:9 **יין ושכר** *Wine or strong drink* – One of the rabbinic explanations of Nadav and Avihu's sin is that they had been drinking alcohol (Vayikra Rabba 12:1). The service of the priests touches upon the highest intensity of relationship with God – yet it requires control, decorum, sobriety.

Nadav and Avihu were "enthusiasts," not in the contemporary sense but in the sense in which the word was used in the seventeenth and eighteenth centuries. Enthusiasts then were people who, full of religious passion, believed that God was inspiring them to do deeds in defiance of law and convention. They were very spiritual but they were also potentially very dangerous. David Hume in particular saw that enthusiasm in this sense is diametrically opposed to the mindset of priesthood. In his words, "All enthusiasts have been free from the yoke of ecclesiastics, and have expressed great independence of devotion; with a contempt of forms, ceremonies, and traditions."

Priests understand the power, and thus the potential danger, of the sacred. That is why holy places, times, and rituals must be guarded with precise rules. To bring unauthorized fire to the Tabernacle might seem a small offense, but a single unauthorized act in the realm of the holy causes a breach in the laws around the sacred that can grow in time to a gaping hole. Enthusiasm, harmless though it might be in some of its manifestations, can quickly become extremism, fanaticism, and religiously motivated violence. As Hume observed, "Human reason and even morality are rejected [by enthusiasts] as fallacious guides, and the fanatic madman delivers himself over blindly" to what he believes to be divine inspiration, but what may in fact be overheated self-importance or frenzied rage.

Precisely because it gives rise to such intense passions, religious life in particular needs the constraints of law and ritual, the entire intricate minuet of worship, so that the fire

12 Moshe told Aharon, and Elazar and Itamar, the two sons left to him, "Take the REVI'I
grain offering left over after the fire offerings to the LORD and eat it unleavened
13 beside the altar, for it is holy of holies. You must eat it in a holy place because
it is your share, and that of your sons, from the LORD's fire offerings, for so
14 I have been commanded. But you and your sons and daughters may eat the
breast of the wave offering and the thigh of the upraised gift in any ritually
pure place, for these have been given to you from the peace sacrifices of Israel
15 as your portion and the portion of your children. The thigh for the upraised
gift and the breast for the wave offering are to be brought, with the fat of the
fire offering, to be waved as a wave offering before the LORD. These are to be
your share and that of your children forever, as the LORD has commanded."
16 Moshe inquired about the goat for the purification offering, and discovered HAMISHI
that it had been burned. He was furious with Elazar and Itamar, the two sons
17 left to Aharon. "Why did you not eat the purification offering in the holy area?"
he asked. "It is holy of holies, and it has been given to you to remove the guilt
18 of the community and atone for them before the LORD. Because its blood
was not to be brought into the inner Sanctuary, you should have eaten it in
19 the Sanctuary, as I commanded." It was Aharon who replied to Moshe, "They

רש״י

יב **הַנּוֹתָרִים.** מִן הַמִּיתָה, מְלַמֵּד שֶׁאַף עֲלֵיהֶן נִקְנְסָה מִיתָה עַל עֲוֹן הָעֵגֶל, הוּא שֶׁנֶּאֱמַר: ״וּבְאַהֲרֹן הִתְאַנַּף ה׳ מְאֹד לְהַשְׁמִידוֹ״ (דברים ט, כ), וְאֵין הַשְׁמָדָה אֶלָּא כִּלּוּי בָּנִים, שֶׁנֶּאֱמַר: ״וָאַשְׁמִיד פִּרְיוֹ מִמַּעַל״ (עמוס ב, ט), וּתְפִלָּתוֹ שֶׁל מֹשֶׁה בִּטְּלָה מֶחֱצָה, שֶׁנֶּאֱמַר: ״וָאֶתְפַּלֵּל גַּם בְּעַד אַהֲרֹן בָּעֵת הַהִוא״ (דברים שם): **קְחוּ אֶת הַמִּנְחָה.** אַף עַל פִּי שֶׁאַתֶּם אוֹנְנִין וְאַף עַל פִּי שֶׁהַקֳּדָשִׁים אֲסוּרִים לְאוֹנֵן: **אֶת הַמִּנְחָה.** זוֹ מִנְחַת שְׁמִינִי וּמִנְחַת נַחְשׁוֹן (במדבר ז, ג): **וְאִכְלוּהָ מַצּוֹת.** מַה תַּלְמוּד לוֹמַר? לְפִי שֶׁהִיא מִנְחַת צִבּוּר וּמִנְחַת שָׁעָה וְאֵין כַּיּוֹצֵא בָּהּ לְדוֹרוֹת, הֻצְרַךְ לְפָרֵשׁ בָּהּ דִּין שְׁאָר מְנָחוֹת:

יג **וְחָק בָּנֶיךָ.** אֵין לַבָּנוֹת חֹק בַּקֳּדָשִׁים: **כִּי כֵן צֻוֵּיתִי.** בַּאֲנִינוּת יֹאכְלוּהָ:

יד **וְאֵת חֲזֵה הַתְּנוּפָה.** שֶׁל שַׁלְמֵי צִבּוּר: **תֹּאכְלוּ בְּמָקוֹם טָהוֹר.** וְכִי אֶת הָרִאשׁוֹנִים אָכְלוּ בְּמָקוֹם טָמֵא?! אֶלָּא הָרִאשׁוֹנִים שֶׁהֵם קָדְשֵׁי קָדָשִׁים הֻזְקְקָה אֲכִילָתָם בְּמָקוֹם קָדוֹשׁ, אֲבָל אֵלּוּ אֵין צְרִיכִים תּוֹךְ הַקְּלָעִים, אֲבָל צְרִיכִים הֵם לֵאָכֵל תּוֹךְ מַחֲנֵה יִשְׂרָאֵל, שֶׁהוּא טָהוֹר מִלְּהִכָּנֵס שָׁם מְצֹרָעִים. מִכָּאן שֶׁקָּדָשִׁים קַלִּים נֶאֱכָלִין בְּכָל הָעִיר: **אַתָּה וּבָנֶיךָ וּבְנֹתֶיךָ.** אַתָּה וּבָנֶיךָ בְּחֵלֶק, אֲבָל בְּנוֹתֶיךָ לֹא בְּחֵלֶק, אֶלָּא אִם תִּתְּנוּ לָהֶם מַתָּנוֹת רַשָּׁאוֹת הֵן לֶאֱכֹל בְּחָזֶה וָשׁוֹק. אוֹ אֵינוֹ אֶלָּא אַף הַבָּנוֹת בְּחֵלֶק? תַּלְמוּד לוֹמַר: ״כִּי חָקְךָ וְחָק בָּנֶיךָ נִתְּנוּ״, חֹק לַבָּנִים וְאֵין חֹק לַבָּנוֹת:

טו **עַל אִשֵּׁי הַחֲלָבִים.** מִכָּאן שֶׁהַחֲלָבִים לְמַטָּן בִּשְׁעַת תְּנוּפָה. וְיִשּׁוּב הַמִּקְרָאוֹת שֶׁלֹּא יַכְחִישׁוּ זֶה אֶת זֶה, כְּבָר פֵּרַשְׁתִּי שְׁלָשְׁתָּן בְּ״צַו אֶת אַהֲרֹן״ (לעיל ז, ל):

טז **שְׂעִיר הַחַטָּאת.** שְׂעִיר מוּסְפֵי רֹאשׁ חֹדֶשׁ. וּשְׁלֹשָׁה שְׂעִירֵי חַטָּאוֹת קָרְבוּ בוֹ בַּיּוֹם: ״קְחוּ שְׂעִיר עִזִּים״ (לעיל ט, ג), וּשְׂעִיר נַחְשׁוֹן, וּשְׂעִיר רֹאשׁ חֹדֶשׁ. וּמִכֻּלָּן לֹא נִשְׂרַף אֶלָּא זֶה. וְנֶחְלְקוּ בַּדָּבָר חַכְמֵי יִשְׂרָאֵל: יֵשׁ אוֹמְרִים מִפְּנֵי טֻמְאָה שֶׁנָּגְעָה בּוֹ נִשְׂרַף, וְיֵשׁ אוֹמְרִים מִפְּנֵי אֲנִינוּת נִשְׂרַף, לְפִי שֶׁהוּא קָדְשֵׁי דוֹרוֹת, אֲבָל בְּקָדְשֵׁי שָׁעָה סָמְכוּ עַל מֹשֶׁה שֶׁאָמַר לָהֶם בַּמִּנְחָה: ״וְאִכְלוּהָ מַצּוֹת״ (לעיל פסוק יב): **דָּרֹשׁ דָּרַשׁ.** שְׁתֵּי דְרִישׁוֹת – מִפְּנֵי מָה נִשְׂרַף זֶה, וּמִפְּנֵי מָה נֶאֶכְלוּ אֵלּוּ. כָּךְ הִיא בְּתוֹרַת כֹּהֲנִים (פרק ב, ב): **עַל אֶלְעָזָר וְעַל אִיתָמָר.** בִּשְׁבִיל כְּבוֹדוֹ שֶׁל אַהֲרֹן, הָפַךְ פָּנָיו כְּנֶגֶד הַבָּנִים וְכָעַס: **לֵאמֹר.** אָמַר לָהֶם: הֲשִׁיבוּנִי עַל דְּבָרַי:

יז **מַדּוּעַ לֹא אֲכַלְתֶּם אֶת הַחַטָּאת בִּמְקוֹם הַקֹּדֶשׁ.** וְכִי חוּץ לַקֹּדֶשׁ אֲכָלוּהָ?! וַהֲלֹא שְׂרָפוּהָ! וּמַהוּ אוֹמֵר ״בִּמְקוֹם הַקֹּדֶשׁ״? אֶלָּא אָמַר לָהֶם: שֶׁמָּא חוּץ לַקְּלָעִים יָצְאָה וְנִפְסְלָה? **כִּי קֹדֶשׁ קָדָשִׁים הִוא.** וְנִפְסֶלֶת בְּיוֹצֵא. וְהֵם אָמְרוּ לוֹ: לָאו. אָמַר לָהֶם: הוֹאִיל וּבִמְקוֹם הַקֹּדֶשׁ הָיְתָה, מַדּוּעַ לֹא אֲכַלְתֶּם אוֹתָהּ?: **וְאֹתָהּ נָתַן לָכֶם לָשֵׂאת וְגוֹ׳.** שֶׁהַכֹּהֲנִים אוֹכְלִים וּבְעָלִים מִתְכַּפְּרִים: **לָשֵׂאת אֶת עֲוֹן הָעֵדָה.** מִכָּאן

יב וַיְדַבֵּר מֹשֶׁה אֶל־אַהֲרֹן וְאֶל אֶלְעָזָר וְאֶל־אִיתָמָר ׀ בָּנָיו הַנּוֹתָרִים רביעי
קְחוּ אֶת־הַמִּנְחָה הַנּוֹתֶרֶת מֵאִשֵּׁי יהוה וְאִכְלוּהָ מַצּוֹת אֵצֶל הַמִּזְבֵּחַ
יג כִּי קֹדֶשׁ קָדָשִׁים הִוא: וַאֲכַלְתֶּם אֹתָהּ בְּמָקוֹם קָדוֹשׁ כִּי חָקְךָ וְחָק־
יד בָּנֶיךָ הִוא מֵאִשֵּׁי יהוה כִּי־כֵן צֻוֵּיתִי: וְאֵת חֲזֵה הַתְּנוּפָה וְאֵת ׀ שׁוֹק
הַתְּרוּמָה תֹּאכְלוּ בְּמָקוֹם טָהוֹר אַתָּה וּבָנֶיךָ וּבְנֹתֶיךָ אִתָּךְ כִּי־חָקְךָ
טו וְחָק־בָּנֶיךָ נִתְּנוּ מִזִּבְחֵי שַׁלְמֵי בְּנֵי יִשְׂרָאֵל: שׁוֹק הַתְּרוּמָה וַחֲזֵה
הַתְּנוּפָה עַל אִשֵּׁי הַחֲלָבִים יָבִיאוּ לְהָנִיף תְּנוּפָה לִפְנֵי יהוה וְהָיָה לְךָ
טז וּלְבָנֶיךָ אִתְּךָ לְחָק־עוֹלָם כַּאֲשֶׁר צִוָּה יהוה: וְאֵת ׀ שְׂעִיר הַחַטָּאת חמישי
דָּרֹשׁ דָּרַשׁ מֹשֶׁה וְהִנֵּה שֹׂרָף וַיִּקְצֹף עַל־אֶלְעָזָר וְעַל־אִיתָמָר בְּנֵי
יז אַהֲרֹן הַנּוֹתָרִם לֵאמֹר: מַדּוּעַ לֹא־אֲכַלְתֶּם אֶת־הַחַטָּאת בִּמְקוֹם
הַקֹּדֶשׁ כִּי קֹדֶשׁ קָדָשִׁים הִוא וְאֹתָהּ ׀ נָתַן לָכֶם לָשֵׂאת אֶת־עֲוֹן הָעֵדָה
יח לְכַפֵּר עֲלֵיהֶם לִפְנֵי יהוה: הֵן לֹא־הוּבָא אֶת־דָּמָהּ אֶל־הַקֹּדֶשׁ פְּנִימָה
יט אָכוֹל תֹּאכְלוּ אֹתָהּ בַּקֹּדֶשׁ כַּאֲשֶׁר צִוֵּיתִי: וַיְדַבֵּר אַהֲרֹן אֶל־מֹשֶׁה הֵן

אונקלוס

יב ומליל משה עם אהרן, ועם אלעזר, ועם איתמר בנוהי דאשתארו, סבו ית מנחתא, דאשתארת מקורבניא דיי, ואיכלוהא פטיר בסטר מדבחא, ארי, קדש קודשין היא: יג ותיכלון יתה באתר קדיש, ארי חולקך וחולק בנך היא, מקורבניא דיי, ארי כן אתפקדית: יד וית חדיא דארמותא, וית שקא דאפרשותא, תיכלון באתר דכי, את, ובנך ובנתך עמך, ארי חולקך וחולק בנך אתיהיבו, מנכסת קודשיא דבני ישראל: טו שקא דאפרשותא וחדיא דארמותא, על קורבני תרביא יתיתון, לארמא ארמא קדם יי, ויהי לך, ולבנך עמך לקים עלם, כמא דפקיד יי: טז וית צפירא דחטאתא, מתבע תבעיה, משה והא אתוקד, ורגיז, על אלעזר ועל איתמר בני אהרן, דאשתארו למימר: יז מדין, לא אכלתון ית חטאתא באתר קדיש, ארי, קדש קודשין היא, ויתה יהב לכון, לסלחא על חובי כנשתא, לכפרא עליהון קדם יי: יח הא לא אתעל מדמה, לבית קודשא גואה, מיכל תיכלון יתה, בקודשא כמא דפקידית: יט ומליל אהרן עם משה, הא

רש"י

למדנו ששעיר ראש חדש היה, שהוא מכפר על עון טומאת מקדש וקדשיו, שחטאת שמיני וחטאת נחשון לא לכפרה באו:

יח **הן לא הובא וגו'.** שאלו הובא היה לכם לשרפה, כמו שנאמר: "וכל חטאת אשר יובא מדמה" וגו' (לעיל ו, כג). **אכול תאכלו אותה.** היה לכם לאכלה אף על פי שאתם אוננים: **כאשר צויתי.** לכם במנחה (לעיל פסוק יב).

יט **וידבר אהרן.** אין לשון 'דבור' אלא לשון עז, שנאמר: "וידבר העם" וגו' (במדבר כא, ה). אפשר משה קצף על אלעזר ועל איתמר ואהרן מדבר? הא ידעת שלא היתה אלא מדת כבוד, אמרו: אינו בדין שיהא אבינו יושב ואנו מדברים לפניו, ואינו בדין שיהא תלמיד משיב את רבו. יכול מפני שלא היה באלעזר להשיב? תלמוד לומר: "ויאמר אלעזר הכהן אל אנשי הצבא" וגו' (שם לא, כא), הרי כשרצה דבר לפני משה ולפני הנשיאים. זו מצאתי בספרי של פנים שני (ספרי זוטא לא, כא): **הן היום הקריבו.** מהו אומר? אלא אמר להם משה:

offered their purification offering and their burnt offerings before the LORD
today – but such things have happened to me. Would it really have been right
20 in the LORD's eyes if I had eaten a purification offering today?" Moshe listened;
and it was right in his eyes.
11 1 2 The LORD spoke to Moshe and Aharon, saying to them: "Tell the Israelites: SHISHI
3 These are the creatures that you may eat among the land mammals: You may

רש״י

שמא זרקתם דמה אוננים, שאונן שעבד חלל? אמר לו אהרן: וכי הם הקריבו שהם הדיוטות? אני הקרבתי, שאני כהן גדול ומקריב אונן: **ותקראנה אתי כאלה.** אפלו לא היו המתים בני, אלא שאר קרובים שאני חיב להיות אונן עליהם כאלו, כגון כל האמורים בפרשת כהנים (להלן כא, ב-ג) שהכהן מטמא להם: **ואכלתי חטאת.** ואם אכלתי, "הייטב" וגו'?: **היום.** אבל אנינות לילה מתרה, שאין אונן אלא יום קבורה: **הייטב בעיני ה'.** אם שמעת בקדשי שעה, אין לך להקל בקדשי דורות:

כ **וייטב בעיניו.** הודה, ולא בוש לומר: לא שמעתי:

יא א **אל משה ואל אהרן.** למשה אמר שיאמר לאהרן: **לאמר אלהם.** אמר שיאמר לאלעזר ולאיתמר. או אינו אלא לאמר לישראל? כשהוא אומר: "דברו אל בני ישראל", הרי דבור אמור לישראל, הא מה אני מקים "לאמר אלהם"? לבנים, לאלעזר ולאיתמר:

ב **דברו אל בני ישראל.** את כלם השוה להיות שלוחים בדבור זה, לפי שהשוו בדמימה וקבלו עליהם גזרת המקום מאהבה: **זאת החיה.** לשון חיים, לפי שישראל דבוקים במקום וראויין להיות חיים, לפיכך הבדילם מן הטמאה וגזר עליהם מצות, ולאמות לא אסר כלום. משל לרופא שנכנס לבקר את החולה וכו', כדאיתא במדרש רבי תנחומא (1)[משל למה הדבר דומה? לרופא שהלך לבקר שני חולים, ראה אחד מהם שהיה בסכנה, אמר לבני ביתו: תנו לו כל מאכל שהוא מבקש. ראה האחד שעתיד לחיות, אמר להם: כך וכך מאכל יאכל, כך וכך לא יאכל. אמרו לרופא: מה זה, לזה אתה אומר יאכל כל מאכל שהוא מבקש, ולאחר אמרת לא יאכל כך וכך? אמר להם הרופא: לזה שהוא לחיים אמרתי לו זה אכול וזה לא תאכל, אבל אותו שהוא למיתה אמרתי להם כל מה שהוא מבקש תנו לו, שאינו לחיים]: **זאת החיה.** מלמד שהיה משה אוחז בחיה ומראה אותה לישראל: זאת תאכלו וזאת לא תאכלו. "את זה תאכלו" וגו' (להלן פסוק ט) – אף בשרצי המים אוחז מכל מין ומין ומראה להם, וכן בעוף: "ואת אלה תשקצו מן העוף" (להלן פסוק יג), וכן בשרצים: "וזה לכם הטמא" (להלן פסוק כט): **זאת החיה... מכל הבהמה.** מלמד שהבהמה בכלל חיה:

ג **מפרסת.** כתרגומו: "סדיקא": **פרסה.** פלנט"א בלעז: **ושסעת שסע.** שמבדלת מלמעלה ומלמטה בשתי צפרנים, כתרגומו: "ומטלפן טלפין", שיש שפרסותיו סדוקות מלמעלה ואין שסועות ומבדלות לגמרי, שמלמטה מחברות: **מעלת גרה.** מעלה ומקיאה האכל ממעיה ומחזרת אותו לתוך פיה לכתשו ולטחנו הדק: **גרה.** כך שמו, ויתכן לתתו מגזרת: "מים הנגרים" (שמואל ב' יד, יד), שהוא נגרר אחר הפה. ותרגומו: "פשרא", שעל ידי הגרה האכל נפשר ונמוח: **בבהמה.** תבה יתרה היא לדרשה, להתיר את השליל הנמצא במעי

be holy, for I am holy.... I am the LORD, who brought you up out of Egypt to be your God. Be holy, for I am holy...to distinguish (*lehavdil*) between the impure and the pure and between creatures that may be eaten and those that may not. (Lev. 11:44–47)

A similar statement appears later in Leviticus (20:24–26):

I am the LORD your God, who has set you apart (*hivdalti*) from all other peoples. You, then, shall set pure apart (*vehivdaltem*) from impure animals, pure from impure birds. Do not make yourselves detestable by an animal or bird or anything that creeps upon the ground that I have set apart (*hivdalti*) from you to regard as impure. Be holy to Me, for I the LORD am holy, and I have set you apart (*vaavdil*) from all other peoples to be My own.

The keywords here are "holy" and *lehavdil*, "to distinguish/set apart." Here we encounter an additional dimension of holiness. *To be holy is to make distinctions, to recognize and honor the divine order of creation.* Originally, according to the Torah, human beings (and animals) were to be vegetarians ("I give you all these seed-bearing plants on the face of the earth and every tree with seed-bearing fruit. They shall be yours to eat" [Gen. 1:29]). After the flood, humanity was

הַיּוֹם הִקְרִיבוּ אֶת־חַטָּאתָם וְאֶת־עֹלָתָם לִפְנֵי יהוה וַתִּקְרֶאנָה אֹתִי
כ כָּאֵלֶּה וְאָכַלְתִּי חַטָּאת הַיּוֹם הַיִּיטַב בְּעֵינֵי יהוה׃ וַיִּשְׁמַע מֹשֶׁה וַיִּיטַב
בְּעֵינָיו׃
יא א ב וַיְדַבֵּר יהוה אֶל־מֹשֶׁה וְאֶל־אַהֲרֹן לֵאמֹר אֲלֵהֶם׃ דַּבְּרוּ אֶל־בְּנֵי ו ששי
יִשְׂרָאֵל לֵאמֹר זֹאת הַחַיָּה אֲשֶׁר תֹּאכְלוּ מִכָּל־הַבְּהֵמָה אֲשֶׁר עַל־
ג הָאָרֶץ׃ כֹּל ׀ מַפְרֶסֶת פַּרְסָה וְשֹׁסַעַת שֶׁסַע פְּרָסֹת מַעֲלַת גֵּרָה בַּבְּהֵמָה

אונקלוס

יוֹמָא דֵין, קָרִיבוּ יָת חַטָּוָתְהוֹן וְיָת עֲלָוָתְהוֹן קֳדָם יי, וְעָרְעָא יָתִי עָקָן כְּאִלֵּין, אִלּוּ פוֹן אֲכַלִית חַטָּתָא יוֹמָא דֵין, הֲתַקִּין קֳדָם יי: כ וּשְׁמַע מֹשֶׁה, וּשְׁפַר בְּעֵינוֹהִי: יא א וּמַלִּיל יי, עִם מֹשֶׁה וּלְאַהֲרֹן לְמֵימַר לְהוֹן: ב מַלִּילוּ, עִם בְּנֵי יִשְׂרָאֵל לְמֵימַר, דָּא חַיְתָא דְּתֵיכְלוּן, מִכָּל בְּעִירָא דְּעַל אַרְעָא: ג כָּל דִּסְדִיקָא פַרְסְתַהּ, וּמַטִלְפָן טִלְפִין פַּרְסָתַהּ, מַסְּקָא פִשְׁרָא בִּבְעִירָא,

10:20 וַיִּשְׁמַע מֹשֶׁה וַיִּיטַב בְּעֵינָיו *Moshe listened; and it was right in his eyes* – Aharon is in a state of grief. But, Moshe implies, Aharon is not simply a private person. He is the High Priest. The people need him to perform his duties, whatever his inner feelings. To this Aharon replies: "Would it really have been right in the Lord's eyes if I had eaten a purification offering today?" (Lev. 10:19). The words are opaque and we can only guess at their precise import. Perhaps they mean this: "I know that in general, a High Priest is forbidden to mourn as if he were an ordinary individual. That is the law, and I accept it. But had I acted on this inaugural day as if nothing had happened, as if my sons had not died, would this not seem to the people as if I were heartless, as if the service of God meant a renunciation of my humanity?" This time, Moshe is silent. Aharon is right, and Moshe knows it.

In this exchange between two brothers, a momentous courage is born: the courage of an Aharon who has the strength to grieve and not accept easy consolation, and the courage of a Moshe who has the strength to keep going despite grief. It is almost as if we are present at the birth of an emotional configuration that will characterize the Jewish people in centuries to come. Jews are a people who have had more than their share of suffering. Like Aharon, they did not lose their humanity. But neither did they lose their capacity to continue, to carry on, to hope. Like Moshe, they never lost faith in God. But like Aharon, they never allowed that faith to anaesthetize their feelings, their human vulnerability.

That, it seems to me, is what happened to the Jewish people after the Holocaust. There were, and are, no words to silence the grief or end the tears. Yet, like Moshe, the Jewish people found the strength to continue, to reaffirm hope in the face of despair. A mere three years after coming eye to eye with the angel of death, the Jewish people, by establishing the State of Israel, made the single most powerful affirmation in two thousand years that *am Yisrael ḥai,* the Jewish people lives.

Faith does not render us invulnerable to tragedy, but it gives us the strength to mourn and then, despite everything, to carry on.

THE DIETARY LAWS

Many explanations have been given of the Torah's dietary laws. Some see them as rules of hygiene. Others see them as a discipline of self-restraint. In the words of the talmudic sage Rav: "The commandments were given to refine human beings" (Bereshit Rabba 44:1). Yet others see in them a set of laws that have no logic other than the fact that they were given by God. However, the simplest explanation is the one given here by the Torah itself:

I am the Lord your God. Consecrate yourselves and

4 eat any animal that has divided hoofs, fully split, and chews the cud. Among
those that chew the cud or have divided hoofs you must not eat the following:
the camel, because though it chews the cud, it does not have divided hoofs,
5 and so it is impure for you; the hyrax, though it chews the cud, does not have
6 divided hoofs and so it is impure for you; the hare, though it chews the cud,
7 does not have divided hoofs and so it is impure for you; the pig, though it has
8 fully divided hoofs, does not chew the cud and so it is impure for you. You may
not eat the flesh of these animals or touch their carcasses; they are impure for
9 you. These you may eat among the creatures of the water: anything in the water,
10 whether in sea or in stream, that has fins and scales may be eaten, whereas
anything in the sea or the stream that does not have fins and scales, whether
one of the swarming creatures of the water or any other of living creature there,
11 is detestable to you and will remain so. You may not eat their flesh, and you
12 shall detest their carcasses. Anything in the water that does not have fins or
13 scales is detestable to you. Among the birds, the following you shall regard
as detestable – being detested they shall not be eaten: the griffon vulture,
14 the bearded vulture, the lappet-faced vulture, the kite, any kind of buzzard,

רש״י

אִמּוֹ: **אֹתָהּ תֹּאכֵלוּ.** וְלֹא בְּהֵמָה טְמֵאָה. וַהֲלֹא בְּאַזְהָרָה הִיא (להלן פסוק ח)? אֶלָּא לַעֲבֹר עָלֶיהָ בַּעֲשֵׂה וְלֹא תַעֲשֶׂה:

ח **מִבְּשָׂרָם לֹא תֹאכֵלוּ.** אֵין לִי אֶלָּא אֵלּוּ, שְׁאָר בְּהֵמָה טְמֵאָה שֶׁאֵין לָהּ שׁוּם סִימַן טָהֳרָה, מִנַּיִן? אָמַרְתָּ קַל וָחֹמֶר: וּמָה אֵלּוּ שֶׁיֵּשׁ בָּהֶן קְצָת סִימָנֵי טָהֳרָה אֲסוּרוֹת וְכוּ': **מִבְּשָׂרָם.** עַל בְּשָׂרָם בְּאַזְהָרָה, וְלֹא עַל עֲצָמוֹת וְגִידִין וְקַרְנַיִם וּטְלָפַיִם: **וּבְנִבְלָתָם לֹא תִגָּעוּ.** יָכוֹל יְהוּ יִשְׂרָאֵל מֻזְהָרִים עַל מַגַּע נְבֵלָה? תַּלְמוּד לוֹמַר: "אֱמֹר אֶל הַכֹּהֲנִים" וְגוֹ' (להלן כא, א), כֹּהֲנִים מֻזְהָרִין וְאֵין יִשְׂרָאֵל מֻזְהָרִין. קַל וָחֹמֶר מֵעַתָּה: וּמָה טֻמְאַת מֵת חֲמוּרָה לֹא הִזְהִיר בָּהּ אֶלָּא כֹּהֲנִים, טֻמְאַת נְבֵלָה קַלָּה לֹא כָּל שֶׁכֵּן? וּמַה תַּלְמוּד לוֹמַר "לֹא תִגָּעוּ"? בָּרֶגֶל:

ט **סְנַפִּיר.** אֵלּוּ שֶׁשָּׁט בָּהֶם: **קַשְׂקֶשֶׂת.** אֵלּוּ קְלִפִּין הַקְּבוּעִים בּוֹ, כְּמוֹ שֶׁנֶּאֱמַר: "וְשִׁרְיוֹן קַשְׂקַשִּׂים הוּא לָבוּשׁ" (שמואל א' יז, ה):

י **שֶׁרֶץ.** בְּכָל מָקוֹם מַשְׁמָעוֹ דָּבָר נָמוּךְ שֶׁרוֹחֵשׁ וְנָד עַל הָאָרֶץ:

יא **וְשֶׁקֶץ יִהְיוּ.** לֶאֱסֹר אֶת עֵרוּבֵיהֶם, אִם יֵשׁ בּוֹ בְּנוֹתֵן טַעַם: **מִבְּשָׂרָם.** אֵינוֹ מֻזְהָר עַל הַסְּנַפִּירִים וְעַל הָעֲצָמוֹת: **וְאֶת נִבְלָתָם תְּשַׁקֵּצוּ.** לְרַבּוֹת יַבְחוּשִׁין שֶׁסִּנְנָן. יַבְחוּשִׁין מוּישרונ"ש בְּלַעַז:

יב **כֹּל אֲשֶׁר אֵין לוֹ וְגוֹ'.** מַה תַּלְמוּד לוֹמַר? שֶׁיָּכוֹל אֵין לִי שֶׁיְּהֵא מֻתָּר אֶלָּא הַמַּעֲלֶה סִימָנִין שֶׁלּוֹ לַיַּבָּשָׁה, הִשִּׁירָן בַּמַּיִם מִנַּיִן? תַּלְמוּד לוֹמַר: "כֹּל אֲשֶׁר אֵין לוֹ סְנַפִּיר וְקַשְׂקֶשֶׂת בַּמָּיִם" – הָא אִם הָיוּ לוֹ בַּמַּיִם, אַף עַל פִּי שֶׁהִשִּׁירָן בַּעֲלִיָּתוֹ, מֻתָּר:

יג **לֹא יֵאָכְלוּ.** לְחַיֵּב אֶת הַמַּאֲכִילָן לִקְטַנִּים, שֶׁכָּךְ מַשְׁמָעוֹ: לֹא יְהוּ נֶאֱכָלִין עַל יָדְךָ. אוֹ אֵינוֹ אֶלָּא לְאָסְרָן בַּהֲנָאָה? תַּלְמוּד לוֹמַר: "לֹא תֹאכְלוּ" (דברים יד, יב), בַּאֲכִילָה אֲסוּרִין, בַּהֲנָאָה מֻתָּרִין. כָּל עוֹף שֶׁנֶּאֱמַר בּוֹ 'לְמִינָהּ', 'לְמִינוֹ', 'לְמִינֵהוּ', יֵשׁ בְּאוֹתוֹ הַמִּין שֶׁאֵין דּוֹמִין זֶה לָזֶה לֹא בְּמַרְאֵיהֶם וְלֹא בִּשְׁמוֹתֵיהֶם, וְכֻלָּן מִין אֶחָד:

permitted and forbidden, represent *boundary-making in life*, in the act of eating, the most natural of human activities. This vision epitomizes the priestly voice within Judaism. It is a vision of great beauty. It sees the world as a place of order in which everything has its place and dignity within the richly differentiated tapestry of creation. To be holy is to be a guardian of that order, a task delegated to us by God. That is both an intellectual and ethical challenge: intellectually, to be able to recognize the boundaries and limits of nature; ethically, to have the humility to preserve and conserve the world for the sake of generations yet to come.

ד אֹתָהּ תֹּאכֵלוּ: אַךְ אֶת־זֶה לֹא תֹאכְלוּ מִמַּעֲלֵי הַגֵּרָה וּמִמַּפְרִסֵי הַפַּרְסָה
אֶת־הַגָּמָל כִּי־מַעֲלֵה גֵרָה הוּא וּפַרְסָה אֵינֶנּוּ מַפְרִיס טָמֵא הוּא לָכֶם:
ה וְאֶת־הַשָּׁפָן כִּי־מַעֲלֵה גֵרָה הוּא וּפַרְסָה לֹא יַפְרִיס טָמֵא הוּא לָכֶם:
ו וְאֶת־הָאַרְנֶבֶת כִּי־מַעֲלַת גֵּרָה הִוא וּפַרְסָה לֹא הִפְרִיסָה טְמֵאָה הִוא
ז לָכֶם: וְאֶת־הַחֲזִיר כִּי־מַפְרִיס פַּרְסָה הוּא וְשֹׁסַע שֶׁסַע פַּרְסָה וְהוּא
ח גֵּרָה לֹא־יִגָּר טָמֵא הוּא לָכֶם: מִבְּשָׂרָם לֹא תֹאכֵלוּ וּבְנִבְלָתָם לֹא
ט תִגָּעוּ טְמֵאִים הֵם לָכֶם: אֶת־זֶה תֹּאכְלוּ מִכֹּל אֲשֶׁר בַּמָּיִם כֹּל אֲשֶׁר־
י לוֹ סְנַפִּיר וְקַשְׂקֶשֶׂת בַּמַּיִם בַּיַּמִּים וּבַנְּחָלִים אֹתָם תֹּאכֵלוּ: וְכֹל אֲשֶׁר
אֵין־לוֹ סְנַפִּיר וְקַשְׂקֶשֶׂת בַּיַּמִּים וּבַנְּחָלִים מִכֹּל שֶׁרֶץ הַמַּיִם וּמִכֹּל
יא נֶפֶשׁ הַחַיָּה אֲשֶׁר בַּמָּיִם שֶׁקֶץ הֵם לָכֶם: וְשֶׁקֶץ יִהְיוּ לָכֶם מִבְּשָׂרָם
יב לֹא תֹאכֵלוּ וְאֶת־נִבְלָתָם תְּשַׁקֵּצוּ: כֹּל אֲשֶׁר אֵין־לוֹ סְנַפִּיר וְקַשְׂקֶשֶׂת
יג בַּמָּיִם שֶׁקֶץ הוּא לָכֶם: וְאֶת־אֵלֶּה תְּשַׁקְּצוּ מִן־הָעוֹף לֹא יֵאָכְלוּ שֶׁקֶץ
יד הֵם אֶת־הַנֶּשֶׁר וְאֶת־הַפֶּרֶס וְאֵת הָעָזְנִיָּה: וְאֶת־הַדָּאָה וְאֶת־הָאַיָּה

אונקלוס

יָתַהּ תֵּיכְלוּן: ד בְּרַם יָת דֵּין לָא תֵיכְלוּן, מִמַּסְּקֵי פִשְׁרָא, וּמִסְּדִיקֵי פַרְסְתָא, יָת גַּמְלָא, אֲרֵי מַסֵּיק פִּשְׁרָא הוּא, וּפַרְסְתֵיהּ לָא סְדִיקָא, מְסָאַב הוּא לְכוֹן: ה וְיָת טַבְזָא, אֲרֵי מַסֵּיק פִּשְׁרָא הוּא, וּפַרְסְתֵיהּ לָא סְדִיקָא, מְסָאַב הוּא לְכוֹן: ו וְיָת אַרְנְבָא, אֲרֵי מַסְּקָא פִשְׁרָא הִיא, וּפַרְסְתַהּ לָא סְדִיקָא, מְסָאֲבָא הִיא לְכוֹן: ז וְיָת חֲזִירָא, אֲרֵי סְדִיק פַּרְסְתָא הוּא, וּמְטַלְּפָן טִלְפִין פַּרְסָתֵיהּ, וְהוּא פִשְׁרָא לָא פָשַׁר, מְסָאַב הוּא לְכוֹן: ח מִבִּסְרְהוֹן לָא תֵיכְלוּן, וּבִנְבִילַתְהוֹן לָא תִקְרְבוּן, מְסָאֲבִין אִנּוּן לְכוֹן: ט יָת דֵּין תֵּיכְלוּן, מִכֹּל דִּבְמַיָּא, כֹּל דְּלֵיהּ צִיצִין וְקַלְפִין בְּמַיָּא, בְּיַמְמַיָּא, וּבְנַחְלַיָּא יָתְהוֹן תֵּיכְלוּן: י וְכֹל דְּלֵית לֵיהּ צִיצִין וְקַלְפִין, בְּיַמְמַיָּא וּבְנַחְלַיָּא, מִכֹּל רִחְשָׁא דְמַיָּא, וּמִכֹּל, נַפְשָׁא חַיְתָא דִּבְמַיָּא, שִׁקְצָא אִנּוּן לְכוֹן: יא וְשִׁקְצָא יְהוֹן לְכוֹן, מִבִּסְרְהוֹן לָא תֵיכְלוּן, וְיָת נְבִילַתְהוֹן תְּשַׁקְּצוּן: יב כֹּל דְּלֵית לֵיהּ, צִיצִין וְקַלְפִין בְּמַיָּא, שִׁקְצָא הוּא לְכוֹן: יג וְיָת אִלֵּין תְּשַׁקְּצוּן מִן עוֹפָא, לָא יִתְאַכְלוּן שִׁקְצָא אִנּוּן, נִשְׁרָא וְעָר וְעָזְיָא: יד וְדַיְתָא, וְטָרְפִיתָא לִזְנַהּ: טו יָת כֹּל

permitted to eat meat, with the exception of blood (ch. 9). A concession was made to the human tendency to violence. It is as if God had said: If you must kill, then kill animals, not human beings.

However, the people of Israel were to serve as role models of a higher ideal. They are permitted to kill animals for food, but only those that best exemplify divine order. Amphibians were forbidden because they lack a definite place. Others are forbidden because they lack a clear form – sea creatures that lack a shape defined by fins and scales, and land animals that are not ruminants with clearly defined cloven hoofs. Creatures that prey on others are also forbidden.

The Sanctuary, with its partitions, represents *boundary-making in space*. The dietary laws, with their divisions of

15, 16 any kind of raven, the ostrich, the swallow, the gull, any kind of sparrow hawk,
17, 18 the little owl, the cormorant, the short-eared owl, the barn owl, the pelican,
19 20 the Egyptian vulture, the stork, any kind of heron, the hoopoe, and the bat. All
21 swarming, flying creatures that crawl on fours are detestable to you, but you may
eat those swarming, flying creatures that crawl on four legs, with legs jointed
22 above their feet with which they hop on the ground. Of these you may eat the
23 following: any kind of locust, bald locust, cricket, or grasshopper. Every other
24 swarming, flying, crawling creature on fours is detestable to you. You become
impure through these: whoever touches their carcasses shall be impure until
25 evening, and whoever moves their carcasses shall immerse his clothes and be
26 impure until evening. All livestock with divided hoofs that are not completely
split, or that do not chew the cud, are impure for you; whoever touches them
27 becomes impure. Among four-footed animals, all those that walk on their
paws are impure for you; anyone touching their carcasses shall be impure
28 until evening. One who moves their carcasses shall immerse his clothes and

רש״י

טז **הַנֵּץ.** אושטו״ר:

יז **שָׁלָךְ.** פֵּרְשׁוּ רַבּוֹתֵינוּ, זֶה הַשּׁוֹלֶה דָּגִים מִן הַיָּם, וְזֶהוּ שֶׁתִּרְגֵּם אוּנְקְלוֹס: ״וְשָׁלֵינוּנָא״: **כּוֹס וְיַנְשׁוּף.** הֵם צואיטו״ש הַצּוֹעֲקִים בַּלַּיְלָה, וְיֵשׁ לָהֶם לְסָתוֹת כָּאָדָם. וְעוֹד אַחֵר דּוֹמֶה לוֹ שֶׁקּוֹרִין ייב״ן:

יח **תִּנְשֶׁמֶת.** הִיא קלב״א שורי״ץ, וְדוֹמָה לְעַכְבָּר, וּפוֹרַחַת בַּלַּיְלָה, וְ׳תִנְשֶׁמֶת׳ הָאֲמוּרָה בַּשְּׁרָצִים הִיא דּוֹמָה לָהּ, וְאֵין לָהּ עֵינַיִם, וְקוֹרִין לָהּ טלפ״א:

יט **הַחֲסִידָה.** זוֹ דַּיָּה לְבָנָה, ציגוני״א, וְלָמָּה נִקְרָא שְׁמָהּ ׳חֲסִידָה׳? שֶׁעוֹשָׂה חֲסִידוּת עִם חַבְרוֹתֶיהָ בִּמְזוֹנוֹת: **הָאֲנָפָה.** הִיא דַּיָּה רַגְזָנִית, וְנִרְאֶה לִי, שֶׁהוּא שֶׁקּוֹרִין היירו״ן: **הַדּוּכִיפַת.** תַּרְנְגוֹל הַבָּר, וְכַרְבָּלְתּוֹ כְּפוּלָה, וּבְלַעַז הרופ״א, וְלָמָּה נִקְרָא שְׁמוֹ ׳דּוּכִיפַת׳? שֶׁהוֹדוֹ כָּפוּת, וְזוֹ הִיא כַּרְבָּלְתּוֹ, וְ׳נַגַּר טוּרָא׳ נִקְרָא עַל שֵׁם מַעֲשָׂיו, כְּמוֹ שֶׁפֵּרְשׁוּ רַבּוֹתֵינוּ בְּמַסֶּכֶת גִּטִּין בְּפֶרֶק ׳מִי שֶׁאֲחָזוֹ׳ (דף סח ע״ב):

כ **שֶׁרֶץ הָעוֹף.** הֵם הַדַּקִּים הַנְּמוּכִים הָרוֹחֲשִׁין עַל הָאָרֶץ, כְּגוֹן זְבוּבִים וּצְרָעִין וְיַתּוּשִׁין וַחֲגָבִים:

כא **עַל אַרְבַּע.** עַל אַרְבַּע רַגְלַיִם: **מִמַּעַל לְרַגְלָיו.** סָמוּךְ לְצַוָּארוֹ יֵשׁ לוֹ כְּמִין שְׁתֵּי רַגְלַיִם לְבַד אַרְבַּע רַגְלָיו, וּכְשֶׁרוֹצֶה לָעוּף וְלִקְפֹּץ מִן הָאָרֶץ מִתְחַזֵּק בְּאוֹתָן שְׁתֵּי כְּרָעַיִם וּפוֹרֵחַ. וְיֵשׁ מֵהֶן הַרְבֵּה כְּאוֹתָן שֶׁקּוֹרִין לנגושט״א, אֲבָל אֵין אָנוּ בְּקִיאִין בָּהֶן, שֶׁאַרְבָּעָה סִימָנֵי טָהֳרָה נֶאֶמְרוּ בָּהֶם: אַרְבַּע רַגְלַיִם וְאַרְבַּע כְּנָפַיִם וְקַרְסֻלַּיִן – אֵלּוּ הַכְּתוּבִים כָּאן, וּכְנָפָיו חוֹפִין אֶת רֻבּוֹ. וְכָל סִימָנִים הַלָּלוּ מְצוּיִם בְּאוֹתָן שֶׁבֵּינוֹתֵינוּ, אֲבָל יֵשׁ שֶׁרֹאשָׁן אָרֹךְ, וְיֵשׁ שֶׁאֵין לָהֶם זָנָב, וְצָרִיךְ שֶׁיְּהֵא שְׁמוֹ ׳חָגָב׳, וּבָזֶה אֵין אָנוּ יוֹדְעִים לְהַבְדִּיל בֵּינֵיהֶן:

כג **וְכֹל שֶׁרֶץ הָעוֹף וְגוֹ׳.** בָּא וְלִמֵּד שֶׁאִם יֵשׁ לוֹ חָמֵשׁ טָהוֹר:

כד **וּלְאֵלֶּה.** הָעֲתִידִין לְהֵאָמֵר בָּעִנְיָן לְמַטָּה: **תִּטַּמָּאוּ.** כְּלוֹמַר, בִּנְגִיעָתָם יֵשׁ טֻמְאָה:

כה **וְכָל הַנֹּשֵׂא מִנִּבְלָתָם.** כָּל מָקוֹם שֶׁנֶּאֶמְרָה טֻמְאַת מַשָּׂא, חֲמוּרָה מִטֻּמְאַת מַגָּע, שֶׁהִיא טְעוּנָה כִּבּוּס בְּגָדִים:

כו **מַפְרֶסֶת פַּרְסָה וְשֶׁסַע אֵינֶנָּה שֹׁסַעַת.** כְּגוֹן גָּמָל, שֶׁפַּרְסָתוֹ סְדוּקָה לְמַעְלָה אֲבָל לְמַטָּה הִיא מְחֻבֶּרֶת. כָּאן לִמֶּדְךָ שֶׁנִּבְלַת בְּהֵמָה טְמֵאָה מְטַמְּאָה, וּבָעִנְיָן שֶׁבְּסוֹף הַפָּרָשָׁה (להלן פסוקים לט-מ) פֵּרַשׁ עַל בְּהֵמָה טְהוֹרָה:

כז **עַל כַּפָּיו.** כְּגוֹן כֶּלֶב וְדֹב וְחָתוּל: **טְמֵאִים הֵם לָכֶם.** לְמַגָּע:

one.” How can a bird called “compassion” possibly be unclean? They answered: The *ḥasida* has compassion only for its own kind. Compassion only for your own is not compassion.

טו טז לְמִינָהּ׃ אֵת כָּל־עֹרֵב לְמִינוֹ׃ וְאֵת בַּת הַיַּעֲנָה וְאֶת־הַתַּחְמָס וְאֶת־
יז הַשָּׁחַף וְאֶת־הַנֵּץ לְמִינֵהוּ׃ וְאֶת־הַכּוֹס וְאֶת־הַשָּׁלָךְ וְאֶת־הַיַּנְשׁוּף׃
יח יט וְאֶת־הַתִּנְשֶׁמֶת וְאֶת־הַקָּאָת וְאֶת־הָרָחָם׃ וְאֵת הַחֲסִידָה הָאֲנָפָה
כ לְמִינָהּ וְאֶת־הַדּוּכִיפַת וְאֶת־הָעֲטַלֵּף׃ כֹּל שֶׁרֶץ הָעוֹף הַהֹלֵךְ עַל־
כא אַרְבַּע שֶׁקֶץ הוּא לָכֶם׃ אַךְ אֶת־זֶה תֹּאכְלוּ מִכֹּל שֶׁרֶץ הָעוֹף הַהֹלֵךְ
עַל־אַרְבַּע אֲשֶׁר־לֹא כְרָעַיִם מִמַּעַל לְרַגְלָיו לְנַתֵּר בָּהֵן עַל־הָאָרֶץ׃ לוֹ
כב אֶת־אֵלֶּה מֵהֶם תֹּאכֵלוּ אֶת־הָאַרְבֶּה לְמִינוֹ וְאֶת־הַסָּלְעָם לְמִינֵהוּ
כג וְאֶת־הַחַרְגֹּל לְמִינֵהוּ וְאֶת־הֶחָגָב לְמִינֵהוּ׃ וְכֹל שֶׁרֶץ הָעוֹף אֲשֶׁר־לוֹ
כד אַרְבַּע רַגְלָיִם שֶׁקֶץ הוּא לָכֶם׃ וּלְאֵלֶּה תִּטַּמָּאוּ כָּל־הַנֹּגֵעַ בְּנִבְלָתָם
כה יִטְמָא עַד־הָעָרֶב׃ וְכָל־הַנֹּשֵׂא מִנִּבְלָתָם יְכַבֵּס בְּגָדָיו וְטָמֵא עַד־
כו הָעָרֶב׃ לְכָל־הַבְּהֵמָה אֲשֶׁר הִוא מַפְרֶסֶת פַּרְסָה וְשֶׁסַע ׀ אֵינֶנָּה
שֹׁסַעַת וְגֵרָה אֵינֶנָּה מַעֲלָה טְמֵאִים הֵם לָכֶם כָּל־הַנֹּגֵעַ בָּהֶם יִטְמָא׃
כז וְכֹל ׀ הוֹלֵךְ עַל־כַּפָּיו בְּכָל־הַחַיָּה הַהֹלֶכֶת עַל־אַרְבַּע טְמֵאִים הֵם לָכֶם
כח כָּל־הַנֹּגֵעַ בְּנִבְלָתָם יִטְמָא עַד־הָעָרֶב׃ וְהַנֹּשֵׂא אֶת־נִבְלָתָם יְכַבֵּס

אונקלוס

עוֹרְבָא לִזְנֵיהּ: טז וְיָת בַּת נַעֲמִיתָא, וְצִיצָא וְצִפַּר שַׁחְפָּא, וְנַצָּא לִזְנוֹהִי: יז וְקַדְיָא וְשָׁלֵינוּנָא וְקִפּוֹפָא: יח וּבַוְתָא וְקָתָא וִירַקְרֵיקָא: יט וְחַוָּרִיתָא, וְאִבּוֹ לִזְנַהּ, וְנַגַּר טוּרָא וַעֲטַלֵּיפָא: כ כָּל רִחְשָׁא דְעוֹפָא, דִּמְהַלֵּיךְ עַל אַרְבַּע, שִׁקְצָא הוּא לְכוֹן: כא בְּרַם יָת דֵּין תֵּיכְלוּן, מִכָּל רִחְשָׁא דְעוֹפָא, דִּמְהַלֵּיךְ עַל אַרְבַּע, דְּלֵיהּ קַרְסְלִין מֵעִלָּוֵי רַגְלוֹהִי, לְקַפָּצָא בְהוֹן עַל אַרְעָא: כב יָת אִלֵּין מִנְּהוֹן תֵּיכְלוּן, יָת גּוֹבָא לִזְנֵיהּ, וְיָת רָשׁוֹנָא לִזְנוֹהִי, וְיָת חַרְגְּלָא לִזְנוֹהִי, וְיָת חַגְבָּא לִזְנוֹהִי: כג וְכָל רִחְשָׁא דְעוֹפָא, דְּלֵיהּ אַרְבַּע רַגְלִין, שִׁקְצָא הוּא לְכוֹן: כד וּלְאִלֵּין תִּסְתָּאֲבוּן, כָּל דְּיִקְרַב בְּנִבְלַתְהוֹן יְהֵי מְסָאַב עַד רַמְשָׁא: כה וְכָל דְּיִטּוֹל מִנְּבִילַתְהוֹן, יְצַבַּע לְבוּשׁוֹהִי וִיהֵי מְסָאַב עַד רַמְשָׁא: כו לְכָל בְּעִירָא, דְּהִיא סְדִיקָא פַּרְסְתַהּ, וְטִלְפִין לֵיתַהָא מְטַלְפָא, וּפִשְׁרָא לֵיתַהָא מַסְקָא, מְסָאֲבִין אִנּוּן לְכוֹן, כָּל דְּיִקְרַב בְּהוֹן יְהֵי מְסָאַב: כז וְכָל דִּמְהַלֵּיךְ עַל יְדוֹהִי, בְּכָל חַיְתָא דִּמְהַלְּכָא עַל אַרְבַּע, מְסָאֲבִין אִנּוּן לְכוֹן, כָּל דְּיִקְרַב בְּנִבְלַתְהוֹן יְהֵי מְסָאַב עַד רַמְשָׁא: כח וּדְיִטּוֹל יָת נְבִילַתְהוֹן, יְצַבַּע

11:19 הַחֲסִידָה *The stork* – Ramban links the laws of *kashrut* to the characteristics of different groups of animals. We eat tame herbivores but not predators, because we are affected by what we eat. The Jewish mystics once asked: Why, then, is the *ḥasida*, the stork, an unclean animal? Its name in Hebrew literally means "the compassionate

29 be impure until evening; these animals are impure for you. Among
the creatures that creep along the ground, the following are impure for you:
30 the ferret, the mouse, every kind of spiny-tailed lizard, the legless lizard, the
31 chameleon, the lizard, the skink, and the mole rat. Of all the creatures that
creep along the ground, these are impure for you; whoever touches them when
32 they are dead shall be impure until evening. And if any of these dies and falls on
something – a wooden vessel, clothing, leather goods or sackcloth, any utensil
with which work is done – it renders it impure. The article must be immersed in
water and then remains impure until evening, when it will become pure again.
33 If any of these falls into a pottery jar, everything inside it becomes impure; SHEVI'I
34 you must smash the pot. Edible food becomes impure in such a jar if water
has been poured over; any drinkable beverage in such a jar becomes impure.
35 Anything on which a part of one of their dead bodies falls becomes impure.
If it is an oven or stove, it must be broken into pieces; it is impure for you and
36 will remain so. A spring or cistern holding water remains pure, but anyone who
37 touches one of their dead bodies in it becomes impure. If any part of their dead
38 bodies falls on seed that has been planted, the seed remains pure. But if water

רש"י

כט **וזה לכם הטמא.** כל טמאות הללו אינן לאסור אכילה, אלא לטומאה ממש להיות טמא במגען, ונאסר לאכל תרומה וקדשים ולכנס למקדש: **החלד.** מושטיל"א: **והצב.** פרויי"ט שדומה לצפרדע:

ל **אנקה.** הריצו"ן: **הלטאה.** לוישרד"א: **חמט.** לימצ"א: **תנשמת.** טלפ"א:

לב **במים יובא.** ואף לאחר טבילתו טמא הוא לתרומה "עד הערב", ואחר כך "וטהר" בהערב שמש:

לג **אל תוכו.** אין כלי חרס מטמא אלא מאוירו: **כל אשר בתוכו יטמא.** הכלי חוזר ומטמא מה שבאוירו: **ואתו תשברו.** למד שאין לו טהרה במקוה:

לד **מכל האכל אשר יאכל.** מוסב על מקרא העליון: כל אשר בתוכו יטמא, מכל האכל אשר יאכל אשר בא עליו מים, והוא בתוך כלי חרס הטמא, יטמא. למדנו מכאן דברים הרבה: למדנו שאין אכל מכשר ומתקן לקבל טמאה עד שיבואו עליו מים פעם אחת, ומשבאו עליו מים פעם אחת מקבל טמאה לעולם ואפלו נגוב; והיין והשמן וכל הנקרא משקה מכשיר זרעים לטמאה כמים, שכך יש לדרש המקרא: "אשר יבוא עליו מים" או "כל משקה אשר ישתה בכל כלי, יטמא" האכל. ועוד למדו רבותינו מכאן שאין ולד הטמאה מטמא כלים, שכך שנינו: יכול יהו כל הכלים מטמאין מאויר כלי חרס? תלמוד לומר: "כל אשר בתוכו יטמא... מכל האכל" – אכל ומשקה מטמא מאויר כלי חרס, ואין כל הכלים מטמאין מאויר כלי חרס; לפי שהשרץ אב הטמאה והכלי שנטמא ממנו ולד הטמאה, לפיכך אינו חוזר ומטמא כלים שבתוכו. ולמדנו עוד, שהשרץ שנפל לאויר תנור והפת בתוכו, ולא נגע השרץ בפת, התנור ראשון והפת שניה, ולא נאמר רואין את התנור כאלו מלא טמאה ותהא הפת תחלה, שאם אתה אומר כן, לא נתמעטו כל הכלים מלטמא מאויר כלי חרס, שהרי טמאה עצמה נגעה בהן מגבן. ולמדנו עוד על ביאת מים שאינה מכשרת זרעים אלא אם כן נפלו עליהן משנתלשו, שאם אתה אומר מקבלין הכשר במחבר, אין לך שלא באו עליו מים, ומהו אומר: "אשר יבוא עליו מים"? ולמדנו עוד שאין אכל מטמא אחרים אלא אם כן יש בו כביצה, שנאמר: "אשר יאכל" – אכל הנאכל בבת אחת, ושערו חכמים אין בית הבליעה מחזיק יותר מביצת תרנגלת:

לה **תנור וכירים.** כלים המטלטלין הן, והן של חרס ויש להן תוך, ושופת על נקב החלל את הקדרה, ושניהם פיהם למעלה: **יתץ.** שאין לכלי חרס טהרה בטבילה: **וטמאים יהיו לכם.** שלא תאמר מצוה אני לנתצם, תלמוד לומר: "וטמאים יהיו לכם", אם רצה לקימן בטמאתן – רשאי:

כט בְּגָדָיו וְטָמֵא עַד־הָעָרֶב טְמֵאִים הֵמָּה לָכֶם׃ וְזֶה לָכֶם
הַטָּמֵא בַּשֶּׁרֶץ הַשֹּׁרֵץ עַל־הָאָרֶץ הַחֹלֶד וְהָעַכְבָּר וְהַצָּב לְמִינֵהוּ׃
ל לא וְהָאֲנָקָה וְהַכֹּחַ וְהַלְּטָאָה וְהַחֹמֶט וְהַתִּנְשָׁמֶת׃ אֵלֶּה הַטְּמֵאִים לָכֶם
לב בְּכָל־הַשָּׁרֶץ כָּל־הַנֹּגֵעַ בָּהֶם בְּמֹתָם יִטְמָא עַד־הָעָרֶב׃ וְכֹל אֲשֶׁר־יִפֹּל
עָלָיו מֵהֶם ׀ בְּמֹתָם יִטְמָא מִכָּל־כְּלִי־עֵץ אוֹ בֶגֶד אוֹ־עוֹר אוֹ שָׂק כָּל־
כְּלִי אֲשֶׁר־יֵעָשֶׂה מְלָאכָה בָּהֶם בַּמַּיִם יוּבָא וְטָמֵא עַד־הָעֶרֶב וְטָהֵר׃
לג וְכָל־כְּלִי־חֶרֶשׂ אֲשֶׁר־יִפֹּל מֵהֶם אֶל־תּוֹכוֹ כֹּל אֲשֶׁר בְּתוֹכוֹ יִטְמָא וְאֹתוֹ שביעי
לד תִשְׁבֹּרוּ׃ מִכָּל־הָאֹכֶל אֲשֶׁר יֵאָכֵל אֲשֶׁר יָבוֹא עָלָיו מַיִם יִטְמָא וְכָל־
לה מַשְׁקֶה אֲשֶׁר יִשָּׁתֶה בְּכָל־כְּלִי יִטְמָא׃ וְכֹל אֲשֶׁר־יִפֹּל מִנִּבְלָתָם ׀ עָלָיו
לו יִטְמָא תַּנּוּר וְכִירַיִם יֻתָּץ טְמֵאִים הֵם וּטְמֵאִים יִהְיוּ לָכֶם׃ אַךְ מַעְיָן
לז וּבוֹר מִקְוֵה־מַיִם יִהְיֶה טָהוֹר וְנֹגֵעַ בְּנִבְלָתָם יִטְמָא׃ וְכִי יִפֹּל מִנִּבְלָתָם
לח עַל־כָּל־זֶרַע זֵרוּעַ אֲשֶׁר יִזָּרֵעַ טָהוֹר הוּא׃ וְכִי יֻתַּן־מַיִם עַל־זֶרַע וְנָפַל

אונקלוס

לְבוּשׁוֹהִי וִיהֵי מְסָאַב עַד רַמְשָׁא, מְסָאֲבִין אִנּוּן לְכוֹן: כט וְדֵין לְכוֹן דִּמְסָאַב, בְּרִחְשָׁא דְּרָחֵישׁ עַל אַרְעָא, חֻלְדָּא וְעַכְבְּרָא וְצַבָּא לִזְנוֹהִי: ל וְיַלָּא וְכוֹחָא וְהַלְטָתָא, וְחֻמְטָא וְאָשׁוּתָא: לא אִלֵּין, דִּמְסָאֲבִין לְכוֹן בְּכָל רִחְשָׁא, כָּל דְּיִקְרַב בְּהוֹן, בְּמוֹתְהוֹן יְהֵי מְסָאַב עַד רַמְשָׁא: לב וְכָל דְּיִפּוֹל עֲלוֹהִי מִנְּהוֹן בְּמוֹתְהוֹן יְהֵי מְסָאַב, מִכָּל מָן דְּאָע אוֹ לְבוּשׁ אוֹ מְשַׁךְ אוֹ סַק, כָּל מָן, דְּיִתְעֲבֵיד עֲבִידְתָּא בְּהוֹן, בְּמַיָּא יִתָּעַל, וִיהֵי מְסָאַב עַד רַמְשָׁא וְיִדְכֵּי: לג וְכָל מָן דַּחֲסַף, דְּיִפּוֹל מִנְּהוֹן לְגַוֵּיהּ, כֹּל דִּבְגַוֵּיהּ, יְהֵי מְסָאַב וְיָתֵיהּ תְּתַבְּרוּן: לד מִכָּל מֵיכַל דְּמִתְאֲכִיל, דְּיֵיעוֹל עֲלוֹהִי, מַיָּא יְהֵי מְסָאַב, וְכָל מַשְׁקְיָא דְּיִשְׁתְּתֵי, בְּכָל מָן יְהֵי מְסָאַב: לה וְכֹל, דְּיִפּוֹל מִנְּבִילַתְהוֹן עֲלוֹהִי יְהֵי מְסָאַב, תַּנּוּר וְכִירַיִם, יִתָּרְעוּן מְסָאֲבִין אִנּוּן, וּמְסָאֲבִין יְהוֹן לְכוֹן: לו בְּרַם מַעְיַן וְגוּב, בֵּית כְּנִישַׁת מַיָּא יְהֵי דְּכֵי, וּדְיִקְרַב בִּנְבִילַתְהוֹן יְהֵי מְסָאַב: לז וַאֲרֵי יִפּוֹל מִנְּבִילַתְהוֹן, עַל כָּל בַּר זְרַע זֵרוּעַ דְּיִזְדְּרַע, דְּכֵי הוּא: לח וַאֲרֵי יִתְיְהָבוּן מַיָּא עַל בַּר זַרְעָא, וְיִפּוֹל

רש"י

לו) אַךְ מַעְיָן וּבוֹר מִקְוֵה מַיִם. הַמְחֻבָּרִים לַקַּרְקַע, אֵין מְקַבְּלִין טֻמְאָה. וְעוֹד יֵשׁ לְךָ לִלְמֹד, "יִהְיֶה טָהוֹר" הַטּוֹבֵל בָּהֶם מִטֻּמְאָתוֹ: וְנֹגֵעַ בְּנִבְלָתָם יִטְמָא. אֲפִלּוּ הוּא בְּתוֹךְ מַעְיָן וּבוֹר וְנוֹגֵעַ בְּטֻמְאָתָם – יִטְמָא, שֶׁלֹּא תֹּאמַר קַל וָחֹמֶר: אִם מְטַהֵר אֶת הַטְּמֵאִים מִטֻּמְאָתָם, קַל וָחֹמֶר שֶׁיָּגֵן אֶת הַטָּהוֹר מִלִּטָּמֵא, לְכָךְ נֶאֱמַר: "וְנֹגֵעַ בְּנִבְלָתָם יִטְמָא":

לז) זֶרַע זֵרוּעַ. זְרִיעָה שֶׁל מִינֵי זֵרְעוֹנִין. 'זֵרוּעַ' שֵׁם דָּבָר הוּא, כְּמוֹ: "וְיִתְּנוּ לָנוּ מִן הַזֵּרֹעִים" (דניאל א, יב): טָהוֹר הוּא. לִמֶּדְךָ הַכָּתוּב שֶׁלֹּא הֻכְשַׁר וְנִתְקַן לִקְרוֹת אֹכֶל לְקַבֵּל טֻמְאָה עַד שֶׁיָּבוֹאוּ עָלָיו מַיִם:

לח) וְכִי יֻתַּן מַיִם עַל זֶרַע. לְאַחַר שֶׁנִּתְלַשׁ, שֶׁאִם תֹּאמַר יֵשׁ הֶכְשֵׁר בִּמְחֻבָּר, אֵין לְךָ זֶרַע שֶׁלֹּא הֻכְשַׁר: מַיִם עַל זֶרַע. בֵּין מַיִם בֵּין שְׁאָר מַשְׁקִין, בֵּין הֵם עַל הַזֶּרַע בֵּין זֶרַע נוֹפֵל לְתוֹכָן, הַכֹּל נִדְרָשׁ בְּתוֹרַת כֹּהֲנִים (פרק יא, ו, ט): וְנָפַל מִנִּבְלָתָם עָלָיו. אַף מִשֶּׁנִּגַּב מִן הַמַּיִם, שֶׁלֹּא הִקְפִּידָה תּוֹרָה אֶלָּא לִהְיוֹת עָלָיו שֵׁם אֹכֶל, וּמִשֶּׁיָּרַד לוֹ הֶכְשֵׁר קַבָּלַת טֻמְאָה פַּעַם אַחַת, שׁוּב אֵינוֹ נֶעֱקָר הֵימֶנּוּ:

לט) בְּנִבְלָתָהּ. וְלֹא בַּעֲצָמוֹת וְגִידִים וְלֹא בְּקַרְנַיִם וּטְלָפַיִם וְלֹא בָּעוֹר:

has been poured over the seed and afterward any part of their dead bodies falls
39 upon it, it is rendered impure for you. If an animal of a kind that you
are allowed to eat dies naturally, one who touches its carcass shall be impure
40 until evening. Anyone who eats of its carcass must immerse his clothes, and he
remains impure until evening. Anyone who moves the carcass must immerse
41 his clothes, and he remains impure until evening. All creatures that swarm on
42 the earth are detested; they shall not be eaten. Of these swarming things you
shall not eat any, those that move on their bellies or crawl on all fours or on
43 many feet – for they are all detestable. Do not make yourselves detestable by
contact with any of these swarming creatures. Do not defile yourselves with
44 them or be defiled by them. I am the LORD your God. Consecrate yourselves
and be holy, for I am holy. Do not defile yourselves with any swarming creature
45 that crawls on the ground. I am the LORD, who brought you up out of Egypt to MAFTIR
46 be your God. Be holy, for I am holy." This is the law concerning animals, birds,

רש״י

מ | **וְהַנֹּשֵׂא אֶת נִבְלָתָהּ.** חֲמוּרָה טֻמְאַת מַשָּׂא מִטֻּמְאַת מַגָּע, שֶׁהַנּוֹשֵׂא מְטַמֵּא בְּגָדִים, וְהַנּוֹגֵעַ אֵין בְּגָדָיו טְמֵאִין, שֶׁלֹּא נֶאֱמַר בּוֹ: "יְכַבֵּס בְּגָדָיו": **וְהָאֹכֵל מִנִּבְלָתָהּ.** יָכוֹל תְּטַמְּאֶנּוּ אֲכִילָתוֹ? כְּשֶׁהוּא אוֹמֵר בְּנִבְלַת עוֹף טָהוֹר: "לֹא יֹאכַל לְטָמְאָה בָהּ" (להלן כב, ח), בָּהּ אַתָּה מְטַמֵּא בְּגָדִים בַּאֲכִילָתָהּ, וְאֵין נִבְלַת בְּהֵמָה מְטַמְּאָה בְּגָדִים בַּאֲכִילָתָהּ בְּלֹא מַגָּע אוֹ בְּלֹא מַשָּׂא, כְּגוֹן אִם תְּחָבָהּ לוֹ חֲבֵרוֹ בְּבֵית הַבְּלִיעָה. אִם כֵּן, מַה תַּלְמוּד לוֹמַר: "הָאֹכֵל"? לִתֵּן שִׁעוּר לַנּוֹשֵׂא וְלַנּוֹגֵעַ כְּדֵי אֲכִילָה, וְהוּא כַּזַּיִת: **וְטָמֵא עַד הָעָרֶב.** אַף עַל פִּי שֶׁטָּבַל, צָרִיךְ הַעֲרֵב שֶׁמֶשׁ:

מא | **הַשֹּׁרֵץ עַל הָאָרֶץ.** לְהוֹצִיא אֶת הַיַּתּוּשִׁין שֶׁבַּכְּלִיסִין וְשֶׁבַּפּוֹלִין וְאֶת הַזִּיזִין שֶׁבַּעֲדָשִׁים, שֶׁהֲרֵי לֹא שָׁרְצוּ עַל הָאָרֶץ אֶלָּא בְּתוֹךְ הָאֹכֶל, אֲבָל מִשֶּׁיָּצְאוּ לַאֲוִיר וְשָׁרְצוּ הֲרֵי נֶאֶסְרוּ: **לֹא יֵאָכֵל.** לְחַיֵּב עַל הַמַּאֲכִיל כָּאוֹכֵל. וְאֵין קָרוּי שֶׁרֶץ אֶלָּא דָּבָר נָמוּךְ קְצַר רַגְלַיִם שֶׁאֵינוֹ נִרְאֶה אֶלָּא כְּרוֹחֵשׁ וְנָד:

מב | **הוֹלֵךְ עַל גָּחוֹן.** זֶה נָחָשׁ, וּלְשׁוֹן 'גָּחוֹן' – שְׁחִיָּה, שֶׁהוֹלֵךְ שַׁח וְנוֹפֵל עַל מֵעָיו: **וְכֹל הוֹלֵךְ.** לְהָבִיא הַשִּׁלְשׁוּלִין וְאֶת הַדּוֹמֶה לַדּוֹמֶה: **הוֹלֵךְ עַל אַרְבַּע.** זֶה עַקְרָב: **כֹּל.** לְהָבִיא אֶת הַחִפּוּשִׁית, אשקרבו״ט בְּלַעַ״ז, וְאֶת הַדּוֹמֶה לַדּוֹמֶה: **מַרְבֵּה רַגְלַיִם.** זֶה נָדָל, שֶׁרֶץ שֶׁיֵּשׁ לוֹ רַגְלַיִם מֵרֹאשׁוֹ וְעַד זְנָבוֹ לְכָאן וּלְכָאן, וְקוֹרִין צינטפיד״ש:

מג | **אַל תְּשַׁקְּצוּ.** בַּאֲכִילָתָן, שֶׁהֲרֵי כְּתִיב: "נַפְשֹׁתֵיכֶם", וְאֵין שִׁקּוּץ נֶפֶשׁ בְּמַגָּע, וְכֵן: אַל תִּטַּמְּאוּ בַּאֲכִילָתָן: **וְנִטְמֵתֶם בָּם.** אִם אַתֶּם מִטַּמְּאִין בָּהֶם בָּאָרֶץ, אַף אֲנִי מְטַמֵּא אֶתְכֶם בָּעוֹלָם הַבָּא וּבִישִׁיבַת מַעְלָה:

מד | **כִּי אֲנִי ה׳ אֱלֹהֵיכֶם.** כְּשֵׁם שֶׁאֲנִי קָדוֹשׁ שֶׁאֲנִי ה׳ אֱלֹהֵיכֶם, כָּךְ "וְהִתְקַדִּשְׁתֶּם", קַדְּשׁוּ עַצְמְכֶם לְמַטָּה: **וִהְיִיתֶם קְדֹשִׁים.** לְפָנַי, שֶׁאֲנִי אֲקַדֵּשׁ אֶתְכֶם לְמַעְלָה וּבָעוֹלָם הַבָּא: **וְלֹא תְטַמְּאוּ וְגוֹ׳.** לַעֲבֹר עֲלֵיהֶם בְּלָאוִין הַרְבֵּה, וְכָל לָאו – מַלְקוּת. וְזֶהוּ שֶׁאָמְרוּ בַּתַּלְמוּד: אָכַל פּוּטִיתָא לוֹקֶה אַרְבַּע, נְמָלָה לוֹקֶה חָמֵשׁ, צִרְעָה לוֹקֶה שֵׁשׁ:

מה | **כִּי אֲנִי ה׳ הַמַּעֲלֶה אֶתְכֶם.** עַל מְנָת שֶׁתְּקַבְּלוּ מִצְוֹתַי הֶעֱלֵיתִי אֶתְכֶם:

11:46 **זֹאת תּוֹרַת הַבְּהֵמָה וְהָעוֹף וְכֹל נֶפֶשׁ הַחַיָּה** *This is the law concerning... all creatures* – We owe our translations of the species listed here to the scholarship of natural historians such as Yehuda Feliks and Zohar Amar. This passage is perhaps the most overt example of a much broader principle: we cannot apply Torah to the world unless we understand the world.

To fully apply the Torah's dietary laws, we need an understanding of zoology. To apply Torah to the human mind, one must understand psychology and psychiatry. To apply it to society, we must understand sociology and anthropology. To cure poverty, we must understand economics. To avoid environmental catastrophe, we need to understand botany, biology, climatology, and much else

לט מִנִּבְלָתָם עָלָיו טָמֵא הוּא לָכֶם׃ וְכִי יָמוּת מִן־הַבְּהֵמָה
מ אֲשֶׁר־הִיא לָכֶם לְאָכְלָה הַנֹּגֵעַ בְּנִבְלָתָהּ יִטְמָא עַד־הָעָרֶב׃ וְהָאֹכֵל
מִנִּבְלָתָהּ יְכַבֵּס בְּגָדָיו וְטָמֵא עַד־הָעָרֶב וְהַנֹּשֵׂא אֶת־נִבְלָתָהּ יְכַבֵּס
מא בְּגָדָיו וְטָמֵא עַד־הָעָרֶב׃ וְכָל־הַשֶּׁרֶץ הַשֹּׁרֵץ עַל־הָאָרֶץ שֶׁקֶץ הוּא לֹא
מב יֵאָכֵל׃ כֹּל הוֹלֵךְ עַל־גָּחוֹן וְכֹל ׀ הוֹלֵךְ עַל־אַרְבַּע עַד כָּל־מַרְבֵּה רַגְלַיִם
מג לְכָל־הַשֶּׁרֶץ הַשֹּׁרֵץ עַל־הָאָרֶץ לֹא תֹאכְלוּם כִּי־שֶׁקֶץ הֵם׃ אַל־תְּשַׁקְּצוּ
אֶת־נַפְשֹׁתֵיכֶם בְּכָל־הַשֶּׁרֶץ הַשֹּׁרֵץ וְלֹא תִטַּמְּאוּ בָּהֶם וְנִטְמֵתֶם בָּם׃
מד כִּי אֲנִי יהוה אֱלֹהֵיכֶם וְהִתְקַדִּשְׁתֶּם וִהְיִיתֶם קְדֹשִׁים כִּי קָדוֹשׁ אָנִי וְלֹא
מה תְטַמְּאוּ אֶת־נַפְשֹׁתֵיכֶם בְּכָל־הַשֶּׁרֶץ הָרֹמֵשׂ עַל־הָאָרֶץ׃ כִּי ׀ אֲנִי יהוה מפטיר
הַמַּעֲלֶה אֶתְכֶם מֵאֶרֶץ מִצְרַיִם לִהְיֹת לָכֶם לֵאלֹהִים וִהְיִיתֶם קְדֹשִׁים
מו כִּי קָדוֹשׁ אָנִי׃ זֹאת תּוֹרַת הַבְּהֵמָה וְהָעוֹף וְכֹל נֶפֶשׁ הַחַיָּה הָרֹמֶשֶׂת

אונקלוס

מִנְּבִילַתְהוֹן עֲלוֹהִי, מְסָאַב הוּא לְכוֹן: לט וַאֲרֵי יְמוּת מִן בְּעִירָא, דְּהִיא לְכוֹן לְמֵיכַל, דְּיִקְרַב בִּנְבִילְתַהּ יְהֵי מְסָאַב עַד רַמְשָׁא: מ וּדְיֵיכוֹל מִנְּבִילְתַהּ, יְצַבַּע לְבוּשׁוֹהִי וִיהֵי מְסָאַב עַד רַמְשָׁא, וּדְיִטּוֹל יָת נְבִילְתַהּ, יְצַבַּע לְבוּשׁוֹהִי וִיהֵי מְסָאַב עַד רַמְשָׁא: מא וְכָל רִחְשָׁא דְּרָחֵישׁ עַל אַרְעָא, שִׁקְצָא הוּא לָא יִתְאֲכִיל: מב כָּל דִּמְהַלֵּיךְ עַל מְעוֹהִי, וְכָל דִּמְהַלֵּיךְ עַל אַרְבַּע, עַד כָּל סַגִּיוּת רַגְלִין, לְכָל רִחְשָׁא דְּרָחֵישׁ עַל אַרְעָא, לָא תֵיכְלוּנוּן אֲרֵי שִׁקְצָא אִנּוּן:

מג לָא תְשַׁקְּצוּן יָת נַפְשָׁתְכוֹן, בְּכָל רִחְשָׁא דְּרָחֵישׁ, וְלָא תִסְתָּאֲבוּן בְּהוֹן, וְתִסְתָּאֲבוּן פּוֹן בְּהוֹן: מד אֲרֵי אֲנָא יי אֱלָהֲכוֹן, וְתִתְקַדְּשׁוּן וּתְהוֹן קַדִּישִׁין, אֲרֵי קַדִּישׁ אֲנָא, וְלָא תְסָאֲבוּן יָת נַפְשָׁתְכוֹן, בְּכָל רִחְשָׁא דְּרָחֵישׁ עַל אַרְעָא: מה אֲרֵי אֲנָא יי, דְּאַסֵּיק יָתְכוֹן מֵאַרְעָא דְּמִצְרָיִם, לְמֶהֱוֵי לְכוֹן לֶאֱלָהּ, וּתְהוֹן קַדִּישִׁין, אֲרֵי קַדִּישׁ אֲנָא: מו דָּא אוֹרָיְתָא דִּבְעִירָא וּדְעוֹפָא, וּלְכָל נַפְשָׁא חַיְתָא, דְּרָחֲשָׁא

11:44 וִהְיִיתֶם קְדֹשִׁים כִּי קָדוֹשׁ אָנִי *Be holy, for I am holy* – Eating and procreation are the most primal activities, shared with most other forms of life. Without sexual relations there is no continuation of the species. Without food, even the individual cannot survive. These have been approached in radically different ways by human cultures.

On the one hand, there are hedonistic cultures in which food and sexuality are seen as pleasures and pursued as such. On the other are ascetic cultures – marked by monastic seclusion – in which sexual relations are avoided and eating kept to a minimum. The former emphasize the body, the latter the soul.

Judaism, by contrast, sees the human situation in terms of integration and balance. We are body *and* soul. Hence the Judaic imperative, neither hedonistic nor ascetic, but transformative: we are commanded to *sanctify* both eating and sexual relations. From this flow the dietary laws and the laws of family purity (*nidda* and *mikveh*), two key elements of *kedusha*, the life of holiness. Here we have discussed eating; we will turn to family purity in the coming *parashot*.

47 all creatures that live in water and all that swarm on the earth, to distinguish
between the impure and the pure and between creatures that may be eaten and
those that may not.

The haftara for Parashat Shemini is on page 1562.
On the Shabbat of Parashat HaḤodesh read the haftara on page 1650.

רש״י

מז) **לְהַבְדִּיל.** לֹא בִּלְבַד הַשּׁוֹנֶה, אֶלָּא שֶׁתְּהֵא יוֹדֵעַ וּמַכִּיר וּבָקִי בָּהֶן: **בֵּין הַטָּמֵא וּבֵין הַטָּהֹר.** צָרִיךְ לוֹמַר בֵּין חֲמוֹר לְפָרָה? וַהֲלֹא כְּבָר מְפֹרָשִׁים הֵם! אֶלָּא בֵּין טְמֵאָה לְךָ לִטְהוֹרָה לְךָ, בֵּין נִשְׁחַט חֶצְיוֹ שֶׁל קָנֶה לְנִשְׁחַט רֻבּוֹ: **וּבֵין הַחַיָּה הַנֶּאֱכֶלֶת וְגוֹ׳.** צָרִיךְ לוֹמַר בֵּין צְבִי לְעָרוֹד? וַהֲלֹא כְּבָר מְפֹרָשִׁים הֵם! אֶלָּא בֵּין שֶׁנּוֹלַד בָּהּ סִימָנֵי טְרֵפָה כְּשֵׁרָה לְנוֹלַד בָּהּ סִימָנֵי טְרֵפָה פְּסוּלָה:

see the wisdom of God's creation. It led, said Rambam, to the love and fear of God. I have argued that within the logic of Judaism as a whole, there is another reason. To realize the Torah's vision we need *ḥokhma*. To repair the world, you have to understand it.

מז בַּמָּ֑יִם וּלְכָל־נֶ֖פֶשׁ הַשֹּׁרֶ֥צֶת עַל־הָאָֽרֶץ׃ לְהַבְדִּ֕יל בֵּ֥ין הַטָּמֵ֖א וּבֵ֣ין
הַטָּהֹ֑ר וּבֵ֤ין הַֽחַיָּה֙ הַֽנֶּאֱכֶ֔לֶת וּבֵין֙ הַֽחַיָּ֔ה אֲשֶׁ֖ר לֹ֥א תֵאָכֵֽל׃

The הפטרה *for* פרשת שמיני *is on page 1563.*
On the שבת *of* פרשת החודש *read the* הפטרה *on page 1651.*

אונקלוס

בְּמַיָּא, וּלְכָל נַפְשָׁא דְּרָחֲשָׁא עַל אַרְעָא׃ מז לְאַפְרָשָׁא, בֵּין מְסָאֲבָא וּבֵין דָּכְיָא, וּבֵין חַיְתָא דְּמִתְאַכְלָא, וּבֵין חַיְתָא, דְּלָא מִתְאַכְלָא׃

There was a time when a purely instrumental reason was given for Jews pursuing secular studies. You needed it to get a job and earn a living. The Sages gave another reason. It gave Jews, and by implication Judaism, respect in the eyes of the world. There was a deeper reason still. It allowed us to besides. All these things come under the general heading of *ḥokhma*, "wisdom," which I define as the knowledge that helps us see the universe as God's work and the human person as God's image – in other words, the sciences and humanities broadly conceived.

Parashat Tazria

12 1 2 The LORD spoke to Moshe: "Tell the Israelites: If a woman conceives and gives
birth to a son, she shall be impure for seven days, as she is during her menstrual
3 4 period. On the eighth day, the child's foreskin shall be circumcised. For thirty-
three days she shall wait, bleeding pure blood, but until her time of purification

רש״י

יב ב **אִשָּׁה כִּי תַזְרִיעַ.** אָמַר רַבִּי שִׂמְלַאי: כְּשֵׁם שֶׁיְּצִירָתוֹ שֶׁל אָדָם אַחַר כָּל בְּהֵמָה חַיָּה וָעוֹף בְּמַעֲשֵׂה בְרֵאשִׁית, כָּךְ תּוֹרָתוֹ נִתְפָּרְשָׁה אַחַר תּוֹרַת בְּהֵמָה חַיָּה וָעוֹף: **כִּי תַזְרִיעַ.** לְרַבּוֹת שֶׁאֲפִלּוּ יְלָדַתּוּ מָחוּי, שֶׁנִּמּוֹחָה וְנַעֲשָׂה כְּעֵין זֶרַע, אִמּוֹ טְמֵאָה לֵדָה: **כִּימֵי נִדַּת דְּוֹתָהּ תִּטְמָא.** כְּסֵדֶר כָּל טֻמְאָה הָאֲמוּרָה בְּנִדָּה מְטַמְּאָה בְּטֻמְאַת לֵדָה, וַאֲפִלּוּ נִפְתַּח הַקֶּבֶר בְּלֹא דָם: **דְּוֹתָהּ.** לְשׁוֹן דָּבָר הַזָּב מִגּוּפָהּ. לָשׁוֹן אַחֵר, לְשׁוֹן מַדְוֶה וְחֹלִי, שֶׁאֵין אִשָּׁה רוֹאָה דָם שֶׁלֹּא תֶּחֱלֶה, וְרֹאשָׁהּ וְאֵבָרֶיהָ כְּבֵדִין עָלֶיהָ:

ד **תֵּשֵׁב.** אֵין 'תֵּשֵׁב' אֶלָּא לְשׁוֹן עַכָּבָה, כְּמוֹ: "וַתֵּשְׁבוּ בְקָדֵשׁ" (דברים א, מו), "וַיֵּשֶׁב בְּאֵלֹנֵי מַמְרֵא" (בראשית יג, יח): **בִּדְמֵי טָהֳרָה.** אַף עַל פִּי שֶׁרוֹאָה

of danger – and the danger is always rooted in an absence of sexual ethics. There are six such episodes: Sara and then Rivka (twice) are threatened with being abducted into a royal harem because of their beauty; two visitors come to Lot's house in Sedom and the local populace threatens to rape them; Dina is raped by the local prince, Shekhem. Finally, Potifar's wife attempts to seduce Yosef and falsely accuses him of rape.

Hence, the conclusion that a key difference between the matriarchs and patriarchs of Genesis and their neighbors was their sexual ethics. Note that the problem is violence around sexuality, and the abuse of power, rather than sexuality itself. When some humans became richer and more powerful than others, kings, rulers, and pharaohs – human alpha males – could command almost open-ended gratification of sexual desire, hence Avraham and Yitzhak's fears that they would be killed so that their wives could be taken into a harem.

The Torah views this cluster of behaviors with abhorrence. Such behavior privileges some people against others. It turns women into instruments of male desire. It places power, not love, at the heart of human relationships. It treats women as objects rather than as subjects with equal dignity and integrity. It divorces sex from compassion and dishonors the most intimate human bond.

Now we understand why the sign of the covenant is circumcision. *Brit mila* is the consecration of sexual desire. Our instincts are not evil in themselves. The religious life is not a matter of self-denial and renunciation. But neither is it hedonism, the unrestrained pursuit of pleasure. Instinct has its darker side, which culminates in violence. For faith to be more than the worship of power, it must affect the most intimate relationship between men and women. In a society founded on covenant, male-female relationships must be built on something other and gentler than male dominance, masculine power, sexual desire, and the drive to own, control, possess. The alpha male must become the caring husband. Sex must be sanctified and tempered by mutual respect. The sexual drive must be circumcised and circumscribed so that it no longer seeks to possess and is instead content to love.

12:3 **יִמּוֹל בְּשַׂר עָרְלָתוֹ** *The child's foreskin shall be circumcised* – Why is the commandment of *brit mila*, already given to Avraham, repeated here? Rambam gives an explanation in his commentary on the Mishna (Ḥullin 7:6). Although Avraham was given the command of circumcision as the sign of God's covenant with him, the covenant God made with the Israelites at Mount Sinai superseded all previous commands. Therefore, *our* performing circumcision today is not because of the command to Avraham, but because it was repeated as part of the covenant at Sinai. The command is historically linked with Avraham but legislatively with the revelation to Moshe.

פרשת תזריע

יב א ב וַיְדַבֵּר יְהוָה אֶל־מֹשֶׁה לֵּאמֹר׃ דַּבֵּר אֶל־בְּנֵי יִשְׂרָאֵל לֵאמֹר אִשָּׁה כִּי ז
תַזְרִיעַ וְיָלְדָה זָכָר וְטָמְאָה שִׁבְעַת יָמִים כִּימֵי נִדַּת דְּוֺתָהּ תִּטְמָא׃
ג ד וּבַיּוֹם הַשְּׁמִינִי יִמּוֹל בְּשַׂר עָרְלָתוֹ׃ וּשְׁלֹשִׁים יוֹם וּשְׁלֹשֶׁת יָמִים תֵּשֵׁב
בִּדְמֵי טָהֳרָה בְּכָל־קֹדֶשׁ לֹא־תִגָּע וְאֶל־הַמִּקְדָּשׁ לֹא תָבֹא עַד־מְלֹאת

אונקלוס

יב א וּמַלֵּיל יי עִם מֹשֶׁה לְמֵימַר: ב מַלֵּיל, עִם בְּנֵי יִשְׂרָאֵל לְמֵימַר, אִתְּתָא אֲרֵי תְעַדֵּי, וּתְלִיד דְּכַר, וּתְהֵי מְסָאֲבָא שִׁבְעָא יוֹמִין, כְּיוֹמֵי, רִיחוּק סְאוֹבְתַהּ תְּהֵי מְסָאֲבָא: ג וּבְיוֹמָא תְּמִינָאָה, יִתְגְּזַר בִּסְרָא דְעָרְלְתֵיהּ: ד וּתְלָתִין וּתְלָתָא יוֹמִין, תְּתֵיב בִּדַם דְּכוּ, בְּכָל קֻדְשָׁא לָא תִקְרַב, וּלְמַקְדְּשָׁא לָא תֵיעוֹל, עַד מִשְׁלַם

TAZRIA

Parashat Tazria continues the laws of purity and impurity begun in Parashat Shemini. One of the key roles of the priest was to distinguish *tahor* from *tameh*, pure from impure, the latter debarring an individual from entering the sacred space of the Sanctuary.

These categories flow from the contrast between God and human beings. God is immortal; humans are mortal. God is spiritual; humans are also physical. And whatever is physical is subject to disease and decay. Conditions that render a person *tameh* are those that testify to our mortality and physicality. People who had a reminder of mortality in ways specified by the Torah may not enter holy space until they are healed and purified.

The *parasha* begins with laws relating to childbirth – the impurity it brings, and also the command to circumcise a male child on the eighth day. It continues with laws relating to a still-unidentified disease, *tzaraat*, often translated as leprosy, but referring to something other and larger than the disease because it affects not only people but also clothes and houses. The *parasha* describes some of the symptoms, which may appear following a skin inflammation. It is the task of the priest to examine such symptoms, declaring the person clean or unclean or to be quarantined until a clearer diagnosis can be made. The Sages see *tzaraat* as a punishment for the sin of evil speech.

CIRCUMCISION

Parashat Tazria opens with the command that, for males, is the distinguishing mark of Jewish identity: circumcision. The question arises: Why this sign above all others? Why a physical mark on the flesh, and why this part of the flesh? What does it tell us about the nature of Jewish identity?

There is no explicit answer to these questions in the Torah, and the commentators offer several explanations. According to Midrash Sekhel Tov (on Gen. 17:11) and *Sefer HaḤinukh* (positive command 2), it serves as an outward sign to differentiate Jews from gentiles. It is like the other signs such as tzitzit, tefillin, and mezuza, different in that it is actually a part of one's body. Rambam (*Guide for the Perplexed* III:49) explains that it is a unifying mark that identifies Jews as part of a nation. Ramban (on Gen. 17:11) sees it as a way of conferring *kedusha*, sanctity, on the act of procreation.

Each of these is an important part of the answer, but there may be a way of understanding the command in the wider context of the Torah as a whole.

To see why this might be, we must look back to the first book of the Torah, Genesis. What makes the patriarchs different? How do Avraham and his family mark a new beginning? The book, as we noted there, gives us an inescapable clue. Whenever a member of the covenantal family finds him- or herself entering another society, there is always a moment

5 is completed, she must not touch anything holy or enter the Sanctuary. If she
gives birth to a daughter, she shall be impure – as she is during her menstrual
6 period – for two weeks, and bleeds in purity for sixty-six days. When the days
of her purification are complete, whether for a son or a daughter, she shall bring
a yearling sheep to the priest at the entrance to the Tent of Meeting as a burnt
7 offering and a pigeon or dove as a purification offering. The priest shall present
it before the LORD and make atonement for her; so shall she be purified of her

רש"י

דָּם, טְהוֹרָה: **בִּדְמֵי טָהֳרָה.** לֹא מַפִּיק הֵ"א, וְהוּא שֵׁם דָּבָר, כְּמוֹ 'טֹהַר': **יְמֵי טָהֳרָהּ.** מַפִּיק הַ"א, יְמֵי טֹהַר שֶׁלָּהּ: **לֹא תִגָּע.** אַזְהָרָה לָאוֹכֵל, כְּמוֹ שֶׁשְּׁנוּיָה בִּיבָמוֹת (דף עה ע"א): **בְּכָל קֹדֶשׁ וְגוֹ'.** לְרַבּוֹת אֶת הַתְּרוּמָה, לְפִי שֶׁזּוֹ טְבוּלַת יוֹם אָרֹךְ, שֶׁטָּבְלָה לְסוֹף שִׁבְעָה, וְאֵין שִׁמְשָׁהּ מַעֲרִיב לְטַהֲרָהּ עַד שְׁקִיעַת הַחַמָּה שֶׁל יוֹם אַרְבָּעִים, שֶׁלְּמָחָר תָּבִיא אֶת כַּפָּרַת טָהֳרָתָהּ:

ז **וְהִקְרִיבוֹ.** לִמֵּד שֶׁאֵין מְעַכְּבָהּ לֶאֱכֹל בְּקָדָשִׁים אֶלָּא אֶחָד מֵהֶם, וְאֵי זֶה הוּא? זֶה חַטָּאת, שֶׁנֶּאֱמַר: "וְכִפֶּר עָלֶיהָ הַכֹּהֵן וְטָהֵרָה" (להלן פסוק ח), מִי שֶׁהוּא בָּא לְכַפֵּר, בּוֹ הַטָּהֳרָה תְּלוּיָה: **וְטָהֵרָה.** מִכְלָל שֶׁעַד כָּאן קְרוּיָה טְמֵאָה:

experiencing it yourself, directly and with every fiber of your being. Days, weeks, from now you will come and give thanks before Me (together with offerings for having come through a moment of danger). But for now, look upon your child with wonder." Childbirth exempts the new mother from attendance at the Temple because her bedside replicates the experience of the Temple. She knows what it is for love to beget life and in the midst of mortality to be touched by an intimation of immortality.

12:7 **זֹאת תּוֹרַת הַיֹּלֶדֶת** *The law for a woman who bears a child* – It is common to divide the religious life in Judaism into two dimensions. On the one side, the priesthood and the Sanctuary, and on the other, the prophets and the people. The priests focused on the relationship between the people and God, *mitzvot bein adam laMakom*. Prophets focused on the relationship between the people and one another, *mitzvot bein adam leḥavero*. The priests supervised ritual and the prophets spoke about ethics. One group was concerned with holiness, the other with virtue. You don't need to be holy to be good. You need to be good to be holy, but that is an entrance requirement, not what being holy is about. Pharaoh's daughter, who rescued Moshe when he was a baby, was good but not holy. These are two separate ideas.

I would like to challenge that conception. The prophetic virtues of *ḥesed* and *mishpat* are close to those that prevail today in the liberal democracies of the West – kindness, or protection from harm, and fairness. That is a measure of the impact of the Hebrew Bible on the West, but that is another story for another time. The point is that kindness and fairness are about relationships between individuals. The priesthood and the Sanctuary, however, also made a moral difference. The priestly values of loyalty, respect, and sanctity, though frequently neglected in secularized societies, have been shown to be important, even essential, in sustaining community over time.

Sanctity involves the need to ring-fence certain values we regard as non-negotiable. They are not mine to do with as I wish. These are the things we call *sacred*, sacrosanct, not to be treated lightly or defiled. Reverence is what gives power to social conventions, civilities, ceremony, and ritual.

Not all societies see a need for rituals after birth. Nothing is more "natural" than procreation. Every living thing engages in it. Sociobiologists go so far as to argue that a human being is a gene's way of creating another gene. In the Torah, childbirth is wondrous. To be a parent is the closest any of us come to God Himself. Women, unlike men, know what it is to bring new life out of themselves, as God brings life out of Himself. The idea is beautifully captured in the verse in which, leaving Eden, Adam turns to his wife and calls her Ḥava "for she would become the mother of all life" (Gen. 3:20).

ה יְמֵי טָהֳרָהּ׃ וְאִם־נְקֵבָה תֵלֵד וְטָמְאָה שְׁבֻעַיִם כְּנִדָּתָהּ וְשִׁשִּׁים יוֹם
ו וְשֵׁשֶׁת יָמִים תֵּשֵׁב עַל־דְּמֵי טָהֳרָה׃ וּבִמְלֹאת ׀ יְמֵי טָהֳרָהּ לְבֵן אוֹ
לְבַת תָּבִיא כֶּבֶשׂ בֶּן־שְׁנָתוֹ לְעֹלָה וּבֶן־יוֹנָה אוֹ־תֹר לְחַטָּאת אֶל־
ז פֶּתַח אֹהֶל־מוֹעֵד אֶל־הַכֹּהֵן׃ וְהִקְרִיבוֹ לִפְנֵי יהוה וְכִפֶּר עָלֶיהָ וְטָהֲרָה

אונקלוס

יוֹמֵי דְכוּתַהּ: ה וְאִם נֻקְבְּתָא תְלִיד, וּתְהֵי מְסָאֲבָא אַרְבְּעַת עֲסַר
כְּרִיחוּקַהּ, וְשִׁתִּין וְשִׁתָּא יוֹמִין, תְּתֵיב עַל דַּם דְּכוּ: ו וּבְמִשְׁלַם
יוֹמֵי דְכוּתַהּ, לִבְרָא אוֹ לִבְרַתָּא, תַּיְתֵי, אִמַּר בַּר שַׁתֵּיהּ לַעֲלָתָא,
וּבַר יוֹנָה אוֹ שַׁפְנִינָא לְחַטָּתָא, לִתְרַע מַשְׁכַּן זִמְנָא לְוָת כָּהֲנָא: ז
וִיקָרְבִנֵּיהּ, לִקְדָם יי וִיכַפַּר עֲלַהּ, וְתִדְכֵּי

OFFERINGS AFTER CHILDBIRTH

The laws at the start of this *parasha,* about the sacrifices brought by a woman who has given birth, have challenged and puzzled the commentators. We could easily understand if she had to bring a thanksgiving offering. But instead she must bring a burnt offering, together with a purification offering. Why does she need atonement? Here are some of the suggestions of the commentators:

Ibn Ezra (on Lev. 21:6) says that during the anguish of labor, the woman may have thought or expressed ideas that were sinful or that she now regrets (such as vowing not to have future relations with her husband). Ramban (on Lev. 12:7) explains that the sacrifices are a kind of "ransom" for having survived the dangers of childbirth, as well as a form of prayer for a full recovery. Rabbi Meir Simḥa of Dvinsk suggests that the burnt offering is like an *olat re'iya,* an offering brought when appearing at the Temple on festivals. The woman thus celebrates her ability to appear before God at the Temple (*Meshekh Ḥokhma* on Lev. 12:6).

Without displacing any of these ideas, we might suggest another perspective. This is related to the words *tameh* and *tahor,* impure and pure. *Tameh* does not mean "defiled." It is a technical term referring to people being in a condition that prevents them from entering the Tabernacle or Temple. *Tahor* means the opposite, that they may enter.

As we have noted, the Tabernacle, and later the Temple, were symbols of the presence of God within the human domain. God is eternal and spiritual. We and the universe are physical, and whatever is physical is subject to birth, growth, decline, decay, and death. It is these things that must be excluded from the Sanctuary if we are to have the experience of standing in the presence of eternity.

What bars us, therefore, from entering the holy is anything that reminds us or others of our mortality. Hence the supreme source of impurity is death: contact with or proximity to a dead body. Paradoxically, childbirth defiles, even though it represents new life. The reason may be that until recently, it was a hazard fraught with the risk of death. Many babies were stillborn, many died young, and many mothers died giving birth. The very loss of blood was dangerous. So childbirth may render one impure because it is an encounter with the risk of death. Alternatively, it may simply be that it defiles because it is a reminder of the passing of the generations. Birth, like death, is a signal of mortality. The Tabernacle, and later the Temple, is the space set aside for consciousness of eternity.

12:6 **וּבִמְלֹאת יְמֵי טָהֳרָהּ** *When the days of her purification are complete* – There is a halakhic principle: "One who is engaged in a mitzva is exempt from other *mitzvot*" (Sukka 25a). It is as if God were saying to the mother: "For forty days in the case of a boy, and doubly so in the case of a girl (for the daughter herself contains the potential to beget and nurture future life), I exempt you from coming before Me in the place of holiness because you are fully engaged in one of the holiest acts of all, nurturing and caring for your child. Unlike others, you do not need to visit the Temple to be attached to life in all its sacred splendor. You are

source of blood." This is the law for a woman who bears a child, male or female.
8 "But if she cannot afford a sheep, she may bring two doves or two pigeons –
one for the burnt offering and the other for the purification offering. The priest
will then make atonement for her, and she shall be pure."
13 1 2 The LORD spoke to Moshe and Aharon: "When a person has a swelling, a rash,
or a bright patch on his skin, and it develops on his skin into what seems to be
an impure blight, he shall be brought to the priests, to Aharon or one of his
3 sons. The priest shall examine the disease on his skin. If hair in the diseased part
has turned white and the disease appears to be deeper than the skin, then it is
the disease of an impure blight. When the priest sees this, he shall declare the
4 person impure. But if the bright patch on the skin is white but does not appear
to be deeper than the skin and the hair in it has not turned white, the priest

רש״י

ח **אֶחָד לְעֹלָה וְאֶחָד לְחַטָּאת.** לֹא הִקְדִּימָהּ הַכָּתוּב אֶלָּא לְמִקְרָאָהּ, אֲבָל לְהַקְרָבָה חַטָּאת קוֹדֶם לְעוֹלָה. כָּךְ שָׁנִינוּ בִּזְבָחִים בְּפֶרֶק ׳כָּל הַתָּדִיר׳ (דף צ ע״א):

יג ב **שְׂאֵת אוֹ סַפַּחַת וְגוֹ׳.** שְׁמוֹת נְגָעִים הֵם, וּלְבָנוֹת זוֹ מִזּוֹ: **בַּהֶרֶת.** חֲבַרְבּוּרוֹת, טיי״א בְּלַעַז, וְכֵן: ״בָּהִיר הוּא בַּשְּׁחָקִים״ (איוב לז, כא): **אֶל אַהֲרֹן וְגוֹ׳.** גְּזֵרַת הַכָּתוּב הִיא שֶׁאֵין טֻמְאַת נְגָעִים וְטָהֳרָתָן אֶלָּא עַל פִּי כֹהֵן:

ג **הָפַךְ לָבָן.** מִתְּחִלָּה שָׁחוֹר וְהָפַךְ לְלָבָן בְּתוֹךְ הַנֶּגַע. וּמִעוּט שֵׂעָר – שְׁנַיִם: **עָמֹק מֵעוֹר בְּשָׂרוֹ.** כָּל מַרְאֶה לָבָן עָמֹק הוּא, כְּמַרְאֵה חַמָּה עֲמֻקָּה מִן הַצֵּל: **וְטִמֵּא אֹתוֹ.** יֹאמַר לוֹ: ׳טָמֵא אַתָּה׳, שֶׁשֵּׂעָר לָבָן סִימַן טֻמְאָה הוּא גְּזֵרַת הַכָּתוּב:

ד **וְעָמֹק אֵין מַרְאֶהָ.** לֹא יָדַעְתִּי פֵּרוּשׁוֹ:

In similar fashion, Ḥana dedicated her child, Shmuel, to God (I Sam. 1), as did the wife of Manoaḥ, mother of Shimshon (Judges 13). In each case, the mother brought a burnt offering, as did Avraham, in lieu of the child. By so doing she acknowledged that she was not the owner of the child, merely its guardian. In bringing the offering it was as if she had said: "God, I know I should dedicate this child entirely to Your service. Please accept this offering in his place."

TZARAAT: THE IMPURE BLIGHT

Much of Parashat Tazria and the following *parasha*, Metzora, are about the condition known as *tzaraat*. The Septuagint, the early Greek translation of the Hebrew Bible, translated the word as *lepra*, giving rise to a long tradition identifying it with leprosy, now known as Hansen's disease.

Some such disease, involving skin discoloration and sores, is implied in the stories of Miriam and Naaman, both of whom were smitten by *tzaraat*. However, this cannot be the meaning of the term, at least in the present context. As Rambam (*Hilkhot Tumat Tzaraat* 16:10) and Sforno (on Lev. 13:2) – both of whom were doctors – point out, the symptoms described in the Torah correspond neither to leprosy nor to any other known disease.

Tzaraat as described in Parashot Tazria and Metzora refers not only to various skin conditions but also to discolorations on clothes and the walls of houses. Rambam (ibid.) emphasizes this when he writes:

> *Tzaraat* is a comprehensive term covering a number of dissimilar conditions. So, whiteness in a person's skin is called *tzaraat*. The falling off of some of his hair on the head or the chin is called *tzaraat*. A change of color in garments or in houses is called *tzaraat*.

There is no disease that affects not only people but also clothes and walls.

Moreover, the Torah is not a book of medicine. It was priests, not doctors, who supervised cases of *tzaraat*. The

ח מִמְּקֹר דָּמֶיהָ זֹאת תּוֹרַת הַיֹּלֶדֶת לַזָּכָר אוֹ לַנְּקֵבָה: וְאִם־לֹא תִמְצָא
יָדָהּ דֵּי שֶׂה וְלָקְחָה שְׁתֵּי־תֹרִים אוֹ שְׁנֵי בְּנֵי יוֹנָה אֶחָד לְעֹלָה וְאֶחָד
לְחַטָּאת וְכִפֶּר עָלֶיהָ הַכֹּהֵן וְטָהֵרָה:
יג א ב וַיְדַבֵּר יהוה אֶל־מֹשֶׁה וְאֶל־אַהֲרֹן לֵאמֹר: אָדָם כִּי־יִהְיֶה בְעוֹר־
בְּשָׂרוֹ שְׂאֵת אוֹ־סַפַּחַת אוֹ בַהֶרֶת וְהָיָה בְעוֹר־בְּשָׂרוֹ לְנֶגַע צָרָעַת
ג וְהוּבָא אֶל־אַהֲרֹן הַכֹּהֵן אוֹ אֶל־אַחַד מִבָּנָיו הַכֹּהֲנִים: וְרָאָה הַכֹּהֵן
אֶת־הַנֶּגַע בְּעוֹר־הַבָּשָׂר וְשֵׂעָר בַּנֶּגַע הָפַךְ ׀ לָבָן וּמַרְאֵה הַנֶּגַע עָמֹק
ד מֵעוֹר בְּשָׂרוֹ נֶגַע צָרַעַת הוּא וְרָאָהוּ הַכֹּהֵן וְטִמֵּא אֹתוֹ: וְאִם־בַּהֶרֶת
לְבָנָה הִוא בְּעוֹר בְּשָׂרוֹ וְעָמֹק אֵין־מַרְאֶהָ מִן־הָעוֹר וּשְׂעָרָה לֹא־הָפַךְ

אונקלוס

מְסוֹאֲבַת דְּמַהָא, דָּא אוֹרָיְתָא דִּילֵידְתָּא, לִדְכַר אוֹ לְנֻקְבָּא: ח וְאִם לָא תַשְׁכַּח יְדַהּ כְּמִסַּת אִמְּרָא, וְתִסַּב תַּרְתֵּין שַׁפְנִינִין, אוֹ תְּרֵין בְּנֵי יוֹנָה, חַד לַעֲלָתָא וְחַד לְחַטָּתָא, וִיכַפַּר עֲלַהּ, כָּהֲנָא וְתִדְכֵּי: יג א וּמַלִּיל יְיָ, עִם מֹשֶׁה וּלְאַהֲרֹן לְמֵימַר: ב אֱנָשׁ, אֲרֵי יְהֵי בִמְשַׁךְ בִּסְרֵיהּ עָמְקָא אוֹ עַדְיָא אוֹ בַהֲרָא, וִיהֵי בִמְשַׁךְ בִּסְרֵיהּ לְמַכְתָּשׁ סְגִירוּ, וְיִתֵּיתֵי לְוָת אַהֲרֹן כָּהֲנָא, אוֹ, לְוָת חַד מִבְּנוֹהִי כָּהֲנַיָּא: ג וְיִחְזֵי כָהֲנָא יָת מַכְתָּשָׁא בִּמְשַׁךְ בִּסְרָא, וְסַעֲרָא בְמַכְתָּשָׁא אִתְהֲפֵיךְ לְמִחְוַר, וּמֶחֱזֵי מַכְתָּשָׁא עַמִּיק מִמְּשַׁךְ בִּסְרֵיהּ, מַכְתַּשׁ סְגִירוּתָא הוּא, וְיִחְזֵינֵיהּ כָּהֲנָא וִיסָאֵיב יָתֵיהּ: ד וְאִם בַּהֲרָא חִוָּרָא הִיא בִמְשַׁךְ בִּסְרֵיהּ, וְעַמִּיק לֵית מֶחֱזָהָא מִן מַשְׁכָּא, וְסַעֲרַהּ לָא אִתְהֲפֵיךְ

The Torah makes an implicit comment on this in its account of the name given to the first human child. Ḥava called him Kayin – from the Hebrew meaning "ownership" – saying, "With the Lord's help I have made [literally, 'acquired'] a man" (Gen. 4:1). Treat your child as a possession and you may inadvertently turn him into a murderer, the text implies.

The narrative of the binding of Yitzḥak is a statement that parents do not own their children. The story of Yitzḥak's birth also points in that direction. He was born when Sara was already post-menopausal (18:11), incapable of having a child naturally. Yitzḥak was clearly a special gift of God. As the first Jewish child, he became the precedent for subsequent generations. The binding was intended to establish that children belong to God. Parents are merely their guardians. The same idea lies behind the ritual of the redemption of the firstborn.

And so, in Temple times, mothers would offer a sacrifice after the birth of a child (Lev. 12:6–8). No record exists of a formal prayer offered on such occasions; there may have been no fixed text. Ḥana's prayer after the birth of Shmuel (I Sam. 2:1–10) is, however, a powerful example of such a song of thanksgiving. Ritual is what we use to declare the sanctity of life and its milestones. It gives public, collective expression to one of the essential underpinnings of morality.

12:8 אֶחָד לְעֹלָה *One for the burnt offering* – This offering is a reminder of *akedat Yitzḥak* (the binding of Yitzḥak), and of the animal sacrificed in his place (Gen. 22:13). I argued there that *akedat Yitzḥak* was intended as a protest against the absolute power parents had over children in the ancient world – *patria potestas*, as it was called in Roman law. The child was regarded as the property of his parents. A father had total legal power over a child, even to the extent of life and death.

5 shall quarantine the patient for seven days. On the seventh day the priest shall
examine him again. If the disease has remained the same in appearance and not
spread on the patient's skin, the priest shall quarantine him for another seven
6 days. On the seventh day the priest shall examine it again. If the diseased area SHENI
has receded and not spread over the skin, the priest shall declare the patient
7 pure; it was only a rash. He shall immerse his clothes, and he shall be pure. But
if the rash does spread over the skin after he has appeared before the priest for
8 purification, he must appear before the priest again. If the priest sees that the
rash has indeed spread over the skin, he shall declare the person impure; it is a
blight.
9 10 When a person has a blight-like disease, he shall be brought to the priest, and
the priest shall look. If there is a white swelling in the skin that has turned the
11 hair white, and within the swelling there is healthy flesh, it is a chronic blight
on the skin of his body, and the priest shall pronounce the patient impure; he

רש״י

וְהִסְגִּיר. יַסְגִּירֶנּוּ בְּבַיִת אֶחָד וְלֹא יֵרָאֶה עַד סוֹף הַשָּׁבוּעַ, וְיוֹכִיחוּ סִימָנִים עָלָיו:

ה **בְּעֵינָיו.** בְּמַרְאֵהוּ וּבְשִׁעוּרוֹ הָרִאשׁוֹן: **וְהִסְגִּירוֹ שֵׁנִית.** הָא אִם פָּשָׂה בַּשָּׁבוּעַ רִאשׁוֹן – טָמֵא מֻחְלָט (נגעים ג, ג):

ו **כֵּהָה.** הָכְהָה מִמַּרְאִיתוֹ. הָא אִם עָמַד בְּמַרְאִיתוֹ אוֹ פָּשָׂה – טָמֵא: **מִסְפַּחַת.** שֵׁם נֶגַע טָהוֹר: **וְכִבֶּס בְּגָדָיו וְטָהֵר.** הוֹאִיל וְנִזְקַק לְהִסָּגֵר נִקְרָא טָמֵא וְצָרִיךְ טְבִילָה:

ח **וְטִמְּאוֹ הַכֹּהֵן.** וּמִשֶּׁטִּמְּאוֹ הֲרֵי הוּא מֻחְלָט, וְזָקוּק לְצִפֳּרִים וּלְתִגְלַחַת וּלְקָרְבָּן הָאָמוּר בְּפָרָשַׁת ׳זֹאת תִּהְיֶה׳ (להלן יד, ח-לב): **צָרַעַת הִוא.** הַמִּסְפַּחַת הַזֹּאת: **צָרַעַת.** לְשׁוֹן נְקֵבָה, ״נֶגַע״ לְשׁוֹן זָכָר:

י **וּמִחְיַת.** סיינמי״ט בְּלַעַז, שֶׁנֶּהְפַּךְ מִקְצַת הַלֹּבֶן שֶׁבְּתוֹךְ הַשְּׂאֵת לְמַרְאֵה בָשָׂר, אַף הוּא סִימַן טֻמְאָה, שֵׂעָר לָבָן בְּלֹא מִחְיָה, וּמִחְיָה בְּלֹא שֵׂעָר לָבָן. וְאַף עַל פִּי שֶׁלֹּא נֶאֶמְרָה מִחְיָה אֶלָּא בִּשְׂאֵת, אַף בְּכָל הַמַּרְאוֹת וְתוֹלְדוֹתֵיהֶן הוּא סִימַן טֻמְאָה:

יא **צָרַעַת נוֹשֶׁנֶת הִוא.** מַכָּה יְשָׁנָה הִיא תַּחַת הַמִּחְיָה, וַחֲבוּרָה זוֹ נִרְאֵית בְּרִיאָה מִלְמַעְלָה וְתַחְתֶּיהָ מְלֵאָה לֵחָה, שֶׁלֹּא תֹּאמַר הוֹאִיל וְעָלְתָה מִחְיָה אֲטַהֲרֶנָּה:

13:10 **וְרָאָה הַכֹּהֵן** *The priest shall look* – A priest is not a doctor, and an impure blight is not a natural disease. Yet from this lengthy passage we see that diagnosing it requires repeated careful examinations. Expertise is needed – and so is care. The priest must make minute observations and remember the patient so that he can note changes in his or her symptoms. We may imagine the elements of a doctor-patient relationship.

The dazzling assertion at the heart of the Hebrew Bible is that God "raise[s] His face toward us" (Num. 6:26), knowing, loving, and challenging each of us in our singularity. If the religious voice has one thing to say above all others, it is that each of us counts. One line in the book of Psalms always inspires in me a certain awe. It says of God that "He counts the number of the stars, calling each by name" (Ps. 147:4). To call someone or something by a name is to endow it with significance for what it uniquely is. Even a blighted person is not subjected to exclusion before he receives the priest's individual close attention and care.

ה לָבָן וְהִסְגִּיר הַכֹּהֵן אֶת־הַנֶּגַע שִׁבְעַת יָמִים: וְרָאָהוּ הַכֹּהֵן בַּיּוֹם הַשְּׁבִיעִי
וְהִנֵּה הַנֶּגַע עָמַד בְּעֵינָיו לֹא־פָשָׂה הַנֶּגַע בָּעוֹר וְהִסְגִּירוֹ הַכֹּהֵן שִׁבְעַת
ו יָמִים שֵׁנִית: וְרָאָה הַכֹּהֵן אֹתוֹ בַּיּוֹם הַשְּׁבִיעִי שֵׁנִית וְהִנֵּה כֵּהָה הַנֶּגַע שני
וְלֹא־פָשָׂה הַנֶּגַע בָּעוֹר וְטִהֲרוֹ הַכֹּהֵן מִסְפַּחַת הִוא וְכִבֶּס בְּגָדָיו וְטָהֵר:
ז וְאִם־פָּשֹׂה תִפְשֶׂה הַמִּסְפַּחַת בָּעוֹר אַחֲרֵי הֵרָאֹתוֹ אֶל־הַכֹּהֵן לְטָהֳרָתוֹ
ח וְנִרְאָה שֵׁנִית אֶל־הַכֹּהֵן: וְרָאָה הַכֹּהֵן וְהִנֵּה פָּשְׂתָה הַמִּסְפַּחַת בָּעוֹר
וְטִמְּאוֹ הַכֹּהֵן צָרַעַת הִוא:
ט י נֶגַע צָרַעַת כִּי תִהְיֶה בְּאָדָם וְהוּבָא אֶל־הַכֹּהֵן: וְרָאָה הַכֹּהֵן וְהִנֵּה
שְׂאֵת־לְבָנָה בָּעוֹר וְהִיא הָפְכָה שֵׂעָר לָבָן וּמִחְיַת בָּשָׂר חַי בַּשְׂאֵת:
יא צָרַעַת נוֹשֶׁנֶת הִוא בְּעוֹר בְּשָׂרוֹ וְטִמְּאוֹ הַכֹּהֵן לֹא יַסְגִּרֶנּוּ כִּי טָמֵא הוּא:

אונקלוס

לְמִחְוַר, וְיַסְגַּר כָּהֲנָא, יָת מַכְתָּשָׁא שִׁבְעָא יוֹמִין: ה וְיֶחֱזֵינֵיהּ כָּהֲנָא בְּיוֹמָא שְׁבִיעָאָה, וְהָא מַכְתָּשָׁא קָם כַּד הֲוָה, לָא אוֹסֵיף מַכְתָּשָׁא בְּמַשְׁכָּא, וְיַסְגְּרִנֵּיהּ כָּהֲנָא, שִׁבְעָא יוֹמִין תִּנְיָנוּת: ו וְיֶחֱזֵי כָּהֲנָא יָתֵיהּ, בְּיוֹמָא שְׁבִיעָאָה תִּנְיָנוּת, וְהָא עֲמָא מַכְתָּשָׁא, וְלָא אוֹסֵיף מַכְתָּשָׁא בְּמַשְׁכָּא, וִידַכֵּינֵיהּ כָּהֲנָא עֲדִיתָא הִיא, וִיצַבַּע לְבוּשׁוֹהִי וְיִדְכֵּי: ז וְאִם אוֹסָפָא תוֹסֵיף עֲדִיתָא בְּמַשְׁכָּא, בָּתַר דְּאִתַּחְזִי, לְכָהֲנָא לְדָכוּתֵיהּ, וְיִתַּחְזֵי תִּנְיָנוּת לְכָהֲנָא: ח וְיֶחֱזֵי כָּהֲנָא, וְהָא, אוֹסֵיפַת עֲדִיתָא בְּמַשְׁכָּא, וִיסָאֲבִנֵּיהּ כָּהֲנָא סְגִירוּתָא הִיא: ט מַכְתָּשׁ סְגִירוּ, אֲרֵי תְהֵי בַּאֲנָשָׁא, וְיִתַּיְתֵי לְוָת כָּהֲנָא: י וְיֶחֱזֵי כָּהֲנָא, וְהָא עֲמְקָא חִוָּרָא בְּמַשְׁכָּא, וְהִיא, הֲפַכַת סַעֲרָא לְמִחְוַר, וְרוֹשֶׁם, בְּסַר חַי בְּעַמִּיקְתָא: יא סְגִירוּת עַתִּיקָא הִיא בִּמְשַׁךְ בִּסְרֵיהּ, וִיסַאֲבִנֵּיהּ כָּהֲנָא, לָא יַסְגְּרִנֵּיהּ, אֲרֵי מְסָאַב הוּא:

language of *tuma* and *tahara,* impurity and purity, in which the whole section is couched, is quite different from the concepts of sickness and health, being ill and being cured. The category of *tuma* relates to mortality, and skin disease is the most publicly visible reminder of our physicality. "A *metzora* [an individual with *tzaraat*] is like one who is dead," say the Sages (Nedarim 64b).

What are we to make of a phenomenon that does not correspond to anything in our experience? How could there be a condition that makes sense to Moshe and the Israelites, but not to us?

The Sages were guided here by the principle that "the word of Torah may be poor in one place but rich in another" (Yerushalmi, Rosh HaShana 3:5), meaning that an obscure text can sometimes be understood by considering other passages elsewhere. The most obvious clue is Moshe's warning in Deuteronomy:

> "Take great care in cases of impure blight. Carefully do whatever the Levitical priests instruct you.... Remember what the Lord your God did to Miriam on your way when you left Egypt." (Deut. 24:8–9)

The connection between *tzaraat* and "what the Lord your God did to Miriam" lies in an episode in the book of Numbers (12:1–2) when Miriam and Aharon spoke disparagingly about Moshe. This juxtaposition provides grounding for the link between *tzaraat* and evil speech, a theme that we will continue to explore below.

12 need not quarantine him, for he is definitely impure. If, however, the blight has
spread over the skin, so that it covers all of the patient's skin from head to foot,
13 wherever the priest can see, the priest shall make an examination, and if the
blight has covered all his body, he shall pronounce him pure of the disease; if
14 he has turned completely white, he is pure. But as soon as healthy flesh appears,
15 the patient is impure. The priest shall examine the healthy flesh and pronounce
16 him impure; the healthy flesh is impure, for it indicates a blight. But if the
17 healthy flesh turns white again, the patient shall come back to the priest. The
priest shall examine him, and if the disease has indeed whitened, the priest
shall pronounce the patient pure, and he shall be pure.
18 19 When one has a boil on his skin and it heals, and in the place of the boil there SHELISHI
comes a white swelling or a bright patch of white and reddish color, this shall
20 be shown to the priest. The priest shall then make an examination, and if the
area appears lower than the rest of the skin and its hair has turned white, the
priest shall declare the patient impure: it is a case of blight that has broken out
21 in the boil. But if the priest examines it and there is no white hair in it and it
does not appear lower than the skin, but it has not receded, then the priest shall
22 quarantine the patient for seven days. If it spreads in the skin, the priest shall

רש״י

יב| **מֵרֹאשׁוֹ.** שֶׁל אָדָם ״וְעַד רַגְלָיו״: **לְכָל מַרְאֵה עֵינֵי הַכֹּהֵן.** פְּרָט לְכֹהֵן שֶׁחָשַׁךְ מְאוֹרוֹ:

יד| **וּבְיוֹם הֵרָאוֹת בּוֹ בָּשָׂר חַי.** אִם צָמְחָה בּוֹ מִחְיָה הֲרֵי כְּבָר פֵּרַשׁ שֶׁהַמִּחְיָה סִימַן טֻמְאָה, אֶלָּא הֲרֵי שֶׁהָיָה הַנֶּגַע בְּאֶחָד מֵעֶשְׂרִים וְאַרְבָּעָה רָאשֵׁי אֵבָרִים שֶׁאֵין מְטַמְּאִין מִשּׁוּם מִחְיָה, לְפִי שֶׁאֵין נִרְאֶה הַנֶּגַע כֻּלּוֹ כְּאֶחָד שֶׁשּׁוֹפְעִין אֵילָךְ וְאֵילָךְ, וְחָזַר רֹאשׁ הָאֵבָר וְנִתְגַּלָּה שִׁפּוּעוֹ עַל יְדֵי שֻׁמָּן, כְּגוֹן שֶׁהִבְרִיא וְנַעֲשָׂה רָחָב וְנִרְאֵית בּוֹ הַמִּחְיָה, לִמְּדָנוּ הַכָּתוּב שֶׁתְּטַמֵּא: **וּבְיוֹם.** מַה תַּלְמוּד לוֹמַר? יֵשׁ יוֹם שֶׁאַתָּה רוֹאֶה בּוֹ וְיֵשׁ יוֹם שֶׁאֵין אַתָּה רוֹאֶה בּוֹ; מִכָּאן אָמְרוּ, חָתָן נוֹתְנִין לוֹ כָּל שִׁבְעַת יְמֵי הַמִּשְׁתֶּה לוֹ וּלְאִצְטְלִיתוֹ וְלִכְסוּתוֹ, וְכֵן בָּרֶגֶל נוֹתְנִין לוֹ כָּל יְמֵי הָרֶגֶל:

טו| **צָרַעַת הוּא.** הַבָּשָׂר הַהוּא, ״בָּשָׂר״ לְשׁוֹן זָכָר:

יח| **שְׁחִין.** לְשׁוֹן חִמּוּם, שֶׁנִּתְחַמֵּם הַבָּשָׂר בְּלִקּוּי הַבָּא לוֹ מֵחֲמַת מַכָּה שֶׁלֹּא מֵחֲמַת הָאוּר: **וְנִרְפָּא.** הַשְּׁחִין הֶעֱלָה אֲרוּכָה, וּבִמְקוֹמוֹ הֶעֱלָה נֶגַע אַחֵר:

יט| **אוֹ בַהֶרֶת לְבָנָה אֲדַמְדָּמֶת.** שֶׁאֵין הַנֶּגַע לָבָן חָלָק, אֶלָּא פָּתוּךְ וּמְעֹרָב בִּשְׁתֵּי מַרְאוֹת – לֹבֶן וְאֹדֶם:

כ| **מַרְאֶהָ שָׁפָל.** וְאֵין מַמָּשָׁהּ שָׁפָל, אֶלָּא מִתּוֹךְ לַבְנוּנִיתוֹ הוּא נִרְאֶה שָׁפָל וְעָמֹק, כְּמַרְאֵה חַמָּה עֲמֻקָּה מִן הַצֵּל:

being that words conveyed confidentially will stay confidential. The punishment is the most public possible. The nature of *tzaraat* testified to the kind of sin that provoked it.

The Sages spoke more dramatically about *lashon hara* than any other offense. They said that it was as bad as committing all three cardinal sins: idolatry, incest, and murder. They said that it kills three people: the one who says it, the one he says it about, and the one who listens to it (Arakhin 15b). We do not say, "Sticks and stones may break my bones but words will never harm me." To the contrary, words can cause emotional injuries that are as painful as physical ones, perhaps more so.

The negative force of *lashon hara*, however, has grown exponentially in the age of social media. It is far easier to be critical, offensive, scathing, and destructive when communicating electronically because of the so-called

יב וְאִם־פָּרוֹחַ תִּפְרַח הַצָּרַעַת בָּעוֹר וְכִסְּתָה הַצָּרַעַת אֵת כָּל־עוֹר הַנֶּגַע
יג מֵרֹאשׁוֹ וְעַד־רַגְלָיו לְכָל־מַרְאֵה עֵינֵי הַכֹּהֵן׃ וְרָאָה הַכֹּהֵן וְהִנֵּה כִסְּתָה
הַצָּרַעַת אֶת־כָּל־בְּשָׂרוֹ וְטִהַר אֶת־הַנָּגַע כֻּלּוֹ הָפַךְ לָבָן טָהוֹר הוּא׃
יד טו וּבְיוֹם הֵרָאוֹת בּוֹ בָּשָׂר חַי יִטְמָא׃ וְרָאָה הַכֹּהֵן אֶת־הַבָּשָׂר הַחַי וְטִמְּאוֹ
טז הַבָּשָׂר הַחַי טָמֵא הוּא צָרַעַת הוּא׃ אוֹ כִי יָשׁוּב הַבָּשָׂר הַחַי וְנֶהְפַּךְ
יז לְלָבָן וּבָא אֶל־הַכֹּהֵן׃ וְרָאָהוּ הַכֹּהֵן וְהִנֵּה נֶהְפַּךְ הַנֶּגַע לְלָבָן וְטִהַר
הַכֹּהֵן אֶת־הַנֶּגַע טָהוֹר הוּא׃
יח יט וּבָשָׂר כִּי־יִהְיֶה בוֹ־בְעֹרוֹ שְׁחִין וְנִרְפָּא׃ וְהָיָה בִּמְקוֹם הַשְּׁחִין שְׂאֵת שלישי
כ לְבָנָה אוֹ בַהֶרֶת לְבָנָה אֲדַמְדָּמֶת וְנִרְאָה אֶל־הַכֹּהֵן׃ וְרָאָה הַכֹּהֵן וְהִנֵּה
מַרְאֶהָ שָׁפָל מִן־הָעוֹר וּשְׂעָרָהּ הָפַךְ לָבָן וְטִמְּאוֹ הַכֹּהֵן נֶגַע־צָרַעַת הִוא
כא בַּשְּׁחִין פָּרָחָה׃ וְאִם ׀ יִרְאֶנָּה הַכֹּהֵן וְהִנֵּה אֵין־בָּהּ שֵׂעָר לָבָן וּשְׁפָלָה
כב אֵינֶנָּה מִן־הָעוֹר וְהִיא כֵהָה וְהִסְגִּירוֹ הַכֹּהֵן שִׁבְעַת יָמִים׃ וְאִם־פָּשֹׂה

אונקלוס

יב וְאִם מִסְגָּא תִסְגֵּי סְגִירוּתָא בְּמַשְׁכָּא, וְתַחְפֵּי סְגִירוּתָא, יָת כָּל מְשַׁךְ מַכְתָּשָׁא, מֵרֵישֵׁיהּ וְעַד רַגְלוֹהִי, לְכָל חֵיזוּ עֵינֵי כַּהֲנָא: יג וְיֶחֱזֵי כַּהֲנָא, וְהָא חֲפַת סְגִירוּתָא יָת כָּל בִּסְרֵיהּ, וִידַכֵּי יָת מַכְתָּשָׁא, כֻּלֵּיהּ, אִתְהֲפֵיךְ לְמִחוַר דְּכֵי הוּא: יד וּבְיוֹמָא דְּיִתַּחְזֵי בֵיהּ, בִּסְרָא חַיָּא יְהֵי מְסָאַב: טו וְיֶחֱזֵי כַּהֲנָא, יָת בִּסְרָא חַיָּא וִיסָאֲבִנֵּיהּ, בִּסְרָא חַיָּא, מְסָאַב הוּא סְגִירוּתָא הוּא: טז אוֹ אֲרֵי יְתוּב, בִּסְרָא חַיָּא וְיִתְהֲפֵיךְ לְמִחוַר, וְיֵיתֵי לְוָת כַּהֲנָא: יז וְיֶחֱזֵינֵּיהּ כַּהֲנָא, וְהָא, אִתְהֲפֵיךְ מַכְתָּשָׁא לְמִחוַר, וִידַכֵּי כַּהֲנָא, יָת מַכְתָּשָׁא דְּכֵי הוּא: יח וֶאֱנָשׁ, אֲרֵי יְהֵי בֵיהּ בְּמַשְׁכֵּיהּ שִׁחְנָא, וְיִתַּסֵּי: יט וִיהֵי, בַּאֲתַר שִׁחְנָא עָמְקָא חִוָּרָא, אוֹ בַהֲרָא חִוָּרָא סָמְקָא, וְיִתַּחְזֵי לְוָת כַּהֲנָא: כ וְיֶחֱזֵי כַּהֲנָא, וְהָא מֶחֱזָהָא מַכִּיךְ מִן מַשְׁכָּא, וְסַעֲרַהּ אִתְהֲפֵיךְ לְמִחוַר, וִיסָאֲבִנֵּיהּ כַּהֲנָא, מַכְתַּשׁ סְגִירוּתָא הִיא בְּשִׁחְנָא סְגִיאַת: כא וְאִם יֶחֱזֵינַהּ כַּהֲנָא, וְהָא לֵית בַּהּ סְעַר חִוָּר, וּמַכִּיכָא לָיְתַהָא, מִן מַשְׁכָּא וְהִיא עַמְיָא, וְיַסְגְּרִנֵּיהּ כַּהֲנָא שִׁבְעָא יוֹמִין: כב וְאִם אוֹסָפָא

13:21 וְהִסְגִּירוֹ הַכֹּהֵן שִׁבְעַת יָמִים *Shall quarantine the patient for seven days* – Why was the *metzora* required to quarantine outside the camp? Again, the episode in which Miriam will be struck with *tzaraat* for seven days for speaking ill of Moshe informs the Sages' astonishing insight of seeing the disfiguring blight as a symbol and symptom of evil speech. The Talmud takes the word *metzora* to be an abbreviated form of the phrase *motzi shem ra,* meaning slander (Arakhin 15b).

Identifying a connection between *tzaraat* and evil speech helps us understand certain other features of the phenomenon. The most obvious sign of *tzaraat* was a whitening of the skin. The phrase the Sages used to describe shaming someone was *malbin penei ḥavero,* someone who "causes his fellow's face to turn white" (Bava Metzia 59a). Thus, the punishment was measure for measure. Negative words that could turn someone else's face white are punished by the skin of the speaker turning white. Moreover, malicious speech is usually spoken in private, the fiction

23 declare him impure; it is a blight. But if the bright patch remains in one place
and does not spread, it is scar tissue from the boil, and the priest shall declare
24 the patient pure. When one has a burn on his skin and the raw flesh REVI'I /SHENI/
of the burn becomes a bright patch, either white and reddish or only white,
25 the priest shall examine it, and if the hair in the bright patch has turned white
and it appears to be deeper than the skin, then it is a blight. It has broken out in
26 the burn, and the priest shall pronounce the patient impure: it is a blight. But
if the priest examines it and there is no white hair in the spot and it appears no
deeper than the skin, but it has not receded, the priest shall quarantine him for
27 seven days. The priest shall examine him on the seventh day. If the disease is
spreading on the skin, then the priest shall declare him impure; it is a blight.
28 But if the spot remains in its place and has not spread on the skin, but has
receded, then it was a swelling from the burn, and the priest shall pronounce
him pure; it is merely scar tissue from the burn.
29 30 When a man or woman has a disease on the scalp or beard, and the priest ḤAMISHI
examines the disease and finds that it appears to be deeper than the skin, and
has fine blond hairs in it, the priest shall declare the person impure. It is a scaling
31 eruption, a blight of the head or beard. If the priest examines the scaling and it
appears no deeper than the skin but there is no black hair in it, then the priest
32 shall quarantine the person with the scaling eruption for seven days, and on the
seventh day the priest shall examine the disease. If the scaling has not spread,

אונקלוס

תּוֹסִיף בְּמַשְׁכָּא, וִיסָאֵב כָּהֲנָא, יָתֵיהּ מַכְתָּשָׁא הִיא: כג וְאִם בְּאַתְרַהּ, קָמַת בַּהֲרָתָא לָא אוֹסִיפַת, רוֹשֶׁם שִׁחְנָא הִיא, וִידַכֵּינֵיהּ כָּהֲנָא: כד אוֹ אֱנָשׁ, אֲרֵי יְהֵי בְמַשְׁכֵּיהּ כְּוָאָה דְנוּר, וִיהֵי רוֹשֶׁם כְּוָאָה, בַּהֲרָא, חִוָּרָא סָמְקָא אוֹ חִוָּרָא: כה וְיִחְזֵי יָתַהּ כָּהֲנָא, וְהָא אִתְהֲפֵיךְ סַעֲרָא לְמִחְוַר בְּבַהֲרָתָא, וּמִחְזַהָא עַמִּיק מִן מַשְׁכָּא, סְגִירוּתָא הִיא, בִּכְוָאָה סְגִיאַת, וִיסַאֵיב יָתֵיהּ כָּהֲנָא, מַכְתַּשׁ סְגִירוּתָא הִיא: כו וְאִם יִחְזֵינַהּ

רש״י

כב **נֶגַע הִוא.** הַשְּׂאֵת הַזֹּאת אוֹ הַבַּהֶרֶת:

כג **תַּחְתֶּיהָ.** בִּמְקוֹמָהּ: **צָרֶבֶת הַשְּׁחִין.** כְּתַרְגּוּמוֹ: "רוֹשֶׁם שִׁחְנָא", אֵינוֹ אֶלָּא רֹשֶׁם הַחִמּוּם הַנִּכָּר בַּבָּשָׂר. כָּל 'צָרֶבֶת' לְשׁוֹן רְגִיעַת עוֹר הַנִּרְגָּע מֵחֲמַת חִמּוּם, כְּמוֹ: "וְנִצְרְבוּ בָהּ כָּל פָּנִים" (יחזקאל כא, ג), רייטרי"ר בְּלַעַז: **צָרֶבֶת.** רטריחמנ"ט בְּלַעַז:

כד **מִחְיַת הַמִּכְוָה.** סנמנ"ט, כְּשֶׁחָיְתָה הַמִּכְוָה, נֶהֶפְכָה לְבַהֶרֶת פְּתוּכָה אוֹ לְבָנָה חֲלָקָה:

כט **בְּרֹאשׁ אוֹ בְזָקָן.** בָּא הַכָּתוּב לְחַלֵּק בֵּין נֶגַע שֶׁבִּמְקוֹם שֵׂעָר לְנֶגַע שֶׁבִּמְקוֹם בָּשָׂר, שֶׁזֶּה סִימָנוֹ בְּשֵׂעָר לָבָן וְזֶה סִימָנוֹ בְּשֵׂעָר צָהֹב:

ל **וּבוֹ שֵׂעָר צָהֹב.** שֶׁנֶּהְפַּךְ שֵׂעָר שָׁחוֹר שֶׁבּוֹ לְצָהֹב: **נֶתֶק הוּא.** כָּךְ שְׁמוֹ שֶׁל נֶגַע שֶׁבִּמְקוֹם שֵׂעָר:

לא **וְשֵׂעָר שָׁחֹר אֵין בּוֹ.** הָא אִם הָיָה בוֹ שֵׂעָר שָׁחוֹר – טָהוֹר וְאֵין צָרִיךְ לְהַסְגֵּר, שֶׁשֵּׂעָר שָׁחוֹר סִימַן טָהֳרָה הוּא בִּנְתָקִים, כְּמוֹ שֶׁנֶּאֱמַר: "וְשֵׂעָר שָׁחֹר צָמַח בּוֹ" וְגוֹ' (להלן פסוק לז):

לב **וְהִנֵּה לֹא פָשָׂה וְגוֹ'.** הָא אִם פָּשָׂה אוֹ הָיָה בוֹ שֵׂעָר צָהֹב – טָמֵא:

כג תִּפְשֶׂה בָּעוֹר וְטִמֵּא הַכֹּהֵן אֹתוֹ נֶגַע הִוא: וְאִם־תַּחְתֶּיהָ תַּעֲמֹד
כד הַבַּהֶרֶת לֹא פָשָׂתָה צָרֶבֶת הַשְּׁחִין הִוא וְטִהֲרוֹ הַכֹּהֵן: אוֹ רביעי /שני/
בָשָׂר כִּי־יִהְיֶה בְעֹרוֹ מִכְוַת־אֵשׁ וְהָיְתָה מִחְיַת הַמִּכְוָה בַּהֶרֶת לְבָנָה
כה אֲדַמְדֶּמֶת אוֹ לְבָנָה: וְרָאָה אֹתָהּ הַכֹּהֵן וְהִנֵּה נֶהְפַּךְ שֵׂעָר לָבָן בַּבַּהֶרֶת
וּמַרְאֶהָ עָמֹק מִן־הָעוֹר צָרַעַת הִוא בַּמִּכְוָה פָּרָחָה וְטִמֵּא אֹתוֹ הַכֹּהֵן
כו נֶגַע צָרַעַת הִוא: וְאִם ׀ יִרְאֶנָּה הַכֹּהֵן וְהִנֵּה אֵין־בַּבַּהֶרֶת שֵׂעָר לָבָן
וּשְׁפָלָה אֵינֶנָּה מִן־הָעוֹר וְהִוא כֵהָה וְהִסְגִּירוֹ הַכֹּהֵן שִׁבְעַת יָמִים:
כז וְרָאָהוּ הַכֹּהֵן בַּיּוֹם הַשְּׁבִיעִי אִם־פָּשֹׂה תִפְשֶׂה בָּעוֹר וְטִמֵּא הַכֹּהֵן
כח אֹתוֹ נֶגַע צָרַעַת הִוא: וְאִם־תַּחְתֶּיהָ תַעֲמֹד הַבַּהֶרֶת לֹא־פָשְׂתָה
בָעוֹר וְהִוא כֵהָה שְׂאֵת הַמִּכְוָה הִוא וְטִהֲרוֹ הַכֹּהֵן כִּי־צָרֶבֶת הַמִּכְוָה
הִוא:
כט ל וְאִישׁ אוֹ אִשָּׁה כִּי־יִהְיֶה בוֹ נָגַע בְּרֹאשׁ אוֹ בְזָקָן: וְרָאָה הַכֹּהֵן אֶת־הַנֶּגַע ח חמישי
וְהִנֵּה מַרְאֵהוּ עָמֹק מִן־הָעוֹר וּבוֹ שֵׂעָר צָהֹב דָּק וְטִמֵּא אֹתוֹ הַכֹּהֵן נֶתֶק
לא הוּא צָרַעַת הָרֹאשׁ אוֹ הַזָּקָן הוּא: וְכִי־יִרְאֶה הַכֹּהֵן אֶת־נֶגַע הַנֶּתֶק
וְהִנֵּה אֵין־מַרְאֵהוּ עָמֹק מִן־הָעוֹר וְשֵׂעָר שָׁחֹר אֵין בּוֹ וְהִסְגִּיר הַכֹּהֵן
לב אֶת־נֶגַע הַנֶּתֶק שִׁבְעַת יָמִים: וְרָאָה הַכֹּהֵן אֶת־הַנֶּגַע בַּיּוֹם הַשְּׁבִיעִי

אונקלוס

כהנא, והא לית בבהרתא סער חיור, ומכיכא ליתהא, מן משכא והיא עמיא, ויסגרניה כהנא שבעא יומין: כז ויחזיניה כהנא ביומא שביעאה, אם אוספא תוסיף במשכא, ויסאיב כהנא יתיה, מכתש סגירותא היא: כח ואם באתרה קמת בהרתא, לא אוסיפת במשכא והיא עמיא, עומק כואה היא, וידכיניה כהנא, ארי רושם כואה היא: כט וגבר או אתא, ארי יהי ביה מכתשא, בריש או בדקן: ל ויחזי כהנא ית מכתשא, והא מחזוהי עמיק מן משכא, וביה, סער סמק דעדק, ויסאיב יתיה כהנא נתקא הוא, סגירות רישא, או דקנא הוא: לא וארי יחזי כהנא ית מכתש נתקא, והא לית מחזוהי עמיק מן משכא, וסער אכם לית ביה, ויסגר כהנא, ית מכתש נתקא שבעא יומין: לב ויחזי כהנא ית מכתשא ביומא שביעאה,

"disinhibition effect" which occurs when people are not speaking face to face. Imagine a world in which those who posted negative, hurtful, or malicious remarks about others carried a visible mark of shame, and for a period were excluded from public places and the company of others – in short, suffered the fate of the *metzora*. This would be a world in which people would think twice before using speech to harm others.

and there is no blond hair among it, and the scaling appears to be no deeper
33 than the skin, then the patient shall shave himself, but shall not shave the scaled
part; and the priest shall quarantine the person with the scaling eruption for
34 a further seven days. On the seventh day the priest shall examine the scaling,
and if it has not spread in the skin and it appears to be no deeper than the skin,
then the priest shall pronounce the patient pure; he shall immerse his clothes
35 36 and be pure. But if the scaling spreads in the skin after he is declared pure, and
when the priest examines him, if the scaling has spread in the skin, the priest
37 need not seek the blond hair; he is impure. But if it appears to him that the
scaling is unchanged and if black hair has grown in among it, the eruption is
38 healed and is pure, and the priest shall declare the person pure. When
39 a man or a woman has white patches on the skin of his or her body, the priest
shall examine them, and if the patches on the skin are dull white, it is merely
40 a rash breaking out on the skin; the person is pure. If a man loses SHISHI /SHELISHI/
41 the hair on his head, it is merely baldness; he is pure. If he loses the hair from
42 his forehead, it is merely a receding hairline; he is pure. But if there is a white
and reddish diseased area on his bald spot or receding hairline, it is a blight
43 erupting in his bald spot or at his receding hairline. The priest shall examine
him, and if the diseased swelling is a white and reddish area on his bald spot or
44 receding hairline, resembling a blight in the skin of the body, he is a blighted
person; he is impure. The priest shall declare him impure; he has a blight on

רש״י

לג **והתגלח.** סביבות הנתק: **ואת הנתק לא יגלח.** מניח שתי שערות סמוך לו סביב, כדי שיהא נכר אם פשה, שאם יפשה יעבר השערות ויצא למקום הגלוח:

לה **אחרי טהרתו.** אין לי אלא פושה לאחר הפטור. מנין אף בסוף שבוע ראשון ובסוף שבוע שני? תלמוד לומר: ״פשה יפשה״:

לז **ושער שחר.** מנין אף הירק והאדם שאינו צהב? תלמוד לומר: ״ושער״; ולמה צהב דומה? לתבנית הזהב: **טהור הוא וטהרו הכהן.** הא טמא שטהרו הכהן לא טהר:

לח **בהרת.** חברבורות:

לט **כהות לבנת.** שאין לבן שלהן עז אלא כהה: **בהק.** כמין לבן הנראה בבשר אדם אדם שקורין רו״ס בין חברבורות אדמימותו, קרוי בהק, כאיש עדשן, שבין עדשה לעדשה מבהיק הבשר בלבן צח:

מ **קרח הוא טהור הוא.** מטמאת נתקין, שאין נדון בסימני ראש וזקן שהם מקום שער, אלא בסימני נגעי עור בשר – מחיה ופשיון:

מא **ואם מפאת פניו.** משפוע קדקד כלפי פניו קרוי ׳גבחת׳, ואף הצדעין שמכאן ומכאן בכלל, ומשפוע קדקד כלפי אחוריו קרוי ׳קרחת׳:

מב **נגע לבן אדמדם.** פתוך. מנין שאף המראות? תלמוד לומר: ״נגע״:

מג **כמראה צרעת עור בשר.** כמראה הצרעת האמור בפרשת עור בשר: ״אדם כי יהיה בעור בשרו״ (לעיל פסוק ב), ומה אמור בו? שמטמא בארבעה מראות ונדון בשני שבועות, ולא כמראה צרעת האמור בשחין ומכוה שהוא נדון בשבוע אחד, ולא כמראה נתקין של מקום שער שאין מטמאין בארבע מראות:

מד **בראשו נגעו.** אין לי אלא נתקין. מנין לרבות שאר המנגעים? תלמוד לומר: ״טמא יטמאנו״, לרבות את כלן, על כלן הוא אומר: ״בגדיו יהיו פרמים״ וגו׳ (להלן פסוק מה):

וְהִנֵּה לֹא־פָשָׂה הַנֶּתֶק וְלֹא־הָיָה בוֹ שֵׂעָר צָהֹב וּמַרְאֵה הַנֶּתֶק אֵין עָמֹק
לג מִן־הָעוֹר׃ וְהִתְגַּלָּח וְאֶת־הַנֶּתֶק לֹא יְגַלֵּחַ וְהִסְגִּיר הַכֹּהֵן אֶת־הַנֶּתֶק
לד שִׁבְעַת יָמִים שֵׁנִית׃ וְרָאָה הַכֹּהֵן אֶת־הַנֶּתֶק בַּיּוֹם הַשְּׁבִיעִי וְהִנֵּה לֹא־
פָשָׂה הַנֶּתֶק בָּעוֹר וּמַרְאֵהוּ אֵינֶנּוּ עָמֹק מִן־הָעוֹר וְטִהַר אֹתוֹ הַכֹּהֵן
לה וְכִבֶּס בְּגָדָיו וְטָהֵר׃ וְאִם־פָּשֹׂה יִפְשֶׂה הַנֶּתֶק בָּעוֹר אַחֲרֵי טָהֳרָתוֹ׃
לו וְרָאָהוּ הַכֹּהֵן וְהִנֵּה פָּשָׂה הַנֶּתֶק בָּעוֹר לֹא־יְבַקֵּר הַכֹּהֵן לַשֵּׂעָר הַצָּהֹב
לז טָמֵא הוּא׃ וְאִם־בְּעֵינָיו עָמַד הַנֶּתֶק וְשֵׂעָר שָׁחֹר צָמַח־בּוֹ נִרְפָּא הַנֶּתֶק
לח טָהוֹר הוּא וְטִהֲרוֹ הַכֹּהֵן׃ וְאִישׁ אוֹ־אִשָּׁה כִּי־יִהְיֶה בְעוֹר־
לט בְּשָׂרָם בֶּהָרֹת בֶּהָרֹת לְבָנֹת׃ וְרָאָה הַכֹּהֵן וְהִנֵּה בְעוֹר־בְּשָׂרָם בֶּהָרֹת
מ כֵּהוֹת לְבָנֹת בֹּהַק הוּא פָּרַח בָּעוֹר טָהוֹר הוּא׃ וְאִישׁ כִּי ששי /שלישי/
מא יִמָּרֵט רֹאשׁוֹ קֵרֵחַ הוּא טָהוֹר הוּא׃ וְאִם מִפְּאַת פָּנָיו יִמָּרֵט רֹאשׁוֹ גִּבֵּחַ
מב הוּא טָהוֹר הוּא׃ וְכִי־יִהְיֶה בַקָּרַחַת אוֹ בַגַּבַּחַת נֶגַע לָבָן אֲדַמְדָּם צָרַעַת
מג פֹּרַחַת הִוא בְּקָרַחְתּוֹ אוֹ בְגַבַּחְתּוֹ׃ וְרָאָה אֹתוֹ הַכֹּהֵן וְהִנֵּה שְׂאֵת־
הַנֶּגַע לְבָנָה אֲדַמְדֶּמֶת בְּקָרַחְתּוֹ אוֹ בְגַבַּחְתּוֹ כְּמַרְאֵה צָרַעַת עוֹר
מד בָּשָׂר׃ אִישׁ־צָרוּעַ הוּא טָמֵא הוּא טַמֵּא יְטַמְּאֶנּוּ הַכֹּהֵן בְּרֹאשׁוֹ נִגְעוֹ׃

אונקלוס

וְהָא לָא אוֹסֵיף נִתְקָא, וְלָא הֲוָה בֵיהּ סְעַר סֻמָּק, וּמֶחֱזֵי נִתְקָא, לֵית עֲמִיק מִן מַשְׁכָּא: לג וְיִגַּלַּח סַחְרָנֵי נִתְקָא, וּדְעִם נִתְקָא לָא יְגַלַּח, וְיַסְגַּר כָּהֲנָא יָת נִתְקָא, שִׁבְעָא יוֹמִין תִּנְיָנוּת: לד וְיִחְזֵי כָהֲנָא יָת נִתְקָא בְּיוֹמָא שְׁבִיעָאָה, וְהָא, לָא אוֹסֵיף נִתְקָא בְּמַשְׁכָּא, וּמֶחֱזוֹהִי, לֵיתוֹהִי עֲמִיק מִן מַשְׁכָּא, וִידַכֵּי יָתֵיהּ כָּהֲנָא, וִיצַבַּע לְבוּשׁוֹהִי וְיִדְכֵּי: לה וְאִם אוֹסָפָא יוֹסֵיף, נִתְקָא בְּמַשְׁכָּא, בָּתַר דְּכוּתֵיהּ: לו וְיִחְזְנֵיהּ כָּהֲנָא, וְהָא, אוֹסֵיף נִתְקָא בְּמַשְׁכָּא, לָא יְבַקַּר כָּהֲנָא, לִסְעַר סֻמָּק מְסָאַב הוּא: לז וְאִם כַּד הֲוָה קָם נִתְקָא, וּסְעַר אֻכָּם צְמַח בֵּיהּ, אִתַּסִּי נִתְקָא דְּכֵי הוּא, וִידַכֵּינֵיהּ כָּהֲנָא: לח וּגְבַר אוֹ אִתָּא, אֲרֵי יְהֵי בִמְשַׁךְ בִּסְרְהוֹן בַּהֲרָן, בַּהֲרָן חִוָּרָן: לט וְיִחְזֵי כָהֲנָא, וְהָא בִמְשַׁךְ בִּסְרְהוֹן, בַּהֲרָן עָמְיָן חִוָּרָן, בֻּהֲקָא הוּא, סְגִי בְּמַשְׁכָּא דְּכֵי הוּא: מ וּגְבַר, אֲרֵי יִתַּר סְעַר רֵישֵׁיהּ, קָרִיחַ הוּא דְּכֵי הוּא: מא וְאִם מִקֳּבֵיל אַפּוֹהִי, יִתַּר סְעַר רֵישֵׁיהּ, גְּלִישׁ הוּא דְּכֵי הוּא: מב וַאֲרֵי יְהֵי בְקָרַחוּתָא אוֹ בִגְלִישׁוּתָא, מַכְתַּשׁ חִוַּר סָמוֹק, סְגִירוּת סָגְיָא הִיא, בְּקָרַחוּתֵיהּ אוֹ בִגְלִישׁוּתֵיהּ: מג וְיִחְזֵי יָתֵיהּ כָּהֲנָא, וְהָא עֲמִיק מַכְתָּשָׁא חִוַּר סָמוֹק, בְּקָרַחוּתֵיהּ אוֹ בִגְלִישׁוּתֵיהּ, כְּמֶחֱזֵי סְגִירוּת מְשַׁךְ בִּסְרָא: מד גְּבַר סְגִיר הוּא מְסָאַב הוּא, סַאָבָא יְסַאֲבִנֵּיהּ, כָּהֲנָא בְּרֵישֵׁיהּ מַכְתָּשֵׁיהּ:

45 his scalp. And a blighted person, one bearing the disease – his clothes shall be
torn and the hair of his head disarrayed. And he shall cover his upper lip as he
46 cries out, 'Impure, impure.' He shall be in a state of impurity for as long as he
has the disease; he is impure. He shall live apart; outside the camp shall be his
47 dwelling. When a blight appears in a garment, whether the garment
48 is of wool or of linen, or in the warp or in the weft of the linen or wool cloth,
49 in leather or anything made of leather, if the infection shows as green or red
in the garment, the leather, the warp or the weft, or the article of leather, it
50 is a case of the impure blight and shall be shown to the priest. And the priest
shall examine the disease and quarantine the diseased article for seven days.
51 He shall examine the disease on the seventh day. If the disease has spread in
the garment, the warp or the weft, or the leather, whatever the leather is used
52 for, the infection is a malignant disease blight; it is impure. The garment shall

רש״י

מה פְּרֻמִים. קְרוּעִים: פָּרוּעַ. מְגֻדָּל שֵׂעָר: וְעַל שָׂפָם יַעְטֶה. כְּאָבֵל: שָׂפָם. שֵׂעַר הַשְּׂפָתַיִם, גרנו״ן בְּלַעַז: וְטָמֵא טָמֵא יִקְרָא. מַשְׁמִיעַ שֶׁהוּא טָמֵא וְיִפְרְשׁוּ מִמֶּנּוּ:

מו בָּדָד יֵשֵׁב. שֶׁלֹּא יִהְיוּ טְמֵאִים יוֹשְׁבִים עִמּוֹ. וְאָמְרוּ רַבּוֹתֵינוּ: מַה נִּשְׁתַּנָּה מִשְּׁאָר טְמֵאִים לֵישֵׁב בָּדָד? הוֹאִיל וְהוּא הִבְדִּיל בִּלְשׁוֹן הָרָע בֵּין אִישׁ לְאִשְׁתּוֹ, בֵּין אִישׁ לְרֵעֵהוּ, אַף הוּא יִבָּדֵל: מִחוּץ לַמַּחֲנֶה. חוּץ לְשָׁלֹשׁ מַחֲנוֹת:

מח לַפִּשְׁתִּים וְלַצָּמֶר. שֶׁל פִּשְׁתִּים אוֹ שֶׁל צֶמֶר: אוֹ בְעוֹר. זֶה עוֹר שֶׁלֹּא נַעֲשָׂה בּוֹ מְלָאכָה: אוֹ בְּכָל מְלֶאכֶת עוֹר. עוֹר שֶׁנַּעֲשָׂה בּוֹ מְלָאכָה:

מט יְרַקְרַק. יָרֹק שֶׁבִּירוּקִין: אֲדַמְדָּם. אָדֹם שֶׁבַּאֲדֻמִּים:

נא צָרַעַת מַמְאֶרֶת. לְשׁוֹן ״סִלּוֹן מַמְאִיר״ (יחזקאל כח, כד), פוינ״ט בְּלַעַז. וּמִדְרָשׁוֹ, תֵּן בּוֹ מְאֵרָה, שֶׁלֹּא תֵּהָנֶה הֵימֶנּוּ:

stigmatizing feelings. It relates, for example, that R. Shimon b. Elazar was once on a journey when he saw an individual who was disfigured. He asked the man, "Are all the people in your town as deformed as you are?" The man replied, "If you do not like the pot, go and complain to the potter [i.e., to God who made me this way]." When they arrived at R. Shimon b. Elazar's town, his disciples came to greet him. The man who had been insulted said to them, "Is this the person you call a great man? May there not be many more like him in Israel." When the disciples discovered what their rabbi had said, they agreed that he had done wrong, but added, "Forgive him because he is a great scholar." The man did so on the condition that R. Shimon would agree not to speak likewise in the future (Taanit 20b). The fact that the Talmud records such episodes, critical of the Sages, is eloquent of the need to wrestle with prejudice and the difficulty we have in coming to terms with disability, illness, and physical difference.

Against this, Judaism directs us to integrate people with disabilities into the community. We must reach out to those who have a family member affected by illness and make them feel that they are full participants in the community. The behavioral model here is *avelut*, mourning. When faced with grief, the natural reaction is what halakha defines as *aninut* (the period of mourning before the burial). This is a time of trauma, in which we are emotionally isolated by distress. In the Torah, the appearance of a person with an impure blight, with torn clothes and covered face, is like that of a mourner (Moed Katan 15a), and this is not accidental. The whole thrust of the Jewish laws of mourning and of comforting the bereaved is to lead the mourner back from isolation to reintegration into the community. If this applies to the bereaved, all the more so does it apply to those who are concerned with life.

מה וְהַצָּרוּעַ אֲשֶׁר־בּוֹ הַנֶּגַע בְּגָדָיו יִהְיוּ פְרֻמִים וְרֹאשׁוֹ יִהְיֶה פָרוּעַ וְעַל־
מו שָׂפָם יַעְטֶה וְטָמֵא ׀ טָמֵא יִקְרָא׃ כָּל־יְמֵי אֲשֶׁר הַנֶּגַע בּוֹ יִטְמָא טָמֵא
מז הוּא בָּדָד יֵשֵׁב מִחוּץ לַמַּחֲנֶה מוֹשָׁבוֹ׃ וְהַבֶּגֶד כִּי־יִהְיֶה
מח בוֹ נֶגַע צָרָעַת בְּבֶגֶד צֶמֶר אוֹ בְּבֶגֶד פִּשְׁתִּים׃ אוֹ בִשְׁתִי אוֹ בְעֵרֶב
מט לַפִּשְׁתִּים וְלַצָּמֶר אוֹ בְעוֹר אוֹ בְּכָל־מְלֶאכֶת עוֹר׃ וְהָיָה הַנֶּגַע יְרַקְרַק ׀
אוֹ אֲדַמְדָּם בַּבֶּגֶד אוֹ בָעוֹר אוֹ־בַשְּׁתִי אוֹ־בָעֵרֶב אוֹ בְכָל־כְּלִי־עוֹר נֶגַע
נ צָרַעַת הוּא וְהָרְאָה אֶת־הַכֹּהֵן׃ וְרָאָה הַכֹּהֵן אֶת־הַנֶּגַע וְהִסְגִּיר אֶת־
נא הַנֶּגַע שִׁבְעַת יָמִים׃ וְרָאָה אֶת־הַנֶּגַע בַּיּוֹם הַשְּׁבִיעִי כִּי־פָשָׂה הַנֶּגַע
בַּבֶּגֶד אוֹ־בַשְּׁתִי אוֹ־בָעֵרֶב אוֹ בָעוֹר לְכֹל אֲשֶׁר־יֵעָשֶׂה הָעוֹר לִמְלָאכָה
נב צָרַעַת מַמְאֶרֶת הַנֶּגַע טָמֵא הוּא׃ וְשָׂרַף אֶת־הַבֶּגֶד אוֹ אֶת־הַשְּׁתִי ׀

אונקלוס

מה וּסְגִירָא דְּבֵיהּ מַכְתָּשָׁא, לְבוּשׁוֹהִי, יְהוֹן מְבַזְּעִין וְרֵישֵׁיהּ יְהֵי פְרִיעַ, וְעַל שָׂפָם כְּאָבִילָא יִתְעַטַּף, וְלָא תִסְתַּאֲבוּ וְלָא תִסְתַּאֲבוּ יִקְרֵי: מו כָּל יוֹמִין, דְּמַכְתָּשָׁא בֵיהּ, יְהֵי מְסָאַב מְסָאַב הוּא, בִּלְחוֹדוֹהִי יְתִיב, מִבָּרָא לְמַשְׁרִיתָא מוֹתְבֵיהּ: מז וּלְבוּשָׁא, אֲרֵי יְהֵי בֵיהּ מַכְתַּשׁ סְגִירוּ, בִּלְבוּשׁ עֲמַר, אוֹ בִּלְבוּשׁ כִּתָּן: מח אוֹ בְשִׁתְיָא אוֹ בְעִרְבָּא, לְכִתָּנָא וּלְעַמְרָא, אוֹ בְמַשְׁכָּא, אוֹ בְּכָל עֲבִידַת מְשַׁךְ: מט וִיהֵי מַכְתָּשָׁא, יָרוֹק אוֹ סָמוֹק, בִּלְבוּשָׁא אוֹ בְמַשְׁכָּא, אוֹ בְשִׁתְיָא אוֹ בְעִרְבָּא אוֹ בְכָל מָן דִּמְשַׁךְ, מַכְתַּשׁ סְגִירוּתָא הוּא, וְיִתַּחְזֵי לְוָת כָּהֲנָא: נ וְיִחְזֵי כָהֲנָא יָת מַכְתָּשָׁא, וְיַסְגַּר יָת מַכְתָּשָׁא שִׁבְעָא יוֹמִין: נא וְיִחְזֵי יָת מַכְתָּשָׁא בְּיוֹמָא שְׁבִיעָאָה, אֲרֵי אוֹסֵיף מַכְתָּשָׁא בִּלְבוּשָׁא, אוֹ בְשִׁתְיָא אוֹ בְעִרְבָּא אוֹ בְמַשְׁכָּא, לְכֹל, דְּיִתְעֲבֵיד מַשְׁכָּא לַעֲבִידְתָּא, סְגִירוּת מַחְסְרָא, מַכְתָּשָׁא מְסָאַב הוּא: נב וְיוֹקֵיד יָת לְבוּשָׁא, אוֹ יָת שִׁתְיָא

ILLNESS AND OSTRACIZATION

This passage details quintessential expressions of shame to which the blighted individual is subjected. First is the *stigma*: the public marks of disgrace or dishonor (the torn clothes, unkempt hair). Then comes the *ostracism:* temporary exclusion from the normal affairs of society. These have nothing to do with illness and everything to do with social disapproval. This is what makes the law of *tzaraat* so hard to understand at first: it is one of the rare appearances of public shaming in a non-shame, guilt-based culture. It happened, though, not because society had expressed its disapproval but because God was signaling that it should do so. Malicious gossip, *lashon hara,* undermines relationships, erodes the social bond, and damages trust. It, uniquely in Jewish culture, deserves to be exposed and shamed.

For centuries, Hansen's disease sufferers enacted, with variations, the scene described here. The mistranslation of *tzaraat* as leprosy amplified the stigma they anyway suffered. The stigmatization of disease and disability, however, is something all societies must grapple with. Often we do not know what to do when faced by someone with a severe disability or illness. To avoid our own awkwardness we may shun the affected family, or on the other hand try too hard. Through our own embarrassment, we may create embarrassment in others.

The Talmud, with great candor, tells us of the difficulty some of the Sages had in overcoming their instinctive

be burned – or the warp or weft, wool or linen, or any article of leather that
53 is infected – for it is a malignant disease blight; it must be burned in fire. If,
however, the priest examines it and the disease has not spread in the garment,
54 the warp or the weft, or the article of leather, then the priest shall command the
article in which the disease appears to be washed, and he shall quarantine it for
55 another seven days. After this washing the priest shall once more examine the SHEVI'I /REVI'I/
diseased article. If the diseased area has not changed color, though the disease
has not spread, it is impure. You shall burn it in fire, whether the mark of decay
56 is on the inside or on the outside. But if the priest examines it and the diseased MAFTIR
area has faded after washing, he shall tear it out of the garment or the leather
57 or the warp or the weft. If it appears again in the garment, in the warp or weft,
or in the leather article, it is erupting. Whatever has the disease, you shall burn
58 with fire. But the garment, or the warp or weft, or the leather article from which
the disease departs after you have washed it shall be washed a second time and
59 then be pure." This is the law concerning the disease blight in a garment of wool
or of linen, in warp or in weft, or in any article made of leather, to determine
whether it is pure or impure.

The haftara for Parashat Tazria is on page 1566.
When Tazria and Metzora are read together, read the haftara on page 1568.
On the Shabbat of Parashat HaḤodesh read the haftara on page 1650.

רש״י

נב **בַּצֶּמֶר אוֹ בַפִּשְׁתִּים.** שֶׁל צֶמֶר אוֹ שֶׁל פִּשְׁתִּים, זֶהוּ פְּשׁוּטוֹ. וּמִדְרָשׁוֹ, יָכוֹל יָבִיא גִּזֵּי צֶמֶר וַאֲנִיצֵי פִשְׁתָּן וְיִשְׂרְפֵם עִמּוֹ? תַּלְמוּד לוֹמַר: "הִוא בָּאֵשׁ תִּשָּׂרֵף", אֵינָהּ צְרִיכָה דָּבָר אַחֵר עִמָּהּ. אִם כֵּן מַה תַּלְמוּד לוֹמַר: "בַּצֶּמֶר אוֹ בַפִּשְׁתִּים"? לְהוֹצִיא אֶת הָאִמְרָיוֹת שֶׁבּוֹ שֶׁהֵן מִמִּין אַחֵר. 'אִמְרָיוֹת' לְשׁוֹן שָׂפָה, כְּמוֹ: 'אִמְרָא':

נד **אֵת אֲשֶׁר בּוֹ הַנָּגַע.** יָכוֹל מְקוֹם הַנֶּגַע בִּלְבַד? תַּלְמוּד לוֹמַר: "אֵת אֲשֶׁר בּוֹ הַנָּגַע". יָכוֹל כָּל הַבֶּגֶד כֻּלּוֹ טָעוּן כִּבּוּס? תַּלְמוּד לוֹמַר: "הַנֶּגַע". הָא כֵּיצַד? יְכַבֵּס מִן הַבֶּגֶד עִמּוֹ:

נה **אַחֲרֵי הֻכַּבֵּס.** לְשׁוֹן הֵעָשׂוֹת: **לֹא הָפַךְ הַנֶּגַע אֶת עֵינוֹ.** לֹא הֻכְהָה מִמַּרְאִיתוֹ: **וְהַנֶּגַע לֹא פָשָׂה.** שָׁמַעְנוּ שֶׁאִם לֹא הָפַךְ וְלֹא פָשָׂה טָמֵא, וְאֵין צָרִיךְ לוֹמַר לֹא הָפַךְ וּפָשָׂה. הָפַךְ וְלֹא פָשָׂה אֵינִי יוֹדֵעַ מַה יֵּעָשֶׂה לוֹ? תַּלְמוּד לוֹמַר: "וְהִסְגִּיר אֶת הַנֶּגַע", מִכָּל מָקוֹם, דִּבְרֵי רַבִּי יְהוּדָה. וַחֲכָמִים אוֹמְרִים וְכוּ', כִּדְאִיתָא בְּתוֹרַת כֹּהֲנִים (פרק טו, ז), וּרְמַזְתִּיהָ כָּאן לְיַשֵּׁב הַמִּקְרָא עַל אָפְנָיו: **פְּחֶתֶת הִוא.** לְשׁוֹן גֻּמָּא, כְּמוֹ: "בְּאַחַת הַפְּחָתִים" (שמואל ב׳ יז, ט), כְּלוֹמַר שְׁפָלָה הִיא, נֶגַע שֶׁמַּרְאָיו שׁוֹקְעִין: **בְּקָרַחְתּוֹ אוֹ בְגַבַּחְתּוֹ.** כְּתַרְגּוּמוֹ: "בִּשְׁחִיקוּתֵיהּ אוֹ בְחַדָּתוּתֵיהּ": קָרַחְתּוֹ. שְׁחָקִים, יְשָׁנִים. וּמִפְּנֵי הַמִּדְרָשׁ שֶׁהֻצְרַךְ לִגְזֵרָה שָׁוָה: מִנַּיִן לִפְרִיחָה בִּבְגָדִים שֶׁהִיא טְהוֹרָה? נֶאֶמְרָה קָרַחַת וְגַבַּחַת בְּאָדָם (לעיל פסוק מב) וְנֶאֶמְרָה קָרַחַת וְגַבַּחַת בִּבְגָדִים, מַה לְּהַלָּן פָּרַח בְּכֻלּוֹ טָהוֹר (לעיל פסוק יג) אַף כָּאן פָּרַח בְּכֻלּוֹ טָהוֹר – לְכָךְ אָחַז הַכָּתוּב לְשׁוֹן קָרַחַת וְגַבַּחַת. וּלְעִנְיַן פֵּרוּשׁוֹ וְתַרְגּוּמוֹ זֶהוּ מַשְׁמָעוֹ, קָרַחַת לְשׁוֹן יְשָׁנִים וְגַבַּחַת לְשׁוֹן חֲדָשִׁים, כְּאִלּוּ נִכְתַּב: 'בְּאַחֲרִיתוֹ אוֹ בְּקַדְמוּתוֹ', שֶׁהַקָּרַחַת לְשׁוֹן אֲחוֹרַיִם וְהַגַּבַּחַת לְשׁוֹן פָּנִים, כְּמוֹ שֶׁכָּתוּב: "וְאִם מִפְּאַת פָּנָיו" וְגוֹ' (לעיל פסוק מא), וְהַקָּרַחַת כָּל שֶׁשּׁוֹפֵעַ וְיוֹרֵד מִן הַקָּדְקֹד וּלְאַחֲרָיו. כָּךְ מְפֹרָשׁ בְּתוֹרַת כֹּהֲנִים (פרק טו, ט):

נו **וְקָרַע אֹתוֹ.** יִקְרַע מְקוֹם הַנֶּגַע מִן הַבֶּגֶד וְיִשְׂרְפֶנּוּ:

נז **פֹּרַחַת הִוא.** דָּבָר הַחוֹזֵר וְצוֹמֵחַ: **בָּאֵשׁ תִּשְׂרְפֶנּוּ.** אֶת כָּל הַבֶּגֶד:

נח **וְסָר מֵהֶם הַנָּגַע.** אִם כְּשֶׁכִּבְּסוּהוּ בַּתְּחִלָּה עַל פִּי כֹהֵן סָר מִמֶּנּוּ הַנֶּגַע לְגַמְרֵי: **וְכֻבַּס שֵׁנִית.** לְשׁוֹן טְבִילָה. תַּרְגּוּם שֶׁל כִּבּוּסִין שֶׁבַּפָּרָשָׁה זוֹ לְשׁוֹן לִבּוּן, 'וְיִתְחַוַּר', חוּץ מִזֶּה שֶׁאֵינוֹ לְלִבּוּן אֶלָּא לִטְבֹּל, לְכָךְ תַּרְגּוּמוֹ: "וְיִצְטְבַע". וְכֵן כָּל כִּבּוּסֵי בְגָדִים שֶׁהֵן לִטְבִילָה מְתֻרְגָּמִין: 'וְיִצְטְבַע':

אוֹ אֶת־הָעֵרֶב בַּצֶּמֶר אוֹ בַפִּשְׁתִּים אוֹ אֶת־כָּל־כְּלִי הָעוֹר אֲשֶׁר־יִהְיֶה
נג בּוֹ הַנָּגַע כִּי־צָרַעַת מַמְאֶרֶת הִוא בָּאֵשׁ תִּשָּׂרֵף׃ וְאִם יִרְאֶה הַכֹּהֵן
וְהִנֵּה לֹא־פָשָׂה הַנֶּגַע בַּבֶּגֶד אוֹ בַשְּׁתִי אוֹ בָעֵרֶב אוֹ בְּכָל־כְּלִי־עוֹר׃
נד וְצִוָּה הַכֹּהֵן וְכִבְּסוּ אֵת אֲשֶׁר־בּוֹ הַנָּגַע וְהִסְגִּירוֹ שִׁבְעַת־יָמִים שֵׁנִית׃
נה וְרָאָה הַכֹּהֵן אַחֲרֵי ׀ הֻכַּבֵּס אֶת־הַנֶּגַע וְהִנֵּה לֹא־הָפַךְ הַנֶּגַע אֶת־עֵינוֹ שביעי /רביעי/
וְהַנֶּגַע לֹא־פָשָׂה טָמֵא הוּא בָּאֵשׁ תִּשְׂרְפֶנּוּ פְּחֶתֶת הִוא בְּקָרַחְתּוֹ אוֹ
נו בְגַבַּחְתּוֹ׃ וְאִם רָאָה הַכֹּהֵן וְהִנֵּה כֵּהָה הַנֶּגַע אַחֲרֵי הֻכַּבֵּס אֹתוֹ וְקָרַע
נז אֹתוֹ מִן־הַבֶּגֶד אוֹ מִן־הָעוֹר אוֹ מִן־הַשְּׁתִי אוֹ מִן־הָעֵרֶב׃ וְאִם־תֵּרָאֶה מפטיר
עוֹד בַּבֶּגֶד אוֹ־בַשְּׁתִי אוֹ־בָעֵרֶב אוֹ בְכָל־כְּלִי־עוֹר פֹּרַחַת הִוא בָּאֵשׁ
נח תִּשְׂרְפֶנּוּ אֵת אֲשֶׁר־בּוֹ הַנָּגַע׃ וְהַבֶּגֶד אוֹ־הַשְּׁתִי אוֹ־הָעֵרֶב אוֹ־כָל־כְּלִי
נט הָעוֹר אֲשֶׁר תְּכַבֵּס וְסָר מֵהֶם הַנָּגַע וְכֻבַּס שֵׁנִית וְטָהֵר׃ זֹאת תּוֹרַת
נֶגַע־צָרַעַת בֶּגֶד הַצֶּמֶר ׀ אוֹ הַפִּשְׁתִּים אוֹ הַשְּׁתִי אוֹ הָעֵרֶב אוֹ כָּל־
כְּלִי־עוֹר לְטַהֲרוֹ אוֹ לְטַמְּאוֹ׃

The הפטרה *for* פרשת תזריע *is on page 1567.*
When תזריע *and* מצרע *are read together, read the haftara on page 1569.*
On the שבת *of* פרשת החודש *read the* הפטרה *on page 1651.*

אונקלוס

או ית ערבא, בעמרא או בכתנא, או ית כל מן דמשך, דיהי ביה מכתשא, ארי סגירות מחסרא היא, בנורא תתוקד: נג ואם יחזי כהנא, והא לא אוסיף מכתשא, בלבושא, או בשתיא או בערבא, או בכל מן דמשך: נד ויפקיד כהנא, ויחורון, ית דביה מכתשא, ויסגרניה שבעא יומין תנינות: נה ויחזי כהנא, בתר דחורו ית מכתשא, והא, לא שנא מכתשא מן כד הוה ומכתשא לא אוסיף, מסאב הוא, בנורא תוקדניה, תברא היא, בשחיקותיה או בחדתותיה: נו ואם חזא כהנא, והא עמא מכתשא, בתר דחורו יתיה, ויבזע יתיה, מן לבושא או מן משכא, או מן שתיא או מן ערבא: נז ואם תתחזי עוד, בלבושא, או בשתיא או בערבא או בכל מן דמשך, סגיא היא, בנורא תוקדניה, ית דביה מכתשא: נח ולבושא, או שתיא או ערבא, או כל מן דמשך דתחור, ויעדי מנהון מכתשא, ויצטבע תנינות וידכי: נט דא, אוריתא דמכתש סגירו, לבוש עמר או כתנא, או שתיא או ערבא, או כל מן דמשך, לדכאותיה או לסאבותיה:

Parashat Metzora

14 1 2 The Lord spoke to Moshe: "This shall be the law of the person with an impure
3 blight on the day he is to be purified. He shall be brought to see the priest, and
the priest shall go out of the camp to examine him. If the disease is healed in
4 the blighted person, the priest shall command two living ritually pure birds,
and cedarwood, scarlet wool, and hyssop to be brought for the one who is to
5 be purified. The priest shall command one of the birds to be slaughtered into
6 an earthen vessel, over living water. Then he shall take the living bird, together
with the cedarwood, the scarlet wool, and the hyssop, and dip them and the

רש״י

יד ב **זֹאת תִּהְיֶה תּוֹרַת הַמְּצֹרָע בְּיוֹם טָהֳרָתוֹ.** מְלַמֵּד שֶׁאֵין מְטַהֲרִין אוֹתוֹ בַּלַּיְלָה:

ג **אֶל מִחוּץ לַמַּחֲנֶה.** חוּץ לְשָׁלֹשׁ מַחֲנוֹת שֶׁנִּשְׁתַּלַּח שָׁם בִּימֵי חִלּוּטוֹ:

ד **חַיּוֹת.** פְּרָט לִטְרֵפוֹת: **טְהֹרוֹת.** פְּרָט לְעוֹף טָמֵא. לְפִי שֶׁהַנְּגָעִים בָּאִין עַל לָשׁוֹן הָרָע שֶׁהוּא מַעֲשֵׂה פִטְפּוּטֵי דְבָרִים, לְפִיכָךְ הֻזְקְקוּ לְטָהֳרָתוֹ צִפֳּרִים, שֶׁמְּפַטְפְּטִין תָּמִיד בְּצִפְצוּף קוֹל: **וְעֵץ אֶרֶז.** לְפִי שֶׁהַנְּגָעִים בָּאִין עַל גַּסּוּת הָרוּחַ: **וּשְׁנִי תוֹלַעַת וְאֵזֹב.** מַה תַּקָּנָתוֹ וְיִתְרַפֵּא? יַשְׁפִּיל עַצְמוֹ מִגַּאֲוָתוֹ כְּתוֹלַעַת וּכְאֵזוֹב: **עֵץ אֶרֶז.** מַקֵּל שֶׁל אֶרֶז: **וּשְׁנִי תוֹלַעַת.** לָשׁוֹן שֶׁל צֶמֶר צָבוּעַ זְהוֹרִית:

ה **עַל מַיִם חַיִּים.** נוֹתֵן אוֹתָם תְּחִלָּה בִּכְלִי כְּדֵי שֶׁיְּהֵא דַּם צִפּוֹר נִכָּר בָּהֶם, וְכַמָּה הֵם? רְבִיעִית:

ו **אֶת הַצִּפֹּר הַחַיָּה יִקַּח אֹתָהּ.** מְלַמֵּד שֶׁאֵינוֹ אוֹגְדָהּ עִמָּהֶם, אֶלָּא מַפְרִישָׁהּ לְעַצְמָהּ, אֲבָל הָעֵץ וְהָאֵזוֹב כְּרוּכִין יַחַד בִּלְשׁוֹן הַזְּהוֹרִית, כָּעִנְיָן שֶׁנֶּאֱמַר: "וְאֶת עֵץ הָאֶרֶז וְאֶת שְׁנִי הַתּוֹלַעַת וְאֶת הָאֵזֹב", לְקִיחָה אַחַת לִשְׁלָשְׁתָּן. יָכוֹל כְּשֵׁם שֶׁאֵינָהּ בִּכְלַל אֲגֻדָּה כָּךְ לֹא תִהְיֶה בִּכְלַל טְבִילָה? תַּלְמוּד לוֹמַר: "וְטָבַל אוֹתָם וְאֵת הַצִּפֹּר הַחַיָּה", הֶחְזִיר אֶת הַצִּפּוֹר לִכְלַל טְבִילָה:

gossip and *lashon hara* are so often honored in the breach, not the observance. So common is *lashon hara* that one of the giants of modern Jewry, Rabbi Yisrael Meir HaKohen (the Chofetz Chaim) devoted much of his life to combatting it. Yet it persists, as anyone who has ever been part of a human group knows from personal experience. You can know it is wrong, yet you and others do it anyway.

In our *parasha* the bearer of *lashon hara* is temporarily separated from the rest of society, condemned to live outside the camp as long as the condition lasts. The primary way to avoid *lashon hara* is to practice silence, and indeed the Sages were eloquent on the importance of silence (Mishna Avot 1:17, 3:13). Silence saves us from evil speech but in and of itself it achieves nothing positive. The challenge is to step back and see whether another form of "grooming speech" can create a more healthy community bond. Alongside the grave sin of *lashon hara*, there must in principle be a concept of *lashon hatov*, good speech, and it must be more than a mere negation of its opposite.

One of the most important tasks of a leader, a parent, or a friend is focused praise. In any relationship that matters to you, deliver praise daily. Seeing and praising the good in people makes them better people, makes you a better person, and strengthens the bond between you. Praise an act, a word, a gesture that was kind or sensitive or generous or thoughtful. The praise must be focused on that one act, not generalized. It must be genuine: it must come from the heart. And as a recipient, learn also to accept the praise.

Language is the air we breathe as social beings. Hence the statement in Proverbs (18:21), "Death and life" – both – "are in the power of the tongue." Evil speech destroys relationships. Good speech mends them.

פרשת מצרע

יד א ב וַיְדַבֵּר יְהוָה אֶל־מֹשֶׁה לֵּאמֹר׃ זֹאת תִּהְיֶה תּוֹרַת הַמְּצֹרָע בְּיוֹם טָהֳרָתוֹ ט
ג וְהוּבָא אֶל־הַכֹּהֵן׃ וְיָצָא הַכֹּהֵן אֶל־מִחוּץ לַמַּחֲנֶה וְרָאָה הַכֹּהֵן וְהִנֵּה
ד נִרְפָּא נֶגַע־הַצָּרַעַת מִן־הַצָּרוּעַ׃ וְצִוָּה הַכֹּהֵן וְלָקַח לַמִּטַּהֵר שְׁתֵּי־
ה צִפֳּרִים חַיּוֹת טְהֹרוֹת וְעֵץ אֶרֶז וּשְׁנִי תוֹלַעַת וְאֵזֹב׃ וְצִוָּה הַכֹּהֵן וְשָׁחַט
ו אֶת־הַצִּפּוֹר הָאֶחָת אֶל־כְּלִי־חֶרֶשׂ עַל־מַיִם חַיִּים׃ אֶת־הַצִּפֹּר הַחַיָּה
יִקַּח אֹתָהּ וְאֶת־עֵץ הָאֶרֶז וְאֶת־שְׁנִי הַתּוֹלַעַת וְאֶת־הָאֵזֹב וְטָבַל אוֹתָם

אונקלוס

יד א וּמַלֵּיל יי עִם מֹשֶׁה לְמֵימַר: ב דָּא תְהֵי אוֹרָיְתָא דִסְגִירָא, בְּיוֹמָא דִּדְכוּתֵיהּ, וְיִתֵּיתֵי לְוָת כָּהֲנָא: ג וְיִפּוֹק כָּהֲנָא, לְמִבָּרָא לְמַשְׁרִיתָא, וְיִחְזֵי כָּהֲנָא, וְהָא, אִתַּסִּי מַכְתָּשׁ סְגִירוּתָא מִן סְגִירָא: ד וִיפַקֵּיד כָּהֲנָא, וְיִסַּב לְדְמִדַּכֵּי, תַּרְתֵּין צִפְּרִין חַיִּין דָּכְיָן, וְאָעָא דְאַרְזָא, וּצְבַע זְהוֹרִי וְאֵיזוֹבָא: ה וִיפַקֵּיד כָּהֲנָא, וְיִכּוֹס יָת צִפְּרָא חֲדָא, לְמָן דַּחֲסַף עַל מֵי מַבּוּעַ: ו יָת צִפְּרָא חַיְתָא יִסַּב יָתַהּ, וְיָת אָעָא דְאַרְזָא, וְיָת צְבַע זְהוֹרִי וְיָת אֵיזוֹבָא, וְיִטְבּוֹל יָתְהוֹן,

METZORA

Parashat Metzora opens by continuing the description of the process of purification for the phenomenon known as *tzaraat*, the decay that causes skin disease in humans and discoloration in garments and the walls of houses.

In the previous *parasha*, Tazria, we noted the connection, already hinted at in the Torah, between *tzaraat* and *lashon hara*, evil speech. We shall continue to delve into this connection in Parashat Metzora. The second part of the *parasha* discusses the rules of impurity from bodily discharges, which help us grasp the concepts of *tuma* and *tahara*, impurity and purity, in general.

REINTEGRATION

If *tzaraat* were a disease, then the sufferer's temporary removal from the camp (Lev. 13:46) would clearly be a form of quarantine. But if it is a punishment for malicious speech, then we understand it differently. High morale was essential to the Israelites' survival in the desert. Evil speech creates division between one person and another, undermining trust, weakening community bonds, and destroying morale. The entire community suffers.

Yet there is a reason why it is hard to cure people of *lashon hara*. Robin Dunbar, in his famous book *Grooming, Gossip, and the Evolution of Language* argues that, in nature, groups are held together by devoting a considerable amount of time to building relationships and alliances. Nonhuman primates do this by "grooming," stroking and cleaning one another's skin. But this is very time-consuming and puts a limit on the size of the group.

Humans developed language as a more effective form of grooming. You can only stroke one animal or person at a time, but you can talk to several at a time. The specific form of language that bonds a group together, says Dunbar, is gossip – because this is the way members of the group can learn who to trust and who not to. So gossip is not one form of speech among others. According to Dunbar, it is the most primal of all uses of speech. It is why humans developed language in the first place.

If this is so, it explains why the prohibitions against

7 living bird in the blood of the bird that was killed over living water. With these
he shall sprinkle seven times over the one who is to be purified of the blight to
8 purify him; and he shall set the living bird free into the open field. The one who
is to be purified shall then wash his clothes, shave off all his hair, and immerse
himself in water; then he shall be purified. After that he may come into the
9 camp, but he shall dwell outside his tent for seven days. On the seventh day he
shall shave all the hair from his head, his beard, and his eyebrows. When he has
shaved off all his hair, he shall wash his clothes and immerse his body in water,
10 and he shall be pure. On the eighth day he shall take two unblemished male
lambs and one unblemished ewe lamb in its first year, with three-tenths of an
11 ephah of fine flour mixed with oil as a grain offering, and one *log* of oil. The
priest who purifies shall present the one to be purified, together with these,
12 to the LORD at the entrance to the Tent of Meeting. The priest shall take one
of the male lambs and offer it as a guilt offering, along with the *log* of oil; he
13 shall display these, this way and that, as a wave offering before the LORD. He SHENI
shall slaughter the lamb in the place where purification offerings and burnt
offerings are slaughtered within the holy place. For the guilt offering, like the
14 purification offering, belongs to the priest and is holy of holies. The priest shall
take some of the blood of the guilt offering and apply it to the ridge of the
right ear, to the right thumb, and to the right big toe of the one who is to be
15 16 purified. The priest shall pour some of the *log* of oil into his own left palm, dip
his right finger into the oil in his left hand, and sprinkle of the oil with his finger
17 seven times before the LORD. The priest shall apply some of the remaining oil

רש״י

ח **וַיָּשַׁב מִחוּץ לְאָהֳלוֹ.** מְלַמֵּד שֶׁאָסוּר בְּתַשְׁמִישׁ הַמִּטָּה:

ט **אֶת כָּל שְׂעָרוֹ וְגוֹ׳.** כְּלָל וּפְרָט וּכְלָל, לְהָבִיא כָּל מְקוֹם כְּנוּס שֵׂעָר וְנִרְאֶה:

י **וְכַבְשָׂה אַחַת.** לְחַטָּאת: **וּשְׁלֹשָׁה עֶשְׂרֹנִים.** לְנִסְכֵּי שְׁלֹשָׁה כְּבָשִׂים הַלָּלוּ, שֶׁחַטָּאתוֹ וַאֲשָׁמוֹ שֶׁל מְצֹרָע טְעוּנִין נְסָכִים: **וְלֹג אֶחָד שָׁמֶן.** לְהַזּוֹת עָלָיו שֶׁבַע וְלִתֵּן מִמֶּנּוּ עַל תְּנוּךְ אָזְנוֹ וּמַתַּן בְּהוֹנוֹת:

יא **לִפְנֵי ה׳.** בְּשַׁעַר נִיקָנוֹר וְלֹא בָּעֲזָרָה עַצְמָהּ, לְפִי שֶׁהוּא מְחֻסַּר כִּפּוּרִים:

יב **וְהִקְרִיב אֹתוֹ לְאָשָׁם.** יַקְרִיבֶנּוּ לְתוֹךְ הָעֲזָרָה לְשֵׁם אָשָׁם: **וְהֵנִיף.** שֶׁהוּא טָעוּן תְּנוּפָה חַי: **וְהֵנִיף אֹתָם.** אֶת הָאָשָׁם וְאֶת הַלֹּג:

יג **בִּמְקוֹם אֲשֶׁר יִשְׁחַט וְגוֹ׳.** עַל יֶרֶךְ הַמִּזְבֵּחַ בַּצָּפוֹן. וּמַה תַּלְמוּד לוֹמַר? וַהֲלֹא כְּבָר נֶאֱמַר בְּתוֹרַת אָשָׁם בְּפָרָשַׁת ״צַו אֶת אַהֲרֹן״ שֶׁהָאָשָׁם טָעוּן שְׁחִיטָה בַּצָּפוֹן (לעיל ז, ב)? לְפִי שֶׁיָּצָא זֶה מִכְּלַל אֲשָׁמוֹת לִדּוֹן בְּהַעֲמָדָה, יָכוֹל תְּהֵא שְׁחִיטָתוֹ בִּמְקוֹם הַעֲמָדָתוֹ? לְכָךְ נֶאֱמַר: ״וְשָׁחַט בִּמְקוֹם אֲשֶׁר יִשְׁחַט״ וְגוֹ׳: **כִּי כַּחַטָּאת.** כִּי כְּכָל הַחַטָּאוֹת הָאָשָׁם הַזֶּה הוּא לַכֹּהֵן, בְּכָל עֲבוֹדוֹת הַתְּלוּיוֹת בַּכֹּהֵן הֻשְׁוָה אָשָׁם זֶה לְחַטָּאת, שֶׁלֹּא תֹּאמַר הוֹאִיל וְיָצָא דָּמוֹ מִכְּלַל שְׁאָר אֲשָׁמוֹת לִנָּתֵן עַל תְּנוּךְ וּבְהוֹנוֹת, לֹא יְהֵא טָעוּן מַתַּן דָּמִים וְאֵמוּרִים לְגַבֵּי מִזְבֵּחַ, לְכָךְ נֶאֱמַר: ״כִּי כַּחַטָּאת הָאָשָׁם הוּא לַכֹּהֵן״. יָכוֹל יְהֵא דָּמוֹ נִתָּן לְמַעְלָה כְּחַטָּאת? תַּלְמוּד לוֹמַר וְכוּ׳. בְּתוֹרַת כֹּהֲנִים (פרק ג, ח):

יד **תְּנוּךְ.** גֵּדֶר אֶמְצָעִי שֶׁבָּאֹזֶן, וּלְשׁוֹן ׳תְּנוּךְ׳ לֹא נוֹדַע לִי, וְהַפּוֹתְרִים קוֹרִים לוֹ טנדרו״ס: **בֹּהֶן.** גּוּדָל:

טז **לִפְנֵי ה׳.** כְּנֶגֶד בֵּית קָדְשֵׁי הַקֳּדָשִׁים:

ז וְאֶת ׀ הַצִּפֹּר הַחַיָּה בְּדַם הַצִּפֹּר הַשְּׁחֻטָה עַל הַמַּיִם הַחַיִּים׃ וְהִזָּה עַל
הַמִּטַּהֵר מִן־הַצָּרַעַת שֶׁבַע פְּעָמִים וְטִהֲרוֹ וְשִׁלַּח אֶת־הַצִּפֹּר הַחַיָּה
ח עַל־פְּנֵי הַשָּׂדֶה׃ וְכִבֶּס הַמִּטַּהֵר אֶת־בְּגָדָיו וְגִלַּח אֶת־כָּל־שְׂעָרוֹ וְרָחַץ
בַּמַּיִם וְטָהֵר וְאַחַר יָבוֹא אֶל־הַמַּחֲנֶה וְיָשַׁב מִחוּץ לְאָהֳלוֹ שִׁבְעַת יָמִים׃
ט וְהָיָה בַיּוֹם הַשְּׁבִיעִי יְגַלַּח אֶת־כָּל־שְׂעָרוֹ אֶת־רֹאשׁוֹ וְאֶת־זְקָנוֹ וְאֵת
גַּבֹּת עֵינָיו וְאֶת־כָּל־שְׂעָרוֹ יְגַלֵּחַ וְכִבֶּס אֶת־בְּגָדָיו וְרָחַץ אֶת־בְּשָׂרוֹ
י בַּמַּיִם וְטָהֵר׃ וּבַיּוֹם הַשְּׁמִינִי יִקַּח שְׁנֵי־כְבָשִׂים תְּמִימִם וְכַבְשָׂה אַחַת
בַּת־שְׁנָתָהּ תְּמִימָה וּשְׁלֹשָׁה עֶשְׂרֹנִים סֹלֶת מִנְחָה בְּלוּלָה בַשֶּׁמֶן וְלֹג
יא אֶחָד שָׁמֶן׃ וְהֶעֱמִיד הַכֹּהֵן הַמְטַהֵר אֵת הָאִישׁ הַמִּטַּהֵר וְאֹתָם לִפְנֵי
יב יהוה פֶּתַח אֹהֶל מוֹעֵד׃ וְלָקַח הַכֹּהֵן אֶת־הַכֶּבֶשׂ הָאֶחָד וְהִקְרִיב
יג אֹתוֹ לְאָשָׁם וְאֶת־לֹג הַשָּׁמֶן וְהֵנִיף אֹתָם תְּנוּפָה לִפְנֵי יהוה׃ וְשָׁחַט שני
אֶת־הַכֶּבֶשׂ בִּמְקוֹם אֲשֶׁר יִשְׁחַט אֶת־הַחַטָּאת וְאֶת־הָעֹלָה בִּמְקוֹם
יד הַקֹּדֶשׁ כִּי כַּחַטָּאת הָאָשָׁם הוּא לַכֹּהֵן קֹדֶשׁ קָדָשִׁים הוּא׃ וְלָקַח הַכֹּהֵן
מִדַּם הָאָשָׁם וְנָתַן הַכֹּהֵן עַל־תְּנוּךְ אֹזֶן הַמִּטַּהֵר הַיְמָנִית וְעַל־בֹּהֶן יָדוֹ
טו הַיְמָנִית וְעַל־בֹּהֶן רַגְלוֹ הַיְמָנִית׃ וְלָקַח הַכֹּהֵן מִלֹּג הַשָּׁמֶן וְיָצַק עַל־כַּף
טז הַכֹּהֵן הַשְּׂמָאלִית׃ וְטָבַל הַכֹּהֵן אֶת־אֶצְבָּעוֹ הַיְמָנִית מִן־הַשֶּׁמֶן אֲשֶׁר
יז עַל־כַּפּוֹ הַשְּׂמָאלִית וְהִזָּה מִן־הַשֶּׁמֶן בְּאֶצְבָּעוֹ שֶׁבַע פְּעָמִים לִפְנֵי יהוה׃

אונקלוס

וְיָת צִפְּרָא חַיְתָא, בִּדְמָא דְּצִפְּרָא דִּנְכִיסְתָּא, עַל מֵי מַבּוּעַ: ז וְיַדֵּי, עַל דְּמִדַּכֵּי, מִן סְגִירוּתָא שְׁבַע זִמְנִין, וִידַכֵּינֵיהּ, וִישַׁלַּח, יָת צִפְּרָא חַיְתָא עַל אַפֵּי חַקְלָא: ח וִיצַבַּע דְּמִדַּכֵּי יָת לְבוּשׁוֹהִי וִיגַלַּח יָת כָּל סַעֲרֵיהּ, וְיַסְחֵי בְמַיָּא וְיִדְכֵּי, וּבָתַר כֵּן יֵיעוֹל לְמַשְׁרִיתָא, וִיתִיב, מִבָּרָא לְמַשְׁכְּנֵיהּ שִׁבְעָא יוֹמִין: ט וִיהֵי בְיוֹמָא שְׁבִיעָאָה יְגַלַּח יָת כָּל סַעֲרֵיהּ, יָת רֵישֵׁיהּ וְיָת דִּקְנֵיהּ וְיָת גְּבִינֵי עֵינוֹהִי, וְיָת כָּל סַעֲרֵיהּ יְגַלַּח, וִיצַבַּע יָת לְבוּשׁוֹהִי, וְיַסְחֵי יָת בִּסְרֵיהּ, בְּמַיָּא וְיִדְכֵּי: י וּבְיוֹמָא תְמִינָאָה, יִסַּב תְּרֵין אִמְּרִין שַׁלְמִין, וְאִמַּרְתָּא חֲדָא, בַּת שַׁתַּהּ שַׁלְמָתָא, וּתְלָתָא עֶסְרוֹנִין, סֻלְתָּא מִנְחָתָא דְּפִילָא בִמְשַׁח, וְלֻגָּא חַד דִּמְשַׁח: יא וִיקִים כַּהֲנָא דִּמְדַכֵּי, יָת, גַּבְרָא דְּמִדַּכֵּי וְיָתְהוֹן, קֳדָם יְיָ, בִּתְרַע מַשְׁכַּן זִמְנָא: יב וְיִסַּב כַּהֲנָא יָת אִמְּרָא חַד, וִיקָרֵיב יָתֵיהּ, לַאֲשָׁמָא וְיָת לוּגָּא דִּמְשְׁחָא, וִירִים יָתְהוֹן, אֲרָמָא קֳדָם יְיָ: יג וְיִכּוֹס יָת אִמְּרָא, בְּאַתְרָא, דְּיִכּוֹס יָת חַטָּתָא, וְיָת עֲלָתָא בַּאֲתַר קַדִּישׁ, אֲרֵי, כְּחַטָּתָא, אֲשָׁמָא הוּא לְכַהֲנָא, קֹדֶשׁ קֻדְשִׁין הוּא: יד וְיִסַּב כַּהֲנָא מִדְּמָא דַּאֲשָׁמָא, וְיִתֵּין כַּהֲנָא, עַל רוּם, אֻדְנָא דְּמִדַּכֵּי דְּיַמִּינָא, וְעַל אִלְיוֹן יְדֵיהּ דְּיַמִּינָא, וְעַל אִלְיוֹן רִגְלֵיהּ דְּיַמִּינָא: טו וְיִסַּב כַּהֲנָא מִלּוּגָּא דִּמְשְׁחָא, וְיָרִיק, עַל יְדָא דְּכַהֲנָא דִּסְמָאלָא: טז וְיִטְבּוֹל כַּהֲנָא יָת אֶצְבְּעֵיהּ דְּיַמִּינָא, מִן מִשְׁחָא, דְּעַל יְדֵיהּ דִּסְמָאלָא, וְיַדֵּי מִן מִשְׁחָא בְּאֶצְבְּעֵיהּ, שְׁבַע זִמְנִין קֳדָם

in his hand to the ridge of the right ear, to the right thumb, and to the right
18 big toe of the one who is to be purified, over the guilt offering blood. What
remains of the oil in his hand the priest shall pour on the head of the one to be
19 purified. Thus shall the priest make his atonement before the LORD. Then the
priest shall offer the purification offering to make atonement for the one to be
20 purified of his defilement. Then he shall slaughter the burnt offering. The priest
shall offer the burnt offering and the grain offering on the altar. Thus shall the
21 priest make his atonement, and he shall be purified. If, however, the SHELISHI /ḤAMISHI/
person is poor and cannot afford so much, he shall take one male lamb as a
guilt offering to be made a wave offering to make his atonement, and one-tenth
22 of an ephah of fine flour mixed with oil as a grain offering, and a *log* of oil, and
two doves or two pigeons, such as he can afford; one shall be a purification
23 offering and the other a burnt offering. On the eighth day of his purification,

רש״י

כ| **וְאֶת הַמִּנְחָה.** מִנְחַת נְסָכִים שֶׁל בְּהֵמָה:

כא| **וְעִשָּׂרוֹן סֹלֶת אֶחָד.** לְכֶבֶשׂ זֶה שֶׁהוּא אֶחָד, יָבִיא עִשָּׂרוֹן אֶחָד לִנְסָכָיו: **וְלֹג שָׁמֶן.** לָתֵת מִמֶּנּוּ עַל הַבְּהוֹנוֹת. וְשֶׁמֶן שֶׁל נִסְכֵּי הַמִּנְחָה לֹא הֻזְקַק הַכָּתוּב לְפָרֵשׁ:

one would have to recognize that charity is only part of the answer. In the Talmud we find that fundamental to the Rabbis' conception of Judaism was the idea that its practice should never impoverish or be beyond the reach of the poor. This was not a theoretical issue. Judaism did make economic demands, and it is important that these should not be divisive. Hence, for instance, the institutions that burials should be as simple as possible (Moed Katan 27b), and that on the special festive days when the girls of Jerusalem danced before the boys and wives were chosen, they would wear borrowed clothes "so as not to put to shame those who did not have" (Mishna Taanit 4:8).

Another example: The festival of Passover involves a major upheaval in the running of a household. No leavened ingredient may be eaten or even kept in the home. If one uses earthenware vessels, different utensils must be used for cooking and eating (metal utensils, by contrast, can be made kosher for Passover). The third-century Babylonian community followed the rulings of their great leader, Rav. But one of his rulings had severe implications. Any earthenware pot that had been used for cooking during the year, and so had absorbed some leaven, must not merely be put away during Passover, but actually broken and disposed of. In effect this meant that families had to buy complete new sets of cooking equipment each year. This created a concentrated seasonal demand for earthenware pots, and in the free market, traders were quick to take advantage and raise their prices. It was the kind of situation of exploitation familiar to us from the prophetic literature.

Rav's contemporary and friend, Shmuel, responded immediately. He gathered the merchants together and informed them that unless they held their prices steady, he would pronounce in accordance with the more lenient tradition, which held that old pots need not be broken, simply stored away. It worked (Pesaḥim 30a).

Many, perhaps most, of the innovations of the Rabbis had a similar motive. They were guardians of the tradition, but they were also guardians of the unity of the people, and they were aware that nothing could be more destructive of that unity than a Judaism that was identified with a particular economic class.

וּמִיֶּתֶר הַשֶּׁמֶן אֲשֶׁר עַל־כַּפּוֹ יִתֵּן הַכֹּהֵן עַל־תְּנוּךְ אֹזֶן הַמִּטַּהֵר הַיְמָנִית
יח וְעַל־בֹּהֶן יָדוֹ הַיְמָנִית וְעַל־בֹּהֶן רַגְלוֹ הַיְמָנִית עַל דַּם הָאָשָׁם׃ וְהַנּוֹתָר
בַּשֶּׁמֶן אֲשֶׁר עַל־כַּף הַכֹּהֵן יִתֵּן עַל־רֹאשׁ הַמִּטַּהֵר וְכִפֶּר עָלָיו הַכֹּהֵן
יט לִפְנֵי יהוה׃ וְעָשָׂה הַכֹּהֵן אֶת־הַחַטָּאת וְכִפֶּר עַל־הַמִּטַּהֵר מִטֻּמְאָתוֹ
כ וְאַחַר יִשְׁחַט אֶת־הָעֹלָה׃ וְהֶעֱלָה הַכֹּהֵן אֶת־הָעֹלָה וְאֶת־הַמִּנְחָה
כא הַמִּזְבֵּחָה וְכִפֶּר עָלָיו הַכֹּהֵן וְטָהֵר׃ וְאִם־דַּל הוּא (שלישי /חמישי/)
וְאֵין יָדוֹ מַשֶּׂגֶת וְלָקַח כֶּבֶשׂ אֶחָד אָשָׁם לִתְנוּפָה לְכַפֵּר עָלָיו וְעִשָּׂרוֹן
כב סֹלֶת אֶחָד בָּלוּל בַּשֶּׁמֶן לְמִנְחָה וְלֹג שָׁמֶן׃ וּשְׁתֵּי תֹרִים אוֹ שְׁנֵי בְּנֵי
כג יוֹנָה אֲשֶׁר תַּשִּׂיג יָדוֹ וְהָיָה אֶחָד חַטָּאת וְהָאֶחָד עֹלָה׃ וְהֵבִיא אֹתָם

אונקלוס

יי: יז ומשאר משחא דעל ידיה, יתין כהנא על רום, אדנא דמדכי דימינא, ועל אליון ידיה דימינא, ועל אליון רגליה דימינא, על דמא דאשמא: יח ודישתאר, במשחא דעל ידא דכהנא, יתין על רישא דמדכי, ויכפר עלוהי, כהנא קדם יי: יט ויעביד כהנא ית חטתא, ויכפר, על דמדכי מסאובתיה, ובתר כן יכוס ית עלתא:

כ ויסיק כהנא, ית עלתא וית מנחתא למדבחא, ויכפר עלוהי, כהנא וידכי: כא ואם מסכין הוא, ולית ידיה מדבקא, ויסב, אמר חד אשמא, לארמא לכפרא עלוהי, ועסרונא סלתא, חד דפיל במשח, למנחתא ולוגא דמשחא: כב ותרתין שפנינין, או תרין בני יונה, דתדביק ידיה, ויהי חד חטתא, וחד עלתא: כג וייתי יתהון,

14:20 וְכִפֶּר עָלָיו הַכֹּהֵן וְטָהֵר *Thus shall the priest make his atonement, and he shall be purified* – *Lehakriv,* as we have noted, means "to bring close." The key element of a sacrifice is bringing something close to God. The animal, or *behema,* sacrificed represents the animal, instinctual element within us to be brought close to God and transformed through the divine fire that burned on the altar.

By an irony of history, this idea has become suddenly contemporary. Darwinism, the decoding of the human genome, and scientific materialism (the idea that the material is all there is) have led to the widespread conclusion that we are all animals, nothing more, nothing less. We share 98 percent of our genes with the primates. On this view, *Homo sapiens* exists by mere accident. We are the result of a random series of genetic mutations and just happened to be more adapted to survival than other species. The *nefesh habahamit,* the animal soul, is all there is.

The refutation of this idea lies in the very act of sacrifice itself. We can redirect our animal instincts and rise above mere survival. We can transcend the *behema* in us. No animal is capable of self-transformation, but we are. By bringing that which is animal within us close to God, we allow the material to be suffused with the spiritual and we become something else: no longer slaves of nature but servants of the living God.

14:22 אֲשֶׁר תַּשִּׂיג יָדוֹ *Such as he can afford* – Tabernacle requirements should not put the person recovering from a blight in the position of a beggar. If we were to ask what a religious tradition can contribute to the problem of poverty,

he shall bring them to the priest at the entrance to the Tent of Meeting before
24 the Lord. The priest shall take the lamb of the guilt offering, together with the
log of oil, and move them this way and that as a wave offering before the Lord.
25 Then he shall slaughter the guilt offering lamb. The priest shall take some of the
blood of the guilt offering and apply it to the ridge of the right ear, to the right
26 thumb, and to the right big toe of the one who is to be purified. The priest shall
27 then pour some of the oil into his own left palm, and, using his right finger,
28 shall sprinkle of the oil that is in his left hand seven times before the Lord. He
shall apply some of the oil remaining in his hand to the ridge of the right ear,
to the right thumb, and to the right big toe of the person to be purified, over
29 the guilt offering blood. What remains of the oil in his hand the priest shall
pour on the head of the one to be purified, to make his atonement before the
30 Lord. He shall then offer up one of the doves or pigeons the person could
31 afford; whatever he can afford, one as a purification offering, and the other
as a burnt offering, together with the grain offering; and thus shall the priest
32 make atonement for the person who is to be purified before the Lord." This
is the law for a person who has an impure blight and cannot afford the regular
offerings for his purification.
33 34 The Lord spoke to Moshe and to Aharon: "When you enter the land of Canaan REVI'I /SHISHI/
that I am giving you as a possession, and I afflict a house in the land you possess

רש״י

כג **בַּיּוֹם הַשְּׁמִינִי לְטָהֳרָתוֹ.** שְׁמִינִי לִצִפֳּרִים וּלְהַזָּאַת עֵץ אֶרֶז וְאֵזוֹב וּשְׁנִי תוֹלַעַת:

כח **עַל מְקוֹם דַּם הָאָשָׁם.** אֲפִלּוּ נִתְקַנֵּחַ הַדָּם. לִמֵּד שֶׁאֵין הַדָּם גּוֹרֵם אֶלָּא הַמָּקוֹם גּוֹרֵם:

לד **וְנָתַתִּי נֶגַע צָרַעַת.** בְּשׂוֹרָה הִיא לָהֶם שֶׁהַנְּגָעִים בָּאִים עֲלֵיהֶם, לְפִי שֶׁהִטְמִינוּ אֱמוֹרִיִּים מַטְמוֹנִיּוֹת שֶׁל זָהָב בְּקִירוֹת בָּתֵּיהֶם כָּל אַרְבָּעִים שָׁנָה שֶׁהָיוּ יִשְׂרָאֵל בַּמִּדְבָּר, וְעַל יְדֵי הַנֶּגַע נוֹתֵץ הַבַּיִת וּמוֹצְאָן:

14:34 **וְנָתַתִּי נֶגַע צָרַעַת בְּבֵית אֶרֶץ אֲחֻזַּתְכֶם** *And I afflict a house in the land you possess* – Rambam, on the basis of rabbinic traditions, gives a remarkable account of why *tzaraat* afflicts both inanimate objects like walls and clothes, and human beings:

> It [*tzaraat*] was a sign and wonder among the Israelites to warn them against slanderous speaking. For if a man uttered slander, the walls of his house would suffer a change. If he repented, the house would again become clean. But if he continued in his wickedness until the house was torn down, leather objects in his house on which he sat or lay would suffer a change. If he repented they would again become clean. But if he continued in his wickedness until they were burned, the garments that he wore would suffer a change. If he repented they would again become clean. But if he continued in his wickedness until they were burned, his skin would suffer a change and he would become infected by *tzaraat* and be set apart and alone until he no longer engaged in the conversation of the wicked which is scoffing and slander. (*Hilkhot Tumat Tzaraat* 16:10)

Evil speech is subversive: it is a sin that seeks to conceal itself. People who speak badly about others do so in private, in

בַּיּוֹם הַשְּׁמִינִי לְטׇהֳרָתוֹ אֶל־הַכֹּהֵן אֶל־פֶּתַח אֹהֶל־מוֹעֵד לִפְנֵי יְהֹוָה׃
כד וְלָקַח הַכֹּהֵן אֶת־כֶּבֶשׂ הָאָשָׁם וְאֶת־לֹג הַשָּׁמֶן וְהֵנִיף אֹתָם הַכֹּהֵן
כה תְּנוּפָה לִפְנֵי יְהֹוָה׃ וְשָׁחַט אֶת־כֶּבֶשׂ הָאָשָׁם וְלָקַח הַכֹּהֵן מִדַּם הָאָשָׁם
וְנָתַן עַל־תְּנוּךְ אֹזֶן־הַמִּטַּהֵר הַיְמָנִית וְעַל־בֹּהֶן יָדוֹ הַיְמָנִית וְעַל־בֹּהֶן
כו כז רַגְלוֹ הַיְמָנִית׃ וּמִן־הַשֶּׁמֶן יִצֹק הַכֹּהֵן עַל־כַּף הַכֹּהֵן הַשְּׂמָאלִית׃ וְהִזָּה
הַכֹּהֵן בְּאֶצְבָּעוֹ הַיְמָנִית מִן־הַשֶּׁמֶן אֲשֶׁר עַל־כַּפּוֹ הַשְּׂמָאלִית שֶׁבַע
כח פְּעָמִים לִפְנֵי יְהֹוָה׃ וְנָתַן הַכֹּהֵן מִן־הַשֶּׁמֶן ׀ אֲשֶׁר עַל־כַּפּוֹ עַל־תְּנוּךְ
אֹזֶן הַמִּטַּהֵר הַיְמָנִית וְעַל־בֹּהֶן יָדוֹ הַיְמָנִית וְעַל־בֹּהֶן רַגְלוֹ הַיְמָנִית
כט עַל־מְקוֹם דַּם הָאָשָׁם׃ וְהַנּוֹתָר מִן־הַשֶּׁמֶן אֲשֶׁר עַל־כַּף הַכֹּהֵן יִתֵּן
ל עַל־רֹאשׁ הַמִּטַּהֵר לְכַפֵּר עָלָיו לִפְנֵי יְהֹוָה׃ וְעָשָׂה אֶת־הָאֶחָד מִן־
לא הַתֹּרִים אוֹ מִן־בְּנֵי הַיּוֹנָה מֵאֲשֶׁר תַּשִּׂיג יָדוֹ׃ אֵת אֲשֶׁר־תַּשִּׂיג יָדוֹ אֶת־
הָאֶחָד חַטָּאת וְאֶת־הָאֶחָד עֹלָה עַל־הַמִּנְחָה וְכִפֶּר הַכֹּהֵן עַל הַמִּטַּהֵר
לב לִפְנֵי יְהֹוָה׃ זֹאת תּוֹרַת אֲשֶׁר־בּוֹ נֶגַע צָרָעַת אֲשֶׁר לֹא־תַשִּׂיג יָדוֹ
בְּטׇהֳרָתוֹ׃
לג לד וַיְדַבֵּר יְהֹוָה אֶל־מֹשֶׁה וְאֶל־אַהֲרֹן לֵאמֹר׃ כִּי תָבֹאוּ אֶל־אֶרֶץ כְּנַעַן י רביעי /ששי/
אֲשֶׁר אֲנִי נֹתֵן לָכֶם לַאֲחֻזָּה וְנָתַתִּי נֶגַע צָרַעַת בְּבֵית אֶרֶץ אֲחֻזַּתְכֶם׃

אונקלוס

בְּיוֹמָא תְּמִינָאָה, לְדִכוּתֵיהּ לְוָת כָּהֲנָא, לִתְרַע מַשְׁכַּן זִמְנָא לִקְדָם יְיָ: כד וְיִסַּב כָּהֲנָא, יָת אִמְּרָא דַּאֲשָׁמָא וְיָת לוּגָא דִּמְשַׁחָא, וִירִים יָתְהוֹן כָּהֲנָא, אֲרָמָא קֳדָם יְיָ: כה וְיִכּוֹס יָת אִמְּרָא דַּאֲשָׁמָא, וְיִסַּב כָּהֲנָא מִדְּמָא דַּאֲשָׁמָא, וְיִתֵּין, עַל רוּם אֻדְנָא דְּמִדַּכֵּי דְּיַמִּינָא, וְעַל אִלְיוֹן יְדֵיהּ דְּיַמִּינָא, וְעַל אִלְיוֹן רַגְלֵיהּ דְּיַמִּינָא: כו וּמִן מִשְׁחָא יְרִיק כָּהֲנָא, עַל יְדָא דְּכָהֲנָא דִּסְמָאלָא: כז וְיַדֵּי כָּהֲנָא בְּאֶצְבְּעֵיהּ דְּיַמִּינָא, מִן מִשְׁחָא, דְּעַל יְדֵיהּ דִּסְמָאלָא, שְׁבַע זִמְנִין קֳדָם יְיָ: כח וְיִתֵּין כָּהֲנָא, מִן מִשְׁחָא דְּעַל יְדֵיהּ, עַל רוּם, אֻדְנָא דְּמִדַּכֵּי דְּיַמִּינָא, וְעַל אִלְיוֹן יְדֵיהּ דְּיַמִּינָא, וְעַל אִלְיוֹן רַגְלֵיהּ דְּיַמִּינָא, עַל אֲתַר דְּמָא דַּאֲשָׁמָא: כט וּדְיִשְׁתְּאַר, מִן מִשְׁחָא דְּעַל יְדָא דְּכָהֲנָא, יִתֵּין עַל רֵישָׁא דְּמִדַּכֵּי, לְכַפָּרָא עֲלוֹהִי קֳדָם יְיָ: ל וְיַעֲבֵיד יָת חַד מִן שַׁפְנִינַיָּא, אוֹ מִן בְּנֵי יוֹנָה, מִדְּתַדְבֵּיק יְדֵיהּ: לא יָת דְּתַדְבֵּיק יְדֵיהּ, יָת חַד חַטָּתָא, וְיָת חַד עֲלָתָא עַל מִנְחָתָא, וִיכַפַּר כָּהֲנָא, עַל דְּמִדַּכֵּי קֳדָם יְיָ: לב דָּא אוֹרָיְתָא, דִּבֵיהּ מַכְתַּשׁ סְגִירוּ, דְּלָא תַדְבֵּיק יְדֵיהּ בְּדִכוּתֵיהּ: לג וּמַלֵּיל יְיָ, עִם מֹשֶׁה וּלְאַהֲרֹן לְמֵימַר: לד אֲרֵי תֵיעֲלוּן לְאַרְעָא דִּכְנַעַן, דַּאֲנָא, יָהֵיב לְכוֹן לְאַחְסָנָא, וְאֶתֵּין מַכְתַּשׁ סְגִירוּ, בְּבֵית אֲרַע אַחְסָנַתְכוֹן:

35 with an impure blight, the owner of the house shall come and tell the priest, ‘It
36 looks to me as if there were some disease in the house.’ The priest shall instruct
them to empty the house before he goes to examine the disease, to prevent
everything in the house from becoming impure. After that, the priest shall go
37 to examine the house. He shall look at the disease. If the disease is in the walls
of the house with greenish or reddish spots that appear to go deep into the
38 wall, the priest shall go out to the door of the house and shut the house up for
39 seven days. On the seventh day, the priest shall return; he shall examine the
40 disease and, if it has spread in the walls of the house, the priest shall order the
stones in which the disease appears to be removed and thrown into a ritually
41 impure place outside the town. He shall have the inside of the house scraped
all around, and the plaster that they scrape off shall be poured out in an impure
42 place outside the city. They shall take other stones and put them in the place of
43 those stones, and take new plaster and replaster the house. If the disease breaks
out again in the house after the stones have been removed and the house has
44 been scraped and plastered, the priest shall come back and examine it. If the

רש״י

לה **כְּנֶגַע נִרְאָה לִי בַּבָּיִת.** שֶׁאֲפִלּוּ הוּא חָכָם שֶׁיּוֹדֵעַ שֶׁהוּא נֶגַע וַדַּאי, לֹא יִפְסֹק דָּבָר בָּרוּר לוֹמַר: 'נֶגַע נִרְאָה לִי', אֶלָּא: "כְּנֶגַע נִרְאָה לִי":

לו **בְּטֶרֶם יָבֹא הַכֹּהֵן וְגוֹ'.** שֶׁכָּל זְמַן שֶׁאֵין כֹּהֵן נִזְקָק לוֹ אֵין שָׁם תּוֹרַת טֻמְאָה: **וְלֹא יִטְמָא כָּל אֲשֶׁר בַּבָּיִת.** שֶׁאִם לֹא יְפַנֵּהוּ וְיָבֹא הַכֹּהֵן וְיִרְאֶה הַנֶּגַע, נִזְקָק לְהֶסְגֵּר, וְכָל מַה שֶּׁבְּתוֹכוֹ יִטְמָא. וְעַל מֶה חָסָה תוֹרָה? אִם עַל כְּלֵי שֶׁטֶף, יַטְבִּילֵם וְיִטְהֲרוּ, וְאִם עַל אֳכָלִין וּמַשְׁקִין, יֹאכְלֵם בִּימֵי טֻמְאָתוֹ, הָא לֹא חָסָה תוֹרָה אֶלָּא עַל כְּלֵי חֶרֶס שֶׁאֵין לָהֶם טָהֳרָה בְּמִקְוֶה:

לז **שְׁקַעֲרוּרֹת.** שׁוֹקְעוֹת בְּמַרְאֵיהֶן:

מ **וְחִלְּצוּ אֶת הָאֲבָנִים.** כְּתַרְגּוּמוֹ "וִישַׁלְּפוּן", יִטְּלוּם מִשָּׁם, כְּמוֹ "וְחָלְצָה נַעֲלוֹ" (דברים כה, ט), לְשׁוֹן הֲסָרָה: **אֶל מָקוֹם טָמֵא.** מָקוֹם שֶׁאֵין טְהָרוֹת מִשְׁתַּמְּשׁוֹת שָׁם. לִמֶּדְךָ הַכָּתוּב שֶׁהָאֲבָנִים הַלָּלוּ מְטַמְּאוֹת מְקוֹמָן בְּעוֹדָן בּוֹ:

מא **יַקְצִעַ.** רדוני"ר בְּלַעַז, וּבִלְשׁוֹן מִשְׁנָה יֵשׁ הַרְבֵּה: **מִבַּיִת.** מִבִּפְנִים: **סָבִיב.** סְבִיבוֹת הַנֶּגַע, בְּתוֹרַת כֹּהֲנִים נִדְרַשׁ כֵּן (פרק ד, ה), שֶׁיְּקַלֵּף הַטִּיחַ שֶׁסָּבִיב אַבְנֵי הַנֶּגַע: **הִקְצוּ.** לְשׁוֹן קָצֶה, אֲשֶׁר קִצְּעוּ בִּקְצוֹת הַנֶּגַע סָבִיב:

מג **הִקְצוֹת.** לְשׁוֹן הֵעָשׂוֹת, וְכֵן "הִטּוֹחַ", אֲבָל "חִלֵּץ אֶת הָאֲבָנִים" מוּסָב הַלָּשׁוֹן אֶל הָאָדָם שֶׁחִלְּצָן, וְהוּא מִשְׁקַל לָשׁוֹן כָּבֵד, כְּמוֹ 'כִּפֵּר', 'דִּבֵּר': **וְאִם יָשׁוּב הַנֶּגַע וְגוֹ'.** יָכוֹל חָזַר בּוֹ בַּיּוֹם יְהֵא טָמֵא? תַּלְמוּד לוֹמַר: "וְשָׁב הַכֹּהֵן", "וְאִם יָשׁוּב", מַה 'שִׁיבָה' הָאֲמוּרָה לְהַלָּן בְּסוֹף שָׁבוּעַ, אַף 'שִׁיבָה' הָאֲמוּרָה כָּאן בְּסוֹף שָׁבוּעַ:

מד **וּבָא הַכֹּהֵן וְרָאָה וְהִנֵּה פָּשָׂה.** יָכוֹל לֹא יְהֵא הַחוֹזֵר טָמֵא אֶלָּא אִם כֵּן פָּשָׂה? נֶאֱמַר: "צָרַעַת מַמְאֶרֶת" בְּבָתִּים, וְנֶאֱמַר: "צָרַעַת מַמְאֶרֶת" בִּבְגָדִים (לעיל יג, נא-נב), מַה לְּהַלָּן טִמֵּא אֶת הַחוֹזֵר אַף עַל פִּי שֶׁאֵינוֹ פוֹשֶׂה, אַף כָּאן טִמֵּא אֶת הַחוֹזֵר אַף עַל פִּי שֶׁאֵינוֹ פוֹשֶׂה. אִם כֵּן, מַה תַּלְמוּד לוֹמַר: "וְהִנֵּה פָּשָׂה"? אֵין כָּאן מְקוֹמוֹ שֶׁל מִקְרָא זֶה, אֶלָּא: "וְנָתַץ אֶת הַבַּיִת" הָיָה לוֹ לִכְתֹּב אַחַר: "וְאִם יָשׁוּב הַנֶּגַע", "וְרָאָה וְהִנֵּה פָּשָׂה" הָא לֹא בָא לְלַמֵּד אֶלָּא עַל נֶגַע הָעוֹמֵד בְּעֵינָיו בְּשָׁבוּעַ רִאשׁוֹן, וּבָא בְּסוֹף שָׁבוּעַ שֵׁנִי וּמְצָאוֹ שֶׁפָּשָׂה, שֶׁלֹּא פֵרַשׁ בּוֹ הַכָּתוּב לְמַעְלָה (לעיל פסוק לט) כְּלוּם בְּעוֹמֵד בְּעֵינָיו בְּשָׁבוּעַ רִאשׁוֹן, וְלִמֶּדְךָ כָּאן בְּפִשְׂיוֹן זֶה, שֶׁאֵינוֹ מְדַבֵּר אֶלָּא בְּעוֹמֵד בָּרִאשׁוֹן וּפָשָׂה בַּשֵּׁנִי. וּמַה יַּעֲשֶׂה לוֹ? יָכוֹל יִתְּצֶנּוּ כְּמוֹ שֶׁסָּמַךְ לוֹ: "וְנָתַץ אֶת הַבַּיִת"? תַּלְמוּד לוֹמַר: "וְשָׁב הַכֹּהֵן" (לעיל פסוק לט) "וּבָא הַכֹּהֵן", נִלְמַד בִּיאָה מִשִּׁיבָה, מַה שִּׁיבָה חוֹלֵץ וְקוֹצֶה וְטָח וְנוֹתֵן לוֹ שָׁבוּעַ, אַף בִּיאָה חוֹלֵץ וְקוֹצֶה וְטָח וְנוֹתֵן לוֹ שָׁבוּעַ, וְאִם חוֹזֵר – נוֹתֵץ, לֹא חָזַר – טָהוֹר. וּמִנַּיִן שֶׁאִם עָמַד בָּזֶה וּבָזֶה חוֹלֵץ וְקוֹצֶה וְטָח וְנוֹתֵן לוֹ שָׁבוּעַ? תַּלְמוּד לוֹמַר: "וּבָא" "וְאִם בֹּא יָבֹא" (להלן פסוק מח) בַּמֶּה הַכָּתוּב מְדַבֵּר? אִם בְּפוֹשֶׂה בָּרִאשׁוֹן – הֲרֵי כְּבָר אָמוּר, אִם בְּפוֹשֶׂה בַּשֵּׁנִי – הֲרֵי כְּבָר אָמוּר, הָא אֵינוֹ אוֹמֵר "וּבָא" "וְאִם בֹּא יָבֹא" אֶלָּא אֶת שֶׁבָּא בְּסוֹף שָׁבוּעַ רִאשׁוֹן וּבָא בְּסוֹף שָׁבוּעַ שֵׁנִי "וְרָאָה וְהִנֵּה לֹא פָשָׂה". זֶה הָעוֹמֵד – מַה יַּעֲשֶׂה לוֹ? יָכוֹל יִפָּטֵר וְיֵלֵךְ, כְּמוֹ שֶׁכָּתוּב כָּאן: "וְטִהַר אֶת הַבַּיִת"? תַּלְמוּד לוֹמַר: "כִּי נִרְפָּא הַנָּגַע", לֹא טִהַרְתִּי אֶלָּא אֶת הָרָפוּי. מַה יַּעֲשֶׂה לוֹ? בִּיאָה אֲמוּרָה לְמַעְלָה

לה לו וּבָא אֲשֶׁר־לוֹ הַבַּיִת וְהִגִּיד לַכֹּהֵן לֵאמֹר כְּנֶגַע נִרְאָה לִי בַּבָּיִת: וְצִוָּה
הַכֹּהֵן וּפִנּוּ אֶת־הַבַּיִת בְּטֶרֶם יָבֹא הַכֹּהֵן לִרְאוֹת אֶת־הַנֶּגַע וְלֹא יִטְמָא
לז כָּל־אֲשֶׁר בַּבָּיִת וְאַחַר כֵּן יָבֹא הַכֹּהֵן לִרְאוֹת אֶת־הַבָּיִת: וְרָאָה אֶת־
הַנֶּגַע וְהִנֵּה הַנֶּגַע בְּקִירֹת הַבַּיִת שְׁקַעֲרוּרֹת יְרַקְרַקֹּת אוֹ אֲדַמְדַּמֹּת
לח וּמַרְאֵיהֶן שָׁפָל מִן־הַקִּיר: וְיָצָא הַכֹּהֵן מִן־הַבַּיִת אֶל־פֶּתַח הַבָּיִת
לט וְהִסְגִּיר אֶת־הַבַּיִת שִׁבְעַת יָמִים: וְשָׁב הַכֹּהֵן בַּיּוֹם הַשְּׁבִיעִי וְרָאָה וְהִנֵּה
מ פָּשָׂה הַנֶּגַע בְּקִירֹת הַבָּיִת: וְצִוָּה הַכֹּהֵן וְחִלְּצוּ אֶת־הָאֲבָנִים אֲשֶׁר בָּהֵן
מא הַנָּגַע וְהִשְׁלִיכוּ אֶתְהֶן אֶל־מִחוּץ לָעִיר אֶל־מָקוֹם טָמֵא: וְאֶת־הַבַּיִת
יַקְצִעַ מִבַּיִת סָבִיב וְשָׁפְכוּ אֶת־הֶעָפָר אֲשֶׁר הִקְצוּ אֶל־מִחוּץ לָעִיר
מב אֶל־מָקוֹם טָמֵא: וְלָקְחוּ אֲבָנִים אֲחֵרוֹת וְהֵבִיאוּ אֶל־תַּחַת הָאֲבָנִים
מג וְעָפָר אַחֵר יִקַּח וְטָח אֶת־הַבָּיִת: וְאִם־יָשׁוּב הַנֶּגַע וּפָרַח בַּבַּיִת אַחַר
מד חִלֵּץ אֶת־הָאֲבָנִים וְאַחֲרֵי הִקְצוֹת אֶת־הַבַּיִת וְאַחֲרֵי הִטּוֹחַ: וּבָא הַכֹּהֵן
וְרָאָה וְהִנֵּה פָּשָׂה הַנֶּגַע בַּבָּיִת צָרַעַת מַמְאֶרֶת הִוא בַּבַּיִת טָמֵא הוּא:

אונקלוס

לה וְיֵיתֵי דְּדִילֵיהּ בֵּיתָא, וִיחַוֵּי לְכָהֲנָא לְמֵימַר, כְּמַכְתָּשָׁא, אִתַּחְזִי
לִי בְּבֵיתָא: לו וִיפַקֵּיד כָּהֲנָא וִיפַנּוֹן יָת בֵּיתָא, עַד לָא יֵיעוֹל כָּהֲנָא
לְמִחְזֵי יָת מַכְתָּשָׁא, וְלָא יִסְתָּאַב כָּל דִּבְבֵיתָא, וּבָתַר כֵּן, יֵיעוֹל
כָּהֲנָא לְמִחְזֵי יָת בֵּיתָא: לז וְיִחְזֵי יָת מַכְתָּשָׁא, וְהָא מַכְתָּשָׁא
בְּכָתְלֵי בֵיתָא, פַּחְתִּין יָרְקָן, אוֹ סָמְקָן, וּמֶחֱזֵיהוֹן מַכִּיךְ מִן כָּתְלָא:
לח וְיִפּוֹק כָּהֲנָא, מִן בֵּיתָא לִתְרַע בֵּיתָא, וְיַסְגַּר יָת בֵּיתָא שִׁבְעָא
יוֹמִין: לט וִיתוּב כָּהֲנָא בְּיוֹמָא שְׁבִיעָאָה, וְיִחְזֵי, וְהָא, אוֹסֵיף
מַכְתָּשָׁא בְּכָתְלֵי בֵיתָא: מ וִיפַקֵּיד כָּהֲנָא, וִישַׁלְּפוּן יָת אַבְנַיָּא,
דִּבְהוֹן מַכְתָּשָׁא, וְיִרְמוֹן יָתְהוֹן לְמִבָּרָא לְקַרְתָּא, לַאֲתַר מְסָאַב:
מא וְיָת בֵּיתָא, יְקַלְּפוּן מִגָּיו סְחוֹר סְחוֹר, וְיִרְמוֹן, יָת עַפְרָא דְּקַלִּיפוּ,
לְמִבָּרָא לְקַרְתָּא, לַאֲתַר מְסָאַב: מב וְיִסְּבוּן אַבְנִין אָחֳרָנִין, וְיַעֲלוּן
לַאֲתַר אַבְנַיָּא, וַעֲפַר אָחֳרָן, יִסַּב וְישׁוּעַ יָת בֵּיתָא: מג וְאִם יְתוּב
מַכְתָּשָׁא וְיִסְגֵּי בְּבֵיתָא, בָּתַר דְּשַׁלִּיפוּ יָת אַבְנַיָּא, וּבָתַר, דְּקַלִּיפוּ
יָת בֵּיתָא וּבָתַר דְּאִתְּשַׁע: מד וְיֵיעוֹל כָּהֲנָא, וְיִחְזֵי, וְהָא, אוֹסֵיף
מַכְתָּשָׁא בְּבֵיתָא, סְגִירוּת מְחַסְּרָא הִיא, בְּבֵיתָא מְסָאַב הוּא:

hushed, conspiratorial tones, and often deny that they have done so. What connects the different types of *tzaraat* – garments, the walls of houses, and skin – is that they themselves are boundaries between inside and outside, and holiness depends on the health and strength of boundaries.

That is why, as long as the condition of *tzaraat* existed, what had been done in private was broadcast in public, first by the walls of the offender's house, then by his clothes, and finally by his skin. It was not just a punishment. It was a public shaming. Never say or do in private what you would be ashamed to read about on the front page of tomorrow's newspapers. That is the basic theme of the law of *tzaraat*.

45 disease has spread, then there is malignant blight in the house; it is impure. He
shall have the house torn down, its stones, timber, and all the plaster from the
46 house, and have them all taken outside the town to an impure place. Anyone
who entered the house while it was shut up shall be impure until the evening.
47 Anyone who slept in the house shall wash his clothes; anyone who ate in the
48 house shall wash his clothes. If, however, the priest comes and examines it and
the disease has not spread in the house after its plastering, then the priest shall
49 pronounce the house pure; the disease is healed. He shall take two birds, and
50 cedarwood, scarlet wool, and hyssop to purify the house. He shall slaughter one
51 of the birds in an earthen vessel over living water. He shall take the cedarwood,
the hyssop, the scarlet wool, and the living bird and dip them in the blood of
the slaughtered bird, in the living water, and sprinkle the house seven times.
52 He shall purify the house with the blood of the bird and the living water, with
53 the living bird, the cedarwood, the hyssop, and the scarlet wool. And he shall
send the living bird forth free outside the city, into the open field. Thus shall
54 he make atonement for the house, and it shall be purified." This is the law for HAMISHI
55 every impure blight of disease, for a scaling eruption, for blight of a garment
56 57 or a house, and for swellings, eruptions, and bright patches on the skin, to
determine when they are impure and when they are pure. This is the law of the
blight.
15 1 2 The LORD spoke to Moshe and Aharon: "Speak to the Israelites. Say: When any

רש״י

וּבִיאָה חֲמוּרָה לְמַטָּה (להלן פסוק מח), מַה בָּעֶלְיוֹנָה חוֹלֵץ וְקוֹצֶה וְטָח וְנוֹתֵן לוֹ שָׁבוּעַ, דְּגָמַר לָהּ זֶהוּ שִׁיבָה זֶהוּ בִּיאָה, אַף בַּתַּחְתּוֹנָה כֵּן וְכוּ׳, כִּדְאִיתָא בְּתוֹרַת כֹּהֲנִים (פרשתא ז, ד-ט). גָּמְרוֹ שֶׁל דָּבָר, אֵין נְתִיצָה אֶלָּא בְּנֶגַע הַחוֹזֵר אַחַר חֲלִיצָה וְקִצּוּעַ וְטִיחָה, וְאֵין הַחוֹזֵר צָרִיךְ פִּשְׂיוֹן. וְסֵדֶר הַמִּקְרָאוֹת כָּךְ הוּא, "וְאִם יָשׁוּב" (מג), "וְנָתַץ" (מה), "וְהַבָּא אֶל הַבַּיִת" (מו), "וְהָאֹכֵל בַּבַּיִת" (מז), "וּבָא הַכֹּהֵן וְרָאָה וְהִנֵּה פָּשָׂה" (מד), וְדִבֶּר הַכָּתוּב בְּעוֹמֵד בָּרִאשׁוֹן שֶׁנּוֹתֵן לוֹ שָׁבוּעַ שֵׁנִי לְהֶסְגֵּרוֹ, וּבְסוֹף שָׁבוּעַ שֵׁנִי לְהֶסְגֵּרוֹ בָּא וְרָאָהוּ שֶׁפָּשָׂה, וּמַה יֵּעָשֶׂה לוֹ? חוֹלֵץ וְקוֹצֶה וְטָח וְנוֹתֵן לוֹ שָׁבוּעַ. חָזַר – נוֹתֵץ, לֹא חָזַר – טָעוּן צִפֳּרִים, שֶׁאֵין בִּנְגָעִים יוֹתֵר מִשְּׁלֹשָׁה שָׁבוּעוֹת. "וְאִם בֹּא יָבֹא" (מח) לְסוֹף שָׁבוּעַ שֵׁנִי, "וְרָאָה וְהִנֵּה לֹא פָשָׂה", מִקְרָא זֶה בָּא לְלַמֵּד בְּעוֹמֵד בְּעֵינָיו בָּרִאשׁוֹן וּבַשֵּׁנִי. וּמַה יֵּעָשֶׂה לוֹ? יָכוֹל יְטַהֲרֶנּוּ כְּמַשְׁמָעוֹ שֶׁל מִקְרָא "וְטִהַר הַכֹּהֵן אֶת הַבַּיִת"? תַּלְמוּד לוֹמַר: "כִּי נִרְפָּא הַנָּגַע", לֹא טִהַרְתִּי אֶלָּא אֶת הָרָפוּי, וְאֵין רִפּוּי אֶלָּא הַבַּיִת שֶׁהֻקְצָה וְהוּטַח וְלֹא חָזַר הַנֶּגַע, אֲבָל זֶה טָעוּן חֲלִיצָה וְקִצּוּי וְטִיחָה וְשָׁבוּעַ שְׁלִישִׁי. וְכֵן הַמִּקְרָא נִדְרָשׁ: "וְאִם בֹּא יָבֹא" בַּשֵּׁנִי "וְרָאָה וְהִנֵּה לֹא פָשָׂה", יְטִיחֶנּוּ, וְאֵין טִיחָה בְּלֹא חִלּוּץ וְקִצּוּי. וְ"אַחֲרֵי הִטּוֹחַ אֶת הַבַּיִת, וְטִהַר הַכֹּהֵן אֶת הַבַּיִת" אִם לֹא חָזַר לְסוֹף הַשָּׁבוּעַ, "כִּי נִרְפָּא הַנָּגַע", וְאִם חָזַר, כְּבָר פֵּרַשׁ עַל הַחוֹזֵר שֶׁטָּעוּן נְתִיצָה:

מו **כָּל יְמֵי הִסְגִּיר אֹתוֹ.** וְלֹא יָמִים שֶׁקָּלַף אֶת נִגְעוֹ. יָכוֹל שֶׁאֲנִי מוֹצִיא הַמֻּחְלָט שֶׁקָּלַף אֶת נִגְעוֹ? תַּלְמוּד לוֹמַר: "כָּל יְמֵי": **יִטְמָא עַד הָעָרֶב.** מְלַמֵּד שֶׁאֵין מְטַמֵּא בְגָדִים. יָכוֹל אֲפִלּוּ שָׁהָה בִּכְדֵי אֲכִילַת פְּרָס? תַּלְמוּד לוֹמַר: "וְהָאֹכֵל בַּבַּיִת יְכַבֵּס אֶת בְּגָדָיו" (להלן פסוק מז), אֵין לִי אֶלָּא אוֹכֵל, שׁוֹכֵב מִנַּיִן? תַּלְמוּד לוֹמַר: "וְהַשֹּׁכֵב". אֵין לִי אֶלָּא אוֹכֵל וְשׁוֹכֵב, לֹא אוֹכֵל וְלֹא שׁוֹכֵב מִנַּיִן? תַּלְמוּד לוֹמַר: "יְכַבֵּס" "יְכַבֵּס" רִבָּה. אִם כֵּן לָמָּה נֶאֱמַר: ׳אוֹכֵל׳ וְ׳שׁוֹכֵב׳? לִתֵּן שִׁעוּר לַשּׁוֹכֵב כְּדֵי אֲכִילַת פְּרָס:

נז **לְהוֹרֹת בְּיוֹם הַטָּמֵא וְגוֹ׳.** אֵיזֶה יוֹם מְטַהֲרוֹ וְאֵיזֶה יוֹם מְטַמְּאוֹ:

מה וְנָתַ֣ץ אֶת־הַבַּ֗יִת אֶת־אֲבָנָיו֙ וְאֶת־עֵצָ֔יו וְאֵ֖ת כָּל־עֲפַ֣ר הַבָּ֑יִת וְהוֹצִיא֙
מו אֶל־מִח֣וּץ לָעִ֔יר אֶל־מָק֖וֹם טָמֵֽא׃ וְהַבָּא֙ אֶל־הַבַּ֔יִת כָּל־יְמֵ֖י הִסְגִּ֣יר
מז אֹת֑וֹ יִטְמָ֖א עַד־הָעָֽרֶב׃ וְהַשֹּׁכֵ֣ב בַּבַּ֔יִת יְכַבֵּ֖ס אֶת־בְּגָדָ֑יו וְהָאֹכֵ֣ל
מח בַּבַּ֔יִת יְכַבֵּ֖ס אֶת־בְּגָדָֽיו׃ וְאִם־בֹּ֨א יָבֹ֜א הַכֹּהֵ֗ן וְרָאָה֙ וְהִנֵּ֨ה לֹא־פָשָׂ֤ה
הַנֶּ֙גַע֙ בַּבַּ֔יִת אַחֲרֵ֖י הִטֹּ֣חַ אֶת־הַבָּ֑יִת וְטִהַ֤ר הַכֹּהֵן֙ אֶת־הַבַּ֔יִת כִּ֥י נִרְפָּ֖א
מט הַנָּֽגַע׃ וְלָקַ֛ח לְחַטֵּ֥א אֶת־הַבַּ֖יִת שְׁתֵּ֣י צִפֳּרִ֑ים וְעֵ֣ץ אֶ֔רֶז וּשְׁנִ֥י תוֹלַ֖עַת
נ וְאֵזֹֽב׃ וְשָׁחַ֖ט אֶת־הַצִּפֹּ֣ר הָאֶחָ֑ת אֶל־כְּלִי־חֶ֖רֶשׂ עַל־מַ֥יִם חַיִּֽים׃
נא וְלָקַ֣ח אֶת־עֵֽץ־הָ֠אֶרֶז וְאֶת־הָאֵזֹ֜ב וְאֵ֣ת ׀ שְׁנִ֣י הַתּוֹלַ֗עַת וְאֵת֮ הַצִּפֹּ֣ר
הַחַיָּה֒ וְטָבַ֣ל אֹתָ֗ם בְּדַם֙ הַצִּפֹּ֣ר הַשְּׁחוּטָ֔ה וּבַמַּ֖יִם הַחַיִּ֑ים וְהִזָּ֥ה אֶל־
נב הַבַּ֖יִת שֶׁ֥בַע פְּעָמִֽים׃ וְחִטֵּ֣א אֶת־הַבַּ֔יִת בְּדַם֙ הַצִּפּ֔וֹר וּבַמַּ֖יִם הַחַיִּ֑ים
נג וּבַצִּפֹּ֣ר הַחַיָּ֗ה וּבְעֵ֥ץ הָאֶ֛רֶז וּבָאֵזֹ֖ב וּבִשְׁנִ֥י הַתּוֹלָֽעַת׃ וְשִׁלַּ֞ח אֶת־הַצִּפֹּ֧ר
נד הַחַיָּ֛ה אֶל־מִח֥וּץ לָעִ֖יר אֶל־פְּנֵ֣י הַשָּׂדֶ֑ה וְכִפֶּ֥ר עַל־הַבַּ֖יִת וְטָהֵֽר׃ זֹ֖את חמישי
נה נו הַתּוֹרָ֑ה לְכָל־נֶ֥גַע הַצָּרַ֖עַת וְלַנָּֽתֶק׃ וּלְצָרַ֥עַת הַבֶּ֖גֶד וְלַבָּֽיִת׃ וְלַשְׂאֵ֥ת
נז וְלַסַּפַּ֖חַת וְלַבֶּהָֽרֶת׃ לְהוֹרֹ֕ת בְּי֥וֹם הַטָּמֵ֖א וּבְי֣וֹם הַטָּהֹ֑ר זֹ֥את תּוֹרַ֖ת
הַצָּרָֽעַת׃

טו א ב וַיְדַבֵּ֣ר יהוה אֶל־מֹשֶׁ֥ה וְאֶֽל־אַהֲרֹ֖ן לֵאמֹֽר׃ דַּבְּרוּ֙ אֶל־בְּנֵ֣י יִשְׂרָאֵ֔ל יא

אונקלוס

מה וִיתָרַע יָת בֵּיתָא, יָת אַבְנוֹהִי וְיָת אָעוֹהִי, וְיָת כָּל עֲפַר בֵּיתָא, וְיַפֵּיק לְמִבָּרָא לְקַרְתָּא, לַאֲתַר מְסָאַב: מו וּדְיֵיעוֹל לְבֵיתָא, כָּל יוֹמִין דְּיַסְגַּר יָתֵיהּ, יְהֵי מְסָאַב עַד רַמְשָׁא: מז וּדְיִשְׁכּוֹב בְּבֵיתָא, יְצַבַּע יָת לְבוּשׁוֹהִי, וּדְיֵיכוֹל בְּבֵיתָא, יְצַבַּע יָת לְבוּשׁוֹהִי: מח וְאִם מֵיעַל יֵיעוֹל כָּהֲנָא, וְיִחְזֵי וְהָא, לָא אוֹסֵיף מַכְתָּשָׁא בְּבֵיתָא, בָּתַר דְּאִתְּשַׁע יָת בֵּיתָא, וִידַכֵּי כָּהֲנָא יָת בֵּיתָא, אֲרֵי אִתַּסִּי מַכְתָּשָׁא: מט וְיִסַּב, לְדַכָּאָה יָת בֵּיתָא תַּרְתֵּין צִפְּרִין, וְאָעָא דְאַרְזָא, וּצְבַע זְהוֹרִי וְאֵיזוֹבָא: נ וְיִכּוֹס יָת צִפְּרָא חֲדָא, לְמָן דַּחֲסַף עַל מֵי מַבּוּעַ: נא וְיִסַּב יָת אָעָא דְאַרְזָא, וְיָת אֵיזוֹבָא, וְיָת צְבַע זְהוֹרִי, וְיָת צִפְּרָא חַיְתָא, וְיִטְבּוֹל יָתְהוֹן, בִּדְמָא דְּצִפְּרָא דִּנְכִיסְתָּא, וּבְמֵי מַבּוּעַ, וְיַדֵּי לְבֵיתָא שְׁבַע זִמְנִין: נב וִידַכֵּי יָת בֵּיתָא, בִּדְמָא דְּצִפְּרָא, וּבְמֵי מַבּוּעַ, וּבְצִפְּרָא חַיְתָא, וּבְאָעָא דְאַרְזָא, וּבְאֵיזוֹבָא וּבִצְבַע זְהוֹרִי: נג וִישַׁלַּח, יָת צִפְּרָא חַיְתָא, לְמִבָּרָא לְקַרְתָּא עַל אַפֵּי חַקְלָא, וִיכַפַּר עַל בֵּיתָא וְיִדְכֵּי: נד דָּא אוֹרָיְתָא, לְכָל מַכְתָּשׁ סְגִירוּתָא וּלְנִתְקָא: נה וְלִסְגִירוּת לְבוּשָׁא וּלְבֵיתָא: נו וּלְעָמְקָא וּלְעַדְיָא וּלְבַהֲרָא: נז לְאַלָּפָא, בְּיוֹם מְסָאֲבָא וּבְיוֹם דָּכְיָא, דָּא אוֹרָיְתָא דִּסְגִירוּתָא: טו א וּמַלֵּיל יְיָ, עִם מֹשֶׁה וּלְאַהֲרֹן לְמֵימַר: ב מַלִּילוּ עִם בְּנֵי

3 man has a genital discharge, he is rendered impure. This is the impurity brought
about by his discharge: whether his member allows the discharge to flow or
4 whether it blocks it, the discharge renders him impure, so that any bed he lies
5 upon and any object he sits upon becomes impure. Anyone who touches his
bed shall wash his clothes, immerse in water, and remain impure until evening.
6 Anyone who sits on something he has sat upon shall wash his clothes, immerse
7 in water, and remain impure until evening. Anyone who touches his body shall
8 wash his clothes, immerse in water, and remain impure until evening. If the
man with the discharge spits on a person who is pure, that person shall wash
9 his clothes, immerse in water, and remain impure until evening. Any saddle on
10 which the man with the discharge rides becomes impure. Anyone who touches
anything that was underneath him shall be impure until evening. Anyone who
moves such an item shall wash his clothes, immerse in water, and be impure
11 until evening. If the man with the discharge touches someone without first
washing his hands with water, that person shall wash his clothes, immerse in
12 water, and remain impure until evening. Any earthen vessel that the man with
the discharge touches shall be broken, any wooden vessel immersed in water.

רש״י

טו ב **כי יהיה זב.** יכול זב מכל מקום יהא טמא? תלמוד לומר: "מבשרו", ולא כל בשרו. אחר שחלק הכתוב בין בשר לבשר, זכיתי לדון: טמא בזב וטמא בזבה, מה זבה ממקום שהיא מטמאה טומאה קלה – נדה, מטמאה טומאה חמורה – זיבה, אף הזב ממקום שמטמא טומאה קלה – קרי, מטמא טומאה חמורה – זיבה: **זובו טמא.** למד על הטפה שהיא מטמאה. זוב דומה למי בצק של שעורין, ודחוי, ודומה ללבן ביצה המוזרת. שכבת זרע, קשור כלבן ביצה שאינה מוזרת:

ג **רר.** לשון ריר, שזב בשרו "את זובו", כמו ריר שיוצא צלול: **או החתים.** שיוצא עב וסותם את פי האמה, ונסתם בשרו מטפת זובו, זהו פשוטו. ומדרשו, מנה הכתוב הראשון ראיות שתים וקראו טמא, שנאמר: "זב מבשרו זובו טמא הוא", ומנה הכתוב השני ראיות שלש וקראו טמא, שנאמר: "טמאתו בזובו רר בשרו את זובו או החתים בשרו מזובו טמאתו הוא", הא כיצד? שתים לטומאה והשלישית מזקיקתו לקרבן:

ד **כל המשכב.** הראוי למשכב. יכול אפילו מיוחד למלאכה אחרת? תלמוד לומר: "אשר ישכב", 'אשר שכב' לא נאמר, אלא "אשר ישכב", המיוחד תמיד לכך, יצא זה שאומרין לו: 'עמוד ונעשה מלאכתנו': **אשר ישב.** 'ישב' לא נאמר, אלא "אשר ישב עליו" הזב, במיוחד תמיד לכך:

ה **ואיש אשר יגע במשכבו.** למד על המשכב שחמור מן המגע, שזה נעשה אב הטומאה לטמא אדם לטמא בגדים, והמגע שאינו משכב אינו אלא ולד הטומאה, ואינו מטמא אלא אוכלין ומשקין:

ו **והישב על הכלי.** אפילו לא נגע, אפילו עשרה כלים זה על זה כלן מטמאין משום מושב, וכן במשכב:

ח **וכי ירק הזב בטהור.** ונגע בו או נשאו, שהרוק מטמא במשא:

ט **וכל המרכב.** אף על פי שלא ישב עליו, כגון התפוס של סרגא שקורין ארצו״ן, טמא משום מרכב, והאוכף שקורין אלוי״ש טמא טומאת מושב:

י **וכל הנגע בכל אשר יהיה תחתיו.** של זב, בא ולמד על המרכב שיהא הנוגע בו טמא ואין טעון כבוס בגדים, והוא חומר במשכב ממרכב: **והנושא אותם.** כל האמור בענין הזב, זובו ורקו ושכבת זרעו ומימי רגליו והמשכב והמרכב, משאן מטמא אדם לטמא בגדים:

יא **וידיו לא שטף במים.** בעוד שלא טבל מטומאתו, ואפילו פסק מזובו וספר שבעה ומחסר טבילה, מטמא בכל טומאותיו. וזה שהוציא הכתוב טבילת גופו של זב בלשון שטיפת ידים, ללמדך שאין בית הסתרים טעון ביאת מים, אלא אבר הגלוי כמו הידים:

יב **וכלי חרש אשר יגע בו הזב.** יכול אפילו נגע בו מאחוריו וכו׳,

ג וַאֲמַרְתֶּם אֲלֵהֶם אִישׁ אִישׁ כִּי יִהְיֶה זָב מִבְּשָׂרוֹ זוֹבוֹ טָמֵא הוּא: וְזֹאת
תִּהְיֶה טֻמְאָתוֹ בְּזוֹבוֹ רָר בְּשָׂרוֹ אֶת־זוֹבוֹ אוֹ־הֶחְתִּים בְּשָׂרוֹ מִזּוֹבוֹ
ד טֻמְאָתוֹ הִוא: כָּל־הַמִּשְׁכָּב אֲשֶׁר יִשְׁכַּב עָלָיו הַזָּב יִטְמָא וְכָל־הַכְּלִי
ה אֲשֶׁר־יֵשֵׁב עָלָיו יִטְמָא: וְאִישׁ אֲשֶׁר יִגַּע בְּמִשְׁכָּבוֹ יְכַבֵּס בְּגָדָיו וְרָחַץ
ו בַּמַּיִם וְטָמֵא עַד־הָעָרֶב: וְהַיֹּשֵׁב עַל־הַכְּלִי אֲשֶׁר־יֵשֵׁב עָלָיו הַזָּב יְכַבֵּס
ז בְּגָדָיו וְרָחַץ בַּמַּיִם וְטָמֵא עַד־הָעָרֶב: וְהַנֹּגֵעַ בִּבְשַׂר הַזָּב יְכַבֵּס בְּגָדָיו
ח וְרָחַץ בַּמַּיִם וְטָמֵא עַד־הָעָרֶב: וְכִי־יָרֹק הַזָּב בַּטָּהוֹר וְכִבֶּס בְּגָדָיו
ט וְרָחַץ בַּמַּיִם וְטָמֵא עַד־הָעָרֶב: וְכָל־הַמֶּרְכָּב אֲשֶׁר יִרְכַּב עָלָיו הַזָּב
י יִטְמָא: וְכָל־הַנֹּגֵעַ בְּכֹל אֲשֶׁר יִהְיֶה תַחְתָּיו יִטְמָא עַד־הָעָרֶב וְהַנּוֹשֵׂא
יא אוֹתָם יְכַבֵּס בְּגָדָיו וְרָחַץ בַּמַּיִם וְטָמֵא עַד־הָעָרֶב: וְכֹל אֲשֶׁר יִגַּע־בּוֹ
הַזָּב וְיָדָיו לֹא־שָׁטַף בַּמָּיִם וְכִבֶּס בְּגָדָיו וְרָחַץ בַּמַּיִם וְטָמֵא עַד־
יב הָעָרֶב: וּכְלִי־חֶרֶשׂ אֲשֶׁר־יִגַּע־בּוֹ הַזָּב יִשָּׁבֵר וְכָל־כְּלִי־עֵץ יִשָּׁטֵף בַּמָּיִם:

אונקלוס

יִשְׂרָאֵל, וְתֵימְרוּן לְהוֹן, גְּבַר גְּבַר, אֲרֵי יְהֵי דָּאֵיב מִבִּסְרֵיהּ, דּוֹבֵיהּ מְסָאַב הוּא: ג וְדָא, תְּהֵי סָאוֹבְתֵיהּ בְּדוֹבֵיהּ, רִיר בִּסְרֵיהּ יָת דּוֹבֵיהּ, אוֹ חֲתִים בִּסְרֵיהּ מִדּוֹבֵיהּ, סָאוֹבְתֵיהּ הִיא: ד כָּל מִשְׁכְּבָא, דְּיִשְׁכּוֹב עֲלוֹהִי, דּוֹבָנָא יְהֵי מְסָאַב, וְכָל מָנָא, דְּיִתֵּיב עֲלוֹהִי יְהֵי מְסָאַב: ה וּגְבַר, דְּיִקְרַב בְּמִשְׁכְּבֵיהּ, יְצַבַּע לְבוּשׁוֹהִי, וְיִסְחֵי בְמַיָּא וִיהֵי מְסָאַב עַד רַמְשָׁא: ו וּדְיִתֵּיב עַל מָנָא, דְּיִתֵּיב עֲלוֹהִי דּוֹבָנָא, יְצַבַּע לְבוּשׁוֹהִי, וְיִסְחֵי בְמַיָּא וִיהֵי מְסָאַב עַד רַמְשָׁא: ז וּדְיִקְרַב בִּבְסַר דּוֹבָנָא, יְצַבַּע לְבוּשׁוֹהִי, וְיִסְחֵי בְמַיָּא וִיהֵי מְסָאַב עַד רַמְשָׁא: ח וַאֲרֵי יְרוֹק דּוֹבָנָא בְּדַכְיָא, וִיצַבַּע לְבוּשׁוֹהִי, וְיִסְחֵי בְמַיָּא וִיהֵי מְסָאַב עַד רַמְשָׁא: ט וְכָל מֶרְכְּבָא, דְּיִרְכּוֹב עֲלוֹהִי, דּוֹבָנָא יְהֵי מְסָאַב: י וְכָל דְּיִקְרַב, בְּכֹל דִּיהֵי תְחוֹתוֹהִי, יְהֵי מְסָאַב עַד רַמְשָׁא, וּדְיִטּוֹל יָתְהוֹן, יְצַבַּע לְבוּשׁוֹהִי, וְיִסְחֵי בְמַיָּא וִיהֵי מְסָאַב עַד רַמְשָׁא: יא וְכֹל דְּיִקְרַב בֵּיהּ דּוֹבָנָא, וִידוֹהִי לָא שְׁטִיף בְּמַיָּא, וִיצַבַּע לְבוּשׁוֹהִי, וְיִסְחֵי בְמַיָּא וִיהֵי מְסָאַב עַד רַמְשָׁא: יב וּמָן דַּחֲסַף, דְּיִקְרַב בֵּיהּ דּוֹבָנָא יִתְּבַר, וְכָל מָן דְּאָע, יִשְׁתְּטִיף בְּמַיָּא:

15:2 **זָב מִבְּשָׂרוֹ** *A genital discharge* – The supreme source of impurity is death: contact with or proximity to a dead body. Likewise, the flow of menstrual blood and the reproductive cycle is a sign of human mortality. It may be that the appearance of menstrual blood was a sign that the woman was not pregnant, so it represented a kind of death, the death of the unfertilized egg and of the possibility that month of new life. Seminal and other discharges likewise defiled because they too were signs of the body functioning in non-normal ways.

13 When the man with the discharge is purified of it, he shall count seven days
for his purification. Then he shall wash his clothes and immerse his body in
14 flowing water; then he is pure. On the eighth day he shall take two doves or two
pigeons before the LORD to the entrance of the Tent of Meeting and give them
15 to the priest. The priest shall offer them, one as a purification offering, the other
as a burnt offering. Thus shall the priest make the man's atonement before the
16 LORD after his discharge. If a man has an emission of semen, he shall SHISHI /SHEVI'I/
17 immerse his entire body in water, and he remains impure until evening. Any
clothing or leather on which there is an emission of semen shall be washed in
18 water and shall be impure until evening. And any woman with whom a man
lies carnally – both partners shall immerse in water and remain impure until
evening.

19 When a woman has a discharge of blood that is her usual bodily discharge,
she retains her menstrual status for seven days. Any person who touches her
20 then shall be impure until evening. Anything on which she lies or sits during
21 her menstrual time becomes impure. Whoever touches her bed shall wash his
22 clothes, immerse in water, and remain impure until evening. Whoever touches
any object she has sat upon shall wash his clothes, immerse in water, and remain
23 impure until evening. Whether it be a bed or any object she sits upon, when

רש״י

כִּדְאִיתָא בְּתוֹרַת כֹּהֲנִים (פרשתא ג, א-ב), עַד אֵיזֶהוּ מַגָּעוֹ שֶׁהוּא בְּכֻלּוֹ, הֱוֵי אוֹמֵר זֶה הֶסֵּטוֹ:

יג **וְכִי יִטְהַר.** כְּשֶׁיִּפְסֹק: **שִׁבְעַת יָמִים לְטָהֳרָתוֹ.** שִׁבְעַת יָמִים טְהוֹרִים מִטֻּמְאַת זִיבָה, שֶׁלֹּא יִרְאֶה זוֹב, וְכֻלָּן רְצוּפִין:

יח **וְרָחֲצוּ בַמַּיִם.** גְּזֵרַת מֶלֶךְ הִיא שֶׁתִּטְמָא הָאִשָּׁה בְּבִיאָה, וְאֵין הַטַּעַם מִשּׁוּם נוֹגֵעַ בְּשִׁכְבַת זֶרַע, שֶׁהֲרֵי מַגַּע בֵּית הַסְּתָרִים הוּא:

יט **כִּי תִהְיֶה זָבָה.** יָכוֹל מֵאֶחָד מִכָּל אֵיבָרֶיהָ? תַּלְמוּד לוֹמַר "וְהִוא גִּלְּתָה אֶת מְקוֹר דָּמֶיהָ" (להלן כ, יח), אֵין דָּם מְטַמֵּא אֶלָּא הַבָּא מִן הַמָּקוֹר: **דָּם יִהְיֶה זֹבָהּ בִּבְשָׂרָהּ.** אֵין זוֹבָהּ קָרוּי זוֹב לְטַמֵּא אֶלָּא אִם כֵּן הוּא אָדֹם: **בְּנִדָּתָהּ.** כְּמוֹ "וּמִתֵּבֵל יְנִדֻּהוּ" (איוב יח, יח), שֶׁהִיא מְנֻדָּה מִמַּגַּע כָּל אָדָם: **תִּהְיֶה בְנִדָּתָהּ.** אֲפִלּוּ לֹא רָאֲתָה אֶלָּא רְאִיָּה רִאשׁוֹנָה:

כג **וְאִם עַל הַמִּשְׁכָּב הוּא.** הַשּׁוֹכֵב אוֹ הַיּוֹשֵׁב עַל מִשְׁכָּבָהּ אוֹ עַל מוֹשָׁבָהּ, אֲפִלּוּ לֹא נָגַע בּוֹ, אַף הוּא בְּדַת טֻמְאָה הָאֲמוּרָה בַּמִּקְרָא

respect is the book of Ezekiel. Yeḥezkel was both a prophet and a priest, and his is the most identifiably priestly voice in the non-Mosaic books. How does the priestly domain of regulatory order touch upon the prophetic domain of love and justice?

It was failure to observe the boundary between permitted and forbidden that caused Adam and Ḥava to be exiled from Eden. Within a generation, the first murder had taken place, and before long "the earth had become… full with violence" (Gen. 6:11).

This is the Torah's form of chaos theory: as the beating of a butterfly's wing can cause a typhoon on the other side of the earth, so small breaches in boundaries can lead, in time, to anarchy and tyranny. Knowing how rapid the descent can be from civilization to barbarism, the priestly sensibility is vigilant in maintaining what Wallace Stevens called the "blessed rage for order." That "a man… cleaves to his wife and they become one flesh" (Gen. 2:24) is part of the order of Eden. Yet that bond too requires the clear drawing of boundaries, its space set apart.

יג וְכִֽי־יִטְהַ֤ר הַזָּב֙ מִזּוֹב֔וֹ וְסָ֨פַר ל֜וֹ שִׁבְעַ֥ת יָמִ֛ים לְטׇהֳרָת֖וֹ וְכִבֶּ֣ס בְּגָדָ֑יו
יד וְרָחַ֧ץ בְּשָׂר֛וֹ בְּמַ֥יִם חַיִּ֖ים וְטָהֵֽר׃ וּבַיּ֣וֹם הַשְּׁמִינִ֗י יִֽקַּֽח־לוֹ֙ שְׁתֵּ֣י תֹרִ֔ים א֥וֹ
שְׁנֵ֖י בְּנֵ֣י יוֹנָ֑ה וּבָ֣א ׀ לִפְנֵ֣י יהוה אֶל־פֶּ֨תַח֙ אֹ֣הֶל מוֹעֵ֔ד וּנְתָנָ֖ם אֶל־הַכֹּהֵֽן׃
טו וְעָשָׂ֤ה אֹתָם֙ הַכֹּהֵ֔ן אֶחָ֣ד חַטָּ֔את וְהָאֶחָ֖ד עֹלָ֑ה וְכִפֶּ֨ר עָלָ֧יו הַכֹּהֵ֛ן לִפְנֵ֥י
טז יהוה מִזּוֹבֽוֹ׃ וְאִ֕ישׁ כִּֽי־תֵצֵ֥א מִמֶּ֖נּוּ שִׁכְבַת־זָ֑רַע וְרָחַ֤ץ בַּמַּ֙יִם֙ ששי /שביעי/
יז אֶת־כׇּל־בְּשָׂר֖וֹ וְטָמֵ֥א עַד־הָעָֽרֶב׃ וְכׇל־בֶּ֣גֶד וְכׇל־ע֔וֹר אֲשֶׁר־יִהְיֶ֥ה עָלָ֖יו
יח שִׁכְבַת־זָ֑רַע וְכֻבַּ֥ס בַּמַּ֖יִם וְטָמֵ֥א עַד־הָעָֽרֶב׃ וְאִשָּׁ֕ה אֲשֶׁ֨ר יִשְׁכַּ֥ב אִ֛ישׁ
אֹתָ֖הּ שִׁכְבַת־זָ֑רַע וְרָחֲצ֣וּ בַמַּ֔יִם וְטָמְא֖וּ עַד־הָעָֽרֶב׃
יט וְאִשָּׁה֙ כִּֽי־תִהְיֶ֣ה זָבָ֔ה דָּ֛ם יִהְיֶ֥ה זֹבָ֖הּ בִּבְשָׂרָ֑הּ שִׁבְעַ֤ת יָמִים֙ תִּהְיֶ֣ה
כ בְנִדָּתָ֔הּ וְכׇל־הַנֹּגֵ֥עַ בָּ֖הּ יִטְמָ֥א עַד־הָעָֽרֶב׃ וְכֹל֩ אֲשֶׁ֨ר תִּשְׁכַּ֥ב עָלָ֛יו בְּנִדָּתָ֖הּ
כא יִטְמָ֑א וְכֹ֛ל אֲשֶׁר־תֵּשֵׁ֥ב עָלָ֖יו יִטְמָֽא׃ וְכׇל־הַנֹּגֵ֖עַ בְּמִשְׁכָּבָ֑הּ יְכַבֵּ֥ס בְּגָדָ֛יו
כב וְרָחַ֥ץ בַּמַּ֖יִם וְטָמֵ֥א עַד־הָעָֽרֶב׃ וְכׇל־הַנֹּגֵ֔עַ בְּכׇל־כְּלִ֖י אֲשֶׁר־תֵּשֵׁ֣ב עָלָ֑יו
כג יְכַבֵּ֧ס בְּגָדָ֛יו וְרָחַ֥ץ בַּמַּ֖יִם וְטָמֵ֥א עַד־הָעָֽרֶב׃ וְאִ֨ם עַ֤ל הַמִּשְׁכָּב֙ ה֔וּא

אונקלוס

יג וַאֲרֵי יִדְכֵּי דּוֹבָנָא מִדּוֹבֵיהּ, וְיִמְנֵי לֵיהּ, שִׁבְעָא יוֹמִין, לְדִכוּתֵיהּ וִיצַבַּע לְבוּשׁוֹהִי, וְיַסְחֵי בִּסְרֵיהּ, בְּמֵי מַבּוּעַ וְיִדְכֵּי: יד וּבְיוֹמָא תְּמִינָאָה, יִסַּב לֵיהּ תַּרְתֵּין שַׁפְנִינִין, אוֹ תְּרֵין בְּנֵי יוֹנָה, וְיֵיתֵי לִקְדָם יי, לִתְרַע מַשְׁכַּן זִמְנָא, וְיִתְּנִנּוּן לְכָהֲנָא: טו וְיַעֲבֵיד יָתְהוֹן כָּהֲנָא, חַד חַטָּתָא, וְחַד עֲלָתָא, וִיכַפַּר עֲלוֹהִי כָּהֲנָא, קֳדָם יי מִדּוֹבֵיהּ: טז וּגְבַר, אֲרֵי תִפּוֹק מִנֵּיהּ שִׁכְבַת זַרְעָא, וְיַסְחֵי בְמַיָּא, יָת כָּל בִּסְרֵיהּ וִיהֵי מְסָאַב עַד רַמְשָׁא: יז וְכָל לְבוּשׁ וְכָל מְשַׁךְ, דִּיהֵי עֲלוֹהִי שִׁכְבַת זַרְעָא, וְיִצְטְבַע בְּמַיָּא וִיהֵי מְסָאַב עַד רַמְשָׁא: יח וְאִתְּתָא, דְּיִשְׁכּוּב גְּבַר, יָתַהּ שִׁכְבַת זַרְעָא, וְיַסְחוּן בְּמַיָּא, וִיהוֹן מְסָאֲבִין עַד רַמְשָׁא: יט וְאִתְּתָא אֲרֵי תְהֵי דַּיְבָא, דַּם, יְהֵי דּוֹבַהּ בִּבְסָרַהּ, שִׁבְעָא יוֹמִין תְּהֵי בְרִיחוּקַהּ, וְכָל דְּיִקְרַב בַּהּ יְהֵי מְסָאַב עַד רַמְשָׁא: כ וְכֹל דְּתִשְׁכּוּב עֲלוֹהִי, בְּרִיחוּקַהּ יְהֵי מְסָאַב, וְכֹל, דְּתִתֵּיב עֲלוֹהִי יְהֵי מְסָאַב: כא וְכָל דְּיִקְרַב בְּמִשְׁכְּבַהּ, יְצַבַּע לְבוּשׁוֹהִי, וְיַסְחֵי בְמַיָּא וִיהֵי מְסָאַב עַד רַמְשָׁא: כב וְכָל דְּיִקְרַב, בְּכָל מָנָא דְּתִתֵּיב עֲלוֹהִי, יְצַבַּע לְבוּשׁוֹהִי, וְיַסְחֵי בְמַיָּא וִיהֵי מְסָאַב עַד רַמְשָׁא: כג וְאִם עַל מִשְׁכְּבָא הוּא,

15:18 וְטָמְאוּ עַד־הָעָרֶב *Remain impure until evening* – God does not ask of us to sacrifice or devalue our physicality. To the contrary, we are part of the physical world He created, and this is where He wants us to serve Him. Nonetheless, lines have to be drawn and boundaries maintained between God's domain and ours. This is the function of the purity laws.

▶

The word *tameh* in one or other of its forms appears no less than 106 times in Leviticus, while the root *tahor* appears 62 times. The root *tameh* appears only 285 times in Tanakh as a whole, and *tahor* 207 times, so that Leviticus accounts for around one-third of the occurrences of these words in the Hebrew Bible's thirty-nine books. The only rival in this

24 one touches it he shall be impure until evening. If a man has sexual relations
with her, her menstrual status is extended to him; he too shall be impure for
25 seven days, and any bed he lies upon is rendered impure. Whenever
a woman has a discharge of blood for many days at a time other than her
menstrual period, or if she has a discharge beyond her menstrual period, she
shall be impure as long as she has the discharge, as she is in her menstrual time.
26 Any bed she lies upon while she has this discharge shall be treated like the
bed she uses during her menstruation, and any object she sits upon becomes
27 impure, as during her menstrual time. Whoever touches these things is rendered
impure; he shall wash his clothes, immerse in water, and remain impure until
28 evening. When the woman's discharge ends, she shall count seven days; after
29 that, she will be purified. On the eighth day she shall take two doves or two SHEVI'I
pigeons and bring them to the priest at the entrance to the Tent of Meeting.
30 The priest shall prepare one as a purification offering and the other as a burnt
offering. Thus shall the priest make her atonement before the LORD following
31 her impure discharge. You must separate the Israelites from their own impurity MAFTIR
so that they do not die in their impurity by making My Tabernacle impure in

רש״י

הָעֶלְיוֹן, שֶׁטָּעוּן כִּבּוּס בְּגָדִים: **עַל הַכְּלִי.** לְרַבּוֹת אֶת הַמֶּרְכָּב: **בְּנָגְעוֹ בוֹ יִטְמָא.** אֵינוֹ מְדַבֵּר אֶלָּא עַל הַמֶּרְכָּב שֶׁנִּתְרַבָּה מֵ״עַל הַכְּלִי״: **בְּנָגְעוֹ בוֹ יִטְמָא.** וְאֵינוֹ טָעוּן כִּבּוּס בְּגָדִים, שֶׁהַמֶּרְכָּב אֵין מַגָּעוֹ מְטַמֵּא אָדָם לְטַמֵּא בְּגָדִים:

כד **וּתְהִי נִדָּתָהּ עָלָיו.** יָכוֹל יַעֲלֶה לְרַגְלָהּ, שֶׁאִם בָּא עָלֶיהָ בַּחֲמִישִׁי לְנִדָּתָהּ לֹא יִטְמָא אֶלָּא שְׁלֹשָׁה יָמִים כְּמוֹתָהּ? תַּלְמוּד לוֹמַר: ״וְטָמֵא שִׁבְעַת יָמִים״. וּמַה תַּלְמוּד לוֹמַר: ״וּתְהִי נִדָּתָהּ עָלָיו״? מַה הִיא מְטַמְּאָה אָדָם וּכְלִי חֶרֶס, אַף הוּא מְטַמֵּא אָדָם וּכְלִי חֶרֶס:

כה **יָמִים רַבִּים.** שְׁלֹשָׁה יָמִים: **בְּלֹא עֶת נִדָּתָהּ.** אַחַר שֶׁיָּצְאוּ שִׁבְעַת יְמֵי נִדָּתָהּ: **אוֹ כִי תָזוּב.** אֶת שְׁלֹשֶׁת הַיָּמִים הַלָּלוּ: **עַל נִדָּתָהּ.** מֻפְלָג מִנִּדָּתָהּ יוֹם אֶחָד, זוֹ הִיא זָבָה, וּמִשְׁפָּטָהּ חָרוּץ בְּפָרָשָׁה זוֹ, וְלֹא כְּדַת הַנִּדָּה, שֶׁזּוֹ טְעוּנָה סְפִירַת שִׁבְעָה נְקִיִּים וְקָרְבָּן, וְהַנִּדָּה אֵינָהּ טְעוּנָה סְפִירַת שִׁבְעָה נְקִיִּים, אֶלָּא ״שִׁבְעַת יָמִים תִּהְיֶה בְנִדָּתָהּ״ (לעיל פסוק יט), בֵּין רוֹאָה בֵּין שֶׁאֵינָהּ רוֹאָה. וְדָרְשׁוּ בְּפָרָשָׁה זוֹ אַחַד עָשָׂר יוֹם שֶׁבֵּין סוֹף נִדָּה לִתְחִלַּת נִדָּה, שֶׁכָּל שְׁלֹשָׁה רְצוּפִין שֶׁתִּרְאֶה בְּאַחַד עָשָׂר יוֹם הַלָּלוּ תְּהֵא זָבָה:

לא **וְהִזַּרְתֶּם.** אֵין נְזִירָה אֶלָּא פְּרִישָׁה, וְכֵן ״נָזֹרוּ אָחוֹר״ (ישעיה א, ד), וְכֵן ״נְזִיר אֶחָיו״ (בראשית מט, כו): **וְלֹא יָמֻתוּ בְּטֻמְאָתָם.** הֲרֵי הַכָּרֵת שֶׁל מְטַמֵּא מִקְדָּשׁ קָרוּי מִיתָה:

The concepts of holiness and purity, the two organizing principles of the priestly mind, are about the intense and vigilant preparation we must make before entering God's space. God is that which is not mortal, finite, and physical. Therefore, whatever inescapably reminds us of our physicality and mortality – whether it be birth or death, or a skin disease, or the flow of menstrual blood, or the unusual discharge of some bodily fluid, or contact with the carcass of a repulsive animal – conveys *tuma*, that is, a state from which we must be cleansed before entering the domain of the holy.

There is nothing intrinsically defiling about our physicality. To the contrary, the Torah asks us to seek God within the physical world, to sanctify rather than forswear physical pleasures such as eating and drinking and the marital bond. There is nothing ascetic or otherworldly about the Torah's ethic.

אוֹ עַל־הַכְּלִי אֲשֶׁר־הִוא יֹשֶׁבֶת־עָלָיו בְּנָגְעוֹ־בוֹ יִטְמָא עַד־הָעָרֶב׃
כד וְאִם שָׁכֹב יִשְׁכַּב אִישׁ אֹתָהּ וּתְהִי נִדָּתָהּ עָלָיו וְטָמֵא שִׁבְעַת יָמִים
כה וְכָל־הַמִּשְׁכָּב אֲשֶׁר־יִשְׁכַּב עָלָיו יִטְמָא׃ וְאִשָּׁה כִּי־יָזוּב זוֹב יב
דָּמָהּ יָמִים רַבִּים בְּלֹא עֶת־נִדָּתָהּ אוֹ כִי־תָזוּב עַל־נִדָּתָהּ כָּל־יְמֵי זוֹב
כו טֻמְאָתָהּ כִּימֵי נִדָּתָהּ תִּהְיֶה טְמֵאָה הִוא׃ כָּל־הַמִּשְׁכָּב אֲשֶׁר־תִּשְׁכַּב
עָלָיו כָּל־יְמֵי זוֹבָהּ כְּמִשְׁכַּב נִדָּתָהּ יִהְיֶה־לָּהּ וְכָל־הַכְּלִי אֲשֶׁר תֵּשֵׁב
כז עָלָיו טָמֵא יִהְיֶה כְּטֻמְאַת נִדָּתָהּ׃ וְכָל־הַנּוֹגֵעַ בָּם יִטְמָא וְכִבֶּס בְּגָדָיו
כח וְרָחַץ בַּמַּיִם וְטָמֵא עַד־הָעָרֶב׃ וְאִם־טָהֲרָה מִזּוֹבָהּ וְסָפְרָה־לָּהּ
כט שִׁבְעַת יָמִים וְאַחַר תִּטְהָר׃ וּבַיּוֹם הַשְּׁמִינִי תִּקַּח־לָהּ שְׁתֵּי תֹרִים אוֹ שביעי
ל שְׁנֵי בְּנֵי יוֹנָה וְהֵבִיאָה אוֹתָם אֶל־הַכֹּהֵן אֶל־פֶּתַח אֹהֶל מוֹעֵד׃ וְעָשָׂה
הַכֹּהֵן אֶת־הָאֶחָד חַטָּאת וְאֶת־הָאֶחָד עֹלָה וְכִפֶּר עָלֶיהָ הַכֹּהֵן לִפְנֵי
לא יְהוָה מִזּוֹב טֻמְאָתָהּ׃ וְהִזַּרְתֶּם אֶת־בְּנֵי־יִשְׂרָאֵל מִטֻּמְאָתָם וְלֹא יָמֻתוּ מפטיר

אונקלוס

אוֹ עַל מָנָא, דְּהִיא יָתְבָא עֲלוֹהִי בְּמִקְרְבֵיהּ בֵּיהּ, יְהֵי מְסָאַב עַד רַמְשָׁא: כד וְאִם, מִשְׁכַּב יִשְׁכּוּב גְּבַר יָתַהּ, וּתְהֵי רִיחוּקַהּ עֲלוֹהִי, וִיהֵי מְסָאַב שִׁבְעָא יוֹמִין, וְכָל מִשְׁכְּבָא, דְּיִשְׁכּוּב עֲלוֹהִי יְהֵי מְסָאַב: כה וְאִתְּתָא, אֲרֵי יְדוּב דּוֹב דְּמַהּ יוֹמִין סַגִּיאִין, בְּלָא עִדָּן רִיחוּקַהּ, אוֹ אֲרֵי תְדוּב עַל רִיחוּקַהּ, כָּל יוֹמֵי דּוֹב סְאוֹבְתַהּ, כְּיוֹמֵי רִיחוּקַהּ, תְּהֵי מְסָאֲבָא הִיא: כו כָּל מִשְׁכְּבָא, דְּתִשְׁכּוּב עֲלוֹהִי כָּל יוֹמֵי דּוֹבַהּ, כְּמִשְׁכַּב רִיחוּקַהּ יְהֵי לַהּ, וְכָל מָנָא דְּתֵתֵיב עֲלוֹהִי, מְסָאַב יְהֵי, כִּסְאוֹבַת רִיחוּקַהּ: כז וְכָל דְּיִקְרַב בְּהוֹן יְהֵי מְסָאַב, וִיצַבַּע לְבוּשׁוֹהִי, וְיַסְחֵי בְמַיָּא וִיהֵי מְסָאַב עַד רַמְשָׁא: כח וְאִם דְּכִיאַת מִדּוֹבַהּ, וְתִמְנֵי לַהּ, שִׁבְעָא יוֹמִין וּבָתַר כֵּן תִּדְכֵּי: כט וּבְיוֹמָא תְּמִינָאָה, תִּסַּב לַהּ תַּרְתֵּין שַׁפְנִינִין, אוֹ תְרֵין בְּנֵי יוֹנָה, וְתַיְתֵי יָתְהוֹן לְוָת כַּהֲנָא, לִתְרַע מַשְׁכַּן זִמְנָא: ל וְיַעֲבֵיד כַּהֲנָא יָת חַד חַטָּתָא, וְיָת חַד עֲלָתָא, וִיכַפַּר עֲלַהּ כַּהֲנָא קֳדָם יְיָ, מִדּוֹב סְאוֹבְתַהּ: לא וְתַפְרְשׁוּן יָת בְּנֵי יִשְׂרָאֵל מִסּוֹאֲבָתְהוֹן, וְלָא יְמוּתוּן בְּסוֹאֲבָתְהוֹן,

15:31 בְּטַמְּאָם אֶת־מִשְׁכָּנִי *Making My Tabernacle impure* – The concepts of purity and impurity, as we know, have their main application in relation to the holy space of the Sanctuary. To enter its precincts one has to be pure, or purified. The chief exception is a woman's issue of menstrual blood, from which she had to be purified not only to enter the Temple, but also to resume physical relations with her husband. In general, "pure" and "impure" are not categories applying to life as a whole. They are not ethical terms like good and bad, right and wrong, which apply to secular as well as sacred space and time. They only exist because God has stipulated that they exist, just as, for example, the Sabbath only exists because God so ordered it. You cannot tell that a certain day was the Sabbath because, say, of the quality of the light or the air or the temperature. So the concept of impurity is not like the idea of uncleanliness, which could have physical manifestations. *Tuma* and *tahara* are spiritual categories brought into being by God's command.

32 their midst." This is the law concerning the man who is impure because of a
33 discharge or seminal emission, the woman during her menstrual period, the
man or woman who has a discharge, and the man who has sexual relations with
a woman who is impure.

The haftara for Parashat Metzora is on page 1568 (even when Tazria and Metzora are read together).
On Shabbat HaGadol read the haftara on page 1652.
On Rosh Ḥodesh Iyar read the haftara on page 1634.
On Erev Rosh Ḥodesh Iyar read the haftara on page 1636.

רש״י

לב **זֹאת תּוֹרַת הַזָּב.** בַּעַל רְאִיָּה אַחַת, וּמַהוּ תּוֹרָתוֹ? **וַאֲשֶׁר תֵּצֵא מִמֶּנּוּ שִׁכְבַת זֶרַע.** הֲרֵי הוּא כְּבַעַל קֶרִי, טָמֵא טֻמְאַת עֶרֶב:

לג **וְהַזָּב אֶת זוֹבוֹ.** בַּעַל שְׁתֵּי רְאִיּוֹת וּבַעַל שָׁלֹשׁ רְאִיּוֹת, שֶׁתּוֹרָתָן מְפֹרֶשֶׁת לְמַעְלָה:

we should deny them, but simply to remind ourselves that God utterly transcends all such accidents and attributes of materiality. In the Temple we are in the presence of radical transcendence.

לב בְּטֻמְאָתָם בְּטַמְּאָם אֶת־מִשְׁכָּנִי אֲשֶׁר בְּתוֹכָם: זֹאת תּוֹרַת הַזָּב וַאֲשֶׁר
לג תֵּצֵא מִמֶּנּוּ שִׁכְבַת־זֶרַע לְטָמְאָה־בָהּ: וְהַדָּוָה בְּנִדָּתָהּ וְהַזָּב אֶת־זוֹבוֹ
לַזָּכָר וְלַנְּקֵבָה וּלְאִישׁ אֲשֶׁר יִשְׁכַּב עִם־טְמֵאָה:

The הפטרה *for* פרשת מצרע *is on page 1569 (even when* תזריע *and* מצרע *are read together).*
On שבת הגדול *read the* הפטרה *on page 1653.*
On ראש חודש אייר *read the* הפטרה *on page 1635.*
On ערב ראש חודש אייר *read the* הפטרה *on page 1637.*

אונקלוס

בְּסַאוֹבֵיהוֹן יָת מַשְׁכְּנִי דְּבֵינֵיהוֹן: לב דָּא אוֹרָיְתָא דְּדוֹבָנָא, וּדְתִפּוֹק מִנֵּיהּ, שִׁכְבַת זַרְעָא לְאִסְתַּאָבָא בַהּ: לג וְלִדְסְאוֹבְתַהּ בְּרִיחוּקַהּ, וְלִדְדָאֵיב יָת דּוֹבֵיהּ, לִדְכַר וּלְנֻקְבָּא, וּלְגְבַר, דְּיִשְׁכּוֹב עִם מְסָאַבְתָּא:

Rather, we have to ensure that we have divested ourselves of all lingering traces of that which reminds us of our mortality and physicality, our vulnerability to disease, decay, and death, not because we can escape them, nor that

Parashat Aḥarei Mot

16 1 After the deaths of Aharon's two sons – when they came close to the Lord
2 and died – the Lord spoke to Moshe. "Tell your brother Aharon," said the
Lord to Moshe, "that he may not come at any time into the holy place inside
the inner curtain in front of the cover on the Ark, or he will die – for in a cloud
3 above the cover I appear. This is how Aharon is to enter the holy place: with a
4 young bull as a purification offering and a ram as a burnt offering; he shall put

רש״י

טז א **וַיְדַבֵּר ה׳ אֶל מֹשֶׁה אַחֲרֵי מוֹת שְׁנֵי בְּנֵי אַהֲרֹן וְגוֹ׳.** מַה תַּלְמוּד לוֹמַר? הָיָה רַבִּי אֶלְעָזָר בֶּן עֲזַרְיָה מוֹשְׁלוֹ מָשָׁל, לְחוֹלֶה שֶׁנִּכְנַס אֶצְלוֹ רוֹפֵא, אָמַר לוֹ: אַל תֹּאכַל צוֹנֵן וְאַל תִּשְׁכַּב בְּטַחַב. בָּא אַחֵר וְאָמַר לוֹ: אַל תֹּאכַל צוֹנֵן וְאַל תִּשְׁכַּב בְּטַחַב, שֶׁלֹּא תָּמוּת כְּדֶרֶךְ שֶׁמֵּת פְּלוֹנִי; זֶה זֵרְזוֹ יוֹתֵר מִן הָרִאשׁוֹן, לְכָךְ נֶאֱמַר: "אַחֲרֵי מוֹת שְׁנֵי בְּנֵי אַהֲרֹן":

ב **וַיֹּאמֶר ה׳ אֶל מֹשֶׁה דַּבֵּר אֶל אַהֲרֹן אָחִיךָ וְאַל יָבֹא.** שֶׁלֹּא יָמוּת כְּדֶרֶךְ שֶׁמֵּתוּ בָּנָיו: **וְלֹא יָמוּת.** שֶׁאִם בָּא, הוּא מֵת: **כִּי בֶּעָנָן אֵרָאֶה.** כִּי תָמִיד אֲנִי נִרְאֶה שָׁם עִם עַמּוּד עֲנָנִי. וּלְפִי שֶׁגִּלּוּי שְׁכִינָתִי שָׁם, יִזָּהֵר שֶׁלֹּא יַרְגִּיל לָבֹא, זֶהוּ פְּשׁוּטוֹ. וּמִדְרָשׁוֹ, אַל יָבֹא כִּי אִם בַּעֲנַן הַקְּטֹרֶת בְּיוֹם הַכִּפּוּרִים:

ג **בְּזֹאת.** גִּימַטְרִיָּא שֶׁלּוֹ אַרְבַּע מֵאוֹת וְעֶשֶׂר, רֶמֶז לְבַיִת רִאשׁוֹן: **בְּזֹאת יָבֹא אַהֲרֹן וְגוֹ׳.** וְאַף זוֹ לֹא בְּכָל עֵת, כִּי אִם בְּיוֹם הַכִּפּוּרִים, כְּמוֹ שֶׁמְּפֹרָשׁ בְּסוֹף הַפָּרָשָׁה: "בַּחֹדֶשׁ הַשְּׁבִיעִי בֶּעָשׂוֹר לַחֹדֶשׁ" (להלן פסוק כט):

ד **כְּתֹנֶת בַּד וְגוֹ׳.** מַגִּיד שֶׁאֵינוֹ מְשַׁמֵּשׁ לִפְנִים בִּשְׁמוֹנָה בְּגָדִים שֶׁהוּא מְשַׁמֵּשׁ בָּהֶן בַּחוּץ, שֶׁיֵּשׁ בָּהֶן זָהָב, לְפִי שֶׁאֵין קָטֵגוֹר נַעֲשֶׂה סָנֵגוֹר,

responsibility. "All of Israel," says the Talmud, "are sureties for one another." Ours is not a religion of hermits, living apart from society and communing solely with God. The heroes and heroines of the Torah are fathers and mothers, people set in the context of their families and societies. On Yom Kippur we confess together, publicly and aloud. We say not "I have sinned" but "We have sinned."

Yom Kippur is a day of awe. Yet the Talmud calls it one of the most joyous days of the year. Rightly so, for its message is that as long as we breathe, there is no final verdict on our lives. "Prayer, penitence and charity have the power to turn aside the evil decree."

Throughout our history, on Yom Kippur, Jews who have grown distant, Jews who were forced to disavow their faith in public, even those who had been excommunicated, joined the congregation in prayer. It is the moment when the doors of belonging are opened, and those who have been estranged return.

The Hebrew word *teshuva*, usually translated as "penitence," in fact means returning, retracing our steps, coming home. *Teshuva* as a "return" belongs to the biblical vision in which sin means dislocation, and punishment is exile: Adam and Ḥava's exile from Eden, Israel's exile from its land (see Lev. 24:28). A sin is an act that does not belong, one that transgresses the moral boundaries of the world. Those who act in ways that do not belong find eventually that they do not belong. Increasingly, they place themselves outside the relationships – of family, of community, and of being at one with history – that make them who they are. The most characteristic sense of sin is less one of guilt than of being lost. *Teshuva* means finding your way back home again. On this day of days we hear His voice, gently calling us to come home.

16:4 כְּתֹנֶת־בַּד קֹדֶשׁ יִלְבָּשׁ *Sacred linen tunic* – In public, the High Priest appears in garments of gold, "for glory and for splendor" (Ex. 28:2). Alone with God, however, he is to dress in the simplest linen garments. In the encounter with God, honesty, simplicity, and humility are needed. Some say that it is in memory of this that many men wear a kittel, a plain white robe, on Yom Kippur.

פרשת אחרי מות

טז א וַיְדַבֵּר יְהוָה אֶל־מֹשֶׁה אַחֲרֵי מוֹת שְׁנֵי בְּנֵי אַהֲרֹן בְּקָרְבָתָם לִפְנֵי־
ב יְהוָה וַיָּמֻתוּ: וַיֹּאמֶר יְהוָה אֶל־מֹשֶׁה דַּבֵּר אֶל־אַהֲרֹן אָחִיךָ וְאַל־יָבֹא
בְכָל־עֵת אֶל־הַקֹּדֶשׁ מִבֵּית לַפָּרֹכֶת אֶל־פְּנֵי הַכַּפֹּרֶת אֲשֶׁר עַל־הָאָרֹן
ג וְלֹא יָמוּת כִּי בֶּעָנָן אֵרָאֶה עַל־הַכַּפֹּרֶת: בְּזֹאת יָבֹא אַהֲרֹן אֶל־הַקֹּדֶשׁ
ד בְּפַר בֶּן־בָּקָר לְחַטָּאת וְאַיִל לְעֹלָה: כְּתֹנֶת־בַּד קֹדֶשׁ יִלְבָּשׁ וּמִכְנְסֵי־

אונקלוס

טז א וּמַלֵּיל יי עִם מֹשֶׁה, בָּתַר דְּמִיתוּ, תְּרֵין בְּנֵי אַהֲרֹן, בְּקָרוֹבֵיהוֹן
אִישָּׁתָא נֻכְרֵיתָא קֳדָם יי וּמִיתוּ: ב וַאֲמַר יי לְמֹשֶׁה, מַלֵּיל עִם אַהֲרֹן
אֲחוּךְ, וְלָא יְהֵי עָלֵיל בְּכָל עִדָּן לְקֻדְשָׁא, מִגָּיו לְפָרֻכְתָּא, לִקֳדָם
כַּפֻּרְתָּא, דְּעַל אֲרוֹנָא וְלָא יְמוּת, אֲרֵי בַּעֲנָנָא, אֲנָא מִתְגְּלֵי עַל
בֵּית כַּפּוּרֵי: ג בְּדָא, יְהֵי עָלֵיל אַהֲרֹן לְקֻדְשָׁא, בְּתוֹר בַּר תּוֹרֵי,
לְחַטָּתָא וּדְכַר לַעֲלָתָא: ד כִּתּוּנָא דְבוּצָא דְּקֻדְשָׁא יִלְבַּשׁ, וּמִכְנְסִין

AḤAREI MOT

Parashat Aḥarei Mot describes the service of the High Priest on the Day of Atonement. This is a dramatic and highly charged ritual during which he casts lots on two identical goats, one of which is offered as a sacrifice, while the other is sent into the wilderness to die, the so-called "scapegoat." The entry of the High Priest into the Holy of Holies marks the spiritual high point of the Jewish year.

The *parasha* also outlines the prohibition against eating blood, and the laws of forbidden sexual relations, both of them aspects of the life of purity God asks of the Jewish people. Beginning, then, "after the deaths of Aharon's two sons [Nadav and Avihu] – when they came close to the LORD and died," the *parasha* closes a cycle that deals with the boundaries that protect lives lived in the presence of God.

YOM KIPPUR

Yom Kippur, the Day of Atonement, is the supreme moment of Jewish time, a day of fasting and prayer, introspection and self-judgment. At no other time are we so sharply conscious of standing before God, of *being known*.

The Torah speaks of holy places. The land of Israel is holy. Holier still is Jerusalem, and in Jerusalem the holiest site will be the Temple. Within the Temple – then within the Tabernacle – is the supremely sacred place known as the Holy of Holies.

There is holy time. There are the festivals. Above them is the Sabbath. Above even that is the one day in the year known as *Shabbat Shabbaton*, the most holy day of all, Yom Kippur.

There are holy people. Israel is called a "holy people" (Deut. 7:6). Among them is a tribe of special sanctity, the Levites, and within it are individuals who are holier still, the *kohanim* or priests. Among them is a person who is supremely holy, the High Priest.

In the Tabernacle, the holiest man is to enter the holiest place on the holiest day of the year and seek atonement for his people. Since the destruction of the Temple, we no longer have the holiest place and person. But we still have the day itself: holy time, along with the possibility of repentance and purification.

At the core of the day's service is *vidui*, confession (Lev. 16:21). How can the High Priest confess and atone for the sins of all Israel, sins he did not commit? The answer, surely, is that while Judaism has a strong sense of individual dignity and responsibility, it has an equally strong sense of collective

on the sacred linen tunic with linen undergarments covering his body. He shall
bind the linen sash around himself and wrap a linen turban about his head.
These are sacred vestments; he shall immerse himself in water and only then
5 put them on. From the community of Israel he shall take two male goats for
6 a purification offering and a ram for a burnt offering. And Aharon shall bring
close the bull for his purification offering, to make atonement for him and for
7 his family. He shall take the two goats and set them before the LORD at the
8 entrance to the Tent of Meeting. Aharon shall cast lots over the two goats, one

רש״י

אֶלָּא כְּאַרְבָּעָה כְּכֹהֵן הֶדְיוֹט, וְכֻלָּן שֶׁל בּוּץ: **קֹדֶשׁ יִלְבָּשׁ.** שֶׁיִּהְיוּ מִשֶּׁל הֶקְדֵּשׁ: **יִצְנֹף.** כְּתַרְגּוּמוֹ 'יַחֵית בְּרֵישֵׁיהּ', יַנִּיחַ בְּרֹאשׁוֹ, כְּמוֹ: "וַתַּנַּח בִּגְדוֹ" (בראשית לט, טז) 'וַאֲחֵיתְתֵיהּ': **וְרָחַץ בַּמַּיִם.** אוֹתוֹ הַיּוֹם טָעוּן טְבִילָה בְּכָל חֲלִיפוֹתָיו, וְחָמֵשׁ פְּעָמִים הָיָה מַחֲלִיף מֵעֲבוֹדַת פְּנִים לַעֲבוֹדַת חוּץ וּמִחוּץ לִפְנִים, וּמְשַׁנֶּה מִבִּגְדֵי זָהָב לְבִגְדֵי לָבָן וּמִבִּגְדֵי לָבָן לְבִגְדֵי זָהָב, וּבְכָל חֲלִיפָה טָעוּן טְבִילָה וּשְׁנֵי קִדּוּשֵׁי יָדַיִם וְרַגְלַיִם מִן הַכִּיּוֹר:

ו **אֶת פַּר הַחַטָּאת אֲשֶׁר לוֹ.** הָאָמוּר לְמַעְלָה (פסוק ג), וּלְמֶדְךָ כָּאן שֶׁמִּשֶּׁלּוֹ הוּא בָּא וְלֹא מִשֶּׁל צִבּוּר: **וְכִפֶּר בַּעֲדוֹ וּבְעַד בֵּיתוֹ.** מִתְוַדֶּה עָלָיו עֲוֹנוֹתָיו וַעֲוֹנוֹת בֵּיתוֹ:

ח **וְנָתַן אַהֲרֹן עַל שְׁנֵי הַשְּׂעִירִם גֹּרָלוֹת.** מַעֲמִיד אֶחָד לְיָמִין וְאֶחָד לִשְׂמֹאל, וְנוֹתֵן שְׁתֵּי יָדָיו בַּקַּלְפִּי, וְנוֹטֵל גּוֹרָל בְּיָמִין וַחֲבֵרוֹ בִּשְׂמֹאל וְנוֹתֵן עֲלֵיהֶם, אֶת שֶׁכָּתוּב בּוֹ לַשֵּׁם הוּא לַשֵּׁם, וְאֶת שֶׁכָּתוּב בּוֹ לַעֲזָאזֵל מִשְׁתַּלֵּחַ לַעֲזָאזֵל: **עֲזָאזֵל.** הוּא הַר עַז וְקָשֶׁה, צוּק גָּבוֹהַּ, שֶׁנֶּאֱמַר: "אֶרֶץ גְּזֵרָה" (להלן פסוק כב), חֲתוּכָה:

Who are you? That is the question Yom Kippur forces us to ask ourselves, as Yitzḥak asked Yaakov (27:18). To be Yaakov, we have to release and relinquish the Esav within us, the impulsiveness that can lead us to sell our birthright for a bowl of soup, to lose eternity in the pursuit of desire.

16:6 **פַּר הַחַטָּאת אֲשֶׁר־לוֹ** *His purification* – The bull is designated as a purification offering for the High Priest himself. Rashi learns from the words "his purification" that the bull must be purchased with his own money. This is in contrast to the two goats, which atone for the whole Jewish people and are bought with public funds. The High Priest is required to confess his sins and those of his family. This is the first of three acts of atonement by the High Priest on this day: first for himself and his family, then for the priesthood as a whole (v. 11), and only then for the whole nation (v. 21). The message is clear: we must purify ourselves before we can purify others.

16:8 **לַעֲזָאזֵל** *For Azazel* – What is the meaning of "Azazel," to which the second goat was sent? It appears nowhere else in Scripture. Three major theories emerged as to its meaning. According to the Sages and Rashi, it means "a steep, rocky, or hard place." In other words, the word is a description of its destination.

The second, suggested by Ibn Ezra and Ramban (see note on 17:7), is that Azazel represented a realm of spirits, demons, or fallen angels. In this sense it is like the word "Gehinnom," often understood as "hell," though in fact it was merely a valley outside of Jerusalem. The craggy, angular desert, hostile to human habitation, was a symbol of chaos and danger.

The third interpretation is that the word simply means "the goat [*ez*] that was sent away [*azal*]." This led to the addition of a new word to the English language. In 1530, William Tyndale produced the first printed English translation of the Hebrew Bible, an act then illegal and for which he paid with his life. Seeking to translate "Azazel" into English, he called it "the escapegoat," i.e., the goat that was sent away and released. In the course of time, the first letter was dropped, and the word "scapegoat" was born.

"Scapegoating," as we use the word today, means blaming someone else for our troubles. Faced with problems that it cannot solve, all too often a group ensures its psychic survival by projecting its inner conflicts onto an external

בַּד יִהְי֣וּ עַל־בְּשָׂר֗וֹ וּבְאַבְנֵ֥ט בַּד֙ יַחְגֹּ֔ר וּבְמִצְנֶ֥פֶת בַּ֖ד יִצְנֹ֑ף בִּגְדֵי־קֹ֣דֶשׁ
ה הֵ֔ם וְרָחַ֥ץ בַּמַּ֛יִם אֶת־בְּשָׂר֖וֹ וּלְבֵשָֽׁם׃ וּמֵאֵ֗ת עֲדַת֙ בְּנֵ֣י יִשְׂרָאֵ֔ל יִקַּ֛ח
ו שְׁנֵֽי־שְׂעִירֵ֥י עִזִּ֖ים לְחַטָּ֑את וְאַ֥יִל אֶחָ֖ד לְעֹלָֽה׃ וְהִקְרִ֧יב אַהֲרֹ֛ן אֶת־פַּ֥ר
ז הַֽחַטָּ֖את אֲשֶׁר־ל֑וֹ וְכִפֶּ֥ר בַּֽעֲד֖וֹ וּבְעַ֥ד בֵּיתֽוֹ׃ וְלָקַ֖ח אֶת־שְׁנֵ֣י הַשְּׂעִירִ֑ם
ח וְהֶֽעֱמִ֤יד אֹתָם֙ לִפְנֵ֣י יְהֹוָ֔ה פֶּ֖תַח אֹ֥הֶל מוֹעֵֽד׃ וְנָתַ֧ן אַהֲרֹ֛ן עַל־שְׁנֵ֥י

אונקלוס

דְּבוּץ יְהוֹן עַל בִּסְרֵיהּ, וְהֶמְיָנָא דִּבוּצָא יֵיסַר, וּמַצְנַפְתָּא דִּבוּצָא יַחֵית בְּרֵישֵׁיהּ, לְבוּשֵׁי קֻדְשָׁא אִנּוּן, וְיַסְחֵי בְּמַיָּא, יָת בִּסְרֵיהּ וְיִלְבְּשִׁנּוּן:
ה וּמִן כְּנִשְׁתָּא דִּבְנֵי יִשְׂרָאֵל, יִסַּב, תְּרֵין צְפִירֵי עִזֵּי לְחַטָּתָא, וּדְכַר חַד לַעֲלָתָא:
ו וִיקָרֵיב אַהֲרֹן, יָת תּוֹרָא דְּחַטָּתָא דִּילֵיהּ, וִיכַפַּר עֲלוֹהִי וְעַל אֱנָשׁ בֵּיתֵיהּ:
ז וְיִסַּב יָת תְּרֵין צְפִירִין, וִיקִים יָתְהוֹן קֳדָם יְיָ, בִּתְרַע מַשְׁכַּן זִמְנָא:
ח וְיִתֵּין אַהֲרֹן, עַל תְּרֵין צְפִירִין עַדְבִין, עַדְבָא חַד לִשְׁמָא דַיְיָ, וְעַדְבָא חַד לַעֲזָאזֵל:
ט וִיקָרֵיב אַהֲרֹן יָת צְפִירָא, דִּסְלֵיק עֲלוֹהִי, עַדְבָא לִשְׁמָא דַיְיָ, וְיַעְבְּדִנֵּיהּ

THE RITUAL OF THE TWO GOATS

Central to the Yom Kippur ritual, prescribed in the Torah and expounded in the Mishna, are two goats. They are, for all intents and purposes, indistinguishable from one another; they are chosen to be as similar as possible in size and appearance. They are brought before the High Priest and lots are drawn, one bearing the words "For the LORD," the other, "For Azazel." The first is offered as a sacrifice. Over the second, the High Priest confesses the sins of the nation, and it is then taken away into the desert hills where it plunges to its death. Tradition tells us that a red thread would be attached to its horns, half of which was removed before the animal was sent away. If the rite had been effective, the red thread would turn to white.

Two animals, alike in appearance but different in fate, suggest the idea of twins. This and other clues led classic commentators such as Ramban and Abrabanel to the conclusion that the goats symbolized the most famous of the Torah's twins, Yaakov and Esav. The word *se'ir*, "goat," is associated in the Torah with Esav. He and his descendants lived in the land of Se'ir, while he himself was *sa'ir*, "hairy" (Gen. 27:11). The red thread that is tied to the scapegoat in the Mishna's account recalls Edom – from *adom*, "red" – Esav's other name. The "two male goats" of the High Priest's rites remind us of the "two choice young goats" (27:9) served to Yitzḥak in the scene of Yaakov's deception.

The two goats of the High Priest's service, then, evoke the figures of Yaakov and Esav. What do those brothers represent in the context of Yom Kippur? Midrashic tradition tends to portray Esav as an evildoer. The Torah itself is more nuanced. Esav is not a figure of evil. His father loved him and sought to bless him. Rather, he is the man of impulse (see Gen. 25:34 and the note there; see also the note on Gen. 36:31). Yaakov is the opposite. He acts and thinks long-term. That is what he does when he seizes the opportunity to buy Esav's birthright, when he works for seven years for Raḥel, a period that "seemed to him but a few days" (29:20), and when he fixes terms with Lavan for payment for his labor. Rebuking his son Yosef for the seeming presumptuousness of his dreams, the Torah tells us that the brothers were jealous of Yosef "but his father kept the matter in mind" (37:11). Yaakov never acts impulsively. He thinks long and hard.

The two goats of the High Priest's service symbolize a duality within each of us: "The voice is the voice of Yaakov, but the hands are the hands of Esav" (27:22). The power of ritual is that it does not speak in abstractions. It is gripping, visceral. We each have an inner Esav and Yaakov, the impulsive, emotional brain and the reflective, deliberative one. Our fate, our life script, will be determined by which we choose. Will our life be lived "for the LORD," or rather "for Azazel," left to the random vicissitudes of chance?

9 lot marked 'For the LORD,' the other 'For Azazel.' The goat on which the lot for
the LORD fell, Aharon should bring close and offer up as a purification offering.
10 But the goat on which the lot fell for Azazel shall be presented alive before
the LORD; atonement shall be made over it; it shall be sent forth, away into
11 the wilderness to Azazel. Aharon shall bring close the bull for his purification
offering to make atonement for him and for his family; he shall slaughter the
12 bull as his purification offering. He shall then take a pan full of burning coals
from the altar, from before the LORD, and two handfuls of finely ground fragrant
13 incense, and bring them inside the inner curtain. He shall place the incense on
the fire before the LORD so that the cloud of incense conceals the cover on top
14 of the Ark of the Testimony, so that he does not die. He shall take some of the
bull's blood and sprinkle it with his finger on the cover on the east side. Then,
in front of the cover, he shall sprinkle some of the blood with his finger seven
15 times. He shall then slaughter the goat for the people's purification offering,
bring its blood inside the inner curtain, and do with it as he did with the blood
16 of the bull, sprinkling it on the cover and before the cover. In this way, he shall
make atonement for the Sanctuary – from the impurity of the Israelites, from
their rebellions and all their sins. And he shall do the same for the Tent of

רש"י

ט **וְעָשָׂהוּ חַטָּאת.** כְּשֶׁמַּנִּיחַ הַגּוֹרָל עָלָיו קוֹרֵא לוֹ שֵׁם וְאוֹמֵר: 'לַה' חַטָּאת':

י **יָעֳמַד חַי.** כְּמוֹ 'יָעֳמַד חַי', עַל יְדֵי אֲחֵרִים, וְתַרְגּוּמוֹ: "יִתָּקַם כַּד חַי". מַה תַּלְמוּד לוֹמַר? לְפִי שֶׁנֶּאֱמַר: "לְשַׁלַּח אֹתוֹ לַעֲזָאזֵל", וְאֵינִי יוֹדֵעַ שִׁלּוּחוֹ אִם לְמִיתָה אִם לְחַיִּים, לְכָךְ נֶאֱמַר: "יָעֳמַד חַי", עֲמִידָתוֹ חַי עַד שֶׁיִּשְׁתַּלַּח, מִכָּאן שֶׁשִּׁלּוּחוֹ לְמִיתָה: **לְכַפֵּר עָלָיו.** שֶׁיִּתְוַדֶּה עָלָיו, כִּדְכְתִיב: "וְהִתְוַדָּה עָלָיו" וְגוֹ' (להלן פסוק כא):

יא **וְכִפֶּר בַּעֲדוֹ וְגוֹ'.** וִדּוּי שֵׁנִי, עָלָיו וְעַל אֶחָיו הַכֹּהֲנִים, שֶׁהֵם כֻּלָּם קְרוּיִים 'בֵּיתוֹ', שֶׁנֶּאֱמַר: "בֵּית אַהֲרֹן בָּרְכוּ אֶת ה'" וְגוֹ' (תהלים קלה, יט), מִכָּאן שֶׁהַכֹּהֲנִים מִתְכַּפְּרִים בּוֹ. וְכָל כַּפָּרָתָן אֵינָהּ אֶלָּא עַל טֻמְאַת מִקְדָּשׁ וְקָדָשָׁיו, כְּמוֹ שֶׁנֶּאֱמַר: "וְכִפֶּר עַל הַקֹּדֶשׁ מִטֻּמְאֹת" וְגוֹ' (להלן פסוק טז):

יב **מֵעַל הַמִּזְבֵּחַ.** הַחִיצוֹן: **מִלִּפְנֵי ה'.** מִצַּד שֶׁלִּפְנֵי הַפֶּתַח, וְהוּא צַד מַעֲרָבִי: **דַּקָּה.** מַה תַּלְמוּד לוֹמַר "דַּקָּה"? וַהֲלֹא כָּל הַקְּטֹרֶת דַּקָּה הִיא, שֶׁנֶּאֱמַר: "וְשָׁחַקְתָּ מִמֶּנָּה הָדֵק" (שמות ל, לו)! אֶלָּא שֶׁתְּהֵא דַּקָּה מִן הַדַּקָּה, שֶׁבְּעֶרֶב יוֹם הַכִּפּוּרִים הָיָה מַחֲזִירָהּ לַמַּכְתֶּשֶׁת:

יג **עַל הָאֵשׁ.** שֶׁבְּתוֹךְ הַמַּחְתָּה: **וְלֹא יָמוּת.** הָא אִם לֹא עֲשָׂאָהּ כְּתִקְנָהּ חַיָּב מִיתָה:

יד **וְהִזָּה בְאֶצְבָּעוֹ.** הַזָּאָה אַחַת בְּמַשְׁמָע: **וְלִפְנֵי הַכַּפֹּרֶת יַזֶּה שֶׁבַע.** הֲרֵי אַחַת לְמַעְלָה וְשֶׁבַע לְמַטָּה:

טו **אֲשֶׁר לָעָם.** מַה שֶּׁהַפָּר מְכַפֵּר עַל הַכֹּהֲנִים, מְכַפֵּר הַשָּׂעִיר עַל יִשְׂרָאֵל, וְהוּא הַשָּׂעִיר שֶׁעָלָה עָלָיו הַגּוֹרָל לַשֵּׁם: **כַּאֲשֶׁר עָשָׂה לְדַם הַפָּר.** אַחַת לְמַעְלָה וְשֶׁבַע לְמַטָּה:

טז **מִטֻּמְאֹת בְּנֵי יִשְׂרָאֵל.** עַל הַנִּכְנָסִין לַמִּקְדָּשׁ בְּטֻמְאָה וְלֹא נוֹדַע

an animal, not a person; and (2) that the goat is dedicated by confession (v. 21). This is not an occasion for denying responsibility by blaming the victim, but to the contrary, an acceptance of responsibility in the context of repentance and atonement.

ט הַשְּׂעִירִם גֹּרָלוֹת גּוֹרָל אֶחָד לַיהוָה וְגוֹרָל אֶחָד לַעֲזָאזֵל: וְהִקְרִיב
אַהֲרֹן אֶת־הַשָּׂעִיר אֲשֶׁר עָלָה עָלָיו הַגּוֹרָל לַיהוָה וְעָשָׂהוּ חַטָּאת:
י וְהַשָּׂעִיר אֲשֶׁר עָלָה עָלָיו הַגּוֹרָל לַעֲזָאזֵל יָעֳמַד־חַי לִפְנֵי יְהוָה לְכַפֵּר
יא עָלָיו לְשַׁלַּח אֹתוֹ לַעֲזָאזֵל הַמִּדְבָּרָה: וְהִקְרִיב אַהֲרֹן אֶת־פַּר הַחַטָּאת
אֲשֶׁר־לוֹ וְכִפֶּר בַּעֲדוֹ וּבְעַד בֵּיתוֹ וְשָׁחַט אֶת־פַּר הַחַטָּאת אֲשֶׁר־לוֹ:
יב וְלָקַח מְלֹא־הַמַּחְתָּה גַּחֲלֵי־אֵשׁ מֵעַל הַמִּזְבֵּחַ מִלִּפְנֵי יְהוָה וּמְלֹא חָפְנָיו
יג קְטֹרֶת סַמִּים דַּקָּה וְהֵבִיא מִבֵּית לַפָּרֹכֶת: וְנָתַן אֶת־הַקְּטֹרֶת עַל־
הָאֵשׁ לִפְנֵי יְהוָה וְכִסָּה ׀ עֲנַן הַקְּטֹרֶת אֶת־הַכַּפֹּרֶת אֲשֶׁר עַל־הָעֵדוּת
יד וְלֹא יָמוּת: וְלָקַח מִדַּם הַפָּר וְהִזָּה בְאֶצְבָּעוֹ עַל־פְּנֵי הַכַּפֹּרֶת קֵדְמָה
טו וְלִפְנֵי הַכַּפֹּרֶת יַזֶּה שֶׁבַע־פְּעָמִים מִן־הַדָּם בְּאֶצְבָּעוֹ: וְשָׁחַט אֶת־שְׂעִיר
הַחַטָּאת אֲשֶׁר לָעָם וְהֵבִיא אֶת־דָּמוֹ אֶל־מִבֵּית לַפָּרֹכֶת וְעָשָׂה אֶת־
דָּמוֹ כַּאֲשֶׁר עָשָׂה לְדַם הַפָּר וְהִזָּה אֹתוֹ עַל־הַכַּפֹּרֶת וְלִפְנֵי הַכַּפֹּרֶת:
טז וְכִפֶּר עַל־הַקֹּדֶשׁ מִטֻּמְאֹת בְּנֵי יִשְׂרָאֵל וּמִפִּשְׁעֵיהֶם לְכָל־חַטֹּאתָם וְכֵן

אונקלוס

חַטָּתָא: י וּצְפִירָא, דִּסְלֵיק עֲלוֹהִי עַדְבָא לַעֲזָאזֵל, יִתָּקַם כַּד חַי, קֳדָם יי לְכַפָּרָא עֲלוֹהִי, לְשַׁלָּחָא יָתֵיהּ, לַעֲזָאזֵל לְמַדְבְּרָא: יא וִיקָרֵיב אַהֲרֹן, יָת תּוֹרָא דְּחַטָּתָא דִּילֵיהּ, וִיכַפַּר עֲלוֹהִי וְעַל אֱנָשׁ בֵּיתֵיהּ, וְיִכּוֹס, יָת תּוֹרָא דְּחַטָּתָא דִּילֵיהּ: יב וְיִסַּב מְלֵי מַחְתִּיתָא, גֻּמְרִין דְּאִישָׁא, מֵעִלָּוֵי מַדְבְּחָא מִן קֳדָם יי, וּמְלֵי חָפְנוֹהִי, קְטֹרֶת בֻּסְמִין דַּקִּיקִין, וְיָעֵיל מִגָּיו לְפָרֻכְתָּא: יג וְיִתֵּין יָת קְטֹרֶת בֻּסְמַיָּא, עַל אִישָׁתָא קֳדָם יי, וִיחַפֵּי עֲנַן קְטָרְתָּא, יָת כָּפֻרְתָּא, דְּעַל סָהֲדוּתָא וְלָא יְמוּת: יד וְיִסַּב מִדְּמָא דְּתוֹרָא, וְיַדֵּי בְּאֶצְבְּעֵיהּ, עַל אַפֵּי כָּפֻרְתָּא קִדּוּמָא, וְלִקְדָם כָּפֻרְתָּא, יַדֵּי שְׁבַע זִמְנִין, מִן דְּמָא בְּאֶצְבְּעֵיהּ: טו וְיִכּוֹס, יָת צְפִירָא דְּחַטָּתָא דִּלְעַמָּא, וְיָעֵיל יָת דְּמֵיהּ, לְמִגָּיו לְפָרֻכְתָּא, וְיַעֲבֵיד לִדְמֵיהּ, כְּמָא דַּעֲבַד לִדְמָא דְּתוֹרָא, וְיַדֵּי יָתֵיהּ, עַל כָּפֻרְתָּא וְלִקְדָם כָּפֻרְתָּא: טז וִיכַפַּר עַל קֻדְשָׁא, מִסּוֹאֲבַת בְּנֵי יִשְׂרָאֵל, וּמִמְּרָדֵיהוֹן לְכָל חַטָּאֵיהוֹן, וְכֵן

cause, held to be responsible for the plight of the community. As the French scholar René Girard described the phenomenon:

> The persecutors convince themselves that a small number of people, or even a single individual, despite his relative weakness is extremely harmful to the whole of society.... He will be responsible for the cure, since he was responsible for the sickness.

Hence the demonization that has time and again led to pogroms, massacres, and genocides. Societies find it easier to blame a scapegoat than to face their own problems honestly and openly.

Projecting violence within the group onto an innocent outsider who is held guilty and killed to preserve the group is a vicious idea. The biblical scapegoat is precisely not a scapegoat in Girard's sense. Two features of the High Priest's ritual were crucial in this respect: (1) that the sacrifice was

17 Meeting, which is with them in the midst of their impurity. No one shall be
in the Tent of Meeting from the time Aharon enters to make atonement in the
Sanctuary until he comes out. Thus he shall make atonement for himself, for
18 his house, and for the whole assembly of Israel. He shall then go out to the altar SHENI
that is before the LORD and make its atonement. He shall take some of the bull's
19 blood and some of the goat's blood and apply it to each of the altar's horns. He
shall sprinkle some of the blood upon it with his finger seven times, to purify
20 it and sanctify it from the impurity of the Israelites. When he has finished
making atonement for the Sanctuary, the Tent of Meeting, and the altar, he
21 shall bring close the live goat. Aharon shall lay both his hands on the head of
the live goat and confess over it all the Israelites' iniquities and rebellions, all of
their sins, putting them on the head of the goat and then sending it away into
22 the wilderness with the person designated for the task. The goat shall carry all
their iniquities upon itself to a desolate place, and then the goat shall be sent

רש״י

לָהֶם כַּסּוֹף, שֶׁנֶּאֱמַר: ״לְכָל חַטֹּאתָם״, וְחַטָּאת הִיא שׁוֹגֵג: **וּמִפִּשְׁעֵיהֶם.** אַף הַנִּכְנָסִין מֵזִיד בְּטֻמְאָה: **וְכֵן יַעֲשֶׂה לְאֹהֶל מוֹעֵד.** כְּשֵׁם שֶׁהִזָּה מִשְּׁנֵיהֶם בִּפְנִים אַחַת לְמַעְלָה וְשֶׁבַע לְמַטָּה, כָּךְ מַזֶּה עַל הַפָּרֹכֶת מִבַּחוּץ מִשְּׁנֵיהֶם אַחַת לְמַעְלָה וְשֶׁבַע לְמַטָּה: **הַשֹּׁכֵן אִתָּם בְּתוֹךְ טֻמְאֹתָם.** אַף עַל פִּי שֶׁהֵם טְמֵאִים, שְׁכִינָה בֵּינֵיהֶם:

יח **אֶל הַמִּזְבֵּחַ אֲשֶׁר לִפְנֵי ה׳.** זֶה מִזְבַּח הַזָּהָב שֶׁהוּא לִפְנֵי ה׳ בַּהֵיכָל. וּמַה תַּלְמוּד לוֹמַר ״וְיָצָא״? לְפִי שֶׁהִזָּה הַהַזָּאוֹת עַל הַפָּרֹכֶת וְעָמַד מִן הַמִּזְבֵּחַ וְלִפְנִים וְהִזָּה, וּבְמַתְּנוֹת הַמִּזְבֵּחַ הִזְקִיקוֹ לָצֵאת מִן הַמִּזְבֵּחַ וְלַחוּץ וְיַתְחִיל מִקֶּרֶן מִזְרָחִית צְפוֹנִית: **וְכִפֶּר עָלָיו.** וּמַה הִיא כַּפָּרָתוֹ? ״וְלָקַח מִדַּם הַפָּר וּמִדַּם הַשָּׂעִיר״ – מְעֹרָבִין זֶה לְתוֹךְ זֶה:

יט **וְהִזָּה עָלָיו מִן הַדָּם.** אַחַר שֶׁנָּתַן מַתָּנוֹת בְּאֶצְבָּעוֹ עַל קַרְנוֹתָיו, מַזֶּה שֶׁבַע הַזָּאוֹת עַל גַּגּוֹ: **וְטִהֲרוֹ.** מִמַּה שֶּׁעָבַר: **וְקִדְּשׁוֹ.** לֶעָתִיד לָבֹא:

כא **אִישׁ עִתִּי.** הַמּוּכָן לְכָךְ מִיּוֹם אֶתְמוֹל:

First there is *kappara*, atonement. Second, there is *tahara*, purification, something normally done in a different context altogether, namely the removal of *tuma*, ritual defilement, which could arise from a number of different causes, among them contact with a dead body, skin disease, or nocturnal discharge. Atonement has to do with guilt. Purification has to do with contamination or pollution. These are usually two separate worlds. The difference between guilt cultures and shame cultures is something we have discussed elsewhere (see note on Lev. 5:26). Guilt attaches to the act, not the person. Guilt can be "atoned for" by remorse and restitution, by achieving forgiveness. Shame cannot be removed by forgiveness. We still feel the stigma, the degradation. We feel defiled by the knowledge of our disgrace.

On Yom Kippur, the one day in the year when everyone shares in the process of confession, repentance, atonement, and purification, they are brought together. Yom Kippur confronts our sins as a community bound by mutual responsibility. It deals, in other words, with the social as well as the personal dimension of wrongdoing. Yom Kippur is about shame as well as guilt.

That is why an immensely powerful and dramatic ceremony has to take place during which people can feel and symbolically see their sins carried away to the desert, to no-man's-land. Judaism is a guilt culture, a culture of hope. Nonetheless, it acknowledges the existence of shame. When a whole society confesses its guilt together, individuals can be redeemed from shame.

יז יַעֲשֶׂה לְאֹהֶל מוֹעֵד הַשֹּׁכֵן אִתָּם בְּתוֹךְ טֻמְאֹתָם: וְכׇל־אָדָם לֹא־יִהְיֶה ׀
בְּאֹהֶל מוֹעֵד בְּבֹאוֹ לְכַפֵּר בַּקֹּדֶשׁ עַד־צֵאתוֹ וְכִפֶּר בַּעֲדוֹ וּבְעַד בֵּיתוֹ
יח וּבְעַד כׇּל־קְהַל יִשְׂרָאֵל: וְיָצָא אֶל־הַמִּזְבֵּחַ אֲשֶׁר לִפְנֵי־יְהֹוָה וְכִפֶּר שני
עָלָיו וְלָקַח מִדַּם הַפָּר וּמִדַּם הַשָּׂעִיר וְנָתַן עַל־קַרְנוֹת הַמִּזְבֵּחַ סָבִיב:
יט וְהִזָּה עָלָיו מִן־הַדָּם בְּאֶצְבָּעוֹ שֶׁבַע פְּעָמִים וְטִהֲרוֹ וְקִדְּשׁוֹ מִטֻּמְאֹת
כ בְּנֵי יִשְׂרָאֵל: וְכִלָּה מִכַּפֵּר אֶת־הַקֹּדֶשׁ וְאֶת־אֹהֶל מוֹעֵד וְאֶת־הַמִּזְבֵּחַ
כא וְהִקְרִיב אֶת־הַשָּׂעִיר הֶחָי: וְסָמַךְ אַהֲרֹן אֶת־שְׁתֵּי יָדָו עַל־רֹאשׁ הַשָּׂעִיר
הַחַי וְהִתְוַדָּה עָלָיו אֶת־כׇּל־עֲוֺנֹת בְּנֵי יִשְׂרָאֵל וְאֶת־כׇּל־פִּשְׁעֵיהֶם
לְכׇל־חַטֹּאתָם וְנָתַן אֹתָם עַל־רֹאשׁ הַשָּׂעִיר וְשִׁלַּח בְּיַד־אִישׁ עִתִּי
כב הַמִּדְבָּרָה: וְנָשָׂא הַשָּׂעִיר עָלָיו אֶת־כׇּל־עֲוֺנֹתָם אֶל־אֶרֶץ גְּזֵרָה וְשִׁלַּח

אונקלוס

יַעֲבֵיד לְמַשְׁכַּן זִמְנָא, דְּשָׁרֵי עִמְּהוֹן, בְּגוֹ סוֹאֲבָתְהוֹן: יז וְכָל אֱנָשׁ, לָא יְהֵי בְּמַשְׁכַּן זִמְנָא, בְּמֵיעֲלֵיהּ, לְכַפָּרָא בְּקֻדְשָׁא עַד מִפְּקֵיהּ, וִיכַפַּר עֲלוֹהִי וְעַל אֱנָשׁ בֵּיתֵיהּ, וְעַל כָּל קְהָלָא דְּיִשְׂרָאֵל: יח וְיִפּוֹק, לְמַדְבְּחָא, דִּקְדָם יי וִיכַפַּר עֲלוֹהִי, וְיִסַּב, מִדְּמָא דְּתוֹרָא וּמִדְּמָא דִּצְפִירָא, וְיִתֵּין, עַל קַרְנָת מַדְבְּחָא סְחוֹר סְחוֹר: יט וְיַדֵּי עֲלוֹהִי מִן דְּמָא, בְּאֶצְבְּעֵיהּ שְׁבַע זִמְנִין, וִידַכֵּינֵיהּ וִיקַדְּשִׁנֵּיהּ, מִסּוֹאֲבָת בְּנֵי יִשְׂרָאֵל: כ וִישֵׁיצֵי מִלְּכַפָּרָא עַל קֻדְשָׁא, וְעַל מַשְׁכַּן זִמְנָא וְעַל מַדְבְּחָא, וִיקָרֵיב יָת צְפִירָא חַיָּא: כא וְיִסְמוֹךְ אַהֲרֹן יָת תַּרְתֵּין יְדוֹהִי, עַל רֵישׁ צְפִירָא חַיָּא, וִיוַדֵּי עֲלוֹהִי, יָת כָּל עֲוָיָת בְּנֵי יִשְׂרָאֵל, וְיָת כָּל מָרְדֵיהוֹן לְכָל חֲטָאֵיהוֹן, וְיִתֵּין יָתְהוֹן עַל רֵישׁ צְפִירָא, וִישַׁלַּח, בְּיַד גְּבַר דִּזְמִין לִמְהָךְ לְמַדְבְּרָא: כב וְיִטּוֹל צְפִירָא עֲלוֹהִי, יָת כָּל עֲוָיָתְהוֹן לַאֲרַע דְּלָא יָתְבָא, וִישַׁלַּח יָת צְפִירָא בְּמַדְבְּרָא: כג וְיֵיעוֹל אַהֲרֹן לְמַשְׁכַּן זִמְנָא,

16:21 אֶת־כׇּל־עֲוֺנֹת בְּנֵי יִשְׂרָאֵל *All of their sins* – Purification and guilt offerings are familiar features of the Torah and a normal part of the service of the Tabernacle. The service of Yom Kippur is different, however, in one salient respect. In every other case, the sin is confessed over the animal that is sacrificed. On Yom Kippur, the High Priest confesses the sins of the people over the animal that is not sacrificed, the scapegoat that is sent away, "carry[ing] all their iniquities upon itself" (v. 22). Rambam explains as follows:

> There is no doubt that sins cannot be carried like a burden and taken off the shoulder of one being to be laid on that of another being. But these ceremonies are of a symbolic character, and serve to impress people with a certain idea, and to induce them to repent – as if to say: we have freed ourselves of our previous deeds, cast them behind our backs, and removed them from us as far as possible. (*Guide for the Perplexed* III:46)

Expiation demands a ritual, some dramatic representation of the removal of sin and the wiping clean of the past. Why the unique ritual here? The answer is that two distinct processes are involved in Yom Kippur: "On this day, atonement shall be made for you [*yekhaper*] to purify you [*letaher*]; of all your sins you shall be purified before the Lord" (v. 30).

23 forth into the wilderness. Then Aharon shall enter the Tent of Meeting, take off
the linen vestments he was wearing when he entered the Sanctuary, and leave
24 them there. He shall immerse his body in water in a holy place and put on his
vestments. Then he shall come out and offer his burnt offering and the burnt
25 offering of the people, to make atonement for himself and for the people. And he SHELISHI /SHENI/
26 shall send the fat of the purification offering up in smoke upon the altar. The man
who sent forth the goat for Azazel shall wash his clothes and immerse his body
27 in water; after that he may return to the camp. The purification offering bull and
the purification offering goat, whose blood was brought in to make atonement
in the inner Sanctuary, shall be removed from the camp. Their skin, flesh, and
28 dung shall be burned with fire. The one who burns them shall wash his clothes
29 and immerse his body in water. After that, he too may return to the camp. This
shall be an everlasting statute for you: on the tenth day of the seventh month,
you must afflict yourselves. You shall perform no work at all – neither the native

רש״י

כג **וּבָא אַהֲרֹן אֶל אֹהֶל מוֹעֵד.** אָמְרוּ רַבּוֹתֵינוּ שֶׁאֵין זֶה מְקוֹמוֹ שֶׁל מִקְרָא זֶה, וְנָתְנוּ טַעַם לְדִבְרֵיהֶם בְּמַסֶּכֶת יוֹמָא (דף לב ע״א) וְאָמְרוּ, כָּל הַפָּרָשָׁה כֻּלָּהּ נֶאֶמְרָה עַל הַסֵּדֶר חוּץ מִבִּיאָה זוֹ, שֶׁהִיא אַחַר עֲשִׂיַּת עוֹלָתוֹ וְעוֹלַת הָעָם וְהַקְטָרַת אֵמוּרֵי פַּר וְשָׂעִיר שֶׁנַּעֲשִׂים בַּחוּץ בְּבִגְדֵי זָהָב, וְטוֹבֵל וּמְקַדֵּשׁ וּפוֹשְׁטָן וְלוֹבֵשׁ בִּגְדֵי לָבָן, וּבָא אֶל אֹהֶל מוֹעֵד לְהוֹצִיא אֶת הַכַּף וְאֶת הַמַּחְתָּה שֶׁהִקְטִיר בָּהּ הַקְּטֹרֶת לִפְנַי וְלִפְנִים: **וּפָשַׁט אֶת בִּגְדֵי הַבָּד.** אַחַר שֶׁהוֹצִיאָם, וְלוֹבֵשׁ בִּגְדֵי זָהָב לְתָמִיד שֶׁל בֵּין הָעַרְבַּיִם. וְזֶהוּ סֵדֶר הָעֲבוֹדוֹת: תָּמִיד שֶׁל שַׁחַר בְּבִגְדֵי זָהָב, וַעֲבוֹדַת פַּר וְשָׂעִיר הַפְּנִימִיִּים וּקְטֹרֶת שֶׁל מַחְתָּה בְּבִגְדֵי לָבָן, וְאֵילוֹ וְאֵיל הָעָם וּמִקְצָת הַמּוּסָפִין בְּבִגְדֵי זָהָב, וְהוֹצָאַת כַּף וּמַחְתָּה בְּבִגְדֵי לָבָן, וּשְׁיָרֵי הַמּוּסָפִין וְתָמִיד שֶׁל בֵּין הָעַרְבַּיִם וּקְטֹרֶת הַהֵיכָל שֶׁעַל מִזְבַּח הַפְּנִימִי בְּבִגְדֵי זָהָב. וְסֵדֶר הַמִּקְרָאוֹת לְפִי סֵדֶר הָעֲבוֹדוֹת כָּךְ הוּא: ״וְשִׁלַּח אֶת הַשָּׂעִיר בַּמִּדְבָּר״ (לעיל פסוק כב), ״וְרָחַץ אֶת בְּשָׂרוֹ בַמַּיִם וְגוֹ׳, וְיָצָא וְעָשָׂה אֶת עֹלָתוֹ וְגוֹ׳, וְאֵת חֵלֶב הַחַטָּאת״ וְגוֹ׳, וְכָל הַפָּרָשָׁה עַד ״וְאַחֲרֵי כֵן יָבוֹא אֶל הַמַּחֲנֶה״ (להלן פסוקים כד-כח), וְאַחַר כָּךְ ״וּבָא אַהֲרֹן״ (פסוק כג): **וְהִנִּיחָם שָׁם.** מְלַמֵּד שֶׁטְּעוּנִין גְּנִיזָה, וְלֹא יִשְׁתַּמֵּשׁ בְּאוֹתָן אַרְבָּעָה בְּגָדִים לְיוֹם כִּפּוּרִים אַחֵר:

כד **וְרָחַץ אֶת בְּשָׂרוֹ וְגוֹ׳.** לְמַעְלָה לָמַדְנוּ מִ״וְּרָחַץ... אֶת בְּשָׂרוֹ וּלְבֵשָׁם״ (לעיל פסוק ד) שֶׁכְּשֶׁהוּא מְשַׁנֶּה מִבִּגְדֵי זָהָב לְבִגְדֵי לָבָן טָעוּן טְבִילָה, שֶׁבְּאוֹתָהּ טְבִילָה פָּשַׁט בִּגְדֵי זָהָב שֶׁעָבַד בָּהֶן עֲבוֹדַת תָּמִיד שֶׁל שַׁחַר וְלָבַשׁ בִּגְדֵי לָבָן לַעֲבוֹדַת הַיּוֹם, וְכָאן לָמַדְנוּ שֶׁכְּשֶׁהוּא מְשַׁנֶּה מִבִּגְדֵי לָבָן לְבִגְדֵי זָהָב טָעוּן טְבִילָה: **בְּמָקוֹם קָדוֹשׁ.** הַמְקֻדָּשׁ בִּקְדֻשַּׁת עֲזָרָה, וְהִיא הָיְתָה בְּגַג בֵּית הַפַּרְוָה, וְכֵן אַרְבַּע טְבִילוֹת הַבָּאוֹת חוֹבָה לַיּוֹם, אֲבָל הָרִאשׁוֹנָה הָיְתָה בַּחֹל: **וְלָבַשׁ אֶת בְּגָדָיו.** שְׁמוֹנָה בְּגָדִים שֶׁהוּא עוֹבֵד בָּהֶן כָּל יְמוֹת הַשָּׁנָה: **וְיָצָא.** מִן הַהֵיכָל אֶל הֶחָצֵר, שֶׁמִּזְבַּח הָעוֹלָה שָׁם: **וְעָשָׂה אֶת עֹלָתוֹ.** אַיִל לְעוֹלָה הָאָמוּר לְמַעְלָה, ״בְּזֹאת יָבֹא אַהֲרֹן״ וְגוֹ׳ (לעיל פסוק ג): **וְאֶת עֹלַת הָעָם.** ״וְאַיִל אֶחָד לְעֹלָה״ הָאָמוּר לְמַעְלָה: ״וּמֵאֵת עֲדַת בְּנֵי יִשְׂרָאֵל״ וְגוֹ׳ (לעיל פסוק ה):

כה **וְאֵת חֵלֶב הַחַטָּאת.** אֵמוּרֵי פַּר וְשָׂעִיר: **יַקְטִיר הַמִּזְבֵּחָה.** עַל מִזְבַּח הַחִיצוֹן, דְּאִלּוּ בַּפְּנִימִי כְּתִיב: ״לֹא תַעֲלוּ עָלָיו קְטֹרֶת זָרָה וְעֹלָה וּמִנְחָה״ (שמות ל, ט):

כו **אֲשֶׁר הוּבָא אֶת דָּמָם.** לַהֵיכָל וְלִפְנַי וְלִפְנִים:

to God? Great moments change history. But what changes us is the unspectacular habit of doing certain acts again and again until they reconfigure the brain and change our habits of the heart.

16:29 **תְּעַנּוּ אֶת־נַפְשֹׁתֵיכֶם** *You must afflict yourselves* – Although on Yom Kippur the High Priest atones for the sins of the nation, this does not mean that others are able to leave him to act vicariously on their behalf. They have to enter into the penitential spirit of the day through fasting and other afflictions. The ceremony as a whole is intended to create a national mood of repentance.

כג אֶת־הַשָּׂעִיר בַּמִּדְבָּר: וּבָא אַהֲרֹן אֶל־אֹהֶל מוֹעֵד וּפָשַׁט אֶת־בִּגְדֵי הַבָּד
כד אֲשֶׁר לָבַשׁ בְּבֹאוֹ אֶל־הַקֹּדֶשׁ וְהִנִּיחָם שָׁם: וְרָחַץ אֶת־בְּשָׂרוֹ בַמַּיִם
בְּמָקוֹם קָדוֹשׁ וְלָבַשׁ אֶת־בְּגָדָיו וְיָצָא וְעָשָׂה אֶת־עֹלָתוֹ וְאֶת־עֹלַת
כה הָעָם וְכִפֶּר בַּעֲדוֹ וּבְעַד הָעָם: וְאֵת חֵלֶב הַחַטָּאת יַקְטִיר הַמִּזְבֵּחָה: שלישי /שני/
כו וְהַמְשַׁלֵּחַ אֶת־הַשָּׂעִיר לַעֲזָאזֵל יְכַבֵּס בְּגָדָיו וְרָחַץ אֶת־בְּשָׂרוֹ בַּמָּיִם
כז וְאַחֲרֵי־כֵן יָבוֹא אֶל־הַמַּחֲנֶה: וְאֵת פַּר הַחַטָּאת וְאֵת ׀ שְׂעִיר הַחַטָּאת
אֲשֶׁר הוּבָא אֶת־דָּמָם לְכַפֵּר בַּקֹּדֶשׁ יוֹצִיא אֶל־מִחוּץ לַמַּחֲנֶה וְשָׂרְפוּ
כח בָאֵשׁ אֶת־עֹרֹתָם וְאֶת־בְּשָׂרָם וְאֶת־פִּרְשָׁם: וְהַשֹּׂרֵף אֹתָם יְכַבֵּס בְּגָדָיו
כט וְרָחַץ אֶת־בְּשָׂרוֹ בַּמָּיִם וְאַחֲרֵי־כֵן יָבוֹא אֶל־הַמַּחֲנֶה: וְהָיְתָה לָכֶם
לְחֻקַּת עוֹלָם בַּחֹדֶשׁ הַשְּׁבִיעִי בֶּעָשׂוֹר לַחֹדֶשׁ תְּעַנּוּ אֶת־נַפְשֹׁתֵיכֶם

אונקלוס

וִישַׁלַּח יָת לְבוּשֵׁי בוּצָא, דִּלְבַשׁ בְּמֵיעֲלֵיהּ לְקֻדְשָׁא, וְיַצְנְעִנּוּן תַּמָּן: כד וְיַסְחֵי יָת בִּסְרֵיהּ בְּמַיָּא בַּאֲתַר קַדִּישׁ, וְיִלְבַּשׁ יָת לְבוּשׁוֹהִי, וְיִפּוֹק, וְיַעְבֵּיד יָת עֲלָתֵיהּ וְיָת עֲלַת עַמָּא, וִיכַפַּר עֲלוֹהִי וְעַל עַמָּא: כה וְיָת, תַּרְבֵּי חַטָּתָא יַסֵּיק לְמַדְבְּחָא: כו וּדְמוֹבֵיל יָת צְפִירָא לַעֲזָאזֵל, יְצַבַּע לְבוּשׁוֹהִי, וְיַסְחֵי יָת בִּסְרֵיהּ בְּמַיָּא, וּבָתַר כֵּן יֵיעוֹל לְמַשְׁרִיתָא: כז וְיָת תּוֹרָא דְּחַטָּתָא, וְיָת צְפִירָא דְּחַטָּתָא, דְּאִתָּעַל מִדְּמְהוֹן לְכַפָּרָא בְּקֻדְשָׁא, יִתַּפְּקוּן לְמִבָּרָא לְמַשְׁרִיתָא, וְיוֹקְדוּן בְּנוּרָא, יָת מַשְׁכֵּהוֹן וְיָת בִּסְרְהוֹן וְיָת אֻכְלְהוֹן: כח וּדְמוֹקֵיד יָתְהוֹן, יְצַבַּע לְבוּשׁוֹהִי, וְיַסְחֵי יָת בִּסְרֵיהּ בְּמַיָּא, וּבָתַר כֵּן יֵיעוֹל לְמַשְׁרִיתָא: כט וּתְהֵי לְכוֹן לִקְיָם עָלַם, בְּיַרְחָא שְׁבִיעָאָה, בְּעַסְרָא לְיַרְחָא תְּעַנּוּן יָת נַפְשָׁתְכוֹן,

16:29 לְחֻקַּת עוֹלָם *An everlasting statute* – The move from the first Yom Kippur in the desert to the second was a great transition in Jewish spirituality. The first Yom Kippur was the culmination of Moshe's efforts to secure forgiveness for the people after the sin of the golden calf (Ex. 32–34). The process, which began on the seventeenth of Tammuz, ended on the tenth of Tishrei – the day that later became Yom Kippur. That was the day when Moshe descended the mountain with the second set of tablets, the visible sign that God had reaffirmed His covenant with the people. The second Yom Kippur, one year later, initiates the series of rites set out in this *parasha* (Lev. 16), conducted in the Tabernacle (*Mishkan*) by Aharon in his role as High Priest.

The differences between the two are immense. Moshe acted as a prophet. Aharon functions as a priest. Moshe's encounter was ad hoc, a unique, unrepeatable drama between heaven and earth. Aharon's is the opposite. The rules he follows never changed throughout the generations, so long as the Temple stood.

Moshe's prayers on behalf of the people were full of audacity, what the Sages called *ḥutzpa kelapei Shemaya,* "audacity toward Heaven," reaching a climax in the astonishing words "But now, if only You would forgive their sin – but if not, please blot me out of the book You have written" (Ex. 32:32). Aharon's behavior, by contrast, is marked by obedience, humility, and confession. There are purification rituals, sin offerings, and atonements, for his own sins and those of his "house" as well as those of the people.

Few moments in the Torah rival in intensity the dialogue between Moshe and God after the golden calf. But the question thereafter is: how will we achieve forgiveness in the future, without a Moshe, or prophets, or direct access

30 born nor the migrant living among you. On this day, atonement shall be made
31 for you to purify you; of all your sins you shall be purified before the LORD. It
shall be a Sabbath of complete rest for you, and on it you shall afflict yourselves.
32 This is an everlasting statute. The priest who is anointed and ordained to succeed
his father and serve as priest shall perform the atonement, wearing the sacred
33 linen vestments. He shall make atonement for the innermost Sanctuary, for the
Tent of Meeting, and for the altar. He shall make atonement for the priests and
34 for all the people of the community. This shall be an everlasting statute for you,
making atonement for the Israelites once a year for all their sins." And as the
LORD commanded Moshe, so it was done.
17 1 2 The LORD spoke to Moshe: "Speak to Aharon, his sons, and all the Israelites. REVI'I
3 Say: This is what the LORD has commanded: Any Israelite who slaughters an
4 ox, sheep, or goat inside or outside the camp without then bringing it to the
entrance of the Tent of Meeting to bring close an offering to the LORD before
the LORD's Tabernacle will be considered guilty of bloodshed. He has shed

רש״י

לב) **וְכִפֶּר הַכֹּהֵן אֲשֶׁר יִמְשַׁח וְגוֹ׳.** כַּפָּרָה זוֹ שֶׁל יוֹם הַכִּפּוּרִים אֵינָהּ כְּשֵׁרָה אֶלָּא בְּכֹהֵן גָּדוֹל, לְפִי שֶׁנֶּאֶמְרָה כָּל הַפָּרָשָׁה בְּאַהֲרֹן, הֻצְרַךְ לוֹמַר בְּכֹהֵן גָּדוֹל הַבָּא אַחֲרָיו שֶׁיְּהֵא כָּמוֹהוּ: **וַאֲשֶׁר יְמַלֵּא אֶת יָדוֹ.** אֵין לִי אֶלָּא הַמָּשׁוּחַ בְּשֶׁמֶן הַמִּשְׁחָה, מְרֻבֶּה בְּגָדִים מִנַּיִן? תַּלְמוּד לוֹמַר: "וַאֲשֶׁר יְמַלֵּא אֶת יָדוֹ" וְגוֹ׳, וְהֵם כָּל הַכֹּהֲנִים הַגְּדוֹלִים שֶׁעָמְדוּ מִיֹּאשִׁיָּהוּ וְאֵילָךְ, שֶׁבְּיָמָיו נִגְנְזָה צְלוֹחִית שֶׁל שֶׁמֶן הַמִּשְׁחָה: **לְכַהֵן תַּחַת אָבִיו.** לְלַמֵּד שֶׁאִם בְּנוֹ מְמַלֵּא אֶת מְקוֹמוֹ הוּא קוֹדֵם לְכָל אָדָם:

לד) **וַיַּעַשׂ כַּאֲשֶׁר צִוָּה ה׳ וְגוֹ׳.** כְּשֶׁהִגִּיעַ יוֹם הַכִּפּוּרִים עָשָׂה כַּסֵּדֶר הַזֶּה, וּלְהַגִּיד שִׁבְחוֹ שֶׁל אַהֲרֹן, שֶׁלֹּא הָיָה לוֹבְשָׁן לִגְדֻלָּתוֹ, אֶלָּא כִּמְקַיֵּם גְּזֵרַת הַמֶּלֶךְ:

יז ג) **אֲשֶׁר יִשְׁחַט שׁוֹר אוֹ כֶשֶׂב.** בְּמֻקְדָּשִׁין הַכָּתוּב מְדַבֵּר, שֶׁנֶּאֱמַר: "לְהַקְרִיב קָרְבָּן": **בַּמַּחֲנֶה.** חוּץ לָעֲזָרָה:

ד) **דָּם יֵחָשֵׁב.** כְּשׁוֹפֵךְ דַּם הָאָדָם, שֶׁמִּתְחַיֵּב בְּנַפְשׁוֹ: **דָּם שָׁפָךְ.** לְרַבּוֹת אֶת הַזּוֹרֵק דָּמִים בַּחוּץ:

the institutional base of atonement ceased to exist. The service of Yom Kippur as prescribed in this *parasha* became impossible. How then could the people, individually and collectively, renew and restore their relationship with God? How could they live without an overwhelming sense of guilt? It was a crisis without parallel and went to the very roots of life in the conscious presence of God.

It is from the period of the destruction of the Temple that a remarkable statement appears in the Mishna:

> R. Akiva said: Happy are you, Israel. Who is it before whom you are purified and who purifies you? Your Father in heaven. As it is said: "I will sprinkle over you purifying waters, and you will be cleansed." And it further says: "The hope of Israel is the LORD." Just as a fountain purifies the impure, so does the Holy One, blessed be He, purify Israel. (Yoma 8:9)

This statement embodies a transformative insight. First, note the radical midrashic reading of the text. The words *mikveh Yisrael Adonai* mean "The hope of Israel is the LORD" (Jer. 17:13). However, the root *k-v-h* has two meanings. One is "hope." The other is "a collection or gathering," hence "a gathering of water" and thus *mikveh*, a ritual bath, a place you go to be purified. R. Akiva uses this ambiguity to read the phrase as "God is the ritual bath of Israel," a daringly mystical vision. In his reading, God is the ritual bath into which we plunge ourselves in order to be cleansed. According to R. Akiva, even with no Temple, we may immerse ourselves in God and emerge pure, our sins dissolved.

ל וְכָל־מְלָאכָה לֹא תַעֲשׂוּ הָאֶזְרָח וְהַגֵּר הַגָּר בְּתוֹכְכֶם׃ כִּי־בַיּוֹם הַזֶּה
לא יְכַפֵּר עֲלֵיכֶם לְטַהֵר אֶתְכֶם מִכֹּל חַטֹּאתֵיכֶם לִפְנֵי יהוה תִּטְהָרוּ׃ שַׁבַּת
לב שַׁבָּתוֹן הִיא לָכֶם וְעִנִּיתֶם אֶת־נַפְשֹׁתֵיכֶם חֻקַּת עוֹלָם׃ וְכִפֶּר הַכֹּהֵן
אֲשֶׁר־יִמְשַׁח אֹתוֹ וַאֲשֶׁר יְמַלֵּא אֶת־יָדוֹ לְכַהֵן תַּחַת אָבִיו וְלָבַשׁ אֶת־
לג בִּגְדֵי הַבָּד בִּגְדֵי הַקֹּדֶשׁ׃ וְכִפֶּר אֶת־מִקְדַּשׁ הַקֹּדֶשׁ וְאֶת־אֹהֶל מוֹעֵד
לד וְאֶת־הַמִּזְבֵּחַ יְכַפֵּר וְעַל הַכֹּהֲנִים וְעַל־כָּל־עַם הַקָּהָל יְכַפֵּר׃ וְהָיְתָה־
זֹּאת לָכֶם לְחֻקַּת עוֹלָם לְכַפֵּר עַל־בְּנֵי יִשְׂרָאֵל מִכָּל־חַטֹּאתָם אַחַת
בַּשָּׁנָה וַיַּעַשׂ כַּאֲשֶׁר צִוָּה יהוה אֶת־מֹשֶׁה׃
יז א ב וַיְדַבֵּר יהוה אֶל־מֹשֶׁה לֵּאמֹר׃ דַּבֵּר אֶל־אַהֲרֹן וְאֶל־בָּנָיו וְאֶל כָּל־בְּנֵי יג רביעי
ג יִשְׂרָאֵל וְאָמַרְתָּ אֲלֵיהֶם זֶה הַדָּבָר אֲשֶׁר־צִוָּה יהוה לֵאמֹר׃ אִישׁ אִישׁ
מִבֵּית יִשְׂרָאֵל אֲשֶׁר יִשְׁחַט שׁוֹר אוֹ־כֶשֶׂב אוֹ־עֵז בַּמַּחֲנֶה אוֹ אֲשֶׁר
ד יִשְׁחַט מִחוּץ לַמַּחֲנֶה׃ וְאֶל־פֶּתַח אֹהֶל מוֹעֵד לֹא הֱבִיאוֹ לְהַקְרִיב
קָרְבָּן לַיהוה לִפְנֵי מִשְׁכַּן יהוה דָּם יֵחָשֵׁב לָאִישׁ הַהוּא דָּם שָׁפָךְ

אונקלוס

וְכָל עֲבִידָא לָא תַעְבְּדוּן, יַצִּיבַיָּא, וְגִיּוֹרַיָּא דְּיִתְגַּיְּרוּן בֵּינֵיכוֹן: ל אֲרֵי בְּיוֹמָא הָדֵין, יְכַפַּר עֲלֵיכוֹן לְדַכָּאָה יָתְכוֹן, מִכֹּל חוֹבֵיכוֹן, קֳדָם יי תִּדְכּוֹן: לא שַׁבָּא שַׁבְּתָא הִיא לְכוֹן, וּתְעַנּוֹן יָת נַפְשָׁתְכוֹן, קְיָם עָלַם: לב וִיכַפַּר כָּהֲנָא דִּירַבֵּי יָתֵיהּ, וְדִיקָרֵיב יָת קֻרְבָּנֵיהּ, לְשַׁמָּשָׁא תְּחוֹת אֲבוּהִי, וְיִלְבַּשׁ, יָת לְבוּשֵׁי בוּצָא לְבוּשֵׁי קֻדְשָׁא: לג וִיכַפַּר עַל מַקְדַּשׁ קֻדְשָׁא, וְעַל מַשְׁכַּן זִמְנָא, וְעַל מַדְבְּחָא יְכַפַּר, וְעַל כָּהֲנַיָּא, וְעַל כָּל עַמָּא דִּקְהָלָא יְכַפַּר: לד וּתְהֵי דָא לְכוֹן לִקְיָם עָלַם, לְכַפָּרָא, עַל בְּנֵי יִשְׂרָאֵל מִכָּל חוֹבֵיהוֹן, חֲדָא בְּשַׁתָּא, וַעֲבַד, כְּמָא דְּפַקֵּיד יי יָת מֹשֶׁה: יז א וּמַלֵּיל יי עִם מֹשֶׁה לְמֵימַר: ב מַלֵּיל עִם אַהֲרֹן וְעִם בְּנוֹהִי, וְעִם כָּל בְּנֵי יִשְׂרָאֵל, וְתֵימַר לְהוֹן, דֵּין פִּתְגָּמָא, דְּפַקֵּיד יי לְמֵימַר: ג גְּבַר גְּבַר מִבֵּית יִשְׂרָאֵל, דִּיכּוֹס, תּוֹר אוֹ אִמַּר, אוֹ עֵז בְּמַשְׁרִיתָא, אוֹ דִּיכּוֹס, מִבַּרָא לְמַשְׁרִיתָא: ד וּלְתְרַע, מַשְׁכַּן זִמְנָא לָא אַיְתְיֵהּ, לְקָרָבָא קֻרְבָּנָא קֳדָם יי, קֳדָם מַשְׁכְּנָא דַיי, דְּמָא יִתְחֲשֵׁיב, לְגַבְרָא הַהוּא דְּמָא אֲשַׁד,

16:30 לִפְנֵי יהוה תִּטְהָרוּ *You shall be purified before the LORD* – There is a difference between *kappara*, atonement, and *tahara*, purification (see note on v. 21). Atonement – literally, "erasing" or "covering over" – refers to the sinful act. It is not merely forgiven. It is, as it were, deleted from the record. Purification refers to the person. Sin defiles the sinner. We feel soiled, stained. Yom Kippur, if we have internalized its message, removes the stain, and we are made pure again.

16:34 וְהָיְתָה־זֹּאת לָכֶם לְחֻקַּת עוֹלָם *An everlasting statute for you* – With the loss of the Temple, priesthood, and sacrifices,

5 blood; he shall be severed from his people. For the Israelites must bring the
sacrifices they have been offering in the open fields – to the LORD, to the priest
at the entrance of the Tent of Meeting, and offer them as peace sacrifices to the
6 LORD. The priest shall dash the blood against the LORD's altar at the entrance
to the Tent of Meeting and send the fat up in smoke as a pleasing aroma to the
7 LORD; and no more may they offer sacrifices to the goat demons to whom they
prostitute themselves. This shall be an everlasting statute for them throughout
8 their generations. And you shall tell them: Anyone of the House of Israel or any HAMISHI /SHELISHI/
9 migrant living among you who offers up a burnt offering or other sacrifice and
does not bring it to the entrance of the Tent of Meeting to offer it to the LORD
10 shall be severed from his people. Anyone of the House of Israel, or any migrant
living among you, who eats blood – I will set My face against that person who
11 eats blood and will sever him from his people, for the life of a creature is in its
blood. I have given it to you to make atonement for your lives on the altar, for
12 blood, which is bound up with life, atones. That is why I have told the Israelites:
None of you may eat blood, nor may any migrant living among you eat blood.
13 Any Israelite or migrant living among you who hunts an animal or bird that
14 may be eaten shall pour out its blood and cover it with earth, for the life of all
flesh – its blood is its life. That is why I have said to the Israelites: You must not

רש״י

ה **אֲשֶׁר הֵם זֹבְחִים.** אֲשֶׁר הֵם רְגִילִים לִזְבֹּחַ:

ז **לַשְּׂעִירִם.** לַשֵּׁדִים, כְּמוֹ: "וּשְׂעִירִים יְרַקְּדוּ שָׁם" (ישעיה יג, כא):

ח **אֲשֶׁר יַעֲלֶה עֹלָה.** לְחַיֵּב עַל הַמַּקְטִיר אֵיבָרִים בַּחוּץ כְּשׁוֹחֵט בַּחוּץ, שֶׁאִם שָׁחַט אֶחָד וְהֶעֱלָה חֲבֵרוֹ שְׁנֵיהֶן חַיָּבִין:

ט **וְנִכְרַת.** זַרְעוֹ נִכְרָת וְיָמָיו נִכְרָתִין:

י **כָּל דָּם.** לְפִי שֶׁנֶּאֱמַר: "בַּנֶּפֶשׁ יְכַפֵּר" (פסוק יא), יָכוֹל לֹא יְהֵא חַיָּב אֶלָּא עַל דַּם הַמֻּקְדָּשִׁים? תַּלְמוּד לוֹמַר: "כָּל דָּם": **וְנָתַתִּי פָנַי.** פְּנַאי שֶׁלִּי, פּוֹנֶה אֲנִי מִכָּל עֲסָקַי וְעוֹסֵק בּוֹ:

יא **כִּי נֶפֶשׁ הַבָּשָׂר.** שֶׁל כָּל בְּרִיָּה "בַּדָּם הִיא" תְּלוּיָה, וּלְפִיכָךְ נְתַתִּיו עַל הַמִּזְבֵּחַ לְכַפֵּר עַל נֶפֶשׁ הָאָדָם, תָּבוֹא נֶפֶשׁ וּתְכַפֵּר עַל הַנֶּפֶשׁ:

יב **כָּל נֶפֶשׁ מִכֶּם.** לְהַזְהִיר גְּדוֹלִים עַל הַקְּטַנִּים:

יג **אֲשֶׁר יָצוּד.** אֵין לִי אֶלָּא צַיִד, אֲוָזִין וְתַרְנְגוֹלִין מִנַּיִן? תַּלְמוּד לוֹמַר "צֵיד" – מִכָּל מָקוֹם. אִם כֵּן לָמָּה נֶאֱמַר "אֲשֶׁר יָצוּד"? שֶׁלֹּא יֹאכַל בָּשָׂר אֶלָּא בַּהַזְמָנָה הַזֹּאת: **אֲשֶׁר יֵאָכֵל.** פְּרָט לִטְמֵאִים:

יד **דָּמוֹ בְנַפְשׁוֹ הוּא.** דָּמוֹ הוּא לוֹ בִּמְקוֹם הַנֶּפֶשׁ, שֶׁהַנֶּפֶשׁ תְּלוּיָה בּוֹ:

17:4 **וְנִכְרַת הָאִישׁ הַהוּא מִקֶּרֶב עַמּוֹ** *Severed from his people* – Every commandment in Judaism, every "Thou shalt" and "Thou shalt not," is a way of putting the "we" before the "I." When we rest on the Sabbath, for example, we do not engage *in private* relaxation. If we did, we would spend the seventh day pursuing individual hobbies or whatever else we chose. The Sabbath is instead a day of public rest. It is a day of "we," not "I." Similarly, here, sacrificial slaughter is centralized. One cannot, as in the days of the patriarchs, set up a private altar for private worship. Judaism is a faith less of individual salvation than of collective redemption.

Correspondingly, every transgression in Judaism is a way of putting the "I" before the "we." Whenever we put personal advantage over collective interest, or private inclination before the laws of the community, sooner or later, we sin. That is why the severest punishment in Judaism is one

וְנִכְרַ֛ת הָאִ֥ישׁ הַה֖וּא מִקֶּ֥רֶב עַמּֽוֹ: לְמַ֡עַן אֲשֶׁר֩ יָבִ֨יאוּ בְּנֵ֜י יִשְׂרָאֵ֗ל אֶת־
ה זִבְחֵיהֶם֮ אֲשֶׁ֣ר הֵ֣ם זֹבְחִים֮ עַל־פְּנֵ֣י הַשָּׂדֶה֒ וֶהֱבִיאֻ֣ם לַיהוָ֗ה אֶל־פֶּ֛תַח
ו אֹ֥הֶל מוֹעֵ֖ד אֶל־הַכֹּהֵ֑ן וְזָבְח֗וּ זִבְחֵ֧י שְׁלָמִ֛ים לַיהוָ֖ה אוֹתָֽם: וְזָרַ֨ק הַכֹּהֵ֤ן
אֶת־הַדָּם֙ עַל־מִזְבַּ֣ח יְהוָ֔ה פֶּ֖תַח אֹ֣הֶל מוֹעֵ֑ד וְהִקְטִ֣יר הַחֵ֔לֶב לְרֵ֥יחַ
ז נִיחֹ֖חַ לַיהוָֽה: וְלֹא־יִזְבְּח֥וּ עוֹד֙ אֶת־זִבְחֵיהֶ֔ם לַשְּׂעִירִ֕ם אֲשֶׁ֥ר הֵ֖ם זֹנִ֣ים
ח אַחֲרֵיהֶ֑ם חֻקַּ֥ת עוֹלָ֛ם תִּֽהְיֶה־זֹּ֥את לָהֶ֖ם לְדֹרֹתָֽם: וַאֲלֵהֶ֣ם תֹּאמַ֔ר אִ֥ישׁ חמישי /שלישי/
אִישׁ֙ מִבֵּ֣ית יִשְׂרָאֵ֔ל וּמִן־הַגֵּ֖ר אֲשֶׁר־יָג֣וּר בְּתוֹכָ֑ם אֲשֶׁר־יַעֲלֶ֥ה עֹלָ֖ה אוֹ־
ט זָֽבַח: וְאֶל־פֶּ֜תַח אֹ֤הֶל מוֹעֵד֙ לֹ֣א יְבִיאֶ֔נּוּ לַעֲשׂ֥וֹת אֹת֖וֹ לַיהוָ֑ה וְנִכְרַ֛ת
י הָאִ֥ישׁ הַה֖וּא מֵעַמָּֽיו: וְאִ֨ישׁ אִ֜ישׁ מִבֵּ֣ית יִשְׂרָאֵ֗ל וּמִן־הַגֵּר֙ הַגָּ֣ר בְּתוֹכָ֔ם
אֲשֶׁ֥ר יֹאכַ֖ל כָּל־דָּ֑ם וְנָתַתִּ֣י פָנַ֗י בַּנֶּ֙פֶשׁ֙ הָאֹכֶ֣לֶת אֶת־הַדָּ֔ם וְהִכְרַתִּ֥י אֹתָ֖הּ
יא מִקֶּ֥רֶב עַמָּֽהּ: כִּ֣י נֶ֣פֶשׁ הַבָּשָׂר֮ בַּדָּ֣ם הִוא֒ וַאֲנִ֞י נְתַתִּ֤יו לָכֶם֙ עַל־הַמִּזְבֵּ֔חַ
יב לְכַפֵּ֖ר עַל־נַפְשֹֽׁתֵיכֶ֑ם כִּֽי־הַדָּ֥ם ה֖וּא בַּנֶּ֥פֶשׁ יְכַפֵּֽר: עַל־כֵּ֤ן אָמַ֙רְתִּי֙ לִבְנֵ֣י
יִשְׂרָאֵ֔ל כָּל־נֶ֥פֶשׁ מִכֶּ֖ם לֹא־תֹ֣אכַל דָּ֑ם וְהַגֵּ֛ר הַגָּ֥ר בְּתוֹכְכֶ֖ם לֹא־יֹ֥אכַל
יג דָּֽם: וְאִ֨ישׁ אִ֜ישׁ מִבְּנֵ֣י יִשְׂרָאֵ֗ל וּמִן־הַגֵּר֙ הַגָּ֣ר בְּתוֹכָ֔ם אֲשֶׁ֨ר יָצ֜וּד צֵ֥יד
יד חַיָּ֛ה אוֹ־ע֖וֹף אֲשֶׁ֣ר יֵאָכֵ֑ל וְשָׁפַךְ֙ אֶת־דָּמ֔וֹ וְכִסָּ֖הוּ בֶּעָפָֽר: כִּֽי־נֶ֣פֶשׁ כָּל־
בָּשָׂ֗ר דָּמ֣וֹ בְנַפְשׁוֹ֮ הוּא֒ וָאֹמַר֙ לִבְנֵ֣י יִשְׂרָאֵ֔ל דַּ֥ם כָּל־בָּשָׂ֖ר לֹ֣א תֹאכֵ֑לוּ

אונקלוס

וְישתיצי, אנשא ההוא מגו עמיה: ה בדיל דייתון בני ישראל, ית דבחיהון דאנון דבחין על אפי חקלא, וייתונון לקדם יי, לתרע, משכן זמנא לות כהנא, ויכסון, נכסת קודשין, קדם יי יתהון: ו ויזרוק כהנא ית דמא על מדבחא דיי, בתרע משכן זמנא, ויסיק תרבא, לאתקבלא ברעוא קדם יי: ז ולא ידבחון עוד ית דבחיהון, לשידין, דאנון טען בתריהון, קים עלם, תהי דא להון לדריהון: ח ולהון תימר, גבר גבר מבית ישראל, ומן גיוריא דיתגיירון ביניהון, דיסיק עלתא או נכסת קודשיא: ט ולתרע, משכן זמנא לא ייתיניה, למעבד יתיה קדם יי, וישתיצי, אנשא ההוא מעמיה: י וגבר גבר מבית ישראל, ומן גיוריא דיתגיירון ביניהון, דייכול כל דם, ואתין רוגזי, באנשא דייכול ית דמא, ואשיצי יתיה מגו עמיה: יא ארי נפש בסרא בדמא היא, ואנא, יהבתיה לכון על מדבחא, לכפרא על נפשתכון, ארי דמא הוא על נפשא מכפר: יב על כן אמרית לבני ישראל, כל אנש מנכון לא ייכול דם, וגיוריא, דיתגיירון ביניכון לא ייכלון דם: יג וגבר גבר מבני ישראל, ומן גיוריא דיתגיירון ביניהון, דיצוד, צידא חיתא, או עופא דמתאכיל, ויישוד ית דמיה, ויכסיניה בעפרא: יד ארי נפש כל בסרא, דמיה בנפשיה הוא, ואמרית לבני ישראל, דם כל בסרא לא תיכלון,

eat any creature's blood, because the life of every creature is bound up with its
15 blood. All who eat it will be severed. Anyone, native born or migrant, who eats
an animal that has died of itself or been torn by beasts shall wash his clothes,
16 immerse in water, and remain impure until evening; then he shall be purified. If
he does not wash or immerse his body, he shall bear his guilt."
18 1/2 The LORD spoke to Moshe: "Speak to the Israelites. Say: I am the LORD your
3 God. You shall not do as they do in the land of Egypt where you lived. Nor
shall you do as they do in the land of Canaan where I am bringing you; do not
4 follow their practices. Observe My laws, keep My statutes and follow them;
5 I am the LORD your God. Keep My statutes and laws, for by them a person

רש״י

כי נפש כל בשר דמו הוא. הנפש היא הדם. 'דם' ו'בשר' – לשון זכר, 'נפש' – לשון נקבה:

טו **אשר תאכל נבלה וטרפה.** בנבלת עוף טהור דבר הכתוב, שאין לה טומאה אלא בשעה שנבלעת בבית הבליעה, ולמדך כאן שמטמאה באכילתה. וטרפה האמורה כאן לא נכתב אלא לדרש, וכן שנינו: יכול תהא נבלת עוף טמא מטמאה בבית הבליעה? תלמוד לומר: "טרפה", מי שיש במינו טרפה, יצא עוף טמא שאין במינו טרפה:

טז **ונשא עונו.** אם יאכל קדש או יכנס למקדש, חייב על טומאה זו ככל שאר טומאות: **ובשרו לא ירחץ ונשא עונו.** על רחיצת גופו ענוש כרת, ועל כבוס בגדים במלקות:

יח ב **אני ה' אלהיכם.** אני הוא שאמרתי בסיני: "אנכי ה' אלהיך" (שמות כ, ב), וקבלתם עליכם מלכותי, מעתה קבלו גזרותי. רבי אומר: גלוי וידוע לפניו שסופן לנתק בעריות בימי עזרא, לפיכך בא עליהם בגזרה: "אני ה' אלהיכם", דעו מי גוזר עליכם, דין לפרע ונאמן לשלם שכר:

ג **כמעשה ארץ מצרים.** מגיד שמעשיהם של מצריים ושל כנעניים מקולקלים מכל האמות, ואותו מקום שישבו בו ישראל מקולקל מן הכל: **אשר אני מביא אתכם שמה.** מגיד שאותן עממין שכבשו ישראל, מקולקלים יותר מכלם: **ובחקתיהם לא תלכו.** מה הניח הכתוב שלא אמר? אלא אלו נימוסות שלהן, דברים החקוקין להם, כגון טרטיאות ואצטדיאות. רבי מאיר אומר, אלו דרכי האמורי שמנו חכמים:

ד **את משפטי תעשו.** אלו דברים האמורים בתורה במשפט, שאלו לא נאמרו היו כדאי לאמרן: **ואת חקתי תשמרו.** דברים שהם גזרת המלך, שיצר הרע משיב עליהם למה לנו לשמרן, ואמות העולם משיבין עליהם, כגון אכילת חזיר ולבישת שעטנז וטהרת מי חטאת, לכך נאמר: "אני ה'" – גזרתי עליכם, אי אתה רשאי להפטר: **ללכת בהם.** אל תפטר מתוכם, שלא תאמר: למדתי חכמת ישראל, אלך ואלמד חכמת האמות:

ה **ושמרתם את חקתי וגו'.** לרבות שאר דקדוקי הפרשה, שלא פרט הכתוב בהם. דבר אחר, לתן שמירה ועשיה לחקים ושמירה ועשיה למשפטים, לפי שלא נתן אלא עשיה למשפטים ושמירה לחקים (לעיל פסוק ד):

or wife, and our children. That is why Genesis, the story of our beginnings, deals only cursorily with the creation of the universe, and briefly with politics. Instead, it is a series of narratives about families, marriage partners, parents, children, and siblings.

One of the signs of ancient polytheistic cultures was the absence, subjectivity, or relativity of sexual ethics. Adultery, infidelity, promiscuity, and sexual and child abuse were commonplace. That is the world Genesis contrasts with the life of the covenant. Sexuality is often the primary force behind violence, and sexual decadence the first sign of civilizational decline.

So this passage, despite its seeming remoteness from the themes of Yom Kippur, is telling us a fundamental truth about Judaism as a whole. Holiness is expressed in our most intimate relationships within the family: in the love that is loyal and generous, self-sacrificing and kind, in the sensitivity of marriage partners to one another and their needs, and in our ability to recognize the integrity-of-otherness that lies at the heart of love.

טו כִּי נֶפֶשׁ כָּל־בָּשָׂר דָּמוֹ הִוא כָּל־אֹכְלָיו יִכָּרֵת: וְכָל־נֶפֶשׁ אֲשֶׁר תֹּאכַל
נְבֵלָה וּטְרֵפָה בָּאֶזְרָח וּבַגֵּר וְכִבֶּס בְּגָדָיו וְרָחַץ בַּמַּיִם וְטָמֵא עַד־הָעֶרֶב
טז וְטָהֵר: וְאִם לֹא יְכַבֵּס וּבְשָׂרוֹ לֹא יִרְחָץ וְנָשָׂא עֲוֹנוֹ:
יח א ב וַיְדַבֵּר יהוה אֶל־מֹשֶׁה לֵּאמֹר: דַּבֵּר אֶל־בְּנֵי יִשְׂרָאֵל וְאָמַרְתָּ אֲלֵהֶם יד
ג אֲנִי יהוה אֱלֹהֵיכֶם: כְּמַעֲשֵׂה אֶרֶץ־מִצְרַיִם אֲשֶׁר יְשַׁבְתֶּם־בָּהּ לֹא
תַעֲשׂוּ וּכְמַעֲשֵׂה אֶרֶץ־כְּנַעַן אֲשֶׁר אֲנִי מֵבִיא אֶתְכֶם שָׁמָּה לֹא תַעֲשׂוּ
ד וּבְחֻקֹּתֵיהֶם לֹא תֵלֵכוּ: אֶת־מִשְׁפָּטַי תַּעֲשׂוּ וְאֶת־חֻקֹּתַי תִּשְׁמְרוּ לָלֶכֶת
ה בָּהֶם אֲנִי יהוה אֱלֹהֵיכֶם: וּשְׁמַרְתֶּם אֶת־חֻקֹּתַי וְאֶת־מִשְׁפָּטַי אֲשֶׁר

אונקלוס

אֲרֵי נְפַשׁ כָּל בִּסְרָא דְּמֵיהּ הִיא, כָּל דְּיֵיכְלִנֵּיהּ יִשְׁתֵּיצֵי: טו וְכָל אֱנָשׁ, דְּיֵיכוֹל נְבִילָא וּתְבִירָא, בְּיַצִּיבָא וּבְגִיּוֹרָא, וִיצַבַּע לְבוּשׁוֹהִי, וְיַסְחֵי בְמַיָּא, וִיהֵי מְסָאַב עַד רַמְשָׁא וְיִדְכֵּי: טז וְאִם לָא יְצַבַּע, וּבִסְרֵיהּ לָא יַסְחֵי, וִיקַבֵּיל חוֹבֵיהּ: יח א וּמַלֵּיל יי עִם מֹשֶׁה לְמֵימַר: ב מַלֵּיל עִם בְּנֵי יִשְׂרָאֵל, וְתֵימַר לְהוֹן, אֲנָא יי אֱלָהֲכוֹן: ג כְּעוֹבָדֵי עַמָּא דְאַרְעָא דְמִצְרַיִם, דִּיתֵיבְתּוּן בַּהּ לָא תַעְבְּדוּן, וּכְעוֹבָדֵי עַמָּא דְאַרְעָא דִכְנַעַן, דַּאֲנָא מַעֵיל יָתְכוֹן לְתַמָּן לָא תַעְבְּדוּן, וּבְנִמּוֹסֵיהוֹן לָא תְהָכוּן: ד יָת דִּינַי תַּעְבְּדוּן, וְיָת קְיָמַי תִּטְּרוּן לְהַלָּכָא בְהוֹן, אֲנָא יי אֱלָהֲכוֹן: ה וְתִטְּרוּן יָת קְיָמַי וְיָת דִּינַי, דְּאִם

that is not inflicted by people: *karet*, literally being "severed" from the community.

FORBIDDEN RELATIONSHIPS

This passage on forbidden sexual relationships is the Torah reading for the afternoon of Yom Kippur. Despite the passage directly following the text from the description of the Yom Kippur rituals, the choice of synagogue reading seems arbitrary. Why specifically these prohibitions on a day when we atone for sins of all kinds? Among the classic explanations, Rashi (on Megilla 31a) says that sexual sins are common and the desire to commit them is part of the human condition. Rambam states that sexual desire is, for most people and in all eras, the strongest of all inclinations to sin (*Hilkhot Issurei Bia* 22:18–19).

The passage itself raises questions. Why does it begin with the statement "I am the LORD your God" (Lev. 18:2)? Why the contrast with the behavior of the Egyptians and the Canaanites? Why are sexual sins so serious as to warrant the exile of Israel from its land?

Judaism was and is opposed to a worldview – whether in its ancient forms of myth, or its modern pseudo-scientific counterpart, the neo-Darwinian myth of the "selfish gene" – that the fundamental human drive is to perpetuate one's genes. Against this, Judaism sets an ethic of love and loyalty, whereby two parties, each respecting the integrity of the other, come together in a bond of mutual commitment and fidelity. The human counterpart of the covenant between God and humanity is marriage as a covenant between husband and wife. Essential to the safety of marriage and the family is a strict set of taboos defining who is *not* a potential partner.

A sexual ethic is therefore not just one among many features of Judaism. It is of its essence, for there is the closest possible connection between how we relate to God and how we relate to those to whom we are closest: our husband

6 shall live; I am the Lord. No one among you shall draw close to any SHISHI
7 near relative to expose their nakedness; I am the Lord. You shall not
expose your father's and mother's nakedness. She is your mother; you shall
8 not expose her nakedness. You shall not expose the nakedness of
9 your father's wife; it is your father's nakedness. You shall not expose
the nakedness of your sister – whether she is your father's daughter or your
mother's, whether born into the household or outside, you shall not expose her
10 nakedness. You shall not expose the nakedness of your son's
11 daughter or your daughter's daughter; it is your own nakedness. The
nakedness of your father's wife's daughter, born to your father – she is your sister;
12 do not expose her nakedness. You shall not expose the nakedness
13 of your father's sister; she is of your father's flesh. You shall
not expose the nakedness of your mother's sister, for she is of your mother's
14 flesh. You shall not expose the nakedness of your father's brother –
15 do not draw close to his wife; she is your aunt. You shall not expose
the nakedness of your daughter-in-law: she is your son's wife; do not expose
16 her nakedness. You shall not expose the nakedness of your brother's
17 wife; it is your brother's nakedness. You shall not expose the
nakedness of a woman and her daughter, nor shall you marry her son's daughter
or her daughter's daughter, exposing her nakedness; they are of the same flesh;
18 it would be depravity. Do not marry a woman to be a rival to her sister, exposing

רש"י

וחי בהם. לעולם הבא, שאם תאמר בעולם הזה, והלא סופו הוא מת: **אני ה'.** נאמן לשלם שכר:

ו **לא תקרבו.** להזהיר הנקבה כזכר, לכך נאמר לשון רבים: **אני ה'.** נאמן לשלם שכר:

ז **ערות אביך.** זו אשת אביך. או אינו אלא כמשמעו? נאמר כאן: "ערות אביך", ונאמר להלן: "ערות אביו גלה" (ויקרא כ, יא), מה להלן אשת אביו, אף כאן אשת אביו: **וערות אמך.** להביא אמו שאינה אשת אביו:

ח **ערות אשת אביך.** לרבות לאחר מיתה:

ט **בת אביך.** אף בת אנוסה במשמע: **מולדת בית או מולדת חוץ.** בין שאומרים לו לאביך קיים את אמה, ובין שאומרים לו הוצא את אמה, כגון ממזרת או נתינה:

י **ערות בת בנך וגו'.** בבתו מאנוסתו הכתוב מדבר, ובתו ובת בתו מאשתו אנו למדין מערות אשה ובתה, שנאמר בהן: "לא תגלה" (להלן פסוק יז) בין שהיא ממנו בין שהיא מאיש אחר: **ערות בת בנך.** קל וחומר לבתך, אלא לפי שאין מזהירין מן הדין, למדוה מגזרה שוה במסכת יבמות (דף ג ע"א):

יא **ערות בת אשת אביך.** למד שאינו חייב על אחותו משפחה ונכרית, לכך נאמר: "בת אשת אביך", בראויה לקדושין:

יד **ערות אחי אביך לא תגלה.** ומה היא ערותו? "אל אשתו לא תקרב":

טו **אשת בנך הוא.** לא אמרתי אלא בשיש לבנך אישות בה, פרט לאנוסה ושפחה ונכרית:

יז **ערות אשה ובתה.** לא אסר הכתוב אלא על ידי נשואי הראשונה, לכך נאמר: "לא תקח", לשון קיחה. וכן לענין העונש: "אשר יקח את אשה ואת אמה" (להלן כ, יד) לשון קיחה, אבל אנס אשה, מתר

ו יַעֲשֶׂה אֹתָם הָאָדָם וָחַי בָּהֶם אֲנִי יְהוָה׃ אִישׁ אִישׁ אֶל־כָּל־ ששי
ז שְׁאֵר בְּשָׂרוֹ לֹא תִקְרְבוּ לְגַלּוֹת עֶרְוָה אֲנִי יְהוָה׃ עֶרְוַת אָבִיךָ
ח וְעֶרְוַת אִמְּךָ לֹא תְגַלֵּה אִמְּךָ הִוא לֹא תְגַלֶּה עֶרְוָתָהּ׃ עֶרְוַת
ט אֵשֶׁת־אָבִיךָ לֹא תְגַלֵּה עֶרְוַת אָבִיךָ הִוא׃ עֶרְוַת אֲחוֹתְךָ
בַת־אָבִיךָ אוֹ בַת־אִמֶּךָ מוֹלֶדֶת בַּיִת אוֹ מוֹלֶדֶת חוּץ לֹא תְגַלֶּה
י עֶרְוָתָן׃ עֶרְוַת בַּת־בִּנְךָ אוֹ בַת־בִּתְּךָ לֹא תְגַלֶּה עֶרְוָתָן
יא כִּי עֶרְוָתְךָ הֵנָּה׃ עֶרְוַת בַּת־אֵשֶׁת אָבִיךָ מוֹלֶדֶת אָבִיךָ
יב אֲחוֹתְךָ הִוא לֹא תְגַלֶּה עֶרְוָתָהּ׃ עֶרְוַת אֲחוֹת־אָבִיךָ
יג לֹא תְגַלֵּה שְׁאֵר אָבִיךָ הִוא׃ עֶרְוַת אֲחוֹת־אִמְּךָ לֹא
יד תְגַלֵּה כִּי־שְׁאֵר אִמְּךָ הִוא׃ עֶרְוַת אֲחִי־אָבִיךָ לֹא תְגַלֵּה
טו אֶל־אִשְׁתּוֹ לֹא תִקְרָב דֹּדָתְךָ הִוא׃ עֶרְוַת כַּלָּתְךָ לֹא
טז תְגַלֵּה אֵשֶׁת בִּנְךָ הִוא לֹא תְגַלֶּה עֶרְוָתָהּ׃ עֶרְוַת אֵשֶׁת־
יז אָחִיךָ לֹא תְגַלֵּה עֶרְוַת אָחִיךָ הִוא׃ עֶרְוַת אִשָּׁה וּבִתָּהּ לֹא
תְגַלֵּה אֶת־בַּת־בְּנָהּ וְאֶת־בַּת־בִּתָּהּ לֹא תִקַּח לְגַלּוֹת עֶרְוָתָהּ שַׁאֲרָה
יח הֵנָּה זִמָּה הִוא׃ וְאִשָּׁה אֶל־אֲחֹתָהּ לֹא תִקָּח לִצְרֹר לְגַלּוֹת עֶרְוָתָהּ

אונקלוס

יַעֲבֵיד יָתְהוֹן, אֱנָשָׁא וְיֵיחֵי בְּהוֹן בְּחַיֵּי עָלְמָא, אֲנָא יְיָ׃ ו גְּבַר גְּבַר לְכָל קָרִיב בִּסְרֵיהּ, לָא תִקְרְבוּן לְגַלָּאָה עֶרְיָא, אֲנָא יְיָ׃ ז עֶרְיַת אֲבוּךְ, וְעֶרְיַת אִמָּךְ לָא תְגַלֵּי, אִמָּךְ הִיא, לָא תְגַלֵּי עֶרְיְתַהּ׃ ח עֶרְיַת אִתַּת אֲבוּךְ לָא תְגַלֵּי, עֶרְיְתָא דַאֲבוּךְ הִיא׃ ט עֶרְיַת אֲחָתָךְ בַּת אֲבוּךְ אוֹ בַת אִמָּךְ, דִּילִידָא מִן אֲבוּךְ מִן אִתָּא אָחֳרִי, אוֹ מִן אִמָּךְ מִן גְּבַר אָחֳרָן, לָא תְגַלֵּי עֶרְיַתְהוֹן׃ י עֶרְיַת בַּת בְּרָךְ אוֹ בַת בְּרַתָּךְ, לָא תְגַלֵּי עֶרְיַתְהוֹן, אֲרֵי עֶרְיְתָךְ אִנִּין׃ יא עֶרְיַת בַּת אִתַּת אֲבוּךְ דִּילִידָא מִן אֲבוּךְ, אֲחָתָךְ הִיא, לָא תְגַלֵּי עֶרְיְתַהּ׃ יב עֶרְיַת אֲחָת אֲבוּךְ לָא תְגַלֵּי, קָרִיבַת אֲבוּךְ הִיא׃ יג עֶרְיַת אֲחָת אִמָּךְ לָא תְגַלֵּי, אֲרֵי קָרִיבַת אִמָּךְ הִיא׃ יד עֶרְיַת אַחְבּוּךְ לָא תְגַלֵּי, לְאִתְּתֵיהּ לָא תִקְרַב, אִתַּת אַחְבּוּךְ הִיא׃ טו עֶרְיַת כַּלְּתָךְ לָא תְגַלֵּי, אִתַּת בְּרָךְ הִיא, לָא תְגַלֵּי עֶרְיְתַהּ׃ טז עֶרְיַת אִתַּת אֲחוּךְ לָא תְגַלֵּי, עֶרְיְתָא דַאֲחוּךְ הִיא׃ יז עֶרְיַת אִתְּתָא, וּבְרַתַּהּ לָא תְגַלֵּי, יָת בַּת בְּרַהּ וְיָת בַּת בְּרַתַּהּ, לָא תִסַּב לְגַלָּאָה עֶרְיְתַהּ, קָרִיבָן אִנִּין עֵיצַת חֲטִין הִיא׃ יח וְאִתְּתָא עִם אֲחָתַהּ לָא תִסַּב, לְאַעָקָא לַהּ, לְגַלָּאָה עֶרְיְתַהּ,

רש״י

לִקַּח בִּתָּהּ: שַׁאֲרָה הֵנָּה. קְרוֹבוֹת זוֹ לָזוֹ: זִמָּה. עֵצָה, כְּתַרְגּוּמוֹ: ״עֵצַת חִטְאִין״, שֶׁיִּצְרְךָ יוֹעָצְךָ לַחְטֹא: יח אֶל אֲחֹתָהּ. שְׁתֵּיהֶן כְּאַחַת: לִצְרֹר. לְשׁוֹן צָרָה, לַעֲשׂוֹת אֶת זוֹ צָרָה לָזוֹ:

19 her nakedness while her sister is alive. Do not draw close to a woman to expose
20 her nakedness while she bears the impurity of her menstruation. Do not have
21 carnal relations with your neighbor's wife, becoming impure through her. Do
not give any of your children over to be sacrificed to Molekh, profaning the
22 name of your God; I am the LORD. Do not lie with a male as with a woman; SHEVI'I /REVI'I/
23 this is an abhorrent act. Do not have carnal relations with any animal, through
it making yourself impure; nor may a woman give herself to an animal to
24 mate with it – this is perversion. Do not make yourselves impure in any of
these ways, for it is by all these that the nations I am casting out before you
25 made themselves impure. And so the land itself became impure, and I held it
26 to account for its sins, and the land vomited out its inhabitants. But you shall
keep My statutes and My laws and do none of these abhorrent acts, neither
27 the native born nor the migrant living among you. The people who lived in
the land before you committed all these abhorrent acts and the land became
28 impure. Let the land not vomit you out for making it impure, as it vomited out MAFTIR

רש"י

בְּחַיֶּיהָ. לִמֶּדְךָ שֶׁאִם גֵּרְשָׁהּ, לֹא יִשָּׂא אֶת אֲחוֹתָהּ כָּל זְמַן שֶׁהִיא בַּחַיִּים:

כא **לַמֹּלֶךְ.** עֲבוֹדָה זָרָה הִיא שֶׁשְּׁמָהּ 'מֹלֶךְ', וְזוֹ הִיא עֲבוֹדָתָהּ, שֶׁמּוֹסֵר בְּנוֹ לַכְּמָרִים, וְעוֹשִׂין שְׁתֵּי מְדוּרוֹת גְּדוֹלוֹת, וּמַעֲבִירִין אֶת הַבֵּן בְּרַגְלָיו בֵּין שְׁתֵּי מְדוּרוֹת הָאֵשׁ: **לֹא תִתֵּן.** זוֹ הִיא מְסִירָתוֹ לַכְּמָרִים: **לְהַעֲבִיר לַמֹּלֶךְ.** זוֹ הַעֲבָרַת הָאֵשׁ:

כג **תֶּבֶל הוּא.** לְשׁוֹן קֹדֶשׁ וְעֶרְוָה וְנִאוּף, וְכֵן: "וְאַפִּי עַל תַּבְלִיתָם" (ישעיה י, כה). דָּבָר אַחֵר, "תֶּבֶל הוּא" – לְשׁוֹן בְּלִילָה וְעִרְבּוּב, זֶרַע אָדָם וְזֶרַע בְּהֵמָה:

כח **וְלֹא תָקִיא הָאָרֶץ אֶתְכֶם.** מָשָׁל לְבֶן מֶלֶךְ שֶׁהֶאֱכִילוּהוּ דָּבָר מָאוּס, שֶׁאֵין עוֹמֵד בְּמֵעָיו אֶלָּא מְקִיאוֹ, כָּךְ אֶרֶץ יִשְׂרָאֵל אֵינָהּ מְקַיֶּמֶת עוֹבְרֵי עֲבֵרָה. וְתַרְגּוּמוֹ: 'וְלָא תְרוֹקֵן', לְשׁוֹן רִקּוּן, מְרִיקָה עַצְמָהּ מֵהֶם:

and awaited in the future, when Israel would once again come home and live as God's people in His land.

Taken collectively, the commands of the Torah are a prescription for the construction of a society with the consciousness of God at its center. God asks the Jewish people to become a role model for humanity by the society they build on the principles of justice and the rule of law, and concern for the welfare of the poor and vulnerable – a society in which all have equal dignity under the sovereignty of God.

A society needs a land, a home, a location in space where a nation can shape its own destiny in accord with its deepest aspirations and ideals. *Only in Israel is the fulfillment of the commands a society-building exercise,* shaping the contours of a culture as a whole. Only in Israel can we fulfill the commands in a land, a landscape, and a language saturated with Jewish memories and hopes. Only in Israel does the calendar track the rhythms of the Jewish year. In Israel, Judaism is part of the public square, not just the private, sequestered space of synagogue, school, and home. That is the significance of the return to Zion in modern times. It is the Jewish return to the full terms of the covenant. Jews are the people of the covenant charged with bringing the Divine Presence down to earth in the shared spaces of our collective life, not by force, not by power, but by influence, "'with My spirit,' says the LORD" (Zech. 4:6).

The right to inherit the land, our *parasha* tells us, comes hand in hand with a duty to live individually and collectively by the standards of fidelity, of justice and compassion, of love of family, neighbor, and stranger, which alone constitute our mission and destiny: a holy people in the holy land.

יט עָלֶיהָ בְּחַיֶּיהָ: וְאֶל־אִשָּׁה בְּנִדַּת טֻמְאָתָהּ לֹא תִקְרַב לְגַלּוֹת עֶרְוָתָהּ:
כ כא וְאֶל־אֵשֶׁת עֲמִיתְךָ לֹא־תִתֵּן שְׁכָבְתְּךָ לְזָרַע לְטָמְאָה־בָהּ: וּמִזַּרְעֲךָ
כב לֹא־תִתֵּן לְהַעֲבִיר לַמֹּלֶךְ וְלֹא תְחַלֵּל אֶת־שֵׁם אֱלֹהֶיךָ אֲנִי יְהוָה: וְאֶת־ שביעי /רביעי/
כג זָכָר לֹא תִשְׁכַּב מִשְׁכְּבֵי אִשָּׁה תּוֹעֵבָה הִוא: וּבְכָל־בְּהֵמָה לֹא־תִתֵּן
שְׁכָבְתְּךָ לְטָמְאָה־בָהּ וְאִשָּׁה לֹא־תַעֲמֹד לִפְנֵי בְהֵמָה לְרִבְעָהּ תֶּבֶל
כד הוּא: אַל־תִּטַּמְּאוּ בְּכָל־אֵלֶּה כִּי בְכָל־אֵלֶּה נִטְמְאוּ הַגּוֹיִם אֲשֶׁר־אֲנִי
כה מְשַׁלֵּחַ מִפְּנֵיכֶם: וַתִּטְמָא הָאָרֶץ וָאֶפְקֹד עֲוֺנָהּ עָלֶיהָ וַתָּקִא הָאָרֶץ
כו אֶת־יֹשְׁבֶיהָ: וּשְׁמַרְתֶּם אַתֶּם אֶת־חֻקֹּתַי וְאֶת־מִשְׁפָּטַי וְלֹא תַעֲשׂוּ מִכֹּל
כז הַתּוֹעֵבֹת הָאֵלֶּה הָאֶזְרָח וְהַגֵּר הַגָּר בְּתוֹכְכֶם: כִּי אֶת־כָּל־הַתּוֹעֵבֹת
כח הָאֵל עָשׂוּ אַנְשֵׁי־הָאָרֶץ אֲשֶׁר לִפְנֵיכֶם וַתִּטְמָא הָאָרֶץ: וְלֹא־תָקִיא מפטיר
הָאָרֶץ אֶתְכֶם בְּטַמַּאֲכֶם אֹתָהּ כַּאֲשֶׁר קָאָה אֶת־הַגּוֹי אֲשֶׁר לִפְנֵיכֶם:

אונקלוס

עֲלַהּ בְּחַיַּהָא: יט וּלְאִתְּתָא בְּרִיחוּק סְאוֹבְתַהּ, לָא תִקְרַב, לְגַלָּאָה עֶרְיְתַהּ: כ וּבְאִתַּת חַבְרָךְ, לָא תִתֵּין שְׁכָבְתָּךְ לְזַרְעָא, לְאִסְתַּאָבָא בַהּ: כא וּמִזַּרְעָךְ לָא תִתֵּין לְאַעֲבָרָא לְמֹלֶךְ, וְלָא תַחֵיל, יָת שְׁמָא דֶאֱלָהָךְ אֲנָא יְיָ: כב וְיָת דְּכוּרָא, לָא תִשְׁכּוֹב מִשְׁכְּבֵי אִתָּא, תּוֹעֵיבָא הִיא: כג וּבְכָל בְּעִירָא, לָא תִתֵּין שְׁכָבְתָּךְ לְאִסְתַּאָבָא בַהּ, וְאִתְּתָא, לָא תְקוּם, קֳדָם בְּעִירָא, לְמִשְׁלַט בַּהּ תִּבְלָא הוּא: כד לָא תִסְתַּאֲבוּן בְּכָל אִלֵּין, אֲרֵי בְכָל אִלֵּין אִסְתָּאֲבוּ עַמְמַיָּא, דַּאֲנָא מַגְלֵי מִן קֳדָמֵיכוֹן: כה וְאִסְתָּאֲבַת אַרְעָא, וְאַסְעָרִית חוֹבַהּ עֲלַהּ, וְרוֹקִינַת אַרְעָא יָת יָתְבַהָא: כו וְתִטְּרוּן אַתּוּן, יָת קְיָמַי וְיָת דִּינַי, וְלָא תַעְבְּדוּן, מִכֹּל תּוֹעֵיבָתָא הָאִלֵּין, יַצִּיבַיָּא, וְגִיּוֹרַיָּא דְּיִתְגַּיְּרוּן בֵּינֵיכוֹן: כז אֲרֵי יָת כָּל תּוֹעֵיבָתָא הָאִלֵּין, עֲבַדוּ אֱנָשֵׁי אַרְעָא דְּקֳדָמֵיכוֹן, וְאִסְתָּאֲבַת אַרְעָא: כח וְלָא תְרוֹקֵין אַרְעָא יָתְכוֹן, בְּסָאוֹבֵיכוֹן יָתַהּ, כְּמָא דְרוֹקִינַת, יָת עַמְמַיָּא דִּקְדָמֵיכוֹן:

THE LAW AND THE LAND

This verse raises a question. Reward and punishment in the Torah are often based on the principle of *midda keneged midda*, measure for measure. The punishment fits the crime. So, for example, *Shemitta*, the Sabbatical year, is a commandment relating to the land. The punishment for its non-observance is exile from the land (Lev. 26:35). But sexual offenses have nothing to do with the land. They are commands relating to person, not place. Why should their punishment be exile?

Ramban's answer is that not only some, but *all* the commands, are fundamentally directed to the land of Israel. To be sure, not all of them are conditional on it. But it is there that they receive their main fulfillment. Outside Israel, he says, it is impossible to encounter God directly. Over all other lands, God has set intermediaries (angels, stars, celestial powers). Only in Israel is His providence direct and unmediated. That is what gives the land its primary sanctity. Hence the land does not, in his words, "tolerate the worshippers of idols or those who practice immorality" (commentary on Lev. 18:25).

We may understand Ramban's account non-mystically. Outside Israel, Jews are subject to other powers. They are not under the direct, unmediated rule of God. The commands continue in force, but they are no longer the laws of an independent people. They are like an ongoing rehearsal for a state of affairs no longer experienced, but remembered,

29 the nation there before you, for anyone who performs any of these abhorrent
30 acts shall be severed from his people. Keep My charge and do not follow any of
these abhorrent practices that were followed before you; do not by them make
yourselves impure; I am the Lord your God."

The haftara for Parashat Aḥarei Mot is on page 1570.
When Aḥarei Mot and Kedoshim are read together, read the haftara on page 1572.
On Shabbat HaGadol read the haftara on page 1652.

רש״י

כט **הַנְּפָשׁוֹת הָעֹשֹׂת.** הַזָּכָר וְהַנְּקֵבָה בְּמַשְׁמָע:

ל **וּשְׁמַרְתֶּם אֶת מִשְׁמַרְתִּי.** לְהַזְהִיר בֵּית דִּין עַל כָּךְ: **וְלֹא תִטַּמְּאוּ בָּהֶם אֲנִי ה׳ אֱלֹהֵיכֶם.** הָא אִם תִּטַּמְּאוּ אֵינִי אֱלֹהֵיכֶם וְאַתֶּם נִפְסָלִים מֵאַחֲרַי, וּמָה הֲנָאָה יֵשׁ לִי בָּכֶם וְאַתֶּם מִתְחַיְּבִים כְּלָיָה, לְכָךְ נֶאֱמַר: ״אֲנִי ה׳ אֱלֹהֵיכֶם״:

כט כִּ֚י כׇּל־אֲשֶׁ֣ר יַעֲשֶׂ֔ה מִכֹּ֖ל הַתּוֹעֵבֹ֣ת הָאֵ֑לֶּה וְנִכְרְת֛וּ הַנְּפָשׁ֥וֹת הָעֹשֹׂ֖ת
ל מִקֶּ֥רֶב עַמָּֽם׃ וּשְׁמַרְתֶּ֣ם אֶת־מִשְׁמַרְתִּ֗י לְבִלְתִּ֨י עֲשׂ֜וֹת מֵֽחֻקּ֤וֹת הַתּֽוֹעֵבֹת֙
אֲשֶׁ֣ר נַעֲשׂ֣וּ לִפְנֵיכֶ֔ם וְלֹ֥א תִֽטַּמְּא֖וּ בָּהֶ֑ם אֲנִ֖י יְהֹוָ֥ה אֱלֹהֵיכֶֽם׃

The הפטרה *for* פרשת אחרי מות *is on page 1571.*
When אחרי מות *and* קדשים *are read together, read the haftara on page 1573.*
On שבת הגדול *read the* הפטרה *on page 1653.*

אונקלוס

כט אֲרֵי כָּל דְּיַעֲבֵיד, מִכָּל תּוֹעֵיבָתָא הָאִלֵּין, וְיִשְׁתֵּיצְיָן, נַפְשָׁתָא דְּיַעְבְּדָן מִגּוֹ עַמְּהוֹן: ל וְתִטְּרוּן יָת מַטְּרַת מֵימְרִי, בְּדִיל דְּלָא לְמֶעְבַּד, מִנִּמּוֹסֵי תּוֹעֵיבָתָא דְּאִתְעֲבִידָא קֳדָמֵיכוֹן, וְלָא תִסְתָּאֲבוּן בְּהוֹן, אֲנָא יי אֱלָהֲכוֹן:

PARASHAT KEDOSHIM

19 1/2 The LORD spoke to Moshe: "Speak to all the community of Israel. Say: Be holy,
3 for I am holy; I, the LORD your God. Each one of you, revere your mother and

רש"י

יט ב) **דַּבֵּר אֶל כָּל עֲדַת בְּנֵי יִשְׂרָאֵל.** מְלַמֵּד שֶׁנֶּאֶמְרָה פָּרָשָׁה זוֹ בְּהַקְהֵל, מִפְּנֵי שֶׁרֹב גּוּפֵי תוֹרָה תְּלוּיִין בָּהּ: **קְדֹשִׁים תִּהְיוּ.** הֱווּ פְרוּשִׁים מִן הָעֲרָיוֹת וּמִן הָעֲבֵרָה, שֶׁכָּל מָקוֹם שֶׁאַתָּה מוֹצֵא גֶּדֶר עֶרְוָה אַתָּה מוֹצֵא קְדֻשָּׁה: "אִשָּׁה זֹנָה וַחֲלָלָה" וְגוֹ', "אֲנִי ה' מְקַדִּשְׁכֶם" (ויקרא כא, ז-ח); "וְלֹא יְחַלֵּל זַרְעוֹ... אֲנִי ה' מְקַדְּשׁוֹ" (שם פסוק טו); "קְדֹשִׁים יִהְיוּ", "אִשָּׁה זֹנָה וַחֲלָלָה" וְגוֹ' (שם פסוקים ו-ז):

ג) **אִישׁ אִמּוֹ וְאָבִיו תִּירָאוּ.** כָּל אֶחָד מִכֶּם תִּירָאוּ אָבִיו וְאִמּוֹ, זֶהוּ פְּשׁוּטוֹ. וּמִדְרָשׁוֹ, אֵין לִי אֶלָּא אִישׁ, אִשָּׁה מִנַּיִן? כְּשֶׁהוּא אוֹמֵר: "תִּירָאוּ" הֲרֵי כָּאן שְׁנַיִם. אִם כֵּן לָמָּה נֶאֱמַר "אִישׁ"? שֶׁהָאִישׁ סִפֵּק בְּיָדוֹ לַעֲשׂוֹת, אֲבָל אִשָּׁה – רְשׁוּת אֲחֵרִים עָלֶיהָ: **אִמּוֹ וְאָבִיו תִּירָאוּ.** כָּאן הִקְדִּים אֵם לְאָב, לְפִי שֶׁגָּלוּי לְפָנָיו שֶׁהַבֵּן יָרֵא אֶת אָבִיו יוֹתֵר מֵאִמּוֹ, וּבְכִבּוּד הִקְדִּים אָב לָאֵם, לְפִי שֶׁגָּלוּי לְפָנָיו שֶׁהַבֵּן מְכַבֵּד אֶת אִמּוֹ

applying it specifically to sexual conduct. Ramban reads it more broadly, and holds that it applies more generally to moderation and self-restraint in all matters. The Torah forbids certain activities and permits others. When it says "be holy" it means, according to Ramban, to practice self-restraint even in the domain of the permitted. Don't be a glutton, even if what you are eating is kosher. Don't be an alcoholic even if what you are drinking is kosher wine. Don't be, in his famous phrase, a *naval birshut haTorah,* "a scoundrel with Torah license" (commentary on Lev. 19:2).

Rambam arrives at a similar idea, from a different source:

> The LORD will establish you as His holy people, just as He has sworn to you, if you keep the LORD your God's commandments *and walk in His ways.* (Deut. 28:9)

From this, Rambam infers (*Hilkhot Deot* 1:6) that we are commanded to develop certain traits of character – to be gracious, merciful, and righteous, as God is gracious, merciful, and righteous. To be holy is, as far as we can, to imitate God.

Taking the *parasha* as a whole, however, we may discern an additional aspect of holiness. To be holy, we are taught, is to love your neighbor and to love the stranger. It means not stealing, lying, or deceiving others. It means not standing idly by when someone else's life is in danger. It means not cursing the deaf or putting a stumbling block before the blind, that is, insulting or taking advantage of others even when they are completely unaware of it – because God is not unaware of it.

It means not planting your field with different kinds of seed, not crossbreeding your livestock, or wearing clothes made of a forbidden mixture of wool and linen – or as we would put it nowadays, respecting the integrity of the environment. It means not conforming with whatever happens to be the idolatry of the time – and every age has its idols. It means being honest in business, doing justice, treating your employees well, and sharing your blessings (in those days, parts of the harvest) with others.

Above all, "be holy" means: have the courage to be different. That is the root meaning of *kadosh* in Hebrew. It means, as we saw above, something distinctive and set apart.

To be holy means to bear witness to the presence of God in our, and our people's, lives. Israel – the Jewish people – is the people who in themselves give testimony to One beyond themselves. That is what Judaism's rituals are about: reminding us of the presence of the Divine.

The infinite light of God is hidden in the finite spaces of the physical universe. Indeed, the word *olam,* "universe," is semantically linked to the word *ne'elam,* "hidden." "Holy" is the name we give to those special times, places, people, and deeds that are signals of transcendence, points at which the infinity of God becomes manifest within the finite world. The holiness of Israel, then, refers to the points within our life where we efface ourselves in order to become a vehicle through which God's light flows into the world. "Be holy, for I am holy; I, the LORD your God."

פרשת קדשים

יט א ב וַיְדַבֵּ֥ר יְהוָ֖ה אֶל־מֹשֶׁ֥ה לֵּאמֹֽר׃ דַּבֵּ֞ר אֶל־כׇּל־עֲדַ֧ת בְּנֵי־יִשְׂרָאֵ֛ל וְאָמַרְתָּ֥ טו
ג אֲלֵהֶ֖ם קְדֹשִׁ֣ים תִּהְי֑וּ כִּ֣י קָד֔וֹשׁ אֲנִ֖י יְהוָ֥ה אֱלֹהֵיכֶֽם׃ אִ֣ישׁ אִמּ֤וֹ וְאָבִיו֙

אונקלוס

יט א וּמַלֵּיל יי עִם מֹשֶׁה לְמֵימַר: ב מַלֵּיל, עִם כָּל כְּנִשְׁתָּא דִּבְנֵי יִשְׂרָאֵל, וְתֵימַר לְהוֹן קַדִּישִׁין תְּהוֹן, אֲרֵי קַדִּישׁ, אֲנָא יי אֱלָהֲכוֹן:
ג גְּבַר מִן אִמֵּיהּ וּמִן אֲבוּהִי

KEDOSHIM

Until now Vayikra has been largely about sacrifices, purity, the Sanctuary, and the priesthood. It has been, in short, about a holy place, holy offerings, and the elite of holy people – Aharon and his descendants – who minister there.

With Parashat Kedoshim, the laws of holiness are broadened and democratized from the world of the Sanctuary and priests to that of the Israelites as a whole, commanding them to be holy because "I am holy; I, the Lord your God" (Lev. 19:2). The opening chapter contains the famous commands to love the neighbor and the stranger, the prohibition against taking revenge, as well as other laws more ritual in character. The second half of the *parasha* deals with forbidden sexual relations and other prohibited pagan practices. The apparently unrelated laws in the *parasha* represent a unique moral vision, that of the priestly consciousness.

19:2 דַּבֵּר אֶל־כׇּל *Speak to all* – This is the first and only time in Leviticus that so inclusive an address is commanded. The Sages (Sifra, Kedoshim 1:1) say that it means that the contents of the chapter were proclaimed by Moshe to a formal gathering of the entire nation (*hak'hel*). It is the people as a whole who are commanded to "be holy," not just the priests. This is a radical democratization of holiness. It is life itself that is to be sanctified, as the chapter goes on to make clear. Holiness is to be made manifest in the way the nation makes its clothes and plants its fields, in the way justice is administered, workers are paid, and business conducted. The vulnerable – the deaf, the blind, the elderly, and the stranger – are to be afforded special protection. The whole society is to be governed by love, without resentments or revenge.

The idea, if not the details, had already been hinted at (see Ex. 19:6 and comments there). The first intimation is the monumental assertion in the first chapter of Genesis: "God created humankind in His image: in the image of God He created him; male and female He created them" (Gen. 1:27).

It is striking that these radically egalitarian statements are spoken in the priestly voice that Judaism calls *Torat Kohanim*. On the face of it, priests are not egalitarian. They all come from a single tribe, the Levites, and from a single family within the tribe – that of Aharon. So deep is the concept of equality written into monotheism that it emerges precisely from the priestly voice – from which we would least expect it.

Holiness, we learn here, belongs to all of us when we turn our lives into the service of God, and society into a home for the Divine Presence. That is the moral life as lived by the kingdom of priests: a world where we aspire to come close to God by coming close, in justice and love, to our fellow humans.

BE HOLY

We are commanded to be holy *because God is holy*. Yet surely holiness is precisely what separates God from human beings. "For I am God, I am not a man; within you, My holiness dwells" says the prophet Hoshea (11:9). *Kadosh*, "holy," means "distinct, set apart," above, beyond. Holiness is what makes God, God: transcendent, eternal, beyond imagination. How can we, mere mortals – "this quintessence of dust," as Hamlet put it – be godlike?

The Sages (Sifra, Kedoshim 1:1) understand the command to be holy to mean "be *perushim*" that is, "be separate, practice abstinence, exercise self-restraint." Rashi in his commentary on the Torah understands this narrowly,

4 father and keep My Sabbaths; I am the Lord your God. Do not turn to idols
5 or cast yourselves gods; I am the Lord your God. When you offer a peace
6 sacrifice to the Lord, offer it in such a way that it may be accepted for you. It
shall be eaten on the day you sacrifice it or on the following day; what is left on
7 the third day shall be burned with fire. If any of it is eaten on the third day, it is
8 repugnant; it will not be accepted. Anyone who eats it shall bear his guilt, for he
has desecrated what is holy to the Lord; he shall be severed from his people.
9 When you reap the harvest of your land, do not reap all the way to the edge of
10 your field or gather the gleanings of your harvest. Do not harvest your vineyard
bare or gather the grapes that have fallen there. Leave them for the poor and for
11 the migrant; I am the Lord your God. Do not steal; do not deceive; do not lie
12 to one another. Do not swear falsely by My name, desecrating the name of your
13 God; I am the Lord. Do not defraud or rob your neighbor. Do not hold back
14 the wages of a hired worker until the morning. Do not curse the deaf or put

רש"י

יוֹתֵר מֵאָבִיו, מִפְּנֵי שֶׁמְּשַׁדַּלְתּוֹ בִּדְבָרִים: **וְאֶת שַׁבְּתֹתַי תִּשְׁמֹרוּ.** סָמַךְ שְׁמִירַת שַׁבָּת לְמוֹרָא אָב, לוֹמַר, אַף עַל פִּי שֶׁהִזְהַרְתִּיךָ עַל מוֹרָא אָב, אִם יֹאמַר לְךָ חַלֵּל אֶת הַשַּׁבָּת, אַל תִּשְׁמַע לוֹ, וְכֵן בִּשְׁאָר כָּל הַמִּצְוֹת: **אֲנִי ה׳ אֱלֹהֵיכֶם.** אַתָּה וְאָבִיךָ חַיָּבִים בִּכְבוֹדִי, לְפִיכָךְ לֹא תִּשְׁמַע לוֹ לְבַטֵּל אֶת דְּבָרַי. אֵיזֶהוּ מוֹרָא? לֹא יֵשֵׁב בִּמְקוֹמוֹ וְלֹא יְדַבֵּר בִּמְקוֹמוֹ וְלֹא יִסְתֹּר אֶת דְּבָרָיו. וְאֵיזֶהוּ כָּבוֹד? מַאֲכִיל וּמַשְׁקֶה, מַלְבִּישׁ וּמַנְעִיל, מַכְנִיס וּמוֹצִיא:

ד **אַל תִּפְנוּ אֶל הָאֱלִילִם.** לְעָבְדָם. "אֱלִילִים" לְשׁוֹן 'אַל', כְּלֹא הוּא חָשׁוּב: **וֵאלֹהֵי מַסֵּכָה.** תְּחִלָּתָן אֱלִילִים הֵם, וְאִם אַתָּה פּוֹנֶה אַחֲרֵיהֶם סוֹפְךָ לַעֲשׂוֹתָן אֱלוֹהוֹת: **לֹא תַעֲשׂוּ לָכֶם.** לֹא תַעֲשׂוּ לַאֲחֵרִים וְלֹא אֲחֵרִים לָכֶם, וְאִם תֹּאמַר לֹא תַעֲשׂוּ לְעַצְמְכֶם אֲבָל אֲחֵרִים עוֹשִׂין לָכֶם, הֲרֵי כְּבָר נֶאֱמַר: "לֹא יִהְיֶה לְךָ" (שמות כ, ג), לֹא שֶׁלְּךָ וְלֹא שֶׁל אֲחֵרִים:

ה **וְכִי תִזְבְּחוּ וְגוֹ׳.** לֹא נֶאֶמְרָה פָּרָשָׁה זוֹ אֶלָּא לְלַמֵּד שֶׁלֹּא תְהֵא זְבִיחָתָן אֶלָּא עַל מְנָת לְהֵאָכֵל בְּתוֹךְ הַזְּמַן הַזֶּה, שֶׁאִם לִקְבֹּעַ לָהֶם זְמַן אֲכִילָה, הֲרֵי כְּבָר נֶאֱמַר: "וְאִם נֶדֶר אוֹ נְדָבָה זֶבַח קָרְבָּנוֹ" וְגוֹ׳ (לעיל ז, טז): **לִרְצֹנְכֶם תִּזְבָּחֻהוּ.** תְּחִלַּת זְבִיחָתוֹ תְּהֵא עַל מְנָת נַחַת רוּחַ שֶׁיְּהֵא לָכֶם לְרָצוֹן, שֶׁאִם תַּחְשְׁבוּ עָלָיו מַחְשֶׁבֶת פְּסוּל לֹא יֵרָצֶה עֲלֵיכֶם לְפָנַי: **לִרְצֹנְכֶם.** אפיימינ"ט, זֶהוּ לְפִי פְשׁוּטוֹ. וְרַבּוֹתֵינוּ לָמְדוּ מִכָּאן לְמִתְעַסֵּק בְּקָדָשִׁים שֶׁפָּסוּל, שֶׁצָּרִיךְ שֶׁיִּתְכַּוֵּן לִשְׁחֹט:

ו **בְּיוֹם זִבְחֲכֶם יֵאָכֵל.** כְּשֶׁתִּזְבָּחוּהוּ, תִּשְׁחָטוּהוּ עַל מְנָת זְמַן זֶה שֶׁקָּבַעְתִּי לָכֶם כְּבָר:

ז **וְאִם הֵאָכֹל יֵאָכֵל וְגוֹ׳.** אִם אֵינוֹ עִנְיָן לְחוּץ לִזְמַנּוֹ, שֶׁהֲרֵי כְּבָר נֶאֱמַר: "וְאִם הֵאָכֹל יֵאָכֵל מִבְּשַׂר זֶבַח שְׁלָמָיו" וְגוֹ׳ (לעיל ז, יח), תְּנֵהוּ עִנְיָן לְחוּץ לִמְקוֹמוֹ. יָכוֹל יִהְיוּ חַיָּבִים כָּרֵת עַל אֲכִילָתוֹ? תַּלְמוּד לוֹמַר: "וְהַנֶּפֶשׁ הָאֹכֶלֶת מִמֶּנּוּ עֲוֺנָהּ תִּשָּׂא" (לעיל ז, יח), מִמֶּנּוּ וְלֹא מֵחֲבֵרוֹ, יָצָא הַנִּשְׁחָט בְּמַחְשֶׁבֶת חוּץ לִמְקוֹמוֹ: **פִּגּוּל.** מְתֹעָב, כְּמוֹ: "וּמְרַק פִּגֻּלִים כְּלֵיהֶם" (ישעיה סה, ד):

ח **וְאֹכְלָיו עֲוֺנוֹ יִשָּׂא.** בְּנוֹתָר גָּמוּר הַכָּתוּב מְדַבֵּר, וְאֵינוֹ עָנוּשׁ כָּרֵת עַל הַנִּשְׁחָט חוּץ לִמְקוֹמוֹ, שֶׁכְּבָר מִעֲטוֹ הַכָּתוּב, וְזֶה בְּנוֹתָר גָּמוּר מְדַבֵּר. וּבְמַסֶּכֶת כְּרֵתוֹת (דף ה ע"א) לְמָדוּהוּ מִגְּזֵרָה שָׁוָה:

ט **לֹא תְכַלֶּה פְּאַת שָׂדְךָ.** שֶׁיַּנִּיחַ פֵּאָה בְּסוֹף שָׂדֵהוּ: **וְלֶקֶט קְצִירְךָ.** שִׁבֳּלִים הַנּוֹשְׁרִים בִּשְׁעַת קְצִירָה אַחַת אוֹ שְׁתַּיִם, אֲבָל שָׁלֹשׁ אֵינָן לֶקֶט (פאה ו, ה):

י **לֹא תְעוֹלֵל.** לֹא תִטֹּל עוֹלְלוֹת שֶׁבָּהּ, וְהֵן נִכָּרוֹת. אֵיזֶהוּ עוֹלְלוֹת? כָּל שֶׁאֵין לָהּ לֹא כָתֵף וְלֹא נָטֵף: **וּפֶרֶט כַּרְמְךָ.** גַּרְגְּרֵי עֲנָבִים הַנּוֹשְׁרִים בִּשְׁעַת בְּצִירָה: **אֲנִי ה׳ אֱלֹהֵיכֶם.** דַּיָּן לִפָּרַע, וְאֵינִי גּוֹבֶה מִכֶּם אֶלָּא נְפָשׁוֹת, שֶׁנֶּאֱמַר: "אַל תִּגְזָל דָּל" וְגוֹ׳ "כִּי ה׳ יָרִיב רִיבָם" וְגוֹ׳ (משלי כב, כב-כג):

יא **לֹא תִּגְנֹבוּ.** אַזְהָרָה לְגוֹנֵב מָמוֹן, אֲבָל "לֹא תִּגְנֹב" שֶׁבַּעֲשֶׂרֶת הַדִּבְּרוֹת אַזְהָרָה לְגוֹנֵב נְפָשׁוֹת, דָּבָר הַלָּמֵד מֵעִנְיָנוֹ, דָּבָר שֶׁחַיָּבִין עָלָיו מִיתַת בֵּית דִּין: **וְלֹא תְכַחֲשׁוּ.** לְפִי שֶׁנֶּאֱמַר: "וְכִחֶשׁ בָּהּ" – מְשַׁלֵּם קֶרֶן וְחֹמֶשׁ (לעיל ה, כב-כד), לָמַדְנוּ עֹנֶשׁ, אַזְהָרָה מִנַּיִן? תַּלְמוּד לוֹמַר: "וְלֹא תְכַחֲשׁוּ": **וְלֹא תְשַׁקְּרוּ.** לְפִי שֶׁנֶּאֱמַר: "וְנִשְׁבַּע עַל שָׁקֶר" – יְשַׁלֵּם קֶרֶן וְחֹמֶשׁ (לעיל ה, כב-כד), לָמַדְנוּ עֹנֶשׁ, אַזְהָרָה מִנַּיִן? תַּלְמוּד לוֹמַר "וְלֹא תְשַׁקְּרוּ": **לֹא**

ד תִּירָאוּ וְאֶת־שַׁבְּתֹתַי תִּשְׁמֹרוּ אֲנִי יְהוָה אֱלֹהֵיכֶם: אַל־תִּפְנוּ אֶל־
ה הָאֱלִילִם וֵאלֹהֵי מַסֵּכָה לֹא תַעֲשׂוּ לָכֶם אֲנִי יְהוָה אֱלֹהֵיכֶם: וְכִי תִזְבְּחוּ
ו זֶבַח שְׁלָמִים לַיהוָה לִרְצֹנְכֶם תִּזְבָּחֻהוּ: בְּיוֹם זִבְחֲכֶם יֵאָכֵל וּמִמָּחֳרָת
ז וְהַנּוֹתָר עַד־יוֹם הַשְּׁלִישִׁי בָּאֵשׁ יִשָּׂרֵף: וְאִם הֵאָכֹל יֵאָכֵל בַּיּוֹם
ח הַשְּׁלִישִׁי פִּגּוּל הוּא לֹא יֵרָצֶה: וְאֹכְלָיו עֲוֺנוֹ יִשָּׂא כִּי־אֶת־קֹדֶשׁ יְהוָה
ט חִלֵּל וְנִכְרְתָה הַנֶּפֶשׁ הַהִוא מֵעַמֶּיהָ: וּבְקֻצְרְכֶם אֶת־קְצִיר אַרְצְכֶם לֹא
י תְכַלֶּה פְּאַת שָׂדְךָ לִקְצֹר וְלֶקֶט קְצִירְךָ לֹא תְלַקֵּט: וְכַרְמְךָ לֹא תְעוֹלֵל
וּפֶרֶט כַּרְמְךָ לֹא תְלַקֵּט לֶעָנִי וְלַגֵּר תַּעֲזֹב אֹתָם אֲנִי יְהוָה אֱלֹהֵיכֶם:
יא יב לֹא תִּגְנֹבוּ וְלֹא־תְכַחֲשׁוּ וְלֹא־תְשַׁקְּרוּ אִישׁ בַּעֲמִיתוֹ: וְלֹא־תִשָּׁבְעוּ
יג בִשְׁמִי לַשָּׁקֶר וְחִלַּלְתָּ אֶת־שֵׁם אֱלֹהֶיךָ אֲנִי יְהוָה: לֹא־תַעֲשֹׁק אֶת־רֵעֲךָ
יד וְלֹא תִגְזֹל לֹא־תָלִין פְּעֻלַּת שָׂכִיר אִתְּךָ עַד־בֹּקֶר: לֹא־תְקַלֵּל חֵרֵשׁ

אונקלוס

תְּהוֹן דָּחֲלִין, וְיָת יוֹמֵי שַׁבַּיָּא דִּילִי תִּטְּרוּן, אֲנָא יי אֱלָהֲכוֹן: ד לָא תִתְפְּנוּן בָּתַר טַעֲוָן, וְדַחֲלָן דְּמַתְּכָא, לָא תַעְבְּדוּן לְכוֹן, אֲנָא יי אֱלָהֲכוֹן: ה וַאֲרֵי תִכְּסוּן נִכְסַת קֻדְשִׁין קֳדָם יי, לְרַעֲוָא לְכוֹן תִּכְּסֻנֵּיהּ: ו בְּיוֹמָא דְּיִתְנְכֵיס, יִתְאֲכִיל וּבְיוֹמָא דְּבָתְרוֹהִי, וּדְיִשְׁתְּאַר עַד יוֹמָא תְּלִיתָאָה, בְּנוּרָא יִתּוֹקַד: ז וְאִם, אִתְאֲכָלָא יִתְאֲכִיל בְּיוֹמָא תְּלִיתָאָה, מְרַחַק הוּא לָא יְהֵי לְרַעֲוָא: ח וּדְיֵיכְלִנֵּיהּ חוֹבֵיהּ יְקַבֵּיל, אֲרֵי יָת קֻדְשָׁא דַּיי אַחֵיל, וְיִשְׁתֵּיצֵי, אֲנָשָׁא הַהוּא מֵעַמֵּיהּ: ט וּבְמִחְצַדְכוֹן יָת חֲצָדָא דְּאַרְעֲכוֹן, לָא תְשֵׁיצֵי, פָּתָא דְּחַקְלָךְ לְמִחְצַד, וּלְקָטָא דְּחַצָדָךְ לָא תְלַקֵּיט: י וְכַרְמָךְ לָא תְעֻלֵּיל, וְנִתְרָא דְּכַרְמָךְ לָא תְלַקֵּיט, לְעַנְיֵי וּלְגִיּוֹרֵי תִּשְׁבּוֹק יָתְהוֹן, אֲנָא יי אֱלָהֲכוֹן: יא לָא תִגְנְבוּן, וְלָא תְכַדְּבוּן וְלָא תְשַׁקְּרוּן אֱנָשׁ בְּחַבְרֵיהּ: יב וְלָא תִשְׁתַּבְעוּן בִּשְׁמִי לְשִׁקְרָא, וְתַחֵיל, יָת שְׁמָא דֶּאֱלָהָךְ אֲנָא יי: יג לָא תַעְשׁוֹק יָת חַבְרָךְ וְלָא תֵינוֹס, לָא תְבִית, אַגְרָא דַּאֲגִירָא, לְוָתָךְ עַד צַפְרָא: יד לָא תְלוּט דְּלָא שָׁמַע,

רש״י

תִּגְנֹבוּ וְלֹא תְכַחֲשׁוּ וְלֹא תְשַׁקְּרוּ... וְלֹא תִשָּׁבְעוּ. אִם גָּנַבְתָּ סוֹפְךָ לְכַחֵשׁ, סוֹפְךָ לְשַׁקֵּר, סוֹפְךָ לְהִשָּׁבַע לַשָּׁקֶר:

יב וְלֹא תִשָּׁבְעוּ בִשְׁמִי. לָמָּה נֶאֱמַר? לְפִי שֶׁנֶּאֱמַר: "לֹא תִשָּׂא אֶת שֵׁם ה' אֱלֹהֶיךָ לַשָּׁוְא" (שמות כ, ז), יָכוֹל לֹא יְהֵא חַיָּב אֶלָּא עַל שֵׁם הַמְיֻחָד, מִנַּיִן לְרַבּוֹת כָּל הַכִּנּוּיִין? תַּלְמוּד לוֹמַר: "וְלֹא תִשָּׁבְעוּ בִשְׁמִי לַשָּׁקֶר", כָּל שֵׁם שֶׁיֵּשׁ לִי:

יג לֹא תַעֲשֹׁק. זֶה הַכּוֹבֵשׁ שְׂכַר שָׂכִיר: לֹא תָלִין. לְשׁוֹן נְקֵבָה, מוּסָב עַל הַפְּעֻלָּה: עַד בֹּקֶר. בְּשָׂכִיר יוֹם הַכָּתוּב מְדַבֵּר, שֶׁיְּצִיאָתוֹ מִשֶּׁשָּׁקְעָה הַחַמָּה, לְפִיכָךְ זְמַן גְּבוּי שְׂכָרוֹ כָּל הַלַּיְלָה. וּבְמָקוֹם אַחֵר הוּא אוֹמֵר: "וְלֹא תָבוֹא עָלָיו הַשֶּׁמֶשׁ" (דברים כד, טו), מְדַבֵּר בִּשְׂכִיר לַיְלָה, שֶׁהַשְׁלָמַת פְּעֻלָּתוֹ מִשֶּׁיַּעֲלֶה עַמּוּד הַשַּׁחַר, לְפִיכָךְ זְמַן גְּבוּי שְׂכָרוֹ כָּל הַיּוֹם, לְפִי שֶׁנָּתְנָה תּוֹרָה זְמַן לְבַעַל הַבַּיִת עוֹנָה לְבַקֵּשׁ מָעוֹת:

יד לֹא תְקַלֵּל חֵרֵשׁ. אֵין לִי אֶלָּא חֵרֵשׁ, מִנַּיִן לְרַבּוֹת כָּל אָדָם? תַּלְמוּד לוֹמַר: "בְּעַמְּךָ לֹא תָאֹר" (שמות כב, כז), אִם כֵּן, לָמָּה נֶאֱמַר "חֵרֵשׁ"? מַה

19:14 לֹא־תְקַלֵּל חֵרֵשׁ וְלִפְנֵי עִוֵּר לֹא תִתֵּן מִכְשֹׁל *Do not curse the deaf or put a stumbling-block before the blind* – These are two very different commands. The prohibition against putting a stumbling-block before the blind is readily understandable.

15 a stumbling-block before the blind. Fear your God; I am the Lord. Do not SHENI /ḤAMISHI/
pervert justice: do not show partiality to the poor or deference to the great;
16 judge your fellow man fairly. Do not go around as a gossipmonger among your
people. Do not stand by while your neighbor's life is in danger; I am the Lord.
17 Do not hate your brother in your heart. Admonish your fellow and do not

רש"י

חרש מיוחד שהוא בחיים, אף כל שהוא בחיים, יצא המת שאינו בחיים: **ולפני עור לא תתן מכשל.** לפני הסומא בדבר לא תתן עצה שאינה הוגנת לו, אל תאמר מכור שדך וקח לך חמור, ואתה עוקף עליו ונוטלה הימנו: **ויראת מאלהיך.** לפי שהדבר הזה אינו מסור לבריות לידע אם דעתו של זה לטובה או לרעה, ויכול להשמט ולומר: לטובה נתכונתי, לפיכך נאמר בו: "ויראת מאלהיך", המכיר מחשבותיך. וכן כל דבר המסור ללבו של אדם העושהו, ואין אחר הבריות מכירות בו, נאמר בו: "ויראת מאלהיך":

טו **לא תעשו עול במשפט.** מלמד שהדיין המקלקל את הדין קרוי עול, שנוי ומשקץ, חרם ותועבה, שהעול קרוי תועבה, שנאמר: "כי תועבת ה' וגו' כל עשה עול" (דברים כה, טז), והתועבה קרויה שקץ וחרם, שנאמר: "ולא תביא תועבה אל ביתך והיית חרם כמהו שקץ תשקצנו" וגו' (שם ז, כו): **לא תשא פני דל.** שלא תאמר, עני הוא זה והעשיר חייב לפרנסו, אזכנו בדין ונמצא מתפרנס בנקיות: **ולא תהדר פני גדול.** שלא תאמר, עשיר הוא זה, בן גדולים הוא זה, היאך אביישנו ואראה בבשתו? עונש יש בדבר! לכך נאמר: "ולא תהדר פני גדול": **בצדק תשפט עמיתך.** כמשמעו. דבר אחר, הוי דן את חברך לכף זכות:

טז **לא תלך רכיל.** אני אומר על שם שכל משלחי מדנים ומספרי לשון הרע הולכים בבתי רעיהם לרגל מה יראו רע או מה ישמעו רע לספר בשוק, נקראים הולכי רכיל, הולכי רגילה, אשפיימנ"ט בלע"ז. וראיה לדברי, שלא מצינו רכילות שאין כתוב בלשון הליכה, "לא תלך רכיל", "הלכי רכיל נחשת וברזל" (ירמיה ו, כח). ושאר לשון הרע אין כתוב בו הליכה, "מלשני בסתר רעהו" (תהלים קא, ה), "לשון רמיה" (שם קכ, ב-ג), "לשון מדברת גדלות" (שם יב, ד). לכך אני אומר שהלשון "רכיל" לשון הולך ומרגל, שהכ"ף נחלפת בגימ"ל, שכל האותיות שמוצאיהן ממקום אחד מתחלפות זו בזו: בי"ת בפ"א, וגימ"ל בכ"ף, וקו"ף בכ"ף, ונו"ן בלמ"ד, וזי"ן בצד"י. וכן: "וירגל בעבדך" (שמואל ב' יט, כח), רגל במרמה לאמר עלי רעה, וכן: "לא רגל על לשנו" (תהלים טו, ג), וכן רוכל, הסוחר ומרגל אחר כל סחורה, וכל המוכר בשמים להתקשט בהם הנשים, על שם שמחזר תמיד בעירות נקרא רוכל, לשון רוגל. ותרגומו: "לא תיכול קורצין", כמו "ואכלו קרציהון די יהודיא" (דניאל ג, ח), "אכל ביה קרצא בי מלכא" (ברכות נח ע"א), נראה בעיני שהיה משפטם לאכול בבית המקבל דבריהם שום הלעטה, והוא גמר חזוק שדבריו מקימים ומעמידים על האמת, ואותה הלעטה נקראת 'אכילת קורצין', לשון: "קרץ בעינו" (משלי ו, יג), שכן דרך כל הולכי רכיל לקרץ בעיניהם ולרמז דברי רכילותן, שלא יבינו אחר השומעים: **לא תעמד על דם רעך.** לראות במיתתו ואתה יכול להצילו, כגון טובע בנהר וחיה או לסטים באים עליו: **אני ה'.** נאמן לשלם שכר, ונאמן לפרע:

יז **ולא תשא עליו חטא.** לא תלבין את פניו ברבים:

LAWS OF SOCIAL RELATIONS

Verses 17 and 18, taken as a pair, speak volumes of the biblical concept of love. The Torah does not begin these verses with the command to love. Instead it starts with the hard case: What to do with a neighbor, or brother, whom you dislike, even hate? He may have harmed you, offended you, insulted you. He may have acted in a way that you deeply believe is wrong. Your hatred, let us say, is not irrational. What to do? To command blandly that you must stifle your feelings is naive and unlikely to be effective. Freud coined the phrase "the return of the repressed" to signal that feelings we consciously deny have a way of returning in full and destructive force.

Hence, "Do not hate your brother in your heart" is followed by phrase 2: "Admonish your fellow." Instead of silencing your feelings, verbalize them. You may not hate your brother in your heart; instead, you have to confront the person openly and honestly. As Ramban explains:

> The verse is saying, "Do not hate your brother in your heart when he does something to you against your will, but instead remonstrate with him, saying, 'Why did you do this to me?' And you will not bear sin because of him by covering up your hatred in your heart, for when you remonstrate with him, he will justify himself before you,

טו וְלִפְנֵי עִוֵּר לֹא תִתֵּן מִכְשֹׁל וְיָרֵאתָ מֵּאֱלֹהֶיךָ אֲנִי יהוה׃ לֹא־תַעֲשׂוּ שני /חמישי/
עָוֶל בַּמִּשְׁפָּט לֹא־תִשָּׂא פְנֵי־דָל וְלֹא תֶהְדַּר פְּנֵי גָדוֹל בְּצֶדֶק תִּשְׁפֹּט
טז עֲמִיתֶךָ׃ לֹא־תֵלֵךְ רָכִיל בְּעַמֶּיךָ לֹא תַעֲמֹד עַל־דַּם רֵעֶךָ אֲנִי יהוה׃
יז לֹא־תִשְׂנָא אֶת־אָחִיךָ בִּלְבָבֶךָ הוֹכֵחַ תּוֹכִיחַ אֶת־עֲמִיתֶךָ וְלֹא־תִשָּׂא

אונקלוס

וּקְדָם דְּלָא חָזֵי, לָא תְשִׂים תַּקְלָא, וְתִדְחַל מֵאֱלָהָךְ אֲנָא יְיָ: טו לָא תַעְבְּדוּן שְׁקַר בְּדִין, לָא תִסַּב אַפֵּי מִסְכֵּינָא, וְלָא תֶהְדַּר אַפֵּי רַבָּא, בְּקֻשְׁטָא תְּדִינֵיהּ לְחַבְרָךְ: טז לָא תֵיכוּל קֻרְצִין בְּעַמָּךְ, לָא תְקוּם עַל דְּמָא דְחַבְרָךְ, אֲנָא יְיָ: יז לָא תִסְנֵי יָת אֲחוּךְ בְּלִבָּךְ, אוֹכָחָא תוֹכַח יָת חַבְרָךְ, וְלָא תְקַבֵּיל

Surely throughout history there were times when the righteous were forsaken. Indeed this is one of the questions that, according to the Talmud, Moshe asked God: "Why do the righteous suffer?" (Berakhot 7a). The English writer Edmond Blunden wrote a poem, "Report on Experience," on this theme:

> I have been young, and now am not too old;
> And I have seen the righteous forsaken,
> His health, his honor, and his quality taken.
> This is not what we were formerly told.

I once heard a beautiful explanation from Rabbi Moses Feuerstein of Boston. The key phrase of the verse is *lo ra'iti*, standardly translated as "I have not seen." The verb *ra'iti*, though, occurs twice in the Book of Esther with a quite different meaning. "For how can I live to see (*ra'iti*) the evil that will come upon my people; how can I live to see (*ra'iti*) the loss of those I am born of?" (Esther 8:6). The verb here does not mean literally "to see." It means to stand by and watch, to be a passive witness, a disengaged spectator. *Ra'iti* in this sense means seeing and doing nothing to help. That, for Esther as for the psalmist, is a moral impossibility. You may not, in other words, "stand by while your neighbor's life is in danger." You *are* your brother's keeper. The verse ends the Grace after Meals with a moral commitment. Yes, we have eaten and are satisfied. But that has not made us indifferent to the needs of others.

Especially when interpreted broadly, then, this command is a high moral requirement, and a challenging element of the holiness code.

It warns us against taking advantage of the disabled to cause them harm. The moral offense here is self-evident. But the first command, "Do not curse the deaf," is more far-reaching. On the face of it, cursing the deaf harms no one because the person you are insulting cannot hear what you are saying. Nonetheless, it is morally wrong. If we treat disrespectfully those who are deaf or disabled, even if they are unaware of it, we diminish their humanity and thereby our humanity. Even what may be thought of as a "victimless crime" affects who we are.

19:15 לֹא־תִשָּׂא פְנֵי־דָל *Do not show partiality to the poor* – Precisely because its whole moral code is oriented toward compassion, the Tanakh commands that compassion, the substrate of judgment, must not distort judgment. The preservation of impartiality, the balance of claims, the reciprocity of rights and obligations, and the interdependence of apparently opposed interests are values essential to Jewish legal procedure. These are the characteristics that are often summed up by saying that Judaism is a religion of law. I prefer to describe it as the rule that moral passion must yield to moral rationality if it is to achieve its ends.

19:16 לֹא תַעֲמֹד *Do not stand by* – Alongside the prohibition against murder (Ex. 20:13) we also have an obligation to intervene when we see a person's life endangered. The law has complex implications in the area of charitable giving. Consider this interpretation of a controversial verse in Grace after Meals: "I was once young, now I am old, yet I have not seen the righteous forsaken, with their children begging for bread" (Ps. 37:25).

18 bear guilt on his account. Do not take revenge or bear a grudge against any one
among your people, but love your neighbor as your own self; I am the Lord.

רש״י

יח **לֹא תִקֹּם.** אָמַר לוֹ: הַשְׁאִילֵנִי מַגָּלְךָ, אָמַר לוֹ: לָאו. לְמָחָר אָמַר לוֹ: הַשְׁאִילֵנִי קַרְדֻּמְּךָ, אָמַר לוֹ: אֵינִי מַשְׁאִילְךָ כְּדֶרֶךְ שֶׁלֹּא הִשְׁאַלְתַּנִי, זוֹ הִיא נְקִימָה. וְאֵיזוֹ הִיא נְטִירָה? אָמַר לוֹ: הַשְׁאִילֵנִי קַרְדֻּמְּךָ, אָמַר לוֹ: לָאו. לְמָחָר אָמַר לוֹ: הַשְׁאִילֵנִי מַגָּלְךָ, אָמַר לוֹ: הֵא לְךָ, וְאֵינִי כְּמוֹתְךָ שֶׁלֹּא הִשְׁאַלְתַּנִי, זוֹ הִיא נְטִירָה, שֶׁנּוֹטֵר הָאֵיבָה בְּלִבּוֹ, אַף עַל פִּי שֶׁאֵינוֹ נוֹקֵם: **וְאָהַבְתָּ לְרֵעֲךָ כָּמוֹךָ.** אָמַר רַבִּי עֲקִיבָא: זֶה כְּלָל גָּדוֹל בַּתּוֹרָה:

> [The Torah says] *hokhe'aḥ tokhiaḥ*, meaning "you shall admonish your fellow repeatedly" [because the verb is doubled, it implies you should admonish him more than once]. Might this mean *hokhe'aḥ*, admonish him once, and *tokhiaḥ*, a second time? No, he replied, the word *hokhe'aḥ* means: even a hundred times. Why then does it add the word *tokhiaḥ*? Had there been only a single verb, I would have known that the law applies to a master admonishing his disciple. How do we know that it applies even to a disciple admonishing his master? From the phrase *hokhe'aḥ tokhiaḥ*, implying: under all circumstances (Bava Metzia 31a).

This is significant because it establishes a principle of *critical followership*. Judaism commands almost unlimited respect for teachers. "Let reverence for your teacher be as great as your reverence for Heaven," said the Sages (Avot 4:12). Despite this, the Talmud understands the Torah to be commanding us to remonstrate even with our teacher or leader, should we see him or her doing something wrong. Uncritical followership and habits of silent obedience give rise to the corruptions of power, and sometimes to avoidable catastrophes.

The very act of learning in rabbinic Judaism is conceived as active debate, a kind of gladiatorial contest of the mind: "Even a teacher and disciple, even a father and son, when they sit to study Torah together become enemies to one another. But they do not move from there until they have become beloved to one another" (Kiddushin 30b).

Hence the talmudic saying, "Much wisdom I have learned from my teacher, more from my colleagues, but most from my students" (Taanit 7a). Despite the reverence we owe our teachers, we owe them also our best efforts at questioning and challenging their ideas. This is essential to the rabbinical ideal of learning as a collaborative pursuit of truth.

19:18 **לֹא־תִקֹּם** *Do not take revenge* – There is a fundamental difference between justice and revenge. Revenge is personal, justice impersonal. Revenge involves taking the law into your own hands. Justice is the opposite. It means handing over your cause to an impartial tribunal to examine the evidence and apply the law. The move from revenge to justice is fundamental. When courts and the legal process take the place of retaliation, it is no longer the Montagues against the Capulets but both under the impartial rule of law. Justice is not revenge. It is the only sane alternative to it.

What the prophets mean when they say in the name of God that "vengeance is Mine" is that there are forms of justice that only God can execute. Only for the God of justice are revenge and retribution the same thing. When the psalmist prays, "O God of retribution, Lord – O God of retribution, shine forth" (Ps. 94:1)," he means: God, let there be justice in this world. But You must do it, not us. We can judge individuals in courts of law, but we cannot judge nations. We can wage war to defend ourselves, but we cannot wage war to execute justice: You alone are the Judge of all the earth. *The call for divine vengeance is a renunciation of human vengeance while keeping faith in the ultimate rule of justice in the affairs of humankind.*

Vengeance is a profoundly dangerous human instinct. Wrongs must be righted through the due process of law, and larger questions of ultimate justice belong to God. To commit violence in the name of God is to forget the difference between God and humankind. There are some things, and vengeance is one, that belong to Heaven, not to fallible creatures of earth.

19:18 **וְלֹא־תִטֹּר** *Or bear a grudge* – What is the difference between taking revenge and bearing a grudge? The Sages give the following homely example:

> What is taking vengeance? If X says to Y, "Lend me your sickle," and Y refuses to lend it. The next day, Y says to X,

יח עָלָיו חֵטְא: לֹא־תִקֹּם וְלֹא־תִטֹּר אֶת־בְּנֵי עַמֶּךָ וְאָהַבְתָּ לְרֵעֲךָ כָּמוֹךָ

אונקלוס

עַל דִּילֵיהּ חוֹבָא: יח לָא תִקּוֹם וְלָא תִטַּר דְּבָבוּ לִבְנֵי עַמָּךְ, וְתִרְחֲמֵיהּ לְחַבְרָךְ כְּוָתָךְ,

or he will regret his action and admit his sin, and you will forgive him." (commentary on Lev. 19:17)

A key example of where this did not happen is the story of Yosef and his brothers:

> Now, Yisrael loved Yosef more than all his other sons, for he was a child of his old age; he made him an ornately colored robe. But when his brothers saw that their father loved him more than any of them, they hated him and could not say a peaceful word to him. (Gen. 37:3–4)

On this, Rabbi Yonatan Eybeshutz (c. 1690–1764) comments: "Had they been able to sit together as a group, they would have spoken to one another and remonstrated with each other, and would eventually have made their peace with one another" (*Tiferet Yehonatan* on Gen. 37:4). The tragedy of conflict is that it prevents people from talking together and listening to one another. Thus the bitterest conflicts are self-perpetuating.

The inner logic of the two verses is this: Love your neighbor as yourself. But not all neighbors are lovable. There are those who, out of envy or malice, have done you harm. God does not command you to be angels, without any of the emotions natural to human beings. He does, however, forbid you to hate. That is why, when someone does you wrong, you must confront him. You must tell him of your feelings of hurt and distress. It may be that you misunderstood. Or it may be that he meant to do you harm, but now, faced with the reality of the injury he has done you, he may repent of what he did. If, however, you fail to talk it through, you might bear a grudge and in time, come to take revenge.

The Torah both articulates the highest of ideals, and at the same time speaks to us as human beings. If we were angels it would be easy to love one another. But we are not. An ethic that commands us to love our enemies, without teaching how, is unliveable. Instead, the Torah sets out a realistic program. By being honest with one another, talking things through, we may be able to achieve reconciliation – not always, but often. How much distress and bloodshed might be spared if humanity heeded this command.

19:17 לֹא־תִשְׂנָא אֶת־אָחִיךָ בִּלְבָבֶךָ *Do not hate your brother in your heart* – Jewish law sets a high value on reconciliation and knows the dangers if it is not forthcoming. One of the examples given by Rambam is the biblical story of Avshalom and Amnon. Amnon had raped Avshalom's sister Tamar. At the time, Avshalom said nothing. He appeared to have either forgiven or forgotten the offense. Two years later, however, Avshalom took his revenge and had Amnon killed. Silence is no evidence of forgiveness. Better, concludes Rambam, to confront the wrongdoer directly and "if he repents and requests forgiveness, then one must forgive and not be harsh" (*Hilkhot Deot* 6:6).

This is not always necessary. To forgive without the dialectic of accusation and apology, as an unconditional act of grace, is equally mandated, and a sign of moral greatness:

> If someone is sinned against by another and the offended party does not wish to rebuke him or say anything to him – perhaps because the sinner is simpleminded or distraught – then if one forgives him in his heart and bears no animosity against him and does not rebuke him, this is indeed the way of saintliness [*middat ḥasidut*]. (*Hilkhot Deot* 6:9)

One way or another,

> the wrong done should be completely blotted out from a person's heart and not remembered. This is the appropriate character trait and makes possible the settlement of the earth and social relations among human beings. (*Hilkhot Deot* 7:8)

For Rambam, as for other interpreters of Jewish law, forgiveness is an essential precondition of social existence.

19:17 הוֹכֵחַ תּוֹכִיחַ *Admonish* – One of the Rabbis said to Rabba:

19 Keep My decrees. Do not crossbreed different kinds of animal, do not plant
your field with two kinds of seed intermixed, and do not wear clothing made
20 from two materials combined. If a man has carnal relations with a woman
who is a slave designated for another man, and who has not been redeemed
or given her freedom, there shall be punishment but they shall not be put to
21 death since she has not been freed. The man shall bring his guilt offering to
the LORD at the entrance of the Tent of Meeting: a ram for a guilt offering.
22 The priest shall make his atonement before the LORD with the ram of the
guilt offering for the sin that he committed, and the sin he committed shall be
forgiven.
23 When you enter the land and plant any tree for food, you shall regard its fruit SHELISHI

רש"י

יט **את חקתי תשמרו.** ואלו הן: "בהמתך לא תרביע כלאים" וגו'. חקים אלו גזרת מלך, שאין טעם לדבר: **ובגד כלאים וגו'.** למה נאמר? לפי שנאמר: "לא תלבש שעטנז צמר ופשתים יחדו" (דברים כב, יא), יכול לא ילבש גזי צמר ואניצי פשתן? תלמוד לומר: "בגד", מנין לרבות הלבדים? תלמוד לומר: "שעטנז", דבר שהוא שוע טווי ונוז. ואומר אני, 'נוז' לשון דבר הנמלל ושזור זה עם זה לחברו, מישטיי"ר בלע"ז, כמו "אזין לנאזי דאית בהון" (מועד קטן יב ע"ב), שאנו מפרשין לשון כמוש, פיילשטר"א. ולשון "שעטנז" פרש מנחם, מחברת צמר ופשתים:

כ **נחרפת לאיש.** מיעדת ומיחדת לאיש, ואיני יודע לו דמיון במקרא. ובשפחה כנענית שחציה שפחה וחציה בת חורין המארסת לעבד עברי שמתר בשפחה הכתוב מדבר: **והפדה לא נפדתה.** פדויה ואינה פדויה, וסתם פדיון בכסף: **או חפשה.** בשטר: **בקרת תהיה.** היא לוקה ולא הוא. יש על בית דין לבקר את הדבר שלא לחיבו מיתה, "כי לא חפשה" ואין קדושיה קדושין גמורין. ורבותינו למדו מכאן, שמי שהוא במלקות – תהא בקריאה, שהדינים המלקין קורין על הלוקה: "אם לא תשמר לעשות וגו' והפלא ה' את מכתך" וגו' (דברים כח נח-נט): **כי לא חפשה.** לפיכך אין חיב עליה מיתה, שאין קדושיה קדושין, הא אם חפשה קדושיה קדושין, וחיב מיתה:

כב **ונסלח לו מחטאתו אשר חטא.** לרבות את המזיד כשוגג:

כג **וערלתם ערלתו.** ואטמתם אטימתו, יהא אטום ונסתם מלהנות

can many souls each be a part of something that cannot be split or analyzed into parts? The truth is, at the deepest level, the entire community of Jewish souls is a single unity, standing in relation to one another as do the limbs of the body – many parts but a single entity. (See Tanya, especially chapter 2.)

The radical conclusion of Rabbi Schneur Zalman's mysticism is that, at the level of soul, every Jew is related to every other with complete identity. Between each Jew is a bond closer even than the closest we can speak of in non-mystical terminology, the bond between parent and child. "Love your neighbor as your own self" – because he is yourself. If we could attain this level of perception, then that love would flow unforced and without limits.

But how do we get there? When we think of human beings as bodies, then certainly each is separate and distinct. It is only when we relate to ourselves and others at the level of the soul that we can begin to sense the unity. And hence the task of the mystic – and, in truth, the task of Judaism as a whole – is to move from body to soul, from reactions prompted by ordinary physical stimuli to those wholly spiritual in character and motivation (Tanya, chapter 32).

The result of this approach is a profound emphasis on the love of every Jew – an emphasis that flows not simply from an emotion of benevolence but from a new way of viewing our identity and that of our fellow. It places a simultaneous stress on two things that might, in any other context, seem incompatible: the infinite worth of the individual and the literal unity of the whole Jewish people. The individual, because he is a part of God and every fragment of infinity is infinite. The community, because, at the level of soul, there are no divisions that set person against person.

יט אֲנִי יְהוָה: אֶת־חֻקֹּתַי תִּשְׁמֹרוּ בְּהֶמְתְּךָ לֹא־תַרְבִּיעַ כִּלְאַיִם שָׂדְךָ
כ לֹא־תִזְרַע כִּלְאָיִם וּבֶגֶד כִּלְאַיִם שַׁעַטְנֵז לֹא יַעֲלֶה עָלֶיךָ: וְאִישׁ כִּי־
יִשְׁכַּב אֶת־אִשָּׁה שִׁכְבַת־זֶרַע וְהִוא שִׁפְחָה נֶחֱרֶפֶת לְאִישׁ וְהָפְדֵּה
לֹא נִפְדָּתָה אוֹ חֻפְשָׁה לֹא נִתַּן־לָהּ בִּקֹּרֶת תִּהְיֶה לֹא יוּמְתוּ כִּי־לֹא
כא חֻפָּשָׁה: וְהֵבִיא אֶת־אֲשָׁמוֹ לַיהוָה אֶל־פֶּתַח אֹהֶל מוֹעֵד אֵיל אָשָׁם:
כב וְכִפֶּר עָלָיו הַכֹּהֵן בְּאֵיל הָאָשָׁם לִפְנֵי יְהוָה עַל־חַטָּאתוֹ אֲשֶׁר חָטָא
וְנִסְלַח לוֹ מֵחַטָּאתוֹ אֲשֶׁר חָטָא:
כג וְכִי־תָבֹאוּ אֶל־הָאָרֶץ וּנְטַעְתֶּם כָּל־עֵץ מַאֲכָל וַעֲרַלְתֶּם עָרְלָתוֹ אֶת־ טז שלישי

אונקלוס

אֲנָא יְיָ: יט יָת קְיָמַי תִּטְּרוּן, בְּעִירָךְ לָא תַרְכֵּיב עֵירוּבִין, חַקְלָךְ לָא תִזְרַע עֵירוּבִין, וּלְבוּשׁ עֵירוּבִין שַׁעַטְנֵיזָא, לָא יִסַּק עֲלָךְ: כ וּגְבַר, אֲרֵי יִשְׁכּוּב יָת אִתְּתָא שְׁכְבַת זַרְעָא, וְהִיא אָמָה אֲחִידָא לִגְבַר, וְאִתְפְּרָקָא לָא אִתְפְּרִיקַת בְּכַסְפָּא, אוֹ חֵירוּתָא לָא אִתְיְהִיבַת לַהּ בִּשְׁטָר, בִּקְרִתָּא תְּהֵי בַהּ, לָא יְמוּתוּן אֲרֵי לָא אִתְחָרַרַת: כא וְיַיְתֵי יָת אֲשָׁמֵיהּ לִקְדָם יְיָ, לִתְרַע מַשְׁכַּן זִמְנָא, דִּכְרָא לַאֲשָׁמָא: כב וִיכַפַּר עֲלוֹהִי כָּהֲנָא, בְּדִכְרָא דַאֲשָׁמָא קֳדָם יְיָ, עַל חוֹבְתֵיהּ דְּחָב, וְיִשְׁתְּבֵיק לֵיהּ, מֵחוֹבְתֵיהּ דְּחָב: כג וַאֲרֵי תֵיעֲלוּן לְאַרְעָא, וְתִצְּבוּן כָּל אִילַן דְּמֵיכַל, וּתְרַחֲקוּן רַחָקָא יָת

command not to take revenge. Not only is revenge forbidden but so is anything that might lead to it.

"LOVE YOUR NEIGHBOR AS YOUR OWN SELF"

This iconic command is surely easier said than performed. But there are cases where love flows easily and naturally for most people: for instance, the love of parents for their child. The parents love their child because they stand in a special relationship to the child; the parents have brought the child into being.

In several dazzling passages in the Tanya, the classic statement of Chabad thought, Rabbi Schneur Zalman of Liadi spells out a mystical theology of love. In the Tanya, it is not simply that the soul in its relation to the body is like God in His relation to the world, but that every godly soul is literally a part of God. Man, at his most spiritual level, does more than relate to God: he contains part of the reality of God.

But God, as Rambam lays down as one of the principles of the Jewish faith, is One and indivisible. How then

> "Lend me your axe," and X replies, "I will not lend you an axe, because you refused to lend me a sickle." That is forbidden by "You shall not take vengeance." (Sifra, Kedoshim 2:4 [10])

The prohibition against bearing a grudge is even more demanding:

> Y says to X, "Lend me your sickle," and X replies, "Take it. I am not like you who would not lend me an axe." That is what is forbidden by the law "You shall not bear a grudge." (Sifra, Kedoshim 2:4 [11])

Why is this a sin? On the face of it, the second person has acted correctly. He has *not* taken revenge. Rambam provides an explanation: "One should wipe the offense from his heart and not continue to bear a grudge, for as long as he continues to bear a grudge and remembers [the wrong done to him] he may come to take revenge" (*Hilkhot Deot* 7:8). Animosity is not a safe emotion. It can explode into action at any time. The prohibition against bearing a grudge, implies Rambam, is a kind of "fence," a protective barrier around the

as forbidden. For three years it shall be forbidden to you; it must not be eaten.
24 25 In the fourth year, all its fruit shall be holy, to give praise to the LORD. In the
fifth year you may eat its fruit – and so shall its yield proliferate for you; I am
26 the LORD your God. Do not eat any creature with its blood. Do not practice
27 divination or seek omens. Do not cut off the hair on the sides of your head or
28 destroy the edges of your beard. Do not gash your body for the dead or put
29 tattoo marks on yourself; I am the LORD. Do not profane your daughter by
making her a prostitute, that the land shall not be prostituted, the land filled
30 31 with depravity. Keep My Sabbaths, revere My Sanctuary; I am the LORD. Do not
turn to ghosts or inquire of spirits, rendering yourself impure; I am the LORD
32 your God. Stand up in the presence of the white-haired and show respect to the
33 elderly; revere your God; I am the LORD. When a stranger lives with REVI'I /SHISHI/
34 you in your land, do not wrong him. The stranger living with you shall be like

רש״י

מִמֶּנּוּ: **שָׁלֹשׁ שָׁנִים יִהְיֶה לָכֶם עֲרֵלִים.** מֵאֵימָתַי מוֹנֶה לוֹ? מִשְּׁעַת נְטִיעָתוֹ. יָכוֹל אִם הִצְנִיעוֹ לְאַחַר שָׁלֹשׁ שָׁנִים יְהֵא מֻתָּר? תַּלְמוּד לוֹמַר: ״יִהְיֶה״, בַּהֲוָיָתוֹ יְהֵא:

כד **יִהְיֶה כָּל פִּרְיוֹ קֹדֶשׁ.** כְּמַעֲשֵׂר שֵׁנִי שֶׁכָּתוּב בּוֹ: ״וְכָל מַעְשַׂר הָאָרֶץ וְגוֹ׳ קֹדֶשׁ לַה׳״ (ויקרא כז, ל), מָה מַעֲשֵׂר אֵינוֹ נֶאֱכָל חוּץ לְחוֹמַת יְרוּשָׁלַיִם אֶלָּא בְּפִדְיוֹן, אַף זֶה כֵּן. וְדָבָר זֶה ״הִלּוּלִים לַה׳״ הוּא, שֶׁנּוֹשְׂאוֹ שָׁם לְשַׁבֵּחַ וּלְהַלֵּל לַשָּׁמַיִם:

כה **לְהוֹסִיף לָכֶם תְּבוּאָתוֹ.** הַמִּצְוָה הַזֹּאת שֶׁתִּשְׁמְרוּ תִּהְיֶה ״לְהוֹסִיף לָכֶם תְּבוּאָתוֹ״, שֶׁבִּשְׂכָרָהּ אֲנִי מְבָרֵךְ לָכֶם פֵּרוֹת הַנְּטִיעוֹת. הָיָה רַבִּי עֲקִיבָא אוֹמֵר: דִּבְּרָה תוֹרָה כְּנֶגֶד יֵצֶר הָרָע, שֶׁלֹּא יֹאמַר אָדָם, הֲרֵי אַרְבַּע שָׁנִים אֲנִי מִצְטַעֵר בּוֹ חִנָּם, לְפִיכָךְ נֶאֱמַר: ״לְהוֹסִיף לָכֶם תְּבוּאָתוֹ״: **אֲנִי ה׳.** אֲנִי ה׳ הַמַּבְטִיחַ עַל כָּךְ, וְנֶאֱמָן לִשְׁמֹר הַבְטָחָתִי:

כו **לֹא תֹאכְלוּ עַל הַדָּם.** לְהַרְבֵּה פָּנִים נִדְרָשׁ בְּסַנְהֶדְרִין (דף סג ע״א), אַזְהָרָה שֶׁלֹּא יֹאכַל מִבְּשַׂר קָדָשִׁים לִפְנֵי זְרִיקַת דָּמִים, וְאַזְהָרָה לְאוֹכֵל מִבֶּהֱמַת חֻלִּין טֶרֶם שֶׁתֵּצֵא נַפְשָׁהּ, וְעוֹד הַרְבֵּה: **לֹא תְנַחֲשׁוּ.** כְּגוֹן אֵלּוּ הַמְנַחֲשִׁין בְּחֻלְדָּה וּבְעוֹפוֹת, פִּתּוֹ נָפְלָה מִפִּיו, צְבִי הִפְסִיקוֹ בַּדֶּרֶךְ: **וְלֹא תְעוֹנֵנוּ.** לְשׁוֹן עוֹנוֹת וְשָׁעוֹת, שֶׁאוֹמֵר, יוֹם פְּלוֹנִי יָפֶה לְהַתְחִיל מְלָאכָה, שָׁעָה פְּלוֹנִית קָשָׁה לָצֵאת:

כז **לֹא תַקִּפוּ פְּאַת רֹאשְׁכֶם.** זֶה הַמַּשְׁוֶה צְדָעָיו לַאֲחוֹרֵי אָזְנוֹ וּלְפַדַּחְתּוֹ, וְנִמְצָא הֶקֵּף רֹאשׁוֹ עָגֹל סָבִיב, שֶׁעַל אֲחוֹרֵי אָזְנָיו עִקְּרֵי שְׂעָרוֹ לְמַעְלָה מִצְּדָעָיו הַרְבֵּה: **פְּאַת זְקָנֶךָ.** סוֹף הַזָּקָן וּגְבוּלָיו, וְהֵן חָמֵשׁ: שְׁתַּיִם בְּכָל לְחִי וָלְחִי לְמַעְלָה אֵצֶל הָרֹאשׁ, שֶׁהוּא רָחָב וְיֵשׁ בּוֹ שְׁתֵּי פֵּאוֹת, וְאַחַת לְמַטָּה בְּסַנְטֵרוֹ, מְקוֹם חִבּוּר שְׁנֵי הַלְּחָיַיִם יַחַד:

כח **וְשֶׂרֶט לָנֶפֶשׁ.** כֵּן דַּרְכָּן שֶׁל אֱמוֹרִיִּים לִהְיוֹת מְשָׂרְטִין בְּשָׂרָם כְּשֶׁמֵּת לָהֶם מֵת: **וּכְתֹבֶת קַעֲקַע.** כְּתָב הַמָּחוּקֶה וְשָׁקוּעַ שֶׁאֵינוֹ נִמְחָק לְעוֹלָם, שֶׁמְּקַעְקְעוֹ בְּמַחַט וְהוּא מַשְׁחִיר לְעוֹלָם: **קַעֲקַע.** לְשׁוֹן ״וְהוֹקַע אוֹתָם״ (במדבר כה, ד), ״וְהוֹקַעֲנוּם״ (שמואל ב׳ כא, ו), תּוֹחֲבִין עֵץ בָּאָרֶץ וְתוֹלִין אוֹתָם עֲלֵיהֶם וְנִמְצְאוּ מְחֻקִּין וּתְחוּבִין בַּקַּרְקַע, פורפוינ״ט בְּלַעַ״ז:

כט **אַל תְּחַלֵּל אֶת בִּתְּךָ לְהַזְנוֹתָהּ.** בְּמוֹסֵר בִּתּוֹ פְּנוּיָה לְבִיאָה שֶׁלֹּא לְשֵׁם קִדּוּשִׁין: **וְלֹא תִזְנֶה הָאָרֶץ.** אִם אַתָּה עוֹשֶׂה כֵּן, הָאָרֶץ מְזַנָּה אֶת פֵּרוֹתֶיהָ לַעֲשׂוֹתָן בְּמָקוֹם אַחֵר וְלֹא בְּאַרְצְכֶם, וְכֵן הוּא אוֹמֵר ״וַיִּמָּנְעוּ רְבִבִים״ וְגוֹ׳ (ירמיה ג, ג):

ל **וּמִקְדָּשִׁי תִּירָאוּ.** לֹא יִכָּנֵס לוֹ בְּמַקְלוֹ וּבְמִנְעָלוֹ וּבַאֲפֻנְדָּתוֹ וּבְאָבָק שֶׁעַל רַגְלָיו. וְאַף עַל פִּי שֶׁאֲנִי מַזְהִירְכֶם עַל הַמִּקְדָּשׁ, ״אֶת שַׁבְּתֹתַי תִּשְׁמֹרוּ״, אֵין בִּנְיַן בֵּית הַמִּקְדָּשׁ דּוֹחֶה שַׁבָּת:

לא **אַל תִּפְנוּ אֶל הָאֹבֹת.** אַזְהָרָה לְבַעַל אוֹב וְיִדְּעוֹנִי. בַּעַל אוֹב זֶה פִּיתוֹם הַמְדַבֵּר מִשֶּׁחְיוֹ, וְיִדְּעוֹנִי – הַמַּכְנִיס עֶצֶם חַיָּה שֶׁשְּׁמָהּ ״יַדּוּעַ״ לְתוֹךְ פִּיו וְהָעֶצֶם מְדַבֵּר: **אַל תְּבַקְשׁוּ.** לִהְיוֹת עֲסוּקִים בָּם, שֶׁאִם תַּעַסְקוּ בָּם אַתֶּם מִטַּמְּאִין לְפָנַי וַאֲנִי מְתַעֵב אֶתְכֶם: **אֲנִי ה׳ אֱלֹהֵיכֶם.** דְּעוּ אֶת מִי אַתֶּם מַחֲלִיפִין בְּמִי:

לב **מִפְּנֵי שֵׂיבָה תָּקוּם.** יָכוֹל זָקֵן אַשְׁמַאי? תַּלְמוּד לוֹמַר: ״זָקֵן״, אֵין זָקֵן אֶלָּא שֶׁקָּנָה חָכְמָה: **וְהָדַרְתָּ פְּנֵי זָקֵן.** אֵיזֶהוּ הִדּוּר? לֹא יֵשֵׁב בִּמְקוֹמוֹ וְלֹא יְדַבֵּר בִּמְקוֹמוֹ וְלֹא יִסְתֹּר אֶת דְּבָרָיו. יָכוֹל יַעֲצִים עֵינָיו כְּמִי שֶׁלֹּא רָאָהוּ? לְכָךְ נֶאֱמַר: ״וְיָרֵאתָ מֵּאֱלֹהֶיךָ״, שֶׁהֲרֵי דָּבָר זֶה מָסוּר לְלִבּוֹ שֶׁל עוֹשֵׂהוּ, שֶׁאֵין מַכִּיר בּוֹ אֶלָּא הוּא, וְכָל דָּבָר הַמָּסוּר לַלֵּב נֶאֱמַר בּוֹ: ״וְיָרֵאתָ מֵּאֱלֹהֶיךָ״:

לג **לֹא תוֹנוּ.** אוֹנָאַת דְּבָרִים, לֹא תֹאמַר לוֹ, אֶמֶשׁ הָיִיתָ עוֹבֵד עֲבוֹדָה זָרָה וְעַכְשָׁיו אַתָּה בָּא לִלְמֹד תּוֹרָה שֶׁנִּתְּנָה מִפִּי הַגְּבוּרָה:

לד **כִּי גֵרִים הֱיִיתֶם.** מוּם שֶׁבְּךָ אַל תֹּאמַר לַחֲבֵרְךָ:

כד פִּרְיוֹ שָׁלֹשׁ שָׁנִים יִהְיֶה לָכֶם עֲרֵלִים לֹא יֵאָכֵל׃ וּבַשָּׁנָה הָרְבִיעִת יִהְיֶה
כה כָּל־פִּרְיוֹ קֹדֶשׁ הִלּוּלִים לַיהוָה׃ וּבַשָּׁנָה הַחֲמִישִׁת תֹּאכְלוּ אֶת־פִּרְיוֹ
כו לְהוֹסִיף לָכֶם תְּבוּאָתוֹ אֲנִי יְהוָה אֱלֹהֵיכֶם׃ לֹא תֹאכְלוּ עַל־הַדָּם לֹא
כז תְנַחֲשׁוּ וְלֹא תְעוֹנֵנוּ׃ לֹא תַקִּפוּ פְּאַת רֹאשְׁכֶם וְלֹא תַשְׁחִית אֵת פְּאַת
כח זְקָנֶךָ׃ וְשֶׂרֶט לָנֶפֶשׁ לֹא תִתְּנוּ בִּבְשַׂרְכֶם וּכְתֹבֶת קַעֲקַע לֹא תִתְּנוּ
כט בָּכֶם אֲנִי יְהוָה׃ אַל־תְּחַלֵּל אֶת־בִּתְּךָ לְהַזְנוֹתָהּ וְלֹא־תִזְנֶה הָאָרֶץ
ל וּמָלְאָה הָאָרֶץ זִמָּה׃ אֶת־שַׁבְּתֹתַי תִּשְׁמֹרוּ וּמִקְדָּשִׁי תִּירָאוּ אֲנִי יְהוָה׃
לא אַל־תִּפְנוּ אֶל־הָאֹבֹת וְאֶל־הַיִּדְּעֹנִים אַל־תְּבַקְשׁוּ לְטָמְאָה בָהֶם אֲנִי
לב יְהוָה אֱלֹהֵיכֶם׃ מִפְּנֵי שֵׂיבָה תָּקוּם וְהָדַרְתָּ פְּנֵי זָקֵן וְיָרֵאתָ מֵּאֱלֹהֶיךָ
לג אֲנִי יְהוָה׃ וְכִי־יָגוּר אִתְּךָ גֵּר בְּאַרְצְכֶם לֹא תוֹנוּ אֹתוֹ׃ רביעי /ששי/
לד כְּאֶזְרָח מִכֶּם יִהְיֶה לָכֶם הַגֵּר ׀ הַגָּר אִתְּכֶם וְאָהַבְתָּ לוֹ כָּמוֹךָ כִּי־גֵרִים

אונקלוס

אִבֵּיהּ, תְּלָת שְׁנִין, יְהֵי לְכוֹן, מְרַחַק לְאַבָּדָא לָא יִתְאֲכִיל: כד וּבְשַׁתָּא
רְבִיעֵיתָא, יְהֵי כָּל אִבֵּיהּ, קֹדֶשׁ תֻּשְׁבְּחָן קֳדָם יְיָ: כה וּבְשַׁתָּא
חֲמִישֵׁיתָא, תֵּיכְלוּן יָת אִבֵּיהּ, לְאוֹסָפָא לְכוֹן עֲלַלְתֵּיהּ, אֲנָא יְיָ
אֱלָהֲכוֹן: כו לָא תֵיכְלוּן עַל דְּמָא, לָא תְנַחֲשׁוּן וְלָא תְעָנוּן: כז לָא
תַקְּפוּן, פָּתָא דְּרֵישְׁכוֹן, וְלָא תְחַבֵּיל, יָת פָּתָא דְּדִקְנָךְ: כח וְחִבּוּל עַל
מִית, לָא תִתְּנוּן בִּבְסַרְכוֹן, וְרֻשְׁמִין חֲרִיתִין, לָא תִתְּנוּן בְּכוֹן, אֲנָא
יְיָ: כט לָא תַחֵיל יָת בְּרַתָּךְ לְאַטְעָיוּתַהּ, וְלָא תִטְעֵי אַרְעָא, וְתִתְמְלֵי
אַרְעָא עֵיצַת חֲטִין: ל יָת יוֹמֵי שַׁבַּיָּא דִּילִי תִּטְּרוּן, וּלְבֵית מַקְדְּשִׁי
תְּהוֹן דָּחֲלִין, אֲנָא יְיָ: לא לָא תִתְפְּנוּן בָּתַר בִּדִּין וּזְכוּרוּ, לָא תִתְבְּעוּן
לְאִסְתַּאָבָא בְּהוֹן, אֲנָא יְיָ אֱלָהֲכוֹן: לב מִן קֳדָם דְּסָבַר בְּאוֹרָיְתָא
תְּקוּם, וּתְהַדַּר אַפֵּי סָבָא, וְתִדְחַל מֵאֱלָהָךְ אֲנָא יְיָ: לג וַאֲרֵי יִתְגַּיַּר
עִמְּכוֹן, גִּיּוֹרָא בְּאַרְעֲכוֹן, לָא תוֹנוּן יָתֵיהּ: לד כְּיַצִּיבָא מִנְּכוֹן יְהֵי
לְכוֹן, גִּיּוֹרָא דְּיִתְגַּיַּר עִמְּכוֹן, וְתִרְחַם לֵיהּ כְּוָתָךְ, אֲרֵי דַּיָּרִין הֲוֵיתוֹן

19:32 וְהָדַרְתָּ פְּנֵי זָקֵן *Show respect to the elderly* – The Tanakh takes it as axiomatic that a society is judged by the way it treats the most vulnerable: the very young and the very old. One of the beautiful aspects of Jewish life, in our synagogues, old-age homes, and extended families, is the conversation and friendship between the young and the old, between grandparents and grandchildren, sometimes even into the fourth generation; the young sharing their dreams with the old; the old sharing their memories with the young.

Years ago, the late Alastair Cooke in one of his *Letters from America* radio programs spoke about a remote region whose inhabitants lived to a great old age. A team of researchers went to discover their secret. Was it the climate, or the diet, or their genes? The answer was none of these. It was simply that their society honored the elderly. So should we. It may or may not add years to their life, but it will add life to their years.

19:34 וְאָהַבְתָּ לוֹ כָּמוֹךָ *Love him as your own self* – Leviticus 19 teaches us a third love, in addition to that of God and our neighbor: love for "the stranger living with you." It is easier to love your neighbor as yourself because throughout most of history, your neighbors were often like yourself, in culture,

one of your native born to you: love him as your own self, for you yourselves
35 were strangers in the land of Egypt; I am the LORD your God. Do not falsify
36 measures – not of length, nor of weight, nor of volume. You shall have honest
scales, honest weights, an honest ephah, and an honest hin. I am the LORD
37 your God, who brought you out of the land of Egypt. Keep all My decrees and
laws and fulfill them; I am the LORD."
20 1/2 The LORD spoke to Moshe: "Tell the Israelites: Any person – any Israelite or any HAMISHI
migrant residing among Israel – who sacrifices any of his children to Molekh shall
3 be put to death. The people of the land shall stone him, and I Myself will set My
face against that person; I will sever him from his people because, in sacrificing his
4 children to Molekh, he defiles My Sanctuary; he desecrates My holy name. If the
people of the land close their eyes to a man as he sacrifices his children to Molekh –
5 if they do not put him to death – I Myself will set My face against him and his

רש"י

אני ה' אלהיכם. אלהיך ואלהיו אני:

לה **לא תעשו עול במשפט.** אם לדין, הרי כבר נאמר: "לא תעשו עול במשפט" (לעיל פסוק טו), ומהו "משפט" השנוי כאן? הוא המדה והמשקל והמשורה, מלמד שהמודד נקרא דין, שאם שקר במדה הרי הוא כמקלקל את הדין, וקרוי עול שנוי ומשקץ חרם ותועבה, וגורם לחמשה דברים האמורים בדין: מטמא את הארץ, ומחלל את השם, ומסלק את השכינה, ומפיל את ישראל בחרב, ומגלה אותם מארצם: **במדה.** זו מדת הארץ: **במשקל.** כמשמעו: **ובמשורה.** היא מדת הלח והיבש:

לו **אבני צדק.** הם המשקולות ששוקלין כנגדן: **איפה.** היא מדת היבש: **הין.** זו היא מדת הלח: **אשר הוצאתי אתכם.** על מנת כן. דבר אחר, אני הבחנתי במצרים בין טפה של בכור לטפה שאינה של בכור, ואני הנאמן לפרע ממי שטומן משקלותיו במלח להונות את הבריות שאין מכירים בהם:

כ ב **ואל בני ישראל תאמר.** ענשין על האזהרות: **מות יומת.** בבית דין. ואם אין כח בבית דין, "עם הארץ" מסיעין אותן: **עם הארץ.** שבגינו נבראת הארץ, שעתידין לירש את הארץ על ידי מצות הללו:

ג **אתן את פני.** פנאי שלי, פונה אני מכל עסקי ועוסק בו: **באיש.** ולא בצבור, שאין כל הצבור נכרתין: **כי מזרעו נתן למלך.** לפי שנאמר: "מעביר בנו ובתו באש" (דברים יח, י), בן בנו ובן בתו מנין? תלמוד לומר: "כי מזרעו נתן למלך". זרע פסול מנין? תלמוד לומר: "בתתו מזרעו למלך" (להלן פסוק ד): **למען טמא את מקדשי.** את כנסת ישראל שהיא מקדשת לי, כלשון: "ולא יחלל את מקדשי" (להלן כא, כג):

ד **ואם העלם יעלימו.** אם העלימו בדבר אחד סוף שיעלימו בדברים הרבה, אם העלימו סנהדרי קטנה סוף שיעלימו סנהדרי גדולה:

ה **ובמשפחתו.** אמר רבי שמעון: וכי משפחה מה חטאה? אלא ללמדך שאין לך משפחה שיש בה מוכס שאין כלם מוכסין, שכלן מחפין עליו: **והכרתי אתו.** למה נאמר? לפי שנאמר: "ובמשפחתו",

can we ensure the economy we have is an ethical enterprise?" Economic systems, like political ones, change over time, yet the Torah's concerns are timeless: Within a given system, how can we mitigate its hazards and injustices? How can we protect human dignity? How can we preserve fair dealing and integrity? How can we recognize the exigencies of economic endeavor and at the same time keep alive other and more spacious values? Jewish law and ethics devote great attention, sometimes at the level of broad principle, often in minute detail, to what John Gray calls "the moral foundations of market institutions."

According to Rava, when a person comes to the next world for judgment, the first question he is asked is "Did you deal honestly in business?" (Shabbat 31a). Honest scales and accurate weights and measures are to be a symbol for the hugely important halakhic field of business ethics. The Rabbis established supervisors to check on these measures, just as we now have supervisors of *kashrut*.

לה הֱיִיתֶ֖ם בְּאֶ֣רֶץ מִצְרָ֑יִם אֲנִ֖י יְהֹוָ֥ה אֱלֹהֵיכֶֽם׃ לֹא־תַעֲשׂ֥וּ עָ֖וֶל בַּמִּשְׁפָּ֑ט

לו בַּמִּדָּ֕ה בַּמִּשְׁקָ֖ל וּבַמְּשׂוּרָֽה׃ מֹ֧אזְנֵי צֶ֣דֶק אַבְנֵי־צֶ֗דֶק אֵ֥יפַת צֶ֛דֶק וְהִ֥ין

צֶ֖דֶק יִהְיֶ֣ה לָכֶ֑ם אֲנִי֙ יְהֹוָ֣ה אֱלֹֽהֵיכֶ֔ם אֲשֶׁר־הוֹצֵ֥אתִי אֶתְכֶ֖ם מֵאֶ֥רֶץ

לז מִצְרָֽיִם׃ וּשְׁמַרְתֶּ֤ם אֶת־כׇּל־חֻקֹּתַי֙ וְאֶת־כׇּל־מִשְׁפָּטַ֔י וַעֲשִׂיתֶ֖ם אֹתָ֑ם אֲנִ֖י

יְהֹוָֽה׃

כ א ב וַיְדַבֵּ֥ר יְהֹוָ֖ה אֶל־מֹשֶׁ֥ה לֵּאמֹֽר׃ וְאֶל־בְּנֵ֣י יִשְׂרָאֵל֮ תֹּאמַר֒ אִ֣ישׁ אִ֡ישׁ מִבְּנֵ֣י חמישי

יִשְׂרָאֵ֜ל וּמִן־הַגֵּ֣ר ׀ הַגָּ֣ר בְּיִשְׂרָאֵ֗ל אֲשֶׁ֨ר יִתֵּ֧ן מִזַּרְע֛וֹ לַמֹּ֖לֶךְ מ֣וֹת יוּמָ֑ת

ג עַ֥ם הָאָ֖רֶץ יִרְגְּמֻ֥הוּ בָאָֽבֶן׃ וַאֲנִ֞י אֶתֵּ֤ן אֶת־פָּנַי֙ בָּאִ֣ישׁ הַה֔וּא וְהִכְרַתִּ֥י

אֹת֖וֹ מִקֶּ֣רֶב עַמּ֑וֹ כִּ֤י מִזַּרְעוֹ֙ נָתַ֣ן לַמֹּ֔לֶךְ לְמַ֗עַן טַמֵּא֙ אֶת־מִקְדָּשִׁ֔י

ד וּלְחַלֵּ֖ל אֶת־שֵׁ֥ם קׇדְשִֽׁי׃ וְאִ֡ם הַעְלֵ֣ם יַעְלִ֩ימוּ֩ עַ֨ם הָאָ֜רֶץ אֶת־עֵֽינֵיהֶ֗ם

ה מִן־הָאִ֣ישׁ הַה֔וּא בְּתִתּ֥וֹ מִזַּרְע֖וֹ לַמֹּ֑לֶךְ לְבִלְתִּ֖י הָמִ֥ית אֹתֽוֹ׃ וְשַׂמְתִּ֨י

אֲנִ֧י אֶת־פָּנַ֛י בָּאִ֥ישׁ הַה֖וּא וּבְמִשְׁפַּחְתּ֑וֹ וְהִכְרַתִּ֨י אֹת֜וֹ וְאֵ֣ת ׀ כׇּל־הַזֹּנִ֣ים

אונקלוס

בְּאַרְעָא דְּמִצְרָיִם, אֲנָא יי אֱלָהֲכוֹן: לה לָא תַעְבְּדוּן שְׁקַר בְּדִין, בִּמְשַׁחְתָּא, בְּמַתְקָלָא וּבִמְכִילְתָּא: לו מוֹזְנָוָן דִּקְשׁוֹט מַתְקָלִין דִּקְשׁוֹט, מְכִילָן דִּקְשׁוֹט, וְהִינִין דִּקְשׁוֹט יְהוֹן לְכוֹן, אֲנָא יי אֱלָהֲכוֹן, דְּאַפֵּיקִית יָתְכוֹן מֵאַרְעָא דְּמִצְרָיִם: לז וְתִטְּרוּן יָת כָּל קְיָמַי וְיָת כָּל דִּינַי, וְתַעְבְּדוּן יָתְהוֹן, אֲנָא יי: כ א וּמַלֵּיל יי עִם מֹשֶׁה לְמֵימַר: ב וְעִם בְּנֵי יִשְׂרָאֵל תֵּימַר, גְּבַר גְּבַר מִבְּנֵי יִשְׂרָאֵל, וּמִן גִּיּוֹרַיָּא דְּיִתְגַּיְּרוּן בְּיִשְׂרָאֵל, דְּיִתֵּין מִזַּרְעֵיהּ, לְמֹלֶךְ אִתְקְטָלָא יִתְקְטִיל, עַמָּא בֵּית יִשְׂרָאֵל יִרְגְּמֻנֵּיהּ בְּאַבְנָא: ג וַאֲנָא, אֶתֵּין יָת רֻגְזִי בְּגֻבְרָא הַהוּא, וַאֲשֵׁיצֵי יָתֵיהּ מִגּוֹ עַמֵּיהּ, אֲרֵי מִזַּרְעֵיהּ יְהַב לְמֹלֶךְ, בְּדִיל, לְסַאָבָא יָת מַקְדְּשִׁי, וּלְאַחָלָא יָת שְׁמָא דְּקֻדְשִׁי: ד וְאִם, מִכְבַּשׁ יִכְבְּשׁוּן עַמָּא בֵּית יִשְׂרָאֵל, יָת עֵינֵיהוֹן מִן גֻּבְרָא הַהוּא, בְּדִיהַב מִזַּרְעֵיהּ לְמֹלֶךְ, בְּדִיל דְּלָא לְמִקְטַל יָתֵיהּ: ה וַאֲשַׁוֵּי אֲנָא יָת רֻגְזִי, בְּגֻבְרָא הַהוּא וּבְסַעֲדוֹהִי, וַאֲשֵׁיצֵי יָתֵיהּ, וְיָת כָּל דְּטָעַן

class, nationality, and ethnicity. The challenge is to love the stranger, the one who is not like you.

The Sages noted the repeated emphasis on the stranger in biblical law. According to R. Eliezer, the Torah "warns against the wronging of a *ger* in thirty-six places; others say: in forty-six places" (Bava Metzia 59b). Whatever the precise number, the repetition throughout the Mosaic books is remarkable. Sometimes the stranger is mentioned along with the poor; at others, with the widow and orphan. On several occasions, the Torah specifies: "You shall have the same law for the stranger as for the native born" (Ex. 12:49; Lev. 24:22; Num. 15:16, 29). Not only must the stranger not be wronged, he or she must be included in the positive welfare provisions of Israelite/Jewish society. But here the law goes beyond this; the stranger must be loved.

19:36 מֹאזְנֵי צֶדֶק *Honest scales* – There have been many hypotheses as to the religious origins of the market economy. As we survey the Torah and rabbinic literature, however, we find less concern with the question "What kind of economy should we have?" than with the question "How

family; I will sever him from his people, and with him all who follow him in
6 going astray after Molekh. And anyone who turns to ghosts or spirits, going
astray after them – I will set My face against him and sever him from his people.
7 8 Consecrate yourselves and be holy, for I am the LORD your God. Keep My SHISHI /SHEVI'I/
9 decrees and fulfill them; I am the LORD, who makes you holy. One who curses
his father or mother shall be put to death. Since he has cursed his father or
10 mother, his bloodguilt is upon him. If a man commits adultery with a married
woman, another man's wife, both the adulterer and the adulteress shall be
11 put to death. If a man lies with his father's wife, he has exposed his father's
nakedness; both of them shall be put to death; their bloodguilt is upon them.
12 If a man lies with his daughter-in-law, both of them shall be put to death. They
13 have committed perversion; their bloodguilt is upon them. If a man lies with a
male as he would with a woman, both have performed an abhorrent act; they
14 shall be put to death; their bloodguilt is upon them. If a man marries a woman
and also her mother, it is depravity. He and they shall be burned by fire; there
15 must be no depravity among you. If a man lies with an animal, he shall be put
16 to death and you shall kill the animal. If a woman approaches an animal to
mate with it, you shall kill the woman and the animal; they shall both be put
17 to death; their bloodguilt is upon them. If a man takes his sister – his father's
daughter or his mother's daughter – and they see one another's nakedness, it is a
deep disgrace; they shall be severed in the sight of their people. He has exposed

רש״י

יָכוֹל יִהְיוּ כָּל הַמִּשְׁפָּחָה בְּהִכָּרֵת? תַּלְמוּד לוֹמַר: ״אֹתוֹ״, אוֹתוֹ בְּהִכָּרֵת וְלֹא כָּל הַמִּשְׁפָּחָה בְּהִכָּרֵת אֶלָּא בְּיִסּוּרִין: **לִזְנוֹת אַחֲרֵי הַמֹּלֶךְ.** לְרַבּוֹת שְׁאָר עֲבוֹדָה זָרָה שֶׁעֲבָדָהּ בְּכָךְ, וַאֲפִלּוּ אֵין זוֹ עֲבוֹדָתָהּ:

ז **וְהִתְקַדִּשְׁתֶּם.** זוֹ פְּרִישׁוּת עֲבוֹדָה זָרָה:

ט **אָבִיו וְאִמּוֹ קִלֵּל.** לְרַבּוֹת לְאַחַר מִיתָה: **דָּמָיו בּוֹ.** זוֹ סְקִילָה, וְכֵן כָּל מָקוֹם שֶׁנֶּאֱמַר: ״דָּמָיו בּוֹ״, ״דְּמֵיהֶם בָּם״. וְלָמַדְנוּ מֵאוֹב וְיִדְּעוֹנִי שֶׁנֶּאֱמַר בָּהֶם: ״בָּאֶבֶן יִרְגְּמוּ אֹתָם דְּמֵיהֶם בָּם״ (להלן פסוק כז). וּפְשׁוּטוֹ שֶׁל מִקְרָא, כְּמוֹ: ״דָּמוֹ בְרֹאשׁוֹ״ (יהושע ב, יט), אֵין נֶעֱנָשׁ עַל מִיתָתוֹ אֶלָּא הוּא, שֶׁהוּא גָּרַם לְעַצְמוֹ שֶׁיֵּהָרֵג:

י **וְאִישׁ.** פְּרָט לְקָטָן: **אֲשֶׁר יִנְאַף אֶת אֵשֶׁת אִישׁ.** פְּרָט לְאֵשֶׁת קָטָן, לָמַדְנוּ שֶׁאֵין לְקָטָן קִדּוּשִׁין. וְעַל אֵיזוֹ אֵשֶׁת אִישׁ חִיַּבְתִּי לְךָ? ״אֲשֶׁר יִנְאַף אֶת אֵשֶׁת רֵעֵהוּ״, פְּרָט לְאֵשֶׁת גּוֹי, לָמַדְנוּ שֶׁאֵין קִדּוּשִׁין לְגוֹי: **מוֹת יוּמַת הַנֹּאֵף וְהַנֹּאָפֶת.** כָּל מִיתָה הָאֲמוּרָה בַּתּוֹרָה סְתָם אֵינָהּ אֶלָּא חֶנֶק:

יב **תֶּבֶל עָשׂוּ.** גְּנַאי. לָשׁוֹן אַחֵר, מְבַלְבְּלִין זֶרַע הָאָב בְּזֶרַע הַבֵּן:

יג **מִשְׁכְּבֵי אִשָּׁה.** מַכְנִיס כְּמִכְחוֹל בִּשְׁפוֹפֶרֶת:

יד **יִשְׂרְפוּ אֹתוֹ וְאֶתְהֶן.** אִי אַתָּה יָכוֹל לוֹמַר אִשְׁתּוֹ הָרִאשׁוֹנָה יִשְׂרְפוּ, שֶׁהֲרֵי נְשָׂאָהּ בְּהֶתֵּר וְלֹא נֶאֶסְרָה עָלָיו, אֶלָּא ״אִשָּׁה וְאִמָּהּ״ הַכְּתוּבִין כָּאן שְׁתֵּיהֶן לְאִסּוּר, שֶׁנָּשָׂא חֲמוֹתוֹ וְאִמָּהּ. וְיֵשׁ מֵרַבּוֹתֵינוּ שֶׁאוֹמְרִים, אֵין כָּאן אֶלָּא חֲמוֹתוֹ, וּמַהוּ ״אֶתְהֶן״? אֶת אַחַת מֵהֶן, וְלָשׁוֹן יְוָנִי הוּא: ׳הֵן׳ – אַחַת:

טו **וְאֶת הַבְּהֵמָה תַּהֲרֹגוּ.** אִם אָדָם חָטָא, בְּהֵמָה מֶה חָטְאָה? אֶלָּא מִפְּנֵי שֶׁבָּאָה לָאָדָם תַּקָּלָה עַל יָדָהּ לְפִיכָךְ אָמַר הַכָּתוּב תִּסָּקֵל, קַל וָחֹמֶר לְאָדָם שֶׁיּוֹדֵעַ לְהַבְחִין בֵּין טוֹב לְרָע וְגוֹרֵם רָעָה לַחֲבֵרוֹ לַעֲבֹר עֲבֵרָה. כַּיּוֹצֵא בַּדָּבָר אַתָּה אוֹמֵר: ״אַבֵּד תְּאַבְּדוּן אֶת כָּל הַמְּקֹמוֹת״ (דברים יב, ב), הֲרֵי דְּבָרִים קַל וָחֹמֶר: וּמָה אִילָנוֹת שֶׁאֵינָן רוֹאִין וְאֵינָן שׁוֹמְעִין, עַל שֶׁבָּאת תַּקָּלָה עַל יָדָם אָמְרָה תּוֹרָה הַשְׁחֵת שָׂרֵף וְכַלֵּה, הַמַּטֶּה אֶת חֲבֵרוֹ מִדֶּרֶךְ חַיִּים לְדַרְכֵי מִיתָה עַל אַחַת כַּמָּה וְכַמָּה:

יז **חֶסֶד הוּא.** לָשׁוֹן אֲרַמִּי ״חֶרְפָּה״ (בראשית לד, יד) – ׳חִסּוּדָא׳. וּמִדְרָשׁוֹ: אִם תֹּאמַר, קַיִן נָשָׂא אֲחוֹתוֹ! חֶסֶד עָשָׂה הַמָּקוֹם לִבְנוֹת עוֹלָמוֹ מִמֶּנּוּ, שֶׁנֶּאֱמַר: ״עוֹלָם חֶסֶד יִבָּנֶה״ (תהלים פט, ג):

ו אַחֲרָיו לִזְנוֹת אַחֲרֵי הַמֹּלֶךְ מִקֶּרֶב עַמָּם: וְהַנֶּפֶשׁ אֲשֶׁר תִּפְנֶה אֶל־
הָאֹבֹת וְאֶל־הַיִּדְּעֹנִים לִזְנֹת אַחֲרֵיהֶם וְנָתַתִּי אֶת־פָּנַי בַּנֶּפֶשׁ הַהִוא
ז וְהִכְרַתִּי אֹתוֹ מִקֶּרֶב עַמּוֹ: וְהִתְקַדִּשְׁתֶּם וִהְיִיתֶם קְדֹשִׁים כִּי אֲנִי יְהוָה
ח אֱלֹהֵיכֶם: וּשְׁמַרְתֶּם אֶת־חֻקֹּתַי וַעֲשִׂיתֶם אֹתָם אֲנִי יְהוָה מְקַדִּשְׁכֶם: ששי /שביעי/
ט כִּי־אִישׁ אִישׁ אֲשֶׁר יְקַלֵּל אֶת־אָבִיו וְאֶת־אִמּוֹ מוֹת יוּמָת אָבִיו וְאִמּוֹ
י קִלֵּל דָּמָיו בּוֹ: וְאִישׁ אֲשֶׁר יִנְאַף אֶת־אֵשֶׁת אִישׁ אֲשֶׁר יִנְאַף אֶת־אֵשֶׁת
יא רֵעֵהוּ מוֹת־יוּמַת הַנֹּאֵף וְהַנֹּאָפֶת: וְאִישׁ אֲשֶׁר יִשְׁכַּב אֶת־אֵשֶׁת אָבִיו
יב עֶרְוַת אָבִיו גִּלָּה מוֹת־יוּמְתוּ שְׁנֵיהֶם דְּמֵיהֶם בָּם: וְאִישׁ אֲשֶׁר יִשְׁכַּב
יג אֶת־כַּלָּתוֹ מוֹת יוּמְתוּ שְׁנֵיהֶם תֶּבֶל עָשׂוּ דְּמֵיהֶם בָּם: וְאִישׁ אֲשֶׁר יִשְׁכַּב
אֶת־זָכָר מִשְׁכְּבֵי אִשָּׁה תּוֹעֵבָה עָשׂוּ שְׁנֵיהֶם מוֹת יוּמָתוּ דְּמֵיהֶם בָּם:
יד וְאִישׁ אֲשֶׁר יִקַּח אֶת־אִשָּׁה וְאֶת־אִמָּהּ זִמָּה הִוא בָּאֵשׁ יִשְׂרְפוּ אֹתוֹ
טו וְאֶתְהֶן וְלֹא־תִהְיֶה זִמָּה בְּתוֹכְכֶם: וְאִישׁ אֲשֶׁר יִתֵּן שְׁכָבְתּוֹ בִּבְהֵמָה
טז מוֹת יוּמָת וְאֶת־הַבְּהֵמָה תַּהֲרֹגוּ: וְאִשָּׁה אֲשֶׁר תִּקְרַב אֶל־כָּל־בְּהֵמָה
לְרִבְעָה אֹתָהּ וְהָרַגְתָּ אֶת־הָאִשָּׁה וְאֶת־הַבְּהֵמָה מוֹת יוּמָתוּ דְּמֵיהֶם
יז בָּם: וְאִישׁ אֲשֶׁר־יִקַּח אֶת־אֲחֹתוֹ בַּת־אָבִיו אוֹ בַת־אִמּוֹ וְרָאָה אֶת־
עֶרְוָתָהּ וְהִיא תִרְאֶה אֶת־עֶרְוָתוֹ חֶסֶד הוּא וְנִכְרְתוּ לְעֵינֵי בְּנֵי עַמָּם

אונקלוס

בתרוהי, למטעי, בתר מלך מגו עמהון: ו ואנש, דיתפני בתר בדין וזכורו, למטעי בתריהון, ואתין ית רוגזי באנשא ההוא, ואשיצי יתיה מגו עמיה: ז ותתקדשון, ותהון קדישין, ארי, אנא יי אלהכון: ח ותטרון ית קימי, ותעבדון יתהון, אנא יי מקדשכון: ט ארי גבר גבר, דילוט ית אבוהי, וית אמיה אתקטלא יתקטיל, אבוהי ואמיה, לט קטלא חיב: י וגבר, דיגוף ית אתת גבר, דיגוף ית אתת חבריה, אתקטלא יתקטיל גיפא וגיפתא: יא וגבר, דישכוב ית אתת אבוהי, עריתא דאבוהי גלי, אתקטלא יתקטלון תרויהון קטלא חיבין: יב וגבר, דישכוב ית כלתיה, אתקטלא יתקטלון תרויהון, תבלא עבדו קטלא חיבין:

יג וגבר, דישכוב ית דכורא משכבי אתא, תועיבא עבדו תרויהון, אתקטלא יתקטלון קטלא חיבין: יד וגבר, דיסב ית אתתא, וית אמה עיצת חטין היא, בנורא, יוקדון יתיה ויתהון, ולא תהי עיצת חטין ביניכון: טו וגבר, דיתין שכבתיה, בבעירא אתקטלא יתקטיל, וית בעירא תקטלון: טז ואתתא, דתקרב לות כל בעירא למשלט בה, ותקטול ית אתתא וית בעירא, אתקטלא יתקטלון קטלא חיבין: יז וגבר דיסב ית אחתיה, בת אבוהי או בת אמיה, ויחזי ית עריתה, והיא תחזי ית עריתיה קלנא הוא, וישתיצון, לעיני בני עמהון,

18 his sister's nakedness; he shall bear his guilt. If a man lies with a menstruating
woman and exposes her nakedness, he has laid her hidden source bare; she
has exposed the source of her blood; both of them shall be severed from their
19 people. Do not expose the nakedness of your mother's sister or your father's
sister, because that is to lay bare your own near relative; both shall bear their
20 guilt. If a man lies with his aunt, he has exposed his uncle's nakedness. Both
21 parties shall bear their guilt; they shall die childless. For a man to marry his
brother's wife – that is taboo. He has exposed his brother's nakedness; both
22 parties shall be childless. Keep all My decrees and all My laws and fulfill them,
23 so that the land to which I am bringing you to settle will not vomit you out. Do SHEVI'I
not follow the practices of the nation I am driving out before you, for they did
24 all these things and I was disgusted with them. I have told you: You shall possess
their land; I am giving it to you to possess. It is a land that flows with milk and with
honey. I am the LORD your God, who has set you apart from all other peoples.
25 You, then, shall set pure apart from impure animals, pure from impure birds. Do MAFTIR
not make yourselves detestable by an animal or bird or anything that creeps

רש"י

יח| **הערה.** גלה, וכן כל לשון 'ערוה' גלוי הוא, והוי"ו יורדת בתבה לשם דבר, כמו 'זעוה' (דברים כח, כה) מגזרת "ולא קם ולא זע" (אסתר ה, ט), וכן 'אחוה' (זכריה יא, יד) מגזרת 'אח'. והערה זו נחלקו בה רבותינו: יש אומרים זו נשיקת שמש, ויש אומרים זו הכנסת עטרה:

יט| **וערות אחות אמך.** שנה הכתוב באזהרתן, לומר שהוזהר עליהן בין על אחות אביו ואמו מן האב בין על אחיותיהן מן האם, אבל על ערות אשת אחי אביו לא הוזהר אלא על אשת אחי אביו מן האב:

כ| **אשר ישכב את דדתו.** המקרא הזה בא ללמד על כרת האמור למעלה, שהוא בענש הליכת ערירי: **ערירים.** כתרגומו, בלא ולד, ודומה לו "ואנכי הולך ערירי" (בראשית טו, ב). יש לו בנים – קוברן, אין לו בנים – מת בלא בנים. לכך שנה בשני מקראות אלו, "ערירים ימתו" "ערירים יהיו" (להלן פסוק כא), "ערירים ימתו" – אם יהיו לו בשעת עברה לא יהיו לו כשימות לפי שקוברן בחייו, "ערירים יהיו" – שאם אין לו בשעת עברה יהיה כל ימיו כמו שהוא עכשיו:

כא| **נדה הוא.** השכיבה הזאת מנדה היא ומאוסה. ורבותינו דרשו, לאסר הערלה בה כנדה שהערלה מפלשת בה: "את מקרה הערה" (לעיל פסוק יח):

כג| **ואקץ.** לשון מאוס, כמו: "קצתי בחיי" (בראשית כז, מו), כאדם שהוא קץ במזונו:

כה| **והבדלתם בין הבהמה הטהרה לטמאה.** אין צריך לומר בין פרה לחמור, שהרי מבדלין ונכרין הם, אלא בין טהורה לך לטמאה לך, בין שנשחט רבו של סימן לנשחט חציו. וכמה בין רבו לחציו? מלא שערה: **אשר הבדלתי לכם לטמא.** לאסר:

Our passage lays the foundation of an intricate code of investing the love between husband and wife with a discipline, a structure, a rhythm, turning prose into religious poetry. How do you take an ordinary life and imbue it with the sense of the transcendent? More than any other institution, the family turns the everyday into unselfconscious beauty. Halakha is the genius of taking an ordinary life in ordinary circumstances and making it a home for the Divine Presence.

יח עֶרְוַת אֲחֹתוֹ גִּלָּה עֲוֺנוֹ יִשָּׂא׃ וְאִישׁ אֲשֶׁר־יִשְׁכַּב אֶת־אִשָּׁה דָּוָה וְגִלָּה
אֶת־עֶרְוָתָהּ אֶת־מְקֹרָהּ הֶעֱרָה וְהִוא גִּלְּתָה אֶת־מְקוֹר דָּמֶיהָ וְנִכְרְתוּ
יט שְׁנֵיהֶם מִקֶּרֶב עַמָּם׃ וְעֶרְוַת אֲחוֹת אִמְּךָ וַאֲחוֹת אָבִיךָ לֹא תְגַלֵּה כִּי
כ אֶת־שְׁאֵרוֹ הֶעֱרָה עֲוֺנָם יִשָּׂאוּ׃ וְאִישׁ אֲשֶׁר יִשְׁכַּב אֶת־דֹּדָתוֹ עֶרְוַת דֹּדוֹ
כא גִּלָּה חֶטְאָם יִשָּׂאוּ עֲרִירִים יָמֻתוּ׃ וְאִישׁ אֲשֶׁר יִקַּח אֶת־אֵשֶׁת אָחִיו נִדָּה
כב הִוא עֶרְוַת אָחִיו גִּלָּה עֲרִירִים יִהְיוּ׃ וּשְׁמַרְתֶּם אֶת־כָּל־חֻקֹּתַי וְאֶת־
כָּל־מִשְׁפָּטַי וַעֲשִׂיתֶם אֹתָם וְלֹא־תָקִיא אֶתְכֶם הָאָרֶץ אֲשֶׁר אֲנִי מֵבִיא
כג אֶתְכֶם שָׁמָּה לָשֶׁבֶת בָּהּ׃ וְלֹא תֵלְכוּ בְּחֻקֹּת הַגּוֹי אֲשֶׁר־אֲנִי מְשַׁלֵּחַ שביעי
כד מִפְּנֵיכֶם כִּי אֶת־כָּל־אֵלֶּה עָשׂוּ וָאָקֻץ בָּם׃ וָאֹמַר לָכֶם אַתֶּם תִּירְשׁוּ
אֶת־אַדְמָתָם וַאֲנִי אֶתְּנֶנָּה לָכֶם לָרֶשֶׁת אֹתָהּ אֶרֶץ זָבַת חָלָב וּדְבָשׁ
כה אֲנִי יְהוָה אֱלֹהֵיכֶם אֲשֶׁר־הִבְדַּלְתִּי אֶתְכֶם מִן־הָעַמִּים׃ וְהִבְדַּלְתֶּם בֵּין־ מפטיר
הַבְּהֵמָה הַטְּהֹרָה לַטְּמֵאָה וּבֵין־הָעוֹף הַטָּמֵא לַטָּהֹר וְלֹא־תְשַׁקְּצוּ אֶת־
נַפְשֹׁתֵיכֶם בַּבְּהֵמָה וּבָעוֹף וּבְכֹל אֲשֶׁר תִּרְמֹשׂ הָאֲדָמָה אֲשֶׁר־הִבְדַּלְתִּי

אונקלוס

עֶרְיְתָא דַאֲחָתֵיהּ, גַּלִּי חוֹבֵיהּ יְקַבֵּיל: יח וּגְבַר, דְּיִשְׁכּוּב יָת אִתְּתָא טָמְאָה, וִיגַלֵּי יָת עֶרְיְתַהּ יָת קְלָנַהּ גַּלִּי, וְהִיא, תְּגַלֵּי יָת סוֹאֲבַת דְּמַהָא, וְיִשְׁתֵּיצוּן תַּרְוֵיהוֹן מִגּוֹ עַמְּהוֹן: יט וְעֶרְיַת אֲחַת אִמָּךְ, וַאֲחַת אֲבוּךְ לָא תְגַלֵּי, אֲרֵי יָת קָרִיבְתֵּיהּ, גַּלִּי חוֹבְהוֹן יְקַבְּלוּן: כ וּגְבַר, דְּיִשְׁכּוּב יָת אִתַּת אַחְבּוּהִי, עֶרְיְתָא דַּאֲחְבּוּהִי גַּלִּי, חוֹבְהוֹן יְקַבְּלוּן דְּלָא וְלַד יְמוּתוּן: כא וּגְבַר, דְּיִסַּב, יָת אִתַּת אֲחוּהִי מְרַחֲקָא הִיא, עֶרְיְתָא דַּאֲחוּהִי, גַּלִּי דְּלָא וְלַד יְהוֹן: כב וְתִטְּרוּן יָת כָּל קְיָמַי וְיָת כָּל דִּינַי, וְתַעְבְּדוּן יָתְהוֹן, וְלָא תְרוֹקֵין יָתְכוֹן אַרְעָא, דַּאֲנָא, מַעֵיל יָתְכוֹן, לְתַמָּן לְמִתַּב בַּהּ: כג וְלָא תְהָכוּן בְּנִמּוֹסֵי עַמְמַיָּא, דַּאֲנָא מַגְלֵי מִן קֳדָמֵיכוֹן, אֲרֵי יָת כָּל אִלֵּין עֲבַדוּ, וְרַחֵיק מֵימְרִי יָתְהוֹן: כד וַאֲמָרִית לְכוֹן, אַתּוּן תֵּירְתוּן יָת אַרְעֲהוֹן, וַאֲנָא, אֶתְּנִנַּהּ לְכוֹן לְמֵירַת יָתַהּ, אֲרַע, עָבְדָא חֲלַב וּדְבָשׁ, אֲנָא יי אֱלָהֲכוֹן, דְּאַפְרֵישִׁית יָתְכוֹן מִן עַמְמַיָּא: כה וְתַפְרְשׁוּן, בֵּין בְּעִירָא דָּכְיָא לִמְסָאֲבָא, וּבֵין עוֹפָא מְסָאֲבָא לְדָכְיָא, וְלָא תְשַׁקְּצוּן יָת נַפְשָׁתְכוֹן בִּבְעִירָא וּבְעוֹפָא, וּבְכֹל דְּתַרְחֵישׁ אַרְעָא, דְּאַפְרֵישִׁית

20:18 אֶת־מְקֹרָהּ הֶעֱרָה *He has laid her hidden source bare* – The devaluing of the family and the legitimation of sexual license, whether it takes place in ancient Greece or the contemporary West, is the beginning of the end of a social system. The human person needs to learn a "Thou" before it can coherently pronounce the "I." We need to be cared for before we can learn to care for others. We need the formative experience of personal stability if as adults we are to make the sacrifices necessary to sustain a stable social order. And so, moral agents need to grow within families – families which themselves contain boundaries between free individuals.

26 upon the ground that I have set apart from you to regard as impure. Be holy to
Me, for I the Lord am holy, and I have set you apart from all other peoples to be
27 My own. A man or woman who seeks ghosts or spirits shall be put to death. They
shall be stoned; their bloodguilt is on them."

The haftara for Parashat Kedoshim is on page 1572 (even when Aḥarei Mot and Kedoshim are read together). On Rosh Ḥodesh Iyar read the haftara on page 1635.

רש״י

כו **וָאַבְדִּל אֶתְכֶם מִן הָעַמִּים לִהְיוֹת לִי.** אִם אַתֶּם מֻבְדָּלִים מֵהֶם הֲרֵי אַתֶּם שֶׁלִּי, וְאִם לָאו הֲרֵי אַתֶּם שֶׁל נְבוּכַדְנֶצַּר וַחֲבֵרָיו. רַבִּי אֶלְעָזָר בֶּן עֲזַרְיָה אוֹמֵר, מִנַּיִן שֶׁלֹּא יֹאמַר אָדָם: נַפְשִׁי קָצָה בִּבְשַׂר חֲזִיר, אִי אֶפְשִׁי לִלְבֹּשׁ כִּלְאַיִם, אֲבָל יֹאמַר: אֶפְשִׁי, וּמָה אֶעֱשֶׂה וְאָבִי שֶׁבַּשָּׁמַיִם גָּזַר עָלַי? – תַּלְמוּד לוֹמַר: "וָאַבְדִּל אֶתְכֶם מִן הָעַמִּים לִהְיוֹת לִי", שֶׁתְּהֵא הַבְדָּלַתְכֶם מֵהֶם לִשְׁמִי, פּוֹרֵשׁ מִן הָעֲבֵרָה וּמְקַבֵּל עָלָיו עֹל מַלְכוּת שָׁמַיִם:

כז **כִּי יִהְיֶה בָהֶם אוֹב וְגוֹ׳.** כָּאן נֶאֱמַר בָּהֶם מִיתָה, וּלְמַעְלָה (לעיל פסוק ו) כָּרֵת! – עֵדִים וְהַתְרָאָה בִּסְקִילָה, מֵזִיד בְּלֹא הַתְרָאָה בְּהִכָּרֵת, וּשְׁגָגָתָם חַטָּאת. וְכֵן בְּכָל חַיָּבֵי מִיתוֹת שֶׁנֶּאֱמַר בָּהֶם כָּרֵת:

There is something unique and contemporary about the ethic of holiness. It tells us that morality and ecology are closely related. They both honor creation: the world as God's work and humanity as God's image. The integrity of humanity and the natural environment go together. The natural universe and humanity were both created by God, and we are charged to protect the first and love the second. The *parasha* has expanded this double imperative into numerous detailed guidelines, all under the heading "Be holy."

He knows that different life-forms have their own niche in the environment. That is why the ethic of holiness includes rules like: Don't mate with different kinds of animals, don't plant a field with different kinds of seeds, and don't wear clothing woven from two kinds of material.

The ethic of holiness tells us that God made each of us in love. Therefore, if we seek to imitate God – "Be holy for I am holy, I, the Lord your God" (Lev. 19:2) – we too must love humanity, and not in the abstract but in the concrete form of the neighbor and the stranger.

כו לָכֶ֖ם לְטַמֵּֽא׃ וִהְיִ֤יתֶם לִי֙ קְדֹשִׁ֔ים כִּ֥י קָד֖וֹשׁ אֲנִ֣י יְהוָ֑ה וָאַבְדִּ֥ל אֶתְכֶ֛ם
כז מִן־הָעַמִּ֖ים לִהְי֥וֹת לִֽי׃ וְאִ֣ישׁ אֽוֹ־אִשָּׁ֗ה כִּֽי־יִהְיֶ֨ה בָהֶ֥ם א֛וֹב א֥וֹ יִדְּעֹנִ֖י
מ֣וֹת יוּמָ֑תוּ בָּאֶ֛בֶן יִרְגְּמ֥וּ אֹתָ֖ם דְּמֵיהֶ֥ם בָּֽם׃

The הפטרה for פרשת קדשים is on page page 1573.
(even when אחרי מות and קדשים are read together).
On ראש חודש אייר read the הפטרה on page page 1635.

אונקלוס

לְכוֹן לְסָאָבָא: כו וּתְהוֹן קֳדָמַי קַדִּישִׁין, אֲרֵי קַדִּישׁ אֲנָא יְיָ, וְאַפְרֵישִׁית
יָתְכוֹן, מִן עַמְמַיָּא לְמֶהֱוֵי פָּלְחִין קֳדָמָי: כז וּגְבַר אוֹ אִתָּא, אֲרֵי יְהֵי
בְּהוֹן בִּדִּין, אוֹ זְכוּרוּ אִתְקְטָלָא יִתְקַטְלוּן, בְּאַבְנָא, יִרְגְּמוּן יָתְהוֹן
קַטְלָא חַיָּבִין:

20:26 **וָאַבְדִּל אֶתְכֶם** *I have set you apart* – The verb *b-d-l*, to divide, set apart, separate, distinguish, is a keyword used throughout Tanakh in relation to the priest. That is what a priest does. His task is "to distinguish between sacred and profane" (Lev. 10:10; see comment there) and "to distinguish between the impure and the pure" (Lev. 11:47; see ch. 11, "The Dietary Laws"). This is what God does for His people: "I have set you apart [*vaavdil*] from all other peoples to be My own."

There is one other place in which *b-d-l* is a keyword, namely, the story of creation in Genesis 1, where it occurs five times. God separates light and dark, day and night, upper and lower waters. For three days God demarcates different domains, then for the next three days, He places in each its appropriate objects or life-forms. As His last act of creation, He makes man after His "image and likeness" (see Gen. 1:26). This was clearly an act of love. "Beloved is man," said R. Akiva, "because he was created in [God's] image" (Avot 3:14). Genesis 1 defines the priestly moral imagination, which looks at creation as the work of God. The priest knows that everything has its place: sacred and profane, permitted and forbidden. It is his task to make these distinctions and teach them to others.

Parashat Emor

21 1 The LORD said to Moshe, "Speak to the priests, Aharon's sons. Say: No one of you
2 shall render himself impure for any dead person among his people except for his
3 nearest relatives: his mother, father, son, daughter, or brother; or his virgin sister
who has remained close to him because she has not married – for her, he may
4 render himself impure. But he shall not become impure for those he is related
5 to by marriage, and so become profane. Priests shall not make bald patches on
their heads, or shave off the edges of their beards, or gash wounds into their flesh.
6 They shall be holy to their God and not profane God's name, for they bring close
the LORD's fire offerings, foodstuff offerings to their God; therefore they shall be
7 holy. They may not marry a woman made profane by immorality, nor may they

רש״י

כא א **אמר אל הכהנים.** "אמר" "ואמרת", להזהיר גדולים על הקטנים: **בני אהרן.** יכול חללים? תלמוד לומר: "הכהנים": **בני אהרן.** אף בעלי מומין במשמע: **בני אהרן.** ולא בנות אהרן: **לא יטמא בעמיו.** בעוד שהמת בתוך עמיו, יצא מת מצוה:

ב **כי אם לשארו.** אין "שארו" אלא אשתו:

ג **הקרובה.** לרבות את הארוסה: **אשר לא היתה לאיש.** למשכב: **לה יטמא.** מצוה:

ד **לא יטמא בעל בעמיו להחלו.** לא יטמא לאשתו פסולה שהוא מחולל בה בעודה עמו, וכן פשוטו של מקרא: "לא יטמא בעל" בשארו בעוד שהיא בתוך עמיו, שיש לה קוברין שאינה מת מצוה. ובאיזה שאר אמרתי? באותו שהיא "להחלו", להתחלל הוא מכהנתו:

ה **לא יקרחה קרחה.** על מת. והלא אף ישראל הוזהרו על כך? אלא לפי שנאמר בישראל: "בין עיניכם" (דברים יד, א), יכול לא יהא חייב על כל הראש? תלמוד לומר: "בראשם". וילמדו ישראל מכהנים בגזרה שוה: נאמר כאן "קרחה" ונאמר להלן בישראל "קרחה" (שם), מה כאן כל הראש אף להלן כל הראש במשמע, כל מקום שיקרח בראש. ומה להלן על מת, אף כאן על מת: **ופאת זקנם לא יגלחו.** לפי שנאמר בישראל: "ולא תשחית" (לעיל יט, כז), יכול לקטו במלקט ורהיטני יהא חייב? לכך נאמר: "לא יגלחו", שאינו חייב אלא על דבר הקרוי גלוח ויש בו השחתה, וזהו תער: **ובבשרם לא ישרטו שרטת.** לפי שנאמר בישראל: "ושרט לנפש לא תתנו" (לעיל יט, כח), יכול שרט חמש שריטות לא יהא חייב אלא אחת? תלמוד לומר: "לא ישרטו שרטת", לחייב על כל שריטה ושריטה, שתבה זו יתרה היא לדרש, שהיה לו לכתב "לא ישרטו" ואני יודע שהיא "שרטת":

ו **קדשים יהיו.** על כרחם יקדישום בית דין בכך:

ז **זנה.** שנבעלה בעילת ישראל האסור לה, כגון חייבי כריתות או נתין או ממזר: **חללה.** שנולדה מן הפסולים שבכהנה, כגון בת אלמנה מכהן גדול או בת גרושה מכהן הדיוט, וכן שנתחללה מן הכהנה על ידי ביאת אחד מן הפסולים לכהנה:

at which That-which-is-beyond-time-and-space enters time and space. Just as a highly sensitive experiment has to be conducted without the slightest contamination, so the holy space has to be kept free of conditions that bespeak human mortality.

Tuma should therefore not be thought of as "defilement," as if there were something wrong or sinful about it. *Tuma* is about mortality. Death bespeaks mortality, but so too does birth. A skin disease like *tzaraat* makes us vividly aware of the body. There is nothing wrong about any of these things, but they focus our attention on the physical, the mortal, the fragility of life.

It is notable, however, that a priest, even a High Priest, may perform the rites of a *met mitzva*, that is, one who has no one else to attend to his funeral. Here the basic requirement of human dignity overrides the priestly imperative of purity.

פרשת אמר

כא א וַיֹּאמֶר יהוה אֶל־מֹשֶׁה אֱמֹר אֶל־הַכֹּהֲנִים בְּנֵי אַהֲרֹן וְאָמַרְתָּ אֲלֵהֶם יז
ב לְנֶפֶשׁ לֹא־יִטַּמָּא בְּעַמָּיו: כִּי אִם־לִשְׁאֵרוֹ הַקָּרֹב אֵלָיו לְאִמּוֹ וּלְאָבִיו
ג וְלִבְנוֹ וּלְבִתּוֹ וּלְאָחִיו: וְלַאֲחֹתוֹ הַבְּתוּלָה הַקְּרוֹבָה אֵלָיו אֲשֶׁר לֹא־
ד ה הָיְתָה לְאִישׁ לָהּ יִטַּמָּא: לֹא יִטַּמָּא בַּעַל בְּעַמָּיו לְהֵחַלּוֹ: לֹא־יקרחה יִקְרְחוּ
קָרְחָה בְּרֹאשָׁם וּפְאַת זְקָנָם לֹא יְגַלֵּחוּ וּבִבְשָׂרָם לֹא יִשְׂרְטוּ שָׂרָטֶת:
ו קְדֹשִׁים יִהְיוּ לֵאלֹהֵיהֶם וְלֹא יְחַלְּלוּ שֵׁם אֱלֹהֵיהֶם כִּי אֶת־אִשֵּׁי יהוה
ז לֶחֶם אֱלֹהֵיהֶם הֵם מַקְרִיבִם וְהָיוּ קֹדֶשׁ: אִשָּׁה זֹנָה וַחֲלָלָה לֹא יִקָּחוּ

אונקלוס

כא א וַאֲמַר יי לְמֹשֶׁה, אֵימַר לְכָהֲנַיָּא בְּנֵי אַהֲרֹן, וְתֵימַר לְהוֹן, עַל מִית
לָא יִסְתָּאַב בְּעַמֵּיהּ: ב אֱלָהֵין לְקָרִיבֵיהּ, דְּקָרִיב לֵיהּ, לְאִמֵּיהּ וְלַאֲבוּהִי,
וְלִבְרֵיהּ וְלִבְרַתֵּיהּ וְלַאֲחוּהִי: ג וְלַאֲחָתֵיהּ בְּתוּלְתָא דְּקָרִיבָא לֵיהּ,
דְּלָא הֲוָת לִגְבַר, לַהּ יִסְתָּאַב: ד לָא יִסְתָּאַב בְּרַבָּא בְּעַמֵּיהּ,
לְאַחֲלוּתֵיהּ: ה לָא יְמָרְטוּן מְרַט בְּרֵישֵׁיהוֹן, וּפָתָא דְּדִקְנְהוֹן לָא
יְגַלְּחוּן, וּבִבְסַרְהוֹן, לָא יְחַבְּלוּן חִבּוּל: ו קַדִּישִׁין יְהוֹן קֳדָם אֱלָהֲהוֹן,
וְלָא יְחַלּוּן, שְׁמָא דֶּאֱלָהֲהוֹן, אֲרֵי יָת קֻרְבָּנַיָּא דַּיי, קֻרְבַּן אֱלָהֲהוֹן,
אִנּוּן מְקָרְבִין וִיהוֹן קַדִּישִׁין: ז אִתְּתָא מַטְעֲיָא וּמְחַלְּלָא לָא יִסְּבוּן,

EMOR

Parashat Emor deals with two kinds of holiness: of people and of time. Chapter 21 relates to holy people: priests, and above them, the High Priest. Their close contact with the Sanctuary means that they must live with certain restrictions, namely, on contact with the dead and whom they may marry. Chapter 22 recaps similar laws relating to ordinary Israelites when they seek to enter the Sanctuary, as well as defects in animals that bar them from being offered as sacrifices. Chapter 23 is about holy time, the festivals of the year. Chapter 24 speaks about the candelabrum (menora), lit daily, and the showbread renewed weekly, and ends with a story – one of only two narratives in Leviticus – about the fate of a man who blasphemes in the course of a fight. It is this narrative that draws to a close the long Tabernacle cycle, before we take up the narrative where we left off in Exodus 24, "on Mount Sinai" (Lev. 25:1).

21:1 לְנֶפֶשׁ לֹא־יִטַּמָּא *No one of you shall render himself impure* – A priest may not touch or be under the same roof as a dead body. He must remain aloof from close contact with the dead, with the exception of a close relative. The law for the High Priest is stricter still. He may not allow himself to become ceremonially unclean even for a close relative.

To understand these laws and other purity regulations, we first have to return to the concept of the holy. God is beyond space and time, yet God created space and time as well as the physical entities that occupy space and time. God is therefore "concealed" (*ne'elam*) in our physical world (*olam*). Yet if God were completely and permanently hidden from the world, it would be as if He were absent. From a human perspective there would be no difference between an unknowable God and a nonexistent God. Therefore God established the holy as the point at which the Eternal enters time and the Infinite enters space.

God's eternity stands in the sharpest possible contrast to our mortality. All that lives will one day die. All that is physical will one day erode and cease to be. Hence the extreme delicacy and danger of the Tabernacle or Temple, the point

▶

marry a woman divorced from her husband, for they are holy to their God.
8 You shall treat a priest as holy, for he brings close the offerings of foodstuffs
to your God. And he shall be holy to you, because I, the LORD, am holy and
9 make you holy. If the daughter of a priest profanes herself by immorality, she
10 profanes her father also; she shall be burned with fire. The priest, the
highest among his brothers, on whose head the anointing oil has been poured
and who has been ordained to wear the vestments, shall not dishevel his hair
11 or tear his clothes. He shall not go near the dead; even for his father or mother
12 he shall not render himself impure. He shall not leave the Sanctuary, profaning
his God's Sanctuary, for the crown of his God's anointing oil rests upon him; I
13 14 am the LORD. He may marry a woman only in her virginity. He may not marry
a widow, a divorcée, or one profaned by immorality. He may marry only a
15 virgin from his own people, so that he will not profane his children among
16 his people, for I, the LORD, sanctify him." The LORD spoke to Moshe: SHENI
17 "Tell Aharon: Any of your future descendants who has a physical blemish may
18 not draw close to present foodstuff offerings to his God. No one with a blemish

רש״י

ח| **וְקִדַּשְׁתּוֹ.** עַל כָּרְחוֹ, שֶׁאִם לֹא רָצָה לְגָרֵשׁ הַלְקֵהוּ וְיַסְּרֵהוּ עַד שֶׁיְּגָרֵשׁ: **קָדֹשׁ יִהְיֶה לָּךְ.** נְהֹג בּוֹ קְדֻשָּׁה לִפְתֹּחַ רִאשׁוֹן בְּכָל דָּבָר וּלְבָרֵךְ רִאשׁוֹן בִּסְעוּדָה:

ט| **כִּי תֵחֵל לִזְנוֹת.** כְּשֶׁתִּתְחַלֵּל עַל יְדֵי זְנוּת, שֶׁהָיְתָה בָּהּ זִיקַת בַּעַל וְזָנְתָה אוֹ מִן הָאֵרוּסִין אוֹ מִן הַנִּשּׂוּאִין. וְרַבּוֹתֵינוּ נֶחְלְקוּ בַּדָּבָר, וְהַכֹּל מוֹדִים שֶׁלֹּא דִּבֶּר הַכָּתוּב בִּפְנוּיָה: **אֶת אָבִיהָ הִיא מְחַלֶּלֶת.** חִלְּלָה וּבִזְּתָה אֶת כְּבוֹדוֹ, שֶׁאוֹמְרִים עָלָיו: אָרוּר שֶׁזּוֹ יָלַד, אָרוּר שֶׁזּוֹ גִּדֵּל:

י| **לֹא יִפְרָע.** לֹא יְגַדֵּל פֶּרַע עַל אֵבֶל, וְאֵיזֶהוּ גִּדּוּל פֶּרַע? יוֹתֵר מִשְּׁלֹשִׁים יוֹם:

יא| **וְעַל כָּל נַפְשֹׁת מֵת.** בְּאֹהֶל הַמֵּת: **נַפְשֹׁת מֵת.** לְהָבִיא רְבִיעִית דָּם מִן הַמֵּת שֶׁמְּטַמֵּא בְּאֹהֶל: **לְאָבִיו וּלְאִמּוֹ לֹא יִטַּמָּא.** לֹא בָּא אֶלָּא לְהַתִּיר לוֹ מֵת מִצְוָה:

יב| **וּמִן הַמִּקְדָּשׁ לֹא יֵצֵא.** אֵינוֹ הוֹלֵךְ אַחַר הַמִּטָּה. וְעוֹד, מִכָּאן לָמְדוּ רַבּוֹתֵינוּ שֶׁכֹּהֵן גָּדוֹל מַקְרִיב אוֹנֵן, וְכֵן מַשְׁמָעוֹ: אַף אִם מֵתוּ אָבִיו וְאִמּוֹ אֵינוֹ צָרִיךְ לָצֵאת מִן הַמִּקְדָּשׁ, אֶלָּא עוֹבֵד עֲבוֹדָה: **וְלֹא יְחַלֵּל אֵת מִקְדַּשׁ.** שֶׁאֵינוֹ מְחַלֵּל בְּכָךְ אֶת הָעֲבוֹדָה, שֶׁהִתִּיר לוֹ הַכָּתוּב, הָא כֹּהֵן הֶדְיוֹט שֶׁעָבַד אוֹנֵן, חִלֵּל:

יד| **וַחֲלָלָה.** שֶׁנּוֹלְדָה מִפְּסוּלֵי כְּהֻנָּה:

טו| **וְלֹא יְחַלֵּל זַרְעוֹ.** הָא אִם נָשָׂא אַחַת מִן הַפְּסוּלוֹת, זַרְעוֹ הֵימֶנָּה חָלָל מִדִּין קְדֻשַּׁת כְּהֻנָּה:

יז| **לֶחֶם אֱלֹהָיו.** מַאֲכַל אֱלֹהָיו. כָּל סְעוּדָה קְרוּיָה לֶחֶם, כְּמוֹ: "עֲבַד לְחֶם רַב" (דניאל ה, א):

יח| **כִּי כָל אִישׁ אֲשֶׁר בּוֹ מוּם לֹא יִקְרָב.** אֵינוֹ דִּין שֶׁיִּקְרַב, כְּמוֹ: "הַקְרִיבֵהוּ נָא לְפֶחָתֶךָ" (מלאכי א, ח):

the various types of ritual impurity is that they focus our attention on the physical. Therefore they are incompatible with the holy space of the Tabernacle, which is dedicated to the presence of the nonphysical, the Eternal Infinite that never dies or decays.

This is well illustrated at the beginning of the book of Job. Iyov loses everything: his flocks, his herds, his children. Yet his faith remains intact. Satan then proposes subjecting Iyov to an even greater trial, covering his body with sores (Job 1–2). The logic of this seems absurd. How can a skin disease be a greater trial of faith than losing your children? It isn't. But what the book is saying is that when your body is afflicted, it can be hard, even impossible, to focus on spirituality. This has nothing to do with ultimate truth

ח וְאִשָּׁה גְּרוּשָׁה מֵאִישָׁהּ לֹא יִקָּחוּ כִּי־קָדֹשׁ הוּא לֵאלֹהָיו: וְקִדַּשְׁתּוֹ
כִּי־אֶת־לֶחֶם אֱלֹהֶיךָ הוּא מַקְרִיב קָדֹשׁ יִהְיֶה־לָּךְ כִּי קָדוֹשׁ אֲנִי יהוה
ט מְקַדִּשְׁכֶם: וּבַת אִישׁ כֹּהֵן כִּי תֵחֵל לִזְנוֹת אֶת־אָבִיהָ הִיא מְחַלֶּלֶת
י בָּאֵשׁ תִּשָּׂרֵף: וְהַכֹּהֵן הַגָּדוֹל מֵאֶחָיו אֲשֶׁר־יוּצַק עַל־רֹאשׁוֹ ׀
שֶׁמֶן הַמִּשְׁחָה וּמִלֵּא אֶת־יָדוֹ לִלְבֹּשׁ אֶת־הַבְּגָדִים אֶת־רֹאשׁוֹ לֹא יִפְרָע
יא וּבְגָדָיו לֹא יִפְרֹם: וְעַל כָּל־נַפְשֹׁת מֵת לֹא יָבֹא לְאָבִיו וּלְאִמּוֹ לֹא יִטַּמָּא:
יב וּמִן־הַמִּקְדָּשׁ לֹא יֵצֵא וְלֹא יְחַלֵּל אֵת מִקְדַּשׁ אֱלֹהָיו כִּי נֵזֶר שֶׁמֶן
יג יד מִשְׁחַת אֱלֹהָיו עָלָיו אֲנִי יהוה: וְהוּא אִשָּׁה בִבְתוּלֶיהָ יִקָּח: אַלְמָנָה
וּגְרוּשָׁה וַחֲלָלָה זֹנָה אֶת־אֵלֶּה לֹא יִקָּח כִּי אִם־בְּתוּלָה מֵעַמָּיו יִקַּח
טו טז אִשָּׁה: וְלֹא־יְחַלֵּל זַרְעוֹ בְּעַמָּיו כִּי אֲנִי יהוה מְקַדְּשׁוֹ: וַיְדַבֵּר שני
יז יהוה אֶל־מֹשֶׁה לֵּאמֹר: דַּבֵּר אֶל־אַהֲרֹן לֵאמֹר אִישׁ מִזַּרְעֲךָ לְדֹרֹתָם
יח אֲשֶׁר יִהְיֶה בוֹ מוּם לֹא יִקְרַב לְהַקְרִיב לֶחֶם אֱלֹהָיו: כִּי כָל־אִישׁ

אונקלוס

וְאִתְּתָא, דְּמִתָּרְכָא מִבַּעְלַהּ לָא יִסְּבוּן, אֲרֵי קַדִּישׁ הוּא קֳדָם
אֱלָהֵיהּ: ח וּתְקַדְּשִׁנֵּיהּ, אֲרֵי יָת קֻרְבַּן אֱלָהָךְ הוּא מְקָרֵיב, קַדִּישׁ יְהֵי
לָךְ, אֲרֵי קַדִּישׁ, אֲנָא יי מְקַדִּשְׁכוֹן: ט וּבַת גְּבַר כָּהִין, אֲרֵי תִתַּחַל
לְמִטְעֵי, מְקַדֶּשֶׁת אֲבוּהָא הִיא מִתַּחֲלָא, בְּנוּרָא תִּתּוֹקַד: י וְכָהֲנָא
דְּיִתְרַבָּא מֵאֲחוֹהִי, דְּיִתָּרַק עַל רֵישֵׁיהּ מִשְׁחָא דִּרְבוּתָא וְדִיקָרֵיב יָת
קֻרְבָּנֵיהּ, לְמִלְבַּשׁ יָת לְבוּשַׁיָּא, יָת רֵישֵׁיהּ לָא יְרַבֵּי פֵרוּעַ, וּלְבוּשׁוֹהִי
לָא יְבַזַּע: יא וְעַל, כָּל נַפְשָׁת מִיתָא לָא יֵיעוֹל, לַאֲבוּהִי וּלְאִמֵּיהּ
לָא יִסְתָּאַב: יב וּמִן מַקְדְּשָׁא לָא יִפּוֹק, וְלָא יַחֵיל, יָת מַקְדְּשָׁא
דֶּאֱלָהֵיהּ, אֲרֵי, כְּלִיל, מְשַׁח רְבוּתָא דֶּאֱלָהֵיהּ, עֲלוֹהִי אֲנָא יי:
יג וְהוּא, אִתְּתָא בִּבְתוּלַהָא יִסַּב: יד אַרְמְלָא וּמִתָּרְכָא וַחֲלִילָא
מַטְעִיָא, יָת אִלֵּין לָא יִסַּב, אֱלָהֵין, בְּתוּלְתָא מֵעַמֵּיהּ יִסַּב אִתְּתָא:
טו וְלָא יַחֵיל זַרְעֵיהּ בְּעַמֵּיהּ, אֲרֵי, אֲנָא יי מְקַדְּשֵׁיהּ: טז וּמַלֵּיל יי עִם
מֹשֶׁה לְמֵימַר: יז מַלֵּיל עִם אַהֲרֹן לְמֵימַר, גְּבַר מִבְּנָךְ לְדָרֵיהוֹן, דִּיהֵי
בֵיהּ מוּמָא, לָא יִקְרַב, לְקָרָבָא קֻרְבָּנָא קֳדָם אֱלָהֵיהּ: יח אֲרֵי כָל גְּבַר,

A PRIEST WITH A PHYSICAL BLEMISH

Some forms of physical difference render a priest unfit for service in the Tabernacle. We might assume that this implies that someone who had such a disability is considered less than perfect, and thus debarred from high religious office. But Rambam, in *Guide for the Perplexed* (III:44), gives a quite different explanation. It was, he says, a concession to ill-informed sentiment. People wrongly judge an individual by his physical appearance rather than by his true form. God looks to the heart, but people judge by external appearances. Thus the Torah excludes priests with certain disabilities and physical differences from Temple service to avoid public disrespect. Rambam himself makes it clear that the priest with a physical disability is pleasing before God. The legislation surrounding the Temple, however, involves concessions to human prejudice.

Rambam's understanding of this set of laws emphasizes what human beings lack in empathy. Yet his idea may be taken in a slightly different direction by applying to it what we learned about *tuma* above (v.1). We saw that what unites

▶

shall approach: this includes one who is blind, lame, disfigured, or deformed;
19 20 or who has a broken foot or hand; or who is a hunchback or a dwarf, or who
21 has a growth in his eye, a severe rash, scabs, or crushed testicles. No descendant
of Aharon the priest who has a physical blemish shall draw near to present the
Lord's fire offerings; because of his blemish, he shall not approach to present
22 an offering of foodstuffs to his God. He may eat the foodstuff offerings of
23 his God, the holy of holies as well as the holy. But he may not come close to
the inner curtain or approach the altar, because of his blemish; he shall not
24 profane My Sanctuary; I am the Lord who makes them holy." Moshe told this
to Aharon, his sons, and all the Israelites.
22 1 2 The Lord spoke to Moshe: "Tell Aharon and his sons to take great care with
the sacred offerings that the Israelites consecrate to Me, so that they do not
3 profane My holy name: I am the Lord. Tell them: If any descendant of yours

רש"י

חרם. שחטמו שקוע בין שתי העינים, שכוחל שתי עיניו כאחת: **שרוע.** שאחד מאבריו גדול מחברו, עינו אחת גדולה ועינו אחת קטנה, או שוקו אחת ארכה מחברתה:

כ) **או גבן.** שורצילו"ש בלעז, שגביני עיניו שערן ארך ושוכב: **או דק.** שיש לו בעיניו דק שקורין טייל"א, כמו "הנוטה כדק" (ישעיה מ, כב): **או תבלל.** דבר המבלבל את העין, כגון חוט לבן הנמשך מן הלבן ופוסק בסירא, שהוא עגל המקיף את השחור שקוראים פרוניל"א, והחוט הזה פוסק את העגל ונכנס בשחור. ותרגום "תבלל": "חליז", לשון חלזון, שהוא דומה לתולעת – אותו החוט, וכן כנוהו חכמי ישראל במומי הבכור, חלזון נחש ענב: **גרב או ילפת.** מיני שחין הם. "גרב" זו החרס, שחין היבש מבפנים ומבחוץ. "ילפת" היא חזזית המצרית, ולמה נקראת "ילפת"? שמלפפת והולכת עד יום המיתה, והוא לח מבחוץ ויבש מבפנים. ובמקום אחר קורא לגרב שחין הלח מבחוץ ויבש מבפנים, שנאמר: "ובגרב ובחרס" (דברים כח, כז), כשסמך גרב אצל חרס קורא לילפת "גרב", וכשהוא סמוך אצל ילפת קורא לחרס "גרב", כך מפרש בבכורות (דף מא ע"א): **מרוח אשך.** לפי התרגום "מריס פחדין", שפחדיו מרססין, שביצים שלו כתותין. "פחדין" כמו: "גידי פחדו ישרגו" (איוב מ, יז):

כא) **כל איש אשר בו מום.** לרבות שאר מומין: **מום בו.** בעוד מומו בו פסול, הא אם עבר מומו – כשר: **לחם אלהיו.** כל מאכל קרוי לחם:

כב) **מקדשי הקדשים.** אלו קדשי הקדשים: **ומן הקדשים יאכל.** אלו קדשים קלים. ואם נאמרו קדשי הקדשים למה נאמר קדשים קלים? אם לא נאמר הייתי אומר, בקדשי הקדשים יאכל בעל מום, שמצינו שהתרו לזר, שאכל משה בשר המלואים, אבל בחזה ושוק של קדשים קלים לא יאכל, שלא מצינו זר אוכל בהן, לכך נאמרו קדשים קלים. כך מפרש בזבחים (דף קא ע"ב):

כג) **אך אל הפרכת.** להזות שבע הזאות שעל הפרכת: **ואל המזבח.** החיצון, ושניהם הצרכו לכתב, ומפרש בתורת כהנים (פרק ג, י): **ולא יחלל את מקדשי.** שאם עבד, עבודתו מחללת לפסל:

כד) **וידבר משה.** המצוה הזאת: **אל אהרן וגו' ואל כל בני ישראל.** להזהיר בית דין על הכהנים:

כב ב) **וינזרו.** אין נזירה אלא פרישה, וכן הוא אומר "וינזר מאחרי" (יחזקאל יד, ז), "נזרו אחור" (ישעיה א, ד), יפרשו מן הקדשים בימי טמאתן: וינזרו מקדשי בני ישראל, אשר הם מקדשים לי, ולא יחללו את שם קדשי. סרס המקרא ודרשהו: **אשר הם מקדשים לי.** לרבות קדשי כהנים עצמן:

ג) **כל איש אשר יקרב.** אין קריבה זו אלא אכילה, וכן מצינו שנאמרה אזהרת אכילת קדשים בטמאה בלשון נגיעה: "בכל קדש לא תגע" (ויקרא יב, ד) אזהרה לאוכל, ולמדוה רבותינו מגזרה שוה. ואי אפשר לומר שחייב על הנגיעה, שהרי נאמר כרת על האכילה בזו את

and to give them spiritual satisfaction" (*Mas'at Binyamin* 62). Inclusion of those with disabilities within the faith community was, for him, a significant halakhic factor. If we treat others disrespectfully, we diminish their humanity and thereby ours (see Lev. 19:14 and comment there). This too is part of our halakhic heritage.

יט אֲשֶׁר־בּוֹ מוּם לֹא יִקְרָב אִישׁ עִוֵּר אוֹ פִסֵּחַ אוֹ חָרֻם אוֹ שָׂרוּעַ: אוֹ אִישׁ
כ אֲשֶׁר־יִהְיֶה בוֹ שֶׁבֶר רָגֶל אוֹ שֶׁבֶר יָד: אוֹ־גִבֵּן אוֹ־דַק אוֹ תְּבַלֻּל בְּעֵינוֹ
כא אוֹ גָרָב אוֹ יַלֶּפֶת אוֹ מְרוֹחַ אָשֶׁךְ: כָּל־אִישׁ אֲשֶׁר־בּוֹ מוּם מִזֶּרַע אַהֲרֹן
הַכֹּהֵן לֹא יִגַּשׁ לְהַקְרִיב אֶת־אִשֵּׁי יְהֹוָה מוּם בּוֹ אֵת לֶחֶם אֱלֹהָיו לֹא
כב יִגַּשׁ לְהַקְרִיב: לֶחֶם אֱלֹהָיו מִקָּדְשֵׁי הַקֳּדָשִׁים וּמִן־הַקֳּדָשִׁים יֹאכֵל:
כג אַךְ אֶל־הַפָּרֹכֶת לֹא יָבֹא וְאֶל־הַמִּזְבֵּחַ לֹא יִגַּשׁ כִּי־מוּם בּוֹ וְלֹא יְחַלֵּל
כד אֶת־מִקְדָּשַׁי כִּי אֲנִי יְהֹוָה מְקַדְּשָׁם: וַיְדַבֵּר מֹשֶׁה אֶל־אַהֲרֹן וְאֶל־בָּנָיו
וְאֶל־כָּל־בְּנֵי יִשְׂרָאֵל:
כב א ב וַיְדַבֵּר יְהֹוָה אֶל־מֹשֶׁה לֵּאמֹר: דַּבֵּר אֶל־אַהֲרֹן וְאֶל־בָּנָיו וְיִנָּזְרוּ מִקָּדְשֵׁי
בְנֵי־יִשְׂרָאֵל וְלֹא יְחַלְּלוּ אֶת־שֵׁם קָדְשִׁי אֲשֶׁר הֵם מַקְדִּשִׁים לִי אֲנִי
ג יְהֹוָה: אֱמֹר אֲלֵהֶם לְדֹרֹתֵיכֶם כָּל־אִישׁ ׀ אֲשֶׁר־יִקְרַב מִכָּל־זַרְעֲכֶם

אונקלוס

דְּבֵיהּ מוּמָא לָא יִקְרַב, גְּבַר עֲוִיר אוֹ חֲגִיר, אוֹ חֲרִים אוֹ סְרִיעַ: יט אוֹ גְּבַר, דִּיהֵי בֵיהּ תְּבַר רִגְלָא, אוֹ תְּבַר יְדָא: כ אוֹ גְבִין אוֹ דְקָא, אוֹ חִלִּיז בְּעֵינוֹהִי, אוֹ גַרְבָן אוֹ חֲזָזָן, אוֹ מְרִיס פַּחְדִּין: כא כָּל גְּבַר דְּבֵיהּ מוּמָא, מִזַּרְעָא דְּאַהֲרֹן כָּהֲנָא, לָא יִקְרַב, לְקָרָבָא יָת קֻרְבָּנַיָּא דַּיְיָ, מוּמָא בֵיהּ, יָת קֻרְבַּן אֱלָהֵיהּ, לָא יִקְרַב לְקָרָבָא: כב קֻרְבַּן אֱלָהֵיהּ, מִקֹּדֶשׁ קֻדְשַׁיָּא, וּמִן קֻדְשַׁיָּא יֵיכוֹל: כג בְּרַם לְפָרֻכְתָּא לָא יֵיעוֹל, וּלְמַדְבְּחָא, לָא יִקְרַב אֲרֵי מוּמָא בֵיהּ, וְלָא יַחֵיל יָת מַקְדְּשַׁי, אֲרֵי, אֲנָא יי מְקַדִּשְׁהוֹן: כד וּמַלֵּיל מֹשֶׁה, עִם אַהֲרֹן וְעִם בְּנוֹהִי, וְעִם כָּל בְּנֵי יִשְׂרָאֵל: כב א וּמַלֵּיל יי עִם מֹשֶׁה לְמֵימַר: ב מַלֵּיל עִם אַהֲרֹן וְעִם בְּנוֹהִי, וְיִפְרְשׁוּן מִקֻּדְשַׁיָּא דִּבְנֵי יִשְׂרָאֵל, וְלָא יְחַלְּלוּן יָת שְׁמָא דְקֻדְשִׁי, דְּאִנּוּן מַקְדְּשִׁין, קֳדָמַי אֲנָא יי: ג אֵימַר לְהוֹן, לְדָרֵיכוֹן, כָּל גְּבַר דְּיִקְרַב מִכָּל זַרְעֲכוֹן,

we distance from the operation of holy precincts. Something similar may be said of the appearance of bodily abnormalities in the Tabernacle.

Needless to say, however, our attitudes to disability have changed significantly. The principle of integration, for instance, played a part in a sixteenth-century responsum of Rabbi Aharon Slonik. He had been asked whether a blind man may be called to the reading of the Torah. After citing the authorities who rule affirmatively on the question, he adds the following consideration: "We must allow the blind… to be called to the Torah and to utter blessings, in order to include them in the acceptance of God's dominion

and everything to do with the human mind. You cannot give your mind to meditating on truth when you are hungry or thirsty, homeless or sick (*Guide for the Perplexed* III:27). And a skin disease or a bodily abnormality in one person tends to prompt in others the thought, "This could happen to me." They remind us of the "thousand natural shocks that flesh is heir to."

This is the logic – if logic is the right word – of *tuma*. It has nothing to do with rationality and everything to do with emotion. That which distracts from eternity and infinity by making us forcibly aware of our own mortality, of the fact that we are physical beings in a physical world – that is what

▶

throughout the generations comes near the sacred offerings that the Israelites
have consecrated to the LORD while in an impure state, he shall be severed from
4 My presence; I am the LORD. Any descendant of Aharon who has a defiling
blight of the skin or a discharge may not eat of the sacred offerings until he
becomes pure. One who touches anything made impure by contact with the
5 dead, or who has had a seminal emission, or who has touched any swarming
6 thing or any person who renders him impure – whatever his impurity – the
one who touches these things shall be impure until the evening, and shall not
7 eat of the sacred offerings until he has washed his body in water. When the sun
sets, he shall become pure again and may eat of the sacred offerings, for they
8 are his food. He may not eat an animal found dead or one that was torn by wild
9 animals, becoming impure by doing so; I am the LORD. They shall keep My
charge and not bear guilt and die through it, having profaned it. I am the LORD,
10 who makes them holy. No layman may eat of the sacred offerings, nor may a
11 priest's visitor or hired laborer eat of them. But if a priest acquires a slave for
money, the slave may eat of them, and those born into his household also may
12 eat his food. If a priest's daughter marries a layman, she may no longer eat of
13 the sacred gifts. If a priest's daughter is a widow or a divorcée, has no children,

רש"י

אהרן, שתי כריתות זו אצל זו (לעיל ז, כ-כא), ואם על הנגיעה חייב, לא הוצרך לחייבו על האכילה. וכן נדרש בתורת כהנים (פרשתא ד, ז): וכי יש נוגע חייב? אם כן מה תלמוד לומר: "יקרב"? משיכשר ליקרב, שאין חייבין עליו משום טומאה אלא אם כן קרבו מתיריו. ואם תאמר, שלש כריתות בטומאת כהנים למה? כבר נדרשו במסכת שבועות (דף ז ע"א), אחת לכלל ואחת לפרט וכו': **וטמאתו עליו.** וטומאת האדם עליו. יכול בבשר הכתוב מדבר, וטומאתו של בשר עליו, ובטהור שאכל את הטמא הכתוב מדבר? על כרחך ממשמעו אתה למד, במי שטומאתו פורחת ממנו הכתוב מדבר, וזהו האדם שיש לו טהרה בטבילה: **ונכרתה וגו'.** יכול מצד זה לצד זה, יכרת ממקומו ויתישב במקום אחר? תלמוד לומר: "אני ה'", בכל מקום אני:

ד **בכל טמא נפש.** במי שנטמא במת:

ה **בכל שרץ אשר יטמא לו.** בשיעור הראוי לטמא, בכעדשה: **או באדם.** במת: **אשר יטמא לו.** כשיעורו לטמא, וזהו כזית: **לכל טמאתו.** לרבות נוגע בזב וזבה נדה ויולדת:

ו **נפש אשר תגע בו.** באחד מן הטמאים הללו:

ז **ואחר יאכל מן הקדשים.** נדרש ביבמות (דף עד ע"ב) בתרומה, שמותר לאכלה בהערב השמש: **מן הקדשים.** ולא כל הקדשים:

ח **נבלה וטרפה לא יאכל לטמאה בה.** לענין הטומאה הזהיר כאן, שאם אכל נבלת עוף טהור שאין לה טומאת מגע ומשא אלא טומאת אכילה בבית הבליעה, אסור לאכול בקדשים. וצריך לומר: "וטרפה" – מי שיש במינו טרפה, יצא נבלת עוף טמא שאין במינו טרפה:

ט **ושמרו את משמרתי.** מלאכול תרומה בטומאת הגוף: **ומתו בו.** למדנו שהיא מיתה בידי שמים:

י **לא יאכל קדש.** בתרומה הכתוב מדבר, שכל הענין דבר בה: **תושב כהן ושכיר.** תושבו של כהן ושכירו, לפיכך "תושב" זה נקוד פתח, לפי שהוא דבוק. ואיזהו תושב? זה נרצע שהוא קנוי לו עד היובל; ואיזהו שכיר? זה קנוי קנין שנים שיוצא בשש, בא הכתוב ולמדך כאן שאין גופו קנוי לאדוניו לאכול בתרומתו:

יא **וכהן כי יקנה נפש.** עבד כנעני שקנוי לגופו: **ויליד ביתו.** אלו בני השפחות. ואשת כהן אוכלת בתרומה מן המקרא הזה, שאף היא קנין כספו, ועוד למד ממקרא אחר: "כל טהור בביתך" וגו' (במדבר יח, יא), בספרי (קרח קיז):

יב **לאיש זר.** ללוי וישראל:

יג **אלמנה וגרושה.** מן האיש הזר: **וזרע אין לה.** ממנו: **ושבה.** הא

אֶל־הַקֳּדָשִׁים אֲשֶׁר יַקְדִּישׁוּ בְנֵי־יִשְׂרָאֵל לַיהוָה וְטֻמְאָתוֹ עָלָיו וְנִכְרְתָה
ד הַנֶּפֶשׁ הַהִוא מִלְּפָנַי אֲנִי יהוה: אִישׁ אִישׁ מִזֶּרַע אַהֲרֹן וְהוּא צָרוּעַ אוֹ
זָב בַּקֳּדָשִׁים לֹא יֹאכַל עַד אֲשֶׁר יִטְהָר וְהַנֹּגֵעַ בְּכָל־טְמֵא־נֶפֶשׁ אוֹ אִישׁ
ה אֲשֶׁר־תֵּצֵא מִמֶּנּוּ שִׁכְבַת־זָרַע: אוֹ־אִישׁ אֲשֶׁר יִגַּע בְּכָל־שֶׁרֶץ אֲשֶׁר
ו יִטְמָא־לוֹ אוֹ בְאָדָם אֲשֶׁר יִטְמָא־לוֹ לְכֹל טֻמְאָתוֹ: נֶפֶשׁ אֲשֶׁר תִּגַּע־
בּוֹ וְטָמְאָה עַד־הָעָרֶב וְלֹא יֹאכַל מִן־הַקֳּדָשִׁים כִּי אִם־רָחַץ בְּשָׂרוֹ
ז בַּמָּיִם: וּבָא הַשֶּׁמֶשׁ וְטָהֵר וְאַחַר יֹאכַל מִן־הַקֳּדָשִׁים כִּי לַחְמוֹ הוּא:
ח ט נְבֵלָה וּטְרֵפָה לֹא יֹאכַל לְטָמְאָה־בָהּ אֲנִי יהוה: וְשָׁמְרוּ אֶת־מִשְׁמַרְתִּי
י וְלֹא־יִשְׂאוּ עָלָיו חֵטְא וּמֵתוּ בוֹ כִּי יְחַלְּלֻהוּ אֲנִי יהוה מְקַדְּשָׁם: וְכָל־
יא זָר לֹא־יֹאכַל קֹדֶשׁ תּוֹשַׁב כֹּהֵן וְשָׂכִיר לֹא־יֹאכַל קֹדֶשׁ: וְכֹהֵן כִּי־יִקְנֶה
יב נֶפֶשׁ קִנְיַן כַּסְפּוֹ הוּא יֹאכַל בּוֹ וִילִיד בֵּיתוֹ הֵם יֹאכְלוּ בְלַחְמוֹ: וּבַת־
יג כֹּהֵן כִּי תִהְיֶה לְאִישׁ זָר הִוא בִּתְרוּמַת הַקֳּדָשִׁים לֹא תֹאכֵל: וּבַת־
כֹּהֵן כִּי תִהְיֶה אַלְמָנָה וּגְרוּשָׁה וְזֶרַע אֵין לָהּ וְשָׁבָה אֶל־בֵּית אָבִיהָ

אונקלוס

לְקֻדְשַׁיָּא דִּיקַדְּשׁוּן בְּנֵי יִשְׂרָאֵל קֳדָם יְיָ, וְסוֹאֳבְתֵיהּ עֲלוֹהִי, וְיִשְׁתֵּיצֵי, אֲנָשָׁא הַהוּא, מִן קֳדָמַי אֲנָא יְיָ: ד גְּבַר גְּבַר מִזַּרְעָא דְּאַהֲרֹן, וְהוּא סְגִיר אוֹ דָאִיב, בְּקֻדְשַׁיָּא לָא יֵיכוֹל, עַד דְּיִדְכֵּי, וּדְיִקְרַב בְּכָל טְמֵי נַפְשָׁא, אוֹ גְבַר, דְּתִפּוֹק מִנֵּיהּ שִׁכְבַת זַרְעָא: ה אוֹ גְבַר דְּיִקְרַב, בְּכָל רִחְשָׁא דְּיִסְתְּאַב לֵיהּ, אוֹ בֶאֱנָשָׁא דְּיִסְתְּאַב לֵיהּ, לְכָל סְאוֹבְתֵיהּ: ו אֱנָשׁ דְּיִקְרַב בֵּיהּ, וִיהֵי מְסָאַב עַד רַמְשָׁא, וְלָא יֵיכוֹל מִן קֻדְשַׁיָּא, אֱלָהֵין, אַסְחִי בִסְרֵיהּ בְּמַיָּא: ז וּכְמֵיעַל שִׁמְשָׁא וְיִדְכֵּי, וּבָתַר כֵּן יֵיכוֹל מִן קֻדְשַׁיָּא, אֲרֵי לַחְמֵיהּ הוּא: ח נְבִילָא וּתְבִירָא, לָא יֵיכוֹל לְאִסְתָּאָבָא בַהּ, אֲנָא יְיָ: ט וְיִטְּרוּן יָת מַטְּרַת מֵימְרִי, וְלָא יְקַבְּלוּן עֲלוֹהִי חוֹבָא, וִימוּתוּן בֵּיהּ אֲרֵי יַחֲלְנֵיהּ, אֲנָא יְיָ מְקַדִּשְׁהוֹן: י וְכָל חִילוֹנַי לָא יֵיכוֹל קֻדְשָׁא, תּוֹתָבָא דְּכָהֲנָא, וַאֲגִירָא לָא יֵיכוֹל קֻדְשָׁא: יא וְכָהֵין, אֲרֵי יִקְנֵי נְפַשׁ קִנְיַן כַּסְפֵּיהּ, הוּא יֵיכוֹל בֵּיהּ, וִילִידֵי בֵיתֵיהּ, אִנּוּן יֵיכְלוּן בְּלַחְמֵיהּ: יב וּבַת כָּהֵין, אֲרֵי תְהֵי לִגְבַר חִילוֹנַי, הִיא, בְּאַפְרָשׁוּת קֻדְשַׁיָּא לָא תֵיכוֹל: יג וּבַת כָּהֵין אֲרֵי תְהֵי אַרְמְלָא וּמְתָרְכָא, וּבַר לֵית לַהּ, וּתְתוּב, לְבֵית אֲבוּהָא

22:11 וְכֹהֵן כִּי־יִקְנֶה נֶפֶשׁ *But if a priest acquires a slave* – All members of the priestly household – including slaves – are eligible to eat the sacrificial meats. Visitors, and family members who leave the household, are not. Covenant democratizes society. It is a politics of empowerment. The Torah places a striking emphasis on personal responsibility for the structures of grace within society – above all, the home. Everything dehumanizing about slavery is forbidden. Home is something we build together; though it may have its hierarchies, it still generates a sense of belonging.

and returns to live in her father's house as when she was young, she may eat her
14 father's food again; but no layperson may do so. If someone eats of the sacred
gift unintentionally, he shall make restitution to the priest, adding an extra fifth
15 to its value. The people must not profane the sacred meats that Israelites bring
16 as offerings to the LORD or incur the penalty of iniquity by eating their sacred
offerings; for I, the LORD, make them holy."
17 The LORD spoke to Moshe: "Speak to Aharon, his sons, and all the Israelites. SHELISHI
18 Say: When anyone of the House of Israel or of the migrants living in Israel
presents an offering to the LORD as a burnt offering – whether in fulfillment
19 of a vow or as a freewill offering – to be acceptable on your behalf, it must be
20 an unblemished male from the herd, or of the sheep or goats. Do not offer
21 anything that has a blemish, for it will not be accepted on your behalf. When
someone presents a peace sacrifice to the LORD from the herd or flock – whether
because of a spoken vow or as a freewill offering – it must be unblemished to
22 be acceptable; there shall be no blemish on it. Do not present to the LORD
anything blind, injured, or maimed, or with warts, a severe rash, or scabs. Do
23 not place any of these on the altar as a fire offering to the LORD. You may offer
as a freewill offering an ox or sheep with a limb deformed or uncloven, but
24 they will not be accepted in fulfillment of a vow. Do not offer to the LORD an
animal whose testicles are bruised, crushed, torn, or cut off; and do not do such

רש"י

אִם יֵשׁ לָהּ זֶרַע מִמֶּנּוּ, אֲסוּרָה בִּתְרוּמָה כָּל זְמַן שֶׁהַזֶּרַע קַיָּם: **וְכָל זָר לֹא יֹאכַל בּוֹ.** לֹא בָּא אֶלָּא לְהוֹצִיא אֶת הָאוֹנֵן שֶׁמֻּתָּר בִּתְרוּמָה, זָרוּת אָמַרְתִּי לָךְ וְלֹא אֲנִינוּת:

יד **כִּי יֹאכַל קֹדֶשׁ.** תְּרוּמָה: **וְנָתַן לַכֹּהֵן אֶת הַקֹּדֶשׁ.** דָּבָר הָרָאוּי לִהְיוֹת קֹדֶשׁ, שֶׁאֵינוֹ פּוֹרֵעַ לוֹ מָעוֹת אֶלָּא פֵּרוֹת שֶׁל חֻלִּין, וְהֵן נַעֲשִׂין תְּרוּמָה:

טו **וְלֹא יְחַלְּלוּ וְגוֹ'.** לְהַאֲכִילָם לְזָרִים:

טז **וְהִשִּׂיאוּ אוֹתָם.** אֶת עַצְמָם יַטְעִינוּ עָוֹן, "בְּאָכְלָם אֶת קָדְשֵׁיהֶם" שֶׁהֻבְדְּלוּ לְשֵׁם תְּרוּמָה וְקָדְשׁוּ, וְנֶאֶסְרוּ עֲלֵיהֶן: **וְהִשִּׂיאוּ אוֹתָם.** זֶה אֶחָד מִשְּׁלֹשָׁה אֵתִים שֶׁהָיָה רַבִּי יִשְׁמָעֵאל דּוֹרֵשׁ בַּתּוֹרָה שֶׁמְּדַבְּרִים בָּאָדָם עַצְמוֹ, וְכֵן: "בְּיוֹם מְלֹאת יְמֵי נִזְרוֹ יָבִיא אֹתוֹ" (במדבר ו, יג) – הוּא יָבִיא אֶת עַצְמוֹ, וְכֵן: "וַיִּקְבֹּר אֹתוֹ בַגַּי" (דברים לד, ו) – הוּא קָבַר אֶת עַצְמוֹ. כָּךְ נִדְרָשׁ בְּסִפְרֵי (נשא לב):

יח **נִדְרֵיהֶם.** הֲרֵי עָלַי: **נִדְבוֹתָם.** הֲרֵי זוֹ:

יט **לִרְצֹנְכֶם.** הָבִיאוּ דָּבָר הָרָאוּי לְרַצּוֹת אֶתְכֶם לְפָנַי שֶׁיְּהֵא לָכֶם לְרָצוֹן, אפיימנ"ט בְּלַעַז. וְאֵיזֶהוּ הָרָאוּי לְרָצוֹן? "תָּמִים זָכָר בַּבָּקָר בַּכְּשָׂבִים וּבָעִזִּים". אֲבָל בְּעוֹלַת הָעוֹף אֵין צָרִיךְ תַּמּוּת וְזַכְרוּת, וְאֵינוֹ נִפְסָל בְּמוּם אֶלָּא בְּחֶסְרוֹן אֵבֶר:

כא **לְפַלֵּא נֶדֶר.** לְהַפְרִישׁ בְּדִבּוּרוֹ:

כב **עַוֶּרֶת.** שֵׁם דָּבָר שֶׁל מוּם עִוָּרוֹן בִּלְשׁוֹן נְקֵבָה, שֶׁלֹּא יְהֵא בּוֹ מוּם שֶׁל עַוֶּרֶת: **אוֹ שָׁבוּר.** לֹא יִהְיֶה: **חָרוּץ.** רִיס שֶׁל עַיִן שֶׁנִּסְדַּק אוֹ שֶׁנִּפְגַּם, וְכֵן שְׂפָתוֹ שֶׁנִּסְדְּקָה אוֹ נִפְגְּמָה: **יַבֶּלֶת.** ורוא"ה בְּלַעַז: **גָּרָב.** מִין חֲזָזִית, וְכֵן "יַלֶּפֶת". וּלְשׁוֹן "יַלֶּפֶת" כְּמוֹ "וַיִּלְפֹּת שִׁמְשׁוֹן" (שופטים טז, כט), שֶׁאֲחוּזָה בּוֹ עַד יוֹם מִיתָה, שֶׁאֵין לָהּ רְפוּאָה: **לֹא תַקְרִיבוּ.** שָׁלֹשׁ פְּעָמִים (פסוקים כ, כב, כד), לְהַזְהִיר עַל הַקְדָּשָׁתָן וְעַל שְׁחִיטָתָן וְעַל זְרִיקַת דָּמָן: **וְאִשֶּׁה לֹא תִתְּנוּ.** אַזְהָרַת הַקְטָרָתָן:

כג **שָׂרוּעַ.** אֵיבָר גָּדוֹל מֵחֲבֵרוֹ: **וְקָלוּט.** פַּרְסוֹתָיו קְלוּטוֹת: **נְדָבָה תַּעֲשֶׂה אֹתוֹ.** לְבֶדֶק הַבַּיִת: **וּלְנֵדֶר.** לַמִּזְבֵּחַ: **לֹא יֵרָצֶה.** אֵי זֶה הֶקְדֵּשׁ בָּא לְרַצּוֹת? הֱוֵי אוֹמֵר זֶה הֶקְדֵּשׁ הַמִּזְבֵּחַ:

כד **וּמָעוּךְ וְכָתוּת וְנָתוּק וְכָרוּת.** בַּבֵּיצִים אוֹ בַּגִּיד: **מָעוּךְ.** בֵּיצָיו מְעוּכִין בְּיָד: **כָּתוּת.** כְּתוּשִׁים יוֹתֵר מִמָּעוּךְ: **נָתוּק.** תְּלוּשִׁין בְּיָד עַד שֶׁנִּפְסְקוּ חוּטִים שֶׁתְּלוּיִים בָּהֶן, אֲבָל נְתוּנִים הֵם בְּתוֹךְ הַכִּיס, וְהַכִּיס לֹא נִתְלַשׁ:

יד כִּנְעוּרֶיהָ מִלֶּחֶם אָבִיהָ תֹּאכֵל וְכָל־זָר לֹא־יֹאכַל בּוֹ: וְאִישׁ כִּי־יֹאכַל
טו קֹדֶשׁ בִּשְׁגָגָה וְיָסַף חֲמִשִׁיתוֹ עָלָיו וְנָתַן לַכֹּהֵן אֶת־הַקֹּדֶשׁ: וְלֹא יְחַלְּלוּ
טז אֶת־קָדְשֵׁי בְּנֵי יִשְׂרָאֵל אֵת אֲשֶׁר־יָרִימוּ לַיהוָה: וְהִשִּׂיאוּ אוֹתָם עֲוֺן
אַשְׁמָה בְּאָכְלָם אֶת־קָדְשֵׁיהֶם כִּי אֲנִי יְהוָה מְקַדְּשָׁם:
יז יח וַיְדַבֵּר יְהוָה אֶל־מֹשֶׁה לֵּאמֹר: דַּבֵּר אֶל־אַהֲרֹן וְאֶל־בָּנָיו וְאֶל כָּל־בְּנֵי יח שלישי
יִשְׂרָאֵל וְאָמַרְתָּ אֲלֵהֶם אִישׁ אִישׁ מִבֵּית יִשְׂרָאֵל וּמִן־הַגֵּר בְּיִשְׂרָאֵל
אֲשֶׁר יַקְרִיב קָרְבָּנוֹ לְכָל־נִדְרֵיהֶם וּלְכָל־נִדְבוֹתָם אֲשֶׁר־יַקְרִיבוּ לַיהוָה
יט כ לְעֹלָה: לִרְצֹנְכֶם תָּמִים זָכָר בַּבָּקָר בַּכְּשָׂבִים וּבָעִזִּים: כֹּל אֲשֶׁר־בּוֹ מוּם
כא לֹא תַקְרִיבוּ כִּי־לֹא לְרָצוֹן יִהְיֶה לָכֶם: וְאִישׁ כִּי־יַקְרִיב זֶבַח־שְׁלָמִים
לַיהוָה לְפַלֵּא־נֶדֶר אוֹ לִנְדָבָה בַּבָּקָר אוֹ בַצֹּאן תָּמִים יִהְיֶה לְרָצוֹן
כב כָּל־מוּם לֹא יִהְיֶה־בּוֹ: עַוֶּרֶת אוֹ שָׁבוּר אוֹ־חָרוּץ אוֹ־יַבֶּלֶת אוֹ גָרָב אוֹ
יַלֶּפֶת לֹא־תַקְרִיבוּ אֵלֶּה לַיהוָה וְאִשֶּׁה לֹא־תִתְּנוּ מֵהֶם עַל־הַמִּזְבֵּחַ
כג לַיהוָה: וְשׁוֹר וָשֶׂה שָׂרוּעַ וְקָלוּט נְדָבָה תַּעֲשֶׂה אֹתוֹ וּלְנֵדֶר לֹא יֵרָצֶה:
כד וּמָעוּךְ וְכָתוּת וְנָתוּק וְכָרוּת לֹא תַקְרִיבוּ לַיהוָה וּבְאַרְצְכֶם לֹא תַעֲשׂוּ:

אונקלוס

כְּרַבְיוּתַהּ, מִלַּחְמָא דַּאֲבוּהָא תֵּיכוֹל, וְכָל חִילוֹנַי לָא יֵיכוֹל בֵּיהּ: יד וּגְבַר, אֲרֵי יֵיכוֹל קֻדְשָׁא בְּשָׁלוּ, וְיוֹסֵיף חֻמְשֵׁיהּ עֲלוֹהִי, וְיִתֵּין לְכָהֲנָא יָת קֻדְשָׁא: טו וְלָא יַחֲלוּן, יָת קֻדְשַׁיָּא דִּבְנֵי יִשְׂרָאֵל, יָת דִּיפַרְשׁוּן קֳדָם יְיָ: טז וִיקַבְּלוּן עֲלֵיהוֹן עֲוָיָן וְחוֹבִין, בְּמֵיכַלְהוֹן בְּסָאֳבָא יָת קֻדְשֵׁיהוֹן, אֲרֵי, אֲנָא יְיָ מְקַדֵּשְׁהוֹן: יז וּמַלִּיל יְיָ עִם מֹשֶׁה לְמֵימָר: יח מַלֵּיל עִם אַהֲרֹן וְעִם בְּנוֹהִי, וְעִם כָּל בְּנֵי יִשְׂרָאֵל, וְתֵימַר לְהוֹן, גְּבַר גְּבַר מִבֵּית יִשְׂרָאֵל וּמִן גִּיּוֹרַיָּא בְּיִשְׂרָאֵל, דִּיקָרֵיב קֻרְבָּנֵיהּ לְכָל נִדְרֵיהוֹן וּלְכָל נִדְבָתְהוֹן, דִּיקָרְבוּן קֳדָם יְיָ לַעֲלָתָא: יט לְרַעֲוָא לְכוֹן, שְׁלִים דְּכַר, בְּתוֹרַיָּא, בְּאִמְּרַיָּא וּבְעִזַּיָּא: כ כֹּל, דְּבֵיהּ מוּמָא לָא תְקָרְבוּן, אֲרֵי לָא לְרַעֲוָא יְהֵי לְכוֹן: כא וּגְבַר, אֲרֵי יְקָרֵיב נִכְסַת קֻדְשַׁיָּא קֳדָם יְיָ, לְפָרָשָׁא נִדְרָא אוֹ לִנְדַבְתָּא, בְּתוֹרֵי אוֹ בְעָנָא, שְׁלִים יְהֵי לְרַעֲוָא, כָּל מוּמָא לָא יְהֵי בֵיהּ: כב עֲוִיר אוֹ תְבִיר אוֹ פְסִיק אוֹ יַבְלָן, אוֹ גַרְבָן אוֹ חֲזָזָן, לָא תְקָרְבוּן אִלֵּין קֳדָם יְיָ, וְקֻרְבָּנָא, לָא תִתְּנוּן מִנְּהוֹן, עַל מַדְבְּחָא קֳדָם יְיָ: כג וְתוֹר וְאִמַּר יַתִּיר וְחַסִּיר, נְדַבְתָּא תַּעְבֵיד יָתֵיהּ, וּלְנִדְרָא לָא יִתְרְעֵי: כד וּדְמְרִיס וּדְרִיס וּדְשְׁלִיף וּדְגְזִיר, לָא תְקָרְבוּן קֳדָם יְיָ, וּבְאַרְעֲכוֹן לָא תַעְבְּדוּן:

רש"י

וְכָרוּת. כְּרוּתִין בִּכְלִי וְעוֹדָן בַּכִּיס, שֶׁלֹּא יְהֵא כִּמְחֻסַּר חִיבּוּר: וּמָעוּךְ. תַּרְגּוּם "וְדִימְרִיס" זֶהוּ לְשׁוֹן בַּאֲרַמִּית, לְשׁוֹן כְּתִישָׁה: וְכָתוּת. תַּרְגּוּמוֹ "וְדִירְסִיס", כְּמוֹ "הַבַּיִת הַגָּדוֹל רְסִיסִים" (עמוס ו, יא), בְּקִיעוֹת דַּקּוֹת, וְכֵן "קָנֶה הַמְרֻסָּס" (שבת פ ע"ב) כָּתוּשׁ כְּתִיתִין: וּבְאַרְצְכֶם לֹא תַעֲשׂוּ. דָּבָר זֶה, לְסָרֵס שׁוּם בְּהֵמָה וְחַיָּה וַאֲפִלּוּ טְמֵאָה, לְכָךְ נֶאֱמַר: "בְּאַרְצְכֶם", לְרַבּוֹת כָּל אֲשֶׁר בְּאַרְצְכֶם; שֶׁאִי אֶפְשָׁר לוֹמַר לֹא נִצְטַוּוּ עַל הַסֵּרוּס אֶלָּא בָּאָרֶץ, שֶׁהֲרֵי סֵרוּס חוֹבַת הַגּוּף הוּא, וְכָל חוֹבַת הַגּוּף נוֹהֶגֶת בֵּין בָּאָרֶץ בֵּין בְּחוּצָה לָאָרֶץ:

25 things in your land. Do not accept such animals from a migrant as an offering
of foodstuffs to your God. Because they are mutilated and blemished, they
26 will not be accepted on your behalf." The LORD spoke to Moshe:
27 "When an ox or sheep or goat is born, it shall remain with its mother for seven
days. From the eighth day it is acceptable as a sacrifice, a fire offering to the
28 LORD, but do not slaughter an ox or sheep and its young on the same day.
29 When you sacrifice a thanksgiving offering for the LORD, sacrifice it so that it
30 will be acceptable on your behalf. It shall be eaten on the same day – leave none
31 of it to the morning; I am the LORD. Keep My commands and fulfill them; I
32 am the LORD. Do not profane My holy name – that I may be sanctified in the
33 midst of the Israelites. I am the LORD, who makes you holy, who brought you
out of Egypt to be your God: I am the LORD."

רש"י

כה **ומיד בן נכר.** גוי שהביא קרבן ביד כהן להקריבו לשמים, לא תקריבו לו בעל מום, ואף על פי שלא נאסרו בעלי מומים לקרבן בני נח אלא אם כן מחסרי אבר, זאת נוהגת בבמה שבשדות, אבל על המזבח שבמשכן לא תקריבו; אבל תמימה תקבלו מהם, לכך נאמר למעלה: "איש איש" (פסוק יח), לרבות את הגוים, שנודרים נדרים ונדבות כישראל: **משחתם.** תרגומו: חבולהון: **לא ירצו לכם.** לכפר עליכם:

כז **כי יולד.** פרט ליוצא דפן:

כח **אתו ואת בנו.** נוהג בנקבה, שאסור לשחוט האם והבן או הבת, ואינו נוהג בזכרים, ומותר לשחוט האב והבן: **אתו ואת בנו.** אף בנו ואותו במשמע:

כט **לרצנכם תזבחו.** תחלת זביחתכם הזהרו שתהא לרצון לכם. ומהו הרצון? "ביום ההוא יאכל" (להלן פסוק ל), לא בא להזהיר אלא שתהא שחיטה על מנת כן, אל תשחטוהו על מנת לאכלו למחר, שאם תחשבו בו מחשבת פסול לא יהא לכם לרצון. דבר אחר "לרצנכם", לדעתכם, מכאן למתעסק שפסול בשחיטת קדשים. ואף על פי שפרט באוכלים לשני ימים, חזר ופרט באוכלין ליום אחד, שתהא זביחתן על מנת לאכלן בזמנן:

ל **ביום ההוא יאכל.** לא בא להזהיר אלא שתהא שחיטה על מנת כן, שאם לקבע לה זמן אכילה, כבר כתוב: "ובשר זבח תודת שלמיו" וגו' (לעיל ז, טו): **אני ה'.** דע מי גזר על הדבר ואל יקל בעיניך:

לא **ושמרתם.** זו המשנה: **ועשיתם.** זה המעשה:

לב **ולא תחללו.** לעבר על דברי מזידין. ממשמע שנאמר: "ולא תחללו את שם קדשי", מה תלמוד לומר: "ונקדשתי"? מסר עצמך וקדש שמי. יכול ביחיד? תלמוד לומר: "בתוך בני ישראל". וכשהוא מוסר עצמו ימסר עצמו על מנת למות, שכל המוסר עצמו על מנת הנס אין עושין לו נס, שכן מצינו בחנניה מישאל ועזריה שלא מסרו עצמן על מנת הנס, שנאמר: "והן לא, ידיע להוא לך מלכא" וגו' (דניאל ג, יח), מציל ולא מציל, "ידיע להוא לך" וגו':

לג **המוציא אתכם.** על מנת כן: **אני ה'.** נאמן לשלם שכר:

the midst of" to mean ten men, a minyan, any public gathering of Jews for prayer.

Rabbi Joseph B. Soloveitchik explains this quorum for public prayer using the concept of *sheliḥut*, agency. Just as an agent acts on behalf of and represents the person who has empowered him, so whenever ten Jews assemble for holy purposes they represent not merely a congregation of worshippers but the Jewish people in its totality. They become "the embodiment of the entire *knesset Yisrael*":

something that makes someone grateful that there is a God in heaven who inspires people to do good on earth is perhaps the greatest achievement to which anyone can aspire.

22:32 **בתוך בני ישראל** *In the midst of the Israelites* – In context, the phrase suggests that God will be sanctified through the service of an entire people living in, or journeying to, its land. We encounter here, once again, the inclusive nature of the covenant. The oral tradition, however, understood "in

כה וּמִיַּד בֶּן־נֵכָר לֹא תַקְרִיבוּ אֶת־לֶחֶם אֱלֹהֵיכֶם מִכׇּל־אֵלֶּה כִּי מׇשְׁחָתָם
כו בָּהֶם מוּם בָּם לֹא יֵרָצוּ לָכֶם: וַיְדַבֵּר יהוה אֶל־מֹשֶׁה לֵּאמֹר:
כז שׁוֹר אוֹ־כֶשֶׂב אוֹ־עֵז כִּי יִוָּלֵד וְהָיָה שִׁבְעַת יָמִים תַּחַת אִמּוֹ וּמִיּוֹם
כח הַשְּׁמִינִי וָהָלְאָה יֵרָצֶה לְקׇרְבַּן אִשֶּׁה לַיהוה: וְשׁוֹר אוֹ־שֶׂה אֹתוֹ וְאֶת־
כט בְּנוֹ לֹא תִשְׁחֲטוּ בְּיוֹם אֶחָד: וְכִי־תִזְבְּחוּ זֶבַח־תּוֹדָה לַיהוה לִרְצֹנְכֶם
ל תִּזְבָּחוּ: בַּיּוֹם הַהוּא יֵאָכֵל לֹא־תוֹתִירוּ מִמֶּנּוּ עַד־בֹּקֶר אֲנִי יהוה:
לא לב וּשְׁמַרְתֶּם מִצְוֺתַי וַעֲשִׂיתֶם אֹתָם אֲנִי יהוה: וְלֹא תְחַלְּלוּ אֶת־שֵׁם
לג קׇדְשִׁי וְנִקְדַּשְׁתִּי בְּתוֹךְ בְּנֵי יִשְׂרָאֵל אֲנִי יהוה מְקַדִּשְׁכֶם: הַמּוֹצִיא
אֶתְכֶם מֵאֶרֶץ מִצְרַיִם לִהְיוֹת לָכֶם לֵאלֹהִים אֲנִי יהוה:

אונקלוס

כה וּמִיַּד בַּר עַמְמִין, לָא תְקָרְבוּן, יָת קֻרְבַּן אֱלָהֲכוֹן מִכָּל אִלֵּין, אֲרֵי חִבָּלְהוֹן בְּהוֹן מוּמָא בְהוֹן, לָא לְרַעֲוָא יְהוֹן לְכוֹן: כו וּמַלֵּיל יי עִם מֹשֶׁה לְמֵימַר: כז תּוֹר אוֹ אִמַּר אוֹ עֵז אֲרֵי יִתְיְלֵיד, וִיהֵי, שִׁבְעָא יוֹמִין בָּתַר אִמֵּיהּ, וּמִיּוֹמָא תְּמִינָאָה וּלְהָלְאָה, יִתְרְעֵי, לְקָרָבָא קֻרְבָּנָא קֳדָם יי: כח וְתוֹרְתָא אוֹ סֵיתָא, לַהּ וְלִבְרַהּ, לָא תִכְּסוּן בְּיוֹמָא חַד: כט וַאֲרֵי תִכְּסוּן נִכְסַת תּוֹדְתָא קֳדָם יי, לְרַעֲוָא לְכוֹן תִּכְּסוּן: ל בְּיוֹמָא הַהוּא יִתְאֲכִיל, לָא תַשְׁאֲרוּן מִנֵּיהּ עַד צַפְרָא, אֲנָא יי: לא וְתִטְּרוּן פִּקּוֹדַי, וְתַעְבְּדוּן יָתְהוֹן, אֲנָא יי: לב וְלָא תְחַלּוּן יָת שְׁמָא דְקֻדְשִׁי, וְאֶתְקַדַּשׁ, בְּגוֹ בְּנֵי יִשְׂרָאֵל, אֲנָא יי מְקַדִּשְׁכוֹן: לג דְּאַפֵּיק יָתְכוֹן מֵאַרְעָא דְמִצְרַיִם, לְמֶהֱוֵי לְכוֹן לֶאֱלָהּ, אֲנָא יי:

22:32 וְלֹא תְחַלְּלוּ אֶת־שֵׁם קׇדְשִׁי *Do not profane My holy name* – The two commands, the prohibition against desecrating God's name, *ḥillul Hashem,* and the positive corollary, *kiddush Hashem,* touch on the very nature of Jewish identity. But in what sense can we sanctify or desecrate God's name?

A name is how we are known to others. God's "name" is therefore His standing in the world. Do people acknowledge Him, respect Him, honor Him? The commands of *kiddush Hashem* and *ḥillul Hashem* locate that responsibility in the conduct and fate of the Jewish people. This is what Yeshayahu meant when he said: "'You are My witnesses,' so says the LORD…'that I am He'" (Is. 43:10). Therefore, when we behave in such a way as to evoke admiration for Judaism as a faith and a way of life, that is a *kiddush Hashem,* a sanctification of God's name. When we do the opposite – when we betray that faith and way of life, causing people to have contempt for the God of Israel, and to say: I cannot respect a religion, or a God, that inspires people to behave in such a way – that is a *ḥillul Hashem,* a desecration of God's name.

No nation has ever been given a greater or more fateful responsibility. And we each have a share in this task. As Rambam elaborates in one of the passages from his law code, the *Mishneh Torah,* speaking of *kiddush Hashem*:

> If a person is scrupulous in his conduct, gentle in his conversation, pleasant toward his fellow creatures, affable in manner when receiving, not retorting even when affronted, but showing courtesy to all, even to those who treat him with disdain, conducting his business affairs with integrity…and doing more than his duty in all things, while avoiding extremes and exaggerations – such a person has sanctified God. (*Hilkhot Yesodei HaTorah* 5:11)

God trusts us enough to make us His ambassadors to an often faithless, brutal world. The choice is ours. Will our lives be a *kiddush Hashem,* or God forbid, the opposite? To do

23 1 2 The LORD spoke to Moshe: "Speak to the Israelites. Say: These are the LORD's REVI'I
appointed times that you shall proclaim as sacred assemblies; these are My
3 appointed times. Work shall be done through six days, but the seventh day
shall be a Sabbath of complete rest, a sacred assembly. You shall perform no
work at all; it shall be a Sabbath for the LORD in all your dwellings.

רש״י

כג ב דַּבֵּר אֶל בְּנֵי יִשְׂרָאֵל וְגוֹ׳ מוֹעֲדֵי ה׳. עֲשֵׂה מוֹעֲדוֹת שֶׁיִּהְיוּ יִשְׂרָאֵל מְלֻמָּדִין בָּהֶם, שֶׁמְּעַבְּרִים אֶת הַשָּׁנָה עַל גָּלֻיּוֹת שֶׁנֶּעֶקְרוּ מִמְּקוֹמָן לַעֲלוֹת לָרֶגֶל וַעֲדַיִן לֹא הִגִּיעוּ לִירוּשָׁלַיִם:

ג שֵׁשֶׁת יָמִים. מָה עִנְיַן שַׁבָּת אֵצֶל מוֹעֲדוֹת, לְלַמֶּדְךָ שֶׁכָּל הַמְחַלֵּל אֶת הַמּוֹעֲדוֹת מַעֲלִין עָלָיו כְּאִלּוּ חִלֵּל אֶת הַשַּׁבָּתוֹת, וְכָל הַמְקַיֵּם אֶת הַמּוֹעֲדוֹת מַעֲלִין עָלָיו כְּאִלּוּ קִיֵּם אֶת הַשַּׁבָּתוֹת:

which it does nowhere else. Leviticus 23 is telling its own story – a deeply spiritual one. Recall our argument (made by Yehuda HaLevi and Ibn Ezra) that almost the entire forty chapters between Exodus 24 and Leviticus 25 are a digression (see Ex. 32, "The Golden Calf"). These chapters came about because Moshe argued that the people needed God to be close. They wanted to encounter Him not only at the top of the mountain but also in the midst of the camp – as a constant presence in their lives. That is why God gave the Israelites the Sanctuary (Ex. 25–40) and its service (the book of Leviticus as a whole).

Thus, the list of the festivals in Leviticus emphasizes the dimension of encounter, closeness, the meeting of the human and the Divine. This explains why we find in this chapter, more than in any other, two key expressions. One is *moed*; the other is *mikra kodesh*.

The word *moed* does not just mean "appointed time." We find the same word in the phrase *ohel moed*, meaning "tent of meeting." If the *ohel moed* is the place where man and God meet, then the *moadim* in our chapter are the times when we and God meet. This idea is given beautiful expression in the last line of the mystical song we sing on the Sabbath, *Yedid Nefesh*: "Hurry, beloved, for the appointed time (*moed*) has come." *Moed* here means a tryst – an appointment made between lovers to meet at a certain time and place.

As for the phrase *mikra kodesh*, it comes from the same root as the word that gives the entire book its name: *Vayikra*, meaning "to be summoned in love." A *mikra kodesh* is not just a holy day. It is a meeting to which we have been called in affection by One who holds us close.

Much of the book of Leviticus is about the holiness of place, the Sanctuary. Some of it is about the holiness of people, the priests, and Israel as a whole. In chapter 23, the Torah turns to the holiness of time and the times of holiness.

We are spiritual beings but we are also physical beings. We cannot be spiritual all the time. But one day in seven, we stop working and enter the presence of the God of creation. On certain days of the year, the festivals, we celebrate the God of history. The holiness of the Sabbath is determined by God alone because He alone created the universe. The holiness of the festivals is partially determined by us, by the fixing of the calendar, because history is a partnership between us and God. But in two respects they are the same. They are both times of meeting (*moed*), and they are both times when we feel ourselves called, summoned, invited as God's guests (*mikra kodesh*).

23:3 שַׁבַּת שַׁבָּתוֹן *Sabbath of complete rest* – This is one of several accounts of the Sabbath in the Torah. What do we learn here that we do not learn elsewhere? Famously, two versions of the Ten Commandments, as they appear in Exodus and Deuteronomy, contain two different versions of the Sabbath command. The Exodus account begins with the word *zakhor*, "remember." The Deuteronomy account begins with *shamor*, "keep," "guard," "protect." But they differ more profoundly in their very understanding of the nature and significance of the day. In the Exodus text the Sabbath is a reminder of creation. However, in the Deuteronomy text the Torah speaks about a historical event: the exodus. Deuteronomy teaches us to keep the Sabbath because He took our ancestors out of Egypt, from slavery to freedom. Even greater emphasis is placed on the fact that, one day in seven, no one is a slave.

כג א וַיְדַבֵּר יהוה אֶל־מֹשֶׁה לֵּאמֹר: ב דַּבֵּר אֶל־בְּנֵי יִשְׂרָאֵל וְאָמַרְתָּ אֲלֵהֶם רביעי
ג מוֹעֲדֵי יהוה אֲשֶׁר־תִּקְרְאוּ אֹתָם מִקְרָאֵי קֹדֶשׁ אֵלֶּה הֵם מוֹעֲדָי: שֵׁשֶׁת
יָמִים תֵּעָשֶׂה מְלָאכָה וּבַיּוֹם הַשְּׁבִיעִי שַׁבַּת שַׁבָּתוֹן מִקְרָא־קֹדֶשׁ כָּל־
מְלָאכָה לֹא תַעֲשׂוּ שַׁבָּת הִוא לַיהוה בְּכֹל מוֹשְׁבֹתֵיכֶם:

אונקלוס

כג א וּמַלִּיל יי עִם מֹשֶׁה לְמֵימַר: ב מַלֵּיל, עִם בְּנֵי יִשְׂרָאֵל וְתֵימַר לְהוֹן, מוֹעֲדַיָּא דַּיי, דִּתְעָרְעוּן יָתְהוֹן מְעָרְעֵי קַדִּישׁ, אִלֵּין אִנּוּן מוֹעֲדָי: ג שִׁתָּא יוֹמִין תִּתְעֲבֵיד עֲבִידְתָא, וּבְיוֹמָא שְׁבִיעָאָה, שַׁבָּא שַׁבְּתָא מְעָרַע קַדִּישׁ, כָּל עֲבִידָא לָא תַעְבְּדוּן, שַׁבְּתָא הִיא קֳדָם יי, בְּכָל מוֹתְבָנֵיכוֹן:

> *Knesset Yisrael* is not just a collectivity, a crowd, a herd, or a multitude. It is a separate entity, a living individuality. It embraces not only contemporary Jews but also the entire history of those people who have lived and died with *Shema Yisrael* on their lips. It includes the heroes and the cowards, the great and the small, the well-known historical figures as well as the anonymous people who are buried in unmarked graves. All are part of *knesset Yisrael*. All are personified by ten ordinary Jews who gather together to pray as a *tzibbur* (congregation)....There is only one *knesset Yisrael* and it prays with every minyan of ten.

The synagogue, in this understanding, is the recreation of the Jewish people. Those who gather there are more than a congregation. In a halakhic and mystical sense they are the congregation, the reembodiment here and now of the Jewish people as it stood at Sinai and pledged itself to God. In the synagogue, Jews anticipate not only the rebuilding of Jerusalem but also the physical and spiritual reunification of the Jewish nation. This is a deep and metaphysical idea, but it has been Judaism's genius to translate such ideas into living institutions, never more so than in the case of the synagogue. *Knesset Yisrael*, God's covenantal partner, is the community of all Jews past, present, and future, united as they stand before God in their houses of study and prayer as they once before stood at the foot of Mount Sinai.

22:32 אֲנִי יהוה מְקַדִּשְׁכֶם *I am the Lord, who makes you holy.* It is precisely in our day-to-day relationships, at work or among friends, in our dealings with people and the integrity, sensitivity, and generosity we bring to bear on them, that we most add or subtract to the respect those around us have for the values by which we live. Here, the greatest of biblical commands – to sanctify and not desecrate God's name – have their arena, their impact and influence. "Sanctifying the name" is no mere marginal addendum to the script of Jewish life but its very point: to bring God's presence into the world by making others aware that God's word sanctifies life.

THE JEWISH CALENDAR

There are three lengthy accounts of the festivals in the Torah: one here, a second one in Numbers 28–29, and the third in Deuteronomy 16. What is striking is how different they are. The long section on the festivals in Numbers is wholly dedicated to the special additional sacrifices (the *musafim*) brought on holy days. One of Deuteronomy's most important themes is its insistence that worship be centralized "in the place that the Lord will choose" (for example, Deut. 12:14), which will turn out to be Jerusalem. That is why, when it comes to the festivals, Deuteronomy speaks only of Passover, Shavuot, and Sukkot, and not Rosh HaShana or Yom Kippur, because only on those three was there a duty of *aliya leregel*, pilgrimage to the Temple.

Our passage too is distinctive. Unlike the Exodus and Deuteronomy passages, it includes Rosh HaShana and Yom Kippur. It also tells us about the specific mitzvot of the festivals, most notably Sukkot: it is the only place where the Torah mentions the *arbaa minim*, the four species, and the command to live in a sukka. More puzzling is the fact that the Torah here seems to be calling the Sabbath a *moed*, an appointed time, and a *mikra kodesh*, a sacred assembly,

4 These are the LORD's appointed times, sacred assemblies, which you shall
5 proclaim at their appointed times. In the first month, the fourteenth of the
month in the afternoon is the time for the Passover sacrifice to the LORD.
6 The fifteenth day of this month is the LORD's Festival of Unleavened Bread;
7 for seven days you shall eat unleavened bread. The first day shall be a sacred
8 assembly for you; you shall perform no laborious work. And you shall present
a fire offering for the LORD for seven days; on the seventh day there shall be a
sacred assembly; you shall perform no laborious work."
9 10 The LORD spoke to Moshe: "Speak to the Israelites. Say: When you come
to the land that I am giving you and reap its harvest, bring the first sheaf of
11 your harvest to the priest. He shall display the sheaf this way and that before
the LORD for your acceptance; on the day after the day of rest the priest shall
12 display it. On the day you display the sheaf this way and that, you shall offer

רש״י

ד **אֵלֶּה מוֹעֲדֵי ה׳.** לְמַעְלָה מְדַבֵּר בְּעִבּוּר שָׁנָה, וְכָאן מְדַבֵּר בְּקִדּוּשׁ הַחֹדֶשׁ:

ה **בֵּין הָעַרְבָּיִם.** מִשֵּׁשׁ שָׁעוֹת וּלְמַעְלָה: **פֶּסַח לַה׳.** הַקְרָבַת קָרְבָּן שֶׁשְּׁמוֹ פֶּסַח:

ח **וְהִקְרַבְתֶּם אִשֶּׁה וְגוֹ׳.** הֵם הַמּוּסָפִין הָאֲמוּרִים בְּפָרָשַׁת פִּינְחָס. וְלָמָּה נֶאֶמְרוּ כָּאן? לוֹמַר לְךָ שֶׁאֵין הַמּוּסָפִין מְעַכְּבִין זֶה אֶת זֶה: "וְהִקְרַבְתֶּם אִשֶּׁה לַה׳" – מִכָּל מָקוֹם, אִם אֵין פָּרִים הָבֵא אֵילִים, וְאִם אֵין פָּרִים וְאֵילִים הָבֵא כְּבָשִׂים: **שִׁבְעַת יָמִים.** כָּל מָקוֹם שֶׁנֶּאֱמַר 'שִׁבְעַת' שֵׁם דָּבָר הוּא, שָׁבוּעַ שֶׁל יָמִים, סטיינ"א בְּלַעַז. וְכֵן כָּל לְשׁוֹן שְׁמֹנַת, שֵׁשֶׁת, חֲמֵשֶׁת, שְׁלֹשֶׁת: **מְלֶאכֶת עֲבֹדָה.** אֲפִלּוּ מְלָאכוֹת הַחֲשׁוּבוֹת לָכֶם עֲבוֹדָה וָצֹרֶךְ, שֶׁיֵּשׁ חֶסְרוֹן כִּיס בְּבַטָּלָה שֶׁלָּהֶן, כְּגוֹן דְּבַר הָאָבֵד. כָּךְ הֲבַנְתִּי מִתּוֹרַת כֹּהֲנִים (פרשתא יב, ח), דְּקָתָנֵי: יָכוֹל אַף חֻלּוֹ שֶׁל מוֹעֵד יְהֵא אָסוּר בִּמְלֶאכֶת עֲבוֹדָה? וְכוּ׳:

י **רֵאשִׁית קְצִירְכֶם.** שֶׁתְּהֵא רִאשׁוֹנָה לַקָּצִיר: **עֹמֶר.** עֲשִׂירִית הָאֵיפָה, כָּךְ הָיָה שְׁמָהּ, כְּמוֹ: "וַיָּמֹדּוּ בָעֹמֶר" (שמות טז, יח):

יא **וְהֵנִיף.** כָּל תְּנוּפָה מוֹלִיךְ וּמֵבִיא מַעֲלֶה וּמוֹרִיד, מוֹלִיךְ וּמֵבִיא לַעֲצֹר רוּחוֹת רָעוֹת, מַעֲלֶה וּמוֹרִיד לַעֲצֹר טְלָלִים רָעִים: **לִרְצֹנְכֶם.** אִם תַּקְרִיבוּ כַּמִּשְׁפָּט הַזֶּה יִהְיֶה לְרָצוֹן לָכֶם: **מִמָּחֳרַת הַשַּׁבָּת.** מִמָּחֳרַת יוֹם טוֹב הָרִאשׁוֹן שֶׁל פֶּסַח, שֶׁאִם אַתָּה אוֹמֵר שַׁבַּת בְּרֵאשִׁית, אִי אַתָּה יוֹדֵעַ אֵיזֶהוּ:

יב **וַעֲשִׂיתֶם... כֶּבֶשׂ.** חוֹבָה לָעֹמֶר הוּא בָּא:

the day on which, in the stasis of rest and the silence of the soul, we are invited to hear the call of God.

23:5 פֶּסַח *Passover* – There is a profound difference between the mentalities of ancient Greece and Judaism. Greek thought is *logical* while Jewish thought is *chronological*. Logical systems are ideally timeless. Chronological systems are embedded in time. Logical systems are contemplated. Chronological systems are lived. Thus for Jews the creation of the universe is not a metaphysical truth to be accepted. It is an experience to be lived one day in seven. The exodus from Egypt, likewise, is not a historical truth to be recorded. It is a dramatic episode to be reenacted every year. The calendar – the musical score of the symphony of time – is how we take truths from the abstract heavens or the distant past and make them real in our shared lives.

In the Torah, the festival we call Pesaḥ is consistently described as *Ḥag HaMatzot*, the Festival of Unleavened Bread (*Ḥag HaPesaḥ*, in the Torah, is confined to the fourteenth of Nisan, the day prior to the Seder, when the Paschal sacrifice was brought). Rabbi Levi Yitzḥak of Berdichev gave a beautiful explanation for this dual terminology. The name Pesaḥ signifies the greatness of God, who "passed over" (*pasaḥ*) the houses of the Israelites. The name *Ḥag HaMatzot* suggests the greatness of the Israelites, who followed God into the desert without any provisions. In the Torah God calls the festival *Ḥag HaMatzot* in praise of Israel. The Jewish people, though, calls the festival Pesaḥ in praise of God.

ד ה אֵלֶּה מוֹעֲדֵי יְהוָה מִקְרָאֵי קֹדֶשׁ אֲשֶׁר־תִּקְרְאוּ אֹתָם בְּמוֹעֲדָם: בַּחֹדֶשׁ
ו הָרִאשׁוֹן בְּאַרְבָּעָה עָשָׂר לַחֹדֶשׁ בֵּין הָעַרְבָּיִם פֶּסַח לַיהוָה: וּבַחֲמִשָּׁה
עָשָׂר יוֹם לַחֹדֶשׁ הַזֶּה חַג הַמַּצּוֹת לַיהוָה שִׁבְעַת יָמִים מַצּוֹת תֹּאכֵלוּ:
ז בַּיּוֹם הָרִאשׁוֹן מִקְרָא־קֹדֶשׁ יִהְיֶה לָכֶם כָּל־מְלֶאכֶת עֲבֹדָה לֹא תַעֲשׂוּ:
ח וְהִקְרַבְתֶּם אִשֶּׁה לַיהוָה שִׁבְעַת יָמִים בַּיּוֹם הַשְּׁבִיעִי מִקְרָא־קֹדֶשׁ
כָּל־מְלֶאכֶת עֲבֹדָה לֹא תַעֲשׂוּ:
ט י וַיְדַבֵּר יְהוָה אֶל־מֹשֶׁה לֵּאמֹר: דַּבֵּר אֶל־בְּנֵי יִשְׂרָאֵל וְאָמַרְתָּ אֲלֵהֶם כִּי־
תָבֹאוּ אֶל־הָאָרֶץ אֲשֶׁר אֲנִי נֹתֵן לָכֶם וּקְצַרְתֶּם אֶת־קְצִירָהּ וַהֲבֵאתֶם
יא אֶת־עֹמֶר רֵאשִׁית קְצִירְכֶם אֶל־הַכֹּהֵן: וְהֵנִיף אֶת־הָעֹמֶר לִפְנֵי יְהוָה
יב לִרְצֹנְכֶם מִמָּחֳרַת הַשַּׁבָּת יְנִיפֶנּוּ הַכֹּהֵן: וַעֲשִׂיתֶם בְּיוֹם הֲנִיפְכֶם אֶת־

אונקלוס

ד אִלֵּין מוֹעֲדַיָּא דַּייָ, מְעָרְעֵי קַדִּישׁ, דִּתְעָרְעוּן יָתְהוֹן בְּזִמְנֵיהוֹן: ה בְּיַרְחָא קַדְמָאָה, בְּאַרְבְּעַת עַסְרָא, לְיַרְחָא בֵּין שִׁמְשַׁיָּא, פִּסְחָא קֳדָם יי: ו וּבַחֲמֵישַׁת עַסְרָא יוֹמָא לְיַרְחָא הָדֵין, חַגָּא דְּפַטִּירַיָּא קֳדָם יי, שִׁבְעָא יוֹמִין פַּטִּירָא תֵּיכְלוּן: ז בְּיוֹמָא קַדְמָאָה, מְעָרַע קַדִּישׁ יְהֵי לְכוֹן, כָּל עֲבִידַת פָּלְחַן לָא תַעְבְּדוּן: ח וּתְקָרְבוּן קֻרְבָּנָא, קֳדָם יי שִׁבְעָא יוֹמִין, בְּיוֹמָא שְׁבִיעָאָה מְעָרַע קַדִּישׁ, כָּל עֲבִידַת פָּלְחַן לָא תַעְבְּדוּן: ט וּמַלִּיל יי עִם מֹשֶׁה לְמֵימַר: י מַלֵּיל, עִם בְּנֵי יִשְׂרָאֵל וְתֵימַר לְהוֹן, אֲרֵי תֵיעֲלוּן לְאַרְעָא, דַּאֲנָא יָהֵיב לְכוֹן, וְתַחְצְדוּן יָת חֲצָדַהּ, וְתַיְתוּן יָת עוּמַר, רֵישׁ חֲצָדְכוֹן לְוָת כָּהֲנָא: יא וִירִים יָת עֻמְרָא, קֳדָם יי לְרַעֲוָא לְכוֹן, מִבָּתַר יוֹמָא טָבָא, יְרִימִנֵּיהּ כָּהֲנָא: יב וְתַעְבְּדוּן, בְּיוֹם אֲרָמוּתְכוֹן יָת

We integrate both accounts into the text of the *Kiddush* we make on Friday night. The Sabbath is "a remembrance of creation" (*zikaron lemaaseh bereshit*) as well as a "reminder of the exodus" (*zekher leyetziat Mitzrayim*). However, once we set the Leviticus account in the context of these other two, a richer pattern emerges.

If we play close attention, we can hear three primary voices in the Torah. There are three voices because axiomatic to Jewish faith is the belief that God is encountered in three ways: in creation, revelation, and redemption. Rabbi Shimon ben Tzemaḥ Duran (1366–1441) argued that all of Rambam's Thirteen Principles of Faith could be reduced to these three. They represent the three basic relationships within which Judaism and human life are set. Creation is God's relationship to the world. Revelation is God's relationship with us. When we apply revelation to creation, the result is redemption: the world in which God's will and ours coincide.

We can now understand why the Torah contains three distinct accounts of the Sabbath. The account in the first version of the Ten Commandments, "For in six days the Lord made heaven and earth" (Ex. 20:11), is the Sabbath of creation. The account in the second version, "Remember that you were slaves in Egypt and the Lord, your God, brought you out" (Deut. 5:15), is the Sabbath of redemption. The account here in Emor is the Sabbath of revelation. In revelation, God calls to humankind. That is why the middle book of the Torah begins with the word *vayikra*, "and He called." It is also why the Sabbath is, uniquely here, included in the days "that you shall proclaim (*tikre'u*) as sacred assemblies (*mikra'ei kodesh*)" (Lev. 23:4), with the double emphasis on the verb *k-r-a*, "call," "proclaim," "convoke." The Sabbath is

13 a yearling sheep without blemish as a burnt offering to the LORD. Its grain
offering shall be two-tenths of an ephah of fine flour mixed with oil, a fire
offering for the LORD, a pleasing aroma; and its libation shall be a quarter of
14 a hin of wine. Until that day, until you bring this sacrifice to your God, you
shall eat no bread or roasted grain or ripe grain. This is an everlasting statute
15 throughout your generations, in all your dwellings. And from the
day you bring the sheaf of the wave offering, the day after the day of rest, you
16 shall count for yourselves seven complete weeks. To the day after the seventh
week, you shall count fifty days; and then you shall present a new grain offering
17 to the LORD. You shall bring two loaves of bread from your dwellings made
with two-tenths of an ephah of fine flour baked with leaven, as a wave offering:

רש"י

יג **וּמִנְחָתוֹ.** מִנְחַת נְסָכָיו: **שְׁנֵי עֶשְׂרֹנִים.** כְּפוּלָה הָיְתָה: **וְנִסְכֹּה יַיִן רְבִיעִת הַהִין.** אַף עַל פִּי שֶׁמִּנְחָתוֹ כְּפוּלָה, אֵין נְסָכָיו כְּפוּלִים:

יד **וְקָלִי.** קֶמַח עָשׂוּי מִכַּרְמֶל רַךְ שֶׁמְּיַבְּשִׁין אוֹתוֹ בַּתַּנּוּר: **וְכַרְמֶל.** הֵן קְלָיוֹת שֶׁקּוֹרִין גרניי"ש: **בְּכֹל מֹשְׁבֹתֵיכֶם.** נֶחְלְקוּ בּוֹ חַכְמֵי יִשְׂרָאֵל, יֵשׁ שֶׁלָּמְדוּ מִכָּאן שֶׁהֶחָדָשׁ נוֹהֵג בְּחוּצָה לָאָרֶץ, וְיֵשׁ אוֹמְרִים, לֹא בָא אֶלָּא לְלַמֵּד שֶׁלֹּא נִצְטַוּוּ עַל הֶחָדָשׁ אֶלָּא לְאַחַר יְרֻשָּׁה וִישִׁיבָה מִשֶּׁכְּבָשׁוּ וְחִלְּקוּ:

טו **מִמָּחֳרַת הַשַּׁבָּת.** מִמָּחֳרַת יוֹם טוֹב: **תְּמִימֹת תִּהְיֶינָה.** מְלַמֵּד שֶׁמַּתְחִיל וּמוֹנֶה מִבָּעֶרֶב, שֶׁאִם לֹא כֵן אֵינָן תְּמִימוֹת:

טז **הַשַּׁבָּת הַשְּׁבִיעִת.** כְּתַרְגּוּמוֹ: "שְׁבוּעֲתָא שְׁבִיעֲתָא": **עַד מִמָּחֳרַת הַשַּׁבָּת הַשְּׁבִיעִת תִּסְפְּרוּ.** וְלֹא עַד בִּכְלָל, וְהֵן אַרְבָּעִים וְתִשְׁעָה יוֹם: **חֲמִשִּׁים יוֹם וְהִקְרַבְתֶּם מִנְחָה חֲדָשָׁה לַה'.** בְּיוֹם הַחֲמִשִּׁים תַּקְרִיבוּהָ. וְאוֹמֵר אֲנִי, זֶהוּ מִדְרָשׁוֹ, אֲבָל פְּשׁוּטוֹ: "עַד מִמָּחֳרַת הַשַּׁבָּת הַשְּׁבִיעִת שֶׁהוּא יוֹם חֲמִשִּׁים תִּסְפְּרוּ", וּמִקְרָא מְסֹרָס הוּא: **מִנְחָה חֲדָשָׁה.** הִיא הַמִּנְחָה הָרִאשׁוֹנָה שֶׁהוּבְאָה מִן הֶחָדָשׁ. וְאִם תֹּאמַר, הֲרֵי קָרְבָה מִנְחַת הָעֹמֶר? אֵינָהּ כִּשְׁאָר כָּל הַמְּנָחוֹת, שֶׁהִיא בָּאָה מִן הַשְּׂעוֹרִים:

יז **מִמּוֹשְׁבֹתֵיכֶם.** וְלֹא מִחוּצָה לָאָרֶץ: **לֶחֶם תְּנוּפָה.** לֶחֶם תְּרוּמָה הַמּוּרָם לְשֵׁם גָּבוֹהַּ, וְזוֹ הִיא הַמִּנְחָה הַחֲדָשָׁה הָאֲמוּרָה לְמַעְלָה: **בִּכּוּרִים.** רִאשׁוֹנָה לְכָל הַמְּנָחוֹת, אַף לְמִנְחַת קְנָאוֹת הַבָּאָה מִן הַשְּׂעוֹרִים, לֹא תִקְרַב מִן הֶחָדָשׁ קֹדֶם לִשְׁתֵּי הַלֶּחֶם:

called for its own act of thanksgiving. This is time as R. Ḥai Gaon understood it. "Count fifty days" – each of which is a command in itself, unaffected by the days that came before or after.

But the Omer is also part of historical time. It represents the journey from Egypt to Sinai, from exodus to revelation. This is, in the biblical worldview, a crucial transition. In the exodus the people gained negative liberty: they ceased to be slaves. At Mount Sinai they gained a covenant: the rule of law, a constitution of liberty that made them free.

In this sense, the forty-nine days represent an unbroken historical sequence. There is no way of going directly from escape-from-tyranny to a free society – as we have discovered time and again. Here, time is an ordered sequence of events, a journey, a narrative. Miss one stage, and one may lose everything. This is time as Halakhot Gedolot understood it: "Count… seven complete weeks," with the emphasis on "full, complete, unbroken."

Halakha as we practice it mediates between these two opinions. Out of respect for R. Ḥai, we continue to count after missing a day, but out of respect for the Halakhot Gedolot we do so without a blessing.

Cyclical time is deeply conservative; covenantal time is revolutionary. It was the greatness of the biblical prophets to hear the music of covenant beneath the noise of events, giving history its shape and meaning as the long, slow journey to redemption. Both, however, find their expression in the counting of the Omer.

יג הָעֹמֶר כֶּבֶשׂ תָּמִים בֶּן־שְׁנָתוֹ לְעֹלָה לַיהוָה: וּמִנְחָתוֹ שְׁנֵי עֶשְׂרֹנִים סֹלֶת
יד בְּלוּלָה בַשֶּׁמֶן אִשֶּׁה לַיהוָה רֵיחַ נִיחֹחַ וְנִסְכֹּה יַיִן רְבִיעִת הַהִין: וְלֶחֶם
וְקָלִי וְכַרְמֶל לֹא תֹאכְלוּ עַד־עֶצֶם הַיּוֹם הַזֶּה עַד הֲבִיאֲכֶם אֶת־קָרְבַּן
טו אֱלֹהֵיכֶם חֻקַּת עוֹלָם לְדֹרֹתֵיכֶם בְּכֹל מֹשְׁבֹתֵיכֶם: וּסְפַרְתֶּם יט
לָכֶם מִמָּחֳרַת הַשַּׁבָּת מִיּוֹם הֲבִיאֲכֶם אֶת־עֹמֶר הַתְּנוּפָה שֶׁבַע שַׁבָּתוֹת
טז תְּמִימֹת תִּהְיֶינָה: עַד מִמָּחֳרַת הַשַּׁבָּת הַשְּׁבִיעִת תִּסְפְּרוּ חֲמִשִּׁים יוֹם
יז וְהִקְרַבְתֶּם מִנְחָה חֲדָשָׁה לַיהוָה: מִמּוֹשְׁבֹתֵיכֶם תָּבִיאוּ | לֶחֶם תְּנוּפָה
שְׁתַּיִם שְׁנֵי עֶשְׂרֹנִים סֹלֶת תִּהְיֶינָה חָמֵץ תֵּאָפֶינָה בִּכּוּרִים לַיהוָה:

אונקלוס

עֻמְרָא, אִמַּר שְׁלִים בַּר שַׁתֵּיהּ, לַעֲלָתָא קֳדָם יְיָ: יג וּמִנְחָתֵיהּ תְּרֵין עֶסְרוֹנִין, סֻלְתָּא דְּפִילָא בִמְשַׁח, קֻרְבָּנָא קֳדָם יְיָ לְאִתְקַבָּלָא בְרַעֲוָא, וְנִסְכֵּיהּ חַמְרָא רַבְעוּת הִינָא: יד וּלְחֵים וְקָלֵי וּפֵירוּכָן לָא תֵיכְלוּן, עַד כְּרַן יוֹמָא הָדֵין, עַד אַיְתוֹאֵיכוֹן, יָת קֻרְבָּנָא דֶּאֱלָהֲכוֹן, קְיָם עָלַם לְדָרֵיכוֹן, בְּכֹל מוֹתְבָנֵיכוֹן: טו וְתִמְנוֹן לְכוֹן מִבָּתַר יוֹמָא טָבָא, מִיּוֹם אַיְתוֹאֵיכוֹן, יָת עֻמְרָא דַאֲרָמוּתָא, שְׁבַע שָׁבוּעָן שַׁלְמָן יְהוְיָן: טז עַד מִבָּתַר שָׁבוּעֲתָא שְׁבִיעֵיתָא, תִּמְנוֹן חַמְשִׁין יוֹמִין, וּתְקָרְבוּן, מִנְחֲתָא חֲדַתָּא קֳדָם יְיָ: יז מִמּוֹתְבָנֵיכוֹן, תַּיְתוֹן לְחֵים אֲרָמוּתָא, תַּרְתֵּין גְּרִיצָן תְּרֵין עֶסְרוֹנִין, סֻלְתָּא יְהוְיָן, חֲמִיעַ יִתְאַפְיָן, בִּכּוּרִין קֳדָם יְיָ:

COUNTING THE OMER

This passage was the focus of a halachic disagreement during the period of the *geonim* (eighth to eleventh centuries). What is the law for someone who forgets to count one of the forty-nine days? May he continue to count the rest, or has he forfeited the entire command for that year? There were two views. According to Halakhot Gedolot (a work attributed to Rabbi Shimon Kayyara), the person has indeed forfeited the chance to fulfill the command. According to R. Ḥai Gaon he has not. He continues to count the remaining days, unaffected by his failure to count one of the forty-nine.

How are we to understand this argument? According to the Halakhot Gedolot, the key phrase is "seven *complete* (*temimot*) weeks." One who forgets a day cannot satisfy the requirement of completeness. In this view, the forty-nine days constitute a single religious act, and if one of the parts is missing, the whole is defective. According to R. Ḥai Gaon, however, each day of the forty-nine is a separate command – "To the day after the seventh week, you shall count fifty days." If one fails to keep one of the commands, that is no impediment to keeping the others.

What is at stake here? If we look at the festivals of the Tanakh – Passover, Shavuot, and Sukkot – we see that each has a dual logic. On the one hand, they belong to cyclical time. They celebrate seasons of the year – Passover is the festival of spring, Shavuot of first fruits, and Sukkot of the autumn harvest.

However, they also belong to covenantal, historical time. They commemorate historic events. Passover celebrates the exodus from Egypt, Shavuot the giving of the Torah, and Sukkot the forty years of wandering in the wilderness. Thus, the counting of the Omer also has two temporal dimensions.

On the one hand, it belongs to cyclical time. The forty-nine days represent the period of the grain harvest, the time during which farmers had most to thank God for – for "bringing forth bread from the ground." Each day brought forth its own blessing in the form of new grain, and therefore

18 first produce to the LORD. Together with the bread, you shall present seven
unblemished yearling male lambs, one young bull, and two rams – these shall
be a burnt offering for the LORD with their grain offering and their libations, a
19 fire offering, a pleasing aroma to the LORD. And you shall offer one he-goat as a
20 purification offering and two yearling male sheep as peace sacrifices. The priest
shall display them this way and that with the bread of the first produce as a wave
offering before the LORD together with the two sheep; they shall be holy to the
21 LORD and belong to the priest. On that day you shall make a proclamation; it
shall be a sacred assembly for you; you shall perform no laborious work. This
22 is an everlasting statute throughout your generations in all your dwellings. And
when you reap the harvest of your land, do not reap to the edge of your field
or gather the gleanings of your harvest. Leave them for the poor and for the
migrant; I am the LORD your God."
23 24 Then the LORD spoke to Moshe: "Tell the Israelites: On the first day of the HAMISHI
seventh month, you shall observe a day of rest, a commemoration with the
25 sounding of the ram's horn, a sacred assembly. You shall perform no laborious
26 work, and you shall bring close a fire offering to the LORD." The LORD
27 spoke to Moshe: "Hear: the tenth day of this seventh month is the Day of
Atonement. It shall be a sacred assembly for you, and you shall afflict yourselves
28 and bring a fire offering to the LORD. You shall perform no work at all during
this entire day, for it is the Day of Atonement, there to make atonement for you
29 before the LORD your God. Anyone who does not afflict himself for this whole

רש"י

יח **עַל הַלֶּחֶם.** בִּגְלַל הַלֶּחֶם, חוֹבָה לַלֶּחֶם: **וּמִנְחָתָם וְנִסְכֵּיהֶם.** כְּמִשְׁפַּט מִנְחָה וּנְסָכִים הַמְפֹרָשִׁים בְּכָל בְּהֵמָה בְּפָרָשַׁת נְסָכִים (במדבר טו, ח-טז): שְׁלֹשָׁה עֶשְׂרֹנִים לַפָּר וּשְׁנֵי עֶשְׂרֹנִים לָאַיִל וְעִשָּׂרוֹן לַכֶּבֶשׂ – זוֹ הִיא הַמִּנְחָה. וְהַנְּסָכִים: חֲצִי הַהִין לַפָּר וּשְׁלִישִׁית הַהִין לָאַיִל וּרְבִיעִית הַהִין לַכֶּבֶשׂ:

יט **וַעֲשִׂיתֶם שְׂעִיר עִזִּים.** יָכוֹל שִׁבְעַת הַכְּבָשִׂים וְהַשָּׂעִיר הָאֲמוּרִים כָּאן הֵם שִׁבְעַת הַכְּבָשִׂים וְהַשָּׂעִיר הָאֲמוּרִים בְּחוּמַשׁ הַפְּקוּדִים (שם כח, כז, ל)? כְּשֶׁאַתָּה מַגִּיעַ אֵצֶל פָּרִים וְאֵילִים אֵינָן הֵם, אֱמֹר מֵעַתָּה, אֵלּוּ לְעַצְמָן וְאֵלּוּ לְעַצְמָן, אֵלּוּ קָרְבוּ בִּגְלַל הַלֶּחֶם וְאֵלּוּ לַמּוּסָפִין:

כ **וְהֵנִיף הַכֹּהֵן אֹתָם... תְּנוּפָה.** מְלַמֵּד שֶׁטְּעוּנִין תְּנוּפָה חַיִּים. יָכוֹל כֻּלָּם? תַּלְמוּד לוֹמַר: "עַל שְׁנֵי כְּבָשִׂים": **קֹדֶשׁ יִהְיוּ.** לְפִי שֶׁשַּׁלְמֵי יָחִיד קָדָשִׁים קַלִּים, הֻזְקַק לוֹמַר בְּשַׁלְמֵי צִבּוּר שֶׁהֵם קָדְשֵׁי קָדָשִׁים:

כב **וּבְקֻצְרְכֶם.** חָזַר וְשָׁנָה לַעֲבֹר עֲלֵיהֶם בִּשְׁנֵי לָאוִין. אָמַר רַבִּי אַבְדִּימִי בְּרַבִּי יוֹסֵף, מָה רָאָה הַכָּתוּב לִתְּנָהּ בְּאֶמְצַע הָרְגָלִים, פֶּסַח וַעֲצֶרֶת מִכָּאן וְרֹאשׁ הַשָּׁנָה וְיוֹם הַכִּפּוּרִים מִכָּאן? לְלַמֶּדְךָ שֶׁכָּל הַנּוֹתֵן לֶקֶט שִׁכְחָה וּפֵאָה לֶעָנִי כָּרָאוּי, מַעֲלִין עָלָיו כְּאִלּוּ בָּנָה בֵּית הַמִּקְדָּשׁ וְהִקְרִיב עָלָיו קָרְבְּנוֹתָיו בְּתוֹכוֹ: **תַּעֲזֹב.** הַנַּח לִפְנֵיהֶם וְהֵם יְלַקְּטוּ, וְאֵין לְךָ לְסַיֵּעַ לְאֶחָד מֵהֶם: **אֲנִי ה׳ אֱלֹהֵיכֶם.** נֶאֱמָן לְשַׁלֵּם שָׂכָר:

כד **זִכְרוֹן תְּרוּעָה.** זִכְרוֹן פְּסוּקֵי זִכְרוֹנוֹת וּפְסוּקֵי שׁוֹפָרוֹת, לִזְכֹּר לָכֶם עֲקֵדַת יִצְחָק שֶׁקָּרַב תַּחְתָּיו אַיִל:

כה **וְהִקְרַבְתֶּם אִשֶּׁה.** הַמּוּסָפִים הָאֲמוּרִין בְּחוּמַשׁ הַפְּקֻדִים (במדבר כט, א-ו):

כז **אַךְ.** כָּל אַכִין וְרַקִּין שֶׁבַּתּוֹרָה מִעוּטִין, מְכַפֵּר הוּא לַשָּׁבִין וְאֵינוֹ מְכַפֵּר עַל שֶׁאֵינָם שָׁבִין:

יח וְהִקְרַבְתֶּם עַל־הַלֶּחֶם שִׁבְעַת כְּבָשִׂים תְּמִימִם בְּנֵי שָׁנָה וּפַר בֶּן־בָּקָר
אֶחָד וְאֵילִם שְׁנָיִם יִהְיוּ עֹלָה לַיהֹוָה וּמִנְחָתָם וְנִסְכֵּיהֶם אִשֵּׁה רֵיחַ־
יט נִיחֹחַ לַיהֹוָה: וַעֲשִׂיתֶם שְׂעִיר־עִזִּים אֶחָד לְחַטָּאת וּשְׁנֵי כְבָשִׂים בְּנֵי
כ שָׁנָה לְזֶבַח שְׁלָמִים: וְהֵנִיף הַכֹּהֵן | אֹתָם עַל לֶחֶם הַבִּכֻּרִים תְּנוּפָה
כא לִפְנֵי יְהֹוָה עַל־שְׁנֵי כְּבָשִׂים קֹדֶשׁ יִהְיוּ לַיהֹוָה לַכֹּהֵן: וּקְרָאתֶם בְּעֶצֶם |
הַיּוֹם הַזֶּה מִקְרָא־קֹדֶשׁ יִהְיֶה לָכֶם כָּל־מְלֶאכֶת עֲבֹדָה לֹא תַעֲשׂוּ חֻקַּת
כב עוֹלָם בְּכָל־מוֹשְׁבֹתֵיכֶם לְדֹרֹתֵיכֶם: וּבְקֻצְרְכֶם אֶת־קְצִיר אַרְצְכֶם לֹא־
תְכַלֶּה פְּאַת שָׂדְךָ בְּקֻצְרֶךָ וְלֶקֶט קְצִירְךָ לֹא תְלַקֵּט לֶעָנִי וְלַגֵּר תַּעֲזֹב
אֹתָם אֲנִי יְהֹוָה אֱלֹהֵיכֶם:
כג כד וַיְדַבֵּר יְהֹוָה אֶל־מֹשֶׁה לֵּאמֹר: דַּבֵּר אֶל־בְּנֵי יִשְׂרָאֵל לֵאמֹר בַּחֹדֶשׁ חמישי
הַשְּׁבִיעִי בְּאֶחָד לַחֹדֶשׁ יִהְיֶה לָכֶם שַׁבָּתוֹן זִכְרוֹן תְּרוּעָה מִקְרָא־קֹדֶשׁ:
כה כו כָּל־מְלֶאכֶת עֲבֹדָה לֹא תַעֲשׂוּ וְהִקְרַבְתֶּם אִשֶּׁה לַיהֹוָה: וַיְדַבֵּר
כז יְהֹוָה אֶל־מֹשֶׁה לֵּאמֹר: אַךְ בֶּעָשׂוֹר לַחֹדֶשׁ הַשְּׁבִיעִי הַזֶּה יוֹם הַכִּפֻּרִים
הוּא מִקְרָא־קֹדֶשׁ יִהְיֶה לָכֶם וְעִנִּיתֶם אֶת־נַפְשֹׁתֵיכֶם וְהִקְרַבְתֶּם אִשֶּׁה
כח לַיהֹוָה: וְכָל־מְלָאכָה לֹא תַעֲשׂוּ בְּעֶצֶם הַיּוֹם הַזֶּה כִּי יוֹם כִּפֻּרִים הוּא
כט לְכַפֵּר עֲלֵיכֶם לִפְנֵי יְהֹוָה אֱלֹהֵיכֶם: כִּי כָל־הַנֶּפֶשׁ אֲשֶׁר לֹא־תְעֻנֶּה

אונקלוס

יח ותקרבון על לחמא, שבעא אמרין שלמין בני שנא, ותור בר תורי, חד ודכרין תרין, יהון עלתא קדם יי, ומנחתהון ונסכיהון, קרבן דמתקבל ברעוא קדם יי: יט ותעבדון, צפיר בר עזין חד לחטתא, ותרין אמרין, בני שנא לנכסת קדשיא: כ וירים כהנא יתהון, על לחמא דבכוריא ארמא קדם יי, על תרין אמרין, קדשא, יהון קדם יי לכהנא: כא ותערעון, בכרן יומא הדין, מערע קדיש יהי לכון, כל עבידת פלחן לא תעבדון, קים עלם, בכל מותבניכון לדריכון: כב ובמחצדכון ית חצדא דארעכון, לא תשיצי, פתא דחקלך בחצדך, ולקטא דחצדך לא תלקיט, לעניי ולגיורי

תשבוק יתהון, אנא יי אלהכון: כג ומליל יי עם משה למימר: כד מליל, עם בני ישראל למימר, בירחא שביעאה בחד לירחא, יהי לכון ניחא, דכרן יבבא מערע קדיש: כה כל עבידת פלחן לא תעבדון, ותקרבון קרבנא קדם יי: כו ומליל יי עם משה למימר: כז ברם, בעסרא לירחא שביעאה הדין יומא דכפוריא הוא, מערע קדיש יהי לכון, ותענון ית נפשתכון, ותקרבון קרבנא קדם יי: כח וכל עבידא לא תעבדון, בכרן יומא הדין, ארי יומא דכפוריא הוא, לכפרא עליכון, קדם יי אלהכון: כט ארי כל אנש דלא יתעני,

30 day shall be severed from his people, and if anyone performs any work during
31 this whole day, I will annihilate that person from among his people. No work at
all may you perform; this is an everlasting statute throughout your generations
32 in all your dwellings. It is a Sabbath of complete rest for you, and you shall
afflict yourselves from the evening of the ninth day of the month: from evening
to evening shall you observe your Sabbath."
33 34 The LORD spoke to Moshe: "Tell the Israelites: From the fifteenth day of this SHISHI
seventh month, for seven days shall be the Festival of Tabernacles to the LORD.
35 The first day shall be a sacred assembly; on it, you shall perform no laborious
36 work. For seven days you must bring close a fire offering to the LORD. The
eighth day shall be a sacred assembly for you, and you shall present a fire
offering to the LORD. It is an assembly; you shall perform no laborious work.
37 These are the LORD's festivals, which you shall proclaim, sacred assemblies to
present a fire offering to the LORD: burnt offering, grain offering, sacrifice, and
38 libations, each on its appointed day; in addition to the LORD's Sabbaths, and

רש"י

ל **והאבדתי.** לפי שהוא אומר כרת בכל מקום ואיני יודע מה הוא, כשהוא אומר: "והאבדתי", למד על הכרת שאינו אלא אבדן:

לא **כל מלאכה וגו'.** לעבור עליו בלאוין הרבה, או להזהיר על מלאכת לילה כמלאכת יום: "מקרא קדש" (לעיל פסוק כז) – קדשהו בכסות נקיה ובתפלה, וכל שאר ימים טובים – במאכל ובמשתה ובכסות נקיה ובתפלה:

לו **עצרת הוא.** עצרתי אתכם אצלי, כמלך שזמן את בניו לסעודה לכך וכך ימים, כיון שהגיע זמנן לפטר אמר: בני בבקשה מכם, עכבו עמי עוד יום אחד, קשה עלי פרישתכם: **כל מלאכת עבדה.** אפלו מלאכה שהיא עבודה לכם, שאם לא תעשוה יש חסרון כיס בדבר: **לא תעשו.** יכול אף חלו של מועד יהא אסור במלאכת עבודה? תלמוד לומר: "הוא":

לז **עלה ומנחה.** מנחת נסכים הקרבה עם העולה: **דבר יום ביומו.** חק הכתוב בחומש הפקודים (במדבר כח-כט): **דבר יום ביומו.** הא אם עבר יומו בטל קרבנו:

day's mitzvot. The four species and the rituals associated with them (v. 40) are about rain. They were, says Rambam (*Guide for the Perplexed* III:43), the most readily available products of the land of Israel, reminders of the fertility of the land. Symbolizing nature and the cycle of the seasons – things common to all humanity – the four species represent the universality of the festival. By contrast, the command to live for seven days in huts (v. 42) represents the singular character of Jewish history, with its repeated experiences of exile and homecoming and its long journey across the wilderness of time.

Sukkot celebrates the dual nature of Jewish faith: the *universality of God* and the *particularity of Jewish existence*. We all need rain. We are all part of nature. We are all dependent on the complex ecology of the created world. Hence the four species. But each nation, civilization, religion is different. Whatever God's relationship to other nations (and He *has* a relationship with other nations – so Amos and Yeshayahu insist), Jews know Him through His saving acts in Israel's history. And as Jews, we are heirs to a history unlike that of any other people: small, vulnerable, suffering exile after exile, yet surviving. Hence the sukka.

Humanity is formed out of our commonalities and differences. Our differences give us our identity. Our commonalities give us our humanity. Sukkot brings both together: our uniqueness as a people and our participation in the universal fate of humankind.

בְּעֶצֶם הַיּוֹם הַזֶּה וְנִכְרְתָה מֵעַמֶּיהָ: וְכָל־הַנֶּפֶשׁ אֲשֶׁר תַּעֲשֶׂה כָּל־ ל
מְלָאכָה בְּעֶצֶם הַיּוֹם הַזֶּה וְהַאֲבַדְתִּי אֶת־הַנֶּפֶשׁ הַהִוא מִקֶּרֶב עַמָּהּ:
כָּל־מְלָאכָה לֹא תַעֲשׂוּ חֻקַּת עוֹלָם לְדֹרֹתֵיכֶם בְּכֹל מֹשְׁבֹתֵיכֶם: שַׁבַּת לא לב
שַׁבָּתוֹן הוּא לָכֶם וְעִנִּיתֶם אֶת־נַפְשֹׁתֵיכֶם בְּתִשְׁעָה לַחֹדֶשׁ בָּעֶרֶב
מֵעֶרֶב עַד־עֶרֶב תִּשְׁבְּתוּ שַׁבַּתְּכֶם:
ששי וַיְדַבֵּר יְהוָה אֶל־מֹשֶׁה לֵּאמֹר: דַּבֵּר אֶל־בְּנֵי יִשְׂרָאֵל לֵאמֹר בַּחֲמִשָּׁה לג לד
עָשָׂר יוֹם לַחֹדֶשׁ הַשְּׁבִיעִי הַזֶּה חַג הַסֻּכּוֹת שִׁבְעַת יָמִים לַיהוָה:
בַּיּוֹם הָרִאשׁוֹן מִקְרָא־קֹדֶשׁ כָּל־מְלֶאכֶת עֲבֹדָה לֹא תַעֲשׂוּ: שִׁבְעַת לה לו
יָמִים תַּקְרִיבוּ אִשֶּׁה לַיהוָה בַּיּוֹם הַשְּׁמִינִי מִקְרָא־קֹדֶשׁ יִהְיֶה לָכֶם
וְהִקְרַבְתֶּם אִשֶּׁה לַיהוָה עֲצֶרֶת הִוא כָּל־מְלֶאכֶת עֲבֹדָה לֹא תַעֲשׂוּ:
אֵלֶּה מוֹעֲדֵי יְהוָה אֲשֶׁר־תִּקְרְאוּ אֹתָם מִקְרָאֵי קֹדֶשׁ לְהַקְרִיב אִשֶּׁה לז
לַיהוָה עֹלָה וּמִנְחָה זֶבַח וּנְסָכִים דְּבַר־יוֹם בְּיוֹמוֹ: מִלְּבַד שַׁבְּתֹת יְהוָה לח

אונקלוס

בִּכְרַן יוֹמָא הָדֵין, וְיִשְׁתֵּיצֵי מֵעַמֵּיהּ: ל וְכָל אֱנָשׁ, דְּיַעֲבֵיד כָּל עֲבִידָא, בִּכְרַן יוֹמָא הָדֵין, וְאוֹבֵיד, יָת אֱנָשָׁא הַהוּא מִגּוֹ עַמֵּיהּ: לא כָּל עֲבִידָא לָא תַעְבְּדוּן, קְיָם עָלַם לְדָרֵיכוֹן, בְּכֹל מוֹתְבָנֵיכוֹן: לב שְׁבָא שַׁבָּתָא הוּא לְכוֹן, וּתְעַנּוֹן יָת נַפְשָׁתְכוֹן, בְּתִשְׁעָא לְיַרְחָא בְּרַמְשָׁא, מֵרַמְשָׁא עַד רַמְשָׁא, תְּנוּחוּן נְיָחְכוֹן: לג וּמַלֵּיל יי עִם מֹשֶׁה לְמֵימַר: לד מַלֵּיל, עִם בְּנֵי יִשְׂרָאֵל לְמֵימַר, בַּחֲמֵישַׁת עַסְרָא יוֹמָא, לְיַרְחָא שְׁבִיעָאָה הָדֵין, חַגָּא דִּמְטַלַּיָּא, שִׁבְעָא יוֹמִין קֳדָם יי: לה בְּיוֹמָא קַדְמָאָה מְעָרַע קַדִּישׁ, כָּל עֲבִידַת פָּלְחַן לָא תַעְבְּדוּן: לו שִׁבְעָא יוֹמִין, תְּקָרְבוּן קֻרְבָּנָא קֳדָם יי, בְּיוֹמָא תְּמִינָאָה, מְעָרַע קַדִּישׁ יְהֵי לְכוֹן, וּתְקָרְבוּן קֻרְבָּנָא קֳדָם יי כְּנִישִׁין תְּהוֹן, כָּל עֲבִידַת פָּלְחַן לָא תַעְבְּדוּן: לז אִלֵּין מוֹעֲדַיָּא דַּיי, דִּתְעָרְעוּן יָתְהוֹן מְעָרְעֵי קַדִּישׁ, לְקָרָבָא קֻרְבָּנָא קֳדָם יי, עֲלָתָא וּמִנְחָתָא, נִכְסַת קֻדְשִׁין וְנִסּוּכִין פִּתְגָם יוֹם בְּיוֹמֵיהּ: לח בַּר מִשַּׁבַּיָּא דַּיי, וּבַר

23:34 **חַג הַסֻּכּוֹת** *Festival of Tabernacles* – Although all the festivals are listed together, they in fact represent two different cycles. The first is the cycle of Passover, Shavuot, and Sukkot. These tell the particularistic story of Jewish identity and history: the exodus (Passover), the revelation at Mount Sinai (Shavuot), and the journey through the wilderness (Sukkot). Celebrating them, we reenact the key moments of Jewish memory. We celebrate what it is to be a Jew.

There is, however, a second cycle: the festivals of the seventh month: Rosh HaShana, Yom Kippur, and Sukkot. Rosh HaShana and Yom Kippur are not only about Jews and Judaism. They are about God and humanity as a whole. The language of the prayers is different. We say: "Instill Your awe upon *all* Your works, and fear of You on *all* that You have created." The liturgy is strikingly universalistic. The Days of Awe are about the sovereignty of God over all humankind. On them, we reflect on the *human*, not just the Jewish, condition. On the festival of Sukkot the whole world is judged in the matter of rain (Mishna Rosh HaShana 1:2).

The two cycles to which Sukkot belongs are reflected in the

▶

in addition to your gifts and all your offerings in the fulfillment of vows and
39 all the freewill offerings that you give to the LORD. Hear: on the fifteenth day
of the seventh month, when you have harvested the land's produce, you shall
celebrate a festival to the LORD for seven days. The first day shall be a day of
40 rest; the eighth day shall be a day of rest. On the first day you shall take for
yourselves fruit of the majestic tree, branches of palm trees, boughs of the leafy
tree, and willows of the brook, and rejoice before the LORD your God for seven
41 days. You shall celebrate it as a festival to the LORD for seven days in the year.
It shall be an everlasting statute throughout your generations; celebrate this in
42 the seventh month. For seven days you shall live in huts. All those native born
43 in Israel must live in huts, so that future generations may know that I had the
Israelites live in huts when I brought them out of the land of Egypt; I am the
44 LORD your God." Thus Moshe announced the LORD's appointed times to the
Israelites.

רש״י

לט **אַךְ בַּחֲמִשָּׁה עָשָׂר יוֹם... תָּחֹגּוּ.** קָרְבַּן שְׁלָמִים לַחֲגִיגָה. יָכוֹל תִּדְחֶה אֶת הַשַּׁבָּת? תַּלְמוּד לוֹמַר ״אַךְ״, הוֹאִיל וְיֵשׁ לָהּ תַּשְׁלוּמִין כָּל שִׁבְעָה: **בְּאָסְפְּכֶם אֶת תְּבוּאַת הָאָרֶץ.** שֶׁיְּהֵא חֹדֶשׁ שְׁבִיעִי זֶה בָּא בִּזְמַן אֲסִיפָה, מִכָּאן שֶׁנִּצְטַוּוּ לְעַבֵּר אֶת הַשָּׁנִים, שֶׁאִם אֵין הָעִבּוּר, פְּעָמִים שֶׁהוּא בְּאֶמְצַע הַקַּיִץ אוֹ הַחֹרֶף: **תָּחֹגּוּ.** שַׁלְמֵי חֲגִיגָה: **שִׁבְעַת יָמִים.** אִם לֹא הֵבִיא בָּזֶה יָבִיא בָּזֶה. יָכוֹל יְהֵא מֵבִיא כָּל שִׁבְעָה? תַּלְמוּד לוֹמַר: ״וְחַגֹּתֶם אֹתוֹ״, יוֹם אֶחָד בְּמַשְׁמָע וְלֹא יוֹתֵר. וְלָמָּה נֶאֱמַר שִׁבְעָה? לְתַשְׁלוּמִין:

מ **פְּרִי עֵץ הָדָר.** עֵץ שֶׁטַּעַם עֵצוֹ וּפִרְיוֹ שָׁוֶה: **הָדָר.** הַדָּר בְּאִילָנוֹ מִשָּׁנָה לְשָׁנָה, וְזֶהוּ אֶתְרוֹג: **כַּפֹּת תְּמָרִים.** חָסֵר וָי״ו, לִמֵּד שֶׁאֵינָהּ אֶלָּא אַחַת: **וַעֲנַף עֵץ עָבֹת.** שֶׁעֲנָפָיו קְלוּעִים כַּעֲבוֹתוֹת וְכַחֲבָלִים, וְזֶהוּ הֲדַס הֶעָשׂוּי כְּמִין קְלִיעָה:

מב **הָאֶזְרָח.** זֶה אֶזְרָח: **בְּיִשְׂרָאֵל.** לְרַבּוֹת אֶת הַגֵּרִים:

מג **כִּי בַסֻּכּוֹת הוֹשַׁבְתִּי.** עַנְנֵי כָבוֹד:

and Shavuot represent God's love for the Jewish people, Sukkot represents the Jewish people's love for God. We find this idea in the words of Yirmeyahu that we say on Rosh HaShana. In the Torah, the story of the years in the wilderness is told in terms of the people's rebelliousness and obstinacy. Yirmeyahu, however, describes it quite differently: "I recall on your behalf the devotion of your youth, your bridal love – when you followed Me into the wilderness, a land unseeded" (Jer. 2:2).

It is easy to worship God when you have safety and security. But Israel came of age as a nation long before it knew such things. It was born in the desert, vulnerable, exposed, yet willing to follow the call of God. That was the miracle – faith in the midst of uncertainty. What R. Akiva was saying was: look at the sukka and you will see where our people was born. The sukka was the matrix of Jewish courage, the birthplace of a people obstinate in their loyalty to God.

23:44 מֹעֲדֵי יהוה אֶל־בְּנֵי יִשְׂרָאֵל *The LORD's appointed times to the Israelites* – Chapter 23 of Parashat Emor sets out a weekly, monthly, and yearly schedule of sacred times. This is continued and extended in Parashat Behar to seven- and fifty-year schedules. The Torah forces us to remember what contemporary culture regularly forgets: our lives must have dedicated times when we focus on the things that give life meaning. And because we are social animals, the most important times are the ones we share. The Jewish calendar is precisely that: a structure of shared time.

We all need an identity, and every identity comes with a story. So we need a time when we remind ourselves of the story of where we came from and why we are who we are. That

וּמִלְּבַד מַתְּנוֹתֵיכֶם וּמִלְּבַד כָּל־נִדְרֵיכֶם וּמִלְּבַד כָּל־נִדְבֹתֵיכֶם אֲשֶׁר
לט תִּתְּנוּ לַיהוָה: אַךְ בַּחֲמִשָּׁה עָשָׂר יוֹם לַחֹדֶשׁ הַשְּׁבִיעִי בְּאָסְפְּכֶם
אֶת־תְּבוּאַת הָאָרֶץ תָּחֹגּוּ אֶת־חַג־יְהוָה שִׁבְעַת יָמִים בַּיּוֹם הָרִאשׁוֹן
מ שַׁבָּתוֹן וּבַיּוֹם הַשְּׁמִינִי שַׁבָּתוֹן: וּלְקַחְתֶּם לָכֶם בַּיּוֹם הָרִאשׁוֹן פְּרִי
עֵץ הָדָר כַּפֹּת תְּמָרִים וַעֲנַף עֵץ־עָבֹת וְעַרְבֵי־נָחַל וּשְׂמַחְתֶּם לִפְנֵי
מא יְהוָה אֱלֹהֵיכֶם שִׁבְעַת יָמִים: וְחַגֹּתֶם אֹתוֹ חַג לַיהוָה שִׁבְעַת יָמִים
מב בַּשָּׁנָה חֻקַּת עוֹלָם לְדֹרֹתֵיכֶם בַּחֹדֶשׁ הַשְּׁבִיעִי תָּחֹגּוּ אֹתוֹ: בַּסֻּכֹּת
מג תֵּשְׁבוּ שִׁבְעַת יָמִים כָּל־הָאֶזְרָח בְּיִשְׂרָאֵל יֵשְׁבוּ בַּסֻּכֹּת: לְמַעַן יֵדְעוּ
דֹרֹתֵיכֶם כִּי בַסֻּכּוֹת הוֹשַׁבְתִּי אֶת־בְּנֵי יִשְׂרָאֵל בְּהוֹצִיאִי אוֹתָם מֵאֶרֶץ
מד מִצְרָיִם אֲנִי יְהוָה אֱלֹהֵיכֶם: וַיְדַבֵּר מֹשֶׁה אֶת־מֹעֲדֵי יְהוָה אֶל־בְּנֵי
יִשְׂרָאֵל:

אונקלוס

מִמַּתְּנָתְכוֹן, וּבָר מִכָּל נִדְרֵיכוֹן וּבָר מִכָּל נִדְבָתְכוֹן, דְּתִתְּנוּן קֳדָם יי: לט בְּרַם, בַּחֲמֵישְׁתְּ עַסְרָא יוֹמָא לְיַרְחָא שְׁבִיעָאָה, בְּמִכְנַשְׁכוֹן יָת עֲלַלְתָּא דְאַרְעָא, תֵּיחֲגוּן יָת חַגָּא קֳדָם יי שִׁבְעָא יוֹמִין, בְּיוֹמָא קַדְמָאָה נְיָחָא, וּבְיוֹמָא תְּמִינָאָה נְיָחָא: מ וְתִסְּבוּן לְכוֹן בְּיוֹמָא קַדְמָאָה, פֵּירֵי אִילָנָא אֶתְרוֹגִין לוּלָבִין, וַהֲדַסִּין וְעַרְבִין דִּנְחַל, וְתִחְדּוֹן, קֳדָם יי אֱלָהֲכוֹן שִׁבְעָא יוֹמִין: מא וְתֵיחֲגוּן יָתֵיהּ חַגָּא קֳדָם יי, שִׁבְעָא יוֹמִין בְּשַׁתָּא, קְיָם עָלַם לְדָרֵיכוֹן, בְּיַרְחָא שְׁבִיעָאָה תֵּיחֲגוּן יָתֵיהּ: מב בִּמְטַלַּיָּא תִּתְּבוּן שִׁבְעָא יוֹמִין, כָּל יַצִּיבַיָּא בְּיִשְׂרָאֵל, יִתְּבוּן בִּמְטַלַּיָּא: מג בְּדִיל דִּידְעוּן דָּרֵיכוֹן, אֲרֵי בִּמְטַלַּת עֲנָנֵי, אוֹתֵיבִית יָת בְּנֵי יִשְׂרָאֵל, בְּאַפָּקוּתִי יָתְהוֹן מֵאַרְעָא דְמִצְרָיִם, אֲנָא יי אֱלָהֲכוֹן: מד וּמַלֵּיל מֹשֶׁה, יָת סֵדֶר מוֹעֲדַיָּא דַיי, וְאַלֵּיפִנּוּן לִבְנֵי יִשְׂרָאֵל: כד א וּמַלֵּיל יי עִם מֹשֶׁה לְמֵימַר: ב פַּקֵּיד יָת בְּנֵי יִשְׂרָאֵל, וְיִסְּבוּן לָךְ, מְשַׁח זֵיתָא דָּכְיָא,

23:43 בְּהוֹצִיאִי אוֹתָם מֵאֶרֶץ מִצְרָיִם *I brought them out of the land of Egypt* – We observe Sukkot, says the Torah, "so that your descendants will know that I made the Israelites live in booths when I brought them out of Egypt." What, though, is special or miraculous about this fact? On this, the Talmud records two views (Sukka 11b). According to R. Eliezer, *sukkot* represent the clouds of glory that accompanied the Israelites on their journey. According to R. Akiva, however, *sukkot* represent exactly what they are: temporary dwellings, shacks with a canopy of leaves for a roof.

Regarding R. Eliezer's view, the miracle is self-evident. For forty years, God's sheltering presence protected the Israelites from heat by day, cold by night, and the wild animals and enemies they encountered on the way.

Regarding R. Akiva's view, though, the sukka seems to represent no miracle whatsoever. That the Israelites lived in temporary dwellings for forty years was only to be expected. That is how nomads live.

Perhaps, however, R. Eliezer and R. Akiva differed less on whether there was a miracle than on to whom it belonged. According to R. Eliezer, the miracle was God's. It was He who protected the people on their long walk to freedom. According to R. Akiva, the miracle was that of the Jewish people. Though the journey to the Promised Land took forty years, and the Israelites faced setbacks, they did not give up or lose faith. According to R. Akiva, while Passover

24 1 2 The LORD spoke to Moshe: "Command the Israelites to bring you pure oil SHEVI'I
3 from crushed olives for the light, to kindle the lamp, every night. From evening
to morning, before the LORD, Aharon shall set it up outside the curtain of the
testimony in the Tent of Meeting to burn each night. This shall be a rule for all
4 time, throughout your generations. Aharon shall set out the lamps on the pure
candelabrum each day before the LORD.
5 And you shall take fine flour and bake twelve loaves, two-tenths of an ephah for
6 each loaf. You shall place them in two columns, six to each column, on the pure
7 table before the LORD. Lay pure incense on each stack, as a remembrance for
8 the bread, as a fire offering to the LORD. Every Sabbath he shall set it out, always,
9 before the LORD on behalf of the Israelites: an everlasting covenant. It shall
belong to Aharon and his sons. They shall eat it in a holy place because it is holy
10 of holies among the LORD's fire offerings, their perpetual share." A man
went out among the Israelites, the son of an Israelite woman and an Egyptian
man. And a fight broke out in the camp between this son of an Israelite woman,

רש"י

כד ב) **צו את בני ישראל.** זו פרשת מצות הנרות. ופרשת 'ואתה תצוה' (שמות כז, כ) לא נאמרה אלא על סדר מלאכת המשכן לפרש צרך המנורה, וכן משמע: ואתה סופך לצוות את בני ישראל על כך: **שמן זית זך.** שלשה שמנים יוצאים מן הזית, הראשון קרוי זך, והן מפרשין במנחות (דף פו ע"א) ובתורת כהנים (פרשתא יג, א): **תמיד.** מלילה ללילה, כמו: "עלת תמיד" (במדבר כח, ו) שאינה אלא מיום ליום:

ג) **לפרכת העדת.** שלפני הארון שהוא קרוי עדות. ורבותינו דרשו על נר מערבי, שהוא עדות לכל באי עולם שהשכינה שורה בישראל, שנותן בה שמן כמדת חברותיה, וממנה היה מתחיל ובה היה מסיים: **יערך אתו אהרן מערב עד בקר.** יערך אותו עריכה הראויה למדת כל הלילה, ושערו חכמים חצי לג לכל נר ונר, והן כדאי אף ללילי תקופת טבת, ומדה זו הקבעה להם:

ד) **המנרה הטהרה.** שהיא זהב טהור. דבר אחר, על טהרה של מנורה, שמטהרה ומדשנה תחלה מן האפר:

ו) **שש המערכת.** שש חלות המערכת האחת: **השלחן הטהר.** של זהב טהור. דבר אחר, על טהרו של שלחן, שלא יהיו הסניפין מגביהין את הלחם מעל גבי השלחן:

ז) **ונתת על המערכת.** על כל אחת משתי המערכות; הרי שני בזיכי לבונה, מלא קמץ לכל אחת: **והיתה.** הלבונה הזאת: **ללחם לאזכרה.** שאין מן הלחם לגבוה כלום, אלא הלבונה נקטרת כשמסלקין אותו בכל שבת ושבת, והיא לזכרון ללחם, שעל ידה הוא נזכר למעלה, כקמץ שהוא אזכרה למנחה:

ט) **והיתה.** המנחה הזאת, שכל דבר הבא מן התבואה בכלל מנחה הוא: **ואכלהו.** מוסב על הלחם שהוא לשון זכר:

י) **ויצא בן אשה ישראלית.** מהיכן יצא? רבי לוי אומר: מעולמו יצא. רבי ברכיה אומר: מפרשה שלמעלה יצא, לגלג ואמר: "ביום השבת יערכנו" (לעיל פסוק ח), דרך המלך לאכול פת חמה בכל יום, שמא פת צוננת של תשעה ימים? בתמיה. ומתניתא אמרה: מבית דינו של משה יצא מחיב. בא לטע אהלו בתוך מחנה דן, אמרו לו, מה טיבך לכאן? אמר להם: מבני דן אני. אמרו לו: "איש על דגלו באתת לבית אבתם" כתיב (במדבר ב, ב), נכנס לבית דינו של משה ויצא מחיב, עמד וגדף: **בן איש מצרי.** הוא המצרי שהרג משה: **בתוך בני ישראל.** מלמד שנתגיר: **וינצו במחנה.** על עסקי המחנה: **ואיש הישראלי.** זה שכנגדו, שמחה בו מטע אהלו:

Doubtless, most people know that these things are important. But knowing is not enough. These are elements of life that become real not just when we know them, but when we live them.

And we need, from time to time, to step back from the ceaseless pressures of work and find the rest in which we can celebrate our blessings, renew our relationships, and recover the full vigor of body and mind. That is the Sabbath.

כד א ב וַיְדַבֵּר יְהוָה אֶל־מֹשֶׁה לֵּאמֹר: צַו אֶת־בְּנֵי יִשְׂרָאֵל וְיִקְחוּ אֵלֶיךָ שֶׁמֶן שביעי
ג זַיִת זָךְ כָּתִית לַמָּאוֹר לְהַעֲלֹת נֵר תָּמִיד: מִחוּץ לְפָרֹכֶת הָעֵדֻת בְּאֹהֶל
מוֹעֵד יַעֲרֹךְ אֹתוֹ אַהֲרֹן מֵעֶרֶב עַד־בֹּקֶר לִפְנֵי יְהוָה תָּמִיד חֻקַּת
ד עוֹלָם לְדֹרֹתֵיכֶם: עַל הַמְּנֹרָה הַטְּהֹרָה יַעֲרֹךְ אֶת־הַנֵּרוֹת לִפְנֵי יְהוָה
תָּמִיד:
ה וְלָקַחְתָּ סֹלֶת וְאָפִיתָ אֹתָהּ שְׁתֵּים עֶשְׂרֵה חַלּוֹת שְׁנֵי עֶשְׂרֹנִים יִהְיֶה
ו הַחַלָּה הָאֶחָת: וְשַׂמְתָּ אוֹתָם שְׁתַּיִם מַעֲרָכוֹת שֵׁשׁ הַמַּעֲרָכֶת עַל
ז הַשֻּׁלְחָן הַטָּהֹר לִפְנֵי יְהוָה: וְנָתַתָּ עַל־הַמַּעֲרֶכֶת לְבֹנָה זַכָּה וְהָיְתָה
ח לַלֶּחֶם לְאַזְכָּרָה אִשֶּׁה לַיהוָה: בְּיוֹם הַשַּׁבָּת בְּיוֹם הַשַּׁבָּת יַעַרְכֶנּוּ
ט לִפְנֵי יְהוָה תָּמִיד מֵאֵת בְּנֵי־יִשְׂרָאֵל בְּרִית עוֹלָם: וְהָיְתָה לְאַהֲרֹן
וּלְבָנָיו וַאֲכָלֻהוּ בְּמָקוֹם קָדֹשׁ כִּי קֹדֶשׁ קָדָשִׁים הוּא לוֹ מֵאִשֵּׁי יְהוָה
י חָק־עוֹלָם: וַיֵּצֵא בֶּן־אִשָּׁה יִשְׂרְאֵלִית וְהוּא בֶּן־אִישׁ מִצְרִי
בְּתוֹךְ בְּנֵי יִשְׂרָאֵל וַיִּנָּצוּ בַּמַּחֲנֶה בֶּן הַיִּשְׂרְאֵלִית וְאִישׁ הַיִּשְׂרְאֵלִי:

אונקלוס

כְּתִישָׁא לְאַנְהָרָא, לְאַדְלָקָא בּוֹצִינַיָּא תְּדִירָא: ג מִבָּרָא לְפָרֻכְתָּא
דְּסָהֲדוּתָא בְּמַשְׁכַּן זִמְנָא, יְסַדַּר יָתֵיהּ אַהֲרֹן, מֵרַמְשָׁא עַד צַפְרָא,
קֳדָם יי תְּדִירָא, קְיָם עָלַם לְדָרֵיכוֹן: ד עַל מְנָרְתָּא דָּכִיתָא, יְסַדַּר יָת
בּוֹצִינַיָּא, קֳדָם יי תְּדִירָא: ה וְתִסַּב סֻלְתָּא, וְתֵיפֵי יָתַהּ, תַּרְתַּא עֶסְרֵי
גְּרִיצָן, תְּרֵין עֶסְרוֹנִין, תְּהֵי הָוְיָא גְּרִיצְתָּא חֲדָא: ו וּתְשַׁוֵּי יָתְהוֹן,
תַּרְתֵּין סִדְרִין שֵׁית סִדְרָא, עַל, פָּתוּרָא דָּכְיָא קֳדָם יי: ז וְתִתֵּין עַל
סִדְרָא לְבוֹנְתָא דָּכִיתָא, וּתְהֵי לִלְחֵים לְאַדְכָּרָא, קֻרְבָּנָא קֳדָם יי:
ח בְּיוֹמָא דְשַׁבְּתָא בְּיוֹמָא דְשַׁבְּתָא, יְסַדְּרִנֵּיהּ, קֳדָם יי תְּדִירָא, מִן
בְּנֵי יִשְׂרָאֵל קְיָם עָלַם: ט וּתְהֵי לְאַהֲרֹן וְלִבְנוֹהִי, וְיֵיכְלֻנֵּיהּ בַּאֲתַר
קַדִּישׁ, אֲרֵי, קֹדֶשׁ קֻדְשִׁין הוּא לֵיהּ, מִקֻּרְבָּנַיָּא דַּיי קְיָם עָלַם: י וּנְפַק
בַּר אִתְּתָא בַּת יִשְׂרָאֵל, וְהוּא בַּר גְּבַר מִצְרַאי, בְּגוֹ בְּנֵי יִשְׂרָאֵל,
וְאִתְנְצִיאוּ בְּמַשְׁרִיתָא, בַּר אִתְּתָא בַּת יִשְׂרָאֵל, וְגַבְרָא בַּר יִשְׂרָאֵל:

happens on Passover, when we reenact the founding moment of our people as they began their long walk to freedom.

We need a moral code, an internalized satellite navigation system to guide us through the wilderness of time. That is what we celebrate on Shavuot when we relive the moment when our ancestors stood at Sinai, made their covenant with God, and heard Heaven declare the Ten Commandments.

We need a regular reminder of the brevity of life itself, and hence the need to use time wisely. That is what we do on Rosh HaShana as we stand before God in judgment and pray to be written in the book of life.

We need a time when we confront our faults, apologize for the wrong we have done, make amends, resolve to change, and ask for forgiveness. That is the work of Yom Kippur.

We need to remind ourselves that we are on a journey, that we are "migrants and visitors" (Lev. 25:24) on earth, and that where we live is only a temporary dwelling. That is what we experience on Sukkot.

11 and an Israelite man. The Israelite woman's son blasphemed the Name and
cursed – his mother's name was Shlomit, daughter of Divri, of the tribe of Dan –
12 and they brought him before Moshe. They placed the man in custody until the
Lord's verdict would be pronounced to them.
13 14 And the Lord spoke to Moshe: "Take the one who cursed outside the camp.
All the people who heard him shall lay their hands on his head – and then the
15 whole community shall stone him. Tell the Israelites: Anyone who curses his
16 God shall bear the sin, and anyone who blasphemes the Lord's name shall be
put to death: the whole community shall stone him. Migrant and native born
17 alike: one who blasphemes the Lord's name shall be put to death. One who
18 takes the life of any human being shall be put to death. One who takes the

רש״י

יא **וַיִּקֹּב.** כְּתַרְגּוּמוֹ: ״וּפָרֵשׁ״, שֶׁנָּקַב שֵׁם הַמְיֻחָד וְגִדֵּף, וְהוּא שֵׁם הַמְפֹרָשׁ שֶׁשָּׁמַע מִסִּינַי: **וְשֵׁם אִמּוֹ שְׁלֹמִית בַּת דִּבְרִי.** שִׁבְחָן שֶׁל יִשְׂרָאֵל שֶׁפִּרְסְמָהּ הַכָּתוּב לָזוֹ, לוֹמַר שֶׁהִיא לְבַדָּהּ הָיְתָה זוֹנָה: **שְׁלֹמִית.** דַּהֲוַת פַּטְפְּטָה, שְׁלָם עֲלָךְ, שְׁלָם עֲלַךְ, שְׁלָם עֲלֵיכוֹן, מְפַטְפֶּטֶת בִּדְבָרִים, שׁוֹאֶלֶת בִּשְׁלוֹם הַכֹּל: **בַּת דִּבְרִי.** דַּבְּרָנִית הָיְתָה, מְדַבֶּרֶת עִם כָּל אָדָם, לְפִיכָךְ קִלְקְלָה: **לְמַטֵּה דָן.** מַגִּיד שֶׁהָרָשָׁע גּוֹרֵם גְּנַאי לוֹ, גְּנַאי לְאָבִיו, גְּנַאי לְשִׁבְטוֹ. כַּיּוֹצֵא בוֹ: ״אָהֳלִיאָב בֶּן אֲחִיסָמָךְ לְמַטֵּה דָן״ (שמות לח, כג), שֶׁבַח לוֹ, שֶׁבַח לְאָבִיו, שֶׁבַח לְשִׁבְטוֹ:

יב **וַיַּנִּיחֻהוּ.** לְבַדּוֹ, וְלֹא הִנִּיחוּ מְקוֹשֵׁשׁ עִמּוֹ, שֶׁשְּׁנֵיהֶם הָיוּ בְּפֶרֶק אֶחָד; וְיוֹדְעִים הָיוּ שֶׁהַמְקוֹשֵׁשׁ בְּמִיתָה, אֲבָל לֹא פֹרַשׁ לָהֶם בְּאֵיזוֹ מִיתָה, לְכָךְ נֶאֱמַר: ״כִּי לֹא פֹרַשׁ מַה יֵּעָשֶׂה לוֹ״ (במדבר טו, לד), אֲבָל בַּמְקַלֵּל הוּא אוֹמֵר ״לִפְרֹשׁ לָהֶם״, שֶׁלֹּא הָיוּ יוֹדְעִים אִם חַיָּב מִיתָה אִם לָאו:

יד **הַשֹּׁמְעִים.** אֵלּוּ הָעֵדִים: **כָּל.** לְהָבִיא אֶת הַדַּיָּנִים: **אֶת יְדֵיהֶם.** אוֹמְרִים לוֹ, דָּמְךָ בְּרֹאשְׁךָ, וְאֵין אָנוּ נֶעֱנָשִׁים בְּמִיתָתְךָ שֶׁאַתָּה גָּרַמְתָּ לָךְ: **כָּל הָעֵדָה.** בְּמַעֲמַד כָּל הָעֵדָה, מִכָּאן שֶׁשְּׁלוּחוֹ שֶׁל אָדָם כְּמוֹתוֹ:

טו **וְנָשָׂא חֶטְאוֹ.** בְּכָרֵת, כְּשֶׁאֵין הַתְרָאָה:

טז **וְנֹקֵב שֵׁם.** אֵינוֹ חַיָּב עַד שֶׁיְּפָרֵשׁ אֶת הַשֵּׁם, וְלֹא הַמְקַלֵּל בְּכִנּוּי: **וְנֹקֵב.** לְשׁוֹן קְלָלָה, כְּמוֹ: ״מָה אֶקֹּב״ (במדבר כג, ח):

יז **וְאִישׁ כִּי יַכֶּה.** לְפִי שֶׁנֶּאֱמַר: ״מַכֵּה אִישׁ״ וְגוֹ׳ (שמות כא, יב), אֵין לִי אֶלָּא שֶׁהָרַג אֶת הָאִישׁ, אִשָּׁה וְקָטָן מִנַּיִן? תַּלְמוּד לוֹמַר: ״כָּל נֶפֶשׁ אָדָם״:

become creatures of impulse and desire, and the end of this long road is violence. It is an unpopular truth. The serpent is always waiting in the wings, saying to us as he said to Ḥava: "What harm is there in eating one forbidden fruit?" A world God created and pronounced good can all too easily be destroyed if we forget the concept of boundaries and the habits of self-restraint.

The fundamental issue addressed by the Torah is violence and the misuse of power. There is more than one way of thinking about violence. There is the way of wisdom: Judaism's insights into philosophy and the social sciences. *There is the way of prophecy, focusing on emotion and the* moral sense. And there is the way of priesthood, whose central insight is the connection between sacred order and social order. When human beings lose respect for God, they eventually lose respect for humanity.

The message of Leviticus throughout is that life itself is holy: people, not just priests; the whole of life, not just edited parts of it. So we have to be holy in the way we eat, the way we conduct our most intimate sexual relationships, and the way we use language. We must not curse even the deaf, let alone our parents, let alone God, because verbal abuse leads to physical abuse. Blasphemy injures society by desecrating the sacred. That is why, uniquely in this case, the witnesses are to lay their hands on the sinner, to indicate that this affects everyone. It is a sobering narrative, the negative side of the broader picture of the book: the priestly sanctification of life.

יא וַיִּקֹּב בֶּן־הָֽאִשָּׁה הַיִּשְׂרְאֵלִית אֶת־הַשֵּׁם וַיְקַלֵּל וַיָּבִיאוּ אֹתוֹ אֶל־מֹשֶׁה
יב וְשֵׁם אִמּוֹ שְׁלֹמִית בַּת־דִּבְרִי לְמַטֵּה־דָֽן׃ וַיַּנִּיחֻהוּ בַּמִּשְׁמָר לִפְרֹשׁ
לָהֶם עַל־פִּי יהוה׃
יג יד וַיְדַבֵּר יהוה אֶל־מֹשֶׁה לֵּאמֹֽר׃ הוֹצֵא אֶת־הַֽמְקַלֵּל אֶל־מִחוּץ לַֽמַּחֲנֶה
וְסָמְכוּ כָל־הַשֹּׁמְעִים אֶת־יְדֵיהֶם עַל־רֹאשׁוֹ וְרָגְמוּ אֹתוֹ כָּל־הָעֵדָֽה׃
טו וְאֶל־בְּנֵי יִשְׂרָאֵל תְּדַבֵּר לֵאמֹר אִישׁ אִישׁ כִּֽי־יְקַלֵּל אֱלֹהָיו וְנָשָׂא חֶטְאֽוֹ׃
טז וְנֹקֵב שֵׁם־יהוה מוֹת יוּמָת רָגוֹם יִרְגְּמוּ־בוֹ כָּל־הָעֵדָה כַּגֵּר כָּֽאֶזְרָח
יז יח בְּנָקְבוֹ־שֵׁם יוּמָֽת׃ וְאִישׁ כִּי יַכֶּה כָּל־נֶפֶשׁ אָדָם מוֹת יוּמָֽת׃ וּמַכֵּה

אונקלוס

יא וּפָרֵישׁ, בַּר אִתְּתָא בַת יִשְׂרָאֵל יָת שְׁמָא וְאַרְגֵּיז, וְאַיְתִיאוּ יָתֵיהּ
לְוָת מֹשֶׁה, וְשׁוּם אִמֵּיהּ, שְׁלוֹמִית בַּת דִּבְרִי לְשִׁבְטָא דְדָן: יב וְאַסְרוּהִי
בְּבֵית מַטְּרָא, עַד דְּיִתְפָּרַשׁ לְהוֹן עַל גְּזֵירַת מֵימְרָא דַיָי: יג וּמַלֵּיל יי
עִם מֹשֶׁה לְמֵימַר: יד אַפֵּיק יָת דְּאַרְגֵּיז, לְמִבָּרָא לְמַשְׁרִיתָא, וְיִסְמְכוּן
כָּל דִּשְׁמַעוּ, יָת יְדֵיהוֹן עַל רֵישֵׁיהּ, וְיִרְגְּמוּן יָתֵיהּ כָּל כְּנִשְׁתָּא: טו וְעִם
בְּנֵי יִשְׂרָאֵל תְּמַלֵּיל לְמֵימַר, גְּבַר גְּבַר, אֲרֵי יַרְגֵּיז קֳדָם אֱלָהֵיהּ וִיקַבֵּיל
חוֹבֵיהּ: טז וּדְיִפָרֵישׁ שְׁמָא דַיָי אִתְקְטָלָא יִתְקְטִיל, מִרְגָּם יִרְגְּמוּן בֵּיהּ
כָּל כְּנִשְׁתָּא, גִּיּוֹרָא כְּיַצִּיבָא, בְּפָרָשׁוּתֵיהּ שְׁמָא יִתְקְטִיל: יז וּגְבַר,
אֲרֵי יִקְטוֹל כָּל נַפְשָׁא דֶאֱנָשָׁא, אִתְקְטָלָא יִתְקְטִיל: יח וּדְיִקְטוֹל

THE EXECUTION OF THE BLASPHEMER

Leviticus, a book of law rather than narrative, is suddenly interrupted by a tragic and disturbing story: Two men start fighting. The details of their quarrel appear to be irrelevant. One of the men, however, in the course of the struggle, curses God, or possibly, uses the sacred Name to curse his opponent. Everyone present knows that something serious has happened. Taking God's name in vain is forbidden (Ex. 20:6). Just a few chapters earlier, we read that cursing your parents is a capital sin (Ex. 21:17; Lev. 20:9). Cursing God must surely be more serious still.

What the people are unsure of is whether the law applies to someone of mixed parentage. Hence God's answer: "Migrant and native born alike" (Lev. 24:16). In the course of the revelation, the people learn something else: "All the people who heard him shall lay their hands on his head" (24:14) prior to carrying out the punishment. In no other case of the death sentence, Rambam notes, do the witnesses lay their hands on the condemned man.

This stark episode represents the end of the long sequence of laws which began forty chapters earlier (in Ex. 25:1 – see Lev. 23, "The Jewish Calendar" and Ex. 32, "The Golden Calf"), about the Sanctuary and the code of holiness. Why end this literary unit, which stands at the very center of the Torah, with so negative a note?

The end of the book of Exodus gives us a clue. As we have noted (Ex. 40, "Exodus: The Narrative Structure"), Exodus ends the way Genesis begins: with an act of creation. In Genesis it was God's creation of the universe. In Exodus it was the Israelites' creation of the Sanctuary. The connection is deliberate. In the beginning, God created order. Then He gave humans free will and they proceeded to create chaos. Only with the completion of the Sanctuary do we find humans creating order, symbolized in the holy place they have made for God. We can summarize *Torat Kohanim* in a single sentence: *sacred order leads to social order*. The two are inextricably intertwined. When people lose their fear of God, eventually they lose their other inhibitions. They

19 life of an animal shall make restitution for it: life for life. One who injures his
20 fellow man shall be penalized in proportion to the injury inflicted: the cost of a
broken bone for a broken bone, of an eye for an eye, of a tooth for a tooth. Just
21 as he inflicted injury on another human being, so shall he suffer the loss. One MAFTIR
who kills an animal shall make restitution for it; but one who kills a human
22 being shall be put to death. There shall be one law for you, for migrant and
23 for native born alike, for I am the Lord your God." Moshe told this to the
Israelites, and so they took the blasphemer outside the camp and stoned him.
Thus the Israelites did as the Lord had commanded Moshe.

The haftara for Parashat Emor is on page 1576.

רש״י

כ׳ **כֵּן יִנָּתֶן בּוֹ.** פֵּרְשׁוּ רַבּוֹתֵינוּ שֶׁאֵינוֹ נְתִינַת מוּם מַמָּשׁ, אֶלָּא תַּשְׁלוּמֵי מָמוֹן – שָׁמִין אוֹתוֹ כְּעֶבֶד, לְכָךְ כָּתוּב בּוֹ לְשׁוֹן נְתִינָה, דָּבָר הַנִּתָּן מִיָּד לְיָד:

כא׳ **וּמַכֵּה בְהֵמָה יְשַׁלְּמֶנָּה.** לְמַעְלָה דִּבֵּר בְּהוֹרֵג בְּהֵמָה, וְכָאן דִּבֵּר בְּעוֹשֶׂה בָהּ חַבּוּרָה: **וּמַכֵּה אָדָם יוּמָת.** אֲפִלּוּ לֹא הֲרָגוֹ אֶלָּא עָשָׂה בוֹ חַבּוּרָה, שֶׁלֹּא נֶאֱמַר כָּאן 'נֶפֶשׁ'. וּבְמַכֵּה אָבִיו וְאִמּוֹ דִּבֵּר הַכָּתוּב, וּבָא לְהַקִּישׁוֹ לְמַכֵּה בְהֵמָה, מַה מַּכֵּה בְהֵמָה מֵחַיִּים, אַף מַכֵּה אָבִיו מֵחַיִּים, פְּרָט לְמַכֶּה לְאַחַר מִיתָה, לְפִי שֶׁמָּצִינוּ שֶׁהַמְקַלְּלוֹ לְאַחַר מִיתָה חַיָּב, הֻצְרַךְ לוֹמַר בְּמַכֶּה שֶׁפָּטוּר. וּמָה בִּבְהֵמָה בְּחַבָּלָה, שֶׁאִם אֵין חַבָּלָה אֵין תַּשְׁלוּמִין, אַף מַכֵּה אָבִיו אֵינוֹ חַיָּב עַד שֶׁיַּעֲשֶׂה בוֹ חַבּוּרָה:

כב׳ **אֲנִי ה׳ אֱלֹהֵיכֶם.** אֱלֹהֵי כֻּלְּכֶם, כְּשֵׁם שֶׁאֲנִי מְיַחֵד שְׁמִי עֲלֵיכֶם, כָּךְ אֲנִי מְיַחֲדוֹ עַל הַגֵּרִים:

כג׳ **וּבְנֵי יִשְׂרָאֵל עָשׂוּ.** כָּל הַמִּצְוָה הָאֲמוּרָה בִּסְקִילָה בְּמָקוֹם אַחֵר: דְּחִיָּה, רְגִימָה וּתְלִיָּה:

Avihu, on the day the Sanctuary was consecrated. The story itself seems out of place.

Something is being conveyed here beyond the detailed points of law. The implication seems to be that what begins as an offense in one area, a crossing of boundaries, never ends there. An offense against God eventually leads to assaults against humans. Spiritual sins lead to physical crimes. Leviticus has been about the sanctity of time, person, and place. The Torah now turns to sanctity of speech. The priests have already been warned: "Do not profane My holy name, that I may be sanctified in the midst of the Israelites. I am the Lord who makes you holy" (Lev. 22:32). The story of the blasphemer tells us that the same applies to ordinary Israelites, "migrant and native born alike."

Judaism has been skeptical of the value of capital punishment certainly since the days of the Mishna, eighteen centuries ago, and has rarely practiced it since. But the drama of this incident, paired with the earlier drama of Nadav and Avihu, underscores the point. Once boundaries are disrespected, a process has begun that leads, not immediately but ultimately, to civilizational breakdown.

Sacred and secular, spiritual and physical, offenses against God and crimes against human beings are indissolubly connected. Sacred order and social order go together. Lose one – either one – and you will eventually lose the other. A sense of the sacred is what lifts us above instinct and protects us from our dysfunctional drives. That is the message with which the book of Leviticus draws toward its close.

יט נֶפֶשׁ־בְּהֵמָה יְשַׁלְּמֶנָּה נֶפֶשׁ תַּחַת נָפֶשׁ: וְאִישׁ כִּי־יִתֵּן מוּם בַּעֲמִיתוֹ
כ כַּאֲשֶׁר עָשָׂה כֵּן יֵעָשֶׂה לּוֹ: שֶׁבֶר תַּחַת שֶׁבֶר עַיִן תַּחַת עַיִן שֵׁן תַּחַת
כא שֵׁן כַּאֲשֶׁר יִתֵּן מוּם בָּאָדָם כֵּן יִנָּתֶן בּוֹ: וּמַכֵּה בְהֵמָה יְשַׁלְּמֶנָּה וּמַכֵּה מפטיר
כב אָדָם יוּמָת: מִשְׁפַּט אֶחָד יִהְיֶה לָכֶם כַּגֵּר כָּאֶזְרָח יִהְיֶה כִּי אֲנִי יְהוָה
כג אֱלֹהֵיכֶם: וַיְדַבֵּר מֹשֶׁה אֶל־בְּנֵי יִשְׂרָאֵל וַיּוֹצִיאוּ אֶת־הַמְקַלֵּל אֶל־
מִחוּץ לַמַּחֲנֶה וַיִּרְגְּמוּ אֹתוֹ אָבֶן וּבְנֵי־יִשְׂרָאֵל עָשׂוּ כַּאֲשֶׁר צִוָּה יְהוָה
אֶת־מֹשֶׁה:

The הפטרה *for* פרשת אמר *is on page page 1577.*

אונקלוס

נְפַשׁ בְּעִירָא יְשַׁלְּמִנַּהּ, נַפְשָׁא חֲלָף נַפְשָׁא: יט וּגְבַר, אֲרֵי יִתֵּין מוּמָא בְּחַבְרֵיהּ, כְּמָא דַעֲבַד, כֵּן יִתְעֲבֵיד לֵיהּ: כ תְּבָרָא חֲלָף תְּבָרָא, עֵינָא חֲלָף עֵינָא, שִׁנָּא חֲלָף שִׁנָּא, כְּמָא דִיהַב מוּמָא בַּאֲנָשָׁא, כֵּן יִתְיְהֵיב בֵּיהּ: כא וּדְיִקְטוֹל בְּעִירָא יְשַׁלְּמִנַּהּ, וּדְיִקְטוֹל אֲנָשָׁא יִתְקְטִיל: כב דִּינָא חַד יְהֵי לְכוֹן, גִּיּוֹרָא כְּיַצִּיבָא יְהֵי, אֲרֵי, אֲנָא יי אֱלָהֲכוֹן: כג וּמַלֵּיל מֹשֶׁה עִם בְּנֵי יִשְׂרָאֵל, וְאַפִּיקוּ יָת דְּאַרְגֵּיז, לְמִבָּרָא לְמַשְׁרִיתָא, וּרְגַמוּ יָתֵיהּ אַבְנָא, וּבְנֵי יִשְׂרָאֵל עֲבַדוּ, כְּמָא דְפַקֵּיד יי יָת מֹשֶׁה:

24:20 עַיִן תַּחַת עַיִן *An eye for an eye* – This is the famous and much misunderstood *lex talionis*, the law of retribution. As the Sages make clear, the principle of "an eye for an eye" was never meant literally (Bava Kamma 84a). A world based on a literal practice of an eye for an eye would eventually go blind. Other than in the case of murder, it meant monetary compensation. The principle is simply that the punishment must fit the crime. It was meant restrictively, to forbid either excessive leniency or excessive harshness.

"The widespread belief that the Hebrew Bible is all about vengeance and 'an eye for an eye,' while the Gospels supposedly invent love as an unconditional and universal value, must…count as one of the most extraordinary misunderstandings in all of Western history," writes philosopher Simon May. Because this misconception, focused on our verse, has fueled so much antisemitism over the centuries, we have translated the verse explicitly in line with the rabbinic understanding.

24:22 מִשְׁפַּט אֶחָד יִהְיֶה לָכֶם *There shall be one law* – What are these laws doing here, in the middle of the story of the blasphemer? Seemingly, they have nothing to do with it. The blasphemer has committed a sin against God. The laws that follow his story are about crimes against people or property. Moshe does not ask about injury. He asks about blasphemy. Besides which, he and the people already know the laws about injury and murder (Ex. 21:24–25). Yet they are presented seamlessly as part of a single narrative, as God's answer to Moshe's question. Leviticus, we recall, is not generally a book of narrative. It contains only one other story, about the deaths of two of Aharon's sons, Nadav and

Parashat Behar

25 1/2 On Mount Sinai the Lord spoke to Moshe: "Speak to the Israelites. Say:
When you enter the land that I am giving you, the land shall keep a Sabbath
3 to the Lord. For six years you may plant your fields, prune your vineyards,
4 and harvest their crops. But the seventh year shall be to the land a Sabbath of
complete rest, a Sabbath to the Lord. You shall not sow your fields or prune
5 your vineyards; you shall not harvest what grows of itself or gather the grapes

רש״י

כה א **בהר סיני.** מה ענין שמטה אצל הר סיני? והלא כל המצות נאמרו מסיני? אלא מה שמטה נאמרו כללותיה ופרטותיה ודקדוקיה מסיני, אף כלן נאמרו כללותיהן ודקדוקיהן מסיני. כך שנויה בתורת כהנים (פרשתא א, א). ונראה לי שכך פרושה, לפי שלא מצינו שמטת קרקעות שנשנית בערבות מואב במשנה תורה, למדנו שכללותיה ופרטותיה כלן נאמרו מסיני, ובא הכתוב ולמד כאן על כל דבור שנדבר למשה שמסיני היו כלם כללותיהן ודקדוקיהן, וחזרו ושנאום בערבות מואב:

ב **שבת לה׳.** לשם ה׳, כשם שנאמר בשבת בראשית:

ד **יהיה לארץ.** לשדות ולכרמים: **לא תזמר.** שקוצצין זמורותיה, ותרגומו: "לא תכסח", ודומה לו: "קוצים כסוחים" (ישעיה לג, יב), "שרפה באש כסוחה" (תהלים פ, יז):

ה **את ספיח קצירך.** אפילו לא זרעתה והיא צמחה מן הזרע שנפל בה בעת הקציר, הוא קרוי 'ספיח': **לא תקצור.** להיות מחזיק בו כשאר קציר, אלא הפקר יהיה לכל:

bringing God close, living in the constant presence of the Divine. With this established, we now return to the basic terms of our covenant: the commitment to establish a just, compassionate, and equitable society.

25:4 שַׁבַּת שַׁבָּתוֹן יִהְיֶה לָאָרֶץ *To the land a Sabbath* – We owe to the mathematician Benoit Mandelbrot the concept of fractals, the discovery that phenomena in nature often display the same pattern at different levels of magnitude. A single rock looks like a mountain. Crystals, snowflakes, and ferns are made up of elements that have the same shape as the whole. Fractal geometry is the scientific equivalent of the mystical ability to sense the great in the small: "To see a World in a Grain of Sand / And a Heaven in a Wild Flower / Hold Infinity in the palm of your hand / and Eternity in an hour" (William Blake).

The Vilna Gaon saw this pattern in holy time. Parashat Emor showed, for him, that the structure of the week – six days of work followed by a seventh that is holy – is mirrored in the structure of the year – six festive days of lesser holiness plus a seventh, Yom Kippur, of supreme holiness. The same pattern now appears on an even larger scale: six ordinary years followed by the Sabbatical year of *Shemitta*, "release"; seven cycles of seven years, followed by the Jubilee year, *Yovel*, when the shofar was sounded proclaiming "liberty throughout the land to all its inhabitants" (Lev. 25:10).

At the core of this fractal structure is the original divine act of creation. God made the world in six days, culminating in the creation of man in His image; on the seventh day, He rested. Wherever the Torah wishes to emphasize the dimension of holiness it makes systematic use of the number and concept of seven. The Sabbath was an unprecedented innovation. It meant that one day in seven, all hierarchies of wealth and power were suspended. No one could be forced to work: not employees, or slaves, or even domestic animals. In the seventh year, debts were remitted and slaves sent free. In the Jubilee all ancestral land was returned to its original owners. These laws share a common logic: "For it is to Me that the Israelites are servants; they are My servants whom I brought out of the land of Egypt" (25:55). Those who are servants to God may not be slaves to man (Bava Metzia 10a). This is the idea woven into Jewish time from its very inception.

פרשת בהר

כה א ב וַיְדַבֵּר יהוה אֶל־מֹשֶׁה בְּהַר סִינַי לֵאמֹר: דַּבֵּר אֶל־בְּנֵי יִשְׂרָאֵל וְאָמַרְתָּ
אֲלֵהֶם כִּי תָבֹאוּ אֶל־הָאָרֶץ אֲשֶׁר אֲנִי נֹתֵן לָכֶם וְשָׁבְתָה הָאָרֶץ שַׁבָּת
ג לַיהוה: שֵׁשׁ שָׁנִים תִּזְרַע שָׂדֶךָ וְשֵׁשׁ שָׁנִים תִּזְמֹר כַּרְמֶךָ וְאָסַפְתָּ אֶת־
ד תְּבוּאָתָהּ: וּבַשָּׁנָה הַשְּׁבִיעִת שַׁבַּת שַׁבָּתוֹן יִהְיֶה לָאָרֶץ שַׁבָּת לַיהוה
ה שָׂדְךָ לֹא תִזְרָע וְכַרְמְךָ לֹא תִזְמֹר: אֵת סְפִיחַ קְצִירְךָ לֹא תִקְצוֹר

אונקלוס

כה א וּמַלֵּיל יי עִם מֹשֶׁה, בְּטוּרָא דְסִינַי לְמֵימַר: ב מַלֵּיל, עִם בְּנֵי יִשְׂרָאֵל וְתֵימַר לְהוֹן, אֲרֵי תֵיעֲלוּן לְאַרְעָא, דַּאֲנָא יָהֵיב לְכוֹן, וְתַשְׁמֵיט אַרְעָא, שְׁמִטְּתָא קֳדָם יי: ג שֵׁית שְׁנִין תִּזְרַע חַקְלָךְ, וְשֵׁית שְׁנִין תִּכְסַח כַּרְמָךְ, וְתִכְנוֹשׁ יָת עֲלַלְתַּהּ: ד וּבְשַׁתָּא שְׁבִיעֵיתָא, נְיָח שְׁמִטְּתָא יְהֵי לְאַרְעָא, דְּתַשְׁמֵיט קֳדָם יי, חַקְלָךְ לָא תִזְרַע, וְכַרְמָךְ לָא תִכְסַח: ה יָת כַּתֵּי חֲצָדָךְ לָא תַחְצוֹד,

BEHAR

Our *parasha* consists of a single chapter that, despite its brevity, had a transformative impact on the social structure of ancient Israel and provided a unique solution to the otherwise intractable conflict between two fundamental ideals: freedom and equality. Much of human history has illustrated the fact that you can have freedom without equality (laissez-faire economics), or equality without freedom (Communism, socialism), but not both. The powerful insight of the Torah is that you can have both, but not at the same time. Therefore time itself has to become part of the solution, in the form of the seventh year and, after seven Sabbatical cycles, the Jubilee. These become periodic corrections to the distortions of the free market that allow some to become rich while others suffer the loss of land, home, and even freedom. There is the command to help the needy (Lev. 25:35). And there is the obligation to treat slaves not slavishly but as "a hired worker or a resident worker" (25:40). Through the periodic liberation of slaves, release of debts, and restoration of ancestral lands, the Torah provides a still-inspiring alternative to individualism on the one hand and collectivism on the other.

25:1 בְּהַר סִינַי *On Mount Sinai* – This is not a phrase that shouts for attention, until we recall that the book of Leviticus does not take place on Mount Sinai. It takes place in the wilderness of Sinai, at the foot of the mountain, not the top. The last time Mount Sinai figured in the narrative was when Moshe came down carrying the second set of tablets, the sign that God had reestablished His covenant with the people after the sin of the golden calf (Ex. 34). This verse, then, marks the end of the long digression that comes to repair the rupture caused by that sin (see Ex. 32, "The Golden Calf").

If we look at the substance of the chapter, we discover the same thing. It is not about a subject we immediately associate with Leviticus, which mostly speaks of the relationship between human beings and God. It is, though, precisely the subject we associate with the book of Exodus: social justice – specifically, the Jubilee year, the release of debts, and the liberation of slaves. The obvious place for these laws is immediately after the civil legislation contained in Exodus 21–23, which deals with justice in the relationships between humans. The last forty chapters have forged a new identity for Israel as a people with God in its midst,

6 of your unpruned vine; it is a year of rest for the land. You may eat the land's
Sabbath yield: you, your male and female servants, and the hired worker and
7 resident worker who live with you, your livestock and the wild animals in your
8 land – whatever the land produces is there to be eaten. And you shall
count off seven Sabbaths of years – seven times seven years – so that the seven
9 Sabbath cycles total forty-nine years. Then you shall sound the ram's horn. On
the tenth day of the seventh month, on the Day of Atonement, you shall sound
10 the horn all across your land. You shall consecrate the fiftieth year and proclaim
liberty throughout the land to all its inhabitants. This shall be your Jubilee; each

רש"י

נזירך. שהנזרת והפרשת בני אדם מהם ולא הפקרתם: **לא תבצר.** אותם אינך בוצר, אלא מן המפקר:

ו **והיתה שבת הארץ וגו'.** אף על פי שאסרתים עליך, לא באכילה ולא בהנאה אסרתים, אלא שלא תנהג בהם כבעל הבית, אלא הכל יהיו שוים בה, אתה ושכירך ותושבך: **שבת הארץ לכם לאכלה.** מן השבות אתה אוכל, ואי אתה אוכל מן השמור: **לך ולעבדך ולאמתך.** לפי שנאמר: "ואכלו אביני עמך" (שמות כג, יא), יכול יהיו אסורים באכילה לעשירים? תלמוד לומר: "לך ולעבדך ולאמתך", הרי בעלים ועבדים ושפחות אמורים כאן: **ולשכירך ולתושבך.** אף הגוים:

ז **ולבהמתך ולחיה.** אם חיה אוכלת, בהמה לא כל שכן, שמזונותיה עליך, מה תלמוד לומר: "ולבהמתך"? מקיש בהמה לחיה, כל זמן שחיה אוכלת מן השדה האכל לבהמתך מן הבית, כלה לחיה מן השדה, כלה לבהמתך מן הבית:

ח **שבתת שנים.** שמטות שנים. יכול יעשה שבע שנים רצופות שמטה ויעשה יובל אחריהם? תלמוד לומר: "שבע שנים שבע פעמים", הוי אומר כל שמטה ושמטה בזמנה: **והיו לך ימי שבע וגו'.** מגיד לך שאף על פי שלא עשית שמטות, עשה יובל לסוף ארבעים ותשע שנים. ופשוטו של מקרא: ועלו לך חשבון שנות השמטות למספר ארבעים ותשע שנים:

ט **והעברת.** לשון "ויעבירו קול במחנה" (שמות לו, ו), לשון הכרזה: **ביום הכפרים... בכל ארצכם.** ממשמע שנאמר "ביום הכפרים" איני יודע שהוא בעשור לחדש? אם כן למה נאמר "בעשור לחדש"? אלא לומר לך, תקיעת עשור לחדש דוחה שבת בכל ארצכם, ואין תקיעת ראש השנה דוחה שבת בכל ארצכם, אלא בבית דין בלבד:

י **וקדשתם.** בכניסתה מקדשין אותה בבית דין, ואומרים 'מקדשת השנה': **וקראתם דרור.** לעבדים, בין נרצע בין שלא כלו לו שש שנים משנמכר. אמר רבי יהודה: מהו לשון 'דרור'? כמדיר בי דירא וכו', שדר בכל מקום שהוא רוצה, ואינו ברשות אחרים: **יובל הוא.** שנה זאת מבדלת משאר שנים בנקיבת שם לה לבדה, ומה שמה? 'יובל'

"Who is wise?" Alexander asked the Elders of the Negev. "One who foresees the consequences," they responded (Tamid 32a). Leaders, if they are wise, think about the impact of their decisions many years from now.

THE JUBILEE YEAR

The words "proclaim liberty throughout the land" that appear in this *parasha* (v. 10) are inscribed on the Liberty Bell in Philadelphia. It was the chiming of this bell from the tower of Independence Hall on July 8, 1776, that summoned citizens to hear the first public reading of the American Declaration of Independence. Biblical freedom inspired American freedom, and many other freedoms. Seldom has an ancient idea more effectively proved its relevance to the contemporary world. The social program of Parashat Behar with its concern for economic justice, debt relief, welfare, and humane working conditions speaks with undiminished power to the problems of a global economy.

The Torah – this chapter especially – sets out the parameters of a society based on equality and liberty. These are eternal values. But they conflict. It is hard to pursue both fully at the same time. Communism, for instance, favors equality at the cost of liberty. Free market capitalism favors liberty at the cost of equality. How we construct the balance varies from age to age and place to place. In general the Rabbis favored markets and competition because they generated

ו וְאֶת־עִנְּבֵי נְזִירֶךָ לֹא תִבְצֹר שְׁנַת שַׁבָּתוֹן יִהְיֶה לָאָרֶץ׃ וְהָיְתָה שַׁבַּת
הָאָרֶץ לָכֶם לְאָכְלָה לְךָ וּלְעַבְדְּךָ וְלַאֲמָתֶךָ וְלִשְׂכִירְךָ וּלְתוֹשָׁבְךָ
ז הַגָּרִים עִמָּךְ׃ וְלִבְהֶמְתְּךָ וְלַחַיָּה אֲשֶׁר בְּאַרְצֶךָ תִּהְיֶה כָל־תְּבוּאָתָהּ
ח לֶאֱכֹל׃ וְסָפַרְתָּ לְךָ שֶׁבַע שַׁבְּתֹת שָׁנִים שֶׁבַע שָׁנִים
שֶׁבַע פְּעָמִים וְהָיוּ לְךָ יְמֵי שֶׁבַע שַׁבְּתֹת הַשָּׁנִים תֵּשַׁע וְאַרְבָּעִים שָׁנָה׃
ט וְהַעֲבַרְתָּ שׁוֹפַר תְּרוּעָה בַּחֹדֶשׁ הַשְּׁבִעִי בֶּעָשׂוֹר לַחֹדֶשׁ בְּיוֹם הַכִּפֻּרִים
י תַּעֲבִירוּ שׁוֹפָר בְּכָל־אַרְצְכֶם׃ וְקִדַּשְׁתֶּם אֵת שְׁנַת הַחֲמִשִּׁים שָׁנָה
וּקְרָאתֶם דְּרוֹר בָּאָרֶץ לְכָל־יֹשְׁבֶיהָ יוֹבֵל הִוא תִּהְיֶה לָכֶם וְשַׁבְתֶּם אִישׁ

אונקלוס

וְיָת עִנְּבֵי שְׁבְקָךְ לָא תִקְטוֹף, שְׁנַת שְׁמִטְּתָא יְהֵי לְאַרְעָא׃ ו וּתְהֵי, שְׁמִטַּת אַרְעָא לְכוֹן לְמֵיכַל, לָךְ וּלְעַבְדָּךְ וּלְאַמְתָךְ, וְלַאֲגִירָךְ וּלְתוֹתָבָךְ, דְּדָיְרִין עִמָּךְ׃ ז וְלִבְעִירָךְ, וּלְחַיְתָא דִּבְאַרְעָךְ, תְּהֵי כָל עֲלַלְתַּהּ לְמֵיכַל׃ ח וְתִמְנֵי לָךְ, שְׁבַע שְׁמִטָּן דִּשְׁנִין, שְׁבַע שְׁנִין שְׁבַע זִמְנִין, וִיהוֹן לָךְ, יוֹמֵי שְׁבַע שְׁמִטָּן דִּשְׁנִין, אַרְבְּעִין וּתְשַׁע שְׁנִין׃ ט וְתַעְבַּר, שׁוֹפַר יַבָּבָא בְּיַרְחָא שְׁבִיעָאָה, בְּעַסְרָא לְיַרְחָא, בְּיוֹמָא דְּכִפּוּרַיָּא, תַּעְבְּרוּן שׁוֹפָרָא בְּכָל אַרְעֲכוֹן׃ י וּתְקַדְּשׁוּן, יָת שְׁנַת חַמְשִׁין שְׁנִין, וְתִקְרוֹן חֵירוּתָא, בְּאַרְעָא לְכָל יָתְבַהָא, יוֹבֵילָא הִיא תְּהֵי לְכוֹן, וּתְתוּבוּן, גְּבַר

25:8 וְסָפַרְתָּ לְךָ *And you shall count* – In Parashat Emor and Parashat Behar there are two similar commands, both of which have to do with counting time. In Parashat Emor we read about the counting of the Omer, the forty-nine days between the second day of Passover and Shavuot. In Parashat Behar we read about the counting of the years to the Jubilee. There is, though, one significant difference between the two acts of counting. The counting of the Omer is in the plural: *usfartem lakhem*. The counting of the years is in the singular: *vesafarta lekha*. Oral tradition interpreted the difference as referring to who is to do the counting. In the case of the Omer, the counting is the duty of each individual (Menaḥot 65b); hence the use of the plural. In the case of the Jubilee, the counting is the responsibility of the *beit din*, specifically the Supreme Court, the Sanhedrin (Sifra, Behar 2:2; *Hilkhot Shemitta VeYovel* 10:1). It is the duty of the Jewish people as a whole, performed centrally on their behalf by the court; hence the singular.

Implicit here is an important principle of leadership. As individuals we may count the days, but leaders must count the years. As private persons we can think about tomorrow, but in our role as leaders we must think long-term, focusing our eyes on the far horizon. Jewish history is replete with just such long-term thinking. When Moshe, on the eve of the exodus, focused the attention of the Israelites on how they would tell the story to their children in the years to come, he was taking the first step to making Judaism a religion built on education, study, and the life of the mind.

Throughout the book of Deuteronomy he exhibits stunning insight when he says that the Israelites will find that their real challenge will be not slavery but freedom, not poverty but affluence, and not homelessness but home. Anticipating by two millennia the theory of the fourteenth-century Islamic historian Ibn Khaldun, he predicts that over the course of time, precisely as they succeed, the Israelites will be at risk of losing their social cohesion and solidarity as a group. To prevent this, he sets forth a way of life built on covenant, memory, collective responsibility, justice, welfare, and social inclusion – still, to this day, the most powerful formula ever devised for a strong civil society.

▶

11 person shall return to his hereditary home, each to his family. The fiftieth year
shall be a Jubilee for you. Do not sow, or reap what grows of itself, or harvest
12 the unpruned vines, for it is a Jubilee; it shall be holy to you. You shall eat
13 only directly from the field. And in this Jubilee year, each person shall return
14 to his hereditary home. But when you sell land to your fellow or buy it from SHENI

רש״י

שְׁמָה, עַל שֵׁם תְּקִיעַת שׁוֹפָר: **וְשַׁבְתֶּם אִישׁ אֶל אֲחֻזָּתוֹ.** שֶׁהַשָּׂדוֹת חוֹזְרוֹת לְבַעֲלֵיהֶן: **וְאִישׁ אֶל מִשְׁפַּחְתּוֹ תָּשֻׁבוּ.** לְרַבּוֹת אֶת הַנִּרְצָע:

יא **יוֹבֵל הִוא שְׁנַת הַחֲמִשִּׁים שָׁנָה.** מַה תַּלְמוּד לוֹמַר? לְפִי שֶׁנֶּאֱמַר: "וְקִדַּשְׁתֶּם" וְגוֹ׳, כְּדְאִיתָא בְּרֹאשׁ הַשָּׁנָה (דף ח ע״ב) וּבְתוֹרַת כֹּהֲנִים (פרק ג, א): **אֶת נְזִרֶיהָ.** אֶת הָעֲנָבִים הַמְּשֻׁמָּרִים, אֲבָל בּוֹצֵר אַתָּה מִן הַמֻּפְקָרִים, כְּשֵׁם שֶׁנֶּאֱמַר בַּשְּׁבִיעִית כָּךְ נֶאֱמַר בַּיּוֹבֵל. נִמְצְאוּ שְׁתֵּי שָׁנִים קְדוֹשׁוֹת סְמוּכוֹת זוֹ לָזוֹ, שְׁנַת הָאַרְבָּעִים וְתֵשַׁע שְׁמִטָּה וּשְׁנַת הַחֲמִשִּׁים יוֹבֵל:

יב **קֹדֶשׁ תִּהְיֶה לָכֶם.** תּוֹפֶסֶת דָּמֶיהָ כְּהֶקְדֵּשׁ. יָכוֹל תֵּצֵא הִיא לְחֻלִּין? תַּלְמוּד לוֹמַר: "תִּהְיֶה", בַּהֲוָיָתָהּ תְּהֵא: **מִן הַשָּׂדֶה תֹּאכְלוּ.** עַל יְדֵי הַשָּׂדֶה אַתָּה אוֹכֵל מִן הַבַּיִת, שֶׁאִם כָּלָה לַחַיָּה מִן הַשָּׂדֶה צָרִיךְ אַתָּה לְבַעֵר מִן הַבַּיִת, כְּשֵׁם שֶׁנֶּאֱמַר בַּשְּׁבִיעִית כָּךְ נֶאֱמַר בַּיּוֹבֵל:

יג **תָּשֻׁבוּ אִישׁ אֶל אֲחֻזָּתוֹ.** וַהֲרֵי כְּבָר נֶאֱמַר: "וְשַׁבְתֶּם אִישׁ אֶל אֲחֻזָּתוֹ" (לעיל פסוק י)? אֶלָּא לְרַבּוֹת הַמּוֹכֵר שָׂדֵהוּ וְעָמַד בְּנוֹ וּגְאָלָהּ, שֶׁחוֹזֶרֶת לְאָבִיו בַּיּוֹבֵל:

יד **וְכִי תִמְכְּרוּ וְגוֹ׳.** לְפִי פְּשׁוּטוֹ, כְּמַשְׁמָעוֹ. וְעוֹד יֵשׁ דְּרָשָׁה: מִנַּיִן כְּשֶׁאַתָּה מוֹכֵר, מְכֹר לְיִשְׂרָאֵל חֲבֵרְךָ? תַּלְמוּד לוֹמַר: "וְכִי תִמְכְּרוּ מִמְכָּר – לַעֲמִיתֶךָ" מְכֹר. וּמִנַּיִן שֶׁאִם בָּאתָ לִקְנוֹת, קְנֵה מִיִּשְׂרָאֵל חֲבֵרְךָ? תַּלְמוּד לוֹמַר: "אוֹ קָנֹה – מִיַּד עֲמִיתֶךָ": **אַל תּוֹנוּ.** זוֹ אוֹנָאַת מָמוֹן:

It is the sense of family that has kept Jews linked in a web of mutual obligation despite the fact that they are scattered across the world. The Jewish people remains a family, often divided, always argumentative, but bound in a common bond of fate nonetheless. As our *parasha* reminds us, that person who has fallen is our brother or sister, and ours must be the hand that helps them rise again.

25:14 אַל־תּוֹנוּ אִישׁ אֶת־אָחִיו *Brother must not cheat brother* – On the basis of this command, the Rabbis, expounding and developing halakhot of business, established a threshold for fair profit. An overcharge of more than a sixth above the market price was in most cases sufficient to invalidate the sale. It was forbidden to mislead customers by making old goods look new, or covering bad produce with a layer of good. Jewish law recognizes no concept of *caveat emptor*. The onus of fair representation lies with the vendor, not the purchaser. Giving misleading advice was forbidden under the biblical rubric of not "putting a stumbling-block before the blind" (Lev. 19:14). These and a host of similar provisions legislated for fair dealing and integrity. The Rabbis recognized that a perfect market would not emerge of its own accord. Not everyone had access to full information, and this gave scope for unscrupulous practices and unfair profits, against which they took a strong stand.

The subject of Jewish economic ethics is vast – perhaps a quarter of Jewish law is devoted to it – and much of the literature is highly detailed and case specific. Throughout the centuries, Jewish businesspeople sought rabbinic guidance in difficult cases, as did communal leaders in framing public policies. The glory of Jewish law lies in its concreteness: the Rabbis would have appreciated Mies van der Rohe's dictum that "God is in the details."

What the Tanakh and its rabbinic interpreters understood so well is that the market cannot be sustained by market values alone. It depends on a surrounding matrix of virtue and on the institutions that sustain it: families, communities, beliefs, and traditions. It needs rules of integrity and fair dealing, and a mindset that sees the market as a place not of exploitation, but of mutual gain. Without these, its workings are too arbitrary and abrasive. With them, it is the best way we know of matching one person's talents to another's desires, of encouraging freedom, creativity, and dignity, and of enhancing the conditions of life for all.

If the Jewish experience of economic enterprise teaches one thing it is that ethics and business are not adversaries.

יא אֶל־אֲחֻזָּתוֹ וְאִישׁ אֶל־מִשְׁפַּחְתּוֹ תָּשֻׁבוּ׃ יוֹבֵל הִוא שְׁנַת הַחֲמִשִּׁים
שָׁנָה תִּהְיֶה לָכֶם לֹא תִזְרָעוּ וְלֹא תִקְצְרוּ אֶת־סְפִיחֶיהָ וְלֹא תִבְצְרוּ
יב אֶת־נְזִרֶיהָ׃ כִּי יוֹבֵל הִוא קֹדֶשׁ תִּהְיֶה לָכֶם מִן־הַשָּׂדֶה תֹּאכְלוּ אֶת־
יג יד תְּבוּאָתָהּ׃ בִּשְׁנַת הַיּוֹבֵל הַזֹּאת תָּשֻׁבוּ אִישׁ אֶל־אֲחֻזָּתוֹ׃ וְכִי־תִמְכְּרוּ כ שני
מִמְכָּר לַעֲמִיתֶךָ אוֹ קָנֹה מִיַּד עֲמִיתֶךָ אַל־תּוֹנוּ אִישׁ אֶת־אָחִיו׃

אונקלוס

לְאַחְסַנְתֵּיהּ, וּגְבַר לְזַרְעִיתֵיהּ תְּתוּבוּן: יא יוֹבֵילָא הִיא, שְׁנַת, חַמְשִׁין שְׁנִין תְּהֵי לְכוֹן, לָא תִזְרְעוּן, וְלָא תִחְצְדוּן יָת כַּתַּהָא, וְלָא תִקְטְפוּן יָת שִׁבְקָהָא: יב אֲרֵי יוֹבֵילָא הִיא, קֻדְשָׁא תְּהֵי לְכוֹן, מִן חַקְלָא, תֵּיכְלוּן יָת עֲלַלְתַּהּ: יג בְּשַׁתָּא דְיוֹבֵילָא הָדָא, תְּתוּבוּן, גְּבַר לְאַחְסָנְתֵיהּ: יד וַאֲרֵי תְזַבְּנוּן זְבִינִין לְחַבְרָךְ, אוֹ תִזְבְּנוּן מִיַּד חַבְרָךְ, לָא תוֹנוֹן גְּבַר יָת אֲחוּהִי:

wealth, lowered prices, increased choice, reduced absolute levels of poverty, and in the course of time extended humanity's control over the environment, narrowing the extent to which we are the passive victims of circumstance and fate. They accepted the proposition that the greatest advances are often brought about through quite unspiritual drives. "I saw," says the author of Ecclesiastes, "that all the striving and all the skill: it is all but one man's jealousy of another" (Eccl. 4:4). Or as the talmudic Sages put it, "Were it not for the evil inclination, no one would build a house, marry a wife, have children, or engage in business" (Kohelet Rabba 3:11). To a point, then, free trade and limited government (albeit with due provision for publicly funded education and welfare) are consistent with a biblical vision whose key concerns are freedom, justice, and personal independence. In Judaism, the state exists to serve the individual, not the individual the state.

But the market itself has unintended consequences, among them growing inequality. Poverty creates the need for loans, and the burden of debt can become cumulative and crippling. It can lead people to sell their land and even their freedom; in ancient times this meant selling oneself into slavery. Today it can mean debt bondage, "sweatshop" labor at less-than-subsistence wages, and other inescapable cycles of poverty. Hence the need for periodic redistribution: the cancellation of debts, the liberation of slaves, and the return of ancestral property (other than that within walled cities). That is the logic of the Sabbatical and Jubilee years.

In an age of vast inequalities of income within and between societies – in which, at the time of writing, a billion people lack adequate food and shelter, clean water, and medical facilities, and thirty thousand children die each day from preventable diseases – the vision of Parashat Behar still challenges us with its ideals. To be sure, the Torah is not an economic theory or a political party's program. It is about eternity, whereas politics is about the here and now. But it establishes guiding principles. Wealth and power are not privileges but responsibilities, and we are summoned to become God's partners in building a world less random and capricious, more equitable and humane.

25:14 אָחִיו *[His] brother* – Ten times the laws in Parashat Behar use the word *aḥ*, "brother" (here and vv. 14, 25, 35, 36, 39, 46, 47, and 48).

"Your brother" in these verses is not meant literally. At times it means "your relative," but mostly it means "your fellow Jew." This is a distinctive way of thinking about society and our obligations to others. Jews are not just citizens of the same nation or adherents of the same faith. We are members of the same extended family. On the festivals we relive the same memories. We were forged in the same crucible of suffering. We are more than friends. We are *mishpaḥa*, family.

15 him, brother must not cheat brother: you shall buy from your neighbor by the
number of years since the Jubilee; he shall sell to you by the number of years
16 left for harvesting. You shall increase the price if the remaining years are many,
and lower it if they are few; what is being sold to you is the number of harvests.
17 You shall not cheat one another; you shall hold your God in awe; I am the LORD
18 your God. You shall fulfill My statutes, and keep and act in accordance with
19 My laws – then you will live securely on the land. The land will yield its fruit SHELISHI /SHENI/
20 and you will eat your fill and live securely there. If you should ask, 'What shall
we eat in the seventh year? We may not sow and may not harvest our crops' –
21 I will send My blessing over you in the sixth year and it will yield three years'
22 harvest. As you sow in the eighth year, you will eat of the old harvest; you will
23 still be eating of the old when the crop of the ninth year comes. And the land
shall not be sold in perpetuity, for the land is Mine. You are merely migrants
24 and visitors to Me. Throughout the land that you possess, you must allow land

רש״י

טו **בְּמִסְפַּר שָׁנִים אַחַר הַיּוֹבֵל תִּקְנֶה.** זֶהוּ פְּשׁוּטוֹ לְיַשֵּׁב הַמִּקְרָא עַל אָפְנָיו, עַל הָאוֹנָאָה בָּא לְהַזְהִיר: כְּשֶׁתִּמְכֹּר אוֹ תִּקְנֶה קַרְקַע דְּעוּ כַּמָּה שָׁנִים יֵשׁ עַד הַיּוֹבֵל, וּלְפִי הַשָּׁנִים וּתְבוּאוֹת הַשָּׂדֶה שֶׁהִיא רְאוּיָה לַעֲשׂוֹת יִמְכֹּר הַמּוֹכֵר וְיִקְנֶה הַקּוֹנֶה, שֶׁהֲרֵי סוֹפוֹ לְהַחְזִירָהּ לוֹ בִּשְׁנַת הַיּוֹבֵל. וְאִם יֵשׁ שָׁנִים מוּעָטוֹת וְזֶה מוֹכְרָהּ בְּדָמִים יְקָרִים – הֲרֵי נִתְאַנָּה לוֹקֵחַ, וְאִם יֵשׁ שָׁנִים מְרֻבּוֹת וְאָכַל מִמֶּנָּה תְּבוּאוֹת הַרְבֵּה – הֲרֵי נִתְאַנָּה מוֹכֵר; לְפִיכָךְ צָרִיךְ לִקְנוֹתָהּ לְפִי הַזְּמַן. וְזֶהוּ שֶׁנֶּאֱמַר: "בְּמִסְפַּר שְׁנֵי תְבוּאֹת יִמְכָּר לָךְ" – לְפִי מִנְיַן שְׁנֵי הַתְּבוּאוֹת שֶׁתְּהֵא עוֹמֶדֶת בְּיַד הַלּוֹקֵחַ תִּמְכֹּר לוֹ. וְרַבּוֹתֵינוּ דָּרְשׁוּ מִכָּאן שֶׁהַמּוֹכֵר שָׂדֵהוּ אֵינוֹ רַשַּׁאי לִגְאֹל פָּחוֹת מִשְּׁתֵּי שָׁנִים, שֶׁתַּעֲמֹד שְׁתֵּי שָׁנִים בְּיַד הַלּוֹקֵחַ מִיּוֹם לְיוֹם, וַאֲפִלּוּ יֵשׁ שָׁלֹשׁ תְּבוּאוֹת בְּאוֹתָן שְׁתֵּי שָׁנִים, כְּגוֹן שֶׁמְּכָרָהּ לוֹ בְּקָמוֹתֶיהָ. וּ'שְׁנֵי' אֵינוֹ יוֹצֵא מִפְּשׁוּטוֹ, כְּלוֹמַר, מִסְפַּר שָׁנִים שֶׁל תְּבוּאוֹת וְלֹא שֶׁל שִׁדָּפוֹן, וּמִעוּט 'שָׁנִים' שְׁנַיִם:

טז **תַּרְבֶּה מִקְנָתוֹ.** תִּמְכְּרֶנָּה בְּיֹקֶר: **תַּמְעִיט מִקְנָתוֹ.** תַּמְעִיט בְּדָמֶיהָ:

יז **וְלֹא תוֹנוּ אִישׁ אֶת עֲמִיתוֹ.** כָּאן הִזְהִיר עַל אוֹנָאַת דְּבָרִים, שֶׁלֹּא יַקְנִיט אִישׁ אֶת חֲבֵרוֹ וְלֹא יַשִּׂיאֶנּוּ עֵצָה שֶׁאֵינָהּ הוֹגֶנֶת לוֹ לְפִי דַּרְכּוֹ וַהֲנָאָתוֹ שֶׁל יוֹעֵץ. וְאִם תֹּאמַר, מִי יוֹדֵעַ אִם נִתְכַּוַּנְתִּי לְרָעָה? לְכָךְ נֶאֱמַר: "וְיָרֵאתָ מֵאֱלֹהֶיךָ", הַיּוֹדֵעַ מַחְשָׁבוֹת הוּא יוֹדֵעַ. כָּל דָּבָר הַמָּסוּר לַלֵּב, שֶׁאֵין מַכִּיר אֶלָּא מִי שֶׁהַמַּחְשָׁבָה בְּלִבּוֹ, נֶאֱמַר בּוֹ "וְיָרֵאתָ מֵאֱלֹהֶיךָ":

יח **וִישַׁבְתֶּם עַל הָאָרֶץ לָבֶטַח.** שֶׁבַּעֲוֹן שְׁמִטָּה יִשְׂרָאֵל גּוֹלִים, שֶׁנֶּאֱמַר: "אָז תִּרְצֶה הָאָרֶץ אֶת שַׁבְּתֹתֶיהָ... וְהִרְצָת אֶת שַׁבְּתֹתֶיהָ" (ויקרא כו, לד), וְשִׁבְעִים שָׁנָה שֶׁל גָּלוּת בָּבֶל כְּנֶגֶד שִׁבְעִים שְׁמִטּוֹת שֶׁבִּטְּלוּ הָיוּ (דברי הימים ב׳ לו, כא):

יט **וְנָתְנָה הָאָרֶץ וְגוֹ׳ וִישַׁבְתֶּם לָבֶטַח עָלֶיהָ.** שֶׁלֹּא תִּדְאֲגוּ מִשְּׁנַת בַּצֹּרֶת: **וַאֲכַלְתֶּם לָשֹׂבַע.** אַף בְּתוֹךְ הַמֵּעַיִם תְּהֵא בּוֹ בְּרָכָה:

כ **וְלֹא נֶאֱסֹף.** אֶל הַבַּיִת: **אֶת תְּבוּאָתֵנוּ.** כְּגוֹן יַיִן וּפֵרוֹת הָאִילָן וּסְפִיחִין הַבָּאִים מֵאֲלֵיהֶם:

כא **לִשְׁלֹשׁ הַשָּׁנִים.** לִקְצָת הַשִּׁשִּׁית, מִנִּיסָן וְעַד רֹאשׁ הַשָּׁנָה, וְלַשְּׁבִיעִית וְלַשְּׁמִינִית, שֶׁיִּזְרְעוּ בַּשְּׁמִינִית בְּמַרְחֶשְׁוָן וְיִקְצְרוּ בְּנִיסָן:

כב **עַד הַשָּׁנָה הַתְּשִׁיעִת.** עַד חַג הַסֻּכּוֹת שֶׁל תְּשִׁיעִית, שֶׁהוּא עֵת בּוֹא תְּבוּאָתָהּ שֶׁל שְׁמִינִית לְתוֹךְ הַבַּיִת, שֶׁכָּל יְמוֹת הַקַּיִץ הָיוּ בַּשָּׂדֶה בַּגְּרָנוֹת, וּבְתִשְׁרֵי הוּא עֵת הָאָסִיף לַבַּיִת. וּפְעָמִים שֶׁהָיְתָה צְרִיכָה לַעֲשׂוֹת לְאַרְבַּע שָׁנִים, בַּשִּׁשִּׁית שֶׁלִּפְנֵי הַשְּׁמִטָּה הַשְּׁבִיעִית, שֶׁהֵן בְּטֵלִין מֵעֲבוֹדַת קַרְקַע שְׁתֵּי שָׁנִים רְצוּפוֹת, הַשְּׁבִיעִית וְהַיּוֹבֵל, וּמִקְרָא זֶה נֶאֱמַר בִּשְׁאָר הַשְּׁמִטּוֹת כֻּלָּן:

כג **וְהָאָרֶץ לֹא תִמָּכֵר.** לִתֵּן לָאו עַל חֲזָרַת שָׂדוֹת לַבְּעָלִים בַּיּוֹבֵל, שֶׁלֹּא יְהֵא הַלּוֹקֵחַ כּוֹבְשָׁהּ: **לִצְמִתֻת.** לִפְסִיקָה, לִמְכִירָה פְּסוּקָה עוֹלָמִית: **כִּי לִי הָאָרֶץ.** אַל תֵּרַע עֵינְךָ בָּהּ, שֶׁאֵינָהּ שֶׁלְּךָ:

כד **וּבְכֹל אֶרֶץ אֲחֻזַּתְכֶם.** לְרַבּוֹת בָּתִּים וְעֶבֶד עִבְרִי, וְדָבָר זֶה מְפֹרָשׁ בְּקִדּוּשִׁין בְּפֶרֶק רִאשׁוֹן (דף כא ע״א). וּלְפִי פְּשׁוּטוֹ סָמוּךְ לַפָּרָשָׁה שֶׁלְּאַחֲרָיו,

טו בְּמִסְפַּר שָׁנִים אַחַר הַיּוֹבֵל תִּקְנֶה מֵאֵת עֲמִיתֶךָ בְּמִסְפַּר שְׁנֵי־תְבוּאֹת
טז יִמְכָּר־לָךְ: לְפִי ׀ רֹב הַשָּׁנִים תַּרְבֶּה מִקְנָתוֹ וּלְפִי מְעֹט הַשָּׁנִים תַּמְעִיט
יז מִקְנָתוֹ כִּי מִסְפַּר תְּבוּאֹת הוּא מֹכֵר לָךְ: וְלֹא תוֹנוּ אִישׁ אֶת־עֲמִיתוֹ
יח וְיָרֵאתָ מֵאֱלֹהֶיךָ כִּי אֲנִי יהוה אֱלֹהֵיכֶם: וַעֲשִׂיתֶם אֶת־חֻקֹּתַי וְאֶת־
יט מִשְׁפָּטַי תִּשְׁמְרוּ וַעֲשִׂיתֶם אֹתָם וִישַׁבְתֶּם עַל־הָאָרֶץ לָבֶטַח: וְנָתְנָה שלישי /שני/
כ הָאָרֶץ פִּרְיָהּ וַאֲכַלְתֶּם לָשֹׂבַע וִישַׁבְתֶּם לָבֶטַח עָלֶיהָ: וְכִי תֹאמְרוּ מַה־
כא נֹּאכַל בַּשָּׁנָה הַשְּׁבִיעִת הֵן לֹא נִזְרָע וְלֹא נֶאֱסֹף אֶת־תְּבוּאָתֵנוּ: וְצִוִּיתִי
אֶת־בִּרְכָתִי לָכֶם בַּשָּׁנָה הַשִּׁשִּׁית וְעָשָׂת אֶת־הַתְּבוּאָה לִשְׁלֹשׁ הַשָּׁנִים:
כב וּזְרַעְתֶּם אֵת הַשָּׁנָה הַשְּׁמִינִת וַאֲכַלְתֶּם מִן־הַתְּבוּאָה יָשָׁן עַד ׀ הַשָּׁנָה
כג הַתְּשִׁיעִת עַד־בּוֹא תְּבוּאָתָהּ תֹּאכְלוּ יָשָׁן: וְהָאָרֶץ לֹא תִמָּכֵר לִצְמִתֻת
כד כִּי־לִי הָאָרֶץ כִּי־גֵרִים וְתוֹשָׁבִים אַתֶּם עִמָּדִי: וּבְכֹל אֶרֶץ אֲחֻזַּתְכֶם

אונקלוס

טו בְּמִנְיַן שְׁנַיָּא בָּתַר יוֹבֵילָא, תִּזְבּוֹן מִן חַבְרָךְ, בְּמִנְיַן שְׁנֵי עֲלַלְתָּא יְזַבֵּין לָךְ: טז לְפוּם סַגִּיוּת שְׁנַיָּא, תַּסְגֵּי זְבִינוֹהִי, וּלְפוּם זְעֵירוּת שְׁנַיָּא, תַּזְעַר זְבִינוֹהִי, אֲרֵי מִנְיַן עֲלַלְתָּא, הוּא מְזַבֵּין לָךְ: יז וְלָא תוֹנוֹן גְּבַר יָת חַבְרֵיהּ, וְתִדְחַל מֵאֱלָהָךְ, אֲרֵי, אֲנָא יי אֱלָהֲכוֹן: יח וְתַעְבְּדוּן יָת קְיָמַי, וְיָת דִּינַי תִּטְּרוּן וְתַעְבְּדוּן יָתְהוֹן, וְתִתְּבוּן עַל אַרְעָא לִרְחָצָן: יט וְתִתֵּין אַרְעָא אִבַּהּ, וְתֵיכְלוּן לְמִסְבַּע, וְתִתְּבוּן לִרְחָצָן עֲלַהּ:

כ וַאֲרֵי תֵימְרוּן, מָא נֵיכוֹל בְּשַׁתָּא שְׁבִיעֵיתָא, הָא לָא נִזְרַע, וְלָא נִכְנוֹשׁ יָת עֲלַלְתַּנָא: כא וַאֲפַקֵּיד יָת בִּרְכְתִי לְכוֹן, בְּשַׁתָּא שְׁתִיתֵיתָא, וְתַעֲבֵיד יָת עֲלַלְתָּא, לִתְלָת שְׁנִין: כב וְתִזְרְעוּן, יָת שַׁתָּא תְּמִינֵיתָא, וְתֵיכְלוּן מִן עֲלַלְתָּא עַתִּיקָא, עַד שַׁתָּא תְּשִׁיעֵיתָא, עַד מֵיעַל עֲלַלְתַּהּ, תֵּיכְלוּן עַתִּיקָא: כג וְאַרְעָא, לָא תִזְדַּבַּן לַחֲלוּטִין, אֲרֵי דִילִי אַרְעָא, אֲרֵי דַיָּרִין וְתוֹתָבִין, אַתּוּן קֳדָמַי: כד וּבְכָל אֲרַע אַחְסַנְתְּכוֹן,

than economics and politics. It is a still-revolutionary concept of property and ownership. Ultimately all things belong to God. This is a theological equivalent of the legal concept of eminent domain: the superior dominion of the sovereign power over all lands within its jurisdiction. In the case of Israel, eminent domain – both in relation to persons and to land – is vested in God.

Since God is the ultimate owner of the universe, what we possess, we do not own; we only hold in trust. There are conditions to that trust. The most fundamental, as is demonstrated throughout our *parasha*, is that we must show concern for the good of all, and may not use wealth or power in ways incompatible with human dignity.

In the long run they need one another. It is one of the tasks of religious teaching to show that the long run must always inform the short term, so that economic profit does not lead to moral loss.

25:23 כִּי־לִי הָאָרֶץ *The land is Mine* – Because the land of Israel belongs to God, there can be no permanent freehold. God grants the Israelites possession of it on certain conditions, one of which is that the original owner can buy it back for a fair price at any time he has the money and wishes to do so (see vv. 25–28). The other is that in any case, it returns to the original owner in the Jubilee year.

Underlying these laws is something more fundamental

25 to be redeemed. If your brother grows poor and sells part of REVI'I
his hereditary land, his closest redeeming relative shall come and redeem what
26 his kinsman has sold. If the person lacks a relative to redeem it, but later prospers
27 and can afford to buy it back, he shall calculate the years since its sale and refund
28 the balance to the one to whom he sold it, and return to his hereditary home. If
he cannot afford to recover it, what was sold shall remain in the possession of the
buyer until the Jubilee year; but at the Jubilee it shall be released, and he shall
29 return to his possession. One who sells a house in a walled HAMISHI /SHELISHI/
city retains the right to redeem it until a year after its sale. This is the period of
30 redemption. If it is not redeemed before a full year has passed, the house in the

רש"י

שהמוכר אחזתו רשאי לגאלה לאחר שתי שנים, או הוא או קרובו, ואין הלוקח יכול לעכב:

כה **כי ימוך אחיך ומכר.** מלמד שאין אדם רשאי למכר שדהו אלא מחמת דחק עני: **מאחזתו.** ולא כלה, למד דרך ארץ שישייר שדה לעצמו: **וגאל את ממכר אחיו.** ואין הלוקח יכול לעכב:

כו **ואיש כי לא יהיה לו גאל.** וכי יש לך אדם בישראל שאין לו גואלים? אלא גואל שיוכל לגאל ממכרו:

כז **וחשב את שני ממכרו.** כמה שנים היו עד היובל? כך וכך; ובכמה מכרתיה לך? בכך וכך; עתיד היית להחזירה ביובל, נמצאת קונה מספר התבואות כפי חשבון של כל שנה, אכלת אותה שלש שנים או ארבע, הוצא את דמיהן מן החשבון וטול את השאר; וזהו: "והשיב את העדף" בדמי המקח על האכילה שאכלה, ויתנם ללוקח: **לאיש אשר מכר לו.** המוכר הזה שבא לגאלה:

כח **די השיב לו.** מכאן שאינו גואל לחצאין: **עד שנת היובל.** שלא יכנס לתוך אותה שנה כלום, שהיובל משמט בתחלתו:

כט **בית מושב עיר חומה.** בית בתוך עיר המקפת חומה מימות יהושע בן נון: **והיתה גאלתו.** לפי שנאמר בשדה שיכול לגאלה משתי שנים ואילך כל זמן שירצה, ובתוך שתי שנים הראשונים אינו יכול לגאלה, הצרך לפרש בזה שהוא חלוף, שאם רצה לגאל בשנה ראשונה גואלה, ולאחר מכאן אינו גואלה: **והיתה גאלתו.** של בית: **ימים.** ימי שנה שלמה קרויים 'ימים', וכן: "תשב הנער אתנו ימים" (בראשית כד, נה):

25:29 **ימים תהיה גאלתו** *The period of redemption* – Ramban explains that losing one's home through poverty is deeply painful and may be a source of shame. Because of this, a city home may be redeemed in the first year of being forced to sell it. If, however, the seller recovers his fortunes later, when he has already lived for a time in a new home, his emotional connection to the original home is no longer so strong. The reason why fields and rural homes return to their original owners in the Jubilee year is that they are not only homes, but a source of livelihood.

This relates to the Torah's strong sense of the dignity of labor. God Himself plants a garden and fashions the first human from the earth. The first man is himself charged with serving and protecting the garden. "The sleep of a worker is sweet," says Ecclesiastes (5:11). "You shall eat the

doing more than rescuing people from oppression or liberating slaves. He is engaged in an act of redemption, that is to say, exercising the right and responsibility of a close relative, in this case a father. The fusion here between law, ethics, and narrative, and between God's interventions in history and our duties within society, is complete. In the exodus, God was engaged in more than miracles. He was teaching us how we too ought to behave when people close to us fall into destitution.

This becomes an essential element of a world of hope, not in the trivial sense of wishing or wanting things to be better, but in the grounded confidence that things will become better. We are part of a society in which people know they have a duty to help out family members in distress. Our founding memory is of just such an act performed by God Himself.

כה גְּאֻלָּה תִּתְּנוּ לָאָרֶץ׃ כִּי־יָמוּךְ אָחִיךָ וּמָכַר מֵאֲחֻזָּתוֹ רביעי
כו וּבָא גֹאֲלוֹ הַקָּרֹב אֵלָיו וְגָאַל אֵת מִמְכַּר אָחִיו׃ וְאִישׁ כִּי לֹא יִהְיֶה־לּוֹ
כז גֹּאֵל וְהִשִּׂיגָה יָדוֹ וּמָצָא כְּדֵי גְאֻלָּתוֹ׃ וְחִשַּׁב אֶת־שְׁנֵי מִמְכָּרוֹ וְהֵשִׁיב
כח אֶת־הָעֹדֵף לָאִישׁ אֲשֶׁר מָכַר־לוֹ וְשָׁב לַאֲחֻזָּתוֹ׃ וְאִם לֹא־מָצְאָה יָדוֹ
דֵּי הָשִׁיב לוֹ וְהָיָה מִמְכָּרוֹ בְּיַד הַקֹּנֶה אֹתוֹ עַד שְׁנַת הַיּוֹבֵל וְיָצָא בַּיֹּבֵל
כט וְשָׁב לַאֲחֻזָּתוֹ׃ וְאִישׁ כִּי־יִמְכֹּר בֵּית־מוֹשַׁב עִיר חוֹמָה חמישי /שלישי/
ל וְהָיְתָה גְּאֻלָּתוֹ עַד־תֹּם שְׁנַת מִמְכָּרוֹ יָמִים תִּהְיֶה גְאֻלָּתוֹ׃ וְאִם לֹא־

אונקלוס

פֻּרְקָנָא תִּתְּנוּן לְאַרְעָא: כה אֲרֵי יִתְמַסְכַּן אֲחוּךְ, וִיזַבִּין מֵאַחְסַנְתֵּיהּ, וְיֵיתֵי פָרִיקֵיהּ דְּקָרִיב לֵיהּ, וְיִפְרוֹק, יָת זְבִינֵי אֲחוּהִי: כו וּגְבַר, אֲרֵי, לָא יְהֵי לֵיהּ פָּרִיק, וְתַדְבֵּיק יְדֵיהּ, וְיִשְׁכַּח כְּמִסַּת פֻּרְקָנֵיהּ: כז וִיחַשֵּׁיב יָת שְׁנֵי זְבִינוֹהִי, וְיָתֵיב יָת מוֹתָרָא, לִגְבַר דְּזַבֵּין לֵיהּ, וִיתוּב לְאַחְסַנְתֵּיהּ: כח וְאִם לָא אַשְׁכַּחַת יְדֵיהּ, כְּמִסַּת דְּיָתֵיב לֵיהּ, וִיהֵי זְבִינוֹהִי, בְּיַד דִּזְבַן יָתֵיהּ, עַד שַׁתָּא דְיוֹבֵילָא, וְיִפּוֹק בְּיוֹבֵילָא, וִיתוּב לְאַחְסַנְתֵּיהּ: כט וּגְבַר, אֲרֵי יְזַבֵּין בֵּית מוֹתַב קַרְתָּא מַקְּפָא שׁוּר, וִיהֵי פֻרְקָנֵיהּ, עַד מִשְׁלַם שַׁתָּא דִזְבִינוֹהִי, עִדָּן בְּעִדָּן יְהֵי פֻרְקָנֵיהּ: ל וְאִם לָא

REDEMPTION

The root *g-a-l*, which features in Parashat Behar nineteen times and in the next *parasha*, Beḥukotai, twelve times, means "to redeem." The basic idea of redemption is that the law provides for the possibility of reclaiming land, property, or even liberty itself if one has the means to do so. Our chapter discusses three cases in which an individual finds himself forced, through poverty, to sell something valuable. It may be land, or a house, or himself, sold as a slave. In each case, provision is made for a relative of the seller, or the seller himself should he suddenly find himself with the means to do so, to buy it back by providing the buyer with appropriate compensation. If neither of these is possible then redemption will automatically take place in the Jubilee year (with the exception of a house in a walled city).

In general, the market economy functions on the basis of binding exchange. If I sell something to a purchaser at a price both of us accept as fair, I cannot change my mind tomorrow and say, "I have decided not to sell it after all. Give it back and I will return your money." If the purchaser does not want to do so, I cannot force him. But there are certain things, says the Torah, that should not be left entirely to the vagaries of the market because they are too fundamental to self-respect and human flourishing. When it comes to land, a home, and freedom of employment, a distinction must be made between temporary poverty and permanent deprivation. In such cases, while respecting the integrity of the market – the redeemer must pay the proper market value of what he redeems – a basic law of justice takes priority. No one should be permanently disadvantaged because of temporary misfortune.

Redemption, however, is more than a legal idea. It is the way the Torah describes God's intervention in history to liberate the Israelites from slavery in Egypt. God tells Moshe, "I am the Lord, and I will free you from the forced labor of the Egyptians. I will rescue you from slavery. I will liberate (*vegaalti*) you with an arm stretched forth and with great acts of judgment. I will take you as My people, and I will be your God" (Ex. 6:6–7). At the Sea of Reeds the Israelites sang, "In Your love, You guided out the people You redeemed" (15:13). Only now, given the laws of Parashat Behar, do we understand the significance of the first words God commands Moshe to say to Pharaoh: "This is what the Lord says: 'Israel is My son, My firstborn'" (4:22). God is

walled city shall belong permanently to the buyer and his descendants forever;
31 it is not released at the Jubilee. Houses in villages without surrounding walls,
however, are considered as if they were open country. They may be redeemed,
32 and they are released at the Jubilee. In the Levitical towns – Levites always
33 retain the right to redeem houses in their ancestral towns. Levite property that
can be redeemed – houses sold in towns belonging to them – shall be released at
the Jubilee, because the houses in Levitical towns are their ancestral possession
34 among the Israelites. But the pastureland around their towns can never be
35 sold, because that is their permanent possession. If your brother
becomes poor and is struggling, extend him support – a migrant or visitor also –
36 that he may live among you. Do not take advance or accrued interest from

רש״י

ל| **וְקָם הַבַּיִת... לַצְּמִיתֻת.** יָצָא מִכֹּחוֹ שֶׁל מוֹכֵר וְעוֹמֵד בְּכֹחוֹ שֶׁל קוֹנֶה: **לֹא יֵצֵא בַּיֹּבֵל.** אָמַר רַב סָפְרָא: אִם פָּגַע בּוֹ יוֹבֵל בְּתוֹךְ שְׁנָתוֹ, לֹא יָצָא:

לא| **וּבָתֵּי הַחֲצֵרִים.** כְּתַרְגּוּמוֹ: ״פַּצְחַיָּא״, עֲיָרוֹת פְּתוּחוֹת מֵאֵין חוֹמָה, וְיֵשׁ הַרְבֵּה בְּסֵפֶר יְהוֹשֻׁעַ (פרקים יג-יט) ״הֶעָרִים וְחַצְרֵיהֶם״, ״בְּחַצְרֵיהֶם וּבְטִירֹתָם״ (בראשית כה, טז): **עַל שְׂדֵה הָאָרֶץ יֵחָשֵׁב.** הֲרֵי הֵן כַּשָּׂדוֹת שֶׁנִּגְאָלִים עַד הַיּוֹבֵל, וְיוֹצְאִין בַּיּוֹבֵל לַבְּעָלִים אִם לֹא נִגְאֲלוּ: **גְּאֻלָּה תִּהְיֶה לּוֹ.** מִיָּד, אִם יִרְצֶה, וְזֶה יָפֶה כֹּחוֹ מִכֹּחַ שָׂדוֹת, שֶׁהַשָּׂדוֹת אֵין נִגְאָלוֹת עַד שְׁתֵּי שָׁנִים: **וּבַיֹּבֵל יֵצֵא.** בְּחִנָּם:

לב| **וְעָרֵי הַלְוִיִּם.** אַרְבָּעִים וּשְׁמוֹנֶה עִיר שֶׁנִּתְּנוּ לָהֶם: **גְּאֻלַּת עוֹלָם.** גּוֹאֵל מִיָּד אֲפִלּוּ לִפְנֵי שְׁתֵּי שָׁנִים, אִם מָכְרוּ שָׂדֶה מִשְּׂדוֹתֵיהֶם הַנְּתוּנוֹת לָהֶם בְּאַלְפַּיִם אַמָּה סְבִיבוֹת הֶעָרִים, אוֹ אִם מָכְרוּ בַּיִת בְּעִיר חוֹמָה, גּוֹאֲלִין לְעוֹלָם וְאֵינוֹ חָלוּט לְסוֹף שָׁנָה:

לג| **וַאֲשֶׁר יִגְאַל מִן הַלְוִיִּם.** וְאִם יִקְנֶה בַּיִת אוֹ עִיר מֵהֶם, וְיָצָא בַּיּוֹבֵל אוֹתוֹ מִמְכָּר שֶׁל בַּיִת אוֹ שֶׁל עִיר וְיָשׁוּב לַלֵּוִי שֶׁמְּכָרוֹ, וְלֹא יִהְיֶה חָלוּט כִּשְׁאָר בָּתֵּי עָרֵי חוֹמָה שֶׁל יִשְׂרָאֵל; וּ׳גְאֻלָּה׳ זוֹ לְשׁוֹן מְכִירָה. דָּבָר אַחֵר, לְפִי שֶׁנֶּאֱמַר: ״גְּאֻלַּת עוֹלָם תִּהְיֶה לַלְוִיִּם״ (לעיל פסוק לב), יָכוֹל לֹא דִּבֵּר הַכָּתוּב אֶלָּא בְּלוֹקֵחַ יִשְׂרָאֵל שֶׁקָּנָה בַּיִת בְּעָרֵי הַלְוִיִּם, אֲבָל לֵוִי שֶׁקָּנָה מִלֵּוִי יִהְיֶה חָלוּט? תַּלְמוּד לוֹמַר: ״וַאֲשֶׁר יִגְאַל מִן הַלְוִיִּם״, אַף הַגּוֹאֵל מִיַּד לֵוִי גּוֹאֵל גְּאֻלַּת עוֹלָם. ״וְיָצָא מִמְכַּר בַּיִת״ – הֲרֵי זוֹ מִצְוָה אַחֶרֶת: וְאִם לֹא גְאָלָהּ יוֹצְאָה בַּיּוֹבֵל, וְאֵינוֹ נֶחְלָט לְסוֹף שָׁנָה כְּבַיִת שֶׁל יִשְׂרָאֵל: **כִּי בָתֵּי עָרֵי הַלְוִיִּם הִוא אֲחֻזָּתָם.** לֹא הָיוּ לָהֶם נַחֲלַת שָׂדוֹת וּכְרָמִים אֶלָּא עָרִים לָשֶׁבֶת וּמִגְרְשֵׁיהֶם, לְפִיכָךְ הֵם לָהֶם בִּמְקוֹם שָׂדוֹת וְיֵשׁ לָהֶם גְּאֻלָּה כְּשָׂדוֹת, כְּדֵי שֶׁלֹּא תִּפְקַע נַחֲלָתָם מֵהֶם:

לד| **וּשְׂדֵה מִגְרַשׁ עָרֵיהֶם לֹא יִמָּכֵר.** מֶכֶר גִּזְבָּר, שֶׁאִם הִקְדִּישׁ בֶּן לֵוִי אֶת שָׂדֵהוּ וְלֹא גְאָלָהּ וּמְכָרָהּ גִּזְבָּר, אֵינָהּ יוֹצְאָה לַכֹּהֲנִים בַּיּוֹבֵל, כְּמוֹ שֶׁנֶּאֱמַר בְּיִשְׂרָאֵל: ״וְאִם מָכַר אֶת הַשָּׂדֶה לְאִישׁ אַחֵר לֹא יִגָּאֵל עוֹד״ (ויקרא כז, כ), אֲבָל בֶּן לֵוִי גּוֹאֵל לְעוֹלָם:

לה| **וְהֶחֱזַקְתָּ בּוֹ.** אַל תַּנִּיחֵהוּ שֶׁיֵּרֵד וְיִפֹּל וְיִהְיֶה קָשֶׁה לַהֲקִימוֹ, אֶלָּא חַזְּקֵהוּ מִשְּׁעַת מוֹטַת הַיָּד. לְמָה זֶה דּוֹמֶה? לְמַשּׂאוֹי שֶׁעַל הַחֲמוֹר – עוֹדֵהוּ עַל הַחֲמוֹר, אֶחָד תּוֹפֵס בּוֹ וּמַעֲמִידוֹ; נָפַל לָאָרֶץ, חֲמִשָּׁה אֵין מַעֲמִידִין אוֹתוֹ: **גֵּר וְתוֹשָׁב.** אַף אִם הוּא גֵּר אוֹ תוֹשָׁב. וְאֵיזֶהוּ תוֹשָׁב? כָּל שֶׁקִּבֵּל עָלָיו שֶׁלֹּא לַעֲבֹד עֲבוֹדָה זָרָה וְאוֹכֵל נְבֵלוֹת:

relations and active citizenship in a diverse society. *Ger toshav* legislation cuts deeper. It is based not on pragmatism but religious principle. According to the Torah, you do not have to be Jewish in a Jewish society and land to have many of the rights of citizenship. You simply have to be moral.

Since the days of Moshe, minority rights have been central to the vision of the kind of society God wants us to create in the land of Israel. A strong sense of group identity can coexist with love of, and care for, the people who belong to

resident aliens with the same respect and loving-kindness as one would to a fellow Jew” (*Hilkhot Melakhim* 10:12).

The difference between this and later “ways of peace” legislation (Gittin 61a), which also mandated equal treatment, is that the “ways of peace” apply to non-Jews without regard to their beliefs or religious practice. They date from a time when Jews were a minority in a predominantly non-Jewish, non-monotheistic environment. “Ways of peace” are essentially pragmatic rules of what today we would call good community

יִגָּאֵל עַד־מְלֹאת לוֹ שָׁנָה תְמִימָה וְקָם הַבַּיִת אֲשֶׁר־בָּעִיר אֲשֶׁר־לֹא לוֹ
לא חֹמָה לַצְּמִיתֻת לַקֹּנֶה אֹתוֹ לְדֹרֹתָיו לֹא יֵצֵא בַּיֹּבֵל׃ וּבָתֵּי הַחֲצֵרִים
אֲשֶׁר אֵין־לָהֶם חֹמָה סָבִיב עַל־שְׂדֵה הָאָרֶץ יֵחָשֵׁב גְּאֻלָּה תִּהְיֶה־
לב לּוֹ וּבַיֹּבֵל יֵצֵא׃ וְעָרֵי הַלְוִיִּם בָּתֵּי עָרֵי אֲחֻזָּתָם גְּאֻלַּת עוֹלָם תִּהְיֶה
לג לַלְוִיִּם׃ וַאֲשֶׁר יִגְאַל מִן־הַלְוִיִּם וְיָצָא מִמְכַּר־בַּיִת וְעִיר אֲחֻזָּתוֹ בַּיֹּבֵל
לד כִּי בָתֵּי עָרֵי הַלְוִיִּם הִוא אֲחֻזָּתָם בְּתוֹךְ בְּנֵי יִשְׂרָאֵל׃ וּשְׂדֵה מִגְרַשׁ
לה עָרֵיהֶם לֹא יִמָּכֵר כִּי־אֲחֻזַּת עוֹלָם הוּא לָהֶם׃ וְכִי־יָמוּךְ כא
לו אָחִיךָ וּמָטָה יָדוֹ עִמָּךְ וְהֶחֱזַקְתָּ בּוֹ גֵּר וְתוֹשָׁב וָחַי עִמָּךְ׃ אַל־תִּקַּח

אונקלוס

יִתְפְּרֵיק, עַד מִשְׁלַם לֵיהּ שַׁתָּא שַׁלְמְתָא, וִיקוּם, בֵּיתָא דִּבְקַרְתָּא דְּלֵיהּ שׁוּרָא, לַחֲלוּטִין, לִדְזַבְּנֵיהּ יָתֵיהּ לְדָרוֹהִי, לָא יִפּוֹק בְּיוֹבֵילָא: לא וּבָתֵּי פַּצְחַיָּא, דְּלֵית לְהוֹן שׁוּר מַקַּף סְחוֹר סְחוֹר, עַל חֲקַל אַרְעָא יִתְחַשְׁבוּן, פֻּרְקָנָא תְּהֵי לְהוֹן, וּבְיוֹבֵילָא יִפְקוּן: לב וְקִרְוֵי לֵיוָאֵי, בָּתֵּי קִרְוֵי אַחְסָנַתְהוֹן, פֻּרְקַן עָלַם תְּהֵי לְלֵיוָאֵי: לג וּדְיִפְרוֹק מִן לֵיוָאֵי, וְיִפְּקוּן זְבִינֵי בֵיתָא, וְקִרְוֵי אַחְסַנְתֵיהּ בְּיוֹבֵילָא, אֲרֵי בָתֵּי קִרְוֵי לֵיוָאֵי, אִנּוּן אַחְסַנְתְּהוֹן, בְּגוֹ בְּנֵי יִשְׂרָאֵל: לד וַחֲקַל, רְוַח קִרְוֵיהוֹן לָא יִזְדַּבַּן, אֲרֵי אַחְסָנַת עָלַם, הוּא לְהוֹן: לה וַאֲרֵי יִתְמַסְכַּן אֲחוּךְ, וּתְמוּט יְדֵיהּ עִמָּךְ, וְתַתְקֵיף בֵּיהּ, דַּיָּר וְתוֹתָב, וְיֵיחֵי עִמָּךְ: לו לָא תִסַּב

fruit of your labor; you shall be happy and thriving," says Psalms (128:2). Flay carcasses rather than be dependent on others, says the third-century Rav (Yerushalmi, Berakhot 9:2). Someone who does not engage in *yishuv haolam*, constructive work, is invalid as a witness in Jewish law (Sanhedrin 24b). Work is an important source of dignity and self-respect. It has spiritual value, because earning our food is part of the stature, the creativity of the human condition. Judaism is opposed to the idea of a leisured class, and while a city dweller's attachment to their home is something that must be honored, it does not run as far or as deep as the importance of land to the one who works it.

THE RIGHTS OF STRANGERS

These verses spell out the rights of and obligations toward a *ger*. The Sages hold that the word *ger* (migrant) might mean one of two things. One was a *ger tzedek*, a convert to Judaism who had accepted all its commands and obligations. The other was the *ger toshav*, the "migrant" or "resident alien," who had not adopted the religion of Israel but who lived in the land of Israel. This passage relates to the latter group. There is an obligation to support and sustain a non-Jewish migrant. Not only does he have the right to live in the Holy Land, but he has the right to share in its welfare provisions.

Who then is a *ger toshav*? There are three views in the Talmud (Avoda Zara 64a). According to R. Meir, it is anyone who takes it upon himself not to worship idols. According to the Sages, it is one who commits himself to keep the seven Noahide commands. A third view, more stringent, holds that it is someone who undertakes to keep all the commands of the Torah except one, the prohibition of meat not ritually slaughtered. The law follows the Sages. A *ger toshav* is thus a non-Jew living in Israel who accepts the Noahide laws binding on everyone.

Ger toshav legislation is thus one of the earliest extant forms of minority rights. According to Rambam, there is an obligation on Jews in Israel to establish courts of law for resident aliens to allow them to settle their own disputes – or disputes they have with Jews – according to the provisions of Noahide law. Rambam adds: "One should act toward

37 him; fear your God so that your brother can live with you. Do not lend him
38 your money at interest or provide him with food at a profit. I am the Lord your
God, who brought you out of the land of Egypt to give the land of Canaan to
39 you, to be your God. If your brother becomes poor and sells himself SHISHI /REVI'I/
40 to you, do not work him as a slave. He shall abide with you like a hired worker
41 or a resident worker and work for you until the Jubilee year. Then he and his
children shall be free to leave you and return to their family and their ancestral
42 land. For they are My servants whom I brought out from Egypt: they cannot
43 be sold as slaves. Do not rule them harshly with backbreaking labor; fear your
44 God. As for male or female slaves that you may have: from the nations around

רש״י

לו **נשך ותרבית.** חד שויניהו רבנן, ולעבר עליו בשני לאוין: **ויראת מאלהיך.** לפי שדעתו של אדם נמשכת אחר הרבית וקשה לפרש הימנו, ומורה לעצמו היתר בשביל מעותיו שהיו בטלות אצלו, הצרך לומר "ויראת מאלהיך". או התולה מעותיו בגוי כדי להלוותם לישראל ברבית, הרי זה דבר המסור ללבו של אדם ומחשבתו, לכך הצרך לומר "ויראת מאלהיך":

לח **אשר הוצאתי וגו׳.** והבחנתי בין בכור לשאינו בכור, אף אני יודע ונפרע מן המלוה מעות לישראל ברבית ואומר של גוי הם. דבר אחר: "אשר הוצאתי אתכם מארץ מצרים", על מנת שתקבלו עליכם מצותי ואפלו הן כבדות עליכם: **לתת לכם את ארץ כנען.** בשכר שתקבלו מצותי: **להיות לכם לאלהים.** שכל הדר בארץ ישראל אני לו לאלהים, וכל היוצא ממנה כעובד עבודה זרה:

לט **עבדת עבד.** עבודה של גנאי שיהא נכר בה כעבד, שלא יוליך כליו אחריו לבית המרחץ, ולא ינעל לו מנעליו:

מ **כשכיר כתושב.** עבודת קרקע ומלאכת אמנות, כשאר שכירים התנהג בו: **עד שנת היבל.** אם פגע בו יובל לפני שש שנים, היובל מוציאו:

מא **הוא ובניו עמו.** אמר רבי שמעון: אם הוא נמכר, בניו מי מכרן? אלא מכאן שרבו חיב במזונות בניו: **ואל אחזת אבתיו.** אל כבוד אבותיו, ואין לזלזלו בכך: **אחזת.** חזקת:

מב **כי עבדי הם.** שטרי קודם: **לא ימכרו ממכרת עבד.** בהכרזה: 'כאן יש עבד למכר', ולא יעמידנו על אבן הלקח:

מג **לא תרדה בו בפרך.** מלאכה שלא לצרך כדי לענותו, אל תאמר לו: 'החם לי את הכוס הזה' והוא אינו צריך, 'עדר תחת הגפן עד שאבוא'. שמא תאמר: אין מכיר בדבר אם לצרך אם לאו, ואומר אני לו שהוא לצרך – הרי הדבר הזה מסור ללב, לכך נאמר "ויראת":

מד **ועבדך ואמתך אשר יהיו לך.** אם תאמר, אם כן במה אשתמש? בעבדי איני מושל, באמות איני נוחל, שהרי הזהרתני: "לא תחיה כל נשמה" (דברים כ, טז), אלא מי ישמשני?: **מאת הגוים.** הם יהיו לך

mistreating him. Evidently stuck for a way of opening the conversation, Rabban Gamliel looked around R. Yehoshua's house, noticed that the walls were black, and said: "Judging by the walls, I can see that you must be a blacksmith." R. Yehoshua replied: "Alas for the generation of which you are the leader, seeing that you know nothing of the troubles of the scholars and how they have to make a living" (*Berakhot* 28a).

The story fascinates me, because it is apparent that Rabban Gamliel and R. Yehoshua were able to work and debate together day by day in the academy, one as its head, the other as his deputy, without the wealthy Rabban Gamliel being aware that R. Yehoshua was a poor man. To this day, this rings true as a description of the spirit of the learning community. (Its second implication, no less important, is that ignorance of the real economic difficulties of a people disqualifies a sage from being a leader.) In a covenantal society, anyone who is struggling financially, whether brother or stranger, is to be supported to the extent and in such a manner that they can "live among you": fully as one of you.

25:44 **מהם תקנו עבד ואמה** *Acquire a male or female slave* – Slavery is an assault on the human condition. To be "in the image of God" (Gen. 1:27) means to be summoned to a life

לז מֵאִתּוֹ נֶשֶׁךְ וְתַרְבִּית וְיָרֵאתָ מֵאֱלֹהֶיךָ וְחֵי אָחִיךָ עִמָּךְ׃ אֶת־כַּסְפְּךָ לֹא־
לח תִתֵּן לוֹ בְּנֶשֶׁךְ וּבְמַרְבִּית לֹא־תִתֵּן אָכְלֶךָ׃ אֲנִי יהוה אֱלֹהֵיכֶם אֲשֶׁר־
הוֹצֵאתִי אֶתְכֶם מֵאֶרֶץ מִצְרָיִם לָתֵת לָכֶם אֶת־אֶרֶץ כְּנַעַן לִהְיוֹת לָכֶם
לט לֵאלֹהִים׃ וְכִי־יָמוּךְ אָחִיךָ עִמָּךְ וְנִמְכַּר־לָךְ לֹא־תַעֲבֹד ששי /רביעי/
מ בּוֹ עֲבֹדַת עָבֶד׃ כְּשָׂכִיר כְּתוֹשָׁב יִהְיֶה עִמָּךְ עַד־שְׁנַת הַיֹּבֵל יַעֲבֹד
מא עִמָּךְ׃ וְיָצָא מֵעִמָּךְ הוּא וּבָנָיו עִמּוֹ וְשָׁב אֶל־מִשְׁפַּחְתּוֹ וְאֶל־אֲחֻזַּת
מב אֲבֹתָיו יָשׁוּב׃ כִּי־עֲבָדַי הֵם אֲשֶׁר־הוֹצֵאתִי אֹתָם מֵאֶרֶץ מִצְרָיִם לֹא
מג מד יִמָּכְרוּ מִמְכֶּרֶת עָבֶד׃ לֹא־תִרְדֶּה בוֹ בְּפָרֶךְ וְיָרֵאתָ מֵאֱלֹהֶיךָ׃ וְעַבְדְּךָ
וַאֲמָתְךָ אֲשֶׁר יִהְיוּ־לָךְ מֵאֵת הַגּוֹיִם אֲשֶׁר סְבִיבֹתֵיכֶם מֵהֶם תִּקְנוּ עֶבֶד

אונקלוס

מִנֵּיהּ חִיבְּלְיָא וְרִבִּיתָא, וְתִדְחַל מֵאֱלָהָךְ, וְיֵיחֵי אֲחוּךְ עִמָּךְ: לז יָת כַּסְפָּךְ, לָא תִתֵּין לֵיהּ בְּחִיבְּלְיָא, וּבְרִבִּיתָא לָא תִתֵּין מֵיכְלָךְ: לח אֲנָא, יי אֱלָהֲכוֹן, דְּאַפֵּיקִית יָתְכוֹן מֵאַרְעָא דְּמִצְרָיִם, לְמִתַּן לְכוֹן יָת אַרְעָא דִּכְנַעַן, לְמֶהֱוֵי לְכוֹן לֶאֱלָהּ: לט וַאֲרֵי יִתְמַסְכַּן אֲחוּךְ, עִמָּךְ וְיִזְדַּבַּן לָךְ, לָא תִפְלַח בֵּיהּ פֻּלְחַן עַבְדִּין: מ כַּאֲגִירָא כְּתוֹתָבָא יְהֵי עִמָּךְ, עַד שַׁתָּא דְּיוֹבֵילָא יִפְלַח עִמָּךְ: מא וְיִפּוֹק מֵעִמָּךְ, הוּא וּבְנוֹהִי עִמֵּיהּ, וִיתוּב לְזַרְעִיתֵיהּ, וּלְאַחְסָנַת אֲבָהָתוֹהִי יְתוּב: מב אֲרֵי עַבְדַּי אִנּוּן, דְּאַפֵּיקִית יָתְהוֹן מֵאַרְעָא דְּמִצְרָיִם, לָא יִזְדַּבְּנוּן זְבוּן עַבְדִּין: מג לָא תִפְלַח בֵּיהּ בְּקַשְׁיוּ, וְתִדְחַל מֵאֱלָהָךְ: מד וְעַבְדָּךְ וְאַמְתָךְ דִּיהוֹן לָךְ, מִן עַמְמַיָּא, דִּבְסַחְרָנֵיכוֹן, מִנְּהוֹן תִּקְנוֹן עַבְדִּין

other groups or to none. That is part of *Torat Kohanim,* ethics in the priestly mode: our common humanity precedes our religious differences. Minority rights are the best test of a free and just society.

25:35 וְחֵי עִמָּךְ *That he may live among you* – "The highest degree of charity, exceeded by none," writes Rambam in his famous summary of the eight levels of *tzedaka,* "is that of a person who assists a poor Jew by providing him with a gift or loan or by accepting him into business partnership or by helping him find employment – in a word, by putting him where he can dispense with other people's aid. With reference to such help it is said, 'Extend him support – a migrant or visitor also – that he may live among you' (Lev. 25:35), which means to strengthen him in such a manner that his falling into want is prevented" (*Hilkhot Mattenot Aniyyim* 10:7).

Rambam's exquisitely calibrated ethic is shot through with psychological insight. What matters, he explains in the continuation of the above passage, is not how *much* you give, but *how* you do so. The poor must not be embarrassed. The rich must not be allowed to feel superior. We give, not to take pride in our generosity, still less to emphasize the dependency of others, but because we belong to a covenant of human solidarity.

Especially noteworthy is Rambam's insistence that giving somebody a job, or the means to start a business, is the highest charity of all. What is humiliating about poverty is dependence itself: the feeling of being beholden to others. One of the rules of *tzedaka* is that even the person who subsists through charity must give charity, and be given enough to give it. This concern for dignity, this democratizing tendency, was expressed by the Rabbis most potently in their creation of a culture of study and education, which dominated their lives and to which access was free, universal, and lifelong.

The Talmud tells the story of Rabban Gamliel's visit to the house of his deputy, R. Yehoshua, to apologize for

45 you, you may acquire a male or female slave. You may also acquire them from
among the migrants residing with you and from their families among you who
46 were born in your land; they may be yours, in your possession. They become
hereditary property that you can bequeath to your children; they may be your
47 slaves, but over your brother Israelites you may not rule so harshly. If SHEVI'I
a migrant or temporary resident prospers among you, and your fellow Israelite
becomes poor and is sold to a migrant residing among you or to a branch of a
48 foreign family, the Israelite has the right, subsequent to the sale, to be redeemed;
49 one of his relatives may redeem him. His uncle or cousin or any other blood
relative may redeem him, or if he can afford to do so, he may redeem himself.
50 Together with his owner, he shall calculate the time from the year he was sold
until the Jubilee year. The price of his release shall be based on that number of
51 years, as if he had been there as a hired laborer. If many years remain, he shall
52 pay that proportion of his purchase price for his redemption. If only a few years
remain until the Jubilee year, he shall calculate that and pay for the redemption
53 accordingly. He shall be with him like a worker hired year by year; and never
54 shall he be oppressed in his labors while you look on. And if he is not redeemed

רש״י

לַעֲבָדִים: **אֲשֶׁר סְבִיבֹתֵיכֶם.** וְלֹא שֶׁבְּתוֹךְ גְּבוּל אַרְצְכֶם, שֶׁהֲרֵי בָּהֶם אָמַרְתִּי: ״לֹא תְחַיֶּה כָּל נְשָׁמָה״:

מה **וְגַם מִבְּנֵי הַתּוֹשָׁבִים.** שֶׁבָּאוּ מִסְּבִיבוֹתֵיכֶם לִשָּׂא נָשִׁים בְּאַרְצְכֶם וְיָלְדוּ לָהֶם, הַבֵּן הוֹלֵךְ אַחַר הָאָב וְאֵינוֹ בִּכְלָל ״לֹא תְחַיֶּה״, אֶלָּא אַתָּה מֻתָּר לִקְנוֹתוֹ כְּעֶבֶד: **מֵהֶם תִּקְנוּ.** אוֹתָם תִּקְנוּ:

מו **וְהִתְנַחַלְתֶּם אֹתָם לִבְנֵיכֶם.** הַחֲזִיקוּ בָהֶם לְנַחֲלָה לְצֹרֶךְ בְּנֵיכֶם אַחֲרֵיכֶם. וְלֹא יִתָּכֵן לְפָרֵשׁ ׳הַנְחִילוּם לִבְנֵיכֶם׳, שֶׁאִם כֵּן הָיָה לוֹ לִכְתֹּב ׳וְהִנְחַלְתֶּם אוֹתָם לִבְנֵיכֶם׳: **וְהִתְנַחַלְתֶּם.** כְּמוֹ ׳וְהִתְחַזַּקְתֶּם׳ (במדבר יג, כ): **אִישׁ בְּאָחִיו.** לְהָבִיא נָשִׂיא בְּעַמָּיו וּמֶלֶךְ בִּמְשָׁרְתָיו שֶׁלֹּא לִרְדּוֹת בְּפָרֶךְ:

מז **יַד גֵּר וְתוֹשָׁב.** גֵּר וְהוּא תוֹשָׁב, כְּתַרְגּוּמוֹ: ״עֲרַל וְתוֹתָב״, וְסוֹפוֹ מוֹכִיחַ: ״וְנִמְכַּר לְגֵר תּוֹשָׁב״: **וְכִי תַשִּׂיג יַד גֵּר וְתוֹשָׁב עִמָּךְ.** מִי גָּרַם לוֹ שֶׁיַּעֲשִׁיר? דִּבּוּקוֹ עִמָּךְ: **וּמָךְ אָחִיךָ עִמּוֹ.** מִי גָּרַם לוֹ שֶׁיָּמוּךְ? דִּבּוּקוֹ עִמּוֹ, עַל יְדֵי שֶׁלָּמַד מִמַּעֲשָׂיו: **מִשְׁפַּחַת גֵּר.** זֶה הַגּוֹי. כְּשֶׁהוּא אוֹמֵר ׳לְעֵקֶר׳, זֶה הַנִּמְכָּר לַעֲבוֹדָה זָרָה עַצְמָהּ לִהְיוֹת לָהּ שַׁמָּשׁ, וְלֹא לֶאֱלֹהוּת אֶלָּא לַחְטֹב עֵצִים וְלִשְׁאֹב מַיִם:

מח **גְּאֻלָּה תִּהְיֶה לוֹ.** מִיָּד, אַל תַּנִּיחֵהוּ שֶׁיִּטָּמַע:

נ **עַד שְׁנַת הַיֹּבֵל.** שֶׁהֲרֵי כָּל עַצְמוֹ לֹא קְנָאוֹ אֶלָּא לְעָבְדוֹ עַד הַיּוֹבֵל, שֶׁהֲרֵי בַּיּוֹבֵל יֵצֵא, כְּמוֹ שֶׁנֶּאֱמַר לְמַטָּה: ״וְיָצָא בִּשְׁנַת הַיֹּבֵל״ (להלן פסוק נד). וּבְגוֹי שֶׁתַּחַת יָדְךָ הַכָּתוּב מְדַבֵּר, וְאַף עַל פִּי כֵן לֹא תָבֹא עָלָיו בַּעֲקִיפִין, מִפְּנֵי חִלּוּל הַשֵּׁם, אֶלָּא כְּשֶׁבָּא לִגָּאֵל, יְדַקְדֵּק בַּחֶשְׁבּוֹן, לְפִי הַמַּגִּיעַ בְּכָל שָׁנָה וְשָׁנָה יְנַכֶּה לוֹ הַגּוֹי מִן דָּמָיו – אִם הָיוּ עֶשְׂרִים שָׁנָה מִשֶּׁנִּמְכַּר עַד הַיּוֹבֵל וּקְנָאוֹ בְּעֶשְׂרִים מָנֶה, נִמְצָא שֶׁקָּנָה הַגּוֹי עֲבוֹדַת שָׁנָה בְּמָנֶה, וְאִם שֶׁהָה זֶה אֶצְלוֹ חָמֵשׁ שָׁנִים וּבָא לִגָּאֵל יְנַכֶּה לוֹ חֲמֵשֶׁת מָנִים וְיִתֵּן לוֹ הָעֶבֶד חֲמִשָּׁה עָשָׂר מָנִים, וְזֶהוּ: ״וְהָיָה כֶּסֶף מִמְכָּרוֹ בְּמִסְפַּר שָׁנִים״: **כִּימֵי שָׂכִיר יִהְיֶה עִמּוֹ.** חֶשְׁבּוֹן הַמַּגִּיעַ לְכָל שָׁנָה וְשָׁנָה יְחַשֵּׁב כְּאִלּוּ נִשְׂכַּר עִמּוֹ כָּל שָׁנָה בְּמָנֶה וִינַכֶּה לוֹ:

נא **אִם עוֹד רַבּוֹת בַּשָּׁנִים.** עַד הַיּוֹבֵל: **לְפִיהֶן וְגוֹ׳.** הַכֹּל כְּמוֹ שֶׁפֵּרַשְׁתִּי:

נג **לֹא יִרְדֶּנּוּ בְּפֶרֶךְ לְעֵינֶיךָ.** כְּלוֹמַר, וְאַתָּה רוֹאֶה:

נד **וְאִם לֹא יִגָּאֵל בְּאֵלֶּה.** בְּאֵלֶּה הוּא נִגְאָל, וְאֵינוֹ נִגְאָל בְּשֵׁשׁ:

The answer lay in changing slavery from an ontological condition to a temporary circumstance: from what I am to a situation in which I find myself, now but not forever. No Israelite was allowed to be treated or to see himself as a slave. He might be reduced to slavery for a period of time, but this was a passing plight, not a permanent identity.

מה וְאָמָה: וְגַם מִבְּנֵי הַתּוֹשָׁבִים הַגָּרִים עִמָּכֶם מֵהֶם תִּקְנוּ וּמִמִּשְׁפַּחְתָּם
מו אֲשֶׁר עִמָּכֶם אֲשֶׁר הוֹלִידוּ בְּאַרְצְכֶם וְהָיוּ לָכֶם לַאֲחֻזָּה: וְהִתְנַחַלְתֶּם
אֹתָם לִבְנֵיכֶם אַחֲרֵיכֶם לָרֶשֶׁת אֲחֻזָּה לְעֹלָם בָּהֶם תַּעֲבֹדוּ וּבְאַחֵיכֶם
מז בְּנֵי־יִשְׂרָאֵל אִישׁ בְּאָחִיו לֹא־תִרְדֶּה בּוֹ בְּפָרֶךְ: וְכִי תַשִּׂיג שביעי
יַד גֵּר וְתוֹשָׁב עִמָּךְ וּמָךְ אָחִיךָ עִמּוֹ וְנִמְכַּר לְגֵר תּוֹשָׁב עִמָּךְ אוֹ לְעֵקֶר
מח מִשְׁפַּחַת גֵּר: אַחֲרֵי נִמְכַּר גְּאֻלָּה תִּהְיֶה־לּוֹ אֶחָד מֵאֶחָיו יִגְאָלֶנּוּ:
מט אוֹ־דֹדוֹ אוֹ בֶן־דֹּדוֹ יִגְאָלֶנּוּ אוֹ־מִשְּׁאֵר בְּשָׂרוֹ מִמִּשְׁפַּחְתּוֹ יִגְאָלֶנּוּ אוֹ־
נ הִשִּׂיגָה יָדוֹ וְנִגְאָל: וְחִשַּׁב עִם־קֹנֵהוּ מִשְּׁנַת הִמָּכְרוֹ לוֹ עַד שְׁנַת הַיֹּבֵל
נא וְהָיָה כֶּסֶף מִמְכָּרוֹ בְּמִסְפַּר שָׁנִים כִּימֵי שָׂכִיר יִהְיֶה עִמּוֹ: אִם־עוֹד
נב רַבּוֹת בַּשָּׁנִים לְפִיהֶן יָשִׁיב גְּאֻלָּתוֹ מִכֶּסֶף מִקְנָתוֹ: וְאִם־מְעַט נִשְׁאַר
נג בַּשָּׁנִים עַד־שְׁנַת הַיֹּבֵל וְחִשַּׁב־לוֹ כְּפִי שָׁנָיו יָשִׁיב אֶת־גְּאֻלָּתוֹ: כִּשְׂכִיר
נד שָׁנָה בְּשָׁנָה יִהְיֶה עִמּוֹ לֹא־יִרְדֶּנּוּ בְּפֶרֶךְ לְעֵינֶיךָ: וְאִם־לֹא יִגָּאֵל בְּאֵלֶּה

אונקלוס

וְאַמְהָן: מה וְאַף, מִבְּנֵי תּוֹתָבַיָּא עָרְלַיָּא, דְּדָיְרִין עִמְּכוֹן מִנְּהוֹן תִּקְנוֹן, וּמִזַּרְעִיָּתְהוֹן דְּעִמְּכוֹן, דְּאִתְיְלִדוּ בְּאַרְעֲכוֹן, וִיהוֹן לְכוֹן לְאַחְסָנָא: מו וְתַחְסְנוּן יָתְהוֹן, לִבְנֵיכוֹן בָּתְרֵיכוֹן לְיָרְתַּת אַחְסָנָא, לְעָלַם בְּהוֹן תִּפְלְחוּן, וּבַאֲחֵיכוֹן בְּנֵי יִשְׂרָאֵל גְּבַר בַּאֲחוּהִי, לָא תִפְלַח בֵּיהּ בְּקַשְׁיוּ: מז וַאֲרֵי תַדְבֵּיק, יַד עֲרַל וְתוֹתָב דְּעִמָּךְ, וְיִתְמַסְכַּן אֲחוּךְ עִמֵּיהּ, וְיִזְדַּבַּן, לַעֲרַל תּוֹתָב דְּעִמָּךְ, אוֹ לְאַרְמָאֵי מִזַּרְעִית גִּיּוֹרָא: מח בָּתַר דְּאִזְדַּבַּן, פֻּרְקָנָא תְּהֵי לֵיהּ, חַד מֵאֲחוֹהִי יִפְרְקִנֵּיהּ: מט אוֹ אַחְבּוּהִי, אוֹ בַר אַחְבּוּהִי יִפְרְקִנֵּיהּ, אוֹ מִקָּרִיב בִּסְרֵיהּ, מִזַּרְעִיתֵיהּ יִפְרְקִנֵּיהּ, אוֹ דְתַדְבֵּיק יְדֵיהּ וְיִתְפְּרֵיק: נ וִיחַשֵּׁיב עִם זָבְנֵיהּ, מִשַּׁתָּא דְּאִזְדַּבַּן לֵיהּ, עַד שַׁתָּא דְיוֹבֵילָא, וִיהֵי, כְּסַף זְבִינוֹהִי בְּמִנְיַן שְׁנַיָּא, כְּיוֹמֵי אֲגִירָא יְהֵי עִמֵּיהּ: נא אִם עוֹד סַגִּיוּת בִּשְׁנַיָּא, לְפוּמְהוֹן יָתִיב פֻּרְקָנֵיהּ, מִכְּסַף זְבִינוֹהִי: נב וְאִם זְעֵיר, אִשְׁתְּאַר בִּשְׁנַיָּא, עַד שַׁתָּא דְיוֹבֵילָא וִיחַשֵּׁיב לֵיהּ, כְּפוּם שְׁנוֹהִי, יָתִיב יָת פֻּרְקָנֵיהּ: נג כַּאֲגִיר שְׁנָא, בִּשְׁנָא יְהֵי עִמֵּיהּ, לָא יִפְלַח בֵּיהּ בְּקַשְׁיוּ לְעֵינָךְ: נד וְאִם לָא יִתְפְּרֵיק בְּאִלֵּין,

of freedom (see note on Gen. 5:3). Yet the Torah does not abolish slavery. That is the paradox at the heart of Parashat Behar. Instead, the Torah sets in motion a process that will lead people to come of their own accord to the conclusion that it is wrong. It limits slavery and humanizes it. Every seventh day, slaves are to be granted rest and a taste of freedom. In the seventh year, Israelite slaves are to be set free. If they choose otherwise they are released in the Jubilee year. During their years of service they are to be treated like employees. They are not to be subjected to backbreaking or spirit-crushing labor (v. 43; cf. Ex. 1:13–14 and note on 1:14).

The challenge to which Torah legislation is an answer is: How can one create a social structure in which, of their own accord, people will eventually come to see slavery as wrong and freely choose to abandon it?

55 in any of these ways, he and his children shall be released in the Jubilee year. For MAFTIR
it is to Me that the Israelites are servants. They are My servants whom I brought
26 1 out of the land of Egypt; I am the Lord your God. You shall make no idols,
nor may you erect any divine image or worship pillar. Do not set up any carved
2 stone in your land and bow down to it, for I am the Lord your God. Keep My
Sabbaths, revere My Sanctuary; I am the Lord.

The haftara for Parashat Behar is on page 1576.
When Behar and Beḥukotai are read together, read the haftara on page 1581.

רש״י

נה| **כִּי לִי בְנֵי יִשְׂרָאֵל עֲבָדִים.** שְׁטָרִי קוֹדֵם: **אֲנִי ה׳ אֱלֹהֵיכֶם.** כָּל הַמְשַׁעְבְּדָן מִלְּמַטָּה כְּאִלּוּ מְשַׁעְבֵּד מִלְמַעְלָה:

כו א| **לֹא תַעֲשׂוּ לָכֶם אֱלִילִם.** כְּנֶגֶד זֶה הַנִּמְכָּר לְגוֹי, שֶׁלֹּא יֹאמַר: הוֹאִיל וְרַבִּי מְגַלֶּה עֲרָיוֹת אַף אֲנִי כְּמוֹתוֹ, הוֹאִיל וְרַבִּי עוֹבֵד עֲבוֹדָה זָרָה אַף אֲנִי כְּמוֹתוֹ, הוֹאִיל וְרַבִּי מְחַלֵּל שַׁבָּת אַף אֲנִי כְּמוֹתוֹ, לְכָךְ נֶאֶמְרוּ מִקְרָאוֹת הַלָּלוּ. וְאַף הַפָּרָשִׁיּוֹת הַלָּלוּ נֶאֶמְרוּ עַל הַסֵּדֶר: בַּתְּחִלָּה הִזְהִיר עַל הַשְּׁבִיעִית, וְאִם חָמַד מָמוֹן וְנֶחְשַׁד עַל הַשְּׁבִיעִית סוֹפוֹ לִמְכֹּר מִטַּלְטְלָיו, לְכָךְ סָמַךְ לָהּ: ״וְכִי תִמְכְּרוּ מִמְכָּר״ (לעיל כה, יד). לֹא חָזַר בּוֹ, סוֹף מוֹכֵר אֲחֻזָּתוֹ. לֹא חָזַר בּוֹ, סוֹף מוֹכֵר אֶת בֵּיתוֹ. לֹא חָזַר בּוֹ, סוֹף לוֹוֶה בְּרִבִּית. כָּל אֵלּוּ הָאַחֲרוֹנוֹת קָשׁוֹת מִן הָרִאשׁוֹנוֹת. לֹא חָזַר בּוֹ, סוֹף מוֹכֵר אֶת עַצְמוֹ. לֹא חָזַר בּוֹ, לֹא דַיּוֹ לְיִשְׂרָאֵל אֶלָּא אֲפִלּוּ לְגוֹי: **וְאֶבֶן מַשְׂכִּית.** לְשׁוֹן כִּסּוּי, כְּמוֹ: ״וְשַׂכֹּתִי כַפִּי״ (שמות לג, כב), שֶׁמְּכַסִּין הַקַּרְקַע בְּרִצְפַּת אֲבָנִים: **לְהִשְׁתַּחֲוֹת עָלֶיהָ.** אֲפִלּוּ לַשָּׁמַיִם, לְפִי שֶׁהִשְׁתַּחֲוָאָה בְּפִשּׁוּט יָדַיִם וְרַגְלַיִם הִיא, וְאָסְרָה תּוֹרָה לַעֲשׂוֹת כֵּן חוּץ מִן הַמִּקְדָּשׁ:

ב| **אֲנִי ה׳.** נֶאֱמָן לְשַׁלֵּם שָׂכָר:

respond. He stayed sane by conducting himself as a free man even when all his external freedoms had been taken away.

To be free is to refuse to be defined by circumstance. It is about the action that is not reaction. Our ability to see and do the unexpected is the link between human creativity and freedom. Wittgenstein once said that his aim as a philosopher was "to show the fly the way out of the fly bottle." The fly keeps banging its head against the glass in a vain attempt to get out. The more it tires, the more it fails, until it dies in exhaustion. The one thing it forgets to do is to look up.

The main task of our *parasha* has been to safeguard the functional freedom of those most vulnerable to losing it. Here, however, it reminds us of the deeper significance and responsibility inherent in our own ontological freedom.

נה וְיָצָא בִּשְׁנַת הַיֹּבֵל הוּא וּבָנָיו עִמּוֹ: כִּי־לִי בְנֵי־יִשְׂרָאֵל עֲבָדִים עֲבָדַי מפטיר
כו א הֵם אֲשֶׁר־הוֹצֵאתִי אוֹתָם מֵאֶרֶץ מִצְרָיִם אֲנִי יְהוָה אֱלֹהֵיכֶם: לֹא־
תַעֲשׂוּ לָכֶם אֱלִילִם וּפֶסֶל וּמַצֵּבָה לֹא־תָקִימוּ לָכֶם וְאֶבֶן מַשְׂכִּית לֹא
ב תִתְּנוּ בְּאַרְצְכֶם לְהִשְׁתַּחֲוֺת עָלֶיהָ כִּי אֲנִי יְהוָה אֱלֹהֵיכֶם: אֶת־שַׁבְּתֹתַי
תִּשְׁמֹרוּ וּמִקְדָּשִׁי תִּירָאוּ אֲנִי יְהוָה:

The הפטרה *for* פרשת בהר *is on page page 1577.*
When בהר *and* בחקתי*, read the* הפטרה *on page page 1581.*

אונקלוס

וְיִפּוֹק בְּשַׁתָּא דְיוֹבֵילָא, הוּא וּבְנוֹהִי עִמֵּיהּ: נה אֲרֵי דִילִי בְּנֵי יִשְׂרָאֵל עַבְדִין, עַבְדַי אִנּוּן, דְּאַפֵּיקִית יָתְהוֹן מֵאַרְעָא דְמִצְרָיִם, אֲנָא יי אֱלָהֲכוֹן: כו א לָא תַעְבְּדוּן לְכוֹן טָעֲוָן, וְצֵילֶם וְקָמָא לָא תְקִימוּן לְכוֹן, וְאֶבֶן סִגְדָּא, לָא תִתְּנוּן בְּאַרְעֲכוֹן, לְמִסְגַּד עֲלַהּ, אֲרֵי, אֲנָא יי אֱלָהֲכוֹן: ב יָת יוֹמֵי שַׁבַּיָּא דִילִי תִּטְּרוּן, וּלְבֵית מַקְדְּשִׁי תְּהוֹן דָּחֲלִין, אֲנָא יי:

25:55 כִּי־לִי בְנֵי־יִשְׂרָאֵל עֲבָדִים *For it is to Me that the Israelites are servants* – The Talmud completes the phrase: "For it is to Me that the Israelites are servants; they may not be slaves to slaves" (Bava Metzia 10a). We may not willingly forgo our own freedom. The Midrash (Sifra, Behar 9:6) links the final verses of the *parasha* (Lev. 26:2) to the case of the Jew enslaved to a non-Jew: "He should not say, 'Since my master breaks the Sabbath, I too shall break the Sabbath' – so it says, 'Keep My Sabbaths, revere My Sanctuary; I am the LORD': I am faithful to pay your reward." It may be wishful thinking to imagine a slave able to assert his right to rest on the Sabbath – but it is also a statement of principle.

The idea was perhaps given its most powerful expression by the late Viktor Frankl, a survivor of Auschwitz who, on the basis of his experiences there, founded a new school of psychotherapy. He said that in the camps, they took away everything that made us human except the one thing that can never be taken away – the freedom to decide how to

Parashat Beḥukotai

26 3/4 If you follow My decrees, keep My commands, and fulfill them, then I shall give
you rain in its due time. The land shall yield its crops and the trees of the field
5 shall yield their fruit. Your threshing season shall last until the grape harvest;
the grape harvest shall last until sowing time. You shall eat your bread to the
6 full and live securely in your land. And I will grant peace in the land; when you SHENI
lie down, no one will make you afraid. I will cause dangerous animals to cease

רש״י

ג אִם בְּחֻקֹּתַי תֵּלֵכוּ. יָכוֹל זֶה קִיּוּם הַמִּצְוֹת? כְּשֶׁהוּא אוֹמֵר: "וְאֶת מִצְוֹתַי תִּשְׁמְרוּ" הֲרֵי קִיּוּם הַמִּצְוֹת אָמוּר, הָא מָה אֲנִי מְקַיֵּם: "אִם בְּחֻקֹּתַי תֵּלֵכוּ"? שֶׁתִּהְיוּ עֲמֵלִים בַּתּוֹרָה: וְאֶת מִצְוֹתַי תִּשְׁמְרוּ. הֱווּ עֲמֵלִים בַּתּוֹרָה עַל מְנָת לִשְׁמֹר וּלְקַיֵּם, כְּמוֹ שֶׁנֶּאֱמַר: "וּלְמַדְתֶּם אֹתָם וּשְׁמַרְתֶּם לַעֲשֹׂתָם" (דברים ה, א):

ד בְּעִתָּם. בְּשָׁעָה שֶׁאֵין דֶּרֶךְ בְּנֵי אָדָם לָצֵאת, כְּגוֹן בְּלֵילֵי שַׁבָּתוֹת: וְעֵץ הַשָּׂדֶה. הֵן אִילָנֵי סְרָק, וַעֲתִידִין לַעֲשׂוֹת פֵּרוֹת:

ה וְהִשִּׂיג לָכֶם דַּיִשׁ אֶת בָּצִיר. שֶׁיְּהֵא הַדַּיִשׁ מְרֻבֶּה וְאַתֶּם עֲסוּקִים בּוֹ עַד הַבָּצִיר, וּבַבָּצִיר תַּעַסְקוּ עַד שְׁעַת הַזֶּרַע: וַאֲכַלְתֶּם לַחְמְכֶם לָשֹׂבַע. אוֹכֵל קִמְעָא וְהוּא מִתְבָּרֵךְ בְּמֵעָיו:

ו וְנָתַתִּי שָׁלוֹם. שֶׁמָּא תֹּאמְרוּ: הֲרֵי מַאֲכָל וַהֲרֵי מִשְׁתֶּה, אִם אֵין שָׁלוֹם אֵין כְּלוּם! תַּלְמוּד לוֹמַר אַחַר כָּל זֹאת: "וְנָתַתִּי שָׁלוֹם בָּאָרֶץ", מִכָּאן שֶׁהַשָּׁלוֹם שָׁקוּל כְּנֶגֶד הַכֹּל, וְכֵן הוּא אוֹמֵר: "עוֹשֶׂה שָׁלוֹם וּבוֹרֵא אֶת

yield its fruit, there will be peace, the people will flourish, they will have children, and the Divine Presence will be in their midst. God will make them free.

Covenantal politics is moral politics, driving an elemental connection between the fate of a nation and its vocation. It sees nothing inevitable or even natural about the fate of a people. Israel will not follow the usual laws of the rise and fall of civilizations. Instead, it will be utterly dependent on moral considerations. If Israel stays true to its mission, it will flourish. If it drifts from its vocation, it will suffer.

In this model, statehood is a matter not of power but of ethical responsibility. One might have thought that this kind of politics robbed a nation of its freedom. Spinoza argued just this. "This, then, was the object of the ceremonial law," he wrote, "that men should do nothing of their own free will, but should always act under external authority, and should continually confess by their actions and thoughts that they were not their own masters" (*Tractatus Theologico-Politicus*). However, in this respect, Spinoza was wrong.

Covenant theology is emphatically a politics of liberty. I brought you from slavery to freedom, says God, and I empower you to be free. I will not intervene in your choices, but will instruct you on what choices you ought to make and teach you the constitution of liberty.

The first and most important principle is this: A nation cannot worship itself and survive. Sooner or later, power will corrupt those who wield it. If fortune favors it and it grows rich, it will become self-indulgent and eventually decadent. Its citizens will no longer have the courage to fight for their liberty, and it will fall to another, more Spartan power.

To stay free, a nation must worship something greater than itself, nothing less than God, and must believe that all human beings are created in His image. It rests on the choice Moshe is later to define in these words: "I call heaven and earth as witnesses against you today: I have set before you life and death, the blessing and the curse. Choose life – so that you and your children may live" (Deut. 30:19).

26:6 **וְנָתַתִּי שָׁלוֹם** *I will grant peace* – Against the backdrop of the economic legislation in Parashat Behar, we are reminded that human interaction is not inescapably tragic. It is not destined to be agonistic, conflictual, a matter of victory for some and defeat for others. Market exchange turns difference into a form of blessing from which not only I, but

פרשת בחקתי

כו ג ד אִם־בְּחֻקֹּתַי תֵּלֵכוּ וְאֶת־מִצְוֺתַי תִּשְׁמְרוּ וַעֲשִׂיתֶם אֹתָם׃ וְנָתַתִּי גִשְׁמֵיכֶם כב
ה בְּעִתָּם וְנָתְנָה הָאָרֶץ יְבוּלָהּ וְעֵץ הַשָּׂדֶה יִתֵּן פִּרְיוֹ׃ וְהִשִּׂיג לָכֶם דַּיִשׁ
אֶת־בָּצִיר וּבָצִיר יַשִּׂיג אֶת־זָרַע וַאֲכַלְתֶּם לַחְמְכֶם לָשֹׂבַע וִישַׁבְתֶּם
ו לָבֶטַח בְּאַרְצְכֶם׃ וְנָתַתִּי שָׁלוֹם בָּאָרֶץ וּשְׁכַבְתֶּם וְאֵין מַחֲרִיד וְהִשְׁבַּתִּי שני

אונקלוס

ג אִם בִּקְיָמַי תְּהָכוּן, וְיָת פִּקּוֹדַי תִּטְּרוּן, וְתַעְבְּדוּן יָתְהוֹן: ד וְאֶתֵּין מִטְרֵיכוֹן בְּעִדָּנְהוֹן, וְתִתֵּין אַרְעָא עֲלַלְתַּהּ, וְאִילָן חַקְלָא יִתֵּין אִבֵּיהּ: ה וִיעָרַע לְכוֹן דְּיָשָׁא לִקְטָפָא, וּקְטָפָא יְעָרַע לְאַפּוֹקֵי בַּר זַרְעָא, וְתֵיכְלוּן לַחְמְכוֹן לְמִסְבַּע, וְתִתְּבוּן לְרוּחְצָן בְּאַרְעֲכוֹן: ו וְאֶתֵּין שְׁלָמָא בְּאַרְעָא, וְתִשְׁרוּן וְלֵית דְּמָנִיד, וַאֲבַטֵּיל,

BEḤUKOTAI

This *parasha* is dominated by the passage in which God speaks of the blessings that will be experienced by the Israelites if they are faithful to the covenant and of the curses they will encounter if they are not. The blessings in Parashat Beḥukotai are brief and serene. The curses, by contrast, are long and terrifying. If Israel loses its way spiritually, say the curses, it will lose it physically, economically, and politically also. The nation will experience defeat and disaster. It will forfeit its freedom and its land. The perennial choice between blessing and curse that lies at the heart of Judaism creates a profound ethic of responsibility. So, in a strange way, belief in curses creates blessings.

At the end of the curses, there is a sudden change of key. God promises that even if Israel sins, it may suffer, but it will never die. Israel may betray the covenant but God never will.

26:3 אִם־בְּחֻקֹּתַי תֵּלֵכוּ *If you follow My decrees* – This *parasha*, like Parashat Behar, was stated "on Mount Sinai" (Lev. 27:34), continuing the Sinai revelation after the long insertion of the priestly code (see note on Lev. 25:1). This section is about the blessings and curses that come with the covenant: blessings if the people obey, curses if they do not. We know now, thanks to intensive study by scholars of the ancient Near East, that the covenant the Israelites made with God at Sinai was similar in form if not in substance to the suzerainty treaties of the time – peace agreements between two states, one strong, the other weak. These covenants had a highly formalized structure: preamble, historical prologue, then the terms and conditions, first in general terms and then in specific details. Witnesses are named. Provision is made for the deposition of the treaty and for regular public readings.

An essential element of these treaties was the reward for compliance and the punishment that would follow any breach. Even if we did not know this from the historical record we would know it from the book of Deuteronomy, which is structured as a covenant on a massive scale and which, near the end, details the rewards and punishments in a passage parallel to this one. The closing words of Leviticus – "These are the commands that the Lord gave Moshe" (27:34) – are in fact the closing words of the covenantal revelation at Sinai.

COVENANTAL POLITICS

This chapter sets out, with great clarity, the terms of Jewish life under the covenant. It opens with an idyllic picture of the blessing of divine favor: If Israel follows God's decrees and keeps His commands, there will be rain, the earth will

7 in the land, and through that land no sword shall pass. You shall chase your
8 enemies, and they shall fall before you by the sword. Five of you shall chase away
a hundred, and a hundred of you shall put ten thousand to flight; your enemies
9 shall fall before you by the sword. I will turn to you and make you fruitful, make
10 you numerous, and I will uphold My covenant with you. You shall eat the grain SHELISHI /ḤAMISHI/
11 of long ago and take the old grain out to make space for all the new. I shall set
12 My dwelling among you, and I shall not despise you; I shall walk among you. I
13 shall be your God, and you shall be My people. I am the LORD your God, who
brought you out of Egypt, to be their slaves no more. I broke the bars of your
yoke and led you to walk with your heads held high.
14 But if you do not listen to Me and do not carry out all these commands – if
15 you spurn My decrees and despise My laws, not keeping all My commands;

רש״י

הכל״ (על פי ישעיה מה, ז): **וחרב לא תעבר בארצכם.** אין צריך לומר שלא יבואו למלחמה, אלא אפילו לעבר דרך ארצכם ממדינה למדינה:

ז **לפניכם לחרב.** איש בחרב רעהו:

ח **ורדפו מכם.** מן החלשים שבכם ולא מן הגבורים שבכם: **חמשה מאה ומאה מכם רבבה.** וכי כך הוא החשבון? והלא לא היה צריך לומר אלא ׳ומאה מכם שני אלפים ירדפו׳! אלא אינו דומה מועטין העושין את התורה למרבין העושין את התורה: **ונפלו איביכם וגו׳.** שיהיו נופלין לפניכם שלא כדרך הארץ:

ט **ופניתי אליכם.** אפנה מכל עסקי לשלם שכרכם. משל למה הדבר דומה? למלך ששכר פועלים וכו׳ [הרבה, והיה שם פועל אחד ועשה עמו מלאכה ימים הרבה. נכנסו הפועלים ליטול שכרם ונכנס אותו הפועל עמהם. אמר לו המלך לאותו הפועל: בני, אפנה לך, הרובים הללו שעשו עמי מלאכה ממועטת ואני נותן להם שכר מועט, אבל את – חשבון רב אני עתיד לחשב עמך], כדאיתא בתורת כהנים (ת״כ פרק ב, ה): **והפריתי אתכם.** בפריה ורביה: **והרביתי אתכם.** בקומה זקופה: **והקימתי את בריתי אתכם.** ברית חדשה, לא כברית הראשונה שהפרתם אותה אלא ברית חדשה שלא תופר, שנאמר: ״וכרתי את בית ישראל ואת בית יהודה ברית חדשה... לא כברית״ וגו׳ (ירמיה לא, ל-לא):

י **ואכלתם ישן נושן.** הפרות יהיו משתמרין וטובים להתישן, שיהא ישן הנושן של שלש שנים יפה לאכל משל אשתקד: **וישן מפני חדש תוציאו.** שיהיו הגרנות מלאות חדש והאוצרות מלאות ישן, וצריכים אתם לפנות האוצרות למקום אחר לתת החדש לתוכן:

יא **ונתתי משכני.** זה בית המקדש: **ולא תגעל נפשי.** אין רוחי קצה בכם. כל ׳געילה׳ לשון פליטת דבר הבלוע בדבר, כמו: ״כי שם נגעל מגן גבורים״ (שמואל ב׳ א, כא), לא קבל המשיחה, שמושחין מגן של עור בחלב מבשל כדי להחליק מעליו מכת חץ או חנית, שלא יקב העור:

יב **והתהלכתי בתוככם.** אטייל עמכם בגן עדן כאחד מכם ולא תהיו מזדעזעים ממני. יכול לא תיראו ממני? תלמוד לומר: ״והייתי לכם לאלהים״:

יג **אני ה׳ אלהיכם.** כדאי אני שתאמינו בי שאני יכול לעשות כל אלה, שהרי ״הוצאתי אתכם מארץ מצרים״ ועשיתי לכם נסים גדולים: **מטת.** כמין יתד בשני ראשי העל המעכבים המוסרה שלא תצא מראש השור ויתיר הקשר, כמו: ״עשה לך מוסרות ומטות״ (ירמיה כז, ב), קוניוגל״א בלעז: **קוממיות.** בקומה זקופה:

יד **ואם לא תשמעו לי.** להיות עמלים בתורה ולדעת מדרש חכמים. יכול לקיום המצות? כשהוא אומר: ״ולא תעשו״ וגו׳ הרי קיום מצות אמור, הא מה אני מקיים: ״ואם לא תשמעו לי״? להיות עמלים בתורה. ומה תלמוד לומר: ״לי״? אין ״לי״ אלא זה המכיר את רבונו ומתכון למרד בו, וכן בנמרוד: ״גבר ציד לפני ה׳״ (בראשית י, ט), שמכירו ומתכון למרד בו, וכן באנשי סדום: ״רעים וחטאים לה׳ מאד״ (שם יג, יג), מכירים את רבונם ומתכונים למרד בו: **ולא תעשו.** משלא תלמדו לא תעשו, הרי שתי עברות:

טו **ואם בחקתי תמאסו.** מואס באחרים העושים: **משפטי תגעל נפשכם.** שונא החכמים: **לבלתי עשות.** מונע את אחרים מעשות:

ז חַיָּה רָעָה מִן־הָאָרֶץ וְחֶרֶב לֹא־תַעֲבֹר בְּאַרְצְכֶם: וּרְדַפְתֶּם אֶת־אֹיְבֵיכֶם
ח וְנָפְלוּ לִפְנֵיכֶם לֶחָרֶב: וְרָדְפוּ מִכֶּם חֲמִשָּׁה מֵאָה וּמֵאָה מִכֶּם רְבָבָה
ט יִרְדֹּפוּ וְנָפְלוּ אֹיְבֵיכֶם לִפְנֵיכֶם לֶחָרֶב: וּפָנִיתִי אֲלֵיכֶם וְהִפְרֵיתִי אֶתְכֶם
י וְהִרְבֵּיתִי אֶתְכֶם וַהֲקִימֹתִי אֶת־בְּרִיתִי אִתְּכֶם: וַאֲכַלְתֶּם יָשָׁן נוֹשָׁן וְיָשָׁן שלישי /חמישי/
יא מִפְּנֵי חָדָשׁ תּוֹצִיאוּ: וְנָתַתִּי מִשְׁכָּנִי בְּתוֹכְכֶם וְלֹא־תִגְעַל נַפְשִׁי אֶתְכֶם:
יב וְהִתְהַלַּכְתִּי בְּתוֹכְכֶם וְהָיִיתִי לָכֶם לֵאלֹהִים וְאַתֶּם תִּהְיוּ־לִי לְעָם:
יג אֲנִי יְהוָה אֱלֹהֵיכֶם אֲשֶׁר הוֹצֵאתִי אֶתְכֶם מֵאֶרֶץ מִצְרַיִם מִהְיֹת לָהֶם
עֲבָדִים וָאֶשְׁבֹּר מֹטֹת עֻלְּכֶם וָאוֹלֵךְ אֶתְכֶם קוֹמְמִיּוּת:
יד טו וְאִם־לֹא תִשְׁמְעוּ לִי וְלֹא תַעֲשׂוּ אֵת כָּל־הַמִּצְוֹת הָאֵלֶּה: וְאִם־בְּחֻקֹּתַי
תִּמְאָסוּ וְאִם אֶת־מִשְׁפָּטַי תִּגְעַל נַפְשְׁכֶם לְבִלְתִּי עֲשׂוֹת אֶת־כָּל־

אונקלוס

חַיְתָא בִּשְׁתָּא מִן אַרְעָא, וּדְקָטְלִין בְּחַרְבָּא לָא יִעְדּוֹן בְּאַרְעֲכוֹן: ז וְתִרְדְּפוּן יָת בַּעֲלֵי דְּבָבֵיכוֹן, וְיִפְּלוּן קֳדָמֵיכוֹן לְחַרְבָּא: ח וְיִרְדְּפוּן מִנְּכוֹן חַמְשָׁא לִמְאָה, וּמְאָה מִנְּכוֹן לְרִבּוֹתָא יְעָרְקוּן, וְיִפְּלוּן בַּעֲלֵי דְּבָבֵיכוֹן, קֳדָמֵיכוֹן לְחַרְבָּא: ט וְאֶתְפְּנֵי בְּמֵימְרִי לְאֵיטָבָא לְכוֹן, וְאַפֵּישׁ יָתְכוֹן, וְאַסְגֵּי יָתְכוֹן, וַאֲקֵים יָת קְיָמִי עִמְּכוֹן: י וְתֵיכְלוּן עַתִּיקָא דְּעַתִּיק, וְעַתִּיקָא, מִן קֳדָם חֲדַתָּא תְּפַנּוֹן: יא וְאֶתֵּין מַשְׁכְּנִי בֵּינֵיכוֹן, וְלָא יְרַחֵיק מֵימְרִי יָתְכוֹן: יב וְאַשְׁרֵי שְׁכִינְתִּי בֵּינֵיכוֹן, וְאֶהֱוֵי לְכוֹן לֶאֱלָהּ, וְאַתּוּן תְּהוֹן קֳדָמַי לְעַם: יג אֲנָא יי אֱלָהֲכוֹן, דְּאַפֵּיקִית יָתְכוֹן מֵאַרְעָא דְּמִצְרַיִם, מִלְּמֶהֱוֵי לְהוֹן עַבְדִּין, וְתַבָּרִית נִיר עַמְמַיָּא מִנְּכוֹן, וְדַבָּרִית יָתְכוֹן בְּחֵירוּתָא: יד וְאִם לָא תְקַבְּלוּן לְמֵימְרִי, וְלָא תַעְבְּדוּן, יָת כָּל פִּקּוֹדַיָּא הָאִלֵּין: טו וְאִם בִּקְיָמַי תְּקוּצוּן, וְאִם יָת דִּינַי תְּרַחֵיק נַפְשְׁכוֹן, בְּדִיל דְּלָא לְמֶעְבַּד יָת כָּל

others also, benefit. It follows organically that when the people of Israel obey the laws of fair exchange, and are blessed with abundant harvest, "I will grant peace in the land."

This is in large part what differentiated biblical sensibility from that of ancient Greece. The fact that – individually, collectively, culturally – we are different can have two outcomes. It can lead to war, or it can lead to trade. Greece, with its military virtues, valued the manly arts of war. Jews, with their deep experience of suffering and exile, learned early to prefer peace.

THE CURSES

This passage – traditionally known as the *tokheḥa,* "the admonition" – is one of the most terrifying passages in literature. To this day we read it sotto voce, so fearful is it and so difficult to internalize and imagine. It is all the more fearful given what we know of later Jewish history. The repeated phrases – "If in spite of all this…" "If you still…" "If despite all this…" – come like hammerblows of fate.

Why are the curses almost three times as long as the blessings that precede them? The answer is not because God seeks to punish. The Talmud tells us that God weeps when He allows disaster to strike His people: "Woe to Me, that due to their sins I destroyed My House, burned My Temple and exiled them [My children] among the nations of the world" (Berakhot 3a). The curses are meant as a warning. They are intended to deter, scare, discourage.

Social scientists argue that bad has far more impact on

16 violating My covenant – then I will do this to you: I will appoint over you terror,
consumption, and fever, which make your eyes fail and your spirit languish. In
17 vain shall you sow your seed, for your enemies will eat its yield. I shall set My
face against you. You will be struck down before your enemies. Those who hate
18 you will rule over you; you will flee, though no one chases you. And if, in spite
of all this, you still will not listen to Me, I shall punish you seven times over for

רש"י

את כל מצותי. כופר שלא צויתים, לכך נאמר: "את כל מצותי" ולא נאמר 'את כל המצות': **להפרכם את בריתי.** כופר בעקר. הרי שבע עברות, הראשונה גוררת השניה וכן עד השביעית, ואלו הן: לא למד, ולא עשה, מואס באחרים העושים, שונא את החכמים, מונע את האחרים מעשות, כופר במצות, כופר בעקר:

טז **והפקדתי עליכם.** וצויתי עליכם: **שחפת.** חולי שמשחף את הבשר, אנפולי"ש בלעז, דומה לנפוח שהוקלה נפיחתו, ומראית פניו זעופה: **קדחת.** חולי שמקדיח את הגוף ומחממו ומבעירו, כמו: "כי אש קדחה באפי" (דברים לב, כב): **מכלות עינים ומדיבת נפש.** העינים צופות וכלות לראות שיקל וירפא, וסוף שלא ירפא וידאבו הנפשות של משפחתו במותו. כל תאוה שאינה באה ותוחלת ממשכה קרויה 'כליון עינים': **וזרעתם לריק.** תזרעו ולא תצמח, ואם תצמח "ואכלהו איביכם":

יז **ונתתי פני.** פנאי שלי, פונה אני מכל עסקי להרע לכם: **ורדו בכם שנאיכם.** כמשמעו, ישלטו בכם:

אגדת תורת כהנים מפרשה זו: **אף אני אעשה זאת.** איני מדבר אלא באף, וכן: "והלכתי אף אני עמכם בקרי" (להלן פסוק כד): **והפקדתי עליכם.** שיהיו המכות פוקדות אתכם מזו לזו, עד שהראשונה פקודה אצלכם תביא אחרת ואסמכנה לה: **בהלה.** מכה המבהלת את הבריות, ואי זו? זו מכת מותן: **את השחפת.** יש לך אדם שהוא חולה ומטל במטה אבל בשרו שמור עליו, תלמוד לומר: "שחפת" שהוא נשחף. או עתים שהוא נשחף אבל נוח ואינו מקדיח, תלמוד לומר: "ואת הקדחת", מלמד שהוא מקדיח. או עתים שהוא מקדיח וסבור הוא בעצמו שיחיה, תלמוד לומר: "מכלות עינים". או הוא אינו סבור בעצמו שיחיה אבל אחרים סבורים שיחיה, תלמוד לומר: "ומדיבת נפש" (לעיל פסוק טז): **וזרעתם לריק זרעכם.** זורעה ואינה מצמחת, ומעתה מה אויביכם באים ואוכלים, ומה תלמוד לומר "ואכלהו איביכם"? הא כיצד? זורעה שנה ראשונה ואינה מצמחת, שנה שניה מצמחת, ואויבים באים ומוצאים תבואה לימי המצור, ושבפנים מתים ברעב שלא לקטו תבואה אשתקד. דבר אחר: "וזרעתם לריק זרעכם", כנגד הבנים והבנות הכתוב מדבר, שאתה עמל בהם ומגדלן והחטא בא ומכלה אותם, שנאמר: "אשר טפחתי ורביתי איבי כלם" (איכה ב, כב): **ונתתי פני בכם.** כמו שנאמר בטובה: "ופניתי אליכם", כך נאמר ברעה: "ונתתי פני". משלו משל, למלך שאמר לעבדיו: פונה אני מכל עסקי ועוסק אני עמכם לרעה: **ונגפתם לפני איביכם.** שיהא המות הורג אתכם מבפנים ובעלי דבביכון מקיפין אתכם מבחוץ: **ורדו בכם שנאיכם.** שאיני מעמיד שונאים אלא מכם ובכם, שבשעה שאמות העולם עומדים על ישראל אינם מבקשים אלא מה שבגלוי, שנאמר: "והיה אם זרע ישראל ועלה מדין ועמלק ובני קדם וגו' ויחנו עליהם וישחיתו את יבול הארץ" (שופטים ו, ג-ד), אבל בשעה שאעמיד עליכם מכם ובכם, הם מחפשים אחר המטמוניות שלכם, וכן הוא אומר: "ואשר אכלו שאר עמי ועורם מעליהם הפשיטו" וגו' (מיכה ג, ג): **ונסתם.** מפני אימה: **ואין רדף אתכם.** מבלי כח:

יח **ואם עד אלה.** ואם בעוד אלה לא תשמעו: **ויספתי.** עוד יסורין אחרים: **שבע על חטאתיכם.** שבע פרעניות על שבע עברות האמורות למעלה:

oneself. Someone else is to blame. The attraction of this logic can be overpowering. It calls for, and often evokes, compassion. It is, however, deeply destructive. It leads people to see themselves as objects, not subjects. The results are anger, resentment, rage, and a burning sense of injustice. None of these ever leads to freedom, since by its very logic this mindset abdicates responsibility for the current circumstances in which one finds oneself. Blaming others is the suicide of liberty.

Blaming oneself, by contrast, is difficult. It means living with constant self-criticism. It is not a route to peace of mind. Yet it is profoundly empowering. It implies that, precisely because we accept responsibility for the bad things that have happened, we also have the ability to chart a different course in the future. Within the terms set by covenant, the outcome depends on us.

טז מִצְוֺתַי לְהַפְרְכֶם אֶת־בְּרִיתִי: אַף־אֲנִי אֶעֱשֶׂה־זֹּאת לָכֶם וְהִפְקַדְתִּי
עֲלֵיכֶם בֶּהָלָה אֶת־הַשַּׁחֶפֶת וְאֶת־הַקַּדַּחַת מְכַלּוֹת עֵינַיִם וּמְדִיבֹת
יז נָפֶשׁ וּזְרַעְתֶּם לָרִיק זַרְעֲכֶם וַאֲכָלֻהוּ אֹיְבֵיכֶם: וְנָתַתִּי פָנַי בָּכֶם וְנִגַּפְתֶּם
יח לִפְנֵי אֹיְבֵיכֶם וְרָדוּ בָכֶם שֹׂנְאֵיכֶם וְנַסְתֶּם וְאֵין־רֹדֵף אֶתְכֶם: וְאִם־עַד־
אֵלֶּה לֹא תִשְׁמְעוּ לִי וְיָסַפְתִּי לְיַסְּרָה אֶתְכֶם שֶׁבַע עַל־חַטֹּאתֵיכֶם:

אונקלוס

פִּקּוֹדַי, לְאַשְׁנָיוּתְכוֹן יָת קְיָמִי: טז אַף אֲנָא אַעֲבֵיד דָּא לְכוֹן, וְאַסְעַר עֲלֵיכוֹן בְּיַהֲלְתָא שַׁחֶפְתָּא וְקַדַּחְתָּא, מַחְשְׁכָן עַיְנִין וּמַפְּחָן נְפַשׁ, וְתִזְרְעוּן לְרֵיקָנוּ זַרְעֲכוֹן, וְיֵיכְלֻנֵּיהּ בַּעֲלֵי דְּבָבֵיכוֹן: יז וְאֶתֵּין רָגְזִי בְּכוֹן, וְתִתַּבְרוּן קֳדָם בַּעֲלֵי דְבָבֵיכוֹן, וְיִרְדּוֹן בְּכוֹן סָנְאֵיכוֹן, וְתֵעַרְקוּן וְלֵית דְּרָדֵיף יָתְכוֹן: יח וְאִם עַד אִלֵּין, לָא תְקַבְּלוּן לְמֵימְרִי, וְאוֹסֵיף לְמִרְדֵּי יָתְכוֹן, שְׁבַע עַל חוֹבֵיכוֹן: יט וְאֶתְבַּר יָת יְקָר תָּקְפְּכוֹן, וְאֶתֵּין יָת שְׁמַיָּא דְּעִלָּוֵיכוֹן תַּקִּיפִין כְּבַרְזְלָא מִלְּאַחֲתָא מִטְרָא, וְאַרְעָא דִּתְחוֹתֵיכוֹן חֲסִינָא כִּנְחָשָׁא מִלְּמֶעֱבַד פֵּירִין: כ וְיִסּוֹף לְרֵיקָנוּ חֵילְכוֹן, וְלָא תִתֵּין

us than good. We pay more attention to bad news than good news. Bad health makes more difference to us than good health. Criticism affects us more than praise. Humans are designed to take notice of and rapidly react to threat. Failing to notice a lion is more dangerous than failing to notice a ripened fruit on a tree. Recognizing the kindness of a friend is good and virtuous, but not as significant as ignoring the animosity of an enemy. One traitor can betray an entire nation.

It follows that the stick is a more powerful motivator than the carrot. Fear of the curse is more likely to affect behavior than desire for the blessing.

The central question to which the Torah is the answer is: can there be a society of law-governed liberty, in which the rule of law prevails without the use of human force, in which the rich honor their responsibilities to the poor, justice is impartial, and the principles of welfare are such that extremes of poverty are eliminated? Such is the vision behind the covenant society inaugurated at Mount Sinai. It was essential, therefore, that the promise of reward and the threat of punishment be sufficiently powerful to have an impact on the people as a whole, for it was they who bore responsibility for the fate of the nation. They had to secure the rule of law without relying on a liberty-restricting government to do it for them.

The more people believe that God punishes wrongdoers, the less likely they are to cheat their fellow human beings when no one else is looking. When given the opportunity to punish someone violating a social norm, empirical research finds that believers in a punitive God are less likely to do so than others. In other words, belief that God will punish offenders makes people more forgiving.

The more we internalize the idea that we are accountable to Heaven for what we do, the less likely we are to give way to temptation by cheating or bending the rules. The more social institutions can rely on trust, the less they have to rely on laws, police, regulations, surveillance, and punishment as deterrence. So, in a strange way, belief in curses creates blessings. It gives people the strongest possible motive for self-restraint, promotes trust in society, and secures order while minimizing external constraints on freedom.

26:18 וְאִם־עַד־אֵלֶּה לֹא תִשְׁמְעוּ לִי *And if, in spite of all this, you still will not listen to Me* – In the face of suffering and loss, there are two fundamentally different questions an individual or nation can ask, and they lead to quite different outcomes. The first is "What did I, or we, do wrong?" The second is "Who did this to us?" It is not an exaggeration to say that this is the fundamental choice governing the destinies of people.

The latter leads inescapably to what is today known as the victim culture. It locates the source of evil outside

19 your sins. I will break down the majesty of your power. I will make your sky like
20 iron, your land like brass. Your strength will be spent in vain. Your land will not
21 yield its produce, nor the trees of the land their fruit. If you still walk contrary
to Me and refuse to listen to Me, I will strike you seven times over for your sins:
22 I will send wild animals against you. They will bereave you of your children and
annihilate your cattle. They will make you few in number and your roads will be
23 deserted. If, despite all this, you still do not accept My discipline and still you
24 walk contrary to Me, then I too will walk contrary to you and strike you seven
25 times over for your sins. I will bring a sword against you to avenge the broken
covenant. If you retreat into your cities, I shall send pestilence against you, and
26 you will be delivered up into your enemy's hand. When I cut off your supply of
bread, ten women shall bake bread in a single oven. They will ration it out by

רש״י

יט **וְשָׁבַרְתִּי אֶת גְּאוֹן עֻזְּכֶם.** זֶה בֵּית הַמִּקְדָּשׁ, וְכֵן הוּא אוֹמֵר: "הִנְנִי מְחַלֵּל אֶת מִקְדָּשִׁי גְּאוֹן עֻזְּכֶם" (יחזקאל כד, כא): **וְנָתַתִּי אֶת שְׁמֵיכֶם כַּבַּרְזֶל וְאֶת אַרְצְכֶם כַּנְּחֻשָׁה.** זוֹ קָשָׁה מִשֶּׁל מֹשֶׁה, שֶׁשָּׁם הוּא אוֹמֵר: "וְהָיוּ שָׁמֶיךָ אֲשֶׁר עַל רֹאשְׁךָ נְחֹשֶׁת" וְגוֹ' (דברים כח, כג), שֶׁיִּהְיוּ הַשָּׁמַיִם מַזִּיעִין כְּדֶרֶךְ שֶׁהַנְּחֹשֶׁת מַזִּיעָה, וְהָאָרֶץ אֵינָהּ מַזִּיעָה כְּדֶרֶךְ שֶׁאֵין הַבַּרְזֶל מַזִּיעַ וְהִיא מְשַׁמֶּרֶת פֵּרוֹתֶיהָ; אֲבָל כָּאן הַשָּׁמַיִם לֹא יִהְיוּ מַזִּיעִין כְּדֶרֶךְ שֶׁאֵין הַבַּרְזֶל מַזִּיעַ וִיהֵא חֹרֶב בָּעוֹלָם, וְהָאָרֶץ תְּהֵא מַזִּיעָה כְּדֶרֶךְ שֶׁהַנְּחֹשֶׁת מַזִּיעָה וְהִיא מְאַבֶּדֶת פֵּרוֹתֶיהָ:

כ **וְתַם לָרִיק כֹּחֲכֶם.** הֲרֵי אָדָם שֶׁלֹּא עָמַל, שֶׁלֹּא חָרַשׁ, שֶׁלֹּא זָרַע, שֶׁלֹּא נִכֵּשׁ, שֶׁלֹּא כִּסַּח, שֶׁלֹּא עִדֵּר, וּבִשְׁעַת הַקָּצִיר בָּא שִׁדָּפוֹן וּמַלְקֶה אוֹתוֹ, אֵין בְּכָךְ כְּלוּם. אֲבָל אָדָם שֶׁעָמַל וְחָרַשׁ וְזָרַע וְנִכֵּשׁ וְכִסַּח וְעִדֵּר, וּבָא שִׁדָּפוֹן וּמַלְקֶה אוֹתוֹ, הֲרֵי שִׁנָּיו שֶׁל זֶה קֵהוֹת: **וְלֹא תִתֵּן אַרְצְכֶם אֶת יְבוּלָהּ.** אַף מַה שֶּׁאַתָּה מוֹבִיל לָהּ בִּשְׁעַת הַזֶּרַע: **וְעֵץ הָאָרֶץ.** אֲפִלּוּ מִן הָאָרֶץ יְהֵא לָקוּי, שֶׁלֹּא יַחֲנִיט פֵּרוֹתָיו בִּשְׁעַת הַחֲנָטָה: **לֹא יִתֵּן.** מְשַׁמֵּשׁ לְמַעְלָה וּלְמַטָּה, אַעֵץ וְאַפְּרִי: **לֹא יִתֵּן פִּרְיוֹ.** כְּשֶׁהוּא מַפְרֶה, מַשִּׁיר פֵּרוֹתָיו – הֲרֵי שְׁתֵּי קְלָלוֹת, וְיֵשׁ כָּאן שֶׁבַע פֻּרְעָנִיּוֹת:

כא **וְאִם תֵּלְכוּ עִמִּי קֶרִי.** רַבּוֹתֵינוּ אָמְרוּ: עֲרַאי, בְּמִקְרֶה, שֶׁאֵינוֹ אֶלָּא לִפְרָקִים, כֵּן תֵּלְכוּ עֲרַאי בַּמִּצְוֹת. וּמְנַחֵם פֵּרַשׁ: לְשׁוֹן מְנִיעָה, וְכֵן "הֹקַר רַגְלְךָ" (משלי כה, יז), וְכֵן "יְקַר רוּחַ" (משלי יז, כז); וְקָרוֹב לָשׁוֹן זֶה לְתַרְגּוּמוֹ שֶׁל אוּנְקְלוֹס, לְשׁוֹן קֹשִׁי, שֶׁמַּקְשִׁים לִבָּם לִמָּנַע מֵהִתְקָרֵב אֵלַי: **שֶׁבַע כְּחַטֹּאתֵיכֶם.** שֶׁבַע פֻּרְעָנִיּוֹת אֲחֵרוֹת בְּמִסְפַּר שֶׁבַע, כְּחַטֹּאתֵיכֶם:

כב **וְהִשְׁלַחְתִּי.** לְשׁוֹן גֵּרוּי: **וְשִׁכְּלָה אֶתְכֶם.** אֵין לִי אֶלָּא חַיָּה מְשַׁכֶּלֶת שֶׁדַּרְכָּהּ בְּכָךְ, בְּהֵמָה שֶׁאֵין דַּרְכָּהּ בְּכָךְ מִנַּיִן? תַּלְמוּד לוֹמַר: "וְשֶׁן בְּהֵמֹת אֲשַׁלַּח בָּם" (דברים לב, כד), הֲרֵי שְׁתַּיִם. וּמִנַּיִן שֶׁתְּהֵא מְמִיתָה בִּנְשִׁיכָתָהּ? תַּלְמוּד לוֹמַר: "עִם חֲמַת זֹחֲלֵי עָפָר" (שם), מָה אֵלּוּ נוֹשְׁכִין וּמְמִיתִין, אַף אֵלּוּ נוֹשְׁכִין וּמְמִיתִין, כְּבָר הָיוּ שָׁנִים בְּאֶרֶץ יִשְׂרָאֵל, חֲמוֹר נוֹשֵׁךְ וּמֵמִית, עָרוֹד נוֹשֵׁךְ וּמֵמִית: **וְשִׁכְּלָה אֶתְכֶם.** אֵלּוּ הַקְּטַנִּים: **וְהִכְרִיתָה אֶת בְּהֶמְתְּכֶם.** מִבַּחוּץ: **וְהִמְעִיטָה אֶתְכֶם.** מִבִּפְנִים: **וְנָשַׁמּוּ דַּרְכֵיכֶם.** שְׁבִילִים גְּדוֹלִים וּשְׁבִילִים קְטַנִּים. הֲרֵי שֶׁבַע פֻּרְעָנִיּוֹת: שֶׁן בְּהֵמָה, וְשֶׁן חַיָּה, חֲמַת זוֹחֲלֵי עָפָר, וְשִׁכְּלָה, וְהִכְרִיתָה, וְהִמְעִיטָה, וְנָשַׁמּוּ:

כג **לֹא תִוָּסְרוּ לִי.** לָשׁוּב אֵלַי:

כה **נֹקֶמֶת נְקַם בְּרִית.** וְיֵשׁ נָקָם שֶׁאֵינוֹ בַּבְּרִית כְּדֶרֶךְ שְׁאָר נְקָמוֹת, וְזֶהוּ סִמּוּי עֵינָיו שֶׁל צִדְקִיָּהוּ (מלכים ב׳ כה, ז). דָּבָר אַחֵר: "נְקַם בְּרִית", נִקְמַת בְּרִיתִי אֲשֶׁר עֲבַרְתֶּם. כָּל הֲבָאַת חֶרֶב שֶׁבַּמִּקְרָא הִיא מִלְחֶמֶת חֵילוֹת אוֹיְבִים: **וְנֶאֱסַפְתֶּם.** מִן הַחוּץ אֶל תּוֹךְ הֶעָרִים מִפְּנֵי הַמָּצוֹר: **וְשִׁלַּחְתִּי דֶבֶר בְּתוֹכְכֶם.** וְעַל יְדֵי הַדֶּבֶר "וְנִתַּתֶּם בְּיַד" הָאוֹיְבִים הַצָּרִים עֲלֵיכֶם, לְפִי שֶׁאֵין מְלִינִים אֶת הַמֵּת בִּירוּשָׁלַיִם, וּכְשֶׁהֵם מוֹצִיאִים אֶת הַמֵּת לְקָבְרוֹ נִתָּנִין בְּיַד אוֹיֵב:

כו **מַטֵּה לֶחֶם.** לְשׁוֹן מִשְׁעָן, כְּמוֹ "מַטֵּה עֹז" (ירמיה מח, יז): **בְּשִׁבְרִי לָכֶם מַטֵּה לֶחֶם.** אֶשְׁבֹּר לָכֶם כָּל מִסְעַד אֹכֶל, וְהֵם חָלְיֵי רָעָב: **וְאָפוּ עֶשֶׂר נָשִׁים לַחְמְכֶם בְּתַנּוּר אֶחָד.** מֵחֹסֶר עֵצִים: **וְהֵשִׁיבוּ לַחְמְכֶם בַּמִּשְׁקָל.** שֶׁתְּהֵא הַתְּבוּאָה נִרְקֶבֶת וְנַעֲשֵׂית פַּת נְפוּלָה וּמִשְׁתַּבֶּרֶת בַּתַּנּוּר, וְהֵן

יט וְשָׁבַרְתִּי אֶת־גְּאוֹן עֻזְּכֶם וְנָתַתִּי אֶת־שְׁמֵיכֶם כַּבַּרְזֶל וְאֶת־אַרְצְכֶם
כ כַּנְּחֻשָׁה׃ וְתַם לָרִיק כֹּחֲכֶם וְלֹא־תִתֵּן אַרְצְכֶם אֶת־יְבוּלָהּ וְעֵץ הָאָרֶץ
כא לֹא יִתֵּן פִּרְיוֹ׃ וְאִם־תֵּלְכוּ עִמִּי קֶרִי וְלֹא תֹאבוּ לִשְׁמֹעַ לִי וְיָסַפְתִּי
כב עֲלֵיכֶם מַכָּה שֶׁבַע כְּחַטֹּאתֵיכֶם׃ וְהִשְׁלַחְתִּי בָכֶם אֶת־חַיַּת הַשָּׂדֶה
וְשִׁכְּלָה אֶתְכֶם וְהִכְרִיתָה אֶת־בְּהֶמְתְּכֶם וְהִמְעִיטָה אֶתְכֶם וְנָשַׁמּוּ
כג כד דַּרְכֵיכֶם׃ וְאִם־בְּאֵלֶּה לֹא תִוָּסְרוּ לִי וַהֲלַכְתֶּם עִמִּי קֶרִי׃ וְהָלַכְתִּי
אַף־אֲנִי עִמָּכֶם בְּקֶרִי וְהִכֵּיתִי אֶתְכֶם גַּם־אָנִי שֶׁבַע עַל־חַטֹּאתֵיכֶם׃
כה וְהֵבֵאתִי עֲלֵיכֶם חֶרֶב נֹקֶמֶת נְקַם־בְּרִית וְנֶאֱסַפְתֶּם אֶל־עָרֵיכֶם
כו וְשִׁלַּחְתִּי דֶבֶר בְּתוֹכְכֶם וְנִתַּתֶּם בְּיַד־אוֹיֵב׃ בְּשִׁבְרִי לָכֶם מַטֵּה־לֶחֶם
וְאָפוּ עֶשֶׂר נָשִׁים לַחְמְכֶם בְּתַנּוּר אֶחָד וְהֵשִׁיבוּ לַחְמְכֶם בַּמִּשְׁקָל

אונקלוס

אַרְעֲכוֹן יָת עֲלַלְתַּהּ, וְאִילָן אַרְעָא, לָא יִתֵּין אִבֵּיהּ: כא וְאִם תְּהָכוּן קֳדָמַי בְּקַשְׁיוּ, וְלָא תֵיבוֹן לְקַבָּלָא לְמֵימְרִי, וְאוֹסֵיף לְאֵיתָאָה עֲלֵיכוֹן מַחָא, שְׁבַע כְּחוֹבֵיכוֹן: כב וַאֲגָרֵי בְכוֹן, יָת חֵיוַת בָּרָא וְתַתְכֵּיל יָתְכוֹן, וּתְשֵׁיצֵי יָת בְּעִירְכוֹן, וְתַזְעַר יָתְכוֹן, וְיִצְדְּיָן אוֹרְחָתְכוֹן: כג וְאִם בְּאִלֵּין, לָא תִתְרְדוּן לְמֵימְרִי, וּתְהָכוּן קֳדָמַי בְּקַשְׁיוּ: כד וַאֲהָךְ אַף אֲנָא, עִמְּכוֹן בְּקַשְׁיוּ, וְאַלְקֵי יָתְכוֹן אַף אֲנָא, שְׁבַע עַל חוֹבֵיכוֹן: כה וְאַיְתֵי עֲלֵיכוֹן דְּקָטְלִין בְּחַרְבָּא, וְיִתְפָּרְעוּן מִנְּכוֹן פֻּרְעָנוּתָא עַל דַּעֲבַרְתּוּן עַל אוֹרָיְתָא, וְתִתְכַּנְשׁוּן לְקִרְוֵיכוֹן, וַאֲגָרֵי מוֹתָנָא בֵּינֵיכוֹן, וְתִתְמַסְרוּן בְּיַד סָנְאָה: כו בְּדְאֶתְבַּר לְכוֹן סְעֵיד מֵיכְלָא, וְיֵיפְיָן, עֲסַר נְשִׁין לַחְמְכוֹן בְּתַנּוּרָא חַד, וְיָתִיבוּן לַחְמְכוֹן בְּמַתְקָלָא,

The politics of responsibility is not easy. The curses of this chapter are the very reverse of comforting. Yet the consolations with which they end are not accidental, nor are they wishful thinking. They are testimony to the power of the human spirit when summoned to the highest vocation. A nation that sees itself as responsible for the evils that befall it is also a nation that has an inextinguishable power of recovery and return.

26:21 וְאִם־תֵּלְכוּ עִמִּי קֶרִי *Walk contrary* – The keyword of the curses is *keri*. The word appears here seven times – and nowhere else in the entire Tanakh. The basic principle is clear. "If you act toward Me with *keri* – says God – I will act toward you with *keri*," However, what the word means is not clear. The various translations include rebelliousness, obstinacy, indifference, hard-heartedness and reluctance. Rambam (*Hilkhot Taaniyot* 1:1–3) however, understands *keri* to be related to *mikre*, meaning "chance," the way of the world. To regard something as *mikre* means to see it as if it had no larger significance. It just happened. That, says Rambam, is not how we as Jews should see our fate. It is not mere chance. This means that for Rambam, the curses at the end of Leviticus are not divine retribution as such. It will not be God who makes Israel suffer; it will be other human beings. What will happen is that God will withdraw His protection. Israel will have to face the world without the sheltering presence of God.

This, for Rambam, is an application of the principle of measure for measure, *midda keneged midda*, (Shabbat 105b). If Israel believes in divine providence, it will be blessed by divine providence. If it sees history as mere chance, then indeed they will be left to chance. And since Israel is a small nation surrounded by large empires, chance will not be kind to them.

27 weight, and you will eat but not be full. If, despite all this, you still do
28 not listen to Me – if still you walk contrary to Me – then I, in My fury, will walk
29 contrary to you. I will punish you seven times more for your sins: you shall eat
30 the flesh of your own sons; the flesh of your own daughters you shall eat. I will
destroy your high shrines, cut down your incense altars, and heap your corpses
31 on the corpses of your idols. I shall despise you. I will turn your cities into ruins
32 and make your sanctuaries desolate. I will not savor your pleasing aromas. I
Myself will devastate the land, so that your enemies who settle there will be
33 appalled. I shall scatter you among the nations; I will draw My sword against
34 you. Your land will be desolate; your cities, ruins. Then shall the land make
appeasement for its Sabbaths for as long as it lies desolate and you are in your
enemies' lands. Then the land will rest and make appeasement for its Sabbaths.
35 In its desolation, the land will have the rest it did not have during the Sabbaths
36 when you were dwelling there. As for the survivors, I will bring such insecurity
into their hearts in their enemies' lands that the sound of a windblown leaf will
make them run as if they fled the sword; and they will fall, though no one is

רש"י

יושבות ושוקלות את השברים לחלקם ביניהם: **ואכלתם ולא תשבעו.** זוהי מארה בתוך המעים בלחם. הרי שבע פורעניות: חרב, מזור, דבר, שבר מטה לחם, חסר ענים, פת נפולה, מארה במעים. "ונתתם" אינה מן המנין, היא החרב:

ל **במתיכם.** מגדלים ובירניות: **חמניכם.** מין עבודה זרה שמעמידין על הגגות, ועל שם שמעמידין בחמה קרויין 'חמנים': **ונתתי את פגריכם.** תפוחי רעב היו, ומוציאים יראתם מחיקם ומנשקים אותה, וכרסו נבקעת ונופל עליה: **וגעלה נפשי אתכם.** זה סלוק שכינה:

לא **ונתתי את עריכם חרבה.** יכול מאדם? כשהוא אומר: "והשמתי אני את הארץ" (להלן פסוק לב) הרי אדם אמור, הא מה אני מקיים "חרבה"? מעובר ושב: **והשמותי את מקדשיכם.** יכול מן הקרבנות? כשהוא אומר: "ולא אריח" הרי קרבנות אמורים, הא מה אני מקיים "והשמותי את מקדשיכם"? מן הגדודיות – שיירות של ישראל שהיו מתקדשות ונועדות לבא שם. הרי שבע פורעניות: אכילת בשר בנים ובנות והשמדת במות, הרי שתים. כריתת חמנים אין כאן פורענות, אלא על ידי השמדת הבירניות יפלו החמנים שבראשי הגגות ויכרתו. "ונתתי את פגריכם" וגו', הרי שלש. סלוק שכינה, ארבע. חרבן ערים, שממון מקדש מן הגדודיות, "ולא אריח" קרבנות, הרי שבע:

לב **והשמתי אני את הארץ.** זו מדה טובה לישראל, שלא ימצאו האויבים נחת רוח בארצם, שתהא שוממה מיושביה:

לג **ואתכם אזרה בגוים.** זו מדה קשה, שבשעה שבני מדינה גולים למקום אחד רואים זה את זה ומתנחמין, וישראל נזרו כבמזרה, כאדם הזורה שעורים בנפה ואין אחת מהן דבוקה בחברתה: **והריקתי.** כששולף החרב מתרוקן הנדן. ומדרשו: חרב הנשמטת אחריכם אינה חוזרת מהר, כאדם שמריק את המים ואין סופן לחזור: **והיתה ארצכם שממה.** שלא תמהרו לשוב לתוכה, ומתוך כך "עריכם יהיו חרבה" – נראות לכם חרבות, שבשעה שאדם גולה מביתו ומכרמו ומעירו וסופו לחזור, כאלו אין כרמו וביתו חרבים. כך שנויה בתורת כהנים (פרק ז, ח):

לד **אז תרצה.** תפיס את כעס המקום שכעס על שמטותיה: **והרצת.** למלך את שבתותיה:

לה **את אשר לא שבתה.** שבעים שנה של גלות בבל הן היו כנגד שבעים שנות השמטה ויובל שהיו בשנים שהכעיסו ישראל בארצם לפני המקום, ארבע מאות ושלשים ושש שנה. שלש מאות ותשעים היו שני עונם משנכנסו לארץ עד שגלו עשרת השבטים, ובני יהודה הכעיסו לפניו ארבעים ושש שנה משגלו עשרת השבטים עד חרבות ירושלים. הוא שנאמר ביחזקאל: "ואתה שכב על צדך השמאלי וגו'

כז וַאֲכַלְתֶּם וְלֹא תִשְׂבָּעוּ: וְאִם־בְּזֹאת לֹא תִשְׁמְעוּ לִי וַהֲלַכְתֶּם
כח עִמִּי בְּקֶרִי: וְהָלַכְתִּי עִמָּכֶם בַּחֲמַת־קֶרִי וְיִסַּרְתִּי אֶתְכֶם אַף־אָנִי
כט שֶׁבַע עַל־חַטֹּאתֵיכֶם: וַאֲכַלְתֶּם בְּשַׂר בְּנֵיכֶם וּבְשַׂר בְּנֹתֵיכֶם תֹּאכֵלוּ:
ל וְהִשְׁמַדְתִּי אֶת־בָּמֹתֵיכֶם וְהִכְרַתִּי אֶת־חַמָּנֵיכֶם וְנָתַתִּי אֶת־פִּגְרֵיכֶם
לא עַל־פִּגְרֵי גִּלּוּלֵיכֶם וְגָעֲלָה נַפְשִׁי אֶתְכֶם: וְנָתַתִּי אֶת־עָרֵיכֶם חָרְבָּה
לב וַהֲשִׁמּוֹתִי אֶת־מִקְדְּשֵׁיכֶם וְלֹא אָרִיחַ בְּרֵיחַ נִיחֹחֲכֶם: וַהֲשִׁמֹּתִי אֲנִי
לג אֶת־הָאָרֶץ וְשָׁמְמוּ עָלֶיהָ אֹיְבֵיכֶם הַיֹּשְׁבִים בָּהּ: וְאֶתְכֶם אֱזָרֶה בַגּוֹיִם
וַהֲרִיקֹתִי אַחֲרֵיכֶם חָרֶב וְהָיְתָה אַרְצְכֶם שְׁמָמָה וְעָרֵיכֶם יִהְיוּ חָרְבָּה:
לד אָז תִּרְצֶה הָאָרֶץ אֶת־שַׁבְּתֹתֶיהָ כֹּל יְמֵי הָשַּׁמָּה וְאַתֶּם בְּאֶרֶץ אֹיְבֵיכֶם
לה אָז תִּשְׁבַּת הָאָרֶץ וְהִרְצָת אֶת־שַׁבְּתֹתֶיהָ: כָּל־יְמֵי הָשַּׁמָּה תִּשְׁבֹּת אֵת
לו אֲשֶׁר לֹא־שָׁבְתָה בְּשַׁבְּתֹתֵיכֶם בְּשִׁבְתְּכֶם עָלֶיהָ: וְהַנִּשְׁאָרִים בָּכֶם
וְהֵבֵאתִי מֹרֶךְ בִּלְבָבָם בְּאַרְצֹת אֹיְבֵיהֶם וְרָדַף אֹתָם קוֹל עָלֶה נִדָּף

אונקלוס

ותיכלון ולא תסבעון: כז ואם בדא, לא תקבלון למימרי, ותהכון קדמי בקשיו: כח ואהך עמכון בתקוף רגז, ואדרי יתכון אף אנא, שבע על חוביכון: כט ותיכלון בסר בניכון, ובסר בנתכון תיכלון: ל ואשיצי ית במתכון, ואקציץ ית חנסניסיכון, ואתין ית פגריכון, על פגור טעותכון, ויריחק מימרי יתכון: לא ואתין ית קרויכון חרבא, ואצדי ית מקדשיכון, ולא אקביל ברעוא, קרבן כנישתכון: לב ואצדי אנא ית ארעא, ויצדון עלה בעלי דבביכון, דיתבין בה: לג ויתכון אבדר בינֵי עממיא, ואגרי בתריכון דקטלין בחרבא, ותהי ארעכון צדיא, וקרויכון יהוין חרבא: לד בכן תרעי ארעא ית שמטהא, כל יומין דצדיאת, ואתון בארע בעלי דבביכון, בכן תשמיט ארעא, ותרעי ית שמטהא: לה כל יומין דצדיאת תשמיט, ית דלא שמטת, בשמטיכון כד הויתון יתבין עלה: לו ודישתארון בכון, ואעיל תברא בלבהון, בארעתא דסנאיהון, וירדוף יתהון, קל טרפא דשקיף,

רש"י

וכלית את אלה ושכבת על צדך הימני שנית, ונשאת את עון בית יהודה ארבעים יום" (יחזקאל ד, ד-ו), ונבואה זו נאמרה ליחזקאל בשנה החמישית לגלות המלך יהויכין (שם א, ב) ועוד עשו שש שנים עד גלות צדקיהו, הרי ארבעים ושש. ואם תאמר שנות מנשה חמשים וחמש היו (מלכים ב' כא, א)! מנשה עשה תשובה שלשים ושלש שנה, וכל שנות רשעו עשרים ושתים, כמו שאמרו באגדת 'חלק' (סנהדרין קג ע"א), ושל אמון שתים (מלכים ב' כא, יט) ואחת עשרה ליהויקים (שם כג, לו) וכנגדן לצדקיהו (שם כד, יח). צא וחשב לארבע מאות ושלשים ושש שנה שמטין ויובלות שבהם, והם שש עשרה למאה, ארבע עשרה שמטין ושנים יובלות, הרי לארבע מאות שנה שסים וארבע, לשלשים ושש שנה חמש שמטות, הרי שבעים חסר אחת, ועוד שנה יתרה שנכנסה בשמטה המשלמת לשבעים, ועליהם נגזר שבעים שנה שלמים. וכן הוא אומר: "עד רצתה הארץ את שבתותיה... למלאות שבעים שנה" (דברי הימים ב' לו, כא):

לו) והבאתי מרך. פחד ורך לבב, מ"ם של "מרך" יסוד נופל הוא, כמו מ"ם של 'מועד' ושל 'מוקש':

37 chasing them. They will stumble over one another as if fleeing the sword, when
38 no one chases them. You will have no power to stand before your enemies. You
39 will perish among the nations; your enemies' lands will devour you. Those of
you who survive will waste away in their enemies' lands because of their sins –
40 for their ancestors' sins also, they will waste away. But if they confess their
sins and those of their ancestors – their trespass against Me and their walking
41 contrary to Me, which made Me walk contrary to them, bringing them into
their enemies' lands – if their obstinate hearts are humbled and they atone for
42 their sin, then I will remember My covenant with Yaakov; and My covenant
with Yitzḥak and My covenant with Avraham I will also remember, and I will

רש״י

וְנָסוּ מְנֻסַת חֶרֶב. כְּאִלּוּ רוֹדְפִים הוֹרְגִים אוֹתָם: **עָלֶה נִדָּף.** שֶׁהָרוּחַ דּוֹחֲפוֹ וּמַכֵּהוּ עַל עָלֶה אַחֵר וּמְקַשְׁקֵשׁ וּמוֹצִיא קוֹל, וְכֵן תַּרְגּוּמוֹ: ״קָל טַרְפָּא דְּשָׁקֵיף״, לְשׁוֹן חֲבָטָה, ״שְׁדוּפֹת קָדִים״ (בראשית מא, ו) ׳שְׁקִיפָן קִדּוּם׳, וְהוּא לְשׁוֹן מַשְׁקוֹף (שמות יב, כב) מְקוֹם חֲבָטַת הַדֶּלֶת, וְכֵן תַּרְגּוּמוֹ שֶׁל ״חַבּוּרָה״ (שם כא, כה) ׳מַשְׁקוֹפֵי׳:

לז **וְכָשְׁלוּ אִישׁ בְּאָחִיו.** כְּשֶׁיִּרְצוּ לָנוּס יִכָּשְׁלוּ זֶה בָּזֶה, כִּי יִבָּהֲלוּ לָרוּץ: **כְּמִפְּנֵי חֶרֶב.** כְּאִלּוּ בּוֹרְחִים מִלִּפְנֵי הוֹרְגִים, שֶׁיְּהֵא בְּלִבָּם פַּחַד, וְכָל שָׁעָה סְבוּרִים שֶׁאָדָם רוֹדְפָם. וּמִדְרָשׁוֹ: ״וְכָשְׁלוּ אִישׁ בְּאָחִיו״, זֶה נִכְשָׁל בַּעֲוֹנוֹ שֶׁל זֶה, שֶׁכָּל יִשְׂרָאֵל עֲרֵבִין זֶה לָזֶה:

לח **וַאֲבַדְתֶּם בַּגּוֹיִם.** כְּשֶׁתִּהְיוּ פְּזוּרִים תִּהְיוּ אֲבוּדִים זֶה מִזֶּה: **וְאָכְלָה אֶתְכֶם.** אֵלּוּ הַמֵּתִים בַּגּוֹלָה:

לט **בַּעֲוֹנֹת אֲבֹתָם אִתָּם.** כְּשֶׁאוֹחֲזִים מַעֲשֵׂה אֲבוֹתֵיהֶם בִּידֵיהֶם: **יִמַּקּוּ.** לְשׁוֹן הֲמַסָּה, כְּמוֹ ׳יִמַּסּוּ׳, וְכָמוֹהוּ ״תִּמַּקְנָה בְחוֹרֵיהֶן״ (זכריה יד, יב), ״נָמַקּוּ חַבּוּרֹתָי״ (תהלים לח, ו):

מא **וְהֵבֵאתִי אֹתָם.** אֲנִי בְּעַצְמִי אֲבִיאֵם, זוֹ מִדָּה טוֹבָה לְיִשְׂרָאֵל, שֶׁלֹּא יִהְיוּ אוֹמְרִים, הוֹאִיל וְגָלִינוּ בֵּין הָאֻמּוֹת נַעֲשֶׂה כְּמַעֲשֵׂיהֶם, אֲנִי אֵינִי מַנִּיחָם, אֶלָּא מַעֲמִיד אֲנִי אֶת נְבִיאַי וּמַחֲזִירָן לְתַחַת כְּנָפַי, שֶׁנֶּאֱמַר: ״וְהָעֹלָה עַל רוּחֲכֶם הָיוֹ לֹא תִהְיֶה וְגוֹ׳, חַי אָנִי וְגוֹ׳ אִם לֹא בְּיָד חֲזָקָה״ וְגוֹ׳ (יחזקאל כ, לב-לג): **אוֹ אָז יִכָּנַע.** כְּמוֹ ״אוֹ נוֹדַע כִּי שׁוֹר נַגָּח הוּא״ (שמות כא, לו), אִם אָז יִכָּנַע. לָשׁוֹן אַחֵר: אוּלַי, שֶׁמָּא ״אָז יִכָּנַע לְבָבָם״ וְגוֹ׳: **וְאָז יִרְצוּ אֶת עֲוֹנָם.** יְכַפְּרוּ עַל עֲוֹנָם בְּיִסּוּרֵיהֶם:

מב **וְזָכַרְתִּי אֶת בְּרִיתִי יַעֲקוֹב.** בַּחֲמִשָּׁה מְקוֹמוֹת נִכְתָּב מָלֵא, וְאֵלִיָּהוּ חָסֵר בַּחֲמִשָּׁה מְקוֹמוֹת – יַעֲקֹב נָטַל אוֹת מִשְּׁמוֹ שֶׁל אֵלִיָּהוּ עֵרָבוֹן שֶׁיָּבוֹא וִיבַשֵּׂר גְּאֻלַּת בָּנָיו: **וְזָכַרְתִּי אֶת בְּרִיתִי יַעֲקוֹב.** לָמָּה נִמְנוּ אֲחוֹרַנִּית? כְּלוֹמַר כְּדַי הוּא יַעֲקֹב הַקָּטָן לְכָךְ, וְאִם אֵינוֹ כְּדַי הֲרֵי יִצְחָק עִמּוֹ, וְאִם אֵינוֹ כְּדַאי הֲרֵי אַבְרָהָם כְּדַי. וְלָמָּה לֹא נֶאֶמְרָה ׳זְכִירָה׳ בְּיִצְחָק? אֶלָּא אֶפְרוֹ שֶׁל יִצְחָק נִרְאֶה לְפָנַי צָבוּר וּמֻנָּח עַל הַמִּזְבֵּחַ:

them as a nation and bound them to one another even as it bound them to God. Therefore, even when falling over one another in flight from their enemies, they will still be bound by mutual responsibility. They will still be a nation with a shared fate and destiny.

We can see now why the Sages chose their proof text from the curses of Parashat Beḥukotai. Most other Mosaic texts refer to Israel's fate as a nation in, and journeying toward, its land. But this passage spoke of exile and "the hiding of the face" of God. All Israel are responsible for one another, even in dispersion and defeat, even when they are no longer a nation in any conventional sense. Though they may be scattered across the world, divided by space, language, culture, and outward fortune, Jews remain a people, bound to one another in and through their covenant with God. Though they are parted physically, they remain united spiritually, and that unity will one day give them the strength to return to God and to the land He gave their ancestors.

And so it happened. Thus was a curse turned into a blessing, and a description of weakness turned into a source of indomitable strength.

לז וְנָסוּ מְנֻסַת־חֶרֶב וְנָפְלוּ וְאֵין רֹדֵף׃ וְכָשְׁלוּ אִישׁ־בְּאָחִיו כְּמִפְּנֵי־חֶרֶב
לח וְרֹדֵף אָיִן וְלֹא־תִהְיֶה לָכֶם תְּקוּמָה לִפְנֵי אֹיְבֵיכֶם׃ וַאֲבַדְתֶּם בַּגּוֹיִם
לט וְאָכְלָה אֶתְכֶם אֶרֶץ אֹיְבֵיכֶם׃ וְהַנִּשְׁאָרִים בָּכֶם יִמַּקּוּ בַּעֲוֺנָם בְּאַרְצֹת
מ אֹיְבֵיכֶם וְאַף בַּעֲוֺנֹת אֲבֹתָם אִתָּם יִמָּקּוּ׃ וְהִתְוַדּוּ אֶת־עֲוֺנָם וְאֶת־עֲוֺן
מא אֲבֹתָם בְּמַעֲלָם אֲשֶׁר מָעֲלוּ־בִי וְאַף אֲשֶׁר־הָלְכוּ עִמִּי בְּקֶרִי׃ אַף־אֲנִי
אֵלֵךְ עִמָּם בְּקֶרִי וְהֵבֵאתִי אֹתָם בְּאֶרֶץ אֹיְבֵיהֶם אוֹ־אָז יִכָּנַע לְבָבָם
מב הֶעָרֵל וְאָז יִרְצוּ אֶת־עֲוֺנָם׃ וְזָכַרְתִּי אֶת־בְּרִיתִי יַעֲקוֹב וְאַף אֶת־בְּרִיתִי

אונקלוס

וְיֵעִרְקוּן מִעֲרַק כַּד מִן קֳדָם דְּקָטְלִין בְּחַרְבָּא, וְיִפְּלוּן וְלֵית דְּרָדֵיף: לז וְיִתַּקְלוּן גְּבַר בַּאֲחוּהִי, כַּד מִן קֳדָם דְּקָטְלִין בְּחַרְבָּא וְרָדֵיף לֵית, וְלָא תְהֵי לְכוֹן תְּקוּמָה, קֳדָם בַּעֲלֵי דְּבָבֵיכוֹן: לח וְתֵיבְדוּן בֵּינֵי עַמְמַיָּא, וּתְגַמַּר יָתְכוֹן, אֲרַע בַּעֲלֵי דְּבָבֵיכוֹן: לט וּדְיִשְׁתְּאֲרוּן בְּכוֹן, יִתְמַסְּוּן בְּחוֹבֵיהוֹן, בְּאַרְעָתָא דְּסָנְאֵיכוֹן, וְאַף, בְּחוֹבֵי אֲבָהָתְהוֹן בִּישַׁיָּא דַּאֲחִידִין בִּידֵיהוֹן יִתְמַסּוּן: מ וִיוַדּוּן יָת חוֹבֵיהוֹן וְיָת חוֹבֵי אֲבָהָתְהוֹן, בְּשִׁקְרְהוֹן דְּשַׁקַּרוּ בְמֵימְרִי, וְאַף, דְּהַלִּיכוּ קֳדָמַי בְּקַשְׁיוּ: מא אַף אֲנָא, אֶהָךְ עִמְּהוֹן בְּקַשְׁיוּ, וְאַעֵיל יָתְהוֹן, בַּאֲרַע בַּעֲלֵי דְבָבֵיהוֹן, אוֹ בְכֵן יִתְּבַר, לִבְּהוֹן טַפְשָׁא, וּבְכֵן יִרְעוֹן יָת חוֹבֵיהוֹן: מב וּדְכִירְנָא יָת קְיָמִי דְּעִם יַעֲקֹב, וְאַף יָת קְיָמִי דְּעִם

COLLECTIVE RESPONSIBILITY

There is, on the face of it, nothing positive in this nightmare scenario. But the Sages learned from it a fundamental idea: "'They will stumble over one another' – read this as 'stumble because of one another's sins': this teaches that all Israelites are responsible for one another" (Sifra ad loc.; Shevuot 39a).

The rule of *kol Yisrael arevin zeh bazeh,* all Israel are responsible for one another, not just individually, but before God – is one of the great principles of rabbinic Judaism. We are all in the same boat. My actions do not affect me alone. They have consequences for the whole of society. The idea of collective destiny and responsibility is more than just a metaphor. It is constitutive of Jewish identity.

But why locate this principle here? "Stumbling over one another" is not a description of a nation bound by mutual suretyship. It is an account of panic. In their hurry to escape, people fall over one another. Each is concerned with his own safety, not the common good. Whatever prompted the rabbinic interpretation, it was not the plain sense of the verse. Conversely, the notion that Jews have collective responsibility, that their fate and destiny are interlinked, could have been found in many places throughout the Torah. The Torah, from Exodus onward, is dedicated to this principle. It is basic to Moshe's vision and to the people's experience. They suffered slavery together. They experienced liberation together. The second paragraph of the *Shema* (Deut. 11:13–17) teaches that the people will prosper together or suffer together. Why locate the principle of mutual responsibility among the Torah's curses?

To understand this, note first that there is nothing unique to Judaism in the idea that we are all implicated in one another's fate. That is true of the citizens of any nation under the same political system and sovereign power. Our horizons of possibility are shaped by the society and culture within which we live. What is unusual about Judaism is that the principle applies to a people scattered throughout the world. Jews are linked to one another by the same ties of mutual responsibility that they had in the land – for it was the covenant that formed

43 remember the land. The land will be deserted, making appeasement for its
Sabbaths, lying desolate of them, while they will be making appeasement for
their sins, because they rejected My laws, because they despised My statutes.
44 Yet even then, when they are in the land of their enemies, I will not reject them
nor despise them and annihilate them, will not break My covenant with them,
45 for I am the Lord their God. I will remember for them the covenant with
their ancestors whom I brought out of Egypt in the sight of the nations, to be

רש״י

מג | **יַעַן וּבְיַעַן.** גְּמוּל וּבִגְמוּל אֲשֶׁר בְּמִשְׁפָּטַי מָאָסוּ:

מד | **וְאַף גַּם זֹאת.** וַאֲפִלּוּ אֲנִי עוֹשֶׂה עִמָּהֶם זֹאת הַפֻּרְעָנוּת אֲשֶׁר אָמַרְתִּי, בִּהְיוֹתָם בְּאֶרֶץ אוֹיְבֵיהֶם לֹא אֶמְאָסֵם לְכַלֹּתָם וּלְהָפֵר בְּרִיתִי אֲשֶׁר אִתָּם:

מה | **בְּרִית רִאשֹׁנִים.** שֶׁל שְׁבָטִים:

sensitive to its message can abandon hope. Without belief in the covenant and its insistence of "Yet even then…" there might have been no Jewish people today.

26:44 **כִּי אֲנִי יהוה אֱלֹהֵיהֶם** *For I am the Lord their God* – This is a fundamental statement upon which Judaism rests. It says that though the people may be faithless to God, God will never be faithless to the people. He may judge them harshly but He will not forget their ancestors who followed Him. God does not break His promises even if we break ours.

This verse testifies against the traditional Christian doctrine known as supersessionism or replacement theology, which maintains that Christianity represents God's rejection of the Jewish people, the "old Israel." It says that God once had a covenant with the Jewish people, but no longer. His new chosen people are not Jews but Christians. That doctrine is incompatible with this passage in Parashat Beḥukotai. God may send His people into exile but they remain His people.

It is not an isolated verse. Examination of the Torah as a whole reveals an underlying principle, namely the *rejection of rejection*. At first, God rejects humanity, saving only Noaḥ, when He sees the world full of violence. Yet after the flood He vows: "Never again will I curse the land because of man; the devisings of the human heart are evil from its youth. And never again will I destroy all life as I have done" (Gen. 8:21). That is the first *rejection of rejection*.

Then come a series of sibling rivalries. The covenant passes through Yitzḥak not Yishmael, Yaakov not Esav. But God sees Hagar's and Yishmael's tears. Evidently, He sees Esav's also, for He later commands, "Do not despise an Edomite [i.e., a descendant of Esav], for he is your kin" (Deut. 23:8). Finally God brings it about that Levi, one of the children Yaakov curses on his deathbed – "Cursed be their anger, for it is most fierce, and their fury, for it is most cruel" (Gen. 49:7) – becomes the father of Israel's spiritual leaders, Moshe, Aharon, and Miriam. From now on, all Israel are chosen. That is the second rejection of rejection.

Even when Israel suffer exile and find themselves "in the land of their enemies," they will remain the children of God's covenant, which He will not break, because God does not abandon His people. They may be faithless to Him. He will not be faithless to them. That is the third rejection of rejection, stated in this *parasha*. The God of Avraham keeps His promises.

26:45 **אֲנִי יהוה** *I am the Lord* – Many attempts have been made to prove the existence of God. Theologians have argued on the basis of philosophy, and in some cases the natural sciences (the "argument from design"). Yet the Torah speaks of a different kind of proof altogether: the history of Israel.

The great mathematician and theologian Blaise Pascal wrote this:

> The Jewish people… is not only of remarkable antiquity but has also lasted for a singularly long time.… For

מג יִצְחָק וְאַף אֶת־בְּרִיתִי אַבְרָהָם אֶזְכֹּר וְהָאָרֶץ אֶזְכֹּר׃ וְהָאָרֶץ תֵּעָזֵב
מֵהֶם וְתִרֶץ אֶת־שַׁבְּתֹתֶיהָ בָּהְשַׁמָּה מֵהֶם וְהֵם יִרְצוּ אֶת־עֲוֺנָם יַעַן
מד וּבְיַעַן בְּמִשְׁפָּטַי מָאָסוּ וְאֶת־חֻקֹּתַי גָּעֲלָה נַפְשָׁם׃ וְאַף גַּם־זֹאת בִּהְיוֹתָם
בְּאֶרֶץ אֹיְבֵיהֶם לֹא־מְאַסְתִּים וְלֹא־גְעַלְתִּים לְכַלֹּתָם לְהָפֵר בְּרִיתִי אִתָּם
מה כִּי אֲנִי יְהוָה אֱלֹהֵיהֶם׃ וְזָכַרְתִּי לָהֶם בְּרִית רִאשֹׁנִים אֲשֶׁר הוֹצֵאתִי־
אֹתָם מֵאֶרֶץ מִצְרַיִם לְעֵינֵי הַגּוֹיִם לִהְיוֹת לָהֶם לֵאלֹהִים אֲנִי יְהוָה׃

אונקלוס

יִצְחָק, וְאַף יָת קְיָמִי דְּעִם אַבְרָהָם, אֲנָא דָּכִיר וְאַרְעָא אֲנָא דָּכִיר׃
מג וְאַרְעָא תִּתְרְטֵישׁ מִנְּהוֹן וְתִרְעֵי יָת שְׁמִטַּהָא, בְּדִצְדִיאַת מִנְּהוֹן,
וְאִנּוּן יִרְעוֹן יָת חוֹבֵיהוֹן, לְוָטִין חֲלָף בִּרְכָן אַיְתִי עֲלֵיהוֹן דִּבְדִינַי קַצוּ,
וְיָת קְיָמַי רַחֵיקַת נַפְשְׁהוֹן׃ מד וְאַף בְּרַם דָּא, בְּמִהֲוֵיהוֹן בַּאֲרַע בַּעֲלֵי
דְּבָבֵיהוֹן, לָא אֲרַטֵּישִׁנּוּן וְלָא אֲרַחֵיקִנּוּן לְשֵׁיצָיוּתְהוֹן, לְאַשְׁנָאָה קְיָמִי
עִמְּהוֹן, אֲרֵי, אֲנָא יי אֱלָהֲהוֹן׃ מה וּדְכַרְנָא לְהוֹן קְיָם קַדְמָאֵי, דְּאַפֵּיקִית
יָתְהוֹן מֵאַרְעָא דְּמִצְרַיִם לְעֵינֵי עַמְמַיָּא, לְמִהְוֵי לְהוֹן, לֶאֱלָהּ אֲנָא יי׃

THE BIRTH OF HOPE

After the terrifying curses warning that if Israel betrays its divine mission, it will forfeit its freedom and land, there is a sudden change of key. The end of the chapter holds a turning point. It is the birth of hope: not hope as a dream, a wish, a desire, but as the very shape of history. God is just. He may punish. He may hide His face. But He will not break His word. He will fulfill His promise and redeem His children.

Hope is one of the great Jewish contributions to Western civilization. In the ancient world, there were tragic cultures in which people believed that the gods were at best indifferent to our existence, at worst actively malevolent. Then there is the secular culture of the contemporary West in which the universe is seen as a series of meaningless accidents with no redeeming purpose. Hope is not unknown in these cultures, but it is what Aristotle called "a waking dream," a private wish that things may be otherwise. Seen through the eyes of ancient Greece or contemporary science, there is nothing in the texture of reality to justify belief that the human condition could be other or better than it is.

There is nothing inevitable or even rational about hope. It cannot be inferred from any facts about the past or present. Those with a tragic sense of life hold that hope is an illusion and that a mature response to our place in the universe is to accept its meaninglessness and cultivate stoic acceptance. Judaism insists otherwise: that the reality that underlies the universe is not deaf to our prayers, blind to our aspirations, indifferent to our existence.

We hear this note at several points in the Torah. It occurs twice, for instance, at the end of Genesis when first Yaakov and then Yosef assure the other members of the covenantal family that their stay in Egypt will not be endless. God will honor His promise and bring them back to the Promised Land.

But the key text is here at the end of the curses of Leviticus. This is where God promises that even if Israel sins, it may suffer, but it will never have reason to utterly despair. It may experience exile, but eventually it will return.

Hope emerged as part of the spiritual landscape of Western civilization through this quite specific set of beliefs: that God exists, that He cares about us, that He has made a covenant with humanity and a further covenant with the people He chose to be a living example of faith. The covenant transforms our understanding of history. God has given His word and will not break it. Without these beliefs we would have no reason to hope.

History as conceived in this *parasha* is not utopian. No one reading this chapter can be an optimist. Yet no one

46 their God; I am the LORD." These are the statutes, laws, and instructions that
the LORD established between Himself and the Israelites, through Moshe, on
Mount Sinai.
27 1/2 The LORD spoke to Moshe: "Speak to the Israelites. Say: When a person makes REVI'I /SHISHI/
3 a spoken vow to the LORD to give the equivalent of the value of a person – if it is
a male from twenty to sixty years old, his equivalent is fifty silver shekel by the
4/5 Sanctuary weight. If it is a female, the equivalent is thirty shekel. If the person's
age is between five and twenty years, the equivalent for a male is twenty shekel,
6 and for a female, ten shekel. If the age is between one month and five years,
the equivalent for a male is five silver shekel; for a female, three silver shekel.
7 If the age is sixty years or more, the equivalent for a male is fifteen shekel, and
8 for a female, ten shekel. But if the person is too poor to pay the full amount,
he shall be presented to the priest, who will assess him. The priest shall assess
9 him with reference to the means of the person making the vow. If the
vow concerns an animal of a type that may be offered to the LORD, any such
10 animal given to the LORD becomes sacred. One may not exchange it or offer a
substitute for it, either better for worse or worse for better; and if one animal

רש״י

מו **וְהַתּוֹרֹת.** אַחַת בִּכְתָב וְאַחַת בְּעַל פֶּה, מַגִּיד שֶׁכֻּלָּם נִתְּנוּ לְמֹשֶׁה בְּסִינַי:

כז ב **כִּי יַפְלִא.** יַפְרִישׁ בְּפִיו: **בְּעֶרְכְּךָ נְפָשֹׁת.** לִתֵּן עֵרֶךְ נַפְשׁוֹ, לוֹמַר עֵרֶךְ דָּבָר שֶׁנַּפְשׁוֹ תְּלוּיָה בּוֹ עָלַי:

ג **וְהָיָה עֶרְכְּךָ וְגוֹ׳.** אֵין ׳עֵרֶךְ׳ זֶה לְשׁוֹן דָּמִים, אֶלָּא בֵּין שֶׁהוּא יָקָר בֵּין שֶׁהוּא זוֹל, כְּפִי שָׁנָיו הוּא הָעֵרֶךְ הַקָּצוּב עָלָיו בְּפָרָשָׁה זוֹ: **עֶרְכְּךָ.** כְּמוֹ ׳עֵרֶךְ׳, וְכֵפֶל הַכָּפִי״ן לֹא יָדַעְתִּי מֵאֵיזֶה לָשׁוֹן הוּא:

ה **וְאִם מִבֶּן חָמֵשׁ שָׁנִים.** לֹא שֶׁיְּהֵא הַנּוֹדֵר קָטָן, שֶׁאֵין בְּדִבְרֵי קָטָן כְּלוּם, אֶלָּא גָּדוֹל שֶׁאָמַר: ׳עֵרֶךְ קָטָן זֶה שֶׁהוּא בֶּן חָמֵשׁ שָׁנִים, עָלַי׳:

ז **וְאִם מִבֶּן שִׁשִּׁים שָׁנָה וְגוֹ׳.** כְּשֶׁמַּגִּיעַ לִימֵי הַזִּקְנָה הָאִשָּׁה קְרוֹבָה לְהֵחָשֵׁב כְּאִישׁ, לְפִיכָךְ הָאִישׁ פּוֹחֵת בְּהִזְדַּקְנוֹ יוֹתֵר מִשְּׁלִישׁ בְּעֶרְכּוֹ וְהָאִשָּׁה אֵינָהּ פּוֹחֶתֶת אֶלָּא שְׁלִישׁ בְּעֶרְכָּהּ, דְּאָמְרֵי אֱנָשֵׁי: סָבָא בְּבֵיתָא פַּחָא בְּבֵיתָא, סַבְתָּא בְּבֵיתָא סִימָא בְּבֵיתָא וְסִימָנָא טָבָא בְּבֵיתָא:

ח **וְאִם מָךְ הוּא.** שֶׁאֵין יָדוֹ מַשֶּׂגֶת לִתֵּן הָעֵרֶךְ הַזֶּה: **עַל פִּי אֲשֶׁר תַּשִּׂיג.** לְפִי מַה שֶּׁיֵּשׁ לוֹ יְסַדְּרֶנּוּ, וְיַשְׁאִיר לוֹ כְּדֵי חַיָּיו, מִטָּה כַּר וָכֶסֶת וּכְלֵי אֻמָּנוּת, אִם הָיָה חַמָּר מַשְׁאִיר לוֹ חֲמוֹרוֹ:

ט **כֹּל אֲשֶׁר יִתֵּן מִמֶּנּוּ.** אָמַר: ׳רַגְלָהּ שֶׁל זוֹ עוֹלָה׳, דְּבָרָיו קַיָּמִין, וְתִמָּכֵר לְצָרְכֵי עוֹלָה, וְדָמֶיהָ חֻלִּין חוּץ מִדְּמֵי אוֹתוֹ הָאֵיבָר:

י **טוֹב בְּרָע.** תָּם בְּבַעַל מוּם: **אוֹ רַע בְּטוֹב.** וְכָל שֶׁכֵּן טוֹב בְּטוֹב וְרַע בְּרָע:

such a long spell of years. They have always been preserved, however, and their preservation was foretold.… My encounter with this people amazes me.

There is pain in this history. Yet it remains astonishing. The curses of the *tokheḥa* came true – but so did the consolation. No nation was attacked so often. Empire after empire pronounced their destruction. Yet the empires vanished into oblivion while the people Israel still lives, small, vulnerable, yet still there, defying all the natural laws that govern the history of nations. There is a mystery here, as Pascal so clearly saw. Yet its basic formulation is clear, and despite all the odds it came true: the people of the eternal God became the people of eternity.

מו אֵלֶּה הַחֻקִּים וְהַמִּשְׁפָּטִים וְהַתּוֹרֹת אֲשֶׁר נָתַן יהוה בֵּינוֹ וּבֵין בְּנֵי
יִשְׂרָאֵל בְּהַר סִינַי בְּיַד־מֹשֶׁה׃
כז א ב וַיְדַבֵּר יְהוָה אֶל־מֹשֶׁה לֵּאמֹר׃ דַּבֵּר אֶל־בְּנֵי יִשְׂרָאֵל וְאָמַרְתָּ אֲלֵהֶם כג רביעי /ששי/
ג אִישׁ כִּי יַפְלִא נֶדֶר בְּעֶרְכְּךָ נְפָשֹׁת לַיהוָה׃ וְהָיָה עֶרְכְּךָ הַזָּכָר מִבֶּן
עֶשְׂרִים שָׁנָה וְעַד בֶּן־שִׁשִּׁים שָׁנָה וְהָיָה עֶרְכְּךָ חֲמִשִּׁים שֶׁקֶל כֶּסֶף
ד ה בְּשֶׁקֶל הַקֹּדֶשׁ׃ וְאִם־נְקֵבָה הִוא וְהָיָה עֶרְכְּךָ שְׁלֹשִׁים שָׁקֶל׃ וְאִם מִבֶּן־
חָמֵשׁ שָׁנִים וְעַד בֶּן־עֶשְׂרִים שָׁנָה וְהָיָה עֶרְכְּךָ הַזָּכָר עֶשְׂרִים שְׁקָלִים
ו וְלַנְּקֵבָה עֲשֶׂרֶת שְׁקָלִים׃ וְאִם מִבֶּן־חֹדֶשׁ וְעַד בֶּן־חָמֵשׁ שָׁנִים וְהָיָה
עֶרְכְּךָ הַזָּכָר חֲמִשָּׁה שְׁקָלִים כָּסֶף וְלַנְּקֵבָה עֶרְכְּךָ שְׁלֹשֶׁת שְׁקָלִים
ז כָּסֶף׃ וְאִם מִבֶּן־שִׁשִּׁים שָׁנָה וָמַעְלָה אִם־זָכָר וְהָיָה עֶרְכְּךָ חֲמִשָּׁה
ח עָשָׂר שָׁקֶל וְלַנְּקֵבָה עֲשָׂרָה שְׁקָלִים׃ וְאִם־מָךְ הוּא מֵעֶרְכֶּךָ וְהֶעֱמִידוֹ
לִפְנֵי הַכֹּהֵן וְהֶעֱרִיךְ אֹתוֹ הַכֹּהֵן עַל־פִּי אֲשֶׁר תַּשִּׂיג יַד הַנֹּדֵר יַעֲרִיכֶנּוּ
ט הַכֹּהֵן׃ וְאִם־בְּהֵמָה אֲשֶׁר יַקְרִיבוּ מִמֶּנָּה קָרְבָּן לַיהוָה
י כֹּל אֲשֶׁר יִתֵּן מִמֶּנּוּ לַיהוָה יִהְיֶה־קֹּדֶשׁ׃ לֹא יַחֲלִיפֶנּוּ וְלֹא־יָמִיר אֹתוֹ
טוֹב בְּרָע אוֹ־רַע בְּטוֹב וְאִם־הָמֵר יָמִיר בְּהֵמָה בִּבְהֵמָה וְהָיָה־הוּא

אונקלוס

מו אִלֵּין, קְיָמַיָּא וְדִינַיָּא וְאוֹרָיָתָא, דִּיהַב יְיָ, בֵּין מֵימְרֵיהּ, וּבֵין בְּנֵי יִשְׂרָאֵל, בְּטוּרָא דְסִינַי בִּידָא דְמֹשֶׁה: כז א וּמַלֵּיל יְיָ עִם מֹשֶׁה לְמֵימַר: ב מַלֵּיל, עִם בְּנֵי יִשְׂרָאֵל וְתֵימַר לְהוֹן, גְּבַר, אֲרֵי יַפְרֵישׁ נְדַר, בְּפֻרְסַן נַפְשָׁתָא קֳדָם יְיָ: ג וִיהֵי פֻּרְסָנֵיהּ דִּדְכוּרָא, מִבַּר עַסְרִין שְׁנִין, וְעַד בַּר שִׁתִּין שְׁנִין, וִיהֵי פֻרְסָנֵיהּ, חַמְשִׁין, סִלְעִין דִּכְסַף בְּסִלְעֵי קֻדְשָׁא: ד וְאִם נֻקְבְּתָא הִיא, וִיהֵי פֻּרְסָנַהּ תְּלָתִין סִלְעִין: ה וְאִם מִבַּר חֲמֵשׁ שְׁנִין, וְעַד בַּר עַסְרִין שְׁנִין, וִיהֵי פֻּרְסָנֵיהּ, דִּדְכוּרָא עַסְרִין סִלְעִין, וּלְנֻקְבְּתָא עֲסַר סִלְעִין: ו וְאִם מִבַּר יַרְחָא, וְעַד בַּר חֲמֵשׁ שְׁנִין, וִיהֵי פֻּרְסָנֵיהּ דִּדְכוּרָא, חֲמֵשׁ סִלְעִין דִּכְסַף, וּלְנֻקְבְּתָא פֻּרְסָנַהּ, תְּלָת סִלְעִין דִּכְסַף: ז וְאִם, מִבַּר שִׁתִּין שְׁנִין וּלְעֵילָא אִם דְּכוּרָא, וִיהֵי פֻּרְסָנֵיהּ, חֲמֵשׁ עֲסַר סִלְעִין, וּלְנֻקְבְּתָא עֲסַר סִלְעִין: ח וְאִם מִסְכֵּין הוּא מִפֻּרְסָנֵיהּ, וִיקִימִנֵּיהּ קֳדָם כָּהֲנָא, וְיִפְרוֹס יָתֵיהּ כָּהֲנָא, עַל פּוּם, דְּתַדְבֵּיק יַד נָדְרָא, יִפְרְסִנֵּיהּ כָּהֲנָא: ט וְאִם בְּעִירָא, דִּיקָרְבוּן מִנַּהּ, קֻרְבָּנָא קֳדָם יְיָ, כֹּל דְּיִתֵּין מִנֵּיהּ, קֳדָם יְיָ יְהֵי קֻדְשָׁא: י לָא יַחְלְפִנֵּיהּ, וְלָא יַעְבַּר יָתֵיהּ, טָב בְּבִישׁ אוֹ בִישׁ בְּטָב, וְאִם חַלָּפָא יְחַלֵּיף בְּעִירָא בִּבְעִירָא, וִיהֵי הוּא

of so many powerful kings who have tried a hundred times to wipe them out, as their historians testify, and as can easily be judged by the natural order of things over whereas the peoples of Greece and Italy, of Sparta, Athens, and Rome, and others who came so much later have perished so long ago, these still exist, despite the efforts

11 is substituted for another, both it and the substitute become holy. If the vow
involves any type of impure animal, which cannot be offered to the LORD, the
12 animal shall be brought to stand before the priest. The priest shall assess it,
13 whether good or bad, and its value shall accord to the priest's assessment. If
14 the donor wishes to redeem it, a fifth shall be added to its valuation. When
someone consecrates his house to be sacred to the LORD, the priest shall assess
15 it, whether good or bad, and its value shall accord to the priest's assessment. If the
donor wishes to redeem it, he shall add a fifth to its valuation, and it shall be his
16 again. If someone consecrates part of his hereditary land to the LORD, its value HAMISHI /SHEVI'I/
shall be set in relation to the seed needed to sow it: fifty silver shekel for each
17 homer of barley seed. If the person consecrates his field from the Jubilee year,
18 the value that has been set stands. But if the person consecrates the field after
the Jubilee, the priest shall calculate its value in relation to the number of years
left until the next Jubilee year, and the valuation shall be reduced accordingly.

רש״י

יא **וְאִם כָּל בְּהֵמָה טְמֵאָה.** בְּבַעֲלַת מוּם הַכָּתוּב מְדַבֵּר שֶׁהִיא טְמֵאָה לְהַקְרָבָה, וְלִמֶּדְךָ הַכָּתוּב שֶׁאֵין קָדָשִׁים תְּמִימִים יוֹצְאִין לְחֻלִּין בְּפִדְיוֹן, אֶלָּא אִם כֵּן הוּמְמוּ:

יב **כְּעֶרְכְּךָ הַכֹּהֵן כֵּן יִהְיֶה.** לִשְׁאָר כָּל אָדָם הַבָּא לִקְנוֹתָהּ מִיַּד הֶקְדֵּשׁ:

יג **וְאִם גָּאֹל יִגְאָלֶנָּה.** בַּבְּעָלִים הֶחְמִיר הַכָּתוּב לְהוֹסִיף חֹמֶשׁ, וְכֵן בְּמַקְדִּישׁ בַּיִת, וְכֵן בְּמַקְדִּישׁ אֶת הַשָּׂדֶה, וְכֵן בְּפִדְיוֹן מַעֲשֵׂר שֵׁנִי, הַבְּעָלִים מוֹסִיפִין חֹמֶשׁ וְלֹא שְׁאָר כָּל אָדָם:

טז **וְהָיָה עֶרְכְּךָ לְפִי זַרְעוֹ.** וְלֹא כְּפִי שָׁוְיָהּ; אַחַת שָׂדֶה טוֹבָה וְאַחַת שָׂדֶה רָעָה פִּדְיוֹן הֶקְדֵּשָׁן שָׁוֶה, בֵּית כּוֹר שְׂעוֹרִים בַּחֲמִשִּׁים שְׁקָלִים, כָּךְ גְּזֵרַת הַכָּתוּב. וְהוּא שֶׁבָּא לְגָאֳלָהּ בִּתְחִלַּת הַיּוֹבֵל. וְאִם בָּא לְגָאֳלָהּ בְּאֶמְצָעוֹ נוֹתֵן לְפִי הַחֶשְׁבּוֹן, סֶלַע וּפֻנְדְּיוֹן לְשָׁנָה, לְפִי שֶׁאֵינָהּ הֶקְדֵּשׁ אֶלָּא לְמִנְיַן שְׁנוֹת הַיּוֹבֵל, שֶׁאִם נְגָאֳלָהּ הֲרֵי טוֹב, וְאִם לָאו – הַגִּזְבָּר מוֹכְרָהּ בְּדָמִים הַלָּלוּ לְאַחֵר וְעוֹמֶדֶת בְּיַד הַלּוֹקֵחַ עַד הַיּוֹבֵל כִּשְׁאָר כָּל הַשָּׂדוֹת הַמְּכוּרוֹת, וּכְשֶׁהִיא יוֹצְאָה מִיָּדוֹ חוֹזֶרֶת לַכֹּהֲנִים שֶׁל אוֹתוֹ מִשְׁמָר שֶׁהַיּוֹבֵל פּוֹגֵעַ בּוֹ, וּמִתְחַלֶּקֶת בֵּינֵיהֶם. זֶהוּ הַמִּשְׁפָּט הָאָמוּר בְּמַקְדִּישׁ שָׂדֶה. וְעַכְשָׁיו אֲפָרְשֶׁנּוּ עַל סֵדֶר הַמִּקְרָאוֹת:

יז **אִם מִשְּׁנַת הַיֹּבֵל יַקְדִּישׁ וְגוֹ׳.** אִם מִשֶּׁעָבְרָה שְׁנַת הַיּוֹבֵל מִיָּד הִקְדִּישָׁהּ, וּבָא זֶה לְגָאֳלָהּ מִיָּד: **כְּעֶרְכְּךָ יָקוּם.** כָּעֵרֶךְ הַזֶּה הָאָמוּר יִהְיֶה, חֲמִשִּׁים כֶּסֶף יִתֵּן:

יח **וְאִם אַחַר הַיֹּבֵל יַקְדִּישׁ.** וְכֵן אִם הִקְדִּישָׁהּ מִשְּׁנַת הַיּוֹבֵל וְנִשְׁתַּהָת בְּיַד גִּזְבָּר, וּבָא זֶה לְגָאֳלָהּ אַחַר הַיּוֹבֵל: **וְחִשַּׁב לוֹ הַכֹּהֵן אֶת הַכֶּסֶף עַל פִּי הַשָּׁנִים הַנּוֹתָרֹת.** כְּפִי חֶשְׁבּוֹן. כֵּיצַד? הֲרֵי קָצַב דָּמֶיהָ שֶׁל אַרְבָּעִים וְתֵשַׁע שָׁנָה חֲמִשִּׁים שֶׁקֶל, הֲרֵי שֶׁקֶל לְכָל שָׁנָה וְשֶׁקֶל יָתֵר עַל כֻּלָּן, וְהַשֶּׁקֶל – אַרְבָּעִים וּשְׁמוֹנָה פֻּנְדְּיוֹן, הֲרֵי סֶלַע וּפֻנְדְּיוֹן לְשָׁנָה, אֶלָּא שֶׁחָסֵר פֻּנְדְּיוֹן אֶחָד לְכֻלָּן, וְאָמְרוּ רַבּוֹתֵינוּ שֶׁאוֹתוֹ פֻּנְדְּיוֹן קָלְבּוֹן לִפְרוֹטְרוֹט, וְהַבָּא לִגְאֹל יִתֵּן סֶלַע וּפֻנְדְּיוֹן לְכָל שָׁנָה לַשָּׁנִים הַנּוֹתָרוֹת עַד שְׁנַת הַיּוֹבֵל: **וְנִגְרַע מֵעֶרְכֶּךָ.** מִנְיַן הַשָּׁנִים שֶׁמִּשְּׁנַת הַיּוֹבֵל עַד שְׁנַת הַפִּדְיוֹן:

is your meaning and mission in life. This is what you were placed on earth to do.

And why does the word appear at the beginning of the central book of the Torah? Because the book of Leviticus is about sacrifices, and a vocation is about sacrifice. *We are willing to make sacrifices when we feel they are part of the task we are called on to do.*

Not everyone who finds meaning in life does so in moral terms. But they almost always do so in terms of some project involving challenge, dedication, commitment, and effort that takes them beyond themselves. A world dominated by the self leads ultimately to meaninglessness. In Leviticus, God sets out an alternative: the mystery and majesty of holiness, summoning the people with whom He covenanted to

יא וּתְמוּרָתוֹ יִהְיֶה־קֹּדֶשׁ׃ וְאִם כׇּל־בְּהֵמָה טְמֵאָה אֲשֶׁר לֹא־יַקְרִיבוּ
יב מִמֶּנָּה קׇרְבָּן לַיהֹוָה וְהֶעֱמִיד אֶת־הַבְּהֵמָה לִפְנֵי הַכֹּהֵן׃ וְהֶעֱרִיךְ הַכֹּהֵן
יג אֹתָהּ בֵּין טוֹב וּבֵין רָע כְּעֶרְכְּךָ הַכֹּהֵן כֵּן יִהְיֶה׃ וְאִם־גָּאֹל יִגְאָלֶנָּה
יד וְיָסַף חֲמִישִׁתוֹ עַל־עֶרְכֶּךָ׃ וְאִישׁ כִּי־יַקְדִּשׁ אֶת־בֵּיתוֹ קֹדֶשׁ לַיהֹוָה
וְהֶעֱרִיכוֹ הַכֹּהֵן בֵּין טוֹב וּבֵין רָע כַּאֲשֶׁר יַעֲרִיךְ אֹתוֹ הַכֹּהֵן כֵּן יָקוּם׃
טו וְאִם־הַמַּקְדִּישׁ יִגְאַל אֶת־בֵּיתוֹ וְיָסַף חֲמִישִׁית כֶּסֶף־עֶרְכְּךָ עָלָיו וְהָיָה
טז לוֹ׃ וְאִם ׀ מִשְּׂדֵה אֲחֻזָּתוֹ יַקְדִּישׁ אִישׁ לַיהֹוָה וְהָיָה עֶרְכְּךָ לְפִי זַרְעוֹ חמישי /שביעי/
יז זֶרַע חֹמֶר שְׂעֹרִים בַּחֲמִשִּׁים שֶׁקֶל כָּסֶף׃ אִם־מִשְּׁנַת הַיֹּבֵל יַקְדִּישׁ
יח שָׂדֵהוּ כְּעֶרְכְּךָ יָקוּם׃ וְאִם־אַחַר הַיֹּבֵל יַקְדִּישׁ שָׂדֵהוּ וְחִשַּׁב־לוֹ הַכֹּהֵן
אֶת־הַכֶּסֶף עַל־פִּי הַשָּׁנִים הַנּוֹתָרֹת עַד שְׁנַת הַיֹּבֵל וְנִגְרַע מֵעֶרְכֶּךָ׃

אונקלוס

וְחִלּוּפֵיהּ יְהֵי קֻדְשָׁא: יא וְאִם כָּל בְּעִירָא מְסָאֲבָא, דְּלָא יְקָרְבוּן מִנַּהּ, קֻרְבָּנָא קֳדָם יְיָ, וִיקִים יָת בְּעִירָא קֳדָם כָּהֲנָא: יב וְיִפְרוֹס כָּהֲנָא יָתַהּ, בֵּין טָב וּבֵין בִּישׁ, כְּפֻרְסָן כָּהֲנָא כֵּן יְהֵי: יג וְאִם מִפְרַק יִפְרְקִנַּהּ, וְיוֹסֵיף חֻמְשֵׁיהּ עַל פֻּרְסָנֵיהּ: יד וּגְבַר, אֲרֵי יַקְדֵּישׁ יָת בֵּיתֵיהּ קֻדְשָׁא קֳדָם יְיָ, וְיִפְרְסִנֵּיהּ כָּהֲנָא, בֵּין טָב וּבֵין בִּישׁ, כְּמָא דְּיִפְרוֹס יָתֵיהּ, כָּהֲנָא כֵּן יְקוּם: טו וְאִם דְּאַקְדֵּישׁ, יִפְרוֹק יָת בֵּיתֵיהּ, וְיוֹסֵיף, חוֹמֶשׁ כְּסַף פֻּרְסָנֵיהּ, עֲלוֹהִי וִיהֵי לֵיהּ: טז וְאִם מֵחֲקַל אַחְסָנְתֵיהּ, יַקְדֵּישׁ גְּבַר קֳדָם יְיָ, וִיהֵי פֻּרְסָנֵיהּ לְפוּם זַרְעֵיהּ, בַּר זְרַע כּוֹר סְעָרִין, בְּחַמְשִׁין סִלְעִין דִּכְסַף: יז אִם מִשַּׁתָּא דְיוֹבֵילָא יַקְדֵּישׁ חַקְלֵיהּ, כְּפֻרְסָנֵיהּ יְקוּם: יח וְאִם בָּתַר יוֹבֵילָא יַקְדֵּישׁ חַקְלֵיהּ, וִיחַשֵּׁיב לֵיהּ כָּהֲנָא יָת כַּסְפָּא, עַל פּוּם שְׁנַיָּא דְּאִשְׁתְּאָרָא, עַד שַׁתָּא דְּיוֹבֵילָא, וְיִתְמְנַע מִפֻּרְסָנֵיהּ:

LAWS OF CONSECRATION

The closing passage of Leviticus delineates some of the rules of *hekdesh*, "consecrating" – the process of setting a house, a field, an animal, or even oneself aside to be "sacred to the Lord." Our passage presupposes that in many cases the consecration will be symbolic, and a monetary donation to the Tabernacle will substitute for the person, animal, or place set aside. But sometimes the consecration was quite literal.

One example is the story of the young Shmuel, dedicated by his mother Ḥana to serve in the Sanctuary at Shiloh where he acted as an assistant to Eli the priest. In bed one night Shmuel heard a voice calling his name. He assumed it was Eli. He ran to see what he wanted but Eli told him he had not called. This happened a second time and then a third, and by then Eli realized that it was God calling the child. He told Shmuel that the next time the voice called his name, he should reply, "Speak, O Lord, for Your servant is listening" (I Sam. 3:9). It did not occur to the child that it might be God summoning him to a mission, but it was. In his case, consecration was linked to an audible calling.

In a subtle way, then, the ending of the book recalls the beginning. *Vayikra*, Rashi told us then, means *to be called to a task in love.* This is the source of one of the key ideas of Western thought, namely, the concept of a *vocation* or a *calling*, that is, the choice of a career or way of life not just because you want to do it, or because it offers certain benefits, but because you feel *summoned* to it. You feel this

19 If the person who consecrated the field wishes to redeem it, he shall add a fifth
20 to its valuation, and it shall be his again. But if he does not redeem the field, or
21 if it has been sold to someone else, it can no longer be redeemed. When the
field is released in the Jubilee, it shall be holy to the LORD like devoted land;
22 it comes into the priest's possession. If the person consecrates to the LORD SHISHI
23 a field he has purchased – not part of his hereditary land – the priest shall
calculate its proportionate value until the Jubilee year, and the donor shall pay
24 its valuation on that day, as a sacred donation to the LORD. In the Jubilee year
the field shall return to the person from whom it was bought, whose hereditary
25 land it was. All assessments shall follow the Sanctuary standard, by which a
26 shekel is twenty gerah. A person cannot consecrate a firstborn animal, whether
27 ox or sheep, because, being a firstling, it already belongs to the LORD. If it is an
impure animal, it may be redeemed for its valuation with a fifth added. If it is
28 not redeemed, it shall be sold at its assessed value. Nothing that a person owns
that has been devoted to the LORD – be it a person, an animal, or inherited
land – may be sold or redeemed. Every devoted thing is holy of holies to the
29 LORD. And no person condemned to utter destruction may be ransomed; he SHEVI'I

רש״י

יט **וְאִם גָּאֹל יִגְאַל... הַמַּקְדִּישׁ אֹתוֹ.** יוֹסִיף חֹמֶשׁ עַל הַקִּצְבָה הַזֹּאת:

כ **וְאִם לֹא יִגְאַל אֶת הַשָּׂדֶה.** הַמַּקְדִּישׁ: **וְאִם מָכַר.** הַגִּזְבָּר: **אֶת הַשָּׂדֶה לְאִישׁ אַחֵר לֹא יִגָּאֵל עוֹד.** לָשׁוּב לְיַד הַמַּקְדִּישׁ:

כא **וְהָיָה הַשָּׂדֶה בְּצֵאתוֹ בַיֹּבֵל.** מִיַּד הַלּוֹקְחוֹ מִן הַגִּזְבָּר, כְּדֶרֶךְ שְׁאָר שָׂדוֹת הַיּוֹצְאוֹת מִיַּד לוֹקְחֵיהֶם בַּיּוֹבֵל: **קֹדֶשׁ לַה׳.** לֹא שֶׁיָּשׁוּב לְהֶקְדֵּשׁ בֶּדֶק הַבַּיִת לְיַד הַגִּזְבָּר, אֶלָּא ״כִּשְׂדֵה הַחֵרֶם״ הַנָּתוּן לַכֹּהֲנִים, שֶׁנֶּאֱמַר ״כָּל חֵרֶם בְּיִשְׂרָאֵל לְךָ יִהְיֶה״ (במדבר יח, יד), אַף זוֹ תִּתְחַלֵּק לַכֹּהֲנִים שֶׁל אוֹתוֹ מִשְׁמָר שֶׁיּוֹם הַכִּפּוּרִים שֶׁל יוֹבֵל פּוֹגֵעַ בּוֹ:

כב **וְאִם אֶת שְׂדֵה מִקְנָתוֹ וְגוֹ׳.** חִלּוּק יֵשׁ בֵּין שְׂדֵה מִקְנָה לִשְׂדֵה אֲחֻזָּה, שֶׁשְּׂדֵה מִקְנָה לֹא תִתְחַלֵּק לַכֹּהֲנִים בַּיּוֹבֵל, לְפִי שֶׁאֵינוֹ יָכוֹל לְהַקְדִּישָׁהּ אֶלָּא עַד הַיּוֹבֵל, שֶׁהֲרֵי בַּיּוֹבֵל הָיְתָה עֲתִידָה לָצֵאת מִיָּדוֹ וְלָשׁוּב לַבְּעָלִים. לְפִיכָךְ אִם בָּא לְגָאֳלָהּ, יִגְאַל בַּדָּמִים הַלָּלוּ הַקְּצוּבִים לִשְׂדֵה אֲחֻזָּה. וְאִם לֹא יִגְאַל וּמְכָרָהּ הַגִּזְבָּר לְאַחֵר, אוֹ אִם יִגְאַל הוּא, ״בִּשְׁנַת הַיּוֹבֵל יָשׁוּב הַשָּׂדֶה לַאֲשֶׁר קָנָהוּ מֵאִתּוֹ״ (להלן פסוק כד), אוֹתוֹ שֶׁהִקְדִּישָׁהּ. וְשֶׁמָּא תֹּאמַר: ״לַאֲשֶׁר קָנָהוּ״ הַלּוֹקֵחַ הַזֶּה הָאַחֲרוֹן ״מֵאִתּוֹ״, וְזֶהוּ הַגִּזְבָּר, לְכָךְ הֻצְרַךְ לוֹמַר: ״לַאֲשֶׁר לוֹ אֲחֻזַּת הָאָרֶץ״ (שם) מִירֻשַּׁת אָבוֹת, וְזֶהוּ בְּעָלִים הָרִאשׁוֹנִים שֶׁמְּכָרוּהָ לַמַּקְדִּישׁ:

כה **וְכָל עֶרְכְּךָ יִהְיֶה בְּשֶׁקֶל הַקֹּדֶשׁ.** כָּל עֵרֶךְ שֶׁכָּתוּב בּוֹ ׳שְׁקָלִים׳ יִהְיֶה בְּשֶׁקֶל הַקֹּדֶשׁ: **עֶשְׂרִים גֵּרָה.** עֶשְׂרִים מָעוֹת, כָּךְ הָיוּ מִתְּחִלָּה, וּלְאַחַר מִכָּאן הוֹסִיפוּ שְׁתוּת, וְאָמְרוּ רַבּוֹתֵינוּ: שֵׁשׁ מָעָה כֶּסֶף דִּינָר, עֶשְׂרִים וְאַרְבַּע מָעוֹת לְסֶלַע:

כו **לֹא יַקְדִּישׁ אִישׁ אֹתוֹ.** לְשֵׁם קָרְבָּן אַחֵר, לְפִי שֶׁאֵינוֹ שֶׁלּוֹ:

כז **וְאִם בַּבְּהֵמָה הַטְּמֵאָה וְגוֹ׳.** אֵין הַמִּקְרָא הַזֶּה מוּסָב עַל הַבְּכוֹר, שֶׁאֵין לוֹמַר בִּבְכוֹר בְּהֵמָה טְמֵאָה ״וּפָדָה בְעֶרְכֶּךָ״, וַהֲמוֹר אֵין זֶה, שֶׁהֲרֵי אֵין פִּדְיוֹן פֶּטֶר חֲמוֹר אֶלָּא טָלֶה, וְהוּא מַתָּנָה לַכֹּהֵן וְאֵינוֹ לַהֶקְדֵּשׁ; אֶלָּא הַכָּתוּב מוּסָב עַל הַהֶקְדֵּשׁ, שֶׁהַכָּתוּב שֶׁל מַעְלָה דִּבֶּר בְּפִדְיוֹן בְּהֵמָה טְהוֹרָה שֶׁהוּמְמָה, וְכָאן דִּבֶּר בְּמַקְדִּישׁ בְּהֵמָה טְמֵאָה לְבֶדֶק הַבַּיִת: **וּפָדָה בְעֶרְכֶּךָ.** כְּפִי מַה שֶּׁיַּעֲרִיכֶנָּה הַכֹּהֵן: **וְאִם לֹא יִגָּאֵל.** עַל יְדֵי בְּעָלִים: **וְנִמְכַּר בְּעֶרְכֶּךָ.** לַאֲחֵרִים:

כח **אַךְ כָּל חֵרֶם וְגוֹ׳.** נֶחְלְקוּ רַבּוֹתֵינוּ בַּדָּבָר: יֵשׁ אוֹמְרִים סְתָם חֲרָמִים לַהֶקְדֵּשׁ, וּמָה אֲנִי מְקַיֵּם: ״כָּל חֵרֶם בְּיִשְׂרָאֵל לְךָ יִהְיֶה״ (במדבר יח, יד)? בְּחֶרְמֵי כֹּהֲנִים, שֶׁפֵּרֵשׁ וְאָמַר: ׳הֲרֵי זֶה חֵרֶם לַכֹּהֵן׳; וְיֵשׁ שֶׁאָמְרוּ סְתָם חֲרָמִים לַכֹּהֲנִים: **לֹא יִמָּכֵר וְלֹא יִגָּאֵל.** אֶלָּא יִנָּתֵן לַכֹּהֵן. לְדִבְרֵי הָאוֹמֵר סְתָם חֲרָמִים לַכֹּהֲנִים, מְפָרֵשׁ מִקְרָא זֶה בִּסְתָם חֲרָמִים, וְהָאוֹמֵר סְתָם חֲרָמִים לְבֶדֶק הַבַּיִת, מְפָרֵשׁ מִקְרָא זֶה בְּחֶרְמֵי כֹּהֲנִים, שֶׁהַכֹּל מוֹדִים שֶׁחֶרְמֵי כֹּהֲנִים אֵין לָהֶם פִּדְיוֹן עַד שֶׁיָּבֹאוּ לְיַד כֹּהֵן, וְחֶרְמֵי גָּבוֹהַּ נִפְדִּים: **כָּל חֵרֶם קֹדֶשׁ קָדָשִׁים הוּא.** הָאוֹמֵר סְתָם חֲרָמִים לְבֶדֶק הַבַּיִת מֵבִיא רְאָיָה מִכָּאן, וְהָאוֹמֵר סְתָם חֲרָמִים לַכֹּהֲנִים, מְפָרֵשׁ: ״כָּל חֵרֶם קֹדֶשׁ קָדָשִׁים הוּא לַה׳״ – לְלַמֵּד שֶׁחֶרְמֵי כֹּהֲנִים חָלִים עַל

יט וְאִם־גָּאֹל יִגְאַל אֶת־הַשָּׂדֶה הַמַּקְדִּישׁ אֹתוֹ וְיָסַף חֲמִשִׁית כֶּסֶף־עֶרְכְּךָ
כ עָלָיו וְקָם לוֹ: וְאִם־לֹא יִגְאַל אֶת־הַשָּׂדֶה וְאִם־מָכַר אֶת־הַשָּׂדֶה לְאִישׁ
כא אַחֵר לֹא־יִגָּאֵל עוֹד: וְהָיָה הַשָּׂדֶה בְּצֵאתוֹ בַיֹּבֵל קֹדֶשׁ לַיהוָה כִּשְׂדֵה
כב הַחֵרֶם לַכֹּהֵן תִּהְיֶה אֲחֻזָּתוֹ: וְאִם אֶת־שְׂדֵה מִקְנָתוֹ אֲשֶׁר לֹא מִשְּׂדֵה ששי
כג אֲחֻזָּתוֹ יַקְדִּישׁ לַיהוָה: וְחִשַּׁב־לוֹ הַכֹּהֵן אֵת מִכְסַת הָעֶרְכְּךָ עַד שְׁנַת
כד הַיֹּבֵל וְנָתַן אֶת־הָעֶרְכְּךָ בַּיּוֹם הַהוּא קֹדֶשׁ לַיהוָה: בִּשְׁנַת הַיּוֹבֵל
כה יָשׁוּב הַשָּׂדֶה לַאֲשֶׁר קָנָהוּ מֵאִתּוֹ לַאֲשֶׁר־לוֹ אֲחֻזַּת הָאָרֶץ: וְכָל־
כו עֶרְכְּךָ יִהְיֶה בְּשֶׁקֶל הַקֹּדֶשׁ עֶשְׂרִים גֵּרָה יִהְיֶה הַשָּׁקֶל: אַךְ־בְּכוֹר
אֲשֶׁר יְבֻכַּר לַיהוָה בִּבְהֵמָה לֹא־יַקְדִּישׁ אִישׁ אֹתוֹ אִם־שׁוֹר אִם־שֶׂה
כז לַיהוָה הוּא: וְאִם בַּבְּהֵמָה הַטְּמֵאָה וּפָדָה בְעֶרְכֶּךָ וְיָסַף חֲמִשִׁתוֹ
כח עָלָיו וְאִם־לֹא יִגָּאֵל וְנִמְכַּר בְּעֶרְכֶּךָ: אַךְ כָּל־חֵרֶם אֲשֶׁר יַחֲרִם אִישׁ
לַיהוָה מִכָּל־אֲשֶׁר־לוֹ מֵאָדָם וּבְהֵמָה וּמִשְּׂדֵה אֲחֻזָּתוֹ לֹא יִמָּכֵר וְלֹא
כט יִגָּאֵל כָּל־חֵרֶם קֹדֶשׁ־קָדָשִׁים הוּא לַיהוָה: כָּל־חֵרֶם אֲשֶׁר יָחֳרַם שביעי

אונקלוס

יט ואם מפרק יפרוק ית חקלא, דאקדיש יתיה, ויוסיף, חומש כסף פרסניה, עלוהי ויקום ליה: כ ואם לא יפרוק ית חקלא, ואם זבין ית חקלא לגבר אחרן, לא יתפריק עוד: כא ויהי חקלא במפקיה ביובילא, קודשא קדם יי כחקל חרמא, לכהנא תהי אחסנתיה: כב ואם ית חקל זבינוהי, דלא מחקל אחסנתיה, יקדיש קדם יי: כג ויחשיב ליה כהנא, ית נסיב פרסניה, עד שתא דיובילא, ויתין ית פרסניה ביומא ההוא, קודשא קדם יי: כד בשתא דיובילא יתוב חקלא, לדזבניה מניה, לדדיליה אחסנת ארעא: כה וכל פרסניה, יהי בסלעי קודשא, עסרין מעין יהי סלעא: כו ברם בוכרא, דיתבכר קדם יי בבעירא, לא יקדיש גבר יתיה, אם תור אם אמר, דיי הוא: כז ואם בבעירא מסאבא ויפרוק בפרסניה, ויוסיף חומשיה עלוהי, ואם לא יתפריק ויזדבן בפרסניה: כח ברם כל חרמא, דיחרים גבר קדם יי מכל דליה, מאנשא ובעירא ומחקל אחסנתיה, לא יזדבן ולא יתפריק, כל חרמא, קודש קודשין הוא קדם יי: כט כל חרמא,

a life driven by its energy, transformed by its alignment with the will and word of the Creator.

The end of the book, like its beginning, invites us to consider what it would mean for us to live a consecrated, dedicated life. We can suggest this as a guide: where what we want to do meets what needs to be done, that is where God wants us to be. For each of us God has a task: work to perform, a kindness to show, a gift to give, love to share, loneliness to ease, pain to heal, or broken lives to help mend. One of the great spiritual challenges for each of us is discerning that task, hearing *Vayikra*, God's call.

30 must be put to death. All tithes from the land, whether seed from the ground
31 or fruit of the tree, belong to the LORD; they are sacred to the LORD. If a person
32 wishes to redeem part of his tithe, he shall add a fifth to its value. All tithes MAFTIR
from the herd or flock – every tenth animal that passes under the shepherd's
33 staff – shall be sacred to the LORD. One should not pick out the good from
the bad or make any substitution. But if a substitution is made, both the item
34 and its substitute shall be sacred; they cannot be redeemed." These are the
commands that the LORD gave Moshe, on Mount Sinai, for the people of Israel.

The haftara for Parashat Beḥukotai is on page 1580 (even when Behar and Beḥukotai are read together).

רש"י

קָדְשֵׁי קָדָשִׁים וְעַל קָדָשִׁים קַלִּים, וְנוֹתֵן לַכֹּהֵן, כְּמוֹ שֶׁשָּׁנִינוּ בְּמַסֶּכֶת עֲרָכִין (דף כח ע"ב): אִם נֶדֶר נוֹתֵן דְּמֵיהֶם, וְאִם נְדָבָה נוֹתֵן אֶת טוֹבָתָהּ: **מֵאָדָם.** כְּגוֹן שֶׁהֶחֱרִים עֲבָדָיו וְשִׁפְחוֹתָיו הַכְּנַעֲנִים:

כט **כָּל חֵרֶם אֲשֶׁר יָחֳרַם וְגוֹ'.** הַיּוֹצֵא לֵהָרֵג וְאָמַר אֶחָד: 'עֶרְכּוֹ עָלַי', לֹא אָמַר כְּלוּם: **מוֹת יוּמָת.** הֲרֵי הוֹלֵךְ לָמוּת, לְפִיכָךְ "לֹא יִפָּדֶה", אֵין לוֹ דָּמִים וְלֹא עֵרֶךְ:

ל **וְכָל מַעְשַׂר הָאָרֶץ.** בְּמַעֲשֵׂר שֵׁנִי הַכָּתוּב מְדַבֵּר: **מִזֶּרַע הָאָרֶץ.** דָּגָן: **מִפְּרִי הָעֵץ.** תִּירוֹשׁ וְיִצְהָר: **לַה' הוּא.** קְנָאוֹ הַשֵּׁם, וּמִשֻּׁלְחָנוֹ צִוָּה לְךָ לַעֲלוֹת וְלֶאֱכֹל בִּירוּשָׁלַיִם, כְּמוֹ שֶׁנֶּאֱמַר: "וְאָכַלְתָּ לִפְנֵי ה' אֱלֹהֶיךָ... מַעְשַׂר דְּגָנְךָ תִּירֹשְׁךָ" וְגוֹ' (דברים יד, כג):

לא **מִמַּעַשְׂרוֹ.** וְלֹא מִמַּעֲשַׂר חֲבֵרוֹ; הַפּוֹדֶה מַעֲשֵׂר שֶׁל חֲבֵרוֹ אֵין מוֹסִיף חֹמֶשׁ. וּמַה הִיא גְּאֻלָּתוֹ? כְּדֵי לְהַתִּירוֹ בַּאֲכִילָה בְּכָל מָקוֹם, וְהַמָּעוֹת יַעֲלֶה וְיֹאכַל בִּירוּשָׁלַיִם, כְּמוֹ שֶׁכָּתוּב: "וְנָתַתָּה בַּכָּסֶף" וְגוֹ' (שם פסוק כה):

לב **תַּחַת הַשָּׁבֶט.** כְּשֶׁבָּא לְעַשְּׂרָן מוֹצִיאָן בַּפֶּתַח זֶה אַחַר זֶה, וְהָעֲשִׂירִי מַכֶּה בְּשֵׁבֶט צְבוּעָה בְּסִיקְרָא, לִהְיוֹת נִכָּר שֶׁהוּא מַעֲשֵׂר, כֵּן עוֹשֶׂה לַטְּלָאִים וְלָעֲגָלִים שֶׁל כָּל שָׁנָה וְשָׁנָה: **יִהְיֶה קֹּדֶשׁ.** לִקָּרֵב לַמִּזְבֵּחַ דָּמוֹ וְאֵמוּרָיו, וְהַבָּשָׂר נֶאֱכָל לַבְּעָלִים, שֶׁהֲרֵי לֹא נִמְנָה עִם שְׁאָר מַתְּנוֹת כְּהֻנָּה, וְלֹא מָצִינוּ שֶׁיְּהֵא נִתָּן לַכֹּהֲנִים:

לג **לֹא יְבַקֵּר וְגוֹ'.** לְפִי שֶׁנֶּאֱמַר: "וְכֹל מִבְחַר נִדְרֵיכֶם" (שם יב, יא), יָכוֹל יְהֵא בּוֹרֵר וּמוֹצִיא אֶת הַיָּפֶה? תַּלְמוּד לוֹמַר: "לֹא יְבַקֵּר בֵּין טוֹב לָרַע", בֵּין תָּם בֵּין בַּעַל מוּם חָלָה עָלָיו קְדֻשָּׁה. וְלֹא שֶׁיִּקְרַב בַּעַל מוּם, אֶלָּא יֵאָכֵל בְּתוֹרַת מַעֲשֵׂר, וְאָסוּר לְגָזֵז וְלֵעָבֵד:

ל מִן־הָאָדָם לֹא יִפָּדֶה מוֹת יוּמָת׃ וְכָל־מַעְשַׂר הָאָרֶץ מִזֶּרַע הָאָרֶץ
לא מִפְּרִי הָעֵץ לַיהוָה הוּא קֹדֶשׁ לַיהוָה׃ וְאִם־גָּאֹל יִגְאַל אִישׁ מִמַּעַשְׂרוֹ
לב חֲמִשִׁיתוֹ יֹסֵף עָלָיו׃ וְכָל־מַעְשַׂר בָּקָר וָצֹאן כֹּל אֲשֶׁר־יַעֲבֹר תַּחַת מפטיר
לג הַשָּׁבֶט הָעֲשִׂירִי יִהְיֶה־קֹּדֶשׁ לַיהוָה׃ לֹא יְבַקֵּר בֵּין־טוֹב לָרַע וְלֹא
יְמִירֶנּוּ וְאִם־הָמֵר יְמִירֶנּוּ וְהָיָה־הוּא וּתְמוּרָתוֹ יִהְיֶה־קֹּדֶשׁ לֹא יִגָּאֵל׃
לד אֵלֶּה הַמִּצְוֹת אֲשֶׁר צִוָּה יְהוָה אֶת־מֹשֶׁה אֶל־בְּנֵי יִשְׂרָאֵל בְּהַר סִינָי׃

The הפטרה *for* פרשת בחקתי *is on page page 1581
(even when* בהר *and* בחקתי *are read together).*

אונקלוס

דִּיתַּחְרַם, מִן אֲנָשָׁא לָא יִתְפְּרֵיק, אִתְקְטָלָא יִתְקְטִיל: ל וְכָל מַעְסַר אַרְעָא, מִזַּרְעָא דְּאַרְעָא מִפֵּירֵי אִילָנָא, דַּיי הוּא, קֻדְשָׁא קֳדָם יי: לא וְאִם מִפְרַק יִפְרוֹק, גְּבַר מִמַּעַסְרֵיהּ, חֻמְשֵׁיהּ יוֹסֵיף עֲלוֹהִי: לב וְכָל מַעְסַר תּוֹרִין וְעָן, כֹּל דְּיִעְבַּר תְּחוֹת חֻטְרָא, עֲסִירָאָה, יְהֵי קֻדְשָׁא קֳדָם יי: לג לָא יְבַקַּר, בֵּין טָב לְבִישׁ וְלָא יְחַלְפִנֵּיהּ, וְאִם חַלָּפָא יְחַלְפִנֵּיהּ, וִיהֵי הוּא וְחִלּוּפֵיהּ, יְהֵי קֻדְשָׁא לָא יִתְפְּרֵיק: לד אִלֵּין פִּקּוֹדַיָּא, דְּפַקֵּיד יי, יָת מֹשֶׁה לְוָת בְּנֵי יִשְׂרָאֵל, בְּטוּרָא דְּסִינָי:

במדבר
NUMBERS

THE BOOK OF NUMBERS

Numbers is not an easy book to read. It is among the most self-critical books about what Nelson Mandela called "the long walk to freedom." Its message is that there is no shortcut to liberty. Numbers is a sober warning set in the midst of a text – the Torah – that remains the master narrative of hope.

The Mosaic books, especially Exodus and Numbers, are about the journey from slavery to freedom and from oppression to law-governed liberty. On the map, the distance traveled from Egypt to the Promised Land is not far. But the message of Numbers is that it always takes longer than you think. For the journey is not just physical, a walk across the desert. It is psychological, moral, and spiritual. It takes as long as the time needed for human beings to change.

Political change cannot be brought about by politics alone. It needs human transformation, brought about by rituals, habits of the heart, and a strenuous process of education. It comes along with knowledge born out of painful experience, preserved for future generations by acts of remembering. You cannot arrive at freedom merely by escaping from slavery. It is won only when a nation takes upon itself the responsibilities of self-restraint, courage, and patience.

Exodus and Numbers have much in common. Both tell of distances traversed and battles fought. Both tell of a series of breakdowns of morale. In both books the people romanticize the past, thinking of Egypt not as a land of oppression but as a place of safety where they had food and security. In both, there is a major sin that threatens the entire future of the people: in Exodus, the golden calf, in Numbers, the episode of the spies.

A key difference is in the nature of the journey itself. In Exodus, it is a journey from; it is the story of an escape. In Numbers, it is a journey to, a story of approach and preparation. These are not just two halves of a single story. Exodus and Numbers represent two different kinds of liberty. Exodus is about negative freedom, *ḥofesh* in Hebrew. Numbers is about positive freedom, for which the Sages coined the word *ḥerut*. Negative freedom is what a slave acquires when he or she is liberated. There is no one to give you orders. But a society in which everyone is free to do what they choose is not a free society. It is anarchy. A free society requires codes and disciplines of self-restraint so that my freedom is not bought at the cost of yours. It is a society of law-governed liberty, or positive freedom. What matters in Exodus is how the people escape from Pharaoh. What matters in Numbers is how they rise to the challenge of self-rule and responsibility.

PARASHAT BEMIDBAR

1 1 The LORD spoke to Moshe in the Sinai Desert, in the Tent of Meeting, on the
first of the second month, in the second year since their coming out from the
2 land of Egypt. He said: "Take a census of the entire community of Israel by
their clans and their ancestral houses, listing every male by name individually,
3 twenty years of age and upward: everyone in Israel who is capable of active

רש״י

א א| בְּמִדְבַּר סִינַי בְּאֶחָד לַחֹדֶשׁ. מִתּוֹךְ חִבָּתָן לְפָנָיו מוֹנֶה אוֹתָם כָּל שָׁעָה. כְּשֶׁיָּצְאוּ מִמִּצְרַיִם מְנָאָן (שמות יב, לז), וּכְשֶׁנָּפְלוּ בָּעֵגֶל מְנָאָן לֵידַע הַנּוֹתָרִים. וּכְשֶׁבָּא לְהַשְׁרוֹת שְׁכִינָתוֹ עֲלֵיהֶם מְנָאָם. בְּאֶחָד בְּנִיסָן הוּקַם הַמִּשְׁכָּן וּבְאֶחָד בְּאִיָּר מְנָאָם:

ב| לְמִשְׁפְּחֹתָם. דַּע מִנְיַן כָּל שֵׁבֶט וָשֵׁבֶט: לְבֵית אֲבֹתָם. מִי שֶׁאָבִיו מִשֵּׁבֶט אֶחָד וְאִמּוֹ מִשֵּׁבֶט אַחֵר יָקוּם עַל שֵׁבֶט אָבִיו: לְגֻלְגְּלֹתָם. עַל יְדֵי שְׁקָלִים, בֶּקַע לַגֻּלְגֹּלֶת:

ג| כָּל יֹצֵא צָבָא. מַגִּיד שֶׁאֵין יוֹצֵא בַּצָּבָא פָּחוֹת מִבֶּן עֶשְׂרִים:

Israelites as a whole who experienced the wilderness years. This too is essential to the distributed and democratized nature of Jewish spirituality.

The way to the Holy Land lies through the wilderness. The desert was the place where the people could be alone with God. There, undistracted by the sight of natural or man-made beauty, they could hear God's voice directly. What they heard was a counterintuitive challenge: to take the pain of suffering in Egypt forward with them and redirect it into creating a society that would be the opposite of Egypt, not an empire built on power but a society of individuals of equal dignity under the sovereignty of God.

1:2 שְׂאוּ אֶת־רֹאשׁ כָּל־עֲדַת בְּנֵי־יִשְׂרָאֵל *Take a census* – The book of Numbers begins with a census of the Israelites. That is why this book is known in English as Numbers, rather than "In the Desert" or similar, as in Hebrew. This raises a number of questions: What is the significance of this act of counting? And why here at the beginning of the book? Rashi notes that this is not the first time the people have been counted. Their number was already given as they prepared to leave Egypt (Ex. 12:37). A more precise calculation was made when the adult males each gave a half shekel toward the building of the Sanctuary (ch. 30, 38:26). In Numbers, a third and fourth count took place. Why so often?

Rashi's answer is simple and moving:

> Because they [the children of Israel] are dear to Him, God counts them often. He counted them when they were about to leave Egypt. He counted them after the golden calf to establish how many were left. When He was about to cause His presence to rest on them [with the inauguration of the Sanctuary], He counted them again. (Rashi on Num. 1:1)

For Rashi, the counting of the people was an act of divine love.

The phrase the Torah uses to describe the act of counting: *se'u et rosh*, literally, to "lift the head," is a strange, indirect expression. Biblical Hebrew contains many verbs meaning "to count": *limnot, lifkod, lispor, laḥshov*. Why does the Torah not use one of these words, choosing instead the roundabout expression "lift the heads" of the people?

In any census, head count, or roll call there is a tendency to focus on the total: the crowd, the multitude, the mass. Counting a group devalues the individual and tends to make him or her replaceable. If one soldier dies in battle, another will take his place. If one person leaves the organization, someone else can be hired to do his or her job. There is therefore a danger, when counting a nation, that each individual will feel insignificant. "What am I? What difference can I make? I am only one of millions, a mere wave in the ocean, a grain of sand on the seashore, dust on the surface

פרשת במדבר

א א וַיְדַבֵּ֨ר יְהוָ֧ה אֶל־מֹשֶׁ֛ה בְּמִדְבַּ֥ר סִינַ֖י בְּאֹ֣הֶל מוֹעֵ֑ד בְּאֶחָד֩ לַחֹ֨דֶשׁ הַשֵּׁנִ֜י א
ב בַּשָּׁנָ֣ה הַשֵּׁנִ֗ית לְצֵאתָ֛ם מֵאֶ֥רֶץ מִצְרַ֖יִם לֵאמֹֽר׃ שְׂא֗וּ אֶת־רֹאשׁ֙ כָּל־
עֲדַ֣ת בְּנֵֽי־יִשְׂרָאֵ֔ל לְמִשְׁפְּחֹתָ֖ם לְבֵ֣ית אֲבֹתָ֑ם בְּמִסְפַּ֣ר שֵׁמ֔וֹת כָּל־זָכָ֖ר
ג לְגֻלְגְּלֹתָֽם׃ מִבֶּ֨ן עֶשְׂרִ֤ים שָׁנָה֙ וָמַ֔עְלָה כָּל־יֹצֵ֥א צָבָ֖א בְּיִשְׂרָאֵ֑ל תִּפְקְד֧וּ

אונקלוס

א א וּמַלֵּיל יי עִם מֹשֶׁה, בְּמַדְבְּרָא דְסִינַי בְּמַשְׁכַּן זִמְנָא, בְּחַד לְיַרְחָא תִנְיָנָא בְּשַׁתָּא תִנְיֵיתָא, לְמִפַּקְהוֹן, מֵאַרְעָא דְמִצְרַיִם לְמֵימַר: ב קַבִּילוּ, יָת חֻשְׁבַּן כָּל כְּנִשְׁתָּא דִבְנֵי יִשְׂרָאֵל, לְזַרְעִיָתְהוֹן לְבֵית אֲבָהָתְהוֹן, בְּמִנְיַן שְׁמָהָן, כָּל דְכוּרָא לְגֻלְגְּלָתְהוֹן: ג מִבַּר עַסְרִין שְׁנִין וּלְעֵילָא, כָּל נָפֵיק חֵילָא בְּיִשְׂרָאֵל, תִּמְנוֹן

BEMIDBAR

The central theme of the book of Numbers is the second stage of the Israelites' journey, physically from Egypt to the Promised Land, mentally from slavery to freedom. This *parasha* and the following one are about the preparations for that journey, the first of which is to take a census. To inherit the land, the Israelites will have to fight battles. Hence the census, specifically of men between the ages of twenty and sixty – that is, those eligible to serve in war. The Levites are counted separately because it is not their role to fight but to minister in the Sanctuary.

Instructions are given as to the layout of the camp, which is to be arranged in a square with the Sanctuary in the middle. Three tribes are to set up their tents and banners on each side, while the Levites form an inner square. The order in which they encamp is also the order in which they will journey.

The duties of the family of Kehat – which also includes Moshe, Aharon, and Miriam, who have other roles – are spelled out. It is their task to carry the sacred objects, the Ark, table, candelabrum (menora), altars, curtains, and holy vessels used in the sacrificial service, when the Israelites journey. This task demands special care.

The name of our *parasha* underscores the fact that the founding drama of the Israelites as a nation under the sovereignty of God is enacted, not in the Promised Land, but in the wilderness on the way.

1:1 בְּמִדְבַּר סִינַי *The Sinai Desert* – The Egyptian-French poet Edmond Jabès (1912–91) noted the connection between *d-b-r*, "word," and *m-d-b-r*, "desert." For him, the wilderness experience is an essential and continuing feature of what it is to be a Jew: "With exemplary regularity the Jew chooses to set out for the desert, to go toward a renewed world that has become his origin." For Jabès, the desert – with its unearthly silence and emptiness – is the condition in which the Word can be heard. There, between sand and sky, the unmediated encounter takes place between God and His people. There is something stark and austere about the wilderness, as there is about Judaism. In no other religion do God and humanity stand in such direct closeness, engaging in such frank and direct dialogue. Judaism is faith stripped of all accretions of myth.

Note also what is unique about the Jewish story. It is not unknown in the history of religion for founders to spend time alone – their "wilderness years" – during which their understanding of their mission takes shape. There are such stories told of the heroes of Buddhism, Christianity, and Islam. What is unique to the Jewish experience is that *this happened to an entire people*. It was not Moshe alone but the

4 service. You and Aharon shall number them by their divisions. And one man
from each tribe shall join you in the task, each the head of his ancestral house.
5 These are the names of the men who will assist you: from Reuven, Elitzur son of
6 7 Shedeiur; from Shimon, Shelumiel son of Tzurishadai; from Yehuda, Naḥshon
8 9 son of Aminadav; from Yissakhar, Netanel son of Tzuar; from Zevulun, Eliav
10 son of Ḥelon. For the sons of Yosef: from Efrayim, Elishama son of Amihud;
11 from Menashe, Gamliel son of Pedatzur. From Binyamin, Avidan son of Gidoni;
12 13, 14 from Dan, Aḥiezer son of Amishadai; from Asher, Pagiel son of Okhran; from
15, 16 Gad, Elyasaf son of Deuel; and from Naftali, Aḥira son of Einan." These were
the ones chosen from the community, princes of their ancestral tribes; they
17 are the heads of Israel's clans. Moshe and Aharon took these men, those who
18 had been marked out by name, and they convened the entire community on
the first day of the second month. And the people declared themselves by their
clans and their ancestral houses. All those over twenty years old were counted

רש״י

ד| **וְאִתְּכֶם יִהְיוּ.** כְּשֶׁתִּפְקְדוּ אוֹתָם יִהְיוּ עִמָּכֶם נְשִׂיא כָּל שֵׁבֶט וָשֵׁבֶט:
טז| **אֵלֶּה קְרוּאֵי הָעֵדָה.** הַנִּקְרָאִים לְכָל דְּבַר חֲשִׁיבוּת שֶׁבָּעֵדָה:
יז| **אֵת הָאֲנָשִׁים הָאֵלֶּה.** אֵת שְׁנֵים עָשָׂר נְשִׂיאִים הַלָּלוּ: **אֲשֶׁר נִקְּבוּ.** לוֹ כָּאן בְּשֵׁמוֹת:
יח| **וַיִּתְיַלְדוּ עַל מִשְׁפְּחֹתָם.** הֵבִיאוּ סִפְרֵי יִחוּסֵיהֶם וְעֵדֵי חֶזְקַת לֵדָתָם, כָּל אֶחָד וְאֶחָד לְהִתְיַחֵס עַל הַשֵּׁבֶט:

In Judaism, by stark contrast, political leadership had little or no ritual function (other than the king's recital of the book of the covenant every seven years in the ritual known as *hak'hel*). Indeed, the chief objection to the Hasmonean kings on the part of the Sages was that they broke this ancient rule, some of them declaring themselves High Priests also. The Talmud records the objection: "Let the crown of kingship be sufficient for you. Leave the crown of priesthood to the sons of Aharon" (Kiddushin 66a). The effect of this principle was to *secularize power*.

No less fundamental was the division of religious leadership itself into two distinct functions: that of the prophet and the priest. Priests constituted a religious establishment. The prophets, at least those whose messages have been eternalized in Tanakh, were not an establishment but an anti-establishment, critical of the powers that be. It is the fate of establishments, especially those whose membership is a matter of birth, to become corrupt. That is why the prophets were essential. They were the world's first social critics, mandated by God to speak truth to power. The essential lesson of the Torah is that leadership can never be confined to one class or role. It must always be distributed and divided. In ancient Israel, kings dealt with power, priests with holiness, and prophets with the integrity and faithfulness of society as a whole. In Judaism, leadership is less a *function* than a *field of tensions* between different roles, each with its own perspective and voice.

Leadership in Judaism is *counterpoint*, a musical form defined as "the technique of combining two or more melodic lines in such a way that they establish a harmonic relationship while retaining their linear individuality." In Leviticus, Moshe and Aharon lead the people side by side; in Numbers, the people's own representatives step forward, bringing an added layer of complexity to the dynamics of the people. It is this internal complexity that is ultimately to give Jewish leadership its vigor, saving it from entropy, the loss of energy over time.

ד אֹתָם לְצִבְאֹתָם אַתָּה וְאַהֲרֹן׃ וְאִתְּכֶם יִהְיוּ אִישׁ אִישׁ לַמַּטֶּה אִישׁ רֹאשׁ
ה לְבֵית־אֲבֹתָיו הוּא׃ וְאֵלֶּה שְׁמוֹת הָאֲנָשִׁים אֲשֶׁר יַעַמְדוּ אִתְּכֶם לִרְאוּבֵן
ו ז אֱלִיצוּר בֶּן־שְׁדֵיאוּר׃ לְשִׁמְעוֹן שְׁלֻמִיאֵל בֶּן־צוּרִישַׁדָּי׃ לִיהוּדָה נַחְשׁוֹן
ח ט בֶּן־עַמִּינָדָב׃ לְיִשָּׂשכָר נְתַנְאֵל בֶּן־צוּעָר׃ לִזְבוּלֻן אֱלִיאָב בֶּן־חֵלֹן׃
י לִבְנֵי יוֹסֵף לְאֶפְרַיִם אֱלִישָׁמָע בֶּן־עַמִּיהוּד לִמְנַשֶּׁה גַּמְלִיאֵל בֶּן־
יא יב יג פְּדָהצוּר׃ לְבִנְיָמִן אֲבִידָן בֶּן־גִּדְעֹנִי׃ לְדָן אֲחִיעֶזֶר בֶּן־עַמִּישַׁדָּי׃ לְאָשֵׁר
יד טו פַּגְעִיאֵל בֶּן־עָכְרָן׃ לְגָד אֶלְיָסָף בֶּן־דְּעוּאֵל׃ לְנַפְתָּלִי אֲחִירַע בֶּן־עֵינָן׃
טז אֵלֶּה קריאֵי הָעֵדָה נְשִׂיאֵי מַטּוֹת אֲבוֹתָם רָאשֵׁי אַלְפֵי יִשְׂרָאֵל הֵם׃ קְרוּאֵי
יז יח וַיִּקַּח מֹשֶׁה וְאַהֲרֹן אֵת הָאֲנָשִׁים הָאֵלֶּה אֲשֶׁר נִקְּבוּ בְּשֵׁמוֹת׃ וְאֵת
כָּל־הָעֵדָה הִקְהִילוּ בְּאֶחָד לַחֹדֶשׁ הַשֵּׁנִי וַיִּתְיַלְדוּ עַל־מִשְׁפְּחֹתָם
לְבֵית אֲבֹתָם בְּמִסְפַּר שֵׁמוֹת מִבֶּן עֶשְׂרִים שָׁנָה וָמַעְלָה לְגֻלְגְּלֹתָם׃

אונקלוס

יָתְהוֹן, לְחֵילֵיהוֹן אַתְּ וְאַהֲרֹן: ד וְעִמְּכוֹן יְהוֹן, גְּבְרָא גְּבְרָא לְשִׁבְטָא, גְּבַר, רֵישׁ לְבֵית אֲבָהָתוֹהִי הוּא: ה וְאִלֵּין שְׁמָהָת גֻּבְרַיָּא, דִּיקוּמוּן עִמְּכוֹן, לִרְאוּבֵן, אֱלִיצוּר בַּר שְׁדֵיאוּר: ו לְשִׁמְעוֹן, שְׁלוּמִיאֵל בַּר צוּרִישַׁדָּי: ז לִיהוּדָה, נַחְשׁוֹן בַּר עַמִּינָדָב: ח לְיִשָּׂשכָר, נְתַנְאֵל בַּר צוּעָר: ט לִזְבוּלוּן, אֱלִיאָב בַּר חֵלוֹן: י לִבְנֵי יוֹסֵף, לְאֶפְרַיִם, אֱלִישָׁמָע בַּר עַמִּיהוּד, לִמְנַשֶּׁה, גַּמְלִיאֵל בַּר פְּדָהצוּר: יא לְבִנְיָמִין, אֲבִידָן בַּר גִּדְעוֹנִי: יב לְדָן, אֲחִיעֶזֶר בַּר עַמִּישַׁדָּי: יג לְאָשֵׁר, פַּגְעִיאֵל בַּר עָכְרָן: יד לְגָד, אֶלְיָסָף בַּר דְּעוּאֵל: טו לְנַפְתָּלִי, אֲחִירַע בַּר עֵינָן: טז אִלֵּין מְעָרְעֵי כְּנִשְׁתָּא, רַבְרְבֵי שִׁבְטֵי אֲבָהָתְהוֹן, רֵישֵׁי, אַלְפַיָּא דְּיִשְׂרָאֵל אִנּוּן: יז וּדְבַר מֹשֶׁה וְאַהֲרֹן, יָת גֻּבְרַיָּא הָאִלֵּין, דְּאִתְפָּרַשׁוּ בִּשְׁמָהָן: יח וְיָת כָּל כְּנִשְׁתָּא כְּנַשׁוּ, בְּחַד לְיַרְחָא תִּנְיָנָא, וְאִתְיַחַסוּ עַל זַרְעִיָּתְהוֹן לְבֵית אֲבָהָתְהוֹן, בְּמִנְיַן שְׁמָהָן, מִבַּר עֶסְרִין שְׁנִין, וּלְעֵילָּא לְגֻלְגְּלָתְהוֹן:

powers." Neither authority nor power was to be located in a single individual or office. Instead, leadership was divided between different kinds of roles.

One of the key divisions – anticipating by millennia the "separation of church and state" – was between the king, the head of state, on the one hand, and the High Priest, the most senior religious office, on the other.

This was revolutionary. The kings of Mesopotamian city-states and the pharaohs of Egypt were considered demigods or chief intermediaries with the gods. They officiated at supreme religious festivals. They were regarded as the representatives of heaven on earth.

of infinity." So God tells Moshe to "lift people's heads" and to show them that they each count; they all matter as individuals. To lift someone's head means to show them favor, to recognize them. If a census is taken in this way, it is a gesture of love.

PRINCES OF THE TRIBES

For the first time here, we meet those "chosen from the community" as representatives, "princes" of the tribes. One of the most important Jewish contributions to our understanding of leadership is its early insistence of what, in the eighteenth century, Montesquieu called "the separation of

▶

19 individually by name, as the Lord had commanded Moshe; so it was that he
20 counted them in the Sinai Desert. The children of Reuven, Yisrael's SHENI
firstborn – his descendants by their clans and their ancestral families – the
tally of their names, each male aged twenty years and above: everyone capable
21 of active service, all counted individually – those counted from the tribe of
Reuven numbered 46,500.
22 Of the children of Shimon – his descendants by their clans and their ancestral
families – the tally of their names, each male aged twenty years and above:
23 everyone capable of active service, all counted individually – those counted
from the tribe of Shimon numbered 59,300.
24 Of the children of Gad – his descendants by their clans and their ancestral
families – the tally of their names, each male aged twenty years and above:
25 everyone capable of active service, all counted individually – those counted
from the tribe of Gad numbered 45,650.
26 Of the children of Yehuda – his descendants by their clans and their ancestral
families – the tally of their names, each male aged twenty years and above:
27 everyone capable of active service, all counted individually – those counted
from the tribe of Yehuda numbered 74,600.

---

end of the book, with a shock you see that that empty page has your name on it. And you realize that is the chapter that you have to write.

Can you just put that book back on the shelf and walk away and forget it? If you did, all those two hundred generations of your ancestors would have kept that book going in vain, because it would have stopped with you. You have to write your chapter in that book, and when the time comes, hand that book on to your children and grandchildren.

The Baal Shem Tov used a similar image. He said that the Jewish people are a living *sefer Torah*, and every Jew is one of its letters. It is an image that invites a question – *the* question: will we, in our lifetime, be letters in the scroll of the Jewish people?

At some stage, each of us must decide how to live our lives. We have many options, and no generation in history has had a wider choice. We can live for work or success or wealth or fame or power. We can have a whole series of lifestyles and relationships. We can explore any of a myriad of faiths, mysticisms, or therapies. There is only one constraint – namely, that however much of anything else we have, we have only one life, and it is short. How we live and what we live for are the most fateful decisions we ever make.

We can live life as a succession of moments spent, like coins, in return for pleasures of various kinds. Or we can see our life as though it were a letter of the alphabet. A letter on its own has no meaning, yet when letters are joined to others they make a word, words combine with others to make a sentence, sentences connect to make a paragraph, and paragraphs join to make a story. That is how the Baal Shem Tov understood life. Every Jew is a letter. Each Jewish family is a word, every community a sentence, and the Jewish people at any one time are a paragraph. The Jewish people through time constitute a story, the strangest and most moving story in the annals of mankind. Every one of us has our part to write in that story before handing the book on. The men of Moshe's census, reporting as fit for service if required, are shrouded in the past, together with their sisters, elders, and children. Yet we carry them all in our DNA, our names, and our story. We too are counted – individually, yet as part of the whole.

יט כ כַּאֲשֶׁר צִוָּה יְהוָה אֶת־מֹשֶׁה וַיִּפְקְדֵם בְּמִדְבַּר סִינָי׃ וַיִּהְיוּ שני
בְנֵי־רְאוּבֵן בְּכֹר יִשְׂרָאֵל תּוֹלְדֹתָם לְמִשְׁפְּחֹתָם לְבֵית אֲבֹתָם בְּמִסְפַּר
שֵׁמוֹת לְגֻלְגְּלֹתָם כָּל־זָכָר מִבֶּן עֶשְׂרִים שָׁנָה וָמַעְלָה כֹּל יֹצֵא צָבָא׃
כא פְּקֻדֵיהֶם לְמַטֵּה רְאוּבֵן שִׁשָּׁה וְאַרְבָּעִים אֶלֶף וַחֲמֵשׁ מֵאוֹת׃
כב לִבְנֵי שִׁמְעוֹן תּוֹלְדֹתָם לְמִשְׁפְּחֹתָם לְבֵית אֲבֹתָם פְּקֻדָיו בְּמִסְפַּר שֵׁמוֹת
כג לְגֻלְגְּלֹתָם כָּל־זָכָר מִבֶּן עֶשְׂרִים שָׁנָה וָמַעְלָה כֹּל יֹצֵא צָבָא׃ פְּקֻדֵיהֶם
לְמַטֵּה שִׁמְעוֹן תִּשְׁעָה וַחֲמִשִּׁים אֶלֶף וּשְׁלֹשׁ מֵאוֹת׃
כד לִבְנֵי גָד תּוֹלְדֹתָם לְמִשְׁפְּחֹתָם לְבֵית אֲבֹתָם בְּמִסְפַּר שֵׁמוֹת מִבֶּן
כה עֶשְׂרִים שָׁנָה וָמַעְלָה כֹּל יֹצֵא צָבָא׃ פְּקֻדֵיהֶם לְמַטֵּה גָד חֲמִשָּׁה
וְאַרְבָּעִים אֶלֶף וְשֵׁשׁ מֵאוֹת וַחֲמִשִּׁים׃
כו לִבְנֵי יְהוּדָה תּוֹלְדֹתָם לְמִשְׁפְּחֹתָם לְבֵית אֲבֹתָם בְּמִסְפַּר שֵׁמֹת מִבֶּן
כז עֶשְׂרִים שָׁנָה וָמַעְלָה כֹּל יֹצֵא צָבָא׃ פְּקֻדֵיהֶם לְמַטֵּה יְהוּדָה אַרְבָּעָה
וְשִׁבְעִים אֶלֶף וְשֵׁשׁ מֵאוֹת׃

אונקלוס

יט כְּמָא דְפַקֵּיד יי יָת מֹשֶׁה, וּמְנַנּוּן בְּמַדְבְּרָא דְסִינָי: כ וַהֲווֹ בְנֵי רְאוּבֵן
בֻּכְרָא דְיִשְׂרָאֵל, תּוּלְדָתְהוֹן לְזַרְעֲיָתְהוֹן לְבֵית אֲבָהָתְהוֹן, בְּמִנְיַן
שְׁמָהָן לְגֻלְגְּלָתְהוֹן, כָּל דְּכוּרָא, מִבַּר עַסְרִין שְׁנִין וּלְעֵילָא, כָּל נָפֵיק
חֵילָא: כא מִנְיָנֵיהוֹן לְשִׁבְטָא דִרְאוּבֵן, אַרְבְּעִין וְשִׁתָּא אַלְפִין וַחֲמֵשׁ
מְאָה: כב לִבְנֵי שִׁמְעוֹן, תּוּלְדָתְהוֹן לְזַרְעֲיָתְהוֹן לְבֵית אֲבָהָתְהוֹן,
מִנְיָנוֹהִי, בְּמִנְיַן שְׁמָהָן לְגֻלְגְּלָתְהוֹן, כָּל דְּכוּרָא, מִבַּר עַסְרִין שְׁנִין
וּלְעֵילָא, כָּל נָפֵיק חֵילָא: כג מִנְיָנֵיהוֹן לְשִׁבְטָא דְשִׁמְעוֹן, חַמְשִׁין
וְתִשְׁעָא אַלְפִין וּתְלָת מְאָה: כד לִבְנֵי גָד, תּוּלְדָתְהוֹן לְזַרְעֲיָתְהוֹן
לְבֵית אֲבָהָתְהוֹן, בְּמִנְיַן שְׁמָהָן, מִבַּר עַסְרִין שְׁנִין וּלְעֵילָא, כָּל
נָפֵיק חֵילָא: כה מִנְיָנֵיהוֹן לְשִׁבְטָא דְגָד, אַרְבְּעִין וַחֲמִשָּׁא אַלְפִין,
וְשֵׁית מְאָה וְחַמְשִׁין: כו לִבְנֵי יְהוּדָה, תּוּלְדָתְהוֹן לְזַרְעֲיָתְהוֹן לְבֵית
אֲבָהָתְהוֹן, בְּמִנְיַן שְׁמָהָן, מִבַּר עַסְרִין שְׁנִין וּלְעֵילָא, כָּל נָפֵיק חֵילָא:
כז מִנְיָנֵיהוֹן לְשִׁבְטָא דִיהוּדָה, שִׁבְעִין וְאַרְבְּעָא אַלְפִין וְשֵׁית מְאָה:

TO BE COUNTED

Each man in the census is "counted individually by name" (Num. 1:18), a person in his own right within the tally. We can picture an allegory for this passage. Imagine that you are in an enormous library. You are wandering through, looking at all the titles of the books, and then suddenly you stop dead. There is a book and the cover has your name on it. You take it out, you open it up, and you see that there are several hundred pages of that book written by many different hands in different languages. And you try to work out what this book is. And with a shock, you realize that this book has been written by your ancestors. Every single one of them has written a chapter in this book telling their story and handing it on to their children. And as you get to the

28 Of the children of Yissakhar – his descendants by their clans and their ancestral
families – the tally of their names, each male aged twenty years and above:
29 everyone capable of active service, all counted individually – those counted
from the tribe of Yissakhar numbered 54,400.
30 Of the children of Zevulun – his descendants by their clans and their ancestral
families – the tally of their names, each male aged twenty years and above:
31 everyone capable of active service, all counted individually – those counted
from the tribe of Zevulun numbered 57,400.
32 Of the children of Yosef: of the children of Efrayim – his descendants by
their clans and their ancestral families – the tally of their names, each male
aged twenty years and above: everyone capable of active service, all counted
33 individually – those counted from the tribe of Efrayim numbered 40,500.
34 Of the children of Menashe – his descendants by their clans and their ancestral
families – the tally of their names, each male aged twenty years and above:
35 everyone capable of active service, all counted individually – those counted
from the tribe of Menashe numbered 32,200.
36 Of the children of Binyamin – his descendants by their clans and their ancestral
families – the tally of their names, each male aged twenty years and above:
37 everyone capable of active service, all counted individually – those counted
from the tribe of Binyamin numbered 35,400.
38 Of the children of Dan – his descendants by their clans and their ancestral
families – the tally of their names, each male aged twenty years and above:
39 everyone capable of active service, all counted individually – those counted
from the tribe of Dan numbered 62,700.
40 Of the children of Asher – his descendants by their clans and their ancestral
families – the tally of their names, each male aged twenty years and above:

אונקלוס

כח לִבְנֵי יִשָּׂשכָר, תּוֹלְדָתְהוֹן לְזַרְעֲיָתְהוֹן לְבֵית אֲבָהָתְהוֹן, בְּמִנְיַן שְׁמָהָן, מִבַּר עֶסְרִין שְׁנִין וּלְעֵילָא, כָּל נָפֵיק חֵילָא: כט מִנְיָנֵיהוֹן לְשִׁבְטָא דְיִשָּׂשכָר, חַמְשִׁין וְאַרְבְּעָא אַלְפִין וְאַרְבַּע מְאָה: ל לִבְנֵי זְבוּלוּן, תּוֹלְדָתְהוֹן לְזַרְעֲיָתְהוֹן לְבֵית אֲבָהָתְהוֹן, בְּמִנְיַן שְׁמָהָן, מִבַּר עֶסְרִין שְׁנִין וּלְעֵילָא, כָּל נָפֵיק חֵילָא: לא מִנְיָנֵיהוֹן לְשִׁבְטָא דִזְבוּלוּן, חַמְשִׁין וְשִׁבְעָא אַלְפִין וְאַרְבַּע מְאָה: לב לִבְנֵי יוֹסֵף לִבְנֵי אֶפְרַיִם, תּוֹלְדָתְהוֹן לְזַרְעֲיָתְהוֹן לְבֵית אֲבָהָתְהוֹן, בְּמִנְיַן שְׁמָהָן, מִבַּר עֶסְרִין שְׁנִין וּלְעֵילָא, כָּל נָפֵיק חֵילָא: לג מִנְיָנֵיהוֹן לְשִׁבְטָא דְאֶפְרַיִם, אַרְבְּעִין אַלְפִין וַחֲמֵשׁ מְאָה: לד לִבְנֵי מְנַשֶּׁה, תּוֹלְדָתְהוֹן לְזַרְעֲיָתְהוֹן לְבֵית אֲבָהָתְהוֹן, בְּמִנְיַן שְׁמָהָן, מִבַּר עֶסְרִין שְׁנִין וּלְעֵילָא, כָּל נָפֵיק חֵילָא: לה מִנְיָנֵיהוֹן לְשִׁבְטָא דִמְנַשֶּׁה, תְּלָתִין וּתְרֵין אַלְפִין וּמָאתַן: לו לִבְנֵי בִנְיָמִין, תּוֹלְדָתְהוֹן לְזַרְעֲיָתְהוֹן לְבֵית אֲבָהָתְהוֹן, בְּמִנְיַן שְׁמָהָן, מִבַּר

כח לִבְנֵ֣י יִשָּׂשכָ֔ר תּוֹלְדֹתָ֥ם לְמִשְׁפְּחֹתָ֖ם לְבֵ֣ית אֲבֹתָ֑ם בְּמִסְפַּ֣ר שֵׁמֹ֗ת מִבֶּ֨ן
כט עֶשְׂרִ֤ים שָׁנָה֙ וָמַ֔עְלָה כֹּ֖ל יֹצֵ֥א צָבָֽא׃ פְּקֻדֵיהֶ֖ם לְמַטֵּ֣ה יִשָּׂשכָ֑ר אַרְבָּעָ֥ה
וַחֲמִשִּׁ֛ים אֶ֖לֶף וְאַרְבַּ֥ע מֵאֽוֹת׃
ל לִבְנֵ֣י זְבוּלֻ֔ן תּוֹלְדֹתָ֥ם לְמִשְׁפְּחֹתָ֖ם לְבֵ֣ית אֲבֹתָ֑ם בְּמִסְפַּ֣ר שֵׁמֹ֗ת מִבֶּ֨ן
לא עֶשְׂרִ֤ים שָׁנָה֙ וָמַ֔עְלָה כֹּ֖ל יֹצֵ֥א צָבָֽא׃ פְּקֻדֵיהֶ֖ם לְמַטֵּ֣ה זְבוּלֻ֑ן שִׁבְעָ֧ה
וַחֲמִשִּׁ֛ים אֶ֖לֶף וְאַרְבַּ֥ע מֵאֽוֹת׃
לב לִבְנֵ֤י יוֹסֵף֙ לִבְנֵ֣י אֶפְרַ֔יִם תּוֹלְדֹתָ֥ם לְמִשְׁפְּחֹתָ֖ם לְבֵ֣ית אֲבֹתָ֑ם בְּמִסְפַּ֣ר
לג שֵׁמֹ֗ת מִבֶּ֨ן עֶשְׂרִ֤ים שָׁנָה֙ וָמַ֔עְלָה כֹּ֖ל יֹצֵ֥א צָבָֽא׃ פְּקֻדֵיהֶ֖ם לְמַטֵּ֣ה אֶפְרָ֑יִם
אַרְבָּעִ֥ים אֶ֖לֶף וַחֲמֵ֥שׁ מֵאֽוֹת׃
לד לִבְנֵ֣י מְנַשֶּׁ֔ה תּוֹלְדֹתָ֥ם לְמִשְׁפְּחֹתָ֖ם לְבֵ֣ית אֲבֹתָ֑ם בְּמִסְפַּ֣ר שֵׁמ֗וֹת מִבֶּ֨ן
לה עֶשְׂרִ֤ים שָׁנָה֙ וָמַ֔עְלָה כֹּ֖ל יֹצֵ֥א צָבָֽא׃ פְּקֻדֵיהֶ֖ם לְמַטֵּ֣ה מְנַשֶּׁ֑ה שְׁנַ֧יִם
וּשְׁלֹשִׁ֛ים אֶ֖לֶף וּמָאתָֽיִם׃
לו לִבְנֵ֣י בִנְיָמִ֔ן תּוֹלְדֹתָ֥ם לְמִשְׁפְּחֹתָ֖ם לְבֵ֣ית אֲבֹתָ֑ם בְּמִסְפַּ֣ר שֵׁמֹ֗ת מִבֶּ֨ן
לז עֶשְׂרִ֤ים שָׁנָה֙ וָמַ֔עְלָה כֹּ֖ל יֹצֵ֥א צָבָֽא׃ פְּקֻדֵיהֶ֖ם לְמַטֵּ֣ה בִנְיָמִ֑ן חֲמִשָּׁ֧ה
וּשְׁלֹשִׁ֛ים אֶ֖לֶף וְאַרְבַּ֥ע מֵאֽוֹת׃
לח לִבְנֵ֣י דָ֔ן תּוֹלְדֹתָ֥ם לְמִשְׁפְּחֹתָ֖ם לְבֵ֣ית אֲבֹתָ֑ם בְּמִסְפַּ֣ר שֵׁמֹ֗ת מִבֶּ֨ן עֶשְׂרִ֤ים
לט שָׁנָה֙ וָמַ֔עְלָה כֹּ֖ל יֹצֵ֥א צָבָֽא׃ פְּקֻדֵיהֶ֖ם לְמַטֵּ֣ה דָ֑ן שְׁנַ֧יִם וְשִׁשִּׁ֛ים אֶ֖לֶף
וּשְׁבַ֥ע מֵאֽוֹת׃
מ לִבְנֵ֣י אָשֵׁ֔ר תּוֹלְדֹתָ֥ם לְמִשְׁפְּחֹתָ֖ם לְבֵ֣ית אֲבֹתָ֑ם בְּמִסְפַּ֣ר שֵׁמֹ֗ת מִבֶּ֨ן

אונקלוס

עֶסְרִין שְׁנִין וּלְעֵילָא, כָּל נָפֵיק חֵילָא: לז מִנְיָנֵיהוֹן לְשִׁבְטָא דְבִנְיָמִין, תְּלָתִין וְחַמְשָׁא אַלְפִין וְאַרְבַּע מְאָה: לח לִבְנֵי דָן, תּוֹלְדָתְהוֹן לְזַרְעִיָתְהוֹן לְבֵית אֲבָהָתְהוֹן, בְּמִנְיַן שְׁמָהָן, מִבַּר עֶסְרִין שְׁנִין וּלְעֵילָא, כָּל נָפֵיק חֵילָא: לט מִנְיָנֵיהוֹן לְשִׁבְטָא דְדָן, שִׁתִּין וּתְרֵין אַלְפִין וּשְׁבַע מְאָה: מ לִבְנֵי אָשֵׁר, תּוֹלְדָתְהוֹן לְזַרְעִיָתְהוֹן לְבֵית אֲבָהָתְהוֹן, בְּמִנְיַן שְׁמָהָן, מִבַּר

41 everyone capable of active service, all counted individually – those counted
from the tribe of Asher numbered 41,500.
42 The children of Naftali – his descendants by their clans and their ancestral
families – the tally of their names, each male aged twenty years and above:
43 everyone capable of active service, all counted individually – those counted
from the tribe of Naftali numbered 53,400.
44 These were the ones counted by Moshe, Aharon, and the twelve princes of
45 Israel, one from each ancestral house. Thus the total number of the Israelites
counted, by their ancestral houses, aged twenty years and above – everyone
46 47 in Israel capable of active service – was 603,550. The ancestral house of the
Levites, however, was not counted among them.
48 49 For the Lord had spoken to Moshe and said, "You shall not count the tribe of
50 Levi, nor take a census of them among the Israelites. Instead, you shall appoint
the Levites over the Tabernacle of the Testimony, over all its utensils and all that
belongs to it. For they are to carry the Tabernacle and all its utensils; they are to
51 tend to it, and around the Tabernacle they shall encamp. When the Tabernacle
is to move onward, the Levites shall take it down, and when the Tabernacle is
to encamp, the Levites shall erect it. Any outsider who draws close to it shall
52 be put to death. The Israelites shall encamp in their respective camps, each
53 by his own banner, in his division. But the Levites shall encamp around the

רש"י

מט) **אַךְ אֶת מַטֵּה לֵוִי לֹא תִפְקֹד.** כְּדַאי הוּא לִגְיוֹן שֶׁל מֶלֶךְ לִהְיוֹת נִמְנֶה לְבַדּוֹ. דָּבָר אַחֵר, צָפָה הַקָּדוֹשׁ בָּרוּךְ הוּא שֶׁעֲתִידָה לַעֲמֹד גְּזֵרָה עַל כָּל הַנִּמְנִין מִבֶּן עֶשְׂרִים שָׁנָה וָמַעְלָה שֶׁיָּמוּתוּ בַּמִּדְבָּר, אָמַר: אַל יִהְיוּ אֵלּוּ בִּכְלָל, לְפִי שֶׁהֵם שֶׁלִּי, שֶׁלֹּא טָעוּ בָּעֵגֶל:

נ) **וְאַתָּה הַפְקֵד אֶת הַלְוִיִּם.** כְּתַרְגּוּמוֹ "מַנִּי", לְשׁוֹן מִנּוּי שְׂרָרָה עַל דָּבָר שֶׁהוּא מְמֻנֶּה עָלָיו, כְּמוֹ "וְיַפְקֵד הַמֶּלֶךְ פְּקִידִים" (אסתר ב, ג):

נא) **יוֹרִידוּ אֹתוֹ.** כְּתַרְגּוּמוֹ: "יְפָרְקוּן", כְּשֶׁבָּאִין לִסַּע בַּמִּדְבָּר מִמַּסָּע לְמַסָּע הָיוּ מְפָרְקִין אוֹתוֹ מֵהֲקָמָתוֹ, וְנוֹשְׂאִין אוֹתוֹ עַד מְקוֹם אֲשֶׁר יִשְׁכֹּן שָׁם הֶעָנָן וְיַחֲנוּ שָׁם, וּמְקִימִין אוֹתוֹ: **וְהַזָּר הַקָּרֵב.** לַעֲבוֹדָתָם זוֹ: **יוּמָת.** בִּידֵי שָׁמַיִם:

נב) **וְאִישׁ עַל דִּגְלוֹ.** כְּמוֹ שֶׁהַדְּגָלִים סְדוּרִים בְּסֵפֶר זֶה, שְׁלֹשָׁה שְׁבָטִים לְכָל דֶּגֶל:

1:46 **שֵׁשׁ־מֵאוֹת אֶלֶף וּשְׁלֹשֶׁת אֲלָפִים וַחֲמֵשׁ מֵאוֹת וַחֲמִשִּׁים** *603,550* – The number six hundred thousand, an approximation of the Torah's total here, became a proverbial quantity for a great number of Jews. For example, there is a wonderful blessing mentioned in the Talmud to be said on seeing six hundred thousand Israelites together in one place. It is: "Blessed are You, Lord… who discerns secrets" (Berakhot 58a; Rashi ad loc.). The Talmud explains that every person is different. We each have different attributes. We all think our own thoughts. Only God can enter the minds of each of us and know what we are thinking, and this is what the blessing refers to. In other words, even in a massive crowd where, to human eyes, faces blur into a mass, God still relates to us as individuals, not as members of a crowd.

מא עֶשְׂרִים שָׁנָה וָמַעְלָה כֹּל יֹצֵא צָבָא׃ פְּקֻדֵיהֶם לְמַטֵּה אָשֵׁר אֶחָד
וְאַרְבָּעִים אֶלֶף וַחֲמֵשׁ מֵאוֹת׃
מב בְּנֵי נַפְתָּלִי תּוֹלְדֹתָם לְמִשְׁפְּחֹתָם לְבֵית אֲבֹתָם בְּמִסְפַּר שֵׁמֹת מִבֶּן
מג עֶשְׂרִים שָׁנָה וָמַעְלָה כֹּל יֹצֵא צָבָא׃ פְּקֻדֵיהֶם לְמַטֵּה נַפְתָּלִי שְׁלֹשָׁה
וַחֲמִשִּׁים אֶלֶף וְאַרְבַּע מֵאוֹת׃
מד אֵלֶּה הַפְּקֻדִים אֲשֶׁר פָּקַד מֹשֶׁה וְאַהֲרֹן וּנְשִׂיאֵי יִשְׂרָאֵל שְׁנֵים עָשָׂר
מה אִישׁ אִישׁ־אֶחָד לְבֵית־אֲבֹתָיו הָיוּ׃ וַיִּהְיוּ כָּל־פְּקוּדֵי בְנֵי־יִשְׂרָאֵל לְבֵית
מו אֲבֹתָם מִבֶּן עֶשְׂרִים שָׁנָה וָמַעְלָה כָּל־יֹצֵא צָבָא בְּיִשְׂרָאֵל׃ וַיִּהְיוּ כָּל־
הַפְּקֻדִים שֵׁשׁ־מֵאוֹת אֶלֶף וּשְׁלֹשֶׁת אֲלָפִים וַחֲמֵשׁ מֵאוֹת וַחֲמִשִּׁים׃
מז וְהַלְוִיִּם לְמַטֵּה אֲבֹתָם לֹא הָתְפָּקְדוּ בְּתוֹכָם׃
מח מט וַיְדַבֵּר יהוה אֶל־מֹשֶׁה לֵּאמֹר׃ אַךְ אֶת־מַטֵּה לֵוִי לֹא תִפְקֹד וְאֶת־
נ רֹאשָׁם לֹא תִשָּׂא בְּתוֹךְ בְּנֵי יִשְׂרָאֵל׃ וְאַתָּה הַפְקֵד אֶת־הַלְוִיִּם עַל־
מִשְׁכַּן הָעֵדֻת וְעַל כָּל־כֵּלָיו וְעַל כָּל־אֲשֶׁר־לוֹ הֵמָּה יִשְׂאוּ אֶת־הַמִּשְׁכָּן
נא וְאֶת־כָּל־כֵּלָיו וְהֵם יְשָׁרְתֻהוּ וְסָבִיב לַמִּשְׁכָּן יַחֲנוּ׃ וּבִנְסֹעַ הַמִּשְׁכָּן יוֹרִידוּ
נב אֹתוֹ הַלְוִיִּם וּבַחֲנֹת הַמִּשְׁכָּן יָקִימוּ אֹתוֹ הַלְוִיִּם וְהַזָּר הַקָּרֵב יוּמָת׃ וְחָנוּ
נג בְנֵי יִשְׂרָאֵל אִישׁ עַל־מַחֲנֵהוּ וְאִישׁ עַל־דִּגְלוֹ לְצִבְאֹתָם׃ וְהַלְוִיִּם יַחֲנוּ

אונקלוס

עֶסְרִין שְׁנִין וּלְעֵילָא, כָּל נָפֵיק חֵילָא: מא מִנְיָנֵיהוֹן לְשִׁבְטָא דְאָשֵׁר, אַרְבְּעִין וְחַד אַלְפִין וַחֲמֵשׁ מְאָה: מב בְּנֵי נַפְתָּלִי, תּוֹלְדָתְהוֹן לְזַרְעִיָתְהוֹן לְבֵית אֲבָהָתְהוֹן, בְּמִנְיַן שְׁמָהָן, מִבַּר עֶסְרִין שְׁנִין וּלְעֵילָא, כָּל נָפֵיק חֵילָא: מג מִנְיָנֵיהוֹן לְשִׁבְטָא דְנַפְתָּלִי, חַמְשִׁין וּתְלָתָא אַלְפִין וְאַרְבַּע מְאָה: מד אִלֵּין מִנְיָנַיָּא, דִּמְנָא מֹשֶׁה וְאַהֲרֹן וְרַבְרְבֵי יִשְׂרָאֵל, תְּרֵי עֲסַר גֻּבְרִין, גַּבְרָא חַד לְבֵית אֲבָהָתוֹהִי הֲווֹ: מה וַהֲווֹ, כָּל מִנְיָנֵי בְנֵי יִשְׂרָאֵל לְבֵית אֲבָהָתְהוֹן, מִבַּר עֶסְרִין שְׁנִין וּלְעֵילָא, כָּל נָפֵיק חֵילָא בְּיִשְׂרָאֵל: מו וַהֲווֹ כָּל מִנְיָנַיָּא, שֵׁית מְאָה וּתְלָתָא אַלְפִין, וַחֲמֵשׁ מְאָה וְחַמְשִׁין: מז וְלֵיוָאֵי לְשִׁבְטָא דַאֲבָהָתְהוֹן, לָא אִתְמְנִיאוּ בֵּינֵיהוֹן: מח וּמַלֵּיל יי עִם מֹשֶׁה לְמֵימַר: מט בְּרַם יָת שִׁבְטָא דְלֵוִי לָא תִמְנֵי, וְיָת חֻשְׁבַּנְהוֹן לָא תְקַבֵּיל, בְּגוֹ בְּנֵי יִשְׂרָאֵל: נ וְאַתְּ, מַנִּי יָת לֵיוָאֵי עַל מַשְׁכְּנָא דְסָהֲדוּתָא, וְעַל כָּל מָנוֹהִי וְעַל כָּל דְּלֵיהּ, אִנּוּן, יִטְּלוּן יָת מַשְׁכְּנָא וְיָת כָּל מָנוֹהִי, וְאִנּוּן יְשַׁמְּשֻׁנֵּיהּ, וּסְחוֹר סְחוֹר לְמַשְׁכְּנָא יִשְׁרוֹן: נא וּבְמִטַּל מַשְׁכְּנָא, יְפָרְקוּן יָתֵיהּ לֵיוָאֵי, וּבְמִשְׁרֵי מַשְׁכְּנָא, יְקִימוּן יָתֵיהּ לֵיוָאֵי, וְחִילוֹנַי דְּיִקְרַב יִתְקְטֵיל: נב וְיִשְׁרוֹן בְּנֵי יִשְׂרָאֵל, גְּבַר עַל מַשְׁרוֹהִי, וּגְבַר עַל טִקְסֵיהּ לְחֵילֵיהוֹן: נג וְלֵיוָאֵי, יִשְׁרוֹן

Tabernacle of the Testimony, so that fury does not engulf the community of
the Israelites; the Levites shall keep watch faithfully over the Tabernacle of the
54 Testimony." The Israelites did so; all that the LORD had commanded Moshe,
they fulfilled.
2 1 2 The LORD spoke to Moshe and Aharon: "The Israelites shall camp, each by his SHELISHI
banner, the ensign of his ancestral house, positioned around the Tent of Meeting
3 at a distance. Camping to the east, toward the sunrise, shall be the divisions
under the banner of Yehuda. The leader of Yehuda's descendants is Naḥshon
4 5 son of Aminadav. And his division numbers 74,600. Camping next to them
shall be the tribe of Yissakhar. The leader of Yissakhar's descendants is Netanel
6 7 son of Tzuar. And his division numbers 54,400. Then the tribe of Zevulun. The
8 leader of Zevulun's descendants is Eliav son of Ḥelon. His division numbers
9 57,400. The total number in Yehuda's camp, in their divisions, is 186,400. They
10 shall be the first to set out. The divisions under the banner of Reuven's

רש"י

נג] **וְלֹא יִהְיֶה קֶצֶף.** אִם תַּעֲשׂוּ כְּמִצְוָתִי לֹא יִהְיֶה קֶצֶף, וְאִם לָאו, שֶׁיִּכָּנְסוּ זָרִים בַּעֲבוֹדָתָם זוֹ, יִהְיֶה קֶצֶף, כְּמוֹ שֶׁמָּצִינוּ בְּמַעֲשֵׂה קֹרַח: "כִּי יָצָא הַקֶּצֶף" וְגוֹ' (להלן יז, יא):

ב ב] **בְּאֹתֹת.** כָּל דֶּגֶל יִהְיֶה לוֹ אוֹת, מַפָּה צְבוּעָה תְּלוּיָה בוֹ, צִבְעוֹ שֶׁל זֶה לֹא כְּצִבְעוֹ שֶׁל זֶה, צֶבַע כָּל אֶחָד כְּגוֹן אַבְנוֹ הַקְּבוּעָה בַּחֹשֶׁן, וּמִתּוֹךְ כָּךְ יַכִּיר כָּל אֶחָד אֶת דִּגְלוֹ. דָּבָר אַחֵר, "בְּאֹתֹת לְבֵית אֲבֹתָם", בָּאוֹת שֶׁמָּסַר לָהֶם יַעֲקֹב אֲבִיהֶם כְּשֶׁנְּשָׂאוּהוּ מִמִּצְרַיִם, שֶׁנֶּאֱמַר: "וַיַּעֲשׂוּ בָנָיו לוֹ כֵּן כַּאֲשֶׁר צִוָּם" (בראשית נ, יב) – יְהוּדָה וְיִשָּׂשכָר וּזְבוּלֻן יִשָּׂאוּהוּ מִן הַמִּזְרָח, וּרְאוּבֵן וְשִׁמְעוֹן וְגָד מִן הַדָּרוֹם וְכוּ', כִּדְאִיתָא בְּתַנְחוּמָא בְּפָרָשָׁה זוֹ (יב): **מִנֶּגֶד.** מֵרָחוֹק מִיל, כְּמוֹ שֶׁנֶּאֱמַר בִּיהוֹשֻׁעַ: "אַךְ רָחוֹק יִהְיֶה בֵּינֵיכֶם וּבֵינָו כְּאַלְפַּיִם אַמָּה" (יהושע ג, ד), שֶׁיּוּכְלוּ לָבֹא בְּשַׁבָּת. מֹשֶׁה וְאַהֲרֹן וּבָנָיו וְהַלְוִיִּם חוֹנִים בְּסָמוּךְ לוֹ:

ג] **קֵדְמָה.** לִפְנֵי הַקְּרוּיִים 'קֶדֶם', וְאֵיזוֹ? זוֹ רוּחַ מִזְרָחִית, וְהַמַּעֲרָב קָרוּי אָחוֹר:

ט] **רִאשֹׁנָה יִסָּעוּ.** כְּשֶׁרוֹאִין הֶעָנָן מִסְתַּלֵּק, תּוֹקְעִין הַכֹּהֲנִים בַּחֲצוֹצְרוֹת וְנוֹסֵעַ מַחֲנֵה יְהוּדָה תְּחִלָּה; וּכְשֶׁהוֹלְכִין – הוֹלְכִין כְּדֶרֶךְ חֲנִיָּתָן, הַלְוִיִּם וְהָעֲגָלוֹת בָּאֶמְצַע, דֶּגֶל יְהוּדָה בַּמִּזְרָח, וְשֶׁל רְאוּבֵן בַּדָּרוֹם, וְשֶׁל אֶפְרַיִם בַּמַּעֲרָב, וְשֶׁל דָּן בַּצָּפוֹן:

infatuated lovers. The Zohar, key text of Jewish mysticism, uses the most daring language of passion, as does *Yedid Nefesh*, the poem attributed to the sixteenth-century Tzefat kabbalist Rabbi Elazar Azikri.

That is one of the striking differences between the synagogues and the cathedrals of the Middle Ages. In a cathedral you sense the vastness of God and the smallness of humankind. But in the Altneushul in Prague or the synagogues of the Ari and Rabbi Yosef Karo in Tzefat, you sense the closeness of God and the potential greatness of humankind.

2:2 **מִנֶּגֶד סָבִיב לְאֹהֶל־מוֹעֵד** *Positioned around the Tent of Meeting at a distance* – Immediately after the census we read of how the twelve tribes are to encamp, each equidistant from the Sanctuary. Each tribe is different, but (with the exception of the Levites) all are equal. They eat the same food; they drink the same water. None yet has lands of their own, for the desert has no owners. There is no economic or territorial conflict between them.

They have not yet begun building a society with all the inequalities to which society gives rise. For the moment, they are together, their tents forming a perfect square with the Sanctuary at its center.

2:9 **רִאשֹׁנָה יִסָּעוּ** *They shall be the first to set out* – A significant part of what faith is in Judaism is to have the courage to "be the first to set out," to pioneer, to do something new, to venture out into the unknown. That is what Avraham

סָבִיב לְמִשְׁכַּן הָעֵדֻת וְלֹא־יִהְיֶה קֶצֶף עַל־עֲדַת בְּנֵי יִשְׂרָאֵל וְשָׁמְרוּ
נד הַלְוִיִּם אֶת־מִשְׁמֶרֶת מִשְׁכַּן הָעֵדוּת׃ וַיַּעֲשׂוּ בְּנֵי יִשְׂרָאֵל כְּכֹל אֲשֶׁר
צִוָּה יהוה אֶת־מֹשֶׁה כֵּן עָשׂוּ׃
ב א ב וַיְדַבֵּר יהוה אֶל־מֹשֶׁה וְאֶל־אַהֲרֹן לֵאמֹר׃ אִישׁ עַל־דִּגְלוֹ בְאֹתֹת שלישי ב
ג לְבֵית אֲבֹתָם יַחֲנוּ בְּנֵי יִשְׂרָאֵל מִנֶּגֶד סָבִיב לְאֹהֶל־מוֹעֵד יַחֲנוּ׃ וְהַחֹנִים
קֵדְמָה מִזְרָחָה דֶּגֶל מַחֲנֵה יְהוּדָה לְצִבְאֹתָם וְנָשִׂיא לִבְנֵי יְהוּדָה
ד נַחְשׁוֹן בֶּן־עַמִּינָדָב׃ וּצְבָאוֹ וּפְקֻדֵיהֶם אַרְבָּעָה וְשִׁבְעִים אֶלֶף וְשֵׁשׁ
ה מֵאוֹת׃ וְהַחֹנִים עָלָיו מַטֵּה יִשָּׂשכָר וְנָשִׂיא לִבְנֵי יִשָּׂשכָר נְתַנְאֵל
ו בֶּן־צוּעָר׃ וּצְבָאוֹ וּפְקֻדָיו אַרְבָּעָה וַחֲמִשִּׁים אֶלֶף וְאַרְבַּע מֵאוֹת׃
ז ח מַטֵּה זְבוּלֻן וְנָשִׂיא לִבְנֵי זְבוּלֻן אֱלִיאָב בֶּן־חֵלֹן׃ וּצְבָאוֹ וּפְקֻדָיו
ט שִׁבְעָה וַחֲמִשִּׁים אֶלֶף וְאַרְבַּע מֵאוֹת׃ כָּל־הַפְּקֻדִים לְמַחֲנֵה יְהוּדָה
מְאַת אֶלֶף וּשְׁמֹנִים אֶלֶף וְשֵׁשֶׁת־אֲלָפִים וְאַרְבַּע־מֵאוֹת לְצִבְאֹתָם
י רִאשֹׁנָה יִסָּעוּ׃ דֶּגֶל מַחֲנֵה רְאוּבֵן תֵּימָנָה לְצִבְאֹתָם

אונקלוס

סְחוֹר סְחוֹר לְמַשְׁכְּנָא דְסַהֲדוּתָא, וְלָא יְהֵי רָגְזָא, עַל כְּנִשְׁתָּא דִבְנֵי יִשְׂרָאֵל, וְיִטְּרוּן לֵיוָאֵי, יָת מַטְּרַת מַשְׁכְּנָא דְסַהֲדוּתָא: נד וַעֲבַדוּ בְּנֵי יִשְׂרָאֵל, כְּכֹל, דְּפַקֵּיד יְיָ, יָת מֹשֶׁה כֵּן עֲבַדוּ: ב א וּמַלֵּיל יְיָ, עִם מֹשֶׁה וּלְאַהֲרֹן לְמֵימָר: ב גְּבַר עַל טִקְסֵיהּ בְּאָתְוָן לְבֵית אֲבָהָתְהוֹן, יִשְׁרוֹן בְּנֵי יִשְׂרָאֵל, מִקֳּבֵיל, סְחוֹר סְחוֹר לְמַשְׁכַּן זִמְנָא יִשְׁרוֹן: ג וּדְשָׁרַן קִדּוּמָא מַדִּנְחָא, טִיקַס, מַשְׁרִית יְהוּדָה לְחֵילֵיהוֹן, וְרַבָּא לִבְנֵי יְהוּדָה, נַחְשׁוֹן בַּר עַמִּינָדָב: ד וְחֵילֵיהּ וּמִנְיָנֵיהוֹן, שִׁבְעִין וְאַרְבְּעָא אַלְפִין וְשִׁית מְאָה: ה וּדְשָׁרַן סְמִיכִין עֲלוֹהִי שִׁבְטָא דְיִשָּׂשכָר, וְרַבָּא לִבְנֵי יִשָּׂשכָר, נְתַנְאֵל בַּר צוּעָר: ו וְחֵילֵיהּ וּמִנְיָנוֹהִי, חַמְשִׁין וְאַרְבְּעָא אַלְפִין וְאַרְבַּע מְאָה: ז שִׁבְטָא דִזְבוּלוּן, וְרַבָּא לִבְנֵי זְבוּלוּן, אֱלִיאָב בַּר חֵלוֹן: ח וְחֵילֵיהּ וּמִנְיָנוֹהִי, חַמְשִׁין וְשִׁבְעָא אַלְפִין וְאַרְבַּע מְאָה: ט כָּל מִנְיָנַיָּא לְמַשְׁרִית יְהוּדָה, מְאָה וּתְמָנַן, וְשִׁתָּא אַלְפִין וְאַרְבַּע מְאָה לְחֵילֵיהוֹן, בְּקַדְמֵיתָא נָטְלִין: י טֵיקַס מַשְׁרִית רְאוּבֵן, דָּרוֹמָא לְחֵילֵיהוֹן, וְרַבָּא

1:53 יַחֲנוּ סָבִיב לְמִשְׁכַּן הָעֵדֻת *Encamp around the Tabernacle of the Testimony* – The book of Numbers is about a people with the Divine Presence in its midst. God is no longer simply the distant, majestic creator of the universe and intervener in history. He is also close, the *Shekhina*, God as immanent as well as transcendent: God-as-neighbor. Jewish spirituality conceives of God in abstract and awe-inspiring ways: God is more distant than the furthest star and more eternal than time itself. Yet no religion has ever felt God to be closer. In Tanakh, the prophets argue with God. In the book of Psalms, King David speaks to Him in terms of utmost intimacy. In the Talmud, God listens to the debates between the Sages and accepts their rulings even when they go against a heavenly voice. God's relationship with Israel, said the prophets, is like that between a parent and a child, or between a husband and a wife. In Song of Songs, it is like that between two

camp shall be to the south. The leader of Reuven's descendants is Elitzur son
11 12 of Shedeiur. And his division numbers 46,500. Camping next to them shall be
the tribe of Shimon. The leader of Shimon's descendants is Shelumiel son of
13 14 Tzurishadai. His division numbers 59,300. Then the tribe of Gad: the leader of
15 Gad's descendants is Elyasaf son of Reuel. And his division numbers 45,650.
16 The total number in Reuven's camp, in their divisions, is 151,450. They shall
17 set out second. And the Tent of Meeting and the Levite camp shall set
out in the midst of the camps. All shall set out as they encamp, each in his own
18 place under his banner. The divisions under the banner of Efrayim
shall be to the west. The leader of Efrayim's descendants is Elishama son of
19 20 Amihud. And his division numbers 40,500. Next to them shall be the tribe of
21 Menashe. The leader of Menashe's descendants is Gamliel son of Pedatzur. His
22 division numbers 32,200. Then the tribe of Binyamin: the leader of Binyamin's
23 24 descendants is Avidan son of Gidoni. His division numbers 35,400. The total
number of men in Efrayim's camp, in their divisions, is 108,100. They shall set
25 out third. The divisions under the banner of Dan shall be to the north.
26 The leader of Dan's descendants is Aḥiezer son of Amishadai. His division
27 numbers 62,700. Camping next to them shall be the tribe of Asher. The leader
28 of Asher's descendants is Pagiel son of Okhran. His division numbers 41,500.

אונקלוס

לִבְנֵי רְאוּבֵן, אֱלִיצוּר בַּר שְׁדֵיאוּר: יא וְחֵילֵיהּ וּמִנְיָנוֹהִי, אַרְבְּעִין וְשִׁתָּא אַלְפִין וַחֲמֵשׁ מְאָה: יב וְדִשְׁרַן סְמִיכִין עֲלוֹהִי שִׁבְטָא דְשִׁמְעוֹן, וְרַבָּא לִבְנֵי שִׁמְעוֹן, שְׁלוּמִיאֵל בַּר צוּרִישַׁדָּי: יג וְחֵילֵיהּ וּמִנְיָנֵיהוֹן, חַמְשִׁין וּתְשְׁעָא אַלְפִין וּתְלָת מְאָה: יד וְשִׁבְטָא דְגָד, וְרַבָּא לִבְנֵי גָד, אֶלְיָסָף בַּר רְעוּאֵל: טו וְחֵילֵיהּ וּמִנְיָנֵיהוֹן, אַרְבְּעִין וַחֲמְשָׁא אַלְפִין, וְשֵׁית מְאָה וְחַמְשִׁין: טז כָּל מִנְיָנַיָּא לְמַשְׁרִית רְאוּבֵן, מְאָה וְחַמְשִׁין וְחַד אַלְפִין,

רש״י

יז וְנָסַע אֹהֶל מוֹעֵד. לְאַחַר שְׁנֵי דְגָלִים הַלָּלוּ: כַּאֲשֶׁר יַחֲנוּ כֵּן יִסָּעוּ. כְּמוֹ שֶׁפֵּרַשְׁתִּי, הֲלִיכָתָן כַּחֲנִיָּתָן, כָּל דֶּגֶל מְהַלֵּךְ לָרוּחַ הַקְּבוּעַ לוֹ: עַל יָדוֹ. עַל מְקוֹמוֹ, וְאֵין לְשׁוֹן 'יָד' זָז מִמַּשְׁמָעוֹ, רוּחַ שֶׁל צִדּוֹ קָרוּי "עַל יָדוֹ", הַסְּמוּכָה לוֹ לְכָל הוֹשָׁטַת יָדוֹ, אינשו"ן אי"ש"ח בְּלַעַז:

כ וְעָלָיו. כְּתַרְגּוּמוֹ: "וְדִסְמִיכִין עֲלוֹהִי":

and Sara did when they left their land, their home, and their father's house. It is what the Israelites did in the days of Moshe when they journeyed forth into the wilderness, guided only by a pillar of cloud by day and fire by night. It took faith to challenge the religions of the ancient world, especially when they were embodied in the greatest empires of their time. Faith is the courage to take a risk for the sake of God or the Jewish people; to begin a journey to a distant destination knowing that there will be hazards along the way, but knowing also that God is with us, giving us strength if we align our will with His.

יא וּנְשִׂיא לִבְנֵי רְאוּבֵן אֱלִיצוּר בֶּן־שְׁדֵיאוּר: וּצְבָאוֹ וּפְקֻדָיו שִׁשָּׁה
יב וְאַרְבָּעִים אֶלֶף וַחֲמֵשׁ מֵאוֹת: וְהַחוֹנִם עָלָיו מַטֵּה שִׁמְעוֹן וְנָשִׂיא לִבְנֵי
יג שִׁמְעוֹן שְׁלֻמִיאֵל בֶּן־צוּרִישַׁדָּי: וּצְבָאוֹ וּפְקֻדֵיהֶם תִּשְׁעָה וַחֲמִשִּׁים
יד אֶלֶף וּשְׁלֹשׁ מֵאוֹת: וּמַטֵּה גָּד וְנָשִׂיא לִבְנֵי גָד אֶלְיָסָף בֶּן־רְעוּאֵל:
טו טז וּצְבָאוֹ וּפְקֻדֵיהֶם חֲמִשָּׁה וְאַרְבָּעִים אֶלֶף וְשֵׁשׁ מֵאוֹת וַחֲמִשִּׁים: כָּל־
הַפְּקֻדִים לְמַחֲנֵה רְאוּבֵן מְאַת אֶלֶף וְאֶחָד וַחֲמִשִּׁים אֶלֶף וְאַרְבַּע־
יז מֵאוֹת וַחֲמִשִּׁים לְצִבְאֹתָם וּשְׁנִיִּם יִסָּעוּ: וְנָסַע אֹהֶל־
מוֹעֵד מַחֲנֵה הַלְוִיִּם בְּתוֹךְ הַמַּחֲנֹת כַּאֲשֶׁר יַחֲנוּ כֵּן יִסָּעוּ אִישׁ עַל־יָדוֹ
יח לְדִגְלֵיהֶם: דֶּגֶל מַחֲנֵה אֶפְרַיִם לְצִבְאֹתָם יָמָּה וְנָשִׂיא
יט לִבְנֵי אֶפְרַיִם אֱלִישָׁמָע בֶּן־עַמִּיהוּד: וּצְבָאוֹ וּפְקֻדֵיהֶם אַרְבָּעִים אֶלֶף
כ וַחֲמֵשׁ מֵאוֹת: וְעָלָיו מַטֵּה מְנַשֶּׁה וְנָשִׂיא לִבְנֵי מְנַשֶּׁה גַּמְלִיאֵל בֶּן־
כא כב פְּדָהצוּר: וּצְבָאוֹ וּפְקֻדֵיהֶם שְׁנַיִם וּשְׁלֹשִׁים אֶלֶף וּמָאתָיִם: וּמַטֵּה
כג בִּנְיָמִן וְנָשִׂיא לִבְנֵי בִנְיָמִן אֲבִידָן בֶּן־גִּדְעֹנִי: וּצְבָאוֹ וּפְקֻדֵיהֶם חֲמִשָּׁה
כד וּשְׁלֹשִׁים אֶלֶף וְאַרְבַּע מֵאוֹת: כָּל־הַפְּקֻדִים לְמַחֲנֵה אֶפְרַיִם מְאַת אֶלֶף
כה וּשְׁמֹנַת־אֲלָפִים וּמֵאָה לְצִבְאֹתָם וּשְׁלִשִׁים יִסָּעוּ: דֶּגֶל
כו מַחֲנֵה דָן צָפֹנָה לְצִבְאֹתָם וְנָשִׂיא לִבְנֵי דָן אֲחִיעֶזֶר בֶּן־עַמִּישַׁדָּי: וּצְבָאוֹ
כז וּפְקֻדֵיהֶם שְׁנַיִם וְשִׁשִּׁים אֶלֶף וּשְׁבַע מֵאוֹת: וְהַחֹנִים עָלָיו מַטֵּה אָשֵׁר
כח וְנָשִׂיא לִבְנֵי אָשֵׁר פַּגְעִיאֵל בֶּן־עָכְרָן: וּצְבָאוֹ וּפְקֻדֵיהֶם אֶחָד וְאַרְבָּעִים

אונקלוס

וְאַרְבַּע מְאָה וְחַמְשִׁין לְחֵילֵיהוֹן, בְּתִנְיֵיתָא נָטְלִין: יז וְנָטֵיל מַשְׁכַּן זִמְנָא, מַשְׁרִית לֵיוָאֵי בְּגוֹ מַשְׁרְיָתָא, כְּמָא דְשָׁרַן כֵּן נָטְלִין, גְּבַר עַל אַתְרֵיהּ לְטִקְסֵיהוֹן: יח טֵיקַס מַשְׁרִית אֶפְרַיִם, לְחֵילֵיהוֹן מַעַרְבָא, וְרַבָּא לִבְנֵי אֶפְרַיִם, אֱלִישָׁמָע בַּר עַמִּיהוּד: יט וְחֵילֵיהּ וּמִנְיָנֵיהוֹן, אַרְבְּעִין אַלְפִין וַחֲמֵשׁ מְאָה: כ וּדְסָמְכִין עֲלוֹהִי שִׁבְטָא דִמְנַשֶּׁה, וְרַבָּא לִבְנֵי מְנַשֶּׁה, גַּמְלִיאֵל בַּר פְּדָהצוּר: כא וְחֵילֵיהּ וּמִנְיָנֵיהוֹן, תְּלָתִין וּתְרֵין אַלְפִין וּמָאתָן: כב וְשִׁבְטָא דְבִנְיָמִין, וְרַבָּא לִבְנֵי בִנְיָמִין, אֲבִידָן בַּר גִּדְעוֹנִי: כג וְחֵילֵיהּ וּמִנְיָנֵיהוֹן, תְּלָתִין וַחֲמְשָׁא אַלְפִין וְאַרְבַּע מְאָה: כד כָּל מִנְיָנַיָּא לְמַשְׁרִית אֶפְרַיִם, מְאָה וּתְמָנְיָא אַלְפִין וּמְאָה לְחֵילֵיהוֹן, בִּתְלִיתֵיתָא נָטְלִין: כה טֵיקַס מַשְׁרִית דָּן, צִפּוּנָא לְחֵילֵיהוֹן, וְרַבָּא לִבְנֵי דָן, אֲחִיעֶזֶר בַּר עַמִּישַׁדָּי: כו וְחֵילֵיהּ וּמִנְיָנֵיהוֹן, שִׁתִּין וּתְרֵין אַלְפִין וּשְׁבַע מְאָה: כז וּדְשָׁרַן סְמִיכִין עֲלוֹהִי שִׁבְטָא דְאָשֵׁר, וְרַבָּא לִבְנֵי אָשֵׁר, פַּגְעִיאֵל בַּר עָכְרָן: כח וְחֵילֵיהּ וּמִנְיָנֵיהוֹן, אַרְבְּעִין וְחַד

29 Then the tribe of Naftali: the leader of Naftali's descendants is Aḥira son of
30 31 Einan. His division numbers 53,400. The total number in Dan's camp, in their
divisions, is 157,600. They shall set out last, by their banners."
32 These were the numbers of the Israelites by their ancestral houses. The total
33 number in the camps by their divisions was 603,550. As the LORD had
commanded Moshe, the Levites were not counted among the other Israelites.
34 And so the Israelites did all that the LORD had commanded Moshe. Thus they
camped by their banners, and thus they set out, each amid his clan and his
ancestral house.
3 1 These were the descendants of Aharon and Moshe at the time when the LORD REVI'I
2 spoke to Moshe at Mount Sinai. The names of Aharon's sons were Nadav, the
3 firstborn, Avihu, Elazar, and Itamar. These were the names of Aharon's sons,
4 the anointed priests, ordained for priestly service. But Nadav and Avihu died
before the LORD when, before the LORD, they offered unauthorized fire in the
Wilderness of Sinai; they had had no sons. And Elazar and Itamar served as
priests while their father Aharon lived.
5 6 The LORD said to Moshe, "Bring close the tribe of Levi and set them before

רש"י

ג א **וְאֵלֶּה תּוֹלְדֹת אַהֲרֹן וּמֹשֶׁה.** וְאֵינוֹ מַזְכִּיר אֶלָּא בְּנֵי אַהֲרֹן, וְנִקְרְאוּ תּוֹלְדוֹת מֹשֶׁה, לְפִי שֶׁלִּמְּדָן תּוֹרָה, מְלַמֵּד שֶׁכָּל הַמְלַמֵּד אֶת בֶּן חֲבֵרוֹ תּוֹרָה מַעֲלֶה עָלָיו הַכָּתוּב כְּאִלּוּ יְלָדוֹ: **בְּיוֹם דִּבֶּר ה' אֶת מֹשֶׁה.** נַעֲשׂוּ אֵלּוּ הַתּוֹלָדוֹת שֶׁלּוֹ, שֶׁלִּמְּדָן מַה שֶּׁלָּמַד מִפִּי הַגְּבוּרָה:

ד **עַל פְּנֵי אַהֲרֹן.** בְּחַיָּיו:

3:1 **תּוֹלְדֹת אַהֲרֹן וּמֹשֶׁה** *Descendants of Aharon and Moshe* – The genealogy begins with the words "These were the descendants of Aharon and Moshe" but goes on to list only Aharon's children. On this, the Rabbis say that because Moshe taught Aharon's children they were regarded as his own. In general, "disciples" are called "children" (see Rashi on Num. 3:1). Teachers open our eyes to the world. They give us curiosity and confidence. They connect us to our past and future. They are the guardians of our social heritage. We have many heroes today, and they are often celebrities. They come, they have their fifteen minutes of fame, and they go. But the influence of good teachers stays with us. They are the people who really shape our lives.

basic shape of the narrative is roughly: First God creates order. Then people create chaos. Terrible consequences follow. God begins again, sometimes deeply grieved, but never losing His faith in the one life-form on which He set His image. As the book of Numbers opens, then, we see that there is to be an order to the way the tribes are encamped around the Tabernacle, and to the way they proceed when traveling. Each person has his or her place within the family, the tribe, and the nation. Everyone has been counted and each person counts. It is as if God is saying to the Israelites: This is what order looks like. Preserve and protect this order, for without it you cannot enter the land, fight its battles, and create a society that is both just and free.

כט אֶלֶף וַחֲמֵשׁ מֵאוֹת: וּמַטֵּה נַפְתָּלִי וְנָשִׂיא לִבְנֵי נַפְתָּלִי אֲחִירַע בֶּן־עֵינָן:
ל לא וּצְבָאוֹ וּפְקֻדֵיהֶם שְׁלֹשָׁה וַחֲמִשִּׁים אֶלֶף וְאַרְבַּע מֵאוֹת: כָּל־הַפְּקֻדִים
לַמַּחֲנֵה דָן מְאַת אֶלֶף וְשִׁבְעָה וַחֲמִשִּׁים אֶלֶף וְשֵׁשׁ מֵאוֹת לָאַחֲרֹנָה
יִסְעוּ לְדִגְלֵיהֶם:
לב אֵלֶּה פְּקוּדֵי בְנֵי־יִשְׂרָאֵל לְבֵית אֲבֹתָם כָּל־פְּקוּדֵי הַמַּחֲנֹת לְצִבְאֹתָם
לג שֵׁשׁ־מֵאוֹת אֶלֶף וּשְׁלֹשֶׁת אֲלָפִים וַחֲמֵשׁ מֵאוֹת וַחֲמִשִּׁים: וְהַלְוִיִּם לֹא
לד הָתְפָּקְדוּ בְּתוֹךְ בְּנֵי יִשְׂרָאֵל כַּאֲשֶׁר צִוָּה יהוה אֶת־מֹשֶׁה: וַיַּעֲשׂוּ בְּנֵי
יִשְׂרָאֵל כְּכֹל אֲשֶׁר־צִוָּה יהוה אֶת־מֹשֶׁה כֵּן־חָנוּ לְדִגְלֵיהֶם וְכֵן נָסָעוּ
אִישׁ לְמִשְׁפְּחֹתָיו עַל־בֵּית אֲבֹתָיו:
ג א וְאֵלֶּה תּוֹלְדֹת אַהֲרֹן וּמֹשֶׁה בְּיוֹם דִּבֶּר יהוה אֶת־מֹשֶׁה בְּהַר סִינָי: ג רביעי
ב ג וְאֵלֶּה שְׁמוֹת בְּנֵי־אַהֲרֹן הַבְּכֹר ׀ נָדָב וַאֲבִיהוּא אֶלְעָזָר וְאִיתָמָר: אֵלֶּה
ד שְׁמוֹת בְּנֵי אַהֲרֹן הַכֹּהֲנִים הַמְּשֻׁחִים אֲשֶׁר־מִלֵּא יָדָם לְכַהֵן: וַיָּמָת נָדָב
וַאֲבִיהוּא לִפְנֵי יהוה בְּהַקְרִבָם אֵשׁ זָרָה לִפְנֵי יהוה בְּמִדְבַּר סִינַי וּבָנִים
לֹא־הָיוּ לָהֶם וַיְכַהֵן אֶלְעָזָר וְאִיתָמָר עַל־פְּנֵי אַהֲרֹן אֲבִיהֶם:
ה ו וַיְדַבֵּר יהוה אֶל־מֹשֶׁה לֵּאמֹר: הַקְרֵב אֶת־מַטֵּה לֵוִי וְהַעֲמַדְתָּ אֹתוֹ

אונקלוס

אַלְפִין וַחֲמֵשׁ מְאָה: כט וְשִׁבְטָא דְנַפְתָּלִי, וְרַבָּא לִבְנֵי נַפְתָּלִי, אֲחִירַע בַּר עֵינָן: ל וְחֵילֵיהּ וּמִנְיָנֵיהוֹן, חַמְשִׁין וּתְלָתָא אַלְפִין וְאַרְבַּע מְאָה: לא כָּל מִנְיָנַיָּא לְמַשְׁרִית דָּן, מְאָה וְחַמְשִׁין, וְשִׁבְעָא אַלְפִין וְשִׁית מְאָה, בְּבַתְרֵיתָא נָטְלִין לְטִקְסֵיהוֹן: לב אִלֵּין, מִנְיָנֵי בְנֵי יִשְׂרָאֵל לְבֵית אֲבָהָתְהוֹן, כָּל מִנְיָנֵי מַשְׁרְיָתָא לְחֵילֵיהוֹן, שִׁית מְאָה וּתְלָתָא אַלְפִין, וַחֲמֵשׁ מְאָה וְחַמְשִׁין: לג וְלֵיוָאֵי, לָא אִתְמְנִיאוּ, בְּגוֹ בְּנֵי יִשְׂרָאֵל, כְּמָא דְפַקֵּיד יי יָת מֹשֶׁה: לד וַעֲבַדוּ בְּנֵי יִשְׂרָאֵל, כְּכֹל, דְּפַקֵּיד יי יָת מֹשֶׁה, כֵּן שָׁרַן לְטִקְסֵיהוֹן וְכֵן נָטְלִין, גְּבַר לְזַרְעִיתֵיהּ

עַל בֵּית אֲבָהָתוֹהִי: ג א וְאִלֵּין, תּוֹלְדָת אַהֲרֹן וּמֹשֶׁה, בְּיוֹמָא, דְּמַלֵּיל יי, עִם מֹשֶׁה בְּטוּרָא דְסִינָי: ב וְאִלֵּין, שְׁמָהָת בְּנֵי אַהֲרֹן בֻּכְרָא נָדָב, וַאֲבִיהוּא, אֶלְעָזָר וְאִיתָמָר: ג אִלֵּין, שְׁמָהָת בְּנֵי אַהֲרֹן, כָּהֲנַיָּא דְּאִתְרַבִּיאוּ, דְּאִתְקָרַב קֻרְבָּנְהוֹן לְשַׁמָּשָׁא: ד וּמִית נָדָב וַאֲבִיהוּא קֳדָם יי, בְּקָרוֹבֵיהוֹן אִישָׁתָא נֻכְרֵיתָא, קֳדָם יי בְּמַדְבְּרָא דְסִינַי, וּבְנִין לָא הֲווֹ לְהוֹן, וְשַׁמֵּישׁ אֶלְעָזָר וְאִיתָמָר, עַל אַפֵּי אַהֲרֹן אֲבוּהוֹן: ה וּמַלֵּיל יי עִם מֹשֶׁה לְמֵימַר: ו קָרֵיב יָת שִׁבְטָא דְלֵוִי, וּתְקֵים יָתֵיהּ,

2:34 כֵּן־חָנוּ לְדִגְלֵיהֶם *They camped by their banners* – The drama to which the whole Torah is a commentary is: *how can freedom co-exist with order*? This drama is set on the stage of history, and it plays itself out through multiple scenes. The

7 Aharon the priest to assist him. They shall keep his charge and that of the whole
community at the Tent of Meeting, carrying out the service of the Tabernacle.
8 Theirs shall be the charge of all the utensils of the Tent of Meeting, and they
shall keep, too, the charge of the Israelites by performing the service of the
9 Tabernacle. Give the Levites over to Aharon and his sons; they among the
10 Israelites are to be dedicated wholly to him. Appoint Aharon and his sons to
attend to the priestly duties; any outsider who draws close will die."
11 12 And the Lord spoke to Moshe: "In place of the firstborn, the first to emerge
from every womb among the Israelites, I have taken the Levites from among the
13 Israelites; the Levites shall be Mine, for all the firstborn are Mine. On the day I
struck down all the firstborn in Egypt, I consecrated every firstborn in Israel to
Myself, man and animal. They are to be Mine; I am the Lord."
14 15 Then the Lord spoke to Moshe in the Sinai Desert: "Count the Levites by their HAMISHI
ancestral houses and their clans. Count every male a month old or more."

רש״י

ו **ושרתו אתו.** ומהו השרות? "ושמרו את משמרתו". לפי ששמירת המקדש עליו שלא יקרב זר, כמו שנאמר: "אתה ובניך ובית אביך אתך תשאו את עון המקדש" (להלן יח, א), והלוים הללו מסייעין אותם, זו היא השרות:

ז **ושמרו את משמרתו.** כל מנוי שהאדם ממנה עליו ומוטל עליו לעשותו קרוי 'משמרת' בכל המקרא ובלשון משנה, כמו שאמרו בבגתן ותרש: "והלא אין משמרתי ומשמרתך שוה", וכן משמרות כהנה ולויה:

ח **ואת משמרת בני ישראל.** שכלן היו זקוקין לצרכי המקדש, אלא שהלוים באים תחתיהם בשליחותם, לפיכך לוקחים מהם המעשרות בשכרן, שנאמר: "כי שכר הוא לכם חלף עבדתכם" (להלן יח, לא):

ט **נתונם המה לו.** לעזרה: **מאת בני ישראל.** כמו 'מתוך בני ישראל', כלומר מאחר כל העדה נבדלו לכך בגזרת המקום והוא נתנם לו, שנאמר: "ואתנה את הלוים נתנים" וגו' (להלן ח, יט):

י **ואת אהרן ואת בניו תפקד.** לשון פקידות, ואינו לשון מנין: **ושמרו את כהנתם.** קבלת דמים וזריקה והקטרה ועבודות המסורות לכהנים:

יב **ואני הנה לקחתי.** ואני מהיכן זכיתי בהן "מתוך בני ישראל", שיהיו ישראל שוכרין אותן לשרות שלי? על ידי הבכורות זכיתי בהם ולקחתים תמורתם. לפי שהיתה העבודה בבכורות, וכשחטאו בעגל נפסלו, והלוים שלא עבדו עבודה זרה נבחרו תחתיהם:

טו **מבן חדש ומעלה.** משיצא מכלל נפלים הוא נמנה לקרא שומר משמרת הקדש. אמר רבי יהודה ברבי שלום: למוד הוא אותו השבט להיות נמנה מן הבטן, שנאמר: "אשר ילדה אתה ללוי במצרים" (להלן כו, נט), עם כניסתה בפתח מצרים ילדה אותה ונמנית בשבעים נפש, שכשאתה מונה חשבונם לא תמצאם אלא שבעים חסר אחת, והיא השלימה את המנין:

confrontation with the prophets of Baal, he encountered God not in the whirlwind, or the fire, or the earthquake, but in the *kol demama daka*, the still, small voice, literally "the sound of a slender silence" (I Kings 19:9–12). I define this as the sound you can hear only if you are listening.

In the silence of the *midbar*, the desert, you can hear the *Medaber*, the Speaker, and the *medubar*, that which is spoken. To hear the voice of God you need a listening silence in the soul.

nothing to enter – so the Torah is free. It is God's gift to us (*Midrash Lekaḥ Tov*, Yitro 20:2).

But there is another, more spiritual reason. The desert is a place of silence. There is nothing visual to distract you, and there is no ambient noise to muffle sound. To be sure, when the Israelites received the Torah, there was thunder and lightning and the sound of a shofar. The earth felt as if it were shaking at its foundations. But in a later age, when the prophet Eliyahu stood at the same mountain after his

ז לִפְנֵי אַהֲרֹן הַכֹּהֵן וְשֵׁרְתוּ אֹתוֹ׃ וְשָׁמְרוּ אֶת־מִשְׁמַרְתּוֹ וְאֶת־מִשְׁמֶרֶת
ח כָּל־הָעֵדָה לִפְנֵי אֹהֶל מוֹעֵד לַעֲבֹד אֶת־עֲבֹדַת הַמִּשְׁכָּן׃ וְשָׁמְרוּ אֶת־
כָּל־כְּלֵי אֹהֶל מוֹעֵד וְאֶת־מִשְׁמֶרֶת בְּנֵי יִשְׂרָאֵל לַעֲבֹד אֶת־עֲבֹדַת
ט הַמִּשְׁכָּן׃ וְנָתַתָּה אֶת־הַלְוִיִּם לְאַהֲרֹן וּלְבָנָיו נְתוּנִם נְתוּנִם הֵמָּה לוֹ
י מֵאֵת בְּנֵי יִשְׂרָאֵל׃ וְאֶת־אַהֲרֹן וְאֶת־בָּנָיו תִּפְקֹד וְשָׁמְרוּ אֶת־כְּהֻנָּתָם
וְהַזָּר הַקָּרֵב יוּמָת׃
יא יב וַיְדַבֵּר יְהוָה אֶל־מֹשֶׁה לֵּאמֹר׃ וַאֲנִי הִנֵּה לָקַחְתִּי אֶת־הַלְוִיִּם מִתּוֹךְ
בְּנֵי יִשְׂרָאֵל תַּחַת כָּל־בְּכוֹר פֶּטֶר רֶחֶם מִבְּנֵי יִשְׂרָאֵל וְהָיוּ לִי הַלְוִיִּם׃
יג כִּי לִי כָּל־בְּכוֹר בְּיוֹם הַכֹּתִי כָל־בְּכוֹר בְּאֶרֶץ מִצְרַיִם הִקְדַּשְׁתִּי לִי כָל־
בְּכוֹר בְּיִשְׂרָאֵל מֵאָדָם עַד־בְּהֵמָה לִי יִהְיוּ אֲנִי יְהוָה׃
יד טו וַיְדַבֵּר יְהוָה אֶל־מֹשֶׁה בְּמִדְבַּר סִינַי לֵאמֹר׃ פְּקֹד אֶת־בְּנֵי לֵוִי לְבֵית חמישי
אֲבֹתָם לְמִשְׁפְּחֹתָם כָּל־זָכָר מִבֶּן־חֹדֶשׁ וָמַעְלָה תִּפְקְדֵם׃

אונקלוס

קֳדָם אַהֲרֹן כָּהֲנָא, וִישַׁמְשׁוּן יָתֵיהּ: ז וְיִטְּרוּן יָת מַטַּרְתֵּיהּ, וְיָת מַטְּרַת כָּל כְּנִשְׁתָּא, קֳדָם מַשְׁכַּן זִמְנָא, לְמִפְלַח יָת פָּלְחַן מַשְׁכְּנָא: ח וְיִטְּרוּן, יָת כָּל מָנֵי מַשְׁכַּן זִמְנָא, וְיָת מַטְּרַת בְּנֵי יִשְׂרָאֵל, לְמִפְלַח יָת פָּלְחַן מַשְׁכְּנָא: ט וְתִתֵּין יָת לֵיוָאֵי, לְאַהֲרֹן וְלִבְנוֹהִי, מְסִירִין יְהִיבִין אִנּוּן לֵיהּ, מִן בְּנֵי יִשְׂרָאֵל: י וְיָת אַהֲרֹן וְיָת בְּנוֹהִי תְּמַנֵּי, וְיִטְּרוּן יָת כְּהֻנַּתְהוֹן, וְחִילוֹנַי דְּיִקְרַב יִתְקְטִיל: יא וּמַלֵּיל יי עִם מֹשֶׁה לְמֵימַר: יב וַאֲנָא הָא קָרֵיבִית יָת לֵיוָאֵי, מִגּוֹ בְּנֵי יִשְׂרָאֵל, חֲלָף כָּל בֻּכְרָא, פָּתַח וַלְדָּא מִבְּנֵי יִשְׂרָאֵל, וִיהוֹן מְשַׁמְּשִׁין קֳדָמַי לֵיוָאֵי: יג אֲרֵי דִילִי כָּל בֻּכְרָא, בְּיוֹמָא דִּקְטָלִית כָּל בֻּכְרָא בְּאַרְעָא דְמִצְרַיִם, אַקְדֵּישִׁית קֳדָמַי כָּל בֻּכְרָא בְּיִשְׂרָאֵל, מֵאֱנָשָׁא עַד בְּעִירָא, דִּילִי יְהוֹן אֲנָא יי: יד וּמַלֵּיל יי עִם מֹשֶׁה, בְּמַדְבְּרָא דְסִינַי לְמֵימַר: טו מְנִי יָת בְּנֵי לֵוִי, לְבֵית אֲבָהָתְהוֹן לְזַרְעִיָּתְהוֹן, כָּל דְּכוּרָא, מִבַּר יַרְחָא וּלְעֵילָא תִּמְנֵינוּן:

3:14 וַיְדַבֵּר יְהוָה אֶל־מֹשֶׁה בְּמִדְבַּר סִינַי לֵאמֹר *Then the Lord spoke to Moshe in the Sinai Desert* – Parashat Bemidbar is usually read on the Sabbath before Shavuot. Shavuot is the time of the giving of the Torah. *Bemidbar* means "in the desert." Why, in the fixing of the Torah reading cycle, was a link forged between the giving of the Torah and the particular fact of its emergence from the wilderness?

The Sages gave several interpretations. According to the Mekhilta, the Torah was given publicly, openly, and in a place no one owns because had it been given in the land of Israel, Jews would have said to the nations of the world, "You have no share in it." Instead, God seems to say, whoever wants to come and accept it, let them come and accept it (*Mekhilta*, Yitro, *BaḤodesh* 1).

Another explanation: Had the Torah been given in Israel, the national homeland of the Israelites, the nations of the world would have had an excuse for not accepting it. This follows the rabbinic tradition that before God gave the Torah to the Israelites, He offered it to all the other nations and each found a reason to decline (ibid., *BaḤodesh* 5).

Yet another: Just as the wilderness is free – it costs

16 17 So Moshe counted them at the LORD's word as he was commanded. These were
18 the names of Levi's sons: Gershon, Kehat, and Merari. These were the names
19 of Gershon's sons with their clans: Livni and Shimi. Kehat's sons with their
20 clans: Amram, Yitzhar, Ḥevron, and Uziel. Merari's sons with their clans: Maḥli
21 and Mushi. These were the Levite clans by their ancestral houses. Gershon
encompassed the clans of Livni and Shimi; these were the Gershonite clans.
22 23 Their total number of males a month old and upward was 7,500. The Gershonite
24 families were to camp behind the Tabernacle to the west. And the leader of the
25 Gershonite families was Elyasaf son of Lael. The charge of the sons of Gershon
at the Tent of Meeting was the Tabernacle and the tent, its covering, the screen
26 at the entrance to the Tent of Meeting, the curtains of the courtyard, the screen
at the entrance to the courtyard surrounding the Tabernacle and altar, and its
27 ropes – and all the service related to these. Kehat encompassed the
clans of Amram, Yitzhar, Ḥevron, and Uziel; these were the Kohatite clans.
28 Their total number of males a month old and upward was 8,600; these kept the
29 charge of the Sanctuary. The Kohatite families were to camp on the south side
30 of the Tabernacle. The leader of the ancestral house of the Kohatite families was
31 Elitzafan son of Uziel. Their charge was the Ark, the table, the candelabrum,
the altars, and the sacred utensils used in their service, and the screen and
32 everything pertaining to it. Chief of the leaders of the Levites was Elazar son of
Aharon the priest; he was appointed over those responsible for keeping charge

אונקלוס

טז ומנא יתהון, משה על מימרא דיי, כמא דאתפקד: יז והוו אלין בני לוי בשמהתהון, גרשון, וקהת ומררי: יח ואלין, שמהת בני גרשון לזרעיתהון, לבני ושמעי: יט ובני קהת לזרעיתהון, עמרם ויצהר, חברון ועזיאל: כ ובני מררי, לזרעיתהון מחלי ומושי, אלין אנון,

רש״י

טז על פי ה׳. אמר משה לפני הקדוש ברוך הוא: היאך אני נכנס לתוך אהליהם לדעת מנין יונקיהם? אמר לו הקדוש ברוך הוא: עשה אתה שלך ואני אעשה שלי. הלך משה ועמד על פתח האהל, והשכינה מקדמת לפניו, ובת קול יוצאת מן האהל ואומרת: כך וכך תינוקות יש באהל זה; לכך נאמר: ״על פי ה׳״:

כא לגרשון משפחת הלבני. כלומר, לגרשון היו הפקודים משפחת הלבני ומשפחת השמעי, פקודיהם כך וכך:

כה המשכן. יריעות התחתונות: והאהל. יריעות עזים העשויות לגג: מכסהו. עורות אילים ותחשים: ומסך פתח. הוא הוילון:

כו ואת מיתריו. של משכן והאהל, ולא של חצר:

כט משפחת בני קהת יחנו... תימנה. וסמוכין להם דגל ראובן החונים תימנה, אוי לרשע ואוי לשכנו, לכך לקו מהם דתן ואבירם ומאתים וחמשים איש עם קרח ועדתו, שנמשכו עמהם במחלקתם:

לא והמסך. היא הפרכת, שאף היא קרויה ״פרכת המסך״ (להלן ד, ה):

לב ונשיא נשיאי הלוי. ממנה על כלם, ועל מה היא נשיאותו? ״פקדת שמרי משמרת״, על ידו היא פקדת כלם:

טז יז וַיִּפְקֹד אֹתָם מֹשֶׁה עַל־פִּי יְהוָה כַּאֲשֶׁר צֻוָּה: וַיִּהְיוּ־אֵלֶּה בְנֵי־לֵוִי
יח בִּשְׁמֹתָם גֵּרְשׁוֹן וּקְהָת וּמְרָרִי: וְאֵלֶּה שְׁמוֹת בְּנֵי־גֵרְשׁוֹן לְמִשְׁפְּחֹתָם
יט לִבְנִי וְשִׁמְעִי: וּבְנֵי קְהָת לְמִשְׁפְּחֹתָם עַמְרָם וְיִצְהָר חֶבְרוֹן וְעֻזִּיאֵל:
כ וּבְנֵי מְרָרִי לְמִשְׁפְּחֹתָם מַחְלִי וּמוּשִׁי אֵלֶּה הֵם מִשְׁפְּחֹת הַלֵּוִי לְבֵית
כא אֲבֹתָם: לְגֵרְשׁוֹן מִשְׁפַּחַת הַלִּבְנִי וּמִשְׁפַּחַת הַשִּׁמְעִי אֵלֶּה הֵם מִשְׁפְּחֹת
כב הַגֵּרְשֻׁנִּי: פְּקֻדֵיהֶם בְּמִסְפַּר כָּל־זָכָר מִבֶּן־חֹדֶשׁ וָמָעְלָה פְּקֻדֵיהֶם
כג שִׁבְעַת אֲלָפִים וַחֲמֵשׁ מֵאוֹת: מִשְׁפְּחֹת הַגֵּרְשֻׁנִּי אַחֲרֵי הַמִּשְׁכָּן יַחֲנוּ
כד כה יָמָּה: וּנְשִׂיא בֵית־אָב לַגֵּרְשֻׁנִּי אֶלְיָסָף בֶּן־לָאֵל: וּמִשְׁמֶרֶת בְּנֵי־גֵרְשׁוֹן
כו בְּאֹהֶל מוֹעֵד הַמִּשְׁכָּן וְהָאֹהֶל מִכְסֵהוּ וּמָסַךְ פֶּתַח אֹהֶל מוֹעֵד: וְקַלְעֵי
הֶחָצֵר וְאֶת־מָסַךְ פֶּתַח הֶחָצֵר אֲשֶׁר עַל־הַמִּשְׁכָּן וְעַל־הַמִּזְבֵּחַ סָבִיב
כז וְאֵת מֵיתָרָיו לְכֹל עֲבֹדָתוֹ: וְלִקְהָת מִשְׁפַּחַת הָעַמְרָמִי
וּמִשְׁפַּחַת הַיִּצְהָרִי וּמִשְׁפַּחַת הַחֶבְרֹנִי וּמִשְׁפַּחַת הָעָזִּיאֵלִי אֵלֶּה הֵם
כח מִשְׁפְּחֹת הַקְּהָתִי: בְּמִסְפַּר כָּל־זָכָר מִבֶּן־חֹדֶשׁ וָמָעְלָה שְׁמֹנַת אֲלָפִים
כט וְשֵׁשׁ מֵאוֹת שֹׁמְרֵי מִשְׁמֶרֶת הַקֹּדֶשׁ: מִשְׁפְּחֹת בְּנֵי־קְהָת יַחֲנוּ עַל
ל יֶרֶךְ הַמִּשְׁכָּן תֵּימָנָה: וּנְשִׂיא בֵית־אָב לְמִשְׁפְּחֹת הַקְּהָתִי אֱלִיצָפָן
לא בֶּן־עֻזִּיאֵל: וּמִשְׁמַרְתָּם הָאָרֹן וְהַשֻּׁלְחָן וְהַמְּנֹרָה וְהַמִּזְבְּחֹת וּכְלֵי
לב הַקֹּדֶשׁ אֲשֶׁר יְשָׁרְתוּ בָּהֶם וְהַמָּסָךְ וְכֹל עֲבֹדָתוֹ: וּנְשִׂיא נְשִׂיאֵי הַלֵּוִי

אונקלוס

זַרְעִית לֵוִי לְבֵית אֲבָהָתְהוֹן: כא לְגֵרְשׁוֹן, זַרְעִית לִבְנִי, וְזַרְעִית שִׁמְעִי, אִלֵּין אִנּוּן, זַרְעִית גֵּרְשׁוֹן: כב מִנְיָנֵיהוֹן בְּמִנְיַן כָּל דְּכוּרָא, מִבַּר יַרְחָא וּלְעֵילָּא, מִנְיָנֵיהוֹן, שִׁבְעָא אַלְפִין וַחֲמֵשׁ מְאָה: כג זַרְעִית גֵּרְשׁוֹן, אֲחוֹרֵי מַשְׁכְּנָא, יִשְׁרוֹן מַעַרְבָא: כד וְרַב בֵּית אַבָּא לְבֵית גֵּרְשׁוֹן, אֶלְיָסָף בַּר לָאֵל: כה וּמַטְּרַת בְּנֵי גֵרְשׁוֹן בְּמַשְׁכַּן זִמְנָא, מַשְׁכְּנָא וּפְרָסָא, חוֹפָאֵיהּ, וּפְרָסָא, דִּתְרַע מַשְׁכַּן זִמְנָא: כו וּסְרָדֵי דָרְתָא, וְיָת פְּרָסָא דִּתְרַע דָּרְתָא, דְּעַל מַשְׁכְּנָא, וְעַל מַדְבְּחָא סְחוֹר סְחוֹר, וְיָת אֲטוּנוֹהִי, לְכָל פָּלְחָנֵיהּ: כז וְלִקְהָת, זַרְעִית עַמְרָם וְזַרְעִית יִצְהָר, וְזַרְעִית חֶבְרוֹן, וְזַרְעִית עֻזִּיאֵל, אִלֵּין אִנּוּן זַרְעִית קְהָת: כח בְּמִנְיַן כָּל דְּכוּרָא, מִבַּר יַרְחָא וּלְעֵילָּא, תְּמָנְיָא אַלְפִין וְשִׁית מְאָה, נָטְרֵי מַטְּרַתָּא דְּקֻדְשָׁא: כט זַרְעִית בְּנֵי קְהָת יִשְׁרוֹן, עַל שִׁדָּא דְּמַשְׁכְּנָא דָּרוֹמָא: ל וְרַב בֵּית אַבָּא לְזַרְעִית קְהָת, אֱלִיצָפָן בַּר עֻזִּיאֵל: לא וּמַטְּרַתְהוֹן, אֲרוֹנָא וּפָתוּרָא וּמְנָרְתָא וּמַדְבְּחַיָּא, וּמָנֵי קֻדְשָׁא, דִּישַׁמְּשׁוּן בְּהוֹן, וּפְרָסָא, וְכָל פָּלְחָנֵיהּ: לב וְאַמַּרְכְּלָא דִּמְמַנָּא עַל רַבְרְבֵי לֵיוָאֵי,

33 of the Sanctuary. Merari encompassed the clans of Maḥli and Mushi; these
34 were the Merarite families. The total number of their males a month old and
35 upward was 6,200. The leader of the ancestral house of the Merarite families
was Tzuriel son of Aviḥayil; and they were to camp on the north side of the
36 Tabernacle. The Merarites were appointed to take care of the frames, bars,
37 posts, and bases of the Tabernacle, all its utensils and accessories, as well as the
38 posts of the surrounding courtyard with their bases, pegs, and ropes. Those
who were to camp to the east of the Tabernacle in front of the Tent of Meeting
toward the sunrise were Moshe, Aharon, and his sons. They were charged, on
the Israelites' behalf, to keep faithful watch over the Sanctuary. Any outsider
39 who drew close would die. The total number of Levites counted by Moshe and
Aharon at the LORD's command, by their clans, all the males a month old and
40 upward, was 22,000. Then the LORD said to Moshe, "Count all the SHISHI
firstborn Israelite males a month of age and upward, taking a census of their
41 names. Take the Levites for Me – I am the LORD – in place of all the firstborn
of the Israelites, and the livestock of the Levites in place of all the firstborn of

רש״י

לח] **משֶׁה וְאַהֲרֹן וּבָנָיו.** וּסְמוּכִין לָהֶם דֶּגֶל מַחֲנֵה יְהוּדָה וְהַחוֹנִים עָלָיו יִשָּׂשכָר וּזְבוּלֻן, טוֹב לַצַּדִּיק טוֹב לִשְׁכֵנוֹ, לְפִי שֶׁהָיוּ שְׁכֵנָיו שֶׁל משֶׁה שֶׁהָיָה עוֹסֵק בַּתּוֹרָה, נַעֲשׂוּ גְּדוֹלִים בַּתּוֹרָה, שֶׁנֶּאֱמַר: "יְהוּדָה מְחֹקְקִי" (תהלים ס, ט), "וּמִבְּנֵי יִשָּׂשכָר יוֹדְעֵי בִינָה" וְגוֹ' (דברי הימים א' יב, לג) מָאתַיִם רָאשֵׁי סַנְהֶדְרָאוֹת, "וּמִזְּבוּלֻן מֹשְׁכִים בְּשֵׁבֶט סֹפֵר" (שופטים ה, יד):

לט] **אֲשֶׁר פָּקַד משֶׁה וְאַהֲרֹן.** נָקוּד עַל וְאַהֲרֹן, לוֹמַר שֶׁלֹּא הָיָה בְּמִנְיַן הַלְוִיִּם: **שְׁנַיִם וְעֶשְׂרִים אָלֶף.** וּבִפְרָטָן אַתָּה מוֹצֵא שְׁלֹשׁ מֵאוֹת יְתֵרִים: בְּנֵי גֵרְשׁוֹן שִׁבְעַת אֲלָפִים וַחֲמֵשׁ מֵאוֹת, בְּנֵי קְהָת שְׁמֹנַת אֲלָפִים וְשֵׁשׁ מֵאוֹת, בְּנֵי מְרָרִי שֵׁשֶׁת אֲלָפִים וּמָאתָיִם! וְלָמָּה לֹא כְּלָלָן עִם הַשְּׁאָר וְיִפְדּוּ אֶת הַבְּכוֹרוֹת, וְלֹא יִהְיוּ זְקוּקִים הַשְּׁלֹשָׁה וְשִׁבְעִים וּמָאתַיִם בְּכוֹרוֹת הָעוֹדְפִים עַל הַמִּנְיָן לְפִדְיוֹן? אָמְרוּ רַבּוֹתֵינוּ בְּמַסֶּכֶת בְּכוֹרוֹת (דף ה ע"א): אוֹתָן שְׁלֹשׁ מֵאוֹת לְוִיִּם בְּכוֹרוֹת הָיוּ, וְדַיָּם שֶׁיַּפְקִיעוּ עַצְמָם מִן הַפִּדְיוֹן:

מ] **פְּקֹד כָּל בְּכֹר זָכָר וְגוֹ' מִבֶּן חֹדֶשׁ וָמָעְלָה.** מִשֶּׁיָּצָא מִכְּלַל סְפֵק נְפָלִים:

been the firstborns – those who were saved from the last of the Ten Plagues – who were charged with special holiness as the ministers of God. It was after the sin of the golden calf, in which only the tribe of Levi did not participate, that the change was made.

Even as a role reserved specifically for firstborn males, the priesthood would have been an elite. However, it is not the priests alone who are to be holy; the people as a whole are commanded to "be holy" (Lev. 19:1–2). Life itself is to be sanctified. Holiness is to be made manifest in the way the nation makes its clothes and plants its fields, in the way justice is administered, workers are paid, and business conducted. The vulnerable – the deaf, the blind, the elderly, and the stranger – are to be afforded special protection. The whole society is to be governed by love, without resentments or revenge.

This is a radical democratization of holiness. When we turn our lives into the service of God, and society into a home for the Divine Presence, holiness belongs to all of us.

לג אֶלְעָזָר בֶּן־אַהֲרֹן הַכֹּהֵן פְּקֻדַּת שֹׁמְרֵי מִשְׁמֶרֶת הַקֹּדֶשׁ׃ לִמְרָרִי
לד מִשְׁפַּחַת הַמַּחְלִי וּמִשְׁפַּחַת הַמּוּשִׁי אֵלֶּה הֵם מִשְׁפְּחֹת מְרָרִי׃ וּפְקֻדֵיהֶם
לה בְּמִסְפַּר כָּל־זָכָר מִבֶּן־חֹדֶשׁ וָמָעְלָה שֵׁשֶׁת אֲלָפִים וּמָאתָיִם׃ וּנְשִׂיא
בֵית־אָב לְמִשְׁפְּחֹת מְרָרִי צוּרִיאֵל בֶּן־אֲבִיחָיִל עַל יֶרֶךְ הַמִּשְׁכָּן יַחֲנוּ
לו צָפֹנָה׃ וּפְקֻדַּת מִשְׁמֶרֶת בְּנֵי מְרָרִי קַרְשֵׁי הַמִּשְׁכָּן וּבְרִיחָיו וְעַמֻּדָיו
לז וַאֲדָנָיו וְכָל־כֵּלָיו וְכֹל עֲבֹדָתוֹ׃ וְעַמֻּדֵי הֶחָצֵר סָבִיב וְאַדְנֵיהֶם וִיתֵדֹתָם
לח וּמֵיתְרֵיהֶם׃ וְהַחֹנִים לִפְנֵי הַמִּשְׁכָּן קֵדְמָה לִפְנֵי אֹהֶל־מוֹעֵד ׀ מִזְרָחָה
מֹשֶׁה ׀ וְאַהֲרֹן וּבָנָיו שֹׁמְרִים מִשְׁמֶרֶת הַמִּקְדָּשׁ לְמִשְׁמֶרֶת בְּנֵי יִשְׂרָאֵל
לט וְהַזָּר הַקָּרֵב יוּמָת׃ כָּל־פְּקוּדֵי הַלְוִיִּם אֲשֶׁר פָּקַד מֹשֶׁה וְאַהֲרֹן עַל־
פִּי יהוה לְמִשְׁפְּחֹתָם כָּל־זָכָר מִבֶּן־חֹדֶשׁ וָמַעְלָה שְׁנַיִם וְעֶשְׂרִים
מ אָלֶף׃ וַיֹּאמֶר יהוה אֶל־מֹשֶׁה פְּקֹד כָּל־בְּכֹר זָכָר לִבְנֵי ששי
מא יִשְׂרָאֵל מִבֶּן־חֹדֶשׁ וָמָעְלָה וְשָׂא אֵת מִסְפַּר שְׁמֹתָם׃ וְלָקַחְתָּ אֶת־
הַלְוִיִּם לִי אֲנִי יהוה תַּחַת כָּל־בְּכֹר בִּבְנֵי יִשְׂרָאֵל וְאֵת בֶּהֱמַת הַלְוִיִּם

אונקלוס

אֶלְעָזָר בַּר אַהֲרֹן כַּהֲנָא, מִתְּחוֹת יְדוֹהִי מְמַנַּן, נָטְרֵי מַטַּרְתָּא
דְקֻדְשָׁא׃ לג לִמְרָרִי, זַרְעִית מַחְלִי, וְזַרְעִית מוּשִׁי, אִלֵּין אִנּוּן זַרְעִית
מְרָרִי׃ לד וּמִנְיָנֵיהוֹן בְּמִנְיַן כָּל דְּכוּרָא, מִבַּר יַרְחָא וּלְעֵילָא, שִׁתָּא
אַלְפִין וּמָאתַן׃ לה וְרַב בֵּית בָּא לְזַרְעִית מְרָרִי, צוּרִיאֵל בַּר אֲבִיחָיִל,
עַל שִׁדָּא דְמַשְׁכְּנָא, יִשְׁרוֹן צִפּוּנָא׃ לו וּדְמַסִּיר לְמַטַּר לִבְנֵי מְרָרִי, דַּפֵּי
מַשְׁכְּנָא, וְעַבְּרוֹהִי וְעַמּוּדוֹהִי וְסָמְכוֹהִי, וְכָל מָנוֹהִי, וְכָל פָּלְחָנֵיהּ׃
לז וְעַמּוּדֵי דָּרְתָא, סְחוֹר סְחוֹר וְסָמְכֵיהוֹן, וְסִכֵּיהוֹן וְאַטּוּנֵיהוֹן׃

לח וְדִשְׁרַן קֳדָם מַשְׁכְּנָא, קִדּוּמָא קֳדָם מַשְׁכַּן זִמְנָא מַדִּנְחָא, מֹשֶׁה
וְאַהֲרֹן וּבְנוֹהִי, נָטְרֵי מַטְּרַת מַקְדְּשָׁא, לְמַטְּרַת בְּנֵי יִשְׂרָאֵל, וְחִילוֹנַי
דְּיִקְרַב יִתְקְטִיל׃ לט כָּל מִנְיָנֵי לֵיוָאֵי, דִּמְנָא מֹשֶׁה וְאַהֲרֹן, עַל מֵימְרָא
דַּיי לְזַרְעֲיָתְהוֹן, כָּל דְּכוּרָא מִבַּר יַרְחָא וּלְעֵילָּא, עֶסְרִין וּתְרֵין אַלְפִין׃
מ וַאֲמַר יי לְמֹשֶׁה, מְנִי כָּל בְּכוֹרַיָּא דְכוּרַיָּא לִבְנֵי יִשְׂרָאֵל, מִבַּר
יַרְחָא וּלְעֵילָּא, וְקַבֵּיל, יָת חֻשְׁבַּן שְׁמָהָתְהוֹן׃ מא וּתְקָרֵיב יָת לֵיוָאֵי
קֳדָמַי אֲנָא יי, חֲלַף כָּל בְּכֻרָא בִּבְנֵי יִשְׂרָאֵל, וְיָת בְּעִירָא דְלֵיוָאֵי,

3:41 תַּחַת כָּל־בְּכֹר בִּבְנֵי יִשְׂרָאֵל *In place of all the firstborn of the Israelites* – On the face of it, the priesthood was not egalitarian. We have encountered four instances in the Torah thus far of non-Israelite priests: Malkitzedek, Avraham's contemporary, described as a priest of God Most High; Potifera, Yosef's father-in-law; the Egyptian priests as a whole, whose land Yosef did not nationalize; and Yitro, Moshe's father-in-law, a Midianite priest. The priesthood was not unique to Israel, and everywhere it was an elite. In Israel too, priests all came from a single tribe, the Levites, and from a single family within the tribe – that of Aharon. The Torah tells us that this was not God's original intention. Initially it was to have

42 the Israelites' livestock." So Moshe counted all the firstborn of the Israelites, as
43 the LORD had commanded him. The total number of firstborn males a month
of age and upward, the full tally of their names, was 22,273.
44 45 Then the LORD spoke to Moshe: "Take the Levites in place of all the firstborn of
Israel, and the livestock of the Levites in place of their livestock. The Levites shall
46 be Mine; I am the LORD. As for the redemption of the 273 firstborn Israelites
47 who exceed the number of the Levites, collect five shekel for each, according
48 to the Sanctuary weight – a shekel being twenty gerah. Give the money to
49 Aharon and his sons as a redemption for the additional Israelites." Moshe took
the redemption money from those who were over and above those redeemed
50 by the Levites; from the firstborn of the Israelites he took silver weighing 1,365
51 shekel by the Sanctuary weight. Moshe gave the redemption money to Aharon
and his sons, at the LORD's word, as the LORD had commanded Moshe.
4 1 2 The LORD spoke to Moshe and Aharon: "Take a census of the Kohatites among SHEVI'I
3 the Levites, by their families and their ancestral houses, from thirty to fifty
years old: all those able to go into service to perform the work of the Tent
4 of Meeting. This will be the service of the Kohatites in the Tent of Meeting:
5 the most sacred objects; when the camp is about to set out, Aharon and his

אונקלוס

חֲלָף כָּל בֻּכְרָא, בִּבְעִירָא דִּבְנֵי יִשְׂרָאֵל: מב וּמְנָא מֹשֶׁה, כְּמָא דְּפַקֵּיד יי יָתֵיהּ, יָת כָּל בֻּכְרָא בִּבְנֵי יִשְׂרָאֵל: מג וַהֲווֹ כָּל בֻּכְרַיָּא דְּכוּרַיָּא, בְּמִנְיַן שְׁמָהָן, מִבַּר יַרְחָא וּלְעֵילָּא לְמִנְיָנֵיהוֹן, עֶסְרִין וּתְרֵין אַלְפִין, מָאתַן וְשִׁבְעִין וּתְלָתָא: מד וּמַלֵּיל יי עִם מֹשֶׁה לְמֵימַר: מה קָרֵיב יָת

רש״י

מה **וְאֶת בֶּהֱמַת הַלְוִיִּם וְגוֹ׳.** לֹא פָּדוּ בַּהֲמוֹת הַלְוִיִּם אֶת בְּכוֹרֵי בְּהֵמָה טְהוֹרָה שֶׁל יִשְׂרָאֵל, אֶלָּא אֶת פִּטְרֵי חֲמוֹרֵיהֶם, וְשֶׂה אֶחָד שֶׁל בֶּן לֵוִי פָּטַר כַּמָּה פִּטְרֵי חֲמוֹרִים שֶׁל יִשְׂרָאֵל. תֵּדַע, שֶׁהֲרֵי מָנָה הָעוֹדְפִים בָּאָדָם וְלֹא מָנָה הָעוֹדְפִים בַּבְּהֵמָה:

מו-מז **וְאֵת פְּדוּיֵי הַשְּׁלֹשָׁה וְגוֹ׳.** וְאֶת הַבְּכוֹרוֹת הַצְּרִיכִין לְהִפָּדוֹת בָּהֶם, אֵלּוּ שְׁלֹשָׁה וְשִׁבְעִים וּמָאתַיִם הָעוֹדְפִים בָּהֶם יְתֵרִים עַל הַלְוִיִּם, מֵהֶם תִּקַּח חֲמֵשֶׁת שְׁקָלִים לַגֻּלְגֹּלֶת. כָּךְ הָיְתָה מְכִירָתוֹ שֶׁל יוֹסֵף, עֶשְׂרִים כֶּסֶף, שֶׁהָיָה בְּכוֹרָהּ שֶׁל רָחֵל:

מט **הָעֹדְפִים עַל פְּדוּיֵי הַלְוִיִּם.** עַל אוֹתָן שֶׁפָּדוּ הַלְוִיִּם בְּגוּפָן:

נ **חֲמִשָּׁה וְשִׁשִּׁים וּשְׁלֹשׁ מֵאוֹת וָאֶלֶף.** כָּךְ סְכוּם הַחֶשְׁבּוֹן: חֲמֵשֶׁת שְׁקָלִים לַגֻּלְגֹּלֶת, לְמָאתַיִם בְּכוֹרוֹת – אֶלֶף שֶׁקֶל, לְשִׁבְעִים בְּכוֹרוֹת – שְׁלֹשׁ מֵאוֹת וַחֲמִשִּׁים שֶׁקֶל, לִשְׁלֹשָׁה בְּכוֹרוֹת – חֲמִשָּׁה עָשָׂר שֶׁקֶל. אָמַר: כֵּיצַד אֶעֱשֶׂה? בְּכוֹר שֶׁאֹמַר לוֹ: תֵּן חֲמֵשֶׁת שְׁקָלִים! יֹאמַר לִי: אֲנִי מִפְּדוּיֵי הַלְוִיִּם. מֶה עָשָׂה? הֵבִיא שְׁנַיִם וְעֶשְׂרִים אֶלֶף פִּתְקִין וְכָתַב עֲלֵיהֶם ׳בֶּן לֵוִי׳, וּמָאתַיִם וְשִׁבְעִים וּשְׁלֹשָׁה פִּתְקִין כָּתַב עֲלֵיהֶן ׳חֲמֵשֶׁת שְׁקָלִים׳. בְּלָלָן וּנְתָנָן בְּקַלְפֵּי. אָמַר לָהֶם: בּוֹאוּ וּטְלוּ פִּתְקֵיכֶם לְפִי הַגּוֹרָל:

ד ב **נָשֹׂא אֶת רֹאשׁ וְגוֹ׳.** מְנֵה מֵהֶם אֶת הָרְאוּיִין לַעֲבוֹדַת מַשָּׂא, וְהֵם מִבֶּן שְׁלֹשִׁים וְעַד בֶּן חֲמִשִּׁים שָׁנָה, וְהַפָּחוֹת מִשְּׁלֹשִׁים לֹא נִתְמַלֵּא כֹּחוֹ, מִכָּאן אָמְרוּ: ״בֶּן שְׁלֹשִׁים לַכֹּחַ״ (אבות ה, כא), וְהַיּוֹתֵר עַל בֶּן חֲמִשִּׁים כֹּחוֹ מַכְחִישׁ מֵעַתָּה:

ד **קֹדֶשׁ הַקֳּדָשִׁים.** הַמְקֻדָּשׁ שֶׁבְּכֻלָּן, הָאָרוֹן וְהַשֻּׁלְחָן וְהַמְּנוֹרָה וְהַמִּזְבְּחוֹת וְהַפָּרֹכֶת וּכְלֵי שָׁרֵת:

ה **וּבָא אַהֲרֹן וּבָנָיו וְגוֹ׳.** יַכְנִיסוּ כָּל כְּלִי וּכְלִי לְנַרְתִּיקוֹ הַמְפֹרָשׁ לוֹ בְּפָרָשָׁה זוֹ, וְלֹא יִצְטָרְכוּ הַלְוִיִּם בְּנֵי קְהָת אֶלָּא לָשֵׂאת: **בִּנְסֹעַ הַמַּחֲנֶה.** כְּשֶׁהֶעָנָן מִסְתַּלֵּק, הֵן יוֹדְעִין שֶׁיִּסְעוּ:

מב תַּחַת כָּל־בְּכוֹר בִּבְהֶמַת בְּנֵי יִשְׂרָאֵל: וַיִּפְקֹד מֹשֶׁה כַּאֲשֶׁר צִוָּה יְהוָה
מג אֹתוֹ אֶת־כָּל־בְּכוֹר בִּבְנֵי יִשְׂרָאֵל: וַיְהִי כָל־בְּכוֹר זָכָר בְּמִסְפַּר שֵׁמֹת
מִבֶּן־חֹדֶשׁ וָמַעְלָה לִפְקֻדֵיהֶם שְׁנַיִם וְעֶשְׂרִים אֶלֶף שְׁלֹשָׁה וְשִׁבְעִים
וּמָאתָיִם:
מד מה וַיְדַבֵּר יְהוָה אֶל־מֹשֶׁה לֵּאמֹר: קַח אֶת־הַלְוִיִּם תַּחַת כָּל־בְּכוֹר בִּבְנֵי
יִשְׂרָאֵל וְאֶת־בֶּהֱמַת הַלְוִיִּם תַּחַת בְּהֶמְתָּם וְהָיוּ־לִי הַלְוִיִּם אֲנִי יְהוָה:
מו וְאֵת פְּדוּיֵי הַשְּׁלֹשָׁה וְהַשִּׁבְעִים וְהַמָּאתָיִם הָעֹדְפִים עַל־הַלְוִיִּם מִבְּכוֹר
מז בְּנֵי יִשְׂרָאֵל: וְלָקַחְתָּ חֲמֵשֶׁת חֲמֵשֶׁת שְׁקָלִים לַגֻּלְגֹּלֶת בְּשֶׁקֶל הַקֹּדֶשׁ
מח תִּקָּח עֶשְׂרִים גֵּרָה הַשָּׁקֶל: וְנָתַתָּה הַכֶּסֶף לְאַהֲרֹן וּלְבָנָיו פְּדוּיֵי הָעֹדְפִים
מט בָּהֶם: וַיִּקַּח מֹשֶׁה אֵת כֶּסֶף הַפִּדְיוֹם מֵאֵת הָעֹדְפִים עַל פְּדוּיֵי הַלְוִיִּם:
נ מֵאֵת בְּכוֹר בְּנֵי יִשְׂרָאֵל לָקַח אֶת־הַכָּסֶף חֲמִשָּׁה וְשִׁשִּׁים וּשְׁלֹשׁ מֵאוֹת
נא וָאֶלֶף בְּשֶׁקֶל הַקֹּדֶשׁ: וַיִּתֵּן מֹשֶׁה אֶת־כֶּסֶף הַפְּדֻיִם לְאַהֲרֹן וּלְבָנָיו
עַל־פִּי יְהוָה כַּאֲשֶׁר צִוָּה יְהוָה אֶת־מֹשֶׁה:
ד א ב וַיְדַבֵּר יְהוָה אֶל־מֹשֶׁה וְאֶל־אַהֲרֹן לֵאמֹר: נָשֹׂא אֶת־רֹאשׁ בְּנֵי קְהָת שביעי
ג מִתּוֹךְ בְּנֵי לֵוִי לְמִשְׁפְּחֹתָם לְבֵית אֲבֹתָם: מִבֶּן שְׁלֹשִׁים שָׁנָה וָמַעְלָה
וְעַד בֶּן־חֲמִשִּׁים שָׁנָה כָּל־בָּא לַצָּבָא לַעֲשׂוֹת מְלָאכָה בְּאֹהֶל מוֹעֵד:
ד ה זֹאת עֲבֹדַת בְּנֵי־קְהָת בְּאֹהֶל מוֹעֵד קֹדֶשׁ הַקֳּדָשִׁים: וּבָא אַהֲרֹן וּבָנָיו

אונקלוס

לֵיוָאֵי, חֲלָף כָּל בֻּכְרָא בִּבְנֵי יִשְׂרָאֵל, וְיָת בְּעִירָא דְּלֵיוָאֵי חֲלָף בְּעִירְהוֹן, וִיהוֹן מְשַׁמְּשִׁין קֳדָמַי לֵיוָאֵי אֲנָא יי: מו וְיָת פֻּרְקַן מָאתַן, וְשַׁבְעִין וּתְלָתָא, דְּיַתִּירִין עַל לֵיוָאֵי, מִבֻּכוֹרַיָּא דִּבְנֵי יִשְׂרָאֵל: מז וְתִסַּב, חֲמֵשׁ חֲמֵשׁ, סִלְעִין לְגֻלְגַּלְתָּא, בְּסִלְעֵי קֻדְשָׁא תִּסַּב, עֶסְרִין מָעִין סִלְעָא: מח וְתִתֵּין כַּסְפָּא, לְאַהֲרֹן וְלִבְנוֹהִי, פֻּרְקַן, דְּיַתִּירִין דִּבְהוֹן: מט וּנְסֵיב מֹשֶׁה, יָת כְּסַף פֻּרְקָנְהוֹן, מִן דְּיַתִּירִין, עַל פְּרִיקֵי לֵיוָאֵי: נ מִן בֻּכוֹרַיָּא, דִּבְנֵי יִשְׂרָאֵל נְסֵיב יָת כַּסְפָּא, אֶלֶף וּתְלָת מְאָה, וְשִׁתִּין וַחֲמֵשׁ, סִלְעִין בְּסִלְעֵי קֻדְשָׁא: נא וִיהַב מֹשֶׁה, יָת כְּסַף פְּרִיקַיָּא, לְאַהֲרֹן וְלִבְנוֹהִי עַל מֵימְרָא דַּיי, כְּמָא דְּפַקֵּיד יי יָת מֹשֶׁה: ד א וּמַלֵּיל יי, עִם מֹשֶׁה וּלְאַהֲרֹן לְמֵימַר: ב קַבִּילוּ, יָת חֻשְׁבַּן בְּנֵי קְהָת, מִגּוֹ בְּנֵי לֵוִי, לְזַרְעֲיָתְהוֹן לְבֵית אֲבָהָתְהוֹן: ג מִבַּר תְּלָתִין שְׁנִין וּלְעֵילָא, וְעַד בַּר חַמְשִׁין שְׁנִין, כָּל דְּאָתֵי לְחֵילָא, לְמֶעְבַּד עֲבִידְתָּא בְּמַשְׁכַּן זִמְנָא: ד דֵּין, פֻּלְחַן בְּנֵי קְהָת בְּמַשְׁכַּן זִמְנָא, קוֹדֶשׁ קֻדְשַׁיָּא: ה וְיֵיעוֹל אַהֲרֹן וּבְנוֹהִי

sons shall come and take down the screening curtain and cover the Ark of
6 the Testimony with it. Then they shall put over it a covering of fine leather,
7 and over that a cloth of pure blue, and then they shall insert its poles. On the
table of the showbread they shall spread a blue cloth, and on it place the bowls,
spoons, jars, and the libation pitchers; and the bread of the Presence shall be
8 on it constantly. They shall spread over them a scarlet cloth, and then cover it
9 with a covering of fine leather; and then they shall insert its poles. They shall
take a blue cloth and cover the candelabrum and its lamps, tongs, pans, and all
10 the oil vessels used in its service. Then they must put it and all its utensils into a
11 covering of fine leather, and place them on a carrying frame. They shall spread
a blue cloth on the golden altar, and cover it with a covering of fine leather;
12 and then they shall insert its poles. Then they shall take all the service utensils,
with which they serve in the Sanctuary, put them into a blue cloth, cover them
13 with a covering of fine leather, and place them on a carrying frame. They shall
14 remove the ashes from the altar and spread a purple cloth over it. Then they
shall place upon it all the special implements with which they serve there – the
pans, the forks, the shovels, the basins, and all the altar's utensils – and spread
15 over it all a covering of fine leather, and then insert its poles. When Aharon
and his sons have finished covering the Sanctuary and all the furnishings of the
Sanctuary, when the camp is ready to set out, then the Kohatites shall come to

רש״י

ז **קְעָרוֹת וְכַפּוֹת וּקְשָׂוֹת וּמְנַקִּיּוֹת.** כְּבָר פֵּרַשְׁתִּים בִּמְלֶאכֶת הַמִּשְׁכָּן (שמות כה, כט): **הַנָּסֶךְ.** הַכִּסּוּי, לְשׁוֹן מָסָךְ, כְּדִכְתִיב: "אֲשֶׁר יֻסַּךְ בָּהֵן" (שם):

ט **מַלְקָחֶיהָ.** כְּמִין צְבָת שֶׁמּוֹשֵׁךְ בָּהּ אֶת הַפְּתִילָה לְכָל צַד שֶׁיִּרְצֶה: **מַחְתֹּתֶיהָ.** כְּמִין כַּף קְטַנָּה וְשׁוּלֶיהָ פְּשׁוּטִין וְלֹא סְגַלְגַּלִּים וְאֵין לָהּ מְחִצָּה לְפָנֶיהָ אֶלָּא מִצִּדֶּיהָ, וְחוֹתֶה בָּהּ אֶת דֶּשֶׁן הַנֵּרוֹת כְּשֶׁמֵּטִיבָן: **נֵרֹתֶיהָ.** לוצ"ש בְּלַעַז, שֶׁנּוֹתְנִים בָּהֶן הַשֶּׁמֶן וְהַפְּתִילוֹת:

י **אֶל מִכְסֵה עוֹר תָּחַשׁ.** כְּמִין מַרְצוּף:

יב **אֶת כָּל כְּלֵי הַשָּׁרֵת אֲשֶׁר יְשָׁרְתוּ בָם בַּקֹּדֶשׁ.** בְּתוֹךְ הַמִּשְׁכָּן שֶׁהוּא קֹדֶשׁ, וְהֵן כְּלֵי הַקְּטֹרֶת שֶׁמְּשָׁרְתִין בָּהֶם בַּמִּזְבֵּחַ הַפְּנִימִי:

יג **וְדִשְּׁנוּ אֶת הַמִּזְבֵּחַ.** מִזְבַּח הַנְּחֹשֶׁת: **וְדִשְּׁנוּ.** יִטְּלוּ אֶת הַדֶּשֶׁן מֵעָלָיו: **וּפָרְשׂוּ עָלָיו בֶּגֶד אַרְגָּמָן.** וְאֵשׁ שֶׁיָּרְדָה מִן הַשָּׁמַיִם רְבוּצָה תַּחַת הַבֶּגֶד כַּאֲרִי בִּשְׁעַת הַמַּסָּעוֹת, וְאֵינָהּ שׂוֹרַפְתּוֹ, שֶׁהָיוּ כּוֹפִין עָלֶיהָ פְּסַכְתֵּר שֶׁל נְחֹשֶׁת:

יד **מַחְתֹּת.** שֶׁבָּהֶן חוֹתִים גֶּחָלִים לִתְרוּמַת הַדֶּשֶׁן. עֲשׂוּיָה כְּמִין מַחֲבַת שֶׁאֵין לָהּ אֶלָּא שָׁלֹשׁ מְחִצּוֹת, וּמִלְּפָנֶיהָ שׁוֹאֶבֶת אֶת הַגֶּחָלִים: **מִזְלָגֹת.** צִנּוֹרוֹת שֶׁל נְחֹשֶׁת שֶׁבָּהֶן מַכִּין בָּאֵיבָרִים שֶׁעַל הַמִּזְבֵּחַ לְהַפְּכָן כְּדֵי שֶׁיִּתְעַכְּלוּ יָפֶה וּמַהֵר: **יָעִים.** הֵם מַגְרֵפוֹת, וּבְלַעַז וודי"ל, וְהֵן שֶׁל נְחֹשֶׁת, וּבָהֶן מְכַבְּדִין אֶת הַדֶּשֶׁן מֵעַל הַמִּזְבֵּחַ:

טו **לְכַסֹּת אֶת הַקֹּדֶשׁ.** הָאָרוֹן וְהַמִּזְבֵּחַ: **וְאֶת כָּל כְּלֵי הַקֹּדֶשׁ.** הַמְּנוֹרָה וּכְלֵי שָׁרֵת: **וָמֵתוּ.** שֶׁאִם יִגְּעוּ חַיָּבִין מִיתָה בִּידֵי שָׁמַיִם:

בִּנְסֹעַ הַמַּחֲנֶה וְהוֹרִדוּ אֵת פָּרֹכֶת הַמָּסָךְ וְכִסּוּ־בָהּ אֵת אֲרֹן הָעֵדֻת׃
ו וְנָתְנוּ עָלָיו כְּסוּי עוֹר תַּחַשׁ וּפָרְשׂוּ בֶגֶד־כְּלִיל תְּכֵלֶת מִלְמָעְלָה
ז וְשָׂמוּ בַּדָּיו׃ וְעַל ׀ שֻׁלְחַן הַפָּנִים יִפְרְשׂוּ בֶּגֶד תְּכֵלֶת וְנָתְנוּ עָלָיו אֶת־
הַקְּעָרֹת וְאֶת־הַכַּפֹּת וְאֶת־הַמְּנַקִּיֹּת וְאֵת קְשׂוֹת הַנָּסֶךְ וְלֶחֶם הַתָּמִיד
ח עָלָיו יִהְיֶה׃ וּפָרְשׂוּ עֲלֵיהֶם בֶּגֶד תּוֹלַעַת שָׁנִי וְכִסּוּ אֹתוֹ בְּמִכְסֵה עוֹר
ט תָּחַשׁ וְשָׂמוּ אֶת־בַּדָּיו׃ וְלָקְחוּ ׀ בֶּגֶד תְּכֵלֶת וְכִסּוּ אֶת־מְנֹרַת הַמָּאוֹר
וְאֶת־נֵרֹתֶיהָ וְאֶת־מַלְקָחֶיהָ וְאֶת־מַחְתֹּתֶיהָ וְאֵת כָּל־כְּלֵי שַׁמְנָהּ אֲשֶׁר
י יְשָׁרְתוּ־לָהּ בָּהֶם׃ וְנָתְנוּ אֹתָהּ וְאֶת־כָּל־כֵּלֶיהָ אֶל־מִכְסֵה עוֹר תָּחַשׁ
יא וְנָתְנוּ עַל־הַמּוֹט׃ וְעַל ׀ מִזְבַּח הַזָּהָב יִפְרְשׂוּ בֶּגֶד תְּכֵלֶת וְכִסּוּ אֹתוֹ
יב בְּמִכְסֵה עוֹר תָּחַשׁ וְשָׂמוּ אֶת־בַּדָּיו׃ וְלָקְחוּ אֶת־כָּל־כְּלֵי הַשָּׁרֵת אֲשֶׁר
יְשָׁרְתוּ־בָם בַּקֹּדֶשׁ וְנָתְנוּ אֶל־בֶּגֶד תְּכֵלֶת וְכִסּוּ אוֹתָם בְּמִכְסֵה עוֹר
יג תָּחַשׁ וְנָתְנוּ עַל־הַמּוֹט׃ וְדִשְּׁנוּ אֶת־הַמִּזְבֵּחַ וּפָרְשׂוּ עָלָיו בֶּגֶד אַרְגָּמָן׃
יד וְנָתְנוּ עָלָיו אֶת־כָּל־כֵּלָיו אֲשֶׁר יְשָׁרְתוּ עָלָיו בָּהֶם אֶת־הַמַּחְתֹּת אֶת־
הַמִּזְלָגֹת וְאֶת־הַיָּעִים וְאֶת־הַמִּזְרָקֹת כֹּל כְּלֵי הַמִּזְבֵּחַ וּפָרְשׂוּ עָלָיו
טו כְּסוּי עוֹר תַּחַשׁ וְשָׂמוּ בַדָּיו׃ וְכִלָּה אַהֲרֹן־וּבָנָיו לְכַסֹּת אֶת־הַקֹּדֶשׁ
וְאֶת־כָּל־כְּלֵי הַקֹּדֶשׁ בִּנְסֹעַ הַמַּחֲנֶה וְאַחֲרֵי־כֵן יָבֹאוּ בְנֵי־קְהָת לָשֵׂאת

אונקלוס

בְּמִטַּל מַשְׁרִיתָא, וִיפָרְקוּן, יָת פָּרֻכְתָּא דִּפְרָסָא, וִיכַסּוּן בַּהּ, יָת
אֲרוֹנָא דְּסַהֲדוּתָא: ו וְיִתְּנוּן עֲלוֹהִי, חוֹפָאָה דִּמְשַׁךְ סַסְגּוֹנָא, וְיִפְרְסוּן
לְבוּשׁ גְּמִיר, תַּכְלָא מִלְעֵילָא, וִישַׁוּוֹן אֲרִיחוֹהִי: ז וְעַל פָּתוֹרָא דִּלְחֵים
אַפַּיָּא, יִפְרְסוּן לְבוּשׁ תַּכְלָא, וְיִתְּנוּן עֲלוֹהִי, יָת מְגִסַּיָּא וְיָת בָּזִכַּיָּא וְיָת
מְכִילָתָא, וְיָת קְסְוָת נִסּוּכָא, וְלַחְמָא תְּדִירָא עֲלוֹהִי יְהֵי: ח וְיִפְרְסוּן
עֲלֵיהוֹן, לְבוּשׁ צְבַע זְהוֹרִי, וִיכַסּוּן יָתֵיהּ, בְּחוֹפָאָה דִּמְשַׁךְ סַסְגּוֹנָא,
וִישַׁוּוֹן יָת אֲרִיחוֹהִי: ט וְיִסְּבוּן לְבוּשׁ תַּכְלָא, וִיכַסּוּן, יָת מְנָרְתָא
דְּאַנְהוֹרֵי וְיָת בּוֹצִינַהָא, וְיָת צֵיבְתַהָא וְיָת מַחְתְּיָתַהָא, וְיָת כָּל מָנֵי
שִׁמּוּשַׁהּ, דִּישַׁמְּשׁוּן לַהּ בְּהוֹן: י וְיִתְּנוּן יָתַהּ וְיָת כָּל מָנַהָא, לְחוֹפָאָה
דִּמְשַׁךְ סַסְגּוֹנָא, וְיִתְּנוּן עַל אֲרִיחָא: יא וְעַל מַדְבְּחָא דְּדַהֲבָא, יִפְרְסוּן
לְבוּשׁ תַּכְלָא, וִיכַסּוּן יָתֵיהּ, בְּחוֹפָאָה דִּמְשַׁךְ סַסְגּוֹנָא, וִישַׁוּוֹן יָת
אֲרִיחוֹהִי: יב וְיִסְּבוּן יָת כָּל מָנֵי שִׁמּוּשָׁא דִּישַׁמְּשׁוּן בְּהוֹן בְּקֻדְשָׁא,
וְיִתְּנוּן לִלְבוּשׁ תַּכְלָא, וִיכַסּוּן יָתְהוֹן, בְּחוֹפָאָה דִּמְשַׁךְ סַסְגּוֹנָא,
וְיִתְּנוּן עַל אֲרִיחָא: יג וְיִסְפּוֹן יָת קִטְמָא דְּמַדְבְּחָא, וְיִפְרְסוּן עֲלוֹהִי,
לְבוּשׁ אַרְגְּוָן: יד וְיִתְּנוּן עֲלוֹהִי, יָת כָּל מָנוֹהִי דִּישַׁמְּשׁוּן עֲלוֹהִי בְּהוֹן,
יָת מַחְתְּיָתָא יָת צִנּוֹרְיָתָא וְיָת מַגְרוֹפְיָתָא וְיָת מִזְרְקַיָּא, כָּל מָנֵי
מַדְבְּחָא, וְיִפְרְסוּן עֲלוֹהִי, חוֹפָאָה, דִּמְשַׁךְ סַסְגּוֹנָא וִישַׁוּוֹן אֲרִיחוֹהִי:
טו וִישֵׁיצֵי אַהֲרֹן וּבְנוֹהִי, לְכַסָּאָה יָת קֻדְשָׁא, וְיָת כָּל מָנֵי קֻדְשָׁא
בְּמִטַּל מַשְׁרִיתָא, וּבָתַר כֵּן, יֵיעֲלוּן בְּנֵי קְהָת לְמִטַּל, וְלָא יִקְרְבוּן

carry them; but they must not touch the sacred objects lest they die. These are
16 what the Kohatites must carry for the Tent of Meeting. The responsibility of
Elazar son of Aharon the priest is for the lighting oil, the fragrant incense, the
daily grain offering, and the anointing oil. He is also responsible for the whole
Tabernacle and all that is in it, for the Sanctuary and all its utensils."
17 18 Again the LORD spoke to Moshe and Aharon: "Do not let the tribe of the clans MAFTIR
19 of Kehat be cut off from among the Levites. So that they may live and not die
when they come close to the most sacred things, they must do this: let Aharon
and his sons go in and assign each man his duties and what he must carry;
20 but they themselves must not go in and watch while the holy things are being
covered, for they would die."

The haftara for Parashat Bemidbar is on page 1584.
On Erev Rosh Ḥodesh Sivan read the haftara on page 1636.

רש״י

טז **וּפְקֻדַּת אֶלְעָזָר.** שֶׁהוּא מְמֻנֶּה עֲלֵיהֶם לָשֵׂאת אוֹתָם, שֶׁמֶן וּקְטֹרֶת וְשֶׁמֶן הַמִּשְׁחָה וּמִנְחַת הַתָּמִיד, עָלָיו מֻטָּל לְצַוּוֹת וּלְזָרֵז וּלְהַקְרִיב בְּעֵת חֲנִיָּתָן: **פְּקֻדַּת כָּל הַמִּשְׁכָּן.** וְעוֹד הָיָה מְמֻנֶּה עַל מַשָּׂא בְּנֵי קְהָת, לְצַוּוֹת אִישׁ אִישׁ עַל עֲבוֹדָתוֹ וְעַל מַשָּׂאוֹ, וְהוּא הַמִּשְׁכָּן וְכָל אֲשֶׁר בּוֹ, כָּל הַסְּדוּרִים לְמַעְלָה בְּפָרָשָׁה זוֹ. אֲבָל מַשָּׂא בְּנֵי גֵרְשׁוֹן וּמְרָרִי, שֶׁאֵינָן מִקֹּדֶשׁ הַקֳּדָשִׁים, עַל פִּי אִיתָמָר הָיָה, כְּמוֹ שֶׁכָּתוּב בְּפָרָשַׁת ׳נָשֹׂא׳ (להלן ד, כח; לג):

יח **אַל תַּכְרִיתוּ.** אַל תִּגְרְמוּ לָהֶם שֶׁיָּמוּתוּ:

כ **וְלֹא יָבֹאוּ לִרְאוֹת כְּבַלַּע אֶת הַקֹּדֶשׁ.** לְתוֹךְ נַרְתִּיק שֶׁלּוֹ, כְּמוֹ שֶׁפֵּרַשְׁתִּי לְמַעְלָה בְּפָרָשָׁה זוֹ (פסוק ה), וּפָרְשׂוּ עָלָיו בֶּגֶד פְּלוֹנִי וְכִסּוּ אוֹתוֹ בְּמִכְסֵה פְּלוֹנִי, וּבִלּוּעַ שֶׁלּוֹ הוּא כִּסּוּיוֹ:

Torah, with great realism, is telling us something counter-intuitive and of great significance. *The journey from is always easier than the journey to.*

It may take a revolution to depose a tyrant, but it is easier to do that than to create a genuinely free society with the rule of law and respect for human rights. Likewise in the life of individuals. We all know of bad habits we have to cure. But the real challenge is to know where God wants us to travel to. What task were we put in the world, in this time and place, with these gifts, to do?

There is a biological reason why this is so. We are genetically predisposed to react strongly to danger. Our deepest instincts are aroused. We move into the fight-or-flight mode, with our senses alert, our attention focused, and our adrenalin levels high. When it comes to *fleeing from*, we often find ourselves accessing strengths we did not know we had.

But *fleeing to* is something else entirely. It means making a home in a place where, literally or metaphorically, we have not been before. We become "strangers in a strange land." We need to learn new skills, shoulder new responsibilities, acquire new strengths. That calls for imagination and willpower. It involves the most unique of all human abilities: envisaging a future that has not yet been and acting to bring it about. Fleeing to is a journey into the unknown.

To be a Jew is to know that, in some sense, life is a journey. Hence the importance of knowing at the outset where we are traveling to, and never forgetting, never giving up.

The Israelites, in their journey, make a series of mistakes. They focus too much on the present (the food, the water) and too little on the future. When they face difficulties, they have too much fear and too little faith. They keep looking back to how things were instead of looking forward to how they might be. The result will be that almost an entire generation will experience exodus but not entry. Leaving is easy. Arriving is formidably hard.

וְלֹא־יִגְּעוּ אֶל־הַקֹּדֶשׁ וָמֵתוּ אֵלֶּה מַשָּׂא בְנֵי־קְהָת בְּאֹהֶל מוֹעֵד׃
טז וּפְקֻדַּת אֶלְעָזָר ׀ בֶּן־אַהֲרֹן הַכֹּהֵן שֶׁמֶן הַמָּאוֹר וּקְטֹרֶת הַסַּמִּים וּמִנְחַת
הַתָּמִיד וְשֶׁמֶן הַמִּשְׁחָה פְּקֻדַּת כָּל־הַמִּשְׁכָּן וְכָל־אֲשֶׁר־בּוֹ בְּקֹדֶשׁ
וּבְכֵלָיו׃
יז יח וַיְדַבֵּר יהוה אֶל־מֹשֶׁה וְאֶל־אַהֲרֹן לֵאמֹר׃ אַל־תַּכְרִיתוּ אֶת־שֵׁבֶט ד מפטיר
יט מִשְׁפְּחֹת הַקְּהָתִי מִתּוֹךְ הַלְוִיִּם׃ וְזֹאת ׀ עֲשׂוּ לָהֶם וְחָיוּ וְלֹא יָמֻתוּ
בְּגִשְׁתָּם אֶת־קֹדֶשׁ הַקֳּדָשִׁים אַהֲרֹן וּבָנָיו יָבֹאוּ וְשָׂמוּ אוֹתָם אִישׁ אִישׁ
כ עַל־עֲבֹדָתוֹ וְאֶל־מַשָּׂאוֹ׃ וְלֹא־יָבֹאוּ לִרְאוֹת כְּבַלַּע אֶת־הַקֹּדֶשׁ וָמֵתוּ׃

The הפטרה *for* פרשת במדבר *is on page 1585.*
On ערב ראש חודש סיון *read the* הפטרה *on page 1637.*

אונקלוס

לְקֻדְשָׁא וְלָא יְמוּתוּן, אִלֵּין, מַטּוּל בְּנֵי קְהָת בְּמַשְׁכַּן זִמְנָא: טז וּדְמְסִיר, לְאֶלְעָזָר בַּר אַהֲרֹן כָּהֲנָא, מִשְׁחָא דְאַנְהָרוּתָא וּקְטֹרֶת בֻּסְמַיָּא, וּמִנְחָתָא תְּדִירָא וּמִשְׁחָא דִרְבוּתָא, מַסְרַת, כָּל מַשְׁכְּנָא וְכָל דְּבֵיהּ, בְּקֻדְשָׁא וּבְמָנוֹהִי: יז וּמַלֵּיל יְיָ, עִם מֹשֶׁה וּלְאַהֲרֹן לְמֵימַר: יח לָא תְשֵׁיצוֹן, יָת שֵׁיבֶט זַרְעִית קְהָת, מִגּוֹ לֵיוָאֵי: יט וְדָא עֲבִידוּ לְהוֹן, וְיֵיחוֹן וְלָא יְמוּתוּן, בְּמִקְרַבְהוֹן לְקֹדֶשׁ קֻדְשַׁיָּא, אַהֲרֹן וּבְנוֹהִי יֵיעֲלוּן, וִימַנּוֹן יָתְהוֹן, גְּבַר גְּבַר, עַל פָּלְחָנֵיהּ וּלְמַטּוּלֵיהּ: כ וְלָא יֵיעֲלוּן לְמִחְזֵי, כַּד מְכַסַּן יָת מָנֵי קֻדְשָׁא וְלָא יְמוּתוּן:

THE JOURNEY ONWARD

The books of Exodus and Numbers have some striking similarities. They are both about journeys. They both portray the Israelites as quarrelsome and ungrateful. Both contain stories about the people complaining about food and water. In both the Israelites commit a major sin: in Exodus, the golden calf, in Numbers, the episode of the spies. In both, God threatens to destroy them and begin again with Moshe. Both times, Moshe's passionate appeal persuades God to forgive the people.

But, as we noted at the beginning of Numbers, there is a difference. Exodus is about a journey *from*. Numbers is about a journey *to*. By now, the people have already left Egypt far behind. They have received the Torah and built the Sanctuary. Now they are ready to move on. This time they are looking forward, not back. They are thinking not of the danger they are fleeing from but of the destination they are traveling toward, the Promised Land.

If we had never read the Torah before, we might have assumed that the second half of the journey would be more relaxed, the mood more hopeful. After all, the great dangers have passed. Pharaoh has let the people go. They have been saved at the Sea of Reeds. They have fought and defeated the Amalekites. What else do they have to worry about? They know that when God is with them, no force can prevail against them.

In fact, though, the opposite is the case. The mood of Numbers is palpably darker than it is in Exodus. The rebellions are more serious. Moshe's leadership is more hesitant. We see him giving way, at times, to anger and despair. The

Parashat Naso

4 21 22 Then the Lord spoke to Moshe: "Take a census too of the Gershonites, by
23 their clans and their ancestral houses, from thirty years old to fifty: all who
24 go into service to carry out the work of the Tent of Meeting. This will be the
25 service of the clans of Gershon, serving and carrying: they shall carry the
curtains of the Tabernacle and the Tent of Meeting, its covering, the covering
of fine leather that is over it, the screen at the entrance to the Tent of Meeting,
26 the hangings for the courtyard, the curtain for the entrance of the gate to the
courtyard around the Tabernacle and the altar, and their ropes, together with

רש״י

כב **נָשֹׂא אֶת רֹאשׁ בְּנֵי גֵרְשׁוֹן גַּם הֵם.** כְּמוֹ שֶׁצִּוִּיתִיךָ עַל בְּנֵי קְהָת, לִרְאוֹת כַּמָּה יֵשׁ שֶׁהִגִּיעוּ לִכְלַל עֲבוֹדָה:

כה **אֶת יְרִיעֹת הַמִּשְׁכָּן.** עֶשֶׂר תַּחְתּוֹנוֹת: **וְאֶת אֹהֶל מוֹעֵד.** יְרִיעוֹת עִזִּים הָעֲשׂוּיוֹת לְאֹהֶל עָלָיו: **מִכְסֵהוּ.** עוֹרוֹת אֵילִים מְאָדָּמִים: **מָסַךְ פֶּתַח.** וִילוֹן הַמִּזְרָחִי:

כו **אֲשֶׁר עַל הַמִּשְׁכָּן.** כְּלוֹמַר: הַקְּלָעִים וְהַמָּסָךְ שֶׁל חָצֵר, הַסּוֹכְכִים וּמְגִנִּים עַל הַמִּשְׁכָּן וְעַל מִזְבַּח הַנְּחֹשֶׁת סָבִיב: **וְאֵת כָּל אֲשֶׁר יֵעָשֶׂה לָהֶם.** כְּתַרְגּוּמוֹ: ״וְיָת כָּל דְּיִתְמְסַר לְהוֹן״, לִבְנֵי גֵּרְשׁוֹן:

The religion of Israel is a principled protest against this view. At this distance in time, it is hard to fully appreciate the transformative potential of a single radical idea – that the human person as such, man or woman, rich or poor, powerful or powerless, is the image of God and therefore of non-negotiable, unquantifiable value. We stand equal in the presence of God. This idea is fundamental to Judaism. In Greek thought and throughout the European Enlightenment, what mattered were universals. In Judaism, what matters to God are individuals. There is a verse in Psalms (147:4) which says that God "counts the number of the stars, calling each by name." A name is a marker of uniqueness. Collective nouns group things together; proper names distinguish them as individuals. Only what we value do we name. (One of the most chilling acts of dehumanization in the extermination camps of Nazi Germany was that those who entered were never addressed by their names. Instead they were given a number, inscribed on their skin.)

God gives even the stars their names. All the more so does this apply to human beings. When God calls, He calls our name, to which the reply is simply *Hineni*, "Here I am." God – one and alone – meets us, one and alone, endowing us with a significance that cannot be quantified or measured by a census.

That is the nature of the censuses in the book of Numbers. There is a difference between a census commanded by God, who cherishes and holds special each individual, and a census undertaken by a human being, who merely assumes that there is strength in numbers. The phrase *naso et rosh*, translated idiomatically as "take a census," literally means that those being counted have "their heads raised" – the same verb as that used later in the priestly blessing: "May the Lord raise His face toward you" (Num. 6:26). God "raises our head" in the most profound way known to humankind, by assuring each of us of His special, enduring, unquantifiable love. As the Israelites prepare to become a society with the Divine Presence at its center, they have to be reminded that they are to become the pioneers of a new social order, whose most famous definition was given by the prophet Zekharya (4:6): "Not with valor and not with strength, but with My spirit, says the Lord of Hosts."

פרשת נשא

ד כא וַיְדַבֵּר יְהוָה אֶל־מֹשֶׁה לֵּאמֹר: כב נָשֹׂא אֶת־רֹאשׁ בְּנֵי גֵרְשׁוֹן גַּם־הֵם
כג לְבֵית אֲבֹתָם לְמִשְׁפְּחֹתָם: מִבֶּן שְׁלֹשִׁים שָׁנָה וָמַעְלָה עַד בֶּן־חֲמִשִּׁים
שָׁנָה תִּפְקֹד אוֹתָם כָּל־הַבָּא לִצְבֹא צָבָא לַעֲבֹד עֲבֹדָה בְּאֹהֶל
כד כה מוֹעֵד: זֹאת עֲבֹדַת מִשְׁפְּחֹת הַגֵּרְשֻׁנִּי לַעֲבֹד וּלְמַשָּׂא: וְנָשְׂאוּ אֶת־
יְרִיעֹת הַמִּשְׁכָּן וְאֶת־אֹהֶל מוֹעֵד מִכְסֵהוּ וּמִכְסֵה הַתַּחַשׁ אֲשֶׁר־עָלָיו
כו מִלְמָעְלָה וְאֶת־מָסַךְ פֶּתַח אֹהֶל מוֹעֵד: וְאֵת קַלְעֵי הֶחָצֵר וְאֶת־
מָסַךְ ׀ פֶּתַח ׀ שַׁעַר הֶחָצֵר אֲשֶׁר עַל־הַמִּשְׁכָּן וְעַל־הַמִּזְבֵּחַ סָבִיב וְאֵת

אונקלוס

כא וּמַלֵּיל יי עִם מֹשֶׁה לְמֵימַר: כב קַבֵּיל, יָת חֻשְׁבַּן, בְּנֵי גֵרְשׁוֹן אַף אִנּוּן, לְבֵית אֲבָהָתְהוֹן לְזַרְעֲיָתְהוֹן: כג מִבַּר תְּלָתִין שְׁנִין וּלְעֵילָא, עַד, בַּר חַמְשִׁין שְׁנִין תִּמְנֵי יָתְהוֹן, כָּל דְּאָתֵי לְחַיָּלָא חֵילָא, לְמִפְלַח פֻּלְחָנָא בְּמַשְׁכַּן זִמְנָא: כד דֵּין פֻּלְחַן, זַרְעֲיַת גֵּרְשׁוֹן, לְמִפְלַח וּלְמִטַּל:

כה וְיִטְּלוּן, יָת יְרִיעָת מַשְׁכְּנָא וְיָת מַשְׁכַּן זִמְנָא, חוֹפָאֵיהּ, וְחוֹפָאָה, דְּסַסְגוֹנָא דַּעֲלוֹהִי מִלְעֵילָא, וְיָת פְּרָסָא, דִּתְרַע מַשְׁכַּן זִמְנָא: כו וְיָת סְרָדֵי דָּרְתָא, וְיָת פְּרָסָא דְּמַעֲלָנָא דִּתְרַע דָּרְתָא, דְּעַל מַשְׁכְּנָא וְעַל מַדְבְּחָא סְחוֹר סְחוֹר, וְיָת

THE CENSUS

Parashat Naso begins with a continuation of the census that gives the entire book its English name, "Numbers," itself based on the old rabbinic name, *Ḥumash HaPekudim*, the book of "counting" or "numbering."

In the ancient world, and to some extent still today, a census represented the principle that there is power in numbers. Specifically, counting the people was a way of knowing the size of the army a nation could muster. Numbers also determined a people's capacity to build monumental buildings like the Tower of Bavel spoken about in Genesis, or the giant pyramid of Giza, undertaken by Pharaoh Khufu around 2500 BCE, before even the birth of Avraham. In such a world, with the exception of the ruler and the elite, life was cheap. The Sages said about the Tower of Bavel that if a person fell and died, no one noticed. If a brick fell, they wept (Pirkei DeRabbi Eliezer 24). Size meant strength, military or economic. Life was measured in the mass.

NASO

Continuing the preparations for the Israelites' journey from Sinai to the Holy Land, Parashat Naso contains a mélange of subjects whose inner connection is not immediately obvious: the roles of two of the Levitical clans, Gershon and Merari; the census of the Levites as a group; rules about the purity of the camp; the law of the *sota* (the woman suspected of adultery); the nazirite; and the priestly blessing. The *parasha* concludes with a lengthy and repetitive account of the offerings brought by the tribes at the dedication of the Tabernacle. There is a logic holding together this apparently disconnected series. It lies in the last word of the priestly blessing (Num. 6:26): *shalom*, "peace." Much of the rest of the book of Numbers is a set of variations on the theme of internal dissension and strife. The theme that binds the laws and narrative of this *parasha*, we shall see, is that of making special efforts to preserve or restore peace between people.

all the utensils for their service and everything made for them; and they will
27 serve. All the carrying and service of the Gershonites shall be performed at
Aharon and his sons' command; you shall assign to their charge all that they
28 are to carry. This is the service of the families of the Gershonites for the
Tent of Meeting. Their charge will be under the authority of Itamar son of
29 Aharon the priest. As for the sons of Merari, you shall number them
30 by their clans and ancestral houses, from thirty years old to fifty, all who go
31 into service to carry out the work of the Tent of Meeting. This is what they
are charged to carry as the whole of their service in the Tent of Meeting: the
32 boards of the Tabernacle, its crossbars, its posts, its sockets; and the posts of
the surrounding courtyard with their sockets, pegs, and ropes, together with
all their furnishings and everything for their service. You shall assign each
33 object by name to the man charged with carrying it. This is the service of the
families of the Merarites, the whole of their service for the Tent of Meeting,
34 under the authority of Itamar son of Aharon the priest." So Moshe and Aharon
and the leaders of the community counted the Kohatites by their clans and
35 their ancestral houses, from thirty years old to fifty, all who went into the
36 service of the Tent of Meeting; and those numbered by their clans were
37 2,750. These were the ones numbered from the clans of Kehat, all who served
in the Tent of Meeting, whom Moshe and Aharon numbered at the LORD's
38 command through Moshe. Those numbered of the Gershonites, by SHENI
39 their families and ancestral houses, from thirty years old to fifty: all who went
40 into the service of the Tent of Meeting – those numbered by their clans and

אונקלוס

אֲטוּנֵיהוֹן, וְיָת כָּל מָנֵי פָלְחָנְהוֹן, וְיָת כָּל דְּיִתְמְסַר, לְהוֹן וְיִפְלְחוּן: כז עַל מֵימַר אַהֲרֹן וּבְנוֹהִי תְּהֵי, כָּל פָּלְחַן בְּנֵי גֵרְשׁוֹן, לְכָל מַטּוּלְהוֹן, וּלְכָל פָּלְחָנְהוֹן, וְתִמְנוּן עֲלֵיהוֹן בְּמַטְּרָא, יָת כָּל מַטּוּלְהוֹן: כח דֵּין פָּלְחַן, זַרְעִיַת, בְּנֵי גֵרְשׁוֹן בְּמַשְׁכַּן זִמְנָא, וּמַטַּרְתְּהוֹן, בִּידָא דְאִיתָמָר, בַּר אַהֲרֹן כָּהֲנָא: כט בְּנֵי מְרָרִי, לְזַרְעִיָתְהוֹן לְבֵית אֲבָהָתְהוֹן תִּמְנֵי יָתְהוֹן: ל מִבַּר תְּלָתִין שְׁנִין וּלְעֵילָא, וְעַד, בַּר חַמְשִׁין שְׁנִין תִּמְנִינוּן, כָּל דְּאָתֵי לְחֵילָא, לְמִפְלַח, יָת פָּלְחַן מַשְׁכַּן זִמְנָא: לא וְדָא מַטְּרַת מַטּוּלְהוֹן, לְכָל פָּלְחָנְהוֹן בְּמַשְׁכַּן זִמְנָא, דַּפֵּי מַשְׁכְּנָא, וְעַבְרוֹהִי וְעַמּוּדוֹהִי וְסָמְכוֹהִי: לב וְעַמּוּדֵי דָרְתָא סְחוֹר סְחוֹר וְסָמְכֵיהוֹן, וְסִכֵּיהוֹן וַאֲטוּנֵיהוֹן, לְכָל מָנֵיהוֹן, וּלְכָל פָּלְחָנְהוֹן, וּבִשְׁמָהָן

רש״י

כו עַל פִּי אַהֲרֹן וּבָנָיו. וְאֵי זֶה מֵהַבָּנִים מְמֻנֶּה עֲלֵיהֶם? "בְּיַד אִיתָמָר בֶּן אַהֲרֹן הַכֹּהֵן" (להלן פסוק כח).

לב וִיתֵדֹתָם וּמֵיתְרֵיהֶם. שֶׁל עַמּוּדִים, שֶׁהֲרֵי יִתְדוֹת וּמֵיתְרֵי הַקְּלָעִים בְּמַשָּׂא בְּנֵי גֵרְשׁוֹן הָיוּ, וִיתֵדוֹת וּמֵיתָרִים הָיוּ לַיְרִיעוֹת וְלַקְּלָעִים מִלְמַטָּה שֶׁלֹּא תַּגְבִּיהֵם הָרוּחַ, וִיתֵדוֹת וּמֵיתָרִים הָיוּ לָעַמּוּדִים סָבִיב לִתְלוֹת בָּהֶם הַקְּלָעִים בִּשְׂפָתָם הָעֶלְיוֹנָה בִּכְלוֹנְסוֹת וְקֻנְטִיסִין, כְּמוֹ שֶׁשְּׁנוּיָה בִּמְלֶאכֶת הַמִּשְׁכָּן (ברייתא דמלאכת המשכן פרק ה).

מֵיתְרֵיהֶם וְאֶת־כָּל־כְּלֵי עֲבֹדָתָם וְאֵת כָּל־אֲשֶׁר יֵעָשֶׂה לָהֶם וְעָבָדוּ׃
כז עַל־פִּי אַהֲרֹן וּבָנָיו תִּהְיֶה כָּל־עֲבֹדַת בְּנֵי הַגֵּרְשֻׁנִּי לְכָל־מַשָּׂאָם וּלְכֹל
כח עֲבֹדָתָם וּפְקַדְתֶּם עֲלֵהֶם בְּמִשְׁמֶרֶת אֵת כָּל־מַשָּׂאָם׃ זֹאת עֲבֹדַת
מִשְׁפְּחֹת בְּנֵי הַגֵּרְשֻׁנִּי בְּאֹהֶל מוֹעֵד וּמִשְׁמַרְתָּם בְּיַד אִיתָמָר בֶּן־אַהֲרֹן
כט הַכֹּהֵן׃ בְּנֵי מְרָרִי לְמִשְׁפְּחֹתָם לְבֵית־אֲבֹתָם תִּפְקֹד
ל אֹתָם׃ מִבֶּן שְׁלֹשִׁים שָׁנָה וָמַעְלָה וְעַד בֶּן־חֲמִשִּׁים שָׁנָה תִּפְקְדֵם
לא כָּל־הַבָּא לַצָּבָא לַעֲבֹד אֶת־עֲבֹדַת אֹהֶל מוֹעֵד׃ וְזֹאת מִשְׁמֶרֶת
מַשָּׂאָם לְכָל־עֲבֹדָתָם בְּאֹהֶל מוֹעֵד קַרְשֵׁי הַמִּשְׁכָּן וּבְרִיחָיו וְעַמּוּדָיו
לב וַאֲדָנָיו׃ וְעַמּוּדֵי הֶחָצֵר סָבִיב וְאַדְנֵיהֶם וִיתֵדֹתָם וּמֵיתְרֵיהֶם לְכָל־
כְּלֵיהֶם וּלְכֹל עֲבֹדָתָם וּבְשֵׁמֹת תִּפְקְדוּ אֶת־כְּלֵי מִשְׁמֶרֶת מַשָּׂאָם׃
לג זֹאת עֲבֹדַת מִשְׁפְּחֹת בְּנֵי מְרָרִי לְכָל־עֲבֹדָתָם בְּאֹהֶל מוֹעֵד בְּיַד
לד אִיתָמָר בֶּן־אַהֲרֹן הַכֹּהֵן׃ וַיִּפְקֹד מֹשֶׁה וְאַהֲרֹן וּנְשִׂיאֵי הָעֵדָה אֶת־
לה בְּנֵי הַקְּהָתִי לְמִשְׁפְּחֹתָם וּלְבֵית אֲבֹתָם׃ מִבֶּן שְׁלֹשִׁים שָׁנָה וָמַעְלָה
לו וְעַד בֶּן־חֲמִשִּׁים שָׁנָה כָּל־הַבָּא לַצָּבָא לַעֲבֹדָה בְּאֹהֶל מוֹעֵד׃ וַיִּהְיוּ
לז פְקֻדֵיהֶם לְמִשְׁפְּחֹתָם אַלְפַּיִם שְׁבַע מֵאוֹת וַחֲמִשִּׁים׃ אֵלֶּה פְקוּדֵי
מִשְׁפְּחֹת הַקְּהָתִי כָּל־הָעֹבֵד בְּאֹהֶל מוֹעֵד אֲשֶׁר פָּקַד מֹשֶׁה וְאַהֲרֹן
לח עַל־פִּי יְהוָה בְּיַד־מֹשֶׁה׃ וּפְקוּדֵי בְּנֵי גֵּרְשׁוֹן לְמִשְׁפְּחוֹתָם שני
לט וּלְבֵית אֲבֹתָם׃ מִבֶּן שְׁלֹשִׁים שָׁנָה וָמַעְלָה וְעַד בֶּן־חֲמִשִּׁים שָׁנָה
מ כָּל־הַבָּא לַצָּבָא לַעֲבֹדָה בְּאֹהֶל מוֹעֵד׃ וַיִּהְיוּ פְּקֻדֵיהֶם לְמִשְׁפְּחֹתָם

אונקלוס

תִמנוֹן, יָת מָנֵי מַטְרַת מַטּוּלְהוֹן: לג דָּא פָּלְחַן, זַרְעִית בְּנֵי מְרָרִי, לְכָל פָּלְחָנְהוֹן בְּמַשְׁכַּן זִמְנָא, בִּידָא דְּאִיתָמָר, בַּר אַהֲרֹן כָּהֲנָא: לד וּמְנָא מֹשֶׁה וְאַהֲרֹן, וְרַבְרְבֵי כְּנִשְׁתָּא יָת בְּנֵי קְהָת, לְזַרְעֲיָתְהוֹן וּלְבֵית אֲבָהָתְהוֹן: לה מִבַּר תְּלָתִין שְׁנִין וּלְעֵילָא, וְעַד בַּר חַמְשִׁין שְׁנִין, כָּל דְּאָתֵי לְחֵילָא, לְפָלְחָנָא בְּמַשְׁכַּן זִמְנָא: לו וַהֲווֹ מִנְיָנֵיהוֹן לְזַרְעֲיָתְהוֹן, תְּרֵין אַלְפִין, שְׁבַע מְאָה וְחַמְשִׁין: לז אִלֵּין מִנְיָנֵי זַרְעִית קְהָת, כָּל דְּפָלַח בְּמַשְׁכַּן זִמְנָא, דִּמְנָא מֹשֶׁה וְאַהֲרֹן, עַל מֵימְרָא דַּייָ בִּידָא דְמֹשֶׁה: לח וּמִנְיָנֵי בְּנֵי גֵרְשׁוֹן, לְזַרְעֲיָתְהוֹן וּלְבֵית אֲבָהָתְהוֹן: לט מִבַּר תְּלָתִין שְׁנִין וּלְעֵילָא, וְעַד בַּר חַמְשִׁין שְׁנִין, כָּל דְּאָתֵי לְחֵילָא, לְפָלְחָנָא בְּמַשְׁכַּן זִמְנָא: מ וַהֲווֹ מִנְיָנֵיהוֹן, לְזַרְעֲיָתְהוֹן

41 ancestral houses were 2,630. These were the ones numbered from the families
of the Gershonites, all who served in the Tent of Meeting, whom Moshe and
42 Aharon numbered at the command of the Lord. Those numbered from the
43 clans of the Merarites, by their clans and ancestral houses, from thirty years old
44 to fifty, all who went into the service of the Tent of Meeting – those numbered
45 by their clans were 3,200. These were the ones numbered from the clans of
the Merarites, whom Moshe and Aharon numbered at the Lord's command
46 through Moshe. All the Levites, whom Moshe, Aharon, and the leaders of
47 Israel numbered by their clans and ancestral houses, from thirty years old to
fifty: all who entered to do the work of service and the work of carrying relating
48 49 to the Tent of Meeting – those numbered were 8,580. At the command of the
Lord they were listed, and by the authority of Moshe, each according to his
service and to what he was to carry; thus was each one numbered as the Lord
had commanded Moshe.
5 1 2 Then the Lord spoke to Moshe: "Command the Israelites to send away from SHELISHI

רש״י

מז | עבדת עבדה. הוא השיר במצלתים וכנורות, שהיא עבודה לעבודה אחרת: ועבדת משא. כמשמעו:

מט | ופקדיו אשר צוה ה׳ את משה. ואותן הפקודים היו במנין מבן שלשים שנה ועד בן חמשים:

ה ב | צו את בני ישראל וגו׳. פרשה זו נאמרה ביום שהוקם המשכן, ושמונה פרשיות נאמרו בו ביום, כדאיתא במסכת גטין בפרק הניזקין (דף ס ע״א): וישלחו מן המחנה. שלש מחנות היו שם בשעת חנייתן: תוך הקלעים היא מחנה שכינה, חניית הלוים סביב כמו שמפורש בפרשת במדבר סיני (לעיל א, נג) היא מחנה לויה, ומשם ועד סוף מחנה הדגלים לכל ארבע הרוחות היא מחנה ישראל. הצרוע נשתלח חוץ לכלם, הזב מותר במחנה ישראל ומשולח מן השתים, והטמא לנפש מותר אף בשל לויה ואינו משולח אלא משל שכינה. וכל זה דרשו רבותינו

What is the importance, here in the midst of the census, of defining the separate roles of the Levite families? Envy is a constant throughout history. Aeschylus said, "It is in the character of very few men to honor without envy a friend who has prospered." Even when people accept, in theory, the equal dignity of all, and even when they see leadership as service, the old dysfunctional passions die hard. People still resent the success of others. R. Elazar HaKappar said: "Envy, lust, and the pursuit of honor drive a person out of the world" (Avot 4:21). The Levites have reason to resent the fact that the priesthood has gone to just one man and his descendants: Aharon, Moshe's brother. Later in the *parasha* Moshe will turn to the toxic effects of jealousy in a marriage; to individuals who aspire to a higher level of holiness without having been born into the priesthood; to the leadership of the tribes, which could so easily fall into a trap of rivalry.

There is no way of eliminating entirely the danger of jealousy and envy, but Moshe gives us some pointers. Honor everyone equally. Pay special attention to potentially disaffected groups. Make each feel valued. Give everyone a moment in the limelight. Find ways in which those with a particular passion can express it, and ensure that everyone has a chance to contribute. Though there is no fail-safe way to avoid the politics of envy, leaders can and must strive to minimize it.

מא לְבֵית אֲבֹתָם אַלְפַּיִם וְשֵׁשׁ מֵאוֹת וּשְׁלֹשִׁים׃ אֵלֶּה פְקוּדֵי מִשְׁפְּחֹת
בְּנֵי גֵרְשׁוֹן כָּל־הָעֹבֵד בְּאֹהֶל מוֹעֵד אֲשֶׁר פָּקַד מֹשֶׁה וְאַהֲרֹן עַל־פִּי
מב מג יְהוָה׃ וּפְקוּדֵי מִשְׁפְּחֹת בְּנֵי מְרָרִי לְמִשְׁפְּחֹתָם לְבֵית אֲבֹתָם׃ מִבֶּן
שְׁלֹשִׁים שָׁנָה וָמַעְלָה וְעַד בֶּן־חֲמִשִּׁים שָׁנָה כָּל־הַבָּא לַצָּבָא לַעֲבֹדָה
מד בְּאֹהֶל מוֹעֵד׃ וַיִּהְיוּ פְקֻדֵיהֶם לְמִשְׁפְּחֹתָם שְׁלֹשֶׁת אֲלָפִים וּמָאתָיִם׃
מה אֵלֶּה פְקוּדֵי מִשְׁפְּחֹת בְּנֵי מְרָרִי אֲשֶׁר פָּקַד מֹשֶׁה וְאַהֲרֹן עַל־פִּי יְהוָה
מו בְּיַד־מֹשֶׁה׃ כָּל־הַפְּקֻדִים אֲשֶׁר פָּקַד מֹשֶׁה וְאַהֲרֹן וּנְשִׂיאֵי יִשְׂרָאֵל
מז אֶת־הַלְוִיִּם לְמִשְׁפְּחֹתָם וּלְבֵית אֲבֹתָם׃ מִבֶּן שְׁלֹשִׁים שָׁנָה וָמַעְלָה
וְעַד בֶּן־חֲמִשִּׁים שָׁנָה כָּל־הַבָּא לַעֲבֹד עֲבֹדַת עֲבֹדָה וַעֲבֹדַת מַשָּׂא
מח בְּאֹהֶל מוֹעֵד׃ וַיִּהְיוּ פְּקֻדֵיהֶם שְׁמֹנַת אֲלָפִים וַחֲמֵשׁ מֵאוֹת וּשְׁמֹנִים׃
מט עַל־פִּי יְהוָה פָּקַד אוֹתָם בְּיַד־מֹשֶׁה אִישׁ אִישׁ עַל־עֲבֹדָתוֹ וְעַל־מַשָּׂאוֹ
וּפְקֻדָיו אֲשֶׁר־צִוָּה יְהוָה אֶת־מֹשֶׁה׃
ה א ב וַיְדַבֵּר יְהוָה אֶל־מֹשֶׁה לֵּאמֹר׃ צַו אֶת־בְּנֵי יִשְׂרָאֵל וִישַׁלְּחוּ מִן־הַמַּחֲנֶה שלישי

אונקלוס

לְבֵית אֲבָהָתְהוֹן, תְּרֵין אַלְפִין, וְשֵׁית מְאָה וּתְלָתִין: מא אִלֵּין מִנְיָנֵי, זַרְעִיַּת בְּנֵי גֵרְשׁוֹן, כָּל דְּפָלַח בְּמַשְׁכַּן זִמְנָא, דִּמְנָא מֹשֶׁה, וְאַהֲרֹן עַל מֵימְרָא דַּיי: מב וּמִנְיָנֵי, זַרְעִיַּת בְּנֵי מְרָרִי, לְזַרְעִיָּתְהוֹן לְבֵית אֲבָהָתְהוֹן: מג מִבַּר תְּלָתִין שְׁנִין וּלְעֵילָא, וְעַד בַּר חַמְשִׁין שְׁנִין, כָּל דְּאָתֵי לְחֵילָא, לְפָלְחָנָא בְּמַשְׁכַּן זִמְנָא: מד וַהֲווֹ מִנְיָנֵיהוֹן לְזַרְעִיָּתְהוֹן, תְּלָתָא אַלְפִין וּמָאתַן: מה אִלֵּין מִנְיָנֵי, זַרְעִיַּת בְּנֵי מְרָרִי, דִּמְנָא מֹשֶׁה וְאַהֲרֹן, עַל מֵימְרָא דַּיי בִּידָא דְמֹשֶׁה: מו כָּל מִנְיָנַיָּא, דִּמְנָא מֹשֶׁה וְאַהֲרֹן, וְרַבְרְבֵי יִשְׂרָאֵל יָת לֵיוָאֵי, לְזַרְעִיָּתְהוֹן וּלְבֵית אֲבָהָתְהוֹן: מז מִבַּר תְּלָתִין שְׁנִין וּלְעֵילָא, וְעַד בַּר חַמְשִׁין שְׁנִין, כָּל דְּאָתֵי, לְמִפְלַח פָּלְחַן פָּלְחָנָא, וּפָלְחַן מַטּוּל בְּמַשְׁכַּן זִמְנָא: מח וַהֲווֹ מִנְיָנֵיהוֹן, תְּמָנְיָא אַלְפִין, וַחֲמֵשׁ מְאָה וּתְמָנַן: מט עַל מֵימְרָא דַּיי, מְנָא יָתְהוֹן בִּידָא דְמֹשֶׁה, גְּבַר גְּבַר, עַל פָּלְחָנֵיהּ וְעַל מַטּוּלֵיהּ, וּמִנְיָנוֹהִי, דְּפַקֵּיד יי יָת מֹשֶׁה: ה א וּמַלֵּיל יי עִם מֹשֶׁה לְמֵימַר: ב פַּקֵּיד יָת בְּנֵי יִשְׂרָאֵל, וִישַׁלְּחוּן מִן מַשְׁרִיתָא,

4:46 כָּל־הַפְּקֻדִים *All the Levites* – Moshe has now given each Levitical clan a special role in carrying the vessels, furnishings, and framework of the Tabernacle whenever the people journeyed from place to place. The most sacred objects are to be carried by the clan of Kehat. The Gershonites are to carry the cloths, coverings, and curtains. The Merarites are to carry the boards, crossbars, posts, and sockets that make up the Tabernacle's framework. Each clan is, in other words, to have a special role and place in the solemn procession as the House of God is carried through the desert.

the camp anyone who has an impure blight, or has had a discharge, or anyone
3 made impure by contact with the dead. Male or female, you must send them
away – send them away outside the camp, so that they do not defile their camps,
4 in the midst of which I dwell." The Israelites did so: outside the camp they sent
them. As the LORD spoke to Moshe, so the Israelites did.
5 6 And the LORD spoke to Moshe: "Tell the Israelites: When one man or woman
commits any sin against another, breaking faith with the LORD and incurring
7 guilt, then he or she shall confess the sin committed and make restitution,
adding a fifth to its value, and giving it all to the one whom he has wronged.
8 But if there is no relative to whom restitution can be made for the wrong, the
restitution for that wrong shall go to the LORD, to the priest, in addition to
9 the ram of atonement by which atonement is made on his behalf. All gifts the
10 Israelites present to the priest as sacred offerings shall be his. Each priest's sacred
offerings will be his; whatever anyone gives him shall be his."
11 12 The LORD spoke to Moshe: "Speak to the Israelites and tell them: If any man's REVI'I

רש״י

מִן הַמִּקְרָאוֹת בְּמַסֶּכֶת פְּסָחִים (דף סז ע״א): **טָמֵא לָנָפֶשׁ.** ׳לִטְמֵי נַפְשָׁא דֶּאֱנָשָׁא׳, אוֹמֵר אֲנִי שֶׁהוּא לְשׁוֹן עַצְמוֹת אָדָם בִּלְשׁוֹן אֲרַמִּי. וְהַרְבֵּה יֵשׁ בִּבְרֵאשִׁית רַבָּה: ״אַדְרִיָּנוּס שְׁחִיק טַמַיָּא״, שְׁחִיק עֲצָמוֹת:

ו **לִמְעֹל מַעַל בַּה׳.** הֲרֵי חָזַר וְכָתַב כָּאן פָּרָשַׁת גּוֹזֵל וְנִשְׁבָּע עַל שֶׁקֶר, הִיא הָאֲמוּרָה בְּפָרָשַׁת וַיִּקְרָא: ״וּמָעֲלָה מַעַל בַּה׳ וְכִחֵשׁ בַּעֲמִיתוֹ״ וְגוֹ׳ (ויקרא ה, כא); וְנִשְׁנֵית כָּאן בִּשְׁבִיל שְׁנֵי דְּבָרִים שֶׁנִּתְחַדְּשׁוּ בָּהּ: הָאֶחָד – שֶׁכָּתַב ״וְהִתְוַדּוּ״ (להלן פסוק ז), לִמֵּד שֶׁאֵינוֹ חַיָּב חֹמֶשׁ וְאָשָׁם עַל פִּי עֵדִים עַד שֶׁיּוֹדֶה בַּדָּבָר; וְהַשֵּׁנִי – שֶׁפֵּרַשׁ עַל גֶּזֶל הַגֵּר שֶׁהוּא נִתָּן לַכֹּהֲנִים:

ז **אֶת אֲשָׁמוֹ בְּרֹאשׁוֹ.** הוּא הַקֶּרֶן שֶׁנִּשְׁבַּע עָלָיו: **לַאֲשֶׁר אָשַׁם לוֹ.** לְמִי שֶׁנִּתְחַיֵּב לוֹ:

ח **וְאִם אֵין לָאִישׁ גֹּאֵל.** שֶׁמֵּת הַתּוֹבֵעַ שֶׁהִשְׁבִּיעוֹ וְאֵין לוֹ יוֹרְשִׁים: **לְהָשִׁיב הָאָשָׁם אֵלָיו.** כְּשֶׁנִּמְלַךְ זֶה לְהִתְוַדּוֹת עַל עֲוֹנוֹ. וְאָמְרוּ רַבּוֹתֵינוּ: וְכִי יֵשׁ לְךָ אָדָם בְּיִשְׂרָאֵל שֶׁאֵין לוֹ גּוֹאֲלִים, אוֹ בֵּן אוֹ בַּת אוֹ אָח אוֹ שְׁאֵר בָּשָׂר הַקָּרוֹב מִמִּשְׁפַּחַת אָבִיו לְמַעְלָה עַד יַעֲקֹב? אֶלָּא זֶה הַגֵּר שֶׁמֵּת וְאֵין לוֹ יוֹרְשִׁים: **הָאָשָׁם הַמּוּשָׁב.** זֶה הַקֶּרֶן וְהַחֹמֶשׁ: **לַה׳ לַכֹּהֵן.** קְנָאוֹ הַשֵּׁם וּנְתָנוֹ לַכֹּהֵן שֶׁבְּאוֹתוֹ מִשְׁמָר: **מִלְּבַד אֵיל הַכִּפֻּרִים.** הָאָמוּר בְּוַיִּקְרָא (ה, כה) שֶׁהוּא צָרִיךְ לְהָבִיא:

ט **וְכָל תְּרוּמָה וְגוֹ׳.** אָמַר רַבִּי יִשְׁמָעֵאל, וְכִי תְּרוּמָה מַקְרִיבִין לַכֹּהֵן? וַהֲלֹא הוּא הַמְחַזֵּר אַחֲרֶיהָ לְבֵית הַגְּרָנוֹת, וּמַה תַּלְמוּד לוֹמַר: ״אֲשֶׁר יַקְרִיבוּ לַכֹּהֵן״? אֵלּוּ הַבִּכּוּרִים, שֶׁנֶּאֱמַר בָּהֶם: ״תָּבִיא בֵּית ה׳ אֱלֹהֶיךָ״ (שמות כג, יט), וְאֵינִי יוֹדֵעַ מַה יֵּעָשֶׂה בָּהֶם, תַּלְמוּד לוֹמַר: ״לַכֹּהֵן לוֹ יִהְיֶה״, בָּא הַכָּתוּב וְלִמֵּד עַל הַבִּכּוּרִים שֶׁיִּהְיוּ נִתָּנִין לַכֹּהֵן:

י **וְאִישׁ אֶת קֳדָשָׁיו לוֹ יִהְיוּ.** לְפִי שֶׁנֶּאֶמְרוּ מַתְּנוֹת כְּהֻנָּה וּלְוִיָּה, יָכוֹל יָבוֹאוּ וְיִטְּלוּם בִּזְרוֹעַ? תַּלְמוּד לוֹמַר: ״וְאִישׁ אֶת קֳדָשָׁיו לוֹ יִהְיוּ״, מַגִּיד שֶׁטּוֹבַת הֲנָאָתָן לַבְּעָלִים. וְעוֹד מִדְרָשִׁים הַרְבֵּה דָּרְשׁוּ בוֹ בְּסִפְרֵי (ו). וּמִדְרַשׁ אַגָּדָה: ״וְאִישׁ אֶת קֳדָשָׁיו לוֹ יִהְיוּ״, מִי שֶׁמְּעַכֵּב מַעַשְׂרוֹתָיו וְאֵינוֹ נוֹתְנָן, לוֹ יִהְיוּ הַמַּעַשְׂרוֹת, סוֹף שֶׁאֵין שָׂדֵהוּ עוֹשָׂה אֶלָּא אֶחָד מֵעֲשָׂרָה שֶׁהָיְתָה לְמוּדָה לַעֲשׂוֹת. ״אִישׁ אֲשֶׁר יִתֵּן לַכֹּהֵן״ מַתָּנוֹת הָרְאוּיוֹת לוֹ, ״לוֹ יִהְיֶה״ מָמוֹן הַרְבֵּה:

willing to renounce His own honor, allowing His name to be effaced, "in order to make peace between husband and wife" by clearing an innocent woman from suspicion (Sifrei, Naso 42). Though the ordeal was eventually abolished by Rabban Yoḥanan b. Zakkai after the destruction of the Second Temple, the law served as a reminder as to how important domestic peace is in the Jewish scale of values. Peace and truth, the two objectives of the ritual, are often elusive in relationships between people:

R. Shimon said: When God was about to create Adam, the ministering angels split into contending groups.

ג כָּל־צָרוּעַ וְכָל־זָב וְכֹל טָמֵא לָנָפֶשׁ׃ מִזָּכָר עַד־נְקֵבָה תְּשַׁלֵּחוּ אֶל־
מִחוּץ לַמַּחֲנֶה תְּשַׁלְּחוּם וְלֹא יְטַמְּאוּ אֶת־מַחֲנֵיהֶם אֲשֶׁר אֲנִי שֹׁכֵן
ד בְּתוֹכָם׃ וַיַּעֲשׂוּ־כֵן בְּנֵי יִשְׂרָאֵל וַיְשַׁלְּחוּ אוֹתָם אֶל־מִחוּץ לַמַּחֲנֶה
כַּאֲשֶׁר דִּבֶּר יהוה אֶל־מֹשֶׁה כֵּן עָשׂוּ בְּנֵי יִשְׂרָאֵל׃
ה ו וַיְדַבֵּר יהוה אֶל־מֹשֶׁה לֵּאמֹר׃ דַּבֵּר אֶל־בְּנֵי יִשְׂרָאֵל אִישׁ אוֹ־אִשָּׁה
כִּי יַעֲשׂוּ מִכָּל־חַטֹּאת הָאָדָם לִמְעֹל מַעַל בַּיהוה וְאָשְׁמָה הַנֶּפֶשׁ
ז הַהִוא׃ וְהִתְוַדּוּ אֶת־חַטָּאתָם אֲשֶׁר עָשׂוּ וְהֵשִׁיב אֶת־אֲשָׁמוֹ בְּרֹאשׁוֹ
ח וַחֲמִישִׁתוֹ יֹסֵף עָלָיו וְנָתַן לַאֲשֶׁר אָשַׁם לוֹ׃ וְאִם־אֵין לָאִישׁ גֹּאֵל לְהָשִׁיב
הָאָשָׁם אֵלָיו הָאָשָׁם הַמּוּשָׁב לַיהוה לַכֹּהֵן מִלְּבַד אֵיל הַכִּפֻּרִים אֲשֶׁר
ט יְכַפֶּר־בּוֹ עָלָיו׃ וְכָל־תְּרוּמָה לְכָל־קָדְשֵׁי בְנֵי־יִשְׂרָאֵל אֲשֶׁר־יַקְרִיבוּ
י לַכֹּהֵן לוֹ יִהְיֶה׃ וְאִישׁ אֶת־קֳדָשָׁיו לוֹ יִהְיוּ אִישׁ אֲשֶׁר־יִתֵּן לַכֹּהֵן לוֹ
יִהְיֶה׃
יא יב וַיְדַבֵּר יהוה אֶל־מֹשֶׁה לֵּאמֹר׃ דַּבֵּר אֶל־בְּנֵי יִשְׂרָאֵל וְאָמַרְתָּ אֲלֵהֶם ה רביעי

אונקלוס

כָּל דִּסְגִיר וְכָל דְּדָאִיב, וְכֹל דְּמִסְאַב לִטְמֵי נַפְשָׁא: ג מִדְּכַר עַד נֻקְבָּא תְּשַׁלְּחוּן, לְמִבָּרָא לְמַשְׁרִיתָא תְּשַׁלְּחוּנוּן, וְלָא יְסָאֲבוּן יָת מַשְׁרְיָתְהוֹן, דִּשְׁכִינְתִּי שָׁרְיָא בֵּינֵיהוֹן: ד וַעֲבַדוּ כֵן בְּנֵי יִשְׂרָאֵל, וְשַׁלַּחוּ יָתְהוֹן, לְמִבָּרָא לְמַשְׁרִיתָא, כְּמָא דְּמַלֵּיל יי עִם מֹשֶׁה, כֵּן עֲבַדוּ בְּנֵי יִשְׂרָאֵל: ה וּמַלֵּיל יי עִם מֹשֶׁה לְמֵימַר: ו מַלֵּיל עִם בְּנֵי יִשְׂרָאֵל, גְּבַר אוֹ אִתְּתָא, אֲרֵי יַעְבְּדוּן מִכָּל חוֹבֵי אֱנָשָׁא, לְשַׁקָּרָא שְׁקַר קֳדָם יי, וִיחוּב אֲנָשָׁא הַהוּא: ז וִיוַדּוֹן, יָת חוֹבֵיהוֹן דַּעֲבַדוּ, וְיָתֵיב יָת חוֹבְתֵיהּ בְּרֵישֵׁיהּ, וְחֻמְשֵׁיהּ יוֹסֵיף עֲלוֹהִי, וְיִתֵּין, לִדְחַיָּב לֵיהּ: ח וְאִם לֵית לְגַבְרָא פָּרִיק, לְאָתָבָא חוֹבְתָא לֵיהּ, חוֹבְתָא, דְּמָתִיב קֳדָם יי לְכָהֲנָא, בָּר, מִדְּכַר כִּפּוּרַיָּא, דִּיכַפַּר בֵּיהּ עֲלוֹהִי: ט וְכָל אַפְרָשׁוּתָא, לְכָל קֻדְשַׁיָּא דִּבְנֵי יִשְׂרָאֵל, דִּיקָרְבוּן לְכָהֲנָא דִּילֵיהּ יְהֵי: י וּגְבַר יָת מַעְסַר קֻדְשׁוֹהִי דִּילֵיהּ יְהֵי, גְּבַר, דְּיִתֵּין לְכָהֲנָא דִּילֵיהּ יְהֵי: יא וּמַלֵּיל יי עִם מֹשֶׁה לְמֵימַר: יב מַלֵּיל עִם בְּנֵי יִשְׂרָאֵל, וְתֵימַר לְהוֹן,

THE RITUAL OF THE ACCUSED WIFE

The case of the *sota* concerns the woman suspected by her husband of adultery – a situation fraught with danger of violence and abuse. The Mishna (Sota 1:5) clarifies that the woman in this predicament has the choice either to divorce her husband, or to prove her innocence beyond equivocation. What struck the Sages most forcibly about the ritual of the *sota* is the fact that it involved obliterating the name of God, something strictly forbidden under other circumstances. The officiating priest recites a curse including God's name, writes it on a parchment scroll, and then dissolves the writing into specially prepared water. The results of the woman drinking this water will publicly indicate her guilt or innocence of her husband's charge. The Sages inferred from this that God was

13 wife goes astray and is unfaithful to him; if another man has sexual relations
with her, and this happens without the husband's knowledge because she
defiled herself in secret, there was no witness against her, and she was not
14 caught in the act – if a fit of jealousy overcomes him, making him jealous over
his wife who has defiled herself, or a fit of jealousy overcomes him, making him
15 jealous over his wife who has not defiled herself – then the man shall bring
his wife to the priest together with the prescribed offering for her, one-tenth
of an ephah of barley flour. He shall not pour oil on it or place frankincense
upon it, for it is a grain offering of jealousy, a grain offering of remembrance,
16 calling attention to a wrong. The priest shall bring the woman close and have
17 her stand before the Lord. He shall then take sacred water in an earthenware
vessel, and pick up some earth from the floor of the Tabernacle and place it in

רש"י

יב **אִישׁ אִישׁ כִּי תִשְׂטֶה אִשְׁתּוֹ.** מַה כָּתוּב לְמַעְלָה מִן הָעִנְיָן? "וְאִישׁ אֶת קֳדָשָׁיו לוֹ יִהְיוּ" (לעיל פסוק י), אִם אַתָּה מְעַכֵּב מַתְּנוֹת הַכֹּהֵן, חַיֶּיךָ שֶׁתִּצְטָרֵךְ לָבֹא אֶצְלוֹ לְהָבִיא לוֹ אֶת הַסּוֹטָה: **כִּי תִשְׂטֶה.** תֵּט מִדַּרְכֵי צְנִיעוּת וְתֵחָשֵׁד בְּעֵינָיו, כְּמוֹ: "שְׂטֵה מֵעָלָיו וַעֲבֹר" (משלי ד, טו), "אַל יֵשְׂטְ אֶל דְּרָכֶיהָ לִבֶּךָ" (שם ז, כה): **וּמָעֲלָה בוֹ מָעַל.** וּמַהוּ הַמַּעַל? "וְשָׁכַב אִישׁ אֹתָהּ":

יג **וְנֶעְלַם מֵעֵינֵי אִישָׁהּ.** הָא אִם הָיָה רוֹאֶה וּמְעַמְעֵם, אֵין הַמַּיִם בּוֹדְקִין אוֹתָהּ: **וְנִסְתְּרָה.** שִׁעוּר שֶׁתֵּרָאֶה לְטֻמְאַת בִּיאָה: **וְעֵד אֵין בָּהּ.** הָא אִם יֵשׁ בָּהּ אֲפִלּוּ עֵד אֶחָד שֶׁאָמַר 'נִטְמֵאת', לֹא הָיְתָה שׁוֹתָה: **וְעֵד אֵין בָּהּ.** בַּטֻּמְאָה, אֲבָל יֵשׁ עֵדִים לַסְּתִירָה: **נִתְפָּשָׂה.** נֶאֶנְסָה, כְּמוֹ: "וּתְפָשָׂהּ וְשָׁכַב עִמָּהּ" (דברים כב, כח):

יד **וְעָבַר עָלָיו.** קֹדֶם לַסְּתִירָה: **רוּחַ קִנְאָה וְקִנֵּא.** פֵּרְשׁוּ רַבּוֹתֵינוּ לְשׁוֹן הַתְרָאָה, שֶׁמַּתְרֶה בָּהּ: 'אַל תִּסָּתְרִי עִם אִישׁ פְּלוֹנִי': **וְהוּא נִטְמָאָה אוֹ עָבַר עָלָיו וְגוֹ'.** כְּלוֹמַר, הוּא הִתְרָה בָהּ וְעָבְרָה עַל הַתְרָאָתוֹ, וְאֵין יָדוּעַ אִם נִטְמְאָה אִם לָאו:

טו **קֶמַח.** שֶׁלֹּא יְהֵא מִסֹּלֶת: **שְׂעֹרִים.** וְלֹא חִטִּים, הִיא עָשְׂתָה מַעֲשֵׂה בְּהֵמָה וְקָרְבָּנָהּ מַאֲכַל בְּהֵמָה: **לֹא יִצֹק עָלָיו שֶׁמֶן.** שֶׁלֹּא יְהֵא קָרְבָּנָהּ מְהֻדָּר, שֶׁהַשֶּׁמֶן קָרוּי 'אוֹר' וְהִיא עָשְׂתָה בַּחֹשֶׁךְ: **וְלֹא יִתֵּן עָלָיו לְבֹנָה.** שֶׁהָאִמָּהוֹת נִקְרָאוֹת לְבוֹנָה, שֶׁנֶּאֱמַר: "אֶל גִּבְעַת הַלְּבוֹנָה" (שיר השירים ד, ו), וְהִיא פֵּרְשָׁה מִדַּרְכֵיהֶן: **כִּי מִנְחַת קְנָאֹת הוּא.** הַקֶּמַח הַזֶּה, 'קֶמַח' לְשׁוֹן זָכָר: **מִנְחַת קְנָאֹת.** מְעוֹרֶרֶת עָלֶיהָ שְׁתֵּי קְנָאוֹת, קִנְאַת הַמָּקוֹם וְקִנְאַת הַבַּעַל:

יז **מַיִם קְדֹשִׁים.** שֶׁקָּדְשׁוּ בַּכִּיּוֹר. לְפִי שֶׁנַּעֲשָׂה הַכִּיּוֹר מִנְּחֹשֶׁת מַרְאוֹת הַצּוֹבְאוֹת, וְזוֹ פֵּרְשָׁה מִדַּרְכֵיהֶן, שֶׁהָיוּ נִבְעָלוֹת לְבַעֲלֵיהֶן בְּמִצְרַיִם תַּחַת הַתַּפּוּחַ וְזוֹ קִלְקְלָה לְאַחֵר, תִּבָּדֵק בּוֹ: **בִּכְלִי חָרֶשׂ.** הִיא הִשְׁקְתָה אֶת הַנּוֹאֵף יַיִן מְשֻׁבָּח בְּכוֹסוֹת מְשֻׁבָּחִים, לְפִיכָךְ תִּשְׁתֶּה מַיִם הַמָּרִים בִּמְקֻדָּה בְּזוּיָה שֶׁל חֶרֶס:

Fragments of it lie everywhere. Each person, culture, and language has part of it; none has it all.

In many cases, truth and peace are conflicting values. Holding on to my conception of truth makes it hard for me to concede space to yours. A tradition is what it is, not only in virtue of the ideals it espouses, but also how it resolves conflicts between those values, and the Rabbis articulated an ethic heavily weighted toward peace. Heroism, they said, meant conquering oneself, not others. Lights of peace (the Sabbath candles) took precedence over lights of victory (the Ḥanukka candles) (Shabbat 23b; *Hilkhot Ḥanukka* 4:14). In the case of the husband possessed by jealousy, establishing truth is a prerequisite for peace. If the wife has been unfaithful, they are forbidden to continue to live as husband and wife. If she has not, the husband's withdrawal and anger would be unacceptably harsh. The doubt must be resolved, and we have to go the extra mile to achieve that end.

יג אִישׁ אִישׁ כִּי־תִשְׂטֶה אִשְׁתּוֹ וּמָעֲלָה בוֹ מָעַל׃ וְשָׁכַב אִישׁ אֹתָהּ
שִׁכְבַת־זֶרַע וְנֶעְלַם מֵעֵינֵי אִישָׁהּ וְנִסְתְּרָה וְהִיא נִטְמָאָה וְעֵד אֵין
יד בָּהּ וְהִוא לֹא נִתְפָּשָׂה׃ וְעָבַר עָלָיו רוּחַ־קִנְאָה וְקִנֵּא אֶת־אִשְׁתּוֹ
וְהִוא נִטְמָאָה אוֹ־עָבַר עָלָיו רוּחַ־קִנְאָה וְקִנֵּא אֶת־אִשְׁתּוֹ וְהִיא לֹא
טו נִטְמָאָה׃ וְהֵבִיא הָאִישׁ אֶת־אִשְׁתּוֹ אֶל־הַכֹּהֵן וְהֵבִיא אֶת־קָרְבָּנָהּ
עָלֶיהָ עֲשִׂירִת הָאֵיפָה קֶמַח שְׂעֹרִים לֹא־יִצֹק עָלָיו שֶׁמֶן וְלֹא־יִתֵּן עָלָיו
טז לְבֹנָה כִּי־מִנְחַת קְנָאֹת הוּא מִנְחַת זִכָּרוֹן מַזְכֶּרֶת עָוֺן׃ וְהִקְרִיב אֹתָהּ
יז הַכֹּהֵן וְהֶעֱמִדָהּ לִפְנֵי יהוה׃ וְלָקַח הַכֹּהֵן מַיִם קְדֹשִׁים בִּכְלִי־חָרֶשׂ
וּמִן־הֶעָפָר אֲשֶׁר יִהְיֶה בְּקַרְקַע הַמִּשְׁכָּן יִקַּח הַכֹּהֵן וְנָתַן אֶל־הַמָּיִם׃

אונקלוס

גְּבַר גְּבַר אֲרֵי תִסְטֵי אִתְּתֵיהּ, וּתְשַׁקַּר בֵּיהּ שְׁקָר: יג וְיִשְׁכּוּב גְּבַר יָתַהּ שִׁכְבַת זַרְעָא, וִיהֵי מְכַסָּא מֵעֵינֵי בַעְלַהּ, וּמִטַּמְּרָא וְהִיא מְסָאֲבָא, וְסָהִיד לֵית בַּהּ, וְהִיא לָא אִתְּאַחֲדַת: יד וְיִעְבַּר עֲלוֹהִי רוּחַ קִנְאָה, וִיקַנֵּי יָת אִתְּתֵיהּ וְהִיא מְסָאֲבָא, אוֹ עֲבַר עֲלוֹהִי רוּחַ קִנְאָה וִיקַנֵּי יָת אִתְּתֵיהּ, וְהִיא לָא מְסָאֲבָא: טו וְיַיְתֵי גַּבְרָא יָת אִתְּתֵיהּ לְוָת כָּהֲנָא, וְיַיְתֵי יָת קֻרְבָּנַהּ עֲלַהּ, חַד מִן עַסְרָא בִּתְלָת סְאִין קְמַח סְעָרִין, לָא יְרִיק עֲלוֹהִי מִשְׁחָא, וְלָא יִתֵּין עֲלוֹהִי לְבוֹנְתָא, אֲרֵי מִנְחַת קִנְאָתָא הוּא, מִנְחַת דֻּכְרָנָא מְדַכְּרַת חוֹבִין: טז וִיקָרֵיב יָתַהּ כָּהֲנָא, וִיקִימִנַּהּ קֳדָם יְיָ: יז וְיִסַּב כָּהֲנָא, מֵי כִיּוֹר בְּמָן דַּחֲסַף, וּמִן עַפְרָא, דִּיהֵי בְּאִיסוֹדֵי מַשְׁכְּנָא, יִסַּב כָּהֲנָא וְיִתֵּין לְמַיָּא:

Some said, "Let him be created." Others said, "Let him not be created." That is why it is written: "Mercy and truth collided; righteousness and peace clashed" (Ps. 85:11).

Mercy said, "Let him be created, because he will do merciful deeds."

Truth said, "Let him not be created, for he will be full of falsehood."

Righteousness said, "Let him be created, for he will do righteous deeds."

Peace said, "Let him not be created, for he will never cease quarreling."

What did the Holy One, blessed be He, do? He took truth and threw it to the ground. The angels said, "Sovereign of the Universe, why do You do thus to Your own seal, truth? Let truth arise from the ground." (Bereshit Rabba 8:5)

This midrash clothes in a story an audacious theological interpretation. God, it suggests, was in two minds before creating mankind. Yes, humanity is capable of great acts of altruism and self-sacrifice, but it is also constantly at war. Human beings tell lies and are full of strife. God takes truth and throws it to the ground, meaning: for life to be livable, truth on earth cannot be what it is in heaven. Truth in heaven may be platonic – eternal, harmonious, radiant. But man cannot aspire to such truth, and if he does, he will create conflict, not peace. In that case, says God, throwing truth to the ground, let human beings live by a different standard of truth, one that is human and thus conscious of its limitations. Truth on the ground is multiple, partial.

18 the water. He shall have the woman stand before the Lord, and loosen the hair
of the woman's head, placing on her palms the grain offering of remembrance,
the grain offering of jealousy. His hand shall hold the bitter water that gives rise
19 to a curse. And the priest shall administer an oath to her, saying to the woman,
'If no man has had sexual relations with you, and if you have not gone astray,
letting yourself be defiled while married to your husband, may your innocence
20 be established by this bitter, cursing water. But if you have gone astray while
married to your husband, and if you have let yourself be defiled and a man
other than your husband has had relations with you' – the priest shall here put
the woman under the oath of the curse, and say to her – 'the Lord make you
a curse and an oath among your people, when the Lord makes your thigh sag
22 and your belly swell; may this curse-causing water enter your intestines and
make your belly swell and your thigh sag.' And the woman shall say, 'Amen,
23 Amen.' Then the priest shall write these curses on a scroll and wash them off
24 into the bitter water. He shall make the woman drink the bitter water that causes

רש״י

יח **וְהֶעֱמִיד הַכֹּהֵן וְגוֹ׳.** וַהֲלֹא כְּבָר נֶאֱמַר: "וְהֶעֱמִדָהּ לִפְנֵי ה׳" (לעיל פסוק טז)? אֶלָּא מְסִיעִין הָיוּ אוֹתָהּ מִמָּקוֹם לְמָקוֹם, כְּדֵי לְיַגְּעָהּ וְתִטָּרֵף דַּעְתָּהּ וְתוֹדֶה: **וּפָרַע.** סוֹתֵר אֶת קְלִיעַת שְׂעָרָהּ כְּדֵי לְבַזּוֹתָהּ, מִכָּאן לִבְנוֹת יִשְׂרָאֵל שֶׁגִּלּוּי הָרֹאשׁ גְּנַאי לָהֶן: **לִפְנֵי ה׳.** בְּשַׁעַר נִיקָנוֹר, הוּא שַׁעַר הָעֲזָרָה הַמִּזְרָחִי, דֶּרֶךְ כָּל הַנִּכְנָסִים: **וְנָתַן עַל כַּפֶּיהָ.** לְיַגְּעָהּ, אוּלַי תִּטָּרֵף דַּעְתָּהּ וְתוֹדֶה, וְלֹא יִמָּחֶה שֵׁם הַמְיֻחָד עַל הַמַּיִם: **הַמָּרִים.** עַל שֵׁם סוֹפָן, שֶׁהֵם מָרִים לָהּ: **הַמְאָרְרִים.** הַמְחַסְּרִים אוֹתָהּ מִן הָעוֹלָם, לְשׁוֹן "סִלּוֹן מַמְאִיר" (יחזקאל כח, כד). וְלֹא יִתָּכֵן לְפָרֵשׁ מַיִם אֲרוּרִים שֶׁהֲרֵי קְדוֹשִׁים הֵן, וְלֹא 'אֲרוּרִים' כָּתַב הַכָּתוּב אֶלָּא "מְאָרְרִים" אֶת אֲחֵרִים. וְאַף אוּנְקְלוֹס לֹא תִרְגֵּם 'לִיטַיָּא' אֶלָּא "מְלַטְטַיָּא", שֶׁמַּאֲרוֹת קְלָלָה בְּגוּפָהּ שֶׁל זוֹ:

יט **וְהִשְׁבִּיעַ וְגוֹ׳.** וּמַה הִיא הַשְּׁבוּעָה? "אִם לֹא שָׁכַב הִנָּקִי", הָא אִם שָׁכַב – חִנָּקִי, שֶׁמִּכְּלַל לָאו אַתָּה שׁוֹמֵעַ הֵן, אֶלָּא שֶׁמִּצְוָה לִפְתֹּחַ בְּדִינֵי נְפָשׁוֹת תְּחִלָּה לִזְכוּת:

כ **וְאַתְּ כִּי שָׂטִית.** "כִּי" מְשַׁמֵּשׁ בִּלְשׁוֹן 'אִם':

כא **בִּשְׁבֻעַת הָאָלָה.** שְׁבוּעָה שֶׁל קְלָלָה: **יִתֵּן ה׳ אוֹתָךְ לְאָלָה וְגוֹ׳.** שֶׁיִּהְיוּ הַכֹּל מְקַלְּלִין בִּיךְ: יְבוֹאֵךְ כְּדֶרֶךְ שֶׁבָּא לִפְלוֹנִית: **וְלִשְׁבֻעָה.** שֶׁיִּהְיוּ הַכֹּל נִשְׁבָּעִין בִּיךְ, אִם לֹא יֶאֱרַע לִי כְּדֶרֶךְ שֶׁאֵרַע לִפְלוֹנִית, וְכֵן הוּא אוֹמֵר: "וְהִנַּחְתֶּם שִׁמְכֶם לִשְׁבוּעָה לִבְחִירַי" (ישעיהו סה, טו), שֶׁהַצַּדִּיקִים נִשְׁבָּעִים בְּפֻרְעָנוּתָן שֶׁל רְשָׁעִים. וְכֵן לְעִנְיַן הַבְּרָכָה: "וְנִבְרְכוּ" וְגוֹ׳ (בראשית יב, ג), "בְּךָ יְבָרֵךְ יִשְׂרָאֵל לֵאמֹר" (שם מח, כ): **אֶת יְרֵכֵךְ.** בַּקְּלָלָה הִקְדִּים יָרֵךְ לַבֶּטֶן, לְפִי שֶׁבָּהּ הִתְחִילָה בַּעֲבֵרָה תְּחִלָּה: **צָבָה.** כְּתַרְגּוּמוֹ, נְפוּחָה:

כב **לַצְבּוֹת בֶּטֶן.** כְּמוֹ לְהַצְבּוֹת בֶּטֶן, זֶהוּ שִׁמּוּשׁ פַּתָּח שֶׁהַלָּמֶ"ד נְקוּדָה בּוֹ. וְכֵן "לַנְחֹתָם הַדֶּרֶךְ" (שמות יג, כא), "לַרְאֹתְכֶם בַּדֶּרֶךְ אֲשֶׁר תֵּלְכוּ בָהּ" (דברים א, לג), וְכֵן "לַנְפִּל יָרֵךְ" לְהַנְפִּיל יָרֵךְ, שֶׁהַמַּיִם מַצְבִּים אֶת הַבֶּטֶן וּמַפִּילִים אֶת הַיָּרֵךְ: **לַצְבּוֹת בֶּטֶן וְלַנְפִּל יָרֵךְ.** בִּטְנוֹ וִירֵכוֹ שֶׁל בּוֹעֵל. אוֹ אֵינוֹ אֶלָּא שֶׁל נִבְעֶלֶת? כְּשֶׁהוּא אוֹמֵר: "אֶת יְרֵכֵךְ נֹפֶלֶת וְאֶת בִּטְנֵךְ צָבָה" (לעיל פסוק כא), הֲרֵי שֶׁל נִבְעֶלֶת אָמוּר: **אָמֵן אָמֵן.** קַבָּלַת שְׁבוּעָה, אָמֵן אִם מֵאִישׁ זֶה אָמֵן אִם מֵאִישׁ אַחֵר, אָמֵן עַל הָאָלָה אָמֵן עַל הַשְּׁבוּעָה:

כד **וְהִשְׁקָה אֶת הָאִשָּׁה.** אֵין זֶה סֵדֶר הַמַּעֲשֶׂה, שֶׁהֲרֵי בַּתְּחִלָּה מַקְרִיב מִנְחָתָהּ; אֶלָּא הַכָּתוּב מְבַשֶּׂרְךָ שֶׁכְּשֶׁיַּשְׁקֶנָּה יָבוֹאוּ בָהּ לְמָרִים. לְפִי שֶׁנֶּאֱמַר בֶּטֶן וְיָרֵךְ, מִנַּיִן לִשְׁאָר כָּל הַגּוּף? תַּלְמוּד לוֹמַר: "וּבָאוּ בָהּ", בְּכֻלָּהּ. אִם כֵּן מַה תַּלְמוּד לוֹמַר בֶּטֶן וְיָרֵךְ? לְפִי שֶׁהֵן הִתְחִילוּ

Peace is easily damaged and hard to repair. The doubt cast within this couple's marriage renders their coexistence impossible. To resolve this, the Sages noted, and to rehabilitate the couple's mutual trust, God is willing to let His own name be blotted out.

יח וְהֶעֱמִיד הַכֹּהֵן אֶת־הָאִשָּׁה לִפְנֵי יהוה וּפָרַע אֶת־רֹאשׁ הָאִשָּׁה וְנָתַן
עַל־כַּפֶּיהָ אֵת מִנְחַת הַזִּכָּרוֹן מִנְחַת קְנָאֹת הִוא וּבְיַד הַכֹּהֵן יִהְיוּ מֵי
יט הַמָּרִים הַמְאָרְרִים: וְהִשְׁבִּיעַ אֹתָהּ הַכֹּהֵן וְאָמַר אֶל־הָאִשָּׁה אִם־לֹא
שָׁכַב אִישׁ אֹתָךְ וְאִם־לֹא שָׂטִית טֻמְאָה תַּחַת אִישֵׁךְ הִנָּקִי מִמֵּי
כ הַמָּרִים הַמְאָרְרִים הָאֵלֶּה: וְאַתְּ כִּי שָׂטִית תַּחַת אִישֵׁךְ וְכִי נִטְמֵאת
כא וַיִּתֵּן אִישׁ בָּךְ אֶת־שְׁכָבְתּוֹ מִבַּלְעֲדֵי אִישֵׁךְ: וְהִשְׁבִּיעַ הַכֹּהֵן אֶת־
הָאִשָּׁה בִּשְׁבֻעַת הָאָלָה וְאָמַר הַכֹּהֵן לָאִשָּׁה יִתֵּן יהוה אוֹתָךְ לְאָלָה
וְלִשְׁבֻעָה בְּתוֹךְ עַמֵּךְ בְּתֵת יהוה אֶת־יְרֵכֵךְ נֹפֶלֶת וְאֶת־בִּטְנֵךְ צָבָה:
כב וּבָאוּ הַמַּיִם הַמְאָרְרִים הָאֵלֶּה בְּמֵעַיִךְ לַצְבּוֹת בֶּטֶן וְלַנְפִּל יָרֵךְ וְאָמְרָה
כג הָאִשָּׁה אָמֵן ׀ אָמֵן: וְכָתַב אֶת־הָאָלֹת הָאֵלֶּה הַכֹּהֵן בַּסֵּפֶר וּמָחָה
כד אֶל־מֵי הַמָּרִים: וְהִשְׁקָה אֶת־הָאִשָּׁה אֶת־מֵי הַמָּרִים הַמְאָרְרִים

אונקלוס

יח וִיקִים כָּהֲנָא יָת אִתְּתָא קֳדָם יְיָ, וְיִפְרַע יָת רֵישָׁא דְּאִתְּתָא, וְיִתֵּין עַל יְדַהָא, יָת מִנְחַת דִּכְרָנָא, מִנְחַת קִנְאָתָא הִיא, וּבִידָא דְּכָהֲנָא יְהוֹן, מַיָּא מְרִירַיָּא מְלַטְטַיָּא: יט וְיוֹמֵי יָתַהּ כָּהֲנָא, וְיֵימַר לְאִתְּתָא אִם לָא שְׁכֵיב גְּבַר יָתִיךְ, וְאִם לָא סְטֵית, לְאִסְתָּאָבָא בַּר מִבַּעְלִיךְ, הֲוַאי זַכָּאָה, מִמַּיָּא, מְרִירַיָּא מְלַטְטַיָּא הָאִלֵּין: כ וְאַתְּ, אֲרֵי סְטֵית, בַּר מִבַּעְלִיךְ וַאֲרֵי אִסְתְּאַבְתְּ, וִיהַב גְּבַר בִּיךְ יָת שְׁכָבְתֵּיהּ, בַּר מִבַּעְלִיךְ: כא וְיוֹמֵי כָּהֲנָא יָת אִתְּתָא בְּמוֹמָתָא דִּלְוָטָא, וְיֵימַר כָּהֲנָא לְאִתְּתָא, יִתֵּין יְיָ יָתִיךְ, לִלְוָט וּלְמוֹמֵי בְּגוֹ עַמִּיךְ, בְּדִיִתֵּין יְיָ יָת יַרְכִּיךְ מַסְיָא, וְיָת מְעַכִי נְפִיחִין: כב וְיֵיעֲלוּן, מַיָּא מְלַטְטַיָּא הָאִלֵּין בִּמְעַכִי, לְאַפָּחָא מְעִין וּלְאַמְסָאָה יַרְכָּא, וְתֵימַר אִתְּתָא אָמֵן אָמֵן: כג וְיִכְתּוֹב, יָת לְוָטַיָּא הָאִלֵּין, כָּהֲנָא בְּסִפְרָא, וְיִמְחוֹק לְמַיָּא מְרִירַיָּא: כד וְיַשְׁקֵי יָת אִתְּתָא, יָת מַיָּא מְרִירַיָּא מְלַטְטַיָּא,

5:23 וּמָחָה אֶל־מֵי הַמָּרִים *Wash them off into the bitter water* – In a long analysis, the fifteenth-century Spanish commentator Rabbi Yitzḥak Arama explains that *shalom* does not mean merely the absence of strife. It means completeness, the harmonious working of a complex system, a state in which everything is in its proper place and all is at one with the physical and ethical laws governing the universe: "Peace is the thread of grace issuing from Him, may He be exalted, stringing together all beings.... It underlies and sustains the reality and unique existence of each" (*Akedat Yitzḥak*, ch. 74).

Similarly, Rabbi Yitzḥak Abrabanel writes, "That is why God is called 'Peace,' because it is He who binds the world together and orders all things according to their particular character and posture. For when things are in their proper order, peace will reign" (commentary on Avot 2:12).

This is a concept of peace heavily dependent on the vision of Genesis 1, in which God brings order out of *tohu vavohu*, chaos, creating a world in which each object and life-form has its place. Peace exists where each element in the system is valued as a vital part of the system as a whole and where there is no discord between them.

25 a curse, and the curse-causing water will enter into her and turn bitter. The
priest shall take the grain offering of jealousy from the woman's hand, wave the
26 grain offering before the LORD, and bring it close to the altar. Then the priest
shall take a handful of the grain offering as a token, and burn it on the altar, after
27 which he shall make the woman drink the water. He having given her the water
to drink, then, if she has let herself be defiled and behaved unfaithfully toward
her husband, the curse-causing water will turn bitter, her belly will swell, her
28 thigh will sag, and the woman will become a curse among her people. But if the
woman has not let herself be defiled and is pure, then she shall be cleared and
29 will conceive children." This is the law for cases of jealousy, when a woman goes
30 astray with someone in place of her husband and becomes defiled, or when a fit
of jealousy overcomes a man and he grows jealous over his wife. He shall have
the woman stand before the LORD, and the priest will deal with her as all this
31 law prescribes. No guilt will attach to the husband, but the woman in question
will bear the punishment of her offense.
6 1 2 Then the LORD spoke to Moshe: "Speak to the Israelites. Say: When a man or
a woman takes a special vow, the vow of a nazirite, to separate him or herself
3 to the LORD, he must separate himself from wine and strong drink. He must

רש"י

בַּעֲבֵרָה תְּחִלָּה, לְפִיכָךְ הִתְחִיל מֵהֶם הַפֻּרְעָנוּת: **לְמָרִים.** לִהְיוֹת לָהּ רָעִים וּמָרִים:

כה **וְהֵנִיף.** מוֹלִיךְ וּמֵבִיא מַעֲלֶה וּמוֹרִיד, וְאַף הִיא מְנִיפָה עִמּוֹ, שֶׁיָּדָהּ לְמַעְלָה מִיָּדוֹ שֶׁל כֹּהֵן: **וְהִקְרִיב אֹתָהּ.** זוֹ הִיא הַגָּשָׁתָהּ בְּקֶרֶן דְּרוֹמִית מַעֲרָבִית שֶׁל מִזְבֵּחַ קֹדֶם קְמִיצָה, כִּשְׁאָר מְנָחוֹת:

כו **אַזְכָּרָתָהּ.** הוּא הַקֹּמֶץ, שֶׁעַל יְדֵי הַקְטָרָתוֹ הַמִּנְחָה בָּאָה לְזִכָּרוֹן לַגָּבוֹהַּ:

כז **וְהִשְׁקָהּ אֶת הַמַּיִם.** לְרַבּוֹת שֶׁאִם אָמְרָה 'אֵינִי שׁוֹתָה' לְאַחַר שֶׁנִּמְחֲקָה הַמְּגִלָּה, מְעַרְעֲרִין אוֹתָהּ וּמַשְׁקִין אוֹתָהּ בְּעַל כָּרְחָהּ, אֶלָּא אִם כֵּן אָמְרָה 'טְמֵאָה אֲנִי': **וְצָבְתָה בִטְנָהּ וְגוֹ'.** אַף עַל פִּי שֶׁבַּקְּלָלָה הִזְכִּיר יָרֵךְ תְּחִלָּה, הַמַּיִם אֵינָן בּוֹדְקִין אֶלָּא כְּדֶרֶךְ כְּנִיסָתָן בָּהּ: **וְהָיְתָה הָאִשָּׁה לְאָלָה.** כְּמוֹ שֶׁפֵּרַשְׁתִּי, שֶׁיִּהְיוּ הַכֹּל אָלִין בָּהּ: **בְּקֶרֶב עַמָּהּ.** הֶפְרֵשׁ יֵשׁ בֵּין אָדָם הַמִּתְנַוֵּל בְּמָקוֹם שֶׁנִּכָּר לְאָדָם הַמִּתְנַוֵּל בְּמָקוֹם שֶׁאֵינוֹ נִכָּר:

כח **וְאִם לֹא נִטְמְאָה הָאִשָּׁה.** בִּסְתִירָה זוֹ: **וּטְהֹרָה הִוא.** מִמָּקוֹם אַחֵר: **וְנִקְּתָה.** מִמַּיִם הַמְאָרְרִים, וְלֹא עוֹד אֶלָּא "וְנִזְרְעָה זָרַע", אִם הָיְתָה יוֹלֶדֶת בְּצַעַר תֵּלֵד בְּרֶוַח, אִם הָיְתָה יוֹלֶדֶת שְׁחוֹרִים יוֹלֶדֶת לְבָנִים:

ל **אוֹ אִישׁ.** כְּמוֹ "אוֹ נוֹדַע" (שמות כא, לו), כְּלוֹמַר, אִם אִישׁ קַנַּאי הוּא, לְכָךְ "וְהֶעֱמִיד אֶת הָאִשָּׁה":

לא **וְנִקָּה הָאִישׁ מֵעָוֹן.** אִם בְּדָקוּהָ הַמַּיִם, אַל יִדְאַג לוֹמַר 'חָבְתִּי בְּמִיתָתָהּ', נָקִי הוּא מִן הָעֹנֶשׁ. דָּבָר אַחֵר, מִשֶּׁיַּשְׁקֶנָּה תְּהֵא אֶצְלוֹ בְּהֶתֵּר וְנִקָּה מֵעָוֹן, שֶׁהַסּוֹטָה אֲסוּרָה לְבַעְלָהּ:

ו ב **כִּי יַפְלִא.** "יַפְרִישׁ". לָמָּה נִסְמְכָה פָּרָשַׁת נָזִיר לְפָרָשַׁת סוֹטָה? לוֹמַר לְךָ שֶׁכָּל הָרוֹאֶה סוֹטָה בְּקִלְקוּלָהּ יַזִּיר עַצְמוֹ מִן הַיַּיִן שֶׁהוּא מֵבִיא לִידֵי נִאוּף: **נֶדֶר נָזִיר.** אֵין נְזִירָה בְּכָל מָקוֹם אֶלָּא פְּרִישָׁה, אַף כָּאן שֶׁפּוֹרֵשׁ מִן הַיַּיִן: **לְהַזִּיר לַה'.** לְהַבְדִּיל עַצְמוֹ מִן הַיַּיִן לְשֵׁם שָׁמַיִם:

ג **מִיַּיִן וְשֵׁכָר.** כְּתַרְגּוּמוֹ: "מֵחֲמַר חֲדַת וְעַתִּיק", שֶׁהַיַּיִן מְשַׁכֵּר כְּשֶׁהוּא

opinion. For them the sin lay in becoming a nazirite in the first place and thereby denying himself some of the pleasures God created and declared good. R. Eliezer added: "From this we may infer that if one who denies himself the enjoyment of wine is called a sinner, all the more so one who denies himself other pleasures of life" (Taanit 11a; Nedarim 10a).

כה וּבָאוּ בָהּ הַמַּיִם הַמְאָרְרִים לְמָרִים׃ וְלָקַח הַכֹּהֵן מִיַּד הָאִשָּׁה אֵת
מִנְחַת הַקְּנָאֹת וְהֵנִיף אֶת־הַמִּנְחָה לִפְנֵי יהוה וְהִקְרִיב אֹתָהּ אֶל־
כו הַמִּזְבֵּחַ׃ וְקָמַץ הַכֹּהֵן מִן־הַמִּנְחָה אֶת־אַזְכָּרָתָהּ וְהִקְטִיר הַמִּזְבֵּחָה
כז וְאַחַר יַשְׁקֶה אֶת־הָאִשָּׁה אֶת־הַמָּיִם׃ וְהִשְׁקָהּ אֶת־הַמַּיִם וְהָיְתָה
אִם־נִטְמְאָה וַתִּמְעֹל מַעַל בְּאִישָׁהּ וּבָאוּ בָהּ הַמַּיִם הַמְאָרְרִים לְמָרִים
כח וְצָבְתָה בִטְנָהּ וְנָפְלָה יְרֵכָהּ וְהָיְתָה הָאִשָּׁה לְאָלָה בְּקֶרֶב עַמָּהּ׃ וְאִם־
כט לֹא נִטְמְאָה הָאִשָּׁה וּטְהֹרָה הִוא וְנִקְּתָה וְנִזְרְעָה זָרַע׃ זֹאת תּוֹרַת
ל הַקְּנָאֹת אֲשֶׁר תִּשְׂטֶה אִשָּׁה תַּחַת אִישָׁהּ וְנִטְמָאָה׃ אוֹ אִישׁ אֲשֶׁר
תַּעֲבֹר עָלָיו רוּחַ קִנְאָה וְקִנֵּא אֶת־אִשְׁתּוֹ וְהֶעֱמִיד אֶת־הָאִשָּׁה לִפְנֵי
לא יהוה וְעָשָׂה לָהּ הַכֹּהֵן אֵת כָּל־הַתּוֹרָה הַזֹּאת׃ וְנִקָּה הָאִישׁ מֵעָוֺן
וְהָאִשָּׁה הַהִוא תִּשָּׂא אֶת־עֲוֺנָהּ׃
ו א ב וַיְדַבֵּר יהוה אֶל־מֹשֶׁה לֵּאמֹר׃ דַּבֵּר אֶל־בְּנֵי יִשְׂרָאֵל וְאָמַרְתָּ אֲלֵהֶם
ג אִישׁ אוֹ־אִשָּׁה כִּי יַפְלִא לִנְדֹּר נֶדֶר נָזִיר לְהַזִּיר לַיהוה׃ מִיַּיִן וְשֵׁכָר

אונקלוס

וְיֵיעֲלוּן בַּהּ, מַיָּא מְלַטְטַיָּא לִלְוָט: כה וְיִסַּב כָּהֲנָא מִידָא דְאִתְּתָא, יָת
מִנְחַת קִנְאָתָא, וִירִים יָת מִנְחָתָא קֳדָם יְיָ, וִיקָרֵיב יָתַהּ לְמַדְבְּחָא: כו
וְיִקְמוֹץ כָּהֲנָא מִן מִנְחָתָא יָת אַדְכָּרְתַהּ, וְיַסֵּיק לְמַדְבְּחָא, וּבָתַר כֵּן,
יַשְׁקֵי יָת אִתְּתָא יָת מַיָּא: כז וְיַשְׁקֵינַהּ יָת מַיָּא, וּתְהֵי אִם אִסְתָּאָבַת
וְשַׁקָּרַת שְׁקַר בְּבַעְלַהּ, וְיֵיעֲלוּן בַּהּ, מַיָּא מְלַטְטַיָּא לִלְוָט, וְיִפְּחוּן
מְעַהָא, וְתִתְמְסֵי יַרְכַּהּ, וּתְהֵי אִתְּתָא, לִלְוָטָא בְּגוֹ עַמַּהּ: כח וְאִם
לָא אִסְתָּאָבַת אִתְּתָא, וְדַכְיָא הִיא, וְתִפּוֹק זַכָּאָה וּתְעַדֵּי עִדּוּי: כט
דָּא אוֹרָיְתָא דְקִנְאָתָא, דְּתִסְטֵי אִתְּתָא, בַּר מִבַּעְלַהּ וְתִסְתָּאַב: ל אוֹ
גְבַר, דְּתִעְבַּר עֲלוֹהִי, רוּחַ קִנְאָה וִיקַנֵּי יָת אִתְּתֵיהּ, וִיקִים יָת אִתְּתָא
קֳדָם יְיָ, וְיַעֲבֵיד לַהּ כָּהֲנָא, יָת כָּל אוֹרָיְתָא הָדָא: לא וִיהֵי זַכָּאָה גֻּבְרָא
מֵחוֹבִין, וְאִתְּתָא הַהִיא, תְּקַבֵּיל יָת חוֹבַהּ: ו א וּמַלֵּיל יְיָ עִם מֹשֶׁה
לְמֵימַר: ב מַלֵּיל עִם בְּנֵי יִשְׂרָאֵל, וְתֵימַר לְהוֹן, גְּבַר אוֹ אִתָּא, אֲרֵי
יַפְרֵישׁ לְמִדַּר נְדַר נְזִירוּ, לְמַזַּר קֳדָם יְיָ: ג מֵחֲמַר חֲדַת וְעַתִּיק יַזַּר,

THE NAZIRITE

The nazirite is an individual who undertakes the special rules of holiness and abstinence: not to drink alcohol (or anything made from grapes), not to have his hair cut, and to avoid contact with the dead. Living as a nazirite was usually undertaken for a limited time period; the standard length was thirty days. The Torah calls the nazirite "holy to the Lord" (Num. 6:8). Intriguingly, however, it requires him, at the end of the period of his vow, to bring a purification offering, as if he had sinned (6:13–14).

This led to an ongoing disagreement between the Rabbis. According to R. Elazar, and later Ramban, the nazirite is praiseworthy. He has voluntarily undertaken a higher level of holiness. The reason he had to bring a sin offering was that he was now returning to ordinary life. His sin lay in *ceasing* to be a nazirite. R. Eliezer HaKappar and Shmuel held the opposite

drink neither vinegar made from wine nor vinegar made from any other strong
drink, nor may he drink any juice made with grapes, nor eat fresh grapes or
4 raisins. All the days of his separation he must not eat anything that comes from
5 the grapevine, from seed to skin. All the days of his separation vow, no razor
shall touch his head. Until the completion of the time for which he separated
himself to the Lord, he shall be holy, and must let the locks of his hair grow
6 long. All the days of his separation to the Lord, he must not come near a
7 dead body. Even for his father or mother or brother or sister, if they die, he
8 must not defile himself, for his vow of separation to his God is on his head. All
9 the days of his separation he is holy to the Lord. If someone dies suddenly
beside him, defiling his consecrated head, he shall shave his head on the day

רש״י

יָשָׁן: **וְכָל מִשְׁרַת.** לְשׁוֹן שְׁרִיָּה בַּמַּיִם אוֹ בְּכָל מַשְׁקֶה, וּבִלְשׁוֹן מִשְׁנָה יֵשׁ הַרְבֵּה: ״אֵין שׁוֹרִין דְּיוֹ וְסַמָּנִים״ (שבת יז ע״ב), ״נָזִיר שֶׁשָּׁרָה פִּתּוֹ בְּיַיִן״ (נזיר לז ע״א):

ד **חַרְצַנִּים.** הֵם הַגַּרְעִינִין: **זָג.** הֵם קְלִפּוֹת שֶׁמִּבַּחוּץ, שֶׁהַחַרְצַנִּים בְּתוֹכָן כְּעִנְבָּל בַּזּוּג:

ה **קָדֹשׁ יִהְיֶה.** הַשֵּׂעָר שֶׁלּוֹ, לְגַדֵּל הַפֶּרַע שֶׁל שְׂעַר רֹאשׁוֹ: **פֶּרַע שְׂעַר.** נָקוּד פַּתָּח לְפִי שֶׁהוּא דָּבוּק לִ״שְׂעַר רֹאשׁוֹ״, פֶּרַע שֶׁל שֵׂעָר. וּפֵרוּשׁוֹ שֶׁל ״פֶּרַע״ גִּדּוּל שֶׁל שֵׂעָר. וְכֵן ״אֶת רֹאשׁוֹ לֹא יִפְרָע״ (ויקרא כא, י), וְאֵין קָרוּי פֶּרַע פָּחוֹת מִשְּׁלֹשִׁים יוֹם:

ח **כֹּל יְמֵי נִזְרוֹ קָדֹשׁ הוּא.** זוֹ קְדֻשַּׁת הַגּוּף מִלִּטַּמֵּא לְמֵתִים:

ט **פֶּתַע.** זֶה אֹנֶס: **פִּתְאֹם.** זֶה שׁוֹגֵג. וְיֵשׁ אוֹמְרִים: ״פֶּתַע פִּתְאֹם״ דָּבָר אֶחָד הוּא, מִקְרֶה שֶׁל פִּתְאֹם:

self-denial. He has adopted the path of personal perfection. That is noble, commendable, and exemplary. That is why Rambam calls him "praiseworthy" and "the equal of a prophet."

But it is not the way of the sage – and if you seek to perfect society, you need sages. The sage is not an extremist – because he or she realizes that there are other people at stake. There are one's family, colleagues, and community. There is a country to defend and a society to help build. The sage knows he or she cannot leave all these commitments behind to pursue a life of solitary virtue. We are called on by God to live in the world and to strive toward a balance among the conflicting pressures on us – in society, not in seclusion.

6:4 מִכֹּל אֲשֶׁר יֵעָשֶׂה מִגֶּפֶן הַיַּיִן *Anything that comes from the grapevine* – "He makes... wine to cheer people's hearts," says the psalmist (Ps. 104:14–15), celebrating one of the sources of enjoyment God created for our benefit. Nonetheless, almost every religion knows the phenomenon of people who, in pursuit of spiritual purity, withdraw from the pleasures and temptations of the world. The ambivalence of Jews toward the life of self-denial may lie in the suspicion that it entered Judaism from the outside. There were ascetic movements in the first centuries of the Common Era in both the West (Greece) and the East (Iran) that saw the physical world as a place of corruption and strife. They were, in fact, dualists, holding that the true God was not the creator of the universe. The physical world was the work of a lesser, and evil, deity. Therefore God – the true God – is not to be found in the physical world and its enjoyments but rather in disengagement from them.

We have seen that Judaism is in two minds about the nazirite. At least some of the negative evaluation of the nazirite among the Rabbis may have been driven by a desire to discourage Jews from imitating non-Jewish practices. Judaism strongly believes that God is to be found in the midst of the physical world that He created that is, in the first chapter of Genesis, seven times pronounced "good." According to many, it believes not in renouncing pleasure but in sanctifying it.

יַזִּ֔יר חֹ֥מֶץ יַ֛יִן וְחֹ֥מֶץ שֵׁכָ֖ר לֹ֣א יִשְׁתֶּ֑ה וְכָל־מִשְׁרַ֤ת עֲנָבִים֙ לֹ֣א יִשְׁתֶּ֔ה
ד וַעֲנָבִ֥ים לַחִ֛ים וִיבֵשִׁ֖ים לֹ֥א יֹאכֵֽל׃ כֹּ֖ל יְמֵ֣י נִזְר֑וֹ מִכֹּל֩ אֲשֶׁ֨ר יֵעָשֶׂ֜ה מִגֶּ֣פֶן
ה הַיַּ֗יִן מֵחַרְצַנִּ֛ים וְעַד־זָ֖ג לֹ֥א יֹאכֵֽל׃ כָּל־יְמֵי֙ נֶ֣דֶר נִזְר֔וֹ תַּ֖עַר לֹא־יַעֲבֹ֣ר
עַל־רֹאשׁ֑וֹ עַד־מְלֹ֨את הַיָּמִ֜ם אֲשֶׁר־יַזִּ֤יר לַֽיהוה֙ קָדֹ֣שׁ יִהְיֶ֔ה גַּדֵּ֥ל פֶּ֖רַע
ו שְׂעַ֥ר רֹאשֽׁוֹ׃ כָּל־יְמֵ֥י הַזִּיר֖וֹ לַֽיהוה עַל־נֶ֥פֶשׁ מֵ֖ת לֹ֥א יָבֹֽא׃ לְאָבִ֣יו וּלְאִמּ֗וֹ
ח לְאָחִיו֙ וּלְאַ֣חֹת֔וֹ לֹא־יִטַּמָּ֥א לָהֶ֖ם בְּמֹתָ֑ם כִּ֛י נֵ֥זֶר אֱלֹהָ֖יו עַל־רֹאשֽׁוֹ׃ כֹּ֖ל
ט יְמֵ֣י נִזְר֑וֹ קָדֹ֥שׁ ה֖וּא לַֽיהוה׃ וְכִֽי־יָמ֨וּת מֵ֤ת עָלָיו֙ בְּפֶ֣תַע פִּתְאֹ֔ם וְטִמֵּ֖א

אונקלוס

חַל דַּחֲמַר חֲדַת, וְחַל דַּחֲמַר עַתִּיק לָא יִשְׁתֵּי, וְכָל מַתְרוּת עִנְּבִין לָא יִשְׁתֵּי, וְעִנְּבִין, רַטִּיבִין וִיבִישִׁין לָא יֵיכוֹל: ד כָּל יוֹמֵי נְזִרֵיהּ, מִכֹּל דְּיִתְעֲבֵיד מִגֻּפְנָא דְּחַמְרָא, מִפֻּרְצְנִין, וְעַד עֻצּוּרִין לָא יֵיכוֹל: ה כָּל יוֹמֵי נְדַר נְזִרֵיהּ, מַסְפַּר לָא יִעְבַּר עַל רֵישֵׁיהּ, עַד מִשְׁלַם יוֹמַיָּא, דִּנְזִיר קֳדָם יי קַדִּישׁ יְהֵי, יְרַבֵּי פֵּירוּעַ סְעַר רֵישֵׁיהּ: ו כָּל יוֹמִין דִּנְזִיר קֳדָם יי, עַל נַפְשַׁת מִיתָא לָא יֵיעוֹל: ז לַאֲבוּהִי וּלְאִמֵּיהּ, לַאֲחוּהִי וּלְאַחָתֵיהּ, לָא יִסְתָּאַב לְהוֹן בְּמוֹתְהוֹן, אֲרֵי, נְזָרָא דֶּאֱלָהֵיהּ עַל רֵישֵׁיהּ: ח כָּל יוֹמֵי נְזִרֵיהּ, קַדִּישׁ הוּא קֳדָם יי: ט וַאֲרֵי יְמוּת מִיתָא עֲלוֹהִי בִּתְכֵיף שָׁלוּ, וִיסָאֵיב

Rambam, surprisingly, holds *both* views regarding the nazirite, positive and negative, in the same book – his law code the *Mishneh Torah*. In the section *Hilkhot Deot*, he adopts the negative position of R. Eliezer:

> A person may say: "Desire, honor, and the like are bad paths to follow and remove a person from the world; therefore I will completely separate myself from them and go to the other extreme." As a result, he does not eat meat or drink wine or take a wife or live in a decent house or wear decent clothing.... This too is bad, and it is forbidden to choose this way. (*Hilkhot Deot* 3:1)

Yet in *Hilkhot Nezirut* he rules in accordance with the positive evaluation of R. Elazar: "Whoever vows to God [to become a nazirite] by way of holiness, he does well and is praiseworthy.... Indeed Scripture considers him the equal of a prophet" (*Hilkhot Nezirut* 10:14).

The resolution of these two contradictory opinions lies in a remarkable insight into the nature of the moral life. What Rambam saw is that there is not a single model of the virtuous life. He identifies two, calling them the way of the saint (*ḥasid*) and the way of the sage (*ḥakham*).

The saint is a person of extremes. Rambam defines *ḥesed* as extreme behavior – good behavior, to be sure, but conduct in excess of what strict justice requires (*Guide for the Perplexed* III:52). So, for example, "if one avoids haughtiness to the utmost extent and becomes exceedingly humble, he is termed a saint (*ḥasid*)" (*Hilkhot Deot* 1:5).

The sage is a different kind of person altogether. He or she follows the "golden mean," the "middle way," the way of moderation and balance. He or she avoids the extremes of cowardice on the one hand, recklessness on the other, and thus acquires the virtue of courage. He or she avoids miserliness in one direction, prodigality in the other, and instead chooses the middle way of generosity. The sage weighs the conflicting pressures and avoids the extremes.

Is the aim of the moral life to achieve personal perfection? Or is it to create gracious relationships and a decent, just, compassionate society? The intuitive answer of most people would be to say: both. Rambam realized that they are in fact different enterprises.

It was this insight that led Rambam to his seemingly contradictory evaluations of the nazirite. The nazirite has chosen, at least for a period, to adopt a life of extreme

10 of his purification; on the seventh day he shall shave it. Then, on the eighth
day, he shall bring two turtledoves or two young pigeons to the priest, to the
11 entrance of the Tent of Meeting. The priest will offer one as a purification
offering and the other as a burnt offering, and make atonement for him for
the guilt he incurred through contact with the dead body. He shall consecrate
12 his head anew on that day. He must rededicate himself to the LORD for the
full term of his vow, and bring a yearling lamb as a guilt offering. The former
13 days are discounted because his separation was defiled. This is the law of the
nazirite: On the day that the term of his nazirite vow is completed, he shall be
14 brought to the entrance to the Tent of Meeting. He shall present his offering
to the LORD: one male yearling lamb without blemish for a burnt offering, one
yearling ewe lamb without blemish for a purification offering, one ram without
15 blemish for a peace offering, and a basket of unleavened bread, loaves of fine
flour mixed with olive oil, and unleavened wafers smeared with olive oil, along
16 with their grain offering and libations. The priest shall present these before the
17 LORD and offer up his purification offering and his burnt offering. He shall
then offer the ram as a sacrifice, a peace offering to the LORD, together with
the basket of unleavened bread. The priest shall also offer his grain offering and
18 his libation. The nazirite shall shave his consecrated hair at the entrance to the
Tent of Meeting and take the hair of his consecrated head and place it on the
19 fire beneath the peace offering. The priest shall take the boiled foreleg of the
ram, one unleavened loaf from the basket, and one unleavened wafer, and place

רש״י

וְכִי יָמוּת מֵת עָלָיו. בָּאֹהֶל שֶׁהוּא בוֹ: **בְּיוֹם טָהֳרָתוֹ.** בְּיוֹם הַזָּאָתוֹ. אוֹ אֵינוֹ אֶלָּא בַּשְּׁמִינִי שֶׁהוּא טָהוֹר לְגַמְרֵי? תַּלְמוּד לוֹמַר: ״בַּיּוֹם הַשְּׁבִיעִי״. אִי שְׁבִיעִי, יָכוֹל אֲפִלּוּ לֹא הִזָּה? תַּלְמוּד לוֹמַר: ״בְּיוֹם טָהֳרָתוֹ״:

י **וּבַיּוֹם הַשְּׁמִינִי יָבִא שְׁתֵּי תֹרִים.** לְהוֹצִיא אֶת הַשְּׁבִיעִי. אוֹ אֵינוֹ אֶלָּא לְהוֹצִיא אֶת הַתְּשִׁיעִי? קָבַע זְמַן לַקָּרְבָּן וְקָבַע זְמַן לַמַּקְרִיבִין, מַה קָּרְבָּן הִכְשִׁיר שְׁמִינִי וּמִשְּׁמִינִי וָהָלְאָה, אַף מַקְרִיבִין שְׁמִינִי וּמִשְּׁמִינִי וָהָלְאָה:

יא **מֵאֲשֶׁר חָטָא עַל הַנָּפֶשׁ.** שֶׁלֹּא נִזְהַר מִטֻּמְאַת הַמֵּת. רַבִּי אֶלְעָזָר הַקַּפָּר אוֹמֵר: שֶׁצִּעֵר עַצְמוֹ מִן הַיַּיִן: **וְקִדַּשׁ אֶת רֹאשׁוֹ.** לַחֲזֹר וּלְהַתְחִיל מִנְיַן נְזִירוּתוֹ:

יב **וְהִזִּיר לַה׳ אֶת יְמֵי נִזְרוֹ.** יַחֲזֹר וְיִמְנֶה נְזִירוּתוֹ כְּבַתְּחִלָּה: **וְהַיָּמִים הָרִאשֹׁנִים יִפְּלוּ.** לֹא יַעֲלוּ מִן הַמִּנְיָן:

יג **יָבִיא אֹתוֹ.** יָבִיא אֶת עַצְמוֹ, וְזֶה אֶחָד מִשְּׁלֹשָׁה אֶתִים שֶׁהָיָה רַבִּי יִשְׁמָעֵאל דּוֹרֵשׁ כֵּן. כַּיּוֹצֵא בוֹ: ״וְהִשִּׂיאוּ אוֹתָם עֲוֹן אַשְׁמָה״ (ויקרא כב, טז), אֶת עַצְמָם; כַּיּוֹצֵא בוֹ: ״וַיִּקְבֹּר אֹתוֹ בַגַּי״ (דברים לד, ו), הוּא קָבַר אֶת עַצְמוֹ:

טו **וּמִנְחָתָם וְנִסְכֵּיהֶם.** שֶׁל עוֹלָה וּשְׁלָמִים, לְפִי שֶׁהָיוּ בַּכְּלָל וְיָצְאוּ לִדּוֹן בְּדָבָר חָדָשׁ שֶׁיִּטְעֲנוּ לֶחֶם, הֶחֱזִירָן לִכְלָלָן שֶׁיִּטָּעֲנוּ נְסָכִים כְּדִין עוֹלָה וּשְׁלָמִים: **חַלֹּת בְּלוּלֹת וּרְקִיקֵי מַצּוֹת.** עֶשֶׂר מִכָּל מִין:

יז **זֶבַח שְׁלָמִים לַה׳ עַל סַל הַמַּצּוֹת.** יִשְׁחַט אֶת הַשְּׁלָמִים עַל מְנָת לְקַדֵּשׁ אֶת הַלֶּחֶם: **אֶת מִנְחָתוֹ וְאֶת נִסְכּוֹ.** שֶׁל אַיִל:

יח **וְגִלַּח הַנָּזִיר פֶּתַח אֹהֶל מוֹעֵד.** יָכוֹל יְגַלַּח בָּעֲזָרָה? הֲרֵי זֶה דֶּרֶךְ בִּזָּיוֹן! אֶלָּא ״וְגִלַּח הַנָּזִיר״ לְאַחַר שְׁחִיטַת הַשְּׁלָמִים שֶׁכָּתוּב בָּהֶן: ״וּשְׁחָטוֹ פֶּתַח אֹהֶל מוֹעֵד״ (ויקרא ג, ב): **אֲשֶׁר תַּחַת זֶבַח הַשְּׁלָמִים.** תַּחַת הַדּוּד שֶׁהוּא מְבַשְּׁלָן בּוֹ, לְפִי שֶׁשַּׁלְמֵי נָזִיר הָיוּ מִתְבַּשְּׁלִין בָּעֲזָרָה, שֶׁצָּרִיךְ לִטֹּל הַכֹּהֵן הַזְּרוֹעַ אַחַר שֶׁנִּתְבַּשְּׁלָה וּלְהָנִיף לִפְנֵי ה׳:

יט **הַזְּרֹעַ בְּשֵׁלָה.** לְאַחַר שֶׁנִּתְבַּשְּׁלָה:

רֹאשׁ נִזְרוֹ וְגִלַּח רֹאשׁוֹ בְּיוֹם טָהֳרָתוֹ בַּיּוֹם הַשְּׁבִיעִי יְגַלְּחֶנּוּ׃ וּבַיּוֹם
הַשְּׁמִינִי יָבִא שְׁתֵּי תֹרִים אוֹ שְׁנֵי בְּנֵי יוֹנָה אֶל־הַכֹּהֵן אֶל־פֶּתַח אֹהֶל
יא מוֹעֵד׃ וְעָשָׂה הַכֹּהֵן אֶחָד לְחַטָּאת וְאֶחָד לְעֹלָה וְכִפֶּר עָלָיו מֵאֲשֶׁר
יב חָטָא עַל־הַנָּפֶשׁ וְקִדַּשׁ אֶת־רֹאשׁוֹ בַּיּוֹם הַהוּא׃ וְהִזִּיר לַיהוה אֶת־
יְמֵי נִזְרוֹ וְהֵבִיא כֶּבֶשׂ בֶּן־שְׁנָתוֹ לְאָשָׁם וְהַיָּמִים הָרִאשֹׁנִים יִפְּלוּ כִּי
יג טָמֵא נִזְרוֹ׃ וְזֹאת תּוֹרַת הַנָּזִיר בְּיוֹם מְלֹאת יְמֵי נִזְרוֹ יָבִיא אֹתוֹ אֶל־
יד פֶּתַח אֹהֶל מוֹעֵד׃ וְהִקְרִיב אֶת־קָרְבָּנוֹ לַיהוה כֶּבֶשׂ בֶּן־שְׁנָתוֹ תָמִים
אֶחָד לְעֹלָה וְכַבְשָׂה אַחַת בַּת־שְׁנָתָהּ תְּמִימָה לְחַטָּאת וְאַיִל־אֶחָד
טו תָּמִים לִשְׁלָמִים׃ וְסַל מַצּוֹת סֹלֶת חַלֹּת בְּלוּלֹת בַּשֶּׁמֶן וּרְקִיקֵי מַצּוֹת
טז מְשֻׁחִים בַּשָּׁמֶן וּמִנְחָתָם וְנִסְכֵּיהֶם׃ וְהִקְרִיב הַכֹּהֵן לִפְנֵי יהוה וְעָשָׂה
יז אֶת־חַטָּאתוֹ וְאֶת־עֹלָתוֹ׃ וְאֶת־הָאַיִל יַעֲשֶׂה זֶבַח שְׁלָמִים לַיהוה עַל
יח סַל הַמַּצּוֹת וְעָשָׂה הַכֹּהֵן אֶת־מִנְחָתוֹ וְאֶת־נִסְכּוֹ׃ וְגִלַּח הַנָּזִיר פֶּתַח
אֹהֶל מוֹעֵד אֶת־רֹאשׁ נִזְרוֹ וְלָקַח אֶת־שְׂעַר רֹאשׁ נִזְרוֹ וְנָתַן עַל־הָאֵשׁ
יט אֲשֶׁר־תַּחַת זֶבַח הַשְּׁלָמִים׃ וְלָקַח הַכֹּהֵן אֶת־הַזְּרֹעַ בְּשֵׁלָה מִן־הָאַיִל
וְחַלַּת מַצָּה אַחַת מִן־הַסַּל וּרְקִיק מַצָּה אֶחָד וְנָתַן עַל־כַּפֵּי הַנָּזִיר אַחַר

אונקלוס

רֵישׁ נְזִרֵיהּ, וִיגַלַּח רֵישֵׁיהּ בְּיוֹמָא דִּדְכוּתֵיהּ, בְּיוֹמָא שְׁבִיעָאָה
יְגַלְּחִנֵּיהּ: י וּבְיוֹמָא תְּמִינָאָה, יַיְתֵי תַּרְתֵּין שַׁפְנִינִין, אוֹ תְּרֵין בְּנֵי יוֹנָה,
לְוָת כָּהֲנָא, לִתְרַע מַשְׁכַּן זִמְנָא: יא וְיַעֲבֵיד כָּהֲנָא, חַד לְחַטָּתָא וְחַד
לַעֲלָתָא, וִיכַפַּר עֲלוֹהִי, מִדְּחָב עַל מִיתָא, וִיקַדֵּישׁ יָת רֵישֵׁיהּ בְּיוֹמָא
הַהוּא: יב וְיַזֵּר קֳדָם יְיָ יָת יוֹמֵי נְזִרֵיהּ, וְיַיְתֵי, אִמַּר בַּר שַׁתֵּיהּ לַאֲשָׁמָא,
וְיוֹמַיָּא קַדְמָאֵי יִבְטְלוּן, אֲרֵי אִסְתְּאַב נְזִרֵיהּ: יג וְדָא אוֹרָיְתָא
דִּנְזִירָא, בְּיוֹם, מִשְׁלַם יוֹמֵי נְזִרֵיהּ, יַיְתֵי יָתֵיהּ, לִתְרַע מַשְׁכַּן זִמְנָא:
יד וִיקָרֵיב יָת קֻרְבָּנֵיהּ קֳדָם יְיָ, אִמַּר בַּר שַׁתֵּיהּ שְׁלִים חַד לַעֲלָתָא,
וְאִמַּרְתָּא חֲדָא בַּת שַׁתַּהּ, שַׁלְמְתָא לְחַטָּתָא, וּדְכַר חַד שְׁלִים
לְנִכְסַת קֻדְשַׁיָּא: טו וְסַל פַּטִּיר, סוֹלֶת גְּרִיצָן דְּפִילָן בִּמְשַׁח, וְאֶסְפּוֹגִין
פַּטִּירִין דִּמְשִׁיחִין בִּמְשַׁח, וּמִנְחָתְהוֹן וְנִסְכֵּיהוֹן: טז וִיקָרֵיב כָּהֲנָא
קֳדָם יְיָ, וְיַעֲבֵיד יָת חַטָּתֵיהּ וְיָת עֲלָתֵיהּ: יז וְיָת דִּכְרָא, יַעֲבֵיד נִכְסַת
קֻדְשַׁיָּא קֳדָם יְיָ, עַל סַלָּא דְּפַטִּירַיָּא, וְיַעֲבֵיד כָּהֲנָא, יָת מִנְחָתֵיהּ
וְיָת נִסְכֵּיהּ: יח וִיגַלַּח נְזִירָא, בִּתְרַע, מַשְׁכַּן זִמְנָא יָת רֵישׁ נְזִרֵיהּ,
וְיִסַּב, יָת סְעַר רֵישׁ נְזִרֵיהּ, וְיִתֵּין עַל אִישָׁתָא, דִּתְחוֹת דּוּדָא דְּנִכְסַת
קֻדְשַׁיָּא: יט וְיִסַּב כָּהֲנָא, יָת דְּרָעָא בְּשֵׁילָא מִן דִּכְרָא, וּגְרִיצְתָּא
פַּטִּירְתָּא חֲדָא מִן סַלָּא, וְאֶסְפּוֹג פַּטִּיר חַד, וְיִתֵּין עַל יְדֵי נְזִירָא, בָּתַר

them on the hands of the nazirite after he has shaved his consecrated head.
20 The priest shall wave them as a wave offering before the LORD. It is a sacred
gift for the priest, together with the breast of the wave offering and the thigh of
21 the upraised gift. After this the nazirite may drink wine." This is the law of the
nazirite who vows offerings to the LORD as a nazirite. Whatever he can afford
further and vows to give, beyond what the law of the nazirite obliges him to,
that too shall he fulfill.
22 23 The LORD spoke to Moshe: "Tell Aharon and his sons: This is how you are
24 to bless the Israelites. Say to them: 'May the LORD bless you and

רש״י

כ **קֹדֶשׁ הוּא לַכֹּהֵן.** הַחַלָּה וְהָרָקִיק וְהַזְּרֹעַ תְּרוּמָה הֵן לַכֹּהֵן: **עַל חֲזֵה הַתְּנוּפָה.** מִלְּבַד חָזֶה וָשׁוֹק הָרְאוּיִים לוֹ מִכָּל שְׁלָמִים, מוּסָף עַל שַׁלְמֵי נָזִיר הַזְּרוֹעַ הַזֶּה. לְפִי שֶׁהָיוּ שַׁלְמֵי נָזִיר בִּכְלָל וְיָצְאוּ לִדּוֹן בַּדָּבָר הֶחָדָשׁ לְהַפְרָשַׁת זְרוֹעַ, הֻצְרַךְ לְהַחֲזִירָן לִכְלָלָן לִדּוֹן אַף בְּחָזֶה וָשׁוֹק:

כא **מִלְּבַד אֲשֶׁר תַּשִּׂיג יָדוֹ.** שֶׁאִם אָמַר: 'הֲרֵינִי נָזִיר עַל מְנָת לְגַלֵּחַ עַל מֵאָה עוֹלוֹת וְעַל מֵאָה שְׁלָמִים' – "כְּפִי נִדְרוֹ אֲשֶׁר יִדֹּר כֵּן יַעֲשֶׂה" מוּסָף "עַל תּוֹרַת נִזְרוֹ", עַל תּוֹרַת הַנָּזִיר מוֹסִיף וְלֹא יְחַסֵּר, שֶׁאִם אָמַר: 'הֲרֵינִי נָזִיר חָמֵשׁ נְזִירוֹת עַל מְנָת לְגַלֵּחַ עַל שָׁלֹשׁ בְּהֵמוֹת הַלָּלוּ', אֵין אֲנִי קוֹרֵא בוֹ 'כַּאֲשֶׁר יִדֹּר כֵּן יַעֲשֶׂה':

כג **אָמוֹר לָהֶם.** כְּמוֹ 'זָכוֹר', 'שָׁמוֹר', בְּלַעַז דישנ"ט: **אָמוֹר לָהֶם.** שֶׁיִּהְיוּ כֻּלָּם שׁוֹמְעִים: **אָמוֹר.** מָלֵא, לֹא תְּבָרְכֵם בְּחִפָּזוֹן וּבֶהָלוּת אֶלָּא בְּכַוָּנָה וּבְלֵב שָׁלֵם:

כד **יְבָרֶכְךָ.** שֶׁיִּתְבָּרְכוּ נְכָסֶיךָ:

However, it seems to me that the explanation is this: The Torah explicitly says that, though the priests say the words, it is God who sends the blessing. "They shall set My name upon the Israelites, and I will bless them." Normally when we fulfill a mitzva, we are doing something. But when the *kohanim* bless the people, they are not doing anything in and of themselves. Instead they are acting as channels through which God's blessing flows into the world and into our lives. An ancient midrash says: "The House of Israel said to the Holy One, blessed be He, 'LORD of the Universe, You order the priests to bless us? We need only Your blessing. Look down from Your holy habitation and bless Your people.' The Holy One, blessed be He, replied to them, 'Though I ordered the priests to bless you, I will stand together with them and bless you'" (Tanḥuma, Naso 15). Love enables this to happen. Love means that we are focused not on ourselves but on another. Love is selflessness. And selflessness allows us to be a channel through which flows a force greater than ourselves.

6:24 **יְבָרֶכְךָ יהוה וְיִשְׁמְרֶךָ** *May the LORD bless you and watch over you* – Blessing in the Mosaic books always means material blessing. Against the idea basic to many other faith systems – which embrace poverty, asceticism, or other forms of self-denial – in Judaism, the world as God's creation is fundamentally good. Religion is neither otherworldly nor anti-worldly. It is precisely in the physical world that God's blessings are to be found.

But material blessings can sometimes dull our sensitivities toward God. The irony is that when we have the most to thank God for, often we thank Him least. We tend to remember God in times of crisis rather than in times of prosperity and peace.

This, more than any other factor, has led to the decline and fall of civilizations. In the early, pioneering years they are lifted by a collective vision and energy. Then as people become affluent they begin to lose the very qualities that made earlier generations great. They become less motivated by ideals than by the pursuit of pleasure. They think less of others, more of themselves. They begin to be deaf and blind to those in need. They become decadent. What happens to nations happens also to individuals and families. Hence the first blessing. "May the LORD... watch over you" means: may He protect you from the blessing turning into a curse.

כ הִתְגַּלְּחוֹ אֶת־נִזְרוֹ׃ וְהֵנִיף אוֹתָם הַכֹּהֵן ׀ תְּנוּפָה לִפְנֵי יהוה קֹדֶשׁ הוּא
לַכֹּהֵן עַל חֲזֵה הַתְּנוּפָה וְעַל שׁוֹק הַתְּרוּמָה וְאַחַר יִשְׁתֶּה הַנָּזִיר יָיִן׃
כא זֹאת תּוֹרַת הַנָּזִיר אֲשֶׁר יִדֹּר קָרְבָּנוֹ לַיהוה עַל־נִזְרוֹ מִלְּבַד אֲשֶׁר־תַּשִּׂיג
יָדוֹ כְּפִי נִדְרוֹ אֲשֶׁר יִדֹּר כֵּן יַעֲשֶׂה עַל תּוֹרַת נִזְרוֹ׃
כב כג וַיְדַבֵּר יהוה אֶל־מֹשֶׁה לֵּאמֹר׃ דַּבֵּר אֶל־אַהֲרֹן וְאֶל־בָּנָיו לֵאמֹר כֹּה ו
כד תְבָרְכוּ אֶת־בְּנֵי יִשְׂרָאֵל אָמוֹר לָהֶם׃ יְבָרֶכְךָ יהוה

אונקלוס

דִּיגַלַּח יָת נִזְרֵיהּ׃ כ וִירִים יָתְהוֹן כָּהֲנָא אֲרָמָא קֳדָם יי, קֻדְשָׁא הוּא לְכָהֲנָא, עַל חַדְיָא דַּאֲרָמוּתָא, וְעַל שָׁקָא דְּאַפְרָשׁוּתָא, וּבָתַר כֵּן, יִשְׁתֵּי נְזִירָא חַמְרָא׃ כא דָּא אוֹרָיְתָא דִּנְזִירָא דְּיִדַּר, קֻרְבָּנֵיהּ קֳדָם יי עַל נִזְרֵיהּ, בַּר מִדְּתַדְבֵּיק יְדֵיהּ, כְּפוּם נִדְרֵיהּ דְּיִדַּר, כֵּן יַעֲבֵיד, עַל אוֹרָיְתָא דִּנְזִרֵיהּ׃ כב וּמַלֵּיל יי עִם מֹשֶׁה לְמֵימַר׃ כג מַלֵּיל עִם אַהֲרֹן וְעִם בְּנוֹהִי לְמֵימַר, כְּדֵין תְּבָרְכוּן יָת בְּנֵי יִשְׂרָאֵל, כַּד תֵּימְרוּן לְהוֹן׃ כד יְבָרְכִנָּךְ יי

THE PRIESTLY BLESSING

The priestly blessing is one of the oldest prayers in the world still in continuous use. It has been found in amulets from the early sixth century BCE, the time of the prophet Yirmeyahu. So ancient are these, that they are written not in the Hebrew alphabet as we recognize it today, which dates from the Babylonian exile, but rather in the ancient Paleo-Hebrew script, a direct descendant of the first alphabet known to humankind. The blessing was spoken by the priests in the Temple. It is said today by the priests in the *ḥazan*'s repetition of the *Amida*, in Israel every day, in most of the Diaspora only on festivals. It is used by parents when they bless their children on Friday night. It is often said to the bride and groom under the *ḥuppa*. It is among the shortest of blessings, a mere fifteen words long, but marked by beauty and simplicity.

It has a strong rhythmic structure. The lines contain three, five, and seven words respectively. In each, the second word is "the Lord." In all three verses, the first part refers to an activity on the part of God – "bless," "make His face shine," and "raise His face toward." The second part describes the effect of the blessing on us, giving us protection, grace, and peace.

The verses also travel inward, as it were. The first verse, "May the Lord bless you and watch over you," refers, as the commentators note, to material blessings: sustenance, physical health, and so on. The second, "May the Lord make His face shine on you and be gracious to you," refers to moral blessing. *Ḥen*, grace, is what we show to other people and they to us. The third is the most inward of all. The knowledge that God raises His face toward us – that we are not just an indiscernible face in a crowd but that God relates to us in our uniqueness and singularity – is the most profound and ultimate source of peace.

Before blessing the congregation in the synagogue, *kohanim* utter a benediction, instituted by the Sages, which is unique in its wording: "Blessed are you … who has made us holy with the holiness of Aharon and has commanded us to bless His people Israel with love." The last word, *be'ahava*, is unusual. It appears in no other blessing over the performance of a command. Ideally we should fulfill all the commands with love. But an absence of love does not invalidate any other command. Surely what matters is that the priests recite the blessing; God will do the rest. What difference does it make whether they do so in love or not?

The commentators wrestle with this. Some say that the fact that the priests are facing the people when they bless means that they are like the cherubim in the Tabernacle, who faced each other as a sign of love. Others change the word order. They say that the blessing really means: "who has made us holy with the holiness of Aharon and with love has commanded us to bless His people Israel." "Love" here refers to God's love for Israel, not the love of the priests.

▶

25 watch over you. May the LORD make His face shine upon you and be
26 gracious to you. May the LORD raise His face toward you and grant
27 you peace.' They shall set My name upon the Israelites, and I will bless
7 1 them." On the day when Moshe finished establishing the Tabernacle, ḤAMISHI
he anointed it and consecrated it. He anointed and consecrated the altar, too,
2 and all its utensils. And the princes of Israel, leaders of their ancestral houses,
drew close. They were the princes of the tribes, the ones who had directed the
3 census. And they brought their offerings before the LORD: six covered wagons
and twelve oxen – a wagon for every two leaders, and for each one an ox. They

רש״י

וְיִשְׁמְרֶךָ. שֶׁלֹּא יָבוֹאוּ עָלֶיךָ שׁוֹדְדִים לִטֹּל מָמוֹנְךָ, שֶׁהַנּוֹתֵן מַתָּנָה לְעַבְדּוֹ אֵינוֹ יָכוֹל לְשָׁמְרוֹ מִכָּל אָדָם, וְכֵיוָן שֶׁבָּאִים לִסְטִים עָלָיו וְנוֹטְלִין אוֹתָהּ מִמֶּנּוּ, מָה הֲנָאָה יֵשׁ לוֹ בְּמַתָּנָה זוֹ; אֲבָל הַקָּדוֹשׁ בָּרוּךְ הוּא, הוּא הַנּוֹתֵן הוּא הַשּׁוֹמֵר. וְהַרְבֵּה מִדְרָשִׁים דָּרְשׁוּ בּוֹ בְּסִפְרֵי (מ):

כה יָאֵר ה׳ פָּנָיו אֵלֶיךָ. יַרְאֶה לְךָ פָּנִים שׂוֹחֲקוֹת, פָּנִים צְהֻבּוֹת: וִיחֻנֶּךָּ. יִתֵּן לְךָ חֵן:

כו יִשָּׂא ה׳ פָּנָיו אֵלֶיךָ. יִכְבֹּשׁ כַּעֲסוֹ:

כז וְשָׂמוּ אֶת שְׁמִי. יְבָרְכוּם בְּשֵׁם הַמְפֹרָשׁ: וַאֲנִי אֲבָרְכֵם. לְיִשְׂרָאֵל, וְאַסְכִּים עִם הַכֹּהֲנִים. דָּבָר אַחֵר, ״וַאֲנִי אֲבָרְכֵם״ לַכֹּהֲנִים:

ז א וַיְהִי בְּיוֹם כַּלּוֹת מֹשֶׁה. ׳כַּלַּת׳ כְּתִיב, יוֹם הֲקָמַת הַמִּשְׁכָּן הָיוּ יִשְׂרָאֵל כְּכַלָּה הַנִּכְנֶסֶת לַחֻפָּה: כַּלּוֹת מֹשֶׁה. בְּצַלְאֵל וְאָהֳלִיאָב וְכָל חֲכַם לֵב עָשׂוּ אֶת הַמִּשְׁכָּן וּתְלָאוֹ הַכָּתוּב בְּמֹשֶׁה, לְפִי שֶׁמָּסַר נַפְשׁוֹ עָלָיו לִרְאוֹת תַּבְנִית כָּל דָּבָר וְדָבָר כְּמוֹ שֶׁהֶרְאָהוּ בָּהָר, לְהוֹרוֹת לְעוֹשֵׂי הַמְּלָאכָה, וְלֹא טָעָה בְּתַבְנִית אַחַת. וְכֵן מָצִינוּ בְּדָוִד, לְפִי שֶׁמָּסַר נַפְשׁוֹ עַל בִּנְיַן בֵּית הַמִּקְדָּשׁ, שֶׁנֶּאֱמַר: ״זְכוֹר ה׳ לְדָוִד אֵת כָּל עֻנּוֹתוֹ אֲשֶׁר נִשְׁבַּע לַה׳״ וְגוֹ׳ (תהלים קלב, א-ב), לְפִיכָךְ נִקְרָא עַל שְׁמוֹ, שֶׁנֶּאֱמַר: ״רְאֵה בֵיתְךָ דָּוִד״ (מלכים א׳ יב, טז): בְּיוֹם כַּלּוֹת מֹשֶׁה לְהָקִים. וְלֹא נֶאֱמַר: ׳בְּיוֹם הָקִים׳, מְלַמֵּד שֶׁכָּל שִׁבְעַת יְמֵי הַמִּלּוּאִים הָיָה מֹשֶׁה מַעֲמִידוֹ וּמְפָרְקוֹ, וּבְאוֹתוֹ הַיּוֹם הֶעֱמִידוֹ וְלֹא פֵּרְקוֹ, לְכָךְ נֶאֱמַר: ״בְּיוֹם כַּלּוֹת מֹשֶׁה לְהָקִים״, אוֹתוֹ הַיּוֹם כָּלוּ הֲקָמוֹתָיו, וְרֹאשׁ חֹדֶשׁ נִיסָן הָיָה. בַּשֵּׁנִי – נִשְׂרְפָה הַפָּרָה, בַּשְּׁלִישִׁי – הִזּוּ הַזָּיָה רִאשׁוֹנָה, וּבַשְּׁבִיעִי – גִּלְּחוּ:

ב הֵם נְשִׂיאֵי הַמַּטֹּת. שֶׁהָיוּ שׁוֹטְרִים עֲלֵיהֶם בְּמִצְרַיִם וְהָיוּ מֻכִּים עֲלֵיהֶם, שֶׁנֶּאֱמַר: ״וַיֻּכּוּ שֹׁטְרֵי בְּנֵי יִשְׂרָאֵל״ וְגוֹ׳ (שמות ה, יד): הֵם הָעֹמְדִים עַל הַפְּקֻדִים. שֶׁעָמְדוּ עִם מֹשֶׁה וְאַהֲרֹן כְּשֶׁמָּנוּ אֶת יִשְׂרָאֵל, שֶׁנֶּאֱמַר: ״וְאִתְּכֶם יִהְיוּ״ וְגוֹ׳ (לעיל א, ד):

ג שֵׁשׁ עֶגְלֹת צָב. אֵין ״צָב״ אֶלָּא מְחֻפִּים, וְכֵן: ״בַּצַּבִּים וּבַפְּרָדִים״ (ישעיה

THE OFFERINGS OF THE PRINCES

One of the most visible features of Numbers as a book – conspicuously so in Parashat Naso – is the great attention it pays to tribes. The book begins with the people being counted according to tribe. Then we read about their positioning in the camp around the Tabernacle by tribe. The order in which they traveled in their journeys through the wilderness was also by tribe. In this *parasha*, at inordinate length we are told of the offerings of each tribe at the dedication of the Tabernacle, despite the fact that each brought exactly the same offering (Num. 7:1–89). Later in the book there is an account of how the land was to be allocated tribe by tribe. The book ends with the second half of the story of the daughters of Tzelofḥad, in which the leaders of their tribe bring a case to Moshe to ensure that their rights as a tribe are respected. In light of all this, the question remains insistent. Why tell the story this way? Why place the emphasis on tribes? Why was Israel not conceived as a united nation to begin with? Why orient the entire book of Numbers along the axis of tribal divisions and distinctions?

It seems that the Torah is telling us something compelling and fundamental, relevant not just then but still today. The Torah conceives of politics and identity from the ground up, not from the top down. It is not the ruler, emperor, or king who represents authority and imposes it on the population. To the contrary, the Torah takes us through the slow growth of Israel as an entity – beginning with one couple, Avraham and Sara, who become a family,

כה כו וַיִשְׁמְרֶךָ׃ יָאֵר יהוה ׀ פָּנָיו אֵלֶיךָ וִיחֻנֶּךָּ׃ יִשָּׂא

כז יהוה ׀ פָּנָיו אֵלֶיךָ וְיָשֵׂם לְךָ שָׁלוֹם׃ וְשָׂמוּ אֶת־שְׁמִי עַל־

ז א בְּנֵי יִשְׂרָאֵל וַאֲנִי אֲבָרְכֵם׃ וַיְהִי בְּיוֹם כַּלּוֹת מֹשֶׁה לְהָקִים חמישי

אֶת־הַמִּשְׁכָּן וַיִּמְשַׁח אֹתוֹ וַיְקַדֵּשׁ אֹתוֹ וְאֶת־כָּל־כֵּלָיו וְאֶת־הַמִּזְבֵּחַ

ב וְאֶת־כָּל־כֵּלָיו וַיִּמְשָׁחֵם וַיְקַדֵּשׁ אֹתָם׃ וַיַּקְרִיבוּ נְשִׂיאֵי יִשְׂרָאֵל רָאשֵׁי

ג בֵּית אֲבֹתָם הֵם נְשִׂיאֵי הַמַּטֹּת הֵם הָעֹמְדִים עַל־הַפְּקֻדִים׃ וַיָּבִיאוּ

אֶת־קָרְבָּנָם לִפְנֵי יהוה שֵׁשׁ־עֶגְלֹת צָב וּשְׁנֵי־עָשָׂר בָּקָר עֲגָלָה עַל־

אונקלוס

וְיִטְּרִנָּךְ: כה יַנְהַר יְיָ שְׁכִינְתֵיהּ לְוָתָךְ, וִירַחֵים עֲלָךְ: כו יְקַבֵּיל יְיָ שְׁכִינְתֵיהּ
לְוָתָךְ, וִישַׁוֵּי לָךְ שְׁלָם: כז וִישַׁוּוֹן יָת בִּרְכַּת שְׁמִי עַל בְּנֵי יִשְׂרָאֵל, וַאֲנָא
אֲבָרֵיכִנּוּן: ז א וַהֲוָה, בְּיוֹמָא דְשֵׁיצִי מֹשֶׁה לַאֲקָמָא יָת מַשְׁכְּנָא, וְרַבִּי
יָתֵיהּ, וְקַדֵּישׁ יָתֵיהּ וְיָת כָּל מָנוֹהִי, וְיָת מַדְבְּחָא וְיָת כָּל מָנוֹהִי, וְרַבִּינוּן
וְקַדֵּישׁ יָתְהוֹן: ב וְקָרִיבוּ רַבְרְבֵי יִשְׂרָאֵל, רֵישֵׁי בֵּית אֲבָהָתְהוֹן, אִנּוּן
רַבְרְבֵי שִׁבְטַיָּא, אִנּוּן דְּקָיְמִין עַל מִנְיָנַיָּא: ג וְאֵיתִיאוּ יָת קֻרְבָּנְהוֹן
לִקְדָם יְיָ, שֵׁית עֶגְלָן כַּד מְחַפְּיָן וּתְרֵי עֲסַר תּוֹרִין, עֲגַלְתָּא, עַל

6:25 יָאֵר יהוה פָּנָיו אֵלֶיךָ וִיחֻנֶּךָּ *May the Lord make His face shine upon you and be gracious to you* – Judaism highly values the intellect: study, questioning, ideas, argument, and the life of the mind. Yet in *Kaddish DeRabbanan*, the prayer we say after studying a rabbinic text, we pray for spiritual leaders who have "grace, loving-kindness, and compassion." The power of intellect is secondary to the personal qualities of sensitivity and graciousness. Grace is that quality which sees the best in others and seeks the best for others. It is a combination of gentleness and generosity.

The second priestly blessing is: May God "Make His face shine upon you," meaning, may His presence be evident in you. May He leave a visible trace of His Being on the face you show to others. How is that presence to be recognized? Not in severity, remoteness, or austerity but in the gentle smile that speaks to what Lincoln called "the better angels of our nature." That is grace.

6:26 יִשָּׂא יהוה פָּנָיו אֵלֶיךָ וְיָשֵׂם לְךָ שָׁלוֹם *May the Lord raise His face toward you and grant you peace* – To make peace in the world we must be at peace with ourselves. To be at peace with ourselves we must know that we are unconditionally valued. That does not often happen. People value us for what we can give them. That is conditional value, what the Sages called "love that is dependent on a cause" (Avot 5:16). God values us unconditionally. We are here because He wanted us to be. Our very existence testifies to His love. Unlike others, God never gives up on us. He rejects no one. He never loses faith, however many times we fail. When we fall, He lifts us. He believes in us more than we believe in ourselves. That, in human terms, is the meaning of "May the Lord raise His face toward you and give you peace."

6:27 וַאֲנִי אֲבָרְכֵם *I will bless them* – The most profound element of the blessing lies in the concluding sentence: "They shall set My name upon the Israelites, and I will bless them." In the ancient world, magi, oracles, and religious virtuosi were held to have the power of blessing. It was thought that blessing or curse lay within the power of the holy person. Holiness is not, though it is often confused with, self-importance. This is the meaning of "They shall set My name upon the Israelites, and I will bless them." It is not the priests who bless the people, but God. In themselves, they have no power. They are intermediaries, channels through which God's blessing flows. True holiness is transparency to the Divine.

4 5 presented them before the Tabernacle. The LORD said to Moshe, "Accept
these from them and use them for service in the Tent of Meeting. Give them
6 to the Levites, to each according to his service." Moshe took the wagons and
7 the oxen, and he gave them to the Levites. He gave two wagons and four oxen
8 to the Gershonites as their service required. He gave four wagons and eight
oxen to the Merarites for their service under the supervision of Itamar son of
9 Aharon the priest. But to the Kohatites he gave none, for their responsibility
10 was for the sacred articles that had to be carried on their shoulders. The
princes presented their dedication offering for the altar at the time when it
11 was anointed. The princes brought their offerings before the altar. The LORD
said to Moshe, "Each day one prince is to bring close his offering for the
12 dedication of the altar." The one who presented his offering on the
13 first day was Naḥshon son of Aminadav, from the tribe of Yehuda. His offering
was one silver bowl weighing one hundred and thirty shekel and one silver
basin weighing seventy shekel according to the Sanctuary weight, both filled
14 with fine flour mixed with oil for a grain offering; one golden spoon weighing
15 ten shekel, full of incense; one young bull, one ram, and one yearling sheep

רש״י

(שם, כ), עֲגָלוֹת מְכֻסּוֹת קְרוּיוֹת ׳צַבִּים׳: וַיַּקְרִיבוּ אוֹתָם לִפְנֵי הַמִּשְׁכָּן. שֶׁלֹּא קִבֵּל מֹשֶׁה מִיָּדָם עַד שֶׁנֶּאֱמַר לוֹ מִפִּי הַמָּקוֹם. אָמַר רַבִּי נָתָן: מָה רָאוּ הַנְּשִׂיאִים לְהִתְנַדֵּב כָּאן בַּתְּחִלָּה וּבִמְלֶאכֶת הַמִּשְׁכָּן לֹא הִתְנַדְּבוּ תְּחִלָּה? אֶלָּא כָּךְ אָמְרוּ הַנְּשִׂיאִים: יִתְנַדְּבוּ צִבּוּר מַה שֶּׁיִּתְנַדְּבוּ וּמַה שֶּׁמְּחַסְּרִין אָנוּ מַשְׁלִימִין; כֵּיוָן שֶׁרָאוּ שֶׁהִשְׁלִימוּ צִבּוּר אֶת הַכֹּל, שֶׁנֶּאֱמַר: ״וְהַמְּלָאכָה הָיְתָה דַיָּם״ (שמות לו, ז), אָמְרוּ: מֵעַתָּה מַה לָּנוּ לַעֲשׂוֹת? הֵבִיאוּ אַבְנֵי הַשֹּׁהַם וְאַבְנֵי הַמִּלּוּאִים לָאֵפוֹד וְלַחֹשֶׁן (שם לה, כז), לְכָךְ הִתְנַדְּבוּ כָּאן תְּחִלָּה:

ז׳ כְּפִי עֲבֹדָתָם. שֶׁהָיָה מַשָּׂא בְּנֵי גֵרְשׁוֹן קַל מִשֶּׁל מְרָרִי שֶׁהָיוּ נוֹשְׂאִים הַקְּרָשִׁים וְהָעַמּוּדִים וְהָאֲדָנִים:

ט׳ כִּי עֲבֹדַת הַקֹּדֶשׁ עֲלֵהֶם. מַשָּׂא דְּבַר הַקְּדֻשָּׁה, ״הָאָרֹן וְהַשֻּׁלְחָן״ וְגוֹ׳ (לעיל ג, לא), לְפִיכָךְ ״בַּכָּתֵף יִשָּׂאוּ״:

י׳ וַיַּקְרִיבוּ הַנְּשִׂאִים אֵת חֲנֻכַּת הַמִּזְבֵּחַ. לְאַחַר שֶׁהִתְנַדְּבוּ הָעֲגָלוֹת וְהַבָּקָר לָשֵׂאת הַמִּשְׁכָּן, נְשָׂאָם לִבָּם לְהִתְנַדֵּב קָרְבָּנוֹת הַמִּזְבֵּחַ לְחָנְכוֹ: וַיַּקְרִיבוּ הַנְּשִׂיאִם אֶת קָרְבָּנָם לִפְנֵי הַמִּזְבֵּחַ. כִּי לֹא קִבֵּל מֹשֶׁה מִיָּדָם עַד שֶׁנֶּאֱמַר לוֹ מִפִּי הַגְּבוּרָה:

יא׳ יַקְרִיבוּ אֶת קָרְבָּנָם לַחֲנֻכַּת הַמִּזְבֵּחַ. וַעֲדַיִן לֹא הָיָה יוֹדֵעַ מֹשֶׁה הֵיאַךְ יַקְרִיבוּ, אִם כְּסֵדֶר תּוֹלְדוֹתָם אִם כְּסֵדֶר הַמַּסָּעוֹת, עַד שֶׁנֶּאֱמַר לוֹ מִפִּי הַקָּדוֹשׁ בָּרוּךְ הוּא: יַקְרִיבוּ לַמַּסָּעוֹת אִישׁ יוֹמוֹ:

יב׳ בַּיּוֹם הָרִאשׁוֹן. אוֹתוֹ הַיּוֹם נָטַל עֶשֶׂר עֲטָרוֹת, רִאשׁוֹן לְמַעֲשֵׂה בְרֵאשִׁית, רִאשׁוֹן לַנְּשִׂיאִים וְכוּ׳, כִּדְאִיתָא בְּסֵדֶר עוֹלָם (פרק ז): לְמַטֵּה יְהוּדָה. יִחֲסוֹ הַכָּתוּב עַל שִׁבְטוֹ, וְלֹא שֶׁגָּבָה מִשִּׁבְטוֹ וְהִקְרִיב. אוֹ אֵינוֹ אוֹמֵר ״לְמַטֵּה יְהוּדָה״ אֶלָּא שֶׁגָּבָה מִשִּׁבְטוֹ וְהֵבִיא? תַּלְמוּד לוֹמַר: ״זֶה קָרְבַּן נַחְשׁוֹן״ (להלן פסוק יז), מִשֶּׁלּוֹ הֵבִיא:

יג׳ שְׁנֵיהֶם מְלֵאִים סֹלֶת. לְמִנְחַת נְדָבָה:

יד׳ עֲשָׂרָה זָהָב. כְּתַרְגּוּמוֹ, מִשְׁקַל עֶשֶׂר שִׁקְלֵי הַקֹּדֶשׁ הָיָה בָהּ: מְלֵאָה קְטֹרֶת. לֹא מָצִינוּ קְטֹרֶת לְיָחִיד וְלֹא עַל מִזְבַּח הַחִיצוֹן אֶלָּא זוֹ בִּלְבַד, וְהוֹרָאַת שָׁעָה הָיְתָה:

טו׳ פַּר אֶחָד. מְיֻחָד שֶׁבְּעֶדְרוֹ:

ultimately the human family itself, brothers and sisters under the parenthood of God. The insistence on one identity to the exclusion of all others is the mark of a potentially totalitarian regime. Hence the insistence of the book of Numbers on the continuing significance of the twelve tribes even when Israel is one nation under the One God.

ד שְׁנֵ֧י הַנְּשִׂאִ֛ים וְשׁ֣וֹר לְאֶחָ֑ד וַיַּקְרִ֧יבוּ אוֹתָ֛ם לִפְנֵ֖י הַמִּשְׁכָּֽן׃ וַיֹּ֥אמֶר יְהֹוָ֖ה
ה אֶל־מֹשֶׁ֥ה לֵּאמֹֽר׃ קַ֚ח מֵֽאִתָּ֔ם וְהָי֕וּ לַעֲבֹ֕ד אֶת־עֲבֹדַ֖ת אֹ֣הֶל מוֹעֵ֑ד
ו וְנָתַתָּ֤ה אוֹתָם֙ אֶל־הַלְוִיִּ֔ם אִ֖ישׁ כְּפִ֥י עֲבֹדָתֽוֹ׃ וַיִּקַּ֣ח מֹשֶׁ֔ה אֶת־הָעֲגָלֹ֖ת
ז וְאֶת־הַבָּקָ֑ר וַיִּתֵּ֥ן אוֹתָ֖ם אֶל־הַלְוִיִּֽם׃ אֵ֣ת ׀ שְׁתֵּ֣י הָעֲגָל֗וֹת וְאֵת֙ אַרְבַּ֣עַת
ח הַבָּקָ֔ר נָתַ֖ן לִבְנֵ֣י גֵרְשׁ֑וֹן כְּפִ֖י עֲבֹדָתָֽם׃ וְאֵ֣ת ׀ אַרְבַּ֣ע הָעֲגָלֹ֗ת וְאֵת֙ שְׁמֹנַ֣ת
ט הַבָּקָ֔ר נָתַ֖ן לִבְנֵ֣י מְרָרִ֑י כְּפִי֙ עֲבֹ֣דָתָ֔ם בְּיַד֙ אִֽיתָמָ֔ר בֶּֽן־אַהֲרֹ֖ן הַכֹּהֵֽן׃ וְלִבְנֵ֥י
י קְהָ֖ת לֹ֣א נָתָ֑ן כִּֽי־עֲבֹדַ֤ת הַקֹּ֙דֶשׁ֙ עֲלֵהֶ֔ם בַּכָּתֵ֖ף יִשָּֽׂאוּ׃ וַיַּקְרִ֣יבוּ הַנְּשִׂאִ֗ים
אֵ֚ת חֲנֻכַּ֣ת הַמִּזְבֵּ֔חַ בְּי֖וֹם הִמָּשַׁ֣ח אֹת֑וֹ וַיַּקְרִ֧יבוּ הַנְּשִׂיאִ֛ם אֶת־קָרְבָּנָ֖ם
יא לִפְנֵ֥י הַמִּזְבֵּֽחַ׃ וַיֹּ֥אמֶר יְהֹוָ֖ה אֶל־מֹשֶׁ֑ה נָשִׂ֨יא אֶחָ֜ד לַיּ֗וֹם נָשִׂ֤יא אֶחָד֙
יב לַיּ֔וֹם יַקְרִ֙יבוּ֙ אֶת־קָרְבָּנָ֔ם לַחֲנֻכַּ֖ת הַמִּזְבֵּֽחַ׃ וַיְהִ֗י הַמַּקְרִ֛יב
יג בַּיּ֥וֹם הָרִאשׁ֖וֹן אֶת־קָרְבָּנ֑וֹ נַחְשׁ֥וֹן בֶּן־עַמִּֽינָדָ֖ב לְמַטֵּ֥ה יְהוּדָֽה׃ וְקָרְבָּנ֞וֹ
קַֽעֲרַת־כֶּ֣סֶף אַחַ֗ת שְׁלֹשִׁ֣ים וּמֵאָה֮ מִשְׁקָלָהּ֒ מִזְרָ֤ק אֶחָד֙ כֶּ֔סֶף שִׁבְעִ֥ים
יד שֶׁ֖קֶל בְּשֶׁ֣קֶל הַקֹּ֑דֶשׁ שְׁנֵיהֶ֣ם ׀ מְלֵאִ֗ים סֹ֛לֶת בְּלוּלָ֥ה בַשֶּׁ֖מֶן לְמִנְחָֽה׃ כַּ֥ף
טו אַחַ֛ת עֲשָׂרָ֥ה זָהָ֖ב מְלֵאָ֥ה קְטֹֽרֶת׃ פַּ֣ר אֶחָ֞ד בֶּן־בָּקָ֗ר אַ֧יִל אֶחָ֛ד כֶּֽבֶשׂ־

אונקלוס

תְּרֵין רַבְרְבַיָּא וְתוֹרָא לְחַד, וְקָרִיבוּ יָתְהוֹן לִקְדָם מַשְׁכְּנָא: ד וַאֲמַר יְיָ לְמֹשֶׁה לְמֵימַר: ה קַבֵּיל מִנְּהוֹן, וִיהוֹן, לְמִפְלַח, יָת פָּלְחַן מַשְׁכַּן זִמְנָא, וְתִתֵּין יָתְהוֹן לְלֵיוָאֵי, גְּבַר כְּמִסַּת פָּלְחָנֵיהּ: ו וּנְסֵיב מֹשֶׁה, יָת עֶגְלָתָא וְיָת תּוֹרֵי, וִיהַב יָתְהוֹן לְלֵיוָאֵי: ז יָת תַּרְתֵּין עֶגְלָן, וְיָת אַרְבְּעָא תוֹרִין, יְהַב לִבְנֵי גֵרְשׁוֹן, כְּמִסַּת פָּלְחָנְהוֹן: ח וְיָת אַרְבַּע עֶגְלָן, וְיָת תְּמָנְיָא תוֹרִין, יְהַב לִבְנֵי מְרָרִי, כְּמִסַּת פָּלְחָנְהוֹן, בִּידָא דְּאִיתָמָר, בַּר אַהֲרֹן כָּהֲנָא: ט וְלִבְנֵי קְהָת לָא יְהַב, אֲרֵי פָּלְחַן קֻדְשָׁא עֲלֵיהוֹן, בְּכַתְפָּא נָטְלִין: י וְקָרִיבוּ רַבְרְבַיָּא, יָת חֲנֻכַּת מַדְבְּחָא, בְּיוֹמָא דְּרַבִּיאוּ יָתֵיהּ, וְקָרִיבוּ רַבְרְבַיָּא, יָת קֻרְבָּנְהוֹן לִקְדָם מַדְבְּחָא: יא וַאֲמַר יְיָ לְמֹשֶׁה, רַבָּא חַד לְיוֹמָא, רַבָּא חַד לְיוֹמָא, יְקָרְבוּן יָת קֻרְבָּנְהוֹן, לַחֲנֻכַּת מַדְבְּחָא: יב וַהֲוָה, דִּמְקָרֵיב, בְּיוֹמָא קַדְמָאָה יָת קֻרְבָּנֵיהּ, נַחְשׁוֹן בַּר עַמִּינָדָב לְשִׁבְטָא דִּיהוּדָה: יג וְקֻרְבָּנֵיהּ מְגִסְתָּא דִּכְסַף חֲדָא, מְאָה וּתְלָתִין סִלְעִין הֲוֵי מַתְקָלַהּ, מִזְרְקָא חַד דִּכְסַף, מַתְקָלֵיהּ שִׁבְעִין סִלְעִין בְּסִלְעֵי קֻדְשָׁא, תַּרְוֵיהוֹן מְלַן, סֻלְתָּא, דְּפִילָא בִּמְשַׁח לְמִנְחָתָא: יד בָּזְכָּא חֲדָא, מַתְקָלַהּ עֲסַר סִלְעִין הִיא דִּדְהַב מַלְיָא קְטוֹרֶת בֻּסְמַיָּא: טו תּוֹר חַד בַּר תּוֹרֵי, דְּכַר חַד, אִמַּר

then an extended family, then a tribe, then a series of tribes. They are forged into a nation negatively by the experience of oppression in Egypt, positively by redemption and by the covenant they made with God at Mount Sinai. But those early structures – family, clan, tribe – remain important in the body politic, not just at the beginning but throughout.

We are not one thing. We have multiple identities, as members of this family, that neighborhood, this congregation, that religious faith, this ethnicity, that nation, and

▶

16 17 for a burnt offering; one goat for a purification offering; and for the peace
sacrifice two oxen, five rams, five male goats, and five yearling sheep. This was
the offering of Naḥshon son of Aminadav.
18 On the second day Netanel son of Tzuar, prince of Yissakhar, presented his
19 offering. He presented as his offering one silver bowl weighing one hundred
and thirty shekel and one silver basin weighing seventy shekel according to the
Sanctuary weight, both filled with fine flour mixed with oil for a grain offering;
20 21 one golden spoon weighing ten shekel, full of incense; one young bull, one
22 ram, and one yearling sheep for a burnt offering; one goat for a purification
23 offering; and for the peace sacrifice two oxen, five rams, five male goats, and
five yearling sheep. This was the offering of Netanel son of Tzuar.
24 25 On the third day came Eliav son of Ḥelon, prince of the Zebulunites: His

רש״י

טז **שעיר עזים אחד לחטאת.** לכפר על קבר התהום, טמאת ספק:

יח-יט **הקריב נתנאל בן צוער, הקרב את קרבנו.** מה תלמוד לומר "הקריב" בשבטו של יששכר מה שלא נאמר בכל השבטים? לפי שבא ראובן וערער ואמר: דיי שקדמני יהודה אחי, אקריב אני אחריו. אמר לו משה: מפי הגבורה נאמר לי שיקריבו כסדר מסען לדגליהם, לכך אמר: "הקרב את קרבנו" והוא חסר יו"ד, שהוא משמע 'הקרב' לשון צווי, שמפי הגבורה נצטוה 'הקרב'. ומהו "הקריב הקרב" שני פעמים? שבשביל שני דברים זכה להקריב שני לשבטים: אחת – שהיו יודעים בתורה, שנאמר: "ומבני יששכר יודעי בינה לעתים" (דברי הימים א' יב, לג); ואחת – שהם נתנו עצה לנשיאים להתנדב קרבנות הללו. ובִיסודו של רבי משה הדרשן מצאתי: אמר רבי פנחס בן יאיר: נתנאל בן צוער השיאן עצה זו: **קערת כסף.** מנין אותיותיו בגימטריא תתק"ל, כנגד שנותיו של אדם הראשון: **שלשים ומאה משקלה.** על שם שכשהעמיד תולדות לקיום העולם בן מאה ושלשים שנה היה, שנאמר: "ויחי אדם שלשים ומאת שנה ויולד בדמותו" וגו' (בראשית ה, ג): **מזרק אחד כסף.** בגימטריא תק"כ, על שם נח שהעמיד תולדות בן ת"ק שנה, ועל שם עשרים שנה שנגזרה גזרת המבול קודם תולדותיו, כמו שפרשתי אצל "והיו ימיו מאה ועשרים שנה" (שם ו, ג). לפיכך נאמר: "מזרק אחד כסף" ולא נאמר 'מזרק כסף אחד' כמו שנאמר בקערה, לומר שאף אותיות של 'אחד' מצטרפות למנין: **שבעים שקל.** כנגד שבעים אומות שיצאו מבניו: **כף אחת.** כנגד התורה שנתנה מידו של הקדוש ברוך הוא: **עשרה זהב.** כנגד עשרת הדברות: **מלאה קטרת.** גימטריא של קטרת 'תרי"ג' מצוות, ובלבד שתחליף קו"ף בדל"ת על ידי א"ת ב"ש ג"ר ד"ק: **פר אחד.** כנגד אברהם, שנאמר בו: "ויקח בן בקר" (שם יח, ז): **איל אחד.** כנגד יצחק: "ויקח את האיל" וגו' (שם כב, יג): **כבש אחד.** כנגד יעקב: "והכשבים הפריד יעקב" (שם ל, מ): **שעיר עזים.** לכפר על מכירת יוסף, שנאמר בו: "וישחטו שעיר עזים" (שם לז, לא): **ולזבח השלמים בקר שנים.** כנגד משה ואהרן שנתנו שלום בין ישראל לאביהם שבשמים: **אילם עתדים כבשים.** שלשה מינים, כנגד כהנים ולוים וישראלים, וכנגד תורה נביאים וכתובים. שלש חמישיות, כנגד חמשה חומשין, וחמשת הדברות הכתובין על לוח אחד, וחמשה הכתובין על השני. עד כאן מיסודו של רבי משה הדרשן:

כד **ביום השלישי נשיא וגו'.** ביום השלישי היה הנשיא המקריב לבני זבולן, וכן כלם. אבל בנתנאל שנאמר בו: "הקריב נתנאל" (לעיל פסוק יח) נופל אחריו הלשון לומר: "נשיא יששכר", לפי שכבר הזכיר שמו והקרבתו, ובשאר שלא נאמר בהן 'הקריב' נופל עליהן לשון זה: 'נשיא לבני פלוני', אותו היום היה הנשיא המקריב לשבט פלוני:

serves as a meditation on giving. Contributing to the common good is a constant calling upon each of us. To live a responsible life – a responsive life – is always to ask of yourself, "What is God calling me to do, here, where I am?" There is almost not a day that goes by when you cannot transform someone's life for the better, in some way. The word *ḥesed* means love, but it is the love we do as opposed to the love we feel; it is love-as-deed. That is the kind of love that changes lives. It's when we see the lonely and we reach out to welcome them. It's when we see the hungry and say: Come and eat with me, share my food. Let us eat together.

Someone once asked the great Victorian Anglo-Jew, Sir

אֶחָד בֶּן־שְׁנָתוֹ לְעֹלָה: שְׂעִיר־עִזִּים אֶחָד לְחַטָּאת: וּלְזֶבַח הַשְּׁלָמִים טז יז
בָּקָר שְׁנַיִם אֵילִם חֲמִשָּׁה עַתּוּדִים חֲמִשָּׁה כְּבָשִׂים בְּנֵי־שָׁנָה חֲמִשָּׁה
זֶה קָרְבַּן נַחְשׁוֹן בֶּן־עַמִּינָדָב:
בַּיּוֹם הַשֵּׁנִי הִקְרִיב נְתַנְאֵל בֶּן־צוּעָר נְשִׂיא יִשָּׂשכָר: הִקְרִב אֶת־קָרְבָּנוֹ יח יט
קַעֲרַת־כֶּסֶף אַחַת שְׁלֹשִׁים וּמֵאָה מִשְׁקָלָהּ מִזְרָק אֶחָד כֶּסֶף שִׁבְעִים
שֶׁקֶל בְּשֶׁקֶל הַקֹּדֶשׁ שְׁנֵיהֶם ׀ מְלֵאִים סֹלֶת בְּלוּלָה בַשֶּׁמֶן לְמִנְחָה:
כַּף אַחַת עֲשָׂרָה זָהָב מְלֵאָה קְטֹרֶת: פַּר אֶחָד בֶּן־בָּקָר אַיִל אֶחָד כ כא
כֶּבֶשׂ־אֶחָד בֶּן־שְׁנָתוֹ לְעֹלָה: שְׂעִיר־עִזִּים אֶחָד לְחַטָּאת: וּלְזֶבַח כב כג
הַשְּׁלָמִים בָּקָר שְׁנַיִם אֵילִם חֲמִשָּׁה עַתֻּדִים חֲמִשָּׁה כְּבָשִׂים בְּנֵי־שָׁנָה
חֲמִשָּׁה זֶה קָרְבַּן נְתַנְאֵל בֶּן־צוּעָר:
בַּיּוֹם הַשְּׁלִישִׁי נָשִׂיא לִבְנֵי זְבוּלֻן אֱלִיאָב בֶּן־חֵלֹן: קָרְבָּנוֹ קַעֲרַת־ כד כה

אונקלוס

חַד בַּר שַׁתֵּיהּ לַעֲלָתָא: טז צְפִיר בַּר עִזִּין חַד לְחַטָּתָא: יז וּלְנִכְסַת קֻדְשַׁיָּא תּוֹרֵי תְּרֵין, דִּכְרֵי חַמְשָׁא גַּדְיֵי חַמְשָׁא, אִמְּרִין בְּנֵי שְׁנָא חַמְשָׁא, דֵּין, קֻרְבָּנָא דְּנַחְשׁוֹן בַּר עַמִּינָדָב: יח בְּיוֹמָא תִּנְיָנָא, קָרֵיב נְתַנְאֵל בַּר צוּעָר, רַב שִׁבְטָא דְּיִשָּׂשכָר: יט קָרֵיב יָת קֻרְבָּנֵיהּ מְגִסְתָּא דִּכְסַף חֲדָא, מְאָה וּתְלָתִין סִלְעִין הֲוֵי מַתְקָלַהּ, מִזְרְקָא חַד דִּכְסַף, מַתְקְלֵיהּ שִׁבְעִין סִלְעִין בְּסִלְעֵי קֻדְשָׁא, תַּרְוֵיהוֹן מְלַן, סֻלְתָּא, דְּפִילָא בִּמְשַׁח לְמִנְחָתָא: כ בָּזִכָּא חֲדָא, מַתְקָלַהּ עֲסַר סִלְעִין הִיא דִּדְהַב מְלְיָא קְטֹרֶת בֻּסְמַיָּא: כא תּוֹר חַד בַּר תּוֹרֵי, דְּכַר חַד, אִמַּר חַד בַּר שַׁתֵּיהּ לַעֲלָתָא: כב צְפִיר בַּר עִזִּין חַד לְחַטָּתָא: כג וּלְנִכְסַת קֻדְשַׁיָּא תּוֹרֵי תְּרֵין, דִּכְרֵי חַמְשָׁא גַּדְיֵי חַמְשָׁא, אִמְּרִין בְּנֵי שְׁנָא חַמְשָׁא, דֵּין, קֻרְבָּנָא דִּנְתַנְאֵל בַּר צוּעָר: כד בְּיוֹמָא תְּלִיתָאָה, רַבָּא לִבְנֵי זְבוּלוּן, אֱלִיאָב בַּר חֵלוֹן: כה קֻרְבָּנֵיהּ מְגִסְתָּא

7:18 בַּיּוֹם הַשֵּׁנִי *On the second day* – The gifts brought by the princes of each tribe are described in a series of long paragraphs repeated no less than twelve times, despite the fact that each prince brought an identical offering.

Why does the Torah spend so much time describing an event that could have been stated far more briefly by naming the princes and then simply telling us generically that each brought a silver bowl, a silver basin, and so on? The Rabbis made the assumption that every word of the Torah is meaningful. It tells us something we need to know, and does so in the fewest possible words. So the repetitiousness of this particular passage cries out for explanation.

The long account of the offerings of the princes of the twelve tribes is a dramatic way of indicating that each was considered important enough to merit its own passage in the Torah. People will do destructive things if they feel slighted and not given their due role and recognition. The case of Koraḥ and his allies will be proof of this. By giving the princes of the tribes their share of honor and attention, the Torah is telling us how important it is to preserve the harmony of the nation by honoring all.

A LITANY OF GIFTS

The lengthy, twelvefold repetition of the gifts of the tribes

offering was one silver bowl weighing one hundred and thirty shekel and one
silver basin weighing seventy shekel according to the Sanctuary weight, both
26 filled with fine flour mixed with oil for a grain offering; one golden spoon
27 weighing ten shekel, full of incense; one young bull, one ram, and one yearling
28 29 sheep for a burnt offering; one goat for a purification offering; and for the peace
sacrifice two oxen, five rams, five male goats, and five yearling sheep. This was
the offering of Eliav son of Ḥelon.
30 On the fourth day came Elitzur son of Shedeiur, prince of the Reubenites:
31 His offering was one silver bowl weighing one hundred and thirty shekel and
one silver basin weighing seventy shekel according to the Sanctuary weight,
32 both filled with fine flour mixed with oil for a grain offering; one golden spoon
33 weighing ten shekel, full of incense; one young bull, one ram, and one yearling
34 35 sheep for a burnt offering; one goat for a purification offering; and for the peace
sacrifice two oxen, five rams, five male goats, and five yearling sheep. This was
the offering of Elitzur son of Shedeiur.
36 On the fifth day came Shelumiel son of Tzurishadai, prince of the Simeonites:
37 His offering was one silver bowl weighing one hundred and thirty shekel and
one silver basin weighing seventy shekel according to the Sanctuary weight,
38 both filled with fine flour mixed with oil for a grain offering; one golden spoon
39 weighing ten shekel, full of incense; one young bull, one ram, and one yearling
40 41 sheep for a burnt offering; one goat for a purification offering; and for the peace

אונקלוס

דכסף חדא, מאה ותלתין סלעין הוי מתקלה, מזרקא חד דכספא, מתקליה שבעין סלעין בסלעי קדשא, תרויהון מלן, סלתא, דפילא במשח למנחתא: כו בזכא חדא, מתקלה עסר סלעין היא דדהב מליא קטורת בסמיא: כז תור חד בר תורי, דכר חד, אמר חד בר שתיה לעלתא: כח צפיר בר עזין חד לחטתא: כט ולנכסת קדשיא תורי תרין, דכרי חמשא גדי חמשא, אמרין בני שנא חמשא, דין, קרבנא דאליאב בר חלון: ל ביומא רביעאה, רבא לבני ראובן, אליצור בר שדיאור: לא קרבניה מגסתא דכסף חדא, מאה ותלתין סלעין

הוי מתקלה, מזרקא חד דכספא, מתקליה שבעין סלעין בסלעי קדשא, תרויהון מלן, סלתא, דפילא במשח למנחתא: לב בזכא חדא, מתקלה עסר סלעין היא דדהב מליא קטורת בסמיא: לג תור חד בר תורי, דכר חד, אמר חד בר שתיה לעלתא: לד צפיר בר עזין חד לחטתא: לה ולנכסת קדשיא תורי תרין, דכרי חמשא גדי חמשא, אמרין בני שנא חמשא, דין, קרבנא דאליצור בר שדיאור: לו ביומא חמישאה, רבא לבני שמעון, שלומיאל בר צורישדי: לז קרבניה מגסתא דכסף חדא, מאה ותלתין סלעין הוי מתקלה, מזרקא

The Greeks knew about love as an emotion. In Judaism we propose that the love that changes lives is the love we do, the blessings we share, the offerings we bring.

didn't ask me how much I own. You asked me how much I'm worth. So I calculated the amount I have given to charity this year, and that is the figure I gave you. You see," he said, "we are worth what we are willing to share with others."

כֶּסֶף אַחַת שְׁלֹשִׁים וּמֵאָה מִשְׁקָלָהּ מִזְרָק אֶחָד כֶּסֶף שִׁבְעִים שֶׁקֶל
כו בְּשֶׁקֶל הַקֹּדֶשׁ שְׁנֵיהֶם ׀ מְלֵאִים סֹלֶת בְּלוּלָה בַשֶּׁמֶן לְמִנְחָה: כַּף אַחַת
כז עֲשָׂרָה זָהָב מְלֵאָה קְטֹרֶת: פַּר אֶחָד בֶּן־בָּקָר אַיִל אֶחָד כֶּבֶשׂ־אֶחָד
כח כט בֶּן־שְׁנָתוֹ לְעֹלָה: שְׂעִיר־עִזִּים אֶחָד לְחַטָּאת: וּלְזֶבַח הַשְּׁלָמִים בָּקָר
שְׁנַיִם אֵילִם חֲמִשָּׁה עַתֻּדִים חֲמִשָּׁה כְּבָשִׂים בְּנֵי־שָׁנָה חֲמִשָּׁה זֶה
קָרְבַּן אֱלִיאָב בֶּן־חֵלֹן:
ל לא בַּיּוֹם הָרְבִיעִי נָשִׂיא לִבְנֵי רְאוּבֵן אֱלִיצוּר בֶּן־שְׁדֵיאוּר: קָרְבָּנוֹ קַעֲרַת־
כֶּסֶף אַחַת שְׁלֹשִׁים וּמֵאָה מִשְׁקָלָהּ מִזְרָק אֶחָד כֶּסֶף שִׁבְעִים שֶׁקֶל
לב בְּשֶׁקֶל הַקֹּדֶשׁ שְׁנֵיהֶם ׀ מְלֵאִים סֹלֶת בְּלוּלָה בַשֶּׁמֶן לְמִנְחָה: כַּף אַחַת
לג עֲשָׂרָה זָהָב מְלֵאָה קְטֹרֶת: פַּר אֶחָד בֶּן־בָּקָר אַיִל אֶחָד כֶּבֶשׂ־אֶחָד
לד לה בֶּן־שְׁנָתוֹ לְעֹלָה: שְׂעִיר־עִזִּים אֶחָד לְחַטָּאת: וּלְזֶבַח הַשְּׁלָמִים בָּקָר
שְׁנַיִם אֵילִם חֲמִשָּׁה עַתֻּדִים חֲמִשָּׁה כְּבָשִׂים בְּנֵי־שָׁנָה חֲמִשָּׁה זֶה קָרְבַּן
אֱלִיצוּר בֶּן־שְׁדֵיאוּר:
לו לז בַּיּוֹם הַחֲמִישִׁי נָשִׂיא לִבְנֵי שִׁמְעוֹן שְׁלֻמִיאֵל בֶּן־צוּרִישַׁדָּי: קָרְבָּנוֹ
קַעֲרַת־כֶּסֶף אַחַת שְׁלֹשִׁים וּמֵאָה מִשְׁקָלָהּ מִזְרָק אֶחָד כֶּסֶף שִׁבְעִים
שֶׁקֶל בְּשֶׁקֶל הַקֹּדֶשׁ שְׁנֵיהֶם ׀ מְלֵאִים סֹלֶת בְּלוּלָה בַשֶּׁמֶן לְמִנְחָה:
לח לט כַּף אַחַת עֲשָׂרָה זָהָב מְלֵאָה קְטֹרֶת: פַּר אֶחָד בֶּן־בָּקָר אַיִל אֶחָד
מ מא כֶּבֶשׂ־אֶחָד בֶּן־שְׁנָתוֹ לְעֹלָה: שְׂעִיר־עִזִּים אֶחָד לְחַטָּאת: וּלְזֶבַח

אונקלוס

חַד דִּכְסַף, מַתְקְלֵיהּ שִׁבְעִין סִלְעִין בְּסִלְעֵי קֻדְשָׁא, תַּרְוֵיהוֹן מְלַן, סֻלְתָּא, דְּפִילָא בִמְשַׁח לְמִנְחָתָא: לח בָּזִכָא חֲדָא, מַתְקְלַהּ עֲסַר סִלְעִין הִיא דִּדְהַב מַלְיָא קְטֹרֶת בֻּסְמַיָּא: לט תּוֹר חַד בַּר תּוֹרֵי, דְּכַר חַד, אִמַּר חַד בַּר שַׁתֵּיהּ לַעֲלָתָא: מ צְפִיר בַּר עִזִּין חַד לְחַטָּתָא: מא וּלְנִכְסַת

Moses Montefiore, “Sir Moses, how much are you worth?” Moses thought for a while and named a figure. The other replied, “That can’t be right. It’s a large sum but not large enough. By my calculation you must be worth ten times that amount.”

The reply Sir Moses gave was moving and wise. “You

sacrifice two oxen, five rams, five male goats, and five yearling sheep. This was
the offering of Shelumiel son of Tzurishadai.
42 43 On the sixth day came Elyasaf son of Deuel, prince of the Gadites: His offering SHISHI
was one silver bowl weighing one hundred and thirty shekel and one silver
basin weighing seventy shekel according to the Sanctuary weight, both filled
44 with fine flour mixed with oil for a grain offering; one golden spoon weighing
45 ten shekel, full of incense; one young bull, one ram, and one yearling sheep
46 47 for a burnt offering; one goat for a purification offering; and for the peace
sacrifice two oxen, five rams, five male goats, and five yearling sheep. This was
the offering of Elyasaf son of Deuel.
48 On the seventh day came Elishama son of Amihud, prince of the Efraimites:
49 His offering was one silver bowl weighing one hundred and thirty shekel and
one silver basin weighing seventy shekel according to the Sanctuary weight,
50 both filled with fine flour mixed with oil for a grain offering; one golden spoon
51 weighing ten shekel, full of incense; one young bull, one ram, and one yearling
52 53 sheep for a burnt offering; one goat for a purification offering; and for the peace
sacrifice two oxen, five rams, five male goats, and five yearling sheep. This was
the offering of Elishama son of Amihud.
54 On the eighth day came Gamliel son of Pedatzur, prince of the Manassites:
55 His offering was one silver bowl weighing one hundred and thirty shekel and
one silver basin weighing seventy shekel according to the Sanctuary weight,
56 both filled with fine flour mixed with oil for a grain offering; one golden spoon
57 weighing ten shekel, full of incense; one young bull, one ram, and one yearling
58 59 sheep for a burnt offering; one goat for a purification offering; and for the peace

אונקלוס

קֻדְשַׁיָּא תּוֹרֵי תְּרֵין, דִּכְרֵי חַמְשָׁא גַּדֵּי חַמְשָׁא, אִמְּרִין בְּנֵי שְׁנָא חַמְשָׁא, דֵּין, קֻרְבָּנָא דִּשְׁלוּמִיאֵל בַּר צוּרִישַׁדָּי: מב בְּיוֹמָא שְׁתִיתָאָה, רַבָּא לִבְנֵי גָד, אֶלְיָסָף בַּר דְּעוּאֵל: מג קֻרְבָּנֵיהּ מְגִסְתָּא דִּכְסַף חֲדָא, מְאָה וּתְלָתִין סִלְעִין הֲוֵי מַתְקָלַהּ, מִזְרְקָא חַד דִּכְסַף, מַתְקָלֵיהּ שִׁבְעִין סִלְעִין בְּסִלְעֵי קֻדְשָׁא, תַּרְוֵיהוֹן מְלַן, סֻלְתָּא, דְּפִילָא בִמְשַׁח לְמִנְחָתָא: מד בָּזִכָּא חֲדָא, מַתְקָלַהּ עֲסַר סִלְעִין הִיא דִּדְהַב מַלְיָא קְטֹרֶת בֻּסְמַיָּא: מה תּוֹר חַד בַּר תּוֹרֵי, דְּכַר חַד, אִמַּר חַד בַּר שַׁתֵּיהּ לַעֲלָתָא: מו צְפִיר בַּר עִזִּין חַד לְחַטָּתָא: מז וּלְנִכְסַת קֻדְשַׁיָּא תּוֹרֵי תְּרֵין, דִּכְרֵי חַמְשָׁא גַּדֵּי חַמְשָׁא, אִמְּרִין בְּנֵי שְׁנָא חַמְשָׁא, דֵּין, קֻרְבָּנָא דְּאֶלְיָסָף בַּר דְּעוּאֵל: מח בְּיוֹמָא שְׁבִיעָאָה, רַבָּא לִבְנֵי אֶפְרָיִם, אֱלִישָׁמָע בַּר עַמִּיהוּד: מט קֻרְבָּנֵיהּ מְגִסְתָּא דִּכְסַף חֲדָא, מְאָה וּתְלָתִין סִלְעִין הֲוֵי מַתְקָלַהּ, מִזְרְקָא חַד דִּכְסַף, מַתְקָלֵיהּ שִׁבְעִין סִלְעִין בְּסִלְעֵי קֻדְשָׁא, תַּרְוֵיהוֹן מְלַן, סֻלְתָּא, דְּפִילָא בִמְשַׁח לְמִנְחָתָא: נ בָּזִכָּא חֲדָא, מַתְקָלַהּ עֲסַר סִלְעִין הִיא דִּדְהַב מַלְיָא קְטֹרֶת בֻּסְמַיָּא: נא תּוֹר חַד בַּר תּוֹרֵי, דְּכַר חַד, אִמַּר חַד בַּר שַׁתֵּיהּ לַעֲלָתָא: נב צְפִיר בַּר עִזִּין חַד לְחַטָּתָא: נג וּלְנִכְסַת קֻדְשַׁיָּא תּוֹרֵי תְּרֵין, דִּכְרֵי חַמְשָׁא גַּדֵּי חַמְשָׁא, אִמְּרִין בְּנֵי שְׁנָא חַמְשָׁא, דֵּין, קֻרְבָּנָא דֶּאֱלִישָׁמָע בַּר עַמִּיהוּד: נד בְּיוֹמָא תְּמִינָאָה, רַבָּא לִבְנֵי מְנַשֶּׁה, גַּמְלִיאֵל בַּר פְּדָהצוּר: נה קֻרְבָּנֵיהּ מְגִסְתָּא דִּכְסַף חֲדָא, מְאָה וּתְלָתִין סִלְעִין הֲוֵי מַתְקָלַהּ, מִזְרְקָא חַד דִּכְסַף, מַתְקָלֵיהּ שִׁבְעִין סִלְעִין בְּסִלְעֵי קֻדְשָׁא, תַּרְוֵיהוֹן מְלַן, סֻלְתָּא, דְּפִילָא

הַשְּׁלָמִים בָּקָר שְׁנַיִם אֵילִם חֲמִשָּׁה עַתֻּדִים חֲמִשָּׁה כְּבָשִׂים בְּנֵי־שָׁנָה
חֲמִשָּׁה זֶה קָרְבַּן שְׁלֻמִיאֵל בֶּן־צוּרִישַׁדָּי׃
מב מג בַּיּוֹם הַשִּׁשִּׁי נָשִׂיא לִבְנֵי גָד אֶלְיָסָף בֶּן־דְּעוּאֵל׃ קָרְבָּנוֹ קַעֲרַת־כֶּסֶף ששי
אַחַת שְׁלֹשִׁים וּמֵאָה מִשְׁקָלָהּ מִזְרָק אֶחָד כֶּסֶף שִׁבְעִים שֶׁקֶל בְּשֶׁקֶל
מד הַקֹּדֶשׁ שְׁנֵיהֶם ׀ מְלֵאִים סֹלֶת בְּלוּלָה בַשֶּׁמֶן לְמִנְחָה׃ כַּף אַחַת עֲשָׂרָה
מה זָהָב מְלֵאָה קְטֹרֶת׃ פַּר אֶחָד בֶּן־בָּקָר אַיִל אֶחָד כֶּבֶשׂ־אֶחָד בֶּן־
מו מז שְׁנָתוֹ לְעֹלָה׃ שְׂעִיר־עִזִּים אֶחָד לְחַטָּאת׃ וּלְזֶבַח הַשְּׁלָמִים בָּקָר
שְׁנַיִם אֵילִם חֲמִשָּׁה עַתֻּדִים חֲמִשָּׁה כְּבָשִׂים בְּנֵי־שָׁנָה חֲמִשָּׁה זֶה
קָרְבַּן אֶלְיָסָף בֶּן־דְּעוּאֵל׃
מח מט בַּיּוֹם הַשְּׁבִיעִי נָשִׂיא לִבְנֵי אֶפְרָיִם אֱלִישָׁמָע בֶּן־עַמִּיהוּד׃ קָרְבָּנוֹ ז
קַעֲרַת־כֶּסֶף אַחַת שְׁלֹשִׁים וּמֵאָה מִשְׁקָלָהּ מִזְרָק אֶחָד כֶּסֶף שִׁבְעִים
שֶׁקֶל בְּשֶׁקֶל הַקֹּדֶשׁ שְׁנֵיהֶם ׀ מְלֵאִים סֹלֶת בְּלוּלָה בַשֶּׁמֶן לְמִנְחָה׃
נ נא כַּף אַחַת עֲשָׂרָה זָהָב מְלֵאָה קְטֹרֶת׃ פַּר אֶחָד בֶּן־בָּקָר אַיִל אֶחָד
נב נג כֶּבֶשׂ־אֶחָד בֶּן־שְׁנָתוֹ לְעֹלָה׃ שְׂעִיר־עִזִּים אֶחָד לְחַטָּאת׃ וּלְזֶבַח
הַשְּׁלָמִים בָּקָר שְׁנַיִם אֵילִם חֲמִשָּׁה עַתֻּדִים חֲמִשָּׁה כְּבָשִׂים בְּנֵי־שָׁנָה
חֲמִשָּׁה זֶה קָרְבַּן אֱלִישָׁמָע בֶּן־עַמִּיהוּד׃
נד נה בַּיּוֹם הַשְּׁמִינִי נָשִׂיא לִבְנֵי מְנַשֶּׁה גַּמְלִיאֵל בֶּן־פְּדָהצוּר׃ קָרְבָּנוֹ קַעֲרַת־
כֶּסֶף אַחַת שְׁלֹשִׁים וּמֵאָה מִשְׁקָלָהּ מִזְרָק אֶחָד כֶּסֶף שִׁבְעִים שֶׁקֶל
נו בְּשֶׁקֶל הַקֹּדֶשׁ שְׁנֵיהֶם ׀ מְלֵאִים סֹלֶת בְּלוּלָה בַשֶּׁמֶן לְמִנְחָה׃ כַּף אַחַת
נז עֲשָׂרָה זָהָב מְלֵאָה קְטֹרֶת׃ פַּר אֶחָד בֶּן־בָּקָר אַיִל אֶחָד כֶּבֶשׂ־אֶחָד
נח נט בֶּן־שְׁנָתוֹ לְעֹלָה׃ שְׂעִיר־עִזִּים אֶחָד לְחַטָּאת׃ וּלְזֶבַח הַשְּׁלָמִים בָּקָר

אונקלוס

בִּמְשַׁח לְמִנְחְתָא: נו בָּזִכָא חֲדָא, מַתְקְלַהּ עֲסַר סִלְעִין הִיא דִּדְהַב מַלְיָא קְטוֹרֶת בֻּסְמַיָּא: נז תּוֹר חַד בַּר תּוֹרֵי, דְּכַר חַד, אִמַּר חַד בַּר שַׁתֵּיהּ לַעֲלָתָא: נח צְפִיר בַּר עִזִּין חַד לְחַטָּתָא: נט וּלְנִכְסַת קֻדְשַׁיָּא תּוֹרֵי

sacrifice two oxen, five rams, five male goats, and five yearling sheep. This was
the offering of Gamliel son of Pedatzur.
60 61 On the ninth day came Avidan son of Gidoni, prince of the Benjaminites: His
offering was one silver bowl weighing one hundred and thirty shekel and one
silver basin weighing seventy shekel according to the Sanctuary weight, both
62 filled with fine flour mixed with oil for a grain offering; one golden spoon
63 weighing ten shekel, full of incense; one young bull, one ram, and one yearling
64 65 sheep for a burnt offering; one goat for a purification offering; and for the peace
sacrifice two oxen, five rams, five male goats, and five yearling sheep. This was
the offering of Avidan son of Gidoni.
66 67 On the tenth day came Aḥiezer son of Amishadai, prince of the Danites: His
offering was one silver bowl weighing one hundred and thirty shekel and one
silver basin weighing seventy shekel according to the Sanctuary weight, both
68 filled with fine flour mixed with oil for a grain offering; one golden spoon
69 weighing ten shekel, full of incense; one young bull, one ram, and one yearling
70 71 sheep for a burnt offering; one goat for a purification offering; and for the peace
sacrifice two oxen, five rams, five male goats, and five yearling sheep. This was
the offering of Aḥiezer son of Amishadai.
72 73 On the eleventh day came Pagiel son of Okhran, prince of the Asherites: His SHEVI'I
offering was one silver bowl weighing one hundred and thirty shekel and one
silver basin weighing seventy shekel according to the Sanctuary weight, both
74 filled with fine flour mixed with oil for a grain offering; one golden spoon
75 weighing ten shekel, full of incense; one young bull, one ram, and one yearling
76 77 sheep for a burnt offering; one goat for a purification offering; and for the peace

אונקלוס

תְּרֵין, דִּכְרֵי חַמְשָׁא גְּדֵי חַמְשָׁא, אִמְּרִין בְּנֵי שְׁנָא חַמְשָׁא, דֵּין, קֻרְבָּנָא
דְּגַמְלִיאֵל בַּר פְּדָצוּר: ס בְּיוֹמָא תְּשִׁיעָאָה, רַבָּא לִבְנֵי בִנְיָמִין, אֲבִידָן
בַּר גִּדְעוֹנִי: סא קֻרְבָּנֵיהּ מְגִסְתָּא דִּכְסַף חֲדָא, מְאָה וּתְלָתִין סִלְעִין הֲוֵי
מַתְקָלַהּ, מִזְרְקָא חַד דְּכַסְפָּא, מַתְקָלֵיהּ שִׁבְעִין סִלְעִין בְּסִלְעֵי קֻדְשָׁא,
תַּרְוֵיהוֹן מְלַן, סָלְתָּא, דְּפִילָא בִמְשַׁח לְמִנְחָתָא: סב בָּזִכָּא חֲדָא, מַתְקָלַהּ
עֲסַר סִלְעִין הִיא דִּדְהַב מַלְיָא קְטֹרֶת בֻּסְמַיָּא: סג תּוֹר חַד בַּר תּוֹרֵי,
דְּכַר חַד, אִמַּר חַד בַּר שַׁתֵּיהּ לַעֲלָתָא: סד צְפִיר בַּר עִזִּין חַד לְחַטָּתָא: סה
וּלְנִכְסַת קֻדְשַׁיָּא תּוֹרֵי תְּרֵין, דִּכְרֵי חַמְשָׁא גְּדֵי חַמְשָׁא, אִמְּרִין בְּנֵי שְׁנָא
חַמְשָׁא, דֵּין, קֻרְבָּנָא דַּאֲבִידָן בַּר גִּדְעוֹנִי: סו בְּיוֹמָא עֲסִירָאָה, רַבָּא לִבְנֵי
דָן, אֲחִיעֶזֶר בַּר עַמִּישַׁדָּי: סז קֻרְבָּנֵיהּ מְגִסְתָּא דִּכְסַף חֲדָא, מְאָה וּתְלָתִין
סִלְעִין הֲוֵי מַתְקָלַהּ, מִזְרְקָא חַד דְּכַסְפָּא, מַתְקָלֵיהּ שִׁבְעִין סִלְעִין
בְּסִלְעֵי קֻדְשָׁא, תַּרְוֵיהוֹן מְלַן, סָלְתָּא, דְּפִילָא בִמְשַׁח לְמִנְחָתָא: סח
בָּזִכָּא חֲדָא, מַתְקָלַהּ עֲסַר סִלְעִין הִיא דִּדְהַב מַלְיָא קְטֹרֶת בֻּסְמַיָּא:
סט תּוֹר חַד בַּר תּוֹרֵי, דְּכַר חַד, אִמַּר חַד בַּר שַׁתֵּיהּ לַעֲלָתָא: ע צְפִיר בַּר
עִזִּין חַד לְחַטָּתָא: עא וּלְנִכְסַת קֻדְשַׁיָּא תּוֹרֵי תְּרֵין, דִּכְרֵי חַמְשָׁא גְּדֵי
חַמְשָׁא, אִמְּרִין בְּנֵי שְׁנָא חַמְשָׁא, דֵּין, קֻרְבָּנָא דַּאֲחִיעֶזֶר בַּר עַמִּישַׁדָּי:
עב בְּיוֹם חַד עֲסַר יוֹמִין, רַבָּא לִבְנֵי אָשֵׁר, פַּגְעִיאֵל בַּר עָכְרָן: עג קֻרְבָּנֵיהּ
מְגִסְתָּא דִּכְסַף חֲדָא, מְאָה וּתְלָתִין סִלְעִין הֲוֵי מַתְקָלַהּ, מִזְרְקָא חַד

שְׁנַיִם אֵילִם חֲמִשָּׁה עַתֻּדִים חֲמִשָּׁה כְּבָשִׂים בְּנֵי־שָׁנָה חֲמִשָּׁה זֶה קָרְבַּן
גַּמְלִיאֵל בֶּן־פְּדָהצוּר׃
סא בַּיּוֹם הַתְּשִׁיעִי נָשִׂיא לִבְנֵי בִנְיָמִן אֲבִידָן בֶּן־גִּדְעֹנִי׃ קָרְבָּנוֹ קַעֲרַת־
כֶּסֶף אַחַת שְׁלֹשִׁים וּמֵאָה מִשְׁקָלָהּ מִזְרָק אֶחָד כֶּסֶף שִׁבְעִים שֶׁקֶל
סב בְּשֶׁקֶל הַקֹּדֶשׁ שְׁנֵיהֶם ׀ מְלֵאִים סֹלֶת בְּלוּלָה בַשֶּׁמֶן לְמִנְחָה׃ כַּף אַחַת
סג עֲשָׂרָה זָהָב מְלֵאָה קְטֹרֶת׃ פַּר אֶחָד בֶּן־בָּקָר אַיִל אֶחָד כֶּבֶשׂ־אֶחָד
סד סה בֶּן־שְׁנָתוֹ לְעֹלָה׃ שְׂעִיר־עִזִּים אֶחָד לְחַטָּאת׃ וּלְזֶבַח הַשְּׁלָמִים בָּקָר
שְׁנַיִם אֵילִם חֲמִשָּׁה עַתֻּדִים חֲמִשָּׁה כְּבָשִׂים בְּנֵי־שָׁנָה חֲמִשָּׁה זֶה
קָרְבַּן אֲבִידָן בֶּן־גִּדְעֹנִי׃
סו סז בַּיּוֹם הָעֲשִׂירִי נָשִׂיא לִבְנֵי דָן אֲחִיעֶזֶר בֶּן־עַמִּישַׁדָּי׃ קָרְבָּנוֹ קַעֲרַת־
כֶּסֶף אַחַת שְׁלֹשִׁים וּמֵאָה מִשְׁקָלָהּ מִזְרָק אֶחָד כֶּסֶף שִׁבְעִים שֶׁקֶל
סח בְּשֶׁקֶל הַקֹּדֶשׁ שְׁנֵיהֶם ׀ מְלֵאִים סֹלֶת בְּלוּלָה בַשֶּׁמֶן לְמִנְחָה׃ כַּף אַחַת
סט עֲשָׂרָה זָהָב מְלֵאָה קְטֹרֶת׃ פַּר אֶחָד בֶּן־בָּקָר אַיִל אֶחָד כֶּבֶשׂ־אֶחָד
ע עא בֶּן־שְׁנָתוֹ לְעֹלָה׃ שְׂעִיר־עִזִּים אֶחָד לְחַטָּאת׃ וּלְזֶבַח הַשְּׁלָמִים בָּקָר
שְׁנַיִם אֵילִם חֲמִשָּׁה עַתֻּדִים חֲמִשָּׁה כְּבָשִׂים בְּנֵי־שָׁנָה חֲמִשָּׁה זֶה קָרְבַּן
אֲחִיעֶזֶר בֶּן־עַמִּישַׁדָּי׃
עב עג בְּיוֹם עַשְׁתֵּי עָשָׂר יוֹם נָשִׂיא לִבְנֵי אָשֵׁר פַּגְעִיאֵל בֶּן־עָכְרָן׃ קָרְבָּנוֹ שביעי
קַעֲרַת־כֶּסֶף אַחַת שְׁלֹשִׁים וּמֵאָה מִשְׁקָלָהּ מִזְרָק אֶחָד כֶּסֶף שִׁבְעִים
שֶׁקֶל בְּשֶׁקֶל הַקֹּדֶשׁ שְׁנֵיהֶם ׀ מְלֵאִים סֹלֶת בְּלוּלָה בַשֶּׁמֶן לְמִנְחָה׃
עד עה כַּף אַחַת עֲשָׂרָה זָהָב מְלֵאָה קְטֹרֶת׃ פַּר אֶחָד בֶּן־בָּקָר אַיִל אֶחָד
עו עז כֶּבֶשׂ־אֶחָד בֶּן־שְׁנָתוֹ לְעֹלָה׃ שְׂעִיר־עִזִּים אֶחָד לְחַטָּאת׃ וּלְזֶבַח

אונקלוס

דְּכַסְפָּא, מַתְקָלֵיהּ שַׁבְעִין סִלְעִין בְּסִלְעֵי קֻדְשָׁא, תַּרְוֵיהוֹן מְלַן, סֻלְתָּא, דְּפִילָא בִמְשַׁח לְמִנְחָתָא: עד בָּזִכָּא חֲדָא, מַתְקְלַהּ עֲסַר סִלְעִין הִיא דִּדְהַב מַלְיָא קְטֹרֶת בֻּסְמַיָּא: עה תּוֹר חַד בַּר תּוֹרֵי, דְּכַר חַד, אִמַּר חַד בַּר שַׁתֵּיהּ לַעֲלָתָא: עו צְפִיר בַּר עִזִּין חַד לְחַטָּתָא: עז וּלְנִכְסַת

sacrifice two oxen, five rams, five male goats, and five yearling sheep. This was
the offering of Pagiel son of Okhran.
78 79 On the twelfth day came Aḥira son of Einan, prince of the Naftalites: His
offering was one silver bowl weighing one hundred and thirty shekel and one
silver basin weighing seventy shekel according to the Sanctuary weight, both
80 filled with fine flour mixed with oil for a grain offering; one golden spoon
81 weighing ten shekel, full of incense; one young bull, one ram, and one yearling
82 83 sheep for a burnt offering; one goat for a purification offering; and for the peace
sacrifice two oxen, five rams, five male goats, and five yearling sheep. This was
the offering of Aḥira son of Einan.
84 All this was the dedication offering from the princes of Israel for the altar at
the time it was anointed: There were twelve silver bowls, twelve silver basins,
85 and twelve golden spoons, each silver bowl weighing one hundred and thirty
shekel and each basin seventy shekel – so all the silver in the utensils weighed
86 two thousand four hundred shekel according to the Sanctuary weight. There
were twelve gold spoons full of incense weighing ten shekel each according
to the Sanctuary weight – so all the gold of the spoons weighed one hundred
87 and twenty shekel. The total number of the animals for the burnt offerings was MAFTIR
twelve bulls, twelve rams, and twelve yearling sheep, along with their grain
88 offerings. There were also twelve goats for the purification offerings. The total
number of all the animals for the peace sacrifices was twenty-four bulls, sixty

אונקלוס

קודשיא תורי תרין, דכרי חמשא גדי חמשא, אמרין בני שנא חמשא, דין, קורבנא דפגעיאל בר עכרן: עח ביום תרי עסר יומין, רבא לבני נפתלי, אחירע בר עינן: עט קורבניה מגסתא דכסף חדא, מאה ותלתין סלעין הוי מתקלה, מזרקא חד דכספא, מתקליה שבעין סלעין

רש״י

פד) **ביום המשח אתו.** בו ביום שנמשח הקריב, ומה אני מקיים "אחרי המשח" (להלן פסוק פח)? שנמשח תחלה ואחר כך הקריב. או: "אחרי המשח" לאחר זמן, ולא בא ללמד "ביום המשח" אלא לומר שנמשח ביום? כשהוא אומר: "ביום משחו אתם" (ויקרא ז, לו), למדנו שנמשח ביום, ומה תלמוד לומר: "ביום המשח אתו"? ביום שנמשח הקריב: **קערת כסף שתים עשרה.** הם הם שהתנדבו, ולא אירע בהם פסול:

פה) **שלשים ומאה הקערה האחת וגו'.** מה תלמוד לומר? לפי שנאמר: "שלשים ומאה משקלה" ולא פירש באיזו שקל, לכך חזר ושנאה כאן וכלל בכלן: "כל כסף הכלים... בשקל הקדש": **כל כסף הכלים וגו'.** למדך שהיו כלי המקדש מכוונים במשקלן, שוקלן אחד אחד ושוקלן כלן כאחד, לא רבה ולא מעט:

פו) **כפות זהב שתים עשרה.** למה נאמר? לפי שנאמר: "כף אחת עשרה זהב", היא של זהב ומשקלה עשרה שקלים של כסף; או אינו אלא כף אחת של כסף ומשקלה עשרה שקלי זהב – ושקלי זהב אין משקלם שוה לשל כסף? תלמוד לומר: "כפות זהב", של זהב היו:

הַשְּׁלָמִים בָּקָר שְׁנַיִם אֵילִם חֲמִשָּׁה עַתֻּדִים חֲמִשָּׁה כְּבָשִׂים בְּנֵי־שָׁנָה
חֲמִשָּׁה זֶה קָרְבַּן פַּגְעִיאֵל בֶּן־עָכְרָן׃
עח עט בְּיוֹם שְׁנֵים עָשָׂר יוֹם נָשִׂיא לִבְנֵי נַפְתָּלִי אֲחִירַע בֶּן־עֵינָן׃ קָרְבָּנוֹ
קַעֲרַת־כֶּסֶף אַחַת שְׁלֹשִׁים וּמֵאָה מִשְׁקָלָהּ מִזְרָק אֶחָד כֶּסֶף שִׁבְעִים
שֶׁקֶל בְּשֶׁקֶל הַקֹּדֶשׁ שְׁנֵיהֶם ׀ מְלֵאִים סֹלֶת בְּלוּלָה בַשֶּׁמֶן לְמִנְחָה׃
פ פא כַּף אַחַת עֲשָׂרָה זָהָב מְלֵאָה קְטֹרֶת׃ פַּר אֶחָד בֶּן־בָּקָר אַיִל אֶחָד
פב פג כֶּבֶשׂ־אֶחָד בֶּן־שְׁנָתוֹ לְעֹלָה׃ שְׂעִיר־עִזִּים אֶחָד לְחַטָּאת׃ וּלְזֶבַח
הַשְּׁלָמִים בָּקָר שְׁנַיִם אֵילִם חֲמִשָּׁה עַתֻּדִים חֲמִשָּׁה כְּבָשִׂים בְּנֵי־שָׁנָה
חֲמִשָּׁה זֶה קָרְבַּן אֲחִירַע בֶּן־עֵינָן׃
פד זֹאת ׀ חֲנֻכַּת הַמִּזְבֵּחַ בְּיוֹם הִמָּשַׁח אֹתוֹ מֵאֵת נְשִׂיאֵי יִשְׂרָאֵל קַעֲרֹת
כֶּסֶף שְׁתֵּים עֶשְׂרֵה מִזְרְקֵי־כֶסֶף שְׁנֵים עָשָׂר כַּפּוֹת זָהָב שְׁתֵּים עֶשְׂרֵה׃
פה שְׁלֹשִׁים וּמֵאָה הַקְּעָרָה הָאַחַת כֶּסֶף וְשִׁבְעִים הַמִּזְרָק הָאֶחָד כֹּל כֶּסֶף
פו הַכֵּלִים אַלְפַּיִם וְאַרְבַּע־מֵאוֹת בְּשֶׁקֶל הַקֹּדֶשׁ׃ כַּפּוֹת זָהָב שְׁתֵּים־עֶשְׂרֵה
מְלֵאֹת קְטֹרֶת עֲשָׂרָה עֲשָׂרָה הַכַּף בְּשֶׁקֶל הַקֹּדֶשׁ כָּל־זְהַב הַכַּפּוֹת
פז עֶשְׂרִים וּמֵאָה׃ כָּל־הַבָּקָר לָעֹלָה שְׁנֵים עָשָׂר פָּרִים אֵילִם שְׁנֵים־עָשָׂר מפטיר
כְּבָשִׂים בְּנֵי־שָׁנָה שְׁנֵים עָשָׂר וּמִנְחָתָם וּשְׂעִירֵי עִזִּים שְׁנֵים עָשָׂר
פח לְחַטָּאת׃ וְכֹל בְּקַר ׀ זֶבַח הַשְּׁלָמִים עֶשְׂרִים וְאַרְבָּעָה פָּרִים אֵילִם

אונקלוס

בסלעי קודשא, תרויהון מלן, סולתא, דפילא במשח למנחתא: פ בזכא חדא, מתקלה עסר סלעין היא דדהב מליא קטורת בסמיא: פא תור חד בר תורי, דכר חד, אמר חד בר שתיה לעלתא: פב צפיר בר עזין חד לחטאתא: פג ולנכסת קודשיא תורי תרין, דכרי חמשא גדי חמשא, אמרין בני שנא חמשא, דין, קורבנא דאחירע בר עינן: פד דא חנכת מדבחא, ביומא דרביאו יתיה, מן רברבי ישראל, מגסי כספא תרתא עסרי, מזרקי כספא תרי עסר, בזכי דדהבא תרתא עסרי: פה מאה ותלתין סלעין הוי מתקלה, דמגסתא חדא דכספא, ושבעין דמזרקא חד, כל כסף מניא, תרין אלפין וארבע מאה בסלעי קודשא: פו בזכי דדהבא תרתא עסרי מלין קטורת בסמיא, מתקל עסר סלעין הוי מתקלה, דבזכא בסלעי קודשא, כל דהב בזכיא מאה ועסרין: פז כל תורי לעלתא תרי עסר תורין, דכרין תרי עסר אמרין בני שנא, תרי עסר ומנחתהון, וצפירי בני עזי, תרי עסר לחטאתא: פח וכל, תורי לנכסת קודשיא, עסרין וארבעא תורין, דכרין

rams, sixty goats, and sixty yearling sheep. This was the dedication offering for
89 the altar after it was anointed. When Moshe entered the Tent of Meeting to
speak with the LORD, he would hear the Voice speaking to him from above the
cover over the Ark of the Covenant, from between the two cherubim. Thus did
He speak to him.

The haftara for Parashat Naso is on page 1586.

רש״י

פט **ובבא משה.** שני כתובים המכחישים זה את זה, בא שלישי והכריע ביניהם. כתוב אחד אומר: "וידבר ה' אליו מאהל מועד" (ויקרא א, א) והוא חוץ לפרכת, וכתוב אחד אומר: "ודברתי אתך מעל הכפרת" (שמות כה, כב), בא זה והכריע ביניהם: משה בא אל אהל מועד, ושם שומע את הקול הבא מעל הכפרת מבין שני הכרבים, הקול יוצא מן השמים לבין שני הכרובים, ומשם יוצא לאהל מועד:

מדבר. כמו 'מתדבר', כבודו של מעלה לומר כן, מדבר בינו לבין עצמו, ומשה שומע מאליו: **וידבר אליו.** למעט את אהרן מן הדברות: **וישמע את הקול.** יכול קול נמוך? תלמוד לומר: "את הקול", הוא הקול שנדבר עמו בסיני, וכשמגיע לפתח היה נפסק ולא היה יוצא חוץ לאהל:

within striking distance. The people Moshe leads, like many of us today, are still prone to ambition, aspiration, vanity. They still have the human desire for honor, status, and respect. This is to be one of the primary themes of the book of Numbers.

Throughout Parashat Naso, we have seen Moshe dealing sequentially with several of these potential dangers, implicit in the "second-best" status of the Levites, in the longing that a layman may have for special sanctity, and in the parallel primacy of the tribal leaders. The fact that corrective measures are laid out *before* the narratives of conflict that dominate many of the later chapters of Numbers is an instance of the principle that "God creates the cure before the disease" (*Midrash Lekaḥ Tov,* Shemot 3:1). Rambam writes that the whole Torah was given to make peace in the world (*Hilkhot Ḥanukka* 4:14). Parashat Naso is a series of practical lessons in how to ensure, as far as possible, that everyone feels recognized and respected, and that suspicion is defused and dissolved. It is not enough to pray for peace; we have to work for it.

שִׁשִּׁים עַתֻּדִים שִׁשִּׁים כְּבָשִׂים בְּנֵי־שָׁנָה שִׁשִּׁים זֹאת חֲנֻכַּת הַמִּזְבֵּחַ
פט אַחֲרֵי הִמָּשַׁח אֹתוֹ: וּבְבֹא מֹשֶׁה אֶל־אֹהֶל מוֹעֵד לְדַבֵּר אִתּוֹ וַיִּשְׁמַע
אֶת־הַקּוֹל מִדַּבֵּר אֵלָיו מֵעַל הַכַּפֹּרֶת אֲשֶׁר עַל־אֲרֹן הָעֵדֻת מִבֵּין שְׁנֵי
הַכְּרֻבִים וַיְדַבֵּר אֵלָיו:

The הפטרה *for* פרשת נשא *is on page 1587.*

אונקלוס

שִׁתִּין גַּדֵּי שִׁתִּין, אִמְּרִין בְּנֵי שְׁנָא שִׁתִּין, דָּא חֲנֻכַּת מַדְבְּחָא, בָּתַר דְּרַבִּיאוּ יָתֵיהּ: פט וְכַד עָלֵיל מֹשֶׁה, לְמַשְׁכַּן זִמְנָא לְמַלָּלָא עִמֵּיהּ, וְשָׁמַע יָת קָלָא דְּמִתְמַלַּל עִמֵּיהּ, מֵעִלָּוֵי כָּפֻּרְתָּא דְּעַל אֲרוֹנָא דְּסָהֲדוּתָא, מִבֵּין תְּרֵין כְּרוּבַיָּא, וּמִתְמַלַּל עִמֵּיהּ:

7:89 **וּבְבֹא מֹשֶׁה** *When Moshe entered* – In the Torah, which lays as its conceptual foundation the idea that all of us, regardless of color, culture, creed, or class, are in the image and likeness of God, God summons His people, Israel, to take the first steps to create what might eventually become a truly egalitarian society – or to put it more precisely, a society in which dignity, *kavod*, does not depend on power or wealth or an accident of birth.

Hence the concept, which we will explore more fully in Parashat Koraḥ, of *leadership as service*. The highest title accorded to Moshe in the Torah is that of *eved Hashem*, "the LORD's own servant" (Deut. 34:5). His highest praise is that he was "very humble, more so than any other man on earth" (Num. 12:3). To lead is to serve. Greatness is humility. As the book of Proverbs puts it, "A man's pride will bring him down; he who is lowly in spirit will grasp honor" (29:23).

The Torah points us in the direction of an ideal world, but it does not assume that we have reached it yet or are

PARASHAT BEHAALOTEKHA

8 1 2 And the LORD spoke to Moshe: "Speak to Aharon; say to him: When you raise
up the lamps, the seven lamps shall light the space in front of the candelabrum."
3 Aharon did so; he mounted the lamps toward the front of the candelabrum as

רש״י

ח ב| **בְּהַעֲלֹתְךָ**. לָמָּה נִסְמְכָה פָּרָשַׁת הַמְּנוֹרָה לְפָרָשַׁת הַנְּשִׂיאִים? לְפִי שֶׁכְּשֶׁרָאָה אַהֲרֹן חֲנֻכַּת הַנְּשִׂיאִים חָלְשָׁה דַּעְתּוֹ, שֶׁלֹּא הָיָה עִמָּהֶם בַּחֲנֻכָּה לֹא הוּא וְלֹא שִׁבְטוֹ, אָמַר לוֹ הַקָּדוֹשׁ בָּרוּךְ הוּא: חַיֶּיךָ, שֶׁלְּךָ גְּדוֹלָה מִשֶּׁלָּהֶם, שֶׁאַתָּה מַדְלִיק וּמֵטִיב אֶת הַנֵּרוֹת: **בְּהַעֲלֹתְךָ**. עַל שֵׁם שֶׁהַלַּהַב עוֹלֶה, כָּתוּב בְּהַדְלָקָתָן לְשׁוֹן עֲלִיָּה, שֶׁצָּרִיךְ לְהַדְלִיק עַד שֶׁתְּהֵא שַׁלְהֶבֶת עוֹלָה מֵאֵלֶיהָ. וְעוֹד דָּרְשׁוּ רַבּוֹתֵינוּ מִכָּאן שֶׁמַּעֲלָה הָיְתָה לִפְנֵי הַמְּנוֹרָה שֶׁעָלֶיהָ הַכֹּהֵן עוֹמֵד וּמֵטִיב: **אֶל מוּל פְּנֵי הַמְּנוֹרָה**. אֶל מוּל נֵר הָאֶמְצָעִי, שֶׁאֵינוֹ בַּקָּנִים אֶלָּא בַּגּוּף שֶׁל מְנוֹרָה: **יָאִירוּ שִׁבְעַת הַנֵּרוֹת**. שִׁשָּׁה שֶׁעַל שֵׁשֶׁת הַקָּנִים, שְׁלֹשָׁה הַמִּזְרָחִיִּים פּוֹנִים לְמוּל הָאֶמְצָעִי הַפְּתִילוֹת שֶׁבָּהֶן, וְכֵן שְׁלֹשָׁה הַמַּעֲרָבִיִּים רָאשֵׁי הַפְּתִילוֹת לְמוּל הָאֶמְצָעִי. וְלָמָּה? כְּדֵי שֶׁלֹּא יֹאמְרוּ: לָאוֹרָה הוּא צָרִיךְ:

ג| **וַיַּעַשׂ כֵּן אַהֲרֹן**. לְהַגִּיד שִׁבְחוֹ שֶׁל אַהֲרֹן שֶׁלֹּא שִׁנָּה:

defilements of the Temple, just enough to light the candelabrum until more oil could be sourced.

To defend a country physically, as the Maccabees did, you need an army, but to defend a civilization you need education, educators, and schools. Those are the things that kept the Jewish spirit alive and the menora of Jewish values burning in an everlasting light throughout the centuries. In the hindsight of history, military victory is often secondary to the cultural victory of handing your values on to the next generation, and making sure that your children, and theirs, light up the world. The service of God first requires light. This is reflected in the ritual of the candelabrum here, remembered in the synagogue in the *ner tamid*, the everlasting light, and celebrated on Ḥanukka in the growing light of the *ḥanukiya*.

8:3 **וַיַּעַשׂ כֵּן אַהֲרֹן** *Aharon did so* – The simplicity of this daily ritual epitomizes the role of the priest. A priest engages in rites that in essence never change. One symbol of this was the candelabrum, tended each day so that a *ner tamid*, an everlasting light, burned in the Sanctuary as a sign of the presence of the eternal God. Priestly rituals followed a daily, weekly, monthly, and yearly cycle that never changed. Barring tragedies such as the destruction of the Temple, they could be calculated in advance until the end of time.

On the phrase "Aharon did so… *as the LORD had commanded Moshe*," Rashi comments, "This is stated *in order to praise Aharon*, that he did so [i.e., followed Moshe's instructions] without making any change." On the face of it, this is a very odd comment. Do we need to be told every occasion on which a priest – or anyone else, for that matter – did what God commanded? Is that an occasion for praise? It ought to be the norm. Only the exceptions are newsworthy.

I would suggest that Rashi is alluding to an earlier drama: the inauguration of the Tabernacle at which two of Aharon's sons, Nadav and Avihu, offered up "unauthorized fire before the LORD: fire He had not commanded," and they died (Lev. 10:1–2). Nadav and Avihu were doing what they had seen Moshe do at moments of great spiritual intensity, namely, act on his own initiative. What they failed to understand was that he was a prophet; they were priests. A prophet responds to the unique circumstances of the here and now. The essence of priestly service is to do what you are commanded "without making any change" (Deut. 28:14). What the Torah is saying about Aharon at this point is that he understands his role. He is Aharon, not Moshe – a priest, not a prophet. He epitomizes *that which does not change.*

פרשת בהעלתך

ח א ב וַיְדַבֵּר יְהֹוָה אֶל־מֹשֶׁה לֵּאמֹר: דַּבֵּר אֶל־אַהֲרֹן וְאָמַרְתָּ אֵלָיו ח
בְּהַעֲלֹתְךָ אֶת־הַנֵּרֹת אֶל־מוּל פְּנֵי הַמְּנוֹרָה יָאִירוּ שִׁבְעַת הַנֵּרוֹת:
ג וַיַּעַשׂ כֵּן אַהֲרֹן אֶל־מוּל פְּנֵי הַמְּנוֹרָה הֶעֱלָה נֵרֹתֶיהָ כַּאֲשֶׁר צִוָּה יְהֹוָה

אונקלוס

ח א וּמַלֵּיל יי עִם מֹשֶׁה לְמֵימַר: ב מַלֵּיל עִם אַהֲרֹן, וְתֵימַר לֵיהּ, בְּאַדְלָקוּתָךְ יָת בּוֹצִינַיָּא, לָקֳבֵיל אַפֵּי מְנָרְתָא, יְהוֹן מְנַהֲרִין שִׁבְעָא בּוֹצִינַיָּא: ג וַעֲבַד כֵּן אַהֲרֹן, לָקֳבֵיל אַפֵּי מְנָרְתָא, אַדְלֵיק בּוֹצִינַהָא, כְּמָא דְּפַקֵּיד יי

BEHAALOTEKHA

Parashat Behaalotekha begins with the final preparations for the Israelites' journey from the Sinai Desert to the Promised Land. There are instructions for Aharon, the High Priest, to tend to the lighting of the candelabrum (menora), and for consecrating the Levites into their special role as guardians of the sacred. Before setting out, the Israelites celebrate Passover, one year after the exodus itself, and provisions are made so that those who are unable to celebrate it at its proper time may do so a month later. Details are given about the cloud that signals when to encamp and when to move on. Moshe is commanded to make two silver trumpets to summon the people. The narrative then changes tone. The Israelites set out after their long stay in the Sinai Desert, but almost immediately there are problems, protests, and complaints. Moshe suffers his deepest emotional crisis. He prays to God to die. God tells him to gather seventy elders who will help him with the burdens of leadership. In the last scene of the *parasha*, Moshe's own sister and brother speak against him. Miriam is punished. Moshe, here described as the humblest of men, prays on her behalf. After a week's wait for Miriam to be healed, the people move on. Rare markings found in the Torah scroll in the middle of the *parasha* can be viewed as hints to a distinct division within the *parasha*. The two halves focus respectively on Aharon the priest and Moshe the prophet, and the uniqueness and challenges that accompany each role.

LIGHTING THE CANDELABRUM

The first instruction Aharon receives at the dedication of the Tabernacle is on the lighting of the candelabrum. Similarly, Ḥanukka, the festival named for the rededication of the Temple after its desecration by the Greeks, celebrates the moment when the Maccabees relit the candelabrum. Over time, Ḥanukka became associated with *ḥinukh*, a word meaning "education." What we rededicated after the battle with the Hellenizers was not a physical building – the Temple – but living embodiments of Judaism, namely, our children, our students, the people to whom we teach and hand on our heritage and values. History itself has a history, and what began as the festival of a military victory, recorded in the first and second books of Maccabees, became predominantly the festival of a spiritual and civilizational victory. Tradition ruled that the two books of Maccabees, and others under the same title, should be called *sefarim ḥitzoni'im*, apocryphal works, while the festival we celebrate focuses on one symbolic detail of the original chain of events, not mentioned in the books of the Maccabees at all: that one cruse of pure, undefiled oil was found by the Maccabees among the wreckage and

4 the Lord had commanded Moshe. This is how the candelabrum was made: of
hammered gold, hammered from its base to its flowers. According to the vision
that the Lord had shown Moshe, so was the lampstand made.
5 6 The Lord spoke to Moshe: "Take the Levites from among the Israelites and
7 purify them. This is what you shall do to them to purify them: Sprinkle upon
them the water of purification, and have them shave their whole bodies and
8 wash their clothes; then they will be purified. They shall take a young bull
with its grain offering of fine flour mixed with oil. You, meanwhile, shall take
9 a second young bull for a purification offering. You shall bring the Levites
10 before the Tent of Meeting and assemble all the community of Israel. Then
you shall bring the Levites forward before the Lord, and the Israelites shall
11 lay their hands upon the Levites. Aharon shall then present the Levites before
the Lord like a wave offering from the Israelites, so that they may perform
12 the Lord's service. The Levites shall then lay their hands upon the heads of
the bulls, and Aharon shall offer one as a purification offering and the other
13 as a burnt offering to the Lord, to make atonement for the Levites. You shall
have the Levites stand before Aharon and his sons, and then present them like
14 a wave offering to the Lord. Thus you shall separate the Levites from among
15 the other Israelites; the Levites shall become Mine. After that, the Levites shall SHENI

רש"י

ד **וְזֶה מַעֲשֵׂה הַמְּנֹרָה.** שֶׁהֶרְאָהוּ הַקָּדוֹשׁ בָּרוּךְ הוּא בָּאֶצְבַּע לְפִי שֶׁנִּתְקַשָּׁה בָּהּ, לְכָךְ נֶאֱמַר: "וְזֶה": **מִקְשָׁה.** בטדי"ץ בְּלַעַז, לְשׁוֹן: "דָּא לְדָא נָקְשָׁן" (דניאל ה, ו). עֶשֶׁת שֶׁל כִּכַּר זָהָב הָיְתָה, וּמַקִּישׁ בְּקֻרְנָס וְחוֹתֵךְ בְּכַשִּׁיל לְפַשֵּׁט אֵיבָרֶיהָ כְּתִקּוּנָן, וְלֹא נַעֲשֵׂית אֵיבָרִים אֵיבָרִים עַל יְדֵי חִבּוּר: **עַד יְרֵכָהּ עַד פִּרְחָהּ.** יְרֵכָהּ הִיא הַשִּׁדָּה שֶׁעַל הָרַגְלַיִם, חָלוּל, כְּדֶרֶךְ מְנוֹרוֹת כֶּסֶף שֶׁלִּפְנֵי הַשָּׂרִים: **עַד יְרֵכָהּ עַד פִּרְחָהּ.** כְּלוֹמַר גּוּפָהּ שֶׁל מְנוֹרָה כֻּלָּהּ וְכָל הַתָּלוּי בָּהּ: **עַד יְרֵכָהּ.** שֶׁהוּא אֵיבָר גָּדוֹל: **עַד פִּרְחָהּ.** שֶׁהוּא מַעֲשֶׂה דַּק שֶׁבָּהּ, הַכֹּל "מִקְשָׁה". וְדֶרֶךְ 'עַד' לְשַׁמֵּשׁ בְּלָשׁוֹן זֶה, כְּמוֹ: "מִגָּדִישׁ וְעַד קָמָה וְעַד כֶּרֶם זָיִת" (שופטים טו, ה): **כַּמַּרְאֶה אֲשֶׁר הֶרְאָה וְגוֹ'.** כְּתַבְנִית אֲשֶׁר הֶרְאָהוּ בָּהָר, כְּמוֹ שֶׁנֶּאֱמַר: "וּרְאֵה וַעֲשֵׂה בְּתַבְנִיתָם" וְגוֹ' (שמות כה, מ): **כֵּן עָשָׂה אֶת הַמְּנֹרָה.** מִי שֶׁעֲשָׂאָהּ. וּמִדְרַשׁ אַגָּדָה: עַל יְדֵי הַקָּדוֹשׁ בָּרוּךְ הוּא נַעֲשֵׂית מֵאֵלֶיהָ:

ו **קַח אֶת הַלְוִיִּם.** קָחֵם בִּדְבָרִים: 'אַשְׁרֵיכֶם שֶׁתִּזְכּוּ לִהְיוֹת שַׁמָּשִׁים לַמָּקוֹם':

ז **הַזֵּה עֲלֵיהֶם מֵי חַטָּאת.** שֶׁל אֵפֶר הַפָּרָה, מִפְּנֵי טְמֵאֵי מֵתִים שֶׁבָּהֶם: **וְהֶעֱבִירוּ תַעַר.** מָצָאתִי בְּדִבְרֵי רַבִּי מֹשֶׁה הַדַּרְשָׁן, לְפִי שֶׁנִּתְּנוּ כַּפָּרָה עַל הַבְּכוֹרוֹת שֶׁעָבְדוּ עֲבוֹדָה זָרָה, וְהִיא קְרוּיָה 'זִבְחֵי מֵתִים' (תהלים קו, כח), וְהַמְּצֹרָע קָרוּי 'מֵת' (להלן יב, יב), הִזְקִיקָם תִּגְלַחַת כִּמְצֹרָעִים:

ח **וְלָקְחוּ פַּר בֶּן בָּקָר.** וְהוּא עוֹלָה, כְּמוֹ שֶׁכָּתוּב: "וַעֲשֵׂה אֶת הָאֶחָד... עֹלָה" (להלן פסוק יב), וְהוּא קָרְבַּן צִבּוּר בַּעֲבוֹדָה זָרָה (להלן טו, כד): **וּפַר שֵׁנִי.** מַה תַּלְמוּד לוֹמַר "שֵׁנִי"? לוֹמַר לְךָ, מָה עוֹלָה לֹא נֶאֱכֶלֶת אַף חַטָּאת לֹא נֶאֱכֶלֶת, וּבְזוֹ יֵשׁ סֶמֶךְ לִדְבָרָיו בְּתוֹרַת כֹּהֲנִים (חובה פרק ג, ד). וְאוֹמֵר אֲנִי שֶׁהוֹרָאַת שָׁעָה הָיְתָה, שֶׁשָּׂעִיר הָיָה לָהֶם לְהָבִיא לְחַטָּאת עֲבוֹדָה זָרָה עִם פַּר הָעוֹלָה:

ט **וְהִקְהַלְתָּ אֶת כָּל עֲדַת.** לְפִי שֶׁהַלְוִיִּם נְתוּנִים קָרְבַּן כַּפָּרָה תַּחְתֵּיהֶם, יָבוֹאוּ וְיַעַמְדוּ עַל קָרְבָּנָם וְיִסְמְכוּ אֶת יְדֵיהֶם עֲלֵיהֶם:

יא **וְהֵנִיף אַהֲרֹן אֶת הַלְוִיִּם תְּנוּפָה.** כְּדֶרֶךְ שֶׁאָשָׁם מְצֹרָע טָעוּן תְּנוּפָה חַי (ויקרא יד, יב). שָׁלֹשׁ תְּנוּפוֹת נֶאֶמְרוּ בְּפָרָשָׁה זוֹ: הָרִאשׁוֹנָה לִבְנֵי קְהָת, לְכָךְ נֶאֱמַר בָּם: "וְהָיוּ לַעֲבֹד אֶת עֲבֹדַת ה'", לְפִי שֶׁעֲבוֹדַת קֹדֶשׁ הַקֳּדָשִׁים עֲלֵיהֶם, "הָאָרֹן וְהַשֻּׁלְחָן" וְגוֹ' (לעיל ג, לא); הַשְּׁנִיָּה לִבְנֵי גֵּרְשׁוֹן, לְכָךְ נֶאֱמַר בָּם: "תְּנוּפָה לַה'" (להלן פסוק יג), שֶׁאַף עֲלֵיהֶם הָיְתָה עֲבוֹדַת הַקֹּדֶשׁ – יְרִיעוֹת וּקְרָסִים הַנִּרְאִים בְּבֵית קֹדֶשׁ הַקֳּדָשִׁים; וְהַשְּׁלִישִׁית לִבְנֵי מְרָרִי (להלן פסוק טו):

ד אֶת־מֹשֶׁה׃ וְזֶה מַעֲשֵׂה הַמְּנֹרָה מִקְשָׁה זָהָב עַד־יְרֵכָהּ עַד־פִּרְחָהּ
מִקְשָׁה הִוא כַּמַּרְאֶה אֲשֶׁר הֶרְאָה יהוה אֶת־מֹשֶׁה כֵּן עָשָׂה אֶת־
הַמְּנֹרָה׃
ה ו וַיְדַבֵּר יהוה אֶל־מֹשֶׁה לֵּאמֹר׃ קַח אֶת־הַלְוִיִּם מִתּוֹךְ בְּנֵי יִשְׂרָאֵל
ז וְטִהַרְתָּ אֹתָם׃ וְכֹה־תַעֲשֶׂה לָהֶם לְטַהֲרָם הַזֵּה עֲלֵיהֶם מֵי חַטָּאת
ח וְהֶעֱבִירוּ תַעַר עַל־כָּל־בְּשָׂרָם וְכִבְּסוּ בִגְדֵיהֶם וְהִטֶּהָרוּ׃ וְלָקְחוּ פַּר בֶּן־
בָּקָר וּמִנְחָתוֹ סֹלֶת בְּלוּלָה בַשָּׁמֶן וּפַר־שֵׁנִי בֶן־בָּקָר תִּקַּח לְחַטָּאת׃
ט וְהִקְרַבְתָּ אֶת־הַלְוִיִּם לִפְנֵי אֹהֶל מוֹעֵד וְהִקְהַלְתָּ אֶת־כָּל־עֲדַת בְּנֵי
י יִשְׂרָאֵל׃ וְהִקְרַבְתָּ אֶת־הַלְוִיִּם לִפְנֵי יהוה וְסָמְכוּ בְנֵי־יִשְׂרָאֵל אֶת־
יא יְדֵיהֶם עַל־הַלְוִיִּם׃ וְהֵנִיף אַהֲרֹן אֶת־הַלְוִיִּם תְּנוּפָה לִפְנֵי יהוה מֵאֵת
יב בְּנֵי יִשְׂרָאֵל וְהָיוּ לַעֲבֹד אֶת־עֲבֹדַת יהוה׃ וְהַלְוִיִּם יִסְמְכוּ אֶת־יְדֵיהֶם
עַל רֹאשׁ הַפָּרִים וַעֲשֵׂה אֶת־הָאֶחָד חַטָּאת וְאֶת־הָאֶחָד עֹלָה לַיהוה
יג לְכַפֵּר עַל־הַלְוִיִּם׃ וְהַעֲמַדְתָּ אֶת־הַלְוִיִּם לִפְנֵי אַהֲרֹן וְלִפְנֵי בָנָיו וְהֵנַפְתָּ
יד אֹתָם תְּנוּפָה לַיהוה׃ וְהִבְדַּלְתָּ אֶת־הַלְוִיִּם מִתּוֹךְ בְּנֵי יִשְׂרָאֵל וְהָיוּ לִי
טו הַלְוִיִּם׃ וְאַחֲרֵי־כֵן יָבֹאוּ הַלְוִיִּם לַעֲבֹד אֶת־אֹהֶל מוֹעֵד וְטִהַרְתָּ אֹתָם שני

אונקלוס

יָת מֹשֶׁה׃ ד וְדֵין עוֹבָד מְנָרְתָא נְגִידָא דִּהַב, עַד שִׁדַּהּ עַד שׁוֹשַׁנַּהּ נְגִידָא הִיא, כְּחֶזְוָא, דְּאַחְזִי יְיָ יָת מֹשֶׁה, כֵּן עֲבַד יָת מְנָרְתָא׃ ה וּמַלֵּיל יְיָ עִם מֹשֶׁה לְמֵימַר׃ ו קָרֵיב יָת לֵיוָאֵי, מִגּוֹ בְּנֵי יִשְׂרָאֵל, וּתְדַכֵּי יָתְהוֹן׃ ז וּכְדֵין תַּעֲבֵיד לְהוֹן לְדַכּוֹאֵיהוֹן, אַדִּי עֲלֵיהוֹן מַיָּא דְּחַטָּתָא, וְיַעְבְּרוּן מִסְפָּר עַל כָּל בִּסְרְהוֹן, וִיחַוְּרוּן לְבוּשֵׁיהוֹן וְיִדַּכּוֹן׃ ח וְיִסְּבוּן תּוֹר בַּר תּוֹרֵי, וּמִנְחָתֵיהּ, סֻלְתָּא דְּפִילָא בִמְשַׁח, וְתוֹר תִּנְיָן בַּר תּוֹרֵי תִּסַּב לְחַטָּתָא׃ ט וּתְקָרֵיב יָת לֵיוָאֵי, לִקְדָם מַשְׁכַּן זִמְנָא, וְתִכְנוֹשׁ, יָת כָּל כְּנִשְׁתָּא דִּבְנֵי יִשְׂרָאֵל׃ י וּתְקָרֵיב יָת לֵיוָאֵי קֳדָם יְיָ, וְיִסְמְכוּן בְּנֵי יִשְׂרָאֵל, יָת יְדֵיהוֹן עַל לֵיוָאֵי׃ יא וִירִים אַהֲרֹן יָת לֵיוָאֵי אֲרָמָא קֳדָם יְיָ, מִן בְּנֵי יִשְׂרָאֵל, וִיהוֹן, לְמִפְלַח יָת פָּלְחָנָא דַּייָ׃ יב וְלֵיוָאֵי יִסְמְכוּן יָת יְדֵיהוֹן, עַל רֵישׁ תּוֹרַיָּא, וַעֲבֵיד, יָת חַד חַטָּתָא, וְיָת חַד עֲלָתָא קֳדָם יְיָ, לְכַפָּרָא עַל לֵיוָאֵי׃ יג וּתְקִים יָת לֵיוָאֵי, קֳדָם אַהֲרֹן וּקְדָם בְּנוֹהִי, וּתְרִים יָתְהוֹן, אֲרָמָא קֳדָם יְיָ׃ יד וְתַפְרֵישׁ יָת לֵיוָאֵי, מִגּוֹ בְּנֵי יִשְׂרָאֵל, וִיהוֹן מְשַׁמְּשִׁין קֳדָמַי לֵיוָאֵי׃ טו וּבָתַר כֵּן יֵיעֲלוּן לֵיוָאֵי, לְמִפְלַח יָת מַשְׁכַּן זִמְנָא, וּתְדַכֵּי יָתְהוֹן,

enter to perform the service of the Tent of Meeting, once you have purified
16 them and presented them as a wave offering. They are wholly given over to Me
from among the Israelites. I have taken them for Myself in place of the first to
17 emerge from every womb, the firstborn of all the Israelites. For all the firstborn
among the Israelites, man and beast alike, are Mine; on the day that I struck
18 down the firstborn in Egypt, I consecrated them to Myself. But I have now
19 taken the Levites in place of all the firstborn among the Israelites, and I have
given the Levites to Aharon and his sons from among the Israelites, to perform
the service of the Israelites in the Tent of Meeting and to make atonement for
the Israelites, so that no plague will come among the Israelites for drawing too
20 close to the Sanctuary." Moshe, Aharon, and all the community of Israel did
this for the Levites; all that the Lord commanded Moshe with regard to the
21 Levites, so the Israelites did. The Levites purified themselves and washed their
clothes. Aharon presented them as a wave offering before the Lord, and made
22 atonement for them in order to purify them. And after that, the Levites went
in to perform their service in the Tent of Meeting before Aharon and his sons.
As the Lord had commanded Moshe regarding the Levites, so they did for
23 24 them. And the Lord spoke to Moshe: "The Levites: From twenty-
25 five years upward they shall go into the service of the Tent of Meeting. At fifty
26 years old they shall retire from the service and serve no longer. They may assist
their fellow Levites in carrying out their duties in the Tent of Meeting, but shall
not perform the service itself. This is how you shall conduct the Levites with
regard to their duties."

רש״י

טז **נְתֻנִים נְתֻנִים.** נְתוּנִים לְמַשָּׂא, נְתוּנִים לְשִׁיר: **פִּטְרַת.** פְּתִיחַת:

יז **כִּי לִי כָל בְּכוֹר.** שֶׁלִּי הָיוּ הַבְּכוֹרוֹת בְּקַו הַדִּין, שֶׁהֵגַנְתִּי עֲלֵיהֶם בֵּין בְּכוֹרֵי מִצְרַיִם וְלָקַחְתִּי אוֹתָם לִי, עַד שֶׁטָּעוּ בָּעֵגֶל, וְעַכְשָׁיו: "וָאֶקַּח אֶת הַלְוִיִּם" וְגוֹ' (להלן פסוק יח):

יט **וָאֶתְּנָה וְגוֹ'.** חֲמִשָּׁה פְּעָמִים נֶאֱמַר 'בְּנֵי יִשְׂרָאֵל' בְּמִקְרָא זֶה, לְהוֹדִיעַ חִבָּתָן שֶׁתּוֹכֵף אַזְכָּרוֹתֵיהֶן בְּמִקְרָא אֶחָד כְּמִנְיַן חֲמִשָּׁה חֻמְשֵׁי תוֹרָה, כָּךְ רָאִיתִי בִּבְרֵאשִׁית רַבָּה (ג, ה): **וְלֹא יִהְיֶה בִּבְנֵי יִשְׂרָאֵל נֶגֶף.** שֶׁלֹּא יִצְטָרְכוּ לָגֶשֶׁת אֶל הַקֹּדֶשׁ, שֶׁאִם יִגְּשׁוּ יִהְיֶה נֶגֶף:

כ **וַיַּעַשׂ מֹשֶׁה וְאַהֲרֹן וְכָל עֲדַת וְגוֹ'.** מֹשֶׁה הֶעֱמִידָן, וְאַהֲרֹן הֵנִיף, וְיִשְׂרָאֵל סָמְכוּ אֶת יְדֵיהֶם:

כב **כַּאֲשֶׁר צִוָּה ה' וְגוֹ' כֵּן עָשׂוּ.** לְהַגִּיד שֶׁבַח הָעוֹשִׂין וְהַנַּעֲשָׂה בָּהֶן, שֶׁאֶחָד מֵהֶם לֹא עִכֵּב:

כד **זֹאת אֲשֶׁר לַלְוִיִּם.** שָׁנִים פּוֹסְלִים בָּהֶם, וְאֵין הַמּוּמִין פּוֹסְלִים בָּהֶם: **מִבֶּן חָמֵשׁ וְעֶשְׂרִים.** וּבְמָקוֹם אַחֵר אוֹמֵר: "מִבֶּן שְׁלֹשִׁים שָׁנָה" (לעיל ד, ג), הָא כֵּיצַד? מִבֶּן עֶשְׂרִים וְחָמֵשׁ בָּא לִלְמֹד הִלְכוֹת עֲבוֹדָה וְלוֹמֵד חָמֵשׁ שָׁנִים, וּבֶן שְׁלֹשִׁים עוֹבֵד. מִכָּאן לְתַלְמִיד שֶׁלֹּא רָאָה סִימָן יָפֶה בְּמִשְׁנָתוֹ בְּחָמֵשׁ שָׁנִים, שׁוּב אֵינוֹ רוֹאֶה:

כה **וְלֹא יַעֲבֹד עוֹד.** עֲבוֹדַת מַשָּׂא בַּכָּתֵף, אֲבָל חוֹזֵר הוּא לִנְעִילַת שְׁעָרִים וְלָשִׁיר וְלִטְעֹן עֲגָלוֹת, וְזֶהוּ: "וְשֵׁרֵת אֶת אֶחָיו" (להלן פסוק כו), "עִם אֲחוֹהִי", כְּתַרְגּוּמוֹ:

כו **לִשְׁמֹר מִשְׁמֶרֶת.** לַחֲנוֹת סָבִיב לָאֹהֶל וּלְהָקִים וּלְהוֹרִיד בִּשְׁעַת הַמַּסָּעוֹת:

טז וְהֵנַפְתָּ אֹתָם תְּנוּפָה: כִּי נְתֻנִים נְתֻנִים הֵמָּה לִי מִתּוֹךְ בְּנֵי יִשְׂרָאֵל
יז תַּחַת פִּטְרַת כָּל־רֶחֶם בְּכוֹר כֹּל מִבְּנֵי יִשְׂרָאֵל לָקַחְתִּי אֹתָם לִי: כִּי
לִי כָל־בְּכוֹר בִּבְנֵי יִשְׂרָאֵל בָּאָדָם וּבַבְּהֵמָה בְּיוֹם הַכֹּתִי כָל־בְּכוֹר
יח בְּאֶרֶץ מִצְרַיִם הִקְדַּשְׁתִּי אֹתָם לִי: וָאֶקַּח אֶת־הַלְוִיִּם תַּחַת כָּל־בְּכוֹר
יט בִּבְנֵי יִשְׂרָאֵל: וָאֶתְּנָה אֶת־הַלְוִיִּם נְתֻנִים ׀ לְאַהֲרֹן וּלְבָנָיו מִתּוֹךְ בְּנֵי
יִשְׂרָאֵל לַעֲבֹד אֶת־עֲבֹדַת בְּנֵי־יִשְׂרָאֵל בְּאֹהֶל מוֹעֵד וּלְכַפֵּר עַל־בְּנֵי
יִשְׂרָאֵל וְלֹא יִהְיֶה בִּבְנֵי יִשְׂרָאֵל נֶגֶף בְּגֶשֶׁת בְּנֵי־יִשְׂרָאֵל אֶל־הַקֹּדֶשׁ:
כ וַיַּעַשׂ מֹשֶׁה וְאַהֲרֹן וְכָל־עֲדַת בְּנֵי־יִשְׂרָאֵל לַלְוִיִּם כְּכֹל אֲשֶׁר־צִוָּה
כא יהוה אֶת־מֹשֶׁה לַלְוִיִּם כֵּן־עָשׂוּ לָהֶם בְּנֵי יִשְׂרָאֵל: וַיִּתְחַטְּאוּ הַלְוִיִּם
וַיְכַבְּסוּ בִּגְדֵיהֶם וַיָּנֶף אַהֲרֹן אֹתָם תְּנוּפָה לִפְנֵי יהוה וַיְכַפֵּר עֲלֵיהֶם
כב אַהֲרֹן לְטַהֲרָם: וְאַחֲרֵי־כֵן בָּאוּ הַלְוִיִּם לַעֲבֹד אֶת־עֲבֹדָתָם בְּאֹהֶל
מוֹעֵד לִפְנֵי אַהֲרֹן וְלִפְנֵי בָנָיו כַּאֲשֶׁר צִוָּה יהוה אֶת־מֹשֶׁה עַל־הַלְוִיִּם
כג כד כֵּן עָשׂוּ לָהֶם: וַיְדַבֵּר יהוה אֶל־מֹשֶׁה לֵּאמֹר: זֹאת אֲשֶׁר
לַלְוִיִּם מִבֶּן חָמֵשׁ וְעֶשְׂרִים שָׁנָה וָמַעְלָה יָבוֹא לִצְבֹא צָבָא בַּעֲבֹדַת
כה אֹהֶל מוֹעֵד: וּמִבֶּן חֲמִשִּׁים שָׁנָה יָשׁוּב מִצְּבָא הָעֲבֹדָה וְלֹא יַעֲבֹד עוֹד:
כו וְשֵׁרֵת אֶת־אֶחָיו בְּאֹהֶל מוֹעֵד לִשְׁמֹר מִשְׁמֶרֶת וַעֲבֹדָה לֹא יַעֲבֹד כָּכָה
תַּעֲשֶׂה לַלְוִיִּם בְּמִשְׁמְרֹתָם:

אונקלוס

וּתְרִים יָתְהוֹן אֲרָמָא: טז אֲרֵי אַפְרָשָׁא מַפְרְשִׁין אִנּוּן קֳדָמַי, מִגּוֹ בְּנֵי יִשְׂרָאֵל, חֲלָף פָּתַח כָּל וַלְדָּא, בְּכָרָא כּוֹלָא מִבְּנֵי יִשְׂרָאֵל, קָרֵיבִית יָתְהוֹן קֳדָמָי: יז אֲרֵי דִּילִי כָּל בְּכָרָא בִּבְנֵי יִשְׂרָאֵל, בַּאֲנָשָׁא וּבִבְעִירָא, בְּיוֹמָא, דְּקַטָלִית כָּל בְּכָרָא בְּאַרְעָא דְּמִצְרַיִם, אַקְדֵּישִׁית יָתְהוֹן קֳדָמָי: יח וְקָרֵיבִית יָת לֵיוָאֵי, חֲלָף כָּל בְּכָרָא בִּבְנֵי יִשְׂרָאֵל: יט וִיהַבִית יָת לֵיוָאֵי, מְסִירִין לְאַהֲרֹן וְלִבְנוֹהִי, מִגּוֹ בְּנֵי יִשְׂרָאֵל, לְמִפְלַח, יָת פָּלְחַן בְּנֵי יִשְׂרָאֵל בְּמַשְׁכַּן זִמְנָא, וּלְכַפָּרָא עַל בְּנֵי יִשְׂרָאֵל, וְלָא יְהֵי, בִּבְנֵי יִשְׂרָאֵל מוֹתָא, בְּמִקְרַב בְּנֵי יִשְׂרָאֵל לְקֻדְשָׁא: כ וַעֲבַד מֹשֶׁה וְאַהֲרֹן, וְכָל כְּנִשְׁתָּא דִּבְנֵי יִשְׂרָאֵל לְלֵיוָאֵי,

כְּכֹל, דְּפַקֵּיד יי יָת מֹשֶׁה לְלֵיוָאֵי, כֵּן עֲבַדוּ לְהוֹן בְּנֵי יִשְׂרָאֵל: כא וְאִדַּכִּיאוּ לֵיוָאֵי, וְחַוַּרוּ לְבוּשֵׁיהוֹן, וַאֲרֵים אַהֲרֹן יָתְהוֹן, אֲרָמָא קֳדָם יי, וְכַפַּר עֲלֵיהוֹן, אַהֲרֹן לְדַכּוֹאֵיהוֹן: כב וּבָתַר כֵּן עָאלוּ לֵיוָאֵי, לְמִפְלַח יָת פָּלְחָנְהוֹן בְּמַשְׁכַּן זִמְנָא, קֳדָם אַהֲרֹן וּקְדָם בְּנוֹהִי, כְּמָא דְּפַקֵּיד יי יָת מֹשֶׁה עַל לֵיוָאֵי, כֵּן עֲבַדוּ לְהוֹן: כג וּמַלֵּיל יי עִם מֹשֶׁה לְמֵימַר: כד דָּא דִּלְלֵיוָאֵי, מִבַּר עַסְרִין וְחָמֵשׁ שְׁנִין וּלְעֵילָא, יֵיתֵי לְחַיָּלָא חֵילָא, בְּפָלְחַן מַשְׁכַּן זִמְנָא: כה וּמִבַּר חַמְשִׁין שְׁנִין, יְתוּב מֵחֵיל פָּלְחָנָא, וְלָא יִפְלַח עוֹד: כו וִישַׁמֵּישׁ עִם אֲחוֹהִי, בְּמַשְׁכַּן זִמְנָא לְמִטַּר מַטְּרָא, וּפָלְחָנָא לָא יִפְלַח, כְּדֵין, תַּעֲבֵיד לְלֵיוָאֵי בְּמַטְּרָתְהוֹן:

9 1 The LORD spoke to Moshe in the Sinai Desert in the first month of the second SHELISHI
2 year after they had left Egypt: "Let the Israelites offer the Passover sacrifice at
3 its appointed time. On the fourteenth day of this month in the afternoon you
shall offer it at its appointed time. Bring it in accordance with all its decrees
4 and laws." And so Moshe instructed the Israelites to offer the Passover sacrifice.
5 On the afternoon of the fourteenth day of the first month they offered the
Passover sacrifice in the Sinai Desert. Just as the LORD commanded Moshe, so
6 the Israelites did. But there were people who were impure because of contact
with the dead, and they were unable to offer the Passover sacrifice on that day.
7 That very day they approached Moshe and Aharon: "We have become impure
because of contact with the dead," these people said to him, "but must we be
debarred from presenting the LORD's offering at its appointed time among
8 all the Israelites?" "Wait," Moshe replied, "and let me hear what the LORD
commands concerning you."
9 10 And the LORD spoke to Moshe: "Tell the Israelites: When any of you or your
future descendants are impure because of contact with the dead, or away on

רש״י

ט א| **בַּחֹדֶשׁ הָרִאשׁוֹן.** פָּרָשָׁה שֶׁבְּרֹאשׁ הַסֵּפֶר לֹא נֶאֶמְרָה עַד אִיָּר, לִמַּדְתָּ שֶׁאֵין סֵדֶר מֻקְדָּם וּמְאֻחָר בַּתּוֹרָה. וְלָמָּה לֹא פָּתַח בְּזוֹ? מִפְּנֵי שֶׁהוּא גְּנוּתָן שֶׁל יִשְׂרָאֵל, שֶׁכָּל אַרְבָּעִים שָׁנָה שֶׁהָיוּ יִשְׂרָאֵל בַּמִּדְבָּר לֹא הִקְרִיבוּ אֶלָּא פֶּסַח זֶה בִּלְבַד:

ב| **בְּמֹעֲדוֹ.** אַף בְּשַׁבָּת, אַף בְּטֻמְאָה:

ג| **כְּכָל חֻקֹּתָיו.** אֵלּוּ מִצְוֹת שֶׁבְּגוּפוֹ: "שֶׂה תָמִים זָכָר בֶּן שָׁנָה" (שמות יב, ה): **וּכְכָל מִשְׁפָּטָיו.** אֵלּוּ מִצְוֹת שֶׁעַל גּוּפוֹ מִמָּקוֹם אַחֵר: לְשִׁבְעַת יָמִים לְמַצָּה וּלְבִעוּר חָמֵץ:

ד| **וַיְדַבֵּר מֹשֶׁה וְגוֹ׳.** מַה תַּלְמוּד לוֹמַר? וַהֲלֹא כְּבָר נֶאֱמַר: "וַיְדַבֵּר מֹשֶׁה אֶת מֹעֲדֵי ה׳" (ויקרא כג, מד)? אֶלָּא כְּשֶׁשָּׁמַע פָּרָשַׁת מוֹעֲדִים מִסִּינַי אֲמָרָהּ לָהֶם, וְחָזַר וְהִזְהִירָם בִּשְׁעַת מַעֲשֶׂה:

ו| **לִפְנֵי מֹשֶׁה וְלִפְנֵי אַהֲרֹן.** כְּשֶׁשְּׁנֵיהֶם יוֹשְׁבִין בְּבֵית הַמִּדְרָשׁ בָּאוּ וְשָׁאֲלוּם. וְלֹא יִתָּכֵן לוֹמַר זֶה אַחַר זֶה, שֶׁאִם מֹשֶׁה לֹא הָיָה יוֹדֵעַ, אַהֲרֹן מִנַּיִן לוֹ?:

ז| **לָמָּה נִגָּרַע.** אָמַר לָהֶם: אֵין קָדָשִׁים קְרֵבִים בְּטֻמְאָה. אָמְרוּ לוֹ: יִזָּרֵק הַדָּם עָלֵינוּ בְּכֹהֲנִים טְהוֹרִים וְיֵאָכֵל הַבָּשָׂר לִטְהוֹרִים, אָמַר לָהֶם: "עִמְדוּ וְאֶשְׁמְעָה" (להלן פסוק ח), כְּתַלְמִיד הַמֻּבְטָח לִשְׁמֹעַ מִפִּי רַבּוֹ. אַשְׁרֵי יְלוּד אִשָּׁה שֶׁכָּךְ מֻבְטָח, שֶׁכָּל זְמַן שֶׁהָיָה רוֹצֶה הָיָה מְדַבֵּר עִם הַשְּׁכִינָה. וּרְאוּיָה הָיְתָה פָּרָשָׁה זוֹ לְהֵאָמֵר עַל יְדֵי מֹשֶׁה כִּשְׁאָר כָּל הַתּוֹרָה כֻּלָּהּ, אֶלָּא שֶׁזָּכוּ אֵלּוּ שֶׁתֵּאָמֵר עַל יְדֵיהֶן, שֶׁמְּגַלְגְּלִין זְכוּת עַל יְדֵי זַכַּאי:

י| **אוֹ בְדֶרֶךְ רְחֹקָה.** נָקוּד עָלָיו, לוֹמַר לֹא שֶׁרְחוֹקָה וַדַּאי, אֶלָּא שֶׁהָיָה חוּץ לְאַסְקֻפַּת הָעֲזָרָה כָּל זְמַן שְׁחִיטָה. פֶּסַח שֵׁנִי – מַצָּה וְחָמֵץ עִמּוֹ בַּבַּיִת, וְאֵין שָׁם יוֹם טוֹב, וְאֵין אִסּוּר חָמֵץ אֶלָּא עִמּוֹ בַּאֲכִילָתוֹ:

going, missing the mark and recalculating the route. Because even the Torah acknowledges this, we know that in the inner reaches of our soul we can be honest with ourselves, we can acknowledge the ways in which we've fallen short. Those who cannot offer the Passover sacrifice, whether due to lack of planning or to circumstances beyond their control, are eager for another chance. They know that, in His forgiveness, God gives us the strength to heal what we have harmed, to try again, and to become the person He wants us to be.

ט א וַיְדַבֵּר יהוה אֶל־מֹשֶׁה בְמִדְבַּר־סִינַי בַּשָּׁנָה הַשֵּׁנִית לְצֵאתָם מֵאֶרֶץ שלישי
ב מִצְרַיִם בַּחֹדֶשׁ הָרִאשׁוֹן לֵאמֹר: וְיַעֲשׂוּ בְנֵי־יִשְׂרָאֵל אֶת־הַפָּסַח
ג בְּמוֹעֲדוֹ: בְּאַרְבָּעָה עָשָׂר־יוֹם בַּחֹדֶשׁ הַזֶּה בֵּין הָעַרְבַּיִם תַּעֲשׂוּ אֹתוֹ
ד בְּמֹעֲדוֹ כְּכָל־חֻקֹּתָיו וּכְכָל־מִשְׁפָּטָיו תַּעֲשׂוּ אֹתוֹ: וַיְדַבֵּר מֹשֶׁה אֶל־בְּנֵי
ה יִשְׂרָאֵל לַעֲשֹׂת הַפָּסַח: וַיַּעֲשׂוּ אֶת־הַפֶּסַח בָּרִאשׁוֹן בְּאַרְבָּעָה עָשָׂר
יוֹם לַחֹדֶשׁ בֵּין הָעַרְבַּיִם בְּמִדְבַּר סִינָי כְּכֹל אֲשֶׁר צִוָּה יהוה אֶת־מֹשֶׁה
ו כֵּן עָשׂוּ בְּנֵי יִשְׂרָאֵל: וַיְהִי אֲנָשִׁים אֲשֶׁר הָיוּ טְמֵאִים לְנֶפֶשׁ אָדָם וְלֹא־
יָכְלוּ לַעֲשֹׂת־הַפֶּסַח בַּיּוֹם הַהוּא וַיִּקְרְבוּ לִפְנֵי מֹשֶׁה וְלִפְנֵי אַהֲרֹן בַּיּוֹם
ז הַהוּא: וַיֹּאמְרוּ הָאֲנָשִׁים הָהֵמָּה אֵלָיו אֲנַחְנוּ טְמֵאִים לְנֶפֶשׁ אָדָם
לָמָּה נִגָּרַע לְבִלְתִּי הַקְרִיב אֶת־קָרְבַּן יהוה בְּמֹעֲדוֹ בְּתוֹךְ בְּנֵי יִשְׂרָאֵל:
ח וַיֹּאמֶר אֲלֵהֶם מֹשֶׁה עִמְדוּ וְאֶשְׁמְעָה מַה־יְצַוֶּה יהוה לָכֶם:
ט וַיְדַבֵּר יהוה אֶל־מֹשֶׁה לֵּאמֹר: דַּבֵּר אֶל־בְּנֵי יִשְׂרָאֵל לֵאמֹר אִישׁ אִישׁ
י כִּי־יִהְיֶה טָמֵא ׀ לָנֶפֶשׁ אוֹ בְדֶרֶךְ רְחֹקָה לָכֶם אוֹ לְדֹרֹתֵיכֶם וְעָשָׂה פֶסַח

אונקלוס

ט א וּמַלֵּיל יי עִם מֹשֶׁה בְּמַדְבְּרָא דְסִינַי, בְּשַׁתָּא תִּנְיֵיתָא, לְמִפַּקְהוֹן
מֵאַרְעָא דְמִצְרַיִם, בְּיַרְחָא קַדְמָאָה לְמֵימַר: ב וְיַעְבְּדוּן בְּנֵי יִשְׂרָאֵל,
יָת פִּסְחָא בְּזִמְנֵיהּ: ג בְּאַרְבְּעַת עַסְרָא יוֹמָא, בְּיַרְחָא הָדֵין, בֵּין
שִׁמְשַׁיָּא, תַּעְבְּדוּן יָתֵיהּ בְּזִמְנֵיהּ, כְּכָל גְּזֵירָתֵיהּ וּכְכָל דְּחָזֵי לֵיהּ
תַּעְבְּדוּן יָתֵיהּ: ד וּמַלֵּיל מֹשֶׁה, עִם בְּנֵי יִשְׂרָאֵל לְמֶעְבַּד פִּסְחָא: ה
וַעֲבַדוּ יָת פִּסְחָא, בְּנִיסָן, בְּאַרְבְּעַת עַסְרָא יוֹמָא לְיַרְחָא, בֵּין שִׁמְשַׁיָּא
בְּמַדְבְּרָא דְסִינַי, כְּכֹל, דְּפַקֵּיד יי יָת מֹשֶׁה, כֵּן עֲבַדוּ בְּנֵי יִשְׂרָאֵל:
ו וַהֲווֹ גֻּבְרַיָּא, דַּהֲווֹ מְסָאֲבִין לִטְמֵי נַפְשָׁא דֶאֱנָשָׁא, וְלָא יְכִילוּ
לְמֶעְבַּד פִּסְחָא בְּיוֹמָא הַהוּא, וּקְרִיבוּ, קֳדָם מֹשֶׁה, וּקְדָם אַהֲרֹן
בְּיוֹמָא הַהוּא: ז וַאֲמַרוּ, גֻּבְרַיָּא הָאִנּוּן לֵיהּ, אֲנַחְנָא מְסָאֲבִין לִטְמֵי
נַפְשָׁא דֶאֱנָשָׁא, לְמָא נִתְמְנַע, בְּדִיל דְּלָא לְקָרָבָא, יָת קֻרְבָּנָא דַיי
בְּזִמְנֵיהּ, בְּגוֹ בְּנֵי יִשְׂרָאֵל: ח וַאֲמַר לְהוֹן מֹשֶׁה, אוֹרִיכוּ עַד דְּאֶשְׁמַע,
מָא דְאִתְפַּקַּד מִן קֳדָם יי עַל דִּילְכוֹן: ט וּמַלֵּיל יי עִם מֹשֶׁה לְמֵימַר:
י מַלֵּיל, עִם בְּנֵי יִשְׂרָאֵל לְמֵימַר, גְּבַר גְּבַר אֲרֵי יְהֵי מְסָאַב לִטְמֵי
נַפְשָׁא דֶאֱנָשָׁא, אוֹ בְאוֹרַח רַחִיקָא לְכוֹן, אוֹ לְדָרֵיכוֹן, וְיַעְבֵּיד פִּסְחָא

My favorite sentence in the English language is Winston Churchill's definition of success: "Going from failure to failure without loss of enthusiasm." The real difference is not between failure and success. The real difference is between failing and giving up and failing and keeping on

9:1 בַּשָּׁנָה הַשֵּׁנִית לְצֵאתָם מֵאֶרֶץ מִצְרַיִם בַּחֹדֶשׁ הָרִאשׁוֹן *The first month of the second year* – The first commemorative Passover, as opposed to the original Passover in Egypt, already presents the issue of people unable to fulfill the command as given.

11 a journey, they may still offer a Passover sacrifice to the LORD. They shall offer
it in the afternoon of the fourteenth day of the second month; then shall they
12 eat it with unleavened bread and bitter herbs. They shall not leave any of it
over until morning, nor shall they break any of its bones. They shall offer it in
13 compliance with all the rules of the Passover sacrifice. But anyone who is ritually
pure and not on a journey, but still fails to offer the Passover sacrifice, that person
shall be severed from his people, because he did not offer the LORD's sacrifice
14 at its appointed time; he will bear his guilt. If there is a migrant living among
you and he offers a Passover sacrifice to the LORD, he shall do so in compliance
with all its rules and laws. You shall have one law for migrant and native born
15 alike." On the day when the Tabernacle was erected, the cloud covered REVI'I
the Tabernacle, the Tent of the Testimony, and from evening until morning it
16 hung over the Tabernacle with the appearance of fire. It was always there; the
17 cloud covered the Tent, appearing at night as fire. Whenever the cloud rose
above the Tent, the Israelites would set out, and wherever the cloud settled, the
18 Israelites would encamp. At the LORD's command, the Israelites set out, and at
the LORD's command they would encamp; for as long as the cloud rested on the
19 Tabernacle, they continued to camp there. Even when the cloud lingered over
the Tabernacle for many days, the Israelites kept the LORD's charge and did not
20 journey on. Sometimes the cloud would be over the Tabernacle for just a few
days; at the LORD's command they would camp, and at the LORD's command
21 they would set out. Sometimes the cloud stayed only from evening to morning,
and in the morning it rose, and they set out. Day or night, they would set out when

רש״י

יד **וְכִי יָגוּר אִתְּכֶם גֵּר וְעָשָׂה פֶסַח.** יָכוֹל כָּל הַמִּתְגַּיֵּר יַעֲשֶׂה פֶסַח מִיָּד? תַּלְמוּד לוֹמַר: "חֻקָּה אַחַת" וְגוֹ׳, אֶלָּא כָּךְ מַשְׁמָעוֹ: "וְכִי יָגוּר אִתְּכֶם גֵּר" וּבָא עֵת לַעֲשׂוֹת פֶּסַח עִם חֲבֵרָיו, כַּחֻקָּה וְכַמִּשְׁפָּט יַעֲשֶׂה:

טו **הַמִּשְׁכָּן לְאֹהֶל הָעֵדֻת.** הַמִּשְׁכָּן הֶעָשׂוּי לִהְיוֹת אֹהֶל לְלוּחוֹת הָעֵדוּת: **יִהְיֶה עַל הַמִּשְׁכָּן.** כְּמוֹ ׳הוֹוֶה עַל הַמִּשְׁכָּן׳, וְכֵן לְשׁוֹן כָּל הַפָּרָשָׁה:

יז **הֵעָלוֹת הֶעָנָן.** כְּתַרְגּוּמוֹ: "אִסְתַּלָּקוּת", וְכֵן: "וְנַעֲלָה הֶעָנָן" (להלן פסוק כא). וְלֹא יִתָּכֵן לִכְתֹּב: ׳וּלְפִי עֲלוֹת הֶעָנָן וְעָלָה הֶעָנָן׳, שֶׁאֵין זֶה לְשׁוֹן סִלּוּק אֶלָּא גִּמּוּהַּ וַעֲלִיָּה, כְּמוֹ: "הִנֵּה עָב קְטַנָּה כְּכַף אִישׁ עֹלָה מִיָּם" (מלכים א׳ יח, מד):

יח **עַל פִּי ה׳ יִסָּעוּ.** שָׁנִינוּ בִּמְלֶאכֶת הַמִּשְׁכָּן (ברייתא דמלאכת המשכן פי״ג): כֵּיוָן שֶׁהָיוּ יִשְׂרָאֵל נוֹסְעִים, הָיָה עַמּוּד הֶעָנָן מִתְקַפֵּל וְנִמְשָׁךְ עַל גַּבֵּי בְּנֵי יְהוּדָה כְּמִין קוֹרָה, תָּקְעוּ וְהֵרִיעוּ וְתָקְעוּ, וְלֹא הָיָה מְהַלֵּךְ עַד שֶׁמֹּשֶׁה אוֹמֵר: "קוּמָה ה׳" (להלן י, לה), וְנָסַע דֶּגֶל מַחֲנֵה יְהוּדָה. זוֹ בְּסִפְרֵי (פד): **וְעַל פִּי ה׳ יַחֲנוּ.** כֵּיוָן שֶׁהָיוּ יִשְׂרָאֵל חוֹנִים, עַמּוּד הֶעָנָן מִתַּמֵּר וְעוֹלֶה וְנִמְשָׁךְ עַל גַּבֵּי בְּנֵי יְהוּדָה כְּמִין סֻכָּה, וְלֹא הָיָה נִפְרָשׂ עַד שֶׁמֹּשֶׁה אוֹמֵר: "שׁוּבָה ה׳ רִבְבוֹת אַלְפֵי יִשְׂרָאֵל" (להלן י, לו), הֱוֵי אוֹמֵר: עַל פִּי ה׳ וּבְיַד מֹשֶׁה (ראה להלן פסוק כג):

כ **וְיֵשׁ.** כְּלוֹמַר, וּפְעָמִים: **יָמִים מִסְפָּר.** יָמִים מוּעָטִים:

יא לַיהוָה: בַּחֹדֶשׁ הַשֵּׁנִי בְּאַרְבָּעָה עָשָׂר יוֹם בֵּין הָעַרְבַּיִם יַעֲשׂוּ אֹתוֹ
יב עַל־מַצּוֹת וּמְרֹרִים יֹאכְלֻהוּ: לֹא־יַשְׁאִירוּ מִמֶּנּוּ עַד־בֹּקֶר וְעֶצֶם לֹא
יג יִשְׁבְּרוּ־בוֹ כְּכָל־חֻקַּת הַפֶּסַח יַעֲשׂוּ אֹתוֹ: וְהָאִישׁ אֲשֶׁר־הוּא טָהוֹר
וּבְדֶרֶךְ לֹא־הָיָה וְחָדַל לַעֲשׂוֹת הַפֶּסַח וְנִכְרְתָה הַנֶּפֶשׁ הַהִוא מֵעַמֶּיהָ
יד כִּי | קָרְבַּן יהוה לֹא הִקְרִיב בְּמֹעֲדוֹ חֶטְאוֹ יִשָּׂא הָאִישׁ הַהוּא: וְכִי־
יָגוּר אִתְּכֶם גֵּר וְעָשָׂה פֶסַח לַיהוָה כְּחֻקַּת הַפֶּסַח וּכְמִשְׁפָּטוֹ כֵּן יַעֲשֶׂה
טו חֻקָּה אַחַת יִהְיֶה לָכֶם וְלַגֵּר וּלְאֶזְרַח הָאָרֶץ: וּבְיוֹם רביעי
הָקִים אֶת־הַמִּשְׁכָּן כִּסָּה הֶעָנָן אֶת־הַמִּשְׁכָּן לְאֹהֶל הָעֵדֻת וּבָעֶרֶב
טז יִהְיֶה עַל־הַמִּשְׁכָּן כְּמַרְאֵה־אֵשׁ עַד־בֹּקֶר: כֵּן יִהְיֶה תָמִיד הֶעָנָן יְכַסֶּנּוּ
יז וּמַרְאֵה־אֵשׁ לָיְלָה: וּלְפִי הֵעָלֹת הֶעָנָן מֵעַל הָאֹהֶל וְאַחֲרֵי כֵן יִסְעוּ
בְּנֵי יִשְׂרָאֵל וּבִמְקוֹם אֲשֶׁר יִשְׁכָּן־שָׁם הֶעָנָן שָׁם יַחֲנוּ בְּנֵי יִשְׂרָאֵל:
יח עַל־פִּי יהוה יִסְעוּ בְּנֵי יִשְׂרָאֵל וְעַל־פִּי יהוה יַחֲנוּ כָּל־יְמֵי אֲשֶׁר יִשְׁכֹּן
יט הֶעָנָן עַל־הַמִּשְׁכָּן יַחֲנוּ: וּבְהַאֲרִיךְ הֶעָנָן עַל־הַמִּשְׁכָּן יָמִים רַבִּים
כ וְשָׁמְרוּ בְנֵי־יִשְׂרָאֵל אֶת־מִשְׁמֶרֶת יהוה וְלֹא יִסָּעוּ: וְיֵשׁ אֲשֶׁר יִהְיֶה
הֶעָנָן יָמִים מִסְפָּר עַל־הַמִּשְׁכָּן עַל־פִּי יהוה יַחֲנוּ וְעַל־פִּי יהוה יִסָּעוּ:
כא וְיֵשׁ אֲשֶׁר יִהְיֶה הֶעָנָן מֵעֶרֶב עַד־בֹּקֶר וְנַעֲלָה הֶעָנָן בַּבֹּקֶר וְנָסָעוּ אוֹ

אונקלוס

קֳדָם יְיָ: יא בְּיַרְחָא תִּנְיָנָא, בְּאַרְבְּעַת עַסְרָא יוֹמָא, בֵּין שִׁמְשַׁיָּא יַעְבְּדוּן יָתֵיהּ, עַל פַּטִּיר וּמְרָרִין יֵיכְלֻנֵּיהּ: יב לָא יַשְׁאֲרוּן מִנֵּיהּ עַד צַפְרָא, וְגַרְמָא לָא יִתְבְּרוּן בֵּיהּ, כְּכָל גְּזֵירַת פִּסְחָא יַעְבְּדוּן יָתֵיהּ: יג וְגֻבְרָא דְּהוּא דְּכֵי וּבְאוֹרַח לָא הֲוָה, וְיִתְמְנַע מִלְּמֶעְבַּד פִּסְחָא, וְיִשְׁתֵּיצֵי, אֲנָשָׁא הַהוּא מֵעַמֵּיהּ, אֲרֵי קֻרְבָּנָא דַּייָ, לָא קָרֵיב בְּזִמְנֵיהּ, חוֹבֵיהּ יְקַבֵּיל גֻּבְרָא הַהוּא: יד וַאֲרֵי יִתְגַּיַּר עִמְּכוֹן גִּיּוֹרָא, וְיַעְבֵּיד פִּסְחָא קֳדָם יְיָ, כִּגְזֵירַת פִּסְחָא, וּכְדַחֲזֵי לֵיהּ כֵּן יַעְבֵּיד, קְיָמָא חַד יְהֵי לְכוֹן, וּלְגִיּוֹרַיָּא וּלְיַצִּיבַיָּא דְּאַרְעָא: טו וּבְיוֹמָא דְּאִתָּקַם מַשְׁכְּנָא, חֲפָא עֲנָנָא יָת מַשְׁכְּנָא, לְמַשְׁכְּנָא דְּסָהֲדוּתָא, וּבְרַמְשָׁא, הֲוֵי עַל מַשְׁכְּנָא, כְּחֵיזוּ אִישָּׁתָא עַד צַפְרָא:

טז כֵּן הֲוֵי תְּדִירָא, עֲנָנָא חָפֵי לֵיהּ, וְחֵיזוּ אִישָּׁתָא בְּלֵילְיָא: יז וּלְפוּם, אִסְתַּלָּקוּת עֲנָנָא מֵעִלָּוֵי מַשְׁכְּנָא, וּבָתַר כֵּן, נָטְלִין בְּנֵי יִשְׂרָאֵל, וּבְאַתְרָא, דְּשָׁרֵי תַּמָּן עֲנָנָא, תַּמָּן שָׁרַן בְּנֵי יִשְׂרָאֵל: יח עַל מֵימְרָא דַּייָ, נָטְלִין בְּנֵי יִשְׂרָאֵל, וְעַל מֵימְרָא דַּייָ שָׁרַן, כָּל יוֹמִין, דְּשָׁרֵי עֲנָנָא, עַל מַשְׁכְּנָא שָׁרַן: יט וּבְאוֹרָכוּת עֲנָנָא, עַל מַשְׁכְּנָא יוֹמִין סַגִּיאִין, וְיִטְּרוּן בְּנֵי יִשְׂרָאֵל, יָת מַטְּרַת מֵימְרָא דַּייָ וְלָא נָטְלִין: כ וְאִית, דְּהָוֵי עֲנָנָא, יוֹמִין דְּמִנְיָן עַל מַשְׁכְּנָא, עַל מֵימְרָא דַּייָ שָׁרַן, וְעַל מֵימְרָא דַּייָ נָטְלִין: כא וְאִית, דְּהָוֵי עֲנָנָא מֵרַמְשָׁא עַד צַפְרָא, וּמִסְתַּלַּק עֲנָנָא, בְּצַפְרָא וְנָטְלִין, אוֹ יֵימָם וְלֵילֵי, וּמִסְתַּלַּק עֲנָנָא וְנָטְלִין: כב אוֹ תְּרֵין יוֹמִין אוֹ יַרְחָא אוֹ עִדָּן בְּעִדָּן, בְּאוֹרָכוּת עֲנָנָא עַל מַשְׁכְּנָא לְמִשְׁרֵי

22 the cloud rose. Whether it was two days, or a month, or for many days together,
the Israelites would camp as long as the cloud rested over the Tabernacle, and
23 would not move on. They journeyed only when the cloud rose. At the LORD's
command they camped, and at the LORD's command they set out. And they kept
the LORD's charge, the LORD's word through Moshe.
10 1 2 The LORD spoke to Moshe: "Make two silver trumpets; make them of
hammered metal. Use them for summoning the community and for having the
3 camps set out. When both are blown with a long note, the entire community
4 shall assemble before you at the entrance to the Tent of Meeting. If only one is
5 blown, the princes, leaders of Israel's divisions, shall assemble before you. When
6 you blow a series of short blasts, the camps on the east side shall march, and
when you blow a second series of short blasts, the camps on the south side will
7 march; thus shall a series of short blasts signal them to move on. To assemble

רש״י

כב| **אוֹ יָמִים.** שָׁנָה, כְּמוֹ: ״יָמִים תִּהְיֶה גְּאֻלָּתוֹ״ (ויקרא כה, כט):

י ב| **לְמִקְרָא הָעֵדָה.** כְּשֶׁתִּרְצֶה לְדַבֵּר עִם הַסַּנְהֶדְרִין וּשְׁאָר הָעָם וְתִקְרָאֵם לֶאֱסֹף אֵלֶיךָ, תִּקְרָאֵם עַל יְדֵי חֲצוֹצְרוֹת: **וּלְמַסַּע אֶת הַמַּחֲנוֹת.** בִּשְׁעַת סִלּוּק מַסָּעוֹת תִּתְקְעוּ בָּהֶם לְסִימָן. נִמְצֵאתָ אַתָּה אוֹמֵר, עַל פִּי שְׁלֹשָׁה הָיוּ נוֹסְעִים: עַל פִּי הַקָּדוֹשׁ בָּרוּךְ הוּא וְעַל פִּי מֹשֶׁה וְעַל פִּי חֲצוֹצְרוֹת: **מִקְשָׁה.** מִן הָעֶשֶׁת תַּעֲשֶׂה בְּהַקָּשַׁת הַקֻּרְנָס:

ג| **וְתָקְעוּ בָּהֵן.** בִּשְׁתֵּיהֶן, וְהוּא סִימָן לְמִקְרָא הָעֵדָה, שֶׁנֶּאֱמַר: ״וְנוֹעֲדוּ אֵלֶיךָ כָּל הָעֵדָה אֶל פֶּתַח אֹהֶל מוֹעֵד״:

ד| **וְאִם בְּאַחַת יִתְקָעוּ.** הוּא סִימָן לְמִקְרָא הַנְּשִׂיאִים, שֶׁנֶּאֱמַר: ״וְנוֹעֲדוּ אֵלֶיךָ הַנְּשִׂיאִים״, וְאַף הֵן יְעִידָתָן אֶל פֶּתַח אֹהֶל מוֹעֵד, וּמִגְּזֵרָה שָׁוָה הוּא בָּא בְּסִפְרֵי (עג):

ה| **וּתְקַעְתֶּם תְּרוּעָה.** סִימָן מַסַּע הַמַּחֲנוֹת: תְּקִיעָה תְּרוּעָה וּתְקִיעָה, כָּךְ הוּא נִדְרָשׁ בְּסִפְרֵי מִן הַמִּקְרָאוֹת הַיְתֵרִים (שם):

ז| **וּבְהַקְהִיל אֶת הַקָּהָל וְגוֹ׳.** לְפִי שֶׁהוּא אוֹמֵר: ״וְהָיוּ לְךָ לְמִקְרָא הָעֵדָה וּלְמַסַּע אֶת הַמַּחֲנוֹת״ (לעיל פסוק ב), מַה מִּקְרָא הָעֵדָה תּוֹקֵעַ בִּשְׁנֵי כֹּהֲנִים וּבִשְׁתֵּיהֶן, שֶׁנֶּאֱמַר: ״וְתָקְעוּ בָּהֵן״ וְגוֹ׳ (לעיל פסוק ג), אַף מַסַּע הַמַּחֲנוֹת בִּשְׁתֵּיהֶם. יָכוֹל מַה מַּסַּע הַמַּחֲנוֹת תּוֹקֵעַ וּמֵרִיעַ וְתוֹקֵעַ, אַף מִקְרָא הָעֵדָה תּוֹקֵעַ וּמֵרִיעַ וְתוֹקֵעַ, וּמֵעַתָּה אֵין חִלּוּק בֵּין מִקְרָא

since, Jews have known that we are thrown together by circumstance. We share a history all too often written in tears. Rabbi Soloveitchik calls this the covenant of fate (*brit goral*). This is not a purely negative phenomenon. It gives rise to a powerful sense that we are part of a single story – that what we have in common is stronger than the things that separate us. The covenant of fate was born in the experience of slavery in Egypt.

But there is an additional element of Jewish identity. Rabbi Soloveitchik calls this the covenant of destiny (*brit yiud*), entered into at Mount Sinai. This defines the people of Israel not as the object of persecution but the subject of a unique vocation, to become "a kingdom of priests and a holy nation" (Ex. 19:6). Our task as a people of destiny is to bear witness to the presence of God through the way we lead our lives (Torah) and the path we chart as a people across the centuries (history) – a camp and a congregation. Sometimes the clarion call speaks to our sense of faith. We are God's people, His emissaries and ambassadors, charged with making His presence real in the world through healing deeds and leading holy lives. At other times the trumpet that sounds and summons us is the call of fate: Jewish lives endangered in Israel or the Diaspora. Whichever sound the silver instruments make, they call on that duality that makes Jews and Judaism inseparable. However deep the divisions between us, we remain one family in fate and faith.

כב יוֹמָם וָלַיְלָה וְנַעֲלָה הֶעָנָן וְנָסָעוּ: אוֹ־יֹמַיִם אוֹ־חֹדֶשׁ אוֹ־יָמִים בְּהַאֲרִיךְ
הֶעָנָן עַל־הַמִּשְׁכָּן לִשְׁכֹּן עָלָיו יַחֲנוּ בְנֵי־יִשְׂרָאֵל וְלֹא יִסָּעוּ וּבְהֵעָלֹתוֹ
כג יִסָּעוּ: עַל־פִּי יהוה יַחֲנוּ וְעַל־פִּי יהוה יִסָּעוּ אֶת־מִשְׁמֶרֶת יהוה שָׁמָרוּ
עַל־פִּי יהוה בְּיַד־מֹשֶׁה:
י א ב וַיְדַבֵּר יהוה אֶל־מֹשֶׁה לֵּאמֹר: עֲשֵׂה לְךָ שְׁתֵּי חֲצוֹצְרֹת כֶּסֶף מִקְשָׁה ט
ג תַּעֲשֶׂה אֹתָם וְהָיוּ לְךָ לְמִקְרָא הָעֵדָה וּלְמַסַּע אֶת־הַמַּחֲנוֹת: וְתָקְעוּ
ד בָּהֵן וְנוֹעֲדוּ אֵלֶיךָ כָּל־הָעֵדָה אֶל־פֶּתַח אֹהֶל מוֹעֵד: וְאִם־בְּאַחַת
ה יִתְקָעוּ וְנוֹעֲדוּ אֵלֶיךָ הַנְּשִׂיאִים רָאשֵׁי אַלְפֵי יִשְׂרָאֵל: וּתְקַעְתֶּם תְּרוּעָה
ו וְנָסְעוּ הַמַּחֲנוֹת הַחֹנִים קֵדְמָה: וּתְקַעְתֶּם תְּרוּעָה שֵׁנִית וְנָסְעוּ הַמַּחֲנוֹת
ז הַחֹנִים תֵּימָנָה תְּרוּעָה יִתְקְעוּ לְמַסְעֵיהֶם: וּבְהַקְהִיל אֶת־הַקָּהָל

אונקלוס

עֲלוֹהִי, שָׁרַן בְּנֵי יִשְׂרָאֵל וְלָא נָטְלִין, וּבְאִסְתַּלָּקוּתֵיהּ נָטְלִין: כג עַל מֵימְרָא דַּייָ שָׁרַן, וְעַל מֵימְרָא דַּייָ נָטְלִין, יָת מַטְּרַת מֵימְרָא דַּייָ נָטְרִין, עַל מֵימְרָא דַּייָ בִּידָא דְמֹשֶׁה: י א וּמַלֵּיל יי עִם מֹשֶׁה לְמֵימַר: ב עֲבֵיד לָךְ, תַּרְתֵּין חֲצוֹצְרָן דִּכְסַף, נְגִיד תַּעְבֵּיד יָתְהוֹן, וִיהוֹן לָךְ לְעָרָעָא כְּנִשְׁתָּא, וּלְאַטָּלָא יָת מַשְׁרְיָתָא: ג וְיִתְקְעוּן בְּהוֹן, וְיִזְדַּמְּנוּן לְוָתָךְ כָּל כְּנִשְׁתָּא, לִתְרַע מַשְׁכַּן זִמְנָא: ד וְאִם בַּחֲדָא יִתְקְעוּן, וְיִזְדַּמְּנוּן לְוָתָךְ רַבְרְבַיָּא, רֵישֵׁי אַלְפַיָּא דְיִשְׂרָאֵל: ה וְתִתְקְעוּן יַבָּבְתָּא, וְיִטְּלוּן מַשְׁרְיָתָא, דִּשְׁרַן קִדּוּמָא: ו וְתִתְקְעוּן יַבָּבְתָּא תִּנְיָנוּת, וְיִטְּלוּן מַשְׁרְיָתָא, דִּשְׁרַן דָּרוֹמָא, יַבָּבְתָּא יִתְקְעוּן לְמַטְּלָנֵיהוֹן: ז וּבְמִכְנַשׁ יָת קְהָלָא,

CONGREGATION AND CAMP

This passage, with its juxtaposition of the words "congregation," *eda*, and "camp," *maḥaneh*, became a springboard for one of the most profound meditations of Rabbi Joseph B. Soloveitchik (1903–93). We have seen (see note on Ex. 12:3) that for Rabbi Soloveitchik (*Kol Dodi Dofek*), there are two ways in which people become a group – a community, society, or nation. The first is when they face a common enemy. They band together for mutual protection, knowing that only by so doing can they survive. Such a group is a *maḥaneh* – a camp, a defensive formation. Alternatively, people can come together because they share a vision, a set of ideals. This is what it means to be an *eda*, congregation. (*Eda* is related to the word *ed*, "witness.") A society built around a shared project is not a *maḥaneh* but an *eda* – not a camp but a congregation. A camp is brought into being by what happens to it from the outside. A congregation comes into existence by internal decision. The first is a response to what has happened to the group in the past. The second represents what the group seeks to achieve in the future. This duality was given its first expression with this command: "Make two silver trumpets; make them of hammered metal. Use them for summoning the community (*eda*), and for having the camps (*maḥanot*) set out."

The two types of groups represent, in the most profound sense, two different ways of existing and relating to the world. Our ancestors became a *maḥaneh* in Egypt, forged together by a crucible of slavery and suffering. Ever

8 the community, blow a long blast, not a series of short blasts. Aharon's sons
the priests shall blow the trumpets. This shall be for you an everlasting decree
9 throughout your generations. When you go to war against an enemy who is
attacking you in your land, you shall blow short blasts on the trumpets to be
remembered before the LORD your God, to be delivered from your enemies.
10 And on your days of rejoicing, your festivals and New Moons, you shall blow
the trumpets over your burnt offerings and your peace offerings. They will be a
reminder of you before your God. I am the LORD your God."
11 On the twentieth day of the second month in the second year, the cloud rose HAMISHI
12 above the Tabernacle of the Covenant. The Israelites set out on their journey
from the Sinai Desert, and the cloud came to rest in the Wilderness of Paran.
13 14 For the first time, at the LORD's command through Moshe, they set out. The
divisions of Yehuda's camp set out first, under their banner. Leading that
15 division was Naḥshon son of Aminadav. Netanel son of Tzuar was in charge
16 of the division of the tribe of Yissakhar. Eliav son of Ḥelon was in charge of
17 the division of the tribe of Zevulun. The Tabernacle was taken down, and
18 the Gershonites and the Merarites, who carried it, set out. The divisions of
the camp of Reuven set out next, under their banner. Leading that division
19 was Elitzur son of Shedeiur. Shelumiel son of Tzurishadai was in charge of
20 the division of the tribe of Shimon. Elyasaf son of Deuel was in charge of the
21 division of the tribe of Gad. Then the Kohatites, who carried the sacred objects,

רש״י

הָעֵדָה לְמַסַּע אֶת הַמַּחֲנוֹת? תַּלְמוּד לוֹמַר: "וּבְהַקְהִיל אֶת הַקָּהָל" וְגוֹ', לוֹמַר שֶׁאֵין תְּרוּעָה לְמִקְרָא הָעֵדָה, וְהוּא הַדִּין לַנְּשִׂיאִים. הֲרֵי סִימָן לִשְׁלָשְׁתָּם: מִקְרָא הָעֵדָה בִּשְׁתַּיִם, וְשֶׁל נְשִׂיאִים בְּאַחַת, וְזוֹ וָזוֹ אֵין בָּהֶם תְּרוּעָה, וּמַסַּע הַמַּחֲנוֹת בִּשְׁתַּיִם עַל יְדֵי תְּרוּעָה וּתְקִיעָה:

ח **וּבְנֵי אַהֲרֹן יִתְקְעוּ.** בַּמִּקְרָאוֹת וּבַמַּסָּעוֹת הַלָּלוּ:

י **עַל עֹלֹתֵיכֶם.** בְּקָרְבַּן צִבּוּר הַכָּתוּב מְדַבֵּר: **אֲנִי ה' אֱלֹהֵיכֶם.** מִכָּאן לָמַדְנוּ מַלְכֻיּוֹת עִם זִכְרוֹנוֹת וְשׁוֹפָרוֹת, שֶׁנֶּאֱמַר: "וּתְקַעְתֶּם" – הֲרֵי שׁוֹפָרוֹת, "לְזִכָּרוֹן" – הֲרֵי זִכְרוֹנוֹת, "אֲנִי ה' אֱלֹהֵיכֶם" – זוֹ מַלְכֻיּוֹת וְכוּ':

יא **בַּחֹדֶשׁ הַשֵּׁנִי.** נִמְצֵאתָ אַתָּה אוֹמֵר, שְׁנֵים עָשָׂר חֹדֶשׁ חָסֵר עֲשָׂרָה יָמִים עָשׂוּ בְּחוֹרֵב, שֶׁהֲרֵי בְּרֹאשׁ חֹדֶשׁ סִיוָן חָנוּ שָׁם (שמות יט, א) וְלֹא נָסְעוּ עַד עֶשְׂרִים בְּאִיָּר לַשָּׁנָה הַבָּאָה:

יב **לְמַסְעֵיהֶם.** כְּמִשְׁפָּט הַמְפֹרָשׁ לְמַסַּע דִּגְלֵיהֶם מִי רִאשׁוֹן וּמִי אַחֲרוֹן: **בְּמִדְבַּר פָּארָן.** קִבְרוֹת הַתַּאֲוָה בְּמִדְבַּר פָּארָן הָיָה, וְשָׁם חָנוּ מִמַּסָּע זֶה:

יז **וְהוּרַד הַמִּשְׁכָּן.** כֵּיוָן שֶׁנּוֹסֵעַ דֶּגֶל יְהוּדָה, נִכְנְסוּ אַהֲרֹן וּבָנָיו וּפֵרְקוּ אֶת הַפָּרֹכֶת וְכִסּוּ בָהּ אֶת הָאָרוֹן, שֶׁנֶּאֱמַר: "וּבָא אַהֲרֹן וּבָנָיו בִּנְסֹעַ הַמַּחֲנֶה" (לעיל ד, ה), וּבְנֵי גֵרְשׁוֹן וּבְנֵי מְרָרִי פּוֹרְקִין הַמִּשְׁכָּן וְטוֹעֲנִין אוֹתוֹ בָּעֲגָלוֹת, וְהָאָרוֹן וּכְלֵי הַקֹּדֶשׁ שֶׁל מַשָּׂא בְּנֵי קְהָת עוֹמְדִים מְכֻסִּין וּנְתוּנִין עַל הַמּוֹטוֹת, עַד שֶׁנָּסַע דֶּגֶל מַחֲנֵה רְאוּבֵן, וְאַחַר כָּךְ "וְנָסְעוּ הַקְּהָתִים" (להלן פסוק כא):

כא **נֹשְׂאֵי הַמִּקְדָּשׁ.** נוֹשְׂאֵי דְּבָרִים הַמְקֻדָּשִׁים: **וְהֵקִימוּ אֶת הַמִּשְׁכָּן.** בְּנֵי גֵרְשׁוֹן וּבְנֵי מְרָרִי, שֶׁהָיוּ קוֹדְמִים לָהֶם מַסַּע שְׁנֵי דְּגָלִים, הָיוּ מְקִימִין אֶת הַמִּשְׁכָּן כְּשֶׁהָיָה הֶעָנָן שׁוֹכֵן, וְסִימַן הַחֲנִיָּה נִרְאֶה בְּדֶגֶל מַחֲנֵה יְהוּדָה וְהֵם חוֹנִים, וַעֲדַיִן בְּנֵי קְהָת בָּאִים מֵאַחֲרֵיהֶם עִם שְׁנֵי דְּגָלִים הָאַחֲרוֹנִים, הָיוּ בְּנֵי גֵרְשׁוֹן וּבְנֵי מְרָרִי מְקִימִין אֶת הַמִּשְׁכָּן, וּכְשֶׁבָּאִים בְּנֵי קְהָת מוֹצְאִים אוֹתוֹ עַל מְכוֹנוֹ, וּמַכְנִיסִין בּוֹ הָאָרוֹן וְהַשֻּׁלְחָן וְהַמְּנוֹרָה וְהַמִּזְבְּחוֹת. וְזֶהוּ מַשְׁמָעוּת הַמִּקְרָא: "וְהֵקִימוּ" מְקִימֵי הַמִּשְׁכָּן אוֹתוֹ, "עַד" – טֶרֶם "בֹּאָם" שֶׁל בְּנֵי קְהָת:

ח תִּתְקְעוּ וְלֹא תָרִיעוּ׃ וּבְנֵי אַהֲרֹן הַכֹּהֲנִים יִתְקְעוּ בַּחֲצֹצְרוֹת וְהָיוּ לָכֶם
ט לְחֻקַּת עוֹלָם לְדֹרֹתֵיכֶם׃ וְכִי־תָבֹאוּ מִלְחָמָה בְּאַרְצְכֶם עַל־הַצַּר הַצֹּרֵר
אֶתְכֶם וַהֲרֵעֹתֶם בַּחֲצֹצְרֹת וְנִזְכַּרְתֶּם לִפְנֵי יהוה אֱלֹהֵיכֶם וְנוֹשַׁעְתֶּם
י מֵאֹיְבֵיכֶם׃ וּבְיוֹם שִׂמְחַתְכֶם וּבְמוֹעֲדֵיכֶם וּבְרָאשֵׁי חָדְשֵׁכֶם וּתְקַעְתֶּם
בַּחֲצֹצְרֹת עַל עֹלֹתֵיכֶם וְעַל זִבְחֵי שַׁלְמֵיכֶם וְהָיוּ לָכֶם לְזִכָּרוֹן לִפְנֵי
אֱלֹהֵיכֶם אֲנִי יהוה אֱלֹהֵיכֶם׃
יא וַיְהִי בַּשָּׁנָה הַשֵּׁנִית בַּחֹדֶשׁ הַשֵּׁנִי בְּעֶשְׂרִים בַּחֹדֶשׁ נַעֲלָה הֶעָנָן מֵעַל חמישי
יב מִשְׁכַּן הָעֵדֻת׃ וַיִּסְעוּ בְנֵי־יִשְׂרָאֵל לְמַסְעֵיהֶם מִמִּדְבַּר סִינָי וַיִּשְׁכֹּן הֶעָנָן
יג יד בְּמִדְבַּר פָּארָן׃ וַיִּסְעוּ בָּרִאשֹׁנָה עַל־פִּי יהוה בְּיַד־מֹשֶׁה׃ וַיִּסַּע דֶּגֶל
מַחֲנֵה בְנֵי־יְהוּדָה בָּרִאשֹׁנָה לְצִבְאֹתָם וְעַל־צְבָאוֹ נַחְשׁוֹן בֶּן־עַמִּינָדָב׃
טו טז וְעַל־צְבָא מַטֵּה בְּנֵי יִשָּׂשכָר נְתַנְאֵל בֶּן־צוּעָר׃ וְעַל־צְבָא מַטֵּה בְּנֵי
יז זְבוּלֻן אֱלִיאָב בֶּן־חֵלֹן׃ וְהוּרַד הַמִּשְׁכָּן וְנָסְעוּ בְנֵי־גֵרְשׁוֹן וּבְנֵי מְרָרִי
יח נֹשְׂאֵי הַמִּשְׁכָּן׃ וְנָסַע דֶּגֶל מַחֲנֵה רְאוּבֵן לְצִבְאֹתָם וְעַל־צְבָאוֹ אֱלִיצוּר
יט בֶּן־שְׁדֵיאוּר׃ וְעַל־צְבָא מַטֵּה בְּנֵי שִׁמְעוֹן שְׁלֻמִיאֵל בֶּן־צוּרִישַׁדָּי׃
כ כא וְעַל־צְבָא מַטֵּה בְנֵי־גָד אֶלְיָסָף בֶּן־דְּעוּאֵל׃ וְנָסְעוּ הַקְּהָתִים נֹשְׂאֵי

אונקלוס

תִּתְקְעוּן וְלָא תְיַבְּבוּן: ח וּבְנֵי אַהֲרֹן כָּהֲנַיָּא, יִתְקְעוּן בַּחֲצוֹצְרָתָא, וִיהוֹן לְכוֹן, לִקְיָם עָלַם לְדָרֵיכוֹן: ט וַאֲרֵי תֵיעֲלוּן לְאַגָּחָא קְרָבָא בְּאַרְעֲכוֹן, עַל מְעִיקֵי דִּמְעִיקִין לְכוֹן, וּתְיַבְּבוּן בַּחֲצוֹצְרָתָא, וְיֵיעוֹל דָּכְרָנְכוֹן לְטָבָא, קֳדָם יי אֱלָהֲכוֹן, וְתִתְפָּרְקוּן מִסָּנְאֵיכוֹן: י וּבְיוֹם חֶדְוַתְכוֹן וּבְמוֹעֲדֵיכוֹן וּבְרֵישֵׁי יַרְחֵיכוֹן, וְתִתְקְעוּן בַּחֲצוֹצְרָתָא, עַל עֲלָוָתְכוֹן, וְעַל נִכְסַת קֻדְשֵׁיכוֹן, וִיהוֹן לְכוֹן לְדָכְרָנָא קֳדָם אֱלָהֲכוֹן, אֲנָא יי אֱלָהֲכוֹן: יא וַהֲוָה, בְּשַׁתָּא תִנְיֵתָא, בְּיַרְחָא תִנְיָנָא בְּעַסְרִין בְּיַרְחָא, אִסְתַּלַּק עֲנָנָא, מֵעִלָּוֵי מַשְׁכְּנָא דְסָהֲדוּתָא: יב וּנְטַלוּ בְנֵי יִשְׂרָאֵל, לְמַטְלָנֵיהוֹן מִמַּדְבְּרָא דְסִינָי, וּשְׁרָא עֲנָנָא בְּמַדְבְּרָא דְפָארָן:

יג וּנְטַלוּ בְּקַדְמֵיתָא, עַל מֵימְרָא דַּיי בִּידָא דְמֹשֶׁה: יד וּנְטַל, טִיקַס מַשְׁרִית בְּנֵי יְהוּדָה, בְּקַדְמֵיתָא לְחֵילֵיהוֹן, וְעַל חֵילֵיהּ, נַחְשׁוֹן בַּר עַמִּינָדָב: טו וְעַל חֵילָא, דְּשִׁבְטָא דִּבְנֵי יִשָּׂשכָר, נְתַנְאֵל בַּר צוּעָר: טז וְעַל חֵילָא, דְּשִׁבְטָא דִּבְנֵי זְבוּלוּן, אֱלִיאָב בַּר חֵלוֹן: יז וּמִתְפָּרַק מַשְׁכְּנָא, וְנָטְלִין בְּנֵי גֵרְשׁוֹן וּבְנֵי מְרָרִי, נָטְלֵי מַשְׁכְּנָא: יח וּנְטַל, טִיקַס, מַשְׁרִית רְאוּבֵן לְחֵילֵיהוֹן, וְעַל חֵילֵיהּ, אֱלִיצוּר בַּר שְׁדֵיאוּר: יט וְעַל חֵילָא, דְּשִׁבְטָא דִּבְנֵי שִׁמְעוֹן, שְׁלֻמִיאֵל בַּר צוּרִישַׁדָּי: כ וְעַל חֵילָא דְּשִׁבְטָא דִּבְנֵי גָד, אֶלְיָסָף בַּר דְּעוּאֵל: כא וְנָטְלִין בְּנֵי קְהָת, נָטְלֵי

22 set out. By the time they arrived, the Tabernacle would have been erected. The
divisions of the camp of Efrayim set out next, under their banner. Leading that
23 division was Elishama son of Amihud. Gamliel son of Pedatzur was in charge
24 of the division of the tribe of Menashe. Avidan son of Gidoni was in charge of
25 the division of the tribe of Binyamin. Then, at the rear of the whole camp, the
divisions of the camp of Dan set out under their banner. Leading that division
26 was Aḥiezer son of Amishadai. Pagiel son of Okhran was in charge of the
27 division of the tribe of Asher. Aḥira son of Einan was in charge of the division
28 of the tribe of Naftali. This was the order in which the Israelites set out in their
29 divisions. Moshe said to Ḥovav son of Reuel the Midianite, Moshe's
father-in-law, "We are setting out to the place that the Lord said He would give
us. Come with us and we will be good to you, for the Lord has promised good
30 things to Israel." But he replied, "I will not come; I must go back to my own land
31 and my own people." "Please do not leave us," said Moshe, "for you know where
32 we should camp in the wilderness; you would be our eyes. If you come with us,
33 whatever good the Lord does for us, we will do for you." They journeyed from

רש״י

כה| **מְאַסֵּף לְכָל הַמַּחֲנֹת.** תַּלְמוּד יְרוּשַׁלְמִי (עירובין ה, א), לְפִי שֶׁהָיָה שִׁבְטוֹ שֶׁל דָּן מְרֻבֶּה בְּאֻכְלוּסִין הָיָה נוֹסֵעַ בָּאַחֲרוֹנָה, וְכָל מִי שֶׁהָיָה מְאַבֵּד דָּבָר הָיָה מַחֲזִירוֹ לוֹ. אָתְיָא כְּמַאן דַּאֲמַר כְּתֵבָה הָיוּ מְהַלְּכִין, וּמַפִּיק לֵיהּ מִן "כַּאֲשֶׁר יַחֲנוּ כֵּן יִסָּעוּ" (לעיל ב, יז), וְאִית דְּאָמְרֵי: כְּקוֹרָה הָיוּ מְהַלְּכִין, וּמַפִּיק לֵיהּ מִן "מְאַסֵּף לְכָל הַמַּחֲנֹת":

כח| **אֵלֶּה מַסְעֵי.** זֶה סֵדֶר מַסְעֵיהֶם: **וַיִּסָּעוּ.** בַּיּוֹם הַהוּא נָסְעוּ:

כט| **חֹבָב.** הוּא יִתְרוֹ, שֶׁנֶּאֱמַר: "מִבְּנֵי חֹבָב חֹתֵן מֹשֶׁה" (שופטים ד, יא), וּמַה תַּלְמוּד לוֹמַר: "וַתָּבֹאנָה אֶל רְעוּאֵל אֲבִיהֶן" (שמות ב, יח)? מְלַמֵּד שֶׁהַתִּינוֹקוֹת קוֹרִין לַאֲבִי אֲבִיהֶן 'אַבָּא'. וְשֵׁמוֹת הַרְבֵּה הָיוּ לוֹ: יִתְרוֹ – עַל שֵׁם שֶׁיִּתֵּר פָּרָשָׁה אַחַת בַּתּוֹרָה, חוֹבָב – עַל שֶׁחִבֵּב אֶת הַתּוֹרָה וְכוּ': **נֹסְעִים אֲנַחְנוּ אֶל הַמָּקוֹם.** מִיָּד עַד שְׁלֹשָׁה יָמִים אָנוּ נִכְנָסִין לָאָרֶץ, שֶׁבְּמַסָּע זֶה הָרִאשׁוֹן נָסְעוּ עַל מְנָת לְהִכָּנֵס לְאֶרֶץ יִשְׂרָאֵל, אֶלָּא שֶׁחָטְאוּ בַּמִּתְאוֹנְנִים. וּמִפְּנֵי מָה שִׁתֵּף מֹשֶׁה עַצְמוֹ עִמָּהֶם? שֶׁעֲדַיִן לֹא נִגְזְרָה גְּזֵרָה עָלָיו וּכְסָבוּר שֶׁהוּא נִכְנָס:

ל| **אֶל אַרְצִי וְאֶל מוֹלַדְתִּי.** אִם בִּשְׁבִיל נְכָסַי אִם בִּשְׁבִיל מִשְׁפַּחְתִּי:

לא| **אַל נָא תַּעֲזֹב.** אֵין 'נָא' אֶלָּא לְשׁוֹן בַּקָּשָׁה, שֶׁלֹּא יֹאמְרוּ לֹא נִתְגַּיֵּר יִתְרוֹ מֵחִבָּה, סָבוּר הָיָה שֶׁיֵּשׁ לַגֵּרִים חֵלֶק בָּאָרֶץ, עַכְשָׁיו שֶׁרָאָה שֶׁאֵין לָהֶם חֵלֶק הִנִּיחָם וְהָלַךְ לוֹ: **כִּי עַל כֵּן יָדַעְתָּ חֲנֹתֵנוּ בַּמִּדְבָּר.** כִּי נָאֶה לְךָ לַעֲשׂוֹת זֹאת, עַל אֲשֶׁר יָדַעְתָּ חֲנִיָּתֵנוּ בַּמִּדְבָּר וְרָאִיתָ נִסִּים וּגְבוּרוֹת שֶׁנַּעֲשׂוּ לָנוּ: **כִּי עַל כֵּן יָדַעְתָּ.** כְּמוֹ: 'עַל אֲשֶׁר יָדַעְתָּ', כְּמוֹ: "כִּי עַל כֵּן לֹא נְתַתִּיהָ לְשֵׁלָה בְנִי" (בראשית לח, כו), "כִּי עַל כֵּן בָּאוּ" (שם יט, ח), "כִּי עַל כֵּן רָאִיתִי פָנֶיךָ" (שם לג, י): **וְהָיִיתָ לָּנוּ לְעֵינָיִם.** לְשׁוֹן עָבָר, כְּתַרְגּוּמוֹ. דָּבָר אַחֵר לְשׁוֹן עָתִיד, כָּל דָּבָר וְדָבָר שֶׁיִּתְעַלֵּם מֵעֵינֵינוּ תִּהְיֶה מֵאִיר עֵינֵינוּ. דָּבָר אַחֵר, שֶׁתְּהֵא חָבִיב עָלֵינוּ כְּגַלְגַּל עֵינֵינוּ, שֶׁנֶּאֱמַר: "וַאֲהַבְתֶּם אֶת הַגֵּר" (דברים י, יט):

לב| **וְהָיָה הַטּוֹב הַהוּא וְגוֹ'.** מַה טּוֹבָה הֵיטִיבוּ לוֹ? אָמְרוּ, כְּשֶׁהָיוּ יִשְׂרָאֵל מְחַלְּקִין אֶת הָאָרֶץ הָיָה דֻּשְׁנָהּ שֶׁל יְרִיחוֹ חֲמֵשׁ מֵאוֹת אַמָּה עַל חֲמֵשׁ מֵאוֹת אַמָּה, וְהִנִּיחוּהוּ מִלְּחַלֵּק. אָמְרוּ, מִי שֶׁיִּבָּנֶה בֵּית הַמִּקְדָּשׁ בְּחֶלְקוֹ הוּא יִטְּלֶנּוּ, וּבֵין כָּךְ וּבֵין כָּךְ נְתָנוּהוּ לִבְנֵי יִתְרוֹ לְיוֹנָדָב בֶּן רֵכָב:

לג| **דֶּרֶךְ שְׁלֹשֶׁת יָמִים.** מַהֲלַךְ שְׁלֹשֶׁת יָמִים הָלְכוּ בְּיוֹם אֶחָד, שֶׁהָיָה

It seems that in their different ways, Yitro and Miriam are essential emotional supports for Moshe. When they are there, he copes. When they are not, he loses his poise. Leaders need soulmates, people who lift their spirits and give them the strength to carry on. No one can lead alone.

כב הַמִּקְדָּשׁ וְהֵקִימוּ אֶת־הַמִּשְׁכָּן עַד־בֹּאָם: וְנָסַע דֶּגֶל מַחֲנֵה בְנֵי־אֶפְרַיִם
כג לְצִבְאֹתָם וְעַל־צְבָאוֹ אֱלִישָׁמָע בֶּן־עַמִּיהוּד: וְעַל־צְבָא מַטֵּה בְּנֵי
כד מְנַשֶּׁה גַּמְלִיאֵל בֶּן־פְּדָהצוּר: וְעַל־צְבָא מַטֵּה בְּנֵי בִנְיָמִן אֲבִידָן בֶּן־
כה גִּדְעוֹנִי: וְנָסַע דֶּגֶל מַחֲנֵה בְנֵי־דָן מְאַסֵּף לְכָל־הַמַּחֲנֹת לְצִבְאֹתָם
כו וְעַל־צְבָאוֹ אֲחִיעֶזֶר בֶּן־עַמִּישַׁדָּי: וְעַל־צְבָא מַטֵּה בְּנֵי אָשֵׁר פַּגְעִיאֵל
כז כח בֶּן־עָכְרָן: וְעַל־צְבָא מַטֵּה בְּנֵי נַפְתָּלִי אֲחִירַע בֶּן־עֵינָן: אֵלֶּה מַסְעֵי
כט בְנֵי־יִשְׂרָאֵל לְצִבְאֹתָם וַיִּסָּעוּ: וַיֹּאמֶר מֹשֶׁה לְחֹבָב בֶּן־
רְעוּאֵל הַמִּדְיָנִי חֹתֵן מֹשֶׁה נֹסְעִים ׀ אֲנַחְנוּ אֶל־הַמָּקוֹם אֲשֶׁר אָמַר
יהוה אֹתוֹ אֶתֵּן לָכֶם לְכָה אִתָּנוּ וְהֵטַבְנוּ לָךְ כִּי־יהוה דִּבֶּר־טוֹב עַל־
ל יִשְׂרָאֵל: וַיֹּאמֶר אֵלָיו לֹא אֵלֵךְ כִּי אִם־אֶל־אַרְצִי וְאֶל־מוֹלַדְתִּי אֵלֵךְ:
לא וַיֹּאמֶר אַל־נָא תַּעֲזֹב אֹתָנוּ כִּי ׀ עַל־כֵּן יָדַעְתָּ חֲנֹתֵנוּ בַּמִּדְבָּר וְהָיִיתָ
לב לָּנוּ לְעֵינָיִם: וְהָיָה כִּי־תֵלֵךְ עִמָּנוּ וְהָיָה ׀ הַטּוֹב הַהוּא אֲשֶׁר יֵיטִיב
לג יהוה עִמָּנוּ וְהֵטַבְנוּ לָךְ: וַיִּסְעוּ מֵהַר יהוה דֶּרֶךְ שְׁלֹשֶׁת יָמִים וַאֲרוֹן

אונקלוס

מקדשא, ומקימין ית משכנא עד מיתיהון: כב ונטיל, טיקס, משרית בני אפרים לחיליהון, ועל חיליה, אלישמע בר עמיהוד: כג ועל חילא, דשבטא דבני מנשה, גמליאל בר פדצור: כד ועל חילא, דשבטא דבני בנימין, אבידן בר גדעוני: כה ונטיל, טיקס משרית בני דן, מכניש לכל משריתא לחיליהון, ועל חיליה, אחיעזר בר עמישדי: כו ועל חילא, דשבטא דבני אשר, פגעיאל בר עכרן: כז ועל חילא, דשבטא דבני נפתלי, אחירע בר עינן: כח אלין, מטלני בני ישראל לחיליהון, ונטלו: כט ואמר משה, לחובב, בר רעואל מדינאה חמוהי דמשה, נטלין אנחנא, לאתרא דאמר יי, יתיה אתין לכון, איתא עמנא ונוטיב לך, ארי יי מליל לאיתאה טבתא על ישראל: ל ואמר ליה לא איזיל, אלהין לארעי, ולילדותי איזיל: לא ואמר, לא כען תשבוק יתנא, ארי על כן ידעתא, כד הוינא שרן במדברא, וגבורן דאתעבידא לנא חזיתא בעינך: לב ויהי ארי תיזיל עמנא, ויהי טבא ההוא, דיוטיב יי, עמנא ונוטיב לך: לג ונטלו מטורא דאתגלי עלוהי יקרא דיי, מהלך תלתא יומין, וארון

10:30 לֹא אֵלֵךְ *I will not come* – It is perhaps not by coincidence that immediately after we read of Yitro's departure (Reuel is another name for Yitro), Moshe experiences burnout and despair (Num. 11:10–15). Something very similar will happen later in Parashat Ḥukat (ch. 20), where first we read of the death of Miriam, followed immediately by the scene in which the people ask for water and Moshe loses his temper and strikes the rock. This act costs him the chance to lead the people across the Jordan into the Promised Land.

the LORD's mountain for three days; and the Ark of the LORD's Covenant went
34 ahead of them for those three days to find a resting place for them. The LORD's
35 cloud was over them by day as they journeyed from the camp. When SHISHI
the Ark set out, Moshe would say, "Arise, LORD; let Your enemies be scattered,
36 and Your foes flee before You." When it came to rest, he would say, "Bring back,
O LORD, the myriad thousands of Israel."
11 1 The people began to rail bitterly in the LORD's presence. And the LORD heard
and was incensed; fire from the LORD blazed against them, consuming at the

רש״י

הַקָּדוֹשׁ בָּרוּךְ הוּא חָפֵץ לְהַכְנִיסָם לָאָרֶץ מִיָּד: **וַאֲרוֹן בְּרִית ה׳ נֹסֵעַ לִפְנֵיהֶם דֶּרֶךְ שְׁלֹשֶׁת יָמִים.** זֶה הָאָרוֹן הַיּוֹצֵא עִמָּהֶם לַמִּלְחָמָה וּבוֹ שִׁבְרֵי לוּחוֹת מֻנָּחִים, וּמַקְדִּים לִפְנֵיהֶם דֶּרֶךְ שְׁלֹשֶׁת יָמִים לְתַקֵּן לָהֶם מְקוֹם חֲנִיָּה:

לד **וַעֲנַן ה׳ עֲלֵיהֶם יוֹמָם.** שִׁבְעָה עֲנָנִים כְּתוּבִים בְּמַסְעֵיהֶם, אַרְבָּעָה מֵאַרְבַּע רוּחוֹת, וְאֶחָד לְמַעְלָה וְאֶחָד לְמַטָּה, וְאֶחָד לִפְנֵיהֶם, מַנְמִיךְ אֶת הַגָּבוֹהַּ וּמַגְבִּיהַּ אֶת הַנָּמוּךְ וְהוֹרֵג נְחָשִׁים וְעַקְרַבִּים:

לה **וַיְהִי בִּנְסֹעַ הָאָרֹן.** עָשָׂה לוֹ סִימָנִיּוֹת מִלְּפָנָיו וּמִלְּאַחֲרָיו לוֹמַר שֶׁאֵין זֶה מְקוֹמוֹ; וְלָמָּה נִכְתַּב כָּאן? כְּדֵי לְהַפְסִיק בֵּין פֻּרְעָנוּת לְפֻרְעָנוּת וְכוּ׳, כִּדְאִיתָא בְּ״כָל כִּתְבֵי הַקֹּדֶשׁ״ (שבת קטו ע״ב – קטז ע״א): **קוּמָה ה׳.** לְפִי שֶׁהָיָה מַקְדִּים לִפְנֵיהֶם מַהֲלַךְ שְׁלֹשֶׁת יָמִים, הָיָה מֹשֶׁה אוֹמֵר: עֲמֹד וְהַמְתֵּן לָנוּ וְאַל תִּתְרַחֵק יוֹתֵר. בְּמִדְרַשׁ תַּנְחוּמָא בְּוַיַּקְהֵל (ז): **וְיָפֻצוּ אֹיְבֶיךָ.** הַמְכֻנָּסִין: **וְיָנֻסוּ מְשַׂנְאֶיךָ.** אֵלּוּ הָרוֹדְפִים: **מְשַׂנְאֶיךָ.** אֵלּוּ שׂוֹנְאֵי יִשְׂרָאֵל, שֶׁכָּל הַשּׂוֹנֵא אֶת יִשְׂרָאֵל שׂוֹנֵא אֶת מִי שֶׁאָמַר וְהָיָה הָעוֹלָם, שֶׁנֶּאֱמַר: ״וּמְשַׂנְאֶיךָ נָשְׂאוּ רֹאשׁ״ (תהלים פג, ג), וּמִי הֵם? ״עַל עַמְּךָ יַעֲרִימוּ סוֹד״ (שם ד):

לו **שׁוּבָה ה׳.** מְנַחֵם תִּרְגְּמוֹ לְשׁוֹן מַרְגּוֹעַ, וְכֵן: ״בְּשׁוּבָה וָנַחַת תִּוָּשֵׁעוּן״ (ישעיה ל, טו): **רִבְבוֹת אַלְפֵי יִשְׂרָאֵל.** מַגִּיד שֶׁאֵין הַשְּׁכִינָה שׁוֹרָה בְּיִשְׂרָאֵל פְּחוּתִים מִשְּׁנֵי אֲלָפִים וּשְׁתֵּי רְבָבוֹת:

יא א **וַיְהִי הָעָם כְּמִתְאֹנְנִים.** אֵין ׳הָעָם׳ אֶלָּא רְשָׁעִים, וְכֵן הוּא אוֹמֵר: ״מָה אֶעֱשֶׂה לָעָם הַזֶּה״ (שמות יז, ד), וְאוֹמֵר: ״הָעָם הַזֶּה הָרָע״ (ירמיה יג, י). וּכְשֶׁהֵם כְּשֵׁרִים קְרוּאִים ׳עַמִּי׳, שֶׁנֶּאֱמַר: ״שַׁלַּח עַמִּי״ (שמות ח, טז), ״עַמִּי מֶה עָשִׂיתִי לְךָ״ (מיכה ו, ג): **כְּמִתְאֹנְנִים.** אֵין ׳מִתְאוֹנְנִים׳ אֶלָּא לְשׁוֹן עֲלִילָה, מְבַקְּשִׁים עֲלִילָה הֵיאַךְ לִפְרֹשׁ מֵאַחֲרֵי הַמָּקוֹם, וְכֵן הוּא אוֹמֵר בְּשִׁמְשׁוֹן: ״כִּי תֹאֲנָה הוּא מְבַקֵּשׁ״ (שופטים יד, ד): **רַע בְּאָזְנֵי ה׳.** תּוֹאֲנָה שֶׁהִיא רָעָה בְּאָזְנֵי ה׳, שֶׁמִּתְכַּוְּנִים שֶׁתָּבוֹא בְּאָזְנָיו וְיַקְנִיט.

and it is time to move on. History beckons. Destiny calls. For God exists within, not just beyond, time and space and we have to engage in the world as it is, even as we aspire to the world as it ought to be.

These are the two books of Jewish life: the Judaism-of-eternity and the Judaism-of-history. Nowhere is the line between them clearer than it is here, as the long stay at Sinai comes to an end and the people have to gather their belongings and travel on. These two verses, flanked by an inverted *nun*, are the interlude between two movements of the symphony, the *adagio* of the stay and the *allegro* of the journey. What it tells us is simply this: that whether setting out or halting, the Ark must always be there at the heart of Jewish life, reminding us that God is to be found both in eternity and history, stasis and change, beyond time and within time, joining His fate to ours, the God of both priest and prophet, who gives us the patience to rest and the courage to move on.

10:35 **וַיְהִי בִּנְסֹעַ הָאָרֹן** *When the Ark set out* – The Israelites are about to begin the second half of their journey through the wilderness. They travel, tribe by tribe, in the order specified earlier in the book, with the Ark, symbolizing the Divine Presence, in their midst. So at the beginning and end of each stage on the way, Moshe will remind the people that they are not alone, nor are they defenseless. God is with them, giving them strength in battle and security in their resting places. We still say these verses in the synagogue when we take the *sefer Torah* out of the ark, and when we replace it.

11:1 **וַיְהִי הָעָם כְּמִתְאֹנְנִים רַע** *The people began to rail bitterly* – The Torah gives us no indication of what the people are complaining about. Usually we are told exactly what the issue is – but not here. The Torah seems to be implying that they are complaining because that is what they have become accustomed to doing, even when they have nothing specific

בְּרִית־יְהוָה נֹסֵעַ לִפְנֵיהֶם דֶּרֶךְ שְׁלֹשֶׁת יָמִים לָתוּר לָהֶם מְנוּחָה׃

לד לה וַעֲנַן יְהוָה עֲלֵיהֶם יוֹמָם בְּנָסְעָם מִן־הַמַּחֲנֶה׃ ׆ וַיְהִי בִּנְסֹעַ ששי

הָאָרֹן וַיֹּאמֶר מֹשֶׁה קוּמָה ׀ יְהוָה וְיָפֻצוּ אֹיְבֶיךָ וְיָנֻסוּ מְשַׂנְאֶיךָ מִפָּנֶיךָ׃

לו וּבְנֻחֹה יֹאמַר שׁוּבָה יְהוָה רִבְבוֹת אַלְפֵי יִשְׂרָאֵל׃ ׆

יא א וַיְהִי הָעָם כְּמִתְאֹנְנִים רַע בְּאָזְנֵי יְהוָה וַיִּשְׁמַע יְהוָה וַיִּחַר אַפּוֹ וַתִּבְעַר־

אונקלוס

קְיָמָא דַּיי נְטִיל קֳדָמֵיהוֹן, מַהֲלַךְ תְּלָתָא יוֹמִין, לְאַתְקָנָא לְהוֹן אֲתַר בֵּית מַשְׁרֵי: לד וַעֲנַן יְקָרָא דַּיי, מְטַל עֲלֵיהוֹן בִּימָמָא, בְּמִטַּלְהוֹן מִן מַשְׁרִיתָא: לה וַהֲוָה, בְּמִטַּל אֲרוֹנָא וַאֲמַר מֹשֶׁה, אִתְגְּלִי יי, וְיִתְבַּדְּרוּן סָנְאָךְ, וְיִעֲרְקוּן בַּעֲלֵי דְּבָבָךְ מִן קֳדָמָךְ: לו וּבְמִשְׁרוֹהִי אֲמַר, תּוּב יי שְׁרֵי בִּיקָרָךְ, בְּגוֹ רִבְוָת אַלְפַיָּא דְּיִשְׂרָאֵל: יא א וַהֲוָה עַמָּא כַּד מִסְתַּקְפִין, בִּישׁ קֳדָם יי, וּשְׁמִיעַ קֳדָם יי וּתְקֵיף רֻגְזֵיהּ, וּדְלֵיקַת בְּהוֹן

A BOOK BETWEEN THE BOOKS

This passage is separated from the rest of the text by two inverted Hebrew letters, each a *nun*. The Rabbis proposed that they form a set of brackets, parentheses, separating this one paragraph from the words that precede and follow it. Some rabbis went so far as to say that this shows that *these two sentences are a book in their own right*. In other words, Numbers is not one book but three (Soferim 6:1; Bereshit Rabba 64:8).

To consider the significance of this we must take it in the context of the structure of the three central books of the Torah: Exodus, Leviticus, and Numbers. The outer sections – the first nineteen chapters of Exodus and the last twenty-five of Numbers – are full of incidents. The Israelites leave Egypt and travel through the desert. There are dangers, battles, and miracles. We are in the presence of history. This is the world of the prophet. Here the dominant figure is Moshe.

However, within this outer wrapping are fifty-nine chapters – the last part of Exodus, the whole of Leviticus, and the first ten chapters of Numbers – in which the Israelites stay in the Sinai Desert. Time slows to a standstill. This is the world of the Tabernacle and the Temple, the universe of *kedusha*, holiness, in which the dominant figures are Aharon the High Priest and his descendants. Now, in our *parasha*, we have read, "The LORD spoke to Moshe in the Sinai Desert in the first month of the second year after they had left Egypt" (Num. 9:1). The historical narrative resumes.

There are aspects of Judaism – the laws of purity and impurity, permitted and forbidden, sacred and secular – that have barely changed through the centuries. This is where we encounter the holiness, the otherness, the eternity of God. But there are other aspects that are deeply enmeshed in time. Most of the books in Tanakh are about this dimension. They tell a story about the faithfulness or faithlessness of the people to their covenant with God. It is about politics and economics, battles won or lost, about Israel as a nation in a world of nations, and about its ability to stay true to its founding principles through the rapids of history.

If Israel were only a people of eternity, it would never have had an impact on history. Jews would have been a priestly sect like the one known to us from the Dead Sea Scrolls, holy and harmless, secluded and serene, in touch with the ethereal music of the spheres but not the substance of everyday life. If, on the other hand, Jews had been only a people of history, they would have disappeared in exile. They would have been like the Jebusites and Perizzites, a brief footnote in the history of a long-vanished past. Judaism lives in the creative tension between these two essential elements of its being.

Our passage, then, is set at a dividing line between two kinds of books. In two verses, it encapsulates Jewish history. There are times when Jews halt and encamp, when time itself seems to stop and the people feel close to eternity as they did in their prolonged stay in the desert of Sinai. And there are moments when the cloud shifts, the trumpet sounds,

2 edge of the camp. The people cried out to Moshe – Moshe prayed to the LORD –
3 and the fire subsided. And so that place was named Tavera, because the LORD's
4 fire had blazed against them. The rabble in their midst began to have strong
cravings, and once again the Israelites began to weep, saying, "Who will give us
5 meat to eat? We remember the fish we ate in Egypt at no cost, the cucumbers,
6 and the melons, and the leeks, and the onions, and the garlic. But now our
7 throats are dry. There is nothing at all but this manna to look at." The manna
8 was like coriander seed, and like bdellium in color. The people went around
gathering it. Then they would grind it in a mill or crush it in a mortar. They
cooked it in a pot and they made cakes from it; it tasted like cakes made with

רש״י

אָמְרוּ: אוֹי לָנוּ, כַּמָּה לִבְּטָנוּ בַּדֶּרֶךְ הַזֶּה, שְׁלֹשָׁה יָמִים שֶׁלֹּא נַחְנוּ מֵעִנּוּי הַדֶּרֶךְ: **וַיִּחַר אַפּוֹ.** אֲנִי הָיִיתִי מִתְכַּוֵּן לְטוֹבַתְכֶם שֶׁתִּכָּנְסוּ לָאָרֶץ מִיָּד: **בִּקְצֵה הַמַּחֲנֶה.** בַּמֻּקְצִין שֶׁבָּהֶם לְשִׁפְלוּת, אֵלּוּ עֵרֶב רַב. רַבִּי שִׁמְעוֹן בֶּן מְנַסְיָא אוֹמֵר: בַּקְּצִינִים שֶׁבָּהֶם וּבַגְּדוֹלִים:

ב **וַיִּצְעַק הָעָם אֶל מֹשֶׁה.** מָשָׁל לְמֶלֶךְ בָּשָׂר וָדָם שֶׁכָּעַס עַל בְּנוֹ, וְהָלַךְ הַבֵּן אֵצֶל אוֹהֲבוֹ שֶׁל אָבִיו וְאָמַר לוֹ: צֵא וּבַקֵּשׁ עָלַי מֵאַבָּא: **וַתִּשְׁקַע הָאֵשׁ.** שָׁקְעָה בִּמְקוֹמָהּ בָּאָרֶץ, שֶׁאִלּוּ חָזְרָה לְאַחַת הָרוּחוֹת הָיְתָה מְקַפֶּלֶת וְהוֹלֶכֶת כָּל אוֹתוֹ הָרוּחַ:

ד **וְהָאסַפְסֻף.** אֵלּוּ עֵרֶב רַב שֶׁנֶּאֶסְפוּ עֲלֵיהֶם בְּצֵאתָם מִמִּצְרַיִם: **וַיָּשֻׁבוּ.** גַּם בְּנֵי יִשְׂרָאֵל וַיִּבְכּוּ עִמָּהֶם: **מִי יַאֲכִלֵנוּ בָּשָׂר.** וְכִי לֹא הָיָה לָהֶם בָּשָׂר? וַהֲלֹא כְּבָר נֶאֱמַר: "וְגַם עֵרֶב רַב עָלָה אִתָּם וְצֹאן וּבָקָר" וְגוֹ׳ (שמות יב, לח), וְאִם תֹּאמַר אֲכָלוּם, וַהֲלֹא בִּכְנִיסָתָם לָאָרֶץ נֶאֱמַר: "וּמִקְנֶה רַב הָיָה לִבְנֵי רְאוּבֵן" וְגוֹ׳ (להלן לב, א), אֶלָּא שֶׁמְּבַקְּשִׁים עֲלִילָה:

ה **אֲשֶׁר נֹאכַל בְּמִצְרַיִם חִנָּם.** אִם תֹּאמַר שֶׁמִּצְרִים נוֹתְנִים לָהֶם דָּגִים חִנָּם, וַהֲלֹא כְּבָר נֶאֱמַר: "וְתֶבֶן לֹא יִנָּתֵן לָכֶם" (שמות ה, יח), אִם תֶּבֶן לֹא הָיוּ נוֹתְנִים לָהֶם חִנָּם, דָּגִים הָיוּ נוֹתְנִין לָהֶם חִנָּם?! וּמַהוּ אוֹמֵר: "חִנָּם"? חִנָּם מִן הַמִּצְוֹת: **אֵת הַקִּשֻּׁאִים.** אָמַר רַבִּי שִׁמְעוֹן: מִפְּנֵי מָה הַמָּן מִשְׁתַּנֶּה לְכָל דָּבָר חוּץ מֵאֵלּוּ? מִפְּנֵי שֶׁהֵן קָשִׁים לַמֵּינִיקוֹת, אוֹמְרִים לְאִשָּׁה: אַל תֹּאכְלִי שׁוּם וּבָצָל, מִפְּנֵי הַתִּינוֹק. מָשָׁל לְמֶלֶךְ כו׳ [בשר ודם שמסר בנו לפידגוג, והיה יושב ומפקדו ואומר לו, הנראה שלא יאכל מאכל רע ולא ישתה משקה רע. ובכל כך היה הבן ההוא מתרעם על אביו לומר, לא מפני שאוהבני, אלא מפני שאי אפשר לו שאוכל], כִּדְאִיתָא בְּסִפְרֵי (פז): **הַקִּשֻּׁאִים.** הֵם קוקומבר״ש בְּלַעַז: **אֲבַטִּחִים.** בודיק״ש: **הֶחָצִיר.** כְּרֵישִׁין, פוריל״ש, וְתַרְגּוּמוֹ: "יָת בּוּצִינַיָּא" וְכוּ׳:

ו **אֶל הַמָּן עֵינֵינוּ.** מָן בַּשַּׁחַר, מָן בָּעֶרֶב:

ז **וְהַמָּן כִּזְרַע גַּד.** מִי שֶׁאָמַר זֶה לֹא אָמַר זֶה. יִשְׂרָאֵל אוֹמְרִים: "בִּלְתִּי אֶל הַמָּן עֵינֵינוּ", וְהַקָּדוֹשׁ בָּרוּךְ הוּא הִכְתִּיב בַּתּוֹרָה: "וְהַמָּן כִּזְרַע גַּד" וְגוֹ׳, כְּלוֹמַר, רְאוּ בָּאֵי עוֹלָם עַל מַה מִּתְלוֹנְנִים בָּנַי, וְהַמָּן כָּךְ וְכָךְ הוּא חָשׁוּב: **כִּזְרַע גַּד.** עָגֹל כְּגִדָּא, זֶרַע קוליינדר״ו: **בְּדֹלַח.** שֵׁם אֶבֶן טוֹבָה, קריסט״ל:

ח **שָׁטוּ.** אֵין 'שַׁיִט' אֶלָּא לְשׁוֹן טִיּוּל, אישבנ״ייר, בְּלֹא עָמָל: **וְטָחֲנוּ בָרֵחַיִם וְגוֹ׳.** לֹא יָרַד בָּרֵחַיִם וְלֹא בַּקְּדֵרָה וְלֹא בַּמְּדוֹכָה, אֶלָּא מִשְׁתַּנֶּה הָיָה טַעְמוֹ לַנִּטְחָנִין וְלַנִּדּוֹכִין וְלַמְּבֻשָּׁלִין: **בַּפָּרוּר.** קְדֵרָה:

manna. Their complaint is that it is boring. They have lost their appetite. They have reached the spiritual heights but they remain the same recalcitrant, ungrateful, small-minded people they were before.

The song *Dayeinu,* which we sing at the Passover Seder, is structured as a *tikkun,* a making right, for the ingratitude of the Israelites in the wilderness. A series of fifteen praises punctuated by the refrain *dayeinu,* "that would have been enough," it enumerates the kindnesses of God on the long journey from slavery to freedom. It is as if the poet were saying: Where they complained, let us give thanks. Each stage was a miracle. Each would have been enough to convince us that there is a Providence at work in our fate.

As the philosopher Hegel points out, slavery gives rise to a culture of ressentiment, a generalized discontent; and the Israelites were newly released slaves. One sign of freedom is the capacity for gratitude. Only a free person can give thanks with a full heart.

ב בם אש יהוה ותאכל בקצה המחנה: ויצעק העם אל־משה ויתפלל
ג משה אל־יהוה ותשקע האש: ויקרא שם־המקום ההוא תבערה
ד כי־בערה בם אש יהוה: והאספסף אשר בקרבו התאוו תאוה וישבו
ה ויבכו גם בני ישראל ויאמרו מי יאכלנו בשר: זכרנו את־הדגה אשר־
נאכל במצרים חנם את הקשאים ואת האבטחים ואת־החציר ואת־
ו הבצלים ואת־השומים: ועתה נפשנו יבשה אין כל בלתי אל־המן
ז ח עינינו: והמן כזרע־גד הוא ועינו כעין הבדלח: שטו העם ולקטו
וטחנו ברחים או דכו במדכה ובשלו בפרור ועשו אתו עגות והיה

אונקלוס

אישתא מן קדם יי, ושיציאת בסיפי משריתא: ב וצוח עמא על משה, וצלי משה קדם יי, ואשתקעת אישתא: ג וקרא, שמיה דאתרא ההוא דליקתא, ארי דליקת בהון אישתא מן קדם יי: ד ועירברבין דביניהון, שאילו שאילתא, ותבו ובכו, אף בני ישראל, ואמרו, מאן יוכילננא בסרא: ה דכירין אנחנא ית נוניא, דהוינא אכלין במצרים מגן, ית בוציניא, וית אבטיחיא, וכרתי ובצלי ותומי: ו וכען, נפשנא תאיבא לית כל מדעם, אלהין למנא עיננא: ז ומנא, כבר זרע גדא הוא, וחזויה כחיזו בדלחא: ח שיטין עמא ולקטין דצבי טחין ברחיא, ודצבי דאיך במדוכתא, ומבשלין ליה בקדרא, ועבדין יתיה גריצן, והוי

to complain about. When that happens, the whole mood of the group is badly affected.

We are social animals. We are affected by those around us. Consciously or unconsciously, we conform to the norms of the group. Social phenomena are contagious. Already in the twelfth century, Rambam had codified social contagion as an axiom of Jewish law, writing that "it is in the nature of human beings to be influenced in their deeds and characters by their friends and companions and to act like the people of their country" (*Hilkhot Deot* 6:1).

The Torah – as understood by the Sages in the light of Jewish history from the days of Moshe to their own – attaches huge significance to the tone of conversation within a society as a whole, within communities, and even within families. Freedom depends on civility, on people speaking courteously of and to one another. Free people do not blame others for their misfortune. They accept and practice responsibility. They assume that if something bad has happened, they must work together to put it right. When criticism is necessary, and it often is, they do so constructively. In any group, where the predominant tone is one of complaint, criticism, envy, backbiting, cynicism, and mutual suspicion, not only is the group itself weakened; a profound disempowerment also takes place. The ability to challenge leaders is essential, but generalized, unconstructive complaint is potentially disastrous.

11:6 אין כל בלתי אל־המן *Nothing at all but this manna* – Moshe has faced a similar challenge before. Back in the book of Exodus the people made the same complaint: "If only we had died by the Lord's hand in Egypt, when we sat by the fleshpots and ate our fill of bread. Instead, you have brought us out into this desert to kill the entire assembly by starvation" (Ex. 16:3).

Moshe, on that occasion, experienced no crisis. The people were hungry and needed food. That was a legitimate request. Since then, though, they have experienced the twin peaks of the revelation at Mount Sinai and the construction of the Tabernacle. They have come closer to God than any nation has ever done before. Nor are they starving. Their complaint is not that they have no food. They have the

9 oil. When the dew fell over the camp at night, the manna would fall upon that.
10 Moshe heard the people weeping clan by clan, each one at his tent's opening.
11 The LORD's anger blazed intensely, and Moshe was distressed. "Why have You
treated Your servant so badly?" asked Moshe of the LORD. "Why have I found
so little favor in Your sight that You lay all the burden of this people upon me?
12 Was it I who conceived all this people? Was it I who gave birth to them all,
that You should say to me, 'Carry them in your bosom, as a nursemaid carries
13 a baby,' to the land that You swore to their fathers? Where am I to get meat
14 to give all this people when they come wailing to me, 'Give us meat to eat'? I
15 cannot bear all this people alone; the burden is too heavy for me. If this is how
You treat me, kill me now, if I find any favor in Your sight, and let me not see
my own misery."

רש"י

לְשַׁד הַשָּׁמֶן. לִחְלוּחַ שֶׁל שֶׁמֶן, כָּךְ פֵּרְשׁוֹ דּוּנַשׁ. וְדוֹמֶה לוֹ: "נֶהְפַּךְ לְשַׁדִּי בְּחַרְבֹנֵי קַיִץ" (תהלים לב, ד), וְהַלָּמֶ"ד יְסוֹד, נֶהְפַּךְ לִחְלוּחִי בְּחַרְבוֹנֵי קַיִץ. וְרַבּוֹתֵינוּ פֵּרְשׁוּהוּ לְשׁוֹן שָׁדַיִם, אַךְ אֵין עִנְיַן שָׁדַיִם אֵצֶל שֶׁמֶן. וְאִי אֶפְשָׁר לוֹמַר "לְשַׁד הַשָּׁמֶן" לְשׁוֹן "וַיִּשְׁמַן יְשֻׁרוּן" (דברים לב, טו), שֶׁאִם כֵּן הָיָה הַמֵּ"ם נָקוּד קָמָץ קָטָן (צירי) וְטַעְמוֹ לְמַטָּה תַּחַת הַמֵּ"ם, עַכְשָׁיו שֶׁהַמֵּ"ם נָקוּד פַּתָּח קָטָן (סגול) וְהַטַּעַם תַּחַת הַשִּׁי"ן, לְשׁוֹן שֶׁמֶן הוּא, וְהַשִּׁי"ן הַנְּקוּדָה בְּקָמָץ גָּדוֹל וְאֵינָהּ נְקוּדָה בְּפַתָּח קָטָן מִפְּנֵי שֶׁהוּא סוֹף פָּסוּק. דָּבָר אַחֵר, "לְשַׁד" לְשׁוֹן נוֹטָרִיקוֹן לִישׁ שֶׁמֶן דְּבַשׁ, כְּעִסָּה הַנִּלּוֹשָׁה בְּשֶׁמֶן וּקְטוּפָה בִּדְבַשׁ. וְתַרְגּוּם שֶׁל אוּנְקְלוֹס דִּמְתַרְגֵּם: "דְּלִישׁ בְּמִשְׁחָא" נוֹטֶה לְפִתְרוֹנוֹ שֶׁל דּוּנַשׁ, שֶׁהָעִסָּה הַנִּלּוֹשָׁה בְּשֶׁמֶן לַחְלוּחִית שֶׁמֶן יֵשׁ בָּהּ:

י **בֹּכֶה לְמִשְׁפְּחֹתָיו.** מִשְׁפָּחוֹת מִשְׁפָּחוֹת נֶאֱסָפִים וּבוֹכִים, לְפַרְסֵם תַּרְעֻמְתָּן בְּגָלוּי. וְרַבּוֹתֵינוּ אָמְרוּ: "לְמִשְׁפְּחֹתָיו", עַל עִסְקֵי מִשְׁפָּחוֹת, עַל עֲרָיוֹת הַנֶּאֱסָרוֹת לָהֶם:

יב **כִּי תֹאמַר אֵלַי.** שֶׁאַתָּה אוֹמֵר אֵלַי: שָׂאֵהוּ בְחֵיקֶךָ, וְהֵיכָן אָמַר לוֹ כֵן? "לֵךְ נְחֵה אֶת הָעָם" (שמות לב, לד), וְאוֹמֵר: "וַיְצַוֵּם אֶל בְּנֵי יִשְׂרָאֵל" (שם ו, יג), עַל מְנָת שֶׁיִּהְיוּ סוֹקְלִים אֶתְכֶם וּמְחָרְפִין אֶתְכֶם: **עַל הָאֲדָמָה אֲשֶׁר נִשְׁבַּעְתָּ לַאֲבֹתָיו.** אַתָּה אוֹמֵר לִי לְשָׂאתָם בְּחֵיקִי:

טו **וְאִם כָּכָה אַתְּ עֹשֶׂה לִּי.** תָּשַׁשׁ כֹּחוֹ שֶׁל מֹשֶׁה כִּנְקֵבָה כְּשֶׁהֶרְאָהוּ הַקָּדוֹשׁ בָּרוּךְ הוּא הַפֻּרְעָנוּת שֶׁהוּא עָתִיד לְהָבִיא עֲלֵיהֶם עַל זֹאת, אָמַר לְפָנָיו: אִם כֵּן, הָרְגֵנִי תְּחִלָּה: **וְאַל אֶרְאֶה בְּרָעָתִי.** 'בְּרָעָתָם' הָיָה לוֹ לִכְתֹּב, אֶלָּא שֶׁכִּנָּה הַכָּתוּב, וְזֶה אֶחָד מִתִּקּוּנֵי סוֹפְרִים בַּתּוֹרָה לְכִנּוּי וּלְתִקּוּן לָשׁוֹן:

leader is a parent, then the followers remain children. They are totally dependent on him. They do not develop skills of their own. They do not acquire a sense of responsibility or the self-confidence that comes from exercising it.

Perhaps this is what God is hinting to Moshe when He tells him to take seventy elders to stand with him in the Tent of Meeting. He is telling Moshe that his task is not to solve the crisis of the people's demand for meat. His task is to inspire others with his spirit – delegating, empowering, guiding, and encouraging. God is telling Moshe that great leaders do not create followers; they create leaders. They share their inspiration. They give of their spirit to others. They do not see the people they lead as children who need a father-mother-nursemaid, but as adults who need to be educated to take individual and collective responsibility for their own future.

People become what their leader gives them the space to become. When that space is large, they grow into greatness.

ט טַעְמוֹ כְּטַעַם לְשַׁד הַשָּׁמֶן: וּבְרֶדֶת הַטַּל עַל־הַמַּחֲנֶה לָיְלָה יֵרֵד הַמָּן
י עָלָיו: וַיִּשְׁמַע מֹשֶׁה אֶת־הָעָם בֹּכֶה לְמִשְׁפְּחֹתָיו אִישׁ לְפֶתַח אָהֳלוֹ
יא וַיִּחַר־אַף יהוה מְאֹד וּבְעֵינֵי מֹשֶׁה רָע: וַיֹּאמֶר מֹשֶׁה אֶל־יהוה לָמָה
הֲרֵעֹתָ לְעַבְדֶּךָ וְלָמָּה לֹא־מָצָתִי חֵן בְּעֵינֶיךָ לָשׂוּם אֶת־מַשָּׂא כָּל־הָעָם
יב הַזֶּה עָלָי: הֶאָנֹכִי הָרִיתִי אֵת כָּל־הָעָם הַזֶּה אִם־אָנֹכִי יְלִדְתִּיהוּ כִּי־
תֹאמַר אֵלַי שָׂאֵהוּ בְחֵיקֶךָ כַּאֲשֶׁר יִשָּׂא הָאֹמֵן אֶת־הַיֹּנֵק עַל הָאֲדָמָה
יג אֲשֶׁר נִשְׁבַּעְתָּ לַאֲבֹתָיו: מֵאַיִן לִי בָּשָׂר לָתֵת לְכָל־הָעָם הַזֶּה כִּי־יִבְכּוּ
יד עָלַי לֵאמֹר תְּנָה־לָּנוּ בָשָׂר וְנֹאכֵלָה: לֹא־אוּכַל אָנֹכִי לְבַדִּי לָשֵׂאת
טו אֶת־כָּל־הָעָם הַזֶּה כִּי כָבֵד מִמֶּנִּי: וְאִם־כָּכָה ׀ אַתְּ־עֹשֶׂה לִּי הָרְגֵנִי נָא
הָרֹג אִם־מָצָאתִי חֵן בְּעֵינֶיךָ וְאַל־אֶרְאֶה בְּרָעָתִי:

אונקלוס

טַעְמֵיהּ, כִּטְעֵים דְּלִישׁ בְּמִשְׁחָא: ט וְכַד נָחֵית טַלָּא, עַל מַשְׁרִיתָא בְּלֵילְיָא, נָחֵית מַנָּא עֲלוֹהִי: י וּשְׁמַע מֹשֶׁה יָת עַמָּא, בָּכַן לְזַרְעֲיָתְהוֹן, גְּבַר בִּתְרַע מַשְׁכְּנֵיהּ, וּתְקֵיף רֻגְזָא דַּייָ לַחְדָּא, וּבְעֵינֵי מֹשֶׁה בִּישׁ: יא וַאֲמַר מֹשֶׁה קֳדָם יְיָ, לְמָא אַבְאֵישְׁתָּא לְעַבְדָּךְ, וּלְמָא לָא אַשְׁכַּחִית רַחֲמִין קֳדָמָךְ, לְשַׁוָּאָה, יָת מָטוֹל, כָּל עַמָּא הָדֵין עֲלָי: יב הַאֲבָא אֲנָא, לְכָל עַמָּא הָדֵין, אִם בְּנַי אִנּוּן, דַּאֲמַרְתְּ לִי סוֹבַרְהִי בְּתָקְפָּךְ, כְּמָא דִּמְסוֹבַר תְּרָבְיָנָא יָת יָנְקָא, עַל אַרְעָא, דְּקַיֵּימְתָּא לַאֲבָהָתוֹהִי: יג מְנָן לִי בִּסְרָא, לְמִתַּן לְכָל עַמָּא הָדֵין, אֲרֵי בָכַן עֲלַי לְמֵימַר, הַב לָנָא בִּסְרָא וְנֵיכוֹל: יד לֵית אֲנָא יָכֵיל בִּלְחוֹדַי, לְסוֹבָרָא יָת כָּל עַמָּא הָדֵין, אֲרֵי יַקִּיר מִנִּי: טו וְאִם כְּדֵין אַתְּ עָבֵיד לִי, קְטוֹלְנִי כְּעַן מִקְטָל, אִם אַשְׁכַּחִית רַחֲמִין קֳדָמָךְ, וְלָא אֶחֱזֵי בְּבִשְׁתִּי:

11:12 כַּאֲשֶׁר יִשָּׂא הָאֹמֵן אֶת־הַיֹּנֵק *As a nursemaid carries a baby* – Inevitably, when we read Moshe's anguished plea, our attention focuses on his wish to die. But this is not the most interesting part of his speech. Moshe is not the only Jewish leader to pray to die. So does Eliyahu. So does Yirmeyahu. So does Yona.

What is singular here is his statement that God told him to carry the people in his arms "as a nursemaid carries a baby." God never used those words or even remotely implied such a thing. He asked Moshe to lead but did not tell him how to lead. He told Moshe what to do, but never discussed with him his leadership style.

It seems that the Torah is here hinting that *the way Moshe conceives the role of leader is itself part of the problem.* His is the language of the leader-as-parent. Moshe is not a typical charismatic leader. He says of himself, "I am not a man of words" (Ex. 4:10). He is not particularly close to the people. Aharon is. Perhaps Miriam is also. Kalev has the power to calm the people, at least temporarily. Moshe has neither the gift nor the desire to sway crowds, attract a mass following, or win popularity. But Moshe, especially here, seems to feel that *the leader must do it all.* He must be the people's father, mother, and nursemaid. He must be the doer, the problem solver, omniscient and omnipotent. The trouble is that if the

16 Then the LORD said to Moshe, "Gather for Me seventy of Israel's elders, whom
you know to be the people's elders and officers, and bring them to the Tent of
17 Meeting. Let them stand there with you. I will come down and speak with you
there, and I will take some of the spirit that is on you and place it upon them;
they will share the burden of the people with you, and you will not have to bear
18 it alone. And say to the people: Consecrate yourselves for tomorrow; you will
then have meat to eat, for you have been wailing in the presence of the LORD,
'Who will give us meat to eat? It was better for us in Egypt.' The LORD will give
19 you meat, and you will eat. You will eat it not just for one day, or two days, or

רש״י

טז **אֶסְפָה לִּי.** הֲרֵי תְּשׁוּבָה לִתְלוּנָתְךָ שֶׁאָמַרְתָּ: "לֹא אוּכַל אָנֹכִי לְבַדִּי" (לעיל פסוק יד). וְהַזְּקֵנִים הָרִאשׁוֹנִים הֵיכָן הָיוּ? וַהֲלֹא אַף בְּמִצְרַיִם יָשְׁבוּ עִמָּהֶם, שֶׁנֶּאֱמַר: "לֵךְ וְאָסַפְתָּ אֶת זִקְנֵי יִשְׂרָאֵל" (שמות ג, טז), אֶלָּא בְּאֵשׁ תַּבְעֵרָה מֵתוּ. וּרְאוּיִים הָיוּ לְכָךְ מִסִּינַי, דִּכְתִיב: "וַיֶּחֱזוּ אֶת הָאֱלֹהִים" (שמות כד, יא), שֶׁנָּהֲגוּ קַלּוּת רֹאשׁ כְּנוֹשֵׁךְ פִּתּוֹ וּמְדַבֵּר בִּפְנֵי הַמֶּלֶךְ, וְזֶהוּ: "וַיֹּאכְלוּ וַיִּשְׁתּוּ" (שם), וְלֹא רָצָה הַקָּדוֹשׁ בָּרוּךְ הוּא לִתֵּן אֲבֵלוּת בְּמַתַּן תּוֹרָה, וּפָרַע לָהֶם כָּאן: **אֲשֶׁר יָדַעְתָּ כִּי הֵם וְגוֹ׳.** אוֹתָן שֶׁאַתָּה מַכִּיר שֶׁנִּתְמַנּוּ עֲלֵיהֶם שׁוֹטְרִים בְּמִצְרַיִם בַּעֲבוֹדַת פֶּרֶךְ, וְהָיוּ מְרַחֲמִים עֲלֵיהֶם וּמֻכִּים עַל יָדָם, שֶׁנֶּאֱמַר: "וַיֻּכּוּ שֹׁטְרֵי בְּנֵי יִשְׂרָאֵל" (שמות ה, יד), עַתָּה יִתְמַנּוּ בִּגְדֻלָּתָן, כְּדֶרֶךְ שֶׁנִּצְטַעֲרוּ בְּצָרָתָן: **וְלָקַחְתָּ אֹתָם.** קָחֵם בִּדְבָרִים, אַשְׁרֵיכֶם שֶׁנִּתְמַנִּיתֶם פַּרְנָסִים עַל בָּנָיו שֶׁל מָקוֹם: **וְהִתְיַצְּבוּ שָׁם עִמָּךְ.** כְּדֵי שֶׁיִּרְאוּ יִשְׂרָאֵל וְיִנְהֲגוּ בָּהֶם גְּדֻלָּה וְכָבוֹד, וְיֹאמְרוּ: חֲבִיבִין אֵלּוּ שֶׁנִּכְנְסוּ עִם מֹשֶׁה לִשְׁמוֹעַ דִּבּוּר מִפִּי הַקָּדוֹשׁ בָּרוּךְ הוּא:

יז **וְיָרַדְתִּי.** זוֹ אַחַת מֵעֶשֶׂר יְרִידוֹת הַכְּתוּבוֹת בַּתּוֹרָה: **וְדִבַּרְתִּי עִמְּךָ.** וְלֹא עִמָּהֶם: **וְאָצַלְתִּי.** כְּתַרְגּוּמוֹ: "וַאֲרַבֵּי", כְּמוֹ: "וְאֶל אֲצִילֵי בְּנֵי יִשְׂרָאֵל" (שמות כד, יא): **וְשַׂמְתִּי עֲלֵיהֶם.** לְמָה מֹשֶׁה דּוֹמֶה בְּאוֹתָהּ שָׁעָה? לְנֵר שֶׁמֻּנָּח עַל גַּבֵּי מְנוֹרָה, וְהַכֹּל מַדְלִיקִין הֵימֶנּוּ וְאֵין אוֹרוֹ חָסֵר כְּלוּם: **וְנָשְׂאוּ אִתְּךָ.** הַתְנֵה עִמָּהֶם, עַל מְנָת שֶׁיְּקַבְּלוּ עֲלֵיהֶם טֹרַח בָּנַי, שֶׁהֵם טַרְחָנִים וְסַרְבָנִים: **וְלֹא תִשָּׂא אַתָּה לְבַדֶּךָ.** הֲרֵי תְּשׁוּבָה לְמַה שֶּׁאָמַרְתָּ "לֹא אוּכַל אָנֹכִי לְבַדִּי" (לעיל פסוק יד):

יח **הִתְקַדְּשׁוּ.** הַזְמִינוּ עַצְמְכֶם לְפֻרְעָנוּת, וְכֵן הוּא אוֹמֵר: "וְהַקְדִּשֵׁם לְיוֹם הֲרֵגָה" (ירמיה יב, ג):

Little can he know that he – who encounters little in his lifetime but complaints and rebellions – will have so decisive an influence that the people of Israel thirty-three centuries later would still be studying and living by the words he transmitted. He is helping forge an identity that would prove more tenacious than any other in the history of mankind. He cannot know these things; he does not *need* to know these things. All he needs is to see that seventy elders have internalized his spirit and made his message their own. Then he knows that his life is not in vain. He has disciples. His vision is not his alone. He has planted it in others. Others, too, will continue his work after his lifetime. That was enough for him, as it must be for us. Once Moshe knows this, he can face the future with equanimity.

11:17 **וְלֹא־תִשָּׂא אַתָּה לְבַדֶּךָ** *You will not have to bear it alone* – It is as if God were saying to Moshe, "Remember what your father-in-law Yitro told you. Do not try to lead alone. Even you, the greatest of the prophets, are still human, and humans are social animals. Enlist others."

What is moving about this episode is that, at the moment of Moshe's maximum emotional vulnerability, God Himself speaks to Moshe as a friend. God is not (merely) the creator of the universe, Lord of history, sovereign, lawgiver, and redeemer. He is also close, tender, loving: "He heals the brokenhearted and binds up their wounds" (Ps. 147:3). He is always there: "The LORD is close to all who call on Him – to all who truly call on Him" (145:18). *Faith is the redemption of solitude.* It is about relationships – between us and God, us and our family, us and our neighbors, us and our people, us and humankind. Judaism is not about the lonely soul. It is about the bonds that bind us to one another and to the Author of all. It is, in the highest sense, about friendship.

טז וַיֹּאמֶר יְהוָה אֶל־מֹשֶׁה אֶסְפָה־לִּי שִׁבְעִים אִישׁ מִזִּקְנֵי יִשְׂרָאֵל אֲשֶׁר י
יָדַעְתָּ כִּי־הֵם זִקְנֵי הָעָם וְשֹׁטְרָיו וְלָקַחְתָּ אֹתָם אֶל־אֹהֶל מוֹעֵד וְהִתְיַצְּבוּ
יז שָׁם עִמָּךְ׃ וְיָרַדְתִּי וְדִבַּרְתִּי עִמְּךָ שָׁם וְאָצַלְתִּי מִן־הָרוּחַ אֲשֶׁר עָלֶיךָ
וְשַׂמְתִּי עֲלֵיהֶם וְנָשְׂאוּ אִתְּךָ בְּמַשָּׂא הָעָם וְלֹא־תִשָּׂא אַתָּה לְבַדֶּךָ׃
יח וְאֶל־הָעָם תֹּאמַר הִתְקַדְּשׁוּ לְמָחָר וַאֲכַלְתֶּם בָּשָׂר כִּי בְּכִיתֶם בְּאָזְנֵי
יְהוָה לֵאמֹר מִי יַאֲכִלֵנוּ בָּשָׂר כִּי־טוֹב לָנוּ בְּמִצְרָיִם וְנָתַן יְהוָה לָכֶם
יט בָּשָׂר וַאֲכַלְתֶּם׃ לֹא יוֹם אֶחָד תֹּאכְלוּן וְלֹא יוֹמָיִם וְלֹא ׀ חֲמִשָּׁה יָמִים

אונקלוס

טו וַאֲמַר יי לְמֹשֶׁה, כְּנוֹשׁ קֳדָמַי, שִׁבְעִין גֻּבְרָא מִסָּבֵי יִשְׂרָאֵל, דִּידַעְתָּא,
אֲרֵי אִנּוּן, סָבֵי עַמָּא וְסָרְכוֹהִי, וְתִדְבַּר יָתְהוֹן לְמַשְׁכַּן זִמְנָא, וְיִתְעַתְּדוּן
תַּמָּן עִמָּךְ: יז וְאֶתְגְּלֵי, וַאֲמַלֵּיל עִמָּךְ תַּמָּן, וַאֲרַבֵּי, מִן רוּחָא דַּעֲלָךְ
וַאֲשַׁוֵּי עֲלֵיהוֹן, וִיסוֹבְרוּן עִמָּךְ בְּמַטּוּל עַמָּא, וְלָא תְסוֹבַר אַתְּ בִּלְחוֹדָךְ:

יח וּלְעַמָּא תֵּימַר, אִזְדַּמַּנוּ לִמְחַר וְתֵיכְלוּן בִּסְרָא, אֲרֵי, בְּכֵיתוּן קֳדָם יי
לְמֵימַר, מַאן יוֹכְלִנַנָא בִּסְרָא, אֲרֵי טָב לַנָא בְּמִצְרָיִם, וְיִתֵּין יי לְכוֹן, בִּסְרָא
וְתֵיכְלוּן: יט לָא יוֹמָא חַד, תֵּיכְלוּן וְלָא תְּרֵין יוֹמִין, וְלָא חַמְשָׁא יוֹמִין,

THE SEVENTY ELDERS

The people's complaint about food has been the worst crisis in Moshe's life. Why? It was an appalling show of ingratitude, but not the first time the Israelites had behaved this way. He had faced and overcome such difficulties before. Each time, God had answered the people's requests. Moshe knew this. Why did this outburst of the people induce in him a complete breakdown?

Equally strange is God's reaction here. To be sure, it is a response to Moshe's complaint: "I cannot bear all this people alone" (Num. 11:14). Nevertheless, how will the appointment of elders address the crisis? He does not need deputies to help him find meat. Either it will appear by a miracle, or it will not appear at all. Nor does he need help in sharing the burdens of leadership. Already, on Yitro's advice, he has created a leadership infrastructure: heads of thousands, hundreds, fifties, and tens. How would a new appointment of seventy elders make a difference?

And why the emphasis on spirit in God's reply: "I will take some of the spirit that is on you and place it upon them" (Num. 11:17)? The elders do not need to become prophets to help Moshe in carrying out the burdens of leadership. Prophets help only in knowing what guidance to give the people – and for this, one prophet, Moshe, is sufficient. To put it bluntly: Either the seventy elders will deliver the same message as Moshe or they will not. If they do, they will be superfluous. If they do not, they will undermine his authority.

Yet it works. From this moment onward, Moshe's despair disappears. When Eldad and Meidad prophesy not in the Tent of Meeting but in the camp, Yehoshua senses a threat to Moshe's authority – yet Moshe responds with surpassing generosity of spirit, "Would that all the LORD's people were prophets" (11:29). In the next chapter, when his own brother and sister start complaining about him, he does nothing. The despair is gone. The crisis has passed. How?

God let Moshe see the influence he had on others. All the evidence seemed to suggest that he had none. When he heard the people complain of boredom after all they had received, Moshe was staring at his own defeat. There was no point in carrying on. If the people have not changed by now, it is a reasonable assumption that they never will. And so, for a brief moment, God would take "some of the spirit that is on you and place it upon them" so that Moshe can see the difference he has made to this one group. He needs a glimpse of how his spirit has communicated itself to them. Then he knows he has made a difference.

20 five, or ten, or twenty days, but for a whole month, until it comes out at your
nostrils and becomes nauseating to you; for you have rejected the LORD who
is among you and have come wailing in His presence, 'Why ever did we leave
21 Egypt?'" But Moshe said, "Here I am among six hundred thousand men on
22 foot, and You say, 'I will give them meat to eat for a whole month'! If whole
flocks and herds were slaughtered for them, would there be enough? If all the
fish of the sea were caught for them, would there be enough?!"
23 The LORD said to Moshe, "Does the LORD's hand fall short? Soon you shall see
24 whether what I say comes true or not." Moshe went out and told the people
what the LORD had said. He gathered seventy of the people's elders and had
25 them stand surrounding the Tent. Then the LORD came down in the cloud
and spoke to him, and took some of the spirit that was upon him and placed
it on the seventy elders. When the spirit rested upon them, they prophesied –
26 but they did not do so again. Two men, one named Eldad and the other
Meidad, had remained in the camp, yet the spirit rested upon them. Though
they were among those listed, they had not gone out to the Tent – and they
27 spoke prophecy in the camp. A young man ran and told Moshe, "Eldad and

רש"י

כ **עַד חֹדֶשׁ יָמִים.** זוֹ בַּכְּשֵׁרִים שֶׁמִּתְמַהְּנִין עַל מִטּוֹתֵיהֶן וְאַחַר כָּךְ נִשְׁמָתָן יוֹצְאָה; וּבָרְשָׁעִים הוּא אוֹמֵר "הַבָּשָׂר עוֹדֶנּוּ בֵּין שִׁנֵּיהֶם" (להלן פסוק לג), כָּךְ הִיא שְׁנוּיָה בְּסִפְרֵי (צג). אֲבָל בִּמְכִילְתָּא (ויסע פ"ד) שְׁנוּיָה חִלּוּף: הָרְשָׁעִים אוֹכְלִין וּמִצְטַעֲרִין שְׁלֹשִׁים יוֹם, וְהַכְּשֵׁרִים – "הַבָּשָׂר עוֹדֶנּוּ בֵּין שִׁנֵּיהֶם": **עַד אֲשֶׁר יֵצֵא מֵאַפְּכֶם.** כְּתַרְגּוּמוֹ: "דְּתִקּוּצוּן בֵּיהּ", יְהֵא דוֹמֶה לָכֶם כְּאִלּוּ אֲכַלְתֶּם מִמֶּנּוּ יוֹתֵר מִדַּאי עַד שֶׁיּוֹצֵא וְנִגְעָל לַחוּץ דֶּרֶךְ הָאַף: **וְהָיָה לָכֶם לְזָרָא.** שֶׁתִּהְיוּ מְרַחֲקִין אוֹתוֹ יוֹתֵר מִמַּה שֶּׁקֵּרַבְתֶּם. וּבְדִבְרֵי רַבִּי מֹשֶׁה הַדַּרְשָׁן רָאִיתִי, שֶׁיֵּשׁ לָשׁוֹן שֶׁקּוֹרִין לַחֶרֶב 'זָרָא': **אֶת ה' אֲשֶׁר בְּקִרְבְּכֶם.** אִם לֹא שֶׁנָּטַעְתִּי שְׁכִינָתִי בֵּינֵיכֶם, לֹא גָּבַהּ לִבַּבְכֶם לִכָּנֵס לְכָל הַדְּבָרִים הַלָּלוּ:

כא **שֵׁשׁ מֵאוֹת אֶלֶף רַגְלִי.** לֹא חָשׁ לִמְנוֹת אֶת הַפְּרָט, שְׁלֹשֶׁת אֲלָפִים הַיְּתֵרִים (לעיל א, מו). וְרַבִּי מֹשֶׁה הַדַּרְשָׁן פֵּרֵשׁ, שֶׁלֹּא בָּכוּ אֶלָּא אוֹתָן שֶׁיָּצְאוּ מִמִּצְרַיִם:

כב-כג **הֲצֹאן וּבָקָר יִשָּׁחֵט.** זֶה אֶחָד מֵאַרְבָּעָה דְּבָרִים שֶׁהָיָה רַבִּי עֲקִיבָא דּוֹרֵשׁ וְאֵין רַבִּי שִׁמְעוֹן דּוֹרֵשׁ כְּמוֹתוֹ. רַבִּי עֲקִיבָא אוֹמֵר: "שֵׁשׁ מֵאוֹת אֶלֶף רַגְלִי, וְאַתָּה אָמַרְתָּ בָּשָׂר אֶתֵּן לָהֶם וְאָכְלוּ חֹדֶשׁ יָמִים, הֲצֹאן וּבָקָר" וְגוֹ', הַכֹּל כְּמַשְׁמָעוֹ, מִי מַסְפִּיק לָהֶם? כָּעִנְיָן שֶׁנֶּאֱמַר: "וּמָצָא כְּדֵי גְאֻלָּתוֹ" (ויקרא כה, כו). וְאֵיזוֹ קָשָׁה, זוֹ אוֹ "שִׁמְעוּ נָא הַמֹּרִים" (להלן כ, י)? אֶלָּא לְפִי שֶׁלֹּא אָמַר בָּרַבִּים, חָסַךְ לוֹ הַכָּתוּב וְלֹא נִפְרַע מִמֶּנּוּ, וְזוֹ שֶׁל מְרִיבָה הָיְתָה בַּגָּלוּי, לְפִיכָךְ לֹא חָסַךְ לוֹ הַכָּתוּב. רַבִּי שִׁמְעוֹן אוֹמֵר: חַס וְשָׁלוֹם, לֹא עָלְתָה עַל דַּעְתּוֹ שֶׁל אוֹתוֹ צַדִּיק כָּךְ! מִי שֶׁכָּתוּב בּוֹ: "בְּכָל בֵּיתִי נֶאֱמָן הוּא" (להלן יב, ז) יֹאמַר: 'אֵין הַמָּקוֹם מַסְפִּיק לָנוּ'?! אֶלָּא, כָּךְ אָמַר: "שֵׁשׁ מֵאוֹת אֶלֶף רַגְלִי וְגוֹ', וְאַתָּה אָמַרְתָּ בָּשָׂר אֶתֵּן" לְחֹדֶשׁ יָמִים, וְאַחַר כָּךְ תַּהֲרֹג אֻמָּה גְּדוֹלָה כָּזוֹ, "הֲצֹאן וּבָקָר יִשָּׁחֵט לָהֶם" כְּדֵי שֶׁיֵּהָרְגוּ וּתְהֵא אֲכִילָה זוֹ מַסְפַּקְתָּן עַד עוֹלָם? וְכִי שִׁבְחֲךָ הוּא זֶה? אוֹמְרִים לוֹ לַחֲמוֹר: טֹל כֹּר שְׂעוֹרִים וְנַחְתֹּךְ רֹאשְׁךָ? הֱשִׁיבוֹ הַקָּדוֹשׁ בָּרוּךְ הוּא: וְאִם לֹא אֶתֵּן, יֹאמְרוּ שֶׁקָּצְרָה יָדִי, הֲטוֹב בְּעֵינֶיךָ שֶׁיַּד ה' תִּקְצַר בְּעֵינֵיהֶם? יֹאבְדוּ הֵם וּמֵאָה כַּיּוֹצֵא בָּהֶם וְאַל תְּהִי יָדִי קְצָרָה לִפְנֵיהֶם אֲפִלּוּ שָׁעָה אַחַת, "עַתָּה תִרְאֶה הֲיִקְרְךָ דְבָרִי". רַבָּן גַּמְלִיאֵל בְּנוֹ שֶׁל רַבִּי יְהוּדָה הַנָּשִׂיא אוֹמֵר: אִי אֶפְשָׁר לַעֲמֹד עַל הַטָּפֵל, מֵאַחַר שֶׁאֵינָן מְבַקְּשִׁים אֶלָּא עֲלִילָה לֹא תַסְפִּיק לָהֶם, סוֹפָן לָדוּן אַחֲרֶיךָ, אִם אַתָּה נוֹתֵן לָהֶם בְּשַׂר בְּהֵמָה גַּסָּה, יֹאמְרוּ: דַּקָּה בִּקַּשְׁנוּ, וְאִם אַתָּה נוֹתֵן לָהֶם דַּקָּה, יֹאמְרוּ: גַּסָּה בִּקַּשְׁנוּ, חַיָּה וָעוֹף בִּקַּשְׁנוּ, דָּגִים וַחֲגָבִים בִּקַּשְׁנוּ. אָמַר לוֹ: אִם כֵּן יֹאמְרוּ שֶׁקָּצְרָה יָדִי. אָמַר לְפָנָיו: הֲרֵינִי הוֹלֵךְ וּמְפַיְּסָן. אָמַר לוֹ: "עַתָּה תִרְאֶה הֲיִקְרְךָ דְבָרִי", שֶׁלֹּא יִשְׁמְעוּ לָךְ. הָלַךְ מֹשֶׁה לְפַיְּסָן, אָמַר לָהֶם: "הֲיַד ה' תִּקְצָר", "הֵן הִכָּה צוּר וַיָּזוּבוּ מַיִם וְגוֹ' הֲגַם לֶחֶם יוּכַל תֵּת" (תהלים עח, כ). אָמְרוּ: פְּשָׁרָה הִיא זוֹ, אֵין בּוֹ כֹּחַ לְמַלֹּאת שְׁאֵלָתֵנוּ, וְזֶהוּ שֶׁנֶּאֱמַר: "וַיֵּצֵא מֹשֶׁה וַיְדַבֵּר אֶל הָעָם" (להלן פסוק כד), כֵּיוָן שֶׁלֹּא שָׁמְעוּ לוֹ, "וַיֶּאֱסֹף שִׁבְעִים אִישׁ" וְגוֹ' (שם):

כ וְלֹא עֲשָׂרָה יָמִים וְלֹא עֶשְׂרִים יוֹם: עַד ׀ חֹדֶשׁ יָמִים עַד אֲשֶׁר־יֵצֵא
מֵאַפְּכֶם וְהָיָה לָכֶם לְזָרָא יַעַן כִּי־מְאַסְתֶּם אֶת־יהוה אֲשֶׁר בְּקִרְבְּכֶם
כא וַתִּבְכּוּ לְפָנָיו לֵאמֹר לָמָּה זֶּה יָצָאנוּ מִמִּצְרָיִם: וַיֹּאמֶר מֹשֶׁה שֵׁשׁ־
מֵאוֹת אֶלֶף רַגְלִי הָעָם אֲשֶׁר אָנֹכִי בְּקִרְבּוֹ וְאַתָּה אָמַרְתָּ בָּשָׂר אֶתֵּן
כב לָהֶם וְאָכְלוּ חֹדֶשׁ יָמִים: הֲצֹאן וּבָקָר יִשָּׁחֵט לָהֶם וּמָצָא לָהֶם אִם
אֶת־כָּל־דְּגֵי הַיָּם יֵאָסֵף לָהֶם וּמָצָא לָהֶם:
כג וַיֹּאמֶר יהוה אֶל־מֹשֶׁה הֲיַד יהוה תִּקְצָר עַתָּה תִרְאֶה הֲיִקְרְךָ דְבָרִי יא
כד אִם־לֹא: וַיֵּצֵא מֹשֶׁה וַיְדַבֵּר אֶל־הָעָם אֵת דִּבְרֵי יהוה וַיֶּאֱסֹף שִׁבְעִים
כה אִישׁ מִזִּקְנֵי הָעָם וַיַּעֲמֵד אֹתָם סְבִיבֹת הָאֹהֶל: וַיֵּרֶד יהוה ׀ בֶּעָנָן וַיְדַבֵּר
אֵלָיו וַיָּאצֶל מִן־הָרוּחַ אֲשֶׁר עָלָיו וַיִּתֵּן עַל־שִׁבְעִים אִישׁ הַזְּקֵנִים
כו וַיְהִי כְּנוֹחַ עֲלֵיהֶם הָרוּחַ וַיִּתְנַבְּאוּ וְלֹא יָסָפוּ: וַיִּשָּׁאֲרוּ שְׁנֵי־אֲנָשִׁים ׀
בַּמַּחֲנֶה שֵׁם הָאֶחָד ׀ אֶלְדָּד וְשֵׁם הַשֵּׁנִי מֵידָד וַתָּנַח עֲלֵהֶם הָרוּחַ
כז וְהֵמָּה בַּכְּתֻבִים וְלֹא יָצְאוּ הָאֹהֱלָה וַיִּתְנַבְּאוּ בַּמַּחֲנֶה: וַיָּרָץ הַנַּעַר

אונקלוס

וְלָא עַסְרָא יוֹמִין, וְלָא עַסְרִין יוֹם: כ עַד יְרַח יוֹמִין, עַד דְּתִקוּצוּן בֵּיהּ, וִיהֵי לְכוֹן לְתַקְלָא, חֲלָף, דְּקַצְתּוּן בְּמֵימְרָא דַּייָ דִּשְׁכִינְתֵּיהּ שָׁרְיָא בֵּינֵיכוֹן, וּבְכֵיתוּן קֳדָמוֹהִי לְמֵימַר, לְמָא דְנַן נְפַקְנָא מִמִּצְרָיִם: כא וַאֲמַר מֹשֶׁה, שִׁית מְאָה אַלְפִין גַּבְרָא רִגְלָאָה, עַמָּא, דַּאֲנָא בֵּינֵיהוֹן, וְאַתְּ אֲמַרְתְּ, בִּסְרָא אֶתֵּין לְהוֹן, וְיֵיכְלוּן יְרַח יוֹמִין: כב הֲעָן וְתוֹרִין, יִתְנַכְסוּן לְהוֹן הַיִסְפְּקוּן לְהוֹן, אִם יָת כָּל נוּנֵי יַמָּא, יִתְכַּנְשׁוּן לְהוֹן הַיִסְפְּקוּן לְהוֹן: כג וַאֲמַר יְיָ לְמֹשֶׁה, הֲמֵימְרָא דַּייָ מִתְעַכַּב, כְּעַן תֶּחֱזֵי, הַיְעָרְעִנָּךְ פִּתְגָּמִי אִם לָא: כד וּנְפַק מֹשֶׁה, וּמַלֵּיל עִם עַמָּא, יָת פִּתְגָּמַיָּא דַּייָ, וּכְנַשׁ, שִׁבְעִין גֻּבְרָא מִסָּבֵי עַמָּא, וַאֲקִים יָתְהוֹן סְחוֹר סְחוֹר לְמַשְׁכְּנָא: כה וְאִתְגְּלִי יְיָ בַּעֲנָנָא וּמַלֵּיל עִמֵּיהּ, וְרַבִּי, מִן רוּחָא דַּעֲלוֹהִי, וִיהַב, עַל שִׁבְעִין גֻּבְרָא סָבַיָּא, וַהֲוָה, כַּד שְׁרַת עֲלֵיהוֹן רוּחַ נְבוּאָה, וּמִתְנַבַּן וְלָא פָסְקִין: כו וְאִשְׁתְּאַרוּ תְּרֵין גֻּבְרִין בְּמַשְׁרִיתָא, שׁוּם חַד אֶלְדָּד, וְשׁוּם תִּנְיָנָא מֵידָד וּשְׁרַת עֲלֵיהוֹן רוּחַ נְבוּאָה, וְאִנּוּן בִּכְתִיבַיָּא, וְלָא נְפַקוּ לְמַשְׁכְּנָא, וְאִתְנַבִּיאוּ בְּמַשְׁרִיתָא: כז וּרְהַט עוּלֵימָא,

רש״י

כה) וְלֹא יָסָפוּ. לֹא נִתְנַבְּאוּ אֶלָּא אוֹתוֹ הַיּוֹם לְבַדּוֹ, כָּךְ מְפֹרָשׁ בְּסִפְרֵי (פה), וְאוּנְקְלוֹס תִּרְגֵּם: "וְלָא פָסְקִין", שֶׁלֹּא פָּסְקָה נְבוּאָה מֵהֶם:

כו) וַיִּשָּׁאֲרוּ שְׁנֵי אֲנָשִׁים. מֵאוֹתָן שֶׁנִּבְחֲרוּ, אָמְרוּ: אֵין אָנוּ כְּדַאי לִגְדֻלָּה זוֹ: וְהֵמָּה בַּכְּתֻבִים. בַּמְבֹרָרִים שֶׁבָּהֶם לְסַנְהֶדְרִין. וְנִכְתְּבוּ כֻּלָּם נְקוּבִים בְּשֵׁמוֹת וְעַל יְדֵי גּוֹרָל, לְפִי שֶׁהַחֶשְׁבּוֹן עוֹלֶה לִשְׁנֵים עָשָׂר שְׁבָטִים שִׁשָּׁה שִׁשָּׁה לְכָל שֵׁבֶט וָשֵׁבֶט, חוּץ מִשְּׁנֵי שְׁבָטִים שֶׁאֵין מַגִּיעַ אֲלֵיהֶם אֶלָּא חֲמִשָּׁה חֲמִשָּׁה. אָמַר מֹשֶׁה: אֵין שֵׁבֶט שׁוֹמֵעַ לִי לִפְחֹת מִשִּׁבְטוֹ זָקֵן אֶחָד. מֶה עָשָׂה? נָטַל שִׁבְעִים וּשְׁנַיִם פְּתָקִין וְכָתַב עַל שִׁבְעִים 'זָקֵן' וְעַל שְׁנַיִם חָלָק, וּבֵרֵר מִכָּל שֵׁבֶט וָשֵׁבֶט שִׁשָּׁה, וְהָיוּ שִׁבְעִים וּשְׁנַיִם. אָמַר לָהֶם: טְלוּ פִּתְקֵיכֶם מִתּוֹךְ קַלְפִּי. מִי שֶׁעָלָה בְּיָדוֹ 'זָקֵן' נִתְקַדֵּשׁ; מִי שֶׁעָלָה בְּיָדוֹ חָלָק, אָמַר לוֹ: הַמָּקוֹם לֹא חָפֵץ בְּךָ:

כז) וַיָּרָץ הַנַּעַר. יֵשׁ אוֹמְרִים: גֵּרְשׁוֹם בֶּן מֹשֶׁה הָיָה:

28 Meidad are speaking prophecy in the camp!" Yehoshua son of Nun, who had
29 been Moshe's disciple since his youth, said, "My lord Moshe, stop them!" But
Moshe replied, "Are you jealous for me? Would that all the LORD's people were
30 prophets, that the LORD would put His spirit upon them all!" And Moshe SHEVI'I
31 returned to the camp together with the elders of Israel. Then a wind from
the LORD sprang up, sweeping quail in from the sea and letting them fall near
the camp, about a day's journey on one side and a day's journey on the other,
32 around the camp and piled up two cubits above the ground. All that day, all
night, and all the next day, the people went out and gathered quail. Even those
who gathered least gathered ten omer, and they spread them out all around
33 the camp. While the meat was still between their teeth, before it was eaten,
the LORD's anger blazed against the people, and the LORD struck the people

רש"י

כח) **כלאם.** הטל עליהם צרכי צבור והם כלים מאליהם. דבר אחר, תנם אל בית הכלא, לפי שהיו מתנבאים: משה מת ויהושע מכניס את ישראל לארץ:

כט) **המקנא אתה לי.** "הקנאתי את מקנא": לי. כמו בשבילי. כל לשון קנאה, אדם הנותן לב על הדבר או לנקום או לעזר, אנפרנמ"ט בלעז, אוחז בעבי המשא:

ל) **ויאסף משה.** מפתח אהל מועד: **אל המחנה.** נכנסו איש לאהלו: **ויאסף.** לשון כניסה אל הבית, כמו: "ואספתו אל תוך ביתך" (דברים כב, ב), ואב לכלם: "יצבר ולא ידע מי אספם" (תהלים לט, ז). מלמד שלא הביא עליהם פרענות עד שנכנסו הצדיקים איש לאהלו:

לא) **ויגז.** ויפריח, וכן: "כי גז חיש" (תהלים צ, י), "וכן נגזו ועבר" (נחום א, יב): **ויטש.** ויפשט, כמו "והנה נטשים על פני כל הארץ" (שמואל א' ל, טז), "ונטשתיך המדברה" (יחזקאל כט, ה): **וכאמתים.** פורחות בגבה עד שהן כנגד לבו של אדם, כדי שלא יהא טרח באסיפתן לא להגביה ולא לשחות:

לב) **הממעיט.** מי שאוסף פחות מכלם, העצלים והחגרים, "אסף עשרה חמרים": **וישטחו.** עשו אותן משטחין משטחין:

לג) **טרם יכרת.** כתרגומו: "עד לא פסק". דבר אחר, אינו מספיק לפסקו בשניו עד שנשמתו יוצאה:

forms of leadership come not with position, title, or robes of office, not with prestige and power, but with the willingness to work with others to achieve what we cannot do alone; to speak, to listen, to teach, to learn, to treat other people's views with respect even if they disagree with us; to explain patiently and cogently why we believe what we believe and do what we do; to encourage others, praise their best endeavors, and challenge them to do better still. One should always choose influence rather than power. It helps change people into people who can change the world.

11:30 **הוא וזקני ישראל** *Together with the elders of Israel* – God has spoken directly to Moshe's concerns. He tells him he will not have to lead alone in the future. There will be others to help him.

The Sages said, "A prisoner cannot release himself from prison" (Berakhot 5b). It takes someone else to lift you from depression. That is why Judaism is so insistent on not leaving people alone at times of maximum vulnerability. Hence the principles of visiting the sick, comforting mourners, including the lonely ("the migrant, the orphan, and the widow") in festive celebrations, and offering hospitality – an act said to be "greater than receiving the *Shekhina*" (Shabbat 127a). Precisely because depression isolates you from others, remaining alone intensifies the despair. What the seventy elders will subsequently do to help Moshe is unclear. But simply *being there with him* is part of the cure.

כח וַיַּגֵּד לְמֹשֶׁה וַיֹּאמַר אֶלְדָּד וּמֵידָד מִתְנַבְּאִים בַּמַּחֲנֶה׃ וַיַּעַן יְהוֹשֻׁעַ
כט בִּן־נוּן מְשָׁרֵת מֹשֶׁה מִבְּחֻרָיו וַיֹּאמַר אֲדֹנִי מֹשֶׁה כְּלָאֵם׃ וַיֹּאמֶר לוֹ
מֹשֶׁה הַמְקַנֵּא אַתָּה לִי וּמִי יִתֵּן כָּל־עַם יהוה נְבִיאִים כִּי־יִתֵּן יהוה
ל לא אֶת־רוּחוֹ עֲלֵיהֶם׃ וַיֵּאָסֵף מֹשֶׁה אֶל־הַמַּחֲנֶה הוּא וְזִקְנֵי יִשְׂרָאֵל׃ וְרוּחַ שביעי
נָסַע ׀ מֵאֵת יהוה וַיָּגָז שַׂלְוִים מִן־הַיָּם וַיִּטֹּשׁ עַל־הַמַּחֲנֶה כְּדֶרֶךְ יוֹם
לב כֹּה וּכְדֶרֶךְ יוֹם כֹּה סְבִיבוֹת הַמַּחֲנֶה וּכְאַמָּתַיִם עַל־פְּנֵי הָאָרֶץ׃ וַיָּקָם
הָעָם כָּל־הַיּוֹם הַהוּא וְכָל־הַלַּיְלָה וְכֹל ׀ יוֹם הַמָּחֳרָת וַיַּאַסְפוּ אֶת־
הַשְּׂלָו הַמַּמְעִיט אָסַף עֲשָׂרָה חֳמָרִים וַיִּשְׁטְחוּ לָהֶם שָׁטוֹחַ סְבִיבוֹת
לג הַמַּחֲנֶה׃ הַבָּשָׂר עוֹדֶנּוּ בֵּין שִׁנֵּיהֶם טֶרֶם יִכָּרֵת וְאַף יהוה חָרָה בָעָם וַיַּךְ

אונקלוס

וְחַוִּי לְמשֶׁה וַאֲמַר, אֶלְדָּד וּמֵידָד, מִתְנַבַּן בְּמַשְׁרִיתָא: כח וַאֲתֵיב יְהוֹשֻׁעַ בַּר נוּן, מְשֻׁמְשָׁנֵיהּ דְּמשֶׁה, מֵעוּלֵימוּהִי וַאֲמַר, רִבּוֹנִי משֶׁה אֲסַרְנוּן: כט וַאֲמַר לֵיהּ משֶׁה, הֲקַנְאָתִי אַתְּ מְקַנֵּי, רְעֵינָא פוֹן, דִּיהוֹן כָּל עַמֵּיהּ דַּיי נְבִיִּין, אֲרֵי יִתֵּין יי, יָת רוּחַ נְבוּאֲתֵיהּ עֲלֵיהוֹן: ל וְאִתְכְּנֵישׁ משֶׁה לְמַשְׁרִיתָא, הוּא וְסָבֵי יִשְׂרָאֵל: לא וְרוּחָא, נְטַל מִן קֳדָם יי, וְאַפְרַח שְׂלָו מִן יַמָּא, וּרְמָא עַל מַשְׁרִיתָא כְּמַהֲלַךְ יוֹמָא לְכָא, וּכְמַהֲלַךְ יוֹמָא לְכָא, סְחוֹר סְחוֹר לְמַשְׁרִיתָא, וּכְרוּם תַּרְתֵּין אַמִּין עַל אַפֵּי אַרְעָא: לב וְקָם עַמָּא, כָּל יוֹמָא הַהוּא וְכָל לֵילְיָא, וְכָל יוֹמָא דְּבָתְרוֹהִי, וּכְנַשׁוּ יָת שְׂלָו, דְּאַזְעַר, כְּנַשׁ עַסְרָא דְּגוֹרִין, וּשְׁטַחוּ לְהוֹן מַשְׁטְחִין, סְחוֹר סְחוֹר לְמַשְׁרִיתָא: לג בִּסְרָא, עַד כְּעַן בֵּין שִׁנֵּיהוֹן, עַד לָא פְסַק, וְרֻגְזָא דַּיי תְּקֵיף בְּעַמָּא, וּקְטַל

11:29 כִּי־יִתֵּן יהוה אֶת־רוּחוֹ עֲלֵיהֶם *The Lord would put His spirit upon them all* – Compare this magnanimous response to Moshe's conduct later when his leadership is challenged by Koraḥ and his followers. On that occasion, in effect, he prays that the ground swallow them up, that "they go down alive to Sheol [the netherworld]" (Num. 16:28–30). He is sharp, decisive, and unforgiving.

To understand the difference between Koraḥ on the one hand, and Eldad and Meidad on the other, it is essential to grasp the difference between two concepts often confused, namely power and influence. Power works by division ("divide and conquer"), influence by multiplication. Eldad and Meidad seek and receive no power. They merely receive the same influence – the divine spirit that has emanated from Moshe. They become prophets. That is why Moshe says, "Would that all the Lord's people were prophets, that the Lord would put His spirit upon them all!" (11:29). Prophecy is not a zero-sum game. When it comes to leadership as influence, the more we share, the more we have. Koraḥ, or at least some of his followers, sought power, and power is a zero-sum game. Moshe could not let the challenge of Koraḥ go unopposed without fatefully compromising his own authority.

Judaism is a sustained protest against what Hobbes in *The Leviathan* called the "general inclination of all mankind," namely "a perpetual and restless desire of power after power, that ceaseth only in death." That may be the reason why Jews have seldom exercised power for prolonged periods but have had an influence on the world out of all proportion to their numbers.

Not all of us have power, but we all have influence. That is why we can each be a leader. The most important

34 with a very great plague. The place was named Kivrot HaTaava, because there
35 they buried the people who had craved. And from Kivrot HaTaava the people
journeyed to Ḥatzerot, and at Ḥatzerot they stayed.
12 1 Once, Miriam and Aharon spoke against Moshe because of his Kushite wife;
2 he had married a Kushite woman. "Has the Lord spoken only through
Moshe?" they said. "Has He not spoken through us also?" The Lord heard
3 this. Now the man Moshe was very humble, more so than any other man on

רש״י

יב א **ותדבר.** אין דבור בכל מקום אלא לשון קשה, וכן הוא אומר: "דבר האיש אדני הארץ אתנו קשות" (בראשית מב, ל). ואין אמירה בכל מקום אלא לשון תחנונים, וכן הוא אומר: "ויאמר אל נא אחי תרעו" (בראשית יט, ז), "ויאמר שמעו נא דברי" (להלן פסוק ו), כל "נא" לשון בקשה: **ותדבר מרים ואהרן.** היא פתחה בדבור תחלה, לפיכך הקדימה הכתוב. ומנין היתה יודעת מרים שפרש משה מן האשה? רבי נתן אומר: מרים היתה בצד צפורה בשעה שנאמר למשה: "אלדד ומידד מתנבאים במחנה" (לעיל יא, כז), כיון ששמעה צפורה אמרה: אוי לנשותיהן של אלו אם הם נזקקים לנבואה, שיהיו פורשין מנשותיהן כדרך שפרש בעלי ממני. ומשם ידעה מרים והגידה לאהרן. ומה מרים שלא נתכונה לגנותו, כך נענשה, קל וחומר למספר בגנותו של חברו: **האשה הכשית.** מגיד שהכל מודים ביפיה, כשם שהכל מודים בשחרותו של כושי. **כושית.** בגימטריא 'יפת מראה': **על אדות האשה.** על אודות גרושיה: **כי אשה כשית לקח.** מה תלמוד לומר? אלא יש לך אשה נאה ביפיה ואינה נאה במעשיה, במעשיה ולא ביפיה, אבל זאת נאה בכל: **האשה הכשית.** על שם נויה נקראת 'כושית', כאדם הקורא את בנו נאה 'כושי' כדי שלא תשלט בו עין רעה: **כי אשה כשית לקח.** ועתה גרשה:

ב **הרק אך במשה.** עמו לבדו "דבר ה'": **הלא גם בנו דבר.** ולא פרשנו מדרך ארץ:

ג **ענו.** שפל וסבלן:

Moshe's wife because, like Kushite women generally, she has dark skin (see Jer. 13:23). If so, this is one of the first recorded instances of color prejudice, and for this sin too Miriam is struck with leprosy.

Jews have been subjected to racism more and longer than any other nation on earth. Therefore we should be doubly careful never to be guilty of it ourselves. We believe that God created each of us, regardless of color, class, culture, or creed, in His image. If we look down on other people because of their race, then we are demeaning God's image and failing to treat others with *kevod habriyot*, human dignity.

According to this understanding of the verse, if we think less of a person because of the color of his or her skin, we are repeating the sin of Aharon and Miriam. "First correct yourself; then [seek to] correct others," says the Talmud (Bava Metzia 107b). The Tanakh contains negative evaluations of some other nations, but always and only because of their moral failures, never because of ethnicity or skin color.

12:3 **וְהָאִישׁ מֹשֶׁה עָנָו מְאֹד** *Now the man Moshe was very humble* – This is a novum in history. The idea that a leader's highest virtue is humility must have seemed absurd, almost self-contradictory, in the ancient world. Leaders were proud, magnificent, distinguished by their dress, appearance, and regal manner. They built temples in their own honor. They had triumphant inscriptions engraved for posterity. Their role was not to serve but to be served. Everyone else was expected to be humble, not they. Humility and majesty could not coexist.

In Judaism, this entire configuration was overturned. Leaders were to serve, not to be served. Moshe's highest accolade was to be called *eved Hashem*, God's servant. The architectural symbolism of the two great empires of the ancient world, the Mesopotamian ziggurat (Tower of Bavel) and the pyramids of Egypt, visually represented a hierarchical society, broad at the base, narrow at the top. The Jewish symbol, the candelabrum (menora), was the opposite, broad at the top, narrow at the base, as if to say that in Judaism the leader serves the people, not vice versa. Moshe's first response to God's call at the burning bush was one of humility: "Who am I…to

לד יהוה בָּעָם מַכָּה רַבָּה מְאֹד׃ וַיִּקְרָא אֶת־שֵׁם־הַמָּקוֹם הַהוּא קִבְרוֹת
לה הַתַּאֲוָה כִּי־שָׁם קָבְרוּ אֶת־הָעָם הַמִּתְאַוִּים׃ מִקִּבְרוֹת הַתַּאֲוָה נָסְעוּ
הָעָם חֲצֵרוֹת וַיִּהְיוּ בַּחֲצֵרוֹת׃
יב א וַתְּדַבֵּר מִרְיָם וְאַהֲרֹן בְּמֹשֶׁה עַל־אֹדוֹת הָאִשָּׁה הַכֻּשִׁית אֲשֶׁר לָקָח כִּי־
ב אִשָּׁה כֻשִׁית לָקָח׃ וַיֹּאמְרוּ הֲרַק אַךְ־בְּמֹשֶׁה דִּבֶּר יהוה הֲלֹא גַּם־בָּנוּ
ג דִבֵּר וַיִּשְׁמַע יהוה׃ וְהָאִישׁ מֹשֶׁה עָנָו מְאֹד מִכֹּל הָאָדָם אֲשֶׁר עַל־פְּנֵי

אונקלוס

יי בְּעַמָּא, קְטוֹל סַגִּי לַחֲדָא: לד וּקְרָא, יָת שְׁמֵיהּ דְּאַתְרָא הַהוּא קִבְרֵי דִּמְשַׁאֲלֵי, אֲרֵי תַמָּן קְבַרוּ, יָת עַמָּא דְּשַׁאִילוּ: לה מִקִּבְרֵי דִּמְשַׁאֲלֵי, נְטַלוּ עַמָּא לַחֲצֵרוֹת, וַהֲווֹ בַּחֲצֵרוֹת: יב א וּמַלֵּילַת מִרְיָם וְאַהֲרֹן בְּמֹשֶׁה, עַל עֵיסַק, אִתְּתָא שַׁפִּירְתָּא דִּנְסֵיב, אֲרֵי אִתְּתָא שַׁפִּירְתָּא דִּנְסֵיב רַחֵיק: ב וַאֲמַרוּ, הַלְחוֹד בְּרַם עִם מֹשֶׁה מַלֵּיל יי, הֲלָא אַף עִמַּנָא מַלֵּיל, וּשְׁמִיעַ קֳדָם יי: ג וְגַבְרָא מֹשֶׁה עִנְוְתָן לַחֲדָא, מִכֹּל אֱנָשָׁא, דְּעַל אַפֵּי

MIRIAM AND AHARON SPEAK ABOUT MOSHE

One of the fundamental themes of Genesis is sibling rivalry. It appears, with variations, five times: in the stories of Kayin and Hevel, Yitzḥak and Yishmael, Yaakov and Esav, Yosef and his brothers, and the two sisters Leah and Raḥel. Until now we have had no reason to associate this theme with life after the exodus. Miriam and Aharon, Moshe's siblings, have been until now admirably free of rivalry. Miriam watched over her brother's fate as a baby. Aharon has shared with Moshe the burden of leadership from the outset of his mission. Neither has uttered a word of criticism, still less of envy, until now.

What, then, is their complaint? A midrash tells us that Miriam said, in effect: "I am sorry for the wives of the elders, for if they have been filled with Moshe's spirit, they are likely to do what Moshe has done, namely discontinue marital relations." Miriam is critical of this, saying that God has spoken not just to Moshe, but to her and Aharon also, yet they have not discontinued marital relations with their spouses. Evidently she is making the complaint, not out of malice, but out of sympathy for the wives of the elders. Miriam and Aharon do not know what it means to be the unique individual that Moshe is. One can sympathize with Miriam's concern if she believes, as the midrash suggests, that Moshe's wife (and perhaps his children also) suffer from a lack of attention. That is one of the burdens of leadership in general (see note on Num. 27:13) – all the more so in the case of one who felt the need to be perpetually ready for a communication from God Himself. Miriam is expressing her concern for the wives of Moshe's newly inspired leadership group. Her motives are honorable. Miriam is never less than a heroic and compassionate human being.

Yet because others less noble might derive the wrong lesson from her behavior, because – as we have seen – complaint is a social contagion, she is stigmatized for seven days by an unsightly skin condition. Many years later, Moshe is to recall this incident to remind the people how dangerous it is to "judge the judges" and heap unjustified criticism on leaders. Speech does not always have to be positive. The prophets of Israel were deeply critical of the failings of the generation. But speech does have to be constructive, creative, in intent.

Never give way to sibling rivalry. Never speak badly of others. Never underestimate the damaging effect of words. And the lead has to be given by the leaders. That is why God is angry with Miriam and Aharon. If leaders speak like this, how can one blame the people for doing likewise?

12:1 עַל־אֹדוֹת הָאִשָּׁה הַכֻּשִׁית *Because of his Kushite wife* – There are midrashic interpretations that read this passage differently, but it may be that Miriam and Aharon look down on

▶

4 earth. And suddenly the LORD said to Moshe and Aharon and
Miriam: "All three of you, come out to the Tent of Meeting." So the three of
5 them went. The LORD came down in a column of cloud, and, standing at the
entrance to the Tent, called, "Aharon and Miriam." The two of them came
6 forward. The LORD said: "Now listen to My words: When there is a prophet
among you, I make Myself known to him in a vision, I speak to him in a dream.
7 8 Not so with Moshe My servant: he is trusted in all My House: With him I
speak mouth to mouth, clearly, never in riddles. He sees the LORD's form. Why,
9 then, are you not afraid to speak against My servant Moshe?" The LORD's anger
10 flared against them; and He departed. When the cloud withdrew from the Tent,

רש״י

ד **פִּתְאֹם.** נִגְלָה עֲלֵיהֶם פִּתְאֹם וְהֵם טְמֵאִים בְּדֶרֶךְ אֶרֶץ, וְהָיוּ צוֹעֲקִים: מַיִם מַיִם, לְהוֹדִיעָם שֶׁיָּפֶה עָשָׂה מֹשֶׁה שֶׁפֵּרַשׁ מִן הָאִשָּׁה, מֵאַחַר שֶׁנִּגְלֵית עָלָיו שְׁכִינָה תָּדִיר, וְאֵין עֵת קְבוּעָה לַדִּבּוּר: **צְאוּ שְׁלָשְׁתְּכֶם.** מַגִּיד שֶׁשְּׁלָשְׁתָּן נִקְרְאוּ בְּדִבּוּר אֶחָד, מַה שֶּׁאִי אֶפְשָׁר לַפֶּה לוֹמַר וְלָאֹזֶן לִשְׁמֹעַ:

ה **בְּעַמּוּד עָנָן.** יָצָא יְחִידִי, שֶׁלֹּא כְמִדַּת בָּשָׂר וָדָם; מֶלֶךְ בָּשָׂר וָדָם כְּשֶׁיּוֹצֵא לַמִּלְחָמָה יוֹצֵא בְּאֻכְלוּסִין וּכְשֶׁיּוֹצֵא לְשָׁלוֹם יוֹצֵא בְּמֻעָטִין, וּמִדַּת הַקָּדוֹשׁ בָּרוּךְ הוּא יוֹצֵא לַמִּלְחָמָה יְחִידִי, שֶׁנֶּאֱמַר: "ה' אִישׁ מִלְחָמָה" (שמות טו, ג), וְיוֹצֵא לְשָׁלוֹם בְּאֻכְלוּסִין, שֶׁנֶּאֱמַר: "רֶכֶב אֱלֹהִים רִבֹּתַיִם אַלְפֵי שִׁנְאָן" (תהלים סח, יח): **וַיִּקְרָא אַהֲרֹן וּמִרְיָם.** שֶׁיִּהְיוּ נִמְשָׁכִין וְיוֹצְאִין מִן הֶחָצֵר לִקְרַאת הַדִּבּוּר: **וַיֵּצְאוּ שְׁנֵיהֶם.** וּמִפְּנֵי מָה מְשָׁכָן וְהִפְרִידָן מִמֹּשֶׁה, לְפִי שֶׁאוֹמְרִים מִקְצָת שִׁבְחוֹ שֶׁל אָדָם בְּפָנָיו וְכֻלּוֹ שֶׁלֹּא בְּפָנָיו. וְכֵן מָצִינוּ בְּנֹחַ, שֶׁלֹּא בְּפָנָיו נֶאֱמַר: "אִישׁ צַדִּיק תָּמִים" (בראשית ו, ט), וּבְפָנָיו נֶאֱמַר: "כִּי אֹתְךָ רָאִיתִי צַדִּיק לְפָנַי" (שם ז, א). דָּבָר אַחֵר, שֶׁלֹּא יִשְׁמַע בִּנְזִיפָתוֹ שֶׁל אַהֲרֹן:

ו **שִׁמְעוּ נָא דְבָרָי.** אֵין 'נָא' אֶלָּא לְשׁוֹן בַּקָּשָׁה: **אִם יִהְיֶה נְבִיאֲכֶם.** אִם יִהְיוּ לָכֶם נְבִיאִים: **ה' בַּמַּרְאָה אֵלָיו אֶתְוַדָּע.** שְׁכִינַת שְׁמִי אֵין נִגְלֵית עָלָיו בְּאַסְפַּקְלַרְיָא הַמְּאִירָה, אֶלָּא בַּחֲלוֹם וְחִזָּיוֹן:

ח **פֶּה אֶל פֶּה.** אָמַרְתִּי לוֹ לִפְרֹשׁ מִן הָאִשָּׁה. וְהֵיכָן אָמַרְתִּי לוֹ? בְּסִינַי: "לֵךְ אֱמֹר לָהֶם שׁוּבוּ לָכֶם לְאָהֳלֵיכֶם וְאַתָּה פֹּה עֲמֹד עִמָּדִי" (דברים ה, כז-כח): **וּמַרְאֶה וְלֹא בְחִידֹת.** 'וּמַרְאֶה' זֶה מַרְאֵה דִּבּוּר, שֶׁאֲנִי מְפָרֵשׁ לוֹ דִּבּוּרִי בְּמַרְאִית פָּנִים שֶׁבּוֹ וְאֵינִי סוֹתְמוֹ לוֹ בְּחִידוֹת, כָּעִנְיָן שֶׁנֶּאֱמַר לִיחֶזְקֵאל: "חוּד חִידָה" וְגוֹ' (יחזקאל יז, ב). יָכוֹל מַרְאֵה שְׁכִינָה? תַּלְמוּד לוֹמַר: "לֹא תוּכַל לִרְאֹת אֶת פָּנָי" (שמות לג, כ): **וּתְמֻנַת ה' יַבִּיט.** זֶה מַרְאֵה אֲחוֹרַיִם, כָּעִנְיָן שֶׁנֶּאֱמַר: "וְרָאִיתָ אֶת אֲחֹרָי" (שמות לג, כג): **בְּעַבְדִּי בְמֹשֶׁה.** אֵינוֹ אוֹמֵר 'בְּעַבְדִּי מֹשֶׁה' אֶלָּא "בְּעַבְדִּי בְּמֹשֶׁה", בְּעַבְדִּי אַף עַל פִּי שֶׁאֵינוֹ מֹשֶׁה, בְּמֹשֶׁה אֲפִלּוּ אֵינוֹ עַבְדִּי, כְּדַאי הֱיִיתֶם לִירֹא מִפָּנָיו, וְכָל שֶׁכֵּן שֶׁהוּא עַבְדִּי, וְעֶבֶד מֶלֶךְ – מֶלֶךְ, וְהָיָה לָכֶם לוֹמַר: אֵין הַמֶּלֶךְ אוֹהֲבוֹ חִנָּם. וְאִם תֹּאמְרוּ: אֵינִי מַכִּיר בְּמַעֲשָׂיו – זוֹ קָשָׁה מִן הָרִאשׁוֹנָה:

ט **וַיִּחַר אַף ה' בָּם וַיֵּלַךְ.** מֵאַחַר שֶׁהוֹדִיעָם סִרְחוֹנָם גָּזַר עֲלֵיהֶם נִדּוּי, קַל וָחֹמֶר לְבָשָׂר וָדָם, שֶׁלֹּא יִכְעֹס עַל חֲבֵרוֹ עַד שֶׁיּוֹדִיעֶנּוּ סִרְחוֹנוֹ:

י **וְהֶעָנָן סָר.** וְאַחַר כָּךְ "וְהִנֵּה מִרְיָם מְצֹרַעַת כַּשָּׁלֶג", מָשָׁל לְמֶלֶךְ שֶׁאָמַר לַפֵּדָגוֹג: רְדֵה אֶת בְּנִי, אֲבָל לֹא תִרְדֶּנּוּ עַד שֶׁאֵלֵךְ מֵאֶצְלְךָ, שֶׁרַחֲמַי עָלָיו:

and to the abode of loneliness." A sense of loneliness permeates Rabbi Soloveitchik's work, whether or not he is talking explicitly about it. His modern "halakhic man" has friends: but they are people of the mind. He "embraces the entire company of the sages of the *mesora*.... He walks alongside Rambam, listens to R. Akiva, senses the presence of Abaye and Rava." But his peers are of the past; the present offers him little. The people around him are impatient, secular. There is little in *Halakhic Man*, where there could have been so much, about the delights of intellectual companionship, *ḥevruta*. This is in strange contrast to talmudic Judaism itself, which has nothing positive to say about isolation. "There is either companionship or death" (Taanit 23a), said the Rabbis; "A sword is upon those who sit alone and study Torah" (Berakhot 63b). Nothing in the classic literature of rabbinic Judaism dwells in this land of anguish, conflict, isolation. When Rabbi Soloveitchik seeks a precedent he finds it in the Tanakh – in the prophets, or the voice of the lover in Song of Songs, or in the image of Adam and Ḥava alone in the universe.

ד הָאֲדָמָה: וַיֹּאמֶר יְהוָה פִּתְאֹם אֶל־מֹשֶׁה וְאֶל־אַהֲרֹן
ה וְאֶל־מִרְיָם צְאוּ שְׁלָשְׁתְּכֶם אֶל־אֹהֶל מוֹעֵד וַיֵּצְאוּ שְׁלָשְׁתָּם: וַיֵּרֶד
יְהוָה בְּעַמּוּד עָנָן וַיַּעֲמֹד פֶּתַח הָאֹהֶל וַיִּקְרָא אַהֲרֹן וּמִרְיָם וַיֵּצְאוּ
ו שְׁנֵיהֶם: וַיֹּאמֶר שִׁמְעוּ־נָא דְבָרָי אִם־יִהְיֶה נְבִיאֲכֶם יְהוָה בַּמַּרְאָה
ז אֵלָיו אֶתְוַדָּע בַּחֲלוֹם אֲדַבֶּר־בּוֹ: לֹא־כֵן עַבְדִּי מֹשֶׁה בְּכָל־בֵּיתִי נֶאֱמָן
ח הוּא: פֶּה אֶל־פֶּה אֲדַבֶּר־בּוֹ וּמַרְאֶה וְלֹא בְחִידֹת וּתְמֻנַת יְהוָה יַבִּיט
ט וּמַדּוּעַ לֹא יְרֵאתֶם לְדַבֵּר בְּעַבְדִּי בְמֹשֶׁה: וַיִּחַר־אַף יְהוָה בָּם וַיֵּלַךְ:
י וְהֶעָנָן סָר מֵעַל הָאֹהֶל וְהִנֵּה מִרְיָם מְצֹרַעַת כַּשָּׁלֶג וַיִּפֶן אַהֲרֹן אֶל־

אונקלוס

אַרְעָא: ד וַאֲמַר יי בִּתְכֵּיף, לְמשֶׁה וּלְאַהֲרֹן וּלְמִרְיָם, פּוּקוּ תְּלָתֵיכוֹן
לְמַשְׁכַּן זִמְנָא, וּנְפַקוּ תְּלָתֵיהוֹן: ה וְאִתְגְּלִי יי בְּעַמּוּדָא דַעֲנָנָא, וְקָם
בִּתְרַע מַשְׁכְּנָא, וּקְרָא אַהֲרֹן וּמִרְיָם, וּנְפַקוּ תַּרְוֵיהוֹן: ו וַאֲמַר שְׁמַעוּ
כְּעַן פִּתְגָמַי, אִם יְהוֹן לְכוֹן נְבִיִּין, אֲנָא יי, בְּחֶזְוְין אֲנָא מִתְגְּלֵי
לְהוֹן, בְּחֶלְמִין אֲנָא מְמַלֵּיל עִמְּהוֹן: ז לָא כֵן עַבְדִּי משֶׁה, בְּכָל
עַמִּי מְהֵימַן הוּא: ח מְמַלַּל עִם מְמַלַּל מַלֵּילְנָא עִמֵּיהּ, בְּחֶזְוּ וְלָא
בְחֶדְוָן, וּדְמוּת יְקָרָא דַּיי מִסְתַּכַּל, וּמָדֵין לָא דְחֵילְתּוּן, לְמַלָּלָא
בְּעַבְדִּי בְמשֶׁה: ט וּתְקֵיף רוּגְזָא דַּיי, בְּהוֹן וְאִסְתַּלַּק: י וַעֲנָנָא, אִסְתַּלַּק
מֵעִלָּוֵי מַשְׁכְּנָא, וְהָא מִרְיָם חִוְּרָא כְּתַלְגָּא, וְאִתְפְּנִי אַהֲרֹן, לְוָת

bring the Israelites out of Egypt?" (Ex. 3:11). It was precisely this humility that qualified him to lead.

Humility is not what it is sometimes taken to be – a low estimate of oneself. True humility is mindlessness of self. An *anav* (the biblical word used in this chapter) is one who never thinks about himself because he has more important things to think about. I once heard someone say about a religious leader: "He took God so seriously that he didn't need to take himself seriously at all." That is biblical humility.

Humility is not self-abasement. It is not "self" anything. It is the ability to stand in silent awe in the presence of otherness – the Thou of God, the otherness of other people, the majesty of creation, the beauty of the world, the power of great ideas, the call of great ideals. Humility is the silence of the self in the presence of that which is greater than the self.

Humility – true humility – is one of the most expansive and life-enhancing of all virtues. It does not mean undervaluing yourself. It means valuing other people. It signals an openness to life's grandeur and the willingness to be surprised, uplifted, by goodness wherever one finds it.

Humility, then, is more than just a virtue; it is a form of perception, a language in which the "I" is silent so that I can hear the "Thou," the unspoken call beneath human speech, the divine whisper within all that moves, the voice of otherness that calls me to redeem its loneliness with the touch of love. Humility is what opens us to the world.

12:7 לֹא־כֵן עַבְדִּי מֹשֶׁה *Not so with Moshe My servant* – This description of Moshe's unique experience, coupled with Miriam's concern, if we accept that interpretation, for his neglected wife (see above, "Miriam and Aharon Speak about Moshe"), paint a poignantly ambivalent picture of the prophetic experience. It struck a chord with Rabbi Joseph B. Soloveitchik. "When the hour of estrangement strikes, the ordeal of the man of faith begins and he starts his withdrawal from society," he writes in his classic *The Lonely Man of Faith*. "He returns, like Moses of old, to his solitary hiding

Miriam had been struck with an impure blight, white as snow. Aharon turned
11 toward Miriam and saw that she was blighted. Aharon said to Moshe, "Please,
12 my lord, do not hold against us the sin that we have foolishly committed! Let
her not be like a stillborn child emerging from its mother's womb with half its
13 flesh eaten away!" And Moshe cried out to the Lord, "Please, God, heal her
now!"
14 But the Lord said to Moshe: "If her father had spat in her face, would she not MAFTIR
be shamed for seven days? Let her be shut out of the camp for seven days;
15 after that, she may be brought back." So Miriam was shut out of the camp for
seven days, and the people did not move on until Miriam was brought back.
16 After that, the people set out from Ḥatzerot and encamped in the Wilderness
of Paran.

The haftara for Parashat Behaalotekha is on page 1588.

רש״י

יא **נוֹאַלְנוּ.** כְּתַרְגּוּמוֹ, לְשׁוֹן אֱוִיל:

יב **אַל נָא תְהִי.** אֲחוֹתֵנוּ זוֹ: **כַּמֵּת.** שֶׁהַמְּצֹרָע חָשׁוּב כַּמֵּת, מַה מֵּת מְטַמֵּא בְּבִיאָה אַף מְצֹרָע מְטַמֵּא בְּבִיאָה: **אֲשֶׁר בְּצֵאתוֹ מֵרֶחֶם אִמּוֹ.** 'אִמֵּנוּ' הָיָה לוֹ לוֹמַר, אֶלָּא שֶׁכִּנָּה הַכָּתוּב. וְכֵן 'חֲצִי בְּשָׂרֵנוּ' הָיָה לוֹ לוֹמַר, אֶלָּא שֶׁכִּנָּה הַכָּתוּב. מֵאַחַר שֶׁיָּצָאת מֵרֶחֶם אִמֵּנוּ, הִיא לָנוּ כְּאִלּוּ נֶאֱכַל חֲצִי בְּשָׂרֵנוּ, כָּעִנְיָן שֶׁנֶּאֱמַר: "כִּי אָחִינוּ בְשָׂרֵנוּ הוּא" (בראשית לז, כז). וּלְפִי מַשְׁמָעוֹ, אַף הוּא נִרְאֶה כֵּן, אֵין רָאוּי לְאָח לְהַנִּיחַ אֶת אֲחוֹתוֹ לִהְיוֹת כַּמֵּת: **אֲשֶׁר בְּצֵאתוֹ.** מֵאַחַר שֶׁיָּצָא זֶה מֵרֶחֶם אִמּוֹ שֶׁל זֶה שֶׁיֵּשׁ כֹּחַ בְּיָדוֹ לַעֲזֹר וְאֵינוֹ עוֹזְרוֹ, הֲרֵי נֶאֱכַל חֲצִי בְּשָׂרוֹ, שֶׁאָחִיו בְּשָׂרוֹ הוּא. דָּבָר אַחֵר, "אַל נָא תְהִי כַּמֵּת" – אִם אֵינְךָ רוֹפְאָהּ בִּתְפִלָּה, מִי מַסְגִּירָהּ אוֹ מִי מְטַהֲרָהּ? אֲנִי אִי אֶפְשָׁר לִרְאוֹתָהּ, שֶׁאֲנִי קָרוֹב וְאֵין קָרוֹב רוֹאֶה אֶת הַנְּגָעִים, וְכֹהֵן אַחֵר אֵין בָּעוֹלָם. וְזֶהוּ "אֲשֶׁר בְּצֵאתוֹ מֵרֶחֶם אִמּוֹ":

יג **אֵל נָא רְפָא נָא לָהּ.** בָּא הַכָּתוּב לְלַמֶּדְךָ דֶּרֶךְ אֶרֶץ, שֶׁהַשּׁוֹאֵל דָּבָר מֵחֲבֵרוֹ צָרִיךְ לוֹמַר שְׁנַיִם אוֹ שְׁלֹשָׁה דִּבְרֵי תַחֲנוּנִים, וְאַחַר כָּךְ יְבַקֵּשׁ שְׁאֵלוֹתָיו: **לֵאמֹר.** מַה תַּלְמוּד לוֹמַר? אָמַר לוֹ: הֲשִׁיבֵנִי אִם אֲתָּה מְרַפֵּא אוֹתָהּ אִם לָאו, עַד שֶׁהֱשִׁיבוֹ: "וְאָבִיהָ יָרֹק יָרַק" וְגוֹ'. רַבִּי אֶלְעָזָר בֶּן עֲזַרְיָה אוֹמֵר: בְּאַרְבָּעָה מְקוֹמוֹת בִּקֵּשׁ מֹשֶׁה מִלִּפְנֵי הַקָּדוֹשׁ בָּרוּךְ הוּא לַהֲשִׁיבוֹ אִם יַעֲשֶׂה שְׁאֵלוֹתָיו אִם לָאו. כַּיּוֹצֵא בוֹ: "וַיְדַבֵּר מֹשֶׁה לִפְנֵי ה' לֵאמֹר" וְגוֹ' (שמות ו, יב), מַה תַּלְמוּד לוֹמַר: "לֵאמֹר"? הֲשִׁיבֵנִי אִם גּוֹאֲלָם אַתָּה אִם לָאו, עַד שֶׁהֱשִׁיבוֹ: "עַתָּה תִרְאֶה" וְגוֹ' (שם פסוק א). כַּיּוֹצֵא בוֹ: "וַיְדַבֵּר מֹשֶׁה אֶל ה' לֵאמֹר יִפְקֹד ה' אֱלֹהֵי הָרוּחֹת לְכָל בָּשָׂר" (להלן כז, טו-טז), הֱשִׁיבוֹ: "קַח לְךָ" (שם פסוק יח). כַּיּוֹצֵא בוֹ: "וָאֶתְחַנַּן אֶל ה' בָּעֵת הַהִוא לֵאמֹר" (דברים ג, כג), הֱשִׁיבוֹ: "רַב לָךְ" (שם פסוק כו): **רְפָא נָא לָהּ.** מִפְּנֵי מָה לֹא הֶאֱרִיךְ מֹשֶׁה בִּתְפִלָּה? שֶׁלֹּא יִהְיוּ יִשְׂרָאֵל אוֹמְרִים, אֲחוֹתוֹ עוֹמֶדֶת בְּצָרָה וְהוּא עוֹמֵד וּמַרְבֶּה בִּתְפִלָּה:

יד **וְאָבִיהָ יָרֹק יָרַק בְּפָנֶיהָ.** וְאִם אָבִיהָ הֶרְאָה לָהּ פָּנִים זוֹעֲפוֹת "הֲלֹא תִכָּלֵם שִׁבְעַת יָמִים", קַל וָחֹמֶר לַשְּׁכִינָה אַרְבָּעָה עָשָׂר יוֹם, אֶלָּא דַּיּוֹ לַבָּא מִן הַדִּין לִהְיוֹת כַּנִּדּוֹן, לְפִיכָךְ אַף בִּנְזִיפָתִי "תִּסָּגֵר שִׁבְעַת יָמִים": **וְאַחַר תֵּאָסֵף.** אוֹמֵר אֲנִי, כָּל הָאֲסִיפוֹת הָאֲמוּרוֹת בַּמְּצֹרָעִים, עַל שֵׁם שֶׁהוּא מְשֻׁלָּח מִחוּץ לַמַּחֲנֶה וּכְשֶׁהוּא נִרְפָּא נֶאֱסָף אֶל הַמַּחֲנֶה, לְכָךְ כָּתוּב בּוֹ אֲסִיפָה, לְשׁוֹן הַכְנָסָה:

טו **וְהָעָם לֹא נָסַע.** זֶה הַכָּבוֹד חָלַק לָהּ הַמָּקוֹם בִּשְׁבִיל שָׁעָה אַחַת שֶׁנִּתְעַכְּבָה לְמֹשֶׁה כְּשֶׁהֻשְׁלַךְ לַיְאוֹר, שֶׁנֶּאֱמַר: "וַתֵּתַצַּב אֲחֹתוֹ מֵרָחֹק" וְגוֹ' (שמות ב, ד):

grows worse and one will give up hope of praying for him" (*Yoreh De'ah* 335). There is an understanding here that sincere prayer, like Moshe's prayer for Miriam, emerges from a deep identification with the patient's fate, despite the gulf in experience that illness creates. *Hesed* is the redemption of solitude, the bridge we build across the ontological abyss between I and Thou.

יא מִרְיָם וְהִנֵּה מְצֹרָעַת: וַיֹּאמֶר אַהֲרֹן אֶל־מֹשֶׁה בִּי אֲדֹנִי אַל־נָא תָשֵׁת
יב עָלֵינוּ חַטָּאת אֲשֶׁר נוֹאַלְנוּ וַאֲשֶׁר חָטָאנוּ: אַל־נָא תְהִי כַּמֵּת אֲשֶׁר
יג בְּצֵאתוֹ מֵרֶחֶם אִמּוֹ וַיֵּאָכֵל חֲצִי בְשָׂרוֹ: וַיִּצְעַק מֹשֶׁה אֶל־יְהוָה לֵאמֹר
אֵל נָא רְפָא נָא לָהּ:
יד וַיֹּאמֶר יְהוָה אֶל־מֹשֶׁה וְאָבִיהָ יָרֹק יָרַק בְּפָנֶיהָ הֲלֹא תִכָּלֵם שִׁבְעַת מפטיר
טו יָמִים תִּסָּגֵר שִׁבְעַת יָמִים מִחוּץ לַמַּחֲנֶה וְאַחַר תֵּאָסֵף: וַתִּסָּגֵר מִרְיָם
טז מִחוּץ לַמַּחֲנֶה שִׁבְעַת יָמִים וְהָעָם לֹא נָסַע עַד הֵאָסֵף מִרְיָם: וְאַחַר
נָסְעוּ הָעָם מֵחֲצֵרוֹת וַיַּחֲנוּ בְּמִדְבַּר פָּארָן:

The הפטרה *for* פרשת בהעלתך *is on page 1589.*

אונקלוס

מִרְיָם וְהָא סְגִירָא: יא וַאֲמַר אַהֲרֹן לְמֹשֶׁה, בְּבָעוּ רִבּוֹנִי, לָא כְעַן
תְּשַׁוֵּי עֲלַנָא חוֹבָא, דְּאִטְפַּשְׁנָא וְדִסְרַחְנָא: יב לָא כְעַן תִּתְרְחֵק דָּא
מִבֵּינַנָא, אֲרֵי אֲחָתַנָא הִיא, צַלִּי כְעַן, עַל בִּסְרָא מִיתָא הָדֵין דְּבַהּ
וְיִתַּסֵּי: יג וְצַלִּי מֹשֶׁה, קֳדָם יי לְמֵימַר, אֱלָהָא, בְּבָעוּ, אַסִּי כְעַן יָתַהּ: יד
וַאֲמַר יי לְמֹשֶׁה, וְאִלּוּ אֲבוּהָא מִנְזָף נְזַף בַּהּ, הֲלָא תִתְכְּלֵים שִׁבְעָא
יוֹמִין, תִּסְתְּגַר, שִׁבְעָא יוֹמִין מִבָּרָא לְמַשְׁרִיתָא, וּבָתַר כֵּן תִּתְכְּנֵישׁ:
טו וְאִסְתְּגַרַת מִרְיָם, מִבָּרָא לְמַשְׁרִיתָא שִׁבְעָא יוֹמִין, וְעַמָּא לָא
נְטַל, עַד דְּאִתְכְּנֵישַׁת מִרְיָם: טז וּבָתַר כֵּן, נְטַלוּ עַמָּא מֵחֲצֵרוֹת, וּשְׁרוֹ
בְּמַדְבְּרָא דְפָארָן:

12:13 רְפָא נָא לָהּ *Heal her now* – Moshe prays on Miriam's behalf one of the shortest prayers in Tanakh, a mere five words: "Please God, heal her now"– literally, "God, please, heal, please, her." God refuses to remove the punishment, but He does mitigate it, limiting the disfigurement to a week. When she is ready to return to the camp, the Israelites move on.

Historically, Jews have always regarded the treatment of the sick as a fundamental priority. Doctors would treat the poor without charge. Communal funds – they came to be known as *hekdesh*, the same term used in an earlier age for donations to the Temple – were put aside for the maintenance of hospices. In late medieval times the Jewish communities of Turkey, Italy, Germany, Poland, and the Netherlands supported hospitals, communal physicians, nurses, midwives, and visitation societies. The latter were by no means an afterthought. Particular concern was always taken to visit the sick, an activity invested with immense sensitivity and religious depth. The detailed guidelines in the *Shulkhan Arukh*, Rabbi Yosef Karo's authoritative code of law, give some sense of the reverence in which the command was held – for instance, "One should not visit the sick during the first three hours of the day, for every patient's illness is alleviated in the morning, and consequently he [the visitor] will not trouble himself to pray for him; and not during the last three hours of the day, for then his illness

Parashat Shelaḥ

13 1/2 Then the Lord spoke to Moshe: "Send out men to scout the land of Canaan,
which I am going to give to the Israelites, one man from each of their ancestral
3 tribes, each a leader among them." So Moshe sent them at the Lord's command
from the Wilderness of Paran. They were all leading men among the Israelites.
4/5 These were their names: from the tribe of Reuven, Shamua son of Zakur; from
6 the tribe of Shimon, Shafat son of Ḥori; from the tribe of Yehuda, Kalev son

רש״י

יג ב| שְׁלַח לְךָ אֲנָשִׁים. לָמָּה נִסְמְכָה פָּרָשַׁת מְרַגְּלִים לְפָרָשַׁת מִרְיָם? לְפִי שֶׁלָּקְתָה עַל עִסְקֵי דִבָּה שֶׁדִּבְּרָה בְאָחִיהָ, וּרְשָׁעִים הַלָּלוּ רָאוּ וְלֹא לָקְחוּ מוּסָר: שְׁלַח לְךָ. לְדַעְתְּךָ, אֲנִי אֵינִי מְצַוֶּה לְךָ, אִם תִּרְצֶה שְׁלַח. לְפִי שֶׁבָּאוּ יִשְׂרָאֵל וְאָמְרוּ: "נִשְׁלְחָה אֲנָשִׁים לְפָנֵינוּ" (דברים א, כב), כְּמָה שֶׁנֶּאֱמַר: "וַתִּקְרְבוּן אֵלַי כֻּלְּכֶם" וְגוֹ׳ (שם), וּמֹשֶׁה נִמְלַךְ בַּשְּׁכִינָה, אָמַר: אֲנִי אָמַרְתִּי לָהֶם שֶׁהִיא טוֹבָה, שֶׁנֶּאֱמַר: "אַעֲלֶה אֶתְכֶם מֵעֳנִי מִצְרַיִם" וְגוֹ׳ (שמות ג, יז), חַיֵּיהֶם שֶׁאֲנִי נוֹתֵן לָהֶם מָקוֹם לִטְעוֹת בְּדִבְרֵי הַמְרַגְּלִים, לְמַעַן לֹא יִירָשׁוּהָ:

ג| עַל פִּי ה׳. בִּרְשׁוּתוֹ, שֶׁלֹּא עִכֵּב עַל יָדוֹ: כֻּלָּם אֲנָשִׁים. כָּל ׳אֲנָשִׁים׳ שֶׁבַּמִּקְרָא לְשׁוֹן חֲשִׁיבוּת, וְאוֹתָהּ שָׁעָה כְּשֵׁרִים הָיוּ:

God. He sent them manna from heaven, water from a rock, and surrounded them with clouds of glory. He guided them; His presence dwelt amongst them in the Tabernacle. The divine hand surrounded them like a protective wall.

Canaan meant practical responsibility, the work of building up a nation. They would have to plow the land, and create and sustain an army, an economy, and a welfare system. They would have to do what every other nation does: live in the real world. What then would happen to their relationship with God? Yes, He would still be present in the rain that made crops grow, in the blessings of field and town, and in the Temple in Jerusalem that they would visit three times a year, but not intimately and miraculously, as He was in the desert. This is what the spies feared: not failure but success.

This, said the Rebbe, was a noble sin but still a sin. God wants us to live in the real world of nations, economies, and armies. God wants us, as He put it, to create "a dwelling place in the lower world." This is what Kalev saw. He knew that the Sanctuary was mere preparation and that redemption is its fulfillment: God wants us to bring the *Shekhina*, the Divine Presence, into everyday life. It is easy to find God in total seclusion and escape from responsibility. It is hard to find God in the office, in business, in farms and fields and factories and finance. But it is that challenge to which we are summoned: to create a space for God in the midst of this physical world that He created and seven times pronounced good. That is what ten of the spies failed to understand, and it was a spiritual failure that condemned an entire generation to forty years of futile wandering.

13:2 אֲנָשִׁים *Men* – Ten of these men are to come back with a negative report. The people will be demoralized, and as a result will lose their chance to enjoy their inheritance in the land promised to their ancestors. The daughters of Tzelofḥad, by contrast, love the land and do inherit it, as we will read in Parashat Pinḥas. What we love, we inherit. Comparing these two stories, Rabbi Ephrayim Luntschitz of Prague argued that God was not *commanding* Moshe to send men, but permitting him. God was saying, "From My perspective, seeing the future, it would have been better to send women, because they love and cherish the land and would never come to speak negatively about it. However, since you are convinced that these men are worthy and do indeed value the land, I give you permission to go ahead and send them" (*Keli Yakar* on Num. 13:2). Clearly, Moshe's calculation was wrong. And what we fail to love, we lose.

פרשת שלח

יג א ב וַיְדַבֵּר יְהוָה אֶל־מֹשֶׁה לֵּאמֹר: שְׁלַח־לְךָ אֲנָשִׁים וְיָתֻרוּ אֶת־אֶרֶץ יב
כְּנַעַן אֲשֶׁר־אֲנִי נֹתֵן לִבְנֵי יִשְׂרָאֵל אִישׁ אֶחָד אִישׁ אֶחָד לְמַטֵּה אֲבֹתָיו
ג תִּשְׁלָחוּ כֹּל נָשִׂיא בָהֶם: וַיִּשְׁלַח אֹתָם מֹשֶׁה מִמִּדְבַּר פָּארָן עַל־פִּי
ד יְהוָה כֻּלָּם אֲנָשִׁים רָאשֵׁי בְנֵי־יִשְׂרָאֵל הֵמָּה: וְאֵלֶּה שְׁמוֹתָם לְמַטֵּה
ה ו רְאוּבֵן שַׁמּוּעַ בֶּן־זַכּוּר: לְמַטֵּה שִׁמְעוֹן שָׁפָט בֶּן־חוֹרִי: לְמַטֵּה יְהוּדָה

אונקלוס

יג א וּמַלֵּיל יי עִם מֹשֶׁה לְמֵימַר: ב שְׁלַח לָךְ גֻּבְרִין, וִיאַלְּלוּן יָת
אַרְעָא דִכְנַעַן, דַּאֲנָא יָהֵיב לִבְנֵי יִשְׂרָאֵל, גֻּבְרָא חַד גֻּבְרָא חַד,
לְשִׁבְטָא דַּאֲבָהָתוֹהִי תִּשְׁלְחוּן, כָּל רַבָּא דִבְהוֹן: ג וּשְׁלַח יָתְהוֹן
מֹשֶׁה, מִמַּדְבְּרָא דְפָארָן עַל מֵימְרָא דַייָ, כֻּלְּהוֹן גֻּבְרִין, רֵישֵׁי בְּנֵי
יִשְׂרָאֵל אִנּוּן: ד וְאִלֵּין שְׁמָהָתְהוֹן, לְשִׁבְטָא דִרְאוּבֵן, שַׁמּוּעַ בַּר זַכּוּר:
ה לְשִׁבְטָא דְשִׁמְעוֹן, שָׁפָט בַּר חוֹרִי: ו לְשִׁבְטָא דִיהוּדָה,

THE SENDING OF THE SPIES

Who sends the spies and to what end is not entirely clear. In our *parasha*, the text says that it is God who tells Moshe to do so (Num. 13:1–2). In Deuteronomy (1:22), Moshe says that it was the people who made the request. Either way, the result will be that an entire generation, demoralized by the spies' negative report, is deprived of the chance to enter the Promised Land.

In *Torah Studies*, Rabbi Menachem Mendel Schneerson offered a remarkable commentary on the episode of the spies. He raised the obvious question: The Torah emphasizes that the spies are all leaders, princes, heads of tribes. They know that God is with them, that with His help there is nothing they cannot do and that God would not promise them a land they could not conquer. Why then do they come back with a negative report?

His answer turns the conventional understanding of the spies upside down. They were, he said, not afraid of defeat. *They were afraid of victory*. What they said to the people was one thing, but what led them to say it was another thing entirely.

In the desert, they lived closely and continuously with

SHELAḤ

Parashat Shelaḥ tells the story of the spies sent by Moshe to survey the land. Ten return with an ambivalent report: the land is good but the people are giants and their cities are impregnable. Two, Yehoshua and Kalev, argue to the contrary but their confidence is ignored and the people, fearful and demoralized, say, "Let us appoint a leader and go back to Egypt" (Num. 14:4).

God is angry and threatens to destroy the people and start again with Moshe. Moshe intercedes and succeeds in averting this fate, but God insists that the people will be punished by having to spend forty years in the desert. Their children, not they, will enter the land. There then follows a series of laws about sacrifices, challah, and forgiveness for sins committed inadvertently. The legal section is interrupted by a brief section about a Sabbath desecrator. The *parasha* ends with the law about tzitzit, fringes on the corners of garments, a text recited daily as the third paragraph of the *Shema*. This constant reminder to control our responses to temptation emphasizes the difficulty of freedom – something that the desert generation will take forty years to overcome.

7 8 of Yefuneh; from the tribe of Yissakhar, Yigal son of Yosef; from the tribe of
9 Efrayim, Hoshea son of Nun; from the tribe of Binyamin, Palti son of Rafu;
10 11 from the tribe of Zevulun, Gadiel son of Sodi; from the tribe of Yosef, from
12 the tribe of Menashe, Gadi son of Susi; from the tribe of Dan, Amiel son of
13 14 Gemali; from the tribe of Asher, Setur son of Mikhael; from the tribe of Naftali,
15 16 Naḥbi son of Vofsi; from the tribe of Gad, Geuel son of Makhi. These were the
names of the men Moshe sent to scout the land. And Moshe named Hoshea
17 son of Nun Yehoshua. When Moshe sent them to scout the land of Canaan,
he told them, "Ascend there into the Negev; then go up into the hill country.
18 See what the land is like. Are the people who live there strong or weak, few
19 or many? Is the land in which they live a good place or bad? Are the cities in
20 which they live open or fortified? Is the soil rich or poor? Are there trees in
it or not? Take courage and bring back some of the fruit of the land" – it was
21 the season of the first ripe grapes. So they went up and scouted the land from SHENI
22 the Wilderness of Tzin to Reḥov, near Levo Ḥamat. They went up through the

רש״י

טז **ויקרא משה להושע וגו'.** התפלל עליו: יה יושיעך מעצת מרגלים:

יז **עלו זה בנגב.** הוא היה הפסולת של ארץ ישראל, שכן דרך התגרים, מראים את הפסולת תחלה ואחר כך מראים את השבח:

יח **את הארץ מה הוא.** יש ארץ מגדלת גבורים ויש ארץ מגדלת חלשים, יש מגדלת אוכלוסין ויש ממעטת אוכלוסין: **החזק הוא הרפה.** סימן מסר להם, אם בפרזים יושבין – חזקים הם, שסומכין על גבורתם, ואם בערים בצורות הם יושבין – חלשים הם:

יט **הבמחנים.** תרגומו: "הבפצחין", כרכין פצוחין ופתוחין מאין חומה: **הטובה הוא.** במעינות ותהומות טובים ובריאים:

כ **היש בה עץ.** אם יש בהם אדם כשר שיגן עליהם בזכותו: **בכורי ענבים.** ימים שהענבים מתבשלין בבכור:

כא **ממדבר צן עד רחב לבא חמת.** הלכו בגבוליה באורך וברוחב כמין 'גאם', הלכו רוח גבול דרומית ממקצוע מזרח עד מקצוע מערב, כמו שצוה משה: "עלו זה בנגב" (לעיל פסוק יז) דרך גבול דרומית מזרחית, עד הים, שהים הוא גבול מערבי, ומשם חזרו והלכו כל גבול מערבי על שפת הים עד לבא חמת, שהוא אצל הר ההר במקצוע מערבית צפונית, כמו שמפורש בגבולות הארץ בפרשת אלה מסעי (להלן לד, ז):

Anyone who, like Yehoshua, has experienced a name change has likewise been inducted into what Carol Dweck calls a growth mindset. They know their qualities are not predetermined; they can change and grow. People with a growth mindset do not fear failure. They relish challenges. They know that if they fail, they will try again until they succeed. I do not think it is coincidence that the two spies with a growth mindset are also the two who are unafraid of the risks and trials of conquering the land.

God does not ask us never to fail. He asks of us that we give of our best, and He forgives us when we fail. All He asks is that *we acknowledge our failures*. This gives us the courage to take risks. That is what Yehoshua and Kalev know, one through his name change, the other through the experience of his ancestor Yehuda.

Alone among the twelve spies, Yehoshua and Kalev show leadership. They tell the people that the conquest of the land is eminently achievable, not because they are all-powerful, but because God is with them. It is a paradoxical but deeply liberating truth: Fear of failure causes us to fail. It is the willingness to fail that allows us to succeed.

ז ח כָּלֵב בֶּן־יְפֻנֶּה׃ לְמַטֵּה יִשָּׂשכָר יִגְאָל בֶּן־יוֹסֵף׃ לְמַטֵּה אֶפְרָיִם הוֹשֵׁעַ
ט י בִּן־נוּן׃ לְמַטֵּה בִנְיָמִן פַּלְטִי בֶּן־רָפוּא׃ לְמַטֵּה זְבוּלֻן גַּדִּיאֵל בֶּן־סוֹדִי׃
יא יב לְמַטֵּה יוֹסֵף לְמַטֵּה מְנַשֶּׁה גַּדִּי בֶּן־סוּסִי׃ לְמַטֵּה דָן עַמִּיאֵל בֶּן־גְּמַלִּי׃
יג יד טו לְמַטֵּה אָשֵׁר סְתוּר בֶּן־מִיכָאֵל׃ לְמַטֵּה נַפְתָּלִי נַחְבִּי בֶּן־וָפְסִי׃ לְמַטֵּה
טז גָד גְּאוּאֵל בֶּן־מָכִי׃ אֵלֶּה שְׁמוֹת הָאֲנָשִׁים אֲשֶׁר־שָׁלַח מֹשֶׁה לָתוּר
יז אֶת־הָאָרֶץ וַיִּקְרָא מֹשֶׁה לְהוֹשֵׁעַ בִּן־נוּן יְהוֹשֻׁעַ׃ וַיִּשְׁלַח אֹתָם מֹשֶׁה
לָתוּר אֶת־אֶרֶץ כְּנָעַן וַיֹּאמֶר אֲלֵהֶם עֲלוּ זֶה בַּנֶּגֶב וַעֲלִיתֶם אֶת־הָהָר׃
יח וּרְאִיתֶם אֶת־הָאָרֶץ מַה־הִוא וְאֶת־הָעָם הַיֹּשֵׁב עָלֶיהָ הֶחָזָק הוּא
יט הֲרָפֶה הַמְעַט הוּא אִם־רָב׃ וּמָה הָאָרֶץ אֲשֶׁר־הוּא יֹשֵׁב בָּהּ הֲטוֹבָה
הִוא אִם־רָעָה וּמָה הֶעָרִים אֲשֶׁר־הוּא יוֹשֵׁב בָּהֵנָּה הַבְּמַחֲנִים אִם
כ בְּמִבְצָרִים׃ וּמָה הָאָרֶץ הַשְּׁמֵנָה הִוא אִם־רָזָה הֲיֵשׁ־בָּהּ עֵץ אִם־אַיִן
כא וְהִתְחַזַּקְתֶּם וּלְקַחְתֶּם מִפְּרִי הָאָרֶץ וְהַיָּמִים יְמֵי בִּכּוּרֵי עֲנָבִים׃ וַיַּעֲלוּ שני
כב וַיָּתֻרוּ אֶת־הָאָרֶץ מִמִּדְבַּר־צִן עַד־רְחֹב לְבֹא חֲמָת׃ וַיַּעֲלוּ בַנֶּגֶב

אונקלוס

כָּלֵב בַּר יְפֻנֶּה: ז לְשִׁבְטָא דְיִשָּׂשכָר, יִגְאָל בַּר יוֹסֵף: ח לְשִׁבְטָא דְאֶפְרָיִם הוֹשֵׁעַ בַּר נוּן: ט לְשִׁבְטָא דְבִנְיָמִין, פַּלְטִי בַּר רָפוּא: י לְשִׁבְטָא דִזְבוּלוּן, גַּדִּיאֵל בַּר סוֹדִי: יא לְשִׁבְטָא דְיוֹסֵף לְשִׁבְטָא דִמְנַשֶּׁה, גַּדִּי בַּר סוּסִי: יב לְשִׁבְטָא דְדָן, עַמִּיאֵל בַּר גְּמַלִּי: יג לְשִׁבְטָא דְאָשֵׁר, סְתוּר בַּר מִיכָאֵל: יד לְשִׁבְטָא דְנַפְתָּלִי, נַחְבִּי בַּר וָפְסִי: טו לְשִׁבְטָא דְגָד, גְּאוּאֵל בַּר מָכִי: טז אִלֵּין שְׁמָהָת גֻּבְרַיָּא, דִּשְׁלַח מֹשֶׁה לְאַלָּלָא יָת אַרְעָא, וּקְרָא מֹשֶׁה, לְהוֹשֵׁעַ בַּר נוּן יְהוֹשֻׁעַ: יז וּשְׁלַח יָתְהוֹן מֹשֶׁה, לְאַלָּלָא יָת אַרְעָא דִּכְנָעַן, וַאֲמַר לְהוֹן, סַקוּ דָא בְּדָרוֹמָא, וְתִסְּקוּן לְטוּרָא: יח וְתִחְזוֹן יָת אַרְעָא מָא הִיא, וְיָת עַמָּא דְיָתֵיב עֲלַהּ, הֲתַקִּיף הוּא אִם חַלָּשׁ, הַזְעֵיר הוּא אִם סַגִּי: יט וּמָא אַרְעָא, דְהוּא יָתֵיב בַּהּ, הֲטָבָא הִיא אִם בִּישָׁא, וּמָא קִרְוַיָּא, דְהוּא יָתֵיב בְּהוֹן, הַבִּפְצִחִין אִם בִּכְרַכִּין: כ וּמָא אַרְעָא, הַעֲתִירָא הִיא אִם מִסְכֵּינָא, הַאִית בַּהּ אִילָנִין אִם לָא, וְתִתַּקְפוּן, וְתִסְּבוּן מֵאִבָּא דְאַרְעָא, וְיוֹמַיָּא, יוֹמֵי בִכּוּרֵי עִנְבִין: כא וּסְלִיקוּ וְאַלִּילוּ יָת אַרְעָא, מִמַּדְבְּרָא דְצִין עַד רְחוֹב לְמֵטֵי חֲמָת: כב וּסְלִיקוּ בְדָרוֹמָא

13:16 וַיִּקְרָא מֹשֶׁה לְהוֹשֵׁעַ... יְהוֹשֻׁעַ *And Moshe named Hoshea… Yehoshua* – A change of name in the Torah always implies a change of character or calling. Avram became Avraham. Yaakov became Yisrael. When our name changes, says Rambam in his discussion of repentance (*Hilkhot Teshuva* 2:4), it is as if we or someone else were saying, "You are not the same person as you were before."

Could this hint at what gift, what strength of character, Yehoshua and Kalev possess that the other ten spies do not? Kalev comes from the tribe of Yehuda, and Yehuda, we learn in the book of Genesis, was the first *baal teshuva*, the first penitent (see Gen. 38:26 and the note there, and Gen. 34, "Yehuda's Test"). He matured. He was taught a lesson by his daughter-in-law, Tamar. Yehuda is the clearest example in Genesis of someone who takes adversity as a learning experience rather than as failure.

Negev and came to Ḥevron, where Aḥiman, Sheshai, and Talmai, descendants
of Anak, were dwelling. Ḥevron had been built seven years before the Egyptian
23 city of Tzoan. Then they came to the Eshkol Ravine and there they cut down
a vine branch, and on it one cluster of grapes, which they carried on a pole
24 between two men. They also took some pomegranates and figs. That place was
named the Eshkol Ravine, because of the cluster that the Israelites cut there.
25 26 They returned from scouting the land when forty days had passed. As soon as
they arrived they came to Moshe and Aharon and to all the community of Israel
at Kadesh in the Wilderness of Paran, and brought their report to them and to
27 all the community, and showed them the fruit of the land. They told Moshe,
"We came to the land you sent us to, and it is indeed flowing with milk and with
28 honey, and this is its fruit. But the people who live in the land are fierce, and the
cities are fortified and very large indeed. We even saw the descendants of Anak

רש״י

כב **וַיָּבֹא עַד חֶבְרוֹן.** כָּלֵב לְבַדּוֹ הָלַךְ שָׁם, וְנִשְׁתַּטֵּחַ עַל קִבְרֵי אָבוֹת שֶׁלֹּא יְהֵא נִסָּת לַחֲבֵרָיו לִהְיוֹת בַּעֲצָתָם, וְכֵן הוּא אוֹמֵר: "וְלוֹ אֶתֵּן אֶת הָאָרֶץ אֲשֶׁר דָּרַךְ בָּהּ" (דברים א, לו), וּכְתִיב: "וַיִּתְּנוּ לְכָלֵב אֶת חֶבְרוֹן" (שופטים א, כ): **שֶׁבַע שָׁנִים נִבְנְתָה.** אֶפְשָׁר שֶׁבָּנָה חָם אֶת חֶבְרוֹן לִכְנַעַן בְּנוֹ הַקָּטָן קֹדֶם שֶׁיִּבְנֶה אֶת צֹעַן לְמִצְרַיִם בְּנוֹ הַגָּדוֹל? אֶלָּא שֶׁהָיְתָה מְבֻנָּה בְּכָל טוּב עַל אֶחָד מִשִּׁבְעָה בְּצֹעַן, וּבָא לְהוֹדִיעֲךָ שִׁבְחָהּ שֶׁל אֶרֶץ יִשְׂרָאֵל, שֶׁאֵין לְךָ טְרָשִׁין בְּאֶרֶץ יִשְׂרָאֵל יוֹתֵר מֵחֶבְרוֹן, לְפִיכָךְ הִקְצוּהָ לִקְבֻרַת מֵתִים, וְאֵין לְךָ מְעֻלָּה בְּכָל הָאֲרָצוֹת כְּמִצְרַיִם, שֶׁנֶּאֱמַר: "כְּגַן ה׳ כְּאֶרֶץ מִצְרַיִם" (בראשית יג, י), וְצֹעַן הִיא הַמְעֻלָּה שֶׁבְּאֶרֶץ מִצְרַיִם, שֶׁשָּׁם מוֹשַׁב הַמְּלָכִים, שֶׁנֶּאֱמַר: "כִּי הָיוּ בְצֹעַן שָׂרָיו" (ישעיה ל, ד), וְהָיְתָה חֶבְרוֹן טוֹבָה מִמֶּנָּה שִׁבְעָה חֲלָקִים:

כג **זְמוֹרָה.** שׁוֹכַת גֶּפֶן, וְאֶשְׁכּוֹל שֶׁל עֲנָבִים תָּלוּי בָּהּ: **וַיִּשָּׂאֻהוּ בַמּוֹט בִּשְׁנָיִם.** מִמַּשְׁמַע שֶׁנֶּאֱמַר: "וַיִּשָּׂאֻהוּ בַמּוֹט", אֵינִי יוֹדֵעַ שֶׁהוּא בִּשְׁנַיִם? מַה תַּלְמוּד לוֹמַר "בִּשְׁנָיִם"? בִּשְׁנֵי מוֹטוֹת. הָא כֵּיצַד? שְׁמוֹנָה נָטְלוּ אֶשְׁכּוֹל, אֶחָד נָטַל תְּאֵנָה וְאֶחָד רִמּוֹן. יְהוֹשֻׁעַ וְכָלֵב לֹא נָטְלוּ כְּלוּם, לְפִי שֶׁכָּל עַצְמָם לְהוֹצִיא דִּבָּה נִתְכַּוְּנוּ: כְּשֵׁם שֶׁפִּרְיָהּ מְשֻׁנֶּה כָּךְ עַמָּהּ מְשֻׁנֶּה. וְאִם תָּפֵץ אַתָּה לֵידַע כַּמָּה מַשּׂאוֹי אֶחָד מֵהֶם, צֵא וּלְמַד מֵאֲבָנִים שֶׁהֵקִימוּ בַּגִּלְגָּל, הֵרִימוּ לָהֶם אִישׁ אֶבֶן אַחַת מִן הַיַּרְדֵּן עַל שִׁכְמוֹ וֶהֱקִימוּהָ בַּגִּלְגָּל, וּשְׁקָלוּם רַבּוֹתֵינוּ מִשְׁקַל כָּל אַחַת אַרְבָּעִים סְאָה, וּגְמִירֵי, טוּנָא דְּמַדְלֵי אֱנָשׁ עַל כַּתְפֵּיהּ אֵינוֹ אֶלָּא שְׁלִישׁ מַשּׂאוֹי כְּמַשּׂאוֹי שֶׁמְּסַיְּעִין אוֹתוֹ לַהֲרִים:

כה **וַיָּשֻׁבוּ מִתּוּר הָאָרֶץ מִקֵּץ אַרְבָּעִים יוֹם.** וַהֲלֹא אַרְבַּע מֵאוֹת פַּרְסָה עַל אַרְבַּע מֵאוֹת פַּרְסָה הִיא, וּמַהֲלַךְ אָדָם בֵּינוֹנִי עֲשָׂרָה פַּרְסָאוֹת לַיּוֹם, הֲרֵי מַהֲלַךְ אַרְבָּעִים יוֹם מִן הַמִּזְרָח לַמַּעֲרָב, וְהֵם הָלְכוּ אָרְכָּהּ וְרָחְבָּהּ! אֶלָּא שֶׁגָּלוּי לִפְנֵי הַקָּדוֹשׁ בָּרוּךְ הוּא שֶׁיִּגְזֹר עֲלֵיהֶם יוֹם לַשָּׁנָה, קִצֵּר לִפְנֵיהֶם אֶת הַדֶּרֶךְ:

כו **וַיֵּלְכוּ וַיָּבֹאוּ.** מַהוּ "וַיֵּלְכוּ", לְהַקִּישׁ הֲלִיכָתָן לְבִיאָתָן, מַה בִּיאָתָן בְּעֵצָה רָעָה, אַף הֲלִיכָתָן בְּעֵצָה רָעָה: **וַיָּשִׁיבוּ אֹתָם דָּבָר.** אֶת מֹשֶׁה וְאֶת אַהֲרֹן:

כז **זָבַת חָלָב וּדְבַשׁ.** כָּל דְּבַר שֶׁקֶר שֶׁאֵין אוֹמְרִים בּוֹ קְצָת אֱמֶת בִּתְחִלָּתוֹ, אֵין מִתְקַיֵּם בְּסוֹפוֹ:

Rambam. He showed that one could be a supreme exponent of Jewish law while at the same time contributing to philosophy, medicine, and many other disciplines of his time. Of course, there was only one Rambam, and not everyone has the strength to live in a world without walls. But the story of the spies tells us that our fears are sometimes exaggerated. Judaism is strong enough to withstand any challenge if we have the confidence of our faith. People who are strong do not have to live behind defensive walls.

וַיָּבֹא עַד־חֶבְרוֹן וְשָׁם אֲחִימַן שֵׁשַׁי וְתַלְמַי יְלִידֵי הָעֲנָק וְחֶבְרוֹן שֶׁבַע
כג שָׁנִים נִבְנְתָה לִפְנֵי צֹעַן מִצְרָיִם׃ וַיָּבֹאוּ עַד־נַחַל אֶשְׁכֹּל וַיִּכְרְתוּ מִשָּׁם
זְמוֹרָה וְאֶשְׁכּוֹל עֲנָבִים אֶחָד וַיִּשָּׂאֻהוּ בַמּוֹט בִּשְׁנָיִם וּמִן־הָרִמֹּנִים
כד וּמִן־הַתְּאֵנִים׃ לַמָּקוֹם הַהוּא קָרָא נַחַל אֶשְׁכּוֹל עַל אֹדוֹת הָאֶשְׁכּוֹל
כה אֲשֶׁר־כָּרְתוּ מִשָּׁם בְּנֵי יִשְׂרָאֵל׃ וַיָּשֻׁבוּ מִתּוּר הָאָרֶץ מִקֵּץ אַרְבָּעִים
כו יוֹם׃ וַיֵּלְכוּ וַיָּבֹאוּ אֶל־מֹשֶׁה וְאֶל־אַהֲרֹן וְאֶל־כָּל־עֲדַת בְּנֵי־יִשְׂרָאֵל
אֶל־מִדְבַּר פָּארָן קָדֵשָׁה וַיָּשִׁיבוּ אֹתָם דָּבָר וְאֶת־כָּל־הָעֵדָה וַיַּרְאוּם
כז אֶת־פְּרִי הָאָרֶץ׃ וַיְסַפְּרוּ־לוֹ וַיֹּאמְרוּ בָּאנוּ אֶל־הָאָרֶץ אֲשֶׁר שְׁלַחְתָּנוּ
כח וְגַם זָבַת חָלָב וּדְבַשׁ הִוא וְזֶה־פִּרְיָהּ׃ אֶפֶס כִּי־עַז הָעָם הַיֹּשֵׁב בָּאָרֶץ

אונקלוס

וַאֲתָא עַד חֶבְרוֹן, וְתַמָּן אֲחִימַן שֵׁשַׁי וְתַלְמַי, בְּנֵי גִּבָּרָא, וְחֶבְרוֹן, שְׁבַע שְׁנִין אִתְבְּנִיאַת, קֳדָם טָנִיס דְּמִצְרָיִם: כג וַאֲתוֹ עַד נַחְלָא דְּאֶתְכָּלָא, וְקָצוּ מִתַּמָּן עוֹבַרְתָּא וְאֶתְכָּל דְּעִנְּבִין חַד, וְנַטְלוּהִי בַּאֲרִיחָא בִּתְרֵין, וּמִן רִמּוֹנַיָּא וּמִן תְּאֵנַיָּא: כד לְאַתְרָא הַהוּא, קְרָא נַחְלָא דְּאֶתְכָּלָא, עַל עֵיסַק אֶתְכָּלָא, דְּקָצוּ מִתַּמָּן בְּנֵי יִשְׂרָאֵל: כה וְתָבוּ מִלְּאַלָּלָא אַרְעָא, מִסּוֹף אַרְבְּעִין יוֹמִין: כו וַאֲזַלוּ, וַאֲתוֹ לְוָת מֹשֶׁה וּלְוָת אַהֲרֹן, וּלְוָת כָּל כְּנִשְׁתָּא דִּבְנֵי יִשְׂרָאֵל, לְמַדְבְּרָא דְּפָארָן לִרְקָם, וַאֲתִיבוּ יָתְהוֹן פִּתְגָּמָא וְיָת כָּל כְּנִשְׁתָּא, וְאַחְזִיאוּנוּן יָת אִבָּא דְאַרְעָא: כז וְאִשְׁתַּעִיאוּ לֵיהּ וַאֲמַרוּ, אֲתֵינָא, לְאַרְעָא דִּשְׁלַחְתָּנָא, וְאַף, עָבְדָא חֲלַב וּדְבַשׁ, הִיא וְדֵין אִבַּהּ: כח לְחוֹד אֲרֵי תַּקִּיף עַמָּא, דְּיָתֵיב בְּאַרְעָא,

13:28 **וְהֶעָרִים בְּצֻרוֹת** *The cities are fortified* – There is a fascinating passage from Midrash Tanḥuma – cited by Rashi in his commentary – with far-reaching implications.

> How were they [the spies] to know [the people's] strength? [By looking at their cities:] Are they unwalled or fortified? If they live in unwalled cities, they are strong and trust in their own strength. If, however, they live in fortified cities, they are weak and insecure.

The spies report back, "But the people who live in the land are fierce, and the cities are fortified and very large indeed" (Num. 13:28). They said: the people are strong and so are the cities. Hence their conclusion: We cannot win. We should not even try.

Clearly, the sight of the cities made a deep impression on the spies. This makes psychological sense, and it accords with historical fact. The cities in ancient Canaan were indeed surrounded by high, thick walls, which made them seem impregnable. However, according to the Midrash, the spies drew precisely the wrong conclusion: the cities are strong; therefore the people are strong. In fact the opposite was the case: the cities are strong; therefore the people are weak.

There is a commentary here on the experience of Jews in the modern age. Two centuries ago, Jews in Europe were not ready for the challenge of an integrated society and some chose instead segregation and the voluntary ghetto. Ours, by contrast, is not the age of the spies but of their descendants, born in freedom. We have had time enough to realize that we can be at home in Western culture without it calling into question Jewish faith or Jewish life. Those who are strong do not need to live behind defensive walls. The model is

29 there. In the Negev region, Amalek lives; the Hittites, Jebusites, and Amorites
live in the hill country, and the Canaanites live by the sea and by the Jordan."
30 But Kalev silenced the people around Moshe and said, "Let us go up at once
31 and take possession of it, for certainly we are able." The men who had gone up
with him said, "We cannot go up against those people, for they are stronger
32 than us." So they gave the Israelites an adverse report of the land that they had
scouted: "The land which we have journeyed through and scouted is a land
that consumes its inhabitants; the people we saw in it were tall and broad to a
33 man. There we saw the Nefilim – the descendants of Anak are from the Nefilim.
14 1 We looked to our own eyes like grasshoppers, and so we were in theirs." All the
2 community lifted their heads and cried out – that night the people wept. And

רש״י

כח **בְּצֻרוֹת.** לְשׁוֹן חֹזֶק, וְתַרְגּוּמוֹ: ״כְּרִיכָן״, לְשׁוֹן בִּירָנִיּוֹת עֲגֻלּוֹת, וּבִלְשׁוֹן אֲרַמִּי ׳כְּרִיךְ׳ – עָגֹל:

כט **עֲמָלֵק יוֹשֵׁב וְגוֹ׳.** לְפִי שֶׁנִּכְווּ בַּעֲמָלֵק כְּבָר, הִזְכִּירוּהוּ מְרַגְּלִים כְּדֵי לְיָרְאָם: **וְעַל יַד הַיַּרְדֵּן.** ׳יַד׳ כְּמַשְׁמָעוֹ, אֵצֶל הַיַּרְדֵּן, וְלֹא תוּכְלוּ לַעֲבֹר:

ל **וַיַּהַס כָּלֵב.** הִשְׁתִּיק אֶת כֻּלָּם: **אֶל מֹשֶׁה.** לִשְׁמֹעַ מַה שֶּׁיְּדַבֵּר בְּמֹשֶׁה, צָוַח וְאָמַר: וְכִי זוֹ בִּלְבַד עָשָׂה לָנוּ בֶּן עַמְרָם? הַשּׁוֹמֵעַ הָיָה סָבוּר שֶׁבָּא לְסַפֵּר בִּגְנוּתוֹ, וּמִתּוֹךְ שֶׁהָיָה בְּלִבָּם עַל מֹשֶׁה בִּשְׁבִיל דִּבְרֵי הַמְרַגְּלִים שָׁתְקוּ כֻּלָּם לִשְׁמֹעַ גְּנוּתוֹ. אָמַר: וַהֲלֹא קָרַע לָנוּ אֶת הַיָּם, וְהוֹרִיד לָנוּ אֶת הַמָּן, וְהֵגִיז לָנוּ אֶת הַשְּׂלָו: **עָלֹה נַעֲלֶה.** אֲפִלּוּ בַּשָּׁמַיִם, וְהוּא אוֹמֵר: עֲשׂוּ סֻלָּמוֹת וַעֲלוּ שָׁם! נַצְלִיחַ בְּכָל דְּבָרָיו: **וַיַּהַס.** לְשׁוֹן שְׁתִיקָה, וְכֵן: ״הַס כָּל בָּשָׂר״ (זכריה ב, יז), ״הַס כִּי לֹא לְהַזְכִּיר״ (עמוס ו, י), כֵּן דֶּרֶךְ בְּנֵי אָדָם, הָרוֹצֶה לְשַׁתֵּק אֲגֻדַּת אֲנָשִׁים אוֹמֵר שי״ט:

לא **חָזָק הוּא מִמֶּנּוּ.** כִּבְיָכוֹל כְּלַפֵּי מַעְלָה אָמְרוּ:

לב **אֹכֶלֶת יוֹשְׁבֶיהָ.** בְּכָל מָקוֹם שֶׁעָבַרְנוּ מְצָאנוּם קוֹבְרֵי מֵתִים, וְהַקָּדוֹשׁ בָּרוּךְ הוּא עָשָׂה לְטוֹבָה כְּדֵי לְטָרְדָם בְּאֶבְלָם וְלֹא יִתְּנוּ לֵב לָאֵלּוּ: **אַנְשֵׁי מִדּוֹת.** גְּדוֹלִים וּגְבוֹהִים וְצָרִיךְ לָתֵת לָהֶם מִדָּה, כְּגוֹן גָּלְיָת: ״גָּבְהוֹ שֵׁשׁ אַמּוֹת וָזָרֶת״ (שמואל א׳ יז, ד), וְכֵן: ״אִישׁ מָדוֹן״ (שמואל ב׳ כא, כ), ״אִישׁ מִדָּה״ (דברי הימים א׳ יא, כג):

לג **הַנְּפִילִים.** עֲנָקִים, מִבְּנֵי שַׁמְחֲזַאי וַעֲזָאֵל שֶׁנָּפְלוּ מִן הַשָּׁמַיִם בִּימֵי דוֹר אֱנוֹשׁ: **וְכֵן הָיִינוּ בְּעֵינֵיהֶם.** שָׁמַעְנוּ אוֹמְרִים זֶה לָזֶה: נְמָלִים יֵשׁ בַּכְּרָמִים כַּאֲנָשִׁים: **עֲנָק.** שֶׁמַּעֲנִיקִים חַמָּה בְּקוֹמָתָן:

words appear in our *parasha*. Instead, no less than twelve times, we encounter the rare verb *latur*. This word was revived in Modern Hebrew, where it means (and sounds like) "to tour." *Tayar* is a tourist. There is all the difference between a tourist and a spy.

Malbim (1809–79) explains the difference simply. *Latur* means to seek out the good. That is what tourists do. They go to the beautiful, the majestic, the inspiring (compare, for instance, Eccl. 1:13). They don't spend their time trying to find out what is bad. *Laḥpor* and *leragel* are the opposite. They are about searching out a place's weaknesses and vulnerabilities. That is spying. In Genesis 42, when the brothers come before Yosef in Egypt to buy food, he accuses them of being *meraglim*, "spies," a word that appears seven times in that one chapter. He also defines what it is to be a spy: "You have come to see where our land is exposed" (i.e., where it is undefended). The exclusive use of the verb *latur* in our *parasha* – repeated twelve times – is there to tell us that the twelve men are not being sent to spy. But only two of them understand this.

The reason ten of the twelve men come back with a negative report, then, is because they have misunderstood their mission. They believe it is their role to find out where the "land is exposed," where it is vulnerable, where its defenses could be overcome. They look and cannot find. The people are strong, and the cities impregnable.

In fact, they are meant to see what is good about the land, not what is bad. So, if they are not meant to be spies, what is the purpose of this mission? I suggest that the answer is to be found in a passage in the Talmud (Kiddushin 41a) that

כט וְהֶעָרִים בְּצֻרוֹת גְּדֹלֹת מְאֹד וְגַם־יְלִדֵי הָעֲנָק רָאִינוּ שָׁם: עֲמָלֵק יוֹשֵׁב
בְּאֶרֶץ הַנֶּגֶב וְהַחִתִּי וְהַיְבוּסִי וְהָאֱמֹרִי יוֹשֵׁב בָּהָר וְהַכְּנַעֲנִי יוֹשֵׁב עַל־
ל הַיָּם וְעַל יַד הַיַּרְדֵּן: וַיַּהַס כָּלֵב אֶת־הָעָם אֶל־מֹשֶׁה וַיֹּאמֶר עָלֹה נַעֲלֶה
לא וְיָרַשְׁנוּ אֹתָהּ כִּי־יָכוֹל נוּכַל לָהּ: וְהָאֲנָשִׁים אֲשֶׁר עָלוּ עִמּוֹ אָמְרוּ לֹא
לב נוּכַל לַעֲלוֹת אֶל־הָעָם כִּי־חָזָק הוּא מִמֶּנּוּ: וַיֹּצִיאוּ דִּבַּת הָאָרֶץ אֲשֶׁר
תָּרוּ אֹתָהּ אֶל־בְּנֵי יִשְׂרָאֵל לֵאמֹר הָאָרֶץ אֲשֶׁר עָבַרְנוּ בָהּ לָתוּר אֹתָהּ
אֶרֶץ אֹכֶלֶת יוֹשְׁבֶיהָ הִוא וְכָל־הָעָם אֲשֶׁר־רָאִינוּ בְתוֹכָהּ אַנְשֵׁי מִדּוֹת:
לג וְשָׁם רָאִינוּ אֶת־הַנְּפִילִים בְּנֵי עֲנָק מִן־הַנְּפִלִים וַנְּהִי בְעֵינֵינוּ כַּחֲגָבִים
יד א וְכֵן הָיִינוּ בְּעֵינֵיהֶם: וַתִּשָּׂא כָּל־הָעֵדָה וַיִּתְּנוּ אֶת־קוֹלָם וַיִּבְכּוּ הָעָם

אונקלוס

וְקִרְוַיָּא, כְּרִיכָן רַבְרְבָן לַחְדָּא, וְאַף בְּנֵי גִּבָּרָא חֲזֵינָא תַמָּן: כט עֲמָלְקָאָה יָתֵיב בַּאֲרַע דָּרוֹמָא, וְחִתָּאָה, וִיבוּסָאָה וֶאֱמוֹרָאָה יָתֵיב בְּטוּרָא, וּכְנַעֲנָאָה יָתֵיב עַל יַמָּא, וְעַל כֵּיף יַרְדְּנָא: ל וְאַצֵּית כָּלֵב, יָת עַמָּא לְמֹשֶׁה, וַאֲמַר, מִסָּק נִסַּק וְנֵירַת יָתַהּ, אֲרֵי מִכָּל נִכּוֹל לַהּ: לא וְגֻבְרַיָּא, דִּסְלִיקוּ עִמֵּיהּ אֲמַרוּ, לָא נִכּוֹל לְמִסַּק לְוָת עַמָּא, אֲרֵי תַקִּיף הוּא מִנַּנָא: לב וְאַפִּיקוּ שׁוּם בִּישׁ, עַל אַרְעָא דְּאַלִּילוּ יָתַהּ, לְוָת בְּנֵי יִשְׂרָאֵל לְמֵימַר, אַרְעָא, דַּעֲבַרְנָא בַהּ לְאַלָּלָא יָתַהּ, אֲרַע מְקַטְּלָא יָתְבַהָא הִיא, וְכָל עַמָּא, דַּחֲזֵינָא בְגַוַּהּ אֱנָשִׁין דִּמְשַׁחְן: לג וְתַמָּן חֲזֵינָא, יָת גִּבָּרַיָּא, בְּנֵי עֲנָק מִן גִּבָּרַיָּא, וַהֲוֵינָא בְּעֵינֵי נַפְשַׁנָא כְּקַמְצִין, וְכֵן הֲוֵינָא בְּעֵינֵיהוֹן: יד א וַאֲרֵימַת כָּל כְּנִשְׁתָּא, וִיהַבוּ יָת קָלְהוֹן, וּבְכוֹ עַמָּא

13:33 וְכֵן הָיִינוּ בְּעֵינֵיהֶם *And so we were in theirs* – Rabbi Menachem Mendel of Kotzk pointed out that the spies make one statement that is completely unwarranted. They are entitled to say, "We looked to our own eyes like grasshoppers." It accurately describes how they felt. But they are not entitled to say the second half of the sentence. They have no idea how they appeared in the eyes of the inhabitants of the land; they merely inferred it and were wrong.

They should have known this. They had even sung, along their fellow Israelites, a song at the sea that contained the words "Nations heard and they trembled.... the people of Canaan melted away" (Ex. 15:14–15). They should have known that the people of the land were afraid of them. And so it was, as Raḥav is to tell the spies sent by Yehoshua forty years later: "I know that the LORD has given you the land, and that dread of you has fallen upon us, for all the inhabitants of the land quake before you. For we have heard that the LORD dried up the waters of the Sea of Reeds before you" (Josh. 2:9–11).

Yet they assumed that others saw them as they saw themselves, projecting their sense of inadequacy onto the external world, with the result that they misinterpreted what they saw. Instead of ordinary people, they saw giants. Instead of towns, they saw impregnable fortresses, and they were afraid. The spies' confirmation bias meant that they paid selective attention to phenomena that gave them reasons to be afraid. Their perception was not in the world but in the mind.

THE SPIES' REPORT

The disastrous outcome of the twelve men's report invites us to re-examine the purpose of their mission. Biblical Hebrew has two verbs that mean "to spy": *laḥpor* and *leragel* (from which we get the word *meraglim*, "spies"). Neither of these

all the Israelites railed against Moshe and Aharon; all the community said to
them, "If only we had died in Egypt, if only we had died in this wilderness!
3 Why is the LORD bringing us as far as this land only to fall by the sword? Our
wives and children will be made plunder. Would it not be better for us to go
4 back to Egypt?" So they said to one another, "Let us appoint a leader and go
5 back to Egypt." Moshe and Aharon fell facedown before all the assembled
6 community of Israel. Yehoshua son of Nun and Kalev son of Yefuneh, who
7 were among those who scouted the land, tore their clothes and said before the
entire community of Israel: "The land we journeyed through and scouted is a
8 very, very good land. If the LORD favors us, He will bring us into this land, a SHELISHI
9 land flowing with milk and with honey, and He will give it to us. Do not rebel
against the LORD, and do not be afraid of the people of the land, for they are
no more than bread for us. They have been stripped of their protection and the
10 LORD is with us. Do not be afraid of them!" The community, all, threatened
to stone them to death – but then the LORD's glory was revealed to all the
Israelites at the Tent of Meeting.
11 The LORD said to Moshe, "How long will these people provoke Me? How long
will they fail to have faith in Me in spite of all the signs I have performed among

רש״י

יד ב לוּ מַתְנוּ. הַלְוַאי וּמַתְנוּ:

ד נִתְּנָה רֹאשׁ. כְּתַרְגּוּמוֹ: "נְמַנֵּי רֵישָׁא", נָשִׂים עָלֵינוּ מֶלֶךְ. וְרַבּוֹתֵינוּ פֵּרְשׁוּ, לְשׁוֹן עֲבוֹדָה זָרָה:

ט אַל תִּמְרֹדוּ. וְשׁוּב "וְאַתֶּם אַל תִּירְאוּ": כִּי לַחְמֵנוּ הֵם. נֹאכְלֵם כַּלֶּחֶם: סָר צִלָּם. מְגִנָּם וְחָזְקָם, כְּשֵׁרִים שֶׁבָּהֶם מֵתוּ, אִיּוֹב שֶׁהָיָה מֵגֵן עֲלֵיהֶם. דָּבָר אַחֵר, צִלּוֹ שֶׁל הַמָּקוֹם סָר מֵעֲלֵיהֶם:

י לִרְגּוֹם אֹתָם. אֶת יְהוֹשֻׁעַ וְכָלֵב: וּכְבוֹד ה׳. הֶעָנָן יָרַד שָׁם:

יא עַד אָנָה. עַד הֵיכָן: יְנַאֲצֻנִי. יַרְגִּיזוּנִי: בְּכֹל הָאֹתוֹת. בִּשְׁבִיל כָּל הַנִּסִּים שֶׁעָשִׂיתִי לָהֶם הָיָה לָהֶם לְהַאֲמִין שֶׁהַיְּכֹלֶת בְּיָדִי לְקַיֵּם הַבְטָחָתִי:

land. The Israelites are traveling to the country promised to their ancestors. But none of them have ever seen it. How then can they be expected to muster the energies necessary to fight the coming battles? They are about to marry a land they have not seen.

The twelve are sent *latur*: their mission is to be the eyes of the congregation, letting them know the beauty and goodness of what lies ahead, the land that has been their destiny since the days of their ancestor Avraham.

Moshe has told them that the land is good. It is "flowing with milk and honey." But Moshe has never seen the land. They need the independent testimony of eyewitnesses. And in fact, all twelve fulfill that mission. When they return, the first thing they say is: "We came to the land you sent us to, and it is indeed flowing with milk and with honey, and this is its fruit" (Num. 13:27). But because ten of them think their task is to be spies, they go on to say that the conquest is impossible – and disaster ensues. Only Yehoshua and Kalev have in fact understood the mission.

ב בַּלַּיְלָה הַהוּא: וַיִּלֹּנוּ עַל־מֹשֶׁה וְעַל־אַהֲרֹן כֹּל בְּנֵי יִשְׂרָאֵל וַיֹּאמְרוּ
אֲלֵהֶם כָּל־הָעֵדָה לוּ־מַתְנוּ בְּאֶרֶץ מִצְרַיִם אוֹ בַּמִּדְבָּר הַזֶּה לוּ־מָתְנוּ:
ג וְלָמָה יהוה מֵבִיא אֹתָנוּ אֶל־הָאָרֶץ הַזֹּאת לִנְפֹּל בַּחֶרֶב נָשֵׁינוּ וְטַפֵּנוּ
ד יִהְיוּ לָבַז הֲלוֹא טוֹב לָנוּ שׁוּב מִצְרָיְמָה: וַיֹּאמְרוּ אִישׁ אֶל־אָחִיו נִתְּנָה
ה רֹאשׁ וְנָשׁוּבָה מִצְרָיְמָה: וַיִּפֹּל מֹשֶׁה וְאַהֲרֹן עַל־פְּנֵיהֶם לִפְנֵי כָּל־קְהַל
ו עֲדַת בְּנֵי יִשְׂרָאֵל: וִיהוֹשֻׁעַ בִּן־נוּן וְכָלֵב בֶּן־יְפֻנֶּה מִן־הַתָּרִים אֶת־
ז הָאָרֶץ קָרְעוּ בִּגְדֵיהֶם: וַיֹּאמְרוּ אֶל־כָּל־עֲדַת בְּנֵי־יִשְׂרָאֵל לֵאמֹר
ח הָאָרֶץ אֲשֶׁר עָבַרְנוּ בָהּ לָתוּר אֹתָהּ טוֹבָה הָאָרֶץ מְאֹד מְאֹד: אִם־חָפֵץ שלישי
בָּנוּ יהוה וְהֵבִיא אֹתָנוּ אֶל־הָאָרֶץ הַזֹּאת וּנְתָנָהּ לָנוּ אֶרֶץ אֲשֶׁר־הִוא
ט זָבַת חָלָב וּדְבָשׁ: אַךְ בַּיהוה אַל־תִּמְרֹדוּ וְאַתֶּם אַל־תִּירְאוּ אֶת־עַם
הָאָרֶץ כִּי לַחְמֵנוּ הֵם סָר צִלָּם מֵעֲלֵיהֶם וַיהוה אִתָּנוּ אַל־תִּירָאֻם:
י וַיֹּאמְרוּ כָּל־הָעֵדָה לִרְגּוֹם אֹתָם בָּאֲבָנִים וּכְבוֹד יהוה נִרְאָה בְּאֹהֶל
מוֹעֵד אֶל־כָּל־בְּנֵי יִשְׂרָאֵל:
יא וַיֹּאמֶר יהוה אֶל־מֹשֶׁה עַד־אָנָה יְנַאֲצֻנִי הָעָם הַזֶּה וְעַד־אָנָה לֹא־ יג

אונקלוס

בְּלֵילְיָא הַהוּא: ב וְאִתְרַעַמוּ עַל מֹשֶׁה וְעַל אַהֲרֹן, כֹּל בְּנֵי יִשְׂרָאֵל, וַאֲמַרוּ לְהוֹן כָּל כְּנִשְׁתָּא, לְוַי דְּמִיתְנָא בְּאַרְעָא דְּמִצְרַיִם, אוֹ, בְּמַדְבְּרָא הָדֵין לְוַי דְּמִיתְנָא: ג וּלְמָא יְיָ, מַעֵיל יָתַנָא, לְאַרְעָא הָדָא לְמִפַּל בְּחַרְבָּא, נְשַׁנָא וְטַפְלַנָא יְהוֹן לְבִזָּא, הֲלָא טָב לַנָא דְּנְתוּב לְמִצְרָיִם: ד וַאֲמַרוּ גְּבַר לַאֲחוּהִי, נְמַנֵּי רֵישָׁא וּנְתוּב לְמִצְרָיִם: ה וּנְפַל מֹשֶׁה, וְאַהֲרֹן עַל אַפֵּיהוֹן, קֳדָם, כָּל קְהָלָא כְּנִשְׁתָּא דִּבְנֵי יִשְׂרָאֵל: ו וִיהוֹשֻׁעַ בַּר נוּן, וְכָלֵב בַּר יְפֻנֶּה, מִן מְאַלְּלֵי אַרְעָא, בַּזַּעוּ לְבוּשֵׁיהוֹן: ז וַאֲמַרוּ, לְכָל כְּנִשְׁתָּא דִּבְנֵי יִשְׂרָאֵל לְמֵימַר, אַרְעָא, דַּעֲבַרְנָא בַהּ לְאַלָּלָא יָתַהּ, טָבָא אַרְעָא לַחֲדָא לַחֲדָא: ח אִם רַעֲוָא בַנָא קֳדָם יְיָ, וְיָעֵיל יָתַנָא לְאַרְעָא הָדָא, וְיִתְּנַהּ לַנָא, אַרְעָא, דְּהִיא, עָבְדָא חֲלַב וּדְבָשׁ: ט בְּרַם בְּמֵימְרָא דַּייָ לָא תִמְרְדוּן, וְאַתּוּן, לָא תִדְחֲלוּן מִן עַמָּא דְּאַרְעָא, אֲרֵי בִּידַנָא מְסִירִין אִנּוּן, עֲדָא תֻּקְפְּהוֹן מִנְּהוֹן, וּמֵימְרָא דַּייָ בְּסַעֲדַנָא לָא תִדְחֲלוּן מִנְּהוֹן: י וַאֲמַרוּ כָּל כְּנִשְׁתָּא, לְמִרְגַּם יָתְהוֹן בְּאַבְנַיָּא, וִיקָרָא דַּייָ, אִתְגְּלִי בְּמַשְׁכַּן זִמְנָא, לְכָל בְּנֵי יִשְׂרָאֵל: יא וַאֲמַר יְיָ לְמֹשֶׁה, עַד אֵמָתַי יְהוֹן מַרְגְּזִין קֳדָמַי עַמָּא הָדֵין, וְעַד אֵמָתַי לָא יְהֵימְנוּן בְּמֵימְרִי, בְּכָל אָתַיָּא, דַּעֲבַדִית בֵּינֵיהוֹן:

states that it is forbidden for a man to marry a woman without seeing her first. The reason? Were he to marry without having seen her first, he might, when he does see her, find he is not attracted to her. Tensions will inevitably arise. Hence the idea: first see, then love.

The same applies to a marriage between a people and its

12 them? I will strike them with a plague now and disinherit them, and make you
13 into a nation greater and mightier than they." But Moshe said to the LORD,
"The Egyptians will hear about it, for by Your power You brought this people
14 up from among them, and they will tell the inhabitants of this land. They have
heard that You, LORD, are among these people, that You, LORD, are seen face-
to-face, that Your cloud stands over them, that You go before them in a pillar of
15 cloud by day and in a pillar of fire by night. If You kill this people like a single
16 man, the nations that have heard of Your fame will say, 'It was because the LORD
was unable to bring this people into the land He swore to them; that is why
17 He slaughtered them in the wilderness.' So now, let my LORD's power be great,
18 as You declared when You said: 'The LORD is slow to anger and abounding
in kindness, forgiving sin and rebellion, though He does not acquit the guilty,
but holds the descendants to account for the sins of the fathers; children and
19 grandchildren to the third and fourth generation.' Please – pardon the sin of
this people in Your great kindness, as You have forgiven this people from the

רש״י

יב **ואורשנו.** כתרגומו, ותרוכין. ואם תאמר: מה אעשה לשבועת אבות? "ואעשה אתך לגוי גדול", שאתה מזרעם:

יג-יד **ושמעו מצרים.** ושמעו את אשר הרגת: **כי העלית.** 'כי' משמש בלשון 'אשר'. והם ראו את אשר העלית בכחך הגדול אותם מקרבם, וכשישמעו שאתה הורגם, לא יאמרו שחטאו לך, אלא יאמרו שכנגדם יכלת להלחם אבל כנגד יושבי הארץ לא יכלת להלחם, וזו היא: **ואמרו אל יושב הארץ הזאת.** כמו 'על יושב הארץ הזאת'. ומה יאמרו עליהם? מה שאמור בסוף הענין: "מבלתי יכלת ה'" (להלן פסוק טז), בשביל ש"שמעו כי אתה ה'" שוכן בקרבם ועין בעין אתה נראה להם, והכל כדרך חבה, ולא הכירו בך שנתקה אהבתך מהם עד הנה:

טו **והמתה את העם הזה כאיש אחד.** פתאם, ומתוך כך: "ואמרו הגוים אשר שמעו את שמעך" וגו':

טז **מבלתי יכלת וגו'.** לפי שיושבי הארץ חזקים וגבורים, ואינו דומה פרעה לשלשים ואחד מלכים, זאת יאמרו על יושבי הארץ הזאת: "מבלתי יכלת", מתוך שלא היה יכלת בידו להביאם, שחטם: **יכלת.** שם דבר הוא:

יז-יח **כאשר דברת לאמר.** ומהו הדבור? **ה' ארך אפים. לצדיקים** ולרשעים. כשעלה משה למרום מצאו להקדוש ברוך הוא שהיה יושב וכותב: "ה' ארך אפים", אמר לו: לצדיקים? אמר לו הקדוש ברוך הוא: אף לרשעים. אמר לו: רשעים יאבדו. אמר לו הקדוש ברוך הוא: חייך שתצטרך לדבר. כשחטאו ישראל בעגל ובמרגלים התפלל משה לפניו ב'ארך אפים', אמר לו הקדוש ברוך הוא: והלא אמרת לי 'לצדיקים'! אמר לו: והלא אתה אמרת לי 'אף לרשעים': **יגדל נא כח אדני.** לעשות דבורך: **ונקה.** לשבים: **לא ינקה.** לשאינן שבים:

commandments and Your laws" (Dan. 9:4–5). Others were said by Ezra (Ezra 9:10–11:15) and Neḥemya (Neh. 1:6–7). All three of these were composed in the aftermath of the Babylonian exile and the later return of Jews to a devastated land of Israel, and they represent the authentic Jewish response to calamity: "When sufferings come, search your deeds and return in repentance" (Berakhot 5a). All renewal, whether in the life of an individual or a nation, begins with spiritual and moral renewal, and this in turn begins with *seliḥa*, the act of saying sorry to God. These, and in particular the Thirteen Attributes, became the model for the *Seliḥot* we say today.

יב יַאֲמִינוּ בִּי בְּכֹל הָאֹתוֹת אֲשֶׁר עָשִׂיתִי בְּקִרְבּוֹ: אַכֶּנּוּ בַדֶּבֶר וְאוֹרִשֶׁנּוּ
יג וְאֶעֱשֶׂה אֹתְךָ לְגוֹי־גָּדוֹל וְעָצוּם מִמֶּנּוּ: וַיֹּאמֶר מֹשֶׁה אֶל־יהוה וְשָׁמְעוּ
יד מִצְרַיִם כִּי־הֶעֱלִיתָ בְכֹחֲךָ אֶת־הָעָם הַזֶּה מִקִּרְבּוֹ: וְאָמְרוּ אֶל־יוֹשֵׁב
הָאָרֶץ הַזֹּאת שָׁמְעוּ כִּי־אַתָּה יהוה בְּקֶרֶב הָעָם הַזֶּה אֲשֶׁר־עַיִן בְּעַיִן
נִרְאָה ׀ אַתָּה יהוה וַעֲנָנְךָ עֹמֵד עֲלֵהֶם וּבְעַמֻּד עָנָן אַתָּה הֹלֵךְ לִפְנֵיהֶם
טו יוֹמָם וּבְעַמּוּד אֵשׁ לָיְלָה: וְהֵמַתָּה אֶת־הָעָם הַזֶּה כְּאִישׁ אֶחָד וְאָמְרוּ
טז הַגּוֹיִם אֲשֶׁר־שָׁמְעוּ אֶת־שִׁמְעֲךָ לֵאמֹר: מִבִּלְתִּי יְכֹלֶת יהוה לְהָבִיא
יז אֶת־הָעָם הַזֶּה אֶל־הָאָרֶץ אֲשֶׁר־נִשְׁבַּע לָהֶם וַיִּשְׁחָטֵם בַּמִּדְבָּר: וְעַתָּה
יח יִגְדַּל־נָא כֹּחַ אֲדֹנָי כַּאֲשֶׁר דִּבַּרְתָּ לֵאמֹר: יהוה אֶרֶךְ אַפַּיִם וְרַב־חֶסֶד
נֹשֵׂא עָוֺן וָפָשַׁע וְנַקֵּה לֹא יְנַקֶּה פֹּקֵד עֲוֺן אָבוֹת עַל־בָּנִים עַל־שִׁלֵּשִׁים
יט וְעַל־רִבֵּעִים: סְלַח־נָא לַעֲוֺן הָעָם הַזֶּה כְּגֹדֶל חַסְדֶּךָ וְכַאֲשֶׁר נָשָׂאתָה

אונקלוס

יב אֲמַחֵינוּן בְּמוֹתָא וַאֲשֵׁיצֵינוּן, וְאַעֲבֵיד יָתָךְ, לְעַם רַב וְתַקִּיף מִנְּהוֹן: יג וַאֲמַר מֹשֶׁה קֳדָם יְיָ, וְיִשְׁמְעוּן מִצְרָאֵי, אֲרֵי אַסֵּיקְתָּא בְחֵילָךְ, יָת עַמָּא הָדֵין מִבֵּינֵיהוֹן: יד וְיֵימְרוּן, לְיָתֵיב אַרְעָא הָדָא, דִּשְׁמַעוּ אֲרֵי אַתְּ יְיָ, שְׁכִינְתָךְ שָׁרְיָא בְּגוֹ עַמָּא הָדֵין, דִּבְעֵינֵיהוֹן חֲזַן שְׁכִינַת יְקָרָךְ יְיָ, וַעֲנָנָךְ מַטֵּל עֲלֵיהוֹן, וּבְעַמּוּדָא דַעֲנָנָא, אַתְּ מְדַבַּר קֳדָמֵיהוֹן בִּימָמָא, וּבְעַמּוּדָא דְּאִשָּׁתָא בְּלֵילְיָא: טו וּתְקַטֵּיל, יָת עַמָּא הָדֵין כִּגְבַר חַד, וְיֵימְרוּן עַמְמַיָּא, דִּשְׁמַעוּ יָת שֵׁימַע גְּבוּרְתָךְ לְמֵימַר: טז מִדְּלֵית יְכֹלָא קֳדָם יְיָ, לְאַעָלָא יָת עַמָּא הָדֵין, לְאַרְעָא דְּקַיֵּים לְהוֹן, וְקַטֵּילִנּוּן בְּמַדְבְּרָא: יז וּכְעַן, סַגֵּי כְעַן חֵילָא קֳדָמָךְ יְיָ, כְּמָא דְּמַלֵּילְתָּא לְמֵימַר: יח יְיָ, מַרְחִיק רְגַז וּמַסְגֵּי לְמֶעְבַּד טַבְוָן, שָׁבֵיק לַעֲוָיָן וְלִמְרוֹד, סָלַח לִדְתָיְבִין לְאוֹרָיְתֵיהּ וְלִדְלָא תָּיְבִין לָא מְזַכֵּי, מַסְעַר, חוֹבֵי אֲבָהָן עַל בְּנִין מָרָדִין, עַל דָּר תְּלִיתָאֵי וְעַל דָּר רְבִיעָאֵי: יט שְׁבוֹק כְּעַן, לְחוֹבֵי, עַמָּא הָדֵין כִּסְגִיאוּת טַבְוָתָךְ, וּכְמָא דִּשְׁבַקְתָּא לְעַמָּא הָדֵין, מִמִּצְרַיִם וְעַד כְּעַן: כ וַאֲמַר יְיָ, שְׁבַקִית

14:18 אֶרֶךְ אַפַּיִם *The Lord is slow to anger* – In this verse, Moshe is paraphrasing back to God the words (known as the Thirteen Attributes of Mercy) that God said to him on Mount Sinai (see Ex. 34:5–7 and the notes there). From this the Rabbis inferred:

> This teaches us that God, as it were, robed Himself as if He were a leader of prayer, and said to Moshe: "Whenever Israel sins, let them perform this rite before Me and I shall forgive them."... R. Yehuda said: There is a covenant that the Thirteen Attributes do not return unanswered. (Rosh HaShana 17b)

In Exodus, God taught Moshe how to pray.

We have records of a number of penitential pleas long before Jewish prayer was formalized. One, moving and eloquent, was said by Daniel in exile: "O Lord, the great and awesome God, who keeps the covenant and the love with those who love Him and keep His commandments: we have sinned, offended, done evil and rebelled, straying from Your

20 time of Egypt until now." And the LORD said, "I have forgiven them at your
21 22 word. Yet as surely as I live and as the LORD's glory fills the whole earth, none
of those who have seen My glory and the signs I performed in Egypt and in
23 the wilderness, and have tested Me these ten times and not obeyed Me, shall
see the land I swore to their fathers. None of those who have provoked Me will
24 see it. But My servant Kalev, because he was filled with a different spirit and
has followed Me wholeheartedly – him I will bring into the land he came to,
25 and his descendants will inherit it. The Amalekites and Canaanites are living
in the valleys; so turn tomorrow and head for the wilderness by way of the Sea
of Reeds."
26 27 Then the LORD spoke to Moshe and Aharon: "How long shall this wicked REVI'I
community keep railing against Me? I have heard the Israelites' complaints
28 with which they rail against Me. Tell them: 'As surely as I live,' says the LORD,
29 'I will do to you the very thing I heard you say. In this wilderness your corpses

רש״י

כ| **כדברך.** בשביל מה שאמרת, פן יאמרו: "מבלתי יכלת ה'" (לעיל פסוק טז):

כא-כג| **ואולם.** כמו 'אבל', זאת אעשה להם: **חי אני.** לשון שבועה, כשם שאני חי וכבודי ימלא את כל הארץ, כך אקים להם, "כי כל האנשים הראים וגו' אם יראו את הארץ"; הרי זה מקרא מסרס: חי אני כי כל האנשים אם יראו את הארץ, וכבודי ימלא את כל הארץ, שלא יתחלל שמי במגפה הזאת לאמר: 'מבלתי יכלת ה'' להביאם, שלא אמיתם פתאם כאיש אחד, אלא באחור ארבעים שנה מעט מעט:

כב| **וינסו.** כמשמעו: **זה עשר פעמים.** שנים בים ושנים במן ושנים בשלו וכו', כדאיתא במסכת ערכין (דף טו ע"א – טו ע"ב):

כג| **אם יראו.** לא יראו:

כד| **רוח אחרת.** שתי רוחות, אחת בפה ואחת בלב. למרגלים אמר: אני עמכם בעצה, ובלבו היה לומר האמת, ועל ידי כן היה בו כח להשתיקם, כמו שנאמר: "ויהס כלב" (לעיל יג, ל), שהיו סבורים שיאמר כמותם. זהו שנאמר בספר יהושע: "ואשב אותו דבר כאשר עם לבבי" (יהושע יד, ז), ולא כאשר עם פי: **וימלא אחרי.** וימלא את לבו אחרי, וזה מקרא קצר: **אשר בא שמה.** חברון תנתן לו: **יורשנה.** כתרגומו: "יתרכנה", יורישו את הענקים ואת העם אשר בה, ואין לתרגמו 'ירתנה' אלא במקום 'יירשנה':

כה| **והעמלקי וגו'.** אם תלכו שם יהרגו אתכם, מאחר שאיני עמכם: **מחר פנו.** לאחוריכם, "וסעו לכם" וגו':

כו| **לעדה הרעה וגו'.** אלו המרגלים, מכאן ל'עדה' שהיא עשרה: **אשר המה מלינים.** את ישראל "עלי": **את תלנות בני ישראל אשר המה.** המרגלים, "מלינים" אותם "עלי, שמעתי":

כח| **חי אני.** לשון שבועה, אם לא כן אעשה – כביכול איני חי: **כאשר דברתם.** שבקשתם ממני: "או במדבר הזה לו מתנו" (לעיל פסוק ב):

of the desert, untrammeled by habits of servitude. *Liberty is the work of more than one generation*. The forty years of wandering in the wilderness prefigure a much larger, longer journey that will eventuate in a society that sanctifies human life as the gift of God and the human person as the image of God.

is a consequence of human nature. People long deprived of their freedom grow used to their chains.

It takes more than a few days or weeks to turn a population of slaves into a nation capable of handling the responsibilities of freedom. In the case of the Israelites it needs a generation born in liberty, hardened by the experience

כ כא לָעָ֥ם הַזֶּ֖ה מִמִּצְרַ֥יִם וְעַד־הֵֽנָּה׃ וַיֹּ֣אמֶר יְהוָ֔ה סָלַ֖חְתִּי כִּדְבָרֶֽךָ׃ וְאוּלָ֖ם
כב חַי־אָ֑נִי וְיִמָּלֵ֥א כְבוֹד־יְהוָ֖ה אֶת־כָּל־הָאָֽרֶץ׃ כִּ֣י כָל־הָאֲנָשִׁ֗ים הָרֹאִ֤ים
אֶת־כְּבֹדִי֙ וְאֶת־אֹ֣תֹתַ֔י אֲשֶׁר־עָשִׂ֥יתִי בְמִצְרַ֖יִם וּבַמִּדְבָּ֑ר וַיְנַסּ֣וּ אֹתִ֗י
כג זֶ֚ה עֶ֣שֶׂר פְּעָמִ֔ים וְלֹ֥א שָׁמְע֖וּ בְּקוֹלִֽי׃ אִם־יִרְאוּ֙ אֶת־הָאָ֔רֶץ אֲשֶׁ֥ר
כד נִשְׁבַּ֖עְתִּי לַאֲבֹתָ֑ם וְכָל־מְנַאֲצַ֖י לֹ֥א יִרְאֽוּהָ׃ וְעַבְדִּ֣י כָלֵ֗ב עֵ֣קֶב הָֽיְתָ֞ה
ר֤וּחַ אַחֶ֙רֶת֙ עִמּ֔וֹ וַיְמַלֵּ֖א אַחֲרָ֑י וַהֲבִֽיאֹתִ֗יו אֶל־הָאָ֙רֶץ֙ אֲשֶׁר־בָּ֣א שָׁ֔מָּה
כה וְזַרְע֖וֹ יוֹרִשֶֽׁנָּה׃ וְהָעֲמָלֵקִ֥י וְהַֽכְּנַעֲנִ֖י יוֹשֵׁ֣ב בָּעֵ֑מֶק מָחָ֗ר פְּנ֨וּ וּס֥עוּ לָכֶ֛ם
הַמִּדְבָּ֖ר דֶּ֥רֶךְ יַם־סֽוּף׃
כו כז וַיְדַבֵּ֣ר יְהוָ֔ה אֶל־מֹשֶׁ֥ה וְאֶֽל־אַהֲרֹ֖ן לֵאמֹֽר׃ עַד־מָתַ֗י לָעֵדָ֤ה הָֽרָעָה֙ רביעי
הַזֹּ֔את אֲשֶׁ֛ר הֵ֥מָּה מַלִּינִ֖ים עָלָ֑י אֶת־תְּלֻנּ֞וֹת בְּנֵ֣י יִשְׂרָאֵ֗ל אֲשֶׁ֥ר הֵ֛מָּה
כח מַלִּינִ֥ים עָלַ֖י שָׁמָֽעְתִּי׃ אֱמֹ֣ר אֲלֵהֶ֗ם חַי־אָ֙נִי֙ נְאֻם־יְהוָ֔ה אִם־לֹ֕א כַּאֲשֶׁ֥ר
כט דִּבַּרְתֶּ֖ם בְּאָזְנָ֑י כֵּ֖ן אֶֽעֱשֶׂ֥ה לָכֶֽם׃ בַּמִּדְבָּ֣ר הַ֠זֶּה יִפְּל֨וּ פִגְרֵיכֶ֜ם וְכָל־

אונקלוס

כְּפִתְגָמָךְ: כא וּבְרַם קַיָּם אֲנָא, וּמַלְיָא יְקָרָא דַייָ יָת כָּל אַרְעָא: כב אֲרֵי כָּל גֻּבְרַיָּא, דַּחֲזוֹ יָת יְקָרִי וְיָת אָתְוָתִי, דַּעֲבַדִית בְּמִצְרַיִם וּבְמַדְבְּרָא, וְנַסִּיאוּ קֳדָמַי, דְּנַן עֲסַר זִמְנִין, וְלָא קַבִּילוּ לְמֵימְרִי: כג אִם יֶחֱזוֹן יָת אַרְעָא, דְּקַיֵּימִית לַאֲבָהָתְהוֹן, וְכָל דְּאַרְגִּיזוּ קֳדָמַי לָא יֶחֱזוֹנַהּ: כד וְעַבְדִּי כָלֵב, חֲלָף דַּהֲוָת, רוּחַ אָחֳרִי עִמֵּיהּ, וְאַשְׁלֵים בָּתַר דַּחַלְתִּי, וְאַעֵילִנֵּיהּ, לְאַרְעָא דְּעָאל לְתַמָּן, וּבְנוֹהִי יְתָרְכִנַּהּ: כה וַעֲמַלְקָאָה וּכְנַעֲנָאָה יָתֵיב בְּמֵישְׁרָא, מְחַר, אִתְפְּנוֹ וְטוּלוּ לְכוֹן, לְמַדְבְּרָא אוֹרַח יַמָּא דְסוּף: כו וּמַלֵּיל יְיָ, עִם מֹשֶׁה וּלְאַהֲרֹן לְמֵימָר: כז עַד אִמָּתַי, לִכְנִשְׁתָּא בִּשְׁתָּא הָדָא, דְּאִנּוּן מִתְרַעֲמִין עֲלַי, יָת תֻּרְעֲמַת בְּנֵי יִשְׂרָאֵל, דְּאִנּוּן מִתְרַעֲמִין, עֲלַי שְׁמִיעַ קֳדָמָי: כח אֵימַר לְהוֹן, קַיָּם אֲנָא אֲמַר יְיָ, אִם לָא, כְּמָא דְמַלֵּילְתּוּן קֳדָמַי, כֵּן אַעֲבֵיד לְכוֹן: כט בְּמַדְבְּרָא הָדֵין, יִפְּלוּן פִּגְרֵיכוֹן, וְכָל מִנְיָנְכוֹן לְכָל חֻשְׁבָּנְכוֹן, מִבַּר,

14:35 בַּמִּדְבָּר הַזֶּה יִתַּמּוּ *In this wilderness they shall come to their end* – We have already seen (Ex. 13, "The Journey Begins") that for Rambam the entry into the land was delayed for a generation so that it could be undertaken by those who had been born in the desert, since "it is a well-known fact that traveling in the wilderness deprived of bodily enjoyments like bathing produces courage, while the opposite produces faintheartedness. Besides, another generation arose during the wanderings that had not been accustomed to degradation and slavery" (*Guide for the Perplexed* III:32).

This is an unusual position, because *Rambam does not mention the spies at all*. It was, he implies, a given of the state of the people at the time and of the constraints of human nature. People cannot change overnight. It takes time to move from slavery to the responsibilities of freedom. It can take an entire generation, sometimes longer still. This is a radical suggestion because it implies that the negative report of the spies is only the precipitating factor, not the underlying cause. Nor is the divine verdict, that the people are condemned to spend forty years in the wilderness, a punishment as such. It

will fall, all of your number, all those listed in the census, from twenty years
30 old and upward: all those who have railed against Me. None of you will enter
the land that I promised to settle you in, except for Kalev son of Yefuneh and
31 Yehoshua son of Nun. I will bring in your children, whom you said would be
32 taken captive, and they will know the land you rejected. But as for you, your
33 corpses will fall in this wilderness. Your children will shepherd in the wilderness
for forty years, suffering for your faithlessness until the last of your corpses lies
34 here in the wilderness. For the number of the days in which you scouted the
land, forty days, you shall bear your sins – for every day a year: forty years.
35 You will know what it is to oppose Me. I, the Lord, have spoken.' This will
I do to this entire wicked community that has gathered together against Me.
36 In this wilderness they shall come to their end, and there they shall die." So
the men Moshe sent to scout the land, and who came back and caused all the
37 community to rail against him by giving an adverse report of the land – those
men who gave the adverse report of the land died by a plague before the Lord.
38 And only Yehoshua son of Nun and Kalev son of Yefuneh remained alive of all
39 those men who went to scout the land. When Moshe reported these words to
40 all the Israelites, the people were overcome with grief. They rose early the next
morning and climbed up to the heights of the hill country, saying, "We are

רש״י

כט **וְכָל פְּקֻדֵיכֶם לְכָל מִסְפַּרְכֶם.** כָּל הַנִּמְנֶה לְכָל מִסְפָּר שֶׁאַתֶּם נִמְנִין בּוֹ, כְּגוֹן לָצֵאת וְלָבֹא לַצָּבָא וְלָתֵת שְׁקָלִים, כָּל הַמְּנוּיִים לְכָל אוֹתָן מִסְפָּרוֹת יָמוּתוּ, וְאֵלּוּ הֵן: "מִבֶּן עֶשְׂרִים שָׁנָה" וְגוֹ׳ – לְהוֹצִיא שִׁבְטוֹ שֶׁל לֵוִי שֶׁאֵין פְּקוּדֵיהֶם מִבֶּן עֶשְׂרִים:

לב **וּפִגְרֵיכֶם אַתֶּם.** כְּתַרְגּוּמוֹ, לְפִי שֶׁדִּבֵּר עַל הַבָּנִים לְהַכְנִיסָם לָאָרֶץ וּבִקֵּשׁ לוֹמַר: ׳וְאַתֶּם תָּמוּתוּ׳, נוֹפֵל לָשׁוֹן זֶה כָּאן לוֹמַר "אַתֶּם":

לג **אַרְבָּעִים שָׁנָה.** לֹא מֵת אֶחָד מֵהֶם פָּחוֹת מִבֶּן שִׁשִּׁים, לְכָךְ נִגְזַר אַרְבָּעִים, כְּדֵי שֶׁיִּהְיוּ אוֹתָם שֶׁל בְּנֵי עֶשְׂרִים מַגִּיעִין לִכְלַל שִׁשִּׁים. וְשָׁנָה רִאשׁוֹנָה הָיְתָה בַּכְּלָל, וְאַף עַל פִּי שֶׁקָּדְמָה לְשִׁלּוּחַ הַמְרַגְּלִים, לְפִי שֶׁמִּשֶּׁעָשׂוּ אֶת הָעֵגֶל עָלְתָה גְּזֵרָה זוֹ בְּמַחֲשָׁבָה, אֶלָּא שֶׁהִמְתִּין לָהֶם עַד שֶׁתִּתְמַלֵּא סְאָתָם, וְזֶהוּ שֶׁנֶּאֱמַר: "וּבְיוֹם פָּקְדִי", בַּמְרַגְּלִים, "וּפָקַדְתִּי עֲלֵהֶם חַטָּאתָם" (שמות לב, לד), וְאַף כָּאן נֶאֱמַר: "תִּשְׂאוּ אֶת עֲוֹנֹתֵיכֶם", שְׁתֵּי עֲוֹנוֹת, שֶׁל עֵגֶל וְשֶׁל תְּלוּנָה, וְחִשֵּׁב לָהֶם בְּמִנְיַן חַיֵּיהֶם מִקְצָת שָׁנָה כְּכֻלָּהּ, וּכְשֶׁנִּכְנְסוּ לִשְׁנַת שִׁשִּׁים מֵתוּ אוֹתָם שֶׁל בְּנֵי עֶשְׂרִים: **וְנָשְׂאוּ אֶת זְנוּתֵיכֶם.** כְּתַרְגּוּמוֹ, יִסְבְּלוּ אֶת חַטָּאתְכֶם:

לד **אֶת תְּנוּאָתִי.** שֶׁהֱנִיאוֹתֶם אֶת לְבַבְכֶם מֵאַחֲרַי. ׳תְּנוּאָה׳ לְשׁוֹן הֲסָרָה, כְּמוֹ: "כִּי הֵנִיא אָבִיהָ אֹתָהּ" (להלן ל, ו):

לו **וַיָּשֻׁבוּ וַיַּלִּינוּ עָלָיו.** וּכְשֶׁשָּׁבוּ מִתּוּר הָאָרֶץ הִרְעִימוּ עָלָיו אֶת כָּל הָעֵדָה בְּהוֹצָאַת דִּבָּה, אוֹתָן הָאֲנָשִׁים "וַיָּמֻתוּ" (להלן פסוק לז). כָּל הוֹצָאַת דִּבָּה לְשׁוֹן אִנּוּךְ דְּבָרִים, שֶׁמַּלְקִיאִים לְשׁוֹנָם לְאָדָם לְדַבֵּר בּוֹ, כְּמוֹ: "דּוֹבֵב שִׂפְתֵי יְשֵׁנִים" (שיר השירים ז, י), וְיֶשְׁנָהּ לְטוֹבָה וְיֶשְׁנָהּ לְרָעָה, לְכָךְ נֶאֱמַר כָּאן: "מוֹצִאֵי דִבַּת הָאָרֶץ רָעָה" (להלן פסוק לז), שֶׁיֵּשׁ דִּבָּה שֶׁהִיא טוֹבָה: **דִּבָּה.** פרלדי״ץ בְּלַעַז:

לז **בַּמַּגֵּפָה לִפְנֵי ה׳.** בְּאוֹתָהּ מִיתָה הַהֲגוּנָה לָהֶם, מִדָּה כְּנֶגֶד מִדָּה. הֵם חָטְאוּ בַּלָּשׁוֹן, וְנִשְׁתַּרְבֵּב לְשׁוֹנָם עַד טַבּוּרָם, וְתוֹלָעִים יוֹצְאִים מִלְּשׁוֹנָם וּבָאִין לְתוֹךְ טַבּוּרָם, לְכָךְ נֶאֱמַר: "בַּמַּגֵּפָה" וְלֹא ׳בְּמַגֵּפָה׳, וְזֶהוּ "לִפְנֵי ה׳", בְּאוֹתָהּ הָרְאוּיָה לָהֶם עַל פִּי מִדּוֹתָיו שֶׁל הַקָּדוֹשׁ בָּרוּךְ הוּא שֶׁהוּא מוֹדֵד מִדָּה כְּנֶגֶד מִדָּה:

לח **וִיהוֹשֻׁעַ וְכָלֵב חָיוּ וְגוֹ׳.** מַה תַּלְמוּד לוֹמַר: "חָיוּ מִן הָאֲנָשִׁים הָהֵם"? אֶלָּא מְלַמֵּד שֶׁנָּטְלוּ חֶלְקָם שֶׁל מְרַגְּלִים בָּאָרֶץ וְקָמוּ תַּחְתֵּיהֶם לְחַיִּים:

מ **אֶל רֹאשׁ הָהָר.** הִיא הַדֶּרֶךְ הָעוֹלָה לְאֶרֶץ יִשְׂרָאֵל: **הִנֶּנּוּ וְעָלִינוּ אֶל הַמָּקוֹם.** לְאֶרֶץ יִשְׂרָאֵל: **אֲשֶׁר אָמַר ה׳.** לְתִתָּהּ לָנוּ, שָׁם נַעֲלֶה: **כִּי חָטָאנוּ.** עַל אֲשֶׁר אָמַרְנוּ: "הֲלוֹא טוֹב לָנוּ שׁוּב מִצְרָיְמָה" (לעיל פסוק ג):

פִּקְדֵיכֶם לְכָל־מִסְפַּרְכֶם מִבֶּן עֶשְׂרִים שָׁנָה וָמָעְלָה אֲשֶׁר הֲלִינֹתֶם עָלָי׃
ל אִם־אַתֶּם תָּבֹאוּ אֶל־הָאָרֶץ אֲשֶׁר נָשָׂאתִי אֶת־יָדִי לְשַׁכֵּן אֶתְכֶם בָּהּ
לא כִּי אִם־כָּלֵב בֶּן־יְפֻנֶּה וִיהוֹשֻׁעַ בִּן־נוּן׃ וְטַפְּכֶם אֲשֶׁר אֲמַרְתֶּם לָבַז יִהְיֶה
לב וְהֵבֵיאתִי אֹתָם וְיָדְעוּ אֶת־הָאָרֶץ אֲשֶׁר מְאַסְתֶּם בָּהּ׃ וּפִגְרֵיכֶם אַתֶּם
לג יִפְּלוּ בַּמִּדְבָּר הַזֶּה׃ וּבְנֵיכֶם יִהְיוּ רֹעִים בַּמִּדְבָּר אַרְבָּעִים שָׁנָה וְנָשְׂאוּ
לד אֶת־זְנוּתֵיכֶם עַד־תֹּם פִּגְרֵיכֶם בַּמִּדְבָּר׃ בְּמִסְפַּר הַיָּמִים אֲשֶׁר־תַּרְתֶּם
אֶת־הָאָרֶץ אַרְבָּעִים יוֹם יוֹם לַשָּׁנָה יוֹם לַשָּׁנָה תִּשְׂאוּ אֶת־עֲוֺנֹתֵיכֶם
לה אַרְבָּעִים שָׁנָה וִידַעְתֶּם אֶת־תְּנוּאָתִי׃ אֲנִי יהוה דִּבַּרְתִּי אִם־לֹא ׀ זֹאת
אֶעֱשֶׂה לְכָל־הָעֵדָה הָרָעָה הַזֹּאת הַנּוֹעָדִים עָלָי בַּמִּדְבָּר הַזֶּה יִתַּמּוּ
לו וְשָׁם יָמֻתוּ׃ וְהָאֲנָשִׁים אֲשֶׁר־שָׁלַח מֹשֶׁה לָתוּר אֶת־הָאָרֶץ וַיָּשֻׁבוּ
לז וילונו עָלָיו אֶת־כָּל־הָעֵדָה לְהוֹצִיא דִבָּה עַל־הָאָרֶץ׃ וַיָּמֻתוּ הָאֲנָשִׁים וַיַּלִּינוּ
לח מוֹצִאֵי דִבַּת־הָאָרֶץ רָעָה בַּמַּגֵּפָה לִפְנֵי יהוה׃ וִיהוֹשֻׁעַ בִּן־נוּן וְכָלֵב
לט בֶּן־יְפֻנֶּה חָיוּ מִן־הָאֲנָשִׁים הָהֵם הַהֹלְכִים לָתוּר אֶת־הָאָרֶץ׃ וַיְדַבֵּר
מֹשֶׁה אֶת־הַדְּבָרִים הָאֵלֶּה אֶל־כָּל־בְּנֵי יִשְׂרָאֵל וַיִּתְאַבְּלוּ הָעָם מְאֹד׃
מ וַיַּשְׁכִּמוּ בַבֹּקֶר וַיַּעֲלוּ אֶל־רֹאשׁ־הָהָר לֵאמֹר הִנֶּנּוּ וְעָלִינוּ אֶל־הַמָּקוֹם

אונקלוס

עֶסְרִין שְׁנִין וּלְעֵילָא, דְּאִתְרַעַמְתּוּן עֲלָי: ל אִם אַתּוּן תֵּיעֲלוּן לְאַרְעָא, דְּקַיֵּימִית בְּמֵימְרִי, לְאַשְׁרָאָה יָתְכוֹן בַּהּ, אֱלָהֵין כָּלֵב בַּר יְפֻנֶּה, וִיהוֹשֻׁעַ בַּר נוּן: לא וְטַפְלְכוֹן, דַּאֲמַרְתּוּן לְבִזָּא יְהוֹן, וְאַעֵיל יָתְהוֹן, וְיִדְּעוּן יָת אַרְעָא, דְּקַצְתּוּן בַּהּ: לב וּפִגְרֵיכוֹן דִּילְכוֹן, יִפְּלוּן בְּמַדְבְּרָא הָדֵין: לג וּבְנֵיכוֹן, יְהוֹן מְאַחֲרִין בְּמַדְבְּרָא אַרְבְּעִין שְׁנִין, וִיקַבְּלוּן יָת חוֹבֵיכוֹן, עַד דִּיסוּפוּן פִּגְרֵיכוֹן בְּמַדְבְּרָא: לד בְּמִנְיַן יוֹמַיָּא, דְּאַלֵּילְתּוּן יָת אַרְעָא אַרְבְּעִין יוֹמִין, יוֹמָא לְשַׁתָּא יוֹמָא לְשַׁתָּא, תְּקַבְּלוּן יָת חוֹבֵיכוֹן, אַרְבְּעִין שְׁנִין, וְתִדְּעוּן יָת דְּאִתְרַעַמְתּוּן עֲלָי: לה אֲנָא יי גְּזָרִית בְּמֵימְרִי, אִם לָא דָּא אַעֲבֵיד, לְכָל כְּנִשְׁתָּא בִשְׁתָּא הָדָא, דְּאִזְדַּמַּנוּ עֲלָי, בְּמַדְבְּרָא הָדֵין, יְסוּפוּן וְתַמָּן יְמוּתוּן: לו וְגֻבְרַיָּא, דִּשְׁלַח מֹשֶׁה לְאַלָּלָא יָת אַרְעָא, וְתָבוּ, וְאַרְעִימוּ עֲלוֹהִי יָת כָּל כְּנִשְׁתָּא, לְאַפָּקָא שׁוּם בִּישׁ עַל אַרְעָא: לז וּמִיתוּ גֻבְרַיָּא, דְּאַפִּיקוּ שׁוּם בִּישׁ עַל אַרְעָא, בְּמוֹתָנָא קֳדָם יי: לח וִיהוֹשֻׁעַ בַּר נוּן, וְכָלֵב בַּר יְפֻנֶּה, אִתְקַיָּמוּ מִן גֻבְרַיָּא הָאִנּוּן, דַּאֲזַלוּ לְאַלָּלָא יָת אַרְעָא: לט וּמַלֵּיל מֹשֶׁה יָת פִּתְגָמַיָּא הָאִלֵּין, לְכָל בְּנֵי יִשְׂרָאֵל, וְאִתְאַבַּלוּ עַמָּא לַחֲדָא: מ וְאַקְדִּימוּ בְצַפְרָא, וּסְלִיקוּ לְרֵישׁ טוּרָא לְמֵימַר, הָאֲנַחְנָא סָלְקִין, לְאַתְרָא,

41 ready to go up to the place that the LORD spoke of; we were wrong." But Moshe
42 said, "Why are you transgressing the LORD's command? It will not work. Do
not go up; the LORD is not with you. Do not be struck down by your enemies.
43 Ahead of you are the Amalekites and Canaanites, and you will fall by the sword.
Because you have turned away from following the LORD, the LORD will not be
44 with you." Defiantly, they went up to the heights of the hill country. Neither the
45 Ark of the LORD's Covenant nor Moshe left the camp. And the Amalekites and
Canaanites who lived in that hill country came down, and fought them, and
crushed them, all the way to Ḥorma.
15 1 2 The LORD spoke to Moshe: "Speak to the Israelites. Say: When you come to
3 the land that I am giving you to live in, and you present a fire offering from the
herd or from the flock for a pleasing aroma to the LORD – whether it be a burnt
offering or a sacrifice to fulfill a spoken vow, or brought as a freewill offering,
4 or a festival offering – the one who brings this offering to the LORD shall bring
with it a grain offering of a tenth of a measure of fine flour mixed with a quarter
5 of a hin of oil, and with the burnt offering or the sacrifice, a quarter of a hin of

רש״י

מא **וְהִוא לֹא תִצְלָח.** זוֹ שֶׁאַתֶּם עוֹשִׂים לֹא תִּצְלָח:

מג **כִּי עַל כֵּן שַׁבְתֶּם.** כְּלוֹמַר, כִּי זֹאת תָּבֹא לָכֶם עַל אֲשֶׁר שַׁבְתֶּם וְגוֹ׳:

מד **וַיַּעְפִּלוּ.** לְשׁוֹן חֹזֶק, וְכֵן: "הִנֵּה עֻפְּלָה" (חבקוק ב, ד), אינגרי"ש בְּלַעַז, לְשׁוֹן עַזּוּת, וְכֵן: "עֹפֶל בַּת צִיּוֹן" (מיכה ד, ח), "עֹפֶל וָבַחַן" (ישעיה לב, יד). וּמִדְרַשׁ תַּנְחוּמָא מְפָרְשׁוֹ לְשׁוֹן אֹפֶל, הָלְכוּ חֲשֵׁכִים שֶׁלֹּא בִּרְשׁוּת:

מה **וַיַּכְּתוּם.** כְּמוֹ: "וָאֶכֹּת אֹתוֹ טָחוֹן" (דברים ט, כא), מַכָּה אַחַר מַכָּה: **עַד הַחָרְמָה.** שֵׁם הַמָּקוֹם נִקְרָא עַל שֵׁם הַמְּאֹרָע:

טו ב **כִּי תָבֹאוּ.** בִּשֵּׂר לָהֶם שֶׁיִּכָּנְסוּ לָאָרֶץ:

ג **וַעֲשִׂיתֶם אִשֶּׁה.** אֵין זֶה צִוּוּי, אֶלָּא כְּשֶׁתָּבוֹאוּ שָׁם וְתַעֲלֶה עַל לְבַבְכֶם לַעֲשׂוֹת אִשֶּׁה לַה׳: **רֵיחַ נִיחֹחַ.** נַחַת רוּחַ לְפָנַי: **לְפַלֵּא נֶדֶר אוֹ בִנְדָבָה.** אוֹ שֶׁתַּעֲשׂוּ הָאִשֶּׁה בִּשְׁבִיל חוֹבַת מוֹעֲדֵיכֶם, שֶׁחִיַּבְתִּי אֶתְכֶם לַעֲשׂוֹת בַּמּוֹעֵד:

ד **וְהִקְרִיב הַמַּקְרִיב.** תַּקְרִיבוּ נְסָכִים וּמִנְחָה לְכָל בְּהֵמָה, הַמִּנְחָה כָּלִיל וְהַשֶּׁמֶן נִבְלָל בְּתוֹכָהּ, וְהַיַּיִן לַסְּפָלִים, כְּמוֹ שֶׁשָּׁנִינוּ בְּמַסֶּכֶת סֻכָּה (דף מח ע״ב):

service on Passover begins: "This year, slaves, next year free; this year here, next year in Israel." A tradition can be evolutionary without being revolutionary.

That is the lesson of the spies. Despite the divine anger, the people are not condemned to permanent exile. But they have to face the fact that their children will achieve what they themselves are not ready for.

People still forget this. Wars have been undertaken, at least in part, in the name of democracy and freedom. Yet that is the work not of a war, but of education, society-building, and the slow acceptance of responsibility. It takes generations. Sometimes it never happens at all. The people – like the Israelites immediately after the spies' report – lose heart and want to go back to the predictable past ("Let us appoint a leader and go back to Egypt" – Num. 14:4), not the unseen, hazardous, demanding future. That is why, historically, there have been more tyrannies than democracies.

The politics of liberty demands patience. It needs years of struggle without giving up hope. The late Emmanuel Levinas spoke about "difficult freedom" – and freedom always is difficult. The story of the spies tells us that the generation who left Egypt was not yet ready for it. That is their tragedy.

But their children will be. That is their consolation.

מא אֲשֶׁר־אָמַר יְהוָה כִּי חָטָאנוּ: וַיֹּאמֶר מֹשֶׁה לָמָּה זֶּה אַתֶּם עֹבְרִים אֶת־
מב פִּי יְהוָה וְהִוא לֹא תִצְלָח: אַל־תַּעֲלוּ כִּי אֵין יְהוָה בְּקִרְבְּכֶם וְלֹא תִּנָּגְפוּ
מג לִפְנֵי אֹיְבֵיכֶם: כִּי הָעֲמָלֵקִי וְהַכְּנַעֲנִי שָׁם לִפְנֵיכֶם וּנְפַלְתֶּם בֶּחָרֶב כִּי־
מד עַל־כֵּן שַׁבְתֶּם מֵאַחֲרֵי יְהוָה וְלֹא־יִהְיֶה יְהוָה עִמָּכֶם: וַיַּעְפִּלוּ לַעֲלוֹת
אֶל־רֹאשׁ הָהָר וַאֲרוֹן בְּרִית־יְהוָה וּמֹשֶׁה לֹא־מָשׁוּ מִקֶּרֶב הַמַּחֲנֶה:
מה וַיֵּרֶד הָעֲמָלֵקִי וְהַכְּנַעֲנִי הַיֹּשֵׁב בָּהָר הַהוּא וַיַּכּוּם וַיַּכְּתוּם עַד־הַחָרְמָה:
טו א ב וַיְדַבֵּר יְהוָה אֶל־מֹשֶׁה לֵּאמֹר: דַּבֵּר אֶל־בְּנֵי יִשְׂרָאֵל וְאָמַרְתָּ אֲלֵהֶם יד
ג כִּי תָבֹאוּ אֶל־אֶרֶץ מוֹשְׁבֹתֵיכֶם אֲשֶׁר אֲנִי נֹתֵן לָכֶם: וַעֲשִׂיתֶם אִשֶּׁה
לַיהוָה עֹלָה אוֹ־זֶבַח לְפַלֵּא־נֶדֶר אוֹ בִנְדָבָה אוֹ בְּמֹעֲדֵיכֶם לַעֲשׂוֹת
ד רֵיחַ נִיחֹחַ לַיהוָה מִן־הַבָּקָר אוֹ מִן־הַצֹּאן: וְהִקְרִיב הַמַּקְרִיב קָרְבָּנוֹ
ה לַיהוָה מִנְחָה סֹלֶת עִשָּׂרוֹן בָּלוּל בִּרְבִעִית הַהִין שָׁמֶן: וְיַיִן לַנֶּסֶךְ

אונקלוס

דַּאֲמַר יי אֲרֵי חַבְנָא: מא וַאֲמַר מֹשֶׁה, לְמָא דְנַן, אַתּוּן עָבְרִין עַל גְּזֵירַת מֵימְרָא דַיי, וְהִיא לָא תַצְלַח: מב לָא תִסְּקוּן, אֲרֵי, לֵית שְׁכִינְתָא דַיי בֵּינֵיכוֹן, וְלָא תִתַּבְרוּן, קֳדָם בַּעֲלֵי דְבָבֵיכוֹן: מג אֲרֵי עֲמַלְקָאָה וּכְנַעֲנָאָה תַּמָּן קֳדָמֵיכוֹן, וְתִפְּלוּן בְּחַרְבָּא, אֲרֵי עַל כֵּן תַּבְתּוּן מִבָּתַר פָּלְחָנָא דַיי, וְלָא יְהֵי מֵימְרָא דַיי בְּסַעְדְּכוֹן: מד וְאַרְשַׁעוּ, לְמִסַּק לְרֵישׁ טוּרָא, וַאֲרוֹן קְיָמָא דַיי וּמֹשֶׁה, לָא עֲדוֹ מִגּוֹ מַשְׁרִיתָא: מה וּנְחַת עֲמַלְקָאָה וּכְנַעֲנָאָה, דְּיָתֵיב בְּטוּרָא הַהוּא, וּמְחוֹנוּן וּטְרָדוּנוּן עַד חָרְמָה: טו א וּמַלֵּיל יי עִם מֹשֶׁה לְמֵימַר: ב מַלֵּיל עִם בְּנֵי יִשְׂרָאֵל, וְתֵימַר לְהוֹן, אֲרֵי תֵיעֲלוּן, לְאַרַע מוֹתְבָנֵיכוֹן, דַּאֲנָא יָהֵיב לְכוֹן: ג וְתַעְבְּדוּן קֻרְבָּנָא קֳדָם יי עֲלָתָא אוֹ נִכְסַת קֻדְשַׁיָּא, לְפָרָשָׁא נִדְרָא אוֹ בִנְדַבְתָּא, אוֹ בְּמוֹעֲדֵיכוֹן, לְמֶעְבַּד, לְאִתְקַבָּלָא בְרַעֲוָא קֳדָם יי, מִן תּוֹרֵי אוֹ מִן עָנָא: ד וִיקָרֵיב, דִּמְקָרֵיב קֻרְבָּנֵיהּ קֳדָם יי, מִנְחָתָא סֻלְתָּא עֶסְרוֹנָא, דְּפִיל, בִּרְבַעוּת הִינָא מִשְׁחָא: ה וְחַמְרָא לְנִסְכָּא

14:41 וְהִוא לֹא תִצְלָח *It will not work* – Many philosophers tend to cluster at the extremes: either rigidly conservative or profoundly revolutionary. The current social order is either right or wrong. If it is right, we should not change it. If it is wrong, we should overthrow it. The fact that change takes time, even many generations, is not an idea easy to square with philosophy (even those philosophers, like Hegel and Marx, who factored in time, did so mechanically, speaking about "historical inevitability" rather than the unpredictable exercise of freedom). What we see playing out in this incident, however, is what I call the chronological imagination, as opposed to the Greek logical imagination. Logic lacks the dimension of time. Narrative holds a different kind of wisdom.

One of the odd facts about Western civilization in recent centuries is that the people who have been most eloquent about tradition have been deeply conservative, defenders of the status quo. Yet there is no reason why a tradition should be conservative. We can hand on to our children not only our past but also our unrealized ideals. We can want them to go beyond us, to travel further on the road to freedom than we were able to do. That, for example, is how the Seder

6 wine as a libation for every lamb. In the case of a ram, you shall bring a grain
offering of two-tenths of a measure of fine flour mixed with a third of a hin
7 of oil. You shall also offer a third of a hin of wine as a libation, for a pleasing
8 aroma to the LORD. If, however, you offer an animal from the herd as a burnt HAMISHI
offering or as a sacrifice to fulfill a spoken vow, or as a peace offering to the
9 LORD, then you shall bring with each animal a grain offering of three-tenths
10 of a measure of fine flour mixed with half a hin of oil. You shall also offer half a
11 hin of wine as a libation; it is a fire offering, a pleasing aroma to the LORD. So
12 shall it be with each ox, each ram, and with any sheep or goat. However many
13 you offer, you shall do the same for each. Every native-born person, presenting
a fire offering as a pleasing aroma to the LORD, shall perform them in this way.
14 And whensoever, through the generations, a migrant joins you or lives among
you, and he too prepares a fire offering for a pleasing aroma to the LORD, he
15 shall do just as you do. There shall be one law for the congregation: as for you,
so for any migrant. It shall be an eternal decree throughout the generations:
16 you and the migrant shall be the same before the LORD. One law and one rule
for you and for the migrant who lives among you."
17 18 The LORD spoke to Moshe: "Speak to the Israelites. Say: When you come to SHISHI
19 the land to which I am bringing you, and eat the bread of the land, you shall set

רש״י

ה **לַכֶּבֶשׂ הָאֶחָד.** עַל כָּל הָאָמוּר לְמַעְלָה הוּא מוּסָב, עַל הַמִּנְחָה וְעַל הַשֶּׁמֶן וְעַל הַיַּיִן:

ו **אוֹ לָאַיִל.** וְאִם אַיִל הוּא. וְרַבּוֹתֵינוּ דָּרְשׁוּ: "אוֹ" לְרַבּוֹת אֶת הַפַּלְגָּס לִנְסָכֵי אַיִל:

י **אִשֵּׁה רֵיחַ.** אֵינוֹ מוּסָב אֶלָּא עַל הַמִּנְחָה וְהַשֶּׁמֶן, אֲבָל הַיַּיִן אֵינוֹ אִשֶּׁה, שֶׁאֵינוֹ נִתָּן עַל הָאֵשׁ:

יא **אוֹ לַשֶּׂה.** בֵּין שֶׁהוּא בַּכְּבָשִׂים בֵּין שֶׁהוּא בָּעִזִּים. 'כֶּבֶשׂ' וָ'שֶׂה' קְרוּיִם בְּתוֹךְ שְׁנָתָם, 'אַיִל' בֶּן שְׁלֹשָׁה עָשָׂר חֹדֶשׁ וְיוֹם אֶחָד:

יב **כַּמִּסְפָּר אֲשֶׁר תַּעֲשׂוּ.** כְּמִסְפַּר הַבְּהֵמוֹת אֲשֶׁר תַּקְרִיבוּ לְקָרְבָּן, כָּכָה תַּעֲשׂוּ נְסָכִים לְכָל אֶחָד מֵהֶם, כְּמִסְפָּרָם שֶׁל בְּהֵמוֹת מִסְפָּרָם שֶׁל נְסָכִים:

טו **כָּכֶם כַּגֵּר.** כְּמוֹתְכֶם כֵּן גֵּר, וְכֵן דֶּרֶךְ לָשׁוֹן עִבְרִית: "כְּגַן ה' כְּאֶרֶץ מִצְרַיִם" (בראשית יג, י) כֵּן אֶרֶץ מִצְרַיִם, "כָּמוֹנִי כָמוֹךָ כְּעַמִּי כְעַמֶּךָ" (מלכים א' כב, ד):

יח **בְּבֹאֲכֶם אֶל הָאָרֶץ.** מְשֻׁנָּה בִּיאָה זוֹ מִכָּל בִּיאוֹת שֶׁבַּתּוֹרָה, שֶׁבְּכֻלָּן נֶאֱמַר: "כִּי תָבֹא" "כִּי תָבֹאוּ", לְפִיכָךְ כֻּלָּן לְמֵדוֹת זוֹ מִזּוֹ, וְכֵיוָן שֶׁפֵּרַט לְךָ הַכָּתוּב בְּאַחַת מֵהֶן שֶׁאֵינָהּ אֶלָּא לְאַחַר יְרֻשָּׁה וִישִׁיבָה, אַף כֻּלָּן כֵּן. אֲבָל זוֹ נֶאֱמַר בָּהּ: "בְּבֹאֲכֶם", מִשֶּׁנִּכְנְסוּ בָהּ וְאָכְלוּ מִלַּחְמָהּ נִתְחַיְּבוּ בַחַלָּה:

been less intelligible to them than the principle that "there shall be one law for the congregation: as for you, so for any migrant.… You and the migrant shall be the same before the LORD." This is part of Israel's moral struggle against tribalism and its modern successor, xenophobic nationalism. Strangers, too, have rights and make a legitimate claim on our humanity, for we are all strangers to someone else. This is something Israel is expected not merely to know abstractly but to feel in the deepest recesses of its collective memory. "You yourselves were strangers in the land of Egypt" (Lev. 19:34).

רְבִיעִ֥ית הַהִ֖ין תַּעֲשֶׂ֣ה עַל־הָעֹלָ֑ה א֣וֹ לַזָּ֔בַח לַכֶּ֖בֶשׂ הָאֶחָֽד׃ א֤וֹ לָאַ֙יִל֙
ו תַּעֲשֶׂ֣ה מִנְחָ֔ה סֹ֖לֶת שְׁנֵ֣י עֶשְׂרֹנִ֑ים בְּלוּלָ֥ה בַשֶּׁ֖מֶן שְׁלִשִׁ֥ית הַהִֽין׃ וְיַ֥יִן
ז לַנֶּ֖סֶךְ שְׁלִשִׁ֣ית הַהִ֑ין תַּקְרִ֥יב רֵֽיחַ־נִיחֹ֖חַ לַֽיהוָֽה׃ וְכִֽי־תַעֲשֶׂ֥ה בֶן־בָּקָ֖ר חמישי
ח עֹלָ֣ה אוֹ־זָ֑בַח לְפַלֵּא־נֶ֛דֶר אֽוֹ־שְׁלָמִ֖ים לַֽיהוָֽה׃ וְהִקְרִ֤יב עַל־בֶּן־הַבָּקָר֙
ט מִנְחָ֔ה סֹ֖לֶת שְׁלֹשָׁ֣ה עֶשְׂרֹנִ֑ים בָּל֥וּל בַּשֶּׁ֖מֶן חֲצִ֥י הַהִֽין׃ וְיַ֛יִן תַּקְרִ֥יב לַנֶּ֖סֶךְ
י חֲצִ֣י הַהִ֑ין אִשֵּׁ֥ה רֵֽיחַ־נִיחֹ֖חַ לַֽיהוָֽה׃ כָּ֣כָה יֵעָשֶׂ֗ה לַשּׁוֹר֙ הָֽאֶחָ֔ד א֖וֹ לָאַ֣יִל
יא הָאֶחָ֑ד אֽוֹ־לַשֶּׂ֥ה בַכְּבָשִׂ֖ים א֥וֹ בָעִזִּֽים׃ כַּמִּסְפָּ֖ר אֲשֶׁ֣ר תַּעֲשׂ֑וּ כָּ֛כָה תַּעֲשׂ֥וּ
יב לָאֶחָ֖ד כְּמִסְפָּרָֽם׃ כָּל־הָאֶזְרָ֥ח יַעֲשֶׂה־כָּ֖כָה אֶת־אֵ֑לֶּה לְהַקְרִ֛יב אִשֵּׁ֥ה
יג רֵֽיחַ־נִיחֹ֖חַ לַֽיהוָֽה׃ וְכִֽי־יָג֨וּר אִתְּכֶ֜ם גֵּ֣ר א֤וֹ אֲשֶֽׁר־בְּתֽוֹכְכֶם֙ לְדֹרֹ֣תֵיכֶ֔ם
יד וְעָשָׂ֛ה אִשֵּׁ֥ה רֵֽיחַ־נִיחֹ֖חַ לַֽיהוָ֑ה כַּאֲשֶׁ֥ר תַּעֲשׂ֖וּ כֵּ֥ן יַעֲשֶֽׂה׃ הַקָּהָ֕ל חֻקָּ֥ה
אַחַ֛ת לָכֶ֖ם וְלַגֵּ֣ר הַגָּ֑ר חֻקַּ֤ת עוֹלָם֙ לְדֹרֹ֣תֵיכֶ֔ם כָּכֶ֛ם כַּגֵּ֥ר יִהְיֶ֖ה לִפְנֵ֥י יְהוָֽה׃
טו תּוֹרָ֥ה אַחַ֛ת וּמִשְׁפָּ֥ט אֶחָ֖ד יִהְיֶ֣ה לָכֶ֑ם וְלַגֵּ֖ר הַגָּ֥ר אִתְּכֶֽם׃
טז יז וַיְדַבֵּ֥ר יְהוָ֖ה אֶל־מֹשֶׁ֥ה לֵּאמֹֽר׃ דַּבֵּר֙ אֶל־בְּנֵ֣י יִשְׂרָאֵ֔ל וְאָמַרְתָּ֖ אֲלֵהֶ֑ם ששי
יח בְּבֹאֲכֶם֙ אֶל־הָאָ֔רֶץ אֲשֶׁ֥ר אֲנִ֛י מֵבִ֥יא אֶתְכֶ֖ם שָֽׁמָּה׃ וְהָיָ֕ה בַּאֲכָלְכֶ֖ם

אונקלוס

רִבְעוּת הִינָא, תַּעֲבֵיד עַל עֲלָתָא אוֹ לְנִכְסַת קֻדְשַׁיָּא, לְאִמְּרָא חַד: ו אוֹ לְדִכְרָא תַּעֲבֵיד מִנְחָתָא, סֻלְתָּא תְּרֵין עֶסְרוֹנִין, דְּפִילָא בִּמְשַׁח תַּלְתּוּת הִינָא: ז וְחַמְרָא לְנִסְכָּא תַּלְתּוּת הִינָא, תְּקָרֵיב לְאִתְקַבָּלָא בְּרַעֲוָא קֳדָם יְיָ: ח וַאֲרֵי תַעֲבֵיד בַּר תּוֹרֵי עֲלָתָא אוֹ נִכְסַת קֻדְשַׁיָּא, לְפָרָשָׁא נִדְרָא אוֹ נִכְסַת קֻדְשַׁיָּא קֳדָם יְיָ: ט וִיקָרֵיב עַל בַּר תּוֹרֵי מִנְחָתָא, סֻלְתָּא תְּלָתָא עֶסְרוֹנִין, דְּפִיל בִּמְשַׁח פַּלְגוּת הִינָא: י וְחַמְרָא, תְּקָרֵיב לְנִסְכָּא פַּלְגוּת הִינָא, לְאִתְקַבָּלָא בְרַעֲוָא קֳדָם יְיָ: יא כְּדֵין יִתְעֲבֵיד, לְתוֹרָא חַד, אוֹ לְדִכְרָא חַד, אוֹ לְאִמַּר בְּאִמְּרַיָּא אוֹ בְעִזַּיָּא: יב כְּמִנְיָן דְּתַעְבְּדוּן, כְּדֵין, תַּעְבְּדוּן לְחַד כְּמִנְיָנֵיהוֹן: יג כָּל יַצִּיבָא יַעֲבֵיד כְּדֵין יָת אִלֵּין, לְקָרָבָא, קֻרְבַּן דְּמִתְקַבַּל בְּרַעֲוָא קֳדָם יְיָ: יד וַאֲרֵי יִתְגַּיַּר עִמְּכוֹן גִּיּוֹרָא, אוֹ דְבֵינֵיכוֹן לְדָרֵיכוֹן, וְיַעֲבֵיד, קֻרְבַּן דְּמִתְקַבַּל בְּרַעֲוָא קֳדָם יְיָ, כְּמָא דְתַעְבְּדוּן כֵּן יַעֲבֵיד: טו קְהָלָא, קְיָמָא חַד, לְכוֹן וּלְגִיּוֹרַיָּא דְּיִתְגַּיְּרוּן, קְיָם עָלַם לְדָרֵיכוֹן, כְּוָתְכוֹן, גִּיּוֹרָא יְהֵי קֳדָם יְיָ: טז אוֹרָיְתָא חֲדָא, וְדִינָא חַד יְהֵי לְכוֹן, וּלְגִיּוֹרַיָּא דְּיִתְגַּיְּרוּן עִמְּכוֹן: יז וּמַלֵּיל יְיָ עִם מֹשֶׁה לְמֵימַר: יח מַלֵּיל עִם בְּנֵי יִשְׂרָאֵל, וְתֵימַר לְהוֹן, בְּמֵיעַלְכוֹן לְאַרְעָא, דַּאֲנָא, מַעֵיל יָתְכוֹן לְתַמָּן: יט וִיהֵי,

15:15 כָּכֶם כַּגֵּר יִהְיֶה לִפְנֵי יהוה *You and the migrant shall be the same before the* LORD – The Mosaic books never tire of this theme (see, for instance, Ex. 22:20 and the note there). For the ancient world generally, even for Plato and Aristotle, strangers were aliens, beyond the radius of concern, unentitled to civil rights or citizenship. Few things would have

20 some aside as an offering to the LORD. As the first portion of your kneading,
you shall set aside a loaf as an offering, like the offering you present from the
21 threshing floor. You shall present to the LORD an offering from the first of your
22 kneading throughout your generations. If, without intention, you
fail to perform any of these commandments that the LORD gave to Moshe,
23 anything that the LORD has commanded you through Moshe from the day
24 the LORD commanded it and onward – in all generations to come – if it is
done unintentionally by the community, the entire community must offer one
bull from the herd as a burnt offering, a pleasing aroma to the LORD, with its
prescribed grain offering and libation, and one goat as a purification offering.
25 The priest shall then make atonement for all the community of Israel and they
will be forgiven, because it was an accidental failing, and because they brought
their sacrifice, a fire offering to the LORD and the purification offering for their
26 error before the LORD. The community of Israel and the migrants living among
27 them will all be forgiven, because all the people acted in error. If it is SHEVI'I
an individual who sins inadvertently, he shall offer a year-old female goat as a
28 purification offering. The priest shall make atonement before the LORD for the
person who sinned inadvertently, to atone for his sin, and he will be forgiven.
29 There shall be one law for one who inadvertently commits a sin, whether he is

רש״י

כ| **רֵאשִׁית עֲרִסֹתֵכֶם.** כְּשֶׁתָּלוּשׁוּ כְּדֵי עֲרִיסוֹתֵיכֶם שֶׁאַתֶּם רְגִילִין לָלוּשׁ בַּמִּדְבָּר, וְכַמָּה הִיא? ״וַיָּמֹדּוּ בָעֹמֶר״ (שמות טז, יח), ״עֹמֶר לַגֻּלְגֹּלֶת״ (שם פסוק טז), תָּרִימוּ מֵרֵאשִׁיתָהּ, כְּלוֹמַר, קֹדֶם שֶׁתֹּאכְלוּ מִמֶּנָּה, רֵאשִׁית חֶלְקָהּ חַלָּה אַחַת מִמֶּנָּה ״תָּרִימוּ תְרוּמָה״ לְשֵׁם ה׳: **חַלָּה.** טורטי״ל בְּלַעַז: **כִּתְרוּמַת גֹּרֶן.** שֶׁלֹּא נֶאֱמַר בָּהּ שִׁעוּר, וְלֹא כִּתְרוּמַת מַעֲשֵׂר שֶׁנֶּאֱמַר בָּהּ שִׁעוּר. אֲבָל חֲכָמִים נָתְנוּ שִׁעוּר, לְבַעַל הַבַּיִת אֶחָד מֵעֶשְׂרִים וְאַרְבָּעָה, וְלַנַּחְתּוֹם אֶחָד מֵאַרְבָּעִים וּשְׁמוֹנָה:

כא| **מֵרֵאשִׁית עֲרִסֹתֵיכֶם.** לָמָּה נֶאֱמַר? לְפִי שֶׁנֶּאֱמַר: ״רֵאשִׁית עֲרִסֹתֵכֶם״ (לעיל פסוק כ), שׁוֹמֵעַ אֲנִי רִאשׁוֹנָה שֶׁבָּעִסּוֹת? תַּלְמוּד לוֹמַר: ״מֵרֵאשִׁית״, מִקְצָתָהּ וְלֹא כֻּלָּהּ: **תִּתְּנוּ לַה׳ תְּרוּמָה.** לְפִי שֶׁלֹּא שָׁמַעְנוּ שִׁעוּר לְחַלָּה נֶאֱמַר: ״תִּתְּנוּ״, שֶׁיְּהֵא בָּהּ כְּדֵי נְתִינָה:

כב| **וְכִי תִשְׁגּוּ וְלֹא תַעֲשׂוּ.** עֲבוֹדָה זָרָה הָיְתָה בִּכְלַל כָּל הַמִּצְוֹת שֶׁהַצִּבּוּר מְבִיאִין עָלֶיהָ פַּר, וַהֲרֵי הַכָּתוּב מוֹצִיאָהּ כָּאן מִכְּלָלָהּ לָדוּן בְּפַר לְעוֹלָה וְשָׂעִיר לְחַטָּאת: **וְכִי תִשְׁגּוּ וְגוֹ׳.** בַּעֲבוֹדָה זָרָה הַכָּתוּב מְדַבֵּר, אוֹ אֵינוֹ אֶלָּא בְּאַחַת מִכָּל הַמִּצְוֹת? תַּלְמוּד לוֹמַר: ״אֵת כָּל הַמִּצְוֹת הָאֵלֶּה״, מִצְוָה אַחַת שֶׁהִיא כְּכָל הַמִּצְוֹת. מַה הָעוֹבֵר עַל כָּל הַמִּצְוֹת פּוֹרֵק עֹל וּמֵפֵר בְּרִית וּמְגַלֶּה פָנִים, אַף מִצְוָה זוֹ פּוֹרֵק בָּהּ עֹל וּמֵפֵר בְּרִית וּמְגַלֶּה פָּנִים, וְאֵיזוֹ זוֹ? זוֹ עֲבוֹדָה זָרָה: **אֲשֶׁר דִּבֶּר ה׳ אֶל מֹשֶׁה.** ״אָנֹכִי״ וְ״לֹא יִהְיֶה לְךָ״ מִפִּי הַגְּבוּרָה שְׁמַעְנוּם. ״אַחַת דִּבֶּר אֱלֹהִים שְׁתַּיִם זוּ שָׁמָעְתִּי״ (תהלים סב, יב):

כג| **אֵת כָּל אֲשֶׁר צִוָּה וְגוֹ׳.** מַגִּיד שֶׁכָּל הַמּוֹדֶה בַּעֲבוֹדָה זָרָה כְּכוֹפֵר בְּכָל הַתּוֹרָה כֻּלָּהּ וּבְכָל מַה שֶּׁנִּתְנַבְּאוּ הַנְּבִיאִים, שֶׁנֶּאֱמַר: ״מִן הַיּוֹם אֲשֶׁר צִוָּה ה׳ וָהָלְאָה״:

כד| **אִם מֵעֵינֵי הָעֵדָה נֶעֶשְׂתָה לִשְׁגָגָה.** אִם מֵעֵינֵי הָעֵדָה נֶעֶשְׂתָה עֲבֵרָה זוֹ עַל יְדֵי שׁוֹגֵג, כְּגוֹן שֶׁשָּׁגְגוּ וְהוֹרוּ עַל אַחַת מִן הָעֲבוֹדוֹת שֶׁהִיא מֻתֶּרֶת לַעֲבֹד עֲבוֹדָה זָרָה בְּכָךְ: **לְחַטָּת.** חָסֵר אָלֶ״ף, שֶׁאֵינוֹ כִּשְׁאָר חַטָּאוֹת, שֶׁכָּל חַטָּאוֹת שֶׁבַּתּוֹרָה הַבָּאוֹת עִם עוֹלָה, הַחַטָּאת קוֹדֶמֶת לָעוֹלָה, שֶׁנֶּאֱמַר: ״וְאֶת הַשֵּׁנִי יַעֲשֶׂה עֹלָה״ (ויקרא ה, י), וְזוֹ עוֹלָה קוֹדֶמֶת לְחַטָּאת:

כה| **הֵבִיאוּ אֶת קָרְבָּנָם אִשֶּׁה לַה׳.** זֶה הָאָמוּר בַּפָּרָשָׁה, הוּא פַּר הָעוֹלָה, שֶׁנֶּאֱמַר: ״אִשֶּׁה לַה׳״: **וְחַטָּאתָם.** זֶה הַשָּׂעִיר:

כז| **תֶּחֱטָא בִשְׁגָגָה.** בַּעֲבוֹדָה זָרָה: **עֵז בַּת שְׁנָתָהּ.** שְׁאָר עֲבֵרוֹת יָחִיד מֵבִיא כִּשְׂבָּה אוֹ שְׂעִירָה, וּבְזוֹ קָבַע לָהּ שְׂעִירָה:

כ מִלֶּחֶם הָאָרֶץ תָּרִימוּ תְרוּמָה לַיהוָה׃ רֵאשִׁית עֲרִסֹתֵכֶם חַלָּה תָּרִימוּ
כא תְרוּמָה כִּתְרוּמַת גֹּרֶן כֵּן תָּרִימוּ אֹתָהּ׃ מֵרֵאשִׁית עֲרִסֹתֵיכֶם תִּתְּנוּ
כב לַיהוָה תְּרוּמָה לְדֹרֹתֵיכֶם׃ וְכִי תִשְׁגּוּ וְלֹא תַעֲשׂוּ אֵת
כג כָּל־הַמִּצְוֺת הָאֵלֶּה אֲשֶׁר־דִּבֶּר יְהוָה אֶל־מֹשֶׁה׃ אֵת כָּל־אֲשֶׁר צִוָּה
יְהוָה אֲלֵיכֶם בְּיַד־מֹשֶׁה מִן־הַיּוֹם אֲשֶׁר צִוָּה יְהוָה וָהָלְאָה לְדֹרֹתֵיכֶם׃
כד וְהָיָה אִם מֵעֵינֵי הָעֵדָה נֶעֶשְׂתָה לִשְׁגָגָה וְעָשׂוּ כָל־הָעֵדָה פַּר בֶּן־בָּקָר
אֶחָד לְעֹלָה לְרֵיחַ נִיחֹחַ לַיהוָה וּמִנְחָתוֹ וְנִסְכּוֹ כַּמִּשְׁפָּט וּשְׂעִיר־עִזִּים
כה אֶחָד לְחַטָּת׃ וְכִפֶּר הַכֹּהֵן עַל־כָּל־עֲדַת בְּנֵי יִשְׂרָאֵל וְנִסְלַח לָהֶם
כִּי־שְׁגָגָה הִוא וְהֵם הֵבִיאוּ אֶת־קָרְבָּנָם אִשֶּׁה לַיהוָה וְחַטָּאתָם לִפְנֵי
כו יְהוָה עַל־שִׁגְגָתָם׃ וְנִסְלַח לְכָל־עֲדַת בְּנֵי יִשְׂרָאֵל וְלַגֵּר הַגָּר בְּתוֹכָם
כז כִּי לְכָל־הָעָם בִּשְׁגָגָה׃ וְאִם־נֶפֶשׁ אַחַת תֶּחֱטָא בִשְׁגָגָה שביעי
כח וְהִקְרִיבָה עֵז בַּת־שְׁנָתָהּ לְחַטָּאת׃ וְכִפֶּר הַכֹּהֵן עַל־הַנֶּפֶשׁ הַשֹּׁגֶגֶת
כט בְּחֶטְאָה בִשְׁגָגָה לִפְנֵי יְהוָה לְכַפֵּר עָלָיו וְנִסְלַח לוֹ׃ הָאֶזְרָח בִּבְנֵי

אונקלוס

בְּמֵיכַלְכוֹן מִלַּחְמָא דְּאַרְעָא, תַּפְרְשׁוּן אַפְרָשׁוּתָא קֳדָם יי: כ רֵישׁ אֲצְוָתְכוֹן, חַלְּתָא תַּפְרְשׁוּן אַפְרָשׁוּתָא, כְּמָא דְּמַפְרְשִׁין מִן אִדְּרָא, כֵּן תַּפְרְשׁוּן יָתַהּ: כא מֵרֵישׁ אֲצְוָתְכוֹן, תִּתְּנוּן קֳדָם יי אַפְרָשׁוּתָא, לְדָרֵיכוֹן: כב וַאֲרֵי תִשְׁתְּלוּן, וְלָא תַעְבְּדוּן, יָת כָּל פִּקּוֹדַיָּא הָאִלֵּין, דְּמַלֵּיל יי עִם מֹשֶׁה: כג יָת כָּל דְּפַקֵּיד יי, לְכוֹן בִּידָא דְּמֹשֶׁה, מִן יוֹמָא, דְּפַקֵּיד יי, וּלְהַלְאָה לְדָרֵיכוֹן: כד וִיהֵי, אִם מֵעֵינֵי כְנִשְׁתָּא אִתְעֲבֵידַת לְשָׁלוּ, וְיַעְבְּדוּן כָּל כְּנִשְׁתָּא, תּוֹר בַּר תּוֹרֵי חַד לַעֲלָתָא, לְאִתְקַבָּלָא בְרַעֲוָא קֳדָם יי, וּמִנְחָתֵיהּ וְנִסְכֵּיהּ כִּדְחָזֵי, וּצְפִיר בַּר עִזִּין חַד לְחַטָּתָא: כה וִיכַפַּר כָּהֲנָא, עַל כָּל כְּנִשְׁתָּא, דִּבְנֵי יִשְׂרָאֵל וְיִשְׁתְּבֵיק לְהוֹן, אֲרֵי שָׁלוּתָא הִיא, וְאִנּוּן אֵיתִיאוּ יָת קֻרְבָּנְהוֹן קֻרְבָּנָא קֳדָם יי, וְחוֹבַתְהוֹן, קֳדָם יי עַל שָׁלוּתְהוֹן: כו וְיִשְׁתְּבֵיק, לְכָל כְּנִשְׁתָּא דִּבְנֵי יִשְׂרָאֵל, וּלְגִיּוֹרַיָּא דְּיִתְגַּיְּרוּן בֵּינֵיהוֹן, אֲרֵי לְכָל עַמָּא בְּשָׁלוּתָא: כז וְאִם אֱנָשׁ חַד יְחוּב בְּשָׁלוּ, וִיקָרֵיב, עִזָּא בַּת שַׁתַּהּ לְחַטָּתָא: כח וִיכַפַּר כָּהֲנָא, עַל אֱנָשׁ דְּאִשְׁתְּלִי, בְּמֵיחֲבֵיהּ בְּשָׁלוּ קֳדָם יי, לְכַפָּרָא עֲלוֹהִי וְיִשְׁתְּבֵיק לֵיהּ: כט יַצִּיבָא בִּבְנֵי

15:26 כִּי לְכָל־הָעָם בִּשְׁגָגָה *Because all the people acted in error* – This verse, which today is part of the *Kol Nidrei* liturgy, is interpreted by the Sages to signal two things for the generations: (1) that we can come together as a community to seek forgiveness, and (2) that through repentance, even deliberate sins come to be regarded as unintentional ones (Yoma 86b) and can thus be forgiven. The importance of the first is that we should never rely on our own personal merits. Judaism is the faith of a people and its communities, not just of individuals in their private lives. The second reminds us that by expressing remorse for the past, we may not cancel the wrong we have done but we revoke the intention with which we did it.

30 a native-born Israelite or a migrant living among them. However, if a person
commits a sin high-handedly, whether he is native born or a migrant, he reviles
31 the LORD and shall be severed from the people. Because he despises the LORD's
word and violates His commandments, he will be severed utterly and must
bear his guilt."
32 When the Israelites were in the wilderness, they encountered a man gathering
33 wood on the Sabbath. Those who found him gathering wood brought him
34 before Moshe and Aharon, and before the whole community, and he was
placed in custody, because it had not been specified what should be done to
35 him. And the LORD said to Moshe, "The man shall be put to death.
36 The whole community must stone him outside the camp." And so, as the LORD
had commanded Moshe, the whole community took him outside the camp
and stoned him to death.
37 38 The LORD said to Moshe: "Speak to the Israelites; tell them to make fringes MAFTIR
on the corners of their garments throughout the generations. To the fringe

רש״י

ל **בְּיָד רָמָה.** בְּמֵזִיד: **מְגַדֵּף.** מְחָרֵף, כְּמוֹ: ״וְהָיְתָה חֶרְפָּה וּגְדוּפָה״ (יחזקאל ה, טו), ״חֲשֶׁר גִּדְּפוּ נַעֲרֵי מֶלֶךְ חַשּׁוּר״ (ישעיה לז, ו). וְעוֹד דָּרְשׁוּ רַבּוֹתֵינוּ, מִכָּחן לַמְּבָרֵךְ חֶת הַשֵּׁם שֶׁהוּח בְּכָרֵת:

לא **דְּבַר ה׳.** חַזְהָרַת עֲבוֹדָה זָרָה מִפִּי הַגְּבוּרָה, וְהַשְּׁחָר מִפִּי מֹשֶׁה: **עֲוֹנָה בָהּ.** בִּזְמַן שֶׁעֲוֹנָהּ בָּהּ, שֶׁלֹּח עָשָׂה תְּשׁוּבָה:

לב **וַיִּהְיוּ בְנֵי יִשְׂרָאֵל בַּמִּדְבָּר וַיִּמְצְאוּ.** בִּגְנוּתָן שֶׁל יִשְׂרָחֵל דִּבֵּר הַכָּתוּב, שֶׁלֹּח שָׁמְרוּ חֶלָּח שַׁבָּת רִחשׁוֹנָה, וּבַשְּׁנִיָּה בָּח זֶה וְחִלְּלָהּ:

לג **הַמֹּצְאִים אֹתוֹ מְקֹשֵׁשׁ.** שֶׁהִתְרוּ בוֹ, וְלֹח הִנִּיחַ מִלְּקוֹשֵׁשׁ חַף מִשֶּׁמְּנָחוּהוּ וְהִתְרוּ בוֹ:

לד **כִּי לֹא פֹרַשׁ מַה יֵּעָשֶׂה לוֹ.** לֹח הָיוּ יוֹדְעִים בְּחֵיזוֹ מִיתָה יָמוּת, חֲבָל יוֹדְעִים הָיוּ שֶׁהַמְחַלֵּל שַׁבָּת בְּמִיתָה:

לה **רָגוֹם.** עָשֹׂה, פייסנ״ט בְּלַעַז, וְכֵן: ״הָלוֹךְ״ חלנ״ט, וְכֵן: ״זָכוֹר״ (שמות כ, ח) וְ״שָׁמוֹר״ (דברים ה, יב):

לו **וַיֹּצִיאוּ אֹתוֹ.** מִכָּחן שֶׁבֵּית הַסְּקִילָה חוּץ וְרָחוֹק מִבֵּית דִּין:

pariah image that antisemitism seemed to impose. The Sabbath created the coherence of the religious community. It also, perhaps, was decisive in preserving the attitudes which made the Jews so adaptable and socially mobile. It was, if you like, the insertion into the world of an alternative identity, in which the white tablecloth, the silver candlesticks, the leisurely meals, the assembled family, enacted rather than symbolized a freedom from the existing economic and social order.

The Sabbath still has enormous importance as "a public good," central to the shared culture of Judaism. Perhaps this is why this narrative comes to complement that of the blasphemer in Leviticus: reverence for the Sabbath, like reverence for God, protects the social fabric that unites us.

The scene of "religious coercion" and capital punishment feels foreign to Judaism at least since the time of the Mishna. Perhaps the Torah itself hints at a certain discomfort, for immediately after this story we turn to the laws of tzitzit. Part of what makes religion a force for honest and altruistic behavior is the daily remembrance that God sees what we do. Studies in social science posit that "watched people are nice people"; even a picture of eyes on the wall makes people act with more integrity and generosity. It is no coincidence that, as belief in a personal God has waned in the West, surveillance by CCTV and other means has increased. The gentle reminder of the tzitzit stands in contrast to the harsh enforcement of criminal law.

יִשְׂרָאֵל וְלַגֵּר הַגָּר בְּתוֹכָם תּוֹרָה אַחַת יִהְיֶה לָכֶם לָעֹשֶׂה בִּשְׁגָגָה׃
ל וְהַנֶּפֶשׁ אֲשֶׁר־תַּעֲשֶׂה ׀ בְּיָד רָמָה מִן־הָאֶזְרָח וּמִן־הַגֵּר אֶת־יהוה הוּא
לא מְגַדֵּף וְנִכְרְתָה הַנֶּפֶשׁ הַהִוא מִקֶּרֶב עַמָּהּ׃ כִּי דְבַר־יהוה בָּזָה וְאֶת־
מִצְוָתוֹ הֵפַר הִכָּרֵת ׀ תִּכָּרֵת הַנֶּפֶשׁ הַהִוא עֲוֺנָה בָהּ׃
לב וַיִּהְיוּ בְנֵי־יִשְׂרָאֵל בַּמִּדְבָּר וַיִּמְצְאוּ אִישׁ מְקֹשֵׁשׁ עֵצִים בְּיוֹם הַשַּׁבָּת׃
לג וַיַּקְרִיבוּ אֹתוֹ הַמֹּצְאִים אֹתוֹ מְקֹשֵׁשׁ עֵצִים אֶל־מֹשֶׁה וְאֶל־אַהֲרֹן
לד וְאֶל כָּל־הָעֵדָה׃ וַיַּנִּיחוּ אֹתוֹ בַּמִּשְׁמָר כִּי לֹא פֹרַשׁ מַה־יֵּעָשֶׂה
לה לוֹ׃ וַיֹּאמֶר יהוה אֶל־מֹשֶׁה מוֹת יוּמַת הָאִישׁ רָגוֹם
לו אֹתוֹ בָאֲבָנִים כָּל־הָעֵדָה מִחוּץ לַמַּחֲנֶה׃ וַיֹּצִיאוּ אֹתוֹ כָּל־הָעֵדָה
אֶל־מִחוּץ לַמַּחֲנֶה וַיִּרְגְּמוּ אֹתוֹ בָּאֲבָנִים וַיָּמֹת כַּאֲשֶׁר צִוָּה יהוה אֶת־
מֹשֶׁה׃
לז לח וַיֹּאמֶר יהוה אֶל־מֹשֶׁה לֵּאמֹר׃ דַּבֵּר אֶל־בְּנֵי יִשְׂרָאֵל וְאָמַרְתָּ אֲלֵהֶם מפטיר
וְעָשׂוּ לָהֶם צִיצִת עַל־כַּנְפֵי בִגְדֵיהֶם לְדֹרֹתָם וְנָתְנוּ עַל־צִיצִת הַכָּנָף

אונקלוס

יִשְׂרָאֵל, וּלְגִיּוֹרַיָּא דְּיִתְגַּיְּרוּן בֵּינֵיהוֹן, אוֹרַיְתָא חֲדָא יְהֵי לְכוֹן, לִדְיַעֲבֵיד בְּשָׁלוּ: ל וֶאֱנָשׁ, דְּיַעֲבֵיד בְּרֵישׁ גְּלֵי, מִן יַצִּיבַיָּא וּמִן גִּיּוֹרַיָּא, קֳדָם יי הוּא מַרְגִּיז, וְיִשְׁתֵּיצֵי, אֱנָשָׁא הַהוּא מִגּוֹ עַמֵּיהּ: לא אֲרֵי עַל פִּתְגָמָא דַיי בְּסַר, וְיָת פִּקּוֹדוֹהִי אַשְׁנִי, אִשְׁתֵּיצָאָה יִשְׁתֵּיצֵי, אֱנָשָׁא הַהוּא חוֹבֵיהּ בֵּיהּ: לב וַהֲווֹ בְנֵי יִשְׂרָאֵל בְּמַדְבְּרָא, וְאַשְׁכַּחוּ, גְּבַר, כַּד מְגַבֵּיב אָעִין בְּיוֹמָא דְּשַׁבְּתָא: לג וְקָרִיבוּ יָתֵיהּ, דְּאַשְׁכַּחוּ יָתֵיהּ כַּד מְגַבֵּיב אָעִין, לְוָת מֹשֶׁה וּלְוָת אַהֲרֹן, וּלְוָת כָּל כְּנִשְׁתָּא: לד וְאַצְנְעוּ יָתֵיהּ בְּבֵית מַטְּרָא, אֲרֵי לָא אִתְפָּרַשׁ לְהוֹן, מָא דְּיַעְבְּדוּן לֵיהּ: לה וַאֲמַר יי לְמֹשֶׁה, אִתְקְטָלָא יִתְקְטִיל גַּבְרָא, רְגוּמוּ יָתֵיהּ בְּאַבְנַיָּא כָּל כְּנִשְׁתָּא, מִבָּרָא לְמַשְׁרִיתָא: לו וְאַפִּיקוּ יָתֵיהּ כָּל כְּנִשְׁתָּא, לְמִבָּרָא לְמַשְׁרִיתָא, וּרְגַמוּ יָתֵיהּ, בְּאַבְנַיָּא וּמִית, כְּמָא דְּפַקֵּיד יי יָת מֹשֶׁה: לז וַאֲמַר יי לְמֹשֶׁה לְמֵימַר: לח מַלֵּיל, עִם בְּנֵי יִשְׂרָאֵל וְתֵימַר לְהוֹן, וְיַעְבְּדוּן לְהוֹן כְּרוּסְפְּדִין, עַל כַּנְפֵי כְּסוּתְהוֹן לְדָרֵיהוֹן, וְיִתְּנוּן, עַל כְּרוּסְפַּד כַּנְפָא

15:32 אִישׁ מְקֹשֵׁשׁ עֵצִים בְּיוֹם הַשַּׁבָּת *A man gathering wood on the Sabbath* – This incident recalls the case of the blasphemer, which arose in Leviticus 24. We noted there ("The Execution of the Blasphemer") that the erosion of reverence for God in a society has implications in the social arena; hence the need for a decisive public response. What, then, is the critical social importance of the Sabbath?

The Sabbath is one of the most potent of all religious institutions. Few will disagree with Ahad Ha'am's famous judgment that "more than the Jews kept the Sabbath, the Sabbath kept the Jews." It created an alternative world in which differentiations based on work, income, or expenditure had no room in which to operate. At all times, even in those many Jewish communities that lived in grinding poverty, one saved in order to dress and eat well on the seventh day. It was impossible, on the Sabbath, to internalize the

39 on each corner they should attach a blue cord. And this shall be your fringe:
seeing it, you shall remember all the LORD's commands and keep them. You

רש"י

לח **וְעָשׂוּ לָהֶם צִיצִת.** עַל שֵׁם הַפְּתִילִים הַתְּלוּיִים בָּהּ, כְּמוֹ: "וַיִּקָּחֵנִי
בְּצִיצִת רֹאשִׁי" (יחזקאל ח, ג). דָּבָר אַחֵר, "צִיצִת" עַל שֵׁם "וּרְאִיתֶם אֹתוֹ",
כְּמוֹ "מֵצִיץ מִן הַחֲרַכִּים" (שיר השירים ב, ט): **תְּכֵלֶת.** צֶבַע יָרֹק שֶׁל חִלָּזוֹן:
לט **וּזְכַרְתֶּם אֶת כָּל מִצְוֹת ה'.** שֶׁמִּנְיַן גִּימַטְרִיָּא שֶׁל צִיצִית שֵׁשׁ מֵאוֹת,
וּשְׁמוֹנָה חוּטִים וַחֲמִשָּׁה קְשָׁרִים הֲרֵי תרי"ג: **וְלֹא תָתוּרוּ אַחֲרֵי לְבַבְכֶם.**
כְּמוֹ "מִתּוּר הָאָרֶץ" (לעיל יג, כה), הַלֵּב וְהָעֵינַיִם הֵם מְרַגְּלִים לַגּוּף,
מְסַרְסְרִים לוֹ אֶת הָעֲבֵרוֹת, הָעַיִן רוֹאָה וְהַלֵּב חוֹמֵד וְהַגּוּף עוֹשֶׂה
אֶת הָעֲבֵרוֹת:

undergarment, worn *beneath* our outer clothing throughout the day.

My teacher Rabbi Nachum Rabinovitch gave this explanation: There are two kinds of clothing. There are the clothes we wear to project an image. A king, a judge, a soldier all wear clothing that conceals the individual and instead proclaims a role, an office, a rank. Such are the clothes we wear in public when we want to create a certain impression. But there are other clothes we wear when we are alone that may convey more powerfully than anything else the kind of person we really are: the artist in his studio, the writer at his desk, the gardener tending the roses. They are not dressed to create an impression. To the contrary, these people dress as they do because of what they are, not because of what they wish to seem.

In this striking way, tzitzit represents the dual nature of Judaism. On the one hand it is a way of life that is public, communal, shared with others across the world and through the ages. We keep the Sabbath, celebrate the festivals, and observe the dietary laws in a way that has hardly varied for many centuries. That is the public face of Judaism – the tallit we wear, the cloak woven out of the 613 threads, each a command.

But there is also our inner life as people of faith. There are things we can say to God that we can say to no one else. He knows our thoughts, hopes, fears, better than we know them ourselves. We speak to Him in the privacy of the soul, and He listens. That internal conversation – the opening of our heart to the One who brought us into existence in love – is not for public show. Like the fringed undergarment, it stays hidden. But it is no less real an aspect of Jewish spirituality. The two types of fringed garments represent the two dimensions of the life of faith – the outer persona and the inner person, the image we present to the world and the face we show only to God.

15:39 **וּזְכַרְתֶּם** *You shall remember* – Wittgenstein once said that "the work of the philosopher consists in assembling reminders for a particular purpose" (*Philosophical Investigations*). In the case of Judaism the purpose of the outward signs – tzitzit, mezuza, and tefillin – is precisely that: to assemble reminders, on our clothes, our homes, our arms and head, that certain things are wrong, and that even if no other human being sees us, God sees us and will call us to account.

"More devious is the heart than all else, and it is hopelessly sick. Who can know it?" said Yirmeyahu (Jer. 17:9). One of the blessings and curses of human nature is that we use our power of reason not always and only to act rationally, but also to rationalize and make excuses for the things we do, even when we know we should not have done them. The moral sense, wrote the social psychologist James Q. Wilson, "is not a strong beacon light radiating outward to illuminate in sharp outline all that it touches." It is, rather, "a small candle flame, casting vague and multiple shadows, flickering and sputtering in the strong winds of power and passion, greed and ideology." He added: "But brought close to the heart" it "dispels the darkness and warms the soul."

That, perhaps, is one of the lessons the Torah wishes us to draw from the story of the spies. Had they recalled what God had done to Egypt, the mightiest empire of the ancient world, they would not have said, "We cannot attack those people; they are stronger than we are" (Num. 13:31). But they were in the grip of fear. Strong emotion – fear especially – distorts our perception. It activates the amygdala, the source of our most primal reactions, causing it

לט פְּתִיל תְּכֵלֶת: וְהָיָה לָכֶם לְצִיצִת וּרְאִיתֶם אֹתוֹ וּזְכַרְתֶּם אֶת־כָּל־מִצְוֹת
יְהוָה וַעֲשִׂיתֶם אֹתָם וְלֹא תָתֻרוּ אַחֲרֵי לְבַבְכֶם וְאַחֲרֵי עֵינֵיכֶם אֲשֶׁר־

אונקלוס

חוּטָא דִתְכִילְתָא: לט וִיהוֹן לְכוֹן לִכְרֻסְפְּדִין, וְתִחְזוֹן יָתֵיהּ, וְתִדְכְּרוּן
יָת כָּל פִּקּוֹדַיָּא דַיי, וְתַעְבְּדוּן יָתְהוֹן, וְלָא תִטְעוֹן, בָּתַר הַרְהוֹר לִבְּכוֹן
וּבָתַר חֵיזוּ עֵינֵיכוֹן,

TZITZIT

Parashat Shelaḥ begins with the story of the spies. It ends with the laws of tzitzit, the fringes with their cord of blue to be placed on the corners of garments so the people will "remember all the Lord's commands and keep them" (Num. 15:39). This passage became the third paragraph of the *Shema*.

On the face of it, there is no connection between these bookends of the *parasha*. One is a historical incident, the other a timeless law. One concerns the fate of the nation, the other has to do with individual dress. However, a close reading reveals that the two are very much related. They are an instance of intertextuality – the interrelationship between two texts that shed light on one another. Their juxtaposition tells us something about both the narrative and the law.

Intertextuality is often signaled in the Torah by use of the same word or words in two passages. Our *parasha* never, as we noted above (ch. 14, "The Spies' Report"), uses the standard Hebrew word, based on the root *r-g-l*, that means "spy." Instead the word used is *latur*, which means not "to spy" but rather "to see," "to explore." It is this verb, in verse 39, that explains what the fringes are intended to prevent: "You shall remember all the Lord's commands and keep them. You will not then go astray (*velo taturu*), following the lusts of your heart or of your eyes."

The verbal connection is usually missed in translation. In Hebrew, however, the echo is unmistakable – *veyaturu* in the case of the spies, *velo taturu* in the case of tzitzit.

Similarly, the word *u're'item*, "and you shall see," appears only three times in the Torah, two of them in this *parasha*. The first occurs in Moshe's briefing of the spies, translated as: "See what the land is like" (13:18). The second is in the command of the tzitzit, translated as: "Seeing it, you shall remember all the Lord's commands" (15:39).

What these connections have in common is that *t-u-r* and *u're'item* are both verbs of seeing. At stake is the testimony of our eyes. The spies saw, but misunderstood what they saw, because they doubted their ability to overcome their opponents. They attributed to objective reality what was in fact subjective self-doubt. Had that been rare, the Torah would not have legislated against it. It is, however, a common and fateful error.

Rabbi Joseph B. Soloveitchik taught that *tekhelet* and *lavan*, blue and white, the two colors of the tzitzit, represent two ways of viewing and understanding the world. In Hebrew, *lavan* signifies not only the color white but also clarity, rationality, and openness. The Torah wants us to understand the world, exploring natural phenomena with the methods of science, not to live in ignorance and obscurity. *Tekhelet*, the Sages said, resembles the sea, which is like the sky, which represents the celestial throne (Sota 17a). Blue represents distance, inapproachability, the ineffable – those elements of reality that are beyond our rational understanding and control, numinous, awe-inspiring. We seek to understand what can be understood, while what lies beyond the horizon of human understanding we interpret through an act of faith.

Tzitzit is, as the Torah says, a way of remembering the commandments. But it is significantly more than this. It is a call from God to see the world through Jewish eyes. Faith does not mean seeing the world as we would like it to be. Nor is it a matter of blaming the world for not being as we would wish. Faith is the courage to see the world precisely as it is while refusing to be intimidated by it.

15:38 לְדֹרֹתָם *Throughout the generations* – In the course of time, the custom has evolved to fulfill the command of tzitzit in two quite different ways: the first, in the form of a tallit (robe, shawl) which is worn *over* our other clothes, specifically while we pray; the second, in the form of an

40 will not then go astray, following the lusts of your heart or of your eyes. This
41 is to remind you to keep all My commands, to remain holy to your God. I am
the LORD your God, who brought you out of Egypt to be your God. I am the
LORD your God."

The haftara for Parashat Shelaḥ is on page 1590.

רש״י

מא| **אני ה׳.** נאמן לשלם שכר: **אלהיכם.** נאמן להפרע: **אשר הוצאתי אתכם.** על מנת כן פדיתי אתכם שתקבלו עליכם גזרותי: **אני ה׳ אלהיכם.** עוד למה נאמר? כדי שלא יאמרו ישראל: מפני מה אמר המקום, לא שנעשה ונטול שכר? אנו לא עושים ולא נוטלים שכר! על כרחכם אני מלככם. וכן הוא אומר: "אם לא ביד חזקה... אמלוך עליכם" (יחזקאל כ, לג). דבר אחר, למה נאמר יציאת מצרים? אני הוא שהבחנתי במצרים בין טפה של בכור לשאינה של בכור, אני הוא עתיד להבחין ולהפרע מן התולה קלא אילן בבגדו ואומר: תכלת היא. ומיסודו של רבי משה הדרשן העתקתי: למה נסמכה פרשת מקושש לפרשת עבודה זרה? לומר שהמחלל את השבת כעובד עבודה זרה, שאף היא שקולה ככל המצות. וכן הוא אומר בעזרא: "ועל הר סיני ירדת..." ותתן לעמך תורה ומצות "ואת שבת קדשך הודעת להם" (נחמיה ט, יג-יד). ואף פרשת ציצית לכך נסמכה לאלו, לפי שאף היא שקולה כנגד כל המצות, שנאמר: "ועשיתם את כל מצותי" (לעיל פסוק מ): **על כנפי בגדיהם.** כנגד "ואשא אתכם על כנפי נשרים" (שמות יט, ד). על ארבע כנפות, ולא בעלת שלש ולא בעלת חמש, כנגד ארבע לשונות של גאלה שנאמרו במצרים: "והוצאתי", "והצלתי", "וגאלתי", "ולקחתי" (שמות ו, ו-ז): **פתיל תכלת.** על שם שכול בכורות, תרגומו של שכול: 'תכלא'. ומכתם היתה בלילה, וכן צבע התכלת דומה לרקיע המשחיר לעת ערב. ושמונה חוטים שבה, כנגד שמונה ימים ששהו ישראל משיצאו ממצרים עד שאמרו שירה על הים:

to learned helplessness. They see themselves as powerless to change. They are the passive victims of forces beyond their control.

Applying cognitive behavioral therapy to the story of the spies reminds us how easy it is to fall into these and other forms of cognitive distortion. The result can be depression and despair – dangerous states of mind that need immediate medical or therapeutic attention.

What I find profoundly moving is the therapy the Torah itself prescribes. We have already noted the linguistic links between the story of the spies and our passage on tzitzit (see above, "Tzitzit"). The blue thread in the tzitzit, says the Talmud (Sota 17a), is there to remind us of the sea, the sky, and God's throne of glory. *Tekhelet*, the blue itself, was in the ancient world the mark of royalty. Thus the tzitzit is itself a form of cognitive behavioral therapy, saying: "Do not be afraid. God is with you. And do not give way to your emotions, because you are royalty: you are children of the King."

Never let negative emotions distort your perceptions. You are not a grasshopper. Those who oppose you are not giants. To see the world as it is, not as you are afraid it might be, let faith banish fear.

מ אַתֶּם זֹנִים אַחֲרֵיהֶם: לְמַעַן תִּזְכְּרוּ וַעֲשִׂיתֶם אֶת־כׇּל־מִצְוֺתָי וִהְיִיתֶם
מא קְדֹשִׁים לֵאלֹהֵיכֶם: אֲנִי יהוה אֱלֹהֵיכֶם אֲשֶׁר הוֹצֵאתִי אֶתְכֶם מֵאֶרֶץ
מִצְרַיִם לִהְיוֹת לָכֶם לֵאלֹהִים אֲנִי יהוה אֱלֹהֵיכֶם:

The הפטרה *for* פרשת שלח *is on page 1591.*

אונקלוס

דְּאַתּוּן טָעַן בָּתְרֵיהוֹן: מ בְּדִיל דְּתִדְכְּרוּן, וְתַעְבְּדוּן יָת כׇּל פִּקּוֹדָי, וּתְהוֹן קַדִּישִׁין קֳדָם אֱלָהֲכוֹן: מא אֲנָא יי אֱלָהֲכוֹן, דְּאַפֵּיקִית יָתְכוֹן מֵאַרְעָא דְמִצְרַיִם, לְמֶהֱוֵי לְכוֹן לֶאֱלָהּ, אֲנָא יי אֱלָהֲכוֹן:

to override the prefrontal cortex that allows us to think rationally about the consequences of our decisions and to follow the right path.

Tzitzit, with their thread of blue, remind us of Heaven, and that is what we most need if we are consistently to act in accordance with the better angels of our nature.

15:39 אַחֲרֵי לְבַבְכֶם וְאַחֲרֵי עֵינֵיכֶם *Your heart or of your eyes* – Note the strange order of the parts of the body. Normally we would expect it to be the other way around, as Rashi says in his commentary on the verse "The eye sees and the heart desires." First we see, then we feel. But in fact the Torah reverses the order, thus anticipating the point Adam T. Beck later made in developing cognitive behavioral therapy, which is that often our feelings distort our perception. The heart determines what the eye sees. We interpret events in accordance with our feelings – often in negative ways that can be fatalistic and damaging to our self-respect. We can think ourselves into "learned helplessness."

The spies have clearly demonstrated this effect. One negative thought pattern identified by Beck is *all-or-nothing thinking*. Everything is either black or white, good or bad, easy or impossible. That was the spies' verdict on the possibility of conquest: it couldn't be done. They could have said, "It will be difficult, we will need courage and skill, but with God's help we will prevail." But they did not. Their thinking was a polarized either-or.

Another negative thought pattern is *mind-reading*. We assume we know what other people are thinking, when usually we are completely wrong because we are jumping to conclusions about them based on our own feelings, not theirs. That is what the spies did when they said, "We looked to our own eyes like grasshoppers, and *so we were in theirs*" (Num. 13:33).

A third is *blame*. In the wake of the spies' report, the people "railed against Moshe and Aharon" (14:1), as if to say, "It is all your fault. If only you had let us stay in Egypt!" People who blame others have already begun down the road

Parashat Koraḥ

16 1 Koraḥ, son of Yitzhar son of Kehat son of Levi, together with Datan and
Aviram sons of Eliav and On son of Pelet – descendants of Reuven – took
2 two hundred fifty Israelite men, leaders of the community, chosen from the

רש"י

טז א **ויקח קרח.** פרשה זו יפה נדרשת במדרש רבי תנחומא: **ויקח קרח.** לקח את עצמו לצד אחד להיות נחלק מתוך העדה לעורר על הכהנה, וזהו שתרגם אונקלוס: "ואתפליג", נחלק משאר העדה להחזיק במחלקת. וכן: "מה יקחך לבך" (איוב טו, יב), לוקח אותך להפליגך משאר בני אדם. דבר אחר, "ויקח קרח", משך ראשי סנהדראות שבהם בדברים, כמו שנאמר: "קח את אהרן" (ויקרא ח, ב), "קחו עמכם דברים" (הושע יד, ג): **בן יצהר בן קהת בן לוי.** ולא הזכיר 'בן יעקב', שבקש רחמים על עצמו שלא יזכר שמו על מחלקתם, שנאמר: "בקהלם אל תחד כבדי" (בראשית מט, ו). והיכן נזכר שמו על קרח? בהתיחסם על הדוכן בדברי הימים, שנאמר: "בן אביסף בן קרח בן יצהר בן קהת בן לוי בן ישראל" (דברי הימים א' ו, כב-כג): **ודתן ואבירם.** בשביל שהיה שבט ראובן שרוי בחנייתם תימנה, שכן לקהת ובניו החונים תימנה, נשתתפו עם קרח במחלקתו, אוי לרשע אוי לשכנו. ומה ראה קרח לחלק עם משה? נתקנא על נשיאותו של אליצפן בן עזיאל, שמנהו משה נשיא על בני קהת על פי הדבור. אמר קרח: אחי אבא ארבעה היו, שנאמר: "ובני קהת" וגו' (שמות ו, יח), עמרם הבכור נטלו שני בניו גדלה, אחד מלך ואחד כהן גדול, מי ראוי לטל את השניה? לא אני, שאני בן יצהר שהוא שני לעמרם? והוא מנה נשיא את בן אחיו הקטן מכלם! הריני חולק עליו ומבטל את דבריו. מה עשה? עמד וכנס מאתים וחמשים ראשי סנהדראות, רבן משבט ראובן שכניו, והם אליצור בן שדיאור וחבריו וכיוצא בו, שנאמר: "נשיאי עדה קראי מועד" (להלן פסוק ב), ולהלן הוא אומר: "אלה קרואי העדה" (לעיל א, טז), והלבישן טליתות שכלן תכלת, באו ועמדו לפני משה, אמרו לו: טלית שכלה של תכלת חיבת בציצית או פטורה? אמר להם: חיבת. התחילו לשחק עליו: אפשר טלית של מין אחר, חוט אחד של תכלת פוטרה, זו שכלה תכלת לא תפטר את עצמה?!: **בני ראובן.** דתן ואבירם ואון בן פלת:

16:1 **וַיִּקַּח** *Took* – The verb does not have an object in the Hebrew. What did Koraḥ take? Rashi begins his commentary (on Num. 16:1) by stating what he believes to be the plain sense: "Koraḥ took himself to one side." He separated himself from the community and prepared to start a revolt.

Rashi cites Midrash Tanḥuma, which seeks to fill gaps in the narrative and elucidate its subtler levels. In this vein, Tanḥuma (Koraḥ, 2) answers the question "What did Koraḥ take?" by saying that he took a blue cloak and asked, "Does a cloak made entirely of blue wool require tzitzit, or is it exempt?"

Koraḥ knows that even a blue cloak requires tzitzit, a set of fringes that contain a cord of blue; and that it would be difficult to explain this convincingly to a large and skeptical public. Koraḥ's aim is to make Moshe seem absurd, whatever he answers.

Clearly this is not the plain sense of the text. Neither Koraḥ nor any of his fellow rebels mention tzitzit. Their complaints are that Moshe acted high-handedly, appointed his brother as High Priest, and failed in his central mission of bringing the people to the Promised Land. Yet the Midrash is teaching something deep about leadership. Recall Koraḥ's opening words to Moshe and Aharon: "You have gone too far! All the community is holy, every one of them, and the Lord is in their midst. Why then do you set yourselves above the Lord's people?" (Num. 16:3). Was Koraḥ right? Is all the community holy? Our midrash does not answer this directly, but does so implicitly.

Commanding all men to wear tzitzit with their thread of blue, the color associated with royalty and Aharon's priestly robe, meant that they were all holy, noble, and worthy to be priests. Had not God Himself summoned

פרשת קרח

טז א וַיִּקַּח קֹרַח בֶּן־יִצְהָר בֶּן־קְהָת בֶּן־לֵוִי וְדָתָן וַאֲבִירָם בְּנֵי אֱלִיאָב טו
ב וְאוֹן בֶּן־פֶּלֶת בְּנֵי רְאוּבֵן: וַיָּקֻמוּ לִפְנֵי מֹשֶׁה וַאֲנָשִׁים מִבְּנֵי־יִשְׂרָאֵל

אונקלוס

טז א וְאִתְפְּלֵיג קֹרַח, בַּר יִצְהָר בַּר קְהָת בַּר לֵוִי, וְדָתָן וַאֲבִירָם, בְּנֵי אֱלִיאָב, וְאוֹן בַּר פֶּלֶת בְּנֵי רְאוּבֵן: ב וְקָמוּ לְאַפֵּי מֹשֶׁה, וְגֻבְרַיָּא מִבְּנֵי יִשְׂרָאֵל

KORAḤ

The rebellion of Koraḥ, which dominates this *parasha*, is the most devastating challenge to Moshe's leadership in the Torah. Building on the unrest and shattered hopes of the people following the incident of the spies, Koraḥ assembles a heterogeneous group of malcontents – some from his own tribe, some from that of Reuven, yet others who have leadership positions elsewhere – and renounces the leadership of Moshe and Aharon.

The rebellion fails – ended by the ground opening and swallowing the chief rebels – yet the complaints of the people continue. These end only when Aharon's staff, alone among the staffs for each tribe, buds, blossoms, and brings forth almonds, a paradigm of peaceful conflict resolution. The *parasha* ends with a legal section detailing the duties of the priests and Levites and the offerings to be given to them by the rest of the people.

THE KORAḤ REBELLION

The Koraḥ rebellion is not just the worst of many in the wilderness years. It is also different in kind. It is not about a problem the Israelites have encountered – a lack of food or water or a way through the sea or the prospect of having to fight a battle against giants. It is an ad hominem attack on Moshe and Aharon. Koraḥ and his fellow rebels accuse Moshe of nepotism, of failure, and above all of being a fraud – of attributing to God decisions and laws that Moshe has devised himself for his own ends.

In contemporary terms, the Koraḥ rebellion is a populist movement. Populism is the politics of anger. It appears when there is widespread discontent with political leaders, when people feel that heads of institutions are working in their own interest rather than that of the general public. People come to feel that the distribution of rewards is unfair: a few gain disproportionately and the many stay static or lose. Discontent takes the form of the rejection of current political and cultural elites. Populist politicians claim that they, and they alone, are the true voice of the people. Populists stir up resentment against the establishment. They are deliberately divisive and confrontational. They promise strong leadership that will give the people back what has been taken from them. Ramban is undoubtedly correct (commentary on Num. 16:1) when he says that such a challenge to Moshe's leadership would have been impossible at any earlier point. Only in the aftermath of the episode of the spies, when the people realized that they would not see the Promised Land in their lifetime, could discontent be stirred by Koraḥ and his assorted fellow travelers. They felt they had nothing to lose. It was easy to tap into their disappointment, resentment, and fear.

Moshe wins the argument against Koraḥ, but only at the cost of invoking a miracle in which the earth opens up and swallows his opponents. Yet this does not end the argument. The next day the people gather against Moshe, saying: "You have killed the LORD's people!" (Num. 17:6). In this kind of confrontation, there is no benign outcome. You can only aim at minimizing the tragedy.

There is a warning here to stay far from people, movements, and parties that demonize their opponents. A healthy culture welcomes argument and respects dissenting views. Resist with all your heart and soul any attempt to substitute power for truth.

3 assembly, men of repute, and confronted Moshe and Aharon together. They
said to them, "You have gone too far. All the community is holy, every one
of them, and the LORD is in their midst. Why then do you set yourselves
4 above the LORD's people?" When Moshe heard this, he fell upon his face.

רש״י

ג| רַב לָכֶם. הַרְבֵּה יוֹתֵר מִדַּאי לְקַחְתֶּם לְעַצְמְכֶם גְּדֻלָּה: כֻּלָּם קְדֹשִׁים. כֻּלָּם שָׁמְעוּ דְּבָרִים בְּסִינַי מִפִּי הַגְּבוּרָה: וּמַדּוּעַ תִּתְנַשְּׂאוּ. אִם לָקַחְתָּ אַתָּה מַלְכוּת, לֹא הָיָה לְךָ לִבְרֹר לְאָחִיךָ כְּהֻנָּה. לֹא אַתֶּם לְבַדְּכֶם שְׁמַעְתֶּם בְּסִינַי: "אָנֹכִי ה׳ אֱלֹהֶיךָ", כָּל הָעֵדָה שָׁמְעוּ:

ד| וַיִּפֹּל עַל פָּנָיו. מִפְּנֵי הַמַּחְלֹקֶת, שֶׁכְּבָר זֶה בְּיָדָם סִרְחוֹן רְבִיעִי. [חָטְאוּ בָּעֵגֶל, "וַיְחַל מֹשֶׁה" (שמות לב, יא); בַּמִּתְאוֹנְנִים, "וַיִּתְפַּלֵּל מֹשֶׁה" (לעיל יא, ב); בַּמְרַגְּלִים, "וַיֹּאמֶר מֹשֶׁה אֶל ה׳ וְשָׁמְעוּ מִצְרַיִם" (לעיל יד, יג). בְּמַחְלָקְתּוֹ שֶׁל קֹרַח נִתְרַשְּׁלוּ יָדָיו]. מָשָׁל לְבֶן מֶלֶךְ שֶׁסָּרַח עַל אָבִיו,

script, traveling in the same direction, acting as an ensemble rather than a collection of prima donnas.

We are *all* God's servants. As the Torah says, "For it is to Me that the Israelites are servants; they are My servants whom I brought out of the land of Egypt" (Lev. 25:55). It is not that Moshe is a different kind of being than we are all called on to be. It is that he epitomized true service of God to the utmost degree. *The less there is of self in one who serves God, the more there is of God.* Moshe was the supreme exemplar of R. Yoḥanan's principle that "where you find humility, there you find greatness" (*Midrash Lekaḥ Tov*, Ekev 15a). The greatest achievement of a leader is to have served God and helped others to do so. That is what Moshe understood, and what Koraḥ and his fellow rebels did not.

16:3 **כָּל־הָעֵדָה כֻּלָּם קְדֹשִׁים** *All the community is holy, every one of them* – How should we understand Koraḥ's fundamental claim here? Ramban (on Num. 16:1) suggests that Koraḥ was protesting the transfer of priestly and Levitical duties to the tribe of Levi after the sin of the golden calf. Until then, that role had gone to the firstborn males in every family and tribe (see Ex. 34:20; Num. 3:12). Koraḥ was saying not that everyone was equally holy, but that the original plan, in which the firstborns were consecrated as holy, was fairer than the system that replaced it. In transferring priestly functions to a single tribe, Moshe was in danger of creating a dynastic elite set apart from the rest of the population.

Yeshayahu Leibowitz argued for a different interpretation. Koraḥ said, "All the community *is* holy." He was basing himself on Moshe's own words in the command of tzitzit, "This is to remind you to keep all My commands, to *remain* holy to your God" (Num. 15:40). One is a statement of fact, the other is a command. Koraḥ was confusing the two.

A third possibility is that Koraḥ made the mistake of thinking that what applies to a community as a whole applies to each of its members. In Judaism, holiness is primarily collective, not individual. The community is holy, but that does not mean that everyone within it has the same level of holiness.

On each of these three interpretations, Koraḥ's core claim is wrong. I would argue, however, that Koraḥ's mistake lies not in saying that all members of the congregation are holy. Rather, it lies in his assertions – first that a group of people of equal dignity do not need a leader; second, that leaders "set themselves above" those they lead; and third, that there was no need to change the structures of holiness after the sin of the golden calf.

A profound egalitarian impulse exists at the heart of Judaism. It is grounded in the first chapter of the Torah, where God created human beings in His image and likeness. The Sages (Sanhedrin 4:5) derive from this first that we are each of infinite value: "an entire world." We each have the same ancestry; we are all children of Adam and Ḥava. No one is entitled to say, "My ancestors were greater than yours." Koraḥ and his fellow rebels, then, are wrong in their attempt to seize power – they are not good men – but in one basic thing they are correct: all the congregation is holy, every one of them, and the LORD is in their midst.

16:4 **וַיִּפֹּל עַל־פָּנָיו** *He fell upon his face* – Moshe's first response is to fall facedown. Rashi says this was in near despair. Moshe had already prayed to God to forgive the people three times.

ג חֲמִשִּׁים וּמָאתָיִם נְשִׂיאֵי עֵדָה קְרִאֵי מוֹעֵד אַנְשֵׁי־שֵׁם׃ וַיִּקָּהֲלוּ עַל־
מֹשֶׁה וְעַל־אַהֲרֹן וַיֹּאמְרוּ אֲלֵהֶם רַב־לָכֶם כִּי כָל־הָעֵדָה כֻּלָּם קְדֹשִׁים
ד וּבְתוֹכָם יְהוָה וּמַדּוּעַ תִּתְנַשְּׂאוּ עַל־קְהַל יְהוָה׃ וַיִּשְׁמַע מֹשֶׁה וַיִּפֹּל

אונקלוס

מָאתַן וְחַמְשִׁין, רַבְרְבֵי כְּנִשְׁתָּא, מְעָרְעֵי זְמַן אֱנָשִׁין דִּשְׁמָא: ג וְאִתְכְּנִישׁוּ עַל מֹשֶׁה וְעַל אַהֲרֹן, וַאֲמַרוּ לְהוֹן סַגִּי לְכוֹן, אֲרֵי כָל כְּנִשְׁתָּא כֻּלְּהוֹן קַדִּישִׁין, וּבֵינֵיהוֹן שָׁרְיָא שְׁכִינְתָא דַיְיָ, וּמָדֵין אַתּוּן מִתְרַבְרְבִין עַל קְהָלָא דַיְיָ: ד וּשְׁמַע מֹשֶׁה, וּנְפַל

with their two supreme leaders, Moshe and Aharon, this further rejection is the final insult. He feels humiliated and is determined to bring Moshe and Aharon down.

16:1 בְּנֵי רְאוּבֵן *Descendants of Reuven* – Koraḥ's allies include two disaffected groups: the Reubenites, among them Datan and Aviram, and "two hundred fifty Israelite men, leaders of the community, chosen from the assembly, men of repute" (v. 2).

The Reubenites, suggests Ibn Ezra, felt that as descendants of Yaakov's firstborn, they were entitled to leadership positions, yet the tribe was systematically passed over when it came to leadership roles, leaving its members with a sense of grievance. Ibn Ezra adds that the final straw may have been Moshe's appointment of Yehoshua as his successor. Yehoshua came from the tribe of Efrayim, the son of Yosef. This may have revived memories of the old conflict between the children of Leah (of whom Reuven was the firstborn) and those of Raḥel, whose first child was Yosef.

The 250 other rebels, Ibn Ezra conjectures, were firstborns, still unreconciled to the fact that after the sin of the golden calf, the role of special service to God passed from the firstborn to the tribe of Levi.

The rebels share the mistake of seeing leadership in terms of status: the one before whom others prostrate themselves and to whom others defer. That is what leaders are in hierarchical societies. That is not what leadership is in the Torah. Of Moshe it says that he was "very humble, more so than any other man on earth" (Num. 12:3). A true leader is a servant, not a master. Seeking to set oneself above others is a moral failing, not a mark of stature. A leader is one who coordinates, giving structure and shape to the enterprise, making sure that everyone is following the same

Israel to be a "kingdom of priests and a holy nation" (Ex. 19:6)? Koraḥ's mistake is saying that a robe that is entirely blue does not need tzitzit and, by analogy, saying that a congregation of leaders does not need a leader. The truth is otherwise. A holy people still needs a leader, just as a garment, every thread of which is blue, still needs a fringe. A garment that is entirely blue but which lacks tzitzit has no special sanctity. A blue cloak is still only a cloak. The function of the tzitzit is not to diminish the significance of the garment but to endow it with a special and recognizable character.

Koraḥ does, though, have one virtue. He sees that the Jewish people should aspire to be a "cloak that is entirely blue." He dies for his sins, but his sons survive, and many centuries later their descendants are to sing psalms in the Temple – a whole series of psalms bear their name (see Psalms 42, 44–49, 84–88). If ambition had not corrupted him, Koraḥ might have been a genuine leader. For though his claim is self-serving, he sees a real and moving truth, that if a people dedicates itself to God it can become a robe every strand of which is royal blue.

16:1 בֶּן־קְהָת בֶּן־לֵוִי *Son of Kehat son of Levi* – The genealogy given in the opening verse of the *parasha*: "Koraḥ son of Yitzhar son of Kehat son of Levi" – suggested to the Sages (Bemidbar Rabba 18:2) the nature of his discontent. Koraḥ was aggrieved that he had been passed over when leaders were appointed for the various clans. In Numbers 3:30 we read that "the leader of the ancestral house of the Kohatite families was Elitzafan son of Uziel." Uziel was the youngest of the four sons of Kehat. Koraḥ is the son of Yitzhar, the second eldest of the brothers. Having already felt slighted that his father's elder brother, Amram, provided the Israelites

5 Then he spoke to Koraḥ and all his company. "In the morning," he said, "the
Lord will make known who is His and who is holy, and will bring that one
close to Him. The one He chooses will be the one He will allow to come close.
6 7 Do this: Let Koraḥ and his company take censers. Tomorrow light fire in them
and place incense upon them before the Lord. The man whom the Lord
8 chooses – he is holy. It is you, sons of Levi, who have gone too far!" Moshe said
9 to Koraḥ, "Listen now, you sons of Levi. Is it not enough for you that the God
of Israel has separated you from the Israelite community, enabling you to come
close to Him, to serve in the Lord's Tabernacle, and stand in the presence of
10 the community to minister to them? He has brought you, and with you all
your fellow Levites, to be close to Him, and yet you seek the priesthood also?
11 And so you and all your company have assembled to defy the Lord. Aharon
12 – who is he that you should have grievances against him?" After this, Moshe

רש״י

ופיס עליו אוהבו פעם ושתים ושלש, כשפרח רביעית נתרשלו ידי האוהב ההוא, אמר: עד מתי אטריח על המלך? שמא לא יקבל עוד ממני:

ה **בקר וידע וגו׳.** עתה עת שכרות הוא לנו ולא נכון להראות לפניו. והוא היה מתכוין לדחותם, שמא יחזרו בהם: **בקר וידע ה׳ את אשר לו.** לעבודת לויה: **ואת הקדוש.** לכהנה: **והקריב.** אותם ״אליו״:

ו–ז [תוספת מאיגרת רבינו שמעיה: **זאת עשו קחו לכם מחתות.** מה ראה לומר להם כך? אמר להם: בדרכי הגוים יש נימוסים הרבה וכמרים הרבה, ואין כלם מתקבצים בבית אחד. אנו אין לנו אלא ה׳ אחד, ארון אחד ותורה אחת ומזבח אחד וכהן גדול אחד, ואתם חמשים ומאתים איש מבקשים כהנה גדולה? אף אני רוצה בכך. הא לכם תשמיש חביב מכל, היא הקטרת החביבה מכל הקרבנות, וסם המות נתון בתוכו שבו נשרפו נדב ואביהוא, לפיכך התרה בהם: ״והיה האיש אשר יבחר ה׳ הוא הקדוש״ (להלן פסוק ז), כבר הוא בקדשתו, וכי אין אנו יודעים שמי שיבחר הוא הקדוש? אלא אמר להם משה: הריני אומר לכם, שלא תתחיבו: מי שיבחר בו יצא חי וכלכם אובדים: **רב לכם בני לוי.** דבר גדול אמרתי לכם. ולא טפשים היו שככך התרה בהם וקבלו עליהם לקרב, אלא הם חטאו על נפשותם, שנאמר: ״את מחתות החטאים האלה בנפשתם״ (להלן יז, ג). וקרח שפקח היה, מה ראה לשטות זו? עינו הטעתו, ראה שלשלת גדולה יוצאה ממנו – שמואל ששקול כנגד משה ואהרן, אמר: בשבילו אני נמלט; ועשרים וארבע משמרות עומדות לבני בניו כלם מתנבאים ברוח הקדש, שנאמר: ״כל אלה בנים להימן״ (דברי הימים א׳ כה, ה), אמר: אפשר כל הגדלה הזאת עתידה לעמד ממני ואני אדם? לכך נשתתף לבא לאותה חזקה, ששמע מפי משה שכלם אובדים ואחד נמלט – ״אשר יבחר ה׳ הוא הקדוש״, טעה ותלה בעצמו. ולא ראה יפה, לפי שבניו עשו תשובה, ומשה היה רואה. תנחומא (ה):] **מחתות.** כלים שאותן בהם גחלים ויש להם בית יד: **רב לכם.** דבר גדול נטלתם בעצמכם, לחלק על הקדוש ברוך הוא:

ח **ויאמר משה אל קרח שמעו נא בני לוי.** התחיל לדבר עמו דברים רכים, כיון שראהו קשה ערף, אמר: עד שלא ישתתפו שאר השבטים ויאבדו עמו אדבר גם אל כלם. התחיל לזרז בהם: ״שמעו נא בני לוי״:

ט **ולעמד לפני העדה.** לשיר על הדוכן:

י **ויקרב אתך.** לאותו שרות שהרחיק ממנו שאר עדת ישראל:

יא **לכן.** בשביל כך, ״אתה וכל עדתך הנעדים״ אתך ״על ה׳״, כי בשליחותו עשיתי לתת כהנה לאהרן, ולא לנו הוא המחלקת הזה:

יב **וישלח משה וגו׳.** מכאן שאין מחזיקין במחלקת, שהיה משה מחזר אחריהם להשלימם בדברי שלום: **לא נעלה.** פיהם הכשילם, שאין להם אלא ירידה:

the God of Israel has separated you from the Israelite community? ... He has brought you, and with you all your fellow Levites, to be close to Him, and yet you seek the priesthood also?" (Num. 16:9–10).

ה עַל־פָּנָיו: וַיְדַבֵּר אֶל־קֹרַח וְאֶל־כָּל־עֲדָתוֹ לֵאמֹר בֹּקֶר וְיֹדַע יהוה אֶת־
אֲשֶׁר־לוֹ וְאֶת־הַקָּדוֹשׁ וְהִקְרִיב אֵלָיו וְאֵת אֲשֶׁר יִבְחַר־בּוֹ יַקְרִיב אֵלָיו:
ו ז זֹאת עֲשׂוּ קְחוּ־לָכֶם מַחְתּוֹת קֹרַח וְכָל־עֲדָתוֹ: וּתְנוּ־בָהֵן ׀ אֵשׁ וְשִׂימוּ
עֲלֵיהֶן ׀ קְטֹרֶת לִפְנֵי יהוה מָחָר וְהָיָה הָאִישׁ אֲשֶׁר־יִבְחַר יהוה הוּא
ח הַקָּדוֹשׁ רַב־לָכֶם בְּנֵי לֵוִי: וַיֹּאמֶר מֹשֶׁה אֶל־קֹרַח שִׁמְעוּ־נָא בְּנֵי לֵוִי:
ט הַמְעַט מִכֶּם כִּי־הִבְדִּיל אֱלֹהֵי יִשְׂרָאֵל אֶתְכֶם מֵעֲדַת יִשְׂרָאֵל לְהַקְרִיב
אֶתְכֶם אֵלָיו לַעֲבֹד אֶת־עֲבֹדַת מִשְׁכַּן יהוה וְלַעֲמֹד לִפְנֵי הָעֵדָה
י לְשָׁרְתָם: וַיַּקְרֵב אֹתְךָ וְאֶת־כָּל־אַחֶיךָ בְנֵי־לֵוִי אִתָּךְ וּבִקַּשְׁתֶּם גַּם־
יא כְּהֻנָּה: לָכֵן אַתָּה וְכָל־עֲדָתְךָ הַנֹּעָדִים עַל־יהוה וְאַהֲרֹן מַה־הוּא כִּי
יב תלונו עָלָיו: וַיִּשְׁלַח מֹשֶׁה לִקְרֹא לְדָתָן וְלַאֲבִירָם בְּנֵי אֱלִיאָב וַיֹּאמְרוּ תַּלִּינוּ

אונקלוס

עַל אַפּוֹהִי: ה וּמַלֵּיל עִם קֹרַח, וְעִם כָּל כְּנִשְׁתֵּיהּ לְמֵימַר, בְּצַפְרָא, וִיהוֹדַע יי יָת דְּכָשַׁר לֵיהּ, וְיָת דְּקַדִּישׁ וִיקָרֵיב לִקְדָמוֹהִי, וְיָת דְּיִתְרְעֵי בֵיהּ יְקָרֵיב לְשִׁמּוּשֵׁיהּ: ו דָּא עֲבִידוּ, סַבוּ לְכוֹן מַחְתְּיָן, קֹרַח וְכָל כְּנִשְׁתֵּיהּ: ז וְהַבוּ בְהוֹן אִישָׁתָא, וְשַׁווּ עֲלֵיהוֹן קְטוֹרֶת בֻּסְמִין, קֳדָם יי מְחַר, וִיהֵי, גֻּבְרָא, דְּיִתְרְעֵי יי הוּא קַדִּישׁ, סַגִּי לְכוֹן בְּנֵי לֵוִי: ח וַאֲמַר מֹשֶׁה לְקֹרַח, שְׁמַעוּ כְעַן בְּנֵי לֵוִי: ט הַזְעֵיר לְכוֹן, אֲרֵי אַפְרֵישׁ אֱלָהָא דְיִשְׂרָאֵל יָתְכוֹן מִכְּנִשְׁתָּא דְיִשְׂרָאֵל, לְקָרָבָא יָתְכוֹן לִקְדָמוֹהִי, לְמִפְלַח, יָת פָּלְחַן מַשְׁכְּנָא דַיי, וּלְמְקָם, קֳדָם כְּנִשְׁתָּא לְשַׁמָּשׁוּתְהוֹן: י וְקָרֵיב יָתָךְ, וְיָת כָּל אַחָךְ בְּנֵי לֵוִי עִמָּךְ, וּבָעַן אַתּוּן אַף כְּהֻנְּתָא רַבְּתָא: יא בְּכֵן, אַתְּ וְכָל כְּנִשְׁתָּךְ, דְּאִזְדַּמַּנְתּוּן עַל יי, וְאַהֲרֹן מָא הוּא, אֲרֵי מִתְרָעֲמִתּוּן עֲלוֹהִי: יב וּשְׁלַח מֹשֶׁה, לְמִקְרֵי, לְדָתָן וְלַאֲבִירָם בְּנֵי אֱלִיאָב, וַאֲמַרוּ

He did not know how he could succeed a fourth time. Rashbam says he fell in prayer. Saadia Gaon and Ibn Ezra say he did so to receive prophetic guidance from God. Immediately after, in any case, he stands, composed.

16:5 בֹּקֶר *In the morning* – By deferring the test to the next day, Moshe is giving Koraḥ and his followers a chance to think again and back down. By choosing the test he does, he is warning the rebels of the risk they are taking. The people still vividly recall what had happened to Aharon's two sons, Nadav and Avihu, when they offered up incense and fire that "He had not commanded" (Lev. 10:1–2): they died. Once Moshe has proposed this test, Koraḥ and his fellows know that they are risking their lives.

16:10 וּבִקַּשְׁתֶּם גַּם־כְּהֻנָּה *Yet you seek the priesthood also* – Moshe speaks to Koraḥ directly. He knows that not all the rebels share the same discontent. He knows also that their apparent egalitarianism – "all the community is holy" (Num. 16:3) – is a veneer for personal ambition: Koraḥ wants Aharon's position as High Priest. Koraḥ is Moshe and Aharon's cousin and feels that the second leadership role, the high priesthood, should have gone to him. Moshe now reasons with him firmly: "Is it not enough for you that

sent for Datan and Aviram, sons of Eliav. But they said, "We will not come up.
13 Is it not enough that you have brought us out of a land flowing with milk and
14 with honey to kill us in the desert, that you insist on lording it over us? And SHENI
more: you have not brought us to a land flowing with milk and with honey, nor
have you given us an inheritance of cropland and vineyard. Would you pull out
15 these people's eyes?! We will not come up!" Moshe became very angry and
said to the LORD, "Pay no attention to their offering. I have not taken a single
16 donkey from them, nor have I wronged any one of them." Moshe said to Koraḥ,
"You and your entire company shall appear before the LORD tomorrow: you,

רש״י

יד] **ותתן לנו.** הדבר מוסב על 'לא' האמור למעלה, כלומר: לא הביאותנו ולא נתת לנו נחלת שדה וכרם. אמרת לנו: אעלה אתכם מעני מצרים אל ארץ טובה וגו' (שמות ג, ח; יז), משם הוצאתנו, ולא אל ארץ זבת חלב ודבש הביאתנו, אלא גזרת עלינו להמיתנו במדבר, שאמרת לנו: "במדבר הזה יפלו פגריכם" (לעיל יד, כט): **העיני האנשים ההם תנקר** וגו'. אפילו אתה שולח לנקר את עינינו אם לא נעלה אליך, לא נעלה: **האנשים ההם.** כאדם התולה קללתו בחברו:

טו] **אל תפן אל מנחתם.** לפי פשוטו, הקטרת שהם מקריבין לפניך מחר אל תפן אליהם. והמדרש אומר: יודע אני שיש להם חלק בתמידי צבור, אף חלקם לא יקבל לפניך לרצון, תניחנו האש ולא תאכלנו: **לא חמור אחד מהם נשאתי.** לא חמורו של אחד מהם נטלתי. אפילו כשהלכתי ממדין למצרים והרכבתי את אשתי ואת בני על החמור, והיה לי ליטול אותו החמור משלהם, לא נטלתי אלא משלי. "שחרית", לשון ארמי, כך נקראת אנגריא של מלך 'שחור':

טז] **והם.** עדתך:

Whose ox have I seized, and whose donkey have I seized? Whom have I cheated, and whom have I oppressed, and from whose hand have I taken a bribe and averted my eyes from him? Let me repay you" (I Sam. 12:3). Shmuel is experiencing the same emotion as Moshe: the shame and humiliation of feeling accused of something he did not do, after a lifetime of self-sacrificing service to others.

Koraḥ's rebellion is bound up in issues that are real and substantive. There are the repercussions of the sin of the golden calf. There was the crushing sense of loss after the episode of the spies. At such moments, a leader will be attacked and blamed personally. He will bear the brunt of people's anger. Moshe surely takes the right course of action in proposing the test of the incense offering. That will resolve the question of the priesthood. As for the resentments of the rebels, however, there is nothing Moshe can do.

Of all the challenges of leadership, not taking criticism personally and staying calm when the people you lead are angry with you may be the hardest of all. Depersonalizing attacks is the best way to deal with them. People get angry when leaders cannot magically make harsh realities disappear. Leaders in such circumstances are called on to accept that anger with grace.

THE NATURE OF THE ARGUMENT

It is striking how the Sages framed the conflict with Koraḥ. They insisted on the validity of argument in the public domain. They said that what was wrong with Koraḥ and his fellows was not the fact that they argued with Moshe and Aharon, or even the content of their claims, but rather the nature of their dispute:

> Every argument for the sake of Heaven will in the end be of permanent value, but every argument not for the sake of Heaven will not endure. Which is an argument for the sake of Heaven? The argument between Hillel and Shammai. Which is an argument not for the sake of Heaven? The argument of Koraḥ and his company. (Avot 5:17)

Meiri (*Beit HaBeḥira* ad loc.) and other medieval commentators understood the Sages to be distinguishing here between an argument for the sake of *truth* and one for the sake of *victory*. The Sages Hillel and Shammai argued for the

יג לֹא נַעֲלֶה: הַמְעַט כִּי הֶעֱלִיתָנוּ מֵאֶרֶץ זָבַת חָלָב וּדְבַשׁ לַהֲמִיתֵנוּ
יד בַּמִּדְבָּר כִּי־תִשְׂתָּרֵר עָלֵינוּ גַּם־הִשְׂתָּרֵר: אַף לֹא אֶל־אֶרֶץ זָבַת חָלָב שני
וּדְבַשׁ הֲבִיאֹתָנוּ וַתִּתֶּן־לָנוּ נַחֲלַת שָׂדֶה וָכָרֶם הַעֵינֵי הָאֲנָשִׁים הָהֵם
טו תְּנַקֵּר לֹא נַעֲלֶה: וַיִּחַר לְמֹשֶׁה מְאֹד וַיֹּאמֶר אֶל־יהוה אַל־תֵּפֶן אֶל־
מִנְחָתָם לֹא חֲמוֹר אֶחָד מֵהֶם נָשָׂאתִי וְלֹא הֲרֵעֹתִי אֶת־אַחַד מֵהֶם:
טז וַיֹּאמֶר מֹשֶׁה אֶל־קֹרַח אַתָּה וְכָל־עֲדָתְךָ הֱיוּ לִפְנֵי יהוה אַתָּה וָהֵם

אונקלוס

לָא נִסַּק: יג הַזְעִיר, אֲרֵי אַסֵּיקְתַּנָא מֵאֲרַע עָבְדָא חֲלַב וּדְבַשׁ, לְקַטָּלוּתַנָא בְּמַדְבְּרָא, אֲרֵי אִתְרָבַבְתְּ עֲלַנָא אַף אִתְרַבְרְבָא: יד בְּרַם, לָא לַאֲרַע עָבְדָא חֲלַב וּדְבַשׁ אַעֵילְתַּנָא, וִיהַבְתְּ לַנָא, אַחְסָנַת חַקְלִין וְכַרְמִין, הַעֵינֵי, גֻּבְרַיָּא הָאִנּוּן, תְּשַׁלַּח לְעַוָּרָא לָא נִסַּק: טו וּתְקֵיף לְמֹשֶׁה לַחְדָא, וַאֲמַר קֳדָם יְיָ, לָא תְקַבֵּיל בְּרַעֲוָא קֻרְבָּנְהוֹן, לָא, חֲמָרָא דְחַד מִנְּהוֹן שַׁחֲרִית, וְלָא אַבְאֵישִׁית לְחַד מִנְּהוֹן: טז וַאֲמַר מֹשֶׁה לְקֹרַח, אַתְּ וְכָל כְּנִשְׁתָּךְ, הֲווֹ זְמִינִין לִקְדָם יְיָ, אַתְּ וְאִנּוּן,

16:13 מֵאֶרֶץ זָבַת חָלָב וּדְבַשׁ *Out of a land flowing with milk and with honey* – Koraḥ has made classic populist claims. The establishment, represented by Moshe and Aharon, is corrupt. Moshe has kept the leadership roles within his immediate family instead of sharing them out more widely. Koraḥ has presented himself as the people's champion. The whole community, he says, is holy. There is nothing special about you, Moshe and Aharon. We have all seen God's miracles and heard His voice. We all helped build His Sanctuary. Koraḥ poses as the democrat – so that he can become the autocrat.

Next, he and his fellow rebels have mounted an impressive campaign of fake news. We have to infer this indirectly. When Moshe says to God, "I have not taken a single donkey from them, nor have I wronged any one of them" (Num. 16:15), it is clear that he has been accused of just that: exploiting his office for personal gain. When he says, "By this you will know that the LORD sent me to do these deeds; it was not my idea" (Num. 16:28), it is equally clear that he has been accused of presenting his own decisions as the will and word of God.

Most blatant, however, is the manipulative claim of Datan and Aviram: "Is it not enough that you have brought us out of a land flowing with milk and with honey to kill us in the desert, that you insist on lording it over us?" (Num. 16:13). This is the most tendentious speech in the Torah. It combines false nostalgia for Egypt as a "land flowing with milk and with honey," replacing their slavery there with the image of God's promised plenty for them in the Holy Land, blaming Moshe for the report of the spies, and accusing him of holding on to leadership for his own personal prestige. All three are outrageous lies.

16:15 אַל־תֵּפֶן אֶל־מִנְחָתָם *Pay no attention to their offering* – Moshe, as Israel's leader, had always prayed on behalf of the people, even for his sister Miriam when she was struck with leprosy for speaking badly about him. It is an extraordinary thing to pray to God *not* to accept someone's offering. Sforno (on Num. 16:15) explains his behavior by saying that there is a rule that offenses against other people are atoned for only when they have forgiven you. "I," Moshe is saying to God, "refuse to forgive them."

16:15 לֹא חֲמוֹר אֶחָד מֵהֶם נָשָׂאתִי *I have not taken a single donkey from them* – Jewish tradition focuses on this specific moment in the Koraḥ story, by pairing this *parasha* with a *haftara* taken from the book of Samuel, in which the prophet, having anointed Sha'ul as king, says to the people: "Here I am. Testify against me in front of the LORD and in front of His anointed.

17 they, and Aharon. Each one shall take his censer, place incense upon it, and
present it before the LORD, each holding his censer, two hundred fifty censers
18 in all, and you and Aharon likewise with yours." Each took his censer, placed
fire in it, put incense upon it, and stood at the entrance to the Tent of Meeting,
19 as did Moshe and Aharon. Koraḥ gathered all his company against them to the
entrance to the Tent of Meeting. Then the glory of the LORD was revealed to the
20 21 entire community. The LORD spoke to Moshe and Aharon: "Separate SHELISHI
22 yourselves from this community and let Me consume them in a moment." They
fell on their faces and said, "God, the God of the spirit of all flesh, if one man
23 sins, will You rage against the entire community?" The LORD spoke
24 to Moshe: "Tell the community to move away from the dwellings of Koraḥ,
25 Datan, and Aviram." Moshe rose and went to Datan and Aviram. Israel's elders
26 followed him. He spoke to the community, saying: "Turn away now from the
tents of these wicked men. Do not touch anything of theirs, lest you be swept
27 away for all their sins." So they moved away from around the dwellings of Koraḥ,
Datan, and Aviram. Datan and Aviram came out and stood at the openings of

רש"י

יז **וְהִקְרַבְתֶּם... אִישׁ מַחְתָּתוֹ.** הַחֲמִשִּׁים וּמָאתַיִם אִישׁ שֶׁבָּכֶם:

יט **וַיַּקְהֵל עֲלֵיהֶם קֹרַח.** בְּדִבְרֵי לֵיצָנוּת. כָּל הַלַּיְלָה הַהוּא הָלַךְ אֵצֶל הַשְּׁבָטִים וּפִתָּה אוֹתָם: כִּסְבוּרִין אַתֶּם שֶׁעָלַי לְבַדִּי אֲנִי מַקְפִּיד? אֵינִי מַקְפִּיד אֶלָּא בִּשְׁבִיל כֻּלְּכֶם, אֵלּוּ בָּאִין וְנוֹטְלִין כָּל הַגְּדֻלּוֹת, לוֹ הַמַּלְכוּת וּלְאָחִיו הַכְּהֻנָּה! עַד שֶׁנִּתְפַּתּוּ כֻּלָּם: **וַיֵּרָא כְבוֹד ה'.** בָּא בְּעַמּוּד עָנָן:

כב **אֵל אֱלֹהֵי הָרוּחֹת.** יוֹדֵעַ מַחְשָׁבוֹת. אֵין מִדָּתְךָ כְּמִדַּת בָּשָׂר וָדָם, מֶלֶךְ בָּשָׂר וָדָם שֶׁסָּרְחָה עָלָיו מִקְצָת מְדִינָה אֵינוֹ יוֹדֵעַ מִי הַחוֹטֵא, לְפִיכָךְ כְּשֶׁהוּא כּוֹעֵס נִפְרָע מִכֻּלָּם. אֲבָל אַתָּה, לְפָנֶיךָ גְּלוּיוֹת כָּל הַמַּחְשָׁבוֹת וְיוֹדֵעַ אַתָּה מִי הַחוֹטֵא: **הָאִישׁ אֶחָד.** הוּא הַחוֹטֵא וְאַתָּה "עַל כָּל הָעֵדָה תִּקְצֹף"? אָמַר הַקָּדוֹשׁ בָּרוּךְ הוּא: יָפֶה אֲמַרְתֶּם, אֲנִי יוֹדֵעַ וּמוֹדִיעַ מִי חָטָא וּמִי לֹא חָטָא:

כד **הֵעָלוּ וְגוֹ'.** כְּתַרְגּוּמוֹ, "אִסְתַּלַּקוּ" מִסְּבִיבוֹת מִשְׁכַּן קֹרַח:

כה **וַיָּקָם מֹשֶׁה.** כִּסָבוּר שֶׁיִּשְּׂאוּ לוֹ פָּנִים וְלֹא עָשׂוּ:

כז **יָצְאוּ נִצָּבִים.** בְּקוֹמָה זְקוּפָה לְחָרֵף וּלְגַדֵּף, כְּמוֹ: "וַיִּתְיַצֵּב אַרְבָּעִים

but if you lose, you also win, because being defeated by the truth is the only defeat that is also a victory. We are enlarged thereby. As R. Shimon HaAmsoni said: "Just as I received reward for the exposition, so I will receive reward for the retraction" (Kiddushin 57a). In an argument for the sake of victory, if you lose, you lose, but if you win, you also lose, for by diminishing your opponents, you diminish yourself.

The concept of "argument for the sake of Heaven" allowed the Sages to reframe disagreement as a unifying, not just a divisive, force. That is implicit in the radical idea that each of two opposing opinions can represent "the words of the living God" (Eiruvin 13b).

A free society depends on the dignity of dissent. We see it in rabbinic dialogues between Hillel and Shammai and their descendants. Dismiss a contrary view and you impoverish the entire culture. Knowing this does not stop politics from being abrasive, sometimes brutal. But it does mean that people recognize the humanity of their opponents, listen to them, and realize that other viewpoints have integrity. Great leaders seek not power but truth, not victory but healing. Koraḥ, as the antithesis of this approach, forever represents for Judaism the danger of "arguments not for the sake of Heaven."

יז וְאַהֲרֹ֖ן מָחָֽר׃ וּקְח֣וּ ׀ אִ֣ישׁ מַחְתָּת֗וֹ וּנְתַתֶּ֤ם עֲלֵיהֶם֙ קְטֹ֔רֶת וְהִקְרַבְתֶּ֞ם
לִפְנֵ֣י יהוה֙ אִ֣ישׁ מַחְתָּת֔וֹ חֲמִשִּׁ֥ים וּמָאתַ֖יִם מַחְתֹּ֑ת וְאַתָּ֥ה וְאַהֲרֹ֖ן
יח אִ֥ישׁ מַחְתָּתֽוֹ׃ וַיִּקְח֞וּ אִ֣ישׁ מַחְתָּת֗וֹ וַיִּתְּנ֤וּ עֲלֵיהֶם֙ אֵ֔שׁ וַיָּשִׂ֥ימוּ עֲלֵיהֶ֖ם
יט קְטֹ֑רֶת וַיַּֽעַמְד֗וּ פֶּ֛תַח אֹ֥הֶל מוֹעֵ֖ד וּמֹשֶׁ֥ה וְאַהֲרֹֽן׃ וַיַּקְהֵ֨ל עֲלֵיהֶ֥ם
קֹ֙רַח֙ אֶת־כָּל־הָ֣עֵדָ֔ה אֶל־פֶּ֖תַח אֹ֣הֶל מוֹעֵ֑ד וַיֵּרָ֥א כְבוֹד־יהוה אֶל־
כ כָּל־הָעֵדָֽה׃ וַיְדַבֵּ֣ר יהוה אֶל־מֹשֶׁ֥ה וְאֶֽל־אַהֲרֹ֖ן לֵאמֹֽר׃ שלישי
כא כב הִבָּ֣דְל֔וּ מִתּ֖וֹךְ הָעֵדָ֣ה הַזֹּ֑את וַאֲכַלֶּ֥ה אֹתָ֖ם כְּרָֽגַע׃ וַיִּפְּל֤וּ עַל־פְּנֵיהֶם֙
וַיֹּ֣אמְר֔וּ אֵ֕ל אֱלֹהֵ֥י הָרוּחֹ֖ת לְכָל־בָּשָׂ֑ר הָאִ֤ישׁ אֶחָד֙ יֶֽחֱטָ֔א וְעַ֥ל כָּל־
כג כד הָעֵדָ֖ה תִּקְצֹֽף׃ וַיְדַבֵּ֥ר יהוה אֶל־מֹשֶׁ֥ה לֵּאמֹֽר׃ דַּבֵּ֥ר
כה אֶל־הָעֵדָ֖ה לֵאמֹ֑ר הֵֽעָלוּ֙ מִסָּבִ֔יב לְמִשְׁכַּן־קֹ֖רַח דָּתָ֥ן וַאֲבִירָֽם׃ וַיָּ֣קָם
כו מֹשֶׁ֔ה וַיֵּ֖לֶךְ אֶל־דָּתָ֣ן וַאֲבִירָ֑ם וַיֵּלְכ֥וּ אַחֲרָ֖יו זִקְנֵ֥י יִשְׂרָאֵֽל׃ וַיְדַבֵּ֨ר אֶל־
הָעֵדָ֜ה לֵאמֹ֗ר ס֣וּרוּ נָ֡א מֵעַל֩ אָהֳלֵ֨י הָאֲנָשִׁ֤ים הָֽרְשָׁעִים֙ הָאֵ֔לֶּה וְאַל־
כז תִּגְּע֖וּ בְּכָל־אֲשֶׁ֣ר לָהֶ֑ם פֶּן־תִּסָּפ֖וּ בְּכָל־חַטֹּאתָֽם׃ וַיֵּעָל֗וּ מֵעַ֧ל מִשְׁכַּן־
קֹ֛רַח דָּתָ֥ן וַאֲבִירָ֖ם מִסָּבִ֑יב וְדָתָ֨ן וַאֲבִירָ֜ם יָצְא֣וּ נִצָּבִ֗ים פֶּ֚תַח אָהֳלֵיהֶ֔ם

אונקלוס

וְאַהֲרֹן מְחַר: יז וְסַבוּ גְּבַר מַחְתִּיתֵיהּ, וְתִתְּנוּן עֲלֵיהוֹן קְטוֹרֶת בֻּסְמִין, וּתְקָרְבוּן, קֳדָם יי גְּבַר מַחְתִּיתֵיהּ, מָאתַן וְחַמְשִׁין מַחְתְּיָן, וְאַתְּ וְאַהֲרֹן גְּבַר מַחְתִּיתֵיהּ: יח וּנְסִיבוּ גְּבַר מַחְתִּיתֵיהּ, וִיהַבוּ עֲלֵיהוֹן אִישָּׁתָא, וְשַׁוִּיאוּ עֲלֵיהוֹן קְטוֹרֶת בֻּסְמִין, וְקָמוּ, בִּתְרַע, מַשְׁכַּן זִמְנָא וּמֹשֶׁה וְאַהֲרֹן: יט וְאַכְנֵישׁ עֲלֵיהוֹן קֹרַח יָת כָּל כְּנִשְׁתָּא, לִתְרַע מַשְׁכַּן זִמְנָא, וְאִתְגְּלִי יְקָרָא דַּיי לְכָל כְּנִשְׁתָּא: כ וּמַלֵּיל יי, עִם מֹשֶׁה וּלְאַהֲרֹן לְמֵימַר: כא אִתְפָּרְשׁוּ, מִגּוֹ כְּנִשְׁתָּא הָדָא, וַאֲשֵׁיצֵי יָתְהוֹן כְּשָׁעָא: כב וּנְפַלוּ עַל אַפֵּיהוֹן וַאֲמַרוּ, אֵל, אֱלָהּ רוּחַיָּא לְכָל בִּסְרָא, גַּבְרָא חַד יְחוּב, וְעַל כָּל כְּנִשְׁתָּא יְהֵי רְגָזָא: כג וּמַלֵּיל יי עִם מֹשֶׁה לְמֵימַר: כד מַלֵּיל עִם כְּנִשְׁתָּא לְמֵימַר, אִסְתַּלַּקוּ מִסְּחוֹר סְחוֹר, לְמַשְׁכְּנָא דְּקֹרַח דָּתָן וַאֲבִירָם: כה וְקָם מֹשֶׁה, וַאֲזַל לְוָת דָּתָן וַאֲבִירָם, וַאֲזַלוּ בָּתְרוֹהִי סָבֵי יִשְׂרָאֵל: כו וּמַלֵּיל עִם כְּנִשְׁתָּא לְמֵימַר, זוּרוּ כְּעַן, מֵעִלָּוֵי מַשְׁכְּנֵי גֻּבְרַיָּא חַיָּבַיָּא הָאִלֵּין, וְלָא תִקְרְבוּן בְּכָל דִּילְהוֹן, דִּלְמָא תִלְקוֹן בְּכָל חוֹבֵיהוֹן: כז וְאִסְתַּלַּקוּ, מֵעִלָּוֵי מַשְׁכְּנָא דְּקֹרַח, דָּתָן וַאֲבִירָם מִסְּחוֹר סְחוֹר, וְדָתָן וַאֲבִירָם נְפַקוּ קָיְמִין, בִּתְרַע מַשְׁכְּנֵיהוֹן,

sake of truth, the determination of God's will. The school of Hillel knew that more than one interpretation can be given. They studied the views of their opponents alongside, and even before, their own. They were "kindly and modest" (Eiruvin 13b) because they realized that truth is not an all-or-nothing affair. It is a conversation, scored for a multiplicity of voices. Koraḥ, who challenged Moshe and Aharon for leadership, was arguing for the sake not of truth, but of victory; he wanted to be a leader too.

In an argument for the sake of truth, if you win, you win,

28 their tents with their wives, children, and infants. Moshe said, "By this you
29 will know that the LORD sent me to do these deeds; it was not my idea. If all
these men die as others do, and share the common fate of all humanity, then
30 the LORD has not sent me. But if the LORD creates something entirely new, so
that the ground opens its mouth and swallows them and all they have, and
they go down alive to Sheol, then you will know that these men have provoked
31 the LORD." As soon as he had finished speaking these words, the ground
32 beneath them split open. The earth opened its mouth and swallowed them
and their households, with all the people who pertained to Koraḥ and all their
33 possessions – they and all that was theirs descended alive to Sheol – the earth
34 closed over them – and they perished from the midst of the assembly. At their
cry, all the Israelites around them fled, for they said, "The earth could swallow
35 us." And fire came forth from the LORD and consumed the two hundred fifty
17 1 men who were offering incense. Then the LORD spoke to Moshe:
2 "Tell Elazar son of Aharon the priest to remove the censers from the fire, for
3 they have become holy. Scatter the burning coals far and wide. And the censers
of those who committed a mortal sin – make them into hammered plates as a
covering for the altar. Having been offered before the LORD, they have become

רש״י

יוֹס" דִּגְלִית (שמואל א׳ יז, טז): **וּנְשֵׁיהֶם וּבְנֵיהֶם וְטַפָּם.** בֹּא וּרְאֵה כַּמָּה קָשָׁה הַמַּחְלֹקֶת, שֶׁהֲרֵי בֵּית דִּין שֶׁל מַטָּה אֵין עוֹנְשִׁין אֶלָּא עַד שֶׁיָּבִיא שְׁתֵּי שְׂעָרוֹת, וּבֵית דִּין שֶׁל מַעְלָה עַד עֶשְׂרִים שָׁנָה, וְכָאן אָבְדוּ אַף יוֹנְקֵי שָׁדַיִם:

כח **לַעֲשׂוֹת אֵת כָּל הַמַּעֲשִׂים הָאֵלֶּה.** שֶׁעָשִׂיתִי עַל פִּי הַדִּבּוּר, לָתֵת לְאַהֲרֹן כְּהֻנָּה גְּדוֹלָה, וּבָנָיו סְגָנֵי כְהֻנָּה, וֶאֱלִיצָפָן נְשִׂיא הַקְּהָתִי:

כט **לֹא ה׳ שְׁלָחָנִי.** אֶלָּא אֲנִי עָשִׂיתִי הַכֹּל מִדַּעְתִּי, וּבְדִין הוּא חוֹלֵק עָלַי:

ל **וְאִם בְּרִיאָה.** חֲדָשָׁה: **יִבְרָא ה׳.** לְהָמִית אוֹתָם בְּמִיתָה שֶׁלֹּא מֵת בָּהּ אָדָם עַד הֵנָּה, וּמַה הִיא הַבְּרִיאָה? "וּפָצְתָה הָאֲדָמָה אֶת פִּיהָ" וְתִבְלָעֵם, אָז "וִידַעְתֶּם כִּי נִאֲצוּ" הֵם, וַאֲנִי מִפִּי הַגְּבוּרָה אָמַרְתִּי. וְרַבּוֹתֵינוּ פֵּרְשׁוּ: "אִם בְּרִיאָה" – פֶּה לָאָרֶץ מִשֵּׁשֶׁת יְמֵי בְרֵאשִׁית, מוּטָב, וְאִם לָאו – "יִבְרָא ה׳":

לד **נָסוּ לְקֹלָם.** בִּשְׁבִיל הַקּוֹל הַיּוֹצֵא עַל בְּלִיעָתָן:

יז ב **וְאֶת הָאֵשׁ.** שֶׁבְּתוֹךְ הַמַּחְתּוֹת: **זְרֵה הָלְאָה.** לָאָרֶץ מֵעַל הַמַּחְתּוֹת: **כִּי קָדֵשׁוּ.** הַמַּחְתּוֹת, וַאֲסוּרִין בַּהֲנָאָה, שֶׁהֲרֵי עֲשָׂאוּם כְּלֵי שָׁרֵת:

ג **הַחַטָּאִים הָאֵלֶּה בְּנַפְשֹׁתָם.** שֶׁנַּעֲשׂוּ פּוֹשְׁעִים בְּנַפְשׁוֹתָם, שֶׁנֶּחְלְקוּ עַל הַקָּדוֹשׁ בָּרוּךְ הוּא: **רִקֻּעֵי.** רְדוּדִין: **פַּחִים.** טַסִּים מְרֻדָּדִין, טינבי״ש בְּלַעַז: **צִפּוּי לַמִּזְבֵּחַ.** לְמִזְבַּח הַנְּחֹשֶׁת: **וְיִהְיוּ לְאוֹת.** לְזִכָּרוֹן, שֶׁיֹּאמְרוּ: אֵלּוּ הָיוּ מֵאוֹתָן שֶׁנֶּחְלְקוּ עַל הַכְּהֻנָּה וְנִשְׂרְפוּ:

events which involve temporary suspension of natural or scientific law. The Mishna teaches that these events were programmed into nature at the outset. In general, Judaism emphasizes the law-like structure of the physical universe, as it says in Ecclesiastes, "There is nothing new beneath the sun" (1:9).

we will encounter more of these, including "the mouth of [Miriam's] well," which accompanied the Israelites on their journey (a midrashic tradition – Taanit 9a – arising from the juxtaposition of Miriam's death and the people's thirst; Num. 20:1–4), and "the mouth of [Bilam's] donkey," which spoke (Num. 22:28). These are all miraculous

כח וּנְשֵׁיהֶם וּבְנֵיהֶם וְטַפָּם: וַיֹּאמֶר מֹשֶׁה בְּזֹאת תֵּדְעוּן כִּי־יְהוָה שְׁלָחַנִי
כט לַעֲשׂוֹת אֵת כָּל־הַמַּעֲשִׂים הָאֵלֶּה כִּי־לֹא מִלִּבִּי: אִם־כְּמוֹת כָּל־הָאָדָם
ל יְמֻתוּן אֵלֶּה וּפְקֻדַּת כָּל־הָאָדָם יִפָּקֵד עֲלֵיהֶם לֹא יְהוָה שְׁלָחָנִי: וְאִם־
בְּרִיאָה יִבְרָא יְהוָה וּפָצְתָה הָאֲדָמָה אֶת־פִּיהָ וּבָלְעָה אֹתָם וְאֶת־כָּל־
אֲשֶׁר לָהֶם וְיָרְדוּ חַיִּים שְׁאֹלָה וִידַעְתֶּם כִּי נִאֲצוּ הָאֲנָשִׁים הָאֵלֶּה אֶת־
לא יְהוָה: וַיְהִי כְּכַלֹּתוֹ לְדַבֵּר אֵת כָּל־הַדְּבָרִים הָאֵלֶּה וַתִּבָּקַע הָאֲדָמָה
לב אֲשֶׁר תַּחְתֵּיהֶם: וַתִּפְתַּח הָאָרֶץ אֶת־פִּיהָ וַתִּבְלַע אֹתָם וְאֶת־בָּתֵּיהֶם
לג וְאֵת כָּל־הָאָדָם אֲשֶׁר לְקֹרַח וְאֵת כָּל־הָרְכוּשׁ: וַיֵּרְדוּ הֵם וְכָל־אֲשֶׁר
לד לָהֶם חַיִּים שְׁאֹלָה וַתְּכַס עֲלֵיהֶם הָאָרֶץ וַיֹּאבְדוּ מִתּוֹךְ הַקָּהָל: וְכָל־
יִשְׂרָאֵל אֲשֶׁר סְבִיבֹתֵיהֶם נָסוּ לְקֹלָם כִּי אָמְרוּ פֶּן־תִּבְלָעֵנוּ הָאָרֶץ:
לה וְאֵשׁ יָצְאָה מֵאֵת יְהוָה וַתֹּאכַל אֵת הַחֲמִשִּׁים וּמָאתַיִם אִישׁ מַקְרִיבֵי
יז א ב הַקְּטֹרֶת: וַיְדַבֵּר יְהוָה אֶל־מֹשֶׁה לֵּאמֹר: אֱמֹר אֶל־אֶלְעָזָר
בֶּן־אַהֲרֹן הַכֹּהֵן וְיָרֵם אֶת־הַמַּחְתֹּת מִבֵּין הַשְּׂרֵפָה וְאֶת־הָאֵשׁ זְרֵה־
ג הָלְאָה כִּי קָדֵשׁוּ: אֵת מַחְתּוֹת הַחַטָּאִים הָאֵלֶּה בְּנַפְשֹׁתָם וְעָשׂוּ
אֹתָם רִקֻּעֵי פַחִים צִפּוּי לַמִּזְבֵּחַ כִּי־הִקְרִיבֻם לִפְנֵי־יְהוָה וַיִּקְדָּשׁוּ

אונקלוס

ונשיהון ובניהון וטפלהון: כח ואמר משה, בדא תדעון, ארי יי שלחני, למעבד, ית כל עובדיא האלין, ארי לא מרעותי: כט אם כמותא דכל אנשא ימותון אלין, וסעורא דכל אנשא, יסתער עליהון, לא יי שלחני: ל ואם בריאה יברי יי, ותפתח ארעא ית פמה ותבלע יתהון וית כל דילהון, ויחתון כד חיין לשאול, ותדעון, ארי ארגיזו, גבריא האלין קדם יי: לא והוה כד שיצי, למללא, ית כל פתגמיא האלין, ואתבזעת ארעא דתחותיהון: לב ופתחת ארעא ית פמה, ובלעת יתהון וית אנש בתיהון, וית כל אנשא דלקרח, וית כל קנינא: לג ונחתו, אנון וכל דילהון, כד חיין לשאול, וחפת עליהון ארעא, ואבדו מגו קהלא: לד וכל ישראל, דבסחרניהון ערקו לקלהון, ארי אמרו, דלמא תבלעננא ארעא: לה ואישתא נפקת מן קדם יי, ואכלת, ית מאתן וחמשין גברא, מקרבי קטורת בסמיא: יז א ומליל יי עם משה למימר: ב אימר לאלעזר בר אהרן כהנא, ויפריש ית מחתיתא מבין יקידיא, וית אישתא ירחיק להלאה, ארי אתקדשא: ג ית, מחתית חיביא האלין דאתחיבו בנפשתהון, ויעבדון יתהון, טסין רדידין חופאה למדבחא, ארי קריבונין קדם יי ואתקדשא.

16:32 וַתִּפְתַּח הָאָרֶץ אֶת־פִּיהָ *The earth opened its mouth* – "The mouth of the earth," which opens to swallow Koraḥ, is listed in the Mishna as one of the "ten things created on the eve of the Sabbath at sunset" (Avot 5:6). In the coming *parashot*

4 holy. And they will be a sign for the Israelites." Elazar the priest took the bronze
censers that the men consumed by fire had presented, and hammered them
5 into a covering for the altar, as the LORD had said to him through Moshe –
a reminder for the Israelites that no outsider, no one not descended from
Aharon, should offer incense before the LORD, and become like Koraḥ and his
company.
6 The next day the entire Israelite community complained to Moshe and Aharon,
7 "You have killed the LORD's people!" As the community assembled against
Moshe and Aharon, they turned toward the Tent of Meeting. A cloud was
8 covering it, and the glory of the LORD appeared. Moshe and Aharon came
9 to the front of the Tent of Meeting. And the LORD spoke to Moshe: REVI'I
10 "Get away from this community; let Me consume them in an instant." They
11 fell on their faces, and Moshe said to Aharon, "Take the censer, put fire from
the altar into it, place incense upon it, and go quickly to the community and
make atonement for them. Fury has come forth from the LORD; the plague has
12 begun." Aharon took it as Moshe said and ran into the midst of the assembly,
for the plague had already begun among the people. He offered incense and

רש"י

ד **וַיְרַקְּעוּם.** אינטינבירינ"ט בְּלַעַז:

ה **וְלֹא יִהְיֶה כְקֹרַח.** כְּדֵי שֶׁלֹּא יִהְיֶה כְּקֹרַח: **כַּאֲשֶׁר דִּבֶּר ה' בְּיַד מֹשֶׁה לוֹ.** כְּמוֹ 'עָלָיו', עַל אַהֲרֹן דִּבֶּר אֶל מֹשֶׁה שֶׁיִּהְיֶה הוּא וּבָנָיו כֹּהֲנִים, לְפִיכָךְ "לֹא יִקְרַב אִישׁ זָר אֲשֶׁר לֹא מִזֶּרַע אַהֲרֹן" וְגוֹ'. וְכֵן כָּל 'לִי' וְ'לוֹ' וְ'לָהֶם' הַסְּמוּכִים אֵצֶל דִּבּוּר, פִּתְרוֹנָם כְּמוֹ 'עַל'. וּמִדְרָשׁוֹ, עַל קֹרַח. וּמַהוּ "בְּיַד מֹשֶׁה" וְלֹא כָּתַב 'אֶל מֹשֶׁה'? רֶמֶז לַחוֹלְקִים עַל הַכְּהֻנָּה שֶׁלּוֹקִין בְּצָרַעַת כְּמוֹ שֶׁלָּקָה מֹשֶׁה בְּיָדוֹ, שֶׁנֶּאֱמַר: "וַיּוֹצִאָהּ וְהִנֵּה יָדוֹ מְצֹרַעַת כַּשָּׁלֶג" (שמות ד, ו), וְעַל כֵּן לָקָה עֻזִּיָּהוּ בְּצָרַעַת (דברי הימים ב' כו, טז-כ):

יא **וְכַפֵּר עֲלֵיהֶם.** רָז זֶה מָסַר לוֹ מַלְאַךְ הַמָּוֶת כְּשֶׁעָלָה לָרָקִיעַ, שֶׁהַקְּטֹרֶת עוֹצֶרֶת הַמַּגֵּפָה, כִּדְאִיתָא בְּמַסֶּכֶת שַׁבָּת (דף פט ע"א):

entire Israelite community complained to Moshe and Aharon, 'You have killed the LORD's people'" (17:6). You may be right, they imply, and Koraḥ may have been wrong. But is this a way to win an argument?

17:11 **וְהוֹלֵךְ מְהֵרָה... הֵחֵל הַנָּגֶף** *Go quickly.... The plague has begun* – The plague is a punishment for the people's rebellion against Moshe and Aharon, yet the leaders' response is to rush to the people's defense. The voice of Heaven often speaks in the language of justice. The people have sinned and must be punished. But at the same time, God sends His prophets to speak in the people's defense. If the prophet adopts the perspective of justice and he too condemns the people, then he has betrayed his mission.

This will not be the last time that punishment takes the form of a plague. We remember this poignantly in the *Taḥanun* prayer as we quote words spoken by David during a moment of crisis (II Sam. 24:14). The king had sinned by taking a census of the people. God, through the prophet Gad, offered him a choice: famine, war, or punishment directly from Heaven. David replied: "I am in grave torment.... Let us fall into the hand of the LORD, for His mercy is great." God's punishment, even a deadly epidemic, is better than suffering the cruelty of man.

ד וְיִהְיוּ לְאוֹת לִבְנֵי יִשְׂרָאֵל׃ וַיִּקַּח אֶלְעָזָר הַכֹּהֵן אֵת מַחְתּוֹת הַנְּחֹשֶׁת
ה אֲשֶׁר הִקְרִיבוּ הַשְּׂרֻפִים וַיְרַקְּעוּם צִפּוּי לַמִּזְבֵּחַ׃ זִכָּרוֹן לִבְנֵי יִשְׂרָאֵל
לְמַעַן אֲשֶׁר לֹא־יִקְרַב אִישׁ זָר אֲשֶׁר לֹא מִזֶּרַע אַהֲרֹן הוּא לְהַקְטִיר
קְטֹרֶת לִפְנֵי יהוה וְלֹא־יִהְיֶה כְקֹרַח וְכַעֲדָתוֹ כַּאֲשֶׁר דִּבֶּר יהוה בְּיַד־
מֹשֶׁה לוֹ׃
ו וַיִּלֹּנוּ כָּל־עֲדַת בְּנֵי־יִשְׂרָאֵל מִמָּחֳרָת עַל־מֹשֶׁה וְעַל־אַהֲרֹן לֵאמֹר
ז אַתֶּם הֲמִתֶּם אֶת־עַם יהוה׃ וַיְהִי בְּהִקָּהֵל הָעֵדָה עַל־מֹשֶׁה וְעַל־
אַהֲרֹן וַיִּפְנוּ אֶל־אֹהֶל מוֹעֵד וְהִנֵּה כִסָּהוּ הֶעָנָן וַיֵּרָא כְּבוֹד יהוה׃
ח ט וַיָּבֹא מֹשֶׁה וְאַהֲרֹן אֶל־פְּנֵי אֹהֶל מוֹעֵד׃ וַיְדַבֵּר רביעי
י יהוה אֶל־מֹשֶׁה לֵּאמֹר׃ הֵרֹמּוּ מִתּוֹךְ הָעֵדָה הַזֹּאת וַאֲכַלֶּה אֹתָם
יא כְּרָגַע וַיִּפְּלוּ עַל־פְּנֵיהֶם׃ וַיֹּאמֶר מֹשֶׁה אֶל־אַהֲרֹן קַח אֶת־הַמַּחְתָּה
וְתֶן־עָלֶיהָ אֵשׁ מֵעַל הַמִּזְבֵּחַ וְשִׂים קְטֹרֶת וְהוֹלֵךְ מְהֵרָה אֶל־הָעֵדָה
יב וְכַפֵּר עֲלֵיהֶם כִּי־יָצָא הַקֶּצֶף מִלִּפְנֵי יהוה הֵחֵל הַנָּגֶף׃ וַיִּקַּח אַהֲרֹן
כַּאֲשֶׁר ׀ דִּבֶּר מֹשֶׁה וַיָּרָץ אֶל־תּוֹךְ הַקָּהָל וְהִנֵּה הֵחֵל הַנֶּגֶף בָּעָם וַיִּתֵּן

אונקלוס

וִיהוֹן לְאָת לִבְנֵי יִשְׂרָאֵל: ד וּנְסֵיב אֶלְעָזָר כָּהֲנָא, יָת מַחְתְּיָת נְחָשָׁא, דְּקָרִיבוּ יְקִידַיָּא, וְרַדִּידוּנִין חוּפָאָה לְמַדְבְּחָא: ה דָּכְרָנָא לִבְנֵי יִשְׂרָאֵל, בְּדִיל, דְּלָא יִקְרַב גְּבַר חִילוֹנַי, דְּלָא מִזַּרְעָא דְאַהֲרֹן הוּא, לְאַסָּקָא קְטוֹרֶת בֻּסְמִין קֳדָם יְיָ, וְלָא יְהֵי כְקֹרַח וְכִכְנִשְׁתֵּיהּ, כְּמָא דְמַלֵּיל יְיָ, בִּידָא דְמֹשֶׁה לֵיהּ: ו וְאִתְרָעֲמוּ, כָּל כְּנִשְׁתָּא דִבְנֵי יִשְׂרָאֵל מִיּוֹמָא דְבָתְרוֹהִי, עַל מֹשֶׁה וְעַל אַהֲרֹן לְמֵימַר, אַתּוּן גְּרַמְתּוּן דְּמִית עַמָּא דַייָ: ז וַהֲוָה, בְּאִתְכַּנָּשׁוּת כְּנִשְׁתָּא עַל מֹשֶׁה וְעַל אַהֲרֹן, וְאִתְפְּנִיאוּ לְמַשְׁכַּן זִמְנָא, וְהָא חֲפָהִי עֲנָנָא, וְאִתְגְּלִי יְקָרָא דַייָ: ח וְעָאל מֹשֶׁה וְאַהֲרֹן, לִקְדָם מַשְׁכַּן זִמְנָא: ט וּמַלֵּיל יְיָ עִם מֹשֶׁה לְמֵימַר: י אִתְפְּרַשׁוּ, מִגּוֹ כְּנִשְׁתָּא הָדָא, וַאֲשֵׁיצֵי יָתְהוֹן כְּשָׁעָה, וּנְפַלוּ עַל אַפֵּיהוֹן: יא וַאֲמַר מֹשֶׁה לְאַהֲרֹן, סַב יָת מַחְתִּיתָא, וְהַב עֲלַהּ אִישָׁתָא, מֵעִלָּוֵי מַדְבְּחָא וְשַׁו קְטוֹרֶת בֻּסְמִין, וְאוֹבֵיל בִּפְרִיעַ, לִכְנִשְׁתָּא וְכַפַּר עֲלֵיהוֹן, אֲרֵי נְפַק רֻגְזָא, מִן קֳדָם יְיָ שָׁרֵי מוֹתָנָא: יב וּנְסֵיב אַהֲרֹן, כְּמָא דְמַלֵּיל מֹשֶׁה, וּרְהַט לְגוֹ קְהָלָא, וְהָא, שָׁרֵי מוֹתָנָא בְּעַמָּא, וִיהַב

17:6 אַתֶּם הֲמִתֶּם אֶת־עַם יהוה *You have killed the Lord's people* – No sooner has Moshe finished than "the ground beneath them split open. The earth opened its mouth and swallowed them" (Num. 16:31–32). One cannot imagine a more dramatic vindication. God has shown, beyond possibility of doubt, that Moshe is right and the rebels wrong. Yet far from being apologetic and repentant, the people return the next morning still complaining – this time, not about who should lead whom but about the way Moshe has chosen to end the dispute: "The next day the

13 made atonement for the people; he stood between the dead and the living, and
14 the plague was halted; 14,700 died from that plague, in addition to those who
15 died on account of Koraḥ. And Aharon returned to Moshe at the entrance to
the Tent of Meeting – for the plague had stopped.
16 17 Then the LORD spoke to Moshe: "Speak to the Israelites and take from them HAMISHI
twelve staffs, one for each ancestral house, from all the leaders of their ancestral
18 houses. Write each man's name on his staff, and on Levi's staff write Aharon's
19 name, for there shall be one staff for the head of each ancestral house. Place
them in the Tent of Meeting in front of the Ark of the Covenant, where I meet
20 with you. The staff of the man I choose – that will give flower. Thus I will rid
21 Myself of the incessant railings of the Israelites against you." Moshe spoke to
the Israelites, and each of their leaders gave him a staff, one for each leader,
according to their ancestral houses, twelve staffs with Aharon's staff among
22 them. Moshe placed the staffs before the LORD in the Tent of the Testimony.

רש״י

יג **ויעמד בין המתים וגו׳.** אחז את המלאך והעמידו על כרחו. אמר לו המלאך: הנח לי לעשות שליחותי. אמר לו: משה צוני לעכב על ידך. אמר לו: אני שלוחו של מקום ואתה שלוחו של משה. אמר לו: אין משה אומר כלום מלבו אלא מפי הגבורה, אם אין אתה מאמין, הרי הקדוש ברוך הוא ומשה אל פתח אהל מועד, בא עמי ושאל. וזהו שנאמר: "וישב אהרן אל משה" (להלן פסוק טו). דבר אחר, למה בקטרת? לפי שהיו ישראל מליזים ומרננים אחר הקטרת לומר: סם המות הוא, על ידו מתו נדב ואביהוא, על ידו נשרפו חמשים ומאתים איש. אמר הקדוש ברוך הוא: תראו שעוצר מגפה הוא, והחטא הוא הממית:

יח **כי מטה אחד.** אף על פי שחלקתים לשתי משפחות, משפחת כהנה לבד ולויה לבד, מכל מקום שבט אחד הוא:

כ **והשכתי.** כמו: "וישכו המים" (בראשית ח, א), "וחמת המלך שככה" (אסתר ז, י):

כא **בתוך מטותם.** הניחו באמצע, שלא יאמרו: מפני שהניחו בצד שכינה פרח:

the land of Israel. After the debacle of the spies, that hope has died. The stick that comes to life again (like Yeḥezkel's vision of the valley of dry bones, Ezek. 37) symbolizes that hope is not dead, merely deferred. The next generation will live and reach the destination. God is a God of life. What He touches does not die.

The episode of Koraḥ teaches us that there are two ways of resolving conflict: by force and by persuasion. The first negates your opponent. The second enlists your opponent, taking his or her challenge seriously and addressing it. Force never ends conflict – not even in the case of Moshe, not even when the force is miraculous. There never was a more decisive intervention than the miracle that swallowed up Koraḥ and his fellow rebels. Yet it does not end the conflict. It deepens it.

What ends it is the quiet, gentle miracle that shows that Aharon is the true emissary of the God of life. Not by accident is the verse that calls Torah a "tree of life" preceded by these words: "Its ways are the ways of pleasantness, and all of its paths are peaceful" (Prov. 3:17). This is the preferred form of conflict resolution in Judaism – not by force, but by pleasantness and peace.

יג אֶת־הַקְּטֹרֶת וַיְכַפֵּר עַל־הָעָם׃ וַיַּעֲמֹד בֵּין־הַמֵּתִים וּבֵין הַחַיִּים וַתֵּעָצַר
יד הַמַּגֵּפָה׃ וַיִּהְיוּ הַמֵּתִים בַּמַּגֵּפָה אַרְבָּעָה עָשָׂר אֶלֶף וּשְׁבַע מֵאוֹת מִלְּבַד
טו הַמֵּתִים עַל־דְּבַר־קֹרַח׃ וַיָּשָׁב אַהֲרֹן אֶל־מֹשֶׁה אֶל־פֶּתַח אֹהֶל מוֹעֵד
וְהַמַּגֵּפָה נֶעֱצָרָה׃
טז יז וַיְדַבֵּר יהוה אֶל־מֹשֶׁה לֵּאמֹר׃ דַּבֵּר ׀ אֶל־בְּנֵי יִשְׂרָאֵל וְקַח מֵאִתָּם טז חמישי
מַטֶּה מַטֶּה לְבֵית אָב מֵאֵת כָּל־נְשִׂיאֵהֶם לְבֵית אֲבֹתָם שְׁנֵים עָשָׂר
יח מַטּוֹת אִישׁ אֶת־שְׁמוֹ תִּכְתֹּב עַל־מַטֵּהוּ׃ וְאֵת שֵׁם אַהֲרֹן תִּכְתֹּב עַל־
יט מַטֵּה לֵוִי כִּי מַטֶּה אֶחָד לְרֹאשׁ בֵּית אֲבוֹתָם׃ וְהִנַּחְתָּם בְּאֹהֶל מוֹעֵד
כ לִפְנֵי הָעֵדוּת אֲשֶׁר אִוָּעֵד לָכֶם שָׁמָּה׃ וְהָיָה הָאִישׁ אֲשֶׁר אֶבְחַר־בּוֹ
מַטֵּהוּ יִפְרָח וַהֲשִׁכֹּתִי מֵעָלַי אֶת־תְּלֻנּוֹת בְּנֵי יִשְׂרָאֵל אֲשֶׁר הֵם מַלִּינִם
כא עֲלֵיכֶם׃ וַיְדַבֵּר מֹשֶׁה אֶל־בְּנֵי יִשְׂרָאֵל וַיִּתְּנוּ אֵלָיו ׀ כָּל־נְשִׂיאֵיהֶם מַטֶּה
לְנָשִׂיא אֶחָד מַטֶּה לְנָשִׂיא אֶחָד לְבֵית אֲבֹתָם שְׁנֵים עָשָׂר מַטּוֹת
כב וּמַטֵּה אַהֲרֹן בְּתוֹךְ מַטּוֹתָם׃ וַיַּנַּח מֹשֶׁה אֶת־הַמַּטֹּת לִפְנֵי יהוה בְּאֹהֶל

אונקלוס

יָת קְטוֹרֶת בֻּסְמַיָּא, וְכַפַּר עַל עַמָּא: יג וְקָם בֵּין מִיתַיָּא וּבֵין חַיַּיָּא, וְאִתְכְּלִי מוֹתָנָא: יד וַהֲווֹ, דְּמִיתוּ בְּמוֹתָנָא, אַרְבְּעַת עֲסַר אַלְפִין וּשְׁבַע מְאָה, בָּר מִדְּמִיתוּ עַל פַּלְגּוּתָא דְקֹרַח: טו וְתָב אַהֲרֹן לְוָת מֹשֶׁה, לִתְרַע מַשְׁכַּן זִמְנָא, וּמוֹתָנָא אִתְכְּלִי: טז וּמַלֵּיל יְיָ עִם מֹשֶׁה לְמֵימַר: יז מַלֵּיל עִם בְּנֵי יִשְׂרָאֵל, וְסַב מִנְּהוֹן, חֻטְרָא חֻטְרָא לְבֵית אַבָּא, מִן כָּל רַבְרְבָנֵיהוֹן לְבֵית אֲבָהַתְהוֹן, תְּרֵי עֲסַר חֻטְרִין, גְּבַר יָת שְׁמֵיהּ, תִּכְתּוֹב עַל חֻטְרֵיהּ: יח וְיָת שְׁמָא דְאַהֲרֹן, תִּכְתּוֹב עַל חֻטְרָא דְלֵוִי, אֲרֵי חֻטְרָא חַד, לְרֵישׁ בֵּית אֲבָהַתְהוֹן: יט וְתַצְנְעִנּוּן בְּמַשְׁכַּן זִמְנָא, קֳדָם סָהֲדוּתָא, דַּאֲזַמֵּן מֵימְרִי לְכוֹן תַּמָּן: כ וִיהֵי, גֻּבְרָא, דְּאֶתְרְעֵי בֵיהּ חֻטְרֵיהּ יַנְעֵי, וַאֲנִיחַ מִן קֳדָמַי, יָת תֻּרְעֲמַת בְּנֵי יִשְׂרָאֵל, דְּאִנּוּן מִתְרַעֲמִין עֲלֵיכוֹן: כא וּמַלֵּיל מֹשֶׁה עִם בְּנֵי יִשְׂרָאֵל, וִיהַבוּ לֵיהּ כָּל רַבְרְבָנֵיהוֹן, חֻטְרָא לְרַבָּא חַד, חֻטְרָא לְרַבָּא חַד לְבֵית אֲבָהַתְהוֹן, תְּרֵי עֲסַר חֻטְרִין, וְחֻטְרָא דְאַהֲרֹן בְּגוֹ חֻטְרֵיהוֹן: כב וְאַצְנַע מֹשֶׁה, יָת חֻטְרַיָּא קֳדָם יְיָ, בְּמַשְׁכְּנָא דְסָהֲדוּתָא:

THE SIGN OF THE STAFFS

The use of force never ends a conflict. It merely adds grievance to injury. What ends this conflict is not the miracle of the ground opening up and swallowing Moshe's opponents, but something else altogether: the visible symbol that Aharon is the chosen vehicle of the God of life. The gentle miracle of the dead wood that comes to life again, flowering and bearing fruit, anticipates the famous words of the book of Proverbs about the Torah: "It is a tree of life for those who grasp it; those who hold fast to it are fortunate" (3:18). Moshe and Aharon stand accused of failing in their mission. They have brought the people out of Egypt to bring them to

▶

23 And the following day Moshe entered the Tent of the Testimony, and Aharon's
staff, representing the House of Levi, had given flower. It had budded, produced
24 blossoms, and was now bearing almonds. Moshe brought out all the staffs
from before the LORD to all the Israelites. They saw. And each man took back
his staff.
25 Then the LORD said to Moshe, "Put back Aharon's staff in front of the Ark of SHISHI
the Covenant to serve as a sign to rebels so that their railings against Me end,
26 and they will not die." Moshe did so. As the LORD commanded him, so he did.
27 The Israelites said to Moshe, "We are going to die. We are lost; all of us are
28 lost. Whoever approaches the LORD's Tabernacle is to die. Will we die out
18 1 completely?" The LORD said to Aharon: "You, your sons, and your
ancestral house shall bear any guilt connected with the Sanctuary, and you and
2 your sons will bear any guilt connected with your priesthood. Bring with you
also your brothers from the tribe of Levi, your father's tribe. Let them join you
3 and minister to you and your sons before the Tent of the Testimony. They shall
discharge their duties to you and to the Tent as a whole, but they must not
draw close to the utensils of the Sanctuary or the altar, or both they and you

רש״י

כג **וַיֹּצֵא פֶרַח.** כְּמַשְׁמָעוֹ: **צִיץ.** הוּא חֲנָטַת הַפְּרִי כְּשֶׁהַפֶּרַח נוֹפֵל: **וַיִּגְמֹל שְׁקֵדִים.** כְּשֶׁהֻכַּר הַפְּרִי הֻכַּר שֶׁהֵן שְׁקֵדִים, לְשׁוֹן: "וַיִּגְדַּל הַיֶּלֶד וַיִּגָּמַל" (בראשית כא, ח), וְלָשׁוֹן זֶה מָצוּי בְּפֵרוֹת הָאִילָן, כְּמוֹ: "וּבֹסֶר גֹּמֵל יִהְיֶה נִצָּה" (ישעיה יח, ה). וְלָמָּה שְׁקֵדִים? הוּא הַפְּרִי הַמְמַהֵר לְהַפְרִיחַ מִכָּל הַפֵּרוֹת; אַף הַמְעוֹרֵר עַל הַכְּהֻנָּה פֻּרְעָנוּתוֹ מְמַהֶרֶת לָבֹא, כְּמוֹ שֶׁמָּצִינוּ בְּעֻזִּיָּהוּ: "וְהַצָּרַעַת זָרְחָה בְמִצְחוֹ" (דברי הימים ב׳ כו, יט). וְתַרְגּוּמוֹ: "וְכַפִּית שִׁגְדִּין", כְּמִין אֶשְׁכּוֹל שְׁקֵדִים יַחַד כְּפוּתִים זֶה עַל זֶה:

כה **וּתְכַל תְּלוּנֹּתָם.** כְּמוֹ 'וְתִכְלֶה תְּלוּנָּתָם', לְשׁוֹן שֵׁם מִפְעָל יָחִיד לִנְקֵבָה כְּמוֹ מורמורדי״ן בְּלַעַז: **לְמִשְׁמֶרֶת לְאוֹת.** לְזִכָּרוֹן שֶׁבָּחַרְתִּי בְּאַהֲרֹן לְכֹהֵן, וְלֹא יַלִּינוּ עוֹד עַל הַכְּהֻנָּה:

כח **כֹּל הַקָּרֵב הַקָּרֵב וְגוֹ׳.** אֵין אָנוּ יְכוֹלִין לִהְיוֹת זְהִירִין בְּכָךְ, כֻּלָּנוּ רַשָּׁאִין לְהִכָּנֵס לַחֲצַר אֹהֶל מוֹעֵד, וְאֶחָד שֶׁיַּקְרִיב עַצְמוֹ יוֹתֵר מֵחֲבֵרָיו וְיִכָּנֵס לְתוֹךְ אֹהֶל מוֹעֵד יָמוּת: **הַאִם תַּמְנוּ לִגְוֹעַ.** שֶׁמָּא הֻפְקַרְנוּ לְמִיתָה?!:

יח א **וַיֹּאמֶר ה׳ אֶל אַהֲרֹן.** לְמֹשֶׁה אָמַר שֶׁיֹּאמַר לְאַהֲרֹן, לְהַזְהִירוֹ עַל תַּקָּנַת יִשְׂרָאֵל שֶׁלֹּא יִכָּנְסוּ לַמִּקְדָּשׁ: **אַתָּה וּבָנֶיךָ וּבֵית אָבִיךָ.** הֵם בְּנֵי קְהָת אֲבִי עַמְרָם: **תִּשְׂאוּ אֶת עֲוֹן הַמִּקְדָּשׁ.** עֲלֵיכֶם אֲנִי מַטִּיל עֹנֶשׁ הַזָּרִים שֶׁיֶּחֶטְאוּ בְּעִסְקֵי הַדְּבָרִים הַמְקֻדָּשִׁים הַמְּסוּרִים לָכֶם, הוּא הָאֹהֶל וְהָאָרוֹן וְהַשֻּׁלְחָן וּכְלֵי הַקֹּדֶשׁ, אַתֶּם תֵּשְׁבוּ וְתַזְהִירוּ עַל כָּל זָר הַבָּא לִגַּע: **וְאַתָּה וּבָנֶיךָ.** הַכֹּהֲנִים: **תִּשְׂאוּ אֶת עֲוֹן כְּהֻנַּתְכֶם.** שֶׁאֵינָהּ מְסוּרָה לַלְוִיִּם, וְתַזְהִירוּ הַלְוִיִּם הַשּׁוֹגְגִים שֶׁלֹּא יִגְּעוּ אֲלֵיכֶם בַּעֲבוֹדַתְכֶם:

ב **וְגַם אֶת אַחֶיךָ.** בְּנֵי גֵרְשׁוֹן וּבְנֵי מְרָרִי: **וְיִלָּווּ.** וְיִתְחַבְּרוּ אֲלֵיכֶם, לְהַזְהִיר גַּם אֶת הַזָּרִים מִלִּקְרַב אֲלֵיהֶם: **וִישָׁרְתוּךָ.** בִּשְׁמִירַת הַשְּׁעָרִים וּלְמַנּוֹת מֵהֶם גִּזְבָּרִין וַאֲמַרְכָּלִין:

symbol of life, light, holiness, and the watchful presence of God.

After the episode of the spies, Moshe faces an almost impossible task. How do you lead a people when they know they will not reach their destination in their lifetime? In the end, what stills the rebellion is the sight of Aharon's staff, a piece of dry wood coming to life again, bearing flowers and fruit. Having thought of themselves as condemned to die in the desert, they now realize that they too have borne fruit – their children – and that those children will complete the journey their parents began.

כג הָעֵדֻת: וַיְהִי מִמָּחֳרָת וַיָּבֹא מֹשֶׁה אֶל־אֹהֶל הָעֵדוּת וְהִנֵּה פָּרַח מַטֵּה־
כד אַהֲרֹן לְבֵית לֵוִי וַיֹּצֵא פֶרַח וַיָּצֵץ צִיץ וַיִּגְמֹל שְׁקֵדִים: וַיֹּצֵא מֹשֶׁה
אֶת־כָּל־הַמַּטֹּת מִלִּפְנֵי יהוה אֶל־כָּל־בְּנֵי יִשְׂרָאֵל וַיִּרְאוּ וַיִּקְחוּ אִישׁ
מַטֵּהוּ:
כה וַיֹּאמֶר יהוה אֶל־מֹשֶׁה הָשֵׁב אֶת־מַטֵּה אַהֲרֹן לִפְנֵי הָעֵדוּת לְמִשְׁמֶרֶת ששי
כו לְאוֹת לִבְנֵי־מֶרִי וּתְכַל תְּלוּנֹּתָם מֵעָלַי וְלֹא יָמֻתוּ: וַיַּעַשׂ מֹשֶׁה כַּאֲשֶׁר
צִוָּה יהוה אֹתוֹ כֵּן עָשָׂה:
כז וַיֹּאמְרוּ בְּנֵי יִשְׂרָאֵל אֶל־מֹשֶׁה לֵאמֹר הֵן גָּוַעְנוּ אָבַדְנוּ כֻּלָּנוּ
כח אָבָדְנוּ: כֹּל הַקָּרֵב ׀ הַקָּרֵב אֶל־מִשְׁכַּן יהוה יָמוּת הַאִם תַּמְנוּ
יח א לִגְוֹעַ: וַיֹּאמֶר יהוה אֶל־אַהֲרֹן אַתָּה וּבָנֶיךָ וּבֵית־אָבִיךָ אִתָּךְ
תִּשְׂאוּ אֶת־עֲוֺן הַמִּקְדָּשׁ וְאַתָּה וּבָנֶיךָ אִתָּךְ תִּשְׂאוּ אֶת־עֲוֺן כְּהֻנַּתְכֶם:
ב וְגַם אֶת־אַחֶיךָ מַטֵּה לֵוִי שֵׁבֶט אָבִיךָ הַקְרֵב אִתָּךְ וְיִלָּווּ עָלֶיךָ וִישָׁרְתוּךָ
ג וְאַתָּה וּבָנֶיךָ אִתָּךְ לִפְנֵי אֹהֶל הָעֵדֻת: וְשָׁמְרוּ מִשְׁמַרְתְּךָ וּמִשְׁמֶרֶת
כָּל־הָאֹהֶל אַךְ אֶל־כְּלֵי הַקֹּדֶשׁ וְאֶל־הַמִּזְבֵּחַ לֹא יִקְרָבוּ וְלֹא־יָמֻתוּ

אונקלוס

כג וַהֲוָה בְּיוֹמָא דְּבָתְרוֹהִי, וְעָאל מֹשֶׁה לְמַשְׁכְּנָא דְסָהֲדוּתָא, וְהָא, יְעָא חֻטְרָא דְּאַהֲרֹן לְבֵית לֵוִי, וְאַפֵּיק לַבְלְבִין וְאָנֵיץ נֵץ, וְכַפִּית שִׁגְדִּין: כד וְאַפֵּיק מֹשֶׁה יָת כָּל חֻטְרַיָּא מִן קֳדָם יי, לְכָל בְּנֵי יִשְׂרָאֵל, וְאִשְׁתְּמוֹדָעוּ וּנְסִיבוּ גְּבַר חֻטְרֵיהּ: כה וַאֲמַר יי לְמֹשֶׁה, אֲתֵיב, יָת חֻטְרָא דְּאַהֲרֹן לִקְדָם סָהֲדוּתָא, לְמַטְּרָא לְאָת לְעַמָּא סָרְבָנָא, וִיסוּפוּן תְּרַעֲמָתְהוֹן, מִן קֳדָמַי וְלָא יְמוּתוּן: כו וַעֲבַד מֹשֶׁה, כְּמָא דְּפַקֵּיד יי, יָתֵיהּ כֵּן עֲבַד: כז וַאֲמַרוּ בְּנֵי יִשְׂרָאֵל, לְמֹשֶׁה לְמֵימַר, הָא מִנַּנָא קְטִילַת חַרְבָּא, הָא מִנַּנָא בְּלַעַת אַרְעָא, הָא מִנַּנָא מִיתוּ בְּמוֹתָנָא: כח כָּל דְּקָרֵיב מִקְרַב, לְמַשְׁכְּנָא דַּיי מָאִית, הָא אֲנַחְנָא סָיְפִין לִמְמָת: יח א וַאֲמַר יי לְאַהֲרֹן, אַתְּ, וּבְנָךְ וּבֵית אֲבוּךְ עִמָּךְ, תְּסַלְחוּן עַל חוֹבֵי מַקְדְּשָׁא, וְאַתְּ וּבְנָךְ עִמָּךְ, תְּסַלְחוּן עַל חוֹבֵי כְּהֻנַּתְכוֹן: ב וְאַף יָת אֲחָךְ שִׁבְטָא דְלֵוִי, שִׁבְטָא דַּאֲבוּךְ קָרֵיב לְוָתָךְ, וְיִתּוֹסְפוּן עֲלָךְ וִישַׁמְּשֻׁנָּךְ, וְאַתְּ וּבְנָךְ עִמָּךְ, קֳדָם מַשְׁכְּנָא דְסָהֲדוּתָא: ג וְיִטְּרוּן מַטַּרְתָּךְ, וּמַטְּרַת כָּל מַשְׁכְּנָא, בְּרַם לְמָנֵי קֻדְשָׁא וּלְמַדְבְּחָא לָא יִקְרְבוּן, וְלָא יְמוּתוּן

17:23 וַיִּגְמֹל שְׁקֵדִים *Bearing almonds* – In the Near East, the almond is the first tree to blossom, its white flowers signaling the end of winter and the emergence of new life. The almond flowers also recall the gold flowers on the candelabrum (menora), lit daily by Aharon in the Sanctuary (Ex. 25:31, 37:17). The Hebrew word *tzitz,* used here to mean "blossom," recalls the *tzitz,* the headplate of pure gold worn as part of Aharon's headdress, on which were inscribed the words "Holy to the Lord" (28:36). The sprouting almond branch is therefore more than a sign. It is a multifaceted

4 will die. They will join you in discharging the duties of the Tent of Meeting for
5 all the service of the Tent; no outsider shall draw near you. You shall discharge
the duties of the Sanctuary and the altar, so that fury may never again fall upon
6 the Israelites. I have singled out your brothers, the Levites, from among the
Israelites as a gift to you, dedicated to the LORD to perform the service of the
7 Tent of Meeting. You and your sons shall take care to perform the duties of
your priesthood in all matters pertaining to the altar and inside the curtain. I
give you your priestly service as a gift, but any outsider who draws close will
die."
8 The LORD spoke to Aharon: "I place in your charge the offerings made to
Me, all the sacred gifts of the Israelites. I give them to you and your sons as an
9 anointed right; this is an everlasting decree. This is what belongs to you among

רש"י

ד **וזר לא יקרב אליכם.** אתכם אני מזהיר על כך:

ה **ולא יהיה עוד קצף.** כמו שהיה כבר, שנאמר: "כי יצא הקצף" (לעיל יז, יא):

ו **לכם מתנה נתנים.** יכול לעבודתכם של הדיוט? תלמוד לומר: "לה'", כמו שמפרש למעלה, לשמר משמרת גזברין ואמרכלין:

ז **עבדת מתנה.** במתנה נתתיה לכם:

ח **ואני הנה נתתי לך.** בשמחה. לשון שמחה הוא זה, כמו: "הנה הוא יצא לקראתך וראך ושמח בלבו" (שמות ד, יד). משל למלך שנתן שדה לאוהבו ולא כתב ולא חתם ולא העלה בערכאין. בא אחד וערער על השדה, אמר לו המלך: כל מי שירצה יבא ויערער לנגדך, הריני כותב וחותם לך ומעלה בערכאין. אף כאן, לפי שבא קרח וערער כנגד אהרן על הכהנה, בא הכתוב ונתן לו עשרים וארבע מתנות כהנה בברית מלח עולם, ולכך נסמכה פרשה זו לכאן: **משמרת תרומתי.** שאתה צריך לשמרן בטהרה: **למשחה.** לגדלה:

ט **מן האש.** לאחר הקטרת האשים: **כל קרבנם.** כגון זבחי שלמי צבור:

Above all, though, came the belief that status was conferred by scholarship, Torah study. On this, the rabbis' remarks were forceful and unambiguous:

> With three crowns was Israel crowned.... The crown of priesthood was bestowed on Aharon and his descendants. The crown of kingship was conferred on David and his successors. But the crown of Torah is for all Israel. Whoever wishes, let him come and take it.... A Torah scholar of illegitimate birth takes precedence over an ignorant High Priest. (*Hilkhot Talmud Torah* 3:1–2)

Alongside statements like these went the creation of the world's first system of community-funded, universal education (Bava Batra 21a).

Significantly, the Rabbis traced their descent not from kings or priests – the two dynastic roles in Judaism – but to the prophets:

> Moshe received the Torah from Sinai and handed it on to Yehoshua, who handed it on to the elders, the elders to the prophets, and the prophets to the Men of the Great Assembly. (Avot 1:1)

Prophecy was not a dynasty. It was available to anyone of the right character, dedication, and spirituality. The Rabbis also understood that since knowledge is power, and the distribution of power is the central concern of politics, the distribution of knowledge is the single greatest issue affecting the structure of society. It was not on the streets or behind the barricades but in the house of study that the Rabbis achieved the revolutionary ideal of a society of equal dignity under the sovereignty of God.

ד גַּם־הֵם גַּם־אַתֶּם׃ וְנִלְווּ עָלֶיךָ וְשָׁמְרוּ אֶת־מִשְׁמֶרֶת אֹהֶל מוֹעֵד לְכֹל
ה עֲבֹדַת הָאֹהֶל וְזָר לֹא־יִקְרַב אֲלֵיכֶם׃ וּשְׁמַרְתֶּם אֵת מִשְׁמֶרֶת הַקֹּדֶשׁ
ו וְאֵת מִשְׁמֶרֶת הַמִּזְבֵּחַ וְלֹא־יִהְיֶה עוֹד קֶצֶף עַל־בְּנֵי יִשְׂרָאֵל׃ וַאֲנִי הִנֵּה
לָקַחְתִּי אֶת־אֲחֵיכֶם הַלְוִיִּם מִתּוֹךְ בְּנֵי יִשְׂרָאֵל לָכֶם מַתָּנָה נְתֻנִים
ז לַיהוה לַעֲבֹד אֶת־עֲבֹדַת אֹהֶל מוֹעֵד׃ וְאַתָּה וּבָנֶיךָ אִתְּךָ תִּשְׁמְרוּ
אֶת־כְּהֻנַּתְכֶם לְכָל־דְּבַר הַמִּזְבֵּחַ וּלְמִבֵּית לַפָּרֹכֶת וַעֲבַדְתֶּם עֲבֹדַת
מַתָּנָה אֶתֵּן אֶת־כְּהֻנַּתְכֶם וְהַזָּר הַקָּרֵב יוּמָת׃
ח וַיְדַבֵּר יהוה אֶל־אַהֲרֹן וַאֲנִי הִנֵּה נָתַתִּי לְךָ אֶת־מִשְׁמֶרֶת תְּרוּמֹתָי
לְכָל־קָדְשֵׁי בְנֵי־יִשְׂרָאֵל לְךָ נְתַתִּים לְמָשְׁחָה וּלְבָנֶיךָ לְחָק־עוֹלָם׃
ט זֶה יִהְיֶה לְךָ מִקֹּדֶשׁ הַקֳּדָשִׁים מִן־הָאֵשׁ כָּל־קָרְבָּנָם לְכָל־מִנְחָתָם

אונקלוס

אַף אִנּוּן אַף אַתּוּן: ד וְיִתּוֹסְפוּן עֲלָךְ, וְיִטְּרוּן, יָת מַטְּרַת מַשְׁכַּן זִמְנָא, לְכָל פֻּלְחַן מַשְׁכְּנָא, וְחִילוֹנַי לָא יִקְרַב לְוָתְכוֹן: ה וְתִטְּרוּן, יָת מַטְּרַת קֻדְשָׁא, וְיָת מַטְּרַת מַדְבְּחָא, וְלָא יְהֵי עוֹד, רֻגְזָא עַל בְּנֵי יִשְׂרָאֵל: ו וַאֲנָא, הָא קָרֵיבִית יָת אֲחֵיכוֹן לֵיוָאֵי, מִגּוֹ בְּנֵי יִשְׂרָאֵל, לְכוֹן, מַתְּנָא יְהִיבִין קֳדָם יי, לְמִפְלַח, יָת פֻּלְחַן מַשְׁכַּן זִמְנָא: ז וְאַתְּ וּבְנָךְ עִמָּךְ, תִּטְּרוּן יָת כְּהֻנַּתְכוֹן, לְכָל פִּתְגָם מַדְבְּחָא, וּלְמִגָּיו לְפָרֻכְתָּא וְתִפְלְחוּן, פֻּלְחַן מַתְּנָא, אֶתֵּין יָת כְּהֻנַּתְכוֹן, וְחִילוֹנַי דְּיִקְרַב יִתְקְטִיל: ח וּמַלֵּיל יי עִם אַהֲרֹן, וַאֲנָא הָא יְהַבִית לָךְ, יָת מַטְּרַת אַפְרָשׁוּתַי, לְכָל קֻדְשַׁיָּא דִּבְנֵי יִשְׂרָאֵל, לָךְ יְהַבְתִּנּוּן לִרְבוּ, וְלִבְנָךְ לִקְיָם עָלַם: ט דֵּין יְהֵי לָךְ, מִקֹּדֶשׁ קֻדְשַׁיָּא מוֹתַר מִן אִישָׁתָא, כָּל קֻרְבָּנְהוֹן, לְכָל מִנְחָתְהוֹן וּלְכָל

18:6 הִנֵּה לָקַחְתִּי אֶת־אֲחֵיכֶם הַלְוִיִּם *I have singled out your brothers* – Stepping back from the Koraḥ revolt and looking at Tanakh and Jewish history as a whole, we see that hierarchy was introduced into Judaism only in response to crisis. The restriction of priesthood to the sons of Aharon, and of secondary holiness to the Levites, only happened according to the Torah because of the sin of the golden calf. Had that not happened, sacred duties would have stayed the prerogative of the firstborn of all the tribes. The event highlighted the need for a new arrangement of sacred and profane, and the Levitical status became "a gift" for the tribe who were not involved in the sin. Monarchy was introduced only after the breakdown of law and order in the last days of the judges (I Sam. 8). Despite the fact that the Torah contains a command to appoint a king, still God said that in seeking a king the people had "rejected" Him (v. 7). It can be argued that neither monarchy nor the special status of the tribe of Levi and the family of Aharon were part of the original plan. They were responses to human weakness and failure.

Only thus can we understand the direction taken by Judaism after the destruction of the Second Temple. What emerged from this period was, by historical standards, an extraordinarily egalitarian structure, based not on kings and priests but on Torah study and the dignity of *knesset Yisrael*, the congregation of Israel as a whole. In place of sacrifices offered by priests came prayer offered by everyone. In place of rule by kings came governance by "the townsfolk" or "the notables" (*tovei ha'ir*) – not quite representative democracy but a move in that direction nonetheless.

the holiest offerings, from the fire: all their offerings, their grain offerings,
their purification offerings, and their guilt offerings. The holiest offerings that
10 they bring to Me will be yours and your sons'. You shall eat them in the way
11 of the holiest things. All your males may eat it; it is holy to you. This too will
be yours: as an everlasting statute I give the upraised gifts of all the Israelites'
wave offerings to you, together with your sons and daughters. Anyone who is
12 ritually pure in your household may eat of them. All the best of the oil, wine,
13 and grain, the choice produce that they give to the LORD, I give to you. The
first fruits of all that is in their land that they bring to the LORD will be yours.
14 Anyone who is pure in your household may eat it. Everything that is set aside
15 in Israel shall be yours. All the first to emerge from the womb of any creature,
human or animal, that is offered to the LORD shall be yours. You must, however,
16 redeem firstborn boys and the firstborn of impure animals. Their redemption
price from the age of one month shall be set at five shekel of silver according
17 to the Sanctuary weight: twenty gerah per shekel. You must not redeem the
firstborn of an ox, sheep, or goat; they are sacred. You must dash their blood
on the altar and send their fat up in smoke for a pleasing aroma to the LORD.
18 But their meat is yours. It shall be yours like the breast of the wave offering

רש״י

מִנְחָתָם חַטָּאתָם וַאֲשָׁמָם. כְּמַשְׁמָעוֹ: **אֲשֶׁר יָשִׁיבוּ לִי.** זֶה גֶּזֶל הַגֵּר:

י **בְּקֹדֶשׁ הַקֳּדָשִׁים תֹּאכְלֶנּוּ וְגוֹ׳.** לִמֵּד עַל קָדְשֵׁי קָדָשִׁים שֶׁאֵין נֶאֱכָלִין אֶלָּא בָּעֲזָרָה וּלְזִכְרֵי כְהֻנָּה:

יא **תְּרוּמַת מַתָּנָם.** הַמּוּרָם מִן הַתּוֹדָה וּמֵהַשְּׁלָמִים וּמֵאֵיל נָזִיר: **לְכָל תְּנוּפֹת.** שֶׁהֲרֵי אֵלּוּ טְעוּנִין תְּנוּפָה: **כָּל טָהוֹר.** וְלֹא טְמֵאִים. דָּבָר אַחֵר, "כָּל טָהוֹר" לְרַבּוֹת אִשְׁתּוֹ:

יב **רֵאשִׁיתָם.** הִיא תְּרוּמָה גְּדוֹלָה:

יח **כַּחֲזֵה הַתְּנוּפָה וּכְשׁוֹק הַיָּמִין.** שֶׁל שְׁלָמִים, שֶׁנֶּאֱכָלִים לַכֹּהֲנִים וְלִנְשֵׁיהֶם לִבְנֵיהֶם וּלְעַבְדֵיהֶם לִשְׁנֵי יָמִים וְלַיְלָה אֶחָד, אַף הַבְּכוֹר נֶאֱכָל לִשְׁנֵי יָמִים וְלַיְלָה אֶחָד: **לְךָ יִהְיֶה.** בָּא רַבִּי עֲקִיבָא וְלִמֵּד: הוֹסִיף לְךָ הַכָּתוּב הֲוָיָה אַחֶרֶת, שֶׁלֹּא תֹאמַר, כֶּחָזֶה וָשׁוֹק שֶׁל תּוֹדָה שֶׁאֵינוֹ נֶאֱכָל אֶלָּא לְיוֹם וָלַיְלָה:

apart to serve and to know God ... he is sanctified as holy of holies, and God is his portion and inheritance forever. (*Hilkhot Shemitta VeYovel* 13:12–13)

The hasidic master Rabbi Shlomo of Karlin (1738–92) said something beautiful and unexpected: "The greatest *yetzer hara* [inhibition against doing good] is that *we forget that we are children of the King*." All of us are here because God brought us into being in love and gave us work to do, saying in His still, small voice: "Bring a fragment of My presence into other lives." Not only Levites, not only kings, but every person. What made Moshe and Yirmeyahu and David special was not that they had a high opinion of themselves – the opposite was the case – but that they heard and heeded the cry of human suffering. For them, injustice was not a fact but a call. They believed, not in themselves, but in the cause. They knew that when someone is drowning, you don't stop to ask who is the best swimmer. You jump in. Leadership is response-ability, the ability to respond. How different is this conception of greatness to Koraḥ's – and yet how much more profound a recognition of the dignity of every human life.

וּלְכָל־חַטָּאתָם וּלְכָל־אֲשָׁמָם אֲשֶׁר יָשִׁיבוּ לִי קֹדֶשׁ קָדָשִׁים לְךָ הוּא
י וּלְבָנֶיךָ׃ בְּקֹדֶשׁ הַקֳּדָשִׁים תֹּאכְלֶנּוּ כָּל־זָכָר יֹאכַל אֹתוֹ קֹדֶשׁ יִהְיֶה־
יא לָּךְ׃ וְזֶה־לְּךָ תְּרוּמַת מַתָּנָם לְכָל־תְּנוּפֹת בְּנֵי יִשְׂרָאֵל לְךָ נְתַתִּים
וּלְבָנֶיךָ וְלִבְנֹתֶיךָ אִתְּךָ לְחָק־עוֹלָם כָּל־טָהוֹר בְּבֵיתְךָ יֹאכַל אֹתוֹ׃
יב כֹּל חֵלֶב יִצְהָר וְכָל־חֵלֶב תִּירוֹשׁ וְדָגָן רֵאשִׁיתָם אֲשֶׁר־יִתְּנוּ לַיהוָה
יג לְךָ נְתַתִּים׃ בִּכּוּרֵי כָּל־אֲשֶׁר בְּאַרְצָם אֲשֶׁר־יָבִיאוּ לַיהוָה לְךָ יִהְיֶה
יד טו כָּל־טָהוֹר בְּבֵיתְךָ יֹאכְלֶנּוּ׃ כָּל־חֵרֶם בְּיִשְׂרָאֵל לְךָ יִהְיֶה׃ כָּל־פֶּטֶר
רֶחֶם לְכָל־בָּשָׂר אֲשֶׁר־יַקְרִיבוּ לַיהוָה בָּאָדָם וּבַבְּהֵמָה יִהְיֶה־לָּךְ אַךְ ׀
פָּדֹה תִפְדֶּה אֵת בְּכוֹר הָאָדָם וְאֵת בְּכוֹר־הַבְּהֵמָה הַטְּמֵאָה תִּפְדֶּה׃
טז וּפְדוּיָו מִבֶּן־חֹדֶשׁ תִּפְדֶּה בְּעֶרְכְּךָ כֶּסֶף חֲמֵשֶׁת שְׁקָלִים בְּשֶׁקֶל הַקֹּדֶשׁ
יז עֶשְׂרִים גֵּרָה הוּא׃ אַךְ בְּכוֹר־שׁוֹר אוֹ־בְכוֹר כֶּשֶׂב אוֹ־בְכוֹר עֵז לֹא
תִפְדֶּה קֹדֶשׁ הֵם אֶת־דָּמָם תִּזְרֹק עַל־הַמִּזְבֵּחַ וְאֶת־חֶלְבָּם תַּקְטִיר
יח אִשֶּׁה לְרֵיחַ נִיחֹחַ לַיהוָה׃ וּבְשָׂרָם יִהְיֶה־לָּךְ כַּחֲזֵה הַתְּנוּפָה וּכְשׁוֹק

אונקלוס

חַטָּוָתְהוֹן, וּלְכָל אֲשָׁמְהוֹן דִּיתִיבוּן קֳדָמַי, קֹדֶשׁ קֻדְשִׁין דִּילָךְ, הוּא וְלִבְנָךְ: י בְּקֹדֶשׁ קֻדְשִׁין תֵּיכְלִנֵּיהּ, כָּל דְּכוּרָא יֵיכוֹל יָתֵיהּ, קֻדְשָׁא יְהֵי לָךְ: יא וְדֵין לָךְ אַפְרָשׁוּת מַתְּנָתְהוֹן, לְכָל אֲרָמוּת בְּנֵי יִשְׂרָאֵל, לָךְ יְהַבְתִּנּוּן, וְלִבְנָךְ וְלִבְנָתָךְ, עִמָּךְ לִקְיָם עָלַם, כָּל דִּדְכֵי בְּבֵיתָךְ יֵיכוֹל יָתֵיהּ: יב כָּל טוּב מְשַׁח, וְכָל טוּב חֲמַר וַעֲבוּר, רֵישִׁיתְהוֹן, דְּיִתְּנוּן קֳדָם יי לָךְ יְהַבְתִּנּוּן: יג בִּכּוּרֵי, כָּל דִּבְאַרְעֲהוֹן, דְּיַיְתוֹן קֳדָם יי דִּילָךְ יְהֵי, כָּל דִּדְכֵי בְּבֵיתָךְ יֵיכְלִנֵּיהּ: יד כָּל חֶרְמָא בְּיִשְׂרָאֵל דִּילָךְ יְהֵי: טו כָּל פְּתַח וַלְדָּא, לְכָל בִּסְרָא, דִּיקָרְבוּן קֳדָם יי, בַּאֲנָשָׁא וּבִבְעִירָא יְהֵי לָךְ, בְּרַם מִפְרַק תִּפְרוֹק, יָת בְּכוֹרָא דַאֲנָשָׁא, וְיָת, בְּכוֹרָא דִּבְעִירָא מְסָאֲבָא תִּפְרוֹק: טז וּפֻרְקָנֵיהּ מִבַּר יַרְחָא תִּפְרוֹק, בְּפֻרְסָנֵיהּ, כְּסַף, חֲמֵשׁ סִלְעִין בְּסִלְעֵי קֻדְשָׁא, עַסְרִין מָעִין הוּא: יז בְּרַם בְּכוֹרָא דְתוֹרָא, אוֹ בְּכוֹרָא דְאִמְּרָא, אוֹ בְּכוֹרָא דְעִזָּא, לָא תִפְרוֹק קֻדְשָׁא אִנּוּן, יָת דִּמְהוֹן, תִּזְרוֹק עַל מַדְבְּחָא וְיָת תַּרְבְּהוֹן תַּסֵּיק, קֻרְבַּן לְאִתְקַבָּלָא בְּרַעֲוָא קֳדָם יי: יח וּבִסְרְהוֹן יְהֵי לָךְ, כְּחֶדְיָא דַאֲרָמוּתָא, וּכְשָׁקָא

18:20 אֲנִי חֶלְקְךָ וְנַחֲלָתְךָ *I am your share, your inheritance* – As the *parasha* ends we return to the special status of the Levites, against which Koraḥ rebelled. Interestingly, however, when Rambam comes to codify this idea, he brings us back to the universal element in Judaism's vision of spiritual aristocracy. Having established that the tribe of Levi was chosen to serve, to know God, and "to teach His upright ways and righteous laws," Rambam adds this:

> And not only the tribe of Levi, but any person in the world whose spirit stirs him, and he reaches an understanding from his own mind that he should set himself

▶

19 and the right thigh. All the sacred gifts that the Israelites raise up to the LORD
I give to you, your sons, and your daughters as an everlasting statute. It is an
everlasting covenant of salt before the LORD, for you and for your descendants."
20 The LORD said to Aharon: "You will have no inheritance in their land, nor shall
you have any share among them. I am your share, your inheritance, among the
21 Israelites. And I give to the Levites all tithes in Israel as an inheritance SHEVI'I
22 in return for the service they perform, the service in the Tent of Meeting. From
now the Israelites shall no longer come close to the Tent of Meeting, or they
23 will incur guilt and die. Instead, the Levites will perform the service of the
Tent of Meeting, and they will bear responsibility for their own sins; this is an
everlasting decree through all your generations. But among the Israelites they
24 will not inherit land, because I have given as an inheritance to the Levites the
tithe of the Israelites which they have lifted up to the LORD as an upraised gift.
That is why I have said of them that they shall have no land inheritance among
the Israelites."
25 26 The LORD spoke to Moshe: "Speak to the Levites and say to them: When
you receive from the Israelites the tithe that I have given you from them as
your inheritance, you shall lift up a tenth of it as an offering to the LORD, a
27 tithe of the tithe. It will be considered your own upraised gift, like the grain
28 of the threshing floor or the flow from the winepress. So shall you set aside an
offering to the LORD from all the tithes that you take from the Israelites, and
29 you shall give it as an upraised gift to the LORD for Aharon the priest. From

אונקלוס

דְּיַמִּינָא דִּילָךְ יְהֵי: יט כָּל אַפְרָשׁוּת קֻדְשַׁיָּא, דְּיַפְרְשׁוּן בְּנֵי יִשְׂרָאֵל קֳדָם יְיָ, יְהַבִית לָךְ, וְלִבְנָךְ וְלִבְנָתָךְ, עִמָּךְ לִקְיָם עָלַם, קְיָם מְלַח עָלְמָא

רש״י

יט כל תרומת הקדשים. מֵחִבָּתָהּ שֶׁל פָּרָשָׁה זוֹ, כְּלָלָהּ בַּתְּחִלָּה וּכְלָלָהּ בַּסּוֹף וּפֵרַט בָּאֶמְצַע: ברית מלח עולם. כָּרַת בְּרִית עִם אַהֲרֹן בְּדָבָר הַבָּרִיא וּמִתְקַיֵּם וּמַבְרִיא אֶת אֲחֵרִים: ברית מלח. כַּבְּרִית הַכְּרוּתָה לַמֶּלַח, שֶׁאֵינוֹ מַסְרִיחַ לְעוֹלָם:

כ וחלק לא יהיה לך בתוכם. אַף בַּבִּזָּה:

כג והם. הַלְוִיִּם, "יִשְׂאוּ עֲוֹנָם" שֶׁל יִשְׂרָאֵל, שֶׁעֲלֵיהֶם לְהַזְהִיר הַזָּרִים מִגֶּשֶׁת אֲלֵיהֶם:

כד אשר ירימו לה׳ תרומה. הַכָּתוּב קְרָאוֹ 'תְּרוּמָה' עַד שֶׁיַּפְרִישׁ מִמֶּנּוּ תְּרוּמַת מַעֲשֵׂר:

כז ונחשב לכם תרומתכם כדגן מן הגרן. תְּרוּמַת מַעֲשֵׂר שֶׁלָּכֶם אֲסוּרָה לְזָרִים וְלִטְמֵאִים, וְחַיָּבִין עָלֶיהָ מִיתָה וְחֹמֶשׁ, כִּתְרוּמָה גְּדוֹלָה שֶׁנִּקְרֵאת רֵאשִׁית דָּגָן מִן הַגֹּרֶן: וכמלאה מן היקב. כִּתְרוּמַת תִּירוֹשׁ וְיִצְהָר הַנִּטֶּלֶת מִן הַיְקָבִים: מלאה. לְשׁוֹן בִּשּׁוּל תְּבוּאָה שֶׁנִּתְמַלֵּאת: יקב. הוּא הַבּוֹר שֶׁלִּפְנֵי הַגַּת שֶׁהַיַּיִן יוֹרֵד לְתוֹכוֹ. וְכָל לְשׁוֹן 'יֶקֶב' חֲפִירַת קַרְקַע הוּא, וְכֵן: "יִקְבֵי הַמֶּלֶךְ" (זכריה יד, י), הוּא יָם אוֹקְיָנוֹס, חֲפִירָה שֶׁחָפַר מַלְכּוֹ שֶׁל עוֹלָם:

כח כן תרימו גם אתם. כְּמוֹ שֶׁיִּשְׂרָאֵל מְרִימִים מִגָּרְנָם וּמִיִּקְבֵיהֶם תָּרִימוּ אַתֶּם מִמַּעֲשֵׂר שֶׁלָּכֶם, כִּי הוּא נַחֲלַתְכֶם:

כט מכל מתנתיכם תרימו את כל תרומת ה׳. בִּתְרוּמָה גְּדוֹלָה הַכָּתוּב

יט הַיָּמִין לְךָ יִהְיֶה: כֹּל ׀ תְּרוּמֹת הַקֳּדָשִׁים אֲשֶׁר יָרִימוּ בְנֵי־יִשְׂרָאֵל
לַיהוָה נָתַתִּי לְךָ וּלְבָנֶיךָ וְלִבְנֹתֶיךָ אִתְּךָ לְחָק־עוֹלָם בְּרִית מֶלַח עוֹלָם
כ הִוא לִפְנֵי יְהוָה לְךָ וּלְזַרְעֲךָ אִתָּךְ: וַיֹּאמֶר יְהוָה אֶל־אַהֲרֹן בְּאַרְצָם
לֹא תִנְחָל וְחֵלֶק לֹא־יִהְיֶה לְךָ בְּתוֹכָם אֲנִי חֶלְקְךָ וְנַחֲלָתְךָ בְּתוֹךְ בְּנֵי
כא יִשְׂרָאֵל: וְלִבְנֵי לֵוִי הִנֵּה נָתַתִּי כָּל־מַעֲשֵׂר בְּיִשְׂרָאֵל לְנַחֲלָה שביעי
כב חֵלֶף עֲבֹדָתָם אֲשֶׁר־הֵם עֹבְדִים אֶת־עֲבֹדַת אֹהֶל מוֹעֵד: וְלֹא־יִקְרְבוּ
כג עוֹד בְּנֵי יִשְׂרָאֵל אֶל־אֹהֶל מוֹעֵד לָשֵׂאת חֵטְא לָמוּת: וְעָבַד הַלֵּוִי
הוּא אֶת־עֲבֹדַת אֹהֶל מוֹעֵד וְהֵם יִשְׂאוּ עֲוֺנָם חֻקַּת עוֹלָם לְדֹרֹתֵיכֶם
כד וּבְתוֹךְ בְּנֵי יִשְׂרָאֵל לֹא יִנְחֲלוּ נַחֲלָה: כִּי אֶת־מַעְשַׂר בְּנֵי־יִשְׂרָאֵל אֲשֶׁר
יָרִימוּ לַיהוָה תְּרוּמָה נָתַתִּי לַלְוִיִּם לְנַחֲלָה עַל־כֵּן אָמַרְתִּי לָהֶם בְּתוֹךְ
בְּנֵי יִשְׂרָאֵל לֹא יִנְחֲלוּ נַחֲלָה:
כה כו וַיְדַבֵּר יְהוָה אֶל־מֹשֶׁה לֵּאמֹר: וְאֶל־הַלְוִיִּם תְּדַבֵּר וְאָמַרְתָּ אֲלֵהֶם יז
כִּי־תִקְחוּ מֵאֵת בְּנֵי־יִשְׂרָאֵל אֶת־הַמַּעֲשֵׂר אֲשֶׁר נָתַתִּי לָכֶם מֵאִתָּם
כז בְּנַחֲלַתְכֶם וַהֲרֵמֹתֶם מִמֶּנּוּ תְּרוּמַת יְהוָה מַעֲשֵׂר מִן־הַמַּעֲשֵׂר: וְנֶחְשַׁב
כח לָכֶם תְּרוּמַתְכֶם כַּדָּגָן מִן־הַגֹּרֶן וְכַמְלֵאָה מִן־הַיָּקֶב: כֵּן תָּרִימוּ גַם־
אַתֶּם תְּרוּמַת יְהוָה מִכֹּל מַעְשְׂרֹתֵיכֶם אֲשֶׁר תִּקְחוּ מֵאֵת בְּנֵי יִשְׂרָאֵל
כט וּנְתַתֶּם מִמֶּנּוּ אֶת־תְּרוּמַת יְהוָה לְאַהֲרֹן הַכֹּהֵן: מִכֹּל מַתְּנֹתֵיכֶם

אונקלוס

הִיא קֳדָם יְיָ, לָךְ וְלִבְנָךְ עִמָּךְ: כ וַאֲמַר יְיָ לְאַהֲרֹן, בְּאַרְעֲהוֹן לָא תַחְסִין, וְחוּלָק, לָא יְהֵי לָךְ בֵּינֵיהוֹן, מַתְּנָן דִּיהַבִית לָךְ אִנּוּן חוּלָקָךְ וְאַחְסַנְתָּךְ, בְּגוֹ בְּנֵי יִשְׂרָאֵל: כא וְלִבְנֵי לֵוִי, הָא יְהַבִית, כָּל מַעְסְרָא בְּיִשְׂרָאֵל לְאַחְסָנָא, חֲלַף פָּלְחָנְהוֹן דְּאִנּוּן פָּלְחִין, יָת פָּלְחַן מַשְׁכַּן זִמְנָא: כב וְלָא יִקְרְבוּן עוֹד, בְּנֵי יִשְׂרָאֵל לְמַשְׁכַּן זִמְנָא, לְקַבָּלָא חוֹבָא לִמְמָת: כג וְיִפְלְחוּן לֵיוָאֵי אִנּוּן, יָת פָּלְחַן מַשְׁכַּן זִמְנָא, וְאִנּוּן יְקַבְּלוּן חוֹבֵיהוֹן, קְיָם עָלַם לְדָרֵיכוֹן, וּבְגוֹ בְּנֵי יִשְׂרָאֵל, לָא יַחְסְנוּן אַחְסָנָא: כד אֲרֵי יָת מַעְסְרָא דִּבְנֵי יִשְׂרָאֵל, דְּיַפְרְשׁוּן קֳדָם יְיָ אַפְרָשׁוּתָא, יְהַבִית לְלֵיוָאֵי לְאַחְסָנָא, עַל כֵּן אֲמָרִית לְהוֹן, בְּגוֹ בְּנֵי יִשְׂרָאֵל, לָא יַחְסְנוּן אַחְסָנָא: כה וּמַלִּיל יְיָ עִם מֹשֶׁה לְמֵימָר: כו וְעִם לֵיוָאֵי תְּמַלֵּיל וְתֵימַר לְהוֹן, אֲרֵי תִסְּבוּן, מִן בְּנֵי יִשְׂרָאֵל יָת מַעְסְרָא, דִּיהַבִית לְכוֹן, מִנְּהוֹן בְּאַחְסַנְתְּכוֹן, וְתַפְרְשׁוּן מִנֵּיהּ אַפְרָשׁוּתָא קֳדָם יְיָ, מַעְסְרָא מִן מַעְסְרָא: כז וְיִתְחֲשֵׁיב לְכוֹן אַפְרָשׁוּתְכוֹן, כַּעֲבוּרָא מִן אִדְּרָא, וּכְמַלְאֲתָא מִן מַעְצַרְתָּא: כח כֵּן תַּפְרְשׁוּן אַף אַתּוּן אַפְרָשׁוּתָא קֳדָם יְיָ, מִכָּל מַעְסְרֵיכוֹן, דְּתִסְּבוּן, מִן בְּנֵי יִשְׂרָאֵל, וְתִתְּנוּן מִנֵּיהּ יָת אַפְרָשׁוּתָא קֳדָם יְיָ, לְאַהֲרֹן כָּהֲנָא: כט מִכָּל מַתְּנָתְכוֹן, תַּפְרְשׁוּן,

all your gifts, you shall set aside an offering to the Lord; of each the finest
30 portion shall be consecrated. Say to the Levites: When you have presented the MAFTIR
best portion of it, it will be reckoned to you as the yield of the threshing floor
31 and the winepress. You and your household may eat of it anywhere, because
32 this is your payment for your service in the Tent of Meeting. You will not bear
guilt for it once you have separated out the finest portion; then you will not be
profaning the sacred offerings of the Israelites, and will not die."

The haftara for Parashat Koraḥ is on page 1592.
On Rosh Ḥodesh Tamuz read the haftara on page 1634.

רש״י

מְדַבֵּר, שֶׁאִם הִקְדִּים לֵוִי אֶת הַכֹּהֵן בַּכְּרִי וְקִבֵּל מַעַשְׂרוֹתָיו קֹדֶם שֶׁיִּטֹּל כֹּהֵן תְּרוּמָה גְּדוֹלָה מִן הַכְּרִי, צָרִיךְ לְהַפְרִישׁ הַלֵּוִי מִן הַמַּעֲשֵׂר תְּחִלָּה אֶחָד מֵחֲמִשִּׁים לִתְרוּמָה גְּדוֹלָה, וְיַחֲזֹר וְיַפְרִישׁ תְּרוּמַת מַעֲשֵׂר:

ל) **בַּהֲרִימְכֶם אֶת חֶלְבּוֹ מִמֶּנּוּ.** לְאַחַר שֶׁתָּרִימוּ תְּרוּמַת מַעֲשֵׂר מִמֶּנּוּ, "וְנֶחְשַׁב" הַמּוֹתָר "לַלְוִיִּם" חֻלִּין גְּמוּרִין, "כִּתְבוּאַת גֹּרֶן" לְיִשְׂרָאֵל. שֶׁלֹּא תֹּאמַר: הוֹאִיל וּקְרָאוֹ הַכָּתוּב 'תְּרוּמָה', שֶׁנֶּאֱמַר: "כִּי אֶת מַעְשַׂר בְּנֵי יִשְׂרָאֵל אֲשֶׁר יָרִימוּ לַה' תְּרוּמָה" (לעיל פסוק כד), יָכוֹל יְהֵא כֻּלּוֹ אָסוּר? תַּלְמוּד לוֹמַר: "וְנֶחְשַׁב לַלְוִיִּם כִּתְבוּאַת גֹּרֶן", מַה שֶּׁל יִשְׂרָאֵל חֻלִּין, אַף שֶׁל לֵוִי חֻלִּין:

לא) **בְּכָל מָקוֹם.** אֲפִלּוּ בְּבֵית הַקְּבָרוֹת:

לב) **וְלֹא תִשְׂאוּ עָלָיו חֵטְא וְגוֹ'.** הָא אִם לֹא תָּרִימוּ, תִּשְׂאוּ חֵטְא: **וְלֹא תָמוּתוּ.** הָא אִם תְּחַלְּלוּ, תָּמוּתוּ:

מפטיר

ל תָּרִ֥ימוּ אֶת־כׇּל־תְּרוּמַ֣ת יְהֹוָ֔ה מִכׇּל־חֶלְבּ֔וֹ אֶת־מִקְדְּשׁ֖וֹ מִמֶּֽנּוּ׃ וְאָמַרְתָּ֖
אֲלֵהֶ֑ם בַּהֲרִֽימְכֶ֤ם אֶת־חֶלְבּוֹ֙ מִמֶּ֔נּוּ וְנֶחְשַׁב֙ לַלְוִיִּ֔ם כִּתְבוּאַ֥ת גֹּ֖רֶן
לא וְכִתְבוּאַ֥ת יָֽקֶב׃ וַאֲכַלְתֶּ֤ם אֹתוֹ֙ בְּכׇל־מָק֔וֹם אַתֶּ֖ם וּבֵיתְכֶ֑ם כִּֽי־שָׂכָ֥ר
לב הוּא֙ לָכֶ֔ם חֵ֥לֶף עֲבֹדַתְכֶ֖ם בְּאֹ֥הֶל מוֹעֵֽד׃ וְלֹֽא־תִשְׂא֤וּ עָלָיו֙ חֵ֔טְא
בַּהֲרִֽימְכֶ֥ם אֶת־חֶלְבּ֖וֹ מִמֶּ֑נּוּ וְאֶת־קׇדְשֵׁ֧י בְנֵֽי־יִשְׂרָאֵ֛ל לֹ֥א תְחַלְּל֖וּ
וְלֹ֥א תָמֽוּתוּ׃

The הפטרה *for* פרשת קרח *is on page 1593.*
On ראש חודש תמוז *read the* הפטרה *on page 1635.*

אונקלוס

יָת כָּל אַפְרָשׁוּתָא קֳדָם יְיָ, מִכָּל שְׁפַר רֵיהּ, יָת קֻדְשֵׁיהּ מִנֵּיהּ: ל וְתֵימַר לְהוֹן, בְּאַפְרָשׁוּתְכוֹן יָת שְׁפַר רֵיהּ מִנֵּיהּ, וְיִתְחֲשֵׁיב לְלֵיוָאֵי, כְּעַלְלַת אִדְּרָא וּכְעַלְלַת מַעְצַרְתָּא: לא וְתֵיכְלוּן יָתֵיהּ בְּכָל אֲתַר, אַתּוּן וֶאֱנָשׁ בָּתֵּיכוֹן, אֲרֵי אַגְרָא הוּא לְכוֹן, חֲלָף פֻּלְחָנְכוֹן בְּמַשְׁכַּן זִמְנָא: לב וְלָא תְקַבְּלוּן עֲלוֹהִי חוֹבָא, בְּאַפְרָשׁוּתְכוֹן יָת שְׁפַר רֵיהּ מִנֵּיהּ, וְיָת קֻדְשַׁיָּא דִּבְנֵי יִשְׂרָאֵל, לָא תַחֲלוּן וְלָא תְמוּתוּן:

Parashat Ḥukat

19 1 2 The Lord spoke to Moshe and Aharon: "This is the decree of the Law that
the Lord commands. Tell the Israelites to bring you a cow, completely red,

רש"י

יט ב זאת חקת התורה. לְפִי שֶׁהַשָּׂטָן וְאֻמּוֹת הָעוֹלָם מוֹנִין אֶת יִשְׂרָאֵל, לוֹמַר: מָה הַמִּצְוָה הַזֹּאת וּמָה טַעַם יֵשׁ בָּהּ? לְפִיכָךְ כָּתַב בָּהּ 'חֻקָּה' – גְּזֵרָה הִיא מִלְּפָנַי, אֵין לְךָ רְשׁוּת לְהַרְהֵר אַחֲרֶיהָ: וְיִקְחוּ אֵלֶיךָ. לְעוֹלָם הִיא נִקְרֵאת עַל שִׁמְךָ, פָּרָה שֶׁעָשָׂה מֹשֶׁה בַּמִּדְבָּר: אֲדֻמָּה תְּמִימָה. שֶׁתְּהֵא תְמִימָה בַּאֲדְמִימוּת, שֶׁאִם הָיוּ בָהּ שְׁתֵּי שְׂעָרוֹת שְׁחוֹרוֹת פְּסוּלָה:

(wool) and vegetable (linen) textiles, or mix animal life (milk) and animal death (meat). As for the red heifer, Rabbi Hirsch says that the ritual is to cleanse humans from depression brought about by proximity to death.

My own view is that *ḥukim* are *commands deliberately intended to bypass the rational brain,* the prefrontal cortex. The root from which the word *ḥok* comes is *ḥ-k-k,* meaning "to engrave." Rituals cut deep below the surface of the mind, and for an important reason. We are not fully rational animals, and we can make momentous mistakes if we think we are. We have a limbic system, an emotional brain. We also have an extremely powerful set of reactions to potential danger, located in the amygdala, that lead us to flee, freeze, or fight. A moral system, to be adequate to the human condition, must recognize the nature of the human condition. It must speak to our fears.

The most profound fear most of us have is of death. Death defiles in the simplest, starkest sense. It makes mockery of virtue: the hero may die young while the coward lives to old age. And bereavement is tragic in a different way. To lose those we love is to have the fabric of our life torn, perhaps irreparably. Mortality opens an abyss between us and God's eternity.

It is this fear, existential and elemental, to which the rite of the heifer is addressed. Faith can rescue life from meaninglessness. "Rational knowledge," Tolstoy noted, "negates the meaning of life." Something, then, other than rational knowledge is needed. "Faith is the force of life. If a man lives, then he must believe in something.…Without faith it is impossible to live."

To defeat the defilement of contact with death, there must be a ritual that bypasses rational knowledge. Hence the rite of the red heifer, in which death is dissolved in the waters of life, and those on whom they are sprinkled are made pure again so that they can, after a time, enter the precincts of the *Shekhina* and reestablish contact with eternity.

THE RED HEIFER

In Parashat Ḥukat we read of the death of two of Israel's three great leaders in the wilderness, Miriam and Aharon, and the sentence of death decreed against Moshe, the greatest of them all. To counter that sense of loss and bereavement, the Torah employs one of Judaism's great principles: the Holy One, blessed be He, creates the remedy before the disease (Megilla 13b). Before any of the deaths are mentioned, we read about the strange ritual of the red heifer, which purifies people who have been in contact with death – the archetypal source of impurity.

Why this ritual? Even though the red heifer is a *ḥok,* as we saw above, it can also have a dimension of symbolic import. The red heifer itself is the starkest symbol of pure, animal life, untamed, undomesticated. The red, like the scarlet of the wool, is the color of blood, the essence of life. The cedar, tallest of trees, represents vegetative life. The hyssop symbolizes purity. All these are reduced to ash in the fire, a powerful drama of mortality. The ash itself is then dissolved in "living" – flowing – water (Num. 19:17), symbolizing continuity, the flow of life, and the potential of rebirth. The body dies but the spirit flows on. A generation dies but another is born. Lives may end but life does not. Those who live after us continue what we

פרשת חקת

יט א ב וַיְדַבֵּר יְהוָה אֶל־מֹשֶׁה וְאֶל־אַהֲרֹן לֵאמֹר: זֹאת חֻקַּת הַתּוֹרָה אֲשֶׁר־
צִוָּה יְהוָה לֵאמֹר דַּבֵּר ׀ אֶל־בְּנֵי יִשְׂרָאֵל וְיִקְחוּ אֵלֶיךָ פָרָה אֲדֻמָּה תְּמִימָה

אונקלוס

יט א וּמַלֵּיל יי, עִם מֹשֶׁה וּלְאַהֲרֹן לְמֵימַר: ב דָּא גְּזֵירַת אוֹרָיְתָא,
דְּפַקֵּיד יי לְמֵימַר, מַלֵּיל עִם בְּנֵי יִשְׂרָאֵל, וְיִסְּבוּן לָךְ תּוֹרְתָא
סְמוֹקְתָא שַׁלְמְתָא,

ḤUKAT

Parashat Ḥukat begins with the law of the red heifer, judged by the Sages to be the most incomprehensible in the Torah. It became a classic example of a *ḥok*, a "statute," often understood as a law that has no reason, or at least none we can understand. The text then shifts from law to narrative. After the death of Miriam, the people find themselves without water. They complain to Moshe and Aharon, who turn to God. They then respond to the people in a way that seems to suggest anger. They are judged to have acted wrongly, and both are told they will not enter the land. Aharon dies. The people complain again and are attacked by venomous snakes. Moshe, at God's command, places a brass serpent on a pole, so that all who look up to it will be healed. The people sing a song about a miraculous well that gave them water. Moshe then leads the people into successful battles against Siḥon, king of the Emorites, and Og, king of Bashan.

The *parasha* demonstrates, as we shall see, one of the recurring themes in Numbers, the close connection between law and narrative, in this case between the law of the red heifer and the story that follows. The ideas of purification from death embodied in the law of the heifer preempt the deaths of Miriam and Aharon and the foreshadowing of Moshe's death in the wilderness. After this study in mortality, the Israelites meet hostile nations in battle, and despite their earlier fears, emerge triumphant.

THE DECREE OF THE LAW

Though the ritual of the red heifer has not been practiced since the days of the Temple, it nonetheless remains significant, in itself and for an understanding of what a *ḥok*, "statute," actually is. Other instances include the prohibitions against eating meat and milk together, wearing clothes of mixed wool and linen (*shaatnez*), and sowing a field with two kinds of grain (*kilayim*). The Sages recognized that whereas non-Jews might understand Jewish laws based on social justice (*mishpatim*) or historical memory (*edot*), commands such as the prohibition of eating meat and milk together seemed irrational and superstitious. The *ḥukim* were laws of which "Satan and the nations of the world made fun" (Yoma 67b).

There have been several very different explanations of *ḥukim*. The most famous is that a *ḥok* is a law whose logic we cannot understand. It makes sense to God, but it makes no sense to us. Or perhaps, as Saadia Gaon put it, it is a command issued for no other reason than to reward us for obeying it (Emunot VeDeot, book III).

Rambam had a quite different view. He believed that no divine command was irrational. The *ḥukim* only appear to be inexplicable because we have forgotten the original context in which they were ordained. Each of them was a rejection of, and education against, some idolatrous practice, since forgotten, which is why we now find the commands hard to understand (*Guide for the Perplexed* III:31).

A third view, adopted by Ramban (commentary on Lev. 19:19) and further articulated by Rabbi Samson Raphael Hirsch, is that the *ḥukim* are laws designed to teach the integrity of nature. Nature has its own domains and boundaries; to cross them is to dishonor the divinely created order and to threaten nature itself. So we do not combine animal

3 without blemish, on which no yoke has been laid. Give this to Elazar the priest;
4 it shall be taken outside the camp and slaughtered in his presence. Elazar the
priest shall take some of its blood with his finger and sprinkle it seven times
5 toward the front of the Tent of Meeting. The cow shall then be burned in front
6 of him; its skin, flesh, and blood shall be burned, together with its dung. The
priest shall take cedarwood, hyssop, and scarlet cloth and throw them into
7 the fire where the cow is burning. Then the priest shall wash his clothes and
bathe his body in water. Afterward he may enter the camp, but he will remain
8 impure until that evening. The one who burned it shall wash his clothes in
water and bathe his body in water, but he too will remain impure until evening.
9 Meanwhile, one who is pure shall gather up the ashes of the cow and place
them outside the camp in a pure place. And they shall be kept by the Israelite
10 community for the water of lustration, as a purification offering. The one who
gathers the ashes of the cow shall likewise wash his clothes but remains impure
until evening. This shall be an everlasting decree for the Israelites and for any
11 migrant living among them. Whoever touches the dead body of any person
12 shall be impure for seven days. He must purify himself with the water on the
third and seventh days to become pure. If he does not purify himself on the

רש״י

ג **אֶלְעָזָר.** מִצְוָתָהּ בַּסְּגָן: **אֶל מִחוּץ לַמַּחֲנֶה.** חוּץ לְשָׁלֹשׁ מַחֲנוֹת: **וְשָׁחַט אֹתָהּ לְפָנָיו.** זָר שׁוֹחֵט וְאֶלְעָזָר רוֹאֶה:

ד **אֶל נֹכַח פְּנֵי אֹהֶל מוֹעֵד.** עוֹמֵד בְּמִזְרָחָהּ שֶׁל יְרוּשָׁלַיִם וּמִתְכַּוֵּן וְרוֹאֶה פִּתְחוֹ שֶׁל הֵיכָל בִּשְׁעַת הַזָּאַת הַדָּם:

ז **אֶל הַמַּחֲנֶה.** לְמַחֲנֵה שְׁכִינָה, שֶׁאֵין טָמֵא מְשֻׁלָּח חוּץ לִשְׁתֵּי מַחֲנוֹת אֶלָּא זָב וּבַעַל קֶרִי וּמְצֹרָע: **וְטָמֵא הַכֹּהֵן עַד הָעָרֶב.** סָרְסֵהוּ וְדָרְשֵׁהוּ: וְטָמֵא עַד הָעֶרֶב וְאַחַר יָבֹא אֶל הַמַּחֲנֶה:

ט **וְהִנִּיחַ מִחוּץ לַמַּחֲנֶה.** לִשְׁלֹשָׁה חֲלָקִים מְחַלְּקָהּ: אֶחָד נִתַּן בְּהַר הַמִּשְׁחָה, וְאֶחָד מִתְחַלֵּק לְכָל הַמִּשְׁמָרוֹת, וְאֶחָד נִתַּן בַּחֵיל. זֶה שֶׁל מִשְׁמָרוֹת הָיָה חוּץ לָעֲזָרָה, לִטֹּל מִמֶּנּוּ בְּנֵי הָעֲיָרוֹת וְכָל הַצְּרִיכִין לְהִטַּהֵר. וְזֶה שֶׁבְּהַר הַמִּשְׁחָה כֹּהֲנִים גְּדוֹלִים לְפָרוֹת אֲחֵרוֹת מְקַדְּשִׁין הֵימֶנָּה. וְזֶה שֶׁבַּחֵיל נָתוּן לְמִשְׁמֶרֶת מִגְּזֵרַת הַכָּתוּב, שֶׁנֶּאֱמַר: "וְהָיְתָה לַעֲדַת בְּנֵי יִשְׂרָאֵל לְמִשְׁמֶרֶת": **לְמֵי נִדָּה.** לְמֵי הַזָּיָה, כְּמוֹ: "וַיַּדּוּ אֶבֶן בִּי" (איכה ג, נג), "לְיַדּוֹת אֶת קַרְנוֹת הַגּוֹיִם" (זכריה ב, ד), לְשׁוֹן זְרִיקָה: **חַטָּאת הִוא.** לְשׁוֹן חִטּוּי כִּפְשׁוּטוֹ. וּלְפִי הִלְכוֹתָיו קְרָאָהּ הַכָּתוּב 'חַטָּאת', לוֹמַר שֶׁהִיא כְּקָדָשִׁים לֵאָסֵר בַּהֲנָאָה:

יב **הוּא יִתְחַטָּא בוֹ.** בְּאֵפֶר הַפָּרָה:

in the form of his disciples who studied and lived by his words, and as it did for Miriam in the lives of all those she led and taught. For good or bad, our lives have an impact on other lives, and the ripples of our deeds spread ever outward across space and time. We are part of the undying river of life. So we may be mortal, but that does not reduce our life to insignificance, for we are part of something larger than ourselves, characters in a story that began early in the history of civilization and that will last as long as humankind.

19:11 **שבעת ימים** *Seven days* – We no longer have the red heifer and the seven-day purification ritual to help us confront death, but we do have the shiva, the seven days of mourning during which we are comforted by others and thereby reconnected with life. Our grief is gradually dissolved by the contact with friends and family who come to console us, as the ashes of the heifer were dissolved in the "living water" (Num. 19:17), and we emerge, still bereaved, but in some measure cleansed, purified, able again to face life.

ג אֲשֶׁר אֵין־בָּהּ מוּם אֲשֶׁר לֹא־עָלָה עָלֶיהָ עֹל׃ וּנְתַתֶּם אֹתָהּ אֶל־
אֶלְעָזָר הַכֹּהֵן וְהוֹצִיא אֹתָהּ אֶל־מִחוּץ לַמַּחֲנֶה וְשָׁחַט אֹתָהּ לְפָנָיו׃
ד וְלָקַח אֶלְעָזָר הַכֹּהֵן מִדָּמָהּ בְּאֶצְבָּעוֹ וְהִזָּה אֶל־נֹכַח פְּנֵי אֹהֶל־מוֹעֵד
ה מִדָּמָהּ שֶׁבַע פְּעָמִים׃ וְשָׂרַף אֶת־הַפָּרָה לְעֵינָיו אֶת־עֹרָהּ וְאֶת־בְּשָׂרָהּ
ו וְאֶת־דָּמָהּ עַל־פִּרְשָׁהּ יִשְׂרֹף׃ וְלָקַח הַכֹּהֵן עֵץ אֶרֶז וְאֵזוֹב וּשְׁנִי תוֹלָעַת
ז וְהִשְׁלִיךְ אֶל־תּוֹךְ שְׂרֵפַת הַפָּרָה׃ וְכִבֶּס בְּגָדָיו הַכֹּהֵן וְרָחַץ בְּשָׂרוֹ
ח בַּמַּיִם וְאַחַר יָבֹא אֶל־הַמַּחֲנֶה וְטָמֵא הַכֹּהֵן עַד־הָעָרֶב׃ וְהַשֹּׂרֵף אֹתָהּ
ט יְכַבֵּס בְּגָדָיו בַּמַּיִם וְרָחַץ בְּשָׂרוֹ בַּמָּיִם וְטָמֵא עַד־הָעָרֶב׃ וְאָסַף ׀ אִישׁ
טָהוֹר אֵת אֵפֶר הַפָּרָה וְהִנִּיחַ מִחוּץ לַמַּחֲנֶה בְּמָקוֹם טָהוֹר וְהָיְתָה
י לַעֲדַת בְּנֵי־יִשְׂרָאֵל לְמִשְׁמֶרֶת לְמֵי נִדָּה חַטָּאת הִוא׃ וְכִבֶּס הָאֹסֵף
אֶת־אֵפֶר הַפָּרָה אֶת־בְּגָדָיו וְטָמֵא עַד־הָעָרֶב וְהָיְתָה לִבְנֵי יִשְׂרָאֵל
יא וְלַגֵּר הַגָּר בְּתוֹכָם לְחֻקַּת עוֹלָם׃ הַנֹּגֵעַ בְּמֵת לְכָל־נֶפֶשׁ אָדָם וְטָמֵא
יב שִׁבְעַת יָמִים׃ הוּא יִתְחַטָּא־בוֹ בַּיּוֹם הַשְּׁלִישִׁי וּבַיּוֹם הַשְּׁבִיעִי יִטְהָר

אונקלוס

דְּלֵית בַּהּ מוּמָא, דְּלָא סְלֵיק עֲלַהּ נִירָא: ג וְתִתְּנוּן יָתַהּ, לְאֶלְעָזָר כָּהֲנָא, וְיַפֵּיק יָתַהּ לְמִבָּרָא לְמַשְׁרִיתָא, וְיִכּוֹס יָתַהּ קֳדָמוֹהִי: ד וְיִסַּב, אֶלְעָזָר כָּהֲנָא, מִדְּמַהּ בְּאֶצְבְּעֵיהּ, וְיַדֵּי, לָקֳבֵיל אַפֵּי מַשְׁכַּן זִמְנָא, מִדְּמַהּ שְׁבַע זִמְנִין: ה וְיוֹקֵיד יָת תּוֹרְתָא לְעֵינוֹהִי, יָת מַשְׁכַּהּ וְיָת בִּסְרַהּ וְיָת דְּמַהּ, עַל אֻכְלַהּ יוֹקֵיד: ו וְיִסַּב כָּהֲנָא, אָעָא דְאַרְזָא, וְאֵיזוֹבָא וּצְבַע זְהוֹרִי, וְיִרְמֵי, לְגוֹ יְקֵידַת תּוֹרְתָא: ז וִיצַבַּע לְבוּשׁוֹהִי כָּהֲנָא, וְיַסְחֵי בִּסְרֵיהּ בְּמַיָּא, וּבָתַר כֵּן יֵיעוֹל לְמַשְׁרִיתָא, וִיהֵי מְסָאַב כָּהֲנָא עַד רַמְשָׁא: ח וּדְמוֹקֵיד יָתַהּ, יְצַבַּע לְבוּשׁוֹהִי בְּמַיָּא, וְיַסְחֵי בִּסְרֵיהּ בְּמַיָּא, וִיהֵי מְסָאַב עַד רַמְשָׁא: ט וְיִכְנוֹשׁ גְּבַר דְּכֵי, יָת קִטְמָא דְּתוֹרְתָא, וְיַצְנַע, מִבָּרָא לְמַשְׁרִיתָא בַּאֲתַר דְּכֵי, וּתְהֵי, לִכְנִשְׁתָּא דִּבְנֵי יִשְׂרָאֵל לְמַטְּרָא, לְמֵי אַדָּיוּתָא חַטָּתָא הִיא: י וִיצַבַּע, דְּכָנֵישׁ יָת קִטְמָא דְּתוֹרְתָא יָת לְבוּשׁוֹהִי, וִיהֵי מְסָאַב עַד רַמְשָׁא, וּתְהֵי לִבְנֵי יִשְׂרָאֵל, וּלְגִיּוֹרַיָּא, דְּיִתְגַּיְּרוּן בֵּינֵיהוֹן לִקְיָם עָלַם: יא דְּיִקְרַב בְּמִיתָא לְכָל נַפְשָׁא דַאֲנָשָׁא, וִיהֵי מְסָאַב שִׁבְעָא יוֹמִין: יב הוּא יְדֵי עֲלוֹהִי, בְּיוֹמָא תְּלִיתָאָה, וּבְיוֹמָא שְׁבִיעָאָה יִדְכֵּי,

began, and we live on in them. Life is a never-ending stream, and a trace of us is carried onward to the future.

As physical beings, we all one day "return to dust" (Gen. 3:19), but we are reminded of two consolations. The first is that we are not just physical beings. God made the first human "from the dust of the land" (2:7), but He breathed into him the breath of life. "The dust returns to the earth where it began, and the spirit returns to God who gave it" (Eccl. 12:7).

The second is that, even down here on earth, something of us lives on, as it did for Aharon in the form of his sons who carry the name of the priesthood, as it did for Moshe

13 third and seventh days, he will not be pure. Whoever touches a corpse of a
person who has died, and fails to purify himself, defiles the LORD's Tabernacle.
He shall be severed from Israel because, since the water of lustration was not
14 sprinkled on him, he remains impure; his impurity is still with him. This is the
law: when a person dies in a tent, whoever enters that tent and whoever is in
15 it shall remain impure for seven days. Any open vessel not sealed with a cover
16 shall be impure. Anyone in the open field who touches a person killed by the
sword, or who died naturally, or a human bone or a grave, shall be impure for
17 seven days. For this impure person they shall take some of the ashes of the
18 burnt purification offering, and place living water along with it into a vessel. A SHENI
person who is pure shall then take hyssop, dip it into the water, and sprinkle
it on the tent, on all the vessels, on the people who were there, and on anyone
19 who touched the bone, the slain person, or any other corpse, or a grave. On
the third day and seventh day the person who is pure shall sprinkle it on the
one who is impure, thus purifying him on the seventh day. He shall then wash
20 his clothes and immerse in water, and at evening he will be pure. Anyone who
becomes impure and fails to purify himself shall be severed from the assembly,

רש״י

יג **בְּמֵת בְּנֶפֶשׁ.** וְאֵיזֶה מֵת? שֶׁל "נֶפֶשׁ הָאָדָם", לְהוֹצִיא נֶפֶשׁ בְּהֵמָה שֶׁאֵין טֻמְאָתָהּ צְרִיכָה הַזָּאָה. דָּבָר אַחֵר, "בְּנֶפֶשׁ" זוֹ רְבִיעִית דָּם: **אֶת מִשְׁכַּן ה׳ טִמֵּא.** אִם נִכְנַס לָעֲזָרָה, אֲפִלּוּ בִּטְבִילָה, בְּלֹא הַזָּאַת שְׁלִישִׁי וּשְׁבִיעִי: **עוֹד טֻמְאָתוֹ בוֹ.** אַף עַל פִּי שֶׁטָּבַל:

יד **כָּל הַבָּא אֶל הָאֹהֶל.** בְּעוֹד שֶׁהַמֵּת בְּתוֹכוֹ:

טו **וְכֹל כְּלִי פָתוּחַ.** בִּכְלִי חֶרֶס הַכָּתוּב מְדַבֵּר, שֶׁאֵין מְקַבֵּל טֻמְאָה מִגַּבּוֹ אֶלָּא מִתּוֹכוֹ, לְפִיכָךְ אִם אֵין מְגוּפַת צְמִידָתוֹ פְּתוּלָה עָלָיו יָפֶה בְּחִבּוּר "טָמֵא הוּא", הָא אִם יֵשׁ צָמִיד פָּתִיל עָלָיו – טָהוֹר. "פָּתִיל" לְשׁוֹן מְחֻבָּר בִּלְשׁוֹן עֲרָבִי, וְכֵן: "נַפְתּוּלֵי אֱלֹהִים נִפְתַּלְתִּי" (בראשית ל, ח), נִתְחַבַּרְתִּי עִם אֲחוֹתִי:

טז **עַל פְּנֵי הַשָּׂדֶה.** רַבּוֹתֵינוּ דָּרְשׁוּ לְרַבּוֹת גּוֹלֵל וְדוֹפֵק. וּפְשׁוּטוֹ: "עַל פְּנֵי הַשָּׂדֶה", שֶׁאֵין שָׁם אֹהֶל, מְטַמֵּא הַמֵּת שָׁם בִּנְגִיעָה:

יט **וְחִטְּאוֹ בַּיּוֹם הַשְּׁבִיעִי.** הוּא גְּמַר טָהֳרָתוֹ:

כ **וְאִישׁ אֲשֶׁר יִטְמָא וְגוֹ׳.** אִם נֶאֱמַר 'מִקְדָּשׁ' לָמָּה נֶאֱמַר 'מִשְׁכָּן' (לעיל פסוק יג)? כו׳ כִּדְאִיתָא בִּשְׁבוּעוֹת (דף טז ע״ב):

will be written in the earth, for they have forsaken the source of living waters" (Jer. 17:13). We may understand the symbolic significance of the fact that when Miriam died, the flow of water to the Israelites ceased (see Num. 20:1–2). As long as she was alive, there was water, i.e., life. Her death marked the beginning of the end of Moshe's generation, and the sign of this was the drying up of the well that had served the people until then.

We die, but life goes on – that is the symbolic statement of the red heifer rite. So long as there is a covenant between the dead, the living, and those not yet born, mortality is redeemed from tragedy. We will live on in our children or in those whose lives we touch. As dust dissolves in living water, so death dissolves in the stream of life itself.

The law of the red heifer is thus intimately related to the narrative that follows. Before we are exposed to the death of Miriam and Aharon and the decree of death against Moshe, the Torah provides us with metaphysical comfort. They died, but what they lived for did not die. The water ceased, but after an interval, it returned. We are destined to mourn the death of those close to us, but eventually we reconnect with (the water of) life. Law informs the narrative, and narrative explains the law.

וְאִם־לֹא יִתְחַטָּא בַּיּוֹם הַשְּׁלִישִׁי וּבַיּוֹם הַשְּׁבִיעִי לֹא יִטְהָר׃ כׇּל־הַנֹּגֵעַ יג
בְּמֵת בְּנֶפֶשׁ הָאָדָם אֲשֶׁר־יָמוּת וְלֹא יִתְחַטָּא אֶת־מִשְׁכַּן יהוה טִמֵּא
וְנִכְרְתָה הַנֶּפֶשׁ הַהִוא מִיִּשְׂרָאֵל כִּי מֵי נִדָּה לֹא־זֹרַק עָלָיו טָמֵא יִהְיֶה
עוֹד טֻמְאָתוֹ בוֹ׃ זֹאת הַתּוֹרָה אָדָם כִּי־יָמוּת בְּאֹהֶל כׇּל־הַבָּא אֶל־ יד
הָאֹהֶל וְכׇל־אֲשֶׁר בָּאֹהֶל יִטְמָא שִׁבְעַת יָמִים׃ וְכֹל כְּלִי פָתוּחַ אֲשֶׁר טו
אֵין־צָמִיד פָּתִיל עָלָיו טָמֵא הוּא׃ וְכֹל אֲשֶׁר־יִגַּע עַל־פְּנֵי הַשָּׂדֶה טז
בַּחֲלַל־חֶרֶב אוֹ בְמֵת אוֹ־בְעֶצֶם אָדָם אוֹ בְקָבֶר יִטְמָא שִׁבְעַת יָמִים׃
וְלָקְחוּ לַטָּמֵא מֵעֲפַר שְׂרֵפַת הַחַטָּאת וְנָתַן עָלָיו מַיִם חַיִּים אֶל־כֶּלִי׃ יז
וְלָקַח אֵזוֹב וְטָבַל בַּמַּיִם אִישׁ טָהוֹר וְהִזָּה עַל־הָאֹהֶל וְעַל־כׇּל־הַכֵּלִים יח שני
וְעַל־הַנְּפָשׁוֹת אֲשֶׁר הָיוּ־שָׁם וְעַל־הַנֹּגֵעַ בַּעֶצֶם אוֹ בֶחָלָל אוֹ בַמֵּת
אוֹ בַקָּבֶר׃ וְהִזָּה הַטָּהֹר עַל־הַטָּמֵא בַּיּוֹם הַשְּׁלִישִׁי וּבַיּוֹם הַשְּׁבִיעִי יט
וְחִטְּאוֹ בַּיּוֹם הַשְּׁבִיעִי וְכִבֶּס בְּגָדָיו וְרָחַץ בַּמַּיִם וְטָהֵר בָּעָרֶב׃ וְאִישׁ כ
אֲשֶׁר־יִטְמָא וְלֹא יִתְחַטָּא וְנִכְרְתָה הַנֶּפֶשׁ הַהִוא מִתּוֹךְ הַקָּהָל כִּי

אונקלוס

וְאִם לָא יַדֵּי עֲלוֹהִי, בְּיוֹמָא תְּלִיתָאָה, וּבְיוֹמָא שְׁבִיעָאָה לָא יִדְכֵּי: יג כָּל דְּיִקְרַב, בְּמִיתָא בְּנַפְשָׁא דַּאֲנָשָׁא דִּימוּת וְלָא יַדֵּי עֲלוֹהִי, יָת מַשְׁכְּנָא דַּיי סַאֵיב, וְיִשְׁתֵּיצֵי, אֲנָשָׁא הַהוּא מִיִּשְׂרָאֵל, אֲרֵי מֵי אַדָּיוּתָא, לָא אִזְדְּרִיקוּ עֲלוֹהִי מְסָאַב יְהֵי, עוֹד סְאוֹבְתֵיהּ בֵּיהּ: יד דָּא אוֹרָיְתָא, אֱנָשׁ אֲרֵי יְמוּת בְּמַשְׁכְּנָא, כָּל דְּעָלֵיל לְמַשְׁכְּנָא וְכָל דִּבְמַשְׁכְּנָא, יְהֵי מְסָאַב שִׁבְעָא יוֹמִין: טו וְכֹל מָן דַּחֲסַף פְּתִיחַ, דְּלֵית מְגוּפַת שְׁיָע מַקַּף עֲלוֹהִי, מְסָאַב הוּא: טז וְכֹל דְּיִקְרַב עַל אַפֵּי חַקְלָא, בִּקְטִיל חַרְבָּא אוֹ בְמִיתָא, אוֹ בְגַרְמָא דַּאֲנָשָׁא אוֹ בְקִבְרָא, יְהֵי מְסָאַב שִׁבְעָא יוֹמִין: יז וְיִסְּבוּן לִדְמְסָאַב, מֵעֲפַר יְקֵידַת חַטָּתָא, וְיִתֵּין עֲלוֹהִי, מֵי מַבּוּעַ לְמָן: יח וְיִסַּב אֵיזוֹבָא, וְיִטְבּוֹל בְּמַיָּא גְּבַר דְּכֵי, וְיַדֵּי עַל מַשְׁכְּנָא וְעַל כָּל מָנַיָּא, וְעַל נַפְשָׁתָא דַּהֲווֹ תַמָּן, וְעַל דְּיִקְרַב, בְּגַרְמָא אוֹ בִקְטִילָא, אוֹ בְמִיתָא אוֹ בְקִבְרָא: יט וְיַדֵּי דָּכְיָא עַל מְסָאֲבָא, בְּיוֹמָא תְּלִיתָאָה וּבְיוֹמָא שְׁבִיעָאָה, וִידַכֵּינֵיהּ בְּיוֹמָא שְׁבִיעָאָה, וִיצַבַּע לְבוּשׁוֹהִי, וְיַסְחֵי בְמַיָּא וְיִדְכֵּי בְרַמְשָׁא: כ וּגְבַר דְּיִסְתָּאַב וְלָא יַדֵּי עֲלוֹהִי, וְיִשְׁתֵּיצֵי, אֲנָשָׁא הַהוּא מִגּוֹ קְהָלָא, אֲרֵי

19:17 מַיִם חַיִּים *Living water* – The phrase "living water" is an explicit metaphor. Water is the source of all life – plant, animal, and human. In the desert, or more generally in the Middle East, you feel this with a peculiar vividness. Hence it became the symbol of God-who-is-life. Speaking in God's name, Yirmeyahu says of his generation, "Those who stray from Me

We can emerge from the shadow of death if we allow ourselves to be healed by the God of life. Faith leads us back into life. To allow this to happen, however, we often need the help of others. It took a priest to sprinkle the waters of cleansing. In a different sense, it takes comforters to lift our grief during our period of mourning.

for he has defiled the Lord's Sanctuary. Since water of lustration was not
21 sprinkled on him, he is impure. This is an everlasting decree for them. The
one who sprinkles the water of lustration shall wash his own clothes. Anyone
who had contact with the water of lustration shall remain impure until evening.
22 Anything the impure person touches is rendered impure, and one who touches
him remains impure until evening."
20 1 The Israelites, all the community, arrived at the Wilderness of Tzin in the first
month, and the people stayed at Kadesh. There Miriam died and was buried.
2 And there was no water for the community, and together they confronted
3 Moshe and Aharon. The people contended with Moshe: "If only we had died
4 when our brothers died before the Lord! Why have you brought the Lord's
5 assembly into this wilderness only for us and our livestock to die here? Why
did you take us up out of Egypt to bring us to this dreadful place with no grain,

רש״י

כא **וּמַזֵּה מֵי הַנִּדָּה.** רַבּוֹתֵינוּ אָמְרוּ שֶׁהַמַּזֶּה טָהוֹר, וְזֶה בָּא לְלַמֵּד שֶׁהַנּוֹשֵׂא מֵי חַטָּאת טָמֵא טֻמְאָה חֲמוּרָה לְטַמֵּא בְּגָדִים שֶׁעָלָיו, מַה שֶּׁאֵין כֵּן בַּנּוֹגֵעַ. וְזֶה שֶׁהוֹצִיא בִּלְשׁוֹן 'מַזֶּה', לוֹמַר לְךָ שֶׁאֵינָן מְטַמְּאִין עַד שֶׁיְּהֵא בָּהֶן שִׁעוּר הַזָּאָה: **וְהַנֹּגֵעַ... יִטְמָא.** וְאֵין טָעוּן כִּבּוּס בְּגָדִים:

כב **וְכֹל אֲשֶׁר יִגַּע בּוֹ הַטָּמֵא.** הַזֶּה שֶׁנִּטְמָא בְּמֵת, "יִטְמָא": **וְהַנֶּפֶשׁ הַנֹּגַעַת.** בּוֹ בְּטָמֵא מֵת: **תִּטְמָא עַד הָעָרֶב.** כָּאן לָמַדְנוּ שֶׁהַמֵּת אֲבִי אֲבוֹת הַטֻּמְאָה, וְהַנּוֹגֵעַ בּוֹ אַב הַטֻּמְאָה וּמְטַמֵּא אָדָם. זֶהוּ פֵּרוּשָׁהּ לְפִי מַשְׁמָעָהּ וְהִלְכוֹתֶיהָ: וּמִדְרַשׁ אַגָּדָה הֶעְתַּקְתִּי מִיסוֹדוֹ שֶׁל רַבִּי מֹשֶׁה הַדַּרְשָׁן. וְזֶהוּ:

ב **וְיִקְחוּ אֵלֶיךָ.** מִשֶּׁלָּהֶם. כְּשֵׁם שֶׁהֵם פֵּרְקוּ נִזְמֵי הַזָּהָב לָעֵגֶל מִשֶּׁלָּהֶם, כָּךְ יָבִיאוּ זוֹ לְכַפָּרָה מִשֶּׁלָּהֶם: **פָּרָה אֲדֻמָּה.** מָשָׁל לְבֶן שִׁפְחָה שֶׁטִּנֵּף פַּלָּטִין שֶׁל מֶלֶךְ, אָמְרוּ: תָּבֹא אִמּוֹ וּתְקַנֵּחַ הַצּוֹאָה; כָּךְ תָּבֹא פָּרָה וּתְכַפֵּר עַל הָעֵגֶל: **אֲדֻמָּה.** עַל שֵׁם: "אִם יַאְדִּימוּ כַתּוֹלָע" (ישעיה א, יח), שֶׁהַחֵטְא קָרוּי אָדֹם: **תְּמִימָה.** עַל שֵׁם יִשְׂרָאֵל שֶׁהָיוּ תְּמִימִים וְנַעֲשׂוּ בּוֹ בַּעֲלֵי מוּמִין, תָּבֹא זוֹ וּתְכַפֵּר עֲלֵיהֶם וְיַחְזְרוּ לְתַמּוּתָם: **לֹא עָלָה עָלֶיהָ עֹל.** כְּשֵׁם שֶׁפָּרְקוּ מֵעֲלֵיהֶם עֹל שָׁמַיִם:

ג **אֶל אֶלְעָזָר הַכֹּהֵן.** כְּשֵׁם שֶׁנִּקְהֲלוּ עַל אַהֲרֹן, שֶׁהוּא כֹּהֵן, לַעֲשׂוֹת הָעֵגֶל. וּלְפִי שֶׁאַהֲרֹן עָשָׂה אֶת הָעֵגֶל לֹא נַעֲשֵׂית עֲבוֹדָה זוֹ עַל יָדוֹ, שֶׁאֵין קַטֵּגוֹר נַעֲשֶׂה סַנֵּגוֹר:

your emotions. You find yourself angry when the situation calls for calm. You hit when you should speak, and speak when you should be silent. Rambam, in another context, mentions that the *Shekhina* does not rest upon us when we are in a state of grief (*Shemona Perakim*, ch. 7). The loss of a sibling can be less expected and more profoundly disorienting than even the loss of a parent. And Miriam was no ordinary sibling. Moshe owes her his life and his identity.

Without Miriam, Moshe could never have become the human face of God to the Israelites, lawgiver, liberator, and prophet. Losing her, he not only lost his sister. He lost the human foundation of his life. This is why, despite facing the rock and the thirst twice before, Moshe for the first time loses emotional control.

[*ḥaver habitaḥon*] and describes it as having someone in whom "you have absolute trust and with whom you are completely open and unguarded," knowing that the other person will neither take advantage of the confidences shared, nor share them with others. A careful reading of this episode within the broader context of Moshe's early life suggests that Miriam was Moshe's "trusted friend," the source of his emotional stability.

Yet only in this week's *parasha* do we begin to get a full sense of her influence, and this only by implication. For the first time, when the people complain of thirst, Moshe faces a challenge without Miriam, and for the first time he loses emotional control in the presence of the people. This is one of the effects of bereavement. Bereaved, you lose control of

אֶת־מִקְדַּ֤שׁ יְהוָה֙ טִמֵּ֔א מֵ֥י נִדָּ֛ה לֹא־זֹרַ֥ק עָלָ֖יו טָמֵ֥א הֽוּא׃ כא וְהָיְתָ֥ה
לָהֶ֖ם לְחֻקַּ֣ת עוֹלָ֑ם וּמַזֵּ֤ה מֵֽי־הַנִּדָּה֙ יְכַבֵּ֣ס בְּגָדָ֔יו וְהַנֹּגֵ֙עַ֙ בְּמֵ֣י הַנִּדָּ֔ה
יִטְמָ֖א עַד־הָעָֽרֶב׃ כב וְכֹ֧ל אֲשֶׁר־יִגַּע־בּ֛וֹ הַטָּמֵ֖א יִטְמָ֑א וְהַנֶּ֥פֶשׁ הַנֹּגַ֖עַת
תִּטְמָ֥א עַד־הָעָֽרֶב׃

כ א וַיָּבֹ֣אוּ בְנֵֽי־יִ֠שְׂרָאֵל כָּל־הָ֨עֵדָ֤ה מִדְבַּר־צִן֙ בַּחֹ֣דֶשׁ הָֽרִאשׁ֔וֹן וַיֵּ֥שֶׁב הָעָ֖ם
בְּקָדֵ֑שׁ וַתָּ֤מָת שָׁם֙ מִרְיָ֔ם וַתִּקָּבֵ֖ר שָֽׁם׃ ב וְלֹא־הָ֥יָה מַ֖יִם לָעֵדָ֑ה וַיִּקָּ֣הֲל֔וּ
עַל־מֹשֶׁ֖ה וְעַל־אַהֲרֹֽן׃ ג וַיָּ֥רֶב הָעָ֖ם עִם־מֹשֶׁ֑ה וַיֹּאמְר֣וּ לֵאמֹ֔ר וְל֥וּ גָוַ֛עְנוּ
בִּגְוַ֥ע אַחֵ֖ינוּ לִפְנֵ֥י יְהוָֽה׃ ד וְלָמָ֤ה הֲבֵאתֶם֙ אֶת־קְהַ֣ל יְהוָ֔ה אֶל־הַמִּדְבָּ֖ר
הַזֶּ֑ה לָמ֣וּת שָׁ֔ם אֲנַ֖חְנוּ וּבְעִירֵֽנוּ׃ ה וְלָמָ֤ה הֶֽעֱלִיתֻ֙נוּ֙ מִמִּצְרַ֔יִם לְהָבִ֣יא אֹתָ֔נוּ

אונקלוס

יָת מַקְדְּשָׁא דַּייָ סַאֵיב, מֵי אַדָּיוּתָא, לָא אִזְדְּרִיקוּ עֲלוֹהִי מְסָאַב הוּא: כא וּתְהֵי לְהוֹן לִקְיָם עָלַם, וּדְמַדֵּי מֵי אַדָּיוּתָא יְצַבַּע לְבוּשׁוֹהִי, וּדְיִקְרַב בְּמֵי אַדָּיוּתָא, יְהֵי מְסָאַב עַד רַמְשָׁא: כב וְכֹל, דְּיִקְרַב בֵּיהּ מְסָאֲבָא יְהֵי מְסָאַב, וֶאֱנָשׁ דְּיִקְרַב בֵּיהּ יְהֵי מְסָאַב עַד רַמְשָׁא: כ א וַאֲתוֹ בְּנֵי יִשְׂרָאֵל, כָּל כְּנִשְׁתָּא לְמַדְבְּרָא דְּצִין בְּיַרְחָא קַדְמָאָה, וִיתֵיב עַמָּא בִּרְקַם, וּמֵיתַת תַּמָּן מִרְיָם, וְאִתְקְבַרַת תַּמָּן: ב וְלָא הֲוָה מַיָּא לִכְנִשְׁתָּא, וְאִתְכְּנִישׁוּ, עַל מֹשֶׁה וְעַל אַהֲרֹן: ג וּנְצָא עַמָּא עִם מֹשֶׁה, וַאֲמַרוּ לְמֵימַר, לְוֵי דְּמֵיתְנָא, בְּמוֹתָא דַּאֲחַנָא קֳדָם יְיָ: ד וּלְמָא אֲתֵיתוֹן יָת קְהָלָא דַּייָ, לְמַדְבְּרָא הָדֵין, לִמְמָת תַּמָּן, אֲנַחְנָא וּבְעִירַנָא: ה וּלְמָא אַסֵּיקְתוּנָא מִמִּצְרַיִם, לְאֵיתָאָה יָתָנָא,

MOSHE AND MIRIAM

Immediately after the account of Miriam's death we read: "And there was no water for the community, and together they confronted Moshe and Aharon" (Num. 20:2). A famous talmudic passage (Taanit 9a) explains that it was in Miriam's merit that the Israelites had a well of water that miraculously accompanied them through their desert journeys. When Miriam died, the water ceased. This interpretation reads the sequence of events supernaturally. Miriam died. Then there was no water. From this, you can infer that until then there was water because Miriam was alive. It was a miracle in her merit (see note on v. 1).

However, there is another way of reading the passage. The connection between Miriam's death and the events that follow it may have less to do with a miraculous well and more to do with Moshe's response to the complaints of the Israelites.

Let us recall who Miriam was, for Moshe. She was his elder sister, who watched over his fate as he floated down the Nile in a pitched basket. She had the presence of mind, and the audacity, to speak to Pharaoh's daughter and arrange for the child to be nursed by an Israelite woman, Moshe's own mother Yokheved. Without Miriam, Moshe would have grown up not knowing who he was.

Miriam is a background presence throughout much of the narrative. We see her leading the women in song at the Sea of Reeds, so it is clear that she, like Aharon, has a leadership role. We gain a sense of how much she means to Moshe when she is punished after she and Aharon "spoke against Moshe because of his Kushite wife; he had married a Kushite woman" (Num. 12:1). Aharon turns helplessly to Moshe and asks him to intervene on her behalf, which he does. Moshe still cares deeply for her.

Leaders need confidants. Rambam, in his Commentary on the Mishna (Avot 1:6), counts this as one of the four kinds of friendship. He calls it the "friendship of trust"

6 no figs, no vines or pomegranates – there is no water to drink!" Moshe and
Aharon went away from the assembly to the entrance of the Tent of Meeting.
They fell on their faces, and the LORD's glory was revealed to them.
7 8 And the LORD spoke to Moshe: "Take the staff, you and your brother Aharon, SHELISHI /SHENI/
and assemble the community. Speak to the rock before their eyes and it will
give forth water. You shall bring forth water for them from the rock, giving
9 the community and their animals to drink." Moshe took the staff from before
10 the LORD, as He had commanded him. And Moshe and Aharon gathered the
assembly together before the rock. He said to them, "Listen now, rebels! Shall
11 we produce water for you from this rock?" Then Moshe raised his hand and
struck the rock twice with his staff. Water gushed out, and the community
12 and their animals drank. But the LORD said to Moshe and Aharon,

רש״י

ה **וְשָׂרַף אֶת הַפָּרָה.** כְּשֵׁם שֶׁנִּשְׂרַף הָעֵגֶל:

ו **עֵץ אֶרֶז וְאֵזוֹב וּשְׁנִי תוֹלַעַת.** שְׁלֹשָׁה מִינִין הַלָּלוּ כְּנֶגֶד שְׁלֹשֶׁת אַלְפֵי אִישׁ שֶׁנָּפְלוּ בָּעֵגֶל. וְאֶרֶז הוּא הַגָּבוֹהַּ מִכָּל הָאִילָנוֹת, וְאֵזוֹב נָמוּךְ מִכֻּלָּם, סִימָן שֶׁהַגָּבוֹהַּ שֶׁנִּתְגָּאָה וְחָטָא יַשְׁפִּיל אֶת עַצְמוֹ כְּאֵזוֹב וְתוֹלַעַת וְיִתְכַּפֵּר לוֹ:

ט **לְמִשְׁמֶרֶת.** כְּמוֹ שֶׁפֶּשַׁע הָעֵגֶל שָׁמוּר לְדוֹרוֹת לְפֻרְעָנוּת, וְאֵין לְךָ פְּקֻדָּה שֶׁאֵין בָּהּ מִפְּקֻדַּת הָעֵגֶל, שֶׁנֶּאֱמַר: "וּבְיוֹם פָּקְדִי וּפָקַדְתִּי" וְגוֹ׳ (שמות לב, לד). וּכְשֵׁם שֶׁהָעֵגֶל מְטַמֵּא כָּל הָעוֹסְקִין בּוֹ, כָּךְ פָּרָה מְטַמְּאָה כָּל הָעוֹסְקִין בָּהּ, וּכְשֵׁם שֶׁנִּטַּהֲרוּ בְּאֶפְרוֹ, שֶׁנֶּאֱמַר: "וַיִּזֶר עַל פְּנֵי הַמַּיִם" וְגוֹ׳ (שמות לב, כ), כָּךְ: "וְלָקְחוּ לַטָּמֵא מֵעֲפַר שְׂרֵפַת הַחַטָּאת" וְגוֹ׳ (להלן פסוק יז):

כ א **כָּל הָעֵדָה.** עֵדָה הַשְּׁלֵמָה, שֶׁכְּבָר מֵתוּ מֵתֵי מִדְבָּר וְאֵלּוּ פָּרְשׁוּ לַחַיִּים: **וַתָּמָת שָׁם מִרְיָם.** לָמָּה נִסְמְכָה מִיתַת מִרְיָם לְפָרָשַׁת פָּרָה אֲדֻמָּה? לוֹמַר לְךָ, מָה קָרְבָּנוֹת מְכַפְּרִין, אַף מִיתַת צַדִּיקִים מְכַפֶּרֶת: **וַתָּמָת שָׁם מִרְיָם.** אַף הִיא בִּנְשִׁיקָה מֵתָה, וּמִפְּנֵי מָה לֹא נֶאֱמַר בָּהּ: 'עַל פִּי ה״'? שֶׁאֵינוֹ דֶּרֶךְ כָּבוֹד שֶׁל מַעְלָה. וּבְאַהֲרֹן נֶאֱמַר: "עַל פִּי ה״ בְּאֵלֶה מַסְעֵי" (להלן לג, לח):

ב **וְלֹא הָיָה מַיִם לָעֵדָה.** מִכָּאן שֶׁכָּל אַרְבָּעִים שָׁנָה הָיָה לָהֶם הַבְּאֵר בִּזְכוּת מִרְיָם:

ג **וְלוּ גָוַעְנוּ.** הַלְוַאי שֶׁגָּוַעְנוּ: **בִּגְוַע אַחֵינוּ.** בְּמִיתַת אַחֵינוּ בַּדֶּבֶר, לִמֵּד שֶׁמִּיתַת צָמָא מְגֻנָּה מִמֶּנָּה: **בִּגְוַע.** שֵׁם דָּבָר הוּא, כְּמוֹ: 'בְּמִיתַת אַחֵינוּ'. וְלֹא יִתָּכֵן לְפָרְשׁוֹ כְּשֶׁמֵּתוּ אַחֵינוּ, שֶׁאִם כֵּן הָיָה לוֹ לְהִנָּקֵד 'בִּגְוֹעַ':

ח **וְאֶת בְּעִירָם.** מִכָּאן שֶׁחָס הַקָּדוֹשׁ בָּרוּךְ הוּא עַל מָמוֹנָם שֶׁל יִשְׂרָאֵל:

י **וַיַּקְהִלוּ וְגוֹ׳.** זֶה אֶחָד מִן הַמְּקוֹמוֹת שֶׁהֶחֱזִיק מוּעָט אֶת הַמְרֻבֶּה: **הֲמִן הַסֶּלַע הַזֶּה נוֹצִיא.** לְפִי שֶׁלֹּא הָיוּ מַכִּירִין אוֹתוֹ, לְפִי שֶׁהָלַךְ הַסֶּלַע וְיָשַׁב לוֹ בֵּין הַסְּלָעִים כְּשֶׁנִּסְתַּלֵּק הַבְּאֵר, וְהָיוּ יִשְׂרָאֵל אוֹמְרִים לָהֶם: מָה לָכֶם, מֵאֵיזֶה סֶלַע תּוֹצִיאוּ לָנוּ מַיִם? לְכָךְ אָמַר לָהֶם: 'הַמֹּרִים', סַרְבָנִים, לְשׁוֹן יְוָנִי שׁוֹטִים, מוֹרִים אֶת מוֹרֵיהֶם, "הֲמִן הַסֶּלַע הַזֶּה" שֶׁלֹּא נִצְטַוִּינוּ עָלָיו, "נוֹצִיא לָכֶם מָיִם"?:

יא **פַּעֲמָיִם.** לְפִי שֶׁבָּרִאשׁוֹנָה לֹא הוֹצִיא אֶלָּא טִפִּין, לְפִי שֶׁלֹּא צִוָּה הַמָּקוֹם לְהַכּוֹתוֹ, אֶלָּא "וְדִבַּרְתֶּם אֶל הַסֶּלַע", וְהֵמָּה דִּבְּרוּ אֶל סֶלַע אַחֵר וְלֹא הוֹצִיא, אָמְרוּ: שֶׁמָּא צָרִיךְ לְהַכּוֹתוֹ כְּבָרִאשׁוֹנָה, שֶׁנֶּאֱמַר: "וְהִכִּיתָ בַצּוּר" (שמות יז, ו), וְנִזְדַּמֵּן לָהֶם אוֹתוֹ סֶלַע וְהִכָּהוּ:

so too was God. Yet they had done no more than ask for water. Giving the people the impression that God was angry with them was a failure to sanctify God's name. In anyone else, it would have been considered a minor offense. However, the greater the person, the more exacting are the standards God sets.

Thus, one moment's anger was sufficient to deprive Moshe of the reward surely most precious to him, of seeing the culmination of his work by leading the people across the Jordan and into the Promised Land.

אֶל־הַמָּקוֹם הָרָע הַזֶּה לֹא ׀ מְקוֹם זֶרַע וּתְאֵנָה וְגֶפֶן וְרִמּוֹן וּמַיִם אַיִן
ו לִשְׁתּוֹת: וַיָּבֹא מֹשֶׁה וְאַהֲרֹן מִפְּנֵי הַקָּהָל אֶל־פֶּתַח אֹהֶל מוֹעֵד וַיִּפְּלוּ
עַל־פְּנֵיהֶם וַיֵּרָא כְבוֹד־יְהוָה אֲלֵיהֶם:
ז ח וַיְדַבֵּר יְהוָה אֶל־מֹשֶׁה לֵּאמֹר: קַח אֶת־הַמַּטֶּה וְהַקְהֵל אֶת־הָעֵדָה שלישי /שני/
אַתָּה וְאַהֲרֹן אָחִיךָ וְדִבַּרְתֶּם אֶל־הַסֶּלַע לְעֵינֵיהֶם וְנָתַן מֵימָיו וְהוֹצֵאתָ
ט לָהֶם מַיִם מִן־הַסֶּלַע וְהִשְׁקִיתָ אֶת־הָעֵדָה וְאֶת־בְּעִירָם: וַיִּקַּח מֹשֶׁה
י אֶת־הַמַּטֶּה מִלִּפְנֵי יְהוָה כַּאֲשֶׁר צִוָּהוּ: וַיַּקְהִלוּ מֹשֶׁה וְאַהֲרֹן אֶת־
הַקָּהָל אֶל־פְּנֵי הַסָּלַע וַיֹּאמֶר לָהֶם שִׁמְעוּ־נָא הַמֹּרִים הֲמִן־הַסֶּלַע
יא הַזֶּה נוֹצִיא לָכֶם מָיִם: וַיָּרֶם מֹשֶׁה אֶת־יָדוֹ וַיַּךְ אֶת־הַסֶּלַע בְּמַטֵּהוּ
יב פַּעֲמָיִם וַיֵּצְאוּ מַיִם רַבִּים וַתֵּשְׁתְּ הָעֵדָה וּבְעִירָם: וַיֹּאמֶר

אונקלוס

לְאַתְרָא בִּישָׁא הָדֵין, לָא אֲתַר כְּשַׁר לְבֵית זְרַע, וְאַף לָא תֵּינִין וְגוּפְנִין וְרִמּוֹנִין, וּמַיָּא לֵית לְמִשְׁתֵּי: ו וְעָאל מֹשֶׁה וְאַהֲרֹן מִן קֳדָם קְהָלָא, לִתְרַע מַשְׁכַּן זִמְנָא, וּנְפַלוּ עַל אַפֵּיהוֹן, וְאִתְגְּלִי יְקָרָא דַּייָ לְהוֹן: ז וּמַלִּיל ייָ עִם מֹשֶׁה לְמֵימַר: ח סַב יָת חֻטְרָא, וְתִכְנוֹשׁ יָת כְּנִשְׁתָּא אַתְּ וְאַהֲרֹן אֲחוּךְ, וּתְמַלְּלוּן עִם כֵּיפָא, לְעֵינֵיהוֹן וְיִתֵּין מוֹהִי, וְתַפֵּיק לְהוֹן מַיָּא מִן כֵּיפָא, וְתַשְׁקֵי יָת כְּנִשְׁתָּא וְיָת בְּעִירְהוֹן: ט וּנְסֵיב מֹשֶׁה, יָת חֻטְרָא מִן קֳדָם יְיָ, כְּמָא דְּפַקְדֵיהּ: י וּכְנַשׁוּ, מֹשֶׁה וְאַהֲרֹן, יָת קְהָלָא לִקְדָם כֵּיפָא, וַאֲמַר לְהוֹן, שְׁמַעוּ כְעַן סָרְבָנַיָּא, הֲמִן כֵּיפָא הָדֵין, נַפֵּיק לְכוֹן מַיָּא: יא וַאֲרֵים מֹשֶׁה יָת יְדֵיהּ, וּמְחָא יָת כֵּיפָא, בְּחֻטְרֵיהּ תַּרְתֵּין זִמְנִין, וּנְפַקוּ מַיָּא סַגִּיאֵי, וּשְׁתִיאַת כְּנִשְׁתָּא וּבְעִירְהוֹן: יב וַאֲמַר

20:10 שִׁמְעוּ־נָא הַמֹּרִים *Listen now, rebels* – Rambam writes in his work *Shemona Perakim* (ch. 4) that Moshe's sin lay in his anger – his intemperate words to the people, "Listen now, rebels!" To be sure, there were other occasions on which he lost his temper – or at least appeared to lose it. His reaction to the sin of the golden calf, for instance, was hardly relaxed. But that case was different. The Israelites had committed a sin. God Himself was threatening to destroy the people. Moshe had to act decisively and with sufficient force to restore order to a people wildly out of control.

Here, though, the people had not sinned. They were thirsty. God was not angry with them. Moshe's intemperate reaction was therefore wrong, says Rambam. In general, Rambam advocated moderation. Like Aristotle, he believed that emotional intelligence exists in striking a balance between excess and deficiency, too much and too little. Too much fear makes me a coward; too little makes me rash and foolhardy, taking unnecessary risks. The middle way is courage. There are, however, two exceptions, says Rambam: pride and anger. Even a little pride is too much. Likewise, even a little anger is wrong. Moshe is not only a leader but the supreme role model of the Israelites. Seeing his behavior, the people may have concluded that anger is permissible.

In addition, says Rambam, by losing his temper Moshe failed to respect the people and might have demoralized them. Knowing that Moshe was God's emissary, the people might have concluded that if Moshe was angry with them,

"Because you did not put your trust in Me to demonstrate My holiness in the
Israelites' eyes, you shall not bring this assembly into the land that I am giving
13 them." These were the waters of Meriva, where the Israelites quarreled with
14 the LORD and where He showed them His holiness. Moshe sent REVI'I
messengers from Kadesh to the king of Edom: "This is what your brother Israel
15 says: 'You know all the hardship we have encountered, how our ancestors
went down to Egypt and lived in Egypt for a long time. And the Egyptians
16 oppressed us and our forebears, and we cried out to the LORD. He heard our
voice, sent a messenger, and He brought us out of Egypt. Now here we are in
17 Kadesh, a town adjoining your border. Please, let us pass through your land.

רש"י

יב **להקדישני.** שאלו דברתם אל הסלע והוציא, הייתי מקודש לעיני העדה, ואומרים: מה סלע זה, שאינו מדבר ואינו שומע ואינו צריך לפרנסה, מקיים דבורו של מקום, קל וחומר אנו: **לכן לא תביאו.** בשבועה, נשבע בקפיצה, שלא ירבו בתפלה על כך: **יען לא האמנתם בי.** גלה הכתוב שאלולי חטא זה בלבד היו נכנסין לארץ, כדי שלא יאמרו עליהם: כעון שאר דור המדבר שנגזר עליהם שלא יכנסו לארץ, כך היה עון משה ואהרן. והלא "הצאן ובקר ישחט" קשה מזו? אלא לפי שבסתר חסך עליו הכתוב, וכאן שבמעמד כל ישראל לא חסך עליו הכתוב, מפני קדוש השם:

יג **המה מי מריבה.** הם הנזכרים במקום אחר, את אלו ראו אצטגניני פרעה שמושיען של ישראל לוקה במים, לכך גזרו: "כל הבן הילוד היארה תשליכהו" (שמות א, כב): **ויקדש בם.** שמתו משה ואהרן על ידם, שכשהקדוש ברוך הוא עושה דין במקדשיו הוא יראוי ומתקדש על הבריות, וכן הוא אומר: "נורא אלהים ממקדשיך" (תהלים סח, לו), וכן הוא אומר: "בקרבי אקדש" (ויקרא י, ג):

יד **אחיך ישראל.** מה ראה להזכיר כאן אחוה? אלא אמר לו: אחים אנחנו בני אברהם, שנאמר לו: "כי גר יהיה זרעך" (בראשית טו, יג) ועל שנינו היה אותו החוב לפרעו: **אתה ידעת את כל התלאה.** לפיכך פרש אביכם מעל אבינו, שנאמר: "וילך אל ארץ מפני יעקב אחיו" (שם לו, ו), מפני השטר חוב המטל עליהם, והטילו על יעקב:

טו **וירעו לנו.** סבלנו צרות רבות: **ולאבתינו.** מכאן שהאבות מצטערים בקבר כשפורענות באה על ישראל:

טז **וישמע קלנו.** בברכה שברכנו אבינו: "הקל קול יעקב" (בראשית כז, כב), שאנו צועקים ונענים: **מלאך.** זה משה, מכאן שהנביאים קרויין מלאכים, ואומר: "ויהיו מלעבים במלאכי האלהים" (דברי הימים ב' לו, טז):

יז **נעברה נא בארצך.** אין לך לעורר על הירשה של ארץ ישראל,

time were those who had spent much of their lives as slaves in Egypt. Those he now faces were born in freedom in the wilderness.

There is a critical difference between slaves and free human beings. Slaves respond to orders. Free people do not. They must be educated, informed, instructed, taught – for if not, they will not learn to take responsibility. Slaves understand that a stick is used for striking. That is how slave masters compel obedience. But free human beings must not be struck. They respond not to power but persuasion. They need to be spoken to. What Moshe fails to hear is that the difference between God's command then and now ("strike the rock" and "speak to the rock") is of the essence. The symbolism in each case is precisely calibrated to the mentalities of two different generations.

A figure capable of leading slaves to freedom is not the same as one able to lead free human beings from a nomadic existence in the wilderness to the conquest and settlement of a land. Each age produces its leaders, and each leader is a function of an age. At the dawn of time, said the Rabbis, God showed Adam each generation and its searchers, each generation and its leaders (Avoda Zara 5a) – meaning, no two generations are alike. The world changes and leaders need to help us to adapt to the new without breaking faith with the old.

יְהוָה֮ אֶל־מֹשֶׁ֣ה וְאֶל־אַהֲרֹן֒ יַ֚עַן לֹא־הֶאֱמַנְתֶּ֣ם בִּ֔י לְהַ֨קְדִּישֵׁ֔נִי לְעֵינֵ֖י
בְּנֵ֣י יִשְׂרָאֵ֑ל לָכֵ֗ן לֹ֤א תָבִ֙יאוּ֙ אֶת־הַקָּהָ֣ל הַזֶּ֔ה אֶל־הָאָ֖רֶץ אֲשֶׁר־נָתַ֥תִּי
יג לָהֶֽם׃ הֵ֚מָּה מֵ֣י מְרִיבָ֔ה אֲשֶׁר־רָב֥וּ בְנֵֽי־יִשְׂרָאֵ֖ל אֶת־יְהוָ֑ה וַיִּקָּדֵ֖שׁ
יד בָּֽם׃ וַיִּשְׁלַ֨ח מֹשֶׁ֧ה מַלְאָכִ֛ים מִקָּדֵ֖שׁ אֶל־מֶ֣לֶךְ אֱד֑וֹם כֹּ֤ה יח רביעי
אָמַר֙ אָחִ֣יךָ יִשְׂרָאֵ֔ל אַתָּ֣ה יָדַ֔עְתָּ אֵ֥ת כָּל־הַתְּלָאָ֖ה אֲשֶׁ֥ר מְצָאָֽתְנוּ׃
טו וַיֵּרְד֤וּ אֲבֹתֵ֙ינוּ֙ מִצְרַ֔יְמָה וַנֵּ֥שֶׁב בְּמִצְרַ֖יִם יָמִ֣ים רַבִּ֑ים וַיָּרֵ֥עוּ לָ֛נוּ מִצְרַ֖יִם
טז וְלַאֲבֹתֵֽינוּ׃ וַנִּצְעַ֤ק אֶל־יְהוָה֙ וַיִּשְׁמַ֣ע קֹלֵ֔נוּ וַיִּשְׁלַ֣ח מַלְאָ֔ךְ וַיֹּצִאֵ֖נוּ
יז מִמִּצְרָ֑יִם וְהִנֵּה֙ אֲנַ֣חְנוּ בְקָדֵ֔שׁ עִ֖יר קְצֵ֥ה גְבוּלֶֽךָ׃ נַעְבְּרָה־נָּ֣א בְאַרְצֶ֗ךָ

אונקלוס

יב לְמשֶׁה וּלְאַהֲרֹן, חֲלָף דְּלָא הֵימַנְתּוּן בְּמֵימְרִי, לְקַדָּשׁוּתִי, לְעֵינֵי בְּנֵי
יִשְׂרָאֵל, בְּכֵן, לָא תַעֲלוּן יָת קְהָלָא הָדֵין, לְאַרְעָא דִּיהַבִית לְהוֹן: יג
אִנּוּן מֵי מַצּוּתָא, דִּנְצוֹ בְּנֵי יִשְׂרָאֵל קֳדָם יְיָ, וְאִתְקַדַּשׁ בְּהוֹן: יד וּשְׁלַח
מֹשֶׁה אִזְגַּדִּין, מֵרְקַם לְוָת מַלְכָּא דֶאֱדוֹם, כִּדְנַן אֲמַר אֲחוּךְ יִשְׂרָאֵל,
אַתְּ יְדַעְתְּ, יָת כָּל עָקְתָא דְּאַשְׁכַּחְתַנָא: טו וּנְחַתוּ אֲבָהָתַנָא לְמִצְרַיִם,
וִיתֵיבְנָא בְּמִצְרַיִם יוֹמִין סַגִּיאִין, וְאַבְאִישׁוּ לַנָא, מִצְרָאֵי וְלַאֲבָהָתַנָא:
טז וְצַלֵּינָא קֳדָם יְיָ וְקַבֵּיל צְלוֹתַנָא, וּשְׁלַח מַלְאֲכָא, וְאַפְּקַנָא מִמִּצְרַיִם,
וְהָא אֲנַחְנָא בִּרְקַם, קַרְתָּא דְּבִסְטַר תְּחוּמָךְ: יז נִעְבַּר כְּעַן בְּאַרְעָךְ,

MOSHE'S PUNISHMENT

It is one of the most perplexing passages in the Torah. Moshe the faithful shepherd, who has led the Israelites for forty years, is told that he will not enter the Promised Land.

What offense could warrant so great a punishment? Because the text does not make it clear, the commentators offer numerous theories, among them that of Rambam (see note on v. 10 above). Rashi (in his commentary here) says that Moshe's sin lay in striking the rock rather than speaking to it. Had Moshe done as he was commanded, the people would have learned an unforgettable lesson: "If a rock, which neither speaks nor hears nor is in need of sustenance, obeys the word of God, how much more so should we." Ramban (on Num. 20:8) says that the sin lay in saying, "Shall we bring forth water for you from this rock?" implying that what was at issue was human ability rather than divine miracle. Rabbi Yosef Albo (*Sefer HaIkkarim* IV:22) suggests that the sin lay in the fact that Moshe and Aharon fled from the congregation and fell on their faces rather than standing their ground, confident that God would answer their prayers. The nineteenth-century Italian exegete Rabbi Shmuel David Luzzatto was moved to remark, "Moshe committed one sin, yet the commentators have accused him of thirteen or more – each inventing some new iniquity."

However we identify Moshe's sin, there is a disproportion between it and its punishment. Could God not forgive Moshe? To deprive him of seeing the culmination of a lifetime's efforts appears unduly harsh.

It is difficult to hazard a different explanation of so debated a text, but there may be a way of seeing the entire episode that makes sense of what otherwise seems like a mystery.

The remarkable fact about Moshe and the rock is the way he observes precedent. Almost forty years earlier, in similar circumstances, God told him to take his staff and strike the rock. Now too, God tells him to take his staff. Evidently Moshe now infers that he is being told to act this time as he did before, which is what he does. He strikes the rock. But time has changed one essential detail. He is facing a new generation. The people he confronted the first

We will not pass through any field or vineyard, nor will we drink water from
any well. We will go along the King's Highway and not turn from it to the right
18 or the left until we have passed through your territory.'" But Edom said to him,
19 "You shall not pass through, or I will come out against you with the sword." The
Israelites said, "We will keep to the beaten track. If we or our livestock drink
any of your water, we will pay for it. It is such a small matter; we only want to
20 pass through on foot." But they said, "You will not pass through." And Edom
21 came out against them with a large fighting force, heavily armed. Edom refused
to let Israel pass through their territory, and Israel turned away.
22 They set out from Kadesh, and all the Israelite community arrived at Mount ḤAMISHI /SHELISHI/
23 Hor. There at Mount Hor, by the border of the land of Edom, the LORD said
24 to Moshe and Aharon, "Aharon is to be gathered to his people. He shall not
enter the land that I have given to the Israelites, because you disobeyed My
25 command at the waters of Meriva. Take Aharon and his son Elazar, and bring
26 them up onto Mount Hor. Strip Aharon of his vestments and put them on
27 his son Elazar. There will Aharon be gathered in and he will die." Moshe did
as the LORD commanded. They ascended Mount Hor in the sight of all the
28 community. Moshe stripped Aharon of his vestments and put them on his
son Elazar. And there, Aharon died, at the top of the mountain; and Moshe

רש״י

כְּשֵׁם שֶׁלֹּא פָּרַעְתָּ הַחוֹב, עֲשֵׂה לָנוּ עֵזֶר מְעַט לַעֲבֹר דֶּרֶךְ אַרְצְךָ: **וְלֹא נִשְׁתֶּה מֵי בְאֵר.** ׳מֵי בוֹרוֹת׳ הָיָה צָרִיךְ לוֹמַר, אֶלָּא כָּךְ אָמַר מֹשֶׁה: אַף עַל פִּי שֶׁיֵּשׁ בְּיָדֵינוּ מָן לֶאֱכֹל וּבְאֵר לִשְׁתּוֹת, לֹא נִשְׁתֶּה מִמֶּנּוּ, אֶלָּא נִקְנֶה מִכֶּם אֹכֶל וּמַיִם לַהֲנָאַתְכֶם. מִכָּאן לְאַכְסְנַאי שֶׁאַף עַל פִּי שֶׁיֵּשׁ בְּיָדוֹ לֶאֱכֹל יִקְנֶה מִן הַחֶנְוָנִי, כְּדֵי לְהַנּוֹת אֶת אֻשְׁפִּיזוֹ: **דֶּרֶךְ הַמֶּלֶךְ נֵלֵךְ וְגוֹ׳.** אָנוּ חוֹסְמִים אֶת בְּהֶמְתֵּנוּ וְלֹא יִטּוּ לְכָאן וּלְכָאן לֶאֱכֹל:

יח **פֶּן בַּחֶרֶב אֵצֵא לִקְרָאתֶךָ.** אַתֶּם מִתְגָּאִים בַּקּוֹל שֶׁהוֹרִישְׁכֶם אֲבִיכֶם, וְאוֹמְרִים: "וַנִּצְעַק אֶל ה׳ וַיִּשְׁמַע קֹלֵנוּ" (לעיל פסוק טז), וַאֲנִי אֵצֵא עֲלֵיכֶם בְּמָה שֶׁהוֹרִישַׁנִי אָבִי: "וְעַל חַרְבְּךָ תִחְיֶה" (בראשית כז, מ):

יט **רַק אֵין דָּבָר.** אֵין שׁוּם דָּבָר מַזִּיקְךָ:

כ **וּבְיָד חֲזָקָה.** בְּהַבְטָחַת זְקֵנֵנוּ: "וְהַיָּדַיִם יְדֵי עֵשָׂו" (בראשית כז, כב):

כב **כָּל הָעֵדָה.** כֻּלָּם שְׁלֵמִים וְעוֹמְדִים לְהִכָּנֵס לָאָרֶץ, שֶׁלֹּא הָיָה בָּהֶן אֶחָד מֵאוֹתָם שֶׁנִּגְזְרָה גְּזֵרָה עֲלֵיהֶם, שֶׁכְּבָר כָּלוּ מֵתֵי מִדְבָּר, וְאֵלּוּ מֵאוֹתָן שֶׁכָּתוּב בָּהֶן: "חַיִּים כֻּלְּכֶם הַיּוֹם" (דברים ד, ד): **הֹר הָהָר.** הַר עַל גַּבֵּי הַר, כְּתַפּוּחַ קָטָן עַל גַּבֵּי תַפּוּחַ גָּדוֹל. וְאַף עַל פִּי שֶׁהֶעָנָן הוֹלֵךְ לִפְנֵיהֶם וּמַשְׁוֶה אֶת הֶהָרִים, שְׁלֹשָׁה נִשְׁאֲרוּ בָהֶן: הַר סִינַי לַתּוֹרָה, הֹר הָהָר לִקְבוּרַת אַהֲרֹן, וְהַר נְבוֹ לִקְבוּרַת מֹשֶׁה:

כג **עַל גְּבוּל אֶרֶץ אֱדוֹם.** מַגִּיד שֶׁמִּפְּנֵי שֶׁנִּתְחַבְּרוּ כָּאן לְהִתְקָרֵב לְעֵשָׂו הָרָשָׁע נִפְרְצוּ מַעֲשֵׂיהֶם וְחָסְרוּ הַצַּדִּיק הַזֶּה:

כה **קַח אֶת אַהֲרֹן.** בִּדְבָרִים שֶׁל נִחוּמִים, אֱמֹר לוֹ: אַשְׁרֶיךָ שֶׁתִּרְאֶה כִּתְרְךָ נָתוּן לִבְנְךָ, מַה שֶּׁאֵין אֲנִי זַכַּאי לְכָךְ:

כו **אֶת בְּגָדָיו.** בִּגְדֵי כְהֻנָּה גְדוֹלָה הַלְבִּישֵׁהוּ וְהַפְשִׁיטֵם מֵעָלָיו לְתִתָּם עַל בְּנוֹ בְּפָנָיו. אָמַר לוֹ: הִכָּנֵס לַמְּעָרָה, וְנִכְנַס. רָאָה מִטָּה מֻצַּעַת וְנֵר דָּלוּק. אָמַר לוֹ: עֲלֵה לַמִּטָּה, וְעָלָה. פְּשֹׁט יָדֶיךָ, וּפָשַׁט. קְמֹץ פִּיךָ, וְקָמַץ. עֲצֹם עֵינֶיךָ, וְעָצַם. מִיָּד חָמַד מֹשֶׁה לְאוֹתָהּ מִיתָה. וְזֶהוּ שֶׁנֶּאֱמַר לוֹ: "כַּאֲשֶׁר מֵת אַהֲרֹן אָחִיךָ" (דברים לב, נ), מִיתָה שֶׁנִּתְאַוִּיתָ לָהּ:

כז **וַיַּעַשׂ מֹשֶׁה.** אַף עַל פִּי שֶׁהַדָּבָר קָשֶׁה לוֹ, לֹא עִכֵּב:

לֹא נַעֲבֹר בְּשָׂדֶה וּבְכֶרֶם וְלֹא נִשְׁתֶּה מֵי בְאֵר דֶּרֶךְ הַמֶּלֶךְ נֵלֵךְ לֹא נִטֶּה
יח יָמִין וּשְׂמֹאול עַד אֲשֶׁר־נַעֲבֹר גְּבֻלֶךָ׃ וַיֹּאמֶר אֵלָיו אֱדוֹם לֹא תַעֲבֹר
יט בִּי פֶּן־בַּחֶרֶב אֵצֵא לִקְרָאתֶךָ׃ וַיֹּאמְרוּ אֵלָיו בְּנֵי־יִשְׂרָאֵל בַּמְסִלָּה
נַעֲלֶה וְאִם־מֵימֶיךָ נִשְׁתֶּה אֲנִי וּמִקְנַי וְנָתַתִּי מִכְרָם רַק אֵין־דָּבָר
כ בְּרַגְלַי אֶעֱבֹרָה׃ וַיֹּאמֶר לֹא תַעֲבֹר וַיֵּצֵא אֱדוֹם לִקְרָאתוֹ בְּעַם כָּבֵד
כא וּבְיָד חֲזָקָה׃ וַיְמָאֵן ׀ אֱדוֹם נְתֹן אֶת־יִשְׂרָאֵל עֲבֹר בִּגְבֻלוֹ וַיֵּט יִשְׂרָאֵל
מֵעָלָיו׃
כב כג וַיִּסְעוּ מִקָּדֵשׁ וַיָּבֹאוּ בְנֵי־יִשְׂרָאֵל כָּל־הָעֵדָה הֹר הָהָר׃ וַיֹּאמֶר יְהֹוָה חמישי /שלישי/
כד אֶל־מֹשֶׁה וְאֶל־אַהֲרֹן בְּהֹר הָהָר עַל־גְּבוּל אֶרֶץ־אֱדוֹם לֵאמֹר׃ יֵאָסֵף
אַהֲרֹן אֶל־עַמָּיו כִּי לֹא יָבֹא אֶל־הָאָרֶץ אֲשֶׁר נָתַתִּי לִבְנֵי יִשְׂרָאֵל
כה עַל אֲשֶׁר־מְרִיתֶם אֶת־פִּי לְמֵי מְרִיבָה׃ קַח אֶת־אַהֲרֹן וְאֶת־אֶלְעָזָר
כו בְּנוֹ וְהַעַל אֹתָם הֹר הָהָר׃ וְהַפְשֵׁט אֶת־אַהֲרֹן אֶת־בְּגָדָיו וְהִלְבַּשְׁתָּם
כז אֶת־אֶלְעָזָר בְּנוֹ וְאַהֲרֹן יֵאָסֵף וּמֵת שָׁם׃ וַיַּעַשׂ מֹשֶׁה כַּאֲשֶׁר צִוָּה יְהֹוָה
כח וַיַּעֲלוּ אֶל־הֹר הָהָר לְעֵינֵי כָּל־הָעֵדָה׃ וַיַּפְשֵׁט מֹשֶׁה אֶת־אַהֲרֹן אֶת־
בְּגָדָיו וַיַּלְבֵּשׁ אֹתָם אֶת־אֶלְעָזָר בְּנוֹ וַיָּמָת אַהֲרֹן שָׁם בְּרֹאשׁ הָהָר וַיֵּרֶד

אונקלוס

לָא נִעְבַּר בַּחֲקַל וּבִכְרַם, וְלָא נִשְׁתֵּי מֵי גוֹב, בְּאוֹרַח מַלְכָּא נֵיזֵיל, לָא נִסְטֵי לְיַמִּינָא וְלִסְמָאלָא, עַד דְּנִעְבַּר תְּחוּמָךְ: יח וַאֲמַר לֵיהּ אֱדוֹמָאָה, לָא תִעְבַּר בִּתְחוּמִי, דִּלְמָא בִּדְקָטְלִין בְּחַרְבָּא אֶפּוֹק לְקַדָּמוּתָךְ: יט וַאֲמַרוּ לֵיהּ בְּנֵי יִשְׂרָאֵל בְּאוֹרַח כְּבִישָׁא נִסַּק, וְאִם מַיָּךְ נִשְׁתֵּי אֲנָא וּבְעִירַי, וְאֶתֵּין דְּמֵיהוֹן, לְחוֹד לֵית פִּתְגָם בִּישׁ בְּרַגְלַי אֶעְבַּר: כ וַאֲמַר לָא תִעְבַּר, וּנְפַק אֱדוֹמָאָה לְקַדָּמוּתֵיהּ, בְּחֵיל רַב וּבְיַד תַּקִּיפָא: כא וְסָרֵיב אֱדוֹמָאָה, לָא שְׁבַק יָת יִשְׂרָאֵל, לְמִעְבַּר בִּתְחוּמֵיהּ, וּסְטָא יִשְׂרָאֵל מִלְּוָתֵיהּ: כב וּנְטַלוּ מֵרְקַם, וַאֲתוֹ בְנֵי יִשְׂרָאֵל, כָּל כְּנִשְׁתָּא לְהוֹר טוּרָא: כג וַאֲמַר יְיָ, לְמֹשֶׁה וּלְאַהֲרֹן בְּהוֹר טוּרָא, עַל תְּחוּם אַרְעָא דֶאֱדוֹם לְמֵימַר: כד יִתְכְּנֵישׁ אַהֲרֹן לְעַמֵּיהּ, אֲרֵי לָא יֵיעוֹל לְאַרְעָא, דִּיהַבִית לִבְנֵי יִשְׂרָאֵל, עַל, דְּסָרֵיבְתּוּן עַל מֵימְרִי לְמֵי מַצּוּתָא: כה דְּבַר יָת אַהֲרֹן, וְיָת אֶלְעָזָר בְּרֵיהּ, וְתַסֵּיק יָתְהוֹן לְהוֹר טוּרָא: כו וְתַשְׁלַח יָת אַהֲרֹן יָת לְבוּשׁוֹהִי, וְתַלְבֵּישִׁנּוּן יָת אֶלְעָזָר בְּרֵיהּ, וְאַהֲרֹן יִתְכְּנֵישׁ וִימוּת תַּמָּן: כז וַעֲבַד מֹשֶׁה, כְּמָא דְּפַקֵּיד יְיָ, וּסְלִיקוּ לְהוֹר טוּרָא, לְעֵינֵי כָּל כְּנִשְׁתָּא: כח וְאַשְׁלַח מֹשֶׁה יָת אַהֲרֹן יָת לְבוּשׁוֹהִי, וְאַלְבֵּישׁ יָתְהוֹן יָת אֶלְעָזָר בְּרֵיהּ, וּמִית אַהֲרֹן, תַּמָּן בְּרֵישׁ טוּרָא, וּנְחַת

29 and Elazar came down from the mountain. When all the community saw that
Aharon had perished, the whole House of Israel wept for Aharon for thirty
21 1 days. When the Canaanite king of Arad, dwelling in the Negev, heard
that the Israelites were coming by the way of Atarim, he attacked the Israelites
2 and took captives. And the Israelites vowed to the LORD: "If You give this people
3 over into our hands, we will utterly destroy their towns." The LORD listened to
Israel's plea and gave over the Canaanites. They completely destroyed them
and their cities; and so the place was named Ḥorma.
4 They set out from Mount Hor by the way to the Reed Sea, going around the
5 land of Edom. But the people became restive along the way. The people spoke
out against God and Moshe: "Why did you bring us up from Egypt to die in
the desert? There is no bread, there is no water; we detest this miserable food!"
6 The LORD sent venomous snakes among the people; they bit the people, and

רש״י

כט **וַיִּרְאוּ כָּל הָעֵדָה וגו׳.** כְּשֶׁרָאוּ מֹשֶׁה וְאֶלְעָזָר יוֹרְדִים וְאַהֲרֹן לֹא יָרַד, אָמְרוּ: הֵיכָן הוּא אַהֲרֹן? אָמַר לָהֶם: מֵת. אָמְרוּ: אֶפְשָׁר מִי שֶׁעָמַד כְּנֶגֶד הַמַּלְאָךְ וְעָצַר אֶת הַמַּגֵּפָה (במדבר יז, יג) יִשְׁלֹט בּוֹ מַלְאַךְ הַמָּוֶת?! מִיָּד בִּקֵּשׁ מֹשֶׁה רַחֲמִים וְהֶרְאוּהוּ מַלְאֲכֵי הַשָּׁרֵת לָהֶם מֻטָּל בְּמִטָּה, רָאוּ וְהֶאֱמִינוּ: **כֹּל בֵּית יִשְׂרָאֵל.** הָאֲנָשִׁים וְהַנָּשִׁים, לְפִי שֶׁהָיָה אַהֲרֹן רוֹדֵף שָׁלוֹם וּמֵטִיל אַהֲבָה בֵּין בַּעֲלֵי מְרִיבָה וּבֵין אִישׁ לְאִשְׁתּוֹ: **כִּי גָוַע.** אוֹמֵר אֲנִי שֶׁהַמְתַרְגֵּם: 'דְּהָא מִית' טוֹעֶה הוּא, אֶלָּא אִם כֵּן מְתַרְגֵּם: 'וַיִּרְאוּ' – 'וְאִתְחֲזִיאוּ', שֶׁלֹּא אָמְרוּ רַבּוֹתֵינוּ זִכְרוֹנָם לִבְרָכָה 'כִּי' זֶה מְשַׁמֵּשׁ בִּלְשׁוֹן 'דְּהָא', אֶלָּא עַל מִדְרָשׁ שֶׁנִּסְתַּלְּקוּ עַנְנֵי כָבוֹד, וּכְדְאָמַר רַבִּי אַבָּהוּ: אַל תִּקְרֵי 'וַיִּרְאוּ' אֶלָּא 'וַיֵּרָאוּ', וְעַל לָשׁוֹן זֶה נוֹפֵל לָשׁוֹן 'דְּהָא', לְפִי שֶׁהִיא נְתִינַת טַעַם לְמָה שֶׁלְּמַעְלָה הֵימֶנּוּ: לָמָּה וַיֵּרָאוּ? לְפִי שֶׁהֲרֵי מֵת אַהֲרֹן. אֲבָל עַל תַּרְגּוּם: "וַחֲזוֹ כָּל כְּנִשְׁתָּא" אֵין לְשׁוֹן 'דְּהָא' נוֹפֵל, אֶלָּא לְשׁוֹן 'אֲשֶׁר', שֶׁהוּא מִגִּזְרַת שִׁמּוּשׁ 'אִי', שֶׁמָּצִינוּ 'אִם' מְשַׁמֵּשׁ בִּלְשׁוֹן 'אֲשֶׁר', כְּמוֹ: "וְאִם מַדּוּעַ לֹא תִקְצַר רוּחִי" (איוב כא, ד), וְהַרְבֵּה מְפֹרָשִׁים מִזֶּה הַלָּשׁוֹן: "אִם חֲרוּצִים יָמָיו" (שם יד, ה):

כא א **וַיִּשְׁמַע הַכְּנַעֲנִי.** שָׁמַע שֶׁמֵּת אַהֲרֹן וְנִסְתַּלְּקוּ עַנְנֵי כָבוֹד כו׳, כִּדְאִיתָא בְּרֹאשׁ הַשָּׁנָה (דף ג ע״א). וַעֲמָלֵק מֵעוֹלָם רְצוּעַת מַרְדּוּת לְיִשְׂרָאֵל, מְזֻמָּן בְּכָל עֵת לְפֻרְעָנוּת: **יֹשֵׁב הַנֶּגֶב.** זֶה עֲמָלֵק, שֶׁנֶּאֱמַר: "עֲמָלֵק יוֹשֵׁב בְּאֶרֶץ הַנֶּגֶב" (לעיל יג, כט), וְשִׁנָּה אֶת לְשׁוֹנוֹ לְדַבֵּר בִּלְשׁוֹן כְּנַעַן, כְּדֵי שֶׁיִּהְיוּ יִשְׂרָאֵל מִתְפַּלְּלִים לְהַקָּדוֹשׁ בָּרוּךְ הוּא לָתֵת כְּנַעֲנִים בְּיָדָם, וְהֵם אֵינָן כְּנַעֲנִים. רָאוּ יִשְׂרָאֵל לְבוּשֵׁיהֶם כִּלְבוּשֵׁי עֲמָלֵקִים וּלְשׁוֹנָם לְשׁוֹן כְּנַעַן, אָמְרוּ: נִתְפַּלֵּל סְתָם, שֶׁנֶּאֱמַר: "אִם נָתֹן תִּתֵּן אֶת הָעָם הַזֶּה בְּיָדִי" (להלן פסוק ב): **דֶּרֶךְ הָאֲתָרִים.** דֶּרֶךְ הַנֶּגֶב שֶׁהָלְכוּ בָהּ מְרַגְּלִים, שֶׁנֶּאֱמַר: "וַיַּעֲלוּ בַנֶּגֶב" (לעיל יג, כב). דָּבָר אַחֵר, "דֶּרֶךְ הָאֲתָרִים", דֶּרֶךְ הַתַּיָּר הַגָּדוֹל הַנּוֹסֵעַ לִפְנֵיהֶם, שֶׁנֶּאֱמַר: "דֶּרֶךְ שְׁלֹשֶׁת יָמִים לָתוּר לָהֶם מְנוּחָה" (לעיל י, לג): **וַיִּשְׁבְּ מִמֶּנּוּ שֶׁבִי.** אֵינָהּ אֶלָּא שִׁפְחָה אַחַת:

ב **וְהַחֲרַמְתִּי.** אַקְדִּישׁ שְׁלָלָם לַגָּבוֹהַּ:

ג **וַיַּחֲרֵם אֶתְהֶם.** בַּהֲרִיגָה: **וְאֶת עָרֵיהֶם.** חֶרְמֵי גָבוֹהַּ:

ד **דֶּרֶךְ יַם סוּף.** כֵּיוָן שֶׁמֵּת אַהֲרֹן וּבָאת עֲלֵיהֶם מִלְחָמָה זוֹ, חָזְרוּ לַאֲחוֹרֵיהֶם דֶּרֶךְ יַם סוּף, הוּא הַדֶּרֶךְ שֶׁחָזְרוּ לָהֶם כְּשֶׁנִּגְזְרָה עֲלֵיהֶם גְּזֵרַת מְרַגְּלִים, שֶׁנֶּאֱמַר: "וּסְעוּ הַמִּדְבָּרָה דֶּרֶךְ יַם סוּף" (דברים א, מ). וְכָאן חָזְרוּ לַאֲחוֹרֵיהֶם שֶׁבַע מַסָּעוֹת, שֶׁנֶּאֱמַר: "וּבְנֵי יִשְׂרָאֵל נָסְעוּ מִבְּאֵרֹת בְּנֵי יַעֲקָן מוֹסֵרָה שָׁם מֵת אַהֲרֹן" (שם י, ו), וְכִי בְּמוֹסֵרָה מֵת? וַהֲלֹא בְּהֹר הָהָר מֵת! אֶלָּא שָׁם חָזְרוּ וְהִתְאַבְּלוּ עָלָיו וְהִסְפִּידוּהוּ כְּאִלּוּ הוּא בִּפְנֵיהֶם. וְצֵא וּבְדֹק בְּמַסָּעוֹת וְתִמְצָאֵם שֶׁבַע מַסָּעוֹת מִן מוֹסֵרָה עַד הֹר הָהָר: **לִסְבֹב אֶת אֶרֶץ אֱדוֹם.** שֶׁלֹּא נְתָנָם לַעֲבֹר בְּאַרְצוֹ: **וַתִּקְצַר נֶפֶשׁ הָעָם בַּדָּרֶךְ.** בְּטֹרַח הַדֶּרֶךְ שֶׁהֻקְשָׁה לָהֶם, אָמְרוּ: עַכְשָׁיו הָיִינוּ קְרוֹבִים לִכָּנֵס לָאָרֶץ וְאָנוּ חוֹזְרִים לַאֲחוֹרֵינוּ, כָּךְ חָזְרוּ אֲבוֹתֵינוּ וְנִשְׁתַּהוּ שְׁלֹשִׁים וּשְׁמוֹנֶה שָׁנָה עַד הַיּוֹם, לְפִיכָךְ קָצְרָה נַפְשָׁם בְּעִנּוּי הַדֶּרֶךְ. וּבִלְשׁוֹן לַעַז אנקרוטלו״ר. וְלֹא יִתָּכֵן לוֹמַר "וַתִּקְצַר נֶפֶשׁ הָעָם בַּדָּרֶךְ" בִּהְיוֹתָם בַּדֶּרֶךְ וְלֹא פֵרַשׁ בּוֹ בַּמֶּה קָצְרָה, שֶׁכָּל מָקוֹם שֶׁתִּמְצָא קִצּוּר נֶפֶשׁ בַּמִּקְרָא מְפֹרָשׁ שָׁם בַּמֶּה קָצְרָה, כְּגוֹן: "וַתִּקְצַר נַפְשִׁי בָּהֶם" (זכריה יא, ח), וּכְגוֹן: "וַתִּקְצַר נַפְשׁוֹ בַּעֲמַל יִשְׂרָאֵל" (שופטים י, טז), וְכָל דָּבָר הַקָּשֶׁה עַל אָדָם נוֹפֵל בּוֹ לְשׁוֹן קִצּוּר נֶפֶשׁ, כְּאָדָם שֶׁהַטֹּרַח בָּא עָלָיו וְאֵין דַּעְתּוֹ רְחָבָה לְקַבֵּל אוֹתוֹ הַדָּבָר, וְאֵין לוֹ מָקוֹם בְּתוֹךְ לִבּוֹ לָגוּר שָׁם אוֹתוֹ הַצַּעַר, וּבְדָבָר הַמַּטְרִיחַ נוֹפֵל לְשׁוֹן גֹּדֶל, שֶׁגָּדוֹל הוּא וְכָבֵד עַל הָאָדָם, כְּגוֹן: "וְגַם נַפְשָׁם בָּחֲלָה בִי" (זכריה שם), גָּדְלָה עָלַי, "וְיִגְאֶה כַּשַּׁחַל תְּצוּדֵנִי" (איוב י, טז). כְּלָלוֹ שֶׁל פֵּרוּשׁ: כָּל לְשׁוֹן קִצּוּר נֶפֶשׁ בְּדָבָר, לְשׁוֹן 'שֶׁאֵין יָכוֹל לְסָבְלוֹ' הוּא, שֶׁאֵין הַדַּעַת סוֹבַלְתּוֹ:

כט מֹשֶׁה וְאֶלְעָזָר מִן־הָהָר: וַיִּרְאוּ כָּל־הָעֵדָה כִּי גָוַע אַהֲרֹן וַיִּבְכּוּ אֶת־
כא א אַהֲרֹן שְׁלֹשִׁים יוֹם כֹּל בֵּית יִשְׂרָאֵל: וַיִּשְׁמַע הַכְּנַעֲנִי
מֶלֶךְ־עֲרָד יֹשֵׁב הַנֶּגֶב כִּי בָּא יִשְׂרָאֵל דֶּרֶךְ הָאֲתָרִים וַיִּלָּחֶם בְּיִשְׂרָאֵל
ב וַיִּשְׁבְּ ׀ מִמֶּנּוּ שֶׁבִי: וַיִּדַּר יִשְׂרָאֵל נֶדֶר לַיהוָה וַיֹּאמַר אִם־נָתֹן תִּתֵּן אֶת־
ג הָעָם הַזֶּה בְּיָדִי וְהַחֲרַמְתִּי אֶת־עָרֵיהֶם: וַיִּשְׁמַע יהוה בְּקוֹל יִשְׂרָאֵל
וַיִּתֵּן אֶת־הַכְּנַעֲנִי וַיַּחֲרֵם אֶתְהֶם וְאֶת־עָרֵיהֶם וַיִּקְרָא שֵׁם־הַמָּקוֹם
חָרְמָה:
ד וַיִּסְעוּ מֵהֹר הָהָר דֶּרֶךְ יַם־סוּף לִסְבֹב אֶת־אֶרֶץ אֱדוֹם וַתִּקְצַר נֶפֶשׁ־
ה הָעָם בַּדָּרֶךְ: וַיְדַבֵּר הָעָם בֵּאלֹהִים וּבְמֹשֶׁה לָמָה הֶעֱלִיתֻנוּ מִמִּצְרַיִם
לָמוּת בַּמִּדְבָּר כִּי אֵין לֶחֶם וְאֵין מַיִם וְנַפְשֵׁנוּ קָצָה בַּלֶּחֶם הַקְּלֹקֵל:
ו וַיְשַׁלַּח יהוה בָּעָם אֵת הַנְּחָשִׁים הַשְּׂרָפִים וַיְנַשְּׁכוּ אֶת־הָעָם וַיָּמָת

אונקלוס

מֹשֶׁה, וְאֶלְעָזָר מִן טוּרָא: כט וַחֲזוֹ כָּל כְּנִשְׁתָּא, אֲרֵי מִית אַהֲרֹן, וּבְכוֹ יָת אַהֲרֹן תְּלָתִין יוֹמִין, כֹּל בֵּית יִשְׂרָאֵל: כא א וּשְׁמַע, כְּנַעֲנָאָה מַלְכָּא דַעֲרָד יָתֵיב דָּרוֹמָא, אֲרֵי אֲתָא יִשְׂרָאֵל, אוֹרַח מְאַלְלַיָּא, וַאֲגִיחַ קְרָבָא בְּיִשְׂרָאֵל, וּשְׁבָא מִנֵּיהּ שִׁבְיָא: ב וְקַיֵּים יִשְׂרָאֵל קְיָם, קֳדָם יי וַאֲמַר, אִם מִמְסַר תִּמְסַר, יָת עַמָּא הָדֵין בִּידִי, וַאֲגַמַּר יָת קִרְוֵיהוֹן: ג וְקַבֵּיל יי צְלוֹתֵיהּ דְּיִשְׂרָאֵל, וּמְסַר יָת כְּנַעֲנָאָה, וְגַמַּר יָתְהוֹן וְיָת קִרְוֵיהוֹן, וּקְרָא שְׁמֵיהּ דְּאַתְרָא חָרְמָה: ד וּנְטַלוּ, מֵהוֹר טוּרָא אוֹרַח יַמָּא דְסוּף, לְאַקָּפָא יָת אַרְעָא דֶאֱדוֹם, וַעֲקַת נַפְשָׁא דְעַמָּא בְּאוֹרְחָא: ה וְאִתְרַעַם עַמָּא, קֳדָם יי וְעִם מֹשֶׁה נְצוֹ, לְמָא אַסֵּיקְתּוּנָא מִמִּצְרַיִם, לִמְמָת בְּמַדְבְּרָא, אֲרֵי לֵית לַחְמָא וְלֵית מַיָּא, וְנַפְשַׁנָא עָקַת, בְּמַנָּא הָדֵין דְּמֵיכְלֵיהּ קְלִיל: ו וְגָרֵי יי בְּעַמָּא, יָת חִיוָון קָלַן, וְנַכִּיתוּ יָת עַמָּא, וּמִית

רש״י

ה בֵּאלֹהִים וּבְמֹשֶׁה. הִשְׁווּ עֶבֶד לְקוֹנוֹ: לָמָה הֶעֱלִיתֻנוּ. שְׁנֵיהֶם שָׁוִים: וְנַפְשֵׁנוּ קָצָה. אַף זֶה לְשׁוֹן קִצּוּר נֶפֶשׁ וּמִאוּס: בַּלֶּחֶם הַקְּלֹקֵל. לְפִי שֶׁהַמָּן נִבְלָע בָּאֵיבָרִים קְרָאוּהוּ 'קְלֹקֵל', אָמְרוּ: עָתִיד הַמָּן הַזֶּה שֶׁיִּתְפַּח בְּמֵעֵינוּ, כְּלוּם יֵשׁ יְלוּד אִשָּׁה שֶׁמַּכְנִיס וְאֵינוֹ מוֹצִיא?

ו אֵת הַנְּחָשִׁים הַשְּׂרָפִים. שֶׁשּׂוֹרְפִים אֶת הָאָדָם בְּאֶרֶס שִׁנֵּיהֶם: וַיְנַשְּׁכוּ אֶת הָעָם. יָבֹא נָחָשׁ שֶׁלָּקָה עַל הוֹצָאַת דִּבָּה וְיִפָּרַע מִמּוֹצִיאֵי דִבָּה, יָבֹא נָחָשׁ שֶׁכָּל הַמִּינִין נִטְעָמִין לוֹ טַעַם אֶחָד וְיִפָּרַע מִכְּפוּיֵי טוֹבָה שֶׁדָּבָר אֶחָד מִשְׁתַּנֶּה לָהֶם לְכַמָּה טְעָמִים:

20:29 וַיִּבְכּוּ אֶת־אַהֲרֹן שְׁלֹשִׁים יוֹם כֹּל בֵּית יִשְׂרָאֵל *The whole House of Israel wept for Aharon for thirty days* – Aharon dies, and the people mourn profoundly. Moshe too knows that his days are numbered. He will not live to cross the Jordan. He will die in sight of the land but without setting foot on it. Parashat Ḥukat is thus about mortality. It is about the death of an entire generation, symbolized in the fate of its three leaders (and in the ritual of the red heifer, as we saw above). It is about the discovery of a painful truth, most famously expressed by R. Tarfon in the Mishna: It is not for you to complete the task, but neither are you free to desist from it (Avot 2:16). The great challenges of humanity are too large to be completed in a single generation.

7 many Israelites died. The people came to Moshe and said, "We sinned when
we spoke against the LORD and you. Pray to the LORD to take the snakes away
8 from us." Moshe prayed for the people. The LORD then said to Moshe, "Fashion
a snake and place it on a pole. Anyone who is bitten shall look at that and live."
9 Moshe fashioned a bronze snake and placed it on a pole. When anyone was
10 bitten by a snake, he would look at the bronze snake and live. The Israelites SHISHI
11 moved on and camped at Ovot. Then they moved on from Ovot, and camped
12 at Iyei HaAvarim in the wilderness bordering Moav to the east. From there they
13 moved on and camped at the Zered Stream. From there they moved on and
camped beyond the Arnon, in the wilderness that extends from the border of
the Amorites, for the Arnon marks the border of Moav, between Moav and the
14 Amorites. That is why the Book of the Wars of the LORD records: "Vahev in Sufa
15 and the wadis, Arnon and the wadi slopes that lead to the settlement of Ar and

רש"י

ז **ויתפלל משה.** מכאן למי שמבקשים ממנו מחילה שלא יהא אכזרי מלמחול:

ח **על נס.** על כלונס שקורין פירק"א בלעז, וכן: "וכנס על הגבעה" (ישעיה ל, יז), "ארים נסי" (שם מט, כב), "שאו נס" (שם יג, ב). ולפי שהוא גבוה לאות ולראיה קוראו 'נס': **כל הנשוך.** אפילו כלב או חמור נושכו היה נזוק ומתנונה והולך, אלא שנשיכת הנחש ממהרת להמית, לכך נאמר כאן: "וראה אתו" – ראיה בעלמא, ובנשיכת הנחש נאמר: "והביט", "והיה אם נשך הנחש את איש והביט" וגו' (להלן פסוק ט), שלא היה ממהר נשוך הנחש להתרפאות אלא אם כן מביט בו בכוונה. ואמרו רבותינו: וכי נחש ממית או מחיה? אלא בזמן שהיו ישראל מסתכלין כלפי מעלה ומשעבדין את לבם לאביהם שבשמים היו מתרפאים, ואם לאו היו נמוקים:

ט **נחש נחשת.** לא נאמר לו לעשותו של נחשת, אלא אמר משה: הקדוש ברוך הוא קוראו נחש ואני אעשנו של נחשת, לשון נופל על לשון:

יא **בעיי העברים.** לא ידעתי למה נקרא שמם עיים, ו'עי' לשון חרבה הוא, דבר הטאוט במטאטא, והעי"ן בו יסוד לבדה, והוא מלשון "יעים" (לעיל ד, יד), "ויעה ברד" (ישעיה כח, יז): **העברים.** דרך מעבר העוברים שם את הר נבו אל ארץ כנען, שהוא מפסיק בין ארץ מואב לארץ אמורי: **על פני מואב ממזרח השמש.** במזרחה של ארץ מואב:

יג **מגבל האמרי.** תחום סוף מצר שלהם, וכן "גבול מואב", לשון קצה וסוף: **מעבר ארנון.** הקיפו ארץ מואב כל דרומה ומזרחה, עד שבאו מעבר השני לארנון בתוך ארץ האמורי, בצפונה של ארץ מואב: **היצא מגבל האמרי.** רצועה יוצאה מגבול האמורי והיא של אמוריים, ונכנסת לגבול מואב עד ארנון שהוא גבול מואב, ושם חנו ישראל ולא באו לגבול מואב, "כי ארנון גבול מואב", והם לא נתנו להם רשות לעבור בארצם. ואף על פי שלא פרשה משה, פרשה יפתח, כמו שאמר יפתח: "וגם אל מלך מואב שלח ולא אבה" (שופטים יא, יז), ומשה רמזה: "כאשר עשו לי בני עשו היושבים בשעיר והמואבים היושבים בער" (דברים ב, כט), מה אלו לא נתנום לעבור בתוך ארצם אלא הקיפום סביב, אף מואב כן:

יד-טו **על כן.** על חניה זו ונסים שנעשו בה "יאמר בספר מלחמת ה'", כשמספרים נסים שנעשו לאבותינו, יספרו: "את והב" וגו': **את והב.** כמו 'את יהב', כמו שיאמר מן 'יעד' 'ועד', כן יאמר מן יהב 'והב', והוי"ו יסוד הוא, כלומר את אשר יהב להם והרבה נסים בים סוף: **ואת הנחלים ארנון.** כשם שמספרים בנסי ים סוף, כך יש לספר בנסי נחלי ארנון, שאף כאן נעשו נסים גדולים, ומה הם הנסים? **ואשד הנחלים.** תרגום של שפך – 'אשד', שפך הנחלים, שנשפך שם דם אמוריים שהיו נחבאים שם; לפי שהיו ההרים גבוהים והנחל עמק וקצר וההרים סמוכים זה לזה, אדם עומד על ההר מזה ומדבר עם חברו בהר מזה, והדרך עובר בתוך הנחל,

Even a teacher and disciple, even a father and son, when they sit to study Torah together become enemies to one another. But they do not move from there until they have become beloved to one another. Therefore it says, "*Vahev in sufa*," meaning "There is love in the end." (Kiddushin 30b)

ז עַם־רָב מִיִּשְׂרָאֵל: וַיָּבֹא הָעָם אֶל־מֹשֶׁה וַיֹּאמְרוּ חָטָאנוּ כִּי־דִבַּרְנוּ
בַיהוה וָבָךְ הִתְפַּלֵּל אֶל־יהוה וְיָסֵר מֵעָלֵינוּ אֶת־הַנָּחָשׁ וַיִּתְפַּלֵּל
ח מֹשֶׁה בְּעַד הָעָם: וַיֹּאמֶר יהוה אֶל־מֹשֶׁה עֲשֵׂה לְךָ שָׂרָף וְשִׂים אֹתוֹ
ט עַל־נֵס וְהָיָה כָּל־הַנָּשׁוּךְ וְרָאָה אֹתוֹ וָחָי: וַיַּעַשׂ מֹשֶׁה נְחַשׁ נְחֹשֶׁת
וַיְשִׂמֵהוּ עַל־הַנֵּס וְהָיָה אִם־נָשַׁךְ הַנָּחָשׁ אֶת־אִישׁ וְהִבִּיט אֶל־נְחַשׁ
י יא הַנְּחֹשֶׁת וָחָי: וַיִּסְעוּ בְּנֵי יִשְׂרָאֵל וַיַּחֲנוּ בְּאֹבֹת: וַיִּסְעוּ מֵאֹבֹת וַיַּחֲנוּ ששי
יב בְּעִיֵּי הָעֲבָרִים בַּמִּדְבָּר אֲשֶׁר עַל־פְּנֵי מוֹאָב מִמִּזְרַח הַשָּׁמֶשׁ: מִשָּׁם
יג נָסָעוּ וַיַּחֲנוּ בְּנַחַל זָרֶד: מִשָּׁם נָסָעוּ וַיַּחֲנוּ מֵעֵבֶר אַרְנוֹן אֲשֶׁר בַּמִּדְבָּר
הַיֹּצֵא מִגְּבֻל הָאֱמֹרִי כִּי אַרְנוֹן גְּבוּל מוֹאָב בֵּין מוֹאָב וּבֵין הָאֱמֹרִי:
יד עַל־כֵּן יֵאָמַר בְּסֵפֶר מִלְחֲמֹת יהוה אֶת־וָהֵב בְּסוּפָה וְאֶת־הַנְּחָלִים
טו אַרְנוֹן: וְאֶשֶׁד הַנְּחָלִים אֲשֶׁר נָטָה לְשֶׁבֶת עָר וְנִשְׁעַן לִגְבוּל מוֹאָב:

אונקלוס

עַם סַגִּי מִיִּשְׂרָאֵל: ז וַאֲתָא עַמָּא לְוָת מֹשֶׁה וַאֲמַרוּ חַבְנָא, אֲרֵי אִתְרַעֲמְנָא קֳדָם יי וְעִמָּךְ נְצֵינָא, צַלִּי קֳדָם יי, וְיַעְדֵּי מִנַּנָא יָת חִוְיָא, וְצַלִּי מֹשֶׁה עַל עַמָּא: ח וַאֲמַר יי לְמֹשֶׁה, עֲבֵיד לָךְ קַלְיָא, וְשַׁוִּי יָתֵיהּ עַל אָת, וִיהֵי כָּל דְּיִתְנְכֵית, וְיֶחֱזֵי יָתֵיהּ וְיִתְקַיַּם: ט וַעֲבַד מֹשֶׁה חִוְיָא דִנְחָשָׁא, וְשַׁוְיֵהּ עַל אָת, וַהֲוֵי, כַּד נָכֵית חִוְיָא יָת גֻּבְרָא, וּמִסְתַּכַּל, בְּחִוְיָא דִּנְחָשָׁא וּמִתְקַיַּם: י וּנְטַלוּ בְּנֵי יִשְׂרָאֵל, וּשְׁרוֹ בְּאוֹבוֹת: יא וּנְטַלוּ מֵאוֹבוֹת, וּשְׁרוֹ בִּמְגָזַת עִבְרָאֵי, בְּמַדְבְּרָא דְּעַל אַפֵּי מוֹאָב, מִמַּדְנַח שִׁמְשָׁא: יב מִתַּמָּן נְטַלוּ, וּשְׁרוֹ בְּנַחְלָא דְּזָרֶד: יג מִתַּמָּן נְטַלוּ, וּשְׁרוֹ, מֵעִבְרָא דְּאַרְנוֹן דִּבְמַדְבְּרָא, דְּנָפֵיק מִתְּחוּם אֱמוֹרָאָה, אֲרֵי אַרְנוֹן תְּחוּם מוֹאָב, בֵּין מוֹאָב וּבֵין אֱמוֹרָאָה: יד עַל כֵּן יִתְאֲמַר, בְּסִפְרָא קְרָבִין עֲבַד יי עַל יַמָּא דְסוּף, וּגְבוּרָן עַל נַחֲלֵי אַרְנוֹן: טו וְשָׁפוֹךְ לְנַחְלַיָּא, דִּמְדַבְּרִין לְקֳבֵיל לְחָיַת, וּמִסְתְּמִיךְ לִתְחוּם מוֹאָב:

THE BOOK OF THE WARS OF THE LORD

The *parasha* tells three stories of hostile encounters with other nations. In the first, Edom meets Israel's peaceful overtures with aggression, and Israel retreats. In this, the second, Arad also aggressively denies Israel passage through their land, but Israel appeals to God for support, and they destroy or "dedicate" the kingdom to God. The third and fourth times the situation arises, Israel conquers the lands of Amor and Bashan and settles there.

It is clear that we are moving into a new phase in the history of Israel's relations with other powers. What is meant here by "the Book of the Wars of the Lord"? Ḥizkuni holds that it was a book that existed in ancient times and was lost. For Rashi it was a list of miracles performed by God for Israel. Ibn Ezra says it was a record of the Israelites' history begun in the time of Avraham. Some modern scholars suggest that it was a collection of epic poems telling of Israel's battles. The Torah is not the only ancient account of Israel's history; others were composed and later lost (see also I Kings 14:19 among other places).

The brief quotation from this work is cryptic, its meaning almost unintelligible. The Sages gave a midrashic interpretation that laid no claim to being the plain meaning of the verse but is nevertheless fascinating:

16 lie along the border of Moav." And from there to Be'er, the well where the LORD
17 said to Moshe, "Gather the people, and I will give them water." Then
18 the Israelites sang this song: "Spring up, well – sing to her – that the nobles of
the people carved out with their scepter and their staffs." They went from the
19 20 desert to Matana, from Matana to Naḥaliel, from Naḥaliel to Bamot, and from
Bamot to the valley in the fields of Moav, to the top of Pisga, overlooking the
wasteland.
21 22 Then the Israelites sent messengers to Siḥon, king of the Amorites: "Let us pass SHEVI'I /REVI'I/
through your land. We will not turn aside into any field or vineyard, nor will we
drink water from any well. We will walk on the King's Highway until we have

רש״י

אָמְרוּ אֱמוֹרִיִּים: כְּשֶׁיִּכָּנְסוּ יִשְׂרָאֵל לְתוֹךְ הַנַּחַל לַעֲבֹר, נֵצֵא מִן הַמְּעָרוֹת שֶׁבֶּהָרִים שֶׁלְּמַעְלָה מֵהֶם וְנַהַרְגֵם בְּחִצִּים וְאַבְנֵי בַּלִּיסְטְרָאוֹת, וְהָיוּ אוֹתָן הַנְּקָעִים בָּהָר שֶׁל צַד מוֹאָב, וּבָהָר שֶׁל צַד אֱמוֹרִיִּים הָיוּ כְּנֶגֶד אוֹתָן נְקָעִים כְּמִין קְרָנוֹת וְשָׁדַיִם בּוֹלְטִין לַחוּץ, כֵּיוָן שֶׁבָּאוּ יִשְׂרָאֵל לַעֲבֹר, נִזְדַּעְזַע הָהָר שֶׁל אֶרֶץ יִשְׂרָאֵל כְּשִׁפְחָה הַיּוֹצֵאת לְהַקְבִּיל פְּנֵי גְבִרְתָּהּ, וְנִתְקָרֵב לְצַד הַר שֶׁל מוֹאָב, וְנִכְנְסוּ אוֹתָן הַשָּׁדַיִם לְתוֹךְ אוֹתָן נְקָעִים וַהֲרָגוּם, וְזֶהוּ: "אֲשֶׁר נָטָה לְשֶׁבֶת עָר", שֶׁהָהָר נָטָה מִמְּקוֹמוֹ וְנִתְקָרֵב לְצַד מוֹאָב וְנִדְבַּק בּוֹ, וְזֶהוּ: "וְנִשְׁעַן לִגְבוּל מוֹאָב":

טז **וּמִשָּׁם בְּאֵרָה.** מִשָּׁם בָּא הָאֶשֶׁד אֶל הַבְּאֵר. כֵּיצַד? אָמַר הַקָּדוֹשׁ בָּרוּךְ הוּא, מִי מוֹדִיעַ לְבָנַי הַנִּסִּים הַלָּלוּ? הַמָּשָׁל אוֹמֵר: נָתַתָּ פַּת לְתִינוֹק, הוֹדַע לְאִמּוֹ. לְאַחַר שֶׁעָבְרוּ חָזְרוּ הֶהָרִים לִמְקוֹמָם, וְהַבְּאֵר יָרְדָה לְתוֹךְ הַנַּחַל וְהֶעֶלְתָה מִשָּׁם דַּם הַהֲרוּגִים וּזְרוֹעוֹת וְאֵיבָרִים וּמוֹלִיכָתָן סְבִיב הַמַּחֲנֶה, וְיִשְׂרָאֵל רָאוּ וְאָמְרוּ שִׁירָה:

יז **עֲלִי בְאֵר.** מִתּוֹךְ הַנַּחַל וְהַעֲלִי מַה שֶּׁאַתְּ מַעֲלָה. וּמִנַּיִן שֶׁהַבְּאֵר הוֹדִיעָה לָהֶם? שֶׁנֶּאֱמַר: "וּמִשָּׁם בְּאֵרָה", וְכִי מִשָּׁם הָיְתָה? וַהֲלֹא מִתְּחִלַּת אַרְבָּעִים שָׁנָה הָיְתָה עִמָּהֶם! אֶלָּא שֶׁיָּרְדָה לְפַרְסֵם אֶת הַנִּסִּים. וְכֵן "אָז יָשִׁיר", הַשִּׁירָה הַזֹּאת נֶאֶמְרָה בְּסוֹף אַרְבָּעִים, וְהַבְּאֵר נִתְּנָה לָהֶם מִתְּחִלַּת אַרְבָּעִים, מָה רָאָה לִכְתֹּב כָּאן? אֶלָּא הָעִנְיָן הַזֶּה נִדְרָשׁ לְמַעְלָה הֵימֶנּוּ:

יח-כ **בְּאֵר חֲפָרוּהָ.** זֹאת הִיא הַבְּאֵר אֲשֶׁר "חֲפָרוּהָ שָׂרִים", מֹשֶׁה וְאַהֲרֹן: **בְּמִשְׁעֲנֹתָם.** בְּמַטֶּה: **וּמִמִּדְבָּר.** נִתְּנָה לָהֶם: **וּמִמַּתָּנָה נַחֲלִיאֵל.** כְּתַרְגּוּמוֹ: **וּמִבָּמוֹת הַגַּיְא אֲשֶׁר בִּשְׂדֵה מוֹאָב.** כִּי שָׁם מֵת מֹשֶׁה וְשָׁם בָּטְלָה הַבְּאֵר. דָּבָר אַחֵר, **כָּרוּהָ נְדִיבֵי הָעָם.** כָּל נָשִׂיא וְנָשִׂיא כְּשֶׁהָיוּ חוֹנִים נוֹטֵל מַקְלוֹ וּמוֹשֵׁךְ אֵצֶל דִּגְלוֹ וּמַחֲנֵהוּ, וּמֵי הַבְּאֵר נִמְשָׁכִין דֶּרֶךְ אוֹתוֹ סִימָן וּבָאִין לִפְנֵי חֲנִיַּת כָּל שֵׁבֶט וָשֵׁבֶט: **בִּמְחֹקֵק.** עַל פִּי מֹשֶׁה שֶׁנִּקְרָא מְחוֹקֵק, שֶׁנֶּאֱמַר: "כִּי שָׁם חֶלְקַת מְחֹקֵק סָפוּן" (דברים לג, כא). וְלָמָּה לֹא נִזְכַּר מֹשֶׁה בַּשִּׁירָה זוֹ? לְפִי שֶׁלָּקָה עַל יְדֵי הַבְּאֵר. וְכֵיוָן שֶׁלֹּא נִזְכַּר שְׁמוֹ שֶׁל מֹשֶׁה לֹא נִזְכַּר שְׁמוֹ שֶׁל הַקָּדוֹשׁ בָּרוּךְ הוּא. מָשָׁל לְמֶלֶךְ שֶׁהָיוּ מְזַמְּנִין אוֹתוֹ לִסְעוּדָה, אָמַר: אִם אוֹהֲבִי שָׁם אֲנִי שָׁם, וְאִם לָאו אֵינִי הוֹלֵךְ: **רֹאשׁ הַפִּסְגָּה.** כְּתַרְגּוּמוֹ: "רֵישׁ רָמָתָא": **פִּסְגָּה.** לְשׁוֹן גֹּבַהּ, וְכֵן "פַּסְּגוּ אַרְמְנוֹתֶיהָ" (תהלים מח, יד), הַגְבִּיהוּ אַרְמְנוֹתֶיהָ: **וְנִשְׁקָפָה.** אוֹתָהּ הַפִּסְגָּה, עַל פְּנֵי הַמָּקוֹם שֶׁשְּׁמוֹ "יְשִׁימֹן", וְהוּא לְשׁוֹן מִדְבָּר שֶׁהוּא שָׁמֵם. דָּבָר אַחֵר, "וְנִשְׁקָפָה" הַבְּאֵר "עַל פְּנֵי הַיְשִׁימֹן", שֶׁנִּגְנְזָה בְּיַמָּהּ שֶׁל טְבֶרְיָא, וְהָעוֹמֵד עַל הַיְשִׁימוֹן מַבִּיט וְרוֹאֶה כְּמִין כְּבָרָה בַּיָּם וְהִיא הַבְּאֵר. כָּךְ דָּרַשׁ רַבִּי תַּנְחוּמָא (כח):

כא **וַיִּשְׁלַח יִשְׂרָאֵל מַלְאָכִים.** וּבְמָקוֹם אַחֵר תּוֹלֶה הַשְּׁלִיחוּת בְּמֹשֶׁה, שֶׁנֶּאֱמַר: "וָאֶשְׁלַח מַלְאָכִים מִמִּדְבַּר קְדֵמוֹת" (דברים ב, כו), וְכֵן: "וַיִּשְׁלַח מֹשֶׁה מַלְאָכִים מִקָּדֵשׁ אֶל מֶלֶךְ אֱדוֹם" (לעיל כ, יד), וּבְיִפְתָּח הוּא אוֹמֵר: "וַיִּשְׁלַח יִשְׂרָאֵל מַלְאָכִים אֶל מֶלֶךְ אֱדוֹם" וְגוֹ' (שופטים יא, יז); הַכְּתוּבִים הַלָּלוּ צְרִיכִים זֶה לָזֶה, זֶה נוֹעֵל וְזֶה פּוֹתֵחַ, שֶׁמֹּשֶׁה הוּא יִשְׂרָאֵל וְיִשְׂרָאֵל הֵם מֹשֶׁה, לוֹמַר לְךָ שֶׁנְּשִׂיא הַדּוֹר הוּא כְּכָל הַדּוֹר, כִּי הַנָּשִׂיא הוּא הַכֹּל:

כב **אֶעְבְּרָה בְאַרְצֶךָ.** אַף עַל פִּי שֶׁלֹּא נִצְטַוּוּ לִפְתֹּחַ לָהֶם בְּשָׁלוֹם בִּקְּשׁוּ מֵהֶם שָׁלוֹם:

gravitational pull of the earth, it modulates into song. Poetry, music, love, wonder – the things that have no survival value but which speak to our deepest sense of being – all tell us that we are not mere animals, assemblages of selfish genes.

A song – even a spontaneous one – can capture the fleeting moment, so that even if the narrative is lost, the wonder of the event remains.

טז וּמִשָּׁם בְּאֵרָה הִוא הַבְּאֵר אֲשֶׁר אָמַר יהוה לְמֹשֶׁה אֱסֹף אֶת־הָעָם
יז וְאֶתְּנָה לָהֶם מָיִם׃ אָז יָשִׁיר יִשְׂרָאֵל אֶת־הַשִּׁירָה הַזֹּאת
יח עֲלִי בְאֵר עֱנוּ־לָהּ׃ בְּאֵר חֲפָרוּהָ שָׂרִים כָּרוּהָ נְדִיבֵי הָעָם בִּמְחֹקֵק
יט בְּמִשְׁעֲנֹתָם וּמִמִּדְבָּר מַתָּנָה׃ וּמִמַּתָּנָה נַחֲלִיאֵל וּמִנַּחֲלִיאֵל בָּמוֹת׃
כ וּמִבָּמוֹת הַגַּיְא אֲשֶׁר בִּשְׂדֵה מוֹאָב רֹאשׁ הַפִּסְגָּה וְנִשְׁקָפָה עַל־פְּנֵי
הַיְשִׁימֹן׃
כא כב וַיִּשְׁלַח יִשְׂרָאֵל מַלְאָכִים אֶל־סִיחֹן מֶלֶךְ־הָאֱמֹרִי לֵאמֹר׃ אֶעְבְּרָה שביעי /רביעי/
בְאַרְצֶךָ לֹא נִטֶּה בְּשָׂדֶה וּבְכֶרֶם לֹא נִשְׁתֶּה מֵי בְאֵר בְּדֶרֶךְ הַמֶּלֶךְ

אונקלוס

טז וּמִתַּמָּן אִתְיְהֵיבַת לְהוֹן בֵּירָא, הִיא בֵּירָא, דַּאֲמַר יי לְמֹשֶׁה, כְּנוֹשׁ יָת עַמָּא, וְאֶתֵּין לְהוֹן מַיָּא: יז בְּכֵן שַׁבַּח יִשְׂרָאֵל, יָת תֻּשְׁבַּחְתָּא הָדָא, סַקִּי בֵירָא שַׁבַּחוּ לַהּ: יח בֵּירָא דְּחַפְרוּהָא רַבְרְבַיָּא, כְּרוּהָא רֵישֵׁי עַמָּא, סָפְרַיָּא בְּחֻטְרֵיהוֹן, וּמִמַּדְבְּרָא אִתְיְהֵיבַת לְהוֹן: יט וּמִדְּאִתְיְהֵיבַת לְהוֹן נַחֲתָא עִמְּהוֹן לְנַחֲלַיָּא, וּמִנַּחֲלַיָּא סָלְקָא עִמְּהוֹן לְרָמָתָא: כ וּמֵרָמָתָא, לְחִלַּיָּא דִּבְחַקְלֵי מוֹאָב, רֵישׁ רָמְתָא, וּמִסְתַּכְיָא עַל אַפֵּי בֵּית יְשִׁימוֹן: כא וּשְׁלַח יִשְׂרָאֵל אִזְגַּדִּין, לְוָת סִיחוֹן מַלְכָּא אֱמוֹרָאָה לְמֵימַר: כב אֶעְבַּר בְּאַרְעָךְ, לָא נִסְטֵי בַּחֲקַל וּבִכְרַם, לָא נִשְׁתֵּי מֵי גוֹב, בְּאוֹרַח מַלְכָּא

The Rabbis read *vahev* as a derivative of the root *a-h-b*, meaning "to love," and *sufa* as related to the word *sof*, "an end." "*Vahev in sufa*" then means: there is love at the end. It is intriguing that the Sages interpret the phrase "the Wars of the Lord" as a reference to the debates within the house of study, the dialogue and disputation about Jewish law and the meaning of sacred texts. By the time this interpretation was offered, Jews no longer fought wars on the battlefield. The wars they were familiar with were intellectual, spiritual; they took place in the mind, their weapons were reason and tradition, their arena was the study hall, and their aim was to establish the meaning of God's word.

Yet there is more to the statement than this. There is an awareness of human conflict. The Sages do not speak of the house of study as an environment of peace and harmony. In Parashat Koraḥ, we saw the name – argument for the sake of Heaven – that the Sages gave this conflict, thus attaching to it a spiritual dignity of its own. They went so far as to portray God as saying about the protagonists and their divergent views, "These and those are the words of the living God" (Eiruvin 13b; Gittin 6b). God *lives* in the cut and thrust of the house of study. He does not deliver the verdict in the debate; He empowers His sages to do that.

When two sides fight, not with weapons but with ideas, they recognize that their very disagreement presupposes an agreement – about the value of the argument itself. Two sages who dispute the interpretation of a text nonetheless agree on fundamentals: that the text is holy and binding, and we, who interpret it, revere both God and His word. Thus, in the "wars of the Lord," they attested, "there is love in the end."

21:17 אָז יָשִׁיר יִשְׂרָאֵל אֶת־הַשִּׁירָה הַזֹּאת *Then the Israelites sang this song* – The song Israel sings at the well is one of ten songs the Rabbis enumerated that were sung at key moments in the life of the nation. There is something profoundly spiritual about music. When language aspires to the transcendent, and the soul longs to break free of the

23 passed through your territory." But Siḥon would not allow the Israelites to pass
through his territory. He gathered all his people and went out to confront the
Israelites in the wilderness. When he arrived at Yahatz, he launched an attack
24 on the Israelites. The Israelites struck him down with their swords and took
possession of his land from the Arnon to the Yabok, as far as the Amonites, for
25 the border of the Amonites was strong. The Israelites took all these cities, and
they settled in all the cities of the Amorites, in Ḥeshbon and all its surrounding
26 settlements. Ḥeshbon was the city of Siḥon, king of the Amorites, who had
fought against the former king of Moav and had taken all his land from him as
27 far as the Arnon. That is why the ballad singers sing: "Come to Ḥeshbon, build

רש״י

כג **וְלֹא נָתַן סִיחֹן וְגוֹ׳.** לְפִי שֶׁכָּל מַלְכֵי כְנַעַן הָיוּ מַעֲלִין לוֹ מַס, שֶׁהָיָה שׁוֹמְרָם שֶׁלֹּא יַעַבְרוּ עֲלֵיהֶם גְּיָסוֹת, כֵּיוָן שֶׁאָמְרוּ לוֹ יִשְׂרָאֵל: ״אֶעְבְּרָה בְאַרְצֶךָ״, אָמַר לָהֶם: כָּל עַצְמִי אֵינִי יוֹשֵׁב כָּאן אֶלָּא לְשָׁמְרָם מִפְּנֵיכֶם, וְאַתֶּם אוֹמְרִים כָּךְ?!: **וַיֵּצֵא לִקְרַאת יִשְׂרָאֵל.** אִלּוּ הָיְתָה חֶשְׁבּוֹן מְלֵאָה יַתּוּשִׁין אֵין כָּל בְּרִיָּה יְכוֹלָה לְכָבְשָׁהּ, וְאִם הָיָה סִיחוֹן בִּכְפָר חַלָּשׁ אֵין כָּל אָדָם יָכוֹל לְכָבְשׁוֹ, וְכָל שֶׁכֵּן שֶׁהָיָה בְּחֶשְׁבּוֹן. אָמַר הַקָּדוֹשׁ בָּרוּךְ הוּא: מָה אֲנִי מַטְרִיחַ עַל בָּנַי כָּל זֹאת לָצוּר עַל כָּל עִיר וָעִיר, נָתַן בְּלֵב כָּל אַנְשֵׁי הַמִּלְחָמָה לָצֵאת מִן הָעֲיָרוֹת, וְנִתְקַבְּצוּ כֻלָּם לְמָקוֹם אֶחָד, וְשָׁם נָפְלוּ, וּמִשָּׁם הָלְכוּ יִשְׂרָאֵל אֶל הֶעָרִים וְאֵין עוֹמֵד לְנֶגְדָּם, כִּי אֵין שָׁם אִישׁ אֶלָּא נָשִׁים וָטָף:

כד **כִּי עַז.** וּמַהוּ חָזְקוֹ? הַתְרָאָתוֹ שֶׁל הַקָּדוֹשׁ בָּרוּךְ הוּא שֶׁאָמַר לָהֶם: ״אַל תְּצֻרֵם״ וְגוֹ׳ (דברים ב, יט):

כה **בְּנֹתֶיהָ.** כְּפָרִים הַסְּמוּכִים לָהּ:

כו **וְהוּא נִלְחַם וְגוֹ׳.** לָמָּה הֻצְרַךְ לִכָּתֵב? לְפִי שֶׁנֶּאֱמַר: ״אַל תָּצַר אֶת מוֹאָב״ (דברים ב, ט), וְחֶשְׁבּוֹן מִשֶּׁל מוֹאָב הָיְתָה, כָּתַב לָנוּ שֶׁסִּיחוֹן לְקָחָהּ מֵהֶם וְעַל יָדוֹ טָהֲרָה לְיִשְׂרָאֵל: **מִיָּדוֹ.** מֵרְשׁוּתוֹ:

כז **עַל כֵּן.** עַל אוֹתָהּ מִלְחָמָה שֶׁנִּלְחַם סִיחוֹן בְּמוֹאָב:

The Sages in the Mishna text cite a biblical verse in support of their view. R. Eliezer does not. Clearly, though, he must have had another biblical verse in mind. The Talmud (Shabbat 63a) fills in the gap:

> Abaye asked R. Dimi: "What is R. Eliezer's reason for maintaining that [weapons] are ornaments?"
>
> [He replied]: "Because it is written, 'Fasten your sword on your thigh, mighty one, in your majesty and splendor' (Ps. 45:4)."
>
> R. Kahana raised an objection to Mar, son of R. Huna: "But this refers to the words of the Torah!"
>
> He replied: "A verse cannot depart from its plain meaning."
>
> R. Kahana said: "When I was eighteen I knew the whole six orders [of the Mishna] yet I did not know until today that a verse cannot depart from its plain meaning."

Some two centuries after the original Mishna teaching, R. Kahana can *no longer understand* that when a psalm refers to a sword it actually means a sword. For him it is self-evident that it means "words," teachings, texts. With what else does the Jewish people defend itself, if not its sacred merits achieved by devotion to religious learning? To understand R. Eliezer's view a mere two or three centuries earlier, R. Kahana has to be exposed to a principle he had never considered before, namely, that one cannot ignore the literal meaning of a biblical text. Whatever else a verse means, it also means what it says. Reading Ḥukat today, we hear two voices intertwined: that of biblical Israel rising to independence and singing its own song. And that of the Sages and their heirs, searching the text for its fundamental truths, renewed in every generation, as of old.

כג נֵלֵךְ עַד אֲשֶׁר־נַעֲבֹר גְּבֻלֶךָ׃ וְלֹא־נָתַן סִיחֹן אֶת־יִשְׂרָאֵל עֲבֹר בִּגְבֻלוֹ
וַיֶּאֱסֹף סִיחֹן אֶת־כָּל־עַמּוֹ וַיֵּצֵא לִקְרַאת יִשְׂרָאֵל הַמִּדְבָּרָה וַיָּבֹא
כד יָהְצָה וַיִּלָּחֶם בְּיִשְׂרָאֵל׃ וַיַּכֵּהוּ יִשְׂרָאֵל לְפִי־חָרֶב וַיִּירַשׁ אֶת־אַרְצוֹ
כה מֵאַרְנֹן עַד־יַבֹּק עַד־בְּנֵי עַמּוֹן כִּי עַז גְּבוּל בְּנֵי עַמּוֹן׃ וַיִּקַּח יִשְׂרָאֵל
אֵת כָּל־הֶעָרִים הָאֵלֶּה וַיֵּשֶׁב יִשְׂרָאֵל בְּכָל־עָרֵי הָאֱמֹרִי בְּחֶשְׁבּוֹן
כו וּבְכָל־בְּנֹתֶיהָ׃ כִּי חֶשְׁבּוֹן עִיר סִיחֹן מֶלֶךְ הָאֱמֹרִי הִוא וְהוּא נִלְחַם
כז בְּמֶלֶךְ מוֹאָב הָרִאשׁוֹן וַיִּקַּח אֶת־כָּל־אַרְצוֹ מִיָּדוֹ עַד־אַרְנֹן׃ עַל־כֵּן

אונקלוס

נֵיזֵיל, עַד דְּנִעְבַּר תְּחוּמָךְ׃ כג וְלָא שְׁבַק סִיחוֹן יָת יִשְׂרָאֵל לְמִעְבַּר בִּתְחוּמֵיהּ, וּכְנַשׁ סִיחוֹן יָת כָּל עַמֵּיהּ, וּנְפַק, לְקַדָּמוּת יִשְׂרָאֵל לְמַדְבְּרָא, וַאֲתָא לְיָהָץ, וַאֲגִיחַ קְרָבָא בְּיִשְׂרָאֵל׃ כד וּמְחָהִי יִשְׂרָאֵל לְפִתְגָם דְּחָרֶב, וִירִיתוּ יָת אַרְעֵיהּ מֵאַרְנוֹנָא, עַד יֻבְקָא עַד בְּנֵי עַמּוֹן, אֲרֵי תַקִּיף, תְּחוּמָא דִּבְנֵי עַמּוֹן׃ כה וּכְבַשׁ יִשְׂרָאֵל, יָת כָּל קִרְוַיָּא הָאִלֵּין, וִיתֵיב יִשְׂרָאֵל בְּכָל קִרְוֵי אֱמוֹרָאָה, בְּחֶשְׁבּוֹן וּבְכָל כַּפְרָנָהָא׃ כו אֲרֵי חֶשְׁבּוֹן, קַרְתָּא, דְּסִיחוֹן, מַלְכָּא אֱמוֹרָאָה הִיא, וְהוּא אֲגִיחַ קְרָבָא, בְּמַלְכָּא דְּמוֹאָב קַדְמָאָה, וּנְסֵיב יָת כָּל אַרְעֵיהּ, מִנֵּיהּ עַד אַרְנוֹן׃ כז עַל כֵּן, יֵימְרוּן מַתְלַיָּא עוּלוּ לְחֶשְׁבּוֹן, תִּתְבְּנֵי וְתִשְׁתַּכְלַל קַרְתָּא דְּסִיחוֹן׃ כח אֲרֵי קְדוֹם תַּקִּיף כְּאִישָׁא נְפַק מֵחֶשְׁבּוֹן,

THE FIRST CONQUEST OF LAND

The third time the Israelites are attacked, they fight back fearlessly and make their first territorial conquest. To understand the transformation this demonstrates in the people, it is illustrative to see the further cultural metamorphosis that took place in Judaism between the biblical era and the age of the Rabbis. We see it, for instance, in an extraordinary conversation, reported in the Talmud, between the Jewish Sages in the late first century CE. The subject under discussion is a detail in the laws of the Sabbath. In Jewish law one may not carry objects on the seventh day, whether from a private domain into the street or in the street itself. Wearing clothes, however, is clearly not carrying. Here, the Sages debate a borderline case: wearing a sword. Is this *wearing*, in which case it is permitted, or is it *carrying*, in which case it is forbidden?

What is at stake in fact goes to the heart of the value system of Jews between the two great rebellions against Rome in the first and second centuries. Are weapons an ornament, as some cultures regarded them, and thus an item of clothing, or are they negative testimony to the existence of armed conflict, and thus a burden? At stake is how the Sages saw the war against the Romans, and something deeper: how they viewed the very culture of military valor. The Mishna (Shabbat 6:4) records the following disagreement:

> A man must not go out with a sword, bow, shield, lance, or spear, and if he does go out, he incurs a sin offering. R. Eliezer, however, said: They are ornaments for him. But the Sages maintain that they are merely shameful, for it is said, "They shall beat their swords into plowshares, their spears into pruning hooks. Nation shall not raise sword against nation" (Is. 2:4).

For R. Eliezer, weapons are "ornaments." There is honor in fighting for your freedom and resisting an imperial power. We can hear this sentiment in the victory songs recorded in our *parasha*. The Sages – the majority – disagree. Their proof text is the famous verse from Isaiah in which the prophet envisions a world without war. Military confrontation may sometimes be necessary in self-defense but it is not, in Judaism, a positive value. In the Messianic age there will be no more weapons; therefore they are not a badge of honor but a burden and may not be worn on the Sabbath.

28 and refound the town of Siḥon. For fire went forth from Ḥeshbon, a flame from
the town of Siḥon. It consumed Ar of Moav the masters of Arnon's high shrines.
29 Woe for you, Moav! You are destroyed, men of Kemosh! He made his sons
30 fugitives, his daughters fugitives, to Siḥon the Amorite king. Yet we – we threw
them wholly down, from Ḥeshbon to Divon, laid waste as far as Nofaḥ, as far as
31 32 Meideva." So Israel settled in the land of the Amorites. And Moshe sent spies
to Yazer. And Israel captured its surrounding settlements and dispossessed
33 the Amorites who were there. Then they turned and journeyed along the road
toward Bashan. Og, king of Bashan, with all his people came out to Edrei to
34 engage them in battle. But the LORD said to Moshe: "Do not be afraid of him, MAFTIR
for I have given him into your hand, with all his people and his land. Do to him
35 what you did to Siḥon, king of the Amorites, who lived in Ḥeshbon." So they
struck him down, together with his sons and all his people until there were no
22 1 survivors, and they took possession of his land. The Israelites moved on and
encamped in the plains of Moav across the Jordan from Yeriḥo.

The haftara for Parashat Ḥukat is on page 1594.
When Ḥukat and Balak are read together, read the haftara on page 1598.
On Rosh Ḥodesh Tamuz read the haftara on page 1634.

רש״י

יֹאמְרוּ הַמֹּשְׁלִים. בִּלְעָם, שֶׁנֶּאֱמַר בּוֹ: ״וַיִּשָּׂא מְשָׁלוֹ״ (להלן כג, ז): **הַמֹּשְׁלִים.** בִּלְעָם וּבְעוֹר, וְהֵם אָמְרוּ: ״בֹּאוּ חֶשְׁבּוֹן״, שֶׁלֹּא הָיָה סִיחוֹן יָכוֹל לְכָבְשָׁהּ וְהָלַךְ וְשָׂכַר אֶת בִּלְעָם לְקַלְּלוֹ, וְזֶהוּ שֶׁאָמַר לוֹ בָּלָק: ״כִּי יָדַעְתִּי אֵת אֲשֶׁר תְּבָרֵךְ מְבֹרָךְ״ וְגוֹ׳ (להלן כב, ו): **תִּבָּנֶה וְתִכּוֹנֵן.** חֶשְׁבּוֹן בְּשֵׁם סִיחוֹן לִהְיוֹת עִירוֹ:

כח **כִּי אֵשׁ יָצְאָה מֵחֶשְׁבּוֹן.** מִשֶּׁכְּבָשָׁהּ סִיחוֹן: **אָכְלָה עָר מוֹאָב.** שֵׁם אוֹתָהּ הַמְּדִינָה קָרוּי ׳עָר׳ בְּלָשׁוֹן עִבְרִי וּ׳לְחָיַת׳ בְּלָשׁוֹן אֲרַמִּי: **עָר מוֹאָב.** עָר שֶׁל מוֹאָב:

כט **אוֹי לְךָ מוֹאָב.** שֶׁקִּלְּלוּ אֶת מוֹאָב שֶׁיִּמָּסְרוּ בְּיָדוֹ: **כְּמוֹשׁ.** שֵׁם אֱלֹהֵי מוֹאָב (שופטים יא, כד): **נָתַן.** הַנּוֹתֵן אֶת בָּנָיו שֶׁל מוֹאָב: **פְּלֵיטִם.** נָסִים וּפְלֵטִים מֵחֶרֶב, וְאֶת בְּנֹתָיו בַּשְּׁבִית וְגוֹ׳:

ל **וַנִּירָם אָבַד.** מַלְכוּת שֶׁלָּהֶם: **אָבַד חֶשְׁבּוֹן עַד דִּיבֹן.** מַלְכוּת וְעֹל שֶׁהָיָה לְמוֹאָב בְּחֶשְׁבּוֹן אָבַד מִשָּׁם, וְכֵן ״עַד דִּיבֹן״, תַּרְגּוּם שֶׁל ׳סָר׳ – ׳עַד׳, כְּלוֹמַר סָר נִיר מִדִּיבֹן. ׳נִיר׳ לְשׁוֹן מַלְכוּת וְעֹל מֶמְשֶׁלֶת אִישׁ, כְּמוֹ: ״לְמַעַן הֱיוֹת נִיר לְדָוִיד עַבְדִּי״ (מלכים א׳ יא, לו): **וַנַּשִּׁים.** שִׁי״ן דְּגוּשָׁה, לְשׁוֹן שְׁמָמָה. כָּךְ יֹאמְרוּ הַמּוֹשְׁלִים: ״וַנַּשִּׁים״ אוֹתָם ״עַד נֹפַח״, הַשְּׁמָמוֹת עַד נֹפַח:

לב **וַיִּשְׁלַח מֹשֶׁה לְרַגֵּל אֶת יַעְזֵר וְגוֹ׳.** הַמְרַגְּלִים לְכָדוּהָ, אָמְרוּ: לֹא נַעֲשֶׂה כָּרִאשׁוֹנִים, בְּטוּחִים אָנוּ בְּכֹחַ תְּפִלָּתוֹ שֶׁל מֹשֶׁה לְהִלָּחֵם:

לד **אַל תִּירָא אֹתוֹ.** שֶׁהָיָה מֹשֶׁה יָרֵא לְהִלָּחֵם, שֶׁמָּא תַּעֲמֹד לוֹ זְכוּתוֹ שֶׁל אַבְרָהָם, שֶׁנֶּאֱמַר: ״וַיָּבֹא הַפָּלִיט״ (בראשית יד, יג), הוּא עוֹג שֶׁפָּלַט מִן הָרְפָאִים שֶׁהִכּוּ כְּדָרְלָעֹמֶר וַחֲבֵרָיו בְּעַשְׁתְּרוֹת קַרְנַיִם, שֶׁנֶּאֱמַר: ״רַק עוֹג מֶלֶךְ הַבָּשָׁן נִשְׁאַר מִיֶּתֶר הָרְפָאִים״ (דברים ג, יא):

לה **וַיַּכּוּ אֹתוֹ.** מֹשֶׁה הֲרָגוֹ, כִּדְאִיתָא בִּבְרָכוֹת בְּ׳הָרוֹאֶה׳ (דף נד ע״ב): עֲקַר טוּרָא בַּר תְּלָתָא פַּרְסֵי וְכוּ׳:

כח יֹאמְרוּ הַמֹּשְׁלִים בֹּאוּ חֶשְׁבּוֹן תִּבָּנֶה וְתִכּוֹנֵן עִיר סִיחוֹן׃ כִּי־אֵשׁ יָצְאָה
מֵחֶשְׁבּוֹן לֶהָבָה מִקִּרְיַת סִיחֹן אָכְלָה עָר מוֹאָב בַּעֲלֵי בָּמוֹת אַרְנֹן׃
כט אוֹי־לְךָ מוֹאָב אָבַדְתָּ עַם־כְּמוֹשׁ נָתַן בָּנָיו פְּלֵיטִם וּבְנֹתָיו בַּשְּׁבִית
ל לְמֶלֶךְ אֱמֹרִי סִיחוֹן׃ וַנִּירָם אָבַד חֶשְׁבּוֹן עַד־דִּיבֹן וַנַּשִּׁים עַד־נֹפַח
לא לב אֲשֶׁר עַד־מֵידְבָא׃ וַיֵּשֶׁב יִשְׂרָאֵל בְּאֶרֶץ הָאֱמֹרִי׃ וַיִּשְׁלַח מֹשֶׁה לְרַגֵּל
לג אֶת־יַעְזֵר וַיִּלְכְּדוּ בְּנֹתֶיהָ ויירש אֶת־הָאֱמֹרִי אֲשֶׁר־שָׁם׃ וַיִּפְנוּ וַיַּעֲלוּ וַיּוֹרֶשׁ
דֶּרֶךְ הַבָּשָׁן וַיֵּצֵא עוֹג מֶלֶךְ־הַבָּשָׁן לִקְרָאתָם הוּא וְכָל־עַמּוֹ לַמִּלְחָמָה
לד אֶדְרֶעִי׃ וַיֹּאמֶר יהוה אֶל־מֹשֶׁה אַל־תִּירָא אֹתוֹ כִּי בְיָדְךָ נָתַתִּי אֹתוֹ מפטיר
וְאֶת־כָּל־עַמּוֹ וְאֶת־אַרְצוֹ וְעָשִׂיתָ לּוֹ כַּאֲשֶׁר עָשִׂיתָ לְסִיחֹן מֶלֶךְ הָאֱמֹרִי
לה אֲשֶׁר יוֹשֵׁב בְּחֶשְׁבּוֹן׃ וַיַּכּוּ אֹתוֹ וְאֶת־בָּנָיו וְאֶת־כָּל־עַמּוֹ עַד־בִּלְתִּי
כב א הִשְׁאִיר־לוֹ שָׂרִיד וַיִּירְשׁוּ אֶת־אַרְצוֹ׃ וַיִּסְעוּ בְּנֵי יִשְׂרָאֵל וַיַּחֲנוּ בְּעַרְבוֹת
מוֹאָב מֵעֵבֶר לְיַרְדֵּן יְרֵחוֹ׃

The הפטרה *for* פרשת חקת *is on page 1595.*
When חקת *and* בלק *are read together, read the* הפטרה *on page 1599.*
On ראש חודש תמוז *read the* הפטרה *on page 1635.*

אונקלוס

עָבְדֵי קְרָבָא כְּשַׁלְהָבִיתָא מִקַּרְתָּא דְּסִיחוֹן, קְטִילוּ עַמָּא דְּשָׁרוֹ
בִּלְחָיַת מוֹאָב, כֻּמְרַיָּא דְּפָלְחִין בֵּית דַּחְלַת רָמָתָא דְּאַרְנוֹן׃ כט וַי
לְכוֹן מוֹאֲבָאֵי, אֲבַדְתּוּן עַמָּא דְּפָלְחִין לִכְמוֹשׁ, מְסַר בְּנוֹהִי צִירִין
וּבְנָתֵיהּ בְּשִׁבְיָא, לְמַלְכָּא אֱמוֹרָאָה סִיחוֹן׃ ל פְּסַקַת מַלְכוּ מֵחֶשְׁבּוֹן
עֲדָא שָׁלְטָן מִדִּיבוֹן, וְצַדִּיאוּ עַד נוֹפַח, דִּסְמִיךְ עַד מֵידְבָא׃ לא
וִיתֵיב יִשְׂרָאֵל, בַּאֲרַע אֱמוֹרָאָה׃ לב וּשְׁלַח מֹשֶׁה לְאַלָּלָא יָת יַעְזֵר,
וּכְבַשׁוּ כַּפְרָנַהָא, וְתָרֵיךְ יָת אֱמוֹרָאָה דְּתַמָּן׃ לג וְאִתְפְּנִיאוּ וּסְלִיקוּ,
לְאוֹרַח מַתְנַן, וּנְפַק עוֹג מַלְכָּא דְּמַתְנַן לְקַדָּמוּתְהוֹן, הוּא וְכָל עַמֵּיהּ,
לְאַגָּחָא קְרָבָא לְאֶדְרֶעִי׃ לד וַאֲמַר יי לְמֹשֶׁה לָא תִדְחַל מִנֵּיהּ, אֲרֵי
בִידָךְ, מְסָרִית יָתֵיהּ, וְיָת כָּל עַמֵּיהּ וְיָת אַרְעֵיהּ, וְתַעְבֵּיד לֵיהּ, כְּמָא
דַּעֲבַדְתָּא, לְסִיחוֹן מַלְכָּא אֱמוֹרָאָה, דְּיָתֵיב בְּחֶשְׁבּוֹן׃ לה וּמְחוֹ יָתֵיהּ
וְיָת בְּנוֹהִי וְיָת כָּל עַמֵּיהּ, עַד דְּלָא אִשְׁתְּאַר לֵיהּ מְשֵׁיזֵיב, וִירִיתוּ יָת
אַרְעֵיהּ׃ כב א וּנְטַלוּ בְּנֵי יִשְׂרָאֵל, וּשְׁרוֹ בְּמֵישְׁרַיָּא דְּמוֹאָב, מֵעִבְרָא
לְיַרְדְּנָא דִּירִיחוֹ׃

Parashat Balak

22 2 And Balak son of Tzipor had seen all that the Israelites had done to the
3 Amorites. The Moabites were in deep dread of the people because they were
4 so numerous. Fearful of the Israelites, the Moabites said to the elders of
Midyan, "This horde will now lick up everything around us, as an ox licks up
5 grass in the field." Balak son of Tzipor was king of Moav at that time. He sent
messengers to summon Bilam son of Beor who was at Petor near the River in

רש״י

כב ב **וַיַּרְא בָּלָק בֶּן צִפּוֹר אֵת כָּל אֲשֶׁר עָשָׂה יִשְׂרָאֵל לָאֱמֹרִי.** אָמַר: אֵלּוּ שְׁנֵי מְלָכִים שֶׁהָיִינוּ בְּטוּחִים עֲלֵיהֶם לֹא עָמְדוּ בִּפְנֵיהֶם, אָנוּ עַל אַחַת כַּמָּה וְכַמָּה, לְפִיכָךְ: "וַיָּגָר מוֹאָב":

ג **וַיָּגָר.** לְשׁוֹן מוֹרָא, כְּמוֹ: "גּוּרוּ לָכֶם" (איוב יט, כט): **וַיָּקָץ מוֹאָב.** קָצוּ בְּחַיֵּיהֶם:

ד **אֶל זִקְנֵי מִדְיָן.** וַהֲלֹא מֵעוֹלָם הָיוּ שׂוֹנְאִים זֶה אֶת זֶה, שֶׁנֶּאֱמַר: "הַמַּכֶּה אֶת מִדְיָן בִּשְׂדֵה מוֹאָב" (בראשית לו, לה), שֶׁבָּאוּ מִדְיָן עַל מוֹאָב לַמִּלְחָמָה! אֶלָּא מִיִּרְאָתָן שֶׁל יִשְׂרָאֵל עָשׂוּ שָׁלוֹם בֵּינֵיהֶם. וּמָה רָאָה מוֹאָב לִטֹּל עֵצָה מִמִּדְיָן? כֵּיוָן שֶׁרָאוּ אֶת יִשְׂרָאֵל נוֹצְחִים שֶׁלֹּא כְּמִנְהַג הָעוֹלָם, אָמְרוּ: מַנְהִיגָם שֶׁל אֵלּוּ בְּמִדְיָן נִתְגַּדֵּל, נִשְׁאַל מֵהֶם מַה מִּדָּתוֹ. אָמְרוּ לָהֶם: אֵין כֹּחוֹ אֶלָּא בְּפִיו. אָמְרוּ: אַף אָנוּ נָבוֹא עֲלֵיהֶם בְּאָדָם שֶׁכֹּחוֹ בְּפִיו: **כִּלְחֹךְ הַשּׁוֹר.** כָּל מַה שֶּׁהַשּׁוֹר מְלַחֵךְ אֵין בּוֹ בְּרָכָה: **בָּעֵת הַהִוא.** לֹא הָיָה רָאוּי לְמַלְכוּת, מִנְּסִיכֵי מִדְיָן הָיָה, וְכֵיוָן שֶׁמֵּת סִיחוֹן מִנּוּהוּ עֲלֵיהֶם לְצֹרֶךְ שָׁעָה:

ה **פְּתוֹרָה.** כְּשֻׁלְחָנִי הַזֶּה שֶׁהַכֹּל מְרִיצִין לוֹ מָעוֹת, כָּךְ כָּל הַמְּלָכִים מְרִיצִין לוֹ אִגְּרוֹתֵיהֶם. וּלְפִי פְשׁוּטוֹ שֶׁל מִקְרָא כָּךְ שֵׁם הַמָּקוֹם: **אֶרֶץ**

What is his flaw? There are many speculations, but one suggestion given in the Talmud infers the answer from his name. What is the meaning of Bilam? Answers the Talmud (Sanhedrin 105a): it means "a man without a people" (*belo am*). This is a fine insight. Bilam is a prophet for hire, a man without loyalties. He has supernatural powers. He can bless someone and that person will succeed. He can curse and that person will be blighted by misfortune. But there is no hint in any of the reports, biblical or otherwise, that Bilam is a prophet in the moral sense: that he is concerned with justice, desert, the rights and wrongs of those whose lives he affects. Bilam has skills, and he uses them with devastating effect. But he has no commitments, no loyalties, no rootedness in humanity. He is the man *belo am*, without a people. Moshe is the opposite. God Himself says of him, "He is trusted [literally, 'loyal'] in all My House" (Num. 12:7). The Hebrew word *emuna* is usually translated as "faith," and that is what it came to mean in the Middle Ages. But in Biblical Hebrew it is better translated as faithfulness, reliability, loyalty. It means not walking away from the other party when times are tough. It is a key covenantal virtue. There are people with great gifts, intellectual and sometimes even spiritual, who nonetheless fail to achieve what they might have done. They lack the basic moral qualities of integrity, honesty, humility, and above all, loyalty. What they do, they do brilliantly. But often they do the wrong things. Conscious of their unusual endowments, they give way to pride, arrogance and a belief that they can somehow get away with great crimes. Bilam is the classic example.

Prophecy is a form of leadership – but leadership without loyalty is not leadership. Skills alone cannot substitute for the moral qualities that make people follow those who demonstrate them. We follow those we trust, because they have acted so as to earn our trust. That was what made Moshe the great leader Bilam might have been but never was.

פרשת בלק

כב ב וַיַּרְא בָּלָק בֶּן־צִפּוֹר אֵת כָּל־אֲשֶׁר־עָשָׂה יִשְׂרָאֵל לָאֱמֹרִי׃ ג וַיָּגָר מוֹאָב יט
ד מִפְּנֵי הָעָם מְאֹד כִּי רַב־הוּא וַיָּקָץ מוֹאָב מִפְּנֵי בְּנֵי יִשְׂרָאֵל׃ וַיֹּאמֶר
מוֹאָב אֶל־זִקְנֵי מִדְיָן עַתָּה יְלַחֲכוּ הַקָּהָל אֶת־כָּל־סְבִיבֹתֵינוּ כִּלְחֹךְ
הַשּׁוֹר אֵת יֶרֶק הַשָּׂדֶה וּבָלָק בֶּן־צִפּוֹר מֶלֶךְ לְמוֹאָב בָּעֵת הַהִוא׃
ה וַיִּשְׁלַח מַלְאָכִים אֶל־בִּלְעָם בֶּן־בְּעוֹר פְּתוֹרָה אֲשֶׁר עַל־הַנָּהָר אֶרֶץ

אונקלוס

כב ב וַחֲזָא בָּלָק בַּר צִפּוֹר, יָת, כָּל דַּעֲבַד יִשְׂרָאֵל לֶאֱמוֹרָאָה: ג וּדְחֵיל מוֹאֲבָאָה, מִן קֳדָם עַמָּא, לַחֲדָא אֲרֵי סַגִּי הוּא, וְעָקַת לְמוֹאֲבָאֵי, מִן קֳדָם בְּנֵי יִשְׂרָאֵל: ד וַאֲמַר מוֹאָב לְסָבֵי מִדְיָן, כְּעַן, יְשֵׁיצוֹן קְהָלָא יָת כָּל סַחְרָנַנָא, כְּמָא דִּמְלַחֵיךְ תּוֹרָא, יָת יָרוֹקָא דְּחַקְלָא, וּבָלָק בַּר צִפּוֹר, מַלְכָּא לְמוֹאָב בְּעִדָּנָא הַהוּא: ה וּשְׁלַח אִזְגַּדִּין לְוָת בִּלְעָם בַּר בְּעוֹר, לִפְתוֹר, אֲרָם דְּעַל פְּרָת, אֲרַע

BALAK

The Israelites are approaching the end of their forty years in the wilderness. Already they have fought and won wars against Siḥon, king of the Amorites, and Og, king of Bashan. They have arrived at the plains of Moav – today, southern Jordan at the point where it touches the Dead Sea. Balak, king of Moav is concerned, and he shares his distress with the elders of Midyan. The strategy Balak adopts is to seek the help of the seer and diviner Bilam.

Three times at different places they prepare altars and sacrifices, but each time, Bilam utters blessings instead of curses. Balak leaves in anger and frustration. Having been spared Bilam's curses, however, the Israelites bring disaster on themselves through adultery and idolatry, seduced by the local women. Twenty-four thousand people die in a plague that strikes the camp until Pinḥas, in an act of zealotry, rises up against one of the wrongdoers.

The character of Bilam remains ambiguous, both in the Torah and subsequent Jewish tradition. Is he a diviner (reading omens and signs) or a sorcerer (practicing occult arts)? Is he a genuine prophet or a fraud? Does he assent to the divine blessings placed in his mouth, or does he wish to curse Israel? The causal link between the blessings of Bilam and the catastrophic story at the end of the *parasha* will be fully explained only in Parashat Matot.

BILAM THE PROPHET

We are introduced to Bilam as a religious virtuoso in his society, a sought-after shaman, magus, spellbinder, and miracle worker. On the phrase "there has never arisen a prophet in Israel like Moshe, whom the Lord knew face to face" (Deut. 34:10), the Sages went so far as to say: "In Israel there was no other prophet as great as Moshe, but among the nations there was. Who was he? Bilam" (Sifrei, Devarim 357). Yet the ultimate verdict on Bilam is negative. The picture that emerges from the Jewish sources is of a man with great gifts, a genuine prophet, a man whom the Sages compared with Moshe himself – yet at the same time a figure of flawed character that eventually led to his downfall and to his reputation as an evildoer – one of those mentioned by the Mishna as having been denied a share in the World to Come.

his native land: "A people has come out of Egypt, and now they cover the face
6 of the land – and they have settled down alongside me. Please, come now and
curse this people for me, for they are stronger than I. Perhaps then I will be able
to defeat them and drive them from the land, for I know that whomsoever you
7 bless is blessed and whomsoever you curse is cursed." So the elders of Moav
and Midyan went, carrying with them payment for divination. They came to
8 Bilam and repeated Balak's words to him. "Spend the night here," he said, "and
I will give you your reply that the LORD speaks to me." So the princes of Moav
9 stayed the night with Bilam. God came to Bilam and said, "Who are these men
10 with you?" And Bilam replied to God, "Balak son of Tzipor, king of Moav, has
11 sent me a message: 'A people has come out of Egypt and covers the face of the
land. Now come and curse them for me. Perhaps I will be able to fight against
12 them and drive them away.'" "Do not go with them," said God to Bilam. "Do
13 not curse this people, for they are blessed." Then Bilam arose in the morning SHENI /ḤAMISHI/
and said to Balak's princes, "Go back to your land, because the LORD has
14 refused to let me go with you." The princes of Moav rose and went to Balak and

רש״י

בְּנֵי עַמּוֹ. שֶׁל בָּלָק. מִשָּׁם הָיָה, וְזֶה הָיָה מִתְנַבֵּא וְאוֹמֵר לוֹ: עָתִיד אַתָּה לִמְלֹךְ. וְאִם תֹּאמַר: מִפְּנֵי מָה הִשְׁרָה הַקָּדוֹשׁ בָּרוּךְ הוּא שְׁכִינָתוֹ עַל גּוֹי רָשָׁע? כְּדֵי שֶׁלֹּא יִהְיֶה פִּתְחוֹן פֶּה לָאֻמּוֹת לוֹמַר: אִלּוּ הָיוּ לָנוּ נְבִיאִים חָזַרְנוּ לְמוּטָב. הֶעֱמִיד לָהֶם נְבִיאִים, וְהֵם פָּרְצוּ גֶּדֶר הָעוֹלָם, שֶׁבַּתְּחִלָּה הָיוּ גְּדוּרִים בַּעֲרָיוֹת, וְזֶה נָתַן לָהֶם עֵצָה לְהַפְקִיר עַצְמָן לִזְנוּת: **לִקְרֹא לוֹ.** הַקְּרִיאָה הָיְתָה שֶׁלּוֹ וְלַהֲנָאָתוֹ, שֶׁהָיָה פּוֹסֵק לוֹ מָמוֹן הַרְבֵּה: **עַם יָצָא מִמִּצְרַיִם.** וְאִם תֹּאמַר: מַה מַּזִּיקְךָ? **הִנֵּה כִסָּה אֶת עֵין הָאָרֶץ.** סִיחוֹן וְעוֹג שֶׁהָיוּ שׁוֹמְרִים אוֹתָנוּ, עָמְדוּ עֲלֵיהֶם וַהֲרָגוּם: **וְהוּא יֹשֵׁב מִמֻּלִי.** חָסֵר כְּתִיב, קְרוֹבִים הֵם לְהַכְרִיתֵנִי, כְּמוֹ: "כִּי אֲמִילַם" (תהלים קיח, י):

ו **נַכֶּה בּוֹ.** אֲנִי וְעַמִּי נַכֶּה בָּהֶם. דָּבָר אַחֵר, לְשׁוֹן מִשְׁנָה הוּא: "מְנַכֶּה לוֹ מִן הַדָּמִים" (חולין קלב ע"א), לְחַסֵּר מֵהֶם מְעַט: **כִּי יָדַעְתִּי וְגוֹ׳.** עַל יְדֵי מִלְחֶמֶת סִיחוֹן שֶׁעֲזַרְתּוֹ לְהַכּוֹת אֶת מוֹאָב:

ז **וּקְסָמִים בְּיָדָם.** כָּל מִינֵי קְסָמִים, שֶׁלֹּא יֹאמַר: אֵין כְּלֵי תַּשְׁמִישִׁי עִמִּי. דָּבָר אַחֵר, קֶסֶם זֶה נָטְלוּ בְיָדָם זִקְנֵי מִדְיָן, אָמְרוּ: אִם יָבֹא עִמָּנוּ בַּפַּעַם הַזֹּאת יֵשׁ בּוֹ מַמָּשׁ, וְאִם יְדַחֵנוּ אֵין בּוֹ תּוֹעֶלֶת. לְפִיכָךְ כְּשֶׁאָמַר לָהֶם: "לִינוּ פֹה הַלַּיְלָה" (להלן פסוק ח) אָמְרוּ: אֵין בּוֹ תִּקְוָה, הִנִּיחוּהוּ וְהָלְכוּ לָהֶם, שֶׁנֶּאֱמַר: "וַיֵּשְׁבוּ שָׂרֵי מוֹאָב עִם בִּלְעָם" (שם), אֲבָל זִקְנֵי מִדְיָן הָלְכוּ לָהֶם:

ח **לִינוּ פֹה הַלַּיְלָה.** אֵין רוּחַ הַקֹּדֶשׁ שׁוֹרָה עָלָיו אֶלָּא בַּלַּיְלָה, וְכֵן לְכָל נְבִיאֵי אֻמּוֹת הָעוֹלָם, וְכֵן לָבָן בַּחֲלוֹם הַלַּיְלָה, שֶׁנֶּאֱמַר: "וַיָּבֹא אֱלֹהִים אֶל לָבָן הָאֲרַמִּי בַּחֲלֹם הַלָּיְלָה" (בראשית לא, כד), כְּאָדָם הַהוֹלֵךְ אֵצֶל פִּילַגְשׁוֹ בְּהֵחָבֵא: **כַּאֲשֶׁר יְדַבֵּר ה׳ אֵלָי.** אִם יַמְלִיכֵנִי לָלֶכֶת עִם בְּנֵי אָדָם כְּמוֹתְכֶם אֵלֵךְ עִמָּכֶם, שֶׁמָּא אֵין כְּבוֹדוֹ לְתִתִּי לַהֲלֹךְ אֶלָּא עִם שָׂרִים גְּדוֹלִים: **וַיֵּשְׁבוּ.** לְשׁוֹן עַכָּבָה:

ט **מִי הָאֲנָשִׁים הָאֵלֶּה עִמָּךְ.** לְהַטְעוֹתוֹ בָּא, אָמַר: פְּעָמִים שֶׁאֵין הַכֹּל גָּלוּי לְפָנָיו, אֵין דַּעְתּוֹ שָׁוָה עָלָיו, אַף אֲנִי אֶרְאֶה עֵת שֶׁאוּכַל לְקַלֵּל וְלֹא יָבִין:

י **בָּלָק בֶּן צִפֹּר מֶלֶךְ מוֹאָב.** אַף עַל פִּי שֶׁאֵינִי חָשׁוּב בְּעֵינֶיךָ, חָשׁוּב אֲנִי בְּעֵינֵי הַמְּלָכִים:

יא **קָבָה לִּי.** זוֹ קָשָׁה מֵ"אָרָה לִּי", שֶׁהוּא נוֹקֵב וּמְפָרֵשׁ: **וְגֵרַשְׁתִּיו.** מִן הָעוֹלָם, וּבָלָק לֹא אָמַר אֶלָּא "וַאֲגָרְשֶׁנּוּ מִן הָאָרֶץ" (לעיל פסוק ו), אֵינִי מְבַקֵּשׁ אֶלָּא לְהַסִּיעָם מֵעָלַי, וּבִלְעָם הָיָה שׂוֹנְאָם יוֹתֵר מִבָּלָק:

יב **לֹא תֵלֵךְ עִמָּהֶם.** אָמַר לוֹ: אִם כֵּן אֲקַלְּלֵם בִּמְקוֹמִי. אָמַר לוֹ: "לֹא תָאֹר אֶת הָעָם". אָמַר לוֹ: אִם כֵּן אֲבָרְכֵם. אָמַר לוֹ: אֵינָם צְרִיכִים לְבִרְכָתְךָ "כִּי בָרוּךְ הוּא". מָשָׁל אוֹמְרִים לַצִּרְעָה: לֹא מִדֻּבְשֵׁךְ וְלֹא מֵעֻקְצֵךְ:

יג **לַהֲלֹךְ עִמָּכֶם.** אֶלָּא עִם שָׂרִים גְּדוֹלִים מִכֶּם. לָמַדְנוּ שֶׁרוּחוֹ גְבוֹהָה, וְלֹא רָצָה לְגַלּוֹת שֶׁהוּא בִּרְשׁוּתוֹ שֶׁל מָקוֹם אֶלָּא בִּלְשׁוֹן גַּסּוּת, לְפִיכָךְ "וַיֹּסֶף עוֹד בָּלָק" (להלן פסוק טו):

בְּנֵי־עַמּוֹ לִקְרֹא־לוֹ לֵאמֹר הִנֵּה עַם יָצָא מִמִּצְרַיִם הִנֵּה כִסָּה אֶת־עֵין
ו הָאָרֶץ וְהוּא יֹשֵׁב מִמֻּלִי׃ וְעַתָּה לְכָה־נָּא אָרָה־לִּי אֶת־הָעָם הַזֶּה
כִּי־עָצוּם הוּא מִמֶּנִּי אוּלַי אוּכַל נַכֶּה־בּוֹ וַאֲגָרְשֶׁנּוּ מִן־הָאָרֶץ כִּי יָדַעְתִּי
ז אֵת אֲשֶׁר־תְּבָרֵךְ מְבֹרָךְ וַאֲשֶׁר תָּאֹר יוּאָר׃ וַיֵּלְכוּ זִקְנֵי מוֹאָב וְזִקְנֵי
ח מִדְיָן וּקְסָמִים בְּיָדָם וַיָּבֹאוּ אֶל־בִּלְעָם וַיְדַבְּרוּ אֵלָיו דִּבְרֵי בָלָק׃ וַיֹּאמֶר
אֲלֵיהֶם לִינוּ פֹה הַלַּיְלָה וַהֲשִׁבֹתִי אֶתְכֶם דָּבָר כַּאֲשֶׁר יְדַבֵּר יְהוָה אֵלָי
ט וַיֵּשְׁבוּ שָׂרֵי־מוֹאָב עִם־בִּלְעָם׃ וַיָּבֹא אֱלֹהִים אֶל־בִּלְעָם וַיֹּאמֶר מִי
י הָאֲנָשִׁים הָאֵלֶּה עִמָּךְ׃ וַיֹּאמֶר בִּלְעָם אֶל־הָאֱלֹהִים בָּלָק בֶּן־צִפֹּר מֶלֶךְ
יא מוֹאָב שָׁלַח אֵלָי׃ הִנֵּה הָעָם הַיֹּצֵא מִמִּצְרַיִם וַיְכַס אֶת־עֵין הָאָרֶץ
יב עַתָּה לְכָה קָבָה־לִּי אֹתוֹ אוּלַי אוּכַל לְהִלָּחֶם בּוֹ וְגֵרַשְׁתִּיו׃ וַיֹּאמֶר
אֱלֹהִים אֶל־בִּלְעָם לֹא תֵלֵךְ עִמָּהֶם לֹא תָאֹר אֶת־הָעָם כִּי בָרוּךְ הוּא׃
יג וַיָּקָם בִּלְעָם בַּבֹּקֶר וַיֹּאמֶר אֶל־שָׂרֵי בָלָק לְכוּ אֶל־אַרְצְכֶם כִּי מֵאֵן שני
יד יְהוָה לְתִתִּי לַהֲלֹךְ עִמָּכֶם׃ וַיָּקוּמוּ שָׂרֵי מוֹאָב וַיָּבֹאוּ אֶל־בָּלָק וַיֹּאמְרוּ /חמישי/

אונקלוס

בְּנֵי עַמֵּיהּ לְמִקְרֵי לֵיהּ, לְמֵימַר, הָא, עַמָּא נְפַק מִמִּצְרַיִם הָא חֲפָא יָת עֵין שִׁמְשָׁא דְּאַרְעָא, וְהוּא שָׁרֵי מִלְּקִבְלִי: ו וּכְעַן אֵיתָא כְּעַן לוּט לִי יָת עַמָּא הָדֵין, אֲרֵי תַקִּיף הוּא מִנִּי, מָאִם אִכּוּל לְאַגָּחָא בֵּיהּ קְרָב, וַאֲתָרְכִנֵּיהּ מִן אַרְעָא, אֲרֵי יָדַעְנָא, יָת דִּתְבָרֵיךְ מְבָרַךְ, וּדְתֵלוּט לִיט: ז וַאֲזַלוּ, סָבֵי מוֹאָב וְסָבֵי מִדְיָן, וְקִסְמַיָּא בִּידֵיהוֹן, וַאֲתוֹ לְוָת בִּלְעָם, וּמַלִּילוּ עִמֵּיהּ פִּתְגָמֵי בָלָק: ח וַאֲמַר לְהוֹן, בִּיתוּ הָכָא בְּלֵילְיָא, וַאֲתֵיב יָתְכוֹן פִּתְגָמָא, כְּמָא דִּימַלֵּיל יי עִמִּי, וְאוֹרִיכוּ רַבְרְבֵי מוֹאָב עִם בִּלְעָם: ט וַאֲתָא מֵימַר מִן קֳדָם יי לְוָת בִּלְעָם,

וַאֲמַר, מַאן גֻּבְרַיָּא הָאִלֵּין דְּעִמָּךְ: י וַאֲמַר בִּלְעָם קֳדָם יי, בָּלָק בַּר צִפּוֹר, מַלְכָּא דְמוֹאָב שְׁלַח לְוָתִי: יא הָא עַמָּא דִּנְפַק מִמִּצְרַיִם, וַחֲפָא יָת עֵין שִׁמְשָׁא דְּאַרְעָא, כְּעַן, אֵיתָא לוּט לִי יָתֵיהּ, מָאִם אִכּוּל, לְאַגָּחָא בֵיהּ קְרָב וַאֲתָרְכִנֵּיהּ: יב וַאֲמַר יי לְבִלְעָם, לָא תֵיזֵיל עִמְּהוֹן, לָא תְלוּט יָת עַמָּא, אֲרֵי בְרִיךְ הוּא: יג וְקָם בִּלְעָם בְּצַפְרָא, וַאֲמַר לְרַבְרְבֵי בָלָק, אִיזִילוּ לְאַרְעֲכוֹן, אֲרֵי רַעֲוָא קֳדָם יי, דְּלָא לְמִשְׁבְּקִי לְמֵיזַל עִמְּכוֹן: יד וְקָמוּ רַבְרְבֵי מוֹאָב, וַאֲתוֹ לְוָת בָּלָק, וַאֲמַרוּ,

22:6 **עָצוּם הוּא מִמֶּנִּי** *Stronger than I* – The language the Torah uses here and in verse 3 is reminiscent of the reaction of the Egyptians at the beginning of the book of Exodus: "'The Israelite people are *many* (*rav*) and more *powerful* (*atzum*) than we.'… And the Egyptians *came to dread* (*vayakutzu*) the Israelites" (Ex. 1:9, 12). Again we are given an insight into the perspective of other nations on Israel, which may differ from Israel's experience of themselves.

15 said, "Bilam refuses to go with us." Balak then sent other princes, yet more
16 numerous and eminent than the first. They came to Bilam and said to him,
"This is what Balak son of Tzipor says: 'Do not let anything prevent you from
17 coming to me, for I will do you great honor, and whatever else you ask of me.
18 Please – come and curse this people for me.'" Bilam replied to Balak's servants,
"Even if Balak were to give me his palace full of silver and gold, I could not do
19 anything, small or great, to transgress the word of the LORD my God. But now,
you too remain here tonight so that I may know what else the LORD may tell
20 me." God came to Bilam that night and said to him, "If the men have come to
summon you, you may get up and go with them; but do only what I tell you to
21 do." So Bilam rose in the morning, saddled his donkey, and went along with the SHELISHI
22 princes of Moav. God was furious at his going, and an angel of the LORD stood
in the road to oppose him as he was riding on his donkey, his two servants with

רש״י

יז **כי כבד אכבדך מאד.** יותר ממה שהיית נוטל לשעבר אני נותן לך:

יח **מלא ביתו כסף וזהב.** למדנו שנפשו רחבה ומחמד ממון אחרים. אמר: ראוי לו לתן לי כל כסף וזהב שלו, שהרי צריך לשכר חילות רבות, ספק נוצח ספק אינו נוצח, ואני ודאי נוצח: **לא אוכל לעבר.** על כרחו גלה שהוא ברשות אחרים, ונתנבא כאן שאינו יכול לבטל הברכות שנתברכו האבות מפי השכינה:

יט **גם אתם.** פיו הכשילו, "גם אתם" סופכם לילך בפחי נפש כראשונים: **מה יסף.** לא ישנה דבריו מברכה לקללה, הלואי שלא יוסיף לברך. כאן נתנבא שעתיד להוסיף להם ברכות על ידו:

כ **אם לקרא לך.** אם הקריאה שלך וסבור אתה לטל עליה שכר, "קום לך אתם": **ואך.** על כרחך "את הדבר אשר אדבר אליך אתו תעשה", ואף על פי כן: "וילך בלעם", אמר: שמא אפתנו וירצה:

כא **ויחבש את אתנו.** מכאן שהשנאה מקלקלת את השורה, שחבש הוא בעצמו. אמר הקדוש ברוך הוא: רשע, כבר קדמך אברהם אביהם, שנאמר: "וישכם אברהם בבקר ויחבש את חמרו" (בראשית כב, ג): **עם שרי מואב.** לבו כלבם שוה:

כב **כי הולך הוא.** ראה שהדבר רע בעיני המקום ונתאוה לילך:

their plans. *Itam* means "with them physically but not mentally"; in other words, Bilam could accompany them but not share their purpose or intention. God is angry when Bilam goes, because he identifies with their mission.

There is another possible answer. The hardest word to hear in any language is the word "no." Bilam asked God once. God said no. That should have sufficed. Yet now Bilam asks a second time. God does not change His mind. Therefore Bilam's delay says something not about God but about himself. He has not accepted the divine refusal. He wants to hear the answer "yes" – and that is indeed what he hears. Not because God wants him to go, but because God speaks once, and if we refuse to accept what He says, God does not force His will upon us. As the Sages of the Talmud put it: "Man is led down the path he chooses to tread" (Makkot 10b).

The true meaning of God's second reply, "Go with them," is: "If you insist, then I cannot stop you going – but I am angry that you should have asked a second time."

If God speaks and we do not listen, He does not intervene to save us from our choices. But God is not prepared to let Bilam proceed as if he has divine consent. This is to be Bilam's lesson, and what we, too, must discover if we are to be open to the voice of God.

טו מֵאֵן בִּלְעָם הֲלֹךְ עִמָּנוּ: וַיֹּסֶף עוֹד בָּלָק שְׁלֹחַ שָׂרִים רַבִּים וְנִכְבָּדִים
טז מֵאֵלֶּה: וַיָּבֹאוּ אֶל־בִּלְעָם וַיֹּאמְרוּ לוֹ כֹּה אָמַר בָּלָק בֶּן־צִפּוֹר אַל־נָא
יז תִמָּנַע מֵהֲלֹךְ אֵלָי: כִּי־כַבֵּד אֲכַבֶּדְךָ מְאֹד וְכֹל אֲשֶׁר־תֹּאמַר אֵלַי
יח אֶעֱשֶׂה וּלְכָה־נָּא קָבָה לִּי אֵת הָעָם הַזֶּה: וַיַּעַן בִּלְעָם וַיֹּאמֶר אֶל־עַבְדֵי
בָלָק אִם־יִתֶּן־לִי בָלָק מְלֹא בֵיתוֹ כֶּסֶף וְזָהָב לֹא אוּכַל לַעֲבֹר אֶת־פִּי
יט יְהוָה אֱלֹהָי לַעֲשׂוֹת קְטַנָּה אוֹ גְדוֹלָה: וְעַתָּה שְׁבוּ נָא בָזֶה גַּם־אַתֶּם
כ הַלָּיְלָה וְאֵדְעָה מַה־יֹּסֵף יְהוָה דַּבֵּר עִמִּי: וַיָּבֹא אֱלֹהִים ׀ אֶל־בִּלְעָם
לַיְלָה וַיֹּאמֶר לוֹ אִם־לִקְרֹא לְךָ בָּאוּ הָאֲנָשִׁים קוּם לֵךְ אִתָּם וְאַךְ אֶת־
כא הַדָּבָר אֲשֶׁר־אֲדַבֵּר אֵלֶיךָ אֹתוֹ תַעֲשֶׂה: וַיָּקָם בִּלְעָם בַּבֹּקֶר וַיַּחֲבֹשׁ שלישי
כב אֶת־אֲתֹנוֹ וַיֵּלֶךְ עִם־שָׂרֵי מוֹאָב: וַיִּחַר־אַף אֱלֹהִים כִּי־הוֹלֵךְ הוּא
וַיִּתְיַצֵּב מַלְאַךְ יְהוָה בַּדֶּרֶךְ לְשָׂטָן לוֹ וְהוּא רֹכֵב עַל־אֲתֹנוֹ וּשְׁנֵי נְעָרָיו

אונקלוס

סָרִיב בִּלְעָם לְמֵיתֵי עִמַּנָא: טו וְאוֹסִיף עוֹד בָּלָק, שְׁלַח רַבְרְבִין, סַגִּיאִין וִיקִירִין מֵאִלֵּין: טז וַאֲתוֹ לְוָת בִּלְעָם, וַאֲמַרוּ לֵיהּ, כִּדְנַן אֲמַר בָּלָק בַּר צִפּוֹר, לָא כְעַן תִּתְמְנַע מִלְּמֵיתֵי לְוָתִי: יז אֲרֵי יַקָּרָא אֲיַקְּרִנָּךְ לַחְדָּא, וְכֹל, דְּתֵימַר לִי אַעֲבֵיד, וְאִיתָא כְעַן לוּט לִי, יָת עַמָּא הָדֵין: יח וַאֲתֵיב בִּלְעָם, וַאֲמַר לְעַבְדֵי בָלָק, אִם יִתֵּין לִי בָלָק, מְלֵי בֵיתֵיהּ כְּסַף וּדְהַב, לֵית לִי רְשׁוּ, לְמִעְבַּר עַל גְּזֵירַת מֵימְרָא דַּייָ אֱלָהִי, לְמֶעְבַּד זְעֵירְתָּא אוֹ רַבְּתָא: יט וּכְעַן, אוֹרִיכוּ כְעַן הָכָא, אַף אַתּוּן בְּלֵילְיָא, וְאֶדַּע, מָא יוֹסֵיף יי לְמַלָּלָא עִמִּי: כ וַאֲתָא מֵימַר מִן קֳדָם יי לְוָת בִּלְעָם בְּלֵילְיָא, וַאֲמַר לֵיהּ, אִם לְמִקְרֵי לָךְ אֲתוֹ גֻּבְרַיָּא, קוּם אִיזֵיל עִמְּהוֹן, וּבְרַם, יָת פִּתְגָּמָא, דַּאֲמַלֵּיל עִמָּךְ יָתֵיהּ תַּעֲבֵיד: כא וְקָם בִּלְעָם בְּצַפְרָא, וְזָרֵיז יָת אֲתָנֵיהּ, וַאֲזַל עִם רַבְרְבֵי מוֹאָב: כב וּתְקֵיף רֻגְזָא דַּייָ אֲרֵי אָזֵיל הוּא, וְאִתְעַתַּד, מַלְאֲכָא דַּייָ, בְּאוֹרְחָא לְשָׂטָן לֵיהּ, וְהוּא רָכֵיב עַל אֲתָנֵיהּ, וּתְרֵין עוּלֵימוֹהִי

22:20 **קוּם לֵךְ אִתָּם** *You may…go with them* – At first God said, "Do not go." Now He says, "Go." Then immediately, "God was furious at his going" (v. 22). Does God change His mind – not once but twice in the course of a single narrative?

The commentators offer various ways of resolving the apparent contradictions. According to Ramban (on Num. 22:20), God's first statement, "Don't go with them" meant "Don't curse the Israelites." His second – "Go with them" – meant "Go but make it clear that you will only say the words I put in your mouth, even if they are words of blessing." God was angry with Bilam, not because he went but because he did not tell them of the proviso.

In the nineteenth century, Malbim and Rabbi Tzvi Hirsch Mecklenberg suggested another, ingenious answer (Malbim on Num. 22:21; *HaKetav VeHaKabbala* on Num. 22:12). The Torah uses two different words for "with them" in the first and second divine replies. When God says, "Don't go with them," the Hebrew is *imahem*. When He later says, "Go with them," the corresponding word is *itam*. The two prepositions have subtly different meanings. *Imahem* means "with them mentally as well as physically," going along with

23 him. The donkey saw the angel of the LORD standing in the road, drawn sword
in hand, and she swerved from the road into a field. And Bilam beat the donkey
24 to urge her back onto the road. Then the angel of the LORD was standing in a
25 narrow path between vineyards with a wall on either side. When the donkey
saw the angel of the LORD, she pressed against the wall, crushing Bilam's foot
26 against it. He beat her once again. And the angel of the LORD went ahead and
stood in a narrow place where there was no room at all to turn right or left.
27 When the donkey saw the angel of the LORD, she lay down under Bilam. Bilam
28 was furious and beat the donkey with his stick. Then the LORD opened the
donkey's mouth and – "What have I done to you," she said to Bilam, "that you
29 have struck me these three times?" "You are playing games with me," said Bilam
to the donkey. "If only I had a sword in my hand, I would kill you here and now."
30 But the donkey said to Bilam, "Am I not your donkey on whom you have always
ridden to this day? Have I been in the habit of doing this to you?" "No," he
31 replied. Then the LORD uncovered Bilam's eyes, and he saw the angel of the
LORD standing in the road, drawn sword in hand. He bowed and prostrated

רש"י

לשטן לו. מלאך של רחמים היה, והיה רוצה למנעו מלחטוא שלא יחטא ויאבד: **ושני נעריו עמו.** מכאן לאדם חשוב היוצא לדרך יוליך עמו שני אנשים לשמשו, וחוזרים ומשמשים זה את זה:

כג **ותרא האתון.** והוא לא ראה, שנתן הקדוש ברוך הוא רשות לבהמה לראות יותר מן האדם, שמתוך שיש בו דעת תטרף דעתו כשיראה מזיקין: **וחרבו שלופה בידו.** אמר: רשע זה הניח כלי אמנותו, שכלי זינן של אמות העולם בחרב, והוא בא עליהם בפיו שהוא אמנות שלהם, אף אני אתפוש את שלו ואבא עליו באמנותו, וכן היה סופו: "ואת בלעם בן בעור הרגו בחרב" (להלן לא, ח):

כד **במשעול.** כתרגומו: "בשביל", וכן: "אם ישפק עפר שמרון לשעלים" (מלכים א' כ, י), עפר הנדבק בכפות הרגלים בהלוכן. וכן: "מי מדד בשעלו מים" (ישעיה מ, יב), ברגליו ובהלוכו: **גדר מזה וגדר מזה.** סתם 'גדר' של אבנים הוא:

כה **ותלחץ.** היא עצמה: **ותלחץ.** את אחרים, את רגל בלעם:

כו **ויוסף מלאך ה' עבור.** לעבור עוד לפניו להלך להיות לפניו במקום אחר, כמו: "והוא עבר לפניהם" (בראשית לג, ג). ומדרש אגדה יש בתנחומא, מה ראה לעמד בשלשה מקומות? סימני אבות הראהו:

כח **זה שלש רגלים.** רמזה לו, אתה מבקש לעקר אמה החוגגת שלש רגלים בשנה:

כט **התעללת.** כתרגומו, לשון גנאי ובזיון: **לו יש חרב בידי.** גנות גדולה היה לו דבר זה בעיני השרים, זה הולך להרג אמה שלמה בפיו, ולאתון זו צריך לכלי זין:

ל **ההסכן הסכנתי.** כתרגומו, וכן: "הלאל יסכן גבר" (איוב כב, ב). ורבותינו דרשו מקרא זה בתלמוד: אמרו ליה: מאי טעמא לא רכבת אסוסיא? אמר להון: ברטיבא שדאי ליה כו', כדאיתא במסכת עבודה זרה (דף ד ע"ב):

in which rulers engaged in endless projects of self-aggrandizement, Israel produced a literature in which they attributed their successes to God and their failures to themselves. Far from making them weak, this made them strong. So it is with us as individuals. Pagan prophets like Bilam had not yet learned the lesson we must all one day learn: that what matters is not that God does what we want, but that we do what He wants. God laughs at those who think they have godlike powers. The smaller we see ourselves, the greater we become.

כג עִמּוֹ: וַתֵּרֶא הָאָתוֹן אֶת־מַלְאַךְ יְהוָה נִצָּב בַּדֶּרֶךְ וְחַרְבּוֹ שְׁלוּפָה בְּיָדוֹ
וַתֵּט הָאָתוֹן מִן־הַדֶּרֶךְ וַתֵּלֶךְ בַּשָּׂדֶה וַיַּךְ בִּלְעָם אֶת־הָאָתוֹן לְהַטֹּתָהּ
כד הַדָּרֶךְ: וַיַּעֲמֹד מַלְאַךְ יְהוָה בְּמִשְׁעוֹל הַכְּרָמִים גָּדֵר מִזֶּה וְגָדֵר מִזֶּה:
כה וַתֵּרֶא הָאָתוֹן אֶת־מַלְאַךְ יְהוָה וַתִּלָּחֵץ אֶל־הַקִּיר וַתִּלְחַץ אֶת־רֶגֶל
כו בִּלְעָם אֶל־הַקִּיר וַיֹּסֶף לְהַכֹּתָהּ: וַיּוֹסֶף מַלְאַךְ־יְהוָה עֲבוֹר וַיַּעֲמֹד
כז בְּמָקוֹם צָר אֲשֶׁר אֵין־דֶּרֶךְ לִנְטוֹת יָמִין וּשְׂמֹאול: וַתֵּרֶא הָאָתוֹן אֶת־
מַלְאַךְ יְהוָה וַתִּרְבַּץ תַּחַת בִּלְעָם וַיִּחַר־אַף בִּלְעָם וַיַּךְ אֶת־הָאָתוֹן
כח בַּמַּקֵּל: וַיִּפְתַּח יְהוָה אֶת־פִּי הָאָתוֹן וַתֹּאמֶר לְבִלְעָם מֶה־עָשִׂיתִי
כט לְךָ כִּי הִכִּיתַנִי זֶה שָׁלֹשׁ רְגָלִים: וַיֹּאמֶר בִּלְעָם לָאָתוֹן כִּי הִתְעַלַּלְתְּ
ל בִּי לוּ יֶשׁ־חֶרֶב בְּיָדִי כִּי עַתָּה הֲרַגְתִּיךְ: וַתֹּאמֶר הָאָתוֹן אֶל־בִּלְעָם
הֲלוֹא אָנֹכִי אֲתֹנְךָ אֲשֶׁר־רָכַבְתָּ עָלַי מֵעוֹדְךָ עַד־הַיּוֹם הַזֶּה הַהַסְכֵּן
לא הִסְכַּנְתִּי לַעֲשׂוֹת לְךָ כֹּה וַיֹּאמֶר לֹא: וַיְגַל יְהוָה אֶת־עֵינֵי בִלְעָם וַיַּרְא
אֶת־מַלְאַךְ יְהוָה נִצָּב בַּדֶּרֶךְ וְחַרְבּוֹ שְׁלֻפָה בְּיָדוֹ וַיִּקֹּד וַיִּשְׁתַּחוּ לְאַפָּיו:

אונקלוס

עִמֵּיהּ: כג וַחֲזַת אֲתָנָא יָת מַלְאֲכָא דַּייָ מְעַתַּד בְּאוֹרְחָא, וְחַרְבֵּיהּ שְׁלִיפָא בִּידֵיהּ, וּסְטַת אֲתָנָא מִן אוֹרְחָא, וַאֲזָלַת בְּחַקְלָא, וּמְחָא בִלְעָם יָת אֲתָנָא, לְאַסְטָיוּתַהּ לְאוֹרְחָא: כד וְקָם מַלְאֲכָא דַּייָ, בִּשְׁבִיל כַּרְמַיָּא, אַתְרָא דְּגָדֵירָא מִכָּא וְגָדֵירָא מִכָּא: כה וַחֲזַת אֲתָנָא יָת מַלְאֲכָא דַּייָ, וְאִדְּחֵיקַת עִם כָּתְלָא, וּדְחָקַת, יָת רִגְלָא דְּבִלְעָם לְכָתְלָא, וְאוֹסֵיף לְמִמְחַהּ: כו וְאוֹסֵיף מַלְאֲכָא דַּייָ עֲבַר, וְקָם בַּאֲתַר עָק, דְּלֵית אוֹרַח לְמִסְטֵי לְיַמִּינָא וְלִסְמָאלָא: כז וַחֲזַת אֲתָנָא יָת מַלְאֲכָא דַּייָ, וּרְבַעַת תְּחוֹת בִּלְעָם, וּתְקֵיף רֻגְזָא דְּבִלְעָם, וּמְחָא יָת אֲתָנָא בְּחֻטְרָא: כח וּפְתַח יְיָ יָת פֻּמָּא דַּאֲתָנָא, וַאֲמָרַת לְבִלְעָם מָא עֲבָדִית לָךְ, אֲרֵי מְחֵיתַנִי, דְּנָן תְּלָת זִמְנִין: כט וַאֲמַר בִּלְעָם לַאֲתָנָא, אֲרֵי חַיֵּיכְתְּ בִּי, אִלּוּ פוֹן אִית חַרְבָּא בִּידִי, אֲרֵי כְעַן קְטַלְתִּיךְ: ל וַאֲמָרַת אֲתָנָא לְבִלְעָם, הֲלָא אֲנָא אֲתָנָךְ דִּרְכֵיבְתְּ עֲלַי, מִדְּאִיתָךְ עַד יוֹמָא הָדֵין, הֲמֵילַף אֲלֵיפְנָא, לְמֶעֱבַד לָךְ כְּדֵין, וַאֲמַר לָא: לא וּגְלָא יְיָ יָת עֵינֵי בִלְעָם, וַחֲזָא, יָת מַלְאֲכָא דַּייָ מְעַתַּד בְּאוֹרְחָא, וְחַרְבֵּיהּ שְׁלִיפָא בִּידֵיהּ, וּכְרַע וּסְגִיד לְאַפּוֹהִי:

22:33 וַתִּרְאַנִי הָאָתוֹן *The donkey saw me* – One thing provokes divine laughter in the Tanakh, namely human pretension. It can be heard between the lines of the story of the Tower of Bavel, in the defeat of Egypt's hubris, and in our *parasha*. There is deliberate humor in the episode of the talking donkey. Bilam is known as the man who held the secrets of blessing and curse. His fame has spread to Moav and Midyan. Yet God now proceeds to show Bilam that when He so chooses, even a donkey is a greater prophet than he. God humbles the self-important, just as He grants importance to the humble.

Hubris always eventually becomes nemesis. In a world

32 himself facedown. The angel of the LORD said to him, "Why have you beaten
your donkey these three times? It was I who came out here to oppose you,
33 because your way is perverse to me. The donkey saw me and turned away from
me these three times. If she had not turned away from me, I would certainly
34 have killed you by now and let her live." Bilam said to the angel of the LORD, "I
have sinned, for I did not know that you were standing against me in the road.
35 Now, if you consider it wrong, I will go back." The angel of the LORD said to
Bilam, "Go with the men, but say nothing except what I tell you." So Bilam
36 continued on with Balak's princes. When Balak heard that Bilam was coming,
he went out to meet him at the city of Moav, at the Arnon border on the edge
37 of his territory. Balak said to Bilam, "Did I not send to summon you? Why did
38 you not come to me? Am I really not able to offer you any honor?" Bilam
replied to Balak, "Well, I have come to you now. But can I speak any words I
39 choose? I can only say the word God puts into my mouth." Then Bilam went REVI'I /SHISHI/
40 with Balak and they came to Kiryat Ḥutzot. Balak sacrificed oxen and sheep
41 and sent them to Bilam and the princes who were with him. In the morning
Balak took Bilam up to Bamot Baal, where he could see part of the people.
23 1 Bilam said to Balak, "Build me seven altars here and prepare for me seven bulls

רש״י

לב) **כִּי יָרַט הַדֶּרֶךְ לְנֶגְדִּי.** רַבּוֹתֵינוּ חַכְמֵי הַמִּשְׁנָה דְּרָשׁוּהוּ נוֹטָרִיקוֹן: יָרְאָה, רָאֲתָה, נָטְתָה, בִּשְׁבִיל שֶׁהַדֶּרֶךְ לְנֶגְדִּי, כְּלוֹמַר לְקִנְאָתִי וּלְהַקְנִיטֵנִי. וּלְפִי מַשְׁמָעוֹ, כִּי חָרַד הַדֶּרֶךְ לְנֶגְדִּי, לְשׁוֹן רֶטֶט, כִּי רָאִיתִי בַּעַל הַדֶּרֶךְ שֶׁחָרַד וּמִהֵר הַדֶּרֶךְ שֶׁהוּא לְכַעֲסִי וּלְהַמְרוֹתִי, וּמִקְרָא קָצָר הוּא, כְּמוֹ: "וַתְּכַל דָּוִד" (שמואל ב׳ יג, לט) שֶׁרוֹצֶה לוֹמַר: וַתְּכַל נֶפֶשׁ דָּוִד. לָשׁוֹן אַחֵר, 'יָרַט' לְשׁוֹן רָצוֹן, וְכֵן: "וְעַל יְדֵי רְשָׁעִים יִרְטֵנִי" (איוב טז, יא), מְפַיֵּס וּמְנַחֵם אוֹתִי עַל יְדֵי רְשָׁעִים, שֶׁאֵינָן אֶלָּא מַקְנִיטִים:

לג) **אוּלַי נָטְתָה.** כְּמוֹ לוּלֵא, פְּעָמִים שֶׁ'אוּלַי' מְשַׁמֵּשׁ בִּלְשׁוֹן לוּלֵא: **גַּם אֹתְכָה הָרַגְתִּי.** הֲרֵי זֶה מִקְרָא מְסֹרָס, וְהוּא כְּמוֹ: 'גַּם הָרַגְתִּי אוֹתְךָ'. כְּלוֹמַר, לֹא הָעַכָּבָה בִּלְבַד קָרַאתְךָ עַל יָדִי, כִּי גַּם הַהֲרִיגָה: **וְאוֹתָהּ הֶחֱיֵיתִי.** וְעַתָּה מִפְּנֵי שֶׁדִּבְּרָה וְהוֹכִיחַתְךָ, וְלֹא יָכֹלְתָּ לַעֲמֹד בְּתוֹכַחְתָּהּ, כְּמוֹ שֶׁכָּתוּב: "וַיֹּאמֶר לֹא" (לעיל פסוק ל) – הֲרַגְתִּיהָ, שֶׁלֹּא יֹאמְרוּ: זוֹ הִיא שֶׁסִּלְּקָה אֶת בִּלְעָם בְּתוֹכַחְתָּהּ וְלֹא יָכֹל לְהָשִׁיב, שֶׁחָס הַמָּקוֹם עַל כְּבוֹד הַבְּרִיּוֹת. וְכֵן: "וְאֶת הַבְּהֵמָה תַּהֲרֹגוּ" (ויקרא כ, טו), וְכֵן: "וְהָרַגְתָּ אֶת הָאִשָּׁה וְאֶת הַבְּהֵמָה" (שם פסוק טז):

לד) **כִּי לֹא יָדַעְתִּי.** גַּם זֶה גְּנוּתוֹ, וְעַל כָּרְחוֹ הוֹדָה, שֶׁהוּא הָיָה מִשְׁתַּבֵּחַ שֶׁיּוֹדֵעַ דַּעַת עֶלְיוֹן, וּפִיו הֵעִיד: "לֹא יָדַעְתִּי": **אִם רַע בְּעֵינֶיךָ אָשׁוּבָה** לִי. לְהִתְרִיס נֶגֶד הַמָּקוֹם הִיא תְּשׁוּבָה זוֹ. אָמַר לוֹ: הוּא בְּעַצְמוֹ צִוַּנִי לָלֶכֶת וְאַתָּה מַלְאָךְ מְבַטֵּל אֶת דְּבָרָיו, לָמוּד הוּא בְּכָךְ שֶׁאוֹמֵר דָּבָר וּמַלְאָךְ מַחֲזִירוֹ, אָמַר לְאַבְרָהָם: "קַח נָא אֶת בִּנְךָ" וְגוֹ׳ (בראשית כב, ב) וְעַל יְדֵי מַלְאָךְ בִּטֵּל אֶת דְּבָרוֹ, אַף אֲנִי אִם רַע בְּעֵינֶיךָ צָרִיךְ אֲנִי לָשׁוּב:

לה) **לֵךְ עִם הָאֲנָשִׁים.** בְּדֶרֶךְ שֶׁאָדָם רוֹצֶה לֵילֵךְ בָּהּ מוֹלִיכִין אוֹתוֹ: **לֵךְ עִם הָאֲנָשִׁים.** כִּי חֶלְקְךָ עִמָּהֶם וְסוֹפְךָ לֵאָבֵד מִן הָעוֹלָם: **וְאֶפֶס.** עַל כָּרְחֲךָ, "אֶת הַדָּבָר אֲשֶׁר אֲדַבֵּר" וְגוֹ׳: **עִם שָׂרֵי בָלָק.** שָׂמֵחַ לְקַלְּלָם כְּמוֹתָם:

לו) **וַיִּשְׁמַע בָּלָק.** שָׁלַח שְׁלוּחִים לְבַשְּׂרוֹ: **אֶל עִיר מוֹאָב.** אֶל מֶטְרוֹפּוֹלִין שֶׁלּוֹ, עִיר הַחֲשׁוּבָה שֶׁלּוֹ, לוֹמַר: רְאֵה מָה אֵלּוּ מְבַקְשִׁים לַעֲקֹר:

לז) **הַאֻמְנָם לֹא אוּכַל כַּבְּדֶךָ.** נִתְנַבֵּא שֶׁסּוֹפוֹ לָצֵאת מֵעִמּוֹ בְּקָלוֹן:

לט) **קִרְיַת חֻצוֹת.** עִיר מְלֵאָה שְׁוָקִים אֲנָשִׁים נָשִׁים וָטַף בְּחוּצוֹתֶיהָ, לוֹמַר: רְאֵה וְרַחֵם שֶׁלֹּא יֵעָקְרוּ אֵלּוּ:

מ) **בָּקָר וָצֹאן.** דָּבָר מוּעָט, בָּקָר אֶחָד וְצֹאן אֶחָד בִּלְבַד:

מא) **בָּמוֹת בָּעַל.** כְּתַרְגּוּמוֹ: "לְרָמַת דַּחַלְתֵּיהּ", שֵׁם עֲבוֹדָה זָרָה:

לב וַיֹּאמֶר אֵלָיו מַלְאַךְ יְהוָה עַל־מָה הִכִּיתָ אֶת־אֲתֹנְךָ זֶה שָׁלוֹשׁ רְגָלִים
לג הִנֵּה אָנֹכִי יָצָאתִי לְשָׂטָן כִּי־יָרַט הַדֶּרֶךְ לְנֶגְדִּי: וַתִּרְאַנִי הָאָתוֹן וַתֵּט
לְפָנַי זֶה שָׁלֹשׁ רְגָלִים אוּלַי נָטְתָה מִפָּנַי כִּי עַתָּה גַּם־אֹתְכָה הָרַגְתִּי
לד וְאוֹתָהּ הֶחֱיֵיתִי: וַיֹּאמֶר בִּלְעָם אֶל־מַלְאַךְ יְהוָה חָטָאתִי כִּי לֹא יָדַעְתִּי
לה כִּי אַתָּה נִצָּב לִקְרָאתִי בַּדָּרֶךְ וְעַתָּה אִם־רַע בְּעֵינֶיךָ אָשׁוּבָה לִּי: וַיֹּאמֶר
מַלְאַךְ יְהוָה אֶל־בִּלְעָם לֵךְ עִם־הָאֲנָשִׁים וְאֶפֶס אֶת־הַדָּבָר אֲשֶׁר־
לו אֲדַבֵּר אֵלֶיךָ אֹתוֹ תְדַבֵּר וַיֵּלֶךְ בִּלְעָם עִם־שָׂרֵי בָלָק: וַיִּשְׁמַע בָּלָק
כִּי־בָא בִלְעָם וַיֵּצֵא לִקְרָאתוֹ אֶל־עִיר מוֹאָב אֲשֶׁר עַל־גְּבוּל אַרְנֹן
לז אֲשֶׁר בִּקְצֵה הַגְּבוּל: וַיֹּאמֶר בָּלָק אֶל־בִּלְעָם הֲלֹא שָׁלֹחַ שָׁלַחְתִּי אֵלֶיךָ
לח לִקְרֹא־לָךְ לָמָּה לֹא־הָלַכְתָּ אֵלָי הַאֻמְנָם לֹא אוּכַל כַּבְּדֶךָ: וַיֹּאמֶר
בִּלְעָם אֶל־בָּלָק הִנֵּה־בָאתִי אֵלֶיךָ עַתָּה הֲיָכֹל אוּכַל דַּבֵּר מְאוּמָה
לט הַדָּבָר אֲשֶׁר יָשִׂים אֱלֹהִים בְּפִי אֹתוֹ אֲדַבֵּר: וַיֵּלֶךְ בִּלְעָם עִם־בָּלָק רביעי /ששי/
מ וַיָּבֹאוּ קִרְיַת חֻצוֹת: וַיִּזְבַּח בָּלָק בָּקָר וָצֹאן וַיְשַׁלַּח לְבִלְעָם וְלַשָּׂרִים
מא אֲשֶׁר אִתּוֹ: וַיְהִי בַבֹּקֶר וַיִּקַּח בָּלָק אֶת־בִּלְעָם וַיַּעֲלֵהוּ בָּמוֹת בָּעַל
כג א וַיַּרְא מִשָּׁם קְצֵה הָעָם: וַיֹּאמֶר בִּלְעָם אֶל־בָּלָק בְּנֵה־לִי בָזֶה שִׁבְעָה

אונקלוס

לב וַאֲמַר לֵיהּ מַלְאֲכָא דַייָ, עַל מָא, מְחֵיתָא יָת אֲתָנָךְ, דְּנַן תְּלָת זִמְנִין, הָא אֲנָא נְפָקִית לְשָׂטָן, אֲרֵי גְּלֵי קֳדָמַי דְּאַתְּ רָעֵי לְמֵיזַל בְּאוֹרְחָא לְקִבְלִי: לג וַחֲזַתְנִי אֲתָנָא, וּסְטַת מִן קֳדָמַי, דְּנַן תְּלָת זִמְנִין, אִלּוּ פּוֹן לָא סְטַת מִן קֳדָמַי, אֲרֵי כְעַן, אַף יָתָךְ קְטָלִית וְיָתַהּ קַיֵּימִית: לד וַאֲמַר בִּלְעָם, לְמַלְאֲכָא דַייָ חַבִית, אֲרֵי לָא יְדַעִית, אֲרֵי אַתְּ, מְעַתַּד לִקְדָמוּתִי בְּאוֹרְחָא, וּכְעַן, אִם בִּישׁ בְּעֵינָךְ אֲתוּב לִי: לה וַאֲמַר מַלְאֲכָא דַייָ לְבִלְעָם, אִיזֵיל עִם גֻּבְרַיָּא, וּבְרַם, יָת פִּתְגָּמָא, דַּאֲמַלֵּיל עִמָּךְ יָתֵיהּ תְּמַלֵּיל, וַאֲזַל בִּלְעָם עִם רַבְרְבֵי בָלָק: לו וּשְׁמַע בָּלָק אֲרֵי אֲתָא בִלְעָם, וּנְפַק לְקַדָּמוּתֵיהּ לְקַרְתָּא דְּמוֹאָב, דְּעַל תְּחוּם אַרְנוֹן, דְּבִסְטַר תְּחוּמָא: לז וַאֲמַר בָּלָק לְבִלְעָם, הֲלָא מִשְׁלַח שְׁלַחִית לְוָתָךְ לְמִקְרֵי לָךְ, לְמָא לָא אֲתֵיתָא לְוָתִי, הַבְקֻשְׁטָא הֲוֵיתָא אָמַר, לֵית אֲנָא יָכֵיל לְיַקָּרוּתָךְ: לח וַאֲמַר בִּלְעָם לְבָלָק, הָא אֲתֵיתִי לְוָתָךְ, כְּעַן, הֲמֵיכַל יָכֵילְנָא לְמַלָּלָא מִדְּעַם, פִּתְגָּמָא, דִּישַׁוֵּי יְיָ, בְּפֻמִּי יָתֵיהּ אֲמַלֵּיל: לט וַאֲזַל בִּלְעָם עִם בָּלָק, וְאַעֲלֵיהּ לְקִרְיַת מַחְוְזוֹהִי: מ וּנְכַס בָּלָק תּוֹרִין וְעָן, וְשַׁלַּח לְבִלְעָם, וּלְרַבְרְבַיָּא דְּעִמֵּיהּ: מא וַהֲוָה בְצַפְרָא, וּדְבַר בָּלָק יָת בִּלְעָם, וְאַסְּקֵיהּ לְרָמַת דַּחַלְתֵּיהּ, וַחֲזָא מִתַּמָּן קְצָת מִן עַמָּא: כג א וַאֲמַר בִּלְעָם לְבָלָק, בְּנֵי לִי הָכָא שִׁבְעָא

2 and seven rams." Balak did as Bilam said, and Balak and Bilam offered a bull
3 and a ram on each altar. Then Bilam said to Balak, "Stand by your offerings and
I will go; perhaps the Lord will come to meet me. Whatever He shows me, I
4 will tell you." And he went off alone. God met Bilam, who said to Him, "I have
5 prepared seven altars; on each altar I have offered a bull and a ram." And the
6 Lord put a word in Bilam's mouth, "Go back to Balak and say this." He went
back to him, and found him standing by his offering together with all the
7 princes of Moav. And Bilam took up his oracle and said: "Balak brought me
from Aram, the king of Moav from the eastern hills. 'Go: curse Yaakov for me;
8 go: denounce Israel.' How can I curse whom God has not cursed? How can I

רש״י

כג ג **אולי יקרה ה׳ לקראתי.** אינו רגיל לדבר עמי ביום: **וילך שפי.** כתרגומו: "יחידי", לשון שפי ושקט, שאין עמו אלא שתיקה:

ד **ויקר.** לשון עראי, לשון גנאי, לשון טומאת קרי, כלומר בקושי ובבזיון, ולא היה נגלה עליו ביום אלא בשביל להראות חבתן של ישראל: **את שבעת המזבחת.** 'שבעה מזבחות ערכתי' אין כתיב כאן אלא "את שבעת המזבחות", אמר לפניו: אבותיהם של אלו בנו לפניך שבעה מזבחות, ואני ערכתי כנגד כלן. אברהם בנה ארבעה: "ויבן שם מזבח לה׳ הנראה אליו" (בראשית יב, ז), "ויעתק משם ההרה" וגו׳ (שם פסוק ח), "ויאהל אברם" וגו׳ (שם יג, יח), ואחד בהר המוריה (שם כב, ט); ויצחק בנה אחד, "ויבן שם מזבח וגו׳ ויכרו שם עבדי יצחק באר" (שם כו, כה). ויעקב בנה שנים: אחד בשכם (שם לג, כ) ואחד בבית אל (שם לה, ז): **ואעל פר ואיל במזבח.** ואברהם לא העלה אלא איל אחד:

ז **ארה לי יעקב ולכה זעמה ישראל.** בשני שמותיהם אמר לו לקללם, שמא אחד מהם אינו מבהק:

ח **מה אקב לא קבה אל.** כשהיו ראויים להתקלל לא נתקללו, כשהזכיר אביהם את עוונם: "כי באפם הרגו איש" (בראשית מט, ו), לא קלל אלא אפם, שנאמר: "ארור אפם" (שם פסוק ז), כשנכנס אביהם במרמה אצל אביו היה ראוי להתקלל; מה נאמר שם – "גם ברוך יהיה" (שם כז, לג). במברכים נאמר: "אלה יעמדו לברך את העם" (דברים כז, יב), במקללים לא נאמר: 'ואלה יעמדו לקלל את העם', אלא "ואלה יעמדו על הקללה" (שם פסוק יג), לא רצה להזכיר עליהם שם קללה: **לא זעם ה׳.** אני אין כחי אלא שאני יודע לכוין השעה שהקדוש ברוך הוא כועס בה, והוא לא כעס כל הימים הללו שבאתי אליך, וזהו שנאמר: "עמי זכר נא מה יעץ וגו׳ ומה ענה אתו בלעם וגו׳ למען דעת צדקות ה׳" (מיכה ו, ה):

the nations, says the Lord of Hosts. Yet you desecrate it. (Mal. 1:11–12)

Why then choose Israel? Moshe is to answer explicitly: "The Lord your God chose not to listen to Bilam; the Lord your God turned the curse into a blessing for you – *because the Lord your God loves you*" (Deut. 23:6).

God is often exasperated by Israel's conduct, but He cannot relinquish that love for them. Where in the Torah does God express this love? In the blessings of Bilam. That is where He gives voice to His feelings for this people. "Who can number the dust of Yaakov, count even a fourth of Israel?" (Num. 23:10). "A people – see – rises like a lioness, lifts itself up like a lion" (23:24). "How good are your tents, Yaakov, your homes, O Israel!" (24:5). These famous words are not Bilam's. They are God's – the most eloquent expression of His love for this small, otherwise undistinguished people. Bilam, the pagan prophet, is the most unlikely vehicle for God's blessings. But that is God's way. He chose an aged, infertile couple to be the grandparents of the Jewish people. He chose a man who couldn't speak to be the mouthpiece of His word. He chose Bilam, an indifferent man in the service of a hateful one, to express His love.

That is what the story is about: not Balak, or Bilam, or Moav, or Midyan, or what happened next. It is about God's love for a people, their strength, resilience, their willingness to be different, their family life (tents, homes), and their ability to outlive empires. Bilam's poetry bears a message rarely so clearly conveyed in prose. *Love can turn curses into blessings. Love heals the wounds of the world.*

ב מִזְבְּחֹת וְהָכֵן לִי בָּזֶה שִׁבְעָה פָרִים וְשִׁבְעָה אֵילִים: וַיַּעַשׂ בָּלָק
ג כַּאֲשֶׁר דִּבֶּר בִּלְעָם וַיַּעַל בָּלָק וּבִלְעָם פָּר וָאַיִל בַּמִּזְבֵּחַ: וַיֹּאמֶר בִּלְעָם
לְבָלָק הִתְיַצֵּב עַל־עֹלָתֶךָ וְאֵלְכָה אוּלַי יִקָּרֵה יהוה לִקְרָאתִי וּדְבַר
ד מַה־יַּרְאֵנִי וְהִגַּדְתִּי לָךְ וַיֵּלֶךְ שֶׁפִי: וַיִּקָּר אֱלֹהִים אֶל־בִּלְעָם וַיֹּאמֶר
ה אֵלָיו אֶת־שִׁבְעַת הַמִּזְבְּחֹת עָרַכְתִּי וָאַעַל פָּר וָאַיִל בַּמִּזְבֵּחַ: וַיָּשֶׂם
ו יהוה דָּבָר בְּפִי בִלְעָם וַיֹּאמֶר שׁוּב אֶל־בָּלָק וְכֹה תְדַבֵּר: וַיָּשָׁב אֵלָיו
ז וְהִנֵּה נִצָּב עַל־עֹלָתוֹ הוּא וְכָל־שָׂרֵי מוֹאָב: וַיִּשָּׂא מְשָׁלוֹ וַיֹּאמַר מִן־
אֲרָם יַנְחֵנִי בָלָק מֶלֶךְ־מוֹאָב מֵהַרְרֵי־קֶדֶם לְכָה אָרָה־לִּי יַעֲקֹב וּלְכָה
ח זֹעֲמָה יִשְׂרָאֵל: מָה אֶקֹּב לֹא קַבֹּה אֵל וּמָה אֶזְעֹם לֹא זָעַם יהוה:

אונקלוס

מַדְבְּחִין, וְאַתְקֵין לִי הָכָא, שִׁבְעָא תוֹרִין וְשִׁבְעָא דִכְרִין: ב וַעֲבַד
בָּלָק, כְּמָא דְּמַלֵּיל בִּלְעָם, וְאַסֵּיק בָּלָק וּבִלְעָם, תּוֹר וּדְכַר עַל כָּל
מַדְבַּח: ג וַאֲמַר בִּלְעָם לְבָלָק, אִתְעַתַּד עַל עֲלָתָךְ, וַאֲהָךְ, מָאִם,
יְעָרַע מֵימַר מִן קֳדָם יי לְקַדָּמוּתִי, וּפִתְגָּמָא דְּיִחַזֵּינַנִי וַאֲחַוֵּי לָךְ,
וַאֲזַל יְחִידִי: ד וְעָרַע מֵימַר מִן קֳדָם יי בְּבִלְעָם, וַאֲמַר קֳדָמוֹהִי,
יָת שִׁבְעָא מַדְבְּחִין סַדָּרִית, וְאַסֵּיקִית, תּוֹר וּדְכַר עַל כָּל מַדְבַּח:
ה וְשַׁוִּי יי, פִּתְגָּמָא בְּפֻמָּא דְבִלְעָם, וַאֲמַר, תּוּב לְוָת בָּלָק וּכְדֵין
תְּמַלֵּיל: ו וְתָב לְוָתֵיהּ, וְהָא מְעַתַּד עַל עֲלָתֵיהּ, הוּא וְכָל רַבְרְבֵי
מוֹאָב: ז וּנְטַל מַתְלֵיהּ וַאֲמַר, מִן אֲרָם, דַּבְּרַנִי בָלָק מַלְכָּא דְמוֹאָב
מִטּוּרֵי מַדִּנְחָא, אֵיתָא לוּט לִי יַעֲקֹב, וְאֵיתָא תָּרֵיךְ לִי יִשְׂרָאֵל:
ח מָא אֲלוּטֵיהּ, דְּלָא לָטֵיהּ אֵל, וּמָא אֲתָרְכֵיהּ, דְּלָא תָּרְכֵיהּ יי:

BILAM'S BLESSINGS

God puts into Bilam's mouth the extraordinary poetry that makes this among the most lyrical passages in the Torah. Why? All He really needs Bilam to say – and Bilam does eventually say it (Num. 24:9) – is the promise He gave to Avraham: "I will bless those who bless you, and those who curse you I will curse" (Gen. 12:3). In Bilam's blessings, the Israelites are rescued from a danger they know nothing about by a deliverance they know nothing about. Even Moshe would not know what had happened, were God not to tell him. Yet the story leaves a deep impression. Moshe will remind the people of it in Deuteronomy 23:4–5. Yehoshua, at Gilgal, giving an abridged summary of Jewish history, is to single out this event for attention (Josh. 24:9–10). At the culmination of the reforms instituted by Ezra and Neḥemya after the Babylonian exile, Neḥemya reminds the people that an Amonite or Moabite may not enter "the congregation of God" because they "hired Bilam to curse them" (Neh. 13:2). Why the resonance of an event that seemingly had no impact on any of the parties involved (see Num. 25:1 and note there) and made no difference to what happened thereafter?

The answer may lie in the very misdemeanors that precede and follow the story. God has threatened twice to destroy the people, after the golden calf and the episode of the spies. Toward the end of our *parasha*, He sends a plague against them. A generation has passed in the desert. This is the new generation in which all the hopes of the future are invested. Yet they too stumble at the first fence, fall in the first trial. Malakhi, last of the prophets, speaks aptly:

> From one end of the earth to the other, My name is great among the nations. Incense is offered in My name, a pure offering everywhere, for My name is great among

9 denounce whom the LORD has not denounced? From the tops of crags I see
him; from the hills I gaze down: a people that dwells alone; not reckoning itself
10 among nations. Who can number the dust of Yaakov, count even a fourth of
11 Israel? Let me die the death of the upright, and let me end be like his." And
Balak said to Bilam, "What have you done to me? I brought you to curse my
12 enemies, and you have blessed them." He answered, "Am I not obliged to speak
13 strictly the words the LORD puts in my mouth?" Then Balak said to him, "Come HAMISHI
with me to another place where you will see them. You will see only part of
14 them; you will not see them all. Curse them for me from there." He took him
to the field of Tzofim, to the top of Pisga. He built seven altars and on each altar

רש״י

ט **כִּי מֵרֹאשׁ צֻרִים אֶרְאֶנּוּ.** אֲנִי מִסְתַּכֵּל בְּרֵאשִׁיתָם וּבִתְחִלַּת שָׁרְשֵׁיהֶם, וַאֲנִי רוֹאֶה אוֹתָם מְיֻסָּדִים וַחֲזָקִים כְּצוּרִים וּגְבָעוֹת הַלָּלוּ, עַל יְדֵי אָבוֹת וְאִמָּהוֹת: **הֶן עָם לְבָדָד יִשְׁכֹּן.** הוּא אֲשֶׁר זָכוּ לוֹ אֲבוֹתָיו לִשְׁכֹּן בָּדָד, כְּתַרְגּוּמוֹ: **וּבַגּוֹיִם לֹא יִתְחַשָּׁב.** כְּתַרְגּוּמוֹ, לֹא יִהְיוּ נַעֲשִׂין כָּלָה עִם שְׁאָר הָאֻמּוֹת, שֶׁנֶּאֱמַר: "כִּי אֶעֱשֶׂה כָלָה בְּכָל הַגּוֹיִם" וְגוֹ' (ירמיה ל, יא), אֵינָן נִמְנִין עִם הַשְּׁאָר. דָּבָר אַחֵר, כְּשֶׁהֵן שְׂמֵחִין אֵין אֻמָּה שְׂמֵחָה עִמָּהֶם, שֶׁנֶּאֱמַר: "ה' בָּדָד יַנְחֶנּוּ" (דברים לב, יב). וּכְשֶׁהָאֻמּוֹת בְּטוֹבָה הֵם אוֹכְלִין עִם כָּל אֶחָד וְאֶחָד וְאֵין עוֹלֶה לָהֶם מִן הַחֶשְׁבּוֹן, וְזֶהוּ: "וּבַגּוֹיִם לֹא יִתְחַשָּׁב":

י **מִי מָנָה עֲפַר יַעֲקֹב וְגוֹ'.** כְּתַרְגּוּמוֹ: "דַּעְדְּקַיָּא דְּבֵית יַעֲקֹב כּוּ' מֵאַרְבַּע מַשִּׁרְיָתָא" מֵאַרְבָּעָה דְּגָלִים. דָּבָר אַחֵר, "עֲפַר יַעֲקֹב", אֵין חֶשְׁבּוֹן בַּמִּצְוֹת שֶׁהֵם מְקַיְּמִין בֶּעָפָר: "לֹא תַחֲרֹשׁ בְּשׁוֹר וּבַחֲמֹר" (דברים כב, י), "לֹא תִזְרַע כִּלְאָיִם" (ויקרא יט, יט), אֵפֶר פָּרָה (לעיל יט, ט) וַעֲפַר סוֹטָה (לעיל ה, יז) וְכַיּוֹצֵא בָּהֶם: **וּמִסְפָּר אֶת רֹבַע יִשְׂרָאֵל.** רְבִיעוֹתֵיהֶן, זֶרַע הַיּוֹצֵא מִן הַתַּשְׁמִישׁ שֶׁלָּהֶם: **תָּמֹת נַפְשִׁי מוֹת יְשָׁרִים.** שֶׁבָּהֶם:

יג **וְקָבְנוֹ לִי.** לְשׁוֹן צִוּוּי, קַלְּלֵהוּ לִי:

יד **שְׂדֵה צֹפִים.** מָקוֹם גָּבוֹהַּ הָיָה, שֶׁשָּׁם הַצּוֹפֶה עוֹמֵד לִשְׁמֹר אִם יָבֹא חַיִל עַל הָעִיר: **רֹאשׁ הַפִּסְגָּה.** בִּלְעָם לֹא הָיָה קוֹסֵם כְּבָלָק, רָאָה בָלָק שֶׁעֲתִידָה פִּרְצָה לְהִפָּרֵץ בְּיִשְׂרָאֵל מִשָּׁם, שֶׁשָּׁם מֵת מֹשֶׁה, כַּסָּבוּר שֶׁשָּׁם תָּחוּל עֲלֵיהֶם הַקְּלָלָה וְזוֹ הִיא הַפִּרְצָה שֶׁאֲנִי רוֹאֶה:

nuance between "people" (*am*) and "nation" (*goy*) – or as we might say nowadays, "society" and "state" (commentary on Num. 23:9). Israel uniquely became a society before it was a state. It had laws before it had a land. It was a people – a group bound together by a common code and culture – before it was a nation, that is, a political entity.

Jews, certainly from the Babylonian exile onward, had none of the conventional attributes of a nation. They did not live in the same land. Some lived in Israel, others in Babylon, yet others in Egypt. Later they would be scattered throughout the world. They did not share a language of everyday speech. There were many Jewish vernaculars. They did not live under the same political dispensation. They did not share the same cultural environment. Nor did they experience the same fate. Despite all their many differences though, they always saw themselves and were seen by others as one nation: the world's first, and for long the world's only, global people.

What makes Jews "a people that dwells alone, not reckoning itself among nations" is that their nationhood is not a matter of geography, politics, or ethnicity. It is a matter of religious vocation as God's covenant partners, summoned to be a living example of a nation among the nations made distinctive by its faith and way of life. Israel's strength lies not in nationalism but in building a society based on justice and human dignity.

This verse, then, expresses the uniqueness of the Jewish people – its isolation on the one hand, its defiance and resilience on the other. Though it has faced opposition and persecution from some of the greatest superpowers the world has ever known, it has so far outlived them all.

ט כִּי־מֵרֹאשׁ צֻרִים אֶרְאֶנּוּ וּמִגְּבָעוֹת אֲשׁוּרֶנּוּ הֶן־עָם לְבָדָד יִשְׁכֹּן וּבַגּוֹיִם
י לֹא יִתְחַשָּׁב: מִי מָנָה עֲפַר יַעֲקֹב וּמִסְפָּר אֶת־רֹבַע יִשְׂרָאֵל תָּמֹת כ
יא נַפְשִׁי מוֹת יְשָׁרִים וּתְהִי אַחֲרִיתִי כָּמֹהוּ: וַיֹּאמֶר בָּלָק אֶל־בִּלְעָם מֶה
יב עָשִׂיתָ לִי לָקֹב אֹיְבַי לְקַחְתִּיךָ וְהִנֵּה בֵּרַכְתָּ בָרֵךְ: וַיַּעַן וַיֹּאמַר הֲלֹא
יג אֵת אֲשֶׁר יָשִׂים יהוה בְּפִי אֹתוֹ אֶשְׁמֹר לְדַבֵּר: וַיֹּאמֶר אֵלָיו בָּלָק לְךָ־ חמישי
נָּא אִתִּי אֶל־מָקוֹם אַחֵר אֲשֶׁר תִּרְאֶנּוּ מִשָּׁם אֶפֶס קָצֵהוּ תִרְאֶה וְכֻלּוֹ
יד לֹא תִרְאֶה וְקָבְנוֹ־לִי מִשָּׁם: וַיִּקָּחֵהוּ שְׂדֵה צֹפִים אֶל־רֹאשׁ הַפִּסְגָּה

אונקלוס

ט אֲרֵי מֵרֵישׁ טוּרַיָּא חֲזֵיתֵיהּ, וּמֵרָמָתָא סְכֵיתֵיהּ, הָא עַמָּא בִּלְחוֹדֵיהוֹן
עֲתִידִין דְּיַחְסְנוּן עָלְמָא, וּבְעַמְמַיָּא לָא יִתְדָּנוּן גְּמִירָא: י מָאן יִכּוֹל
לְמִמְנֵי דַעְדְקַיָּא דְּבֵית יַעֲקֹב, דַּאֲמִיר עֲלֵיהוֹן יִסְגּוֹן כְּעַפְרָא דְאַרְעָא,
אוֹ חֲדָא מֵאַרְבַּע מַשְׁרְיָתָא דְּיִשְׂרָאֵל, תְּמוּת נַפְשִׁי מוֹתָא דְקַשִּׁיטוֹהִי,
וִיהֵי סוֹפִי כְּוָתְהוֹן: יא וַאֲמַר בָּלָק לְבִלְעָם, מָא עֲבַדְתְּ לִי, לְמִלַּט
סָנְאַי דְּבַרְתָּךְ, וְהָא בָרָכָא מְבָרֵיכְתְּ לְהוֹן: יב וַאֲתֵיב וַאֲמַר, הֲלָא, יָת
דִּישַׁוֵּי יי בְּפֻמִּי, יָתֵיהּ אֶטַּר לְמַלָּלָא: יג וַאֲמַר לֵיהּ בָּלָק, אִיתָא כְעַן
עִמִּי, לַאֲתַר אָחֳרָן דְּתִחְזֵינֵיהּ מִתַּמָּן, לְחוֹד קְצָתֵיהּ תִּחְזֵי, וְכֻלֵּיהּ לָא
תִחְזֵי, וּתְלוּטֵיהּ לִי מִתַּמָּן: יד וְדַבְּרֵיהּ לַחֲקַל סָכוּתָא, לְרֵישׁ רָמָתָא,

23:9 עָם לְבָדָד יִשְׁכֹּן *A people that dwells alone* – This is a very ambiguous blessing. Being alone, from a Torah perspective, is not a good thing. The first time the words "not good" appear in the Torah is in the verse "It is not good for man to be alone" (Gen. 2:18). The second time is when Moshe's father-in-law Yitro sees him leading alone and says, "What you are doing is not good" (Ex. 18:17). We cannot live and thrive alone. Isolation is not a blessing – quite the opposite.

The word *badad* appears in two other profoundly negative contexts. First is the case of the leper: "He shall live apart; outside the camp shall be his dwelling" (Lev. 13:46). The second is the opening line of the book of Lamentations, "How the city that overflowed with people sits alone" (Lam. 1:1). The only context in which *badad* has a positive sense is when it is applied to God (Deut. 32:12), for obvious theological reasons. In the Rabbis' view, "a people that dwells alone" eventually became not a blessing but a curse.

What is more, "a people that dwells alone" risks turning from an ambiguous prophecy to a self-fulfilling one. Why bother to make friends and allies if you know in advance that you will fail? Those who take refuge in solitude compound their problems rather than solving them.

Nowhere in Tanakh are we told that it will be the fate of Israel, or Jews, to be hated. To the contrary, the prophets foresaw that there would come a time when the nations would turn to Israel for inspiration. Isolation may at times be the Jewish condition, but it is not the Jewish vocation. We must treat this pronouncement with caution. It is Bilam's curse, not God's blessing.

23:9 וּבַגּוֹיִם לֹא יִתְחַשָּׁב *Not reckoning itself among nations* – Ibn Ezra interprets this verse as meaning that unlike all other nations, Jews, even when they are a minority in a non-Jewish culture, will not assimilate. Ramban says that their culture and creed will remain pure, not a cosmopolitan mix of multiple traditions and nationalities. Netziv gives the sharp interpretation, clearly directed against the Jews of his time, that "if Jews live distinctive and apart from others they will dwell safely, but if they seek to emulate 'the nations' they 'will not be reckoned' as anything special at all." Rabbi Samson Raphael Hirsch offered a fine insight by focusing on the

▶

15 offered a bull and a ram. Then Bilam said to Balak, "Stand here beside your
16 offering, while I seek a meeting there." The LORD met Bilam and put a word in
17 his mouth. "Go back to Balak," He said, "and tell him this." He came to him and
found him standing by his offering together with the princes of Moav. Balak
18 asked him, "What did the LORD say?" So he took up his oracle and said: "Stand
19 up, Balak, listen; pay attention, son of Tzipor. Not man is God, to lie; no mortal,
to change His mind. Would He speak and not fulfill, would He promise and
20 21 not keep? I received an order to bless. He has blessed; I cannot revoke it. He
has glimpsed no wrong in Yaakov, He has seen no sin in Israel. The LORD their
22 God is with them, in them the King's horn blasts sounds. God, who freed them
23 from Egypt, is like the oryx's proud horn for them. There is no divination over

רש״י

טו **אִקָּרֶה כֹּה.** מֵאֵת הַקָּדוֹשׁ בָּרוּךְ הוּא. 'אִקָּרֶה' לְשׁוֹן אֶתְפַּעֵל:

טז **וַיָּשֶׂם דָּבָר בְּפִיו.** וּמָה הָיְתָה הַשִּׂימָה הַזֹּאת, וּמֶה חָסֵר הַמִּקְרָא בְּאָמְרוֹ: "שׁוּב אֶל בָּלָק וְכֹה תְדַבֵּר"? אֶלָּא כְּשֶׁהָיָה שׁוֹמֵעַ שֶׁאֵינוֹ נִרְשֶׁה לְקַלֵּל, אָמַר: מָה אֲנִי חוֹזֵר אֵצֶל בָּלָק לְצַעֲרוֹ, וְנָתַן לוֹ הַקָּדוֹשׁ בָּרוּךְ הוּא רֶסֶן וְחַכָּה בְּפִיו כְּאָדָם הַפּוֹקֵס בְּהֵמָה בְּחַכָּה לְהוֹלִיכָהּ אֶל אֲשֶׁר יִרְצֶה, אָמַר לוֹ: עַל כָּרְחֲךָ תָּשׁוּב אֶל בָּלָק:

יז **וְשָׂרֵי מוֹאָב אִתּוֹ.** וּלְמַעְלָה הוּא אוֹמֵר: "וְכָל שָׂרֵי מוֹאָב" (לעיל פסוק ו), כֵּיוָן שֶׁרָאוּ שֶׁאֵין בּוֹ תִּקְוָה הָלְכוּ לָהֶם מִקְצָתָם, וְלֹא נִשְׁאֲרוּ אֶלָּא מִקְצָתָם: **מַה דִּבֶּר ה׳.** לְשׁוֹן צְחוֹק הוּא זֶה, כְּלוֹמַר אֵינְךָ בִּרְשׁוּתְךָ:

יח **קוּם בָּלָק.** כֵּיוָן שֶׁרָאָהוּ מְצַחֵק בּוֹ, נִתְכַּוֵּן לְצַעֲרוֹ: עֲמֹד עַל רַגְלֶיךָ, אֵינְךָ רַשַּׁאי לֵישֵׁב וַאֲנִי שָׁלוּחַ אֵלֶיךָ בִּשְׁלִיחוּתוֹ שֶׁל מָקוֹם: **בְּנוֹ צִפֹּר.** לְשׁוֹן מִקְרָא הוּא כֵּן, כְּמוֹ: "חַיְתוֹ יָעַר" (תהלים נ, י), "וְחַיְתוֹ אֶרֶץ" (בראשית א, כד), "לְמַעְיְנוֹ מָיִם" (תהלים קיד, ח):

יט **לֹא אִישׁ אֵל וְגוֹ׳.** כְּבָר נִשְׁבַּע לָהֶם לַהֲבִיאָם וּלְהוֹרִישָׁם אֶרֶץ שִׁבְעָה עֲמָמִים, וְאַתָּה סָבוּר לַהֲמִיתָם בַּמִּדְבָּר? **הַהוּא אָמַר וְגוֹ׳.** בִּלְשׁוֹן תְּמִיהָ, וְתַרְגּוּמוֹ: "תָּיְבִין וּמִתְמַלְכִין", חוֹזְרִים וְנִמְלָכִין לַחֲזֹר בָּהֶם:

כ **הִנֵּה בָרֵךְ לָקָחְתִּי.** אַתָּה שׁוֹאֲלֵנִי: "מַה דִּבֶּר ה׳" (לעיל פסוק יז), קִבַּלְתִּי מִמֶּנּוּ לְבָרֵךְ אוֹתָם: **וּבֵרֵךְ וְלֹא אֲשִׁיבֶנָּה.** הוּא בֵּרַךְ אוֹתָם, וַאֲנִי לֹא אָשִׁיב אֶת בִּרְכָתוֹ: **וּבֵרֵךְ.** כְּמוֹ 'וּבֵרַךְ' וְכֵן הוּא גִּזְרַת רי״שׁ, כְּמוֹ: "אוֹיֵב חֵרֵף" (תהלים עד, יח) כְּמוֹ 'חֵרַף', וְכֵן: "וּבֹצֵעַ בֵּרֵךְ" (שם י, ג), הַמְהַלֵּל וּמְבָרֵךְ אֶת הַגּוֹזֵל וְאוֹמֵר לוֹ: אַל תִּירָא כִּי לֹא תֵעָנֵשׁ, שָׁלוֹם יִהְיֶה לָּךְ, מַרְגִּיז הוּא לְהַקָּדוֹשׁ בָּרוּךְ הוּא. וְאֵין לוֹמַר 'בֵּרֵךְ' שֵׁם דָּבָר, שֶׁאִם כֵּן הָיָה נָקוּד בְּפַתָּח קָטָן (סגול) וְטַעְמוֹ לְמַעְלָה, אֲבָל לְפִי שֶׁהוּא לְשׁוֹן פִּעֵל, הוּא נָקוּד קָמָץ קָטָן (צירי) וְטַעְמוֹ לְמַטָּה:

כא **לֹא הִבִּיט אָוֶן וְגוֹ׳.** כְּתַרְגּוּמוֹ. דָּבָר אַחֵר, אַחֲרֵי פְּשׁוּטוֹ הוּא נִדְרָשׁ מִדְרָשׁ נָאֶה: "לֹא הִבִּיט" הַקָּדוֹשׁ בָּרוּךְ הוּא אָוֶן שֶׁבְּיַעֲקֹב, שֶׁכְּשֶׁהֵן עוֹבְרִין עַל דְּבָרָיו, אֵינוֹ מְדַקְדֵּק אַחֲרֵיהֶם לְהִתְבּוֹנֵן בְּאוֹנִיּוֹת שֶׁלָּהֶם וּבַעֲמָלָן שֶׁהֵן עוֹבְרִין עַל דָּתוֹ: **עָמָל.** לְשׁוֹן עֲבֵרָה, כְּמוֹ: "הָרֹה עָמָל" (איוב טו, לה), "כִּי אַתָּה עָמָל וָכַעַס תַּבִּיט" (תהלים י, יד), לְפִי שֶׁהָעֲבֵרָה הִיא עָמָל לִפְנֵי הַמָּקוֹם: **ה׳ אֱלֹהָיו עִמּוֹ.** אֲפִלּוּ מַכְעִיסִין וּמַמְרִים לְפָנָיו אֵינוֹ זָז מִתּוֹכָן: **וּתְרוּעַת מֶלֶךְ בּוֹ.** לְשׁוֹן חִבָּה וְרֵעוּת, כְּמוֹ: "רֵעֶה דָוִד" (שמואל ב׳ טו, לז), אוֹהֵב דָּוִד, "וַתִּתְּנָהּ לְמֵרֵעֵהוּ" (שופטים טו, ו). וְכֵן תִּרְגֵּם אוּנְקְלוֹס: "וּשְׁכִינַת מַלְכְּהוֹן בֵּינֵיהוֹן":

כב **אֵל מוֹצִיאָם מִמִּצְרָיִם.** אַתָּה אָמַרְתָּ: "הִנֵּה עַם יָצָא מִמִּצְרַיִם" (לעיל כב, ה), לֹא יָצָא מֵעַצְמוֹ אֶלָּא הָאֱלֹהִים הוֹצִיאָם: **כְּתוֹעֲפֹת רְאֵם לוֹ.** כְּתֹקֶף רוּם וְגֹבַהּ שֶׁלּוֹ, וְכֵן: "וְכֶסֶף תּוֹעָפוֹת" (איוב כב, כה), לְשׁוֹן מָעוֹז הֵמָּה. וְאוֹמֵר אֲנִי שֶׁהוּא לְשׁוֹן: "וְעוֹף יְעוֹפֵף" (בראשית א, כ), הַמְעוֹפֵף בְּרוּם וָגֹבַהּ, וְתֹקֶף רַב הוּא זֶה, "וְתוֹעֲפֹת רְאֵם" עֲפִיפַת גֹּבַהּ. דָּבָר אַחֵר, "תּוֹעֲפֹת רְאֵם", תֹּקֶף רְאֵמִים, וְאָמְרוּ רַבּוֹתֵינוּ: אֵלּוּ הַשֵּׁדִים:

כג **כִּי לֹא נַחַשׁ בְּיַעֲקֹב.** כִּי רְאוּיִם הֵם לִבְרָכָה, שֶׁאֵין בָּהֶם מְנַחֲשִׁים וְקוֹסְמִים: **כָּעֵת יֵאָמֵר לְיַעֲקֹב וְגוֹ׳.** עוֹד עָתִיד לִהְיוֹת עֵת כָּעֵת הַזֹּאת אֲשֶׁר תִּגָּלֶה חִבָּתָן לְעֵין כֹּל, שֶׁהֵן יוֹשְׁבִין לְפָנָיו וְלוֹמְדִים תּוֹרָה מִפִּיו

has come directly from God – since there is nothing in Bilam's character and conduct that would explain it in any other way. Bilam is, if one can say such a thing, God's way of fulfilling Proverbs's principle: "Let another person praise you, not your own mouth; a stranger, not your own lips" (Prov. 27:2).

Bilam is the most unlikely messenger but the one who delivers the most beautiful of messages.

טו וַיִּבֶן שִׁבְעָה מִזְבְּחֹת וַיַּעַל פָּר וָאַיִל בַּמִּזְבֵּחַ: וַיֹּאמֶר אֶל־בָּלָק הִתְיַצֵּב
טז כֹּה עַל־עֹלָתֶךָ וְאָנֹכִי אִקָּרֶה כֹּה: וַיִּקָּר יהוה אֶל־בִּלְעָם וַיָּשֶׂם דָּבָר
יז בְּפִיו וַיֹּאמֶר שׁוּב אֶל־בָּלָק וְכֹה תְדַבֵּר: וַיָּבֹא אֵלָיו וְהִנּוֹ נִצָּב עַל־עֹלָתוֹ
יח וְשָׂרֵי מוֹאָב אִתּוֹ וַיֹּאמֶר לוֹ בָּלָק מַה־דִּבֶּר יהוה: וַיִּשָּׂא מְשָׁלוֹ וַיֹּאמַר
יט קוּם בָּלָק וּשֲׁמָע הַאֲזִינָה עָדַי בְּנוֹ צִפֹּר: לֹא אִישׁ אֵל וִיכַזֵּב וּבֶן־אָדָם
כ וְיִתְנֶחָם הַהוּא אָמַר וְלֹא יַעֲשֶׂה וְדִבֶּר וְלֹא יְקִימֶנָּה: הִנֵּה בָרֵךְ לָקָחְתִּי
כא וּבֵרֵךְ וְלֹא אֲשִׁיבֶנָּה: לֹא־הִבִּיט אָוֶן בְּיַעֲקֹב וְלֹא־רָאָה עָמָל בְּיִשְׂרָאֵל
כב יהוה אֱלֹהָיו עִמּוֹ וּתְרוּעַת מֶלֶךְ בּוֹ: אֵל מוֹצִיאָם מִמִּצְרָיִם כְּתוֹעֲפֹת
כג רְאֵם לוֹ: כִּי לֹא־נַחַשׁ בְּיַעֲקֹב וְלֹא־קֶסֶם בְּיִשְׂרָאֵל כָּעֵת יֵאָמֵר לְיַעֲקֹב

אונקלוס

וּבְנָא שִׁבְעָא מַדְבְּחִין, וְאַסֵּיק, תּוֹר וּדְכַר עַל כָּל מַדְבְּחָא: טו וַאֲמַר לְבָלָק, אִתְעַתַּד הָכָא עַל עֲלָתָךְ, וַאֲנָא אִתְמְטֵי עַד כָּא: טז וְעָרַע מֵימַר מִן קֳדָם יי בְּבִלְעָם, וְשַׁוִּי פִּתְגָּמָא בְּפוּמֵּיהּ, וַאֲמַר, תּוּב לְוָת בָּלָק וּכְדֵין תְּמַלֵּיל: יז וַאֲתָא לְוָתֵיהּ, וְהָא מְעַתַּד עַל עֲלָתֵיהּ, וְרַבְרְבֵי מוֹאָב עִמֵּיהּ, וַאֲמַר לֵיהּ בָּלָק, מָא מַלֵּיל יי: יח וּנְטַל מַתְלֵיהּ וַאֲמַר, קוּם בָּלָק וּשְׁמַע, אַצֵּית לְמֵימְרִי בַּר צִפּוֹר: יט לָא כְמִלֵּי בְנֵי אֱנָשָׁא מֵימַר אֱלָהָא, בְּנֵי אֱנָשָׁא אָמְרִין וּמְכַדְּבִין, וְאַף לָא כְעוֹבָדֵי בְנֵי בִסְרָא דְּאִנּוּן גָּזְרִין לְמֶעְבַּד תָּיְבִין וּמִתְמַלְּכִין, הוּא אָמַר וְעָבֵיד, וְכָל מֵימְרֵיהּ מִתְקַיַּם: כ הָא בִרְכָן קַבֵּילִית אֲבָרְכִנֵּיהּ לְיִשְׂרָאֵל, וְלָא אָתֵיב בִּרְכְתִי מִנֵּיהּ: כא אִסְתַּכָּלִית וְלֵית פָּלְחֵי גִלּוּלִין בִּדְבֵית יַעֲקֹב, וְאַף לָא עָבְדֵי לֵיאוּת שְׁקַר בְּיִשְׂרָאֵל, מֵימְרָא דַיי אֱלָהֲהוֹן בְּסַעְדְּהוֹן, וּשְׁכִינַת מַלְכְּהוֹן בֵּינֵיהוֹן: כב אֵל דְּאַפֵּיקִנּוּן מִמִּצְרַיִם, תֻּקְפָּא וְרוּמָא דִּילֵיהּ: כג אֲרֵי לָא נַחֲשָׁיָא צָבַן דְּיֵיטַב לִדְבֵית יַעֲקֹב, וְאַף לָא קַסָּמַיָּא רָעַן בִּרְבוּת בֵּית יִשְׂרָאֵל, כְּעִדָּן, יִתְאֲמַר לְיַעֲקֹב

23:21 לֹא־רָאָה עָמָל בְּיִשְׂרָאֵל *He has seen no sin in Israel* – From the beginning of Exodus to the end of Numbers, not a word is spoken in praise of the Israelites – *except by Bilam*. Nor are these faint praises. This verse is a prime example, suggesting that the people are almost flawless. Who said these words? Ostensibly Bilam. But we know he is only speaking the words God put in his mouth. A comment in Midrash Rabba adds:

> It would have been appropriate for the reprimands [delivered to Israel] to be delivered by Bilam and the blessings by Moshe. However, if Bilam had spoken the reprimands, the Israelites would have said, "Our enemy is reprimanding us." And had Moshe delivered the blessings, the nations of the world would have said, "One who loves them is blessing them." Therefore, said the Holy One, blessed be He, "Let Moshe who loves them reprimand them, and let Bilam who hates them bless them, so that both the reprimands and the blessings make a clear impression on Israel." (Devarim Rabba 1:4)

When people say what they are expected to say, their words tend to be discounted. Friends praise and bless. Enemies criticize and curse. To make an impression, to be credible, the order had to be reversed.

Might this be the explanation for the remarkable fact that more than any other national literature, the Hebrew Bible records Israel's failings, its shortcomings, its sins, its faults? It is a literature of unparalleled self-criticism. Yet somehow, somewhere, the people must be assured that they are loved not just for their ancestors but for themselves.

Bilam is God's messenger delivering a love letter to His people in such a way as to leave no doubt that the message

Yaakov, no spell against Israel can hold. It will now be said of Yaakov, of Israel,
24 'See what God has done.' A people – see – rises like a lioness, lifts itself up like
a lion. It will not lie down until it eats its meat and drinks the blood of the slain."
25 Balak said to Bilam, "Do not curse or bless them." But Bilam answered, "Did I
26
27 not tell you, 'I must do whatever the LORD says'?" Then Balak said to Bilam, SHISHI /SHEVI'I/
"Come now and I will take you to another place. Perhaps God will deem it right
28 to let you curse them for me there." So Balak took Bilam to the top of Peor,
29 overlooking the wasteland. Bilam said to Balak, "Build me seven altars here
30 and prepare for me seven bulls and seven rams." Balak did as Bilam had said,
24 1 and offered a bull and a ram on each altar. When Bilam saw that it pleased the
LORD to bless the Israelites, he did not go as at other times to seek omens.
2 Instead, he turned toward the wilderness. And Bilam raised his eyes and saw
3 Israel encamped there tribe by tribe, and God's spirit came upon him. He took
up his oracle and said: "The word of Bilam, son of Beor; the word of the man

רש״י

וּמְחִזָּתָן לִפְנִים מִמַּלְאֲכֵי הַשָּׁרֵת, וְהֵם יִשְׁאֲלוּ לָהֶם: "מַה פָּעַל אֵל", וְזֶהוּ שֶׁנֶּאֱמַר: "וְהָיוּ עֵינֶיךָ רֹאוֹת אֶת מוֹרֶיךָ" (ישעיה ל, כ). דָּבָר אַחֵר, "יֵאָמֵר לְיַעֲקֹב" אֵינוֹ לְשׁוֹן עָתִיד אֶלָּא לְשׁוֹן הֹוֶה, אֵינָן צְרִיכִים לִמְנַחֵשׁ וְקוֹסֵם, כִּי בְּכָל עֵת שֶׁצָּרִיךְ לְהֵאָמֵר לְיַעֲקֹב וּלְיִשְׂרָאֵל מַה פָּעַל הַקָּדוֹשׁ בָּרוּךְ הוּא וּמַה גְּזֵרוֹתָיו בַּמָּרוֹם, אֵינָן מְנַחֲשִׁים וְקוֹסְמִים, אֶלָּא נֶאֱמָר לָהֶם עַל פִּי נְבִיאֵיהֶם מַה הִיא גְּזֵרַת הַמָּקוֹם, אוֹ אוּרִים וְתֻמִּים מַגִּידִים לָהֶם. וְאוּנְקְלוֹס לֹא תִּרְגֵּם כֵּן:

כד **הֵן עָם כְּלָבִיא יָקוּם וְגוֹ׳.** כְּשֶׁהֵן עוֹמְדִין מִשְּׁנָתָם שַׁחֲרִית הֵן מִתְגַּבְּרִים כְּלָבִיא וְכַאֲרִי לַחֲטֹף אֶת הַמִּצְוֹת, לִלְבֹּשׁ טַלִּית, לִקְרֹא אֶת שְׁמַע וּלְהָנִיחַ תְּפִלִּין: **לֹא יִשְׁכַּב.** בַּלַּיְלָה עַל מִטָּתוֹ עַד שֶׁהוּא אוֹכֵל וּמְחַבֵּל כָּל מַזִּיק הַבָּא לְטָרְפוֹ. כֵּיצַד? קוֹרֵא אֶת שְׁמַע עַל מִטָּתוֹ וּמַפְקִיד רוּחוֹ בְּיַד הַמָּקוֹם. בָּא מַחֲנֶה וְגַיִס לְהַזִּיקָם, הַקָּדוֹשׁ בָּרוּךְ הוּא שׁוֹמְרָם וְנִלְחָם מִלְחֲמוֹתֵיהֶם וּמַפִּילָם חֲלָלִים. דָּבָר אַחֵר, "הֵן עָם כְּלָבִיא יָקוּם" וְגוֹ׳, כְּתַרְגּוּמוֹ: **וְדַם חֲלָלִים יִשְׁתֶּה.** נִתְנַבֵּא שֶׁאֵין מֹשֶׁה מֵת עַד שֶׁיַּפִּיל מַלְכֵי מִדְיָן חֲלָלִים וְיֵהָרֵג הוּא עִמָּהֶם, שֶׁנֶּאֱמַר: "וְאֶת בִּלְעָם בֶּן בְּעוֹר הַקּוֹסֵם הָרְגוּ בְנֵי יִשְׂרָאֵל בַּחֶרֶב אֶל חַלְלֵיהֶם" (יהושע יג, כב):

כה **גַּם קֹב לֹא תִקֳּבֶנּוּ.** "גַּם" רִאשׁוֹן מוּסָף עַל "גַּם" הַשֵּׁנִי וְ"גַם" שֵׁנִי עַל "גַּם" רִאשׁוֹן, וְכֵן: "גַּם לִי גַּם לָךְ לֹא יִהְיֶה" (מלכים א׳ ג, כו), וְכֵן: "גַּם בָּחוּר גַּם בְּתוּלָה" (דברים לב, כה):

כז **וְקַבֹּתוֹ לִי.** אֵין זֶה לְשׁוֹן צִוּוּי כְּמוֹ "וְקָבְנוֹ" (לעיל פסוק יג), אֶלָּא לְשׁוֹן עָתִיד, אוּלַי יִישַׁר בְּעֵינָיו וְתִקְּבֶנּוּ לִי מִשָּׁם. מלדיר״ש לו״י בְּלַעַ״ז:

כח **רֹאשׁ הַפְּעוֹר.** קוֹסֵם גָּדוֹל הָיָה בָּלָק, וְרָאָה שֶׁהֵן עֲתִידִין לִלְקוֹת עַל יְדֵי פְעוֹר, וְלֹא הָיָה יוֹדֵעַ בַּמָּה. אָמַר: שֶׁמָּא הַקְּלָלָה תָּחוּל עֲלֵיהֶם מִשָּׁם. וְכֵן כָּל הַחוֹזִים בַּכּוֹכָבִים רוֹאִים וְאֵין יוֹדְעִין מָה רוֹאִים:

כד א **וַיַּרְא בִּלְעָם כִּי טוֹב וְגוֹ׳.** אָמַר: אֵינִי צָרִיךְ לִבְדֹּק עוֹד בְּהַקָּדוֹשׁ בָּרוּךְ הוּא, כִּי לֹא יַחְפֹּץ לְקַלְּלָם: **וְלֹא הָלַךְ כְּפַעַם בְּפַעַם.** כַּאֲשֶׁר עָשָׂה שְׁתֵּי פְעָמִים: **לִקְרַאת נְחָשִׁים.** לְנַחֵשׁ אוּלַי יִקָּרֶה ה׳ לִקְרָאתוֹ כִּרְצוֹנוֹ. אָמַר: רוֹצֶה וְלֹא רוֹצֶה לְקַלְּלָם, אַזְכִּיר עֲוֹנוֹתֵיהֶם, וְהַקְּלָלָה עַל הַזְכָּרַת עֲוֹנוֹתֵיהֶם תָּחוּל: **וַיָּשֶׁת אֶל הַמִּדְבָּר פָּנָיו.** כְּתַרְגּוּמוֹ:

ב **וַיִּשָּׂא בִלְעָם אֶת עֵינָיו.** בִּקֵּשׁ לְהַכְנִיס בָּהֶם עַיִן רָעָה. וַהֲרֵי יֵשׁ לְךָ שָׁלֹשׁ מִדּוֹתָיו: עַיִן רָעָה, וְרוּחַ גְּבוֹהָה וְנֶפֶשׁ רְחָבָה הָאֲמוּרִים לְמַעְלָה: **שֹׁכֵן לִשְׁבָטָיו.** רָאָה כָּל שֵׁבֶט וָשֵׁבֶט שׁוֹכֵן לְעַצְמוֹ וְאֵינָן מְעֹרָבִין, רָאָה שֶׁאֵין פִּתְחֵיהֶם מְכֻוָּנִין זֶה כְּנֶגֶד זֶה, שֶׁלֹּא יָצִיץ לְתוֹךְ אֹהֶל חֲבֵרוֹ: **וַתְּהִי עָלָיו רוּחַ אֱלֹהִים.** עָלָה בְלִבּוֹ שֶׁלֹּא יְקַלְּלֵם:

ג **בְּנוֹ בְעֹר.** כְּמוֹ: "לְמַעְיְנוֹ מָיִם" (תהלים קיד, ח). וּמִדְרַשׁ אַגָּדָה, שְׁנֵיהֶם

an eye made quiet by the power / of harmony, and the deep power of joy, / we see into the life of things" (Wordsworth, *Lines Composed a Few Miles Above Tintern Abbey*).

This is what Bilam experiences against his will. Far from the uproar of the camp, viewing it from above, he is "a man whose eye is opened." He sees Israel momentarily from the perspective of God, and cannot do otherwise than bless them.

כד וּלְיִשְׂרָאֵל מַה־פָּעַל אֵל: הֶן־עָם כְּלָבִיא יָקוּם וְכַאֲרִי יִתְנַשָּׂא לֹא יִשְׁכַּב
כה עַד־יֹאכַל טֶרֶף וְדַם־חֲלָלִים יִשְׁתֶּה: וַיֹּאמֶר בָּלָק אֶל־בִּלְעָם גַּם־קֹב
כו לֹא תִקֳּבֶנּוּ גַּם־בָּרֵךְ לֹא תְבָרְכֶנּוּ: וַיַּעַן בִּלְעָם וַיֹּאמֶר אֶל־בָּלָק הֲלֹא
כז דִּבַּרְתִּי אֵלֶיךָ לֵאמֹר כֹּל אֲשֶׁר־יְדַבֵּר יהוה אֹתוֹ אֶעֱשֶׂה: וַיֹּאמֶר בָּלָק ששי /שביעי/
אֶל־בִּלְעָם לְכָה־נָּא אֶקָּחֲךָ אֶל־מָקוֹם אַחֵר אוּלַי יִישַׁר בְּעֵינֵי הָאֱלֹהִים
כח וְקַבֹּתוֹ לִי מִשָּׁם: וַיִּקַּח בָּלָק אֶת־בִּלְעָם רֹאשׁ הַפְּעוֹר הַנִּשְׁקָף עַל־פְּנֵי
כט הַיְשִׁימֹן: וַיֹּאמֶר בִּלְעָם אֶל־בָּלָק בְּנֵה־לִי בָזֶה שִׁבְעָה מִזְבְּחֹת וְהָכֵן
ל לִי בָּזֶה שִׁבְעָה פָרִים וְשִׁבְעָה אֵילִים: וַיַּעַשׂ בָּלָק כַּאֲשֶׁר אָמַר בִּלְעָם
כד א וַיַּעַל פַּר וָאַיִל בַּמִּזְבֵּחַ: וַיַּרְא בִּלְעָם כִּי טוֹב בְּעֵינֵי יהוה לְבָרֵךְ אֶת־
יִשְׂרָאֵל וְלֹא־הָלַךְ כְּפַעַם־בְּפַעַם לִקְרַאת נְחָשִׁים וַיָּשֶׁת אֶל־הַמִּדְבָּר
ב פָּנָיו: וַיִּשָּׂא בִלְעָם אֶת־עֵינָיו וַיַּרְא אֶת־יִשְׂרָאֵל שֹׁכֵן לִשְׁבָטָיו וַתְּהִי
ג עָלָיו רוּחַ אֱלֹהִים: וַיִּשָּׂא מְשָׁלוֹ וַיֹּאמַר נְאֻם בִּלְעָם בְּנוֹ בְעֹר וּנְאֻם

אונקלוס

וּלְיִשְׂרָאֵל, מָא עֲבַד אֱלָהָא: כד הָא עַמָּא כְּלֵיתָא שָׁרֵי, וּכְאַרְיָא יִתְנַטַּל, לָא יִשְׁרֵי בְּאַרְעֵיהּ עַד דְּיִקְטוֹל קְטוֹל, וְנִכְסֵי עַמְמַיָּא יֵירַת: כה וַאֲמַר בָּלָק לְבִלְעָם, אַף מְלַט לָא תְלוּטִנּוּן, אַף בָּרָכָא לָא תְבָרֵיכִנּוּן: כו וַאֲתֵיב בִּלְעָם, וַאֲמַר לְבָלָק, הֲלָא, מַלֵּילִית עִמָּךְ לְמֵימַר, כֹּל, דִּימַלֵּיל יי יָתֵיהּ אַעֲבֵיד: כז וַאֲמַר בָּלָק לְבִלְעָם, אֵיתָא כְעַן אֲדַבְּרִנָּךְ, לַאֲתַר אָחֳרָן, מָאִם תְּהֵי רַעֲוָא מִן קֳדָם יי, וּתְלוּטֵיהּ לִי מִתַּמָּן: כח וּדְבַר בָּלָק יָת בִּלְעָם, רֵישׁ רָמְתָא, דְּמִסְתַּכְיָא עַל אַפֵּי בֵית יְשִׁימוֹן: כט וַאֲמַר בִּלְעָם לְבָלָק, בְּנֵי לִי הָכָא שִׁבְעָא מַדְבְּחִין, וְאַתְקֵין לִי הָכָא, שִׁבְעָא תוֹרִין וְשִׁבְעָא דִכְרִין: ל וַעֲבַד בָּלָק, כְּמָא דַּאֲמַר בִּלְעָם, וְאַסֵּיק, תּוֹר וּדְכַר עַל כָּל מַדְבַּח: כד א וַחֲזָא בִּלְעָם, אֲרֵי תָקִין, קֳדָם יי לְבָרָכָא יָת יִשְׂרָאֵל, וְלָא הֲלֵיךְ כִּזְמַן בִּזְמַן אֱלָהֵין לִקְדָמוּת נַחֲשַׁיָּא, וְשַׁוִּי לְמַדְבְּרָא אַפּוֹהִי: ב וּזְקַף בִּלְעָם יָת עֵינוֹהִי, וַחֲזָא יָת יִשְׂרָאֵל, שָׁרַן לְשִׁבְטֵיהוֹן, וּשְׁרַת עֲלוֹהִי רוּחַ נְבוּאָה מִן קֳדָם יי: ג וּנְטַל מַתְלֵיהּ וַאֲמַר, אֵימַר בִּלְעָם בַּר בְּעוֹר, וְאֵימַר

24:2 וַיִּשָּׂא בִלְעָם אֶת־עֵינָיו וַיַּרְא *Bilam raised his eyes and saw* – Blessing, prayer, is a way of seeing, not unlike the account Iris Murdoch gives of the aesthetic sense:

> I am looking out of my window in an anxious and resentful frame of mind, oblivious of my surroundings, brooding perhaps on some damage done to my prestige. Then suddenly I observe a hovering kestrel. In a moment, everything is altered. The brooding self with its hurt vanity has disappeared. There is nothing now but kestrel. And when I return to the thinking of the other matter it seems less important. (*The Sovereignty of Good*)

She calls this "unselfing," and sees it as essential to the moral life. This is what happens, or ought to happen, when we pray. The relentless first-person singular falls silent and we become aware that we are not the center of the universe. There is a reality outside. That is a moment of transformation. For a moment we still the clamor of desire and experience instead "that serene and blessed mood, / in which… with

▶

4 whose eye is opened. The word of one who hears God's speech, who sees a
5 vision of Shaddai, who falls, but with eyes unveiled. How good are your tents,
6 Yaakov, your homes, O Israel. Like palm groves stretching forth, like gardens by
7 the river, like aloes the LORD planted, like cedars by the waters. Water will drip
from his branches; his seed has abundant water; his king will be higher than
8 Agag, his kingdom exalted. God, who freed him from Egypt, is the oryx's proud
horn to him. He will devour enemy nations, break their bones, pierce them
9 with arrows. Like a lion he crouches, lies down, like a lioness; who dares to
10 rouse him? Blessing on all who bless you, on those who curse you, curse." Balak
was furious with Bilam. He struck his hands together. Balak said to Bilam, "I
summoned you to curse my enemies. Instead you have blessed them these
11 three times over. Now get away from here and go home. I said that I would
12 honor you, but the LORD has denied you all honor." Bilam replied to Balak,
13 "Did I not tell the messengers whom you sent to me, 'Even if Balak were to give

רש"י

היו גדולים מאבותיהם: בלק "בנו צפר" (לעיל כג, יח), אביו בנו הוא במלכות, ובלעם גדול מאביו בנביאות, מנה בן פרס היה: **שתם העין.** עינו נקורה ומוצאת לחוץ וחור שלה נראה פתוח. ולשון משנה הוא: "כדי שישתום ויסתום ויגוב" (עבודה זרה סט ע"א). ורבותינו אמרו: לפי שאמר: "ומספר את רבע ישראל" (לעיל כג, י) שהקדוש ברוך הוא יושב ומונה רביעותיהן של ישראל מתי תבוא טפה שנולד הצדיק ממנה, אמר בלבו, מי שהוא קדוש ומשרתיו קדושים יסתכל בדברים הללו, ועל דבר זה נסמית עינו של בלעם. ויש מפרשים "שתם העין" פתוח העין, כמו שתרגם אונקלוס, ועל שאמר "שתם העין" ולא אמר "שתם העינים" למדנו שסומא באחת מעיניו היה:

ד **נפל וגלוי עינים.** פשוטו כתרגומו, שאין נראה עליו אלא בלילה כשהוא שוכב. ומדרשו: כשהיה נגלה עליו לא היה בו כח לעמוד על רגליו ונופל על פניו, לפי שהיה ערל, ומאוס להיות נגלה עליו בקומה זקופה לפניו:

ה **מה טבו אהליך.** על שראה פתחיהם שאינן מכוונין זה מול זה: **משכנתיך.** חניותיך, כתרגומו. דבר אחר, "מה טבו אהליך", מה טבו אהל שילה ובית עולמים בישובן, שמקריבין בהן קרבנות לכפר עליכם: **משכנתיך.** אף כשהן חרבין, לפי שהן משכון עליהן וחרבנן כפרה על הנפשות, שנאמר: "כלה ה' את חמתו" (איכה ד, יא), ובמה כלה? "ויצת אש בציון":

ו **כנחלים נטיו.** שנארכו ונמשכו לנטות למרחוק. אמרו רבותינו: מברכותיו של אותו רשע אנו למדים מה היה בלבו לקללם כשאמר להשית אל המדבר פניו, וכשהפך המקום את פיו ברכם מעין אותם קללות שבקש לומר כו', כדאיתא ב'חלק' (סנהדרין קה ע"ב): **כאהלים.** כתרגומו, לשון "מר ואהלות" (תהלים מה, ט): **נטע ה'.** כגן עדן. לשון אחר, "כאהלים נטע ה'", כבשמים המתוחין כאהל, שנאמר: "וימתחם כאהל לשבת" (ישעיה מ, כב): **נטע ה'.** לשון נטיעה מצינו באהלים, שנאמר: "ויטע אהלי אפדנו" (דניאל יא, מה):

ז **מדליו.** מבארותיו, ופרושו כתרגומו: **וזרעו במים רבים.** לשון הצלחה הוא זה, כזרע הזרוע על פני המים: **וירם מאגג מלכו.** מלך ראשון שלהם יכבש את אגג מלך עמלק: **ותנשא מלכתו.** של יעקב יותר ויותר, שיבא אחריו דוד ושלמה:

ח **אל מוציאו ממצרים.** מי גורם להם הגדלה הזאת? אל המוציאם ממצרים, בתקף ורום שלו "יאכל" את הגוים שהם "צריו": **ועצמתיהם.** של צרים: **יגרם.** מנחם פתר בו לשון שבירה, וכן: "לא גרמו לבקר" (צפניה ג, ג), וכן: "ואת חרשיה תגרמי" (יחזקאל כג, לד). ואני אומר, לשון עצם הוא, שמגרר הבשר בשניו מסביב והמח שבפנים, ומעמיד העצם על ערמימותו: **וחציו ימחץ.** אונקלוס תרגם "חציו" של צרים, חלקה שלהם, כמו: "בעלי חצים" (בראשית מט, כג), מרי פלגותא – לשון חלקה וחציה. וכן "ימחץ" לשון "ומחצה וחלפה רקתו" (שופטים ה, כו), שיחצו את ארצם. ויש לפתר לשון חצים ממש, "חציו" של הקדוש ברוך הוא ימחץ בדמם של צרים, יטבל ויצטבע בדמם, כמו: "למען

ד הַגֶּבֶר שְׁתֻם הָעָיִן׃ נְאֻם שֹׁמֵעַ אִמְרֵי־אֵל אֲשֶׁר מַחֲזֵה שַׁדַּי יֶחֱזֶה נֹפֵל
ה ו וּגְלוּי עֵינָיִם׃ מַה־טֹּבוּ אֹהָלֶיךָ יַעֲקֹב מִשְׁכְּנֹתֶיךָ יִשְׂרָאֵל׃ כִּנְחָלִים נִטָּיוּ
ז כְּגַנֹּת עֲלֵי נָהָר כַּאֲהָלִים נָטַע יְהוָה כַּאֲרָזִים עֲלֵי־מָיִם׃ יִזַּל־מַיִם מִדָּלְיָו
ח וְזַרְעוֹ בְּמַיִם רַבִּים וְיָרֹם מֵאֲגַג מַלְכּוֹ וְתִנַּשֵּׂא מַלְכֻתוֹ׃ אֵל מוֹצִיאוֹ
מִמִּצְרַיִם כְּתוֹעֲפֹת רְאֵם לוֹ יֹאכַל גּוֹיִם צָרָיו וְעַצְמֹתֵיהֶם יְגָרֵם וְחִצָּיו
ט יִמְחָץ׃ כָּרַע שָׁכַב כַּאֲרִי וּכְלָבִיא מִי יְקִימֶנּוּ מְבָרְכֶיךָ בָרוּךְ וְאֹרְרֶיךָ
י אָרוּר׃ וַיִּחַר־אַף בָּלָק אֶל־בִּלְעָם וַיִּסְפֹּק אֶת־כַּפָּיו וַיֹּאמֶר בָּלָק אֶל־
יא בִּלְעָם לָקֹב אֹיְבַי קְרָאתִיךָ וְהִנֵּה בֵּרַכְתָּ בָרֵךְ זֶה שָׁלֹשׁ פְּעָמִים׃ וְעַתָּה
בְּרַח־לְךָ אֶל־מְקוֹמֶךָ אָמַרְתִּי כַּבֵּד אֲכַבֶּדְךָ וְהִנֵּה מְנָעֲךָ יְהוָה מִכָּבוֹד׃
יב וַיֹּאמֶר בִּלְעָם אֶל־בָּלָק הֲלֹא גַּם אֶל־מַלְאָכֶיךָ אֲשֶׁר־שָׁלַחְתָּ אֵלַי
יג דִּבַּרְתִּי לֵאמֹר׃ אִם־יִתֶּן־לִי בָלָק מְלֹא בֵיתוֹ כֶּסֶף וְזָהָב לֹא אוּכַל

אונקלוס

גְּבַרָא דְּשַׁפִּיר חָזֵי: ד אֵימַר, דִּשְׁמַע מֵימַר מִן קֳדָם אֵל, דְּחֵיזוּ מִן קֳדָם שַׁדַּי חָזֵי, שָׁכֵיב וּמִתְגְּלֵי לֵיהּ: ה מָא טָבָא אַרְעָךְ יַעֲקֹב, בֵּית מִשְׁרָךְ יִשְׂרָאֵל: ו כִּנְחָלִין דְּמִדַּבְּרִין, כְּגִנַּת שַׁקְיָא דְּעַל פְּרָת, כְּבֻסְמַיָּא דִּנְצַב יי, כְּאַרְזִין דִּנְצִיבִין עַל מַיָּא: ז יִסְגֵּי מַלְכָּא דְּיִתְרַבָּא מִבְּנוֹהִי, וְיִשְׁלוֹט בְּעַמְמִין סַגִּיאִין, וְיִתַּקַּף מֵאֲגַג מַלְכֵּיהּ, וְתִנַּטַּל מַלְכוּתֵיהּ: ח אֵל דְּאַפֵּיקִנּוּן מִמִּצְרַיִם, תָּקְפָּא וְרוּמָא דִּילֵיהּ, יֵיכְלוּן בֵּית יִשְׂרָאֵל נִכְסֵי עַמְמַיָּא סָנְאֵיהוֹן, וּבְבִזַּת מַלְכֵיהוֹן יִתְפַּנְּקוּן וְאַרְעֲתְהוֹן יַחְסְנוּן: ט יְנוּחַ יִשְׁרֵי בִּתְקוֹף כְּאַרְיָא, וּכְלֵיתָא וְלֵית דִּיקִימִנֵּיהּ, בְּרִיכָךְ יְהוֹן בְּרִיכִין, וְלִיטָךְ יְהוֹן לִיטִין: י וּתְקֵיף רָגְזָא דְּבָלָק בְּבִלְעָם, וּשְׁקַפִנּוּן לִידוֹהִי, וַאֲמַר בָּלָק לְבִלְעָם, לְמֶלָּט סָנְאַי קְרֵיתָךְ, וְהָא בָּרָכָא מְבָרֵיכְתְּ לְהוֹן, דְּנָן תְּלָת זִמְנִין: יא וּכְעַן אִיזֵיל לָךְ לְאַתְרָךְ, אֲמָרִית יַקָּרָא אֲיַקְּרִנָּךְ, וְהָא, מַנְעָךְ יי מִן יְקָר: יב וַאֲמַר בִּלְעָם לְבָלָק, הֲלָא, אַף עִם אִזְגַּדָּךְ, דִּשְׁלַחְתָּא לְוָתִי מַלֵּילִית לְמֵימַר: יג אִם יִתֵּין לִי בָלָק, מְלֵי בֵיתֵיהּ כְּסַף וּדְהַב, לֵית לִי רְשׁוּ,

רש״י

תִּמְחַץ רַגְלְךָ בְּדָם" (תהלים סח, כד), וְאֵינוֹ זָז מִלְּשׁוֹן מַכָּה, כְּמוֹ "מָחַצְתִּי" (דברים לב, לט), שֶׁהַצָּבוּעַ בְּדָם נִרְאֶה כְּאִלּוּ מָחוּץ וְנָגוּעַ:

ט כָּרַע שָׁכַב כַּאֲרִי. כְּתַרְגּוּמוֹ, יִתְיַשְּׁבוּ בְּאַרְצָם בְּכֹחַ וּבִגְבוּרָה:

י וַיִּסְפֹּק. הִכָּה זוֹ עַל זוֹ:

24:5 מִשְׁכְּנֹתֶיךָ יִשְׂרָאֵל *Your homes, O Israel* – This blessing, as understood by the Rabbis, was prophetic. "How good are your tents, Yaakov, your homes, O Israel." The home, *mishkan,* meant the synagogue, home of both the community and the Divine Presence. The Rabbis added to this interpretation a further note. They said: All of Bilam's blessings eventually turned into curses, except this. Israel lost all its earthly glory, but it never lost its synagogues. Because of this, it survived. No other people maintained its identity through two thousand years of dispersion, but Jews did, because though they had lost their geographic home they preserved their spiritual home, and though they were no longer a sovereign nation they were still a constituted people, the "congregation of Israel."

me his palace full of silver and gold, I could not do anything to transgress the
word of the LORD, doing either good or bad of my own accord. What the LORD
14 says is what I must say.' So now that I am going back to my people, let me advise SHEVI'I
15 you what this people will do to your people in days to come." He took up his
oracle, saying: "The word of Bilam son of Beor, the word of a man whose eye is
16 opened. The word of one who hears God's speech, and has knowledge from
the Most High, who sees a vision of Shaddai, who falls, but with eyes unveiled.
17 I see him, but not now; I gaze upon him, though not near: A star will shoot
forth from Yaakov; a scepter will arise from Israel, and smash the brow of Moav,
18 and devastate all children of Shet. Edom will become a possession, Se'ir the
19 possession of its foes. But Israel will act valiantly. From Yaakov will come forth
20 a ruler and empty the city of survivors." He looked at Amalek; he took up his
oracle and said: "Amalek is first among nations, but its end will be death forever."
21 He looked at the Kenites; he took up his oracle and said: "Invincible your
22 dwelling, your nest set in the rock. Yet Kayin is destined for burning, when
23 Assyria seizes you captive." And he took up his oracle and said, "Alas! Who will
24 live when God does this? Ships from the coast of Kitim will afflict Assyria,

רש"י

יג **לַעֲבֹר אֶת פִּי ה'.** כָּאן לֹא נֶאֱמַר 'אֱלֹהָי', כְּמוֹ שֶׁאָמַר בָּרִאשׁוֹנָה, לְפִי שֶׁיָּדַע שֶׁנִּגְאַשׁ בְּהַקָּדוֹשׁ בָּרוּךְ הוּא וְנִטְרַד:

יד **הוֹלֵךְ לְעַמִּי.** מֵעַתָּה הֲרֵינִי כִּשְׁאָר עַמִּי, שֶׁנִּסְתַּלֵּק הַקָּדוֹשׁ בָּרוּךְ הוּא מֵעָלָיו: **לְכָה אִיעָצְךָ.** מַה לְּךָ לַעֲשׂוֹת, וּמַה הִיא הָעֵצָה? אֱלֹהֵיהֶם שֶׁל אֵלּוּ שׂוֹנֵא זִמָּה הוּא כו', כִּדְאִיתָא בְּ'חֵלֶק' (סנהדרין קו ע"א). תֵּדַע שֶׁבִּלְעָם הֵשִׂיא עֵצָה זוֹ לְהַכְשִׁילָם בְּזִמָּה, שֶׁהֲרֵי נֶאֱמַר: "הֵן הֵנָּה הָיוּ לִבְנֵי יִשְׂרָאֵל בִּדְבַר בִּלְעָם" (להלן לא, טז): **אֲשֶׁר יַעֲשֶׂה הָעָם הַזֶּה לְעַמְּךָ.** מִקְרָא קָצָר הוּא זֶה, אִיעָצְךָ לְהַכְשִׁילָם, וְאֹמַר לְךָ מַה שֶּׁהֵן עֲתִידִין לְהָרַע לְמוֹאָב בְּאַחֲרִית הַיָּמִים: "וּמָחַץ פַּאֲתֵי מוֹאָב" (להלן פסוק יז). הַתַּרְגּוּם מְפָרֵשׁ קֹצֶר הָעִבְרִי:

טז **וְיֹדֵעַ דַּעַת עֶלְיוֹן.** לְכַוֵּן הַשָּׁעָה שֶׁכּוֹעֵס בָּהּ:

יז **אֶרְאֶנּוּ.** רוֹאֶה אֲנִי שִׁבְחוֹ שֶׁל יַעֲקֹב וּגְדֻלָּתוֹ, אַךְ לֹא עַתָּה הוּא אֶלָּא לְאַחַר זְמַן: **דָּרַךְ כּוֹכָב מִיַּעֲקֹב.** כְּתַרְגּוּמוֹ, לְשׁוֹן: "דָּרַךְ קַשְׁתּוֹ" (איכה ב, ד), שֶׁהַכּוֹכָב עוֹבֵר כַּחֵץ, וּבְלַעַז דישטינ"ט, כְּלוֹמַר יָקוּם מַזָּל: **וְקָם שֵׁבֶט.** מֶלֶךְ רוֹדֶה וּמוֹשֵׁל: **וּמָחַץ פַּאֲתֵי מוֹאָב.** זֶה דָּוִד, שֶׁנֶּאֱמַר בּוֹ: "הַשְׁכֵּב אוֹתָם אַרְצָה וַיְמַדֵּד שְׁנֵי חֲבָלִים לְהָמִית" וְגוֹ' (שמואל ב' ח, ב): **וְקַרְקַר.** לְשׁוֹן כּוֹרֶה, כְּמוֹ: "אֲנִי קַרְתִּי" (מלכים ב' יט, כד), "מַקֶּבֶת בּוֹר נֻקַּרְתֶּם" (ישעיה נא, א), "יִקְּרוּהָ עֹרְבֵי נַחַל" (משלי ל, יז), פורייי"ר בְּלַעַז: **כָּל בְּנֵי שֵׁת.** כָּל הָאֻמּוֹת, שֶׁכֻּלָּם יָצְאוּ מִן שֵׁת בְּנוֹ שֶׁל אָדָם הָרִאשׁוֹן:

יח **וְהָיָה יְרֵשָׁה שֵׂעִיר אֹיְבָיו.** לְאוֹיְבָיו יִשְׂרָאֵל:

יט **וְיֵרְדְּ מִיַּעֲקֹב.** וְעוֹד יִהְיֶה מוֹשֵׁל אַחֵר מִיַּעֲקֹב: **וְהֶאֱבִיד שָׂרִיד מֵעִיר.** הַחֲשׁוּבָה שֶׁל אֱדוֹם, הִיא רוֹמִי. וְעַל מֶלֶךְ הַמָּשִׁיחַ אוֹמֵר כֵּן, שֶׁנֶּאֱמַר בּוֹ: "וְיֵרְדְּ מִיָּם עַד יָם" (תהלים עב, ח), "וְלֹא יִהְיֶה שָׂרִיד לְבֵית עֵשָׂו" (עובדיה א, יח):

כ **וַיַּרְא אֶת עֲמָלֵק.** נִסְתַּכֵּל בְּפֻרְעָנוּתוֹ שֶׁל עֲמָלֵק: **רֵאשִׁית גּוֹיִם עֲמָלֵק.** הוּא קָדַם אֶת כֻּלָּם לְהִלָּחֵם בְּיִשְׂרָאֵל, וְכָךְ תִּרְגֵּם אוּנְקְלוֹס, "וְאַחֲרִיתוֹ" לֹאבַד בְּיָדָם, שֶׁנֶּאֱמַר: "תִּמְחֶה אֶת זֵכֶר עֲמָלֵק" (דברים כה, יט):

כא **וַיַּרְא אֶת הַקֵּינִי.** לְפִי שֶׁהָיָה קֵינִי תָּקוּעַ אֵצֶל עֲמָלֵק, כָּעִנְיָן שֶׁנֶּאֱמַר: "וַיֹּאמֶר שָׁאוּל אֶל הַקֵּינִי" וְגוֹ' (שמואל א' טו, ו), הִזְכִּירוֹ אַחַר עֲמָלֵק. נִסְתַּכֵּל בִּגְדֻלָּתָם שֶׁל בְּנֵי יִתְרוֹ שֶׁנֶּאֱמַר בָּהֶם: "תִּרְעָתִים שִׁמְעָתִים שׂוּכָתִים" (דברי הימים א' ב, נה): **אֵיתָן מוֹשָׁבֶךָ.** תָּמֵהַּ אֲנִי מֵהֵיכָן זָכִיתָ לְכָךְ, הֲלֹא אַתָּה עִמִּי הָיִיתָ בַּעֲצַת "הָבָה נִתְחַכְּמָה לוֹ" (שמות א, י), וְעַתָּה נִתְיַשַּׁבְתָּ בְּאֵיתָן וּמָעוֹז שֶׁל יִשְׂרָאֵל:

כב **כִּי אִם יִהְיֶה לְבָעֵר קָיִן וְגוֹ'.** אַשְׁרֶיךָ שֶׁנִּתְקַעְתָּ לְתֹקֶף זֶה, שֶׁאֵינְךָ

לַעֲבֹר אֶת־פִּי יְהוָה לַעֲשׂוֹת טוֹבָה אוֹ רָעָה מִלִּבִּי אֲשֶׁר־יְדַבֵּר יְהוָה
יד אֹתוֹ אֲדַבֵּר׃ וְעַתָּה הִנְנִי הוֹלֵךְ לְעַמִּי לְכָה אִיעָצְךָ אֲשֶׁר יַעֲשֶׂה הָעָם שביעי
טו הַזֶּה לְעַמְּךָ בְּאַחֲרִית הַיָּמִים׃ וַיִּשָּׂא מְשָׁלוֹ וַיֹּאמַר נְאֻם בִּלְעָם בְּנוֹ
טז בְעֹר וּנְאֻם הַגֶּבֶר שְׁתֻם הָעָיִן׃ נְאֻם שֹׁמֵעַ אִמְרֵי־אֵל וְיֹדֵעַ דַּעַת עֶלְיוֹן
יז מַחֲזֵה שַׁדַּי יֶחֱזֶה נֹפֵל וּגְלוּי עֵינָיִם׃ אֶרְאֶנּוּ וְלֹא עַתָּה אֲשׁוּרֶנּוּ וְלֹא
קָרוֹב דָּרַךְ כּוֹכָב מִיַּעֲקֹב וְקָם שֵׁבֶט מִיִּשְׂרָאֵל וּמָחַץ פַּאֲתֵי מוֹאָב
יח וְקַרְקַר כָּל־בְּנֵי־שֵׁת׃ וְהָיָה אֱדוֹם יְרֵשָׁה וְהָיָה יְרֵשָׁה שֵׂעִיר אֹיְבָיו
יט כ וְיִשְׂרָאֵל עֹשֶׂה חָיִל׃ וְיֵרְדְּ מִיַּעֲקֹב וְהֶאֱבִיד שָׂרִיד מֵעִיר׃ וַיַּרְא אֶת־
עֲמָלֵק וַיִּשָּׂא מְשָׁלוֹ וַיֹּאמַר רֵאשִׁית גּוֹיִם עֲמָלֵק וְאַחֲרִיתוֹ עֲדֵי אֹבֵד׃
כא וַיַּרְא אֶת־הַקֵּינִי וַיִּשָּׂא מְשָׁלוֹ וַיֹּאמַר אֵיתָן מוֹשָׁבֶךָ וְשִׂים בַּסֶּלַע
כב כג קִנֶּךָ׃ כִּי אִם־יִהְיֶה לְבָעֵר קָיִן עַד־מָה אַשּׁוּר תִּשְׁבֶּךָּ׃ וַיִּשָּׂא מְשָׁלוֹ
כד וַיֹּאמַר אוֹי מִי יִחְיֶה מִשֻּׂמוֹ אֵל׃ וְצִים מִיַּד כִּתִּים וְעִנּוּ אַשּׁוּר וְעִנּוּ־עֵבֶר

אונקלוס

לְמִעְבַּר עַל גְּזֵירַת מֵימְרָא דַיְיָ, לְמֶעֱבַד טָבְתָא, אוֹ בִישְׁתָא מֵרְעוּתִי, דִּימַלֵּיל יְיָ יָתֵיהּ אֲמַלֵּיל: יד וּכְעַן, הָאֲנָא אָזֵיל לְעַמִּי, אֵיתַא אֶמְלְכִנָּךְ מָא דְתַעֲבֵיד, וַאֲחַוֵּי לָךְ, מָא דְיַעֲבֵיד, עַמָּא הָדֵין, לְעַמָּךְ בְּסוֹף יוֹמַיָּא: טו וּנְטַל מַתְלֵיהּ וַאֲמַר, אֵימַר בִּלְעָם בַּר בְּעוֹר, וְאֵימַר גַּבְרָא דְשַׁפִּיר חָזֵי: טז אֵימַר, דְּשָׁמַע מֵימַר מִן קֳדָם אֵל, וְיָדַע מַדַּע מִן קֳדָם עִלָּאָה, חֵיזוּ מִן קֳדָם שַׁדַּי חָזֵי, שָׁכֵיב וּמִתְגְּלֵי לֵיהּ: יז חֲזֵיתֵיהּ וְלָא כְעַן, סְכֵיתֵיהּ וְלָא אִיתוֹהִי קָרִיב, כַּד יְקוּם מַלְכָּא מִיַּעֲקֹב, וְיִתְרַבָּא מְשִׁיחָא מִיִּשְׂרָאֵל, וְיִקַטֵּיל רַבְרְבֵי מוֹאָב, וְיִשְׁלוֹט בְּכָל בְּנֵי אֲנָשָׁא:

יח וִיהֵי אֱדוֹם יָרְתָא, וִיהֵי יָרְתָא, שֵׂעִיר לְבַעֲלֵי דְבָבוֹהִי, וְיִשְׂרָאֵל יַצְלַח בְּנִכְסִין: יט וְיֵיחוֹת חַד מִדְּבֵית יַעֲקֹב, וְיוֹבֵיד מְשֵׁיזֵיב מִקִּרְיַת עַמְמַיָּא: כ וַחֲזָא יָת עֲמַלְקָאָה, וּנְטַל מַתְלֵיהּ וַאֲמַר, רֵישׁ קְרָבַיָּא דְיִשְׂרָאֵל הֲוָה עֲמָלֵק, וְסוֹפֵיהּ לְעָלְמָא יֵיבַד: כא וַחֲזָא יָת שַׁלְמָאָה, וּנְטַל מַתְלֵיהּ וַאֲמַר, תַּקִּיף בֵּית מוֹתְבָךְ, וְשַׁוִּי בִּכְרַךְ תַּקִּיף מְדוֹרָךְ: כב אֲרֵי אִם יְהֵי לְשֵׁיצָאָה שַׁלְמָאָה, עַד מָא אַתּוּרָאָה יִשְׁבְּנָךְ: כג וּנְטַל מַתְלֵיהּ וַאֲמַר, וַי לְחַיָּבַיָּא דְיֵיחוֹן, כַּד יַעֲבֵיד אֱלָהָא יָת אִלֵּין: כד וְסִיעָן יִצְטָרְחָן מֵרוֹמָאֵי, וִיעַנּוּן לְאַתּוּר וִישַׁעְבְּדוּן לְעֵיבֶר פְּרָת,

רש״י

נִטְרָד עוֹד מִן הָעוֹלָם, כִּי אַף אִם חַיָּה עָתִיד לִגְלוֹת עִם עֲשֶׂרֶת הַשְּׁבָטִים וְתִהְיֶה לְבָעֵר מִמָּקוֹם שֶׁנִּתְיַשַּׁבְתָּ שָׁם, מַה בְּכָךְ?: **עַד מָה אַשּׁוּר תִּשְׁבֶּךָּ.** עַד הֵיכָן הוּא מַגְלֶה אוֹתְךָ, שֶׁמָּא לַחְלַח וְחָבוֹר, אֵין זֶה טֵרוּד מִן הָעוֹלָם, אֶלָּא טִלְטוּל מִמָּקוֹם לְמָקוֹם, וְתָשׁוּב עִם שְׁאָר הַגָּלֻיּוֹת:

כג-כד **וַיִּשָּׂא מְשָׁלוֹ וְגוֹ׳.** כֵּיוָן שֶׁהִזְכִּיר אֶת שְׁבִיַּת אַשּׁוּר, אָמַר: **אוֹי מִי יִחְיֶה מִשֻּׂמוֹ אֵל.** מִי יָכוֹל לְהַחֲיוֹת אֶת עַצְמוֹ מִשּׂוּמוֹ אֶת אֵלֶּה, שֶׁלֹּא יָשִׂים עָלָיו הַגּוֹזֵר אֶת אֵלֶּה, שֶׁיַּעֲמֹד סַנְחֵרִיב וִיבַלְבֵּל אֶת כָּל הָאֻמּוֹת, וְעוֹד יָבוֹאוּ "צִים מִיַּד כִּתִּים" וְיַעַבְרוּ כִּתִּיִּים שֶׁהֵן רוֹמִיִּים בְּבִירָנִיּוֹת גְּדוֹלוֹת עַל אַשּׁוּר: **וְעִנּוּ עֵבֶר.** וְעִנּוּ אוֹתָם שֶׁבְּעֵבֶר הַנָּהָר:

25 afflict Ever; they too will perish for all time." Then Bilam rose and returned
home, and Balak also set off upon his way.
25 1 Israel was dwelling at Shitim. And the men began to consort with Moabite
2 women, who invited the people to join the sacrifices to their god; the men ate,
3 and then they worshipped the women's god. Israel allied itself with Baal Peor,
4 and the LORD was filled with fury against Israel. "Take all the people's leaders,"
said the LORD to Moshe, "and have them impaled before the LORD in broad
5 daylight, so that the LORD's fury with Israel may be allayed." Moshe said to
Israel's judges, "Each of you kill those of your men who have allied themselves
6 with Baal Peor." At that moment, an Israelite man brought a Midianite woman
to his friends before the eyes of Moshe and the entire Israelite community,
7 who were weeping at the entrance to the Tent of Meeting. When Pinḥas son MAFTIR
of Elazar son of Aharon the priest saw this, he rose from the midst of the

רש"י

וגם הוא עדי אבד. וכן פירש דניאל: "עד די קטילת חיותא והובד גשמה" (דניאל ז, יא): **וצים.** ספינות גדולות, כדכתיב: "וצי אדיר" (ישעיה לג, כא), תרגומו "ובורני רבתא":

כה א **בשטים.** כך שמה: **לזנות אל בנות מואב.** על ידי עצת בלעם, כדאיתא ב'חלק' (סנהדרין קו ע"א):

ב **וישתחוו לאלהיהן.** כשתקף יצרו עליו ואומר לה: השמעי לי! והיא מוציאה לו דמות פעור מחיקה ואומרת לו השתחוה לזה:

ג **פעור.** על שם שפוערין לפניו פי הטבעת ומוציאין רעי, וזו היא עבודתו: **ויחר אף ה' בישראל.** שלח בם מגפה:

ד **קח את כל ראשי העם.** לשפט את העובדים לפעור: **והוקע אותם.** את העובדים: **והוקע.** היא תליה, כמו שמצינו בבני שאול: "והוקענום לה'" (שמואל ב' כא, ו), ושם תליה מפורשת, עבודה זרה בסקילה, וכל הנסקלים נתלין: **נגד השמש.** לעין כל. ומדרש אגדה: השמש מודיע את החוטאים, הענן נקפל מכנגדו והחמה זורחת עליו:

ה **הרגו איש אנשיו.** כל אחד ואחד מדייני ישראל היה הורג שנים, ודייני ישראל שמונה רבוא ושמונת אלפים, כדאיתא בסנהדרין (דף יח ע"א):

ו **והנה איש וגו'.** נתקבצו שבטו של שמעון אצל זמרי שהיה נשיא שלהם, אמרו לו: אנו נדונין במיתה ואתה יושב? וכו', כדאיתא ב'אלו הן הנשרפין' (סנהדרין פב ע"א): **את המדינית.** כזבי בת צור: **לעיני משה.** אמר לו: משה, זו אסורה או מותרת? אם תאמר אסורה, בת יתרו מי התירה לך? כו', כדאיתא התם: **והמה בכים.** נתעלמה ממנו הלכה, געו כלם בבכיה. בעגל עמד משה כנגד ששים רבוא, שנאמר: "ויטחן עד אשר דק" וגו' (שמות לב, כ), וכאן רפו ידיו? אלא כדי שיבא פינחס ויטל את הראוי לו:

ז **וירא פינחס.** ראה מעשה ונזכר הלכה. אמר לו למשה: מקבלני ממך: הבועל ארמית קנאין פוגעין בו. אמר לו: קרינא דאגרתא איהו להוי פרונקא. מיד – "ויקח רמח בידו" וגו':

counterintuitive point, between Pinḥas's act (Num. 25:6–9) and the divine verdict on the act (25:10–15). The result is that we are forced to wait a week before hearing whether he did right or wrong. It is as if the Sages wanted us to live with that ambiguity so that we would not too readily conclude that Pinḥas is a hero. His act is fraught with moral hazard.

married to a Midianite woman, the daughter of one of their priests (Sanhedrin 82a). Any attempt on Moshe's part to do what Pinḥas does would expose him to the charge of hypocrisy, and make the situation worse, not better. Pinḥas, then, acts on his own initiative.

Not by accident did tradition fix the *parasha* break between Parashat Balak and Parashat Pinḥas at the most

כה וְגַם־הוּא עֲדֵי אֹבֵד: וַיָּקׇם בִּלְעָם וַיֵּלֶךְ וַיָּשׇׁב לִמְקֹמוֹ וְגַם־בָּלָק הָלַךְ
לְדַרְכּוֹ:
כה א ב וַיֵּשֶׁב יִשְׂרָאֵל בַּשִּׁטִּים וַיָּחֶל הָעָם לִזְנוֹת אֶל־בְּנוֹת מוֹאָב: וַתִּקְרֶאןָ כא
ג לָעָם לְזִבְחֵי אֱלֹהֵיהֶן וַיֹּאכַל הָעָם וַיִּשְׁתַּחֲווּ לֵאלֹהֵיהֶן: וַיִּצָּמֶד יִשְׂרָאֵל
ד לְבַעַל פְּעוֹר וַיִּחַר־אַף יהוה בְּיִשְׂרָאֵל: וַיֹּאמֶר יהוה אֶל־מֹשֶׁה קַח
אֶת־כׇּל־רָאשֵׁי הָעָם וְהוֹקַע אוֹתָם לַיהוה נֶגֶד הַשָּׁמֶשׁ וְיָשֹׁב חֲרוֹן אַף־
ה יהוה מִיִּשְׂרָאֵל: וַיֹּאמֶר מֹשֶׁה אֶל־שֹׁפְטֵי יִשְׂרָאֵל הִרְגוּ אִישׁ אֲנָשָׁיו
ו הַנִּצְמָדִים לְבַעַל פְּעוֹר: וְהִנֵּה אִישׁ מִבְּנֵי יִשְׂרָאֵל בָּא וַיַּקְרֵב אֶל־אֶחָיו
אֶת־הַמִּדְיָנִית לְעֵינֵי מֹשֶׁה וּלְעֵינֵי כׇּל־עֲדַת בְּנֵי־יִשְׂרָאֵל וְהֵמָּה בֹכִים
ז פֶּתַח אֹהֶל מוֹעֵד: וַיַּרְא פִּינְחָס בֶּן־אֶלְעָזָר בֶּן־אַהֲרֹן הַכֹּהֵן וַיָּקׇם מפטיר

אונקלוס

וְאַף אִנּוּן לְעָלְמָא יֵיבְדוּן: כה וְקָם בִּלְעָם, וַאֲזַל וְתָב לְאַתְרֵיהּ, וְאַף בָּלָק אֲזַל לְאוֹרְחֵיהּ: כה א וִיתֵיב יִשְׂרָאֵל בְּשִׁטִּין, וְשָׁרִי עַמָּא, לְמִטְעֵי בָּתַר בְּנָת מוֹאָב: ב וּקְרָאָה לְעַמָּא, לְדִבְחֵי טַעֲוָתְהוֹן, וַאֲכַל עַמָּא, וּסְגִידוּ לְטַעֲוָתְהוֹן: ג וְאִתְחַבַּר יִשְׂרָאֵל לְבַעְלָא פְעוֹר, וּתְקֵיף רֻגְזָא דַּיי בְּיִשְׂרָאֵל: ד וַאֲמַר יי לְמֹשֶׁה, דְּבַר יָת כָּל רֵישֵׁי עַמָּא, וְדוּן וּקְטוֹל דְּחַיָּב קְטוֹל, קֳדָם יי לְקָבֵיל שִׁמְשָׁא, וִיתוּב, תְּקוֹף רֻגְזָא דַּיי מִיִּשְׂרָאֵל: ה וַאֲמַר מֹשֶׁה, לְדַיָּנֵי יִשְׂרָאֵל, קְטוּלוּ גְּבַר גֻּבְרוֹהִי, דְּאִתְחַבַּרוּ לְבַעְלָא פְעוֹר: ו וְהָא, גֻּבְרָא מִבְּנֵי יִשְׂרָאֵל אֲתָא, וְקָרֵיב לְוָת אֲחוֹהִי יָת מִדְיָנֵיתָא, לְעֵינֵי מֹשֶׁה, וּלְעֵינֵי כָּל כְּנִשְׁתָּא דִּבְנֵי יִשְׂרָאֵל, וְאִנּוּן בָּכַן, בִּתְרַע מַשְׁכַּן זִמְנָא: ז וַחֲזָא, פִּינְחָס בַּר אֶלְעָזָר, בַּר אַהֲרֹן כָּהֲנָא, וְקָם

25:1 לִזְנוֹת אֶל־בְּנוֹת מוֹאָב *To consort with Moabite women* – Bilam's failure to curse Israel does not, in the end, affect the Moabites. They proceed to enlist their women to successfully entice the Israelite men. A plague then strikes the Israelites, taking twenty-four thousand lives.

It does not affect the Midianites, whose hostility to Israel will later cause God to instruct Moshe to take military vengeance against them (Num. 31).

It does not affect Bilam himself; we will find this out in chapter 31. We see immediately here that it has not changed the Israelites either. Had the Israelites known the danger they were in, and how they were saved from it, it would have given them pause for thought before engaging in immorality and idol worship with the Moabite women. They would have known that the Moabites were not their friends.

In the story of Bilam, fearing that the Israelites derive strength from a supernatural force, the Moabites tried to counter it with another supernatural force. The plan failed and "Bilam rose and returned home, and Balak also set off upon his way" (24:25). It quickly becomes clear, however, that no supernatural means were needed. The Israelites bring their own downfall upon themselves.

25:7 וַיָּקׇם מִתּוֹךְ הָעֵדָה *He rose from the midst of the community* – The Rabbis suggest that Moshe's own background renders him powerless in this situation, for he is himself

8 community, took a spear in his hand, went after the Israelite man into the
tent, and stabbed both of them, the Israelite man and the woman, through the
9 stomach – and the plague among the Israelites ended. Those who had died by
the plague numbered twenty-four thousand.

The haftara for Parashat Balak is on page 1598 (even when Ḥukat and Balak are read together).

רש״י

ח **אֶל הַקֻּבָּה.** אֶל הָאֹהֶל: **אֶל קֳבָתָהּ.** כְּמוֹ: ״וְהַלְּחָיַיִם וְהַקֵּבָה״ (דברים יח, ג), כִּוֵּן בְּתוֹךְ זַכְרוּת שֶׁל זִמְרִי וְנַקְבוּת שֶׁלָּהּ, וְרָאוּ כֻלָּם שֶׁלֹּא לְחִנָּם הֲרָגָם, וְהַרְבֵּה נִסִּים נַעֲשׂוּ לוֹ וְכוּ׳, כִּדְאִיתָא הָתָם (סנהדרין פב ע״ב):

to restore order to the camp. One of the tribal leaders, Zimri from the tribe of Shimon, brings a Midianite woman into the center of the camp and cohabits with her in full view of the people, as brazen an offense as we have seen since Datan and Aviram joined the Koraḥ rebellion. Only the human zealousness of Pinḥas – killing them both as they are cavorting – saves the day.

It is a shocking awakening. God saves Israel from its enemies but even God cannot save Israel from itself. To be defended by the Holy One, Israel must be holy, and that includes – as Leviticus insists in chapters 18 and 20 – a strict sexual ethic. Lose that and the nation will lose everything. If the Israelites act like the Canaanites, they will suffer the fate of the Canaanites. If, on the other hand, it honors and sanctifies fidelity between husband and wife and tender care between parents and children, then Israel will eventually be blessed even by its enemies. If unworthy, it can expect no special indulgence from God. Loyalty begins in our most intimate relationships and extends outward to the nation and upward to God. Disloyalty, as the Israelites showed in Shitim, can only end in disaster.

The book of Numbers has been a counterpoint between order and chaos, law and narrative, God's faith and the people's faithlessness, the blessings God brings forth from the mouth of an enemy and the curses the people bring upon themselves. It is a story of innocence lost and responsibility to be gained – less a chronicle of what happened in the course of forty years than a tutorial in what it is to find or lose direction in the wilderness of time. The enduring lesson remains. God may save us from our enemies, but only we can save us from ourselves.

ח מִתּוֹךְ הָעֵדָה וַיִּקַּח רֹמַח בְּיָדוֹ: וַיָּבֹא אַחַר אִישׁ־יִשְׂרָאֵל אֶל־הַקֻּבָּה
וַיִּדְקֹר אֶת־שְׁנֵיהֶם אֵת אִישׁ יִשְׂרָאֵל וְאֶת־הָאִשָּׁה אֶל־קֳבָתָהּ וַתֵּעָצַר
ט הַמַּגֵּפָה מֵעַל בְּנֵי יִשְׂרָאֵל: וַיִּהְיוּ הַמֵּתִים בַּמַּגֵּפָה אַרְבָּעָה וְעֶשְׂרִים
אָלֶף:

The הפטרה *for* פרשת בלק *is on page 1599 (even when* חקת *and* בלק *are read together).*

אונקלוס

מִגּוֹ כְּנִשְׁתָּא, וּנְסֵיב רֻמְחָא בִּידֵיהּ: ח וְעָאל בָּתַר גֻּבְרָא בַּר
יִשְׂרָאֵל לְקֻבְּתָא, וּבְזַע יָת תַּרְוֵיהוֹן, יָת גֻּבְרָא בַּר יִשְׂרָאֵל, וְיָת
אִתְּתָא בִּמְעַהָא, וְאִתְכְּלִי מוֹתָנָא, מֵעַל בְּנֵי יִשְׂרָאֵל: ט וַהֲווֹ, דְּמִיתוּ
בְּמוֹתָנָא, עֶסְרִין וְאַרְבְּעָא אַלְפִין:

THE END OF THE BAAL PEOR AFFAIR

This may be the first time the Israelites have committed the cardinal sin of idolatry. Most of the commentators do not regard the golden calf as an idol. It was intended as a substitute Moshe – a vehicle for receiving divine messages – rather than an object of worship in its own right. But the idolatry at Shitim is real. For the first time we see the Israelites bowing down to Baal, the Canaanite god. It is a betrayal of everything they should stand for.

What is more, this is the first time the Israelites have sinned gratuitously. Previously they have been driven by fear or hunger or thirst or disappointment. None of these is operative in the case of the Moabite women. This is sheer sexual self-indulgence, yielding to temptation unthinkingly. Even the idolatrous act is undertaken not in any spirit of rebelliousness, but almost as an afterthought: they "began to *consort* with Moabite women … *ate*, and then they *worshipped* the women's god" (vv. 1–2). If the first, why not the second and the third?

Idolatry and adultery are closely related. Idolatry is worship of power – and in human terms the worship of power translates into the untrammeled pursuit of sexual desire. To paraphrase Thucydides, the strong do what they wish and the weak suffer as they must. For Israel to slip into the same sin at the first opportunity bodes ill for the future. It also makes a nonsense of Bilam's blessing, "How good are your tents, Yaakov, your homes, O Israel" (Num. 24:5), if, as the rabbis thought, this refers to the modesty of Israel's family life (Rashi on Num. 24:5). That they could fall so quickly is a frightening sign of how little they have learned about the nature of their mission as an exemplary people.

God issues a sharp and painful punishment. But it fails

Parashat Pinḥas

25 10 11 The Lord spoke to Moshe: "Pinḥas son of Elazar son of Aharon the priest has
allayed My rage against the Israelites. Because he was passionate on My behalf
12 among you, I did not destroy the Israelites in My own passion. Therefore, say

רש״י

כה יא **פִּינְחָס בֶּן אֶלְעָזָר בֶּן אַהֲרֹן הַכֹּהֵן.** לְפִי שֶׁהָיוּ הַשְּׁבָטִים מְבַזִּים אוֹתוֹ, הַרְאִיתֶם בֶּן פּוּטִי זֶה שֶׁפִּטֵּם אֲבִי אִמּוֹ עֲגָלִים לַעֲבוֹדָה זָרָה וְהָרַג נְשִׂיא שֵׁבֶט מִיִּשְׂרָאֵל, לְפִיכָךְ בָּא הַכָּתוּב וְיִחֲסוֹ אַחַר אַהֲרֹן: **בְּקַנְאוֹ אֶת קִנְאָתִי.** בְּנָקְמוֹ אֶת נִקְמָתִי, בְּקָצְפּוֹ אֶת הַקֶּצֶף שֶׁהָיָה לִי לִקְצֹף. כָּל לְשׁוֹן 'קִנְאָה' הוּא הַמִּתְחָרֶה לִנְקֹם נִקְמַת דָּבָר, אנפרנמנ״ט בְּלַעַז:

יב **אֶת בְּרִיתִי שָׁלוֹם.** שֶׁתְּהֵא לוֹ לִבְרִית שָׁלוֹם, כְּאָדָם הַמַּחֲזִיק טוֹבָה וְחַנּוּת לְמִי שֶׁעוֹשֶׂה עִמּוֹ טוֹבָה, אַף כָּאן פֵּרֵשׁ לוֹ הַקָּדוֹשׁ בָּרוּךְ הוּא שְׁלוֹמוֹתָיו:

to be found in violent confrontation, but in gentleness. God then tells him to appoint Elisha as his successor.

What is great about the zealot is also what is dangerous. *The zealot acts the part of God.* Rashi, commenting on the phrase "Pinḥas…has allayed My rage against the Israelites, because he was passionate on My behalf" (Num. 25:11), interprets this to mean that God was saying that Pinḥas had "executed My vengeance and showed the anger that was for Me to show." He had done what normally only God would do. The zealot, on his own initiative, acts on behalf of God. But human beings are not God. They do not know what God knows.

Pinḥas and Eliyahu are heroes of the spiritual life. Yet both are implicitly reprimanded by God. God does not say that they are wrong to do what they do. To the contrary, God praises Pinḥas and answers Eliyahu's prayer. But He also makes it clear that once is enough. Pinḥas is now to take on the role of priesthood and the way of peace. Eliyahu is to appoint his successor. There are forms of justice that, in essence, are God's domain, not ours.

25:12 **בְּרִיתִי שָׁלוֹם** *My covenant of peace* – To any onlooker, Pinḥas might have seemed simply a man of violence. On the one hand, he saved countless lives; no more people died of the plague. On the other hand, he could not have known that in advance. Is he then a hero or a murderer? Parashat Balak ends with this ambiguity unresolved. Only in our *parasha* do we hear God's answer. Pinḥas, we are assured, is a hero. He has saved the Israelites from destruction, showed the zeal that counterbalanced the people's faithlessness, and as a reward, God makes a personal covenant with him.

Halakha, however, dramatically circumscribes his act in multiple ways. First, it rules that if Zimri had turned and killed Pinḥas in self-defense, he would be declared innocent in a court of law (Sanhedrin 82a). Second, it rules that if Pinḥas had killed Zimri and Kozbi just before or after they were engaged in cohabitation, he would have been guilty of murder (Sanhedrin 81b). Third, had Pinḥas consulted a *beit din* and asked whether he was permitted to do what he was proposing to do, the answer would have been no (Sanhedrin 82a).

This is one of the rare cases where we say: *Halakha ve'ein morin ken*, "It is the law, but it should not be taught." That is why it is hedged with qualifications. It only applied when the offense was committed in public, when the sentence was carried out while the sin or crime was being committed, and only when the person carrying it out was a "zealot."

An act like that of Pinḥas can only be justified in retrospect, when it does actually produce the consequences it was intended to achieve. What is more, it is essential that it never becomes the basis of a general rule. Rare indeed are the circumstances in which Pinḥas-like zealotry is justified, and if anyone asks whether he may do the same, the answer must always be: no.

פרשת פינחס

כה יא וַיְדַבֵּ֥ר יְהוָ֖ה אֶל־מֹשֶׁ֥ה לֵּאמֹֽר׃ פִּֽינְחָ֨ס בֶּן־אֶלְעָזָ֜ר בֶּן־אַהֲרֹ֣ן הַכֹּהֵ֗ן כב
הֵשִׁ֤יב אֶת־חֲמָתִי֙ מֵעַ֣ל בְּנֵֽי־יִשְׂרָאֵ֔ל בְּקַנְא֥וֹ אֶת־קִנְאָתִ֖י בְּתוֹכָ֑ם וְלֹא־
יב כִלִּ֥יתִי אֶת־בְּנֵֽי־יִשְׂרָאֵ֖ל בְּקִנְאָתִֽי׃ לָכֵ֖ן אֱמֹ֑ר הִנְנִ֨י נֹתֵ֥ן ל֛וֹ אֶת־בְּרִיתִ֖י

אונקלוס

כה י וּמַלֵּיל יְיָ עִם מֹשֶׁה לְמֵימָר: יא פִּינְחָס בַּר אֶלְעָזָר בַּר אַהֲרֹן
כָּהֲנָא, אֲתֵיב יָת חֵמְתִּי מֵעַל בְּנֵי יִשְׂרָאֵל, בִּדְקַנִּי יָת קִנְאָתִי בֵּינֵיהוֹן,
וְלָא שֵׁיצִיתִי יָת בְּנֵי יִשְׂרָאֵל בְּקִנְאָתִי: יב בְּכֵן אֵימַר, הָאֲנָא גָּזַר לֵיהּ,
יָת קְיָמִי

PINḤAS

Parashat Pinḥas begins by completing the episode that began in Parashat Balak: Pinḥas ends the plague, which was the result of the Israelites' seduction into idolatry by the Moabite and Midianite women. Pinḥas's reward for his zealotry is a "covenant of peace" (Num. 25:12) and "everlasting priesthood" (25:13).

The *parasha* then moves on to the second census in the book, this time of the new generation, the one to enter the land. There then follow two narratives, one about the daughters of Tzelofḥad and God's positive reply to their request for a share in the land, and the second about Moshe's request that God appoint a successor. The narrative in which Yehoshua is chosen as Moshe's successor raises questions about the fact that Moshe is unable to hand on his leadership role to his children. The *parasha* ends with two chapters about the sacrifices to be brought at different times, daily, weekly, monthly, and on festivals. Not for the first time in the Torah, stories of chaos and disruption give way to a detailed account of priestly order.

PINḤAS THE ZEALOT

With Pinḥas, a new type of character enters the world of Israel: the zealot (translated here as "passionate"). Through his passion for God, Pinḥas succeeds in allaying God's passion. He is to be followed, many centuries later, by the one other figure in Tanakh described as a zealot, the prophet Eliyahu. Asked by God on Mount Ḥorev, "Why are you here, Eliyahu?" Eliyahu replies, "I acted out of fervor, out of passion for the Lord, God of Hosts" (I Kings 19:9–10). In fact, tradition identifies these two men with each other: "Pinḥas *is* Eliyahu," say the Sages (*Yalkut Shimoni* I:771).

Pinḥas and Eliyahu are religious heroes. They step into the breach at a time when the nation is facing religious and moral crisis and palpable divine anger. They risk their lives by so doing. And God Himself is called "zealous" many times in the Torah. Zealousness must therefore be a virtue, or so it seems.

Yet the treatment of the two men in both the Written and Oral Torah is ambivalent. God rewards Pinḥas by giving him "My covenant of peace" (Num. 25:12), intimating that God will ensure that he never again acts the part of a zealot. Indeed, some years later, in the days of Yehoshua, he is to play a vital role as a diplomatic man of peace by averting a civil war between the rest of the Israelites and the two and a half tribes – Reuven, Gad, and half of Menashe – who have settled to the east of the Jordan (Josh. 22).

As for Eliyahu, he is implicitly rebuked by God in one of the great scenes of the Bible. Standing at Ḥorev, God shows him a whirlwind, an earthquake, and a fire, but God is not in any of these. Then He comes to Eliyahu in a "faint sound of silence" (I Kings 19:11–12). He asks Eliyahu, for the second time, "Why are you here?" and Eliyahu replies with exactly the same words he had used before: "I acted out of fervor, out of passion for the Lord, God of Hosts" (19:13–14). He has not understood that God has been trying to tell him that He is not

13 this: I grant him My covenant of peace. For him and for his descendants, it
shall be a covenant of everlasting priesthood, because he was passionate for his
14 God and made atonement on the part of the Israelites." The name of the slain
Israelite man who was killed with the Midianite woman was Zimri son of Salu,
15 leader of the ancestral House of Shimon. The name of the Midianite woman
who was killed was Kozbi, daughter of Tzur the tribal leader of a Midianite
ancestral house.
16 17, 18 And the LORD spoke to Moshe: "Attack the Midianites and defeat them, for
they attacked you by the deception they practiced against you in the Peor affair,
and in the affair of their sister Kozbi, daughter of a Midianite leader, who was
26 1 killed on the day of the plague in the Peor affair." After the plague –
2 the LORD said to Moshe and Elazar son of Aharon the priest: "Take a census
of the entire Israelite community, from twenty years of age and upward, by

רש״י

יג| **וְהָיְתָה לּוֹ.** בְּרִיתִי זֹאת: **בְּרִית כְּהֻנַּת עוֹלָם.** שֶׁאַף עַל פִּי שֶׁכְּבָר נִתְּנָה כְּהֻנָּה לְזַרְעוֹ שֶׁל אַהֲרֹן, לֹא נִתְּנָה אֶלָּא לְאַהֲרֹן וּלְבָנָיו שֶׁנִּמְשְׁחוּ עִמּוֹ וּלְתוֹלְדוֹתֵיהֶם שֶׁיּוֹלִידוּ אַחַר הִמָּשְׁחָתָן, אֲבָל פִּינְחָס שֶׁנּוֹלַד קֹדֶם לָכֵן וְלֹא נִמְשַׁח, לֹא בָּא לִכְלַל כְּהֻנָּה עַד כָּאן. וְכֵן שָׁנִינוּ בִּזְבָחִים: לֹא נִתְכַּהֵן פִּינְחָס עַד שֶׁהֲרָגוֹ לְזִמְרִי (זבחים קא ע״ב): **לֵאלֹהָיו.** בִּשְׁבִיל אֱלֹהָיו, כְּמוֹ: "הַמְקַנֵּא אַתָּה לִי" (לעיל יא, כט), "קִנֵּאתִי לְצִיּוֹן" (זכריה ח, ב), בִּשְׁבִיל צִיּוֹן:

יד| **וְשֵׁם אִישׁ יִשְׂרָאֵל וְגוֹ׳.** בְּמָקוֹם שֶׁיִּחֵס אֶת הַצַּדִּיק לְשֶׁבַח, יִחֵס אֶת הָרָשָׁע לִגְנַאי: **נְשִׂיא בֵית אָב לַשִּׁמְעֹנִי.** לְאֶחָד מֵחֲמֵשֶׁת בָּתֵּי אָבוֹת שֶׁהָיוּ לְשֵׁבֶט שִׁמְעוֹן. דָּבָר אַחֵר, לְהוֹדִיעַ שִׁבְחוֹ שֶׁל פִּינְחָס, שֶׁאַף עַל פִּי שֶׁזֶּה הָיָה נָשִׂיא, לֹא מָנַע אֶת עַצְמוֹ מִלְּקַנֵּא לְחִלּוּל הַשֵּׁם, לְכָךְ הוֹדִיעֲךָ הַכָּתוּב מִי הוּא הַמֻּכֶּה:

טו| **וְשֵׁם הָאִשָּׁה הַמֻּכָּה וְגוֹ׳.** לְהוֹדִיעֲךָ שִׂנְאָתָן שֶׁל מִדְיָנִים, שֶׁהִפְקִירוּ בַּת מֶלֶךְ לִזְנוּת כְּדֵי לְהַחֲטִיא אֶת יִשְׂרָאֵל: **רֹאשׁ אֻמּוֹת.** אֶחָד מֵחֲמֵשֶׁת מַלְכֵי מִדְיָן: "אֶת אֱוִי וְאֶת רֶקֶם וְאֶת צוּר" וְגוֹ׳ (להלן לא, ח), וְהוּא הָיָה חָשׁוּב מִכֻּלָּם, שֶׁנֶּאֱמַר: "רֹאשׁ אֻמּוֹת", וּלְפִי שֶׁנָּהַג בִּזָּיוֹן בְּעַצְמוֹ לְהַפְקִיר בִּתּוֹ מְנָאוֹ שְׁלִישִׁי: **בֵּית אָב.** חֲמִשָּׁה בָּתֵּי אָבוֹת הָיוּ לְמִדְיָן: "עֵיפָה וָעֵפֶר וַחֲנֹךְ וַאֲבִידָע וְאֶלְדָּעָה" (בראשית כה, ד), וְזֶה הָיָה מֶלֶךְ לְאֶחָד מֵהֶם:

יז| **צָרוֹר.** כְּמוֹ: 'זָכוֹר', 'שָׁמוֹר', לְשׁוֹן הֹוֶה, עֲלֵיכֶם לְאַיֵּב אוֹתָם:

יח| **כִּי צֹרְרִים הֵם לָכֶם וְגוֹ׳ עַל דְּבַר פְּעוֹר.** שֶׁהִפְקִירוּ בְּנוֹתֵיהֶם לִזְנוּת כְּדֵי לְהַטְעוֹתְכֶם אַחַר פְּעוֹר. וְאֶת מוֹאָב לֹא צִוָּה לְהַשְׁמִיד, מִפְּנֵי רוּת שֶׁהָיְתָה עֲתִידָה לָצֵאת מֵהֶם, כִּדְאָמְרִינַן בְּבָבָא קַמָּא (דף לח ע״ב):

כו א| **וַיְהִי אַחֲרֵי הַמַּגֵּפָה וְגוֹ׳.** מָשָׁל לְרוֹעֶה שֶׁנִּכְנְסוּ זְאֵבִים לְתוֹךְ עֶדְרוֹ וְהָרְגוּ בָּהֶן, וְהוּא מוֹנֶה אוֹתָן לֵידַע מִנְיַן הַנּוֹתָרוֹת. דָּבָר אַחֵר, כְּשֶׁיָּצְאוּ מִמִּצְרַיִם וְנִמְסְרוּ לְמֹשֶׁה, נִמְסְרוּ לוֹ בְּמִנְיָן, עַכְשָׁיו שֶׁקָּרַב לָמוּת וּלְהַחֲזִיר צֹאנוֹ, מַחֲזִירָם בְּמִנְיָן:

ב| **לְבֵית אֲבֹתָם.** עַל שֵׁבֶט הָאָב יִתְיַחֲסוּ וְלֹא אַחַר הָאֵם:

Crisis in Jewish history has always led to renewal, not to despair. "Whenever you find the word *vayehi,* 'and it came to pass,' this is always a sign of suffering"; conversely, "whenever you find the phrase *vehaya,* 'and it shall come to pass,' this is always a sign of joy" (Bemidbar Rabba 13:5). The Jewish way of telling a story, the Mishna instructs us, is *mathil bigenut umesayem beshevaḥ,* to "begin with the bad and end with the good" (Pesaḥim 10:4). This is also a mode of being in the world. Leaders don't wait for things to come to pass. They say not *vayehi* but *yehi,* "Let there be." That was the word with which God created the universe. It is also the word with which we create the micro-universe that is our life. The past might give us cause for lamentation, but the future still holds its promise.

The first census in Numbers documented the people of Israel who had recently left Egypt. The census taken now, "after the plague," shows the population that, having survived all the hazards and hardships of the desert, will take possession of the Promised Land.

יג שָׁלוֹם׃ וְהָיְתָה לּוֹ וּלְזַרְעוֹ אַחֲרָיו בְּרִית כְּהֻנַּת עוֹלָם תַּחַת אֲשֶׁר קִנֵּא
יד לֵאלֹהָיו וַיְכַפֵּר עַל־בְּנֵי יִשְׂרָאֵל׃ וְשֵׁם אִישׁ יִשְׂרָאֵל הַמֻּכֶּה אֲשֶׁר
טו הֻכָּה אֶת־הַמִּדְיָנִית זִמְרִי בֶּן־סָלוּא נְשִׂיא בֵית־אָב לַשִּׁמְעֹנִי׃ וְשֵׁם
הָאִשָּׁה הַמֻּכָּה הַמִּדְיָנִית כָּזְבִּי בַת־צוּר רֹאשׁ אֻמּוֹת בֵּית־אָב בְּמִדְיָן
הוּא׃
טז יז וַיְדַבֵּר יהוה אֶל־מֹשֶׁה לֵּאמֹר׃ צָרוֹר אֶת־הַמִּדְיָנִים וְהִכִּיתֶם אוֹתָם׃
יח כִּי־צֹרְרִים הֵם לָכֶם בְּנִכְלֵיהֶם אֲשֶׁר־נִכְּלוּ לָכֶם עַל־דְּבַר פְּעוֹר וְעַל־
דְּבַר כָּזְבִּי בַת־נְשִׂיא מִדְיָן אֲחֹתָם הַמֻּכָּה בְיוֹם־הַמַּגֵּפָה עַל־דְּבַר
כו א פְּעוֹר׃ וַיְהִי אַחֲרֵי הַמַּגֵּפָה
ב וַיֹּאמֶר יהוה אֶל־מֹשֶׁה וְאֶל אֶלְעָזָר בֶּן־אַהֲרֹן הַכֹּהֵן לֵאמֹר׃ שְׂאוּ אֶת־
רֹאשׁ ׀ כָּל־עֲדַת בְּנֵי־יִשְׂרָאֵל מִבֶּן עֶשְׂרִים שָׁנָה וָמַעְלָה לְבֵית אֲבֹתָם

אונקלוס

שְׁלָם: יג וּתְהֵי לֵיהּ וְלִבְנוֹהִי בָּתְרוֹהִי, קְיָם כְּהֻנַּת עָלַם, חֲלָף, דְּקַנִּי קֳדָם אֱלָהֵיהּ, וְכַפַּר עַל בְּנֵי יִשְׂרָאֵל: יד וְשׁוּם גֻּבְרָא בַּר יִשְׂרָאֵל קְטִילָא, דְּאִתְקְטִיל עִם מִדְיָנֵיתָא, זִמְרִי בַּר סָלוּא, רַב בֵּית בָּא לְבֵית שִׁמְעוֹן: טו וְשׁוּם אִתְּתָא דְּאִתְקְטֵילַת, מִדְיָנֵיתָא כָּזְבִּי בַת צוּר, רֵישׁ אֻמֵּי, בֵּית אַבָּא, בְּמִדְיָן הוּא: טז וּמַלֵּיל יי עִם מֹשֶׁה לְמֵימַר: יז אַעֵיק לְמִדְיָנָאֵי, וְתִקַטֵּיל יָתְהוֹן: יח אֲרֵי מְעִיקִין אִנּוּן לְכוֹן, בְּנִכְלֵיהוֹן, דְּנַכִּילוּ לְכוֹן עַל עֵיסַק פְּעוֹר, וְעַל עֵיסַק, כָּזְבִּי בַת רַבָּא דְּמִדְיָן אֲחָתְהוֹן, דְּאִתְקְטֵילַת בְּיוֹמָא דְּמוֹתָנָא עַל עֵיסַק פְּעוֹר: כו א וַהֲוָה בָּתַר מוֹתָנָא, וַאֲמַר יי לְמֹשֶׁה, וּלְאֶלְעָזָר, בַּר אַהֲרֹן כָּהֲנָא לְמֵימַר: ב קַבִּילוּ, יָת חֻשְׁבַּן כָּל כְּנִשְׁתָּא דִּבְנֵי יִשְׂרָאֵל, מִבַּר עֶסְרִין שְׁנִין, וּלְעֵילָא לְבֵית אֲבָהָתְהוֹן,

PREFACE TO THE SECOND CENSUS

The Rabbis said: "Whenever you find the word *vayehi*, 'and it came to pass,' this is always a sign of suffering" (Megilla 10b). They could hear this in the very sound of the word – "*Vai, vayehi*" (Shemot Rabba 20:1), and nowhere is it better illustrated than in this preface to the second census in the book of Numbers.

The previous chapter described the terrible events at Shitim, where God saved the Israelites from their enemies, only to see them commit the ultimate betrayal. Twenty-four thousand people died in a plague. God tells Moshe to take revenge against the Midianites (Num. 25:17). Immediately after, we read: "*Vayehi* after the plague." At this point, there is a *piska be'emtza pasuk*, a paragraph break in the middle of a sentence. It is a moment of radical discontinuity, one of the rare occasions when the Torah signals a break in the sequence of words. In a Torah scroll, the rest of the line is left empty. The sentence continues on the next line. This creates a deliberate pause until we can begin to take in the enormity of the offense. There is an audible silence in which the absence of words speaks more powerfully than any words could. Seeing what His people had done, God might have destroyed them.

Yet now, after the silence, comes a new beginning. It may be that the space in the middle of a sentence is there not to break but to join. The Torah wants us to understand that it is not merely after the plague but also because of it that God orders a new census. There are acts that are unforgivable, but the story must continue somehow.

3 their ancestral houses: everyone in Israel capable of active service." Moshe and
Elazar the priest spoke to them in the plains of Moav by the Jordan opposite
4 Yeriḥo: "Take a census of those twenty years of age and upward just as the LORD
5 commanded Moshe and the Israelites who came out of Egypt." Reuven was SHENI
Yisrael's firstborn. Reuven's descendants: of Ḥanokh, the clan of Ḥanokh; of Palu,
6 the clan of Palu; of Ḥetzron, the clan of Ḥetzron; of Karmi, the clan of Karmi.
7 8 These are the Reubenite clans. Their tally was 43,730. Palu's descendants: Eliav.
9 Eliav's descendants: Nemuel, Datan, and Aviram. These were the same Datan
and Aviram, elect of the community, who rebelled against Moshe and Aharon in
10 the company of Koraḥ, when they rebelled against the LORD. The earth opened
its mouth and swallowed them, along with Koraḥ, when the company died and
11 fire consumed the two hundred fifty men; and they became a sign. But the sons
12 of Koraḥ did not die. Shimon's descendants by their clans: of Nemuel,
the clan of Nemuel; of Yamin, the clan of Yamin; of Yakhin, the clan of Yakhin;
13 14 of Zeraḥ, the clan of Zeraḥ; of Sha'ul, the clan of Sha'ul. These are the Simeonite
15 clans: 22,200. Gad's descendants by their clans: of Tzefon, the clan of
16 Tzefon; of Ḥagi, the clan of Ḥagi; of Shuni, the clan of Shuni; of Ozni, the clan
17 of Ozni; of Eri, the clan of Eri; of Arod, the clan of Arod; of Areli, the clan of

רש״י

ג **וַיְדַבֵּר מֹשֶׁה וְאֶלְעָזָר הַכֹּהֵן אֹתָם.** דִּבְּרוּ עִמָּם עַל זֹאת, שֶׁצִּוָּה הַמָּקוֹם לִמְנוֹתָם: **לֵאמֹר.** אָמְרוּ לָהֶם צְרִיכִים אַתֶּם לְהִמָּנוֹת:

ד **מִבֶּן עֶשְׂרִים שָׁנָה וָמָעְלָה כַּאֲשֶׁר צִוָּה וְגוֹ׳.** שֶׁיְּהֵא מִנְיָנָם מִבֶּן עֶשְׂרִים שָׁנָה וָמַעְלָה, שֶׁנֶּאֱמַר: "כֹּל הָעֹבֵר עַל הַפְּקֻדִים" וְגוֹ׳ (שמות ל, יג):

ה **מִשְׁפַּחַת הַחֲנֹכִי.** לְפִי שֶׁהָיוּ הָאֻמּוֹת מְבַזִּין אוֹתָם וְאוֹמְרִים, מָה אֵלּוּ מִתְיַחֲסִין עַל שִׁבְטֵיהֶם? סְבוּרִין הֵם שֶׁלֹּא שָׁלְטוּ הַמִּצְרִים בְּאִמּוֹתֵיהֶם? אִם בְּגוּפָם הָיוּ מוֹשְׁלִים קַל וָחֹמֶר בִּנְשׁוֹתֵיהֶם! לְפִיכָךְ הִטִּיל הַקָּדוֹשׁ בָּרוּךְ הוּא שְׁמוֹ עֲלֵיהֶם, הֵ״א מִצַּד זֶה וְיוּ״ד מִצַּד זֶה, לוֹמַר, מֵעִיד אֲנִי עֲלֵיהֶם שֶׁהֵם בְּנֵי אֲבוֹתֵיהֶם. וְזֶה הוּא שֶׁמְּפֹרָשׁ עַל יְדֵי דָּוִד: "שִׁבְטֵי יָהּ עֵדוּת לְיִשְׂרָאֵל" (תהלים קכב, ד), הַשֵּׁם הַזֶּה מֵעִיד עֲלֵיהֶם לְשִׁבְטֵיהֶם. לְפִיכָךְ בְּכֻלָּם כְּתִיב: "הַחֲנֹכִי", "הַפַּלֻּאִי", אֲבָל בְּ"יִמְנָה" (להלן פסוק מד) לֹא הֻצְרַךְ לוֹמַר 'מִשְׁפַּחַת הַיִּמְנִי', לְפִי שֶׁהַשֵּׁם קָבוּעַ בּוֹ, יוּ״ד בָּרֹאשׁ וְהֵ״א בַּסּוֹף:

ט **אֲשֶׁר הִצּוּ.** אֶת יִשְׂרָאֵל "עַל מֹשֶׁה": **בְּהַצֹּתָם.** אֶת הָעָם "עַל ה׳": **הִצּוּ.** הִשִּׂיאוּ אֶת יִשְׂרָאֵל לָרִיב "עַל מֹשֶׁה", לְשׁוֹן הִפְעִילוּ:

י **וַיִּהְיוּ לְנֵס.** לְאוֹת וּלְזִכָּרוֹן, לְמַעַן אֲשֶׁר לֹא יִקְרַב אִישׁ זָר לַחֲלֹק עוֹד עַל הַכְּהֻנָּה:

יא **וּבְנֵי קֹרַח לֹא מֵתוּ.** הֵם הָיוּ בָּעֵצָה תְּחִלָּה, וּבִשְׁעַת הַמַּחְלֹקֶת הִרְהֲרוּ תְּשׁוּבָה בְּלִבָּם, לְפִיכָךְ נִתְבַּצֵּר לָהֶם מָקוֹם גָּבוֹהַּ בַּגֵּיהִנֹּם וְיָשְׁבוּ שָׁם:

יג **לְזֶרַח.** הוּא צֹחַר (שמות ו, טו), לְשׁוֹן צֹהַר, אֲבָל מִשְׁפַּחַת אֹהַד בָּטְלָה. וְכֵן חָמֵשׁ מִשֵּׁבֶט בִּנְיָמִין, שֶׁהֲרֵי בַּעֲשָׂרָה בָּנִים יָרַד לְמִצְרַיִם (בראשית מו, כא) וְכָאן לֹא מָנָה אֶלָּא חֲמִשָּׁה, וְכֵן אֶצְבּוֹן לְגָד, הֲרֵי שֶׁבַע מִשְׁפָּחוֹת. וּמָצָאתִי בְּתַלְמוּד יְרוּשַׁלְמִי (סוטה א, י) שֶׁכְּשֶׁמֵּת אַהֲרֹן נִסְתַּלְּקוּ עַנְנֵי כָבוֹד וּבָאוּ הַכְּנַעֲנִים לְהִלָּחֵם בְּיִשְׂרָאֵל, וְנָתְנוּ לֵב לַחֲזֹר לְמִצְרַיִם, וְחָזְרוּ לַאֲחוֹרֵיהֶם שְׁמוֹנָה מַסָּעוֹת מֵהֹר הָהָר לְמוֹסֵרָה, שֶׁנֶּאֱמַר: "וּבְנֵי יִשְׂרָאֵל נָסְעוּ מִבְּאֵרֹת בְּנֵי יַעֲקָן מוֹסֵרָה, שָׁם מֵת אַהֲרֹן" (דברים י, ו), וַהֲלֹא בְּהֹר הָהָר מֵת, וּמִמּוֹסֵרָה עַד הֹר הָהָר שְׁמוֹנָה מַסָּעוֹת יֵשׁ לְמַפְרֵעַ? אֶלָּא שֶׁחָזְרוּ לַאֲחוֹרֵיהֶם, וְרָדְפוּ בְּנֵי לֵוִי אַחֲרֵיהֶם לְהַחֲזִירָם, וְהָרְגוּ מֵהֶם שֶׁבַע מִשְׁפָּחוֹת, וּמִבְּנֵי לֵוִי נָפְלוּ אַרְבַּע מִשְׁפָּחוֹת: מִשְׁפַּחַת שִׁמְעִי, וְעָזִּיאֵלִי, וּמִבְּנֵי יִצְהָר לֹא נִמְנוּ כָּאן אֶלָּא מִשְׁפַּחַת הַקָּרְחִי, וְהָרְבִיעִית לֹא יָדַעְתִּי מַה הִיא. וְרַבִּי תַּנְחוּמָא דָּרַשׁ שֶׁמֵּתוּ בַּמַּגֵּפָה בִּדְבַר בִּלְעָם (מדרש תנחומא ה), אֲבָל לְפִי הַחֶסְרוֹן שֶׁחָסֵר מִשֵּׁבֶט שִׁמְעוֹן בְּמִנְיָן זֶה מִמִּנְיָן הָרִאשׁוֹן שֶׁבְּמִדְבַּר סִינַי, נִרְאֶה שֶׁכָּל עֶשְׂרִים וְאַרְבָּעָה אֶלֶף נָפְלוּ מִשִּׁבְטוֹ שֶׁל שִׁמְעוֹן:

ג כָּל־יֹצֵא צָבָא בְּיִשְׂרָאֵל׃ וַיְדַבֵּר מֹשֶׁה וְאֶלְעָזָר הַכֹּהֵן אֹתָם בְּעַרְבֹת
ד מוֹאָב עַל־יַרְדֵּן יְרֵחוֹ לֵאמֹר׃ מִבֶּן עֶשְׂרִים שָׁנָה וָמָעְלָה כַּאֲשֶׁר צִוָּה
ה יהוה אֶת־מֹשֶׁה וּבְנֵי יִשְׂרָאֵל הַיֹּצְאִים מֵאֶרֶץ מִצְרָיִם׃ רְאוּבֵן בְּכוֹר שני
יִשְׂרָאֵל בְּנֵי רְאוּבֵן חֲנוֹךְ מִשְׁפַּחַת הַחֲנֹכִי לְפַלּוּא מִשְׁפַּחַת הַפַּלֻּאִי׃
ו ז לְחֶצְרֹן מִשְׁפַּחַת הַחֶצְרוֹנִי לְכַרְמִי מִשְׁפַּחַת הַכַּרְמִי׃ אֵלֶּה מִשְׁפְּחֹת
הָרֻאוּבֵנִי וַיִּהְיוּ פְקֻדֵיהֶם שְׁלֹשָׁה וְאַרְבָּעִים אֶלֶף וּשְׁבַע מֵאוֹת וּשְׁלֹשִׁים׃
ח ט וּבְנֵי פַלּוּא אֱלִיאָב׃ וּבְנֵי אֱלִיאָב נְמוּאֵל וְדָתָן וַאֲבִירָם הוּא־דָתָן
וַאֲבִירָם קרואי הָעֵדָה אֲשֶׁר הִצּוּ עַל־מֹשֶׁה וְעַל־אַהֲרֹן בַּעֲדַת־קֹרַח קְרִיאֵי
י בְּהַצֹּתָם עַל־יהוה׃ וַתִּפְתַּח הָאָרֶץ אֶת־פִּיהָ וַתִּבְלַע אֹתָם וְאֶת־קֹרַח
בְּמוֹת הָעֵדָה בַּאֲכֹל הָאֵשׁ אֵת חֲמִשִּׁים וּמָאתַיִם אִישׁ וַיִּהְיוּ לְנֵס׃
יא יב וּבְנֵי־קֹרַח לֹא־מֵתוּ׃ בְּנֵי שִׁמְעוֹן לְמִשְׁפְּחֹתָם לִנְמוּאֵל
מִשְׁפַּחַת הַנְּמוּאֵלִי לְיָמִין מִשְׁפַּחַת הַיָּמִינִי לְיָכִין מִשְׁפַּחַת הַיָּכִינִי׃
יג יד לְזֶרַח מִשְׁפַּחַת הַזַּרְחִי לְשָׁאוּל מִשְׁפַּחַת הַשָּׁאוּלִי׃ אֵלֶּה מִשְׁפְּחֹת
טו הַשִּׁמְעֹנִי שְׁנַיִם וְעֶשְׂרִים אֶלֶף וּמָאתָיִם׃ בְּנֵי גָד לְמִשְׁפְּחֹתָם
לִצְפוֹן מִשְׁפַּחַת הַצְּפוֹנִי לְחַגִּי מִשְׁפַּחַת הַחַגִּי לְשׁוּנִי מִשְׁפַּחַת הַשּׁוּנִי׃
טז יז לְאָזְנִי מִשְׁפַּחַת הָאָזְנִי לְעֵרִי מִשְׁפַּחַת הָעֵרִי׃ לַאֲרוֹד מִשְׁפַּחַת הָאֲרוֹדִי

אונקלוס

כָּל נָפֵיק חֵילָא בְּיִשְׂרָאֵל׃ ג וּמַלִּיל מֹשֶׁה, וְאֶלְעָזָר כָּהֲנָא, אֲמַרוּ לְמִמְנֵי יָתְהוֹן בְּמֵישְׁרַיָּא דְמוֹאָב, עַל יַרְדְּנָא דִירֵיחוֹ לְמֵימָר׃ ד מִבַּר עַסְרִין שְׁנִין וּלְעֵילָא, כְּמָא דְפַקֵּיד יי יָת מֹשֶׁה וּבְנֵי יִשְׂרָאֵל, דִּנְפַקוּ מֵאַרְעָא דְמִצְרָיִם׃ ה רְאוּבֵן בְּכְרֵיהּ דְיִשְׂרָאֵל, בְּנֵי רְאוּבֵן, חֲנוֹךְ זַרְעִית חֲנוֹךְ, לְפַלּוּא, זַרְעִית פַּלּוּא׃ ו לְחֶצְרוֹן, זַרְעִית חֶצְרוֹן, לְכַרְמִי, זַרְעִית כַּרְמִי׃ ז אִלֵּין זַרְעִית רְאוּבֵן, וַהֲווֹ מִנְיָנֵיהוֹן, אַרְבְּעִין וּתְלָתָא אַלְפִין, וּשְׁבַע מְאָה וּתְלָתִין׃ ח וּבְנֵי פַלּוּא אֱלִיאָב׃ ט וּבְנֵי אֱלִיאָב, נְמוּאֵל וְדָתָן וַאֲבִירָם, הוּא דָתָן וַאֲבִירָם מְעַרְעֵי כְּנִשְׁתָּא, דְּאִתְכְּנִישׁוּ, עַל מֹשֶׁה וְעַל אַהֲרֹן בִּכְנִשְׁתָּא דְקֹרַח, בְּאִתְכַּנּוֹשֵׁיהוֹן עַל יי׃ י וּפְתַחַת אַרְעָא יָת פֻּמַּהּ, וּבְלַעַת יָתְהוֹן, וְיָת קֹרַח בְּמוֹתָא דִּכְנִשְׁתָּא, כַּד אֲכַלַת אִישָׁתָא, יָת מָאתַן וְחַמְשִׁין גֻּבְרָא, וַהֲווֹ לְאָת׃ יא וּבְנֵי קֹרַח לָא מִיתוּ׃ יב בְּנֵי שִׁמְעוֹן לְזַרְעִיָתְהוֹן, לִנְמוּאֵל, זַרְעִית נְמוּאֵל, לְיָמִין, זַרְעִית יָמִין, לְיָכִין, זַרְעִית יָכִין׃ יג לְזֶרַח, זַרְעִית זֶרַח, לְשָׁאוּל, זַרְעִית שָׁאוּל׃ יד אִלֵּין זַרְעִית שִׁמְעוֹן, עַסְרִין וּתְרֵין אַלְפִין וּמָאתַן׃ טו בְּנֵי גָד לְזַרְעִיָתְהוֹן, לִצְפוֹן, זַרְעִית צְפוֹן, לְחַגִּי, זַרְעִית חַגִּי, לְשׁוּנִי, זַרְעִית שׁוּנִי׃ טז לְאָזְנִי, זַרְעִית אָזְנִי, לְעֵרִי, זַרְעִית עֵרִי׃ יז לַאֲרוֹד, זַרְעִית אֲרוֹד,

18 19 Areli. These are the Gadite clans. Their tally was 40,500. Among
Yehuda's sons were Er and Onan; Er and Onan died in the land of Canaan.
20 Yehuda's descendants by their clans: of Shela, the clan of Shela; of Peretz, the
21 clan of Peretz; of Zeraḥ, the clan of Zeraḥ. Peretz's descendants: of Ḥetzron, the
22 clan of Ḥetzron; of Ḥamul, the clan of Ḥamul. These are the clans of Yehuda.
23 Their tally was 76,500. Yissakhar's descendants by their clans: of Tola,
24 the clan of Tola; of Puva, the clan of Puva; of Yashuv, the clan of Yashuv; of
25 Shimron, the clan of Shimron. These are the clans of Yissakhar. Their tally was
26 64,300. Zevulun's descendants by their clans: of Sered, the clan of
27 Sered; of Elon, the clan of Elon; of Yaḥle'el, the clan of Yaḥle'el. These are the
28 Zebulunite clans. Their tally was 60,500. Yosef's descendants by
29 their clans: Menashe and Efrayim – Menashe's descendants: of Makhir, the clan

רש"י

טז **לְאָזְנִי.** אוֹמֵר אֲנִי שֶׁזּוֹ מִשְׁפַּחַת אֶצְבּוֹן, וְאֵינִי יוֹדֵעַ לָמָּה לֹא נִקְרֵאת מִשְׁפַּחְתּוֹ עַל שְׁמוֹ:

כד **לְיָשׁוּב.** הוּא יוֹב הָאָמוּר בְּיוֹרְדֵי מִצְרַיִם, כִּי כָּל הַמִּשְׁפָּחוֹת נִקְרְאוּ עַל שֵׁם יוֹרְדֵי מִצְרַיִם, וְהַנּוֹלָדִין מִשָּׁם וָהָלְאָה לֹא נִקְרְאוּ הַמִּשְׁפָּחוֹת עַל שְׁמָם, חוּץ מִמִּשְׁפְּחוֹת אֶפְרַיִם וּמְנַשֶּׁה שֶׁנּוֹלְדוּ כֻּלָּם בְּמִצְרַיִם, וְאַרְדְּ וְנַעֲמָן בְּנֵי בֶלַע בֶּן בִּנְיָמִין. וּמָצָאתִי בִּיסוֹדוֹ שֶׁל רַבִּי מֹשֶׁה הַדַּרְשָׁן, שֶׁיָּרְדָה אִמָּן לְמִצְרַיִם כְּשֶׁהָיְתָה מְעֻבֶּרֶת מֵהֶם, לְכָךְ נֶחְלְקוּ לְמִשְׁפָּחוֹת, כְּחֶצְרוֹן וְחָמוּל שֶׁהָיוּ בְּנֵי בָנִים לִיהוּדָה, וְחֶבֶר וּמַלְכִּיאֵל שֶׁהָיוּ בְּנֵי בָנִים שֶׁל אָשֵׁר. וְאִם אַגָּדָה הִיא הֲרֵי טוֹב, וְאִם לָאו אוֹמֵר אֲנִי שֶׁהָיוּ לְבֶלַע בְּנֵי בָנִים הַרְבֵּה, וּמִשְּׁנַיִם הַלָּלוּ אַרְדְּ וְנַעֲמָן יָצְאָה מִכָּל אֶחָד מִשְׁפָּחָה רַבָּה, וְנִקְרְאוּ תּוֹלְדוֹת שְׁאָר הַבָּנִים עַל שֵׁם בֶּלַע, וְתוֹלְדוֹת הַשְּׁנַיִם הַלָּלוּ נִקְרְאוּ עַל שְׁמָם. וְכֵן אֲנִי אוֹמֵר בִּבְנֵי מָכִיר שֶׁנֶּחְלְקוּ לִשְׁתֵּי מִשְׁפָּחוֹת, אַחַת נִקְרֵאת עַל שְׁמוֹ וְאַחַת נִקְרֵאת עַל שֵׁם גִּלְעָד בְּנוֹ. חָמֵשׁ מִשְׁפָּחוֹת חָסְרוּ מִבָּנָיו שֶׁל בִּנְיָמִין, כָּאן נִתְקַיְּמָה מִקְצָת נְבוּאַת אִמּוֹ שֶׁקְּרָאַתּוּ "בֶּן אוֹנִי" (בראשית לה, יח), בֶּן אֲנִינוּתִי, וּבְפִילֶגֶשׁ בַּגִּבְעָה נִתְקַיְּמָה כֻּלָּהּ. זוֹ מָצָאתִי בִּיסוֹדוֹ שֶׁל רַבִּי מֹשֶׁה הַדַּרְשָׁן:

Ruth. Theirs are in fact the only stories told in any detail about David's female forebears.

The heroes in David's background are two women who stand at the very edge of Israelite society. In the biblical era there were no more vulnerable individuals than childless widows. But Tamar and Ruth were in a far worse situation still. They came from groups traditionally despised by the Israelites: the Canaanites and the Moabites. They had no natural place in the society in which they found themselves. *It was these two women, Tamar and Ruth, whose loyalty and steadfastness were the key factors in giving birth eventually to King David,* the man who became king of Israel, united the nation, initiated the plans for building the Temple, and wrote some of the finest poetry in the religious history of humankind.

This is worthy of serious reflection. Otto Rank, in his classic *The Myth of the Birth of the Hero*, points out that there are common elements in the stories told about the heroes of myth. Though raised by lowly adoptive parents, they are of noble birth. They have royal blood or are descended from the gods. The story of David turns this convention on its head. David has the kind of family background most people would seek to hide. His unlikely rise to greatness is due, not to any hidden divinity, but to the unexpected courage of his foremothers' love.

It is interesting too that this reminder of Tamar and foreshadowing of Ruth appear in the same census as the daughters of Tzelofḥad (Num. 26:33). They too are courageous women who find their way to insist that the family line will not be broken despite the absence of sons. Their path is to be easier, however. They are able to challenge the law to secure their place in the land.

יח לְאַרְאֵלִי מִשְׁפַּחַת הָאַרְאֵלִי: אֵלֶּה מִשְׁפְּחֹת בְּנֵי־גָד לִפְקֻדֵיהֶם אַרְבָּעִים
יט אֶלֶף וַחֲמֵשׁ מֵאוֹת: בְּנֵי יְהוּדָה עֵר וְאוֹנָן וַיָּמָת עֵר
כ וְאוֹנָן בְּאֶרֶץ כְּנָעַן: וַיִּהְיוּ בְנֵי־יְהוּדָה לְמִשְׁפְּחֹתָם לְשֵׁלָה מִשְׁפַּחַת
כא הַשֵּׁלָנִי לְפֶרֶץ מִשְׁפַּחַת הַפַּרְצִי לְזֶרַח מִשְׁפַּחַת הַזַּרְחִי: וַיִּהְיוּ בְנֵי־פֶרֶץ
כב לְחֶצְרֹן מִשְׁפַּחַת הַחֶצְרֹנִי לְחָמוּל מִשְׁפַּחַת הֶחָמוּלִי: אֵלֶּה מִשְׁפְּחֹת
כג יְהוּדָה לִפְקֻדֵיהֶם שִׁשָּׁה וְשִׁבְעִים אֶלֶף וַחֲמֵשׁ מֵאוֹת: בְּנֵי
יִשָּׂשכָר לְמִשְׁפְּחֹתָם תּוֹלָע מִשְׁפַּחַת הַתּוֹלָעִי לְפֻוָּה מִשְׁפַּחַת הַפּוּנִי:
כד כה לְיָשׁוּב מִשְׁפַּחַת הַיָּשֻׁבִי לְשִׁמְרֹן מִשְׁפַּחַת הַשִּׁמְרֹנִי: אֵלֶּה מִשְׁפְּחֹת
כו יִשָּׂשכָר לִפְקֻדֵיהֶם אַרְבָּעָה וְשִׁשִּׁים אֶלֶף וּשְׁלֹשׁ מֵאוֹת: בְּנֵי
זְבוּלֻן לְמִשְׁפְּחֹתָם לְסֶרֶד מִשְׁפַּחַת הַסַּרְדִּי לְאֵלוֹן מִשְׁפַּחַת הָאֵלֹנִי
כז לְיַחְלְאֵל מִשְׁפַּחַת הַיַּחְלְאֵלִי: אֵלֶּה מִשְׁפְּחֹת הַזְּבוּלֹנִי לִפְקֻדֵיהֶם
כח שִׁשִּׁים אֶלֶף וַחֲמֵשׁ מֵאוֹת: בְּנֵי יוֹסֵף לְמִשְׁפְּחֹתָם מְנַשֶּׁה
כט וְאֶפְרָיִם: בְּנֵי מְנַשֶּׁה לְמָכִיר מִשְׁפַּחַת הַמָּכִירִי וּמָכִיר הוֹלִיד אֶת־

אונקלוס

לְאַרְאֵלִי, זַרְעִית אַרְאֵלִי: יח אִלֵּין, זַרְעֲיַת בְּנֵי גָד לְמִנְיָנֵיהוֹן, אַרְבְּעִין אַלְפִין וַחֲמֵשׁ מְאָה: יט בְּנֵי יְהוּדָה עֵר וְאוֹנָן, וּמִית עֵר, וְאוֹנָן בְּאַרְעָא דִכְנָעַן: כ וַהֲווֹ בְנֵי יְהוּדָה לְזַרְעֲיָתְהוֹן, לְשֵׁלָה, זַרְעִית שֵׁלָה, לְפֶרֶץ, זַרְעִית פֶּרֶץ, לְזֶרַח, זַרְעִית זָרַח: כא וַהֲווֹ בְנֵי פֶרֶץ, לְחֶצְרוֹן, זַרְעִית חֶצְרוֹן, לְחָמוּל, זַרְעִית חָמוּל: כב אִלֵּין, זַרְעֲיַת יְהוּדָה לְמִנְיָנֵיהוֹן, שִׁבְעִין וְשִׁתָּא אַלְפִין וַחֲמֵשׁ מְאָה: כג בְּנֵי יִשָּׂשכָר לְזַרְעֲיָתְהוֹן, תּוֹלָע, זַרְעִית תּוֹלָע, לְפֻוָּה, זַרְעִית פֻּוָּה: כד לְיָשׁוּב, זַרְעִית יָשׁוּב, לְשִׁמְרוֹן, זַרְעִית שִׁמְרוֹן: כה אִלֵּין, זַרְעֲיַת יִשָּׂשכָר לְמִנְיָנֵיהוֹן, שִׁתִּין וְאַרְבְּעָא אַלְפִין וּתְלָת מְאָה: כו בְּנֵי זְבוּלוּן לְזַרְעֲיָתְהוֹן, לְסֶרֶד, זַרְעִית סֶרֶד, לְאֵלוֹן, זַרְעִית אֵלוֹן, לְיַחְלְאֵל, זַרְעִית יַחְלְאֵל: כז אִלֵּין, זַרְעֲיַת זְבוּלוּן לְמִנְיָנֵיהוֹן, שִׁתִּין אַלְפִין וַחֲמֵשׁ מְאָה: כח בְּנֵי יוֹסֵף לְזַרְעֲיָתְהוֹן, מְנַשֶּׁה וְאֶפְרָיִם: כט בְּנֵי מְנַשֶּׁה, לְמָכִיר זַרְעִית מָכִיר, וּמָכִיר אוֹלֵיד יָת

26:21 בְּנֵי־פֶרֶץ *Peretz's descendants* – The text has obliquely reminded us of the narrative that led to Peretz's birth – Tamar's courageous plot to form an unorthodox Levirate relationship with her father-in-law (see Gen. 38 and comments there). Later, Ruth's relationship with Peretz's descendent, Boaz, will in many ways reflect the heroism of Tamar.

The book of Ruth ends with a family tree listing ten generations from Peretz to the birth of David. A ten-generation genealogy is a highly charged phenomenon in the Bible. There are ten generations from Adam to Noaḥ, and ten from Noaḥ to Avraham. The ten generations from Peretz to David carry the same sense of preordained destiny. The beginning of such a family tree is significant. So too is the seventh, the number associated with holiness. *David's family tree begins with Peretz, the son born to Yehuda and Tamar. The seventh generation is Oved, the son born to Ruth and Boaz.* The key progenitors of Israel's great and future king are Tamar and

30 of Makhir. Makhir had a son Gilad. Of Gilad, the clan of Gilad. These are Gilad's
31 descendants: of I'ezer, the clan of I'ezer; of Ḥelek, the clan of Ḥelek; of Asriel, the
32 clan of Asriel; of Shekhem, the clan of Shekhem; of Shemida, the clan of Shemida;
33 and of Ḥefer, the clan of Ḥefer. But Tzelofḥad son of Ḥefer had no sons, only
daughters. The names of Tzelofḥad's daughters were Maḥla, Noa, Ḥogla, Milka,
34 35 and Tirtza. These are the clans of Menashe. Their tally was 52,700. These
are Efrayim's descendants by their clans: of Shutelaḥ, the clan of Shutelaḥ; of
36 Bekher, the clan of Bekher; of Taḥan, the clan of Taḥan. These are Shutelaḥ's
37 descendants: of Eran, the clan of Eran. These are the clans of Efrayim. Their tally
38 was 32,500. All these are Yosef's descendants by their clans. Binyamin's
descendants by their clans: of Bela, the clan of Bela; of Ashbel, the clan of Ashbel;
39 of Aḥiram, the clan of Aḥiram; of Shefufam, the clan of Shefufam; of Ḥufam, the
40 clan of Ḥufam. Bela's descendants were Ard and Naaman: the clan of Ard; of
41 Naaman, the clan of Naaman. These are the clans of Binyamin. Their tally was
42 45,600. These are Dan's descendants by their clans: of Shuḥam, the clan
43 of Shuḥam. These are the clans of Dan; all the Shuhamite clans according to their
44 tally were 64,400. Asher's descendants by their clans: of Yimna, the
45 clan of Yimna; of Yishvi, the clan of Yishvi; of Beria, the clan of Beria. Of Beria's
46 descendants: of Ḥever, the clan of Ḥever; of Malkiel, the clan of Malkiel. The

אונקלוס

גִּלְעָד, לְגִלְעָד, זַרְעִית גִּלְעָד: ל אִלֵּין בְּנֵי גִלְעָד, אִיעֶזֶר, זַרְעִית אִיעֶזֶר, לְחֵלֶק, זַרְעִית חֵלֶק: לא וְאַשְׂרִיאֵל, זַרְעִית אַשְׂרִיאֵל, וְשֶׁכֶם, זַרְעִית שֶׁכֶם: לב וּשְׁמִידָע, זַרְעִית שְׁמִידָע, וְחֵפֶר, זַרְעִית חֵפֶר: לג וּצְלָפְחָד בַּר חֵפֶר, לָא הֲווֹ לֵיהּ, בְּנִין אֱלָהֵין בְּנָן, וְשׁוּם בְּנָת צְלָפְחָד, מַחְלָה וְנוֹעָה, חָגְלָה מִלְכָּה וְתִרְצָה: לד אִלֵּין זַרְעֲיָת מְנַשֶּׁה, וּמִנְיָנֵיהוֹן, חַמְשִׁין וּתְרֵין אַלְפִין וּשְׁבַע מְאָה: לה אִלֵּין בְּנֵי אֶפְרַיִם לְזַרְעֲיָתְהוֹן, לְשׁוּתֶלַח, זַרְעִית שׁוּתֶלַח, לְבֶכֶר, זַרְעִית בֶּכֶר, לְתַחַן, זַרְעִית תַּחַן: לו וְאִלֵּין בְּנֵי שׁוּתָלַח, לְעֵרָן, זַרְעִית עֵרָן: לז אִלֵּין זַרְעֲיָת בְּנֵי אֶפְרַיִם לְמִנְיָנֵיהוֹן, תְּלָתִין וּתְרֵין אַלְפִין וַחֲמֵשׁ מְאָה, אִלֵּין בְּנֵי יוֹסֵף לְזַרְעֲיָתְהוֹן: לח בְּנֵי בִנְיָמִין לְזַרְעֲיָתְהוֹן, לְבֶלַע, זַרְעִית בֶּלַע, לְאַשְׁבֵּל, זַרְעִית אַשְׁבֵּל, לַאֲחִירָם, זַרְעִית אֲחִירָם: לט לִשְׁפוּפָם, זַרְעִית שְׁפוּפָם, לְחוּפָם, זַרְעִית חוּפָם: מ וַהֲווֹ בְנֵי בֶלַע אַרְדְּ וְנַעֲמָן, זַרְעִית אַרְדְּ, לְנַעֲמָן, זַרְעִית נַעֲמָן: מא אִלֵּין בְּנֵי בִנְיָמִין לְזַרְעֲיָתְהוֹן, וּמִנְיָנֵיהוֹן, אַרְבְּעִין וַחֲמִשָּׁא אַלְפִין וְשֵׁית מְאָה: מב אִלֵּין בְּנֵי דָן לְזַרְעֲיָתְהוֹן, לְשׁוּחָם, זַרְעִית שׁוּחָם, אִלֵּין,

רש״י

לו וְאֵלֶּה בְּנֵי שׁוּתֶלַח וְגוֹ'. אַחַר בְּנֵי שׁוּתֶלַח נִקְרְאוּ תּוֹלְדוֹתֵיהֶם עַל שֵׁם שׁוּתֶלַח, וּמֵעֵרָן יָצְאָה מִשְׁפָּחָה רַבָּה וְנִקְרֵאת עַל שְׁמוֹ, וְנֶחְשְׁבוּ בְּנֵי שׁוּתֶלַח לִשְׁתֵּי מִשְׁפָּחוֹת. צֵא וַחֲשֹׁב, וְתִמְצָא בְּפָרָשָׁה זוֹ חֲמִשִּׁים וְשֶׁבַע מִשְׁפָּחוֹת וּמִבְּנֵי לֵוִי שְׁמוֹנֶה, הֲרֵי שִׁשִּׁים וְחָמֵשׁ, וְזֶהוּ שֶׁנֶּאֱמַר: ״כִּי אַתֶּם הַמְעַט״ וְגוֹ' (דברים ז, ז), הֵ״א מְעַט, חָמֵשׁ אַתֶּם חֲסֵרִים מִמִּשְׁפְּחוֹת כָּל הָעַמִּים שֶׁהֵן שִׁבְעִים. אַף זֶה הֵבַנְתִּי מִיסוֹדוֹ שֶׁל רַבִּי מֹשֶׁה הַדַּרְשָׁן, אַךְ הֻצְרַכְתִּי לִפְחֹת וּלְהוֹסִיף בִּדְבָרָיו:

לח לַאֲחִירָם. הוּא אֵחִי שֶׁיָּרַד לְמִצְרַיִם (בראשית מו, כא), וּלְפִי שֶׁנִּקְרָא עַל שֵׁם יוֹסֵף שֶׁהָיָה אָחִיו וְרָם מִמֶּנּוּ נִקְרָא אֲחִירָם:

לט לִשְׁפוּפָם. הוּא מֻפִּים (בראשית שם), עַל שֵׁם שֶׁהָיָה יוֹסֵף שָׁפוּף בֵּין הָאֻמּוֹת:

מב לְשׁוּחָם. הוּא חֻשִׁים (שם כג):

מו וְשֵׁם בַּת אָשֵׁר שָׂרַח. לְפִי שֶׁהָיְתָה קַיֶּמֶת בַּחַיִּים מְנָאָהּ כָּאן:

ל גִּלְעָד לְגִלְעָד מִשְׁפַּחַת הַגִּלְעָדִי׃ אֵלֶּה בְּנֵי גִלְעָד אִיעֶזֶר מִשְׁפַּחַת
לא הָאִיעֶזְרִי לְחֵלֶק מִשְׁפַּחַת הַחֶלְקִי׃ וְאַשְׂרִיאֵל מִשְׁפַּחַת הָאַשְׂרִאֵלִי
לב וְשֶׁכֶם מִשְׁפַּחַת הַשִּׁכְמִי׃ וּשְׁמִידָע מִשְׁפַּחַת הַשְּׁמִידָעִי וְחֵפֶר מִשְׁפַּחַת
לג הַחֶפְרִי׃ וּצְלָפְחָד בֶּן־חֵפֶר לֹא־הָיוּ לוֹ בָּנִים כִּי אִם־בָּנוֹת וְשֵׁם בְּנוֹת
לד צְלָפְחָד מַחְלָה וְנֹעָה חָגְלָה מִלְכָּה וְתִרְצָה׃ אֵלֶּה מִשְׁפְּחֹת מְנַשֶּׁה
לה וּפְקֻדֵיהֶם שְׁנַיִם וַחֲמִשִּׁים אֶלֶף וּשְׁבַע מֵאוֹת׃ אֵלֶּה בְנֵי־
אֶפְרַיִם לְמִשְׁפְּחֹתָם לְשׁוּתֶלַח מִשְׁפַּחַת הַשֻּׁתַלְחִי לְבֶכֶר מִשְׁפַּחַת
לו הַבַּכְרִי לְתַחַן מִשְׁפַּחַת הַתַּחֲנִי׃ וְאֵלֶּה בְּנֵי שׁוּתָלַח לְעֵרָן מִשְׁפַּחַת
לז הָעֵרָנִי׃ אֵלֶּה מִשְׁפְּחֹת בְּנֵי־אֶפְרַיִם לִפְקֻדֵיהֶם שְׁנַיִם וּשְׁלֹשִׁים אֶלֶף
לח וַחֲמֵשׁ מֵאוֹת אֵלֶּה בְנֵי־יוֹסֵף לְמִשְׁפְּחֹתָם׃ בְּנֵי בִנְיָמִן
לְמִשְׁפְּחֹתָם לְבֶלַע מִשְׁפַּחַת הַבַּלְעִי לְאַשְׁבֵּל מִשְׁפַּחַת הָאַשְׁבֵּלִי
לט לַאֲחִירָם מִשְׁפַּחַת הָאֲחִירָמִי׃ לִשְׁפוּפָם מִשְׁפַּחַת הַשּׁוּפָמִי לְחוּפָם
מ מִשְׁפַּחַת הַחוּפָמִי׃ וַיִּהְיוּ בְנֵי־בֶלַע אַרְדְּ וְנַעֲמָן מִשְׁפַּחַת הָאַרְדִּי
מא לְנַעֲמָן מִשְׁפַּחַת הַנַּעֲמִי׃ אֵלֶּה בְנֵי־בִנְיָמִן לְמִשְׁפְּחֹתָם וּפְקֻדֵיהֶם
מב חֲמִשָּׁה וְאַרְבָּעִים אֶלֶף וְשֵׁשׁ מֵאוֹת׃ אֵלֶּה בְנֵי־דָן
לְמִשְׁפְּחֹתָם לְשׁוּחָם מִשְׁפַּחַת הַשּׁוּחָמִי אֵלֶּה מִשְׁפְּחֹת דָּן לְמִשְׁפְּחֹתָם׃
מג כָּל־מִשְׁפְּחֹת הַשּׁוּחָמִי לִפְקֻדֵיהֶם אַרְבָּעָה וְשִׁשִּׁים אֶלֶף וְאַרְבַּע
מד מֵאוֹת׃ בְּנֵי אָשֵׁר לְמִשְׁפְּחֹתָם לְיִמְנָה מִשְׁפַּחַת הַיִּמְנָה
מה לְיִשְׁוִי מִשְׁפַּחַת הַיִּשְׁוִי לִבְרִיעָה מִשְׁפַּחַת הַבְּרִיעִי׃ לִבְנֵי בְרִיעָה
מו לְחֶבֶר מִשְׁפַּחַת הַחֶבְרִי לְמַלְכִּיאֵל מִשְׁפַּחַת הַמַּלְכִּיאֵלִי׃ וְשֵׁם בַּת־

אונקלוס

זַרְעִית דָּן לְזַרְעֲיָתְהוֹן: מג כָּל זַרְעִית שׁוּחָם לְמִנְיָנֵיהוֹן, שִׁתִּין וְאַרְבְּעָא אַלְפִין וְאַרְבַּע מְאָה: מד בְּנֵי אָשֵׁר לְזַרְעֲיָתְהוֹן, לְיִמְנָה, זַרְעִית יִמְנָה, לְיִשְׁוִי, זַרְעִית יִשְׁוִי, לִבְרִיעָה, זַרְעִית בְּרִיעָה: מה לִבְנֵי בְרִיעָה, לְחֶבֶר, זַרְעִית חֶבֶר, לְמַלְכִּיאֵל, זַרְעִית מַלְכִּיאֵל: מו וְשׁוּם בַּת

47 name of Asher's daughter was Seraḥ. These are the clans of Asher; their tally
48 was 53,400. Naftali's descendants by their clans: of Yaḥtze'el, the clan
49 of Yaḥtze'el; of Guni, the clan of Guni; of Yetzer, the clan of Yetzer; of Shilem,
50 51 the clan of Shilem. These are all the clans of Naftali. Their tally was 45,400. The
total number of those Israelite men was 601,730.
52 53 The LORD spoke to Moshe: "The land shall be apportioned to them for SHELISHI
54 inheritance by the tally of their names. To those who are many, give a large
inheritance; to those who are few, a small inheritance. Let each be given its
55 inheritance in keeping with its number. The land must be apportioned by lot.
56 By the names of their ancestral tribes they shall inherit. Whether large or small,
57 each tribe will inherit by means of the lot." These are the numbers of
the Levites by their clans: of Gershon, the clan of Gershon; of Kehat, the clan
58 of Kehat; of Merari, the clan of Merari. These are the Levite clans: the clan of
Livna, the clan of Ḥevron, the clan of Maḥli, the clan of Mushi, and the clan
59 of Koraḥ. Kehat had a son Amram. The name of Amram's wife was Yokheved
daughter of Levi; she had been born to Levi in Egypt. She bore to Amram
60 Aharon, Moshe, and their sister Miriam. To Aharon were born Nadav, Avihu,
61 Elazar, and Itamar. Nadav and Avihu died when they offered unauthorized fire

רש״י

נג] **לָאֵלֶּה תֵּחָלֵק הָאָרֶץ.** וְלֹא לִפְחוּתִים מִבֶּן עֶשְׂרִים, אַף עַל פִּי שֶׁבָּאוּ לִכְלַל עֶשְׂרִים בְּטֶרֶם חִלּוּק הָאָרֶץ, שֶׁהֲרֵי שֶׁבַע שָׁנִים כָּבְשׁוּ וְשֶׁבַע חִלְּקוּ, לֹא נָטְלוּ חֵלֶק בָּאָרֶץ אֶלָּא אֵלּוּ שֵׁשׁ מֵאוֹת אֶלֶף וָאֶלֶף, וְאִם הָיוּ לְאֶחָד מֵהֶם שִׁשָּׁה בָּנִים, לֹא נָטְלוּ אֶלָּא חֵלֶק אֲבִיהֶם לְבַדּוֹ:

נד] **לָרַב תַּרְבֶּה נַחֲלָתוֹ.** לְשֵׁבֶט שֶׁהָיָה מְרֻבֶּה בְּאוּכְלוּסִין נָתְנוּ חֵלֶק רָב. וְאַף עַל פִּי שֶׁלֹּא הָיוּ הַחֲלָקִים שָׁוִים, שֶׁהֲרֵי הַכֹּל לְפִי רִבּוּי הַשֵּׁבֶט חִלְּקוּ הַחֲלָקִים, לֹא עָשׂוּ אֶלָּא עַל יְדֵי גוֹרָל, וְהַגּוֹרָל הָיָה עַל פִּי רוּחַ הַקֹּדֶשׁ, כְּמוֹ שֶׁמְּפֹרָשׁ בְּבָבָא בַּתְרָא (דף קכב ע״א): אֶלְעָזָר הַכֹּהֵן הָיָה מְלֻבָּשׁ בְּאוּרִים וְתֻמִּים וְאוֹמֵר בְּרוּחַ הַקֹּדֶשׁ: אִם שֵׁבֶט פְּלוֹנִי עוֹלֶה, תְּחוּם פְּלוֹנִי עוֹלֶה עִמּוֹ. וְהַשְּׁבָטִים הָיוּ כְּתוּבִים בִּשְׁנֵים עָשָׂר פְּתָקִין וּשְׁנֵים עָשָׂר גְּבוּלִין בִּשְׁנֵים עָשָׂר פְּתָקִין, וּבְלָלוּם בְּקַלְפִּי, וְהַנָּשִׂיא מַכְנִיס יָדוֹ לְתוֹכָהּ וְנוֹטֵל שְׁנֵי פְתָקִין. עוֹלֶה בְּיָדוֹ פֶּתֶק שֶׁל שֵׁם שִׁבְטוֹ וּפֶתֶק שֶׁל גְּבוּל הַמְפֹרָשׁ לוֹ, וְהַגּוֹרָל עַצְמוֹ הָיָה צוֹוֵחַ וְאוֹמֵר: אֲנִי הַגּוֹרָל עָלִיתִי לִגְבוּל פְּלוֹנִי לְשֵׁבֶט פְּלוֹנִי, שֶׁנֶּאֱמַר: "עַל פִּי הַגּוֹרָל". וְלֹא נִתְחַלְּקָה הָאָרֶץ בְּמִדָּה, לְפִי שֶׁיֵּשׁ גְּבוּל מְשֻׁבָּח מֵחֲבֵרוֹ, אֶלָּא בְּשׁוּמָא: בֵּית כּוֹר רַע כְּנֶגֶד בֵּית סְאָה טוֹב, הַכֹּל לְפִי הַדָּמִים:

נה] **לִשְׁמוֹת מַטּוֹת אֲבֹתָם.** אֵלּוּ יוֹצְאֵי מִצְרַיִם. שִׁנָּה הַכָּתוּב נַחֲלָה זוֹ מִכָּל הַנְּחָלוֹת שֶׁבַּתּוֹרָה, שֶׁכָּל הַנְּחָלוֹת, הַחַיִּים יוֹרְשִׁים אֶת הַמֵּתִים, וְכָאן מֵתִים יוֹרְשִׁים אֶת הַחַיִּים. כֵּיצַד? שְׁנֵי אַחִים מִיּוֹצְאֵי מִצְרַיִם שֶׁהָיוּ לָהֶם בָּנִים בְּבָאֵי הָאָרֶץ, לָזֶה אֶחָד וְלָזֶה שְׁלֹשָׁה, הָאֶחָד נָטַל חֵלֶק אֶחָד, וְהַשְּׁלֹשָׁה נָטְלוּ שְׁלֹשָׁה, שֶׁנֶּאֱמַר: "לָאֵלֶּה תֵּחָלֵק הָאָרֶץ", חָזְרָה נַחֲלָתָן אֵצֶל אֲבִי אֲבִיהֶן וְחִלְּקוּ הַכֹּל בְּשָׁוֶה, וְזֶהוּ שֶׁנֶּאֱמַר: "לִשְׁמוֹת מַטּוֹת אֲבֹתָם יִנְחָלוּ", שֶׁאַחַר שֶׁנָּטְלוּ הַבָּנִים חִלְּקוּהָ לְפִי הָאָבוֹת שֶׁיָּצְאוּ מִמִּצְרַיִם. וְאִלּוּ מִתְּחִלָּה חִלְּקוּהָ לְמִנְיַן יוֹצְאֵי מִצְרַיִם, לֹא הָיוּ נוֹטְלִין אֵלּוּ הָאַרְבָּעָה אֶלָּא שְׁנֵי חֲלָקִים, עַכְשָׁיו נָטְלוּ אַרְבָּעָה חֲלָקִים:

נו] **עַל פִּי הַגּוֹרָל.** הַגּוֹרָל הָיָה מְדַבֵּר כְּמוֹ שֶׁפֵּרַשְׁתִּי לְמַעְלָה, מַגִּיד שֶׁנִּתְחַלְּקָה בְּרוּחַ הַקֹּדֶשׁ, וְכֵן הוּא אוֹמֵר: "וַיִּתְּנוּ לְכָלֵב אֶת חֶבְרוֹן (עַל פִּי ה׳) [כַּאֲשֶׁר דִּבֶּר מֹשֶׁה]" (שופטים א, כ), וְאוֹמֵר: "עַל פִּי ה׳ נָתְנוּ לוֹ אֶת הָעִיר אֲשֶׁר שָׁאָל" (יהושע יט, נ): **מַטּוֹת אֲבֹתָם.** יָצְאוּ גֵּרִים וַעֲבָדִים:

נח] **אֵלֶּה מִשְׁפְּחֹת לֵוִי.** חָסֵר כָּאן מִשְׁפְּחוֹת הַשִּׁמְעִי וְהָעֻזִּיאֵלִי וּקְצָת מִן הַיִּצְהָרִי:

נט] **אֲשֶׁר יָלְדָה אֹתָהּ לְלֵוִי בְּמִצְרָיִם.** אִשְׁתּוֹ יְלָדַתָּה בְּמִצְרַיִם וְאֵין הוֹרָתָהּ בְּמִצְרַיִם, כְּשֶׁנִּכְנְסוּ לְתוֹךְ הַחוֹמָה יְלָדַתָּה, וְהִיא הִשְׁלִימָה מִנְיַן שִׁבְעִים, שֶׁהֲרֵי בִּפְרָטָן אִי אַתָּה מוֹצֵא אֶלָּא שִׁשִּׁים וָתֵשַׁע:

מז אֲשֶׁר שָׂרַח׃ אֵלֶּה מִשְׁפְּחֹת בְּנֵי־אָשֵׁר לִפְקֻדֵיהֶם שְׁלֹשָׁה וַחֲמִשִּׁים
מח אֶלֶף וְאַרְבַּע מֵאוֹת׃ בְּנֵי נַפְתָּלִי לְמִשְׁפְּחֹתָם לְיַחְצְאֵל
מט מִשְׁפַּחַת הַיַּחְצְאֵלִי לְגוּנִי מִשְׁפַּחַת הַגּוּנִי׃ לְיֵצֶר מִשְׁפַּחַת הַיִּצְרִי לְשִׁלֵּם
נ מִשְׁפַּחַת הַשִּׁלֵּמִי׃ אֵלֶּה מִשְׁפְּחֹת נַפְתָּלִי לְמִשְׁפְּחֹתָם וּפְקֻדֵיהֶם חֲמִשָּׁה
נא וְאַרְבָּעִים אֶלֶף וְאַרְבַּע מֵאוֹת׃ אֵלֶּה פְּקוּדֵי בְּנֵי יִשְׂרָאֵל שֵׁשׁ־מֵאוֹת
אֶלֶף וָאָלֶף שְׁבַע מֵאוֹת וּשְׁלֹשִׁים׃
נב נג וַיְדַבֵּר יהוה אֶל־מֹשֶׁה לֵּאמֹר׃ לָאֵלֶּה תֵּחָלֵק הָאָרֶץ בְּנַחֲלָה בְּמִסְפַּר כג שלישי
נד שֵׁמוֹת׃ לָרַב תַּרְבֶּה נַחֲלָתוֹ וְלַמְעַט תַּמְעִיט נַחֲלָתוֹ אִישׁ לְפִי פְקֻדָיו
נה יֻתַּן נַחֲלָתוֹ׃ אַךְ־בְּגוֹרָל יֵחָלֵק אֶת־הָאָרֶץ לִשְׁמוֹת מַטּוֹת־אֲבֹתָם
נו נז יִנְחָלוּ׃ עַל־פִּי הַגּוֹרָל תֵּחָלֵק נַחֲלָתוֹ בֵּין רַב לִמְעָט׃ וְאֵלֶּה
פְקוּדֵי הַלֵּוִי לְמִשְׁפְּחֹתָם לְגֵרְשׁוֹן מִשְׁפַּחַת הַגֵּרְשֻׁנִּי לִקְהָת מִשְׁפַּחַת
נח הַקְּהָתִי לִמְרָרִי מִשְׁפַּחַת הַמְּרָרִי׃ אֵלֶּה ׀ מִשְׁפְּחֹת לֵוִי מִשְׁפַּחַת
הַלִּבְנִי מִשְׁפַּחַת הַחֶבְרֹנִי מִשְׁפַּחַת הַמַּחְלִי מִשְׁפַּחַת הַמּוּשִׁי מִשְׁפַּחַת
נט הַקָּרְחִי וּקְהָת הוֹלִד אֶת־עַמְרָם׃ וְשֵׁם ׀ אֵשֶׁת עַמְרָם יוֹכֶבֶד בַּת־לֵוִי
אֲשֶׁר יָלְדָה אֹתָהּ לְלֵוִי בְּמִצְרָיִם וַתֵּלֶד לְעַמְרָם אֶת־אַהֲרֹן וְאֶת־מֹשֶׁה
ס וְאֵת מִרְיָם אֲחֹתָם׃ וַיִּוָּלֵד לְאַהֲרֹן אֶת־נָדָב וְאֶת־אֲבִיהוּא אֶת־אֶלְעָזָר
סא וְאֶת־אִיתָמָר׃ וַיָּמָת נָדָב וַאֲבִיהוּא בְּהַקְרִיבָם אֵשׁ־זָרָה לִפְנֵי יהוה׃

אונקלוס

אֲשֶׁר שָׂרַח: מז אִלֵּין, זַרְעִית בְּנֵי אָשֵׁר לְמִנְיָנֵיהוֹן, חַמְשִׁין וּתְלָתָא אַלְפִין וְאַרְבַּע מְאָה: מח בְּנֵי נַפְתָּלִי לְזַרְעֲיָתְהוֹן, לְיַחְצְאֵל, זַרְעִית יַחְצְאֵל, לְגוּנִי, זַרְעִית גּוּנִי: מט לְיֵצֶר, זַרְעִית יֵצֶר, לְשִׁלֵּם, זַרְעִית שִׁלֵּם: נ אִלֵּין, זַרְעִית נַפְתָּלִי לְזַרְעֲיָתְהוֹן, וּמִנְיָנֵיהוֹן, אַרְבְּעִין וַחֲמֵשָׁא אַלְפִין וְאַרְבַּע מְאָה: נא אִלֵּין, מִנְיָנֵי בְּנֵי יִשְׂרָאֵל, שִׁית מְאָה וְחַד אַלְפִין, שְׁבַע מְאָה וּתְלָתִין: נב וּמַלִּיל יְיָ עִם מֹשֶׁה לְמֵימַר: נג לְאִלֵּין, תִּתְפְּלֵיג אַרְעָא, בְּאַחְסָנָא בְּמִנְיַן שְׁמָהָן: נד לְסַגִּיאֵי, תַּסְגּוֹן אַחְסַנְתְּהוֹן, וְלִזְעֵירֵי, תַּזְעֲרוּן אַחְסַנְתְּהוֹן, גְּבַר לְפוּם מִנְיָנוֹהִי, תִּתְיְהֵיב אַחְסַנְתֵּיהּ: נה בְּרַם בְּעַדְבָא, תִּתְפְּלֵיג אַרְעָא, לִשְׁמָהַת שִׁבְטֵי אֲבָהָתְהוֹן יַחְסְנוּן:

נו עַל פּוּם עַדְבָא, תִּתְפְּלֵיג אַחְסַנְתְּהוֹן, בֵּין סַגִּיאֵי לִזְעֵירֵי: נז וְאִלֵּין מִנְיָנֵי לֵיוָאֵי לְזַרְעֲיָתְהוֹן, לְגֵרְשׁוֹן, זַרְעִית גֵּרְשׁוֹן, לִקְהָת, זַרְעִית קְהָת, לִמְרָרִי, זַרְעִית מְרָרִי: נח אִלֵּין זַרְעִית לֵוִי, זַרְעִית לִבְנִי, זַרְעִית חֶבְרוֹן זַרְעִית מַחְלִי זַרְעִית מוּשִׁי, זַרְעִית קֹרַח, וּקְהָת אוֹלֵיד יָת עַמְרָם: נט וְשׁוּם אִתַּת עַמְרָם, יוֹכֶבֶד בַּת לֵוִי, דִּילֵידַת יָתַהּ, לְלֵוִי בְּמִצְרָיִם, וִילֵידַת לְעַמְרָם, יָת אַהֲרֹן וְיָת מֹשֶׁה, וְיָת מִרְיָם אֲחָתְהוֹן: ס וְאִתְיְלִיד לְאַהֲרֹן, יָת נָדָב וְיָת אֲבִיהוּא, יָת אֶלְעָזָר וְיָת אִיתָמָר: סא וּמִית נָדָב וַאֲבִיהוּא, בְּקָרוֹבֵיהוֹן אִישָׁתָא נֻכְרֵיתָא קֳדָם יְיָ:

62 before the Lord. Their number was 23,000, this including every male one
month of age and upward. They were not numbered along with the Israelites
63 because no land inheritance was given to them in the Israelites' midst. This was
the census that Moshe and Elazar the priest took of the Israelites on the plains
64 of Moav by the Jordan opposite Yeriḥo. It contained not one man who had been
counted by Moshe and Aharon the priest when they took the census of the
65 Israelites in the Sinai Desert. For the Lord had said of those, "They shall die in
the wilderness." Not one of them was left now except for Kalev son of Yefuneh
27 1 and Yehoshua son of Nun. Then the daughters of Tzelofḥad son of
Ḥefer son of Gilad son of Makhir son of Menashe, of the clans of Menashe
son of Yosef, came forward; the daughters' names were Maḥla, Noa, Ḥogla,
2 Milka, and Tirtza. And they stood before Moshe, Elazar the priest, the princes,

רש״י

סב **כִּי לֹא הָתְפָּקְדוּ בְּתוֹךְ בְּנֵי יִשְׂרָאֵל.** לִהְיוֹת נִמְנִין בְּנֵי עֶשְׂרִים שָׁנָה, מַה טַּעַם? ״כִּי לֹא נִתַּן לָהֶם נַחֲלָה״, וְהַנִּמְנִין מִבֶּן עֶשְׂרִים שָׁנָה הָיוּ בְּנֵי נַחֲלָה, שֶׁנֶּאֱמַר: ״אִישׁ לְפִי פְקֻדָיו יֻתַּן נַחֲלָתוֹ״ (לעיל פסוק נד):

סד **וּבְאֵלֶּה לֹא הָיָה אִישׁ וְגוֹ׳.** אֲבָל עַל הַנָּשִׁים לֹא נִגְזְרָה גְּזֵרַת הַמְרַגְּלִים, לְפִי שֶׁהֵן הָיוּ מְחַבְּבוֹת אֶת הָאָרֶץ, הָאֲנָשִׁים אוֹמְרִים: ״נִתְּנָה רֹאשׁ וְנָשׁוּבָה מִצְרָיְמָה״ (לעיל יד, ד), וְהַנָּשִׁים אוֹמְרוֹת: ״תְּנָה לָּנוּ אֲחֻזָּה״ (להלן כז, ד), לְכָךְ נִסְמְכָה פָּרָשַׁת בְּנוֹת צְלָפְחָד לְכָאן:

כז א **לְמִשְׁפְּחֹת מְנַשֶּׁה בֶן יוֹסֵף.** לָמָּה נֶאֱמַר? וַהֲלֹא כְּבָר נֶאֱמַר: ״בֶּן מְנַשֶּׁה״, אֶלָּא לוֹמַר לְךָ, יוֹסֵף חִבֵּב אֶת הָאָרֶץ, שֶׁנֶּאֱמַר: ״וְהַעֲלִתֶם אֶת עַצְמֹתַי״ וְגוֹ׳ (בראשית נ, כה), וּבְנוֹתָיו חִבְּבוּ אֶת הָאָרֶץ, שֶׁנֶּאֱמַר: ״תְּנָה לָּנוּ אֲחֻזָּה״ (להלן פסוק ד). וּלְלַמֶּדְךָ שֶׁהָיוּ כֻּלָּם צַדִּיקִים, שֶׁכָּל מִי שֶׁמַּעֲשָׂיו וּמַעֲשֵׂה אֲבוֹתָיו סְתוּמִים וּפֵרַט לְךָ הַכָּתוּב בְּאֶחָד מֵהֶם לְיַחֲסוֹ לְשֶׁבַח, הֲרֵי זֶה צַדִּיק בֶּן צַדִּיק, וְאִם יִחֲסוֹ לִגְנַאי, כְּגוֹן: ״בָּא יִשְׁמָעֵאל בֶּן נְתַנְיָה בֶּן אֱלִישָׁמָע״ (מלכים ב׳ כה, כה), בְּיָדוּעַ שֶׁכָּל הַנִּזְכָּרִים עִמּוֹ רְשָׁעִים הָיוּ: **מַחְלָה נֹעָה וְגוֹ׳.** וּלְהַלָּן (לו, יא) הוּא אוֹמֵר: ״וַתִּהְיֶינָה מַחְלָה תִרְצָה״, מַגִּיד שֶׁכֻּלָּן שְׁקוּלוֹת זוֹ כְּזוֹ, לְפִיכָךְ שִׁנָּה אֶת סִדְרָן:

ב **לִפְנֵי מֹשֶׁה וְלִפְנֵי אֶלְעָזָר.** מַגִּיד שֶׁלֹּא עָמְדוּ לִפְנֵיהֶם אֶלָּא בִּשְׁנַת הָאַרְבָּעִים אַחַר מִיתַת אַהֲרֹן: **לִפְנֵי מֹשֶׁה.** וְאַחַר כָּךְ ״לִפְנֵי אֶלְעָזָר״, אֶפְשָׁר אִם מֹשֶׁה לֹא יָדַע אֶלְעָזָר יוֹדֵעַ? אֶלָּא סָרֵס הַמִּקְרָא וְדָרְשֵׁהוּ, דִּבְרֵי רַבִּי יֹאשִׁיָּה. אַבָּא חָנָן מִשּׁוּם רַבִּי אֱלִיעֶזֶר אוֹמֵר: בְּבֵית הַמִּדְרָשׁ הָיוּ יוֹשְׁבִים, וְעָמְדוּ לִפְנֵי כֻלָּם:

The incident is also significant in the history of halakha. As Jews we believe that there is a *Torah Shebikhtav*, a Written Torah which never changes, and a *Torah Shebe'al Peh*, an Oral Torah which is, as it were, subject to ongoing interpretation. This is a highly sensitive process and it is entrusted to the great sages of each generation. Their task is to hear in the word of God for all time, the word of God for this time. In many cases the process begins, as with the daughters of Tzelofḥad, with a challenging question respectfully asked.

In halakha, as in other areas, there is a difference between change, or *shinui*, and *ḥiddush*. *Ḥiddush* means not change, but renewal. I call this "homeostatic change." Homeostatic temperature control will be continually changing, switching the air-conditioning on or off to maintain an even temperature. An airliner on automatic pilot is making adjustments every microsecond to stay on course. Change takes place in Judaism, but its aim is to stay true to the essential principles.

When the five daughters of Tzelofḥad come to Moshe, he is able to ask God their question directly. Yet it is an early instance of what we now call the Oral Torah: Torah applied to a time or a circumstance that is different from the one where it was given. This is the ongoing process that gives Judaism its unbroken continuity while at the same time relating to the challenge of each age, in each age.

סב וַיִּהְי֣וּ פְקֻדֵיהֶ֗ם שְׁלֹשָׁ֤ה וְעֶשְׂרִים֙ אֶ֔לֶף כָּל־זָכָ֖ר מִבֶּן־חֹ֣דֶשׁ וָמָ֑עְלָה
כִּ֣י ׀ לֹ֣א הָתְפָּקְד֗וּ בְּתוֹךְ֙ בְּנֵ֣י יִשְׂרָאֵ֔ל כִּ֠י לֹא־נִתַּ֤ן לָהֶם֙ נַחֲלָ֔ה בְּת֖וֹךְ
סג בְּנֵ֥י יִשְׂרָאֵֽל׃ אֵ֚לֶּה פְּקוּדֵ֣י מֹשֶׁ֔ה וְאֶלְעָזָ֖ר הַכֹּהֵ֑ן אֲשֶׁ֨ר פָּקְד֜וּ אֶת־בְּנֵ֤י
סד יִשְׂרָאֵל֙ בְּעַרְבֹ֣ת מוֹאָ֔ב עַ֖ל יַרְדֵּ֥ן יְרֵחֽוֹ׃ וּבְאֵ֙לֶּה֙ לֹא־הָ֣יָה אִ֔ישׁ מִפְּקוּדֵ֣י
סה מֹשֶׁ֔ה וְאַהֲרֹ֖ן הַכֹּהֵ֑ן אֲשֶׁ֨ר פָּקְד֧וּ אֶת־בְּנֵ֛י יִשְׂרָאֵ֖ל בְּמִדְבַּ֥ר סִינָֽי׃ כִּֽי־אָמַ֤ר
יהוה֙ לָהֶ֔ם מ֥וֹת יָמֻ֖תוּ בַּמִּדְבָּ֑ר וְלֹֽא־נוֹתַ֤ר מֵהֶם֙ אִ֔ישׁ כִּ֚י אִם־כָּלֵ֣ב בֶּן־
כז א יְפֻנֶּ֔ה וִיהוֹשֻׁ֖עַ בִּן־נֽוּן׃ וַתִּקְרַ֜בְנָה בְּנ֣וֹת צְלָפְחָ֗ד בֶּן־חֵ֤פֶר
בֶּן־גִּלְעָד֙ בֶּן־מָכִ֣יר בֶּן־מְנַשֶּׁ֔ה לְמִשְׁפְּחֹ֖ת מְנַשֶּׁ֣ה בֶן־יוֹסֵ֑ף וְאֵ֙לֶּה֙ שְׁמ֣וֹת
ב בְּנֹתָ֔יו מַחְלָ֣ה נֹעָ֔ה וְחָגְלָ֥ה וּמִלְכָּ֖ה וְתִרְצָֽה׃ וַֽתַּעֲמֹ֜דְנָה לִפְנֵ֣י מֹשֶׁ֗ה
וְלִפְנֵי֙ אֶלְעָזָ֣ר הַכֹּהֵ֔ן וְלִפְנֵ֥י הַנְּשִׂיאִ֖ם וְכָל־הָעֵדָ֑ה פֶּ֥תַח אֹֽהֶל־מוֹעֵ֖ד

אונקלוס

סב וַהֲווֹ מִנְיָנֵיהוֹן, עַסְרִין וּתְלָתָא אַלְפִין, כָּל דְּכוּרָא מִבַּר יַרְחָא וּלְעֵילָא, אֲרֵי לָא אִתְמְנִיאוּ, בְּגוֹ בְּנֵי יִשְׂרָאֵל, אֲרֵי, לָא אִתְיְהִיבַת לְהוֹן אַחְסָנָא, בְּגוֹ בְּנֵי יִשְׂרָאֵל: סג אִלֵּין מִנְיָנֵי מֹשֶׁה, וְאֶלְעָזָר כַּהֲנָא, דִּמְנוֹ, יָת בְּנֵי יִשְׂרָאֵל בְּמֵישְׁרַיָּא דְּמוֹאָב, עַל יַרְדְּנָא דִּירִיחוֹ: סד וּבְאִלֵּין לָא הֲוָה גְּבַר, מִמִּנְיָנֵי מֹשֶׁה, וְאַהֲרֹן כַּהֲנָא, דִּמְנוֹ, יָת בְּנֵי יִשְׂרָאֵל בְּמַדְבְּרָא דְּסִינָי: סה אֲרֵי אֲמַר יי לְהוֹן, מְמָת יְמוּתוּן בְּמַדְבְּרָא, וְלָא אִשְׁתְּאַר מִנְּהוֹן אֱנָשׁ, אֱלָהֵין כָּלֵב בַּר יְפֻנֶּה, וִיהוֹשֻׁעַ בַּר נוּן: כז א וּקְרִיבָא בְּנָת צְלָפְחָד, בַּר חֵפֶר בַּר גִּלְעָד בַּר מָכִיר בַּר מְנַשֶּׁה, לְזַרְעִית מְנַשֶּׁה בַר יוֹסֵף, וְאִלֵּין שְׁמָהָת בְּנָתֵיהּ, מַחְלָה נוֹעָה, וְחָגְלָה וּמִלְכָּה וְתִרְצָה: ב וְקָמָא קֳדָם מֹשֶׁה, וְקֳדָם אֶלְעָזָר כַּהֲנָא, וְקֳדָם רַבְרְבַיָּא וְכָל כְּנִשְׁתָּא, בִּתְרַע מַשְׁכַּן זִמְנָא לְמֵימַר:

THE DAUGHTERS OF TZELOFḤAD

Tzelofḥad, of the tribe of Menashe, died in the wilderness before the allocation of the land, leaving five daughters. Now the daughters come before Moshe, arguing that it would be unjust for his family to be denied their share in the land simply because he had daughters but not sons. Moshe brings their case before God, who tells him: "What Tzelofḥad's daughters say is right. You must certainly give them a heritable portion of land along with their father's kin. Transfer their father's portion to them" (Num. 27:7). And so it comes to pass.

The Sages spoke of Tzelofḥad's daughters in terms of highest praise. They were, they said, very wise and chose the right time to present their request. They knew how to interpret Scripture, and they were perfectly virtuous (Bava Batra 110b). Even more consequentially, their love of the land of Israel was in striking contrast to that of the men. The spies had come back with a negative report about the land, and the people had said, "Let us appoint a [new] leader and go back to Egypt" (Num. 14:4). But Tzelofḥad's daughters wanted to have a share in the land, which they were duly granted. We have seen Rabbi Ephrayim Luntschitz's reading of this in his *Keli Yakar* (commentary on Num. 13:2). We can lose a priceless legacy simply because, not loving it, we do not come to appreciate its true value. What we love, we inherit.

3 and all the community at the entrance to the Tent of Meeting, and said, "Our
father died in the wilderness. He was not among the company of those who
gathered together against the LORD in the company of Koraḥ; he died in his
4 own sin, and had no sons. Why should our father's name be lost to his family
only because he had no son? Give us a portion of land along with our father's
5 brothers." Moshe brought their case before the LORD.
6 7 And the LORD said to Moshe: "What Tzelofḥad's daughters say is right. You REVI'I
must certainly give them a heritable portion of land along with their father's
8 kin. Transfer their father's portion to them. Speak to the Israelites; tell them: If
9 a man dies and has no son, you shall transfer his property to his daughters. If
10 he does not have a daughter, you shall give his property to his brothers. If he
11 has no brothers, you shall give his property to his father's brothers. If his father
had no brothers, give his property to the closest relative in his clan, and that
person shall inherit it." This shall be a decree of law for the Israelites, as the
LORD commanded Moshe.
12 The LORD said to Moshe, "Ascend this mountain of Avarim, and gaze upon

רש״י

ג **וְהוּא לֹא הָיָה וְגוֹ׳.** לְפִי שֶׁהָיוּ בָּאוֹת לוֹמַר "בְּחֶטְאוֹ מֵת", נִזְקְקוּ לוֹמַר: לֹא בְּחֵטְא מִתְלוֹנְנִים וְלֹא בַּעֲדַת קֹרַח שֶׁהִצּוּ עַל הַקָּדוֹשׁ בָּרוּךְ הוּא, אֶלָּא בְּחֶטְאוֹ לְבַדּוֹ מֵת וְלֹא הֶחֱטִיא אֶת אֲחֵרִים עִמּוֹ. רַבִּי עֲקִיבָא אוֹמֵר: מְקוֹשֵׁשׁ עֵצִים הָיָה; וְרַבִּי שִׁמְעוֹן אוֹמֵר: מִן הַמַּעְפִּילִים הָיָה:

ד **לָמָּה יִגָּרַע שֵׁם אָבִינוּ.** אָנוּ בִּמְקוֹם בֵּן עוֹמְדוֹת, וְאִם אֵין הַנְּקֵבוֹת חֲשׁוּבוֹת זֶרַע תִּתְיַבֵּם אִמֵּנוּ לְיָבָם: **כִּי אֵין לוֹ בֵּן.** הָא אִם הָיָה לוֹ בֵּן לֹא הָיוּ תּוֹבְעוֹת כְּלוּם, מַגִּיד שֶׁחַכְמָנִיּוֹת הָיוּ:

ה **וַיַּקְרֵב מֹשֶׁה אֶת מִשְׁפָּטָן.** נִתְעַלְּמָה הֲלָכָה מִמֶּנּוּ. וְכָאן נִפְרַע עַל שֶׁנָּטַל עֲטָרָה לוֹמַר: "וְהַדָּבָר אֲשֶׁר יִקְשֶׁה מִכֶּם תַּקְרִבוּן אֵלַי" (דברים א, יז). דָּבָר אַחֵר, רְאוּיָה הָיְתָה פָּרָשָׁה זוֹ לְהִכָּתֵב עַל יְדֵי מֹשֶׁה, אֶלָּא שֶׁזָּכוּ בְּנוֹת צְלָפְחָד וְנִכְתְּבָה עַל יָדָן:

ז **כֵּן בְּנוֹת צְלָפְחָד דֹּבְרֹת.** כְּתַרְגּוּמוֹ: "יָאוּת". כָּךְ כְּתוּבָה פָּרָשָׁה זוֹ לְפָנַי בַּמָּרוֹם, מַגִּיד שֶׁרָאֲתָה עֵינָן מַה שֶּׁלֹּא רָאֲתָה עֵינוֹ שֶׁל מֹשֶׁה: **כֵּן בְּנוֹת צְלָפְחָד דֹּבְרֹת.** יָפֶה תָּבְעוּ, אַשְׁרֵי אָדָם שֶׁהַקָּדוֹשׁ בָּרוּךְ הוּא מוֹדֶה לִדְבָרָיו: **נָתֹן תִּתֵּן.** שְׁנֵי חֲלָקִים, חֵלֶק אֲבִיהֶן שֶׁהָיָה מִיּוֹצְאֵי מִצְרַיִם, וְחֶלְקוֹ עִם אֶחָיו בְּנִכְסֵי חֵפֶר: **וְהַעֲבַרְתָּ.** לְשׁוֹן עֶבְרָה הוּא, בְּמִי שֶׁאֵינוֹ מַנִּיחַ בֵּן לְיָרְשׁוֹ. דָּבָר אַחֵר, עַל שֵׁם שֶׁהַבַּת מַעֲבֶרֶת נַחֲלָה מִשֵּׁבֶט לְשֵׁבֶט, שֶׁבְּנָהּ וּבַעְלָהּ יוֹרְשִׁין אוֹתָהּ, שֶׁ"לֹּא תִסֹּב נַחֲלָה" (להלן לו, ז) לֹא נִצְטַוָּה אֶלָּא לְאוֹתוֹ הַדּוֹר בִּלְבַד, וְכֵן: "וְהַעֲבַרְתֶּם אֶת נַחֲלָתוֹ לְבִתּוֹ" (להלן פסוק ח), בְּכֻלָּן הוּא אוֹמֵר: "וּנְתַתֶּם" (להלן פסוקים ט-יא) וּבְבַת הוּא אוֹמֵר: "וְהַעֲבַרְתֶּם":

יא **לִשְׁאֵרוֹ הַקָּרֹב אֵלָיו מִמִּשְׁפַּחְתּוֹ.** וְאֵין מִשְׁפָּחָה קְרוּיָה אֶלָּא מִשְׁפַּחַת הָאָב:

יב **עֲלֵה אֶל הַר הָעֲבָרִים.** לָמָּה נִסְמְכָה לְכָאן? כֵּיוָן שֶׁאָמַר הַקָּדוֹשׁ בָּרוּךְ הוּא: "נָתֹן תִּתֵּן לָהֶם" (לעיל פסוק ז), אָמַר: אוֹתִי צִוָּה הַמָּקוֹם לְהַנְחִיל, שֶׁמָּא הֻתְּרָה הַגְּזֵרָה וְאֶכָּנֵס לָאָרֶץ, אָמַר לוֹ הַקָּדוֹשׁ בָּרוּךְ הוּא: גְּזֵרָתִי בִּמְקוֹמָהּ עוֹמֶדֶת. דָּבָר אַחֵר, כֵּיוָן שֶׁנִּכְנַס מֹשֶׁה לְנַחֲלַת בְּנֵי גָד וּבְנֵי רְאוּבֵן, שָׂמַח וְאָמַר: כִּמְדֻמֶּה שֶׁהֻתַּר לִי נִדְרִי. מָשָׁל לְמֶלֶךְ שֶׁגָּזַר עַל בְּנוֹ שֶׁלֹּא יִכָּנֵס לְפֶתַח פָּלָטִין שֶׁלּוֹ, נִכְנַס לַשַּׁעַר וְהוּא אַחֲרָיו, לֶחָצֵר וְהוּא אַחֲרָיו, לַטְרַקְלִין וְהוּא אַחֲרָיו, כֵּיוָן שֶׁבָּא לְהִכָּנֵס לַקִּיטוֹן אָמַר לוֹ: בְּנִי, מִכָּאן וְאֵילַךְ אַתָּה אָסוּר לִכָּנֵס:

tonight that we as a people will get to the Promised Land." King knew what the Rabbis knew: "It is not for you to complete the task, but neither are you free to stand aside from it" (Avot 2:16). The Jewish story, in many ways, is the West's meta-narrative of hope.

ג לֵאמֹר׃ אָבִינוּ מֵת בַּמִּדְבָּר וְהוּא לֹא־הָיָה בְּתוֹךְ הָעֵדָה הַנּוֹעָדִים
ד עַל־יהוה בַּעֲדַת־קֹרַח כִּי־בְחֶטְאוֹ מֵת וּבָנִים לֹא־הָיוּ לוֹ׃ לָמָּה יִגָּרַע
שֵׁם־אָבִינוּ מִתּוֹךְ מִשְׁפַּחְתּוֹ כִּי אֵין לוֹ בֵּן תְּנָה־לָּנוּ אֲחֻזָּה בְּתוֹךְ אֲחֵי
ה אָבִינוּ׃ וַיַּקְרֵב מֹשֶׁה אֶת־מִשְׁפָּטָן לִפְנֵי יהוה׃
ו ז וַיֹּאמֶר יהוה אֶל־מֹשֶׁה לֵּאמֹר׃ כֵּן בְּנוֹת צְלָפְחָד דֹּבְרֹת נָתֹן תִּתֵּן לָהֶם רביעי
אֲחֻזַּת נַחֲלָה בְּתוֹךְ אֲחֵי אֲבִיהֶם וְהַעֲבַרְתָּ אֶת־נַחֲלַת אֲבִיהֶן לָהֶן׃
ח וְאֶל־בְּנֵי יִשְׂרָאֵל תְּדַבֵּר לֵאמֹר אִישׁ כִּי־יָמוּת וּבֵן אֵין לוֹ וְהַעֲבַרְתֶּם
ט אֶת־נַחֲלָתוֹ לְבִתּוֹ׃ וְאִם־אֵין לוֹ בַּת וּנְתַתֶּם אֶת־נַחֲלָתוֹ לְאֶחָיו׃
י יא וְאִם־אֵין לוֹ אַחִים וּנְתַתֶּם אֶת־נַחֲלָתוֹ לַאֲחֵי אָבִיו׃ וְאִם־אֵין אַחִים
לְאָבִיו וּנְתַתֶּם אֶת־נַחֲלָתוֹ לִשְׁאֵרוֹ הַקָּרֹב אֵלָיו מִמִּשְׁפַּחְתּוֹ וְיָרַשׁ
אֹתָהּ וְהָיְתָה לִבְנֵי יִשְׂרָאֵל לְחֻקַּת מִשְׁפָּט כַּאֲשֶׁר צִוָּה יהוה אֶת־
מֹשֶׁה׃
יב וַיֹּאמֶר יהוה אֶל־מֹשֶׁה עֲלֵה אֶל־הַר הָעֲבָרִים הַזֶּה וּרְאֵה אֶת־הָאָרֶץ

אונקלוס

ג אֲבוּנָא מִית בְּמַדְבְּרָא, וְהוּא לָא הֲוָה בְּגוֹ כְּנִשְׁתָּא, דְּאִזְדַּמַּנוּ, עַל יי בִּכְנִשְׁתָּא דְּקֹרַח, אֲרֵי בְחוֹבֵיהּ מִית, וּבְנִין לָא הֲווֹ לֵיהּ: ד לְמָא יִתְמְנַע שְׁמָא דַּאֲבוּנָא מִגּוֹ זַרְעִיתֵיהּ, אֲרֵי, לֵית לֵיהּ בַּר, הַב לַנָא אַחְסָנָא, בְּגוֹ אֲחֵי אֲבוּנָא: ה וְקָרֵיב מֹשֶׁה, יָת דִּינְהוֹן לִקְדָם יי: ו וַאֲמַר יי לְמֹשֶׁה לְמֵימַר: ז יָאוּת, בְּנָת צְלָפְחָד מְמַלְּלָן, מִתַּן תִּתֵּין לְהוֹן אֲחֻדַת אַחְסָנָא, בְּגוֹ אֲחֵי אֲבוּהוֹן, וְתַעְבַּר, יָת אַחְסָנַת אֲבוּהוֹן לְהוֹן: ח וְעִם בְּנֵי יִשְׂרָאֵל תְּמַלֵּיל לְמֵימַר, גְּבַר אֲרֵי יְמוּת, וּבַר לֵית לֵיהּ, וְתַעְבְּרוּן יָת אַחְסָנְתֵיהּ לִבְרַתֵּיהּ: ט וְאִם לֵית לֵיהּ בְּרַתָּא, וְתִתְּנוּן יָת אַחְסָנְתֵיהּ לַאֲחוֹהִי: י וְאִם לֵית לֵיהּ אַחִין, וְתִתְּנוּן יָת אַחְסָנְתֵיהּ לַאֲחֵי אֲבוּהִי: יא וְאִם לֵית אַחִין לַאֲבוּהִי, וְתִתְּנוּן יָת אַחְסָנְתֵיהּ, לְקָרִיבֵיהּ, דְּקָרִיב לֵיהּ, מִזַּרְעִיתֵיהּ וְיֵירַת יָתַהּ, וּתְהֵי, לִבְנֵי יִשְׂרָאֵל לִגְזֵירַת דִּין, כְּמָא דְּפַקֵּיד יי יָת מֹשֶׁה: יב וַאֲמַר יי לְמֹשֶׁה, סַק, לְטוּרָא דְּעִבְרָאֵי הָדֵין, וַחְזִי יָת אַרְעָא,

27:12 עֲלֵה אֶל־הַר הָעֲבָרִים הַזֶּה *Ascend this mountain* – God grants Moshe one last gift: not entry into the land, but a glimpse of it from afar, from a mountaintop on the other side of the river. Moshe's life has not been in vain. He has taken the people almost all the way, but it will be a new generation who will complete the journey.

Martin Luther King reminded his audience of the last day of Moshe's life on what turned out to be the last day of his. "We've got some difficult times ahead. But it doesn't matter with me now. Because I've been to the mountaintop.... And I've looked over. And I've seen the Promised Land. I may not get there with you. But I want you to know

▶

13 the land that I have given to the Israelites. After you have seen it, you too
14 will be gathered to your people, like Aharon your brother, because when the
community rebelled in the Wilderness of Tzin, you disobeyed Me, failing to
affirm My sanctity in their eyes through the water." These were the waters
15 of Merivat Kadesh in the Wilderness of Tzin. Moshe spoke to the
16 LORD: "Let the LORD, God of the spirit of all flesh, appoint a man over the

רש"י

יג **כאשר נאסף אהרן אחיך.** מכאן שנתאוה משה למיתתו של אהרן. דבר אחר, אין אתה טוב ממנו. "על אשר לא קדשתם" (דברים לב, נא), הא אם קדשתם אותי עדין לא הגיע זמנכם להפטר מן העולם. בכל מקום שכתב מיתתם כתב סרחונם, לפי שנגזרה גזרה על דור המדבר למות במדבר בעון שלא האמינו, לכך בקש משה שיכתב סרחונו, שלא יאמרו: אף הוא מן הממרים היה. משל לשתי נשים שלוקות בבית דין, אחת קלקלה ואחת אכלה פגי שביעית וכו' [אמרה להן אותה שאכלה פגי שביעית: בבקשה מכם, הודיעו על מה היא לוקה, שלא יאמרו על מה שזו לוקה זו לוקה. הביאו פגי שביעית ותלו בצוארה, והיו מכריזין לפניה ואומרין: על עסקי שביעית היא לוקה] (יומא פו ע"ב), אף כאן בכל מקום שהזכיר מיתתן הזכיר סרחונן, להודיע שלא היתה בהם אלא זו בלבד:

יד **הם מי מריבת קדש.** הם לבדם, אין בהם עון אחר. דבר אחר, הם שהמרו במרה, הם היו שהמרו בים סוף, הם עצמם שהמרו במדבר צין:

טו **וידבר משה אל ה' וגו'.** להודיע שבחן של צדיקים, שכשנפטרים מן העולם מניחין צרכן ועוסקין בצרכי צבור: **לאמר.** אמר לו: השיבני אם אתה ממנה להם פרנס אם לאו:

טז **יפקד ה'.** כיון ששמע משה שאמר לו המקום: תן נחלת צלפחד לבנותיו, אמר: הגיע שעה שאתבע צרכי שיירשו בני את גדלתי. אמר לו הקדוש ברוך הוא: לא כך עלתה במחשבה לפני, כדאי הוא יהושע לטול שכר שמושו, שלא מש מתוך האהל. וזהו שאמר שלמה: "נצר תאנה יאכל פריה" (משלי כז, יח). **אלהי הרוחת.** למה

27:16 **יִפְקֹד יהוה... אִישׁ** *Appoint a man* – We might reasonably conclude that Moshe is talking about gender, meaning a man, not a woman. However, Jewish tradition did not read it this way. There were female prophets as well as male. There was a woman tribal and military leader, Devora, in the era of the judges. *Ish* in this context does not mean a man as opposed to a woman. What it does mean can be inferred from the two places in the Torah where we find the phrase *ha'ish Moshe*, "the man Moshe." One occurs in the story of the exodus: "The man Moshe, too, was held in high regard (*gadol meod*, literally, 'very great') in the land of Egypt, among both Pharaoh's officials and the people" (Ex. 11:3). The other appears in the episode in which his own sister and brother, Miriam and Aharon, criticize him: "Now the man Moshe was very humble (*anav meod*), more so than any other man on earth" (Num. 12:3).

These two characteristics – greatness and humility – often appear to be opposed. People whom the world considers great are rarely humble, and those who are humble rarely achieve greatness, at least in the public eye. But Moshe was

asked the Sages, did Moshe add the phrase "God of the spirit of all flesh"? The answer, given by Rashi quoting a midrash, is that he was signaling what he saw as an essential quality of anyone leading the Jewish people: "Master of the Universe, the character of each person is revealed to You, and no two are alike. Appoint over them a leader *who will bear with each person according to his individual character*" (Rashi on Num. 27:16, based on Tanḥuma, Pinḥas 11). A true leader, even as he or she seeks to communicate a shared vision and common purpose, is nonetheless sensitive to the differences between people. One of the most striking facts about Judaism is its insistence on *the dignity of difference*. No two human beings are exactly alike. This, we believe, is not something to be lamented, but to be honored. It is the basis of one of the most striking sentences in the Mishna, that "a single soul is like a whole universe" (Sanhedrin 4:5), meaning that none of us is substitutable for any other. Leaders honor diversity. They recognize our distinctive gifts and help us realize them. They understand our role in the team. They help us make the contribution only we can make to the project we all share.

יג אֲשֶׁר נָתַתִּי לִבְנֵי יִשְׂרָאֵל: וְרָאִיתָה אֹתָהּ וְנֶאֱסַפְתָּ אֶל־עַמֶּיךָ גַּם־אָתָּה
יד כַּאֲשֶׁר נֶאֱסַף אַהֲרֹן אָחִיךָ: כַּאֲשֶׁר מְרִיתֶם פִּי בְמִדְבַּר־צִן בִּמְרִיבַת
הָעֵדָה לְהַקְדִּישֵׁנִי בַמַּיִם לְעֵינֵיהֶם הֵם מֵי־מְרִיבַת קָדֵשׁ מִדְבַּר־
טו טז צִן: וַיְדַבֵּר מֹשֶׁה אֶל־יְהוָה לֵאמֹר: יִפְקֹד יְהוָה אֱלֹהֵי הָרוּחֹת כד

אונקלוס

דִיהַבִית לִבְנֵי יִשְׂרָאֵל: יג וְתִחְזֵי יָתַהּ, וְתִתְכְּנֵישׁ לְעַמָּךְ אַף אַתְּ, כְּמָא דְאִתְכְּנֵישׁ אַהֲרֹן אֲחוּךְ: יד כְּמָא דְסָרֵיבְתּוּן עַל מֵימְרִי בְּמַדְבְּרָא דְצִין, בְּמַצּוּת כְּנִשְׁתָּא, לְקַדָּשׁוּתִי בְמַיָּא לְעֵינֵיהוֹן, אִנּוּן, מֵי מַצּוּת רְקַם מַדְבְּרָא דְצִין: טו וּמַלֵּיל מֹשֶׁה, קֳדָם יי לְמֵימַר: טז יְמַנֵּי יי, אֱלָה

MOSHE'S CONTINUITY

Seven chapters earlier, God told Moshe and Aharon that they would die without entering the land, and shortly thereafter we read of the death of Aharon. Why then is Moshe now told "You too will be gathered to your people, like Aharon your brother," and why does Moshe now pray for a successor?

The Sages sensed two clues. The first is that this story appears immediately after the episode in which the daughters of Tzelofhad sought and were granted their father's share in the land. A midrash explains:

> Moshe reasoned: The time is right for me to make my own request. If daughters are allowed to inherit, it is surely right that my sons should inherit my glory. (Bemidbar Rabba 21:14)

The second clue lies in the words "like Aharon your brother" (Num. 27:13). The midrash says: "This teaches us that Moshe wanted to die the way Aharon did." *Ktav Sofer* explains: Aharon had the privilege of knowing that his children would follow in his footsteps. To this day, *kohanim* are direct descendants of Aharon. Moshe likewise longed to see one of his sons, Gershom or Eliezer, take his place as leader of the people. It was not to be. That is the story beneath the story.

It had an aftermath. In the book of Judges we read of a man named Mikha who established an idolatrous cult in the territory of Efrayim and hired a Levite to officiate in the shrine. Some men from the tribe of Dan, moving north to find more suitable land for themselves, came upon Mikha's house and seized both the idolatrous artifacts and the Levite, whom they persuaded to become their priest, saying, "Come with us.... Would you rather be the priest of one man's household or the priest of a whole tribal clan in Israel?" (Judges 18:19).

Only at the end of the story (18:30) are we told the name of this priest: Yonatan son of Gershom son of Moshe. In our texts, the letter *nun* has been inserted into the last of these names, so that it can be read as Menashe rather than Moshe. However, the letter, unusually, is written above the line, as a superscription. The Talmud says that the *nun* was added to avoid besmirching the name of Moshe himself, by disclosing that his grandson had become an idolator.

How are we to explain Moshe's apparent failure to pass on his Torah? There are hints here and there that Moshe was so preoccupied with leading the people that he did not have time to attend to the spiritual needs of his family. The Sages, however, offered a quite different explanation. God did not want the "crown of Torah" to pass from parent to child in automatic succession. Kingship and priesthood did. But the crown of Torah, the Sages said, belongs to anyone who chooses to take hold of it. "Moshe charged us with the Law, heritage of Yaakov's assembly" (Deut. 33:4), meaning that it belongs to all of us. If the crown of Torah were hereditary, it might become the prerogative of the rich. Children of great scholars might take their inheritance for granted. It could lead to arrogance and contempt for others. Learning might become a mere intellectual pursuit rather than a spiritual exercise.

Moshe's tragedy, then, was Israel's consolation. The fact that his successor was not his son but his disciple meant that one form of leadership – historically and spiritually the most important one – could be aspired to by everyone.

27:16 אֱלֹהֵי הָרוּחֹת לְכָל־בָּשָׂר *God of the spirit of all flesh* – Why,

17 community who will go out before them and come in before them, who will
lead them out and bring them home. Let not the Lord's community be like
18 sheep without a shepherd." The Lord said to Moshe, "Take Yehoshua son of
19 Nun, a man infused with My spirit, and lay your hand upon him. Have him
stand before Elazar the priest and the entire community, and in their sight,
20 give him this charge. Give over to him some of your majesty, so that the entire

רש"י

נֶאֱמַר? אָמַר לְפָנָיו: רִבּוֹנוֹ שֶׁל עוֹלָם, גָּלוּי לְפָנֶיךָ דַּעְתּוֹ שֶׁל כָּל אֶחָד וְאֶחָד וְאֵינָן דּוֹמִין זֶה לָזֶה, מַנֵּה עֲלֵיהֶם מַנְהִיג שֶׁיְּהֵא סוֹבֵל כָּל אֶחָד וְאֶחָד לְפִי דַעְתּוֹ:

יז אֲשֶׁר יֵצֵא לִפְנֵיהֶם. לֹא כְדֶרֶךְ מַלְכֵי הָאֻמּוֹת שֶׁיּוֹשְׁבִים בְּבָתֵּיהֶם וּמְשַׁלְּחִין אֶת חֵילוֹתֵיהֶם לַמִּלְחָמָה, אֶלָּא כְּמוֹ שֶׁעָשִׂיתִי אֲנִי, שֶׁנִּלְחַמְתִּי בְּסִיחוֹן וְעוֹג, שֶׁנֶּאֱמַר: "אַל תִּירָא אֹתוֹ" (במדבר כא, לד), וּכְדֶרֶךְ שֶׁעָשָׂה יְהוֹשֻׁעַ, שֶׁנֶּאֱמַר: "וַיֵּלֶךְ יְהוֹשֻׁעַ אֵלָיו וַיֹּאמֶר לוֹ הֲלָנוּ אַתָּה" וְגוֹ' (יהושע ה, יג), וְכֵן בְּדָוִד הוּא אוֹמֵר: "כִּי הוּא יוֹצֵא וָבָא לִפְנֵיהֶם" (שמואל א' יח, טז), יוֹצֵא בָּרֹאשׁ וְנִכְנָס בָּרֹאשׁ: וַאֲשֶׁר יוֹצִיאֵם. בִּזְכֻיּוֹתָיו: וַאֲשֶׁר יְבִיאֵם. בִּזְכֻיּוֹתָיו. דָּבָר אַחֵר, "וַאֲשֶׁר יְבִיאֵם", שֶׁלֹּא תַעֲשֶׂה לוֹ כְּדֶרֶךְ שֶׁאַתָּה עוֹשֶׂה לִי, שֶׁאֵינִי מַכְנִיסָן לָאָרֶץ:

יח קַח לְךָ. קָחֶנּוּ בִּדְבָרִים, אַשְׁרֶיךָ שֶׁזָּכִיתָ לְהַנְהִיג בָּנָיו שֶׁל מָקוֹם: לְךָ. אֶת שֶׁבָּדוּק לְךָ, אֶת זֶה אַתָּה מַכִּיר: אֲשֶׁר רוּחַ בּוֹ. כַּאֲשֶׁר שָׁאַלְתָּ, שֶׁיּוּכַל לַהֲלֹךְ כְּנֶגֶד רוּחוֹ שֶׁל כָּל אֶחָד וְאֶחָד: וְסָמַכְתָּ אֶת יָדְךָ עָלָיו. תֵּן לוֹ מְתֻרְגְּמָן שֶׁיִּדְרֹשׁ בְּחַיֶּיךָ, שֶׁלֹּא יֹאמְרוּ עָלָיו: לֹא הָיָה לוֹ לְהָרִים רֹאשׁ בִּימֵי מֹשֶׁה:

יט וְצִוִּיתָה אֹתוֹ. עַל יִשְׂרָאֵל: דַּע שֶׁטַּרְחָנִין הֵם, סַרְבָנִים הֵם, עַל מְנָת שֶׁתְּקַבֵּל עָלֶיךָ:

כ וְנָתַתָּה מֵהוֹדְךָ עָלָיו. זֶה קֵרוּן עוֹר פָּנִים: מֵהוֹדְךָ. וְלֹא כָּל הוֹדְךָ, נִמְצֵינוּ לְמֵדִין, פְּנֵי מֹשֶׁה כַּחַמָּה, פְּנֵי יְהוֹשֻׁעַ כַּלְּבָנָה:

they are unable to keep up. He or she must be impatient and patient all at once – a difficult balancing act. Leaders must not go on ahead so far and fast that, nearing their destination, they find themselves alone.

27:18 **קַח־לְךָ אֶת־יְהוֹשֻׁעַ בִּן־נוּן** *Take Yehoshua son of Nun* – On this phrase, Rashi says, "Persuade him, saying, 'Happy are you to merit leading the children of God'" (Rashi, quoting Sifrei, Pinḥas 23). In the end, leadership is a privilege. It is one of the richest sources of meaning in life.

Walter Lippmann once wrote, "The final test of a leader is that he leaves behind him in other men the conviction and the will to carry on." The measure of Moshe's greatness is that he not only inspired Yehoshua to continue the task he had begun, but did so to an unending flow of prophets, sages, and people of spirit who, lifted by his vision, carried it forward in generation after generation. In his lifetime he knew the bitterness of failure, but few if any have inspired so many for so long.

27:19 **וְצִוִּיתָה אֹתוֹ** *Give him this charge* – Rashi here makes a startling comment: "You shall command him about the Israelites, saying, 'Be aware that they are troublesome and obstinate. [You may be their leader only] on condition that you accept this'" (based on Shemot Rabba 7:3 and Sifrei, Behaalotekha 91).

This comment is a rabbinic anticipation of Ronald Heifetz's theory of adaptive leadership. Adaptive leadership is needed when, to meet a new challenge, the people have to change. This cannot be done by the leader alone. He or she has to educate the people and hand the challenge back to them.

People resist change, especially when it means giving up long-standing habits that have become deeply embedded in their character. They can go through all the emotions associated with loss: denial, anger, bargaining, and depression. That is one of the bass notes of Numbers: the people's anger at Moshe for forcing them to face the responsibilities of freedom. Hence their frequent false nostalgia about how things were in Egypt, and their regret that they ever left.

Moshe lived through this time and again. Perhaps this is

יז לְכָל־בָּשָׂר אִישׁ עַל־הָעֵדָה: אֲשֶׁר־יֵצֵא לִפְנֵיהֶם וַאֲשֶׁר יָבֹא לִפְנֵיהֶם
וַאֲשֶׁר יוֹצִיאֵם וַאֲשֶׁר יְבִיאֵם וְלֹא תִהְיֶה עֲדַת יְהוָה כַּצֹּאן אֲשֶׁר אֵין־
יח לָהֶם רֹעֶה: וַיֹּאמֶר יְהוָה אֶל־מֹשֶׁה קַח־לְךָ אֶת־יְהוֹשֻׁעַ בִּן־נוּן אִישׁ
יט אֲשֶׁר־רוּחַ בּוֹ וְסָמַכְתָּ אֶת־יָדְךָ עָלָיו: וְהַעֲמַדְתָּ אֹתוֹ לִפְנֵי אֶלְעָזָר
כ הַכֹּהֵן וְלִפְנֵי כָּל־הָעֵדָה וְצִוִּיתָה אֹתוֹ לְעֵינֵיהֶם: וְנָתַתָּה מֵהוֹדְךָ עָלָיו

אונקלוס

רוּחַיָּא לְכָל בִּסְרָא, גְּבַר עַל כְּנִשְׁתָּא: יז דְּיִפּוֹק קֳדָמֵיהוֹן, וּדְיֵיעוֹל
קֳדָמֵיהוֹן, וּדְיַפֵּיקִנּוּן וּדְיַעֵילִנּוּן, וְלָא תְהֵי כְּנִשְׁתָּא דַּייָ, כְּעָנָא, דְּלֵית
לְהוֹן רָעֵי: יח וַאֲמַר יי לְמֹשֶׁה, דְּבַר לָךְ יָת יְהוֹשֻׁעַ בַּר נוּן, גְּבַר דְּרוּחַ
נְבוּאָה בֵּיהּ, וְתִסְמוֹךְ יָת יְדָךְ עֲלוֹהִי: יט וּתְקִים יָתֵיהּ, קֳדָם אֶלְעָזָר
כָּהֲנָא, וּקְדָם כָּל כְּנִשְׁתָּא, וּתְפַקֵּיד יָתֵיהּ לְעֵינֵיהוֹן: כ וְתִתֵּין מִזִּיוָךְ
עֲלוֹהִי, בְּדִיל דִּיקַבְּלוּן מִנֵּיהּ, כָּל כְּנִשְׁתָּא דִּבְנֵי יִשְׂרָאֵל: כא וּקְדָם

both. The Torah goes out of its way to apply the same adverb, *meod*, "very," to both attributes. He was very great and at the same time very humble.

The word *ish* in the context of leadership does not mean "a man" but rather, "a mensch," one whose greatness is lightly worn, who cares about the people others often ignore, "the fatherless, the widow, and the stranger," who spends as much time with the people at the margins of society as with the elites, who is courteous to everyone equally and who receives respect because he or she gives respect.

Humility is one of the most important qualities of a leader. That humility was palpable in the case of Yehoshua. After the making of the golden calf, he was waiting for Moshe at the foot of the mountain so he could inform him about what had happened in his absence (Ex. 32:17). When Eldad and Meidad began prophesying, which Yehoshua saw as a potential threat to Moshe's leadership, his concern for Moshe was immediate and deeply felt (Num. 11:28). Yet when Moshe told him to assemble a military force and fight the Amalekites, he did so without demur, and won (Ex. 17:9–13).

27:17 אֲשֶׁר־יֵצֵא לִפְנֵיהֶם וַאֲשֶׁר יָבֹא לִפְנֵיהֶם *Who will lead them out and bring them home* – The first phrase in this verse, "who will go out before them and come in before them," is clear enough. It means one who will lead from the front, who will not send his people into battle while staying behind in safety himself. Rashi quotes a verse (I Sam. 18:16) in which the Torah says: "All of Israel and Yehuda loved David, *for he went out and came in before them.*"

It is the second phrase that is difficult: "who will lead them out and bring them home." Surely that follows from the first without saying anything new. Rashi offers two different explanations. One is that it means "who will lead them [to victory] *through his merits*" (Rashi, quoting Sifrei ad loc.). The other is that Moshe is protesting to God: "Do not do to my successor what You did to me, denying me the chance to lead the people into the land" (based on Tanḥuma, Buber, ad loc.). Let Yehoshua, unlike me, reach his destination. This is striking, but not the plain sense of the verse.

There is another interpretation. A leader must indeed lead from the front. But he or she must also understand the pace at which people can go. Leadership is not effective if leaders are so far ahead of those they lead that when they turn their heads round, they discover that there is no one following. Leaders must go out in front and come back in front. But they must also "lead the people out and bring them home," meaning, they must take people with them.

A leader must have vision, but also realism. He or she must think the impossible but know the possible. People are slow to change. A leader of the people must go at the people's pace. He or she must educate them, prepare them for the challenges ahead, listen to their grievances, give them courage, lift their sights, and be prepared to slow down if

21 Israelite community will obey him. Let him stand before Elazar the priest, who
shall seek the decision of the Urim before the LORD on his behalf. By this word
they will go out and by this word they will return, he and all Israel, the entire
22 community." Moshe did as the LORD commanded him. He took Yehoshua and
23 had him stand before Elazar the priest and the entire community. And he laid
his hands upon him and commissioned him, as the LORD had spoken through
Moshe.
28 1 2 The LORD spoke to Moshe: "Command the Israelites; say to them: Take care ḤAMISHI
to present My offering of foodstuffs – fire offerings of pleasing aroma to Me –
3 at its appointed times. Say to them: This is the fire offering you must present
to the LORD: two yearling lambs without blemish as a regular burnt offering

רש״י

לְמַעַן יִשְׁמְעוּ כָּל עֲדַת בְּנֵי יִשְׂרָאֵל. שֶׁיִּהְיוּ נוֹהֲגִין בּוֹ כָּבוֹד וְיִרְאָה כְּדֶרֶךְ שֶׁנּוֹהֲגִין בְּךָ:

כא| **וְלִפְנֵי אֶלְעָזָר הַכֹּהֵן יַעֲמֹד.** הֲרֵי שְׁאֵלָתְךָ שֶׁשָּׁאַלְתָּ, שֶׁאֵין הַכָּבוֹד הַזֶּה זָז מִבֵּית אָבִיךָ, שֶׁאַף יְהוֹשֻׁעַ יְהֵא צָרִיךְ לְאֶלְעָזָר: **וְשָׁאַל לוֹ.** כְּשֶׁיִּצְטָרֵךְ לָצֵאת לַמִּלְחָמָה: **עַל פִּיו.** שֶׁל אֶלְעָזָר: **וְכָל הָעֵדָה.** סַנְהֶדְרִין:

כב| **וַיִּקַּח אֶת יְהוֹשֻׁעַ.** לְקָחוֹ בִּדְבָרִים, וְהוֹדִיעוֹ מַתַּן שְׂכַר פַּרְנָסֵי יִשְׂרָאֵל לָעוֹלָם הַבָּא:

כג| **וַיִּסְמֹךְ אֶת יָדָיו.** בְּעַיִן יָפָה, יוֹתֵר וְיוֹתֵר מִמַּה שֶּׁנִּצְטַוָּה, שֶׁהַקָּדוֹשׁ בָּרוּךְ הוּא אָמַר לוֹ: "וְסָמַכְתָּ אֶת יָדְךָ" (לעיל פסוק יח) וְהוּא עָשָׂה בִּשְׁתֵּי יָדָיו, וַעֲשָׂאוֹ כִּכְלִי מָלֵא וְגָדוּשׁ וּמִלְּאוֹ חָכְמָתוֹ בְּעַיִן יָפָה: **כַּאֲשֶׁר דִּבֶּר ה׳.** אַף לְעִנְיַן הַהוֹד, נָתַן מֵהוֹדוֹ עָלָיו:

כח ב| **צַו אֶת בְּנֵי יִשְׂרָאֵל.** מָה אָמוּר לְמַעְלָה? "יִפְקֹד ה׳" (לעיל כז, טז), אָמַר לוֹ הַקָּדוֹשׁ בָּרוּךְ הוּא: עַד שֶׁאַתָּה מְצַוֵּנִי עַל בָּנַי, צַוֵּה אֶת בָּנַי עָלַי. מָשָׁל לְבַת מֶלֶךְ שֶׁהָיְתָה נִפְטֶרֶת מִן הָעוֹלָם וְהָיְתָה מְפַקֶּדֶת לְבַעְלָהּ עַל בָּנֶיהָ וְכוּ׳ [אָמְרָה לוֹ: בְּבַקָּשָׁה מִמְּךָ הִזָּהֵר לִי בְּבָנַי. אָמַר לָהּ: עַד שֶׁאַתְּ מְפַקְּדֵתְנִי עַל בָּנַי פַּקְּדִי אֶת בָּנַי עָלַי, שֶׁלֹּא יִמְרְדוּ בִּי וְשֶׁלֹּא יִנְהֲגוּ בִּי מִנְהַג בִּזָּיוֹן], כִּדְאִיתָא בְּסִפְרֵי (קמב): **קָרְבָּנִי.** זֶה הַדָּם: **לַחְמִי.** אֵלּוּ אֵמוּרִין, וְכֵן הוּא אוֹמֵר: "וְהִקְטִירָם הַכֹּהֵן הַמִּזְבֵּחָה לֶחֶם אִשֶּׁה" (ויקרא ג, טז): **לְאִשַּׁי.** הַנִּתָּנִין לְאִשֵּׁי מִזְבְּחִי: **תִּשְׁמְרוּ.** שֶׁיִּהְיוּ כֹּהֲנִים וּלְוִיִּם וְיִשְׂרְאֵלִים עוֹמְדִין עַל גַּבָּיו, מִכָּאן לָמְדוּ וְתִקְּנוּ מַעֲמָדוֹת: **בְּמוֹעֲדוֹ.** בְּכָל יוֹם הוּא מוֹעֵד הַתְּמִידִים:

ג| **וְאָמַרְתָּ לָהֶם.** אַזְהָרָה לְבֵית דִּין: **שְׁנַיִם לַיּוֹם.** כִּפְשׁוּטוֹ. וְעִקָּרוֹ בָּא לְלַמֵּד שֶׁיִּהְיוּ נִשְׁחָטִין כְּנֶגֶד הַיּוֹם, תָּמִיד שֶׁל שַׁחַר בַּמַּעֲרָב וְשֶׁל בֵּין הָעַרְבַּיִם בַּמִּזְרָח שֶׁל טַבָּעוֹת:

in the afternoon'" (Num. 28:4) – the routine of daily service. The midrash concludes: "A certain rabbi stood up and declared: 'The law is in accordance with Ben Pazi.'"

Judaism, suggests Ben Pazi, is not just poetry but also prose, not just the fire of romantic love but the daily kindnesses of a successful marriage, not just an exalted faith in the transcendent God but the way it takes faith and translates it into everyday life.

This account of the yearly calendar of sacrifices begins with ordinary days, then the Sabbath, then the New Moon, and finally the annual cycle of festivals. The order is reflected in the general rule in Judaism that "when a frequent obligation coincides with a rare one, the more frequent one takes precedence" (Berakhot 51b). When a festival falls on the Sabbath, for instance, the Sabbath takes priority, and its additions to the prayers are said before those of the festival. This is in itself an expression of Jewish values. In many faiths, a sense of holiness and spirituality belongs to moments that are rare, unusual, exceptional. In Judaism what is holy is the texture of everyday life itself. It is the religious drama of daily deeds, words, and relationships. God is not distant but in the here and now – if we create space in our hearts for His presence. We encounter Him, as the journey through the desert nears its end, not in the thunder and lightning of Sinai but every morning and evening in ritual and routine. That is what life is and what faith transfigures.

כא לְמַעַן יִשְׁמְעוּ כׇּל־עֲדַת בְּנֵי יִשְׂרָאֵל׃ וְלִפְנֵי אֶלְעָזָר הַכֹּהֵן יַעֲמֹד וְשָׁאַל
לוֹ בְּמִשְׁפַּט הָאוּרִים לִפְנֵי יהוה עַל־פִּיו יֵצְאוּ וְעַל־פִּיו יָבֹאוּ הוּא וְכׇל־
כב בְּנֵי־יִשְׂרָאֵל אִתּוֹ וְכׇל־הָעֵדָה׃ וַיַּעַשׂ מֹשֶׁה כַּאֲשֶׁר צִוָּה יהוה אֹתוֹ וַיִּקַּח
כג אֶת־יְהוֹשֻׁעַ וַיַּעֲמִדֵהוּ לִפְנֵי אֶלְעָזָר הַכֹּהֵן וְלִפְנֵי כׇּל־הָעֵדָה׃ וַיִּסְמֹךְ
אֶת־יָדָיו עָלָיו וַיְצַוֵּהוּ כַּאֲשֶׁר דִּבֶּר יהוה בְּיַד־מֹשֶׁה׃
כח א ב וַיְדַבֵּר יהוה אֶל־מֹשֶׁה לֵּאמֹר׃ צַו אֶת־בְּנֵי יִשְׂרָאֵל וְאָמַרְתָּ אֲלֵהֶם אֶת־ חמישי
ג קׇרְבָּנִי לַחְמִי לְאִשַּׁי רֵיחַ נִיחֹחִי תִּשְׁמְרוּ לְהַקְרִיב לִי בְּמוֹעֲדוֹ׃ וְאָמַרְתָּ
לָהֶם זֶה הָאִשֶּׁה אֲשֶׁר תַּקְרִיבוּ לַיהוה כְּבָשִׂים בְּנֵי־שָׁנָה תְמִימִם שְׁנַיִם

אונקלוס

אֶלְעָזָר כָּהֲנָא יְקוּם, וְיִשְׁאַל לֵיהּ, בְּדִין אוּרַיָּא קֳדָם יי, עַל מֵימְרֵיהּ יְהוֹן נָפְקִין וְעַל מֵימְרֵיהּ יְהוֹן עָאלִין, הוּא, וְכָל בְּנֵי יִשְׂרָאֵל עִמֵּיהּ וְכָל כְּנִשְׁתָּא: כב וַעֲבַד מֹשֶׁה, כְּמָא דְּפַקֵּיד יי יָתֵיהּ, וּדְבַר יָת יְהוֹשֻׁעַ, וַאֲקִימֵיהּ קֳדָם אֶלְעָזָר כָּהֲנָא, וּקֳדָם כָּל כְּנִשְׁתָּא: כג וּסְמַךְ יָת יְדוֹהִי, עֲלוֹהִי וּפַקְּדֵיהּ, כְּמָא דְּמַלֵּיל יי בִּידָא דְמֹשֶׁה: כח א וּמַלֵּיל יי עִם מֹשֶׁה לְמֵימַר: ב פַּקֵּיד יָת בְּנֵי יִשְׂרָאֵל, וְתֵימַר לְהוֹן, יָת קֻרְבָּנִי לְחֵים סְדוּר לְקֻרְבָּנַי, לְאִתְקַבָּלָא בְרַעֲוָא, תִּטְּרוּן, לְקָרָבָא קֳדָמַי בְּזִמְנֵיהּ: ג וְתֵימַר לְהוֹן, דֵּין קֻרְבָּנָא, דִּתְקָרְבוּן קֳדָם יי, אִמְּרִין בְּנֵי שְׁנָא שַׁלְמִין, תְּרֵין

why he was initially so reluctant to accept the role of leader. Being exposed to people's anger is the price leaders have to pay if they are to move a people from where they are to where they need to be. The highest form of leadership is the kind that changes people by a combination of vision, education, and giving people a sense of possibility and responsibility – helping them to achieve greatness. When the leader is good, people say, "The leader did it." When the leader is great, they say, "We did it ourselves."

This always carries a price because people often want the leader to do it for them. When they realize that the leader cannot relieve people of responsibility, there is anger. That is what the Sages meant when they said that God told Moshe to inform Yehoshua that the people "are troublesome and obstinate" and that being their leader came with the condition that "you accept this."

Learning to "take the heat" and live with people's anger is one of the hardest tasks of leadership, but it is essential. The leader has to hold steady, be respectful of people's pain, and defend the vision without becoming personally defensive. "Receiving anger" is, in Heifetz's words, "a sacred task."

THE SACRIFICIAL YEAR

As the rupture and disorder of the Baal Peor incident and its aftermath give way to the order and structure that characterize the rest of the book of Numbers, Moshe recaps the Jewish calendar, viewed entirely through the prism of the sacrificial rituals of each day.

We have already encountered the astonishing midrashic passage (quoted in the preface to *Ein Yaakov*, 6b; see Ex. 29, "The Regular Burnt Offering") in which the Sages discuss the question: What is the one sentence that summarizes Judaism?

Ben Zoma holds that it is "Listen, Israel…" (Deut. 6:4) – faith in the One God. Ben Nannas chooses, "Love your neighbor as your own self" (Lev. 19:18) – Judaism's ethic of love. But Ben Pazi says, "There is a more embracing verse still: 'Offer one lamb in the morning and the second

4 5 each day. Offer one lamb in the morning and the second in the afternoon, with
a tenth of an ephah of fine flour as a grain offering mixed with a quarter of a hin
6 of beaten oil. This is the regular burnt offering instituted at Mount Sinai, as a
7 pleasing aroma, a fire offering to the Lord. Its libation shall be a quarter of a
hin for each lamb, to be poured out in the Sanctuary as a libation of fermented
8 drink to the Lord. Offer the other lamb in the afternoon together with a grain
offering and libation as in the morning; a fire offering, a pleasing aroma to the
Lord.

9 On the Sabbath day: two yearling lambs without blemish and two-tenths of a
10 measure of fine flour as a grain offering, mixed with oil, and its libation. This is
the burnt offering for every Sabbath, to be brought in addition to the regular
daily burnt offering and its libation.

11 On your New Moons you shall present a burnt offering to the Lord: two
12 young bulls, one ram, and seven yearling lambs, all without blemish. There
shall be a grain offering of three-tenths of a measure of fine flour mixed with
oil for each bull, a grain offering of two-tenths of fine flour mixed with oil
13 for each ram, and a grain offering of one-tenth of fine flour mixed with oil
for each lamb. This shall be a burnt offering of pleasing aroma, a fire offering
14 to the Lord. Their libations shall be half a hin of wine for a bull, a third of

רש״י

ד **אֶת הַכֶּבֶשׂ אֶחָד.** אַף עַל פִּי שֶׁכְּבָר נֶאֱמַר בְּפָרָשַׁת וְאַתָּה תְּצַוֶּה: "וְזֶה אֲשֶׁר תַּעֲשֶׂה" וְגוֹ' (שמות כט, לח-לט), הִיא הָיְתָה אַזְהָרָה לִימֵי הַמִּלּוּאִים, וְכָאן צִוָּה לְדוֹרוֹת:

ה **סֹלֶת לְמִנְחָה.** מִנְחַת נְסָכִים:

ו **הָעֲשֻׂיָה בְּהַר סִינַי.** כְּאוֹתָן שֶׁנַּעֲשׂוּ בִּימֵי הַמִּלּוּאִים. דָּבָר אַחֵר, "הָעֲשֻׂיָה בְּהַר סִינַי", מַקִּישׁ עוֹלַת תָּמִיד לְעוֹלַת הַר סִינַי, אוֹתָהּ שֶׁקָּרְבָה לִפְנֵי מַתַּן תּוֹרָה שֶׁכָּתוּב בָּהּ: "וַיָּשֶׂם בָּאַגָּנֹת" (שמות כד, ו), מְלַמֵּד שֶׁטְּעוּנָה כְּלִי:

ז **וְנִסְכּוֹ.** יַיִן: **בַּקֹּדֶשׁ הַסֵּךְ.** עַל הַמִּזְבֵּחַ יִתְנַסְּכוּ: **נֶסֶךְ שֵׁכָר.** יַיִן הַמְשַׁכֵּר, פְּרָט לְיַיִן מִגִּתּוֹ:

ח **רֵיחַ נִיחֹחַ.** נַחַת רוּחַ לְפָנַי שֶׁאָמַרְתִּי וְנַעֲשָׂה רְצוֹנִי:

י **עֹלַת שַׁבַּת בְּשַׁבַּתּוֹ.** וְלֹא עוֹלַת שַׁבָּת בְּשַׁבָּת אַחֶרֶת, הֲרֵי שֶׁלֹּא הִקְרִיב בְּשַׁבָּת זוֹ, שׁוֹמֵעַ אֲנִי יַקְרִיב שְׁתַּיִם לְשַׁבָּת הַבָּאָה? תַּלְמוּד לוֹמַר: "בְּשַׁבַּתּוֹ", מַגִּיד שֶׁאִם עָבַר יוֹמוֹ בָּטֵל קָרְבָּנוֹ: **עַל עֹלַת הַתָּמִיד.** אֵלּוּ מוּסָפִין, לְבַד אוֹתָן שְׁנֵי כְבָשִׂים שֶׁל עוֹלַת הַתָּמִיד. וּמַגִּיד שֶׁאֵין קְרֵבִין אֶלָּא בֵּין שְׁנֵי הַתְּמִידִין, וְכֵן בְּכָל הַמּוּסָפִין נֶאֱמַר: "עַל עוֹלַת הַתָּמִיד" לְתַלְמוּד זֶה:

יב **וּשְׁלֹשָׁה עֶשְׂרֹנִים.** כְּמִשְׁפַּט נִסְכֵּי פָר, שֶׁכֵּן הֵן קְצוּבִין בְּפָרָשַׁת נְסָכִים (לעיל טו, ח-י):

prayer for the restoration of the Temple and its sacrifices. Our *parasha* is cited, describing the offering of the day. On Rosh Ḥodesh, we pray that the new month be blessed for good.

A midrashic tradition associates Rosh Ḥodesh with Jewish women, as a tribute to their faithfulness and to their generosity in providing gifts for the construction of the Tabernacle. From the first month of the second year after the exodus, the day the Tabernacle was dedicated, it became a women's festival (Rashi, Megilla 22b; *Shulkhan Arukh, Oraḥ Ḥayim* 417:1).

ד לַיּוֹם עֹלָה תָמִיד׃ אֶת־הַכֶּבֶשׂ אֶחָד תַּעֲשֶׂה בַבֹּקֶר וְאֵת הַכֶּבֶשׂ הַשֵּׁנִי
ה תַּעֲשֶׂה בֵּין הָעַרְבָּיִם׃ וַעֲשִׂירִית הָאֵיפָה סֹלֶת לְמִנְחָה בְּלוּלָה בְּשֶׁמֶן
ו כָּתִית רְבִיעִת הַהִין׃ עֹלַת תָּמִיד הָעֲשֻׂיָה בְּהַר סִינַי לְרֵיחַ נִיחֹחַ אִשֶּׁה
ז לַיהוָה׃ וְנִסְכּוֹ רְבִיעִת הַהִין לַכֶּבֶשׂ הָאֶחָד בַּקֹּדֶשׁ הַסֵּךְ נֶסֶךְ שֵׁכָר
ח לַיהוָה׃ וְאֵת הַכֶּבֶשׂ הַשֵּׁנִי תַּעֲשֶׂה בֵּין הָעַרְבָּיִם כְּמִנְחַת הַבֹּקֶר וּכְנִסְכּוֹ
תַּעֲשֶׂה אִשֵּׁה רֵיחַ נִיחֹחַ לַיהוָה׃
ט וּבְיוֹם הַשַּׁבָּת שְׁנֵי־כְבָשִׂים בְּנֵי־שָׁנָה תְּמִימִם וּשְׁנֵי עֶשְׂרֹנִים סֹלֶת
י מִנְחָה בְּלוּלָה בַשֶּׁמֶן וְנִסְכּוֹ׃ עֹלַת שַׁבַּת בְּשַׁבַּתּוֹ עַל־עֹלַת הַתָּמִיד
וְנִסְכָּהּ׃
יא וּבְרָאשֵׁי חָדְשֵׁיכֶם תַּקְרִיבוּ עֹלָה לַיהוָה פָּרִים בְּנֵי־בָקָר שְׁנַיִם וְאַיִל
יב אֶחָד כְּבָשִׂים בְּנֵי־שָׁנָה שִׁבְעָה תְּמִימִם׃ וּשְׁלֹשָׁה עֶשְׂרֹנִים סֹלֶת מִנְחָה
בְּלוּלָה בַשֶּׁמֶן לַפָּר הָאֶחָד וּשְׁנֵי עֶשְׂרֹנִים סֹלֶת מִנְחָה בְּלוּלָה בַשֶּׁמֶן
יג לָאַיִל הָאֶחָד׃ וְעִשָּׂרֹן עִשָּׂרוֹן סֹלֶת מִנְחָה בְּלוּלָה בַשֶּׁמֶן לַכֶּבֶשׂ הָאֶחָד
יד עֹלָה רֵיחַ נִיחֹחַ אִשֶּׁה לַיהוָה׃ וְנִסְכֵּיהֶם חֲצִי הַהִין יִהְיֶה לַפָּר וּשְׁלִישִׁת

אונקלוס

לְיוֹמָא עֲלָתָא תְּדִירָא: ד יָת אִמְּרָא חַד תַּעֲבֵיד בְּצַפְרָא, וְיָת אִמְּרָא תִּנְיָנָא, תַּעֲבֵיד בֵּין שִׁמְשַׁיָּא: ה וְחַד מִן עַסְרָא בִּתְלָת סְאִין, סֻלְתָּא לְמִנְחָתָא, דְּפִילָא, בִּמְשַׁח כְּתִישָׁא רַבְעוּת הִינָא: ו עֲלַת תְּדִירָא, דְּאִתְעֲבִידַת בְּטוּרָא דְסִינַי, לְאִתְקַבָּלָא בְרַעֲוָא, קֻרְבָּנָא קֳדָם יְיָ: ז וְנִסְכֵּיהּ רַבְעוּת הִינָא, לְאִמְּרָא חַד, בְּקֻדְשָׁא, יִתְנַסַּךְ, נְסוּךְ דַּחֲמַר עַתִּיק קֳדָם יְיָ: ח וְיָת אִמְּרָא תִּנְיָנָא, תַּעֲבֵיד בֵּין שִׁמְשַׁיָּא, כְּמִנְחַת צַפְרָא וּכְנִסְכֵּיהּ תַּעֲבֵיד, קֻרְבַּן דְּמִתְקַבַּל בְּרַעֲוָא קֳדָם יְיָ: ט וּבְיוֹמָא דְּשַׁבְּתָא, תְּרֵין אִמְּרִין בְּנֵי שְׁנָא שַׁלְמִין, וּתְרֵין עֶסְרוֹנִין, סֻלְתָּא מִנְחָתָא, דְּפִילָא בִּמְשַׁח וְנִסְכֵּיהּ: י עֲלַת שַׁבָּא תִּתְעֲבֵיד בְּשַׁבָּא, עַל עֲלַת תְּדִירָא וְנִסְכַּהּ: יא וּבְרֵישֵׁי יַרְחֵיכוֹן, תְּקָרְבוּן עֲלָתָא קֳדָם יְיָ, תּוֹרֵי בְּנֵי תוֹרֵי תְּרֵין וּדְכַר חַד, אִמְּרִין בְּנֵי שְׁנָא, שִׁבְעָא שַׁלְמִין: יב וּתְלָתָא עֶסְרוֹנִין, סֻלְתָּא מִנְחָתָא דְּפִילָא בִּמְשַׁח, לְתוֹרָא חַד, וּתְרֵין עֶסְרוֹנִין, סֻלְתָּא מִנְחָתָא דְּפִילָא בִּמְשַׁח, לִדְכְרָא חַד: יג וְעֶסְרוֹנָא עֶסְרוֹנָא, סֻלְתָּא מִנְחָתָא דְּפִילָא בִּמְשַׁח, לְאִמְּרָא חַד, עֲלָתָא לְאִתְקַבָּלָא בְּרַעֲוָא, קֻרְבָּנָא קֳדָם יְיָ: יד וְנִסְכֵּיהוֹן, פַּלְגוּת הִינָא יְהֵי לְתוֹרָא וּתְלָתוּת

28:11 וּבְרָאשֵׁי חָדְשֵׁיכֶם *On your New Moons* – Rosh Ḥodesh (the New Moon), like the new year, is understood in Judaism as a time of renewal and rededication, in which we pray for forgiveness and atonement and seek to begin again. As with the festivals, the Musaf prayer now commemorates the special offerings that were brought for the occasion in the Tabernacle and Temple. The central blessings of Musaf begin with a brief statement of the nature of the day and a

a hin of wine for a ram, and a quarter of a hin of wine for a lamb. This is the
15 monthly burnt offering for each New Moon of the year. One male goat shall be
brought as a purification offering to the LORD, in addition to the regular burnt
16 offering and its libation. On the fourteenth day of the first month, a SHISHI
17 Passover sacrifice shall be brought to the LORD. And the fifteenth day of this
18 month will be a festival. For seven days unleavened bread shall be eaten. The
19 first day shall be a sacred assembly; you shall perform no laborious work. You
shall offer a burnt fire offering to the LORD: two young bulls, one ram, and
20 seven yearling lambs, all unblemished. Their grain offering shall be fine flour
mixed with oil: three-tenths of a measure for each bull, two-tenths for the ram,
21 22 and one-tenth for each of the seven lambs, together with one male goat as a
23 purification offering to make your atonement. These you shall offer in addition
24 to the morning burnt offering, the regular daily offering. In the same way you
shall offer daily for seven days the foodstuffs of a fire offering, a pleasing aroma
to the LORD. It shall be offered in addition to the regular burnt offering and its
25 libation. The seventh day shall be for you a sacred assembly; you shall perform
26 no laborious work. The day of first produce, when you bring an

רש״י

יד **זֹאת עֹלַת חֹדֶשׁ בְּחָדְשׁוֹ.** שֶׁאִם עָבַר יוֹמוֹ בָּטֵל קָרְבָּנוֹ וְשׁוּב אֵין לוֹ תַּשְׁלוּמִין:

טו **וּשְׂעִיר עִזִּים וְגוֹ׳.** כָּל שְׂעִירֵי הַמּוּסָפִין בָּאִין לְכַפֵּר עַל טֻמְאַת מִקְדָּשׁ וְקָדָשָׁיו, הַכֹּל כְּמוֹ שֶׁמְּפֹרָשׁ בְּמַסֶּכֶת שְׁבוּעוֹת (דף ב ע״א-ע״ב). וְנִשְׁתַּנָּה שְׂעִיר רֹאשׁ חֹדֶשׁ שֶׁנֶּאֱמַר בּוֹ: ״לַה׳״, לְלַמֶּדְךָ שֶׁמְּכַפֵּר עַל שֶׁאֵין בּוֹ יְדִיעָה לֹא בַּתְּחִלָּה וְלֹא בַּסּוֹף, שֶׁאֵין מַכִּיר בַּחֵטְא אֶלָּא הַקָּדוֹשׁ בָּרוּךְ הוּא בִּלְבַד, וּשְׁאָר הַשְּׂעִירִין לְמֵדִין מִמֶּנּוּ. וּמִדְרָשׁוֹ בָּאַגָּדָה: אָמַר הַקָּדוֹשׁ בָּרוּךְ הוּא: הָבִיאוּ כַּפָּרָה עָלַי עַל שֶׁמִּעַטְתִּי אֶת הַיָּרֵחַ: **עַל עֹלַת הַתָּמִיד יֵעָשֶׂה.** כָּל הַקָּרְבָּן הַזֶּה: **וְנִסְכּוֹ.** אֵין ׳וְנִסְכּוֹ׳ מוּסָב עַל הַשָּׂעִיר, שֶׁאֵין נְסָכִים לְחַטָּאת:

יח **כָּל מְלֶאכֶת עֲבֹדָה.** אֲפִלּוּ מְלָאכָה הַצְּרִיכָה לָכֶם, כְּגוֹן דָּבָר הָאָבֵד הַמֻּתָּר בְּחֻלּוֹ שֶׁל מוֹעֵד, אֲסוּרָה בְּיוֹם טוֹב:

יט **פָּרִים.** כְּנֶגֶד אַבְרָהָם, שֶׁנֶּאֱמַר: ״וְאֶל הַבָּקָר רָץ אַבְרָהָם״ (בראשית יח, ז): **אֵילִים.** כְּנֶגֶד אֵילוֹ שֶׁל יִצְחָק (שם כב, יג): **כְּבָשִׂים.** כְּנֶגֶד יַעֲקֹב, שֶׁנֶּאֱמַר: ״וְהַכְּשָׂבִים הִפְרִיד יַעֲקֹב״ (שם ל, מ). בִּיסוֹדוֹ שֶׁל רַבִּי מֹשֶׁה הַדַּרְשָׁן רָאִיתִי זֹאת:

כד **כָּאֵלֶּה תַּעֲשׂוּ לַיּוֹם.** שֶׁלֹּא יִהְיוּ פּוֹחֲתִין וְהוֹלְכִין כְּפָרֵי הֶחָג:

כו **וּבְיוֹם הַבִּכּוּרִים.** חַג הַשָּׁבוּעוֹת קָרוּי: ״בִּכּוּרֵי קְצִיר חִטִּים״ (שמות לד, כב), עַל שֵׁם שְׁתֵּי הַלֶּחֶם שֶׁהֵם רִאשׁוֹנִים לְמִנְחַת חִטִּים הַבָּאָה מִן הֶחָדָשׁ:

start of the journey from Egypt. Sukkot recalls the forty years of the journey itself. What is missing is a festival of celebrating the journey's end, the arrival at the destination. Logic would suggest that this was Shavuot. Were it not so, there would have been no annual celebration of the single most important fact about Israel's existence as a nation, namely, that it lived in the land given by God in fulfilment of the promise He had made to their ancestors at the dawn of their history. Shavuot completes the cycle of the three pilgrimage festivals by being the festival of homecoming. That was its historical dimension, made explicit in the *vidui bikkurim* (Deut. 26:1–11), the declaration accompanying the first fruits, and symbolized in the two loaves of wheat (Lev. 23:17) that were the special offering of Shavuot.

It would also follow that the three pilgrimage festivals correspond to three different kinds of bread. Passover is

הַהִין לָאַיִל וּרְבִיעִת הַהִין לַכֶּבֶשׂ יָיִן זֹאת עֹלַת חֹדֶשׁ בְּחָדְשׁוֹ לְחָדְשֵׁי
טו הַשָּׁנָה: וּשְׂעִיר עִזִּים אֶחָד לְחַטָּאת לַיהוָה עַל־עֹלַת הַתָּמִיד יֵעָשֶׂה
טז וְנִסְכּוֹ: וּבַחֹדֶשׁ הָרִאשׁוֹן בְּאַרְבָּעָה עָשָׂר יוֹם לַחֹדֶשׁ ששי
יז פֶּסַח לַיהוָה: וּבַחֲמִשָּׁה עָשָׂר יוֹם לַחֹדֶשׁ הַזֶּה חָג שִׁבְעַת יָמִים מַצּוֹת
יח יֵאָכֵל: בַּיּוֹם הָרִאשׁוֹן מִקְרָא־קֹדֶשׁ כָּל־מְלֶאכֶת עֲבֹדָה לֹא תַעֲשׂוּ:
יט וְהִקְרַבְתֶּם אִשֶּׁה עֹלָה לַיהוָה פָּרִים בְּנֵי־בָקָר שְׁנַיִם וְאַיִל אֶחָד וְשִׁבְעָה
כ כְבָשִׂים בְּנֵי שָׁנָה תְּמִימִם יִהְיוּ לָכֶם: וּמִנְחָתָם סֹלֶת בְּלוּלָה בַשָּׁמֶן
כא שְׁלֹשָׁה עֶשְׂרֹנִים לַפָּר וּשְׁנֵי עֶשְׂרֹנִים לָאַיִל תַּעֲשׂוּ: עִשָּׂרוֹן עִשָּׂרוֹן
כב תַּעֲשֶׂה לַכֶּבֶשׂ הָאֶחָד לְשִׁבְעַת הַכְּבָשִׂים: וּשְׂעִיר חַטָּאת אֶחָד לְכַפֵּר
כג עֲלֵיכֶם: מִלְּבַד עֹלַת הַבֹּקֶר אֲשֶׁר לְעֹלַת הַתָּמִיד תַּעֲשׂוּ אֶת־אֵלֶּה:
כד כָּאֵלֶּה תַּעֲשׂוּ לַיּוֹם שִׁבְעַת יָמִים לֶחֶם אִשֵּׁה רֵיחַ־נִיחֹחַ לַיהוָה עַל־
כה עוֹלַת הַתָּמִיד יֵעָשֶׂה וְנִסְכּוֹ: וּבַיּוֹם הַשְּׁבִיעִי מִקְרָא־קֹדֶשׁ יִהְיֶה לָכֶם
כו כָּל־מְלֶאכֶת עֲבֹדָה לֹא תַעֲשׂוּ: וּבְיוֹם הַבִּכּוּרִים כה

אונקלוס

הִינָא לְדִכְרָא, וְרַבְעוּת הִינָא, לְאִמְּרָא חֲמַר, דָּא עֲלַת רֵישׁ יַרְחָא בְּאִתְחַדָּתוּתֵיהּ, כֵּן לְכָל רֵישֵׁי יַרְחֵי שַׁתָּא: טו וּצְפִיר בַּר עִזִּין חַד, לְחַטָּתָא קֳדָם יְיָ, עַל עֲלַת תְּדִירָא, יִתְעֲבֵיד וְנִסְכֵּיהּ: טז וּבְיַרְחָא קַדְמָאָה, בְּאַרְבְּעַת עַסְרָא, יוֹמָא לְיַרְחָא, פִּסְחָא קֳדָם יְיָ: יז וּבַחֲמֵישַׁת עַסְרָא יוֹמָא, לְיַרְחָא הָדֵין חַגָּא, שִׁבְעָא יוֹמִין, פַּטִּירָא יִתְאֲכִיל: יח בְּיוֹמָא קַדְמָאָה מְעָרַע קַדִּישׁ, כָּל עֲבִידַת פָּלְחַן לָא תַעְבְּדוּן: יט וּתְקָרְבוּן קֻרְבָּנָא עֲלָתָא קֳדָם יְיָ, תּוֹרֵי בְּנֵי תוֹרֵי, תְּרֵין וְדִכַר חַד, וְשִׁבְעָא אִמְּרִין בְּנֵי שְׁנָא, שַׁלְמִין יְהוֹן לְכוֹן: כ וּמִנְחַתְהוֹן, סֻלְתָּא דְּפִילָא בִּמְשַׁח, תְּלָתָא עֶסְרוֹנִין לְתוֹרָא, וּתְרֵין עֶסְרוֹנִין, לְדִכְרָא תַּעְבְּדוּן: כא עֶסְרוֹנָא עֶסְרוֹנָא תַּעְבֵּיד, לְאִמְּרָא חַד, כֵּן לְשִׁבְעָא אִמְּרִין: כב וּצְפִירָא דְּחַטָּתָא חַד, לְכַפָּרָא עֲלֵיכוֹן: כג בַּר מֵעֲלַת צַפְרָא, דְּהִיא עֲלַת תְּדִירָא, תַּעְבְּדוּן יָת אִלֵּין: כד כְּאִלֵּין, תַּעְבְּדוּן לְיוֹמָא שִׁבְעָא יוֹמִין, לְחֵים, קֻרְבַּן דְּמִתְקַבַּל בְּרַעֲוָא קֳדָם יְיָ, עַל עֲלַת תְּדִירָא, יִתְעֲבֵיד וְנִסְכֵּיהּ: כה וּבְיוֹמָא שְׁבִיעָאָה, מְעָרַע קַדִּישׁ יְהֵי לְכוֹן, כָּל עֲבִידַת פָּלְחַן לָא תַעְבְּדוּן: כו וּבְיוֹמָא דְּבִכּוּרַיָּא,

28:26 **וּבְיוֹם הַבִּכּוּרִים** *The day of the first produce* – Nowhere does the Torah link Shavuot to a specific historical event. Passover and Sukkot both, like Shavuot, are agricultural and seasonal. Passover is the festival of spring. Sukkot is the festival of ingathering, the autumn harvest. But each also has a historical dimension. Passover recalls the exodus from Egypt. Sukkot is a reminder of the forty years in the desert when the Israelites lived in temporary dwellings. What, then, is the historical dimension of Shavuot in the Torah? Shavuot, I would speculate, was the day, commanded in the desert, that was to celebrate the Promised Land.

There is evidence to support this. Passover is about the

offering of new grain to the LORD on your Festival of Weeks, shall be a sacred
27 assembly for you. On it you shall perform no laborious work. You shall present
a burnt offering as a pleasing aroma to the LORD: two young bulls, one ram,
28 and seven yearling lambs. Their grain offering shall be fine flour mixed with oil:
29 three-tenths of a measure for each bull, two-tenths for the one ram, and one-
30 31 tenth for each of the seven lambs. Offer one male goat to atone for you. These
you shall offer in addition to the regular burnt offering, its grain offering and
libations. They shall be without blemish.

29 1 The first day of the seventh month shall be a sacred assembly for you; you
shall perform no laborious work on it. It shall be for you a day of the horn's
2 sounding. You shall present a burnt offering as a pleasing aroma to the LORD:

רש״י

לא| תְּמִימִם יִהְיוּ לָכֶם וְנִסְכֵּיהֶם. אַף הַנְּסָכִים יִהְיוּ תְּמִימִים, לָמְדוּ רַבּוֹתֵינוּ מִכָּאן שֶׁהַיַּיִן שֶׁהֶעֱלָה קְמָחִין פָּסוּל לִנְסָכִים:

commemoration or remembrance of *terua*" (Lev. 23:24), are the only hints we are given of what the day represents. Nor does the Torah specify what instrument is to be used for the "sounding." It might be a horn. But equally it might refer to the silver trumpets the Israelites were commanded to make to summon the people. Sometimes the word refers to a shout or cry on the part of a crowd. Furthermore, we do not know what the sound of *terua* symbolizes. Is it the sound of celebration, of warning, of fear or tears? We are not told.

The Sages ultimately identified *terua* with the shofar for a simple reason. Rosh HaShana is not the only time that a *terua* was sounded in the seventh month. It was also sounded on Yom Kippur of the Jubilee year, when slaves went free and ancestral land returned to its original owners. There (25:9) the instrument is specified: "Then you shall sound the ram's horn (*shofar terua*)." It became a simple inference to conclude that this applied to the *terua* of the first day of the seventh month as well.

What was special about the shofar? In several places in Tanakh it is the sound of battle (see, for example, Josh. 6; I Sam. 4; Jer. 4:19, 49:2). It could also be the sound of celebration (see II Sam. 6:15). But in a number of places, especially the historical books, the shofar was sounded at the coronation of a king. So we find, for instance, at the proclamation of Shlomo as king. "Tzadok … anointed Shlomo. They sounded the ram's horn, and all the people cried, 'Long live King Shlomo!'" (I Kings 1:39).

The book of Psalms associates the shofar not with a human king but with the declaration of God as king. A key text is Psalm 47, said in many congregations before the shofar blowing on Rosh HaShana: "God ascends amid shouts of joy – the LORD – to the blast of the ram's horn…. For God is King over all the earth" (Ps. 47:6, 8).

Psalm 98 makes a clear connection between God's kingship and His judgment:

> With trumpets and the sound of the ram's horn, shout for joy before the LORD, the King…. For He is coming to judge the earth. He will judge the world with justice and the peoples with equity. (Ps. 98:6, 9)

Rosh HaShana, then, is the day we celebrate God not just as creator of the world, but as its ruler also. Rabbi Joseph B. Soloveitchik told the story of his first Hebrew teacher, who made an indelible impression on him as a child by telling him that Rosh HaShana was God's coronation. "And who puts the crown on His head?" asked the teacher. "We do."

בְּהַקְרִיבְכֶם מִנְחָה חֲדָשָׁה לַיהוָה בְּשָׁבֻעֹתֵיכֶם מִקְרָא־קֹדֶשׁ יִהְיֶה

כז לָכֶם כָּל־מְלֶאכֶת עֲבֹדָה לֹא תַעֲשׂוּ: וְהִקְרַבְתֶּם עוֹלָה לְרֵיחַ נִיחֹחַ

לַיהוָה פָּרִים בְּנֵי־בָקָר שְׁנַיִם אַיִל אֶחָד שִׁבְעָה כְבָשִׂים בְּנֵי שָׁנָה:

כח וּמִנְחָתָם סֹלֶת בְּלוּלָה בַשָּׁמֶן שְׁלֹשָׁה עֶשְׂרֹנִים לַפָּר הָאֶחָד שְׁנֵי עֶשְׂרֹנִים

כט ל לָאַיִל הָאֶחָד: עִשָּׂרוֹן עִשָּׂרוֹן לַכֶּבֶשׂ הָאֶחָד לְשִׁבְעַת הַכְּבָשִׂים: שְׂעִיר

לא עִזִּים אֶחָד לְכַפֵּר עֲלֵיכֶם: מִלְּבַד עֹלַת הַתָּמִיד וּמִנְחָתוֹ תַּעֲשׂוּ תְּמִימִם

יִהְיוּ־לָכֶם וְנִסְכֵּיהֶם:

כט א וּבַחֹדֶשׁ הַשְּׁבִיעִי בְּאֶחָד לַחֹדֶשׁ מִקְרָא־קֹדֶשׁ יִהְיֶה לָכֶם כָּל־מְלֶאכֶת

ב עֲבֹדָה לֹא תַעֲשׂוּ יוֹם תְּרוּעָה יִהְיֶה לָכֶם: וַעֲשִׂיתֶם עֹלָה לְרֵיחַ נִיחֹחַ

לַיהוָה פַּר בֶּן־בָּקָר אֶחָד אַיִל אֶחָד כְּבָשִׂים בְּנֵי־שָׁנָה שִׁבְעָה תְּמִימִם:

אונקלוס

בְּקָרוֹבֵיכוֹן, מִנְחָתָא חֲדַתָּא קֳדָם יְיָ, בְּעַצְרָתְכוֹן, מְעָרַע קַדִּישׁ יְהֵי לְכוֹן, כָּל עֲבִידַת פָּלְחַן לָא תַעְבְּדוּן: כז וּתְקָרְבוּן עֲלָתָא, לְאִתְקַבָּלָא בְרַעֲוָא קֳדָם יְיָ, תּוֹרֵי בְּנֵי תּוֹרֵי, תְּרֵין דְּכַר חַד, שִׁבְעָא אִמְּרִין בְּנֵי שְׁנָא: כח וּמִנְחָתְהוֹן, סֻלְתָּא דְּפִילָא בִמְשַׁח, תְּלָתָא עֶסְרוֹנִין לְתוֹרָא חַד, תְּרֵין עֶסְרוֹנִין, לְדִכְרָא חַד: כט עֶסְרוֹנָא עֶסְרוֹנָא, לְאִמְּרָא חַד, כֵּן לְשִׁבְעָא אִמְּרִין: ל צְפִיר בַּר עִזִּין חַד, לְכַפָּרָא עֲלֵיכוֹן: לא בָּר מֵעֲלַת תְּדִירָא, וּמִנְחָתֵיהּ תַּעְבְּדוּן, שַׁלְמִין יְהוֹן לְכוֹן וְנִסְכֵּיהוֹן: כט א וּבְיַרְחָא שְׁבִיעָאָה בְּחַד לְיַרְחָא, מְעָרַע קַדִּישׁ יְהֵי לְכוֹן, כָּל עֲבִידַת פָּלְחַן לָא תַעְבְּדוּן, יוֹם יַבָּבָא יְהֵי לְכוֹן: ב וְתַעְבְּדוּן עֲלָתָא, לְאִתְקַבָּלָא בְרַעֲוָא קֳדָם יְיָ, תּוֹר בַּר תּוֹרֵי, חַד דְּכַר חַד, אִמְּרִין בְּנֵי שְׁנָא, שִׁבְעָא שַׁלְמִין:

about "the bread of affliction" (Deut. 16:3) that our ancestors ate in Egypt. Sukkot is about the manna, the "bread from heaven" (Ex. 16:4) that they ate for forty years in the wilderness, the sukka itself symbolizing the clouds of glory that appeared just before the manna fell for the first time (13:21, 16:10). Shavuot, "the day of first produce," is about the bread of freedom made with the grain of the land itself.

In the Talmud, Shavuot became known as *zeman matan Torateinu*, "the time of the giving of our Torah," the anniversary of the revelation at Mount Sinai (see, for example, Pesaḥim 68b, among others). At Mount Sinai, a mere seven weeks after leaving Egypt, the Israelites underwent a unique experience that transformed their identity. They made a covenant with God. They pledged themselves to live by His laws. This was their foundational moment as a body politic – uniquely in the history of nations, first came the law, and only then the land.

It seems to me that only when they lost the land but knew they still had the law did Jews fully realize that this – a deeper source of identity even than the land – is what Shavuot had been about from the very beginning.

29:1 **יוֹם תְּרוּעָה** *A day of the horn's sounding* – The Torah does not use the phrase *Rosh HaShana*, the beginning or "head" of the year, and the only time that expression appears in Tanakh (Ezek. 40:1), it refers to Yom Kippur. In fact, the Torah seems to make it clear that Rosh HaShana is *not* the beginning of the year. The first month is not Tishrei, but Nisan. The biblical names for the festival, *Yom Terua* and *Zikhron Terua*, literally "the day of *terua*" and "a

▶

3 one young bull, one ram, and seven yearling lambs, all without blemish. Their
grain offering shall be fine flour mixed with oil, three-tenths of a measure for
4 5 the bull, two-tenths for the ram, and one-tenth for each of the seven lambs; and
6 there shall be one male goat as a purification offering to atone for you. This will
be in addition to the monthly burnt offering with its grain offering, and the
regular burnt offering with its grain offering and libations as prescribed. It shall
7 be a pleasing aroma, a fire offering to the LORD. The tenth day of this
seventh month shall be a sacred assembly for you; you shall afflict yourselves
8 on it and perform no work at all. You shall present a burnt offering to the LORD
for a pleasing aroma: one young bull, one ram, and seven yearling lambs, all
9 without blemish. Their grain offering shall be fine flour mixed with oil, three-
10 tenths of a measure for the bull, two-tenths for the single ram, and one-tenth for
11 each of the seven sheep. There shall be one male goat as a purification offering,
in addition to the special purification offering of atonement and the regular
12 burnt offering with its grain offering and libations. The fifteenth day SHEVI'I
of the seventh month shall be a sacred assembly for you; you shall perform no
laborious work on it; you shall celebrate a festival to the LORD for seven days.
13 And you shall present a burnt offering, a fire offering, for a pleasing aroma to
the LORD: thirteen young bulls, two rams, and fourteen yearling lambs, all
14 without blemish. Their grain offering shall be fine flour mixed with oil: three-
tenths of a measure for each of the thirteen bulls, two-tenths for each of the

רש״י

כט ו **מִלְּבַד עֹלַת הַחֹדֶשׁ.** מוּסְפֵי רֹאשׁ חֹדֶשׁ שֶׁהוּא בְּיוֹם רֹאשׁ הַשָּׁנָה: יא **מִלְּבַד חַטַּאת הַכִּפֻּרִים.** שָׂעִיר הַנַּעֲשֶׂה בִּפְנִים הָאָמוּר בְּאַחֲרֵי מוֹת (ויקרא טז, ט; טו), שֶׁגַּם הוּא חַטָּאת: **וְעֹלַת הַתָּמִיד.** וּמִלְּבַד עוֹלַת הַתָּמִיד תַּעֲשׂוּ עוֹלוֹת הַלָּלוּ: **וְנִסְכֵּיהֶם.** מוּסָב עַל הַמּוּסָפִין הַכְּתוּבִין וְעַל "תַּעֲשׂוּ", וְהוּא לְשׁוֹן צִוּוּי, מִלְּבַד עוֹלַת הַתָּמִיד וּמִנְחָתָהּ תַּעֲשׂוּ אֶת אֵלֶּה וְנִסְכֵּיהֶם. וְכֵן כָּל 'וְנִסְכֵּיהֶם' הָאֲמוּרִים בְּכָל הַמּוֹעֲדוֹת, חוּץ מִשֶּׁל קָרְבְּנוֹת הֶחָג, שֶׁכָּל 'וְנִסְכָּהּ', 'וְנִסְכֵּיהֶם', 'וּנְסָכֶיהָ' שֶׁבָּהֶם מוּסַבִּים עַל הַתָּמִיד וְאֵינָן לְשׁוֹן צִוּוּי, שֶׁהֲרֵי נִסְכֵּיהֶם שֶׁל מוּסָפִין כְּתוּבִין לְעַצְמָן בְּכָל יוֹם וָיוֹם:

29:13 **פָּרִים בְּנֵי־בָקָר שְׁלֹשָׁה עָשָׂר** *Thirteen young bulls* – On the seven days of Sukkot, seventy young bulls were offered. Connecting this to Zekharya's prophecy that in the Messianic age all nations would celebrate Sukkot, the Sages concluded that the seventy sacrifices of Sukkot represented the seventy nations of the world as described in Genesis 10. Zekharya foresaw a day when

> all those remaining from all the nations who came up against Jerusalem will go up year after year to bow down to the King, LORD of Hosts, and to celebrate the Festival of Tabernacles. (Zech. 14:16)

Even though Zekharya's vision had not yet been realized, sacrifices were already to be made on behalf of the seventy nations of the world. Furthermore, the Sages said that on Sukkot, the world is judged for rain (Rosh HaShana 1:2). All peoples, especially in the Middle East, need rain. These facets make Sukkot the most universalistic of all festivals.

ג וּמִנְחָתָם סֹלֶת בְּלוּלָה בַשָּׁמֶן שְׁלֹשָׁה עֶשְׂרֹנִים לַפָּר שְׁנֵי עֶשְׂרֹנִים
ד ה לָאָיִל: וְעִשָּׂרוֹן אֶחָד לַכֶּבֶשׂ הָאֶחָד לְשִׁבְעַת הַכְּבָשִׂים: וּשְׂעִיר־
ו עִזִּים אֶחָד חַטָּאת לְכַפֵּר עֲלֵיכֶם: מִלְּבַד עֹלַת הַחֹדֶשׁ וּמִנְחָתָהּ
וְעֹלַת הַתָּמִיד וּמִנְחָתָהּ וְנִסְכֵּיהֶם כְּמִשְׁפָּטָם לְרֵיחַ נִיחֹחַ אִשֶּׁה
ז לַיהוָה: וּבֶעָשׂוֹר לַחֹדֶשׁ הַשְּׁבִיעִי הַזֶּה מִקְרָא־קֹדֶשׁ
ח יִהְיֶה לָכֶם וְעִנִּיתֶם אֶת־נַפְשֹׁתֵיכֶם כָּל־מְלָאכָה לֹא תַעֲשׂוּ: וְהִקְרַבְתֶּם
עֹלָה לַיהוָה רֵיחַ נִיחֹחַ פַּר בֶּן־בָּקָר אֶחָד אַיִל אֶחָד כְּבָשִׂים בְּנֵי־שָׁנָה
ט שִׁבְעָה תְּמִימִם יִהְיוּ לָכֶם: וּמִנְחָתָם סֹלֶת בְּלוּלָה בַשָּׁמֶן שְׁלֹשָׁה
י עֶשְׂרֹנִים לַפָּר שְׁנֵי עֶשְׂרֹנִים לָאַיִל הָאֶחָד: עִשָּׂרוֹן עִשָּׂרוֹן לַכֶּבֶשׂ
יא הָאֶחָד לְשִׁבְעַת הַכְּבָשִׂים: שְׂעִיר־עִזִּים אֶחָד חַטָּאת מִלְּבַד חַטַּאת
יב הַכִּפֻּרִים וְעֹלַת הַתָּמִיד וּמִנְחָתָהּ וְנִסְכֵּיהֶם: וּבַחֲמִשָּׁה שביעי
עָשָׂר יוֹם לַחֹדֶשׁ הַשְּׁבִיעִי מִקְרָא־קֹדֶשׁ יִהְיֶה לָכֶם כָּל־מְלֶאכֶת עֲבֹדָה
יג לֹא תַעֲשׂוּ וְחַגֹּתֶם חַג לַיהוָה שִׁבְעַת יָמִים: וְהִקְרַבְתֶּם עֹלָה אִשֵּׁה
רֵיחַ נִיחֹחַ לַיהוָה פָּרִים בְּנֵי־בָקָר שְׁלֹשָׁה עָשָׂר אֵילִם שְׁנָיִם כְּבָשִׂים
יד בְּנֵי־שָׁנָה אַרְבָּעָה עָשָׂר תְּמִימִם יִהְיוּ: וּמִנְחָתָם סֹלֶת בְּלוּלָה בַשָּׁמֶן
שְׁלֹשָׁה עֶשְׂרֹנִים לַפָּר הָאֶחָד לִשְׁלֹשָׁה עָשָׂר פָּרִים שְׁנֵי עֶשְׂרֹנִים לָאָיִל

אונקלוס

ג וּמִנְחַתְהוֹן, סֻלְתָּא דְּפִילָא בִּמְשַׁח, תְּלָתָא עֶסְרוֹנִין לְתוֹרָא, תְּרֵין עֶסְרוֹנִין לְדִכְרָא: ד וְעֶסְרוֹנָא חַד, לְאִמְּרָא חַד, כֵּן לְשִׁבְעָא אִמְּרִין: ה וּצְפִיר בַּר עִזִּין חַד חַטָּתָא, לְכַפָּרָא עֲלֵיכוֹן: ו בַּר מֵעֲלַת יַרְחָא וּמִנְחָתַהּ, וַעֲלַת תְּדִירָא וּמִנְחָתַהּ, וְנִסְכֵּיהוֹן כְּדַחֲזֵי לְהוֹן, לְאִתְקַבָּלָא בְּרַעֲוָא, קֻרְבָּנָא קֳדָם יְיָ: ז וּבְעַסְרָא לְיַרְחָא שְׁבִיעָאָה הָדֵין, מְעָרַע קַדִּישׁ יְהֵי לְכוֹן, וּתְעַנּוֹן יָת נַפְשָׁתְכוֹן, כָּל עֲבִידָא לָא תַעְבְּדוּן: ח וּתְקָרְבוּן עֲלָתָא קֳדָם יְיָ לְאִתְקַבָּלָא בְרַעֲוָא, תּוֹר בַּר תּוֹרֵי, חַד דְּכַר חַד, אִמְּרִין בְּנֵי שְׁנָא שִׁבְעָא, שַׁלְמִין יְהוֹן לְכוֹן: ט וּמִנְחַתְהוֹן, סֻלְתָּא דְּפִילָא בִּמְשַׁח, תְּלָתָא עֶסְרוֹנִין לְתוֹרָא, תְּרֵין עֶסְרוֹנִין, לְדִכְרָא חַד: י עֶסְרוֹנָא עֶסְרוֹנָא, לְאִמְּרָא חַד, כֵּן לְשִׁבְעָא אִמְּרִין: יא צְפִיר בַּר עִזִּין חַד חַטָּתָא, בָּר, מֵחַטַּאת כִּפּוּרַיָּא וַעֲלַת תְּדִירָא, וּמִנְחָתַהּ וְנִסְכֵּיהוֹן: יב וּבַחֲמֵישַׁת עַסְרָא יוֹמָא לְיַרְחָא שְׁבִיעָאָה, מְעָרַע קַדִּישׁ יְהֵי לְכוֹן, כָּל עֲבִידַת פֻּלְחָן לָא תַעְבְּדוּן, וְתֵיחֲגוּן חַגָּא, קֳדָם יְיָ שִׁבְעָא יוֹמִין: יג וּתְקָרְבוּן עֲלָתָא, קֻרְבַּן דְּמִתְקַבַּל בְּרַעֲוָא קֳדָם יְיָ, תּוֹרֵי בְּנֵי תוֹרֵי, תְּלָת עֲסַר דִּכְרִין תְּרֵין, אִמְּרִין בְּנֵי שְׁנָא, אַרְבְּעַת עֲסַר שַׁלְמִין יְהוֹן: יד וּמִנְחַתְהוֹן, סֻלְתָּא דְּפִילָא בִּמְשַׁח, תְּלָתָא עֶסְרוֹנִין לְתוֹרָא חַד, לִתְלָת עֲסַר תּוֹרִין, תְּרֵין עֶסְרוֹנִין לְדִכְרָא

15
16 two rams, and one-tenth for each of the fourteen lambs. There shall be one
male goat as a purification offering, in addition to the regular burnt offering
17 with its grain offering and libation. On the second day: twelve young
18 bulls, two rams, and fourteen yearling lambs, all without blemish. The grain
offering and libations for the bulls, rams, and sheep shall be as prescribed for
19 their number. There shall be one male goat as a purification offering, in addition
20 to the regular burnt offering with its grain offering and libations. On
the third day: eleven bulls, two rams, and fourteen yearling lambs, all without
21 blemish. The grain offering and libations for the bulls, rams, and lambs shall be
22 as prescribed for their number. There shall be one male goat as a purification
offering, in addition to the regular burnt offering with its grain offering and
23 libation. On the fourth day: ten bulls, two rams, and fourteen yearling
24 lambs, all without blemish. The grain offering and libations for the bulls, rams,
25 and sheep shall be as prescribed for their number. And there shall be one male
goat as a purification offering, in addition to the regular burnt offering with its
26 grain offering and libation. On the fifth day: nine bulls, two rams, and
27 fourteen yearling lambs, all without blemish. The grain offering and libations
28 for the bulls, rams, and lambs shall be as prescribed for their number. And there
shall be one male goat as a purification offering, in addition to the regular burnt
29 offering with its grain offering and libation. On the sixth day: eight bulls,
30 two rams, and fourteen yearling lambs, all without blemish. The grain offering
and libations for the bulls, rams, and lambs shall be as prescribed for their
31 number. And there shall be one male goat as a purification offering, in addition
32 to the regular burnt offering with its grain offering and libations. On the

אונקלוס

חַד, לִתְרֵין דִּכְרִין: טו וְעִסְרוֹנָא עִסְרוֹנָא, לְאִמְּרָא חַד, כֵּן לְאַרְבְּעַת עֲסַר אִמְּרִין: טז וּצְפִיר בַּר עִזִּין חַד חַטָּתָא, בָּר מֵעֲלַת תְּדִירָא, מִנְחֲתַהּ וְנִסְכַּהּ: יז וּבְיוֹמָא תִנְיָנָא, תּוֹרֵי בְּנֵי תוֹרֵי, תְּרֵי עֲסַר דִּכְרִין תְּרֵין, אִמְּרִין בְּנֵי שְׁנָא, אַרְבְּעַת עֲסַר שַׁלְמִין: יח וּמִנְחָתְהוֹן וְנִסְכֵּיהוֹן, לְתוֹרֵי, לְדִכְרֵי וּלְאִמְּרֵי, בְּמִנְיָנֵיהוֹן כְּדַחְזֵי: יט וּצְפִיר בַּר עִזִּין חַד חַטָּתָא, בָּר מֵעֲלַת תְּדִירָא, וּמִנְחֲתַהּ וְנִסְכֵּיהוֹן: כ וּבְיוֹמָא תְּלִיתָאָה, תּוֹרֵי חַד עֲסַר דִּכְרִין תְּרֵין, אִמְּרִין בְּנֵי שְׁנָא, אַרְבְּעַת עֲסַר שַׁלְמִין: כא וּמִנְחָתְהוֹן וְנִסְכֵּיהוֹן, לְתוֹרֵי, לְדִכְרֵי וּלְאִמְּרֵי, בְּמִנְיָנֵיהוֹן כְּדַחְזֵי: כב וּצְפִירָא דְּחַטָּתָא חַד, בָּר מֵעֲלַת ◀

רש״י

יח וּמִנְחָתָם וְנִסְכֵּיהֶם לַפָּרִים. פָּרֵי הֶחָג שִׁבְעִים הֵם, כְּנֶגֶד שִׁבְעִים אֻמּוֹת, שֶׁמִּתְמַעֲטִים וְהוֹלְכִים, סִימַן כְּלָיָה הוּא לָהֶם, וּבִימֵי הַמִּקְדָּשׁ הָיוּ מְגִנִּים עֲלֵיהֶם מִן הַיִּסּוּרִין, וְהַכְּבָשִׂים כְּנֶגֶד יִשְׂרָאֵל שֶׁנִּקְרְאוּ: "שֶׂה פְזוּרָה" (ירמיה נ, יז), וְהֵם קְבוּעִים, וּמִנְיָנָם תִּשְׁעִים וּשְׁמוֹנָה, לְכַלּוֹת מֵהֶם תִּשְׁעִים וּשְׁמוֹנָה קְלָלוֹת שֶׁבְּמִשְׁנֵה תוֹרָה. בַּשֵּׁנִי נֶאֱמַר: "וְנִסְכֵּיהֶם" (להלן פסוק יט) עַל שְׁנֵי תְמִידֵי הַיּוֹם, וְלֹא שִׁנָּה הַלָּשׁוֹן אֶלָּא לִדְרֹשׁ, כְּמוֹ שֶׁאָמְרוּ רַבּוֹתֵינוּ זִכְרוֹנָם לִבְרָכָה: בַּשֵּׁנִי "וְנִסְכֵּיהֶם", בַּשִּׁשִּׁי "וּנְסָכֶיהָ" (להלן פסוק לא), בַּשְּׁבִיעִי "כְּמִשְׁפָּטָם" (להלן פסוק לג), מ"ם יו"ד מ"ם, הֲרֵי כָּאן 'מַיִם', רֶמֶז לְנִסּוּךְ הַמַּיִם מִן הַתּוֹרָה בֶּחָג:

טו הָאֶחָד לִשְׁנֵי הָאֵילִם: וְעִשָּׂרוֹן עִשָּׂרוֹן לַכֶּבֶשׂ הָאֶחָד לְאַרְבָּעָה עָשָׂר
טז כְּבָשִׂים: וּשְׂעִיר־עִזִּים אֶחָד חַטָּאת מִלְּבַד עֹלַת הַתָּמִיד מִנְחָתָהּ
יז וְנִסְכָּהּ: וּבַיּוֹם הַשֵּׁנִי פָּרִים בְּנֵי־בָקָר שְׁנֵים עָשָׂר אֵילִם
יח שְׁנָיִם כְּבָשִׂים בְּנֵי־שָׁנָה אַרְבָּעָה עָשָׂר תְּמִימִם: וּמִנְחָתָם וְנִסְכֵּיהֶם
יט לַפָּרִים לָאֵילִם וְלַכְּבָשִׂים בְּמִסְפָּרָם כַּמִּשְׁפָּט: וּשְׂעִיר־עִזִּים אֶחָד
כ חַטָּאת מִלְּבַד עֹלַת הַתָּמִיד וּמִנְחָתָהּ וְנִסְכֵּיהֶם: וּבַיּוֹם
הַשְּׁלִישִׁי פָּרִים עַשְׁתֵּי־עָשָׂר אֵילִם שְׁנָיִם כְּבָשִׂים בְּנֵי־שָׁנָה אַרְבָּעָה
כא עָשָׂר תְּמִימִם: וּמִנְחָתָם וְנִסְכֵּיהֶם לַפָּרִים לָאֵילִם וְלַכְּבָשִׂים בְּמִסְפָּרָם
כב כַּמִּשְׁפָּט: וּשְׂעִיר חַטָּאת אֶחָד מִלְּבַד עֹלַת הַתָּמִיד וּמִנְחָתָהּ
כג וְנִסְכָּהּ: וּבַיּוֹם הָרְבִיעִי פָּרִים עֲשָׂרָה אֵילִם שְׁנָיִם כְּבָשִׂים
כד בְּנֵי־שָׁנָה אַרְבָּעָה עָשָׂר תְּמִימִם: מִנְחָתָם וְנִסְכֵּיהֶם לַפָּרִים לָאֵילִם
כה וְלַכְּבָשִׂים בְּמִסְפָּרָם כַּמִּשְׁפָּט: וּשְׂעִיר־עִזִּים אֶחָד חַטָּאת מִלְּבַד עֹלַת
כו הַתָּמִיד מִנְחָתָהּ וְנִסְכָּהּ: וּבַיּוֹם הַחֲמִישִׁי פָּרִים תִּשְׁעָה אֵילִם
כז שְׁנָיִם כְּבָשִׂים בְּנֵי־שָׁנָה אַרְבָּעָה עָשָׂר תְּמִימִם: וּמִנְחָתָם וְנִסְכֵּיהֶם
כח לַפָּרִים לָאֵילִם וְלַכְּבָשִׂים בְּמִסְפָּרָם כַּמִּשְׁפָּט: וּשְׂעִיר חַטָּאת אֶחָד
כט מִלְּבַד עֹלַת הַתָּמִיד וּמִנְחָתָהּ וְנִסְכָּהּ: וּבַיּוֹם הַשִּׁשִּׁי פָּרִים
ל שְׁמֹנָה אֵילִם שְׁנָיִם כְּבָשִׂים בְּנֵי־שָׁנָה אַרְבָּעָה עָשָׂר תְּמִימִם: וּמִנְחָתָם
לא וְנִסְכֵּיהֶם לַפָּרִים לָאֵילִם וְלַכְּבָשִׂים בְּמִסְפָּרָם כַּמִּשְׁפָּט: וּשְׂעִיר חַטָּאת
לב אֶחָד מִלְּבַד עֹלַת הַתָּמִיד מִנְחָתָהּ וּנְסָכֶיהָ: וּבַיּוֹם

אונקלוס

תְּדִירָא, וּמִנְחָתַהּ וְנִסְכַּהּ: כג וּבְיוֹמָא רְבִיעָאָה, תּוֹרֵי עַסְרָא דִּכְרִין תְּרֵין, אִמְּרִין בְּנֵי שְׁנָא, אַרְבְּעַת עֲסַר שַׁלְמִין: כד מִנְחַתְהוֹן וְנִסְכֵּיהוֹן, לְתוֹרֵי, לְדִכְרֵי וּלְאִמְּרֵי, בְּמִנְיָנֵיהוֹן כְּדַחְזֵי: כה וּצְפִיר בַּר עִזִּין חַד חַטָּתָא, בַּר מֵעֲלַת תְּדִירָא, מִנְחָתַהּ וְנִסְכַּהּ: כו וּבְיוֹמָא חֲמִישָׁאָה, תּוֹרֵי תִּשְׁעָא דִּכְרִין תְּרֵין, אִמְּרִין בְּנֵי שְׁנָא, אַרְבְּעַת עֲסַר שַׁלְמִין: כז וּמִנְחַתְהוֹן וְנִסְכֵּיהוֹן, לְתוֹרֵי, לְדִכְרֵי וּלְאִמְּרֵי, בְּמִנְיָנֵיהוֹן כְּדַחְזֵי: כח וּצְפִירָא דְּחַטָּתָא חַד, בַּר מֵעֲלַת תְּדִירָא, וּמִנְחָתַהּ וְנִסְכַּהּ: כט וּבְיוֹמָא שְׁתִיתָאָה, תּוֹרֵי תְּמָנְיָא דִּכְרִין תְּרֵין, אִמְּרִין בְּנֵי שְׁנָא, אַרְבְּעַת עֲסַר שַׁלְמִין: ל וּמִנְחַתְהוֹן וְנִסְכֵּיהוֹן, לְתוֹרֵי, לְדִכְרֵי וּלְאִמְּרֵי, בְּמִנְיָנֵיהוֹן כְּדַחְזֵי: לא וּצְפִירָא דְּחַטָּתָא חַד, בַּר מֵעֲלַת תְּדִירָא, מִנְחָתַהּ וְנִסְכַּהּ: לב וּבְיוֹמָא

seventh day: seven bulls, two rams, and fourteen yearling lambs, all without
33 blemish. The grain offering and libation for the bulls, rams, and lambs shall
34 be as prescribed for their number. And there shall be one male goat as a
purification offering, in addition to the regular burnt offering with its grain
35 offering and libation. On the eighth day you shall hold an assembly; MAFTIR
36 you shall perform no laborious work on it. You shall present a burnt offering,
a fire offering, for a pleasing aroma to the LORD: one bull, one ram, and seven
37 yearling lambs, all without blemish. The grain offering and libations for the bull,
38 ram, and lambs shall be as prescribed for their number. And there shall be one
male goat as a purification offering, in addition to the regular burnt offering
39 with its grain offering and libation. These you shall offer to the LORD on your
festivals, in addition to your vows and freewill offerings: your burnt offerings,
30 1 grain offerings, libations, and peace offerings." And Moshe told the Israelites all
that the LORD had commanded him.

The haftara for Parashat Pinḥas is on page 1598. If the parasha falls before the Seventeeth of Tamuz, read this haftara. If it falls after, read the haftara on page 1600.

רש"י

לה **עצרת תהיה לכם.** עצורים בעשית מלאכה. דבר אחר, "עצרת", עצרו מלאכת, מלמד שטעון לינה. ומדרשו באגדה: לפי שכל ימות הרגל הקריבו כנגד שבעים אמות, וכאין ללכת, אמר להם המקום: בבקשה מכם עשו לי סעודה קטנה, כדי שאהנה מכם:

לו **פר אחד איל אחד.** אלו כנגד ישראל, התעכבו לי מעט עוד, ולשון חבה הוא זה, כבנים הנפטרים מאביהם והוא אומר להם: קשה עלי פרדתכם, עכבו עוד יום אחד. משל למלך שעשה סעודה וכו', כדאיתא במסכת סכה (דף נה ע"ב) [משל למלך בשר ודם שאמר לעבדיו: עשו לי סעודה גדולה. ליום אחרון אמר לאוהבו: עשה לי סעודה קטנה, כדי שאהנה ממך]. ובמדרש רבי תנחומא (יז) למדה תורה דרך ארץ, שמי שיש לו אכסנאי, יום ראשון יאכילנו פטומות, למחר יאכילנו דגים, למחר יאכילנו בשר בהמה, למחר מאכילו קטניות, למחר מאכילו ירק, פוחת והולך כפרי החג:

לט **אלה תעשו לה' במועדיכם.** דבר הקצוב לחובה: **לבד מנדריכם.** אם באתם לדר קרבנות ברגל, מצוה היא בידכם, או נדרים או נדבות שנדרתם כל השנה הקריבום ברגל, שמא יקשה לו לחזור ולעלות לירושלים ולהקריב נדריו, ונמצא עובר בבל תאחר:

ל א **ויאמר משה אל בני ישראל.** להפסיק הענין, דברי רבי ישמעאל. לפי שעד כאן דבריו של מקום ופרשת נדרים מתחלת בדבורו של משה, הצרך להפסיק תחלה ולומר שחזר משה ואמר פרשה זו לישראל, שאם לא כן יש במשמע שלא אמר להם זו, אלא בפרשת נדרים התחיל דבריו:

Even though the Temple has not been rebuilt, its sacrificial rituals are gone, Israel remains surrounded by enemies, and all we have of the Temple Mount is a wall, the most abstract of all religious symbols, still today in Jerusalem you can feel the Divine Presence as nowhere else on earth – a presence that does not have to be announced with clarions, robes, and rituals. We know that though God is God of all the world, to us He is also father, husband, neighbor, shepherd, king, and we are His children, and this is our private time together, breathing each other's being, blessed by the gift of being present to one another.

symphony. It is quiet time with God. We are reluctant to leave, and we dare to think that He is reluctant to see us go. There are some things we share because we are human. But there are other things, constitutive of our identity, that are uniquely ours – most importantly, our relationships to those who form our family. On Sukkot we are among strangers and friends. On Shemini Atzeret we are with family.

When the Temple stood, it was as if God had said to His people: "Stop. Pause. Stand in My courtyard, in Jerusalem the holy city, and feel My presence in the quiet of the day, the still blue sky, and the breeze gently rustling the trees."

הַשְּׁבִיעִ֗י פָּרִ֥ים שִׁבְעָ֛ה אֵילִ֥ם שְׁנָ֖יִם כְּבָשִׂ֧ים בְּנֵי־שָׁנָ֛ה אַרְבָּעָ֥ה עָשָׂ֖ר
לג תְּמִימִֽם׃ וּמִנְחָתָ֣ם וְנִסְכֵּהֶ֡ם לַ֠פָּרִים לָאֵילִ֧ם וְלַכְּבָשִׂ֛ים בְּמִסְפָּרָ֖ם
לד כְּמִשְׁפָּטָֽם׃ וּשְׂעִ֥יר חַטָּ֖את אֶחָ֑ד מִלְּבַד֙ עֹלַ֣ת הַתָּמִ֔יד מִנְחָתָ֖הּ
לה וְנִסְכָּֽהּ׃ בַּיּוֹם֙ הַשְּׁמִינִ֔י עֲצֶ֖רֶת תִּהְיֶ֣ה לָכֶ֑ם כָּל־מְלֶ֥אכֶת עֲבֹדָ֖ה מפטיר
לו לֹ֥א תַעֲשֽׂוּ׃ וְהִקְרַבְתֶּ֨ם עֹלָ֜ה אִשֵּׁ֨ה רֵ֤יחַ נִיחֹ֙חַ֙ לַֽיהוָ֔ה פַּ֥ר אֶחָ֖ד אַ֣יִל
לז אֶחָ֑ד כְּבָשִׂ֧ים בְּנֵי־שָׁנָ֛ה שִׁבְעָ֖ה תְּמִימִֽם׃ מִנְחָתָ֣ם וְנִסְכֵּיהֶ֗ם לַפָּ֨ר לָאַ֧יִל
לח וְלַכְּבָשִׂ֛ים בְּמִסְפָּרָ֖ם כַּמִּשְׁפָּֽט׃ וּשְׂעִ֥יר חַטָּ֖את אֶחָ֑ד מִלְּבַד֙ עֹלַ֣ת הַתָּמִ֔יד
לט וּמִנְחָתָ֖הּ וְנִסְכָּֽהּ׃ אֵ֛לֶּה תַּעֲשׂ֥וּ לַיהוָ֖ה בְּמוֹעֲדֵיכֶ֑ם לְבַ֨ד מִנִּדְרֵיכֶ֜ם
ל א וְנִדְבֹתֵיכֶ֗ם לְעֹלֹֽתֵיכֶם֙ וּלְמִנְחֹ֣תֵיכֶ֔ם וּלְנִסְכֵּיכֶ֖ם וּלְשַׁלְמֵיכֶֽם׃ וַיֹּ֥אמֶר
מֹשֶׁ֖ה אֶל־בְּנֵ֣י יִשְׂרָאֵ֑ל כְּכֹ֛ל אֲשֶׁר־צִוָּ֥ה יְהוָ֖ה אֶת־מֹשֶֽׁה׃

The הפטרה *for* פרשת פינחס *is on page 1599. If the* פרשה *falls before the Seventeeth of* תמוז*, read this* הפטרה*. If it falls after, read the* הפטרה *on page 1601.*

אונקלוס

שְׁבִיעָאָה, תּוֹרֵי שִׁבְעָא דִּכְרִין תְּרֵין, אִמְּרִין בְּנֵי שְׁנָא, אַרְבְּעַת עֲסַר
שַׁלְמִין: לג וּמִנְחָתְהוֹן וְנִסְכֵּיהוֹן, לְתוֹרֵי, לְדִכְרֵי וּלְאִמְּרֵי, בְּמִנְיָנְהוֹן
כְּדַחְזֵי לְהוֹן: לד וּצְפִירָא דְּחַטָּתָא חַד, בַּר מֵעֲלַת תְּדִירָא, מִנְחָתַהּ
וְנִסְכַּהּ: לה בְּיוֹמָא תְּמִינָאָה, כְּנִישִׁין תְּהוֹן לְכוֹן, כָּל עֲבִידַת פֻּלְחַן
לָא תַעְבְּדוּן: לו וּתְקָרְבוּן עֲלָתָא, קֻרְבַּן דְּמִתְקַבַּל בְּרַעֲוָא קֳדָם יי,
תּוֹר חַד דְּכַר חַד, אִמְּרִין בְּנֵי שְׁנָא, שִׁבְעָא שַׁלְמִין: לז מִנְחָתְהוֹן
וְנִסְכֵּיהוֹן, לְתוֹרָא לְדִכְרָא וּלְאִמְּרֵי, בְּמִנְיָנֵיהוֹן כִּדְחָזֵי: לח וּצְפִירָא
דְּחַטָּתָא חַד, בַּר מֵעֲלַת תְּדִירָא, וּמִנְחָתַהּ וְנִסְכַּהּ: לט אִלֵּין, תַּעְבְּדוּן
קֳדָם יי בְּמוֹעֲדֵיכוֹן, בַּר מִנִּדְרֵיכוֹן וְנִדְבָתְכוֹן, לַעֲלָוָתְכוֹן וּלְמִנְחָוָתְכוֹן,
וּלְנִסְכֵּיכוֹן וּלְנִכְסַת קֻדְשֵׁיכוֹן: ל א וַאֲמַר מֹשֶׁה לִבְנֵי יִשְׂרָאֵל, כְּכֹל,
דְּפַקֵּיד יי יָת מֹשֶׁה:

29:35 עֲצֶרֶת תִּהְיֶה לָכֶם *You shall hold an assembly* – Shemini Atzeret is a strange, even unique day in the Jewish calendar. It is described as the eighth day, and thus part of Sukkot, but it is also designated by a name, Atzeret, of its own. Is it, or is it not, a separate festival in its own right? It seems to be both. How are we to understand this fact?

What guided the Sages was the detail that whereas on the seven days of Sukkot seventy young bulls were offered (see note on v. 13), on Atzeret, the eighth day, there was only one. It was as if all humanity were in some sense present in Jerusalem on Sukkot. On the eighth day, as they were leaving, it was as if God were inviting the Jewish people to a small private reception. The word *atzeret* itself was interpreted to mean, "Stop, stay a while." Shemini Atzeret was private time between God and His people. It was a day of particularity after the universality of the seven days of Sukkot.

In some versions of this narrative, the emphasis was on the length of time before the people would return to the Temple, virtually half a year until Passover. Others stressed the sudden shift from seventy sacrifices to one. The memorable phrase that shines through, though, is the one mentioned by Rashi (on Lev. 23:36), in which God says to Israel, "It is hard for Me to see you go." This is the language of intimacy.

So, when all the universality of Judaism has been expressed, there remains something that cannot be universalized: that sense of intimacy with and closeness to God that we feel on Shemini Atzeret, when all the other guests have left. Shemini Atzeret is chamber music, not a

Parashat Matot

30 2 Moshe spoke to the tribal heads of the Israelites: "This is what the Lord has
3 commanded: When a man makes a vow to the Lord or takes an oath binding
himself to an obligation, he must not break his word; whatever he speaks, that

רש״י

ב׳ רָאשֵׁי הַמַּטּוֹת. חָלַק כָּבוֹד לַנְּשִׂיאִים לְלַמְּדָם תְּחִלָּה, וְאַחַר כָּךְ לְכָל בְּנֵי יִשְׂרָאֵל. וּמִנַּיִן שֶׁאַף שְׁאָר הַדִּבְּרוֹת כֵּן? תַּלְמוּד לוֹמַר: "וַיָּשֻׁבוּ אֵלָיו אַהֲרֹן וְכָל הַנְּשִׂאִים בָּעֵדָה וַיְדַבֵּר מֹשֶׁה אֲלֵיהֶם, וְאַחֲרֵי כֵן נִגְּשׁוּ כָּל בְּנֵי יִשְׂרָאֵל" (שמות לד, לא-לב). וּמָה רָאָה לְאָמְרָהּ כָּאן? לִמֵּד שֶׁהֲפָרַת נְדָרִים בְּיָחִיד מֻמְחֶה, וְאִם אֵין יָחִיד מֻמְחֶה מֵפֵר בִּשְׁלֹשָׁה הֶדְיוֹטוֹת. אוֹ יָכוֹל שֶׁלֹּא אָמַר מֹשֶׁה פָּרָשָׁה זוֹ אֶלָּא לַנְּשִׂיאִים בִּלְבַד? נֶאֱמַר כָּאן: "זֶה הַדָּבָר", וְנֶאֱמַר בִּשְׁחוּטֵי חוּץ: "זֶה הַדָּבָר" (ויקרא יז, ב), מַה לְּהַלָּן נֶאֶמְרָה לְאַהֲרֹן וּלְבָנָיו וּלְכָל בְּנֵי יִשְׂרָאֵל, שֶׁנֶּאֱמַר: "דַּבֵּר אֶל אַהֲרֹן וְגוֹ׳" (שם), אַף זוֹ נֶאֶמְרָה לְכֻלָּן: זֶה הַדָּבָר. מֹשֶׁה נִתְנַבֵּא בְּ"כֹה אָמַר ה׳ כַּחֲצֹת הַלַּיְלָה" (שמות יא, ד) וְהַנְּבִיאִים נִתְנַבְּאוּ בְּ"כֹה אָמַר ה׳", מוּסָף עֲלֵיהֶם מֹשֶׁה, שֶׁנִּתְנַבֵּא בִּלְשׁוֹן "זֶה הַדָּבָר". דָּבָר אַחֵר, "זֶה הַדָּבָר" מִעוּט הוּא, לוֹמַר שֶׁהֶחָכָם בִּלְשׁוֹן הַתָּרָה וּבַעַל בִּלְשׁוֹן הֲפָרָה, כִּלְשׁוֹן הַכָּתוּב כָּאן, וְאִם חִלְּפוּ אֵין מֻתָּר וְאֵין מוּפָר:

ג׳ נֶדֶר. הָאוֹמֵר: הֲרֵי עָלַי קוֹנָם שֶׁלֹּא אֹכַל אוֹ שֶׁלֹּא אֶעֱשֶׂה דָּבָר פְּלוֹנִי. יָכוֹל אֲפִלּוּ נִשְׁבַּע שֶׁיֹּאכַל נְבֵלוֹת אֲנִי קוֹרֵא עָלָיו: "כְּכָל הַיֹּצֵא מִפִּיו יַעֲשֶׂה"? תַּלְמוּד לוֹמַר: "לֶאְסֹר אִסָּר", לֶאֱסֹר אֶת הַמֻּתָּר וְלֹא

30:3 **אוֹ־הִשָּׁבַע שְׁבֻעָה** *Or takes an oath* – Vows and oaths are obligations created by words. The difference between them is that a vow, *neder*, affects the status of an object (*ḥeftza*). It dedicates it in such a way as to render it inaccessible to me for my personal use. However, an oath, *shevua*, affects the person (*gavra*), not the object.

This distinction led Rabbi Joseph B. Soloveitchik into a fascinating reflection. The difference between *gavra* and *ḥeftza*, he suggests, is the difference between subject and object. "When I say that I am writing a letter, I am the *gavra*, the subject of the action, while the letter is the *ḥeftza*." A *gavra* acts; a *ḥeftza* is acted on. A judge passes sentence; a prisoner is sentenced. These are two different modes of being. Sometimes we are one, sometimes the other.

Rabbi Soloveitchik quotes the statement in the Gemara that an oath is administered to each of us before we are born, saying, "Be righteous and not wicked" (Nidda 30b). The fact that this is an oath requires us to be a *gavra*, not a *ḥeftza*, to be a free and responsible choosing subject, not the passive object of other people's acts. "If a human being is to act as an emissary of God, then they must be a *gavra*, constantly moving upward."

The difference between a vow and an oath thus becomes a metaphor for two different kinds of life, one defined by others and one self-created. One kind of person, Rabbi Soloveitchik says, is "receptive, passive… wholly under the influence of other people and their views." The other is "not passive but active.… He does not simply abandon himself to the rule of the species but blazes his own individual trail."

Things happen to us and they affect us, sometimes very deeply. To that extent, we are a *ḥeftza*. We are the object of events, and of other people's deeds, and we are shaped by them. But the challenge of faith is to become a *gavra*, to be our best self, undeflected and undefeated by what others do or say. It is not easy; it is never less than challenging. Faith is the call to be not an object but a subject, to influence more than to be influenced by our environment. We are called on to be more than others make us.

30:3 **נֶדֶר... שְׁבֻעָה... לֶאְסֹר אִסָּר עַל־נַפְשׁוֹ** *Vow… oath… obligation* – This vocabulary is to be adopted and adapted as the annulment of vows that marks the start of the holiest day of the year, Yom Kippur. As the *ḥazan* sings *Kol Nidrei*, we hear in that ancient tune the deepest music of the Jewish soul, elegiac yet striving, pained but resolute, the music of our ancestors which stretches out to us from the past and enfolds us in its cadences, making us and them one. The music is pure poetry, but the words are prosaic prose.

פרשת מטות

ל ב וַיְדַבֵּר מֹשֶׁה אֶל־רָאשֵׁי הַמַּטּוֹת לִבְנֵי יִשְׂרָאֵל לֵאמֹר זֶה הַדָּבָר אֲשֶׁר כו
ג צִוָּה יהוָה: אִישׁ כִּי־יִדֹּר נֶדֶר לַיהוָה אוֹ־הִשָּׁבַע שְׁבֻעָה לֶאְסֹר אִסָּר

אונקלוס

ב וּמַלֵּיל מֹשֶׁה עִם רֵישֵׁי שִׁבְטַיָּא, לִבְנֵי יִשְׂרָאֵל לְמֵימַר, דֵּין פִּתְגָּמָא, דְּפַקֵּיד יי: ג גְּבַר אֲרֵי יִדַּר נְדַר קֳדָם יי, אוֹ יְקַיֵּים קְיָם לְמֵיסַר אִסָּר

MATOT

Parashat Matot opens with an account of Moshe instructing the leaders of the tribes on the laws of vows and oaths. The Israelites are then commanded to wage war against the Midianites because of their hostility. There is an account of what is to be done with the spoils of war. Two tribes, Reuven and Gad, together with half the tribe of Menashe, ask permission to stay east of the Jordan where the land is ideal pasture for their cattle. Moshe is initially angered but eventually agrees on condition that they first join and lead in the battles for the land west of the Jordan.

As Numbers draws toward its close, there is a new tone to the narrative. We no longer hear the querulous complaints that had been the bass note of so much of the wilderness years. That undertone was the sound of the generation born into slavery that had left Egypt. By now, the people of the generation born in freedom and toughened by conditions in the desert have a more purposeful feel about them. Battle-tried, they no longer doubt their ability, with God's help, to fight and win. The problems they face now are of a different kind, and they are newly equipped to deal with them.

VOWS AND OATHS

The laws of vows and oaths represent one of the most distinctive features of Judaism as a way of life, namely, its intense focus on the way we create or destroy worlds by words. With words, God created the world: "God said, 'Let there be…' and there was" (Gen. 2:19). One of the gifts God gave the first human was language: the ability to name the animals. When the Torah says that "the Lord God formed man from the dust of the land and breathed the breath of life into his nostrils, and the man became a living being" (2:7), the Targum translates the last phrase as "and the man became a speaking being." For Judaism, speaking is life itself.

If trust in others' words breaks down, social relationships break down. Society will then depend on law enforcement agencies or some other use of force. When force is widely used, society is no longer free. The only way free human beings can form collaborative and cooperative relationships without recourse to force is by the use of verbal undertakings honored by those who make them.

The insistence on honoring your word is axiomatic to the creation of the kind of society the Torah envisages in Israel, and the moral is still relevant today. A free society depends on trust, and trust depends on keeping your word. Only under very special and precisely formulated circumstances can you be released from your undertakings.

If you seek liberty, treat words as holy, vows and oaths as sacrosanct. When that happens, then, just as God used words to create the natural universe, so we use words to create a social universe. Words create moral obligations, and moral obligations, undertaken responsibly and honored faithfully, create the possibility of a free society.

This accounts for the appearance of the laws of vows and oaths prior to the episode of the tribes of Reuven and Gad. Just like the appearance of the laws of the red heifer (purification after contact with the dead) before the story of the deaths of Miriam and Aharon and the announcement of the death of Moshe, it is an instance of the rule that "God provides the cure before the disease" (Megilla 13b; see ch. 19, "The Red Heifer"). The law is stated before the narrative to which it applies.

4 he must fulfill. When a woman makes a vow to the Lord or takes an oath
5 binding herself to an obligation while still a girl in her father's house, and her
father hears of her vow or self-imposed obligation and remains silent, then all
6 her vows and self-imposed obligations stand. But if her father restrains her on
the day he hears her, none of her vows or self-imposed obligations shall stand.
7 The Lord will forgo them for her, because her father has restrained her. If she

רש״י

לְהַתִּיר אֶת הָאִסּוּר: **לֹא יַחֵל דְּבָרוֹ.** כְּמוֹ: לֹא יְחַלֵּל דְּבָרוֹ, לֹא יַעֲשֶׂה דְּבָרָיו חֻלִּין:

ד **בְּבֵית אָבִיהָ.** בִּרְשׁוּת אָבִיהָ, וַאֲפִלּוּ אֵינָהּ בְּבֵיתוֹ: **בִּנְעֻרֶיהָ.** וְלֹא קְטַנָּה וְלֹא בּוֹגֶרֶת, שֶׁהַקְּטַנָּה אֵין נִדְרָהּ נֶדֶר, וְהַבּוֹגֶרֶת אֵינָהּ בִּרְשׁוּתוֹ שֶׁל אָבִיהָ לְהָפֵר נְדָרֶיהָ. וְאֵי זוֹ הִיא קְטַנָּה? אָמְרוּ רַבּוֹתֵינוּ: בַּת אַחַת עֶשְׂרֵה שָׁנָה וְיוֹם אֶחָד נְדָרֶיהָ נִבְדָּקִין, אִם יָדְעָה לְשֵׁם מִי נָדְרָה וּלְשֵׁם מִי הִקְדִּישָׁה, נִדְרָהּ נֶדֶר. בַּת שְׁתֵּים עֶשְׂרֵה שָׁנָה וְיוֹם אֶחָד אֵינָהּ צְרִיכָה לִבָּדֵק:

ו **וְאִם הֵנִיא אָבִיהָ אֹתָהּ.** אִם מָנַע אוֹתָהּ מִן הַנֶּדֶר, כְּלוֹמַר שֶׁהֵפֵר לָהּ. הֲנָאָה זוֹ אֵינִי יוֹדֵעַ מַה הִיא, כְּשֶׁהוּא אוֹמֵר: "וְאִם בְּיוֹם שְׁמֹעַ אִישָׁהּ יָנִיא אוֹתָהּ וְהֵפֵר" (להלן פסוק ט), הֱוֵי אוֹמֵר הֲנָאָה זוֹ הֲפָרָה. וּפְשׁוּטוֹ, לְשׁוֹן מְנִיעָה וַהֲסָרָה, וְכֵן: "וְלָמָּה תְנִיאוּן" (להלן לב, ז), וְכֵן: "שֶׁמֶן רֹאשׁ אַל יָנִי רֹאשִׁי" (תהלים קמא, ה), וְכֵן: "וִידַעְתֶּם אֶת תְּנוּאָתִי" (לעיל יד, לד), אֶת אֲשֶׁר סַרְתֶּם מֵעָלַי: **וַה׳ יִסְלַח לָהּ.** בַּמָּה הַכָּתוּב מְדַבֵּר? בְּאִשָּׁה שֶׁנָּדְרָה בְּנָזִיר וְשָׁמַע בַּעְלָהּ וְהֵפֵר לָהּ וְהִיא לֹא יָדְעָה, וְעוֹבֶרֶת עַל נִדְרָהּ וְשׁוֹתָה יַיִן וּמִטַּמְּאָה לַמֵּתִים, זוֹ הִיא שֶׁצְּרִיכָה סְלִיחָה וְאַף עַל פִּי שֶׁהוּא מוּפָר. וְאִם הַמּוּפָרִין צְרִיכִין סְלִיחָה, קַל וָחֹמֶר לְשֶׁאֵינָן מוּפָרִין:

ז **וְאִם הָיוֹ תִהְיֶה לְאִישׁ.** זוֹ אֲרוּסָה; אוֹ אֵינוֹ אֶלָּא נְשׂוּאָה? כְּשֶׁהוּא אוֹמֵר: "וְאִם בֵּית אִישָׁהּ נָדָרָה" (להלן פסוק יח), הֲרֵי נְשׂוּאָה אָמוּר, וְכָאן

specific circumstances. The passage highlights the fact, however, that commitments are not made in a vacuum but within a web of social connections. Our *parasha* is addressed, uniquely, not to "all Israel" but to "the tribal heads," hinting at the concentric circles of commitment which are the background of the specific commitments we undertake as individuals.

In stable families, nurtured by those who brought us into existence, we learn to give and receive love. There is no greater crucible of trust than the family bond. There we find, if we are lucky, that love given is not given in vain.

Communities are our closest approximation to the extended families of the Torah, where the concept of virtue was born and our ethical tradition has its origins. Communities are where we acquire a sense of place and belonging. They are usually small enough to allow us to recognize one another, to value the contribution of each to the welfare of all.

Families and communities are in turn undergirded by faith. Religious faith suggests that our commitments to fidelity and interdependence are not arbitrary. They mirror the deep structure of reality. The bonds between husband and wife, parent and child, and us and our neighbors partake of the covenantal bond between God and humanity. The moral rules and virtues which constrain and enlarge our aspirations are not mere subjective devices and desires. They are "out there" as well as "in here."

All this is the background and training ground for commitments undertaken, trust given and earned. In a passage on speech, Ecclesiastes moves from relationships between humans to those between us and God. The same rule applies to both: say little, do much, and always do what you said you would. Vows can be annulled, but "better not to vow" (Eccl. 5:4) than to vow and then annul, for the latter causes an erosion of trust that devalues the sanctity of the commitment implicit in a vow.

There is such a thing as an ecology of hope – a web of circumstances that teaches us that it is worth working together for a better tomorrow. There are environments in which hope flourishes and others in which it dies. Hope is born with trust, and has its being in the context of family, community, and faith.

ד עַל־נַפְשׁוֹ לֹא יַחֵל דְּבָרוֹ כְּכָל־הַיֹּצֵא מִפִּיו יַעֲשֶׂה׃ וְאִשָּׁה כִּי־תִדֹּר נֶדֶר
ה לַיהוָה וְאָסְרָה אִסָּר בְּבֵית אָבִיהָ בִּנְעֻרֶיהָ׃ וְשָׁמַע אָבִיהָ אֶת־נִדְרָהּ
וֶאֱסָרָהּ אֲשֶׁר אָסְרָה עַל־נַפְשָׁהּ וְהֶחֱרִישׁ לָהּ אָבִיהָ וְקָמוּ כָּל־נְדָרֶיהָ
ו וְכָל־אִסָּר אֲשֶׁר־אָסְרָה עַל־נַפְשָׁהּ יָקוּם׃ וְאִם־הֵנִיא אָבִיהָ אֹתָהּ בְּיוֹם
שָׁמְעוֹ כָּל־נְדָרֶיהָ וֶאֱסָרֶיהָ אֲשֶׁר־אָסְרָה עַל־נַפְשָׁהּ לֹא יָקוּם וַיהוָה
ז יִסְלַח־לָהּ כִּי־הֵנִיא אָבִיהָ אֹתָהּ׃ וְאִם־הָיוֹ תִהְיֶה לְאִישׁ וּנְדָרֶיהָ עָלֶיהָ

אונקלוס

עַל נַפְשֵׁיהּ, לָא יְבַטֵּיל פִּתְגָמֵיהּ, כְּכָל דְּיִפּוֹק מִפּוּמֵיהּ יַעֲבֵיד׃ ד וְאִתְּתָא, אֲרֵי תִדַּר נְדַר קֳדָם יְיָ, וְתֵיסַר אֱסָר, בְּבֵית אֲבוּהָא בְּרַבְיוּתַהּ׃ ה וְיִשְׁמַע אֲבוּהָא יָת נִדְרַהּ, וֶאֱסָרַהּ דַּאֲסַרַת עַל נַפְשַׁהּ, וְיִשְׁתּוֹק לַהּ אֲבוּהָא, וִיקוּמוּן כָּל נִדְרַהָא, וְכָל אֱסָרֵי, דַּאֲסַרַת עַל נַפְשַׁהּ יְקוּמוּן׃ ו וְאִם אַעְדֵּי אֲבוּהָא יָתְהוֹן בְּיוֹמָא דִשְׁמַע, כָּל נִדְרַהָא, וֶאֱסָרַהָא, דַּאֲסַרַת עַל נַפְשַׁהּ לָא יְקוּמוּן, וּמִן קֳדָם יְיָ יִשְׁתְּבֵיק לַהּ, אֲרֵי אַעְדֵּי אֲבוּהָא יָתְהוֹן׃ ז וְאִם מֶהֱוָא תְהֵוֵי לִגְבַר, וְנִדְרַהָא עֲלַהּ,

Kol nidrei literally means "all vows." The passage itself is not a prayer at all, but a dry legal formula annulling in advance all vows, oaths, and promises between us and God in the coming year, or in some traditions, retroactively annulling those of the previous year. Nothing could be more incongruous, less apparently in keeping with the solemnity of the day. Indeed, for more than a thousand years there have been attempts to remove it from the liturgy. Why annul vows? Better not to make them in the first place if they could not be kept. Besides which, though Jewish law admits the possibility of annulment, it does so only after patient examination of individual cases. To do so globally for the whole community was difficult to justify. From the eighth century onward we read of *geonim*, rabbinic leaders, who condemned the prayer and sought to have it abolished. Five centuries later, a new note of concern was added. In the Christian-Jewish disputation in Paris in 1240, the Christian protagonist Nicholas Donin attacked *Kol Nidrei* as evidence that Jews did not feel themselves bound by their word, a claim later repeated by antisemitic writers. In vain, Jews explained that the prayer had nothing to do with promises between man and man. It referred only to private commitments between man and God. All in all, it was and is a strange way to begin the holiest of days.

Yet the prayer survived all attempts to have it dislodged. One theory is that it had its origins in the forced conversion of Spanish Jews to Christianity under the Visigoths in the seventh century. These Jews, the first Marranos, publicly abandoned their faith rather than face torture and death, but they remained Jews in secret. On the Day of Atonement they made their way back to the synagogue and prayed to have their vow of conversion annulled. That, surely, is the significance of *Kol Nidrei* in the Jewish imagination. It is the moment when the doors of belonging are opened, and when those who have been estranged return. During the year – albeit less dramatically than their medieval predecessors – they may have been Marranos, hidden Jews. They have worn other masks, carried different identities. But tonight the music of *Kol Nidrei* has spoken to them and they have said: Here is where I belong. Among my people and its faith. I am a Jew.

30:6 וְאִם־הֵנִיא אָבִיהָ אֹתָהּ *If her father restrains her* – The text appears to give a father or husband power of veto over a woman's vows. This jars with our sense of women's autonomy. There is no hint, for instance, that Elkana was consulted over Ḥana's vow (1 Sam. 1:11). Indeed, the Sages expounded the law to limit men's power of veto to very

8 marries, having made vows or verbally bound herself, and her husband hears of
it and on the day he does so keeps silent, then her vow or any pledge by which
9 she has bound herself shall stand. But if, on the day her husband hears of it,
he restrains her, he can annul her vow or the pledge by which she has bound
10 herself, and the LORD will forgo them for her. The vow of a widow or a divorcée –
11 whatever she binds herself by – stands. If, while in her husband's house, a
12 woman makes a vow or takes an oath binding herself to an obligation and her
husband hears and keeps silent, and does not restrain her, then all her vows and
13 the obligations by which she binds herself shall stand. But if her husband annuls
them on the day when he hears them, then the words she spoke as a vow or the
obligation by which she bound herself will not stand. Her husband has annulled
14 them, and the LORD will forgo them for her. Every vow or binding by oath may
15 be upheld by her husband or else annulled by her husband. But if her husband
keeps silent from that day to the next, then he has upheld all her vows and the
obligations by which she has bound herself. He has upheld them by remaining
16 silent on the day when he heard them. If he nullifies them some time after he
17 has heard of them, he shall bear her guilt." These are the decrees that the LORD
issued to Moshe, between a husband and his wife and between a father and his
daughter while she is a girl in her father's home.
31 1 2 The LORD spoke to Moshe: "Take revenge for the Israelites against the SHENI

רש"י

בַּאֲרוּסָה, וּבָא לַחֲלֹק בָּהּ, שֶׁאָבִיהָ וּבַעְלָהּ מְפִירִין נְדָרֶיהָ. הֵפֵר הָאָב וְלֹא הֵפֵר הַבַּעַל, אוֹ הֵפֵר הַבַּעַל וְלֹא הֵפֵר הָאָב, הֲרֵי זֶה אֵינוֹ מוּפָר, וְאֵין צָרִיךְ לוֹמַר אִם קִיֵּם אֶחָד מֵהֶם: **וּנְדָרֶיהָ עָלֶיהָ.** שֶׁנָּדְרָה בְּבֵית אָבִיהָ וְלֹא שָׁמַע בָּהֶן אָבִיהָ, וְלֹא הוּפְרוּ וְלֹא הוּקְמוּ:

ח **וְשָׁמַע אִישָׁהּ וְגוֹ׳.** הֲרֵי לְךָ שֶׁאִם קִיֵּם הַבַּעַל שֶׁהוּא קַיָּם:

ט **וְהֵפֵר אֶת נִדְרָהּ אֲשֶׁר עָלֶיהָ.** יָכוֹל אֲפִלּוּ לֹא הֵפֵר הָאָב? תַּלְמוּד לוֹמַר: "בִּנְעֻרֶיהָ בֵּית אָבִיהָ" (להלן פסוק יז), כָּל שֶׁבִּנְעוּרֶיהָ בִּרְשׁוּת אָבִיהָ הִיא:

י **אֲשֶׁר אָסְרָה עַל נַפְשָׁהּ יָקוּם עָלֶיהָ.** לְפִי שֶׁאֵינָהּ לֹא בִּרְשׁוּת אָב וְלֹא בִּרְשׁוּת בַּעַל, וּבְאַלְמָנָה מִן הַנִּשּׂוּאִין הַכָּתוּב מְדַבֵּר, אֲבָל אַלְמָנָה מִן הָאֵרוּסִין, מֵת הַבַּעַל, נִתְרוֹקְנָה וְחָזְרָה לִרְשׁוּת לָאָב:

יא **וְאִם בֵּית אִישָׁהּ נָדָרָה.** בִּנְשׂוּאָה הַכָּתוּב מְדַבֵּר:

יד **כָּל נֵדֶר וְכָל שְׁבֻעַת אִסָּר וְגוֹ׳.** לְפִי שֶׁאָמַר שֶׁהַבַּעַל מֵפֵר, יָכוֹל כָּל נְדָרִים בַּמַּשְׁמָע? תַּלְמוּד לוֹמַר: "לְעַנֹּת נָפֶשׁ", אֵינוֹ מֵפֵר אֶלָּא נִדְרֵי עִנּוּי נֶפֶשׁ בִּלְבַד, וְהֵם מְפֹרָשִׁים בְּמַסֶּכֶת נְדָרִים (דף עט ע"א ואילך):

טו **מִיּוֹם אֶל יוֹם.** שֶׁלֹּא תֹאמַר מֵעֵת לְעֵת, לְכָךְ נֶאֱמַר: "מִיּוֹם אֶל יוֹם", לְלַמֶּדְךָ שֶׁאֵין מֵפֵר אֶלָּא עַד שֶׁתֶּחְשַׁךְ:

טז **אַחֲרֵי שָׁמְעוֹ.** אַחֲרֵי שֶׁשָּׁמַע וְקִיֵּם, שֶׁאָמַר: אֶפְשִׁי בּוֹ, וְחָזַר וְהֵפֵר לָהּ, אֲפִלּוּ בּוֹ בַּיּוֹם: **וְנָשָׂא אֶת עֲוֺנָהּ.** הוּא מִכְנָס תַּחְתֶּיהָ. לָמַדְנוּ מִכָּאן שֶׁהַגּוֹרֵם תַּקָּלָה לַחֲבֵרוֹ הוּא נִכְנָס תַּחְתָּיו לְכָל עֳנָשִׁין:

לא ב **מֵאֵת הַמִּדְיָנִים.** וְלֹא מֵאֵת הַמּוֹאָבִים, שֶׁהַמּוֹאָבִים נִכְנְסוּ לַדָּבָר מֵחֲמַת יִרְאָה, שֶׁהָיוּ יְרֵאִים מֵהֶם שֶׁיִּהְיוּ שׁוֹלְלִים אוֹתָם, שֶׁלֹּא נֶאֱמַר

A WAR OF RETRIBUTION

Religions, especially religions of the Book, have hard texts: verses, commands, episodes, narratives that if understood literally and applied directly would not merely offend our moral sense. They would also go against our best understanding of the religion itself. The war of revenge against

ח אוֹ מִבְטָא שְׂפָתֶיהָ אֲשֶׁר אָסְרָה עַל־נַפְשָׁהּ׃ וְשָׁמַע אִישָׁהּ בְּיוֹם שָׁמְעוֹ
וְהֶחֱרִישׁ לָהּ וְקָמוּ נְדָרֶיהָ וֶאֱסָרֶהָ אֲשֶׁר־אָסְרָה עַל־נַפְשָׁהּ יָקֻמוּ׃
ט וְאִם בְּיוֹם שְׁמֹעַ אִישָׁהּ יָנִיא אוֹתָהּ וְהֵפֵר אֶת־נִדְרָהּ אֲשֶׁר עָלֶיהָ וְאֵת
י מִבְטָא שְׂפָתֶיהָ אֲשֶׁר אָסְרָה עַל־נַפְשָׁהּ וַיהוָה יִסְלַח־לָהּ׃ וְנֵדֶר אַלְמָנָה
יא וּגְרוּשָׁה כֹּל אֲשֶׁר־אָסְרָה עַל־נַפְשָׁהּ יָקוּם עָלֶיהָ׃ וְאִם־בֵּית אִישָׁהּ
יב נָדָרָה אוֹ־אָסְרָה אִסָּר עַל־נַפְשָׁהּ בִּשְׁבֻעָה׃ וְשָׁמַע אִישָׁהּ וְהֶחֱרִשׁ לָהּ
לֹא הֵנִיא אֹתָהּ וְקָמוּ כָּל־נְדָרֶיהָ וְכָל־אִסָּר אֲשֶׁר־אָסְרָה עַל־נַפְשָׁהּ
יג יָקוּם׃ וְאִם־הָפֵר יָפֵר אֹתָם ׀ אִישָׁהּ בְּיוֹם שָׁמְעוֹ כָּל־מוֹצָא שְׂפָתֶיהָ
לִנְדָרֶיהָ וּלְאִסַּר נַפְשָׁהּ לֹא יָקוּם אִישָׁהּ הֲפֵרָם וַיהוָה יִסְלַח־לָהּ׃
יד כָּל־נֵדֶר וְכָל־שְׁבֻעַת אִסָּר לְעַנֹּת נָפֶשׁ אִישָׁהּ יְקִימֶנּוּ וְאִישָׁהּ יְפֵרֶנּוּ׃
טו וְאִם־הַחֲרֵשׁ יַחֲרִישׁ לָהּ אִישָׁהּ מִיּוֹם אֶל־יוֹם וְהֵקִים אֶת־כָּל־נְדָרֶיהָ אוֹ
אֶת־כָּל־אֱסָרֶיהָ אֲשֶׁר עָלֶיהָ הֵקִים אֹתָם כִּי־הֶחֱרִשׁ לָהּ בְּיוֹם שָׁמְעוֹ׃
טז יז וְאִם־הָפֵר יָפֵר אֹתָם אַחֲרֵי שָׁמְעוֹ וְנָשָׂא אֶת־עֲוֺנָהּ׃ אֵלֶּה הַחֻקִּים
אֲשֶׁר צִוָּה יְהוָה אֶת־מֹשֶׁה בֵּין אִישׁ לְאִשְׁתּוֹ בֵּין־אָב לְבִתּוֹ בִּנְעֻרֶיהָ
בֵּית אָבִיהָ׃

לא א ב וַיְדַבֵּר יְהוָה אֶל־מֹשֶׁה לֵּאמֹר׃ נְקֹם נִקְמַת בְּנֵי יִשְׂרָאֵל מֵאֵת הַמִּדְיָנִים כז שני

אונקלוס

אוֹ פֵּירוּשׁ סִפְוָתַהָא, דַּאֲסָרַת עַל נַפְשַׁהּ: ח וְיִשְׁמַע בַּעְלַהּ, בְּיוֹמָא דְּיִשְׁמַע וְיִשְׁתּוֹק לַהּ, וִיקוּמוּן נִדְרַהָא, וֶאֱסָרַהָא, דַּאֲסָרַת עַל נַפְשַׁהּ יְקוּמוּן: ט וְאִם, בְּיוֹמָא דְּשָׁמַע בַּעְלַהּ אַעְדִּי יָתְהוֹן, וּבַטֵּיל, יָת נִדְרַהּ דַּעֲלַהּ, וְיָת פֵּירוּשׁ סִפְוָתַהָא, דַּאֲסָרַת עַל נַפְשַׁהּ, וּמִן קֳדָם יי יִשְׁתְּבֵיק לַהּ: י וּנְדַר אַרְמְלָא וּמְתָרְכָא, כֹּל, דַּאֲסָרַת עַל נַפְשַׁהּ קַיָּם עֲלַהּ: יא וְאִם בֵּית בַּעְלַהּ נְדַרַת, אוֹ אֲסָרַת אֱסָר, עַל נַפְשַׁהּ בְּקִיּוּם: יב וְיִשְׁמַע בַּעְלַהּ וְיִשְׁתּוֹק לַהּ, לָא אַעְדִּי יָתְהוֹן, וִיקוּמוּן כָּל נִדְרַהָא, וְכָל אֱסָרֵי, דַּאֲסָרַת עַל נַפְשַׁהּ יְקוּמוּן: יג וְאִם בַּטָּלָא יְבַטֵּיל יָתְהוֹן בַּעְלַהּ בְּיוֹמָא דִּשְׁמַע, כָּל אַפָּקוּת סִפְוָתַהָא לְנִדְרַהָא, וּלְאֱסָר נַפְשַׁהּ לָא יְקוּמוּן, בַּעְלַהּ בַּטֵּילִנּוּן, וּמִן קֳדָם יי יִשְׁתְּבֵיק לַהּ: יד כָּל נְדַר, וְכָל קְיוּמַת אֱסָר לְסַגָּפָא נְפַשׁ, בַּעְלַהּ יְקַיְּמִנּוּן וּבַעְלַהּ יְבַטֵּילִנּוּן: טו וְאִם מִשְׁתָּק יִשְׁתּוֹק לַהּ בַּעְלַהּ מִיּוֹם לְיוֹם, וִיקַיֵּים יָת כָּל נִדְרַהָא, אוֹ יָת כָּל אֱסָרַהָא דַּעֲלַהּ, קַיֵּים יָתְהוֹן, אֲרֵי שְׁתֵיק לַהּ בְּיוֹמָא דִּשְׁמַע: טז וְאִם בַּטָּלָא יְבַטֵּיל, יָתְהוֹן בָּתַר דִּשְׁמַע, וִיקַבֵּיל יָת חוֹבַהּ: יז אִלֵּין קְיָמַיָּא, דְּפַקֵּיד יי יָת מֹשֶׁה, בֵּין גְּבַרָא לְאִתְּתֵיהּ, בֵּין אַבָּא לִבְרַתֵּיהּ, בִּרְבִיוּתַהּ בֵּית אֲבוּהָא: לא א וּמַלֵּיל יי עִם מֹשֶׁה לְמֵימַר: ב אִתְפְּרַע, פֻּרְעֲנוּת בְּנֵי יִשְׂרָאֵל, מִן מִדְיָנָאֵי,

3 Midianites; after that you will be gathered in to your people." Moshe spoke to
the people: "Equip men from among you for active service, to go out against
4 Midyan, to execute the LORD's vengeance against Midyan. For this service, call
5 up one thousand from each of Israel's tribes." And so, of the thousands of Israel,
one thousand men were selected from each tribe, twelve thousand in all, all
6 armed for battle. Moshe sent them, a thousand from each tribe, into service,
together with Pinḥas son of Elazar the priest, who was in charge of the sacred
7 utensils and the trumpets for sounding the blast. And they did battle against
8 Midyan as the LORD had commanded Moshe, and killed every male. And,
among the slain, they killed the kings of Midyan: Evi, Rekem, Tzur, Ḥur, and
Reva – all five kings of Midyan. At the sword's edge they also killed Bilam son of
9 Beor. The Israelites took captive the Midianite women and children, and took

רש״י

אֶלָּא "אַל תִּתְגָּר בָּם מִלְחָמָה" (דברים ב, ט), אֲבָל מִדְיָנִים נִתְעַבְּרוּ עַל רִיב לֹא לָהֶם. דָּבָר אַחֵר, מִפְּנֵי שְׁתֵּי פְּרֵידוֹת טוֹבוֹת שֶׁיֵּשׁ לִי לְהוֹצִיא מֵהֶם, רוּת הַמּוֹאֲבִיָּה וְנַעֲמָה הָעַמּוֹנִית:

ג **וַיְדַבֵּר מֹשֶׁה וְגוֹ׳.** אַף עַל פִּי שֶׁשָּׁמַע שֶׁמִּיתָתוֹ תְּלוּיָה בַּדָּבָר, עָשָׂה בְּשִׂמְחָה וְלֹא אֵחַר: **הֵחָלְצוּ.** כְּתַרְגּוּמוֹ, לְשׁוֹן חֲלוּצֵי צָבָא, מְזֻיָּנִים: **אֲנָשִׁים.** צַדִּיקִים, וְכֵן: "בְּחַר לָנוּ אֲנָשִׁים" (שמות יז, ט), וְכֵן: "אֲנָשִׁים חֲכָמִים וּנְבֹנִים" (דברים א, יג): **נִקְמַת ה׳.** שֶׁהָעוֹמֵד כְּנֶגֶד יִשְׂרָאֵל כְּאִלּוּ עוֹמֵד כְּנֶגֶד הַקָּדוֹשׁ בָּרוּךְ הוּא:

ד **לְכֹל מַטּוֹת יִשְׂרָאֵל.** לְרַבּוֹת שֵׁבֶט לֵוִי:

ה **וַיִּמָּסְרוּ.** לְהוֹדִיעֲךָ שִׁבְחָן שֶׁל רוֹעֵי יִשְׂרָאֵל, כַּמָּה הֵם חֲבִיבִים עַל יִשְׂרָאֵל. עַד שֶׁלֹּא שָׁמְעוּ בְּמִיתָתוֹ, מַה הוּא אוֹמֵר? "עוֹד מְעַט וּסְקָלֻנִי" (שמות יז, ד), וּמִשֶּׁשָּׁמְעוּ שֶׁמִּיתַת מֹשֶׁה תְּלוּיָה בְּנִקְמַת מִדְיָן, לֹא רָצוּ לָלֶכֶת עַד שֶׁנִּמְסְרוּ עַל כָּרְחָן:

ו **אֹתָם וְאֶת פִּינְחָס.** מַגִּיד שֶׁהָיָה פִּינְחָס שָׁקוּל כְּנֶגֶד כֻּלָּם. וּמִפְּנֵי מָה הָלַךְ פִּינְחָס וְלֹא הָלַךְ אֶלְעָזָר? אָמַר הַקָּדוֹשׁ בָּרוּךְ הוּא: מִי שֶׁהִתְחִיל בַּמִּצְוָה, שֶׁהָרַג כָּזְבִּי בַּת צוּר, יִגְמֹר. דָּבָר אַחֵר, שֶׁהָלַךְ לִנְקֹם נִקְמַת יוֹסֵף אֲבִי אִמּוֹ, שֶׁנֶּאֱמַר: "וְהַמְּדָנִים מָכְרוּ אֹתוֹ" (בראשית לז, לו). וּמִנַּיִן שֶׁהָיְתָה אִמּוֹ שֶׁל פִּינְחָס מִשֶּׁל יוֹסֵף? שֶׁנֶּאֱמַר: "מִבְּנוֹת פּוּטִיאֵל" (שמות ו, כה), מִזֶּרַע יִתְרוֹ שֶׁפִּטֵּם עֲגָלִים לַעֲבוֹדָה זָרָה, וּמִזֶּרַע יוֹסֵף שֶׁפִּטְפֵּט בְּיִצְרוֹ. דָּבָר אַחֵר, שֶׁהָיָה מְשׁוּחַ מִלְחָמָה: **וּכְלֵי הַקֹּדֶשׁ.** זֶה הָאָרוֹן וְהַצִּיץ, שֶׁהָיָה בִּלְעָם עִמָּהֶם וּמַפְרִיחַ מַלְכֵי מִדְיָן בִּכְשָׁפִים, וְהוּא עַצְמוֹ פּוֹרֵחַ עִמָּהֶם; הֶרְאָה לָהֶם אֶת הַצִּיץ שֶׁהַשֵּׁם חָקוּק בּוֹ, וְהֵם נוֹפְלִים, לְכָךְ נֶאֱמַר: "עַל חַלְלֵיהֶם" (להלן פסוק ח) בְּמַלְכֵי מִדְיָן, שֶׁנּוֹפְלִים עַל הַחֲלָלִים מִן הָאֲוִיר. וְכֵן בְּבִלְעָם כְּתִיב: "אֶל חַלְלֵיהֶם" בְּסֵפֶר יְהוֹשֻׁעַ (יג, כב): **בְּיָדָם.** בִּרְשׁוּתוֹ, וְכֵן: "וַיִּקַּח אֶת כָּל אַרְצוֹ מִיָּדוֹ" (במדבר כא, כו):

ח **חֲמֵשֶׁת מַלְכֵי מִדְיָן.** וְכִי אֵינִי רוֹאֶה שֶׁחֲמִשָּׁה מָנָה הַכָּתוּב? לָמָּה הֻזְקַק לוֹמַר 'חֲמֵשֶׁת'? אֶלָּא לְלַמֶּדְךָ שֶׁשָּׁווּ כֻּלָּם בְּעֵצָה וְהֻשְׁווּ כֻּלָּם

contemporary audience. In each case, the issue is how to apply the-word-then to the-world-now, bridging the hermeneutical abyss of time and change. Religions develop rules of interpretation and structures of authority. Without these, any group can do almost anything in the name of religion, selecting texts, taking them out of context, reading them literally, and ignoring the rest. Without rules, principles, and authority, sacred texts provide the charisma of seemingly divine authority for purposes that are all too human. As Shakespeare said, "The devil can cite Scripture for his purpose."

Never say, then, "I hate, I kill, because my religion says so." Every text needs interpretation. Every interpretation needs wisdom. Every wisdom needs careful negotiation between the timeless and time. Fundamentalism reads texts as if God were as simple as we are. That is unlikely to be true. Hard texts need interpreting; without it, they lead to violence. God has given us both the mandate and the responsibility to do just that. We are guardians of His word for the sake of His world.

ג אַחַר תֵּאָסֵף אֶל־עַמֶּיךָ: וַיְדַבֵּר מֹשֶׁה אֶל־הָעָם לֵאמֹר הֵחָלְצוּ מֵאִתְּכֶם
ד אֲנָשִׁים לַצָּבָא וְיִהְיוּ עַל־מִדְיָן לָתֵת נִקְמַת־יהוה בְּמִדְיָן: אֶלֶף לַמַּטֶּה
ה אֶלֶף לַמַּטֶּה לְכֹל מַטּוֹת יִשְׂרָאֵל תִּשְׁלְחוּ לַצָּבָא: וַיִּמָּסְרוּ מֵאַלְפֵי
ו יִשְׂרָאֵל אֶלֶף לַמַּטֶּה שְׁנֵים־עָשָׂר אֶלֶף חֲלוּצֵי צָבָא: וַיִּשְׁלַח אֹתָם
מֹשֶׁה אֶלֶף לַמַּטֶּה לַצָּבָא אֹתָם וְאֶת־פִּינְחָס בֶּן־אֶלְעָזָר הַכֹּהֵן לַצָּבָא
ז וּכְלֵי הַקֹּדֶשׁ וַחֲצֹצְרוֹת הַתְּרוּעָה בְּיָדוֹ: וַיִּצְבְּאוּ עַל־מִדְיָן כַּאֲשֶׁר
ח צִוָּה יהוה אֶת־מֹשֶׁה וַיַּהַרְגוּ כָּל־זָכָר: וְאֶת־מַלְכֵי מִדְיָן הָרְגוּ עַל־
חַלְלֵיהֶם אֶת־אֱוִי וְאֶת־רֶקֶם וְאֶת־צוּר וְאֶת־חוּר וְאֶת־רֶבַע חֲמֵשֶׁת
ט מַלְכֵי מִדְיָן וְאֵת בִּלְעָם בֶּן־בְּעוֹר הָרְגוּ בֶּחָרֶב: וַיִּשְׁבּוּ בְנֵי־יִשְׂרָאֵל

אונקלוס

בָּתַר כֵּן תִּתְכְּנֵישׁ לְעַמָּךְ: ג וּמַלֵּיל מֹשֶׁה עִם עַמָּא לְמֵימַר, זָרִיזוּ מִנְּכוֹן, גֻּבְרִין לְחֵילָא, וִיהוֹן עַל מִדְיָן, לְמִתַּן פֻּרְעָנוּת דִּין עַמֵּיהּ דַּיי בְּמִדְיָן: ד אַלְפָא לְשִׁבְטָא, אַלְפָא לְשִׁבְטָא, לְכֹל שִׁבְטַיָּא דְּיִשְׂרָאֵל, תִּשְׁלְחוּן לְחֵילָא: ה וְאִתְבְּחַרוּ מֵאַלְפַיָּא דְּיִשְׂרָאֵל, אַלְפָא לְשִׁבְטָא, תְּרֵי עֲסַר אַלְפִין מְזָרְזֵי חֵילָא: ו וּשְׁלַח יָתְהוֹן מֹשֶׁה, אַלְפָא לְשִׁבְטָא לְחֵילָא, יָתְהוֹן, וְיָת פִּינְחָס, בַּר אֶלְעָזָר כַּהֲנָא לְחֵילָא, וּמָנֵי קֻדְשָׁא, וַחֲצוֹצְרָת יַבָּבְתָא בִּידֵיהּ: ז וְאִתְחַיַּלוּ עַל מִדְיָן, כְּמָא דְּפַקֵּיד יי יָת מֹשֶׁה, וּקְטַלוּ כָּל דְּכוּרָא: ח וְיָת מַלְכֵי מִדְיָן קְטַלוּ עַל קְטִילֵיהוֹן, יָת אֱוִי וְיָת רֶקֶם וְיָת צוּר וְיָת חוּר וְיָת רֶבַע, חַמְשָׁא מַלְכֵי מִדְיָן, וְיָת בִּלְעָם בַּר בְּעוֹר, קְטַלוּ בְּחַרְבָּא: ט וּשְׁבוֹ בְנֵי יִשְׂרָאֵל,

the Midianites is one. The war mandated against the seven nations in the land is another. They strike us as barbaric and out of key with an ethic of compassion and with the just-war doctrine that is to emerge in the Jewish tradition.

These texts – and there are notorious examples in the holy texts of most religions – require the most careful interpretation if they are not to do great harm. That is why every text-based religion develops its own traditions of interpretation. Rabbinic Judaism declared Biblicism – accepting the authority of the written word while rejecting oral tradition, the position of the Sadducees and Karaites – as heresy. The Rabbis said: 'One who translates a verse literally is a liar' (Kiddushin 49a). The point is clear: no text without interpretation; no interpretation without tradition.

Why must it be so? One reason is that these ancient texts were originally directed to times and conditions quite unlike ours. The war commands of Deuteronomy and the book of Joshua, for example, belong to a time when warfare was systemic, endemic, and brutal. The massacre of populations, such as we read of here, was commonplace. Another reason is that we are dealing with sacred Scripture, texts invested with the ultimate authority of God Himself. How do you take the word of eternity and apply it to the here and now? That is never simple and self-understood. For much of the biblical era, ancient Israel had its prophets who delivered, not the word of the Lord for all time, but the word of the Lord for *this* time. There are things – including a revenge attack such as this – that may be justified in an age of prophecy that are wholly unjustifiable at other times.

As a general rule, the application of every ancient text to another age involves an act of interpretation, and there is nothing inherently religious about this. It is a central problem in secular law and jurisprudence, deliberated over in every Supreme Court. How is a law enacted then to be understood now? It is a problem every theatrical director faces in deciding how, for example, to stage *The Merchant of Venice* for a

10 as booty all their cattle, flocks, and wealth. They burned all the towns where
11 they lived and their encampments. They gathered all the spoil and plunder,
12 people and animals, and they brought the captives and the plunder and spoil
to Moshe, Elazar the priest, and the Israelite community, at the camp on the
13 plains of Moav by the Jordan across from Yeriḥo. Moshe, Elazar the SHELISHI /SHENI/
priest, and all the community princes went to meet them outside the camp.
14 And Moshe grew furious with the commanders of the forces, the officers of
15 thousands and of hundreds, now returned from the service of war. "Have you
16 left all the women alive?" Moshe demanded. "These were the very ones who,
on Bilam's advice, induced the Israelites to betray the Lord during the Peor
17 affair, so that a plague struck down the Lord's community. Now, therefore, kill
18 every male child and kill every woman who has had relations with a man. All
the young girls who have not had relations with any man – them you may spare
19 alive. You must stay outside the camp for seven days. Every one among you or

רש"י

בַּפֻּרְעָנוּת. בִּלְעָם הָלַךְ שָׁם לִטֹּל שְׂכַר עֶשְׂרִים וְאַרְבָּעָה אֶלֶף שֶׁהִפִּיל מִיִּשְׂרָאֵל בַּעֲצָתוֹ, וְיָצָא מִמִּדְיָן לִקְרַאת יִשְׂרָאֵל וּמַשִּׂיאָן עֵצָה רָעָה, אָמַר לָהֶם: אִם כְּשֶׁהֱיִיתֶם שִׁשִּׁים רִבּוֹא לֹא יְכָלְתֶּם לָהֶם, עַתָּה בִּשְׁנֵים עָשָׂר אֶלֶף אַתֶּם בָּאִים לְהִלָּחֵם? נָתְנוּ לוֹ שְׂכָרוֹ מִשְׁלָם וְלֹא קִפְּחוּהוּ:

בֶּחָרֶב. הוּא בָּא עַל יִשְׂרָאֵל וְהֶחֱלִיף אֻמָּנוּתוֹ בְּאֻמָּנוּתָם, שֶׁאֵין נוֹשָׁעִים אֶלָּא בְּפִיהֶם עַל יְדֵי תְּפִלָּה וּבַקָּשָׁה, וּבָא הוּא וְתָפַשׂ אֻמָּנוּתָם לְקַלְּלָם בְּפִיו, אַף הֵם בָּאוּ עָלָיו וְהֶחֱלִיפוּ אֻמָּנוּתָם בְּאֻמָּנוּת הָאֻמּוֹת שֶׁבָּאִין בַּחֶרֶב, שֶׁנֶּאֱמַר: "וְעַל חַרְבְּךָ תִחְיֶה" (בראשית כז, מ):

י טִירֹתָם. מְקוֹם פַּלְטֵרִין שֶׁלָּהֶם, שֶׁהוּא לְשׁוֹן מוֹשַׁב כְּמָרִים יוֹדְעֵי חֻקֵּיהֶם. דָּבָר אַחֵר, לְשׁוֹן מוֹשַׁב שָׂרֵיהֶם, כְּמוֹ שֶׁמְּתֻרְגָּם "סַרְנֵי פְלִשְׁתִּים" (יהושע יג, ג) – "טוּרְנֵי פְלִשְׁתָּאֵי":

יא וַיִּקְחוּ אֶת כָּל הַשָּׁלָל וְגוֹ'. מַגִּיד שֶׁהָיוּ כְּשֵׁרִים וְצַדִּיקִים, וְלֹא נֶחְשְׁדוּ עַל הַגָּזֵל לִשְׁלֹחַ יָד בַּבִּזָּה שֶׁלֹּא בִּרְשׁוּת, שֶׁנֶּאֱמַר: "אֶת כָּל הַשָּׁלָל" וְגוֹ', וַעֲלֵיהֶם מְפֹרָשׁ בַּקַּבָּלָה: "שִׁנַּיִךְ כְּעֵדֶר הָרְחֵלִים" וְגוֹ' (שיר השירים ו, ו), אַף אַנְשֵׁי הַמִּלְחָמָה שֶׁבָּךְ כֻּלָּם צַדִּיקִים: שָׁלָל. הֵן מִטַּלְטְלִין שֶׁל מַלְבּוּשׁ וְתַכְשִׁיטִין: "בַּז" הוּא בִּזַּת מִטַּלְטְלִין שֶׁאֵינָם תַּכְשִׁיטִין:

מַלְקוֹחַ. אָדָם וּבְהֵמָה. וּבְמָקוֹם שֶׁכָּתוּב 'שְׁבִי' אֵצֶל 'מַלְקוֹחַ', 'שְׁבִי' בְּאָדָם וּ'מַלְקוֹחַ' בִּבְהֵמָה:

יג וַיֵּצְאוּ מֹשֶׁה וְאֶלְעָזָר הַכֹּהֵן. לְפִי שֶׁרָאוּ אֶת נַעֲרֵי יִשְׂרָאֵל יוֹצְאִים לַחֲטֹף מִן הַבִּזָּה:

יד וַיִּקְצֹף מֹשֶׁה עַל פְּקוּדֵי הֶחָיִל. מְמֻנִּים עַל הַחַיִל, לְלַמֶּדְךָ שֶׁכָּל סִרְחוֹן הַדּוֹר תָּלוּי בַּגְּדוֹלִים, שֶׁיֵּשׁ כֹּחַ בְּיָדָם לִמְחוֹת:

טז הֵן הֵנָּה. מַגִּיד שֶׁהָיוּ מַכִּירִים אוֹתָן, זוֹ הִיא שֶׁנִּכְשַׁל פְּלוֹנִי בָּהּ: בִּדְבַר בִּלְעָם. אָמַר לָהֶם: אֲפִלּוּ אַתֶּם מַכְנִיסִים כָּל הֲמוֹנוֹת שֶׁבָּעוֹלָם אֵין אַתֶּם יְכוֹלִים לָהֶם, שֶׁמָּא מְרֻבִּים אַתֶּם מִן הַמִּצְרִים שֶׁהָיוּ שֵׁשׁ מֵאוֹת רֶכֶב בָּחוּר (שמות יד, ז)? בּוֹאוּ וְאַשִּׂיאֲכֶם עֵצָה: אֱלֹהֵיהֶם שֶׁל אֵלּוּ שׂוֹנֵא זִמָּה הוּא וְכוּ', כִּדְאִיתָא בְּ'חֵלֶק' (סנהדרין קו ע"א) וּבְסִפְרֵי (קנז):

יז וְכָל אִשָּׁה יֹדַעַת אִישׁ. רְאוּיָה לְהִבָּעֵל, אַף עַל פִּי שֶׁלֹּא נִבְעֲלָה, וְלִפְנֵי הַצִּיץ הֶעֱבִירוּם, וְהָרְאוּיָה לְהִבָּעֵל פָּנֶיהָ מוֹרִיקוֹת: הֲרֹגוּ. לָמָּה חָזַר וְאָמַר? לְהַפְסִיק הָעִנְיָן, דִּבְרֵי רַבִּי יִשְׁמָעֵאל, שֶׁאִם אֲנִי קוֹרֵא: "הִרְגוּ כָל זָכָר בַּטָּף וְכָל אִשָּׁה יֹדַעַת אִישׁ... וְכֹל הַטַּף בַּנָּשִׁים" וְגוֹ', אֵינִי יוֹדֵעַ אִם לַהֲרֹג עִם הַזְּכָרִים אוֹ לְהַחֲיוֹת עִם הַטַּף, לְכָךְ נֶאֱמַר: "הֲרֹגוּ":

the plan to have the women seduce the Israelite men.

The real effect of concealing the information about Bilam, though, is to focus attention on the Israelites. It is they who sinned. Had Bilam's name been mentioned at the outset, we would have focused on him. It would have been his malice, his cunning, his defiance of God's purposes that would have been the story. The Torah is signaling to us that it was not the story. God saves Israel from its enemies but only we can save us from ourselves.

אֶת־נְשֵׁי מִדְיָן וְאֶת־טַפָּם וְאֵת כָּל־בְּהֶמְתָּם וְאֶת־כָּל־מִקְנֵהֶם וְאֶת־
י כָּל־חֵילָם בָּזָזוּ: וְאֵת כָּל־עָרֵיהֶם בְּמוֹשְׁבֹתָם וְאֵת כָּל־טִירֹתָם שָׂרְפוּ
יא בָּאֵשׁ: וַיִּקְחוּ אֶת־כָּל־הַשָּׁלָל וְאֵת כָּל־הַמַּלְקוֹחַ בָּאָדָם וּבַבְּהֵמָה:
יב וַיָּבִאוּ אֶל־מֹשֶׁה וְאֶל־אֶלְעָזָר הַכֹּהֵן וְאֶל־עֲדַת בְּנֵי־יִשְׂרָאֵל אֶת־הַשְּׁבִי
וְאֶת־הַמַּלְקוֹחַ וְאֶת־הַשָּׁלָל אֶל־הַמַּחֲנֶה אֶל־עַרְבֹת מוֹאָב אֲשֶׁר עַל־
יג יַרְדֵּן יְרֵחוֹ: וַיֵּצְאוּ מֹשֶׁה וְאֶלְעָזָר הַכֹּהֵן וְכָל־ שלישי /שני/
יד נְשִׂיאֵי הָעֵדָה לִקְרָאתָם אֶל־מִחוּץ לַמַּחֲנֶה: וַיִּקְצֹף מֹשֶׁה עַל פְּקוּדֵי
טו הֶחָיִל שָׂרֵי הָאֲלָפִים וְשָׂרֵי הַמֵּאוֹת הַבָּאִים מִצְּבָא הַמִּלְחָמָה: וַיֹּאמֶר
טז אֲלֵיהֶם מֹשֶׁה הַחִיִּיתֶם כָּל־נְקֵבָה: הֵן הֵנָּה הָיוּ לִבְנֵי יִשְׂרָאֵל בִּדְבַר
בִּלְעָם לִמְסָר־מַעַל בַּיהוָה עַל־דְּבַר פְּעוֹר וַתְּהִי הַמַּגֵּפָה בַּעֲדַת יהוה:
יז וְעַתָּה הִרְגוּ כָל־זָכָר בַּטָּף וְכָל־אִשָּׁה יֹדַעַת אִישׁ לְמִשְׁכַּב זָכָר הֲרֹגוּ:
יח יט וְכֹל הַטַּף בַּנָּשִׁים אֲשֶׁר לֹא־יָדְעוּ מִשְׁכַּב זָכָר הַחֲיוּ לָכֶם: וְאַתֶּם חֲנוּ

אונקלוס

יָת נְשֵׁי מִדְיָן וְיָת טַפְלְהוֹן, וְיָת כָּל בְּעִירְהוֹן וְיָת כָּל גֵּיתֵיהוֹן, וְיָת כָּל נִכְסֵיהוֹן בַּזּוּ: י וְיָת כָּל קִרְוֵיהוֹן בְּמוֹתְבָנֵיהוֹן, וְיָת כָּל בֵּית סִגְדַּתְהוֹן, אוֹקִידוּ בְּנוּרָא: יא וּשְׁבוֹ יָת כָּל עֲדָאָה, וְיָת כָּל דִּבַרְתָּא, בֶּאֱנָשָׁא וּבִבְעִירָא: יב וְאַיְתִיאוּ, לְוָת מֹשֶׁה וּלְוָת אֶלְעָזָר כָּהֲנָא וּלְוָת כְּנִשְׁתָּא דִּבְנֵי יִשְׂרָאֵל, יָת שִׁבְיָא וְיָת דִּבַרְתָּא, וְיָת עֲדָאָה לְמַשְׁרִיתָא, לְמֵישְׁרַיָּא דְּמוֹאָב, דְּעַל יַרְדְּנָא דִּירִיחוֹ: יג וּנְפַקוּ, מֹשֶׁה וְאֶלְעָזָר כָּהֲנָא, וְכָל רַבְרְבֵי כְּנִשְׁתָּא לְקַדָּמוּתְהוֹן, לְמִבָּרָא לְמַשְׁרִיתָא: יד וּרְגִיז מֹשֶׁה, עַל דִּמְמַנַּן עַל חֵילָא, רַבָּנֵי אַלְפֵי וְרַבָּנֵי מָאוָתָא, דַּאֲתוֹ מֵחֵיל קְרָבָא: טו וַאֲמַר לְהוֹן מֹשֶׁה, הֲקַיֵּימְתּוּן כָּל נֻקְבָּא: טז הָא אִנִּין, הֲוָאָה לִבְנֵי יִשְׂרָאֵל בְּעֵיצַת בִּלְעָם, לְשַׁקָּרָא שְׁקַר קֳדָם יי עַל עֵיסַק פְּעוֹר, וַהֲוָת מַחְתָּא בִּכְנִשְׁתָּא דַּיי: יז וּכְעַן, קְטוּלוּ כָל דְּכוּרָא בְּטַפְלָא, וְכָל אִתְּתָא, דִּידַעַת גְּבַר, לְמִשְׁכְּבֵי דְּכוּרָא קְטוּלוּ: יח וְכָל טַפְלָא בִּנְשַׁיָּא, דְּלָא יְדַעָא מִשְׁכְּבֵי דְּכוּרָא, קַיִּימוּ לְכוֹן: יט וְאַתּוּן, שְׁרוֹ,

31:16 בִּדְבַר בִּלְעָם *On Bilam's advice* – In chapter 25, we read of the sequel to the episode of Bilam's curses/blessings. The Israelites, having been saved by God from the would-be curses of Moav and Midyan, suffered a self-inflicted tragedy by allowing themselves to be enticed by the women of the land. God's anger burned against them. Here, several chapters later, it emerges that it was Bilam who devised this strategy. Having failed to curse the Israelites, Bilam eventually succeeds in doing them great harm.

When the Torah withholds a fact essential to understanding a passage and reveals it only later, it is forcing us to realize that events are not always what they first seem. In this case, certain puzzling aspects of the Bilam story become clear. We now understand why God was angry with Bilam for going along with the Moabites and Midianites despite the fact that He had given him permission to do so. Evidently, God detected in Bilam's mind a persisting malevolence toward Israel, which eventually found expression in

your captives who has killed a person or touched a corpse must purify himself
20 or herself on the third and seventh days. You must also purify every garment, as
21 well as every article of leather, goats' hair, or wood." Elazar the priest
said to the soldiers returning from war, "This is the Law's decree that the LORD
22 23 commanded Moshe: Gold, silver, bronze, iron, tin, and lead – anything that can
withstand fire – you shall pass through the fire and it will be purified, though
it must also be purified with the water of lustration. Anything that cannot
24 withstand fire, you must immerse in water. You shall wash your clothes on the
25 seventh day and you will then be pure, and may enter the camp." The REVI'I
26 LORD said to Moshe: "Together with Elazar the priest and the family heads

רש״י

יט **מִחוּץ לַמַּחֲנֶה.** שֶׁלֹּא יִכָּנְסוּ לָעֲזָרָה: **כֹּל הֹרֵג נֶפֶשׁ.** רַבִּי מֵאִיר אוֹמֵר: בְּהוֹרֵג בְּדָבָר הַמְקַבֵּל טֻמְאָה הַכָּתוּב מְדַבֵּר, וּלְמֶדְךָ הַכָּתוּב, שֶׁהַכְּלִי מְטַמֵּא אָדָם בְּחִבּוּרֵי הַמֵּת, כְּאִלּוּ נוֹגֵעַ בַּמֵּת עַצְמוֹ. אוֹ אֲפִלּוּ זָרַק בּוֹ חֵץ וַהֲרָגוֹ? תַּלְמוּד לוֹמַר: "וְכֹל נֹגֵעַ בֶּחָלָל", הִקִּישׁ הוֹרֵג לְנוֹגֵעַ, מַה נּוֹגֵעַ עַל יְדֵי חִבּוּרוֹ, אַף הוֹרֵג עַל יְדֵי חִבּוּרוֹ: **תִּתְחַטְּאוּ.** בְּמֵי נִדָּה, כְּדִין שְׁאָר טְמֵאֵי מֵתִים, שֶׁאַף לְדִבְרֵי הָאוֹמֵר קִבְרֵי גוֹיִם אֵינָם מְטַמְּאִין בְּאֹהֶל, שֶׁנֶּאֱמַר: "וְאַתֵּן צֹאנִי צֹאן מַרְעִיתִי אָדָם אַתֶּם" (יחזקאל לד, לא), מוֹדֶה הוּא שֶׁהַגּוֹיִם מְטַמְּאִין בְּמַגָּע וּבְמַשָּׂא, שֶׁלֹּא נֶאֱמַר 'אָדָם' אֶלָּא אֵצֶל טֻמְאַת אֹהָלוֹת, שֶׁנֶּאֱמַר: "אָדָם כִּי יָמוּת בְּאֹהֶל" (לעיל יט, יד): **אַתֶּם וּשְׁבִיכֶם.** לֹא שֶׁהַגּוֹיִם מְקַבְּלִין טֻמְאָה וּצְרִיכִין הַזָּאָה, אֶלָּא מָה אַתֶּם בְּנֵי בְרִית, אַף שְׁבִיכֶם כְּשֶׁיָּבוֹאוּ לַבְּרִית וְיִטַּמְּאוּ צְרִיכִין הַזָּאָה:

כ **וְכָל מַעֲשֵׂה עִזִּים.** לְהָבִיא כְּלֵי הַקַּרְנַיִם וְהַטְּלָפַיִם וְהָעֲצָמוֹת:

כא **וַיֹּאמֶר אֶלְעָזָר הַכֹּהֵן וְגוֹ׳.** לְפִי שֶׁבָּא מֹשֶׁה לִכְלַל כַּעַס בָּא לִכְלַל טָעוּת, שֶׁנִּתְעַלְּמוּ מִמֶּנּוּ הִלְכוֹת גִּעוּלֵי גוֹיִם. וְכֵן אַתָּה מוֹצֵא בַּשְּׁמִינִי לַמִּלּוּאִים, שֶׁנֶּאֱמַר: "וַיִּקְצֹף עַל אֶלְעָזָר וְעַל אִיתָמָר" (ויקרא י, טז), בָּא לִכְלַל כַּעַס, בָּא לִכְלַל טָעוּת. וְכֵן בִּ'שִׁמְעוּ נָא הַמֹּרִים' – "וַיַּךְ אֶת הַסֶּלַע" (לעיל כ, יא), עַל יְדֵי הַכַּעַס טָעָה: **אֲשֶׁר צִוָּה ה׳ וְגוֹ׳.** תָּלָה הַהוֹרָאָה בְּרַבּוֹ:

כב **אַךְ אֶת הַזָּהָב וְגוֹ׳.** אַף עַל פִּי שֶׁלֹּא הִזְהִיר לָכֶם מֹשֶׁה אֶלָּא עַל הִלְכוֹת טֻמְאָה, עוֹד יֵשׁ לְהַזְהִיר לָכֶם עַל הִלְכוֹת גִּעוּל, וְ'אַךְ' לְשׁוֹן מִעוּט, כְּלוֹמַר מְמֻעָטִין אַתֶּם מִלְּהִשְׁתַּמֵּשׁ בַּכֵּלִים, אֲפִלּוּ לְאַחַר טָהֳרָתָן מִטֻּמְאַת הַמֵּת, עַד שֶׁיִּטָהֲרוּ מִבְּלִיעַת אִסּוּר נְבֵלוֹת. וְרַבּוֹתֵינוּ אָמְרוּ: "אַךְ אֶת הַזָּהָב", לוֹמַר, שֶׁצָּרִיךְ לְהַעֲבִיר חֲלֻדָּה שֶׁלּוֹ קֹדֶם שֶׁיַּגְעִילֶנּוּ, וְזֶהוּ לְשׁוֹן 'אַךְ', שֶׁלֹּא יְהֵא שָׁם חֲלֻדָּה, אַךְ הַמַּתֶּכֶת יִהְיֶה כְּמוֹת שֶׁהוּא:

כג **כָּל דָּבָר אֲשֶׁר יָבֹא בָאֵשׁ.** לְבַשֵּׁל בּוֹ כְּלוּם: **תַּעֲבִירוּ בָאֵשׁ.** כְּדֶרֶךְ תַּשְׁמִישׁוֹ הַגְעָלָתוֹ, מַה שֶּׁתַּשְׁמִישׁוֹ עַל יְדֵי חַמִּין יַגְעִילֶנּוּ בְּחַמִּין, וּמַה שֶּׁתַּשְׁמִישׁוֹ עַל יְדֵי צָלִי, כְּגוֹן הַשַּׁפּוּד וְהָאַסְכָּלָה, יְלַבְּנֶנּוּ בָּאוּר: **אַךְ בְּמֵי נִדָּה יִתְחַטָּא.** לְפִי פְשׁוּטוֹ, חִטּוּי זֶה לְטַהֲרוֹ מִטֻּמְאַת מֵת; אָמַר לָהֶם: צְרִיכִין הַכֵּלִים גִּעוּל לְטַהֲרָם מִן הָאִסּוּר וְחִטּוּי לְטַהֲרָן מִן הַטֻּמְאָה. וְרַבּוֹתֵינוּ דָּרְשׁוּ מִכָּאן שֶׁאַף לְהַכְשִׁירָן מִן הָאִסּוּר הִטְעִין טְבִילָה לִכְלֵי מַתָּכוֹת, וּ"מֵי נִדָּה" הַכְּתוּבִין כָּאן דָּרְשׁוּ: מַיִם הָרְאוּיִם לִטְבֹּל בָּהֶם נִדָּה, וְכַמָּה הֵם? אַרְבָּעִים סְאָה:

כד **אֶל הַמַּחֲנֶה.** לְמַחֲנֵה שְׁכִינָה, שֶׁאֵין טְמֵא מֵת טָעוּן שִׁלּוּחַ מִמַּחֲנֵה לְוִיָּה וּמִמַּחֲנֵה יִשְׂרָאֵל:

כו **שָׂא אֵת רֹאשׁ.** קַח אֶת חֶשְׁבּוֹן:

Perhaps it was speaking from his own experience that Reish Lakish had said: Great is repentance, because *through it deliberate sins are accounted as though they were merits* (Yoma 86b). Any act we perform has multiple consequences, some good, some bad. When we intend evil, the bad consequences are attributed to us because they are what we sought to achieve. The good consequences are not; they are mere unintended outcomes. However, once one has undergone complete repentance, their original intent is canceled out. It is then possible to see the good, as well as the bad, consequences of the original act – and to be accredited with the former. There are two concepts of the past. The first is what happened. That is something we cannot change. The second is the *significance*, the *meaning*, of what happened. That is something we *can* change. Though we may need to pass through fire and water, we can reclaim our past through our choices for the future.

מִחוּץ לַמַּחֲנֶה שִׁבְעַת יָמִים כֹּל הֹרֵג נֶפֶשׁ וְכֹל ׀ נֹגֵעַ בֶּחָלָל תִּתְחַטְּאוּ
כ בַּיּוֹם הַשְּׁלִישִׁי וּבַיּוֹם הַשְּׁבִיעִי אַתֶּם וּשְׁבִיכֶם: וְכָל־בֶּגֶד וְכָל־כְּלִי־עוֹר
כא וְכָל־מַעֲשֵׂה עִזִּים וְכָל־כְּלִי־עֵץ תִּתְחַטָּאוּ: וַיֹּאמֶר אֶלְעָזָר
הַכֹּהֵן אֶל־אַנְשֵׁי הַצָּבָא הַבָּאִים לַמִּלְחָמָה זֹאת חֻקַּת הַתּוֹרָה אֲשֶׁר־
כב צִוָּה יהוה אֶת־מֹשֶׁה: אַךְ אֶת־הַזָּהָב וְאֶת־הַכָּסֶף אֶת־הַנְּחֹשֶׁת אֶת־
כג הַבַּרְזֶל אֶת־הַבְּדִיל וְאֶת־הָעֹפָרֶת: כָּל־דָּבָר אֲשֶׁר־יָבֹא בָאֵשׁ תַּעֲבִירוּ
בָאֵשׁ וְטָהֵר אַךְ בְּמֵי נִדָּה יִתְחַטָּא וְכֹל אֲשֶׁר לֹא־יָבֹא בָּאֵשׁ תַּעֲבִירוּ
כד בַמָּיִם: וְכִבַּסְתֶּם בִּגְדֵיכֶם בַּיּוֹם הַשְּׁבִיעִי וּטְהַרְתֶּם וְאַחַר תָּבֹאוּ אֶל־
כה כו הַמַּחֲנֶה: וַיֹּאמֶר יהוה אֶל־מֹשֶׁה לֵּאמֹר: שָׂא אֵת רֹאשׁ כח רביעי
מַלְקוֹחַ הַשְּׁבִי בָּאָדָם וּבַבְּהֵמָה אַתָּה וְאֶלְעָזָר הַכֹּהֵן וְרָאשֵׁי אֲבוֹת

אונקלוס

מִבָּרָא לְמַשְׁרִיתָא שִׁבְעָא יוֹמִין, כָּל דִּקְטַל נַפְשָׁא, וְכָל דִּקְרֵב בִּקְטִילָא, תַּדּוֹן עֲלוֹהִי, בְּיוֹמָא תְלִיתָאָה וּבְיוֹמָא שְׁבִיעָאָה, אַתּוּן וּשְׁבִיכוֹן: כ וְכָל לְבוּשׁ וְכָל מָן דִּמְשַׁךְ, וְכָל עוֹבַד דִּמְעַזֵּי וְכָל מָן דְּאָע, תַּדּוֹן עֲלוֹהִי: כא וַאֲמַר אֶלְעָזָר כָּהֲנָא לְגֻבְרֵי חֵילָא, דַּאֲתוֹ לִקְרָבָא, דָּא גְזֵירַת אוֹרַיְתָא, דְּפַקֵּיד יי יָת מֹשֶׁה: כב בְּרַם יָת דַּהֲבָא וְיָת כַּסְפָּא, יָת נְחָשָׁא יָת בַּרְזְלָא, יָת עֲבָצָא וְיָת אֲבָרָא:

כג כָּל מִדַּעַם דְּמִתָּעַל בְּנוּרָא, תַּעְבְּרוּנֵּיהּ בְּנוּרָא וְיִדְכֵּי, בְּרַם, בְּמֵי אַדָּיוּתָא יִתַּדֵּי, וְכָל דְּלָא מִתָּעַל, בְּנוּרָא תַּעְבְּרוּנֵּיהּ בְּמַיָּא: כד וּתְחַוְּרוּן לְבוּשֵׁיכוֹן, בְּיוֹמָא שְׁבִיעָאָה וְתִדְכּוֹן, וּבָתַר כֵּן תֵּיעֲלוּן לְמַשְׁרִיתָא: כה וַאֲמַר יי לְמֹשֶׁה לְמֵימַר: כו קַבֵּיל, יָת חֻשְׁבַּן דִּבְרַת שִׁבְיָא, בַּאֲנָשָׁא וּבִבְעִירָא, אַתְּ וְאֶלְעָזָר כָּהֲנָא, וְרֵישֵׁי אֲבָהָת

31:23 תַּעֲבִירוּ בָאֵשׁ וְטָהֵר *Pass through the fire and it will be purified* – The spoils of war, which had been used as vessels and tools of idolatry, must undergo a ritual of renewal, passing through fire and water, before they can be used by the people. The process is echoed in a poignant debate in the Talmud between R. Yoḥanan and his learning partner, Reish Lakish (Bava Metzia 84a). According to tradition, Reish Lakish was originally a robber or highwayman, who was persuaded by R. Yoḥanan, the leading Sage in the land of Israel at the time, to devote his life to talmudic study.

One day, in the house of study, the question arose as to when instruments like swords, spears, daggers, and knives are considered complete, and thus capable of becoming ritually unclean. R. Yoḥanan said they are complete when they have been tempered in a furnace. Reish Lakish said they are not complete until they have been quenched in water. In the heat of the argument, R. Yoḥanan said, "Trust a robber to be expert in his trade."

Reish Lakish, wounded by the jibe, turned on R. Yoḥanan and said, "What benefit have you conferred on me by persuading me to give up robbery and become a rabbi? There, among robbers, I was called master, and here in the house of study I am called a master."

R. Yoḥanan responded, "I conferred on you the benefit of bringing you under the wings of the Divine Presence."

Scarred by this encounter, Reish Lakish became ill and eventually died and R. Yoḥanan grieved for him deeply. Reminding a penitent of his past is forbidden; once he has undergone a true repentance, he is no longer the same person he was.

of the community, you must make an inventory of the plunder that was taken,
27 people and animals, giving half to the soldiers who went into battle and half
28 to the rest of the community. Levy a tribute to the LORD. From the soldiers
who took part in the battle, take one part of every five hundred, be it of people,
29 oxen, donkeys, or flocks. Take this from their half and give it to Elazar the
30 priest as an upraised gift to the LORD. From the Israelites' half, take one out
of every fifty, be it of people, cattle, donkeys, or flock – all the animals – and
give them to the Levites who carry out the duties of the LORD's Tabernacle."
31, 32 Moshe and Elazar the priest did as the LORD commanded Moshe. The plunder,
33 aside from the spoil the troops had taken, was 675,000 sheep, 72,000 oxen,
34, 35 61,000 donkeys, and 32,000 women who had not had relations with a man.
36, 37 The half share of those who had served in battle was 337,500 sheep, of which
38 the LORD's tribute was 675. The cattle were 36,000, of which the LORD's tribute
39, 40 was 72. The donkeys were 30,500, of which the LORD's tribute was 61. There
41 were 16,000 people, of which the LORD's tribute was 32 persons. Moshe gave
the tribute, an upraised gift for the LORD, to Elazar the priest, as the LORD
42 had commanded Moshe. The half share that Moshe took for the Israelites from HAMISHI
43 those who had served in battle as the community's half consisted of 337,500
44, 45, 46, 47 sheep, 36,000 heads of cattle, 30,500 donkeys, and 16,000 people. Moshe took

אונקלוס

כְּנִשְׁתָּא: כו וְתַפְלֵיג יָת דִּבַרְתָּא, בֵּין גֻּבְרֵי מְגִיחֵי קְרָבָא, דִּנְפַקוּ לְחֵילָא, וּבֵין כָּל כְּנִשְׁתָּא: כח וְתַפְרֵישׁ נְסִיבָא קֳדָם יְיָ, מִן גֻּבְרֵי מְגִיחֵי קְרָבָא דִּנְפַקוּ לְחֵילָא, חֲדָא נַפְשָׁא, מֵחֲמֵשׁ מְאָה, מִן אֱנָשָׁא וּמִן תּוֹרֵי, וּמִן חֲמָרֵי וּמִן עָנָא: כט מִפַּלְגּוּתְהוֹן תִּסְּבוּן, וְתִתֵּין, לְאֶלְעָזָר כָּהֲנָא אַפְרָשׁוּתָא קֳדָם יְיָ: ל וּמִפַּלְגּוּת בְּנֵי יִשְׂרָאֵל, תִּסַּב חַד דְּאִתְּאֲחַד מִן חַמְשִׁין, מִן אֱנָשָׁא מִן תּוֹרֵי, מִן חֲמָרֵי וּמִן עָנָא מִכָּל בְּעִירָא, וְתִתֵּין יָתְהוֹן לְלֵיוָאֵי, נָטְרֵי, מַטְּרַת מַשְׁכְּנָא דַּייָ: לא וַעֲבַד מֹשֶׁה, וְאֶלְעָזָר כָּהֲנָא, כְּמָא דְּפַקֵּיד יְיָ יָת מֹשֶׁה: לב וַהֲוָת דִּבַרְתָּא, שְׁאָר בִּזָּא, דְּבַזּוּ עַמָּא דִּנְפַקוּ לְחֵילָא, עָנָא, שֵׁית מְאָה וְשִׁבְעִין וְחַמְשָׁא אַלְפִין:

לג וְתוֹרֵי, שִׁבְעִין וּתְרֵין אַלְפִין: לד וַחֲמָרֵי, שִׁתִּין וְחַד אַלְפִין: לה וְנַפְשָׁא דַּאֲנָשָׁא, מִן נְשַׁיָּא, דְּלָא יְדַעָא מִשְׁכְּבֵי דְּכוּרָא, כָּל נַפְשָׁתָא, תְּלָתִין וּתְרֵין אַלְפִין: לו וַהֲוָת פַּלְגּוּתָא, חוּלָק, גֻּבְרַיָּא דִּנְפַקוּ לְחֵילָא, מִנְיַן עָנָא, תְּלָת מְאָה וּתְלָתִין, וְשִׁבְעָא אַלְפִין וַחֲמֵשׁ מְאָה: לז וַהֲוָה, נְסִיבָא קֳדָם יְיָ מִן עָנָא, שֵׁית מְאָה וְשִׁבְעִין וַחֲמֵשׁ: לח וְתוֹרֵי, תְּלָתִין וְשִׁתָּא אַלְפִין, וּנְסִיבְהוֹן קֳדָם יְיָ שִׁבְעִין וּתְרֵין: לט וַחֲמָרֵי, תְּלָתִין אַלְפִין וַחֲמֵשׁ מְאָה, וּנְסִיבְהוֹן קֳדָם יְיָ שִׁתִּין וְחַד: מ וְנַפְשָׁא דַּאֲנָשָׁא, שִׁתַּת עֲסַר אַלְפִין, וּנְסִיבְהוֹן קֳדָם יְיָ, תְּלָתִין וּתְרֵין נַפְשָׁן: מא וִיהַב מֹשֶׁה, יָת נְסִיב אַפְרָשׁוּתָא קֳדָם יְיָ, לְאֶלְעָזָר כָּהֲנָא, כְּמָא דְּפַקֵּיד יְיָ יָת מֹשֶׁה:

רש״י

כז וְחָצִיתָ אֶת הַמַּלְקוֹחַ בֵּין תֹּפְשֵׂי הַמִּלְחָמָה וְגוֹ׳. חֶצְיוֹ לְאֵלּוּ וְחֶצְיוֹ לְאֵלּוּ:

לב וַיְהִי הַמַּלְקוֹחַ יֶתֶר הַבָּז. לְפִי שֶׁלֹּא נִצְטַוּוּ לְהָרִים מֶכֶס מִן הַמִּטַּלְטְלִין אֶלָּא מִן הַמַּלְקוֹחַ, כָּתַב אֶת הַלָּשׁוֹן הַזֶּה: "וַיְהִי הַמַּלְקוֹחַ" שֶׁבָּא לִכְלַל חֲלֻקָּה וְלִכְלַל מֶכֶס, שֶׁהָיָה עוֹדֵף עַל בַּז הַמִּטַּלְטְלִין "אֲשֶׁר בָּזְזוּ עַם הַצָּבָא" אִישׁ לוֹ וְלֹא בָּא לִכְלַל חֲלֻקָּה, מִסְפַּר הַצֹּאן וְגוֹ׳:

מב וּמִמַּחֲצִית בְּנֵי יִשְׂרָאֵל אֲשֶׁר חָצָה מֹשֶׁה. לָעֵדָה, וְהוֹצִיאָהּ לָהֶם "מִן הָאֲנָשִׁים הַצֹּבְאִים":

מג-מז וַתְּהִי מֶחֱצַת הָעֵדָה. כָּךְ וְכָךְ, "וַיִּקַּח מֹשֶׁה" וְגוֹ׳:

כז הָעֵדָה׃ וְחָצִיתָ אֶת־הַמַּלְקוֹחַ בֵּין תֹּפְשֵׂי הַמִּלְחָמָה הַיֹּצְאִים לַצָּבָא
כח וּבֵין כָּל־הָעֵדָה׃ וַהֲרֵמֹתָ מֶכֶס לַיהוָה מֵאֵת אַנְשֵׁי הַמִּלְחָמָה הַיֹּצְאִים
לַצָּבָא אֶחָד נֶפֶשׁ מֵחֲמֵשׁ הַמֵּאוֹת מִן־הָאָדָם וּמִן־הַבָּקָר וּמִן־הַחֲמֹרִים
כט וּמִן־הַצֹּאן׃ מִמַּחֲצִיתָם תִּקָּחוּ וְנָתַתָּה לְאֶלְעָזָר הַכֹּהֵן תְּרוּמַת יְהוָה׃
ל וּמִמַּחֲצִת בְּנֵי־יִשְׂרָאֵל תִּקַּח ׀ אֶחָד ׀ אָחֻז מִן־הַחֲמִשִּׁים מִן־הָאָדָם
מִן־הַבָּקָר מִן־הַחֲמֹרִים וּמִן־הַצֹּאן מִכָּל־הַבְּהֵמָה וְנָתַתָּה אֹתָם לַלְוִיִּם
לא שֹׁמְרֵי מִשְׁמֶרֶת מִשְׁכַּן יְהוָה׃ וַיַּעַשׂ מֹשֶׁה וְאֶלְעָזָר הַכֹּהֵן כַּאֲשֶׁר צִוָּה
לב יְהוָה אֶת־מֹשֶׁה׃ וַיְהִי הַמַּלְקוֹחַ יֶתֶר הַבָּז אֲשֶׁר בָּזְזוּ עַם הַצָּבָא צֹאן
לג שֵׁשׁ־מֵאוֹת אֶלֶף וְשִׁבְעִים אֶלֶף וַחֲמֵשֶׁת אֲלָפִים׃ וּבָקָר שְׁנַיִם וְשִׁבְעִים
לד לה אָלֶף׃ וַחֲמֹרִים אֶחָד וְשִׁשִּׁים אָלֶף׃ וְנֶפֶשׁ אָדָם מִן־הַנָּשִׁים אֲשֶׁר לֹא־
לו יָדְעוּ מִשְׁכַּב זָכָר כָּל־נֶפֶשׁ שְׁנַיִם וּשְׁלֹשִׁים אָלֶף׃ וַתְּהִי הַמֶּחֱצָה חֵלֶק
הַיֹּצְאִים בַּצָּבָא מִסְפַּר הַצֹּאן שְׁלֹשׁ־מֵאוֹת אֶלֶף וּשְׁלֹשִׁים אֶלֶף וְשִׁבְעַת
לז אֲלָפִים וַחֲמֵשׁ מֵאוֹת׃ וַיְהִי הַמֶּכֶס לַיהוָה מִן־הַצֹּאן שֵׁשׁ מֵאוֹת חָמֵשׁ
לח וְשִׁבְעִים׃ וְהַבָּקָר שִׁשָּׁה וּשְׁלֹשִׁים אָלֶף וּמִכְסָם לַיהוָה שְׁנַיִם וְשִׁבְעִים׃
לט מ וַחֲמֹרִים שְׁלֹשִׁים אֶלֶף וַחֲמֵשׁ מֵאוֹת וּמִכְסָם לַיהוָה אֶחָד וְשִׁשִּׁים׃ וְנֶפֶשׁ
מא אָדָם שִׁשָּׁה עָשָׂר אָלֶף וּמִכְסָם לַיהוָה שְׁנַיִם וּשְׁלֹשִׁים נָפֶשׁ׃ וַיִּתֵּן מֹשֶׁה
אֶת־מֶכֶס תְּרוּמַת יְהוָה לְאֶלְעָזָר הַכֹּהֵן כַּאֲשֶׁר צִוָּה יְהוָה אֶת־מֹשֶׁה׃
מב מג וּמִמַּחֲצִית בְּנֵי יִשְׂרָאֵל אֲשֶׁר חָצָה מֹשֶׁה מִן־הָאֲנָשִׁים הַצֹּבְאִים׃ וַתְּהִי חמישי
מֶחֱצַת הָעֵדָה מִן־הַצֹּאן שְׁלֹשׁ־מֵאוֹת אֶלֶף וּשְׁלֹשִׁים אֶלֶף שִׁבְעַת
מד מה אֲלָפִים וַחֲמֵשׁ מֵאוֹת׃ וּבָקָר שִׁשָּׁה וּשְׁלֹשִׁים אָלֶף׃ וַחֲמֹרִים שְׁלֹשִׁים
מו מז אֶלֶף וַחֲמֵשׁ מֵאוֹת׃ וְנֶפֶשׁ אָדָם שִׁשָּׁה עָשָׂר אָלֶף׃ וַיִּקַּח מֹשֶׁה מִמַּחֲצִת

אונקלוס

מב וּמִפַּלְגוּת בְּנֵי יִשְׂרָאֵל, דִּפְלַג מֹשֶׁה, מִן גֻּבְרַיָּא דִּנְפַקוּ לְחֵילָא: מג וַהֲוָת, פַּלְגוּת כְּנִשְׁתָּא מִן עָנָא, תְּלָת מְאָה וּתְלָתִין, וְשִׁבְעָא אַלְפִין וַחֲמֵשׁ מְאָה: מד וְתוֹרֵי, תְּלָתִין וְשִׁתָּא אַלְפִין: מה וּחְמָרֵי, תְּלָתִין אַלְפִין וַחֲמֵשׁ מְאָה: מו וְנַפְשָׁא דַּאֲנָשָׁא, שִׁתַּת עֲסַר אַלְפִין: מז וּנְסֵיב מֹשֶׁה מִפַּלְגוּת

from the Israelites' half one out of every 50 humans and animals. These he gave
to the Levites who keep the charge of the LORD's Tabernacle, as the LORD had
48 commanded Moshe. The commanders over the thousands of the warriors –
49 officers over thousands and officers over hundreds – approached Moshe and
said to him, "Your servants have counted the warriors in our charge; not one of
50 us is missing. And so we make an offering to the LORD of the gold articles each
man found – anklets, bracelets, signet rings, earrings, and pendants – to make
51 our atonement before the LORD." Moshe and Elazar the priest took all the gold
52 from them, all the crafted objects. All the gold for the upraised gift presented
to the LORD by the officers of thousands and the officers of hundreds was
53 worth 16,750 shekel. Yet the men of the army each kept plunder for themselves.
54 Moshe and Elazar the priest took the gold from the officers of thousands and
of hundreds, and brought it to the Tent of Meeting as a remembrance for the
Israelites before the LORD.
32 1 The people of Reuven and Gad had much cattle – in this they were very rich. SHISHI /SHELISHI/
And seeing the lands of Yazer and Gilad they noticed that this was cattle
2 country. So the people of Gad and Reuven came to Moshe, Elazar the priest,
3 and the princes of the community and said: "Atarot, Divon, Yazer, Nimra,

רש״י

מח הַפְּקֻדִים. הַמְמֻנִּים:

מט וְלֹא נִפְקַד. לֹא נֶחְסַר. וְתַרְגּוּמוֹ: "וְלָא שְׁגָא", אַף הוּא בִּלְשׁוֹן אֲרַמִּי חֶסְרוֹן, כְּמוֹ: "אָנֹכִי אֲחַטֶּנָּה" (בראשית לא, לט), תַּרְגּוּמוֹ: "דַּהֲוָת שָׁגְיָא מִמִּנְיָנָא", וְכֵן: "כִּי יִפָּקֵד מוֹשָׁבֶךָ" (שמואל א' כ, יח), יֶחְסַר מְקוֹם מוֹשָׁבְךָ, אִישׁ הָרָגִיל לֵישֵׁב שָׁם. וְכֵן: "וַיִּפָּקֵד מְקוֹם דָּוִד" (שם פסוק כז), נֶחְסַר מְקוֹמוֹ וְאֵין אִישׁ יוֹשֵׁב שָׁם:

נ אֶצְעָדָה. אֵלּוּ צְמִידִים שֶׁל רֶגֶל: וְצָמִיד. שֶׁל יָד: עָגִיל. נִזְמֵי אֹזֶן: וְכוּמָז. דְּפוּס שֶׁל בֵּית הָרֶחֶם, לְכַפֵּר עַל הִרְהוּר הַלֵּב שֶׁל בְּנוֹת מִדְיָן:

לב ג עֲטָרוֹת וְדִיבֹן וְגוֹ'. מֵאֶרֶץ סִיחוֹן וְעוֹג הָיוּ:

THE NEGOTIATION

At this stage in the journey, the people have their attention focused on the destination: the land west of the river Jordan, the place that even the spies confirmed to be "flowing with milk and with honey" (Num. 13:27). Yet it is at just this point that a problem arises, different in kind from those that came before.

The members of the tribes of Reuven and Gad begin to have different thoughts. Seeing that the land through which they are traveling is ideal for raising cattle, they decide that they would prefer to stay there, to the east of the Jordan, and they propose this to Moshe. Unsurprisingly, he is angry at the suggestion. The two tribes are putting their own interests above those of the nation as a whole. As Moshe put it to the tribes: "Are your brothers to go to war while you stay here? Why would you discourage the Israelites from crossing into the land the LORD has given them?" (32:6–7). The proposal is potentially disastrous.

Moshe reminds the men of Reuven and Gad what happened in the incident of the spies. The spies demoralized the people, ten of them saying that they could not conquer the land. The result of that one moment was to condemn an entire generation to die in the wilderness and to delay the eventual conquest by forty years.

בְּנֵי־יִשְׂרָאֵל אֶת־הָאָחֻז אֶחָד מִן־הַחֲמִשִּׁים מִן־הָאָדָם וּמִן־הַבְּהֵמָה
וַיִּתֵּן אֹתָם לַלְוִיִּם שֹׁמְרֵי מִשְׁמֶרֶת מִשְׁכַּן יהוה כַּאֲשֶׁר צִוָּה יהוה אֶת־
מח מֹשֶׁה: וַיִּקְרְבוּ אֶל־מֹשֶׁה הַפְּקֻדִים אֲשֶׁר לְאַלְפֵי הַצָּבָא שָׂרֵי הָאֲלָפִים
מט וְשָׂרֵי הַמֵּאוֹת: וַיֹּאמְרוּ אֶל־מֹשֶׁה עֲבָדֶיךָ נָשְׂאוּ אֶת־רֹאשׁ אַנְשֵׁי
נ הַמִּלְחָמָה אֲשֶׁר בְּיָדֵנוּ וְלֹא־נִפְקַד מִמֶּנּוּ אִישׁ: וַנַּקְרֵב אֶת־קָרְבַּן יהוה
אִישׁ אֲשֶׁר מָצָא כְלִי־זָהָב אֶצְעָדָה וְצָמִיד טַבַּעַת עָגִיל וְכוּמָז לְכַפֵּר
נא עַל־נַפְשֹׁתֵינוּ לִפְנֵי יהוה: וַיִּקַּח מֹשֶׁה וְאֶלְעָזָר הַכֹּהֵן אֶת־הַזָּהָב מֵאִתָּם
נב כֹּל כְּלִי מַעֲשֶׂה: וַיְהִי ׀ כָּל־זְהַב הַתְּרוּמָה אֲשֶׁר הֵרִימוּ לַיהוה שִׁשָּׁה
עָשָׂר אֶלֶף שְׁבַע־מֵאוֹת וַחֲמִשִּׁים שָׁקֶל מֵאֵת שָׂרֵי הָאֲלָפִים וּמֵאֵת
נג נד שָׂרֵי הַמֵּאוֹת: אַנְשֵׁי הַצָּבָא בָּזְזוּ אִישׁ לוֹ: וַיִּקַּח מֹשֶׁה וְאֶלְעָזָר הַכֹּהֵן
אֶת־הַזָּהָב מֵאֵת שָׂרֵי הָאֲלָפִים וְהַמֵּאוֹת וַיָּבִאוּ אֹתוֹ אֶל־אֹהֶל מוֹעֵד
זִכָּרוֹן לִבְנֵי־יִשְׂרָאֵל לִפְנֵי יהוה:
לב א וּמִקְנֶה ׀ רַב הָיָה לִבְנֵי רְאוּבֵן וְלִבְנֵי־גָד עָצוּם מְאֹד וַיִּרְאוּ אֶת־אֶרֶץ כט ששי /שלישי/
ב יַעְזֵר וְאֶת־אֶרֶץ גִּלְעָד וְהִנֵּה הַמָּקוֹם מְקוֹם מִקְנֶה: וַיָּבֹאוּ בְנֵי־גָד
וּבְנֵי רְאוּבֵן וַיֹּאמְרוּ אֶל־מֹשֶׁה וְאֶל־אֶלְעָזָר הַכֹּהֵן וְאֶל־נְשִׂיאֵי הָעֵדָה
ג לֵאמֹר: עֲטָרוֹת וְדִיבֹן וְיַעְזֵר וְנִמְרָה וְחֶשְׁבּוֹן וְאֶלְעָלֵה וּשְׂבָם וּנְבוֹ וּבְעֹן:

אונקלוס

בְּנֵי יִשְׂרָאֵל, יָת דְּאִתְּחַד חַד מִן חַמְשִׁין, מִן אֱנָשָׁא וּמִן בְּעִירָא, וִיהַב יָתְהוֹן לְלֵיוָאֵי, נָטְרֵי מַטְּרַת מַשְׁכְּנָא דַּייָ, כְּמָא דְּפַקִּיד יְיָ יָת מֹשֶׁה: מח וְקָרִיבוּ לְוָת מֹשֶׁה, דִּמְמַנַּן עַל אַלְפֵי חֵילָא, רַבָּנֵי אַלְפֵי וְרַבָּנֵי מָאוָתָא: מט וַאֲמַרוּ לְמֹשֶׁה, עַבְדָּךְ קַבִּילוּ, יָת חֻשְׁבַּן, גֻּבְרֵי מְגִיחֵי קְרָבָא דְּעִמַּנָא, וְלָא שְׁגָא מִנַּנָא אֱנָשׁ: נ וְקָרֵיבְנָא יָת קֻרְבָּנָא דַּייָ, גְּבַר דְּאַשְׁכַּח מָן דִּדְהַב שֵׁירִין וְשַׁבְּין, עִזְקָן קְדָשִׁין וּמָחוֹךְ, לְכַפָּרָא עַל נַפְשָׁתַנָא קֳדָם יְיָ: נא וּנְסֵיב מֹשֶׁה, וְאֶלְעָזָר כָּהֲנָא, יָת דַּהֲבָא מִנְּהוֹן, כָּל מָן דְּעוֹבָדָא: נב וַהֲוָה כָּל דְּהַב אַפְרָשׁוּתָא, דְּאַפְרִישׁוּ קֳדָם יְיָ, שִׁתַּת עֲסַר אַלְפִין, שְׁבַע מְאָה וְחַמְשִׁין סִלְעִין, מִן רַבָּנֵי אַלְפֵי, וּמִן רַבָּנֵי מָאוָתָא: נג גֻּבְרִין דְּחֵילָא, בַּזּוּ גְּבַר לְנַפְשֵׁיהּ: נד וּנְסֵיב מֹשֶׁה, וְאֶלְעָזָר כָּהֲנָא יָת דַּהֲבָא, מִן רַבָּנֵי אַלְפֵי וּמָאוָתָא, וְאַיְתִיאוּ יָתֵיהּ לְמַשְׁכַּן זִמְנָא, דָּכְרָנָא לִבְנֵי יִשְׂרָאֵל קֳדָם יְיָ: לב א וּבְעִיר סַגִּי, הֲוָה, לִבְנֵי רְאוּבֵן, וְלִבְנֵי גָד תַּקִּיף לַחֲדָא, וַחֲזוֹ, יָת אֲרַע יַעְזֵר וְיָת אֲרַע גִּלְעָד, וְהָא אַתְרָא אֲתַר כְּשַׁר לְבֵית בְּעִיר: ב וַאֲתוֹ בְּנֵי גָד וּבְנֵי רְאוּבֵן, וַאֲמַרוּ לְמֹשֶׁה וּלְאֶלְעָזָר כָּהֲנָא, וּלְרַבְרְבֵי כְּנִשְׁתָּא לְמֵימַר: ג עֲטָרוֹת וְדִיבוֹן וְיַעְזֵר וְנִמְרָה, וְחֶשְׁבּוֹן וְאֶלְעָלֵה, וּשְׂבָם וּנְבוֹ וּבְעוֹן:

4 Ḥeshbon, Elaleh, Sevam, Nevo, and Beon, the land that the Lord struck down
before the community of Israel, is good cattle country, and your servants keep
5 cattle." They said, "If we have found favor with you, let this land be
6 given to your servants as our possession. Do not make us cross the Jordan." But
Moshe asked the Gadites and Reubenites, "Are your brothers to go to war while
7 you stay here? Why would you discourage the Israelites from crossing into the
8 land the Lord has given them? That is what your fathers did when I sent them
9 from Kadesh Barnea to see the land. They went as far as the Eshkol Ravine and
saw the land, but they discouraged the Israelites from entering the land the
10 Lord had given them, and on that day the Lord's rage burned, and He swore:
11 None of the men twenty years of age or above who left Egypt will see the land
that I swore to give Avraham, Yitzḥak, and Yaakov, because they did not follow
12 Me wholeheartedly – none except Kalev son of Yefuneh the Kenizzite and
13 Yehoshua son of Nun, because they wholeheartedly followed the Lord. The
Lord was incensed at Israel, and He made them wander in the wilderness for

רש״י

ו| **הַאַחֵיכֶם.** לְשׁוֹן תְּמִיהָה הוּא:

ז| **וְלָמָּה תְנִיאוּן.** תָּסִירוּ וְתַמְנִיעוּ לִבָּם "מֵעֲבֹר", שֶׁיִּהְיוּ סְבוּרִים שֶׁאַתֶּם יְרֵאִים לַעֲבֹר מִפְּנֵי הַמִּלְחָמָה וְחֹזֶק הֶעָרִים וְהָעָם:

ח| **מִקָּדֵשׁ בַּרְנֵעַ.** כָּךְ שְׁמָהּ, וּשְׁתֵּי קָדֵשׁ הָיוּ:

יב| **הַקְּנִזִּי.** חוֹרְגוֹ שֶׁל קְנַז הָיָה, וְיָלְדָה לוֹ אִמּוֹ שֶׁל כָּלֵב אֶת עָתְנִיאֵל:

יג| **וַיְנִעֵם.** וַיְטַלְטְלֵם, מִן "נָע וָנָד" (בראשית ד, יב):

because he is willing to compromise on the integrity of the nation as a whole, not because he uses honeyed words and diplomatic evasions, but because he is honest, principled, and focused on the common good. We all face conflicts in our lives. This is how to resolve them.

32:6 **הַאַחֵיכֶם יָבֹאוּ לַמִּלְחָמָה וְאַתֶּם תֵּשְׁבוּ פֹה** *Are your brothers to go… while you stay here?* – The extent to which Moshe's concerns for the unity of the nation are justified will become apparent many years later. The Reubenites and Gadites do indeed fulfill their promise in the days of Yehoshua. The rest of the tribes conquer and settle the land of Israel while they (together with half the tribe of Menashe) establish their presence in Transjordan. Despite this, within a brief space of time there is almost civil war.

Chapter 22 of the book of Joshua describes how, after returning to their families and settling their land, the Reubenites and Gadites build "an altar" (Josh. 22:10) on the east side of the Jordan. Seeing this as an act of secession, the rest of the Israelites prepare to do battle against them. Yehoshua, in a striking act of diplomacy, sends Pinḥas, the former zealot, now man of peace, to negotiate. He warns them of the terrible consequences of what they have done by, in effect, creating a religious center outside the land of Israel. It will split the nation in two.

The Reubenites and Gadites make it clear that this was not their intention at all. To the contrary, they themselves were worried that in the future, the rest of the Israelites would see them living across the Jordan and conclude that they no longer want to be part of the nation. That is why they have built the altar, not to offer sacrifices, not as a rival to the nation's Sanctuary, but merely as a symbol and a sign to future generations that they too are Israelites. Pinḥas and the rest of the delegation are satisfied with this answer, and once again civil war is averted.

ד הָאָרֶץ אֲשֶׁר הִכָּה יהוה לִפְנֵי עֲדַת יִשְׂרָאֵל אֶרֶץ מִקְנֶה הִוא וְלַעֲבָדֶיךָ
ה מִקְנֶה: וַיֹּאמְרוּ אִם־מָצָאנוּ חֵן בְּעֵינֶיךָ יֻתַּן אֶת־הָאָרֶץ
ו הַזֹּאת לַעֲבָדֶיךָ לַאֲחֻזָּה אַל־תַּעֲבִרֵנוּ אֶת־הַיַּרְדֵּן: וַיֹּאמֶר מֹשֶׁה לִבְנֵי־
ז גָד וְלִבְנֵי רְאוּבֵן הַאַחֵיכֶם יָבֹאוּ לַמִּלְחָמָה וְאַתֶּם תֵּשְׁבוּ פֹה: וְלָמָּה
תנואון אֶת־לֵב בְּנֵי יִשְׂרָאֵל מֵעֲבֹר אֶל־הָאָרֶץ אֲשֶׁר־נָתַן לָהֶם יהוה: תְנִיאוּן
ח כֹּה עָשׂוּ אֲבֹתֵיכֶם בְּשָׁלְחִי אֹתָם מִקָּדֵשׁ בַּרְנֵעַ לִרְאוֹת אֶת־הָאָרֶץ:
ט וַיַּעֲלוּ עַד־נַחַל אֶשְׁכּוֹל וַיִּרְאוּ אֶת־הָאָרֶץ וַיָּנִיאוּ אֶת־לֵב בְּנֵי יִשְׂרָאֵל
י לְבִלְתִּי־בֹא אֶל־הָאָרֶץ אֲשֶׁר־נָתַן לָהֶם יהוה: וַיִּחַר־אַף יהוה בַּיּוֹם
יא הַהוּא וַיִּשָּׁבַע לֵאמֹר: אִם־יִרְאוּ הָאֲנָשִׁים הָעֹלִים מִמִּצְרַיִם מִבֶּן עֶשְׂרִים
שָׁנָה וָמַעְלָה אֵת הָאֲדָמָה אֲשֶׁר נִשְׁבַּעְתִּי לְאַבְרָהָם לְיִצְחָק וּלְיַעֲקֹב
יב כִּי לֹא־מִלְאוּ אַחֲרָי: בִּלְתִּי כָּלֵב בֶּן־יְפֻנֶּה הַקְּנִזִּי וִיהוֹשֻׁעַ בִּן־נוּן כִּי
יג מִלְאוּ אַחֲרֵי יהוה: וַיִּחַר־אַף יהוה בְּיִשְׂרָאֵל וַיְנִעֵם בַּמִּדְבָּר אַרְבָּעִים

אונקלוס

ד אַרְעָא, דִּמְחָא יי יָת יָתְבַהָא קֳדָם כְּנִשְׁתָּא דְיִשְׂרָאֵל, אֲרַע כָּשְׁרָא לְבֵית בְּעִיר הִיא, וּלְעַבְדָּךְ אִית בְּעִיר: ה וַאֲמַרוּ, אִם אַשְׁכַּחְנָא רַחֲמִין בְּעֵינָךְ, תִּתְיְהֵיב, אַרְעָא הָדָא, לְעַבְדָּךְ לְאַחְסָנָא, לָא תַעְבְּרִנָּנָא יָת יַרְדְּנָא: ו וַאֲמַר מֹשֶׁה, לִבְנֵי גָד וְלִבְנֵי רְאוּבֵן, הַאֲחֵיכוֹן, יֵיתוֹן לְאַגָּחָא קְרָבָא, וְאַתּוּן תְּתִבוּן הָכָא: ז וּלְמָא תוֹנוֹן, יָת לִבָּא דִבְנֵי יִשְׂרָאֵל, מִלְּמִעְבַּר לְאַרְעָא, דִּיהַב לְהוֹן יי: ח כְּדֵין עֲבַדוּ אֲבָהָתְכוֹן, כַּד שְׁלַחִית יָתְהוֹן, מֵרְקַם גֵּיאָה לְמִחְזֵי יָת אַרְעָא:

ט וּסְלִיקוּ עַד נַחְלָא דְאֶתְכָּלָא, וַחֲזוֹ יָת אַרְעָא, וְאוֹנִיאוּ, יָת לִבָּא דִבְנֵי יִשְׂרָאֵל, בְּדִיל דְּלָא לְמֵיעַל לְאַרְעָא, דִּיהַב לְהוֹן יי: י וּתְקֵיף רֻגְזָא דַיי בְּיוֹמָא הַהוּא, וְקַיֵּים לְמֵימַר: יא אִם יִחְזוֹן גֻּבְרַיָּא דִּסְלִיקוּ מִמִּצְרַיִם, מִבַּר עַסְרִין שְׁנִין וּלְעֵילָא, יָת אַרְעָא, דְּקַיֵּימִית, לְאַבְרָהָם לְיִצְחָק וּלְיַעֲקֹב, אֲרֵי לָא אַשְׁלִימוּ בָּתַר דַּחַלְתִּי: יב אֱלָהֵין, כָּלֵב בַּר יְפֻנֶּה קְנִזָּאָה, וִיהוֹשֻׁעַ בַּר נוּן, אֲרֵי אַשְׁלִימוּ בָּתַר דַּחַלְתָּא דַיי: יג וּתְקֵיף רֻגְזָא דַיי בְּיִשְׂרָאֵל, וְאוֹחַרְנוּן בְּמַדְבְּרָא, אַרְבְּעִין

> And here you are, a brood of sinners, taking your fathers' places and bringing yet more of the LORD's burning rage down upon Israel. If you turn back from following Him, He will once again leave them in the wilderness, and you will destroy this entire people. (Num. 32:14–15)

Moshe is blunt, honest, and confrontational.

One of the hardest tasks of any leader – from prime ministers to parents – is conflict resolution. Yet it is also the most vital. Where there is leadership, there is long-term cohesiveness within the group, whatever the short-term problems. Where there is a lack of leadership – where leaders lack authority, grace, generosity of spirit, and the ability to respect positions other than their own – then there is divisiveness, rancor, backbiting, resentment, internal politics, and a lack of trust. True leaders are the people who put the interests of the group above those of any subsection of the group. Moshe succeeds here, not because he is weak, not

forty years until the whole generation that had done evil in the LORD's sight
14 was gone. And here you are, a brood of sinners, taking your fathers' places and
15 bringing yet more of the LORD's burning rage down upon Israel. If you turn
back from following Him, He will once again leave them in the wilderness, and
16 you will destroy this entire people." Then they set forward and said to
him, "Let us build sheep pens here for our livestock and towns for our children.
17 But we will arm ourselves and go ahead of the Israelites until we have seen
them safely to their place. Meanwhile, our children will remain in the fortified
18 towns, protected from the inhabitants of the land. We will not return to our
homes until every one of the Israelites has taken possession of his inheritance.
19 We, however, will not take possession with them on the far side of the Jordan,
for our inheritance will be on the east side of the Jordan."
20 Moshe replied to them, "If you do this – if you arm yourselves for battle before SHEVI'I /REVI'I/
21 the LORD, and each of your armed men crosses the Jordan before the LORD
22 until He has driven out His enemies before Him, and the land has been subdued

רש״י

יד **לספות.** כמו: "ספו שנה על שנה" (ישעיה כט, א), "עולותיכם ספו" וגו' (ירמיה ז, כא), לשון תוספת:

טז **נבנה למקננו פה.** חסים היו על ממונם יותר מבניהם ובנותיהם, שהקדימו מקניהם לטפם. אמר להם משה: לא כן, עשו העקר עקר והטפל טפל, בנו לכם תחלה ערים לטפכם ואחר כך גדרות לצאנכם (להלן פסוק כד):

יז **ואנחנו נחלץ חשים.** נזדין מהירים, כמו: "מהר שלל חש בז" (ישעיה ח, א), "ימהר יחישה" (שם ה, יט): [**לפני בני ישראל.** בראשי גיסות, מתוך שגבורים היו, שכן נאמר בגד: "וטרף זרוע אף קדקד" (דברים לג, כ). ואף משה חזר ופרש להם באלה הדברים: "ואצו אתכם בעת ההוא וגו' חלוצים תעברו לפני אחיכם בני ישראל כל בני חיל" (דברים ג, יח), וביריחו כתיב: "והחלוץ הלך לפניהם" (יהושע ו, יג), זה ראובן וגד שקימו תנאם: – תוספת מדפיס שמעיה שהעיד: "אני רבי להגיה"] **וישב טפנו.** בעודנו אצל אחינו: **בערי המבצר.** שנבנה עכשיו:

יט **מעבר לירדן וגו'.** בעבר המערבי: **כי באה נחלתנו.** כבר קבלנוה בעבר המזרחי:

a double condition, both positive and negative: if we do this, these will be the consequences, but if we fail to do this, those will be the consequences. They agree on objective criteria to assess the fulfillment of the conditions, and Moshe leaves them no escape from their commitment. The Reubenites and Gadites will not return to the east bank of the Jordan until all the other tribes are safely settled in their territories. And so it happens, as narrated in the book of Joshua:

> Then Yehoshua summoned the Reubenites, the Gadites, and half the tribe of Menashe and said to them, "You have performed everything that Moshe, the LORD's servant, commanded you, and you have obeyed me in all that I commanded you. You have not abandoned your brothers all this time – to this very day – and you have fulfilled the charge of the LORD your God's command. Now the LORD your God has granted rest to your brothers, as He promised them, so turn now and make your way home to the lands of your holding, which Moshe, the LORD's servant, assigned to you beyond the Jordan. (Josh. 22:1–4)

Conflict has been averted. The Reubenites and Gadites achieve what they want but the interests of the other tribes and of the nation as a whole are secured.

יד שָׁנָה עַד־תֹּם כָּל־הַדּוֹר הָעֹשֶׂה הָרַע בְּעֵינֵי יהוה: וְהִנֵּה קַמְתֶּם תַּחַת
אֲבֹתֵיכֶם תַּרְבּוּת אֲנָשִׁים חַטָּאִים לִסְפּוֹת עוֹד עַל חֲרוֹן אַף־יהוה
טו אֶל־יִשְׂרָאֵל: כִּי תְשׁוּבֻן מֵאַחֲרָיו וְיָסַף עוֹד לְהַנִּיחוֹ בַּמִּדְבָּר וְשִׁחַתֶּם
טז לְכָל־הָעָם הַזֶּה: וַיִּגְּשׁוּ אֵלָיו וַיֹּאמְרוּ גִּדְרֹת צֹאן נִבְנֶה
יז לְמִקְנֵנוּ פֹּה וְעָרִים לְטַפֵּנוּ: וַאֲנַחְנוּ נֵחָלֵץ חֻשִׁים לִפְנֵי בְּנֵי יִשְׂרָאֵל עַד
אֲשֶׁר אִם־הֲבִיאֹנֻם אֶל־מְקוֹמָם וְיָשַׁב טַפֵּנוּ בְּעָרֵי הַמִּבְצָר מִפְּנֵי יֹשְׁבֵי
יח יט הָאָרֶץ: לֹא נָשׁוּב אֶל־בָּתֵּינוּ עַד הִתְנַחֵל בְּנֵי יִשְׂרָאֵל אִישׁ נַחֲלָתוֹ: כִּי
לֹא נִנְחַל אִתָּם מֵעֵבֶר לַיַּרְדֵּן וָהָלְאָה כִּי בָאָה נַחֲלָתֵנוּ אֵלֵינוּ מֵעֵבֶר
הַיַּרְדֵּן מִזְרָחָה:
כ וַיֹּאמֶר אֲלֵיהֶם מֹשֶׁה אִם־תַּעֲשׂוּן אֶת־הַדָּבָר הַזֶּה אִם־תֵּחָלְצוּ לִפְנֵי שביעי /רביעי/
כא יהוה לַמִּלְחָמָה: וְעָבַר לָכֶם כָּל־חָלוּץ אֶת־הַיַּרְדֵּן לִפְנֵי יהוה עַד
כב הוֹרִישׁוֹ אֶת־אֹיְבָיו מִפָּנָיו: וְנִכְבְּשָׁה הָאָרֶץ לִפְנֵי יהוה וְאַחַר תָּשֻׁבוּ

אונקלוס

שְׁנִין, עַד דִּסַף כָּל דָּרָא, דַּעֲבַד דְּבִישׁ קֳדָם יְיָ: יד וְהָא קַמְתּוּן, בָּתַר אֲבָהָתְכוֹן, תַּלְמִידֵי גֻּבְרַיָּא חַיָּבַיָּא, לְאוֹסָפָא עוֹד, עַל תְּקוֹף רֻגְזָא דַּיְיָ עַל יִשְׂרָאֵל: טו אֲרֵי תְתוּבוּן מִבָּתַר דַּחְלְתֵיהּ, וְיוֹסֵיף עוֹד, לְאוֹחָרוּתְהוֹן בְּמַדְבְּרָא, וּתְחַבְּלוּן לְכָל עַמָּא הָדֵין: טז וּקְרִיבוּ לְוָתֵיהּ וַאֲמַרוּ, חַטְרִין דְּעָן, נִבְנֵי לִבְעִירַנָא הָכָא, וְקִרְוִין לְטַפְלַנָא: יז וַאֲנַחְנָא נִזְדָּרֵז מְבַעִין, קֳדָם בְּנֵי יִשְׂרָאֵל, עַד דְּנָעֵילִנּוּן לְאַתְרְהוֹן, וְיִתֵּיב טַפְלַנָא בְּקִרְוִין כְּרִיכָן, מִן קֳדָם יָתְבֵי אַרְעָא: יח לָא נְתוּב לְבָתַּנָא, עַד דְּיַחְסְנוּן בְּנֵי יִשְׂרָאֵל, גְּבַר אַחְסַנְתֵּיהּ: יט אֲרֵי לָא נַחְסֵין עִמְּהוֹן, מֵעִבְרָא לְיַרְדְּנָא וּלְהַלְאָה, אֲרֵי קַבֵּילְנָא אַחְסַנְתָּנָא לָנָא, מֵעִבְרָא לְיַרְדְּנָא מַדִּנְחָא: כ וַאֲמַר לְהוֹן מֹשֶׁה, אִם תַּעְבְּדוּן יָת פִּתְגָּמָא הָדֵין, אִם תִּזְדָּרְזוּן, קֳדָם עַמָּא דַּיְיָ לִקְרָבָא: כא וְיִעְבַּר לְכוֹן כָּל דִּמְזָרַז, יָת יַרְדְּנָא קֳדָם עַמָּא דַּיְיָ, עַד דִּיתָרֵיךְ, יָת בַּעֲלֵי דְּבָבוֹהִי מִן קֳדָמוֹהִי: כב וְתִתְכְּבֵישׁ אַרְעָא, קֳדָם

32:16 וַיִּגְּשׁוּ אֵלָיו *Then they set forward* – The tribes do not argue with Moshe's claim. They accept its validity, but they point out that his concern is not incompatible with their own objectives. They are able to invent an option for mutual gain. If you allow us to make temporary provisions for our cattle and children, they say, we will not only fight in the army. We will be its advance guard. We will benefit, knowing that our request has been granted. The nation will benefit by our willingness to take on the most demanding military task.

32:20 אִם־תַּעֲשׂוּן אֶת־הַדָּבָר הַזֶּה *If you do this* – Moshe recognizes the fact that the two and a half tribes have met his objections. He restates their position to make sure he and they have understood the proposal and they are ready to stand by it. He extracts from them agreement to a *tenai kaful*,

before the LORD – then you may return and be clear before the LORD and
23 before Israel, and this land will be yours as a possession before the LORD. But if
you do not do this, you will have sinned against the LORD, and know that your
24 sin will find you. Build towns for your children and pens for your flocks, but
25 do what you have promised." The people of Gad and Reuven replied to Moshe,
26 "Your servants will do just as my lord charges us. Our children, wives, livestock,
27 and all our animals will remain here in the towns of Gilad, but your servants, all
equipped for war, will cross over to do battle before the LORD, as my lord has
28 said." Moshe gave instructions concerning them to Elazar the priest, Yehoshua

רש"י

כד) **לְצֹנַאֲכֶם.** תֵּבָה זוֹ מִגִּזְרַת "צֹנֶה וַאֲלָפִים כֻּלָּם" (תהלים ח, ח), שֶׁאֵין בּוֹ אָלֶ"ף מַפְסִיק בֵּין נוּ"ן לַצַּדִ"י, וְאָלֶ"ף שֶׁבָּא כָּאן אַחַר הַנּוּ"ן, בִּמְקוֹם הֵ"א שֶׁל "צֹנֶה" הוּא. מִיסוֹדוֹ שֶׁל רַבִּי מֹשֶׁה לָמַדְתִּי: **וְהַיֹּצֵא מִפִּיכֶם תַּעֲשׂוּ.** לַגָּבֹהַּ, שֶׁקִּבַּלְתֶּם עֲלֵיכֶם לַעֲבֹר לַמִּלְחָמָה עַד כִּבּוּשׁ וְחִלּוּק, שֶׁמֹּשֶׁה לֹא בִקֵּשׁ מֵהֶם אֶלָּא "וְנִכְבְּשָׁה... וְאַחַר תָּשֻׁבוּ" (לעיל פסוק כב), וְהֵם קִבְּלוּ עֲלֵיהֶם "עַד הִתְנַחֵל" (לעיל פסוק יח), הֲרֵי הוֹסִיפוּ לְהִתְעַכֵּב שֶׁבַע שֶׁחִלְּקוּ, וְכֵן עָשׂוּ:

כה) **וַיֹּאמֶר בְּנֵי גָד.** כֻּלָּם כְּאִישׁ אֶחָד:

כח) **וַיְצַו לָהֶם.** כְּמוֹ 'עֲלֵיהֶם', וְעַל תְּנָאָם מִנָּה אֶלְעָזָר וִיהוֹשֻׁעַ, כְּמוֹ: "ה' יִלָּחֵם לָכֶם" (שמות יד, יד):

said to him, 'Let us build sheep pens here for our livestock and towns for our children'" (Num. 32:16). Moshe replied: "Build towns for your children, and pens for your flocks, but do what you have promised" (32:24).

Note the ordering of the nouns here. The men of Reuven and Gad put property before people: they speak of their flocks first, their children second. Moshe reverses the order. As Rashi notes (on Num. 32:16):

> They paid more regard to their property than to their sons and daughters, because they mentioned their cattle before the children. Moshe said to them: "Not so. Make the main thing primary and the subordinate thing secondary. First build cities for your children, and only then, folds for your flocks."

A midrash (Bemidbar Rabba 22:9) makes the same point through an ingenious interpretation of a verse in Ecclesiastes: "A wise man's mind is to his right, as the mind of a fool is to his left" (Eccl. 10:2). The midrash identifies "right" with Torah and life: "At his right hand, darting fire" (Deut. 33:2). "Left," by contrast, refers to worldly goods: "Long life is in its right hand; in its left hand is wealth and honor" (Prov. 3:16).

Hence, infers the midrash, the men of Reuven and Gad put "wealth and honor" before faith and posterity. Moshe hints that their priorities are wrong. The midrash continues: "The Holy One, blessed be He, said to them: 'Seeing that you have shown greater love for your cattle than for human souls, by your life, there will be no blessing in it.'"

This will turn out to be not a minor incident in the wilderness long ago, but a consistent pattern throughout Jewish history. The fate of Jewish communities was determined by their decision to put children and their education first. The Rabbis ruled that "any town that lacks children at school is to be excommunicated" (Shabbat 119b). Already in the first century, the Jewish community in Israel had established a network of schools at which attendance was compulsory (Bava Batra 21a) – the first such system in history.

Moshe's implied rebuke to the tribes of Reuven and Gad is a fundamental statement of Jewish priorities. Property is secondary, children primary. Those who invest in the future have a future. It is not what we own that gives us a share in eternity, but those to whom we give birth and the effort we make to ensure that they carry our faith and way of life into the next generation.

וִהְיִיתֶם נְקִיִּם מֵיהוָה וּמִיִּשְׂרָאֵל וְהָיְתָה הָאָרֶץ הַזֹּאת לָכֶם לַאֲחֻזָּה
כג לִפְנֵי יְהוָה: וְאִם־לֹא תַעֲשׂוּן כֵּן הִנֵּה חֲטָאתֶם לַיהוָה וּדְעוּ חַטַּאתְכֶם
כד אֲשֶׁר תִּמְצָא אֶתְכֶם: בְּנוּ־לָכֶם עָרִים לְטַפְּכֶם וּגְדֵרֹת לְצֹנַאֲכֶם וְהַיֹּצֵא
כה מִפִּיכֶם תַּעֲשׂוּ: וַיֹּאמֶר בְּנֵי־גָד וּבְנֵי רְאוּבֵן אֶל־מֹשֶׁה לֵאמֹר עֲבָדֶיךָ
כו יַעֲשׂוּ כַּאֲשֶׁר אֲדֹנִי מְצַוֶּה: טַפֵּנוּ נָשֵׁינוּ מִקְנֵנוּ וְכָל־בְּהֶמְתֵּנוּ יִהְיוּ־שָׁם
כז בְּעָרֵי הַגִּלְעָד: וַעֲבָדֶיךָ יַעַבְרוּ כָּל־חֲלוּץ צָבָא לִפְנֵי יְהוָה לַמִּלְחָמָה
כח כַּאֲשֶׁר אֲדֹנִי דֹּבֵר: וַיְצַו לָהֶם מֹשֶׁה אֵת אֶלְעָזָר הַכֹּהֵן וְאֵת יְהוֹשֻׁעַ

אונקלוס

עַמָּא דַיי וּבָתַר כֵּן תְּתוּבוּן, וּתְהוֹן זַכָּאִין, קֳדָם יי וּמִיִּשְׂרָאֵל, וּתְהֵי, אַרְעָא הָדָא לְכוֹן, לְאַחְסָנָא קֳדָם יי: כג וְאִם לָא תַעְבְּדוּן כֵּן, הָא חַבְתּוּן קֳדָם יי, וְדַעוּ חוֹבַתְכוֹן, דְּתַשְׁכַּח יָתְכוֹן: כד בְּנוֹ לְכוֹן קִרְוִין לְטַפְלְכוֹן, וְחַטְרִין לְעָנְכוֹן, וּדְיִפּוֹק מִפֻּמְכוֹן תַּעְבְּדוּן: כה וַאֲמַר בְּנֵי גָד וּבְנֵי רְאוּבֵן, לְמֹשֶׁה לְמֵימַר, עַבְדָּךְ יַעְבְּדוּן, כְּמָא דְּרִבּוֹנִי מְפַקֵּיד: כו טַפְלַנָא נְשַׁנָא, גֵּיתָנָא וְכָל בְּעִירַנָא, יְהוֹן תַּמָּן בְּקִרְוֵי גִלְעָד: כז וְעַבְדָּךְ יִעְבְּרוּן, כָּל מְזָרַז חֵילָא, קֳדָם עַמָּא דַיי לִקְרָבָא, כְּמָא דְּרִבּוֹנִי מְמַלֵּיל: כח וּפַקֵּיד לְהוֹן מֹשֶׁה, יָת אֶלְעָזָר כָּהֲנָא, וְיָת יְהוֹשֻׁעַ

32:22 וִהְיִיתֶם נְקִיִּם מֵיהוָה וּמִיִּשְׂרָאֵל *Be clear before the* Lord *and before Israel* – We learn from this that it is not enough to do what is right in the eyes of God. One must also act in such a way as to be seen to have done right in the eyes of one's fellow man. That is the rule of *viheyitem nekiyim*, "Be clear before the Lord and before Israel."

This concern became the basis of two halakhic principles. The first is known as *ḥashad*, "suspicion," namely, that certain acts, permitted in themselves, are forbidden on the grounds that performing them may lead others to suspect one of doing something forbidden. A closely related halakhic principle is the idea known as *marit haayin*, "appearances." These twin principles of *ḥashad* and *marit haayin* mean that we should act in such a way as to be held as a role model and that, just as a book of instructions should be unambiguous, so should be our conduct. People should be able to observe the way we behave and learn from us how a Jew should live.

These rules apply to every Jew, not just to religious leaders. Each of us is bidden to become a role model. We are not allowed to say, when we have acted in a way conducive to suspicion, "I have done nothing wrong; to the contrary, the other person, by harboring doubts about me, is in the wrong." To be sure, he is. But that does not relieve us of the responsibility to conduct our lives in a way that is above suspicion. Each of us must play our part in constructing a society of mutual respect.

Suspicion is a pervasive feature of social life. Judaism – a central project of which is the construction of a gracious society built on responsibility and trust – confronts the problem from both directions. On the one hand, it commands us not to harbor suspicions but to judge people generously. On the other, it bids each of us to act in a way that is above suspicion, keeping (as the rabbis put it) "far from unseemly conduct, from whatever resembles it, and from what may merely appear to resemble it" (Bemidbar Rabba 10:8).

We will not always succeed. Despite our best endeavors, others may still accuse us (as they accused Moshe) of things of which we are genuinely innocent. Yet we must do our best, by being charitable in our judgment of others and scrupulous in the way we conduct ourselves.

32:24 עָרִים לְטַפְּכֶם וּגְדֵרֹת לְצֹנַאֲכֶם *Towns for your children and pens for your flocks* – Let us listen carefully to what the Reubenites and Gadites said: "Then they set forward and

29 son of Nun, and the family heads of the Israelite tribes. Moshe said to them, "If
the men of Gad and Reuven cross the Jordan with you, each equipped for battle
before the LORD, and the land is subdued before you, then you shall give them
30 the land of Gilad as a possession. But if they do not cross with you, equipped
for war, then they must have their possession with you in the land of Canaan."
31 The Gadites and the Reubenites answered, "What the LORD has spoken to your
32 servants, we will do. We will cross into the land of Canaan equipped for war
before the LORD, and we shall then have our hereditary land across the Jordan."
33 So Moshe gave to them – the people of Gad and Reuven, and half the tribe of
Menashe son of Yosef – the kingdom of Siḥon, king of the Amorites, and the
kingdom of Og, king of Bashan, the land along with its towns and the territory of
34 35 the surrounding towns. The Gadites rebuilt Divon, Atarot, Aroer, Atrot Shofan,
36 Yazer, Yogbeha, Beit Nimra, and Beit Haran, as fortified towns and enclosures for
37 38 flocks. The Reubenites built Ḥeshbon, Elaleh, Kiryatayim, Nevo and Baal Meon
– the names of which were changed – and Sivma. They named the cities that they
39 built up. The descendants of Makhir son of Menashe went to Gilad and captured
40 it, driving out the Amorites who were there. So Moshe gave Gilad to Makhir son MAFTIR
41 of Menashe, and he settled there. Yair son of Menashe went and captured their
42 villages, naming them Hamlets of Yair. Novaḥ went and captured Kenat and its
surrounding villages, renaming it Novaḥ after himself.

The haftara for Parashat Matot is on page 1600.
Read this haftara on the first Shabbat after the Seventeenth of Tamuz.

אונקלוס

בַּר נוּן, וְיָת רֵישֵׁי, אֲבָהָת שִׁבְטַיָּא לִבְנֵי יִשְׂרָאֵל: כט וַאֲמַר מֹשֶׁה לְהוֹן, אִם יִעְבְּרוּן בְּנֵי גָד וּבְנֵי רְאוּבֵן עִמְּכוֹן, יָת יַרְדְּנָא, כָּל דִּמְזָרַז לִקְרָבָא קֳדָם עַמָּא דַיְיָ, וְתִתְכְּבֵישׁ אַרְעָא קֳדָמֵיכוֹן, וְתִתְּנוּן לְהוֹן, יָת אֲרַע גִּלְעָד לְאַחְסָנָא: ל וְאִם לָא יִעְבְּרוּן, מְזָרְזִין עִמְּכוֹן, וְיַחְסְנוּן בֵּינֵיכוֹן בְּאַרְעָא דִכְנָעַן: לא וַאֲתִיבוּ בְּנֵי גָד, וּבְנֵי רְאוּבֵן לְמֵימַר, יָת דְּמַלֵּיל יְיָ, לְעַבְדָּךְ כֵּן נַעְבֵּיד: לב נַחְנָא נִעְבַּר מְזָרְזִין, קֳדָם עַמָּא דַיְיָ לְאַרְעָא דִכְנָעַן, וְעִמַּנָא אֲחֻדַת אַחְסָנְתָנָא, מֵעִבְרָא לְיַרְדְּנָא: לג וִיהַב לְהוֹן מֹשֶׁה, לִבְנֵי גָד וְלִבְנֵי רְאוּבֵן, וּלְפַלְגוּת שִׁבְטָא דִמְנַשֶּׁה

רש״י

לב וְאִתָּנוּ אֲחֻזַּת נַחֲלָתֵנוּ. כְּלוֹמַר, בְּיָדֵנוּ וּבִרְשׁוּתֵנוּ תְּהִי אֲחֻזַּת נַחֲלָתֵנוּ מֵעֵבֶר הַזֶּה:

לו עָרֵי מִבְצָר וְגִדְרֹת צֹאן. זֶה סוֹף פָּסוּק מוּסָב עַל תְּחִלַּת הָעִנְיָן, "וַיִּבְנוּ בְנֵי גָד" אֶת הֶעָרִים הַלָּלוּ לִהְיוֹת "עָרֵי מִבְצָר וְגִדְרֹת צֹאן":

לח וְאֶת נְבוֹ וְאֶת בַּעַל מְעוֹן מוּסַבֹּת שֵׁם. נְבוֹ וּבַעַל מְעוֹן שְׁמוֹת עֲבוֹדָה זָרָה הֵם, וְהָיוּ הָאֱמוֹרִיִּים קוֹרִים עָרֵיהֶם עַל שֵׁם עֲבוֹדָה זָרָה שֶׁלָּהֶם, וּבְנֵי רְאוּבֵן הֵסֵבּוּ אֶת שְׁמָם לְשֵׁמוֹת אֲחֵרִים, וְזֶהוּ: "מוּסַבֹּת שֵׁם", נְבוֹ וּבַעַל מְעוֹן מוּסַבּוֹת לְשֵׁם אַחֵר: וְאֶת שִׂבְמָה. הִיא שְׂבָם הָאֲמוּרָה לְמַעְלָה (פסוק ג):

לט וַיּוֹרֶשׁ. כְּתַרְגּוּמוֹ: "וְתָרִיךְ", שֶׁתֵּיבַת 'רֵישׁ' מְשַׁמֶּשֶׁת שְׁתֵּי מַחְלָקוֹת: לְשׁוֹן יְרֻשָּׁה וּלְשׁוֹן הוֹרָשָׁה, שֶׁהוּא טֵרוּד וְתֵרוּךְ:

מא חַוֹּתֵיהֶם. "כַּפְרָנֵיהוֹן": וַיִּקְרָא אֶתְהֶן חַוֹּת יָאִיר. לְפִי שֶׁלֹּא הָיוּ לוֹ בָּנִים קְרָאָם בִּשְׁמוֹ לְזִכָּרוֹן:

מב וַיִּקְרָא לָה נֹבַח. "לָה" אֵינוֹ מַפִּיק הֵ"א, וְרָאִיתִי בִּיסוֹדוֹ שֶׁל רַבִּי מֹשֶׁה, לְפִי שֶׁלֹּא נִתְקַיֵּם לָהּ שֵׁם זֶה לְפִיכָךְ הוּא רָפֶה, שֶׁמַּשְׁמָעוּת מִדְרָשׁוֹ כְּמוֹ 'לֹא'. וְתָמֵהַּ אֲנִי, מַה יִּדְרֹשׁ בִּשְׁתֵּי תֵבוֹת הַדּוֹמִין לָהּ, "וַיֹּאמֶר לָה בֹעַז" (רות ב, יד), "לִבְנוֹת לָה בַיִת" (זכריה ה, יא):

כט בִּן־נוּן וְאֶת־רָאשֵׁי אֲבוֹת הַמַּטּוֹת לִבְנֵי יִשְׂרָאֵל: וַיֹּאמֶר מֹשֶׁה אֲלֵהֶם
אִם־יַעַבְרוּ בְנֵי־גָד וּבְנֵי־רְאוּבֵן ׀ אִתְּכֶם אֶת־הַיַּרְדֵּן כׇּל־חָלוּץ לַמִּלְחָמָה
לִפְנֵי יהוה וְנִכְבְּשָׁה הָאָרֶץ לִפְנֵיכֶם וּנְתַתֶּם לָהֶם אֶת־אֶרֶץ הַגִּלְעָד
ל לַאֲחֻזָּה: וְאִם־לֹא יַעַבְרוּ חֲלוּצִים אִתְּכֶם וְנֹאחֲזוּ בְתֹכְכֶם בְּאֶרֶץ כְּנָעַן:
לא וַיַּעֲנוּ בְנֵי־גָד וּבְנֵי רְאוּבֵן לֵאמֹר אֵת אֲשֶׁר דִּבֶּר יהוה אֶל־עֲבָדֶיךָ
לב כֵּן נַעֲשֶׂה: נַחְנוּ נַעֲבֹר חֲלוּצִים לִפְנֵי יהוה אֶרֶץ כְּנָעַן וְאִתָּנוּ אֲחֻזַּת
לג נַחֲלָתֵנוּ מֵעֵבֶר לַיַּרְדֵּן: וַיִּתֵּן לָהֶם ׀ מֹשֶׁה לִבְנֵי־גָד וְלִבְנֵי רְאוּבֵן וְלַחֲצִי ׀
שֵׁבֶט ׀ מְנַשֶּׁה בֶן־יוֹסֵף אֶת־מַמְלֶכֶת סִיחֹן מֶלֶךְ הָאֱמֹרִי וְאֶת־מַמְלֶכֶת
לד עוֹג מֶלֶךְ הַבָּשָׁן הָאָרֶץ לְעָרֶיהָ בִּגְבֻלֹת עָרֵי הָאָרֶץ סָבִיב: וַיִּבְנוּ בְנֵי־
לה גָד אֶת־דִּיבֹן וְאֶת־עֲטָרֹת וְאֵת עֲרֹעֵר: וְאֶת־עַטְרֹת שׁוֹפָן וְאֶת־יַעְזֵר
לו וְיׇגְבְּהָה: וְאֶת־בֵּית נִמְרָה וְאֶת־בֵּית הָרָן עָרֵי מִבְצָר וְגִדְרֹת צֹאן:
לז לח וּבְנֵי רְאוּבֵן בָּנוּ אֶת־חֶשְׁבּוֹן וְאֶת־אֶלְעָלֵא וְאֵת קִרְיָתָיִם: וְאֶת־נְבוֹ
וְאֶת־בַּעַל מְעוֹן מוּסַבֹּת שֵׁם וְאֶת־שִׂבְמָה וַיִּקְרְאוּ בְשֵׁמֹת אֶת־שְׁמוֹת
לט הֶעָרִים אֲשֶׁר בָּנוּ: וַיֵּלְכוּ בְּנֵי מָכִיר בֶּן־מְנַשֶּׁה גִּלְעָדָה וַיִּלְכְּדֻהָ וַיּוֹרֶשׁ
מ אֶת־הָאֱמֹרִי אֲשֶׁר־בָּהּ: וַיִּתֵּן מֹשֶׁה אֶת־הַגִּלְעָד לְמָכִיר בֶּן־מְנַשֶּׁה מפטיר
מא וַיֵּשֶׁב בָּהּ: וְיָאִיר בֶּן־מְנַשֶּׁה הָלַךְ וַיִּלְכֹּד אֶת־חַוֹּתֵיהֶם וַיִּקְרָא אֶתְהֶן
מב חַוֹּת יָאִיר: וְנֹבַח הָלַךְ וַיִּלְכֹּד אֶת־קְנָת וְאֶת־בְּנֹתֶיהָ וַיִּקְרָא לָה נֹבַח
בִּשְׁמוֹ:

The הפטרה *for* פרשת מטות *is on page 1601.*
Read this הפטרה *on the first* שבת *after the Seventeeth of* תמוז*.*

אונקלוס

בַּר יוֹסֵף, יָת מַלְכוּתֵיהּ דְּסִיחוֹן מַלְכָּא אֱמוֹרָאָה, וְיָת מַלְכוּתֵיהּ, דְּעוֹג מַלְכָּא דְמַתְנַן, אַרְעָא, לְקִרְוַהָא בִּתְחוּמִין, קִרְוֵי אַרְעָא סְחוֹר סְחוֹר: לד וּבְנוֹ בְנֵי גָד, יָת דִּיבוֹן וְיָת עֲטָרוֹת, וְיָת עֲרוֹעֵר: לה וְיָת עַטְרוֹת שׁוֹפָן, וְיָת יַעְזֵר וְרָמָתָא: לו וְיָת בֵּית נִמְרָה וְיָת בֵּית הָרָן, קִרְוִין כְּרִיכָן וְחַטְרִין דְּעָן: לז וּבְנֵי רְאוּבֵן בְּנוֹ, יָת חֶשְׁבּוֹן וְיָת אֶלְעָלֵא, וְיָת קִרְיָתָיִם: לח וְיָת נְבוֹ, וְיָת בַּעַל מְעוֹן, מַקְּפָן שְׁמָהָן וְיָת שִׂבְמָה, וּקְרוֹ בִשְׁמָהָן, יָת שְׁמָהָת קִרְוַיָּא דִּבְנוֹ: לט וַאֲזַלוּ, בְּנֵי מָכִיר בַּר מְנַשֶּׁה, לְגִלְעָד וְכַבְשׁוּהָא, וְתָרִיךְ יָת אֱמוֹרָאָה דְּבַהּ: מ וִיהַב מֹשֶׁה יָת גִּלְעָד, לְמָכִיר בַּר מְנַשֶּׁה, וִיתֵיב בַּהּ: מא וְיָאִיר בַּר מְנַשֶּׁה אֲזַל, וּכְבַשׁ יָת כַּפְרָנֵיהוֹן, וּקְרָא יָתְהוֹן כַּפְרָנֵי יָאִיר: מב וְנֹבַח אֲזַל, וּכְבַשׁ יָת קְנָת וְיָת כַּפְרָנַהָא, וּקְרָא לַהּ נֹבַח בִּשְׁמֵיהּ:

Parashat Masei

33 1 These were the journeys of the Israelites when they left Egypt by their divisions
2 under the leadership of Moshe and Aharon. Moshe recorded the places of their
setting out on every journey at the Lord's command. These are their journeys,

רש״י

לג א **אֵלֶּה מַסְעֵי.** לָמָּה נִכְתְּבוּ הַמַּסָּעוֹת הַלָּלוּ? לְהוֹדִיעַ חֲסָדָיו שֶׁל מָקוֹם, שֶׁאַף עַל פִּי שֶׁגָּזַר עֲלֵיהֶם לְטַלְטְלָם וְלַהֲנִיעָם בַּמִּדְבָּר, לֹא תֹאמַר שֶׁהָיוּ נָעִים וּמְטֻלְטָלִים מִמַּסָּע לְמַסָּע כָּל אַרְבָּעִים שָׁנָה וְלֹא הָיְתָה לָהֶם מְנוּחָה, שֶׁהֲרֵי אֵין כָּאן אֶלָּא אַרְבָּעִים וּשְׁתַּיִם מַסָּעוֹת, צֵא מֵהֶם אַרְבַּע עֶשְׂרֵה שֶׁכֻּלָּם הָיוּ בְּשָׁנָה רִאשׁוֹנָה קֹדֶם גְּזֵרָה, מִשֶּׁנָּסְעוּ מֵרַעְמְסֵס עַד שֶׁבָּאוּ לְרִתְמָה, שֶׁמִּשָּׁם נִשְׁתַּלְּחוּ מְרַגְּלִים, שֶׁנֶּאֱמַר: "וְאַחַר נָסְעוּ הָעָם מֵחֲצֵרוֹת" וְגוֹ' (לעיל יב, טז), "שְׁלַח לְךָ אֲנָשִׁים" וְגוֹ' (שם יג, ב), וְכָאן הוּא אוֹמֵר: "וַיִּסְעוּ מֵחֲצֵרֹת וַיַּחֲנוּ בְּרִתְמָה" (להלן פסוק יח), לָמַדְתָּ שֶׁהָיְתָה בְּמִדְבַּר פָּארָן. וְעוֹד הוֹצֵא מִשָּׁם שְׁמוֹנָה מַסָּעוֹת, שֶׁהָיוּ לְאַחַר מִיתַת אַהֲרֹן, מֵהֹר הָהָר עַד עַרְבוֹת מוֹאָב בִּשְׁנַת הָאַרְבָּעִים, נִמְצָא שֶׁכָּל שְׁמוֹנֶה וּשְׁלֹשִׁים שָׁנָה לֹא נָסְעוּ אֶלָּא עֶשְׂרִים מַסָּעוֹת. זֶה מִיסוֹדוֹ שֶׁל רַבִּי מֹשֶׁה. וְרַבִּי תַּנְחוּמָא דָּרַשׁ בּוֹ דְּרָשָׁה אַחֶרֶת: מָשָׁל לְמֶלֶךְ שֶׁהָיָה בְּנוֹ חוֹלֶה וְהוֹלִיכוֹ לְמָקוֹם רָחוֹק לְרַפְּאוֹתוֹ. כֵּיוָן שֶׁהָיוּ חוֹזְרִין, הִתְחִיל אָבִיו מוֹנֶה כָּל הַמַּסָּעוֹת. אָמַר לוֹ: כָּאן יָשַׁנְנוּ, כָּאן הוּקַרְנוּ, כָּאן חָשַׁשְׁתָּ אֶת רֹאשְׁךָ וְכוּ' (תנחומא ג):

33:2 **לְמַסְעֵיהֶם עַל־פִּי יהוה** *Every journey at the Lord's command* – The Jewish story began when Avraham first heard the words *lekh lekha,* with their call to leave where he was and travel "to the land that I will show you" (Gen. 12:1). We are the people who travel. We are the people who do not stand still. We are the people for whom time itself is a journey through the wilderness in search of the Promised Land.

This is a familiar theme from the world of myth. In many cultures, stories are told about the journey of the hero. Joseph Campbell analyzed these tales in his book *The Hero with a Thousand Faces*. Nonetheless, the Jewish story is different in significant ways:

1. The journey, set out in the books of Exodus and Numbers, is undertaken by everyone – men, women, and children. It is as if, in Judaism, we are all heroes, or at least all summoned to a heroic challenge.
2. It takes longer than a single generation. Perhaps, had the spies not demoralized the nation with their report, it might have taken only a short while. But there is a deeper truth here. The Jewish journey began before we were born and it is our responsibility to hand it on to those who will continue it after us.
3. In myth, the hero usually encounters a major trial: an

The road from slavery to freedom is as long or short as it takes for people to develop the habits of responsibility for their and their children's future. Freedom means making sacrifices in the present for the sake of peace and prosperity in the future. It means obeying laws for the sake of the common good. It requires virtue, courage, and discipline. Parashat Masei is about the many small journeys it took before the people were ready to enter the land and begin to construct a society of freedom under the sovereignty of God.

The journey is Judaism's first metaphor for a life worth living. Judaism is not a state of being; it is about walking, about the way, about following the call of God. For Avraham, it was following the call. For Moshe and the Israelites it was following that pillar of cloud by day, and fire by night, across the wilderness. It is this journey that has inspired men and women throughout human history to dedicate their lives to the uncertain proposition that by constant struggle we can reduce suffering and enhance dignity not for ourselves alone but for all those amongst whom we live; that our lives have a moral purpose, that redemption can be sought in this world with all its imperfections, and that by our efforts we can leave society better than we found it. None of this is the work of a moment – it is a journey, stage by stage and step by step.

פרשת מסעי

לג א אֵלֶּה מַסְעֵי בְנֵי־יִשְׂרָאֵל אֲשֶׁר יָצְאוּ מֵאֶרֶץ מִצְרַיִם לְצִבְאֹתָם בְּיַד־ ל
ב מֹשֶׁה וְאַהֲרֹן׃ וַיִּכְתֹּב מֹשֶׁה אֶת־מוֹצָאֵיהֶם לְמַסְעֵיהֶם עַל־פִּי יְהוָה

אונקלוס

לג א אִלֵּין מַטְלָנֵי בְנֵי יִשְׂרָאֵל, דִּנְפַקוּ, מֵאַרְעָא דְמִצְרַיִם לְחֵילֵיהוֹן,
בִּידָא דְמֹשֶׁה וְאַהֲרֹן׃ ב וּכְתַב מֹשֶׁה, יָת מַפְּקָנֵיהוֹן, לְמַטְלָנֵיהוֹן
עַל מֵימְרָא דַייָ,

MASEI

Parashat Masei begins with an itinerary of the forty-two stopping points of the Israelites on their forty-year journey through the wilderness, culminating in their encampment on the plains of Moav, where they will stay until the death of Moshe. As we shall see, there is great significance to the lengthy descriptions of all their travels and sojourns. With their destination already close, the *parasha* sets out the boundaries of the Promised Land. It also specifies certain places that will become cities of refuge where people guilty of manslaughter are to be protected against possible vengeance on the part of a relative of the person who died. The *parasha*, and with it the book of Numbers, ends with a claim by the leaders of the tribe of Menashe that the ruling that the daughters of Tzelofḥad were entitled to inherit their late father's share in the land could mean that the land will be lost to the tribe if any of them marries members of another tribe. A divine decision resolves the conflict: the daughters have a right to inherit the land but must marry only within the tribe. This seemingly strange conclusion to the book of Numbers sheds important light on the theme of the book in its entirety.

THESE WERE THE JOURNEYS

"They set out from X and camped at Y. They set out from Y and camped at Z." The *parasha* begins with a recitation of the forty-two journeys the Israelites made during their years in the wilderness. It is for the most part a tedious recitation, deliberately so.

This is puzzling. The word "Torah," the name given to the five Mosaic books, means "instruction," "teaching," "guidance." It does not record events merely because they happened. Nowhere is this more manifest than in the book of Numbers, where almost thirty-eight of the forty wilderness years are passed over in silence, evidently because, although things happened in those years, they were mere events with no teaching to be drawn for the generations. Where then is the teaching in this list of place-names?

Look at a map and you will see that the distance between Egypt and the land of Israel is not far. In Genesis 12 we read of how Avraham traveled there after arriving in the land of Canaan because there was a famine and he needed to buy food. The physical journey is a matter of weeks, not years. The forty-year itinerary of Israel's travels, then, is a reminder for all time of what Nelson Mandela called "the long walk to freedom." The real journey to freedom is not a physical one. It is a mental, moral, and spiritual one. It is long, arduous, and demanding, and there are challenges and failures along the way. That is what the book of Numbers has been all about.

Rambam saw the journey through the desert not as a diversion, but as a necessary stage: a situation where, by sheer necessity, the people would acquire strength and endurance. He made this point in the course of his larger argument that it is impossible in human nature to go from one extreme to another, from the established way of doing things to a completely new one. If so, then the forty-two stopping points on the way may be a literary device to communicate just how many stages we must go through to get from here to there when the destination is liberty itself.

3 by the places from which they set out. They set out from Ramesses on the
fifteenth day of the first month. On the day after the Passover the Israelites
4 went out defiantly, before all the Egyptians' eyes, while the Egyptians were
burying their firstborns, whom the Lord had struck down, every one. The
5 Lord had executed judgments even against their gods. The Israelites set out
6 from Ramesses and camped at Sukkot. They set out from Sukkot and camped
7 at Etam on the edge of the wilderness. They set out from Etam and turned
8 back to Pi HaḤirot, which faces Baal Tzefon, and camped before Migdol. They
set out from Pi HaḤirot and passed through the sea into the wilderness – and
they made a three-day journey through the Wilderness of Etam and camped at
9 Mara. They set out from Mara and came to Eilim. At Eilim there were twelve
10 springs and seventy date palms, and they encamped there. They set out from
11 Eilim and camped by the Sea of Reeds. They set out from the Sea of Reeds SHENI
12 and camped in the Wilderness of Sin. They set out from the wilderness of Sin
13 14 and camped at Dofka. They set out from Dofka and camped at Alush. They
set out from Alush and camped at Refidim, where there was no water for the

but reality itself, seen as a journey we must all undertake, each with our own strengths and contributions to our people and to humanity.

33:5 סֻכֹּת *Sukkot* – The first stop on the journey is apparently named for the structures the freed Israelites were to live in for the rest of their lives. There is no more potent symbol of Jewish history than the sukka, the temporary dwelling. For that, for the greater part of four thousand years, is where Jews have lived. Our story has been one of exiles and dispersions, as if wandering in the wilderness was not just the fate of Moshe's generation but a recurring theme of Jewish life. In the Middle Ages alone, Jews were expelled from England in 1290, Vienna in 1421, Cologne in 1424, Bavaria in 1442, Milan in 1489, and most traumatically from Spain in 1492. In the late nineteenth century, the wave of pogroms in Eastern Europe sent millions of Jews into flight to the West, and these great migrations continue even today. Jewish history reads like a vast continuation of the stages of the Israelites' journey in this chapter: "They set out... and camped.... They set out... and camped." More than most, Jews have known insecurity, whether in the land of Israel or elsewhere. Too often, home turned out to be no more than a temporary dwelling, a sukka.

Yet with its genius for the unexpected, Judaism declared the festival of Sukkot to be not a time of sadness but the "season of our rejoicing." For the sukka in all its vulnerability symbolizes faith: the faith of a people who set out long ago on a risk-laden journey across a desert of space and time with no more protection than the sheltering Divine Presence. Sitting in the sukka underneath its canopy of leaves, I often think of my ancestors and their wanderings across Europe in search of safety, and I begin to understand how faith was their only home. It was fragile, chillingly exposed to the storms of prejudice and hate. But it proved stronger. Faith survived. The Jewish people has outlived all its persecutors.

To know that life is full of risk and yet to affirm it, to sense the full insecurity of the human situation and yet to rejoice: this, for me, is the essence of faith. Judaism is no comforting illusion that all is well in this dark world. It is instead the courage to celebrate in the midst of uncertainty and to rejoice even in the transitory shelter of the sukka, the Jewish symbol of home.

ג וְאֵ֥לֶּה מַסְעֵיהֶ֖ם לְמוֹצָאֵיהֶֽם׃ וַיִּסְע֤וּ מֵרַעְמְסֵס֙ בַּחֹ֣דֶשׁ הָֽרִאשׁ֔וֹן
בַּחֲמִשָּׁ֥ה עָשָׂ֛ר י֖וֹם לַחֹ֣דֶשׁ הָרִאשׁ֑וֹן מִמָּחֳרַ֣ת הַפֶּ֗סַח יָצְא֤וּ בְנֵֽי־יִשְׂרָאֵל֙
ד בְּיָ֣ד רָמָ֔ה לְעֵינֵ֖י כׇּל־מִצְרָֽיִם׃ וּמִצְרַ֣יִם מְקַבְּרִ֗ים אֵת֩ אֲשֶׁ֨ר הִכָּ֧ה יְהֹוָ֛ה
ה בָּהֶ֖ם כׇּל־בְּכ֑וֹר וּבֵאלֹ֣הֵיהֶ֔ם עָשָׂ֥ה יְהֹוָ֖ה שְׁפָטִֽים׃ וַיִּסְע֥וּ בְנֵֽי־יִשְׂרָאֵ֖ל
ו מֵֽרַעְמְסֵ֑ס וַֽיַּחֲנ֖וּ בְּסֻכֹּֽת׃ וַיִּסְע֖וּ מִסֻּכֹּ֑ת וַיַּחֲנ֣וּ בְאֵתָ֔ם אֲשֶׁ֖ר בִּקְצֵ֥ה
ז הַמִּדְבָּֽר׃ וַיִּסְעוּ֙ מֵֽאֵתָ֔ם וַיָּ֙שׇׁב֙ עַל־פִּ֣י הַחִירֹ֔ת אֲשֶׁ֥ר עַל־פְּנֵ֖י בַּ֣עַל צְפ֑וֹן
ח וַֽיַּחֲנ֖וּ לִפְנֵ֥י מִגְדֹּֽל׃ וַיִּסְעוּ֙ מִפְּנֵ֣י הַחִירֹ֔ת וַיַּעַבְר֥וּ בְתוֹךְ־הַיָּ֖ם הַמִּדְבָּ֑רָה
ט וַ֠יֵּלְכ֠וּ דֶּ֣רֶךְ שְׁלֹ֤שֶׁת יָמִים֙ בְּמִדְבַּ֣ר אֵתָ֔ם וַֽיַּחֲנ֖וּ בְּמָרָֽה׃ וַיִּסְעוּ֙ מִמָּרָ֔ה
וַיָּבֹ֖אוּ אֵילִ֑מָה וּ֠בְאֵילִ֠ם שְׁתֵּ֨ים עֶשְׂרֵ֜ה עֵינֹ֥ת מַ֛יִם וְשִׁבְעִ֥ים תְּמָרִ֖ים
י יא וַיַּחֲנוּ־שָֽׁם׃ וַיִּסְע֖וּ מֵאֵילִ֑ם וַֽיַּחֲנ֖וּ עַל־יַם־סֽוּף׃ וַיִּסְע֖וּ מִיַּם־ס֑וּף וַיַּחֲנ֖וּ שני
יב יג בְּמִדְבַּר־סִֽין׃ וַיִּסְע֖וּ מִמִּדְבַּר־סִ֑ין וַֽיַּחֲנ֖וּ בְּדׇפְקָֽה׃ וַיִּסְע֖וּ מִדׇּפְקָ֑ה
יד וַֽיַּחֲנ֖וּ בְּאָלֽוּשׁ׃ וַיִּסְעוּ֙ מֵֽאָל֔וּשׁ וַֽיַּחֲנוּ֙ בִּרְפִידִ֔ם וְלֹא־הָ֨יָה שָׁ֥ם מַ֛יִם

אונקלוס

וְאִלֵּין מַטְּלָנֵיהוֹן לְמַפְּקָנֵיהוֹן: ג וּנְטַלוּ מֵרַעְמְסֵס בְּיַרְחָא קַדְמָאָה, בַּחֲמֵישְׁתְּ עַסְרָא, יוֹמָא לְיַרְחָא קַדְמָאָה, מִבָּתַר פִּסְחָא, נְפַקוּ בְנֵי יִשְׂרָאֵל בְּרֵישׁ גְּלֵי, לְעֵינֵי כָּל מִצְרָאֵי: ד וּמִצְרָאֵי מְקַבְּרִין, יָת דִּקְטַל יְיָ, בְּהוֹן כָּל בֻּכְרָא, וּבְטַעֲוָתְהוֹן, עֲבַד יְיָ דִּינִין: ה וּנְטַלוּ בְנֵי יִשְׂרָאֵל מֵרַעְמְסֵס, וּשְׁרוֹ בְּסֻכּוֹת: ו וּנְטַלוּ מִסֻּכּוֹת, וּשְׁרוֹ בְּאֵיתָם, דִּבְסְטַר מַדְבְּרָא: ז וּנְטַלוּ מֵאֵיתָם, וְתָב עַל פּוּם חִירָתָא, דִּקְדָם בְּעֵיל צְפוֹן, וּשְׁרוֹ קֳדָם מִגְדּוֹל: ח וּנְטַלוּ מִן קֳדָם חִירָתָא, וַעֲבַרוּ בְּגוֹ יַמָּא בְּמַדְבְּרָא, וַאֲזַלוּ, מַהֲלַךְ תְּלָתָא יוֹמִין בְּמַדְבְּרָא דְּאֵיתָם, וּשְׁרוֹ בְּמָרָה: ט וּנְטַלוּ מִמָּרָה, וַאֲתוֹ לְאֵילִים, וּבְאֵילִים, תַּרְתֵּי עֲסַר, מַבּוּעִין דְּמַיִין, וְשַׁבְעִין דִּקְלִין וּשְׁרוֹ תַמָּן: י וּנְטַלוּ מֵאֵילִים, וּשְׁרוֹ עַל יַמָּא דְּסוּף: יא וּנְטַלוּ מִיַּמָּא דְּסוּף, וּשְׁרוֹ בְּמַדְבְּרָא דְּסִין: יב וּנְטַלוּ מִמַּדְבְּרָא דְּסִין, וּשְׁרוֹ בְּדָפְקָה: יג וּנְטַלוּ מִדָּפְקָה, וּשְׁרוֹ בְּאָלוּשׁ: יד וּנְטַלוּ מֵאָלוּשׁ, וּשְׁרוֹ בִּרְפִידִים, וְלָא הֲוָה תַמָּן מַיָּא,

adversary, a dragon, a dark force. He (it is usually a he) may even die and be resurrected. As Campbell puts it:

> A hero ventures forth from the world of common day into a region of supernatural wonder: fabulous forces are there encountered.…The hero comes back from this mysterious adventure with the power to bestow boons on his fellow man.

The Jewish story is different. The main adversary the Israelites encounter is themselves: their fears, their weaknesses, their constant urge to return and regress.

The Torah here is not myth but anti-myth. It focuses relentlessly on the human drama of courage versus fear and hope versus despair. It emphasizes the call, not to some larger-than-life hero but to all-of-us-together, given strength by our ties to our people's past and the bonds between us in the present. The Torah is not some fabled escape from reality

15 people to drink. They set out from Refidim and camped in the Sinai Desert.
16 17 They set out from the Sinai Desert and camped at Kivrot HaTaava. They set out
18 from Kivrot HaTaava and camped at Ḥatzerot. They set out from Ḥatzerot and
19 20 camped at Ritma. They set out from Ritma and camped at Rimon Peretz. They
21 set out from Rimon Peretz and camped at Livna. They set out from Livna and
22 23 camped at Risa. They set out from Risa and camped at Kehelata. They set out
24 from Kehelata and camped at Mount Shefer. They set out from Mount Shefer
25 and camped at Ḥarada. They set out from Ḥarada and camped at Mak'helot.
26 27 They set out from Mak'helot and camped at Taḥat. They set out from Taḥat
28 29 and camped at Teraḥ. They set out from Teraḥ and camped at Mitka. They set
30 out from Mitka and camped at Ḥashmona. They set out from Ḥashmona and
31 camped at Moserot. They set out from Moserot and camped at Benei Yaakan.
32 33 They set out from Benei Yaakan and camped at Ḥor HaGidgad. They set out
34 from Ḥor HaGidgad and camped at Yotvata. They set out from Yotvata and
35 camped at Avrona. They set out from Avrona and camped at Etzyon Gever.
36 They set out from Etzyon Gever and camped in the Wilderness of Tzin, that is,

רש״י

יח | וַיַּחֲנוּ בְּרִתְמָה. עַל שֵׁם לָשׁוֹן הָרָע שֶׁל מְרַגְּלִים, שֶׁנֶּאֱמַר: "מַה יִּתֵּן לְךָ וּמַה יֹּסִיף לָךְ לָשׁוֹן רְמִיָּה, חִצֵּי גִבּוֹר שְׁנוּנִים עִם גַּחֲלֵי רְתָמִים" (תהלים קכ, ג-ד):

recalcitrant, obstinate people complaining and rebelling against God. Yet the prophets in retrospect saw things differently. The wilderness was a kind of *yiḥud*, an alone-togetherness, in which the people and God bonded in love.

We can sharpen our understanding of the Israelites' desert period with reference to the work of anthropologist Arnold van Gennep, who focused attention on the importance of *rites of passage*. Societies develop rituals to mark the transition from one state to the next – from childhood to adulthood, for example, or from being single to being married – and they involve three stages. The first is *separation*, a symbolic break with the past. The last is *incorporation*, reentering society with a new identity. Between the two comes the crucial stage of *transition* when, having cast off one identity but not yet donned another, you are remade, reborn, refashioned.

Van Gennep used the term *liminal*, from the Latin word for "threshold," to describe this transitional state when you are in a kind of no-man's-land between the old and the new. That is what the wilderness signifies for Israel: liminal space between slavery and freedom, past and future, exile and return, Egypt and the Promised Land. The desert was the space that made transition and transformation possible. There, in no-man's-land, the Israelites, alone with God and with one another, could cast off one identity and assume another. There they could be reborn, no longer slaves to Pharaoh, instead servants of God, summoned to become "a kingdom of priests and a holy nation" (Ex. 19:6).

The desert thus became the birthplace of a wholly new relationship between God and humankind, a relationship built on covenant. Distant from the great centers of civilization, a people found themselves alone with God and there consummated a bond that neither exile nor tragedy could break. That is the moral truth at the beating heart of our faith: that it is not power or politics that link us to God, but love.

טו טז לָעָם לִשְׁתּוֹת׃ וַיִּסְעוּ מֵרְפִידִם וַיַּחֲנוּ בְּמִדְבַּר סִינָי׃ וַיִּסְעוּ מִמִּדְבַּר
יז סִינָי וַיַּחֲנוּ בְּקִבְרֹת הַתַּאֲוָה׃ וַיִּסְעוּ מִקִּבְרֹת הַתַּאֲוָה וַיַּחֲנוּ בַּחֲצֵרֹת׃
יח יט וַיִּסְעוּ מֵחֲצֵרֹת וַיַּחֲנוּ בְּרִתְמָה׃ וַיִּסְעוּ מֵרִתְמָה וַיַּחֲנוּ בְּרִמֹּן פָּרֶץ׃
כ כא כב וַיִּסְעוּ מֵרִמֹּן פָּרֶץ וַיַּחֲנוּ בְּלִבְנָה׃ וַיִּסְעוּ מִלִּבְנָה וַיַּחֲנוּ בְּרִסָּה׃ וַיִּסְעוּ
כג כד מֵרִסָּה וַיַּחֲנוּ בִּקְהֵלָתָה׃ וַיִּסְעוּ מִקְּהֵלָתָה וַיַּחֲנוּ בְּהַר־שָׁפֶר׃ וַיִּסְעוּ
כה כו מֵהַר־שָׁפֶר וַיַּחֲנוּ בַּחֲרָדָה׃ וַיִּסְעוּ מֵחֲרָדָה וַיַּחֲנוּ בְּמַקְהֵלֹת׃ וַיִּסְעוּ
כז כח מִמַּקְהֵלֹת וַיַּחֲנוּ בְּתָחַת׃ וַיִּסְעוּ מִתָּחַת וַיַּחֲנוּ בְּתָרַח׃ וַיִּסְעוּ מִתָּרַח
כט ל וַיַּחֲנוּ בְּמִתְקָה׃ וַיִּסְעוּ מִמִּתְקָה וַיַּחֲנוּ בְּחַשְׁמֹנָה׃ וַיִּסְעוּ מֵחַשְׁמֹנָה וַיַּחֲנוּ
לא לב בְּמֹסֵרוֹת׃ וַיִּסְעוּ מִמֹּסֵרוֹת וַיַּחֲנוּ בִּבְנֵי יַעֲקָן׃ וַיִּסְעוּ מִבְּנֵי יַעֲקָן וַיַּחֲנוּ
לג לד בְּחֹר הַגִּדְגָּד׃ וַיִּסְעוּ מֵחֹר הַגִּדְגָּד וַיַּחֲנוּ בְּיָטְבָתָה׃ וַיִּסְעוּ מִיָּטְבָתָה
לה לו וַיַּחֲנוּ בְּעַבְרֹנָה׃ וַיִּסְעוּ מֵעַבְרֹנָה וַיַּחֲנוּ בְּעֶצְיֹן גָּבֶר׃ וַיִּסְעוּ מֵעֶצְיֹן

אונקלוס

לְעַמָּא לְמִשְׁתֵּי: טו וּנְטַלוּ מֵרְפִידִים, וּשְׁרוֹ בְּמַדְבְּרָא דְסִינָי: טז וּנְטַלוּ
מִמַּדְבְּרָא דְסִינָי, וּשְׁרוֹ בְּקִבְרֵי דִמְשַׁאֲלֵי: יז וּנְטַלוּ מִקִּבְרֵי דִמְשַׁאֲלֵי,
וּשְׁרוֹ בַּחֲצֵרוֹת: יח וּנְטַלוּ מֵחֲצֵרוֹת, וּשְׁרוֹ בְּרִתְמָה: יט וּנְטַלוּ מֵרִתְמָה,
וּשְׁרוֹ בְּרִמּוֹן פָּרֶץ: כ וּנְטַלוּ מֵרִמּוֹן פָּרֶץ, וּשְׁרוֹ בְּלִבְנָה: כא וּנְטַלוּ מִלִּבְנָה,
וּשְׁרוֹ בְּרִסָּה: כב וּנְטַלוּ מֵרִסָּה, וּשְׁרוֹ בִּקְהֵלָתָה: כג וּנְטַלוּ מִקְּהֵלָתָה,
וּשְׁרוֹ בְּטוּרָא דְשָׁפֶר: כד וּנְטַלוּ מִטּוּרָא דְשָׁפֶר, וּשְׁרוֹ בַּחֲרָדָה: כה
וּנְטַלוּ מֵחֲרָדָה, וּשְׁרוֹ בְּמַקְהֵלוֹת: כו וּנְטַלוּ מִמַּקְהֵלוֹת, וּשְׁרוֹ בְּתָחַת:
כז וּנְטַלוּ מִתָּחַת, וּשְׁרוֹ בְּתָרַח: כח וּנְטַלוּ מִתָּרַח, וּשְׁרוֹ בְּמִתְקָה: כט
וּנְטַלוּ מִמִּתְקָה, וּשְׁרוֹ בְּחַשְׁמוֹנָה: ל וּנְטַלוּ מֵחַשְׁמוֹנָה, וּשְׁרוֹ בְּמוֹסֵרוֹת:
לא וּנְטַלוּ מִמּוֹסֵרוֹת, וּשְׁרוֹ בִּבְנֵי יַעֲקָן: לב וּנְטַלוּ מִבְּנֵי יַעֲקָן, וּשְׁרוֹ בְּחוֹר
גִּדְגָּד: לג וּנְטַלוּ מֵחוֹר גִּדְגָּד, וּשְׁרוֹ בְּיָטְבָתָה: לד וּנְטַלוּ מִיָּטְבָתָה, וּשְׁרוֹ
בְּעַבְרוֹנָה: לה וּנְטַלוּ מֵעַבְרוֹנָה, וּשְׁרוֹ בְּעֶצְיוֹן גָּבֶר: לו וּנְטַלוּ מֵעֶצְיוֹן

33:16 קִבְרֹת הַתַּאֲוָה *Kivrot HaTaava* – Difficult memories hide behind this place-name (see ch. 11). Yet including it as merely one element in a list has removed the sting, as hindsight often does. In later generations, the prophets remembered the wilderness years as the formative time in which the Israelites, having left Egypt and not yet entered the land, were alone with God. Their prophecies speak of the desert period as a honeymoon in which God and the people, imagined as bridegroom and bride, were alone together, consummating their union in love. Hoshea, speaking in God's name regarding a future second honeymoon with the Israelites, says:

> I will lead her back to the open desert and I will speak to her heart….
>
> She will return to Me in song as in the first days of her youth,
>
> As on the day when she came up out of the land of Egypt. (Hos. 2:16–17)

Yirmeyahu says in God's name:

> I recall on your behalf the devotion of your youth, your bridal love, when you followed Me into the wilderness, a land unseeded. (Jer. 2:2)

To be sure, in the Torah itself we see the Israelites as a

37 Kadesh. They set out from Kadesh and camped at Mount Hor, at the edge of
38 the land of Edom. And Aharon the priest ascended Mount Hor at the Lord's
command, and he died there in the fortieth year, on the first day of the fifth
39 month after the Israelites left Egypt. Aharon was one hundred and twenty-
40 three years old when he died on Mount Hor. And the Canaanite king
of Arad, who lived in the Negev in the land of Canaan, heard that the Israelites
41 42 were coming. They set out from Mount Hor and camped at Tzalmona. They
43 set out from Tzalmona and camped at Punon. They set out from Punon and
44 camped at Ovot. They set out from Ovot and camped at Iyei HaAvarim in the
45 46 territory of Moav. They set out from Iyim and camped at Divon Gad. They
47 set out from Divon Gad and camped at Almon Divlatayma. They set out
from Almon Divlatayma and camped in the Mountains of Avarim, before
48 Nevo. They set out from the Mountains of Avarim and camped in the plains
49 of Moav by the Jordan across from Yeriḥo. And they camped by the Jordan
50 from Beit HaYeshimot to Avel HaShitim in the plains of Moav. And SHELISHI /ḤAMISHI/
the Lord spoke to Moshe on the plains of Moav by the Jordan across from
51 Yeriḥo: "Speak to the Israelites. Say: When you cross the Jordan into the land
52 of Canaan, you shall drive out all the inhabitants of the land before you. You

רש״י

לח) **עַל פִּי ה׳.** מְלַמֵּד שֶׁמֵּת בִּנְשִׁיקָה:

מ) **וַיִּשְׁמַע הַכְּנַעֲנִי.** לְלַמֶּדְךָ שֶׁמִּיתַת אַהֲרֹן הִיא הַשְּׁמוּעָה, שֶׁנִּסְתַּלְּקוּ עַנְנֵי כָבוֹד, וְכַסָּבוּר שֶׁנִּתְּנָה רְשׁוּת לְהִלָּחֵם בְּיִשְׂרָאֵל, לְפִיכָךְ חָזַר וּכְתָבָהּ:

מד) **בְּעִיֵּי הָעֲבָרִים.** לְשׁוֹן חֲרָבוֹת וְגַלִּים, כְּמוֹ: "לְעִי הַשָּׂדֶה" (מיכה א, ו), "שָׂמוּ אֶת יְרוּשָׁלַםִ לְעִיִּים" (תהלים עט, א):

מט) **מִבֵּית הַיְשִׁמֹת עַד אָבֵל הַשִּׁטִּים.** כָּאן לִמֶּדְךָ שִׁעוּר מַחֲנֵה יִשְׂרָאֵל שְׁנֵים עָשָׂר מִיל, דְּאָמַר רַבָּה בַּר בַּר חָנָה: לְדִידִי חֲזֵי לִי הַהוּא אַתְרָא וְכוּ׳: **אָבֵל הַשִּׁטִּים.** מִישׁוֹר שֶׁל שִׁטִּים 'אָבֵל' שְׁמוֹ:

נא-נב) **כִּי אַתֶּם עֹבְרִים אֶת הַיַּרְדֵּן וְגוֹ׳ וְהוֹרַשְׁתֶּם וְגוֹ׳.** וַהֲלֹא כַּמָּה פְעָמִים הֻזְהֲרוּ עַל כָּךְ! אֶלָּא כָּךְ אָמַר לָהֶם מֹשֶׁה: כְּשֶׁאַתֶּם עוֹבְרִים

the encampments, we suffer burnout. Without the journey, we do not grow. Rabbi Aharon Lichtenstein illustrated this idea with a beautiful reading of Robert Frost's poem, "Stopping by Woods on a Snowy Evening":

> The woods are lovely, dark, and deep.
> But I have promises to keep,
> And miles to go before I sleep,
> And miles to go before I sleep.

Rabbi Lichtenstein analyzes the poem in terms of Kierkegaard's distinction between the aesthetic and ethical dimensions of life. The poet is enchanted by the aesthetic beauty of the scene, the soft silence of the falling snow, the dark dignity of the tall trees. He would love to stay here in this timeless moment, this eternity-in-an-hour. But he knows that life has an ethical dimension also, and this demands action, not just contemplation. He has promises to keep; he has duties toward the world. So he must walk on despite his fatigue. He has miles to go before he sleeps: he has work to do while the breath of life is within him.

For us as Jews, as for Robert Frost the poet, ethics takes priority over aesthetics. Yes, there are moments when we should, indeed must, pause to see the beauty of the world, but then, like the Israelites in Parashat Masei, we must move on, for – to ourselves and to God – we have promises to keep.

לז גֶּבֶר וַיַּחֲנוּ בְמִדְבַּר־צִן הִוא קָדֵשׁ: וַיִּסְעוּ מִקָּדֵשׁ וַיַּחֲנוּ בְּהֹר הָהָר
לח בִּקְצֵה אֶרֶץ אֱדוֹם: וַיַּעַל אַהֲרֹן הַכֹּהֵן אֶל־הֹר הָהָר עַל־פִּי יְהוָה וַיָּמָת
שָׁם בִּשְׁנַת הָאַרְבָּעִים לְצֵאת בְּנֵי־יִשְׂרָאֵל מֵאֶרֶץ מִצְרַיִם בַּחֹדֶשׁ
לט הַחֲמִישִׁי בְּאֶחָד לַחֹדֶשׁ: וְאַהֲרֹן בֶּן־שָׁלֹשׁ וְעֶשְׂרִים וּמְאַת שָׁנָה בְּמֹתוֹ
מ בְּהֹר הָהָר: וַיִּשְׁמַע הַכְּנַעֲנִי מֶלֶךְ עֲרָד וְהוּא־יֹשֵׁב
מא בַּנֶּגֶב בְּאֶרֶץ כְּנָעַן בְּבֹא בְּנֵי יִשְׂרָאֵל: וַיִּסְעוּ מֵהֹר הָהָר וַיַּחֲנוּ בְּצַלְמֹנָה:
מב מג מד וַיִּסְעוּ מִצַּלְמֹנָה וַיַּחֲנוּ בְּפוּנֹן: וַיִּסְעוּ מִפּוּנֹן וַיַּחֲנוּ בְּאֹבֹת: וַיִּסְעוּ מֵאֹבֹת
מה וַיַּחֲנוּ בְּעִיֵּי הָעֲבָרִים בִּגְבוּל מוֹאָב: וַיִּסְעוּ מֵעִיִּים וַיַּחֲנוּ בְּדִיבֹן גָּד:
מו מז וַיִּסְעוּ מִדִּיבֹן גָּד וַיַּחֲנוּ בְּעַלְמֹן דִּבְלָתָיְמָה: וַיִּסְעוּ מֵעַלְמֹן דִּבְלָתָיְמָה
מח וַיַּחֲנוּ בְּהָרֵי הָעֲבָרִים לִפְנֵי נְבוֹ: וַיִּסְעוּ מֵהָרֵי הָעֲבָרִים וַיַּחֲנוּ בְּעַרְבֹת
מט מוֹאָב עַל יַרְדֵּן יְרֵחוֹ: וַיַּחֲנוּ עַל־הַיַּרְדֵּן מִבֵּית הַיְשִׁמֹת עַד אָבֵל הַשִּׁטִּים
נ בְּעַרְבֹת מוֹאָב: וַיְדַבֵּר יְהוָה אֶל־מֹשֶׁה בְּעַרְבֹת מוֹאָב שלישי /חמישי/
נא עַל־יַרְדֵּן יְרֵחוֹ לֵאמֹר: דַּבֵּר אֶל־בְּנֵי יִשְׂרָאֵל וְאָמַרְתָּ אֲלֵהֶם כִּי אַתֶּם
נב עֹבְרִים אֶת־הַיַּרְדֵּן אֶל־אֶרֶץ כְּנָעַן: וְהוֹרַשְׁתֶּם אֶת־כָּל־יֹשְׁבֵי הָאָרֶץ

אונקלוס

גְּבַר, וּשְׁרוֹ בְּמַדְבְּרָא דְּצִין הִיא רְקָם: לז וּנְטַלוּ מֵרְקָם, וּשְׁרוֹ בְּהוֹר טוּרָא, בִּסְיָפֵי אֲרַעָא דֶּאֱדוֹם: לח וּסְלֵיק אַהֲרֹן כָּהֲנָא, לְהוֹר טוּרָא, עַל מֵימְרָא דַּייָ וּמִית תַּמָּן, בִּשְׁנַת אַרְבְּעִין, לְמִפַּק בְּנֵי יִשְׂרָאֵל מֵאַרְעָא דְּמִצְרַיִם, בְּיַרְחָא חֲמִישָׁאָה בְּחַד לְיַרְחָא: לט וְאַהֲרֹן, בַּר מְאָה וְעַסְרִין וּתְלָת שְׁנִין, כַּד מִית בְּהוֹר טוּרָא: מ וּשְׁמַע, כְּנַעֲנָאָה מַלְכָּא דַּעֲרָד, וְהוּא יָתֵיב בְּדָרוֹמָא בְּאַרְעָא דִּכְנָעַן, בְּמֵיתֵי בְּנֵי יִשְׂרָאֵל: מא וּנְטַלוּ מֵהוֹר טוּרָא, וּשְׁרוֹ בְּצַלְמוֹנָה: מב וּנְטַלוּ מִצַּלְמוֹנָה, וּשְׁרוֹ בְּפוּנוֹן: מג וּנְטַלוּ מִפּוּנוֹן, וּשְׁרוֹ בְּאוֹבוֹת: מד וּנְטַלוּ מֵאוֹבוֹת, וּשְׁרוֹ, בִּמְגִזַּת עִבְרָאֵי בִּתְחוּם מוֹאָב: מה וּנְטַלוּ מִמְּגִזָּתָא, וּשְׁרוֹ בְּדִיבוֹן גָּד: מו וּנְטַלוּ מִדִּיבוֹן גָּד, וּשְׁרוֹ בְּעַלְמוֹן דִּבְלָתָיְמָה: מז וּנְטַלוּ מֵעַלְמוֹן דִּבְלָתָיְמָה, וּשְׁרוֹ, בְּטוּרָא דְּעִבְרָאֵי קֳדָם נְבוֹ: מח וּנְטַלוּ מִטּוּרָא דְּעִבְרָאֵי, וּשְׁרוֹ בְּמֵישְׁרַיָּא דְּמוֹאָב, עַל יַרְדְּנָא דִּירֵיחוֹ: מט וּשְׁרוֹ עַל יַרְדְּנָא מִבֵּית יְשִׁימוֹת, עַד מֵישַׁר שִׁטִּין, בְּמֵישְׁרַיָּא דְּמוֹאָב: נ וּמַלֵּיל יְיָ, עִם מֹשֶׁה בְּמֵישְׁרַיָּא דְּמוֹאָב, עַל יַרְדְּנָא דִּירֵיחוֹ לְמֵימַר: נא מַלֵּיל עִם בְּנֵי יִשְׂרָאֵל, וְתֵימַר לְהוֹן, אֲרֵי אַתּוּן, עָבְרִין יָת יַרְדְּנָא לְאַרְעָא דִּכְנָעַן: נב וּתְתָרְכוּן, יָת כָּל יָתְבֵי אַרְעָא

33:48 וַיִּסְעוּ...וַיַּחֲנוּ *They set out... and camped* – The dialectic between setting out and encamping, walking and standing still, is part of the rhythm of Jewish life. Rabbi Avraham HaKohen Kook spoke of the two symbols in Bilam's blessing, "How good are your tents, Yaakov, your homes, O Israel" (Num. 24:5). Tents are for people on a journey. Homes are for people who have found permanence.

In life, there are journeys and encampments. Without

shall destroy all their carved images and all their molten idols and demolish all
53 their high shrines. You shall take possession of the land and settle there, for I
54 have given you the land to possess. You shall divide up the land by lot among
your clans: to a large clan give a large inheritance, and to a small one a small
inheritance. Whatever falls to them by lot will be theirs. According to your
55 ancestral tribes you shall inherit. But if you do not drive the inhabitants out
of the land before you, then those you allow to remain will be barbs in your

רש״י

בַּיַּרְדֵּן בַּיַּבָּשָׁה, עַל מְנָת כֵּן תַּעַבְרוּ, וְאִם לָאו, בָּאִים מַיִם וְשׁוֹטְפִין אֶתְכֶם. וְכֵן מָצִינוּ שֶׁאָמַר לָהֶם יְהוֹשֻׁעַ עוֹדָם בַּיַּרְדֵּן (יהושע ד, י). בְּמַסֶּכֶת סוֹטָה (לד ע״א) וּבְתוֹסֶפְתָּא דְּסוֹטָה (ח, ה):

נב) **וְהוֹרַשְׁתֶּם.** וְגֵרַשְׁתֶּם: **מַשְׂכִּיֹּתָם.** כְּתַרְגּוּמוֹ: ״בֵּית סִגְדַּתְהוֹן״, עַל שֵׁם שֶׁהָיוּ מְסוֹכְכִין אֶת הַקַּרְקַע בְּרִצְפַּת אַבְנֵי שַׁיִשׁ לְהִשְׁתַּחֲווֹת עָלֶיהָ בְּפִשּׁוּט יָדַיִם וְרַגְלַיִם, כִּדְכְתִיב: ״וְאֶבֶן מַשְׂכִּית... לְהִשְׁתַּחֲוֹת עָלֶיהָ״ (ויקרא כו, א): **מַסֵּכֹתָם.** כְּתַרְגּוּמוֹ: ״מַתְּכָתְהוֹן״:

נג) **וְהוֹרַשְׁתֶּם אֶת הָאָרֶץ.** וְהוֹרַשְׁתֶּם אוֹתָהּ מִיּוֹשְׁבֶיהָ, וְאָז ״וִישַׁבְתֶּם בָּהּ״ – תּוּכְלוּ לְהִתְקַיֵּם בָּהּ, וְאִם לָאו – לֹא תוּכְלוּ לְהִתְקַיֵּם בָּהּ:

נד) **אֶל אֲשֶׁר יֵצֵא לוֹ שָׁמָּה.** מִקְרָא קָצָר הוּא זֶה, אֶל מָקוֹם אֲשֶׁר יֵצֵא לוֹ שָׁמָּה הַגּוֹרָל לוֹ יִהְיֶה: **לְמַטּוֹת אֲבֹתֵיכֶם.** לְפִי חֶשְׁבּוֹן יוֹצְאֵי מִצְרַיִם. דָּבָר אַחֵר, בִּשְׁנֵים עָשָׂר גְּבוּלִין כְּמִנְיַן הַשְּׁבָטִים:

נה) **וְהָיָה אֲשֶׁר תּוֹתִירוּ מֵהֶם.** יִהְיוּ לָכֶם לְרָעָה: **לְשִׂכִּים בְּעֵינֵיכֶם.** לִיתֵדוֹת הַמְנַקְּרוֹת עֵינֵיכֶם. תַּרְגּוּם שֶׁל יְתֵדוֹת: ״סִכַּיָּא״: **וְלִצְנִנִים.** פּוֹתְרִים בּוֹ הַפּוֹתְרִים לְשׁוֹן מְשׂוּכַת קוֹצִים הַסּוֹכֶכֶת אֶתְכֶם, לִסְגֹּר וְלִכְלֹא אֶתְכֶם מֵאֵין יוֹצֵא וָבָא: **וְצָרְרוּ אֶתְכֶם.** כְּתַרְגּוּמוֹ:

is possible outside Israel, but it is a pale shadow of what it is in the land. There is a way of stating this non-mystically, in concepts and categories closer to ordinary experience.

The Torah is not merely a code of personal perfection. It is the framework for the construction of a society, a nation, a culture. Israel is the sole place on earth where Jews have had the sustained chance to create an entire society on Jewish lines. Only there are they able to construct a political system, an economy, and an environment on the template of Jewish values. There alone can Judaism be what it is meant to be – not just a code of conduct for individuals, but also and essentially the architectonics of a society.

But why Israel specifically? Because it has always been a key strategic location where three continents – Europe, Africa, and Asia – meet. Lacking the extended flat and fertile space of the Nile Delta or the Tigris-Euphrates valley, it could never be the base of an empire, but because of its location it was always sought after by empires. So it was politically vulnerable.

It was and is ecologically vulnerable, dependent on rains that are always unpredictable. Its existence could never be taken for granted. Small geographically and demographically, it would depend on outstanding achievement on the part of its people. This would depend, in turn, on their morale and sense of mission. Thus the prophets knew that without social justice and a sense of divine vocation, the nation would eventually fall and suffer exile again.

These are, as it were, the empirical foundations of the mysticism of HaLevi and Ramban. History tells us that the project of constructing a society under divine sovereignty in a vulnerable land is the highest of high-risk strategies. Yet the risk was worth taking. For only in Israel is God so close that you can feel Him in the sun and wind, sense Him just beyond the hills, hear Him in the inflections of everyday speech, breathe His presence in the early morning air and live, dangerously but confidently, under the shadow of His wings.

מִפְּנֵיכֶם וְאִבַּדְתֶּם אֵת כָּל־מַשְׂכִּיֹּתָם וְאֵת כָּל־צַלְמֵי מַסֵּכֹתָם תְּאַבֵּדוּ
נג וְאֵת כָּל־בָּמוֹתָם תַּשְׁמִידוּ׃ וְהוֹרַשְׁתֶּם אֶת־הָאָרֶץ וִישַׁבְתֶּם־בָּהּ כִּי
נד לָכֶם נָתַתִּי אֶת־הָאָרֶץ לָרֶשֶׁת אֹתָהּ׃ וְהִתְנַחַלְתֶּם אֶת־הָאָרֶץ בְּגוֹרָל
לְמִשְׁפְּחֹתֵיכֶם לָרַב תַּרְבּוּ אֶת־נַחֲלָתוֹ וְלַמְעַט תַּמְעִיט אֶת־נַחֲלָתוֹ
אֶל אֲשֶׁר־יֵצֵא לוֹ שָׁמָּה הַגּוֹרָל לוֹ יִהְיֶה לְמַטּוֹת אֲבֹתֵיכֶם תִּתְנֶחָלוּ׃
נה וְאִם־לֹא תוֹרִישׁוּ אֶת־יֹשְׁבֵי הָאָרֶץ מִפְּנֵיכֶם וְהָיָה אֲשֶׁר תּוֹתִירוּ
מֵהֶם לְשִׂכִּים בְּעֵינֵיכֶם וְלִצְנִינִם בְּצִדֵּיכֶם וְצָרְרוּ אֶתְכֶם עַל־הָאָרֶץ

אונקלוס

מִן קֳדָמֵיכוֹן, וּתְאַבְּדוּן, יָת כָּל בֵּית סִגְדַּתְהוֹן, וְיָת כָּל צַלְמֵי מַתְּכָתְהוֹן תְּאַבְּדוּן, וְיָת כָּל בָּמָתְהוֹן תְּשֵׁיצוֹן: נג וּתְתָרְכוּן יָת יָתְבֵי אַרְעָא וְתִתְּבוּן בַּהּ, אֲרֵי לְכוֹן, יְהַבִית יָת אַרְעָא לְמֵירַת יָתַהּ: נד וְתַחְסְנוּן יָת אַרְעָא בְּעַדְבָּא לְזַרְעֲיָתְכוֹן, לְסַגִּיאֵי, תַּסְגּוֹן יָת אַחְסַנְתְּהוֹן וְלִזְעֵירֵי תַּזְעֲרוּן יָת אַחְסַנְתְּהוֹן, לִדְיִפּוֹק לֵיהּ תַּמָּן, עַדְבָּא דִּילֵיהּ יְהֵי, לְשִׁבְטֵי אֲבָהָתְכוֹן תַּחְסְנוּן: נה וְאִם לָא תְתָרְכוּן, יָת יָתְבֵי אַרְעָא מִן קֳדָמֵיכוֹן, וִיהֵי דְּתַשְׁאֲרוּן מִנְּהוֹן, לְסִיעָן נָטְלִין זֵין לְקִבְלְכוֹן, וּלְמַשְׁרְיָן מַקְּפָנֵיכוֹן, וִיעִיקוּן לְכוֹן, עַל אַרְעָא,

THE LAND OF ISRAEL

The long journey is nearing its close. The Jordan is almost within sight. Finally we are reaching the end of the list of encampments, and God tells Moshe: "Take possession of the land and settle there" (Num. 33:53). This, according to Ramban (on Num. 33:53), is the source of the command to dwell in the land of Israel.

The centrality of the land of Israel to Judaism cannot be doubted. Whatever the subplots and subsidiary themes of Tanakh, its overarching narrative is the promise of and journey to the land. Jewish history begins with Avraham and Sara's journey to it. Tanakh as a whole ends with Koresh, king of Persia, granting permission to Jews, exiled in Babylon, to return to their land (II Chr. 36:23).

The paradox of Jewish history is that although a specific territory, the Holy Land, is at its heart, Jews have spent more time longing for it than dwelling in it. On the one hand, monotheism must understand God as non-territorial. The God of *everywhere* can be found *anywhere*. On the other hand, it must be impossible to live fully as a Jew outside Israel, for if not, Jews would not have been commanded to go there initially, or to return subsequently. On this tension, the Jewish existence is built.

What then is special about Israel? In *The Kuzari*, Rabbi Yehuda HaLevi says that different environments have different ecologies. Just as there are some countries, climates, and soils particularly suited to growing vines, so there is a country, Israel, particularly suited to growing prophets – indeed a whole divinely inspired people (*Kuzari* II:9–12). Ramban (on Lev. 18:25) gives a different explanation:

> Though every land and nation is under the overarching sovereignty of God, only Israel is *directly* so. Others are ruled by intermediaries earthly and heavenly. Their fate is governed by other factors. Only in the land and people of Israel do we find a nation's fortunes and misfortunes directly attributable to their relationship with God.

HaLevi and Ramban both expound what we might call *mystical geography*. For both of them, religious experience

eyes and thorns in your sides. They will harass you in the land where you settle.
56 Then, what I intended to do to them, I will do instead to you."
34 1/2 The LORD said to Moshe: "Command the Israelites. Say to them: As you enter
the land of Canaan – this is the land that will become your possession, the
3 land of Canaan with its borders: Your southern sector shall extend from the
Wilderness of Tzin alongside Edom; your southern border to the east begins
4 at the end of the Dead Sea. The border shall then turn south of Scorpion
Ascent and cross toward Tzin. Its outer limit shall be south of Kadesh Barnea,
5 extending to Ḥatzar Adar and continuing toward Atzmon. The border shall
6 then turn from Atzmon to the Ravine of Egypt and end at the sea. Your
western border will be the Great Sea and its coast; this shall be your western
7 border. This shall be your northern border: from the Great Sea, mark a line to
8 Mount Hor. From Mount Hor mark a line to Levo Ḥamat. The outer limit of

רש״י

לד ב **זֹאת הָאָרֶץ אֲשֶׁר תִּפֹּל לָכֶם וְגוֹ׳.** לְפִי שֶׁהַרְבֵּה מִצְוֹת נוֹהֲגוֹת בָּאָרֶץ וְאֵין נוֹהֲגוֹת בְּחוּצָה לָאָרֶץ, הֻצְרַךְ לִכְתֹּב מִצְרָנֵי גְבוּלֵי רוּחוֹתֶיהָ סָבִיב, לוֹמַר לְךָ, מִן הַגְּבוּלִים הַלָּלוּ וְלִפְנִים הַמִּצְוֹת נוֹהֲגוֹת: **תִּפֹּל לָכֶם.** עַל שֵׁם שֶׁנֶּחְלְקָה בְּגוֹרָל נִקְרֵאת חֲלֻקָּה לְשׁוֹן נְפִילָה. וּמִדְרַשׁ אַגָּדָה אוֹמֵר: עַל יְדֵי שֶׁהִפִּיל הַקָּדוֹשׁ בָּרוּךְ הוּא שָׂרֵיהֶם שֶׁל שִׁבְעָה אֻמּוֹת מִן הַשָּׁמַיִם וּכְפָתָן לִפְנֵי מֹשֶׁה, אָמַר לוֹ: רְאֵה אֵין בָּהֶם עוֹד כֹּחַ:

ג **וְהָיָה לָכֶם פְּאַת נֶגֶב.** רוּחַ דְּרוֹמִית אֲשֶׁר מִן הַמִּזְרָח לַמַּעֲרָב: **מִמִּדְבַּר צִן.** אֲשֶׁר אֵצֶל אֱדוֹם, מַתְחִיל מִקְצוֹעַ דְּרוֹמִית מִזְרָחִית שֶׁל אֶרֶץ תִּשְׁעַת הַמַּטּוֹת. כֵּיצַד? שָׁלֹשׁ אֲרָצוֹת יוֹשְׁבוֹת בִּדְרוֹמָהּ שֶׁל אֶרֶץ יִשְׂרָאֵל זוֹ אֵצֶל זוֹ: קְצָת אֶרֶץ מִצְרַיִם, וְאֶרֶץ אֱדוֹם כֻּלָּהּ, וְאֶרֶץ מוֹאָב כֻּלָּהּ. אֶרֶץ מִצְרַיִם בְּמִקְצוֹעַ דְּרוֹמִית מַעֲרָבִית, שֶׁנֶּאֱמַר בְּפָרָשָׁה זוֹ: "מֵעַצְמוֹן נַחְלָה מִצְרָיִם וְהָיוּ תוֹצְאֹתָיו הַיָּמָּה" (להלן פסוק ה), וְנַחַל מִצְרַיִם הָיָה מְהַלֵּךְ עַל פְּנֵי כָּל אֶרֶץ מִצְרַיִם, שֶׁנֶּאֱמַר: "מִן הַשִּׁיחוֹר אֲשֶׁר עַל פְּנֵי מִצְרַיִם" (יהושע יג, ג), וּמַפְסִיק בֵּין אֶרֶץ מִצְרַיִם לְאֶרֶץ יִשְׂרָאֵל. וְאֶרֶץ אֱדוֹם אֶצְלָהּ לְצַד הַמִּזְרָח, וְאֶרֶץ מוֹאָב אֵצֶל אֶרֶץ אֱדוֹם, בְּסוֹף הַדָּרוֹם לַמִּזְרָח. וּכְשֶׁיָּצְאוּ יִשְׂרָאֵל מִמִּצְרַיִם, אִם רָצָה הַמָּקוֹם לְקָרֵב אֶת כְּנִיסָתָם לָאָרֶץ, הָיָה מַעֲבִירָם אֶת הַנִּילוּס לְצַד צָפוֹן וּבָאִין לְאֶרֶץ יִשְׂרָאֵל, וְלֹא עָשָׂה כֵן, וְזֶהוּ שֶׁנֶּאֱמַר: "וְלֹא נָחָם אֱלֹהִים דֶּרֶךְ אֶרֶץ פְּלִשְׁתִּים" (שמות יג, יז) שֶׁהֵם יוֹשְׁבִים עַל הַיָּם בְּמַעֲרָבָהּ שֶׁל אֶרֶץ כְּנַעַן, כָּעִנְיָן שֶׁנֶּאֱמַר בַּפְּלִשְׁתִּים: "יֹשְׁבֵי חֶבֶל הַיָּם גּוֹי כְּרֵתִים" (צפניה ב, ה), וְלֹא נָחָם אוֹתוֹ הַדֶּרֶךְ, אֶלָּא הִסֵּבָן וְהוֹצִיאָם דֶּרֶךְ דְּרוֹמָהּ אֶל הַמִּדְבָּר, וְהוּא שֶׁקְּרָאוֹ יְחֶזְקֵאל: "מִדְבַּר הָעַמִּים" (יחזקאל כ, לה) לְפִי שֶׁהָיוּ כַּמָּה אֻמּוֹת יוֹשְׁבִים בְּצִדּוֹ. וְהוֹלְכִין אֵצֶל דְּרוֹמָהּ מִן הַמַּעֲרָב כְּלַפֵּי מִזְרָח תָּמִיד, עַד שֶׁבָּאוּ לִדְרוֹמָהּ שֶׁל אֶרֶץ אֱדוֹם, וּבִקְּשׁוּ מִמֶּלֶךְ אֱדוֹם שֶׁיַּנִּיחֵם לַעֲבֹר דֶּרֶךְ אַרְצוֹ וּלְהִכָּנֵס לָאָרֶץ דֶּרֶךְ רָחְבָּהּ, וְלֹא רָצָה, וְהֻצְרְכוּ לִסְבֹּב אֶת כָּל דְּרוֹמָהּ שֶׁל אֱדוֹם עַד בּוֹאָם לִדְרוֹמָהּ שֶׁל אֶרֶץ מוֹאָב, שֶׁנֶּאֱמַר: "וְגַם אֶל מֶלֶךְ מוֹאָב שָׁלַח וְלֹא אָבָה" (שופטים יא, יז), וְהָלְכוּ כָּל דְּרוֹמָהּ שֶׁל מוֹאָב עַד סוֹפָהּ, וּמִשָּׁם הָפְכוּ פְּנֵיהֶם לַצָּפוֹן עַד שֶׁסָּבְבוּ כָּל מֶצֶר מִזְרָחִי שֶׁלָּהּ לְרָחְבָּהּ, וּכְשֶׁכָּלוּ אֶת מִזְרָחָהּ מָצְאוּ אֶת אֶרֶץ סִיחוֹן וְעוֹג שֶׁהָיוּ יוֹשְׁבִין בְּמִזְרָחָהּ שֶׁל אֶרֶץ כְּנַעַן, וְהַיַּרְדֵּן מַפְסִיק בֵּינֵיהֶם, וְזֶהוּ שֶׁנֶּאֱמַר בְּיִפְתָּח: "וַיֵּלֶךְ בַּמִּדְבָּר וַיָּסָב אֶת אֶרֶץ אֱדוֹם וְאֶת אֶרֶץ מוֹאָב וַיָּבֹא מִמִּזְרַח שֶׁמֶשׁ לְאֶרֶץ מוֹאָב" (שם פסוק יח), וְכָבְשׁוּ אֶת אֶרֶץ סִיחוֹן וְעוֹג שֶׁהָיְתָה בִּצְפוֹנָהּ שֶׁל אֶרֶץ מוֹאָב, וְקָרְבוּ עַד הַיַּרְדֵּן, וְהוּא כְּנֶגֶד מִקְצוֹעַ צְפוֹנִית מַעֲרָבִית שֶׁל אֶרֶץ מוֹאָב. נִמְצָא שֶׁאֶרֶץ כְּנַעַן שֶׁבְּעֵבֶר הַיַּרְדֵּן לַמַּעֲרָב, הָיָה מִקְצוֹעַ דְּרוֹמִית מִזְרָחִית שֶׁלָּהּ אֵצֶל אֱדוֹם:

ד **וְנָסַב לָכֶם הַגְּבוּל מִנֶּגֶב לְמַעֲלֵה עַקְרַבִּים.** כָּל מָקוֹם שֶׁנֶּאֱמַר: 'וְנָסַב' אוֹ 'וְיָצָא', מְלַמֵּד שֶׁלֹּא הָיָה הַמֶּצֶר שָׁוֶה, אֶלָּא הוֹלֵךְ וְיוֹצֵא לַחוּץ. יוֹצֵא הַמֶּצֶר וְעוֹקֵם לְצַד צְפוֹנוֹ שֶׁל עוֹלָם בַּאֲלַכְסוֹן לַמַּעֲרָב, וְעוֹבֵר הַמֶּצֶר בִּדְרוֹמָהּ שֶׁל מַעֲלֵה עַקְרַבִּים, נִמְצָא מַעֲלֵה עַקְרַבִּים לִפְנִים מִן הַמֶּצֶר: **וְעָבַר צִנָה.** אֶל צִן, כְּמוֹ: 'מִצְרַיְמָה': **וְהָיוּ תּוֹצְאֹתָיו.** קְצוֹתָיו, בִּדְרוֹמָהּ שֶׁל קָדֵשׁ בַּרְנֵעַ: **וְיָצָא חֲצַר אַדָּר.** מִתְפַּשֵּׁט הַמֶּצֶר וּמַרְחִיב לְצַד צָפוֹן, וְנִמְשָׁךְ עוֹד בַּאֲלַכְסוֹן לַמַּעֲרָב, וּבָא לוֹ לַחֲצַר אַדָּר וּמִשָּׁם לְעַצְמוֹן וּמִשָּׁם לְנַחַל מִצְרַיִם. וּלְשׁוֹן 'וְנָסַב' הָאָמוּר כָּאן, לְפִי שֶׁכָּתַב: "וְיָצָא חֲצַר אַדָּר", שֶׁהִתְחִיל לְהַרְחִיב מִשֶּׁעָבַר אֶת קָדֵשׁ בַּרְנֵעַ, וְרֹחַב אוֹתָהּ רְצוּעָה שֶׁבָּלְטָה לְצַד צָפוֹן הָיְתָה מִקָּדֵשׁ עַד עַצְמוֹן, וּמִשָּׁם וָהָלְאָה נִתְקַצֵּר הַמֶּצֶר וְנָסַב לְצַד הַדָּרוֹם וּבָא לוֹ לְנַחַל מִצְרַיִם, וּמִשָּׁם לְצַד

נו אֲשֶׁר אַתֶּם יֹשְׁבִים בָּהּ: וְהָיָה כַּאֲשֶׁר דִּמִּיתִי לַעֲשׂוֹת לָהֶם אֶעֱשֶׂה
לָכֶם:
לד א ב וַיְדַבֵּר יְהוָה אֶל־מֹשֶׁה לֵּאמֹר: צַו אֶת־בְּנֵי יִשְׂרָאֵל וְאָמַרְתָּ אֲלֵהֶם לא
כִּי־אַתֶּם בָּאִים אֶל־הָאָרֶץ כְּנָעַן זֹאת הָאָרֶץ אֲשֶׁר תִּפֹּל לָכֶם בְּנַחֲלָה
ג אֶרֶץ כְּנַעַן לִגְבֻלֹתֶיהָ: וְהָיָה לָכֶם פְּאַת־נֶגֶב מִמִּדְבַּר־צִן עַל־יְדֵי אֱדוֹם
ד וְהָיָה לָכֶם גְּבוּל נֶגֶב מִקְצֵה יָם־הַמֶּלַח קֵדְמָה: וְנָסַב לָכֶם הַגְּבוּל מִנֶּגֶב
לְמַעֲלֵה עַקְרַבִּים וְעָבַר צִנָה והיה תּוֹצְאֹתָיו מִנֶּגֶב לְקָדֵשׁ בַּרְנֵעַ וְיָצָא וְהָיוּ
ה חֲצַר־אַדָּר וְעָבַר עַצְמֹנָה: וְנָסַב הַגְּבוּל מֵעַצְמוֹן נַחְלָה מִצְרָיִם וְהָיוּ
ו תוֹצְאֹתָיו הַיָּמָּה: וּגְבוּל יָם וְהָיָה לָכֶם הַיָּם הַגָּדוֹל וּגְבוּל זֶה־יִהְיֶה
ז לָכֶם גְּבוּל יָם: וְזֶה־יִהְיֶה לָכֶם גְּבוּל צָפוֹן מִן־הַיָּם הַגָּדֹל תְּתָאוּ לָכֶם
ח הֹר הָהָר: מֵהֹר הָהָר תְּתָאוּ לְבֹא חֲמָת וְהָיוּ תּוֹצְאֹת הַגְּבֻל צְדָדָה:

אונקלוס

דאתון יתבין בה: נו ויהי, כמא דחשיבית, למעבד להון אעביד לכון: לד א ומליל יי עם משה למימר: ב פקיד, ית בני ישראל ותימר להון, ארי אתון עאלין לארעא דכנען, דא ארעא, דתתפליג לכון באחסנא, ארעא דכנען לתחומהא: ג ויהי לכון רוח דרומא, ממדברא דצין על תחומי אדום, ויהי לכון תחום דרומא, מסיפי ימא דמלחא קדומא: ד ויסחר לכון תחומא מדרומא, למסקנא דעקרבין ויעבר לצין, ויהון מפקנוהי, מדרומא לרקם גיאה, ויפוק לחצר אדר ויעבר לעצמון: ה ויסחר תחומא, מעצמון לנחלא דמצרים, ויהון מפקנוהי לימא: ו ותחום מערבא, ויהי לכון, ימא רבא ותחומיה, דין יהי לכון תחום מערבא: ז ודין יהי לכון תחום צפונא, מן ימא רבא, תכוונון לכון להור טורא: ח מהור טורא, תכוונון למטי חמת, ויהון מפקנוהי דתחומא לצדד:

רש״י

המערב אל הים הגדול, שהוא מצר מערבה של כל ארץ ישראל, נמצא שנחל מצרים במקצוע מערבית דרומית:

ה והיו תוצאתיו הימה. אל מצר המערב, שאין עוד גבול נגב מאריך לצד המערב משם והלאה:

ו וגבול ים. ומצר מערבי מהו? והיה לכם הים הגדול. למצר: וגבול. הנסין שבתוך הים אף הם מן הגבול, והם איים שקורין איסל״ש:

ז וגבול צפון. מצר צפון: מן הים הגדל תתאו לכם הר ההר. שהוא במקצוע צפונית מערבית, וראשו משפיע ונכנס לתוך הים, ויש מרחב הים לפנים הימנו וחוצה הימנו: תתאו. תשפעו לכם לנטות ממערב לצפון אל הר ההר: תתאו. לשון סבה, כמו: ״אל תא הרצים״ (דברי הימים ב׳ יב, יא), ״ותאי השער״ (יחזקאל מ, י), היציע שקורין אפנדי״ץ, שהוא מוסב ומשפע:

ח מהר ההר. תסבו ותלכו אל מצר הצפון לצד המזרח, ותפגעו ב״לבא חמת״, זו אנטוכיא: תוצאת הגבל. סופי הגבול. כל מקום שנאמר: ׳תוצאות הגבול׳, או המצר כלה שם לגמרי ואינו עובר להלן כלל, או משם מתפשט ומרחיב ויוצא לאחוריו להמשך להלן באלכסון יותר מן הרחב הראשון, ולענין רחב המדה הראשון קרוי ׳תוצאות׳, שמשם כלתה אותה מדה:

9 the border shall be at Tzedad; the border shall then extend to Zifron, and its
10 outer limit shall be Ḥatzar Einan. This shall be your northern border. Mark
11 your eastern border from Ḥatzar Einan to Shefam. The border will run down
from Shefam to Rivla on the east side of Ayin. It will then continue down to
12 reach the eastern slope of the Sea of Galilee. From there the border will run
down along the Jordan, ending at the Dead Sea. This is to be your land with
13 its borders on all sides." Moshe commanded the Israelites: "This is the land of
which you take possession by lot, which the Lord has commanded to give to
14 the nine and a half tribes – for the tribe of Reuven by its ancestral houses, and
the tribe of Gad by its ancestral houses, and half the tribe of Menashe have

רש״י

ט-יב | **וְהָיוּ תוֹצְאֹתָיו חֲצַר עֵינָן.** הוּא הָיָה סוֹף הַמֵּצַר הַצְּפוֹנִי, וְנִמְצָא חֲצַר עֵינָן בְּמִקְצוֹעַ צְפוֹנִית מִזְרָחִית, וּמִשָּׁם "וְהִתְאַוִּיתֶם לָכֶם" אֶל מֵצַר הַמִּזְרָחִי: **וְהִתְאַוִּיתֶם.** לְשׁוֹן הֲסִבָּה וּנְטִיָּה, כְּמוֹ: "תְּתָאוּ": **שְׁפָמָה.** בַּמֵּצַר הַמִּזְרָחִי, וּמִשָּׁם הָרִבְלָה: **מִקֶּדֶם לָעָיִן.** שֵׁם מָקוֹם, וְהַמֵּצַר הוֹלֵךְ בְּמִזְרָחוֹ, נִמְצָא הָעַיִן לִפְנִים מִן הַמֵּצַר, וּמֵאֶרֶץ יִשְׂרָאֵל הוּא: **וְיָרַד הַגְּבֻל.** כָּל שֶׁהַגְּבוּל הוֹלֵךְ מִצָּפוֹן לְדָרוֹם, הוּא יוֹרֵד וְהוֹלֵךְ: **וּמָחָה עַל כֶּתֶף יָם כִּנֶּרֶת קֵדְמָה.** שֶׁיְּהֵא יָם כִּנֶּרֶת תּוֹךְ לַגְּבוּל בַּמַּעֲרָב, וְהַגְּבוּל בְּמִזְרַח יָם כִּנֶּרֶת, וּמִשָּׁם יָרַד אֶל הַיַּרְדֵּן, וְהַיַּרְדֵּן מוֹשֵׁךְ וּבָא מִן הַצָּפוֹן לַדָּרוֹם בַּאֲלַכְסוֹן, נוֹטֶה לְצַד מִזְרָח, וּמִתְקָרֵב לְצַד אֶרֶץ כְּנַעַן כְּנֶגֶד יָם כִּנֶּרֶת, וּמוֹשֵׁךְ לְצַד מִזְרָחָהּ שֶׁל אֶרֶץ יִשְׂרָאֵל כְּנֶגֶד יָם כִּנֶּרֶת, עַד שֶׁנּוֹפֵל בְּיָם הַמֶּלַח, וּמִשָּׁם כָּלֶה הַגְּבוּל בְּתוֹצְאוֹתָיו אֶל יָם הַמֶּלַח, שֶׁמִּמֶּנּוּ הִתְחַלְתָּ מֵצַר מִקְצוֹעַ דְּרוֹמִית מִזְרָחִית, הֲרֵי סִבַּבְתָּ אוֹתָהּ לְאַרְבַּע רוּחוֹתֶיהָ:

The desire for revenge exists. But given free rein, it will reduce societies to violence and bloodshed without end. The alternative is to channel it through the operation of law, fair trial, and then either punishment or protection. That is what was introduced into civilization by the law of the cities of refuge, allowing retribution to take the place of revenge, and justice the place of retaliation.

34:11 עָרֵי מִקְלָט *Refuge cities* – The purpose of the cities of refuge was to make sure that someone judged innocent of murder was safe from being killed. This apparently simple concept was given a remarkable interpretation by the Talmud: "The Sages taught: If a student was exiled, his teacher was exiled with him, as it is said: 'That man may flee to one of these cities and live' (Deut. 19:5), meaning: do the things for him that will enable him to live" (Makkot 10a).

As Rambam explains: "Life without study is like death for scholars who seek wisdom" (*Hilkhot Rotze'aḥ UShmirat HaNefesh* 7:1). In Judaism, study is life itself, and study without a teacher is impossible. Teachers are like parents, only more so. Parents give us physical life; teachers give us spiritual life (*Hilkhot Talmud Torah* 5:1). Physical life is mortal, transient. Spiritual life is eternal. Therefore, we owe our teacher our life in its deepest sense.

Judaism made a wise decision when it made teachers its heroes and lifelong education its passion. We do not worship power or wealth. These things have their place, but not at the top of the hierarchy of values. Power forces us. Wealth induces us. But teachers develop us. They open us to the wisdom of the ages, helping us to see the world more clearly, think more deeply, argue more cogently, and decide more wisely.

34:12 וְהָיוּ תוֹצְאֹתָיו יָם הַמֶּלַח *Ending at the Dead Sea* – There are two seas in Israel: the Dead Sea and the Sea of Galilee. The latter is full of life: fish, birds, vegetation. The former, as its name suggests, contains no life at all. Yet they are both fed by the same river, the Jordan. The difference, says the Midrash, is that the Sea of Galilee receives water at one end and gives out water at the other. The Dead Sea receives but does not give. The Jordan ends there. To receive without reciprocating is a kind of death. To live is to give.

ט וְיָצָא הַגְּבֻל זִפְרֹנָה וְהָיוּ תוֹצְאֹתָיו חֲצַר עֵינָן זֶה־יִהְיֶה לָכֶם גְּבוּל צָפוֹן׃
יא וְהִתְאַוִּיתֶם לָכֶם לִגְבוּל קֵדְמָה מֵחֲצַר עֵינָן שְׁפָמָה׃ וְיָרַד הַגְּבֻל מִשְּׁפָם
הָרִבְלָה מִקֶּדֶם לָעָיִן וְיָרַד הַגְּבֻל וּמָחָה עַל־כֶּתֶף יָם־כִּנֶּרֶת קֵדְמָה׃
יב וְיָרַד הַגְּבוּל הַיַּרְדֵּנָה וְהָיוּ תוֹצְאֹתָיו יָם הַמֶּלַח זֹאת תִּהְיֶה לָכֶם הָאָרֶץ
יג לִגְבֻלֹתֶיהָ סָבִיב׃ וַיְצַו מֹשֶׁה אֶת־בְּנֵי יִשְׂרָאֵל לֵאמֹר זֹאת הָאָרֶץ אֲשֶׁר
תִּתְנַחֲלוּ אֹתָהּ בְּגוֹרָל אֲשֶׁר צִוָּה יהוה לָתֵת לְתִשְׁעַת הַמַּטּוֹת וַחֲצִי
יד הַמַּטֶּה׃ כִּי לָקְחוּ מַטֵּה בְנֵי הָראוּבֵנִי לְבֵית אֲבֹתָם וּמַטֵּה בְנֵי־הַגָּדִי

אונקלוס

ט וְיִפּוֹק תְּחוּמָא לְזִפְרוֹן, וִיהוֹן מַפְּקָנוֹהִי לַחֲצַר עֵינָן, דֵּין יְהֵי לְכוֹן
תְּחוּם צִפּוּנָא: י וּתְכַוְּנוּן לְכוֹן לִתְחוּם קִדּוּמָא, מֵחֲצַר עֵינָן לִשְׁפָם:
יא וְיֵיחוֹת תְּחוּמָא מִשְּׁפָם, לְרִבְלָה מִמַּדְנַח לְעַיִן, וְיֵיחוֹת תְּחוּמָא,
וְיִמְטֵי, עַל כֵּיף יַם גְּנֵיסַר קִדּוּמָא: יב וְיֵיחוֹת תְּחוּמָא לְיַרְדְּנָא, וִיהוֹן
מַפְּקָנוֹהִי לְיַמָּא דְּמִלְחָא, דָּא תְּהֵי לְכוֹן אַרְעָא, לִתְחוּמַהָא סְחוֹר
סְחוֹר: יג וּפַקֵּיד מֹשֶׁה, יָת בְּנֵי יִשְׂרָאֵל לְמֵימַר, דָּא אַרְעָא, דְּתַחְסְנוּן
יָתַהּ בְּעַדְבָא, דְּפַקֵּיד יי, לְמִתַּן, לְתִשְׁעַת שִׁבְטִין וּפַלְגוּת שִׁבְטָא:
יד אֲרֵי קַבִּילוּ, שִׁבְטָא דִּבְנֵי רְאוּבֵן לְבֵית אֲבָהָתְהוֹן, וְשִׁבְטָא דִּבְנֵי גָד

CITIES OF REFUGE

As the book of Numbers draws to a close, we encounter the law of the cities of refuge: three cities to the east of the Jordan and, later, three more within the land of Israel itself. There, people who commit homicide can flee and find protection until their case is heard by a court of law. If they are found guilty of murder (in biblical times), they are sentenced to death. If found innocent – if the death happened by accident or inadvertently, with neither deliberation nor malice – then they are to stay in a city of refuge "until the death of the High Priest" (Num. 35:25). By residing there, they are protected against revenge on the part of the *goel hadam*, the blood redeemer, usually the closest relative of the person who was killed.

Though the Torah rejects revenge except when commanded by God, something of the idea survives in the concept of the *goel hadam*. The desire for revenge is basic. It exists in all societies. The Torah recognizes the pain, the loss, and the moral indignation of the victim's family, understands that the desire for revenge is natural, and yet tames it. Torah legislates for people with all their passions, not for saints. It is a realistic code, not a utopian one.

Yet the Torah inserts one vital element *between* the killer and the victim's family: the principle of justice. There must be no direct act of revenge. The killer must be protected until his case has been heard in a court of law. If found guilty, he must pay the price. If he is found innocent of deliberate murder, though the vengeful instinct of the victim's family may be no less acute, he is given refuge from it. This due process turns revenge into retribution, which makes all the difference.

People often find it difficult to distinguish between retribution and revenge, yet they are completely different concepts. Revenge is personal. You killed a member of my family so I will kill you. Retribution, by contrast, is *im*personal. Indeed, the best definition of the society the Torah seeks to create is *nomocracy*: the rule of laws, not men.

Retribution is the principled rejection of revenge. It says that we are not free to take the law into our own hands. Passion may not override the due process of the law, for that is a sure route to anarchy and bloodshed. Wrong must be punished, but only after it has been established by a fair trial, and only on behalf not just of the victim but of society as a whole. The cities of refuge were part of this process, by which vengeance was subordinated to, and replaced by, retributive justice.

15 taken their possession. The two and a half tribes have taken their possession
across the Jordan from Yeriḥo to the east as the sun rises."
16 17 And the Lord spoke to Moshe: "These are the names of the men who shall REVI'I /SHISHI/
apportion the land to you for possession: Elazar the priest and Yehoshua son of
18 Nun. And you shall also take one leader from each tribe to apportion the land.
19 These are the names of the men: for the tribe of Yehuda, Kalev son of Yefuneh;
20 21 for the tribe of the Simeonites, Shmuel son of Amihud; for the tribe of Binyamin,
22 23 Elidad son of Kislon; for the tribe of the Danites, a leader, Buki son of Yogli. For
the descendants of Yosef: for the tribe of the Manassites a leader, Ḥaniel son
24 25 of Efod; for the tribe of the Efraimites a leader, Kemuel son of Shiftan. For the
26 tribe of the Zebulunites a leader, Elitzafan son of Parnakh. For the tribe of the
27 Issakharites a leader, Paltiel son of Azan. For the tribe of the Asherites a leader,
28 Aḥihud son of Shelomi. For the tribe of the Naftalites a leader, Pedahel son of
29 Amihud." These were the ones whom the Lord commanded to apportion the
possession for the Israelites in the land of Canaan.
35 1 The Lord spoke to Moshe in the plains of Moav by the Jordan across from ḤAMISHI
2 Yeriḥo: "Command the Israelites to grant the Levites towns to live in, among the
inheritance they will possess. Grant them also pasturelands around the towns.
3 The towns shall be theirs to live in, and the pasturelands shall be for their cattle,
4 all that they own, and all their animals. The pasturelands of the towns that you
shall give to the Levites shall extend from the town wall outward for a thousand
5 cubits in all directions; you shall measure out from the town, two thousand

אונקלוס

לְבֵית אֲבָהָתְהוֹן, וּפַלְגוּת שִׁבְטָא דִמְנַשֶּׁה, קַבִּילוּ אַחְסַנְתְּהוֹן: טו תְּרֵין שִׁבְטִין וּפַלְגוּת שִׁבְטָא, קַבִּילוּ אַחְסַנְתְּהוֹן, מֵעִבְרָא, לְיַרְדְּנָא דִירִיחוֹ קִדּוּמָא מַדִּנְחָא: טז וּמַלֵּיל יְיָ עִם מֹשֶׁה לְמֵימַר: יז אִלֵּין שְׁמָהָת גֻּבְרַיָּא, דְּיַחְסְנוּן לְכוֹן יָת אַרְעָא, אֶלְעָזָר כָּהֲנָא, וִיהוֹשֻׁעַ בַּר נוּן: יח וְרַבָּא חַד, רַבָּא חַד מִשִּׁבְטָא, תְּדַבְּרוּן לְאַחְסָנָא יָת אַרְעָא: יט וְאִלֵּין שְׁמָהָת גֻּבְרַיָּא, לְשִׁבְטָא דִיהוּדָה, כָּלֵב בַּר יְפֻנֶּה: כ וּלְשִׁבְטָא דִבְנֵי

רש״י

טו קֵדְמָה מִזְרָחָה. אֶל פְּנֵי הָעוֹלָם שֶׁהֵם בַּמִּזְרָח, שֶׁרוּחַ מִזְרָחִית קְרוּיָה פָּנִים וּמַעֲרָבִית קְרוּיָה אָחוֹר, לְפִיכָךְ דָּרוֹם לַיָּמִין וְצָפוֹן לַשְּׂמֹאל:

יז אֲשֶׁר יִנְחֲלוּ לָכֶם. בִּשְׁבִילְכֶם, כָּל נָשִׂיא וְנָשִׂיא אַפּוֹטְרוֹפּוֹס לְשִׁבְטוֹ, וּמְחַלֵּק נַחֲלַת הַשֵּׁבֶט לְמִשְׁפָּחוֹת וְלִגְבָרִים, וּבוֹרֵר לְכָל אֶחָד וְאֶחָד חֵלֶק הָגוּן, וּמַה שֶּׁהֵם עוֹשִׂים יִהְיֶה עָשׂוּי כְּאִלּוּ עֲשָׂאוּם שְׁלוּחִים. וְלֹא יִתָּכֵן לְפָרֵשׁ 'לָכֶם' זֶה כְּכָל 'לָכֶם' שֶׁבַּמִּקְרָא, שֶׁאִם כֵּן הָיָה לוֹ לִכְתֹּב: 'יַנְחִילוּ לָכֶם', "יִנְחֲלוּ" מַשְׁמָע שֶׁהֵם נוֹחֲלִים לָכֶם בִּשְׁבִילְכֶם וּבִמְקוֹמְכֶם, כְּמוֹ: "ה' יִלָּחֵם לָכֶם" (שמות יד, יד):

יח לִנְחֹל אֶת הָאָרֶץ. שֶׁיְּהֵא נוֹחֵל וְחוֹלֵק אוֹתָהּ בִּמְקוֹמְכֶם:

כט לְנַחֵל אֶת בְּנֵי יִשְׂרָאֵל. שֶׁהֵם יַנְחִילוּ אוֹתָהּ לָהֶם לְמַחְלְקוֹתֶיהָ:

לה ב וּמִגְרָשׁ. רֶוַח מָקוֹם חָלָק חוּץ לָעִיר סָבִיב לִהְיוֹת לְנוֹי לָעִיר, וְאֵין רַשָּׁאִין לִבְנוֹת שָׁם בַּיִת וְלֹא לִנְטֹעַ כֶּרֶם וְלֹא לִזְרֹעַ זְרִיעָה:

ג וּלְכֹל חַיָּתָם. לְכָל צָרְכֵיהֶם:

ד אֶלֶף אַמָּה סָבִיב. וְאַחֲרָיו הוּא אוֹמֵר: "אַלְפַּיִם בָּאַמָּה" (פסוק ה), הָא כֵּיצַד? אַלְפַּיִם הוּא נוֹתֵן לָהֶם סָבִיב, וּמֵהֶם אֶלֶף הַפְּנִימִיִּים לְמִגְרָשׁ וְהַחִיצוֹנִיִּים לְשָׂדוֹת וּכְרָמִים:

טו לְבֵית אֲבֹתָם וַחֲצִי מַטֵּה מְנַשֶּׁה לָקְחוּ נַחֲלָתָם׃ שְׁנֵי הַמַּטּוֹת וַחֲצִי
הַמַּטֶּה לָקְחוּ נַחֲלָתָם מֵעֵבֶר לְיַרְדֵּן יְרֵחוֹ קֵדְמָה מִזְרָחָה׃
טז יז וַיְדַבֵּר יְהוָה אֶל־מֹשֶׁה לֵּאמֹר׃ אֵלֶּה שְׁמוֹת הָאֲנָשִׁים אֲשֶׁר־יִנְחֲלוּ רביעי /ששי/
יח לָכֶם אֶת־הָאָרֶץ אֶלְעָזָר הַכֹּהֵן וִיהוֹשֻׁעַ בִּן־נוּן׃ וְנָשִׂיא אֶחָד נָשִׂיא
יט אֶחָד מִמַּטֶּה תִּקְחוּ לִנְחֹל אֶת־הָאָרֶץ׃ וְאֵלֶּה שְׁמוֹת הָאֲנָשִׁים לְמַטֵּה
כ יְהוּדָה כָּלֵב בֶּן־יְפֻנֶּה׃ וּלְמַטֵּה בְּנֵי שִׁמְעוֹן שְׁמוּאֵל בֶּן־עַמִּיהוּד׃
כא כב לְמַטֵּה בִנְיָמִן אֱלִידָד בֶּן־כִּסְלוֹן׃ וּלְמַטֵּה בְנֵי־דָן נָשִׂיא בֻּקִּי בֶּן־יָגְלִי׃
כג כד לִבְנֵי יוֹסֵף לְמַטֵּה בְנֵי־מְנַשֶּׁה נָשִׂיא חַנִּיאֵל בֶּן־אֵפֹד׃ וּלְמַטֵּה בְנֵי־
כה אֶפְרַיִם נָשִׂיא קְמוּאֵל בֶּן־שִׁפְטָן׃ וּלְמַטֵּה בְנֵי־זְבוּלֻן נָשִׂיא אֱלִיצָפָן
כו בֶּן־פַּרְנָךְ׃ וּלְמַטֵּה בְנֵי־יִשָּׂשכָר נָשִׂיא פַּלְטִיאֵל בֶּן־עַזָּן׃ וּלְמַטֵּה בְנֵי־
כח אָשֵׁר נָשִׂיא אֲחִיהוּד בֶּן־שְׁלֹמִי׃ וּלְמַטֵּה בְנֵי־נַפְתָּלִי נָשִׂיא פְּדַהְאֵל
כט בֶּן־עַמִּיהוּד׃ אֵלֶּה אֲשֶׁר צִוָּה יְהוָה לְנַחֵל אֶת־בְּנֵי־יִשְׂרָאֵל בְּאֶרֶץ
כְּנָעַן׃

לה א ב וַיְדַבֵּר יְהוָה אֶל־מֹשֶׁה בְּעַרְבֹת מוֹאָב עַל־יַרְדֵּן יְרֵחוֹ לֵאמֹר׃ צַו אֶת־ חמישי
בְּנֵי יִשְׂרָאֵל וְנָתְנוּ לַלְוִיִּם מִנַּחֲלַת אֲחֻזָּתָם עָרִים לָשָׁבֶת וּמִגְרָשׁ לֶעָרִים
ג סְבִיבֹתֵיהֶם תִּתְּנוּ לַלְוִיִּם׃ וְהָיוּ הֶעָרִים לָהֶם לָשָׁבֶת וּמִגְרְשֵׁיהֶם יִהְיוּ
ד לִבְהֶמְתָּם וְלִרְכֻשָׁם וּלְכֹל חַיָּתָם׃ וּמִגְרְשֵׁי הֶעָרִים אֲשֶׁר תִּתְּנוּ לַלְוִיִּם
ה מִקִּיר הָעִיר וָחוּצָה אֶלֶף אַמָּה סָבִיב׃ וּמַדֹּתֶם מִחוּץ לָעִיר אֶת־פְּאַת־

אונקלוס

שִׁמְעוֹן, שְׁמוּאֵל בַּר עַמִּיהוּד: כא לְשִׁבְטָא דְבִנְיָמִין, אֱלִידָד בַּר כִּסְלוֹן: כב וּלְשִׁבְטָא דִבְנֵי דָן רַבָּא, בֻּקִּי בַּר יָגְלִי: כג לִבְנֵי יוֹסֵף, לְשִׁבְטָא דִּבְנֵי מְנַשֶּׁה רַבָּא, חַנִּיאֵל בַּר אֵפוֹד: כד וּלְשִׁבְטָא דִּבְנֵי אֶפְרַיִם רַבָּא, קְמוּאֵל בַּר שִׁפְטָן: כה וּלְשִׁבְטָא דִּבְנֵי זְבוּלוּן רַבָּא, אֱלִיצָפָן בַּר פַּרְנָךְ: כו וּלְשִׁבְטָא דִּבְנֵי יִשָּׂשכָר רַבָּא, פַּלְטִיאֵל בַּר עַזָּן: כז וּלְשִׁבְטָא דִּבְנֵי אָשֵׁר רַבָּא, אֲחִיהוּד בַּר שְׁלוֹמִי: כח וּלְשִׁבְטָא דִּבְנֵי נַפְתָּלִי רַבָּא, פְּדַהְאֵל בַּר עַמִּיהוּד: כט אִלֵּין, דְּפַקֵּיד יי, לְאַחְסָנָא יָת בְּנֵי יִשְׂרָאֵל בְּאַרְעָא דִּכְנָעַן: לה א וּמַלֵּיל יי, עִם מֹשֶׁה בְּמֵישְׁרַיָּא דְמוֹאָב, עַל יַרְדְּנָא דִּירִיחוֹ לְמֵימַר: ב פַּקֵּיד יָת בְּנֵי יִשְׂרָאֵל, וְיִתְּנוּן לְלֵיוָאֵי, מֵאַחְסָנַת, אֲחָדַּתְהוֹן קִרְוִין לְמִתַּב, וְרֵוַח, לְקִרְוַיָּא סַחְרָנֵיהוֹן, תִּתְּנוּן לְלֵיוָאֵי: ג וִיהוֹן קִרְוַיָּא, לְהוֹן לְמִתַּב, וְרַוְחֵיהוֹן, יְהוֹן לִבְעִירְהוֹן וּלְקִנְיָנְהוֹן, וּלְכָל חֵיוַתְהוֹן: ד וְרַוְחֵי קִרְוַיָּא, דְּתִתְּנוּן לְלֵיוָאֵי, מִכּוֹתֶל קַרְתָּא וּלְבָרָא, אֲלַף אַמִּין סְחוֹר סְחוֹר: ה וְתִמְשְׁחוּן מִבָּרָא לְקַרְתָּא, יָת רוּחַ

cubits on the east side, two thousand cubits on the south side, two thousand
cubits on the west side, and two thousand cubits on the north side, with the
town in the middle, and this shall belong to them as pastureland for their towns.
6 Six of the towns that you give to the Levites shall be towns of refuge, which
you will designate as places to which a manslayer may flee. In addition to these,
7 you shall give them forty-two more towns. Thus the total number of towns you
8 shall give to the Levites shall be forty-eight, along with their pastureland. As for
the towns that you give from the possession of the Israelites, take more from
the larger tribes and fewer from the smaller so that each grants towns to the
Levites in proportion to its own inheritance."
9 10 The LORD spoke to Moshe: "Speak to the Israelites. Tell them: When you cross SHISHI /SHEVI'I/
11 the Jordan into the land of Canaan, select towns to be your refuge cities, to
12 which a person who kills another unintentionally may flee. The cities shall be
a refuge for you from avengers, so that no person who has killed another may
13 die without standing trial before the community. The towns that you designate
14 shall be six cities of refuge for you; you shall designate three towns across the
15 Jordan and three in the land of Canaan as cities of refuge. These six towns shall
be a place of refuge for Israelites, migrants, and temporary residents alike, so
16 that anyone who kills a person unintentionally may flee there. If a person strikes
another with an iron object, however, and he dies, that person is a murderer;
17 the murderer must be put to death. If he strikes him with a handheld stone
that could cause death and he dies, that person is a murderer; the murderer

אונקלוס

קִדּוּמָא תְּרֵין אַלְפִין אַמִּין, וְיָת רוּחַ דָּרוֹמָא תְּרֵין אַלְפִין אַמִּין, וְיָת רוּחַ מַעְרְבָא תְּרֵין אַלְפִין אַמִּין, וְיָת רוּחַ צִפּוּנָא, תְּרֵין אַלְפִין אַמִּין וְקַרְתָּא בִּמְצִיעַ, דֵּין יְהֵי לְהוֹן, רְוָחֵי קִרְוַיָּא: ו וְיָת קִרְוַיָּא, דְּתִתְּנוּן לְלֵיוָאֵי, יָת שֵׁית קִרְוֵי שֵׁיזָבוּתָא, דְּתִתְּנוּן, לְמֶעְרַק לְתַמָּן קָטוֹלָא,

רש"י

יא **וְהִקְרִיתֶם.** אֵין הַקְרָיָה אֶלָּא לְשׁוֹן הַזְמָנָה, וְכֵן הוּא אוֹמֵר: "כִּי הִקְרָה ה' אֱלֹהֶיךָ לְפָנָי" (בראשית כז, כ):

יב **מִגֹּאֵל.** מִפְּנֵי גּוֹאֵל הַדָּם שֶׁהוּא קָרוֹב לַנִּרְצָח:

יג **שֵׁשׁ עָרֵי מִקְלָט.** מַגִּיד שֶׁאַף עַל פִּי שֶׁהִבְדִּיל מֹשֶׁה בְּחַיָּיו שָׁלֹשׁ עָרִים בְּעֵבֶר הַיַּרְדֵּן, לֹא הָיוּ קוֹלְטוֹת עַד שֶׁנִּבְחֲרוּ שָׁלֹשׁ שֶׁנָּתַן יְהוֹשֻׁעַ בְּאֶרֶץ כְּנַעַן:

יד **אֵת שְׁלֹשׁ הֶעָרִים וְגוֹ'.** אַף עַל פִּי שֶׁבְּאֶרֶץ כְּנַעַן תִּשְׁעָה שְׁבָטִים וְכָאן אֵינָן אֶלָּא שְׁנַיִם, הִשְׁוָה מִנְיַן עָרֵי מִקְלָט שֶׁלָּהֶם, מִשּׁוּם דְּבְגִלְעָד נְפִישֵׁי רוֹצְחִים, דִּכְתִיב: "גִּלְעָד קִרְיַת פֹּעֲלֵי אָוֶן עֲקֻבָּה מִדָּם" (הושע ו, ח):

טז **וְאִם בִּכְלִי בַרְזֶל הִכָּהוּ.** אֵין זֶה מְדַבֵּר בְּהוֹרֵג בְּשׁוֹגֵג אֶלָּא בְּהוֹרֵג בְּמֵזִיד, וּבָא לְלַמֵּד שֶׁהַהוֹרֵג בְּכָל דָּבָר צָרִיךְ שֶׁיְּהֵא בּוֹ שִׁעוּר כְּדֵי לְהָמִית, שֶׁנֶּאֱמַר בְּכֻלָּם: "אֲשֶׁר יָמוּת בּוֹ", כְּדִמְתַרְגְּמִינָן: "דְּהִיא כְמִסַּת דִּימוּת בַּהּ", חוּץ מִן הַבַּרְזֶל, שֶׁגָּלוּי וְיָדוּעַ לִפְנֵי הַקָּדוֹשׁ בָּרוּךְ הוּא שֶׁהַבַּרְזֶל מֵמִית בְּכָל שֶׁהוּא, אֲפִלּוּ מַחַט, לְפִיכָךְ לֹא נָתְנָה בּוֹ תּוֹרָה שִׁעוּר לִכְתֹּב בּוֹ: 'אֲשֶׁר יָמוּת בּוֹ'. וְאִם תֹּאמַר בְּהוֹרֵג בְּשׁוֹגֵג הַכָּתוּב מְדַבֵּר, הֲרֵי הוּא אוֹמֵר לְמַטָּה: "אוֹ בְכָל אֶבֶן אֲשֶׁר יָמוּת בָּהּ בְּלֹא רְאוֹת" וְגוֹ' (להלן פסוק כג), לָמַד עַל הָאֲמוּרִים לְמַעְלָה שֶׁבְּהוֹרֵג בְּמֵזִיד הַכָּתוּב מְדַבֵּר:

יז **בְּאֶבֶן יָד.** שֶׁיֵּשׁ בָּהּ מְלֹא יָד:

קִדְמָה אַלְפַּיִם בָּאַמָּה וְאֶת־פְּאַת־נֶגֶב אַלְפַּיִם בָּאַמָּה וְאֶת־פְּאַת־יָם ׀
אַלְפַּיִם בָּאַמָּה וְאֵת פְּאַת צָפוֹן אַלְפַּיִם בָּאַמָּה וְהָעִיר בַּתָּוֶךְ זֶה יִהְיֶה
ו לָהֶם מִגְרְשֵׁי הֶעָרִים: וְאֵת הֶעָרִים אֲשֶׁר תִּתְּנוּ לַלְוִיִּם אֵת שֵׁשׁ־עָרֵי
הַמִּקְלָט אֲשֶׁר תִּתְּנוּ לָנֻס שָׁמָּה הָרֹצֵחַ וַעֲלֵיהֶם תִּתְּנוּ אַרְבָּעִים וּשְׁתַּיִם
ז עִיר: כָּל־הֶעָרִים אֲשֶׁר תִּתְּנוּ לַלְוִיִּם אַרְבָּעִים וּשְׁמֹנֶה עִיר אֶתְהֶן
ח וְאֶת־מִגְרְשֵׁיהֶן: וְהֶעָרִים אֲשֶׁר תִּתְּנוּ מֵאֲחֻזַּת בְּנֵי־יִשְׂרָאֵל מֵאֵת
הָרַב תַּרְבּוּ וּמֵאֵת הַמְעַט תַּמְעִיטוּ אִישׁ כְּפִי נַחֲלָתוֹ אֲשֶׁר יִנְחָלוּ יִתֵּן
מֵעָרָיו לַלְוִיִּם:
ט וַיְדַבֵּר יְהוָה אֶל־מֹשֶׁה לֵּאמֹר: דַּבֵּר אֶל־בְּנֵי יִשְׂרָאֵל וְאָמַרְתָּ אֲלֵהֶם לב ששי /שביעי/
יא כִּי אַתֶּם עֹבְרִים אֶת־הַיַּרְדֵּן אַרְצָה כְּנָעַן: וְהִקְרִיתֶם לָכֶם עָרִים
יב עָרֵי מִקְלָט תִּהְיֶינָה לָכֶם וְנָס שָׁמָּה רֹצֵחַ מַכֵּה־נֶפֶשׁ בִּשְׁגָגָה: וְהָיוּ
לָכֶם הֶעָרִים לְמִקְלָט מִגֹּאֵל וְלֹא יָמוּת הָרֹצֵחַ עַד־עָמְדוֹ לִפְנֵי הָעֵדָה
יג יד לַמִּשְׁפָּט: וְהֶעָרִים אֲשֶׁר תִּתֵּנוּ שֵׁשׁ־עָרֵי מִקְלָט תִּהְיֶינָה לָכֶם: אֵת ׀
שְׁלֹשׁ הֶעָרִים תִּתְּנוּ מֵעֵבֶר לַיַּרְדֵּן וְאֵת שְׁלֹשׁ הֶעָרִים תִּתְּנוּ בְּאֶרֶץ
טו כְּנָעַן עָרֵי מִקְלָט תִּהְיֶינָה: לִבְנֵי יִשְׂרָאֵל וְלַגֵּר וְלַתּוֹשָׁב בְּתוֹכָם תִּהְיֶינָה
טז שֵׁשׁ־הֶעָרִים הָאֵלֶּה לְמִקְלָט לָנוּס שָׁמָּה כָּל־מַכֵּה־נֶפֶשׁ בִּשְׁגָגָה: וְאִם־
יז בִּכְלִי בַרְזֶל ׀ הִכָּהוּ וַיָּמֹת רֹצֵחַ הוּא מוֹת יוּמַת הָרֹצֵחַ: וְאִם בְּאֶבֶן יָד

אונקלוס

וַעֲלֵיהוֹן תִּתְּנוּן, אַרְבְּעִין וְתַרְתֵּין קִרְוִין: ז כָּל קִרְוַיָּא, דְּתִתְּנוּן לְלֵיוָאֵי, אַרְבְּעִין וְתַמְנֵי קִרְוִין, יָתְהוֹן וְיָת רְוַחֵיהוֹן: ח וְקִרְוַיָּא, דְּתִתְּנוּן מֵאַחְסָנַת בְּנֵי יִשְׂרָאֵל, מִן סַגִּיאֵי תַּסְגּוֹן, וּמִן זְעִירֵי תַּזְעֲרוּן, גְּבַר, כְּפוּם אַחְסַנְתֵּיהּ דְּיַחְסְנוּן, יִתֵּין מִקִּרְווֹהִי לְלֵיוָאֵי: ט וּמַלֵּיל יי עִם מֹשֶׁה לְמֵימָר: י מַלֵּיל עִם בְּנֵי יִשְׂרָאֵל, וְתֵימַר לְהוֹן, אֲרֵי אַתּוּן, עָבְרִין יָת יַרְדְּנָא לְאַרְעָא דִּכְנָעַן: יא וּתְזַמְּנוּן לְכוֹן קִרְוִין, קִרְוֵי שֵׁיזָבוּתָא יְהֶוְיָן לְכוֹן, וְיֵעְרוֹק לְתַמָּן קָטוֹלָא, דְּיִקְטוֹל נַפְשָׁא בְּשָׁלוּ: יב וִיהוֹן לְכוֹן קִרְוַיָּא, לְשֵׁיזָבָא מִגָּאֵיל דְּמָא, וְלָא יְמוּת קָטוֹלָא, עַד דִּיקוּם, קֳדָם כְּנִשְׁתָּא לְדִינָא: יג וְקִרְוַיָּא דְּתִתְּנוּן, שֵׁית קִרְוֵי שֵׁיזָבוּתָא יְהֶוְיָן לְכוֹן: יד יָת תְּלָת קִרְוַיָּא, תִּתְּנוּן מֵעִבְרָא לְיַרְדְּנָא, וְיָת תְּלָת קִרְוַיָּא, תִּתְּנוּן בְּאַרְעָא דִּכְנָעַן, קִרְוֵי שֵׁיזָבוּתָא יְהֶוְיָן: טו לִבְנֵי יִשְׂרָאֵל, וּלְגִיּוֹרַיָּא וּלְתוֹתָבַיָּא דְּבֵינֵיהוֹן, יְהֶוְיָן, שֵׁית קִרְוַיָּא הָאִלֵּין לְשֵׁיזָבָא, לְמֵעְרַק לְתַמָּן, כָּל דְּיִקְטוֹל נַפְשָׁא בְּשָׁלוּ: טז וְאִם בְּמָן דְּבַרְזֶל מַחְהִי, וְקַטְלֵיהּ קָטוֹלָא הוּא, אִתְקְטָלָא יִתְקְטִיל קָטוֹלָא: יז וְאִם, בְּאַבְנָא דְמִתְנַסְבָא בִּיד

18 must be put to death. Likewise, if he strikes him with a wooden tool that could
cause death and he dies, that person is a murderer; the murderer must be
19 put to death. The blood avenger shall put the murderer to death; whenever
20 he meets him, he may put him to death. So too if one person pushes another
in hate, or throws something at him with prior intent, he shall be put to
21 death. If in enmity someone strikes a person with his hand and he dies, the
one who struck the blow is a murderer and shall be put to death. The blood
22 avenger shall put the murderer to death whenever they meet. If, however, one
person pushes another suddenly, without enmity, or throws an object at him
23 unintentionally, or drops a fatal stone on him without seeing him and he dies –
24 they were not enemies, he intended him no harm – then the community must
judge between the killer and the blood avenger in accordance with these laws.
25 And the community must protect the manslayer from the avenger of blood
and return him to the refuge city to which he fled. There he shall live until the

רש"י

אשר ימות בה. שיש בה שעור להמית, כתרגומו. לפי שנאמר: "והכה איש את רעהו באבן" (שמות כא, יח) ולא נתן בה שעור, יכול כל שהוא? לכך נאמר: "אשר ימות בה":

יח **או בכלי עץ יד.** לפי שנאמר: "וכי יכה איש את עבדו או את אמתו בשבט" (שם פסוק כ), יכול כל שהוא? לכך נאמר בעץ: "אשר ימות בו", שיהא בו כדי להמית:

יט **בפגעו בו.** אפילו בתוך ערי מקלט:

כ **בצדיה.** כתרגומו: "בכמנא", במארב:

כב **בפתע.** באונס, ותרגומו: "בתכיף", שהיה סמוך לו, ולא היה לו שהות להזהר עליו:

כג **או בכל אבן אשר ימות בה.** הכהו: **בלא ראות.** שלא ראהו: **ויפל עליו.** מכאן אמרו, ההורג דרך ירידה – גולה, דרך עליה – אינו גולה:

כה **עד מות הכהן הגדל.** שהוא בא להשרות שכינה בישראל ולהאריך ימיהם, והרוצח בא לסלק את השכינה מישראל ומקצר את ימי החיים, אינו כדאי שיהא לפני כהן גדול. דבר אחר, לפי שהיה לו לכהן גדול להתפלל שלא תארע תקלה זו לישראל בחייו:

atonement, but simply with the fact that it causes great collective grief, in which people forget their own misfortunes in the face of larger national loss. That is when people let go of their individual sense of injustice and desire for revenge. It then becomes safe for the person found guilty of manslaughter to return home.

Rambam does not understand the law of the cities of refuge in terms of guilt or punishment. For him, the only relevant consideration is safety. The person guilty of manslaughter goes into exile, not because it is a form of atonement or expiation, but simply because it is safer for him to be a long way from those who might be seeking vengeance. He stays there until the death of the High Priest, because only after national tragedy can you assume that people have given up thoughts of taking revenge for their own lost family member.

This is a fundamentally different way to conceptualize the cities of refuge. The Talmud's explanation operates on the supernatural level; had the High Priest prayed hard and devotedly enough, there would have been no accidental deaths. Rambam's explanation is not supernatural. It is what we would call social psychology. There are events that evoke widespread and deep national grief, when our personal grievances seem simply too small to worry about. These collective sorrows bring the people together and move them beyond the resentments of the past.

יח אֲשֶׁר־יָמוּת בָּהּ הִכָּהוּ וַיָּמֹת רֹצֵחַ הוּא מוֹת יוּמַת הָרֹצֵחַ׃ אוֹ בִּכְלִי
יט עֵץ־יָד אֲשֶׁר־יָמוּת בּוֹ הִכָּהוּ וַיָּמֹת רֹצֵחַ הוּא מוֹת יוּמַת הָרֹצֵחַ׃ גֹּאֵל
כ הַדָּם הוּא יָמִית אֶת־הָרֹצֵחַ בְּפִגְעוֹ־בוֹ הוּא יְמִתֶנּוּ׃ וְאִם־בְּשִׂנְאָה
כא יֶהְדָּפֶנּוּ אוֹ־הִשְׁלִיךְ עָלָיו בִּצְדִיָּה וַיָּמֹת׃ אוֹ בְאֵיבָה הִכָּהוּ בְיָדוֹ וַיָּמֹת
מוֹת־יוּמַת הַמַּכֶּה רֹצֵחַ הוּא גֹּאֵל הַדָּם יָמִית אֶת־הָרֹצֵחַ בְּפִגְעוֹ־בוֹ׃
כב וְאִם־בְּפֶתַע בְּלֹא־אֵיבָה הֲדָפוֹ אוֹ־הִשְׁלִיךְ עָלָיו כָּל־כְּלִי בְּלֹא צְדִיָּה׃
כג אוֹ בְכָל־אֶבֶן אֲשֶׁר־יָמוּת בָּהּ בְּלֹא רְאוֹת וַיַּפֵּל עָלָיו וַיָּמֹת וְהוּא
כד לֹא־אוֹיֵב לוֹ וְלֹא מְבַקֵּשׁ רָעָתוֹ׃ וְשָׁפְטוּ הָעֵדָה בֵּין הַמַּכֶּה וּבֵין גֹּאֵל
כה הַדָּם עַל הַמִּשְׁפָּטִים הָאֵלֶּה׃ וְהִצִּילוּ הָעֵדָה אֶת־הָרֹצֵחַ מִיַּד גֹּאֵל
הַדָּם וְהֵשִׁיבוּ אֹתוֹ הָעֵדָה אֶל־עִיר מִקְלָטוֹ אֲשֶׁר־נָס שָׁמָּה וְיָשַׁב

אונקלוס

דְּהִיא כְּמִסַּת דִּימוּת בַּהּ מְחָהִי, וְקַטְלֵיהּ קָטוֹלָא הוּא, אִתְקְטָלָא
יִתְקְטִיל קָטוֹלָא: יח אוֹ, בְּמָן דְּאָע דְּמִתְנְסֵיב בְּיַד דְּהוּא כְּמִסַּת
דִּימוּת בֵּיהּ מְחָהִי, וְקַטְלֵיהּ קָטוֹלָא הוּא, אִתְקְטָלָא יִתְקְטִיל
קָטוֹלָא: יט גָּאֵיל דְּמָא, הוּא יִקְטוֹל יָת קָטוֹלָא, כַּד אִתְחַיַּב לֵיהּ
מִן דִּינָא הוּא יִקְטְלִנֵּיהּ: כ וְאִם בְּסִנְאָה דְּחָהִי, אוֹ רְמָא עֲלוֹהִי,
בְּכְמָנָא וְקַטְלֵיהּ: כא אוֹ בִּדְבָבוּ, מְחָהִי בִּידֵיהּ וְקַטְלֵיהּ, אִתְקְטָלָא
יִתְקְטִיל מָחְיָא קָטוֹלָא הוּא, גָּאֵיל דְּמָא, יִקְטוֹל, יָת קָטוֹלָא כַּד
אִתְחַיַּב לֵיהּ: כב וְאִם בִּתְכֵּיף בְּלָא דְּבָבוּ דְּחָהִי, אוֹ רְמָא עֲלוֹהִי,
כָּל מָן בְּלָא כְמָן לֵיהּ: כג אוֹ בְּכָל אַבְנָא, דְּהִיא כְּמִסַּת דִּימוּת
בַּהּ בְּלָא חָזֵי, וּרְמָא עֲלוֹהִי וְקַטְלֵיהּ, וְהוּא לָא סָנֵי לֵיהּ, וְלָא
תָבַע בִּשְׁתֵּיהּ: כד וִידִינוּן כְּנִשְׁתָּא, בֵּין מָחְיָא, וּבֵין גָּאֵיל דְּמָא, עַל
דִּינַיָּא הָאִלֵּין: כה וִישֵׁיזְבוּן כְּנִשְׁתָּא יָת קָטוֹלָא, מִיַּד גָּאֵיל דְּמָא,
וִיתִיבוּן יָתֵיהּ כְּנִשְׁתָּא, לְקִרְיַת שֵׁיזָבוּתֵיהּ דַּעֲרַק לְתַמָּן, וְיִתֵּיב

35:25 עַד־מוֹת הַכֹּהֵן הַגָּדֹל *Until the death of the High Priest* – There seems no connection between manslaughter, blood vengeance, and the High Priest, let alone his death. One explanation offered in the Talmud for the connection made in the law is that the death of the High Priest atoned for the lost life of the victim (Makkot 11b). To be sure, there was no malice aforethought. The killing was unintended. But it is precisely for unintended acts – sins committed *beshogeg*, unknowingly or unwittingly – that a purification offering had to be brought (Lev. 4). In the case of manslaughter, no purification offering is adequate. What has been lost is a life, and one life is like a universe. In the case of manslaughter, it seems as if it is the death of the High Priest that atones.

A second explanation – or it may be a variant on the first – is that in some way the High Priest shared in the responsibility for the death: "A venerable old scholar said: I heard an explanation at one of the sessional lectures of Rava that the High Priest should have implored divine grace for the generation, which he failed to do" (Makkot 11a).

According to this approach, the High Priest had a share, however small, in the guilt for the fact that someone died, albeit unintentionally. Manslaughter, because it is unintentional, is an event that might have been averted by the prayers of the High Priest. Therefore it is not fully atoned for until the High Priest dies. Only then can the manslaughterer go free.

Rambam offers a completely different kind of explanation in *Guide for the Perplexed* (III:40). According to him, the death of the High Priest has nothing to do with guilt or

26 death of the High Priest anointed with the sacred oil. But if the manslayer ever
27 goes outside the limits of the city of refuge to which he fled and the blood
avenger finds him outside the limits of his city of refuge and kills him, the
28 avenger is not liable for murder; the manslayer must stay in his city of refuge
until the High Priest dies. After the death of the High Priest the manslayer
29 may return to his own hereditary land. These shall be a decree of law for you
30 throughout your generations, wherever you should live. If anyone kills a human
being, the murderer shall be put to death on the evidence of eyewitnesses. No
31 one shall be put to death on the testimony of one witness alone. You may not
accept a ransom for the life of a murderer found guilty of a capital crime; he
32 must be put to death. Nor may you accept a ransom for someone who has fled
to his city of refuge, to allow him to return and live on his land before the priest
33 dies. You shall not pollute the land in which you live; blood pollutes the land.
And the land can have no atonement for the blood that is shed in it – except
34 through the blood of the one who shed it. Do not defile the land in which
you live, and in the midst of which I dwell – for I the LORD dwell in the midst
of Israel."

רש״י

אֲשֶׁר מָשַׁח אֹתוֹ בְּשֶׁמֶן הַקֹּדֶשׁ. לְפִי פְשׁוּטוֹ, מִן הַמִּקְרָאוֹת הַקְּצָרִים הוּא שֶׁלֹּא פֵרַשׁ מִי מְשָׁחוֹ, אֶלָּא כְמוֹ: אֲשֶׁר מְשָׁחוֹ הַמּוֹשֵׁחַ אוֹתוֹ בְּשֶׁמֶן הַקֹּדֶשׁ. וְרַבּוֹתֵינוּ דְּרָשׁוּהוּ בְּמַסֶּכֶת מַכּוֹת (דף יא ע״ב) לִרְאָיַת דָּבָר, לְלַמֵּד שֶׁאִם עַד שֶׁלֹּא נִגְמַר דִּינוֹ מֵת הַכֹּהֵן הַגָּדוֹל וּמִנּוּ אַחֵר תַּחְתָּיו, וּלְאַחַר מִכָּאן נִגְמַר דִּינוֹ, חוֹזֵר בְּמִיתָתוֹ שֶׁל שֵׁנִי, שֶׁנֶּאֱמַר: "אֲשֶׁר מָשַׁח אֹתוֹ", וְכִי הוּא מְשָׁחוֹ לַכֹּהֵן, אוֹ הַכֹּהֵן מָשַׁח אוֹתוֹ? אֶלָּא לְהָבִיא אֶת הַנִּמְשָׁח בְּיָמָיו שֶׁמַּחֲזִירוֹ בְּמִיתָתוֹ:

כז **אֵין לוֹ דָּם.** הֲרֵי הוּא כְּהוֹרֵג אֶת הַמֵּת, שֶׁאֵין לוֹ דָּם:

כט **בְּכֹל מוֹשְׁבֹתֵיכֶם.** לִמֵּד שֶׁתְּהֵא סַנְהֶדְרִין נוֹהֶגֶת בְּחוּצָה לָאָרֶץ כָּל זְמַן שֶׁנּוֹהֶגֶת בְּאֶרֶץ יִשְׂרָאֵל:

ל **כָּל מַכֵּה נֶפֶשׁ וְגוֹ׳.** הַבָּא לְהָרְגוֹ עַל שֶׁהִכָּה אֶת הַנֶּפֶשׁ: **לְפִי עֵדִים יִרְצַח.** שֶׁיָּעִידוּ שֶׁבְּמֵזִיד וּבְהַתְרָאָה הֲרָגוֹ:

לא **וְלֹא תִקְחוּ כֹפֶר.** לֹא יִפָּטֵר בְּמָמוֹן:

לב **וְלֹא תִקְחוּ כֹפֶר לָנוּס אֶל עִיר מִקְלָטוֹ.** לְמִי שֶׁנָּס אֶל עִיר מִקְלָט, שֶׁהָרַג בְּשׁוֹגֵג, אֵינוֹ נִפְטָר מִגָּלוּת בְּמָמוֹן לִתֵּן כֹּפֶר "לָשׁוּב לָשֶׁבֶת בָּאָרֶץ" בְּטֶרֶם יָמוּת הַכֹּהֵן: **לָנוּס.** כְּמוֹ 'לַנָּס', כְּמוֹ: "שׁוּבֵי מִלְחָמָה" (מיכה ב, ח), שֶׁשָּׁבוּ מִן הַמִּלְחָמָה, "נוּגֵי מִמּוֹעֵד" (צפניה ג, יח), "כִּי מְלִים הָיוּ" (יהושע ה, ה), כַּאֲשֶׁר תֹּאמַר 'שׁוּב' עַל מִי שֶׁשָּׁב כְּבָר, וּ'מוּל' עַל שֶׁמָּל כְּבָר, כֵּן תֹּאמַר 'לָנוּס' עַל מִי שֶׁנָּס כְּבָר, וְקוֹרֵהוּ 'נוּס' – מְבֹרָח. וְאִם תֹּאמַר 'לָנוּס' – לִבְרֹחַ, וּתְפָרְשֵׁהוּ: לֹא תִקְחוּ כֹפֶר לְמִי שֶׁיֵּשׁ לוֹ לִבְרֹחַ לְפָטְרוֹ מִן הַגָּלוּת, לֹא יָדַעְתִּי הֵיאַךְ יֹאמַר: "לָשׁוּב לָשֶׁבֶת בָּאָרֶץ", הֲרֵי עֲדַיִן לֹא נָס, וּמֵהֵיכָן יָשׁוּב?:

לג **וְלֹא תַחֲנִיפוּ.** וְלֹא תַרְשִׁיעוּ, כְּתַרְגּוּמוֹ: "וְלָא תְחַיְּבוּן":

לד **אֲשֶׁר אֲנִי שֹׁכֵן בְּתוֹכָהּ.** שֶׁלֹּא תַשְׁכִּינוּ אוֹתִי בְּטֻמְאָתָהּ: **כִּי אֲנִי ה׳ שֹׁכֵן בְּתוֹךְ בְּנֵי יִשְׂרָאֵל.** אַף בִּזְמַן שֶׁהֵם טְמֵאִים, שְׁכִינָה בֵּינֵיהֶם:

Since the human person is the image of God, murder is not merely a crime; it is sacrilege. It defiles the land. It desecrates something holy, namely human life itself.

4:10). Likewise we recall the central law of the covenant with Noaḥ: "One who sheds the blood of man, by man shall his blood be shed, for in God's image man was made" (9:6).

כו בָּ֔הּ עַד־מוֹת֙ הַכֹּהֵ֣ן הַגָּדֹ֔ל אֲשֶׁר־מָשַׁ֥ח אֹת֖וֹ בְּשֶׁ֥מֶן הַקֹּֽדֶשׁ׃ וְאִם־יָצֹ֥א
כז יֵצֵ֖א הָרֹצֵ֑חַ אֶת־גְּבוּל֙ עִ֣יר מִקְלָט֔וֹ אֲשֶׁ֥ר יָנ֖וּס שָֽׁמָּה׃ וּמָצָ֤א אֹתוֹ֙ גֹּאֵ֣ל
הַדָּ֔ם מִח֕וּץ לִגְב֖וּל עִ֣יר מִקְלָט֑וֹ וְרָצַ֞ח גֹּאֵ֤ל הַדָּם֙ אֶת־הָרֹצֵ֔חַ אֵ֥ין ל֖וֹ
כח דָּֽם׃ כִּ֣י בְעִ֤יר מִקְלָטוֹ֙ יֵשֵׁ֔ב עַד־מ֖וֹת הַכֹּהֵ֣ן הַגָּדֹ֑ל וְאַחֲרֵי־מוֹת֙ הַכֹּהֵ֣ן
כט הַגָּדֹ֔ל יָשׁוּב֙ הָרֹצֵ֔חַ אֶל־אֶ֖רֶץ אֲחֻזָּתֽוֹ׃ וְהָי֨וּ אֵ֧לֶּה לָכֶ֛ם לְחֻקַּ֥ת מִשְׁפָּ֖ט
ל לְדֹרֹתֵיכֶ֑ם בְּכֹ֖ל מוֹשְׁבֹתֵיכֶֽם׃ כָּל־מַכֵּה־נֶ֕פֶשׁ לְפִ֣י עֵדִ֔ים יִרְצַ֖ח אֶת־
לא הָרֹצֵ֑חַ וְעֵ֣ד אֶחָ֔ד לֹא־יַעֲנֶ֥ה בְנֶ֖פֶשׁ לָמֽוּת׃ וְלֹֽא־תִקְח֥וּ כֹ֙פֶר֙ לְנֶ֣פֶשׁ רֹצֵ֔חַ
לב אֲשֶׁר־ה֥וּא רָשָׁ֖ע לָמ֑וּת כִּי־מ֖וֹת יוּמָֽת׃ וְלֹא־תִקְח֣וּ כֹ֔פֶר לָנ֖וּס אֶל־עִ֣יר
לג מִקְלָט֑וֹ לָשׁוּב֙ לָשֶׁ֣בֶת בָּאָ֔רֶץ עַד־מ֖וֹת הַכֹּהֵֽן׃ וְלֹא־תַחֲנִ֣יפוּ אֶת־הָאָ֗רֶץ
אֲשֶׁ֤ר אַתֶּם֙ בָּ֔הּ כִּ֣י הַדָּ֔ם ה֥וּא יַחֲנִ֖יף אֶת־הָאָ֑רֶץ וְלָאָ֣רֶץ לֹֽא־יְכֻפַּ֗ר לַדָּם֙
לד אֲשֶׁ֣ר שֻׁפַּךְ־בָּ֔הּ כִּי־אִ֖ם בְּדַ֥ם שֹׁפְכֽוֹ׃ וְלֹ֤א תְטַמֵּא֙ אֶת־הָאָ֔רֶץ אֲשֶׁ֤ר
אַתֶּם֙ יֹשְׁבִ֣ים בָּ֔הּ אֲשֶׁ֥ר אֲנִ֖י שֹׁכֵ֣ן בְּתוֹכָ֑הּ כִּ֚י אֲנִ֣י יהוה שֹׁכֵ֕ן בְּת֖וֹךְ בְּנֵ֥י
יִשְׂרָאֵֽל׃

אונקלוס

בַּהּ, עַד דִּימוּת כָּהֲנָא רַבָּא, דְּרַבִּי יָתֵיהּ בִּמְשַׁח קֻדְשָׁא: כו וְאִם מִפָּק יִפּוֹק קָטוֹלָא, יָת תְּחוּם קִרְיַת שֵׁיזָבוּתֵיהּ, דִּיעְרוֹק לְתַמָּן: כז וְיַשְׁכַּח יָתֵיהּ גָּאֵיל דְּמָא, מִבָּרָא, לִתְחוּם קִרְיַת שֵׁיזָבוּתֵיהּ, וְיִקְטוֹל, גָּאֵיל דְּמָא יָת קָטוֹלָא, לֵית לֵיהּ דַּם: כח אֲרֵי בְּקִרְיַת שֵׁיזָבוּתֵיהּ יִתֵּיב, עַד דִּימוּת כָּהֲנָא רַבָּא, וּבָתַר דִּימוּת כָּהֲנָא רַבָּא, יְתוּב קָטוֹלָא, לַאֲרַע אַחְסָנְתֵיהּ: כט וִיהוֹן אִלֵּין לְכוֹן, לִגְזֵירַת דִּין לְדָרֵיכוֹן, בְּכָל מוֹתְבָנֵיכוֹן: ל כָּל דְּיִקְטוֹל נַפְשָׁא, לְפוּם סָהֲדִין, יִקְטוֹל יָת קָטוֹלָא, וְסָהִיד חַד, לָא יַסְהֵיד בֶּאֱנָשׁ לְמִקְטַל: לא וְלָא תְקַבְּלוּן מָמוֹן עַל אֱנָשׁ קָטוֹל, דְּהוּא חַיָּב לִמְמָת, אֲרֵי אִתְקְטָלָא יִתְקְטִיל: לב וְלָא תְקַבְּלוּן מָמוֹן, לְמִעְרַק לְקִרְיַת שֵׁיזָבוּתֵיהּ, לִמְתָב לְמִתַּב בְּאַרְעָא, עַד דִּימוּת כָּהֲנָא: לג וְלָא תְחַיְּבוּן יָת אַרְעָא, דְּאַתּוּן בַּהּ, אֲרֵי דְמָא, הוּא מְחַיֵּיב יָת אַרְעָא, וּלְאַרְעָא לָא מִתְכַּפַּר, עַל דַּם זַכַּאי דְּאִתְאֲשַׁד בַּהּ, אֱלָהֵין בִּדַם אַשְׁדֵיהּ: לד וְלָא תְסָאֲבוּן יָת אַרְעָא, דְּאַתּוּן יָתְבִין בַּהּ, דִּשְׁכִינְתִּי שָׁרְיָא בְּגַוַּהּ, אֲרֵי אֲנָא יי, שְׁכִינְתִּי שָׁרְיָא, בְּגוֹ בְּנֵי יִשְׂרָאֵל:

35:33 הַדָּם הוּא יַחֲנִיף אֶת־הָאָרֶץ *Blood pollutes the land* – The root *ḥ-n-f*, which appears twice in this verse and nowhere else in the Mosaic books, means "to pollute," "to soil," "to dirty," "to defile." There is something fundamentally blemished about a world in which murder goes unpunished. The book of Numbers draws to a close, then, with a statement of one of the fundamentals of Judaism: the sanctity of human life. As the people approach the land that will become holy, they are reminded: "You shall not pollute the land in which you live; blood pollutes the land" (Num. 35:33). With these words we are brought back almost to the beginning of the human story, to the scene in which the first child, Kayin, murders the second, Hevel, and is told by God, "The voice of your brother's blood cries out to Me from the land" (Gen.

36 1 The heads of the ancestral houses of the descendants of Gilad son of Makhir SHEVI'I
son of Menashe, one of the families of Yosef's sons, came forward and spoke
before Moshe and the leaders, the heads of the ancestral houses of the Israelites.
2 "The Lord," they said, "commanded my lord to give the land as an inheritance
to the Israelites by lot. But my lord was also commanded by the Lord to give
3 the inheritance of our brother Tzelofḥad to his daughters. If they marry men
from another Israelite tribe, their share will be taken away from our ancestral
inheritance and given to the tribe into which they marry. It will be taken away
4 from the allotted portion of our inheritance. When the Israelites observe the
Jubilee, their inheritance will be added to that of the tribe into which they
married; their inheritance will be taken away from the inheritance of our
5 forefathers' tribe." Then Moshe, at the Lord's word, commanded the Israelites:
6 "What the tribe of Yosef's descendants say is right. This is the word that the
Lord has commanded to Tzelofḥad's daughters: They may marry whomever
7 they wish as long as they marry within a clan of their father's tribe, so that

רש"י

לו ג **וְנוֹסַף עַל נַחֲלַת הַמַּטֶּה.** שֶׁהֲרֵי בְּנָהּ יוֹרְשָׁהּ, וְהַבֵּן מִתְיַחֵס עַל שֵׁבֶט אָבִיו:

ד **וְאִם יִהְיֶה הַיֹּבֵל.** מִכָּאן הָיָה רַבִּי יְהוּדָה אוֹמֵר: עָתִיד הַיּוֹבֵל שֶׁיִּפָּסֵק: **וְאִם יִהְיֶה הַיֹּבֵל.** כְּלוֹמַר, אֵין זוֹ מְכִירָה שֶׁחוֹזֶרֶת בַּיּוֹבֵל, שֶׁהַיְרֻשָּׁה אֵינָהּ חוֹזֶרֶת, וַאֲפִלּוּ אִם יִהְיֶה הַיּוֹבֵל לֹא תַּחְזֹר הַנַּחֲלָה לְשִׁבְטוֹ, וְנִמְצָא שֶׁנּוֹסְפָה "עַל נַחֲלַת הַמַּטֶּה אֲשֶׁר תִּהְיֶינָה לָהֶם":

each count (see note on Num. 1:2). The book also focuses on the psychology of individuals. We read of Moshe's despair, of Aharon and Miriam's criticism of him, of the spies who lacked the courage to come back with a positive report, and of the malcontents, led by Koraḥ, who challenged Moshe's leadership. We read of Yehoshua and Kalev, Eldad and Meidad, Datan and Aviram, Zimri and Pinḥas, Balak and Bilam.

Against this backdrop we can understand the claim of Tzelofḥad's daughters. They were invoking their rights as individuals. Recognizing the justice of the women's cause, God affirmed their rights as individuals. But society is not built on individuals alone. We each have a series of identities, based partly on family background, partly on occupation, partly on locality and community. These "mediating structures," larger than the individual but smaller than the state, are where we develop our complex, vivid, face-to-face interactions and identities. This domain is known as civil society and a strong civil society is essential to liberty. We have rights as individuals; we have identities as members of communities. The existence of something like tribes is fundamental to a free society.

That is the Torah's point in dividing the story of the daughters of Tzelofḥad. The first part, in Pinḥas, is about individual rights, the rights of Tzelofḥad's daughters to a share in the land. The second, at the end of the book, is about group rights, the right of the tribe of Menashe to its territory.

A culture based solely on individual rights will undermine families, communities, traditions, loyalties, and shared codes of reverence and restraint. We should be free to live, worship, and identify as we choose. But despite its emphasis on the individual, Judaism also insists on the value of those institutions that preserve and protect our identities as members of groups. Honoring both is delicate, difficult, and necessary. Numbers ends by showing us how.

לו א וַיִּקְרְבוּ רָאשֵׁי הָאָבוֹת לְמִשְׁפַּחַת בְּנֵי־גִלְעָד בֶּן־מָכִיר בֶּן־מְנַשֶּׁה שביעי
מִמִּשְׁפְּחֹת בְּנֵי יוֹסֵף וַיְדַבְּרוּ לִפְנֵי מֹשֶׁה וְלִפְנֵי הַנְּשִׂאִים רָאשֵׁי אָבוֹת
ב לִבְנֵי יִשְׂרָאֵל: וַיֹּאמְרוּ אֶת־אֲדֹנִי צִוָּה יהוה לָתֵת אֶת־הָאָרֶץ בְּנַחֲלָה
בְּגוֹרָל לִבְנֵי יִשְׂרָאֵל וַאדֹנִי צֻוָּה בַיהוה לָתֵת אֶת־נַחֲלַת צְלָפְחָד
ג אָחִינוּ לִבְנֹתָיו: וְהָיוּ לְאֶחָד מִבְּנֵי שִׁבְטֵי בְנֵי־יִשְׂרָאֵל לְנָשִׁים וְנִגְרְעָה
נַחֲלָתָן מִנַּחֲלַת אֲבֹתֵינוּ וְנוֹסַף עַל נַחֲלַת הַמַּטֶּה אֲשֶׁר תִּהְיֶינָה לָהֶם
ד וּמִגֹּרַל נַחֲלָתֵנוּ יִגָּרֵעַ: וְאִם־יִהְיֶה הַיֹּבֵל לִבְנֵי יִשְׂרָאֵל וְנוֹסְפָה נַחֲלָתָן
עַל נַחֲלַת הַמַּטֶּה אֲשֶׁר תִּהְיֶינָה לָהֶם וּמִנַּחֲלַת מַטֵּה אֲבֹתֵינוּ יִגָּרַע
ה נַחֲלָתָן: וַיְצַו מֹשֶׁה אֶת־בְּנֵי יִשְׂרָאֵל עַל־פִּי יהוה לֵאמֹר כֵּן מַטֵּה בְנֵי־
ו יוֹסֵף דֹּבְרִים: זֶה הַדָּבָר אֲשֶׁר־צִוָּה יהוה לִבְנוֹת צְלָפְחָד לֵאמֹר לַטּוֹב

אונקלוס

לו א וְקָרִיבוּ רֵישֵׁי אֲבָהָתָא, לְזַרְעִית בְּנֵי גִלְעָד בַּר מָכִיר בַּר מְנַשֶּׁה, מִזַּרְעִית בְּנֵי יוֹסֵף, וּמַלִּילוּ, קֳדָם מֹשֶׁה וּקְדָם רַבְרְבַיָּא, רֵישֵׁי אֲבָהָתָא לִבְנֵי יִשְׂרָאֵל: ב וַאֲמַרוּ, יָת רִבּוֹנִי פַּקֵּיד יְיָ, לְמִתַּן יָת אַרְעָא בְּאַחְסָנָא, בְּעַדְבָא לִבְנֵי יִשְׂרָאֵל, וְרִבּוֹנִי אִתְפַּקַּד בְּמֵימְרָא דַּייָ, לְמִתַּן, יָת אַחְסָנַת, צְלָפְחָד אֲחוּנָא לִבְנָתֵיהּ: ג וִיהֶוְיָן, לְחַד, מִבְּנֵי שִׁבְטֵי בְּנֵי יִשְׂרָאֵל לִנְשִׁין, וְתִתְמְנַע אַחְסָנַתְהוֹן מֵאַחְסָנַת אֲבָהָתַנָא, וְתִתּוֹסַף, עַל אַחְסָנַת שִׁבְטָא, דִּיהֶוְיָן לְהוֹן, וּמֵעֲדַב אַחְסָנְתַנָא יִתְמְנַע: ד וְאִם יְהֵי יוֹבֵילָא לִבְנֵי יִשְׂרָאֵל, וְתִתּוֹסַף אַחְסָנַתְהוֹן, עַל אַחְסָנַת שִׁבְטָא, דִּיהֶוְיָן לְהוֹן, וּמֵאַחְסָנַת שִׁבְטָא דַּאֲבָהָתַנָא, תִּתְמְנַע אַחְסָנַתְהוֹן: ה וּפַקֵּיד מֹשֶׁה יָת בְּנֵי יִשְׂרָאֵל, עַל מֵימְרָא דַּייָ לְמֵימַר, יָאוּת, שִׁבְטָא דִּבְנֵי יוֹסֵף מְמַלְּלִין: ו דֵּין פִּתְגָמָא דְּפַקֵּיד יְיָ, לִבְנָת צְלָפְחָד לְמֵימַר, לִדְתָקֵין בְּעֵינֵיהוֹן יְהֶוְיָן

THE DAUGHTERS OF TZELOFḤAD – EPILOGUE

In Parashat Pinḥas we read of how the five daughters of Tzelofḥad came to Moshe with a request to be permitted to inherit their father's land based on the principles of justice. Now, at the end of the book, the Torah reports on another event arising from that case. Leaders of Tzelofḥad's tribe, Menashe, make the following complaint: If the land were to pass to Tzelofḥad's daughters and they married men from another tribe, the land would eventually pass to their husbands, and thus to their husbands' tribes. Thus, land that had initially been granted to the tribe of Menashe might be lost to it in perpetuity.

Again, Moshe takes the case to God, who offers a solution. The daughters of Tzelofḥad are entitled to the land, but so too is the tribe. If they wish to take possession of the land, they must marry men from within their own tribe. That way both claims can be honored. The daughters do not lose their right to the land but they do lose some freedom in choosing a marriage partner.

The two passages are intimately related. Why then are they separated in the text, and why does the book of Numbers end on this seemingly anticlimactic note? Numbers as a book is about individuals. It begins with a census, whose purpose is to "lift the heads" (in the literal Hebrew) of the Israelites. This is the unusual locution the Torah uses to convey that God orders a census to tell the people that they

the Israelites' inheritance does not pass from one tribe to another. Thus
the Israelites will each stay attached to the inheritance of their ancestral
8 tribes. Every daughter among the Israelite tribes who inherits land must
marry a member of her father's tribe, so that the Israelites may possess the
9 inheritance of their ancestors. No inheritance may pass from one tribe to
another; each Israelite tribe shall remain attached to its own inheritance."
10 11 Tzelofḥad's daughters did as the LORD commanded Moshe. Maḥla, Tirtza, MAFTIR
Ḥogla, Milka, and Noa, Tzelofḥad's daughters, were each married to men
12 who were their cousins. They thus married into the families of Menashe son
of Yosef, and their inheritance remained within the tribe of their father's clan.
13 All these are the commandments and laws that the LORD gave through Moshe
to the Israelites on the plains of Moav, by the Jordan, across from Yeriḥo.

The haftara for Parashat Masei is on page 1602.
Read this haftara even when it is Rosh Ḥodesh Av.

רש״י

ח וְכָל בַּת יֹרֶשֶׁת נַחֲלָה. שֶׁלֹּא הָיָה בֵּן לְאָבִיהָ:
יא מַחְלָה תִרְצָה וְגוֹ׳. כָּאן מְנָאָן לְפִי גְּדֻלָּתָן זוֹ מִזּוֹ בְּשָׁנִים, וְנִשְּׂאוּ כְּסֵדֶר תּוֹלְדוֹתָן, וּבְכָל הַמִּקְרָא מְנָאָן לְפִי חָכְמָתָן, וּמַגִּיד שֶׁשְּׁקוּלוֹת זוֹ כָּזוֹ:

favoritism. It is almost as if the Torah were describing the Israelites the way it describes the cosmos in the first chapter of Genesis, everything in its due proportion and proper place.

Then, in chapters 11–25, comes the chaos: dissension in the camp, complaints and criticism. The attempt to prepare the people for entry into the land by sending spies ends in disaster. The people panic and rebel. Kalev and Yehoshua attempt to calm them and fail. Next comes the story of the Koraḥ rebellion, a tale of the chaos that results when authority is challenged and ceases to command respect. Finally, after the story of Bilam, comes the absolute nadir, when the Israelite men bring disaster on themselves by acts of immorality and idolatry. Complete chaos reigns in the camp, ended only by an act of violent zealotry on the part of Pinḥas.

After this stark contrast between order and chaos comes part 3, chapters 26–36, in which a new beginning is made, starting symbolically with a new census and a new generation. From here on, there are no rebellions. Order prevails. There are provisions for the sacrifices to be brought at their appointed times. The land is apportioned between the tribes. Levitical towns and cities of refuge are designated. Claims such as those of Tzelofḥad's daughters (ch. 27) and the heads of their tribe (ch. 36) are resolved peaceably, as is a potential conflict between the rest of the people and the Reubenites and Gadites. There is an orderly transition from Moshe's leadership to his successor Yehoshua. Battles are fought and won. The long journey is nearing its end, all its stages enumerated and recorded. For all the intervening chaos, order wins in the end.

The journey has not been only physical, a walk across the desert. It has been psychological, moral, and spiritual. It has taken as long as the time needed for human beings to change. Freedom, the Torah candidly acknowledges, is immensely demanding. It is *avoda,* "hard work." It is striking that the Torah uses the same Hebrew word to describe slavery to Pharaoh and servitude to God. There is all the difference in the world between being enslaved to a human ruler and serving the Creator of the universe who made us all in His image, but the difference is not that the one is hard and the other is easy. They are both hard work, but one breaks the spirit, the other lifts and exalts it. A free society is a spiritual achievement. Maintaining liberty is as challenging today as it was in the days of Moshe. The book of Numbers remains one of its classic texts.

בְּעֵינֵיהֶם תִּהְיֶינָה לְנָשִׁים אַךְ לְמִשְׁפַּחַת מַטֵּה אֲבִיהֶם תִּהְיֶינָה לְנָשִׁים׃
ז וְלֹא־תִסֹּב נַחֲלָה לִבְנֵי יִשְׂרָאֵל מִמַּטֶּה אֶל־מַטֶּה כִּי אִישׁ בְּנַחֲלַת מַטֵּה
ח אֲבֹתָיו יִדְבְּקוּ בְּנֵי יִשְׂרָאֵל׃ וְכָל־בַּת יֹרֶשֶׁת נַחֲלָה מִמַּטּוֹת בְּנֵי יִשְׂרָאֵל
לְאֶחָד מִמִּשְׁפַּחַת מַטֵּה אָבִיהָ תִּהְיֶה לְאִשָּׁה לְמַעַן יִירְשׁוּ בְּנֵי יִשְׂרָאֵל
ט אִישׁ נַחֲלַת אֲבֹתָיו׃ וְלֹא־תִסֹּב נַחֲלָה מִמַּטֶּה לְמַטֶּה אַחֵר כִּי־אִישׁ
י בְּנַחֲלָתוֹ יִדְבְּקוּ מַטּוֹת בְּנֵי יִשְׂרָאֵל׃ כַּאֲשֶׁר צִוָּה יְהוָה אֶת־מֹשֶׁה כֵּן
יא עָשׂוּ בְּנוֹת צְלָפְחָד׃ וַתִּהְיֶינָה מַחְלָה תִרְצָה וְחָגְלָה וּמִלְכָּה וְנֹעָה בְּנוֹת מפטיר
יב צְלָפְחָד לִבְנֵי דֹדֵיהֶן לְנָשִׁים׃ מִמִּשְׁפְּחֹת בְּנֵי־מְנַשֶּׁה בֶן־יוֹסֵף הָיוּ לְנָשִׁים
יג וַתְּהִי נַחֲלָתָן עַל־מַטֵּה מִשְׁפַּחַת אֲבִיהֶן׃ אֵלֶּה הַמִּצְוֺת וְהַמִּשְׁפָּטִים
אֲשֶׁר צִוָּה יְהוָה בְּיַד־מֹשֶׁה אֶל־בְּנֵי יִשְׂרָאֵל בְּעַרְבֹת מוֹאָב עַל יַרְדֵּן יְרֵחוֹ׃

The הפטרה *for* פרשת מסעי *is on page 1603.*
Read this הפטרה *even when it is* ראש חודש אב.

אונקלוס

לִנְשִׁין, בְּרַם, לְזַרְעִית, שִׁבְטָא דַּאֲבוּהוֹן יְהֶוְיָן לִנְשִׁין: ז וְלָא תַסְחַר אַחְסָנָא לִבְנֵי יִשְׂרָאֵל, מִשִּׁבְטָא לְשִׁבְטָא, אֲרֵי גְּבַר, בְּאַחְסָנַת שִׁבְטָא דַּאֲבָהָתוֹהִי, יִדְבְּקוּן בְּנֵי יִשְׂרָאֵל: ח וְכָל בְּרַתָּא יָרְתַת אַחְסָנָא, מִשִּׁבְטַיָּא דִּבְנֵי יִשְׂרָאֵל, לְחַד, מִזַּרְעִית, שִׁבְטָא דַּאֲבוּהָא תְּהֵי לְאִתּוּ, בְּדִיל, דְּיֵירְתוּן בְּנֵי יִשְׂרָאֵל, גְּבַר אַחְסָנַת אֲבָהָתוֹהִי: ט וְלָא תַסְחַר אַחְסָנָא, מִשִּׁבְטָא לְשִׁבְטָא אָחֳרָנָא, אֲרֵי גְּבַר בְּאַחְסָנְתֵיהּ, יִדְבְּקוּן, שִׁבְטַיָּא דִּבְנֵי יִשְׂרָאֵל: י כְּמָא דְּפַקֵּיד יי יָת מֹשֶׁה, כֵּן עֲבַדָא בְּנָת צְלָפְחָד: יא וַהֲוָאָה מַחְלָה תִּרְצָה, וְחָגְלָה וּמִלְכָּה, וְנוֹעָה בְּנָת צְלָפְחָד, לִבְנֵי אֲחֵי אֲבוּהוֹן לִנְשִׁין: יב מִזַּרְעִית, בְּנֵי מְנַשֶּׁה בַר יוֹסֵף הֲוָאָה לִנְשִׁין, וַהֲוָת אַחְסָנְתְהוֹן, עַל שֵׁיבֶט זַרְעִית אֲבוּהוֹן: יג אִלֵּין פִּקּוֹדַיָּא וְדִינַיָּא, דְּפַקֵּיד יי, בִּידָא דְמֹשֶׁה לְוָת בְּנֵי יִשְׂרָאֵל, בְּמֵישְׁרַיָּא דְמוֹאָב, עַל יַרְדְּנָא דִירֵיחוֹ:

NUMBERS: THE NARRATIVE STRUCTURE

There have been times when the book of Numbers has resembled a bricolage of texts pasted together with no overarching structure or theme. Many of its laws read as if they more properly belong to Leviticus. Other passages read like repetitions of stories we encountered in the book of Exodus. Then there is the sheer overwhelming negativity of the narratives, culminating at Baal Peor in a complete breakdown of all that was supposed to characterize the Israelites as "a kingdom of priests and a holy nation" (Ex. 19:6). What is Numbers about? What hope is there to be rescued from this cumulative tale of failure and faithlessness? What is its overarching theme?

The central question of the Torah is how freedom and order, the essential elements in God's creation of the universe, can coexist in the universes human beings create (see Ex. 40, "Exodus: The Narrative Structure").

Understanding this, we notice that the book of Numbers is divided into three sections. The first, chapters 1–10, shows the Israelites preparing to begin the second half of their journey. The tribes are numbered. They are encamped, in precise formation, around the Sanctuary. There is a series of laws designed to maintain the purity of the camp and ward off potential threats to its peace. There is a lengthy account of the offerings brought by the tribes at the inauguration of the Sanctuary, each stated in the same words as if to avoid any

דברים
DEUTERONOMY

THE BOOK OF DEUTERONOMY

The Hebrew names of the Mosaic books convey important insights into the nature of the book. The fifth book of the Torah is named in Hebrew *Devarim*, "words," taken from the opening verse. The whole of Torah is "words." What, then, is the connection between the title of this particular book and its contents?

The first connection is Moshe himself. He is a man transformed. Recall his words to God at the burning bush at the very outset of his mission: "Then Moshe said to the Lord, 'Please, my Lord, I am not a man of words (*ish devarim*).... I am slow of speech and tongue'" (Ex. 4:10). Of Moshe alone – "very humble, more so than any other man on earth" (Num. 12:3) – could it be said that his words, *devarim*, were the words of God. It was precisely because he said, "I am not a man of words" that he became the man of Devarim, the one whose words were not his own but those of the Divine Presence, the *Shekhina*, speaking through his lips – the most eloquent spokesman of God in all history.

The second significance of *devarim*, "words," is that it is the supreme expression of the politics of the word: a society founded on the basis of a covenant, a text, a set of mutual promises, by which God and His people pledge themselves in loyalty to one another.

The third significance is that Israel's existence as a nation is not based on power or a land (though it longs for and is promised both) but on words – the words of God to Israel and the acceptance of those words by Israel. *So long as the word exists, Israel exists; and because God is eternal and never revokes His word, Israel will always exist.* Because Israel's very being as a nation is constituted by *devarim*, the "words" of God, there is always the possibility and promise of return. Israel, alone among the nations of the world, survives the loss of power and land because there is something it will never lose: God's word given and received in love. "Take words..." – the words of the covenant – "with you and return to the Lord" (Hos. 14:3). Israel survived because it never lost the words that bound it to God and God to it. That was the basis of its survival in exile. Those "words" were never rescinded. Hence Israel never lost the promise of return.

So the decision to call the fifth and final book of the Torah *Devarim* brought together in a single word the three main themes of the book: the uniqueness of Moshe as a prophet, the uniqueness of Israel as a nation, and the uniqueness of Jewish history as a narrative of exile and return. The book of *Devarim*, "words," is the supreme expression of the power of the word to link heaven and earth, God and a people, in an unbreakable bond of mutual loyalty.

Parashat Devarim

1 1 These are the words that Moshe spoke to all Israel east of the Jordan, in the

רש"י

א א אֵלֶּה הַדְּבָרִים. לְפִי שֶׁהֵן דִּבְרֵי תוֹכָחוֹת, וּמָנָה כָּאן כָּל הַמְּקוֹמוֹת שֶׁהִכְעִיסוּ לִפְנֵי הַמָּקוֹם בָּהֶן, לְפִיכָךְ סָתַם אֶת הַדְּבָרִים וְהִזְכִּירָם בְּרֶמֶז, מִפְּנֵי כְּבוֹדָן שֶׁל יִשְׂרָאֵל: אֶל כָּל יִשְׂרָאֵל. אִלּוּ הוֹכִיחַ מִקְצָתָן, הָיוּ אֵלּוּ שֶׁבַּשּׁוּק אוֹמְרִים: אַתֶּם הֱיִיתֶם שׁוֹמְעִים מִבֶּן עַמְרָם וְלֹא הֲשִׁיבוֹתֶם דָּבָר, מִכָּךְ וְכָךְ, אִלּוּ הָיִינוּ שָׁם הָיִינוּ מְשִׁיבִין אוֹתוֹ; לְכָךְ כִּנְּסָם כֻּלָּם וְאָמַר לָהֶם: הֲרֵי כֻּלְּכֶם כָּאן, כָּל מִי שֶׁיֵּשׁ לוֹ תְּשׁוּבָה יָשִׁיב: **בַּמִּדְבָּר.** לֹא בַּמִּדְבָּר הָיוּ אֶלָּא בְּעַרְבוֹת מוֹאָב, וּמַהוּ "בַּמִּדְבָּר"? אֶלָּא בִּשְׁבִיל מַה שֶּׁהִכְעִיסוּהוּ בַּמִּדְבָּר, שֶׁאָמְרוּ: "מִי יִתֵּן מוּתֵנוּ" וְגוֹ' (שמות טז, ג): **בָּעֲרָבָה.** בִּשְׁבִיל הָעֲרָבָה, שֶׁחָטְאוּ בְּבַעַל פְּעוֹר בְּשִׁטִּים בְּעַרְבוֹת מוֹאָב:

Despite the fact that the Jewish people agreed three times to accept the terms on which God was to become their sovereign, they were not yet ready for such responsibility. The story of the golden calf demonstrated that they were still in an age of magical thinking in which people do what the gods require and gods produce the outcome the people desire. It took the long journey through the desert to grow into an *ethic of responsibility*.

The covenants of Noaḥ, Avraham, and Sinai began with an act of divine initiative. The fourth, which comprises the whole of the book of Deuteronomy, is undertaken by human initiative. It is Moshe who rehearses and recites the whole content and context of the covenant. That is why Deuteronomy is the turning point in Jewish history. It marks the move from divine initiative to human responsibility.

Deuteronomy is the book of the covenant, the center point of Jewish theology. It aims at the construction of a society worthy of being a home for the Divine Presence – one that will moralize its members, inspire others, and serve as a role model of what might be achieved were humanity as a whole to worship the God who made us all in His image. "These are the words" of the covenant initiated by Moshe.

1:1 כָּל־יִשְׂרָאֵל *All Israel* – Rabbi Efrayim Luntschitz (1550–1619), in his commentary *Keli Yakar,* noted that the phrase *kol Yisrael,* which appears eleven times in Deuteronomy, exists nowhere else in the Mosaic books. Until now the Israelites have been described as *Bnei Yisrael,* literally "the children of Israel." Now for the first time they are no longer "the children of Israel" – they are simply "Israel." Until now, they have been linked by biological descent. They have a common ancestor: Yaakov, who was given the name Yisrael. They are part of the same family tree.

Now, Moshe is preparing the Israelites for a new mode of existence. They are no longer children, but are about to become moral adults. Their unity is no longer simply a matter of a common past; rather, they are to create a shared future. They are no longer to exist in a state of dependency – relying on Moshe and through him, God, to provide for their needs, welfare, and safety. Henceforth, they will have to take responsibility for one another.

Through this subtle linguistic shift, Moshe indicates that once the Israelites cross the Jordan they will become a nation, not just a family. They will have to fight wars, defend themselves, institute systems of justice and welfare, and learn the necessity for, as well as the limits of, politics.

None of that is necessary in the wilderness. God provided their needs, fought their battles, sent them food and water, and gave them shelter. In the land of Israel, God will still be with them, but only rarely in the form of miracles. No longer will it be God serving the people, giving them all they need. It will be the people serving God. The nation will be defined by the covenant their parents made at Mount Sinai. It will be their constitution, their mission, their task, their destiny. They are about to change from a group of individuals with a common ancestry to a nation bound by collective responsibility. God does not choose, nor does He make a covenant with, individuals as individuals. He makes a covenant with an entire people, righteous and not-yet-righteous

פרשת דברים

א א אֵ֣לֶּה הַדְּבָרִ֗ים אֲשֶׁ֨ר דִּבֶּ֤ר מֹשֶׁה֙ אֶל־כָּל־יִשְׂרָאֵ֔ל בְּעֵ֖בֶר הַיַּרְדֵּ֑ן בַּמִּדְבָּ֡ר א

אונקלוס

א א אִלֵּין פִּתְגָמַיָּא, דְּמַלֵּיל מֹשֶׁה עִם כָּל יִשְׂרָאֵל, בְּעִבְרָא דְּיַרְדְּנָא, אוֹכַח יָתְהוֹן עַל דְּחָבוּ בְּמַדְבְּרָא, וְעַל דְּאַרְגִּיזוּ

DEVARIM

The book of Deuteronomy as a whole is structured on the model of a covenant, and represents Moshe's renewal of the Sinai covenant with the next generation, who would enter the Promised Land and there create a covenant-based society. Accordingly, our *parasha* opens with the first two elements of a covenant document: a preamble identifying the speaker and context (Deut. 1:1–5) and a historical prologue recalling the events that led to the covenant and its renewal (beginning at 1:6).

The preamble identifies the time and place: the last weeks of Moshe's life, with the people encamped by the banks of the Jordan. Moshe recalls his appointments of leaders, the sending of the spies, and the people's failure of nerve that led to the forty-year stay in the wilderness. Moving to more recent episodes, he reminds the people of their victories over Moav and Ammon and the settlement of their land by the tribes of Reuven and Gad and part of Menashe. The *parasha* ends with Moshe's description of his appointment of, and encouragement to, Yehoshua as his successor. Moshe's role changes, in these last weeks of his life, as he becomes the great exemplar of the teacher as hero.

"THESE ARE THE WORDS"

The last book of the Ḥumash is the foundational text of covenantal politics, that is, a political order created out of words. Daniel Elazar, the political scientist who pioneered the study of covenantal politics, explains that there are three fundamental types of political structure, differentiated by the way they come into existence. The first is by conquest, the second is by organic development, and the third, born in ancient Israel, is covenant. "Covenantal foundings" suggests Elazar, "emphasize the deliberate coming together of humans as equals to establish bodies politic in such a way that all reaffirm their fundamental equality and retain their basic rights."

If conquest represents the politics of power, and organic development the politics of the elite, covenant is the politics of the word. It involves a document to which all sides agree to be bound. Deuteronomy defines Israel as a nation uniquely brought into being by a mutually binding pledge between a people and God in which God adopts the people as His own, and the people in turn agree to be bound to His authority and word.

Covenant is central to the emergence of free societies in the West. It is no accident that covenantal politics – movements rooted in the equality of dignity and shared responsibility of all citizens – emerged in the seventeenth century. It was then, under the twin influence of the Reformation and the spread of printing, that Europeans for the first time read the Hebrew Bible for themselves, in their homes and in their own language. Western freedom is biblical freedom.

Covenantal responsibility does not arise all at once. God makes one covenant with Noaḥ. He makes a further one with Avraham, and He makes a third with the Israelites at Sinai. The covenant with Noaḥ is entirely unilateral. God speaks, issuing certain rules, and nothing more is required from Noaḥ himself. The covenant with Avraham requires Avraham to perform an act – circumcision – for himself and the male members of his family. The covenant with the Israelites at Sinai is more demanding still in that God insists that Moshe indicate the nature of the agreement to the Israelites, and only when they agree, which they do three times (Ex. 19:8; 24:3, 7), does the covenant have force.

This is the key covenant of the Torah, and in principle should be its culmination. But it turned out not to be so.

wilderness; in the Arava across from Suf, between Paran and Tofel, Lavan,
2 Ḥatzerot, and Di Zahav. By way of Mount Se'ir, it takes eleven days to cross
3 from Ḥorev to Kadesh Barnea. In the fortieth year, on the first day of the
eleventh month, Moshe spoke to the Israelites exactly as the Lord had
4 commanded him regarding them, after he had defeated Siḥon, king of the
Amorites, who lived in Ḥeshbon, and Og, king of Bashan, who lived in Ashtarot
5 and in Edre'i. On the east bank of the Jordan, in the land of Moav, Moshe began

רש"י

מול סוף. על מה שהמרו בים סוף, בבואם לים סוף, שאמרו: "המבלי אין קברים במצרים" (שמות יד, יא), וכן בנסעם מתוך הים, שנאמר: "וימרו על ים בים סוף" (תהלים קו, ז), כדאיתא בערכין (דף טו ע"א): **בין פארן ובין תפל ולבן.** אמר רבי יוחנן: חזרנו על כל המקרא ולא מצינו מקום ששמו תפל ולבן, אלא הוכיחן על הדברים שתפלו על המן שהוא לבן, שאמרו: "ונפשנו קצה בלחם הקלקל" (במדבר כא, ה), ועל מה שעשו במדבר פארן על ידי המרגלים: **וחצרת.** במחלקתו של קרח. דבר אחר, אמר להם: היה לכם ללמד ממה שעשיתי למרים בחצרות בשביל לשון הרע, ואתם נדברתם במקום: **ודי זהב.** הוכיחן על העגל שעשו בשביל רב זהב שהיה להם, שנאמר: "וכסף הרביתי לה וזהב עשו לבעל" (הושע ב, י):

ב **אחד עשר יום מחרב.** אמר להם משה: ראו מה גרמתם, אין לכם דרך קצרה מחורב לקדש ברנע כדרך הר שעיר, ואף היא מהלך אחד עשר יום ואתם הלכתם אותה בשלשה ימים, שהרי בעשרים באייר נסעו מחורב, שנאמר: "ויהי בשנה השנית בחדש השני בעשרים בחדש" וגו' (במדבר י, יא), ובעשרים ותשעה בסיון שלחו את המרגלים מקדש ברנע, צא מהם שלשים יום שעשו בקברות התאוה שאכלו הבשר חדש ימים, ושבעה ימים שעשו בחצרות להסגר של מרים, נמצא בשלשה ימים הלכו כל אותו הדרך, וכל כך היתה השכינה מתלבטת בשבילכם למהר ביאתכם לארץ דרך הר שעיר, ובשביל שקלקלתם הסב אתכם סביבות הר שעיר ארבעים שנה:

ג **ויהי בארבעים שנה בעשתי עשר חדש באחד לחדש.** מלמד שלא הוכיחן אלא סמוך למיתה. ממי למד? מיעקב, שלא הוכיח את בניו אלא סמוך למיתה. אמר: ראובן בני, אני אומר לך מפני מה לא הוכחתיך כל השנים הללו, כדי שלא תניחני ותלך ותדבק בעשו אחי. ומפני ארבעה דברים אין מוכיחין את האדם אלא סמוך למיתה: כדי שלא יהא מוכיחו וחוזר ומוכיחו, ושלא יהא חברו רואהו ומתבייש ממנו וכו', כדאיתא בספרי (ב). וכן יהושע לא הוכיח את ישראל אלא סמוך למיתה. וכן שמואל, שנאמר: "הנני ענו בי" (שמואל א' יב, ג). וכן דוד את שלמה בנו:

ד **אחרי הכתו.** אמר משה: אם אני מוכיחם קדם שיכנסו לקצות הארץ, יאמרו: מה לזה עלינו, מה היטיב לנו, אינו בא אלא לקנתר ולמצא עלה, שאין בו כח להכניסנו לארץ. לפיכך המתין עד שהפיל סיחון ועוג לפניהם והורישם את ארצם, ואחר כך הוכיחן: סיחן... **אשר יושב בחשבון.** אלו לא היה סיחון קשה והיה שרוי בחשבון, היה קשה, שהמדינה קשה. ואלו היתה עיר אחרת וסיחון שרוי בתוכה, היה קשה, שהמלך קשה. על אחת כמה וכמה שהמלך קשה והמדינה קשה: **אשר יושב בעשתרת.** המלך קשה והמדינה קשה: **עשתרת.** הוא לשון צוקין וקשי, כמו: "עשתרת קרנים" (בראשית יד, ה), ו'עשתרת' זה הוא עשתרת קרנים שהיו שם רפאים שהכה אמרפל, שנאמר: "ויכו את רפאים בעשתרת קרנים" (שם), ועוג נמלט מהם, והוא שנאמר: "ויבא הפליט" (שם פסוק יג), ואומר: "כי רק עוג מלך הבשן נשאר מיתר הרפאים" (להלן ג, יא): **באדרעי.** שם המלכות:

ה **הואיל.** התחיל, כמו: "הנה נא הואלתי" (בראשית יח, כז): **באר את התורה.** בשבעים לשון פרשה להם:

1:5 **הואיל משה באר את־התורה הזאת** *Moshe began to expound this Law* – Over the last month of his life, Moshe, so to speak, changes career. He shifts his relationship with the people. Moshe the liberator, the lawgiver, the worker of miracles, the intermediary between the Israelites and God, now becomes the figure known to Jewish memory: *Moshe Rabbeinu*, "Moshe, our teacher." That is how Deuteronomy begins – "Moshe began to expound this Law" (Deut. 1:5). Scripture uses a verb, *be'er*, that we have not encountered in this sense in the Torah and which appears only one more time, toward the end of the book: "On the boulders you shall write very clearly (*ba'er hetev*) all the words of this Law" (27:8). Moshe wants to explain, to make clear. He wants the people to understand that Judaism is not a religion

ב בַּעֲרָבָה מוֹל סוּף בֵּין־פָּארָן וּבֵין־תֹּפֶל וְלָבָן וַחֲצֵרֹת וְדִי זָהָב׃ אַחַד
ג עָשָׂר יוֹם מֵחֹרֵב דֶּרֶךְ הַר־שֵׂעִיר עַד קָדֵשׁ בַּרְנֵעַ׃ וַיְהִי בְּאַרְבָּעִים שָׁנָה
בְּעַשְׁתֵּי־עָשָׂר חֹדֶשׁ בְּאֶחָד לַחֹדֶשׁ דִּבֶּר מֹשֶׁה אֶל־בְּנֵי יִשְׂרָאֵל כְּכֹל
ד אֲשֶׁר צִוָּה יהוה אֹתוֹ אֲלֵהֶם׃ אַחֲרֵי הַכֹּתוֹ אֵת סִיחֹן מֶלֶךְ הָאֱמֹרִי
אֲשֶׁר יוֹשֵׁב בְּחֶשְׁבּוֹן וְאֵת עוֹג מֶלֶךְ הַבָּשָׁן אֲשֶׁר־יוֹשֵׁב בְּעַשְׁתָּרֹת
ה בְּאֶדְרֶעִי׃ בְּעֵבֶר הַיַּרְדֵּן בְּאֶרֶץ מוֹאָב הוֹאִיל מֹשֶׁה בֵּאֵר אֶת־הַתּוֹרָה

אונקלוס

בְּמֵישְׁרָא לָקֳבֵיל יַם סוּף, בְּפָארָן אִתַּפַּלוּ עַל מַנָּא, וּבַחֲצֵרוֹת אַרְגִּיזוּ עַל בִּסְרָא וְעַל דַּעֲבַדוּ עֵיגַל דִּדְהַב: ב מַהֲלַךְ חַד עֲסַר יוֹמִין מֵחוֹרֵב, אוֹרַח טוּרָא דְּשֵׂעִיר, עַד רְקַם גֵּיאָה: ג וַהֲוָה בְּאַרְבְּעִין שְׁנִין, בְּחַד עֲסַר יַרְחִין בְּחַד לְיַרְחָא, מַלֵּיל מֹשֶׁה עִם בְּנֵי יִשְׂרָאֵל, כְּכֹל, דְּפַקֵּיד יְיָ, יָתֵיהּ לְוָתְהוֹן: ד בָּתַר דִּמְחָא, יָת סִיחוֹן מַלְכָּא אֱמוֹרָאָה, דְּיָתֵיב בְּחֶשְׁבּוֹן, וְיָת, עוֹג מַלְכָּא דְּמַתְנָן, דְּיָתֵיב בְּעַשְׁתְּרוֹת בְּאֶדְרֶעִי: ה בְּעִבְרָא דְיַרְדְּנָא בְּאַרְעָא דְמוֹאָב, שָׁרִי מֹשֶׁה, פָּרֵישׁ, יָת אֻלְפַן אוֹרָיְתָא

alike. This is the "all Israel" being addressed for the first time here.

1:1 **דִּי זָהָב** *Di Zahav* – Di Zahav is the name of a place, but it has not been mentioned before. However, the name itself is suggestive. Di Zahav means "enough gold." Might there not be a subtle reference here to an episode which involved gold – namely, the golden calf, the worst sin of the previous generation? On this slender basis, the Sages (Berakhot 32a) built a daring interpretation.

Moshe, in this dramatic rereading, has been transformed into counsel for the defense. Yes, he says to God, the people committed a sin. But it was You who gave them the opportunity and the temptation. Without gold, they could not have made the calf. Who told them to ask their Egyptian neighbors for gold? It was You (Ex. 3:22, 11:2, 12:35). This was not something they did of their own accord. Therefore You must not blame them. Please, instead, forgive them.

We hear, in this aggadic passage, one of the most striking and humane motifs in rabbinic thought. It is called *limmud zekhut*, the act of judging favorably or arguing the case for the defense. It means placing a positive construction on events, pleading a cause, setting forth the case for mercy, or at least mitigation of sentence.

The Sages arranged for this *limmud zekhut* to occur specifically on *Shabbat Ḥazon*, the Sabbath before the Ninth of Av. They introduced into their reading of the first verse of *Devarim*, the *parasha* always read at this time of the year, a note of defense. It is true that Israel sinned, nowhere more so than when they made the golden calf, but do not blame them, says Moshe. They had gold only because You told them to take it. Moshe, often the Israelites' greatest critic, here becomes attorney for the defense. Thus the Sages brought a note of hope into what otherwise might have been the Sabbath of despair.

We are a self-critical people. The Tanakh is the most self-critical of all national literatures. We know our failings, and there is something admirable about this honesty. But it must never leave us bereft of hope. Jewish leadership, as the Sages understood it, is about giving expression to love, respect, and even awe for the Jewish people, who – though it has come through an unparalleled history of suffering – still survives, still flourishes, and still bears witness to the living God. We are not short of critics, internal and external. What we need by way of balance is the voice of those who are *melamed zekhut*, who see our faults but see our virtues also.

6 to expound this Law: "The LORD our God spoke to us at Ḥorev; He said: You
7 have settled long enough at this mountain. Start out and advance into the hill
country of the Amorites and all the neighboring regions – the Arava, the hill
country, the lowlands, the Negev, and the seacoast – the land of the Canaanites
8 and the Lebanon, as far as the Euphrates River. See: I have set the land before
you. Go in and take possession of the land that the LORD swore He would give
to your ancestors – to Avraham, Yitzḥak, and Yaakov – and to their descendants
9 after them. At that time I said to you, 'I cannot bear the burden of you alone.
10 The LORD your God has increased your numbers: today you are as numerous
11 as the stars of the heavens. May the LORD, God of your ancestors, multiply you SHENI
12 again a thousandfold and bless you, as He has promised. But how can I bear

רש״י

ו **רַב לָכֶם שֶׁבֶת.** כִּפְשׁוּטוֹ. וְיֵשׁ מִדְרַשׁ אַגָּדָה: הַרְבֵּה גְּדֻלָּה לָכֶם וְשָׂכָר עַל יְשִׁיבַתְכֶם בָּהָר הַזֶּה, עֲשִׂיתֶם מִשְׁכָּן מְנוֹרָה וְכֵלִים, קִבַּלְתֶּם תּוֹרָה, מִנִּיתֶם לָכֶם סַנְהֶדְרִין שָׂרֵי אֲלָפִים וְשָׂרֵי מֵאוֹת:

ז **פְּנוּ וּסְעוּ לָכֶם.** זוֹ דֶּרֶךְ עֲרָד וְחָרְמָה: **וּבֹאוּ הַר הָאֱמֹרִי.** כְּמַשְׁמָעוֹ: **וְאֶל כָּל שְׁכֵנָיו.** עַמּוֹן וּמוֹאָב וְהַר שֵׂעִיר: **בָּעֲרָבָה.** זֶה מִישׁוֹר שֶׁל יַעַר: **בָהָר.** זֶה הַר הַמֶּלֶךְ: **וּבַשְּׁפֵלָה.** זוֹ שְׁפֵלַת דָּרוֹם: **וּבַנֶּגֶב וּבְחוֹף הַיָּם.** אַשְׁקְלוֹן וְעַזָּה וְקֵסָרִי וְכוּ', כִּדְאִיתָא בְּסִפְרֵי (ו): **עַד הַנָּהָר הַגָּדֹל.** מִפְּנֵי שֶׁנִּזְכָּר עִם אֶרֶץ יִשְׂרָאֵל קוֹרֵהוּ גָּדוֹל, מְשַׁל הֶדְיוֹט אוֹמֵר: עֶבֶד מֶלֶךְ מֶלֶךְ, הִדָּבֵק לַשַּׁחוּר וְיִשְׁתַּחֲווּ לָךְ, קְרַב לְגַבֵּי דְּהִינָא וְאִדְּהַן:

ח **רְאֵה נָתַתִּי.** בְּעֵינֵיכֶם אַתֶּם רוֹאִים, אֵינִי אוֹמֵר לָכֶם מֵאֹמֶד וּמִשְּׁמוּעָה: **בֹּאוּ וּרְשׁוּ.** אֵין מְעַרְעֵר בַּדָּבָר וְאֵינְכֶם צְרִיכִים לְמִלְחָמָה, אִלּוּ לֹא שָׁלְחוּ מְרַגְּלִים לֹא הָיוּ צְרִיכִים לִכְלֵי זַיִן: **לַאֲבֹתֵיכֶם.** לָמָּה הִזְכִּיר שׁוּב "לְאַבְרָהָם לְיִצְחָק וּלְיַעֲקֹב"? אֶלָּא אַבְרָהָם כְּדַאי לְעַצְמוֹ, יִצְחָק כְּדַאי לְעַצְמוֹ, יַעֲקֹב כְּדַאי לְעַצְמוֹ:

ט **וָאֹמַר אֲלֵכֶם בָּעֵת הַהִוא לֵאמֹר.** מַהוּ 'לֵאמֹר'? אָמַר לָהֶם מֹשֶׁה: לֹא מֵעַצְמִי אֲנִי אוֹמֵר לָכֶם אֶלָּא מִפִּי הַקָּדוֹשׁ בָּרוּךְ הוּא: **לֹא אוּכַל לְבַדִּי וְגוֹ'.** אֶפְשָׁר שֶׁלֹּא הָיָה מֹשֶׁה יָכוֹל לָדוּן אֶת יִשְׂרָאֵל? אָדָם שֶׁהוֹצִיאָם מִמִּצְרַיִם, וְקָרַע לָהֶם אֶת הַיָּם, וְהוֹרִיד אֶת הַמָּן, וְהֵגִיז אֶת הַשְּׂלָו, לֹא הָיָה יָכוֹל לְדוּנָם? אֶלָּא כָּךְ אָמַר לָהֶם: "ה' אֱלֹהֵיכֶם הִרְבָּה אֶתְכֶם" (להלן פסוק י) – הִגְדִּיל וְהֵרִים אֶתְכֶם עַל דַּיָּנֵיכֶם, נָטַל אֶת הָעֹנֶשׁ מִכֶּם וּנְתָנוֹ עַל הַדַּיָּנִים. וְכֵן אָמַר שְׁלֹמֹה: "כִּי מִי יוּכַל לִשְׁפֹּט אֶת עַמְּךָ הַכָּבֵד הַזֶּה" (מלכים א' ג, ט), אֶפְשָׁר מִי שֶׁכָּתוּב בּוֹ: "וַיֶּחְכַּם מִכָּל הָאָדָם" (שם ה, יא) אוֹמֵר: "מִי יוּכַל לִשְׁפֹּט"? אֶלָּא כָּךְ אָמַר שְׁלֹמֹה: אֵין דַּיָּנֵי אֻמָּה זוֹ כְּדַיָּנֵי שְׁאָר הָאֻמּוֹת, שֶׁאִם דָּן וְהוֹרֵג וּמַכֶּה וְחוֹנֵק וּמַטֶּה אֶת דִּינוֹ וְגוֹזֵל אֵין בְּכָךְ כְּלוּם, אֲנִי אִם חִיַּבְתִּי מָמוֹן שֶׁלֹּא כַּדִּין, נְפָשׁוֹת אֲנִי נִתְבָּע, שֶׁנֶּאֱמַר: "וְקָבַע אֶת קֹבְעֵיהֶם נָפֶשׁ" (משלי כב, כג):

י **וְהִנְּכֶם הַיּוֹם כְּכוֹכְבֵי הַשָּׁמַיִם.** וְכִי כְּכוֹכְבֵי הַשָּׁמַיִם הָיוּ בְּאוֹתוֹ הַיּוֹם? וַהֲלֹא לֹא הָיוּ אֶלָּא שִׁשִּׁים רִבּוֹא, מַהוּ "וְהִנְּכֶם הַיּוֹם"? הִנְּכֶם מְשׁוּלִים כַּיּוֹם, קַיָּמִים לְעוֹלָם כַּחַמָּה וְכַלְּבָנָה וְכַכּוֹכָבִים:

יא **יֹסֵף עֲלֵיכֶם כָּכֶם אֶלֶף פְּעָמִים.** מַהוּ שׁוּב "וִיבָרֵךְ אֶתְכֶם כַּאֲשֶׁר דִּבֶּר לָכֶם"? אֶלָּא אָמְרוּ לוֹ: מֹשֶׁה, אַתָּה נוֹתֵן קִצְבָּה לְבִרְכוֹתֵינוּ, כְּבָר הִבְטִיחַ הַקָּדוֹשׁ בָּרוּךְ הוּא אֶת אַבְרָהָם: "אֲשֶׁר אִם יוּכַל אִישׁ לִמְנוֹת" וְגוֹ' (בראשית יג, טז). אָמַר לָהֶם: זוֹ מִשֶּׁלִּי הִיא, אֲבָל הוּא "יְבָרֵךְ אֶתְכֶם כַּאֲשֶׁר דִּבֶּר לָכֶם":

יב **אֵיכָה אֶשָּׂא לְבַדִּי.** אִם אֹמַר לְקַבֵּל שָׂכָר, לֹא אוּכַל, זוֹ הִיא שֶׁאָמַרְתִּי לָכֶם: לֹא מֵעַצְמִי אֲנִי אוֹמֵר לָכֶם אֶלָּא מִפִּי הַקָּדוֹשׁ בָּרוּךְ הוּא: **טָרְחֲכֶם.** מְלַמֵּד שֶׁהָיוּ יִשְׂרָאֵל טַרְחָנִין, הָיָה אֶחָד מֵהֶם רוֹאֶה אֶת בַּעַל דִּינוֹ נוֹצֵחַ בַּדִּין, אוֹמֵר: יֵשׁ לִי עֵדִים לְהָבִיא, יֵשׁ לִי רְאָיוֹת לְהָבִיא, מוֹסִיף אֲנִי עֲלֵיכֶם דַּיָּנִין: **וּמַשַּׂאֲכֶם.** מְלַמֵּד שֶׁהָיוּ אֶפִּיקוֹרְסִין. הִקְדִּים מֹשֶׁה לָצֵאת, אָמְרוּ: מָה רָאָה בֶּן עַמְרָם לָצֵאת? שֶׁמָּא אֵינוֹ שָׁפוּי בְּתוֹךְ בֵּיתוֹ. אֵחַר לָצֵאת, אָמְרוּ: מָה רָאָה בֶּן עַמְרָם שֶׁלֹּא

soul. It belongs to the life we live together. Where people meet is where God is to be found. As against the hyper-individualism of our late capitalist society, we find God in the "we," not the "I".

ו הַזֹּאת לֵאמֹר׃ יְהוָה אֱלֹהֵינוּ דִּבֶּר אֵלֵינוּ בְּחֹרֵב לֵאמֹר רַב־לָכֶם שֶׁבֶת
ז בָּהָר הַזֶּה׃ פְּנוּ ׀ וּסְעוּ לָכֶם וּבֹאוּ הַר הָאֱמֹרִי וְאֶל־כָּל־שְׁכֵנָיו בָּעֲרָבָה
בָהָר וּבַשְּׁפֵלָה וּבַנֶּגֶב וּבְחוֹף הַיָּם אֶרֶץ הַכְּנַעֲנִי וְהַלְּבָנוֹן עַד־הַנָּהָר
ח הַגָּדֹל נְהַר־פְּרָת׃ רְאֵה נָתַתִּי לִפְנֵיכֶם אֶת־הָאָרֶץ בֹּאוּ וּרְשׁוּ אֶת־
הָאָרֶץ אֲשֶׁר נִשְׁבַּע יְהוָה לַאֲבֹתֵיכֶם לְאַבְרָהָם לְיִצְחָק וּלְיַעֲקֹב לָתֵת
ט לָהֶם וּלְזַרְעָם אַחֲרֵיהֶם׃ וָאֹמַר אֲלֵכֶם בָּעֵת הַהִוא לֵאמֹר לֹא־אוּכַל
י לְבַדִּי שְׂאֵת אֶתְכֶם׃ יְהוָה אֱלֹהֵיכֶם הִרְבָּה אֶתְכֶם וְהִנְּכֶם הַיּוֹם כְּכוֹכְבֵי
יא הַשָּׁמַיִם לָרֹב׃ יְהוָה אֱלֹהֵי אֲבוֹתֵכֶם יֹסֵף עֲלֵיכֶם כָּכֶם אֶלֶף פְּעָמִים שני
יב וִיבָרֵךְ אֶתְכֶם כַּאֲשֶׁר דִּבֶּר לָכֶם׃ אֵיכָה אֶשָּׂא לְבַדִּי טָרְחֲכֶם וּמַשַּׂאֲכֶם

אונקלוס

הָדָא לְמֵימַר׃ ו יי אֱלָהַנָא, מַלֵּיל עִמַּנָא בְּחוֹרֵב לְמֵימַר, סַגִּי לְכוֹן דִּיתֵיבְתּוּן בְּטוּרָא הָדֵין׃ ז אִתְפְּנוּ וְטוּלוּ לְכוֹן, וְעוּלוּ לְטוּרָא דֶּאֱמוֹרָאָה וּלְכָל מְגִירוֹהִי, בְּמֵישְׁרָא בְּטוּרָא, וּבִשְׁפֵילְתָּא וּבְדָרוֹמָא וּבִסְפַר יַמָּא, אֲרַע כְּנַעֲנָאָה וְלִבְנָן, עַד נַהְרָא רַבָּא נַהְרָא פְרָת׃ ח חֲזוֹ, דִּיהַבִית קֳדָמֵיכוֹן יָת אַרְעָא, עוּלוּ וְאַחְסִינוּ יָת אַרְעָא, דְּקַיֵּים יי, לַאֲבָהָתְכוֹן, לְאַבְרָהָם לְיִצְחָק וּלְיַעֲקֹב לְמִתַּן לְהוֹן, וְלִבְנֵיהוֹן בָּתְרֵיהוֹן׃ ט וַאֲמָרִית לְכוֹן, בְּעִדָּנָא הַהוּא לְמֵימַר, לֵית אֲנָא יָכֵיל בִּלְחוֹדִי לְסוֹבָרָא יָתְכוֹן׃ י יי אֱלָהֲכוֹן אַסְגִּי יָתְכוֹן, וְהָא אִיתֵיכוֹן יוֹמָא דֵין, כְּכוֹכְבֵי שְׁמַיָּא לִסְגֵי׃ יא יי אֱלָהָא דַּאֲבָהָתְכוֹן, יוֹסֵיף עֲלֵיכוֹן, כְּוָתְכוֹן אֲלַף זִמְנִין, וִיבָרֵיךְ יָתְכוֹן, כְּמָא דְּמַלֵּיל לְכוֹן׃ יב אֵיכְדֵין אֲסוֹבַר בִּלְחוֹדִי, טָרְחֵיכוֹן וְעִסְקֵיכוֹן

of mysteries intelligible only to the few. It is a "heritage of Yaakov's [entire] assembly" (33:4). Moshe becomes, in the last month of his life, the master educator. At this defining moment of his life, Moshe understands that, though he will not be *physically* with the people when they enter the Promised Land, he can still be with them intellectually and emotionally if he gives them the teachings to take with them into the future. Moshe now becomes the pioneer of perhaps the single greatest contribution of Judaism to the concept of leadership: the idea of *the teacher as hero*.

1:12 **אֵיכָה אֶשָּׂא לְבַדִּי** *How can I bear alone* – As noted, the *parasha* of Devarim is always read on the Sabbath before the Ninth of Av. We can hear the verbal parallel between Moshe's exclamation, "How (*eikha*) can I bear" and the opening outcry of the Book of Lamentations: "How (*eikha*) the city that overflowed with people sits alone!" (Lam. 1:1). *Eikha* is not only the word these two verses have in common. They also share the word *levadi/badad*, meaning "lonely," "alone," "solitary." In both places, aloneness gives rise to a lament, for Judaism is a religion, not of isolated individuals, but of a people. Today's secular culture is highly individualistic, and contemporary forms of spirituality reflect that fact. Nowadays we often think that God is about me, not us. Nor is this new. Religion has often been thought of as a private engagement of the soul. Dean Inge defined it as "what a person does in his solitude." Walter Savage Landor called solitude the "audience chamber of God." Judaism holds the opposite. "It is not good for man to be alone."

Faith does not belong to the private recesses of the

13 alone all your problems, your burdens, your disputes? Choose for yourselves
men who are wise, discerning, and known to your tribes, and I will appoint
14 them as your leaders.' You answered me, 'The plan you propose is a good one.'
15 So I took the leaders of your tribes, wise men and well known, and appointed
them to be leaders over you, chiefs of thousands, chiefs of hundreds, chiefs of
16 fifties, chiefs of tens, and officials, for your tribes. I charged your judges at that
time: 'Hear the disputes among your people and judge fairly, between one
17 person and another, whether Israelite or migrant. Do not show partiality in
judgment: listen equally to the small and the great. Do not be intimidated by
any man, for judgment belongs to God. Any case that is too difficult for you,

רש״י

לָצֵאת? מָה אַתֶּם סְבוּרִים, יוֹשֵׁב וְיוֹעֵץ עֲלֵיכֶם עֵצוֹת רָעוֹת וְחוֹשֵׁב עֲלֵיכֶם מַחֲשָׁבוֹת: **וְרִיבְכֶם.** מְלַמֵּד שֶׁהָיוּ רוֹגְנִים:

יג **הָבוּ לָכֶם.** הַזְמִינוּ עַצְמְכֶם לַדָּבָר: **אֲנָשִׁים.** וְכִי תַּעֲלֶה עַל דַּעְתְּךָ נָשִׁים? מַה תַּלְמוּד לוֹמַר: אֲנָשִׁים? צַדִּיקִים, חֲכָמִים, כְּסוּפִים: **וּנְבֹנִים.** מְבִינִים דָּבָר מִתּוֹךְ דָּבָר. זֶהוּ שֶׁשָּׁאַל אַרְיוֹס אֶת רַבִּי יוֹסֵי: מַה בֵּין חֲכָמִים לִנְבוֹנִים? חָכָם דּוֹמֶה לְשֻׁלְחָנִי עָשִׁיר, כְּשֶׁמְּבִיאִין לוֹ דִּינָרִין לִרְאוֹת רוֹאֶה, וּכְשֶׁאֵין מְבִיאִין לוֹ יוֹשֵׁב וְתוֹהֵא. נָבוֹן דּוֹמֶה לְשֻׁלְחָנִי תַּגָּר, כְּשֶׁמְּבִיאִין לוֹ מָעוֹת לִרְאוֹת רוֹאֶה, וּכְשֶׁאֵין מְבִיאִין לוֹ הוּא מְחַזֵּר וּמֵבִיא מִשֶּׁלּוֹ: **וִידֻעִים לְשִׁבְטֵיכֶם.** שֶׁהֵם נִכָּרִים לָכֶם, שֶׁאִם בָּא לְפָנַי מְעֻטָּף בְּטַלִּיתוֹ אֵינִי יוֹדֵעַ מִי הוּא וּמֵאֵיזֶה שֵׁבֶט הוּא וְאִם הָגוּן הוּא, אֲבָל אַתֶּם מַכִּירִין בּוֹ, שֶׁאַתֶּם גִּדַּלְתֶּם אוֹתוֹ, לְכָךְ נֶאֱמַר: "וִידֻעִים לְשִׁבְטֵיכֶם": **בְּרָאשֵׁיכֶם.** רָאשִׁים וּמְכֻבָּדִים עֲלֵיכֶם, שֶׁתִּהְיוּ נוֹהֲגִין בָּהֶם כָּבוֹד וְיִרְאָה: **וַאֲשִׂמֵם.** חָסֵר יוּ״ד, לִמֵּד שֶׁאַשְׁמוֹתֵיהֶם שֶׁל יִשְׂרָאֵל תְּלוּיוֹת בְּרָאשֵׁי דַּיָּנֵיהֶם, שֶׁהָיָה לָהֶם לִמְחוֹת וּלְכַוֵּן אוֹתָם לַדֶּרֶךְ הַיְשָׁרָה:

יד **וַתַּעֲנוּ אֹתִי וְגוֹ׳.** חֲלַטְתֶּם אֶת הַדָּבָר לְהַנָאַתְכֶם, הָיָה לָכֶם לְהָשִׁיב: רַבֵּנוּ מֹשֶׁה, מִמִּי נָאֶה לִלְמֹד, מִמְּךָ אוֹ מִתַּלְמִידְךָ? לֹא מִמְּךָ שֶׁנִּצְטַעַרְתָּ עָלֶיהָ? אֶלָּא יָדַעְתִּי מַחְשְׁבוֹתֵיכֶם, הֱיִיתֶם אוֹמְרִים: עַכְשָׁיו יִתְמַנּוּ עָלֵינוּ דַּיָּנִין הַרְבֵּה, אִם אֵין מַכִּירֵנוּ, אָנוּ מְבִיאִין לוֹ דּוֹרוֹן וְהוּא נוֹשֵׂא לָנוּ פָּנִים: **לַעֲשׂוֹת.** אִם הָיִיתִי מִתְעַצֵּל, אַתֶּם אוֹמְרִים עֲשֵׂה מְהֵרָה:

טו **וָאֶקַּח אֶת רָאשֵׁי שִׁבְטֵיכֶם.** מְשַׁכְתִּים בִּדְבָרִים: אַשְׁרֵיכֶם, עַל מִי בָּאתֶם לְהִתְמַנּוֹת, עַל בְּנֵי אַבְרָהָם יִצְחָק וְיַעֲקֹב, עַל בְּנֵי אָדָם שֶׁנִּקְרְאוּ אַחִים וְרֵעִים, חֵלֶק וְנַחֲלָה, וְכָל לְשׁוֹן חִבָּה: **אֲנָשִׁים חֲכָמִים וִידֻעִים.** אֲבָל נְבוֹנִים לֹא מָצָאתִי. זוֹ אַחַת מִשֶּׁבַע מִדּוֹת שֶׁאָמַר יִתְרוֹ לְמֹשֶׁה, וְלֹא מָצָא אֶלָּא שָׁלֹשׁ: אֲנָשִׁים צַדִּיקִים, חֲכָמִים וִידֻעִים: **רָאשִׁים עֲלֵיכֶם.** שֶׁתִּנְהֲגוּ בָּהֶם כָּבוֹד, רָאשִׁים בְּמִקָּח, רָאשִׁים בְּמִמְכָּר, רָאשִׁים בְּמַשָּׂא וּמַתָּן, נִכְנָס אַחֲרוֹן וְיוֹצֵא רִאשׁוֹן: **שָׂרֵי אֲלָפִים.** אֶחָד מְמֻנֶּה עַל אֶלֶף: **שָׂרֵי מֵאוֹת.** אֶחָד מְמֻנֶּה עַל מֵאָה: **וְשֹׁטְרִים.** מִנִּיתִי עֲלֵיכֶם "לְשִׁבְטֵיכֶם", אֵלּוּ הַכּוֹפְתִין וְהַמַּכִּין בִּרְצוּעָה עַל פִּי הַדַּיָּנִין:

טז **וָאֲצַוֶּה אֶת שֹׁפְטֵיכֶם.** אָמַרְתִּי לָהֶם: הֱווּ מְתוּנִים בַּדִּין, אִם בָּא דִּין לְפָנֶיךָ פַּעַם אַחַת וּשְׁתַּיִם וְשָׁלֹשׁ, אַל תֹּאמַר: כְּבָר בָּא דִּין זֶה לְפָנַי פְּעָמִים הַרְבֵּה, אֶלָּא הֱיוּ נוֹשְׂאִים וְנוֹתְנִים בּוֹ: **בָּעֵת הַהִוא.** מִשֶּׁמִּנִּיתִים אָמַרְתִּי לָהֶם: אֵין עַכְשָׁיו כִּלְשֶׁעָבַר, לְשֶׁעָבַר הֱיִיתֶם בִּרְשׁוּת עַצְמְכֶם, עַכְשָׁיו הֲרֵי אַתֶּם מְשֻׁעְבָּדִים לַצִּבּוּר: **שָׁמֹעַ.** לְשׁוֹן הֹוֶה, אודנ״ט בְּלַעַז, כְּמוֹ 'זָכוֹר' וְ'שָׁמוֹר': **וּבֵין גֵּרוֹ.** זֶה בַּעַל דִּינוֹ שֶׁאוֹגֵר עָלָיו דְּבָרִים. דָּבָר אַחֵר, "וּבֵין גֵּרוֹ", אַף עַל עִסְקֵי דִּירָה, בֵּין חֲלֻקַּת אַחִים, אֲפִלּוּ בֵּין תַּנּוּר לְכִירַיִם:

יז **לֹא תַכִּירוּ פָנִים בַּמִּשְׁפָּט.** זֶה הַמְמֻנֶּה לְהוֹשִׁיב הַדַּיָּנִים, שֶׁלֹּא יֹאמַר: אִישׁ פְּלוֹנִי נָאֶה אוֹ גִּבּוֹר, אוֹשִׁיבֶנּוּ דַּיָּן, אִישׁ פְּלוֹנִי קְרוֹבִי, אוֹשִׁיבֶנּוּ דַּיָּן בָּעִיר, וְהוּא אֵינוֹ בָּקִי בְּדִינִין, נִמְצָא מְחַיֵּב אֶת הַזַּכַּאי וּמְזַכֶּה אֶת הַחַיָּב, מַעֲלֶה אֲנִי עַל מִי שֶׁמִּנָּהוּ כְּאִלּוּ הִכִּיר פָּנִים בַּדִּין: **כַּקָּטֹן כַּגָּדֹל תִּשְׁמָעוּן.** שֶׁיְּהֵא חָבִיב עָלֶיךָ דִּין שֶׁל פְּרוּטָה כְּדִין שֶׁל מֵאָה מָנֶה, שֶׁאִם קָדַם וּבָא לְפָנֶיךָ לֹא תְּסַלְּקֶנּוּ לָאַחֲרוֹנָה. דָּבָר אַחֵר, "כַּקָּטֹן כַּגָּדֹל תִּשְׁמָעוּן", כְּתַרְגּוּמוֹ, שֶׁלֹּא תֹּאמַר: זֶה עָנִי הוּא וַחֲבֵרוֹ עָשִׁיר וּמִצְוָה לְפַרְנְסוֹ, אֲזַכֶּה אֶת הֶעָנִי וְנִמְצָא מִתְפַּרְנֵס בִּנְקִיּוּת. דָּבָר אַחֵר, שֶׁלֹּא תֹּאמַר: הֵיאַךְ אֲנִי פּוֹגֵם בִּכְבוֹדוֹ שֶׁל עָשִׁיר זֶה בִּשְׁבִיל דִּינָר, אֲזַכֶּנּוּ עַכְשָׁיו, וּכְשֶׁיֵּצֵא לַחוּץ, אֹמַר לוֹ: תֵּן לוֹ, שֶׁאַתָּה חַיָּב לוֹ: **לֹא תָגוּרוּ מִפְּנֵי אִישׁ.** לֹא תִּירְאוּ. דָּבָר אַחֵר, "לֹא תָגוּרוּ", לֹא תַּכְנִיס דְּבָרֶיךָ מִפְּנֵי אִישׁ, לְשׁוֹן: "אֹגֵר בַּקַּיִץ" (משלי י, ה): **כִּי הַמִּשְׁפָּט לֵאלֹהִים הוּא.** מַה שֶּׁאַתָּה נוֹטֵל מִזֶּה שֶׁלֹּא כַּדִּין אַתָּה מַזְקִיקֵנִי לְהַחֲזִיר לוֹ, נִמְצָא שֶׁהִטֵּיתָ עָלַי הַמִּשְׁפָּט:

Torah insists that justice is not a human artifact. Because judgment belongs to God, it must never be compromised – by fear, bribery, or favoritism. Judaism is a religion of love: you shall love the LORD your God; you shall love your neighbor

יג וְרִיבְכֶֽם׃ הָב֣וּ לָכֶ֞ם אֲנָשִׁ֧ים חֲכָמִ֛ים וּנְבֹנִ֖ים וִידֻעִ֣ים לְשִׁבְטֵיכֶ֑ם וַאֲשִׂימֵ֖ם
יד בְּרָאשֵׁיכֶֽם׃ וַֽתַּעֲנ֖וּ אֹתִ֑י וַתֹּ֣אמְר֔וּ טֽוֹב־הַדָּבָ֥ר אֲשֶׁר־דִּבַּ֖רְתָּ לַעֲשֽׂוֹת׃
טו וָאֶקַּ֞ח אֶת־רָאשֵׁ֣י שִׁבְטֵיכֶ֗ם אֲנָשִׁ֤ים חֲכָמִים֙ וִֽידֻעִ֔ים וָאֶתֵּ֥ן אֹתָ֛ם רָאשִׁ֖ים
עֲלֵיכֶ֑ם שָׂרֵ֨י אֲלָפִ֜ים וְשָׂרֵ֣י מֵא֗וֹת וְשָׂרֵ֤י חֲמִשִּׁים֙ וְשָׂרֵ֣י עֲשָׂרֹ֔ת וְשֹׁטְרִ֖ים
טז לְשִׁבְטֵיכֶֽם׃ וָאֲצַוֶּה֙ אֶת־שֹׁ֣פְטֵיכֶ֔ם בָּעֵ֥ת הַהִ֖וא לֵאמֹ֑ר שָׁמֹ֤עַ בֵּין־אֲחֵיכֶם֙
יז וּשְׁפַטְתֶּ֣ם צֶ֔דֶק בֵּֽין־אִ֥ישׁ וּבֵין־אָחִ֖יו וּבֵ֥ין גֵּרֽוֹ׃ לֹֽא־תַכִּ֨ירוּ פָנִ֜ים בַּמִּשְׁפָּ֗ט
כַּקָּטֹ֤ן כַּגָּדֹל֙ תִּשְׁמָע֔וּן לֹ֤א תָג֙וּרוּ֙ מִפְּנֵי־אִ֔ישׁ כִּ֥י הַמִּשְׁפָּ֖ט לֵאלֹהִ֣ים ה֑וּא

אונקלוס

וְדִינְכוֹן: יג הַבוּ לְכוֹן, גֻּבְרִין חַכִּימִין וְסֻכְלְתָנִין, וּמַדְּעָן לְשִׁבְטֵיכוֹן, וַאֲמַנֵּינוּן רֵישִׁין עֲלֵיכוֹן: יד וַאֲתֵיבְתּוּן יָתִי, וַאֲמַרְתּוּן, תַּקִּין פִּתְגָּמָא דְּמַלֵּילְתָּא לְמֶעְבַּד: טו וּדְבַרִית יָת רֵישֵׁי שִׁבְטֵיכוֹן, גֻּבְרִין חַכִּימִין וּמַדְּעָן, וּמַנִּיתִי יָתְהוֹן, רֵישִׁין עֲלֵיכוֹן, רַבָּנֵי אַלְפֵי וְרַבָּנֵי מָאוָתָא, וְרַבָּנֵי חַמְשִׁין וְרַבָּנֵי עֲסוֹרְיָתָא, וְסָרְכִין לְשִׁבְטֵיכוֹן: טז וּפַקֵּידִית יָת דַּיָּנֵיכוֹן, בְּעִדָּנָא הַהוּא לְמֵימַר, שְׁמַעוּ בֵּין אֲחֵיכוֹן וּתְדִינוּן קֻשְׁטָא, בֵּין גֻּבְרָא וּבֵין אֲחוּהִי וּבֵין גִּיּוֹרֵיהּ: יז לָא תִשְׁתְּמוֹדְעוּן אַפֵּי בְּדִינָא, מִלֵּי זְעֵירָא כְּרַבָּא תִּשְׁמְעוּן, לָא תִדְחֲלוּן מִן קֳדָם גֻּבְרָא, אֲרֵי דִינָא דַּייָ הוּא,

1:16 וּשְׁפַטְתֶּם צֶדֶק *Judge fairly* – Three features mark Judaism as a distinctive faith. First is the radical idea that when God reveals Himself to humans He does so in the form of law. In the ancient world, God was power. In Judaism, God is order, and order presupposes law. In the natural world of cause and effect, order takes the form of scientific law. But in the human world, where we have free will, order takes the form of moral law. Torah means "direction," "guidance," "teaching"; it also means "law." The most basic meaning of the most fundamental principle of Judaism, *Torah min haShamayim*, "Torah from Heaven," is that God, not humans, is the source of binding law.

Second, we are charged with being interpreters of the law. That is our responsibility as heirs and guardians of the *Torah Shebe'al Peh*, the Oral Tradition.

The Written Torah is *min haShamayim*, "from Heaven," but about the Oral Torah the Talmud insists: *Lo bashamayim hi*, "It is not in heaven" (Bava Metzia 59b). Judaism is a continuing conversation between the Giver of the law and the interpreters of the law. That is part of what the Talmud means when it says that "every judge who delivers a true judgment becomes a partner with the Holy One, blessed be He, in the work of creation" (Shabbat 10a).

Third, fundamental to Judaism is education, and fundamental to education is instruction in Torah, that is, the law. To be a Jewish child is to be, in the British phrase, "learned in the law." Why? Because Judaism is not just about spirituality. It is not simply a code for the salvation of the soul. It is a set of instructions for the creation of what Rabbi Aharon Lichtenstein called "societal beatitude." It is about bringing God into the shared spaces of our collective life. That needs law: law that represents justice, honoring all humans alike; law that judges impartially between rich and poor, powerful and powerless; law that links God, its giver, to us, its interpreters; law that alone allows freedom to coexist with order, so that my freedom is not bought at the cost of yours.

1:17 לֹא־תַכִּירוּ פָנִים בַּמִּשְׁפָּט *Do not show partiality in judgment* – The literal meaning of the phrase is "Do not recognize faces in judgment." That is to say, do not let kinship distort the course of justice. From the negative we can infer the positive, that when it comes not to justice but compassion, to "recognize a face" requires us to show the kind of care that family members should to one another.

1:17 הַמִּשְׁפָּט לֵאלֹהִים הוּא *Judgment belongs to God* – The

18 bring to me, and I will hear it.' I charged you at that time, with all the things you
19 are to do. Then we set out from Ḥorev and journeyed through all that vast and
fearful wilderness that you have seen, toward the hill country of the Amorites,
20 as the Lord our God had commanded us, until we reached Kadesh Barnea. I
said to you, 'You have reached the hill country of the Amorites, which the
21 Lord our God is giving us. See, the Lord your God has laid the land out before
you. Go up, take possession, as the Lord, God of your ancestors, has promised.
22 Do not fear and do not be dismayed.' Then all of you drew close to me and said, SHELISHI
'Let us send men ahead of us to explore the land and bring back a report to us
23 about the route by which we should go up and the towns we will come to.' The
plan seemed good to me, so I selected twelve of you, one man from each tribe.

רש"י

תקרבון אלי. על דבר זה נסתלק ממנו משפט בנות צלפחד. וכן שמואל אמר לשאול: "אנכי הראה" (שמואל א' ט, יט), אמר לו הקדוש ברוך הוא: חייך שאני מודיעך שאין אתה רואה. ואימתי הודיעו? כשבא למשח את דוד: "וירא את אליאב ויאמר אך נגד ה' משיחו" (שמואל א' טז, ו), אמר לו הקדוש ברוך הוא: ולא אמרת: "אנכי הראה"? "אל תבט אל מראהו" (שם פסוק ז):

יח **את כל הדברים אשר תעשון.** אלו עשרת הדברים שבין דיני ממונות לדיני נפשות:

יט **המדבר הגדול והנורא.** שהיו בו נחשים כקורות ועקרבים כקשתות:

כב **ותקרבון אלי כלכם.** בערבוביא, ולהלן הוא אומר: "ותקרבון אלי כל ראשי שבטיכם וזקניכם, ותאמרו הן הראנו" וגו' (להלן ה, כ-כא), אותה קריבה היתה הוגנת, ילדים מכבדים את הזקנים ושלחום לפניהם, וזקנים מכבדים את הראשים ללכת לפניהם, אבל כאן: "ותקרבון אלי כלכם", בערבוביא, ילדים דוחפין את הזקנים וזקנים דוחפין את הראשים: **וישבו אתנו דבר.** באיזה לשון הם מדברים: **את הדרך אשר נעלה בה.** אין דרך שאין בה עקמימות: **ואת הערים אשר נבא אליהן.** תחלה לכבש:

כג **וייטב בעיני הדבר.** בעיני ולא בעיני המקום. ואם בעיני משה היה טוב, למה אמרה בתוכחות? משל לאדם שאומר לחברו: מכור לי חמורך זה, אמר לו: הן. נותנו אתה לי לנסיון? אמר לו: הן. בהרים וגבעות? אמר לו: הן. כיון שראה שאין מעכבו כלום, אמר הלוקח בלבו: בטוח הוא זה שלא אמצא בו מום. מיד אמר לו: טול מעותיך ואיני מנסה מעתה. אף אני הודיתי לדבריכם, שמא תחזרו בכם כשתראו שאיני מעכב, ואתם לא חזרתם בכם: **ואקח מכם.** מן הברורים שבכם, מן המסלתים שבכם:

the two Hebrew verbs, *laḥpor* and *leragel*, that mean to spy.

But the account in Shelaḥ conspicuously does not mention spying. Instead, thirteen times, it uses the verb *latur*, which means to tour, explore, travel, inspect. According to Malbim, *latur* means to seek out what is good about a place. *Laḥpor* and *leragel* mean to seek out what is weak, vulnerable, exposed, defenseless. Touring and spying are completely different activities, so why does the account in our *parasha* present what happened as a spying mission, while the account in Shelaḥ emphatically does not?

Addressing the discrepancy between the two accounts of the spies, Rabbi David Tzvi Hoffman argued that the account in Shelaḥ tells us what happened. The account in our *parasha*, on the other hand, was meant not to inform but to warn. They belong to different literary genres with different purposes. Parashat Shelaḥ is a historical narrative; our *parasha* is a sermon.

Rashi, however, explains that the two accounts, here and in Shelaḥ, are not two different versions of the same event. They are the same version of the same event split in two, half told there, half here. It was the people who requested spies (as stated here). Moshe took their request to God. God acceded to the request, but as a concession. "You may send," says God, not "You must send."

However, in granting permission, God made a provision.

יח וְהַדָּבָר֙ אֲשֶׁ֣ר יִקְשֶׁ֣ה מִכֶּ֔ם תַּקְרִב֥וּן אֵלַ֖י וּשְׁמַעְתִּֽיו׃ וָאֲצַוֶּ֥ה אֶתְכֶ֖ם בָּעֵ֣ת
יט הַהִ֑וא אֵ֥ת כָּל־הַדְּבָרִ֖ים אֲשֶׁ֥ר תַּעֲשֽׂוּן׃ וַנִּסַּ֣ע מֵחֹרֵ֗ב וַנֵּ֡לֶךְ אֵ֣ת כָּל־
הַמִּדְבָּ֣ר הַגָּדוֹל֩ וְהַנּוֹרָ֨א הַה֜וּא אֲשֶׁ֣ר רְאִיתֶ֗ם דֶּ֚רֶךְ הַ֣ר הָֽאֱמֹרִ֔י כַּאֲשֶׁ֥ר
כ צִוָּ֛ה יְהוָ֥ה אֱלֹהֵ֖ינוּ אֹתָ֑נוּ וַנָּבֹ֕א עַ֖ד קָדֵ֥שׁ בַּרְנֵֽעַ׃ וָאֹמַ֖ר אֲלֵכֶ֑ם בָּאתֶם֙
כא עַד־הַ֣ר הָֽאֱמֹרִ֔י אֲשֶׁר־יְהוָ֥ה אֱלֹהֵ֖ינוּ נֹתֵ֥ן לָֽנוּ׃ רְ֠אֵה נָתַ֨ן יְהוָ֧ה אֱלֹהֶ֛יךָ
לְפָנֶ֖יךָ אֶת־הָאָ֑רֶץ עֲלֵ֣ה רֵ֡שׁ כַּאֲשֶׁר֩ דִּבֶּ֨ר יְהוָ֜ה אֱלֹהֵ֤י אֲבֹתֶ֙יךָ֙ לָ֔ךְ אַל־
כב תִּירָ֖א וְאַל־תֵּחָֽת׃ וַתִּקְרְב֣וּן אֵלַי֮ כֻּלְּכֶם֒ וַתֹּאמְר֗וּ נִשְׁלְחָ֤ה אֲנָשִׁים֙ לְפָנֵ֔ינוּ שלישי
וְיַחְפְּרוּ־לָ֖נוּ אֶת־הָאָ֑רֶץ וְיָשִׁ֤בוּ אֹתָ֙נוּ֙ דָּבָ֔ר אֶת־הַדֶּ֙רֶךְ֙ אֲשֶׁ֣ר נַעֲלֶה־
כג בָּ֔הּ וְאֵת֙ הֶֽעָרִ֔ים אֲשֶׁ֥ר נָבֹ֖א אֲלֵיהֶֽן׃ וַיִּיטַ֥ב בְּעֵינַ֖י הַדָּבָ֑ר וָאֶקַּ֤ח מִכֶּם֙

אונקלוס

וּפִתְגָמָא דְיִקְשֵׁי מִנְּכוֹן, תְּקָרְבוּן לְוָתִי וְאֶשְׁמְעִנֵּיהּ: יח וּפַקֵּידִית יָתְכוֹן בְּעִדָּנָא הַהוּא, יָת כָּל פִּתְגָמַיָּא דְתַעְבְּדוּן: יט וּנְטַלְנָא מֵחוֹרֵב, וְהַלֵּיכְנָא, יָת כָּל מַדְבְּרָא רַבָּא וּדְחִילָא הַהוּא דַּחֲזֵיתוּן, אוֹרַח טוּרָא דֶּאֱמוֹרָאָה, כְּמָא דְּפַקֵּיד, יי אֱלָהַנָא יָתַנָא, וַאֲתֵינָא, עַד רְקַם גֵּיאָה: כ וַאֲמָרִית לְכוֹן, אֲתֵיתוּן עַד טוּרָא דֶּאֱמוֹרָאָה, דַּיי אֱלָהַנָא יָהֵיב לַנָא: כא חֲזִי, דִּיהַב יי אֱלָהָךְ, קֳדָמָךְ יָת אַרְעָא, סַק אַחְסִין, כְּמָא דְּמַלִּיל יי, אֱלָהָא דַּאֲבָהָתָךְ לָךְ, לָא תִדְחַל וְלָא תִתְּבַר: כב וּקְרֵיבְתּוּן לְוָתִי כֻּלְּכוֹן, וַאֲמַרְתּוּן, נִשְׁלַח גֻּבְרִין קֳדָמַנָא, וִיאַלְּלוּן לַנָא יָת אַרְעָא, וִיתִיבוּן יָתַנָא פִּתְגָמָא, יָת אוֹרְחָא דְּנִסַּק בַּהּ, וְיָת קִרְוַיָּא, דְּנֵיעוֹל לְהוֹן: כג וּשְׁפַר בְּעֵינַי פִּתְגָמָא, וּדְבָרִית מִנְּכוֹן

as yourself; you shall love the stranger for you were once strangers. But it is also a religion of justice, for without justice, love corrupts (who would not bend the rules, if he could, to favor those he loves?). It is also a religion of compassion, for without compassion law itself can generate inequity. Justice plus compassion equals *tzedek*, the first precondition of a decent society.

RETELLING THE STORY OF THE SPIES

Early in Moshe's final speech, he recalls the episode of the spies, the reason why the people's parents were denied the opportunity to enter the land, so that the next generation might learn the lessons of that event. But the story of the spies that he tells here is very different from the version in Parashat Shelaḥ (Num. 13–14), which described the events as they happened almost thirty-nine years earlier. The discrepancies between the two accounts are glaring and numerous. I want to focus only on two.

First, who proposed sending the spies? In Parashat Shelaḥ, it was God who told Moshe to do so: "Then the Lord spoke to Moshe: 'Send out men'" (Num. 13:1–2). In our *parasha*, it was the people who requested it: "Then all of you drew close to me and said, 'Let us send men'" (Deut. 1:22). The English does not convey the sense of menace in the original here. They came, says Rashi, "in a crowd," without respect, protocol, or order. They were a mob. This mirrors the people's behavior at the beginning of the story of the golden calf: "When the people saw that Moshe was long delayed in coming down the mountain, they *gathered around Aharon* and said to him…" (Ex. 32:1).

In Numbers (ch. 14, "The Spies' Report") we noted a second discrepancy: In our *parasha*, the people said, "Let us send men ahead of us to explore (*veyaḥperu*) the land" (Deut. 1:22). The twelve men "went up into the hill country. And, arriving at the Eshkol Ravine, they spied it out (*vayeraglu*)" (1:24). In other words, our *parasha* uses

24 They set out and went up into the hill country. And, arriving at the Eshkol
25 Ravine, they spied it out. They took some of the fruit of the land, which they
brought down to us, and they brought us back a report: 'The land that the
26 Lord our God is giving us is good.' But you were unwilling to go up, and you
27 rebelled against the word of the Lord your God. You grumbled in your tents
and said, 'It is because the Lord hates us that He has brought us out of the land
28 of Egypt, to hand us over to the Amorites to destroy us. Where can we go? Our
brothers have melted all the bravado from our hearts by telling us, "The people
are stronger and taller than we are. The cities are large and walled to the sky; we
29 even saw the Anakites there."' And I said to you, 'Do not be terrified and have
30 no fear of them. The Lord your God, who is going before you, He will fight for
31 you, just as He did for you in Egypt before your eyes, and in the wilderness,
where you saw the Lord your God carry you as a man carries his child, all
32 along the way you traveled until you reached this place. And yet despite all this,
33 you show no faith in the Lord your God, who goes ahead of you on your
journey – in fire by night, and cloud by day – to seek out a place for you to

רש"י

שנים עשר אנשים איש אחד לשבט. מגיד שלא היה שבט לוי עמהם:

כד **עד נחל אשכל.** מגיד שנקרא על שם סופו: **וירגלו אתה.** מלמד שהלכו בה ארבעה אומנין שתי וערב:

כה **ויורדו אלינו.** מגיד שארץ ישראל גבוהה מכל הארצות: **ויאמרו טובה הארץ.** מי הם שאמרו טובתה? יהושע וכלב:

כו **ותמרו.** לשון התרסה, התרסתם כנגד מאמרו:

כז **ותרגנו.** לשון הרע, וכן: "דברי נרגן" (משלי יח, ח), אדם המוציא דבה: **בשנאת ה' אתנו.** והוא היה אוהב אתכם, אבל אתם שונאים אותו. משל הדיוט אומר: מה דבלבך על רחמך, מה דבלביה עלך: **בשנאת ה' אתנו הוציאנו מארץ מצרים.** הוצאתו לשנאה היתה. משל למלך בשר ודם שהיו לו שני בנים ויש לו שתי שדות, אחת של שקיא ואחת של בעל, למי שהוא אוהב נותן של שקיא ולמי שהוא שונא נותן לו של בעל. ארץ מצרים של שקיא היא, שנילוס עולה ומשקה אותה, וארץ כנען של בעל, והוציאנו ממצרים לתת לנו את ארץ כנען:

כח **ערים גדלת ובצורת בשמים.** דברו הכתובים לשון הבאי:

כט **לא תערצון.** לשון שבירה כתרגומו, ודומה לו: "בערוץ נחלים" (איוב ל, ו), לשבר הנחלים:

ל **ילחם לכם.** בשבילכם:

לא **ובמדבר אשר ראית.** מוסב על מקרא שלמעלה הימנו: "ככל אשר עשה אתכם במצרים" ועשה אף במדבר, "אשר ראית אשר נשאך" וגו': **כאשר ישא איש את בנו.** כמו שפרשתי אצל "ויסע מלאך האלהים ההלך לפני מחנה ישראל" וגו' (שמות יד, יט-כ), משל למהלך בדרך ובנו לפניו, באו לסטים לשבותו וכו' [נטלו מלפניו נתנו לאחריו. בא זאב מאחריו, נתנו לפניו. באו לסטים לפניו וזאבים מאחריו, נתנו על זרועו ונלחם בהם. כך: "ואנכי תרגלתי לאפרים קחם על זרועתיו" (הושע יא, ג)]:

לב **ובדבר הזה.** שהוא מבטיחכם להביאכם אל הארץ, "אינכם מאמינים" בו:

לג **לראתכם.** כמו 'להראותכם', וכן: "לנחתם הדרך" (שמות יג, כא), וכן: "לשמע בקול תודה" (תהלים כו, ז), וכן: "ללכת לגיד ביזרעאל" (מלכים ב' ט, טו ועיין רש"י שם):

fight. It is because they allowed the news that made them fearful to override that direct testimony to beauty that they were condemned never themselves to "see the good land" (1:35).

כד שנים עשר אנשים איש אחד לשבט: ויפנו ויעלו ההרה ויבאו עד־
כה נחל אשכל וירגלו אתה: ויקחו בידם מפרי הארץ ויורדו אלינו
וישבו אתנו דבר ויאמרו טובה הארץ אשר־יהוה אלהינו נתן לנו:
כו ולא אביתם לעלת ותמרו את־פי יהוה אלהיכם: ותרגנו באהליכם
ותאמרו בשנאת יהוה אתנו הוציאנו מארץ מצרים לתת אתנו
כח ביד האמרי להשמידנו: אנה | אנחנו עלים אחינו המסו את־לבבנו
לאמר עם גדול ורם ממנו ערים גדלת ובצורת בשמים וגם־בני
כט ל ענקים ראינו שם: ואמר אלכם לא־תערצון ולא־תיראון מהם: יהוה
אלהיכם ההלך לפניכם הוא ילחם לכם ככל אשר עשה אתכם
לא במצרים לעיניכם: ובמדבר אשר ראית אשר נשאך יהוה אלהיך
כאשר ישא־איש את־בנו בכל־הדרך אשר הלכתם עד־באכם עד־
לב לג המקום הזה: ובדבר הזה אינכם מאמינם ביהוה אלהיכם: ההלך
לפניכם בדרך לתור לכם מקום לחנתכם באש | לילה לראתכם

אונקלוס

תרי עסר גברין, גברא חד לשבטא: כד ואתפניאו וסליקו לטורא, ואתו עד נחלא דאתכלא, ואלילו יתה: כה ונסיבו בידיהון מאבא דארעא, ואחיתו לנא, ואתיבו יתנא פתגמא ואמרו, טבא ארעא, דיי אלהנא יהיב לנא: כו ולא אביתון למסק, וסריבתון, על מימרא דיי אלהכון: כז ואתרעמתון במשכניכון ואמרתון, בדסני יי יתנא, אפקנא מארעא דמצרים, למימסר יתנא, בידא דאמוראה לשיציותנא: כח לאן אנחנא סלקין, אחנא תברו ית לבנא למימר, עם רב ותקיף מננא, קרוין, רברבן וכריכן עד צית שמיא, ואף בני גברא חזינא תמן: כט ואמרית לכון, לא תתברון ולא תדחלון מנהון: ל יי אלהכון דמדבר קדמיכון, מימריה יגיח לכון, ככל, דעבד עמכון, במצרים לעיניכון: לא ובמדברא דחזיתא, דסוברך יי אלהך, כמא דמסובר גברא ית בריה, בכל אורחא דהליכתון, עד מיתיכון עד אתרא הדין: לב ובפתגמא הדין, ליתיכון מהימנין, במימרא דיי אלהכון: לג דמדבר קדמיכון באורחא, לאתקנא לכון, אתר בית משרי לאשרויותכון, בעמודא דאישתא בליליא, לאחזיותכון

The people asked for spies. But God did not give Moshe permission to send spies. He specifically used the verb *latur*, meaning, He allowed the men to tour the land and testify that it is a good and fertile land, flowing with milk and honey.

The people did not need spies. As Moshe says, throughout the wilderness years God has been going "ahead of you on your journey, in fire by night and cloud by day, to seek out [*latur*] a place for you to camp and show you the way you should go" (1:33). They did, however, need eyewitness testimony of the beauty and fruitfulness of the land to which they had been traveling and for which they would have to

34 camp and show you the way you should go.' Hearing your words, the LORD
35 became furious and swore an oath: 'Not one man of this evil generation shall
36 see the good land that I swore to give your ancestors, except for Kalev son of
Yefuneh. He will see it, and to him and his descendants I will give the land on
37 which he set foot, because he followed the LORD wholeheartedly.' And because
of you, the LORD was enraged even with me, and said, 'You also shall not enter
38 it. Yehoshua son of Nun, who stands before you – he shall enter there. Encourage
39 him, for he will give Israel their possession. As for your little ones, whom you REVI'I
thought would be taken captive, and your children who do not yet know good
from bad, they shall enter, and I will give it to them, and they will take possession
40 of it. But you – turn around and set out into the wilderness by way of the Sea of
41 Reeds.' And you answered me: 'We have sinned against the LORD! We will go
up and fight, as the LORD our God commanded us.' So each of you strapped on
42 your weapons thinking that it would be easy to go up into the hill country. "The
LORD said to me, 'Tell them: Do not go up and do not fight, for I will not be
43 with you. Do not be struck down by your enemies.' And I told you, but you
would not listen. You rebelled against the word of the LORD and willfully went

רש"י

לו אֲשֶׁר דָּרַךְ בָּהּ. חֶבְרוֹן, שֶׁנֶּאֱמַר: "וַיָּבֹא עַד חֶבְרוֹן" (במדבר יג, כב):

לז הִתְאַנַּף. נִתְמַלֵּא רֹגֶז:

מ פְּנוּ לָכֶם. אָמַרְתִּי לְהַעֲבִיר אֶתְכֶם דֶּרֶךְ רֹחַב אֶרֶץ אֱדוֹם לְצַד צָפוֹן לִכָּנֵס לָאָרֶץ, קִלְקַלְתֶּם וּגְרַמְתֶּם לָכֶם עִכּוּב: פְּנוּ לָכֶם. לַאֲחוֹרֵיכֶם, וְתֵלְכוּ בַּמִּדְבָּר לְצַד יַם סוּף, שֶׁהַמִּדְבָּר שֶׁהָיוּ הוֹלְכִים בּוֹ לִדְרוֹמָהּ שֶׁל הַר שֵׂעִיר הָיָה, מַפְסִיק בֵּין יַם סוּף לְהַר שֵׂעִיר, עַתָּה הַמְשִׁכוּ לְצַד הַיָּם וְתִסְבְּבוּ אֶת הַר שֵׂעִיר כָּל דְּרוֹמוֹ מִן הַמַּעֲרָב לַמִּזְרָח:

מא וַתָּהִינוּ. לָשׁוֹן: "הִנֶּנּוּ וְעָלִינוּ אֶל הַמָּקוֹם" (במדבר יד, מ), זֶה הַלָּשׁוֹן שֶׁאֲמַרְתֶּם, לְשׁוֹן הֵן, כְּלוֹמַר נִזְדַּמַּנְתֶּם:

מב לֹא תַעֲלוּ. לֹא עֲלִיָּה תְּהֵא לָכֶם אֶלָּא יְרִידָה:

from their real sins. Aharon's sin was the golden calf. Moshe's mistake was the episode of the spies. The hint to this is in Moshe's words here, "Because of you, the LORD was enraged even with me."

As we saw, different verbs are used here and in Shelaḥ (ch. 1, "Retelling the Story of the Spies," above). God did *not* give Moshe permission to send spies. He specifically used the verb *latur*, meaning, He allowed the men to tour the land and come back and testify to its goodness. Moshe's error, if the analysis here is correct, was a subtle one, failing to make clear the difference between a spying mission and a morale-boosting eyewitness account of the land. In the face of a mob, a leader is not always in control of the situation. True leadership is impossible against the madness of crowds. Moshe implies that God was angry with him for not showing stronger leadership, but it was the people – or rather, their parents – who made that leadership impossible.

There is a famous saying of the Sages: "Make for yourself a teacher and acquire for yourself a friend" (Avot 1:6). You make a teacher by being willing to learn. You make a leader by being willing to follow. When people are unwilling to follow, even the greatest leader cannot lead. That is one reason why Yehoshua was chosen to be Moshe's successor. There were other distinguished candidates. But Yehoshua, serving Moshe throughout the wilderness years, is a role model of what it is to be a follower.

לד בַּדֶּרֶךְ אֲשֶׁר תֵּלְכוּ־בָהּ וּבֶעָנָן יוֹמָם׃ וַיִּשְׁמַע יְהוָה אֶת־קוֹל דִּבְרֵיכֶם
לה וַיִּקְצֹף וַיִּשָּׁבַע לֵאמֹר׃ אִם־יִרְאֶה אִישׁ בָּאֲנָשִׁים הָאֵלֶּה הַדּוֹר הָרָע
לו הַזֶּה אֵת הָאָרֶץ הַטּוֹבָה אֲשֶׁר נִשְׁבַּעְתִּי לָתֵת לַאֲבֹתֵיכֶם׃ זוּלָתִי כָּלֵב
בֶּן־יְפֻנֶּה הוּא יִרְאֶנָּה וְלוֹ־אֶתֵּן אֶת־הָאָרֶץ אֲשֶׁר דָּרַךְ־בָּהּ וּלְבָנָיו יַעַן
לז אֲשֶׁר מִלֵּא אַחֲרֵי יְהוָה׃ גַּם־בִּי הִתְאַנַּף יְהוָה בִּגְלַלְכֶם לֵאמֹר גַּם־אַתָּה
לח לֹא־תָבֹא שָׁם׃ יְהוֹשֻׁעַ בִּן־נוּן הָעֹמֵד לְפָנֶיךָ הוּא יָבֹא שָׁמָּה אֹתוֹ חַזֵּק
לט כִּי־הוּא יַנְחִלֶנָּה אֶת־יִשְׂרָאֵל׃ וְטַפְּכֶם אֲשֶׁר אֲמַרְתֶּם לָבַז יִהְיֶה וּבְנֵיכֶם רביעי
אֲשֶׁר לֹא־יָדְעוּ הַיּוֹם טוֹב וָרָע הֵמָּה יָבֹאוּ שָׁמָּה וְלָהֶם אֶתְּנֶנָּה וְהֵם
מ מא יִירָשׁוּהָ׃ וְאַתֶּם פְּנוּ לָכֶם וּסְעוּ הַמִּדְבָּרָה דֶּרֶךְ יַם־סוּף׃ וַתַּעֲנוּ ׀ וַתֹּאמְרוּ
אֵלַי חָטָאנוּ לַיהוָה אֲנַחְנוּ נַעֲלֶה וְנִלְחַמְנוּ כְּכֹל אֲשֶׁר־צִוָּנוּ יְהוָה
מב אֱלֹהֵינוּ וַתַּחְגְּרוּ אִישׁ אֶת־כְּלֵי מִלְחַמְתּוֹ וַתָּהִינוּ לַעֲלֹת הָהָרָה׃ וַיֹּאמֶר
יְהוָה אֵלַי אֱמֹר לָהֶם לֹא תַעֲלוּ וְלֹא תִלָּחֲמוּ כִּי אֵינֶנִּי בְּקִרְבְּכֶם וְלֹא
מג תִּנָּגְפוּ לִפְנֵי אֹיְבֵיכֶם׃ וָאֲדַבֵּר אֲלֵיכֶם וְלֹא שְׁמַעְתֶּם וַתַּמְרוּ אֶת־פִּי

אונקלוס

בְּאוֹרְחָא דִּתְהָכוּן בַּהּ, וּבְעַמּוּדָא דַּעֲנָנָא בִּימָמָא: לד וּשְׁמִיעַ קֳדָם יי יָת קָל פִּתְגָמֵיכוֹן, וּרְגִיז וְקַיֵּים לְמֵימַר: לה אִם יֶחֱזֵי גְּבַר בְּגֻבְרַיָּא הָאִלֵּין, דָּרָא בִּישָׁא הָדֵין, יָת אַרְעָא טָבְתָא, דְּקַיֵּימִית, לְמִתַּן לַאֲבָהָתְכוֹן: לו אֱלָהֵין, כָּלֵב בַּר יְפֻנֶּה הוּא יֶחְזֵינַהּ, וְלֵיהּ אֶתֵּין יָת אַרְעָא, דִּדְרַךְ בַּהּ וְלִבְנוֹהִי, חֲלַף, דְּאַשְׁלֵים בָּתַר דַּחַלְתָּא דַיי: לז אַף עֲלַי הֲוָה רְגַז מִן קֳדָם יי, בְּדִילְכוֹן לְמֵימַר, אַף אַתְּ לָא תֵיעוֹל לְתַמָּן: לח יְהוֹשֻׁעַ בַּר נוּן דְּקָאֵים קֳדָמָךְ, הוּא יֵיעוֹל לְתַמָּן, יָתֵיהּ תַּקֵּיף, אֲרֵי הוּא יַחְסְנִנַּהּ לְיִשְׂרָאֵל: לט וְטַפְלְכוֹן דַּאֲמַרְתּוּן לְבִזָּא יְהוֹן, וּבְנֵיכוֹן, דְּלָא יְדַעוּ יוֹמָא דֵין טָב וּבִישׁ, אִנּוּן יֵיעֲלוּן לְתַמָּן, וּלְהוֹן אֶתְּנִנַּהּ, וְאִנּוּן יֵרְתֻנַּהּ: מ וְאַתּוּן אִתְפְּנוּ לְכוֹן, וְטוּלוּ לְמַדְבְּרָא אוֹרַח יַמָּא דְסוּף: מא וַאֲתֵיבְתּוּן וַאֲמַרְתּוּן לִי, חַבְנָא קֳדָם יי, אֲנַחְנָא נִסַּק וְנַגִּיחַ קְרָב, כְּכֹל דְּפַקְּדָנָא יי אֱלָהָנָא, וְזָרֵיזְתּוּן, גְּבַר יָת מָנֵי קְרָבֵיהּ, וְשָׁרֵיתוּן לְמִסַּק לְטוּרָא: מב וַאֲמַר יי לִי, אֵימַר לְהוֹן לָא תִסְּקוּן וְלָא תְגִיחוּן קְרָב, אֲרֵי לֵית שְׁכִינְתִּי בֵּינֵיכוֹן, וְלָא תִתַּבְּרוּן, קֳדָם בַּעֲלֵי דְבָבֵיכוֹן: מג וּמַלֵּילִית עִמְּכוֹן וְלָא קַבֵּילְתּוּן, וְסָרֵיבְתּוּן עַל מֵימְרָא

1:37 גַּם־בִּי הִתְאַנַּף יהוה *The LORD was enraged even with me* – How could the episode of the spies have been Moshe's fault? It wasn't he who proposed sending them. Ramban suggests that Moshe was simply saying that, like the spies and the people, he too was condemned to die in the wilderness. Alternatively, he was hinting that no one should be able to say that Moshe avoided the fate of the generation he led.

However, Abrabanel offers a fascinating reading. Perhaps the reason Moshe and Aharon were not permitted to enter the land was not because of the episode of water and the rock at Kadesh. That is intended to distract attention

44 up into the hill country. The Amorites who lived in those hills came out against
you and chased you like a swarm of bees. In Se'ir they struck you down, as far
45 as Ḥorma. You came back and wept before the LORD, but the LORD would not
46 listen to you, nor pay you any heed. And so you remained at Kadesh for a long
2 1 time – all that time that you were there. Then we turned and journeyed back
into the wilderness, by way of the Sea of Reeds, as the LORD had told me and,
2 for a long time, made our way around Mount Se'ir. Then the LORD ḤAMISHI
3 said to me: 'You have circled about this hill country long enough now. Turn to
4 the north. And give the people these orders: You are about to pass through the
territory of your kinsmen, the descendants of Esav, who live in Se'ir. They will
5 be afraid of you, but be very careful. Do not provoke them, for I will not give
you even a foot of their land; I have given Mount Se'ir to Esav as his possession.
6 You shall pay them in silver for the food you eat, pay them silver for the water
7 that you buy from them and drink. For the LORD your God has blessed you in
all the work of your hands. He has watched over your wanderings through this
vast wilderness. These forty years the LORD your God has been with you: you
8 have lacked for nothing.' So we passed by, away from our kinsmen, the
descendants of Esav who live in Se'ir. We turned from the route of the Arava,
away from Eilat and Etzyon Gever, and journeyed in the direction of
9 the Wilderness of Moav. Then the LORD said to me: 'Do not mistreat the

רש״י

מד **כַּאֲשֶׁר תַּעֲשֶׂינָה הַדְּבֹרִים.** מַה הַדְּבוֹרָה הַזֹּאת כְּשֶׁהִיא מַכָּה אֶת הָאָדָם מִיַּד מֵתָה, אַף הֵם כְּשֶׁהָיוּ נוֹגְעִים בָּכֶם מִיָּד מֵתִים:

מה **וְלֹא שָׁמַע ה׳ בְּקֹלְכֶם.** כִּבְיָכוֹל עֲשִׂיתֶם מִדַּת רַחֲמָיו כְּאִלּוּ אַכְזָרִי:

מו **וַתֵּשְׁבוּ בְקָדֵשׁ יָמִים רַבִּים.** תְּשַׁע עֶשְׂרֵה שָׁנָה, שֶׁנֶּאֱמַר: ״כַּיָּמִים אֲשֶׁר יְשַׁבְתֶּם״ בִּשְׁאָר הַמַּסָּעוֹת, וְהֵם הָיוּ שְׁלֹשִׁים וּשְׁמֹנֶה שָׁנָה, תְּשַׁע עֶשְׂרֵה מֵהֶם עָשׂוּ בְּקָדֵשׁ וּתְשַׁע עֶשְׂרֵה שָׁנָה הוֹלְכִים וּמְטֹרָפִים וְחָזְרוּ לְקָדֵשׁ, כְּמוֹ שֶׁנֶּאֱמַר: ״וַיְנִעֵם בַּמִּדְבָּר״ (במדבר לב, יג). כָּךְ מָצָאתִי בְּסֵדֶר עוֹלָם (פרק ח):

ב א **וַנִּסַּע הַמִּדְבָּרָה.** אִלּוּ לֹא חָטְאוּ הָיוּ עוֹבְרִים דֶּרֶךְ הַר שֵׂעִיר לִכָּנֵס לָאָרֶץ מִדְּרוֹמוֹ לִצְפוֹנוֹ, וּבִשְׁבִיל שֶׁקִּלְקְלוּ הִפְנָן לְצַד הַמִּדְבָּר שֶׁהוּא בֵּין יַם סוּף לִדְרוֹמוֹ שֶׁל הַר שֵׂעִיר, וְהָלְכוּ אֵצֶל דְּרוֹמוֹ מִן הַמַּעֲרָב לַמִּזְרָח דֶּרֶךְ יְצִיאָתָן מִמִּצְרַיִם שֶׁהוּא בְּמִקְצוֹעַ דְּרוֹמִית מַעֲרָבִית, מִשָּׁם הָיוּ הוֹלְכִים לְצַד הַמִּזְרָח: **וַנָּסָב אֶת הַר שֵׂעִיר.** כָּל דְּרוֹמוֹ עַד אֶרֶץ מוֹאָב:

ג **פְּנוּ לָכֶם צָפֹנָה.** סְבוּ לָכֶם לְרוּחַ מִזְרָחִית מִן הַדָּרוֹם לַצָּפוֹן פְּנֵיכֶם לַצָּפוֹן, נִמְצְאוּ הוֹלְכִים אֶת רוּחַ מִזְרָחִית, וְזֶהוּ שֶׁנֶּאֱמַר: ״וַיָּבֹא מִמִּזְרַח שֶׁמֶשׁ לְאֶרֶץ מוֹאָב״ (שופטים יא, יח):

ד **וְנִשְׁמַרְתֶּם מְאֹד.** וּמַהוּ הַשְּׁמִירָה? ״אַל תִּתְגָּרוּ בָם״ (להלן פסוק ה):

ה **עַד מִדְרַךְ כַּף רָגֶל.** (אֲפִלּוּ כְּדֵי מִדְרַךְ כַּף רֶגֶל), [כְּלוֹמַר אֲפִלּוּ דְּרִיסַת הָרֶגֶל אֵינִי מַרְשֶׁה לָכֶם לַעֲבֹר בְּאַרְצָם שֶׁלֹּא בִּרְשׁוּת – רַבֵּנוּ שְׁמַעְיָה הֵעִיד: ״כָּךְ מָצָא לְהַגִּיהַּ״]. וּמִדְרַשׁ אַגָּדָה, עַד שֶׁיָּבוֹא יוֹם דְּרִיסַת כַּף רֶגֶל עַל הַר הַזֵּיתִים, שֶׁנֶּאֱמַר: ״וְעָמְדוּ רַגְלָיו״ וְגוֹ׳ (זכריה יד, ד): **יְרֻשָּׁה לְעֵשָׂו.** מֵאַבְרָהָם. עֲשָׂרָה עֲמָמִים נָתַתִּי לוֹ, שִׁבְעָה לָכֶם, וְקֵינִי וּקְנִזִּי וְקַדְמֹנִי הֵן עַמּוֹן וּמוֹאָב וְשֵׂעִיר, אַחַת מֵהֶם לְעֵשָׂו, וְהַשְּׁנַיִם לִבְנֵי לוֹט בִּשְׂכַר שֶׁהָלַךְ אִתּוֹ לְמִצְרַיִם וְשָׁתַק עַל מַה שֶּׁהָיָה אוֹמֵר עַל אִשְׁתּוֹ ׳אֲחוֹתִי הִיא׳, לְפִיכָךְ עֲשָׂאוֹ כִּבְנוֹ:

ו **תִּכְרוּ.** לְשׁוֹן מִקָּח, וְכֵן: ״אֲשֶׁר כָּרִיתִי לִי״ (בראשית נ, ה), שֶׁכֵּן בִּכְרַכֵּי הַיָּם קוֹרִין לִמְכִירָה כִּירָה:

מד יְהוָה וַתָּזִדוּ וַתַּעֲלוּ הָהָרָה: וַיֵּצֵא הָאֱמֹרִי הַיֹּשֵׁב בָּהָר הַהוּא לִקְרַאתְכֶם
וַיִּרְדְּפוּ אֶתְכֶם כַּאֲשֶׁר תַּעֲשֶׂינָה הַדְּבֹרִים וַיַּכְּתוּ אֶתְכֶם בְּשֵׂעִיר עַד־
מה חָרְמָה: וַתָּשֻׁבוּ וַתִּבְכּוּ לִפְנֵי יְהוָה וְלֹא־שָׁמַע יְהוָה בְּקֹלְכֶם וְלֹא הֶאֱזִין
מו א אֲלֵיכֶם: וַתֵּשְׁבוּ בְקָדֵשׁ יָמִים רַבִּים כַּיָּמִים אֲשֶׁר יְשַׁבְתֶּם: וַנֵּפֶן וַנִּסַּע ב
הַמִּדְבָּרָה דֶּרֶךְ יַם־סוּף כַּאֲשֶׁר דִּבֶּר יְהוָה אֵלָי וַנָּסָב אֶת־הַר־שֵׂעִיר
ב ג יָמִים רַבִּים: וַיֹּאמֶר יְהוָה אֵלַי לֵאמֹר: רַב־לָכֶם סֹב ב חמישי
ד אֶת־הָהָר הַזֶּה פְּנוּ לָכֶם צָפֹנָה: וְאֶת־הָעָם צַו לֵאמֹר אַתֶּם עֹבְרִים
בִּגְבוּל אֲחֵיכֶם בְּנֵי־עֵשָׂו הַיֹּשְׁבִים בְּשֵׂעִיר וְיִירְאוּ מִכֶּם וְנִשְׁמַרְתֶּם
ה מְאֹד: אַל־תִּתְגָּרוּ בָם כִּי לֹא־אֶתֵּן לָכֶם מֵאַרְצָם עַד מִדְרַךְ כַּף־רָגֶל
ו כִּי־יְרֻשָּׁה לְעֵשָׂו נָתַתִּי אֶת־הַר שֵׂעִיר: אֹכֶל תִּשְׁבְּרוּ מֵאִתָּם בַּכֶּסֶף
ז וַאֲכַלְתֶּם וְגַם־מַיִם תִּכְרוּ מֵאִתָּם בַּכֶּסֶף וּשְׁתִיתֶם: כִּי יְהוָה אֱלֹהֶיךָ
בֵּרַכְךָ בְּכֹל מַעֲשֵׂה יָדֶךָ יָדַע לֶכְתְּךָ אֶת־הַמִּדְבָּר הַגָּדֹל הַזֶּה זֶה ׀
ח אַרְבָּעִים שָׁנָה יְהוָה אֱלֹהֶיךָ עִמָּךְ לֹא חָסַרְתָּ דָּבָר: וַנַּעֲבֹר מֵאֵת אַחֵינוּ
בְנֵי־עֵשָׂו הַיֹּשְׁבִים בְּשֵׂעִיר מִדֶּרֶךְ הָעֲרָבָה מֵאֵילַת וּמֵעֶצְיֹן
ט גָּבֶר וַנֵּפֶן וַנַּעֲבֹר דֶּרֶךְ מִדְבַּר מוֹאָב: וַיֹּאמֶר יְהוָה

אונקלוס

דַּיְיָ, וְאַרְשַׁעְתּוּן וּסְלֵיקְתּוּן לְטוּרָא: מד וּנְפַק אֱמוֹרָאָה, דְּיָתֵיב בְּטוּרָא הַהוּא לְקַדָּמוּתְכוֹן, וּרְדַפוּ יָתְכוֹן, כְּמָא דְנָתְזָן דַּבְרְיָתָא, וּטְרָדוּ יָתְכוֹן, בְּשֵׂעִיר עַד חָרְמָה: מה וְתַבְתּוּן וּבְכֵיתוּן קֳדָם יְיָ, וְלָא קַבֵּיל יְיָ צְלוֹתְכוֹן, וְלָא אֲצֵית לְמִלֵּיכוֹן: מו וִיתֵיבְתּוּן בִּרְקַם יוֹמִין סַגִּיאִין, כְּיוֹמַיָּא דִּיתֵיבְתּוּן: ב א וְאִתְפְּנֵינָא, וּנְטַלְנָא לְמַדְבְּרָא אוֹרַח יַמָּא דְסוּף, כְּמָא דְּמַלֵּיל יְיָ עִמִּי, וְאַקֵּיפְנָא יָת טוּרָא דְשֵׂעִיר יוֹמִין סַגִּיאִין: ב וַאֲמַר יְיָ לִי לְמֵימָר: ג סַגִּי לְכוֹן, דְּאַקֵּיפְתּוּן יָת טוּרָא הָדֵין, אִתְפְּנוֹ לְכוֹן לְצִפּוּנָא: ד וְיָת עַמָּא פַּקֵּיד לְמֵימָר, אַתּוּן עָבְרִין, בִּתְחוּם אֲחֵיכוֹן בְּנֵי עֵשָׂו, דְּיָתְבִין בְּשֵׂעִיר, וְיִדְחֲלוּן מִנְּכוֹן, וְתִסְתַּמְרוּן לַחֲדָא: ה לָא תִתְגָּרוּן בְּהוֹן, אֲרֵי, לָא אֶתֵּין לְכוֹן מֵאַרְעֲהוֹן, עַד מִדְרַךְ פַּרְסַת רְגַל, אֲרֵי יְרֻתָּא לְעֵשָׂו, יְהָבִית יָת טוּרָא דְשֵׂעִיר: ו עֲבוּרָא תִּזְבְּנוּן מִנְּהוֹן, בְּכַסְפָּא וְתֵיכְלוּן, וְאַף מַיָּא, תִּזְבְּנוּן מִנְּהוֹן, בְּכַסְפָּא וְתִשְׁתּוּן: ז אֲרֵי יְיָ אֱלָהָךְ בָּרְכָךְ, בְּכֹל עוּבָדֵי יְדָךְ, סוֹפֵיק לָךְ צָרְכָךְ בְּמַהֲכָךְ, יָת מַדְבְּרָא רַבָּא הָדֵין, דְּנָן אַרְבְּעִין שְׁנִין, מֵימְרָא דַּייָ אֱלָהָךְ בְּסַעֲדָךְ, לָא חֲסַרְתָּא מִדָּעַם: ח וַעֲבַרְנָא מִלְּוָת אַחָנָא בְּנֵי עֵשָׂו, דְּיָתְבִין בְּשֵׂעִיר, מֵאוֹרַח מֵישְׁרָא, מֵאֵילַת וּמֵעֶצְיוֹן גָּבֶר, וְאִתְפְּנֵינָא וַעֲבַרְנָא, אוֹרַח מַדְבְּרָא דְמוֹאָב: ט וַאֲמַר יְיָ

רש״י

ז כִּי ה' אֱלֹהֶיךָ בֵּרַכְךָ. לְפִיכָךְ לֹא תִכְפּוּ אֶת טוֹבָתוֹ לְהַרְאוֹת כְּאִלּוּ אַתֶּם עֲנִיִּים, אֶלָּא הַרְאוּ עַצְמְכֶם עֲשִׁירִים:

ח וַנֵּפֶן וַנַּעֲבֹר. לְצַד צָפוֹן, הָפַכְנוּ פָּנֵינוּ לָלֶכֶת רוּחַ מִזְרָחִית:

Moabites or provoke them to war, for I will not give you any of their land as a
10 possession: I have given Ar to the descendants of Lot for a possession.'" The
Emim lived there originally – a strong and numerous people, as tall as the
11 Anakites. Like the Anakites, they are considered Refaim, but the Moabites call
12 them Emim. Horites used to live in Se'ir, but the descendants of Esav
dispossessed them, destroying them and settling in their place, as Israel did in
13 the land that the Lord gave them as a possession. "'Now, get up and cross the
14 Zered Stream.' So we crossed the Zered Stream. From the time we left Kadesh
Barnea to the time we crossed the Zered Stream was thirty-eight years – until
the entire generation of warriors had perished from the camp – as the Lord
15 had sworn to them. And the Lord's hand was against them to trouble them
16 from the camp until they had all perished. When all those warriors among the
17 18 people had died, the Lord spoke to me: 'Today you are going to cross
19 the border of Moav at Ar. When you come to the Amonites, do not harass them
or provoke them to war, for I will not give you any of the land of the Amonites

רש״י

ט **ואל תתגר בם.** לא אסר להם על מואב אלא מלחמה, אבל מיראים היו אותם ונראים להם כשהם מזינים, לפיכך כתיב: "ויגר מואב מפני העם" (במדבר כב, ג), שהיו שוללים ובוזזים אותם. אבל בבני עמון נאמר: "ואל תתגר בם" (להלן פסוק יט), שום גרוי, בשכר צניעות אמם שלא פרסמה על אביה כמו שעשתה הבכירה שקראה שם בנה מואב: **ער.** שם המדינה:

י **האמים לפנים וגו'.** אתה סבור שזו ארץ רפאים שנתתי לו לאברהם (בראשית טו, כ), לפי שהאמים שהם רפאים ישבו בה לפנים, אבל לא זו היא, כי אותן רפאים הורשתי מפני בני לוט והושבתים תחתם:

יא-יב **רפאים יחשבו וגו'.** רפאים היו נחשבין אותם אמים, כענקים הנקראים רפאים, על שם שכל הרואה אותם ידיו מתרפות: **אמים.** על שם שאימתם מוטלת על הבריות. וכן: "ובשעיר ישבו החרים" ונתתים לבני עשו: **יירשום.** לשון הוה, כלומר נתתי בהם כח שיהיו מורישים אותם והולכים:

טו **היתה בם.** למהר ולהמם בתוך ארבעים שנה, שלא יגרמו לבניהם עוד להתעכב במדבר:

טז-יז **ויהי כאשר תמו וגו' וידבר ה' אלי וגו'.** אבל משלוח המרגלים עד כאן לא נאמר 'וידבר' בפרשה זו אלא 'ויאמר', ללמדך שכל שלשים ושמונה שנה שהיו ישראל נזופים, לא נתיחד עמו הדבור בלשון חבה פנים אל פנים וישוב, ללמדך שאין השכינה שורה על הנביאים אלא בשביל ישראל: **אנשי המלחמה.** מבן עשרים שנה היוצאים בצבא:

יח-יט **אתה עבר היום את גבול מואב.** אל 'מול בני עמון', מכאן שארץ עמון לצד צפון:

My predecessor as chief rabbi, Lord Jakobovits, pointed out that the word *yizkor*, the name given to the traditional Jewish prayer for the dead, is associated in the Torah with the future. "God remembered Noaḥ" (Gen. 8:1) and brought him out on dry land. He "remembered Avraham" (19:29) and rescued his nephew Lot from the destruction of the cities of the plain. "God remembered Raḥel" (30:23) and gave her a child. We remember for the sake of the future, and for life.

a claim on me. They are the past as past. Memory is the past as present, as it lives on in me. Without memory there can be no identity.

Alzheimer's disease, the progressive atrophying of memory function, is also the disintegration of personality. As with individuals, so with a nation: it has a continuing identity to the extent that it can remember where it came from and who its ancestors were. We remember not what is objectively most remarkable but what shapes who we are.

אֵלַי אַל־תָּצַר אֶת־מוֹאָב וְאַל־תִּתְגָּר בָּם מִלְחָמָה כִּי לֹא־אֶתֵּן לְךָ
י מֵאַרְצוֹ יְרֻשָּׁה כִּי לִבְנֵי־לוֹט נָתַתִּי אֶת־עָר יְרֻשָּׁה: הָאֵמִים לְפָנִים יָשְׁבוּ
יא בָהּ עַם גָּדוֹל וְרַב וָרָם כַּעֲנָקִים: רְפָאִים יֵחָשְׁבוּ אַף־הֵם כַּעֲנָקִים
יב וְהַמֹּאָבִים יִקְרְאוּ לָהֶם אֵמִים: וּבְשֵׂעִיר יָשְׁבוּ הַחֹרִים לְפָנִים וּבְנֵי עֵשָׂו
יִירָשׁוּם וַיַּשְׁמִידוּם מִפְּנֵיהֶם וַיֵּשְׁבוּ תַּחְתָּם כַּאֲשֶׁר עָשָׂה יִשְׂרָאֵל לְאֶרֶץ
יג יְרֻשָּׁתוֹ אֲשֶׁר־נָתַן יְהוָה לָהֶם: עַתָּה קֻמוּ וְעִבְרוּ לָכֶם אֶת־נַחַל זָרֶד
יד וַנַּעֲבֹר אֶת־נַחַל זָרֶד: וְהַיָּמִים אֲשֶׁר־הָלַכְנוּ ׀ מִקָּדֵשׁ בַּרְנֵעַ עַד אֲשֶׁר־
עָבַרְנוּ אֶת־נַחַל זֶרֶד שְׁלֹשִׁים וּשְׁמֹנֶה שָׁנָה עַד־תֹּם כָּל־הַדּוֹר אַנְשֵׁי
טו הַמִּלְחָמָה מִקֶּרֶב הַמַּחֲנֶה כַּאֲשֶׁר נִשְׁבַּע יְהוָה לָהֶם: וְגַם יַד־יְהוָה הָיְתָה
טז בָּם לְהֻמָּם מִקֶּרֶב הַמַּחֲנֶה עַד תֻּמָּם: וַיְהִי כַאֲשֶׁר־תַּמּוּ כָּל־אַנְשֵׁי
יז הַמִּלְחָמָה לָמוּת מִקֶּרֶב הָעָם: וַיְדַבֵּר יְהוָה אֵלַי לֵאמֹר:
יח יט אַתָּה עֹבֵר הַיּוֹם אֶת־גְּבוּל מוֹאָב אֶת־עָר: וְקָרַבְתָּ מוּל בְּנֵי עַמּוֹן
אַל־תְּצֻרֵם וְאַל־תִּתְגָּר בָּם כִּי לֹא־אֶתֵּן מֵאֶרֶץ בְּנֵי־עַמּוֹן לְךָ יְרֻשָּׁה

אונקלוס

לִי, לָא תְצוּר עַל מוֹאֲבָאֵי, וְלָא תִתְגָּרֵי לְמֶעְבַּד עִמְּהוֹן קְרָב, אֲרֵי, לָא אֶתֵּין לָךְ מֵאַרְעֲהוֹן יְרֻתָּא, אֲרֵי לִבְנֵי לוֹט, יְהָבִית יָת לְחָיַת יְרֻתָּא: י אֵימְתָנֵי מִלְּקַדְמִין יְתִיבוּ בַהּ, עַם רַב וְסַגִּי, וְתַקִּיף כְּגִבָּרַיָּא: יא גִּבָּרַיָּא, מִתְחַשְׁבִין אַף אִנּוּן כְּגִבָּרַיָּא, וּמוֹאֲבָאֵי, קָרַן לְהוֹן אֵימְתָנֵי: יב וּבְשֵׂעִיר, יְתִיבוּ חוֹרָאֵי מִלְּקַדְמִין, וּבְנֵי עֵשָׂו תָּרִיכוּנוּן, וְשֵׁיצִיאוּנוּן מִן קֳדָמֵיהוֹן, וִיתִיבוּ בְּאַתְרֵיהוֹן, כְּמָא דַּעֲבַד יִשְׂרָאֵל, לַאֲרַע יְרֻתְּתֵיהּ, דִּיהַב יי לְהוֹן: יג כְּעַן, קוּמוּ, וְעִיבַרוּ לְכוֹן יָת נַחְלָא דְזָרֶד, וַעֲבַרְנָא יָת נַחְלָא דְזָרֶד: יד וְיוֹמַיָּא, דְּהַלֵּיכְנָא מֵרְקַם גֵּיאָה, עַד דַּעֲבַרְנָא יָת נַחְלָא דְזֶרֶד, תְּלָתִין וְתַמְנֵי שְׁנִין, עַד דְּסָף כָּל דָּרָא, גֻּבְרֵי מְגִיחֵי קְרָבָא מִגּוֹ מַשְׁרִיתָא, כְּמָא דְקַיֵּים יי לְהוֹן: טו וְאַף מְחָא מִן קֳדָם יי הֲוָת בְּהוֹן, לְשֵׁיצָיוּתְהוֹן מִגּוֹ מַשְׁרִיתָא, עַד דִּשְׁלִימוּ: טז וַהֲוָה כַּד שְׁלִימוּ, כָּל גֻּבְרֵי מְגִיחֵי קְרָבָא, לִמְמָת מִגּוֹ עַמָּא: יז וּמַלֵּיל יי עִמִּי לְמֵימַר: יח אַתְּ עָבַר יוֹמָא דֵין, יָת תְּחוּם מוֹאָב יָת לְחָיַת: יט וְתִתְקָרַב, לָקֳבֵיל בְּנֵי עַמּוֹן, לָא תְצוּר עֲלֵיהוֹן וְלָא תִתְגָּרֵי לְמֶעְבַּד עִמְּהוֹן קְרָב, אֲרֵי לָא אֶתֵּין, מֵאֲרַע בְּנֵי עַמּוֹן לָךְ יְרֻתָּא,

2:10 **וָרָם כַּעֲנָקִים** *As tall as the Anakites* – The Anakites and Og, so vivid in the legends of the time, are no longer a helpful reference point to us. Moshe's story however, repeated year after year, is as alive to us now as it ever was. The passing references to bygone peoples emphasize the profound difference between history and memory. History is *his* story – an event that happened sometime else to someone else. Memory is *my* story – something that happened to me and is part of who I am. History is information. Memory, by contrast, is part of identity. I can study the history of other peoples, cultures, and civilizations. They deepen my knowledge and broaden my horizons. But they do not make

20 as a possession: I have given it as a possession to the descendants of Lot.'" This
too was considered a land of Refaim. Refaim lived there originally, although the
21 Amonites call them Zamzumim – a strong and numerous people, as tall as the
Anakites. The Lord destroyed them so that the Amonites could dispossess
22 them and settle in their place, just as He did for the descendants of Esav, who
live in Se'ir, by destroying the Horites before them so that they could dispossess
23 them and settle in their place to this day, where they still remain; likewise the
Avim, who had lived in villages as far as Aza – the Caftorites, emerging from
24 Caftor, destroyed them and settled in their place. "'Set out and cross the Arnon
Stream. I have given over Siḥon, the Amorite king of Ḥeshbon, with his land,
25 into your hands. Begin to take possession of it; enter into battle with him. This
day I am beginning to put the terror and fear of you upon the peoples everywhere
under the skies. When they hear reports of you, they will tremble in dread of
26 you.' So I sent messengers from the Kedemot wilderness to Siḥon, king of
27 Ḥeshbon, with an offer of peace: 'Let us pass through your land. We will stay on
28 the main road, turning aside neither to the right nor to the left. Provide us with
food and we will pay for it in silver and eat; give us water and we will pay for it in
29 silver and drink. Only let us pass through on foot – just as the descendants of

רש״י

כ **אֶרֶץ רְפָאִים תֵּחָשֵׁב.** אֶרֶץ רְפָאִים נֶחְשֶׁבֶת אַף הִיא, לְפִי שֶׁהָרְפָאִים יָשְׁבוּ בָהּ לְפָנִים, אֲבָל לֹא זוֹ הִיא שֶׁנָּתַתִּי לְאַבְרָהָם:

כג **וְהָעַוִּים הַיֹּשְׁבִים בַּחֲצֵרִים וְגוֹ׳.** עַוִּים מִפְּלִשְׁתִּים הֵם, שֶׁעִמָּהֶם הֵם נֶחְשָׁבִים בְּסֵפֶר יְהוֹשֻׁעַ, שֶׁנֶּאֱמַר: "חֲמֵשֶׁת סַרְנֵי פְלִשְׁתִּים הָעַזָּתִי וְהָאַשְׁדּוֹדִי הָאֶשְׁקְלוֹנִי הַגִּתִּי וְהָעֶקְרוֹנִי וְהָעַוִּים" (יהושע יג, ג), וּמִפְּנֵי הַשְּׁבוּעָה שֶׁנִּשְׁבַּע אַבְרָהָם לַאֲבִימֶלֶךְ לֹא יָכְלוּ יִשְׂרָאֵל לְהוֹצִיא אַרְצָם מִיָּדָם, וְהֵבֵאתִי עֲלֵיהֶם כַּפְתּוֹרִים וְהִשְׁמִידוּם וְיָשְׁבוּ תַחְתָּם, וְעַכְשָׁיו אַתֶּם מֻתָּרִים לְקַחְתָּהּ מִיָּדָם:

כה **תַּחַת כָּל הַשָּׁמָיִם.** לִמֵּד שֶׁעָמְדָה חַמָּה לְמֹשֶׁה בְּיוֹם מִלְחֶמֶת עוֹג, וְנוֹדַע הַדָּבָר תַּחַת כָּל הַשָּׁמַיִם:

כו **מִמִּדְבַּר קְדֵמוֹת.** אַף עַל פִּי שֶׁלֹּא צִוַּנִי הַמָּקוֹם לִקְרֹא לְסִיחוֹן לְשָׁלוֹם, לָמַדְתִּי מִמִּדְבַּר סִינַי, מִן הַתּוֹרָה שֶׁקָּדְמָה לָעוֹלָם, כְּשֶׁבָּא הַקָּדוֹשׁ בָּרוּךְ הוּא לִתְּנָהּ לְיִשְׂרָאֵל חִזֵּר אוֹתָהּ עַל עֵשָׂו וְיִשְׁמָעֵאל, וְגָלוּי לְפָנָיו שֶׁלֹּא יְקַבְּלוּהָ וְאַף עַל פִּי כֵן פָּתַח לָהֶם בְּשָׁלוֹם, אַף אֲנִי קִדַּמְתִּי אֶת סִיחוֹן בְּדִבְרֵי שָׁלוֹם:

כט **כַּאֲשֶׁר עָשׂוּ לִי בְּנֵי עֵשָׂו.** לֹא לְעִנְיַן לַעֲבֹר בְּאַרְצָם, אֶלָּא לְעִנְיַן מֶכֶר אֹכֶל וּמַיִם:

No war, either permitted or obligatory [such as a war of self-defense] may be initiated without first offering terms of peace.... Joshua sent three messages before entering the land: the first, "Whoever wishes to flee, let him flee"; the second, "Whoever wishes to make peace, let him make peace"; the third, "Whoever wishes to make war, let him make war." (*Hilkhot Melakhim UMilḥemoteihem* 9:1)

War, for Rambam, is never mandated except when the effort to make peace has been tried, and failed. Moshe's actions here express this fundamental principle.

2:29 **כַּאֲשֶׁר עָשׂוּ־לִי בְּנֵי עֵשָׂו הַיֹּשְׁבִים בְּשֵׂעִיר** *Just as the descendants of Esav living in Se'ir... did for us* – There is nothing in this passage to remind us of the eternal strife between the two nations predicted before their birth ("Two nations are

כ כִּי לִבְנֵי־לוֹט נְתַתִּיהָ יְרֻשָּׁה: אֶרֶץ־רְפָאִים תֵּחָשֵׁב אַף־הִוא רְפָאִים
כא יָשְׁבוּ־בָהּ לְפָנִים וְהָעַמֹּנִים יִקְרְאוּ לָהֶם זַמְזֻמִּים: עַם גָּדוֹל וְרַב וָרָם
כב כָּעֲנָקִים וַיַּשְׁמִידֵם יהוה מִפְּנֵיהֶם וַיִּירָשֻׁם וַיֵּשְׁבוּ תַחְתָּם: כַּאֲשֶׁר עָשָׂה
לִבְנֵי עֵשָׂו הַיֹּשְׁבִים בְּשֵׂעִיר אֲשֶׁר הִשְׁמִיד אֶת־הַחֹרִי מִפְּנֵיהֶם וַיִּירָשֻׁם
כג וַיֵּשְׁבוּ תַחְתָּם עַד הַיּוֹם הַזֶּה: וְהָעַוִּים הַיֹּשְׁבִים בַּחֲצֵרִים עַד־עַזָּה
כד כַּפְתֹּרִים הַיֹּצְאִים מִכַּפְתֹּר הִשְׁמִידֻם וַיֵּשְׁבוּ תַחְתָּם: קוּמוּ סְּעוּ וְעִבְרוּ
אֶת־נַחַל אַרְנֹן רְאֵה נָתַתִּי בְיָדְךָ אֶת־סִיחֹן מֶלֶךְ־חֶשְׁבּוֹן הָאֱמֹרִי
כה וְאֶת־אַרְצוֹ הָחֵל רָשׁ וְהִתְגָּר בּוֹ מִלְחָמָה: הַיּוֹם הַזֶּה אָחֵל תֵּת פַּחְדְּךָ
וְיִרְאָתְךָ עַל־פְּנֵי הָעַמִּים תַּחַת כָּל־הַשָּׁמָיִם אֲשֶׁר יִשְׁמְעוּן שִׁמְעֲךָ
כו וְרָגְזוּ וְחָלוּ מִפָּנֶיךָ: וָאֶשְׁלַח מַלְאָכִים מִמִּדְבַּר קְדֵמוֹת אֶל־סִיחוֹן מֶלֶךְ
כז חֶשְׁבּוֹן דִּבְרֵי שָׁלוֹם לֵאמֹר: אֶעְבְּרָה בְאַרְצֶךָ בַּדֶּרֶךְ בַּדֶּרֶךְ אֵלֵךְ לֹא
כח אָסוּר יָמִין וּשְׂמֹאול: אֹכֶל בַּכֶּסֶף תַּשְׁבִּרֵנִי וְאָכַלְתִּי וּמַיִם בַּכֶּסֶף תִּתֶּן־
כט לִי וְשָׁתִיתִי רַק אֶעְבְּרָה בְרַגְלָי: כַּאֲשֶׁר עָשׂוּ־לִי בְּנֵי עֵשָׂו הַיֹּשְׁבִים

אונקלוס

אֲרֵי לִבְנֵי לוֹט יְהַבְתַּהּ יְרֻתָּא: כ אֲרַע גִּבָּרַיָּא מִתְחַשְׁבָא אַף הִיא, גִּבָּרִין יְתִיבוּ בַהּ מִלְקַדְמִין, וְעַמּוֹנָאֵי, קָרַן לְהוֹן חֻשְׁבָּנֵי: כא עַם רַב וְסַגִּי, וְתַקִּיף כְּגִבָּרַיָּא, וְשֵׁיצִינוּן יי מִן קֳדָמֵיהוֹן, וְתָרִיכוּנוּן וִיתִיבוּ בְאַתְרְהוֹן: כב כְּמָא דַעֲבַד לִבְנֵי עֵשָׂו, דְּיָתְבִין בְּשֵׂעִיר, דְּשֵׁיצִי יָת חוֹרָאֵי מִן קֳדָמֵיהוֹן, וְתָרִיכוּנוּן וִיתִיבוּ בְאַתְרְהוֹן, עַד יוֹמָא הָדֵין: כג וְעַוָּאֵי, דְּיָתְבִין בִּרְפִיחַ עַד עַזָּה, קַפּוּטְקָאֵי דִּנְפַקוּ מִקַּפּוּטְקְיָא, שֵׁיצִיאוּנוּן וִיתִיבוּ בְאַתְרְהוֹן: כד קוּמוּ טוּלוּ, וְעִיבַרוּ יָת נַחְלָא דְאַרְנוֹן, חֲזִי דִּמְסָרִית בִּידָךְ, יָת סִיחוֹן מַלְכָּא דְחֶשְׁבּוֹן אֱמוֹרָאָה, וְיָת אַרְעֵיהּ שָׁרִי לְתָרְכוּתֵיהּ, וְתִתְגָּרֵי לְמֶעֱבַד עִמֵּהּ קְרָב: כה יוֹמָא הָדֵין, אֲשָׁרֵי לְמִתַּן זִיעְתָךְ וְדַחֲלְתָךְ, עַל אַפֵּי עַמְמַיָּא, דִּתְחוֹת כָּל שְׁמַיָּא, דִּיִשְׁמְעוּן שִׁמְעָךְ, וְיָזוּעוּן וְיִתַּבְרוּן מִן קֳדָמָךְ: כו וּשְׁלַחִית אִזְגַּדִּין מִמַּדְבְּרָא דִקְדֵמוֹת, לְוָת סִיחוֹן מַלְכָּא דְחֶשְׁבּוֹן, פִּתְגָּמֵי שְׁלָמָא לְמֵימַר: כז אֶעְבַּר בְּאַרְעָךְ, בְּאוֹרְחָא בְאוֹרְחָא אֵיזֵיל, לָא אֶסְטֵי לְיַמִּינָא וְלִסְמָאלָא: כח עֲבוּרָא בְּכַסְפָּא תְּזַבֵּין לִי וְאֵיכוֹל, וּמַיָּא, בְּכַסְפָּא תִּתֵּין לִי וְאֶשְׁתֵּי, לְחוֹד אֶעְבַּר בְּרַגְלָי: כט כְּמָא דַעֲבַדוּ לִי בְּנֵי עֵשָׂו, דְּיָתְבִין

2:26 וָאֶשְׁלַח מַלְאָכִים... אֶל־סִיחוֹן מֶלֶךְ חֶשְׁבּוֹן דִּבְרֵי שָׁלוֹם *I sent messengers… to Siḥon, king of Ḥeshbon, with an offer of peace* – Rashi points out something remarkable here: that even though God does not tell Moshe to offer peace to Siḥon, Moshe takes it upon himself to do so. Despite the apparent militarism of the early texts of Judaism, their underlying value was always peace. Already in Leviticus we find the blessing "I will grant peace in the land… and through that land no sword shall pass" (26:6). The priestly benedictions end with a prayer for peace (Num. 6:26). Rambam summarized the laws about initiating a war as follows:

Esav living in Se'ir and the Moabites living in Ar did for us – until we cross the
30 Jordan into the land that the Lord our God is giving us.' But Siḥon, king of
Ḥeshbon, refused to let us pass through, for the Lord your God had hardened
his spirit and made his heart defiant in order to give him over into your hands,
31 as He has now done. The Lord said to me, 'I have begun to give Siḥon SHISHI
32 and his land over to you. Go: begin to conquer and possess his land.' Then
33 Siḥon and all his people came out to meet us in battle at Yahatz. The Lord our
God gave him over to us, and we struck him down, together with his sons and
34 all his people. At that time we captured all his towns and completely destroyed
35 them, men, women, and children alike, leaving not a single survivor. Only the
livestock and the spoil of the cities we captured did we keep as booty for
36 ourselves. From Aroer on the banks of the Arnon Stream, including the town
in the ravine, as far as Gilad, not one city was unattainable to us. The Lord our
37 God gave us all of them. But you did not touch the land of the Amonites, not
the land around the Yabok Stream, nor the towns of the hill country that the
3 1 Lord our God commanded us to leave. After this, we turned and journeyed
along the road toward Bashan. Og, king of Bashan, with all his people came out
2 to Edre'i to engage us in battle. But the Lord said to me, 'Do not be afraid of
him, for I have given him into your hand, with all his people and his land. Do
3 to him what you did to Siḥon, king of the Amorites, who lived in Ḥeshbon.' So
the Lord our God also gave over to us Og, king of Bashan, and all his people.

רש״י

לב| **וַיֵּצֵא סִיחֹן.** לֹא שָׁלַח בִּשְׁבִיל עוֹג לַעֲזֹר לוֹ, לְלַמֶּדְךָ שֶׁלֹּא הָיוּ צְרִיכִים זֶה לָזֶה:

לג| **וְאֶת בָּנָו.** ׳בְּנוֹ׳ כְּתִיב, שֶׁהָיָה לוֹ בֵּן גִּבּוֹר כְּמוֹתוֹ:

לד| **מְתִם.** נָשִׁים. בְּבִזַּת סִיחוֹן נֶאֱמַר: ״בָּזַזְנוּ לָנוּ״ (להלן פסוק לה), לְשׁוֹן בִּזָּה, שֶׁהָיְתָה חֲבִיבָה עֲלֵיהֶם וּבוֹזְזִים אִישׁ לוֹ, וּכְשֶׁבָּאוּ לְבִזַּת עוֹג כְּבָר הָיוּ שְׂבֵעִים וּמְלֵאִים, וְהָיְתָה בְזוּיָה בְּעֵינֵיהֶם וּמְקָרְעִין וּמַשְׁלִיכִין בְּהֵמָה וּבְגָדִים, כִּי אִם כֶּסֶף וְזָהָב, לְכָךְ נֶאֱמַר: ״בַּזּוֹנוּ לָנוּ״ (להלן ג, ז), לְשׁוֹן בִּזָּיוֹן. כָּךְ נִדְרָשׁ בְּסִפְרֵי בְּפָרָשַׁת ׳וַיֵּשֶׁב יִשְׂרָאֵל בַּשִּׁטִּים׳ (ספרי במדבר קלא):

לז| **כָּל יַד נַחַל יַבֹּק.** כָּל אֵצֶל נַחַל יַבֹּק: **וְכֹל אֲשֶׁר צִוָּה ה׳ אֱלֹהֵינוּ.** שֶׁלֹּא לִכְבֹּשׁ, הִנַּחְנוּ:

ג א| **וַנֵּפֶן וַנַּעַל.** כָּל לְצַד צָפוֹן עֲלִיָּה הִיא:

ב| **אַל תִּירָא אֹתוֹ.** וּבְסִיחוֹן לֹא הֻצְרַךְ לוֹמַר ׳אַל תִּירָא אֹתוֹ׳, אֶלָּא מִתְיָרֵא הָיָה מֹשֶׁה שֶׁלֹּא תַעֲמֹד לוֹ זְכוּת שֶׁשִּׁמֵּשׁ לְאַבְרָהָם, שֶׁנֶּאֱמַר: ״וַיָּבֹא הַפָּלִיט״ (בראשית יד, יג) וְהוּא עוֹג:

inside your womb.... People will overpower people, and the greater shall the younger serve" [Gen. 25:23]). In recording the aid given by Esav's descendants to the Jewish people, the Torah teaches an important message: heroes have their faults and non-heroes their virtues, and these virtues are important to God. "The Holy One, blessed be He, does not withhold the reward of any creature," said the Sages (Pesaḥim 118a).

בַּשֵּׂעִיר וְהַמּוֹאָבִים הַיֹּשְׁבִים בְּעָר עַד אֲשֶׁר־אֶעֱבֹר אֶת־הַיַּרְדֵּן אֶל־
ל הָאָרֶץ אֲשֶׁר־יהוה אֱלֹהֵינוּ נֹתֵן לָנוּ: וְלֹא אָבָה סִיחֹן מֶלֶךְ חֶשְׁבּוֹן
הַעֲבִרֵנוּ בּוֹ כִּי־הִקְשָׁה יהוה אֱלֹהֶיךָ אֶת־רוּחוֹ וְאִמֵּץ אֶת־לְבָבוֹ לְמַעַן
לא תִּתּוֹ בְיָדְךָ כַּיּוֹם הַזֶּה: וַיֹּאמֶר יהוה אֵלַי רְאֵה הַחִלֹּתִי ג ששי
לב תֵּת לְפָנֶיךָ אֶת־סִיחֹן וְאֶת־אַרְצוֹ הָחֵל רָשׁ לָרֶשֶׁת אֶת־אַרְצוֹ: וַיֵּצֵא
לג סִיחֹן לִקְרָאתֵנוּ הוּא וְכָל־עַמּוֹ לַמִּלְחָמָה יָהְצָה: וַיִּתְּנֵהוּ יהוה אֱלֹהֵינוּ
לד לְפָנֵינוּ וַנַּךְ אֹתוֹ וְאֶת־בָּנָו וְאֶת־כָּל־עַמּוֹ: וַנִּלְכֹּד אֶת־כָּל־עָרָיו בָּעֵת
הַהִוא וַנַּחֲרֵם אֶת־כָּל־עִיר מְתִם וְהַנָּשִׁים וְהַטָּף לֹא הִשְׁאַרְנוּ שָׂרִיד:
לה לו רַק הַבְּהֵמָה בָּזַזְנוּ לָנוּ וּשְׁלַל הֶעָרִים אֲשֶׁר לָכָדְנוּ: מֵעֲרֹעֵר אֲשֶׁר
עַל־שְׂפַת־נַחַל אַרְנֹן וְהָעִיר אֲשֶׁר בַּנַּחַל וְעַד־הַגִּלְעָד לֹא הָיְתָה קִרְיָה
לז אֲשֶׁר שָׂגְבָה מִמֶּנּוּ אֶת־הַכֹּל נָתַן יהוה אֱלֹהֵינוּ לְפָנֵינוּ: רַק אֶל־אֶרֶץ
בְּנֵי־עַמּוֹן לֹא קָרָבְתָּ כָּל־יַד נַחַל יַבֹּק וְעָרֵי הָהָר וְכֹל אֲשֶׁר־צִוָּה יהוה
ג א אֱלֹהֵינוּ: וַנֵּפֶן וַנַּעַל דֶּרֶךְ הַבָּשָׁן וַיֵּצֵא עוֹג מֶלֶךְ־הַבָּשָׁן לִקְרָאתֵנוּ הוּא
ב וְכָל־עַמּוֹ לַמִּלְחָמָה אֶדְרֶעִי: וַיֹּאמֶר יהוה אֵלַי אַל־תִּירָא אֹתוֹ כִּי בְיָדְךָ
נָתַתִּי אֹתוֹ וְאֶת־כָּל־עַמּוֹ וְאֶת־אַרְצוֹ וְעָשִׂיתָ לּוֹ כַּאֲשֶׁר עָשִׂיתָ לְסִיחֹן
ג מֶלֶךְ הָאֱמֹרִי אֲשֶׁר יוֹשֵׁב בְּחֶשְׁבּוֹן: וַיִּתֵּן יהוה אֱלֹהֵינוּ בְּיָדֵנוּ גַּם אֶת־

אונקלוס

בְּשֵׂעִיר, וּמוֹאֲבָאֵי, דְּיָתְבִין בִּלְחָיַת, עַד דְּאֶעְבַּר יָת יַרְדְּנָא, לְאַרְעָא, דַּייָ אֱלָהַנָא יָהֵיב לַנָא: ל וְלָא אֲבָא, סִיחוֹן מַלְכָּא דְּחֶשְׁבּוֹן, לְמִשְׁבְּקַנָא לְמֶעְבַּר בִּתְחוּמֵיהּ, אֲרֵי אַקְשִׁי יי אֱלָהָךְ יָת רוּחֵיהּ, וְתַקֵּיף יָת לִבֵּיהּ, בְּדִיל, לְמִמְסְרֵיהּ בִּידָךְ כְּיוֹמָא הָדֵין: לא וַאֲמַר יי לִי, חֲזִי, דְּשָׁרֵיתִי לְמִמְסַר קֳדָמָךְ, יָת סִיחוֹן וְיָת אַרְעֵיהּ, שָׁרִי לְתָרְכוּתֵיהּ, לְמֵירַת יָת אַרְעֵיהּ: לב וּנְפַק סִיחוֹן לְקַדָּמוּתַנָא, הוּא וְכָל עַמֵּיהּ, לְאַגָּחָא קְרָבָא לְיָהָץ: לג וּמַסְרֵיהּ, יי אֱלָהַנָא קֳדָמַנָא, וּמְחֵינָא יָתֵיהּ, וְיָת בְּנוֹהִי וְיָת כָּל עַמֵּיהּ: לד וּכְבַשְׁנָא יָת כָּל קִרְווֹהִי בְּעִדָּנָא הַהוּא, וְגַמַּרְנָא יָת כָּל קִרְוַיָּא גֻּבְרַיָּא, וּנְשַׁיָּא וְטַפְלָא, לָא אַשְׁאַרְנָא מְשֵׁיזֵיב: לה לְחוֹד בְּעִירָא בַּזנָא לַנָא, וַעֲדֵי קִרְוַיָּא דִּכְבַשְׁנָא: לו מֵעֲרוֹעֵר, דְּעַל כֵּיף נַחְלָא דְאַרְנוֹן, וְקַרְתָּא דִּבְנַחְלָא וְעַד גִּלְעָד, לָא הֲוָת קַרְתָּא, דִּתְקֵיפַת מִנַּנָא, יָת כּוֹלָּא, מְסַר, יי אֱלָהַנָא קֳדָמַנָא: לז לְחוֹד, לַאֲרַע בְּנֵי עַמּוֹן לָא קְרֵיבְתָּא, כָּל כֵּיף, נַחַל יֻבְקָא וְקִרְוֵי טוּרָא, וְכֹל דְּפַקֵּיד יי אֱלָהַנָא: ג א וְאִתְפְּנֵינָא וּסְלֵיקְנָא, לְאוֹרַח מַתְנָן, וּנְפַק עוֹג מַלְכָּא דְמַתְנָן לְקַדָּמוּתַנָא, הוּא וְכָל עַמֵּיהּ, לְאַגָּחָא קְרָבָא לְאֶדְרֶעִי: ב וַאֲמַר יי לִי לָא תִדְחַל מִנֵּיהּ, אֲרֵי בִידָךְ, מְסָרִית יָתֵיהּ, וְיָת כָּל עַמֵּיהּ וְיָת אַרְעֵיהּ, וְתַעֲבֵיד לֵיהּ, כְּמָא דַּעֲבַדְתָּא, לְסִיחוֹן מַלְכָּא אֱמוֹרָאָה, דְּיָתֵיב בְּחֶשְׁבּוֹן: ג וּמְסַר יי אֱלָהַנָא בִּידַנָא, אַף, יָת

4 We struck him down until not a single survivor remained. We captured all his
towns at that time; there was not a single town we did not take from them –
5 sixty towns, the entire region of Argov, Og's kingdom in Bashan. And these
were all fortress towns with high walls, gates, and bars – there were a great
6 many unwalled towns besides. And we utterly destroyed them, as we had done
to Siḥon, king of Ḥeshbon, in each town utterly destroying them: men, women,
7 and children. All the livestock and the spoil of the towns we kept as booty for
8 ourselves. At that time, then, we took from the two kings of the Amorites the
9 land beyond the Jordan, from the Arnon Stream to Mount Ḥermon" – the
10 Sidonians call Ḥermon Siryon, and the Amorites call it Senir – "all the towns of
the plateau, the whole of Gilad, and the whole of Bashan, as far as Salkha and
11 Edre'i, towns of Og's kingdom in Bashan." Only Og, king of Bashan, was left
then of the remaining Refaim. His bed, made of iron, is still there, in Raba of
the Amonites: it is nine cubits long and four cubits wide, as measured by a
12 man's forearm. "Of the land that we took possession of at that time, I gave to the
Reubenites and Gadites the territory from Aroer on the edge of the Arnon
13 Stream, as well as half the hill country of Gilad with its towns. To the half tribe
of Menashe I gave the rest of Gilad and all of Bashan, Og's kingdom – the whole

רש״י

ד **חֶבֶל אַרְגֹּב.** מְתַרְגְּמִינַן: ״בֵּית פֶּלֶךְ טְרָכוֹנָא״. וְרָאִיתִי תַּרְגּוּם יְרוּשַׁלְמִי בִּמְגִלַּת אֶסְתֵּר (א, ג) קוֹרֵא פָּלָטִין – טְרָכוֹנִין, לָמַדְתִּי ״חֶבֶל אַרְגֹּב״ – הַפַּרְכִיָּא שֶׁל הֵיכַל הַמֶּלֶךְ, כְּלוֹמַר שֶׁהַמַּלְכוּת נִקְרָא עַל שְׁמָהּ וְכֵן: ״אֶת אַרְגֹּב״ דִּמְלָכִים (ב׳ טו, כה), אֵצֶל הֵיכַל הַמֶּלֶךְ הֲרָגוֹ פֶּקַח לִ[פְקַחְיָה בֶּן] מְנַחֵם:

ה **מֵעָרֵי הַפְּרָזִי.** פְּרוּזוֹת וּפְתוּחוֹת בְּלֹא חוֹמָה, וְכֵן: ״פְּרָזוֹת תֵּשֵׁב יְרוּשָׁלַםִ״ (זכריה ב, ח):

ו **הַחֲרֵם.** לְשׁוֹן הֹוֶה, הָלוֹךְ וְכַלּוֹת:

ח **מִיַּד.** מֵרְשׁוּת:

ט **צִידֹנִים יִקְרְאוּ לְחֶרְמוֹן וְגוֹ׳.** וּבְמָקוֹם אַחֵר הוּא אוֹמֵר: ״וְעַד הַר שִׂיאֹן הוּא חֶרְמוֹן״ (להלן ד, מח), הֲרֵי לוֹ אַרְבָּעָה שֵׁמוֹת. לָמָּה הֻצְרְכוּ לִכָּתֵב? לְהַגִּיד שֶׁבַח אֶרֶץ יִשְׂרָאֵל, שֶׁהָיוּ אַרְבַּע מַלְכֻיּוֹת מִתְפָּאֲרוֹת בְּכָךְ, זוֹ אוֹמֶרֶת עַל שְׁמִי יִקָּרֵא, וְזוֹ אוֹמֶרֶת עַל שְׁמִי יִקָּרֵא: **שְׂנִיר.** הוּא שֶׁלֶג בִּלְשׁוֹן אַשְׁכְּנַז וּבִלְשׁוֹן כְּנַעַן:

יא **מִיֶּתֶר הָרְפָאִים.** שֶׁהָרְגוּ אַמְרָפֶל וַחֲבֵרָיו בְּעַשְׁתְּרוֹת קַרְנַיִם, וְהוּא פָּלַט מִן הַמִּלְחָמָה, שֶׁנֶּאֱמַר: ״וַיָּבֹא הַפָּלִיט״ (בראשית יד, יג), זֶהוּ עוֹג: **בְּאַמַּת אִישׁ.** בְּאַמַּת עוֹג:

יב **וְאֶת הָאָרֶץ הַזֹּאת.** הָאֲמוּרָה לְמַעְלָה מִנַּחַל אַרְנֹן וְעַד הַר חֶרְמוֹן (לעיל פסוק ח), ״יָרַשְׁנוּ בָּעֵת הַהִיא״: **מֵעֲרֹעֵר אֲשֶׁר עַל נַחַל אַרְנֹן.** אֵינוֹ מְחֻבָּר לְרֹאשׁוֹ שֶׁל מִקְרָא אֶלָּא לְסוֹפוֹ, עַל ״נָתַתִּי לָראוּבֵנִי וְלַגָּדִי״, אֲבָל לְעִנְיַן יְרֻשָּׁה עַד הַר חֶרְמוֹן הָיָה:

יג **הַהוּא יִקָּרֵא אֶרֶץ רְפָאִים.** הִיא אוֹתָהּ שֶׁנָּתַתִּי לְאַבְרָהָם:

the fruit of a model negotiation, and a sign of hope after the many destructive conflicts in the book of Numbers.

One of the hardest tasks of any leader – from prime ministers to parents – is conflict resolution. Yet it is also the most vital. Where there is leadership, there is long-term cohesiveness within the group, whatever the short-term problems. True leaders are the people who put the interests of the group above those of any subsection of the group. They care for, and inspire others to care for, the common good. That is why this episode was of the highest consequence.

עוֹג מֶלֶךְ־הַבָּשָׁן וְאֶת־כָּל־עַמּוֹ וַנַּכֵּהוּ עַד־בִּלְתִּי הִשְׁאִיר־לוֹ שָׂרִיד׃
ד וַנִּלְכֹּד אֶת־כָּל־עָרָיו בָּעֵת הַהִוא לֹא הָיְתָה קִרְיָה אֲשֶׁר לֹא־לָקַחְנוּ
ה מֵאִתָּם שִׁשִּׁים עִיר כָּל־חֶבֶל אַרְגֹּב מַמְלֶכֶת עוֹג בַּבָּשָׁן׃ כָּל־אֵלֶּה
עָרִים בְּצֻרֹת חוֹמָה גְבֹהָה דְּלָתַיִם וּבְרִיחַ לְבַד מֵעָרֵי הַפְּרָזִי הַרְבֵּה
ו מְאֹד׃ וַנַּחֲרֵם אוֹתָם כַּאֲשֶׁר עָשִׂינוּ לְסִיחֹן מֶלֶךְ חֶשְׁבּוֹן הַחֲרֵם כָּל־עִיר
ז ח מְתִם הַנָּשִׁים וְהַטָּף׃ וְכָל־הַבְּהֵמָה וּשְׁלַל הֶעָרִים בַּזּוֹנוּ לָנוּ׃ וַנִּקַּח
בָּעֵת הַהִוא אֶת־הָאָרֶץ מִיַּד שְׁנֵי מַלְכֵי הָאֱמֹרִי אֲשֶׁר בְּעֵבֶר הַיַּרְדֵּן
ט מִנַּחַל אַרְנֹן עַד־הַר חֶרְמוֹן׃ צִידֹנִים יִקְרְאוּ לְחֶרְמוֹן שִׂרְיֹן וְהָאֱמֹרִי
י יִקְרְאוּ־לוֹ שְׂנִיר׃ כֹּל ׀ עָרֵי הַמִּישֹׁר וְכָל־הַגִּלְעָד וְכָל־הַבָּשָׁן עַד־סַלְכָה
יא וְאֶדְרֶעִי עָרֵי מַמְלֶכֶת עוֹג בַּבָּשָׁן׃ כִּי רַק־עוֹג מֶלֶךְ הַבָּשָׁן נִשְׁאַר מִיֶּתֶר
הָרְפָאִים הִנֵּה עַרְשׂוֹ עֶרֶשׂ בַּרְזֶל הֲלֹה הִוא בְּרַבַּת בְּנֵי עַמּוֹן תֵּשַׁע
יב אַמּוֹת אָרְכָּהּ וְאַרְבַּע אַמּוֹת רָחְבָּהּ בְּאַמַּת־אִישׁ׃ וְאֶת־הָאָרֶץ הַזֹּאת
יָרַשְׁנוּ בָּעֵת הַהִוא מֵעֲרֹעֵר אֲשֶׁר־עַל־נַחַל אַרְנֹן וַחֲצִי הַר־הַגִּלְעָד
יג וְעָרָיו נָתַתִּי לָראוּבֵנִי וְלַגָּדִי׃ וְיֶתֶר הַגִּלְעָד וְכָל־הַבָּשָׁן מַמְלֶכֶת עוֹג
נָתַתִּי לַחֲצִי שֵׁבֶט הַמְנַשֶּׁה כֹּל חֶבֶל הָאַרְגֹּב לְכָל־הַבָּשָׁן הַהוּא יִקָּרֵא

אונקלוס

עוֹג מַלְכָּא דְמַתְנַן וְיָת כָּל עַמֵּיהּ, וּמְחֵינָנְהִי, עַד דְּלָא אִשְׁתְּאַר לֵיהּ מְשֵׁיזֵיב: ד וּכְבַשְׁנָא יָת כָּל קִרְווֹהִי בְּעִדָּנָא הַהוּא, לָא הֲוָת קַרְתָּא, דְּלָא נְסֵיבְנָא מִנְּהוֹן, שִׁתִּין קִרְוִין כָּל בֵּית פֶּלֶךְ טְרָכוֹנָא, מַלְכוּתֵיהּ דְּעוֹג בְּמַתְנַן: ה כָּל אִלֵּין, קִרְוִין כְּרִיכָן, מַקְּפָן שׁוּר רָם דִּילְהוֹן דַּשִּׁין וְעַבְרִין, בָּר, מִקִּרְוֵי פַּצְחַיָּא דְּסַגִּיאָן לַחֲדָא: ו וְגַמַּרְנָא יָתְהוֹן, כְּמָא דַּעֲבַדְנָא, לְסִיחוֹן מַלְכָּא דְחֶשְׁבּוֹן, גַּמַּרְנָא יָת כָּל קִרְוַיָּא גֻּבְרַיָּא, נְשַׁיָּא וְטַפְלָא: ז וְכָל בְּעִירָא, וַעֲדֵי קִרְוַיָּא בַּזְנָא לָנָא: ח וּכְבַשְׁנָא, בְּעִדָּנָא הַהוּא יָת אַרְעָא, מִיַּד, תְּרֵין מַלְכֵי אֱמוֹרָאָה, דִּבְעִבְרָא דְיַרְדְּנָא, מִנַּחְלָא דְּאַרְנוֹן עַד טוּרָא דְחֶרְמוֹן:

ט צִידוֹנָאֵי, קָרַן לְחֶרְמוֹן שִׂרְיוֹן, וֶאֱמוֹרָאֵי, קָרַן לֵיהּ טוּר תַּלְגָּא: י כָּל קִרְוֵי מֵישְׁרָא, וְכָל גִּלְעָד וְכָל מַתְנַן, עַד סַלְכָה וְאֶדְרֶעִי, קִרְוֵי, מַלְכוּתֵיהּ דְּעוֹג בְּמַתְנַן: יא אֲרֵי לְחוֹד עוֹג מַלְכָּא דְמַתְנַן, אִשְׁתְּאַר מִשְּׁאָר גִּבָּרַיָּא, הָא עַרְסֵיהּ עַרְסָא דְּבַרְזְלָא, הֲלָא הִיא, בְּרַבַּת בְּנֵי עַמּוֹן, תְּשַׁע אַמִּין אָרְכַּהּ, וְאַרְבַּע אַמִּין, פְּתָיַהּ בְּאַמַּת מְלָךְ: יב וְיָת אַרְעָא הָדָא, יְרִיתְנָא בְּעִדָּנָא הַהוּא, מֵעֲרוֹעֵר דְּעַל נַחְלָא דְּאַרְנוֹן, וּפַלְגוּת טוּרָא דְגִלְעָד וְקִרְווֹהִי, יְהַבִית, לְשֵׁיבֶט רְאוּבֵן וּלְשֵׁיבֶט גָּד: יג וּשְׁאָר גִּלְעָד וְכָל מַתְנַן מַלְכוּתֵיהּ דְּעוֹג, יְהַבִית, לְפַלְגוּת שִׁבְטָא דִמְנַשֶּׁה, כָּל בֵּית פֶּלֶךְ טְרָכוֹנָא לְכָל מַתְנַן, הַהוּא מִתְקְרֵי

3:12 וְעָרָיו נָתַתִּי לָראוּבֵנִי וְלַגָּדִי *I gave to the the Reubenites and Gadites the territory* – Moshe here refers back to an immensely significant episode at the end of Parashat Mattot (Num. 32; see commentary there). These words were

region of Argov: all that portion of Bashan that used to be known as the land of
14 the Refaim." Yair of Menashe took the whole region of Argov – that is, Bashan – as
far as the border of the people of Geshur and of Maakha – and named it after
15 16 himself, hamlets of Yair, as it is called to this day. "To Makhir I gave Gilad, and to SHEVI'I
the Reubenites and the Gadites I gave the territory from Gilad as far as the Arnon
Stream, with the middle of the ravine as a border, and up to the Yabok Stream and
17 the Amonites' border. It included also the Arava, with the Jordan and its banks,
from the Sea of Galilee down to the Arava Sea, the Dead Sea, with the lower
18 slopes of Pisga on the east. At that time, I charged you: 'The LORD your God has
given you this land to possess, but all your troops must cross over armed before
19 your fellow Israelites. Only your wives, children, and cattle – I know that you
20 have much cattle – shall stay behind in the towns I have given you, until the LORD MAFTIR
gives rest to your fellows as to you, and they too have taken possession of the land
that the LORD your God is giving them beyond the Jordan. Then you may each
21 return to the land that I have given to you.' And I charged Yehoshua also at that
time: 'Your own eyes have seen all that the LORD your God has done to these two
kings; so will the LORD do to all the kingdoms into which you are about to cross.
22 Do not fear them, for it is the LORD your God who is fighting for you.'

The haftara for Parashat Devarim is on page 1606.

רש"י

טז **תּוֹךְ הַנַּחַל וּגְבֻל.** כָּל הַנַּחַל וְעַד מֵעֵבֶר לִשְׂפָתוֹ, כְּלוֹמַר, עַד וְעַד בִּכְלָל, וְיוֹתֵר מִכָּאן:

יז **כִּנֶּרֶת.** מֵעֵבֶר הַיַּרְדֵּן הַמַּעֲרָבִי הִיא, וְנַחֲלַת בְּנֵי גָּד מֵעֵבֶר הַיַּרְדֵּן הַמִּזְרָחִי, וְנָפַל בְּגוֹרָלָם רֹחַב הַיַּרְדֵּן כְּנֶגְדָּם וְעוֹד מֵעֵבֶר לִשְׂפָתוֹ עַד כִּנֶּרֶת, וְזֶהוּ שֶׁנֶּאֱמַר: "וְהַיַּרְדֵּן וּגְבֻל", הַיַּרְדֵּן וּמֵעֵבֶר לוֹ:

יח **וָאֲצַו אֶתְכֶם.** לִבְנֵי רְאוּבֵן וְגָד הָיָה מְדַבֵּר: **לִפְנֵי אֲחֵיכֶם.** הֵם הָיוּ הוֹלְכִים לִפְנֵי יִשְׂרָאֵל לַמִּלְחָמָה, לְפִי שֶׁהָיוּ גִּבּוֹרִים וְאוֹיְבִים נוֹפְלִים לִפְנֵיהֶם, שֶׁנֶּאֱמַר: "וְטָרַף זְרוֹעַ אַף קָדְקֹד" (דברים לג, כ):

the series of addresses we know as the book of Deuteronomy or Devarim. In these addresses, he reviews the people's past and foresees their future. He gives them laws. Some he has given them before but in a different form. Others are new; he has delayed announcing them until the people are about to enter the land. Linking all these details of law and history into a single overarching vision, he teaches the people to see themselves as an *am kadosh*, a holy people, the only people whose sovereign and lawgiver is God Himself.

Moshe surely knows that some of his greatest achievements will not last forever. The people he has rescued will one day suffer exile and persecution again. The next time, though, they will not have a Moshe to do miracles. So he plants a vision in their minds, hope in their hearts, a discipline in their deeds, and a strength in their souls that will never fade. When leaders become educators they change lives. Judaism, with its acute concern for human dignity, favors leadership as education over leadership as power. And it began with Moshe, at the end of his life.

One of Moshe's final acts as a leader-educator is to appoint his successor, Yehoshua. It will be Yehoshua, whom Moshe has nurtured and educated as his successor, who will lead the people across the Jordan into the Promised Land. Good leaders create followers; great leaders create leaders. The paradigm case is Moshe.

יד אֶרֶץ רְפָאִים: יָאִיר בֶּן־מְנַשֶּׁה לָקַח אֶת־כָּל־חֶבֶל אַרְגֹּב עַד־גְּבוּל
הַגְּשׁוּרִי וְהַמַּעֲכָתִי וַיִּקְרָא אֹתָם עַל־שְׁמוֹ אֶת־הַבָּשָׁן חַוֺּת יָאִיר עַד
טו טז הַיּוֹם הַזֶּה: וּלְמָכִיר נָתַתִּי אֶת־הַגִּלְעָד: וְלָרֽאוּבֵנִי וְלַגָּדִי נָתַתִּי מִן־ שביעי
הַגִּלְעָד וְעַד־נַחַל אַרְנֹן תּוֹךְ הַנַּחַל וּגְבֻל וְעַד יַבֹּק הַנַּחַל גְּבוּל בְּנֵי
יז עַמּוֹן: וְהָעֲרָבָה וְהַיַּרְדֵּן וּגְבֻל מִכִּנֶּרֶת וְעַד יָם הָעֲרָבָה יָם הַמֶּלַח תַּחַת
יח אַשְׁדֹּת הַפִּסְגָּה מִזְרָחָה: וָאֲצַו אֶתְכֶם בָּעֵת הַהִוא לֵאמֹר יהוה אֱלֹהֵיכֶם
נָתַן לָכֶם אֶת־הָאָרֶץ הַזֹּאת לְרִשְׁתָּהּ חֲלוּצִים תַּעַבְרוּ לִפְנֵי אֲחֵיכֶם
יט בְּנֵי־יִשְׂרָאֵל כָּל־בְּנֵי־חָיִל: רַק נְשֵׁיכֶם וְטַפְּכֶם וּמִקְנֵכֶם יָדַעְתִּי כִּי־מִקְנֶה
כ רַב לָכֶם יֵשְׁבוּ בְּעָרֵיכֶם אֲשֶׁר נָתַתִּי לָכֶם: עַד אֲשֶׁר־יָנִיחַ יהוה ׀ לַאֲחֵיכֶם מפטיר
כָּכֶם וְיָרְשׁוּ גַם־הֵם אֶת־הָאָרֶץ אֲשֶׁר יהוה אֱלֹהֵיכֶם נֹתֵן לָהֶם בְּעֵבֶר
כא הַיַּרְדֵּן וְשַׁבְתֶּם אִישׁ לִירֻשָּׁתוֹ אֲשֶׁר נָתַתִּי לָכֶם: וְאֶת־יְהוֹשׁוּעַ צִוֵּיתִי
בָּעֵת הַהִוא לֵאמֹר עֵינֶיךָ הָרֹאֹת אֵת כָּל־אֲשֶׁר עָשָׂה יהוה אֱלֹהֵיכֶם
לִשְׁנֵי הַמְּלָכִים הָאֵלֶּה כֵּן־יַעֲשֶׂה יהוה לְכָל־הַמַּמְלָכוֹת אֲשֶׁר אַתָּה
כב עֹבֵר שָׁמָּה: לֹא תִּירָאוּם כִּי יהוה אֱלֹהֵיכֶם הוּא הַנִּלְחָם לָכֶם:

The הפטרה *for* פרשת דברים *is on page 1607.*

אונקלוס

אֲרַע גִּבָּרַיָּא: יד יָאִיר בַּר מְנַשֶּׁה, נְסֵיב יָת כָּל בֵּית פֶּלֶךְ טְרָכוֹנָא, עַד תְּחוּם גְּשׁוּרָאָה וְאַפִּיקוֹרוֹס, וּקְרָא יָתְהוֹן עַל שְׁמֵיהּ יָת מַתְנַן כַּפְרָנֵי יָאִיר, עַד יוֹמָא הָדֵין: טו וּלְמָכִיר יְהַבִית יָת גִּלְעָד: טז וּלְשִׁבְטָא רְאוּבֵן וּלְשִׁבְטָא גָּד, יְהַבִית מִן גִּלְעָד וְעַד נַחְלָא דְאַרְנוֹן, גּוֹ נַחְלָא וּתְחוּמֵיהּ, וְעַד יֻבְקָא דְּנַחְלָא, תְּחוּמָא דִּבְנֵי עַמּוֹן: יז וּמֵישְׁרָא וְיַרְדְּנָא וּתְחוּמֵיהּ, מִגִּנֵּיסַר, וְעַד יַמָּא דְּמֵישְׁרָא יַמָּא דְמִלְחָא, תְּחוֹת, מַשְׁפַּךְ מֵרָמָתָא מַדִּנְחָא: יח וּפַקֵּידִית יָתְכוֹן, בְּעִדָּנָא הַהוּא לְמֵימַר, יְיָ אֱלָהֲכוֹן, יְהַב לְכוֹן, יָת אַרְעָא הָדָא לְמֵירְתַהּ, מְזָרְזִין תִּעְבְּרוּן, קֳדָם, אֲחֵיכוֹן בְּנֵי יִשְׂרָאֵל כָּל מְזָרְזֵי חֵילָא: יט לְחוֹד, נְשֵׁיכוֹן וְטַפְלְכוֹן וּבְעִירְכוֹן, יָדַעְנָא, אֲרֵי בְעִיר סַגִּי לְכוֹן, יִתְּבוּן בְּקִרְוֵיכוֹן, דִּיהַבִית לְכוֹן: כ עַד, דִּיְנִיחַ יְיָ לַאֲחֵיכוֹן כְּוָתְכוֹן, וְיֵירְתוּן אַף אִנּוּן, יָת אַרְעָא, דַּיְיָ אֱלָהֲכוֹן, יָהֵיב לְהוֹן בְּעִבְרָא דְּיַרְדְּנָא, וּתְתוּבוּן, גְּבַר לִירֻתְּתֵיהּ, דִּיהַבִית לְכוֹן: כא וְיָת יְהוֹשֻׁעַ פַּקֵּידִית, בְּעִדָּנָא הַהוּא לְמֵימַר, עֵינָךְ חֲזָאָה, יָת כָּל דַּעֲבַד, יְיָ אֱלָהֲכוֹן לִתְרֵין מַלְכַיָּא הָאִלֵּין, כֵּן יַעֲבֵיד יְיָ לְכָל מַלְכְוָתָא, דְּאַתְּ עָבַר לְתַמָּן: כב לָא תִדְחֲלוּן מִנְּהוֹן, אֲרֵי יְיָ אֱלָהֲכוֹן, מֵימְרֵיהּ מְגִיחַ לְכוֹן:

3:21 וְאֶת־יְהוֹשׁוּעַ צִוֵּיתִי *I charged Yehoshua* – By the end of the book of Numbers, Moshe's career as a leader appeared to have come to its end. Moshe seemed to have achieved everything he was destined to achieve. For him there would be no more battles to fight, no more miracles to perform, no more prayers to say on behalf of the people. It is what Moshe does next that bears the mark of greatness. For the final month of his life he stands before the assembled people, and delivers

PARASHAT VAETHANAN

3 23 24 At that time, I pleaded with the LORD: 'O Lord GOD, You have begun to show
Your servant Your greatness and Your mighty hand; what force in heaven or
25 earth can do deeds and mighty acts like Yours! Please let me cross over and see
26 the good land beyond the Jordan, that good hill country and the Lebanon.' But
the LORD was enraged with me because of you, and would not listen to me. 'It

רש״י

כג) **ואתחנן.** אין חנון בכל מקום אלא לשון מתנת חנם. אף על פי שיש להם לצדיקים לתלות במעשיהם הטובים, אין מבקשים מאת המקום אלא מתנת חנם. דבר אחר, זה אחד מעשרה לשונות שנקראת תפלה, כדאיתא בספרי (כו): **בעת ההוא.** לאחר שכבשתי ארץ סיחון ועוג, דמיתי שמא הותר הנדר: **לאמר.** זה אחד משלשה מקומות שאמר משה לפני המקום: איני מניחך עד שתודיעני אם תעשה שאלתי אם לאו:

כד) **ה׳ אלהים.** רחום בדין: **אתה החלות להראות את עבדך.** פתח להיות עומד ומתפלל אף על פי שנגזרה גזרה. אמר לו: ממך למדתי, שאמרת לי: "ועתה הניחה לי" (שמות לב, י), וכי תופס הייתי בך? אלא לפתח פתח, שבי היה תלוי להתפלל עליהם: **את גדלך.** זו מדת טובך, וכן הוא אומר: "ועתה יגדל נא כח אדני" (במדבר יד, יז): **ואת ידך.** זו ימינך שהיא פשוטה לכל באי עולם: **החזקה.** שאתה כובש ברחמים את מדת הדין בחזקה: **אשר מי אל וגו׳.** אינך דומה למלך בשר ודם, שיש לו יועצין וסנקתדרין הממחין בידו כשרוצה לעשות חסד ולעבר על מדותיו, אתה אין מי ימחה בידך אם תמחל לי ותבטל גזרתך:

כה) **אעברה נא.** אין ׳נא׳ אלא לשון בקשה: **ההר הטוב הזה.** זו ירושלים: **והלבנן.** זה בית המקדש:

כו) **ויתעבר ה׳.** נתמלא חמה: **למענכם.** אתם גרמתם לי, וכן הוא אומר: "ויקציפו על מי מריבה וירע למשה בעבורם" (תהלים קו, לב): **רב לך.** שלא יאמרו, הרב כמה קשה והתלמיד כמה סרבן ומפציר. דבר אחר, "רב לך", הרבה מזה שמור לך רב טוב הצפון לך:

what to desire. All animals act to satisfy their desires. Only human beings are capable of standing back and passing judgment on their desires. There are some desires we should not satisfy. Junk food is bad for us. So is smoking. So is wealth illicitly obtained. So is ambition achieved by betraying others. And so on. To be humanly mature is to know what to desire.

Prayer is the education of desire. The weekday *Amida*, as an example, teaches us to seek knowledge, wisdom, and understanding – not just material goods. It teaches us to want to return to God when, as happens so often, we drift in the winds of time, blown this way and that by the pressures of today. It teaches us to seek spiritual healing as well as physical health. It teaches us to seek the best not just for ourselves but also for our people and ultimately for all humanity.

Prayer opens our eyes to the wonders of the physical world. It trains us to give thanks for the sheer gift of being alive. Above all, prayer tells us we are not alone in the world.

Without a vessel to contain a blessing, there can be no blessing. If we have no receptacle to catch the rain, the rain may fall, but we will have none to drink. If we have no radio receiver, the sound waves will flow, but we will be unable to convert them into sound. God's blessings flow continuously, but unless we make ourselves into a vessel for them, they will flow elsewhere. Prayer is the act of turning ourselves into a vehicle for the Divine.

And so our *parasha* opens with a prayer that is not answered. "It is enough," says God. It is not time for Moshe to grasp after more life. It is time to climb the mountain, and survey what he has achieved.

פרשת ואתחנן

ג כג כד וָאֶתְחַנַּן אֶל־יְהוָה בָּעֵת הַהִוא לֵאמֹר: אֲדֹנָי יֱהוִה אַתָּה הַחִלּוֹתָ ד
לְהַרְאוֹת אֶת־עַבְדְּךָ אֶת־גָּדְלְךָ וְאֶת־יָדְךָ הַחֲזָקָה אֲשֶׁר מִי־אֵל בַּשָּׁמַיִם
כה וּבָאָרֶץ אֲשֶׁר־יַעֲשֶׂה כְמַעֲשֶׂיךָ וְכִגְבוּרֹתֶךָ: אֶעְבְּרָה־נָּא וְאֶרְאֶה אֶת־
כו הָאָרֶץ הַטּוֹבָה אֲשֶׁר בְּעֵבֶר הַיַּרְדֵּן הָהָר הַטּוֹב הַזֶּה וְהַלְּבָנֹן: וַיִּתְעַבֵּר
יְהוָה בִּי לְמַעַנְכֶם וְלֹא שָׁמַע אֵלָי וַיֹּאמֶר יְהוָה אֵלַי רַב־לָךְ אַל־תּוֹסֶף

אונקלוס

כג וְצַלֵּיתִי קֳדָם יי, בְּעִדָּנָא הַהוּא לְמֵימַר: כד יי אֱלֹהִים, אַתְּ שָׁרֵיתָא לְאַחֲזָאָה יָת עַבְדָּךְ, יָת רְבוּתָךְ, וְיָת יְדָךְ תַּקִּיפְתָּא, דְּאַתְּ הוּא אֱלָהָא דִּשְׁכִינְתָּךְ בִּשְׁמַיָּא מִלְּעֵילָא וְשַׁלִּיט בְּאַרְעָא, לֵית דְּיַעֲבֵיד כְּעוֹבָדָךְ וּכִגְבָרְוָתָךְ: כה אֶעְבַּר כְּעַן, וְאֶחֱזֵי יָת אַרְעָא טָבְתָא, דִּבְעִבְרָא דְיַרְדְּנָא, טוּרָא טָבָא, הָדֵין וּבֵית מַקְדְּשָׁא: כו וַהֲוָה רְגֵז מִן קֳדָם יי עֲלַי בְּדִילְכוֹן, וְלָא קַבֵּיל מִנִּי, וַאֲמַר יי לִי סַגִּי לָךְ, לָא

VAETḤANAN

Parashat Vaetḥanan contains some of the most sublime theological passages in the whole of Judaism. Moshe tells the people that their laws and history are unique, and will be seen as such by other nations. Their laws were given by God; their history was written by God – there is no other nation of which either can be said. Moshe then begins his second great speech. He reminds the people of the Ten Commandments and the revelation at Mount Sinai and commands them to set God at the center of their lives in the passage that became the first paragraph of the *Shema*, the supreme expression of the love of God. This love was to be more than an emotion. It was to be constantly spoken of to children, worn by men in the form of tefillin, and placed as mezuzot "on the doorposts of your houses" (Deut. 6:9).

There is much in Judaism about *what*: what is permitted, what is forbidden, what is sacred, what is secular. There is much, too, about *how*: how to learn, how to pray, how to grow in our relationship with God and with other people. In Parashat Vaetḥanan, Moshe says some of the most inspiring words ever uttered about the *why* of Jewish existence. Abrahamic monotheism believes there is an answer to the question *why*. Neither the universe nor human life is meaningless, an accident, a mere happenstance. Religious faith is faith in the meaningfulness of life.

Vaetḥanan tells us that we were called on to inspire the world. Our vocation is to be God's ambassadors to the world, giving testimony through the way we live that it is possible for a small people to survive and thrive under the most adverse conditions, to construct a society of law-governed liberty for which we all bear collective responsibility. Vaetḥanan is the mission statement of the Jewish people.

3:26 וְלֹא שָׁמַע אֵלָי *And would not listen to me* – When Moshe prayed for God to forgive the Israelites, God forgave them because God forgives. But when he prayed that he, Moshe, be allowed to cross the Jordan and enter the Promised Land, God did not grant him his request. He told him to stop praying. However hard or long Moshe prayed, it was not going to happen. This is the proof that prayer does not change God's mind in any simple sense. If it is good that something happens, God does not need my prayer to make it happen. If it is not good, then God will not bring it about, however hard I pray.

Prayer changes the world *because it changes us*. We pray not simply for God to fulfill our desires but in order to know

27 is enough!' the LORD said to me. 'Never speak to Me about this again! Go up
to the top of Pisga and gaze around you to the west, to the north, to the south,
28 and to the east. See it with your eyes, for you will not cross this Jordan. But
charge Yehoshua, make him strong and determined, for he will be the one to
cross over at the head of this people and who will secure their possession of the
29 land that you may only see.' And we came to rest in the valley beside Beit Peor.
4 1 And now, Israel, listen to the decrees and laws that I am teaching you to keep,
so that you may live to enter and take possession of the land that the LORD,
2 God of your ancestors, is giving to you. Do not add anything to that which
I command you, or subtract from it; keep the commandments of the LORD
3 your God with which I am charging you. You saw with your own eyes what the
LORD did in the affair of Baal Peor – how the LORD your God wiped out from
4 among you everyone who followed Baal Peor, while you, who held firmly to
5 the LORD your God, are all here living today. See: I have taught you decrees SHENI
and laws as the LORD my God commanded me, for you to keep in the land
6 that you are about to enter and possess. Take care to keep them, for this will be
your wisdom and understanding in the eyes of the peoples: when they hear all
these decrees they will say, 'Surely this great nation is a wise and understanding

רש"י

כז **וּרְאֵה בְעֵינֶיךָ.** בִּקַּשְׁתָּ מִמֶּנִּי: "וְאֶרְאֶה אֶת הָאָרֶץ הַטּוֹבָה" (לעיל פסוק כה), אֲנִי מַרְאֶה לְךָ אֶת כֻּלָּהּ, שֶׁנֶּאֱמַר: "וַיַּרְאֵהוּ ה' אֶת כָּל הָאָרֶץ" (להלן לד, א):

כח **וְצַו אֶת יְהוֹשֻׁעַ.** עַל הַטְּרָחוֹת וְעַל הַמַּשָּׂאוֹת וְעַל הַמְּרִיבוֹת: **וְחַזְּקֵהוּ וְאַמְּצֵהוּ.** בִּדְבָרֶיךָ, שֶׁלֹּא יֵרַךְ לִבּוֹ לוֹמַר: כְּשֵׁם שֶׁנֶּעֱנַשׁ רַבִּי עֲלֵיהֶם כָּךְ סוֹפִי לֵעָנֵשׁ עֲלֵיהֶם, מַבְטִיחוֹ אֲנִי כִּי "הוּא יַעֲבֹר וְהוּא יַנְחִיל": **כִּי הוּא יַעֲבֹר.** אִם יַעֲבֹר לִפְנֵיהֶם – יִנְחָלוּ, וְאִם לָאו – לֹא יִנְחָלוּ. וְכֵן אַתָּה מוֹצֵא כְּשֶׁשָּׁלַח מִן הָעָם אֶל הָעַי וְהוּא יָשַׁב: "וַיַּכּוּ מֵהֶם אַנְשֵׁי הָעַי" וְגוֹ' (יהושע ז, ה), וְכֵיוָן שֶׁנָּפַל עַל פָּנָיו, אָמַר לוֹ: "קֻם לָךְ" (שם פסוק י), 'קֻם לְךָ' כְּתִיב, אַתָּה הוּא הָעוֹמֵד בִּמְקוֹמְךָ וּמְשַׁלֵּחַ אֶת בָּנַי לַמִּלְחָמָה, "לָמָּה זֶּה אַתָּה נֹפֵל עַל פָּנֶיךָ", לֹא כָּךְ אָמַרְתִּי לְמֹשֶׁה רַבְּךָ: אִם הוּא עוֹבֵר עוֹבְרִין וְאִם לָאו אֵין עוֹבְרִין?:

כט **וַנֵּשֶׁב בַּגָּיְא וְגוֹ'.** וְנִצְמַדְתֶּם לַעֲבוֹדָה זָרָה, וְאַף עַל פִּי כֵן: "וְעַתָּה יִשְׂרָאֵל שְׁמַע אֶל הַחֻקִּים" (להלן ד, א), וְהַכֹּל מָחוּל לְךָ, וַאֲנִי לֹא זָכִיתִי לִמָּחֵל לִי:

ד ב **לֹא תֹסִפוּ.** כְּגוֹן חָמֵשׁ פָּרָשִׁיּוֹת בַּתְּפִלִּין, חֲמֵשֶׁת מִינִין בַּלּוּלָב וְחָמֵשׁ צִיצִיּוֹת, וְכֵן "לֹא תִגְרְעוּ":

ו **וּשְׁמַרְתֶּם.** זוֹ מִשְׁנָה: **וַעֲשִׂיתֶם.** כְּמַשְׁמָעוֹ: **כִּי הוּא חָכְמַתְכֶם וּבִינַתְכֶם וְגוֹ'.** בְּזֹאת תֵּחָשְׁבוּ חֲכָמִים וּנְבוֹנִים "לְעֵינֵי הָעַמִּים":

other peoples of his time. Moshe's contemporaries would have known far better than we do if this had been the case.... They would say that Israel is a foolish and inferior nation, because its laws were stolen from others." Moshe, suggests Luzzatto, knew that there was something different about the laws of Israel. This could not have been the case if Israel had simply adopted or adapted the practices of its time.

acknowledge the divine source of its laws. The Jewish people will be living proof that God exists and has communicated with mankind.

Rabbi Shmuel David Luzzatto (1800–65), writing in a later age, sees the text from yet a different perspective. "This is a refutation," he writes, "of those who say that the statutes Moshe gave Israel were adopted from the Egyptians and the

כז דַּבֵּר אֵלַי עוֹד בַּדָּבָר הַזֶּה: עֲלֵה ׀ רֹאשׁ הַפִּסְגָּה וְשָׂא עֵינֶיךָ יָמָּה וְצָפֹנָה
כח וְתֵימָנָה וּמִזְרָחָה וּרְאֵה בְעֵינֶיךָ כִּי־לֹא תַעֲבֹר אֶת־הַיַּרְדֵּן הַזֶּה: וְצַו
אֶת־יְהוֹשֻׁעַ וְחַזְּקֵהוּ וְאַמְּצֵהוּ כִּי־הוּא יַעֲבֹר לִפְנֵי הָעָם הַזֶּה וְהוּא
כט יַנְחִיל אוֹתָם אֶת־הָאָרֶץ אֲשֶׁר תִּרְאֶה: וַנֵּשֶׁב בַּגָּיְא מוּל בֵּית פְּעוֹר:
ד א וְעַתָּה יִשְׂרָאֵל שְׁמַע אֶל־הַחֻקִּים וְאֶל־הַמִּשְׁפָּטִים אֲשֶׁר אָנֹכִי מְלַמֵּד
אֶתְכֶם לַעֲשׂוֹת לְמַעַן תִּחְיוּ וּבָאתֶם וִירִשְׁתֶּם אֶת־הָאָרֶץ אֲשֶׁר יְהוָה
ב אֱלֹהֵי אֲבֹתֵיכֶם נֹתֵן לָכֶם: לֹא תֹסִפוּ עַל־הַדָּבָר אֲשֶׁר אָנֹכִי מְצַוֶּה
אֶתְכֶם וְלֹא תִגְרְעוּ מִמֶּנּוּ לִשְׁמֹר אֶת־מִצְוֺת יְהוָה אֱלֹהֵיכֶם אֲשֶׁר אָנֹכִי
ג מְצַוֶּה אֶתְכֶם: עֵינֵיכֶם הָרֹאוֹת אֵת אֲשֶׁר־עָשָׂה יְהוָה בְּבַעַל פְּעוֹר
כִּי כָל־הָאִישׁ אֲשֶׁר הָלַךְ אַחֲרֵי בַעַל־פְּעוֹר הִשְׁמִידוֹ יְהוָה אֱלֹהֶיךָ
ד ה מִקִּרְבֶּךָ: וְאַתֶּם הַדְּבֵקִים בַּיהוָה אֱלֹהֵיכֶם חַיִּים כֻּלְּכֶם הַיּוֹם: רְאֵה ׀ שני
לִמַּדְתִּי אֶתְכֶם חֻקִּים וּמִשְׁפָּטִים כַּאֲשֶׁר צִוַּנִי יְהוָה אֱלֹהָי לַעֲשׂוֹת כֵּן
ו בְּקֶרֶב הָאָרֶץ אֲשֶׁר אַתֶּם בָּאִים שָׁמָּה לְרִשְׁתָּהּ: וּשְׁמַרְתֶּם וַעֲשִׂיתֶם
כִּי הִוא חָכְמַתְכֶם וּבִינַתְכֶם לְעֵינֵי הָעַמִּים אֲשֶׁר יִשְׁמְעוּן אֵת כָּל־

אונקלוס

תּוֹסֵיף, לְמַלָּלָא קֳדָמַי, עוֹד בְּפִתְגָּמָא הָדֵין: כז סַק לְרֵישׁ רָמְתָא, וּזְקַף עֵינָךְ, לְמַעְרְבָא וּלְצִפּוּנָא, וּלְדָרוֹמָא וּלְמַדִנְחָא וַחֲזִי בְעֵינָךְ, אֲרֵי לָא תִעְבַּר יָת יַרְדְּנָא הָדֵין: כח וּפַקֵּיד יָת יְהוֹשֻׁעַ וְתַקֵּיפְהִי וְאַלֵּימְהִי, אֲרֵי הוּא יִעְבַּר, קֳדָם עַמָּא הָדֵין, וְהוּא יַחְסֵין יָתְהוֹן, יָת אַרְעָא דְּתִחְזֵי: כט וִיתֵיבְנָא בְּחֵילְתָא, לָקֳבֵיל בֵּית פְּעוֹר: ד א וּכְעַן יִשְׂרָאֵל, שְׁמַע לִקְיָמַיָּא וּלְדִינַיָּא, דַּאֲנָא, מַלֵּיף יָתְכוֹן לְמֶעֱבַד, בְּדִיל דְּתֵיחוֹן, וְתֵיעֲלוּן וְתֵירְתוּן יָת אַרְעָא, דַּיי, אֱלָהָא דַּאֲבָהָתְכוֹן יָהֵיב לְכוֹן: ב לָא תֵיסְפוּן, עַל פִּתְגָּמָא דַּאֲנָא מְפַקֵּיד יָתְכוֹן, וְלָא תִמְנְעוּן מִנֵּיהּ, לְמִטַּר, יָת פִּקּוֹדַיָּא דַּיי אֱלָהֲכוֹן, דַּאֲנָא מְפַקֵּיד יָתְכוֹן: ג עֵינֵיכוֹן חֲזָאָה, יָת דַּעֲבַד יי בִּפְלָחֵי בַעְלָא פְעוֹר, אֲרֵי כָל גַּבְרָא, דַּהֲלֵיךְ בָּתַר בַּעְלָא פְעוֹר, שֵׁיצְיֵהּ, יי אֱלָהָךְ מִבֵּינָךְ: ד וְאַתּוּן דְּאַדְבֵּיקְתּוּן, בְּדַחַלְתָּא דַּיי אֱלָהֲכוֹן, קַיָּמִין כֻּלְּכוֹן יוֹמָא דֵין: ה חֲזוֹ דְּאַלֵּיפִית יָתְכוֹן, קְיָמִין וְדִינִין, כְּמָא דְּפַקְּדַנִי יי אֱלָהִי, לְמֶעֱבַד כֵּן, בְּגוֹ אַרְעָא, דְּאַתּוּן, עָאלִין לְתַמָּן לְמֵירְתַהּ: ו וְתִטְּרוּן וְתַעְבְּדוּן, אֲרֵי הִיא חָכְמַתְכוֹן וְסָכְלְתָנוּתְכוֹן, לְעֵינֵי עַמְמַיָּא, דְּיִשְׁמְעוּן, יָת כָּל

IN THE EYES OF THE PEOPLES

According to Ramban, the meaning of the phrase "your wisdom and understanding in the eyes of the peoples" is that "the statutes and ordinances have the great benefit that they will bring honor from others to those who observe them. Even their enemies will praise them." Other nations will admire Israel's way of life.

Sforno interprets it differently: through the Torah "you will be able to refute a heretic by intellectual proofs." It is not so much that others will admire Israel as that they will

7 people!' For what other great nation has God so close to it as the LORD our
8 God is to us whenever we call out to Him? And what other great nation has
decrees and laws as just as this entire Torah that I am setting before you today?
9 But take care and be very vigilant not to forget the things that your eyes have
seen, nor to let them fade from your mind, as long as you live. Make known
10 to your children and your children's children, how you once stood before the
LORD your God at Ḥorev, when the LORD said to me, 'Assemble the people for
Me, and I will let them hear My words so that they may learn to be in awe of Me
11 as long as they live on earth, and teach their children likewise.' And you came
close and stood at the foot of the mountain while the mountain was ablaze to
12 high heaven and shrouded in dark clouds. Then the LORD spoke to you out of

רש״י

ח **חֻקִּים וּמִשְׁפָּטִים צַדִּיקִם.** הֲגוּנִים וּמְקֻבָּלִים:

ט **רַק הִשָּׁמֶר לְךָ וְגוֹ׳ פֶּן תִּשְׁכַּח אֶת הַדְּבָרִים.** אָז כְּשֶׁלֹּא תִּשְׁכְּחוּ אוֹתָם וְתַעֲשׂוּם עַל אֲמִתָּתָם, תֵּחָשְׁבוּ חֲכָמִים וּנְבוֹנִים, וְאִם תְּעַוְּתוּ אוֹתָם מִתּוֹךְ שִׁכְחָה, תֵּחָשְׁבוּ שׁוֹטִים:

י **יוֹם אֲשֶׁר עָמַדְתָּ.** מוּסָב עַל מִקְרָא שֶׁלְּמַעְלָה מִמֶּנּוּ: אֲשֶׁר רָאוּ עֵינֶיךָ יוֹם אֲשֶׁר עָמַדְתָּ בְּחֹרֵב, אֲשֶׁר רָאִיתָ אֶת הַקּוֹלוֹת וְאֶת הַלַּפִּידִים. יִלְמְדוּן. לְעַצְמָם:

an obvious choice. They were not large: "It is not because you were more numerous than other peoples that the LORD desired you and chose you, for you are the smallest of all peoples" (Deut. 7:7). Nor were they especially pious: "Not for your righteousness or rectitude" (9:5). The impression we gain of the Israelites throughout is of a fractious, often wayward group, a "stiff-necked people."

Yet Moshe and the prophets were convinced that the message they carried was not for their people alone. It had a universal significance. Moshe said that the laws the Israelites had been commanded will show "your wisdom and understanding in the eyes of the peoples: when they hear all these decrees they will say, 'Surely this great nation is a wise and understanding people!'" (4:6).

4:6 **עַם־חָכָם וְנָבוֹן** *A wise and understanding people* – Judaism recognizes a dual epistemology, that there are two ways of knowing. One is called *ḥokhma*, "wisdom"; the other is Torah, "teaching," "instruction," "law," "guidance." The difference was stated clearly by the Sages: "If you are told that there is wisdom among the nations, believe it. If you are told there is Torah among the nations, do not believe it" (Eikha Rabba 2:13).

Wisdom is a biblical category. The word appears in the Tanakh some 341 times in various inflections. There are entire books dedicated to *ḥokhma*, known generically as the "wisdom literature." Wisdom is universal. We can also see this by examining where the concept of wisdom appears in the Mosaic books. In Genesis it appears solely in connection with Egypt. When Pharaoh dreams his dreams and wants to know what they mean, he summons his "sages" (Gen. 41:8). Yosef uses the word when speaking to Pharaoh, as does Pharaoh in describing Yosef ("There can be no one else as astute or as wise as you" – 41:39). It also appears in the description of Betzalel, the man who made the appurtenances of the Sanctuary. As Rambam notes in the last chapter of *Guide for the Perplexed*, one of the senses of *ḥokhma* is craftsmanship, a cultural universal. Here, when Moshe speaks of the universal significance of Torah itself – as opposed to its particular meaning to Israel – he says, "This will be your wisdom and understanding in the eyes of the peoples" (Deut. 4:6).

ז הַחֻקִּים הָאֵלֶּה וְאָמְרוּ רַק עַם־חָכָם וְנָבוֹן הַגּוֹי הַגָּדוֹל הַזֶּה׃ כִּי מִי־
גוֹי גָּדוֹל אֲשֶׁר־לוֹ אֱלֹהִים קְרֹבִים אֵלָיו כַּיהוָה אֱלֹהֵינוּ בְּכָל־קָרְאֵנוּ
ח אֵלָיו׃ וּמִי גּוֹי גָּדוֹל אֲשֶׁר־לוֹ חֻקִּים וּמִשְׁפָּטִים צַדִּיקִם כְּכֹל הַתּוֹרָה
ט הַזֹּאת אֲשֶׁר אָנֹכִי נֹתֵן לִפְנֵיכֶם הַיּוֹם׃ רַק הִשָּׁמֶר לְךָ וּשְׁמֹר נַפְשְׁךָ
מְאֹד פֶּן־תִּשְׁכַּח אֶת־הַדְּבָרִים אֲשֶׁר־רָאוּ עֵינֶיךָ וּפֶן־יָסוּרוּ מִלְּבָבְךָ
י כֹּל יְמֵי חַיֶּיךָ וְהוֹדַעְתָּם לְבָנֶיךָ וְלִבְנֵי בָנֶיךָ׃ יוֹם אֲשֶׁר עָמַדְתָּ לִפְנֵי
יְהוָה אֱלֹהֶיךָ בְּחֹרֵב בֶּאֱמֹר יְהוָה אֵלַי הַקְהֶל־לִי אֶת־הָעָם וְאַשְׁמִעֵם
אֶת־דְּבָרָי אֲשֶׁר יִלְמְדוּן לְיִרְאָה אֹתִי כָּל־הַיָּמִים אֲשֶׁר הֵם חַיִּים עַל־
יא הָאֲדָמָה וְאֶת־בְּנֵיהֶם יְלַמֵּדוּן׃ וַתִּקְרְבוּן וַתַּעַמְדוּן תַּחַת הָהָר וְהָהָר
יב בֹּעֵר בָּאֵשׁ עַד־לֵב הַשָּׁמַיִם חֹשֶׁךְ עָנָן וַעֲרָפֶל׃ וַיְדַבֵּר יְהוָה אֲלֵיכֶם

אונקלוס

קְיָמַיָּא הָאִלֵּין, וְיֵימְרוּן, לְחוֹד עַם חַכִּים וְסָכְלְתָן, עַמָּא רַבָּא הָדֵין: ז אֲרֵי מַאן עַם רַב, דְּלֵיהּ אֱלָהּ קָרִיב לֵיהּ לְקַבָּלָא צְלוֹתֵיהּ בְּעִדָּן עָקְתֵיהּ, כַּיי אֱלָהַנָא, בְּכָל עִדָּן דַּאֲנַחְנָא מְצַלַּן קֳדָמוֹהִי: ח וּמַאן עַם רַב, דְּלֵיהּ, קְיָמִין וְדִינִין קַשִּׁיטִין, כְּכָל אוֹרָיְתָא הָדָא, דַּאֲנָא, יָהֵיב קֳדָמֵיכוֹן יוֹמָא דֵין: ט לְחוֹד, אִסְתְּמַר לָךְ וְטַר נַפְשָׁךְ לַחְדָּא, דִּלְמָא תִתְנְשֵׁי יָת פִּתְגָמַיָּא דַּחֲזָאָה עֵינָךְ, וְדִלְמָא יִעְדּוּן מִלִּבָּךְ, כָּל יוֹמֵי חַיָּךְ, וּתְהוֹדְעִנּוּן לִבְנָךְ וְלִבְנֵי בְנָךְ: י יוֹמָא, דְּקַמְתָּא, קֳדָם יי אֱלָהָךְ בְּחוֹרֵב, כַּד אֲמַר יי לִי, כְּנוֹשׁ קֳדָמַי יָת עַמָּא, וְאַשְׁמְעִנּוּן יָת פִּתְגָמַי, דְּיֵילְפוּן לְמִדְחַל קֳדָמַי, כָּל יוֹמַיָּא דְּאִנּוּן קַיָּמִין עַל אַרְעָא, וְיָת בְּנֵיהוֹן יַלְּפוּן: יא וּקְרֵיבְתּוּן וְקַמְתּוּן בְּשִׁפּוֹלֵי טוּרָא, וְטוּרָא, בָּעֵר בְּאִישָׁתָא עַד צֵית שְׁמַיָּא, חֲשׁוֹכָא עֲנָנָא וַאֲמִטְתָא: יב וּמַלֵּיל יי, עִמְּכוֹן

and these words have spread to the farthest islands and among many unenlightened peoples, and they discuss these words and the commandments of the Torah. (*Hilkhot Melakhim UMilḥemoteihem* 11:4)

The effect of Christianity and Islam was to spread the Jewish message – albeit in ways with which Jews could not fully agree – throughout the world. At the time of this writing, these religions represent more than half of the people on the face of the earth. The "Judeo-Christian ethic" and the Abrahamic faiths have shaped much of the civilization of the West. The Torah really did become "your wisdom and understanding in the eyes of the peoples."

The people God chose to carry His message were not

Whichever interpretation we take, the implication of Moshe's words is clear. The Torah would have an impact far beyond the boundaries, literal or metaphorical, of Israel. At no time in the biblical era could this be said to be true, but it did come true nonetheless. The Greeks, struck by the intensity with which Jews studied Torah, called them "a nation of philosophers." Then came Christianity and Islam, two faiths tracing their ancestry to Avraham and drawing much of their inspiration from the Hebrew Bible. Already in the twelfth century, Rambam could write (in a passage long censored and only recently restored):

> The whole world is already filled with the words of [the Christian] Messiah and the words of the commandments,

the fire. You heard the sound of words but saw no image; there was only a voice.
13 He announced to you His covenant, which He charged you to keep – the Ten
14 Commandments – and He wrote them on two tablets of stone. And the LORD
charged me at that time to teach you decrees and laws for you to keep in the
15 land that you are about to cross into and possess. You saw no image when the
LORD spoke to you at Ḥorev out of the fire, and so take great care for your own
16 sake not to act in self-destruction, making yourselves any idol, an image of any
17 shape, any form of man or of woman, or in the form of any animal of the land,
18 or any winged bird that flies in the sky, or in the form of anything that crawls
19 on the ground, or of any fish in the waters below the earth. And when you raise
your eyes to the heavens and see the sun, moon, and stars, all the heavenly
array, do not be led astray to bow down to them and worship them; the LORD
20 your God has allotted them to all the other peoples beneath the sky. But you,
the LORD took, and He brought you out of the iron crucible that was Egypt,
21 to become the people of His heritage, as you are on this day. The LORD was

רש״י

יד וְאֹתִי צִוָּה ה׳ בָּעֵת הַהִוא לְלַמֵּד אֶתְכֶם. תּוֹרָה שֶׁבְּעַל פֶּה:

טז סָמֶל. צוּרָה:

יט וּפֶן תִּשָּׂא עֵינֶיךָ. לְהִסְתַּכֵּל בַּדָּבָר וְלָתֵת לֵב לִטְעוֹת אַחֲרֵיהֶם: אֲשֶׁר חָלַק ה׳. לְהָאִיר לָהֶם. דָּבָר אַחֵר, לֶאֱלֹהוֹת, לֹא מְנָעָן מִלִּטְעוֹת אַחֲרֵיהֶם, אֶלָּא הֶחֱלִיקָם בְּדִבְרֵי הַבְלֵיהֶם לְטָרְדָם, וְכֵן הוּא אוֹמֵר: ״כִּי הֶחֱלִיק אֵלָיו בְּעֵינָיו לִמְצֹא עֲוֹנוֹ לִשְׂנֹא״ (תהלים לו, ג):

כ מִכּוּר. כּוּר הוּא כְּלִי שֶׁמְּזַקְּקִים בּוֹ אֶת הַזָּהָב:

כא הִתְאַנַּף. נִתְמַלֵּא רֹגֶז: עַל דִּבְרֵיכֶם. עַל אוֹדוֹתֵיכֶם, עַל עִסְקֵיכֶם:

understanding the world and relating to it is fundamentally different from that of the Greeks and of the philosophical tradition of which they were the founders. A listening culture is not the same as a seeing culture.

To this day, the West, when it speaks of understanding, uses metaphors of sight. We talk of *insight*, *foresight*, and *hindsight*, of making an *observation*, of people of *vision*. When we understand something we say, "I *see*." These come to the West from ancient Greece.

In the Hebrew Bible, by contrast, instead of saying that someone thinks, the verse will say that he "said in his or her heart." Thought is not a form of sight but of speech. This becomes all the more emphatic in the Babylonian Talmud, as the Nazir, Rabbi David Cohen, pointed out in his book *Kol HaNevua*. When the Talmud brings a proof text, it says *Ta shema*, "Come and hear." When it draws an inference, it says *Shema mina*, "Hear from this." When it wants to signal agreement, it says *Shome'a ani*, "I hear." All of these are verbs of listening, attending with the ear. For the Greeks, truth is what we see. For Jews, it is what we hear (see note on Gen. 3:6).

Pagan cultures *saw* God, or rather, the gods. They were there in visible phenomena: the sun, the storm, the earth, the sea, the great forces that surround us and reduce us to a sense of insignificance. The polytheistic imagination views reality as the clash of powerful forces, each of which is indifferent to the fate of humankind. A tidal wave does not stop to think whom it will drown.

A world confined to the visible is an impersonal world, deaf to our prayers, blind to our hopes, a world without overarching meaning. Judaism, by contrast, is the supreme example of a person-centered civilization – and persons communicate by words. They speak and listen. Words bridge the metaphysical abyss between soul and soul.

מִתּ֣וֹךְ הָאֵ֑שׁ ק֤וֹל דְּבָרִים֙ אַתֶּ֣ם שֹׁמְעִ֔ים וּתְמוּנָ֛ה אֵינְכֶ֥ם רֹאִ֖ים זוּלָתִ֥י
יג קֽוֹל׃ וַיַּגֵּ֨ד לָכֶ֜ם אֶת־בְּרִית֗וֹ אֲשֶׁ֨ר צִוָּ֤ה אֶתְכֶם֙ לַעֲשׂ֔וֹת עֲשֶׂ֖רֶת הַדְּבָרִ֑ים
יד וַֽיִּכְתְּבֵ֔ם עַל־שְׁנֵ֖י לֻח֥וֹת אֲבָנִֽים׃ וְאֹתִ֞י צִוָּ֤ה יהוה֙ בָּעֵ֣ת הַהִ֔וא לְלַמֵּ֣ד
אֶתְכֶ֔ם חֻקִּ֖ים וּמִשְׁפָּטִ֑ים לַעֲשֹׂתְכֶ֣ם אֹתָ֔ם בָּאָ֕רֶץ אֲשֶׁ֥ר אַתֶּ֛ם עֹבְרִ֥ים
טו שָׁ֖מָּה לְרִשְׁתָּֽהּ׃ וְנִשְׁמַרְתֶּ֥ם מְאֹ֖ד לְנַפְשֹֽׁתֵיכֶ֑ם כִּ֣י לֹ֤א רְאִיתֶם֙ כָּל־תְּמוּנָ֔ה
טז בְּי֗וֹם דִּבֶּ֨ר יהוה אֲלֵיכֶ֛ם בְּחֹרֵ֖ב מִתּ֥וֹךְ הָאֵֽשׁ׃ פֶּ֨ן־תַּשְׁחִת֔וּן וַעֲשִׂיתֶ֥ם
יז לָכֶ֛ם פֶּ֖סֶל תְּמוּנַ֣ת כָּל־סָ֑מֶל תַּבְנִ֥ית זָכָ֖ר א֥וֹ נְקֵבָֽה׃ תַּבְנִ֕ית כָּל־בְּהֵמָ֖ה
יח אֲשֶׁ֣ר בָּאָ֑רֶץ תַּבְנִית֙ כָּל־צִפּ֣וֹר כָּנָ֔ף אֲשֶׁ֥ר תָּע֖וּף בַּשָּׁמָֽיִם׃ תַּבְנִ֕ית כָּל־
יט רֹמֵ֖שׂ בָּאֲדָמָ֑ה תַּבְנִ֛ית כָּל־דָּגָ֥ה אֲשֶׁר־בַּמַּ֖יִם מִתַּ֥חַת לָאָֽרֶץ׃ וּפֶן־תִּשָּׂ֨א
עֵינֶ֜יךָ הַשָּׁמַ֗יְמָה וְֽ֠רָאִיתָ אֶת־הַשֶּׁ֨מֶשׁ וְאֶת־הַיָּרֵ֜חַ וְאֶת־הַכּֽוֹכָבִ֗ים כֹּ֚ל
צְבָ֣א הַשָּׁמַ֔יִם וְנִדַּחְתָּ֛ וְהִשְׁתַּחֲוִ֥יתָ לָהֶ֖ם וַעֲבַדְתָּ֑ם אֲשֶׁ֨ר חָלַ֜ק יהוה
כ אֱלֹהֶ֙יךָ֙ אֹתָ֔ם לְכֹל֙ הָֽעַמִּ֔ים תַּ֖חַת כָּל־הַשָּׁמָֽיִם׃ וְאֶתְכֶם֙ לָקַ֣ח יהוה
וַיּוֹצִ֥א אֶתְכֶ֛ם מִכּ֥וּר הַבַּרְזֶ֖ל מִמִּצְרָ֑יִם לִהְי֥וֹת ל֛וֹ לְעַ֥ם נַחֲלָ֖ה כַּיּ֥וֹם
כא הַזֶּֽה׃ וַֽיהוה הִתְאַנַּף־בִּ֖י עַל־דִּבְרֵיכֶ֑ם וַיִּשָּׁבַ֗ע לְבִלְתִּ֤י עָבְרִי֙ אֶת־הַיַּרְדֵּ֔ן

אונקלוס

מִגּוֹ אִישָׁתָא, קָל פִּתְגָּמִין אַתּוּן שָׁמְעִין, וּדְמוּ, לֵיתֵיכוֹן חָזַן אֱלָהֵין קָלָא: יג וְחַוִּי לְכוֹן יָת קְיָמֵיהּ, דְּפַקֵּיד יָתְכוֹן לְמֶעְבַּד, עַסְרָא פִתְגָּמִין, וּכְתַבְנוּן, עַל תְּרֵין לוּחֵי אַבְנַיָּא: יד וְיָתִי, פַּקֵּיד יי בְּעִדָּנָא הַהוּא, לְאַלָּפָא יָתְכוֹן, קְיָמִין וְדִינִין, לְמֶעְבַּדְכוֹן יָתְהוֹן, בְּאַרְעָא, דְּאַתּוּן עָבְרִין לְתַמָּן לְמֵירְתַהּ: טו וְתִסְתַּמְרוּן לַחֲדָא לְנַפְשָׁתְכוֹן, אֲרֵי לָא חֲזֵיתוּן כָּל דְּמוּ, בְּיוֹמָא, דְּמַלֵּיל יי עִמְּכוֹן, בְּחוֹרֵב מִגּוֹ אִישָׁתָא: טז דִּלְמָא תְחַבְּלוּן, וְתַעְבְּדוּן לְכוֹן, צֵילֵם דְּמוּת כָּל צוּרָא, דְּמוּת דְּכַר אוֹ נֻקְבָּא: יז דְּמוּת, כָּל בְּעִירָא דְּבְאַרְעָא, דְּמוּת כָּל צִפַּר גַּפָּא, דְּפָרַח בַּאֲוִיר רְקִיעַ שְׁמַיָּא: יח דְּמוּת, כָּל רִחְשָׁא דִּבְאַרְעָא, דְּמוּת, כָּל נוּנֵי דִּבְמַיָּא מִלְּרַע לְאַרְעָא: יט וְדִלְמָא תִזְקוֹף עֵינָךְ לִשְׁמַיָּא, וְתִחְזֵי, יָת שִׁמְשָׁא וְיָת סֵיהֲרָא וְיָת כּוֹכְבַיָּא, כָּל חֵילֵי שְׁמַיָּא, וְתִטְעֵי, וְתִסְגּוֹד לְהוֹן וְתִפְלְחִנּוּן, דִּזְמִין, יי אֱלָהָךְ יָתְהוֹן, לְכָל עַמְמַיָּא, דִּתְחוֹת כָּל שְׁמַיָּא: כ וְיָתְכוֹן קָרֵיב יי לְדַחַלְתֵיהּ, וְאַפֵּיק יָתְכוֹן, מִכּוּרָא דְּבַרְזְלָא מִמִּצְרָיִם, לְמֶהֱוֵי לֵיהּ, לְעַם אַחְסָנָא כְּיוֹמָא הָדֵין: כא וּמִן קֳדָם יי הֲוָה

4:12 זוּלָתִי קוֹל *There was only a voice* – Rabbi Yaakov Leiner (1814–78), leader of the hasidic community in Radzyn, Poland, made a profound point about the differences between the senses of sight and hearing:

> From a human perspective, it often seems as if seeing is a more precise form of knowledge than hearing. In fact, however, hearing has a greater power than seeing. Sight discloses the external aspect of things, but hearing reveals their inwardness. (*Beit Yaakov, Rosh Ḥodesh Menaḥem Av*)

God is not something we see, but a voice we hear. This has deep implications for the whole of Judaism. Its way of

incensed with me because of your words, and He vowed that I would not cross
the Jordan nor enter the good land that the LORD your God is giving you as a
22 heritage. I will die in this land without crossing the Jordan – but you will cross
23 over and take possession of that good land. Take care not to forget the covenant
that the LORD your God has forged with you. Do not make yourselves an idol
24 in any form: the LORD your God has forbidden it. For the LORD your God is a
consuming fire, an impassioned God.
25 When you have had children and grandchildren, and have lived long in the
land, if you act destructively, forming an idol in any image, wreaking evil in
26 the sight of the LORD your God and provoking Him to anger, I call heaven and
earth to witness against you today – to bear witness that you will quickly perish
from the land that you are crossing the Jordan to take possession of. You will
27 not live long there; you will be utterly destroyed. The LORD will scatter you
among the peoples. Only a few of you will remain among the nations that the
28 LORD will drive you away to. There you will worship man-made gods of wood
29 and of stone, ones that do not see, do not hear, do not eat or smell. Yet there, if
you seek the LORD your God, you will find Him: if you search after Him with
30 all your heart and all your soul. In your distress, when all these things have
happened to you, in the days to come, you will finally return to the LORD your
31 God and heed His voice. For the LORD your God is a merciful God. He will
not forsake or destroy you. He will not forget the covenant that He forged on

רש״י

כב **כִּי אָנֹכִי מֵת וְגוֹ׳ אֵינֶנִּי עֹבֵר.** מֵאַחַר שֶׁמֵּת מֵהֵיכָן יַעֲבֹר?! אֶלָּא אַף עַצְמוֹתַי אֵינָם עוֹבְרִים:

כג **תְּמוּנַת כֹּל.** תְּמוּנַת כָּל דָּבָר: **אֲשֶׁר צִוְּךָ ה׳.** אֲשֶׁר צִוְּךָ שֶׁלֹּא לַעֲשׂוֹת:

כד **אֵל קַנָּא.** מְקַנֵּא לִנְקֹם, אנפרנדד״א בְּלַעַז, מִתְחָרֶה עַל רָגְזוֹ לְהִפָּרַע מֵעוֹבְדֵי עֲבוֹדָה זָרָה:

כה **וְנוֹשַׁנְתֶּם.** רָמַז לָהֶם שֶׁיִּגְלוּ מִמֶּנָּה לְסוֹף שְׁמוֹנֶה מֵאוֹת וַחֲמִשִּׁים וּשְׁתַּיִם שָׁנָה כְּמִנְיַן ׳וְנוֹשַׁנְתֶּם׳, וְהוּא הִקְדִּים וְהִגְלָם לְסוֹף שְׁמוֹנֶה מֵאוֹת וַחֲמִשִּׁים, וְהִקְדִּים שְׁתֵּי שָׁנִים לְ׳וְנוֹשַׁנְתֶּם׳, כְּדֵי שֶׁלֹּא יִתְקַיֵּם בָּהֶם: ״כִּי אָבֹד תֹּאבֵדוּן״ (להלן פסוק כו), וְזֶהוּ שֶׁנֶּאֱמַר: ״וַיִּשְׁקֹד ה׳ עַל הָרָעָה וַיְבִיאֶהָ עָלֵינוּ כִּי צַדִּיק ה׳ אֱלֹהֵינוּ״ (דניאל ט, יד), צְדָקָה עָשָׂה עִמָּנוּ שֶׁמִּהֵר לַהֲבִיאָהּ שְׁתֵּי שָׁנִים לִפְנֵי זְמַנָּהּ:

כו **הַעִידֹתִי בָכֶם.** הִנְנִי מַזְמִינָם לִהְיוֹת עֵדִים שֶׁהִתְרֵיתִי בָּכֶם:

כח **וַעֲבַדְתֶּם שָׁם אֱלֹהִים.** כְּתַרְגּוּמוֹ, מִשֶּׁאַתֶּם עוֹבְדִים לְעוֹבְדֵיהֶם כְּאִלּוּ אַתֶּם עוֹבְדִים לָהֶם:

לא **לֹא יַרְפְּךָ.** מִלְּהַחֲזִיק בְּךָ בְּיָדָיו, וּלְשׁוֹן ״לֹא יַרְפְּךָ״ לְשׁוֹן לֹא יַפְעִיל הוּא, לֹא יִתֵּן לְךָ רִפְיוֹן, לֹא יַפְרִישׁ אוֹתְךָ מֵאֶצְלוֹ, וְכֵן: ״אֲחַזְתִּיו וְלֹא אַרְפֶּנּוּ״ (שיר השירים ג, ד), שֶׁלֹּא נִנְקַד ׳אֶרְפֶּנּוּ׳. כָּל לְשׁוֹן רִפְיוֹן מוּסָב עַל לְשׁוֹן מַפְעִיל וּמִתְפַּעֵל, כְּמוֹ ״הַרְפֵּה לָהּ״ (מלכים ב׳ ד, כז), תֵּן לָהּ רִפְיוֹן, ״הֶרֶף מִמֶּנִּי״ (להלן ט, יד), הִתְרַפֵּה מִמֶּנִּי:

כב וּלְבִלְתִּי־בֹא אֶל־הָאָרֶץ הַטּוֹבָה אֲשֶׁר יְהוָה אֱלֹהֶיךָ נֹתֵן לְךָ נַחֲלָה: כִּי
אָנֹכִי מֵת בָּאָרֶץ הַזֹּאת אֵינֶנִּי עֹבֵר אֶת־הַיַּרְדֵּן וְאַתֶּם עֹבְרִים וִירִשְׁתֶּם
כג אֶת־הָאָרֶץ הַטּוֹבָה הַזֹּאת: הִשָּׁמְרוּ לָכֶם פֶּן־תִּשְׁכְּחוּ אֶת־בְּרִית יְהוָה
אֱלֹהֵיכֶם אֲשֶׁר כָּרַת עִמָּכֶם וַעֲשִׂיתֶם לָכֶם פֶּסֶל תְּמוּנַת כֹּל אֲשֶׁר צִוְּךָ
כד יְהוָה אֱלֹהֶיךָ: כִּי יְהוָה אֱלֹהֶיךָ אֵשׁ אֹכְלָה הוּא אֵל קַנָּא:
כה כִּי־תוֹלִיד בָּנִים וּבְנֵי בָנִים וְנוֹשַׁנְתֶּם בָּאָרֶץ וְהִשְׁחַתֶּם וַעֲשִׂיתֶם פֶּסֶל
כו תְּמוּנַת כֹּל וַעֲשִׂיתֶם הָרַע בְּעֵינֵי־יְהוָה אֱלֹהֶיךָ לְהַכְעִיסוֹ: הַעִידֹתִי בָכֶם
הַיּוֹם אֶת־הַשָּׁמַיִם וְאֶת־הָאָרֶץ כִּי־אָבֹד תֹּאבֵדוּן מַהֵר מֵעַל הָאָרֶץ
אֲשֶׁר אַתֶּם עֹבְרִים אֶת־הַיַּרְדֵּן שָׁמָּה לְרִשְׁתָּהּ לֹא־תַאֲרִיכֻן יָמִים עָלֶיהָ
כז כִּי הִשָּׁמֵד תִּשָּׁמֵדוּן: וְהֵפִיץ יְהוָה אֶתְכֶם בָּעַמִּים וְנִשְׁאַרְתֶּם מְתֵי מִסְפָּר
כח בַּגּוֹיִם אֲשֶׁר יְנַהֵג יְהוָה אֶתְכֶם שָׁמָּה: וַעֲבַדְתֶּם־שָׁם אֱלֹהִים מַעֲשֵׂה יְדֵי
אָדָם עֵץ וָאֶבֶן אֲשֶׁר לֹא־יִרְאוּן וְלֹא יִשְׁמְעוּן וְלֹא יֹאכְלוּן וְלֹא יְרִיחֻן:
כט וּבִקַּשְׁתֶּם מִשָּׁם אֶת־יְהוָה אֱלֹהֶיךָ וּמָצָאתָ כִּי תִדְרְשֶׁנּוּ בְּכָל־לְבָבְךָ
ל וּבְכָל־נַפְשֶׁךָ: בַּצַּר לְךָ וּמְצָאוּךָ כֹּל הַדְּבָרִים הָאֵלֶּה בְּאַחֲרִית הַיָּמִים
לא וְשַׁבְתָּ עַד־יְהוָה אֱלֹהֶיךָ וְשָׁמַעְתָּ בְּקֹלוֹ: כִּי אֵל רַחוּם יְהוָה אֱלֹהֶיךָ
לֹא יַרְפְּךָ וְלֹא יַשְׁחִיתֶךָ וְלֹא יִשְׁכַּח אֶת־בְּרִית אֲבֹתֶיךָ אֲשֶׁר נִשְׁבַּע

אונקלוס

רְגַז עֲלַי עַל פִּתְגָמֵיכוֹן, וְקַיֵּים, בְּדִיל דְּלָא לְמֶעְבַּר יָת יַרְדְּנָא, וּבְדִיל דְּלָא לְמֵיעַל לְאַרְעָא טָבְתָא, דַּייָ אֱלָהָךְ, יָהֵיב לָךְ אַחְסָנָא: כב אֲרֵי אֲנָא מָאִית בְּאַרְעָא הָדָא, לֵית אֲנָא עָבַר יָת יַרְדְּנָא, וְאַתּוּן עָבְרִין, וְתֵירְתוּן, יָת אַרְעָא טָבְתָא הָדָא: כג אִסְתַּמַּרוּ לְכוֹן, דִּלְמָא תִתְנְשׁוֹן יָת קְיָמָא דַּייָ אֱלָהֲכוֹן, דִּגְזַר עִמְּכוֹן, וְתַעְבְּדוּן לְכוֹן צֵילַם דְּמוּת כּוֹלָא, דְּפַקְּדָךְ יְיָ אֱלָהָךְ: כד אֲרֵי יְיָ אֱלָהָךְ, מֵימְרֵיהּ אֶישָׁא אָכְלָא הוּא, אֵל קַנָּא: כה אֲרֵי תֵילְדוּן בְּנִין וּבְנֵי בְנִין, וְתִתְעַתְּקוּן בְּאַרְעָא, וּתְחַבְּלוּן, וְתַעְבְּדוּן צֵילַם דְּמוּת כּוֹלָא, וְתַעְבְּדוּן דְּבִישׁ, קֳדָם יְיָ אֱלָהָךְ לְאַרְגָּזָא קֳדָמוֹהִי: כו אַסְהֵידִית בְּכוֹן יוֹמָא דֵין יָת שְׁמַיָּא וְיָת אַרְעָא, אֲרֵי מֵיבַד תֵּיבְדוּן בִּפְרִיעַ, מֵעַל אַרְעָא, דְּאַתּוּן, עָבְרִין יָת יַרְדְּנָא, לְתַמָּן לְמֵירְתַהּ, לָא תֵירְכוּן יוֹמִין עֲלַהּ, אֲרֵי אִשְׁתֵּיצָאָה תִּשְׁתֵּיצוּן: כז וִיבַדַּר יְיָ, יָתְכוֹן בֵּינֵי עַמְמַיָּא, וְתִשְׁתַּאֲרוּן עַם דְּמִנְיָן, בְּעַמְמַיָּא, דִּידַבַּר יְיָ, יָתְכוֹן לְתַמָּן: כח וְתִפְלְחוּן תַּמָּן לְעַמְמַיָּא פָּלְחֵי טַעֲוָתָא, עוֹבָד יְדֵי אֱנָשָׁא, אָעָא וְאַבְנָא, דְּלָא חָזַן וְלָא שָׁמְעִין, וְלָא אָכְלִין וְלָא מְרִיחִין: כט וְתִתְבְּעוּן מִתַּמָּן, יָת דַּחַלְתָּא דַּייָ אֱלָהָךְ וְתִשְׁכַּח, אֲרֵי תִבְעֵי מִן קֳדָמוֹהִי, בְּכָל לִבָּךְ וּבְכָל נַפְשָׁךְ: ל כַּד תֵּיעוֹק לָךְ, וְיַשְׁכְּחֻנָּךְ, כֹּל פִּתְגָמַיָּא הָאִלֵּין, בְּסוֹף יוֹמַיָּא, וּתְתוּב לְדַחַלְתָּא דַּייָ אֱלָהָךְ, וּתְקַבֵּיל לְמֵימְרֵיהּ: לא אֲרֵי אֱלָהָא רַחֲמָנָא יְיָ אֱלָהָךְ, לָא יִשְׁבְּקִנָּךְ וְלָא יְחַבְּלִנָּךְ, וְלָא יִתְנְשֵׁי יָת

32 oath with your ancestors. For ask now about earliest times, times long before
your own, from the day God created humans on the earth; ask from one end of
heaven to the other: Has anything as great as this ever happened before? Has
33 anyone heard of anything like this? Has any people ever heard the voice of God
34 speaking out of fire, as you have, and lived? Has God ever taken one nation to
Himself, by miracles, from the midst of another, by trials, signs, wonders, and
war, with a mighty hand and an arm stretched forth and terrifying displays of
35 power, as the Lord your God did for you in Egypt before your eyes? To you
this was shown – so that you may know that the Lord is God; besides Him,
36 there is no other. From heaven He let you hear His voice to discipline you. On
earth He showed you His great fire, and from within the fire you heard His
37 words. And because He loved your ancestors and chose their descendants after
them He brought you out of Egypt with His own presence and by His great
38 power, driving out from before you nations greater and mightier than you, to
39 bring you in and give you their land as a possession, as it is on this day. Know
today and take to heart that the Lord is God in heaven above and on the earth

רש״י

לב) **לְיָמִים רִאשֹׁנִים.** עַל יָמִים רִאשׁוֹנִים: **וּלְמִקְצֵה הַשָּׁמַיִם.** וְגַם שְׁאַל לְכָל הַבְּרוּאִים אֲשֶׁר מִקָּצֶה אֶל קָצֶה, זֶהוּ פְּשׁוּטוֹ. וּמִדְרָשׁוֹ, מְלַמֵּד עַל קוֹמָתוֹ שֶׁל אָדָם שֶׁהָיְתָה מִן הָאָרֶץ עַד הַשָּׁמַיִם, וְהוּא הַשִּׁעוּר עַצְמוֹ אֲשֶׁר מִקָּצֶה אֶל קָצֶה: **הֲנִהְיָה כַּדָּבָר הַגָּדוֹל הַזֶּה.** מַהוּ הַדָּבָר הַגָּדוֹל? ״הֲשָׁמַע עָם״ וְגוֹ׳ (להלן פסוק לג):

לד) **אוֹ הֲנִסָּה אֱלֹהִים.** הֲכִי עָשָׂה נִסִּים שׁוּם אֱלוֹהַּ ״לָבוֹא לָקַחַת לוֹ גוֹי״ וְגוֹ׳, כָּל הֵהִ״ין הַלָּלוּ תְּמֵיהוֹת הֵן, לְכָךְ נְקוּדוֹת הֵן בַּחֲטַף פַּתָּח: הֲנִהְיָה, הֲנִשְׁמַע, הֲשָׁמַע, הֲנִסָּה: **בְּמַסֹּת.** עַל יְדֵי נִסְיוֹנוֹת הוֹדִיעָם גְּבוּרוֹתָיו, כְּגוֹן: ״הִתְפָּאֵר עָלַי״ (שמות ח, ה) אִם אוּכַל לַעֲשׂוֹת כֵּן, הֲרֵי זֶה נִסָּיוֹן: **בְּאֹתֹת.** בְּסִימָנִים לְהַאֲמִין שֶׁהוּא שְׁלוּחוֹ שֶׁל מָקוֹם, כְּגוֹן: ״מַה זֶּה בְיָדֶךָ״ (שם ד, ב): **וּבְמוֹפְתִים.** הֵם נִפְלָאוֹת, שֶׁהֵבִיא עֲלֵיהֶם מַכּוֹת מֻפְלָאוֹת: **וּבְמִלְחָמָה.** בַּיָּם, שֶׁנֶּאֱמַר: ״כִּי ה׳ נִלְחָם לָהֶם״ (שם יד, כה):

לה) **הָרְאֵתָ.** כְּתַרְגּוּמוֹ: ״אִתַּחְזֵיתָא״, כְּשֶׁנָּתַן הַקָּדוֹשׁ בָּרוּךְ הוּא אֶת הַתּוֹרָה פָּתַח לָהֶם שִׁבְעָה רְקִיעִים וּכְשֵׁם שֶׁקָּרַע אֶת הָעֶלְיוֹנִים כָּךְ קָרַע אֶת הַתַּחְתּוֹנִים וְרָאוּ שֶׁהוּא יְחִידִי, לְכָךְ נֶאֱמַר: ״אַתָּה הָרְאֵתָ לָדַעַת״:

לז) **וְתַחַת כִּי אָהַב.** וְכָל זֶה תַּחַת אֲשֶׁר אָהַב: **וַיּוֹצִאֲךָ בְּפָנָיו.** כְּאָדָם הַמַּנְהִיג בְּנוֹ לְפָנָיו, שֶׁנֶּאֱמַר: ״וַיִּסַּע מַלְאַךְ הָאֱלֹהִים הַהֹלֵךְ וְגוֹ׳ וַיֵּלֶךְ מֵאַחֲרֵיהֶם״ (שמות יד, יט). דָּבָר אַחֵר, ״וַיּוֹצִאֲךָ בְּפָנָיו״, בִּפְנֵי אֲבוֹתָיו, כְּמָה שֶׁנֶּאֱמַר: ״נֶגֶד אֲבוֹתָם עָשָׂה פֶלֶא״ (תהלים עח, יב). וְאַל תִּתְמַהּ עַל שֶׁהִזְכִּירָם בִּלְשׁוֹן יָחִיד, שֶׁהֲרֵי כְּתָבָם בִּלְשׁוֹן יָחִיד, ״וַיִּבְחַר בְּזַרְעוֹ אַחֲרָיו״:

לח) **מִמְּךָ מִפָּנֶיךָ.** סָרְסֵהוּ וְדָרְשֵׁהוּ: לְהוֹרִישׁ מִפָּנֶיךָ גּוֹיִם גְּדֹלִים וַעֲצֻמִים מִמְּךָ: **כַּיּוֹם הַזֶּה.** כַּאֲשֶׁר אַתָּה רוֹאֶה הַיּוֹם:

that there will never be any other people quite like Israel. Turning to the new generation, he asks them this rhetorical question, one that still echoes, gathering force with each successive century. As we survey the breathtaking landscape of Jewish history, we know this: that those who sought to destroy the people of the covenant gather dust in the museums of mankind while *am Yisrael ḥai,* the people Israel lives. Ancient Egypt is no more. The Moabites have long since disappeared. The Assyrians, Babylonians, Persians, Greeks, and Romans successively strode the stage of world dominion. Each empire played its part, and each in turn has gone. In our day, the two great powers which declared, as stated in the Merneptah Stele, "Israel is laid waste – its seed is no more" – the Third Reich and the Soviet Union – have been defeated, dismantled, and have disappeared. But the Jews survive. "Has anything as great as this ever happened before? Has anyone heard of anything like this?"

לב לָהֶם: כִּי שְׁאַל־נָא לְיָמִים רִאשֹׁנִים אֲשֶׁר־הָיוּ לְפָנֶיךָ לְמִן־הַיּוֹם אֲשֶׁר
בָּרָא אֱלֹהִים ׀ אָדָם עַל־הָאָרֶץ וּלְמִקְצֵה הַשָּׁמַיִם וְעַד־קְצֵה הַשָּׁמָיִם
לג הֲנִהְיָה כַּדָּבָר הַגָּדוֹל הַזֶּה אוֹ הֲנִשְׁמַע כָּמֹהוּ: הֲשָׁמַע עָם קוֹל אֱלֹהִים
לד מְדַבֵּר מִתּוֹךְ־הָאֵשׁ כַּאֲשֶׁר־שָׁמַעְתָּ אַתָּה וַיֶּחִי: אוֹ ׀ הֲנִסָּה אֱלֹהִים
לָבוֹא לָקַחַת לוֹ גוֹי מִקֶּרֶב גּוֹי בְּמַסֹּת בְּאֹתֹת וּבְמוֹפְתִים וּבְמִלְחָמָה
וּבְיָד חֲזָקָה וּבִזְרוֹעַ נְטוּיָה וּבְמוֹרָאִים גְּדֹלִים כְּכֹל אֲשֶׁר־עָשָׂה לָכֶם
לה יהוה אֱלֹהֵיכֶם בְּמִצְרַיִם לְעֵינֶיךָ: אַתָּה הָרְאֵתָ לָדַעַת כִּי יהוה הוּא
לו הָאֱלֹהִים אֵין עוֹד מִלְבַדּוֹ: מִן־הַשָּׁמַיִם הִשְׁמִיעֲךָ אֶת־קֹלוֹ לְיַסְּרֶךָּ
וְעַל־הָאָרֶץ הֶרְאֲךָ אֶת־אִשּׁוֹ הַגְּדוֹלָה וּדְבָרָיו שָׁמַעְתָּ מִתּוֹךְ הָאֵשׁ:
לז וְתַחַת כִּי אָהַב אֶת־אֲבֹתֶיךָ וַיִּבְחַר בְּזַרְעוֹ אַחֲרָיו וַיּוֹצִאֲךָ בְּפָנָיו בְּכֹחוֹ
לח הַגָּדֹל מִמִּצְרָיִם: לְהוֹרִישׁ גּוֹיִם גְּדֹלִים וַעֲצֻמִים מִמְּךָ מִפָּנֶיךָ לַהֲבִיאֲךָ
לט לָתֶת־לְךָ אֶת־אַרְצָם נַחֲלָה כַּיּוֹם הַזֶּה: וְיָדַעְתָּ הַיּוֹם וַהֲשֵׁבֹתָ אֶל־לְבָבֶךָ
כִּי יהוה הוּא הָאֱלֹהִים בַּשָּׁמַיִם מִמַּעַל וְעַל־הָאָרֶץ מִתָּחַת אֵין עוֹד:

אונקלוס

קְיָמָא דַאֲבָהָתָךְ, דְּקַיֵּים לְהוֹן: לב אֲרֵי שְׁאַל כְּעַן לְיוֹמַיָּא קַדְמָאֵי דַּהֲווֹ קֳדָמָךְ, לְמִן יוֹמָא דִּבְרָא יי אָדָם עַל אַרְעָא, וּלְמִסְּיָפֵי שְׁמַיָּא וְעַד סְיָפֵי שְׁמַיָּא, הַהֲוָה, כְּפִתְגָּמָא רַבָּא הָדֵין, אוֹ הַאִשְׁתְּמַע דִּכְוָתֵיהּ: לג הֲשְׁמַע עַמָּא קָל מֵימְרָא דַּיי, מְמַלֵּיל מִגּוֹ אִישָּׁתָא, כְּמָא דִּשְׁמַעְתָּא אַתְּ וְאִתְקַיַּמְתָּא: לד אוֹ נִסִּין עֲבַד יי, לְאִתְגְּלָאָה, לְמִפְרַק לֵיהּ עַם מִגּוֹ עַם, בְּנִסִּין בְּאָתִין וּבְמוֹפְתִין וּבִקְרָבָא, וּבְיַד תַּקִּיפָא וּבִדְרָעָא מְרָמְמָא, וּבְחֶזְוָנִין רַבְרְבִין, כְּכֹל, דַּעֲבַד לְכוֹן, יי אֱלָהֲכוֹן, בְּמִצְרַיִם לְעֵינֵיכוֹן: לה אַתְּ אִתַּחְזֵיתָא לְמִדַּע, אֲרֵי יי הוּא אֱלֹהִים, לֵית עוֹד בַּר מִנֵּיהּ: לו מִן שְׁמַיָּא, אַשְׁמְעָךְ יָת קָל מֵימְרֵיהּ לְאַלָּפוּתָךְ, וְעַל אַרְעָא, אַחְזְיָךְ יָת אִישָּׁתֵיהּ רַבְּתָא, וּפִתְגָּמוֹהִי שְׁמַעְתָּא מִגּוֹ אִישָּׁתָא: לז וְחָלַף, אֲרֵי רְחִים יָת אֲבָהָתָךְ, וְאִתְרְעִי בִּבְנֵיהוֹן בָּתְרֵיהוֹן, וְאַפְּקָךְ בְּמֵימְרֵיהּ, בְּחֵילֵיהּ רַבָּא מִמִּצְרָיִם: לח לְתָרָכָא, עַמְמִין, רַבְרְבִין וְתַקִּיפִין, מִנָּךְ מִן קֳדָמָךְ, לְאַעָלוּתָךְ, לְמִתַּן לָךְ יָת אַרְעֲהוֹן, אַחְסָנָא כְּיוֹמָא הָדֵין: לט וְתִדַּע יוֹמָא דֵין, וְתָתֵיב לְלִבָּךְ, אֲרֵי יי הוּא אֱלֹהִים, דִּשְׁכִינְתֵיהּ בִּשְׁמַיָּא מִלְּעֵילָא, וְשַׁלִּיט עַל אַרְעָא מִלְּרַע, לֵית עוֹד:

4:32 הֲנִהְיָה כַּדָּבָר הַגָּדוֹל הַזֶּה *Has anything... happened before* – Israel knows God directly, through its own past. Where other faiths, ancient and modern, saw religion as the flight from history into a world without time, Judaism saw time itself as the arena where God and mankind met. Three-quarters of the Hebrew Bible is made up of historical narratives. Jews were the first to make the momentous claim that history has meaning. It is not merely a sequence of disconnected events, but the long story of humanity's response to, or rebellion against, the voice of God as it echoes in the conscience of mankind.

4:32 הֲנִשְׁמַע כָּמֹהוּ *Has anyone heard of anything like this?* – At the very beginning of our national history Moshe recognizes

40 beneath; there is no other. Keep His decrees and commandments, with which
I am charging you today, so that it may be well for you and your children after
you, and that you may live long in the land that the LORD your God is giving
you for all time."
41 42 Then Moshe designated three cities to the east side of the Jordan to which a SHELISHI
manslayer could flee, someone who had killed a fellow human being without
43 intent or prior enmity. He could flee to one of these cities and live: Betzer in
the wilderness plateau for the people of Reuven, Ramot in Gilad for the people
44 of Gad, and Golan in Bashan for the people of Menashe. This is the Law that
45 Moshe set before the people of Israel. These are the testimonies, decrees, and
46 laws that Moshe spoke to the Israelites when they had come out of Egypt and
were beyond the Jordan in the valley opposite Beit Peor, in the land of Siḥon,
king of the Amorites, who reigned at Ḥeshbon, whom Moshe and the Israelites
47 defeated when they came out of Egypt. They had taken possession of his land
and the land of Og, king of Bashan, the two Amorite kings east of the Jordan:
48 from Aroer on the edge of the Arnon Stream, as far as Mount Siyon – that is,
49 Ḥermon – together with all the Arava on the east bank of the Jordan as far as
the Arava Sea, below the slopes of Pisga.
5 1 Moshe summoned all Israel, and said to them: "Listen, Israel, to the decrees REVI'I
and laws that I shall declare in your hearing today; learn them and carefully
2 3 observe them. The LORD our God forged a covenant with us at Ḥorev. Not
with our ancestors did the LORD forge this covenant, but with us who are here

אונקלוס

מ וְתִטַּר יָת קְיָמוֹהִי וְיָת פִּקּוֹדוֹהִי, דַּאֲנָא מְפַקֵּיד לָךְ יוֹמָא דֵין, דְּיִיטַב לָךְ, וְלִבְנָךְ בָּתְרָךְ, וּבְדִיל דְּתוֹרִיךְ יוֹמִין עַל אַרְעָא, דַּיְיָ אֱלָהָךְ, יָהֵיב לָךְ כָּל יוֹמַיָּא: מא בְּכֵן אַפְרֵישׁ מֹשֶׁה תְּלָת קִרְוִין, בְּעִבְרָא דְּיַרְדְּנָא, מַדְנַח שִׁמְשָׁא: מב לְמֶעְרַק לְתַמָּן קָטוֹלָא, דְּיִקְטוֹל יָת חַבְרֵיהּ בְּלָא מַדְּעֵיהּ, וְהוּא, לָא סָנֵי לֵיהּ מֵאִתְמָלֵי וּמִדְּקַמּוֹהִי, וְיֵעְרוֹק, לַחֲדָא, מִן קִרְוַיָּא הָאִלֵּין וְיִתְקַיַּם: מג יָת בֶּצֶר בְּמַדְבְּרָא, בַּאֲרַע מֵישְׁרָא לְשִׁבְטָא רְאוּבֵן, וְיָת רָמוֹת בְּגִלְעָד לְשִׁבְטָא גָד, וְיָת גּוֹלָן בְּמַתְנַן לְשִׁבְטָא דִּמְנַשֶּׁה: מד וְדָא אוֹרָיְתָא, דְּסַדַּר מֹשֶׁה, קֳדָם בְּנֵי יִשְׂרָאֵל: מה אִלֵּין סָהֲדְוָתָא, וּקְיָמַיָּא וְדִינַיָּא, דְּמַלֵּיל מֹשֶׁה עִם בְּנֵי יִשְׂרָאֵל, בְּמִפַּקְהוֹן מִמִּצְרָיִם: מו בְּעִבְרָא דְּיַרְדְּנָא בְּחֵלְתָּא, לָקֳבֵיל בֵּית

רש״י

מא אָז יַבְדִּיל. נָתַן לֵב לִהְיוֹת חָרֵד לַדָּבָר שֶׁיַּבְדִּילֵם, וְאַף עַל פִּי שֶׁאֵינָן קוֹלְטוֹת עַד שֶׁיֻּבְדְּלוּ אוֹתָן שֶׁבְּאֶרֶץ כְּנַעַן, אָמַר מֹשֶׁה: מִצְוָה שֶׁאֶפְשָׁר לְקַיְּמָהּ אֲקַיְּמֶנָּה: בְּעֵבֶר הַיַּרְדֵּן מִזְרְחָה שָׁמֶשׁ. בְּאוֹתוֹ עֵבֶר שֶׁבְּמִזְרָחוֹ שֶׁל יַרְדֵּן: מִזְרְחָה שָׁמֶשׁ. לְפִי שֶׁהוּא דָּבוּק נְקוּדָה רֵי״שׁ בַּחֲטָף, מִזְרַח שֶׁל שֶׁמֶשׁ, מְקוֹם זְרִיחַת הַשֶּׁמֶשׁ:

מד וְזֹאת הַתּוֹרָה. זוֹ שֶׁהוּא עָתִיד לְסַדֵּר אַחַר פָּרָשָׁה זוֹ:

מה-מו אֵלֶּה הָעֵדֹת וְגוֹ׳ אֲשֶׁר דִּבֶּר. הֵם הֵם אֲשֶׁר דִּבֶּר בְּצֵאתָם מִמִּצְרַיִם, דִּבֵּר לָהֶם בְּעַרְבוֹת מוֹאָב אֲשֶׁר בְּעֵבֶר הַיַּרְדֵּן שֶׁהוּא בַּמִּזְרָח, שֶׁהָעֵבֶר הַשֵּׁנִי הָיָה בַּמַּעֲרָב: בְּעֵבֶר הַיַּרְדֵּן. חָזַר וְשָׁנָה לָהֶם:

ה ג לֹא אֶת אֲבֹתֵינוּ. בִּלְבַד ״כָּרַת ה׳״ וְגוֹ׳:

מ וְשָׁמַרְתָּ אֶת־חֻקָּיו וְאֶת־מִצְוֺתָיו אֲשֶׁר אָנֹכִי מְצַוְּךָ הַיּוֹם אֲשֶׁר יִיטַב לְךָ
וּלְבָנֶיךָ אַחֲרֶיךָ וּלְמַעַן תַּאֲרִיךְ יָמִים עַל־הָאֲדָמָה אֲשֶׁר יְהוָה אֱלֹהֶיךָ
נֹתֵן לְךָ כָּל־הַיָּמִים׃
מא מב אָז יַבְדִּיל מֹשֶׁה שָׁלֹשׁ עָרִים בְּעֵבֶר הַיַּרְדֵּן מִזְרְחָה שָׁמֶשׁ׃ לָנֻס שָׁמָּה ה שלישי
רוֹצֵחַ אֲשֶׁר יִרְצַח אֶת־רֵעֵהוּ בִּבְלִי־דַעַת וְהוּא לֹא־שֹׂנֵא לוֹ מִתְּמֹל
מג שִׁלְשֹׁם וְנָס אֶל־אַחַת מִן־הֶעָרִים הָאֵל וָחָי׃ אֶת־בֶּצֶר בַּמִּדְבָּר בְּאֶרֶץ
הַמִּישֹׁר לָראוּבֵנִי וְאֶת־רָאמֹת בַּגִּלְעָד לַגָּדִי וְאֶת־גּוֹלָן בַּבָּשָׁן לַמְנַשִּׁי׃
מד מה וְזֹאת הַתּוֹרָה אֲשֶׁר־שָׂם מֹשֶׁה לִפְנֵי בְּנֵי יִשְׂרָאֵל׃ אֵלֶּה הָעֵדֹת וְהַחֻקִּים
וְהַמִּשְׁפָּטִים אֲשֶׁר דִּבֶּר מֹשֶׁה אֶל־בְּנֵי יִשְׂרָאֵל בְּצֵאתָם מִמִּצְרָיִם׃
מו בְּעֵבֶר הַיַּרְדֵּן בַּגַּיְא מוּל בֵּית פְּעוֹר בְּאֶרֶץ סִיחֹן מֶלֶךְ הָאֱמֹרִי אֲשֶׁר
יוֹשֵׁב בְּחֶשְׁבּוֹן אֲשֶׁר הִכָּה מֹשֶׁה וּבְנֵי יִשְׂרָאֵל בְּצֵאתָם מִמִּצְרָיִם׃
מז וַיִּירְשׁוּ אֶת־אַרְצוֹ וְאֶת־אֶרֶץ ׀ עוֹג מֶלֶךְ־הַבָּשָׁן שְׁנֵי מַלְכֵי הָאֱמֹרִי
מח אֲשֶׁר בְּעֵבֶר הַיַּרְדֵּן מִזְרַח שָׁמֶשׁ׃ מֵעֲרֹעֵר אֲשֶׁר עַל־שְׂפַת־נַחַל אַרְנֹן
מט וְעַד־הַר שִׂיאֹן הוּא חֶרְמוֹן׃ וְכָל־הָעֲרָבָה עֵבֶר הַיַּרְדֵּן מִזְרָחָה וְעַד יָם
הָעֲרָבָה תַּחַת אַשְׁדֹּת הַפִּסְגָּה׃
ה א וַיִּקְרָא מֹשֶׁה אֶל־כָּל־יִשְׂרָאֵל וַיֹּאמֶר אֲלֵהֶם שְׁמַע יִשְׂרָאֵל אֶת־הַחֻקִּים רביעי
וְאֶת־הַמִּשְׁפָּטִים אֲשֶׁר אָנֹכִי דֹּבֵר בְּאָזְנֵיכֶם הַיּוֹם וּלְמַדְתֶּם אֹתָם
ב ג וּשְׁמַרְתֶּם לַעֲשֹׂתָם׃ יְהוָה אֱלֹהֵינוּ כָּרַת עִמָּנוּ בְּרִית בְּחֹרֵב׃ לֹא אֶת־
אֲבֹתֵינוּ כָּרַת יְהוָה אֶת־הַבְּרִית הַזֹּאת כִּי אִתָּנוּ אֲנַחְנוּ אֵלֶּה פֹה הַיּוֹם

אונקלוס

פְּעוֹר, בְּאַרַע, סִיחוֹן מַלְכָּא אֱמוֹרָאָה, דְּיָתֵיב בְּחֶשְׁבּוֹן, דִּמְחָא מֹשֶׁה וּבְנֵי יִשְׂרָאֵל, בְּמִפַּקְהוֹן מִמִּצְרָיִם: מז וִירִיתוּ יָת אַרְעֵיהּ, וְיָת אֲרַע עוֹג מַלְכָּא דְמַתְנַן, תְּרֵין מַלְכֵי אֱמוֹרָאָה, דִּבְעִבְרָא דְיַרְדְּנָא, מַדְנַח שִׁמְשָׁא: מח מֵעֲרוֹעֵר, דְּעַל כֵּיף נַחְלָא דְאַרְנוֹן, וְעַד טוּרָא דְשִׂיאוֹן הוּא חֶרְמוֹן: מט וְכָל מֵישְׁרָא, עִבְרָא דְיַרְדְּנָא מַדִנְחָא,

וְעַד יַמָּא דְמֵישְׁרָא, תְּחוֹת מַשְׁפַּךְ מְרָמְתָא: ה א וּקְרָא מֹשֶׁה לְכָל יִשְׂרָאֵל, וַאֲמַר לְהוֹן, שְׁמַע יִשְׂרָאֵל יָת קְיָמַיָּא וְיָת דִּינַיָּא, דַּאֲנָא, מְמַלֵּיל קֳדָמֵיכוֹן יוֹמָא דֵין, וְתֵילְפוּן יָתְהוֹן, וְתִטְּרוּן לְמֶעְבַּדְהוֹן: ב יי אֱלָהַנָא, גְּזַר עִמַּנָא, קְיָם בְּחוֹרֵב: ג לָא עִם אֲבָהָתַנָא, גְּזַר יי יָת קְיָמָא הָדֵין, אֱלָהֵין עִמַּנָא, אֲנַחְנָא אִלֵּין כָּא, יוֹמָא דֵין

4 today, all of us, alive. Face-to-face from amid the fire the LORD spoke to you at
5 the mountain. I was standing between the LORD and you at that time to tell
you the word of the LORD, because you were afraid of the fire and did not go
6 up the mountain. He said: I am the LORD your God, who brought
7 you out of the land of Egypt, out of the house of slaves. Have no other gods

רש״י

ד פָּנִים בְּפָנִים. אָמַר רַבִּי בֶּרֶכְיָה: כָּךְ אָמַר מֹשֶׁה: אַל תֹּאמְרוּ אֲנִי מַטְעֶה אֶתְכֶם עַל לֹא דָּבָר כְּדֶרֶךְ שֶׁהַסַּרְסוּר עוֹשֶׂה בֵּין הַמּוֹכֵר לַלּוֹקֵחַ, הֲרֵי (הלוקח) [הַמּוֹכֵר] עַצְמוֹ מְדַבֵּר עִמָּכֶם:

ד-ה לֵאמֹר. מוּסָב עַל ״דִּבֶּר ה׳ עִמָּכֶם בָּהָר מִתּוֹךְ הָאֵשׁ״ לֵאמֹר, וְ״אָנֹכִי עֹמֵד בֵּין ה׳ וּבֵינֵיכֶם״:

ז עַל פָּנָי. בְּכָל מָקוֹם אֲשֶׁר אֲנִי שָׁם, וְזֶהוּ כָּל הָעוֹלָם. דָּבָר אַחֵר, כָּל זְמַן שֶׁאֲנִי קַיָּם:

עֲשֶׂרֶת הַדִּבְּרוֹת כְּבָר פֵּרַשְׁתִּים.

Commandments is an abridged form of preamble ("I am the LORD your God") and historical review ("who brought you out of the land of Egypt, out of the house of slaves"). The verses that follow are the stipulations, or as we would call them, the commands. If so, then Halakhot Gedolot as understood by Ramban may well have been correct in seeing the verse as an introduction to the commands, not a command in its own right. From God's relationship with and redemption of Israel arises our commitment to all the commands that follow.

5:6 מִבֵּית עֲבָדִים *Out of the house of slaves* – For Rambam, as noted above, the first command is to believe in God, creator of heaven and earth:

> The basic principle of all basic principles and the pillar of all sciences is to realize that there is a First Being who brought every existing thing into being.... To acknowledge this truth is a positive command, as it is said: "I am the LORD your God" (Ex. 20:2; Deut. 5:6). (*Hilkhot Yesodei HaTorah* 1:1–5)

Yehuda HaLevi shifted the focus of this commandment. HaLevi was a great medieval Hebrew poet and also wrote one of Judaism's theological masterpieces, the Kuzari. In it, HaLevi draws a portrait diametrically opposed to Rambam's account. Judaism is not about abstract concepts but about concrete experiences: the taste of slavery, the feeling of liberation, the realization on the part of the people that God had heard their cry and set them free. The prophets were not philosophers. Philosophers found God in physics and metaphysics, but the prophets found God in history. This is how HaLevi explains his faith:

> I believe in the God of Avraham, Yitzhak, and Yaakov, who led the children of Israel out of Egypt with signs and miracles, who fed them in the desert and gave them the land, after having brought them through the sea and the Jordan in a miraculous way. (Kuzari I:11)

He goes on to emphasize that God's opening words in the revelation at Mount Sinai were not, "I am the LORD your God, creator of heaven and earth" but "I am the LORD your God, who brought you out of the land of Egypt, out of the house of slaves" (Kuzari I:25). The covenant God made with the Israelites at Mount Sinai was not rooted in the ancient past of creation but in the recent past of the exodus.

What is at stake in this difference of opinion between Rambam and HaLevi? At the heart of Judaism is a twofold understanding of the nature of God and His relationship to the universe. On the one hand, God is creator of the universe and the maker of the human person "in His image." This aspect of God is universal. It is accessible to anyone, Jew or Gentile.

But there is a quite different aspect of God which predominates throughout most of Tanakh. This is God as He is involved in the fate of one family, one nation: the children of Israel. He intervened in their history. He made a highly specific covenant with them at Sinai, covering almost every aspect of life.

ד ה כֻּלָּ֖נוּ חַיִּֽים׃ פָּנִ֣ים ׀ בְּפָנִ֗ים דִּבֶּ֨ר יְהוָ֧ה עִמָּכֶ֛ם בָּהָ֖ר מִתּ֥וֹךְ הָאֵֽשׁ׃ אָֽנֹכִ֞י
עֹמֵ֨ד בֵּין־יְהוָ֤ה וּבֵֽינֵיכֶם֙ בָּעֵ֣ת הַהִ֔וא לְהַגִּ֥יד לָכֶ֖ם אֶת־דְּבַ֣ר יְהוָ֑ה כִּ֤י
ו יְרֵאתֶם֙ מִפְּנֵ֣י הָאֵ֔שׁ וְלֹֽא־עֲלִיתֶ֥ם בָּהָ֖ר לֵאמֹֽר׃ אָֽנֹכִ֖י יְהוָ֣ה
ז אֱלֹהֶ֑יךָ אֲשֶׁ֧ר הוֹצֵאתִ֛יךָ מֵאֶ֥רֶץ מִצְרַ֖יִם מִבֵּ֣ית עֲבָדִ֑ים׃ לֹֽא־יִהְיֶ֥ה לְךָ֛

אונקלוס

כֻּלַּנָא קַיָּמִין: ד מַמְלַל עִם מַמְלַל, מַלֵּיל יי עִמְּכוֹן, בְּטוּרָא מִגּוֹ אִישָׁתָא: ה אֲנָא, הֲוֵיתִי קָאֵים בֵּין מֵימְרָא דַּיי וּבֵינֵיכוֹן בְּעִדָּנָא הַהוּא, לְחַוָּאָה לְכוֹן יָת פִּתְגָּמָא דַּיי, אֲרֵי דְּחֵילְתּוֹן מִן קֳדָם אִישָׁתָא, וְלָא סְלֵיקְתּוֹן בְּטוּרָא לְמֵימַר: ו אֲנָא יי אֱלָהָךְ, דְּאַפֵּיקְתָּךְ, מֵאַרְעָא דְּמִצְרַיִם מִבֵּית עַבְדוּתָא: ז לָא יְהֵי לָךְ

THE TEN COMMANDMENTS

Though the Ten Commandments are a central text of Judaism, scholars have disagreed throughout the ages on how to count them. What was the first commandment? This was debated by, among others, Rambam (1138–1204) and the author of Halakhot Gedolot, probably Rabbi Shimon Kayyara (in the period of the *geonim* in the eighth century), who for the first time enumerated the 613 commands.

Rambam counts the opening line of the Ten Commandments, "I am the LORD your God, who brought you out of the land of Egypt, out of the house of slaves," as a positive command, to believe in God. Halakhot Gedolot does not count it as a command at all. Why not?

Ramban (1194–1270), in defense of Halakhot Gedolot, speculates that its author counted among the 613 commands only the specific laws enjoining us to do this or avoid doing that. The commands are rules of behavior, not items of faith. Faith in the existence of God, or acceptance of the kingship of God, is not itself a command but a prelude to, and presupposition of, the commands. He quotes a passage from Mekhilta:

> "Have no other gods than me." Why is this said? Because it says, "I am the LORD your God." To explain this by way of a parable: A king of flesh and blood entered a province. His servants said to him, "Issue decrees for the people." He, however, told them, "No. When they accept my sovereignty, I will issue decrees. For if they do not accept my sovereignty, how will they carry out my decrees?"

According to Ramban, Halakhot Gedolot must have believed that the verse "I am the LORD your God, who brought you out of the land of Egypt, out of the house of slaves" is not itself a command, but a statement of why the Israelites should be bound by the will of God. He had rescued them, liberated them, and brought them to safety. The first verse of the Decalogue is not a law but a statement of fact, a reason why the Israelites should accept God's sovereignty.

Thanks to recent archaeological discoveries, we now know that the biblical covenant has the same literary structure as ancient Near Eastern political treaties. These treaties usually follow a six-part pattern, of which the first three elements were: (1) the preamble, identifying the initiator of the treaty; (2) a historical review, summarizing the past relationship between the parties; and (3) the stipulations, namely, the terms and conditions of the covenant.

Fundamentally a covenant is a peace treaty. It can exist between states of roughly equivalent power (a parity treaty). But it can also exist between states of radically different power, in which case it is called a suzerainty treaty. Such is the covenant between Israel and God.

This was revolutionary. Covenants were common in the ancient Near East. But covenants between God and a people were unknown, indeed inconceivable. It was unimaginable that God would seek to constrain His own powers in the name of righteousness and justice, or that a supreme power would make a treaty with the supremely powerless.

Seen in this context, the first verse of the Ten

8 than Me. Do not make for yourself a carved image or likeness of any creature in
9 the heavens above or the earth beneath or the water beneath the earth. Do not
bow down to them or worship them, for I the LORD your God demand absolute
loyalty. For those who hate Me, I hold the descendants to account for the sins
10 of the fathers to the third and fourth generation, but to those who love Me and
11 keep My commands – I shall act with faithful love for thousands. Do
not speak the name of the LORD your God in vain, for the LORD will not hold
12 guiltless those who speak His name in vain. Guard the Sabbath to keep
13 it holy, as the LORD your God has commanded you. Six days you shall work and
14 carry out all your labors, but the seventh is a Sabbath to the LORD your God. On
it, do no work at all – neither you, nor your son or daughter, your male or female
servant, your ox, your donkey, nor any of your livestock, or the migrant within
15 your gates, so that your male and female servants may rest as you do. Remember
that you were slaves in Egypt, and the LORD your God brought you out of
there with a mighty hand and an arm stretched forth. That is why the LORD
16 your God has commanded you to keep the Sabbath day. Honor your
father and mother, as the LORD your God has commanded you, so that you may
live long and that it may be well for you in the land that the LORD your God is

רש״י

יב **שָׁמוֹר.** וּבָרִאשׁוֹנוֹת הוּא אוֹמֵר: "זָכוֹר" (שמות כ, ח), שְׁנֵיהֶם בְּדִבּוּר אֶחָד וּבְתֵבָה אַחַת נֶאֶמְרוּ וּבִשְׁמִיעָה אַחַת נִשְׁמְעוּ: **כַּאֲשֶׁר צִוְּךָ.** קֹדֶם מַתַּן תּוֹרָה, בְּמָרָה:

טו **וְזָכַרְתָּ כִּי עֶבֶד הָיִיתָ וְגוֹ׳.** עַל מְנָת כֵּן פְּדָאֲךָ, שֶׁתִּהְיֶה לוֹ עֶבֶד וְתִשְׁמֹר מִצְוֹתָיו:

טז **כַּאֲשֶׁר צִוְּךָ.** אַף עַל כִּבּוּד אָב וָאֵם נִצְטַוּוּ בְּמָרָה, שֶׁנֶּאֱמַר: "שָׁם שָׂם לוֹ חֹק וּמִשְׁפָּט" (שמות טו, כה):

fuses theology, spirituality, morality, and law. The central emphasis is on society rather than the individual and his or her relationship with God. So in the first account of the Ten Commandments in the book of Exodus, the reason for keeping the Sabbath is because God created the universe in six days and rested on the seventh. In Deuteronomy, however, the Sabbath is given a quite different logic, namely the importance of freedom. The Sabbath is the ultimate expression of a free society, the antithesis of slavery in Egypt. On this day, all relationships of dominance and subordination are suspended. We may not work, or command others to work, "so that your male and female servants may rest as you do" (Deut. 5:14). At many times in history, people have dreamed of an ideal world. The name given to such visions is "utopia," meaning "no place," because at no time or place have these dreams been realized on a society-wide basis. The Sabbath is the sole successful utopian experiment in history. It is based on the simple idea that utopia (in Judaism, the Messianic age) is not solely in the future. It is something we can experience in the midst of time, one day in seven. The Sabbath became the weekly rehearsal of an ideal world, one not yet reached but still lived as a goal, of a world at peace with itself, recognizing the createdness, and thus the integrity, of all people and all forms of life. If Egypt meant slavery, the Sabbath is collective freedom, a "foretaste of the World to Come."

ח אֱלֹהִים אֲחֵרִים עַל־פָּנָי: לֹא־תַעֲשֶׂה לְךָ פֶסֶל כָּל־תְּמוּנָה אֲשֶׁר בַּשָּׁמַיִם
ט מִמַּעַל וַאֲשֶׁר בָּאָרֶץ מִתָּחַת וַאֲשֶׁר בַּמַּיִם מִתַּחַת לָאָרֶץ: לֹא־תִשְׁתַּחֲוֶה
לָהֶם וְלֹא תָעָבְדֵם כִּי אָנֹכִי יְהוָה אֱלֹהֶיךָ אֵל קַנָּא פֹּקֵד עֲוֺן אָבוֹת עַל־
י בָּנִים וְעַל־שִׁלֵּשִׁים וְעַל־רִבֵּעִים לְשֹׂנְאָי: וְעֹשֶׂה חֶסֶד לַאֲלָפִים לְאֹהֲבַי
יא וּלְשֹׁמְרֵי מצותו: לֹא תִשָּׂא אֶת־שֵׁם־יְהוָה אֱלֹהֶיךָ לַשָּׁוְא כִּי מִצְוֺתָי
יב לֹא יְנַקֶּה יְהוָה אֵת אֲשֶׁר־יִשָּׂא אֶת־שְׁמוֹ לַשָּׁוְא: שָׁמוֹר
יג אֶת־יוֹם הַשַּׁבָּת לְקַדְּשׁוֹ כַּאֲשֶׁר צִוְּךָ יְהוָה אֱלֹהֶיךָ: שֵׁשֶׁת יָמִים
יד תַּעֲבֹד וְעָשִׂיתָ כָּל־מְלַאכְתֶּךָ: וְיוֹם הַשְּׁבִיעִי שַׁבָּת לַיהוָה אֱלֹהֶיךָ
לֹא־תַעֲשֶׂה כָל־מְלָאכָה אַתָּה ׀ וּבִנְךָ־וּבִתֶּךָ וְעַבְדְּךָ־וַאֲמָתֶךָ וְשׁוֹרְךָ
וַחֲמֹרְךָ וְכָל־בְּהֶמְתֶּךָ וְגֵרְךָ אֲשֶׁר בִּשְׁעָרֶיךָ לְמַעַן יָנוּחַ עַבְדְּךָ וַאֲמָתְךָ
טו כָּמוֹךָ: וְזָכַרְתָּ כִּי עֶבֶד הָיִיתָ בְּאֶרֶץ מִצְרַיִם וַיֹּצִאֲךָ יְהוָה אֱלֹהֶיךָ מִשָּׁם
בְּיָד חֲזָקָה וּבִזְרֹעַ נְטוּיָה עַל־כֵּן צִוְּךָ יְהוָה אֱלֹהֶיךָ לַעֲשׂוֹת אֶת־יוֹם
טז הַשַּׁבָּת: כַּבֵּד אֶת־אָבִיךָ וְאֶת־אִמֶּךָ כַּאֲשֶׁר צִוְּךָ יְהוָה אֱלֹהֶיךָ
לְמַעַן ׀ יַאֲרִיכֻן יָמֶיךָ וּלְמַעַן יִיטַב לָךְ עַל הָאֲדָמָה אֲשֶׁר־יְהוָה אֱלֹהֶיךָ

אונקלוס

אֱלָהּ אָחֳרָן בַּר מִנִּי: ח לָא תַעֲבֵיד לָךְ צְלֵם כָּל דְּמוּ, דְּבִשְׁמַיָּא מִלְּעֵילָא וּדְבְאַרְעָא מִלְּרַע, וּדְבְמַיָּא מִלְּרַע לְאַרְעָא: ט לָא תִסְגּוּד לְהוֹן וְלָא תִפְלְחִנּוּן, אֲרֵי אֲנָא, יי אֱלָהָךְ אֵל קַנָּא, מַסְעַר, חוֹבֵי אֲבָהָן עַל בְּנִין מָרָדִין, וְעַל דָּר תְּלִיתַאי וְעַל דָּר רְבִיעַאי לְסָנְאַי, כַּד מַשְׁלְמִין בְּנַיָּא לְמֶחְטֵי בָּתַר אֲבָהָתְהוֹן: י וְעָבֵיד טֵיבוּ לְאַלְפֵי דָרִין, לְרָחֲמַי וּלְנָטְרֵי פִקּוֹדָי: יא לָא תֵימֵי, בִּשְׁמָא דַּיי אֱלָהָךְ לְמַגָּנָא, אֲרֵי לָא יְזַכֵּי יי, יָת, דְּיֵימֵי בִשְׁמֵיהּ לְשִׁקְרָא: יב טַר יָת יוֹמָא דְשַׁבְּתָא לְקַדָּשׁוּתֵיהּ, כְּמָא דְפַקְדָךְ יי אֱלָהָךְ: יג שִׁתָּא יוֹמִין תִּפְלַח וְתַעֲבֵיד כָּל עֲבִידְתָךְ: יד וְיוֹמָא שְׁבִיעָאָה, שַׁבְּתָא קֳדָם יי אֱלָהָךְ, לָא תַעֲבֵיד כָּל עֲבִידָא, אַתְּ וּבְרָךְ וּבְרַתָּךְ וְעַבְדָּךְ וְאַמְתָךְ, וְתוֹרָךְ וּחְמָרָךְ וְכָל בְּעִירָךְ, וְגִיּוֹרָךְ דִּבְקִרְוָךְ, בְּדִיל, דִּינוּחַ, עַבְדָּךְ וְאַמְתָךְ כְּוָתָךְ: טו וְתִדְכַּר, אֲרֵי עַבְדָּא הֲוֵיתָא בְּאַרְעָא דְמִצְרַיִם, וְאַפְּקָךְ יי אֱלָהָךְ מִתַּמָּן בְּיַד תַּקִּיפָא וּבִדְרָע מְרָמַם, עַל כֵּן, פַּקְדָךְ יי אֱלָהָךְ, לְמֶעְבַּד יָת יוֹמָא דְשַׁבְּתָא: טז יַקַּר יָת אֲבוּךְ וְיָת אִמָּךְ, כְּמָא דְפַקְדָךְ יי אֱלָהָךְ, בְּדִיל דְּיֵירְכוּן יוֹמָךְ, וּבְדִיל דְּיֵיטַב לָךְ, עַל אַרְעָא, דַּיי אֱלָהָךְ

Rambam, the philosopher, emphasized the universal, metaphysical aspect of Judaism and the eternal, unchanging existence of God. Yehuda HaLevi, the poet, was more attuned to the particularistic and prophetic dimension of Judaism: the role of God in the historical drama of the Jewish people.

5:14 לֹא־תַעֲשֶׂה כָל־מְלָאכָה *Do no work at all* – Deuteronomy

17 giving you. Do not murder. Do not
commit adultery. Do not steal. Do not
18 bear false witness against your neighbor. Do not
crave your neighbor's wife. Do not
set your desire on your neighbor's house, or field, or male or female servant,
19 his ox, his donkey, or anything else that is your neighbor's. The Lord HAMISHI
spoke these words with a loud voice to your whole assembly at the mountain
from amid the fire, cloud, and thick darkness, and He added no more. And He
20 wrote them on two stone tablets, and gave them to me. When you heard the
voice out of the darkness, while the mountain was ablaze with fire, your tribal
21 leaders and elders came to me; they said, 'The Lord our God has shown us
His glory and greatness – we have heard His voice from within the fire. Today
22 we have seen that God may speak to a person and that person still live. But
now, must we die? For this great fire will consume us. If we hear the voice of
23 the Lord our God for any longer, we will die. For what mortal has heard the
voice of the Living God speaking from within the fire, as we have, and yet
24 lived? You go near and listen to all that the Lord our God says. Then tell us all
25 that the Lord our God tells you, and we will heed and do it.' The Lord heard

רש״י

יז **וְלֹא תִנְאָף.** אֵין לְשׁוֹן נִאוּף אֶלָּא בְּאֵשֶׁת אִישׁ:

יח **לֹא תִתְאַוֶּה.** "לָא תֵרוֹג", אַף הוּא לְשׁוֹן חֶמְדָּה, כְּמוֹ "נֶחְמָד לְמַרְאֶה" (בראשית ב, ט) דְּמְתַרְגְּמִינַן: "דִּמְרַגַּג לְמִחְזֵי":

יט **וְלֹא יָסָף.** מְתַרְגְּמִינַן "וְלָא פָסִיק", כִּי קוֹלוֹ חָזָק וְקַיָּם לְעוֹלָם. דָּבָר אַחֵר, "וְלֹא יָסָף", לֹא הוֹסִיף לְהֵרָאוֹת בְּאוֹתוֹ פֻּמְבֵּי:

כד **וְאַתְּ תְּדַבֵּר אֵלֵינוּ.** הִתַּשְׁתֶּם אֶת כֹּחִי כִּנְקֵבָה, שֶׁנִּצְטַעַרְתִּי עֲלֵיכֶם וְרִפִּיתֶם אֶת יָדַי, כִּי רָאִיתִי שֶׁאֵינְכֶם חֲרֵדִים לְהִתְקָרֵב אֵלָיו מֵאַהֲבָה. וְכִי לֹא הָיָה יָפֶה לָכֶם לִלְמֹד מִפִּי הַגְּבוּרָה וְלֹא לִלְמֹד מִמֶּנִּי?:

5:19 **וְלֹא יָסָף** *And He added no more* – What was unique, transfiguring, and still hard to understand about this event was that the nation, as a nation, heard the voice of God. God spoke – not just to a prophet, not in a vision or a trance, not as a sound within the soul, but as an event in public space and time. It was a *kol gadol velo yasaf*, a phrase for which Rashi (ad loc.) offers two understandings: a great voice that was never heard again, and a great voice that was ever heard again – it happened once but it reverberated for all time.

How do we reconcile Rashi's two interpretations of this phrase? Note that the wording of the Ten Commandments in Exodus and Deuteronomy is not identical. The first represents the direct revelation at Sinai. In the second, here, Moshe cites the second tablets – the ones he engraved after breaking the first on seeing the golden calf. The second, carved out on the mountain by Moshe's hand, came together with *Torah Shebe'al Peh*, the Oral Law.

We can now grasp how the revelation can be a great voice that happened once and never again and a great voice that never stopped. The voice that was heard once was the Written Torah; the great voice that never ceased was the Oral Torah. The covenant laid out in Deuteronomy is based on a three-thousand-year-old conversation between Israel and God; not only a single revelation, but a voice that resonated forevermore.

יז נָתַן לָךְ׃ לֹא תִרְצָח וְלֹא
תִנְאָף וְלֹא תִגְנֹב וְלֹא־
יח תַעֲנֶה בְרֵעֲךָ עֵד שָׁוְא׃ וְלֹא
תַחְמֹד אֵשֶׁת רֵעֶךָ וְלֹא
תִתְאַוֶּה בֵּית רֵעֶךָ שָׂדֵהוּ וְעַבְדּוֹ וַאֲמָתוֹ שׁוֹרוֹ וַחֲמֹרוֹ וְכֹל אֲשֶׁר
יט לְרֵעֶךָ׃ אֶת־הַדְּבָרִים הָאֵלֶּה דִּבֶּר יהוה אֶל־כָּל־קְהַלְכֶם חמישי
בָּהָר מִתּוֹךְ הָאֵשׁ הֶעָנָן וְהָעֲרָפֶל קוֹל גָּדוֹל וְלֹא יָסָף וַיִּכְתְּבֵם עַל־שְׁנֵי
כ לֻחֹת אֲבָנִים וַיִּתְּנֵם אֵלָי׃ וַיְהִי כְּשָׁמְעֲכֶם אֶת־הַקּוֹל מִתּוֹךְ הַחֹשֶׁךְ וְהָהָר
כא בֹּעֵר בָּאֵשׁ וַתִּקְרְבוּן אֵלַי כָּל־רָאשֵׁי שִׁבְטֵיכֶם וְזִקְנֵיכֶם׃ וַתֹּאמְרוּ הֵן
הֶרְאָנוּ יהוה אֱלֹהֵינוּ אֶת־כְּבֹדוֹ וְאֶת־גָּדְלוֹ וְאֶת־קֹלוֹ שָׁמַעְנוּ מִתּוֹךְ
כב הָאֵשׁ הַיּוֹם הַזֶּה רָאִינוּ כִּי־יְדַבֵּר אֱלֹהִים אֶת־הָאָדָם וָחָי׃ וְעַתָּה לָמָּה
נָמוּת כִּי תֹאכְלֵנוּ הָאֵשׁ הַגְּדֹלָה הַזֹּאת אִם־יֹסְפִים ׀ אֲנַחְנוּ לִשְׁמֹעַ
כג אֶת־קוֹל יהוה אֱלֹהֵינוּ עוֹד וָמָתְנוּ׃ כִּי מִי כָל־בָּשָׂר אֲשֶׁר שָׁמַע קוֹל
כד אֱלֹהִים חַיִּים מְדַבֵּר מִתּוֹךְ־הָאֵשׁ כָּמֹנוּ וַיֶּחִי׃ קְרַב אַתָּה וּשְׁמָע אֵת
כָּל־אֲשֶׁר יֹאמַר יהוה אֱלֹהֵינוּ וְאַתְּ ׀ תְּדַבֵּר אֵלֵינוּ אֵת כָּל־אֲשֶׁר יְדַבֵּר
כה יהוה אֱלֹהֵינוּ אֵלֶיךָ וְשָׁמַעְנוּ וְעָשִׂינוּ׃ וַיִּשְׁמַע יהוה אֶת־קוֹל דִּבְרֵיכֶם

אונקלוס

יְהֵיב לָךְ: יז לָא תִקְטוֹל נְפַשׁ, וְלָא תְגוּף, וְלָא תִגְנוּב, וְלָא תַסְהֵיד בְּחַבְרָךְ סָהֲדוּתָא דְשִׁקְרָא: יח וְלָא תַחְמֵיד אִתַּת חַבְרָךְ, וְלָא תֵירוֹג בֵּית חַבְרָךְ, חַקְלֵיהּ, וְעַבְדֵּיהּ וְאַמְתֵיהּ תּוֹרֵיהּ וּחְמָרֵיהּ, וְכֹל דִּלְחַבְרָךְ: יט יָת פִּתְגָמַיָּא הָאִלֵּין, מַלֵּיל יְיָ עִם כָּל קְהָלְכוֹן בְּטוּרָא, מִגּוֹ אִישָׁתָא עֲנָנָא וַאֲמִטְתָא, קָל רַב וְלָא פְסֵיק, וּכְתַבְנוּן, עַל תְּרֵין לוּחֵי אַבְנַיָּא, וִיהַבְנוּן לִי: כ וַהֲוָה, בְּמִשְׁמַעְכוֹן יָת קָלָא מִגּוֹ חֲשׁוֹכָא, וְטוּרָא בָּעַר בְּאִישָׁתָא, וּקְרֵיבְתּוּן לְוָתִי, כָּל רֵישֵׁי שִׁבְטֵיכוֹן וְסָבֵיכוֹן: כא וַאֲמַרְתּוּן, הָא אַחְזְיַנָא, יְיָ אֱלָהַנָא יָת יְקָרֵיהּ וְיָת רְבוּתֵיהּ, וְיָת קָל מֵימְרֵיהּ שְׁמַעְנָא מִגּוֹ אִישָׁתָא, יוֹמָא הָדֵין חֲזֵינָא, אֲרֵי מְמַלֵּיל יְיָ, עִם אֱנָשָׁא וּמִתְקַיַּם: כב וּכְעַן לְמָא נְמוּת, אֲרֵי תֵיכְלִנַּנָא, אִישָׁתָא רַבְּתָא הָדָא, אִם מוֹסְפִין אֲנַחְנָא, לְמִשְׁמַע, יָת קָל מֵימְרָא דַּייָ אֱלָהַנָא, עוֹד מָיְתִין אֲנַחְנָא: כג אֲרֵי מָאן כָּל בִּסְרָא, דִּשְׁמַע קָל מֵימְרָא דַּייָ קַיָּמָא, מְמַלֵּיל מִגּוֹ אִישָׁתָא, כְּוָתַנָא וְאִתְקַיַּם: כד קְרַב אַתְּ וּשְׁמַע, יָת כָּל דְּיֵימַר יְיָ אֱלָהַנָא, וְאַתְּ תְּמַלֵּיל עִמַּנָא, יָת כָּל דִּימַלֵּיל, יְיָ אֱלָהַנָא, עִמָּךְ וּנְקַבֵּיל וְנַעֲבֵיד: כה וּשְׁמִיעַ קֳדָם יְיָ יָת קָל פִּתְגָמֵיכוֹן,

your words when you spoke to me, and to me the Lord said: 'I have heard the
26 words this people have spoken to you; they did well to speak as they did. If only
they would have such a mind as this always, to hold Me in awe and to keep all
My commandments, so that it might be well for them and for their children
27 28 forever! Go, tell them to go back to their tents. But you stay here by Me, and
I will tell you all the commandments, decrees, and laws that you shall teach
them, so that they may keep them in the land that I am giving them to possess.'
29 Take care to do as the Lord your God has commanded you; do not turn aside –
30 neither to the right nor to the left. Follow only the path that the Lord your
God has commanded you, so that you may live and it may be well for you, and
6 1 your years may be long in the land you are to possess. This is the command –
the decrees and the laws – that the Lord your God charged me to teach you to
2 keep in the land that you are about to cross over into and take possession of, so
that you and your children and grandchildren may remain in awe of the Lord
your God as long as you live, keeping all His decrees and commandments that
3 I am commanding you and so that your years may be long. Listen, Israel, and
take care to keep them, so that it may be well for you, and so that you may be
abundantly fertile in a land flowing with milk and with honey, as the Lord, the
God of your ancestors, promised you.
4 5 Listen, Israel: the Lord our God – the Lord is one. You shall love the Lord SHISHI

רש״י

ו ד **ה׳ אֱלֹהֵינוּ ה׳ אֶחָד.** ה׳ שֶׁהוּא "אֱלֹהֵינוּ" עַתָּה וְלֹא אֱלֹהֵי הָאֻמּוֹת, הוּא עָתִיד לִהְיוֹת "ה׳ אֶחָד", שֶׁנֶּאֱמַר: "כִּי אָז אֶהְפֹּךְ אֶל עַמִּים שָׂפָה בְרוּרָה לִקְרֹא כֻלָּם בְּשֵׁם ה׳" (צפניה ג, ט), וְנֶאֱמַר: "בַּיּוֹם הַהוּא יִהְיֶה ה׳ אֶחָד וּשְׁמוֹ אֶחָד" (זכריה יד, ט):

ה **וְאָהַבְתָּ.** עֲשֵׂה דְּבָרָיו מֵאַהֲבָה. אֵינוֹ דוֹמֶה עוֹשֶׂה מֵאַהֲבָה לְעוֹשֶׂה מִיִּרְאָה. הָעוֹשֶׂה אֵצֶל רַבּוֹ מִיִּרְאָה כְּשֶׁהוּא מַטְרִיחַ עָלָיו מַנִּיחוֹ וְהוֹלֵךְ לוֹ:

LISTEN

"Listen, Israel, the Lord our God – the Lord is one." These words are the supreme testimony of Jewish faith. The keyword of Judaism is *Shema*. God is not something we see, but a voice we hear (see above, 4:12 and note there) The patriarchs and prophets did not see God; they heard Him.

This has implications for the whole of Judaism. It is a way of understanding the world. Judaism, with its belief in the invisible God who transcends the universe, and its prohibition against visual representations of God, is supremely a civilization of the ear. To give dramatic force to the idea that God is heard, not seen, we cover our eyes with our hand as we say these words.

The verb *lishmoa* is a key term of the book of Deuteronomy, where it appears in one or other form some ninety-two times. It conveys a wide range of meanings, clustered around five primary senses:

1. To listen, to pay focused attention, as in "Be still and listen (*u'shema*), Israel" (Deut. 27:9)

בְּדַבֶּרְכֶ֖ם אֵלָ֑י וַיֹּ֨אמֶר יְהוָ֜ה אֵלַ֗י שָׁ֠מַעְתִּי אֶת־ק֨וֹל דִּבְרֵ֜י הָעָ֤ם הַזֶּה֙
כו אֲשֶׁ֣ר דִּבְּר֣וּ אֵלֶ֔יךָ הֵיטִ֖יבוּ כׇּל־אֲשֶׁ֥ר דִּבֵּֽרוּ׃ מִֽי־יִתֵּ֡ן וְהָיָה֩ לְבָבָ֨ם זֶ֜ה
לָהֶ֗ם לְיִרְאָ֥ה אֹתִ֛י וְלִשְׁמֹ֥ר אֶת־כׇּל־מִצְוֺתַ֖י כׇּל־הַיָּמִ֑ים לְמַ֨עַן יִיטַ֥ב
כז כח לָהֶ֛ם וְלִבְנֵיהֶ֖ם לְעֹלָֽם׃ לֵ֖ךְ אֱמֹ֣ר לָהֶ֑ם שׁ֥וּבוּ לָכֶ֖ם לְאׇהֳלֵיכֶֽם׃ וְאַתָּ֗ה
פֹּה֮ עֲמֹ֣ד עִמָּדִי֒ וַאֲדַבְּרָ֣ה אֵלֶ֗יךָ אֵ֤ת כׇּל־הַמִּצְוָה֙ וְהַחֻקִּ֣ים וְהַמִּשְׁפָּטִ֔ים
כט אֲשֶׁ֥ר תְּלַמְּדֵ֖ם וְעָשׂ֣וּ בָאָ֔רֶץ אֲשֶׁ֧ר אָנֹכִ֛י נֹתֵ֥ן לָהֶ֖ם לְרִשְׁתָּֽהּ׃ וּשְׁמַרְתֶּ֣ם
לַעֲשׂ֔וֹת כַּאֲשֶׁ֥ר צִוָּ֛ה יְהוָ֥ה אֱלֹהֵיכֶ֖ם אֶתְכֶ֑ם לֹ֥א תָסֻ֖רוּ יָמִ֥ין וּשְׂמֹֽאל׃
ל בְּכׇל־הַדֶּ֗רֶךְ אֲשֶׁ֨ר צִוָּ֜ה יְהוָ֧ה אֱלֹהֵיכֶ֛ם אֶתְכֶ֖ם תֵּלֵ֑כוּ לְמַ֤עַן תִּֽחְיוּן֙ וְט֣וֹב
ו א לָכֶ֔ם וְהַאַרַכְתֶּ֣ם יָמִ֔ים בָּאָ֖רֶץ אֲשֶׁ֥ר תִּירָשֽׁוּן׃ וְזֹ֣את הַמִּצְוָ֗ה הַֽחֻקִּים֙
וְהַמִּשְׁפָּטִ֔ים אֲשֶׁ֥ר צִוָּ֛ה יְהוָ֥ה אֱלֹהֵיכֶ֖ם לְלַמֵּ֣ד אֶתְכֶ֑ם לַעֲשׂ֣וֹת בָּאָ֔רֶץ
ב אֲשֶׁ֥ר אַתֶּ֛ם עֹבְרִ֥ים שָׁ֖מָּה לְרִשְׁתָּֽהּ׃ לְמַ֨עַן תִּירָ֜א אֶת־יְהוָ֣ה אֱלֹהֶ֗יךָ
לִ֠שְׁמֹר אֶת־כׇּל־חֻקֹּתָ֣יו וּמִצְוֺתָיו֮ אֲשֶׁ֣ר אָנֹכִ֣י מְצַוֶּךָ֒ אַתָּה֙ וּבִנְךָ֣ וּבֶן־בִּנְךָ֔
ג כֹּ֖ל יְמֵ֣י חַיֶּ֑יךָ וּלְמַ֖עַן יַאֲרִכֻ֥ן יָמֶֽיךָ׃ וְשָׁמַעְתָּ֤ יִשְׂרָאֵל֙ וְשָׁמַרְתָּ֣ לַעֲשׂ֔וֹת
אֲשֶׁר֙ יִיטַ֣ב לְךָ֔ וַאֲשֶׁ֥ר תִּרְבּ֖וּן מְאֹ֑ד כַּאֲשֶׁ֨ר דִּבֶּ֜ר יְהוָ֨ה אֱלֹהֵ֤י אֲבֹתֶ֙יךָ֙
לָ֔ךְ אֶ֛רֶץ זָבַ֥ת חָלָ֖ב וּדְבָֽשׁ׃
ד ה שְׁמַ֖ע יִשְׂרָאֵ֑ל יְהוָ֥ה אֱלֹהֵ֖ינוּ יְהוָ֥ה ׀ אֶחָֽד׃ וְאָ֣הַבְתָּ֔ אֵ֖ת יְהוָ֣ה ׀ ששי

אונקלוס

בְּמַלָּלוּתְכוֹן עִמִּי, וַאֲמַר יי לִי, שְׁמִיעַ קֳדָמַי, יָת קָל פִּתְגָמֵי, עַמָּא הָדֵין דְּמַלִּילוּ עִמָּךְ, אַתְקִינוּ כָּל דְּמַלִּילוּ: כו לְוַי, דִּיהֵי לִבָּא הָדֵין לְהוֹן, לְמִדְחַל קֳדָמַי, וּלְמִטַּר יָת כָּל פִּקּוֹדַי כָּל יוֹמַיָּא, בְּדִיל דְּיֵיטַב לְהוֹן, וְלִבְנֵיהוֹן לְעָלַם: כז אִיזֵיל אֵימַר לְהוֹן, תּוּבוּ לְכוֹן לְמַשְׁכְּנֵיכוֹן: כח וְאַתְּ, הָכָא קוּם קֳדָמַי, וַאֲמַלֵּיל עִמָּךְ, יָת כָּל תַּפְקֵידְתָּא, וּקְיָמַיָּא וְדִינַיָּא דְּתַלְּפִנּוּן, וְיַעְבְּדוּן בְּאַרְעָא, דַּאֲנָא, יָהֵיב לְהוֹן לְמֵירְתַהּ: כט וְתִטְּרוּן לְמֶעְבַּד, כְּמָא דְּפַקֵּיד, יי אֱלָהֲכוֹן יָתְכוֹן, לָא תִסְטוּן לְיַמִּינָא וְלִסְמָאלָא: ל בְּכָל אוֹרְחָא, דְּפַקֵּיד, יי אֱלָהֲכוֹן, יָתְכוֹן תְּהָכוּן, בְּדִיל דְּתֵיחוֹן וְיֵיטַב לְכוֹן, וְתֵירְכוּן יוֹמִין, בְּאַרְעָא דְּתֵירְתוּן: ו א וְדָא תַּפְקֵידְתָּא, קְיָמַיָּא וְדִינַיָּא, דְּפַקֵּיד, יי אֱלָהֲכוֹן לְאַלָּפָא יָתְכוֹן, לְמֶעְבַּד בְּאַרְעָא, דְּאַתּוּן, עָבְרִין לְתַמָּן לְמֵירְתַהּ: ב בְּדִיל דְּתִדְחַל קֳדָם יי אֱלָהָךְ, לְמִטַּר, יָת כָּל קְיָמוֹהִי וּפִקּוֹדוֹהִי דַּאֲנָא מְפַקֵּיד לָךְ, אַתְּ וּבְרָךְ וּבַר בְּרָךְ, כֹּל יוֹמֵי חַיָּךְ, וּבְדִיל דְּיֵירְכוּן יוֹמָךְ: ג וּתְקַבֵּיל יִשְׂרָאֵל וְתִטַּר לְמֶעְבַּד, דְּיֵיטַב לָךְ, וּדְתִסְגּוֹן לַחְדָּא, כְּמָא דְּמַלֵּיל יי, אֱלָהָא דַּאֲבָהָתָךְ לָךְ, אֲרַע, עָבְדָא חֲלַב וּדְבַשׁ: ד שְׁמַע יִשְׂרָאֵל, יי אֱלָהַנָא יי חַד: ה וְתִרְחַם, יָת יי

6 your God with all your heart, with all your soul, and with all your might. Let
these words that I charge you with today remain impressed upon your heart.
7 Teach them to your children, speaking of them when you sit at home and when

רש״י

בְּכָל לְבָבְךָ. בִּשְׁנֵי יְצָרֶיךָ. דָּבָר אַחֵר, "בְּכָל לְבָבְךָ", שֶׁלֹּא יְהֵא לִבְּךָ חָלוּק עַל הַמָּקוֹם: **וּבְכָל נַפְשְׁךָ.** אֲפִלּוּ הוּא נוֹטֵל אֶת נַפְשְׁךָ: **וּבְכָל מְאֹדֶךָ.** בְּכָל מָמוֹנְךָ, יֵשׁ לְךָ אָדָם שֶׁמָּמוֹנוֹ חָבִיב עָלָיו מִגּוּפוֹ, לְכָךְ נֶאֱמַר: "בְּכָל מְאֹדֶךָ". דָּבָר אַחֵר, "וּבְכָל מְאֹדֶךָ", בְּכָל מִדָּה וּמִדָּה שֶׁמּוֹדֵד לְךָ, בֵּין בְּמִדָּה טוֹבָה בֵּין בְּמִדַּת פֻּרְעָנוּת, וְכֵן דָּוִד הוּא אוֹמֵר: "כּוֹס יְשׁוּעוֹת אֶשָּׂא וּבְשֵׁם ה' אֶקְרָא" (תהלים קטז, יג) "צָרָה וְיָגוֹן אֶמְצָא וּבְשֵׁם ה' אֶקְרָא" (שם פסוקים ג-ד):

ו **וְהָיוּ הַדְּבָרִים.** מַהוּ הָאַהֲבָה? "וְהָיוּ הַדְּבָרִים הָאֵלֶּה", שֶׁמִּתּוֹךְ כָּךְ אַתָּה מַכִּיר בְּהַקָּדוֹשׁ בָּרוּךְ הוּא וּמִדַּבֵּק בִּדְרָכָיו: **אֲשֶׁר אָנֹכִי מְצַוְּךָ הַיּוֹם.** לֹא יִהְיוּ בְעֵינֶיךָ כְּדְיוֹטַגְמָא יְשָׁנָה שֶׁאֵין אָדָם סוֹפְנָהּ, אֶלָּא כַּחֲדָשָׁה שֶׁהַכֹּל רָצִין לִקְרָאתָהּ. 'דְּיוֹטַגְמָא' – מִצְוַת הַמֶּלֶךְ הַבָּאָה בְּמִכְתָּב:

ז **וְשִׁנַּנְתָּם.** לְשׁוֹן חִדּוּד הוּא, שֶׁיִּהְיוּ מְחֻדָּדִים בְּפִיךָ, שֶׁאִם יִשְׁאָלְךָ אָדָם דָּבָר לֹא תְהֵא צָרִיךְ לְגַמְגֵּם בּוֹ, אֶלָּא אֱמֹר לוֹ מִיָּד: **לְבָנֶיךָ.** אֵלּוּ הַתַּלְמִידִים. מָצִינוּ בְּכָל מָקוֹם שֶׁהַתַּלְמִידִים קְרוּיִים בָּנִים, שֶׁנֶּאֱמַר: "בָּנִים אַתֶּם לַה' אֱלֹהֵיכֶם" (להלן יד, א), וְאוֹמֵר: "בְּנֵי הַנְּבִיאִים אֲשֶׁר בֵּית אֵל" (מלכים ב' ב, ג), וְכֵן בְּחִזְקִיָּהוּ שֶׁלִּמֵּד תּוֹרָה לְכָל יִשְׂרָאֵל וּקְרָאָם בָּנִים, שֶׁנֶּאֱמַר: "בָּנַי עַתָּה אַל תִּשָּׁלוּ" (דברי הימים ב' כט, יא). וּכְשֵׁם שֶׁהַתַּלְמִידִים קְרוּיִים בָּנִים, כָּךְ הָרַב קָרוּי אָב, שֶׁנֶּאֱמַר: "אָבִי אָבִי רֶכֶב יִשְׂרָאֵל" וְגוֹ' (מלכים ב' ב, יב): **וְדִבַּרְתָּ בָּם.** שֶׁלֹּא יְהֵא עִקַּר דִּבּוּרְךָ אֶלָּא בָּם, עֲשֵׂם

How is this vision connected to the legal, halakhic content of much of Deuteronomy? On the one hand we have this passionate declaration of love by God for a people; on the other we have a detailed code of law covering most aspects of life for individuals and the nation as a whole once it enters the land. Law and love are not two things that go obviously together. What has the one to do with the other?

Commitment is falling in love with something and then building a structure of behavior around it to sustain that love over time. Law, the mitzvot, halakha, is that structure of behavior. Love is a passion, an emotion, a heightened state, a peak experience. But an emotional state cannot be guaranteed forever. We wed in poetry but we stay married in prose. Which is why we need laws, rituals, habits of deed. Rituals are the framework that keeps love alive. That is what the vast multiplicity of rituals in Judaism, many of them spelled out in the book of Deuteronomy, actually achieved. They sustained the love between God and a people. Could it have been done without the rituals, the 613 commands, that fill our days with reminders of God's presence? I think not. Without the rituals, eventually love dies. With them, the glowing embers remain and still have the power to burst into flame. Not every day in a long and happy marriage feels like a wedding, but even love grown old will still be strong, if the choreography of fond devotion, the ritual courtesies and kindnesses, are sustained. Jewish law is the structure of behavior built around the love between God and His people, so that the love remains long after the first feelings of passion have grown old.

6:5 בְּכָל־לְבָבְךָ *With all your heart* – It is said that the Rebbe Menachem Mendel of Kotzk once asked his disciples, "Where does God live?" The disciples were perplexed. "What does the Rebbe mean, where does God live? Where does God not live? Surely we have been taught that no place is devoid of His presence? He fills the heavens and the earth." The Rebbe replied, "You have not understood. God lives *where we let Him in*."

On another occasion, he asked, "Why does it say in the *Shema*: 'Let these words…remain impressed upon your heart'? Why 'upon' and not 'in'?" He answered: "The heart is not always open. Therefore the Torah says: Lay these words *on* your heart, so that when your heart opens, they will be there, ready to fall in." In Judaism, spirituality means openness. To one who is open, God is closer than we are to ourselves. To one who is closed, He is farther away than the most distant galaxies. A question, asked with sincerity, is an opening in the soul. The task of education is to teach a child to be open – to the voice of God and the miracle of existence.

6:6 עַל־לְבָבֶךָ *Impressed upon your heart* – The ideal polity, so the Torah implies, is *nomocracy*: the rule not of men or women, but of law – not law carved in stone or written on scrolls but law engraved in the hearts of the people:

ו אֱלֹהֶיךָ בְּכָל־לְבָבְךָ וּבְכָל־נַפְשְׁךָ וּבְכָל־מְאֹדֶךָ: וְהָיוּ הַדְּבָרִים הָאֵלֶּה
ז אֲשֶׁר אָנֹכִי מְצַוְּךָ הַיּוֹם עַל־לְבָבֶךָ: וְשִׁנַּנְתָּם לְבָנֶיךָ וְדִבַּרְתָּ בָּם

אונקלוס

אֱלָהָךְ, בְּכָל לִבָּךְ וּבְכָל נַפְשָׁךְ וּבְכָל נִכְסָךְ: ו וִיהוֹן פִּתְגָמַיָּא הָאִלֵּין, דַּאֲנָא מְפַקֵּיד לָךְ, יוֹמָא דֵין עַל לִבָּךְ: ז וּתְתַנֵּינוּן לִבְנָךְ, וּתְמַלֵּיל בְּהוֹן,

2. To hear, as in "I heard (*shamati*) Your voice in the garden and I was afraid" (Gen. 3:10)
3. To understand, as in "Let us go down and confuse their language so that one will not understand (*yishme'u*) the speech of another" (11:7)
4. To internalize, register, take to heart, as in "As for Yishmael – I have heard you" (17:20), meaning, "I have taken into account what you have said; I will bear it in mind; it is a consideration that weighs with Me"
5. To respond in action, as in "Avram listened (*vayishma*) to Sarai" (16:2). This last sense is the closest *shema* comes to meaning "to obey."

It has yet other meanings in Rabbinic Hebrew, such as "to infer," "to accept," "to take into account as evidence," and "to receive as part of the Oral Tradition." No English word has this range of meanings. Perhaps the closest are "to hearken" and "to heed" – neither of them terms in common use today.

Shema Yisrael, then, does not mean "Hear, Israel." It means something like: "Listen. Concentrate. Give the word of God your most focused attention. Strive to understand. Engage all your faculties, intellectual and emotional. Make His will your own. For what He commands you to do is not irrational or arbitrary but for your welfare, the welfare of your people, and ultimately for the benefit of all humanity."

In Judaism, faith is a form of listening – to the song creation sings to its Creator, and to the message history delivers to those who strive to understand it. That is what Moshe says time and again in Deuteronomy: Stop looking; listen. Stop speaking; listen. Create a silence in the soul. Still the clamor of instinct, desire, fear, anger. Strive to listen to the still, small voice beneath the noise. Then you will know that the universe is the work of the One beyond the furthest star yet closer to you than you are to yourself – and then you will love your God with all your heart, all your soul, and all your might. In God's unity you will find unity, within yourself and between yourself and the world, and you will no longer fear the unknown.

6:4 יהוה אֶחָד *The Lord is one* – This sentence, the heart of Jewish faith, has two distinct meanings. As translated above, it is a theological statement of monotheism: there is but a single God. Equally, though, it can be translated as "Listen, Israel, the Lord is our God, the Lord alone," in which case it is the proclamation of God as the sole sovereign of the people Israel, what the Sages called *kabbalat ol malkhut Shamayim*, "acceptance of the yoke of the kingdom of Heaven," a theological-political statement of Israel as a nation under divine sovereignty. This is how the text is used in our daily prayers.

The words of the *Shema* are the first Hebrew words we learn as children, and the last words we say at the end of our life, the words Jewish martyrs said as they prepared to die for their faith. In these contexts they mean more than that God is One. You, God of the universe, are our God. We have no other. Our ancestors put their faith in You. We put our faith in You. You are the focus of our lives. You are the breath we breathe, the strength we feel, the voice we hear, the horizon of our hopes.

LOVE

Judaism is built around an act of mutual commitment, by God to a people and by the people to God. The commitment itself is an act of love. These famous words, "You shall love the Lord your God with all your heart, with all your soul, and with all your might" (Deut. 6:5), lie at its heart. The Torah is the foundational narrative of the fraught, sometimes tempestuous, marriage between God and an often obstinate people. It is a story of love.

8 you travel on the way, when you lie down and when you rise. Bind them as a
9 sign upon your hand, and have them as an emblem between your eyes. Write
10 them on the doorposts of your houses and on your gates. When the
LORD your God brings you into the land that He swore to your ancestors
Avraham, Yitzhak, and Yaakov that He would give to you, a land with great
11 and goodly towns you did not build, houses full of all good things that you did
not provide, hewn cisterns you did not hew, and vineyards and olive groves
12 that you did not plant – and you eat and are satisfied, take care that you do
not forget the LORD who brought you out of Egypt, out of the house of slaves.
13 It is the LORD your God you must revere, Him you must serve, and only by
14 His name that you must swear. Do not walk after other gods, after gods of the
15 peoples around you, for the LORD your God in your midst demands absolute
loyalty. The anger of the LORD your God would burn against you and He would

רש״י

עִקָּר וְאַל תַּעֲשֵׂם טָפֵל: **וּבְשָׁכְבְּךָ.** יָכוֹל אֲפִלּוּ שָׁכַב בַּחֲצִי הַיּוֹם? תַּלְמוּד לוֹמַר: ״וּבְלֶכְתְּךָ בַדֶּרֶךְ״, דֶּרֶךְ אֶרֶץ דִּבְּרָה תוֹרָה, זְמַן שְׁכִיבָה וּזְמַן קִימָה:

ח **וּקְשַׁרְתָּם לְאוֹת עַל יָדֶךָ.** אֵלּוּ תְּפִלִּין שֶׁבַּזְּרוֹעַ: **וְהָיוּ לְטֹטָפֹת בֵּין עֵינֶיךָ.** אֵלּוּ תְּפִלִּין שֶׁבָּרֹאשׁ. וְעַל שֵׁם מִנְיַן פָּרְשִׁיּוֹתֵיהֶם נִקְרְאוּ טוֹטָפֹת, ׳טַט׳ בְּכַתְפֵּי שְׁתַּיִם, ׳פַּת׳ בְּאַפְרִיקֵי שְׁתַּיִם:

ט **מְזֻזֹת בֵּיתֶךָ.** ׳מְזוּזַת׳ כְּתִיב, שֶׁאֵין צָרִיךְ אֶלָּא אַחַת: **וּבִשְׁעָרֶיךָ.** לְרַבּוֹת שַׁעֲרֵי חֲצֵרוֹת וְשַׁעֲרֵי מְדִינוֹת וְשַׁעֲרֵי עֲיָרוֹת:

יא **חֲצוּבִים.** לְפִי שֶׁהָיוּ מְקוֹם טְרָשִׁין וּסְלָעִים נוֹפֵל בּוֹ לְשׁוֹן חֲצִיבָה:

יב **מִבֵּית עֲבָדִים.** כְּתַרְגּוּמוֹ: ״מִבֵּית עַבְדוּתָא״, מִמָּקוֹם שֶׁהֱיִיתֶם שָׁם עֲבָדִים:

יג **וּבִשְׁמוֹ תִּשָּׁבֵעַ.** אִם יֵשׁ בְּךָ כָּל הַמִּדּוֹת הַלָּלוּ, שֶׁאַתָּה יָרֵא אֶת שְׁמוֹ וְעוֹבֵד אוֹתוֹ, אָז ״בִּשְׁמוֹ תִּשָּׁבֵעַ״, שֶׁמִּתּוֹךְ שֶׁאַתָּה יָרֵא אֶת שְׁמוֹ תְּהֵא זָהִיר בִּשְׁבוּעָתְךָ, וְאִם לָאו לֹא תִּשָּׁבֵעַ:

יד **מֵאֱלֹהֵי הָעַמִּים אֲשֶׁר סְבִיבוֹתֵיכֶם.** הוּא הַדִּין לָרְחוֹקִים, אֶלָּא לְפִי שֶׁאַתָּה רוֹאֶה אֶת סְבִיבוֹתֶיךָ תּוֹעִים אַחֲרֵיהֶם הֻצְרַךְ לְהַזְהִיר עֲלֵיהֶם בְּיוֹתֵר:

translates this verb as "you shall sharpen" (compare Deut. 32:41). Education, in Judaism, is active, not passive. It is about honing the mind, sharpening the intellect, through question and answer, challenge and response. Four times the Torah refers to children asking questions (the "four sons" of the Haggada). Against cultures that see unquestioning obedience as the ideal behavior of a child, Jewish tradition regards the child "who does not know how to ask" as the lowest, not the highest, stage of development.

Judaism is God's perennial question mark against the condition of the world. That things are as they are is a fact, not a value. Should it be so? Why should it be so? Only one who asks whether the world should be as it is, is capable of changing what it is.

6:8 **וּקְשַׁרְתָּם לְאוֹת** *Bind them as a sign* – The word "tefillin" (here called *totafot*) means "emblem," "sign," "insignia," the visible symbol of an abstract idea. Tefillin are our reminder of the commandment "Love the LORD your God with all your heart, with all your soul, and with all your might" (Deut. 6:5). In verse 5, the words "*all your heart*" are understood to refer to the tefillin on the upper arm opposite the heart; "*all your soul*" to the head tefillin opposite the seat of consciousness, the soul; and "*all your might*" to the strap of the hand tefillin, symbolizing action, power, might. Tefillin thus symbolize the love for God in emotion (heart), thought (head), and deed (hand).

ח בְּשִׁבְתְּךָ בְּבֵיתֶךָ וּבְלֶכְתְּךָ בַדֶּרֶךְ וּבְשָׁכְבְּךָ וּבְקוּמֶךָ: וּקְשַׁרְתָּם
ט לְאוֹת עַל־יָדֶךָ וְהָיוּ לְטֹטָפֹת בֵּין עֵינֶיךָ: וּכְתַבְתָּם עַל־מְזֻזוֹת בֵּיתֶךָ
י וּבִשְׁעָרֶיךָ: וְהָיָה כִּי־יְבִיאֲךָ ׀ יְהוָה אֱלֹהֶיךָ אֶל־הָאָרֶץ אֲשֶׁר
נִשְׁבַּע לַאֲבֹתֶיךָ לְאַבְרָהָם לְיִצְחָק וּלְיַעֲקֹב לָתֶת לָךְ עָרִים גְּדֹלֹת
יא וְטֹבֹת אֲשֶׁר לֹא־בָנִיתָ: וּבָתִּים מְלֵאִים כָּל־טוּב אֲשֶׁר לֹא־מִלֵּאתָ
וּבֹרֹת חֲצוּבִים אֲשֶׁר לֹא־חָצַבְתָּ כְּרָמִים וְזֵיתִים אֲשֶׁר לֹא־נָטָעְתָּ
יב וְאָכַלְתָּ וְשָׂבָעְתָּ: הִשָּׁמֶר לְךָ פֶּן־תִּשְׁכַּח אֶת־יְהוָה אֲשֶׁר הוֹצִיאֲךָ
יג מֵאֶרֶץ מִצְרַיִם מִבֵּית עֲבָדִים: אֶת־יְהוָה אֱלֹהֶיךָ תִּירָא וְאֹתוֹ תַעֲבֹד
יד וּבִשְׁמוֹ תִּשָּׁבֵעַ: לֹא תֵלְכוּן אַחֲרֵי אֱלֹהִים אֲחֵרִים מֵאֱלֹהֵי הָעַמִּים
טו אֲשֶׁר סְבִיבוֹתֵיכֶם: כִּי אֵל קַנָּא יְהוָה אֱלֹהֶיךָ בְּקִרְבֶּךָ פֶּן־יֶחֱרֶה

אונקלוס

בְּמִתְּבָךְ בְּבֵיתָךְ וּבְמֶהֱכָךְ בְּאוֹרְחָא, וּבְמִשְׁכְּבָךְ וּבִמְקִימָךְ:
ח וְתִקְטְרִנּוּן לְאָת עַל יְדָךְ, וִיהוֹן לִתְפִלִּין בֵּין עֵינָךְ: ט וְתִכְתְּבִנּוּן עַל מְזוּזִין,
וְתִקְבְּעִנּוּן בְּסִפֵּי בֵיתָךְ וּבְתַרְעָךְ: י וִיהֵי, אֲרֵי יַעֲלִנָּךְ יי אֱלָהָךְ, לְאַרְעָא,
דְּקַיֵּים לַאֲבָהָתָךְ, לְאַבְרָהָם, לְיִצְחָק וּלְיַעֲקֹב לְמִתַּן לָךְ, קִרְוִין, רַבְרְבָן
וְטָבָן דְּלָא בְנֵיתָא: יא וּבָתִּין, מְלַן כָּל טוּב דְּלָא מְלֵיתָא, וְגֻבִּין פְּסִילָן
דְּלָא פְסַלְתָּא, כַּרְמִין וְזֵיתִין דְּלָא נְצַבְתָּא, וְתֵיכוֹל וְתִסְבַּע: יב אִסְתְּמַר
לָךְ, דִּלְמָא תִתְנְשֵׁי יָת דַּחְלְתָא דַיי, דְּאַפְּקָךְ, מֵאַרְעָא דְמִצְרַיִם מִבֵּית
עַבְדוּתָא: יג יָת יי אֱלָהָךְ, תִּדְחַל וְקֳדָמוֹהִי תִּפְלַח, וּבִשְׁמֵיהּ תְּקַיֵּים:
יד לָא תְהָכוּן, בָּתַר טָעֲוַת עַמְמַיָּא, מִטָּעֲוַת עַמְמַיָּא, דִּבְסַחְרָנֵיכוֹן:
טו אֲרֵי אֵל קַנָּא, יי אֱלָהָךְ שְׁכִינְתֵּיהּ בֵּינָךְ, דִּלְמָא יִתְקַף, רֻגְזָא

> "For this covenant, which I will make with the House of Israel after these days," declares the Lord, "I will deliver My teaching into their midst and inscribe it upon their hearts, and I will be their God, and they will be My people." (Jer. 31:32)

It was a utopian aspiration in Deuteronomy, and so it was to Yirmeyahu. It still is. This is why, in the book of Samuel, God says: If you want a king and are prepared to sacrifice some of the freedom I have given you, then appoint a king. But be aware that kings, courts, and governments carry a high price.

At the transition between the Israelites of the book of Judges and the birth of monarchy in the book of Samuel, a social contract formed the Israelite state. But the true foundational moment occurred here, centuries earlier, at Mount Sinai, when a social covenant created a society. God revealed Himself to the people and gave them the Ten Commandments. Unlike any other treaty in the ancient world, it is made not between two rulers but between God and an entire people, the presence, knowledge, and consent of all of whom is essential. This is not democracy in the modern or even the Greek sense. But it is a corollary of the idea that the human person as such is in the image of God. In covenant as the Bible understands it, each individual has significance, dignity, moral worth, the right to be heard, a voice. The connection between the Law and every individual is not imposed by human authority but "impressed upon your heart."

6:7 וְשִׁנַּנְתָּם לְבָנֶיךָ *Teach them to your children* – Rashi

16 annihilate you from the face of the earth. Do not test the LORD your
17 God as you tested Him at Masa. Be very vigilant to keep the commandments
of the LORD your God, and the testimonies and decrees with which He has
18 charged you. Do what is right and what is good in the LORD's eyes, so that it
may go well with you, and you may go in and take possession of the good land
19 that the LORD swore to your ancestors to give you, driving out all your enemies
20 before you, as the LORD promised. And in the future, when your child
asks you, 'What is the meaning of the testimonies, decrees, and laws that the

רש"י

טז **בַּמַּסָּה.** כְּשֶׁיָּצְאוּ מִמִּצְרַיִם שֶׁנִּסּוּהוּ בַּמַּיִם, שֶׁנֶּאֱמַר: "הֲיֵשׁ ה' בְּקִרְבֵּנוּ" (שמות יז, ז):

יח **הַיָּשָׁר וְהַטּוֹב.** זוֹ פְּשָׁרָה לִפְנִים מִשּׁוּרַת הַדִּין:

יט **כַּאֲשֶׁר דִּבֶּר.** וְהֵיכָן דִּבֶּר? "וְהַמֹּתִי אֶת כָּל הָעָם" וְגוֹ' (שמות כג, כז):

כ **כִּי יִשְׁאָלְךָ בִנְךָ מָחָר.** יֵשׁ מָחָר שֶׁהוּא אַחַר זְמַן:

They do more than they are commanded. They go the extra mile. That, according to Rashi, is what the Torah means by "what is right and what is good."

Ramban, while citing Rashi and agreeing with him, goes on to say something different in his commentary on the same passage:

> Now this is a great principle, for it is impossible to mention in the Torah all aspects of man's conduct with his neighbors and friends, all his various transactions and the ordinances of all societies and countries. But since He mentioned many of them, such as "Do not go around as a gossipmonger" (Lev. 19:16), "Do not take revenge or bear a grudge" (19:18), "Do not stand by while your neighbor's life is in danger" (19:16), "Do not curse the deaf" (19:14), "Stand up in the presence of the white-haired" (19:32), and the like, He went on to state in a general way that in all matters one should do what is good and right, including even compromise and going beyond the strict requirement of the law.... Thus one should behave in every sphere of activity, such that one is worthy of being called "good and upright."

It seems as if Ramban is telling us that there are aspects of *the moral life* that are not caught by the concept of law at all. That is what he means by saying, "It is impossible to mention in the Torah all aspects of man's conduct with his neighbors and friends." Moral law is about universals, principles that apply in all places and times: Do not murder. Do not rob. Do not steal. Do not lie. Yet there are important features of the moral life that are not universal at all. They have to do with specific circumstances and the way we respond to them. What is it to be a good husband or wife, a good parent, a good teacher, a good friend? What is it to be a great leader, or follower, or member of a team? When is it right to praise, and when is it appropriate to say, "You could have done better"? There are aspects of the moral life that cannot be reduced to rules of conduct, because what matters is not only what we do, but the way in which we do it – with humility or gentleness or sensitivity or tact. Morality is not just a set of rules, even a code as elaborate as the 613 commandments and their rabbinic extensions. It is also about the way we respond to people as individuals.

This ultimately is the difference between the two great principles of Judaic ethics: justice and love. Justice is universal. It treats all people alike, rich and poor, powerful and powerless, making no distinctions on the basis of color or class. But love is particular. A parent loves his or her children for what makes them each unique. The moral life is a combination of both. That is why it cannot be reduced solely to universal laws. That is what the Torah means when it speaks of "what is right and what is good" over and above the commandments, statutes, and testimonies.

טו אַף־יְהוָה אֱלֹהֶיךָ בָּךְ וְהִשְׁמִידְךָ מֵעַל פְּנֵי הָאֲדָמָה: לֹא
טז תְנַסּוּ אֶת־יְהוָה אֱלֹהֵיכֶם כַּאֲשֶׁר נִסִּיתֶם בַּמַּסָּה: שָׁמוֹר תִּשְׁמְרוּן
יז אֶת־מִצְוֹת יְהוָה אֱלֹהֵיכֶם וְעֵדֹתָיו וְחֻקָּיו אֲשֶׁר צִוָּךְ: וְעָשִׂיתָ הַיָּשָׁר
יח וְהַטּוֹב בְּעֵינֵי יְהוָה לְמַעַן יִיטַב לָךְ וּבָאתָ וְיָרַשְׁתָּ אֶת־הָאָרֶץ הַטֹּבָה
יט אֲשֶׁר־נִשְׁבַּע יְהוָה לַאֲבֹתֶיךָ: לַהֲדֹף אֶת־כָּל־אֹיְבֶיךָ מִפָּנֶיךָ כַּאֲשֶׁר דִּבֶּר
כ יְהוָה: כִּי־יִשְׁאָלְךָ בִנְךָ מָחָר לֵאמֹר מָה הָעֵדֹת וְהַחֻקִּים

אונקלוס

דַּיְיָ אֱלָהָךְ בָּךְ, וִישֵׁיצֵינָךְ, מֵעַל אַפֵּי אַרְעָא: טז לָא תְנַסּוֹן, קֳדָם יְיָ אֱלָהֲכוֹן, כְּמָא דְּנַסֵּיתוֹן בְּנִסֵּיתָא: יז מִטַּר תִּטְּרוּן, יָת פִּקּוֹדַיָּא דַּייָ אֱלָהֲכוֹן, וְסָהֲדְוָתֵיהּ וּקְיָמוֹהִי דְּפַקְּדָךְ: יח וְתַעֲבֵיד, דְּכָשַׁר וּדְתָקֵין קֳדָם יְיָ, בְּדִיל דְּיֵיטַב לָךְ, וְתֵיעוֹל, וְתֵירַת יָת אַרְעָא טָבְתָא, דְּקַיֵּים יְיָ לַאֲבָהָתָךְ: יט לְמִתְבַּר יָת כָּל בַּעֲלֵי דְּבָבָךְ מִן קֳדָמָךְ, כְּמָא דְּמַלֵּיל יְיָ: כ אֲרֵי יִשְׁאֲלִנָּךְ בְּרָךְ, מְחַר לְמֵימַר, מָא סָהֲדְוָתָא, וּקְיָמַיָּא וְדִינַיָּא, דְּפַקֵּיד, יְיָ אֱלָהַנָא יָתְכוֹן: כא וְתֵימַר לִבְרָךְ, עַבְדִּין,

6:16 לֹא תְנַסּוּ אֶת־יְהוָה אֱלֹהֵיכֶם *Do not test the Lord your God* – This verse is the source of the prohibition against "relying on a miracle" – failing to take safety precautions on the basis that God will give supernatural protection.

The Talmud Bavli displays a fascinating attitude toward the miraculous. It tells the story of a man whose wife died giving birth. The man was so poor he was unable to pay for a wet nurse. A miracle happened, says the Talmud, and his own breasts sprouted milk. What is fascinating is what the Talmud says next: "R. Yosef said: Come and see how great is this man that such a miracle was performed for him. Abaye said to him: To the contrary, come and see how lowly was this man, that he needed the natural order to be changed for him" (Shabbat 53b).

Abaye believed, with many of the Sages, that we should not need miracles, nor should we rely on them. Two prophets, Eliyahu and Elisha, both raise the dead to life (I Kings 17:17; II Kings 4:8–37). Yet neither the biblical text nor later Jewish tradition made any great fuss over this. The real miracle in both cases – as it is in the stories of the patriarchs and matriarchs in Genesis, and of Ḥana in the book of Samuel – is that infertile women were able to have children in the first place. In that sense, modern fertility treatments are our miracles. We should not need supernatural intervention to see children as the gift of God.

God is found in order, not in the miraculous suspension of that order; He is there in the law that tells us to provide for those in need, and in the human drive and ability to partner with Him in the work of creation and solve ever more of the problems we face. We are to "keep all these decrees, to revere the Lord our God … so that we might always prosper" (Deut. 6:24), but we are not to demand direct or miraculous connections between the two.

THE RIGHT AND THE GOOD

Verse 17 makes reference to commandments, testimonies, and decrees. This, on the face of it, is the whole of Judaism as far as conduct is concerned. What more then is meant, in the next verse, by the phrase "what is right and what is good"?

Rashi says that it refers to "compromise [that is, not strictly insisting on your rights] and action within or beyond the letter of the law (*lifnim mishurat hadin*)." The law, as it were, lays down a minimum threshold: this we must do. But the moral life aspires to more than simply doing what we must. The saints and heroes of the moral life go beyond.

21 Lord our God has commanded you?' tell him, 'We were slaves to Pharaoh in
22 Egypt, but the Lord brought us out of Egypt with a mighty hand. Before our
eyes the Lord sent great and awesome signs and wonders against Egypt and
23 Pharaoh and his whole household. And He freed us from there, to bring us
24 in and give us the land that He promised on oath to our ancestors. The Lord
commanded us to keep all these decrees, to revere the Lord our God, so that
25 we might always prosper; to keep us alive, as we are today. And if we carefully
keep all this command before the Lord our God, as He has charged us, this
7 1 will be our righteousness.' When the Lord your God brings you into SHEVI'I
the land that you are about to enter and possess, when you drive out many
nations before you – the Hittites, Girgashites, Amorites, Canaanites, Perizzites,
2 Hivites, and Jebusites, seven nations larger and stronger than you – and the
Lord your God gives them over to you and you defeat them, you must utterly
3 destroy them. Make no covenant with them and grant them no mercy. Do not
3 intermarry with them; do not give your daughters to their sons in marriage or
4 take their daughters for your sons. For they will turn your children away from
walking after Me, and bring them to serve other gods. The Lord's anger will
5 burn against you, and He will quickly destroy you. Instead, this is what you
must do to them: tear down their altars, smash their worship pillars, cut down
6 their sacred trees, and burn their idols with fire. For you are a holy people to
the Lord your God. The Lord your God has chosen you, of all the peoples on
7 earth, to be His treasured people. It is not because you were more numerous
than other peoples that the Lord desired you and chose you, for you are the

אונקלוס

הֲוֵינָא לְפַרְעֹה בְּמִצְרָיִם, וְאַפְּקַנָא יְיָ מִמִּצְרַיִם בְּיַד תַּקִּיפָא: כב וִיהַב יְיָ אָתִין וּמוֹפְתִין, רַבְרְבִין וּבִישִׁין בְּמִצְרַיִם, בְּפַרְעֹה וּבְכָל אֱנָשׁ בֵּיתֵיהּ לְעֵינַנָא: כג וְיָתַנָא אַפֵּיק מִתַּמָּן, בְּדִיל לְאַעָלָא יָתַנָא, לְמִתַּן לַנָא יָת אַרְעָא, דְּקַיֵּים לַאֲבָהָתַנָא: כד וּפַקְּדַנָא יְיָ, לְמֶעְבַּד יָת כָּל קְיָמַיָּא הָאִלֵּין, לְמִדְחַל קֳדָם יְיָ אֱלָהַנָא, דְּיֵיטַב לַנָא כָּל יוֹמַיָּא, לְקַיָּמוּתַנָא כְּיוֹמָא הָדֵין: כה וּזְכוּתָא תְּהֵי לַנָא, אֲרֵי נִטַּר לְמֶעְבַּד יָת כָּל תַּפְקֵידְתָּא

רש״י

ז א| וְנָשַׁל. לְשׁוֹן הַשְׁלָכָה וְהַתָּזָה, וְכֵן: ״וְנָשַׁל הַבַּרְזֶל״ (להלן יט, ה):

ב| וְלֹא תְחָנֵּם. לֹא תִּתֵּן לָהֶם חֵן, אָסוּר לוֹ לְאָדָם לוֹמַר: כַּמָּה נָאֶה גּוֹי זֶה. דָּבָר אַחֵר, לֹא תִּתֵּן לָהֶם חֲנָיָה בָּאָרֶץ:

ד| כִּי יָסִיר אֶת בִּנְךָ מֵאַחֲרַי. בְּנוֹ שֶׁל גּוֹי כְּשֶׁיִּשָּׂא אֶת בִּתְּךָ, יָסִיר אֶת בִּנְךָ אֲשֶׁר תֵּלֵד לוֹ בִּתְּךָ מֵאַחֲרַי. לָמַדְנוּ שֶׁבֶּן בִּתְּךָ הַבָּא מִן הַגּוֹי קָרוּי בִּנְךָ, אֲבָל בֶּן בִּנְךָ הַבָּא מִן הַגּוֹיָה אֵינוֹ קָרוּי בִּנְךָ, שֶׁהֲרֵי לֹא נֶאֱמַר עַל בִּתּוֹ: לֹא תִקַּח, כִּי תָסִיר אֶת בִּנְךָ מֵאַחֲרַי:

ה| מִזְבְּחֹתֵיהֶם. שֶׁל לְבֵנִים: וּמַצֵּבֹתָם. אֶבֶן אַחַת: וַאֲשֵׁירֵהֶם. אִילָנוֹת שֶׁעוֹבְדִין אוֹתָן: וּפְסִילֵיהֶם. צְלָמִים:

ז| לֹא מֵרֻבְּכֶם. כִּפְשׁוּטוֹ. וּמִדְרָשׁוֹ, לְפִי שֶׁאֵין אַתֶּם מַגְדִּילִים עַצְמְכֶם

כא והמשפטים אשר צוה יהוה אלהינו אתכם: ואמרת לבנך עבדים
כב היינו לפרעה במצרים ויציאנו יהוה ממצרים ביד חזקה: ויתן יהוה
אתת ומפתים גדלים ורעים | במצרים בפרעה ובכל־ביתו לעינינו:
כג ואותנו הוציא משם למען הביא אתנו לתת לנו את־הארץ אשר
כד נשבע לאבתינו: ויצונו יהוה לעשות את־כל־החקים האלה ליראה
כה את־יהוה אלהינו לטוב לנו כל־הימים לחיתנו כהיום הזה: וצדקה
תהיה־לנו כי־נשמר לעשות את־כל־המצוה הזאת לפני יהוה
ז א אלהינו כאשר צונו: כי יביאך יהוה אלהיך אל־הארץ שביעי
אשר־אתה בא־שמה לרשתה ונשל גוים־רבים | מפניך החתי
והגרגשי והאמרי והכנעני והפרזי והחוי והיבוסי שבעה גוים רבים
ב ועצומים ממך: ונתנם יהוה אלהיך לפניך והכיתם החרם תחרים
ג אתם לא־תכרת להם ברית ולא תחנם: ולא תתחתן בם בתך לא־
ד תתן לבנו ובתו לא־תקח לבנך: כי־יסיר את־בנך מאחרי ועבדו
ה אלהים אחרים וחרה אף־יהוה בכם והשמידך מהר: כי אם־כה
תעשו להם מזבחתיהם תתצו ומצבתם תשברו ואשירהם תגדעון
ו ופסיליהם תשרפון באש: כי עם קדוש אתה ליהוה אלהיך בך
בחר | יהוה אלהיך להיות לו לעם סגלה מכל העמים אשר על־
ז פני האדמה: לא מרבכם מכל־העמים חשק יהוה בכם ויבחר בכם

אונקלוס

הדא, קדם, יי אלהנא כמא דפקדנא: ז א ארי יעלנך יי אלהך,
לארעא, דאת עליל לתמן למירתה, ויתריך עממין סגיאין מן קדמך,
חתאי וגרגשאי ואמוראי וכנענאי ופרזאי, וחואי ויבוסאי, שבעא
עממין, סגיאין ותקיפין מנך: ב וימסרנון, יי אלהך, קדמך ותמחינון,
גמרא תגמר יתהון, לא תגזר להון, קים ולא תרחים עליהון: ג ולא
תתחתן בהון, ברתך לא תתין לבריה, וברתיה לא תסב לברך:

ד ארי יטעין ית ברך מבתר פלחני, ויפלחון לטעות עממיא, ויתקף
רגזא דיי בכון, וישיצינך בפריע: ה ארי אם כדין תעבדון להון,
איגוריהון תתרעון, וקמתהון תתברון, ואשיריהון תקצצון, וצלמיהון
תוקדון בנורא: ו ארי עם קדיש את, קדם יי אלהך, בך, אתרעי
יי אלהך, למהוי ליה לעם חביב, מכל עממיא, דעל אפי ארעא:
ז לא מדסגיאין אתון מכל עממיא, צבי יי, בכון ואתרעי בכון,

8 smallest of all peoples. It was because of the love the LORD had for you, because
of the oath He kept, that He swore to your ancestors, that the LORD freed you
with a mighty hand, and redeemed you from the house of slaves, from the grip
9 of Pharaoh, king of Egypt. Know therefore that only the LORD your God is MAFTIR
God, the faithful God who keeps His covenant and the love to a thousand
10 generations of those who love Him and keep His commandments, and who
instantly repays with destruction those who reject Him, requiting them in a
11 moment. Therefore, carefully keep the command – the decrees and the laws –
that I am charging you with today.

The haftara for Parashat Vaetḥanan is on page 1608.

רש״י

כְּשֶׁאֲנִי מַשְׁפִּיעַ לָכֶם טוֹבָה, לְפִיכָךְ חָשַׁק בָּכֶם: **כִּי אַתֶּם הַמְעַט.** הַמַּמְעִיטִים עַצְמְכֶם, כְּמוֹ: "וְאָנֹכִי עָפָר וָאֵפֶר" (בראשית יח, כז), "וְנַחְנוּ מָה" (שמות טז, ז); לֹא כִּנְבוּכַדְנֶאצַּר שֶׁאָמַר: "אֶדַּמֶּה לְעֶלְיוֹן" (ישעיה יד, יד), וְסַנְחֵרִיב שֶׁאָמַר: "מִי בְּכָל אֱלֹהֵי הָאֲרָצוֹת" (שם לו, כ), וְחִירָם שֶׁאָמַר: "אֵל אָנִי מוֹשַׁב אֱלֹהִים יָשַׁבְתִּי" (יחזקאל כח, ב): **כִּי אַתֶּם הַמְעַט.** הֲרֵי "כִּי" מְשַׁמֵּשׁ בִּלְשׁוֹן "דְּהָא":

ח **כִּי מֵאַהֲבַת ה'.** הֲרֵי 'כִּי' מְשַׁמֵּשׁ בִּלְשׁוֹן 'אֶלָּא', לֹא מֵרָבְכֶם חָשַׁק ה' בָּכֶם אֶלָּא מֵאַהֲבַת ה' אֶתְכֶם: **וּמִשָּׁמְרוֹ אֶת הַשְּׁבֻעָה.** מֵחֲמַת שָׁמְרוֹ אֶת הַשְּׁבוּעָה:

ט **לְאֶלֶף דּוֹר.** וּלְהַלָּן הוּא אוֹמֵר: "לַאֲלָפִים" (לעיל ה, י), כָּאן שֶׁהוּא סָמוּךְ אֵצֶל "לְשֹׁמְרֵי מִצְוֹתָיו" הוּא אוֹמֵר "לְאֶלֶף", וּלְהַלָּן שֶׁהוּא סָמוּךְ אֵצֶל "לְאֹהֲבַי" הוּא אוֹמֵר "לַאֲלָפִים": **לְאֹהֲבָיו.** אֵלּוּ הָעוֹשִׂין מֵאַהֲבָה: **וּלְשֹׁמְרֵי מִצְוֹתָיו.** אֵלּוּ הָעוֹשִׂין מִיִּרְאָה:

י **וּמְשַׁלֵּם לְשֹׂנְאָיו אֶל פָּנָיו.** בְּחַיָּיו מְשַׁלֵּם לוֹ גְּמוּלוֹ הַטּוֹב, כְּדֵי לְהַאֲבִידוֹ מִן הָעוֹלָם הַבָּא:

יא **הַיּוֹם לַעֲשׂוֹתָם.** וּלְמָחָר, לָעוֹלָם הַבָּא, לִטֹּל שְׂכָרָם:

us the willingness to take high ideals and enact them in the real world, unswayed by disappointments and defeats. This small people has outlived all the world's great empires to deliver to humanity a message of hope: You need not be large to be great. What you need is to be open to a power greater than yourself.

7:9 שֹׁמֵר הַבְּרִית וְהַחֶסֶד *His covenant and the love* – The Hebrew phrase here, *shomer habrit vehaḥesed*, "the covenant and the loving kindness," is a puzzling one. If you look, for instance, at the Jewish Publication Society translation, they translate only the word "covenant," because the *ḥesed* is included in the covenant. If you look at the New International version, *habrit vehaḥesed* is translated as "the covenant of love." But of course it doesn't mean that; it means "covenant and love." Everyone had a problem in understanding what else God does for the Jewish people at Mount Sinai, other than make a covenant with them. The answer, I believe, is that a covenant is what sociologists and anthropologists call reciprocal altruism. You do this for me. I will do this for you. "You serve Me," says God, "and I will protect you." Covenant is always reciprocal. But that makes one vulnerable, because what happens if we do not keep the covenant? The covenant is then rendered null and void.

Therefore, even covenant is not enough. God also has a relationship of *ḥesed* with us. An unconditional love, which is translated into deeds of kindness. The covenant is conditional, but *ḥesed* is unconditional. That is what the Rambam meant when he said, in *Guide for the Perplexed*, part III chapter 53, that *ḥesed* means doing something for somebody who has no claim on us.

We received a covenant at Mount Sinai, but we also received something still more long-lasting and profound, which is God's unconditional love.

ח כִּֽי־אַתֶּ֥ם הַמְעַ֖ט מִכׇּל־הָֽעַמִּֽים׃ כִּי֩ מֵאַהֲבַ֨ת יהוה אֶתְכֶ֗ם וּמִשׇּׁמְר֤וֹ
אֶת־הַשְּׁבֻעָה֙ אֲשֶׁ֤ר נִשְׁבַּע֙ לַאֲבֹ֣תֵיכֶ֔ם הוֹצִ֧יא יהוה אֶתְכֶ֖ם בְּיָ֣ד חֲזָקָ֑ה
ט וַֽיִּפְדְּךָ֙ מִבֵּ֣ית עֲבָדִ֔ים מִיַּ֖ד פַּרְעֹ֥ה מֶֽלֶךְ־מִצְרָֽיִם׃ וְיָדַעְתָּ֕ כִּֽי־יהוה מפטיר
אֱלֹהֶ֖יךָ ה֣וּא הָאֱלֹהִ֑ים הָאֵל֙ הַנֶּֽאֱמָ֔ן שֹׁמֵ֧ר הַבְּרִ֣ית וְהַחֶ֗סֶד לְאֹהֲבָ֛יו
י וּלְשֹׁמְרֵ֥י מִצְוֺתָ֖ו לְאֶ֥לֶף דּֽוֹר׃ וּמְשַׁלֵּ֧ם לְשֹׂנְאָ֛יו אֶל־פָּנָ֖יו לְהַֽאֲבִיד֑וֹ לֹ֤א
יא יְאַחֵר֙ לְשֹׂ֣נְא֔וֹ אֶל־פָּנָ֖יו יְשַׁלֶּם־לֽוֹ׃ וְשָׁמַרְתָּ֣ אֶת־הַמִּצְוָ֗ה וְאֶת־הַֽחֻקִּ֛ים
וְאֶת־הַמִּשְׁפָּטִ֥ים אֲשֶׁ֨ר אָנֹכִ֧י מְצַוְּךָ֛ הַיּ֖וֹם לַעֲשׂוֹתָֽם׃

The הפטרה *for* פרשת ואתחנן *is on page 1609.*

אונקלוס

אֲרֵי אַתּוּן זְעֵירִין מִכׇּל עַמְמַיָּא: ח אֲרֵי מִדְּרָחֵים יי יָתְכוֹן, וּמִדְּנָטַר יָת קְיָמָא דְּקַיֵּים לַאֲבָהָתְכוֹן, אַפֵּיק יי, יָתְכוֹן בְּיַד תַּקִּיפָא, וּפָרְקָךְ מִבֵּית עַבְדוּתָא, מִיְּדָא דְּפַרְעֹה מַלְכָּא דְּמִצְרָיִם: ט וְתִדַּע, אֲרֵי יי אֱלָהָךְ הוּא אֱלֹהִים, אֱלָהָא מְהֵימְנָא, נָטַר קְיָמָא וְחִסְדָּא, לְרָחֲמוֹהִי, וּלְנָטְרֵי פִּקּוּדוֹהִי לְאֶלֶף דָּרִין: י וּמְשַׁלֵּים לְסָנְאוֹהִי, טָבְוָן דְּאִנּוּן עָבְדִין קֳדָמוֹהִי בְּחַיֵּיהוֹן לְאוֹבָדֵיהוֹן, לָא מְאַחַר עוֹבַד טָב לְסָנְאוֹהִי, טָבְוָן דְּאִנּוּן עָבְדִין קֳדָמוֹהִי בְּחַיֵּיהוֹן מְשַׁלֵּים לְהוֹן: יא וְתִטַּר יָת תַּפְקֵידְתָּא וְיָת קְיָמַיָּא וְיָת דִּינַיָּא, דַּאֲנָא מְפַקֵּיד לָךְ, יוֹמָא דֵין לְמֶעְבְּדְהוֹן:

7:7 כִּי־אַתֶּם הַמְעַט מִכׇּל־הָעַמִּים *You are the smallest of all peoples* – This remark gives a new complexion to the biblical image of the people Israel. It is not what we have heard thus far. In Genesis, God promised the patriarchs that their descendants would be like the stars of the heaven, the sand on the seashore, the dust of the earth, uncountable. Avraham will be the father, not just of one nation but of many. At the beginning of Exodus we read of how the covenantal family, numbering a mere seventy when they went down to Egypt, "were fruitful and burgeoned, they multiplied and became exceptionally strong, until the land was filled with them" (Ex. 1:7). In these texts and others it is the size, the numerical greatness, of the people that is emphasized. What then are we to make of Moshe's words that speak of its smallness? Targum Yonatan interprets it not to be about numbers at all but about self-image. He translates it not as "the fewest of all peoples" but as "the most lowly and humble of peoples." Rashi gives a similar reading, citing Avraham's words, "I am mere dust and ashes" (Gen. 18:27), and Moshe and Aharon's, "What are we?" (Ex. 16:7).

Whatever the explanation, there is something in this verse that resonates throughout Jewish history. Through the Jewish people, God is telling humankind that you do not need to be numerous to be great. Nations are judged not by their size but by their contribution. Of this the most compelling proof is that a nation as small as the Jews could produce an ever-renewed flow of prophets, priests, poets, philosophers, sages, and saints. It has also yielded some of the world's greatest writers, artists, musicians, filmmakers, intellectuals, doctors, lawyers, and technological innovators. Out of all proportion to their numbers, Jews could and can be found working as lawyers fighting injustice, economists fighting poverty, doctors fighting disease, teachers fighting ignorance, and therapists fighting depression and despair.

You do not need numbers to enlarge the spiritual and moral horizons of humankind. You need other things altogether: a sense of the worth and dignity of the individual, of the power of human possibility to transform the world, of the importance of giving everyone the best education they can have, of making each feel part of a collective responsibility to ameliorate the human condition. Judaism asks of

Parashat Ekev

7 12 If, indeed, you heed these laws, always vigilant to keep them, the Lord your
God will keep with you the covenant and the love He forged on oath with your
13 ancestors. He will love you, bless you, and multiply you. He will bless the fruit
of your womb and the fruit of your land, your grain and wine and oil, the calves
of your herds and the lambs of your flock, in the land that He swore to your
14 ancestors to give you. You shall be blessed above all other peoples, and no male
15 or female among you or your livestock will be barren or childless. The Lord
will keep you free from all sickness. All the terrible diseases of Egypt that you
knew, He will not inflict upon you, but He will lay them upon all those who
16 hate you. You shall devour all the peoples that the Lord your God is giving
over to you. Do not show them pity, and do not worship their gods – for that
17 would be a snare to you. You might say to yourself, 'These nations are

רש״י

יב **וְהָיָה עֵקֶב תִּשְׁמְעוּן.** אִם הַמִּצְוֹת הַקַּלּוֹת שֶׁאָדָם דָּשׁ בַּעֲקֵבָיו תִּשְׁמְעוּן: **וְשָׁמַר ה׳ וְגוֹ׳.** יִשְׁמֹר לְךָ הַבְטָחָתוֹ:

יג **שְׁגַר אֲלָפֶיךָ.** וַלְדֵי בְקָרְךָ שֶׁהַנְּקֵבָה מְשַׁגֶּרֶת מִמֵּעֶיהָ: **וְעַשְׁתְּרֹת צֹאנֶךָ.** מְנַחֵם פֵּרֵשׁ: ״אַבִּירֵי בָשָׁן״ (תהלים כב, יג) מִבְחַר הַצֹּאן, כְּמוֹ: ׳עַשְׁתְּרֹת קַרְנַיִם׳, לְשׁוֹן חֹזֶק, וְאוּנְקְלוֹס תִּרְגֵּם: ״וְעֶדְרֵי עָנָךְ״, וְרַבּוֹתֵינוּ אָמְרוּ: לָמָּה נִקְרָא שְׁמָם ׳עַשְׁתָּרוֹת׳? שֶׁמַּעֲשִׁירוֹת אֶת בַּעֲלֵיהֶן:

יד **עָקָר.** שֶׁאֵינוֹ מוֹלִיד:

יז–יח **כִּי תֹאמַר בִּלְבָבְךָ.** עַל כָּרְחֲךָ לְשׁוֹן ׳דִּלְמָא׳ הוּא, שֶׁמָּא תֹאמַר

Leviticus twice (both in Lev. 19), in Numbers not at all – and in Deuteronomy twenty-three times. Deuteronomy is a book about societal beatitude (see commentary on Deut. 1:16) and the transformative power of love.

This vision was unique in its time. In *Ethical Life: The Past and Present of Ethical Cultures*, philosopher Harry Redner distinguishes four basic visions of the ethical life in the history of civilizations. One he calls civic ethics, the ethics of ancient Greece and Rome. Second is the ethic of duty, which he identifies with Confucianism, Krishnaism, and late Stoicism. Third is the ethic of honor, a distinctive combination of courtly and military decorum to be found among Persians, Arabs, and Turks as well as in medieval Christianity and Islam. The fourth, which he calls simply morality, he traces to Leviticus and Deuteronomy. He defines it simply as "the ethic of love."

What is radical about this idea is that, first, the Torah insists, against virtually the whole of the ancient world, that the elements that constitute reality are neither hostile nor indifferent to humankind. We are here because Someone wanted us to be, One who cares about us, watches over us, and seeks our well-being. Second, the love with which God created the universe is not just divine. It is to serve as the model for us in our humanity. We are bidden to love the neighbor and the stranger, to engage in acts of kindness and compassion, and to build a society based on love (Deut. 10:18–19).

Having created the world in love and forgiveness, God asks us to love and forgive others.

7:17 **רַבִּים הַגּוֹיִם הָאֵלֶּה** *These nations are more numerous* – Not only were the Israelites smaller than the great

פרשת עקב

ז יב וְהָיָה ׀ עֵקֶב תִּשְׁמְעוּן אֵת הַמִּשְׁפָּטִים הָאֵלֶּה וּשְׁמַרְתֶּם וַעֲשִׂיתֶם
אֹתָם וְשָׁמַר יהוה אֱלֹהֶיךָ לְךָ אֶת־הַבְּרִית וְאֶת־הַחֶסֶד אֲשֶׁר נִשְׁבַּע
יג לַאֲבֹתֶיךָ: וַאֲהֵבְךָ וּבֵרַכְךָ וְהִרְבֶּךָ וּבֵרַךְ פְּרִי־בִטְנְךָ וּפְרִי־אַדְמָתֶךָ
דְּגָנְךָ וְתִירֹשְׁךָ וְיִצְהָרֶךָ שְׁגַר־אֲלָפֶיךָ וְעַשְׁתְּרֹת צֹאנֶךָ עַל הָאֲדָמָה
יד אֲשֶׁר־נִשְׁבַּע לַאֲבֹתֶיךָ לָתֶת לָךְ: בָּרוּךְ תִּהְיֶה מִכָּל־הָעַמִּים לֹא־יִהְיֶה
טו בְךָ עָקָר וַעֲקָרָה וּבִבְהֶמְתֶּךָ: וְהֵסִיר יהוה מִמְּךָ כָּל־חֹלִי וְכָל־מַדְוֵי
מִצְרַיִם הָרָעִים אֲשֶׁר יָדַעְתָּ לֹא יְשִׂימָם בָּךְ וּנְתָנָם בְּכָל־שֹׂנְאֶיךָ:
טז וְאָכַלְתָּ אֶת־כָּל־הָעַמִּים אֲשֶׁר יהוה אֱלֹהֶיךָ נֹתֵן לָךְ לֹא־תָחוֹס עֵינְךָ
יז עֲלֵיהֶם וְלֹא תַעֲבֹד אֶת־אֱלֹהֵיהֶם כִּי־מוֹקֵשׁ הוּא לָךְ: כִּי
תֹאמַר בִּלְבָבְךָ רַבִּים הַגּוֹיִם הָאֵלֶּה מִמֶּנִּי אֵיכָה אוּכַל לְהוֹרִישָׁם:

אונקלוס

יב וִיהֵי חֲלַף דְּתְקַבְּלוּן, יָת דִּינַיָּא הָאִלֵּין, וְתִטְּרוּן וְתַעְבְּדוּן יָתְהוֹן, וְיִטַּר יי אֱלָהָךְ לָךְ, יָת קְיָמָא וְיָת חִסְדָּא, דְּקַיֵּים לַאֲבָהָתָךְ: יג וְיִרְחֲמִנָּךְ, וִיבָרְכִנָּךְ וְיַסְגֵּינָךְ, וִיבָרֵיךְ וַלְדָּא דִּמְעָךְ וְאִבָּא דְּאַרְעָךְ, עֲבוּרָךְ וְחַמְרָךְ וּמִשְׁחָךְ, בַּקְרֵי תוֹרָךְ וְעֶדְרֵי עָנָךְ, עַל אַרְעָא, דְּקַיֵּים לַאֲבָהָתָךְ לְמִתַּן לָךְ: יד בְּרִיךְ תְּהֵי מִכָּל עַמְמַיָּא, לָא יְהֵי בָךְ, עֲקַר וְעַקְרָא וּבִבְעִירָךְ: טו וְיַעְדֵּי יי, מִנָּךְ כָּל מַרְעִין, וְכָל מַכְתָּשֵׁי מִצְרַיִם בִּישַׁיָּא דִּידַעְתָּא, לָא יְשַׁוֵּינוּן בָּךְ, וְיִתְּנִנּוּן בְּכָל סָנְאָךְ: טז וּתְגַמַּר יָת כָּל עַמְמַיָּא, דַּיי אֱלָהָךְ יָהֵיב לָךְ, לָא תְחוּס עֵינָךְ עֲלֵיהוֹן, וְלָא תִפְלַח יָת טָעֲוָתְהוֹן, אֲרֵי לְתַקְלָא יְהוֹן לָךְ: יז אֲרֵי תֵימַר בְּלִבָּךְ, סַגִּיאִין, עַמְמַיָּא הָאִלֵּין מִנִּי, אֵיכְדֵין אִכּוּל לְתָרָכוּתְהוֹן: יח לָא

EKEV

In Parashat Ekev, Moshe continues his second address, setting out in broad terms the principles of the covenant the Israelites made with God, and what it demands of them as a chosen nation in a promised land. If they are faithful to the covenant, they will be blessed materially as well as spiritually. But they should not attribute their success to themselves or their righteousness. Moshe reminds them of the people's sins during the wilderness years: the golden calf, the Koraḥ rebellion, and other such episodes. He reminds them, too, of God's forgiveness. Remembering their history, they are to love and revere God and teach their children to do likewise. This entire complex of beliefs is summarized in the passage that became the second paragraph of the *Shema* (Deut. 11:13–21). Israel's fate depends on Israel's faith.

GOD OF LOVE

Something implicit in the Torah from the very beginning becomes explicit in the book of Deuteronomy. God is the God of love. More than we love Him, He loves us.

The book of Deuteronomy is saturated with the language of love. The root *a-h-v* appears in Exodus twice, in

18 more numerous than I. How can I possibly dispossess them?' Do not be afraid
of them. Remember well what the LORD your God did to Pharaoh and to all
19 Egypt. Your own eyes saw the great trials, the signs and wonders, the mighty
hand and the arm stretched forth, with which the LORD your God brought you
20 out. The LORD your God will do the same to all the peoples you fear. The LORD
your God will send the hornet, too, against them until even the survivors who
21 hide from you are destroyed. Do not be terrified of them, for the LORD your
22 God, a great and awesome God, is in your midst. The LORD your God will
drive out these nations before you, little by little. You may not put an end to
23 them at once, or the wild beasts would become too numerous for you. But the
LORD your God will give them over to you, throwing them into great panic
24 until they are destroyed. He will give their kings over to your hands and you
shall wipe out their name from under heaven. No one will be able to stand
25 against you, until you have destroyed them. You shall burn the images of their
gods with fire. Do not covet the silver or gold on them and take it for yourself,

רש״י

בִּלְבָבְךָ מִפְּנֵי שֶׁהֵם רַבִּים לֹא אוּכַל לְהוֹרִישָׁם, אַל תֹּאמַר כֵּן, "לֹא תִירָא מֵהֶם"! וְלֹא יִתָּכֵן לְפָרְשׁוֹ בְּאֶחָד מֵאַרְבַּע לְשׁוֹנוֹת שֶׁל 'כִּי' שֶׁיִּפֹּל עָלָיו שׁוּב "לֹא תִירָא מֵהֶם":

יט **הַמַּסֹּת.** נִסְיוֹנוֹת: **וְהָאֹתֹת.** כְּגוֹן: "וַיְהִי לְנָחָשׁ" (שמות ז, ג), "וְהָיוּ לְדָם בַּיַּבָּשֶׁת" (שם פסוק ט): **וְהַמֹּפְתִים.** הַמַּכּוֹת הַמֻּפְלָאוֹת: **וְהַיָּד הַחֲזָקָה.** זֶה הַדֶּבֶר: **וְהַזְּרֹעַ הַנְּטוּיָה.** זוֹ הַחֶרֶב שֶׁל מַכַּת בְּכוֹרוֹת:

כ **הַצִּרְעָה.** מִין שֶׁרֶץ הָעוֹף, שֶׁהָיְתָה זוֹרֶקֶת בָּהֶם מָרָה וּמְסָרַסְתָּן וּמְסַמְּאָה אֶת עֵינֵיהֶם בְּכָל מָקוֹם שֶׁהָיוּ נִסְתָּרִים שָׁם:

כב **פֶּן תִּרְבֶּה עָלֶיךָ חַיַּת הַשָּׂדֶה.** וַהֲלֹא אִם עוֹשִׂין רְצוֹנוֹ שֶׁל מָקוֹם אֵין מִתְיָרְאִין מִן הַחַיָּה, שֶׁנֶּאֱמַר: "וְחַיַּת הַשָּׂדֶה הָשְׁלְמָה לָךְ" (איוב ה, כג)? אֶלָּא גָּלוּי הָיָה לְפָנָיו שֶׁעֲתִידִין לַחֲטֹא:

כג **וְהָמָם.** נָקוּד קָמַץ כֻּלּוֹ, לְפִי שֶׁאֵין מֵ"ם אַחֲרוֹנָה מִן הַיְסוֹד, וַהֲרֵי הוּא כְּמוֹ: 'וְהָם אוֹתָם', אֲבָל "וְהָמַם גִּלְגַּל עֶגְלָתוֹ" (ישעיה כח, כח) כֻּלּוֹ יְסוֹד, לְפִיכָךְ חֶצְיוֹ קָמַץ וְחֶצְיוֹ פַּתָּח, כִּשְׁאָר פֹּעַל שֶׁל שָׁלֹשׁ אוֹתִיּוֹת:

Remember that you were slaves in Egypt…that is why the LORD your God has commanded you to keep the Sabbath day. (5:15)

Remember that the LORD your God has led you through all this journey of forty years in the wilderness. (8:2)

Remember and never forget how you provoked the LORD your God to fury in the wilderness. (9:7)

Remember what the LORD your God did to Miriam on your way when you left Egypt. (24:9)

Remember what Amalek did to you on your way as you left Egypt. (25:17)

Remember the days of old, consider the years of ages past. (32:7)

As Yosef Hayim Yerushalmi notes in his great treatise, *Zakhor*, "Only in Israel and nowhere else is the injunction to remember felt as a religious imperative to an entire people" (see also commentary on Ex. 16:33). Civilizations begin to die when they forget. Israel was commanded never to forget.

יח לֹא תִירָא מֵהֶם זָכֹר תִּזְכֹּר אֵת אֲשֶׁר־עָשָׂה יהוה אֱלֹהֶיךָ לְפַרְעֹה
יט וּלְכָל־מִצְרָיִם: הַמַּסֹּת הַגְּדֹלֹת אֲשֶׁר־רָאוּ עֵינֶיךָ וְהָאֹתֹת וְהַמֹּפְתִים
וְהַיָּד הַחֲזָקָה וְהַזְּרֹעַ הַנְּטוּיָה אֲשֶׁר הוֹצִאֲךָ יהוה אֱלֹהֶיךָ כֵּן־יַעֲשֶׂה
כ יהוה אֱלֹהֶיךָ לְכָל־הָעַמִּים אֲשֶׁר־אַתָּה יָרֵא מִפְּנֵיהֶם: וְגַם אֶת־הַצִּרְעָה
כא יְשַׁלַּח יהוה אֱלֹהֶיךָ בָּם עַד־אֲבֹד הַנִּשְׁאָרִים וְהַנִּסְתָּרִים מִפָּנֶיךָ: לֹא
כב תַעֲרֹץ מִפְּנֵיהֶם כִּי־יהוה אֱלֹהֶיךָ בְּקִרְבֶּךָ אֵל גָּדוֹל וְנוֹרָא: וְנָשַׁל יהוה
אֱלֹהֶיךָ אֶת־הַגּוֹיִם הָאֵל מִפָּנֶיךָ מְעַט מְעָט לֹא תוּכַל כַּלֹּתָם מַהֵר פֶּן־
כג תִּרְבֶּה עָלֶיךָ חַיַּת הַשָּׂדֶה: וּנְתָנָם יהוה אֱלֹהֶיךָ לְפָנֶיךָ וְהָמָם מְהוּמָה
כד גְדֹלָה עַד הִשָּׁמְדָם: וְנָתַן מַלְכֵיהֶם בְּיָדֶךָ וְהַאֲבַדְתָּ אֶת־שְׁמָם מִתַּחַת
כה הַשָּׁמָיִם לֹא־יִתְיַצֵּב אִישׁ בְּפָנֶיךָ עַד הִשְׁמִדְךָ אֹתָם: פְּסִילֵי אֱלֹהֵיהֶם

אונקלוס

תִדְחַל מִנְּהוֹן, אִדְּכָרָא תִדְכַּר, יָת דַּעֲבַד יי אֱלָהָךְ, לְפַרְעֹה וּלְכָל
מִצְרָאֵי: יט נִסִּין רַבְרְבִין דַּחֲזָאָה עֵינָךְ, וְאָתַיָּא וּמוֹפְתַיָּא וִידָא
תַקִּיפְתָּא וּדְרָעָא מְרָמְמָא, דְּאַפְּקָךְ יי אֱלָהָךְ, כֵּן יַעֲבֵיד, יי אֱלָהָךְ
לְכָל עַמְמַיָּא, דְּאַתְּ דָּחֵיל מִן קֳדָמֵיהוֹן: כ וְאַף יָת עָרָעִיתָא, יְגָרֵי, יי
אֱלָהָךְ בְּהוֹן, עַד דְּיֵיבְדוּן, דְּאִשְׁתְּאָרוּ, וּדְאִטְּמַרוּ מִן קֳדָמָךְ: כא לָא
תִתְּבַר מִן קֳדָמֵיהוֹן, אֲרֵי יי אֱלָהָךְ שְׁכִינְתֵיהּ בֵּינָךְ, אֱלָהָא רַבָּא
וּדְחִילָא: כב וִיתָרֵיךְ יי אֱלָהָךְ, יָת עַמְמַיָּא הָאִלֵּין, מִן קֳדָמָךְ זְעֵיר
זְעֵיר, לָא תִכּוֹל לְשֵׁיצָיוּתְהוֹן בִּפְרִיעַ, דִּלְמָא תִסְגֵּי עֲלָךְ חַיַּת בָּרָא:
כג וְיִמְסְרִנּוּן, יי אֱלָהָךְ קֳדָמָךְ, וִישַׁגֵּשִׁנּוּן שִׁגּוּשׁ רַב, עַד דְּיִשְׁתֵּיצוּן:
כד וְיִמְסַר מַלְכֵיהוֹן בִּידָךְ, וְתוֹבֵיד יָת שׁוּמְהוֹן, מִתְּחוֹת שְׁמַיָּא,
לָא יִתְעַתַּד אֱנָשׁ קֳדָמָךְ, עַד דִּתְשֵׁיצֵי יָתְהוֹן: כה צַלְמֵי טַעֲוָתְהוֹן

empires of the ancient world. They were smaller even than the other nations in the region. Compared to their origins, they had grown, but compared to their neighbors they remained tiny. But Moshe then tells them, "Do not be afraid of them; remember well what the Lord your God did to Pharaoh and to all Egypt" (Deut. 7:18). Israel will be the smallest of the nations for a reason that goes to the very heart of its existence as a nation. It will show the world that a people does not have to be large in order to defeat its enemies. Small groups can make a large difference. Israel's unique history will show that, in the words of the prophet Zekharya (Zech. 4:6), "'Not with valor and not with strength, but with My spirit,' says the Lord of Hosts."

7:18 זָכֹר תִּזְכֹּר *Remember well* – Throughout history there have been many attempts to ground ethics in universal attributes of humanity. Some, like Immanuel Kant, based it on reason. Others based it on duty. Bentham rooted it in consequences ("the greatest happiness for the greatest number"). David Hume attributed it to certain basic emotions: sympathy, empathy, compassion. Adam Smith predicated it on the capacity to stand back from situations and judge them with detachment ("the impartial spectator"). Each of these has its virtues, but none has proved fail-safe.

Judaism took and takes a different view. The guardian of conscience is memory. Time and again the verb *zakhor*, "remember," resonates through Moshe's speeches in Deuteronomy:

because you would be ensnared by it, for it is abhorrent to the Lord your God.
26 Do not bring any abhorrent thing into your house, or you, like it, will be set
apart for utter destruction. Detest and abhor it utterly, for it is set apart for utter
destruction.
8 1 Take care to keep every command that I am charging you with on this day, so
that you may survive and thrive, go in, and take possession of the land that
2 the Lord swore He would give to your ancestors. Remember that the Lord
your God has led you through all this journey of forty years in the wilderness,
to humble you and to test you, and to know what was in your heart: to know
3 whether you would keep His commandments or whether you would fail to. He
humbled you by leaving you hungry, then feeding you manna, which neither
you nor your ancestors had ever known – to teach you that one does not live
4 by bread alone, but by all that comes forth from the mouth of the Lord. Your
5 clothes did not wear out, nor did your feet swell these forty years. Know then
in your heart that just as a parent disciplines his child, so the Lord your God
6 disciplines you. And so keep the commandments of the Lord your God,
7 walking in His ways and revering Him. For the Lord your God is bringing
you into a good land, a land of streams and springs and deep waters gushing
8 out to the valleys and the hills, a land of wheat and barley, vines, fig trees and
9 pomegranates, a land of olive oil and honey, a land where bread will not be

רש״י

ח א **כָּל הַמִּצְוָה.** כִּפְשׁוּטוֹ. וּמִדְרַשׁ אַגָּדָה, אִם הִתְחַלְתָּ בְּמִצְוָה, גְּמֹר אוֹתָהּ, שֶׁאֵינָהּ נִקְרֵאת אֶלָּא עַל שֵׁם הַגּוֹמְרָהּ, שֶׁנֶּאֱמַר: ״וְאֶת עַצְמוֹת יוֹסֵף אֲשֶׁר הֶעֱלוּ בְנֵי יִשְׂרָאֵל מִמִּצְרַיִם קָבְרוּ בִשְׁכֶם״ (יהושע כד, לב), וַהֲלֹא מֹשֶׁה לְבַדּוֹ נִתְעַסֵּק בָּהֶם לְהַעֲלוֹתָם (שמות יג, יט)? אֶלָּא לְפִי שֶׁלֹּא הִסְפִּיק לְגָמְרָהּ וּגְמָרוּהָ יִשְׂרָאֵל, נִקְרֵאת עַל שְׁמָם:

ב **הַתִשְׁמֹר מִצְוֹתָו.** שֶׁלֹּא תְנַסֵּהוּ וְלֹא תְהַרְהֵר אַחֲרָיו:

ד **שִׂמְלָתְךָ לֹא בָלְתָה.** עַנְנֵי כָבוֹד הָיוּ שָׁפִים בִּכְסוּתָם וּמְגַהֲצִים אוֹתָם כְּמִין כֵּלִים מְגֹהָצִים, וְאַף קְטַנֵּיהֶם כְּמוֹ שֶׁהָיוּ גְדֵלִים, הָיָה גָּדֵל לְבוּשָׁן עִמָּהֶם, כַּלְּבוּשׁ הַזֶּה שֶׁל חֹמֶט שֶׁגָּדֵל עִמּוֹ: **לֹא בָצֵקָה.** לֹא נָפְחָה כְּבָצֵק, כְּדֶרֶךְ הוֹלְכֵי יָחֵף שֶׁרַגְלֵיהֶם נְפוּחוֹת:

ח **זֵית שֶׁמֶן.** זֵיתִים הָעוֹשִׂים שֶׁמֶן:

food to all that lives" (Tanḥuma, Lekh Lekha 12). This is more than a beautiful tradition. It is a basic theme of Judaism. It is in the physical that we find the spiritual. God made the world; therefore it is in the world that we find God.

The commentators ask why the Grace after Meals is a biblical command, whereas the blessing *before* meals is only a rabbinic injunction. Their answer is that to thank God when we are hungry is natural. To thank Him when we are sated is more difficult. It is precisely when we are most likely

its emphasis on sanctifying the physical – is particularly concerned to turn the act of eating into a moment of spiritual affirmation.

It is said that Avraham and Sara drew people into the service of the One God by extending them hospitality. After their guests had eaten, they would turn to thank their hosts. Avraham would reply, "Thank not us but God, who provides food for all." "How shall we thank God?" "Say: Blessed is the Lord, who is blessed. Blessed be He who gives bread and

תִּשְׂרְפוּן בָּאֵשׁ לֹא־תַחְמֹד כֶּסֶף וְזָהָב עֲלֵיהֶם וְלָקַחְתָּ לָךְ פֶּן תִּוָּקֵשׁ בּוֹ
כו כִּי תוֹעֲבַת יהוה אֱלֹהֶיךָ הוּא: וְלֹא־תָבִיא תוֹעֵבָה אֶל־בֵּיתֶךָ וְהָיִיתָ
חֵרֶם כָּמֹהוּ שַׁקֵּץ ׀ תְּשַׁקְּצֶנּוּ וְתַעֵב ׀ תְּתַעֲבֶנּוּ כִּי־חֵרֶם הוּא:
ח א כָּל־הַמִּצְוָה אֲשֶׁר אָנֹכִי מְצַוְּךָ הַיּוֹם תִּשְׁמְרוּן לַעֲשׂוֹת לְמַעַן תִּחְיוּן
וּרְבִיתֶם וּבָאתֶם וִירִשְׁתֶּם אֶת־הָאָרֶץ אֲשֶׁר־נִשְׁבַּע יהוה לַאֲבֹתֵיכֶם:
ב וְזָכַרְתָּ אֶת־כָּל־הַדֶּרֶךְ אֲשֶׁר הוֹלִיכְךָ יהוה אֱלֹהֶיךָ זֶה אַרְבָּעִים שָׁנָה
בַּמִּדְבָּר לְמַעַן עַנֹּתְךָ לְנַסֹּתְךָ לָדַעַת אֶת־אֲשֶׁר בִּלְבָבְךָ הֲתִשְׁמֹר
ג מִצְוֺתָו אִם־לֹא: וַיְעַנְּךָ וַיַּרְעִבֶךָ וַיַּאֲכִלְךָ אֶת־הַמָּן אֲשֶׁר לֹא־יָדַעְתָּ וְלֹא
יָדְעוּן אֲבֹתֶיךָ לְמַעַן הוֹדִיעֲךָ כִּי לֹא עַל־הַלֶּחֶם לְבַדּוֹ יִחְיֶה הָאָדָם
ד כִּי עַל־כָּל־מוֹצָא פִי־יהוה יִחְיֶה הָאָדָם: שִׂמְלָתְךָ לֹא בָלְתָה מֵעָלֶיךָ
ה וְרַגְלְךָ לֹא בָצֵקָה זֶה אַרְבָּעִים שָׁנָה: וְיָדַעְתָּ עִם־לְבָבֶךָ כִּי כַּאֲשֶׁר יְיַסֵּר
ו אִישׁ אֶת־בְּנוֹ יהוה אֱלֹהֶיךָ מְיַסְּרֶךָּ: וְשָׁמַרְתָּ אֶת־מִצְוֺת יהוה אֱלֹהֶיךָ
ז לָלֶכֶת בִּדְרָכָיו וּלְיִרְאָה אֹתוֹ: כִּי יהוה אֱלֹהֶיךָ מְבִיאֲךָ אֶל־אֶרֶץ טוֹבָה
ח אֶרֶץ נַחֲלֵי מָיִם עֲיָנֹת וּתְהֹמֹת יֹצְאִים בַּבִּקְעָה וּבָהָר: אֶרֶץ חִטָּה וּשְׂעֹרָה
ט וְגֶפֶן וּתְאֵנָה וְרִמּוֹן אֶרֶץ־זֵית שֶׁמֶן וּדְבָשׁ: אֶרֶץ אֲשֶׁר לֹא בְמִסְכֵּנֻת

אונקלוס

תּוֹקְדוּן בְּנוּרָא, לָא תַחְמֵיד כַּסְפָּא וְדַהֲבָא דַעֲלֵיהוֹן וְתִסַּב לָךְ, דִּלְמָא תִתְּקִיל בֵּיהּ, אֲרֵי מְרַחַק, קֳדָם יי אֱלָהָךְ הוּא: כו וְלָא תָעֵיל דִּמְרַחַק לְבֵיתָךְ, וּתְהֵי חֶרְמָא כְּוָתֵיהּ, שַׁקָּצָא תְּשַׁקְּצִנֵּיהּ, וְרַחָקָא תְּרַחֲקִנֵּיהּ אֲרֵי חֶרְמָא הוּא: ח א כָּל תַּפְקֵידְתָּא, דַּאֲנָא מְפַקֵּיד לָךְ, יוֹמָא דֵין תִּטְּרוּן לְמֶעְבַּד, בְּדִיל דְּתֵיחוּן וְתִסְגּוֹן, וְתֵיעֲלוּן וְתֵירְתוּן יָת אַרְעָא, דְּקַיֵּים יי לַאֲבָהָתְכוֹן: ב וְתִדְכַּר יָת כָּל אוֹרְחָא, דְּדַבְּרָךְ, יי אֱלָהָךְ, דְּנָן, אַרְבְּעִין שְׁנִין בְּמַדְבְּרָא, בְּדִיל לְעַנָּיוּתָךְ לְנַסָּיוּתָךְ, לְמִדַּע, יָת דִּבְלִבָּךְ, הֲתִטַּר פִּקּוֹדוֹהִי אִם לָא: ג וְעַנְּיָךְ וְאַכְפְנָךְ, וְאוֹכְלָךְ יָת מַנָּא דְּלָא יְדַעְתָּא, וְלָא יְדַעוּ אֲבָהָתָךְ, בְּדִיל לְהוֹדָעוּתָךְ, אֲרֵי, לָא עַל לַחְמָא בִּלְחוֹדוֹהִי מִתְקַיַּם אֱנָשָׁא, אֲרֵי, עַל כָּל אַפָּקוּת מֵימַר מִן קֳדָם יי חָיֵי אֱנָשָׁא: ד כְּסוּתָךְ, לָא בְלִיאַת מִנָּךְ, וּמְסָנָךְ לָא יְחֵיפוּ, דְּנָן אַרְבְּעִין שְׁנִין: ה וְתִדַּע עִם לִבָּךְ, אֲרֵי, כְּמָא דְּמַלֵּיף גְּבַר יָת בְּרֵיהּ, יי אֱלָהָךְ מַלֵּיף לָךְ: ו וְתִטַּר, יָת פִּקּוֹדַיָּא דַּיי אֱלָהָךְ, לִמְהָךְ בְּאוֹרְחָן דְּתָקְנָן קֳדָמוֹהִי וּלְמִדְחַל יָתֵיהּ: ז אֲרֵי יי אֱלָהָךְ, מַעֵיל לָךְ לְאַרְעָא טָבְתָא, אֲרַע נָגְדָא נַחְלִין דְּמַיִין, מַבּוּעֵי עֵינָן וּתְהוֹמִין, נָפְקִין בְּבִקְעָן וּבְטוּרִין: ח אֲרַע חִטִּין וְסַעֲרִין, וְגֻפְנִין וְתֵינִין וְרִמּוֹנִין, אֲרַעָא דְּזֵיתַהָא עָבְדִין מִשְׁחָא וְהִיא עָבְדָא דְּבַשׁ: ט אֲרַעָא, דְּלָא בְמִסְכֵּינוּ

8:10 וּבֵרַכְתָּ אֶת־יהוה אֱלֹהֶיךָ *You shall bless the Lord your God* – Grace after Meals is one of the elements of Jewish liturgy already specified in the Bible; it is commanded in this verse. Eating is a biological function. Judaism – with

scarce, where you will lack nothing, a land where the rocks are iron and where
10 you can hew bronze from her hills. And when you eat and are satisfied, you
11 shall bless the LORD your God for the good land that He has given you. Take SHENI
care not to forget the LORD your God, failing to keep His commandments,
12 laws, and decrees, with which I am charging you this day. Otherwise, when
you have eaten and been satisfied, and have built fine houses and lived in
13 them, when your herds and flocks have grown abundant, and your silver and
14 gold is abundant, and all that you have has grown abundant, your heart may
become proud, forgetting the LORD your God who brought you out of Egypt,
15 the house of slaves, who led you through the vast and terrifying wilderness,
an arid wasteland with venomous snakes and scorpions, who brought forth
16 water from flint rock for you, and fed you manna in the wilderness, something
your ancestors did not know, to humble and to test you – so that in the end it
17 would be well for you. You might be tempted to say to yourself, 'My power, the
18 strength of my own hand, have brought me this great wealth.' But remember
the LORD your God, for it is He who gives you the power to do great things,
upholding the covenant that He swore to your ancestors, as He is doing on this
day.

---

universe, shaper of history, and author of the laws of life that directs and facilitates our gratitude. It is hard to feel grateful to a universe that came into existence for no reason and is blind to us and our fate. It is our faith in a personal God that gives force and focus to our thanks.

The nation's history, Moshe asserts, should be engraved on people's souls and reenacted in the annual cycle of festivals; the nation, as a nation, should never attribute its achievements to itself – "my power, the strength of my own hand" – but should always ascribe its victories, indeed its very existence, to something higher than itself: God. This is a dominant theme of Deuteronomy, and it echoes throughout the book time and again.

8:18 **הוּא הַנֹּתֵן לְךָ כֹּחַ** *It is He who gives you the power* – Everything will depend, Moshe teaches, on how the next generation responds to the good things that God promises them. *Either* you will eat and be satisfied and bless God, *remembering* that all things come from Him – *or* you will eat and be satisfied and *forget* to whom you owe all this. You will think it comes entirely from your own efforts: "My power, the strength of my own hand, have brought me this great wealth." Although this may seem a small difference, it will, says Moshe, make *all* the difference.

Moshe's argument is counterintuitive. You may think, he says, that the hard times are behind you. You have wandered for forty years without a home. There were times when you had no water, no food. You were attacked by enemies. You may think this was the test of your strength. It was not. *The real challenge is not poverty but affluence, not slavery but freedom, not homelessness but home.*

Many nations have been lifted to great heights when they faced difficulty and danger. They came through crises – droughts, plagues, recessions, defeats – and were toughened by them. When times are hard, people grow. There is a sense of community and solidarity, of neighbors and strangers pulling together. Many people who have lived through a war remember it as the most vivid time of their life.

The real test of a nation is not if it can survive a crisis but if it can survive the *lack* of a crisis. Can it stay strong

תֹּאכַל־בָּהּ לֶחֶם לֹא־תֶחְסַר כֹּל בָּהּ אֶרֶץ אֲשֶׁר אֲבָנֶיהָ בַרְזֶל וּמֵהֲרָרֶיהָ
י תַּחְצֹב נְחֹשֶׁת: וְאָכַלְתָּ וְשָׂבָעְתָּ וּבֵרַכְתָּ אֶת־יְהוָה אֱלֹהֶיךָ עַל־הָאָרֶץ
יא הַטֹּבָה אֲשֶׁר נָתַן־לָךְ: הִשָּׁמֶר לְךָ פֶּן־תִּשְׁכַּח אֶת־יְהוָה אֱלֹהֶיךָ לְבִלְתִּי שני
יב שְׁמֹר מִצְוֺתָיו וּמִשְׁפָּטָיו וְחֻקֹּתָיו אֲשֶׁר אָנֹכִי מְצַוְּךָ הַיּוֹם: פֶּן־תֹּאכַל
יג וְשָׂבָעְתָּ וּבָתִּים טֹבִים תִּבְנֶה וְיָשָׁבְתָּ: וּבְקָרְךָ וְצֹאנְךָ יִרְבְּיֻן וְכֶסֶף
יד וְזָהָב יִרְבֶּה־לָּךְ וְכֹל אֲשֶׁר־לְךָ יִרְבֶּה: וְרָם לְבָבֶךָ וְשָׁכַחְתָּ אֶת־יְהוָה
טו אֱלֹהֶיךָ הַמּוֹצִיאֲךָ מֵאֶרֶץ מִצְרַיִם מִבֵּית עֲבָדִים: הַמּוֹלִיכְךָ בַּמִּדְבָּר ׀
הַגָּדֹל וְהַנּוֹרָא נָחָשׁ ׀ שָׂרָף וְעַקְרָב וְצִמָּאוֹן אֲשֶׁר אֵין־מָיִם הַמּוֹצִיא לְךָ
טז מַיִם מִצּוּר הַחַלָּמִישׁ: הַמַּאֲכִלְךָ מָן בַּמִּדְבָּר אֲשֶׁר לֹא־יָדְעוּן אֲבֹתֶיךָ
יז לְמַעַן עַנֹּתְךָ וּלְמַעַן נַסֹּתֶךָ לְהֵיטִבְךָ בְּאַחֲרִיתֶךָ: וְאָמַרְתָּ בִּלְבָבֶךָ
יח כֹּחִי וְעֹצֶם יָדִי עָשָׂה לִי אֶת־הַחַיִל הַזֶּה: וְזָכַרְתָּ אֶת־יְהוָה אֱלֹהֶיךָ כִּי
הוּא הַנֹּתֵן לְךָ כֹּחַ לַעֲשׂוֹת חָיִל לְמַעַן הָקִים אֶת־בְּרִיתוֹ אֲשֶׁר־נִשְׁבַּע
לַאֲבֹתֶיךָ כַּיּוֹם הַזֶּה:

אונקלוס

תֵּיכוֹל בַּהּ לַחְמָא, לָא תֶחְסַר כָּל מִדַּעַם בַּהּ, אַרְעָא דְּאַבְנַהָא בַּרְזְלָא, וּמִטּוּרַהָא תִּפְסוֹל נְחָשָׁא: י וְתֵיכוֹל וְתִסְבַּע, וּתְבָרֵיךְ יָת יי אֱלָהָךְ, עַל אַרְעָא טָבְתָא דִּיהַב לָךְ: יא אִסְתְּמַר לָךְ, דִּלְמָא תִתְנְשֵׁי יָת דַּחְלְתָא דַּיי אֱלָהָךְ, בְּדִיל דְּלָא לְמִטַּר פִּקּוֹדוֹהִי וְדִינוֹהִי וּקְיָמוֹהִי, דַּאֲנָא מְפַקֵּיד לָךְ יוֹמָא דֵין: יב דִּלְמָא תֵיכוֹל וְתִסְבַּע, וּבָתִּין שַׁפִּירִין, תִּבְנֵי וְתִתֵּיב: יג וְתוֹרָךְ וְעָנָךְ יִסְגּוֹן, וְכַסְפָּא וְדַהֲבָא יִסְגֵּי לָךְ, וְכֹל דְּלָךְ יִסְגֵּי: יד וְיִרַם לִבָּךְ, וְתִתְנְשֵׁי יָת דַּחְלְתָא דַּיי אֱלָהָךְ, דְּאַפְּקָךְ מֵאַרְעָא דְּמִצְרַיִם מִבֵּית עַבְדוּתָא: טו דְּדַבְּרָךְ, בְּמַדְבְּרָא רַבָּא וּדְחִילָא, אֲתַר דְּחִיוָון קָלָן וְעַקְרַבִּין, וּבֵית צַהֲוָנָא אֲתַר דְּלֵית מַיָּא, דְּאַפֵּיק לָךְ מַיָּא, מִטִּנָּרָא תַּקִּיפָא: טז דְּאוֹכְלָךְ מַנָּא בְּמַדְבְּרָא, דְּלָא יְדַעוּ אֲבָהָתָךְ, בְּדִיל לְעַנְיוּתָךְ, וּבְדִיל לְנַסָּיוּתָךְ, לְאוֹטָבָא לָךְ בְּסוֹפָךְ: יז וְתֵימַר בְּלִבָּךְ, חֵילִי וּתְקוֹף יְדִי, קְנָא לִי יָת נִכְסַיָּא הָאִלֵּין: יח וְתִדְכַּר יָת יי אֱלָהָךְ, אֲרֵי הוּא, יָהֵיב לָךְ, עֵיצָא לְמִקְנֵי נִכְסִין, בְּדִיל לְקַיָּמָא יָת קְיָמֵיהּ, דְּקַיֵּים לַאֲבָהָתָךְ כְּיוֹמָא הָדֵין:

to forget that we need reminding – that what we have, we have from God, creator and sustainer of all.

8:17 כֹּחִי וְעֹצֶם יָדִי *My power, the strength of my own hand* – Gratitude – *hakarat hatov* – is at the heart of what Moshe has to say about the Israelites and their future in the Promised Land. Gratitude has not been their strong point in the desert. They have complained about the lack of food and water, about the manna and the lack of meat and vegetables, about the dangers they faced from the Egyptians as they were leaving, and about the inhabitants of the land they were about to enter. They lacked thankfulness during the difficult times. A greater danger still, says Moshe, would be a lack of gratitude during the good times.

Though you do not have to be religious to be grateful, there is something about belief in God as creator of the

19 If you do forget the LORD your God and follow other gods, serving and
worshipping them, I solemnly warn you today that you will be altogether lost.
20 Like the nations that the LORD will cause to die before you, so shall you be lost,
because you would not listen to the voice of the LORD your God.
9 1 Listen, Israel! You are now about to cross the Jordan, to go in and dispossess
nations larger and mightier than you, with great cities, fortified to high heaven.
2 The people are strong and lofty – Anakites. You know of them; you have heard
3 it said of them, 'Who can stand up against the descendants of Anak?' Know
then today that it is the LORD your God, who is crossing over before you like a
consuming fire: He will wipe them out, subduing them before you, so that you
4 may rapidly dispossess and destroy them, as the LORD promised you. When the SHELISHI
LORD your God drives them out before you, do not say to yourself, 'It is because
of my righteousness that the LORD has brought me in to take possession of this
land.' The LORD is dispossessing these nations before you because of their own
5 wickedness. Not for your righteousness or rectitude are you coming to take

רש״י

ט א גְּדֹלִים וַעֲצֻמִים מִמֶּךָּ. אַתָּה עָצוּם וְהֵם עֲצוּמִים מִמְּךָ:
ד אַל תֹּאמַר בִּלְבָבְךָ. צִדְקָתִי וְרִשְׁעַת הַגּוֹיִם גָּרְמוּ:
ה לֹא בְצִדְקָתְךָ וְגוֹ׳ אַתָּה בָא לָרֶשֶׁת וְגוֹ׳ כִּי בְּרִשְׁעַת הַגּוֹיִם. הֲרֵי ׳כִּי׳ מְשַׁמֵּשׁ בִּלְשׁוֹן ׳אֶלָּא׳:

Philistines up from Kaftor, and Aram from Kir?" God is active in the history of other nations. He sends a prophet, Yona, to Israel's enemy, Assyria, to persuade them to repent and be saved from catastrophe. Yeshayahu even foresees a day when God will do for Israel's other great enemy, Egypt, what He did for the Israelites against Egypt itself – rescue them from oppression:

> On that day, in Egypt's heartlands, an altar to the LORD will stand; at her borders a pillar to the LORD. They will be sign and testament in the land of Egypt to the LORD of Hosts, for the people shall cry out to the LORD because of their oppressors; He will send them a rescuer, a fighter; he will save them. The LORD will be made known to Egypt, and Egypt will know the LORD on that day.... The LORD will plague Egypt – plague it and heal.... On that day a road will run from Egypt to Assyria. Assyria will come to Egypt. Egypt will come to Assyria, and Egypt with Assyria will worship. On that day, Israel will be one with Egypt and Assyria, a blessing on this earth. For the LORD of Hosts has blessed him, saying: Blessed are My people, Egypt, Assyria, work of My hands, and Israel, My own possession. (Is. 19:19–25)

Nor is there any intimation in the Bible that Avraham's family have a monopoly on virtue. One of the heroines of the exodus, without whom there would have been no Moshe, was Pharaoh's daughter. Raḥav, who shelters Yehoshua's spies, is a prostitute from Jericho (Josh. 2). Yael, the heroine who saves Israel from Sisera, is a Kenite (Judges 4). Uriya, whose faithfulness to David contrasts so sharply with David's faithlessness to him, is a Hittite (II Sam. 11). According to many of the Sages, Iyov, the Bible's most conspicuous example of a wholly righteous man, is not an Israelite; his book is also the Tanakh's most focused exploration of the question of individual providence. Just as we do not hold a monopoly on virtue, neither do we hold a monopoly on God's interest and concern.

9:5 לֹא בְצִדְקָתְךָ *Not for your righteousness* – Moshe criticizes the Israelites, telling them, "Not for your righteousness or

יט וְהָיָה אִם־שָׁכֹחַ תִּשְׁכַּח אֶת־יהוה אֱלֹהֶיךָ וְהָלַכְתָּ אַחֲרֵי אֱלֹהִים אֲחֵרִים
כ וַעֲבַדְתָּם וְהִשְׁתַּחֲוִיתָ לָהֶם הַעִדֹתִי בָכֶם הַיּוֹם כִּי אָבֹד תֹּאבֵדוּן׃ כַּגּוֹיִם
אֲשֶׁר יהוה מַאֲבִיד מִפְּנֵיכֶם כֵּן תֹּאבֵדוּן עֵקֶב לֹא תִשְׁמְעוּן בְּקוֹל יהוה
אֱלֹהֵיכֶם׃

ט א שְׁמַע יִשְׂרָאֵל אַתָּה עֹבֵר הַיּוֹם אֶת־הַיַּרְדֵּן לָבֹא לָרֶשֶׁת גּוֹיִם גְּדֹלִים ח
ב וַעֲצֻמִים מִמֶּךָּ עָרִים גְּדֹלֹת וּבְצֻרֹת בַּשָּׁמָיִם׃ עַם־גָּדוֹל וָרָם בְּנֵי עֲנָקִים
ג אֲשֶׁר אַתָּה יָדַעְתָּ וְאַתָּה שָׁמַעְתָּ מִי יִתְיַצֵּב לִפְנֵי בְּנֵי עֲנָק׃ וְיָדַעְתָּ הַיּוֹם
כִּי יהוה אֱלֹהֶיךָ הוּא־הָעֹבֵר לְפָנֶיךָ אֵשׁ אֹכְלָה הוּא יַשְׁמִידֵם וְהוּא
ד יַכְנִיעֵם לְפָנֶיךָ וְהוֹרַשְׁתָּם וְהַאֲבַדְתָּם מַהֵר כַּאֲשֶׁר דִּבֶּר יהוה לָךְ׃ אַל־ שלישי
תֹּאמַר בִּלְבָבְךָ בַּהֲדֹף יהוה אֱלֹהֶיךָ אֹתָם ׀ מִלְּפָנֶיךָ לֵאמֹר בְּצִדְקָתִי
הֱבִיאַנִי יהוה לָרֶשֶׁת אֶת־הָאָרֶץ הַזֹּאת וּבְרִשְׁעַת הַגּוֹיִם הָאֵלֶּה
ה יהוה מוֹרִישָׁם מִפָּנֶיךָ׃ לֹא בְצִדְקָתְךָ וּבְיֹשֶׁר לְבָבְךָ אַתָּה בָא לָרֶשֶׁת

אונקלוס

יט ויהי, אם אתנשאה תתנשי ית דחלתא דיי אלהך, ותהך, בתר טעות עממיא, ותפלחנין ותסגוד להון, אסהידית בכון יומא דין, ארי מיבד תיבדון: כ כעממיא, דיי מוביד מן קדמיכון, כן תיבדון, חלף דלא קבילתון, למימרא דיי אלהכון: ט א שמע ישראל, את עבר יומא דין ית ירדנא, למיעל למירת עממין, רברבין ותקיפין מנך, קרוין, רברבן וכריכן עד צית שמיא: ב עם רב ותקיף בני גבריא, דאת ידעתא ואת שמעתא, מאן יכול למקם, קדם בני גברא: ג ותדע יומא דין, ארי יי אלהך, הוא עבר קדמך מימריה אישא אכלא, הוא ישיצינון, והוא יתברנון קדמך, ותתריכנון ותובידנון בפריע, כמא דמליל יי לך: ד לא תימר בלבך, בדיתבר יי אלהך יתהון מן קדמך למימר, בזכותי אעלני יי, למירת ית ארעא הדא, ובחובי עממיא האלין, יי מתריך להון מן קדמך: ה לא בזכותך, ובקשיטות

during times of ease and plenty, power and prestige? That is the challenge that has defeated every civilization known to history. Let it not, says Moshe, defeat you.

The pages of history are littered with the relics of nations that seemed impregnable in their day, but which eventually declined and fell, always for the reason Moshe foresaw. *They forgot*. Memories fade. People lose sight of the values they once fought for – justice, equality, independence, freedom. The nation, its early battles over, becomes strong. Some of its members grow rich. They become lax, self-indulgent, over-sophisticated, decadent. They lose their sense of social solidarity. They begin to feel that such wealth and position as they have is theirs by right. The bonds of fraternity and collective responsibility begin to fray. That was the danger Moshe foresaw and about which he warned. The politics of free societies depends on the handing on of memory.

9:4 וּבְרִשְׁעַת הַגּוֹיִם הָאֵלֶּה *Because of their own wickedness* – There is no implication in the Tanakh that the Israelites' is the only story. To the contrary, as Amos 9:7 says: "Are you not to Me like the children of Kush, O children of Israel? Did I not bring up Israel from the land of Egypt as I brought the

possession of their land; it is for these nations' wickedness that the LORD your
God is driving them out before you and to fulfill the promise that the LORD
6 made on oath to your ancestors, Avraham, Yitzhak, and Yaakov. Know, then,
that it is not for your righteousness that the LORD your God is giving you this
7 good land to possess, for you are a stiff-necked people. Remember and never
forget how you provoked the LORD your God to fury in the wilderness. From
the day you left Egypt until you arrived here, you have always been rebellious
8 against the LORD. At Horev you provoked the LORD to fury: so incensed was
9 the LORD that He was ready to destroy you. I had ascended the mountain to
receive the stone tablets, the tablets of the Covenant the LORD made with you.
I remained on the mountain forty days and forty nights; I ate no bread and I
10 drank no water. The LORD gave me two stone tablets inscribed by the finger of
God. And upon them were all the words that the LORD had spoken to you at the
11 mountain out of the fire, on the day of that assembly. And when the forty days
and forty nights were at an end, the LORD gave me the two stone tablets, the

רש״י

ט וָאֵשֵׁב בָּהָר. אֵין יְשִׁיבָה אֶלָּא לְשׁוֹן עַכָּבָה:

י לוּחֹת. 'לֻחֹת' כְּתִיב, שֶׁשְּׁתֵיהֶן שָׁווֹת:

people." They submit (eventually) to God, but even then, to almost no one else. In this context can we understand why the Rabbis carefully constructed a culture of "argument for the sake of Heaven" (see Num. 16, "The Nature of the Argument").

The Sages lived through the disaster of the great rebellion against Rome, in which the Temple was destroyed, and in some ways the even greater disaster of the Bar Kokhba rebellion, the greatest human tragedy in Jewish history prior to the Holocaust. They knew they had been defeated because they were divided. How, then, could they continue? Should they encourage conformism and intellectual timidity? That was an option they rejected. What they did instead was to bring difference to the house of study, locate it within the protocols of "argument for the sake of Heaven," and thus create a culture in which strong individuals with strongly held beliefs could disagree without splitting apart. The contrariness identified by Moshe continued through the ages, but over time Judaism developed a culture of constructive dissent, in relation both to God and to other people.

9:7 **ממרים הייתם עם־יהוה** *You have always been rebellious against the LORD* – Criticism is easy to deliver but hard to bear. It is easy for people to close their ears, or even turn the criticism around ("He's blaming us, but he should be blaming himself. After all, he was in charge"). For criticism to be heeded, the people have to know, beyond any doubt, that the critic cares for them, wants the best for them, and is prepared to take personal risks for their sake. Moshe can be as critical as he is in the last month of his life because the people he is talking to know that he has defended them and their parents in his prayers for divine forgiveness, that he has risked challenging God, that he declined God's offer to abandon the Israelites and begin again with him – in short, that Moshe's whole life as a leader was dedicated to what was best for the people. When you know that about someone, you listen to their criticism. If you seek to change someone, make sure that you are willing to help them when they need your help, defend them when they need your defense, and see the good in them, not just the bad. Anyone can complain, but we have to earn the right to criticize.

אֶת־אַרְצָם כִּי בְּרִשְׁעַת ׀ הַגּוֹיִם הָאֵלֶּה יהוה אֱלֹהֶיךָ מוֹרִישָׁם מִפָּנֶיךָ
וּלְמַעַן הָקִים אֶת־הַדָּבָר אֲשֶׁר נִשְׁבַּע יהוה לַאֲבֹתֶיךָ לְאַבְרָהָם לְיִצְחָק
ו וּלְיַעֲקֹב׃ וְיָדַעְתָּ כִּי לֹא בְצִדְקָתְךָ יהוה אֱלֹהֶיךָ נֹתֵן לְךָ אֶת־הָאָרֶץ
ז הַטּוֹבָה הַזֹּאת לְרִשְׁתָּהּ כִּי עַם־קְשֵׁה־עֹרֶף אָתָּה׃ זְכֹר אַל־תִּשְׁכַּח אֵת
אֲשֶׁר־הִקְצַפְתָּ אֶת־יהוה אֱלֹהֶיךָ בַּמִּדְבָּר לְמִן־הַיּוֹם אֲשֶׁר־יָצָאתָ ׀
מֵאֶרֶץ מִצְרַיִם עַד־בֹּאֲכֶם עַד־הַמָּקוֹם הַזֶּה מַמְרִים הֱיִיתֶם עִם־יהוה׃
ח וּבְחֹרֵב הִקְצַפְתֶּם אֶת־יהוה וַיִּתְאַנַּף יהוה בָּכֶם לְהַשְׁמִיד אֶתְכֶם׃
ט בַּעֲלֹתִי הָהָרָה לָקַחַת לוּחֹת הָאֲבָנִים לוּחֹת הַבְּרִית אֲשֶׁר־כָּרַת יהוה
עִמָּכֶם וָאֵשֵׁב בָּהָר אַרְבָּעִים יוֹם וְאַרְבָּעִים לַיְלָה לֶחֶם לֹא אָכַלְתִּי
י וּמַיִם לֹא שָׁתִיתִי׃ וַיִּתֵּן יהוה אֵלַי אֶת־שְׁנֵי לוּחֹת הָאֲבָנִים כְּתֻבִים
בְּאֶצְבַּע אֱלֹהִים וַעֲלֵיהֶם כְּכָל־הַדְּבָרִים אֲשֶׁר דִּבֶּר יהוה עִמָּכֶם בָּהָר
יא מִתּוֹךְ הָאֵשׁ בְּיוֹם הַקָּהָל׃ וַיְהִי מִקֵּץ אַרְבָּעִים יוֹם וְאַרְבָּעִים לַיְלָה נָתַן

אונקלוס

לִבָּךְ, אַתְּ עָלֵיל לְמֵירַת יָת אַרְעֲהוֹן, אֲרֵי, בְּחוֹבֵי עַמְמַיָּא הָאִלֵּין, יי אֱלָהָךְ מְתָרֵיךְ לְהוֹן מִן קֳדָמָךְ, וּבְדִיל לְקַיָּמָא יָת פִּתְגָּמָא, דְּקַיֵּים יי לַאֲבָהָתָךְ, לְאַבְרָהָם לְיִצְחָק וּלְיַעֲקֹב: ו וְתִדַּע, אֲרֵי, לָא בִזְכוּתָךְ יי אֱלָהָךְ, יָהֵיב לָךְ, יָת אַרְעָא טָבְתָא, הָדָא לְמֵירְתַהּ, אֲרֵי עַם קְשֵׁי קְדָל אַתְּ: ז הֱוֵי דְכִיר לָא תִתְנְשֵׁי, יָת דְּאַרְגֵּיזְתָּא, קֳדָם יי אֱלָהָךְ בְּמַדְבְּרָא, לְמִן יוֹמָא, דִּנְפַקְתָּא מֵאַרְעָא דְמִצְרַיִם, עַד מֵיתֵיכוֹן עַד אַתְרָא הָדֵין, מְסָרְבִין הֲוֵיתוֹן קֳדָם יי: ח וּבְחוֹרֵב אַרְגֵּיזְתּוּן קֳדָם יי, וּתְקֵיף רֻגְזָא דַיי, בְּכוֹן לְשֵׁיצָאָה יָתְכוֹן: ט בְּמִסְּקִי לְטוּרָא, לְמִסַּב, לוּחֵי אַבְנַיָּא לוּחֵי קְיָמָא, דִּגְזַר יי עִמְּכוֹן, וִיתֵיבִית בְּטוּרָא, אַרְבְּעִין יְמָמִין וְאַרְבְּעִין לֵילָוָן, לַחְמָא לָא אֲכָלִית, וּמַיָּא לָא שְׁתֵיתִי: י וִיהַב יי לִי, יָת תְּרֵין לוּחֵי אַבְנַיָּא, כְּתִיבִין בְּאֶצְבְּעָא דַיי, וַעֲלֵיהוֹן, כְּכָל פִּתְגָּמַיָּא, דְּמַלֵּיל יי עִמְּכוֹן בְּטוּרָא, מִגּוֹ אִישָׁתָא בְּיוֹמָא דִקְהָלָא: יא וַהֲוָה, מִסּוֹף אַרְבְּעִין יְמָמִין, וְאַרְבְּעִין לֵילָוָן, יְהַב

rectitude are you coming to take possession of their land" (Deut. 9:5). This note is sustained to the end of the prophetic age. Malakhi, last of the prophets, says, "From one end of the earth to the other, My name is great among the nations…yet you desecrate it" (Mal. 1:11–12).

This is a point of immense consequence. A chosen people is the opposite of a master race, first, because it is not a race but a covenant; second, because it exists to serve God, not to master others. A master race worships itself; a chosen people worships something beyond itself. A master race produces monumental buildings, triumphal inscriptions, and a literature of self-congratulation. Israel, to a degree unique in history, produced a literature of almost uninterrupted self-criticism.

9:6 עַם־קְשֵׁה־עֹרֶף אָתָּה *You are a stiff-necked people* – Social cohesion requires a degree of submissiveness, but Jews are described across the Mosaic books as a "stiff-necked

12 tablets of the Covenant. And then the LORD said to me, ‘Get up; go down from
here immediately, because your people whom you brought from Egypt have
acted disastrously; how rapidly they strayed from the path that I commanded
13 them to follow – they have made a molten image for themselves.’ The LORD
14 said to me, ‘I have seen this people, and they are a stiff-necked people. Stand
back from Me and I will destroy them and erase their name from under the
heavens, and I will make of you a nation mightier and more numerous than
15 they.’ I turned and went down from the mountain while it was still ablaze with
16 fire, and the two tablets of the Covenant were in my two hands. When I looked,
I saw that you had indeed sinned against the LORD your God. You had made
for yourselves a molten calf; you had strayed rapidly indeed from the path that
17 the LORD had commanded you to follow. So I took hold of the two tablets and
18 flung them from my hands, smashing them to pieces before your eyes. Then I
threw myself down before the LORD as before, for forty days and forty nights; I
ate no bread and I drank no water, because of the great sin you had committed,
19 angering the LORD by doing what was evil in His eyes. I was terrified of the
LORD’s blazing fury and rage against you, ready to destroy you. But the LORD
20 listened to me that time also. The LORD was so enraged with Aharon that He

רש״י

יח **וָאֶתְנַפַּל לִפְנֵי ה׳ כָּרִאשֹׁנָה אַרְבָּעִים יוֹם.** שֶׁנֶּאֱמַר: ״וְעַתָּה אֶעֱלֶה אֶל ה׳ אוּלַי אֲכַפְּרָה״ (שמות לב, ל), בְּאוֹתָהּ עֲלִיָּה נִתְעַכַּבְתִּי אַרְבָּעִים יוֹם, נִמְנְאוּ כָּלִים בְּעֶשְׂרִים וְתִשְׁעָה בְּאָב, שֶׁהוּא עָלָה בִּשְׁמוֹנָה עָשָׂר בְּתַמּוּז. בּוֹ בַּיּוֹם נִתְרַצָּה הַקָּדוֹשׁ בָּרוּךְ הוּא לְיִשְׂרָאֵל וְאָמַר לְמֹשֶׁה: ״פְּסָל לְךָ שְׁנֵי לֻחֹת״ (שם לד, א), עָשָׂה עוֹד אַרְבָּעִים יוֹם, נִמְנְאוּ כָּלִים בְּיוֹם הַכִּפּוּרִים. בּוֹ בַּיּוֹם נִתְרַצָּה הַקָּדוֹשׁ בָּרוּךְ הוּא לְיִשְׂרָאֵל בְּשִׂמְחָה, וְאָמַר לוֹ לְמֹשֶׁה: ״סָלַחְתִּי כִּדְבָרֶךָ״ (במדבר יד, כ), לְכָךְ הֻקְבַּע לִמְחִילָה וְלִסְלִיחָה.

וּמִנַּיִן שֶׁנִּתְרַצָּה בְּרָצוֹן שָׁלֵם? שֶׁנֶּאֱמַר בָּאַרְבָּעִים שֶׁל לוּחוֹת אַחֲרוֹנוֹת: ״וְאָנֹכִי עָמַדְתִּי בָהָר כַּיָּמִים הָרִאשֹׁנִים״ (להלן י, י), מָה הָרִאשׁוֹנִים בְּרָצוֹן אַף אַחֲרוֹנִים בְּרָצוֹן, אֱמֹר מֵעַתָּה אֶמְצָעִיִּים הָיוּ בְּכַעַס:

כ **וּבְאַהֲרֹן הִתְאַנַּף ה׳.** לְפִי שֶׁשָּׁמַע לָכֶם: **לְהַשְׁמִידוֹ.** זֶה כִּלּוּי בָּנִים, וְכֵן הוּא אוֹמֵר: ״וָאַשְׁמִיד פִּרְיוֹ מִמַּעַל״ (עמוס ב, ט): **וָאֶתְפַּלֵּל גַּם בְּעַד אַהֲרֹן.** וְהוֹעִילָה תְּפִלָּתִי לְכַפֵּר מֶחֱצָה, וּמֵתוּ שְׁנַיִם וְנִשְׁאֲרוּ הַשְּׁנַיִם:

it into the fire, and out came this calf!” (Ex. 32:24). In anyone such evasion is a moral failure; in a leader such as Aharon the High Priest, all the more so.

Yet Aharon was not immediately punished. According to the Torah he was condemned for another sin altogether when, years later, he and Moshe spoke angrily against the people complaining about the lack of water: “Aharon is to be gathered to his people. He shall not enter the land that I have given to the Israelites, because you disobeyed My command at the waters of Meriva” (Num. 20:24).

It is easy to be critical of people who fail the leadership test when, like Aharon, it involves blocking the path the majority are intent on taking. However, it is hard to oppose the mob. They can ignore you, remove you, even assassinate you. Even Moshe was helpless in the face of the people’s demands during the later episode of the spies (14:5).

Tradition, therefore, dealt kindly with Aharon. He is portrayed as a man of peace. Perhaps that is why he was made High Priest. There is more than one kind of leadership, and priesthood does not involve swaying crowds. The fact that Aharon was not a leader in the same mold as Moshe does not mean that he was a failure. He failed when he was

יב יְהוָה אֵלַי אֶת־שְׁנֵי לֻחֹת הָאֲבָנִים לֻחוֹת הַבְּרִית׃ וַיֹּאמֶר יְהוָה אֵלַי
קוּם רֵד מַהֵר מִזֶּה כִּי שִׁחֵת עַמְּךָ אֲשֶׁר הוֹצֵאתָ מִמִּצְרָיִם סָרוּ מַהֵר
יג מִן־הַדֶּרֶךְ אֲשֶׁר צִוִּיתִם עָשׂוּ לָהֶם מַסֵּכָה׃ וַיֹּאמֶר יְהוָה אֵלַי לֵאמֹר
יד רָאִיתִי אֶת־הָעָם הַזֶּה וְהִנֵּה עַם־קְשֵׁה־עֹרֶף הוּא׃ הֶרֶף מִמֶּנִּי וְאַשְׁמִידֵם
וְאֶמְחֶה אֶת־שְׁמָם מִתַּחַת הַשָּׁמָיִם וְאֶעֱשֶׂה אוֹתְךָ לְגוֹי־עָצוּם וָרָב
טו מִמֶּנּוּ׃ וָאֵפֶן וָאֵרֵד מִן־הָהָר וְהָהָר בֹּעֵר בָּאֵשׁ וּשְׁנֵי לוּחֹת הַבְּרִית
טז עַל שְׁתֵּי יָדָי׃ וָאֵרֶא וְהִנֵּה חֲטָאתֶם לַיהוָה אֱלֹהֵיכֶם עֲשִׂיתֶם לָכֶם
יז עֵגֶל מַסֵּכָה סַרְתֶּם מַהֵר מִן־הַדֶּרֶךְ אֲשֶׁר־צִוָּה יְהוָה אֶתְכֶם׃ וָאֶתְפֹּשׂ
יח בִּשְׁנֵי הַלֻּחֹת וָאַשְׁלִכֵם מֵעַל שְׁתֵּי יָדָי וָאֲשַׁבְּרֵם לְעֵינֵיכֶם׃ וָאֶתְנַפַּל ס
לִפְנֵי יְהוָה כָּרִאשֹׁנָה אַרְבָּעִים יוֹם וְאַרְבָּעִים לַיְלָה לֶחֶם לֹא אָכַלְתִּי
וּמַיִם לֹא שָׁתִיתִי עַל כָּל־חַטַּאתְכֶם אֲשֶׁר חֲטָאתֶם לַעֲשׂוֹת הָרַע
יט בְּעֵינֵי יְהוָה לְהַכְעִיסוֹ׃ כִּי יָגֹרְתִּי מִפְּנֵי הָאַף וְהַחֵמָה אֲשֶׁר קָצַף יְהוָה
כ עֲלֵיכֶם לְהַשְׁמִיד אֶתְכֶם וַיִּשְׁמַע יְהוָה אֵלַי גַּם בַּפַּעַם הַהִוא׃ וּבְאַהֲרֹן
הִתְאַנַּף יְהוָה מְאֹד לְהַשְׁמִידוֹ וָאֶתְפַּלֵּל גַּם־בְּעַד אַהֲרֹן בָּעֵת הַהִוא׃

אונקלוס

יי לי, ית תרין, לוחי אבניא לוחי קימא: יב ואמר יי לי, קום חות בפריע מכא, ארי חביל עמך, דאפיקתא ממצרים, סטו בפריע, מן אורחא דפקידתנון, עבדו להון מתכא: יג ואמר יי לי למימר, גלי קדמי עמא הדין, והא עם קשי קדל הוא: יד אנח בעותך מן קדמי ואשיצינון, ואמחי ית שומהון, מתחות שמיא, ואעביד יתך, לעם תקיף וסגי מנהון: טו ואתפניתי, ונחתית מן טורא, וטורא בער באישתא, ותרין לוחי קימא, על תרתין ידי: טז וחזית, והא חבתון קדם יי אלהכון, עבדתון לכון, עיגל מתכא, סטיתון בפריע, מן אורחא, דפקיד יי יתכון: יז ואחדית בתרין לוחיא, ורמיתנון, מעל תרתין ידי, ותברתנון לעיניכון: יח ואשתטחית קדם יי כד בקדמיתא, ארבעין יממין וארבעין לילון, לחמא לא אכלית, ומיא לא שתיתי, על כל חובתכון דחבתון, למעבד דביש, קדם יי לארגזא קדמוהי: יט ארי דחילית, מן קדם רגזא וחמתא, דרגז יי, עליכון לשיצאה יתכון, וקביל יי צלותי, אף בזמנא ההוא: כ ועל אהרן, הוה רגז מן קדם יי, לחדא לשיצאותיה, וצליתי, אף על אהרן בעדנא ההוא:

9:20 וָאֶתְפַּלֵּל גַּם־בְּעַד אַהֲרֹן בָּעֵת הַהִוא *I prayed for Aharon also at that time* – Only now, in the last month of Moshe's life, Moshe tells the people something that he has kept from them until this point: God, according to Moshe, was so angry with Aharon for the sin of the golden calf that He was about to kill him, and would have done so had it not been for Moshe's prayer.

Faced with the sin of the calf, Aharon blamed the people. It was they who made the illegitimate request. He denied responsibility for making the calf. It just happened. "I threw

21 was ready to destroy him, but I prayed for Aharon also at that time. Then I
took that thing of sin you had made, the calf, and burned it in fire. I crushed
it and ground it thoroughly, until it was as fine as dust, and I threw the dust
22 into a stream running down the mountain. At Tavera also, and at Masa and
23 Kivrot HaTaava, you provoked the LORD. And when the LORD sent you from
Kadesh Barnea, saying, 'Go up and take possession of the land that I have given
you,' you rebelled against the command of the LORD your God. You did not
24 have faith in Him and did not obey Him. You have rebelled against the LORD
25 as long as I have known you. I threw myself down before the LORD, and as I
lay prostrate those forty days and forty nights, when the LORD had said He
26 would destroy you, I prayed to the LORD – 'Lord GOD,' I said, 'do not destroy
the people, Your heritage, those whom You redeemed in Your greatness and
27 brought out of Egypt with a mighty hand. Remember Your servants Avraham,
Yitzḥak, and Yaakov; do not attend to the stubbornness of this people, to their

רש"י

כא | טָחוֹן. לְשׁוֹן הֹוֶה, כְּמוֹ "הָלוֹךְ וְגָדוֹל" (שמואל ב' ה, י; דברי הימים א' יא, ט). מולח"נט בְּלַעַז:

כה | וָאֶתְנַפַּל וְגוֹ'. אֵלּוּ הֵן עַצְמָן הָאֲמוּרִים לְמַעְלָה, וּכְפָלָן כָּאן לְפִי שֶׁכָּתוּב כָּאן סֵדֶר תְּפִלָּתוֹ, שֶׁנֶּאֱמַר: "ה' אֱלֹהִים אַל תַּשְׁחֵת עַמְּךָ" וְגוֹ' (להלן פסוק כו):

they reached the end of each section [the psalm was divided into three parts], they blew the shofar and the people prostrated themselves" (Tamid 7:3). We preserve a trace of that gesture, and Moshe's here, by resting our heads on our arms and covering our faces as we say Psalm 6. The *ḥazan*'s repetition of the *Amida* stands in place of the daily sacrifice, which is why we subsequently "fall on our faces."

According to tradition, Moshe began his ascent of Mount Sinai to receive the second tablets on a Thursday and descended forty days later on a Monday (the tenth of Tishrei, Yom Kippur). The second tablets were a sign of God's forgiveness. Hence, these days were seen as "days of favor." They were also market days when people would come from villages to towns. Congregations were larger; the Torah was read; law courts were in session. The heightened atmosphere was the setting for more extended penitential prayer; therefore, on Mondays and Thursdays, *Taḥanun* is longer.

A tradition, found in the geonic literature, dates these prayers to the period of persecution under the Romans. Some passages may have been added in the wake of the Gothic and Frankish persecutions in the seventh century. Their mood bespeaks the tears of Jews throughout the centuries of exile who experienced persecution, expulsion, humiliation, and often bloodshed at the hand of those amongst whom they lived. Even in times of freedom, we continue to say these prayers, keeping faith with our ancestors and remembering their tears.

What is remarkable about the prayers is the absence of anger or despair. If we ever doubt the power of prayer to transform the human situation, here we find an answer. Despite being treated as a pariah people, Jews never allowed themselves to be defined by their enemies. They wept and gave voice to pain: "God, see how low our glory has sunk among the nations. They abhor us as if we were impure." Yet they remained the people of the covenant, children of the divine promise, unbroken and unbreakable. Prayer sustains hope, and hope defeats tragedy. In these profound and moving words, invoking Moshe's loving supplication to God on our behalf, Jews found the strength to survive.

כא וְאֶת־חַטַּאתְכֶם אֲשֶׁר־עֲשִׂיתֶם אֶת־הָעֵגֶל לָקַחְתִּי וָאֶשְׂרֹף אֹתוֹ ׀ בָּאֵשׁ
וָאֶכֹּת אֹתוֹ טָחוֹן הֵיטֵב עַד אֲשֶׁר־דַּק לְעָפָר וָאַשְׁלִךְ אֶת־עֲפָרוֹ אֶל־
כב הַנַּחַל הַיֹּרֵד מִן־הָהָר׃ וּבְתַבְעֵרָה וּבְמַסָּה וּבְקִבְרֹת הַתַּאֲוָה מַקְצִפִים
כג הֱיִיתֶם אֶת־יְהוָה׃ וּבִשְׁלֹחַ יְהוָה אֶתְכֶם מִקָּדֵשׁ בַּרְנֵעַ לֵאמֹר עֲלוּ
וּרְשׁוּ אֶת־הָאָרֶץ אֲשֶׁר נָתַתִּי לָכֶם וַתַּמְרוּ אֶת־פִּי יְהוָה אֱלֹהֵיכֶם וְלֹא
כד הֶאֱמַנְתֶּם לוֹ וְלֹא שְׁמַעְתֶּם בְּקֹלוֹ׃ מַמְרִים הֱיִיתֶם עִם־יְהוָה מִיּוֹם דַּעְתִּי
כה אֶתְכֶם׃ וָאֶתְנַפַּל לִפְנֵי יְהוָה אֶת־אַרְבָּעִים הַיּוֹם וְאֶת־אַרְבָּעִים הַלַּיְלָה
כו אֲשֶׁר הִתְנַפָּלְתִּי כִּי־אָמַר יְהוָה לְהַשְׁמִיד אֶתְכֶם׃ וָאֶתְפַּלֵּל אֶל־יְהוָה
וָאֹמַר אֲדֹנָי יֱהֹוִה אַל־תַּשְׁחֵת עַמְּךָ וְנַחֲלָתְךָ אֲשֶׁר פָּדִיתָ בְּגָדְלֶךָ אֲשֶׁר־
כז הוֹצֵאתָ מִמִּצְרַיִם בְּיָד חֲזָקָה׃ זְכֹר לַעֲבָדֶיךָ לְאַבְרָהָם לְיִצְחָק וּלְיַעֲקֹב

אונקלוס

כא וְיָת חוֹבַתְכוֹן דַּעֲבַדְתּוּן יָת עֶגְלָא, נְסֵיבִית וְאוֹקֵידִית יָתֵיהּ בְּנוּרָא, וְשָׁפֵית יָתֵיהּ בְּשׁוֹפִינָא יָאוּת, עַד דַּהֲוָה דַּקִּיק לְעַפְרָא, וּרְמֵית יָת עַפְרֵיהּ, לְנַחְלָא דְּנָחֵית מִן טוּרָא: כב וּבִדְלֵיקְתָא וּבְנִסֵּיתָא, וּבְקִבְרֵי דִמְשַׁאֲלֵי, מַרְגְּזִין הֲוֵיתוּן קֳדָם יְיָ: כג וְכַד שְׁלַח יְיָ יָתְכוֹן, מֵרְקַם גֵּיאָה לְמֵימַר, סַקוּ וְאַחְסִינוּ יָת אַרְעָא, דִּיהָבִית לְכוֹן, וְסָרֵיבְתּוּן, עַל מֵימְרָא דַּייָ אֱלָהֲכוֹן, וְלָא הֵימֵנְתּוּן לֵיהּ, וְלָא קַבֵּילְתּוּן לְמֵימְרֵיהּ:

כד מְסָרְבִין הֲוֵיתוּן קֳדָם יְיָ, מִיּוֹמָא דִּידַעִית יָתְכוֹן: כה וְאִשְׁתַּטַּחִית קֳדָם יְיָ, יָת אַרְבְּעִין יְמָמִין, וְיָת אַרְבְּעִין לֵילָוָן דְּאִשְׁתַּטַּחִית, אֲרֵי אֲמַר יְיָ לְשֵׁיצָאָה יָתְכוֹן: כו וְצַלֵּיתִי קֳדָם יְיָ וַאֲמָרִית, יְיָ אֱלֹהִים, לָא תְחַבֵּיל עַמָּךְ וְאַחְסַנְתָּךְ, דִּפְרַקְתָּא בְּתָקְפָּךְ, דְּאַפֵּיקְתָּא מִמִּצְרַיִם בְּיַד תַּקִּיפָא: כז אִדְּכַר לְעַבְדָּךְ, לְאַבְרָהָם לְיִצְחָק וּלְיַעֲקֹב,

called on to be a Moshe, but he became a great leader in his own right in a different capacity. There are times when you need someone with the courage to stand against the crowd, others when you need a peacemaker.

MOSHE'S PRAYER

In Exodus we were not told the words of this particular prayer, which are echoed twice weekly in the longer form of the *Taḥanun* prayer, and in some *Seliḥot*: "Remember Your servants Avraham, Yitzḥak, and Yaakov; do not attend to our stubbornness, wickedness, and sinfulness." *Taḥanun*, "plea," is a return to private prayer after the *ḥazan*'s repetition of the *Amida*. Knowing that our time in the direct presence of the supreme King of kings is drawing to an end, we approach Him directly, seeking, as it were, a private audience. Our voices drop; we whisper our deepest thoughts, we express our feelings of inadequacy and vulnerability. We know we are unworthy: we say nothing in our defense except that we have absolute faith in God.

What differentiates *Taḥanun* from other modes of prayer is the extent to which, echoing Moshe, "the humblest of men," we emphasize our failings and our lack of good deeds. We express our dependence on God's unconditional grace and mercy. *Taḥanun* is the chamber music rather than the symphony of the soul, and it has a unique intensity of tone.

The practice of following public prayer with private intercession was formalized in Temple times. After the daily sacrifice, "the Levites sang the psalm [of the day]. When

28 wickedness or sinfulness; otherwise the nation from which You brought us will
say, "It was because the LORD was unable to bring them into the land that He
promised them, and because He hated them, that He took them out to kill
29 them in the wilderness." But they are Your people, Your possession, whom You
freed by Your great power and Your arm stretched forth.'
10 1 And then the LORD said to me, 'Carve two tablets of stone like the first, and REVI'I
2 come up to Me on the mountain. Make, as well, a wooden ark. I will inscribe
upon these tablets the words that were on the first, which you smashed, and
3 you shall place them in the ark.' So I made an ark of acacia wood and carved two
tablets of stone like the first. I ascended the mountain with these two tablets in
4 my hand. And He inscribed on the tablets the same words as before, the Ten
Commandments that the LORD had proclaimed to you on the mountain out
5 of the fire on the day of the assembly; and the LORD gave them to me. I turned,
came down from the mountain, and put the tablets in the ark that I had made.
6 And there they have remained, as the LORD commanded me. And the Israelites
journeyed from Be'erot Benei Yaakan to Mosera. There Aharon died and was
7 buried. Elazar, his son, succeeded him as priest. From there they journeyed to
8 Gudgod, and from Gudgod to Yotvat, a region of flowing streams. At that time
the LORD set the tribe of Levi apart to carry the Ark of the LORD's Covenant,
to stand before the LORD to minister to Him, and to give blessing in His name,
9 as they do to this day. This is why the Levites have no share or inheritance

רש״י

י א **בָּעֵת הַהִוא.** לְסוֹף אַרְבָּעִים יוֹם נִתְרַצָּה לִי וְאָמַר לִי: "פְּסָל לְךָ" וְאַחַר כָּךְ: "וְעָשִׂיתָ לְךָ אֲרוֹן", וַאֲנִי עָשִׂיתִי אָרוֹן תְּחִלָּה, שֶׁכְּשֶׁאָבֹא וְהַלּוּחוֹת בְּיָדִי הֵיכָן אֶתְּנֵם. וְלֹא זֶה הוּא הָאָרוֹן שֶׁעָשָׂה בְּצַלְאֵל, שֶׁהֲרֵי מִשְׁכָּן לֹא נִתְעַסְּקוּ בּוֹ עַד לְאַחַר יוֹם הַכִּפּוּרִים, כִּי בִּרְדְתּוֹ מִן הָהָר צִוָּה לָהֶם עַל מְלֶאכֶת הַמִּשְׁכָּן, וּבְצַלְאֵל עָשָׂה מִשְׁכָּן תְּחִלָּה וְאַחַר כָּךְ אָרוֹן וְכֵלִים, נִמְצָא זֶה אָרוֹן אַחֵר הָיָה, וְזֶהוּ שֶׁהָיָה יוֹצֵא עִמָּהֶם לַמִּלְחָמָה, וְאוֹתוֹ שֶׁעָשָׂה בְּצַלְאֵל לֹא יָצָא לַמִּלְחָמָה אֶלָּא בִּימֵי עֵלִי, וְנֶעֶנְשׁוּ עָלָיו וְנִשְׁבָּה:

ו-ז **וּבְנֵי יִשְׂרָאֵל נָסְעוּ מִבְּאֵרֹת בְּנֵי יַעֲקָן מוֹסֵרָה.** מָה עִנְיָן זֶה לְכָאן? וְעוֹד, וְכִי מִבְּאֵרוֹת בְּנֵי יַעֲקָן נָסְעוּ לְמוֹסֵרָה? וַהֲלֹא מִמּוֹסֵרָה בָּאוּ לִבְנֵי יַעֲקָן, שֶׁנֶּאֱמַר: "וַיִּסְעוּ מִמֹּסֵרוֹת" וְגוֹ' (במדבר לג, לא)! וְעוֹד, "שָׁם מֵת אַהֲרֹן" – וַהֲלֹא בְּהֹר הָהָר מֵת! צֵא וַחֲשֹׁב וְתִמְצָא שְׁמוֹנֶה מַסָּעוֹת מִמּוֹסֵרוֹת לְהֹר הָהָר! אֶלָּא אַף זוֹ מִן הַתּוֹכָחָה: וְעוֹד עֲשִׂיתֶם זֹאת, כְּשֶׁמֵּת אַהֲרֹן בְּהֹר הָהָר לְסוֹף אַרְבָּעִים שָׁנָה וְנִסְתַּלְּקוּ עַנְנֵי כָבוֹד, יְרֵאתֶם לָכֶם מִמִּלְחֶמֶת מֶלֶךְ עֲרָד וּנְתַתֶּם רֹאשׁ לַחֲזֹר לְמִצְרַיִם, וַחֲזַרְתֶּם לַאֲחוֹרֵיכֶם שְׁמוֹנֶה מַסָּעוֹת עַד בְּנֵי יַעֲקָן וּמִשָּׁם לְמוֹסֵרָה, שָׁם נִלְחֲמוּ בָּכֶם בְּנֵי לֵוִי וְהָרְגוּ מִכֶּם וְאַתֶּם מֵהֶם, עַד שֶׁהֶחֱזִירוּ אֶתְכֶם כְּדֶרֶךְ חֲזָרַתְכֶם, וּמִשָּׁם חֲזַרְתֶּם "הַגֻּדְגֹּדָה" הוּא חֹר הַגִּדְגָּד, "וּמִן הַגֻּדְגֹּדָה יָטְבָתָה". וּבְמוֹסֵרָה עֲשִׂיתֶם אֵבֶל כָּבֵד עַל מִיתָתוֹ שֶׁל אַהֲרֹן שֶׁגָּרְמָה לָכֶם זֹאת, וְנִדְמָה לָכֶם כְּאִלּוּ מֵת שָׁם. וְסָמַךְ מֹשֶׁה תּוֹכָחָה זוֹ לִשְׁבִירַת הַלּוּחוֹת, לוֹמַר שֶׁקָּשָׁה מִיתָתָן שֶׁל צַדִּיקִים לִפְנֵי הַקָּדוֹשׁ בָּרוּךְ הוּא כְּיוֹם שֶׁנִּשְׁתַּבְּרוּ בּוֹ הַלּוּחוֹת, וּלְהוֹדִיעֲךָ שֶׁהִקְשָׁה לוֹ מַה שֶּׁנָּתְנוּ רֹאשׁ לִפְרֹשׁ מִמֶּנּוּ, כְּיוֹם שֶׁעָשׂוּ בּוֹ אֶת הָעֵגֶל:

ח **בָּעֵת הַהִוא הִבְדִּיל ה' וְגוֹ'.** מוּסָב לָעִנְיָן הָרִאשׁוֹן, "בָּעֵת הַהִוא" בַּשָּׁנָה הָרִאשׁוֹנָה לְצֵאתְכֶם מִמִּצְרַיִם וּטְעִיתֶם בָּעֵגֶל וּבְנֵי לֵוִי לֹא טָעוּ, הִבְדִּילָם הַמָּקוֹם מִכֶּם. וְסָמַךְ מִקְרָא זֶה לַחֲזָרַת בְּנֵי יַעֲקָן, לוֹמַר שֶׁאַף בְּזוֹ לֹא טָעוּ בָּהּ בְּנֵי לֵוִי אֶלָּא עָמְדוּ בֶּאֱמוּנָתָם: **לָשֵׂאת אֶת אֲרוֹן.** הַלְוִיִּם: לַעֲמֹד... **לְשָׁרְתוֹ וּלְבָרֵךְ בִּשְׁמוֹ.** הַכֹּהֲנִים, וְהוּא נְשִׂיאוּת כַּפַּיִם:

ט **עַל כֵּן לֹא הָיָה לְלֵוִי חֵלֶק.** לְפִי שֶׁהֻבְדְּלוּ לַעֲבוֹדַת מִזְבֵּחַ וְאֵינָן פְּנוּיִין לַחֲרֹשׁ וְלִזְרֹעַ:

כח אַל־תֵּפֶן אֶל־קְשִׁי הָעָם הַזֶּה וְאֶל־רִשְׁעוֹ וְאֶל־חַטָּאתוֹ: פֶּן־יֹאמְרוּ
הָאָרֶץ אֲשֶׁר הוֹצֵאתָנוּ מִשָּׁם מִבְּלִי יְכֹלֶת יהוה לַהֲבִיאָם אֶל־הָאָרֶץ
כט אֲשֶׁר־דִּבֶּר לָהֶם וּמִשִּׂנְאָתוֹ אוֹתָם הוֹצִיאָם לַהֲמִתָם בַּמִּדְבָּר: וְהֵם
עַמְּךָ וְנַחֲלָתֶךָ אֲשֶׁר הוֹצֵאתָ בְּכֹחֲךָ הַגָּדֹל וּבִזְרֹעֲךָ הַנְּטוּיָה:
י א בָּעֵת הַהִוא אָמַר יהוה אֵלַי פְּסָל־לְךָ שְׁנֵי־לוּחֹת אֲבָנִים כָּרִאשֹׁנִים ט רביעי
ב וַעֲלֵה אֵלַי הָהָרָה וְעָשִׂיתָ לְּךָ אֲרוֹן עֵץ: וְאֶכְתֹּב עַל־הַלֻּחֹת אֶת־
הַדְּבָרִים אֲשֶׁר הָיוּ עַל־הַלֻּחֹת הָרִאשֹׁנִים אֲשֶׁר שִׁבַּרְתָּ וְשַׂמְתָּם בָּאָרוֹן:
ג וָאַעַשׂ אֲרוֹן עֲצֵי שִׁטִּים וָאֶפְסֹל שְׁנֵי־לֻחֹת אֲבָנִים כָּרִאשֹׁנִים וָאַעַל
ד הָהָרָה וּשְׁנֵי הַלֻּחֹת בְּיָדִי: וַיִּכְתֹּב עַל־הַלֻּחֹת כַּמִּכְתָּב הָרִאשׁוֹן אֵת
עֲשֶׂרֶת הַדְּבָרִים אֲשֶׁר דִּבֶּר יהוה אֲלֵיכֶם בָּהָר מִתּוֹךְ הָאֵשׁ בְּיוֹם
ה הַקָּהָל וַיִּתְּנֵם יהוה אֵלָי: וָאֵפֶן וָאֵרֵד מִן־הָהָר וָאָשִׂם אֶת־הַלֻּחֹת
ו בָּאָרוֹן אֲשֶׁר עָשִׂיתִי וַיִּהְיוּ שָׁם כַּאֲשֶׁר צִוַּנִי יהוה: וּבְנֵי יִשְׂרָאֵל נָסְעוּ
מִבְּאֵרֹת בְּנֵי־יַעֲקָן מוֹסֵרָה שָׁם מֵת אַהֲרֹן וַיִּקָּבֵר שָׁם וַיְכַהֵן אֶלְעָזָר בְּנוֹ
ז תַּחְתָּיו: מִשָּׁם נָסְעוּ הַגֻּדְגֹּדָה וּמִן־הַגֻּדְגֹּדָה יָטְבָתָה אֶרֶץ נַחֲלֵי־מָיִם:
ח בָּעֵת הַהִוא הִבְדִּיל יהוה אֶת־שֵׁבֶט הַלֵּוִי לָשֵׂאת אֶת־אֲרוֹן בְּרִית־
ט יהוה לַעֲמֹד לִפְנֵי יהוה לְשָׁרְתוֹ וּלְבָרֵךְ בִּשְׁמוֹ עַד הַיּוֹם הַזֶּה: עַל־כֵּן

אונקלוס

לָא תִתְפְּנֵי, לְקַשְׁיוּת עַמָּא הָדֵין, וּלְחוֹבֵיהוֹן וּלְחַטָּאֵיהוֹן: כח דִּלְמָא יֵימְרוּן, דָּיְרֵי אַרְעָא דְּאַפֵּיקְתַּנָא מִתַּמָּן, מִדְּלֵית יְכֹלָא קֳדָם יְיָ, לְאַעָלוּתְהוֹן, לְאַרְעָא דְּמַלֵּיל לְהוֹן, וּמִדְּסָנֵי יָתְהוֹן, אַפֵּיקִנּוּן לְקַטָּלוּתְהוֹן בְּמַדְבְּרָא: כט וְאִנּוּן עַמָּךְ וְאַחְסַנְתָּךְ, דְּאַפֵּיקְתָּא בְּחֵילָךְ רַבָּא, וּבִדְרָעָךְ מְרָמְמָא: א בְּעִדָּנָא הַהוּא אֲמַר יְיָ לִי, פְּסַל לָךְ, תְּרֵין לוּחֵי אַבְנַיָּא כְּקַדְמָאֵי, וְסַק לְקֳדָמַי לְטוּרָא, וְתַעְבֵּיד לָךְ אֲרוֹנָא דְּאָעָא: ב וְאֶכְתּוֹב עַל לוּחַיָּא, יָת פִּתְגָּמַיָּא, דַּהֲווֹ, עַל לוּחַיָּא קַדְמָאֵי דְּתַבַּרְתָּא, וּתְשַׁוֵּינוּן בַּאֲרוֹנָא: ג וַעֲבַדִית אֲרוֹנָא דְּאָעֵי שִׁטִּין, וּפְסָלִית, תְּרֵין לוּחֵי אַבְנַיָּא כְּקַדְמָאֵי, וּסְלֵיקִית לְטוּרָא, וּתְרֵין לוּחַיָּא בִּידִי: ד וּכְתַב עַל לוּחַיָּא כִּכְתָבָא קַדְמָאָה, יָת עַסְרָא פִתְגָּמִין, דְּמַלֵּיל יְיָ עִמְּכוֹן בְּטוּרָא, מִגּוֹ אִישָּׁתָא בְּיוֹמָא דִקְהָלָא, וִיהַבִנּוּן יְיָ לִי: ה וְאִתְפְּנֵיתִי, וּנְחָתִית מִן טוּרָא, וְשַׁוֵּיתִי יָת לוּחַיָּא, בַּאֲרוֹנָא דַּעֲבַדִית, וַהֲווֹ תַמָּן, כְּמָא דְּפַקְּדַנִי יְיָ: ו וּבְנֵי יִשְׂרָאֵל, נְטַלוּ, מִבְּאֵרוֹת בְּנֵי יַעֲקָן לְמוֹסֵרָה, תַּמָּן מִית אַהֲרֹן וְאִתְקְבַר תַּמָּן, וְשַׁמֵּישׁ, אֶלְעָזָר בְּרֵיהּ תְּחוֹתוֹהִי: ז מִתַּמָּן נְטַלוּ לְגֻדְגּוֹד, וּמִן גֻּדְגּוֹד לְיָטְבַת, אֲרַע נָגְדָא נַחְלִין דְּמַיִּין: ח בְּעִדָּנָא הַהוּא, אַפְרֵישׁ יְיָ יָת שִׁבְטָא דְּלֵוִי, לְמִטַּל יָת אֲרוֹן קְיָמָא דַּייָ, לְמֵקָם קֳדָם יְיָ לְשַׁמָּשׁוּתֵיהּ וּלְבָרָכָא בִּשְׁמֵיהּ, עַד יוֹמָא הָדֵין: ט עַל כֵּן,

among their fellow Israelites. The Lord is their inheritance, as the Lord your
10 God promised them. I stayed on the mountain forty days and forty nights, as
I had the first time. And this time too, the Lord listened to me; the Lord did
11 not choose to destroy you. Then the Lord said to me, 'Rise and resume your
journey at the head of the people, so that they may go in and take possession of
the land that I swore to their ancestors to give to them.'
12 So now, Israel, what does the Lord your God ask of you? Only this: to revere HAMISHI
the Lord your God, to walk in all His ways and love Him; to serve the Lord
13 your God with all your heart and all your soul, and to keep the commandments
and decrees of the Lord your God that I am commanding you today, for your
14 own good. Look: the heavens, even the highest heavens, belong to the Lord
15 your God, with the earth and all it contains. Yet it was on your ancestors alone
that the Lord set His heart in love, and it was you, their descendants after

רש״י

ה׳ הוּא נַחֲלָתוֹ. נוֹטֵל פְּרָס מְזֻמָּן מִבֵּית הַמֶּלֶךְ:

י **וְאָנֹכִי עָמַדְתִּי בָהָר.** לְקַבֵּל לוּחוֹת הָאַחֲרוֹנוֹת, וּלְפִי שֶׁלֹּא פֵּרַשׁ לְמַעְלָה כַּמָּה עָמַד בָּהָר בַּעֲלִיָּה אַחֲרוֹנָה זוֹ, חָזַר וְהִתְחִיל בָּהּ: **כַּיָּמִים הָרִאשֹׁנִים.** שֶׁל לוּחוֹת הָרִאשׁוֹנוֹת, מָה הֵם בְּרָצוֹן, אַף אֵלּוּ בְּרָצוֹן, אֲבָל הָאֶמְצָעִיִּים שֶׁעָמַדְתִּי שָׁם לְהִתְפַּלֵּל עֲלֵיכֶם הָיוּ בְּכַעַס:

יא **וַיֹּאמֶר ה׳ אֵלַי וְגוֹ׳.** אַף עַל פִּי שֶׁסַּרְתֶּם מֵאַחֲרָיו וּטְעִיתֶם בָּעֵגֶל, אָמַר לִי: ״לֵךְ נְחֵה אֶת הָעָם״ (שמות לב, לד):

יב **וְעַתָּה יִשְׂרָאֵל.** אַף עַל פִּי שֶׁעֲשִׂיתֶם כָּל זֹאת, עוֹדֶנּוּ רַחֲמָיו וְחִבָּתוֹ עֲלֵיכֶם, וּמִכָּל מַה שֶּׁחֲטָאתֶם לְפָנָיו אֵינוֹ שׁוֹאֵל מִכֶּם ״כִּי אִם לְיִרְאָה״ וְגוֹ׳. וְרַבּוֹתֵינוּ דָּרְשׁוּ מִכָּאן: הַכֹּל בִּידֵי שָׁמַיִם חוּץ מִיִּרְאַת שָׁמַיִם:

יג **לִשְׁמֹר אֶת מִצְוֹת ה׳.** וְאַף הִיא לֹא לְחִנָּם, אֶלָּא ״לְטוֹב לָךְ״, שֶׁתְּקַבְּלוּ שָׂכָר:

יד-טו **הֵן לַה׳ אֱלֹהֶיךָ.** הַכֹּל, וְאַף עַל פִּי כֵן, ״רַק בַּאֲבֹתֶיךָ חָשַׁק ה׳״ מִן הַכֹּל: **בָּכֶם.** כְּמוֹ שֶׁאַתֶּם רוֹאִים אֶתְכֶם חֲשׁוּקִים מִכָּל הָעַמִּים הַיּוֹם הַזֶּה:

A society is thus formed on the basis of love of God, neighbor, and stranger. This is not merely abstract. It is translated into practical imperatives. Provide the poor with food from the corners of the field and the leavings of the harvest. Let them eat freely of the produce of the field in the seventh year and provide them with a tithe on the third and sixth. One year in seven, release debts and Hebrew slaves. Ensure that no one is left out of the festival celebrations, and no one denied access to dignity. Treat employees and debtors ethically and give slaves rest one day in seven. This is a unique vision that shaped the moral horizons of the West. The moral life as Judaism conceives it is a combination of love – *ḥesed* and *raḥamim* – and justice – *tzedek* and *mishpat*. Love is particular; justice is universal. Love is interpersonal; justice is impersonal. Love generates ethics: justice that underlies the love commandment of Leviticus. Not a cold justice in which due deserts are mechanically handed out, but the justice that brings the other, as an individual with needs and interests, into a relationship of respect. All our neighbors are to be recognized as equal to ourselves before the law of love. Justice and love therefore become inseparable.

Love without justice leads to rivalry, and eventually to hate. Justice without love is devoid of the humanizing forces of compassion and mercy. We need both.

Israel is established as a nation and society held together by three loves: You shall love the Lord your God with all your heart, all your soul, and all your might. You shall love your neighbor as yourself. And you shall love the stranger, for you were once strangers in the land of Egypt.

לֹא־הָיָה לְלֵוִי חֵלֶק וְנַחֲלָה עִם־אֶחָיו יְהוָה הוּא נַחֲלָתוֹ כַּאֲשֶׁר דִּבֶּר
י יְהוָה אֱלֹהֶיךָ לוֹ׃ וְאָנֹכִי עָמַדְתִּי בָהָר כַּיָּמִים הָרִאשֹׁנִים אַרְבָּעִים יוֹם
וְאַרְבָּעִים לָיְלָה וַיִּשְׁמַע יְהוָה אֵלַי גַּם בַּפַּעַם הַהִוא לֹא־אָבָה יְהוָה
יא הַשְׁחִיתֶךָ׃ וַיֹּאמֶר יְהוָה אֵלַי קוּם לֵךְ לְמַסַּע לִפְנֵי הָעָם וְיָבֹאוּ וְיִירְשׁוּ
אֶת־הָאָרֶץ אֲשֶׁר־נִשְׁבַּעְתִּי לַאֲבֹתָם לָתֵת לָהֶם׃
יב וְעַתָּה יִשְׂרָאֵל מָה יְהוָה אֱלֹהֶיךָ שֹׁאֵל מֵעִמָּךְ כִּי אִם־לְיִרְאָה אֶת־יְהוָה חמישי
אֱלֹהֶיךָ לָלֶכֶת בְּכָל־דְּרָכָיו וּלְאַהֲבָה אֹתוֹ וְלַעֲבֹד אֶת־יְהוָה אֱלֹהֶיךָ
יג בְּכָל־לְבָבְךָ וּבְכָל־נַפְשֶׁךָ׃ לִשְׁמֹר אֶת־מִצְוֺת יְהוָה וְאֶת־חֻקֹּתָיו אֲשֶׁר
יד אָנֹכִי מְצַוְּךָ הַיּוֹם לְטוֹב לָךְ׃ הֵן לַיהוָה אֱלֹהֶיךָ הַשָּׁמַיִם וּשְׁמֵי הַשָּׁמָיִם
טו הָאָרֶץ וְכָל־אֲשֶׁר־בָּהּ׃ רַק בַּאֲבֹתֶיךָ חָשַׁק יְהוָה לְאַהֲבָה אוֹתָם

אונקלוס

לָא הֲוָה לְלֵוִי, חוּלָק וְאַחְסָנָא עִם אֲחוֹהִי, מַתְּנָן דִּיהַב לֵיהּ יי אִנּוּן אַחְסָנְתֵיהּ, כְּמָא דְּמַלֵּיל, יי אֱלָהָךְ לֵיהּ׃ י וַאֲנָא הֲוֵיתִי קָאֵים בְּטוּרָא, כְּיוֹמַיָּא קַדְמָאֵי, אַרְבְּעִין יְמָמִין, וְאַרְבְּעִין לֵילָוָן, וְקַבֵּיל יי צְלוֹתִי, אַף בְּזִמְנָא הַהוּא, לָא אֲבָא יי לְחַבָּלוּתָךְ׃ יא וַאֲמַר יי לִי, קוּם, אֵיזֵיל לְמַטּוּל קֳדָם עַמָּא, וְיֵיעֲלוּן וְיֵירְתוּן יָת אַרְעָא, דְּקַיֵּימִית לַאֲבָהָתְהוֹן לְמִתַּן לְהוֹן׃ יב וּכְעַן יִשְׂרָאֵל, מָא יי אֱלָהָךְ, תָּבַע מִנָּךְ, אֱלָהֵין לְמִדְחַל, קֳדָם יי אֱלָהָךְ, לִמְהָךְ בְּכָל אוֹרְחָן דְּתַקְנָן קֳדָמוֹהִי וּלְמִרְחַם יָתֵיהּ, וּלְמִפְלַח קֳדָם יי אֱלָהָךְ, בְּכָל לִבָּךְ וּבְכָל נַפְשָׁךְ׃ יג לְמִטַּר, יָת פִּקּוֹדַיָּא דַּיי וְיָת קְיָמוֹהִי, דַּאֲנָא מְפַקֵּיד לָךְ יוֹמָא דֵין, דְּיֵיטַב לָךְ׃ יד הָא דַּיי אֱלָהָךְ, שְׁמַיָּא וּשְׁמֵי שְׁמַיָּא, אַרְעָא וְכָל דְּבַהּ׃ טו לְחוֹד בַּאֲבָהָתָךְ, צְבִי יי לְמִרְחַם יָתְהוֹן, וְאִתְרְעִי

LOVE WITH JUSTICE

Why is it that love is so much stronger a theme in Deuteronomy than in the earlier books of Exodus, Leviticus (with the exception of Lev. 19), and Numbers? To answer this, first note that the book of Genesis contains many references to love. Avraham loves Yitzḥak. Yitzḥak loves Esav. Rivka loves Yaakov. Yaakov loves Raḥel. He also loves Yosef. There is plenty of interpersonal love. But almost all the loves of Genesis turn out to be divisive. They lead to tension between Yaakov and Esav, between Raḥel and Leah, and between Yosef and his brothers. Implicit in Genesis is a profound observation. Love by itself – real love, personal and passionate, the kind of love that suffuses much of the prophetic literature as well as Song of Songs, the greatest love song in the Tanakh, is not sufficient as a basis for society. It can divide as well as unite.

Hence it does not figure as a major motif until we reach the integrated social-moral-political vision of Deuteronomy which combines love and justice. *Tzedek*, justice, is to be another keyword of Deuteronomy, appearing eighteen times. It appears only four times in Exodus, not at all in Numbers, and in Leviticus only in chapter 19, the only chapter that also contains the word "love." In other words, in Judaism love and justice go hand in hand.

This is noted by philosopher Simon May, in his book *Love: A History*:

> [W]hat we must note here, for it is fundamental to the history of Western love, is the remarkable and radical

16 them, that He chose among all the peoples, as He does to this day. And so
17 remove the hardness of your heart, and be stiff-necked no longer. For the LORD
your God is God of gods and Lord of lords, the great, mighty, and awesome
18 God, who shows no partiality and accepts no bribe, who executes justice for
the orphan and the widow, and who loves the stranger, giving him food and
19 clothing. You too must love the stranger, for you yourselves were strangers in
20 the land of Egypt. Revere the LORD your God and worship Him. Hold fast
21 to Him and swear by His name. He is your praise; He is your God, who has
done these great and awesome things for you that your own eyes have seen.
22 When your ancestors went down to Egypt, they were but seventy souls. Now
11 1 the LORD your God has made you as many as the stars of the heavens. And
so – love the LORD your God and keep His charge: His decrees, His laws, and
2 His commands through all your days. Know today that it was not your children
who knew or saw the LORD your God's lesson – His greatness, His mighty

רש״י

טז **עָרְלַת לְבַבְכֶם.** אֹטֶם לְבַבְכֶם וְכִסּוּיוֹ:

יז **וַאֲדֹנֵי הָאֲדֹנִים.** לֹא יוּכַל שׁוּם אָדוֹן לְהַצִּיל אֶתְכֶם מִיָּדוֹ: **לֹא יִשָּׂא פָנִים.** אִם תִּפְרְקוּ עֻלּוֹ: **וְלֹא יִקַּח שֹׁחַד.** לְפַיְּסוֹ בְּמָמוֹן:

יח **עֹשֶׂה מִשְׁפַּט יָתוֹם וְאַלְמָנָה.** הֲרֵי גְּבוּרָה, וְאֵצֶל גְּבוּרָתוֹ אַתָּה מוֹצֵא עַנְוְתָנוּתוֹ: **וְאֹהֵב גֵּר לָתֶת לוֹ לֶחֶם וְשִׂמְלָה.** וְדָבָר חָשׁוּב הוּא זֶה, שֶׁכָּל עַצְמוֹ שֶׁל יַעֲקֹב אָבִינוּ עַל זֶה נִתְפַּלֵּל: "וְנָתַן לִי לֶחֶם לֶאֱכֹל וּבֶגֶד לִלְבֹּשׁ" (בראשית כח, כ):

יט **כִּי גֵרִים הֱיִיתֶם.** מוּם שֶׁבְּךָ אַל תֹּאמַר לַחֲבֵרְךָ:

כ **אֶת ה׳ אֱלֹהֶיךָ תִּירָא.** וְתַעַבְדֵּהוּ וְתִדְבַּק בּוֹ, וּלְאַחַר שֶׁיִּהְיוּ בְּךָ כָּל הַמִּדּוֹת הַלָּלוּ, אָז "בִּשְׁמוֹ תִּשָּׁבֵעַ":

יא ב **וִידַעְתֶּם הַיּוֹם.** תְּנוּ לֵב לָדַעַת וּלְהָבִין וּלְקַבֵּל תּוֹכַחְתִּי: **כִּי לֹא אֶת בְּנֵיכֶם.** אֲנִי מְדַבֵּר עַכְשָׁיו, שֶׁיּוּכְלוּ לוֹמַר: אָנוּ לֹא יָדַעְנוּ וְלֹא רָאִינוּ בְּכָל זֶה:

lords, the great, mighty and awesome God, who shows no partiality and accepts no bribe" (Deut. 10:17). Immediately afterward it is written, "Who executes justice for the orphan and the widow, and who loves the stranger, giving him food and clothing" (10:18). It is repeated in the Prophets, as it says: "Thus says the high, the exalted One, abiding forever, whose name is holy: High and holy I abide, yet I am with the crushed and humbled, giving life to the humbled, giving life to crushed men's hearts" (Is. 57:15). It is stated a third time in the Writings: "Sing to God, sing praises to His name, laud Him who rides the clouds – the LORD is His name – and exult before Him" (Ps. 68:5). Immediately afterward it is written: "Father of orphans, judge of widows, God is in His holy abode" (68:6). (Megilla 31a)

This counterintuitive and life-changing idea is one of the great contributions of the Torah to Western civilization and it is first set out this *parasha*.

Physically, the taller you are the more you look down on others. Morally, the reverse is the case. The more we look up to others, the higher we stand. God's greatness lay not just in the fact that He was creator of the universe and shaper of history, but that He "executes justice for the orphan and the widow, and [He] loves the stranger, giving him food and clothing." Those who emulate Him and do this are the true men and women of God. For us, as for God, greatness is humility.

טז וַיִּבְחַר בְּזַרְעָם אַחֲרֵיהֶם בָּכֶם מִכָּל־הָעַמִּים כַּיּוֹם הַזֶּה׃ וּמַלְתֶּם אֵת
יז עָרְלַת לְבַבְכֶם וְעָרְפְּכֶם לֹא תַקְשׁוּ עוֹד׃ כִּי יהוה אֱלֹהֵיכֶם הוּא אֱלֹהֵי
הָאֱלֹהִים וַאֲדֹנֵי הָאֲדֹנִים הָאֵל הַגָּדֹל הַגִּבֹּר וְהַנּוֹרָא אֲשֶׁר לֹא־יִשָּׂא
יח פָנִים וְלֹא יִקַּח שֹׁחַד׃ עֹשֶׂה מִשְׁפַּט יָתוֹם וְאַלְמָנָה וְאֹהֵב גֵּר לָתֶת
יט לוֹ לֶחֶם וְשִׂמְלָה׃ וַאֲהַבְתֶּם אֶת־הַגֵּר כִּי־גֵרִים הֱיִיתֶם בְּאֶרֶץ מִצְרָיִם׃
כ כא אֶת־יהוה אֱלֹהֶיךָ תִּירָא אֹתוֹ תַעֲבֹד וּבוֹ תִדְבָּק וּבִשְׁמוֹ תִּשָּׁבֵעַ׃ הוּא
תְהִלָּתְךָ וְהוּא אֱלֹהֶיךָ אֲשֶׁר־עָשָׂה אִתְּךָ אֶת־הַגְּדֹלֹת וְאֶת־הַנּוֹרָאֹת
כב הָאֵלֶּה אֲשֶׁר רָאוּ עֵינֶיךָ׃ בְּשִׁבְעִים נֶפֶשׁ יָרְדוּ אֲבֹתֶיךָ מִצְרָיְמָה וְעַתָּה
יא א שָׂמְךָ יהוה אֱלֹהֶיךָ כְּכוֹכְבֵי הַשָּׁמַיִם לָרֹב׃ וְאָהַבְתָּ אֵת יהוה אֱלֹהֶיךָ
ב וְשָׁמַרְתָּ מִשְׁמַרְתּוֹ וְחֻקֹּתָיו וּמִשְׁפָּטָיו וּמִצְוֺתָיו כָּל־הַיָּמִים׃ וִידַעְתֶּם
הַיּוֹם כִּי ׀ לֹא אֶת־בְּנֵיכֶם אֲשֶׁר לֹא־יָדְעוּ וַאֲשֶׁר לֹא־רָאוּ אֶת־מוּסַר

אונקלוס

בִּבְנֵיהוֹן בָּתְרֵיהוֹן, בְּכוֹן, מִכָּל עַמְמַיָּא כְּיוֹמָא הָדֵין: טז וְתַעְדּוֹן, יָת טַפְשׁוּת לִבְּכוֹן, וּקְדָלְכוֹן, לָא תַקְשׁוֹן עוֹד: יז אֲרֵי יי אֱלָהֲכוֹן, הוּא אֱלָהּ דַּיָּנִין, וּמָרֵי מַלְכִין, אֱלָהָא רַבָּא גִּבָּרָא וּדְחִילָא, דְּלֵית קֳדָמוֹהִי מִסַּב אַפִּין, וְאַף לָא לְקַבָּלָא שֹׁחְדָא: יח עָבֵיד, דִּין יִיתַם וְאַרְמְלָא, וְרָחֵים גִּיּוֹרָא, לְמִתַּן לֵיהּ מְזוֹן וּכְסוּ: יט וּתְרַחֲמוּן יָת גִּיּוֹרָא, אֲרֵי דַּיָּרִין הֲוֵיתוֹן בְּאַרְעָא דְמִצְרָיִם: כ יָת יי אֱלָהָךְ, תִּדְחַל וּקְדָמוֹהִי תִּפְלַח, וּלְדַחְלְתֵיהּ תִּתְקָרַב, וּבִשְׁמֵיהּ תְּקַיֵּים: כא הוּא תֻשְׁבַּחְתָּךְ וְהוּא אֱלָהָךְ, דַּעֲבַד עִמָּךְ, יָת רַבְרְבָתָא וְיָת חֲסִינָתָא הָאִלֵּין, דַּחֲזָאָה עֵינָךְ: כב בְּשִׁבְעִין נַפְשָׁן, נְחַתוּ אֲבָהָתָךְ לְמִצְרָיִם, וּכְעַן, שַׁוְּיָךְ יי אֱלָהָךְ, כְּכוֹכְבֵי שְׁמַיָּא לִסְגֵי: יא א וְתִרְחַם, יָת יי אֱלָהָךְ, וְתִטַּר מַטְּרַת מֵימְרֵיהּ, וּקְיָמוֹהִי וְדִינוֹהִי, וּפִקּוֹדוֹהִי כָּל יוֹמַיָּא: ב וְתִדְּעוּן יוֹמָא דֵין, אֲרֵי לָא יָת בְּנֵיכוֹן, דְּלָא יְדַעוּ וּדְלָא חֲזוֹ, יָת אֻלְפָנָא דַּיי אֱלָהֲכוֹן,

cares for the powerless. The Infinitely Great shows concern for the small. The Being at the heart of being listens to those at the margins: the orphan, the widow, the stranger, the poor, the outcast, the neglected.

On this idea, the third-century teacher R. Yoḥanan built the following homily:

> Wherever you find the greatness of the Holy One, blessed be He, there you find His humility. This is written in the Torah, repeated in the Prophets, and stated a third time in the Writings. It is written in the Torah: "For the Lord your God is God of gods and Lord of

the duties we owe those to whom we are bound by kinship or consent. Justice generates morality: the duties we owe everyone because they are human.

This unique ethical vision – based ultimately on the love of God for humans and of humans for God, translated into an ethic of love toward both neighbor and stranger – is the foundation of Western civilization and its abiding glory.

10:19 וַאֲהַבְתֶּם אֶת־הַגֵּר *You too must love the stranger* – The juxtaposition of the two preceding verses – the first about God's supremacy, the second about His care for the low and lonely – could not be more striking. The Power of powers

3 hand, and His arm stretched forth, the signs and the acts that He performed
4 in Egypt against Pharaoh, Egypt's king, and all his land; what He did to the
Egyptian fighting force, their horses and their chariots, how He made the Reed
Sea's water flood over them as they pursued you, so that the LORD destroyed
5 them forever; what He did for you in the wilderness until you came to this
6 place; and what he did to Datan and Aviram, sons of Eliav son of Reuven, in
the midst of all Israel, how the earth opened its mouth and swallowed them,
7 their families, tents, and every living thing in their households: it is your own
8 eyes that have seen all these immense acts, all that the LORD did. And so –
keep all of this command with which I charge you on this day, so that you may
be empowered to go in and take possession of the land that you are crossing
9 over to possess, and so that your years may be long in the land that the LORD
swore to your ancestors to give to them and their descendants, a land flowing

רש״י

ו **בְּקֶרֶב כָּל יִשְׂרָאֵל.** כָּל מָקוֹם שֶׁהָיָה אֶחָד מֵהֶם בּוֹרֵחַ, הָאָרֶץ נִבְקַעַת מִתַּחְתָּיו וּבוֹלַעְתּוֹ, אֵלּוּ דִּבְרֵי רַבִּי יְהוּדָה. אָמַר לוֹ רַבִּי נְחֶמְיָה: וַהֲלֹא כְּבָר נֶאֱמַר: "וַתִּפְתַּח הָאָרֶץ אֶת פִּיהָ" (במדבר טז, לב) וְלֹא 'פִּיּוֹתֶיהָ'? אָמַר לוֹ: וּמָה אֲנִי מְקַיֵּם "בְּקֶרֶב כָּל יִשְׂרָאֵל"? אָמַר לוֹ: שֶׁנַּעֲשֵׂית הָאָרֶץ מִדְרוֹן כְּמַשְׁפֵּךְ, וְכָל מָקוֹם שֶׁהָיָה אֶחָד מֵהֶם, הָיָה מִתְגַּלְגֵּל וּבָא עַד מְקוֹם הַבְּקִיעָה: **וְאֵת כָּל הַיְקוּם אֲשֶׁר בְּרַגְלֵיהֶם.** זֶה מָמוֹנוֹ שֶׁל אָדָם שֶׁמַּעֲמִידוֹ עַל רַגְלָיו:

ז **כִּי עֵינֵיכֶם הָרֹאֹת.** מוּסָב עַל הַמִּקְרָא הָאָמוּר לְמַעְלָה (לעיל פסוק ב): "כִּי לֹא אֶת בְּנֵיכֶם אֲשֶׁר לֹא יָדְעוּ" וְגוֹ', כִּי אִם עִמָּכֶם, אֲשֶׁר "עֵינֵיכֶם הָרֹאֹת" וְגוֹ':

Avraham, then Yitzḥak, then Yaakov and his children into a series of journeys and exiles, a story echoed later in the Book of Ruth.

Life in Israel has never been stable and secure. Those who live there exist in a state of insecurity, never knowing whether the seeds they plant will grow. Israel is the land of promise, but it will always depend on He-who-promises.

The character of a country – its topography and climate – affects the society people build, and hence the culture and ethos that emerge. In Mesopotamia and Egypt, the most powerful reality was the regularity of nature, the succession of the seasons, which seemed to mirror the slow revolution of the stars. The cultures to which both places gave rise were cosmological and their sense of time cyclical. The universe seemed to be ruled by the heavenly bodies whose hierarchy and order were replicated in the hierarchy and order of life on earth. This is the mindset of the world of myth.

In Israel, by contrast, there was no guarantee that next year would be like this, or this year like last, no certainty that the rain would fall and the earth yield its crops or the trees their fruit. Thus in Israel a new sense of time was born – the time we call historical. Those who lived, or live, in Israel exist in a state of radical contingency. They depend on something other than nature. To put it at its simplest: In Egypt, where the source of life was the Nile, you looked down. In Israel, where the source of life is rain, you had no choice but to look up.

When Moshe tells the Israelites about the land, he is telling them – whether or not they understand it at the time – that it is a place where not just wheat and barley but the human spirit also grew. It was the land where people were lifted beyond themselves because, time and again, they would have to believe in something beyond themselves. Not accidentally but essentially, by its climate, topography, and location, Israel is the Holy Land, the place where, merely to survive, the human eye must turn to Heaven and the human ear to Heaven's call.

ג יְהוָה אֱלֹהֵיכֶם אֶת־גָּדְלוֹ אֶת־יָדוֹ הַחֲזָקָה וּזְרֹעוֹ הַנְּטוּיָה׃ וְאֶת־אֹתֹתָיו
וְאֶת־מַעֲשָׂיו אֲשֶׁר עָשָׂה בְּתוֹךְ מִצְרָיִם לְפַרְעֹה מֶלֶךְ־מִצְרַיִם וּלְכָל־
ד אַרְצוֹ׃ וַאֲשֶׁר עָשָׂה לְחֵיל מִצְרַיִם לְסוּסָיו וּלְרִכְבּוֹ אֲשֶׁר הֵצִיף אֶת־מֵי
יַם־סוּף עַל־פְּנֵיהֶם בְּרָדְפָם אַחֲרֵיכֶם וַיְאַבְּדֵם יְהוָה עַד הַיּוֹם הַזֶּה׃
ה ו וַאֲשֶׁר עָשָׂה לָכֶם בַּמִּדְבָּר עַד־בֹּאֲכֶם עַד־הַמָּקוֹם הַזֶּה׃ וַאֲשֶׁר עָשָׂה
לְדָתָן וְלַאֲבִירָם בְּנֵי אֱלִיאָב בֶּן־רְאוּבֵן אֲשֶׁר פָּצְתָה הָאָרֶץ אֶת־פִּיהָ
וַתִּבְלָעֵם וְאֶת־בָּתֵּיהֶם וְאֶת־אָהֳלֵיהֶם וְאֵת כָּל־הַיְקוּם אֲשֶׁר בְּרַגְלֵיהֶם
ז בְּקֶרֶב כָּל־יִשְׂרָאֵל׃ כִּי עֵינֵיכֶם הָרֹאֹת אֵת כָּל־מַעֲשֵׂה יְהוָה הַגָּדֹל אֲשֶׁר
ח עָשָׂה׃ וּשְׁמַרְתֶּם אֶת־כָּל־הַמִּצְוָה אֲשֶׁר אָנֹכִי מְצַוְּךָ הַיּוֹם לְמַעַן תֶּחֶזְקוּ
ט וּבָאתֶם וִירִשְׁתֶּם אֶת־הָאָרֶץ אֲשֶׁר אַתֶּם עֹבְרִים שָׁמָּה לְרִשְׁתָּהּ׃ וּלְמַעַן
תַּאֲרִיכוּ יָמִים עַל־הָאֲדָמָה אֲשֶׁר נִשְׁבַּע יְהוָה לַאֲבֹתֵיכֶם לָתֵת לָהֶם

אונקלוס

יָת רְבוּתֵיהּ, יָת יְדֵיהּ תַּקִּיפְתָּא, וּדְרָעֵיהּ מְרָמְמָא: ג וְיָת אָתְוָתֵיהּ וְיָת
עוֹבָדוֹהִי, דַּעֲבַד בְּגוֹ מִצְרַיִם, לְפַרְעֹה מַלְכָּא דְמִצְרַיִם וּלְכָל אַרְעֵיהּ:
ד וְדַעֲבַד לְמַשִּׁרְיַת מִצְרָאֵי לְסוּסָוָתְהוֹן וּלְרְתִכֵּיהוֹן, דְּאַטֵּיף, יָת מֵי
יַמָּא דְסוּף עַל אַפֵּיהוֹן, בְּמִרְדַּפְהוֹן בָּתְרֵיכוֹן, וְאוֹבֵידִנּוּן יי, עַד יוֹמָא
הָדֵין: ה וְדַעֲבַד לְכוֹן בְּמַדְבְּרָא, עַד מֵיתֵיכוֹן עַד אַתְרָא הָדֵין: ו וְדַעֲבַד
לְדָתָן וְלַאֲבִירָם, בְּנֵי אֱלִיאָב בַּר רְאוּבֵן, דִּפְתַחַת אַרְעָא יָת פֻּמַּהּ,
וּבְלַעֲתִנּוּן וְיָת אֱנָשׁ בָּתֵּיהוֹן וְיָת מַשְׁכְּנֵיהוֹן, וְיָת כָּל יְקוּמָא דְּעִמְּהוֹן,
בְּגוֹ כָּל יִשְׂרָאֵל: ז אֲרֵי עֵינֵיכוֹן חֲזָאָה, יָת כָּל עוֹבָדָא דַיי רַבָּא, דַּעֲבַד:
ח וְתִטְּרוּן יָת כָּל תַּפְקֵידְתָּא, דַּאֲנָא מְפַקֵּיד לָךְ יוֹמָא דֵין, בְּדִיל
דְּתִתַּקְפוּן, וְתֵיעֲלוּן וְתֵירְתוּן יָת אַרְעָא, דְּאַתּוּן, עָבְרִין לְתַמָּן לְמֵירְתַהּ:
ט וּבְדִיל דְּתֵירְכוּן יוֹמִין עַל אַרְעָא, דְּקַיֵּים יי לַאֲבָהָתְכוֹן, לְמִתַּן

THE CONDITIONAL PROSPERITY OF THE LAND

Jewish destiny was to create a society that would honor the proposition that we are all created in the image and likeness of God. It would be a place in which the freedom of some would not lead to the enslavement of others, the opposite of Egypt, whose bread of affliction and bitter herbs of slavery they were to eat every year on the festival of Passover to remind them of what to avoid. Judaism is the code of a self-governing society. It is about the shared spaces of our collective lives, not just an interior drama of the soul. It formalizes the social virtues: righteousness (*tzedek/tzedaka*), justice (*mishpat*), loving-kindness (*ḥesed*), and compassion (*raḥamim*). These structure the template of biblical law, which covers all aspects of the life of society: its economy, its welfare systems, its education and family life. The broad principles driving this elaborate structure, traditionally enumerated as 613 commands, are clear. No one should be left in dire poverty. No one should lack access to justice and the courts. No family should be without its share of the land.

All this must be actualized in a territory. But the land of Israel, says Moshe, is not a fertile plain. It is a land of hills and valleys. It depends on rain – and rain in the Middle East, then and now, is unpredictable. We recall a whole series of earlier episodes in the book of Genesis in which we read the words "There was a famine in the land." This led first

10 with milk and with honey. For the land that you are about to go into SHISHI
and take possession of is not like the land of Egypt you left behind, where you
11 could sow your seed and irrigate by foot as in a vegetable garden. The land that
you are crossing over to possess is a land of hills and valleys; it is watered by the
12 sky's rains. It is a land the LORD your God watches over; the eyes of the LORD
13 your God are always upon it, from the year's opening to its end. And if
you heed My commands, with which I charge you on this day, to love the LORD
14 your God and to serve Him with all your heart and with all your soul, I will

רש״י

י **לֹא כְאֶרֶץ מִצְרַיִם הִוא.** אֶלָּא טוֹבָה הֵימֶנָּה. וְנֶאֶמְרָה הַבְטָחָה זוֹ לְיִשְׂרָאֵל בִּיצִיאָתָם מִמִּצְרַיִם, שֶׁהָיוּ אוֹמְרִים, שֶׁמָּא לֹא נָבוֹא אֶל אֶרֶץ טוֹבָה וְיָפָה כָּזוֹ. יָכוֹל בִּגְנוּתָהּ הַכָּתוּב מְדַבֵּר, וְכָךְ אָמַר לָהֶם: לֹא כְּאֶרֶץ מִצְרַיִם הִיא אֶלָּא רָעָה הֵימֶנָּה? תַּלְמוּד לוֹמַר: "וְחֶבְרוֹן שֶׁבַע שָׁנִים נִבְנְתָה לִפְנֵי צֹעַן מִצְרָיִם" (במדבר יג, כב), אָדָם אֶחָד בָּנָאן, אִם בָּנָה צֹעַן לְמִצְרַיִם בְּנוֹ וְחֶבְרוֹן לִכְנַעַן; דֶּרֶךְ אֶרֶץ אָדָם בּוֹנֶה אֶת הַנָּאֶה וְאַחַר כָּךְ בּוֹנֶה אֶת הַכָּעוּר, שֶׁפְּסָלְתּוֹ שֶׁל רִאשׁוֹן הוּא נוֹתֵן בַּשֵּׁנִי, וּבְכָל מָקוֹם הֶחָבִיב קוֹדֵם, הָא לָמַדְתָּ שֶׁחֶבְרוֹן יָפָה מִצֹּעַן. וּמִצְרַיִם מְשֻׁבַּחַת מִכָּל הָאֲרָצוֹת, שֶׁנֶּאֱמַר: "כְּגַן ה' כְּאֶרֶץ מִצְרַיִם" (בראשית יג, י), וְצֹעַן שֶׁבַח מִצְרַיִם הִיא, שֶׁהָיְתָה מְקוֹם מַלְכוּת, שֶׁכֵּן הוּא אוֹמֵר: "כִּי הָיוּ בְצֹעַן שָׂרָיו" (ישעיה ל, ד), וְחֶבְרוֹן פְּסָלְתָּהּ שֶׁל אֶרֶץ יִשְׂרָאֵל, לְכָךְ הִקְצוּהָ לִקְבוּרַת מֵתִים, וְאַף עַל פִּי כֵן הִיא יָפָה מִצֹּעַן. וּבִכְתֻבּוֹת (דף קיב ע"א) דָּרְשׁוּ בְּעִנְיָן אַחֵר: אֶפְשָׁר אָדָם בּוֹנֶה בַּיִת לִבְנוֹ הַקָּטָן וְאַחַר כָּךְ לִבְנוֹ הַגָּדוֹל? אֶלָּא שֶׁמְּבֻנָּה עַל אֶחָד מִשִּׁבְעָה בְּצֹעַן: **אֲשֶׁר יְצָאתֶם מִשָּׁם.** אֲפִלּוּ אֶרֶץ רַעְמְסֵס אֲשֶׁר יְשַׁבְתֶּם בָּהּ וְהִיא בְּמֵיטַב אֶרֶץ מִצְרַיִם, שֶׁנֶּאֱמַר: "בְּמֵיטַב הָאָרֶץ" וְגוֹ' (בראשית מז, יא), אַף הִיא אֵינָהּ כְּאֶרֶץ יִשְׂרָאֵל: **וְהִשְׁקִיתָ בְרַגְלְךָ.** אֶרֶץ מִצְרַיִם – הָיִיתָ צָרִיךְ לְהָבִיא מַיִם מִנִּילוּס בְּרַגְלְךָ וּלְהַשְׁקוֹתָהּ, וְצָרִיךְ אַתָּה לְנַדֵּד אֶת שְׁנָתְךָ וְלַעֲמֹל, וְהַנָּמוּךְ שׁוֹתֶה וְלֹא הַגָּבוֹהַּ, וְאַתָּה מַעֲלֶה הַמַּיִם מִן הַנָּמוּךְ לַגָּבוֹהַּ. אֲבָל זוֹ – "לִמְטַר הַשָּׁמַיִם תִּשְׁתֶּה מָּיִם" (להלן פסוק יא), אַתָּה יָשֵׁן עַל מִטָּתְךָ וְהַקָּדוֹשׁ בָּרוּךְ הוּא מַשְׁקֶה נָמוּךְ וְגָבוֹהַּ, גָּלוּי וְשֶׁאֵינוֹ גָּלוּי כְּאַחַת: **כְּגַן הַיָּרָק.** שֶׁאֵין דַּי לוֹ בִּגְשָׁמִים וּמַשְׁקִים אוֹתוֹ בָּרֶגֶל וּבַכָּתֵף:

יא **אֶרֶץ הָרִים וּבְקָעֹת.** מְשֻׁבָּח הָהָר מִן הַמִּישׁוֹר, שֶׁהַמִּישׁוֹר בְּבֵית כּוֹר אַתָּה זוֹרֵעַ כּוֹר, אֲבָל הָהָר בֵּית כּוֹר מִמֶּנּוּ חֲמֵשֶׁת כּוֹרִין, אַרְבָּעָה מֵאַרְבָּעָה שִׁפּוּעָיו וְאֶחָד בְּרֹאשׁוֹ: **וּבְקָעֹת.** הֵן מִישׁוֹר:

יב **אֲשֶׁר ה' אֱלֹהֶיךָ דֹּרֵשׁ אֹתָהּ.** וַהֲלֹא כָּל הָאֲרָצוֹת הוּא דּוֹרֵשׁ, שֶׁנֶּאֱמַר: "לְהַמְטִיר עַל אֶרֶץ לֹא אִישׁ" (איוב לח, כו)! אֶלָּא כִּבְיָכוֹל אֵינוֹ דּוֹרֵשׁ אֶלָּא אוֹתָהּ, וְעַל יְדֵי אוֹתָהּ דְּרִישָׁה שֶׁדּוֹרְשָׁהּ דּוֹרֵשׁ אֶת כָּל הָאֲרָצוֹת עִמָּהּ: **תָּמִיד עֵינֵי ה' אֱלֹהֶיךָ בָּהּ.** לִרְאוֹת מַה הִיא צְרִיכָה וּלְחַדֵּשׁ בָּהּ גְּזֵרוֹת, עִתִּים לְטוֹבָה וְעִתִּים לְרָעָה וְכוּ', כִּדְאִיתָא בְּרֹאשׁ הַשָּׁנָה (דף יז ע"ב): **מֵרֵשִׁית הַשָּׁנָה.** מֵרֹאשׁ הַשָּׁנָה נִדּוֹן מַה יְּהֵא בְּסוֹפָהּ:

יג **וְהָיָה אִם שָׁמֹעַ תִּשְׁמְעוּ.** אִם תִּשְׁמַע בַּיָּשָׁן, תִּשְׁמַע בֶּחָדָשׁ, וְכֵן: "וְהָיָה אִם שָׁכֹחַ תִּשְׁכַּח" (לעיל ח, יט), אִם הִתְחַלְתָּ לִשְׁכֹּחַ סוֹפְךָ שֶׁתִּשְׁכַּח כֻּלָּהּ, כְּתִיב בִּמְגִלָּה: אִם תַּעַזְבֵנִי יוֹם, יוֹמַיִם אֶעֶזְבֶךָּ (ראה ספרי מח): **מְצַוֶּה אֶתְכֶם הַיּוֹם.** שֶׁיִּהְיוּ עֲלֵיכֶם חֲדָשִׁים כְּאִלּוּ שְׁמַעְתֶּם בּוֹ בַּיּוֹם: **לְאַהֲבָה אֶת ה'.** שֶׁלֹּא תֹּאמַר: הֲרֵי אֲנִי לָמֵד בִּשְׁבִיל שֶׁאֶהְיֶה עָשִׁיר, בִּשְׁבִיל שֶׁאֶקָּרֵא רַב, בִּשְׁבִיל שֶׁאֲקַבֵּל שָׂכָר, אֶלָּא כָּל מַה שֶּׁתַּעֲשׂוּ עֲשׂוּ מֵאַהֲבָה, וְסוֹף הַכָּבוֹד לָבֹא: **וּלְעָבְדוֹ בְּכָל לְבַבְכֶם.** עֲבוֹדָה שֶׁהִיא בַּלֵּב, וְזוֹ הִיא תְּפִלָּה, שֶׁהַתְּפִלָּה קְרוּיָה עֲבוֹדָה, שֶׁנֶּאֱמַר: "אֱלָהָךְ דִּי אַנְתְּ פָּלַח לֵהּ בִּתְדִירָא" (דניאל ו, יז), וְכִי יֵשׁ פֻּלְחָן בְּבָבֶל? אֶלָּא עַל שֶׁהָיָה מִתְפַּלֵּל, שֶׁנֶּאֱמַר: "וְכַוִּין פְּתִיחָן לֵהּ" וְגוֹ' (שם פסוק יא), וְכֵן בְּדָוִד הוּא אוֹמֵר: "תִּכּוֹן תְּפִלָּתִי קְטֹרֶת לְפָנֶיךָ" (תהלים קמא, ב): **בְּכָל לְבַבְכֶם וּבְכָל נַפְשְׁכֶם.** וַהֲלֹא כְּבָר הִזְהִיר: "בְּכָל לְבָבְךָ וּבְכָל נַפְשְׁךָ" (דברים ו, ה)? אֶלָּא, אַזְהָרָה לַיָּחִיד, אַזְהָרָה לַצִּבּוּר:

יד **וְנָתַתִּי מְטַר אַרְצְכֶם.** עֲשִׂיתֶם מַה שֶּׁעֲלֵיכֶם, אַף אֲנִי אֶעֱשֶׂה מַה שֶּׁעָלַי:

Listening is the greatest gift we can give to another human being. To be listened to, to be heard, is to know that someone else takes me seriously. That is a redemptive act. And it changes not only the one who is heard, but the listener as well.

not like us who make us grow. The bridge between self and other is conversation: speaking and listening. On superficial reading, this passage is a basic text of reward and punishment, obedience and disobedience. But it is addressed not only to our actions, but to the "heart and soul," to an inner act of listening and opening ourselves to influence.

וּלְזַרְעָם אֶרֶץ זָבַת חָלָב וּדְבָשׁ: כִּי הָאָרֶץ אֲשֶׁר אַתָּה בָא־ י ששי
שָׁמָּה לְרִשְׁתָּהּ לֹא כְאֶרֶץ מִצְרַיִם הִוא אֲשֶׁר יְצָאתֶם מִשָּׁם אֲשֶׁר תִּזְרַע
יא אֶת־זַרְעֲךָ וְהִשְׁקִיתָ בְרַגְלְךָ כְּגַן הַיָּרָק: וְהָאָרֶץ אֲשֶׁר אַתֶּם עֹבְרִים
יב שָׁמָּה לְרִשְׁתָּהּ אֶרֶץ הָרִים וּבְקָעֹת לִמְטַר הַשָּׁמַיִם תִּשְׁתֶּה־מָּיִם: אֶרֶץ
אֲשֶׁר־יהוה אֱלֹהֶיךָ דֹּרֵשׁ אֹתָהּ תָּמִיד עֵינֵי יהוה אֱלֹהֶיךָ בָּהּ מֵרֵשִׁית
יג הַשָּׁנָה וְעַד אַחֲרִית שָׁנָה: וְהָיָה אִם־שָׁמֹעַ תִּשְׁמְעוּ אֶל־
מִצְוֹתַי אֲשֶׁר אָנֹכִי מְצַוֶּה אֶתְכֶם הַיּוֹם לְאַהֲבָה אֶת־יהוה אֱלֹהֵיכֶם
יד וּלְעָבְדוֹ בְּכָל־לְבַבְכֶם וּבְכָל־נַפְשְׁכֶם: וְנָתַתִּי מְטַר־אַרְצְכֶם בְּעִתּוֹ

אונקלוס

לְהוֹן וְלִבְנֵיהוֹן, אֲרַע, עָבְדָא חֲלַב וּדְבַשׁ: י אֲרֵי אַרְעָא, דְּאַתְּ עָלֵיל לְתַמָּן לְמֵירְתַהּ, לָא כְאַרְעָא דְמִצְרַיִם הִיא, דִּנְפַקְתּוּן מִתַּמָּן, דְּתִזְרַע יָת זַרְעָךְ, וּמַשְׁקֵית לֵיהּ בְּרַגְלָךְ כְּגִנַּת יַרְקָא: יא וְאַרְעָא, דְּאַתּוּן, עָבְרִין לְתַמָּן לְמֵירְתַהּ, אֲרַע טוּרִין וּבִקְעָן, לִמְטַר שְׁמַיָּא שָׁתְיָא מַיָּא: יב אַרְעָא, דַּיי אֱלָהָךְ תָּבַע יָתַהּ, תְּדִירָא, עֵינֵי יי אֱלָהָךְ בַּהּ, מֵרֵישָׁא דְשַׁתָּא, וְעַד סוֹפָא דְשַׁתָּא: יג וִיהֵי, אִם קַבָּלָא תְקַבְּלוּן לְפִקּוֹדַי, דַּאֲנָא, מְפַקֵּיד יָתְכוֹן יוֹמָא דֵין, לְמִרְחַם, יָת יי אֱלָהֲכוֹן וּלְמִפְלַח קֳדָמוֹהִי, בְּכָל לִבְּכוֹן וּבְכָל נַפְשְׁכוֹן: יד וְאֶתֵּין מְטַר אַרְעֲכוֹן,

11:13 אִם־שָׁמֹעַ תִּשְׁמְעוּ *If you heed* – There is urgency behind Moshe's double emphasis (*shamoa tishme'u* in the Hebrew) in the opening line of this passage, the second paragraph of the *Shema*. A more forceful translation might be: "If you listen – and I mean really listen."

One can almost imagine the Israelites saying to Moshe, "Enough; we hear you," and Moshe replying, "No you don't. You simply do not understand what is happening. The Creator of the entire universe is taking a personal interest in your welfare and destiny. Have you any idea of what that means?" Perhaps we still don't.

The root *sh-m-a* does not have a single direct translation in English (see ch. 6, "Listen"). When you encounter a word in any language that is untranslatable into your own, you are close to the beating pulse of that culture. To understand an untranslatable word, you have to move out of your comfort zone and enter a mindset that is significantly different from yours. We may think, on the face of it, that this is a passage about obedience. Yet throughout Deuteronomy, Moshe tells us that God does not seek blind obedience. There is no word for "obedience" in Biblical Hebrew (Modern Hebrew had to borrow a verb, *letzayet*, from Aramaic). God wants us to listen, not just with our ears but with the deepest resources of our minds.

In making human beings free subjects "in His image," God created otherness. Listening to another human being, let alone God, is an act of opening ourselves up to a mind radically other than our own. This takes courage. To listen is to make myself vulnerable. My deepest certainties may be shaken by entering into the mind of one who thinks quite differently about the world. But it is essential to our humanity. It is the antidote to narcissism: the belief that we are the center of the universe. When we speak, we tell others who and what we are. But when we listen, we allow others to tell us who they are. This is the supremely revelatory moment.

In Judaism we believe that our relationship with God is an ongoing tutorial in our relationships with other people. If we can listen to other people, then we might possibly listen to God, whose otherness is not relative but absolute.

Listening is a profoundly spiritual act. It can also be painful. It is comfortable not to have to listen, not to be challenged, not to be moved outside our comfort zone. But it is the people

grant your land's rain in its season, the early and the late rain; you shall gather
15 in your grain, your wine, your oil. I will grant your fields grass for your cattle,
16 and you will eat and be satisfied. Be vigilant lest your heart be seduced and
17 you go astray and serve other gods and worship them. Then the LORD's rage
will blaze against you, and He will close the skies; there will be no rain. The
land will not yield its crops, and you will swiftly perish from the good land that
18 the LORD is giving you. Therefore set these words of Mine upon your heart
and upon your soul. Bind them as a sign upon your hand, and have them as an
19 emblem between your eyes. Teach them to your children, speaking of them
when you sit at home and when you travel on the way, when you lie down and
20 when you rise. Write them on the doorposts of your house and on your gates,

רש״י

בְּעִתּוֹ. בַּלֵּילוֹת, שֶׁלֹּא יַטְרִיחוּ אֶתְכֶם. דָּבָר אַחֵר, "בְּעִתּוֹ", בְּלֵילֵי שַׁבָּתוֹת, שֶׁהַכֹּל מְצוּיִין בְּבָתֵּיהֶם: **יוֹרֶה.** הִיא רְבִיעָה הַנּוֹפֶלֶת לְאַחַר הַזְּרִיעָה, שֶׁמַּרְוָה אֶת הָאָרֶץ וְאֶת הַזְּרָעִים: **וּמַלְקוֹשׁ.** רְבִיעָה הַיּוֹרֶדֶת סָמוּךְ לַקָּצִיר לְמַלֹּאת הַתְּבוּאָה בְּקַשֶּׁיהָ. וּלְשׁוֹן "מַלְקוֹשׁ" דָּבָר הַמְאַחֵר, כִּדְמִתַּרְגְּמִינַן: "וְהָיָה הָעֲטֻפִים לְלָבָן" – "לַקִּישַׁיָּא" (בראשית ל, מב). דָּבָר אַחֵר, לְכָךְ נִקְרֵאת "מַלְקוֹשׁ", שֶׁיּוֹרֶדֶת עַל הַמְּלִילוֹת וְעַל הַקַּשִּׁין: **וְאָסַפְתָּ דְגָנֶךָ.** אַתָּה תַּאַסְפֶנּוּ אֶל הַבַּיִת וְלֹא אוֹיְבֶיךָ, כְּעִנְיָן שֶׁנֶּאֱמַר: "אִם אֶתֵּן אֶת דְּגָנֵךְ עוֹד מַאֲכָל לְאֹיְבַיִךְ וְגוֹ' כִּי מְאַסְפָיו יֹאכְלֻהוּ" (ישעיה סב, ח-ט), וְלֹא כְּעִנְיָן שֶׁנֶּאֱמַר: "וְהָיָה אִם זָרַע יִשְׂרָאֵל וְעָלָה מִדְיָן וַעֲמָלֵק וּבְנֵי קֶדֶם" וְגוֹ' (שופטים ו, ג):

טו **וְנָתַתִּי עֵשֶׂב בְּשָׂדְךָ.** שֶׁלֹּא תִּצְטָרֵךְ לְהוֹלִיכָהּ לַמִּדְבָּרוֹת. דָּבָר אַחֵר, שֶׁתְּהֵא גּוֹזֵז תְּבוּאָתְךָ כָּל יְמוֹת הַגְּשָׁמִים וּמַשְׁלִיךְ לִפְנֵי בְהֶמְתְּךָ, וְאַתָּה מוֹנֵעַ יָדְךָ מִמֶּנָּה שְׁלֹשִׁים יוֹם קֹדֶם לַקָּצִיר וְאֵינָהּ פּוֹחֶתֶת מִדְּגָנָהּ: **וְאָכַלְתָּ וְשָׂבָעְתָּ.** הֲרֵי זוֹ בְּרָכָה אַחֶרֶת, שֶׁתְּהֵא בְּרָכָה מְצוּיָה בַּפַּת בְּתוֹךְ הַמֵּעַיִם:

טו-טז **וְאָכַלְתָּ וְשָׂבָעְתָּ, הִשָּׁמְרוּ לָכֶם.** כֵּיוָן שֶׁתִּהְיוּ אוֹכְלִים וּשְׂבֵעִים, הִשָּׁמְרוּ לָכֶם שֶׁלֹּא תִּבְעֲטוּ, שֶׁאֵין אָדָם מוֹרֵד בְּהַקָּדוֹשׁ בָּרוּךְ הוּא אֶלָּא מִתּוֹךְ שְׂבִיעָה, שֶׁנֶּאֱמַר: "פֶּן תֹּאכַל וְשָׂבָעְתָּ... וּבְקָרְךָ וְצֹאנְךָ יִרְבְּיֻן" (לעיל ח, יב-יג), מַה הוּא אוֹמֵר אַחֲרָיו? "וְרָם לְבָבֶךָ וְשָׁכַחְתָּ" (שם פסוק יד): **וְסַרְתֶּם.** לִפְרֹשׁ מִן הַתּוֹרָה, וּמִתּוֹךְ כָּךְ: "וַעֲבַדְתֶּם אֱלֹהִים אֲחֵרִים", שֶׁכֵּיוָן שֶׁאָדָם פּוֹרֵשׁ מִן הַתּוֹרָה, הוֹלֵךְ וּמִדַּבֵּק בַּעֲבוֹדָה זָרָה. וְכֵן דָּוִד אוֹמֵר: "כִּי גֵרְשׁוּנִי הַיּוֹם מֵהִסְתַּפֵּחַ בְּנַחֲלַת ה' לֵאמֹר לֵךְ עֲבֹד אֱלֹהִים אֲחֵרִים" (שמואל א' כו, יט), וּמִי אָמַר לוֹ כֵּן? אֶלָּא כֵּיוָן שֶׁאֲנִי מְגֹרָשׁ מִלַּעֲסֹק בַּתּוֹרָה, הֲרֵינִי קָרוֹב לַעֲבֹד אֱלֹהִים אֲחֵרִים: **אֱלֹהִים אֲחֵרִים.** שֶׁהֵם אֲחֵרִים לְעוֹבְדֵיהֶם, צוֹעֵק אֵלָיו וְאֵינוֹ עוֹנֵהוּ, נִמְצָא עָשׂוּי לוֹ כְּנָכְרִי:

יז **אֵת יְבוּלָהּ.** אַף מַה שֶּׁאַתָּה מוֹבִיל לָהּ, כְּעִנְיָן שֶׁנֶּאֱמַר: "זְרַעְתֶּם הַרְבֵּה וְהָבֵא מְעָט" (חגי א, ו): **וַאֲבַדְתֶּם מְהֵרָה.** עַל כָּל שְׁאָר הַיִּסּוּרִין, אַגְלֶה אֶתְכֶם מִן הָאֲדָמָה שֶׁגָּרְמָה לָכֶם לַחְטֹא. מָשָׁל לְמֶלֶךְ שֶׁשָּׁלַח בְּנוֹ לְבֵית הַמִּשְׁתֶּה וְהָיָה יוֹשֵׁב וּמְפַקְּדוֹ: אַל תֹּאכַל יוֹתֵר מִצָּרְכְּךָ שֶׁתָּבוֹא נָקִי לְבֵיתְךָ, וְלֹא הִשְׁגִּיחַ הַבֵּן הַהוּא, אָכַל וְשָׁתָה יוֹתֵר מִצָּרְכּוֹ וְהֵקִיא וְטִנֵּף אֶת כָּל בְּנֵי הַמְּסִבָּה, נְטָלוּהוּ בְּיָדָיו וּבְרַגְלָיו וּזְרָקוּהוּ אֲחוֹרֵי פַלְטֵרִין: **מְהֵרָה.** אֵינִי נוֹתֵן לָכֶם אַרְכָּא. וְאִם תֹּאמְרוּ, וַהֲלֹא נִתְּנָה אַרְכָּא לְדוֹר הַמַּבּוּל, שֶׁנֶּאֱמַר: "וְהָיוּ יָמָיו מֵאָה וְעֶשְׂרִים שָׁנָה" (בראשית ו, ג)? דּוֹר הַמַּבּוּל לֹא הָיָה לָהֶם מִמִּי לִלְמֹד, וְאַתֶּם יֵשׁ לָכֶם מִמִּי לִלְמֹד:

יח **וְשַׂמְתֶּם אֶת דְּבָרַי.** אַף לְאַחַר שֶׁתִּגְלוּ הֱיוּ מְצֻיָּנִים בַּמִּצְוֹת, הַנִּיחוּ תְּפִלִּין עֲשׂוּ מְזוּזוֹת, כְּדֵי שֶׁלֹּא יִהְיוּ לָכֶם חֲדָשִׁים כְּשֶׁתַּחְזְרוּ, וְכֵן הוּא אוֹמֵר: "הַצִּיבִי לָךְ צִיֻּנִים" (ירמיה לא, כ):

יט-כא **לְדַבֵּר בָּם.** מִשָּׁעָה שֶׁהַבֵּן יוֹדֵעַ לְדַבֵּר, לַמְּדֵהוּ "תּוֹרָה צִוָּה לָנוּ מֹשֶׁה" (להלן לג, ד), שֶׁיְּהֵא זֶה לִמּוּד דִּבּוּרוֹ. מִכָּאן אָמְרוּ: כְּשֶׁהַתִּינוֹק מַתְחִיל לְדַבֵּר, אָבִיו מֵשִׂיחַ עִמּוֹ בִּלְשׁוֹן הַקֹּדֶשׁ וּמְלַמְּדוֹ תּוֹרָה, וְאִם לֹא עָשָׂה כֵן הֲרֵי הוּא כְּאִלּוּ קוֹבְרוֹ, שֶׁנֶּאֱמַר: "וְלִמַּדְתֶּם אֹתָם אֶת

society that will bear testimony to something greater than themselves, namely, to God Himself.

But it is clear from the Torah's narrative thus far that the transformation of a people takes a long time. If any change in the human condition takes longer than a generation, education becomes fundamental. We need to hand on our memories, values, ideals, laws, and customs to our children, and they to theirs, if each generation is to continue the journey to a destination not yet reached.

This emphasis on education has given Judaism, from

טו יוֹרֶה וּמַלְקוֹשׁ וְאָסַפְתָּ דְגָנֶךָ וְתִירֹשְׁךָ וְיִצְהָרֶךָ: וְנָתַתִּי עֵשֶׂב בְּשָׂדְךָ
טז לִבְהֶמְתֶּךָ וְאָכַלְתָּ וְשָׂבָעְתָּ: הִשָּׁמְרוּ לָכֶם פֶּן־יִפְתֶּה לְבַבְכֶם וְסַרְתֶּם
יז וַעֲבַדְתֶּם אֱלֹהִים אֲחֵרִים וְהִשְׁתַּחֲוִיתֶם לָהֶם: וְחָרָה אַף־יהוה בָּכֶם
וְעָצַר אֶת־הַשָּׁמַיִם וְלֹא־יִהְיֶה מָטָר וְהָאֲדָמָה לֹא תִתֵּן אֶת־יְבוּלָהּ
יח וַאֲבַדְתֶּם מְהֵרָה מֵעַל הָאָרֶץ הַטֹּבָה אֲשֶׁר יהוה נֹתֵן לָכֶם: וְשַׂמְתֶּם
אֶת־דְּבָרַי אֵלֶּה עַל־לְבַבְכֶם וְעַל־נַפְשְׁכֶם וּקְשַׁרְתֶּם אֹתָם לְאוֹת עַל־
יט יֶדְכֶם וְהָיוּ לְטוֹטָפֹת בֵּין עֵינֵיכֶם: וְלִמַּדְתֶּם אֹתָם אֶת־בְּנֵיכֶם לְדַבֵּר
כ בָּם בְּשִׁבְתְּךָ בְּבֵיתֶךָ וּבְלֶכְתְּךָ בַדֶּרֶךְ וּבְשָׁכְבְּךָ וּבְקוּמֶךָ: וּכְתַבְתָּם

אונקלוס

בְּעִדָּנֵיהּ בַּכִּיר וְלַקִּישׁ, וְתִכְנוֹשׁ עֲבוּרָךְ, וְחַמְרָךְ וּמִשְׁחָךְ: טו וְאֶתֵּין, עִסְבָּא בְּחַקְלָךְ לִבְעִירָךְ, וְתֵיכוּל וְתִסְבַּע: טז אִסְתַּמַּרוּ לְכוֹן, דִּלְמָא יִטְעֵי לִבְּכוֹן, וְתִסְטוֹן, וְתִפְלְחוּן לְטָעֲוַת עַמְמַיָּא, וְתִסְגְּדוּן לְהוֹן: יז וְיִתְקַף רֻגְזָא דַּייָ בְּכוֹן, וְיֵיחוֹד יָת שְׁמַיָּא וְלָא יְהֵי מִטְרָא, וְאַרְעָא, לָא תִתֵּין יָת עֲלַלְתַּהּ, וְתֵיבְדוּן בִּפְרִיעַ, מֵעַל אַרְעָא טָבְתָא, דַּייָ יָהֵיב לְכוֹן: יח וּתְשַׁווֹן יָת פִּתְגָמַי אִלֵּין, עַל לִבְּכוֹן וְעַל נַפְשְׁכוֹן, וְתִקְטְרוּן יָתְהוֹן לְאָת עַל יַדְכוֹן, וִיהוֹן לִתְפִלִּין בֵּין עֵינֵיכוֹן: יט וְתַלְפוּן יָתְהוֹן, יָת בְּנֵיכוֹן לְמַלָּלָא בְהוֹן, בְּמִתְּבָךְ בְּבֵיתָךְ וּבְמַהֲכָךְ בְּאוֹרְחָא, וּבְמִשְׁכְּבָךְ וּבִמְקִימָךְ: כ וְתִכְתּוֹבִנּוּן

11:19 וְלִמַּדְתֶּם אֹתָם *Teach them* – In Deuteronomy, a new word enters the biblical vocabulary: the verb based on the root *l-m-d*, meaning to learn or teach. The verb does not appear even once in Genesis, Exodus, Leviticus, or Numbers. In Deuteronomy it appears seventeen times.

When the Torah speaks about education it does so in a striking and unusual way. It speaks of parents and children and handing on the tradition from one generation to the next. Avraham is chosen – "so that he may direct his children and his household after him to keep the way of the Lord by doing what is right and just" (Gen. 18:19). The *Shema* commands us: "Teach them to your children, speaking of them when you sit at home and when you travel on the way, when you lie down and when you rise." The Seder service on Passover – Judaism's most intense and revolutionary educational experience – involves teaching a child to see himself or herself as part of a people and its memories, and it is achieved not by teachers in classrooms but by parents around the family table. Jewish education is not about the abstract contemplation of truth. It is about introducing the next generation to the covenant which they inherit from their parents and their parents' parents through a family line which stretches back to Sinai. Jewish education is about Jewish continuity.

11:19 אֶת־בְּנֵיכֶם *To your children* – Jews survived because they set as their highest priority handing on their heritage to the next generation. They placed education at the very heart of faith. Their heroes were teachers, their citadels were houses of study, and their passion learning and the life of the mind. And it began, as this passage makes clear, in the context of the home. To be a parent, in Judaism, is to be a teacher. Education is the conversation between the generations.

There is a profound reason for this. The Torah envisages a society that will be more than just a reflection of the values that drive most human groups: the search for wealth and power. Instead, as a holy people in a holy land, Jews are to care about the poor and powerless. They are to become a nation driven by high ideals. They must seek to be an inspiration to others. They are charged with becoming a

21 so that you and your children may live long years in the land that the LORD
swore to your ancestors to give to them for as long as the sky endures above
22 the land. If you carefully keep all of this command with which I am SHEVI'I AND MAFTIR
charging you, loving the LORD your God, walking in all His ways, and holding
23 fast to Him, then the LORD will drive all these nations out before you, and you
24 will dispossess nations larger and mightier than you. Every place where you
set foot shall be yours. Your territory shall stretch from the wilderness to the

רש״י

בְּנֵיכֶם לְדַבֵּר בָּם וְגוֹ׳ לְמַעַן יִרְבּוּ יְמֵיכֶם וִימֵי בְנֵיכֶם״ – אִם עֲשִׂיתֶם כֵּן יִרְבּוּ, וְאִם לָאו לֹא יִרְבּוּ, שֶׁדִּבְרֵי תּוֹרָה נִדְרָשִׁין מִכְּלָל לָאו הֵן וּמִכְּלַל הֵן לָאו: **לָתֵת לָהֶם.** ׳לָתֵת לָכֶם׳ אֵין כְּתִיב כָּאן, אֶלָּא ״לָתֵת לָהֶם״, מִכָּאן מָצִינוּ לְמֵדִים תְּחִיַּת הַמֵּתִים מִן הַתּוֹרָה:

כב **שָׁמֹר תִּשְׁמְרוּן.** אַזְהָרַת שְׁמִירוֹת הַרְבֵּה, לְהִזָּהֵר בְּתַלְמוּדוֹ שֶׁלֹּא יִשְׁתַּכַּח: **לָלֶכֶת בְּכָל דְּרָכָיו.** הוּא רַחוּם וְאַתָּה תְהֵא רַחוּם, הוּא גּוֹמֵל חֲסָדִים וְאַתָּה גּוֹמֵל חֲסָדִים: **וּלְדָבְקָה בוֹ.** אֶפְשָׁר לוֹמַר כֵּן, וַהֲלֹא ״אֵשׁ אֹכְלָה הוּא״ (לעיל ד, כד)? אֶלָּא הִדָּבֵק בַּתַּלְמִידִים וּבַחֲכָמִים, וּמַעֲלֶה אֲנִי עָלֶיךָ כְּאִלּוּ נִדְבַּקְתָּ בוֹ:

כג **וְהוֹרִישׁ ה׳.** עֲשִׂיתֶם מַה שֶּׁעֲלֵיכֶם, אַף אֲנִי אֶעֱשֶׂה מַה שֶּׁעָלַי: **וַעֲצֻמִים מִכֶּם.** אַתֶּם גִּבּוֹרִים וְהֵם גִּבּוֹרִים מִכֶּם, שֶׁאִם לֹא שֶׁיִּשְׂרָאֵל גִּבּוֹרִים, מַה הַשֶּׁבַח הַהוּא שֶׁמְּשַׁבֵּחַ אֶת הָאֱמוֹרִיִּים לוֹמַר: ״וַעֲצֻמִים מִכֶּם״? אֶלָּא אַתֶּם גִּבּוֹרִים מִשְּׁאָר הָאֻמּוֹת, וְהֵם גִּבּוֹרִים מִכֶּם:

We find Rambam's ideas mirrored in the kabbalistic tradition. He who makes *devekut* his aim must sever his contacts with the world and practise a meditative retreat. It is only in Hasidism that we find, as it were, a democratization of Rambam. Cleaving to God in all His ways is removed from Ibn Ezra's category of "mystery." Once one has perceived the implication of the unity of God – that nothing exists except in Him – then one can preserve the state of communion and the not-self even when immersed in the world.

11:23 **גְּדֹלִים וַעֲצֻמִים מִכֶּם** *Larger and mightier than you* – These nations have their own story, which is not Moshe's concern here (see Deut. 9:4 and commentary there). To us as readers, these mighty nations symbolize the insecurity faced by Israel as it emerges into the arena of nations. There is no way of eliminating the objective conditions that create insecurity on many levels, now as then. We have, however, intellectual resources that enable us to cope with it. Of these the most important is a moral vision. We can travel at speed so long as we know where we are going. It is when we lose a sense of vision that we find ourselves, in effect, without a map or a destination. That is when people turn to populist leaders capable of manipulating public fear (see Num. 16, "The Korah Rebellion") or to regressive identities and fundamentalisms that allow them to cope with fear by blaming some group or other for being the cause of the world's ills.

What morality restores to an increasingly uncertain world is the idea of *responsibility* – that what we do, severally and collectively, makes a difference, and that the future lies in our hands. Every era has produced its own philosophies or quasi-scientific systems to show that what happens could not have been otherwise, that the march of history is inevitable, that it is hubris to believe we can fight against fate. All we can do is to align ourselves to its flow, exploit it when we can, and render ourselves stoically indifferent to our fate when we cannot.

This way of thinking is a regression to a view of the universe that is very ancient indeed. It is the world of myth, in which mankind is alone in an environment dominated by irresistible forces blind to our presence, deaf to our prayers and hopes.

The great leap of the biblical imagination was to argue otherwise. There is a personal dimension to existence. Our hopes are not mere dreams, nor are our ideals illusions.

כא עַל־מְזוּזוֹת בֵּיתֶךָ וּבִשְׁעָרֶיךָ׃ לְמַעַן יִרְבּוּ יְמֵיכֶם וִימֵי בְנֵיכֶם עַל
הָאֲדָמָה אֲשֶׁר נִשְׁבַּע יהוה לַאֲבֹתֵיכֶם לָתֵת לָהֶם כִּימֵי הַשָּׁמַיִם עַל־
כב הָאָרֶץ׃ כִּי אִם־שָׁמֹר תִּשְׁמְרוּן אֶת־כָּל־הַמִּצְוָה שביעי ומפטיר
הַזֹּאת אֲשֶׁר אָנֹכִי מְצַוֶּה אֶתְכֶם לַעֲשֹׂתָהּ לְאַהֲבָה אֶת־יהוה אֱלֹהֵיכֶם
כג לָלֶכֶת בְּכָל־דְּרָכָיו וּלְדָבְקָה־בוֹ׃ וְהוֹרִישׁ יהוה אֶת־כָּל־הַגּוֹיִם הָאֵלֶּה
כד מִלִּפְנֵיכֶם וִירִשְׁתֶּם גּוֹיִם גְּדֹלִים וַעֲצֻמִים מִכֶּם׃ כָּל־הַמָּקוֹם אֲשֶׁר תִּדְרֹךְ
כַּף־רַגְלְכֶם בּוֹ לָכֶם יִהְיֶה מִן־הַמִּדְבָּר וְהַלְּבָנוֹן מִן־הַנָּהָר נְהַר־פְּרָת

אונקלוס

עַל מְזוּזַיָּן, וְתִקְבְּעִנּוּן בְּסִפֵּי בֵיתָךְ וּבִתְרָעָךְ: כא בְּדִיל דְּיִסְגּוֹן יוֹמֵיכוֹן
וְיוֹמֵי בְנֵיכוֹן, עַל אַרְעָא, דְּקַיֵּים יי, לַאֲבָהָתְכוֹן לְמִתַּן לְהוֹן, כְּיוֹמֵי
שְׁמַיָּא עַל אַרְעָא: כב אֲרֵי אִם מִטַּר תִּטְּרוּן יָת כָּל תַּפְקֵידְתָּא
הָדָא, דַּאֲנָא, מְפַקֵּיד יָתְכוֹן לְמֶעְבְּדַהּ, לְמִרְחַם, יָת יי אֱלָהֲכוֹן,
לִמְהָךְ בְּכָל אוֹרְחָן דְּתָקְנָן קֳדָמוֹהִי וּלְאִתְקָרָבָא לְדַחַלְתֵיהּ:
כג וִיתָרֵיךְ יי, יָת כָּל עַמְמַיָּא הָאִלֵּין מִן קֳדָמֵיכוֹן, וְתֵירְתוּן
עַמְמִין, רַבְרְבִין וְתַקִּיפִין מִנְּכוֹן: כד כָּל אַתְרָא, דְּתִדְרוֹךְ פַּרְסַת
רַגְלְכוֹן, בֵּיהּ דִּילְכוֹן יְהֵי, מִן מַדְבְּרָא וְלִבְנָן מִן נַהֲרָא נַהֲרָא פְּרָת,

the very beginning, a future orientation that is unusual among the great religions of the world. Jews have always cared about children and placed them as their highest joy. Rather than look back exclusively to a vanished past, they have looked forward to a distant but promised future. A people that places children at the apex of its agenda does not grow old. It learns to see the world through the eyes of a child – with hope and wonder and aspiration unsullied by cynicism and despair.

11:22 וּלְדָבְקָה־בוֹ *Holding fast to Him* – There is a disagreement between Ramban and Ibn Ezra on the interpretation of this verse. Is it possible that man should hold fast to the Almighty, that he be in intimate relation with God at all times? Or must Majesty – the ultimate separateness of God – sometimes interfere with Covenant – the closeness of God?

Ibn Ezra comments, "Holding fast to Him – at the end, for it is a great mystery," implying perhaps that it is a communion reached only at death. Whereas Ramban says: "It is, in fact, the meaning of 'holding fast,' that one should remember God and His love at all times, and not be separated in thought from Him 'when you travel on the way, when you lie down, and when you rise' (Deut. 6:7, 11:19). At such a stage, one may be talking with other people but one's heart is not with (i.e., confined to) them, since one is in the presence of God." The suffusion of man's social existence with his covenantal intimacy with God is for Ramban a this-worldly possibility.

But for whom is it possible? Rambam held that by philosophy and meditation a man may reach the rank of prophecy, and this is the highest natural perfection. But he will still be a divided self. "When you have succeeded in properly performing these acts of divine service, and you have your thought during their performance entirely abstracted from worldly affairs, then take care that you be not disturbed by thinking of your wants or of superfluous things. In short, think of worldly matters when you eat, drink, bathe, talk with your wife and little children, or when you converse with other people" (*Guide for the Perplexed* III:51). *Devekut*, cleaving, is an act of seclusion, and prayer and meditation are its sanctuary. Emerging into everyday life, one relinquishes that union. Only at the highest level of prophecy, where Moshe and the patriarchs stand, does this partition dissolve.

25 Lebanon, from the Euphrates River to the Western Sea. No one will be able to
stand against you. The LORD your God will put the fear and dread of you over
all the land you set foot upon, just as He promised you.

The haftara for Parashat Ekev is on page 1612.

רש״י

כה **לֹא יִתְיַצֵּב אִישׁ וְגוֹ׳.** אֵין לִי אֶלָּא אִישׁ, אֻמָּה וּמִשְׁפָּחָה וְאִשָּׁה בִּכְשָׁפֶיהָ מִנַּיִן? תַּלְמוּד לוֹמַר: ״לֹא יִתְיַצֵּב״, מִכָּל מָקוֹם. אִם כֵּן, מַה תַּלְמוּד לוֹמַר: ״אִישׁ״? אֲפִלּוּ כְּעוֹג מֶלֶךְ הַבָּשָׁן: **פַּחְדְּכֶם וּמוֹרַאֲכֶם.** וַהֲלֹא פַּחַד הוּא מוֹרָא? אֶלָּא ״פַּחְדְּכֶם״ עַל הַקְּרוֹבִים ״וּמוֹרַאֲכֶם״ עַל הָרְחוֹקִים. ׳פַּחַד׳ לְשׁוֹן בְּעִיתַת פִּתְאֹם, ׳מוֹרָא׳ לְשׁוֹן דְּאָגָה מִיָּמִים רַבִּים: **כַּאֲשֶׁר דִּבֶּר לָכֶם.** וְהֵיכָן דִּבֶּר? ״אֶת אֵימָתִי אֲשַׁלַּח לְפָנֶיךָ״ וְגוֹ׳ (שמות כג, כז):

כה וְעַד֙ הַיָּ֣ם הָאַחֲר֔וֹן יִהְיֶ֖ה גְּבֻלְכֶֽם׃ לֹֽא־יִתְיַצֵּ֥ב אִ֖ישׁ בִּפְנֵיכֶ֑ם פַּחְדְּכֶ֨ם
וּמוֹרַאֲכֶ֜ם יִתֵּ֣ן ׀ יהוָ֣ה אֱלֹהֵיכֶ֗ם עַל־פְּנֵ֤י כָל־הָאָ֙רֶץ֙ אֲשֶׁ֣ר תִּדְרְכוּ־בָ֔הּ
כַּאֲשֶׁ֖ר דִּבֶּ֥ר לָכֶֽם׃

The הפטרה *for* פרשת עקב *is on page 1613.*

אונקלוס

וְעַד יַמָּא בַתְרָאָה, יְהֵי תְּחוּמְכוֹן: כה לָא יִתְעַתַּד אֱנָשׁ קֳדָמֵיכוֹן, דַּחְלַתְכוֹן וְאֵימְתְכוֹן, יִתֵּין יי אֱלָהֲכוֹן, עַל אַפֵּי כָל אַרְעָא דְּתִדְרְכוּן בַּהּ, כְּמָא דְּמַלֵּיל לְכוֹן:

Something at the core of being responds to us as persons, inviting us to exercise our freedom by shaping families, communities, and societies in such a way as to honor the image of God that is mankind, investing each human life with ultimate dignity. This view sees choice, agency, and moral responsibility at the heart of the human project. We are not powerless in the face of fate. With every new power come choice, responsibility, and exercise of the moral imagination. It is this sense of responsibility – always opposed by determinisms ancient and modern – that Moshe seeks to impart to Israel in Deuteronomy.

PARASHAT RE'EH

11 26 27 See this: I am setting before you on this day a blessing and a curse: the blessing,
if you obey the commandments of the LORD your God that I am commanding
28 you today; and the curse, if you do not obey the commandments of the LORD
your God, and instead stray from the way I am commanding you this day to
29 follow, to walk after other gods that you have not known. When the

רש"י

כו רְאֵה אָנֹכִי. בְּרָכָה וּקְלָלָה. הָאֲמוּרוֹת בְּהַר גְּרִזִּים וּבְהַר עֵיבָל (להלן כז, טו-כו):

כז אֶת הַבְּרָכָה. עַל מְנָת "אֲשֶׁר תִּשְׁמְעוּ":

כח מִן הַדֶּרֶךְ אֲשֶׁר אָנֹכִי מְצַוֶּה אֶתְכֶם הַיּוֹם לָלֶכֶת וְגוֹ'. הָא לָמַדְתָּ שֶׁכָּל הָעוֹבֵד עֲבוֹדָה זָרָה הֲרֵי הוּא סָר מִכָּל הַדֶּרֶךְ שֶׁנִּצְטַוּוּ יִשְׂרָאֵל. מִכָּאן אָמְרוּ: כָּל הַמּוֹדֶה בַּעֲבוֹדָה זָרָה כְּכוֹפֵר בְּכָל הַתּוֹרָה כֻּלָּהּ:

THE CHOICE

Having set out the broad principles of the covenant, Moshe now turns to the details, which extend over many chapters and several *parashot*. The long review of the laws that will govern Israel in its land begins and ends with Moshe posing a momentous choice.

Rambam (*Hilkhot Teshuva* 5:3) takes these passages as proof of our belief in free will, which indeed they are. But they are more than that. They are also a political statement. The connection between individual freedom (which Rambam is talking about) and collective choice (which Moshe is talking about) is this: if humans are free then they need a free society within which to exercise that freedom. The book of Deuteronomy represents the first attempt in history to create a free society.

Moshe insists on three interconnected things. First, we *are* free. Blessing or curse? Good or evil? Faithfulness or faithlessness? You decide, says Moshe. Never has freedom been so starkly defined, not just for an individual but for a nation as a whole. There is no defense, says Moshe, in protestations of powerlessness, in saying we could not help it, we were outnumbered, we were defeated, it was the fault of our leaders or our enemies. No, says Moshe. Your fate is in your hands. The sovereignty of God does not take away human responsibility. To the contrary, it places it center stage. If you are faithful to God, says Moshe, you will prevail over empires. If you are not, nothing else – neither military strength nor political alliances – will help you. The choice and responsibility are yours alone.

Second, we are collectively responsible. The phrase "All Israelites are responsible for one another" (Shevuot 39b) is rabbinic, but the idea is already present in the Torah. The fate of Israel depends on all Israel, from "the leaders among you, the tribes, the elders and officials" (Deut. 29:9) to your "woodcutters and water drawers" (Josh. 9:23). The people of the covenant did not believe their destiny was determined by a governing elite. It was determined by each of us as moral agents, jointly responsible for the common good.

Third, it is a God-centered politics. To borrow the American phrase, Israel was "one nation under God." It is a powerful, challenging idea. If God is our only sovereign, then all human power is delegated, limited, subject to moral constraints. Jews were the first to believe that an entire nation could govern itself in freedom and equal dignity. This has less to do with political structures (monarchy, oligarchy, democracy – Jews have tried them all), than with collective moral responsibility.

Moshe's words still challenge us today. God has given us freedom; it is for us to use it to create a just, generous, gracious society. God does not do it for us but He teaches us how it is done. As Moshe says: the choice is ours.

פרשת ראה

יא כו כז רְאֵה אָנֹכִי נֹתֵן לִפְנֵיכֶם הַיּוֹם בְּרָכָה וּקְלָלָה: אֶת־הַבְּרָכָה אֲשֶׁר
תִּשְׁמְעוּ אֶל־מִצְוֹת יהוה אֱלֹהֵיכֶם אֲשֶׁר אָנֹכִי מְצַוֶּה אֶתְכֶם הַיּוֹם:
כח וְהַקְּלָלָה אִם־לֹא תִשְׁמְעוּ אֶל־מִצְוֹת יהוה אֱלֹהֵיכֶם וְסַרְתֶּם מִן־
הַדֶּרֶךְ אֲשֶׁר אָנֹכִי מְצַוֶּה אֶתְכֶם הַיּוֹם לָלֶכֶת אַחֲרֵי אֱלֹהִים אֲחֵרִים
כט אֲשֶׁר לֹא־יְדַעְתֶּם: וְהָיָה כִּי יְבִיאֲךָ יהוה אֱלֹהֶיךָ אֶל־הָאָרֶץ

אונקלוס

כו חֲזוֹ, דַּאֲנָא, יָהֵיב קֳדָמֵיכוֹן יוֹמָא דֵין, בִּרְכָן וּלְוָטִין: כז יָת בִּרְכָן, אִם תְּקַבְּלוּן, לְפִקּוֹדַיָּא דַּיי אֱלָהֲכוֹן, דַּאֲנָא, מְפַקֵּיד יָתְכוֹן יוֹמָא דֵין: כח וּלְוָטִין, אִם לָא תְקַבְּלוּן לְפִקּוֹדַיָּא דַּיי אֱלָהֲכוֹן, וְתִסְטוּן מִן אוֹרְחָא, דַּאֲנָא, מְפַקֵּיד יָתְכוֹן יוֹמָא דֵין, לִמְהָךְ, בָּתַר, טָעֲוַת עַמְמַיָּא דְּלָא יְדַעְתּוּן: כט וִיהֵי, אֲרֵי יַעֲלִנָּךְ יי אֱלָהָךְ, לְאַרְעָא,

RE'EH

In Parashat Re'eh, Moshe turns from the general principles of the covenant to the specific details, prefacing them with a warning of the choice that lies before them: blessings if they are faithful to God's laws, curses if they are not. They are to proclaim these to the nation, on Mount Gerizim and Mount Eival, when they enter the land. They must destroy all traces of idolatry, and establish a central site that God will choose where they will worship, offer sacrifices, and eat consecrated food. Moshe then issues further warnings about idolatry, false prophets, clean and unclean animals, tithes, and the Sabbatical year, when debts are to be cancelled and Hebrew slaves set free. The *parasha* concludes with the laws of the three pilgrimage festivals, when the nation is to celebrate and the men "appear before the Lord" at the central place of worship. We learn that not only individually, but also collectively the nation must exercise its free will to choose the good and stay faithful to God. A free society must be a responsible society. And it is not enough to be free; we must also celebrate our freedom.

11:26 רְאֵה *See this – Re'eh*, the first word of the *parasha*, means "see." On the face of it, Moshe is making an appeal to the eye, not the ear. In fact, though, it is about listening to something heard, namely a blessing and a curse. The non sequitur is so marked that some English translations render the verb *re'eh* not as "see" but as "understand."

What are we to make of this apparent anomaly? The revolutionary doctrine known as *Torah min haShamayim*, "Torah from Heaven," maintains that God reveals Himself in speech. All religions have holy places, objects, and times. But in Judaism these are derivative, not primary. Things are holy only because God has said so. Judaism is the religion of holy words.

If you seek God, turn your attention to language. The hidden presence of God is everywhere. But the revealed presence of God is in the words He gave to humanity on the basis of which He made a series of covenants, first with Noaḥ, then with Avraham, then with the Israelites at Mount Sinai. The Mosaic books constitute the covenant binding Heaven and earth, God and mankind. Hence the philosophy of Israel. To meet God is to listen to God.

The apparent counterexample of *re'eh*, "see," turns out to be not a contradiction of this idea but a dramatic reiteration of it. "See this: I am setting before you on this day a blessing and a curse."

What the Israelites are asked to see is words.

LORD your God has brought you into the land that you are entering to possess,
you shall proclaim the blessing on Mount Gerizim and the curse on Mount
30 Eival. They are across the Jordan, westward toward the setting sun, near the
Oaks of Moreh, in the territory of the Canaanites who live in the Arava, near
31 Gilgal. You are about to cross the Jordan, to go into and take possession of the
land that the LORD your God is giving you. When you have possession of it
32 and live there, you must be vigilant to keep all the decrees and laws that I am
12 1 setting before you on this day. These are the decrees and laws that you must
take care to keep in the land that the LORD, God of your ancestors, has given
2 you to possess for as long as you live on this earth. Demolish completely all
the shrines where the nations you are about to dispossess served their gods:
3 on the high mountains, on the hills, and under every leafy tree. Tear down
their altars, smash their worship pillars, burn their sacred trees with fire, and
cut down the statues of their gods, obliterating their names from that place.

רש״י

כט **וְנָתַתָּה אֶת הַבְּרָכָה.** כְּתַרְגּוּמוֹ: ״יָת מְבָרְכַיָּא״, אֶת הַמְבָרְכִים: **עַל הַר גְּרִזִּים.** כְּלַפֵּי הַר גְּרִזִּים הוֹפְכִים פְּנֵיהֶם וּפָתְחוּ בִּבְרָכָה: ׳בָּרוּךְ הָאִישׁ אֲשֶׁר לֹא יַעֲשֶׂה פֶסֶל וּמַסֵּכָה׳ וְגוֹ׳, כָּל הָאֲרוּרִים שֶׁבַּפָּרָשָׁה אָמְרוּ תְּחִלָּה בִּלְשׁוֹן ׳בָּרוּךְ׳, וְאַחַר כָּךְ הָפְכוּ פְּנֵיהֶם כְּלַפֵּי הַר עֵיבָל וּפָתְחוּ בִּקְלָלָה:

ל **הֲלֹא הֵמָּה.** נָתַן בָּהֶם סִימָן: **אַחֲרֵי.** אַחַר הַעֲבָרַת הַיַּרְדֵּן הַרְבֵּה וָהָלְאָה לְמֵרָחוֹק, וְזֶהוּ לְשׁוֹן ׳אַחֲרֵי׳. כָּל מָקוֹם שֶׁנֶּאֱמַר ׳אַחֲרֵי׳ מֻפְלָג הוּא: **דֶּרֶךְ מְבוֹא הַשֶּׁמֶשׁ.** לְהַלָּן מִן הַיַּרְדֵּן לְצַד מַעֲרָב. וְטַעַם הַמִּקְרָא מוֹכִיחַ שֶׁהֵם שְׁנֵי דְּבָרִים, שֶׁנֶּנְקְדוּ בִּשְׁנֵי טְעָמִים, ׳אַחֲרֵי׳ נָקוּד בְּפַשְׁטָא, וְ׳דֶרֶךְ׳ נָקוּד בְּמַשְׁפֵּל וְהוּא דָּגוּשׁ, וְאִם הָיָה ׳אַחֲרֵי דֶרֶךְ׳ דִּבּוּר אֶחָד, הָיָה נָקוּד ׳אַחֲרֵי׳ בִּמְשָׁרֵת, בְּשׁוֹפָר הָפוּךְ, וְ׳דֶרֶךְ׳ בְּפַשְׁטָא וְרָפֶה: **מוּל הַגִּלְגָּל.** רָחוֹק מִן הַגִּלְגָּל: **אֵלוֹנֵי מֹרֶה.** שְׁכֶם הוּא, שֶׁנֶּאֱמַר: ״עַד מְקוֹם שְׁכֶם עַד אֵלוֹן מוֹרֶה״ (בראשית יב, ו):

לא **כִּי אַתֶּם עֹבְרִים אֶת הַיַּרְדֵּן וְגוֹ׳.** נִסִּים שֶׁל יַרְדֵּן יִהְיוּ סִימָן בְּיֶדְכֶם שֶׁתָּבֹאוּ וְתִירְשׁוּ אֶת הָאָרֶץ:

יב ב **אַבֵּד תְּאַבְּדוּן.** ״אַבֵּד״ וְאַחַר כָּךְ ״תְּאַבְּדוּן״, מִכָּאן לְעוֹקֵר עֲבוֹדָה זָרָה שֶׁצָּרִיךְ לְשָׁרֵשׁ אַחֲרֶיהָ: **אֶת כָּל הַמְּקֹמוֹת אֲשֶׁר עָבְדוּ שָׁם וְגוֹ׳.** וּמַה תְּאַבְּדוּן מֵהֶם? ״אֶת אֱלֹהֵיהֶם״ אֲשֶׁר ״עַל הֶהָרִים״:

ג **מִזְבֵּחַ.** שֶׁל אֲבָנִים הַרְבֵּה: **מַצֵּבָה.** שֶׁל אֶבֶן אַחַת, וְהִיא ׳בִּימוֹס׳ שֶׁשָּׁנִינוּ בַּמִּשְׁנָה: ״אֶבֶן שֶׁחֲצָבָהּ מִתְּחִלָּתָהּ לַבִּימוֹס״ (עבודה זרה מז ע״ב): **אֲשֵׁרָה.** אִילָן הַנֶּעֱבָד: **וְאִבַּדְתֶּם אֶת שְׁמָם.** לְכַנּוֹת לָהֶם שֵׁם לִגְנַאי, בֵּית גַּלְיָא קוֹרִין לָהּ בֵּית כַּרְיָא, עֵין כֹּל – עֵין קוֹץ:

The alternative is simple – even though it is demanding and detailed. It means taking God as our sovereign, framer of our laws, author of our liberty, defender of our destiny, object of our worship and our love. If we predicate our existence on something – some One – vastly greater than ourselves then we will be lifted higher than we could reach by ourselves.

nation among nations, worshipping what they worship and living as they live. If we do, we will be subject to the universal law that has governed the fate of nations from the dawn of civilization. Nations are born, they grow, they flourish; they become complacent, then corrupt, then divided, then defeated, then they die. In the case of Israel, small and intensely vulnerable, that fate would happen sooner rather than later. That is what Moshe calls "the curse."

אֲשֶׁר־אַתָּה בָא־שָׁמָּה לְרִשְׁתָּהּ וְנָתַתָּה אֶת־הַבְּרָכָה עַל־הַר גְּרִזִּים
ל וְאֶת־הַקְּלָלָה עַל־הַר עֵיבָל׃ הֲלֹא־הֵמָּה בְּעֵבֶר הַיַּרְדֵּן אַחֲרֵי דֶּרֶךְ
מְבוֹא הַשֶּׁמֶשׁ בְּאֶרֶץ הַכְּנַעֲנִי הַיֹּשֵׁב בָּעֲרָבָה מוּל הַגִּלְגָּל אֵצֶל אֵלוֹנֵי
לא מֹרֶה׃ כִּי אַתֶּם עֹבְרִים אֶת־הַיַּרְדֵּן לָבֹא לָרֶשֶׁת אֶת־הָאָרֶץ אֲשֶׁר־
לב יהוה אֱלֹהֵיכֶם נֹתֵן לָכֶם וִירִשְׁתֶּם אֹתָהּ וִישַׁבְתֶּם־בָּהּ׃ וּשְׁמַרְתֶּם
לַעֲשׂוֹת אֵת כָּל־הַחֻקִּים וְאֶת־הַמִּשְׁפָּטִים אֲשֶׁר אָנֹכִי נֹתֵן לִפְנֵיכֶם
יב א הַיּוֹם׃ אֵלֶּה הַחֻקִּים וְהַמִּשְׁפָּטִים אֲשֶׁר תִּשְׁמְרוּן לַעֲשׂוֹת בָּאָרֶץ אֲשֶׁר
נָתַן יהוה אֱלֹהֵי אֲבֹתֶיךָ לְךָ לְרִשְׁתָּהּ כָּל־הַיָּמִים אֲשֶׁר־אַתֶּם חַיִּים
ב עַל־הָאֲדָמָה׃ אַבֵּד תְּאַבְּדוּן אֶת־כָּל־הַמְּקֹמוֹת אֲשֶׁר עָבְדוּ־שָׁם
הַגּוֹיִם אֲשֶׁר אַתֶּם יֹרְשִׁים אֹתָם אֶת־אֱלֹהֵיהֶם עַל־הֶהָרִים הָרָמִים
ג וְעַל־הַגְּבָעוֹת וְתַחַת כָּל־עֵץ רַעֲנָן׃ וְנִתַּצְתֶּם אֶת־מִזְבְּחֹתָם וְשִׁבַּרְתֶּם
אֶת־מַצֵּבֹתָם וַאֲשֵׁרֵיהֶם תִּשְׂרְפוּן בָּאֵשׁ וּפְסִילֵי אֱלֹהֵיהֶם תְּגַדֵּעוּן

אונקלוס

דְּאַתְּ עָלֵיל לְתַמָּן לְמֵירְתַהּ, וְתִתֵּין יָת מְבָרְכַיָּא עַל טוּרָא דִּגְרִיזִין,
וְיָת מְלָטְטַיָּא עַל טוּרָא דְּעֵיבָל: ל הֲלָא אִנּוּן בְּעִבְרָא דְּיַרְדְּנָא,
אֲחוֹרֵי אוֹרַח מַעֲלָנֵי שִׁמְשָׁא, בַּאֲרַע כְּנַעֲנָאָה, דְּיָתֵיב בְּמֵישְׁרָא,
לָקֳבֵיל גִּלְגְּלָא, בִּסְטַר מֵישְׁרֵי מוֹרֶה: לא אֲרֵי אַתּוּן עָבְרִין יָת יַרְדְּנָא,
לְמֵיעַל לְמֵירַת יָת אַרְעָא, דַּייָ אֱלָהֲכוֹן יָהֵיב לְכוֹן, וְתֵירְתוּן יָתַהּ
וְתִתְּבוּן בַּהּ: לב וְתִטְּרוּן לְמֶעְבַּד, יָת כָּל קְיָמַיָּא וְיָת דִּינַיָּא, דַּאֲנָא,
יָהֵיב קֳדָמֵיכוֹן יוֹמָא דֵין: יב א אִלֵּין, קְיָמַיָּא וְדִינַיָּא דְּתִטְּרוּן לְמֶעְבַּד,
בְּאַרְעָא, דִּיהַב יְיָ, אֱלָהָא דַּאֲבָהָתָךְ, לָךְ לְמֵירְתַהּ, כָּל יוֹמַיָּא, דְּאַתּוּן
קַיָּמִין עַל אַרְעָא: ב אַבָּדָא תְאַבְּדוּן, יָת כָּל אַתְרַיָּא דִּפְלַחוּ תַמָּן
עַמְמַיָּא, דְּאַתּוּן, יָרְתִין יָתְהוֹן יָת טָעֲוָתְהוֹן, עַל טוּרַיָּא רָמַיָּא וְעַל
רָמָתָא, וּתְחוֹת כָּל אִילָן עֲבוֹף: ג וּתְתָרְעוּן יָת אֵיגוֹרֵיהוֹן, וּתְתַבְּרוּן
יָת קָמָתְהוֹן, וַאֲשֵׁירֵיהוֹן תּוֹקְדוּן בְּנוּרָא, וְצַלְמֵי טָעֲוָתְהוֹן תְּקַצְּצוּן,

11:32 וּשְׁמַרְתֶּם לַעֲשׂוֹת אֵת כָּל־הַחֻקִּים וְאֶת־הַמִּשְׁפָּטִים *To keep all the decrees and laws* – Moshe does not want the people to lose the big picture. Jewish law, with its 613 commands, is detailed. It aims at the sanctification of all aspects of life, from daily ritual to the structure of society and its institutions. Its aim is to shape a social world in which we turn even seemingly secular occasions into encounters with the Divine Presence. Despite the details, says Moshe, the choice I set before you is simple.

In effect, Moshe is here defining reality for the next generation and for all generations. We are unique, he tells the next generation. We are a small nation. We have not the numbers, the wealth, nor the sophisticated weaponry of the great empires. As of now we do not even have a land. But we are different, and that difference defines who we are and why. God has chosen to make us His stake in history. He set us free from slavery and took us as His own covenantal partner.

Do not think, says Moshe, that we can survive as a

4 5 Do not make such things for the Lord your God; instead, seek the place that
the Lord your God will choose from among all your tribes to set His name
6 there, to be His dwelling. Go there, bringing your burnt offerings and peace
offerings, your tithes and your offerings, your gifts in fulfillment of vows and
7 your freewill offerings, and the firstborns of your herds and flocks. There you
and your families shall eat in the presence of the Lord your God, rejoicing in
8 all your endeavors in which the Lord your God has granted blessing. Do not
behave as we have been behaving here, now, everyone doing what is right in
9 his own eyes. For you have not yet reached the resting place and inheritance

רש״י

ד **לֹא תַעֲשׂוּן כֵּן.** לְהַקְטִיר לַשָּׁמַיִם בְּכָל מָקוֹם, כִּי אִם בַּמָּקוֹם אֲשֶׁר יִבְחַר (להלן פסוק ה). דָּבָר אַחֵר, "וְנִתַּצְתֶּם אֶת מִזְבְּחֹתָם... וְאִבַּדְתֶּם אֶת שְׁמָם – לֹא תַעֲשׂוּן כֵּן", אַזְהָרָה לַמּוֹחֵק אֶת הַשֵּׁם וְלַנּוֹתֵץ אֶבֶן מִן הַמִּזְבֵּחַ אוֹ מִן הָעֲזָרָה. אָמַר רַבִּי יִשְׁמָעֵאל: וְכִי תַּעֲלֶה עַל דַּעְתְּךָ שֶׁיִּשְׂרָאֵל נוֹתְצִין אֶת הַמִּזְבְּחוֹת? אֶלָּא שֶׁלֹּא תַעֲשׂוּ כְּמַעֲשֵׂיהֶם, וְיִגְרְמוּ עֲוֹנוֹתֵיכֶם לְמִקְדַּשׁ אֲבוֹתֵיכֶם שֶׁיֵּחָרֵב:

ה **לְשִׁכְנוֹ תִדְרְשׁוּ.** זֶה מִשְׁכַּן שִׁילֹה:

ו **וְזִבְחֵיכֶם.** שְׁלָמִים שֶׁל חוֹבָה: **מַעְשְׂרֹתֵיכֶם.** מַעְשַׂר בְּהֵמָה וּמַעֲשֵׂר שֵׁנִי, לֶאֱכֹל לִפְנִים מִן הַחוֹמָה: **תְּרוּמַת יֶדְכֶם.** אֵלּוּ הַבִּכּוּרִים, שֶׁנֶּאֱמַר בָּהֶם: "וְלָקַח הַכֹּהֵן הַטֶּנֶא מִיָּדֶךָ" (להלן כו, ד): **וּבְכֹרֹת בְּקַרְכֶם.** לְתִתָּם לַכֹּהֵן וְיַקְרִיבֵם שָׁם:

ז **אֲשֶׁר בֵּרַכְךָ ה׳.** לְפִי הַבְּרָכָה הָבֵא:

ח **לֹא תַעֲשׂוּן כְּכֹל אֲשֶׁר אֲנַחְנוּ עֹשִׂים וְגוֹ׳.** מוּסָב לְמַעְלָה, עַל "כִּי אַתֶּם עֹבְרִים אֶת הַיַּרְדֵּן" וְגוֹ׳ (לעיל יא, לא), כְּשֶׁתַּעַבְרוּ אֶת הַיַּרְדֵּן מִיָּד מֻתָּרִים אַתֶּם לְהַקְרִיב בַּבָּמָה כָּל אַרְבַּע עֶשְׂרֵה שָׁנָה שֶׁל כִּבּוּשׁ וְחִלּוּק, וּבַבָּמָה לֹא תַקְרִיבוּ כָּל מַה שֶּׁאַתֶּם מַקְרִיבִים פֹּה הַיּוֹם בַּמִּשְׁכָּן שֶׁהוּא עִמָּכֶם וְנִמְשָׁח, וְהוּא כָּשֵׁר לְהַקְרִיב בּוֹ חַטָּאוֹת וַאֲשָׁמוֹת נְדָרִים וּנְדָבוֹת, אֲבָל בַּבָּמָה אֵין קָרֵב אֶלָּא הַנִּדָּר וְהַנִּדָּב, וְזֶהוּ "אִישׁ כָּל הַיָּשָׁר בְּעֵינָיו", נְדָרִים וּנְדָבוֹת שֶׁאַתֶּם מִתְנַדְּבִים עַל יְדֵי שֶׁיָּשָׁר בְּעֵינֵיכֶם לַהֲבִיאָם וְלֹא עַל יְדֵי חוֹבָה, אוֹתָם תַּקְרִיבוּ בַּבָּמָה:

ט **כִּי לֹא בָאתֶם.** כָּל אוֹתָן אַרְבַּע עֶשְׂרֵה שָׁנָה: **עַד עָתָּה.** כְּמוֹ עֲדַיִן: **אֶל הַמְּנוּחָה.** זוֹ שִׁילֹה: **הַנַּחֲלָה.** זוֹ יְרוּשָׁלָיִם:

There is a deep connection between ethics and the human spirit, between *morality* and *morale*. If we lose the former, the latter begins to fail. It was Emile Durkheim in his classic study of suicide who coined the word *anomie* to describe a situation in which the individual loses his moorings in a shared moral order and becomes prone to a sense of meaninglessness and drift. A straight road leads from individualism to cynicism and despair. Individualism narrows the horizons of human happiness.

Moshe's first instruction for a covenant society is a decisive rejection of the idolatrous culture in which "they even offer their sons and daughters up in fire" (Deut. 12:31) to obtain favors from their gods. The God of Israel is to be found less in the "I" of individual devotion and self-interest than in the "we," in the relationships we make, the institutions we fashion, the duties we share, and the moral lives we lead.

individualism takes as the highest virtue – each person doing that which is right in his own eyes – is for the Bible the absence or abdication of virtue, and indeed a way of describing the disintegration of society (see also Judges 17:6, 21:25).

At a certain point in the history of civilizations, a moral consensus breaks down and an attempt is made to solve the problem by conceiving law in minimalist terms. It is there to do no more than to prevent harm to others, to prevent us, in R. Ḥanina's words (Avot 3:2), from swallowing one another alive. The passage of time, however, invariably exposes the contradiction at the heart of this idea. Law is left to solve problems which it cannot solve alone. We then painfully rediscover the ancient truth of the Torah, that the rule of law is compatible with a sense of personal liberty only when supported by at least some collective moral code and by an educational system which allows successive generations to internalize it. Society cannot live by law alone. It needs our common commitment to the common good.

ד וְאִבַּדְתֶּם אֶת־שְׁמָם מִן־הַמָּקוֹם הַהוּא׃ לֹא־תַעֲשׂוּן כֵּן לַיהוָה אֱלֹהֵיכֶם׃
ה כִּי אִם־אֶל־הַמָּקוֹם אֲשֶׁר־יִבְחַר יְהוָה אֱלֹהֵיכֶם מִכָּל־שִׁבְטֵיכֶם לָשׂוּם
ו אֶת־שְׁמוֹ שָׁם לְשִׁכְנוֹ תִדְרְשׁוּ וּבָאתָ שָׁמָּה׃ וַהֲבֵאתֶם שָׁמָּה עֹלֹתֵיכֶם
וְזִבְחֵיכֶם וְאֵת מַעְשְׂרֹתֵיכֶם וְאֵת תְּרוּמַת יֶדְכֶם וְנִדְרֵיכֶם וְנִדְבֹתֵיכֶם
ז וּבְכֹרֹת בְּקַרְכֶם וְצֹאנְכֶם׃ וַאֲכַלְתֶּם־שָׁם לִפְנֵי יְהוָה אֱלֹהֵיכֶם וּשְׂמַחְתֶּם
ח בְּכֹל מִשְׁלַח יֶדְכֶם אַתֶּם וּבָתֵּיכֶם אֲשֶׁר בֵּרַכְךָ יְהוָה אֱלֹהֶיךָ׃ לֹא
תַעֲשׂוּן כְּכֹל אֲשֶׁר אֲנַחְנוּ עֹשִׂים פֹּה הַיּוֹם אִישׁ כָּל־הַיָּשָׁר בְּעֵינָיו׃
ט כִּי לֹא־בָאתֶם עַד־עָתָּה אֶל־הַמְּנוּחָה וְאֶל־הַנַּחֲלָה אֲשֶׁר־יְהוָה

אונקלוס

וְתַבְּדוּן יָת שׁוּמְהוֹן, מִן אַתְרָא הַהוּא: ד לָא תַעְבְּדוּן כֵּן, קֳדָם יי אֱלָהֲכוֹן:
ה אֱלָהֵין, לְאַתְרָא, דְּיִתְרְעֵי יי אֱלָהֲכוֹן מִכָּל שִׁבְטֵיכוֹן, לְאַשְׁרָאָה
שְׁכִינְתֵיהּ תַּמָּן, לְבֵית שְׁכִינְתֵיהּ תִּתְבְּעוּן וְתֵיתוֹן לְתַמָּן: ו וְתַיְתוֹן לְתַמָּן,
עֲלָוָתְכוֹן וְנִכְסַת קֻדְשֵׁיכוֹן, וְיָת מַעְשְׂרֵיכוֹן, וְיָת אַפְרָשׁוּת יְדְכוֹן, וְנִדְרֵיכוֹן
וְנִדְבָתְכוֹן, וּבְכוֹרֵי תוֹרֵיכוֹן וְעָנְכוֹן: ז וְתֵיכְלוּן תַּמָּן, קֳדָם יי אֱלָהֲכוֹן,
וְתִחְדּוּן, בְּכָל אוֹשָׁטוּת יְדְכוֹן, אַתּוּן וֶאֱנָשׁ בָּתֵּיכוֹן, דְּבָרְכָךְ יי אֱלָהָךְ:
ח לָא תַעְבְּדוּן, כְּכֹל, דַּאֲנַחְנָא עָבְדִין, כָּא יוֹמָא דֵין, גְּבַר כָּל דְּכָשַׁר
בְּעֵינוֹהִי: ט אֲרֵי לָא אֲתֵיתוֹן עַד כְּעַן, לְבֵית נְיָחָא וּלְאַחְסַנְתָּא, דַּיי

12:7 וּשְׂמַחְתֶּם *Rejoicing* – The word "joy" (root *s-m-ḥ*) appears only once in Genesis, once in Exodus, once in Leviticus, once in Numbers, and twelve times in Deuteronomy. Moshe says again and again that joy is what we should feel in the land of Israel, the land given to us by God, the place to which the whole of Jewish life since the days of Avraham and Sara has been a journey. It will be there, said Moshe, that the narrative of Jewish history will become lucid, where a whole people will sing together, worship together, and celebrate the festivals together, knowing that history is not about empire or conquest, nor society about hierarchy and power; that commoner and king, Israelite and priest, are all equal in the sight of God, all voices in His holy choir, all dancers in the circle at whose center is the radiance of the Divine. This is what the covenant is about: the transformation of the human condition through what Wordsworth called "the deep power of joy."

Happiness is achieved over a lifetime, but joy lives in the moment. It is hard to feel happy in the midst of uncertainty. But you can still feel joy. King David in the book of Psalms spoke of danger, fear, dejection, sometimes even despair, but his songs usually end in the major key:

> For His wrath lasts but a moment,
> but His favor a lifetime;
> at night there may be weeping,
> but the morning brings joy....
> You have turned my mourning into dancing;
> You have untied my sackcloth
> and clothed me with joy,
> so that my soul may sing to You and not be silent.
> LORD my God, I will praise You forever. (Ps. 30:6–13)

In Judaism joy is the supreme religious emotion. Here we are, in a world filled with beauty. Every breath we breathe is the spirit of God within us. Around us is the love that moves the sun and all the stars. We are here because someone wanted us to be. Robert Louis Stevenson rightly says: "Find out where joy resides and give it a voice far beyond singing. For to miss the joy is to miss all."

12:8 כָּל־הַיָּשָׁר בְּעֵינָיו *Right in his own eyes* – What liberal

10 that the LORD your God is giving you. But you will cross the Jordan and live
in the land that the LORD your God is giving you as an inheritance. When He
gives you rest from all the enemies around you so that you are living in safety,
11 then you shall bring everything that I command you to the place that the LORD SHENI
your God will choose as a dwelling for His name: your burnt offerings and
peace offerings, your tithes and your offerings, and all the choice gifts that you
12 commit by vow to the LORD. And you shall rejoice before the LORD your God,
along with your sons and daughters, your male and female servants, and the
Levites living in your towns, for they have no share or inheritance with you.
13 14 Take care not to offer your burnt offerings in any place you may see. Only in
the place that the LORD will choose of one of your tribes – there you shall

רש״י

י-יא **וַעֲבַרְתֶּם אֶת הַיַּרְדֵּן וִישַׁבְתֶּם בָּאָרֶץ.** שֶׁתַּחְלְקוּהָ וִיהֵא כָּל אֶחָד מַכִּיר אֶת חֶלְקוֹ וְאֶת שִׁבְטוֹ: **וְהֵנִיחַ לָכֶם.** לְאַחַר כִּבּוּשׁ וְחִלּוּק, וּמְנוּחָה מִן "הַגּוֹיִם אֲשֶׁר הִנִּיחַ ה׳ לְנַסּוֹת בָּם אֶת יִשְׂרָאֵל" (שופטים ג, א), וְאֵין זוֹ אֶלָּא בִּימֵי דָוִד, אָז "וְהָיָה הַמָּקוֹם" וְגוֹ׳ – בְּנוּ לָכֶם בֵּית הַבְּחִירָה בִּירוּשָׁלַיִם. וְכֵן הוּא אוֹמֵר בְּדָוִד: "וַיְהִי כִּי יָשַׁב הַמֶּלֶךְ בְּבֵיתוֹ וַה׳ הֵנִיחַ לוֹ מִסָּבִיב מִכָּל אֹיְבָיו, וַיֹּאמֶר הַמֶּלֶךְ אֶל נָתָן הַנָּבִיא, רְאֵה נָא אָנֹכִי יוֹשֵׁב בְּבֵית אֲרָזִים וַאֲרוֹן הָאֱלֹהִים יֹשֵׁב בְּתוֹךְ הַיְרִיעָה" (שמואל ב׳ ז, א-ב): **שָׁמָּה תָבִיאוּ וְגוֹ׳.** לְמַעְלָה אָמוּר לְעִנְיַן שִׁילֹה, וְכָאן אָמוּר לְעִנְיַן יְרוּשָׁלַיִם, וּלְכָךְ חִלְּקָם הַכָּתוּב, לִתֵּן הֶתֵּר בֵּין זוֹ לָזוֹ, מִשֶּׁחָרְבָה שִׁילֹה וּבָאוּ לְנוֹב וְחָרְבָה נוֹב וּבָאוּ לְגִבְעוֹן, הָיוּ הַבָּמוֹת מֻתָּרוֹת, עַד שֶׁבָּאוּ לִירוּשָׁלַיִם: **מִבְחַר נִדְרֵיכֶם.** מְלַמֵּד שֶׁיָּבִיא מִן הַמֻּבְחָר:

יג **הִשָּׁמֶר לְךָ.** לִתֵּן לֹא תַעֲשֶׂה עַל הַדָּבָר: **בְּכָל מָקוֹם אֲשֶׁר תִּרְאֶה.** אֲשֶׁר יַעֲלֶה בְּלִבְּךָ, אֲבָל אַתָּה מַקְרִיב עַל פִּי נָבִיא, כְּגוֹן אֵלִיָּהוּ בְּהַר הַכַּרְמֶל:

יד **בְּאַחַד שְׁבָטֶיךָ.** בְּחֶלְקוֹ שֶׁל בִּנְיָמִין, וּלְמַעְלָה (לעיל פסוק ה) הוּא אוֹמֵר: "מִכָּל שִׁבְטֵיכֶם", הָא כֵּיצַד? כְּשֶׁקָּנָה דָוִד אֶת הַגֹּרֶן מֵאֲרַוְנָה הַיְבוּסִי גָּבָה הַזָּהָב מִכָּל הַשְּׁבָטִים, וּמִכָּל מָקוֹם הַגֹּרֶן בְּחֶלְקוֹ שֶׁל בִּנְיָמִין הָיָה:

humility. They taught that the land belongs to God and we are merely His tenants and guests. The earth yields its produce, not through our power, but only because of God's blessing. Without such regular reminders, societies slowly but inexorably become materialistic and self-satisfied. Rulers and elites forget that their role is to serve the people, and instead they expect the people to serve them.

CENTRALIZED SACRIFICE, "SECULAR" SLAUGHTER

When the Israelites lived grouped around the Tabernacle, meat could be eaten only after sacrificial slaughter in the Sanctuary. There was no "secular" *sheḥita* to obtain kosher meat outside the Tabernacle. Now, our horizons broaden. When "God has enlarged your territory as He has promised" (Deut. 12:20), and established a centralized Temple, it will no longer be convenient to visit the altar whenever the people wish to eat meat. Israel is to build and negotiate, for the first time in its life as a nation, a secular domain.

In 1954, Rabbi Yitzchak Hutner received a letter from a young man who was leaving a religious seminary to begin a secular career. The prospect was causing him distress. In the seminary he had found a sheltered environment within which he felt the intensity of a life devoted uninterruptedly to study. Pursuing a career seemed like a compromise that could only lead to a loss of single-mindedness. He was, he said, fearful of leading a "double life." Rabbi Hutner wrote him a powerful, dissenting reply:

> I would never agree to your leading a double life. One who rents a room in a house in which to live, and [at the same time] pays for a room in a hotel in which to be a guest is certainly leading a double life. But one who rents an apartment with two rooms is not leading a double life but a broad life.

י אֱלֹהֶיךָ נֹתֵן לָךְ: וַעֲבַרְתֶּם אֶת־הַיַּרְדֵּן וִישַׁבְתֶּם בָּאָרֶץ אֲשֶׁר־יְהוָה
אֱלֹהֵיכֶם מַנְחִיל אֶתְכֶם וְהֵנִיחַ לָכֶם מִכָּל־אֹיְבֵיכֶם מִסָּבִיב וִישַׁבְתֶּם־
יא בֶטַח: וְהָיָה הַמָּקוֹם אֲשֶׁר־יִבְחַר יְהוָה אֱלֹהֵיכֶם בּוֹ לְשַׁכֵּן שְׁמוֹ שָׁם שני
שָׁמָּה תָבִיאוּ אֵת כָּל־אֲשֶׁר אָנֹכִי מְצַוֶּה אֶתְכֶם עוֹלֹתֵיכֶם וְזִבְחֵיכֶם
מַעְשְׂרֹתֵיכֶם וּתְרֻמַת יֶדְכֶם וְכֹל מִבְחַר נִדְרֵיכֶם אֲשֶׁר תִּדְּרוּ לַיהוָה:
יב וּשְׂמַחְתֶּם לִפְנֵי יְהוָה אֱלֹהֵיכֶם אַתֶּם וּבְנֵיכֶם וּבְנֹתֵיכֶם וְעַבְדֵיכֶם
וְאַמְהֹתֵיכֶם וְהַלֵּוִי אֲשֶׁר בְּשַׁעֲרֵיכֶם כִּי אֵין לוֹ חֵלֶק וְנַחֲלָה אִתְּכֶם:
יג יד הִשָּׁמֶר לְךָ פֶּן־תַּעֲלֶה עֹלֹתֶיךָ בְּכָל־מָקוֹם אֲשֶׁר תִּרְאֶה: כִּי אִם־בַּמָּקוֹם
אֲשֶׁר־יִבְחַר יְהוָה בְּאַחַד שְׁבָטֶיךָ שָׁם תַּעֲלֶה עֹלֹתֶיךָ וְשָׁם תַּעֲשֶׂה כֹּל

אונקלוס

אֱלָהָךְ יָהֵיב לָךְ: י וְתִעְבְּרוּן יָת יַרְדְּנָא, וְתִתְּבוּן בְּאַרְעָא, דַּיי אֱלָהֲכוֹן מַחְסֵין יָתְכוֹן, וְיָנִיחַ לְכוֹן מִכָּל בַּעֲלֵי דְבָבֵיכוֹן, מִסְּחוֹר סְחוֹר וְתִתְּבוּן לְרֻחְצָן: יא וִיהֵי אַתְרָא, דְּיִתְרְעֵי יי אֱלָהֲכוֹן בֵּיהּ לְאַשְׁרָאָה שְׁכִינְתֵיהּ תַּמָּן, לְתַמָּן תַּיְתוֹן, יָת, כָּל דַּאֲנָא מְפַקֵּיד יָתְכוֹן, עֲלָוָתְכוֹן וְנִכְסַת קֻדְשֵׁיכוֹן, מַעְסְרֵיכוֹן וְאַפְרָשׁוּת יְדְכוֹן, וְכָל שְׁפַר נִדְרֵיכוֹן, דְּתִדְּרוּן קֳדָם יי: יב וְתִחְדּוֹן, קֳדָם יי אֱלָהֲכוֹן, אַתּוּן, וּבְנֵיכוֹן וּבְנָתְכוֹן, וְעַבְדֵיכוֹן וְאַמְהָתְכוֹן, וְלֵיוָאָה דִּבְקִרְוֵיכוֹן, אֲרֵי לֵית לֵיהּ, חוּלָק וְאַחְסָנָא עִמְּכוֹן: יג אִסְתְּמַר לָךְ, דִּלְמָא תַּסֵּיק עֲלָוָתָךְ, בְּכָל אַתְרָא דְּתִחְזֵי: יד אֱלָהֵין בְּאַתְרָא, דְּיִתְרְעֵי יי בְּחַד מִן שִׁבְטָךְ, תַּמָּן תַּסֵּיק עֲלָוָתָךְ, וְתַמָּן תַּעֲבֵיד, כָּל,

12:11 וְכֹל מִבְחַר נִדְרֵיכֶם אֲשֶׁר תִּדְּרוּ לַיהוָה *Choice gifts that you commit by vow to the Lord* – Biblical Israel was a predominantly agricultural society. Accordingly, it was through agriculture that the Torah pursued its religious and social program. This had three fundamental elements.

The first was the alleviation of poverty. The Torah accepts the basic principles of what we now call a market economy. But though the market is good at creating wealth, it is less good at distributing it equitably. Thus the Torah's social legislation aimed, in the words of Henry George, "to lay the foundations of a social state in which deep poverty and degrading want should be unknown." Hence institutions that left parts of the harvest for the poor: *leket, shikheḥa,* and *pe'a* – fallen ears of grain, the forgotten sheaf, and the corners of the field. On the third and sixth year of each septennial cycle, the second tithe, instead of being consumed by its owners in Jerusalem as in other years, is given locally to the poor and known as *maaser ani,* "poor person's tithe."

Shemitta, the seventh year, and *Yovel,* the Jubilee, with their release of debts, manumission of slaves, and return of ancestral property to its original owners, restored essential elements of the economy to their default position of fairness. The first principle was: no one should be desperately poor.

The second element, which included *teruma* and *maaser rishon,* the priestly portion and the first tithe, went to support, respectively, the priests and the Levites. These were a religious elite within the nation in biblical times, whose role was to ensure that the service of God, especially in the Temple, continued at the heart of national life.

The third was more personal and spiritual. There were laws including bringing first fruits to Jerusalem, and the three agricultural pilgrimage festivals – Passover, Shavuot, and Sukkot – that imbued the lessons of gratitude and

15 offer your burnt offerings and there do all that I command you. Whenever you
desire, you may slaughter and eat meat in any of your towns, according to the
blessing that the LORD your God gives you. People both impure and pure may
16 eat of it, as they would of gazelle or of deer. The blood, however, you must not
17 eat. Pour it out on the ground like water. You may not eat the tithe of your
grain, wine, and oil within your towns, or the firstlings of your herds and flocks,
or any of the gifts that you commit by vow, your freewill offerings, or your
18 gifts. These you must eat in the presence of the LORD your God at the place
that the LORD your God will choose, along with your sons and daughters,
your male and female servants, and the Levites living in your towns, rejoicing
19 in all your endeavors in the presence of the LORD your God. Take care not

רש״י

טו **רק בכל אות נפשך.** במה הכתוב מדבר? אם בבשר תאוה להתירה להם בלא הקרבת אימורים, הרי אמור במקום אחר: "כי ירחיב ה'... את גבלך וגו' ואמרת אכלה בשר" וגו' (להלן פסוק כ); במה זה מדבר? בקדשים שנפל בהם מום שיפדו ויאכלו בכל מקום. יכול יפדו על מום עובר? תלמוד לומר: "רק": **תזבח ואכלת.** אין לך בהם היתר גזה וחלב, אלא אכילה על ידי זביחה: **הטמא והטהור.** לפי שבא מכח קדשים שנאמר בהם "והבשר אשר יגע בכל טמא לא יאכל" (ויקרא ז, יט), הצרך להתיר בו שטמא וטהור אוכלים בקערה אחת: **כצבי וכאיל.** שאין קרבן בא מהם: **כצבי וכאיל.** לפטרן מן הזרוע והלחיים והקבה:

טז **רק הדם לא תאכלו.** אף על פי שאמרתי שאין לך בו זריקת דם במזבח, לא תאכלנו: **תשפכנו כמים.** לומר לך שאין צריך כסוי. דבר אחר, הרי הוא כמים להכשיר את הזרעים:

יז **לא תוכל.** בא הכתוב ליתן לא תעשה על הדבר: **לא תוכל.** רבי יהושע בן קרחה אומר: יכול אתה אבל אינך רשאי. כיוצא בו: "ואת היבוסי יושבי ירושלים לא יכלו בני יהודה להורישם" (יהושע טו, סג), יכולים היו אלא שאינן רשאין, לפי שכרת להם אברהם ברית כשלקח מהם מערת המכפלה, ולא יבוסים היו אלא חתיים היו, אלא על שם העיר ששמה 'יבוס'. כך מפרש בפרקי דרבי אליעזר (פ' לו). והוא שנאמר: "כי אם הסירך העורים והפסחים" (שמואל ב' ה, ו), צלמים שכתבו עליהם את השבועה: **ובכרת בקרך.** אזהרה לכהנים: **ותרומת ידך.** אלו הבכורים:

יח **לפני ה'.** לפנים מן החומה: **והלוי אשר בשעריך.** אם אין לך לתת לו מחלקו כגון מעשר ראשון, תן לו מעשר עני, אין לך מעשר עני, הזמינהו על שלמיך:

יט **השמר לך.** לתן לא תעשה על הדבר:

"secular slaughter." It does, however, need to be performed "as I have commanded you" (Deut. 12:21) – referring, as the Rabbis understood, to humane slaughter. Meat need not emerge from the Sanctuary to be kosher, but it must be obtained with compassion.

12:18 **ובנך ובתך ועבדך ואמתך** *Along with your sons and daughters, your male and female servants* – When you rejoice, Moshe says time and again, it must be "you and your sons and daughters, your male and female servants, the Levites, and the migrants, orphans, and widows living in your towns" (Deut. 16:14). A key theme of Parashat Re'eh is the idea of a central Sanctuary in "the place that the LORD your God will choose" (16:7). As we know from later Jewish history, during the reign of King David this was Jerusalem, where David's son Shlomo eventually built the Temple.

Moshe is articulating the idea of *simḥa* as communal, social, and national rejoicing. The nation was to be brought together not just by crisis, catastrophe, or impending war, but by collective celebration in the presence of God. The celebration itself was to be deeply moral. Not only was this a religious act of thanksgiving; it was also to be a form of social inclusion. No one was to be left out: not the stranger, the servant, the orphan, or the widow.

טו אֲשֶׁר אָנֹכִי מְצַוֶּךָּ: רַק בְּכָל־אַוַּת נַפְשְׁךָ תִּזְבַּח ׀ וְאָכַלְתָּ בָשָׂר כְּבִרְכַּת
יהוה אֱלֹהֶיךָ אֲשֶׁר נָתַן־לְךָ בְּכָל־שְׁעָרֶיךָ הַטָּמֵא וְהַטָּהוֹר יֹאכְלֶנּוּ
טז יז כַּצְּבִי וְכָאַיָּל: רַק הַדָּם לֹא תֹאכֵלוּ עַל־הָאָרֶץ תִּשְׁפְּכֶנּוּ כַּמָּיִם: לֹא־
תוּכַל לֶאֱכֹל בִּשְׁעָרֶיךָ מַעְשַׂר דְּגָנְךָ וְתִירֹשְׁךָ וְיִצְהָרֶךָ וּבְכֹרֹת בְּקָרְךָ
יח וְצֹאנֶךָ וְכָל־נְדָרֶיךָ אֲשֶׁר תִּדֹּר וְנִדְבֹתֶיךָ וּתְרוּמַת יָדֶךָ: כִּי אִם־לִפְנֵי
יהוה אֱלֹהֶיךָ תֹּאכְלֶנּוּ בַּמָּקוֹם אֲשֶׁר יִבְחַר יהוה אֱלֹהֶיךָ בּוֹ אַתָּה
וּבִנְךָ וּבִתֶּךָ וְעַבְדְּךָ וַאֲמָתֶךָ וְהַלֵּוִי אֲשֶׁר בִּשְׁעָרֶיךָ וְשָׂמַחְתָּ לִפְנֵי יהוה
יט אֱלֹהֶיךָ בְּכֹל מִשְׁלַח יָדֶךָ: הִשָּׁמֶר לְךָ פֶּן־תַּעֲזֹב אֶת־הַלֵּוִי כָּל־יָמֶיךָ

אונקלוס

דַּאֲנָא מְפַקֵּיד לָךְ: טו לְחוֹד בְּכָל רְעוּת נַפְשָׁךְ, תִּכּוֹס וְתֵיכוֹל בִּסְרָא, כְּבִרְכְּתָא דַּיי אֱלָהָךְ, דִּיהַב לָךְ בְּכָל קִרְוָךְ, מְסָאֲבָא וּדְכֵיָא יֵיכְלִנֵּיהּ, כְּבִסַר טַבְיָא וְאַיְּלָא: טז לְחוֹד דְּמָא לָא תֵיכְלוּן, עַל אַרְעָא תֵּישְׁדְּנֵיהּ כְּמַיָּא: יז לֵית לָךְ רְשׁוּ לְמֵיכַל בְּקִרְוָךְ, מַעְסַר עֲבוּרָךְ וְחַמְרָךְ וּמִשְׁחָךְ, וּבְכוֹרֵי תוֹרָךְ וְעָנָךְ, וְכָל נִדְרָךְ דְּתִדַּר, וְנִדְבָתָךְ וְאַפְרָשׁוּת יְדָךְ: יח אֱלָהֵין, קֳדָם יי אֱלָהָךְ תֵּיכְלִנֵּיהּ, בְּאַתְרָא דְּיִתְרְעֵי, יי אֱלָהָךְ בֵּיהּ, אַתְּ וּבְרָךְ וּבְרַתָּךְ וְעַבְדָּךְ וְאַמְתָךְ, וְלֵיוָאָה דִּבְקִרְוָךְ, וְתֶחְדֵּי, קֳדָם יי אֱלָהָךְ, בְּכָל אוֹשָׁטוּת יְדָךְ: יט אִסְתְּמַר לָךְ, דִּלְמָא תְרַחֵיק יָת לֵיוָאָה, כָּל יוֹמָךְ,

I remember once visiting the hospital in Jerusalem where [a certain Orthodox doctor worked] and I saw him approach a patient who was just about to undergo an operation. He asked him for the name of his mother so that he could say a prayer on his behalf for the success of the operation. When I mentioned this to one of the outstanding Torah sages in Jerusalem, he exclaimed, "How enviable to be such a Jew with so great an opportunity to serve as a vehicle for the glory of Heaven!" Tell me, beloved friend, is a doctor, about to perform an operation on a patient, who says a chapter of Psalms for the safe recovery of his patient, leading a double life?

Beloved friend, God forbid that you should see yourself as leading a double life. [The Sages say that] "Whoever prolongs the word 'One' [in the first verse of the *Shema*, Deut. 6:4] prolongs his days and years" (Berakhot 13b). Therefore throughout your life you should be one of those who "prolongs the 'One'" – focusing on unity, not duality. It would grieve me very much if this point were not apparent to you. Many dots scattered here and there certainly constitute a multiplicity, but the same number of dots ordered around a single point in the center form one circle. This is your duty in life, to place at the center of your life the "One," and then you need have no worry about dualities. Every new dot you acquire will then merely expand the circle, but its unity will remain.

It is all too easy to compartmentalize the religious life. There are sacred times and places: the Sabbath, the festivals, the synagogue, the home. And there are contexts – work, colleagues, the wider society – when we play our allotted roles and live by other rules. The result can be a divided personality and a sense of disconnection between inner and outer worlds. It does not have to be. What we take with us wherever we go is our character. To be gracious, thoughtful, sensitive, attentive; to have integrity, courage, and psychological strength; to be able to respond to different people in different ways, knowing what each needs to fulfill his or her part in the scheme of things – is to come as close as we can to living in the world as God lives in the world. If I were to sum up what faith asks us to be, I would say: a *healing presence*. Deuteronomy makes the concession of allowing

20 to neglect the Levite in all your years living in your land. When the
Lord your God has enlarged your territory as He has promised, and you say,
'I shall eat some meat,' because you have the urge to eat it, you may eat meat
21 whenever you desire it. If the place where the Lord your God chooses to place
His name is too distant from you, you may slaughter animals from the herds
and flocks the Lord has given you, as I have commanded you. These you may
22 eat within your towns whenever you wish. Eat them as you would eat gazelle
23 or a deer; the impure may eat together with the pure. But make sure that you
do not eat the blood, for blood is life, and you must not eat the life with the
24 25 meat. Do not eat it; pour it out onto the ground like water; do not eat it, so
that all may be well for you and your children after you, because you do what
26 is right in the Lord's eyes. But your sacred offerings and the gifts you commit
27 by vow you must bring to the place that the Lord will choose. Present your
burnt offerings – the meat and the blood – on the altar of the Lord your God.
Of your other sacrifices, the blood shall be poured out on the altar of the Lord
28 your God, but you may eat the meat. Take care to heed all these words that I
command you today, so that it may be well for you and for your children after
you forever, because you will be doing what is good and right in the Lord
29 your God's eyes. When the Lord your God has cut down before SHELISHI
you the nations that you are about to come to and dispossess, after you have

רש״י

עַל אַדְמָתֶךָ. אֲבָל בַּגּוֹלָה אֵינְךָ מֻזְהָר עָלָיו יוֹתֵר מֵעֲנִיֵּי יִשְׂרָאֵל:

כ **כִּי יַרְחִיב וְגוֹ׳.** לִמְּדָה תוֹרָה דֶּרֶךְ אֶרֶץ, שֶׁלֹּא יִתְאַוֶּה אָדָם לֶאֱכֹל בָּשָׂר אֶלָּא מִתּוֹךְ רַחֲבַת יָדַיִם וָעֹשֶׁר: **בְּכָל אַוַּת נַפְשְׁךָ וְגוֹ׳.** אֲבָל בַּמִּדְבָּר נֶאֱסַר לָהֶם בְּשַׂר חֻלִּין, אֶלָּא אִם כֵּן מַקְדִּישָׁהּ וּמַקְרִיבָהּ שְׁלָמִים:

כא **כִּי יִרְחַק מִמְּךָ הַמָּקוֹם.** וְלֹא תּוּכַל לָבוֹא וְלַעֲשׂוֹת שְׁלָמִים בְּכָל יוֹם, כְּמוֹ עַכְשָׁיו שֶׁהַמִּשְׁכָּן הוֹלֵךְ עִמָּכֶם: **וְזָבַחְתָּ... כַּאֲשֶׁר צִוִּיתִךָ.** לָמַדְנוּ שֶׁיֵּשׁ צִוּוּי בִּזְבִיחָה הֵיאַךְ יִשְׁחֹט, וְהֵן הִלְכוֹת שְׁחִיטָה שֶׁנֶּאֶמְרוּ לְמֹשֶׁה בְּסִינַי:

כב **אַךְ כַּאֲשֶׁר יֵאָכֵל אֶת הַצְּבִי וְגוֹ׳.** אֵינְךָ מֻזְהָר לְאָכְלָן בְּטָהֳרָה. אִי מָה צְבִי וְאַיָּל חֶלְבָּן מֻתָּר אַף חֻלִּין חֶלְבָּן מֻתָּר? תַּלְמוּד לוֹמַר: ״אַךְ״:

כג **רַק חֲזַק לְבִלְתִּי אֲכֹל הַדָּם.** מִמַּה שֶּׁנֶּאֱמַר ״חֲזַק״ אַתָּה לָמֵד שֶׁהָיוּ שְׁטוּפִים בַּדָּם לְאָכְלוֹ, לְפִיכָךְ הֻצְרַךְ לוֹמַר ״חֲזַק״, דִּבְרֵי רַבִּי יְהוּדָה. רַבִּי שִׁמְעוֹן בֶּן עַזַּאי אוֹמֵר: לֹא בָּא הַכָּתוּב אֶלָּא לְהַזְהִירְךָ וּלְלַמֶּדְךָ עַד כַּמָּה אַתָּה צָרִיךְ לְהִתְחַזֵּק בַּמִּצְוֹת, אִם הַדָּם שֶׁהוּא קַל לְהִשָּׁמֵר מִמֶּנּוּ, שֶׁאֵין אָדָם מִתְאַוֶּה לוֹ, הֻצְרַךְ לְחַזֶּקְךָ בְּאַזְהָרָתוֹ, קַל וָחֹמֶר לִשְׁאָר מִצְוֹת: **וְלֹא תֹאכַל הַנֶּפֶשׁ עִם הַבָּשָׂר.** אַזְהָרָה לְאֵבֶר מִן הַחַי:

כד **לֹא תֹּאכְלֶנּוּ.** אַזְהָרָה לְדַם הַתַּמְצִית:

כה **לֹא תֹּאכְלֶנּוּ.** אַזְהָרָה לְדַם הָאֵבָרִים: **לְמַעַן יִיטַב לְךָ וְגוֹ׳.** צֵא וּלְמַד מַתַּן שְׂכָרָן שֶׁל מִצְוֹת, אִם הַדָּם שֶׁנַּפְשׁוֹ שֶׁל אָדָם קָצָה מִמֶּנּוּ, הַפּוֹרֵשׁ מִמֶּנּוּ זוֹכֶה לוֹ וּלְבָנָיו אַחֲרָיו, קַל וָחֹמֶר לְגָזֵל וַעֲרָיוֹת שֶׁנַּפְשׁוֹ שֶׁל אָדָם מִתְאַוָּה לָהֶם:

כו **רַק קָדָשֶׁיךָ.** אַף עַל פִּי שֶׁשְּׁחִיטָה מֻתֶּרֶת לִשְׁחֹט חֻלִּין, לֹא הִתַּרְתִּי לְךָ לִשְׁחֹט אֶת הַקֳּדָשִׁים וּלְאָכְלָן בִּשְׁעָרֶיךָ בְּלֹא הַקְרָבָה, אֶלָּא הֲבִיאֵם לְבֵית הַבְּחִירָה:

כז **וְעָשִׂיתָ עֹלֹתֶיךָ.** אִם עוֹלוֹת הֵן, תֵּן ״הַבָּשָׂר וְהַדָּם״ עַל גַּבֵּי הַמִּזְבֵּחַ, וְאִם זִבְחֵי שְׁלָמִים הֵם, ״דַּם זְבָחֶיךָ יִשָּׁפֵךְ״ עַל הַמִּזְבֵּחַ תְּחִלָּה, וְאַחַר כָּךְ ״וְהַבָּשָׂר תֹּאכֵל״. וְעוֹד דָּרְשׁוּ רַבּוֹתֵינוּ, ״רַק קָדָשֶׁיךָ״, שֶׁבָּא לְלַמֵּד עַל הַקֳּדָשִׁים שֶׁבְּחוּצָה לָאָרֶץ, וּלְלַמֵּד עַל הַתְּמוּרוֹת וְעַל וַלְדוֹת קָדָשִׁים שֶׁיַּקְרִבֵם:

כח **שְׁמֹר.** זוֹ מִשְׁנָה, שֶׁאַתָּה צָרִיךְ לְשָׁמְרָהּ בְּבִטְנְךָ שֶׁלֹּא תִּשְׁכַּח, כְּעִנְיָן שֶׁנֶּאֱמַר: ״כִּי נָעִים כִּי תִשְׁמְרֵם בְּבִטְנֶךָ״ (משלי כב, יח), וְאִם שָׁנִיתָ, אֶפְשָׁר

כ עַל־אַדְמָתֶךָ׃ כִּי־יַרְחִיב יְהוָה אֱלֹהֶיךָ אֶת־גְּבֻלְךָ כַּאֲשֶׁר יא
דִּבֶּר־לָךְ וְאָמַרְתָּ אֹכְלָה בָשָׂר כִּי־תְאַוֶּה נַפְשְׁךָ לֶאֱכֹל בָּשָׂר בְּכָל־אַוַּת
כא נַפְשְׁךָ תֹּאכַל בָּשָׂר׃ כִּי־יִרְחַק מִמְּךָ הַמָּקוֹם אֲשֶׁר יִבְחַר יְהוָה אֱלֹהֶיךָ
לָשׂוּם שְׁמוֹ שָׁם וְזָבַחְתָּ מִבְּקָרְךָ וּמִצֹּאנְךָ אֲשֶׁר נָתַן יְהוָה לְךָ כַּאֲשֶׁר
כב צִוִּיתִךָ וְאָכַלְתָּ בִּשְׁעָרֶיךָ בְּכֹל אַוַּת נַפְשֶׁךָ׃ אַךְ כַּאֲשֶׁר יֵאָכֵל אֶת־
כג הַצְּבִי וְאֶת־הָאַיָּל כֵּן תֹּאכְלֶנּוּ הַטָּמֵא וְהַטָּהוֹר יַחְדָּו יֹאכְלֶנּוּ׃ רַק חֲזַק
לְבִלְתִּי אֲכֹל הַדָּם כִּי הַדָּם הוּא הַנָּפֶשׁ וְלֹא־תֹאכַל הַנֶּפֶשׁ עִם־הַבָּשָׂר׃
כד כה לֹא תֹּאכְלֶנּוּ עַל־הָאָרֶץ תִּשְׁפְּכֶנּוּ כַּמָּיִם׃ לֹא תֹּאכְלֶנּוּ לְמַעַן יִיטַב
כו לְךָ וּלְבָנֶיךָ אַחֲרֶיךָ כִּי־תַעֲשֶׂה הַיָּשָׁר בְּעֵינֵי יְהוָה׃ רַק קָדָשֶׁיךָ אֲשֶׁר־
כז יִהְיוּ לְךָ וּנְדָרֶיךָ תִּשָּׂא וּבָאתָ אֶל־הַמָּקוֹם אֲשֶׁר־יִבְחַר יְהוָה׃ וְעָשִׂיתָ
עֹלֹתֶיךָ הַבָּשָׂר וְהַדָּם עַל־מִזְבַּח יְהוָה אֱלֹהֶיךָ וְדַם־זְבָחֶיךָ יִשָּׁפֵךְ עַל־
כח מִזְבַּח יְהוָה אֱלֹהֶיךָ וְהַבָּשָׂר תֹּאכֵל׃ שְׁמֹר וְשָׁמַעְתָּ אֵת כָּל־הַדְּבָרִים
הָאֵלֶּה אֲשֶׁר אָנֹכִי מְצַוֶּךָּ לְמַעַן יִיטַב לְךָ וּלְבָנֶיךָ אַחֲרֶיךָ עַד־עוֹלָם כִּי
כט תַעֲשֶׂה הַטּוֹב וְהַיָּשָׁר בְּעֵינֵי יְהוָה אֱלֹהֶיךָ׃ כִּי־יַכְרִית שלישי
יְהוָה אֱלֹהֶיךָ אֶת־הַגּוֹיִם אֲשֶׁר אַתָּה בָא־שָׁמָּה לָרֶשֶׁת אוֹתָם מִפָּנֶיךָ

אונקלוס

על ארעך: כ ארי יפתי יי אלהך ית תחומך כמא דמליל לך, ותימר איכול בסרא, ארי תתרעי נפשך למיכל בסרא, בכל רעות נפשך תיכול בסרא: כא ארי יתרחק מנך אתרא, דיתרעי, יי אלהך לאשראה שכינתיה תמן, ותכוס מתורך ומענך, דיהב יי לך, כמא דפקידתך, ותיכול בקרוך, בכל רעות נפשך: כב ברם, כמא דמתאכיל בסר טביא ואילא, כן תיכלניה, מסאבא ודכיא, כחדא ייכלניה: כג לחוד תקף, בדיל דלא למיכל דמא, ארי דמא הוא נפשא, ולא תיכול נפשא עם בסרא: כד לא תיכלניה, על ארעא תישדניה כמיא: כה לא תיכלניה, בדיל דייטב לך ולבנך בתרך, ארי תעביד דכשר קדם יי: כו לחוד מעסר קודשך, דיהון לך ונדרך, תטול ותיתי, לאתרא דיתרעי יי: כז ותעביד עלותך בסרא ודמא, על מדבחא דיי אלהך, ודם נכסת קודשך, ישתפיך על מדבחא דיי אלהך, ובסרא תיכול: כח טר ותקביל, ית כל פתגמיא האלין, דאנא מפקיד לך, בדיל דייטב לך, ולבנך בתרך עד עלמא, ארי תעביד דתקין ודכשר, קדם יי אלהך: כט ארי ישיצי יי אלהך ית עממיא, דאת עליל לתמן, למירת יתהון מן קדמך,

רש״י

שתשמע ותקים. הא כל שחינו בכלל משנה חינו בכלל מעשה: את כל הדברים. שתהא חביבה עליך מצוה קלה כמצוה חמורה:

הטוב. בעיני השמים: והישר. בעיני אדם:

30 dispossessed them and live in their land, beware being tempted into their ways
after they have been destroyed before you. Do not inquire about their gods,
31 saying, 'How did these nations worship their gods? Let me do the same.' You
must not worship the LORD your God in their way, because they have done
for their gods every abhorrent thing that the LORD hates. They even offer their
13 1 sons and daughters up in fire to their gods. Take care: fulfill all that I command
you. Neither add to it nor subtract from it.
2 If a prophet rises up among you, or one who divines by dreams, and he tells
3 you of some sign or omen, and the sign or omen of which he spoke is realized –
and he had said, 'Let us walk after other gods and worship them' – gods you
4 have not known – do not listen to the words of that prophet or dream diviner.
The LORD your God will be testing you, to know whether you really love the
5 LORD your God with all your heart and with all your soul. Follow the LORD
your God, revere Him, keep His commandments, and listen to His voice.
6 Worship Him; stay close to Him. And that prophet or dream diviner – he shall
be put to death for inciting rebellion against the LORD your God who brought

רש"י

ל **פן תנקש.** אונקלוס תרגם לשון מוקש. ואני אומר שלא חש לדקדק בלשון, שלא מצינו נו"ן בלשון יוקש, ואפלו ליסוד הנופל ממנו. אבל בלשון טרוף וקשקוש מצינו נו"ן: "וארכבתה דא לדא נקשן" (דניאל ה, ו). ואף זה אני אומר, "פן תנקש אחריהם", פן תטרף אחריהם להיות כרוך אחר מעשיהם. וכן: "ינקש נושה לכל אשר לו" (תהלים קט, יא), מקלל את הרשע להיות עליו נושים רבים, ויהיו מחזירין ומתנקשין אחר ממונו: **אחרי השמדם מפניך.** אחר שתראה שאשמידם מפניך, יש לך לתת לב מפני מה נשמדו אלו? מפני מעשים מקלקלים שבידיהם. אף אתה לא תעשה כך, שלא יבואו אחרים וישמידוך: **איכה יעבדו.** לפי שלא ענש על עבודה זרה אלא על זבוח וקטור ונסוך והשתחויה, כמו שכתוב: "בלתי לה' לבדו" (שמות כב, יט) – דברים הנעשים לגבוה, בא ולמדך כאן שאם דרכה של עבודה זרה לעבדה בדבר אחר, כגון פוער לפעור וזורק אבן למרקוליס, זו היא עבודתו וחיב, אבל זבוח וקטור ונסוך והשתחויה אפלו שלא כדרכה חיב:

לא **כי גם את בניהם.** "גם" לרבות את אבותיהם ואמותיהם. אמר רבי עקיבא: אני ראיתי גוי שכפתו לאביו לפני כלבו ואכלו:

יג א **את כל הדבר.** קלה כחמורה: **תשמרו לעשות.** לתן לא תעשה על עשה האמורים בפרשה, שכל 'השמר' לשון לא תעשה הוא, אלא שאין לוקין על 'השמר' של עשה: **לא תסף עליו.** חמש טוטפות, חמשה מינין בלולב, ארבע ברכות בברכת כהנים:

ב **ונתן אליך אות.** בשמים, כענין שנאמר בגדעון: "ועשית לי אות" (שופטים ו, יז), ואומר: "יהי נא חרב אל הגזה" וגו' (שם פסוק לט): **או מופת.** בארץ אף על פי כן לא תשמע לו. ואם תאמר: מפני מה נותן לו הקדוש ברוך הוא ממשלה לעשות אות? "כי מנסה ה' אלהיכם אתכם" (להלן פסוק ד):

ה **ואת מצותיו תשמרו.** תורת משה: **ובקלו תשמעו.** בקול הנביאים: **ואתו תעבדו.** במקדשו: **ובו תדבקון.** הדבק בדרכיו: גמל חסדים, קבר מתים, בקר חולים, כמו שעשה הקדוש ברוך הוא:

ו **סרה.** דבר המוסר מן העולם, שלא היה ולא נברא ולא צויתיו לדבר כן, דיסטולוד"א בלעז:

he was authorized to proclaim Torah: he was Israel's sole legislator. The king and Sanhedrin both had powers to make temporary enactments for the sake of social order. Prophets were given the authority to command specific, time-bound acts. But no one could add to or subtract from the 613 commandments given by God through Moshe. Rather, the other prophets recalled the people to their mission. They reminded them of their duties. They spoke out against corruption and injustice within society. They were social critics, not innovators.

ל וירשת אתם וישבת בארצם: השמר לך פן־תנקש אחריהם אחרי
השמדם מפניך ופן־תדרש לאלהיהם לאמר איכה יעבדו הגוים
לא האלה את־אלהיהם ואעשה־כן גם־אני: לא־תעשה כן ליהוה
אלהיך כי כל־תועבת יהוה אשר שנא עשו לאלהיהם כי גם את־
יג א בניהם ואת־בנתיהם ישרפו באש לאלהיהם: את כל־הדבר אשר
אנכי מצוה אתכם אתו תשמרו לעשות לא־תסף עליו ולא תגרע
ממנו:
ב ג כי־יקום בקרבך נביא או חלם חלום ונתן אליך אות או מופת: ובא
האות והמופת אשר־דבר אליך לאמר נלכה אחרי אלהים אחרים
ד אשר לא־ידעתם ונעבדם: לא תשמע אל־דברי הנביא ההוא או
אל־חולם החלום ההוא כי מנסה יהוה אלהיכם אתכם לדעת
הישכם אהבים את־יהוה אלהיכם בכל־לבבכם ובכל־נפשכם:
ה אחרי יהוה אלהיכם תלכו ואתו תיראו ואת־מצותיו תשמרו ובקלו
ו תשמעו ואתו תעבדו ובו תדבקון: והנביא ההוא או חלם החלום
ההוא יומת כי דבר־סרה על־יהוה אלהיכם המוציא אתכם ׀ מארץ

אונקלוס

ותירת יתהון, ותתיב בארעהון: ל אסתמר לך, דלמא תתקיל בתריהון, בתר דישתיצון מן קדמך, ודלמא תתבע לטעותהון למימר, איכדין פלחין, עממיא האלין ית טעותהון, ואעביד כן אף אנא: לא לא תעביד כן, קדם יי אלהך, ארי כל דמרחק קדם יי דסני, עבדין לטעותהון, ארי אף ית בניהון וית בנתהון, מוקדין בנורא לטעותהון: יג א ית כל פתגמא, דאנא מפקיד יתכון, יתיה תטרון למעבד, לא תיספון עלוהי, ולא תמנעון מניה: ב ארי יקום בינך נביא, או חלים חלמא, ויתין לך, את או מופת: ג וייתי אתא ומופתא, דמליל עמך למימר, נהך, בתר טעות עממיא, דלא ידעתנין ונפלחנין: ד לא תקביל, לפתגמי נביא ההוא, או, מן חלים חלמא ההוא, ארי מנסי, יי אלהכון יתכון, למדע, האיתיכון רחמין ית יי אלהכון, בכל לבכון ובכל נפשכון: ה בתר פלחנא דיי אלהכון, תהכון ויתיה תדחלון, וית פקודוהי תטרון ולמימריה תקבלון, וקדמוהי תפלחון ולדחלתיה תתקרבון: ו ונביא ההוא, או חלים חלמא ההוא יתקטיל, ארי מליל סטיא, על יי אלהכון, דאפיק יתכון מארעא

13:4 לא תשמע אל־דברי הנביא ההוא *Do not listen to the words of that prophet* – In Judaism, what is primary is the covenant between Israel and God. A prophet who seeks to change the covenant or lead the people in a different direction must not be heeded. The classic prophets did not claim the authority to make changes in Judaism. Moshe was unique. Only

you out of Egypt and redeemed you from the house of slaves, seeking to make
you stray from the path the LORD your God commanded you to walk. You
7 must purge the evil from your midst. If anyone, even your brother,
your mother's son, or your own son or daughter, the wife of your embrace,
or the friend who is like your own self to you, secretly tempts you: 'Let us go
and worship other gods' – whom neither you nor your ancestors have known,
8 9 gods of the peoples around you, near or far, end to end of the earth – do not
acquiesce, do not listen to him, do not show him pity or compassion, or cover
10 up for him. You must put him to death. Your own hand shall be first against
11 him to kill him, and after yours, the hand of all the people. Stone him to death
for seeking to make you abandon the LORD your God who brought you out of
12 Egypt, the house of slaves. And all Israel shall hear, and fear, and never commit
13 such an evil again. If you hear it said about one of the towns that the
14 LORD your God is giving you to live in that depraved men among you have
gone out and led the people of the town astray, saying, 'Let us go and worship
15 other gods' – gods you have not known – you shall seek the truth, investigate,

רש"י

והפדך מבית עבדים. אפלו אין לו עליך אלא שפדאך, דיו:

ז **כי יסיתך.** אין הסתה אלא גרוי, שנאמר: "אם ה' הסיתך בי" (שמואל א' כו, יט), אמיטר"א בלעז, שמשיאו לעשות כן: **אחיך.** מאב, או "בן אמך", מאם: **חיקך.** השוכבת בחיקך ומחקה בך, אפיקייד"א בלעז, וכן: "ומחיק הארץ" (יחזקאל מג, יד), מיסוד התקוע בארץ: **אשר כנפשך.** זה אביך. פרש לך הכתוב את החביבין לך, קל וחמר לאחרים: **בסתר.** דבר הכתוב בהוה, שאין דברי מסית אלא בסתר, וכן שלמה הוא אומר: "בנשף בערב יום באישון לילה ואפלה" (משלי ז, ט): **אשר לא ידעת אתה ואבתיך.** דבר זה גנאי גדול הוא לך, שאף האמות אין מניחין מה שמסרו להם אבותיהם, וזה אומר לך: עזב מה שמסרו לך אבותיך:

ח **הקרבים אליך או הרחקים.** למה פרט קרובים ורחוקים? אלא כך אמר הכתוב: מטיבן של קרובים אתה למד טיבן של רחוקים, כשם שאין ממש בקרובים כך אין ממש ברחוקים: **מקצה הארץ.** זו חמה ולבנה וצבא השמים, שהן מהלכין מסוף העולם ועד סופו:

ט **לא תאבה לו.** לא תהא תאב לו, לא תאהבנו, לפי שנאמר: "ואהבת לרעך כמוך" (ויקרא יט, יח), את זה לא תאהב: **ולא תשמע אליו.** בהתחננו על נפשו למחול לו, לפי שנאמר: "עזב תעזב עמו" (שמות כג, ה), לזה לא תעזב: **ולא תחוס עינך עליו.** לפי שנאמר: "לא תעמד על דם רעך" (ויקרא יט, טז), על זה לא תחוס: **ולא תחמל.** לא תהפך בזכותו: **ולא תכסה עליו.** אם אתה יודע לו חובה, אינך רשאי לשתק:

י **כי הרג תהרגנו.** אם יצא מבית דין זכאי החזירהו לחובה, יצא מבית דין חיב אל תחזירהו לזכות: **ידך תהיה בו בראשונה.** מצוה ביד הנסת להמיתו. לא מת בידו – ימות ביד אחרים, שנאמר: "ויד כל העם" וגו':

יג-יד **לשבת שם.** פרט לירושלים שלא נתנה לדירה: **בני בליעל.** בלי על, שפרקו עלו של מקום: **אנשים.** ולא נשים: **ישבי עירם.** ולא יושבי עיר אחרת, מכאן אמרו: אין נעשית עיר הנדחת עד שידיחוה אנשים, ועד שיהיו מדיחיה מתוכה:

טו **ודרשת וחקרת ושאלת היטב.** מכאן למדו שבע חקירות מרבוי המקרא. כאן יש שלש: דרישה וחקירה ו"היטב". "ושאלת" אינו מן המנין, וממנו למדו בדיקות. ובמקום אחר הוא אומר: "ודרשו

land.... Let each man be on guard against his fellow, and let no one trust his own brother, for every brother acts deceitfully, and every friend spreads slander. Each man defrauds his fellows and speaks untruth.... One speaks peaceably to another but secretly plans an ambush. Should I not hold them to account for these things?" demands the LORD. "For a nation such as this, should I not exact retribution?" (Jer. 9:2–8)

מִצְרַ֜יִם וְהַפֹּֽדְךָ֙ מִבֵּ֣ית עֲבָדִ֔ים לְהַדִּֽיחֲךָ֙ מִן־הַדֶּ֔רֶךְ אֲשֶׁ֧ר צִוְּךָ֛ יְהֹוָ֥ה
ז אֱלֹהֶ֖יךָ לָלֶ֣כֶת בָּ֑הּ וּבִֽעַרְתָּ֥ הָרָ֖ע מִקִּרְבֶּֽךָ׃ כִּ֣י יְסִֽיתְךָ֩
אָחִ֨יךָ בֶן־אִמֶּ֜ךָ אֽוֹ־בִנְךָ֨ אֽוֹ־בִתְּךָ֗ א֣וֹ ׀ אֵ֣שֶׁת חֵיקֶ֗ךָ א֧וֹ רֵֽעֲךָ֛ אֲשֶׁ֥ר
כְּנַפְשְׁךָ֖ בַּסֵּ֣תֶר לֵאמֹ֑ר נֵֽלְכָ֗ה וְנַֽעַבְדָה֙ אֱלֹהִ֣ים אֲחֵרִ֔ים אֲשֶׁר֙ לֹ֣א יָדַ֔עְתָּ
ח אַתָּ֖ה וַאֲבֹתֶֽיךָ׃ מֵאֱלֹהֵ֣י הָֽעַמִּ֗ים אֲשֶׁר֙ סְבִיבֹ֣תֵיכֶ֔ם הַקְּרֹבִ֣ים אֵלֶ֔יךָ א֖וֹ
ט הָרְחֹקִ֣ים מִמֶּ֑ךָּ מִקְצֵ֥ה הָאָ֖רֶץ וְעַד־קְצֵ֥ה הָאָֽרֶץ׃ לֹא־תֹאבֶ֣ה ל֔וֹ וְלֹ֥א
י תִשְׁמַ֖ע אֵלָ֑יו וְלֹא־תָח֤וֹס עֵֽינְךָ֙ עָלָ֔יו וְלֹֽא־תַחְמֹ֥ל וְלֹֽא־תְכַסֶּ֖ה עָלָֽיו׃ כִּ֤י
הָרֹ֙ג תַּֽהַרְגֶ֔נּוּ יָֽדְךָ֛ תִּֽהְיֶה־בּ֥וֹ בָרִאשׁוֹנָ֖ה לַהֲמִית֑וֹ וְיַ֥ד כָּל־הָעָ֖ם בָּאַחֲרֹנָֽה׃
יא וּסְקַלְתּ֥וֹ בָאֲבָנִ֖ים וָמֵ֑ת כִּ֣י בִקֵּ֗שׁ לְהַדִּֽיחֲךָ֙ מֵעַל֙ יְהֹוָ֣ה אֱלֹהֶ֔יךָ הַמּוֹצִיאֲךָ֛
יב מֵאֶ֥רֶץ מִצְרַ֖יִם מִבֵּ֥ית עֲבָדִֽים׃ וְכָ֨ל־יִשְׂרָאֵ֔ל יִשְׁמְע֖וּ וְיִרָא֑וּן וְלֹֽא־
יג יוֹסִ֣פוּ לַעֲשׂ֗וֹת כַּדָּבָ֥ר הָרָ֛ע הַזֶּ֖ה בְּקִרְבֶּֽךָ׃ כִּֽי־תִשְׁמַ֞ע בְּאַחַ֣ת
יד עָרֶ֗יךָ אֲשֶׁר֩ יְהֹוָ֨ה אֱלֹהֶ֜יךָ נֹתֵ֥ן לְךָ֛ לָשֶׁ֥בֶת שָׁ֖ם לֵאמֹֽר׃ יָצְא֞וּ אֲנָשִׁ֣ים
בְּנֵֽי־בְלִיַּ֗עַל מִקִּרְבֶּ֔ךָ וַיַּדִּ֛יחוּ אֶת־יֹשְׁבֵ֥י עִירָ֖ם לֵאמֹ֑ר נֵֽלְכָ֗ה וְנַֽעַבְדָ֛ה
טו אֱלֹהִ֥ים אֲחֵרִ֖ים אֲשֶׁ֥ר לֹא־יְדַעְתֶּֽם׃ וְדָרַשְׁתָּ֧ וְחָקַרְתָּ֛ וְשָׁאַלְתָּ֖ הֵיטֵ֑ב

אונקלוס

דְּמִצְרַיִם, וּדְפָרְקָךְ מִבֵּית עַבְדוּתָא, לְאַטְעָיוּתָךְ מִן אוֹרְחָא, דְּפַקְּדָךְ, יְיָ אֱלָהָךְ לִמְהָךְ בַּהּ, וּתְפַלֵּי עָבֵיד דְּבִישׁ מִבֵּינָךְ: ז אֲרֵי יִמְלְכִנָּךְ, אֲחוּךְ בַּר אִמָּךְ, אוֹ בְרָךְ אוֹ בְרַתָּךְ, אוֹ אִתַּת קְיָמָךְ, אוֹ חַבְרָךְ, דִּכְנַפְשָׁךְ בְּסִתְרָא לְמֵימַר, נְהָךְ, וְנִפְלַח לְטָעֲוָת עַמְמַיָּא, דְּלָא יְדַעְתָּא, אַתְּ וַאֲבָהָתָךְ: ח מִטָּעֲוָת עַמְמַיָּא, דִּבְסַחְרָנֵיכוֹן, דְּקָרִיבִין לָךְ, אוֹ דְּרַחִיקִין מִנָּךְ, מִסְּיָפֵי אַרְעָא וְעַד סְיָפֵי אַרְעָא: ט לָא תֵיבֵי לֵיהּ, וְלָא תְקַבֵּיל מִנֵּיהּ, וְלָא תְחוּס עֵינָךְ עֲלוֹהִי, וְלָא תְרַחֵים וְלָא תְכַסֵּי עֲלוֹהִי: י אֲרֵי מִקְטַל תִּקְטְלִנֵּיהּ, יְדָךְ, תְּהֵי בֵיהּ בְּקַדְמֵיתָא לְמִקְטְלֵיהּ, וִידָא דְּכָל עַמָּא בְּבָתְרֵיתָא: יא וְתִרְגְּמִנֵּיהּ בְּאַבְנַיָּא וִימוּת, אֲרֵי בְעָא, לְאַטְעָיוּתָךְ מִדַּחַלְתָּא דַּיְיָ אֱלָהָךְ, דְּאַפְּקָךְ, מֵאַרְעָא דְּמִצְרַיִם מִבֵּית עַבְדוּתָא: יב וְכָל יִשְׂרָאֵל, יִשְׁמְעוּן וְיִדְחֲלוּן, וְלָא יֵיסְפוּן לְמֶעְבַּד, כְּפִתְגָּמָא בִּישָׁא, הָדֵין בֵּינָךְ: יג אֲרֵי תִשְׁמַע בַּחֲדָא מִן קִרְוָךְ, דַּיְיָ אֱלָהָךְ, יָהֵיב לָךְ, לְמִתַּב תַּמָּן לְמֵימַר: יד נְפָקוּ, גֻּבְרִין בְּנֵי רִשְׁעָא מִבֵּינָךְ, וְאַטְעִיאוּ, יָת יָתְבֵי קַרְתְּהוֹן לְמֵימַר, נְהָךְ, וְנִפְלַח, לְטָעֲוָת עַמְמַיָּא דְּלָא יְדַעְתּוּן: טו וְתִתְבַּע וְתִבְדּוֹק, וְתִשְׁאַל יָאוּת,

13:15 וְדָרַשְׁתָּ וְחָקַרְתָּ וְשָׁאַלְתָּ הֵיטֵב *Seek the truth, investigate, and inquire thoroughly* – Essential to the justice system is the pursuit of the truth through careful investigation of evidence. This principle needs protection; the first reference to what could be referred to as a "post-truth society" is twenty-six centuries ago, in the sixth century BCE. This is Yirmeyahu (in chapter 9 of the book that bears his name):

"They have drawn their tongue, their bow is falsehood.
Not for faithfulness have they become powerful in the

and inquire thoroughly abroad. If it is true and is confirmed that this abhorrent
16 thing has been done among you, you shall put the inhabitants of that town to
the sword, destroying it and everything in it; put even its animals to the sword.
17 Gather all its spoil into its public square, then burn with fire the town and all its
spoil, in its entirety, to the LORD your God. It shall be an eternal ruin, never to
18 be rebuilt. Let nothing that has been banned remain in your hands, so that the
LORD may turn away from His flaming rage, show you compassion, and in His
19 compassion increase your numbers, as He swore to your ancestors, for you will
have heeded the voice of the LORD your God, keeping all His commandments
that I am giving you today and doing what is right in the LORD your God's
14 1 eyes. You are children of the LORD your God. Do not lacerate REVI'I

רש"י

הַשֹּׁפְטִים הֵיטֵב" (להלן יט, יח), וּבְמָקוֹם אַחֵר הוּא אוֹמֵר: "וְדָרַשְׁתָּ הֵיטֵב" (להלן יז, ד), וְלָמְדוּ "הֵיטֵב" "הֵיטֵב" לִגְזֵרָה שָׁוָה, לִתֵּן הָאָמוּר שֶׁל זֶה בָּזֶה:

טז **הַכֵּה תַכֶּה.** אִם אֵינְךָ יָכוֹל לַהֲמִיתָם בַּמִּיתָה הַכְּתוּבָה בָּהֶם, הֲמִיתֵם בְּאַחֶרֶת:

יז **לַה׳ אֱלֹהֶיךָ.** לִשְׁמוֹ וּבִשְׁבִילוֹ:

יח **לְמַעַן יָשׁוּב ה׳ מֵחֲרוֹן אַפּוֹ.** שֶׁכָּל זְמַן שֶׁעֲבוֹדָה זָרָה בָּעוֹלָם, חֲרוֹן אַף בָּעוֹלָם:

יד א **לֹא תִתְגֹּדְדוּ.** לֹא תִתְּנוּ גְּדִידָה וְשֶׂרֶט בִּבְשַׂרְכֶם עַל מֵת כְּדֶרֶךְ שֶׁהָאֱמוֹרִיִּים עוֹשִׂין, לְפִי שֶׁאַתֶּם בָּנָיו שֶׁל מָקוֹם, וְאַתֶּם רְאוּיִין לִהְיוֹת נָאִים וְלֹא גְּדוּדִים וּמְקֹרָחִים: **בֵּין עֵינֵיכֶם.** אֵצֶל הַפַּדַּחַת, וּבְמָקוֹם

Why did the Oral Tradition, or at least some of its exponents, narrow the scope of the law in some cases, and broaden it in others? The short answer is: we do not know. The rabbinic literature does not tell us. But we can speculate. A *posek*, seeking to interpret divine law in specific cases, will endeavor to do so in a way consistent with the total structure of biblical teaching. If a text seems to conflict with a basic principle of Jewish law, it will be understood restrictively, at least by some. If it exemplifies such a principle, it will be understood broadly.

The law of the condemned city, where all the inhabitants were sentenced to death, seems to conflict with the principle of individual justice. When Sedom was threatened with such a fate, Avraham argued that if there were only ten innocent people, the destruction of the entire population would be manifestly unfair: "Shall the judge of all the earth not do justice?" (Gen. 18:25). The Sages sought as far as possible to make their individual rulings consistent with the value structure of Jewish law as they understood it. On this view, the law of the condemned city exists to teach us that idolatry, once accepted in public, is contagious, as we see from the history of Israel's kings. Law exists not just to regulate but also to educate.

Living traditions constantly reinterpret their canonical texts. That is what makes fundamentalism – text *without* interpretation – an act of violence against tradition. In fact, fundamentalists and today's atheists share the same approach to texts. They read them directly and literally, ignoring the single most important fact about a sacred text, namely, that its meaning is not self-evident. It has a history and an authority of its own. Hard texts require not only covenantal commitment, but covenantal listening as well.

PROHIBITED MOURNING RITES

To lose a close member of one's family is a shattering experience. It is as if something of ourselves had died too. Yet we are commanded not to engage in excessive rituals of grief. Not to grieve is inhuman: Judaism does not command stoic indifference in the face of death. But to give way to wild expressions of sorrow – lacerating one's flesh, tearing out one's hair – is wrong. It is, the Torah suggests, not fitting

טז וְהִנֵּה אֱמֶת נָכוֹן הַדָּבָר נֶעֶשְׂתָה הַתּוֹעֵבָה הַזֹּאת בְּקִרְבֶּךָ: הַכֵּה תַכֶּה
אֶת־יֹשְׁבֵי הָעִיר הַהִוא לְפִי־חָרֶב הַחֲרֵם אֹתָהּ וְאֶת־כׇּל־אֲשֶׁר־בָּהּ
יז וְאֶת־בְּהֶמְתָּהּ לְפִי־חָרֶב: וְאֶת־כׇּל־שְׁלָלָהּ תִּקְבֹּץ אֶל־תּוֹךְ רְחֹבָהּ
וְשָׂרַפְתָּ בָאֵשׁ אֶת־הָעִיר וְאֶת־כׇּל־שְׁלָלָהּ כָּלִיל לַיהוָה אֱלֹהֶיךָ וְהָיְתָה
יח תֵּל עוֹלָם לֹא תִבָּנֶה עוֹד: וְלֹא־יִדְבַּק בְּיָדְךָ מְאוּמָה מִן־הַחֵרֶם לְמַעַן
יָשׁוּב יְהוָה מֵחֲרוֹן אַפּוֹ וְנָתַן־לְךָ רַחֲמִים וְרִחַמְךָ וְהִרְבֶּךָ כַּאֲשֶׁר נִשְׁבַּע
יט לַאֲבֹתֶיךָ: כִּי תִשְׁמַע בְּקוֹל יְהוָה אֱלֹהֶיךָ לִשְׁמֹר אֶת־כׇּל־מִצְוֺתָיו אֲשֶׁר
יד א אָנֹכִי מְצַוְּךָ הַיּוֹם לַעֲשׂוֹת הַיָּשָׁר בְּעֵינֵי יְהוָה אֱלֹהֶיךָ: בָּנִים יב רביעי
אַתֶּם לַיהוָה אֱלֹהֵיכֶם לֹא תִתְגֹּדְדוּ וְלֹא־תָשִׂימוּ קׇרְחָה בֵּין עֵינֵיכֶם

אונקלוס

וְהָא קְשָׁטָא כֵּיוָן פִּתְגָּמָא, אִתְעֲבִידַת, תּוֹעֵיבְתָא הָדָא בֵּינָךְ: טז מִמְחָא תִמְחֵי, יָת יָתְבֵי, קַרְתָּא הַהִיא לְפִתְגָּם דְּחָרֶב, גַּמַּר יָתַהּ וְיָת כָּל דְּבַהּ, וְיָת בְּעִירַהּ לְפִתְגָּם דְּחָרֶב: יז וְיָת כָּל עֲדָאַהּ, תִּכְנוֹשׁ לְגוֹ פְתָאַהּ, וְתוֹקֵיד בְּנוּרָא, יָת קַרְתָּא וְיָת כָּל עֲדָאַהּ גְּמִיר, קֳדָם יי אֱלָהָךְ, וּתְהֵי תֵּל חָרוּב לְעָלַם, לָא תִתְבְּנֵי עוֹד: יח וְלָא יִדְבַּק בִּידָךְ, מִדְּעַם מִן חֶרְמָא, בְּדִיל דִּיתוּב יי מִתְּקוֹף רֻגְזֵיהּ, וְיִתֵּין לָךְ רַחֲמִין וִירַחֵים עֲלָךְ וְיַסְגֵּינָךְ, כְּמָא דְקַיֵּים לַאֲבָהָתָךְ: יט אֲרֵי תְקַבֵּיל, לְמֵימְרָא דַּיי אֱלָהָךְ, לְמִטַּר יָת כָּל פִּקּוֹדוֹהִי, דַּאֲנָא מְפַקֵּיד לָךְ יוֹמָא דֵין, לְמֶעְבַּד דְּכָשַׁר, קֳדָם יי אֱלָהָךְ: יד א בְּנִין אַתּוּן, קֳדָם יי אֱלָהֲכוֹן, לָא תִתְהַמְמוּן, וְלָא תְשַׁוּוֹן מְרַט, בֵּין עֵינֵיכוֹן

Yirmeyahu's faithful city, now the faithless city of Jerusalem, was indeed eventually conquered by the Babylonians and the people sent into exile. And although he was a moral extremist, Yirmeyahu was, at the same time, a political realist. He knew that in the absence of truth, no society can stand.

Nietzsche, in his book *On the Genealogy of Morality*, speaks about people who think of themselves as free spirits (in other words, atheists like him). He says that they are in fact very far from being free spirits because *they still believe in truth.* "Our faith in science is still based on a metaphysical faith. Even we know, as of today, we godless anti-metaphysicians, still date our fire from the blaze set alight by a faith thousands of years old... that God is truth. That truth is Divine."

In other words, says Nietzsche, our belief in truth and even science ultimately goes back to religious and philosophical foundations. There is nothing in nature that tends toward truth or truthfulness. Every animal that is the potential prey of a predator has to learn to conceal, to hide, to deceive. A free society, however, depends on trust. Trust depends on honesty in public life. And honesty in public life depends on truth as a norm.

13:17 וְהָיְתָה תֵּל עוֹלָם *It shall be an eternal ruin* – There are certain laws that the Rabbis found puzzling and morally problematic. This law of "the town led astray" is a classic example, alongside the law about a wayward and rebellious son who is to be put to death for what appears to us to be no worse than a serious case of juvenile delinquency (Deut. 21:18–21; see commentary there). So incompatible did these laws seem with the principles of justice that the Talmud records the view that they were never put into effect and exist only for didactic purposes, not to be implemented in practice. In the case of the condemned city (see 13:13–19), R. Eliezer said that if it contained a single mezuza, the law was not enforced (Sanhedrin 71a).

▶

2 yourselves or make bald patches in the middle of your heads for the dead. For
you are a people sacred to the LORD your God. The LORD has chosen you of
3 all the peoples on earth to be to Him a treasured people. Do not eat
4 any abhorrent thing. These are the animals you may eat: the ox, the sheep, the
5 goat, the deer, the gazelle, the hartebeest, the ibex, the oryx, the wild ox, and
6 the giraffe. You may eat any animal that has divided hoofs, fully split in two, and
7 chews the cud. Of those that chew the cud or that have a cleft hoof, these you
shall not eat: the camel, the hare, and the hyrax, because they chew the cud but
8 do not have a divided hoof – they are impure for you; and the pig, because it
has a divided hoof but does not chew the cud – it is impure for you. You may
9 not eat their flesh or touch their carcasses. These you may eat among
10 the creatures of the water: anything that has fins and scales. Whatever does not
11 have fins and scales you may not eat; it is impure for you. You may

רש"י

אַחֵר הוּא אוֹמֵר: "לֹא יִקְרְחוּ קָרְחָה בְּרֹאשָׁם" (ויקרא כא, ה), לַעֲשׂוֹת כָּל הָרֹאשׁ כְּבֵין הָעֵינַיִם:

ב **כִּי עַם קָדוֹשׁ אַתָּה.** קְדֻשַּׁת עַצְמְךָ מֵאֲבוֹתֶיךָ, וְעוֹד: "וּבְךָ בָּחַר ה'":

ג **כָּל תּוֹעֵבָה.** כָּל שֶׁתִּעַבְתִּי לְךָ, כְּגוֹן צָרַם אֹזֶן בְּכוֹר כְּדֵי לְשָׁחֲטוֹ בַּמְּדִינָה, הֲרֵי דָּבָר שֶׁתִּעַבְתִּי לְךָ: "כָּל מוּם לֹא יִהְיֶה בּוֹ" (ויקרא כב, כא), בָּא וְלִמֵּד כָּאן שֶׁלֹּא יִשְׁחַט וְיֵאָכֵל עַל אוֹתוֹ הַמּוּם. בִּשֵּׁל בָּשָׂר בְּחָלָב, הֲרֵי דָּבָר שֶׁתִּעַבְתִּי לְךָ, הִזְהִיר כָּאן עַל אֲכִילָתוֹ:

ד-ה **זֹאת הַבְּהֵמָה... אַיָּל וּצְבִי וְיַחְמוּר.** לָמַדְנוּ שֶׁהַחַיָּה בִּכְלַל בְּהֵמָה, וְלָמַדְנוּ שֶׁהַבְּהֵמָה וְחַיָּה טְמֵאָה מְרֻבָּה מִן הַטְּהוֹרָה, שֶׁבְּכָל מָקוֹם פּוֹרֵט אֶת הַמּוּעָט: **וְאַקּוֹ.** מְתֻרְגָּם: "יַעְלָא", "יַעֲלֵי סָלַע" הוּא אשטנבו"ק: **וּתְאוֹ.** "תּוֹרְבָּלָא", שׁוֹר הַיַּעַר, 'בָּאלָא' – יַעַר בִּלְשׁוֹן אֲרַמִּי:

ו **מַפְרֶסֶת.** סְדוּקָה, כְּתַרְגּוּמוֹ: **פַּרְסָה.** פלנט"א: **וְשֹׁסַעַת.** חֲלוּקָה בִּשְׁתֵּי צִפָּרְנַיִם, שֶׁיֵּשׁ סְדוּקָה וְאֵינָהּ חֲלוּקָה בְּצִפָּרְנַיִם וְהִיא טְמֵאָה: **בַּבְּהֵמָה.** מַשְׁמַע מַה שֶּׁנִּמְצָא בַּבְּהֵמָה אֱכֹל, מִכָּאן אָמְרוּ שֶׁהַשְּׁלִיל מֻתָּר בִּשְׁחִיטַת אִמּוֹ:

ז **הַשְּׁסוּעָה.** בְּרִיָּה הִיא שֶׁיֵּשׁ לָהּ שְׁנֵי גַּבִּין וּשְׁתֵּי שִׁדְרָאוֹת. אָמְרוּ רַבּוֹתֵינוּ: לָמָּה נִשְׁנוּ? בַּבְּהֵמָה מִפְּנֵי הַשְּׁסוּעָה וּבָעוֹפוֹת מִפְּנֵי הָרָאָה (להלן פסוק יג), שֶׁלֹּא נֶאֶמְרוּ בְּתוֹרַת כֹּהֲנִים:

ח **וּבְנִבְלָתָם לֹא תִגָּעוּ.** רַבּוֹתֵינוּ פֵּרְשׁוּ: בָּרֶגֶל, שֶׁאָדָם חַיָּב לְטַהֵר אֶת עַצְמוֹ בָּרֶגֶל. יָכוֹל יְהוּ מֻזְהָרִים בְּכָל הַשָּׁנָה? תַּלְמוּד לוֹמַר: "אֱמֹר אֶל הַכֹּהֲנִים" וְגוֹ' (ויקרא כא, א), וּמַה טֻּמְאַת הַמֵּת חֲמוּרָה, כֹּהֲנִים מֻזְהָרִים וְאֵין יִשְׂרָאֵל מֻזְהָרִים, טֻמְאַת נְבֵלָה קַלָּה לֹא כָּל שֶׁכֵּן?:

יא **כָּל צִפּוֹר טְהֹרָה תֹּאכֵלוּ.** לְהַתִּיר מְשֻׁלַּחַת שֶׁבַּמְּצֹרָע:

In this anti-traditional age, with its hostility to ritual and its preference for the public display of private emotion, the idea that grief has its laws and limits sounds strange. Yet many who have had the misfortune to be bereaved testify to the profound healing brought about by observance of the laws of *avelut* (mourning).

Torah and tradition knew how to honor both the dead and the living, sustaining the delicate balance between grief and consolation, the loss of life that gives us pain, and the re-affirmation of life that gives us hope.

14:1 **בָּנִים אַתֶּם לַיהוה אֱלֹהֵיכֶם** *You are children of the LORD your God* – We experience God in two ways: in awe and in love. In awe, for He is our sovereign, the supreme power of the universe. But also in love, for He brought us into being. He is a parent to us. Between a servant and a king there can be estrangement. A king can send a servant into exile. But between a father and a child there can be no permanent estrangement. However far removed they are from one another, the bond between parent and child still holds.

ב לָמֵת: כִּי עַם קָדוֹשׁ אַתָּה לַיהוָה אֱלֹהֶיךָ וּבְךָ בָּחַר יהוה לִהְיוֹת לוֹ
ג לְעַם סְגֻלָּה מִכֹּל הָעַמִּים אֲשֶׁר עַל־פְּנֵי הָאֲדָמָה: לֹא
ד תֹאכַל כָּל־תּוֹעֵבָה: זֹאת הַבְּהֵמָה אֲשֶׁר תֹּאכֵלוּ שׁוֹר שֵׂה כְשָׂבִים
ה ו וְשֵׂה עִזִּים: אַיָּל וּצְבִי וְיַחְמוּר וְאַקּוֹ וְדִישֹׁן וּתְאוֹ וָזָמֶר: וְכָל־בְּהֵמָה
מַפְרֶסֶת פַּרְסָה וְשֹׁסַעַת שֶׁסַע שְׁתֵּי פְרָסוֹת מַעֲלַת גֵּרָה בַּבְּהֵמָה
ז אֹתָהּ תֹּאכֵלוּ: אַךְ אֶת־זֶה לֹא תֹאכְלוּ מִמַּעֲלֵי הַגֵּרָה וּמִמַּפְרִיסֵי
הַפַּרְסָה הַשְּׁסוּעָה אֶת־הַגָּמָל וְאֶת־הָאַרְנֶבֶת וְאֶת־הַשָּׁפָן כִּי־מַעֲלֵה
ח גֵרָה הֵמָּה וּפַרְסָה לֹא הִפְרִיסוּ טְמֵאִים הֵם לָכֶם: וְאֶת־הַחֲזִיר כִּי־
מַפְרִיס פַּרְסָה הוּא וְלֹא גֵרָה טָמֵא הוּא לָכֶם מִבְּשָׂרָם לֹא תֹאכֵלוּ
ט וּבְנִבְלָתָם לֹא תִגָּעוּ: אֶת־זֶה תֹּאכְלוּ מִכֹּל אֲשֶׁר
י בַּמָּיִם כֹּל אֲשֶׁר־לוֹ סְנַפִּיר וְקַשְׂקֶשֶׂת תֹּאכֵלוּ: וְכֹל אֲשֶׁר אֵין־לוֹ
יא סְנַפִּיר וְקַשְׂקֶשֶׂת לֹא תֹאכֵלוּ טָמֵא הוּא לָכֶם: כָּל־צִפּוֹר

אונקלוס

עַל מִית: ב אֲרֵי עַם קַדִּישׁ אַתְּ, קֳדָם יְיָ אֱלָהָךְ, וּבָךְ אִתְרְעִי יְיָ, לְמִהְוֵי לֵיהּ לְעַם חַבִּיב, מִכָּל עַמְמַיָּא, דְּעַל אַפֵּי אַרְעָא: ג לָא תֵיכוֹל כָּל דִּמְרַחַק: ד דֵּין בְּעִירָא דְּתֵיכְלוּן, תּוֹרִין, אִמְּרִין דִּרְחֵלִין וְגַדְיִין דְּעִזִּין: ה אַיְלָא וְטַבְיָא וְיַחְמוּרָא, וְיַעְלָא וְרֵימָא וְתָרְבְּלָא וְדִיצָא: ו וְכָל בְּעִירָא דִּסְדִיקָא פַּרְסָתַהּ, וּמַטִלְפָן טִלְפִין תַּרְתֵּין פַּרְסָתַהּ, מַסְּקָא פִּשְׁרָא בִּבְעִירָא, יָתַהּ תֵּיכְלוּן: ז בְּרַם יָת דֵּין, לָא תֵיכְלוּן מִמַּסְּקֵי פִּשְׁרָא, וּמִסְּדִיקֵי פַרְסָתָא מַטִלְפֵי טִלְפַיָּא, יָת גַּמְלָא, וְיָת אַרְנְבָא וְיָת טַבְזָא אֲרֵי מַסְּקֵי פִשְׁרָא אִנּוּן, וּפַרְסַתְהוֹן לָא סְדִיקָא, מְסָאֲבִין אִנּוּן לְכוֹן: ח וְיָת חֲזִירָא, אֲרֵי סְדִיק פַּרְסְתָא הוּא וְלָא פָשַׁר, מְסָאַב הוּא לְכוֹן, מִבִּסְרְהוֹן לָא תֵיכְלוּן, וּבִנְבִילַתְהוֹן לָא תִקְרְבוּן: ט יָת דֵּין תֵּיכְלוּן, מִכָּל דִּבְמַיָּא, כָּל דְּלֵיהּ, צִיצִין וְקַלְפִין תֵּיכְלוּן: י וְכָל דְּלֵית לֵיהּ, צִיצִין וְקַלְפִין לָא תֵיכְלוּן, מְסָאַב הוּא לְכוֹן: יא כָּל צִפַּר

to a holy people; it is the kind of behavior associated with idolatrous cults.

Here is how Rambam sets out the law: "Whoever does not mourn the dead in the manner enjoined by the Rabbis is cruel (*akhzari*)" (*Hilkhot Evel* 13:12). At the same time, however, "One should not indulge in excessive grief over one's dead, for it is said, 'Weep not for the dead; do not bemoan him' (Jer. 22:10); that is to say, weep not too much, for [death] is the way of the world" (*Hilkhot Evel* 13:11).

Halakha, Jewish law, strives to create a balance between too much and too little grief. Hence the various stages of bereavement: *aninut* (the period between the death and burial), *shiva* (the week of mourning), *sheloshim* (thirty days in the case of other relatives) and *shana* (a year, in the case of parents). Judaism ordains a precisely calibrated sequence of grief, from the initial, numbing moment of loss itself, to the funeral and the return home, to the period of being comforted by friends and members of the community, to a more extended time during which one does not engage in activities associated with joy.

12 eat any pure species of bird. These you may not eat: the griffon vulture, the
13 bearded vulture, the lappet-faced vulture, the glede, the buzzard, the kite of
14 15 any kind, any kind of raven, the ostrich, the swift, the gull, any kind of sparrow
16, 17 hawk, the little owl, the short-eared owl, the barn owl, the pelican, the Egyptian
18 vulture, the cormorant, the stork, any kind of heron, the hoopoe, and the bat.
19 20 All swarming, flying creatures are impure for you; they may not be eaten. You
21 may, however, eat any pure flying creature. Do not eat any creature that has
died of itself. Give it to the migrant in your town to eat, or you may sell it to a
foreigner. For you are a people holy to the LORD your God. Do not boil a kid
in the milk of its mother.

רש״י

יב **וְזֶה אֲשֶׁר לֹא תֹאכְלוּ.** לְחַסֵּר אֶת הַשְּׁחוּטָה:

יג **וְהָרָאָה וְאֶת הָאַיָּה וגו׳.** הִיא רָאָה, הִיא אַיָּה, הִיא דַּיָּה, וְלָמָּה נִקְרָא שְׁמָהּ ׳רָאָה׳? שֶׁרוֹאָה בְּיוֹתֵר. וְלָמָּה הִזְהִירְךָ בְּכָל שְׁמוֹתֶיהָ? שֶׁלֹּא לִתֵּן פִּתְחוֹן פֶּה לְבַעַל דִּין לַחְלֹק, שֶׁלֹּא יְהֵא הָאוֹסְרָהּ קוֹרֵא אוֹתָהּ ׳רָאָה׳ וְהַבָּא לְהַתִּיר אוֹמֵר זוֹ ׳דַּיָּה׳ שְׁמָהּ אוֹ ׳אַיָּה׳ שְׁמָהּ, וְזוֹ לֹא אָסַר הַכָּתוּב. וּבָעוֹפוֹת פֵּרַט לְךָ הַטְּמֵאִים, לְלַמֶּדְךָ שֶׁעוֹפוֹת טְהוֹרִים מְרֻבִּים עַל הַטְּמֵאִים, לְפִיכָךְ פֵּרַט אֶת הַמּוּעָט:

טז **הַתִּנְשָׁמֶת.** קלב״א שורי״ץ:

יז **שָׁלָךְ.** הַשּׁוֹלֶה דָּגִים מִן הַיָּם:

יח **דּוּכִיפַת.** הוּא תַּרְנְגוֹל הַבָּר, וּבְלַעַז הרופ״א וְכַרְבָּלְתּוֹ כְּפוּלָה:

יט **שֶׁרֶץ הָעוֹף.** הֵם הַנְּמוּכִים הָרוֹחֲשִׁים עַל הָאָרֶץ, כְּגוֹן זְבוּבִים וּצְרָעִים וַחֲגָבִים טְמֵאִים, הֵם קְרוּיִים ׳שֶׁרֶץ׳:

כ **כָּל עוֹף טָהוֹר תֹּאכֵלוּ.** וְלֹא אֶת הַטָּמֵא, בָּא לִתֵּן עֲשֵׂה עַל לֹא תַעֲשֶׂה; וְכֵן בַּבְּהֵמָה: ״אֹתָהּ תֹּאכֵלוּ״ (לעיל פסוק ו) וְלֹא בְּהֵמָה טְמֵאָה; לָאו הַבָּא מִכְּלַל עֲשֵׂה עֲשֵׂה, לַעֲבֹר עֲלֵיהֶם בַּעֲשֵׂה וְלֹא תַעֲשֶׂה:

כא **לַגֵּר אֲשֶׁר בִּשְׁעָרֶיךָ.** גֵּר תּוֹשָׁב שֶׁקִּבֵּל עָלָיו שֶׁלֹּא לַעֲבֹד עֲבוֹדָה זָרָה וְאוֹכֵל נְבֵלוֹת: **כִּי עַם קָדוֹשׁ אַתָּה לַה׳.** קַדֵּשׁ אֶת עַצְמְךָ בַּמֻּתָּר לְךָ, דְּבָרִים הַמֻּתָּרִים וַאֲחֵרִים נוֹהֲגִים בָּהֶם אִסּוּר אַל תַּתִּירֵם בִּפְנֵיהֶם: **לֹא תְבַשֵּׁל גְּדִי.** שָׁלֹשׁ פְּעָמִים (שמות כג, יט; שם לד, כו), פְּרָט לְחַיָּה וּלְעוֹפוֹת וְלִבְהֵמָה טְמֵאָה:

nor are we the measure of all things. Some of the most glorious aspects of nature have nothing to do with human needs. One of the few Jewish thinkers to state this clearly was Rambam:

> Consider how vast are the dimensions and how great the number of these corporeal beings. If the whole of the earth would not constitute even the smallest part of the sphere of the fixed stars, what is the relation of the human species to all these created things, and how can any of us imagine that they exist for his sake and that they are instruments for his benefit? (*Guide for the Perplexed* III:14)

We now understand what is at stake in the prohibition of eating certain species of animals, birds, and fish, many of them predators like the creatures described in Job 38–41. They exist for their own sake, not for the sake of humankind. The vast universe, and earth itself with the myriad species it contains, has an integrity of its own. Yes, after the flood, God gave humans permission to eat meat, but this was a concession, as if to say: kill if you must, but let it be animals, not other humans, that you kill. The laws of *kashrut* limit our sense of possession over nature. We are placed in the world "to work it and safeguard it" (Gen. 2:15), but that does not give us license to take from it without exercising restraint.

14:21 **בַּחֲלֵב אִמּוֹ** *In the milk of its mother* – Religions are not philosophical systems. They are embodied truths, made real in the lives of communities. It is one thing to have an abstract conception of ecological responsibility, another to celebrate the Sabbath weekly – to renounce our mastery of nature one day in seven – and to make a blessing, as Jews do, over everything we eat or drink to remind ourselves of God's ownership of the world. Prayer, ritual, and narrative are ways we shape what Tocqueville called "habits of the heart." They form character, create behavioral dispositions,

יב טְהֹרָה תֹּאכֵלוּ: וְזֶה אֲשֶׁר לֹא־תֹאכְלוּ מֵהֶם הַנֶּשֶׁר וְהַפֶּרֶס וְהָעָזְנִיָּה:
יג יד טו וְהָרָאָה וְאֶת־הָאַיָּה וְהַדַּיָּה לְמִינָהּ: וְאֵת כָּל־עֹרֵב לְמִינוֹ: וְאֵת בַּת
טז הַיַּעֲנָה וְאֶת־הַתַּחְמָס וְאֶת־הַשָּׁחַף וְאֶת־הַנֵּץ לְמִינֵהוּ: אֶת־הַכּוֹס וְאֶת־
יז יח הַיַּנְשׁוּף וְהַתִּנְשָׁמֶת: וְהַקָּאָת וְאֶת־הָרָחָמָה וְאֶת־הַשָּׁלָךְ: וְהַחֲסִידָה
יט וְהָאֲנָפָה לְמִינָהּ וְהַדּוּכִיפַת וְהָעֲטַלֵּף: וְכֹל שֶׁרֶץ הָעוֹף טָמֵא הוּא לָכֶם
כ כא לֹא יֵאָכֵלוּ: כָּל־עוֹף טָהוֹר תֹּאכֵלוּ: לֹא־תֹאכְלוּ כָל־נְבֵלָה לַגֵּר אֲשֶׁר־
בִּשְׁעָרֶיךָ תִּתְּנֶנָּה וַאֲכָלָהּ אוֹ מָכֹר לְנָכְרִי כִּי עַם קָדוֹשׁ אַתָּה לַיהוָה
אֱלֹהֶיךָ לֹא־תְבַשֵּׁל גְּדִי בַּחֲלֵב אִמּוֹ:

אונקלוס

דְּכֵי תֵּיכְלוּן: יב וְדֵין, דְּלָא תֵיכְלוּן מִנְּהוֹן, נִשְׁרָא וְעָר וְעָזְיָא: יג וּבַת
כַּנְפָא וְטָרָפִיתָא, וְדַיְתָא לִזְנַהּ: יד וְיָת כָּל עוֹרְבָא לִזְנֵיהּ: טו וְיָת בַּת
נַעֲמִיתָא, וְצִיצָא וְצִפַּר שַׁחְפָּא, וְנַצָּא לִזְנוֹהִי: טז וְקַדְיָא וְקִפּוּפָא
וּבַוְתָא: יז וְקָתָא וִירַקְרֵיקָא וְשָׁלֵינוּנָא: יח וְחַוָּרִיתָא, וְאִבּוֹ לִזְנַהּ,
וְנַגַּר טוּרָא וַעֲטַלֵּיפָא: יט וְכֹל רִחְשָׁא דְעוֹפָא, מְסָאַב הוּא לְכוֹן, לָא
יִתְאַכְלוּן: כ כָּל עוֹף דְּכֵי תֵּיכְלוּן: כא לָא תֵיכְלוּן כָּל נְבִילָא, לְתוֹתַב
עֲרַל דִּבְקִרְוָךְ תִּתְּנִנַּהּ וְיֵיכְלִנַּהּ, אוֹ תְזַבְּנִנַּהּ לְבַר עַמְמִין, אֲרֵי עַם
קַדִּישׁ אַתְּ, קֳדָם יי אֱלָהָךְ, לָא תֵיכְלוּן בְּסַר בַּחֲלָב: כב עַסָּרָא תְעַסַּר,

KOSHER AND NONKOSHER ANIMALS

Moshe returns here to the laws of *kashrut* first laid out in Parashat Shemini. The dietary laws, which seem to defy logical explanation, are as integral to the covenant as the laws of a just society. Why?

We may find some direction in the book of Job. Iyov is the paradigm of the righteous individual who suffers. He loses all he has, for no apparent reason. His companions tell him that he must have sinned. Only this can reconcile his fate with justice. Iyov maintains his innocence and demands a hearing in the heavenly tribunal. For some thirty-seven chapters the argument rages, then in chapter 38 God addresses Iyov "from the whirlwind" (Job 38:1). God offers no answers. Instead, for four chapters, He asks questions of His own, rhetorical questions that have no answer: "Where were you when I laid the earth's foundations?" (38:4); "Have you traveled as far as the sea's depths, walked through them, plumbing the abyss?" (38:16).

God shows Iyov the whole panoply of creation, but it is a very different view of the universe than that set out in Genesis 1–2. There the center of the narrative is the human person. Man and woman were created last, made in God's image, given dominion over all that lives. In Job we see not an anthropocentric, but a *theocentric*, universe. Iyov is the only person in Tanakh who sees the world, as it were, from God's point of view.

Particularly striking is the way these chapters deal with the animal kingdom. What Iyov sees are not domestic animals, but wild, untamable creatures, magnificent in their strength and beauty, living far from and utterly indifferent to humankind:

> Did you endow the horse with his valor? Did you clothe his neck with a mane?
> Do you make him rumble like locusts, neigh in majestic terror?…
> Is it by your wisdom the hawk flies, spreading his wings to head south?
> Does the vulture soar at your bidding? Is that why he builds his nest on high? (39:19–27)

This is the most radically non-anthropocentric passage in the Tanakh. It tells us that man is not the center of the universe,

22 23 Each year, set aside a tenth of the yield of all you have sown in the field. You HAMISHI
shall eat the tithe of your grain, wine, and oil, as well as the firstborn of your
herds and flocks in the presence of the LORD your God in the place that He
will choose as a dwelling for His name, so that you may learn to hold the LORD
24 your God in awe always. But if the distance is too great for you to carry them,
because the place where the LORD your God chooses to set His name is far
25 from you and because the LORD your God has blessed you, then you may
exchange the tithe for money. Wrap up the money in your hand, go to the place
26 that the LORD your God will choose, and spend the money on whatever you
choose: cattle, sheep, wine, strong drink, or whatever else you like. There you
shall eat it in the presence of the LORD your God, and rejoice together with
27 your household. As for the Levites living in your towns, do not neglect them,
28 because they have no share or inheritance as you do. At the end of

רש״י

כא-כב] **לֹא תְבַשֵּׁל גְּדִי. עַשֵּׂר תְּעַשֵּׂר.** מָה עִנְיָן זֶה אֵצֶל זֶה? אָמַר לָהֶם הַקָּדוֹשׁ בָּרוּךְ הוּא לְיִשְׂרָאֵל: אַל תִּגְרְמוּ לִי לְבַשֵּׁל גְּדָיִים שֶׁל תְּבוּאָה עַד שֶׁהֵן בִּמְעֵי אִמּוֹתֵיהֶן, שֶׁאִם אֵין אַתֶּם מְעַשְּׂרִים מַעַשְׂרוֹת כָּרָאוּי, כְּשֶׁהוּא סָמוּךְ לְהִתְבַּשֵּׁל אֲנִי מוֹצִיא רוּחַ קָדִים וְהִיא מְשַׁדַּפְתָּן, שֶׁנֶּאֱמַר: "וּשְׁדֵפָה לִפְנֵי קָמָה" (מלכים ב׳ יט, כו), וְכֵן לְעִנְיַן בִּכּוּרִים: **שָׁנָה שָׁנָה.** מִכָּאן שֶׁאֵין מְעַשְּׂרִין מִן הֶחָדָשׁ עַל הַיָּשָׁן:

כג] **וְאָכַלְתָּ וְגוֹ׳.** זֶה מַעֲשֵׂר שֵׁנִי, שֶׁכְּבָר לָמַדְנוּ לִתֵּן מַעֲשֵׂר אֶחָד לַלְוִיִּם, שֶׁנֶּאֱמַר: "כִּי תִקְחוּ מֵאֵת בְּנֵי יִשְׂרָאֵל" וְגוֹ׳ (במדבר יח, כו), וְנָתַן לָהֶם רְשׁוּת לְאָכְלוֹ בְּכָל מָקוֹם, שֶׁנֶּאֱמַר: "וַאֲכַלְתֶּם אֹתוֹ בְּכָל מָקוֹם" (שם פסוק לא), עַל כָּרְחֲךָ זֶה מַעֲשֵׂר אַחֵר הוּא:

כד] **כִּי יְבָרֶכְךָ.** שֶׁתְּהֵא הַתְּבוּאָה מְרֻבָּה לָשֵׂאת:

כו] **בְּכֹל אֲשֶׁר תְּאַוֶּה נַפְשְׁךָ.** כְּלָל: **בַּבָּקָר וּבַצֹּאן וּבַיַּיִן וּבַשֵּׁכָר.** פְּרָט: **וּבְכֹל אֲשֶׁר תִּשְׁאָלְךָ נַפְשֶׁךָ.** חָזַר וְכָלַל, מַה הַפְּרָט מְפֹרָשׁ וְלַד וַלְדוֹת הָאָרֶץ וְרָאוּי לְמַאֲכַל אָדָם וְכוּ׳:

כז] **וְהַלֵּוִי... לֹא תַעַזְבֶנּוּ.** מִלִּתֵּן לוֹ מַעֲשֵׂר רִאשׁוֹן: **כִּי אֵין לוֹ חֵלֶק וְנַחֲלָה עִמָּךְ.** יָצְאוּ לֶקֶט שִׁכְחָה וּפֵאָה וְהֶפְקֵר, שֶׁאַף הוּא יֵשׁ לוֹ חֵלֶק עִמְּךָ בָּהֶן כָּמוֹךָ, וְאֵינָן חַיָּבִין בְּמַעֲשֵׂר:

כח] **מִקְצֵה שָׁלֹשׁ שָׁנִים.** בָּא וְלִמֵּד שֶׁאִם הִשְׁהָה מַעַשְׂרוֹתָיו שֶׁל שָׁנָה רִאשׁוֹנָה וּשְׁנִיָּה לַשְּׁמִטָּה, שֶׁיְּבַעֲרֵם מִן הַבַּיִת בַּשְּׁלִישִׁית:

other tithes, the "second tithe" described in this verse did not go to the poor, or to the priests and Levites. What then was its logic?

The Sages (Sifrei), focusing on the phrase "So that *you may learn* to hold the LORD your God in awe," said that it was to encourage people to study. Staying in Jerusalem while they consumed the tithe or the food bought with its monetary substitute, they would be influenced by the holy city, with its population engaged in divine service or sacred study.

Rambam gives a different explanation:

> The second tithe was commanded to be spent on food in Jerusalem; in this way the owner was compelled to give part of it away as charity. As he was not able to use it otherwise than by way of eating and drinking, he must have easily been induced to give it gradually away. This rule brought multitudes together in one place, and strengthened the bond of love and brotherhood among the children of men. (*Guide for the Perplexed* III:39)

For Rambam, the second tithe served a social purpose. It strengthened civil society, creating bonds of connectedness and friendship among the people. It encouraged visitors to share the blessings of the harvest with others. Strangers would meet and become friends. There would be a sense of shared citizenship, common belonging, and collective identity. The second tithe served to create social capital, bonds of trust and reciprocal altruism among the population, which came about through sharing food with strangers in the holy precincts of Jerusalem.

כב כג עַשֵּׂר תְּעַשֵּׂר אֵת כָּל־תְּבוּאַת זַרְעֶךָ הַיֹּצֵא הַשָּׂדֶה שָׁנָה שָׁנָה׃ וְאָכַלְתָּ חמישי
לִפְנֵי ׀ יהוה אֱלֹהֶיךָ בַּמָּקוֹם אֲשֶׁר־יִבְחַר לְשַׁכֵּן שְׁמוֹ שָׁם מַעְשַׂר דְּגָנְךָ
תִּירֹשְׁךָ וְיִצְהָרֶךָ וּבְכֹרֹת בְּקָרְךָ וְצֹאנֶךָ לְמַעַן תִּלְמַד לְיִרְאָה אֶת־
כד יהוה אֱלֹהֶיךָ כָּל־הַיָּמִים׃ וְכִי־יִרְבֶּה מִמְּךָ הַדֶּרֶךְ כִּי לֹא תוּכַל שְׂאֵתוֹ
כִּי־יִרְחַק מִמְּךָ הַמָּקוֹם אֲשֶׁר יִבְחַר יהוה אֱלֹהֶיךָ לָשׂוּם שְׁמוֹ שָׁם כִּי
כה יְבָרֶכְךָ יהוה אֱלֹהֶיךָ׃ וְנָתַתָּה בַּכָּסֶף וְצַרְתָּ הַכֶּסֶף בְּיָדְךָ וְהָלַכְתָּ אֶל־
כו הַמָּקוֹם אֲשֶׁר יִבְחַר יהוה אֱלֹהֶיךָ בּוֹ׃ וְנָתַתָּה הַכֶּסֶף בְּכֹל אֲשֶׁר־תְּאַוֶּה
נַפְשְׁךָ בַּבָּקָר וּבַצֹּאן וּבַיַּיִן וּבַשֵּׁכָר וּבְכֹל אֲשֶׁר תִּשְׁאָלְךָ נַפְשֶׁךָ וְאָכַלְתָּ
כז שָּׁם לִפְנֵי יהוה אֱלֹהֶיךָ וְשָׂמַחְתָּ אַתָּה וּבֵיתֶךָ׃ וְהַלֵּוִי אֲשֶׁר־בִּשְׁעָרֶיךָ
כח לֹא תַעַזְבֶנּוּ כִּי אֵין לוֹ חֵלֶק וְנַחֲלָה עִמָּךְ׃ מִקְצֵה ׀ שָׁלֹשׁ

אונקלוס

יָת כָּל עֲלַלַת זַרְעָךְ, דְּיִפֵּיק חַקְלָא שְׁנָא שְׁנָא: כג וְתֵיכוֹל, קֳדָם יי אֱלָהָךְ, בְּאַתְרָא דְּיִתְרְעֵי לְאַשְׁרָאָה שְׁכִינְתֵיהּ תַּמָּן, מַעְסַר עֲבוּרָךְ חַמְרָךְ וּמִשְׁחָךְ, וּבְכוֹרֵי תּוֹרָךְ וְעָנָךְ, בְּדִיל דְּתֵילַף, לְמִדְחַל, קֳדָם יי אֱלָהָךְ כָּל יוֹמַיָּא: כד וַאֲרֵי יִסְגֵּי מִנָּךְ אוֹרְחָא, אֲרֵי לָא תִכּוֹל לְמִטְלֵיהּ, אֲרֵי יִתְרַחַק מִנָּךְ אַתְרָא, דְּיִתְרְעֵי יי אֱלָהָךְ, לְאַשְׁרָאָה שְׁכִינְתֵיהּ תַּמָּן, אֲרֵי יְבָרְכִנָּךְ יי אֱלָהָךְ: כה וְתִתֵּין בְּכַסְפָּא, וּתְצוּר כַּסְפָּא בִּידָךְ, וּתְהָךְ לְאַתְרָא, דְּיִתְרְעֵי, יי אֱלָהָךְ בֵּיהּ: כו וְתִתֵּין כַּסְפָּא, בְּכֹל דְּתִתְרְעֵי נַפְשָׁךְ בְּתוֹרֵי וּבְעָנָא, וּבַחֲמַר חֲדַת וְעַתִּיק, וּבְכֹל, דְּתִשְׁאֲלִנָּךְ נַפְשָׁךְ, וְתֵיכוֹל תַּמָּן, קֳדָם יי אֱלָהָךְ, וְתִחְדֵּי אַתְּ וֶאֱנָשׁ בֵּיתָךְ: כז וְלֵיוָאָה דִּבְקִרְוָךְ לָא תִרְחֲקִנֵּיהּ, אֲרֵי לֵית לֵיהּ, חוּלָק וְאַחְסָנָא עִמָּךְ: כח מִסּוֹף תְּלָת

and educate us in patterns of self-restraint. Roger Scruton makes a fascinating observation in relation to the prohibition against "boiling a kid in the milk of its mother":

> The Jewish law which forbids us to seethe a young animal in its mother's milk may have little sense, when considered from the standpoint of a hard-nosed utilitarianism. But our disposition to hesitate before the mystery of nature, to renounce our presumption of mastery, and to respect the process by which life is made, must surely prompt us to sympathize with such an interdiction. And these very same feelings, had we allowed them to prevail, would have caused us to hesitate before feeding to cows, which live and thrive on pasture, the dead remains of their own and other species.

This practice, adopted to save money, ultimately caused the spread of deadly disease and led to untold damage.

All of the world's great faiths embody a sense of respect for nature, and thus constitute an important counterbalance to the indifference bordering on arrogance that has been one of the less lovely legacies of the Enlightenment. Civilizations at the height of their powers have found it hard to maintain a sense of limits. Each in turn has been captivated by the idea that it alone was immune to the laws of growth and decline, that it could consume resources indefinitely, pursuing present advantage without thought of future depletion. Never is this more likely than when we lose the sense of awe in the face of totality. The great faiths teach a different kind of wisdom: *reverence* in the face of creation, *responsibility* to future generations, and *restraint* in the knowledge that not everything we can do, should we do.

14:23 לְמַעַן תִּלְמַד לְיִרְאָה אֶת־יהוה אֱלֹהֶיךָ כָּל־הַיָּמִים *You may learn to hold the Lord your God in awe always* – Unlike the

every third year, bring out the full tithe of your produce for that year, and leave
29 it within your towns, so that the Levites, who have no share or inheritance
as you have, together with the migrants, orphans, and widows in your towns,
may come and eat and be satisfied, so that the LORD your God will grant you
15 1 blessing in all the work of your hands. At the end of every seventh SHISHI
2 year, you shall grant a remission of debts. This is how the remission is carried
out: every creditor shall relinquish any debt owed by his fellow. He shall not
exact it from his brother, his fellow, because the LORD's remission has been
3 proclaimed. You may require payment from a foreigner, but you must remit any
4 debt owed to you by a brother. There should be no poor among you, because
the LORD will bless you in the land that the LORD your God is giving you
5 to possess as your inheritance, if only you obey the LORD your God, staying

רש"י

כט **וּבָא הַלֵּוִי.** וְיִטֹּל מַעֲשֵׂר רִאשׁוֹן: **וְהַגֵּר וְהַיָּתוֹם.** וְיִטְּלוּ מַעֲשֵׂר שֵׁנִי, שֶׁהוּא שֶׁל עָנִי שֶׁל שָׁנָה זוֹ, וְלֹא תֹאכְלֶנּוּ אַתָּה בִּירוּשָׁלַיִם כְּדֶרֶךְ שֶׁנִּזְקַקְתָּ לֶאֱכֹל מַעֲשֵׂר שֵׁנִי שֶׁל שְׁתֵּי שָׁנִים: **וְאָכְלוּ וְשָׂבֵעוּ.** תֵּן לָהֶם כְּדֵי שָׂבְעָן, מִכָּאן אָמְרוּ: "אֵין פּוֹחֲתִין לֶעָנִי בַּגֹּרֶן" וְכוּ' (ספרי קי). וְאַתָּה הוֹלֵךְ לִירוּשָׁלַיִם בְּמַעֲשַׂר שֶׁל שָׁנָה רִאשׁוֹנָה וּשְׁנִיָּה שֶׁהִשְׁהֵיתָ, וּמִתְוַדֶּה: "בִּעַרְתִּי הַקֹּדֶשׁ מִן הַבַּיִת" (להלן כו, יג) כְּמוֹ שֶׁמְּפֹרָשׁ בְּ'כִי תְכַלֶּה לַעְשֵׂר' (שם פסוק יב):

טו א **מִקֵּץ שֶׁבַע שָׁנִים.** יָכוֹל שֶׁבַע שָׁנִים לְכָל מִלְוָה וּמִלְוָה? תַּלְמוּד לוֹמַר: "קָרְבָה שְׁנַת הַשֶּׁבַע" (להלן פסוק ט), וְאִם אַתָּה אוֹמֵר שֶׁבַע שָׁנִים לְכָל מִלְוָה וּמִלְוָה, לְהַלְוָאַת כָּל אֶחָד וְאֶחָד, הֵיאַךְ הִיא קְרֵבָה? הָא לָמַדְתָּ שֶׁבַע שָׁנִים לְמִנְיַן הַשְּׁמִטִּים:

ב **שָׁמוֹט כָּל בַּעַל מַשֵּׁה יָדוֹ.** שָׁמוֹט אֶת יָדוֹ שֶׁל כָּל בַּעַל מַשֶּׁה:

ד **אֶפֶס כִּי לֹא יִהְיֶה בְּךָ אֶבְיוֹן.** וּלְהַלָּן הוּא אוֹמֵר: "כִּי לֹא יֶחְדַּל אֶבְיוֹן" (להלן פסוק יא)! אֶלָּא בִּזְמַן שֶׁאַתֶּם עוֹשִׂים רְצוֹנוֹ שֶׁל מָקוֹם, אֶבְיוֹנִים בַּאֲחֵרִים וְלֹא בָּכֶם, וּכְשֶׁאֵין אַתֶּם עוֹשִׂים רְצוֹנוֹ שֶׁל מָקוֹם אֶבְיוֹנִים בָּכֶם: **אֶבְיוֹן.** דַּל מֵעָנִי, וּלְשׁוֹן 'אֶבְיוֹן' שֶׁהוּא תָּאֵב לְכָל דָּבָר:

ה **רַק אִם שָׁמוֹעַ תִּשְׁמַע.** אָז לֹא יִהְיֶה בְּךָ אֶבְיוֹן: **שָׁמוֹעַ תִּשְׁמַע.** שָׁמַע קִמְעָא, מַשְׁמִיעִין אוֹתוֹ הַרְבֵּה:

all agricultural work is forbidden, "so that your ox and donkey may rest" (Ex. 23:12). It is a day that sets a limit to our intervention in nature and the pursuit of economic activity. We become conscious of being creations, not creators. The earth is not ours but God's. For six days it is handed over to us, but on the seventh day we symbolically abdicate that power. We may perform no "work," which is to say an act that alters the state of something for human purposes. The Sabbath is a weekly reminder of the integrity of nature and the boundaries of human striving.

What the Sabbath does for human beings and animals, the Sabbatical and Jubilee years do for the land. The earth too is entitled to its periodic rest. The Bible warns that if the Israelites do not respect this, they will suffer exile: "Then shall the land make appeasement for its Sabbaths (referring to Sabbatical years) for as long as it lies desolate and you are in your enemies' lands; then the land will rest and make appeasement for its Sabbaths" (Lev. 26:34). Behind this are two concerns. One is environmental. As Rambam points out (*Guide for the Perplexed* III:39), land which is overexploited is eventually eroded and loses its fertility. The Israelites were therefore commanded to conserve the soil by giving it periodic fallow years and not pursue short-term gain at the cost of long-term desolation. The second, no less significant, is theological: "The land," says God, "is Mine; you are merely migrants and visitors to Me" (Lev. 25:23). We are guests on earth. The same is true of material possessions; the Torah respects private property rights, but our claims over debtors are not absolute and must be relinquished if the poor are unable to pay by the seventh year.

שָׁנִים תּוֹצִיא אֶת־כׇּל־מַעְשַׂר תְּבוּאָתְךָ בַּשָּׁנָה הַהִוא וְהִנַּחְתָּ בִּשְׁעָרֶיךָ׃
כט וּבָא הַלֵּוִי כִּי אֵין־לוֹ חֵלֶק וְנַחֲלָה עִמָּךְ וְהַגֵּר וְהַיָּתוֹם וְהָאַלְמָנָה אֲשֶׁר
בִּשְׁעָרֶיךָ וְאָכְלוּ וְשָׂבֵעוּ לְמַעַן יְבָרֶכְךָ יהוה אֱלֹהֶיךָ בְּכׇל־מַעֲשֵׂה יָדְךָ
טו א ב אֲשֶׁר תַּעֲשֶׂה׃ מִקֵּץ שֶׁבַע־שָׁנִים תַּעֲשֶׂה שְׁמִטָּה׃ וְזֶה דְּבַר ששי
הַשְּׁמִטָּה שָׁמוֹט כׇּל־בַּעַל מַשֵּׁה יָדוֹ אֲשֶׁר יַשֶּׁה בְּרֵעֵהוּ לֹא־יִגֹּשׂ אֶת־
ג רֵעֵהוּ וְאֶת־אָחִיו כִּי־קָרָא שְׁמִטָּה לַיהוה׃ אֶת־הַנׇּכְרִי תִּגֹּשׂ וַאֲשֶׁר
ד יִהְיֶה לְךָ אֶת־אָחִיךָ תַּשְׁמֵט יָדֶךָ׃ אֶפֶס כִּי לֹא יִהְיֶה־בְּךָ אֶבְיוֹן כִּי־בָרֵךְ
ה יְבָרֶכְךָ יהוה בָּאָרֶץ אֲשֶׁר יהוה אֱלֹהֶיךָ נֹתֵן־לְךָ נַחֲלָה לְרִשְׁתָּהּ׃ רַק
אִם־שָׁמוֹעַ תִּשְׁמַע בְּקוֹל יהוה אֱלֹהֶיךָ לִשְׁמֹר לַעֲשׂוֹת אֶת־כׇּל־הַמִּצְוָה

אונקלוס

שְׁנִין, תַּפֵּיק יָת כָּל מַעְסַר עֲלַלְתָּךְ, בְּשַׁתָּא הַהִיא, וְתַצְנַע בְּקִרְוָךְ׃ כט וְיֵיתֵי לֵיוָאָה, אֲרֵי לֵית לֵיהּ חוּלָק וְאַחְסָנָא עִמָּךְ, וְגִיּוֹרָא, וְיַתְמָא וְאַרְמַלְתָּא דִּבְקִרְוָךְ, וְיֵיכְלוּן וְיִסְבְּעוּן, בְּדִיל דִּיבָרְכִנָּךְ יי אֱלָהָךְ, בְּכָל עוֹבָדֵי יְדָךְ דְּתַעֲבֵיד׃ טו א מִסּוֹף שְׁבַע שְׁנִין תַּעֲבֵיד שְׁמִטְּתָא׃ ב וְדֵין פִּתְגָּם שְׁמִטְּתָא, דְּיַשְׁמֵיט, כָּל גְּבַר מָרֵי רְשׁוּ, דְּיִרְשֵׁי בְּחַבְרֵיהּ, לָא יִתְבַּע מִן חַבְרֵיהּ וּמִן אֲחוּהִי, אֲרֵי קְרָא שְׁמִטְּתָא קֳדָם יי׃ ג מִן בַּר עַמְמִין תִּתְבַּע, וְדִיהֵי לָךְ, עִם אֲחוּךְ תַּשְׁמֵיט יְדָךְ׃ ד לְחוֹד, אֲרֵי, לָא יְהֵי בָךְ מִסְכֵּינָא, אֲרֵי בָרָכָא יְבָרְכִנָּךְ יי, בְּאַרְעָא, דַּיי אֱלָהָךְ, יָהֵיב לָךְ אַחְסָנָא לְמֵירְתַהּ׃ ה לְחוֹד אִם קַבָּלָא תְקַבֵּיל, לְמֵימְרָא דַּיי אֱלָהָךְ, לְמִטַּר לְמֶעְבַּד יָת כָּל תַּפְקֵידְתָּא

15:1 שְׁמִטָּה *A remission of debts* – The sequence here – the second and poor person's tithe, followed by the release of debts and slaves in the seventh year – are ways in which we serve God *bekhol meodekha* (Deut. 6:5), which some Sages understand to mean "with all your wealth" (Berakhot 9:5). We use our possessions to serve God when we ensure that those who have more than they need share their blessings with those who have less. In particular, we should ensure that no one in the nation God liberated from slavery is permanently enslaved, either by debt or poverty (the usual reason people sold themselves as slaves).

History is full of ideal worlds, known as utopias. The word means "no place," because no utopias have ever happened. They never happen because they come without a realistic map of how to get from here to there. The Torah has a different approach to ideal worlds. We live them, periodically, in the here and now. The Sabbath is one example (see commentary on Deut. 5:14). Something similar is true of the *Shemitta*, the Sabbatical year, and *Yovel*, the Jubilee year. By cancelling debts, releasing slaves, leaving the produce of the land to be enjoyed by everyone equally, and restoring ancestral property to its original owners, we inhabit a world in which the inequities of the market economy have been redressed. For a year, sometimes two, we suspend the world of competition and live in a world of cooperation and the fellowship of equals.

15:4 בָּאָרֶץ אֲשֶׁר יהוה אֱלֹהֶיךָ נֹתֵן־לְךָ נַחֲלָה לְרִשְׁתָּהּ *The land that the Lord your God is giving you to possess* – Though we must exercise caution when reading twenty-first century concerns into ancient texts, there seems little doubt that much biblical legislation is concerned with what we would nowadays call "sustainability." This is particularly true of the three great commands ordaining periodic rest: the Sabbath, the Sabbatical year, and the Jubilee year. On the Sabbath

6 vigilant to keep all the command with which I am charging you this day. For
the LORD your God will bless you as He has promised you. You will lend to
many nations, but will not borrow. You will rule over many nations, and they
7 will not rule over you. If there be a poor person among your kinsfolk
in any of your towns in the land that the LORD your God is giving you, do
8 not harden your heart or close your hand toward your brother in need. Open
9 your hand generously and freely lend him enough to answer all his needs. Be
vigilant: let your heart not whisper a depraved thought: 'The seventh year, the

רש"י

ו **כאשר דבר לך.** והיכן דבר? "ברוך אתה בעיר" (להלן כח, ג): **והעבטת גוים.** יכול שתהא לוה מזה ומלוה לזה? תלמוד לומר: "ואתה לא תעבט": **ומשלת בגוים רבים.** יכול גוים אחרים מושלים עליך? תלמוד לומר: "ובך לא ימשלו":

ז **כי יהיה בך אביון.** התאב תאב קודם: **מאחד אחיך.** אחיך מאביך קודם לאחיך מאמך: **שעריך.** עניי עירך קודמים: **לא תאמץ.** יש לך אדם שמצטער אם יתן אם לא יתן, לכך נאמר: "לא תאמץ". יש לך אדם שפושט את ידו וקופצה, לכך נאמר: "ולא תקפץ": **מאחיך האביון.** אם לא תתן לו, סופך להיות אחיו של אביון:

ח **פתח תפתח.** אפילו כמה פעמים: **כי פתח תפתח.** הרי 'כי' משמש בלשון 'אלא': **והעבט תעביטנו.** אם לא רצה במתנה, תן לו בהלואה: **די מחסרו.** ואי אתה מצווה לעשרו: **אשר יחסר לו.** אפילו סוס לרכב עליו ועבד לרוץ לפניו: **לו.** זו אשה, וכן הוא אומר: "אעשה לו עזר כנגדו" (בראשית ב, יח):

by knowing that a saint had joined his ranks. He was helped by being given the chance not to be poor.

With its combination of charity and justice, tzedaka is a unique institution. It is deeply humanitarian, but it could not exist without the essentially religious concepts of divine ownership and social covenant. The prophet Yirmeyahu says of King Yoshiyahu, "'He took up the cause of the poor and the destitute with good results. That is the way to know Me,' declares the LORD" (Jer. 22:16). To know God is to act with justice and compassion, to recognize His image in other people, and to hear the silent cry of those in need.

15:8 **דֵּי מַחְסֹרוֹ אֲשֶׁר יֶחְסַר לוֹ** *To answer all his needs* – Judaism conceives poverty not only in material terms, that the poor lack the means of sustenance. It also sees it in psychological terms. Poverty humiliates. It robs people of dignity, makes them dependent on others, and deprives them of self-respect.

So tzedaka is addressed not only to people's physical needs but also to their psychological ones. The Rabbis (Ketubot 67b) based their approach on a finely nuanced understanding of this verse, which contains, in the Hebrew, a double phrasing. The first provision ("to answer all his needs") refers to an absolute subsistence level. In Jewish law this was taken to include food, housing, basic furniture, and, if necessary, funds to pay for a wedding. The second ("that which he lacks") means relative poverty – relative, however, not to others but to the individual's own previous standard of living.

Protecting dignity and avoiding humiliation was a systematic element of rabbinical law. So, for example, the Rabbis ruled that even the richest should be buried plainly so as not to shame the poor. The rabbis intervened to lower the prices of religious necessities so that no one would be excluded from communal celebrations. Work conditions had to be such that employees were treated with basic respect. Freedom presupposes self-respect, and a free society will therefore be one that robs no one of that basic human entitlement.

Rambam teaches that out of concern for recipients' dignity, Jewish law focuses not only on how much we must give but also on the manner in which we do so. Ideally, the donor should not know to whom he or she is giving, nor the recipient know from whom he or she is receiving. If a poor person does not want to accept tzedaka, we should practice a form of benign deception and give it to him under the guise of a loan (*Hilkhot Mattenot Aniyyim* 7:9).

Giving someone a job or making him your partner would not normally be considered charity at all. It costs

ו הַזֹּ֑את אֲשֶׁ֛ר אָנֹכִ֥י מְצַוְּךָ֖ הַיּֽוֹם׃ כִּֽי־יְהוָ֤ה אֱלֹהֶ֙יךָ֙ בֵּֽרַכְךָ֔ כַּאֲשֶׁ֖ר דִּבֶּר־
לָ֑ךְ וְהַעֲבַטְתָּ֞ גּוֹיִ֣ם רַבִּ֗ים וְאַתָּה֙ לֹ֣א תַעֲבֹ֔ט וּמָֽשַׁלְתָּ֙ בְּגוֹיִ֣ם רַבִּ֔ים וּבְךָ֖
ז לֹ֥א יִמְשֹֽׁלוּ׃ כִּֽי־יִהְיֶ֨ה בְךָ֜ אֶבְי֗וֹן מֵאַחַ֤ד אַחֶ֙יךָ֙ בְּאַחַ֣ד יג
שְׁעָרֶ֔יךָ בְּאַ֨רְצְךָ֔ אֲשֶׁר־יְהוָ֥ה אֱלֹהֶ֖יךָ נֹתֵ֣ן לָ֑ךְ לֹ֧א תְאַמֵּ֣ץ אֶת־לְבָבְךָ֗
ח וְלֹ֤א תִקְפֹּץ֙ אֶת־יָ֣דְךָ֔ מֵאָחִ֖יךָ הָאֶבְיֽוֹן׃ כִּֽי־פָתֹ֧חַ תִּפְתַּ֛ח אֶת־יָדְךָ֖ ל֑וֹ
ט וְהַעֲבֵט֙ תַּעֲבִיטֶ֔נּוּ דֵּ֚י מַחְסֹר֔וֹ אֲשֶׁ֥ר יֶחְסַ֖ר לֽוֹ׃ הִשָּׁ֣מֶר לְךָ֡ פֶּן־יִהְיֶ֣ה דָבָר֩

אונקלוס

הָדָא, דַּאֲנָא מְפַקֵּיד לָךְ יוֹמָא דֵין: ו אֲרֵי יְיָ אֱלָהָךְ בָּרְכָךְ, כְּמָא דְּמַלֵּיל לָךְ, וְתוֹזֵיף לְעַמְמִין סַגִּיאִין, וְאַתְּ לָא תְזִיף, וְתִשְׁלוֹט בְּעַמְמִין סַגִּיאִין, וּבָךְ לָא יִשְׁלְטוּן: ז אֲרֵי יְהֵי בָךְ מִסְכֵּינָא, חַד מֵאַחָךְ בַּחֲדָא מִן קִרְוָךְ, בְּאַרְעָךְ, דַּייָ אֱלָהָךְ יָהֵיב לָךְ, לָא תְתַקֵּיף יָת לִבָּךְ, וְלָא תִקְפּוֹץ יָת יְדָךְ, מֵאֲחוּךְ מִסְכֵּינָא: ח אֲרֵי מִפְתַּח תִּפְתַּח, יָת יְדָךְ לֵיהּ, וְאוֹזָפָא תוֹזְפִנֵּיהּ, כְּמִסַּת חֶסְרָנֵיהּ, דְּחַסִּיר לֵיהּ: ט אִסְתְּמַר לָךְ, דִּלְמָא יְהֵי פִתְגָם

LAWS OF TZEDAKA

The focus of the Torah from Exodus onward is the creation of a society in the land of Israel – the society that emerged from the days of Yehoshua to the close of the biblical era. Its economy was primarily agricultural. Therefore, the Torah sets out its program of distributive justice in terms of an agrarian order (see commentary on Deut. 12:11). But the Torah does not predicate its social vision on a single era or economic order. Alongside the specifics is a broad statement of timeless ideals, and this passage is to serve as the basis for extensive rabbinic legislation on tzedaka.

In postbiblical times, when Israel was no longer a nation in its own land, and most of its people no longer worked on farms, tzedaka took on new forms. From earliest rabbinic times there were such institutions as the *tamḥui*, or mobile kitchen, which distributed food daily to whoever applied, and the *kuppa*, or community chest, which distributed money weekly to the poor of the city, together with specific funds for clothing, raising dowries for poor brides, and providing burial expenses for the poor. Thus the Torah established the first form of what came to be known as a welfare state – with one significant difference. It did not depend on a state. It was part of society, implemented not by power but by moral responsibility, not by governments but by individuals and local communities.

Tzedaka was to be constitutive of Jewish community life, the moral bond between people. It is foundational to the concept of covenantal society: society as an ethical enterprise is constructed on the basis of mutual responsibility.

Fundamental to the concept of tzedaka is, firstly, an absolute refusal on the part of the Sages to romanticize poverty. It is not, for them, a blessed state. It is an unmitigated evil. Many of the Sages were poor themselves. Hillel lacked the small sum needed to secure entrance to the house of study (Yoma 35b). Ḥanina ben Dosa is said to have survived on a *kav* of carobs from one week to the next (Berakhot 17b). They knew that poverty does not dignify, nor does it refine the soul. It deadens the sensibilities, turns a person in on himself, crushes the spirit, and humiliates the soul. "If there is no meal," said the Sages, "there can be no Torah" (Avot 3:17). On this the Rabbis would have agreed with Marx, that statements in praise of poverty are indefensible defenses of the status quo by those with privilege and power.

The whole tenor of the Torah is based on the idea that God is to be found in the physical world and its blessings. We are commanded to serve God in joy out of the abundance of good things, not through self-denial. Asceticism – always a temptation in the religious life – was never embraced by the Jewish mainstream. On the contrary, it was an implicit disavowal of this world which God created and pronounced good. Having regard for the poor did not mean in Judaism embracing poverty oneself. No poor person was ever helped

year of remission, is close,' making you miserly toward your brother in need,
giving him nothing. He will cry out to the LORD about you, and you will be
10 held guilty. Give to him generously, and do not let your heart begrudge it, for
by merit of this the LORD your God will grant you blessing in all your work
11 and all your hands' endeavors. There will never cease to be poor people in the
land. And so I command you: open your hand generously to your kinsmen,
12 your poor and needy, who share your land. If a fellow Hebrew, man or
woman, is sold to you, he or she shall work for you for six years; in the seventh
13 year you shall send him or her forth free. And when you send one forth free,
14 do not send him empty-handed. Provide for him liberally from your flock,
your threshing floor, and your winepress, giving him a share in the things with
15 which the LORD your God has blessed you. Remember: you were a slave in
Egypt and the LORD your God redeemed you; and so I give you this command

רש״י

ט **וְקָרָא עָלֶיךָ.** יָכוֹל מִצְוָה? תַּלְמוּד לוֹמַר: "וְלֹא יִקְרָא" (להלן כד, טו): **וְהָיָה בְךָ חֵטְא.** מִכָּל מָקוֹם, אֲפִלּוּ לֹא יִקְרָא. אִם כֵּן לָמָּה נֶאֱמַר: "וְקָרָא עָלֶיךָ"? מְמַהֵר אֲנִי לִפָּרַע עַל יְדֵי הַקּוֹרֵא יוֹתֵר מִמִּי שֶׁאֵינוֹ קוֹרֵא:

י **נָתוֹן תִּתֵּן לוֹ.** אֲפִלּוּ מֵאָה פְעָמִים: **לוֹ.** בֵּינוֹ וּבֵינְךָ: **כִּי בִּגְלַל הַדָּבָר.** אֲפִלּוּ אָמַרְתָּ לִתֵּן, אַתָּה נוֹטֵל שְׂכַר הָאֲמִירָה עִם שְׂכַר הַמַּעֲשֶׂה:

יא **עַל כֵּן.** מִפְּנֵי כֵן: **לֵאמֹר.** עֵצָה לְטוֹבָתְךָ אֲנִי מַשִּׂיאֲךָ: **לְאָחִיךָ לַעֲנִיֶּךָ.** לְאֵי זֶה אָח? לֶעָנִי: **לַעֲנִיֶּךָ.** בְּיוּ"ד אֶחָד – לְשׁוֹן עָנִי אֶחָד הוּא, אֲבָל 'עֲנִיֶּיךָ' בִּשְׁנֵי יוּדִי"ן – שְׁנֵי עֲנִיִּים:

יב **כִּי יִמָּכֵר לְךָ.** עַל יְדֵי אֲחֵרִים, בִּמְכָרוּהוּ בֵּית דִּין בִּגְנֵבָתוֹ הַכָּתוּב מְדַבֵּר. וַהֲרֵי כְּבָר נֶאֱמַר: "כִּי תִקְנֶה עֶבֶד עִבְרִי" (שמות כא, ב), וּבִמְכָרוּהוּ בֵּית דִּין הַכָּתוּב מְדַבֵּר? אֶלָּא מִפְּנֵי שְׁנֵי דְבָרִים שֶׁנִּתְחַדְּשׁוּ כָאן: אֶחָד, שֶׁכָּתוּב "אוֹ הָעִבְרִיָּה" – אַף הִיא תֵצֵא בְּשֵׁשׁ, וְלֹא שֶׁמְּכָרוּהָ בֵּית דִּין, שֶׁאֵין הָאִשָּׁה נִמְכֶּרֶת בִּגְנֵבָתָהּ, שֶׁנֶּאֱמַר "בִּגְנֵבָתוֹ" (שם כב, ב) וְלֹא 'בִּגְנֵבָתָהּ', אֶלָּא בִּקְטַנָּה שֶׁמְּכָרָהּ אָבִיהָ, וְלִמֵּד כָּאן שֶׁאִם יָצְאוּ שֵׁשׁ שָׁנִים קֹדֶם שֶׁתָּבִיא סִימָנִין – תֵּצֵא. וְעוֹד חִדֵּשׁ כָּאן: "הַעֲנֵיק תַּעֲנִיק":

יד **הַעֲנֵיק תַּעֲנִיק.** לְשׁוֹן עֲדִי, בְּגַבַּהּ וּבְמַרְאִית הָעַיִן, דָּבָר שֶׁיְּהֵא נִכָּר שֶׁהֱטִיבוֹתָ לוֹ. וְיֵשׁ מְפָרְשִׁים לְשׁוֹן הַטְעָנָה עַל צַוָּארוֹ: **מִצֹּאנְךָ וּמִגָּרְנְךָ וּמִיִּקְבֶךָ.** יָכוֹל אֵין לִי אֶלָּא אֵלּוּ בִּלְבַד? תַּלְמוּד לוֹמַר: "אֲשֶׁר בֵּרַכְךָ", מִכָּל מַה שֶּׁבֵּרַכְךָ בּוֹרַאֲךָ. וְלָמָּה נֶאֶמְרוּ אֵלּוּ? מָה אֵלּוּ מְיֻחָדִים שֶׁהֵם בִּכְלַל בְּרָכָה, אַף כָּל שֶׁהוּא בִּכְלַל בְּרָכָה, יָצְאוּ פְּרָדוֹת. וְלָמְדוּ רַבּוֹתֵינוּ בְּמַסֶּכֶת קִדּוּשִׁין (דף יז ע"א) בִּגְזֵרָה שָׁוָה, כַּמָּה נוֹתֵן לוֹ מִכָּל מִין וָמִין:

טו **וְזָכַרְתָּ כִּי עֶבֶד הָיִיתָ.** וְהֶעֱנַקְתִּי וְשָׁנִיתִי לְךָ מִבִּזַּת מִצְרַיִם וּבִזַּת הַיָּם, אַף אַתָּה הַעֲנֵק וּשְׁנֵה לוֹ:

How he had the authority to do so is a technical question which need not concern us. But why he should wish to do so is another matter. In effect, he had abrogated an established right of the less well-off. And Hillel was himself a man whose poverty was legendary.

With the transition from an agricultural to a more commercial economy, loans had become less a response to a disastrous harvest than a normal precondition of trading. A moral appeal to cancel debts was accordingly less likely to succeed and less plausible. The biblical law, whose original intent was explicitly to benefit the poor, was now working to their disfavor: they could not obtain loans in certain years. Clearly, forfeiting the redistribution in their favor would be more than compensated by the assistance they would receive in building up their own trade. Here was an instance, drawn from the Second Temple period, of redistribution of wealth yielding to economic growth – on the moral grounds agreed to be strong enough to justify inverting a biblical procedure. Hillel adapted the law dramatically to new circumstances and changing economic systems, still managing to preserve its original intent.

עִם־לְבָבְךָ בְלִיַּעַל לֵאמֹר קָרְבָה שְׁנַת־הַשֶּׁבַע שְׁנַת הַשְּׁמִטָּה וְרָעָה
עֵינְךָ בְּאָחִיךָ הָאֶבְיוֹן וְלֹא תִתֵּן לוֹ וְקָרָא עָלֶיךָ אֶל־יהוה וְהָיָה בְךָ
י חֵטְא׃ נָתוֹן תִּתֵּן לוֹ וְלֹא־יֵרַע לְבָבְךָ בְּתִתְּךָ לוֹ כִּי בִּגְלַל ׀ הַדָּבָר הַזֶּה
יא יְבָרֶכְךָ יהוה אֱלֹהֶיךָ בְּכָל־מַעֲשֶׂךָ וּבְכֹל מִשְׁלַח יָדֶךָ׃ כִּי לֹא־יֶחְדַּל
אֶבְיוֹן מִקֶּרֶב הָאָרֶץ עַל־כֵּן אָנֹכִי מְצַוְּךָ לֵאמֹר פָּתֹחַ תִּפְתַּח אֶת־יָדְךָ
יב לְאָחִיךָ לַעֲנִיֶּךָ וּלְאֶבְיֹנְךָ בְּאַרְצֶךָ׃ כִּי־יִמָּכֵר לְךָ אָחִיךָ
הָעִבְרִי אוֹ הָעִבְרִיָּה וַעֲבָדְךָ שֵׁשׁ שָׁנִים וּבַשָּׁנָה הַשְּׁבִיעִת תְּשַׁלְּחֶנּוּ
יג יד חָפְשִׁי מֵעִמָּךְ׃ וְכִי־תְשַׁלְּחֶנּוּ חָפְשִׁי מֵעִמָּךְ לֹא תְשַׁלְּחֶנּוּ רֵיקָם׃ הַעֲנֵיק
תַּעֲנִיק לוֹ מִצֹּאנְךָ וּמִגָּרְנְךָ וּמִיִּקְבֶךָ אֲשֶׁר בֵּרַכְךָ יהוה אֱלֹהֶיךָ תִּתֶּן־
טו לוֹ׃ וְזָכַרְתָּ כִּי עֶבֶד הָיִיתָ בְּאֶרֶץ מִצְרַיִם וַיִּפְדְּךָ יהוה אֱלֹהֶיךָ עַל־כֵּן

אונקלוס

עִם לִבָּךְ בְּרֶשַׁע לְמֵימַר, קְרִיבַת שַׁתָּא דִשְׁבִיעֵיתָא שַׁתָּא דִשְׁמִטְּתָא, וְתִבְאַשׁ עֵינָךְ, בַּאֲחוּךְ מִסְכֵּינָא, וְלָא תִתֵּין לֵיהּ, וְיִקְרֵי עֲלָךְ קֳדָם יְיָ, וִיהֵי בָךְ חוֹבָא: י מִתַּן תִּתֵּין לֵיהּ, וְלָא יִבְאַשׁ לִבָּךְ בְּמִתְּנָךְ לֵיהּ, אֲרֵי, בְּדִיל פִּתְגָּמָא הָדֵין, יְבָרְכִנָּךְ יְיָ אֱלָהָךְ, בְּכָל עוֹבָדָךְ, וּבְכֹל אוֹשָׁטוּת יְדָךְ: יא אֲרֵי, לָא יִפְסוֹק מִסְכֵּינָא מִגּוֹ אַרְעָא, עַל כֵּן, אֲנָא מְפַקֵּיד לָךְ לְמֵימַר, מִפְתַּח, תִּפְתַּח יָת יְדָךְ, לַאֲחוּךְ לְעַנְיָךְ, וּלְמִסְכֵּינָךְ בְּאַרְעָךְ: יב אֲרֵי יִזְדַּבַּן לָךְ אֲחוּךְ בַּר יִשְׂרָאֵל, אוֹ בַת יִשְׂרָאֵל, וְיִפְלְחִנָּךְ שֵׁית שְׁנִין, וּבְשַׁתָּא שְׁבִיעֵיתָא, תִּפְטְרִנֵּיהּ בַּר חוֹרִין מֵעִמָּךְ: יג וַאֲרֵי תִפְטְרִנֵּיהּ בַּר חוֹרִין מֵעִמָּךְ, לָא תִפְטְרִנֵּיהּ רֵיקָן: יד אַפְרָשָׁא תַּפְרֵישׁ לֵיהּ, מֵעָנָךְ, וּמֵאִדְּרָךְ וּמִמַּעְצַרְתָּךְ, דְּבָרְכָךְ, יְיָ אֱלָהָךְ תִּתֵּין לֵיהּ: טו וְתִדְכַּר, אֲרֵי עַבְדָּא הֲוֵיתָא בְּאַרְעָא דְמִצְרַיִם, וּפָרְקָךְ יְיָ אֱלָהָךְ, עַל כֵּן,

you nothing. But this further serves to show that tzedaka does not mean charity. It means giving people the means to live a dignified life, and any form of employment is more dignified, within the Jewish value system, than dependence (see *Guide for the Perplexed* III:27).

Consider the law that "even a poor person who is dependent on tzedaka is obliged to give tzedaka" (*Hilkhot Mattenot Aniyyim* 7:5). The law seems absurd. Why give money to the poor so that they may give to the poor? It makes sense only on the assumption that giving is essential to human dignity and tzedaka is the obligation to ensure that everyone has that dignity.

15:9 וְהָיָה בְךָ חֵטְא *You will be held guilty* – There is a danger that the wealthy simply will not give loans prior to the seventh year; hence the invocation here of divine concern – always an accompaniment of a law which is difficult for humans to enforce. What happened to this law in a more complex economy? The Mishna records one of the most daring of all rabbinic innovations: "When he saw that the people refrained from giving loans to one another and thus transgressed the biblical warning… Hillel enacted the *pruzbul*" (Gittin 36a). The *pruzbul* was a technical device whereby a loan was transacted through the court, ceased to be an agreement between individuals, and so bypassed the terms of the year of release. Creditors no longer had to relinquish their claims in the seventh year. Hillel – perhaps the founding father of rabbinic Judaism – had set aside the law.

16 today. But if he says to you, 'I do not want to leave you' – because he loves you
17 and your household and he fares well with you, then take an awl and put it
through his ear into the door, and he will be your slave for all time; you shall do
18 the same with a female slave. Do not consider it a hardship when you set him
free, because for six years he has given you twice the service of a hired laborer;
and the LORD your God will bless you in all your work.
19 Every firstborn male among your herd and flock you shall consecrate to the SHEVI'I
LORD your God. Do not work your firstborn ox or shear your firstborn sheep.
20 You and your household shall eat them year by year in the presence of the LORD
21 your God in the place that the LORD will choose. If the animal has a blemish, a
serious blemish such as lameness or blindness, you shall not sacrifice it to the
22 LORD your God. The impure as well as the pure among you shall eat it within
23 your towns, as you would a gazelle or a deer. Its blood, however, you must not
eat. You must pour it out onto the ground like water.
16 1 Observe the month of Aviv by offering a Passover sacrifice to the LORD your

רש״י

יז **עבד עולם.** יכול כמשמעו? תלמוד לומר: "ושבתם איש אל אחזתו ואיש אל משפחתו תשבו" (ויקרא כה, י), הא למדת שאין זה אלא עולמו של יובל: **ואף לאמתך תעשה כן.** הענק לה. יכול אף לרציעה השוה הכתוב אותה? תלמוד לומר: "ואם אמר יאמר העבד" (שמות כא, ה), עבד נרצע ואין אמה נרצעת:

יח **כי משנה שכר שכיר.** מכאן אמרו: עבד עברי עובד בין ביום ובין בלילה, וזהו כפלים שבעבודת שכירי יום. ומהו עבודתו בלילה? רבו מוסר לו שפחה כנענית והולדות לאדון:

יט **כל הבכור... תקדיש.** ובמקום אחר הוא אומר: "לא יקדיש איש אתו" (ויקרא כז, כו)! אינו מקדישו לקרבן אחר, וכאן למד שמצוה לומר: 'הרי את קדוש לבכורה'. דבר אחר, אי אפשר לומר "תקדיש" שכבר נאמר "לא יקדיש", ואי אפשר לומר "לא יקדיש" שהרי כבר נאמר "תקדיש", הא כיצד? מקדישו אתה הקדש עלוי ונותן להקדש כפי טובת הנאה שבו: **לא תעבד בבכר שורך ולא תגז וגו׳.** אף האחוז למדו רבותינו שאסור, אלא שדבר הכתוב בהוה:

כ **לפני ה׳ אלהיך תאכלנו.** לכהן הוא אומר, שכבר מצינו שהוא ממתנות כהנה, אחד תם ואחד בעל מום, שנאמר: "ובשרם יהיה לך" וגו׳ (במדבר יח, יח): **שנה בשנה.** מכאן שאין מאחרין אותו יותר על שנתו. יכול יהא פסול משעברה שנתו? כבר הקיש למעשר, שנאמר: "ואכלת לפני ה׳ אלהיך... מעשר דגנך תירשך ויצהרך ובכרת בקרך וצאנך" (לעיל יד, כג), מה מעשר שני אינו נפסל משנה לחברתה, אף בכור אינו נפסל, אלא שמצוה בתוך שנתו: **שנה בשנה.** אם שחטו בסוף שנתו, אוכלו אותו היום ויום אחד משנה אחרת, למד שנאכל לשני ימים ולילה אחד:

כא **מום.** כלל: **פסח או עור.** פרט: **כל מום רע.** חזר וכלל, מה הפרט מפרש מום הגלוי ואינו חוזר, אף כל מום שבגלוי ואינו חוזר:

כג **רק את דמו לא תאכל.** שלא תאמר: הואיל וכלו היתר הבא מכלל אסור הוא, שהרי קדוש ונשחט בחוץ בלא פדיון ונאכל, יכול יהא אף הדם מתר? תלמוד לומר: "רק את דמו לא תאכל":

טז א **שמור את חדש האביב.** מקדם בואו שמר שיהא ראוי לאביב, להקריב בו את מנחת העמר, ואם לאו – עבר את השנה:

The account in Deuteronomy is about society. Moshe at the end of his life tells the next generation where they came from, where they are going to, and the kind of society they are to construct. It is to be the opposite of Egypt. It must strive for justice, freedom, and human dignity.

One of Deuteronomy's most important themes is its insistence that worship be centralized "in the place that the LORD will choose" (Deut. 12:14). The unity of God is to be mirrored in the unity of the nation, something that could not be achieved if every tribe had its own temple, sanctuary, or shrine. That is why, when it comes to the festivals, Moshe speaks only of Passover, Shavuot, and Sukkot, the three on

טז אָנֹכִי מְצַוְּךָ אֶת־הַדָּבָר הַזֶּה הַיּוֹם: וְהָיָה כִּי־יֹאמַר אֵלֶיךָ לֹא אֵצֵא
יז מֵעִמָּךְ כִּי אֲהֵבְךָ וְאֶת־בֵּיתֶךָ כִּי־טוֹב לוֹ עִמָּךְ: וְלָקַחְתָּ אֶת־הַמַּרְצֵעַ
וְנָתַתָּה בְאָזְנוֹ וּבַדֶּלֶת וְהָיָה לְךָ עֶבֶד עוֹלָם וְאַף לַאֲמָתְךָ תַּעֲשֶׂה־כֵּן:
יח לֹא־יִקְשֶׁה בְעֵינֶךָ בְּשַׁלֵּחֲךָ אֹתוֹ חָפְשִׁי מֵעִמָּךְ כִּי מִשְׁנֶה שְׂכַר שָׂכִיר
עֲבָדְךָ שֵׁשׁ שָׁנִים וּבֵרַכְךָ יהוה אֱלֹהֶיךָ בְּכֹל אֲשֶׁר תַּעֲשֶׂה:
יט כָּל־הַבְּכוֹר אֲשֶׁר יִוָּלֵד בִּבְקָרְךָ וּבְצֹאנְךָ הַזָּכָר תַּקְדִּישׁ לַיהוה אֱלֹהֶיךָ שביעי
כ לֹא תַעֲבֹד בִּבְכֹר שׁוֹרֶךָ וְלֹא תָגֹז בְּכוֹר צֹאנֶךָ: לִפְנֵי יהוה אֱלֹהֶיךָ
כא תֹאכְלֶנּוּ שָׁנָה בְשָׁנָה בַּמָּקוֹם אֲשֶׁר־יִבְחַר יהוה אַתָּה וּבֵיתֶךָ: וְכִי־
יִהְיֶה בוֹ מוּם פִּסֵּחַ אוֹ עִוֵּר כֹּל מוּם רָע לֹא תִזְבָּחֶנּוּ לַיהוה אֱלֹהֶיךָ:
כב כג בִּשְׁעָרֶיךָ תֹּאכְלֶנּוּ הַטָּמֵא וְהַטָּהוֹר יַחְדָּו כַּצְּבִי וְכָאַיָּל: רַק אֶת־דָּמוֹ
לֹא תֹאכֵל עַל־הָאָרֶץ תִּשְׁפְּכֶנּוּ כַּמָּיִם:
טז א שָׁמוֹר אֶת־חֹדֶשׁ הָאָבִיב וְעָשִׂיתָ פֶּסַח לַיהוה אֱלֹהֶיךָ כִּי בְּחֹדֶשׁ הָאָבִיב

אונקלוס

אֲנָא מְפַקֵּיד לָךְ, יָת פִּתְגָּמָא הָדֵין יוֹמָא דֵין: טז וִיהֵי אֲרֵי יֵימַר לָךְ,
לָא אֶפּוֹק מֵעִמָּךְ, אֲרֵי רְחֵמָךְ וְלֶאֱנָשׁ בֵּיתָךְ, אֲרֵי טַב לֵיהּ עִמָּךְ:
יז וְתִסַּב יָת מַרְצְעָא, וְתִתֵּין בְּאֻדְנֵיהּ וּבְדַשָּׁא, וִיהֵי לָךְ עֲבֵד פָּלַח
לְעָלַם, וְאַף לְאַמְתָךְ תַּעֲבֵיד כֵּן: יח לָא יִקְשֵׁי בְעֵינָךְ, בְּמִפְטְרָךְ יָתֵיהּ
בַּר חוֹרִין מֵעִמָּךְ, אֲרֵי, עַל חַד תְּרֵין כַּאֲגַר אֲגִירָא, פַּלְחָךְ שִׁית שְׁנִין,
וִיבָרְכִנָּךְ יי אֱלָהָךְ, בְּכֹל דְּתַעֲבֵיד: יט כָּל בֻּכְרָא, דְּיִתְיְלֵיד בְּתוֹרָךְ
וּבְעָנָךְ דִּכְרִין, תַּקְדֵּישׁ קֳדָם יי אֱלָהָךְ, לָא תִפְלַח בְּבֻכְרָא דְּתוֹרָךְ,
וְלָא תִגּוֹז בֻּכְרָא דְעָנָךְ: כ קֳדָם יי אֱלָהָךְ תֵּיכְלִנֵּיהּ שְׁנָא בִשְׁנָא,
בְּאַתְרָא דְּיִתְרְעֵי יי, אַתְּ וֶאֱנָשׁ בֵּיתָךְ: כא וַאֲרֵי יְהֵי בֵיהּ מוּמָא, חֲגִיר
אוֹ עֲוִיר, כָּל מוּם בִּישׁ, לָא תִכְּסִנֵּיהּ, קֳדָם יי אֱלָהָךְ: כב בְּקִרְוָךְ
תֵּיכְלִנֵּיהּ, מְסָאֲבָא וְדִכְיָא כַּחֲדָא, כִּבְסַר טַבְיָא וְאַיְלָא: כג לְחוֹד
יָת דְּמֵיהּ לָא תֵיכוֹל, עַל אַרְעָא תֵּישְׁדְּנֵיהּ כְּמַיָּא: טז א טַר יָת יַרְחָא
דַאֲבִיבָא, וְתַעֲבֵיד פִּסְחָא, קֳדָם יי אֱלָהָךְ, אֲרֵי בְּיַרְחָא דַאֲבִיבָא,

THE THREE PILGRIMAGE FESTIVALS

There are five passages in the Torah dedicated to the festivals of the Jewish year. Two, both in the book of Exodus (23:14–17 and 34:18, 22–23), are very brief. They refer only to the three pilgrimage festivals, Passover, Shavuot, and Sukkot. They do not specify their dates, merely their rough position in the agricultural year. Nor do they mention the specific commands related to the festivals.

This leaves three other festival accounts, one in Leviticus 23, a second one in Numbers 28–29, and the third here. The three are very different. This is not, as critics maintain, because the Torah is a composite document, but rather because it comes at its subject matter from multiple perspectives – a characteristic of the Torah mindset as a whole.

The long section on the festivals in Numbers is wholly dedicated to the special additional sacrifices (the *musaf*) brought on holy days including the Sabbath and Rosh Ḥodesh. A memory of this is preserved in the Musaf prayers for these days. These are holy times from the perspective of the Tabernacle, the Temple, and later, the synagogue.

God; for in the month of Aviv the LORD your God brought you out of Egypt
2 by night. You shall offer up the Passover sacrifice to the LORD your God, from
the flock and the herd, at the place that the LORD will choose as a dwelling
3 for His name. You must not eat anything leavened with it. For seven days, eat
unleavened bread – the bread of affliction – because you left Egypt in haste.
This is for you to remember the day you left Egypt all the days of your life.
4 For seven days no leaven shall be found with you in all your land. And do not
let any of the meat that you sacrificed on the evening of the first day remain
5 until morning. You may not slaughter the Passover sacrifice in any of the towns
6 that the LORD your God is giving you. Only at the place that the LORD your
God chooses as a dwelling for His name, there shall you slaughter the Passover
7 sacrifice in the evening; at sunset, at the time appointed to leave Egypt, you
shall cook and eat it at the place that the LORD your God will choose, and on
8 the following morning you may set out to your tents. For six days you shall eat
unleavened bread and, on the seventh day, you shall hold an assembly for the
9 LORD your God and perform no work. You shall count seven weeks. At

רש״י

מִמִּצְרַיִם לָיְלָה. וַהֲלֹא בַּיּוֹם יָצְאוּ, שֶׁנֶּאֱמַר: ״מִמָּחֳרַת הַפֶּסַח יָצְאוּ בְנֵי יִשְׂרָאֵל״ וְגוֹ׳ (במדבר לג, ג)? אֶלָּא לְפִי שֶׁבַּלַּיְלָה נָתַן לָהֶם פַּרְעֹה רְשׁוּת לָצֵאת, שֶׁנֶּאֱמַר: ״וַיִּקְרָא לְמֹשֶׁה וּלְאַהֲרֹן לַיְלָה״ וְגוֹ׳ (שמות יב, לא):

ב **וְזָבַחְתָּ פֶּסַח לַה׳ אֱלֹהֶיךָ צֹאן.** שֶׁנֶּאֱמַר: ״מִן הַכְּבָשִׂים וּמִן הָעִזִּים תִּקָּחוּ״ (שמות יב, ה): **וּבָקָר.** תִּזְבַּח לַחֲגִיגָה, שֶׁאִם נִמְנוּ עַל הַפֶּסַח חֲבוּרָה מְרֻבָּה, מְבִיאִים עִמּוֹ חֲגִיגָה כְּדֵי שֶׁיְּהֵא נֶאֱכָל עַל הַשֹּׂבַע. וְעוֹד לָמְדוּ רַבּוֹתֵינוּ דְּבָרִים הַרְבֵּה מִפָּסוּק זֶה:

ג **לֶחֶם עֹנִי.** לֶחֶם שֶׁמַּזְכִּיר אֶת הָעֹנִי שֶׁנִּתְעַנּוּ בְּמִצְרַיִם: **כִּי בְחִפָּזוֹן יָצָאתָ.** וְלֹא הִסְפִּיק בָּצֵק לְהַחֲמִיץ, וְזֶה יִהְיֶה לְךָ לְזִכָּרוֹן. וְחִפָּזוֹן לֹא שֶׁלְּךָ הָיָה אֶלָּא שֶׁל מִצְרַיִם, שֶׁכֵּן הוּא אוֹמֵר: ״וַתֶּחֱזַק מִצְרַיִם עַל הָעָם״ וְגוֹ׳ (שמות יב, לג): **לְמַעַן תִּזְכֹּר.** עַל יְדֵי אֲכִילַת הַפֶּסַח וְהַמַּצָּה ״אֶת יוֹם צֵאתְךָ״:

ד **וְלֹא יָלִין מִן הַבָּשָׂר אֲשֶׁר תִּזְבַּח בָּעֶרֶב בַּיּוֹם הָרִאשׁוֹן לַבֹּקֶר.** אַזְהָרָה לַמּוֹתִיר בְּפֶסַח דּוֹרוֹת, לְפִי שֶׁלֹּא נֶאֱמַר אֶלָּא בְּפֶסַח מִצְרַיִם, וְיוֹם רִאשׁוֹן הָאָמוּר כָּאן הוּא אַרְבָּעָה עָשָׂר בְּנִיסָן, כְּמָה דְּאַתְּ אָמַר: ״אַךְ בַּיּוֹם הָרִאשׁוֹן תַּשְׁבִּיתוּ שְּׂאֹר מִבָּתֵּיכֶם״ (שמות יב, טו). וּלְפִי שֶׁנִּסְתַּלֵּק הַכָּתוּב מֵעִנְיָנוֹ שֶׁל פֶּסַח וְהִתְחִיל לְדַבֵּר בְּחֻקּוֹת שִׁבְעַת יָמִים, כְּגוֹן: ״שִׁבְעַת יָמִים תֹּאכַל עָלָיו מַצּוֹת״, ״וְלֹא יֵרָאֶה לְךָ שְׂאֹר בְּכָל גְּבֻלְךָ״, הֻצְרַךְ לְפָרֵשׁ בְּאֵיזוֹ זְבִיחָה הוּא מַזְהִיר, שֶׁאִם כָּתַב: ׳וְלֹא יָלִין מִן הַבָּשָׂר אֲשֶׁר תִּזְבַּח בָּעֶרֶב לַבֹּקֶר׳, הָיִיתִי אוֹמֵר, שְׁלָמִים הַנִּשְׁחָטִים כָּל שִׁבְעָה כֻּלָּן בְּבַל תּוֹתִירוּ וְאֵינָן נֶאֱכָלִין אֶלָּא לְיוֹם וָלַיְלָה, לְכָךְ כָּתַב: ״בָּעֶרֶב בַּיּוֹם הָרִאשׁוֹן״. דָּבָר אַחֵר, בַּחֲגִיגַת אַרְבָּעָה עָשָׂר הַכָּתוּב מְדַבֵּר, וְלִמֵּד עָלֶיהָ שֶׁנֶּאֱכֶלֶת לִשְׁנֵי יָמִים, וְ״הָרִאשׁוֹן״ הָאָמוּר כָּאן – בְּיוֹם טוֹב הָרִאשׁוֹן הַכָּתוּב מְדַבֵּר, וְכֵן מַשְׁמָעוּת הַמִּקְרָא: בְּשַׂר חֲגִיגָה אֲשֶׁר תִּזְבַּח בָּעֶרֶב לֹא יָלִין בְּיוֹם טוֹב הָרִאשׁוֹן עַד בָּקְרוֹ שֶׁל שֵׁנִי, אֲבָל נֶאֱכֶלֶת הִיא בְּאַרְבָּעָה עָשָׂר וּבַחֲמִשָּׁה עָשָׂר. וְכָךְ הִיא שְׁנוּיָה בְּמַסֶּכֶת פְּסָחִים (דף עא ע״א – עא ע״ב):

ו **בָּעֶרֶב כְּבוֹא הַשֶּׁמֶשׁ מוֹעֵד צֵאתְךָ מִמִּצְרָיִם.** הֲרֵי שְׁלֹשָׁה זְמַנִּים חֲלוּקִים: ׳בָּעֶרֶב׳ מִשֵּׁשׁ שָׁעוֹת וּלְמַעְלָה זָבְחֵהוּ, וּ׳כְבוֹא הַשֶּׁמֶשׁ׳ תֹּאכְלֵהוּ, וּ׳מוֹעֵד צֵאתְךָ׳ אַתָּה שׂוֹרְפֵהוּ, כְּלוֹמַר נַעֲשֶׂה נוֹתָר וְיֵצֵא לְבֵית הַשְּׂרֵפָה:

ז **וּבִשַּׁלְתָּ.** זֶהוּ צְלִי אֵשׁ, שֶׁאַף הוּא קָרוּי בִּשּׁוּל: **וּפָנִיתָ בַבֹּקֶר.** לְבָקְרוֹ שֶׁל שֵׁנִי, מְלַמֵּד שֶׁטָּעוּן לִינָה לֵיל שֶׁל מוֹצָאֵי יוֹם טוֹב:

ח **שֵׁשֶׁת יָמִים תֹּאכַל מַצּוֹת.** וּבְמָקוֹם אַחֵר הוּא אוֹמֵר: ״שִׁבְעַת יָמִים״ (שמות יב, טו)! שִׁבְעָה מִן הַיָּשָׁן וְשִׁשָּׁה מִן הֶחָדָשׁ. דָּבָר אַחֵר, לִמֵּד עַל אֲכִילַת מַצָּה בַּשְּׁבִיעִי שֶׁאֵינָהּ חוֹבָה, וּמִכָּאן אַתָּה לָמֵד לְשֵׁשֶׁת יָמִים, שֶׁהֲרֵי שְׁבִיעִי בִּכְלָל הָיָה וְיָצָא מִן הַכְּלָל לְלַמֵּד שֶׁאֵין אֲכִילַת מַצָּה בּוֹ חוֹבָה אֶלָּא רְשׁוּת, וְלֹא לְלַמֵּד עַל עַצְמוֹ יָצָא אֶלָּא לְלַמֵּד עַל הַכְּלָל כֻּלּוֹ יָצָא, מַה שְּׁבִיעִי רְשׁוּת אַף כֻּלָּם רְשׁוּת, חוּץ מִלַּיְלָה הָרִאשׁוֹן שֶׁהַכָּתוּב קְבָעוֹ חוֹבָה, שֶׁנֶּאֱמַר: ״בָּעֶרֶב תֹּאכְלוּ מַצֹּת״ (שמות יב, יח): **עֲצֶרֶת לַה׳ אֱלֹהֶיךָ.** עֹצֶר עַצְמְךָ מִן הַמְּלָאכָה. דָּבָר אַחֵר, כְּנוּפְיָא שֶׁל מַאֲכָל וּמִשְׁתֶּה, לָשׁוֹן: ״נַעַצְרָה נָּא אוֹתָךְ״ (שופטים יג, טו):

ט **מֵהָחֵל חֶרְמֵשׁ בַּקָּמָה.** מִשֶּׁנִּקְצַר הָעֹמֶר שֶׁהוּא רֵאשִׁית הַקָּצִיר:

ב הוֹצִיאֲךָ יְהוָה אֱלֹהֶיךָ מִמִּצְרַיִם לָיְלָה׃ וְזָבַחְתָּ פֶּסַח לַיהוָה אֱלֹהֶיךָ
ג צֹאן וּבָקָר בַּמָּקוֹם אֲשֶׁר יִבְחַר יְהוָה לְשַׁכֵּן שְׁמוֹ שָׁם׃ לֹא־תֹאכַל עָלָיו
חָמֵץ שִׁבְעַת יָמִים תֹּאכַל־עָלָיו מַצּוֹת לֶחֶם עֹנִי כִּי בְחִפָּזוֹן יָצָאתָ
מֵאֶרֶץ מִצְרַיִם לְמַעַן תִּזְכֹּר אֶת־יוֹם צֵאתְךָ מֵאֶרֶץ מִצְרַיִם כֹּל יְמֵי
ד חַיֶּיךָ׃ וְלֹא־יֵרָאֶה לְךָ שְׂאֹר בְּכָל־גְּבֻלְךָ שִׁבְעַת יָמִים וְלֹא־יָלִין מִן־
ה הַבָּשָׂר אֲשֶׁר תִּזְבַּח בָּעֶרֶב בַּיּוֹם הָרִאשׁוֹן לַבֹּקֶר׃ לֹא תוּכַל לִזְבֹּחַ
ו אֶת־הַפָּסַח בְּאַחַד שְׁעָרֶיךָ אֲשֶׁר־יְהוָה אֱלֹהֶיךָ נֹתֵן לָךְ׃ כִּי אִם־אֶל־
הַמָּקוֹם אֲשֶׁר־יִבְחַר יְהוָה אֱלֹהֶיךָ לְשַׁכֵּן שְׁמוֹ שָׁם תִּזְבַּח אֶת־הַפֶּסַח
ז בָּעָרֶב כְּבוֹא הַשֶּׁמֶשׁ מוֹעֵד צֵאתְךָ מִמִּצְרָיִם׃ וּבִשַּׁלְתָּ וְאָכַלְתָּ בַּמָּקוֹם
ח אֲשֶׁר יִבְחַר יְהוָה אֱלֹהֶיךָ בּוֹ וּפָנִיתָ בַבֹּקֶר וְהָלַכְתָּ לְאֹהָלֶיךָ׃ שֵׁשֶׁת
יָמִים תֹּאכַל מַצּוֹת וּבַיּוֹם הַשְּׁבִיעִי עֲצֶרֶת לַיהוָה אֱלֹהֶיךָ לֹא תַעֲשֶׂה
ט מְלָאכָה׃ שִׁבְעָה שָׁבֻעֹת תִּסְפָּר־לָךְ מֵהָחֵל חֶרְמֵשׁ בַּקָּמָה

אונקלוס

אַפְּקָךְ, יי אֱלָהָךְ, מִמִּצְרַיִם וַעֲבַד לָךְ נִסִּין בְּלֵילְיָא: ב וְתִכּוֹס פִּסְחָא, קֳדָם יי אֱלָהָךְ מִן בְּנֵי עָנָא וְנִכְסַת קֻדְשַׁיָּא מִן תּוֹרֵי, בְּאַתְרָא דְּיִתְרְעֵי יי, לְאַשְׁרָאָה שְׁכִינְתֵּיהּ תַּמָּן: ג לָא תֵיכוּל עֲלוֹהִי חֲמִיעַ, שִׁבְעָא יוֹמִין, תֵּיכוּל עֲלוֹהִי פַּטִּירָא לְחֵים עַנְיֵי, אֲרֵי בִּבְהִילוּ, נְפַקְתָּא מֵאַרְעָא דְּמִצְרַיִם, בְּדִיל דְּתִדְכַּר, יָת יוֹם מִפְּקָךְ מֵאַרְעָא דְּמִצְרַיִם, כָּל יוֹמֵי חַיָּךְ: ד וְלָא יִתַּחְזֵי לָךְ חֲמִיר, בְּכָל תְּחוּמָךְ שִׁבְעָא יוֹמִין, וְלָא יְבִית מִן בִּסְרָא, דְּתִכּוֹס בְּרַמְשָׁא, בְּיוֹמָא קַדְמָאָה לְצַפְרָא: ה לֵית לָךְ רְשׁוּ לְמִכַּס יָת פִּסְחָא, בַּחֲדָא מִן קִרְוָךְ, דַּיי אֱלָהָךְ יָהֵיב לָךְ: ו אֱלָהֵין, בְּאַתְרָא, דְּיִתְרְעֵי יי אֱלָהָךְ לְאַשְׁרָאָה שְׁכִינְתֵּיהּ, תַּמָּן, תִּכּוֹס יָת פִּסְחָא בְּרַמְשָׁא, כְּמֵיעַל שִׁמְשָׁא, זְמַן מִפְּקָךְ מִמִּצְרָיִם: ז וּתְבַשֵּׁיל וְתֵיכוּל, בְּאַתְרָא, דְּיִתְרְעֵי, יי אֱלָהָךְ בֵּיהּ, וְתִתְפְּנֵי בְּצַפְרָא, וּתְהָךְ לְמַשְׁכְּנָךְ: ח שִׁתָּא יוֹמִין תֵּיכוּל פַּטִּירָא, וּבְיוֹמָא שְׁבִיעָאָה, כְּנִישׁ קֳדָם יי אֱלָהָךְ, לָא תַעֲבֵיד עֲבִידָא: ט שִׁבְעָא שָׁבוּעִין תִּמְנֵי לָךְ, מִשֵּׁירָיוּת מִגְּלָא בַּחֲצַד עֻמְרָא דַּאֲרָמוּתָא,

which there is a duty of *aliya laregel*, pilgrimage to the Temple.

Moshe's presentation here has a strong emphasis on the seasons of the agricultural year: Passover is the festival of spring, the countdown to Shavuot begins "at the time when you first put sickle to standing grain" (Deut. 16:9), and Sukkot is celebrated at the time when "you have gathered the produce from your threshing floor and winepress" (16:13). These are dimensions of the festivals the people have not yet experienced as desert nomads, but they will once they enter and make their home in the land which God has blessed.

Equally significant is Deuteronomy's focus – not found elsewhere – on social inclusion: "You and your sons and daughters, your male and female slaves, and the Levites living in your towns, together with the migrants, orphans, and widows among you" (16:11). Deuteronomy is less about individual spirituality than about the kind of society that honors the presence of God by honoring our fellow humans, especially those at the margins of society. The idea that we can serve God while being indifferent to, or dismissive of, our fellow human beings is utterly alien to the vision of Deuteronomy. The festivals are times when people are to invite those at the margins of society. No one is to be left out.

the time when you first put sickle to standing grain, begin your count of seven
10 weeks. And then celebrate the Festival of Weeks to the Lord your God, bringing
a freewill offering, tribute proportionate to the blessing the Lord your God has
11 granted you. And rejoice before the Lord your God – you and your sons and
daughters, your male and female slaves, and the Levites living in your towns,
together with the migrants, orphans, and widows among you – at the place that
12 the Lord your God will choose as a dwelling for His name. Remember that you
were a slave in Egypt, and so take care to fulfill these decrees.
13 You shall keep the Festival of Tabernacles for seven days, after you have gathered MAFTIR
14 the produce from your threshing floor and winepress. Rejoice in your festival,
you and your sons and daughters; your male and female servants; the Levites;
15 and the migrants, orphans, and widows living in your towns. For seven days,
celebrate before the Lord your God at the place that the Lord will choose,
for the Lord your God will grant you blessing in all your harvest and in all the
16 work of your hands, and you shall be wholly joyful. Three times a year, all the
males among you shall appear before the Lord your God in the place that He
will choose: on the Festival of Unleavened Bread, the Festival of Weeks, and the
Festival of Tabernacles. They shall not appear before the Lord empty-handed;
17 each shall bring a gift, in keeping with the blessing that the Lord your God has
given you.

The haftara for Parashat Re'eh is on page 1614.
This haftara is read even on Erev Rosh Ḥodesh Elul. On Rosh Ḥodesh Elul, Ashkenazim read the haftara on page 1634, while Sephardim read this haftara.

רש״י

י **מִסַּת נִדְבַת יָדְךָ.** דֵּי נִדְבַת יָדְךָ, הַכֹּל לְפִי הַבְּרָכָה הָבֵא שַׁלְמֵי שִׂמְחָה וְקַדֵּשׁ קְרוּאִים לֶאֱכֹל:

יא **וְהַלֵּוִי וְהַגֵּר וְהַיָּתוֹם וְהָאַלְמָנָה.** אַרְבָּעָה שֶׁלִּי כְּנֶגֶד אַרְבָּעָה שֶׁלְּךָ: "בִּנְךָ וּבִתֶּךָ וְעַבְדְּךָ וַאֲמָתֶךָ", אִם אַתָּה מְשַׂמֵּחַ אֶת שֶׁלִּי אֲנִי מְשַׂמֵּחַ אֶת שֶׁלְּךָ:

יב **וְזָכַרְתָּ כִּי עֶבֶד הָיִיתָ וְגוֹ'.** עַל מְנָת כֵּן פְּדִיתִיךָ, שֶׁתִּשְׁמֹר וְתַעֲשֶׂה אֶת הַחֻקִּים הָאֵלֶּה:

יג **בְּאָסְפְּךָ.** בִּזְמַן הָאָסִיף, שֶׁאַתָּה מַכְנִיס לַבַּיִת פֵּרוֹת הַקַּיִץ. דָּבָר אַחֵר, "בְּאָסְפְּךָ מִגָּרְנְךָ וּמִיִּקְבֶךָ", לִמֵּד שֶׁמְּסַכְּכִין אֶת הַסֻּכָּה בִּפְסֹלֶת גֹּרֶן וָיֶקֶב:

טו **וְהָיִיתָ אַךְ שָׂמֵחַ.** לְפִי פְּשׁוּטוֹ אֵין זֶה לְשׁוֹן צִוּוּי אֶלָּא לְשׁוֹן הַבְטָחָה. וּלְפִי תַּלְמוּדוֹ לָמְדוּ מִכָּאן לְרַבּוֹת לֵילֵי יוֹם טוֹב הָאַחֲרוֹן לְשִׂמְחָה:

טז **וְלֹא יֵרָאֶה אֶת פְּנֵי ה' רֵיקָם.** אֶלָּא הָבֵא עוֹלוֹת רְאִיָּה וְשַׁלְמֵי חֲגִיגָה:

יז **אִישׁ כְּמַתְּנַת יָדוֹ.** מִי שֶׁיֵּשׁ לוֹ אוֹכְלִין הַרְבֵּה וּנְכָסִים מְרֻבִּים יָבִיא עוֹלוֹת מְרֻבּוֹת וּשְׁלָמִים מְרֻבִּים:

It represents not a positive event, but forty years of wandering in the wilderness without a permanent home. A sukka is, by halakhic definition, a temporary dwelling. Sukkot, when we live for seven days in a hut with only leaves for a roof, exposed to the wind, cold, and rain, is the festival of insecurity. Nonetheless, it is, supremely, the "time of our joy."

There is something profoundly spiritual about our capacity to live in a state of total insecurity and yet feel the joy of simply being, under the shelter of the Divine Presence. Yes, there is danger, risk, uncertainty, vulnerability. But we are here, with a world to live in, family and friends to love and be loved by, and we are not alone, for with us is the Torah, God's unbreakable word, and though we walk through the valley of the shadow, we walk toward the redemptive light.

י תָּחֵל לִסְפֹּר שִׁבְעָה שָׁבֻעוֹת: וְעָשִׂיתָ חַג שָׁבֻעוֹת לַיהוָה אֱלֹהֶיךָ
יא מִסַּת נִדְבַת יָדְךָ אֲשֶׁר תִּתֵּן כַּאֲשֶׁר יְבָרֶכְךָ יהוָה אֱלֹהֶיךָ: וְשָׂמַחְתָּ
לִפְנֵי | יהוָה אֱלֹהֶיךָ אַתָּה וּבִנְךָ וּבִתֶּךָ וְעַבְדְּךָ וַאֲמָתֶךָ וְהַלֵּוִי אֲשֶׁר
בִּשְׁעָרֶיךָ וְהַגֵּר וְהַיָּתוֹם וְהָאַלְמָנָה אֲשֶׁר בְּקִרְבֶּךָ בַּמָּקוֹם אֲשֶׁר יִבְחַר
יב יהוָה אֱלֹהֶיךָ לְשַׁכֵּן שְׁמוֹ שָׁם: וְזָכַרְתָּ כִּי־עֶבֶד הָיִיתָ בְּמִצְרָיִם וְשָׁמַרְתָּ
וְעָשִׂיתָ אֶת־הַחֻקִּים הָאֵלֶּה:
יג יד חַג הַסֻּכֹּת תַּעֲשֶׂה לְךָ שִׁבְעַת יָמִים בְּאָסְפְּךָ מִגָּרְנְךָ וּמִיִּקְבֶךָ: וְשָׂמַחְתָּ מפטיר
בְּחַגֶּךָ אַתָּה וּבִנְךָ וּבִתֶּךָ וְעַבְדְּךָ וַאֲמָתֶךָ וְהַלֵּוִי וְהַגֵּר וְהַיָּתוֹם וְהָאַלְמָנָה
טו אֲשֶׁר בִּשְׁעָרֶיךָ: שִׁבְעַת יָמִים תָּחֹג לַיהוָה אֱלֹהֶיךָ בַּמָּקוֹם אֲשֶׁר־יִבְחַר
יהוָה כִּי יְבָרֶכְךָ יהוָה אֱלֹהֶיךָ בְּכֹל תְּבוּאָתְךָ וּבְכֹל מַעֲשֵׂה יָדֶיךָ וְהָיִיתָ
טז אַךְ שָׂמֵחַ: שָׁלוֹשׁ פְּעָמִים | בַּשָּׁנָה יֵרָאֶה כָל־זְכוּרְךָ אֶת־פְּנֵי | יהוָה אֱלֹהֶיךָ
בַּמָּקוֹם אֲשֶׁר יִבְחָר בְּחַג הַמַּצּוֹת וּבְחַג הַשָּׁבֻעוֹת וּבְחַג הַסֻּכּוֹת וְלֹא
יז יֵרָאֶה אֶת־פְּנֵי יהוָה רֵיקָם: אִישׁ כְּמַתְּנַת יָדוֹ כְּבִרְכַּת יהוָה אֱלֹהֶיךָ אֲשֶׁר
נָתַן־לָךְ:

The הפטרה *for* פרשת ראה *is on page 1615.*
This הפטרה *is read even on* ערב ראש חודש אלול*. On* ראש חודש אלול*,*
אשכנזים *read the* הפטרה *on page 1635, while* ספרדים *read this* הפטרה*.*

אונקלוס

תִּשְׁרֵי לְמִמְנֵי, שִׁבְעָא שָׁבוּעִין: י וְתַעֲבֵיד, חַגָּא דְּשָׁבוּעַיָּא קֳדָם יְיָ אֱלָהָךְ, מִסַּת, נִדְבַת יְדָךְ דְּתִתֵּין, כְּמָא דִּיבָרְכִנָּךְ יְיָ אֱלָהָךְ: יא וְתִחְדֵּי, קֳדָם יְיָ אֱלָהָךְ, אַתְּ וּבְרָךְ וּבְרַתָּךְ וְעַבְדָּךְ וְאַמְתָךְ, וְלֵיוָאָה דִּבְקִרְוָךְ, וְגִיּוֹרָא, וְיַתְמָא וְאַרְמַלְתָּא דְּבֵינָךְ, בְּאַתְרָא, דְּיִתְרְעֵי יְיָ אֱלָהָךְ, לְאַשְׁרָאָה שְׁכִינְתֵיהּ תַּמָּן: יב וְתִדְכַּר, אֲרֵי עַבְדָּא הֲוֵיתָא בְּמִצְרָיִם, וְתִטַּר וְתַעֲבֵיד, יָת קְיָמַיָּא הָאִלֵּין: יג חַגָּא דִמְטַלַּיָּא, תַּעֲבֵיד לָךְ שִׁבְעָא יוֹמִין, בְּמִכְנְשָׁךְ, מֵאִדְּרָךְ וּמִמַּעֲצַרְתָּךְ: יד וְתִחְדֵּי בְּחַגָּךְ, אַתְּ וּבְרָךְ וּבְרַתָּךְ וְעַבְדָּךְ וְאַמְתָךְ, וְלֵיוָאָה, וְגִיּוֹרָא, וְיַתְמָא וְאַרְמַלְתָּא דִּבְקִרְוָךְ: טו שִׁבְעָא יוֹמִין, תֵּיחוֹג קֳדָם יְיָ אֱלָהָךְ, בְּאַתְרָא דְּיִתְרְעֵי יְיָ, אֲרֵי יְבָרְכִנָּךְ יְיָ אֱלָהָךְ, בְּכָל עֲלַלְתָּךְ וּבְכָל עוּבָדֵי יְדָךְ, וּתְהֵי בְּרַם חָדֵי: טז תְּלָת זִמְנִין בְּשַׁתָּא, יִתַּחְזוֹן כָּל דְּכוּרָךְ, קֳדָם יְיָ אֱלָהָךְ, בְּאַתְרָא דְּיִתְרְעֵי, בְּחַגָּא דְפַטִּירַיָּא, וּבְחַגָּא דְּשָׁבוּעַיָּא וּבְחַגָּא דִמְטַלַּיָּא, וְלָא יִתַּחְזוֹן, קֳדָם יְיָ רֵיקָנִין: יז גְּבַר כְּמַתְּנַת יְדֵיהּ, כְּבִרְכְּתָא, דַּייָ אֱלָהָךְ דִּיהַב לָךְ:

16:15 וְהָיִיתָ אַךְ שָׂמֵחַ *You shall be wholly joyful* – The verb "to rejoice" appears three times in the *parasha* in connection with a festival: not at all in connection with Passover, once in relation to Shavuot, but twice in connection with Sukkot: "Rejoice in your festival… and you shall be wholly joyful" (Deut. 16:14–15). It is for this reason that Sukkot (and Shemini Atzeret) are called *zeman simḥatenu*, "the time of our joy."

This is counterintuitive. We could understand why Passover should be a festival of joy: it recalls our ancestors' liberation from slavery. Shavuot celebrates the giving of the Torah, God's great gift to us as a people. But why Sukkot?

▶

Parashat Shofetim

16 18 Appoint judges and officials for your tribes in all the towns that the Lord
19 your God is giving you, to govern the people with equitable justice. Do not
pervert justice or show partiality. Do not take bribes, for bribes blind the
20 eyes of the wise and subvert the cause of the just. Pursue justice, only justice,
so that you may live and possess the land that the Lord your God is giving

רש"י

יח **שֹׁפְטִים וְשֹׁטְרִים.** "שֹׁפְטִים" דַּיָּנִים הַפּוֹסְקִים אֶת הַדִּין, "וְשֹׁטְרִים" הָרוֹדִין אֶת הָעָם אַחַר מִצְוָתָם, שֶׁמַּכִּין וְכוֹפְתִין בְּמַקֵּל וּבִרְצוּעָה עַד שֶׁיְּקַבֵּל עָלָיו אֶת דִּין הַשּׁוֹפֵט: **בְּכָל שְׁעָרֶיךָ.** בְּכָל עִיר וָעִיר: **לִשְׁבָטֶיךָ.** מוּסָב עַל "תִּתֶּן לְךָ": שֹׁפְטִים וְשֹׁטְרִים תִּתֶּן לְךָ לִשְׁבָטֶיךָ בְּכָל שְׁעָרֶיךָ אֲשֶׁר ה' אֱלֹהֶיךָ נֹתֵן לְךָ: **לִשְׁבָטֶיךָ.** מְלַמֵּד שֶׁמּוֹשִׁיבִין דַּיָּנִין לְכָל שֵׁבֶט וָשֵׁבֶט וּבְכָל עִיר וָעִיר: **וְשָׁפְטוּ אֶת הָעָם וְגוֹ'.** מַנֵּה דַּיָּנִין מֻמְחִים וְצַדִּיקִים לִשְׁפֹּט צֶדֶק:

יט **לֹא תַטֶּה מִשְׁפָּט.** כְּמַשְׁמָעוֹ: **לֹא תַכִּיר פָּנִים.** אַף בִּשְׁעַת הַטְּעָנוֹת, שֶׁלֹּא יְהֵא רַךְ לָזֶה וְקָשֶׁה לָזֶה, אֶחָד עוֹמֵד וְאֶחָד יוֹשֵׁב, לְפִי שֶׁכְּשֶׁרוֹאֶה זֶה שֶׁהַדַּיָּן מְכַבֵּד אֶת חֲבֵרוֹ מִסְתַּתְּמִין טַעֲנוֹתָיו: **וְלֹא תִקַּח שֹׁחַד.** אֲפִלּוּ לִשְׁפֹּט צֶדֶק: **כִּי הַשֹּׁחַד יְעַוֵּר.** מִשֶּׁקִּבֵּל שֹׁחַד מִמֶּנּוּ, אִי אֶפְשָׁר שֶׁלֹּא יַטֶּה אֶת לִבּוֹ אֶצְלוֹ לַהֲפֹךְ בִּזְכוּתוֹ: **דִּבְרֵי צַדִּיקִם.** דְּבָרִים הַמְצֻדָּקִים, מִשְׁפְּטֵי אֱמֶת:

כ **צֶדֶק צֶדֶק תִּרְדֹּף.** הֵלֵךְ אַחַר בֵּית דִּין יָפֶה: **לְמַעַן תִּחְיֶה וְיָרַשְׁתָּ.** כְּדַאי הוּא מִנּוּי הַדַּיָּנִין הַכְּשֵׁרִים לְהַחֲיוֹת אֶת יִשְׂרָאֵל וּלְהוֹשִׁיבָן עַל אַדְמָתָן:

another to witness someone committing a crime and fail to prevent it.

Ramban's position, and Yaakov's in Genesis, was that Shimon and Levi may have been right in thinking that the men of Shekhem were guilty of doing nothing when their prince abducted and assaulted Dina, but that does not mean that they were entitled to execute summary justice by killing all the males. Bystander guilt, though real, cannot be reduced to legal categories; this subject will be addressed at the end of the *parasha* (Deut. 21:1–9; see commentary there). On the other hand, the responsibility of society to set up an effective and equitable justice system is so fundamental an ethical principle that it is incumbent not only on Israel, but on all the descendants of Noaḥ.

"Pursue Justice"

For Jews, and not only Jews, the religious voice is above all a moral voice. Avraham is chosen so that he will instruct his children "to do righteousness and justice." Yeshayahu begins his prophetic mission with the most powerful speech ever made against the idea that you can serve God in the house of prayer while ignoring Him in the marketplace. Mikha sums up the religious quest in three imperatives: "To do justice, love goodness, and walk modestly with your God" (Mic. 6:8). And here in the text of the covenant, Moshe tells the Israelites, "Pursue justice, only justice."

No idea in the Hebrew Bible has been more influential than this, that society is founded on a moral covenant between its members, vested in an authority that transcends all earthly powers, and whose most famous symbol is the Ten Commandments engraved in stone. Law as envisaged by the Torah makes no distinction between rich and poor, powerful and powerless, home-born or stranger. Equality before the law is the translation into human terms of equality before God. Time and again the Torah insists that justice is not a human artifact: "Do not be intimidated by any man, for judgment belongs to God" (Deut. 1:17). Because it belongs to God, it must never be compromised – by intimidation, bribery, or favoritism. It is an inalienable right and also an inescapable duty – something that must be pursued actively.

One might suppose that the divinity of justice reduces our accountability for justice on earth. God exists, therefore the universe is just. We, however, are human, and God

פרשת שפטים

טז יח שֹׁפְטִים וְשֹׁטְרִים תִּתֶּן־לְךָ בְּכָל־שְׁעָרֶיךָ אֲשֶׁר יהוה אֱלֹהֶיךָ נֹתֵן לְךָ יד
יט לִשְׁבָטֶיךָ וְשָׁפְטוּ אֶת־הָעָם מִשְׁפַּט־צֶדֶק: לֹא־תַטֶּה מִשְׁפָּט לֹא
תַכִּיר פָּנִים וְלֹא־תִקַּח שֹׁחַד כִּי הַשֹּׁחַד יְעַוֵּר עֵינֵי חֲכָמִים וִיסַלֵּף דִּבְרֵי
כ צַדִּיקִם: צֶדֶק צֶדֶק תִּרְדֹּף לְמַעַן תִּחְיֶה וְיָרַשְׁתָּ אֶת־הָאָרֶץ אֲשֶׁר־

אונקלוס

יח דַּיָּנִין וּפְרְעָנִין, תְּמַנֵּי לָךְ בְּכָל קִרְוָךְ, דַּיי אֱלָהָךְ, יָהֵיב לָךְ
לְשִׁבְטָךְ, וִידִינוּן יָת עַמָּא דִּין דִּקְשׁוֹט: יט לָא תַצְלֵי דִּין, לָא
תִשְׁתְּמוֹדַע אַפִּין, וְלָא תְקַבֵּיל שֹׁחְדָא, אֲרֵי שֹׁחְדָא, מְעַוַּר עֵינֵי
חַכִּימִין, וּמְקַלְקֵיל פִּתְגָּמִין תְּרִיצִין: כ קֻשְׁטָא קֻשְׁטָא תִּרְדּוֹף,
בְּדִיל דְּתֵיחֵי וְתֵירַת יָת אַרְעָא,

SHOFETIM

Having dealt with many of the aspects of worship in the Promised Land, Moshe now turns to the institutions of governance. He begins with the overarching imperative of justice: there must be courts, judges, and officers in every city. Justice must be accessible and impartial. Procedures must be followed for the prosecution of idolatry, and there is to be a supreme court to deal with hard cases.

There are to be three main types of leaders: a king, priests and Levites, and prophets. Warnings are issued against sorcery and witchcraft, and against false prophets. Cities of refuge are to be provided as sanctuaries for those who kill accidentally or unintentionally. Conspiring witnesses who testify falsely are to be punished.

Moshe then turns to the laws of warfare. The *parasha,* which has covered several aspects of the criminal law process, concludes with the atonement procedure to be followed in the case of an unsolved murder.

16:18 שֹׁפְטִים... תִּתֶּן־לְךָ *Appoint judges* – In his law code, the Mishneh Torah, Rambam explains that the establishment of justice and the rule of law is one of the seven Laws of Noaḥ, binding on all humanity:

> And how are the Gentiles commanded to establish law courts? They are required to establish judges and officers in every area of habitation to rule in accordance with the enforcement of the other six commands, to warn the citizenry concerning these laws and to punish any transgressor with death by the sword. And it is on this basis that all the people of Shekhem were liable to execution [at the hands of Shimon and Levi, sons of Yaakov]: because Shekhem [their prince] stole [and raped] Dina, which they saw and knew about, but did not bring him to justice. (*Hilkhot Melakhim UMilḥemoteihem* 9:14)

According to Rambam, the universal requirement to establish courts expresses a principle of collective responsibility. The inhabitants of Shekhem, knowing that their prince had committed a crime and failing to bring him to court, were collectively guilty of injustice. We are responsible not only for our own conduct but for those around us, amongst whom we live. Or perhaps this flows not from the concept of society but simply from the nature of moral obligation. If X is wrong, then not only must I not do it. I must, if I can, stop others from doing it, and if I fail to do so, then I share in the guilt. We would call this nowadays the guilt of the bystander. Clearly, however, the issue is a complex one that needs nuance. There is a difference between a perpetrator and a bystander. It is one thing to commit a crime,

21 you. Do not plant a sacred tree of any kind beside the altar that you
22 make for the LORD your God, and do not erect a worship pillar, for these are
17 1 things that the LORD your God hates. Do not sacrifice an ox or a sheep
that has any blemish, any serious defect, to the LORD your God, for that to the
2 LORD your God would be abhorrent. If a man or woman living among
you in one of the towns the LORD your God is giving you is found doing what is
3 evil in the LORD your God's eyes, breaking His covenant by going off to serve or
bow to other gods – the sun or moon or any of the heavenly host, which I have
4 forbidden – if you have been told of this or have heard about it, then you must
make thorough inquiry. If it is true and is confirmed that this abhorrent deed has
5 been done in Israel, then you shall take the man or woman who has done this

רש״י

כא **לֹא תִטַּע לְךָ אֲשֵׁרָה.** לְחַיְּבוֹ עָלֶיהָ מִשְּׁעַת נְטִיעָתָהּ, וַאֲפִלּוּ לֹא עֲבָדָהּ עוֹבֵר בְּלֹא תַעֲשֶׂה עַל נְטִיעָתָהּ. וְ״לֹא תִטַּע לְךָ... כָּל עֵץ אֵצֶל מִזְבַּח״ – אַזְהָרָה לְנוֹטֵעַ אִילָן וּלְבוֹנֶה בַּיִת בְּהַר הַבַּיִת:

כב **וְלֹא תָקִים לְךָ מַצֵּבָה.** מַצֵּבָה, אֶבֶן אַחַת לְהַקְרִיב עָלֶיהָ, אֲפִלּוּ לַשָּׁמַיִם: **אֲשֶׁר שָׂנֵא.** מִזְבַּח אֲבָנִים וּמִזְבַּח אֲדָמָה צִוָּה לַעֲשׂוֹת, וְאֶת זוֹ שָׂנֵא, כִּי חֹק הָיְתָה לַכְּנַעֲנִים. וְאַף עַל פִּי שֶׁהָיְתָה אֲהוּבָה לוֹ בִּימֵי הָאָבוֹת, עַכְשָׁיו שְׂנֵאָהּ, מֵאַחַר שֶׁעֲשָׂאוּהָ אֵלּוּ חֹק לַעֲבוֹדָה זָרָה:

יז א **לֹא תִזְבַּח וְגוֹ׳ כָּל דָּבָר רָע.** אַזְהָרָה לִמְפַגֵּל בַּקֳּדָשִׁים עַל יְדֵי דִּבּוּר רָע. וְעוֹד נִדְרְשׁוּ בוֹ שְׁאָר דְּרָשׁוֹת בִּשְׁחִיטַת קָדָשִׁים:

ב **לַעֲבֹר בְּרִיתוֹ.** אֲשֶׁר כָּרַת ה׳ אִתְּכֶם שֶׁלֹּא לַעֲבֹד עֲבוֹדָה זָרָה:

ג **אֲשֶׁר לֹא צִוִּיתִי.** לַעֲבֹד:

ד **נָכוֹן.** מְכֻוָּן הָעֵדוּת:

ה **וְהוֹצֵאתָ אֶת הָאִישׁ הַהוּא וְגוֹ׳ אֶל שְׁעָרֶיךָ.** הַמְתַרְגֵּם ״אֶל שְׁעָרֶיךָ״ – ׳לִתְרַע בֵּית דִּינָךְ׳ טוֹעֶה, שֶׁכֵּן שָׁנִינוּ: ״אֶל שְׁעָרֶיךָ״ זֶה שַׁעַר שֶׁעָבַד בּוֹ, אוֹ אֵינוֹ אֶלָּא שַׁעַר שֶׁנִּדּוֹן בּוֹ? נֶאֱמַר ״שְׁעָרֶיךָ״ לְמַטָּה וְנֶאֱמַר ״שְׁעָרֶיךָ״ לְמַעְלָה (לעיל פסוק ב), מָה ״שְׁעָרֶיךָ״ הָאָמוּר לְמַעְלָה שַׁעַר שֶׁעָבַד בּוֹ, אַף ״שְׁעָרֶיךָ״ הָאָמוּר לְמַטָּה שַׁעַר שֶׁעָבַד בּוֹ. וְתַרְגּוּמוֹ: ״לְקִרְוָךְ״:

He has challenged humanity to create a world that will be a home for Him. God lives wherever we treat one another as beings in His image.

17:3 וַיֵּלֶךְ וַיַּעֲבֹד *By going off to serve* – "Evil" in the Torah is often framed not as an act of striking out alone, but as a form of obedience to the wrong gods, an irresistible temptation likely to foster a similar temptation in others. God's call, in contrast, is almost inaudible. But it is there, and if, from time to time throughout our lives, we create a silence in the soul, we will hear it.

Sin is rarely original, but a good deed sometimes is. Just as every life has a task, so every day brings an opportunity. If we are where we are because God wanted us to be, then there must be, in every situation, something He wants us to do, some act of redemption He wants us to perform. I found the best way of knowing what it is, is to turn the situation upside down. I used to hope that people would praise my work; then I realized that what I was here to do was to praise the work of others. There were times when, in crisis, I would await the reassuring word from a friend, until I suddenly saw that I should be the one giving reassurance. The discovery changed my life. That was when I knew that we experience pain to sensitize us to the pain of others. Turning our emotions outward, we can use them as the key to free someone else from the locked room of suffering or disappointment or grief.

God commands in generalities but calls in particulars. He knows our gifts and he knows the needs of the world. That is why we are here. There is an act only we can do, and only at this time, and that is our task. To miss God's quiet call amid the clamour of other temptations would be to overlook the meaning of our life, the purpose of our existence.

כא יְהוָה אֱלֹהֶיךָ נֹתֵן לָךְ׃ לֹא־תִטַּע לְךָ אֲשֵׁרָה כָּל־עֵץ
כב אֵצֶל מִזְבַּח יְהוָה אֱלֹהֶיךָ אֲשֶׁר תַּעֲשֶׂה־לָּךְ׃ וְלֹא־תָקִים לְךָ מַצֵּבָה
יז א אֲשֶׁר שָׂנֵא יְהוָה אֱלֹהֶיךָ׃ לֹא־תִזְבַּח לַיהוָה אֱלֹהֶיךָ
שׁוֹר וָשֶׂה אֲשֶׁר יִהְיֶה בוֹ מוּם כֹּל דָּבָר רָע כִּי תוֹעֲבַת יְהוָה אֱלֹהֶיךָ
ב הוּא׃ כִּי־יִמָּצֵא בְקִרְבְּךָ בְּאַחַד שְׁעָרֶיךָ אֲשֶׁר־יְהוָה
אֱלֹהֶיךָ נֹתֵן לָךְ אִישׁ אוֹ־אִשָּׁה אֲשֶׁר יַעֲשֶׂה אֶת־הָרַע בְּעֵינֵי יְהוָה־
ג אֱלֹהֶיךָ לַעֲבֹר בְּרִיתוֹ׃ וַיֵּלֶךְ וַיַּעֲבֹד אֱלֹהִים אֲחֵרִים וַיִּשְׁתַּחוּ לָהֶם
ד וְלַשֶּׁמֶשׁ ׀ אוֹ לַיָּרֵחַ אוֹ לְכָל־צְבָא הַשָּׁמַיִם אֲשֶׁר לֹא־צִוִּיתִי׃ וְהֻגַּד־לְךָ
וְשָׁמָעְתָּ וְדָרַשְׁתָּ הֵיטֵב וְהִנֵּה אֱמֶת נָכוֹן הַדָּבָר נֶעֶשְׂתָה הַתּוֹעֵבָה
ה הַזֹּאת בְּיִשְׂרָאֵל׃ וְהוֹצֵאתָ אֶת־הָאִישׁ הַהוּא אוֹ אֶת־הָאִשָּׁה הַהִוא
אֲשֶׁר עָשׂוּ אֶת־הַדָּבָר הָרָע הַזֶּה אֶל־שְׁעָרֶיךָ אֶת־הָאִישׁ אוֹ אֶת־

אונקלוס

דַּיי אֱלָהָךְ יָהֵיב לָךְ׃ כא לָא תִצּוֹב לָךְ, אֲשֵׁירַת כָּל אִילָן, בִּסְטַר,
מַדְבְּחָא, דַּיי אֱלָהָךְ דְּתַעְבֵּיד לָךְ׃ כב וְלָא תְקִים לָךְ קָמָא, דְּרָחֵיק
יי אֱלָהָךְ׃ יז א לָא תִכּוֹס קֳדָם יי אֱלָהָךְ תּוֹר וְאִמַּר, דִּיהֵי בֵיהּ
מוּמָא, כָּל מִדַּעַם בִּישׁ, אֲרֵי מְרַחַק, קֳדָם יי אֱלָהָךְ הוּא׃ ב אֲרֵי
יִשְׁתְּכַח בֵּינָךְ בַּחֲדָא מִן קִרְוָךְ, דַּיי אֱלָהָךְ יָהֵיב לָךְ, גְּבַר אוֹ אִתְּא,
דְּיַעְבֵּיד יָת דְּבִישׁ, קֳדָם יי אֱלָהָךְ לְמִעְבַּר עַל קְיָמֵיהּ׃ ג וַאֲזַל,
וּפְלַח לְטָעֲוַת עַמְמַיָּא, וּסְגֵיד לְהוֹן, וּלְשִׁמְשָׁא אוֹ לְסִיהֲרָא, אוֹ,
לְכָל חֵילֵי שְׁמַיָּא דְּלָא פַקֵּידִית׃ ד וְיִתְחַוָּא לָךְ וְתִשְׁמַע, וְתִתְבַּע
יָאוּת, וְהָא קֻשְׁטָא כֵּיוָן פִּתְגָּמָא, אִתְעֲבֵידַת, תּוֹעֵיבְתָּא הָדָא
בְּיִשְׂרָאֵל׃ ה וְתַפֵּיק יָת גַּבְרָא הַהוּא, אוֹ יָת אִתְּתָא הַהִיא,
דַּעֲבַדוּ, יָת פִּתְגָּמָא בִּישָׁא הָדֵין לְקִרְוָךְ, יָת גַּבְרָא, אוֹ יָת

has empowered us to seek the justice that is human – not justice from the point of view of the universe and eternity but from the point of view of the fallible, frail, ephemeral, vulnerable beings that we are. We who live in space and time cannot but see injustice. We cannot know the rewards of a life beyond the grave. Our pain is not made less by the belief that it is necessary for the good of the whole. Still less is it made bearable that it is justified as punishment for sin. That – as Iyov's comforters belatedly discovered – is not a form of comfort but a double affliction. In the book of Job (42:7), the comforters who defend the justice of God are condemned by God Himself, because He asks of us *not* to take His part but to be human, defending one another, as Avraham defended Sedom, in the name of human solidarity.

God in making humanity conferred on us the right and duty to see things from a human point of view. If evil exists within our horizons, then it is real no matter how limited those horizons are. Making us human, not divine, God calls on us to judge and act within the terms of our humanity. "The Torah was not given to ministering angels," said the Sages (Berakhot 25b). It was given to human beings, and the justice it asks us to fight for is human justice.

Underlying all this is a proposition which even today has not lost its power to surprise and inspire. In the beginning God created the world as a home for humanity. Since then

6 evil act out to the town gates and stone that man or that woman to death. The
accused shall be put to death only on the testimony of two or three witnesses; no
7 one shall be put to death on the evidence of one witness alone. The hand of the
witnesses shall be the first against him to kill him, and after theirs, the hand of all
the people. You must purge the evil from your midst.
8 If a case is beyond your judgment, be it a conflict over bloodshed, over civil
claims or over injury – any dispute in your town courts – then you shall go up
9 to the place that the Lord your God will choose. There you shall approach the
Levitical priests or the judge who is in office at that time. Inquire of them and
10 they will give you the verdict. You must act in accordance with the ruling they
give you from the place that the Lord will choose, taking care to do exactly as
11 they instruct you. You shall act in accord with the Law as they interpret it for
you and the judgment as they tell you, not deviating from their declaration to
12 the right or to the left. Should anyone act in wickedness, refusing to listen to
the priest appointed to minister there to the Lord your God, or the judge, that

רש״י

ו **שְׁנַיִם עֵדִים אוֹ שְׁלֹשָׁה.** אִם מִתְקַיֶּמֶת עֵדוּת בִּשְׁנַיִם, לָמָּה פֵּרֵט לְךָ שְׁלֹשָׁה? לְהַקִּישׁ שְׁלֹשָׁה לִשְׁנַיִם, מַה שְּׁנַיִם עֵדוּת אַחַת, אַף שְׁלֹשָׁה עֵדוּת אַחַת, וְאֵין נַעֲשִׂין זוֹמְמִין עַד שֶׁיּוּזַמּוּ כֻּלָּם:

ח **כִּי יִפָּלֵא.** כָּל הַפְלָאָה לְשׁוֹן הַבְדָּלָה וּפְרִישָׁה, שֶׁהַדָּבָר נִבְדָּל וּמְכֻסֶּה מִמְּךָ: **בֵּין דָּם לְדָם.** בֵּין דָּם טָמֵא לְדָם טָהוֹר: **בֵּין דִּין לְדִין.** בֵּין דִּין זַכַּאי לְדִין חַיָּב: **וּבֵין נֶגַע לָנֶגַע.** בֵּין נֶגַע טָמֵא לְנֶגַע טָהוֹר: **דִּבְרֵי רִיבֹת.** שֶׁיִּהְיוּ חַכְמֵי הָעִיר חוֹלְקִים בַּדָּבָר, זֶה מְטַמֵּא וְזֶה מְטַהֵר, זֶה מְחַיֵּב וְזֶה מְזַכֶּה: **וְקַמְתָּ וְעָלִיתָ.** מְלַמֵּד שֶׁבֵּית הַמִּקְדָּשׁ גָּבוֹהַּ מִכָּל הַמְּקוֹמוֹת:

ט **הַכֹּהֲנִים הַלְוִיִּם.** הַכֹּהֲנִים שֶׁיָּצְאוּ מִשֵּׁבֶט לֵוִי: **וְאֶל הַשֹּׁפֵט אֲשֶׁר יִהְיֶה בַּיָּמִים הָהֵם.** אֲפִלּוּ אֵינוֹ כִּשְׁאָר שׁוֹפְטִים שֶׁהָיוּ לְפָנָיו, אַתָּה צָרִיךְ לִשְׁמֹעַ לוֹ, אֵין לְךָ אֶלָּא שׁוֹפֵט שֶׁבְּיָמֶיךָ:

יא **יָמִין וּשְׂמֹאל.** אֲפִלּוּ אוֹמֵר לְךָ עַל יָמִין שֶׁהוּא שְׂמֹאל וְעַל שְׂמֹאל שֶׁהוּא יָמִין, וְכָל שֶׁכֵּן שֶׁאוֹמֵר לְךָ עַל יָמִין יָמִין וְעַל שְׂמֹאל שְׂמֹאל:

forward-looking, the bringing to bear of considered experience on decisions we have to make.

We sometimes confuse this with judgment in a second sense, a metaphorical extension of what judges do, as here, in court. They pass a verdict. They acquit or condemn. Moral judgment in this second sense is, as it were, passing a sentence, outside a court of law, on what we or other people have done. It is backward-looking, after the event. We are reluctant, today, to be judgmental in this second sense. But so we were always taught to be. "Do not judge your fellow human being until you have been in his place," said the Rabbis (Avot 2:4).

There is a difference between righteousness and self-righteousness. The righteous are humble; the self-righteous are proud. The righteous understand doubt, the self-righteous only certainty. The righteous see the good in people, the self-righteous only the bad. The righteous leave you feeling enlarged; the self-righteous make you feel small.

King Shlomo, acceding to the throne, is said by the Bible to have been granted one wish. He asked not for wealth or long life or the defeat of his enemies but simply this: "Grant Your servant an understanding heart to judge Your people, to distinguish between good and evil" (I Kings 3:9). In the siddur, "knowledge, understanding, and discernment" are the things we pray for before all else. This is the "good judgment" we seek in our teachers and leaders, and even in our individualistic age it would be a mistake to dismiss it.

ו הָאִשָּׁה וּסְקַלְתָּם בָּאֲבָנִים וָמֵתוּ׃ עַל־פִּי ׀ שְׁנַיִם עֵדִים אוֹ שְׁלֹשָׁה עֵדִים
ז יוּמַת הַמֵּת לֹא יוּמַת עַל־פִּי עֵד אֶחָד׃ יַד הָעֵדִים תִּהְיֶה־בּוֹ בָרִאשֹׁנָה
לַהֲמִיתוֹ וְיַד כָּל־הָעָם בָּאַחֲרֹנָה וּבִעַרְתָּ הָרָע מִקִּרְבֶּךָ׃
ח כִּי יִפָּלֵא מִמְּךָ דָבָר לַמִּשְׁפָּט בֵּין־דָּם ׀ לְדָם בֵּין־דִּין לְדִין וּבֵין נֶגַע לָנֶגַע
דִּבְרֵי רִיבֹת בִּשְׁעָרֶיךָ וְקַמְתָּ וְעָלִיתָ אֶל־הַמָּקוֹם אֲשֶׁר יִבְחַר יהוה
ט אֱלֹהֶיךָ בּוֹ׃ וּבָאתָ אֶל־הַכֹּהֲנִים הַלְוִיִּם וְאֶל־הַשֹּׁפֵט אֲשֶׁר יִהְיֶה בַּיָּמִים
י הָהֵם וְדָרַשְׁתָּ וְהִגִּידוּ לְךָ אֵת דְּבַר הַמִּשְׁפָּט׃ וְעָשִׂיתָ עַל־פִּי הַדָּבָר
אֲשֶׁר יַגִּידוּ לְךָ מִן־הַמָּקוֹם הַהוּא אֲשֶׁר יִבְחַר יהוה וְשָׁמַרְתָּ לַעֲשׂוֹת
יא כְּכֹל אֲשֶׁר יוֹרוּךָ׃ עַל־פִּי הַתּוֹרָה אֲשֶׁר יוֹרוּךָ וְעַל־הַמִּשְׁפָּט אֲשֶׁר־
יֹאמְרוּ לְךָ תַּעֲשֶׂה לֹא תָסוּר מִן־הַדָּבָר אֲשֶׁר־יַגִּידוּ לְךָ יָמִין וּשְׂמֹאל׃
יב וְהָאִישׁ אֲשֶׁר־יַעֲשֶׂה בְזָדוֹן לְבִלְתִּי שְׁמֹעַ אֶל־הַכֹּהֵן הָעֹמֵד לְשָׁרֶת
שָׁם אֶת־יהוה אֱלֹהֶיךָ אוֹ אֶל־הַשֹּׁפֵט וּמֵת הָאִישׁ הַהוּא וּבִעַרְתָּ הָרָע

אונקלוס

אִתְּתָא, וְתִרְגְּמִנּוּן בְּאַבְנַיָּא וִימוּתוּן: ו עַל מֵימַר תְּרֵין סָהֲדִין, אוֹ, תְּלָתָא סָהֲדִין יִתְקְטִיל דְּחַיָּב קְטוֹל, לָא יִתְקְטִיל, עַל מֵימַר סָהִיד חַד: ז יְדָא דְּסָהֲדַיָּא, תְּהֵי בֵיהּ בְּקַדְמֵיתָא לְמִקְטְלֵיהּ, וִידָא דְּכָל עַמָּא בְּבָתְרֵיתָא, וּתְפַלֵּי עָבֵיד דְּבִישׁ מִבֵּינָךְ: ח אֲרֵי יִתְפָּרַשׁ מִנָּךְ פִּתְגָּמָא לְדִינָא, בֵּין דַּם לְדַם בֵּין דִּין לְדִין, וּבֵין מַכְתַּשׁ סְגִירוּ לְמַכְתַּשׁ סְגִירוּ, פִּתְגָּמֵי פְּלֻגַּת דִּינָא בְּקִרְוָךְ, וּתְקוּם וְתִסַּק, לְאַתְרָא, דְּיִתְרְעֵי, יְיָ אֱלָהָךְ בֵּיהּ: ט וְתֵיתֵי, לְוָת כָּהֲנַיָּא לֵיוָאֵי, וּלְוָת דַּיָּנָא, דִּיהֵי בְּיוֹמַיָּא הָאִנּוּן, וְתִתְבַּע וִיחַוּוֹן לָךְ, יָת פִּתְגָּמָא דְּדִינָא: י וְתַעְבֵּיד, עַל מֵימַר פִּתְגָּמָא דִּיחַוּוֹן לָךְ, מִן אַתְרָא הַהוּא, דְּיִתְרְעֵי יְיָ, וְתִטַּר לְמֶעְבַּד, כְּכֹל דְּיַלְּפֻנָּךְ: יא עַל מֵימַר אוֹרָיְתָא דְּיַלְּפֻנָּךְ, וְעַל דִּינָא, דְּיֵימְרוּן לָךְ תַּעְבֵּיד, לָא תִסְטֵי, מִן פִּתְגָּמָא, דִּיחַוּוֹן לָךְ לְיַמִּינָא וְלִסְמָאלָא: יב וְגַבְרָא דְּיַעְבֵּיד בְּרֶשַׁע, בְּדִיל דְּלָא לְקַבָּלָא מִן כָּהֲנָא דְּקָאֵים, לְשַׁמָּשָׁא תַמָּן קֳדָם יְיָ אֱלָהָךְ, אוֹ מִן דַּיָּנָא, וְיִתְקְטִיל גַּבְרָא הַהוּא, וּתְפַלֵּי עָבֵיד דְּבִישׁ

17:9 וְדָרַשְׁתָּ *Inquire of them* – The Levites were both judges and teachers. The idea of moral authority has become taboo in our society – largely because of a fallacy. The word "judgment" has two distinct, if related, meanings. The first is what we are looking for when we seek advice. Whether the counsel we wish for is moral or practical, we turn to those who have had long and successful encounters with the problem at hand. Whether we go to a tennis coach or a master craftsman or a lawyer, the very act of taking advice presupposes that there is excellence within an activity and that it is learned rather than immediately acquired. If this applies to specialized compartments of human behavior, how much more so does it apply to life itself taken as a whole. There may not be – indeed there is not – a single model of the good life. Even in a world as cohesive and structured as eighteenth-century East European Jewry, you went to Vilna for scholarship, to Mezerich for mysticism, and to Lubavitch for piety. But within each form of life there are exemplars and sages, and consensus tells us who they are. When we seek judgment in this sense, what we want is something

13 person shall be put to death. You must purge the evil from Israel. All the people
14 will hear and fear and will not act in such wickedness again. When SHENI
you enter the land that the Lord your God is giving you, and have taken
possession of it and settled in it, should you say, 'I will set a king over me, like
15 all the surrounding nations,' set over you a king whom the Lord your God
chooses. The king you set over you must be one of your own people. You may
16 not set a foreigner over you, who is not your brother. Further, he must not
acquire many horses for himself, he must not make the people return to Egypt
to acquire more horses, since the Lord has told you: You must not go back
17 that way again. He must not accumulate wives and let his heart be led astray,
18 nor should he amass large amounts of silver and gold. As he presides upon his

רש״י

יג וְכָל הָעָם יִשְׁמְעוּ. מִכָּאן שֶׁמַּמְתִּינִין לוֹ עַד הָרֶגֶל וּמְמִיתִין אוֹתוֹ בָּרֶגֶל:

טז לֹא יַרְבֶּה לוֹ סוּסִים. אֶלָּא כְּדֵי מֶרְכַּבְתּוֹ, שֶׁלֹּא יָשִׁיב אֶת הָעָם מִצְרַיְמָה, שֶׁהַסּוּסִים בָּאִים מִשָּׁם, כְּמָה שֶׁנֶּאֱמַר בִּשְׁלֹמֹה: ״וַתַּעֲלֶה וַתֵּצֵא מֶרְכָּבָה מִמִּצְרַיִם בְּשֵׁשׁ מֵאוֹת כֶּסֶף וְסוּס בַּחֲמִשִּׁים וּמֵאָה״ (מלכים א׳ י, כט):

יז וְלֹא יַרְבֶּה לוֹ נָשִׁים. אֶלָּא שְׁמוֹנֶה עֶשְׂרֵה, שֶׁמָּצִינוּ שֶׁהָיוּ לוֹ לְדָוִד שֵׁשׁ נָשִׁים (שמואל ב׳ ג, ב-ה) וְנֶאֱמַר לוֹ: ״וְאִם מְעָט וְאֹסִפָה לְּךָ כָּהֵנָּה וְכָהֵנָּה״ (שם יב, ח): וְכֶסֶף וְזָהָב לֹא יַרְבֶּה לּוֹ מְאֹד. אֶלָּא כְּדֵי לִתֵּן לְאַפְסַנְיָא:

יח וְהָיָה כְשִׁבְתּוֹ. אִם עָשָׂה כֵן, כְּדַאי הוּא שֶׁתִּתְקַיֵּם מַלְכוּתוֹ:

freedom. He wrote: "Thus the example of the Hebrew nation laid down the parallel lines on which all freedom has been won ... the principle that all political authorities must be tested and reformed according to a code which was not made by man."

Judaism is not an argument for powerlessness. The briefest glance at two thousand years of Jewish history in the Diaspora tells us that there is nothing dignified in powerlessness. Instead, Judaism is an argument for the limitation, secularization, and transformation of power.

Limitation: Israel's kings were the only rulers in the ancient world without the power to legislate. For us, the laws that matter come from God, not from human beings. In Jewish law, kings may issue temporary regulations for the better ordering of society, but so may rabbis or courts.

Secularization: In Judaism, kings were not High Priests and High Priests were not kings. When some of the Hasmonean rulers sought to combine the two offices, the Talmud (Kiddushin 66a) records the objection of the Sages: "Let the royal crown be sufficient for you; leave the priestly crown to the descendants of Aharon."

Transformation: Fundamental to Judaism is the idea of servant leadership. The king must not "consider himself superior to his people, or stray from the commandments to the right or to the left" (Deut. 17:20). Humility is the essence of royalty, because to lead is to serve.

17:17 וְכֶסֶף וְזָהָב לֹא יַרְבֶּה-לּוֹ מְאֹד *Nor should he amass large amounts of silver and gold* – Unique commands are given to the king. He must not accumulate horses so as not to establish trading links with Egypt. He should not have too many wives lest he "let his heart be led astray." He should not accumulate wealth. These were all standing temptations to a king. It was these three prohibitions that Shlomo, wisest of men, broke, marking the beginning of the long, slow slide into corruption that marked much of the history of the monarchy in ancient Israel. It led, after his death, to the division of the kingdom.

But these were symptoms, not the cause. The cause was the feeling on the part of the king that since he is above the people, he is above the law. As the Rabbis said (Sanhedrin 21b), Shlomo justified his breach of these prohibitions by saying:

יג יד מִיִּשְׂרָאֵל: וְכָל־הָעָם יִשְׁמְעוּ וְיִרָאוּ וְלֹא יְזִידוּן עוֹד: כִּי־ טו שני
תָבֹא אֶל־הָאָרֶץ אֲשֶׁר יהוה אֱלֹהֶיךָ נֹתֵן לָךְ וִירִשְׁתָּהּ וְיָשַׁבְתָּה בָּהּ
טו וְאָמַרְתָּ אָשִׂימָה עָלַי מֶלֶךְ כְּכָל־הַגּוֹיִם אֲשֶׁר סְבִיבֹתָי: שׂוֹם תָּשִׂים
עָלֶיךָ מֶלֶךְ אֲשֶׁר יִבְחַר יהוה אֱלֹהֶיךָ בּוֹ מִקֶּרֶב אַחֶיךָ תָּשִׂים עָלֶיךָ
טז מֶלֶךְ לֹא תוּכַל לָתֵת עָלֶיךָ אִישׁ נָכְרִי אֲשֶׁר לֹא־אָחִיךָ הוּא: רַק לֹא־
יַרְבֶּה־לּוֹ סוּסִים וְלֹא־יָשִׁיב אֶת־הָעָם מִצְרַיְמָה לְמַעַן הַרְבּוֹת סוּס
יז וַיהוה אָמַר לָכֶם לֹא תֹסִפוּן לָשׁוּב בַּדֶּרֶךְ הַזֶּה עוֹד: וְלֹא יַרְבֶּה־לּוֹ
יח נָשִׁים וְלֹא יָסוּר לְבָבוֹ וְכֶסֶף וְזָהָב לֹא יַרְבֶּה־לּוֹ מְאֹד: וְהָיָה כְשִׁבְתּוֹ

אונקלוס

מִיִּשְׂרָאֵל: יג וְכָל עַמָּא יִשְׁמְעוּן וְיִדְחֲלוּן, וְלָא יַרְשְׁעוּן עוֹד: יד אֲרֵי תֵיעוֹל לְאַרְעָא, דַּייָ אֱלָהָךְ יָהֵיב לָךְ, וְתֵירְתַהּ וְתֵתֵּיב בַּהּ, וְתֵימַר, אֲמַנֵּי עֲלַי מַלְכָּא, כְּכָל עַמְמַיָּא דִּבְסַחְרָנָי: טו מַנָּאָה תְמַנֵּי עֲלָךְ מַלְכָּא, דְּיִתְרְעֵי, יי אֱלָהָךְ בֵּיהּ, מִגּוֹ אֲחָךְ, תְּמַנֵּי עֲלָךְ מַלְכָּא, לֵית לָךְ רְשׁוּ, לְמַנָּאָה עֲלָךְ גְּבַר נֻכְרַאי, דְּלָא אֲחוּךְ הוּא: טז לְחוֹד לָא יַסְגֵּי לֵיהּ סוּסָוָן, וְלָא יָתִיב יָת עַמָּא לְמִצְרַיִם, בְּדִיל לְאַסְגָּאָה סוּסָוָן, וַייָ אֲמַר לְכוֹן, לָא תֵיסְפוּן, לְמִתַּב, בְּאוֹרְחָא הָדָא עוֹד: יז וְלָא יַסְגֵּי לֵיהּ נְשִׁין, וְלָא יִטְעֵי לִבֵּיהּ, וְכַסְפָּא וְדַהֲבָא, לָא יַסְגֵּי לֵיהּ לַחֲדָא: יח וִיהֵי כְּמִתְבֵיהּ,

SELECTING A MONARCH

In the eighth chapter of I Samuel, as this passage predicts, the people come to the prophet and demand a king. On the instruction of God, Shmuel tells them that if they appoint a king he will eventually seize their children, land, and a percentage of their harvests and cattle. Even constitutional monarchy, in other words, will involve a sacrifice of rights of property and person. "And on that day, you will cry out because of your own king, whom you yourselves chose, but the Lord will not answer you" (I Sam. 8:18).

Is having a king, then, a good thing or a bad thing, from a Jewish perspective? The question turns out to be almost unanswerable.

On the one hand, our *parasha* does say, "Set over you a king." Rambam counts it among the 613 commandments (*Mitzvat Aseh* 173). On the other hand, of no other command anywhere does it say that it is to be acted on when the people say that they want to be "like all the surrounding nations." The Torah doesn't tell us to be like everyone else. Jews are supposed to have the courage to be different.

The episode in the days of Shmuel makes matters no clearer. Shmuel is upset. He thinks the people are rejecting him. Not so, says God, the people are rejecting Me (I Sam. 8:7). Yet God does not command Shmuel to resist the request. He says, in effect: Tell them what monarchy will cost, what the people stand to lose. If they still want a king, give them a king.

If having a king is a good thing, why does God say that it means that the people are rejecting Him? If it is a bad thing, why does God tell Shmuel to give the people what they want even if it is not what God would wish them to want?

The great commentators run the entire spectrum on this issue. For Rambam, having a king was a good thing and a positive command. For Ibn Ezra it was a permission, not an obligation. For Abrabanel it was a concession to human weakness. For Rabbeinu Baḥya, it was its own punishment. Why is the Torah so ambivalent about this central element of its political program?

The simplest answer was given by historian Lord Acton who saw the Hebrew Bible as the world's first tutorial in

royal throne, he must inscribe a copy of this Law for himself upon a scroll in
19 the presence of the Levitical priests. It must always be with him, and he shall
read from it all the days of his life, so that he may learn to revere the LORD
his God, taking care to keep all the words of this commandment and these
20 decrees, not considering himself superior to his people, or straying from the
commandments to the right or to the left. Then he and his descendants will

רש"י

אֶת מִשְׁנֵה הַתּוֹרָה. שְׁתֵּי סִפְרֵי תוֹרוֹת, אַחַת שֶׁהִיא מֻנַּחַת בְּבֵית גְּנָזָיו וְאַחַת שֶׁנִּכְנֶסֶת וְיוֹצְאָה עִמּוֹ:

כ וּלְבִלְתִּי סוּר מִן הַמִּצְוָה. אֲפִלּוּ מִצְוָה קַלָּה שֶׁל נָבִיא: לְמַעַן יַאֲרִיךְ יָמִים. מִכְּלַל הֵן אַתָּה שׁוֹמֵעַ לָאו, וְכֵן מָצִינוּ בְּשָׁאוּל שֶׁאָמַר לוֹ שְׁמוּאֵל: "שִׁבְעַת יָמִים תּוֹחֵל עַד בּוֹאִי אֵלֶיךָ" לְהַעֲלוֹת הָעֹלָה (שמואל א' י, ח), וּכְתִיב: "וַיּוֹחֶל שִׁבְעַת יָמִים" (שם יג, ח), וְלֹא שָׁמַר הַבְטָחָתוֹ לִשְׁמֹר כָּל הַיּוֹם, וְלֹא הִסְפִּיק לְהַעֲלוֹת הָעוֹלָה עַד שֶׁבָּא שְׁמוּאֵל וְאָמַר לוֹ: "נִסְכָּלְתָּ לֹא שָׁמַרְתָּ וְגוֹ' וְעַתָּה מַמְלַכְתְּךָ לֹא תָקוּם" (שם פסוקים יג-יד), הָא לָמַדְתָּ שֶׁבִּשְׁבִיל מִצְוָה קַלָּה שֶׁל נָבִיא נֶעֱנַשׁ: **הוּא וּבָנָיו.** מַגִּיד שֶׁאִם בְּנוֹ הָגוּן לְמַלְכוּת הוּא קוֹדֵם לְכָל אָדָם:

ḥokhma: *ḥokhma* to understand the world as it is, Torah to understand the world as it ought to be.

17:20 **לְבִלְתִּי רוּם־לְבָבוֹ מֵאֶחָיו** *Not considering himself superior to his people* – Consistent with the fundamental Judaic idea that leadership is service, not dominion or power or status or superiority, the king is commanded to be humble: he must constantly read the Torah "so that he may learn to revere the LORD his God… not considering himself superior to his people" (Deut. 17:19–20). It is not easy to be humble when everyone is bowing down before you and when you have the power of life and death over your subjects. If a king, whom all are bound to honor, is commanded to be humble – "not considering himself superior to his people" – how much more so the rest of us. Moshe, the greatest leader the Jewish people ever had, was "very humble, more so than any other man on earth" (Num. 12:3). Was it that he was great because he was humble, or humble because he was great? Either way, as R. Yoḥanan said of God Himself, "Wherever you find His greatness there you find His humility" (Megilla 31a). This is a clear example of how spirituality makes a difference to the way we act, feel, and think. *Believing that there is a God in whose presence we stand means that we are not the center of our world.* Humility means living by the light of that which is greater than me. When God is at the center of our lives, we open ourselves up to the glory of creation and the beauty of other people. The smaller the self, the wider the radius of our world.

17:20 **לְמַעַן יַאֲרִיךְ יָמִים עַל־מַמְלַכְתּוֹ הוּא וּבָנָיו** *Then he and his descendants will reign long* – In the ancient world, the pharaohs of Egypt, like the kings of Mesopotamian city-states, combined temporal and ecclesiastical power. They were both head of state and head of the religion of the state. They claimed to be, and were seen as being, god made manifest or the child of the gods or the chief intercessor with the gods. The Torah's model of leadership is different. There was not to be one leader, but three, each of a very different kind: the king, the priest, and the prophet.

The king recruited an army, levied taxes, and was responsible for civic order. It was his task to defend the nation from enemies outside and lawlessness within. He was immersed in the demands of statecraft, a civil rather than religious leader.

The priest mediated between the people and God. He served in the Temple, offered sacrifices on behalf of the people, and ensured that the holy was at the heart of national life. He was also a teacher and adjudicator of the law. He was the guardian of the holy, preserver of the boundaries between sacred and secular. Yet the priest was not the only kind of spiritual leader in biblical Israel. There was also the prophet. The prophet heard the word of God and conveyed it to the people.

Thus, we have in the Torah an intimation of the doctrine of the separation of powers that would emerge in the West in the eighteenth century, so as to avoid the concentration of power in a single individual or institution.

The Torah does not spell out explicitly why this

עַל כִּסֵּא מַמְלַכְתּוֹ וְכָתַב לוֹ אֶת־מִשְׁנֵה הַתּוֹרָה הַזֹּאת עַל־סֵפֶר
יט מִלִּפְנֵי הַכֹּהֲנִים הַלְוִיִּם: וְהָיְתָה עִמּוֹ וְקָרָא בוֹ כָּל־יְמֵי חַיָּיו לְמַעַן יִלְמַד
לְיִרְאָה אֶת־יהוה אֱלֹהָיו לִשְׁמֹר אֶת־כָּל־דִּבְרֵי הַתּוֹרָה הַזֹּאת וְאֶת־
כ הַחֻקִּים הָאֵלֶּה לַעֲשֹׂתָם: לְבִלְתִּי רוּם־לְבָבוֹ מֵאֶחָיו וּלְבִלְתִּי סוּר מִן־
הַמִּצְוָה יָמִין וּשְׂמֹאול לְמַעַן יַאֲרִיךְ יָמִים עַל־מַמְלַכְתּוֹ הוּא וּבָנָיו בְּקֶרֶב

אונקלוס

עַל כֻּרְסֵי מַלְכוּתֵיהּ, וְיִכְתּוֹב לֵיהּ, יָת פַּתְשֶׁגֶן אוֹרָיְתָא הָדָא עַל סִפְרָא, מִן קֳדָם כָּהֲנַיָּא לֵיוָאֵי: יט וּתְהֵי עִמֵּיהּ, וִיהֵי קָרֵי בֵיהּ כָּל יוֹמֵי חַיּוֹהִי, בְּדִיל דְּיֵילַף, לְמִדְחַל קֳדָם יי אֱלָהֵיהּ, לְמִטַּר, יָת כָּל פִּתְגָּמֵי, אוֹרָיְתָא הָדָא, וְיָת קְיָמַיָּא הָאִלֵּין לְמֶעְבְּדְהוֹן: כ בְּדִיל דְּלָא יִירַם לִבֵּיהּ מֵאֲחוֹהִי, וּבְדִיל, דְּלָא יִסְטֵי מִן תַּפְקֵידְתָּא לְיַמִּינָא וְלִסְמָאלָא, בְּדִיל דְּיוֹרִיךְ יוֹמִין עַל מַלְכוּתֵיהּ, הוּא וּבְנוֹהִי בְּגוֹ

> The only reason that a king may not accumulate wives is that they will lead his heart astray, so I will marry many wives and not let my heart be led astray. And since the only reason not to have many horses is not to establish links with Egypt, I will have many horses but not do business with Egypt. (Sanhedrin 21b)

In both cases he fell into the trap of which the Torah had warned. Shlomo's wives did lead his heart astray (1 Kings 11:3), and his horses were imported from Egypt (10:28–29). The arrogance of power is its downfall. Hence the Torah's insistence on humility, not as merely a good thing to have, but as essential to the role.

17:19 וְקָרָא בוֹ כָּל־יְמֵי חַיָּיו *He shall read from it all the days of his life* – We see that the king is commanded to study constantly. Later, in the book that bears his name, Yehoshua – Moshe's successor – is commanded in very similar terms:

> This book of Torah must never leave your lips; contemplate it day and night, so that you will faithfully uphold all that is written within it. For then your course will succeed; then you will triumph. (Josh. 1:8)

Leaders learn. True, they have advisers, elders, counselors, an inner court of sages and literati. In addition, biblical kings had prophets – Shmuel to Shaul, Natan to David, Yeshayahu to Ḥizkiyahu, and so on – to bring them the word of God. But those on whom the destiny of the nation turns may not delegate the task of thinking, reading, studying, and remembering. They are not entitled to say: I have affairs of state to worry about. I have no time for books. Leaders must be scholars, *benei Torah*, "children of the Book," if they are to direct and lead the people of the Book.

The two greatest kings of early Israel, David and Shlomo, were both authors, David of Psalms, Shlomo (according to tradition) of Song of Songs, Proverbs, and Ecclesiastes. What separates the statesman from the mere politician are reading and writing.

The key biblical word associated with kings is *ḥokhma*, "wisdom." We should note that *ḥokhma* means something slightly different from Torah, which is more commonly associated with priests and prophets than kings. *Ḥokhma* includes worldly wisdom, which is human and universal rather than a special heritage of Jews and Judaism. Broadly speaking, in contemporary terms *ḥokhma* refers to the sciences and humanities – to whatever allows us to see the universe as the work of God and the human person as the image of God. Torah is the specific moral and spiritual heritage of Israel.

Leaders take time to familiarize themselves with the world of ideas. Only thus do they gain the perspective to be able to see farther and clearer than others. To be a Jewish leader means spending time to study both Torah and

18 1 reign long in the midst of Israel. The Levitical priests, the whole tribe SHELISHI
of Levi, will have no share or inheritance with Israel. They will eat the LORD's
2 fire offerings as their inheritance, but will have no inheritance among their
3 kinsfolk. The LORD is their inheritance, as He has promised them. This
shall be the priests' due from the people: those offering a sacrifice – an ox or
a sheep – shall give to the priest the shoulder, the cheeks, and the stomach.
4 You shall give him the first yield of your grain, wine, and oil, and the first wool
5 from the shearing of your sheep. For the LORD your God has chosen him out
of all your tribes to stand and minister in the name of the LORD – him and
6 his sons for all time. If a Levite leaves any of your towns throughout REVI'I
Israel where he has been living, and comes to the place that the LORD will
7 choose – he may do so whenever he wishes – then he may minister in the name
of the LORD his God, alongside any of his brother Levites who serve there
8 before the LORD. They shall have equal portions to eat, regardless of income
9 they may have from the sale of family possessions. When you come
into the land that the LORD your God is giving you, do not learn to partake in
10 the abhorrent practices those nations carry out. Let no one be found among

רש״י

יח א–ב **כָּל שֵׁבֶט לֵוִי.** בֵּין תְּמִימִין בֵּין בַּעֲלֵי מוּמִין: **חֵלֶק.** בַּבִּזָּה: **וְנַחֲלָה.** בָּאָרֶץ: **אִשֵּׁי ה׳.** קָדְשֵׁי הַמִּקְדָּשׁ: **וְנַחֲלָתוֹ.** אֵלּוּ קָדְשֵׁי הַגְּבוּל, תְּרוּמוֹת וּמַעַשְׂרוֹת, אֲבָל "נַחֲלָה" גְּמוּרָה "לֹא יִהְיֶה לּוֹ בְּקֶרֶב אֶחָיו". וּבְסִפְרֵי דָּרְשׁוּ: "וְנַחֲלָה לֹא יִהְיֶה לּוֹ, זוֹ נַחֲלַת שְׁאָר. בְּקֶרֶב אֶחָיו, זוֹ נַחֲלַת חֲמִשָּׁה". וְאֵינִי יוֹדֵעַ מַה הִיא. וְנִרְאֶה לִי שֶׁאֶרֶץ כְּנַעַן שֶׁמֵּעֵבֶר הַיַּרְדֵּן וְאֵילָךְ נִקְרֵאת אֶרֶץ חֲמִשָּׁה עֲמָמִים, וְשֶׁל סִיחוֹן וְעוֹג שְׁנֵי עֲמָמִים, אֱמוֹרִי וּכְנַעֲנִי, וְנַחֲלַת שְׁאָר לְרַבּוֹת קֵינִי וּקְנִזִּי וְקַדְמוֹנִי. וְכֵן דּוֹרֵשׁ בְּפָרָשַׁת מַתָּנוֹת שֶׁנֶּאֶמְרוּ לְאַהֲרֹן: "עַל כֵּן לֹא הָיָה לְלֵוִי" וְגוֹ׳ (לעיל י, ט), לְהַזְהִיר עַל קֵינִי וּקְנִזִּי וְקַדְמוֹנִי: **כַּאֲשֶׁר דִּבֶּר לוֹ.** "בְּאַרְצָם לֹא תִנְחָל וְגוֹ׳ אֲנִי חֶלְקְךָ" (במדבר יח, כ):

ג **מֵאֵת הָעָם.** וְלֹא מֵאֵת הַכֹּהֲנִים: **אִם שׁוֹר אִם שֶׂה.** פְּרָט לְחַיָּה: **הַזְּרֹעַ.** מִן הַפֶּרֶק שֶׁל אַרְכֻּבָּה עַד כַּף שֶׁל יָד שֶׁקּוֹרִין אשפלדו"ן: **וְהַלְּחָיַיִם.** עִם הַלָּשׁוֹן. דּוֹרְשֵׁי רְשׁוּמוֹת הָיוּ אוֹמְרִים: 'זְרוֹעַ' תַּחַת יָד, שֶׁנֶּאֱמַר: "וַיִּקַּח רֹמַח בְּיָדוֹ" (במדבר כה, ז). 'לְחָיַיִם' תַּחַת תְּפִלָּה, שֶׁנֶּאֱמַר: "וַיַּעֲמֹד פִּינְחָס וַיְפַלֵּל" (תהלים קו, ל). 'וְהַקֵּבָה' תַּחַת "הָאִשָּׁה אֶל קֳבָתָהּ" (במדבר כה, ח):

ד **רֵאשִׁית דְּגָנְךָ.** זוֹ תְּרוּמָה, וְלֹא פֵּרַשׁ בָּהּ שִׁעוּר, אֲבָל רַבּוֹתֵינוּ נָתְנוּ בָהּ שִׁעוּר: עַיִן יָפָה אֶחָד מֵאַרְבָּעִים, עַיִן רָעָה אֶחָד מִשִּׁשִּׁים, בֵּינוֹנִית אֶחָד מֵחֲמִשִּׁים. וְסָמְכוּ עַל הַמִּקְרָא שֶׁלֹּא לִפְחֹת מֵאֶחָד מִשִּׁשִּׁים, שֶׁנֶּאֱמַר: "וְשִׁשִּׁיתֶם הָאֵיפָה מֵחֹמֶר הַשְּׂעֹרִים" (יחזקאל מה, יג), שִׁשִּׁית הָאֵיפָה חֲצִי סְאָה, כְּשֶׁאַתָּה נוֹתֵן חֲצִי סְאָה לְכוֹר, הֲרֵי אֶחָד מִשִּׁשִּׁים, שֶׁהַכּוֹר שְׁלֹשִׁים סְאִין: **וְרֵאשִׁית גֵּז צֹאנְךָ.** כְּשֶׁאַתָּה גוֹזֵז צֹאנְךָ בְּכָל שָׁנָה תֵּן מִמֶּנָּה רֵאשִׁית לַכֹּהֵן, וְלֹא פֵּרַשׁ בָּהּ שִׁעוּר. וְרַבּוֹתֵינוּ נָתְנוּ בָהּ שִׁעוּר – אֶחָד מִשִּׁשִּׁים. וְכַמָּה צֹאן חַיָּבוֹת בְּרֵאשִׁית הַגֵּז? חָמֵשׁ רְחֵלוֹת, שֶׁנֶּאֱמַר: "וְחָמֵשׁ צֹאן עֲשׂוּיוֹת" (שמואל א׳ כה, יח):

ה **לַעֲמֹד לְשָׁרֵת.** מִכָּאן שֶׁאֵין שֵׁרוּת אֶלָּא מְעוּמָּד:

ו–ז **וְכִי יָבֹא הַלֵּוִי.** יָכוֹל בְּבֶן לֵוִי וַדַּאי הַכָּתוּב מְדַבֵּר? תַּלְמוּד לוֹמַר: "וְשֵׁרֵת", יָצְאוּ לְוִיִּם שֶׁאֵין רְאוּיִין לְשֵׁרוּת: **וּבָא בְּכָל אַוַּת נַפְשׁוֹ... וְשֵׁרֵת.** לִמֵּד עַל הַכֹּהֵן שֶׁבָּא וּמַקְרִיב קָרְבְּנוֹת נִדְבָתוֹ אוֹ חוֹבָתוֹ, וַאֲפִלּוּ בְּמִשְׁמָר שֶׁאֵינוֹ שֶׁלּוֹ. דָּבָר אַחֵר, עוֹד לִמֵּד עַל הַכֹּהֲנִים הַבָּאִים לָרֶגֶל שֶׁמַּקְרִיבִין בַּמִּשְׁמָר וְעוֹבְדִין בַּקָּרְבָּנוֹת הַבָּאוֹת מֵחֲמַת הָרֶגֶל, כְּגוֹן מוּסְפֵי הָרֶגֶל, וְאַף עַל פִּי שֶׁאֵין הַמִּשְׁמָר שֶׁלָּהֶם:

ח **חֵלֶק כְּחֵלֶק יֹאכֵלוּ.** מְלַמֵּד שֶׁחוֹלְקִין בָּעוֹרוֹת וּבִבְשַׂר שְׂעִירֵי חַטָּאוֹת. יָכוֹל אַף בִּדְבָרִים הַבָּאִים שֶׁלֹּא מֵחֲמַת הָרֶגֶל, כְּגוֹן תְּמִידִים וּמוּסְפֵי שַׁבָּת וּנְדָרִים וּנְדָבוֹת? תַּלְמוּד לוֹמַר: "לְבַד מִמְכָּרָיו עַל הָאָבוֹת", חוּץ מִמַּה שֶּׁמָּכְרוּ הָאָבוֹת, בִּימֵי דָּוִד וּשְׁמוּאֵל שֶׁנִּקְבְּעוּ הַמִּשְׁמָרוֹת וּמָכְרוּ זֶה לָזֶה, טֹל אַתָּה שַׁבַּתְּךָ וַאֲנִי אֶטֹּל שַׁבַּתִּי:

ט **לֹא תִלְמַד לַעֲשׂוֹת.** אֲבָל אַתָּה לָמֵד לְהָבִין וּלְהוֹרוֹת, כְּלוֹמַר לְהָבִין מַעֲשֵׂיהֶם כַּמָּה הֵם מְקֻלְקָלִין וּלְהוֹרוֹת לְבָנֶיךָ לֹא תַעֲשֶׂה כָּךְ וְכָךְ, שֶׁזֶּה הוּא חֹק הַגּוֹיִם:

יח א יִשְׂרָאֵל׃ לֹא־יִהְיֶה לַכֹּהֲנִים הַלְוִיִּם כָּל־שֵׁבֶט לֵוִי חֵלֶק שלישי
ב וְנַחֲלָה עִם־יִשְׂרָאֵל אִשֵּׁי יהוה וְנַחֲלָתוֹ יֹאכֵלוּן׃ וְנַחֲלָה לֹא־יִהְיֶה־לּוֹ
ג בְּקֶרֶב אֶחָיו יהוה הוּא נַחֲלָתוֹ כַּאֲשֶׁר דִּבֶּר־לוֹ׃ וְזֶה
יִהְיֶה מִשְׁפַּט הַכֹּהֲנִים מֵאֵת הָעָם מֵאֵת זֹבְחֵי הַזֶּבַח אִם־שׁוֹר אִם־שֶׂה
ד וְנָתַן לַכֹּהֵן הַזְּרֹעַ וְהַלְּחָיַיִם וְהַקֵּבָה׃ רֵאשִׁית דְּגָנְךָ תִּירֹשְׁךָ וְיִצְהָרֶךָ
ה וְרֵאשִׁית גֵּז צֹאנְךָ תִּתֶּן־לוֹ׃ כִּי בוֹ בָּחַר יהוה אֱלֹהֶיךָ מִכָּל־שְׁבָטֶיךָ
ו לַעֲמֹד לְשָׁרֵת בְּשֵׁם־יהוה הוּא וּבָנָיו כָּל־הַיָּמִים׃ וְכִי־ רביעי
יָבֹא הַלֵּוִי מֵאַחַד שְׁעָרֶיךָ מִכָּל־יִשְׂרָאֵל אֲשֶׁר־הוּא גָּר שָׁם וּבָא בְּכָל־
ז אַוַּת נַפְשׁוֹ אֶל־הַמָּקוֹם אֲשֶׁר־יִבְחַר יהוה׃ וְשֵׁרֵת בְּשֵׁם יהוה אֱלֹהָיו
ח כְּכָל־אֶחָיו הַלְוִיִּם הָעֹמְדִים שָׁם לִפְנֵי יהוה׃ חֵלֶק כְּחֵלֶק יֹאכֵלוּ לְבַד
ט מִמְכָּרָיו עַל־הָאָבוֹת׃ כִּי אַתָּה בָּא אֶל־הָאָרֶץ אֲשֶׁר־יהוה
י אֱלֹהֶיךָ נֹתֵן לָךְ לֹא־תִלְמַד לַעֲשׂוֹת כְּתוֹעֲבֹת הַגּוֹיִם הָהֵם׃ לֹא־יִמָּצֵא

אונקלוס

יִשְׂרָאֵל׃ יח א לָא יְהֵי לְכָהֲנַיָּא לֵיוָאֵי, כָּל שִׁבְטָא דְלֵוִי, חוּלָק וְאַחְסָנָא עִם יִשְׂרָאֵל, קֻרְבָּנַיָּא דַייָ, וְאַחְסָנְתֵיהּ יֵיכְלוּן׃ ב וְאַחְסָנָא לָא יְהֵי לֵיהּ בְּגוֹ אֲחוֹהִי, מַתְּנָן דִּיהַב לֵיהּ יְיָ אִנִּין אַחְסָנְתֵיהּ, כְּמָא דְמַלֵּיל לֵיהּ׃ ג וְדֵין, יְהֵי דַּחֲזֵי לְכָהֲנַיָּא מִן עַמָּא, מִן נָכְסֵי נִכְסְתָא אִם תּוֹר אִם אִמַּר, וְיִתֵּין לְכָהֲנָא, דְּרָעָא וְלוֹעָא וְקֵיבְתָא׃ ד רֵישׁ עֲבוּרָךְ חַמְרָךְ וּמִשְׁחָךְ, וְרֵישׁ, גִּזַּת עָנָךְ תַּפְרֵישׁ לֵיהּ׃ ה אֲרֵי בֵיהּ, אִתְרְעִי, יְיָ אֱלָהָךְ מִכָּל שִׁבְטָךְ, לִמְקָם לְשַׁמָּשָׁא בִּשְׁמָא דַייָ, הוּא וּבְנוֹהִי כָּל יוֹמַיָּא׃ ו וַאֲרֵי יֵיתֵי לֵיוָאָה, מֵחֲדָא מִקִּרְוָךְ מִכָּל יִשְׂרָאֵל, דְּהוּא דָּר תַּמָּן, וְיֵיתֵי בְּכָל רְעוּת נַפְשֵׁיהּ, לְאַתְרָא דְּיִתְרְעֵי יְיָ׃ ז וִישַׁמֵּישׁ, בִּשְׁמָא דַייָ אֱלָהֵיהּ, כְּכָל אֲחוֹהִי לֵיוָאֵי, דִּמְשַׁמְּשִׁין תַּמָּן קֳדָם יְיָ׃ ח חוּלָק כְּחוּלָק יֵיכְלוּן, בָּר מִמַּטַּרְתָּא דְּיֵיתֵהּ שַׁבְּתָא דְּכֵין אַתְקִינוּ אֲבָהָתָא׃ ט אֲרֵי אַתְּ עָלֵיל לְאַרְעָא, דַּייָ אֱלָהָךְ יָהֵיב לָךְ, לָא תֵילַף לְמֶעְבַּד, כְּתוֹעֲבָת עַמְמַיָּא הָאִנּוּן׃ י לָא יִשְׁתְּכַח

power is merely delegated – Heaven's conditional gift to human beings. This means that any attempt by king, priest, or prophet to subvert or contravene the revealed will of God is automatically *ultra vires,* lacking in authority.

18:10 לֹא־יִמָּצֵא בְךָ ... קֹסֵם קְסָמִים *Let no one be found among you…who casts spells* – Witchcraft and magic must be divorced from our reasons for religious belief. On this, Rambam is unequivocal:

separation was important, but we can guess. Power tends to corrupt, therefore no one should have absolute power. Parashat Shofetim signals a radical break from the pagan model of kingship. In Judaism, a king is not a High Priest, and a High Priest is not a king.

The result is a structure which limits the powers of king and priest alike, and which gives prominence to the prophet, who has no power but lasting influence. True power, in the Judaic view of things, belongs to God alone. All earthly

you who makes a son or daughter pass through fire, or who casts spells, or is
11 an augur or diviner or soothsayer, or who practices sorcery, or consults ghosts
12 or spirits, or seeks oracles from the dead. For anyone who does these things
is abhorrent to the LORD; it is because of such abhorrent acts that the LORD
13 your God is driving them out before you. You must be wholly loyal to the
14 LORD your God. The nations that you are driving out listen to augurs and to HAMISHI
those who cast spells. But as for you – the LORD your God does not permit
15 you these. The LORD your God will raise up another prophet like me from
16 among your own people. To him you must listen. For this is what you asked
of the LORD your God at Ḥorev on the day of the assembly when you said: 'If
I hear the voice of the LORD my God any more, or continue to see this great
17 18 fire, I will die.' The LORD said to me: They have spoken well. I will raise up for
them a prophet like you from among their own people. I will put My words in
19 the prophet's mouth and he will tell them all that I command. Anyone who
does not listen to My words that he speaks in My name, I Myself will call him
20 to account. But a prophet who acts in wickedness, speaking anything I have
not commanded in My name, or speaking in the name of other gods – that

רש״י

י **מַעֲבִיר בְּנוֹ וּבִתּוֹ בָּאֵשׁ.** הִיא עֲבוֹדַת הַמֹּלֶךְ, עוֹשֶׂה מְדוּרוֹת אֵשׁ מִכָּאן וּמִכָּאן וּמַעֲבִירוֹ בֵּין שְׁתֵּיהֶם: **קֹסֵם קְסָמִים.** אֵיזֶהוּ קוֹסֵם? הָאוֹחֵז אֶת מַקְלוֹ וְאוֹמֵר: אִם אֵלֵךְ אִם לֹא אֵלֵךְ. וְכֵן הוּא אוֹמֵר: "עַמִּי בְּעֵצוֹ יִשְׁאָל וּמַקְלוֹ יַגִּיד לוֹ" (הושע ד, יב): **מְעוֹנֵן.** רַבִּי עֲקִיבָא אוֹמֵר: אֵלּוּ נוֹתְנֵי עוֹנוֹת שֶׁאוֹמְרִים: עוֹנָה פְּלוֹנִית יָפָה לְהַתְחִיל, וַחֲכָמִים אוֹמְרִים: אֵלּוּ אוֹחֲזֵי הָעֵינַיִם: **מְנַחֵשׁ.** פִּתּוֹ נָפְלָה מִפִּיו, צְבִי הִפְסִיקוֹ בַּדֶּרֶךְ, מַקְלוֹ נָפַל מִיָּדוֹ:

יא **וְחֹבֵר חָבֶר.** שֶׁמְּכַנֵּס נְחָשִׁים וְעַקְרַבִּים אוֹ שְׁאָר חַיּוֹת לְמָקוֹם אֶחָד: **וְשֹׁאֵל אוֹב.** זֶה מְכַשְּׁפוּת שֶׁשְּׁמוֹ פִּיתוֹם וּמְדַבֵּר מִשֶּׁחְיוֹ וּמַעֲלֶה אֶת הַמֵּת בְּבֵית הַשֶּׁחִי שֶׁלּוֹ: **וְיִדְּעֹנִי.** מַכְנִיס עֶצֶם חַיָּה שֶׁשְּׁמָהּ יַדּוּעַ לְתוֹךְ פִּיו, וּמְדַבֵּר הָעֶצֶם עַל יְדֵי מְכַשְּׁפוּת: **וְדֹרֵשׁ אֶל הַמֵּתִים.** כְּגוֹן הַמַּעֲלֶה בִּזְכוּרוֹ וְהַנִּשְׁאָל בְּגֻלְגֹּלֶת:

יב **כָּל עֹשֵׂה אֵלֶּה.** 'עוֹשֵׂה כָל אֵלֶּה' לֹא נֶאֱמַר, אֶלָּא "כָּל עֹשֵׂה אֵלֶּה", אֲפִלּוּ אַחַת מֵהֶן:

יג **תָּמִים תִּהְיֶה עִם ה' אֱלֹהֶיךָ.** הִתְהַלֵּךְ עִמּוֹ בִּתְמִימוּת וּתְצַפֶּה לוֹ וְלֹא תַחְקֹר אַחַר הָעֲתִידוֹת, אֶלָּא כָּל מַה שֶּׁיָּבֹא עָלֶיךָ קַבֵּל בִּתְמִימוּת, וְאָז תִּהְיֶה עִמּוֹ וּלְחֶלְקוֹ:

יד **לֹא כֵן נָתַן לְךָ ה' אֱלֹהֶיךָ.** לִשְׁמֹעַ אֶל מְעוֹנְנִים וְאֶל קוֹסְמִים, שֶׁהֲרֵי הִשְׁרָה שְׁכִינָה עַל הַנְּבִיאִים וְאוּרִים וְתֻמִּים:

טו **מִקִּרְבְּךָ מֵאַחֶיךָ כָּמֹנִי.** כְּמוֹ שֶׁאֲנִי מִקִּרְבְּךָ מֵאַחֶיךָ יָקִים לְךָ תַּחְתַּי, וְכֵן מִנָּבִיא לְנָבִיא:

כ **אֲשֶׁר לֹא צִוִּיתִיו לְדַבֵּר.** אֲבָל צִוִּיתִי לַחֲבֵרוֹ: **וַאֲשֶׁר יְדַבֵּר בְּשֵׁם אֱלֹהִים אֲחֵרִים.** אֲפִלּוּ כִּוֵּן אֶת הַהֲלָכָה לֶאֱסֹר אֶת הָאָסוּר וּלְהַתִּיר

To be sure, God is in the events which, seeming to defy nature, we call miracles. But He is also in nature itself. Science does not displace God: it reveals, in ever more intricate and wondrous ways, the design within nature itself. Far from diminishing our religious sense, science (rightly understood) should enlarge it, teaching us to see "how many are Your works, LORD; You made them all in wisdom" (Ps. 104:24). Above all, however, God is to be found in the voice heard at Sinai, teaching us how to construct a society that will be the opposite of Egypt, in which the few do not enslave the many, nor are strangers mistreated.

בְךָ מַעֲבִיר בְּנוֹ־וּבִתּוֹ בָּאֵשׁ קֹסֵם קְסָמִים מְעוֹנֵן וּמְנַחֵשׁ וּמְכַשֵּׁף:
יא יב וְחֹבֵר חָבֶר וְשֹׁאֵל אוֹב וְיִדְּעֹנִי וְדֹרֵשׁ אֶל־הַמֵּתִים: כִּי־תוֹעֲבַת יהוה
כָּל־עֹשֵׂה אֵלֶּה וּבִגְלַל הַתּוֹעֵבֹת הָאֵלֶּה יהוה אֱלֹהֶיךָ מוֹרִישׁ אוֹתָם
יג יד מִפָּנֶיךָ: תָּמִים תִּהְיֶה עִם יהוה אֱלֹהֶיךָ: כִּי | הַגּוֹיִם הָאֵלֶּה אֲשֶׁר אַתָּה חמישי
יוֹרֵשׁ אוֹתָם אֶל־מְעֹנְנִים וְאֶל־קֹסְמִים יִשְׁמָעוּ וְאַתָּה לֹא כֵן נָתַן לְךָ
טו יהוה אֱלֹהֶיךָ: נָבִיא מִקִּרְבְּךָ מֵאַחֶיךָ כָּמֹנִי יָקִים לְךָ יהוה אֱלֹהֶיךָ אֵלָיו
טז תִּשְׁמָעוּן: כְּכֹל אֲשֶׁר־שָׁאַלְתָּ מֵעִם יהוה אֱלֹהֶיךָ בְּחֹרֵב בְּיוֹם הַקָּהָל
לֵאמֹר לֹא אֹסֵף לִשְׁמֹעַ אֶת־קוֹל יהוה אֱלֹהָי וְאֶת־הָאֵשׁ הַגְּדֹלָה
יז הַזֹּאת לֹא־אֶרְאֶה עוֹד וְלֹא אָמוּת: וַיֹּאמֶר יהוה אֵלָי הֵיטִיבוּ אֲשֶׁר
יח דִּבֵּרוּ: נָבִיא אָקִים לָהֶם מִקֶּרֶב אֲחֵיהֶם כָּמוֹךָ וְנָתַתִּי דְבָרַי בְּפִיו וְדִבֶּר
יט אֲלֵיהֶם אֵת כָּל־אֲשֶׁר אֲצַוֶּנּוּ: וְהָיָה הָאִישׁ אֲשֶׁר לֹא־יִשְׁמַע אֶל־דְּבָרַי
כ אֲשֶׁר יְדַבֵּר בִּשְׁמִי אָנֹכִי אֶדְרֹשׁ מֵעִמּוֹ: אַךְ הַנָּבִיא אֲשֶׁר יָזִיד לְדַבֵּר
דָּבָר בִּשְׁמִי אֵת אֲשֶׁר לֹא־צִוִּיתִיו לְדַבֵּר וַאֲשֶׁר יְדַבֵּר בְּשֵׁם אֱלֹהִים

אונקלוס

בָּךְ, מַעְבַּר בְּרֵיהּ וּבְרַתֵּיהּ בְּנוּרָא, קָסֵים קִסְמִין, מְעָנֵין וּמְנַחֵישׁ וְחָרֵשׁ: יא וְרָטֵין רְטַן, וְשָׁאֵיל בִּדְבִין וּבִזְכוּרוּ, וְתָבַע מִן מִיתַיָּא: יב אֲרֵי מְרַחַק קֳדָם יי כָּל עָבֵיד אִלֵּין, וּבְדִיל תּוֹעֵיבָתָא הָאִלֵּין, יי אֱלָהָךְ, מְתָרֵיךְ יָתְהוֹן מִן קֳדָמָךְ: יג שְׁלִים תְּהֵי, בְּדַחְלְתָא דַּיי אֱלָהָךְ: יד אֲרֵי עַמְמַיָּא הָאִלֵּין, דְּאַתְּ יָרֵית יָתְהוֹן, מִן מְעָנְנַיָּא וּמִן קָסְמַיָּא שָׁמְעִין, וְאַתְּ, לָא כֵן, יְהַב לָךְ יי אֱלָהָךְ: טו נְבִיָּא מִבֵּינָךְ מֵאַחָךְ כְּוָתִי, יְקִים לָךְ יי אֱלָהָךְ, מִנֵּיהּ תְּקַבְּלוּן: טז כְּכֹל דִּשְׁאֵילְתָּא, מִן קֳדָם יי אֱלָהָךְ בְּחוֹרֵב, בְּיוֹמָא דִקְהָלָא לְמֵימַר, לָא אוֹסֵיף, לְמִשְׁמַע יָת קָל מֵימְרָא דַּיי אֱלָהִי, וְיָת אִישָׁתָא רַבְּתָא הָדָא, לָא אֶחְזֵי עוֹד וְלָא אֵמוּת: יז וַאֲמַר יי לִי, אַתְקִינוּ דְּמַלִּילוּ: יח נְבִיָּא אֲקִים לְהוֹן, מִגּוֹ אֲחֵיהוֹן כְּוָתָךְ, וְאֶתֵּין פִּתְגָּמֵי נְבוּאָתִי בְּפֻמֵּיהּ, וִימַלֵּיל עִמְּהוֹן, יָת כָּל דַּאֲפַקְּדִנֵּיהּ: יט וִיהֵי, גֻּבְרָא דְּלָא יְקַבֵּיל לְפִתְגָּמַי, דִּימַלֵּיל בִּשְׁמִי, מֵימְרִי יִתְבַּע מִנֵּיהּ: כ בְּרַם נְבִיָּא, דִּיַרְשַׁע לְמַלָּלָא פִּתְגָּמָא בִּשְׁמִי, יָת דְּלָא פַקֵּידְתֵּיהּ לְמַלָּלָא, וְדִימַלֵּיל, בְּשׁוּם טָעֲוָת

Israel did not believe in Moshe our teacher because of the signs he performed. When faith is predicated on signs, a lurking doubt always remains that these signs may have been performed with the aid of occult arts and witchcraft. All the signs Moshe performed in the wilderness, he did because they were necessary, not to authenticate his status as a prophet.…When we needed food, he brought down manna. When the people were thirsty, he cleaved the rock. When Koraḥ's supporters denied his authority, the earth swallowed them up. So too with all the other signs. What then were our grounds for believing in him? The revelation at Sinai, in which we saw with our own eyes and heard with our own ears. (*Hilkhot Yesodei HaTorah* 8:1)

21 prophet shall die. You may say to yourself, 'How can we recognize a message
22 that the LORD has not spoken?' If what a prophet proclaims in the name of the
LORD does not take place or come true, that is a message that the LORD has
not spoken. The prophet has proclaimed it in wickedness. Do not be afraid
19 1 of him. When the LORD your God has cut down the nations whose
land the LORD your God is giving you, and you have driven them out and are
2 living in their towns and in their houses, you shall set aside three cities in that
3 land that the LORD your God gives you to possess. Determine the distances
and divide the land that the LORD your God is giving you as a heritage into
three equal parts – so that any manslayer will be able to flee to one of these
4 cities. This is the rule for a manslayer who may flee to one of these and live:
it is one who has killed another person unintentionally, without prior hatred.
5 For instance, a man may go into the forest with a neighbor to cut wood, and

רש״י

אֶת הַמֻּתָּר: **וּמֵת.** בְּחֶנֶק. שְׁלֹשָׁה מִיתָתָן בִּידֵי אָדָם: הַמִּתְנַבֵּא מַה שֶּׁלֹּא שָׁמַע, וּמַה שֶּׁלֹּא נֶאֱמַר לוֹ וְנֶאֱמַר לַחֲבֵרוֹ, וְהַמִּתְנַבֵּא בְּשֵׁם עֲבוֹדָה זָרָה. אֲבָל הַכּוֹבֵשׁ אֶת נְבוּאָתוֹ וְהָעוֹבֵר עַל דִּבְרֵי נָבִיא וְהָעוֹבֵר עַל דִּבְרֵי עַצְמוֹ, מִיתָתָן בִּידֵי שָׁמַיִם, שֶׁנֶּאֱמַר: "אָנֹכִי אֶדְרֹשׁ מֵעִמּוֹ" (לעיל פסוק יט):

כא **וְכִי תֹאמַר בִּלְבָבְךָ.** עֲתִידִין אַתֶּם לוֹמַר, כְּשֶׁיָּבֹא חֲנַנְיָה בֶּן עַזּוּר וּמִתְנַבֵּא: "הִנֵּה כְלֵי בֵית ה' מוּשָׁבִים מִבָּבֶלָה עַתָּה מְהֵרָה" (ירמיה כז, טז), וְיִרְמְיָהוּ עוֹמֵד וְצוֹוֵחַ עַל הָעַמּוּדִים וְעַל הַיָּם וְעַל יֶתֶר הַכֵּלִים שֶׁלֹּא גָלוּ עִם יְכָנְיָה: "בָּבֶלָה יוּבָאוּ" (שם פסוק כב) עִם גָּלוּת צִדְקִיָּהוּ:

כב **אֲשֶׁר יְדַבֵּר הַנָּבִיא.** וְיֹאמַר: דָּבָר זֶה עָתִיד לָבוֹא עֲלֵיכֶם, וְתִרְאוּ שֶׁלֹּא יָבוֹא, "הוּא הַדָּבָר אֲשֶׁר לֹא דִבְּרוֹ ה'" וַהֲרֹג אוֹתוֹ. וְאִם תֹּאמַר: זוֹ בְּמִתְנַבֵּא עַל הָעֲתִידוֹת, הֲרֵי שֶׁבָּא וְאָמַר עֲשׂוּ כָּךְ וְכָךְ וּמִפִּי הַקָּדוֹשׁ בָּרוּךְ הוּא אֲנִי אוֹמֵר – כְּבָר נִצְטַוּוּ שֶׁאִם בָּא לְהַדִּיחֲךָ מֵאַחַת מִכָּל הַמִּצְוֹת לֹא תִשְׁמַע לוֹ (דברים יג, ד), אֶלָּא אִם כֵּן מֻמְחֶה הוּא לְךָ שֶׁהוּא צַדִּיק גָּמוּר, כְּגוֹן אֵלִיָּהוּ בְּהַר הַכַּרְמֶל שֶׁהִקְרִיב בַּבָּמָה בִּשְׁעַת אִסּוּר הַבָּמוֹת כְּדֵי לְגַדֵּר אֶת יִשְׂרָאֵל, הַכֹּל לְפִי צֹרֶךְ שָׁעָה וּסְיָג הַפִּרְצָה, לְכָךְ נֶאֱמַר: "אֵלָיו תִּשְׁמָעוּן" (לעיל פסוק טו): **לֹא תָגוּר מִמֶּנּוּ.** לֹא תִמְנַע עַצְמְךָ מִלְּלַמֵּד עָלָיו חוֹבָה, וְלֹא תִירָא לֵעָנֵשׁ עָלָיו:

יט ג **תָּכִין לְךָ הַדֶּרֶךְ.** 'מִקְלָט' 'מִקְלָט' הָיָה כָּתוּב עַל פָּרָשַׁת דְּרָכִים: **וְשִׁלַּשְׁתָּ אֶת גְּבוּל אַרְצְךָ.** שֶׁיְּהֵא מִתְּחִלַּת הַגְּבוּל עַד הָעִיר הָרִאשׁוֹנָה שֶׁל עִיר מִקְלָט כְּשִׁעוּר מַהֲלָךְ שֶׁיֵּשׁ מִמֶּנָּה עַד הַשְּׁנִיָּה, וְכֵן מִשְּׁנִיָּה לַשְּׁלִישִׁית, וְכֵן מִן הַשְּׁלִישִׁית עַד הַגְּבוּל הַשֵּׁנִי שֶׁל אֶרֶץ יִשְׂרָאֵל:

ה **וְנִדְּחָה יָדוֹ.** כְּשֶׁבָּא לְהַפִּיל הַגַּרְזֶן עַל הָעֵץ, וְתַרְגּוּמוֹ: "וְתִתְמְרֵיג יְדֵיהּ", לְשׁוֹן וְנִשְׁמְטָה יָדוֹ לְהַפִּיל מַכַּת הַגַּרְזֶן עַל הָעֵץ. "כִּי שָׁמְטוּ הַבָּקָר" (שמואל ב' ו, ו) תִּרְגֵּם יוֹנָתָן: "אֲרֵי מַרְגּוּהִי תוֹרַיָּא":

his prophetic character. We are not to say, "See, he spoke and his prediction has not come to pass." For God is long-suffering and abounding in kindness and repents of evil.... But if the prophet, in the name of God, assures good fortune, declaring that a particular event would come to pass, and the benefit promised has not been realized, he is unquestionably a false prophet, for no blessing decreed by the Almighty, even if promised conditionally, is ever revoked. (*Hilkhot Yesodei HaTorah* 10:4)

Precisely because Judaism believes in free will, the human future can never be unfailingly predicted. People change. God forgives: "Prayer, penitence, and charity avert the evil decree." There is no decree that cannot be revoked. A prophet does not foretell. He warns. If a prophecy of doom comes true, it has failed.

Calamity, catastrophe, disaster prove nothing. Anyone can foretell these things without risking his reputation or authority. It is only by the realization of a positive vision that prophecy is put to the test. A true prophet is an agent of hope.

כא אַחֲרִים וּמֵת הַנָּבִיא הַהוּא: וְכִי תֹאמַר בִּלְבָבֶךָ אֵיכָה נֵדַע אֶת־הַדָּבָר
כב אֲשֶׁר לֹא־דִבְּרוֹ יהוה: אֲשֶׁר יְדַבֵּר הַנָּבִיא בְּשֵׁם יהוה וְלֹא־יִהְיֶה
הַדָּבָר וְלֹא יָבֹא הוּא הַדָּבָר אֲשֶׁר לֹא־דִבְּרוֹ יהוה בְּזָדוֹן דִּבְּרוֹ הַנָּבִיא
יט א לֹא תָגוּר מִמֶּנּוּ: כִּי־יַכְרִית יהוה אֱלֹהֶיךָ אֶת־הַגּוֹיִם אֲשֶׁר
יהוה אֱלֹהֶיךָ נֹתֵן לְךָ אֶת־אַרְצָם וִירִשְׁתָּם וְיָשַׁבְתָּ בְעָרֵיהֶם וּבְבָתֵּיהֶם:
ב שָׁלוֹשׁ עָרִים תַּבְדִּיל לָךְ בְּתוֹךְ אַרְצְךָ אֲשֶׁר יהוה אֱלֹהֶיךָ נֹתֵן לְךָ
ג לְרִשְׁתָּהּ: תָּכִין לְךָ הַדֶּרֶךְ וְשִׁלַּשְׁתָּ אֶת־גְּבוּל אַרְצְךָ אֲשֶׁר יַנְחִילְךָ
ד יהוה אֱלֹהֶיךָ וְהָיָה לָנוּס שָׁמָּה כָּל־רֹצֵחַ: וְזֶה דְּבַר הָרֹצֵחַ אֲשֶׁר־יָנוּס
שָׁמָּה וָחָי אֲשֶׁר יַכֶּה אֶת־רֵעֵהוּ בִּבְלִי־דַעַת וְהוּא לֹא־שֹׂנֵא לוֹ מִתְּמֹל
ה שִׁלְשֹׁם: וַאֲשֶׁר יָבֹא אֶת־רֵעֵהוּ בַיַּעַר לַחְטֹב עֵצִים וְנִדְּחָה יָדוֹ בַגַּרְזֶן

אונקלוס

עַמְמַיָּא, וְיִתְקְטֵיל נְבִיָּא הַהוּא: כא וַאֲרֵי תֵימַר בְּלִבָּךְ, אֵיכְדֵין נֵדַע
יָת פִּתְגָּמָא, דְּלָא מַלְּלֵיהּ יי: כב דִּימַלֵּיל נְבִיָּא בִּשְׁמָא דַיי, וְלָא יְהֵי
פִתְגָּמָא וְלָא יִתְקַיַּם, הוּא פִתְגָּמָא, דְּלָא מַלְּלֵיהּ יי, בִּרְשַׁע מַלְּלֵיהּ
נְבִיָּא, לָא תִדְחֲלוּן מִנֵּיהּ: יט א אֲרֵי יְשֵׁיצֵי, יי אֱלָהָךְ יָת עַמְמַיָּא,
דַּיי אֱלָהָךְ, יָהֵיב לָךְ יָת אַרְעֲהוֹן, וְתֵירְתִנּוּן, וְתֵתֵּיב בְּקִרְוֵיהוֹן
וּבְבָתֵּיהוֹן: ב תְּלָת קִרְוִין תַּפְרֵישׁ לָךְ, בְּגוֹ אַרְעָךְ, דַּיי אֱלָהָךְ, יָהֵיב לָךְ
לְמֵירְתַהּ: ג תַּתְקֵין לָךְ אוֹרְחָא, וּתְתַלֵּית יָת תְּחוּם אַרְעָךְ, דְּיַחְסְנִנָּךְ
יי אֱלָהָךְ, וִיהֵי, לְמֵעְרַק לְתַמָּן כָּל קָטוֹל: ד וְדֵין פִּתְגָּם קָטוֹלָא,
דְּיֵעְרוֹק לְתַמָּן וְיִתְקַיַּם, דְּיִקְטוֹל יָת חַבְרֵיהּ בְּלָא מַדְּעֵיהּ, וְהוּא,
לָא סָנֵי לֵיהּ מֵאִתְמָלֵי וּמִדְּקַמּוֹהִי: ה וּדְיֵיעוֹל עִם חַבְרֵיהּ בְּחֻרְשָׁא
לְמִקַּץ אָעִין, וְתִתְמְרֵיג יְדֵיהּ בְּבַרְזְלָא לְמִקְצֵיהּ אָעָא, וְיִשְׁתְּלֵיף
בַּרְזְלָא מִן אָעָא, וְיַשְׁכַּח יָת חַבְרֵיהּ וִימוּת, הוּא, יֵעְרוֹק, לַחֲדָא מִן

18:21 **אֵיכָה נֵדַע אֶת־הַדָּבָר אֲשֶׁר לֹא־דִבְּרוֹ יהוה** *How can we recognize a message that the Lord has not spoken?* – How does one tell a true prophet from a false one? On the face of it, if what the prophet predicts comes to pass, he is a true prophet; if not, not. Clearly, though, it is not that simple.

The prophet Yirmeyahu makes a fundamental distinction between prophesies of good news and bad.

> The prophets who were before me and before you long ago – they prophesied war, catastrophe, and pestilence to many lands and to great kingdoms. The prophet who shall prophesy peace, when his words come true, that prophet shall be acknowledged as one whom the Lord has truly sent. (Jer. 28:8–9)

It is easy to prophesy disaster. If the prophecy comes true, then you have spoken the truth. If it does not, then you can say: God relented and forgave. A negative prophecy cannot be refuted, but a positive one can. If the good foreseen comes to pass, then the prophecy is true. If it does not, then you cannot say, "God changed His mind," because God does not retract from a promise He has made of good, or peace, or return.

This is how Rambam puts it:

> As for calamities predicted by a prophet, if, for example, he foretells the death of a certain individual or declares that in a particular year there will be famine or war and so forth, the non-fulfillment of his forecast does not disprove

as he swings the ax to cut down a tree, the ax-head may fly off the handle and
strike the neighbor and kill him; that man may flee to one of these cities and
6 live. Should the distance be too great, the avenger of blood might pursue him
in hot anger, overtake, and kill him even though he did not deserve to die, there
7 having been no prior enmity between the two. That is why I charge you thus:
8 three cities must you set aside. If the Lord your God enlarges your territory,
as He swore to your ancestors, and gives you all of that land that He promised
9 to give your ancestors, if you vigilantly observe all of this commandment with
which I charge you today, loving the Lord your God and walking in all His
10 ways, then you shall add to these three, three cities more so that innocent blood
is not shed, bringing bloodguilt upon you, in the land that the Lord your God
is giving you as a possession.
11 But if one person hates his fellow, lies in wait for him, and attacks and kills

רש״י

וְנָשַׁל הַבַּרְזֶל מִן הָעֵץ. יֵשׁ מֵרַבּוֹתֵינוּ אוֹמְרִים: נִשְׁמַט הַבַּרְזֶל מִקַּתּוֹ, וְיֵשׁ מֵהֶם אוֹמְרִים: שֶׁיַּשַּׁל הַבַּרְזֶל לַחֲתִיכָה מִן הָעֵץ הַמִּתְבַּקֵּעַ וְהִיא נִתְּזָה וְהָרְגָה:

ו **פֶּן יִרְדֹּף גֹּאֵל הַדָּם.** לְכָךְ אֲנִי אוֹמֵר לְהָכִין לְךָ דֶּרֶךְ וְעָרֵי מִקְלָט רַבִּים:

ח **וְאִם יַרְחִיב.** כַּאֲשֶׁר נִשְׁבַּע לָתֵת לְךָ אֶרֶץ קֵינִי וּקְנִזִּי וְקַדְמוֹנִי (בראשית טו, יט):

ט **וְיָסַפְתָּ לְךָ עוֹד שָׁלֹשׁ.** הֲרֵי תֵּשַׁע: שָׁלֹשׁ שֶׁבְּעֵבֶר הַיַּרְדֵּן וְשָׁלֹשׁ שֶׁבְּאֶרֶץ כְּנַעַן וְשָׁלֹשׁ לֶעָתִיד לָבוֹא:

יא **וְכִי יִהְיֶה אִישׁ שֹׂנֵא לְרֵעֵהוּ.** עַל יְדֵי שִׂנְאָתוֹ הוּא בָּא לִידֵי "וְאָרַב לוֹ", מִכָּאן אָמְרוּ: עָבַר אָדָם עַל מִצְוָה קַלָּה סוֹפוֹ לַעֲבֹר עַל מִצְוָה חֲמוּרָה; לְפִי שֶׁעָבַר עַל "לֹא תִשְׂנָא" (ויקרא יט, יז) סוֹפוֹ לָבֹא לִידֵי שְׁפִיכוּת דָּמִים, לְכָךְ נֶאֱמַר: "כִּי יִהְיֶה אִישׁ שֹׂנֵא לְרֵעֵהוּ" וְגוֹ', שֶׁהָיָה לוֹ לִכְתֹּב: 'וְכִי יָקוּם אִישׁ וְאָרַב לְרֵעֵהוּ וְהִכָּהוּ נֶפֶשׁ':

Man was created alone to teach you that whoever destroys a single soul is as if he destroyed an entire world, and whoever saves a single life is as if he had saved an entire world.... And also [he was created alone] to proclaim the greatness of the Holy One, blessed be He, for if a person makes many coins from one mold, they are all the same, but the supreme King of kings, the Holy One, blessed be He, made every person in the stamp of the first man, yet not one of them is identical to another. Therefore every single person is obliged to say: the world was created for my sake. (Sanhedrin 4:5)

The concept of God, singular and alone, gives rise to the concept of the human person, singular and alone. This is the birth of the individual in Western civilization.

It is also vital to Jewish survival in exile. Jews were always a minority, and the minority usually conforms to the majority. Had this been the case among Jews, there would be no Judaism today. Jews, however, have had a long history of valuing the individual over the group. Jews did not bend to the majority. Despite the vital importance of solidarity and communal responsibility, the one is not subsumed into the many.

19:11 **וְכִי־יִהְיֶה אִישׁ שֹׂנֵא לְרֵעֵהוּ** *If one person hates his fellow* – The protection of the city of refuge is given only to those who kill by accident, not to those who "hate" the victim, whose killing, even in the absence of witnesses, cannot be judged to be accidental. This poses an obvious problem for the court. How can human beings know whether the accused hated his victim or not? We cannot look into another person's heart. The law needs a behavioral criterion of hate. The sages ruled that it is deemed to be present if the killer was *not on speaking terms* with the victim ("He had

לִכְרֹת הָעֵץ וְנָשַׁל הַבַּרְזֶל מִן־הָעֵץ וּמָצָא אֶת־רֵעֵהוּ וָמֵת הוּא יָנוּס
ו אֶל־אַחַת הֶעָרִים־הָאֵלֶּה וָחָי׃ פֶּן־יִרְדֹּף גֹּאֵל הַדָּם אַחֲרֵי הָרֹצֵחַ כִּי
יֵחַם לְבָבוֹ וְהִשִּׂיגוֹ כִּי־יִרְבֶּה הַדֶּרֶךְ וְהִכָּהוּ נָפֶשׁ וְלוֹ אֵין מִשְׁפַּט־מָוֶת
ז כִּי לֹא־שֹׂנֵא הוּא לוֹ מִתְּמוֹל שִׁלְשׁוֹם׃ עַל־כֵּן אָנֹכִי מְצַוְּךָ לֵאמֹר
ח שָׁלֹשׁ עָרִים תַּבְדִּיל לָךְ׃ וְאִם־יַרְחִיב יהוה אֱלֹהֶיךָ אֶת־גְּבֻלְךָ כַּאֲשֶׁר
נִשְׁבַּע לַאֲבֹתֶיךָ וְנָתַן לְךָ אֶת־כָּל־הָאָרֶץ אֲשֶׁר דִּבֶּר לָתֵת לַאֲבֹתֶיךָ׃
ט כִּי־תִשְׁמֹר אֶת־כָּל־הַמִּצְוָה הַזֹּאת לַעֲשֹׂתָהּ אֲשֶׁר אָנֹכִי מְצַוְּךָ הַיּוֹם
לְאַהֲבָה אֶת־יהוה אֱלֹהֶיךָ וְלָלֶכֶת בִּדְרָכָיו כָּל־הַיָּמִים וְיָסַפְתָּ לְךָ עוֹד
י שָׁלֹשׁ עָרִים עַל הַשָּׁלֹשׁ הָאֵלֶּה׃ וְלֹא יִשָּׁפֵךְ דָּם נָקִי בְּקֶרֶב אַרְצְךָ אֲשֶׁר
יהוה אֱלֹהֶיךָ נֹתֵן לְךָ נַחֲלָה וְהָיָה עָלֶיךָ דָּמִים׃
יא וְכִי־יִהְיֶה אִישׁ שֹׂנֵא לְרֵעֵהוּ וְאָרַב לוֹ וְקָם עָלָיו וְהִכָּהוּ נֶפֶשׁ וָמֵת וְנָס

אונקלוס

קִרְוַיָּא הָאִלֵּין וְיִתְקַיַּם: ו דִּלְמָא יִרְדּוֹף גָּאֵיל דְּמָא בָּתַר קָטוֹלָא, אֲרֵי יִיחַם לִבֵּיהּ, וְיִדְבְּקִנֵּיהּ, אֲרֵי יִסְגֵּי אוֹרְחָא וְיִקְטְלִנֵּיהּ נְפַשׁ, וְלֵיהּ לֵית חוֹבַת דִּין דִּקְטוֹל, אֲרֵי, לָא סָנֵי הוּא, לֵיהּ מֵאֶתְמָלֵי וּמִדְּקַמּוֹהִי: ז עַל כֵּן, אֲנָא מְפַקֵּיד לָךְ לְמֵימַר, תְּלָת קִרְוִין תַּפְרֵישׁ לָךְ: ח וְאִם יַפְתֵּי, יי אֱלָהָךְ יָת תְּחוּמָךְ, כְּמָא דְּקַיֵּים לַאֲבָהָתָךְ, וְיִתֵּין לָךְ יָת כָּל אַרְעָא, דְּמַלֵּיל לְמִתַּן לַאֲבָהָתָךְ: ט אֲרֵי תִטַּר יָת כָּל תַּפְקֵידְתָּא הָדָא לְמֶעְבְּדַהּ, דַּאֲנָא מְפַקֵּיד לָךְ יוֹמָא דֵין, לְמִרְחַם, יָת יי אֱלָהָךְ, וּלְמְהָךְ בְּאוֹרְחָן דְּתַקְנָן קֳדָמוֹהִי כָּל יוֹמַיָּא, וְתוֹסֵיף לָךְ עוֹד תְּלָת קִרְוִין, עַל תְּלָת אִלֵּין: י וְלָא יִשְׁתְּפֵיךְ דַּם זַכַּאי, בְּגוֹ אַרְעָךְ, דַּיי אֱלָהָךְ, יָהֵיב לָךְ אַחְסָנָא, וִיהֵי עֲלָךְ חוֹבַת דִּין דִּקְטוֹל: יא וַאֲרֵי יְהֵי גְּבַר סָנֵי לְחַבְרֵיהּ, וְיִכְמוֹן לֵיהּ וִיקוּם עֲלוֹהִי, וְיִקְטְלִנֵּיהּ נְפַשׁ וִימוּת, וְיִעְרוֹק,

19:5 **הוּא יָנוּס אֶל־אַחַת הֶעָרִים־הָאֵלֶּה וָחָי** *That man may flee to one of these cities and live* – The cities of refuge were havens, shelters, places of safety designed to protect manslaughterers from "blood vengeance" by a member of the family of the victim. Rambam, following the Talmud, includes the following unexpected detail in his legislation about the cities:

> One who has been exiled does not leave the city of refuge at all, even to perform a mitzva, or to give evidence in a monetary or capital case, or to save someone by his testimony, or to rescue someone from a non-Jew or a river or a fire or a collapsed building. Even if all Israel needs his help, like Yoav ben Tzeruya [King David's chief of staff], he never leaves the city of refuge until the death of the High Priest, and if he leaves, he makes himself vulnerable to death. (*Hilkhot Rotze'aḥ UShmirat HaNefesh* 7:8)

Only within the city of refuge was the manslaughterer safe. To leave the city of refuge was to put his life at risk. No one in Judaism is commanded to put his life at risk to save the life of another – even to save the entire Jewish people ("even if all Israel needs his help"). Despite the fact that Judaism is an intensely communal faith, nonetheless in Jewish law *the individual takes priority over the community.*

This illustrates the supreme importance of the individual in Judaism. This is how a famous Mishna puts it:

12 him, and then flees to one of these cities, the elders of his town shall have him
13 brought back from there and handed over to the avenger of blood to die. Show
him no pity. You must purge the guilt of innocent blood from Israel, so that
14 it may be well for you. Do not move back your neighbor's boundary SHISHI
marker, set up by those long ago in the allotted land that the LORD your God
15 is giving you to possess. One witness alone is not enough to convict
a person of any crime or wrongdoing. A case is to be established only on the
16 evidence of two or three witnesses. If a corrupt witness comes forward to
17 accuse someone of wrongdoing, both parties to the dispute shall appear before
18 the LORD, before the priests and judges in office in that time. The judges shall
make a thorough investigation. If the man who testified proves to be a false
19 witness, having testified falsely against his fellow, then inflict upon the false
witness what the false witness had intended to inflict upon his fellow; you must
20 purge the evil from your midst. Others will hear and fear, and such an evil will
21 not be committed again in your midst. Show no pity: life for life, eye for eye,

רש״י

יג **לֹא תָחוֹס עֵינְךָ.** שֶׁלֹּא תֹּאמַר: הָרִאשׁוֹן כְּבָר נֶהֱרַג, מָה אָנוּ הוֹרְגִים אֶת זֶה וְנִמְצְאוּ שְׁנֵי יִשְׂרְאֵלִים הֲרוּגִים?:

יד **לֹא תַסִּיג גְּבוּל.** לְשׁוֹן: ״נָסֹגוּ אָחוֹר״ (ישעיה מב, יז; ירמיה לח, כב) כְּשֶׁמַּחֲזִיר סִימַן חֶלְקַת הַקַּרְקַע לְאָחוֹר לְתוֹךְ שְׂדֵה חֲבֵרוֹ לְמַעַן הַרְחִיב אֶת שֶׁלּוֹ. וַהֲלֹא כְּבָר נֶאֱמַר: ״וְלֹא תִגְזֹל״ (ויקרא יט, יג), מַה תַּלְמוּד לוֹמַר: ״לֹא תַסִּיג״? לִמֵּד עַל הָעוֹקֵר תְּחוּם חֲבֵרוֹ שֶׁעוֹבֵר בִּשְׁנֵי לָאוִין. יָכוֹל אַף בְּחוּצָה לָאָרֶץ? תַּלְמוּד לוֹמַר: ״בְּנַחֲלָתְךָ אֲשֶׁר תִּנְחַל״ וְגוֹ׳, בְּאֶרֶץ יִשְׂרָאֵל עוֹבֵר בִּשְׁנֵי לָאוִין, בְּחוּצָה לָאָרֶץ אֵינוֹ עוֹבֵר אֶלָּא מִשּׁוּם ״לֹא תִגְזֹל״:

טו **עֵד אֶחָד.** זֶה בָּנָה אָב, כָּל ׳עֵד׳ שֶׁבַּתּוֹרָה שְׁנַיִם, אֶלָּא אִם כֵּן פֵּרַט לְךָ בּוֹ ׳אֶחָד׳: **לְכָל עָוֹן וּלְכָל חַטָּאת.** לִהְיוֹת חֲבֵרוֹ נֶעֱנָשׁ עַל עֵדוּתוֹ, לֹא עֹנֶשׁ גּוּף וְלֹא עֹנֶשׁ מָמוֹן, אֲבָל קָם הוּא לִשְׁבוּעָה. אָמַר לַחֲבֵרוֹ: תֵּן לִי מָנֶה שֶׁהִלְוִיתִיךָ, אָמַר לוֹ: אֵין לְךָ בְּיָדִי כְּלוּם, וְעֵד אֶחָד מְעִידוֹ שֶׁיֵּשׁ לוֹ, חַיָּב לִשָּׁבַע לוֹ: **עַל פִּי שְׁנֵי עֵדִים.** וְלֹא שֶׁיִּכְתְּבוּ עֵדוּתָם בְּאִגֶּרֶת וְיִשְׁלְחוּ לְבֵית דִּין, וְלֹא שֶׁיַּעֲמֹד תֻּרְגְּמָן בֵּין הָעֵדִים וּבֵין הַדַּיָּנִים:

טז **לַעֲנוֹת בּוֹ סָרָה.** דָּבָר שֶׁאֵינוֹ, שֶׁהוּסַר הָעֵד הַזֶּה מִכָּל הָעֵדוּת הַזֹּאת. כֵּיצַד? שֶׁאָמְרוּ לָהֶם: וַהֲלֹא עִמָּנוּ הֱיִיתֶם בְּאוֹתוֹ הַיּוֹם בְּמָקוֹם פְּלוֹנִי:

יז **וְעָמְדוּ שְׁנֵי הָאֲנָשִׁים.** בְּעֵדִים הַכָּתוּב מְדַבֵּר, וְלִמֵּד שֶׁאֵין עֵדוּת בְּנָשִׁים, וְלִמֵּד שֶׁצְּרִיכִין לְהָעִיד עֵדוּתָן מְעוּמָד: **אֲשֶׁר לָהֶם הָרִיב.** אֵלּוּ בַּעֲלֵי הַדִּין: **לִפְנֵי ה׳.** יְהֵא דּוֹמֶה לָהֶם כְּאִלּוּ עוֹמְדִין לִפְנֵי הַמָּקוֹם, שֶׁנֶּאֱמַר: ״בְּקֶרֶב אֱלֹהִים יִשְׁפֹּט״ (תהלים פב, א): **אֲשֶׁר יִהְיוּ בַּיָּמִים הָהֵם.** יִפְתָּח בְּדוֹרוֹ כִּשְׁמוּאֵל בְּדוֹרוֹ, צָרִיךְ אַתָּה לִנְהֹג בּוֹ כָּבוֹד:

יח **וְהִנֵּה עֵד שֶׁקֶר.** כָּל מָקוֹם שֶׁנֶּאֱמַר ׳עֵד׳ בִּשְׁנַיִם הַכָּתוּב מְדַבֵּר: **וְדָרְשׁוּ הַשֹּׁפְטִים הֵיטֵב.** עַל פִּי הַמְּזִמִּים אוֹתָם וּבוֹדְקִים וְחוֹקְרִים אֶת הַבָּאִים לַהֲזִמָּם בִּדְרִישָׁה וּבַחֲקִירָה:

יט **כַּאֲשֶׁר זָמַם.** וְלֹא כַּאֲשֶׁר עָשָׂה, מִכָּאן אָמְרוּ: הָרְגוּ – אֵין נֶהֱרָגִין: **לַעֲשׂוֹת לְאָחִיו.** מַה תַּלְמוּד לוֹמַר: ״לְאָחִיו״? לִמֵּד עַל זוֹמְמֵי בַּת כֹּהֵן נְשׂוּאָה שֶׁאֵינָם בִּשְׂרֵפָה אֶלָּא כְּמִיתַת הַבּוֹעֵל שֶׁהוּא בְּחֶנֶק, שֶׁנֶּאֱמַר: ״בָּאֵשׁ תִּשָּׂרֵף״ (ויקרא כא, ט), הִיא וְלֹא בּוֹעֲלָהּ, לְכָךְ נֶאֱמַר כָּאן: ״לְאָחִיו״, כַּאֲשֶׁר זָמַם לַעֲשׂוֹת לְאָחִיו וְלֹא כַּאֲשֶׁר זָמַם לַעֲשׂוֹת לַאֲחוֹתוֹ. אֲבָל בְּכָל שְׁאָר מִיתוֹת הִשְׁוָה הַכָּתוּב אִשָּׁה לְאִישׁ, וְזוֹמְמֵי אִשָּׁה נֶהֱרָגִין כְּזוֹמְמֵי אִישׁ, כְּגוֹן שֶׁהֱעִידוּהָ שֶׁהָרְגָה אֶת הַנֶּפֶשׁ, שֶׁחִלְּלָה אֶת הַשַּׁבָּת – נֶהֱרָגִין בְּמִיתָתָהּ, שֶׁלֹּא מִעֵט כָּאן אֲחוֹתוֹ אֶלָּא בְּמָקוֹם שֶׁיֵּשׁ לְקַיֵּם בַּהֶן הֲזָמָּה בְּמִיתַת הַבּוֹעֵל:

כ **יִשְׁמְעוּ וְיִרָאוּ.** מִכָּאן שֶׁצְּרִיכִין הַכְרָזָה: אִישׁ פְּלוֹנִי וּפְלוֹנִי נֶהֱרָגִין עַל שֶׁהוּזַמּוּ בְּבֵית דִּין:

כא **עַיִן בְּעַיִן.** מָמוֹן. וְכֵן: ״שֵׁן בְּשֵׁן״ וְגוֹ׳:

Where there is honesty, truth, and truthfulness, there tends to be law, order, and prosperity. A respect for truth is essential for authority, collaborative endeavor, and human graciousness.

יב אֶל־אַחַת הֶעָרִים הָאֵל: וְשָׁלְחוּ זִקְנֵי עִירוֹ וְלָקְחוּ אֹתוֹ מִשָּׁם וְנָתְנוּ
יג אֹתוֹ בְּיַד גֹּאֵל הַדָּם וָמֵת: לֹא־תָחוֹס עֵינְךָ עָלָיו וּבִעַרְתָּ דַם־הַנָּקִי
יד מִיִּשְׂרָאֵל וְטוֹב לָךְ: לֹא תַסִּיג גְּבוּל רֵעֲךָ אֲשֶׁר גָּבְלוּ ששי
רִאשֹׁנִים בְּנַחֲלָתְךָ אֲשֶׁר תִּנְחַל בָּאָרֶץ אֲשֶׁר יְהוָה אֱלֹהֶיךָ נֹתֵן לְךָ
טו לְרִשְׁתָּהּ: לֹא־יָקוּם עֵד אֶחָד בְּאִישׁ לְכָל־עָוֺן וּלְכָל־
חַטָּאת בְּכָל־חֵטְא אֲשֶׁר יֶחֱטָא עַל־פִּי ׀ שְׁנֵי עֵדִים אוֹ עַל־פִּי שְׁלֹשָׁה־
טז עֵדִים יָקוּם דָּבָר: כִּי־יָקוּם עֵד־חָמָס בְּאִישׁ לַעֲנוֹת בּוֹ סָרָה: וְעָמְדוּ
שְׁנֵי־הָאֲנָשִׁים אֲשֶׁר־לָהֶם הָרִיב לִפְנֵי יְהוָה לִפְנֵי הַכֹּהֲנִים וְהַשֹּׁפְטִים
יח אֲשֶׁר יִהְיוּ בַּיָּמִים הָהֵם: וְדָרְשׁוּ הַשֹּׁפְטִים הֵיטֵב וְהִנֵּה עֵד־שֶׁקֶר הָעֵד
יט שֶׁקֶר עָנָה בְאָחִיו: וַעֲשִׂיתֶם לוֹ כַּאֲשֶׁר זָמַם לַעֲשׂוֹת לְאָחִיו וּבִעַרְתָּ
כ הָרָע מִקִּרְבֶּךָ: וְהַנִּשְׁאָרִים יִשְׁמְעוּ וְיִרָאוּ וְלֹא־יֹסִפוּ לַעֲשׂוֹת עוֹד כַּדָּבָר
כא הָרָע הַזֶּה בְּקִרְבֶּךָ: וְלֹא תָחוֹס עֵינֶךָ נֶפֶשׁ בְּנֶפֶשׁ עַיִן בְּעַיִן שֵׁן בְּשֵׁן יָד

אונקלוס

לַחֲדָא מִן קִרְוַיָּא הָאִלֵּין: יב וְיִשְׁלְחוּן סָבֵי קַרְתֵּיהּ, וְיִדְבְּרוּן יָתֵיהּ מִתַּמָּן, וְיִמְסְרוּן יָתֵיהּ, בְּיַד, גָּאֵיל דְּמָא וִימוּת: יג לָא תְחוּס עֵינָךְ עֲלוֹהִי, וּתְפַלֵּי אָשְׁדֵי דַּם זַכַּאי, מִיִּשְׂרָאֵל וְיֵיטַב לָךְ: יד לָא תְשַׁנֵּי תְּחוּמָא דְּחַבְרָךְ, דְּתַחִימוּ קַדְמָאֵי, בְּאַחְסַנְתָּךְ דְּתַחְסִין, בְּאַרְעָא, דַּייָ אֱלָהָךְ, יָהֵיב לָךְ לְמֵירְתַהּ: טו לָא יְקוּם סָהִיד חַד בִּגְבַר, לְכָל עֲוָיָן וּלְכָל חוֹבִין, בְּכָל חֵטְא דְּיֶחְטֵי, עַל מֵימַר תְּרֵין סָהֲדִין, אוֹ, עַל מֵימַר תְּלָתָא סָהֲדִין יִתְקַיַּם פִּתְגָּמָא: טז אֲרֵי יְקוּם סָהִיד שְׁקַר בִּגְבַר, לְאַסְהָדָא בֵיהּ סַטְיָא: יז וִיקוּמוּן תְּרֵין גֻּבְרַיָּא, דִּילְהוֹן דִּינָא קֳדָם יְיָ, קֳדָם כָּהֲנַיָּא וְדַיָּנַיָּא, דִּיהוֹן בְּיוֹמַיָּא הָאִנּוּן: יח וְיִתְבְּעוּן דַּיָּנַיָּא יָאוּת, וְהָא סָהִיד שִׁקְרָא סָהֲדָא, שִׁקְרָא אַסְהֵיד בַּאֲחוּהִי: יט וְתַעְבְּדוּן לֵיהּ, כְּמָא דַּחֲשֵׁיב לְמֶעְבַּד לַאֲחוּהִי, וּתְפַלֵּי עָבֵיד דְּבִישׁ מִבֵּינָךְ: כ וּדְיִשְׁתַּאֲרוּן יִשְׁמְעוּן וְיִדְחֲלוּן, וְלָא יֵיסְפוּן לְמֶעְבַּד עוֹד, כְּפִתְגָּמָא בִישָׁא, הָדֵין בֵּינָךְ: כא וְלָא תְחוּס עֵינָךְ, נַפְשָׁא חֲלָף נַפְשָׁא, עֵינָא חֲלָף עֵינָא שִׁנָּא חֲלָף שִׁנָּא, יְדָא

19:19 וּבִעַרְתָּ הָרָע מִקִּרְבֶּךָ *You must purge the evil from your midst* – The Torah well understands that a culture of truth telling is fundamental to a free society. Where there is a strong moral arena, then truth stands a chance of surviving intact against the assaults that will be made against it. Telling a lie will be a disqualification. A reputation for truth telling will be an essential test of character. A world of truth is a world of trust, and vice versa. Truth becomes the intellectual equivalent of a public space we can all inhabit, whatever our desires and predilections.

not spoken with him for three days because of hatred," says Rambam, *Hilkhot Rotze'aḥ UShmirat HaNefesh* 6:10). We are told (Lev. 19:17): "Do not hate your brother in your heart. Admonish your fellow and do not bear guilt on his account." The second sentence, says Rambam, is the antidote to the first. If someone offends you, say so and do not be silent, for otherwise you will come to hate him in your heart. That has led, most obviously in the case of Avshalom and Amnon (II Sam. 13:22), to murder. Silence incubates hate; speech can heal it.

▶

20 1 tooth for tooth, hand for hand, foot for foot. When you go out to battle
your enemies, and see horses and chariots, an army greater than yours, do not
be afraid of them; for the LORD your God, who brought you out of Egypt, He
2 will be with you. Before you engage in battle, the priest shall come forward and
3 address the men. 'Listen, Israel,' he shall say to them, 'this day you are going
into battle against your enemies. Do not lose heart or be afraid, do not panic
4 or dread them; for it is the LORD your God who goes with you, to fight against
5 your enemies for you, to bring you victory.' Then the officers shall address the
men: 'Is there a man here who has built a new house but not yet dedicated it?
Let him go back home, or he may die in battle and someone else will dedicate
6 it. Is there a man here who has planted a vineyard but not yet harvested it? Let
him go back home, or he may die in the battle and someone else will harvest it.
7 Is there a man here who has betrothed a woman but not yet married her? Let
him go back home, or he may die in battle and someone else will marry her.'
8 And further, 'Is there a man here,' the officers shall say to the men, 'who is afraid
or fainthearted? Let him go back home so that his comrades do not become

רש"י

כ א **כי תצא למלחמה.** סמך הכתוב יציאת מלחמה לכאן, לומר לך שאין מחסר אבר יוצא למלחמה. דבר אחר, לומר לך, אם עשית משפט צדק אתה מבטח שאם תצא למלחמה אתה נוצח, וכן דוד הוא אומר: "עשיתי משפט וצדק בל תניחני לעשקי" (תהלים קיט, קכא): **על איבך.** יהיו בעיניך כאויבים, אל תרחם עליהם כי לא ירחמו עליך: **סוס ורכב.** בעיני כלם כסוס אחד, וכן הוא אומר: "והכית את מדין כאיש אחד" (שופטים ו, טז), וכן הוא אומר: "כי בא סוס פרעה" (שמות טו, יט): **עם רב ממך.** בעיניך הוא רב אבל בעיני אינו רב:

ב **כקרבכם אל המלחמה.** סמוך לצאתכם מן הספר, מגבול ארצכם: **ונגש הכהן.** המשוח לכך, והוא הנקרא 'משוח מלחמה': **ודבר אל העם.** בלשון הקדש:

ג **שמע ישראל.** אפלו אין בכם זכות אלא קריאת שמע בלבד, כדאי אתם שיושיע אתכם: **על איביכם.** אין אלו אחיכם, שאם תפלו בידם אינם מרחמים עליכם, אין זו כמלחמת יהודה עם ישראל, שנאמר: "ויקמו האנשים אשר נקבו בשמות ויחזיקו בשביה וכל מערמיהם הלבישו מן השלל וילבשום וינעלום ויאכלום וישקום ויסכום וינהלום בחמרים לכל כושל ויביאום יריחו עיר התמרים אצל אחיהם וישובו שמרון" (דברי הימים ב' כח, טו), אלא "על אויביכם" אתם הולכים, לפיכך התחזקו למלחמה: **אל ירך לבבכם אל תיראו ואל תחפזו ואל תערצו.** ארבע אזהרות, כנגד ארבעה דברים שמלכי האמות עושין: מגיפין בתריסיהם כדי להקישן זה לזה כדי להשמיע קול שיחפזו אלו שכנגדן וינוסו, ורומסים בסוסיהם ומצהילין אותם להשמיע קול שעטת פרסות סוסיהם, וצווחין בקולם, ותוקעין בשופרות ומיני משמיעי קול. "אל ירך לבבכם", מצהלת סוסים. "אל תיראו", מהגפת התריסין. "ואל תחפזו", מקול הקרנות. "ואל תערצו", מקול הצוחה:

ד **כי ה' אלהיכם וגו'.** הם באים בנצחונו של בשר ודם ואתם באים בנצחונו של מקום. פלשתים באו בנצחונו של גלית, מה היה סופו? נפל ונפלו עמו: **ההלך עמכם.** זה מחנה הארון:

ה **ולא חנכו.** ולא דר בו. 'חנוך' לשון התחלה: **ואיש אחר יחנכנו.** ודבר של עגמת נפש הוא זה:

ו **ולא חללו.** לא פדאו בשנה הרביעית, שהפרות טעונין לאכלן בירושלים, או לחללן בדמים ולאכל הדמים בירושלים:

ז-ח **ויספו השטרים.** למה נאמר כאן "ויספו"? מוסיפין זה על דברי הכהן, כהן מדבר ומשמיע מן "שמע ישראל" עד "להושיע אתכם", ו"מי האיש" ושני ושלישי כהן מדבר ושוטר משמיע, וזה שוטר מדבר ושוטר משמיע: **הירא ורך הלבב.** רבי עקיבא אומר: כמשמעו, שאינו יכול לעמד בקשרי המלחמה ולראות חרב שלופה. רבי יוסי הגלילי

כ א בְּיָד רֶגֶל בְּרָגֶל׃ כִּי־תֵצֵא לַמִּלְחָמָה עַל־אֹיְבֶךָ וְרָאִיתָ סוּס
וָרֶכֶב עַם רַב מִמְּךָ לֹא תִירָא מֵהֶם כִּי־יהוה אֱלֹהֶיךָ עִמָּךְ הַמַּעַלְךָ
ב מֵאֶרֶץ מִצְרָיִם׃ וְהָיָה כְּקָרָבְכֶם אֶל־הַמִּלְחָמָה וְנִגַּשׁ הַכֹּהֵן וְדִבֶּר
ג אֶל־הָעָם׃ וְאָמַר אֲלֵהֶם שְׁמַע יִשְׂרָאֵל אַתֶּם קְרֵבִים הַיּוֹם לַמִּלְחָמָה
עַל־אֹיְבֵיכֶם אַל־יֵרַךְ לְבַבְכֶם אַל־תִּירְאוּ וְאַל־תַּחְפְּזוּ וְאַל־תַּעַרְצוּ
ד מִפְּנֵיהֶם׃ כִּי יהוה אֱלֹהֵיכֶם הַהֹלֵךְ עִמָּכֶם לְהִלָּחֵם לָכֶם עִם־אֹיְבֵיכֶם
ה לְהוֹשִׁיעַ אֶתְכֶם׃ וְדִבְּרוּ הַשֹּׁטְרִים אֶל־הָעָם לֵאמֹר מִי־הָאִישׁ אֲשֶׁר
בָּנָה בַיִת־חָדָשׁ וְלֹא חֲנָכוֹ יֵלֵךְ וְיָשֹׁב לְבֵיתוֹ פֶּן־יָמוּת בַּמִּלְחָמָה
ו וְאִישׁ אַחֵר יַחְנְכֶנּוּ׃ וּמִי־הָאִישׁ אֲשֶׁר נָטַע כֶּרֶם וְלֹא חִלְּלוֹ יֵלֵךְ וְיָשֹׁב
ז לְבֵיתוֹ פֶּן־יָמוּת בַּמִּלְחָמָה וְאִישׁ אַחֵר יְחַלְּלֶנּוּ׃ וּמִי־הָאִישׁ אֲשֶׁר
אֵרַשׂ אִשָּׁה וְלֹא לְקָחָהּ יֵלֵךְ וְיָשֹׁב לְבֵיתוֹ פֶּן־יָמוּת בַּמִּלְחָמָה וְאִישׁ
ח אַחֵר יִקָּחֶנָּה׃ וְיָסְפוּ הַשֹּׁטְרִים לְדַבֵּר אֶל־הָעָם וְאָמְרוּ מִי־הָאִישׁ
הַיָּרֵא וְרַךְ הַלֵּבָב יֵלֵךְ וְיָשֹׁב לְבֵיתוֹ וְלֹא יִמַּס אֶת־לְבַב אֶחָיו כִּלְבָבוֹ׃

אונקלוס

חֲלָף יְדָא רִגְלָא חֲלָף רִגְלָא׃ כ א אֲרֵי תִפּוֹק לְאָגָחָא קְרָבָא עַל בַּעֲלֵי דְבָבָךְ, וְתִחְזֵי, סוּסָוָן וּרְתִכִּין עַם סַגִּי מִנָּךְ, לָא תִדְחַל מִנְּהוֹן, אֲרֵי יי אֱלָהָךְ מֵימְרֵיהּ בְּסַעֲדָךְ, דְאַסְקָךְ מֵאַרְעָא דְמִצְרָיִם׃ ב וִיהֵי, כְּמִקְרַבְכוֹן לְאָגָחָא קְרָבָא, וְיִתְקָרַב כָּהֲנָא וִימַלֵּיל עִם עַמָּא׃ ג וְיֵימַר לְהוֹן שְׁמַע יִשְׂרָאֵל, אַתּוּן מִתְקָרְבִין יוֹמָא דֵין, לְאָגָחָא קְרָבָא עַל בַּעֲלֵי דְבָבֵיכוֹן, לָא יְזוּעַ לִבְּכוֹן, לָא תִדְחֲלוּן וְלָא תִתְבַּעֲתוּן, וְלָא תִתַּבְרוּן מִן קֳדָמֵיהוֹן׃ ד אֲרֵי יי אֱלָהֲכוֹן, דִמְדַבַּר קֳדָמֵיכוֹן, לְאָגָחָא לְכוֹן קְרָב, עִם בַּעֲלֵי דְבָבֵיכוֹן לְמִפְרַק יָתְכוֹן׃ ה וִימַלְּלוּן סָרְכַיָּא עִם עַמָּא לְמֵימַר, מַאן גֻּבְרָא, דִּבְנָא בֵיתָא חֲדַתָּא וְלָא חַנְכֵיהּ, יְהָךְ וִיתוּב לְבֵיתֵיהּ, דִּלְמָא יִתְקְטִיל בִּקְרָבָא, וּגְבַר אָחֳרָן יַחְנְכִנֵּיהּ׃ ו וּמַאן גֻּבְרָא, דִּנְצַב כַּרְמָא וְלָא אַחֲלֵיהּ, יְהָךְ וִיתוּב לְבֵיתֵיהּ, דִּלְמָא יִתְקְטִיל בִּקְרָבָא, וּגְבַר אָחֳרָן יַחֲלִנֵּיהּ׃ ז וּמַאן גֻּבְרָא, דַּאֲרַס אִתְּתָא וְלָא נַסְבַהּ, יְהָךְ וִיתוּב לְבֵיתֵיהּ, דִּלְמָא יִתְקְטִיל בִּקְרָבָא, וּגְבַר אָחֳרָן יִסְּבִנַּהּ׃ ח וְיֵיסְפוּן סָרְכַיָּא לְמַלָּלָא עִם עַמָּא, וְיֵימְרוּן, מַאן גֻּבְרָא דְּדָחֵיל וּתְבִיר לִבָּא, יְהָךְ וִיתוּב לְבֵיתֵיהּ, וְלָא יִתְּבַר, יָת לִבָּא דַאֲחוֹהִי כְּלִבֵּיהּ׃

רש״י

חוֹמֵר: הַיָּרֵא מֵעֲבֵרוֹת שֶׁבְּיָדוֹ, וּלְכָךְ תָּלְתָה לוֹ תּוֹרָה לַחֲזֹר עַל בַּיִת וְכֶרֶם וְאִשָּׁה, לְכַסּוֹת עַל הַחוֹזְרִים בִּשְׁבִיל עֲבֵרוֹת שֶׁבְּיָדָם, שֶׁלֹּא יָבִינוּ שֶׁהֵם בַּעֲלֵי עֲבֵרָה, וְהָרוֹאֵהוּ חוֹזֵר, אוֹמֵר: שֶׁמָּא בָּנָה בַיִת אוֹ נָטַע כֶּרֶם אוֹ אֵרַשׂ אִשָּׁה: פֶּן יָמוּת בַּמִּלְחָמָה. יָשׁוּב פֶּן יָמוּת, שֶׁאִם לֹא יִשְׁמַע לְדִבְרֵי הַכֹּהֵן כְּדַאי הוּא שֶׁיָּמוּת:

9 fainthearted along with him.' When the officers have finished addressing the
10 men, they shall appoint the commanders to lead them. When you SHEVI'I
11 approach a town to fight against it, first offer it peace. If it accepts your terms
of peace and lets you in, all the people found there shall serve you a tribute of
12 forced labor. If it rejects your peace offer and wages war against you, you shall
13 lay siege. When the LORD your God gives it over into your hands, you shall put
14 all its males to the sword. You may, however, take as your plunder the women,
children, livestock, and all else in the town, all its spoil; you may use the spoil
15 of your enemies, which the LORD your God has given you. This is how you are
to treat all the towns that are distant from you and do not belong to the nations
16 nearby. However, in the towns of the nations that the LORD your God is giving
17 you as an inheritance, let nothing that breathes remain alive. These, the Hittites
and Amorites, Canaanites and Perizzites, Hivites and Jebusites, you must utterly
18 destroy as the LORD your God has commanded you, so that they cannot teach
you to do all the abhorrent things that they do for their gods, causing you to sin
19 against your God, the LORD. When you lay siege to a town and wage
war against it for a long time to capture it, do not destroy its trees; do not wield
an ax against them. You may eat from them; you must not cut them down. Are

רש״י

ט **שָׂרֵי צְבָאוֹת.** שֶׁמַּעֲמִידִין זַקָּפִין מִלִּפְנֵיהֶם וּמִלְּאַחֲרֵיהֶם וְכַשִּׁילִים שֶׁל בַּרְזֶל בִּידֵיהֶם, וְכָל מִי שֶׁרוֹצֶה לַחֲזֹר הָרְשׁוּת בְּיָדוֹ לְקַפֵּחַ אֶת שׁוֹקָיו. 'זַקָּפִין' – בְּנֵי אָדָם עוֹמְדִין בִּקְצֵה הַמַּעֲרָכָה לִזְקֹף אֶת הַנּוֹפְלִים וּלְחַזְּקָם בִּדְבָרִים, שׁוּבוּ אֶל הַמִּלְחָמָה וְלֹא תָנוּסוּ, שֶׁתְּחִלַּת נְפִילָה נִיסָה:

י **כִּי תִקְרַב אֶל עִיר.** בְּמִלְחֶמֶת הָרְשׁוּת הַכָּתוּב מְדַבֵּר, כְּמוֹ שֶׁמְּפֹרָשׁ בָּעִנְיָן: "כֵּן תַּעֲשֶׂה לְכָל הֶעָרִים הָרְחֹקֹת" וְגוֹ' (להלן פסוק טו):

יא **כָּל הָעָם הַנִּמְצָא בָהּ.** אֲפִלּוּ אַתָּה מוֹצֵא בָהּ מִשִּׁבְעָה עֲמָמִין שֶׁנִּצְטַוֵּיתָ לְהַחֲרִימָם, אַתָּה רַשַּׁאי לְקַיְּמָם: **לָמַס וַעֲבָדוּךָ.** עַד שֶׁיְּקַבְּלוּ עֲלֵיהֶם מִסִּים וְשִׁעְבּוּד:

יב **וְאִם לֹא תַשְׁלִים עִמָּךְ וְעָשְׂתָה עִמְּךָ מִלְחָמָה.** הַכָּתוּב מְבַשֶּׂרְךָ שֶׁאִם לֹא תַשְׁלִים עִמָּךְ, סוֹפָהּ לְהִלָּחֵם בְּךָ אִם תַּנִּיחֶנָּה וְתֵלֵךְ: **וְצַרְתָּ עָלֶיהָ.** אַף לְהַרְעִיבָהּ וּלְהַצְמִיאָהּ וְלַהֲמִיתָהּ מִיתַת תַּחֲלוּאִים:

יג **וּנְתָנָהּ ה' אֱלֹהֶיךָ בְּיָדֶךָ.** אִם עָשִׂיתָ כָּל הָאָמוּר בָּעִנְיָן, סוֹף שֶׁה' נוֹתְנָהּ בְּיָדֶךָ:

יד **וְהַטַּף.** אַף טַף שֶׁל זְכָרִים, וּמָה אֲנִי מְקַיֵּם: "וְהִכִּיתָ אֶת כָּל זְכוּרָהּ"? בַּגְּדוֹלִים:

יז **כַּאֲשֶׁר צִוְּךָ.** לְרַבּוֹת אֶת הַגִּרְגָּשִׁי:

יח **לְמַעַן אֲשֶׁר לֹא יְלַמְּדוּ.** הָא אִם עָשׂוּ תְשׁוּבָה וּמִתְגַּיְּרִין, אַתָּה רַשַּׁאי לְקַבְּלָם:

יט **יָמִים.** שְׁנַיִם: **רַבִּים.** שְׁלֹשָׁה. מִכָּאן אָמְרוּ: אֵין צָרִין עַל עֲיָרוֹת שֶׁל גּוֹיִם פָּחוֹת מִשְּׁלֹשָׁה יָמִים קֹדֶם לַשַּׁבָּת. וְלִמֵּד שֶׁפּוֹתֵחַ בְּשָׁלוֹם

The sages saw in this command something more than a detail in the laws of war. They saw it as a *binyan av*, a specific example of a more general principle. They called this the rule of *bal tashḥit*, the prohibition against needless destruction of any kind. This is how Rambam summarizes it: "Not only does this apply to trees, but also whoever breaks vessels or tears garments, destroys a building, blocks a wellspring of water, or destructively wastes food transgresses the command of *bal tashḥit*" (*Hilkhot Melakhim UMilḥemoteihem* 6:10). This is the halakhic basis of an ethic of ecological responsibility.

The ruling represents a remarkable constraint on human ownership. Normally, to own something is to be able to

ט וְהָיָה כְּכַלֹּת הַשֹּׁטְרִים לְדַבֵּר אֶל־הָעָם וּפָקְדוּ שָׂרֵי צְבָאוֹת בְּרֹאשׁ
י הָעָם: כִּי־תִקְרַב אֶל־עִיר לְהִלָּחֵם עָלֶיהָ וְקָרָאתָ אֵלֶיהָ טז שביעי
יא לְשָׁלוֹם: וְהָיָה אִם־שָׁלוֹם תַּעַנְךָ וּפָתְחָה לָךְ וְהָיָה כָּל־הָעָם הַנִּמְצָא־בָהּ
יב יִהְיוּ לְךָ לָמַס וַעֲבָדוּךָ: וְאִם־לֹא תַשְׁלִים עִמָּךְ וְעָשְׂתָה עִמְּךָ מִלְחָמָה
יג וְצַרְתָּ עָלֶיהָ: וּנְתָנָהּ יהוה אֱלֹהֶיךָ בְּיָדֶךָ וְהִכִּיתָ אֶת־כָּל־זְכוּרָהּ לְפִי־
יד חָרֶב: רַק הַנָּשִׁים וְהַטַּף וְהַבְּהֵמָה וְכֹל אֲשֶׁר יִהְיֶה בָעִיר כָּל־שְׁלָלָהּ תָּבֹז
טו לָךְ וְאָכַלְתָּ אֶת־שְׁלַל אֹיְבֶיךָ אֲשֶׁר נָתַן יהוה אֱלֹהֶיךָ לָךְ: כֵּן תַּעֲשֶׂה
לְכָל־הֶעָרִים הָרְחֹקֹת מִמְּךָ מְאֹד אֲשֶׁר לֹא־מֵעָרֵי הַגּוֹיִם־הָאֵלֶּה
טז הֵנָּה: רַק מֵעָרֵי הָעַמִּים הָאֵלֶּה אֲשֶׁר יהוה אֱלֹהֶיךָ נֹתֵן לְךָ נַחֲלָה
יז לֹא תְחַיֶּה כָּל־נְשָׁמָה: כִּי־הַחֲרֵם תַּחֲרִימֵם הַחִתִּי וְהָאֱמֹרִי הַכְּנַעֲנִי
יח וְהַפְּרִזִּי הַחִוִּי וְהַיְבוּסִי כַּאֲשֶׁר צִוְּךָ יהוה אֱלֹהֶיךָ: לְמַעַן אֲשֶׁר לֹא־
יְלַמְּדוּ אֶתְכֶם לַעֲשׂוֹת כְּכֹל תּוֹעֲבֹתָם אֲשֶׁר עָשׂוּ לֵאלֹהֵיהֶם וַחֲטָאתֶם
יט לַיהוה אֱלֹהֵיכֶם: כִּי־תָצוּר אֶל־עִיר יָמִים רַבִּים לְהִלָּחֵם
עָלֶיהָ לְתָפְשָׂהּ לֹא־תַשְׁחִית אֶת־עֵצָהּ לִנְדֹּחַ עָלָיו גַּרְזֶן כִּי מִמֶּנּוּ תֹאכֵל

אונקלוס

ט וִיהֵי, כַּד יְשֵׁיצוּן סָרְכַיָּא לְמַלָּלָא עִם עַמָּא, וִימַנּוּן, רַבָּנֵי חֵילָא בְּרֵישׁ עַמָּא: י אֲרֵי תִקְרַב לְקַרְתָּא, לְאַגָּחָא קְרָבָא עֲלַהּ, וְתִקְרֵי לַהּ מִלִּין דִּשְׁלָם: יא וִיהֵי אִם שְׁלָם תַּעֲנֵינָךְ, וְתִפְתַּח לָךְ, וִיהֵי כָּל עַמָּא דְּיִשְׁתְּכַח בַּהּ, יְהוֹן לָךְ, מַסְּקֵי מִסִּין וְיִפְלְחֻנָּךְ: יב וְאִם לָא תַשְׁלֵים עִמָּךְ, וְתַעֲבֵיד עִמָּךְ קְרָב, וּתְצוּר עֲלַהּ: יג וְיִמְסְרִנַּהּ, יי אֱלָהָךְ בִּידָךְ, וְתִמְחֵי יָת כָּל דְּכוּרַהּ לְפִתְגָם דְּחָרֶב: יד לְחוֹד נְשַׁיָּא, וְטַפְלָא וּבְעִירָא, וְכֹל דִּיהֵי בְקַרְתָּא, כָּל עֲדָאַהּ תִּבּוֹז לָךְ, וְתֵיכוֹל יָת עֲדֵי סָנְאָךְ, דִּיהַב, יי אֱלָהָךְ לָךְ: טו כֵּן תַּעֲבֵיד לְכָל קִרְוַיָּא, דְּרַחִיקִין מִנָּךְ לַחֲדָא, דְּלָא מִקִּרְוֵי עַמְמַיָּא הָאִלֵּין אִנּוּן: טז לְחוֹד, מִקִּרְוֵי עַמְמַיָּא הָאִלֵּין, דַּיי אֱלָהָךְ, יָהֵיב לָךְ אַחְסָנָא, לָא תְקַיֵּים כָּל נִשְׁמָא: יז אֲרֵי גַמָּרָא תְגַמְּרִנּוּן, חִתָּאֵי וֶאֱמוֹרָאֵי כְּנַעֲנָאֵי וּפְרִזָּאֵי, חִוָּאֵי וִיבוּסָאֵי, כְּמָא דְּפַקְּדָךְ יי אֱלָהָךְ: יח בְּדִיל, דְּלָא יַלְּפוּן יָתְכוֹן לְמֶעְבַּד, כְּכֹל תּוֹעֵיבָתְהוֹן, דְּעָבְדִין לְטַעֲוָתְהוֹן, וּתְחוּבוּן קֳדָם יי אֱלָהֲכוֹן: יט אֲרֵי תְצוּר עַל קַרְתָּא יוֹמִין סַגִּיאִין לְאַגָּחָא קְרָבָא עֲלַהּ לְמִכְבְּשַׁהּ, לָא תְחַבֵּיל יָת אִילָנַהּ לְאָרָמָא עֲלוֹהִי בַּרְזְלָא, אֲרֵי מִנֵּיהּ תֵּיכוֹל,

THE PROHIBITION ON DESTROYING FRUIT TREES

War is, the Torah implies, inevitably destructive. That is why Judaism's highest value is peace. Nonetheless, there is a difference between necessary and needless destruction. Trees are a source of wood for siege works. But some trees, those that bear fruit, are also a source of food. Therefore, do not destroy them. Do not needlessly deprive yourself and others of a productive resource, or engage in scorched earth tactics.

20 trees of the field human beings that you should besiege them too? Only trees
that you know do not produce food may you cut down for use building siege
works until the town that has made war against you falls.
21 1 If a person is found lying slain in a field on the land that the LORD your God
2 is giving you to possess, and it is not known who killed him, your elders and
judges must go out and measure the distances from the slain person to each
3 of the surrounding towns. The elders of the town nearest the body shall take a
4 female calf that has never been worked or drawn a load with a yoke, and lead it
to a valley with a flowing stream that has not been plowed or planted, and there
5 in the valley the elders of that town shall break the calf's neck. The priests, sons

רש"י

שְׁנַיִם אוֹ שְׁלֹשָׁה יָמִים, וְכֵן הוּא אוֹמֵר: "וַיֵּשֶׁב דָּוִד בְּצִקְלָג יָמִים שְׁנָיִם" (שמואל ב' א, א), וּבְמִלְחֶמֶת הָרְשׁוּת הַכָּתוּב מְדַבֵּר: **כִּי הָאָדָם עֵץ הַשָּׂדֶה.** הֲרֵי "כִּי" מְשַׁמֵּשׁ בִּלְשׁוֹן 'דִּלְמָא', שֶׁמָּא הָאָדָם עֵץ הַשָּׂדֶה לְהִכָּנֵס בְּתוֹךְ הַמָּצוֹר מִפָּנֶיךָ לְהִתְיַסֵּר בְּיִסּוּרֵי רָעָב וְצָמָא כְּאַנְשֵׁי הָעִיר? לָמָּה תַשְׁחִיתֶנּוּ?:

כ **עַד רִדְתָּהּ.** לְשׁוֹן רִדּוּי, שֶׁתְּהֵא כְּפוּפָה לְךָ:

כא ב **וְיָצְאוּ זְקֵנֶיךָ.** סַנְהֶדְרֵי גְּדוֹלָה: **וּמָדְדוּ.** מִמָּקוֹם שֶׁהֶחָלָל שׁוֹכֵב: **אֶל הֶעָרִים אֲשֶׁר סְבִיבֹת הֶחָלָל.** לְכָל צַד, לֵידַע אֵיזוֹ קְרוֹבָה:

ד **אֶל נַחַל אֵיתָן.** קָשֶׁה, שֶׁלֹּא נֶעֱבַד: **וְעָרְפוּ.** קוֹצֵץ עָרְפָּהּ בְּקוֹפִיץ. אָמַר הַקָּדוֹשׁ בָּרוּךְ הוּא: תָּבֹא עֶגְלָה בַּת שְׁנָתָהּ שֶׁלֹּא עָשְׂתָה פֵּרוֹת, וְתֵעָרֵף בְּמָקוֹם שֶׁאֵינוֹ עוֹשֶׂה פֵּרוֹת, לְכַפֵּר עַל הֲרִיגָתוֹ שֶׁל זֶה שֶׁלֹּא הִנִּיחוּהוּ לַעֲשׂוֹת פֵּרוֹת:

20:19 **וְאֹתוֹ לֹא תִכְרֹת** *You must not cut them down* – Václav Havel made a fundamental point in *The Art of the Impossible*: "I believe that we have little chance of averting an environmental catastrophe unless we recognize that we are not the masters of Being, but only a part of Being." That is why a religious vision is so important, reminding us that we are not owners of our resources. They belong not to us but to the Eternal and eternity. Hence we may not needlessly destroy. If that applies even in war, how much more so in times of peace. "The LORD owns the earth and all it contains" (Ps. 24:1). We are its guardians, on behalf of its Creator, for the sake of future generations.

20:19 **כִּי הָאָדָם עֵץ הַשָּׂדֶה** *Are trees of the field human beings* – There is a deep-seated reverence for trees in Judaism, expressed in modern times by the afforestation of Israel and the celebration of Tu BiShvat, the "New Year" for trees. No Jew should be indifferent to the destruction of rain-forests.

The Talmud tells the story of one of the saints of early rabbinic times, Ḥoni the Circle-Drawer:

One day Ḥoni was journeying on the road and saw a man planting a carob tree. He asked him, "How long does it take for a carob tree to bear fruit?" The man replied, "Seventy years." Ḥoni asked, "Are you certain that you will live another seventy years?" The man answered, "I found carob trees in the world. As my forefathers planted them for me, so I too plant these for my children." (Taanit 23a)

Trees are a symbol of the long-term nature of the human enterprise. In the book of Psalms, the wicked grow like grass, the righteous slowly like cedars. Our decisions – economic, political, and military – must be taken on the basis of calculation of distant consequences (the Israelites, for example, are warned against too rapid a conquest "lest the land become desolate and the wild animals too numerous for you" [Ex. 23:29]). The world we inherit is due to the efforts of those who came before us. The world we leave our children is dependent on what we do. Conservation is part of what the philosopher Edmund Burke called the "partnership… between those who are living, those who are dead, and those who are to be born."

כ וְאֹתוֹ לֹא תִכְרֹת כִּי הָאָדָם עֵץ הַשָּׂדֶה לָבֹא מִפָּנֶיךָ בַּמָּצוֹר׃ רַק עֵץ
אֲשֶׁר־תֵּדַע כִּי לֹא־עֵץ מַאֲכָל הוּא אֹתוֹ תַשְׁחִית וְכָרָתָּ וּבָנִיתָ מָצוֹר
עַל־הָעִיר אֲשֶׁר־הִוא עֹשָׂה עִמְּךָ מִלְחָמָה עַד רִדְתָּהּ׃

כא א כִּי־יִמָּצֵא חָלָל בָּאֲדָמָה אֲשֶׁר יהוה אֱלֹהֶיךָ נֹתֵן לְךָ לְרִשְׁתָּהּ נֹפֵל
ב בַּשָּׂדֶה לֹא נוֹדַע מִי הִכָּהוּ׃ וְיָצְאוּ זְקֵנֶיךָ וְשֹׁפְטֶיךָ וּמָדְדוּ אֶל־הֶעָרִים
ג אֲשֶׁר סְבִיבֹת הֶחָלָל׃ וְהָיָה הָעִיר הַקְּרֹבָה אֶל־הֶחָלָל וְלָקְחוּ זִקְנֵי
הָעִיר הַהִוא עֶגְלַת בָּקָר אֲשֶׁר לֹא־עֻבַּד בָּהּ אֲשֶׁר לֹא־מָשְׁכָה בְּעֹל׃
ד וְהוֹרִדוּ זִקְנֵי הָעִיר הַהִוא אֶת־הָעֶגְלָה אֶל־נַחַל אֵיתָן אֲשֶׁר לֹא־יֵעָבֵד
ה בּוֹ וְלֹא יִזָּרֵעַ וְעָרְפוּ־שָׁם אֶת־הָעֶגְלָה בַּנָּחַל׃ וְנִגְּשׁוּ הַכֹּהֲנִים בְּנֵי לֵוִי

אונקלוס

וְיָתֵיהּ לָא תְקוּץ, אֲרֵי לָא כַאֲנָשָׁא אִילָן חַקְלָא, לְמֵיעַל מִן קֳדָמָךְ בִּצְיָרָא׃ כ לְחוֹד אִילָן דְּתִדַּע, אֲרֵי לָא אִילָן דְּמֵיכַל הוּא, יָתֵיהּ תְּחַבֵּיל וּתְקוּץ, וְתִבְנֵי כַּרְקוֹמִין, עַל קַרְתָּא דְּהִיא עָבְדָא עִמָּךְ קְרָב, עַד דְּתִכְבְּשַׁהּ׃ כא א אֲרֵי יִשְׁתְּכַח קְטִילָא, בְּאַרְעָא דַּייָ אֱלָהָךְ, יָהֵיב לָךְ לְמֵירְתַהּ, רְמֵי בְחַקְלָא, לָא יְדִיעַ מַאן קַטְלֵיהּ׃ ב וְיִפְּקוּן סָבָךְ וְדַיָּנָךְ, וְיִמְשְׁחוּן לְקִרְוַיָּא, דִּבְסַחְרָנוּת קְטִילָא׃ ג וּתְהֵי קַרְתָּא, דְּקָרִיבָא לִקְטִילָא, וְיִסְּבוּן, סָבֵי קַרְתָּא הַהִיא עֶגְלַת תּוֹרִין, דְּלָא אִתְפְּלַח בַּהּ, דְּלָא נְגַדַת בְּנִיר׃ ד וְיַחֲתוּן, סָבֵי קַרְתָּא הַהִיא יָת עֶגְלְתָא לְנַחַל בִּיר, דְּלָא יִתְפְּלַח בֵּיהּ וְלָא יִזְדְּרַע, וְיִקְפּוּן תַּמָּן יָת עֶגְלְתָא בְּנַחְלָא׃ ה וְיִתְקָרְבוּן כָּהֲנַיָּא בְּנֵי לֵוִי, אֲרֵי בְהוֹן,

dispose of it as one wishes. Jewish law denies absolute property in this sense. You may not break plates, tear clothes, or set fire to furniture in a spirit of vandalism even if they belong to you and no one else is harmed. Vandalism is a betrayal of the condition on which things are given over to the stewardship of man.

To be sure, conservation is not an absolute value in Jewish law. Halakha permits the destruction of natural resources in the course of constructive projects that will ultimately enhance human welfare. But the onus of proof is on the developer.

Judaism categorically rejects two attitudes to the environment. One, associated with the Stoic tradition, is that we have no moral duties toward nature. The other, drawn from some Eastern religions, is that nature is holy and to interfere with it is sacrilegious. The first allows technology to run rampant while the second turns its back on it altogether. Neither extreme, we believe, does justice to the challenge of human civilization.

God, said Yeshayahu (48:18), did not create the world to be desolate. He formed it to be inhabited. He gave man the intelligence to control nature. Therein lies his dignity. But He charged him with the duty of preserving nature. Therein lies his responsibility.

The rabbis put it simply. They said: When God made the first man, He took him to see all the trees of the Garden of Eden. He said to him: "See how beautiful are My works. All that I have created I have made for you. But be careful that you do not ruin My world, for if you do there is no one else to put right what you have destroyed" (Kohelet Rabba 7). That is as lucid a way as any of stating one of the great imperatives of our time.

of Levi, shall step forward, for it is them the LORD your God has chosen to
minister to Him, to give blessing in the LORD's name, and to decide all cases
6 of dispute and assault. Then all the elders of the town nearest the slain person
7 shall wash their hands over the calf whose neck was broken in the valley and MAFTIR
declare: 'Our hands did not shed this blood and our eyes did not witness it.
8 Absolve Your people Israel, whom You redeemed, LORD, and do not leave
the guilt of innocent blood among Your people Israel.' So shall atonement be
9 made for the bloodshed, and so will you purge the guilt of innocent blood from
yourselves, by doing what is right in the LORD's eyes.

The haftara for Parashat Shofetim is on page 1614.

רש״י

ז **יָדֵינוּ לֹא שָׁפְכוּ.** וְכִי עָלְתָה עַל לֵב שֶׁזִּקְנֵי בֵּית דִּין שׁוֹפְכֵי דָמִים הֵם? אֶלָּא לֹא רְאִינוּהוּ וּפְטַרְנוּהוּ בְּלֹא מְזוֹנוֹת וּבְלֹא לְוָיָה:

ח הַכֹּהֲנִים אוֹמְרִים: **כַּפֵּר לְעַמְּךָ יִשְׂרָאֵל:** **וְנִכַּפֵּר לָהֶם הַדָּם.** הַכָּתוּב מְבַשְּׂרָם, שֶׁמִּשֶּׁעָשׂוּ כֵּן יְכֻפַּר לָהֶם הֶעָוֹן:

ט **וְאַתָּה תְּבַעֵר.** מַגִּיד שֶׁאִם נִמְצָא הַהוֹרֵג אַחַר שֶׁנִּתְעָרְפָה הָעֶגְלָה, הֲרֵי זֶה יֵהָרֵג, וְהוּא ״הַיָּשָׁר בְּעֵינֵי ה׳״:

seized for [the sins of] his fellow citizens; if the whole world, he is seized for [the sins of] the whole world. (Shabbat 54b)

The phrase "is seized" may mean that the bystander is morally guilty. He can be called to account. He may be punished by "the heavenly court" in this world or the next. It does not mean that he can be summoned to an earthly court and sentenced for criminal negligence. We might hold a bystander guilty, but not in the same degree as the perpetrator.

Nonetheless, we have to think long and hard before we can say, "Our hands did not shed this blood." Morality cannot be outsourced. It is about taking responsibility, not handing it away or sloughing it off. It needs for us to think about the "we" and not just the "I." When we assume responsibility for what happens around us, we start to change the moral climate in which we live, move, and have our being. Morality begins with us.

כִּ֣י בָ֗ם בָּחַ֞ר יְהוָ֤ה אֱלֹהֶ֙יךָ֙ לְשָׁ֣רְת֔וֹ וּלְבָרֵ֖ךְ בְּשֵׁ֣ם יְהוָ֑ה וְעַל־פִּיהֶ֥ם יִהְיֶ֖ה
ו כָּל־רִ֥יב וְכָל־נָֽגַע׃ וְכֹ֗ל זִקְנֵי֙ הָעִ֣יר הַהִ֔וא הַקְּרֹבִ֖ים אֶל־הֶחָלָ֑ל יִרְחֲצוּ֙
ז אֶת־יְדֵיהֶ֔ם עַל־הָעֶגְלָ֖ה הָעֲרוּפָ֥ה בַנָּֽחַל׃ וְעָנ֖וּ וְאָמְר֑וּ יָדֵ֗ינוּ לֹ֤א שפכה שָֽׁפְכוּ֙ מפטיר
ח אֶת־הַדָּ֣ם הַזֶּ֔ה וְעֵינֵ֖ינוּ לֹ֥א רָאֽוּ׃ כַּפֵּר֩ לְעַמְּךָ֨ יִשְׂרָאֵ֤ל אֲשֶׁר־פָּדִ֙יתָ֙ יְהוָ֔ה
ט וְאַל־תִּתֵּן֙ דָּ֣ם נָקִ֔י בְּקֶ֖רֶב עַמְּךָ֣ יִשְׂרָאֵ֑ל וְנִכַּפֵּ֥ר לָהֶ֖ם הַדָּֽם׃ וְאַתָּ֗ה תְּבַעֵ֛ר
הַדָּ֥ם הַנָּקִ֖י מִקִּרְבֶּ֑ךָ כִּֽי־תַעֲשֶׂ֥ה הַיָּשָׁ֖ר בְּעֵינֵ֥י יְהוָֽה׃

The הפטרה *for* פרשת שפטים *is on page 1615.*

אונקלוס

אַתְרְעִי, יי אֱלָהָךְ לְשַׁמָּשׁוּתֵיהּ, וּלְבָרָכָא בִּשְׁמָא דַּיי, וְעַל מֵימְרְהוֹן
יְהֵי כָּל דִּין וְכָל מַכְתַּשׁ סְגִירוּ: ו וְכֹל, סָבֵי קַרְתָּא הַהִיא, דְּקָרִיבִין
לְקְטִילָא, יַסְחוֹן יָת יְדֵיהוֹן, עַל עֶגְלְתָא דִּנְקִיפָא בְנַחְלָא: ז וְיָתִיבוּן
וְיֵימְרוּן, יְדָנָא, לָא אֲשַׁדָא יָת דְּמָא הָדֵין, וְעֵינָנָא לָא חֲזָאָה: ח כָּהֲנַיָּא
יֵימְרוּן כַּפַּר לְעַמָּךְ יִשְׂרָאֵל דִּפְרַקְתָּא יי, וְלָא תִתֵּין חוֹבַת דַּם זַכַּאי,
בְּגוֹ עַמָּךְ יִשְׂרָאֵל, וְיִתְכַּפַּר לְהוֹן עַל דְּמָא: ט וְאַתְּ, תְּפַלֵּי, אָשְׁדֵי דַם
זַכַּאי מִבֵּינָךְ, אֲרֵי תַעֲבֵיד דְּכָשַׁר קֳדָם יי:

21:7 יָדֵינוּ לֹא שָׁפְכוּ אֶת־הַדָּם הַזֶּה *Our hands did not shed this blood* – If someone is found murdered outside a town, the elders of the nearest town have to undergo a penitential ritual and say a prayer for absolution that contains the words "Our hands did not shed this blood."

It is odd because no one was accusing them. The Talmud (Sota 46b) elaborates on the nature of the moral concern here. What the elders are really saying is: Did we create an environment in which such a crime could happen? Did we give the victim shelter? Did we protect them? Did we do all we could to make sure the roads were safe at night? We weren't legally responsible for their death, but were we in some larger sense morally responsible? Can we really say, "Our hands did not shed this blood"?

The Talmud discusses the accountability of those in the sphere of influence of a crime:

> Rav and R. Ḥanina, R. Yoḥanan and R. Ḥabiba taught [the following]: Whoever can forbid his household [to commit a sin] but does not, is seized for [the sins of] his household; [if he can forbid] his fellow citizens, he is

Parashat Ki Tetzeh

21 10 When you wage war against your enemies, and the Lord your God gives them
11 into your hand and you take captives, if you see a beautiful woman among the
12 captives, and you desire her and wish to marry her, bring her to your house.
13 Have her shave her head, pare her nails, and remove her captive's garb. She shall
sit in your house mourning for her father and mother for a full month. Only
after that may you go in to her and be her husband, and she shall be your wife.
14 But if you no longer desire her, you must let her go free. You may not sell her

רש״י

י **כִּי תֵצֵא לַמִּלְחָמָה.** בְּמִלְחֶמֶת הָרְשׁוּת הַכָּתוּב מְדַבֵּר, שֶׁבְּמִלְחֶמֶת אֶרֶץ יִשְׂרָאֵל אֵין לוֹמַר "וְשָׁבִיתָ שִׁבְיוֹ", שֶׁהֲרֵי כְּבָר נֶאֱמַר: "לֹא תְחַיֶּה כָּל נְשָׁמָה" (לעיל כ, טז): **וְשָׁבִיתָ שִׁבְיוֹ.** לְרַבּוֹת כְּנַעֲנִים שֶׁבְּתוֹכָהּ, וְאַף עַל פִּי שֶׁהֵן מִשִּׁבְעָה אֻמּוֹת:

יא **וְלָקַחְתָּ לְךָ לְאִשָּׁה.** לֹא דִּבְּרָה תוֹרָה אֶלָּא כְּנֶגֶד יֵצֶר הָרָע, שֶׁאִם אֵין הַקָּדוֹשׁ בָּרוּךְ הוּא מַתִּירָהּ יִשָּׂאֶנָּה בְּאִסּוּר, אֲבָל אִם נְשָׂאָהּ סוֹפוֹ לִהְיוֹת שׂוֹנְאָהּ, שֶׁנֶּאֱמַר אַחֲרָיו: "כִּי תִהְיֶיןָ לְאִישׁ" וְגוֹ' (להלן פסוק טו), וְסוֹפוֹ לְהוֹלִיד מִמֶּנָּה בֵּן סוֹרֵר וּמוֹרֶה (להלן פסוק יח), לְכָךְ נִסְמְכוּ פָּרָשִׁיּוֹת הַלָּלוּ: **אֵשֶׁת.** אֲפִלּוּ אֵשֶׁת אִישׁ:

יב **וְעָשְׂתָה אֶת צִפָּרְנֶיהָ.** תְּגַדְּלֵם כְּדֵי שֶׁתִּתְנַוֵּל:

יג **וְהֵסִירָה אֶת שִׂמְלַת שִׁבְיָהּ.** לְפִי שֶׁהֵם נָאִים, שֶׁהַגּוֹיִם הָאֲרוּרִים בְּנוֹתֵיהֶם מִתְקַשְּׁטוֹת בַּמִּלְחָמָה בִּשְׁבִיל לְהַזְנוֹת אֲחֵרִים עִמָּהֶם: **וְיָשְׁבָה בְּבֵיתֶךָ.** בַּבַּיִת שֶׁמִּשְׁתַּמֵּשׁ בּוֹ. נִכְנָס וְנִתְקָל בָּהּ, יוֹצֵא וְנִתְקָל בָּהּ, רוֹאֶה בִּבְכִיָּתָהּ רוֹאֶה בְּנִוּוּלָהּ, כְּדֵי שֶׁתִּתְגַּנֶּה עָלָיו: **וּבָכְתָה אֶת אָבִיהָ.** כָּל כָּךְ לָמָּה? כְּדֵי שֶׁתְּהֵא בַּת יִשְׂרָאֵל שְׂמֵחָה וְזוֹ עֲצֵבָה, בַּת יִשְׂרָאֵל מִתְקַשֶּׁטֶת וְזוֹ מִתְנַוֶּלֶת:

יד **וְהָיָה אִם לֹא חָפַצְתָּ בָּהּ.** הַכָּתוּב מְבַשֶּׂרְךָ שֶׁסּוֹפְךָ לִשְׂנֹאתָהּ:

angel of peace objected because "man is full of strife." God ignored the angel and created mankind (Bereshit Rabba 8:5). The midrash raises the question that has hovered over human existence since the beginning of time: Why did God create a being capable of destroying all else He had made? Humanity has consistently disrupted the harmony of the world and engaged in violence and war. What answer did God give to the angel of peace? The answer implicit in the midrash is that God had faith that humanity would eventually learn that even a difficult peace is better than an easy war.

There are two words for "strength" in Hebrew: *koaḥ* and *gevura*. But they mean quite different things. *Koaḥ* means the strength to overcome your enemies. *Gevura* means the strength to overcome yourself. Defining *gevura*, the Rabbis said, "Who is strong? One who is capable of self-restraint" (Avot 4:1). *Koaḥ* is the strength to wage war. *Gevura* is the strength to make peace. Israel has needed both to survive.

21:11 בַּשִּׁבְיָה אֵשֶׁת יְפַת־תֹּאַר *A beautiful woman among the captives* – The *parasha*'s opening three laws – a captive woman taken in the course of war, the law about the rights of the firstborn, and the "wayward and rebellious son" (Deut. 21:18) – are all about dysfunction within the family. The Sages said that they were given in this order to hint that someone who takes a captive woman will suffer from strife at home, and the result will be a delinquent son (Sanhedrin 107a). In Judaism, marriage is seen as the foundation of society. Disorder there leads to disorder elsewhere. The Torah did not endorse the taking of the captive woman but rather "spoke only in response to the evil inclination" (Kiddushin 21b), warning by the juxtaposition to the rebellious son that no good would come of it.

פרשת כי תצא

כא י כִּֽי־תֵצֵ֥א לַמִּלְחָמָ֖ה עַל־אֹיְבֶ֑יךָ וּנְתָנ֞וֹ יְהוָ֧ה אֱלֹהֶ֛יךָ בְּיָדֶ֖ךָ וְשָׁבִ֥יתָ שִׁבְיֽוֹ׃
יא וְרָאִיתָ֙ בַּשִּׁבְיָ֔ה אֵ֖שֶׁת יְפַת־תֹּ֑אַר וְחָשַׁקְתָּ֣ בָ֔הּ וְלָקַחְתָּ֥ לְךָ֖ לְאִשָּֽׁה׃
יב וַהֲבֵאתָ֖הּ אֶל־תּ֣וֹךְ בֵּיתֶ֑ךָ וְגִלְּחָה֙ אֶת־רֹאשָׁ֔הּ וְעָשְׂתָ֖ה אֶת־צִפָּרְנֶֽיהָ׃
יג וְהֵסִ֩ירָה֩ אֶת־שִׂמְלַ֨ת שִׁבְיָ֜הּ מֵעָלֶ֗יהָ וְיָֽשְׁבָה֙ בְּבֵיתֶ֔ךָ וּבָכְתָ֛ה אֶת־אָבִ֥יהָ
וְאֶת־אִמָּ֖הּ יֶ֣רַח יָמִ֑ים וְאַ֨חַר כֵּ֜ן תָּב֣וֹא אֵלֶ֗יהָ וּבְעַלְתָּ֔הּ וְהָיְתָ֥ה לְךָ֖ לְאִשָּֽׁה׃
יד וְהָיָ֞ה אִם־לֹ֧א חָפַ֣צְתָּ בָּ֗הּ וְשִׁלַּחְתָּהּ֙ לְנַפְשָׁ֔הּ וּמָכֹ֥ר לֹא־תִמְכְּרֶ֖נָּה בַּכָּ֑סֶף

אונקלוס

י אֲרֵי תִפּוֹק לְאָגָחָא קְרָבָא עַל בַּעֲלֵי דְבָבָךְ, וְיִמְסְרִנּוּן, יי אֱלָהָךְ, בִּידָךְ וְתִשְׁבֵּי שִׁבְיְהוֹן: יא וְתֶחֱזֵי בְּשִׁבְיָא, אִתְּתָא שַׁפִּירַת רֵיו, וְתִתְרְעֵי בַהּ, וְתִסְּבַהּ לָךְ לְאִתּוּ: יב וְתַעֲלִנַּהּ לְגוֹ בֵיתָךְ, וּתְגַלַּח יָת רֵישַׁהּ, וּתְרַבֵּי יָת טֻפְרַהָא: יג וְתַעְדֵּי יָת כְּסוּת שִׁבְיַהּ מִנַּהּ, וְתֵתֵיב בְּבֵיתָךְ, וְתִבְכֵּי, יָת אֲבוּהָא וְיָת אִמַּהּ יְרַח יוֹמִין, וּבָתַר כֵּן, תֵּיעוֹל לְוָתַהּ וְתִבְעֲלִנַּהּ, וּתְהֵי לָךְ לְאִתּוּ: יד וִיהֵי אִם לָא תִתְרְעֵי בַהּ, וְתִפְטְרִנַּהּ לְנַפְשַׁהּ, וְזַבָּנָא לָא תְזַבְּנִנַּהּ בְּכַסְפָּא,

KI TETZEH

Parashat Ki Tetzeh is about relationships: between men and women, parents and children, employers and employees, lenders and borrowers, and humans and animals. In this *parasha*, Moshe reaches the heart of the detailed provisions of the covenant. The *parasha* contains no fewer than seventy-four commands, more than any other in the Torah. Among them are laws about family dysfunction, moral and legal obligations toward neighbors and fellow citizens, sexual misdemeanors, moral behavior in relation to financial matters, and other rules of social responsibility. The *parasha* ends with the command to be eternally vigilant about Amalek, the Torah's paradigm case of hatred and cruelty.

21:10 כִּי־תֵצֵא לַמִּלְחָמָה *When you wage war* – Rambam summarized the Talmud's attitude to war in these words:

> No war, either permitted or obligatory [such as a war of self-defense] may be initiated without first offering terms of peace.... Yehoshua sent three messages before entering the land: the first, "Whoever wishes to flee, let him flee"; the second, "Whoever wishes to make peace, let him make peace"; the third, "Whoever wishes to make war, let him make war." (*Hilkhot Melakhim UMilḥemoteihem* 6:1, 5)

War, for Rambam, is *never* mandated except when the effort to make peace has been tried, and has failed. Even the command at the end of the *parasha* to "blot out the memory of Amalek" (Deut. 25:19), applied, according to Rambam, only if the Amalekites refused to make peace and accept the seven Noahide laws. Even here peace was preferable (*Hilkhot Melakhim UMilḥemoteihem* 6:4).

The Torah teaches a combination of idealism and realism in the political arena. We are neither pacifists nor militarists. We pray for peace, but we are prepared to go to war. We say, "How good and pleasant it is when brothers dwell together" (Ps. 133:1). But we also know, from the very beginning of Torah – from Kayin and Hevel – that brothers are capable of killing one another.

There is a remarkable midrash about the creation of the world. It says that when God came to create man, the

15 for money or treat her as a slave, since you have dishonored her. If a
man has two wives, and loves one but not the other, and if both the loved and
16 the unloved bear him sons, but the firstborn is the son of the one unloved, then
on the day he bequeaths his possessions to his sons, he may not give the rights
of the firstborn to the son of the loved in preference to the son of the unloved,

רש״י

לֹא תִתְעַמֵּר בָּהּ. לֹא תִּשְׁתַּמֵּשׁ בָּהּ, בִּלְשׁוֹן פַּרְסִי קוֹרִין לַעֲבְדוּת וְשִׁמּוּשׁ 'עִימְרָהָא'. מִיסוֹדוֹ שֶׁל רַבִּי מֹשֶׁה הַדַּרְשָׁן לָמַדְתִּי כֵּן:

association *ahuva/senua*, "loved" and "unloved/hated," in precisely the way that it describes Raḥel and Leah – to link the law in this *parasha* with the story of Yaakov and his sons. It is teaching us that law is rooted in the experience of history. Law is itself a *tikkun*, a way of putting right what went wrong in the past. We must learn to love, but we must also know the limits of love, and the importance of justice-as-fairness in families as in society.

21:15 **הָאַחַת אֲהוּבָה וְהָאַחַת שְׂנוּאָה** *Loves one but not the other* – Although the Torah does not outlaw bigamy, it never presents it positively. Monogamy is seen as both the norm (Gen. 2:24) and the ideal (see, for instance, Prov. 31), and although the law protects the rights of the "unloved," marriage is meant to be characterized by love.

Rabbi Yosef Kolon (Maharik, 1420–80), discussing whether a child must obey his parents in his choice of marriage partner, refers to a responsum of Rabbeinu Asher in which the author rules that a son is not bound to obey his father if he tells him not to speak to X, with whom the father is in dispute. The command to love your neighbor overrides the command to obey your parents. Since the love of husband and wife is a supreme example of love-of-neighbor, it too takes priority over a parent's wishes (*Responsa Maharik* 166:3).

Rabbi Eliyahu Capsali (*Me'a She'arim, Shaar* 62) gave the following ruling in a case where a father forbade his son to marry the woman whom "his soul desired":

> Though the command of filial honor and reverence is inexpressibly great … nonetheless it appears in my humble opinion that if the girl about whom you ask is a proper wife for the aforementioned Reuven … then the command of filial honor and reverence is irrelevant, and the son is not to abandon her so as to fulfill his father's command.
>
> For it is nearly certain that this father virtually commands his son to violate the Torah … for we see in the Talmud that a man ought not to marry a woman who does not please him. So that when the father commands his son not to marry this woman, it is as though he commands him to violate the Torah; and it is well known that the son is not to obey his father in such cases. …
>
> Now, if we were to decide that the son is obliged to obey his parents and marry, though his heart is not in the match, we would cause the growth of hatred and strife in the home, which is not the way of our holy Torah – most certainly in this case, where he loves another. Indeed, we can cite in this situation: "Great waters cannot quench love, nor torrents sweep it by" (Song. 8:7).

There is great wisdom in this approach. The Jewish family is based on mutual respect – the children's respect for those who have brought them into the world, and the parents' respect for the right of adult children to make their choices free of excessive parental interference. In this respect, as in so many others, Jewish law is a reflex of Jewish theology. For what we find in the Torah is a profound sense of empowerment of human beings by God. "Walk before Me," says God to Avraham (Gen. 17:1). The prophets, meanwhile, saw marriage as the single most compelling metaphor for the relationship between God and us – because it involves commitment, a mutual pledge of openness and trust, a promise that neither will walk away in difficult times, a covenant of loyalty and love.

טו לֹא־תִתְעַמֵּר בָּהּ תַּחַת אֲשֶׁר עִנִּיתָהּ: כִּי־תִהְיֶיןָ
לְאִישׁ שְׁתֵּי נָשִׁים הָאַחַת אֲהוּבָה וְהָאַחַת שְׂנוּאָה וְיָלְדוּ־לוֹ בָנִים
טז הָאֲהוּבָה וְהַשְּׂנוּאָה וְהָיָה הַבֵּן הַבְּכֹר לַשְּׂנִיאָה: וְהָיָה בְּיוֹם הַנְחִילוֹ
אֶת־בָּנָיו אֵת אֲשֶׁר־יִהְיֶה לוֹ לֹא יוּכַל לְבַכֵּר אֶת־בֶּן־הָאֲהוּבָה עַל־

אונקלוס

לָא תִתַּגַּר בַּהּ, חֲלָף דְּעַנֵּיתַהּ: טו אֲרֵי יְהֶוְיָן לִגְבַר תַּרְתֵּין נְשִׁין, חֲדָא רְחוּמְתָא וַחֲדָא סְנוּאֲתָא, וִילִידָן לֵיהּ בְּנִין, רְחוּמְתָא וּסְנוּאֲתָא, וִיהֵי, בְּרָא בֻּכְרָא לִסְנִיאֲתָא: טז וִיהֵי, בְּיוֹמָא דְּיַחְסֵין לִבְנוֹהִי, יָת דִּיהֵי לֵיהּ, לֵית לֵיהּ רְשׁוּ, לְבַכָּרָא יָת בַּר רְחוּמְתָא, עַל

LAW AND LOVE

In biblical Israel the firstborn was entitled to a double share in his father's inheritance. This passage tells us that the father cannot choose to transfer this privilege from one son to another by favoring the son of the wife he loves most if the firstborn came from another wife. The law seems to be in sharp conflict with the story of Yaakov and his two wives, Leah and Raḥel. Yaakov *did* transfer the right of the firstborn from Reuven, his actual firstborn, son of the less-loved Leah, to Yosef, the firstborn of his beloved Raḥel. Indeed, the Torah itself makes the verbal linkage, using the same pair of opposites, *ahuva/senua*, "loved" and "unloved/hated" both in our verse, and also to describe Raḥel and Leah (Gen. 29:30–31). Yaakov's conduct was the opposite of what is legislated here. How are we to resolve this? Abrabanel's explanation (see his commentary on these verses in Deuteronomy) is that Yaakov transferred the double portion from Reuven to Yosef because God told him to do so. The law in our *parasha* is stated to show that the case of Yosef was an exception, not a precedent. Sforno (on Deut. 21:16) suggests that the prohibition in Deuteronomy applies only when the transfer of the firstborn's rights happens because the father favors one wife over another. It does not apply when the firstborn has been guilty of a sin that forfeits his legal privilege, which is what happened with Reuven. This is stated explicitly in the book of Chronicles, which says that "Reuven … was Yisrael's firstborn, but when he defiled his father's bed, his birthright was granted to the sons of Yosef" (I Chr. 5:1).

There may be a different explanation. The Torah is a book about both law and history. Law answers the question "What may we do or not do?" History is an answer to the question "What happened?" There is no obvious relationship between these two.

In Judaism they are often connected. Especially in *mishpat*, civil law, there is frequently a link between law and history. Much of biblical law, for example, emerges directly from the Israelites' experience of slavery in Egypt, as if to say: This is what our ancestors suffered in Egypt; therefore, do not do likewise. Do not oppress your workers. Do not turn an Israelite into a lifelong slave. And so on.

Such biblical laws represent *truth learned through experience*, justice as it takes shape through history. The Torah takes the past as a guide to the future – often positively but sometimes negatively. Genesis tells us that Yaakov's favoritism toward Raḥel's firstborn, Yosef, over Leah's firstborn, Reuven, was a cause of lingering strife within the family. According to Ibn Ezra, the resentment felt by the descendants of Reuven endured for generations, which is why Datan and Aviram, both Reubenites, became key figures in the Koraḥ rebellion (Ibn Ezra on Num. 16:1).

Yaakov acted out of overwhelming love for Raḥel, and Yosef, her elder son. Love is central to Judaism – love between husband and wife, parent and child, love for God, neighbor, and stranger. But love is not enough. Love unites but it also divides. It leaves the less loved feeling neglected, "hated" (see note on Gen. 29:30). It can leave in its wake strife, envy, and a vortex of violence and revenge. There must also be justice, fairness, and the impartial application of the law.

That is what the Torah is telling us when it uses the verbal

17 the true firstborn. He must acknowledge the son of his unloved wife as the
firstborn, giving him a double portion of all that he has. He is the first fruit of
18 his manhood; the right of the firstborn belongs to him. If a man has a
wayward and rebellious son who does not listen to his father and mother and,
19 though they discipline him, still will not listen, his father and his mother shall
20 take hold of him and bring him out to the elders at the town gate. They shall
say to the town elders, 'This son of ours is wayward and rebellious. He does
21 not listen to us. He is a glutton and a drunkard.' Then all the men of the town
shall stone him to death. Thus you shall purge the evil from your midst, and all
22 Israel will hear, and be afraid. When someone is convicted of a capital SHENI

רש״י

יז **פִּי שְׁנַיִם.** כְּנֶגֶד שְׁנֵי אַחִים: **בְּכֹל אֲשֶׁר יִמָּצֵא לוֹ.** מִכָּאן שֶׁאֵין הַבְּכוֹר נוֹטֵל פִּי שְׁנַיִם בָּרָאוּי לָבֹא לְאַחַר מִיתַת הָאָב כְּבַמֻּחְזָק:

יח **סוֹרֵר.** סָר מִן הַדֶּרֶךְ: **וּמוֹרֶה.** מְסָרֵב בְּדִבְרֵי אָבִיו, לְשׁוֹן "מַמְרִים" (לעיל ט, ז): **וְיִסְּרוּ אֹתוֹ.** מַתְרִין בּוֹ בִּפְנֵי שְׁלֹשָׁה וּמַלְקִין אוֹתוֹ. בֵּן סוֹרֵר וּמוֹרֶה אֵינוֹ חַיָּב עַד שֶׁיִּגְנֹב וְיֹאכַל תַּרְטֵימַר בָּשָׂר וְיִשְׁתֶּה חֲצִי לֹג יַיִן, שֶׁנֶּאֱמַר: "זוֹלֵל וְסֹבֵא" (להלן פסוק כ), וְנֶאֱמַר: "אַל תְּהִי בְסֹבְאֵי יָיִן בְּזֹלְלֵי בָשָׂר לָמוֹ" (משלי כג, כ). וּבֵן סוֹרֵר וּמוֹרֶה נֶהֱרָג עַל שֵׁם סוֹפוֹ, הִגִּיעָה תּוֹרָה לְסוֹף דַּעְתּוֹ, סוֹף שֶׁמְּכַלֶּה מָמוֹן אָבִיו וּמְבַקֵּשׁ לִמּוּדוֹ וְאֵינוֹ מוֹצֵא, וְעוֹמֵד בְּפָרָשַׁת דְּרָכִים וּמְלַסְטֵם אֶת הַבְּרִיּוֹת; אָמְרָה תּוֹרָה, יָמוּת זַכַּאי וְאַל יָמוּת חַיָּב:

כא **וְכָל יִשְׂרָאֵל יִשְׁמְעוּ וְיִרָאוּ.** מִכָּאן שֶׁצָּרִיךְ הַכְרָזָה בְּבֵית דִּין: פְּלוֹנִי נִסְקַל עַל שֶׁהָיָה בֵּן סוֹרֵר וּמוֹרֶה:

כב **וְכִי יִהְיֶה בְאִישׁ חֵטְא מִשְׁפַּט מָוֶת.** סְמִיכוּת הַפָּרָשִׁיּוֹת מַגִּיד שֶׁאִם חָסִים עָלָיו אָבִיו וְאִמּוֹ, סוֹף שֶׁיֵּצֵא לְתַרְבּוּת רָעָה וְיַעֲבֹר עֲבֵרוֹת וְיִתְחַיֵּב

detention, that is to say, putting someone in prison because he or she is judged to be a danger to society.

One of the most significant post-Enlightenment arguments about the nature of ethics was between Kantians and Benthamites. For Kant, ethics was a matter of duty, and justice, of retribution. If a wrong had been done, it had to be set right by wrong being done to the wrongdoer. Bentham, by contrast, developed the theory known as utilitarianism. An act is right if it produces the best consequences for society as a whole. On this view, justice looks less to the past than to the future. If it deters wrongdoing and leads to less crime, it is justified.

According to Bentham, a punishment might be justified even if it were out of proportion to the crime, so long as it deterred others (an "exemplary punishment"). A Kantian would disagree. If it is disproportionate to the crime it is unjust, and no utilitarian benefits can justify injustice. Conversely, Kant considered the hypothetical case of a man who had committed murder on a desert island where the remaining inhabitants were about to leave. Should they sentence him to death and carry out the punishment? There would be no one else on the island to murder. Nonetheless, said Kant, the sentence should be carried out, for if it were not, it would be a failure of justice.

Some such disagreement seems to lie between R. Shimon and R. Yosei. R. Yosei believed that the Torah sometimes prescribes punishment-as-prevention in order to protect society and reduce the incidence of serious crimes. R. Shimon holds that it does not. One cannot preempt a crime in this way, even if lives will be lost in the future as a result. In other words, though the law of the "wayward and rebellious son" represents divine justice, it always encounters the existential reality of divine mercy. We are only judged, like the first wayward and rebellious son, Yishmael, "where we are" now (see Gen. 21:17 and commentary there). And on that basis R. Shimon bar Yoḥai rests his faith that the law never was or will be put into effect.

יז פְּנֵי בֶן־הַשְּׂנוּאָה הַבְּכֹר: כִּי אֶת־הַבְּכֹר בֶּן־הַשְּׂנוּאָה יַכִּיר לָתֶת
לוֹ פִּי שְׁנַיִם בְּכֹל אֲשֶׁר־יִמָּצֵא לוֹ כִּי־הוּא רֵאשִׁית אֹנוֹ לוֹ מִשְׁפַּט
יח הַבְּכֹרָה: כִּי־יִהְיֶה לְאִישׁ בֵּן סוֹרֵר וּמוֹרֶה אֵינֶנּוּ שֹׁמֵעַ
יט בְּקוֹל אָבִיו וּבְקוֹל אִמּוֹ וְיִסְּרוּ אֹתוֹ וְלֹא יִשְׁמַע אֲלֵיהֶם: וְתָפְשׂוּ בוֹ אָבִיו
כ וְאִמּוֹ וְהוֹצִיאוּ אֹתוֹ אֶל־זִקְנֵי עִירוֹ וְאֶל־שַׁעַר מְקֹמוֹ: וְאָמְרוּ אֶל־זִקְנֵי
כא עִירוֹ בְּנֵנוּ זֶה סוֹרֵר וּמֹרֶה אֵינֶנּוּ שֹׁמֵעַ בְּקֹלֵנוּ זוֹלֵל וְסֹבֵא: וּרְגָמֻהוּ כָּל־
אַנְשֵׁי עִירוֹ בָאֲבָנִים וָמֵת וּבִעַרְתָּ הָרָע מִקִּרְבֶּךָ וְכָל־יִשְׂרָאֵל יִשְׁמְעוּ
כב וְיִרָאוּ: וְכִי־יִהְיֶה בְאִישׁ חֵטְא מִשְׁפַּט־מָוֶת וְהוּמָת שני

אונקלוס

אַפֵּי בַר סְנוּאֲתָא בֻּכְרָא: יז אֲרֵי יָת בֻּכְרָא בַּר סְנוּאֲתָא יַפְרֵישׁ, לְמִתַּן לֵיהּ תְּרֵין חוּלָקִין, בְּכֹל דְּיִשְׁתְּכַח לֵיהּ, אֲרֵי הוּא רֵישׁ תָּקְפֵיהּ, לֵיהּ חֲזְיָא בְּכֵירוּתָא: יח אֲרֵי יְהֵי לִגְבַר, בַּר סָטֵי וּמָרוֹד, לָיְתוֹהִי מְקַבֵּיל, לְמֵימַר אֲבוּהִי וּלְמֵימַר אִמֵּיהּ, וּמַלְפִין יָתֵיהּ, וְלָא מְקַבֵּיל מִנְּהוֹן: יט וְיֵחֲדוּן בֵּיהּ אֲבוּהִי וְאִמֵּיהּ, וְיַפְּקוּן יָתֵיהּ, לִקְדָם סָבֵי קַרְתֵּיהּ וְלִתְרַע בֵּית דִּין אַתְרֵיהּ: כ וְיֵימְרוּן לְסָבֵי קַרְתֵּיהּ, בְּרַנָא דֵּין סָטֵי וּמָרוֹד, לָיְתוֹהִי מְקַבֵּיל לְמֵימְרַנָא, זָלֵיל בְּסַר וְסָבֵי חֲמַר: כא וְיִרְגְּמֻנֵּיהּ, כָּל אֲנָשֵׁי קַרְתֵּיהּ בְּאַבְנַיָּא וִימוּת, וּתְפַלֵּי עָבֵיד דְּבִישׁ מִבֵּינָךְ, וְכָל יִשְׂרָאֵל יִשְׁמְעוּן וְיִדְחֲלוּן: כב וַאֲרֵי יְהֵי בִּגְבַר, חוֹבַת, דִּין דִּקְטוֹל וְיִתְקְטֵיל,

THE WAYWARD AND REBELLIOUS SON

The law of the wayward and rebellious son is one that generated considerable debate among the Sages. What was its logic? How was it to be applied? Was it, in fact, ever applied?

Because of the apparent harshness of the law, the whole tendency of rabbinic interpretation was so restrictive as to make it difficult if not impossible for such a case to arise (see the discussion on the "town led astray," Deut. 13:17). The child must be within three months of attaining maturity (younger than that, he was still a minor; older, he was not still a child). He must have stolen money from his parents, used it to buy a specific measure of meat and Italian wine, eaten and drunk it in one go, in a place other than his parents' house, and so on (Sanhedrin 68b–71a). Some Sages suggested conditions that in practice would never be fulfilled. For example, R. Yehuda held that "if his mother is not like his father in voice, appearance, and stature, he does not become a rebellious son" (Sanhedrin 71a). R. Shimon bar Yoḥai firmly declared: There never was and never will be a "wayward and rebellious son" (Sanhedrin 71a.).

Nevertheless, there were those who held that the law was intended to be, and actually was, applied. What, according to them, was the logic of the law? R. Yosei HaGelili said: "The Torah foresaw the ultimate destiny of the wayward and rebellious son. Having dissipated his father's wealth, he would seek to satisfy his wants and be unable to do so. He would then go to a crossroad as a highwayman. Therefore the Torah ordained: Let him die innocent rather than die guilty – for the death of the wicked benefits both themselves and the world" (Sanhedrin 71b).

On this view, the law of the wayward and rebellious son is a form of preemptive punishment for what he is likely to do in the future. The equivalent nowadays would be preventive

23 crime and is executed and you hang him from a post, do not let his corpse
remain all night upon that post. You must bury him that same day, because
a man left hanging is a slur upon God, and you must not defile the land that
22 1 the LORD your God is giving you as your possession. If you see your
kinsman's ox or sheep straying away, do not ignore it; you must return it to its
2 owner. If the owner does not live nearby or you do not know who the owner
is, you must bring it home with you and keep it until the owner claims it; then
3 you must return it. You must do the same with his donkey, the same with his
garment, the same with anything your kinsman loses and you find. You cannot
4 ignore it. You shall not see your kinsman's donkey or ox fallen on the
5 road and ignore it. Help him to lift it. Men's clothing shall not be seen
on a woman, nor shall a man wear women's dress. Whoever does such things is
abhorrent to the LORD your God.
6 If you come across a bird's nest containing fledglings or eggs by the roadside, in

רש״י

מִיתָה בְּבֵית דִּין: **וְתָלִיתָ אֹתוֹ עַל עֵץ.** רַבּוֹתֵינוּ אָמְרוּ: כָּל הַנִּסְקָלִין נִתְלִין, שֶׁנֶּאֱמַר: "כִּי קִלְלַת אֱלֹהִים תָּלוּי", וְהַמְבָרֵךְ ה׳ בִּסְקִילָה:

כג] **כִּי קִלְלַת אֱלֹהִים תָּלוּי.** זִלְזוּלוֹ שֶׁל מֶלֶךְ הוּא, שֶׁאָדָם עָשׂוּי בִּדְמוּת דְּיוֹקָנוֹ וְיִשְׂרָאֵל הֵם בָּנָיו. מָשָׁל לִשְׁנֵי אַחִים תְּאוֹמִים שֶׁהָיוּ דּוֹמִים זֶה לָזֶה, אֶחָד נַעֲשָׂה מֶלֶךְ וְאֶחָד נִתְפַּס לְלִסְטִיּוּת וְנִתְלָה, כָּל הָרוֹאֶה אוֹתוֹ אוֹמֵר: הַמֶּלֶךְ תָּלוּי. כָּל 'קְלָלָה' שֶׁבַּמִּקְרָא לְשׁוֹן הָקֵל וְזִלְזוּל, כְּמוֹ: "וְהוּא קִלְלַנִי קְלָלָה נִמְרֶצֶת" (מלכים א׳ ב, ח):

כב א] **וְהִתְעַלַּמְתָּ.** כּוֹבֵשׁ עַיִן כְּאִלּוּ אֵינוֹ רוֹאֵהוּ: **לֹא תִרְאֶה... וְהִתְעַלַּמְתָּ.** לֹא תִרְאֶה אוֹתוֹ שֶׁתִּתְעַלֵּם מִמֶּנּוּ, זֶהוּ פְּשׁוּטוֹ. וְרַבּוֹתֵינוּ דָּרְשׁוּ: פְּעָמִים שֶׁאַתָּה מִתְעַלֵּם וְכוּ׳:

ב] **עַד דְּרֹשׁ אָחִיךָ.** וְכִי תַּעֲלֶה עַל דַּעְתְּךָ שֶׁיִּתְּנֵהוּ לוֹ קֹדֶם שֶׁיִּדְרְשֵׁהוּ? אֶלָּא דָּרְשֵׁהוּ שֶׁלֹּא יְהֵא רַמַּאי: **וַהֲשֵׁבֹתוֹ לוֹ.** שֶׁתְּהֵא בּוֹ הֲשָׁבָה, שֶׁלֹּא יֹאכַל בְּבֵיתְךָ כְּדֵי דָמָיו וְתִתְבָּעֵם מִמֶּנּוּ. מִכָּאן אָמְרוּ: כָּל דָּבָר שֶׁעוֹשֶׂה וְאוֹכֵל יַעֲשֶׂה וְיֹאכַל, וְשֶׁאֵינוֹ עוֹשֶׂה וְאוֹכֵל יִמָּכֵר:

ג] **לֹא תוּכַל לְהִתְעַלֵּם.** לִכְבֹּשׁ עֵינְךָ כְּאִלּוּ אֵינְךָ רוֹאֶה אוֹתוֹ:

ד] **הָקֵם תָּקִים.** זוֹ טְעִינָה, לְהַטְעִין מַשּׂאוֹי שֶׁנָּפַל מֵעָלָיו: **עִמּוֹ.** עִם בְּעָלָיו, אֲבָל אִם הָלַךְ וְיָשַׁב לוֹ וְאָמַר לוֹ: הוֹאִיל וְעָלֶיךָ מִצְוָה, אִם רָצִיתָ לִטְעֹן טְעֹן, פָּטוּר:

ה] **לֹא יִהְיֶה כְלִי גֶבֶר עַל אִשָּׁה.** שֶׁתְּהֵא דּוֹמָה לְאִישׁ כְּדֵי שֶׁתֵּלֵךְ בֵּין הָאֲנָשִׁים, שֶׁאֵין זוֹ אֶלָּא לְשֵׁם נִאוּף: **וְלֹא יִלְבַּשׁ גֶּבֶר שִׂמְלַת אִשָּׁה.** לֵילֵךְ לֵישֵׁב בֵּין הַנָּשִׁים. דָּבָר אַחֵר, שֶׁלֹּא יָסִיר שֵׂעַר הָעֶרְוָה וְשֵׂעָר שֶׁל בֵּית הַשֶּׁחִי: **כִּי תוֹעֲבַת.** לֹא אָסְרָה תּוֹרָה אֶלָּא לְבוּשׁ הַמֵּבִיא לִידֵי תוֹעֵבָה:

ו] **כִּי יִקָּרֵא.** פְּרָט לִמְזֻמָּן: **לֹא תִקַּח הָאֵם.** בְּעוֹדָהּ עַל בָּנֶיהָ:

in a similar situation. Better still, one should put aside all considerations of honor and go "beyond the limit of the law." Even a prince, he says, should ideally help the lowliest commoner, even if the circumstances do not accord with the dignity of his office or his personal standing (*Hilkhot Rotze'aḥ UShmirat HaNefesh* 13:4).

All of this is part of what sociologists nowadays call social capital. This is the level of trust within a society – the knowledge that you are surrounded by people who have your welfare at heart. They will return your lost property (see the lines immediately prior to the fallen donkey, Deut. 22:1–3), raise the alarm if someone is breaking into your house or car, keep an eye on the safety of your children. High trust levels make society a place where people are good neighbors and are willing to help even a stranger in distress. Its citizens care about the welfare of others. When they see someone in need of help, they do not "see … and ignore"; they do not walk on by.

כג וְתָלִיתָ אֹתוֹ עַל־עֵץ׃ לֹא־תָלִין נִבְלָתוֹ עַל־הָעֵץ כִּי־קָבוֹר תִּקְבְּרֶנּוּ
בַּיּוֹם הַהוּא כִּי־קִלְלַת אֱלֹהִים תָּלוּי וְלֹא תְטַמֵּא אֶת־אַדְמָתְךָ אֲשֶׁר
כב א יְהוָה אֱלֹהֶיךָ נֹתֵן לְךָ נַחֲלָה׃ לֹא־תִרְאֶה אֶת־שׁוֹר אָחִיךָ
ב אוֹ אֶת־שֵׂיוֹ נִדָּחִים וְהִתְעַלַּמְתָּ מֵהֶם הָשֵׁב תְּשִׁיבֵם לְאָחִיךָ׃ וְאִם־לֹא
קָרוֹב אָחִיךָ אֵלֶיךָ וְלֹא יְדַעְתּוֹ וַאֲסַפְתּוֹ אֶל־תּוֹךְ בֵּיתֶךָ וְהָיָה עִמְּךָ עַד
ג דְּרֹשׁ אָחִיךָ אֹתוֹ וַהֲשֵׁבֹתוֹ לוֹ׃ וְכֵן תַּעֲשֶׂה לַחֲמֹרוֹ וְכֵן תַּעֲשֶׂה לְשִׂמְלָתוֹ
וְכֵן תַּעֲשֶׂה לְכָל־אֲבֵדַת אָחִיךָ אֲשֶׁר־תֹּאבַד מִמֶּנּוּ וּמְצָאתָהּ לֹא תוּכַל
ד לְהִתְעַלֵּם׃ לֹא־תִרְאֶה אֶת־חֲמוֹר אָחִיךָ אוֹ שׁוֹרוֹ נֹפְלִים
ה בַּדֶּרֶךְ וְהִתְעַלַּמְתָּ מֵהֶם הָקֵם תָּקִים עִמּוֹ׃ לֹא־יִהְיֶה כְלִי־
גֶבֶר עַל־אִשָּׁה וְלֹא־יִלְבַּשׁ גֶּבֶר שִׂמְלַת אִשָּׁה כִּי תוֹעֲבַת יְהוָה אֱלֹהֶיךָ
כָּל־עֹשֵׂה אֵלֶּה׃
ו כִּי יִקָּרֵא קַן־צִפּוֹר ׀ לְפָנֶיךָ בַּדֶּרֶךְ בְּכָל־עֵץ ׀ אוֹ עַל־הָאָרֶץ אֶפְרֹחִים יז

אונקלוס

וְתִצְלוֹב יָתֵיהּ עַל צְלִיבָא: כג לָא תְבִית נְבִילְתֵיהּ עַל צְלִיבָא, אֲרֵי מִקְבַּר תִּקְבְּרִנֵּיהּ בְּיוֹמָא הַהוּא, אֲרֵי עַל דְּחָב קֳדָם יי אִצְטְלִיב, וְלָא תְסָאֵיב יָת אַרְעָךְ, דַּיי אֱלָהָךְ, יָהֵיב לָךְ אַחְסָנָא: כב א לָא תִחְזֵי יָת תּוֹרָא דַאֲחוּךְ, אוֹ יָת אִמְּרֵיהּ דְּטָעַן, וְתִכְבּוֹשׁ מִנְּהוֹן, אָתָבָא תְּתִיבִנּוּן לַאֲחוּךְ: ב וְאִם לָא קָרִיב אֲחוּךְ, לְוָתָךְ וְלָא יָדַעְתְּ לֵיהּ, וְתִכְנְשִׁנֵּיהּ לְגוֹ בֵּיתָךְ, וִיהֵי עִמָּךְ, עַד דְּיִתְבַּע אֲחוּךְ יָתֵיהּ, וְתָתִיבִנֵּיהּ לֵיהּ: ג וְכֵן תַּעֲבֵיד לַחְמָרֵיהּ, וְכֵן תַּעֲבֵיד לִכְסוּתֵיהּ, וְכֵן תַּעֲבֵיד, לְכָל אֲבֵידְתָא דַאֲחוּךְ, דְּתֵיבַד מִנֵּיהּ וְתַשְׁכְּחִנַּהּ, לֵית לָךְ רְשׁוּ לְכַסָּיוּתַהּ: ד לָא תִחְזֵי יָת חֲמָרָא דַאֲחוּךְ, אוֹ תּוֹרֵיהּ רְמַן בְּאוֹרְחָא, וְתִכְבּוֹשׁ מִנְּהוֹן, אֲקָמָא תָּקִים עִמֵּיהּ: ה לָא יְהֵי תִּקּוּן זֵין דִּגְבַר עַל אִתְּתָא, וְלָא יְתַקַּן גְּבַר בְּתִקּוּנֵי אִתְּתָא, אֲרֵי מְרַחַק, קֳדָם יי אֱלָהָךְ כָּל עָבֵיד אִלֵּין: ו אֲרֵי תְעָרַע קִנָּא דְּצִפְּרָא קֳדָמָךְ, בְּאוֹרְחָא, בְּכָל אִילָן אוֹ עַל אַרְעָא, אֶפְרוֹחִין

22:4 הָקֵם תָּקִים עִמּוֹ *Help him to lift it* – The Sages debated the logic of this command. Some held that it is motivated by concern for the welfare of the animal involved, the ox or the donkey, and that accordingly *tzaar baalei ḥayyim*, prevention of suffering to animals, is a biblical command (Bava Metzia 31a). Others, notably Rambam, held that it had to do with the welfare of the animal's owner, who might be so distressed that he came to stay with the animal at a risk to his own safety – the key word here being "on the road." (*Hilkhot Rotze'aḥ UShmirat HaNefesh* 13:2, 14). The roadside in ancient times was a place of danger.

The Sages also discussed the relationship between this command and the similar but different one in Exodus (23:5): "If you see the donkey of someone who hates you, fallen under its load, resist the impulse to leave it there. Help him to release it." They said that, all other things being equal, if there is a choice between helping an enemy and helping a friend, helping an enemy takes precedence, since it may "overcome the inclination" (Bava Metzia 32b), that is, it may help end the animosity and turn an enemy into a friend.

In general, Rambam states, one should do for someone you find in distress what you would do for yourself

a tree, or on the ground, and the mother is sitting on the fledglings or the eggs, do
7 not take the mother with the young. Let the mother go; only then may you take
8 the young, so that it may be well for you and you may live long. When SHELISHI
you build a new house, erect a parapet for your roof. Otherwise you may bring
9 bloodguilt on your house should anyone fall from it. Do not sow your vineyard
with a second kind of seed, or the whole yield – both the crop you have sown

רש״י

ז **לְמַעַן יִיטַב לָךְ וְגוֹ׳.** אִם מִצְוָה קַלָּה שֶׁאֵין בָּהּ חֶסְרוֹן כִּיס אָמְרָה תוֹרָה: ״לְמַעַן יִיטַב לָךְ וְהַאֲרַכְתָּ יָמִים״, קַל וָחֹמֶר לְמַתַּן שְׂכָרָן שֶׁל מִצְוֹת חֲמוּרוֹת:

ח **כִּי תִבְנֶה בַּיִת חָדָשׁ.** אִם קִיַּמְתָּ מִצְוַת שִׁלּוּחַ הַקֵּן, סוֹפְךָ לִבְנוֹת בַּיִת חָדָשׁ וּתְקַיֵּם מִצְוַת מַעֲקֶה, שֶׁמִּצְוָה גוֹרֶרֶת מִצְוָה (אבות ד, ב), וְתַגִּיעַ לְכֶרֶם וְשָׂדֶה וּלְבְגָדִים נָאִים; לְכָךְ נִסְמְכוּ פָּרָשִׁיּוֹת הַלָּלוּ: **מַעֲקֶה.** גָּדֵר סָבִיב. וְאוּנְקְלוֹס תִּרְגֵּם: ״תְּיָקָא״, כְּגוֹן תִּיק שֶׁמְּשַׁמֵּר מַה שֶּׁבְּתוֹכוֹ: **כִּי יִפֹּל הַנֹּפֵל.** רָאוּי זֶה לִפֹּל, וְאַף עַל פִּי כֵן לֹא תִתְגַּלְגֵּל מִיתָתוֹ עַל יָדְךָ, שֶׁמְּגַלְגְּלִין חוֹבָה עַל יְדֵי חַיָּב:

ט **כִּלְאָיִם.** חִטָּה וּשְׂעוֹרָה וְחַרְצָן בְּמַפֹּלֶת יָד: **פֶּן תִּקְדַּשׁ.** כְּתַרְגּוּמוֹ: ״תִּסְתָּאַב״, כָּל דָּבָר הַנִּתְעָב עַל הָאָדָם, בֵּין לְשֶׁבַח כְּגוֹן הֶקְדֵּשׁ, בֵּין לִגְנַאי כְּגוֹן אִסּוּר, נוֹפֵל בּוֹ לְשׁוֹן קִדּוּשׁ, כְּמוֹ: ״אַל תִּגַּשׁ בִּי כִּי קְדַשְׁתִּיךָ״ (ישעיה סה, ה):

understanding God Himself ("The Lord is my shepherd" [Ps. 23:1]).

Genesis 1 gives us the mandate to "subdue" and "rule" creation, including animals, but Genesis 2 gives us the responsibility to "work" and "safeguard." Animals may not have rights but they have feelings, and we have duties toward them. We must respect them if we are to honor our role as God's partners in creation.

22:9 **כִּלְאָיִם** *A second kind of seed* – The Torah groups together three prohibitions: against crossbreeding livestock, planting a field with mixed seeds, and wearing a garment of mixed wool and linen. It calls these rules *ḥukkim* or "decrees." Ramban and later Rabbi Samson Raphael Hirsch gave this word a novel interpretation.

They understood *ḥukkim* to mean laws which respected the integrity of nature (see Num. 19, "The Decree of the Law"). To mix different species, argued Ramban (on Lev. 19:19), was an affront to the Creator and an assault on the creation. Each species has its own internal laws of development and reproduction, and these must not be tampered with. "One who combines two different species thereby changes and defies the work of creation, as if he believes that the Holy One, blessed be He, has not completely perfected the world and now he wishes to improve it by adding new kinds of creatures." Ramban saw the law against taking the mother bird with its fledglings (vv. 6–7) as motivated by the same concern. Acts like these threaten the continuity of species. Though the Torah permits us to use some (but not all) animals for food, we must not cull them to extinction. (Later authorities were particularly strong in their condemnation of hunting: killing animals *not* for the sake of food; see *Responsa Shemesh Tzedaka* 57. This was wanton and destructive cruelty and had no place in Jewish life.)

No one attached more far-reaching significance to biblical decrees about animals and nature than Rabbi Samson Raphael Hirsch. For him, *ḥukkim* were laws which embodied the principle that "the same regard which you show to man you must also demonstrate to every lower creature, to the earth which bears and sustains all, and to the world of plants and animals." The reason these commandments are difficult to understand is that we approach them from the perspective of man and his needs. If we could put ourselves in the place of animals and plant life, we would find it as easy to comprehend the "decrees" as to understand the Torah's laws of social justice. "They ask you to regard all living things as God's property. Destroy none; abuse none; waste nothing; employ all things wisely.… Look upon all creatures as servants in the household of creation."

Hirsch was what today would be called a "deep"

אוֹ בֵיצִים וְהָאֵם רֹבֶצֶת עַל־הָאֶפְרֹחִים אוֹ עַל־הַבֵּיצִים לֹא־תִקַּח
ז הָאֵם עַל־הַבָּנִים׃ שַׁלֵּחַ תְּשַׁלַּח אֶת־הָאֵם וְאֶת־הַבָּנִים תִּקַּח־לָךְ
ח לְמַעַן יִיטַב לָךְ וְהַאֲרַכְתָּ יָמִים׃ כִּי תִבְנֶה בַּיִת חָדָשׁ וְעָשִׂיתָ שלישי
ט מַעֲקֶה לְגַגֶּךָ וְלֹא־תָשִׂים דָּמִים בְּבֵיתֶךָ כִּי־יִפֹּל הַנֹּפֵל מִמֶּנּוּ׃ לֹא־
תִזְרַע כַּרְמְךָ כִּלְאָיִם פֶּן־תִּקְדַּשׁ הַמְלֵאָה הַזֶּרַע אֲשֶׁר תִּזְרָע וּתְבוּאַת

אונקלוס

אוֹ בֵיעִין, וְאִמָּא רְבִיעָא עַל אֶפְרוֹחִין, אוֹ עַל בֵּיעִין, לָא תִסַּב אִמָּא עַל בְּנַיָּא: ז שַׁלָּחָא תְשַׁלַּח יָת אִמָּא, וְיָת בְּנַיָּא תִּסַּב לָךְ, בְּדִיל דְּיֵיטַב לָךְ, וְתוֹרִיךְ יוֹמִין: ח אֲרֵי תִבְנֵי בֵּיתָא חֲדַתָּא, וְתַעֲבֵיד תְּיָקָא לְאִגָּרָךְ, וְלָא תְשַׁוֵּי חוֹבַת קְטוֹל בְּבֵיתָךְ, אֲרֵי יִפּוֹל דְּנָפֵיל מִנֵּיהּ: ט לָא תִזְרַע כַּרְמָךְ עֵירוּבִין, דִּלְמָא תִסְתְּאַב, דִּמְעַת זַרְעָךְ דְּתִזְרַע, וַעֲלָלַת

LAWS OF A BIRD'S NEST

As mentioned in the commentary at the beginning of the *parasha*, Parashat Ki Tetzeh is about relationships: within families, in the marketplace, between nations. Strikingly, though, it is also about relationships between humans and animals.

Among several pieces of animal legislation in this *parasha*, the law of "letting the mother go" is perhaps the most discussed. Rambam, in his various writings, seems to embrace three different reasons for the command:

(1) The law of the mother bird is a divine decree with no obvious reason. "If the reason for sending the mother bird away were divine compassion toward animals, then, in consistency, God should have forbidden killing animals for food. The law therefore should be understood as a decree without an obvious rationale (*gezerat hakatuv*)" (*Hilkhot Tefilla UVirkat Kohanim* 9:7).

(2) It is intended to spare the mother bird emotional pain. "It is also prohibited to kill an animal with its young on the same day, in order that people should be restrained and prevented from killing the two together in such a manner that the young is killed in the sight of the mother, for the pain of the animals under such circumstances is very great.... The same reason applies to the law which enjoins that we should let the mother bird fly away when we take the young" (*Guide for the Perplexed* III:48).

(3) It is intended to have an effect on us, not the animal. The reason we must not cause animals pain or distress is not because the Torah is concerned about animals but because it is concerned about humans; we should not be cruel (*Guide for the Perplexed* III:17).

We can harmonize these explanations by noting that they answer different questions. The first view explains why we have the laws we have. The Torah forbids certain acts that are cruel to animals but not others. Why these and not those? Because that is the law. Laws will always seem arbitrary. But we observe the law because it is the law, even though, under certain circumstances, we may reason that we know better, or that it does not apply. The second view explains the immediate logic of the law. It exists to prevent needless suffering to animals, because they too feel physical pain and sometimes emotional distress. The third view sets the law in a larger perspective. Cruelty to animals is wrong, not because animals have rights but because we have duties. The duty not to be cruel is intended to promote virtue, and the primary context of virtue is the relationship between human beings. But virtues are indivisible. Those who are cruel to animals often become cruel to people. Hence we have a duty not to cause needless pain to animals because of its effect on us.

This is a nuanced approach. Animals are part of God's creation. They have their own integrity in the scheme of things. This would not have been news to the heroes of the Bible. Avraham, Moshe, and David were all shepherds who lived their formative years caring for animals. That was their first tutorial in leadership. David knew that this was one way of

10 and the yield of the vineyard – will have to be forfeited. Do not plow
11 with an ox and a donkey yoked together. Do not wear clothes made of wool
12 and linen woven together. Make tassels on the four corners of the
13 garment with which you cover yourself. If a man takes a wife and, after
14 sleeping with her, he dislikes her, and he makes up charges against her, sullying
her name, saying, 'I married this woman, but when I lay with her, I did not find
15 her to be a virgin,' the girl's father and mother shall produce the evidence of the
16 girl's virginity before the town elders at the gate. The girl's father shall say to the
17 elders: 'I gave my daughter in marriage to this man but he dislikes her. Now he
has made up charges against her, saying, "I did not find your daughter to be a
virgin." But here is the evidence of my daughter's virginity.' They shall spread
18 out the cloth before the town elders. And then the town elders shall take the
19 man and flog him. They shall fine him one hundred shekel of silver, and give it
to the girl's father, because he has sullied the name of an Israelite virgin. She
shall remain his wife; he does not have the choice to divorce her as long as he
20 lives. If, however, the charge is true, no evidence being found that the
21 girl was a virgin, then the girl shall be brought to the entrance of her father's
house and the men of her town shall stone her to death, for she committed an
outrage in Israel by acting immorally while in her father's house. You shall
22 purge the evil from your midst. If a man is caught lying with the wife
of another, both shall die, the man and the woman with whom he lay. You shall

רש״י

י **לֹא תַחֲרֹשׁ בְּשׁוֹר וּבַחֲמֹר.** הוּא הַדִּין לְכָל שְׁנֵי מִינִים שֶׁבָּעוֹלָם, וְהוּא הַדִּין לְהַנְהִיגָם יַחַד קְשׁוּרִים זוּגִים בְּהוֹלָכַת שׁוּם מַשָּׂא:

יא **שַׁעַטְנֵז.** לְשׁוֹן עֵרוּב, וְרַבּוֹתֵינוּ דָּרְשׁוּ: שׁוּעַ טָווּי וְנוּז:

יב **גְּדִלִים תַּעֲשֶׂה לָּךְ.** אַף מִן הַכִּלְאַיִם, לְכָךְ סְמָכָן הַכָּתוּב:

יג-יד **וּבָא אֵלֶיהָ וּשְׂנֵאָהּ.** סוֹפוֹ: "וְשָׂם לָהּ עֲלִילֹת דְּבָרִים", עֲבֵרָה גוֹרֶרֶת עֲבֵרָה (אבות ד, ב), עָבַר עַל "לֹא תִשְׂנָא" (ויקרא יט, יז), סוֹפוֹ לָבֹא לִידֵי לָשׁוֹן הָרָע: **אֶת הָאִשָּׁה הַזֹּאת.** מִכָּאן שֶׁאֵין אוֹמֵר דָּבָר אֶלָּא בִּפְנֵי בַּעַל דִּין:

טו **אֲבִי הַנַּעֲרָ וְאִמָּהּ.** מִי שֶׁגִּדְּלוּ גִּדּוּלִים הָרָעִים יִתְבַּזּוּ עָלֶיהָ:

טז **וְאָמַר אֲבִי הַנַּעֲרָ.** מְלַמֵּד שֶׁאֵין רְשׁוּת לָאִשָּׁה לְדַבֵּר בִּפְנֵי הָאִישׁ:

יז **וּפָרְשׂוּ הַשִּׂמְלָה.** הֲרֵי זֶה מָשָׁל, מְחֻוָּרִין הַדְּבָרִים כַּשִּׂמְלָה:

יח **וְיִסְּרוּ אֹתוֹ.** מַלְקוּת:

כ **וְאִם אֱמֶת הָיָה הַדָּבָר.** בְּעֵדִים וְהַתְרָאָה שֶׁזִּנְּתָה לְאַחַר אֵרוּסִין:

כא **אֶל פֶּתַח בֵּית אָבִיהָ.** רְאוּ גִּדּוּלִים שֶׁגִּדַּלְתֶּם **לִזְנוֹת בֵּית אָבִיהָ.** כְּמוֹ בְּבֵית אָבִיהָ: **אַנְשֵׁי עִירָהּ.** בְּמַעֲמַד כָּל אַנְשֵׁי עִירָהּ:

כב **וּמֵתוּ גַּם שְׁנֵיהֶם.** לְהוֹצִיא מַעֲשֵׂה חִדּוּדִים שֶׁאֵין הָאִשָּׁה נֶהֱנֵית מֵהֶם: **גַּם.** לְרַבּוֹת הַבָּאִים מֵאַחֲרֵיהֶם. דָּבָר אַחֵר, "גַּם שְׁנֵיהֶם", לְרַבּוֹת אֶת הַוָּלָד, שֶׁאִם הָיְתָה מְעֻבֶּרֶת אֵין מַמְתִּינִין לָהּ עַד שֶׁתֵּלֵד:

ecologist. He believed that there is such a thing as "justice" toward nature and that the world cannot be subordinated to the interests of man. It was an extreme view in Jewish thought, but one shared by the great mystic Rabbi Avraham Kook, who held that animals have rights and that one should not needlessly even pick a flower. "All of creation," he said, "sings a song."

יא הַכָּֽרֶם׃ לֹֽא־תַחֲרֹ֥שׁ בְּשׁוֹר־וּבַחֲמֹ֖ר יַחְדָּֽו׃ לֹ֤א תִלְבַּשׁ֙ שַֽׁעַטְנֵ֔ז
יב צֶ֥מֶר וּפִשְׁתִּ֖ים יַחְדָּֽו׃ גְּדִלִ֖ים תַּעֲשֶׂה־לָּ֑ךְ עַל־אַרְבַּ֛ע
יג כַּנְפ֥וֹת כְּסוּתְךָ֖ אֲשֶׁ֥ר תְּכַסֶּה־בָּֽהּ׃ כִּֽי־יִקַּ֥ח אִ֖ישׁ אִשָּׁ֑ה
יד וּבָ֥א אֵלֶ֖יהָ וּשְׂנֵאָֽהּ׃ וְשָׂ֥ם לָהּ֙ עֲלִילֹ֣ת דְּבָרִ֔ים וְהוֹצִ֥א עָלֶ֖יהָ שֵׁ֣ם רָ֑ע
וְאָמַ֗ר אֶת־הָאִשָּׁ֤ה הַזֹּאת֙ לָקַ֔חְתִּי וָאֶקְרַ֣ב אֵלֶ֔יהָ וְלֹא־מָצָ֥אתִי לָ֖הּ
טו בְּתוּלִֽים׃ וְלָקַ֛ח אֲבִ֥י הַֽנַּעֲרָ֖ וְאִמָּ֑הּ וְהוֹצִ֜יאוּ אֶת־בְּתוּלֵ֧י הַֽנַּעֲרָ֛ אֶל־זִקְנֵ֥י
טז הָעִ֖יר הַשָּֽׁעְרָה׃ וְאָמַ֛ר אֲבִ֥י הַֽנַּעֲרָ֖ אֶל־הַזְּקֵנִ֑ים אֶת־בִּתִּ֗י נָתַ֜תִּי לָאִ֥ישׁ
יז הַזֶּ֛ה לְאִשָּׁ֖ה וַיִּשְׂנָאֶֽהָ׃ וְהִנֵּה־ה֡וּא שָׂם֩ עֲלִילֹ֨ת דְּבָרִ֜ים לֵאמֹ֗ר לֹֽא־
מָצָ֤אתִי לְבִתְּךָ֙ בְּתוּלִ֔ים וְאֵ֖לֶּה בְּתוּלֵ֣י בִתִּ֑י וּפָֽרְשׂוּ֙ הַשִּׂמְלָ֔ה לִפְנֵ֖י זִקְנֵ֥י
יח יט הָעִֽיר׃ וְלָֽקְח֛וּ זִקְנֵ֥י הָֽעִיר־הַהִ֖וא אֶת־הָאִ֑ישׁ וְיִסְּר֖וּ אֹתֽוֹ׃ וְעָֽנְשׁ֨וּ אֹת֜וֹ
מֵ֣אָה כֶ֗סֶף וְנָֽתְנוּ֙ לַאֲבִ֣י הַֽנַּעֲרָ֔ה כִּ֣י הוֹצִיא֙ שֵׁ֣ם רָ֔ע עַ֖ל בְּתוּלַ֣ת יִשְׂרָאֵ֑ל
כ וְלֽוֹ־תִהְיֶ֣ה לְאִשָּׁ֔ה לֹא־יוּכַ֥ל לְשַׁלְּחָ֖הּ כָּל־יָמָֽיו׃ וְאִם־אֱמֶ֣ת
כא הָיָ֔ה הַדָּבָ֖ר הַזֶּ֑ה לֹא־נִמְצְא֥וּ בְתוּלִ֖ים לַֽנַּעֲרָֽ׃ וְהוֹצִ֨יאוּ אֶת־הַֽנַּעֲרָ֜ אֶל־
פֶּ֣תַח בֵּית־אָבִ֗יהָ וּסְקָל֩וּהָ֩ אַנְשֵׁ֨י עִירָ֤הּ בָּאֲבָנִים֙ וָמֵ֔תָה כִּֽי־עָשְׂתָ֤ה
כב נְבָלָה֙ בְּיִשְׂרָאֵ֔ל לִזְנ֖וֹת בֵּ֣ית אָבִ֑יהָ וּבִֽעַרְתָּ֥ הָרָ֖ע מִקִּרְבֶּֽךָ׃ כִּֽי־
יִמָּצֵ֨א אִ֜ישׁ שֹׁכֵ֣ב ׀ עִם־אִשָּׁ֣ה בְעֻֽלַת־בַּ֗עַל וּמֵ֙תוּ֙ גַּם־שְׁנֵיהֶ֔ם הָאִ֛ישׁ

אונקלוס

כַּרְמָא: י לָא תִרְדֵּי בְּתוֹרָא וּבַחֲמָרָא כַּחֲדָא: יא לָא תִלְבַּשׁ שַׁעַטְנֵיזָא, עֲמַר וְכִתָּן מְחֻבָּר כַּחֲדָא: יב כְּרוּסְפְּדִין תַּעְבֵּיד לָךְ, עַל אַרְבַּע, כַּנְפֵי כְּסוּתָךְ דְּתִתְכַּסֵּי בַהּ: יג אֲרֵי יִסַּב גְּבַר אִתְּתָא, וְיֵיעוֹל לְוָתַהּ וְיִסְנְיִנַּהּ: יד וִישַׁוֵּי לַהּ תַּסְקוּפֵי מִלִּין, וְיַפֵּיק עֲלַהּ שׁוּם בִּישׁ, וְיֵימַר, יָת אִתְּתָא הָדָא נְסֵיבִית, וְעָאלִית לְוָתַהּ, וְלָא אַשְׁכַּחִית לַהּ בְּתוּלִין: טו וְיִסַּב, אֲבוּהָא דְּעוּלֵימְתָּא וְאִמַּהּ, וְיַפְּקוּן, יָת בְּתוּלֵי עוּלֵימְתָּא, לִקְדָם סָבֵי קַרְתָּא וְלִתְרַע בֵּית דִּין אַתְרָא: טז וְיֵימַר, אֲבוּהָא דְּעוּלֵימְתָּא לְסָבַיָּא, יָת בְּרַתִּי, יְהָבִית, לְגַבְרָא הָדֵין, לְאִתּוּ וּסְנַהּ: יז וְהָא הוּא, שַׁוֵּי תַּסְקוּפֵי מִלִּין לְמֵימַר, לָא אַשְׁכַּחִית לִבְרַתָּךְ בְּתוּלִין, וְאִלֵּין בְּתוּלֵי בְרַתִּי, וְיִפְרְסוּן שׁוֹשִׁפָא, קֳדָם סָבֵי קַרְתָּא: יח וְיִדְבְּרוּן, סָבֵי קַרְתָּא הַהִיא יָת גַּבְרָא, וְיִלְקוּן יָתֵיהּ: יט וְיִגְבּוֹן מִנֵּיהּ מְאָה סִלְעִין דִּכְסַף, וְיִתְּנוּן לַאֲבוּהָא דְּעוּלֵימְתָּא, אֲרֵי אַפֵּיק שׁוּם בִּישׁ, עַל בְּתוּלְתָּא בַּת יִשְׂרָאֵל, וְלֵיהּ תְּהֵי לְאִתּוּ, לֵית לֵיהּ רְשׁוּ לְמִפְטְרַהּ כָּל יוֹמוֹהִי: כ וְאִם קֻשְׁטָא הֲוָה, פִּתְגָּמָא הָדֵין, לָא אִשְׁתְּכַחוּ בְּתוּלִין לְעוּלֵימְתָּא: כא וְיַפְּקוּן יָת עוּלֵימְתָּא לִתְרַע בֵּית אֲבוּהָא, וְיִרְגְּמֻנַּהּ אֱנָשֵׁי קַרְתַּהּ בְּאַבְנַיָּא וּתְמוּת, אֲרֵי עֲבַדַת קְלָנָא בְּיִשְׂרָאֵל, לְזַנָּאָה בֵּית אֲבוּהָא, וּתְפַלֵּי עָבֵיד דְּבִישׁ מִבֵּינָךְ: כב אֲרֵי יִשְׁתְּכַח גְּבַר, שָׁכֵיב עִם אִתְּתָא אִתַּת גְּבַר, וְיִתְקַטְלוּן אַף תַּרְוֵיהוֹן, גַּבְרָא,

23 purge the evil from Israel. If a virgin is betrothed to be married, and a
24 man encounters her within a town and lies with her, you shall bring them both
to the town gate and stone them to death, the girl because she did not cry for
help in the town, and the man because he violated the wife of his fellow. You
25 shall purge the evil from your midst. But if the man encounters the
betrothed woman in the open country, forces her and lies with her, only the
26 man who did this shall die. You shall do nothing to the girl; she did not commit
the capital offense. Just as one man at times attacks and murders his fellow
27 man, so too here; he came upon her in open country. The betrothed woman
28 may have cried out for help, but no one was there to rescue her. If a
man encounters a virgin who is not betrothed and rapes her, and they are
29 caught in the act, the man who lay with her shall pay the girl's father fifty shekel
of silver, and she shall become his wife. Because he violated her he does not
23 1 have the choice to divorce her as long as he lives. A man cannot marry
2 his father's wife; he must not dishonor his father's bed. No one whose
testicles have been crushed or whose member is severed shall be admitted to
3 the congregation of the Lord. No one born of an illicit union shall be
admitted to the congregation of the Lord; even to the tenth generation, no
descendant of such a union may be admitted to the congregation of the
4 Lord. No Amonite or Moabite shall be admitted to the congregation
of the Lord; even to the tenth generation, none of their descendants shall be
5 admitted to the congregation of the Lord, for they would not greet you with

רש"י

כג **וּמְצָאָהּ אִישׁ בָּעִיר.** לְפִיכָךְ "שָׁכַב עִמָּהּ", פִּרְצָה קוֹרְאָה לַגַּנָּב, הָא אִלּוּ יָשְׁבָה בְּבֵיתָהּ לֹא אֵרַע לָהּ:

כו **כִּי כַּאֲשֶׁר יָקוּם וְגוֹ'.** לְפִי פְּשׁוּטוֹ זֶהוּ מַשְׁמָעוֹ: כִּי אֲנוּסָה הִיא וּבְחָזְקָה עָמַד עָלֶיהָ, כְּאָדָם הָעוֹמֵד עַל חֲבֵרוֹ לְהָרְגוֹ. וְרַבּוֹתֵינוּ דָּרְשׁוּ בּוֹ (פסחים כה ע"ב ועוד): הֲרֵי זֶה בָּא לְלַמֵּד וְנִמְצָא לָמֵד וְכוּ':

כג א **לֹא יִקַּח.** אֵין לוֹ בָּהּ לִקּוּחִין, וְאֵין קִדּוּשִׁין תּוֹפְסִין בָּהּ: **וְלֹא יְגַלֶּה כְּנַף אָבִיו.** שׁוֹמֶרֶת יָבָם שֶׁל אָבִיו הָרְאוּיָה לְאָבִיו. וַהֲרֵי כְּבָר הֻזְהַר עָלֶיהָ מִשּׁוּם "עֶרְוַת אֲחִי אָבִיךָ" (ויקרא יח, יד)? אֶלָּא לַעֲבֹר עַל זוֹ בִּשְׁנֵי לָאוִין, וְלִסְמֹךְ לָהּ: "לֹא יָבֹא מַמְזֵר" (להלן פסוק ג), לְלַמֵּד שֶׁאֵין מַמְזֵר אֶלָּא מֵחַיָּבֵי כְּרֵתוֹת, וְקַל וָחֹמֶר מֵחַיָּבֵי מִיתוֹת בֵּית דִּין, שֶׁאֵין בָּעֲרָיוֹת מִיתַת בֵּית דִּין שֶׁאֵין בָּהּ כָּרֵת:

ב **פְּצוּעַ דַּכָּה.** שֶׁנִּפְצְעוּ אוֹ שֶׁנִּדְכְּאוּ בֵּיצִים שֶׁלּוֹ: **וּכְרוּת שָׁפְכָה.** שֶׁנִּכְרַת הַגִּיד וְשׁוּב אֵינוֹ יוֹרֶה קִלּוּחַ זֶרַע, אֶלָּא שׁוֹפֵךְ וְשׁוֹתֵת וְאֵינוֹ מוֹלִיד:

ג **לֹא יָבֹא מַמְזֵר בִּקְהַל ה'.** לֹא יִשָּׂא יִשְׂרְאֵלִית:

ד **לֹא יָבֹא עַמּוֹנִי.** לֹא יִשָּׂא יִשְׂרְאֵלִית:

ה **עַל דְּבַר.** עַל הָעֵצָה שֶׁיָּעֲצוּ אֶתְכֶם לְהַחֲטִיאֲכֶם כְּדִכְתִיב "בִּדְבַר בִּלְעָם" (במדבר לא, טז):

23:4 **גַּם דּוֹר עֲשִׂירִי** *Even to the tenth generation* – The Torah explicitly excludes Moabites from the "congregation of the Lord even to the tenth generation." Yet, as we read in the Book of Ruth, Ruth herself was a Moabite who pledged herself as part of the Jewish nation. The Rabbis solved this problem simply and ingeniously. The Hebrew for Moabite,

כג הַשֹּׁכֵב עִם־הָאִשָּׁה וְהָאִשָּׁה וּבִעַרְתָּ הָרָע מִיִּשְׂרָאֵל׃ כִּי
יִהְיֶה נַעֲרָ בְתוּלָה מְאֹרָשָׂה לְאִישׁ וּמְצָאָהּ אִישׁ בָּעִיר וְשָׁכַב עִמָּהּ׃
כד וְהוֹצֵאתֶם אֶת־שְׁנֵיהֶם אֶל־שַׁעַר ׀ הָעִיר הַהִוא וּסְקַלְתֶּם אֹתָם בָּאֲבָנִים
וָמֵתוּ אֶת־הַנַּעֲרָ עַל־דְּבַר אֲשֶׁר לֹא־צָעֲקָה בָעִיר וְאֶת־הָאִישׁ עַל־דְּבַר
כה אֲשֶׁר־עִנָּה אֶת־אֵשֶׁת רֵעֵהוּ וּבִעַרְתָּ הָרָע מִקִּרְבֶּךָ׃ וְאִם־
בַּשָּׂדֶה יִמְצָא הָאִישׁ אֶת־הַנַּעֲרָ הַמְאֹרָשָׂה וְהֶחֱזִיק־בָּהּ הָאִישׁ וְשָׁכַב
כו עִמָּהּ וּמֵת הָאִישׁ אֲשֶׁר־שָׁכַב עִמָּהּ לְבַדּוֹ׃ וְלַנַּעֲרָ לֹא־תַעֲשֶׂה דָבָר
אֵין לַנַּעֲרָ חֵטְא מָוֶת כִּי כַּאֲשֶׁר יָקוּם אִישׁ עַל־רֵעֵהוּ וּרְצָחוֹ נֶפֶשׁ כֵּן
כז הַדָּבָר הַזֶּה׃ כִּי בַשָּׂדֶה מְצָאָהּ צָעֲקָה הַנַּעֲרָ הַמְאֹרָשָׂה וְאֵין מוֹשִׁיעַ
כח לָהּ׃ כִּי־יִמְצָא אִישׁ נַעֲרָ בְתוּלָה אֲשֶׁר לֹא־אֹרָשָׂה
כט וּתְפָשָׂהּ וְשָׁכַב עִמָּהּ וְנִמְצָאוּ׃ וְנָתַן הָאִישׁ הַשֹּׁכֵב עִמָּהּ לַאֲבִי הַנַּעֲרָ
חֲמִשִּׁים כָּסֶף וְלוֹ־תִהְיֶה לְאִשָּׁה תַּחַת אֲשֶׁר עִנָּהּ לֹא־יוּכַל שַׁלְּחָהּ
כג א כָּל־יָמָיו׃ לֹא־יִקַּח אִישׁ אֶת־אֵשֶׁת אָבִיו וְלֹא יְגַלֶּה כְּנַף
ב אָבִיו׃ לֹא־יָבֹא פְצוּעַ־דַּכָּה וּכְרוּת שָׁפְכָה בִּקְהַל
ג יְהוָה׃ לֹא־יָבֹא מַמְזֵר בִּקְהַל יְהוָה גַּם דּוֹר עֲשִׂירִי לֹא־יָבֹא
ד לוֹ בִּקְהַל יְהוָה׃ לֹא־יָבֹא עַמּוֹנִי וּמוֹאָבִי בִּקְהַל יְהוָה
ה גַּם דּוֹר עֲשִׂירִי לֹא־יָבֹא לָהֶם בִּקְהַל יְהוָה עַד־עוֹלָם׃ עַל־דְּבַר אֲשֶׁר

אונקלוס

דִּשְׁכֵיב עִם אִתְּתָא וְאִתְּתָא, וּתְפַלֵּי עָבֵיד דְּבִישׁ מִיִּשְׂרָאֵל: כג אֲרֵי תְהֵי עוּלֵימְתָא בְתוּלְתָא, דִּמְאָרְסָא לִגְבַר, וְיַשְׁכְּחִנַּהּ גְּבַר, בְּקַרְתָּא וְיִשְׁכּוּב עִמַּהּ: כד וְתַפְּקוּן יָת תַּרְוֵיהוֹן, לִתְרַע קַרְתָּא הַהִיא, וְתִרְגְּמוּן יָתְהוֹן בְּאַבְנַיָּא וִימוּתוּן, יָת עוּלֵימְתָא, עַל עֵיסַק דְּלָא צְוַחַת בְּקַרְתָּא, וְיָת גַּבְרָא, עַל עֵיסַק דְּעַנִּי יָת אִתַּת חַבְרֵיהּ, וּתְפַלֵּי עָבֵיד דְּבִישׁ מִבֵּינָךְ: כה וְאִם בְּחַקְלָא יַשְׁכַּח גַּבְרָא, יָת עוּלֵימְתָא דִּמְאָרְסָא, וְיִתַקֵּיף בַּהּ גַּבְרָא וְיִשְׁכּוּב עִמַּהּ, וְיִתְקְטִיל, גַּבְרָא, דִּשְׁכֵיב עִמַּהּ בִּלְחוֹדוֹהִי: כו וּלְעוּלֵימְתָא לָא תַעֲבֵיד מִדָּעַם, לֵית לְעוּלֵימְתָא חוֹבַת דִּין דִּקְטוֹל, אֲרֵי, כְּמָא דִּיקוּם גַּבְרָא עַל חַבְרֵיהּ

וְיִקְטְלִנֵּיהּ נְפַשׁ, כֵּן פִּתְגָּמָא הָדֵין: כז אֲרֵי בְחַקְלָא אַשְׁכְּחַהּ, צְוַחַת, עוּלֵימְתָא דִּמְאָרְסָא, וְלֵית דְּפָרֵיק לַהּ: כח אֲרֵי יַשְׁכַּח גְּבַר, עוּלֵימְתָא בְתוּלְתָא דְּלָא מְאָרְסָא, וְיֶחְדִנַּהּ וְיִשְׁכּוּב עִמַּהּ, וְיִשְׁתַּכְחוּן: כט וְיִתֵּין, גַּבְרָא דִּשְׁכֵיב עִמַּהּ, לַאֲבוּהָא דְעוּלֵימְתָא חַמְשִׁין סִלְעִין דִּכְסַף, וְלֵיהּ תְּהֵי לְאִתּוּ, חֲלָף דְּעַנְיַהּ, לֵית לֵיהּ רְשׁוּ לְמִפְטְרַהּ כָּל יוֹמוֹהִי: כג א לָא יִסַּב גְּבַר יָת אִתַּת אֲבוּהִי, וְלָא יְגַלֵּי כַּנְפָא דַּאֲבוּהִי: ב לָא יִדְכֵּי דִּפְסִיק וּדְמִחַבַּל, לְמֵיעַל בִּקְהָלָא דַּיְיָ: ג לָא יִדְכֵּי מַמְזֵירָא לְמֵיעַל בִּקְהָלָא דַּיְיָ, אַף דָּרָא עֲסִירָאָה, לָא יִדְכֵּי לֵיהּ לְמֵיעַל בִּקְהָלָא דַּיְיָ: ד לָא יִדְכּוּן עַמּוֹנָאֵי, וּמוֹאֲבָאֵי לְמֵיעַל בִּקְהָלָא דַּיְיָ,

food and water on your way when you came out of Egypt; and in hostility
against you they hired Bilam son of Beor from Petor of Aram Naharayim to
6 curse you. But the Lord your God chose not to listen to Bilam; the Lord your
God turned the curse into a blessing for you, because the Lord your God loves
7 you. Do not seek their ease or welfare as long as you live. Do not REVI'I
8 despise an Edomite, for he is your kin. Do not despise an Egyptian, for you
9 lived as a stranger in his land. Children born to them may be admitted, in the

רש״י

בַּדֶּרֶךְ. כְּשֶׁהֱיִיתֶם בְּטֵרוּף:

ז **לֹא תִדְרֹשׁ שְׁלֹמָם.** מִכְּלָל שֶׁנֶּאֱמַר: "עִמְּךָ יֵשֵׁב בְּקִרְבְּךָ" (להלן פסוק יז), יָכוֹל אַף זֶה כֵּן? תַּלְמוּד לוֹמַר: "לֹא תִדְרֹשׁ שְׁלֹמָם":

ח-ט **לֹא תְתַעֵב אֲדֹמִי.** לְגַמְרֵי, וְאַף עַל פִּי שֶׁרָאוּי לְךָ לְתַעֲבוֹ, שֶׁיָּצָא בַּחֶרֶב לִקְרָאתְךָ: **לֹא תְתַעֵב מִצְרִי.** מִכֹּל וָכֹל, אַף עַל פִּי שֶׁזָּרְקוּ זְכוּרֵיכֶם לַיְאוֹר, מַה טַּעַם? שֶׁהָיוּ לָכֶם אַכְסַנְיָא בִּשְׁעַת הַדְּחָק, לְפִיכָךְ: **בָּנִים אֲשֶׁר יִוָּלְדוּ לָהֶם דּוֹר שְׁלִישִׁי וְגוֹ'.** וּשְׁאָר אֻמּוֹת מֻתָּרִין מִיָּד. הָא לָמַדְתָּ שֶׁהַמַּחֲטִיא לָאָדָם קָשֶׁה לוֹ מִן הַהוֹרְגוֹ, שֶׁהַהוֹרְגוֹ הוֹרְגוֹ בָּעוֹלָם הַזֶּה, וְהַמַּחֲטִיאוֹ מוֹצִיאוֹ מִן הָעוֹלָם הַזֶּה וּמִן הָעוֹלָם הַבָּא. לְפִיכָךְ אֱדוֹם שֶׁקִּדְּמָם בַּחֶרֶב לֹא נִתְעַב, וְכֵן מִצְרַיִם שֶׁטִּבְּעוּם, וְאֵלּוּ שֶׁהֶחֱטִיאוּם נִתְעֲבוּ:

Moshe's commands against hate are testimony to his greatness as a leader. It is easy to become a leader by mobilizing hate. The language of hate can create enmity between people of different faiths and ethnicities who have lived peaceably together for centuries. It has been the most destructive force in history, and even knowledge of the Holocaust has not ended it. It is the unmistakable mark of toxic leadership.

Great leaders make people better, kinder, nobler than they would otherwise be. The paradigm case was Moshe, the man who had more lasting influence than any other leader in history. A true leader knows: Hate the sin but not the sinner. Do not forget the past but do not be held captive by it. Be willing to fight your enemies but never allow yourself to be defined by them.

23:8 לֹא־תְתַעֵב מִצְרִי כִּי־גֵר הָיִיתָ בְאַרְצוֹ *Do not despise an Egyptian, for you lived as a stranger in his land* – This is a counterintuitive command. Recall what had happened. The Egyptians enslaved the Israelites. They initiated a policy of slow genocide, killing every male Israelite at birth. Moshe begged Pharaoh repeatedly to let the people go and he refused.

Moshe knows that this entire chapter of Israelite history was not accidental or incidental. It is their matrix as a nation, their formative experience. They were commanded

[rule, law, inescapable truth] that Esav hates Yaakov" (Sifrei, Behaalotekha 69). Given this generational hostility, why does Moshe tell us not to despise Esav's descendants?

The answer is: Esav may hate Yaakov, but it does not follow that Yaakov should hate Esav. As Martin Luther King Jr. wrote, "Darkness cannot drive out darkness; only light can do that. Hate cannot drive out hate; only love can do that." Those who quote R. Shimon's aphorism do so selectively. In context it refers to the moment at which Yaakov and Esav meet after their long estrangement. Yaakov has feared that Esav will try to kill him. Then "Esav ran to meet him [Yaakov] and embraced him. He threw his arms around his neck and kissed him, and they [both] wept" (Gen. 33:4). Over the letters of the word "kissed," as it appears in a *sefer Torah*, there are dots, signaling some special meaning. It was in this context that R. Shimon bar Yoḥai said: "Even though it is well known that Esav hates Yaakov, at that moment he was overcome with compassion and kissed him with a full heart" (see Rashi ad loc.). In other words, it is precisely the text cited to show that antisemitism is inevitable that proves the opposite: At the crucial encounter, Esav did *not* feel hate toward Yaakov. They met, embraced, and went their separate ways without ill will. Hate, especially between brothers, is not eternal and inexorable. Always be ready, Moshe seems to imply in our verse, for reconciliation between enemies.

לֹא־קִדְּמוּ אֶתְכֶם בַּלֶּחֶם וּבַמַּיִם בַּדֶּרֶךְ בְּצֵאתְכֶם מִמִּצְרָיִם וַאֲשֶׁר
ו שָׂכַר עָלֶיךָ אֶת־בִּלְעָם בֶּן־בְּעוֹר מִפְּתוֹר אֲרַם נַהֲרַיִם לְקַלְלֶךָּ׃ וְלֹא־
אָבָה יְהוָה אֱלֹהֶיךָ לִשְׁמֹעַ אֶל־בִּלְעָם וַיַּהֲפֹךְ יְהוָה אֱלֹהֶיךָ לְּךָ אֶת־
ז הַקְּלָלָה לִבְרָכָה כִּי אֲהֵבְךָ יְהוָה אֱלֹהֶיךָ׃ לֹא־תִדְרֹשׁ שְׁלֹמָם וְטֹבָתָם
ח כָּל־יָמֶיךָ לְעוֹלָם׃ לֹא־תְתַעֵב אֲדֹמִי כִּי אָחִיךָ הוּא רביעי
ט לֹא־תְתַעֵב מִצְרִי כִּי־גֵר הָיִיתָ בְאַרְצוֹ׃ בָּנִים אֲשֶׁר־יִוָּלְדוּ לָהֶם דּוֹר

אונקלוס

אַף דָּרָא עֲסִירָאָה, לָא יִדְכֵּי לְהוֹן, לְמֵיעַל בִּקְהָלָא דַּיי עַד עָלְמָא: ה עַל עֵיסֶק, דְּלָא עָרַעוּ יָתְכוֹן בְּלַחְמָא וּבְמַיָּא, בְּאוֹרְחָא בְּמִפַּקְכוֹן מִמִּצְרָיִם, וְדַאֲגַר עֲלָךְ יָת בִּלְעָם בַּר בְּעוֹר, מִפְּתוֹר, אֲרָם דְּעַל פְּרָת לְלָטָטוּתָךְ: ו וְלָא אֲבָא, יי אֱלָהָךְ לְקַבָּלָא מִן בִּלְעָם, וַהֲפַךְ יי אֱלָהָךְ לָךְ, יָת לְוָטִין לְבִרְכָן, אֲרֵי רַיחֲמָךְ יי אֱלָהָךְ: ז לָא תִתְבַּע שְׁלָמְהוֹן וְטָבָתְהוֹן, כָּל יוֹמָךְ לְעָלַם: ח לָא תְרַחֵיק אֱדוֹמָאָה, אֲרֵי אֲחוּךְ הוּא, לָא תְרַחֵיק מִצְרָאָה, אֲרֵי דַּיָּר הֲוֵיתָא בְּאַרְעֵיהּ: ט בְּנִין, דְּיִתְיַלְדוּן לְהוֹן דָּרָא

Moavi, is masculine, not feminine. So the prohibition applies to men, not women (Yevamot 76b–77a). This, they said, was one of the rulings given "in the days when the judges ruled" (Ruth 1:1).

This resolved an exegetical problem. In practice, the Rabbis went much further still, and we can identify the period at which they did so. It took place at the time – the late first or early second century CE – when Rabban Gamliel II was deposed as spiritual head of the Jewish community in Israel for his autocratic behavior toward one of his colleagues, and R. Elazar b. Azarya was appointed in his place. At that time many disputed issues were resolved. This is how the Talmud describes one of them:

> On that day, Yehuda, an Amonite proselyte, came before them in the house of study and asked: "Am I permitted to enter the assembly?" R. Yehoshua said, "You are permitted to enter the congregation." Rabban Gamliel said, "Is it not a law that '*no Amonite or Moabite shall be admitted to the congregation of the Lord*'?" R. Yehoshua replied, "Do Amon and Moav still live in their original homes? Long ago, Sanḥeriv, king of Assyria, came and mixed up all the nations, as it says, '*I… sweep away the borders of peoples and take their leaders for plunder; like a wild bull I pull down all who preside*' (Is. 10:13), and anything that parts [from a group] is assumed to part from the majority of the group [in this case, other nations of the empire]." …They then permitted [Yehuda the Amonite] to enter the congregation. (Berakhot 28a)

At a stroke, the entire biblical legislation relating to Israel's neighbors and enemies was declared inoperative, on the grounds that after Sanḥeriv's conquests and population transfers (722–705 BCE), the "nations" could no longer be identified. As Rambam writes about the seven nations against which Israel was commanded to wage war, "Their memory has already perished" (*Hilkhot Melakhim UMilḥemoteihem* 5:4). We no longer know who is who. That chapter in Jewish history is closed.

23:8 לֹא־תְתַעֵב אֲדֹמִי *Do not despise an Edomite* – Edom was another name of Esav. There was a time when Esav hated Yaakov and vowed to kill him. Before the twins were born, Rivka received an oracle (Gen. 25:23) that seemed to imply an eternal conflict between the two brothers and their descendants.

Later, during the Second Temple period, the prophet Malakhi said: "'Is Esav not a brother to Yaakov?' So says the Lord: 'Yet I loved Yaakov and hated Esav'" (Mal. 1:2–3). Centuries later still, R. Shimon bar Yoḥai said, "It is a halakha

10 third generation, to the congregation of the LORD. When you are
11 encamped against your enemies, guard against any impropriety. If one of the
men becomes impure because of a nocturnal emission, he shall go outside the
12 camp and not reenter it. As evening approaches, he shall bathe in water, and at
13 sunset he may reenter the camp. You must designate an area outside the camp
14 where you may relieve yourself. Among your gear you shall have a trowel.
When you relieve yourself outside, you shall dig a hole with it and cover up
15 your excrement. The LORD your God travels with your camp, to protect you

רש״י

י כִּי תֵצֵא מַחֲנֶה וְגוֹ׳ וְנִשְׁמַרְתָּ. שֶׁהַשָּׂטָן מְקַטְרֵג בִּשְׁעַת הַסַּכָּנָה:

יא מִקְּרֵה לָיְלָה. דִּבֶּר הַכָּתוּב בַּהוֶֹה: וְיָצָא אֶל מִחוּץ לַמַּחֲנֶה. זוֹ מִצְוַת עֲשֵׂה: לֹא יָבֹא אֶל תּוֹךְ הַמַּחֲנֶה. זוֹ מִצְוַת לֹא תַעֲשֶׂה. וְאָסוּר לִכָּנֵס לְמַחֲנֵה לְוִיָּה וְכָל שֶׁכֵּן לְמַחֲנֶה שְׁכִינָה:

יב וְהָיָה לִפְנוֹת עֶרֶב. סָמוּךְ לְהַעֲרֵב שִׁמְשׁוֹ יִטְבֹּל, שֶׁאֵינוֹ טָהוֹר בְּלֹא הַעֲרֵב הַשֶּׁמֶשׁ:

יג וְיָד תִּהְיֶה לְךָ. כְּתַרְגּוּמוֹ, כְּמוֹ: ״אִישׁ עַל יָדוֹ״ (במדבר ב, יז): מִחוּץ לַמַּחֲנֶה. חוּץ לֶעָנָן:

יד עַל אֲזֵנֶךָ. לְבַד מִשְּׁאָר כְּלֵי תַּשְׁמִישְׁךָ: אֲזֵנֶךָ. כְּמוֹ כְּלֵי זַיִן:

no longer alive – we feel that more than mere justice is at stake. Only the offended party can forgive, and he or she is no longer alive to be able to forgive. We, the family or friends of the victim, feel the pull of loyalty to the unappeased cry of those who are no longer here. Forgiveness can then come to seem like a betrayal.

How then is it possible? It is possible because, once the impartial processes of law have taken their course, justice done, sentences served, amends made and apologies expressed, a halt must be called to the otherwise endless voice of implacable grief. Forgiveness does not mean forgetting, nor does it mean abandoning the claims of justice. It does mean, however, an acknowledgment that the past is past and must not be allowed to cast its shadow over the future. Forgiveness heals moral wounds the way the body heals physical wounds. At its height it is a process of shared mourning between those who commit and those who suffer the consequences of wrong – the former for harm done, the latter for harm suffered – and like all acts of mourning it is the only bridge from the pain of loss to reintegration with the present and its tasks.

23:13 וְיָד תִּהְיֶה לְךָ מִחוּץ לַמַּחֲנֶה *Designate an area outside the camp* – The rabbis extended the Torah's rule that waste should be disposed of far from human habitation. They banned garbage disposal that interfered with crops or amenities, pollution of the water supply, and activities that would foul the air or create intolerable noise in residential areas. The provision for open space around the Levitical cities is one of the earliest examples of town planning (Num. 35:1–3).

These rulings and others set precedents of environmental legislation as well as commands that educate us in respect for and restraint toward nature as God's creation (see note on Deut. 20:19). Admittedly, environmental ethics has not yet received the same intense halakhic treatment as has medical ethics. Probably that is because medical decisions are taken by individuals while environmental decisions are taken by governments. An individual turns to Jewish law for guidance. Governments rarely do. But it is not because Judaism regards ecological issues lightly. Rambam repeatedly insists that we cannot pursue spiritual ideals without first ensuring our physical survival (for example, *Hilkhot Deot* 4:1). That has always needed long-term planning and the decision to exercise restraint in the present for the sake of the viability of the future. Even in the nomadic days of the wilderness, pollution is understood to threaten the holiness of the camp.

י שְׁלִישִׁי יָבֹא לָהֶם בִּקְהַל יהוה׃ כִּי־תֵצֵא מַחֲנֶה יח
יא עַל־אֹיְבֶיךָ וְנִשְׁמַרְתָּ מִכֹּל דָּבָר רָע׃ כִּי־יִהְיֶה בְךָ אִישׁ אֲשֶׁר לֹא־
יִהְיֶה טָהוֹר מִקְּרֵה־לָיְלָה וְיָצָא אֶל־מִחוּץ לַמַּחֲנֶה לֹא יָבֹא אֶל־תּוֹךְ
יב הַמַּחֲנֶה׃ וְהָיָה לִפְנוֹת־עֶרֶב יִרְחַץ בַּמָּיִם וּכְבֹא הַשֶּׁמֶשׁ יָבֹא אֶל־
יג יד תּוֹךְ הַמַּחֲנֶה׃ וְיָד תִּהְיֶה לְךָ מִחוּץ לַמַּחֲנֶה וְיָצָאתָ שָּׁמָּה חוּץ׃ וְיָתֵד
תִּהְיֶה לְךָ עַל־אֲזֵנֶךָ וְהָיָה בְּשִׁבְתְּךָ חוּץ וְחָפַרְתָּה בָהּ וְשַׁבְתָּ וְכִסִּיתָ
טו אֶת־צֵאָתֶךָ׃ כִּי יהוה אֱלֹהֶיךָ מִתְהַלֵּךְ ׀ בְּקֶרֶב מַחֲנֶךָ לְהַצִּילְךָ וְלָתֵת

אונקלוס

תְּלִיתָאָה, יִדְכֵּי לְהוֹן לְמֵיעַל בִּקְהָלָא דַּיְיָ׃ י אֲרֵי תִפּוֹק מַשְׁרִיתָא עַל בַּעֲלֵי דְּבָבָךְ, וְתִסְתַּמַּר, מִכֹּל מִדַּעַם בִּישׁ׃ יא אֲרֵי יְהֵי בָךְ גְּבַר, דְּלָא יְהֵי דְּכֵי מִקְּרֵי לֵילְיָא, וְיִפּוֹק לְמִבְּרָא לְמַשְׁרִיתָא, לָא יֵיעוֹל לְגוֹ מַשְׁרִיתָא׃ יב וִיהֵי לְמִפְנֵי רַמְשָׁא יַסְחֵי בְמַיָּא, וּכְמֵיעַל שִׁמְשָׁא, יֵיעוֹל לְגוֹ מַשְׁרִיתָא׃ יג וַאֲתַר מְתַקַּן יְהֵי לָךְ, מִבְּרָא לְמַשְׁרִיתָא, וְתִפּוֹק תַּמָּן לְבָרָא׃ יד וְסִכְּתָא, תְּהֵי לָךְ עַל זֵינָךְ, וִיהֵי בְּמִתְּבָךְ בְּבָרָא, וְתַחְפַּר בַּהּ, וְתְתוּב וּתְכַסֵּי יָת מַפְּקָתָךְ׃ טו אֲרֵי יְיָ אֱלָהָךְ, שְׁכִינְתֵיהּ מְהַלְּכָא בְּגוֹ מַשְׁרִיתָךְ, לְשֵׁיזָבוּתָךְ וּלְמִמְסַר סָנְאָךְ קֳדָמָךְ, וּתְהֵי מַשְׁרִיתָךְ קַדִּישָׁא, וְלָא יִתַּחְזֵי בָךְ עֲבֵירַת פִּתְגָם, וִיתוּב מֵימְרֵיהּ מִלְּאֵיטָבָא לָךְ׃ טז לָא תִמְסַר עֶבֶד עַמְמִין לְיַד רִבּוֹנֵיהּ, דְּיִשְׁתֵּיזֵב לְוָתָךְ מִן קֳדָם רִבּוֹנֵיהּ׃ יז

23:9 דּוֹר שְׁלִישִׁי *In the third generation* – Judaism is often portrayed as a religion of justice rather than mercy and forgiveness. That is not the case: Justice and forgiveness go hand in hand. Each is an answer to the problem of revenge, and neither is sufficient on its own. Justice takes the sense of wrong and transforms it from personal retaliation – revenge – to the impersonal processes of law – retribution. Forgiveness is the further acknowledgment that justice alone may not be enough to silence the feelings of the afflicted. Even when the evidence has been taken, the verdict passed, and sentence imposed, there is a residue of pain and grief which has to be discharged. Justice is the impersonal, forgiveness the personal, the restoration of the moral order. Justice rights wrongs; forgiveness rebuilds broken relationships. There is no other way.

It is impossible to understand the force of forgiveness without, at the same time, acknowledging the difficulty. It is hard precisely because it conflicts with our sense of keeping faith with the past. If wrong has been done to me, it is natural to feel that wrong must be done to the wrongdoer in return. When that wrong is historic – when its victims are

to remember it forever, enacting it once a year on Passover, eating the unleavened bread of affliction and the bitter herbs of slavery. All these, on the face of it, are reasons to hate the Egyptians, or at the very least to look back with a sense of grievance, resentment, animosity, and pain. Why does Moshe say the opposite?

Because to be free, you have to let go of hate. If the Israelites continued to hate their erstwhile enemies, Moshe would have succeeded in taking the Israelites out of Egypt, but he would have failed to take Egypt out of the Israelites. Mentally, they would still be there, slaves to the past, prisoners of their memories.

Freedom involves the abandonment of hate, because hate is the abdication of freedom. It is the projection of our conflicts onto an external force whom we can then blame, but only at the cost of denying responsibility. That is Moshe's message to those who are about to enter the Promised Land: that a free society can be built only by people who accept the responsibility of freedom, subjects who refuse to see themselves as objects, people who define themselves by love of God, not hatred of the other.

and to deliver your enemies to you. Therefore your camp must be holy; He
16 must not find any indecent thing among you and turn away from you. If
a slave seeks refuge with you from his master, do not hand him back to his
17 master. He shall live with you in the place he chooses, in whichever of your
18 towns he likes. Do not ill-treat him. No woman of Israel shall
19 be a cult prostitute; no man of Israel shall be a male cult prostitute. Do not
bring wages of prostitution or the payment for a dog into the house of the
Lord your God in fulfillment of any vow, for both are abhorrent to the Lord
20 your God. Do not charge interest on loans to your kinsmen, whether

רש״י

טו **וְלֹא יִרְאֶה בְךָ.** הַקָּדוֹשׁ בָּרוּךְ הוּא, "עֶרְוַת דָּבָר":

טז **לֹא תַסְגִּיר עֶבֶד.** כְּתַרְגּוּמוֹ. דָּבָר אַחֵר, אֲפִלּוּ עֶבֶד כְּנַעֲנִי שֶׁל יִשְׂרָאֵל שֶׁבָּרַח מֵחוּצָה לָאָרֶץ לְאֶרֶץ יִשְׂרָאֵל:

יח **לֹא תִהְיֶה קְדֵשָׁה.** מֻפְקֶרֶת, מְקֻדֶּשֶׁת וּמְזֻמֶּנֶת לִזְנוּת: **וְלֹא יִהְיֶה קָדֵשׁ.** מְזֻמָּן לְמִשְׁכַּב זָכוּר. וְאוּנְקְלוֹס תִּרְגֵּם: "לָא תְהֵי אִתְּתָא מִבְּנָת יִשְׂרָאֵל לִגְבַר עֶבֶד", שֶׁאַף זוֹ מֻפְקֶרֶת לִבְעִילַת זְנוּת הִיא, מֵאַחַר שֶׁאֵין קִדּוּשִׁין תּוֹפְסִין לוֹ בָּהּ, שֶׁהֲרֵי הֻקְשׁוּ לַחֲמוֹר, שֶׁנֶּאֱמַר: "שְׁבוּ לָכֶם פֹּה עִם הַחֲמוֹר" (בראשית כב, ה), עַם הַדּוֹמֶה לַחֲמוֹר, "וְלָא יִסַּב גַּבְרָא מִבְּנֵי יִשְׂרָאֵל אִתְּתָא אֲמָא", שֶׁאַף הוּא נַעֲשָׂה קָדֵשׁ עַל יָדָהּ, שֶׁכָּל בְּעִילוֹתָיו בְּעִילוֹת זְנוּת שֶׁאֵין קִדּוּשִׁין תּוֹפְסִין לוֹ בָּהּ:

יט **אֶתְנַן זוֹנָה.** נָתַן לָהּ טָלֶה בְּאֶתְנַנָּהּ, פָּסוּל לְהַקְרָבָה: **וּמְחִיר כֶּלֶב.** הֶחֱלִיף שֶׂה בְּכֶלֶב: **גַּם שְׁנֵיהֶם.** לְרַבּוֹת שִׁנּוּיֵיהֶם, כְּגוֹן חִטִּים וַעֲשָׂאָן סֹלֶת:

כ **לֹא תַשִּׁיךְ.** אַזְהָרָה לַלֹּוֶה שֶׁלֹּא יִתֵּן רִבִּית לַמַּלְוֶה. וְאַזְהָרָה לַמַּלְוֶה – "אֶת כַּסְפְּךָ לֹא תִתֵּן לוֹ בְּנֶשֶׁךְ" (ויקרא כה, לז):

23:20 לֹא־תַשִּׁיךְ לְאָחִיךָ נֶשֶׁךְ *Do not charge interest on loans to your kinsmen* – Lending to the poor on interest led to inescapable cycles of debt bondage in the ancient world. At the same time, loans and investments are a necessary part of a market economy and often a way for someone without wealth to become self-sustaining. One example of how the Rabbis managed this tension can be found in the commentary on Deut. 15:9. Here we see a distinction in policy between Jewish loan recipients ("kinsmen"), from whom one cannot charge interest, and others, to whom one can lend on interest as long as the usual laws of business integrity are observed. Two forms of relationships are being described.

Political and economic relationships are *contractual*. They presuppose the coming together of self-interested parties, both of whom benefit from the exchange. Contractual relationships, however, are not the only or even the most fundamental forms of association. Family members, for instance, develop an unconscious choreography of mutuality. They help one another; they depend on one another; and that minuet of giving and taking is part of their identity and growth as individuals. In this microcosm of community and its everyday transactions, we see something significant taking place: the making and sustaining of the moral life. I call such relationships – using a keyword of the Torah – *covenantal*. Whereas contracts are about the self, covenants are about the larger groupings in and through which we develop our identity. They are about the "we" in which I discover the "I." Covenant is a bond, not of interest or advantage, but of belonging. Religious communities are bound by covenantal ties; in such a sensitive transaction as a loan to someone in need, a fellow Jew must be treated as a "kinsman." Yet this does not preclude the possibility of lending in a contractual manner, for mutual profit, in an open marketplace.

Covenantal relationships – where we develop the grammar and syntax of reciprocity, where we help others and they help us without calculations of relative advantage – are where trust is born. Contracts, social or economic, mediate relationships between strangers. But if we were always and only strangers to one another, we would have no reason to

אֹיְבֶיךָ לְפָנֶיךָ וְהָיָה מַחֲנֶיךָ קָדוֹשׁ וְלֹא־יִרְאֶה בְךָ עֶרְוַת דָּבָר וְשָׁב
טז מֵאַחֲרֶיךָ׃ לֹא־תַסְגִּיר עֶבֶד אֶל־אֲדֹנָיו אֲשֶׁר־יִנָּצֵל אֵלֶיךָ
יז מֵעִם אֲדֹנָיו׃ עִמְּךָ יֵשֵׁב בְּקִרְבְּךָ בַּמָּקוֹם אֲשֶׁר־יִבְחַר בְּאַחַד שְׁעָרֶיךָ
יח בַּטּוֹב לוֹ לֹא תּוֹנֶנּוּ׃ לֹא־תִהְיֶה קְדֵשָׁה
יט מִבְּנוֹת יִשְׂרָאֵל וְלֹא־יִהְיֶה קָדֵשׁ מִבְּנֵי יִשְׂרָאֵל׃ לֹא־תָבִיא אֶתְנַן זוֹנָה
וּמְחִיר כֶּלֶב בֵּית יְהוָה אֱלֹהֶיךָ לְכָל־נֶדֶר כִּי תוֹעֲבַת יְהוָה אֱלֹהֶיךָ
כ גַּם־שְׁנֵיהֶם׃ לֹא־תַשִּׁיךְ לְאָחִיךָ נֶשֶׁךְ כֶּסֶף נֶשֶׁךְ אֹכֶל נֶשֶׁךְ

אונקלוס

עִמָּךְ יְתֵיב בֵּינָךְ, בְּאַתְרָא דְּיִתְרְעֵי, בַּחֲדָא מִן קִרְוָךְ בִּדְיִיטַב לֵיהּ, לָא תוֹנֵינֵיהּ: יח לָא תְהֵי אִתְּתָא מִבְּנָת יִשְׂרָאֵל לִגְבַר עֶבֶד, וְלָא יִסַּב גְּבַר מִבְּנֵי יִשְׂרָאֵל אִתְּא אָמָה: יט לָא תַעֵיל אֲגַר זָנִיתָא וְחֶלְפַּן כַּלְבָּא, לְבֵית מַקְדְּשָׁא דַּיְיָ אֱלָהָךְ לְכָל נְדַר, אֲרֵי מְרַחַק, קֳדָם יְיָ אֱלָהָךְ אַף תַּרְוֵיהוֹן: כ לָא תְרַבֵּי לַאֲחוּךְ, רִבִּית כְּסַף רִבִּית עֲבוּר, רִבִּית,

23:16 **לֹא־תַסְגִּיר עֶבֶד** *Do not hand him back* – Rashi stresses that the fugitive merits our assistance even if he or she is a non-Jewish slave fleeing a Jewish master. This verse provides the basis of an ethic of assisting refugees. It is also a striking example of the Torah's refusal to see inequalities in society as the will of God. On this, the Talmud (Bava Batra 10a) records a fascinating debate between R. Akiva and the Roman governor of Israel, Turnus Rufus:

> Turnus Rufus asked R. Akiva, "If your God loves the poor, why does He not provide for them?"
>
> R. Akiva replied, "So that we may be saved through them from the punishment of Gehinnom [i.e., charity atones]."
>
> Rufus said, "On the contrary, it is this that will condemn you to Gehinnom. I will make my point clear by a parable. A king of flesh and blood became angry with his slave, put him in prison, and ordered that he be given neither food nor drink. A certain man went [to the prison] and gave him food and drink. When the king hears what that man did, will he not be angry with him? And after all, you are no more than God's servants, as it is written, 'For it is to Me that the Israelites are servants'" (Lev. 25:55).
>
> R. Akiva replied, "I will prove my point with another parable. A king of flesh and blood became angry with his child, put him in prison, and ordered that he be given neither food nor drink. A certain man went [to the prison] and gave him food and drink. When the king hears what the man did, will he not reward him? And after all, we are called [God's] children, as it is written, 'You are children of the Lord your God'" (Deut. 14:1).

There is nothing inevitable or divinely willed about social or economic inequality. Judaism rejects the almost universal belief in antiquity and throughout the Middle Ages that hierarchy and divisions of class are written into the structure of society. What human beings have created, human beings can rectify. It follows that everyone should be provided with the basic requirements of a safe and dignified life.

However complex the application of this principle in a globalized world, it remains one of the Torah's most powerful imperatives: a society is judged by what it contributes to the welfare of the least advantaged, such as the runaway slave, the widow, the orphan, the poor, and the stranger. If someone turns to us for help when fleeing violence, we do not ignore it.

21 on money or food or anything that could earn interest. You may charge interest
on loans to a foreigner, but on loans to your kinsmen do not charge, so that the
Lord your God may bless you in all your endeavors in the land you are entering
22 to possess. When you make a vow to the Lord your God, do not
delay in fulfilling it, for the Lord your God will certainly require it of you; you
23 24 will incur guilt. But if you refrain from vowing you will not incur guilt. Whatever
your lips utter, take care to do, since you have voluntarily vowed to the Lord
25 your God, with your own mouth. When you enter your neighbor's HAMISHI
vineyard, you may eat as many grapes as you wish; eat your fill, but do not put
26 any in a container. When you enter your neighbor's field of standing
grain, you may pluck ears with your hand, but you may not put a sickle to your
24 1 neighbor's grain. If a man takes a wife and becomes her husband, but
begins to dislike her because he finds something indecent in her; if he writes
2 her a bill of divorce, puts it in her hand, and sends her from his house, she may
3 leave his house and become another man's wife. However, if the second
husband rejects her, writes her a bill of divorce, puts it in her hand, and sends
4 her from his house, or the second husband dies, her first husband, who sent her
away, is not permitted to take her again to be his wife after she has been defiled,
for that would be abhorrent to the Lord, and you must not bring sin into the
5 land that the Lord your God is giving you for your possession. When SHISHI

רש״י

כא| **לַנָּכְרִי תַשִּׁיךְ.** וְלֹא לְאָחִיךָ, לָאו הַבָּא מִכְּלַל עֲשֵׂה – עֲשֵׂה, לַעֲבֹר עָלָיו בִּשְׁנֵי לָאוִין וַעֲשֵׂה:

כב| **לֹא תְאַחֵר לְשַׁלְּמוֹ.** שְׁלֹשָׁה רְגָלִים, וּלְמָדוּהוּ רַבּוֹתֵינוּ מִן הַמִּקְרָא:

כד| **מוֹצָא שְׂפָתֶיךָ תִּשְׁמֹר.** לִתֵּן עֲשֵׂה עַל לֹא תַעֲשֶׂה:

כה| **כִּי תָבֹא בְּכֶרֶם רֵעֶךָ.** בְּפוֹעֵל הַכָּתוּב מְדַבֵּר: **וְאֶל כֶּלְיְךָ לֹא תִתֵּן.** מִכָּאן שֶׁלֹּא דִּבְּרָה תוֹרָה אֶלָּא בִּשְׁעַת הַבָּצִיר, בִּזְמַן שֶׁאַתָּה נוֹתֵן לְכֵלָיו שֶׁל בַּעַל הַבַּיִת, אֲבָל אִם בָּא לַעֲדֹר וּלְקַשְׁקֵשׁ אֵינוֹ אוֹכֵל: **כְּנַפְשְׁךָ.** כַּמָּה שֶׁתִּרְצֶה: **שָׂבְעֶךָ.** וְלֹא אֲכִילָה גַּסָּה:

כו| **כִּי תָבֹא בְּקָמַת רֵעֶךָ.** אַף זוֹ בְּפוֹעֵל הַכָּתוּב מְדַבֵּר:

כד א| **כִּי מָצָא בָהּ עֶרְוַת דָּבָר.** מִצְוָה עָלָיו לְגָרְשָׁהּ שֶׁלֹּא תִמְצָא חֵן בְּעֵינָיו:

ב| **לְאִישׁ אַחֵר.** אֵין זֶה בֶּן זוּגוֹ שֶׁל רִאשׁוֹן, הוּא הוֹצִיא רְשָׁעָה מִתּוֹךְ בֵּיתוֹ וְזֶה הִכְנִיסָהּ:

ג| **וּשְׂנֵאָהּ הָאִישׁ הָאַחֲרוֹן.** הַכָּתוּב מְבַשְּׂרוֹ שֶׁסּוֹפוֹ לִשְׂנֹאתָהּ, וְאִם לָאו – קוֹבַרְתּוֹ, שֶׁנֶּאֱמַר: "אוֹ כִי יָמוּת":

ד| **אַחֲרֵי אֲשֶׁר הֻטַּמָּאָה.** לְרַבּוֹת סוֹטָה שֶׁנִּסְתְּרָה:

trust one another. Markets depend on virtues not produced by the market, just as states depend on virtues not created by the state. They depend on a surrounding matrix of virtue and on the institutions that sustain it: families, communities, beliefs, and traditions. They need rules of integrity and fair dealing, and a mindset that sees the market as a place not of exploitation, but of mutual gain. Without these, the workings of the market are too arbitrary and abrasive. With them, it is the best way we know of matching one person's talents to another's desires, of encouraging freedom, creativity, and dignity, and of enhancing the conditions of life for all.

כא כָּל־דָּבָר אֲשֶׁר יִשָּׁךְ׃ לַנָּכְרִי תַשִּׁיךְ וּלְאָחִיךָ לֹא תַשִּׁיךְ לְמַעַן יְבָרֶכְךָ
יְהוָה אֱלֹהֶיךָ בְּכֹל מִשְׁלַח יָדֶךָ עַל־הָאָרֶץ אֲשֶׁר־אַתָּה בָא־שָׁמָּה
כב לְרִשְׁתָּהּ׃ כִּי־תִדֹּר נֶדֶר לַיהוָה אֱלֹהֶיךָ לֹא תְאַחֵר יט
כג לְשַׁלְּמוֹ כִּי־דָרֹשׁ יִדְרְשֶׁנּוּ יְהוָה אֱלֹהֶיךָ מֵעִמָּךְ וְהָיָה בְךָ חֵטְא׃ וְכִי
כד תֶחְדַּל לִנְדֹּר לֹא־יִהְיֶה בְךָ חֵטְא׃ מוֹצָא שְׂפָתֶיךָ תִּשְׁמֹר וְעָשִׂיתָ כַּאֲשֶׁר
כה נָדַרְתָּ לַיהוָה אֱלֹהֶיךָ נְדָבָה אֲשֶׁר דִּבַּרְתָּ בְּפִיךָ׃ כִּי תָבֹא חמישי
בְּכֶרֶם רֵעֶךָ וְאָכַלְתָּ עֲנָבִים כְּנַפְשְׁךָ שָׂבְעֶךָ וְאֶל־כֶּלְיְךָ לֹא
כו תִתֵּן׃ כִּי תָבֹא בְּקָמַת רֵעֶךָ וְקָטַפְתָּ מְלִילֹת בְּיָדֶךָ
כד א וְחֶרְמֵשׁ לֹא תָנִיף עַל קָמַת רֵעֶךָ׃ כִּי־יִקַּח אִישׁ אִשָּׁה וּבְעָלָהּ
וְהָיָה אִם־לֹא תִמְצָא־חֵן בְּעֵינָיו כִּי־מָצָא בָהּ עֶרְוַת דָּבָר וְכָתַב לָהּ
ב סֵפֶר כְּרִיתֻת וְנָתַן בְּיָדָהּ וְשִׁלְּחָהּ מִבֵּיתוֹ׃ וְיָצְאָה מִבֵּיתוֹ וְהָלְכָה וְהָיְתָה
ג לְאִישׁ־אַחֵר׃ וּשְׂנֵאָהּ הָאִישׁ הָאַחֲרוֹן וְכָתַב לָהּ סֵפֶר כְּרִיתֻת וְנָתַן
בְּיָדָהּ וְשִׁלְּחָהּ מִבֵּיתוֹ אוֹ כִי יָמוּת הָאִישׁ הָאַחֲרוֹן אֲשֶׁר־לְקָחָהּ לוֹ
ד לְאִשָּׁה׃ לֹא־יוּכַל בַּעְלָהּ הָרִאשׁוֹן אֲשֶׁר־שִׁלְּחָהּ לָשׁוּב לְקַחְתָּהּ לִהְיוֹת
לוֹ לְאִשָּׁה אַחֲרֵי אֲשֶׁר הֻטַּמָּאָה כִּי־תוֹעֵבָה הִוא לִפְנֵי יְהוָה וְלֹא
ה תַחֲטִיא אֶת־הָאָרֶץ אֲשֶׁר יְהוָה אֱלֹהֶיךָ נֹתֵן לְךָ נַחֲלָה׃ כִּי־ ששי

אונקלוס

כָּל מִדַּעַם דְּמִתְרַבֵּי׃ כא לְבַר עַמְמִין תְּרַבֵּי, וּלְאָחוּךְ לָא תְרַבֵּי, בְּדִיל דִּיבָרְכִנָּךְ יי אֱלָהָךְ, בְּכָל אוֹשָׁטוּת יְדָךְ, עַל אַרְעָא, דְּאַתְּ עָלֵיל לְתַמָּן לְמֵירְתַהּ׃ כב אֲרֵי תִדַּר נְדַר קֳדָם יי אֱלָהָךְ, לָא תְאַחַר לְשַׁלָּמוּתֵיהּ, אֲרֵי מִתְבַּע יִתְבְּעִנֵּיהּ, יי אֱלָהָךְ מִנָּךְ, וִיהֵי בָךְ חוֹבָא׃ כג וַאֲרֵי תִתְמְנַע מִלְּמִדַּר, לָא יְהֵי בָךְ חוֹבָא׃ כד אַפָּקוּת סִפְוָתָךְ תִּטַּר וְתַעְבֵּיד, כְּמָא דִּנְדַרְתָּא, קֳדָם יי אֱלָהָךְ נִדְבְתָא, דְּמַלֵּילְתָּא בְּפֻמָּךְ׃ כה אֲרֵי תֵיתְגַר בְּכַרְמָא דְחַבְרָךְ, וְתֵיכוֹל עִנְבִין, כְּנַפְשָׁךְ סִבְעָךְ, וּלְמָנָךְ לָא תִתֵּין׃ כו אֲרֵי תֵיתְגַר בְּקָמְתָא דְחַבְרָךְ, וְתִקְטוֹף דְּמַלְיָן בִּידָךְ, וּמַגְּלָא לָא תְרִים, עַל קָמְתָא דְחַבְרָךְ׃ כד א אֲרֵי יִסַּב גְּבַר, אִתְּתָא וְיִבְעֲלִנַּהּ, וִיהֵי אִם לָא תַשְׁכַּח רַחֲמִין בְּעֵינוֹהִי, אֲרֵי אַשְׁכַּח בַּהּ עֲבֵירַת פִּתְגָם, וְיִכְתּוֹב לַהּ, גֵּט פִּטּוּרִין וְיִתֵּין בִּידַהּ, וְיִפְטְרִנַּהּ מִבֵּיתֵיהּ׃ ב וְתִפּוֹק מִבֵּיתֵיהּ, וּתְהָךְ וּתְהֵי לִגְבַר אָחֳרָן׃ ג וְיִסְנְיִנַּהּ גַּבְרָא בָּתְרָאָה, וְיִכְתּוֹב לַהּ, גֵּט פִּטּוּרִין וְיִתֵּין בִּידַהּ, וְיִפְטְרִנַּהּ מִבֵּיתֵיהּ, אוֹ אֲרֵי יְמוּת גַּבְרָא בָּתְרָאָה, דְּנַסְבַהּ לֵיהּ לְאִתּוּ׃ ד לֵית לֵיהּ רְשׁוּ לְבַעְלַהּ קַדְמָאָה דְּפַטְרַהּ, לְמִתַּב לְמִסְבַהּ לְמֶהֱוֵי לֵיהּ לְאִתּוּ, בָּתַר דְּאִסְתָּאֲבַת, אֲרֵי מְרַחֲקָא הִיא קֳדָם יי, וְלָא תְחַיֵּיב יָת אַרְעָא, דַּיי אֱלָהָךְ, יָהֵיב לָךְ אַחְסָנָא׃ ה אֲרֵי

a man is newly married, he shall not go out with the army or have any related
duty laid on him. He shall be exempt for one year, to be with his home and
6 bring happiness to the woman he has married. Do not take an upper or lower
millstone as security for a debt, for that would be taking a person's livelihood as
7 security. If someone is found to have kidnapped another Israelite,
enslaving or selling him, the kidnapper shall die. You must purge the evil from
8 your midst. Take great care in cases of impure blight. Carefully do
whatever the Levitical priests instruct you, as I have commanded them.
9 Remember what the LORD your God did to Miriam on your way when you left
10 Egypt. When you make your neighbor a loan of any kind, do not go
11 into his house to take his pledge. Wait outside while the person to whom you
12 are making the loan brings the pledge out to you. If the person is poor, do not
13 go to sleep with the pledge in your possession. You must return his pledge by
sunset, so that he may sleep in his cloak and bless you. This will be accounted
14 to you as a righteous act before the LORD your God. Do not SHEVI'I
take advantage of a poor and destitute laborer, whether he is a kinsman or a

רש"י

ה **אשה חדשה.** שהיא חדשה לו, ואפילו אלמנה, פרט למחזיר גרושתו: **ולא יעבר עליו.** דבר הצבא: **לכל דבר.** שהוא צרך הצבא, לא לספק מים ומזון ולא לתקן דרכים. אבל החוזרים מעורכי המלחמה על פי כהן, כגון בנה בית ולא חנכו או ארש אשה ולא לקחה, מספיקין מים ומזון ומתקנין את הדרכים: **יהיה לביתו.** אף בשביל ביתו, אם בנה בית וחנכו ואם נטע כרם וחללו, אינו זז מביתו בשביל צרכי המלחמה: **לביתו.** זה ביתו: **יהיה.** לרבות את כרמו: **ושמח.** ישמח את אשתו, ותרגומו: "ויחדי ית אתתיה", והמתרגם: 'ויחדי עם אתתיה' טועה הוא, שאין זה תרגום של 'ושמח' אלא של 'ושמח':

ו **רחים.** היא התחתונה: **ורכב.** היא העליונה: **לא יחבל.** אם בא למשכנו על חובו בבית דין, לא ימשכננו בדברים שעושים בהן אכל נפש:

ז **כי ימצא.** בעדים והתראה, וכן כל 'ימצא' שבתורה: **והתעמר בו.** אינו חיב עד שישתמש בו:

ח **השמר בנגע הצרעת.** שלא תתלש סימני טמאה ולא תקץ את הבהרת: **ככל אשר יורו אתכם.** אם להסגיר, אם להחליט, אם לטהר:

ט **זכור את אשר עשה ה' אלהיך למרים.** אם באת להזהר שלא תלקה בצרעת, אל תספר לשון הרע, זכור העשוי למרים שדברה באחיה ולקתה בנגעים:

י **כי תשה ברעך.** תחוב בחברך: **משאת מאומה.** חוב של כלום:

יב **לא תשכב בעבטו.** לא תשכב ועבוטו אצלך:

יג **כבוא השמש.** אם כסות לילה הוא, ואם כסות יום החזירהו בבקר, וכבר כתוב ב'ואלה המשפטים': "עד בא השמש תשיבנו לו" (שמות כב, כה), כל היום תשיבנו לו ובבא השמש תקחנו: **וברכך.** ואם אינו מברכך, מכל מקום "ולך תהיה צדקה":

יד **לא תעשק שכיר.** והלא כבר כתוב? אלא לעבר על האביון בשני לאוין: 'לא תעשק שכר שכיר שהוא עני ואביון', ועל העשיר כבר הזהר: "לא תעשק את רעך" (ויקרא יט, יג): **אביון.** התאב לכל דבר: **מגרך.** זה גר צדק: **בשעריך.** זה גר תושב האוכל נבלות: **אשר בארצך.** לרבות שכר בהמה וכלים:

home on the shared joy of the first year of marriage overrides even the collective interests of a nation going to war.

24:14 לא־תעשק שכיר עני ואביון *Poor and destitute laborer* – The architectonics of biblical liberty are immensely detailed, but they can be summarized under clear themes. One of these is a humane concern for the poor – an insistence that they never suffer hunger, or be humiliated by their economic

יִקַּח אִישׁ אִשָּׁה חֲדָשָׁה לֹא יֵצֵא בַּצָּבָא וְלֹא־יַעֲבֹר עָלָיו לְכָל־דָּבָר
ו נָקִי יִהְיֶה לְבֵיתוֹ שָׁנָה אֶחָת וְשִׂמַּח אֶת־אִשְׁתּוֹ אֲשֶׁר־לָקָח׃ לֹא־יַחֲבֹל
ז רֵחַיִם וָרָכֶב כִּי־נֶפֶשׁ הוּא חֹבֵל׃ כִּי־יִמָּצֵא אִישׁ גֹּנֵב נֶפֶשׁ
מֵאֶחָיו מִבְּנֵי יִשְׂרָאֵל וְהִתְעַמֶּר־בּוֹ וּמְכָרוֹ וּמֵת הַגַּנָּב הַהוּא וּבִעַרְתָּ
ח הָרָע מִקִּרְבֶּךָ׃ הִשָּׁמֶר בְּנֶגַע־הַצָּרַעַת לִשְׁמֹר מְאֹד
וְלַעֲשׂוֹת כְּכֹל אֲשֶׁר־יוֹרוּ אֶתְכֶם הַכֹּהֲנִים הַלְוִיִּם כַּאֲשֶׁר צִוִּיתִם תִּשְׁמְרוּ
ט לַעֲשׂוֹת׃ זָכוֹר אֵת אֲשֶׁר־עָשָׂה יהוה אֱלֹהֶיךָ לְמִרְיָם בַּדֶּרֶךְ בְּצֵאתְכֶם
י מִמִּצְרָיִם׃ כִּי־תַשֶּׁה בְרֵעֲךָ מַשַּׁאת מְאוּמָה לֹא־תָבֹא
יא אֶל־בֵּיתוֹ לַעֲבֹט עֲבֹטוֹ׃ בַּחוּץ תַּעֲמֹד וְהָאִישׁ אֲשֶׁר אַתָּה נֹשֶׁה בוֹ
יב יוֹצִיא אֵלֶיךָ אֶת־הַעֲבוֹט הַחוּצָה׃ וְאִם־אִישׁ עָנִי הוּא לֹא תִשְׁכַּב
יג בַּעֲבֹטוֹ׃ הָשֵׁב תָּשִׁיב לוֹ אֶת־הַעֲבוֹט כְּבוֹא הַשֶּׁמֶשׁ וְשָׁכַב בְּשַׂלְמָתוֹ
יד וּבֵרְכֶךָּ וּלְךָ תִּהְיֶה צְדָקָה לִפְנֵי יהוה אֱלֹהֶיךָ׃ לֹא־ שביעי
תַעֲשֹׁק שָׂכִיר עָנִי וְאֶבְיוֹן מֵאַחֶיךָ אוֹ מִגֵּרְךָ אֲשֶׁר בְּאַרְצְךָ בִּשְׁעָרֶיךָ׃

אונקלוס

יִסַּב גְּבַר אִתְּתָא חֲדַתָּא, לָא יִפּוֹק בְּחֵילָא, וְלָא יִעְבַּר עֲלוֹהִי לְכָל פִּתְגָּם, פְּנֵי, יְהֵי לְבֵיתֵיהּ שַׁתָּא חֲדָא, וִיחַדֵּי יָת אִתְּתֵיהּ דִּנְסִיב: ו לָא יִסַּב מַשְׁכּוֹנָא רֵחְיָא וְרִכְבָּא, אֲרֵי בְהוֹן מִתְעֲבֵיד מְזוֹן לְכָל נְפַשׁ: ז אֲרֵי יִשְׁתְּכַח גְּבַר, גָּנֵיב נַפְשָׁא מֵאֲחוֹהִי מִבְּנֵי יִשְׂרָאֵל, וְיִתַּגַּר בֵּיהּ וִיזַבְּנִנֵּיהּ, וְיִתְקְטִיל גַּנָּבָא הַהוּא, וּתְפַלֵּי עָבֵיד דְּבִישׁ מִבֵּינָךְ: ח אִסְתְּמַר בְּמַכְתַּשׁ סְגִירוּ, לְמִטַּר לַחְדָּא וּלְמֶעְבַּד, כְּכֹל דְּיַלְּפוּן יָתְכוֹן, כָּהֲנַיָּא לֵיוָאֵי, כְּמָא דְּפַקֵּידְתִּנּוּן תִּטְּרוּן לְמֶעְבַּד: ט הֱוֵי דְּכִיר, יָת דַּעֲבַד, יְיָ אֱלָהָךְ לְמִרְיָם, בְּאוֹרְחָא בְּמִפַּקְכוֹן מִמִּצְרָיִם: י אֲרֵי תִרְשֵׁי בְּחַבְרָךְ רְשׁוּת מִדַּעַם, לָא תֵיעוֹל לְבֵיתֵיהּ לְמִסַּב מַשְׁכּוֹנֵיהּ: יא בְּבָרָא תְּקוּם, וְגַבְרָא, דְּאַתְּ רָשֵׁי בֵיהּ, יַפֵּיק לָךְ, יָת מַשְׁכּוֹנָא לְבָרָא: יב וְאִם גְּבַר מִסְכֵּין הוּא, לָא תִשְׁכּוֹב בְּמַשְׁכּוֹנֵיהּ: יג אָתָבָא תָּתֵיב לֵיהּ יָת מַשְׁכּוֹנָא כְּמֵיעַל שִׁמְשָׁא, וְיִשְׁכּוֹב בִּכְסוּתֵיהּ וִיבָרְכִנָּךְ, וְלָךְ תְּהֵי זָכוּ, קֳדָם יְיָ אֱלָהָךְ: יד לָא תַעְשׁוֹק אֲגִירָא עַנְיָא וּמִסְכֵּינָא, מֵאַחָךְ, אוֹ מִגִּיּוֹרָךְ, דִּבְאַרְעָךְ בְּקִרְוָךְ:

24:5 וְשִׂמַּח אֶת־אִשְׁתּוֹ אֲשֶׁר־לָקָח *Bring happiness to the woman he has married* – Not by chance is marriage called *kiddushin*, "sanctification." Like covenant itself, marriage is a pledge of loyalty between two parties, each recognizing the other's integrity, honoring their differences, even as they come together to bring new life into being. Marriage is to society what covenant is to religious faith: a decision to make love – not power, wealth, or *force majeure* – the generative principle of life.

Marriage is the most personal and intimate of all forms of human association, and the deepest matrix of faith. There is no redemption of solitude deeper than to share a life with someone we love and trust, who we know will never desert us, who lifts us when we fall and believes in us even when we fail.

God lives in the unadorned heart of the human situation, in the covenantal love between husband and wife on which the republic of faith is built. Building the foundation of a

15 migrant living in one of the towns in your land. Pay him his wages on the
same day, before sunset, because he is poor and his livelihood depends on it.
Otherwise he will cry out to the LORD against you, and you will bear your
16 guilt. Parents shall not be put to death for their children, nor shall
children be put to death for their parents. A person shall be put to death only
17 for his own sin. Do not deprive a migrant or an orphan of justice. Do
18 not take a widow's garment as a pledge. Remember that you were a slave in
Egypt and the LORD your God redeemed you from there. And so I command

רש״י

טו **וְאֵלָיו הוּא נֹשֵׂא אֶת נַפְשׁוֹ.** אֶל הַשָּׂכָר הַזֶּה הוּא נוֹשֵׂא אֶת נַפְשׁוֹ לָמוּת, עָלָה בַּכֶּבֶשׁ וְנִתְלָה בָּאִילָן: **וְהָיָה בְךָ חֵטְא.** מִכָּל מָקוֹם, אֶלָּא שֶׁמְּמַהֲרִין לִפָּרַע עַל יְדֵי הַקּוֹרֵא:

טז **לֹא יוּמְתוּ אָבוֹת עַל בָּנִים.** בְּעֵדוּת בָּנִים. וְאִם תֹּאמַר בַּעֲוֹן בָּנִים, כְּבָר אָמוּר: "אִישׁ בְּחֶטְאוֹ יוּמָתוּ". אֲבָל מִי שֶׁאֵינוֹ אִישׁ מֵת בַּעֲוֹן אָבִיו, וְהַקְּטַנִּים מֵתִים בַּעֲוֹן אֲבוֹתָם בִּידֵי שָׁמַיִם:

יז **לֹא תַטֶּה מִשְׁפַּט גֵּר יָתוֹם.** וְעַל הֶעָשִׁיר כְּבָר הִזְהִיר: "לֹא תַטֶּה מִשְׁפָּט" (לעיל טז, יט), וְשָׁנָה בֶּעָנִי לַעֲבֹר עָלָיו בִּשְׁנֵי לָאוִין, לְפִי שֶׁנָּקֵל לְהַטּוֹת מִשְׁפַּט עָנִי יוֹתֵר מִשֶּׁל עָשִׁיר, לְכָךְ הִזְהִיר וְשָׁנָה עָלָיו: **וְלֹא תַחֲבֹל.** שֶׁלֹּא בִּשְׁעַת הַלְוָאָה:

יח **וְזָכַרְתָּ.** עַל מְנָת כֵּן פְּדִיתִיךָ, לִשְׁמֹר חֻקּוֹתַי אֲפִלּוּ יֵשׁ חֶסְרוֹן כִּיס בַּדָּבָר:

24:18 **וְזָכַרְתָּ כִּי עֶבֶד הָיִיתָ** *Remember that you were a slave* – The exodus functions not simply as a fact of history, but also and primarily as the fundamental principle of jurisprudence, the logic and justification of the law. The Israelites were commanded to create a society that was opposite to Egypt. It would be a society in which even slaves rested every seventh day and breathed the wide air of freedom. It would be one in which no one became trapped endlessly in debt, or forced irretrievably to sell ancestral property. Everyone would have access to justice.

This made sense because the Israelites had been on the receiving end of Egyptian mores. They knew what it felt like to be poor, to be deprived of justice, to be treated as less than human. They knew from the inside what powerlessness feels like. We can now see something singular about the Jewish experience. For as long as human beings have thought about morality, they have asked the question: Why be moral? Why act for the benefit of others if it is to your advantage to behave otherwise? We are self-seeking creatures, driven by desire. Why desist from something you want to do and can do merely because you ought not to? Plato, in *The Republic* (Book II, 359a–360d), uses a thought experiment. He recalls the legend of Gyges's ring, which had the power to make anyone who wore it invisible. One who had such a ring could commit any crime and get away with it. Why then would such a person be moral?

The Torah gives the most powerful grounding for a moral system. It provides not a veil of ignorance but a sustaining stream of knowledge – acquired through experience, nurtured by memory, enacted in ritual, retold in sacred story, never to be forgotten. Indeed, says God through the prophets from Moshe to Yirmeyahu, if you ever forget it, you will be forced to relive it, through further exiles, other persecutions.

Egypt was, for the Israelites, the school of the soul. They knew what it was like to be on the receiving end of absolute power: Ramesses II, the greatest ruler of the longest-lived empire the world has ever known. They had been rescued by the Creator of heaven and earth, who had brought them from slavery to freedom and then made a covenant with them, not for His sake but for theirs, inviting them under His sovereignty to build a society that would use their God-given freedom to honor the liberty of others. Memory is the driving force of morality.

טו בְּיוֹמוֹ תִתֵּן שְׂכָרוֹ וְלֹא־תָבוֹא עָלָיו הַשֶּׁמֶשׁ כִּי עָנִי הוּא וְאֵלָיו
הוּא נֹשֵׂא אֶת־נַפְשׁוֹ וְלֹא־יִקְרָא עָלֶיךָ אֶל־יהוה וְהָיָה בְךָ
טז חֵטְא: לֹא־יוּמְתוּ אָבוֹת עַל־בָּנִים וּבָנִים לֹא־יוּמְתוּ
יז עַל־אָבוֹת אִישׁ בְּחֶטְאוֹ יוּמָתוּ: לֹא תַטֶּה מִשְׁפַּט
יח גֵּר יָתוֹם וְלֹא תַחֲבֹל בֶּגֶד אַלְמָנָה: וְזָכַרְתָּ כִּי עֶבֶד הָיִיתָ בְּמִצְרַיִם
וַיִּפְדְּךָ יהוה אֱלֹהֶיךָ מִשָּׁם עַל־כֵּן אָנֹכִי מְצַוְּךָ לַעֲשׂוֹת אֶת־הַדָּבָר

אונקלוס

טו בְּיוֹמֵיהּ תִּתֵּין אַגְרֵיהּ וְלָא תֵיעוֹל עֲלוֹהִי שִׁמְשָׁא, אֲרֵי עַנְיָא הוּא, וְלֵיהּ, הוּא מָסַר יָת נַפְשֵׁיהּ, וְלָא יִקְרֵי עֲלָךְ קֳדָם יי, וִיהֵי בָךְ חוֹבָא: טז לָא יְמוּתוּן אֲבָהָן עַל פּוּם בְּנִין, וּבְנִין לָא יְמוּתוּן עַל פּוּם אֲבָהָן, אֱנָשׁ בְּחוֹבֵיהּ יְמוּתוּן: יז לָא תַצְלֵי, דִּין גִּיּוֹר יִיתַם, וְלָא תִסַּב מַשְׁכּוֹנָא, כְּסוּת אַרְמְלָא: יח וְתִדְכַּר, אֲרֵי עַבְדָּא הֲוֵיתָא בְּמִצְרַיִם, וּפַרְקָךְ, יי אֱלָהָךְ מִתַּמָּן, עַל כֵּן, אֲנָא מְפַקֵּיד לָךְ לְמֶעְבַּד, יָת פִּתְגָּמָא

circumstances: There is something extraordinarily humane about these ordinances, and although they speak to an agrarian order more than three thousand years ago, the principle they adumbrate remains true and compelling today. Freedom involves more than an absence of constraints. A society in which the few have wealth and many are on the verge of starvation is not free by the standards of the Torah.

24:16 אִישׁ בְּחֶטְאוֹ יוּמָתוּ *A person shall be put to death only for his own sin* – In general, the Sages rejected the idea that children could be punished, even at the hands of Heaven, for the sins of their parents. As a result, they reinterpreted every passage that gave the opposite impression, that children were indeed being punished for their parents' sins. They explained biblical episodes in which children were punished with their parents by saying that the children "had the power to protest/prevent their parents from sinning, but they failed to do so" (Sanhedrin 27b; *Yalkut Shimoni* I:290).

What, then, is the scope of responsibility we bear in our roles as parents, neighbors, townspeople, citizens, and children of the covenant? Judicially, only the criminal is responsible for his crime. But, implies the Torah, we are also our brother's keeper. We share collective responsibility for the moral and spiritual health of society. "All Israelites," said the Sages, "are responsible for one another" (Shevuot 39a). Legal responsibility is relatively easy to define. But moral responsibility is larger, and necessarily more vague. "Let a person not say, 'I have not sinned, and if someone else commits a sin, that is a matter between him and God.' This is contrary to the Torah," writes Rambam in *Sefer HaMitzvot* (*Mitzvat Aseh* 205).

This is particularly so when it comes to the relationship between parents and children. The duty of parents to teach their children is fundamental to Judaism. It appears in both the first two paragraphs of the *Shema,* as well as passages cited in the Four Sons section of the Haggada. Rambam counts as one of the gravest sins "one who sees his son falling into bad ways and does not stop him." The reason, he says, is that "since his son is under his authority, had he stopped him the son would have desisted." Therefore it is accounted to the father as if he had actively caused his son to sin (*Hilkhot Teshuva* 4:1).

We are not legally responsible for the sins of either our parents or our children. But what we do and how we live do have an effect on the future to the third and fourth generation. If we fail to honor our responsibilities as parents, then – though no law will hold us responsible – our children will pay the price. They will suffer because of our sins.

19 you in this. When you reap the harvest in your field and forget a sheaf
in the field, do not go back to get it. Leave it for the migrant, the orphan, and
the widow, so that the LORD your God may grant you blessing in all the work
20 of your hands. When you beat the fruit from your olive trees, do not
go over them again. Leave what remains for the migrant, the orphan, and the
21 widow. When you gather the grapes of your vineyard, do not go over the vines
again. Leave what remains for the migrant, the orphan, and the widow.
22 Remember that you were a slave in the land of Egypt. And so I command you
25 1 in this. When two people have a dispute they shall go to the court of
justice and the judges shall decide between them, acquitting the innocent and
2 condemning the guilty. If the guilty person is to be flogged, the judge shall
make him lie down and have him flogged there in his presence with the requisite
3 number of lashes. He may be given as many as forty lashes but no more; if he is
given more lashes than this, an excessive flogging, your kinsman will be

רש״י

יט **וְשָׁכַחְתָּ עֹמֶר.** וְלֹא גָּדִישׁ, מִכָּאן אָמְרוּ: עֹמֶר שֶׁיֵּשׁ בּוֹ סָאתַיִם וּשְׁכָחוֹ אֵינוֹ שִׁכְחָה (פאה ו, ו): **בַּשָּׂדֶה.** לְרַבּוֹת שִׁכְחַת קָמָה שֶׁשָּׁכַח מִקְצָתָהּ מִלִּקְצֹר: **לֹא תָשׁוּב לְקַחְתּוֹ.** מִכָּאן אָמְרוּ: שֶׁלְּאַחֲרָיו שִׁכְחָה, שֶׁלְּפָנָיו אֵינוֹ שִׁכְחָה, שֶׁאֵינוֹ בְּבַל תָּשׁוּב (פאה ו, ד): **לְמַעַן יְבָרֶכְךָ.** וְאַף עַל פִּי שֶׁבָּאת לְיָדוֹ שֶׁלֹּא בְּמִתְכַּוֵּן, קַל וָחֹמֶר לְעוֹשֶׂה בְּמִתְכַּוֵּן. אֱמֹר מֵעַתָּה, נָפְלָה סֶלַע מִיָּדוֹ וּמְצָאָהּ עָנִי וְנִתְפַּרְנֵס בָּהּ, הֲרֵי הוּא מִתְבָּרֵךְ עָלֶיהָ:

כ **לֹא תְפַאֵר.** לֹא תִטֹּל תִּפְאַרְתּוֹ מִמֶּנּוּ, מִכָּאן שֶׁמַּנִּיחִין פֵּאָה בָּאִילָן: **אַחֲרֶיךָ.** זוֹ שִׁכְחָה:

כא **לֹא תְעוֹלֵל.** מָצָאתָ בָּהּ עוֹלֶלֶת, לֹא תִקָּחֶנָּה. וְאֵיזוֹ הִיא עוֹלֶלֶת? כָּל שֶׁאֵין לָהּ לֹא כָּתֵף וְלֹא נָטֵף. יֵשׁ לָהּ אֶחָד מֵהֶם, הֲרֵי הִיא לְבַעַל הַבַּיִת. וְרָאִיתִי בְּתַלְמוּד יְרוּשַׁלְמִי (פאה ז, ד): אֵי זוֹ הִיא כָּתֵף? פְּסִיגִין זֶה עַל גַּב זֶה. נָטֵף – אֵלּוּ הַתְּלוּיוֹת בַּשִּׁדְרָה וְיוֹרְדוֹת:

כה א **כִּי יִהְיֶה רִיב.** סוֹפָם לִהְיוֹת נִגָּשִׁים אֶל הַמִּשְׁפָּט. אֱמֹר מֵעַתָּה, אֵין שָׁלוֹם יוֹצֵא מִתּוֹךְ מְרִיבָה; מִי גָּרַם לְלוֹט לִפְרֹשׁ מִן הַצַּדִּיק? הֱוֵי אוֹמֵר זוֹ מְרִיבָה: **וְהִרְשִׁיעוּ אֶת הָרָשָׁע.** יָכוֹל כָּל הַמִּתְחַיְּבִין בַּדִּין לוֹקִין? תַּלְמוּד לוֹמַר: "וְהָיָה אִם בִּן הַכּוֹת הָרָשָׁע" (להלן פסוק ב), פְּעָמִים לוֹקֶה וּפְעָמִים אֵינוֹ לוֹקֶה. וּמִי הוּא הַלּוֹקֶה? לְמֵד מִן הָעִנְיָן: "לֹא תַחְסֹם שׁוֹר בְּדִישׁוֹ" (להלן פסוק ד), לָאו שֶׁלֹּא נִתַּק לַעֲשֵׂה:

ב **וְהִפִּילוֹ הַשֹּׁפֵט.** מְלַמֵּד שֶׁאֵין מַלְקִין אוֹתוֹ לֹא עוֹמֵד וְלֹא יוֹשֵׁב אֶלָּא מֻטֶּה: **לְפָנָיו כְּדֵי רִשְׁעָתוֹ.** וּלְאַחֲרָיו כְּדֵי שְׁתַּיִם, מִכָּאן אָמְרוּ: מַלְקִין אוֹתוֹ שְׁתֵּי יָדוֹת מִלְּאַחֲרָיו וּשְׁלִישׁ מִלְּפָנָיו: **בְּמִסְפָּר.** וְאֵינוֹ נָקוּד 'בַּמִּסְפָּר', לִמֵּד שֶׁהוּא דָּבוּק, לוֹמַר בְּמִסְפַּר אַרְבָּעִים וְלֹא אַרְבָּעִים שְׁלֵמִים, אֶלָּא מִנְיָן שֶׁהוּא סוֹכֵם וּמַשְׁלִים לְאַרְבָּעִים, וְהֵן אַרְבָּעִים חָסֵר אַחַת:

ג **לֹא יֹסִיף.** מִכָּאן אַזְהָרָה לַמַּכֶּה אֶת חֲבֵרוֹ: **וְנִקְלָה אָחִיךָ.** כָּל הַיּוֹם קוֹרֵהוּ 'רָשָׁע', וּמִשֶּׁלָּקָה קוֹרֵהוּ 'אָחִיךָ':

At first sight these rabbinic laws lack the grandeur of the prophets; they are small scale, local, even prosaic. They envisage no transformation of the universe or human sensibility. They seem to be *no more than* pragmatism, generously conceived. They are attempts to avoid the kind of civil strife from which Jews suffered so often during the long night of exile. For these reasons "the ways of peace" has not been seen for the innovation it is. I believe that is a mistake. The prophets articulated utopian peace; the Sages, a *non*-utopian program for peace in the here and now. "The ways of peace" are a program for a peace of small steps, for peace in an unredeemed world.

יט הַזֶּה׃ כִּֽי תִקְצֹר קְצִֽירְךָ בְשָׂדֶךָ וְשָֽׁכַחְתָּ עֹמֶר בַּשָּׂדֶה לֹא כ
תָשׁוּב לְקַחְתּוֹ לַגֵּר לַיָּתוֹם וְלָאַלְמָנָה יִהְיֶה לְמַעַן יְבָרֶכְךָ יְהוָה אֱלֹהֶיךָ
כ בְּכֹל מַעֲשֵׂה יָדֶֽיךָ׃ כִּי תַחְבֹּט זֵֽיתְךָ לֹא תְפַאֵר אַחֲרֶיךָ לַגֵּר
כא לַיָּתוֹם וְלָאַלְמָנָה יִהְיֶֽה׃ כִּי תִבְצֹר כַּרְמְךָ לֹא תְעוֹלֵל אַחֲרֶיךָ לַגֵּר
כב לַיָּתוֹם וְלָאַלְמָנָה יִהְיֶֽה׃ וְזָכַרְתָּ כִּי־עֶבֶד הָיִיתָ בְּאֶרֶץ מִצְרָיִם עַל־כֵּן
כה א אָנֹכִי מְצַוְּךָ לַעֲשׂוֹת אֶת־הַדָּבָר הַזֶּֽה׃ כִּֽי־יִהְיֶה רִיב
בֵּין אֲנָשִׁים וְנִגְּשׁוּ אֶל־הַמִּשְׁפָּט וּשְׁפָטוּם וְהִצְדִּיקוּ אֶת־הַצַּדִּיק
ב וְהִרְשִׁיעוּ אֶת־הָרָשָֽׁע׃ וְהָיָה אִם־בִּן הַכּוֹת הָרָשָׁע וְהִפִּילוֹ הַשֹּׁפֵט
ג וְהִכָּהוּ לְפָנָיו כְּדֵי רִשְׁעָתוֹ בְּמִסְפָּֽר׃ אַרְבָּעִים יַכֶּנּוּ לֹא יֹסִיף פֶּן־יֹסִיף

אונקלוס

הָדֵין׃ יט אֲרֵי תִחְצוֹד חֲצָדָךְ בְּחַקְלָךְ וְתִתְנְשֵׁי עֻמְרָא בְּחַקְלָא, לָא תְתוּב לְמִסְבֵיהּ, לְגִיּוֹרָא, לְיַתְמָא וּלְאַרְמַלְתָּא יְהֵי, בְּדִיל דִּיבָרְכִנָּךְ יי אֱלָהָךְ, בְּכֹל עוֹבָדֵי יְדָךְ׃ כ אֲרֵי תַחְבּוֹט זֵיתָךְ, לָא תְפַלֵּי בָּתְרָךְ, לְגִיּוֹרָא, לְיַתְמָא וּלְאַרְמַלְתָּא יְהֵי׃ כא אֲרֵי תִקְטוֹף כַּרְמָךְ, לָא תְעַלֵּיל בָּתְרָךְ, לְגִיּוֹרָא, לְיַתְמָא וּלְאַרְמַלְתָּא יְהֵי׃ כב וְתִדְכַּר, אֲרֵי עַבְדָּא הֲוֵיתָא בְּאַרְעָא דְמִצְרָיִם, עַל כֵּן, אֲנָא מְפַקֵּיד לָךְ לְמֶעְבַּד, יָת פִּתְגָמָא הָדֵין׃ כה א אֲרֵי יְהֵי דִין בֵּין גֻּבְרַיָּא, וְיִתְקָרְבוּן לְדִינָא וִידִינוּנוּן, וִיזַכּוֹן יָת זַכָּאָה, וִיחַיְּבוּן יָת חַיָּבָא׃ ב וִיהֵי, אִם בַּר חַיָּב לְאַלְקָאָה חַיָּבָא, וְיִרְמֵינֵיהּ דַּיָּנָא וְיִלְקֵינֵיהּ קֳדָמוֹהִי, כְּמִסַּת חוֹבְתֵיהּ בְּמִנְיָן׃ ג אַרְבְּעִין יַלְקֵינֵיהּ לָא יוֹסֵיף, דִּלְמָא יוֹסֵיף לְאַלְקָיוּתֵיהּ עַל

24:19 לַגֵּר לַיָּתוֹם וְלָאַלְמָנָה יִהְיֶה *Leave it for the migrant, the orphan, and the widow* – The language of tzedaka is often that of kinship. And yet a series of statements from the Mishnaic period specifies:

> For the sake of peace, the poor of the heathens should not be prevented from gathering gleanings, forgotten sheaves, and corners of the field. (Gittin 5:8)

> Our masters taught: For the sake of peace, the poor of the heathens should be supported as we support the poor of Israel, the sick of the heathens should be visited as we visit the sick of Israel, and the dead of the heathens should be buried as we bury the dead of Israel. (Gittin 61a)

All of these provisions are ordained because of the principle of *darkhei shalom*, "the ways of peace." The prophets of ancient Israel were the first people in history to conceive of peace as an ideal. They did so in words that have resonated from that day to this, most famously those of Yeshayahu: "They shall beat their swords into plowshares, their spears into pruning hooks. Nation shall not raise sword against nation; no more will they learn to make war" (Is. 2:4). Yeshayahu's younger contemporary, Mikha, repeated these words and added some of his own: "Every man will sit beneath his grapevine, under his fig tree, with none to trouble him" (Mic. 4:4–5).

It is difficult at this distance to sense how revolutionary this was in an age that saw war as inevitable and noble, the arena of virtue and the testing ground of courage. Yet the Rabbis' "ways of peace" are not peace as Yeshayahu or Mikha envisaged it. They are a set of positive obligations promoting social harmony, alongside the negative duties that arise from the corollary principle of *eiva*, "[the avoidance of] animosity" – things we should not do because they endanger peaceful relations.

4 degraded in your eyes. Do not muzzle an ox while it is treading out the
5 grain. When brothers live together, and one of them dies without a
son, his widow shall not be married to a stranger outside the family. Her
husband's brother shall come to her and take her in marriage, fulfilling the duty
6 of a brother-in-law. The firstborn son whom she bears will perpetuate the name
7 of the dead brother, so that his name is not erased from Israel. But if the man
does not wish to marry his brother's widow, she shall go up to the elders at the
gate and say, 'My husband's brother refuses to perpetuate his brother's name in
8 Israel. He does not care to perform the duty of a brother-in-law for me.' The
elders of the town shall summon him and they must talk to him. If he persists
9 in saying, 'I have no desire to marry her,' then his brother's widow shall go up
to him in the presence of the elders, pull the sandal from his foot, spit in his
face, and say, 'This is what is done to the man who will not build up his brother's

רש״י

ד **לֹא תַחְסֹם שׁוֹר.** דִּבֵּר הַכָּתוּב בַּהֹוֶה, וְהוּא הַדִּין לְכָל בְּהֵמָה חַיָּה וָעוֹף וּלְכָל מְלָאכָה שֶׁהִיא בְּדָבָר מַאֲכָל. אִם כֵּן לָמָּה נֶאֱמַר "שׁוֹר"? לְהוֹצִיא אֶת הָאָדָם: **בְּדִישׁוֹ.** יָכוֹל יַחְסְמֶנּוּ מִבַּחוּץ? תַּלְמוּד לוֹמַר: "לֹא תַחְסֹם שׁוֹר", מִכָּל מָקוֹם. וְלָמָּה נֶאֱמַר 'דַּיִשׁ'? לוֹמַר לְךָ מַה 'דַּיִשׁ' מְיֻחָד, דָּבָר שֶׁלֹּא נִגְמְרָה מְלַאכְתּוֹ וְגִדּוּלוֹ מִן הָאָרֶץ, אַף כָּל כַּיּוֹצֵא בּוֹ, יָצָא הַחוֹלֵב וְהַמְגַבֵּן וְהַמְחַבֵּץ שֶׁאֵין גִּדּוּלוֹ מִן הָאָרֶץ, יָצָא הַלָּשׁ וְהַמְקַטֵּף שֶׁנִּגְמְרָה מְלַאכְתּוֹ לְחַלָּה, יָצָא הַבּוֹדֵל בִּתְמָרִים וּבִגְרוֹגָרוֹת שֶׁנִּגְמְרָה מְלַאכְתָּן לְמַעֲשֵׂר:

ה **כִּי יֵשְׁבוּ אַחִים יַחְדָּו.** שֶׁהָיְתָה לָהֶם יְשִׁיבָה אַחַת בָּעוֹלָם, פְּרָט לְאֵשֶׁת אָחִיו שֶׁלֹּא הָיָה בְּעוֹלָמוֹ: **יַחְדָּו.** הַמְיֻחָדִים בְּנַחֲלָה, פְּרָט לְאָחִיו מִן הָאֵם: **וּבֵן אֵין לוֹ.** עַיֵּן עָלָיו, בֵּן אוֹ בַּת אוֹ בֶּן הַבֵּן אוֹ בֶּן הַבַּת אוֹ בַּת הַבֵּן אוֹ בַּת הַבַּת:

ו **וְהָיָה הַבְּכוֹר.** גְּדוֹל הָאַחִים הוּא יְיַבֵּם אוֹתָהּ: **אֲשֶׁר תֵּלֵד.** פְּרָט לְאַיְלוֹנִית שֶׁאֵינָהּ יוֹלֶדֶת: **יָקוּם עַל שֵׁם אָחִיו.** זֶה שֶׁיְּיַבֵּם אֶת אִשְׁתּוֹ יִטֹּל נַחֲלַת הַמֵּת בְּנִכְסֵי אָבִיו: **וְלֹא יִמָּחֶה שְׁמוֹ.** פְּרָט לְאֵשֶׁת סָרִיס שֶׁשְּׁמוֹ מָחוּי:

ז **הַשַּׁעְרָה.** כְּתַרְגּוּמוֹ: "לִתְרַע בֵּית דִּינָא":

ח **וְעָמַד.** בַּעֲמִידָה: **וְאָמַר.** בִּלְשׁוֹן הַקֹּדֶשׁ, וְאַף הִיא דְּבָרֶיהָ בִּלְשׁוֹן הַקֹּדֶשׁ:

ט **וְיָרְקָה בְּפָנָיו.** עַל גַּבֵּי קַרְקַע:

future. Guilt, in Judaism, is about acts, not persons. It is the act, not the person, that is condemned. Once the criminal has served his punishment and repented of his crime, he becomes, once more, "your kinsman."

25:4 **לֹא־תַחְסֹם שׁוֹר בְּדִישׁוֹ** *Do not muzzle an ox while it is treading out the grain* – This law parallels provisions for human beings as well: "When you enter [to work in] your neighbor's vineyard, you may eat as many grapes as you wish, eat your fill.... When you enter [to work in] your neighbor's field of standing grain, you may pluck ears with your hand" (Deut. 23:25–26). The principle is the same in both cases: it is cruel to prevent those working with food from eating some of it. The parallel is instructive. Descartes thought that animals lacked souls. Therefore you could do with them as you pleased. Judaism does not believe that animals lack souls – "The righteous man knows his beast's *nefesh*," says the book of Proverbs (12:10). To be sure, *nefesh* here probably means "life" rather than "soul" (*neshama* in Hebrew). But Tanakh does regard animals as sentient beings. They may not think or speak, but they are capable of distress. Therefore there is such a thing as animal distress, *tzaar baalei ḥayyim*, and as far as possible it should be avoided. Animals, not just humans, have feelings, and they must be respected.

ד לְהַכֹּתוֹ עַל־אֵלֶּה מַכָּה רַבָּה וְנִקְלָה אָחִיךָ לְעֵינֶיךָ׃ לֹא־תַחְסֹם שׁוֹר
ה בְּדִישׁוֹ׃ כִּי־יֵשְׁבוּ אַחִים יַחְדָּו וּמֵת אַחַד מֵהֶם וּבֵן
אֵין־לוֹ לֹא־תִהְיֶה אֵשֶׁת־הַמֵּת הַחוּצָה לְאִישׁ זָר יְבָמָהּ יָבֹא עָלֶיהָ
ו וּלְקָחָהּ לוֹ לְאִשָּׁה וְיִבְּמָהּ׃ וְהָיָה הַבְּכוֹר אֲשֶׁר תֵּלֵד יָקוּם עַל־שֵׁם אָחִיו
ז הַמֵּת וְלֹא־יִמָּחֶה שְׁמוֹ מִיִּשְׂרָאֵל׃ וְאִם־לֹא יַחְפֹּץ הָאִישׁ לָקַחַת אֶת־
יְבִמְתּוֹ וְעָלְתָה יְבִמְתּוֹ הַשַּׁעְרָה אֶל־הַזְּקֵנִים וְאָמְרָה מֵאֵן יְבָמִי לְהָקִים
ח לְאָחִיו שֵׁם בְּיִשְׂרָאֵל לֹא אָבָה יַבְּמִי׃ וְקָרְאוּ־לוֹ זִקְנֵי־עִירוֹ וְדִבְּרוּ אֵלָיו
ט וְעָמַד וְאָמַר לֹא חָפַצְתִּי לְקַחְתָּהּ׃ וְנִגְּשָׁה יְבִמְתּוֹ אֵלָיו לְעֵינֵי הַזְּקֵנִים
וְחָלְצָה נַעֲלוֹ מֵעַל רַגְלוֹ וְיָרְקָה בְּפָנָיו וְעָנְתָה וְאָמְרָה כָּכָה יֵעָשֶׂה

אונקלוס

אִלֵּין מַחָא רַבָּא, וְיֵיקַל אֲחוּךְ לְעֵינָךְ: ד לָא תֵיחוֹד פּוּם תּוֹרָא בְּדִיָשֵׁיהּ: ה אֲרֵי יִתְּבוּן אַחִין כַּחְדָא, וִימוּת חַד מִנְּהוֹן וּבַר לֵית לֵיהּ, לָא תְהֵי אִתַּת מִיתָא, לְבָרָא לִגְבַר אָחֳרָן, יְבָמַהּ יֵיעוֹל עֲלַהּ, וְיִסְּבַהּ לֵיהּ, לְאִתּוּ וְיַבֵּמִנַּהּ: ו וִיהֵי, בֻּכְרָא דִּתְלִיד, יְקוּם, עַל שְׁמָא דַּאֲחוּהִי מִיתָא, וְלָא יִתְמְחֵי שְׁמֵיהּ מִיִּשְׂרָאֵל: ז וְאִם לָא יִצְבֵּי גַּבְרָא, לְמִסַּב יָת יְבִמְתֵּיהּ, וְתִסַּק יְבִמְתֵּיהּ לִתְרַע בֵּית דִּינָא לִקְדָם סָבַיָּא, וְתֵימַר סָרֵיב יְבָמִי, לַאֲקָמָא לַאֲחוּהִי שְׁמָא בְּיִשְׂרָאֵל, לָא אֲבָא לְיַבָּמוּתִי: ח וְיִקְרוֹן לֵיהּ סָבֵי קַרְתֵּיהּ וִימַלְּלוּן עִמֵּיהּ, וִיקוּם וְיֵימַר, לָא רָעֵינָא לְמִסְּבַהּ: ט וְתִתְקָרַב יְבִמְתֵּיהּ לְוָתֵיהּ לִקְדָם סָבַיָּא, וְתִשְׁרֵי סֵינֵיהּ מֵעַל רַגְלֵיהּ, וְתִרוֹק בְּאַנְפּוֹהִי, וְתָתֵיב וְתֵימַר, כְּדֵין יִתְעֲבֵיד

25:3 וְנִקְלָה אָחִיךָ לְעֵינֶיךָ *Your kinsman will be degraded in your eyes* – The Sages derived from this a fundamental principle, namely, *the rehabilitation of an offender* once he has served his punishment. In the earlier part of the passage the offender is called *harasha*, translated here as "the guilty" but which literally means "the wicked." At the end, however, he is called "your kinsman." From this, the Sages drew the conclusion that "once he has been beaten, he becomes [again] your kinsman" (Sifrei ad loc.).

This has both a specific and more general application. The specific rule applies to offenses that carried with them the severe punishment of *karet*, literally, "being cut off" from one's people. In many cases this was interpreted as a divine rather than human punishment; the human punishment was to receive lashes. The principle that "once he has been beaten, he becomes [again] your kinsman" was taken to mean that the human punishment cancels the divine punishment. Once the offender has been beaten, there is no residual guilt (Makkot 3:15).

In addition, the Sages inferred the wider principle that when the guilty has received the punishment his offense deserved, he is restored to his earlier status. For example, he is permitted to be a witness, and his testimony is not invalidated by his having previously been found guilty of an offense. The stain on his character is temporary. Offenders are to be rehabilitated.

Not only were these teachings centuries ahead of their time; they also have much to teach us today. Retributive justice is compatible with a sense of human dignity and freedom. In fact, it is based on them. Jewish law is concerned not only with protecting the rights of those who have been wronged, but also helping wrongdoers rebuild their

10 house.' Throughout Israel his family shall be known as 'the house of the one
11 whose sandal was pulled off.' If two men fight, and the wife of one
comes to defend her husband from the one who does him harm by reaching
12 out and seizing the man's genitals, you shall cut off her hand: show no
13 pity. Do not have two different weights in your bag, one large and the
14 other small. Do not have in your house two different measures, one large and
15 the other small. You must have a full and honest weight and a full and honest
measure, so that your days may be long on the land that the LORD your God is
16 giving you. Whoever does such things, whoever acts dishonestly, is abhorrent
to the LORD your God.
17 18 Remember what Amalek did to you on your way as you left Egypt, how he MAFTIR
attacked you on the way, when you were tired and exhausted, striking down

רש״י

אֲשֶׁר לֹא יִבְנֶה. מִכָּאן לְמִי שֶׁחָלַץ שֶׁלֹּא יַחֲזוֹר וִייַבֵּם, דְּלָא כְּתִיב 'אֲשֶׁר לֹא בָנָה' אֶלָּא "אֲשֶׁר לֹא יִבְנֶה", כֵּיוָן שֶׁלֹּא בָּנָה שׁוּב לֹא יִבְנֶה:

י **וְנִקְרָא שְׁמוֹ וְגוֹ'.** מִצְוָה עַל כָּל הָעוֹמְדִים שָׁם לוֹמַר: "חֲלוּץ הַנַּעַל":

יא **כִּי יִנָּצוּ אֲנָשִׁים.** סוֹפָן לָבֹא לִידֵי מַכּוֹת, כְּמוֹ שֶׁנֶּאֱמַר: "מִיַּד מַכֵּהוּ", אֵין שָׁלוֹם יוֹצֵא מִתַּחַת יְדֵי מַצּוּת:

יב **וְקַצֹּתָה אֶת כַּפָּהּ.** מָמוֹן דְּמֵי בָּשְׁתּוֹ, הַכֹּל לְפִי הַמְבַיֵּשׁ וְהַמִּתְבַּיֵּשׁ. אוֹ אֵינוֹ אֶלָּא יָדָהּ מַמָּשׁ? נֶאֱמַר כָּאן "לֹא תָחוֹס", וְנֶאֱמַר לְהַלָּן בְּעֵדִים זוֹמְמִין "לֹא תָחוֹס" (לעיל יט, כא), מַה לְּהַלָּן מָמוֹן, אַף כָּאן מָמוֹן:

יג **גְּדוֹלָה וּקְטַנָּה.** גְּדוֹלָה שֶׁמַּכְחֶשֶׁת אֶת הַקְּטַנָּה, שֶׁלֹּא יְהֵא נוֹטֵל בַּגְּדוֹלָה וּמַחֲזִיר בַּקְּטַנָּה: **לֹא יִהְיֶה לְךָ.** אִם עָשִׂיתָ כֵּן, לֹא יִהְיֶה לְךָ כְּלוּם: **אֶבֶן וָאָבֶן.** מִשְׁקָלוֹת:

טו **אֶבֶן שְׁלֵמָה וָצֶדֶק יִהְיֶה לָּךְ.** אִם עָשִׂיתָ כֵּן, יִהְיֶה לְךָ הַרְבֵּה:

יז **זָכוֹר אֵת אֲשֶׁר עָשָׂה לְךָ.** אִם שִׁקַּרְתָּ בְּמִדּוֹת וּבְמִשְׁקָלוֹת, הֱוֵי דוֹאֵג מִגֵּרוּי הָאוֹיֵב, שֶׁנֶּאֱמַר: "מֹאזְנֵי מִרְמָה תּוֹעֲבַת ה'" וּכְתִיב בַּתְרֵיהּ: "בָּא זָדוֹן וַיָּבֹא קָלוֹן" (משלי יא, א-ב):

יח **אֲשֶׁר קָרְךָ בַּדֶּרֶךְ.** לְשׁוֹן מִקְרֶה. דָּבָר אַחֵר, לְשׁוֹן קֶרִי וְטֻמְאָה,

there is no need to make the intent explicit in the form of a benediction.

Our good deeds – deeds that make a difference to the lives of our fellow human beings – constitute, as it were, a universal language. Our human situation as embodied souls, physical beings, means that we share needs and vulnerabilities. When it comes to acts that address such needs, it is irrelevant who performs them, for whom they are performed, and with what motive or intention. What matters is that they do good, relieve suffering, bring comfort. They redeem human solitude and bring those who suffer back into "the land of the living."

These universal values are embedded into the particularities of the Jewish covenant. From here the Torah moves on to the commandments of Jewish historical memory, and to the sealing of the covenant anew.

say, a custom, an ethnic folkway, or a habit. Intention gives the act the characteristic essential to a religious deed in Judaism, namely, that it is a response to a command of God. In that minimalist sense, intent is necessary.

An act between us and another human being, however, has a different character. What matters is not the act but its result (in philosophical terms, not the *peula* but the *nifal*). Hence, the Talmud makes the radical remark that "one who gives a sum to charity in order to gain a share in the World to Come or save the life of his child is regarded as perfectly righteous" (Bava Batra 10b). The doer of the deed in this case has ulterior motives, *but the motives are irrelevant to acts the purpose of which is to bring aid to those who are in need.* The religious character of the moment lies not in the act, its intention, or the motive for which it was performed, but the comfort given, the help received, the loneliness lifted. In such cases Judaism does not require specific intent. Hence

י לָאִישׁ אֲשֶׁר לֹא־יִבְנֶה אֶת־בֵּית אָחִיו: וְנִקְרָא שְׁמוֹ בְּיִשְׂרָאֵל בֵּית
יא חֲלוּץ הַנָּעַל: כִּי־יִנָּצוּ אֲנָשִׁים יַחְדָּו אִישׁ וְאָחִיו וְקָרְבָה
אֵשֶׁת הָאֶחָד לְהַצִּיל אֶת־אִישָׁהּ מִיַּד מַכֵּהוּ וְשָׁלְחָה יָדָהּ וְהֶחֱזִיקָה
יב יג בִּמְבֻשָׁיו: וְקַצֹּתָה אֶת־כַּפָּהּ לֹא תָחוֹס עֵינֶךָ: לֹא־יִהְיֶה לְךָ
יד בְּכִיסְךָ אֶבֶן וָאָבֶן גְּדוֹלָה וּקְטַנָּה: לֹא־יִהְיֶה לְךָ בְּבֵיתְךָ אֵיפָה וְאֵיפָה
טו גְּדוֹלָה וּקְטַנָּה: אֶבֶן שְׁלֵמָה וָצֶדֶק יִהְיֶה־לָּךְ אֵיפָה שְׁלֵמָה וָצֶדֶק יִהְיֶה־
טז לָּךְ לְמַעַן יַאֲרִיכוּ יָמֶיךָ עַל הָאֲדָמָה אֲשֶׁר־יְהוָה אֱלֹהֶיךָ נֹתֵן לָךְ: כִּי
תוֹעֲבַת יְהוָה אֱלֹהֶיךָ כָּל־עֹשֵׂה אֵלֶּה כֹּל עֹשֵׂה עָוֶל:
יז יח זָכוֹר אֵת אֲשֶׁר־עָשָׂה לְךָ עֲמָלֵק בַּדֶּרֶךְ בְּצֵאתְכֶם מִמִּצְרָיִם: אֲשֶׁר מפטיר
קָרְךָ בַּדֶּרֶךְ וַיְזַנֵּב בְּךָ כָּל־הַנֶּחֱשָׁלִים אַחֲרֶיךָ וְאַתָּה עָיֵף וְיָגֵעַ וְלֹא יָרֵא

אונקלוס

לְגַבְרָא, דְּלָא יִבְנֵי יָת בֵּיתָא דַּאֲחוּהִי: י וְיִתְקְרֵי שְׁמֵיהּ בְּיִשְׂרָאֵל, בֵּית שְׁרֵי סֵינָא: יא אֲרֵי יִנְצוּן גֻּבְרִין כַּחְדָא גְּבַר וַאֲחוּהִי, וְתִתְקָרַב אִתַּת חַד, לְשֵׁיזָבָא יָת בַּעְלַהּ מִיַּד מָחוֹהִי, וְתוֹשֵׁיט יְדַהּ, וְתַתְקֵיף בְּבֵית בַּהְתְּתֵיהּ: יב וְתִקּוּץ יָת יְדַהּ, לָא תְחוּס עֵינָךְ: יג לָא יְהֵי לָךְ, בְּכִיסָךְ מַתְקַל וּמַתְקַל, רַב וּזְעֵיר: יד לָא יְהֵי לָךְ, בְּבֵיתָךְ מְכִילָא וּמְכִילָא, רַבְּתָא וּזְעֵירְתָא:

טו מַתְקְלִין שַׁלְמִין דִּקְשׁוֹט יְהוֹן לָךְ, מְכִילָן שַׁלְמָן, דִּקְשׁוֹט יְהוֹן לָךְ, בְּדִיל דְּיֵירְכוּן יוֹמָךְ, עַל אַרְעָא, דַּיי אֱלָהָךְ יָהֵיב לָךְ: טז אֲרֵי מְרַחַק, קֳדָם יי אֱלָהָךְ כָּל עָבֵיד אִלֵּין, כָּל עָבֵיד שְׁקַר: יז הֱוִי דְּכִיר, יָת דַּעֲבַד לָךְ עֲמָלֵק, בְּאוֹרְחָא בְּמִפַּקְכוֹן מִמִּצְרָיִם: יח דְּעָרְעָךְ בְּאוֹרְחָא, וְקַטֵּיל בָּךְ כָּל דַּהֲווֹ מִתְאַחֲרִין בָּתְרָךְ, וְאַתְּ מְשַׁלְהֵי וְלָאֵי, וְלָא דָחֵיל מִן קֳדָם

THE LAST OF THE ETHICAL COMMANDMENTS

With this reiteration of the importance of honest weights (see Lev. 19:36 and commentary there), we close Moshe's lengthy summary of the laws *shebein adam laḥavero*, the duties we owe one another. In Jewish law, most commands require a blessing. Its standard form is "Blessed are you, Lord our God… who has sanctified us with His commandments and has commanded us to…." However, there are exceptions. The medieval Jewish sages searched for a general rule to distinguish commandments that require a blessing from those that do not. Various suggestions were made; few were deemed satisfactory. Rabbi Shlomo ibn Aderet (Rashba), among others, doubted whether there was a simple criterion (*Responsa Rashba* III:283). Rambam, however, formulated one of breathtaking simplicity: commands between us and God, *bein adam laMakom*, require a blessing; commands between us and our fellow human beings, *bein adam laḥavero*, do not (*Hilkhot Berakhot* 11:2; *Kesef Mishneh*).

Why should this be so? Some offered the suggestion that commands between us and our fellows are not wholly within our control. In the case of charity, for example, the rich man may wish to give but the poor may not wish to accept. It would be wrong to make a blessing over a command that is not wholly in our power. I believe, however, that a different issue is at stake.

In the case of commands between us and God, what matters is the act and the intention with which it was performed. There is a debate in Jewish law as to whether, in general, commands require specific intent (*kavana*). It is clear, however, that a command between us and God must be directed to God. That is what makes it a religious act as opposed to,

19 all the stragglers in your rear, with no fear of God. And so, when the LORD
your God gives you rest from all the enemies around you in the land that the
LORD your God is giving you as an inheritance to possess, you shall blot out
the memory of Amalek from beneath the sky. Do not forget.

The haftara for Parashat Ki Tetzeh is on page 1616.
If the haftara for Re'eh was not read (because of Rosh Ḥodesh Elul),
it is read at the end of this haftara (see page 1614).

רש״י

שֶׁהָיָה מְטַמְּאָן בְּמִשְׁכַּב זָכוּר. דָּבָר אַחֵר, לְשׁוֹן קֹר וָחֹם, צִנֶּנְךָ וְהִפְשִׁירְךָ מֵרְתִיחָתְךָ, שֶׁהָיוּ הָאֻמּוֹת יְרֵאִים לְהִלָּחֵם בָּכֶם, וּבָא זֶה וְהִתְחִיל וְהֶרְאָה מָקוֹם לַאֲחֵרִים. מָשָׁל לְאַמְבָּטִי רוֹתַחַת שֶׁאֵין כָּל בְּרִיָּה יְכוֹלָה לֵירֵד בְּתוֹכָהּ, בָּא בֶּן בְּלִיַּעַל אֶחָד קָפַץ וְיָרַד לְתוֹכָהּ, אַף עַל פִּי שֶׁנִּכְוָה, הֵקֵרָהּ אוֹתָהּ בִּפְנֵי אֲחֵרִים: **וַיְזַנֵּב בְּךָ.** מַכַּת זָנָב, חוֹתֵךְ מִילוֹת וְזוֹרֵק כְּלַפֵּי מַעְלָה: **כָּל הַנֶּחֱשָׁלִים אַחֲרֶיךָ.** חַסְרֵי כֹחַ מֵחֲמַת חֶטְאָם, שֶׁהָיָה הֶעָנָן פּוֹלְטָן: **וְאַתָּה עָיֵף וְיָגֵעַ.** ׳עָיֵף׳ בַּצָּמָא, דִּכְתִיב: ״וַיִּצְמָא שָׁם הָעָם לַמַּיִם״ (שמות יז, ג), וּכְתִיב אַחֲרָיו: ״וַיָּבֹא עֲמָלֵק״ (שם פסוק ח): **וְיָגֵעַ.** בַּדֶּרֶךְ: **וְלֹא יָרֵא.** עֲמָלֵק, ״אֱלֹהִים״ מִלְּהָרַע לְךָ:

יט **תִּמְחֶה אֶת זֵכֶר עֲמָלֵק.** ״מֵאִישׁ עַד אִשָּׁה מֵעוֹלֵל וְעַד יוֹנֵק מִשּׁוֹר וְעַד שֶׂה״ (שמואל א׳ טו, ג), שֶׁלֹּא יְהֵא שֵׁם עֲמָלֵק נִזְכָּר אֲפִלּוּ עַל הַבְּהֵמָה, לוֹמַר, בְּהֵמָה זוֹ מִשֶּׁל עֲמָלֵק הָיְתָה:

took over the Nile Delta during the Second Intermediate Period of the Egypt of the pharaohs. Eventually they were expelled from Egypt and all traces of their occupation were erased. But the memory persisted. It was not irrational for the Egyptians to fear that the Hebrews were another such population. The fear of the Egyptians was certainly unjustified. The Israelites did not want to take over Egypt. To the contrary, they would have preferred to leave. Not every rational emotion is justified. Yet that rational but unjustified emotion can, in principle, be cured through reasoning.

Precisely the opposite was true of the Amalekites. They attacked the Israelites when they were "tired and exhausted," focused their assault on the "stragglers in your rear." Those who are weak and lagging behind pose no danger. This was irrational, groundless hate. Therefore it may never go away. The hatred symbolized by Amalek lasts "throughout the ages" (Ex. 17:16). All one can do is to remember and not forget, to be constantly vigilant, and to fight it whenever and wherever it appears.

Antisemitism is the paradigm case of irrational hatred. In the Middle Ages, Jews were accused of poisoning wells, spreading the plague, and in one of the most absurd claims ever – the blood libel – they were suspected of killing Christian children to use their blood to make matzot for Passover. This was self-evidently impossible, but that did not stop people from believing it.

Amalek-like, irrational hatred does not die and cannot be reasoned with. But the Jewish people survives as well. Attacked so many times over the centuries, it still lives, and in doing so, gives testimony to the victory of the God of love over the myths and madness of hate.

יט אֱלֹהִֽים׃ וְהָיָ֡ה בְּהָנִ֣יחַ יְהֹוָ֣ה אֱלֹהֶ֣יךָ ׀ לְ֠ךָ֠ מִכָּל־אֹ֨יְבֶ֜יךָ מִסָּבִ֗יב בָּאָ֙רֶץ֙
אֲשֶׁ֣ר־יְהֹוָֽה־אֱ֠לֹהֶ֠יךָ נֹתֵ֨ן לְךָ֤ נַחֲלָה֙ לְרִשְׁתָּ֔הּ תִּמְחֶה֙ אֶת־זֵ֣כֶר עֲמָלֵ֔ק
מִתַּ֖חַת הַשָּׁמָ֑יִם לֹ֖א תִּשְׁכָּֽח׃

The הפטרה *for* פרשת כי תצא *is on page 1617.*
If the הפטרה *for* ראה *was not read (because of* ראש חודש אלול*),*
it is read at the end of this הפטרה *(see page 1615).*

אונקלוס

יי: יט וִיהֵי, כַּד יְנִיחַ יי אֱלָהָךְ לָךְ, מִכָּל בַּעֲלֵי דְּבָבָךְ מִסְּחוֹר סְחוֹר, בְּאַרְעָא דַּיי אֱלָהָךְ, יָהֵיב לָךְ אַחְסָנָא לְמֵירְתַהּ, תִּמְחֵי יָת דֻּכְרָנֵיהּ דַּעֲמָלֵק, מִתְּחוֹת שְׁמַיָּא, לָא תִּתְנְשֵׁי:

AMALEK

The Israelites had two enemies in the days of Moshe: the Egyptians and the Amalekites. The Egyptians enslaved the Israelites. They turned them into a forced labor colony. Pharaoh commanded them to drown every male Israelite child, attempted genocide. Yet about them, as we saw, Moshe commands: "Do not despise an Egyptian, for you lived as a stranger in his land" (Deut. 23:8).

The Amalekites did no more than attack the Israelites once, an attack that was successfully repelled (Ex. 17:13). Yet Moshe commands: "Remember." "Do not forget." "Blot out the memory." In Exodus, the Torah says that "the Lord will be at war with Amalek throughout the ages" (17:16). Why the difference? Why did Moshe tell the Israelites, in effect, to forgive the Egyptians but not the Amalekites?

What is more, the commandment to destroy Amalek no longer has practical application. It is no longer possible to identify the ethnicity of any of the original peoples against whom the Israelites were commanded to fight (see commentary on Deut. 23:4). Rambam added in *Guide for the Perplexed* (III:50) that the command only applied to people of specific biological descent. It is not to be applied in general to enemies or haters of the Jewish people. So the command to wage war against the Amalekites no longer applies, yet the command to remember does. What is it about the memory of Amalek that makes it so different from the memory of Egypt?

The answer may be that when hate is rational, based on some fear or disapproval that – justified or not – has some logic to it, then it can be reasoned with. The Egyptians feared the Israelites because they were numerous. Historians tell us that this fear was not groundless. Egypt had already suffered from one invasion of outsiders, the Hyksos, an Asiatic people with Canaanite names and beliefs who

Parashat Ki Tavo

26 1 "When you have come into the land that the Lord your God is giving you as
2 a possession, and have taken possession and settled in it, you shall take some
of every first fruit of the soil, which you harvest from the land that the Lord
your God is giving you. Put it in a basket and go to the place that the Lord

רש״י

כו א **וְהָיָה כִּי תָבוֹא. וִירִשְׁתָּהּ וְיָשַׁבְתָּ בָּהּ.** מַגִּיד שֶׁלֹּא נִתְחַיְּבוּ בַּבִּכּוּרִים עַד שֶׁכָּבְשׁוּ אֶת הָאָרֶץ וְחִלְּקוּהָ:

ב **מֵרֵאשִׁית.** וְלֹא כָּל רֵאשִׁית, שֶׁאֵין כָּל הַפֵּרוֹת חַיָּבִין בַּבִּכּוּרִים אֶלָּא שִׁבְעַת הַמִּינִין בִּלְבַד, נֶאֱמַר כָּאן "אֶרֶץ" וְנֶאֱמַר לְהַלָּן "אֶרֶץ חִטָּה וּשְׂעֹרָה" וְגוֹ' (לעיל ח, ח), מַה לְּהַלָּן מִשִּׁבְעַת הַמִּינִים שֶׁנִּשְׁתַּבְּחָה בָּהֶן אֶרֶץ יִשְׂרָאֵל, אַף כָּאן שֶׁבַח אֶרֶץ יִשְׂרָאֵל. "זֵית שֶׁמֶן", זַיִת אֲגוֹרִי שֶׁשַּׁמְנוֹ אָגוּר בְּתוֹכוֹ. "וּדְבָשׁ", הוּא דְּבַשׁ תְּמָרִים: **מֵרֵאשִׁית.** אָדָם יוֹרֵד לְתוֹךְ שָׂדֵהוּ וְרוֹאֶה תְּאֵנָה שֶׁבִּכְּרָה, כּוֹרֵךְ עָלֶיהָ גֶּמִי לְסִימָן, וְאוֹמֵר: 'הֲרֵי זוֹ בִּכּוּרִים':

26:2 **מֵרֵאשִׁית כָּל־פְּרִי הָאֲדָמָה** *Some of every first fruit of the soil* – There is a rabbinic aphorism that "God creates the remedy before the disease" (Megilla 13b). Prior to the *tokheḥa* (literally defined as remonstration or rebuke) curses, Moshe outlined the law of bringing first fruits, in celebration, to the Temple. The Torah concludes the passage with the following words: "Then you, with the Levites and the migrants who live among you, shall rejoice in all the good that the Lord your God has bestowed on you and on your household" (Deut. 26:11).

Judaism is a religion of rejoicing; of remembering where we came from, and not taking our blessings for granted; of recalling the source of the good, and therefore not forgetting the larger truth that it comes to us from the hand of God.

Jewish history sometimes seems to have been written in tears. More than most other nations, our collective story is told in terms of exiles and expulsions, persecutions and martyrdoms, inquisitions, pogroms, and holocausts. Yet Jews mourn on the Ninth of Av and the other specified fasts but have not allowed the rest of our days to be darkened by grief. We hold on to the affirmation that finds God in the midst of life and its blessings. Judaism's greatest challenge is to make a blessing over life, turning material satisfactions into spiritual affirmations.

is the story of where I came from and who I am, which led the Sages of the Mishna to say, "In each generation, every person should see himself as if he personally came out of Egypt" (Pesaḥim 10:5).

It is impossible to overestimate the impact this had on the Jewish people from then to now. Identity is not just a matter of who my parents were. It is also a matter of *what they remembered and handed on to me*. Identity is shaped by memory. Telling the story, regularly, as a religious duty, sustained Jewish identity across the centuries, even in the absence of all the normal accompaniments of nationhood – land, geographical proximity, independence, self-determination.

To know who we are is in large part to understand of which story or stories we are a part. That is what makes Jewish identity so rich and resonant. In an age in which computer memories have grown while human memories have become foreshortened, this remains an important message, not just to Jews but also to humanity. Maybe you can delegate history to computers, looking it up when you need it. But you cannot delegate memory. Memory is inherently, inescapably personal. It is what makes us who we are. If you seek to sustain identity, you have to renew memory regularly and teach it to the next generation. Those who tell the story of their past have already begun to build their children's future.

פרשת כי תבוא

כו א וְהָיָה֙ כִּֽי־תָב֣וֹא אֶל־הָאָ֔רֶץ אֲשֶׁר֙ יְהוָ֣ה אֱלֹהֶ֔יךָ נֹתֵ֥ן לְךָ֖ נַחֲלָ֑ה וִֽירִשְׁתָּ֖הּ כא
ב וְיָשַׁ֥בְתָּ בָּֽהּ׃ וְלָקַחְתָּ֞ מֵרֵאשִׁ֣ית ׀ כָּל־פְּרִ֣י הָאֲדָמָ֗ה אֲשֶׁ֨ר תָּבִ֧יא מֵֽאַרְצְךָ֛
אֲשֶׁ֨ר יְהוָ֧ה אֱלֹהֶ֛יךָ נֹתֵ֥ן לָ֖ךְ וְשַׂמְתָּ֣ בַטֶּ֑נֶא וְהָֽלַכְתָּ֙ אֶל־הַמָּק֔וֹם אֲשֶׁ֤ר

אונקלוס

כו א וִיהֵי אֲרֵי תֵיעוֹל לְאַרְעָא, דַּייְ אֱלָהָךְ, יָהֵיב לָךְ אַחְסָנָא, וְתֵירְתַהּ וְתֵיתֵיב בַּהּ: ב וְתִסַּב, מֵרֵישׁ כָּל אִבָּא דְּאַרְעָא, דְּתַעֵיל מֵאַרְעָךְ, דַּייְ אֱלָהָךְ, יָהֵיב לָךְ וּתְשַׁוֵּי בְּסַלָּא, וּתְהָךְ לְאַתְרָא,

KI TAVO

In Parashat Ki Tavo, Moshe reaches the end of the detailed provisions of the covenant, with commands about bringing first fruits to the central Sanctuary, as well as allocating the various tithes. He closes this section with a reminder of what the covenant is: a mutual pledge between the people and God. The people are to give God their total loyalty. God, in turn, will hold the people in special regard.

The text then turns to a distinctive feature of ancient covenants: the blessings and curses that will attend faithfulness on the one hand, disloyalty on the other. Given that Israel's entire existence as a nation is predicated on the covenant, it means that their fate will be an ongoing commentary on their relationship with God and the ideals, both sacred and social, to which the people have dedicated themselves as "a holy people to the LORD your God" (Deut. 7:6).

The *parasha* ends with Moshe summoning the people, at the end of their forty-year journey and in sight of the Promised Land, to renew the covenant their parents made with God at Mount Sinai.

THE CEREMONY OF THE FIRST FRUITS

Parashat Ki Tavo begins with the ceremony of bringing the first fruits to the Temple. The Mishna gives a detailed account of what happened:

> Those who were near to Jerusalem brought fresh figs and grapes, and those who were far away brought dried figs and raisins. Before them went the ox, its horns overlaid with gold, and with a wreath of olive leaves on its head.
>
> The flute was played before them until they came near Jerusalem. When they were near to Jerusalem, they sent messengers before them and bedecked their first fruits. The rulers and the prefects and the treasurers of the Temple went forth to meet them.... All the craftsmen in Jerusalem used to rise up for them and greet them, saying, "Brothers, men of such and such a place, you are welcome." (Bikkurim 3:3)

It was a magnificent celebration. Its most significant aspect was the declaration each individual had to make in the Temple: the well-known passage, beginning "My ancestor was a wandering Aramean" that is still expounded as part of the Haggada on Seder night.

Here for the first time *the retelling of the nation's past becomes an obligation for every citizen of the nation*. The passage, known as *vidui bikkurim*, "the confession made over first fruits," was simple and elemental. It is the entire history of the nation in summary form. Most importantly, it is written in the first person: "*My* ancestor....The LORD brought *us* out of Egypt." History is transformed into memory. This is not a detached tale of some disembodied past. It

3 your God will choose as a dwelling for His name. You shall go to the priest
officiating at that time and say to him, 'I declare today to the LORD your God
that I have come into the land that the LORD swore to our ancestors to give us.'
4 The priest shall take the basket from your hand and set it down before the altar
5 of the LORD your God. You shall then make this declaration before the LORD
your God: 'My ancestor was a wandering Aramean. He went down into Egypt
and lived there as a stranger, just a handful of souls, and there he became a
6 nation – large, mighty, and great. And the Egyptians dealt cruelly with us and
7 oppressed us, subjecting us to harsh labor. We cried out to the LORD, God of
our ancestors. And the LORD heard our voice and He saw our oppression, our
8 toil, and our enslavement. The LORD brought us out of Egypt with a mighty
hand and His arm stretched forth, with terrifying power, with signs, and with
9 wonders. He brought us into this place and He gave us this land, a land flowing

רש״י

ג| **אֲשֶׁר יִהְיֶה בַּיָּמִים הָהֵם.** אֵין לְךָ אֶלָּא כֹּהֵן שֶׁבְּיָמֶיךָ, כְּמוֹ שֶׁהוּא: **וְאָמַרְתָּ אֵלָיו.** שֶׁאֵינְךָ כְּפוּי טוֹבָה: **הִגַּדְתִּי הַיּוֹם.** פַּעַם אַחַת בַּשָּׁנָה וְלֹא שְׁתֵּי פְעָמִים:

ד| **וְלָקַח הַכֹּהֵן הַטֶּנֶא מִיָּדֶךָ.** לְהָנִיף אוֹתוֹ, כֹּהֵן מַנִּיחַ יָדוֹ תַּחַת יַד הַבְּעָלִים וּמֵנִיף:

ה| **וְעָנִיתָ.** לְשׁוֹן הֲרָמַת קוֹל: **אֲרַמִּי אֹבֵד אָבִי.** מַזְכִּיר חַסְדֵי הַמָּקוֹם: "אֲרַמִּי אֹבֵד אָבִי", לָבָן בִּקֵּשׁ לַעֲקֹר אֶת הַכֹּל כְּשֶׁרָדַף אַחַר יַעֲקֹב, וּבִשְׁבִיל שֶׁחָשַׁב לַעֲשׂוֹת, חָשַׁב לוֹ הַמָּקוֹם כְּאִלּוּ עָשָׂה, שֶׁאֻמּוֹת הָעוֹלָם חוֹשֵׁב לָהֶם הַקָּדוֹשׁ בָּרוּךְ הוּא מַחֲשָׁבָה כְּמַעֲשֶׂה: **וַיֵּרֶד מִצְרַיְמָה.** וְעוֹד אֲחֵרִים בָּאוּ לְכַלּוֹתֵנוּ, שֶׁאַחֲרֵי זֹאת יָרַד יַעֲקֹב לְמִצְרַיִם: **בִּמְתֵי מְעָט.** בְּשִׁבְעִים נֶפֶשׁ:

ט| **אֶל הַמָּקוֹם הַזֶּה.** זֶה בֵּית הַמִּקְדָּשׁ: **וַיִּתֶּן לָנוּ אֶת הָאָרֶץ.** כְּמַשְׁמָעוֹ:

clung to his jacket, until the wind gave up, exhausted. Then the sun began to shine. As soon as the farmer felt its heat, he took his jacket off. Warmth is more powerful than wind.

So it was with Israel. Pharaoh and his people afflicted the Israelites, but "the more they were oppressed, the more they increased" (Ex. 1:12). Lavan, in this reading, did not afflict Yaakov. To the contrary, while he was with Lavan, Yaakov grew rich. The danger was that he would remain with Lavan and forget who he was. Throughout Jewish history, the more Jews suffered, the more they prayed, studied, and kept the commands. Paradoxically, the danger to Jewish continuity has been not slavery and suffering, but affluence and freedom.

So Moshe warned at the end of his life: "Take care not to forget the LORD your God.... Otherwise, when you have eaten and been satisfied, and have built fine houses and lived in them...your heart may become proud, forgetting the LORD your God who brought you out of Egypt, the house of slaves" (Deut. 8:11–14).

26:5 **וַיְהִי־שָׁם לְגוֹי** *There he became a nation* – The Vilna Gaon explains that the word *goy*, "nation," is related to the word *geviya*, "body." A group of individuals becomes a nation when it becomes like a single body. R. Shimon bar Yoḥai taught, "Israel is like one body with a single soul. When one is injured, all feel the pain" (Vayikra Rabba 4:6).

Rabbi Joseph B. Soloveitchik (1903–93), in his essay *Kol Dodi Dofek*, spoke of the two covenants that bind Jews to one another: *brit goral*, the "covenant of fate," and *brit yeud*, the "covenant of destiny." The first arises out of shared suffering in the past, the second out of a collective vision of the future (see also commentary on Ex. 12:3 and on Num. 10, "Community and Camp"). In Egypt the Israelites entered into the covenant of fate. They were united by suffering. A midrash states: "In Egypt the Israelites gathered to dwell as a group, all of them becoming as one, and they covenanted to act with loving-kindness toward one another" (Tanna DeVei Eliyahu). That is how they first became a nation.

ג יִבְחַר יְהוָה אֱלֹהֶיךָ לְשַׁכֵּן שְׁמוֹ שָׁם: וּבָאתָ אֶל־הַכֹּהֵן אֲשֶׁר יִהְיֶה
בַּיָּמִים הָהֵם וְאָמַרְתָּ אֵלָיו הִגַּדְתִּי הַיּוֹם לַיהוָה אֱלֹהֶיךָ כִּי־בָאתִי אֶל־
ד הָאָרֶץ אֲשֶׁר נִשְׁבַּע יְהוָה לַאֲבֹתֵינוּ לָתֶת לָנוּ: וְלָקַח הַכֹּהֵן הַטֶּנֶא
ה מִיָּדֶךָ וְהִנִּיחוֹ לִפְנֵי מִזְבַּח יְהוָה אֱלֹהֶיךָ: וְעָנִיתָ וְאָמַרְתָּ לִפְנֵי ׀ יְהוָה
אֱלֹהֶיךָ אֲרַמִּי אֹבֵד אָבִי וַיֵּרֶד מִצְרַיְמָה וַיָּגָר שָׁם בִּמְתֵי מְעָט וַיְהִי־
ו שָׁם לְגוֹי גָּדוֹל עָצוּם וָרָב: וַיָּרֵעוּ אֹתָנוּ הַמִּצְרִים וַיְעַנּוּנוּ וַיִּתְּנוּ עָלֵינוּ
ז עֲבֹדָה קָשָׁה: וַנִּצְעַק אֶל־יְהוָה אֱלֹהֵי אֲבֹתֵינוּ וַיִּשְׁמַע יְהוָה אֶת־קֹלֵנוּ
ח וַיַּרְא אֶת־עָנְיֵנוּ וְאֶת־עֲמָלֵנוּ וְאֶת־לַחֲצֵנוּ: וַיּוֹצִאֵנוּ יְהוָה מִמִּצְרַיִם
ט בְּיָד חֲזָקָה וּבִזְרֹעַ נְטוּיָה וּבְמֹרָא גָּדֹל וּבְאֹתוֹת וּבְמֹפְתִים: וַיְבִאֵנוּ
אֶל־הַמָּקוֹם הַזֶּה וַיִּתֶּן־לָנוּ אֶת־הָאָרֶץ הַזֹּאת אֶרֶץ זָבַת חָלָב וּדְבָשׁ:

אונקלוס

דְּיִתְרְעֵי יי אֱלָהָךְ, לְאַשְׁרָאָה שְׁכִינְתֵיהּ תַּמָּן: ג וְתֵיתֵי לְוָת כָּהֲנָא, דִּיהֵי בְּיוֹמַיָּא הָאִנּוּן, וְתֵימַר לֵיהּ, חַוֵּיתִי יוֹמָא דֵין קֳדָם יי אֱלָהָךְ, אֲרֵי עַאלִית לְאַרְעָא, דְּקַיֵּים יי, לַאֲבָהָתַנָא לְמִתַּן לַנָא: ד וְיִסַּב כָּהֲנָא, סַלָּא מִן יְדָךְ, וְיַחְתְּנֵיהּ, קֳדָם, מַדְבְּחָא דַּיי אֱלָהָךְ: ה וְתָתֵיב וְתֵימַר, קֳדָם יי אֱלָהָךְ, לָבָן אֲרַמָּאָה בְּעָא לְאַבָּדָא יָת אַבָּא, וּנְחַת לְמִצְרַיִם, וְדָר תַּמָּן בְּעַם זְעֵיר, וַהֲוָה תַמָּן, לְעַם רַב תַּקִּיף וְסַגִּי: ו וְאַבְאִישׁוּ לַנָא, מִצְרָאֵי וְעַנִּיוּנָא, וִיהַבוּ עֲלַנָא פָּלְחָנָא קַשְׁיָא: ז וְצַלִּינָא, קֳדָם יי אֱלָהָא דַּאֲבָהָתַנָא, וְקַבֵּיל יי צְלוֹתַנָא, וּגְלֵי קֳדָמוֹהִי עַמְלַנָא, וְלֵיאוּתַנָא וְדֻחְקַנָא: ח וְאַפְּקַנָא יי מִמִּצְרַיִם, בִּיד תַּקִּיפָא וּבִדְרָע מְרָמַם, וּבְחֶזְוָנָא רַבָּא, וּבְאָתִין וּבְמוֹפְתִין: ט וְאַיְתְיַנָא לְאַתְרָא הָדֵין, וִיהַב לַנָא יָת אַרְעָא הָדָא, אֲרַע, עָבְדָא חֲלַב וּדְבָשׁ:

26:5 **אֲרַמִּי אֹבֵד אָבִי** *My ancestor was a wandering Aramean* – The exposition of these four verses constitutes, according to the Mishna (Pesaḥim 10:4), the core of the Passover Haggada. Most scholars take the view that this text was chosen because, as part of the first-fruits ceremony, it would have been well known to most Jews in Temple times, before texts of the Haggada were freely available. Another reason is that the "confession" is preceded by the words "I declare (*higadeti*) today." The verb is from the same root as the word *haggada*, recited on the night of Passover, when we are commanded to "declare" to our children (*vehigadeta levinkha*).

Nonetheless, it is a strange choice. The plain sense of the words *Arami oved avi* is "My ancestor was a wandering Aramean" (meaning Avraham, according to Rashbam; or Yaakov, according to Ibn Ezra and Sforno). The interpretation of the Passover Haggada – "An Aramean sought my ancestor's death" – is not the plain sense. What is more, that interpretation seems to cut across the whole theme of the Haggada, which is about slavery in Egypt. It is strange to begin by saying that what Pharaoh did was bad, but Lavan was worse. Rabbi Z. H. Ferber offered the following explanation:

The sun and the wind were once arguing as to which was stronger. The sun said, "I am stronger, because I give light and warmth to the whole world." The wind said, "I am stronger, because nothing can stand in my way." Just then a farmer began plowing his field. The sun said to the wind, "Let us settle the matter once and for all. Let us see which of us can remove the jacket from the man. That will prove which is the stronger." The wind accepted the challenge and began to blow. But the harder it blew, the more tightly the farmer

10 with milk and with honey. And now I am bringing the first fruit of the land that
You, O LORD, have given me.' Set the basket down before the LORD your God,
11 and then bow down low before the LORD your God. Then you, with the Levites
and the migrants who live among you, shall rejoice in all the good that the LORD
12 your God has bestowed on you and on your household. When you SHENI
have finished setting aside a tenth of all your produce in the third year, the year
of the tithe, and have given it to the Levites, the migrants, the orphans, and the
13 widows, so that they may eat in your towns and be satisfied, you shall declare
before the LORD your God: 'I have removed the consecrated portion from my
house, and I have given it to the Levites and the migrants, the orphans, and the
widows, just as You commanded me. I have not transgressed or forgotten any
14 of Your commandments. I have not eaten of it while in mourning. I have not
removed any of it while impure. I have not offered any of it to the dead. I have
15 obeyed the LORD my God, doing just as You commanded me. Look down from

רש"י

י **וְהִנַּחְתּוֹ.** מַגִּיד שֶׁנּוֹטְלוֹ אַחַר הֲנָפַת הַכֹּהֵן, וְאוֹחֲזוֹ בְּיָדוֹ כְּשֶׁהוּא קוֹרֵא, וְחוֹזֵר וּמֵנִיף:

יא **וְשָׂמַחְתָּ בְכָל הַטּוֹב.** מִכָּאן אָמְרוּ: אֵין קוֹרִין מִקְרָא בִּכּוּרִים אֶלָּא בִּזְמַן שִׂמְחָה, מֵעֲצֶרֶת וְעַד הֶחָג, שֶׁאָדָם מְלַקֵּט תְּבוּאָתוֹ וּפֵרוֹתָיו וְיֵינוֹ וְשַׁמְנוֹ; אֲבָל מִן הֶחָג וְאֵילָךְ מֵבִיא וְאֵינוֹ קוֹרֵא: **אַתָּה וְהַלֵּוִי.** אַף הַלֵּוִי חַיָּב בְּבִכּוּרִים אִם נָטְעוּ בְּתוֹךְ עָרֵיהֶם: **וְהַגֵּר אֲשֶׁר בְּקִרְבֶּךָ.** מֵבִיא וְאֵינוֹ קוֹרֵא, שֶׁאֵינוֹ יָכוֹל לוֹמַר "לַאֲבֹתֵינוּ":

יב **כִּי תְכַלֶּה לַעְשֵׂר אֶת כָּל מַעְשַׂר תְּבוּאָתְךָ בַּשָּׁנָה הַשְּׁלִישִׁת.** כְּשֶׁתִּגְמֹר לְהַפְרִישׁ מַעַשְׂרוֹת שֶׁל שָׁנָה הַשְּׁלִישִׁית, קָבַע זְמַן הַבִּעוּר וְהַוִּדּוּי בְּעֶרֶב הַפֶּסַח שֶׁל שָׁנָה הָרְבִיעִית, שֶׁנֶּאֱמַר: "מִקְצֵה שָׁלֹשׁ שָׁנִים תּוֹצִיא" וְגוֹ' (לעיל יד, כח), נֶאֱמַר כָּאן: "מִקֵּץ" וְנֶאֱמַר לְהַלָּן: "מִקֵּץ שֶׁבַע שָׁנִים" (להלן לא, י) לְעִנְיַן הַקְהֵל, מַה לְּהַלָּן רֶגֶל, אַף כָּאן רֶגֶל. אִי מַה לְּהַלָּן חַג הַסֻּכּוֹת אַף כָּאן חַג הַסֻּכּוֹת? תַּלְמוּד לוֹמַר: "כִּי תְכַלֶּה לַעְשֵׂר" מַעַשְׂרוֹת שֶׁל שָׁנָה הַשְּׁלִישִׁית, רֶגֶל שֶׁהַמַּעַשְׂרוֹת כָּלִין בּוֹ וְזֶהוּ פֶּסַח, שֶׁהַרְבֵּה אִילָנוֹת יֵשׁ שֶׁנִּלְקָטִין אַחַר הַסֻּכּוֹת, נִמְצְאוּ מַעַשְׂרוֹת שֶׁל שְׁלִישִׁית כָּלִין בְּפֶסַח שֶׁל רְבִיעִית, וְכָל מִי שֶׁשִּׁהָה מַעַשְׂרוֹתָיו הִצְרִיכוֹ הַכָּתוּב לְבַעֲרוֹ מִן הַבַּיִת: **שְׁנַת הַמַּעֲשֵׂר.** שָׁנָה שֶׁאֵין נוֹהֵג בָּהּ אֶלָּא מַעֲשֵׂר אֶחָד מִשְּׁנֵי מַעַשְׂרוֹת שֶׁנָּהֲגוּ בִּשְׁתֵּי שָׁנִים שֶׁלְּפָנֶיהָ, שֶׁשָּׁנָה רִאשׁוֹנָה שֶׁל שְׁמִטָּה נוֹהֵג בָּהּ מַעֲשֵׂר רִאשׁוֹן, כְּמוֹ שֶׁנֶּאֱמַר: "כִּי תִקְחוּ מֵאֵת בְּנֵי יִשְׂרָאֵל אֶת הַמַּעֲשֵׂר" (במדבר יח, כו) וּמַעֲשֵׂר שֵׁנִי, שֶׁנֶּאֱמַר: "וְאָכַלְתָּ לִפְנֵי ה' אֱלֹהֶיךָ... מַעְשַׂר דְּגָנְךָ תִּירֹשְׁךָ וְיִצְהָרֶךָ" (לעיל יד, כג), הֲרֵי שְׁתֵּי מַעַשְׂרוֹת; וּבָא וְלִמֶּדְךָ כָּאן בַּשָּׁנָה הַשְּׁלִישִׁית, שֶׁאֵין נוֹהֵג מֵאוֹתָן שְׁתֵּי מַעַשְׂרוֹת אֶלָּא הָאֶחָד, וְאֵי זֶה? זֶה מַעֲשֵׂר רִאשׁוֹן, וְתַחַת מַעֲשֵׂר שֵׁנִי יִתֵּן מַעְשַׂר עָנִי, שֶׁנֶּאֱמַר כָּאן: "וְנָתַתָּה לַלֵּוִי" אֵת אֲשֶׁר לוֹ, הֲרֵי מַעֲשֵׂר רִאשׁוֹן, "לַגֵּר לַיָּתוֹם וְלָאַלְמָנָה" זֶה מַעְשַׂר עָנִי: **וְאָכְלוּ בִשְׁעָרֶיךָ וְשָׂבֵעוּ.** תֵּן לָהֶם כְּדֵי שָׂבְעָן. מִכָּאן אָמְרוּ: אֵין פּוֹחֲתִין לֶעָנִי בַּגֹּרֶן פָּחוֹת מֵחֲצִי קַב חִטִּים וְכוּ':

יג **וְאָמַרְתָּ לִפְנֵי ה' אֱלֹהֶיךָ.** הִתְוַדֵּה שֶׁנָּתַתָּ מַעַשְׂרוֹתֶיךָ: **בִּעַרְתִּי הַקֹּדֶשׁ מִן הַבַּיִת.** זֶה מַעֲשֵׂר שֵׁנִי וְנֶטַע רְבָעִי, וְלִמֶּדְךָ שֶׁאִם שִׁהָה מַעַשְׂרוֹתָיו שֶׁל שְׁתֵּי שָׁנִים וְלֹא הֶעֱלָם לִירוּשָׁלַיִם, שֶׁצָּרִיךְ לְהַעֲלוֹתָם עַכְשָׁיו: **וְגַם נְתַתִּיו לַלֵּוִי.** זֶה מַעֲשֵׂר רִאשׁוֹן: **וְגַם.** לְרַבּוֹת תְּרוּמוֹת וּבִכּוּרִים: **וְלַגֵּר לַיָּתוֹם וְלָאַלְמָנָה.** זֶה מַעְשַׂר עָנִי: **כְּכָל מִצְוָתְךָ.** נְתָתִים כְּסִדְרָן, לֹא הִקְדַּמְתִּי תְּרוּמָה לְבִכּוּרִים וְלֹא מַעֲשֵׂר לִתְרוּמָה וְלֹא שֵׁנִי לָרִאשׁוֹן, שֶׁהַתְּרוּמָה קְרוּיָה "רֵאשִׁית" (לעיל יח, ד), שֶׁהִיא רִאשׁוֹנָה מִשֶּׁנַּעֲשָׂה דָּגָן, וּכְתִיב: "מְלֵאָתְךָ וְדִמְעֲךָ לֹא תְאַחֵר" (שמות כב, כח), לֹא תְשַׁנֶּה אֶת הַסֵּדֶר: **לֹא עָבַרְתִּי מִמִּצְוֹתֶיךָ.** לֹא הִפְרַשְׁתִּי מִמִּין עַל שֶׁאֵינוֹ מִינוֹ, וּמִן הֶחָדָשׁ עַל הַיָּשָׁן: **וְלֹא שָׁכָחְתִּי.** מִלְּבָרֶכְךָ עַל הַפְרָשַׁת מַעַשְׂרוֹת:

יד **לֹא אָכַלְתִּי בְאֹנִי מִמֶּנּוּ.** מִכָּאן שֶׁאָסוּר לְאוֹנֵן: **וְלֹא בִעַרְתִּי מִמֶּנּוּ בְּטָמֵא.** בֵּין שֶׁאֲנִי טָמֵא וְהוּא טָהוֹר בֵּין שֶׁאֲנִי טָהוֹר וְהוּא טָמֵא. וְהֵיכָן הֻזְהַר עַל כָּךְ? "לֹא תוּכַל לֶאֱכֹל בִּשְׁעָרֶיךָ" (לעיל יב, יז) – זוֹ אֲכִילַת טֻמְאָה, כְּמוֹ שֶׁנֶּאֱמַר בִּפְסוּלֵי הַמֻּקְדָּשִׁין: "בִּשְׁעָרֶיךָ תֹּאכְלֶנּוּ הַטָּמֵא וְהַטָּהוֹר" וְגוֹ' (לעיל טו, כב), אֲבָל זֶה לֹא תוּכַל לֶאֱכֹל דֶּרֶךְ אֲכִילַת שְׁעָרֶיךָ הָאָמוּר בְּמָקוֹם אַחֵר: **וְלֹא נָתַתִּי מִמֶּנּוּ לְמֵת.** לַעֲשׂוֹת לוֹ אָרוֹן וְתַכְרִיכִין: **שָׁמַעְתִּי בְּקוֹל ה' אֱלֹהָי.** הֲבִיאוֹתִיו לְבֵית הַבְּחִירָה: **עָשִׂיתִי כְּכֹל אֲשֶׁר צִוִּיתָנִי.** שָׂמַחְתִּי וְשִׂמַּחְתִּי בּוֹ:

טו **הַשְׁקִיפָה מִמְּעוֹן קָדְשְׁךָ.** עָשִׂינוּ מַה שֶּׁגָּזַרְתָּ עָלֵינוּ, עֲשֵׂה אַתָּה מַה שֶּׁעָלֶיךָ לַעֲשׂוֹת, שֶׁאָמַרְתָּ: "אִם בְּחֻקֹּתַי תֵּלֵכוּ... וְנָתַתִּי גִשְׁמֵיכֶם

י וְעַתָּה הִנֵּה הֵבֵאתִי אֶת־רֵאשִׁית פְּרִי הָאֲדָמָה אֲשֶׁר־נָתַתָּה לִּי יהוה
יא וְהִנַּחְתּוֹ לִפְנֵי יהוה אֱלֹהֶיךָ וְהִשְׁתַּחֲוִיתָ לִפְנֵי יהוה אֱלֹהֶיךָ: וְשָׂמַחְתָּ
בְכׇל־הַטּוֹב אֲשֶׁר נָתַן־לְךָ יהוה אֱלֹהֶיךָ וּלְבֵיתֶךָ אַתָּה וְהַלֵּוִי וְהַגֵּר
יב אֲשֶׁר בְּקִרְבֶּךָ: כִּי תְכַלֶּה לַעְשֵׂר אֶת־כׇּל־מַעְשַׂר שני
תְּבוּאָתְךָ בַּשָּׁנָה הַשְּׁלִישִׁת שְׁנַת הַמַּעֲשֵׂר וְנָתַתָּה לַלֵּוִי לַגֵּר לַיָּתוֹם
יג וְלָאַלְמָנָה וְאָכְלוּ בִשְׁעָרֶיךָ וְשָׂבֵעוּ: וְאָמַרְתָּ לִפְנֵי יהוה אֱלֹהֶיךָ בִּעַרְתִּי
הַקֹּדֶשׁ מִן־הַבַּיִת וְגַם נְתַתִּיו לַלֵּוִי וְלַגֵּר לַיָּתוֹם וְלָאַלְמָנָה כְּכׇל־מִצְוָתְךָ
יד אֲשֶׁר צִוִּיתָנִי לֹא־עָבַרְתִּי מִמִּצְוֺתֶיךָ וְלֹא שָׁכָחְתִּי: לֹא־אָכַלְתִּי בְאֹנִי
מִמֶּנּוּ וְלֹא־בִעַרְתִּי מִמֶּנּוּ בְּטָמֵא וְלֹא־נָתַתִּי מִמֶּנּוּ לְמֵת שָׁמַעְתִּי בְּקוֹל
טו יהוה אֱלֹהָי עָשִׂיתִי כְּכֹל אֲשֶׁר צִוִּיתָנִי: הַשְׁקִיפָה מִמְּעוֹן קׇדְשְׁךָ מִן־

אונקלוס

י וּכְעַן, הָא אֵיתֵיתִי יָת רֵישׁ אִבָּא דְּאַרְעָא, דִּיהַבְתְּ לִי יי, וְתַחְתֵּינֵיהּ, קֳדָם יי אֱלָהָךְ, וְתִסְגּוּד, קֳדָם יי אֱלָהָךְ: יא וְתִחְדֵּי בְּכָל טָבְתָא, דִּיהַב לָךְ, יי אֱלָהָךְ וְלֶאֱנָשׁ בֵּיתָךְ, אַתְּ וְלֵיוָאָה, וְגִיּוֹרָא דְּבֵינָךְ: יב אֲרֵי תְשֵׁיצֵי, לְעַסָּרָא, יָת כָּל מַעְסַר עֲלַלְתָּךְ, בְּשַׁתָּא תְּלִיתֵיתָא שְׁנַת מַעְסְרָא, וְתִתֵּין לְלֵיוָאָה, לְגִיּוֹרָא לְיִתַּמָּא וּלְאַרְמַלְתָּא, וְיֵיכְלוּן בְּקִרְוָךְ וְיִסְבְּעוּן:

יג וְתֵימַר, קֳדָם יי אֱלָהָךְ פַּלֵּיתִי קוֹדֶשׁ מַעְסְרָא מִן בֵּיתָא, וְאַף יְהַבְתֵּיהּ לְלֵיוָאָה וּלְגִיּוֹרָא לְיִתַּמָּא וּלְאַרְמַלְתָּא, כְּכָל תַּפְקֵידְתָּךְ דְּפַקֵּידְתָּנִי, לָא עֲבָרִית מִפִּקּוֹדָךְ וְלָא אִתְנְשֵׁיתִי: יד לָא אֲכָלִית בְּאֶבְלִי מִנֵּיהּ, וְלָא חַלֵּיפִית מִנֵּיהּ בִּמְסָאַב, וְלָא יְהָבִית מִנֵּיהּ לְמִית, קַבֵּילִית, לְמֵימְרָא דַּיי אֱלָהִי, עֲבָדִית, כְּכָל דְּפַקֵּידְתָּנִי: טו אִסְתְּכִי מִמְּדוֹר קֻדְשָׁךְ מִן

26:11 וְשָׂמַחְתָּ... אַתָּה וְהַלֵּוִי וְהַגֵּר *Then you, with the Levites and the migrants... shall rejoice* – According to Ibn Ezra this means that "you must bring them to rejoice in the fruit of your land." The description fits the festival tradition we practice to this day. Rambam puts it strongly:

> When one eats and drinks [on a festival], one must also feed the stranger, the orphan, the widow, and others who are distressed and poor. But one who locks the door of his courtyard, and eats and drinks with his children and wife but does not feed the poor and the bitter at heart – this is not joy of a mitzva, but the joy of his belly. (*Hilkhot Yom Tov* 6:18)

The word *simḥa* has in the Torah a nuance untranslatable into English. Joy, happiness, pleasure, and the like are all states of mind, emotions. They belong to the individual. We can feel them alone. *Simḥa*, by contrast, is not a private emotion. It means *happiness shared*. It is a social state, a predicate of "we," not "I." There is no such thing as feeling *simḥa* alone.

Freedom, affluence, and security too often turn a nation into a collection of individuals, each pursuing his or her own happiness, indifferent to the fate of those who have less, the lonely, the marginal, and the excluded. When that happens, societies start to disintegrate.

The only way to avoid it, says Moshe, is to share your happiness with others, and, in the midst of that collective, national celebration, serve God. Blessings are not measured by how much we own or earn or spend or possess but by how much we share. *Simḥa* is the mark of a sacred society. It is a place of collective joy.

Your holy habitation, from heaven, and bless Your people Israel and the land that
You have given us, as You swore to our ancestors – a land flowing with milk and
16 with honey.' The LORD your God is commanding you this day to keep SHELISHI
these decrees and laws. Take care to keep them with all your heart and with all
17 your soul. Today you have proclaimed the LORD to be your God, and that you
will walk in His ways, keep His decrees, commandments, and laws, and listen to
18 His voice. And today the LORD has proclaimed you to be, as He promised you,
19 His treasured people who guard His commands; He will set you high above all
the nations He has made, in praise, fame, and honor. You will be a people holy to
the LORD your God, just as He has promised."
27 1 Then Moshe and the elders of Israel charged the people: "Keep all of the REVI'I
2 command that I charge you with this day. On the day that you cross the Jordan
to the land that the LORD your God is giving you, set up large boulders, and

רש״י

בְּעִתָּם" (ויקרא כו, ג-ד): **אֲשֶׁר נָתַתָּה לָנוּ כַּאֲשֶׁר נִשְׁבַּעְתָּ לַאֲבֹתֵינוּ.** לָתֵת לָנוּ וְקִיַּמְתָּ, "אֶרֶץ זָבַת חָלָב וּדְבָשׁ":

טז **הַיּוֹם הַזֶּה ה' אֱלֹהֶיךָ מְצַוְּךָ.** בְּכָל יוֹם יִהְיוּ בְעֵינֶיךָ חֲדָשִׁים כְּאִלּוּ בּוֹ בַּיּוֹם נִצְטַוֵּיתָ עֲלֵיהֶם: **וְשָׁמַרְתָּ וְעָשִׂיתָ אוֹתָם.** בַּת קוֹל מְבָרַכְתּוֹ: הֵבֵאתָ בִּכּוּרִים הַיּוֹם, תִּשְׁנֶה לַשָּׁנָה הַבָּאָה:

יז-יח **הֶאֱמַרְתָּ, הֶאֱמִירְךָ.** (אֵין לָהֶם עֵד בַּמִּקְרָא, וְלִי נִרְאֶה שֶׁהֵם לְשׁוֹן הַמְשָׁכָה וְהַבְדָּלָה, הִבְדַּלְתּוֹ מֵאֱלֹהֵי הַנֵּכָר "לִהְיוֹת לְךָ לֵאלֹהִים", וְהוּא הִפְרִישְׁךָ אֵלָיו מֵעַמֵּי הָאָרֶץ "לִהְיוֹת לוֹ לְעַם סְגֻלָּה") לְשׁוֹן תִּפְאֶרֶת, כְּמוֹ: "יִתְאַמְּרוּ כָּל פֹּעֲלֵי אָוֶן" (תהלים צד, ד):

יח **כַּאֲשֶׁר דִּבֶּר לָךְ.** "וִהְיִיתֶם לִי סְגֻלָּה" (שמות יט, ה):

יט **וְלִהְיֹתְךָ עַם קָדֹשׁ וגו' כַּאֲשֶׁר דִּבֵּר.** "וִהְיִיתֶם לִי קְדֹשִׁים" (ויקרא כ, כו):

כז א **שָׁמֹר אֶת כָּל הַמִּצְוָה.** לְשׁוֹן הֹוֶה, גרדנ"ט בְּלַעַז:

ב **וַהֲקֵמֹתָ לְךָ.** בַּיַּרְדֵּן, וְאַחַר כָּךְ תּוֹצִיאוּ מִשָּׁם אֲחֵרוֹת וְתִבְנוּ מֵהֶן מִזְבֵּחַ בְּהַר עֵיבָל. נִמְצֵאתָ אַתָּה אוֹמֵר, שְׁלֹשָׁה מִינֵי אֲבָנִים הָיוּ: שְׁתֵּים עֶשְׂרֵה בַּיַּרְדֵּן, וּכְנֶגְדָּן בַּגִּלְגָּל, וּכְנֶגְדָּן בְּהַר עֵיבָל, כִּדְאִיתָא בְּמַסֶּכֶת סוֹטָה (דף לה ע"ב):

Unlike every ancient myth about the beginning of things, there was no struggle, no use of force. Instead, the key verb is *lemor*, "God *said* [*vayomer*], 'Let there be' and there was." Language creates worlds.

That is divine – not human – speech. However, there is a human counterpart. There are things we create with words when we use them in a particular way. J. L. Austin called this use of speech *performative utterance*. So, for example, when a judge says, "This court is now in session," he is not *describing* something but *doing* something.

The most basic type of performative utterance is *making a promise*. This involves the use of language to *create an obligation*. Some promises are unilateral, but others are mutual. Some are specific, others are open-ended. The supreme example of an open-ended mutual pledge between human beings is marriage. The supreme example of an open-ended mutual pledge between human beings and God is a covenant. That is what our two verses state: that God and the people of Israel pledged themselves to one another by making a covenant, a relationship brought into existence by words and sustained by honoring those words.

Language used to create a mutually binding relationship links God and humankind. Our verse means: "Today, through speech, you have made God your God, and God has made you His people." Words, an act of saying, have created an eternally binding relationship.

הַשָּׁמַיִם וּבָרֵךְ אֶת־עַמְּךָ אֶת־יִשְׂרָאֵל וְאֵת הָאֲדָמָה אֲשֶׁר נָתַתָּה לָנוּ
טז כַּאֲשֶׁר נִשְׁבַּעְתָּ לַאֲבֹתֵינוּ אֶרֶץ זָבַת חָלָב וּדְבָשׁ: הַיּוֹם הַזֶּה שלישי
יְהוָה אֱלֹהֶיךָ מְצַוְּךָ לַעֲשׂוֹת אֶת־הַחֻקִּים הָאֵלֶּה וְאֶת־הַמִּשְׁפָּטִים
יז וְשָׁמַרְתָּ וְעָשִׂיתָ אוֹתָם בְּכָל־לְבָבְךָ וּבְכָל־נַפְשֶׁךָ: אֶת־יְהוָה הֶאֱמַרְתָּ
הַיּוֹם לִהְיוֹת לְךָ לֵאלֹהִים וְלָלֶכֶת בִּדְרָכָיו וְלִשְׁמֹר חֻקָּיו וּמִצְוֹתָיו
יח וּמִשְׁפָּטָיו וְלִשְׁמֹעַ בְּקֹלוֹ: וַיהוָה הֶאֱמִירְךָ הַיּוֹם לִהְיוֹת לוֹ לְעַם סְגֻלָּה
יט כַּאֲשֶׁר דִּבֶּר־לָךְ וְלִשְׁמֹר כָּל־מִצְוֹתָיו: וּלְתִתְּךָ עֶלְיוֹן עַל כָּל־הַגּוֹיִם
אֲשֶׁר עָשָׂה לִתְהִלָּה וּלְשֵׁם וּלְתִפְאָרֶת וְלִהְיֹתְךָ עַם־קָדֹשׁ לַיהוָה
אֱלֹהֶיךָ כַּאֲשֶׁר דִּבֵּר:
כז א וַיְצַו מֹשֶׁה וְזִקְנֵי יִשְׂרָאֵל אֶת־הָעָם לֵאמֹר שָׁמֹר אֶת־כָּל־הַמִּצְוָה אֲשֶׁר רביעי
ב אָנֹכִי מְצַוֶּה אֶתְכֶם הַיּוֹם: וְהָיָה בַּיּוֹם אֲשֶׁר תַּעַבְרוּ אֶת־הַיַּרְדֵּן אֶל־
הָאָרֶץ אֲשֶׁר־יְהוָה אֱלֹהֶיךָ נֹתֵן לָךְ וַהֲקֵמֹתָ לְךָ אֲבָנִים גְּדֹלוֹת וְשַׂדְתָּ

אונקלוס

שְׁמַיָּא, וּבָרֵיךְ יָת עַמָּךְ יָת יִשְׂרָאֵל, וְיָת אַרְעָא, דִּיהַבְתְּ לַנָא, כְּמָא דְּקַיֵּימְתָּא לַאֲבָהָתַנָא, אֲרַע, עָבְדָא חֲלַב וּדְבַשׁ: טז יוֹמָא הָדֵין, יי אֱלָהָךְ, מְפַקֵּדָךְ לְמֶעְבַּד, יָת קְיָמַיָּא הָאִלֵּין וְיָת דִּינַיָּא, וְתִטַּר וְתַעְבֵּיד יָתְהוֹן, בְּכָל לִבָּךְ וּבְכָל נַפְשָׁךְ: יז יָת יי חֲטַבְתְּ יוֹמָא דֵין, לְמֶהֱוֵי לָךְ לֶאֱלָהּ וּלִמְהָךְ בְּאוֹרְחָן דְּתָקְנָן קֳדָמוֹהִי, וּלְמִטַּר קְיָמוֹהִי וּפִקּוֹדוֹהִי, וְדִינוֹהִי וּלְקַבָּלָא לְמֵימְרֵיהּ: יח וַיי חַטְבָךְ יוֹמָא דֵין, לְמֶהֱוֵי לֵיהּ לְעַם חֲבִיב, כְּמָא דְּמַלֵּיל לָךְ, וּלְמִטַּר כָּל פִּקּוֹדוֹהִי: יט וּלְמִתְּנָךְ עִלַּאי, עַל כָּל עַמְמַיָּא דַּעֲבַד, לְתֻשְׁבְּחָא וּלְשׁוּם וְלִרְבוּ, וּלְמֶהֱוָךְ עַם קַדִּישׁ, קֳדָם יי אֱלָהָךְ כְּמָא דְּמַלֵּיל: כז א וּפַקֵּיד מֹשֶׁה וְסָבֵי יִשְׂרָאֵל, יָת עַמָּא לְמֵימַר, טְרוּ יָת כָּל תַּפְקֵידְתָּא, דַּאֲנָא, מְפַקֵּיד יָתְכוֹן יוֹמָא דֵין: ב וִיהֵי, בְּיוֹמָא דְּתִעְבְּרוּן יָת יַרְדְּנָא, לְאַרְעָא, דַּיי אֱלָהָךְ יָהֵיב לָךְ, וּתְקִים לָךְ אַבְנִין רַבְרְבָן, וּתְסוּד

26:17 הֶאֱמַרְתָּ *You have proclaimed* – Any translation tends to conceal the difficulty in this key verb, associated with Israel here, and God in the next verse: *lehaamir*. While it is a form of one of the most common of all biblical verbs, *lemor*, "to say," the specific form used here – the *hifil*, causative, form – is unique. It appears nowhere else in this form in the Tanakh. Its meaning is, therefore, obscure.

The JPS translation reads it as "affirmed." Rabbi Aryeh Kaplan, in *The Living Torah*, reads it as "declared allegiance to." Robert Alter, like us, renders it: "proclaimed." Other interpretations include "separated to yourself" (Rashi), "recognized" (Rabbi Saadia Gaon), "betrothed" (Malbim), "exchanged everything else for" (Ḥizkuni), "accepted the uniqueness of" (Rashi on Ḥagiga 3a), or "caused God to declare" (Rabbi Yehuda HaLevi, cited by Ibn Ezra).

In the Torah, the unique bond between humanity and God is formed by *language, speech, words*. Hence the importance here of the verb meaning "to say," "to declare," "to affirm." There is a radical statement of this at the very beginning of the Torah. God *spoke* and the world came into being.

3 coat them with plaster, and write on them all the words of this Law when you
cross over, that you may enter the land that the LORD your God is giving you,
a land flowing with milk and with honey, as the LORD, God of your ancestors,
4 promised you. When you cross the Jordan, set up these stones, as I command
5 you today, on Mount Eival, and coat them with plaster. And there, build an
altar to the LORD your God, an altar of stones. Do not take any iron tool to
6 them: of uncut stones you shall build the altar of the LORD your God. On
7 it, offer burnt offerings to the LORD your God. You shall also sacrifice peace
8 offerings and eat them there, rejoicing before the LORD your God. On the
9 boulders you shall write very clearly all the words of this Law." Then
Moshe and the Levitical priests spoke to all Israel: "Be still and listen, Israel.

רש״י

ח **בַּאֵר הֵיטֵב.** בְּשִׁבְעִים לָשׁוֹן:

ט **הַסְכֵּת.** כְּתַרְגּוּמוֹ: **הַיּוֹם הַזֶּה נִהְיֵיתָ לְעָם.** בְּכָל יוֹם יִהְיוּ בְּעֵינֶיךָ כְּאִלּוּ הַיּוֹם בָּאתָ עִמּוֹ בַּבְּרִית:

being owned by newcomers as well as by those whose families have been here for many generations. Storytelling can bind without dividing. Narrative politics, telling the story, can be egalitarian without being confrontational.

At the border of the land of Israel is to stand, not a gatekeeper, but a set of boulders engraved with a summary of the law (Rabbi Saadia Gaon) or the full text of the Torah from "When God began creating" (Ramban). This will display to all comers that, though we are a disparate collection of tribes and individuals, this covenant, this shared code, accessible to all, makes us together who we are.

27:8 **בַּאֵר הֵיטֵב** *Very clearly* – According to one tradition, the words of the Law on the stones were written in seventy languages. In rabbinic tradition, the phrase *ba'er heitev* came to refer to the need for interpretation to elucidate a text that presents particular difficulty.

Fundamentalism refers to many things in different contexts, but one of them is the tendency to read texts literally and apply them directly: to go straight from revelation to application without interpretation. It is a kind of principled impatience with the interpretative process, emerging when people feel that the world has been allowed to defeat the word. They, by contrast, are determined to defeat the world by means of the word.

In many religions, including Judaism, this is heretical. Every text needs interpretation. Every interpretation needs wisdom. Every wisdom needs careful negotiation between the timeless and time. It needs great wisdom together with a deep grounding in tradition to know how to apply the word to the world. The word, given in love, invites its interpretation in love (see note on Deut. 13:17).

27:9 **הַסְכֵּת וּשְׁמַע** *Be still and listen* – Throughout Deuteronomy, Moshe becomes an educator, explaining to the next generation that the laws God has given them are not just divine decrees. They make sense in human terms. They respect human dignity. They honor the integrity of nature. They give the land the chance to rest and recuperate, and protect Israel against the otherwise inexorable laws of the decline and fall of nations.

That is why Moshe, consistently throughout Deuteronomy, uses the verb *sh-m-a*. He wants the Israelites to obey God, but not blindly or through fear alone. God did not give the Torah to Israel for His sake but for theirs, as partners in the law (see also commentary on Gen. 3:6).

That is the meaning of Moshe's words in our verse: "Be still and listen." Keeping the commands involves an act of listening, not just submission and blind obedience – in all of listening's multiple senses of attending, meditating, and

ג אֹתָם בַּשִּׂיד׃ וְכָתַבְתָּ עֲלֵיהֶן אֶת־כָּל־דִּבְרֵי הַתּוֹרָה הַזֹּאת בְּעָבְרֶךָ
לְמַעַן אֲשֶׁר תָּבֹא אֶל־הָאָרֶץ אֲשֶׁר־יְהוָה אֱלֹהֶיךָ ׀ נֹתֵן לְךָ אֶרֶץ זָבַת
ד חָלָב וּדְבַשׁ כַּאֲשֶׁר דִּבֶּר יְהוָה אֱלֹהֵי־אֲבֹתֶיךָ לָךְ׃ וְהָיָה בְּעָבְרְכֶם אֶת־
הַיַּרְדֵּן תָּקִימוּ אֶת־הָאֲבָנִים הָאֵלֶּה אֲשֶׁר אָנֹכִי מְצַוֶּה אֶתְכֶם הַיּוֹם בְּהַר
ה עֵיבָל וְשַׂדְתָּ אוֹתָם בַּשִּׂיד׃ וּבָנִיתָ שָּׁם מִזְבֵּחַ לַיהוָה אֱלֹהֶיךָ מִזְבַּח
ו אֲבָנִים לֹא־תָנִיף עֲלֵיהֶם בַּרְזֶל׃ אֲבָנִים שְׁלֵמוֹת תִּבְנֶה אֶת־מִזְבַּח יְהוָה
ז אֱלֹהֶיךָ וְהַעֲלִיתָ עָלָיו עוֹלֹת לַיהוָה אֱלֹהֶיךָ׃ וְזָבַחְתָּ שְׁלָמִים וְאָכַלְתָּ
ח שָּׁם וְשָׂמַחְתָּ לִפְנֵי יְהוָה אֱלֹהֶיךָ׃ וְכָתַבְתָּ עַל־הָאֲבָנִים אֶת־כָּל־דִּבְרֵי
ט הַתּוֹרָה הַזֹּאת בַּאֵר הֵיטֵב׃ וַיְדַבֵּר מֹשֶׁה וְהַכֹּהֲנִים הַלְוִיִּם
אֶל־כָּל־יִשְׂרָאֵל לֵאמֹר הַסְכֵּת ׀ וּשְׁמַע יִשְׂרָאֵל הַיּוֹם הַזֶּה נִהְיֵיתָ לְעָם

אונקלוס

יָתְהוֹן בְּסִידָא: ג וְתִכְתּוֹב עֲלֵיהוֹן, יָת כָּל פִּתְגָמֵי, אוֹרָיְתָא הָדָא בְּמִעְבְּרָךְ, בְּדִיל דְּתֵיעוֹל לְאַרְעָא, דַּיְיָ אֱלָהָךְ יָהֵיב לָךְ, אֲרַע עָבְדָא חֲלַב וּדְבַשׁ, כְּמָא דְּמַלֵּיל, יי אֱלָהָא דַּאֲבָהָתָךְ לָךְ: ד וִיהֵי בְּמִעְבַּרְכוֹן יָת יַרְדְּנָא, תְּקִימוּן יָת אַבְנַיָּא הָאִלֵּין, דַּאֲנָא, מְפַקֵּיד יָתְכוֹן, יוֹמָא דֵין בְּטוּרָא דְּעֵיבָל, וּתְסוּד יָתְהוֹן בְּסִידָא: ה וְתִבְנֵי תַּמָּן מַדְבְּחָא, קֳדָם יי אֱלָהָךְ, מַדְבַּח אַבְנִין, לָא תְּרִים עֲלֵיהוֹן בַּרְזְלָא: ו אַבְנִין שַׁלְמָן תִּבְנֵי, יָת מַדְבְּחָא דַּיְיָ אֱלָהָךְ, וְתַסֵּיק עֲלוֹהִי עֲלָוָן, קֳדָם יי אֱלָהָךְ: ז וְתִכּוֹס נִכְסַת קֻדְשִׁין וְתֵיכוֹל תַּמָּן, וְתִחְדֵּי, קֳדָם יי אֱלָהָךְ: ח וְתִכְתּוֹב עַל אַבְנַיָּא, יָת כָּל פִּתְגָמֵי, אוֹרָיְתָא הָדָא פָּרִישׁ יָאוּת: ט וּמַלֵּיל מֹשֶׁה וְכָהֲנַיָּא לֵיוָאֵי, עִם כָּל יִשְׂרָאֵל לְמֵימַר, אַצֵּית וּשְׁמַע יִשְׂרָאֵל, יוֹמָא הָדֵין הֲוֵיתָא לְעַם,

27:3 וְכָתַבְתָּ עֲלֵיהֶן *And write on them* – Whenever I visit Washington, D.C., I make a point of going to see the presidential memorials, Jefferson's, Roosevelt's, and Lincoln's. Each carries inscriptions taken from their words: Jefferson's "We hold these truths to be self-evident," Roosevelt's "The only thing we have to fear is fear itself," and Lincoln's Gettysburg Address and his second inaugural, "With malice toward none; with charity for all." London has no equivalent that I know of. There are memorials and statues everywhere, each with a brief inscription saying who the statue represents, but no speeches, quotations, sound bites. Even the statue of Churchill, whose speeches rivaled Lincoln's in power, carries only one word: "Churchill."

This phenomenon is of a piece with the fact that the clubs and gathering places of Britain's governing elite have no signs or nameplates. You only know where they are if someone in the know shows you. It is as if, if you have to ask, you don't belong. Knowledge that in America is publicly displayed, is in Britain tacit and taken for granted. Those who need to know, know.

America tells national stories; Britain doesn't. The reason is that the two nations have different political cultures. America's is based on covenant, Britain's on hierarchy and tradition. "Telling the story" is at the heart of covenantal politics. It sustains identity and creates a sense of collective belonging. It binds the generations, reminding us of where the nation came from and is going to. It locates national identity in a set of historic events, speaking of the values for which those who came before us fought, and of which we are the guardians for the sake of the future. It must be an inclusive narrative, capable of

10 Today you have become the people of the LORD your God. Therefore listen
to the LORD your God, keeping His commandments and decrees, with which
11 I charge you on this day." On that day Moshe charged the people: HAMISHI
12 "When you have crossed the Jordan, these shall stand on Mount Gerizim to
13 bless the people: Shimon, Levi, Yehuda, Yissakhar, Yosef, and Binyamin. And
these shall stand on Mount Eival for the curse: Reuven, Gad, Asher, Zevulun,
14 Dan, and Naftali. The Levites shall then recite to all the Israelites in a loud
15 voice: 'Cursed be one who makes a graven or molten image, abhorrent
to the LORD, the work of a craftsman, and secretly sets it up.' And all the people
16 shall respond and say, 'Amen!' 'Cursed be one who degrades his father
17 or mother.' And all the people shall say, 'Amen!' 'Cursed be one who
moves back his neighbor's boundary marker.' And all the people shall say,
18 'Amen!' 'Cursed be one who leads a blind person astray along his way.'
19 And all the people shall say, 'Amen!' 'Cursed be one who deprives
the migrant, orphan, or widow of justice.' And all the people shall say, 'Amen!'

רש״י

יב לְבָרֵךְ אֶת הָעָם. כִּדְאִיתָא בְּמַסֶּכֶת סוֹטָה (לז ע״ב): שִׁשָּׁה שְׁבָטִים עָלוּ לְרֹאשׁ הַר גְּרִזִּים וְשִׁשָּׁה לְרֹאשׁ הַר עֵיבָל, וְהַכֹּהֲנִים וְהַלְוִיִּם וְהָאָרוֹן לְמַטָּה בָּאֶמְצַע. הָפְכוּ לְוִיִּם פְּנֵיהֶם כְּלַפֵּי הַר גְּרִזִּים וּפָתְחוּ בַּבְּרָכָה: ׳בָּרוּךְ הָאִישׁ אֲשֶׁר לֹא יַעֲשֶׂה פֶסֶל וּמַסֵּכָה׳ וְגוֹ׳, וְאֵלּוּ וָאֵלּוּ עוֹנִין אָמֵן. חָזְרוּ וְהָפְכוּ פְּנֵיהֶם לְהַר עֵיבָל וּפָתְחוּ בַּקְּלָלָה, וְאוֹמְרִים: ״אָרוּר הָאִישׁ אֲשֶׁר יַעֲשֶׂה פֶסֶל״ וְגוֹ׳, וְכֵן כֻּלָּם עַד ״אָרוּר אֲשֶׁר לֹא יָקִים״:

טז מַקְלֶה אָבִיו. מְזַלְזֵל, לְשׁוֹן: ״וְנִקְלָה אָחִיךָ״ (לעיל כה, ג):

יז מַסִּיג גְּבוּל. מַחֲזִירוֹ לַאֲחוֹרָיו וְגוֹנֵב אֶת הַקַּרְקַע, לְשׁוֹן: ״וְהֻסַּג אָחוֹר״ (ישעיה נט, יד):

יח מַשְׁגֶּה עִוֵּר. הַסּוּמָא בְּדָבָר וּמַשִּׁיאוֹ עֵצָה רָעָה:

wanted those around him to believe in God because then he would be cheated less.

For both researchers, the fundamental problem to be overcome by any society is that of the free rider. We all seek the benefits of cooperative endeavor, while being reluctant to pay the costs. Norenzayan's thesis is that "social surveillance keeps people in line." What moves people to act in prosocial ways is not the idea of God as an abstract creative force, but rather the belief that He sees what we do – and not simply the belief but an active reminder of it. Even being exposed to drawings of human eyes subtly influences our behavior. Religion makes a difference because, through rituals, prayers, and holy days, people are *reminded* that we are seen.

The power of religion, Norenzayan and Johnson argue, is precisely its negative aspect of divine punishment. Norenzayan assembles research evidence that shows, counterintuitively, that those who believe in a punitive God are more law abiding and also more forgiving than those who believe in a forgiving God. His conclusion is that "belief in divine punishment diminishes the motivation for earthly forms of costly punishment." Johnson regards the fear of divine punishment as, historically, a remarkably effective means of deterring free riders and encouraging cooperation on a large scale.

This may be why the tribes, looking one another, as it were, in the eye, repeat the refrain that even if the victim of a crime is unknown, unknowing, or powerless to protest, the people collectively denounce the crime, and God sees and will respond.

י לַיהוָה אֱלֹהֶיךָ׃ וְשָׁמַעְתָּ בְּקוֹל יהוה אֱלֹהֶיךָ וְעָשִׂיתָ אֶת־מִצְוֹתָו
יא וְאֶת־חֻקָּיו אֲשֶׁר אָנֹכִי מְצַוְּךָ הַיּוֹם׃ וַיְצַו מֹשֶׁה אֶת־הָעָם חמישי
יב בַּיּוֹם הַהוּא לֵאמֹר׃ אֵלֶּה יַעַמְדוּ לְבָרֵךְ אֶת־הָעָם עַל־הַר גְּרִזִּים
יג בְּעָבְרְכֶם אֶת־הַיַּרְדֵּן שִׁמְעוֹן וְלֵוִי וִיהוּדָה וְיִשָּׂשכָר וְיוֹסֵף וּבִנְיָמִן׃ וְאֵלֶּה
יַעַמְדוּ עַל־הַקְּלָלָה בְּהַר עֵיבָל רְאוּבֵן גָּד וְאָשֵׁר וּזְבוּלֻן דָּן וְנַפְתָּלִי׃
יד טו וְעָנוּ הַלְוִיִּם וְאָמְרוּ אֶל־כָּל־אִישׁ יִשְׂרָאֵל קוֹל רָם׃ אָרוּר
הָאִישׁ אֲשֶׁר יַעֲשֶׂה פֶסֶל וּמַסֵּכָה תּוֹעֲבַת יהוה מַעֲשֵׂה יְדֵי חָרָשׁ וְשָׂם
טז בַּסָּתֶר וְעָנוּ כָל־הָעָם וְאָמְרוּ אָמֵן׃ אָרוּר מַקְלֶה
יז אָבִיו וְאִמּוֹ וְאָמַר כָּל־הָעָם אָמֵן׃ אָרוּר מַסִּיג גְּבוּל רֵעֵהוּ
יח וְאָמַר כָּל־הָעָם אָמֵן׃ אָרוּר מַשְׁגֶּה עִוֵּר בַּדָּרֶךְ וְאָמַר
יט כָּל־הָעָם אָמֵן׃ אָרוּר מַטֶּה מִשְׁפַּט גֵּר־יָתוֹם וְאַלְמָנָה

אונקלוס

קֳדָם יי אֱלָהָךְ: י וּתְקַבֵּיל לְמֵימְרָא דַּיי אֱלָהָךְ, וְתַעְבֵּיד יָת פִּקּוֹדוֹהִי וְיָת קְיָמוֹהִי, דַּאֲנָא מְפַקֵּיד לָךְ יוֹמָא דֵין: יא וּפַקֵּיד מֹשֶׁה יָת עַמָּא, בְּיוֹמָא הַהוּא לְמֵימַר: יב אִלֵּין, יְקוּמוּן, לְבָרָכָא יָת עַמָּא עַל טוּרָא דִּגְרִיזִין, בְּמִעְבַּרְכוֹן יָת יַרְדְּנָא, שִׁמְעוֹן וְלֵוִי וִיהוּדָה, וְיִשָּׂשכָר וְיוֹסֵף וּבִנְיָמִין: יג וְאִלֵּין, יְקוּמוּן עַל לְוָטַיָּא בְּטוּרָא דְּעֵיבָל, רְאוּבֵן גָּד וְאָשֵׁר, וּזְבוּלוּן דָּן וְנַפְתָּלִי: יד וְיָתִיבוּן לֵיוָאֵי, וְיֵימְרוּן, לְכָל אֱנָשׁ יִשְׂרָאֵל קָל רָם: טו לִיט גֻּבְרָא, דְּיַעְבֵּיד צְלֵם וּמַתְּכָא מְרַחַק קֳדָם יי, עוֹבַד יְדֵי אֻמָּנָא וִישַׁוֵּי בְּסִתְרָא, וְיָתִיבוּן כָּל עַמָּא, וְיֵימְרוּן אָמֵן: טז לִיט, דִּיקַלֵּי אֲבוּהִי וְאִמֵּיהּ, וְיֵימַר כָּל עַמָּא אָמֵן: יז לִיט, דִּישַׁנֵּי תְּחוּמָא דְּחַבְרֵיהּ, וְיֵימַר כָּל עַמָּא אָמֵן: יח לִיט, דְּיַטְעֵי עַוִּירָא בְּאוֹרְחָא, וְיֵימַר כָּל עַמָּא אָמֵן: יט לִיט, דְּיַצְלֵי, דִּין גִּיּוֹר יִיתַם וְאַרְמְלָא,

reflecting. It does not involve abdication of the intellect or silencing of the questioning mind. Israel set it as their highest task to understand why the law is as it is.

Shema, listening, is the Torah's call to moral growth.

CURSES AND BLESSINGS

Here we turn to the sanctions associated with the covenant, namely, the blessings that will follow if it is adhered to, and the curses that will occur if it is broken. Facing one another on two mountainsides, the people hear and denounce a list of clandestine crimes – sins such as incest and "white-collar" theft (pushing back a neighbor's boundary marker) – which cause great social harm but often go undetected.

The research of Ara Norenzayan in *Big Gods* and Dominic Johnson in *God Is Watching You* shed an interesting light on this passage. They focus on the moral impact of the idea that God sees what we do, even in private, that He rewards the good, and more significantly, that He punishes the guilty. It is specifically the punitive dimension of religious belief that is for them the fundamental difference that religion makes to a society. Essentially, they agree with Voltaire, who once said that whatever his personal views on the matter, he

20 'Cursed be one who lies with his father's wife, dishonoring his father's bed.'
21 And all the people shall say, 'Amen!' 'Cursed be one who lies with
22 any animal.' And all the people shall say, 'Amen!' 'Cursed be anyone
who lies with his sister, whether she is the daughter of his father or of his
23 mother.' And all the people shall say, 'Amen!' 'Cursed be one who lies
24 with his mother-in-law.' And all the people shall say, 'Amen!' 'Cursed
be one who strikes down his fellow in secret.' And all the people shall say,
25 'Amen!' 'Cursed be one who accepts a bribe to execute an innocent
26 man.' And all the people shall say, 'Amen!' 'Cursed be one who does
not uphold the words of this Law by keeping them.' And all the people shall
say, 'Amen!'
28 1 If you listen faithfully to the Lord your God, taking care to keep all His
commandments, which I am commanding you today, the Lord your God will
2 set you above all the nations of this earth. All these blessings will come upon
3 you – overtake you – if you listen to the voice of the Lord your God: Blessed
4 shall you be in the town, and blessed shall you be in the field. Blessed shall be
the fruit of your womb, the fruit of your land, and the fruit of your cattle, the
5 calves of your herd, the lambs of your flock. Blessed shall be your basket and
6 your kneading pan. Blessed shall you be when you enter, and blessed shall you
7 be when you leave. The Lord will cause your enemies who rise against you SHISHI
to be vanquished before you. They will come at you from one direction, but

רש״י

כד מַכֵּה רֵעֵהוּ בַּסָּתֶר. עַל לָשׁוֹן הָרָע הוּא אוֹמֵר. רָאִיתִי בִּיסוֹדוֹ שֶׁל רַבִּי מֹשֶׁה הַדַּרְשָׁן: אַחַד עָשָׂר אֲרוּרִים יֵשׁ כָּאן, כְּנֶגֶד אַחַד עָשָׂר שְׁבָטִים, וּכְנֶגֶד שִׁמְעוֹן לֹא כָּתַב אָרוּר, לְפִי שֶׁלֹּא הָיָה בְּלִבּוֹ לְבָרְכוֹ לִפְנֵי מוֹתוֹ כְּשֶׁבֵּרַךְ שְׁאָר הַשְּׁבָטִים, לְכָךְ לֹא רָצָה לְקַלְּלוֹ:

כו אֲשֶׁר לֹא יָקִים. כָּאן כָּלַל אֶת כָּל הַתּוֹרָה כֻּלָּהּ, וְקִבְּלוּהָ עֲלֵיהֶם בְּאָלָה וּבִשְׁבוּעָה:

כח ד שְׁגַר אֲלָפֶיךָ. וַלְדוֹת בְּקָרְךָ שֶׁהַבְּהֵמָה מְשַׁגֶּרֶת מִמֵּעֶיהָ:

וְעַשְׁתְּרוֹת צֹאנֶךָ. כְּתַרְגּוּמוֹ. וְרַבּוֹתֵינוּ אָמְרוּ: לָמָּה נִקְרָא שְׁמָן 'עַשְׁתָּרוֹת'? שֶׁמְּעַשְּׁרוֹת אֶת בַּעֲלֵיהֶן וּמַחֲזִיקוֹת אוֹתָן, כְּעַשְׁתָּרוֹת הַלָּלוּ שֶׁהֵן סְלָעִים חֲזָקִים:

ה בָּרוּךְ טַנְאֲךָ. פֵּרוֹתֶיךָ. דָּבָר אַחֵר, "טַנְאֲךָ", דָּבָר לַח שֶׁאַתָּה מְסַנֵּן בִּסַלִּים: וּמִשְׁאַרְתֶּךָ. דָּבָר יָבֵשׁ שֶׁנִּשְׁאָר בַּכְּלִי וְאֵינוֹ זָב:

ו בָּרוּךְ אַתָּה בְּבֹאֶךָ וּבָרוּךְ אַתָּה בְּצֵאתֶךָ. שֶׁתְּהֵא יְצִיאָתְךָ מִן הָעוֹלָם בְּלֹא חֵטְא כְּבִיאָתְךָ לָעוֹלָם:

self-denial have little place in Jewish spirituality. Rav, the third-century Sage, went so far as to say: "In the World to Come we will face judgment for every legitimate pleasure we denied ourselves in this life" (Yerushalmi, Kiddushin 4:12).

Economic growth has *religious* significance first and foremost because of the degree to which it allows us to alleviate poverty. Throughout history, Judaism resisted any attempt to romanticize, rationalize, or anesthetize the pain of hunger, starvation, or need. One of the recurring themes of the book of Deuteronomy is "Then you ... shall rejoice in all the good that the Lord your God has bestowed on you and on your household" (Deut. 26:10). And joy (as we saw in the note on that verse), is always something we share.

כ וְאָמַר כָּל־הָעָם אָמֵן: אָרוּר שֹׁכֵב עִם־אֵשֶׁת אָבִיו כִּי גִלָּה כְּנַף אָבִיו

כא וְאָמַר כָּל־הָעָם אָמֵן: אָרוּר שֹׁכֵב עִם־כָּל־בְּהֵמָה וְאָמַר

כב כָּל־הָעָם אָמֵן: אָרוּר שֹׁכֵב עִם־אֲחֹתוֹ בַּת־אָבִיו אוֹ בַת־

כג אִמּוֹ וְאָמַר כָּל־הָעָם אָמֵן: אָרוּר שֹׁכֵב עִם־חֹתַנְתּוֹ וְאָמַר

כד כָּל־הָעָם אָמֵן: אָרוּר מַכֵּה רֵעֵהוּ בַּסָּתֶר וְאָמַר כָּל־הָעָם

כה אָמֵן: אָרוּר לֹקֵחַ שֹׁחַד לְהַכּוֹת נֶפֶשׁ דָּם נָקִי וְאָמַר כָּל־

כו הָעָם אָמֵן: אָרוּר אֲשֶׁר לֹא־יָקִים אֶת־דִּבְרֵי הַתּוֹרָה־הַזֹּאת

לַעֲשׂוֹת אוֹתָם וְאָמַר כָּל־הָעָם אָמֵן:

כח א וְהָיָה אִם־שָׁמוֹעַ תִּשְׁמַע בְּקוֹל יהוה אֱלֹהֶיךָ לִשְׁמֹר לַעֲשׂוֹת אֶת־ כב

כָּל־מִצְוֹתָיו אֲשֶׁר אָנֹכִי מְצַוְּךָ הַיּוֹם וּנְתָנְךָ יהוה אֱלֹהֶיךָ עֶלְיוֹן עַל

ב כָּל־גּוֹיֵי הָאָרֶץ: וּבָאוּ עָלֶיךָ כָּל־הַבְּרָכוֹת הָאֵלֶּה וְהִשִּׂיגֻךָ כִּי תִשְׁמַע

ג ד בְּקוֹל יהוה אֱלֹהֶיךָ: בָּרוּךְ אַתָּה בָּעִיר וּבָרוּךְ אַתָּה בַּשָּׂדֶה: בָּרוּךְ

פְּרִי־בִטְנְךָ וּפְרִי אַדְמָתְךָ וּפְרִי בְהֶמְתֶּךָ שְׁגַר אֲלָפֶיךָ וְעַשְׁתְּרוֹת צֹאנֶךָ:

ה ו בָּרוּךְ טַנְאֲךָ וּמִשְׁאַרְתֶּךָ: בָּרוּךְ אַתָּה בְּבֹאֶךָ וּבָרוּךְ אַתָּה בְּצֵאתֶךָ:

ז יִתֵּן יהוה אֶת־אֹיְבֶיךָ הַקָּמִים עָלֶיךָ נִגָּפִים לְפָנֶיךָ בְּדֶרֶךְ אֶחָד יֵצְאוּ ששי

אונקלוס

וְיֵימַר כָּל עַמָּא אָמֵן: כ לִיט, דְּיִשְׁכּוֹב עִם אִתַּת אֲבוּהִי, אֲרֵי גַלִּי כַּנְפָא דַאֲבוּהִי, וְיֵימַר כָּל עַמָּא אָמֵן: כא לִיט, דְּיִשְׁכּוֹב עִם כָּל בְּעִירָא, וְיֵימַר כָּל עַמָּא אָמֵן: כב לִיט, דְּיִשְׁכּוֹב עִם אֲחָתֵיהּ, בַּת אֲבוּהִי אוֹ בַת אִמֵּיהּ, וְיֵימַר כָּל עַמָּא אָמֵן: כג לִיט, דְּיִשְׁכּוֹב עִם חֲמָתֵיהּ, וְיֵימַר כָּל עַמָּא אָמֵן: כד לִיט, דְּיִמְחֵי חַבְרֵיהּ בְּסִתְרָא, וְיֵימַר כָּל עַמָּא אָמֵן: כה לִיט דִּיקַבֵּיל שׁוֹחֲדָא, לְמִקְטַל נְפַשׁ דַּם זַכַּאי, וְיֵימַר כָּל עַמָּא אָמֵן: כו לִיט, דְּלָא יְקַיֵּים, יָת פִּתְגָּמֵי אוֹרָיְתָא הָדָא לְמֶעְבַּד יָתְהוֹן, וְיֵימַר כָּל עַמָּא אָמֵן: כח א וִיהֵי, אִם קַבָּלָא תְקַבֵּיל לְמֵימְרָא

דַּייָ אֱלָהָךְ, לְמִטַּר לְמֶעְבַּד יָת כָּל פִּקּוֹדוֹהִי, דַּאֲנָא מְפַקֵּיד לָךְ יוֹמָא דֵין, וְיִתְּנִנָּךְ, יְיָ אֱלָהָךְ עִלַּאי, עַל כָּל עַמְמֵי אַרְעָא: ב וְיֵיתוֹן עֲלָךְ, כָּל בִּרְכָתָא הָאִלֵּין וְיִדְבְּקֻנָּךְ, אֲרֵי תְקַבֵּיל, לְמֵימְרָא דַּייָ אֱלָהָךְ: ג בְּרִיךְ אַתְּ בְּקַרְתָּא, וּבְרִיךְ אַתְּ בְּחַקְלָא: ד בְּרִיךְ וַלְדָּא דִמְעָךְ, וְאִבָּא דְאַרְעָךְ וּוַלְדָּא דִבְעִירָךְ, בַּקְרֵי תוֹרָךְ וְעֶדְרֵי עָנָךְ: ה בְּרִיךְ סַלָּךְ וְאָצְוָתָךְ: ו בְּרִיךְ אַתְּ בְּמֵיעֲלָךְ, וּבְרִיךְ אַתְּ בְּמִפְּקָךְ: ז יִתֵּין יְיָ יָת בַּעֲלֵי דְבָבָךְ דְּקָיְמִין עֲלָךְ, תְּבִירִין קֳדָמָךְ, בְּאוֹרְחָא חֲדָא יִפְּקוּן

28:5 בָּרוּךְ טַנְאֲךָ וּמִשְׁאַרְתֶּךָ *Your basket and your kneading pan* – These blessings are, by and large, material ones: healthy children, plentiful harvest, safety. Judaism takes a candid view of wealth as God's blessing, to be enjoyed as such. The world is God's creation; therefore it is good, and prosperity is a sign of God's blessing. Asceticism and

▶

8 flee from you in seven. The LORD will send you blessing in your barns and in all
your endeavors. He will bless you in the land that the LORD your God is giving
9 you. The LORD will establish you as His holy people, just as He has sworn to
you, if you keep the LORD your God's commandments and walk in His ways.
10 All the peoples of earth shall see that you are called by the LORD's name, and
11 they shall hold you in awe. The LORD will make you abound in prosperity, in the
fruit of your womb, the fruit of your cattle, and the fruit of your soil in the land
12 that the LORD swore to your ancestors to give you. The LORD will open for you
His treasury of good, the heavens, to give your land rain in its season, to bless all
the work of your hands. You will lend to many nations, and borrow from none.
13 The LORD will make you the head, never the tail. You shall be always above, and
never beneath – if you obey the commandments of the LORD your God that I am
14 charging you with on this day, taking care to keep them, and if you do not stray
from any of the words that I am commanding you today, either to the right or to
the left, to follow other gods and serve them.
15 But if you do not listen to the voice of the LORD your God, taking care to keep
all His commandments and decrees that I am charging you with on this day,
16 all these curses will come upon you and overtake you: Cursed shall you be in
17 the town, and cursed shall you be in the field. Cursed shall be your basket and

רש״י

ז וּבְשִׁבְעָה דְרָכִים יָנוּסוּ לְפָנֶיךָ. כֵּן דֶּרֶךְ הַנִּבְהָלִים לִבְרֹחַ לִהְיוֹת מִתְפַּזְּרִין לְכָל צַד:

gracious, merciful, and holy. He holds that in addition to prescribing or forbidding specific actions, Judaism requires us to develop certain virtues. The Torah is concerned not only with behavior but also with character, not just with *what we do* but also *the kind of person we become*. Ramban (on Leviticus 19:2) locates this idea in the command "Be holy," which, he says, requires us to go beyond the letter of what the law mandates.

Rambam and Ramban believed that there are matters of great religious significance which lie beyond the scope of precise legislation. They cannot be spelled out in terms of exact, exhaustive rules, because life cannot be reduced to an exhaustive list of rules. They have to do with self-restraint, moderation, gentleness, alertness to the suffering of others, and the many other forms of moral literacy which you cannot learn from a book of rules, but only from experience and example.

THE TOKHEḤA

Twice in the Torah – once in Parashat Beḥukotai, the second time here – Moshe voices a series of prophecies of the sufferings that will befall the Jewish people if they fail to honor their mission as the people of God. They are terrifying passages. To this day we read them so quietly that they are hardly audible. Each is known as *tokheḥa*, literally, "remonstration," and that is how we should understand them. Moshe's prophecies take as given that Israel's history is predicated on a covenant with God. Its successes will seem to point to a force greater than itself. On the other hand, if the people break the covenant, the collapse will be dramatic. It will happen because the unity of God is no longer reflected in the unity of the people. The institutions of power will become corrupt. Strains will develop in the social fabric. Prophets will warn of this, but their words will not

ח אֵלֶ֑יךָ וּבְשִׁבְעָ֥ה דְרָכִ֖ים יָנ֥וּסוּ לְפָנֶֽיךָ׃ יְצַ֨ו יְהוָ֤ה אִתְּךָ֙ אֶת־הַבְּרָכָ֔ה
בַּאֲסָמֶ֕יךָ וּבְכֹ֖ל מִשְׁלַ֣ח יָדֶ֑ךָ וּבֵ֣רַכְךָ֔ בָּאָ֕רֶץ אֲשֶׁר־יְהוָ֥ה אֱלֹהֶ֖יךָ נֹתֵ֥ן לָֽךְ׃
ט יְקִֽימְךָ֙ יְהוָ֥ה לוֹ֙ לְעַ֣ם קָד֔וֹשׁ כַּאֲשֶׁ֖ר נִֽשְׁבַּֽע־לָ֑ךְ כִּ֣י תִשְׁמֹ֗ר אֶת־מִצְוֺת֙
י יְהוָ֣ה אֱלֹהֶ֔יךָ וְהָלַכְתָּ֖ בִּדְרָכָֽיו׃ וְרָאוּ֙ כָּל־עַמֵּ֣י הָאָ֔רֶץ כִּ֛י שֵׁ֥ם יְהוָ֖ה נִקְרָ֣א
יא עָלֶ֑יךָ וְיָֽרְא֖וּ מִמֶּֽךָּ׃ וְהוֹתִרְךָ֤ יְהוָה֙ לְטוֹבָ֔ה בִּפְרִ֧י בִטְנְךָ֛ וּבִפְרִ֥י בְהֶמְתְּךָ֖
וּבִפְרִ֣י אַדְמָתֶ֑ךָ עַ֚ל הָֽאֲדָמָ֔ה אֲשֶׁ֨ר נִשְׁבַּ֧ע יְהוָ֛ה לַאֲבֹתֶ֖יךָ לָ֥תֶת לָֽךְ׃
יב יִפְתַּ֣ח יְהוָ֣ה ׀ לְ֠ךָ֠ אֶת־אוֹצָר֨וֹ הַטּ֜וֹב אֶת־הַשָּׁמַ֗יִם לָתֵ֤ת מְטַר־אַרְצְךָ֙
בְּעִתּ֔וֹ וּלְבָרֵ֕ךְ אֵ֖ת כָּל־מַעֲשֵׂ֣ה יָדֶ֑ךָ וְהִלְוִ֙יתָ֙ גּוֹיִ֣ם רַבִּ֔ים וְאַתָּ֖ה לֹ֥א תִלְוֶֽה׃
יג וּנְתָנְךָ֨ יְהוָ֤ה לְרֹאשׁ֙ וְלֹ֣א לְזָנָ֔ב וְהָיִ֙יתָ֙ רַ֣ק לְמַ֔עְלָה וְלֹ֥א תִהְיֶ֖ה לְמָ֑טָּה
כִּֽי־תִשְׁמַ֞ע אֶל־מִצְוֺ֣ת ׀ יְהוָ֣ה אֱלֹהֶ֗יךָ אֲשֶׁ֨ר אָנֹכִ֧י מְצַוְּךָ֛ הַיּ֖וֹם לִשְׁמֹ֥ר
יד וְלַעֲשֽׂוֹת׃ וְלֹ֣א תָס֗וּר מִכָּל־הַדְּבָרִים֙ אֲשֶׁ֨ר אָנֹכִ֜י מְצַוֶּ֥ה אֶתְכֶ֛ם הַיּ֖וֹם
יָמִ֣ין וּשְׂמֹ֑אול לָלֶ֗כֶת אַחֲרֵ֛י אֱלֹהִ֥ים אֲחֵרִ֖ים לְעָבְדָֽם׃
טו וְהָיָ֗ה אִם־לֹ֤א תִשְׁמַע֙ בְּק֨וֹל֙ יְהוָ֣ה אֱלֹהֶ֔יךָ לִשְׁמֹ֤ר לַעֲשׂוֹת֙ אֶת־כָּל־
מִצְוֺתָ֣יו וְחֻקֹּתָ֔יו אֲשֶׁ֛ר אָנֹכִ֥י מְצַוְּךָ֖ הַיּ֑וֹם וּבָ֧אוּ עָלֶ֛יךָ כָּל־הַקְּלָל֥וֹת
טז יז הָאֵ֖לֶּה וְהִשִּׂיגֽוּךָ׃ אָר֥וּר אַתָּ֖ה בָּעִ֑יר וְאָר֥וּר אַתָּ֖ה בַּשָּׂדֶֽה׃ אָר֥וּר טַנְאֲךָ֖

אונקלוס

לְוָתָךְ, וּבְשִׁבְעָא אוֹרְחָן יְעָרְקוּן מִן קֳדָמָךְ: ח יְפַקֵּיד יְיָ לָךְ יָת בִּרְכָן, בְּאוֹצָרָךְ, וּבְכֹל אוֹשָׁטוּת יְדָךְ, וִיבָרְכִנָּךְ, בְּאַרְעָא, דַּייָ אֱלָהָךְ יָהֵיב לָךְ: ט יְקִימִנָּךְ יְיָ קֳדָמוֹהִי לְעַם קַדִּישׁ, כְּמָא דְקַיֵּים לָךְ, אֲרֵי תִטַּר, יָת פִּקּוֹדַיָּא דַּייָ אֱלָהָךְ, וּתְהָךְ בְּאוֹרְחָן דְּתָקְנָן קֳדָמוֹהִי: י וְיִחְזוֹן כָּל עַמְמֵי אַרְעָא, אֲרֵי שְׁמָא דַּייָ אִתְקְרֵי עֲלָךְ, וְיִדְחֲלוּן מִנָּךְ: יא וְיוֹתְרִנָּךְ יְיָ לְטָבָא, בִּוְלָדָא דִּמְעָךְ, וּבִוְלָדָא דִּבְעִירָךְ וּבְאִבָּא דְּאַרְעָךְ, עַל אַרְעָא, דְּקַיֵּים יְיָ, לַאֲבָהָתָךְ לְמִתַּן לָךְ: יב יִפְתַּח יְיָ לָךְ, יָת אוֹצְרֵיהּ טָבָא יָת שְׁמַיָּא, לְמִתַּן מְטַר אַרְעָךְ בְּעִדָּנֵיהּ, וּלְבָרָכָא, יָת כָּל עוֹבָדֵי יְדָךְ, וְתוֹזֵיף לְעַמְמִין סַגִּיאִין, וְאַתְּ לָא תִזִּיף: יג וְיִתְּנִנָּךְ יְיָ תַּקִּיף וְלָא חַלָּשׁ, וּתְהֵי בְּרַם לְעֵילָא, וְלָא תְהֵי לְתַחְתָּא, אֲרֵי תְקַבֵּיל, לְפִקּוֹדַיָּא דַּייָ אֱלָהָךְ, דַּאֲנָא מְפַקְּדָךְ, יוֹמָא דֵין לְמִטַּר וּלְמֶעְבַּד: יד וְלָא תִסְטוֹן, מִכָּל פִּתְגָּמַיָּא דַּאֲנָא מְפַקֵּיד יָתְכוֹן, יוֹמָא דֵין לְיַמִּינָא וְלִסְמָאלָא, לִמְהָךְ, בָּתַר, טָעֲוַת עַמְמַיָּא לְמִפְלַחְהוֹן: טו וִיהֵי, אִם לָא תְקַבֵּיל לְמֵימְרָא דַּייָ אֱלָהָךְ, לְמִטַּר לְמֶעְבַּד יָת כָּל פִּקּוֹדוֹהִי וּקְיָמוֹהִי, דַּאֲנָא מְפַקֵּיד לָךְ יוֹמָא דֵין, וְיֵיתוֹן עֲלָךְ, כָּל לְוָטַיָּא הָאִלֵּין וְיִדְבְּקֻנָּךְ: טז לִיט אַתְּ בְּקַרְתָּא, וְלִיט אַתְּ בְּחַקְלָא: יז לִיט סַלָּךְ,

28:9 **וְהָלַכְתָּ בִּדְרָכָיו** *Walk in His ways* – From this verse, Rambam (*Hilkhot Deot* 1:5), quoting the Talmud (Sota 14a) infers that we are commanded to develop certain traits of character – to be gracious, merciful, and holy, as God is

18 your kneading pan. Cursed shall be the fruit of your womb, the fruit of your
19 land, the calves of your herd, the lambs of your flock. Cursed shall you be when
20 you enter, and cursed shall you be when you leave. The LORD will send upon
you curse, panic, and thwarting in every endeavor you undertake, until you
are destroyed and come to sudden ruin because of the evil you have done in
21 forsaking Me. The LORD will make disease cling to you until it consumes you
22 entirely in the land you are coming into to possess. The LORD will afflict you
with consumption, fever, inflammation, scorching heat and drought, blight and
23 mildew. They will pursue you until you die. The sky over your head will be like
24 bronze, and the earth beneath you iron. The LORD will turn the rain of your
land into powder and dust. It will descend upon you from the sky until you are
25 destroyed. The LORD will cause you to be vanquished before your enemies.

רש"י

כ| **הַמְּאֵרָה.** חִסָּרוֹן, כְּמוֹ "צָרַעַת מַמְאֶרֶת" (ויקרא יג, נא): **הַמְּהוּמָה.** שִׁגּוּשׁ, קוֹל בֶּהָלוֹת:

כב| **בַּשַּׁחֶפֶת.** שֶׁבְּשָׂרוֹ נִשְׁחָף וְנָפוּחַ: **וּבַקַּדַּחַת.** לְשׁוֹן: "כִּי אֵשׁ קָדְחָה בְאַפִּי" (להלן לב, כב), וְהוּא אֵשׁ שֶׁל חוֹלִים, מלוו"י בְּלַעַז, שֶׁהִיא חַמָּה מְאֹד: **וּבַדַּלֶּקֶת.** חַמָּה יוֹתֵר מִקַּדַּחַת, וּמִינֵי חֳלָאִים הֵם: **וּבַחַרְחֻר.** חֹלִי הַמְחַמְּמוֹ תּוֹךְ הַגּוּף וְצָמֵא תָּמִיד לַמַּיִם, וּבְלַעַז אישטרדימנ"ט, לְשׁוֹן: "וְעַצְמִי חָרָה מִנִּי חֹרֶב" (איוב ל, ל), "נָחַר מַפֻּחַ מֵאֵשׁ" (ירמיה ו, כט): **וּבַחֶרֶב.** יָבִיא עָלֶיךָ גְּיָסוֹת: **וּבַשִּׁדָּפוֹן וּבַיֵּרָקוֹן.** מַכַּת תְּבוּאָה שֶׁבַּשָּׂדוֹת: **שִׁדָּפוֹן.** רוּחַ קָדִים, השלי"ד בְּלַעַז: **יֵרָקוֹן.** יֹבֶשׁ, וּפְנֵי הַתְּבוּאָה מַכְסִיפִין וְנֶהֱפָכִין לְיֵרָקוֹן, קרו"א בְּלַעַז: **עַד אָבְדֶךָ.** תַּרְגּוּם: "עַד דְּתֵיבַד", כְּלוֹמַר עַד אַבֵּד אוֹתְךָ, שֶׁתִּכְלֶה מֵאֵלֶיךָ:

כג| **וְהָיוּ שָׁמֶיךָ אֲשֶׁר עַל רֹאשְׁךָ נְחֹשֶׁת.** קְלָלוֹת הַלָּלוּ מֹשֶׁה מִפִּי עַצְמוֹ אֲמָרָן, וְשֶׁבְּתוֹרַת כֹּהֲנִים מִפִּי הַקָּדוֹשׁ בָּרוּךְ הוּא אֲמָרָן כְּמַשְׁמָעָן: "וְאִם לֹא תִשְׁמְעוּ לִי" (ויקרא כו, יד), "וְאִם תֵּלְכוּ עִמִּי קֶרִי" (שם פסוק כא), וְכָאן הוּא אוֹמֵר: "בְּקוֹל ה' אֱלֹהֶיךָ" (לעיל פסוק טו), "יַדְבֵּק ה' בְּךָ" (לעיל פסוק כא), "יַכְּכָה ה'" (לעיל פסוק כב). הֵקֵל מֹשֶׁה בִּקְלָלוֹתָיו לְאָמְרָן בִּלְשׁוֹן יָחִיד, וְגַם כֵּן בִּקְלָלָה זוֹ הֵקֵל, שֶׁבָּרִאשׁוֹנוֹת הוּא אוֹמֵר: "אֶת שְׁמֵיכֶם כַּבַּרְזֶל וְאֶת אַרְצְכֶם כַּנְּחֻשָׁה" (ויקרא כו, יט), שֶׁלֹּא יִהְיוּ הַשָּׁמַיִם מְזִיעִין כְּדֶרֶךְ שֶׁאֵין הַבַּרְזֶל מֵזִיעַ, וּמִתּוֹךְ כָּךְ יְהֵא חֹרֶב בָּעוֹלָם, וְהָאָרֶץ תְּהֵא מְזִיעָה כְּדֶרֶךְ שֶׁהַנְּחֹשֶׁת מֵזִיעַ, וְהִיא מַרְקֶבֶת פֵּרוֹתֶיהָ. וְכָאן הוּא אוֹמֵר: שָׁמֶיךָ נְחֹשֶׁת וְאַרְצְךָ בַּרְזֶל, שֶׁיִּהְיוּ שָׁמַיִם מְזִיעִין, אַף עַל פִּי שֶׁלֹּא יָרִיקוּ מָטָר, מִכָּל מָקוֹם לֹא יִהְיֶה חֹרֶב שֶׁל אֲבַדּוֹן בָּעוֹלָם, וְהָאָרֶץ לֹא תִהְיֶה מְזִיעָה כְּדֶרֶךְ שֶׁאֵין הַבַּרְזֶל מֵזִיעַ, וְאֵין הַפֵּרוֹת מַרְקִיבִין. וּמִכָּל מָקוֹם קְלָלָה הִיא, בֵּין שֶׁהִיא כַּנְּחֹשֶׁת בֵּין שֶׁהִיא כַּבַּרְזֶל לֹא תוֹצִיא פֵּרוֹת, וְכֵן הַשָּׁמַיִם לֹא יָרִיקוּ מָטָר:

כד| **מְטַר אַרְצְךָ אָבָק וְעָפָר.** זִיקָא דְּבָתַר מִטְרָא, מָטָר יוֹרֵד וְלֹא כָל צָרְכּוֹ וְאֵין בּוֹ כְּדֵי לְהַרְבִּיץ אֶת הֶעָפָר, וְהָרוּחַ בָּאָה וּמַעֲלָה אֶת הָאָבָק וּמְכַסֶּה אֶת עֵשֶׂב הַזְּרָעִים שֶׁהֵן לַחִים מִן הַמַּיִם וְנִדְבָּק בָּהֶם, וְנַעֲשֶׂה טִיט וּמִתְיַבֵּשׁ וּמַרְקִיבָן:

The first is the reported speech of God, the second the direct speech of Moshe. The first is directed to the Israelites as a whole; it uses the second-person plural. The second is addressed to individuals, speaking in the singular. The first ends on a note of consolation. Despite the bad things that will happen, God will not abandon the Jewish people. He will remember His covenant with their ancestors. The Jewish people will survive. The second ends bleakly with no consolation offered. The people will be forced back to Egypt, where they will try to sell themselves as slaves but no one will buy them. According to Ramban, the first *tokheḥa* refers to events surrounding the destruction of the First Temple while the second is about the Second Temple and the sufferings of Jews under the Romans. Hope only arises again in Parashat Nitzavim, if Israel "return, you and your children, to the LORD your God, obeying Him with all your heart and all your soul" (30:2).

יח וּמִשְׁאַרְתֶּךָ׃ אָרוּר פְּרִי־בִטְנְךָ וּפְרִי אַדְמָתֶךָ שְׁגַר אֲלָפֶיךָ וְעַשְׁתְּרֹת
יט כ צֹאנֶךָ׃ אָרוּר אַתָּה בְּבֹאֶךָ וְאָרוּר אַתָּה בְּצֵאתֶךָ׃ יְשַׁלַּח יהוה ׀ בְּךָ
אֶת־הַמְּאֵרָה אֶת־הַמְּהוּמָה וְאֶת־הַמִּגְעֶרֶת בְּכָל־מִשְׁלַח יָדְךָ אֲשֶׁר
תַּעֲשֶׂה עַד הִשָּׁמֶדְךָ וְעַד־אֲבָדְךָ מַהֵר מִפְּנֵי רֹעַ מַעֲלָלֶיךָ אֲשֶׁר עֲזַבְתָּנִי׃
כא יַדְבֵּק יהוה בְּךָ אֶת־הַדָּבֶר עַד כַּלֹּתוֹ אֹתְךָ מֵעַל הָאֲדָמָה אֲשֶׁר־אַתָּה
כב בָא־שָׁמָּה לְרִשְׁתָּהּ׃ יַכְּכָה יהוה בַּשַּׁחֶפֶת וּבַקַּדַּחַת וּבַדַּלֶּקֶת וּבַחַרְחֻר
כג וּבַחֶרֶב וּבַשִּׁדָּפוֹן וּבַיֵּרָקוֹן וּרְדָפוּךָ עַד אָבְדֶךָ׃ וְהָיוּ שָׁמֶיךָ אֲשֶׁר עַל־
כד רֹאשְׁךָ נְחֹשֶׁת וְהָאָרֶץ אֲשֶׁר־תַּחְתֶּיךָ בַּרְזֶל׃ יִתֵּן יהוה אֶת־מְטַר אַרְצְךָ
כה אָבָק וְעָפָר מִן־הַשָּׁמַיִם יֵרֵד עָלֶיךָ עַד הִשָּׁמְדָךְ׃ יִתֶּנְךָ יהוה ׀ נִגָּף לִפְנֵי

אונקלוס

וְאָצוּתָךְ: יח לִיט וַלְדָּא דִּמְעָךְ וְאִבָּא דְּאַרְעָךְ, בַּקְרֵי תוֹרָךְ וְעֶדְרֵי
עָנָךְ: יט לִיט אַתְּ בְּמֵיעֲלָךְ, וְלִיט אַתְּ בְּמִפְּקָךְ: כ יְגָרֵי יי בָּךְ, יָת
מְאֵירְתָא יָת שִׁגְשָׁא וְיָת מְזוֹפִיתָא, בְּכָל אוֹשָׁטוּת יְדָךְ דְּתַעֲבֵיד,
עַד דְּתִשְׁתֵּיצֵי וְעַד דְּתֵיבַד בִּפְרִיעַ, מִן קֳדָם, בִּישׁוּת עוֹבָדָךְ
דִּשְׁבַקְתָּא דַּחְלְתִּי: כא יַדְבֵּיק יי, בָּךְ יָת מוֹתָנָא, עַד דִּישֵׁיצֵי יָתָךְ,
מֵעַל אַרְעָא, דְּאַתְּ עָלֵיל לְתַמָּן לְמֵירְתַהּ: כב יִמְחֵינָךְ יי, בְּשַׁחַפְתָּא
וּבְקַדַּחְתָּא וּבְדַלֵּיקְתָא, וּבְחַרְחוּרָא וּבְחַרְבָּא, וּבְשִׁדְפָנָא
וּבְיֵרָקָנָא, וְיִרְדְּפֻנָּךְ עַד דְּתֵיבַד: כג וִיהוֹן שְׁמַיָּא, דְּעִלָּוֵי רֵישָׁךְ
חֲסִינִין כִּנְחָשָׁא מִלְּאַחָתָא מִטְרָא, וְאַרְעָא דִּתְחוֹתָךְ תַּקִּיפָא
כְּבַרְזְלָא מִלְּמֶעְבַּד פֵּירִין: כד יִתֵּין יי, יָת מְטַר אַרְעָךְ אַבְקָא וְעַפְרָא,
מִן שְׁמַיָּא יֵיחוֹת עֲלָךְ, עַד דְּתִשְׁתֵּיצֵי: כה יִתְּנִנָּךְ יי תְּבִיר קֳדָם

be heeded. The people of Israel have always been obstinate. This is both a strength and a weakness. It helped them stand out against the idols of their age. But it also at times made them ungrateful to God, unmindful of their vulnerability, indifferent to their vocation.

The result, Moshe warns, will be catastrophe. The nation that once seemed invincible will be defeated. Worse, it will sometimes seem (as it did to Josephus, witnessing the disastrous revolt against Rome) as if Jews were more intent on fighting other Jews than the enemy at the gates. The people who once seemed to be under the special protection of God will now seem to be abandoned by God. As Moshe puts it in the *tokheḥa*: "You will become an object of horror, a proverb and a byword among all the peoples into whose midst the Lord will lead you" (Deut. 28:37).

The significance of Israel's exile is not merely geographical, but political and spiritual as well. Jews will no longer be under the unmediated, direct sovereignty of God. They will be under the control of the rulers in whose lands they live. Their fate will depend on the whim of a king or the shifting winds of popular opinion. In this sense *galut*, exile, is a metaphysical dislocation – a lack of freedom in every sense of the word. The Torah calls this the "hiding of the face" of God (31:18).

Major Jewish thinkers of the Middle Ages, such as Rabbi Yehuda HaLevi and Ramban, agreed on this: that divine providence governs the affairs of Israel only when they exist as a sovereign people in their own land. This means that *what happens to the Jewish people in exile is not the work of God but of human beings*. Exile is the loss of the protection of God and subjection, instead, to human powers.

There are many differences between the two *tokheḥot*.

You will come at them from one direction but flee before them in seven. You
26 will be an object of horror to all the kingdoms on earth. Your corpses will be
food for all the birds of the sky, for the beasts of the earth; there will be no one
27 to make them afraid. The LORD will afflict you with the boils of Egypt, with
28 hemorrhoids, rashes, and scabs, from which you shall never recover. The LORD
29 will afflict you with insanity, blindness, confusion of mind. You will grope at
noon as a blind man gropes in darkness. Your way will not prosper. Day after
day, you will be abused and looted, and no one will be there to rescue you.
30 You will betroth a woman and some other man will lie with her. You will build
a house, but will not live there. You will plant a vineyard, but not harvest its
31 fruit. Your ox will be slaughtered before your eyes, but you will not eat of it.
Your donkey will be stolen in front of you, and never return. Your sheep will be
32 given to your enemies, and no one will be there to rescue you. Your sons and
daughters will be given over to another people. You will see it with your own
33 eyes and pine for them all through the day but have no power to act. A people
that you do not know will eat the fruit of your land and of your labor. You will
34 be incessantly abused and crushed. The sights you see will drive you to insanity.
35 The LORD will strike your knees and thighs with incurable infection, spreading
36 from the sole of your foot to the crown of your head. The LORD will bring you
and the king you set over you to a nation that neither you nor your ancestors

רש״י

כה) **לְזַעֲוָה.** לְאֵימָה וּלְזִיעַ, שֶׁיָּזוּעוּ כָּל שׁוֹמְעֵי מַכּוֹתֶיךָ מִמְּךָ, וְיֹאמְרוּ: אוֹי לָנוּ שֶׁלֹּא יָבֹא עָלֵינוּ כְּדֶרֶךְ שֶׁבָּא עַל אֵלּוּ:

כז) **בִּשְׁחִין מִצְרַיִם.** רַע הָיָה מְאֹד, לַח מִבַּחוּץ וְיָבֵשׁ מִבִּפְנִים, כִּדְאִיתָא בִּבְכוֹרוֹת (דף מא ע״א): **גָּרָב.** שְׁחִין לַח: **חָרֶס.** שְׁחִין יָבֵשׁ כַּחֶרֶס:

כח) **וּבְתִמְהוֹן לֵבָב.** אֹטֶם הַלֵּב, אשטורדישו״ן בְּלַעַז:

כט) **עָשׁוּק.** בְּכָל מַעֲשֶׂיךָ יְהִי עִרְעָר:

ל) **יִשְׁגָּלֶנָּה.** לְשׁוֹן שֵׁגַל, פִּילֶגֶשׁ, וְהַכָּתוּב כִּנָּהוּ לְשֶׁבַח ״יִשְׁכָּבֶנָּה״, וְתִקּוּן סוֹפְרִים הוּא זֶה: **תְּחַלְּלֶנּוּ.** בַּשָּׁנָה הָרְבִיעִית לֶאֱכֹל פִּרְיוֹ:

לב) **וְכָלוֹת אֲלֵיהֶם.** מְצַפּוֹת אֲלֵיהֶם שֶׁיָּשׁוּבוּ וְאֵינָם שָׁבִים. כָּל תּוֹחֶלֶת שֶׁאֵינָהּ בָּאָה קְרוּיָה כִּלְיוֹן עֵינַיִם:

Aniyyim 9:3). Powerless, stateless, and often living under conditions of great poverty, Jews throughout the centuries of their dispersion created a communal equivalent of a welfare state. They did so voluntarily, because it was a mitzva, because it is what Jews do, and because they knew that no one else would do it for them. As Rambam notes in another aside (*Hilkhot Mattenot Aniyyim* 10:2):

All Jews and those attached to them are like brothers, as it is said, "You are children of the LORD your God" (Deut. 14:1) – and if a brother will not show mercy to his brother, then who else will have mercy on him? And to whom can the poor of Israel look for help? To those nations who hate and persecute them? They can look for help only to their brethren.

Jews were often robbed of sustenance and security, yet they retained the freedom to choose how to respond.

אֹיְבֶיךָ בְּדֶרֶךְ אֶחָד תֵּצֵא אֵלָיו וּבְשִׁבְעָה דְרָכִים תָּנוּס לְפָנָיו וְהָיִיתָ
כו לְזַעֲוָה לְכֹל מַמְלְכוֹת הָאָרֶץ׃ וְהָיְתָה נִבְלָתְךָ לְמַאֲכָל לְכָל־עוֹף
כז הַשָּׁמַיִם וּלְבֶהֱמַת הָאָרֶץ וְאֵין מַחֲרִיד׃ יַכְּכָה יְהוָה בִּשְׁחִין מִצְרַיִם
כח ובעפלים וּבַגָּרָב וּבֶחָרֶס אֲשֶׁר לֹא־תוּכַל לְהֵרָפֵא׃ יַכְּכָה יְהוָה בְּשִׁגָּעוֹן וּבַטְּחֹרִים
כט וּבְעִוָּרוֹן וּבְתִמְהוֹן לֵבָב׃ וְהָיִיתָ מְמַשֵּׁשׁ בַּצָּהֳרַיִם כַּאֲשֶׁר יְמַשֵּׁשׁ הָעִוֵּר
בָּאֲפֵלָה וְלֹא תַצְלִיחַ אֶת־דְּרָכֶיךָ וְהָיִיתָ אַךְ עָשׁוּק וְגָזוּל כָּל־הַיָּמִים
ל וְאֵין מוֹשִׁיעַ׃ אִשָּׁה תְאָרֵשׂ וְאִישׁ אַחֵר ישגלנה בַּיִת תִּבְנֶה וְלֹא־תֵשֵׁב יִשְׁכָּבֶנָּה
לא בּוֹ כֶּרֶם תִּטַּע וְלֹא תְחַלְּלֶנּוּ׃ שׁוֹרְךָ טָבוּחַ לְעֵינֶיךָ וְלֹא תֹאכַל מִמֶּנּוּ
חֲמֹרְךָ גָּזוּל מִלְּפָנֶיךָ וְלֹא יָשׁוּב לָךְ צֹאנְךָ נְתֻנוֹת לְאֹיְבֶיךָ וְאֵין לְךָ
לב מוֹשִׁיעַ׃ בָּנֶיךָ וּבְנֹתֶיךָ נְתֻנִים לְעַם אַחֵר וְעֵינֶיךָ רֹאוֹת וְכָלוֹת אֲלֵיהֶם
לג כָּל־הַיּוֹם וְאֵין לְאֵל יָדֶךָ׃ פְּרִי אַדְמָתְךָ וְכָל־יְגִיעֲךָ יֹאכַל עַם אֲשֶׁר
לד לֹא־יָדָעְתָּ וְהָיִיתָ רַק עָשׁוּק וְרָצוּץ כָּל־הַיָּמִים׃ וְהָיִיתָ מְשֻׁגָּע מִמַּרְאֵה
לה עֵינֶיךָ אֲשֶׁר תִּרְאֶה׃ יַכְּכָה יְהוָה בִּשְׁחִין רָע עַל־הַבִּרְכַּיִם וְעַל־הַשֹּׁקַיִם
לו אֲשֶׁר לֹא־תוּכַל לְהֵרָפֵא מִכַּף רַגְלְךָ וְעַד קָדְקֳדֶךָ׃ יוֹלֵךְ יְהוָה אֹתְךָ

אונקלוס

סְנָאָךְ, בְּאוֹרְחָא חֲדָא תִּפּוֹק לְוָתֵיהּ, וּבְשִׁבְעָא אוֹרְחָן תְּעֵרוֹק מִן קֳדָמוֹהִי, וּתְהֵי לְזִיעַ, לְכֹל מַלְכְוָת אַרְעָא: כו וּתְהֵי נְבִילְתָךְ מְשַׁגְּרָא לְמֵיכַל, לְכָל עוֹפָא דִּשְׁמַיָּא וּלְבְעִירָא דְּאַרְעָא, וְלֵית דְּמָנִיד: כז יִמְחֵינָךְ יְיָ, בְּשִׁחְנָא דְּמִצְרָאֵי וּבִטְחוֹרִין, וּבִגְרַבָּא וּבַחֲרַס יַבִּישׁ, דְּלָא תִכּוֹל לְאִתַּסָּאָה: כח יִמְחֵינָךְ יְיָ, בְּטַפְשׁוּתָא וּבְסַמְיוּתָא, וּבְשַׁעֲמִימוּת לִבָּא: כט וּתְהֵי מְמַשֵּׁישׁ בְּטִיהֲרָא, כְּמָא דִּימַשֵּׁישׁ עַוִּירָא בְּקַבְלָא, וְלָא תַצְלַח יָת אוֹרְחָתָךְ, וּתְהֵי, בְּרַם עֲשִׁיק וַאֲנִיס, כָּל יוֹמַיָּא וְלֵית דְּפָרִיק: ל אִתְּתָא תֵּירוֹס, וּגְבַר אָחֳרָן יִשְׁכְּבִנַּהּ, בֵּיתָא תִבְנֵי וְלָא תֵיתֵב בֵּיהּ, כַּרְמָא תִצּוֹב וְלָא תַחֲלְנֵיהּ: לא תּוֹרָךְ יְהֵי נְכִיס לְעֵינָךְ, וְלָא תֵיכוֹל מִנֵּיהּ, חֲמָרָךְ יְהֵי אָנִיס מִן קֳדָמָךְ, וְלָא יְתוּב לָךְ, עָנָךְ מְסִירָן לְבַעֲלֵי דְּבָבָךְ, וְלֵית לָךְ פָּרִיק: לב בְּנָךְ וּבְנָתָךְ, מְסִירִין לְעַם אָחֳרָן וְעֵינָךְ חָזְיָן, וְיָסוּפָן בְּגַלָּלְהוֹן כָּל יוֹמָא, וְלֵית חֵילָא בִּידָךְ: לג אִבָּא דְאַרְעָךְ וְכָל לֵיאוּתָךְ, יֵיכוֹל עַם דְּלָא יְדַעְתָּא, וּתְהֵי, בְּרַם, עֲשִׁיק וּרְעִיעַ כָּל יוֹמַיָּא: לד וּתְהֵי מִשְׁתַּטֵּי, מֵחֵיזוּ עֵינָךְ דְּתֶהֱוֵי חָזֵי: לה יִמְחֵינָךְ יְיָ בְּשִׁחְנָא בִישָׁא, עַל רְכֻבִּין וְעַל שָׁקַן, דְּלָא תִכּוֹל לְאִתַּסָּאָה, מִפַּרְסַת רַגְלָךְ וְעַד מוֹחָךְ: לו יַגְלֵי יְיָ יָתָךְ,

28:33 פְּרִי אַדְמָתְךָ וְכָל־יְגִיעֲךָ יֹאכַל עַם *A people… will eat the fruit… of your labor* – Rambam, the austere twelfth-century sage, was not a man to confuse law with narrative. Yet in his law code, the *Mishneh Torah,* he is moved to a note of wonder: "We have never seen nor heard of an Israelite community that does not have an alms fund" (*Hilkhot Mattenot*

▷

37 have known. There you will worship other gods, of wood and of stone. You will
become an object of horror, a proverb, and a byword among all the peoples
38 into whose midst the LORD will lead you. You will carry much seed into the
39 field but gather little, because locusts will eat it. You will plant vineyards and
cultivate them, but you will not drink the wine or gather the grapes, because
40 worms will devour them. You will have olive trees throughout your country,
41 but you will have no oil for anointing, because the olives will fall away. You will
bear sons and daughters, but they will not remain yours, for they will be taken
42 into captivity. Crickets will take over all your trees and the fruit of your land.
43 Strangers in your midst will rise ever higher above you, while you descend ever
44 further beneath. They will lend to you but you will be unable to lend to them.
45 They will be the head and you will be the tail. All these curses will come upon
you; they will pursue and overtake you, until you are destroyed – because you
did not listen to the voice of the LORD your God, keeping the commandments
46 and decrees with which He charged you. They will be a sign and portent to
47 you and your descendants forever. Because you did not serve the LORD your
48 God with joy and with a heart content in the abundance of all things, you shall

רש״י

לז **לְשַׁמָּה.** אשטורדישו״ן, כָּל הָרוֹאֶה אוֹתְךָ יִשֹּׁם עָלֶיךָ: **לְמָשָׁל.** כְּשֶׁתָּבֹא מַכָּה רָעָה עַל אָדָם יֹאמְרוּ: זוֹ דוֹמָה לְמַכַּת פְּלוֹנִי: **וְלִשְׁנִינָה.** לְשׁוֹן "וְשִׁנַּנְתָּם" (לעיל ו, ז), יְדַבְּרוּ בְּךָ, וְכֵן תַּרְגּוּמוֹ: "וּלְשׁוֹעִי", לְשׁוֹן סִפּוּר, 'וְאִשְׁתָּעִי':

לח **יַחְסְלֶנּוּ.** יְכַלֶּנּוּ, וְעַל שֵׁם כָּךְ נִקְרָא 'חָסִיל', שֶׁמְּכַלֶּה אֶת הַכֹּל:

מ **כִּי יִשַּׁל.** יַשִּׁיר פֵּרוֹתָיו, לְשׁוֹן: "וְנָשַׁל הַבַּרְזֶל" (לעיל יט, ה):

מב **יְיָרֵשׁ הַצְּלָצַל.** יַעֲשֶׂנּוּ הָאַרְבֶּה רָשׁ מִן הַפְּרִי: **יְיָרֵשׁ.** יַעֲנִי: **הַצְּלָצַל.** מִין אַרְבֶּה. וְאִי אֶפְשָׁר לְפָרֵשׁ 'יְיָרֵשׁ' לְשׁוֹן יְרֻשָּׁה, שֶׁאִם כֵּן הָיָה לוֹ לִכְתֹּב 'יִירַשׁ'; וְלֹא לְשׁוֹן הוֹרָשָׁה וְגֵרוּשִׁין, שֶׁאִם כֵּן הָיָה לוֹ לִכְתֹּב 'יוֹרִישׁ':

מז **מֵרֹב כֹּל.** בְּעוֹד שֶׁהָיָה לְךָ כָּל טוּב:

Joylessness may not be the best way to live, but it is not a sin, let alone one that warrants a litany of curses. Yet the Torah attributes to it a national disaster. Why?

Though our history has been shot through with tragedy, Jews did not lose the ability to rejoice, to sing the LORD's song even in a strange land. There are Eastern faiths that promise peace of mind if we can train ourselves into habits of acceptance. Epicurus taught his disciples to avoid risks like marriage or a career in public life. Neither of these approaches is to be negated, yet Judaism is not a religion of acceptance, nor have Jews tended to seek the risk-free life. We can survive the failures and defeats if we do not lose the capacity for joy. Moshe insists that the capacity for joy is a vital part of the resilience that gives the Jewish people the strength to endure. Without it, we become vulnerable to the multiple disasters set out in the curses in this *parasha*. Celebrating together binds us as a people. Joy connects us to others and to God. It is the ability to celebrate life as such, knowing that whatever tomorrow may bring, we are here today, under God's heaven, in the universe He made, to which He has invited us as His guests.

A people that can know insecurity and still feel joy is one that can never be fully defeated, for its spirit can never be broken nor its hope destroyed.

28:48 **אֹיְבֶיךָ אֲשֶׁר יְשַׁלְּחֶנּוּ יהוה בָּךְ** *The enemies whom the LORD*

וְאֶת־מַלְכְּךָ אֲשֶׁר תָּקִים עָלֶיךָ אֶל־גּוֹי אֲשֶׁר לֹא־יָדַעְתָּ אַתָּה וַאֲבֹתֶיךָ
לז וְעָבַדְתָּ שָּׁם אֱלֹהִים אֲחֵרִים עֵץ וָאָבֶן׃ וְהָיִיתָ לְשַׁמָּה לְמָשָׁל וְלִשְׁנִינָה
לח בְּכֹל הָעַמִּים אֲשֶׁר־יְנַהֶגְךָ יהוה שָׁמָּה׃ זֶרַע רַב תּוֹצִיא הַשָּׂדֶה וּמְעַט
לט תֶּאֱסֹף כִּי יַחְסְלֶנּוּ הָאַרְבֶּה׃ כְּרָמִים תִּטַּע וְעָבָדְתָּ וְיַיִן לֹא־תִשְׁתֶּה וְלֹא
מ תֶאֱגֹר כִּי תֹאכְלֶנּוּ הַתֹּלָעַת׃ זֵיתִים יִהְיוּ לְךָ בְּכָל־גְּבוּלֶךָ וְשֶׁמֶן לֹא
מא תָסוּךְ כִּי יִשַּׁל זֵיתֶךָ׃ בָּנִים וּבָנוֹת תּוֹלִיד וְלֹא־יִהְיוּ לָךְ כִּי יֵלְכוּ בַּשֶּׁבִי׃
מב מג כָּל־עֵצְךָ וּפְרִי אַדְמָתֶךָ יְיָרֵשׁ הַצְּלָצַל׃ הַגֵּר אֲשֶׁר בְּקִרְבְּךָ יַעֲלֶה עָלֶיךָ
מד מַעְלָה מָּעְלָה וְאַתָּה תֵרֵד מַטָּה מָּטָּה׃ הוּא יַלְוְךָ וְאַתָּה לֹא תַלְוֶנּוּ
מה הוּא יִהְיֶה לְרֹאשׁ וְאַתָּה תִּהְיֶה לְזָנָב׃ וּבָאוּ עָלֶיךָ כָּל־הַקְּלָלוֹת הָאֵלֶּה
וּרְדָפוּךָ וְהִשִּׂיגוּךָ עַד הִשָּׁמְדָךְ כִּי־לֹא שָׁמַעְתָּ בְּקוֹל יהוה אֱלֹהֶיךָ
מו לִשְׁמֹר מִצְוֺתָיו וְחֻקֹּתָיו אֲשֶׁר צִוָּךְ׃ וְהָיוּ בְךָ לְאוֹת וּלְמוֹפֵת וּבְזַרְעֲךָ
מז עַד־עוֹלָם׃ תַּחַת אֲשֶׁר לֹא־עָבַדְתָּ אֶת־יהוה אֱלֹהֶיךָ בְּשִׂמְחָה וּבְטוּב
מח לֵבָב מֵרֹב כֹּל׃ וְעָבַדְתָּ אֶת־אֹיְבֶיךָ אֲשֶׁר יְשַׁלְּחֶנּוּ יהוה בָּךְ בְּרָעָב

אונקלוס

וְיָת מַלְכָּךְ דִּתְקִים עֲלָךְ, לְעַם, דְּלָא יְדַעְתָּא אַתְּ וַאֲבָהָתָךְ, וְתִפְלַח תַּמָּן, לְעַמְמַיָּא, פָּלְחֵי טַעֲוָתָא אָעָא וְאַבְנָא: לז וּתְהֵי לְצָדוּ, לְמַתְל וּלְשׁוֹעִי, בְּכֹל עַמְמַיָּא, דִּידַבְּרִנָּךְ יי לְתַמָּן: לח בַּר זְרַע סַגִּי תַּפֵּיק לַחֲקְלָא, וּזְעֵיר תִּכְנוֹשׁ, אֲרֵי יַחְסְלִנֵּיהּ גּוֹבָא: לט כַּרְמִין תִּצּוּב וְתִפְלַח, וַחֲמַר לָא תִשְׁתֵּי וְלָא תִכְנוֹשׁ, אֲרֵי תֵיכְלִנֵּיהּ תּוֹלַעְתָּא: מ זֵיתִין, יְהוֹן לָךְ בְּכָל תְּחוּמָךְ, וּמְשַׁחָא לָא תְסוּךְ, אֲרֵי יִתְּרוּן זֵיתָךְ: מא בְּנִין וּבְנָן תְּלִיד, וְלָא יְהוֹן לָךְ, אֲרֵי יְהָכוּן בְּשִׁבְיָא: מב כָּל אִילָנָךְ וְאִבָּא דְאַרְעָךְ, יַחְסְנִנֵּיהּ סַקָּאָה: מג תּוֹתַב עָרֵל דְּבֵינָךְ, יְהֵי סָלֵיק עֵיל מִנָּךְ לְעֵילָא לְעֵילָא, וְאַתְּ תְּהֵי נָחֵית לְתַחְתָּא לְתַחְתָּא: מד הוּא יוֹזְפִנָּךְ, וְאַתְּ לָא תוֹזְפִנֵּיהּ, הוּא יְהֵי תַקִּיף, וְאַתְּ תְּהֵי חַלָּשׁ: מה וְיֵיתוֹן עֲלָךְ כָּל לְוָטַיָּא הָאִלֵּין, וְיִרְדְּפֻנָּךְ וְיִדְבְּקֻנָּךְ, עַד דְּתִשְׁתֵּיצֵי, אֲרֵי לָא קַבֵּילְתָּא, לְמֵימְרָא דַּיי אֱלָהָךְ, לְמִטַּר, פִּקּוֹדוֹהִי וּקְיָמוֹהִי דְּפַקְּדָךְ: מו וִיהוֹן בָּךְ, לְאָתִין וּלְמוֹפְתִין, וּבִבְנָךְ עַד עָלְמָא: מז חֲלָף, דְּלָא פְלַחְתָּא קֳדָם יי אֱלָהָךְ, בְּחֶדְוָא וּבְשַׁפִּירוּת לִבָּא, מִסַּגִּי כוֹלָא: מח וְתִפְלַח יָת בַּעֲלֵי דְבָבָךְ, דִּיגָרֵינּוּן יי בָּךְ, בְּכַפְנָא

28:47 תַּחַת אֲשֶׁר לֹא־עָבַדְתָּ אֶת־יהוה אֱלֹהֶיךָ בְּשִׂמְחָה *Because you did not serve the* L*ORD your God with joy* – In the *tokheḥa* of Parashat Beḥukotai, God spoke of a fundamental breach between Israel and its Redeemer. The language was harsh: "If you spurn My decrees and despise My laws" (Lev. 26:15); "If you still walk contrary to Me" (26:21). This is an active rebellion of the Israelites against God. In Parashat Ki Tavo, the language is different. It does not speak of a willful, petulant nation deliberately spurning God, but of something that hardly sounds like a sin at all. Why would Israel suffer? "Because you did not serve the LORD your God with joy and with a heart content in the abundance of all things."

serve the enemies whom the LORD will send against you, in hunger and thirst,
in nakedness and the lack of all things. He will lay an iron yoke upon your neck
49 until He has destroyed you. The LORD will bring against you a nation from afar,
from the end of the earth, and it will dart down on you like an eagle; a nation
50 whose language you do not understand, a fierce-faced nation with no respect
51 for the old, no mercy for the young. They will eat the fruit of your cattle and the
fruit of your land until you are destroyed. They will leave you no grain, wine,
or oil, no calves of your herd or lambs of your flock, until they have brought
52 you to death. They will lay siege to you in all the towns throughout your land
until the high, fortified walls in which you placed your trust have fallen. In all
your towns throughout the land the LORD your God has given you, they will
53 lay siege to you. And you will eat the fruit of your womb. When your enemies
besiege you, so fiercely will they crush you that you will eat the flesh of your
54 own sons and daughters whom the LORD your God has given you. Even the
most gentle and sensitive of men among you will begrudge food to his own

רש"י

מט **כַּאֲשֶׁר יִדְאֶה הַנָּשֶׁר.** פִּתְאֹם, וְדֶרֶךְ מַגְלַחַת וְיַקַלּוּ סוּסָיו: **לֹא תִשְׁמַע לְשֹׁנוֹ.** שֶׁלֹּא תַכִּיר לְשׁוֹנוֹ. וְכֵן: "תִּשְׁמַע חֲלוֹם לִפְתֹּר אֹתוֹ" (בראשית מא, טו), וְכֵן: "כִּי שֹׁמֵעַ יוֹסֵף" (שם מב, כג), אינטינדר"א בְּלַעַז:

נב **עַד רֶדֶת חֹמֹתֶיךָ.** לְשׁוֹן רִדּוּי וְכִבּוּשׁ:

נג **וְאָכַלְתָּ... בְּשַׂר בָּנֶיךָ... בְּמָצוֹר.** מֵחֲמַת שֶׁיִּהְיוּ צָרִים עַל הָעִיר וְיִהְיֶה שָׁם "מָצוֹק", עָקַת רְעָבוֹן:

נד **הָרַךְ בְּךָ.** הָרַחְמָנִי וְרַךְ הַלֵּבָב עַל בָּנָיו, תֵּרַע עֵינוֹ בָּהֶם לְהַעֲלִים עֵינוֹ מֵהֶם, מִתֵּת לְאַחַד מֵהֶם מִבְּשַׂר אֲחֵיהֶם אֲשֶׁר יֹאכֵל: **וּבְיֶתֶר בָּנָיו אֲשֶׁר יוֹתִיר.** מִן הַשְּׁחוּטִין שֶׁיִּשְׁחַט לְמַאֲכָלוֹ, תְּהֵא עֵינוֹ רָעָה וְצָרָה בָּהֶם מִלִּתֵּן לָהֶם מִבְּשַׂר הַנִּשְׁחָטִין:

by almost superhuman achievements of national unity and moral purpose will Israel survive as a nation in its land. So it was in biblical times; so it is today.

28:54 **תֵּרַע עֵינוֹ** *Will begrudge food* – The nightmare vision of this passage returns as reportage in the book of Lamentations. The deepest horror of all, we come to understand, is not the suffering inflicted on the people, but what they will discover they have become (compare v. 57 with Lam. 4:10).

Primo Levi survived Auschwitz. In his book *If This Is a Man,* he describes his experiences there. According to Levi, the worst time of all was when the Nazis left in January 1945, fearing the Russian advance. All prisoners who could walk were taken on the brutal death marches. The only people left in the camp were those too ill to move. For ten days they were left alone with only scraps of food and fuel. Levi describes how he worked to light a fire and bring some warmth to his fellow prisoners, many of them dying. He then writes:

> When the broken window was repaired and the stove began to spread its heat, something seemed to relax in everyone, and at that moment Towarowski (a Franco-Pole of twenty-three, typhus) proposed to the others that each of them offer a slice of bread to us three who had been working. And so it was agreed.
>
> Only a day before a similar event would have been inconceivable. The law of the Lager [concentration camps] said: "Eat your own bread, and if you can, that

וּבְצָמָא וּבְעֵירֹם וּבְחֹסֶר כֹּל וְנָתַן עֹל בַּרְזֶל עַל־צַוָּארֶךָ עַד הִשְׁמִידוֹ
אֹתָךְ׃ יִשָּׂא יְהוָה עָלֶיךָ גּוֹי מֵרָחֹק מִקְצֵה הָאָרֶץ כַּאֲשֶׁר יִדְאֶה הַנָּשֶׁר מט
גּוֹי אֲשֶׁר לֹא־תִשְׁמַע לְשֹׁנוֹ׃ גּוֹי עַז פָּנִים אֲשֶׁר לֹא־יִשָּׂא פָנִים לְזָקֵן נ
וְנַעַר לֹא יָחֹן׃ וְאָכַל פְּרִי בְהֶמְתְּךָ וּפְרִי־אַדְמָתְךָ עַד הִשָּׁמְדָךְ אֲשֶׁר נא
לֹא־יַשְׁאִיר לְךָ דָּגָן תִּירוֹשׁ וְיִצְהָר שְׁגַר אֲלָפֶיךָ וְעַשְׁתְּרֹת צֹאנֶךָ עַד
הַאֲבִידוֹ אֹתָךְ׃ וְהֵצַר לְךָ בְּכָל־שְׁעָרֶיךָ עַד רֶדֶת חֹמֹתֶיךָ הַגְּבֹהֹת נב
וְהַבְּצֻרוֹת אֲשֶׁר אַתָּה בֹּטֵחַ בָּהֵן בְּכָל־אַרְצֶךָ וְהֵצַר לְךָ בְּכָל־שְׁעָרֶיךָ
בְּכָל־אַרְצְךָ אֲשֶׁר נָתַן יְהוָה אֱלֹהֶיךָ לָךְ׃ וְאָכַלְתָּ פְרִי־בִטְנְךָ בְּשַׂר נג
בָּנֶיךָ וּבְנֹתֶיךָ אֲשֶׁר נָתַן־לְךָ יְהוָה אֱלֹהֶיךָ בְּמָצוֹר וּבְמָצוֹק אֲשֶׁר־יָצִיק
לְךָ אֹיְבֶךָ׃ הָאִישׁ הָרַךְ בְּךָ וְהֶעָנֹג מְאֹד תֵּרַע עֵינוֹ בְאָחִיו וּבְאֵשֶׁת נד

אונקלוס

וּבִצְהוֹתָא, וּבְעַרְטִלָּיוּתָא וּבַחֲסִירוּת כּוֹלָא, וְיִתֵּין, נִיר דְּפַרְזְלָא עַל
צַוְּרָךְ, עַד דִּישֵׁיצֵי יָתָךְ׃ מט יַיְתֵי יי עֲלָךְ עַם מֵרָחִיק מִסְּיָפֵי אַרְעָא,
כְּמָא דְּמִשְׁתְּדֵי נִשְׁרָא, עַמָּא, דְּלָא תִשְׁמַע לִישָּׁנֵיהּ׃ נ עַם תַּקִּיף
אַפִּין, דְּלָא נָסֵיב אַפֵּי סָבָא, וְעַל יָנְקָא לָא מְרַחֵים׃ נא וְיֵיכוֹל, וַלְדָּא
דִּבְעִירָךְ וְאִבָּא דְּאַרְעָךְ עַד דְּתִשְׁתֵּיצֵי, דְּלָא יַשְׁאַר לָךְ, עֲבוּרָא
חַמְרָא וּמִשְׁחָא, בַּקְרֵי תוֹרָךְ וְעֶדְרֵי עָנָךְ, עַד דְּיוֹבֵיד יָתָךְ׃ נב וִיעִיק
לָךְ בְּכָל קִרְוָךְ, עַד דְּיִכְבּוֹשׁ שׁוּרָךְ רָמַיָּא וּכְרִיכַיָּא, דְּאַתְּ רָחִיץ
לְאִשְׁתֵּיזָבָא בְּהוֹן בְּכָל אַרְעָךְ, וִיעִיק לָךְ בְּכָל קִרְוָךְ, בְּכָל אַרְעָךְ,
דִּיהַב יי אֱלָהָךְ לָךְ׃ נג וְתֵיכוֹל וַלְדָּא דִּמְעָךְ, בְּסַר בְּנָךְ וּבְנָתָךְ,
דִּיהַב לָךְ יי אֱלָהָךְ, בִּצְיָרָא וּבְעָקְתָא, דִּיעִיק לָךְ סָנְאָךְ׃ נד גַּבְרָא
דְּרַכִּיךְ בָּךְ, וּדְמְפַנַּק לַחֲדָא, תִּבְאַשׁ עֵינֵיהּ בַּאֲחוּהִי וּבְאִתַּת

will send against you – It is one of the essential aspects of the Torah, as the Sages and Rambam noted, that it can be read at many levels. The blessings and curses of our *parasha* are both supernatural and natural. On the one hand, the vision of the Torah is that Israel's destiny depends on divine intervention in history. In that sense it is supernatural. On the other hand, there is a sense that there is something natural at work also. Not by chance are the children of Israel and the land of Israel exemplars of the relationship between humanity and God. The people of Israel will always be small: "You are the smallest of all peoples" (Deut. 7:7). The land of Israel will always be vulnerable, occupying as it does a strategic location between three continents – Europe, Africa, and Asia – and two ancient birthplaces of empire, the Nile and Tigris-Euphrates valleys. Israel is a place from which it is impossible to build an empire.

Lacking a constant, predictable water supply, its people will constantly find themselves looking up to the heavens for rain. They will know that (agricultural) prosperity is not entirely in their own hands. They will know also that there will be times of drought and famine during which the poor (small farmers) will be dependent on the generosity of others. The strength of the social bond – tzedaka, the charity which is also justice – will be constantly tested. Any age in which the rich fail in their responsibilities to those less well-off, or in which the sellers exploit the buyers, will be full of danger because the nation can only survive on the basis of a strong sense of collective responsibility. Only

55 brother, his beloved wife, those of his children who survive, and give none
of them any of the flesh of his own children when he eats them, because he
has nothing else left, so fiercely will the besieging enemy crush you in all your
56 towns. The most gentle and sensitive of women among you, so sensitive and
gentle that she would not venture to set the sole of her foot on the ground, will
begrudge food to the husband she loves, and to her own son and daughter,
57 the afterbirth from her womb and the children she bears – she will eat them
in secret for lack of anything else, so fiercely will the besieging enemy crush
58 you in your towns. If you do not take care to keep all the words of this Law,
written in this scroll, to revere this glorious, awesome name, the Lord your
59 God, then the Lord will overwhelm you and your descendants with terrible
60 and relentless plagues, and malignant and chronic diseases. He will bring back
on you all the diseases of Egypt that you dreaded, and they will cling to you.
61 Every other sickness and plague – even those not recorded in this scroll of the
62 Law – the Lord will inflict upon you until you are destroyed. Though you
were once as numerous as the stars in the sky, you will be left but a handful of
63 souls, because you did not listen to the Lord your God. And as the Lord once
delighted in making you prosperous and numerous, so will the Lord delight
in bringing you to ruin and destruction. You will be torn away from the land

רש״י

נו **תֵּרַע עֵינָהּ בְּאִישׁ חֵיקָהּ וּבִבְנָהּ וּבְבִתָּהּ.** הַגְּדוֹלִים:

נז **וּבְשִׁלְיָתָהּ.** בָּנִים הַקְּטַנִּים, בְּכֻלָּן תְּהֵא עֵינָהּ צָרָה כְּשֶׁתֹּאכַל אֶת הָאֶחָד מִלָּתֵת לַאֲשֶׁר אֶצְלָהּ מִן הַבָּשָׂר: **וּבְבָנֶיהָ אֲשֶׁר תֵּלֵד.** תֵּרַע עֵינָהּ לְשָׁחֲטָם וּלְאָכְלָם בְּחֹסֶר כֹּל בַּסָּתֶר:

נט **וְהִפְלָא ה׳ אֶת מַכֹּתְךָ.** מֻפְלָאוֹת וּמֻבְדָּלוֹת מִשְּׁאָר מַכּוֹת: **וְנֶאֱמָנוֹת.** לְיַסֶּרְךָ לְקַיֵּם שְׁלִיחוּתָן:

ס **אֲשֶׁר יָגֹרְתָּ מִפְּנֵיהֶם.** מִפְּנֵי הַמַּכּוֹת. כְּשֶׁהָיוּ יִשְׂרָאֵל רוֹאִים מַכּוֹת מְשֻׁנּוֹת הַבָּאוֹת עַל מִצְרַיִם, הָיוּ יְרֵאִים מֵהֶם שֶׁלֹּא יָבוֹאוּ גַּם עֲלֵיהֶם. תֵּדַע, שֶׁכֵּן כָּתוּב: ״אִם שָׁמוֹעַ תִּשְׁמַע וְגוֹ׳ כָּל הַמַּחֲלָה אֲשֶׁר שַׂמְתִּי בְמִצְרַיִם לֹא אָשִׂים עָלֶיךָ״ (שמות טו, כו), אֵין מְיָרְאִין אֶת הָאָדָם אֶלָּא בְּדָבָר שֶׁהוּא יָגוֹר מִמֶּנּוּ:

סא **יַעְלֵם.** לְשׁוֹן עֲלִיָּה:

סב **וְנִשְׁאַרְתֶּם בִּמְתֵי מְעַט תַּחַת וְגוֹ׳.** מוּעָטִין חִלּוּף מְרֻבִּין:

סג **כֵּן יָשִׂישׂ ה׳.** אֶת אוֹיְבֵיכֶם ״עֲלֵיכֶם, לְהַאֲבִיד״ וְגוֹ׳: **וְנִסַּחְתֶּם.** לְשׁוֹן עֲקִירָה, וְכֵן: ״בֵּית גֵּאִים יִסַּח ה׳״ (משלי טו, כה):

Sharing food is the first act through which slaves become free human beings. One who fears tomorrow does not offer his bread to others. But one who is willing to divide his food with a stranger has already shown himself capable of fellowship and faith, the two things from which hope is born. That is why we begin the Passover Seder by inviting others to join us ("Let all who are hungry come in and eat"). Bread shared is no longer the bread of oppression. Reaching out to others, giving help to the needy and companionship to those who are alone, we bring freedom into the world, and with freedom, God.

נה חֵיקוֹ וּבְיֶתֶר בָּנָיו אֲשֶׁר יוֹתִיר׃ מִתֵּת ׀ לְאַחַד מֵהֶם מִבְּשַׂר בָּנָיו אֲשֶׁר
יֹאכֵל מִבְּלִי הִשְׁאִיר־לוֹ כֹּל בְּמָצוֹר וּבְמָצוֹק אֲשֶׁר יָצִיק לְךָ אֹיִבְךָ
נו בְּכָל־שְׁעָרֶיךָ׃ הָרַכָּה בְךָ וְהָעֲנֻגָּה אֲשֶׁר לֹא־נִסְּתָה כַף־רַגְלָהּ הַצֵּג
עַל־הָאָרֶץ מֵהִתְעַנֵּג וּמֵרֹךְ תֵּרַע עֵינָהּ בְּאִישׁ חֵיקָהּ וּבִבְנָהּ וּבְבִתָּהּ׃
נז וּבְשִׁלְיָתָהּ הַיּוֹצֵת ׀ מִבֵּין רַגְלֶיהָ וּבְבָנֶיהָ אֲשֶׁר תֵּלֵד כִּי־תֹאכְלֵם בְּחֹסֶר־
נח כֹּל בַּסָּתֶר בְּמָצוֹר וּבְמָצוֹק אֲשֶׁר יָצִיק לְךָ אֹיִבְךָ בִּשְׁעָרֶיךָ׃ אִם־לֹא
תִשְׁמֹר לַעֲשׂוֹת אֶת־כָּל־דִּבְרֵי הַתּוֹרָה הַזֹּאת הַכְּתֻבִים בַּסֵּפֶר הַזֶּה
נט לְיִרְאָה אֶת־הַשֵּׁם הַנִּכְבָּד וְהַנּוֹרָא הַזֶּה אֵת יְהוָה אֱלֹהֶיךָ׃ וְהִפְלָא
יְהוָה אֶת־מַכֹּתְךָ וְאֵת מַכּוֹת זַרְעֶךָ מַכּוֹת גְּדֹלֹת וְנֶאֱמָנוֹת וָחֳלָיִם
ס רָעִים וְנֶאֱמָנִים׃ וְהֵשִׁיב בְּךָ אֵת כָּל־מַדְוֵה מִצְרַיִם אֲשֶׁר יָגֹרְתָּ מִפְּנֵיהֶם
סא וְדָבְקוּ בָּךְ׃ גַּם כָּל־חֳלִי וְכָל־מַכָּה אֲשֶׁר לֹא כָתוּב בְּסֵפֶר הַתּוֹרָה הַזֹּאת
סב יַעְלֵם יְהוָה עָלֶיךָ עַד הִשָּׁמְדָךְ׃ וְנִשְׁאַרְתֶּם בִּמְתֵי מְעָט תַּחַת אֲשֶׁר
סג הֱיִיתֶם כְּכוֹכְבֵי הַשָּׁמַיִם לָרֹב כִּי־לֹא שָׁמַעְתָּ בְּקוֹל יְהוָה אֱלֹהֶיךָ׃ וְהָיָה
כַּאֲשֶׁר־שָׂשׂ יְהוָה עֲלֵיכֶם לְהֵיטִיב אֶתְכֶם וּלְהַרְבּוֹת אֶתְכֶם כֵּן יָשִׂישׂ
יְהוָה עֲלֵיכֶם לְהַאֲבִיד אֶתְכֶם וּלְהַשְׁמִיד אֶתְכֶם וְנִסַּחְתֶּם מֵעַל הָאֲדָמָה

אונקלוס

קִיָּמֵיהּ, וּבִשְׁאָר בְּנוֹהִי דִּישְׁאַר: נה מִלְּמִתַּן לְחַד מִנְּהוֹן, מִבְּסַר בְּנוֹהִי דְּיֵיכוּל, מִדְּלָא אִשְׁתְּאַר לֵיהּ כּוֹלָא, בִּצְיָרָא וּבְעָקְתָא, דִּיעִיק לָךְ, סָנְאָךְ בְּכָל קִרְוָךְ: נו דְּרַכִּיכָא בָךְ וְדִמְפַנְּקָא, דְּלָא נַסִּיאַת פַּרְסַת רַגְלַהּ לְאַחָתָא עַל אַרְעָא, מִמְּפַנְּקוּ וּמֵרַכִּיכוּ, תִּבְאַשׁ עֵינַהּ בִּגְבַר קְיָמַהּ, וּבִבְרַהּ וּבִבְרַתַּהּ: נז וּבִזְעֵיר בְּנַהָא, דְּיִפְּקוּן מִבֵּין רַגְלַהָא, וּבִבְנַהָא דִּתְלִיד, אֲרֵי תֵיכְלִנּוּן בְּחַסִּירוּת כּוֹלָא בְּסִתְרָא, בִּצְיָרָא וּבְעָקְתָא, דִּיעִיק לָךְ, סָנְאָךְ בְּקִרְוָךְ: נח אִם לָא תִטַּר לְמֶעְבַּד, יָת כָּל פִּתְגָּמֵי אוֹרַיְתָא הָדָא, דִּכְתִיבִין בְּסִפְרָא הָדֵין, לְמִדְחַל, יָת שְׁמָא, יַקִּירָא וּדְחִילָא הָדֵין, יָת יְיָ אֱלָהָךְ: נט וְיַפְרֵישׁ יְיָ יָת מַחְתָךְ, וְיָת מַחַת בְּנָךְ, מַחָן רַבְרְבָן וּמְהֵימְנָן, וּמַכְתָּשִׁין בִּישִׁין וּמְהֵימְנִין: ס וְיָתֵיב בָּךְ, יָת כָּל מַכְתָּשֵׁי מִצְרַיִם, דִּדְחֵילְתָּא מִן קֳדָמֵיהוֹן, וְיִדְבְּקוּן בָּךְ: סא אַף כָּל מְרַע וְכָל מַחָא, דְּלָא כְתִיבִין, בְּסִפַר אוֹרַיְתָא הָדָא, יַיְתֵינוּן יְיָ עֲלָךְ, עַד דְּתִשְׁתֵּיצֵי: סב וְתִשְׁתָּאֲרוּן בְּעַם זְעֵיר, חֲלָף דַּהֲוֵיתוּן, כְּכוֹכְבֵי שְׁמַיָּא לִסְגֵי, אֲרֵי לָא קַבֵּילְתָּא, לְמֵימְרָא דַּיְיָ אֱלָהָךְ: סג וִיהֵי, כְּמָא דַּחְדִי יְיָ עֲלֵיכוֹן, לְאֵיטָבָא לְכוֹן וּלְאַסְגָּאָה יָתְכוֹן, כֵּן יַחְדֵּי יְיָ עֲלֵיכוֹן, לְאוֹבָדָא יָתְכוֹן וּלְשֵׁיצָאָה יָתְכוֹן, וְתִטַּלְטְלוּן מֵעַל אַרְעָא,

of your neighbor," and left no room for gratitude. It really meant that the law of the Lager was dead.

It was the first human gesture that occurred among us. I believe that that moment can be dated as the beginning of the change by which we who had not died slowly changed from *Haftlinge* [prisoners] to men again.

64 that you are now coming into to possess. The LORD will scatter you among all
nations, from one end of the earth to the other, and there you will serve other
gods, of wood and of stone, which neither you nor your ancestors have known.
65 Yet even among those nations you shall find no ease, no resting place for the
sole of your foot. There the LORD will give you a trembling heart, pining eyes,
66 and a languishing spirit. Your life will hang suspended before you; you will
67 dread both night and day, never sure you will survive. In the morning you will
say, 'Would that it were evening!' In the evening you will say, 'Would that it
were morning!' – because of the dread in your heart that you will dread, the
68 scenes in your eyes that you will see. The LORD will send you back in ships to
Egypt, by a route that I told you that you would never see again. You will offer
yourselves to your enemies for sale as male and female slaves, but none will buy
69 you." These are the words of the covenant that the LORD commanded
Moshe to make with the Israelites in the land of Moav, alongside the covenant
that He had made with them at Ḥorev.

רש״י

סד | **וְעָבַדְתָּ שָּׁם אֱלֹהִים אֲחֵרִים.** כְּתַרְגּוּמוֹ, לֹא עֲבוֹדַת אֱלָהוּת מַמָּשׁ, אֶלָּא מַעֲלִים מַס וְגֻלְגָּלִיּוֹת לְכֻמְרֵי עֲבוֹדָה זָרָה:

סה | **לֹא תַרְגִּיעַ.** לֹא תָנוּחַ, כְּמוֹ: "וְזוֹאת הַמַּרְגֵּעָה" (ישעיה כח, יב): **לֵב רַגָּז.** לֵב חָרֵד, כְּתַרְגּוּמוֹ: "דָּחִיל", כְּמוֹ: "שְׁאוֹל מִתַּחַת רָגְזָה לְךָ" (שם יד, ט), "שָׁמְעוּ עַמִּים יִרְגָּזוּן" (שמות טו, יד), "מוֹסְדוֹת הַשָּׁמַיִם יִרְגָּזוּ" (שמואל ב' כב, ח): **וְכִלְיוֹן עֵינַיִם.** מְצַפֶּה לִישׁוּעָה וְלֹא תָבוֹא:

סו | **חַיֶּיךָ תְּלֻאִים לְךָ.** עַל הַסָּפֵק. כָּל סָפֵק קָרוּי 'תָּלוּי', שֶׁמָּא חָמוּת הַיּוֹם בַּחֶרֶב הַבָּאָה עָלֵינוּ. וְרַבּוֹתֵינוּ דָּרְשׁוּ: זֶה הַלּוֹקֵחַ תְּבוּאָה מִן הַשּׁוּק: **וְלֹא תַאֲמִין בְּחַיֶּיךָ.** זֶה הַסּוֹמֵךְ עַל הַפַּלְטֵר:

סז | **בַּבֹּקֶר תֹּאמַר מִי יִתֵּן.** וְהָיָה עֶרֶב שֶׁל אֶמֶשׁ: **וּבָעֶרֶב תֹּאמַר מִי יִתֵּן בֹּקֶר.** שֶׁל שַׁחֲרִית, שֶׁהַצָּרוֹת מִתְחַזְּקוֹת תָּמִיד, וְכָל שָׁעָה מְרֻבָּה קִלְלָתָהּ מִשֶּׁלְּפָנֶיהָ:

סח | **בָּאֳנִיּוֹת.** בִּסְפִינוֹת בַּשְּׁבִיָּה: **וְהִתְמַכַּרְתֶּם שָׁם לְאֹיְבֶיךָ.** אַתֶּם מְבַקְשִׁים לִהְיוֹת נִמְכָּרִים לָהֶם "לַעֲבָדִים": **וְאֵין קֹנֶה.** כִּי יִגְזְרוּ עָלֶיךָ הֶרֶג וְכִלָּיוֹן: **וְהִתְמַכַּרְתֶּם.** בְּלַעַז אישפורווינדרי"ץ בו"ש. וְלֹא יִתָּכֵן לְפָרֵשׁ "וְהִתְמַכַּרְתֶּם" בִּלְשׁוֹן וְנִמְכַּרְתֶּם עַל יְדֵי מוֹכְרִים אֲחֵרִים:

סט | **לִכְרֹת אֶת בְּנֵי יִשְׂרָאֵל.** שֶׁיְּקַבְּלוּ עֲלֵיהֶם הַתּוֹרָה בְּאָלָה וּבִשְׁבוּעָה: **מִלְּבַד הַבְּרִית.** קְלָלוֹת שֶׁבְּתוֹרַת כֹּהֲנִים שֶׁנֶּאֶמְרוּ בְּסִינַי:

innocent, true at all times, is wrong. There are different historical eras, and these represent different relationships between Israel and God.

The return of Jews to Israel marks the start of an old-new era in the life of the people of the covenant. Once again, as in the days of Yehoshua, Jews are faced with the challenge and opportunity of constructing a society on the principles of the covenant: an arena of justice and compassion, liberty and the rule of law, respect for life and for human dignity. It was never easy. Now, as then, Jews face enemies outside and tensions within. Now, as then, there have been moments when the people must have come close to despair. The principle of "the blessing and the curse" of which Moshe spoke so eloquently has helped Jews emerge from tragedy with hope intact. When Jews have suffered, their first reaction is not to blame others but to examine themselves. That is why bad times – the times spoken of in the *tokheḥa* – have always led to national renewal, and the worse the times, the greater the renewal. A people capable of seeing suffering as a call from God to return to the covenant, choosing and sanctifying life, is one that cannot be defeated because it can never lose hope.

סד אֲשֶׁר־אַתָּה בָא־שָׁמָּה לְרִשְׁתָּהּ: וֶהֱפִיצְךָ יהוה בְּכָל־הָעַמִּים מִקְצֵה
הָאָרֶץ וְעַד־קְצֵה הָאָרֶץ וְעָבַדְתָּ שָּׁם אֱלֹהִים אֲחֵרִים אֲשֶׁר לֹא־יָדַעְתָּ
סה אַתָּה וַאֲבֹתֶיךָ עֵץ וָאָבֶן: וּבַגּוֹיִם הָהֵם לֹא תַרְגִּיעַ וְלֹא־יִהְיֶה מָנוֹחַ
סו לְכַף־רַגְלֶךָ וְנָתַן יהוה לְךָ שָׁם לֵב רַגָּז וְכִלְיוֹן עֵינַיִם וְדַאֲבוֹן נָפֶשׁ: וְהָיוּ
סז חַיֶּיךָ תְּלֻאִים לְךָ מִנֶּגֶד וּפָחַדְתָּ לַיְלָה וְיוֹמָם וְלֹא תַאֲמִין בְּחַיֶּיךָ: בַּבֹּקֶר
תֹּאמַר מִי־יִתֵּן עֶרֶב וּבָעֶרֶב תֹּאמַר מִי־יִתֵּן בֹּקֶר מִפַּחַד לְבָבְךָ אֲשֶׁר
סח תִּפְחָד וּמִמַּרְאֵה עֵינֶיךָ אֲשֶׁר תִּרְאֶה: וֶהֱשִׁיבְךָ יהוה ׀ מִצְרַיִם בָּאֳנִיּוֹת
בַּדֶּרֶךְ אֲשֶׁר אָמַרְתִּי לְךָ לֹא־תֹסִיף עוֹד לִרְאֹתָהּ וְהִתְמַכַּרְתֶּם שָׁם
סט לְאֹיְבֶיךָ לַעֲבָדִים וְלִשְׁפָחוֹת וְאֵין קֹנֶה: אֵלֶּה דִבְרֵי הַבְּרִית
אֲשֶׁר־צִוָּה יהוה אֶת־מֹשֶׁה לִכְרֹת אֶת־בְּנֵי יִשְׂרָאֵל בְּאֶרֶץ מוֹאָב מִלְּבַד
הַבְּרִית אֲשֶׁר־כָּרַת אִתָּם בְּחֹרֵב:

אונקלוס

דַּאַתְּ עָלֵיל לְתַמָּן לְמֵירְתַהּ: סד וִיבַדְּרִנָּךְ יי בְּכָל עַמְמַיָּא, מִסְּיָפֵי אַרְעָא וְעַד סְיָפֵי אַרְעָא, וְתִפְלַח תַּמָּן לְעַמְמַיָּא פָּלְחֵי טָעֲוָתָא, דְּלָא יְדַעְתָּא, אַתְּ וַאֲבָהָתָךְ אָעָא וְאַבְנָא: סה וּבְעַמְמַיָּא הָאִנּוּן לָא תְנוּחַ, וְלָא יְהֵי מְנַח לְפַרְסַת רַגְלָךְ, וְיִתֵּין יי לָךְ תַּמָּן לֵב דָּחִיל, וַחֲשָׁכוּת עַיְנִין וּמַפְּחַן נְפַשׁ: סו וִיהוֹן חַיָּךְ, תְּלַן לָךְ מִקֳּבֵיל, וּתְהֵי תָּוַהּ בְּלֵילְיָא וּבִימָמָא, וְלָא תְהֵימִין בְּחַיָּךְ: סז בְּצַפְרָא תֵּימַר מַאן יִתֵּין רַמְשָׁא, וּבְרַמְשָׁא תֵּימַר מַאן יִתֵּין צַפְרָא, מִתְּוָהַת לִבָּךְ דְּתִהֵי תָּוַהּ, וּמֵחֵיזוּ עֵינָךְ דְּתִהֵי חָזֵי: סח וִיתִיבִנָּךְ יי לְמִצְרַיִם בִּסְפִינָן, בְּאוֹרְחָא דַּאֲמָרִית לָךְ, לָא תוֹסֵיף עוֹד לְמִחְזַהּ, וְתִזְדַּבְּנוּן תַּמָּן לְבַעֲלֵי דְבָבֵיכוֹן, לְעַבְדִּין וּלְאַמְהָן וְלֵית דְּקָנֵי: סט אִלֵּין פִּתְגָּמֵי קְיָמָא דְּפַקֵּיד יי יָת מֹשֶׁה, לְמִגְזַר, עִם בְּנֵי יִשְׂרָאֵל בְּאַרְעָא דְמוֹאָב, בָּר מִקְּיָמָא, דִּגְזַר עִמְּהוֹן בְּחוֹרֵב: כט א וּקְרָא מֹשֶׁה, לְכָל יִשְׂרָאֵל וַאֲמַר לְהוֹן, אַתּוּן חֲזֵיתוּן, יָת כָּל דַּעֲבַד

28:65 וְלֹא־יִהְיֶה מָנוֹחַ *No resting place* – "The righteous have no rest, neither in this world nor the next," says the Talmud (Berakhot 64a). I remain in awe at the challenge God has set us in this imperfect world: to be different, iconoclasts of the politically correct, to be God's question mark against the conventional wisdom of the age, to build, to change, to mend the world until it becomes a place worthy of the Divine Presence because we have learned to honor the image of God that is humankind.

28:69 הַבְּרִית אֲשֶׁר־כָּרַת אִתָּם *The covenant that He had made with them* – The story of the Jewish people is an interweaving of history and prophecy, of the choices of human beings and the overarching tutelage of God. The suffering of Jews in the Diaspora is not to be regarded as divine punishment but rather a consequence of exile itself – the loss of providence, the hiding of the face of God, and being "left to chance" (see commentary on Lev. 26:27). The idea that there is one answer to the problem of evil and the sufferings of the

29 1 Moshe summoned all Israel and said to them: "You have seen all that the LORD SHEVI'I
did before your eyes in the land of Egypt, to Pharaoh, all his officials, and all of
2 his land. Your own eyes saw the great trials, the signs, and the great wonders.
3 But to this day the LORD has not given you a mind that understands, or eyes
4 that see, or ears that hear. For forty years I brought you through the wilderness.
5 The clothes on your back did not wear out, nor the sandals on your feet. You
ate no bread and drank no wine or strong drink, so that you might know that I
6 am the LORD your God. When you came to this place, Siḥon, king of Heshbon, MAFTIR
and Og, king of Bashan, came out to meet us in warfare, but we defeated them.
7 We took their land and gave it as a heritage to the Reubenites, the Gadites, and
8 half the tribe of Menashe. Therefore take great care to keep the words of this
covenant, that you may succeed in all you undertake.

The haftara for Parashat Ki Tavo is on page 1618.

רש״י

כט ג-ח) **וְלֹא נָתַן ה׳ לָכֶם לֵב לָדַעַת.** לְהַכִּיר אֶת חַסְדֵי הַקָּדוֹשׁ בָּרוּךְ הוּא וּלְדָבְקָה בוֹ: **עַד הַיּוֹם הַזֶּה.** שָׁמַעְתִּי שֶׁאוֹתוֹ הַיּוֹם שֶׁנָּתַן מֹשֶׁה סֵפֶר הַתּוֹרָה לִבְנֵי לֵוִי, כְּמוֹ שֶׁכָּתוּב: ״וַיִּתְּנָהּ אֶל הַכֹּהֲנִים בְּנֵי לֵוִי״ (להלן לא, ט), בָּאוּ כָּל יִשְׂרָאֵל לִפְנֵי מֹשֶׁה וְאָמְרוּ לוֹ: מֹשֶׁה רַבֵּנוּ, אַף אָנוּ עָמַדְנוּ בְּסִינַי וְנִתְּנָה לָנוּ, וּמָה אַתָּה מַשְׁלִיט אֶת בְּנֵי שִׁבְטְךָ עָלֶיהָ, וְיֹאמְרוּ לָנוּ יוֹם מָחָר, לֹא לָכֶם נִתְּנָה! וְשָׂמַח מֹשֶׁה עַל הַדָּבָר, וְעַל זֹאת אָמַר לָהֶם: ״הַיּוֹם הַזֶּה נִהְיֵיתָ לְעָם״ וְגוֹ׳ (לעיל כז, ט), הַיּוֹם הַזֶּה הֵבַנְתִּי שֶׁאַתֶּם דְּבֵקִים וַחֲפֵצִים בַּמָּקוֹם: **וַתָּבֹאוּ אֶל הַמָּקוֹם הַזֶּה.** עַתָּה אַתֶּם רוֹאִים עַצְמְכֶם בִּגְדֻלָּה וְכָבוֹד, אַל תִּבְעֲטוּ בַּמָּקוֹם וְאַל יָרוּם לְבַבְכֶם, ״וּשְׁמַרְתֶּם אֶת דִּבְרֵי הַבְּרִית הַזֹּאת״ וְגוֹ׳ (להלן פסוק ח). דָּבָר אַחֵר, ״וְלֹא נָתַן ה׳ לָכֶם לֵב לָדַעַת״, שֶׁאֵין אָדָם עוֹמֵד עַל סוֹף דַּעְתּוֹ שֶׁל רַבּוֹ וְחָכְמַת מִשְׁנָתוֹ עַד אַרְבָּעִים שָׁנָה, וּלְפִיכָךְ לֹא הִקְפִּיד עֲלֵיכֶם הַמָּקוֹם ״עַד הַיּוֹם הַזֶּה״, אֲבָל מִכָּאן וְאֵילַךְ יַקְפִּיד, וּלְפִיכָךְ: ״וּשְׁמַרְתֶּם אֶת דִּבְרֵי הַבְּרִית הַזֹּאת״ וְגוֹ׳:

כט א וַיִּקְרָא מֹשֶׁה אֶל־כָּל־יִשְׂרָאֵל וַיֹּאמֶר אֲלֵהֶם אַתֶּם רְאִיתֶם אֵת כָּל־ שביעי
אֲשֶׁר עָשָׂה יהוה לְעֵינֵיכֶם בְּאֶרֶץ מִצְרַיִם לְפַרְעֹה וּלְכָל־עֲבָדָיו וּלְכָל־
ב אַרְצוֹ: הַמַּסּוֹת הַגְּדֹלֹת אֲשֶׁר רָאוּ עֵינֶיךָ הָאֹתֹת וְהַמֹּפְתִים הַגְּדֹלִים
ג הָהֵם: וְלֹא־נָתַן יהוה לָכֶם לֵב לָדַעַת וְעֵינַיִם לִרְאוֹת וְאָזְנַיִם לִשְׁמֹעַ עַד
ד הַיּוֹם הַזֶּה: וָאוֹלֵךְ אֶתְכֶם אַרְבָּעִים שָׁנָה בַּמִּדְבָּר לֹא־בָלוּ שַׂלְמֹתֵיכֶם
ה מֵעֲלֵיכֶם וְנַעַלְךָ לֹא־בָלְתָה מֵעַל רַגְלֶךָ: לֶחֶם לֹא אֲכַלְתֶּם וְיַיִן וְשֵׁכָר
ו לֹא שְׁתִיתֶם לְמַעַן תֵּדְעוּ כִּי אֲנִי יהוה אֱלֹהֵיכֶם: וַתָּבֹאוּ אֶל־הַמָּקוֹם מפטיר
הַזֶּה וַיֵּצֵא סִיחֹן מֶלֶךְ־חֶשְׁבּוֹן וְעוֹג מֶלֶךְ־הַבָּשָׁן לִקְרָאתֵנוּ לַמִּלְחָמָה
ז וַנַּכֵּם: וַנִּקַּח אֶת־אַרְצָם וַנִּתְּנָהּ לְנַחֲלָה לָרְאוּבֵנִי וְלַגָּדִי וְלַחֲצִי שֵׁבֶט
ח הַמְנַשִּׁי: וּשְׁמַרְתֶּם אֶת־דִּבְרֵי הַבְּרִית הַזֹּאת וַעֲשִׂיתֶם אֹתָם לְמַעַן
תַּשְׂכִּילוּ אֵת כָּל־אֲשֶׁר תַּעֲשׂוּן:

The הפטרה *for* פרשת כי תבוא *is on page 1619.*

אונקלוס

יי לְעֵינֵיכוֹן בְּאַרְעָא דְמִצְרַיִם, לְפַרְעֹה וּלְכָל עַבְדּוֹהִי וּלְכָל אַרְעֵיהּ: ב נִסִּין רַבְרְבִן, דַּחֲזָאָה עֵינָךְ, אָתַיָּא וּמוֹפְתַיָּא, רַבְרְבַיָּא הָאִנּוּן: ג וְלָא יְהַב יי לְכוֹן לִבָּא לְמִדַּע, וְעַיְנִין לְמֶחֱזֵי וְאֻדְנִין לְמִשְׁמַע, עַד יוֹמָא הָדֵין: ד וְדַבָּרִית יָתְכוֹן, אַרְבְּעִין שְׁנִין בְּמַדְבְּרָא, לָא בְלִיאַת כְּסוּתְכוֹן מִנְּכוֹן, וּמְסָנָךְ לָא עֲדוֹ מֵעַל רַגְלָךְ: ה לַחְמָא לָא אֲכַלְתּוּן, וַחֲמַר חֲדַת וְעַתִּיק לָא שְׁתֵיתוּן, בְּדִיל דְּתִדְּעוּן, אֲרֵי, אֲנָא יי אֱלָהֲכוֹן: ו וַאֲתֵיתוֹן לְאַתְרָא הָדֵין, וּנְפַק סִיחוֹן מַלְכָּא דְחֶשְׁבּוֹן, וְעוֹג מַלְכָּא דְמַתְנַן לְקַדָּמוּתַנָא, לְאַגָּחָא קְרָבָא וּמְחֵינָנוּן: ז וּנְסֵיבְנָא יָת אַרְעֲהוֹן, וִיהַבְנַהּ לְאַחְסָנָא, לְשֵׁיבֶט רְאוּבֵן וּלְשֵׁיבֶט גָּד, וּלְפַלְגוּת שִׁבְטָא דִמְנַשֶּׁה: ח וְתִטְּרוּן, יָת פִּתְגָּמֵי קְיָמָא הָדָא, וְתַעְבְּדוּן יָתְהוֹן, בְּדִיל דְּתַצְלְחוּן, יָת כָּל דְּתַעְבְּדוּן:

Parashat Nitzavim

29 9 All of you are standing today before the Lord your God – the leaders among
10 you, the tribes, the elders and officials, all the men of Israel, the children, the
11 women, the strangers in your camp, from woodcutter to water drawer – to
enter into the covenant of the Lord your God, and the oath the Lord your
12 God is making with you today, to establish you today as His people, that He SHENI
may be your God, as He promised you and swore to your ancestors, Avraham,
13 Yitzḥak, and Yaakov. Not with you alone am I making this covenant and oath;
14 with you who are standing here with us today before the Lord our God I

רש"י

כט ט **אתם נצבים היום.** מלמד שכנסם משה לפני הקדוש ברוך הוא ביום מותו להכניסם בברית: **ראשיכם שבטיכם.** ראשיכם לשבטיכם: **זקניכם ושטריכם.** החשוב חשוב קודם, ואחר כך "כל איש ישראל":

י **מחטב עציך.** מלמד שבאו כנעניים להתגיר בימי משה כדרך שבאו גבעונים בימי יהושע, וזהו האמור בגבעונים: "ויעשו גם המה בערמה" (יהושע ט, ד), ונתנם משה חוטבי עצים ושואבי מים:

יא **לעברך בברית.** דרך העברה; כך היו כורתים ברית: עושין מחיצה מכאן ומחיצה מכאן ועוברים בינתים, כמו שנאמר: "העגל אשר כרתו לשנים ויעברו בין בתריו" (ירמיה לד, יח): **לעברך.** להיותך עובר בברית, ולא יתכן לפרשו 'להעבירך', אלא כמו: "לעשתכם אתם" (לעיל ד, יד):

יב **למען הקים אתך היום לו לעם.** כל כך הוא נכנס לטרח למען קים אותך לפניו לעם: **והוא יהיה לך לאלהים.** לפי שדבר לך ונשבע לאבתיך שלא להחליף את זרעם באמה אחרת, לכך הוא אוסר אתכם בשבועות הללו שלא תקניטוהו, אחר שהוא אינו יכול להבדל מכם. עד כאן פרשתי לפי פשוטה של פרשה. ומדרש אגדה: למה נסמכה פרשת "אתם נצבים" לקללות? לפי ששמעו ישראל מאה קללות חסר שתים, חוץ מארבעים ותשע שבתורת כהנים, הוריקו פניהם ואמרו: מי יוכל לעמד באלו? התחיל משה לפיסם: "אתם נצבים היום", הרבה הכעסתם למקום ולא עשה אתכם כליה, והרי אתם קימים לפניו "היום", כיום הזה שהוא קים והוא מאפיל ומאיר, כך האיר לכם וכך עתיד להאיר לכם, והקללות והיסורין מקימין אתכם ומציבין אתכם לפניו. ואף הפרשה שלמעלה מזו פיוסין הם: "אתם ראיתם את כל אשר עשה" וגו' (לעיל פסוק א). דבר אחר, "אתם נצבים", לפי שהיו ישראל יוצאין מפרנס לפרנס, ממשה ליהושע, לפיכך עשה אותם מצבה לזרזם, וכן עשה יהושע (יהושע כד, א), וכן שמואל: "התיצבו ואשפטה אתכם" (שמואל א' יב, ז), כשיצאו מידו ונכנסו לידו של שאול:

יד **ואת אשר איננו פה.** ואף עם דורות העתידים להיות:

A CHOICE FOR THE GENERATIONS

The covenant is forged anew with all the people present, and also "those... who are not with us here today." The commentators point out that this cannot refer to Israelites alive at the time who happened to be somewhere else, as the entire nation was assembled. It can only mean generations not yet born. The covenant is to bind all Jews from that day to this. As the Talmud (Yoma 73b; Nedarim 8a) says, each of us is *mushba veomed meHar Sinai*, "foresworn from Sinai." But how can this be so? How can we be subject to a covenant on the basis of a decision taken long ago by our distant ancestors? The Sages answered the question mystically. They said (Shemot Rabba 28:6) that even the souls of Jews not yet born were present at Sinai and ratified the covenant. Every Jew, in other words, *did* give his or her consent in the days of Moshe even though he or she had not yet been born.

The fifteenth-century Spanish scholar Rabbi Yitzḥak Arama (*Akedat Yitzḥak*, Nitzavim), however, reopened the question. God's covenant is not with souls only, but with embodied human beings. We can understand that the soul,

פרשת נצבים

כט ט אַתֶּם נִצָּבִים הַיּוֹם כֻּלְּכֶם לִפְנֵי יהוה אֱלֹהֵיכֶם רָאשֵׁיכֶם שִׁבְטֵיכֶם כג
י זִקְנֵיכֶם וְשֹׁטְרֵיכֶם כֹּל אִישׁ יִשְׂרָאֵל: טַפְּכֶם נְשֵׁיכֶם וְגֵרְךָ אֲשֶׁר בְּקֶרֶב
יא מַחֲנֶיךָ מֵחֹטֵב עֵצֶיךָ עַד שֹׁאֵב מֵימֶיךָ: לְעָבְרְךָ בִּבְרִית יהוה אֱלֹהֶיךָ
יב וּבְאָלָתוֹ אֲשֶׁר יהוה אֱלֹהֶיךָ כֹּרֵת עִמְּךָ הַיּוֹם: לְמַעַן הָקִים־אֹתְךָ שני
הַיּוֹם ׀ לוֹ לְעָם וְהוּא יִהְיֶה־לְּךָ לֵאלֹהִים כַּאֲשֶׁר דִּבֶּר־לָךְ וְכַאֲשֶׁר
יג נִשְׁבַּע לַאֲבֹתֶיךָ לְאַבְרָהָם לְיִצְחָק וּלְיַעֲקֹב: וְלֹא אִתְּכֶם לְבַדְּכֶם אָנֹכִי
יד כֹּרֵת אֶת־הַבְּרִית הַזֹּאת וְאֶת־הָאָלָה הַזֹּאת: כִּי אֶת־אֲשֶׁר יֶשְׁנוֹ פֹּה
עִמָּנוּ עֹמֵד הַיּוֹם לִפְנֵי יהוה אֱלֹהֵינוּ וְאֵת אֲשֶׁר אֵינֶנּוּ פֹּה עִמָּנוּ הַיּוֹם:

אונקלוס

כט ט אַתּוּן קָיְמִין יוֹמָא דֵין כֻּלְּכוֹן, קֳדָם יי אֱלָהֲכוֹן, רֵישֵׁיכוֹן
שִׁבְטֵיכוֹן, סָבֵיכוֹן וְסָרְכֵיכוֹן, כֹּל אֱנָשׁ יִשְׂרָאֵל: י טַפְלְכוֹן נְשֵׁיכוֹן,
וְגִיּוֹרָךְ, דִּבְגוֹ מַשְׁרִיתָךְ, מִלָּקֵיט אָעָךְ, עַד מָלֵי מַיָּךְ: יא לְאַעֲלוּתָךְ,
בִּקְיָמָא, דַּיי אֱלָהָךְ וּבְמוֹמָתֵיהּ, דַּיי אֱלָהָךְ, גָּזַר עִמָּךְ יוֹמָא דֵין:
יב בְּדִיל לְקַיָּמָא יָתָךְ יוֹמָא דֵין קֳדָמוֹהִי לְעַם, וְהוּא יְהֵי לָךְ לֶאֱלָה,
כְּמָא דְּמַלֵּיל לָךְ, וּכְמָא דְּקַיֵּים לַאֲבָהָתָךְ, לְאַבְרָהָם לְיִצְחָק
וּלְיַעֲקֹב: יג וְלָא עִמְּכוֹן בִּלְחוֹדֵיכוֹן, אֲנָא, גָּזַר יָת קְיָמָא הָדֵין, וְיָת
מוֹמָתָא הָדָא: יד אֲרֵי יָת מַאן דְּאִיתוֹהִי הָכָא, עִמַּנָא קָאֵים יוֹמָא
דֵין, קֳדָם יי אֱלָהַנָא, וְיָת מַאן דְּלֵיתוֹהִי, הָכָא עִמַּנָא יוֹמָא דֵין:

NITZAVIM

Moshe assembles all the people – leaders, elders, officials, children, women, men, and strangers in the camp, from woodcutter to water drawer – to renew the covenant prior to their entry into the land. He warns them solemnly that their future depends on their faithfulness to it. If they break it, they will suffer defeat, devastation, and exile. Yet even then, the covenant and its promise will remain. Even in the midst of dispersion and dislocation, if the people return to God He will return to them and cause them to return to their land. The choice will always be theirs.

29:9 אַתֶּם... כֻּלְּכֶם *All of you* – Judaism is of its essence a collective endeavor. The liturgy, other than occasional meditations, is written in the first-person plural, not the singular. When we pray for an individual we include him or her amongst "all others in Israel" who need healing or consolation. We confess our sins together. When a couple stand under the bridal canopy, the blessings said on the occasion, the *sheva berakhot*, speak of "Zion rejoicing in her children" as if the whole Jewish people past and present joined in the celebration. Jewish mourning customs draw the bereaved gently back into the ambit of community at the very time when they feel most alone. Even the Jewish home is not a closed institution. Jewish teachings emphasize the open house, the extended family, and welcoming the stranger. Hospitality is "greater than welcoming the Divine Presence" (Shabbat 127a). We discover God in our togetherness, not our isolation. Martin Buber misdescribed the faith of Judaism when he spoke of I-and-Thou. The primary relationship in Judaism is We-and-Thou, the Jewish people standing collectively before God.

15 make it, and with those, too, who are not with us here today. You yourselves SHELISHI
know what it was like when we lived in Egypt, and when we passed through the
16 nations we encountered. You saw their detestable things, their abominations of
17 wood and stone, of silver and gold. Let there be among you no man or woman,
family or tribe, whose heart turns away from the LORD our God to serve the
gods of those nations. Let there be among you no root whose fruit is poison
18 and wormwood. When such a person hears the words of this oath, he may
think himself immune, saying, 'I will be safe even if I go my own stubborn way,
19 sweeping away the moist and dry alike,' but the LORD will not be willing to
pardon him. Instead, the LORD's anger and passion will smolder against him;

רש״י

טו-יז **כִּי אַתֶּם יְדַעְתֶּם וגו׳ וַתִּרְאוּ אֶת שִׁקּוּצֵיהֶם.** לְפִי שֶׁרְאִיתֶם הָאֻמּוֹת עוֹבְדֵי עֲבוֹדָה זָרָה, וְשֶׁמָּא הִשִּׂיא לֵב אֶחָד מִכֶּם אוֹתְ לָלֶכֶת אַחֲרֵיהֶם: **פֶּן יֵשׁ בָּכֶם וגו׳.** לְפִיכָךְ אֲנִי צָרִיךְ לְהַשְׁבִּיעֲכֶם:

טז **וַתִּרְאוּ אֶת שִׁקּוּצֵיהֶם.** עַל שֵׁם שֶׁהֵם מְאוּסִים כַּשְּׁקָצִים: **גִּלֻּלֵיהֶם.** מַסְרִיחִים וּמְאוּסִין כַּגָּלָל: **עֵץ וָאֶבֶן.** אוֹתָן שֶׁל עֵצִים וְשֶׁל אֲבָנִים רְאִיתֶם בְּגָלוּי, לְפִי שֶׁאֵין הַגּוֹי יָרֵא שֶׁמָּא יִגָּנְבוּ, אֲבָל שֶׁל כֶּסֶף וְזָהָב, "עִמָּהֶם" בְּחַדְרֵי מַשְׂכִּיתָם הֵם, לְפִי שֶׁהֵם יְרֵאִים שֶׁמָּא יִגָּנְבוּ:

יז **פֶּן יֵשׁ בָּכֶם.** שֶׁמָּא יֵשׁ בָּכֶם: **אֲשֶׁר לְבָבוֹ פֹנֶה הַיּוֹם.** מִלְּקַבֵּל עָלָיו הַבְּרִית: **שֹׁרֶשׁ פֹּרֶה רֹאשׁ וְלַעֲנָה.** שֹׁרֶשׁ מְגַדֵּל עֵשֶׂב מַר, כְּגִידִין שֶׁהֵם מָרִים, כְּלוֹמַר, מַפְרֶה וּמַרְבֶּה רֶשַׁע בְּקִרְבְּכֶם:

יח **וְהִתְבָּרֵךְ בִּלְבָבוֹ.** לְשׁוֹן בְּרָכָה, יַחְשֹׁב בְּלִבּוֹ בִּרְכַּת שָׁלוֹם לְעַצְמוֹ לֵאמֹר, לֹא יְבוֹאוּנִי קְלָלוֹת הַלָּלוּ, אַךְ "שָׁלוֹם יִהְיֶה לִּי": **וְהִתְבָּרֵךְ.** בינדי"א ש"י בְּלַעַז, כְּמוֹ: "וְהִתְגַּלָּח" (ויקרא יג, לג), "וְהִתְפַּלֵּל" (מלכים א׳ ח, מב): **בִּשְׁרִרוּת לִבִּי אֵלֵךְ.** בְּמַרְאִית לִבִּי, כְּמוֹ "אֲשׁוּרֶנּוּ וְלֹא קָרוֹב" (במדבר כד, יז), כְּלוֹמַר, מַה שֶּׁלִּבִּי רוֹאֶה לַעֲשׂוֹת: **לְמַעַן סְפוֹת הָרָוָה.** לְמַעַן שֶׁאוֹסִיף לוֹ פֻּרְעָנוּת עַל מַה שֶּׁעָשָׂה עַד הֵנָּה בְּשׁוֹגֵג וְהָיִיתִי מַעֲבִיר עֲלֵיהֶם, וְגוֹרֵם עַתָּה שֶׁאֲצָרְפֵם עִם הַמֵּזִיד וְאֶפָּרַע מִמֶּנּוּ הַכֹּל. וְכֵן תִּרְגֵּם אוּנְקְלוֹס: "בְּדִיל לְאוֹסָפָא לֵיהּ חֲטָאֵי שָׁלוּתָא עַל זְדָנוּתָא", שֶׁאוֹסִיף אֲנִי לוֹ הַשְּׁגָגוֹת עַל הַזְּדוֹנוֹת: **הָרָוָה.** שׁוֹגֵג, שֶׁהוּא עוֹשֶׂה כְּאָדָם שִׁכּוֹר, שֶׁלֹּא מִדַּעַת: **הַצְּמֵאָה.** שֶׁהוּא עוֹשֶׂה מִדַּעַת וּבְתַאֲוָה:

יט **יֶעְשַׁן אַף ה׳.** עַל יְדֵי כַּעַס, הַגּוּף מִתְחַמֵּם וְהֶעָשָׁן יוֹצֵא מִן הָאַף, וְכֵן: "עָלָה עָשָׁן בְּאַפּוֹ" (שמואל ב׳ כב, ט), וְאַף עַל פִּי שֶׁאֵין זוֹ לִפְנֵי הַמָּקוֹם, הַכָּתוּב מַשְׁמִיעַ אֶת הָאֹזֶן כְּדֶרֶךְ שֶׁהִיא רְגִילָה וִיכוֹלָה לִשְׁמֹעַ, כְּפִי דֶּרֶךְ הָאָרֶץ: **וְקִנְאָתוֹ.** לְשׁוֹן חֵמָה, אנפרטמינ"ט, אֲחִיזַת לְבִישַׁת נְקָמָה, וְאֵינוֹ מַעֲבִיר עַל הַמִּדָּה:

of civilization? Judaism gives us 613 exercises in the power of will to shape our choices. Choosing life, choosing Judaism, is how we, with God, become coauthors of our lives.

29:17 פֶּן־יֵשׁ בָּכֶם שֹׁרֶשׁ *Let there be among you no root* – "All Israel are responsible for one another" (Shevuot 39a). The idea that an individual within Israel – and this applies to a subgroup as well – can "consider himself immune" and depart from the collective morality without consequences is nipped in the bud.

The first philosophers of civil society were the prophets. Unlike the priests, who spoke in terms of holy and profane, permitted and forbidden, pure and impure, the prophets spoke the language of the covenantal virtues: righteousness (*tzedek*), justice (*mishpat*), loving-kindness (*ḥesed*), and compassion (*raḥamim*). Insofar as one can summarize the message of Eliyahu and Elisha, Amos and Hoshea, Yeshayahu and Yirmeyahu, and translate it into secular terms, it would be this: Israel is a small nation surrounded by empires. To survive it needs the strongest possible cohesion and morale. People must feel that they are fighting for something precious, a society whose manifest justice and graciousness are apparent to all. Thus motivated, they will defeat powers greater than themselves. If, however, Israel worships the idols of power or wealth, it will lose its corporate identity. The poor will resent the rich; the weak will feel exploited by the strong. The nation will be divided, and a house divided against itself cannot stand.

טו כִּֽי־אַתֶּם֙ יְדַעְתֶּ֔ם אֵ֥ת אֲשֶׁר־יָשַׁ֖בְנוּ בְּאֶ֣רֶץ מִצְרָ֑יִם וְאֵ֧ת אֲשֶׁר־עָבַ֛רְנוּ שלישי
טז בְּקֶ֥רֶב הַגּוֹיִ֖ם אֲשֶׁ֥ר עֲבַרְתֶּֽם׃ וַתִּרְאוּ֙ אֶת־שִׁקּ֣וּצֵיהֶ֔ם וְאֵ֖ת גִּלֻּלֵיהֶ֑ם
יז עֵ֣ץ וָאֶ֔בֶן כֶּ֥סֶף וְזָהָ֖ב אֲשֶׁ֥ר עִמָּהֶֽם׃ פֶּן־יֵ֣שׁ בָּ֠כֶם אִ֣ישׁ אוֹ־אִשָּׁ֞ה א֧וֹ
מִשְׁפָּחָ֣ה אוֹ־שֵׁ֗בֶט אֲשֶׁר֩ לְבָב֨וֹ פֹנֶ֤ה הַיּוֹם֙ מֵעִם֙ יְהוָ֣ה אֱלֹהֵ֔ינוּ לָלֶ֣כֶת
לַעֲבֹ֔ד אֶת־אֱלֹהֵ֖י הַגּוֹיִ֣ם הָהֵ֑ם פֶּן־יֵ֣שׁ בָּכֶ֗ם שֹׁ֛רֶשׁ פֹּרֶ֥ה רֹ֖אשׁ וְלַעֲנָֽה׃
יח וְהָיָ֡ה בְּשָׁמְעוֹ֩ אֶת־דִּבְרֵ֨י הָאָלָ֜ה הַזֹּ֗את וְהִתְבָּרֵ֨ךְ בִּלְבָב֤וֹ לֵאמֹר֙ שָׁל֣וֹם
יִֽהְיֶה־לִּ֔י כִּ֛י בִּשְׁרִר֥וּת לִבִּ֖י אֵלֵ֑ךְ לְמַ֛עַן סְפ֥וֹת הָרָוָ֖ה אֶת־הַצְּמֵאָֽה׃
יט לֹֽא־יֹאבֶ֣ה יְהוָה֮ סְלֹ֣חַ לוֹ֒ כִּ֣י אָ֠ז יֶעְשַׁ֨ן אַף־יְהוָ֤ה וְקִנְאָתוֹ֙ בָּאִ֣ישׁ הַה֔וּא

אונקלוס

טו אֲרֵי אַתּוּן יְדַעְתּוּן, יָת דִּיתֵיבְנָא בְּאַרְעָא דְּמִצְרָיִם, וְיָת דַּעֲבַרְנָא, בֵּינֵי עַמְמַיָּא דַּעֲבַרְתּוּן: טז וַחֲזֵיתוּן יָת שִׁקּוּצֵיהוֹן, וְיָת טַעֲוָתְהוֹן, אָעָא וְאַבְנָא, כַּסְפָּא וְדַהֲבָא דְּעִמְּהוֹן: יז דִּלְמָא אִית בְּכוֹן, גְּבַר אוֹ אִתְּתָא אוֹ זַרְעִי אוֹ שִׁבְטָא, דְּלִבֵּיהּ פָּנֵי יוֹמָא דֵין מִדַּחְלְתָא דַּייָ אֱלָהַנָא, לִמְהָךְ לְמִפְלַח, יָת טָעֲוָת עַמְמַיָּא הָאִנּוּן, דִּלְמָא אִית בְּכוֹן, גְּבַר, מְהַרְהֵיר חֲטִין אוֹ זְדוֹן: יח וִיהֵי, בְּמִשְׁמְעֵיהּ יָת פִּתְגָּמֵי מוֹמָתָא הָדָא, וְיַחְשֵׁיב בְּלִבֵּיהּ לְמֵימַר שְׁלָמָא יְהֵי לִי, אֲרֵי, בְּהַרְהוֹר לִבִּי אֲנָא אָזֵיל, בְּדִיל, לְאוֹסָפָא לֵיהּ חֲטָאֵי שָׁלוּתָא עַל זֵידָנוּתָא: יט לָא יֵיבֵי יְיָ לְמִשְׁבַּק לֵיהּ, אֲרֵי בְּכֵן, יִתְקַף רֻגְזָא דַּייָ וְחִמְתֵיהּ בְּגֻבְרָא הַהוּא,

which desires closeness to God, would agree to the covenant. But the assent that counts is, surely, that of living, breathing human beings with bodies. We cannot assume that they would agree to the Torah with its many physical restrictions. Only when we understand what is being asked of us can we give our binding consent.

Why, then, be Jewish? When Jews ask this question, we know that we are in the presence of a major crisis in Jewish life. At most times in history, Jewish identity was a fact of birth, a destiny. It was not something you chose, any more than you choose to be born. In Rabbi Arama's day, for the first time Jews converted to another faith in significant numbers. Those who did so seemed to prosper. Those who remained loyal to their faith suffered ever-increasing persecution. In times such as those, what answer could Rabbi Arama give to someone who asked, "Why should I remain a Jew?"

The following was his reply. After thousands of years, Jewish identity was as deeply engraved in the minds of Jews as the instinct of life is in all living creatures. It was no more possible for Jews collectively to desert the covenant than it was for a species to commit suicide. Within all that lives, there is a desire for life, an instinct for survival. And for Jews that instinct is for Jewish survival.

I would like to suggest another answer, which lies in what Moshe himself said at the end of his address: "I call heaven and earth as witnesses against you today. I have set before you life and death, the blessing and the curse. Choose life" (Deut. 30:19). The ancients – with their belief in fate, the influence of the stars, or the arbitrariness of nature – did not fully believe in human freedom. Nor do most scientific atheists believe in it today. We are determined, they say, by our genes. Choice is an illusion of the conscious mind.

Judaism says no. Choice is like a muscle: use it or lose it. Jewish law is an ongoing training regime in willpower. Can you eat this and not that? Can you exercise spiritually three times a day? Can you rest one day in seven? Can you defer the gratification of instinct – what Freud took to be the mark

all the curses written in this scroll will fall on him, and the LORD will erase his
20 name from under the sky. The LORD will single him out for disaster – from
all the tribes of Israel – in line with all the curses of the covenant written in
21 this scroll of the Law. A future generation – your descendants who rise after
you, and foreigners from distant lands – will see the land's devastation and the
22 sicknesses with which the LORD has afflicted it, all its soil a burning waste of
sulfur and salt, nothing planted, nothing sprouting, no vegetation growing on
it, like the ruins of Sedom and Amora, Adma and Tzevoyim, which the LORD
23 overturned in His fierce rage. All the nations will ask, 'Why did the LORD do
24 this to the land? Why this great, blazing anger?' They will say, 'It is because
they abandoned the covenant of the LORD, God of their ancestors, which He
25 made with them when He brought them out of Egypt. They went and served
other gods and worshipped them, gods they did not know and whom He had
26 not allotted to them. So the LORD's anger burned against that land, bringing
27 on it every curse that is written in this scroll. The LORD uprooted them from
their land in anger, rage, and great fury, and threw them into another land,
28 as we now see them.' Hidden things belong to the LORD our God, but as for
overt acts – it is for us and our children to eternity to keep all the words of this

רש״י

כ **הַכְּתוּבָה בְּסֵפֶר הַתּוֹרָה הַזֶּה.** וּלְמַעְלָה הוּא אוֹמֵר: ״בְּסֵפֶר הַתּוֹרָה הַזֹּאת, גַּם כָּל חֳלִי וְכָל מַכָּה וְגוֹ׳״ (לעיל כח, סא), ״הַזֹּאת״ לְשׁוֹן נְקֵבָה, מוּסָב עַל ״הַתּוֹרָה״, ״הַזֶּה״ לְשׁוֹן זָכָר, מוּסָב עַל הַסֵּפֶר, וְעַל יְדֵי פִּסּוּק הַטְּעָמִים הֵן נֶחְלָקִין לִשְׁתֵּי לְשׁוֹנוֹת. בְּפָרָשַׁת קְלָלוֹת הַטִּפְּחָא נְתוּנָה תַּחַת ״בְּסֵפֶר״, וְ״הַתּוֹרָה הַזֹּאת״ דְּבוּקִים זֶה לָזֶה, לְכָךְ אָמַר ״הַזֹּאת״, וְכָאן הַטִּפְּחָא נְתוּנָה תַּחַת ״הַתּוֹרָה״, נִמְצָא ״סֵפֶר הַתּוֹרָה״ דְּבוּקִים זֶה לָזֶה, לְפִיכָךְ לְשׁוֹן זָכָר נוֹפֵל עַל הַסֵּפֶר:

כה **לֹא יְדָעוּם.** לֹא יָדְעוּ בָּהֶם גְּבוּרַת אֱלֹהוּת: **וְלֹא חָלַק לָהֶם.** לֹא נְתָנָם לְחֶלְקָם. וְאוּנְקְלוֹס תִּרְגֵּם: ״וְלָא אוֹטִיבָא לְהוֹן״, לֹא הֵיטִיבוּ לָהֶם שׁוּם טוֹבָה, וּלְשׁוֹן ״לֹא חָלַק״, אוֹתוֹ אֱלוֹהַּ שֶׁבָּחֲרוּ לָהֶם לֹא חָלַק לָהֶם שׁוּם נַחֲלָה וְשׁוּם חֵלֶק:

כז **וַיִּתְּשֵׁם ה׳.** כְּתַרְגּוּמוֹ ״וְטַלְטֵלִנּוּן״, וְכֵן: ״הִנְנִי נֹתְשָׁם מֵעַל אַדְמָתָם״ (ירמיה יב, יד):

כח **הַנִּסְתָּרֹת לַה׳ אֱלֹהֵינוּ.** וְאִם תֹּאמְרוּ, מַה בְּיָדֵנוּ לַעֲשׂוֹת? אַתָּה מַעֲנִישׁ אֶת הָרַבִּים עַל הִרְהוּרֵי הַיָּחִיד, שֶׁנֶּאֱמַר: ״פֶּן יֵשׁ בָּכֶם אִישׁ״ וְגוֹ׳ (לעיל פסוק יז) וְאַחַר כָּךְ: ״וְרָאוּ אֶת מַכּוֹת הָאָרֶץ הַהִוא״ (לעיל פסוק כא), וַהֲלֹא אֵין אָדָם יוֹדֵעַ טְמוּנוֹתָיו שֶׁל חֲבֵרוֹ? אֵין אֲנִי מַעֲנִישׁ אֶתְכֶם עַל ״הַנִּסְתָּרֹת״, שֶׁהֵן ״לַה׳ אֱלֹהֵינוּ״ וְהוּא יִפָּרַע מֵאוֹתוֹ יָחִיד, אֲבָל ״הַנִּגְלֹת לָנוּ וּלְבָנֵינוּ״ לְבַעֵר הָרָע מִקִּרְבֵּנוּ, וְאִם לֹא נַעֲשֶׂה דִּין בָּהֶם יֵעָנְשׁוּ הָרַבִּים. נָקוּד עַל ״לָנוּ״ וְעַל ״לְבָנֵינוּ״ וְעַל ע׳ שֶׁבְּ״עַד״, לִדְרשׁ שֶׁאַף עַל הַנִּגְלוֹת לֹא עָנַשׁ אֶת הָרַבִּים עַד שֶׁעָבְרוּ אֶת הַיַּרְדֵּן, מִשֶּׁקִּבְּלוּ עֲלֵיהֶם אֶת הַשְּׁבוּעָה בְּהַר גְּרִזִּים וּבְהַר עֵיבָל וְנַעֲשׂוּ עֲרֵבִים זֶה לָזֶה:

That is the point of the Torah from the beginning. God gives Adam and Ḥava a command that they are free to obey or disobey. He gives Kayin the freedom to control his negative impulses, and the freedom to capitulate to them. The story of the Tanakh is of God's gift of freedom to humankind. Thus the future is unknown – "hidden things belong to the LORD," and responsibility – for "overt acts" – is ours.

saying that "I, God, am free. What I do, how I appear, how I intervene – none of these things can be predicted or controlled. I am what I choose." God is unknowable and the future is unknowable, and both for the same reason: because of the nature of freedom.

If God is free and He bestows His image on us, then we too, within the limits set by our bodily existence, are free.

וְרָבְצָה בּוֹ כׇּל־הָאָלָה הַכְּתוּבָה בַּסֵּפֶר הַזֶּה וּמָחָה יהוה אֶת־שְׁמוֹ
כ מִתַּחַת הַשָּׁמָיִם׃ וְהִבְדִּילוֹ יהוה לְרָעָה מִכֹּל שִׁבְטֵי יִשְׂרָאֵל כְּכֹל אָלוֹת
כא הַבְּרִית הַכְּתוּבָה בְּסֵפֶר הַתּוֹרָה הַזֶּה׃ וְאָמַר הַדּוֹר הָאַחֲרוֹן בְּנֵיכֶם
אֲשֶׁר יָקוּמוּ מֵאַחֲרֵיכֶם וְהַנׇּכְרִי אֲשֶׁר יָבֹא מֵאֶרֶץ רְחוֹקָה וְרָאוּ אֶת־
כב מַכּוֹת הָאָרֶץ הַהִוא וְאֶת־תַּחֲלֻאֶיהָ אֲשֶׁר־חִלָּה יהוה בָּהּ׃ גׇּפְרִית
וָמֶלַח שְׂרֵפָה כׇל־אַרְצָהּ לֹא תִזָּרַע וְלֹא תַצְמִחַ וְלֹא־יַעֲלֶה בָהּ כׇּל־
עֵשֶׂב כְּמַהְפֵּכַת סְדֹם וַעֲמֹרָה אַדְמָה וצביים אֲשֶׁר הָפַךְ יהוה בְּאַפּוֹ וּצְבוֹיִם
כג וּבַחֲמָתוֹ׃ וְאָמְרוּ כׇּל־הַגּוֹיִם עַל־מֶה עָשָׂה יהוה כָּכָה לָאָרֶץ הַזֹּאת מֶה
כד חֳרִי הָאַף הַגָּדוֹל הַזֶּה׃ וְאָמְרוּ עַל אֲשֶׁר עָזְבוּ אֶת־בְּרִית יהוה אֱלֹהֵי
כה אֲבֹתָם אֲשֶׁר כָּרַת עִמָּם בְּהוֹצִיאוֹ אֹתָם מֵאֶרֶץ מִצְרָיִם׃ וַיֵּלְכוּ וַיַּעַבְדוּ
אֱלֹהִים אֲחֵרִים וַיִּשְׁתַּחֲווּ לָהֶם אֱלֹהִים אֲשֶׁר לֹא־יְדָעוּם וְלֹא חָלַק
כו לָהֶם׃ וַיִּחַר־אַף יהוה בָּאָרֶץ הַהִוא לְהָבִיא עָלֶיהָ אֶת־כׇּל־הַקְּלָלָה
כז הַכְּתוּבָה בַּסֵּפֶר הַזֶּה׃ וַיִּתְּשֵׁם יהוה מֵעַל אַדְמָתָם בְּאַף וּבְחֵמָה
כח וּבְקֶצֶף גָּדוֹל וַיַּשְׁלִכֵם אֶל־אֶרֶץ אַחֶרֶת כַּיּוֹם הַזֶּה׃ הַנִּסְתָּרֹת לַיהוה
אֱלֹהֵינוּ וְהַנִּגְלֹת לָנוּ וּלְבָנֵינוּ עַד־עוֹלָם לַעֲשׂוֹת אֶת־כׇּל־דִּבְרֵי הַתּוֹרָה

אונקלוס

וְיִדְבְּקוּן בֵּיהּ כׇּל לְוָטַיָּא, דִּכְתִיבִין בְּסִפְרָא הָדֵין, וְיִמְחֵי יי יָת שְׁמֵיהּ, מִתְּחוֹת שְׁמַיָּא: כ וְיַפְרְשִׁנֵּיהּ יי לְבִישָׁא, מִכֹּל שִׁבְטַיָּא דְּיִשְׂרָאֵל, כְּכֹל לְוָטֵי קְיָמָא, דִּכְתִיבִין, בְּסִפַר אוֹרָיְתָא הָדֵין: כא וְיֵימַר דָּרָא בָּתְרָאָה, בְּנֵיכוֹן דִּיקוּמוּן מִבָּתְרֵיכוֹן, וּבַר עַמְמִין, דְּיֵיתֵי מֵאֲרַע רְחִיקָא, וְיִחְזוֹן, יָת מַחְתַהּ, דְּאַרְעָא הַהִיא וְיָת מַרְעֲהָא, דְּאַמְרַע יי בַּהּ: כב גׇּפְרֵיתָא וּמִלְחָא תְּהֵי יְקִדָא כׇּל אַרְעַהּ, לָא תִזְדְּרַע וְלָא תַצְמַח, וְלָא יִסַּק בַּהּ כׇּל עִיסַב, כְּהַפֵּיכְתָא, דִּסְדוֹם וַעֲמוֹרָה אַדְמָה וּצְבוֹיִם, דַּהֲפַךְ יי, בְּרוּגְזֵיהּ וּבְחֵמְתֵיהּ: כג וְיֵימְרוּן כׇּל עַמְמַיָּא, עַל מָא עֲבַד יי, כְּדֵין לְאַרְעָא הָדָא, מָא תְקוֹף, רוּגְזָא רַבָּא הָדֵין: כד וְיֵימְרוּן, עַל דִּשְׁבַקוּ, יָת קְיָמָא דַּיי אֱלָהָא דַּאֲבָהָתְהוֹן, דִּגְזַר עִמְּהוֹן, בְּאַפָּקוּתֵיהּ יָתְהוֹן מֵאַרְעָא דְּמִצְרָיִם: כה וַאֲזַלוּ, וּפְלַחוּ לְטָעֲוָת עַמְמַיָּא, וּסְגִידוּ לְהוֹן, דַּחֲלָן דְּלָא יְדַעוּנִין, וְלָא אוֹטִיבָא לְהוֹן: כו וּתְקֵיף רוּגְזָא דַּיי בְּאַרְעָא הַהִיא, לְאֵיתָאָה עֲלַהּ יָת כׇּל לְוָטַיָּא, דִּכְתִיבִין בְּסִפְרָא הָדֵין: כז וְטַלְטֵילִנּוּן יי מֵעַל אַרְעֲהוֹן, בִּרְגַז וּבְחֵמָא וּבִתְקוֹף רַב, וְאַגְלִינוּן, לַאֲרַע אָחֳרִי כְּיוֹמָא הָדֵין: כח דְּמִטַּמְּרָן, קֳדָם יי אֱלָהַנָא, וּדְגַלְיָן, לַנָא וְלִבְנַנָא עַד עָלְמָא, לְמֶעְבַּד, יָת כׇּל פִּתְגָּמֵי אוֹרָיְתָא

29:28 הַנִּסְתָּרֹת לַיהוה *Hidden things belong to the Lord* – If God is not within nature, but is Himself the author of nature, then He is subject to no laws except those by which He chooses to bind Himself. When God says to Moshe, "I will be what I will be" (Ex. 3:14), and later, "I…will show mercy to whom I decide to show mercy" (33:19), He is

30 1 Law. When all these things have come upon you, the blessings and REVI'I /SHENI/
the curses I have set before you, and you – amidst all the nations where the
2 Lord your God has driven you – take them to heart, and return, you and your
children, to the Lord your God, obeying Him with all your heart and all your
3 soul, just as I am commanding you today, then the Lord your God will bring
your captives back and show you compassion. He will bring you back together
4 from all the nations among whom the Lord your God has scattered you. If
you should be expelled to the furthest of horizons, even from there the Lord
5 your God will gather you, from there He will take you back. The Lord your
God will bring you into the land that belonged to your ancestors, and you will
possess it. He will make you yet more prosperous and numerous than your
6 ancestors were. The Lord your God will circumcise your heart and the hearts
of your descendants, so that you may love the Lord your God with all your
7 heart, with all your soul, that you may live. The Lord your God will inflict all ḤAMISHI /SHELISHI/

רש״י

ל ג) **וְשָׁב ה׳ אֱלֹהֶיךָ אֶת שְׁבוּתְךָ.** הָיָה לוֹ לִכְתֹּב: ׳וְהֵשִׁיב אֶת שְׁבוּתְךָ׳, רַבּוֹתֵינוּ לָמְדוּ מִכָּאן כִּבְיָכוֹל שֶׁהַשְּׁכִינָה שְׁרוּיָה עִם יִשְׂרָאֵל בְּצָרַת גָּלוּתָם, וּכְשֶׁנִּגְאָלִין הִכְתִּיב גְּאֻלָּה לְעַצְמוֹ שֶׁהוּא יָשׁוּב עִמָּהֶם. וְעוֹד יֵשׁ לוֹמַר שֶׁגָּדוֹל יוֹם קִבּוּץ גָּלֻיּוֹת וּבְקֹשִׁי, כְּאִלּוּ הוּא עַצְמוֹ צָרִיךְ לִהְיוֹת אוֹחֵז בְּיָדָיו מַמָּשׁ אִישׁ אִישׁ מִמְּקוֹמוֹ, כְּעִנְיָן שֶׁנֶּאֱמַר: ״וְאַתֶּם תְּלֻקְּטוּ לְאַחַד אֶחָד בְּנֵי יִשְׂרָאֵל״ (ישעיה כז, יב), וְאַף בְּגָלֻיּוֹת שְׁאָר הָאֻמּוֹת מָצִינוּ כֵן: ״וְשַׁבְתִּי אֶת שְׁבוּת מִצְרַיִם״ (יחזקאל כט, יד):

land." Hence the double meaning of *teshuva*, most clearly expressed in this *parasha*, but found throughout the entire prophetic literature. It has both a physical and spiritual dimension, and the two are inseparable: it means both *the physical return to the land* and *the spiritual return to God*. *Teshuva* is a double homecoming. In the course of the twentieth century, Jews returned. The State of Israel was reborn. There has been a *physical* homecoming to the land, but not yet a full spiritual homecoming to the faith. That challenge rests with us and our children. The words of the prophets have acquired a new salience in our time.

Unlike Rambam, who traces the imperative of repentance back to sacrificial rituals of atonement (*Hilkhot Teshuva* 1:1), for Ramban, sin and repentance are part of the broader sweep of Jewish history. They belong to the world not of the priest but of the prophet, the figure who heard the voice of God in history, warned the people that public wrongdoing would lead to defeat and exile, and who, when the exile eventually occurred, summoned the people back to their vocation as a prelude to their return to the land.

Every individual act of *teshuva* recapitulates, in some way, this larger pattern of return. *Teshuva* in this sense is less *atonement* than *homecoming* – a subtle difference, but a difference nonetheless. The primary feeling of sin in priestly consciousness is *guilt*; in prophetic consciousness it is a sense of *alienation*. For the priest, *teshuva* is integrally linked with sacrifice. For the prophet, it is associated with behavioral change (*teshuva* as "returning" to the right way) and leads to healing and restoration.

Parashat Nitzavim is always read on the Sabbath before Rosh HaShana, when our thoughts are directed toward *teshuva*. The rituals of atonement are encoded into the Yom Kippur service, but it is worth recalling that *teshuva* has less to do with the Temple, and everything to do with a sense of the divine call ("Where are you?") within the events that happen to us, whether individually as a personal fate or collectively as Jewish history.

ל א הַזֹּאת: וְהָיָה כִי־יָבֹאוּ עָלֶיךָ כָּל־הַדְּבָרִים הָאֵלֶּה הַבְּרָכָה רביעי /שני/
וְהַקְּלָלָה אֲשֶׁר נָתַתִּי לְפָנֶיךָ וַהֲשֵׁבֹתָ אֶל־לְבָבֶךָ בְּכָל־הַגּוֹיִם אֲשֶׁר
ב הִדִּיחֲךָ יהוה אֱלֹהֶיךָ שָׁמָּה: וְשַׁבְתָּ עַד־יהוה אֱלֹהֶיךָ וְשָׁמַעְתָּ בְקֹלוֹ
כְּכֹל אֲשֶׁר־אָנֹכִי מְצַוְּךָ הַיּוֹם אַתָּה וּבָנֶיךָ בְּכָל־לְבָבְךָ וּבְכָל־נַפְשֶׁךָ:
ג וְשָׁב יהוה אֱלֹהֶיךָ אֶת־שְׁבוּתְךָ וְרִחֲמֶךָ וְשָׁב וְקִבֶּצְךָ מִכָּל־הָעַמִּים
ד אֲשֶׁר הֱפִיצְךָ יהוה אֱלֹהֶיךָ שָׁמָּה: אִם־יִהְיֶה נִדַּחֲךָ בִּקְצֵה הַשָּׁמָיִם
ה מִשָּׁם יְקַבֶּצְךָ יהוה אֱלֹהֶיךָ וּמִשָּׁם יִקָּחֶךָ: וֶהֱבִיאֲךָ יהוה אֱלֹהֶיךָ אֶל־
ו הָאָרֶץ אֲשֶׁר־יָרְשׁוּ אֲבֹתֶיךָ וִירִשְׁתָּהּ וְהֵיטִבְךָ וְהִרְבְּךָ מֵאֲבֹתֶיךָ: וּמָל
יהוה אֱלֹהֶיךָ אֶת־לְבָבְךָ וְאֶת־לְבַב זַרְעֶךָ לְאַהֲבָה אֶת־יהוה אֱלֹהֶיךָ
ז בְּכָל־לְבָבְךָ וּבְכָל־נַפְשְׁךָ לְמַעַן חַיֶּיךָ: וְנָתַן יהוה אֱלֹהֶיךָ אֵת כָּל־ חמישי /שלישי/

אונקלוס

הָדָא: ל א וִיהֵי אֲרֵי יֵיתוֹן עֲלָךְ כָּל פִּתְגָּמַיָּא הָאִלֵּין, בִּרְכָן וּלְוָטִין,
דִּיהַבִית קֳדָמָךְ, וְתְתִיב לְלִבָּךְ, בְּכָל עַמְמַיָּא, דְּאַגְלְיָךְ, יי אֱלָהָךְ
לְתַמָּן: ב וּתְתוּב, לְדַחַלְתָּא דַּיי אֱלָהָךְ וּתְקַבֵּיל לְמֵימְרֵיהּ, כְּכֹל,
דַּאֲנָא מְפַקֵּיד לָךְ יוֹמָא דֵּין, אַתְּ וּבְנָךְ, בְּכָל לִבָּךְ וּבְכָל נַפְשָׁךְ:
ג וְיָתִיב יי אֱלָהָךְ, יָת שְׁבֵי גָּלְוָתָךְ וִירַחֵים עֲלָךְ, וִיתוּב, וִיכַנְּשִׁנָּךְ מִכָּל
עַמְמַיָּא, דְּבַדְּרָךְ, יי אֱלָהָךְ לְתַמָּן: ד אִם יְהוֹן גָּלְוָתָךְ בִּסְיָפֵי שְׁמַיָּא,
מִתַּמָּן, יְכַנְּשִׁנָּךְ יי אֱלָהָךְ, וּמִתַּמָּן יְקָרְבִנָּךְ: ה וְיַעֲלִנָּךְ יי אֱלָהָךְ,
לְאַרְעָא, דִּירִיתוּ אֲבָהָתָךְ וְתֵירְתַהּ, וְיוֹטֵיב לָךְ וְיַסְגֵּינָךְ מֵאֲבָהָתָךְ: ו
וְיַעְדֵּי יי אֱלָהָךְ, יָת טַפְשׁוּת לִבָּךְ וְיָת טַפְשׁוּת לִבָּא דִּבְנָךְ, לְמִרְחַם, יָת
יי אֱלָהָךְ, בְּכָל לִבָּךְ וּבְכָל נַפְשָׁךְ בְּדִיל חַיָּךְ: ז וְיִתֵּין יי אֱלָהָךְ, יָת כָּל

RETURN

This passage is a set of variations on the Hebrew verb *lashuv*, which is related to the noun *teshuva*. This is lost in English translation. All the phrases – "take to heart," "return," "bring your captives back," and "turn" – are, in the Hebrew, forms of this verb. The Torah often repeats a word several times to emphasize its significance as a keyword: sometimes three or five times, but usually seven, as in the present instance (taking "bring your captives back," *veshav et shevutekha*, as one composite phrase).

The next passage (Deut. 30:11) continues, "For *this commandment* that I am giving you today is not unattainable to you, neither is it distant." Hence, Ramban identifies our passage as the source of the command of repentance, *teshuva*.

In the Torah, sin is something more than a transaction in the soul, or even an act of wrongdoing narrowly conceived. It is *an act in the wrong place*. It disturbs the moral order of the world. The words for sin – *ḥet* and *avera* – both have this significance. *Ḥet* comes from the same verb as "to miss a target." *Avera*, like the English word "transgression," means to cross a boundary, to enter forbidden territory, to be in a place one should not be.

Because a sin is an act in the wrong place, its consequence is that the one who performs it finds himself in the wrong place – in exile, meaning, not at home. Sin *alienates*; it distances us from God, and so from where we ought to be, where we belong. We become aliens, strangers. We say in our prayers, "Because of our sins we were exiled from our

8 these curses on your enemies and on those who hate and persecute you. Then
you shall turn and heed the LORD's voice, keeping all His commandments
9 with which I am charging you this day, and the LORD your God will grant you
abundant prosperity in all the work of your hands, in the fruit of your womb,
the fruit of your cattle, and the fruit of your land. The LORD will again delight
10 in your well-being as He did in your ancestors', when you heed the LORD your
God, keeping His commandments and decrees that are written in this book of
the Law, and have returned to the LORD your God with all your heart and with
11 all your soul. For this commandment that I am giving you today is SHISHI
12 not unattainable to you, neither is it distant. It is not in heaven, that you should
say, 'Who will go up to heaven for us and bring it to us that we may hear it and
13 keep it?' Nor is it beyond the sea, that you should say, 'Who will cross to the

רש״י

יא **לֹא נִפְלֵאת הִוא מִמְּךָ.** לֹא מְכֻסָּה הִיא מִמְּךָ, כְּמוֹ שֶׁנֶּאֱמַר: "כִּי יִפָּלֵא" (לעיל יז, ח) – "אֲרֵי יִתְכַּסֵּי", "וַתֵּרֶד פְּלָאִים" (איכה א, ט) וַתֵּרֶד בְּמַטְמוֹנִיּוֹת, מְכֻסָּה חֲבוּשָׁה בְּטָמוֹן:

יב **לֹא בַשָּׁמַיִם הִוא.** שֶׁאִלּוּ הָיְתָה בַּשָּׁמַיִם, הָיִיתָ צָרִיךְ לַעֲלוֹת אַחֲרֶיהָ וְלִלְמְדָהּ:

It is "in your mouth" – in the stories we tell: When I take part in a Seder service on Passover, I do not "consume" the story of the exodus; I enact it, making it part of me. It defines me as part of that story. It changes me, for I now know what it feels and tastes like to be oppressed, and I can no longer walk by when others are oppressed.

It is "in your heart" – in the prayers we say. Praying, we hear the universe singing a song to its Creator. We join our ancestors as they sang psalms in the Temple, or as they passed through the divided waters of the Sea of Reeds. Religion is a sustained process of using the deep power of joy to see into the life of things.

"For you to keep it" – in the rituals we perform. A ritual is an *enactment of meaning*. That is what makes a house of worship not a theater, and a congregation something other than an audience. A congregation participates in a ritual, lives the reality it encodes; an audience merely suspends its disbelief while the play is going on, knowing that what it is seeing is a fiction.

Meanings are socially constructed. They belong to the shared life of communities. They involve a living connection to a past to which we feel ourselves to belong, and a future for which we hold ourselves responsible. They are always particular – to this group, that nation, this faith, that tradition. Science may be universal. Meaning never is. *Sacred* meanings are those we make when we covenant with God, listening to His voice, heeding His call.

We could not fully understand God's truth without being gods ourselves. God does not ask us to be anything other than what we are, finite beings whose knowledge is limited, whose lifespan is short, and whose horizons are circumscribed. For God, in creating us, gave our lives significance. Faith, Abrahamic faith, is about God and human beings making meaning in covenant together.

30:12 **לֹא בַשָּׁמַיִם** *Not in heaven* – Here God empowers His children. He gives them His greatest gift: His will as encoded in His word. The Torah is "not in heaven"; it is intelligible to all. Each member of the covenantal community has something to contribute to the totality of its meaning. As Maharsha (Rabbi Shmuel Eliezer Edels, 1555–1631) put it: There are six hundred thousand possible interpretations of the Torah, which is why the Torah was given to six hundred thousand Israelites, so that the revelation would include all possible interpretations (Maharsha, novellae on Berakhot 58a).

ח הָֽאָל֣וֹת הָאֵ֔לֶּה עַל־אֹיְבֶ֥יךָ וְעַל־שֹׂנְאֶ֖יךָ אֲשֶׁ֥ר רְדָפֽוּךָ׃ וְאַתָּ֣ה תָשׁ֔וּב
וְשָׁמַעְתָּ֖ בְּק֣וֹל יהוה וְעָשִׂ֙יתָ֙ אֶת־כָּל־מִצְוֺתָ֔יו אֲשֶׁ֛ר אָנֹכִ֥י מְצַוְּךָ֖ הַיּֽוֹם׃
ט וְהוֹתִֽירְךָ֩ יהוה אֱלֹהֶ֜יךָ בְּכֹ֣ל ׀ מַעֲשֵׂ֣ה יָדֶ֗ךָ בִּפְרִ֨י בִטְנְךָ֜ וּבִפְרִ֧י בְהֶמְתְּךָ֛
וּבִפְרִ֥י אַדְמָתְךָ֖ לְטֹבָ֑ה כִּ֣י ׀ יָשׁ֣וּב יהוה לָשׂ֤וּשׂ עָלֶ֙יךָ֙ לְט֔וֹב כַּאֲשֶׁר־
י שָׂ֖שׂ עַל־אֲבֹתֶֽיךָ׃ כִּ֣י תִשְׁמַ֗ע בְּקוֹל֙ יהוה אֱלֹהֶ֔יךָ לִשְׁמֹ֤ר מִצְוֺתָיו֙
וְחֻקֹּתָ֔יו הַכְּתוּבָ֕ה בְּסֵ֥פֶר הַתּוֹרָ֖ה הַזֶּ֑ה כִּ֤י תָשׁוּב֙ אֶל־יהוה אֱלֹהֶ֔יךָ
יא בְּכָל־לְבָבְךָ֖ וּבְכָל־נַפְשֶֽׁךָ׃ כִּ֚י הַמִּצְוָ֣ה הַזֹּ֔את אֲשֶׁ֛ר אָנֹכִ֥י כד ששי
יב מְצַוְּךָ֖ הַיּ֑וֹם לֹֽא־נִפְלֵ֥את הִוא֙ מִמְּךָ֔ וְלֹֽא־רְחֹקָ֖ה הִֽוא׃ לֹ֥א בַשָּׁמַ֖יִם הִ֑וא
לֵאמֹ֗ר מִ֣י יַעֲלֶה־לָּ֤נוּ הַשָּׁמַ֙יְמָה֙ וְיִקָּחֶ֣הָ לָּ֔נוּ וְיַשְׁמִעֵ֥נוּ אֹתָ֖הּ וְנַעֲשֶֽׂנָּה׃
יג וְלֹֽא־מֵעֵ֥בֶר לַיָּ֖ם הִ֑וא לֵאמֹ֗ר מִ֣י יַעֲבָר־לָ֜נוּ אֶל־עֵ֤בֶר הַיָּם֙ וְיִקָּחֶ֣הָ לָּ֔נוּ

אונקלוס

לְוָטַיָּא הָאִלֵּין, עַל בַּעֲלֵי דְבָבָךְ וְעַל סָנְאָךְ דִּרְדָפוּךְ: ח וְאַתְּ תְּתוּב, וּתְקַבֵּיל לְמֵימְרָא דַיי, וְתַעֲבֵיד יָת כָּל פִּקּוֹדוֹהִי, דַּאֲנָא מְפַקֵּיד לָךְ יוֹמָא דֵין: ט וְיוֹתְרִנָּךְ יי אֱלָהָךְ, בְּכֹל עוֹבָדֵי יְדָךְ, בִּוְלָדָא דִמְעָךְ, וּבִוְלָדָא דִבְעִירָךְ, וּבְאִבָּא דְאַרְעָךְ לְטָבָא, אֲרֵי יְתוּב יי, לְמִחְדֵּי עֲלָךְ לְטָב, כְּמָא דַחְדִי עַל אֲבָהָתָךְ: י אֲרֵי תְקַבֵּיל, לְמֵימְרָא דַיי אֱלָהָךְ, לְמִטַּר פִּקּוֹדוֹהִי וּקְיָמוֹהִי, דִּכְתִיבִין, בְּסִפַר אוֹרָיְתָא הָדֵין, אֲרֵי תְתוּב לְדַחַלְתָּא דַיי אֱלָהָךְ, בְּכָל לִבָּךְ וּבְכָל נַפְשָׁךְ: יא אֲרֵי תַפְקֵידְתָּא הָדָא, דַּאֲנָא מְפַקֵּיד לָךְ יוֹמָא דֵין, לָא מְפָרְשָׁא הִיא מִנָּךְ, וְלָא רַחִיקָא הִיא: יב לָא בִשְׁמַיָּא הִיא, לְמֵימַר, מַאן יִסַּק לַנָא לִשְׁמַיָּא וְיִסְּבַהּ לַנָא, וְיַשְׁמְעִנַּנָא יָתַהּ וְנַעְבְּדִנַּהּ: יג וְלָא מֵעִבְרָא לְיַמָּא הִיא, לְמֵימַר, מַאן יִעְבַּר לַנָא, לְעִיבַר יַמָּא וְיִסְּבַהּ לַנָא,

NOT IN HEAVEN

The Torah "is not in heaven," says Moshe. There is plenary truth in heaven; on earth we live among its reflections and refractions. The Tanakh does not deny that there are ultimate meanings in the universe. There are. That human life is sacred is one of them. But we will always be blind to the truths we do not like, that circumscribe our power or stand in the way of the fulfillment of our desires.

So the Torah turns to covenants. Covenant is about *the meanings we make together* – the agreements God makes with Noaḥ, then Avraham, then the Israelites at Sinai. These are meanings that have ceased to be facts and become instead morally binding commitments. Do not murder, do not rob, do not commit adultery, do not bear false witness. These are part of a total system of meanings, that include the historical memory of liberation from slavery in Egypt, by which a people agreed to bind itself and its descendants, taking on themselves a collective vocation. It is not meaning *discovered* or meaning *invented,* but meaning collectively *made and renewed* in the conscious presence of God – that is to say, an authority beyond ourselves and our merely human devices and desires.

Religion is, for the most part, the constant making and remaking of meaning, by the stories we tell, the prayers we say, and the rituals we perform. Religion is an authentic response to a real presence, but it is also a way of making that presence real by constantly living in response to it. It is truth translated into deed.

14 far side of the sea for us, and bring it to us that we may hear it and keep it?' This
word is very close to you. It is in your mouth and in your heart for you to keep
15 it. See: I have set before you today life and goodness, and death and SHEVI'I AND MAFTIR /REVI'I/
16 evil. For I charge you on this day to love the LORD your God, walk in His ways,
and keep His commandments, decrees, and laws. Then you will survive and
thrive and the LORD your God will bless you in the land you are coming into
17 to possess. But if your heart turns away and you do not listen and are led astray,
18 and bow down to other gods and worship them, then I declare to you today
that you will certainly perish; you will not live long in the land that you are
19 crossing the Jordan to enter and possess. I call heaven and earth as witnesses
against you today: I have set before you life and death, the blessing and the
20 curse. Choose life – so that you and your children may live, loving the LORD

רש״י

יד **כִּי קָרוֹב אֵלֶיךָ.** הַתּוֹרָה נִתְּנָה לָכֶם בִּכְתָב וּבְעַל פֶּה:

טו **אֶת הַחַיִּים וְאֶת הַטּוֹב.** זֶה תָּלוּי בָּזֶה, אִם תַּעֲשֶׂה טוֹב הֲרֵי לְךָ חַיִּים, וְאִם תַּעֲשֶׂה רָע הֲרֵי לְךָ הַמָּוֶת, וְהַכָּתוּב מְפָרֵשׁ וְהוֹלֵךְ הֵיאַךְ:

טז **אֲשֶׁר אָנֹכִי מְצַוְּךָ הַיּוֹם לְאַהֲבָה.** הֲרֵי הַטּוֹב, וּבוֹ תָּלוּי "וְחָיִיתָ וְרָבִיתָ", הֲרֵי הַחַיִּים:

יז **וְאִם יִפְנֶה לְבָבְךָ.** הֲרֵי הָרָע:

יח **כִּי אָבֹד תֹּאבֵדוּן.** הֲרֵי הַמָּוֶת:

יט **הַעִדֹתִי בָכֶם הַיּוֹם אֶת הַשָּׁמַיִם וְאֶת הָאָרֶץ.** שֶׁהֵם קַיָּמִים לְעוֹלָם, וְכַאֲשֶׁר תִּקְרֶה אֶתְכֶם הָרָעָה יִהְיוּ עֵדִים שֶׁאֲנִי הִתְרֵיתִי בָּכֶם בְּכָל זֹאת. דָּבָר אַחֵר, "הַעִדֹתִי בָכֶם הַיּוֹם אֶת הַשָּׁמַיִם" וְגוֹ', אָמַר לָהֶם הַקָּדוֹשׁ בָּרוּךְ הוּא לְיִשְׂרָאֵל: הִסְתַּכְּלוּ בַּשָּׁמַיִם שֶׁבָּרָאתִי לְשַׁמֵּשׁ אֶתְכֶם, שֶׁמָּא שִׁנּוּ אֶת מִדָּתָם? שֶׁמָּא לֹא עָלָה גַּלְגַּל חַמָּה מִן הַמִּזְרָח וְהֵאִיר לְכָל הָעוֹלָם, כְּעִנְיָן שֶׁנֶּאֱמַר: "וְזָרַח הַשֶּׁמֶשׁ וּבָא הַשָּׁמֶשׁ" (קהלת א, ה)? הִסְתַּכְּלוּ בָּאָרֶץ שֶׁבָּרָאתִי לְשַׁמֵּשׁ אֶתְכֶם, שֶׁמָּא שִׁנְּתָה מִדָּתָהּ? שֶׁמָּא זְרַעְתֶּם אוֹתָהּ וְלֹא צָמְחָה, אוֹ שֶׁמָּא זְרַעְתֶּם חִטִּים וְהֶעֱלְתָה שְׂעוֹרִים? וּמָה אֵלּוּ שֶׁנַּעֲשׂוּ לֹא לְשָׂכָר וְלֹא לְהֶפְסֵד, אִם זוֹכִין אֵין מְקַבְּלִין שָׂכָר וְאִם חוֹטְאִין אֵין מְקַבְּלִין פֻּרְעָנוּת – לֹא שִׁנּוּ אֶת מִדָּתָם, אַתֶּם שֶׁאִם זְכִיתֶם תְּקַבְּלוּ שָׂכָר וְאִם חֲטָאתֶם תְּקַבְּלוּ פֻּרְעָנוּת, עַל אַחַת כַּמָּה וְכַמָּה: **וּבָחַרְתָּ בַּחַיִּים.** אֲנִי מוֹרֶה לָכֶם שֶׁתִּבְחֲרוּ בְּחֵלֶק הַחַיִּים,

semantics of the native language of the soul: "This word is very close to you; it is in your mouth and in your heart" (Deut. 30:14). The beauty of Jewish spirituality is precisely that in Judaism God is close. You do not need to climb a mountain or enter an ashram to find the Divine Presence. It is there around the table on the Sabbath, in the light of the candles and the simple holiness of the Kiddush wine, in the blessing of children, in the peace of mind that comes when you leave the world to look after itself for a day while you celebrate the good things that come not from working but resting, not from buying but enjoying – the gifts you have had all along but did not have time to appreciate.

30:16 **וְחָיִיתָ וְרָבִיתָ** *Survive and thrive* – Judaism is about creating spiritual energy, the energy that, if used for the benefit of others, changes lives and begins to change the world. God is our bridge across the abyss that separates me from you, one person from the next. If I learn Torah rightly, then I will want to teach it. If I pray for what I need, I will become aware of what other people need. If I thank God for what He has given me, I will know that He wants me to give part of it to others. Those are litmus paper tests for knowing whether we are on the right or wrong track. Jewish spirituality is not a private starburst of the soul. Jewish life is not the search for personal salvation. It is a restless desire to change the world into a place in which God can feel at home.

30:19 **וּבָחַרְתָּ בַּחַיִּים** *Choose life* – Against all the many determinisms in the history of thought – astrological, philosophical, Spinozist, Marxist, Freudian, neo-Darwinian – Judaism

יד וְיַשְׁמִעֵנוּ אֹתָהּ וְנַעֲשֶׂנָּה׃ כִּי־קָרוֹב אֵלֶיךָ הַדָּבָר מְאֹד בְּפִיךָ וּבִלְבָבְךָ
טו לַעֲשֹׂתוֹ׃ רְאֵה נָתַתִּי לְפָנֶיךָ הַיּוֹם אֶת־הַחַיִּים וְאֶת־הַטּוֹב
טז וְאֶת־הַמָּוֶת וְאֶת־הָרָע׃ אֲשֶׁר אָנֹכִי מְצַוְּךָ הַיּוֹם לְאַהֲבָה אֶת־יהוה
אֱלֹהֶיךָ לָלֶכֶת בִּדְרָכָיו וְלִשְׁמֹר מִצְוֺתָיו וְחֻקֹּתָיו וּמִשְׁפָּטָיו וְחָיִיתָ
וְרָבִיתָ וּבֵרַכְךָ יהוה אֱלֹהֶיךָ בָּאָרֶץ אֲשֶׁר־אַתָּה בָא־שָׁמָּה לְרִשְׁתָּהּ׃
יז וְאִם־יִפְנֶה לְבָבְךָ וְלֹא תִשְׁמָע וְנִדַּחְתָּ וְהִשְׁתַּחֲוִיתָ לֵאלֹהִים אֲחֵרִים
יח וַעֲבַדְתָּם׃ הִגַּדְתִּי לָכֶם הַיּוֹם כִּי אָבֹד תֹּאבֵדוּן לֹא־תַאֲרִיכֻן יָמִים עַל־
יט הָאֲדָמָה אֲשֶׁר אַתָּה עֹבֵר אֶת־הַיַּרְדֵּן לָבוֹא שָׁמָּה לְרִשְׁתָּהּ׃ הַעִדֹתִי
בָכֶם הַיּוֹם אֶת־הַשָּׁמַיִם וְאֶת־הָאָרֶץ הַחַיִּים וְהַמָּוֶת נָתַתִּי לְפָנֶיךָ
כ הַבְּרָכָה וְהַקְּלָלָה וּבָחַרְתָּ בַּחַיִּים לְמַעַן תִּחְיֶה אַתָּה וְזַרְעֶךָ׃ לְאַהֲבָה

שביעי ומפטיר /רביעי/

אונקלוס

וְיַשְׁמְעִנַּנָא יָתַהּ וְנַעְבְּדִנַּהּ׃ יד אֲרֵי קָרִיב לְוָתָךְ, פִּתְגָּמָא לַחֲדָא, בְּפֻמָּךְ וּבְלִבָּךְ לְמֶעְבְּדֵיהּ׃ טו חֲזִי דִּיהָבִית קֳדָמָךְ יוֹמָא דֵין, יָת חַיֵּי וְיָת טָבְתָא, וְיָת מוֹתָא וְיָת בִּשְׁתָּא׃ טז דַּאֲנָא מְפַקֵּיד לָךְ יוֹמָא דֵין, לְמִרְחַם, יָת יי אֱלָהָךְ לִמְהָךְ בְּאוֹרְחָן דְּתָקְנָן קֳדָמוֹהִי, וּלְמִטַּר, פִּקּוֹדוֹהִי וּקְיָמוֹהִי וְדִינוֹהִי, וְתֵיחֵי וְתִסְגֵּי, וִיבָרְכִנָּךְ יי אֱלָהָךְ, בְּאַרְעָא, דְּאַתְּ עָלֵיל לְתַמָּן לְמֵירְתַהּ׃ יז וְאִם יִתְפְּנֵי לִבָּךְ וְלָא תְקַבֵּיל, וְתִטְעֵי, וְתִסְגּוֹד, לְטָעֲוָת עַמְמַיָּא וְתִפְלְחִנּוּן׃ יח חַוֵּיתִי לְכוֹן יוֹמָא דֵין, אֲרֵי מֵיבַד תֵּיבְדוּן, לָא תֵירְכוּן יוֹמִין עַל אַרְעָא, דְּאַתְּ עָבַר יָת יַרְדְּנָא, לְמֵיעַל לְתַמָּן לְמֵירְתַהּ׃ יט אַסְהֵידִית בְּכוֹן יוֹמָא דֵין יָת שְׁמַיָּא וְיָת אַרְעָא, חַיֵּי וּמוֹתָא יְהָבִית קֳדָמָךְ, בִּרְכָן וּלְוָטִין, וְתִתְרְעֵי בְחַיֵּי, בְּדִיל דְּתֵיחֵי אַתְּ וּבְנָךְ׃ כ לְמִרְחַם

GOD IS CLOSE

Over the ages, there have always been Jews who sought inspiration elsewhere – in heaven, across the sea, anywhere but here. During the First Temple period, the people were tempted by the gods of the people around them. Later, they were attracted to Hellenism. It is a strange phenomenon: some Jews have had a tendency to fall in love with people who do not love them and pursue almost any spiritual path but their own. This is debilitating. When those in search of spirituality go elsewhere, Jewish spirituality suffers.

It tends to happen in the paradoxical way that Moshe describes several times in Deuteronomy. It occurs in ages of affluence, not poverty, in eras of freedom, not slavery. The surrounding culture in most of these cases was hostile to Jews and Judaism. Becoming Baal worshippers did not lead to Israelites being welcomed by the Canaanites. Becoming Hellenized did not endear Jews to either the Greeks or the Romans. Abandoning Judaism in the nineteenth century did not end antisemitism; it inflamed it. Yet Jews often preferred to adopt the culture that rejected them rather than embrace the one that was theirs by birth and inheritance, where they had the chance of feeling at home. Was it the failure of Europe to accept the Jewishness of Jews and Judaism? Was it Judaism's failure to confront the challenge? The phenomenon defies any simple explanation. But in the process, we have lost great intellects, spirits, and minds.

Hence the power of Moshe's insistence: to find truth, beauty, and spirituality, you do not have to go elsewhere. The deepest roots of spirituality come from within a culture, a tradition, a sensibility. They come from the syntax and your God, heeding His voice and holding fast to Him, for this is your life and the length of your days, living in the land that the LORD swore to give to your ancestors, to Avraham, Yitzḥak, and Yaakov."

The haftara for Parashat Nitzavim is on page 1620 (even when Nitzavim and Vayelekh are read together).

רש״י

כְּאָדָם הָאוֹמֵר לִבְנוֹ, בְּרֹר לְךָ חֵלֶק יָפֶה בְּנַחֲלָתִי, וּמַעֲמִידוֹ עַל חֵלֶק הַיָּפֶה וְאוֹמֵר לוֹ: אֶת זֶה בְּרֹר לְךָ. וְעַל זֶה נֶאֱמַר: "ה' מְנָת חֶלְקִי וְכוֹסִי אַתָּה תּוֹמִיךְ גּוֹרָלִי" (תהלים טז, ה), הִנַּחְתָּ יָדִי עַל גּוֹרָל הַטּוֹב, לוֹמַר, אֶת זֶה קַח לְךָ:

"Do this. Don't do that." Nor would there be any logic in reward and punishment, both of which presuppose human responsibility for our actions.

"Choose life," our *parasha* teaches. Nothing sounds easier yet nothing has proved more difficult over time. Instead, people choose substitutes for life. They pursue wealth, possessions, status, power, fame, and to these gods they make the supreme sacrifice, realizing too late that true wealth is not what you own but what you are thankful for, that the highest status is not to care about status, and that influence is more powerful than power. That is why, though few faiths are more demanding, Jews have stayed faithful to Judaism, living Jewish lives, building Jewish homes, and continuing the Jewish story.

אֶת־יהוה אֱלֹהֶיךָ לִשְׁמֹעַ בְּקֹלוֹ וּלְדׇבְקָה־בוֹ כִּי הוּא חַיֶּיךָ וְאֹרֶךְ יָמֶיךָ
לָשֶׁבֶת עַל־הָאֲדָמָה אֲשֶׁר נִשְׁבַּע יהוה לַאֲבֹתֶיךָ לְאַבְרָהָם לְיִצְחָק
וּלְיַעֲקֹב לָתֵת לָהֶם׃

The הפטרה *for* פרשת נצבים *is on page 1621*
(even when נצבים *and* וילך *are read together).*

אונקלוס

יָת יי אֱלָהָךְ, לְקַבָּלָא לְמֵימְרֵיהּ וּלְאִתְקָרָבָא לְדַחְלְתֵיהּ, אֲרֵי הוּא חַיָּךְ וְאוֹרְכוּת יוֹמָךְ, לְמִתַּב עַל אַרְעָא, דְּקַיֵּים יי לַאֲבָהָתָךְ, לְאַבְרָהָם, לְיִצְחָק וּלְיַעֲקֹב לְמִתַּן לְהוֹן׃

insists that we are masters of our fate. We are neither programmed nor predestined. We can choose. Rambam leaves us in no doubt that free will is one of the fundamental principles of Judaism:

> Free will is bestowed on every human being. If one desires to turn toward the good way and be righteous, he has the power to do so. If one wishes to turn toward the evil way and be wicked, he is at liberty to do so.... This doctrine is an important principle, the pillar of the law and the commandment.... We have it in us to be as righteous as Moshe or as evil as Yorovam.
>
> If God had decreed that a person should either be righteous or wicked ... what room could there be for the whole of the Torah? By what right or justice could God punish the wicked or reward the righteous? (*Hilkhot Teshuva* 5:1)

Without free will, Judaism would not make sense. If we lacked freedom, there would be no point in God commanding us,

Parashat Vayelekh

31 1 2 Moshe went and spoke these words to all Israel. He told them, "I am a hundred
and twenty years old now, and no longer able to enter and to leave. And the
3 Lord has told me, 'You shall not cross this Jordan.' The Lord your God
Himself will cross ahead of you. He will destroy these nations before you,
and you shall take possession in their place. It is Yehoshua who will lead you
4 across, as the Lord has spoken. The Lord will do to those nations as He did to SHENI
Siḥon and to Og, kings of the Amorites, and to their land, when He destroyed
5 them. The Lord will deliver them to you and you shall deal with them just as
6 I have commanded you. Be strong and be determined. Do not fear or dread
them, for the Lord your God is going with you. He will not fail you or forsake
7 you." Then Moshe summoned Yehoshua and said to him in the sight SHELISHI /ḤAMISHI/
of all Israel: "Be strong and be determined, for it is you who will come with this
people into the land that the Lord has sworn to their ancestors to give them,

רש"י

לא ב **לא אוכל עוד לצאת ולבוא.** יכול שתשש כחו? תלמוד לומר: "לא כהתה עינו ולא נס לחה" (להלן לד, ז), אלא מהו "לא אוכל"? איני רשאי, שנטלה ממני הרשות ונתנה ליהושע: **וה' אמר אלי.** זהו פירוש "לא אוכל עוד לצאת ולבוא", לפי שה' אמר אלי: **אנכי היום.** היום מלאו ימי ושנותי, ביום זה נולדתי וביום זה אמות. דבר אחר, "לצאת ולבוא" בדברי תורה, מלמד שנסתתמו ממנו מסורות ומעינות החכמה:

ו **לא ירפך.** לא יתן לך רפיון להיות נעזב ממנו:

ז **כי אתה תבוא את העם הזה.** כתרגומו: "ארי את תיעול עם עמא הדין". משה אמר לו ליהושע: זקנים שבדור עמהם, הכל לפי דעתן ועצתן. אבל הקדוש ברוך הוא אמר ליהושע: "כי אתה תביא את בני ישראל אל הארץ אשר נשבעתי להם" (להלן פסוק כג), "תביא" על כרחם, הכל תלוי בך, טול מקל והך על קדקדן, דבר אחד לדור ולא שני דברים לדור:

> Be strong and be determined, for it is you who will come with this people into the land. (Deut. 31:7)

And these are God's:

> Be strong, be determined, because you shall bring the Israelites into the land. (31:23)

The difference in Hebrew is even slighter than it is in English. Moshe uses the verb *tavo*, "come with." God uses the verb *tavi*, "bring." It is the slightest of nuances, but Rashi tells us the words refer to two different styles of leadership. Here is Rashi's comment:

> Moshe said to Yehoshua, "Make sure that the elders of the generation are with you. Always act according to their opinion and advice." However, the Holy One, blessed be He, said to Yehoshua, "Because you shall bring the Israelites into the land that I promised them" – meaning, "Bring them even against their will. It all depends on you. If necessary, take a stick and beat them over the head. There is only one leader for a generation, not two." (Rashi on Deut. 31:7)

Moshe advises his successor to lead by consultation and consensus. God tells Yehoshua to lead firmly and with

פרשת וילך

לא א וַיֵּלֶךְ מֹשֶׁה וַיְדַבֵּר אֶת־הַדְּבָרִים הָאֵלֶּה אֶל־כָּל־יִשְׂרָאֵל: ב וַיֹּאמֶר אֲלֵהֶם
בֶּן־מֵאָה וְעֶשְׂרִים שָׁנָה אָנֹכִי הַיּוֹם לֹא־אוּכַל עוֹד לָצֵאת וְלָבוֹא
ג וַיהוה אָמַר אֵלַי לֹא תַעֲבֹר אֶת־הַיַּרְדֵּן הַזֶּה: יהוה אֱלֹהֶיךָ הוּא ׀
עֹבֵר לְפָנֶיךָ הוּא־יַשְׁמִיד אֶת־הַגּוֹיִם הָאֵלֶּה מִלְּפָנֶיךָ וִירִשְׁתָּם יְהוֹשֻׁעַ
ד הוּא עֹבֵר לְפָנֶיךָ כַּאֲשֶׁר דִּבֶּר יהוה: וְעָשָׂה יהוה לָהֶם כַּאֲשֶׁר עָשָׂה שני
ה לְסִיחוֹן וּלְעוֹג מַלְכֵי הָאֱמֹרִי וּלְאַרְצָם אֲשֶׁר הִשְׁמִיד אֹתָם: וּנְתָנָם יהוה
ו לִפְנֵיכֶם וַעֲשִׂיתֶם לָהֶם כְּכָל־הַמִּצְוָה אֲשֶׁר צִוִּיתִי אֶתְכֶם: חִזְקוּ וְאִמְצוּ
אַל־תִּירְאוּ וְאַל־תַּעַרְצוּ מִפְּנֵיהֶם כִּי ׀ יהוה אֱלֹהֶיךָ הוּא הַהֹלֵךְ עִמָּךְ
ז לֹא יַרְפְּךָ וְלֹא יַעַזְבֶךָּ: וַיִּקְרָא מֹשֶׁה לִיהוֹשֻׁעַ וַיֹּאמֶר אֵלָיו שלישי /חמישי/
לְעֵינֵי כָל־יִשְׂרָאֵל חֲזַק וֶאֱמָץ כִּי אַתָּה תָּבוֹא אֶת־הָעָם הַזֶּה אֶל־הָאָרֶץ

אונקלוס

לא א וַאֲזַל מֹשֶׁה, וּמַלֵּיל, יָת פִּתְגָּמַיָּא הָאִלֵּין עִם כָּל יִשְׂרָאֵל: ב וַאֲמַר לְהוֹן, בַּר מְאָה וְעַסְרִין שְׁנִין אֲנָא יוֹמָא דֵין, לֵית אֲנָא יָכֵיל עוֹד לְמִפַּק וּלְמֵיעַל, וַיי אֲמַר לִי, לָא תִעְבַּר יָת יַרְדְּנָא הָדֵין: ג יי אֱלָהָךְ, הוּא עָבַר קֳדָמָךְ, הוּא יְשֵׁיצֵי, יָת עַמְמַיָּא הָאִלֵּין, מִן קֳדָמָךְ וְתֵירְתִנּוּן, יְהוֹשֻׁעַ, הוּא עָבַר קֳדָמָךְ, כְּמָא דְמַלֵּיל יי: ד וְיַעֲבֵיד יי לְהוֹן, כְּמָא דַעֲבַד, לְסִיחוֹן וּלְעוֹג, מַלְכֵי אֱמוֹרָאָה וּלְאַרְעֲהוֹן, דְּשֵׁיצֵי יָתְהוֹן: ה וְיִמְסְרִנּוּן יי קֳדָמֵיכוֹן, וְתַעְבְּדוּן לְהוֹן, כְּכָל תַּפְקֵידְתָּא, דְּפַקֵּידִית יָתְכוֹן: ו תְּקַפוּ וְאִילְמוּ, לָא תִדְחֲלוּן וְלָא תִתַּבְרוּן מִן קֳדָמֵיהוֹן, אֲרֵי יי אֱלָהָךְ, מֵימְרֵיהּ מְדַבַּר קֳדָמָךְ, לָא יִשְׁבְּקִנָּךְ וְלָא יְרַחֲקִנָּךְ: ז וּקְרָא מֹשֶׁה לִיהוֹשֻׁעַ, וַאֲמַר לֵיהּ, לְעֵינֵי כָל יִשְׂרָאֵל תְּקַף וְאִילַם, אֲרֵי אַתְּ, תֵּיעוֹל עִם עַמָּא הָדֵין, לְאַרְעָא,

VAYELEKH

The shortest of all *parashot,* Vayelekh is a mere thirty verses long. Poignantly, Moshe tells the people, "I am a hundred and twenty years old now, and no longer able to enter and to leave" (Deut. 31:2). He will not lead them across the Jordan into the Promised Land. He summons his successor Yehoshua and, in the presence of the people, gives him words of encouragement. He instructs the people to gather every seven years to hear a public reading of the Torah. God appears to Moshe and Yehoshua, warning them that the Israelites may eventually stray from the covenant. He instructs them to write down the Torah and teach it to the people, as permanent testimony of the covenant itself. He then encourages Yehoshua, assuring him that He will be with him as he leads the people.

COMMAND AND CONSENSUS

The great transition is about to take place. Moshe's leadership is coming to an end. Yehoshua's is about to begin. Moshe blesses his successor. Then God does. But they give different blessings. These are Moshe's words:

8 and you will allocate it to them for an inheritance. The LORD Himself will go
before you. He will be with you. He will not fail you or forsake you. Do not fear
9 and do not be dismayed." Then Moshe wrote down this Law and gave it to the
priests, descendants of Levi, who carried the Ark of the Covenant of the LORD,
10 and to all the elders of Israel. Moshe then commanded them: "At the end of REVI'I
every seventh year, the year of remission, during the Festival of Tabernacles,
11 when all Israel comes to appear before the LORD your God at the place that
He will choose, you shall read out this Law in the presence of all Israel, for

רש״י

י **מִקֵּץ שֶׁבַע שָׁנִים.** בַּשָּׁנָה רִאשׁוֹנָה שֶׁל שְׁמִטָּה, הַשְּׁמִינִית. וְלָמָּה קוֹרֵא אוֹתָהּ "שְׁנַת הַשְּׁמִטָּה"? שֶׁעֲדַיִן שְׁבִיעִית נוֹהֶגֶת בָּהּ, בְּקָצִיר שֶׁל שְׁבִיעִית הַיּוֹצֵא לְמוֹצָאֵי שְׁבִיעִית:

יא **תִּקְרָא אֶת הַתּוֹרָה הַזֹּאת.** הַמֶּלֶךְ הָיָה קוֹרֵא מִתְּחִלַּת 'אֵלֶּה הַדְּבָרִים', כִּדְאִיתָא בְּמַסֶּכֶת סוֹטָה (דף מא ע״א), עַל בִּימָה שֶׁל עֵץ שֶׁהָיוּ עוֹשִׂין בָּעֲזָרָה:

Here too, by reading the Torah to the assembled people every seven years, he is to show that the nation as a political entity exists under the sacred canopy of the divine word. We are a people, the king is implicitly saying, formed by covenant. If we keep it, we will flourish; if not, we will fail.

Tanakh gives us vivid descriptions of covenant renewal ceremonies, similar to this one, in the days of Yehoshua (Josh. 24), Yoshiyahu (II Kings 23), Asa (II Chr. 15), and Ezra and Neḥemya (Neh. 8–10). These were historic moments when the nation consciously rededicated itself after a long period of religious relapse. Because of *hak'hel* and covenant renewal, Israel was eternally capable of becoming young again, recovering what Yirmeyahu called "the devotion of your youth" (Jer. 2:2).

What happened to *hak'hel* during the almost two thousand years in which Israel had no king, no country, no Temple? Some scholars have made the intriguing suggestion that the *minhag Eretz Yisrael*, the custom of Jews in and from the land of Israel, which lasted until about the thirteenth century, of reading the Torah not once every year but every three or three and a half years, was intended to create a seven-year cycle, so that the second reading would end at the same time as *hak'hel*, namely on the Sukkot following a Sabbatical year.

Indeed, the institution of the reading of the Torah on Sabbath morning, which goes back to antiquity, acquired new significance at times of exile. It incorporates customs that remind us of *hak'hel*: The Torah is read, as it was by the king at *hak'hel* and Ezra at his assembly, standing on a *bima*, a raised wooden platform. The Torah reader never stands alone; there are usually three people on the *bima*: the *segan* (*gabbai*), the reader, and the person called to the Torah, representing respectively God, Moshe, and the Israelites (see Levush's commentary on *Shulḥan Arukh, Orakh Ḥayyim* 141:4). According to most halakhists, the reading of the Torah is *ḥovat tzibbur*, an obligation of the community, as opposed to the study of Torah, which is *ḥovat yaḥid*, an obligation of the individual. So, I believe, *keriat haTorah* should be translated not as "the *reading* of the Torah" but as "the *proclaiming* of Torah." It is our equivalent of *hak'hel*, transposed from the seventh year to the seventh day.

It is hard for individuals, let alone nations, to stay perennially young. We drift, lose our way, become distracted, lose our sense of purpose and with it our energy and drive. The best way to stay young is never to forget "the devotion of our youth," the defining experiences that made us who we are, the dreams we had long ago of how we might change the world to make it a better, fairer, more spiritually beautiful place. *Hak'hel* was Moshe's parting gift to us, showing us how this might be done.

ח אֲשֶׁר נִשְׁבַּע יְהוָה לַאֲבֹתָם לָתֵת לָהֶם וְאַתָּה תַּנְחִילֶנָּה אוֹתָם: וַיהוָה
הוּא ׀ הַהֹלֵךְ לְפָנֶיךָ הוּא יִהְיֶה עִמָּךְ לֹא יַרְפְּךָ וְלֹא יַעַזְבֶךָּ לֹא תִירָא
ט וְלֹא תֵחָת: וַיִּכְתֹּב מֹשֶׁה אֶת־הַתּוֹרָה הַזֹּאת וַיִּתְּנָהּ אֶל־הַכֹּהֲנִים בְּנֵי
י לֵוִי הַנֹּשְׂאִים אֶת־אֲרוֹן בְּרִית יְהוָה וְאֶל־כָּל־זִקְנֵי יִשְׂרָאֵל: וַיְצַו מֹשֶׁה רביעי
אוֹתָם לֵאמֹר מִקֵּץ ׀ שֶׁבַע שָׁנִים בְּמֹעֵד שְׁנַת הַשְּׁמִטָּה בְּחַג הַסֻּכּוֹת:
יא בְּבוֹא כָל־יִשְׂרָאֵל לֵרָאוֹת אֶת־פְּנֵי יְהוָה אֱלֹהֶיךָ בַּמָּקוֹם אֲשֶׁר יִבְחָר

אונקלוס

דְּקַיֵּים יְיָ לַאֲבָהָתְהוֹן לְמִתַּן לְהוֹן, וְאַתְּ תַּחְסְנִנַּהּ לְהוֹן: ח וַייָ, הוּא מְדַבַּר קֳדָמָךְ, מֵימְרֵיהּ יְהֵי בְּסַעְדָּךְ, לָא יִשְׁבְּקִנָּךְ וְלָא יְרַחֲקִנָּךְ, לָא תִדְחַל וְלָא תִתְּבַר: ט וּכְתַב מֹשֶׁה יָת אוֹרָיְתָא הָדָא, וִיהַבַהּ, לְכָהֲנַיָּא בְּנֵי לֵוִי, דְּנָטְלִין, יָת אֲרוֹן קְיָמָא דַּייָ, וּלְכָל סָבֵי יִשְׂרָאֵל: י וּפַקֵּיד מֹשֶׁה יָתְהוֹן לְמֵימַר, מִסּוֹף שְׁבַע שְׁנִין, בִּזְמַן, שַׁתָּא דִשְׁמִטְתָּא בְּחַגָּא דִמְטַלַּיָּא: יא בְּמֵיתֵי כָל יִשְׂרָאֵל, לְאִתַּחֲזָאָה קֳדָם יְיָ אֱלָהָךְ, בְּאַתְרָא דְיִתְרְעֵי,

authority. Even if people do not agree with you, lead from the front. Be decisive. Be strong.

It is interesting that the person urging consensus is Moshe. This is the man who almost had to drag the people out of Egypt, through the sea, and across a howling desert, the man who did things of his own initiative without even asking God. It seems that at the end of his life, Moshe recognizes one great failure of his leadership. He has taken the Israelites out of Egypt, but he has not taken Egypt out of the Israelites. He now realizes that for them to experience a change of character, there would have to be a different kind of leadership, one that handed back responsibility to the people as a whole, and to the elders in particular.

God, on the other hand, forged the covenant only after Moshe explained to the people what was being proposed (Ex. 19:4–6), and the people – "*as one*" (19:8) – assented to it "*with one voice*" (24:3). It seems that both God and Moshe want Yehoshua to know that true leadership cannot be a one-sided affair, be it the pursuit of consensus or command-and-control. It must be a deft balance of both. They want Yehoshua to hear this in the most striking way, so each says what they are least expected to say.

Leadership is not simple. You have to listen, and you have to lead. You have to strive for consensus, but ultimately, if there is none, you must take the risk of deciding. There is a time to discuss and a time to act, a time to seek agreement and a time to move ahead without waiting for agreement. That is what both God and Moshe are telling Yehoshua in their different ways.

THE *HAK'HEL* CEREMONY

Once every seven years, on the second day of Sukkot in the year after the Sabbatical year, the people are to gather together in the Temple courtyard and hear a public reading of the Torah – specifically, selections from Deuteronomy itself (the details are set out by Rambam in *Hilkhot Ḥagiga* 3).

The Torah does not specify who is to perform the reading, but tradition ascribed the role to the king. To be sure, the Torah tends to separate religion and politics. The king is not High Priest, and the High Priest is not king. But the king is bound by the Torah. He is commanded to have a special Torah scroll written for him; he is to keep it with him when he sits on the throne and to read it "all the days of his life" (see Deut. 17:14–20 and commentary there).

12 them to hear. Assemble the people – men, women, and children, including the
migrants living in your towns – so that they may listen and learn to fear the
13 Lord your God and carefully keep all the words of this Law, and so that their
children, who do not know it, may listen and learn to be in awe of the Lord
your God, as long as you live in the land that you are crossing the Jordan to
possess."

רש"י

יב הָאֲנָשִׁים. לִלְמֹד: וְהַנָּשִׁים. לִשְׁמֹעַ: וְהַטָּף. לָמָּה בָּאִים? לָתֵת שָׂכָר לִמְבִיאֵיהֶם:

31:12 הָאֲנָשִׁים וְהַנָּשִׁים וְהַטַּף וְגֵרְךָ *Men, women, and children… migrants* – Judaism sees universal access to knowledge as fundamental to human dignity and equality. Every other form of equality has been based on either equality of power or of wealth. But there is an inherent problem with these aspirations. Power and wealth are both what I call material goods. The trouble with material goods is the more you share, the less you have. If you have total power but you decide to share it with nine other people, the result is you only have a tenth as much power that you began with. If you have a thousand dollars and share it with nine other people, you're left with only a tenth of the money that you began with. If you have a certain amount of knowledge, however, and you share that with nine others, you do not have less. Maybe you have more. The more we teach our knowledge to others, the more we learn.

Because wealth and power, at least in the short term, are zero-sum games – the more I share, the less I have – wealth and power, the economy and the state, economics and politics, are always arenas of conflict. Knowledge is not, because the more I give away, the more I have.

That is why the Jewish version of an egalitarian society, a society in which everyone reaches his or her own full dignity by having access to education and to knowledge, is the only form of egalitarianism that really has worked. *Hak'hel* establishes a culture that enables and encourages learning, not just for an elite, but for everyone.

31:13 וּבְנֵיהֶם אֲשֶׁר לֹא־יָדְעוּ *Their children, who do not know it* – National narratives can be, indeed must be, inclusive of those of all ages. The book of Deuteronomy as a whole is a restatement of the covenant for a new generation. A similar event is described in the last chapter of the book of Joshua once Yehoshua had fulfilled his mandate as Moshe's successor, bringing the people across the Jordan, leading them in their battles, and settling the land.

Another occurred many centuries later, in very different circumstances, in the reign of King Yoshiyahu. His grandfather Menashe, who reigned for fifty-five years, was one of the worst of Yehuda's kings, introducing idolatry, including child sacrifice. Yoshiyahu sought to return the nation to its faith, ordering the cleansing and repair of the Temple. In the course of this restoration, a copy of the Torah was discovered, sealed in a hiding place, to prevent it being destroyed during the many decades in which the Torah was almost forgotten. The king, deeply affected by this discovery, "summoned all the elders of Yehuda and Jerusalem.… He read out to them all the words of the scroll of the covenant that had been found in the House of the Lord.… And all the people pledged themselves to the covenant" (II Kings 23:1–3).

The most famous *hak'hel*-type ceremony was the national gathering convened by Ezra and Neḥemya after the second wave of returnees from Babylon (Neh. 8–10). Standing on a platform by one of the gates to the Temple, Ezra read the Torah to the assembly. The ceremony began on Rosh HaShana and culminated after Sukkot with the people collectively "binding themselves by an oath, under the penalty of a curse, to follow in the way of God's teaching as given into the hand of God's servant Moshe" (10:30).

Periodically retelling our national story – recalling the nation's history, giving thanks to God, and rededicating ourselves to the terms of our vocation – ensures that this story belongs to latecomers as much as to elders.

יב תִּקְרָא אֶת־הַתּוֹרָה הַזֹּאת נֶגֶד כָּל־יִשְׂרָאֵל בְּאָזְנֵיהֶם: הַקְהֵל אֶת־
הָעָם הָאֲנָשִׁים וְהַנָּשִׁים וְהַטַּף וְגֵרְךָ אֲשֶׁר בִּשְׁעָרֶיךָ לְמַעַן יִשְׁמְעוּ
וּלְמַעַן יִלְמְדוּ וְיָרְאוּ אֶת־יהוה אֱלֹהֵיכֶם וְשָׁמְרוּ לַעֲשׂוֹת אֶת־כָּל־דִּבְרֵי
יג הַתּוֹרָה הַזֹּאת: וּבְנֵיהֶם אֲשֶׁר לֹא־יָדְעוּ יִשְׁמְעוּ וְלָמְדוּ לְיִרְאָה אֶת־
יהוה אֱלֹהֵיכֶם כָּל־הַיָּמִים אֲשֶׁר אַתֶּם חַיִּים עַל־הָאֲדָמָה אֲשֶׁר אַתֶּם
עֹבְרִים אֶת־הַיַּרְדֵּן שָׁמָּה לְרִשְׁתָּהּ:

אונקלוס

תִּקְרֵי, יָת אוֹרָיְתָא הָדָא, קֳדָם כָּל יִשְׂרָאֵל וְתַשְׁמְעִנּוּן: יב כְּנוֹשׁ יָת עַמָּא, גֻּבְרַיָּא וּנְשַׁיָּא וְטַפְלָא, וְגִיּוֹרָךְ דִּבְקִרְוָךְ, בְּדִיל דְּיִשְׁמְעוּן וּבְדִיל דְּיֵילְפוּן, וְיִדְחֲלוּן קֳדָם יי אֱלָהֲכוֹן, וְיִטְּרוּן לְמֶעְבַּד, יָת כָּל פִּתְגָּמֵי אוֹרָיְתָא הָדָא: יג וּבְנֵיהוֹן דְּלָא יְדַעוּ, יִשְׁמְעוּן וְיֵילְפוּן, לְמִדְחַל קֳדָם יי אֱלָהֲכוֹן, כָּל יוֹמַיָּא, דְּאַתּוּן קַיָּמִין עַל אַרְעָא, דְּאַתּוּן, עָבְרִין יָת יַרְדְּנָא, לְתַמָּן לְמֵירְתַהּ:

31:12 **הַקְהֵל אֶת־הָעָם** *Assemble the people* – This is how Rambam describes the ceremony:

> Trumpets were blown throughout Jerusalem to assemble the people; and a high platform, made of wood, was brought and set up in the center of the court of women. The king went up and sat there so that his reading might be heard.…
>
> The *ḥazan* of the synagogue would take a *sefer Torah* and hand it to the head of the synagogue, and the head of the synagogue would hand it to the deputy High Priest, and the deputy High Priest to the High Priest, and the High Priest to the king, to honor him by the service of many persons.…
>
> The king would read the sections we have mentioned until he would come to the end. Then he would roll up the *sefer Torah* and recite a blessing after the reading, the way it is recited in the synagogue.…
>
> Proselytes who did not know Hebrew were required to direct their hearts and listen with utmost awe and reverence, as on the day the Torah was given at Sinai. Even great scholars who knew the entire Torah were required to listen with utmost attention.…
>
> Each had to regard himself as if he had been charged with the Torah now for the first time, and as though he had heard it from the mouth of God, for the king was an ambassador proclaiming the words of God. (*Hilkhot Ḥagiga* 3:4–6)

Apart from giving us a sense of the grandeur of the occasion, Rambam is making a radical suggestion: that *hak'hel* is a reenactment of the giving of the Torah at Sinai – "as on the day the Torah was given," "as though he had heard it from the mouth of God." The comparison almost certainly arises from Moshe's description of the giving of the Torah in Parashat Vaetḥanan:

> Make known… how you once stood before the Lord your God at Ḥorev, when the Lord said to me, "*Assemble* the people for Me, and I will let them *hear My words so that they may learn to be in awe of Me* as long as they live on earth, and *teach their children likewise*." (Deut. 4:9–10)

The italicized words are all echoed here, especially the word *hak'hel* itself, which only appears in one other place in the Torah. Sinai, then, is to be recreated in the Temple in Jerusalem every seven years, renewing the nation, men, women, children, and migrants, in its commitment to its founding principles.

14 The LORD said to Moshe, "Your time to die draws near. Call Yehoshua and come and stand in the Tent of Meeting, so that I may give him his charge." ḤAMISHI /SHISHI/
15 So Moshe and Yehoshua went and stood in the Tent of Meeting. The LORD
appeared in the Tent in a pillar of cloud; and the pillar of cloud stood at the
16 entrance to the Tent. Then the LORD said to Moshe, "Soon, you are going to
rest with your ancestors. And this people will begin to stray after the foreign
gods of the land into which they are going. They will forsake Me and break
17 the covenant I have made with them. My rage will flare against them at that
time. I will abandon them and hide My face from them. They will become easy
prey, and many evils and troubles will come upon them. On that day they will
ask, 'Have not these troubles come upon us because our God is not in our
18 midst?' And I – I will hide My face at that time because of all the evil they have
19 done by turning to other gods. So now write down this song and teach it to the

רש״י

יד| וַאֲצַוֶּנּוּ. וַאֲחַזְּקֶנּוּ:

טו| נֵכַר הָאָרֶץ. גּוֹיֵי הָאָרֶץ:

יז| וְהִסְתַּרְתִּי פָנַי. כְּמוֹ שֶׁאֵינִי רוֹאֶה בְּצָרָתָם:

יט| אֶת הַשִּׁירָה הַזֹּאת. ״הַאֲזִינוּ הַשָּׁמַיִם״ עַד ״וְכִפֶּר אַדְמָתוֹ עַמּוֹ״ (להלן לב, ח-מג):

Then something began to happen. In the midst of darkness, we began to see what looked like the first faint signs of light. One after another, prayers that Jews had said for hundreds of years, more in hope than expectation, began to come true.

"Sound the great shofar for our freedom." The ram's horn sounded and in one country after another Jews left the ghetto and were free.

"Raise the banner to gather our exiles." The banner of Zion was lifted and from across the globe Jews began to return to the land of our ancestors.

"Restore our judges as at first." The State of Israel was born. For the first time in almost two thousand years, Jews could rule over themselves instead of being ruled over by others. They could defend themselves instead of depending on others.

"Return in mercy to Your city, Jerusalem." In 1967, Jerusalem was reunited. Jews could pray again at the Temple wall.

And they streamed into the land. From Yemen, Iraq, and Iran, from Russia and Ethiopia, Jews who had been cut off from their people for decades, for centuries, came home. "If you should be expelled to the furthest of horizons, even from there the LORD your God will gather you, from there He will take you back" (Deut. 30:4).

Rabbi Joseph B. Soloveitchik once said that with the birth of the State of Israel there ended the "hiding of the face" of God. It was the beginning of the end of exile. God had reentered history.

31:18 **בַּיּוֹם הַהוּא** *At that time* – The Torah speaks of the "hiding of the face" of God in a particular context, namely the exile of Jews from their land. From the opening chapters of Genesis to the closing speeches of Deuteronomy, human transgression is seen in terms of dislocation, moral and physical. The divine withdrawal from history is described not as a timeless feature of human freedom but as a specific phase in the history of the covenant. If the children of Israel sin, exile will further deepen the alienation between man and God, until man experiences God in His absence, not His presence.

"WRITE THIS SONG"

The final mitzva is to "write down this song and teach it to

יד וַיֹּאמֶר יהוה אֶל־מֹשֶׁה הֵן קָרְבוּ יָמֶיךָ לָמוּת קְרָא אֶת־יְהוֹשֻׁעַ וְהִתְיַצְּבוּ כה חמישי /ששי/
בְּאֹהֶל מוֹעֵד וַאֲצַוֶּנּוּ וַיֵּלֶךְ מֹשֶׁה וִיהוֹשֻׁעַ וַיִּתְיַצְּבוּ בְּאֹהֶל מוֹעֵד׃
טו וַיֵּרָא יהוה בָּאֹהֶל בְּעַמּוּד עָנָן וַיַּעֲמֹד עַמּוּד הֶעָנָן עַל־פֶּתַח הָאֹהֶל׃
טז וַיֹּאמֶר יהוה אֶל־מֹשֶׁה הִנְּךָ שֹׁכֵב עִם־אֲבֹתֶיךָ וְקָם הָעָם הַזֶּה וְזָנָה ׀
אַחֲרֵי ׀ אֱלֹהֵי נֵכַר־הָאָרֶץ אֲשֶׁר הוּא בָא־שָׁמָּה בְּקִרְבּוֹ וַעֲזָבַנִי וְהֵפֵר
יז אֶת־בְּרִיתִי אֲשֶׁר כָּרַתִּי אִתּוֹ׃ וְחָרָה אַפִּי בוֹ בַיּוֹם־הַהוּא וַעֲזַבְתִּים
וְהִסְתַּרְתִּי פָנַי מֵהֶם וְהָיָה לֶאֱכֹל וּמְצָאֻהוּ רָעוֹת רַבּוֹת וְצָרוֹת וְאָמַר
בַּיּוֹם הַהוּא הֲלֹא עַל כִּי־אֵין אֱלֹהַי בְּקִרְבִּי מְצָאוּנִי הָרָעוֹת הָאֵלֶּה׃
יח וְאָנֹכִי הַסְתֵּר אַסְתִּיר פָּנַי בַּיּוֹם הַהוּא עַל כָּל־הָרָעָה אֲשֶׁר עָשָׂה כִּי
יט פָנָה אֶל־אֱלֹהִים אֲחֵרִים׃ וְעַתָּה כִּתְבוּ לָכֶם אֶת־הַשִּׁירָה הַזֹּאת וְלַמְּדָהּ

אונקלוס

יד וַאֲמַר יי לְמֹשֶׁה, הָא קְרִיבוּ יוֹמָךְ לִמְמָת, קְרִי יָת יְהוֹשֻׁעַ, וְאִתְעַתַּדוּ, בְּמַשְׁכַּן זִמְנָא וַאֲפַקְדִנֵּיהּ, וַאֲזַל מֹשֶׁה וִיהוֹשֻׁעַ, וְאִתְעַתַּדוּ בְּמַשְׁכַּן זִמְנָא: טו וְאִתְגְּלִי יי, בְּמַשְׁכְּנָא בְּעַמּוּדָא דַעֲנָנָא, וְקָם, עַמּוּדָא דַעֲנָנָא עַל תְּרַע מַשְׁכְּנָא: טז וַאֲמַר יי לְמֹשֶׁה, הָא אַתְּ שָׁכֵיב עִם אֲבָהָתָךְ, וִיקוּם עַמָּא הָדֵין, וְיִטְעֵי בָּתַר טָעֲוַת עַמְמֵי אַרְעָא, דְּהוּא עָלֵיל לְתַמָּן בֵּינֵיהוֹן, וְיִשְׁבְּקוּן דַּחְלְתִי, וִישַׁנּוּן יָת קְיָמִי, דִּגְזָרִית עִמְּהוֹן: יז וְיִתְקַף רוּגְזִי בְּהוֹן בְּעִדָּנָא הַהוּא, וַאֲרַחֵיקִנּוּן, וַאֲסַלֵּיק שְׁכִינְתִּי מִנְּהוֹן וִיהוֹן לְמִבַּז, וִיעָרְעָן יָתְהוֹן, בִּישָׁן סַגִּיאָן וְעָקָן, וְיֵימַר בְּעִדָּנָא הַהוּא, הֲלָא, מִדְּלֵית שְׁכִינַת אֱלָהִי בֵּינַי, עָרְעָנִי בִּישָׁתָא הָאִלֵּין: יח וַאֲנָא, סַלָּקָא אֲסַלֵּיק שְׁכִינְתִּי מִנְּהוֹן בְּעִדָּנָא הַהוּא, עַל כָּל בִּשְׁתָּא דַּעֲבַדוּ, אֲרֵי אִתְפְּנִיאוּ, בָּתַר טָעֲוַת עַמְמַיָּא: יט וּכְעַן, כְּתוּבוּ לְכוֹן יָת תֻּשְׁבַּחְתָּא הָדָא, וְאַלְּפַהּ

THE HIDING OF GOD'S FACE

Defeat, exile, suffering, persecution, are full of pain. But perhaps the greatest pain is to seek God and not to be able to find Him. "The LORD is my light and my salvation," said David in the book of Psalms, "whom need I fear?" (Ps. 27:1). "Though I walk through the valley of the shadow of death, I fear no evil, for You are with me" (23:4). But if You are *not* with me – what then? If God's light shines but we cannot see it, if God is close but we cannot feel it, if God speaks and we cannot hear, what then?

Once, in the Garden of Eden, God called out to man and asked, "*Ayeka* – Where are you?" But for nearly two thousand years we have called out to God, "*Ayeka*?" When the Temple was destroyed, where were You? When Your sages and saints were put to death as martyrs, where were You? When Your people were dispersed and forced to wander homeless across the earth, where were You? When they were tortured and murdered for their faith, where were You? Almighty God, when Your people cried out to You from Auschwitz and Bergen-Belsen and Sobibor and Majdanek, where were You? When one million Jewish children were gassed, burned, or buried alive, where were You?

The rabbinic literature contains an extraordinary statement, which by a slight textual emendation turned the phrase "Who is like You, LORD, among the mighty (*ba'elim*)?" (Ex. 15:11) into "Who is like You *ba'ilmim* – among the silent?" "A day will come [says God] when I will hide My face." It came. But it was not a day. It was two thousand years.

Israelites. Place it in their mouths, so that this song may be My witness against
20 them. When I have brought them into the land that flows with milk and with SHISHI /SHEVI'I/
honey, which I promised on oath to their ancestors, they will eat their fill and
grow fat, and they will turn to other gods and worship them, rejecting Me and
21 breaking My covenant. And when they are beset by many evils and troubles,
this song will testify as a witness against them, for it will not be forgotten by
their descendants. For I know what they are inclined to do even now, before I
22 have brought them into the land that I promised them on oath." So, that day,
23 Moshe wrote down this song and taught it to the Israelites. And He charged
Yehoshua son of Nun: "Be strong, be determined, because you shall bring the
24 Israelites into the land that I promised them – and I will be with you." Moshe
25 finished writing down in a scroll the words of this Law to the very end; and SHEVI'I
then Moshe instructed the Levites who carried the Ark of the Covenant of the

רש״י

כ) **וְנִאֲצוּנִי.** וְהִכְעִיסוּנִי, וְכֵן כָּל ׳נִאוּץ׳ לְשׁוֹן כַּעַס:

כא) **וְעָנְתָה הַשִּׁירָה הַזֹּאת לְפָנָיו לְעֵד.** שֶׁהִתְרֵיתִי בּוֹ בְּתוֹכָהּ עַל כָּל הַמּוֹצְאוֹת אוֹתוֹ: **כִּי לֹא תִשָּׁכַח מִפִּי זַרְעוֹ.** הֲרֵי זוֹ הַבְטָחָה לְיִשְׂרָאֵל שֶׁאֵין תּוֹרָה מִשְׁתַּכַּחַת מִזַּרְעָם לְגַמְרֵי:

כג) **וַיְצַו אֶת יְהוֹשֻׁעַ בִּן נוּן.** מוּסָב לְמַעְלָה כְּלַפֵּי שְׁכִינָה, כְּמוֹ שֶׁמְּפֹרָשׁ: "אֶל הָאָרֶץ אֲשֶׁר נִשְׁבַּעְתִּי לָהֶם":

the Torah from me. You must make it new again in every generation." The covenant is not to grow old. It has to be periodically renewed.

If we take the command to refer to the whole Torah and not just one chapter, then what is the significance of the word "song" (*shira*) which appears five times in this passage? It is clearly a keyword. On this, two nineteenth-century scholars offered striking explanations.

The Netziv (Rabbi Naftali Tzvi Yehuda Berlin, 1816–93, one of the great yeshiva heads of the nineteenth century) interprets it to mean that the whole Torah should be read as poetry, not prose; the word *shira* in Hebrew means both a song and a poem. To be sure, most of the Torah is written in prose, but the Netziv argued that it has characteristics of poetry. It is allusive rather than explicit. It leaves unsaid more than is said. Like poetry, it hints at deeper reservoirs of meaning, sometimes by the use of an unusual word or sentence construction. Descriptive prose carries its meaning on the surface. The Torah, like poetry, does not (preface to *Haamek Davar*, 3).

A different aspect is alluded to by Rabbi Yechiel Michel Epstein, author of the halakhic code *Arukh HaShulḥan*. He points out that the rabbinic literature is full of arguments, about which the Sages said: "These and those are the words of the living God" (*Ḥoshen Mishpat*, introduction). This, he says, is one of the reasons the Torah is called a "song" – because a song becomes more beautiful when scored for many voices interwoven in complex harmonies.

When Jews speak they often argue, but when they sing, they sing in harmony, as the Israelites did at the Sea of Reeds, because music is the language of the soul, and at the level of the soul we enter the unity of the Divine, which transcends the oppositions of lower worlds. The Torah is God's song, and we collectively are its singers. It is with a poetic sense of closure, then, that Moshe's life ends with the command to begin again in every generation, writing our own scroll, adding our own commentaries, the people of the book endlessly reinterpreting the book of the people, and singing its song.

אֶת־בְּנֵי־יִשְׂרָאֵל שִׂימָהּ בְּפִיהֶם לְמַעַן תִּהְיֶה־לִּי הַשִּׁירָה הַזֹּאת לְעֵד
כ בִּבְנֵי יִשְׂרָאֵל׃ כִּי־אֲבִיאֶנּוּ אֶל־הָאֲדָמָה ׀ אֲשֶׁר־נִשְׁבַּעְתִּי לַאֲבֹתָיו ששי /שביעי/
זָבַת חָלָב וּדְבַשׁ וְאָכַל וְשָׂבַע וְדָשֵׁן וּפָנָה אֶל־אֱלֹהִים אֲחֵרִים וַעֲבָדוּם
כא וְנִאֲצוּנִי וְהֵפֵר אֶת־בְּרִיתִי׃ וְהָיָה כִּי־תִמְצֶאןָ אֹתוֹ רָעוֹת רַבּוֹת וְצָרוֹת
וְעָנְתָה הַשִּׁירָה הַזֹּאת לְפָנָיו לְעֵד כִּי לֹא תִשָּׁכַח מִפִּי זַרְעוֹ כִּי יָדַעְתִּי
אֶת־יִצְרוֹ אֲשֶׁר הוּא עֹשֶׂה הַיּוֹם בְּטֶרֶם אֲבִיאֶנּוּ אֶל־הָאָרֶץ אֲשֶׁר
כב נִשְׁבָּעְתִּי׃ וַיִּכְתֹּב מֹשֶׁה אֶת־הַשִּׁירָה הַזֹּאת בַּיּוֹם הַהוּא וַיְלַמְּדָהּ
כג אֶת־בְּנֵי יִשְׂרָאֵל׃ וַיְצַו אֶת־יְהוֹשֻׁעַ בִּן־נוּן וַיֹּאמֶר חֲזַק וֶאֱמָץ כִּי אַתָּה
תָּבִיא אֶת־בְּנֵי יִשְׂרָאֵל אֶל־הָאָרֶץ אֲשֶׁר־נִשְׁבַּעְתִּי לָהֶם וְאָנֹכִי אֶהְיֶה
כד עִמָּךְ׃ וַיְהִי ׀ כְּכַלּוֹת מֹשֶׁה לִכְתֹּב אֶת־דִּבְרֵי הַתּוֹרָה־הַזֹּאת עַל־סֵפֶר
כה עַד תֻּמָּם׃ וַיְצַו מֹשֶׁה אֶת־הַלְוִיִּם נֹשְׂאֵי אֲרוֹן בְּרִית־יְהוָה לֵאמֹר׃ שביעי

אונקלוס

לִבְנֵי יִשְׂרָאֵל שַׁוְיַהּ בְּפֻמְּהוֹן, בְּדִיל דִּתְהֵי קֳדָמַי, תֻּשְׁבַּחְתָּא הָדָא, לְסָהִיד בִּבְנֵי יִשְׂרָאֵל: כ אֲרֵי אַעֵילִנּוּן, לְאַרְעָא דְּקַיֵּימִית לַאֲבָהָתְהוֹן, עָבְדָא חֲלַב וּדְבַשׁ, וְיֵיכְלוּן וְיִסְבְּעוּן וְיִתְפַּנְּקוּן, וְיִתְפְּנוּן, בָּתַר טָעֲוַת עַמְמַיָּא וְיִפְלְחוּן לְהוֹן, וְיַרְגְּזוּן קֳדָמַי, וִישַׁנּוּן יָת קְיָמִי: כא וִיהֵי, אֲרֵי יְעָרְעָן יָתְהוֹן, בִּישָׁן סַגִּיאָן וְעָקָן, וְתָתֵיב, תֻּשְׁבַּחְתָּא הָדָא קֳדָמוֹהִי לְסָהִיד, אֲרֵי, לָא תִתְנְשֵׁי מִפּוּם בְּנֵיהוֹן, אֲרֵי גְּלֵי קֳדָמַי יִצְרְהוֹן, דְּאִנּוּן עָבְדִין יוֹמָא דֵין, עַד לָא אַעֵילִנּוּן, לְאַרְעָא דְּקַיֵּימִית: כב וּכְתַב מֹשֶׁה, יָת תֻּשְׁבַּחְתָּא הָדָא בְּיוֹמָא הַהוּא, וְאַלְּפַהּ לִבְנֵי יִשְׂרָאֵל: כג וּפַקֵּיד יָת יְהוֹשֻׁעַ בַּר נוּן, וַאֲמַר תְּקַף וְאִילַם, אֲרֵי אַתְּ, תַּעֵיל יָת בְּנֵי יִשְׂרָאֵל, לְאַרְעָא דְּקַיֵּימִית לְהוֹן, וּמֵימְרִי יְהֵי בְּסַעְדָּךְ: כד וַהֲוָה כַּד שֵׁיצִי מֹשֶׁה, לְמִכְתַּב, יָת פִּתְגָּמֵי אוֹרָיְתָא הָדָא עַל סִפְרָא, עַד דִּשְׁלִימוּ: כה וּפַקֵּיד מֹשֶׁה יָת לֵיוָאֵי, נָטְלֵי, אֲרוֹן קְיָמָא דַּיְיָ לְמֵימַר:

the Israelites. Place it in their mouths, so that this song may be My witness" (Deut. 31:19).

According to the plain sense of the verse, God is speaking to Moshe and Yehoshua and is referring to the song in the following chapter. However, Oral Tradition gave the verse a wider interpretation, understanding it as a command for every Jew to write, or at least take some part in writing, a *sefer Torah*:

> Said Rabba: Even though our ancestors have left us a scroll of the Torah, it is our religious duty to write one for ourselves, as it is said: "So now, write down [literally, 'for yourselves'] this song and teach it to the Israelites. Place it in their mouths, so that this song may be My witness against them." (Sanhedrin 21b)

The logic of this reading seems to be that the phrase "write down for yourselves" could be construed as referring to every Israelite (Ibn Ezra), not just Moshe and Yehoshua. The Talmud offers a further reason. The verse goes on to say: "So that this song may be My witness against them" – implying the Torah as a whole, not just the song in chapter 32 (Nedarim 38a). Thus understood, Moshe's final message to the Israelites is: "It is not enough that you have received

26 LORD: "Take this scroll of the Law and place it beside the Ark of the Covenant
27 of the LORD your God. Let it remain there as a witness to you. For I know how
rebellious and stiff-necked you are. Even now, while I am still living among
you, you have been rebellious toward the LORD; how much more so will you
28 be after my death! Gather to me all the elders of your tribes and your officials, MAFTIR
so that I may proclaim these words in their hearing and call heaven and earth
29 to witness against them. For I know that after my death you will act in self-
destruction, turning away from the path that I have commanded you. In the
days to come evil will befall you, because you will do evil in the sight of the
30 LORD, angering Him with the work of your hands." Then Moshe proclaimed
the words of this song in the hearing of the entire assembly of Israel, to the very
end.

The haftara for Parashat Vayelekh is on page 1622, Shabbat Shuva, the Shabbat between Rosh Hashana and Yom Kippur.

רש״י

כו **לָקֹחַ.** כְּמוֹ: זָכוֹר, שָׁמוֹר, הָלוֹךְ: **מִצַּד אֲרוֹן בְּרִית ה׳.** נֶחְלְקוּ בּוֹ חַכְמֵי יִשְׂרָאֵל בְּבָבָא בַּתְרָא (דף יד ע״ב), יֵשׁ מֵהֶם אוֹמְרִים: דַּף הָיָה בּוֹלֵט מִן הָאָרוֹן מִבַּחוּץ וְשָׁם הָיָה מֻנָּח, וְיֵשׁ אוֹמְרִים: מִצַּד הַלּוּחוֹת הָיָה מֻנָּח בְּתוֹךְ הָאָרוֹן:

כח **הַקְהִילוּ אֵלַי.** וְלֹא תָּקְעוּ אוֹתוֹ הַיּוֹם בַּחֲצוֹצְרוֹת לְהַקְהִיל אֶת הַקָּהָל, לְפִי שֶׁנֶּאֱמַר: "עֲשֵׂה לְךָ" (במדבר י, ב), וְלֹא הִשְׁלִיט יְהוֹשֻׁעַ עֲלֵיהֶם. וְאַף בְּחַיָּיו נִגְנְזוּ קֹדֶם יוֹם מוֹתוֹ, לְקַיֵּם מַה שֶּׁנֶּאֱמַר: "וְאֵין שִׁלְטוֹן בְּיוֹם הַמָּוֶת" (קהלת ח, ח): **וְאָעִידָה בָּם אֶת הַשָּׁמַיִם וְאֶת הָאָרֶץ.** וְאִם תֹּאמַר, הֲרֵי כְּבָר הֵעִיד לְמַעְלָה: "הַעִדֹתִי בָכֶם הַיּוֹם" וְגוֹ׳ (לעיל ל, יט)? לְיִשְׂרָאֵל אָמַר אֲבָל לַשָּׁמַיִם וְלָאָרֶץ לֹא אָמַר, וְעַכְשָׁיו בָּא לוֹמַר: "הַאֲזִינוּ הַשָּׁמַיִם" וְגוֹ׳ (להלן לב, א):

כט **אַחֲרֵי מוֹתִי כִּי הַשְׁחֵת תַּשְׁחִתוּן.** וַהֲרֵי כָּל יְמוֹת יְהוֹשֻׁעַ לֹא הִשְׁחִיתוּ, שֶׁנֶּאֱמַר: "וַיַּעַבְדוּ הָעָם אֶת ה׳ כֹּל יְמֵי יְהוֹשֻׁעַ" (שופטים ב, ז)? מִכָּאן שֶׁתַּלְמִידוֹ שֶׁל אָדָם חָבִיב עָלָיו כְּגוּפוֹ, כָּל זְמַן שֶׁיְּהוֹשֻׁעַ חַי הָיָה נִרְאֶה לְמֹשֶׁה כְּאִלּוּ הוּא חַי:

כו לָקֹחַ אֵת סֵפֶר הַתּוֹרָה הַזֶּה וְשַׂמְתֶּם אֹתוֹ מִצַּד אֲרוֹן בְּרִית־יְהוָה
כז אֱלֹהֵיכֶם וְהָיָה־שָׁם בְּךָ לְעֵד׃ כִּי אָנֹכִי יָדַעְתִּי אֶת־מֶרְיְךָ וְאֶת־עָרְפְּךָ
הַקָּשֶׁה הֵן בְּעוֹדֶנִּי חַי עִמָּכֶם הַיּוֹם מַמְרִים הֱיִתֶם עִם־יְהוָה וְאַף כִּי־
כח אַחֲרֵי מוֹתִי׃ הַקְהִילוּ אֵלַי אֶת־כָּל־זִקְנֵי שִׁבְטֵיכֶם וְשֹׁטְרֵיכֶם וַאֲדַבְּרָה מפטיר
בְאָזְנֵיהֶם אֵת הַדְּבָרִים הָאֵלֶּה וְאָעִידָה בָּם אֶת־הַשָּׁמַיִם וְאֶת־הָאָרֶץ׃
כט כִּי יָדַעְתִּי אַחֲרֵי מוֹתִי כִּי־הַשְׁחֵת תַּשְׁחִתוּן וְסַרְתֶּם מִן־הַדֶּרֶךְ אֲשֶׁר
צִוִּיתִי אֶתְכֶם וְקָרָאת אֶתְכֶם הָרָעָה בְּאַחֲרִית הַיָּמִים כִּי־תַעֲשׂוּ אֶת־
ל הָרַע בְּעֵינֵי יְהוָה לְהַכְעִיסוֹ בְּמַעֲשֵׂה יְדֵיכֶם׃ וַיְדַבֵּר מֹשֶׁה בְּאָזְנֵי כָּל־
קְהַל יִשְׂרָאֵל אֶת־דִּבְרֵי הַשִּׁירָה הַזֹּאת עַד תֻּמָּם׃

The הפטרה *for* פרשת וילך *is on page 1623,* שבת שובה*,*
the שבת *between* ראש השנה *and* יום כיפור*.*

אונקלוס

כו סְבוּ, יָת סִפְרָא דְאוֹרָיְתָא הָדֵין, וּתְשַׁוּוֹן יָתֵיהּ, מִסְּטַר, אֲרוֹן קְיָמָא דַּייָ אֱלָהֲכוֹן, וִיהֵי תַמָּן בָּךְ לְסָהִיד: כז אֲרֵי אֲנָא יְדַעְנָא יָת סָרְבָנוּתָךְ, וְיָת קְדָלָךְ קַשְׁיָא, הָא עַד דַּאֲנָא קַיָּם עִמְּכוֹן יוֹמָא דֵין, מְסָרְבִין הֲוֵיתוֹן קֳדָם יְיָ, וְאַף בָּתַר דְּאֵמוּת: כח כְּנוּשׁוּ לְוָתִי, יָת כָּל סָבֵי שִׁבְטֵיכוֹן וְסָרְכֵיכוֹן, וַאֲמַלֵּיל קֳדָמֵיהוֹן, יָת פִּתְגָּמַיָּא הָאִלֵּין, וְאַסְהֵיד בְּהוֹן, יָת שְׁמַיָּא וְיָת אַרְעָא: כט אֲרֵי יְדַעְנָא, בָּתַר דְּאֵמוּת אֲרֵי חַבָּלָא תְחַבְּלוּן, וְתִסְטוּן מִן אוֹרְחָא, דְּפַקֵּידִית יָתְכוֹן, וּתְעָרַע יָתְכוֹן בִּישְׁתָא בְּסוֹף יוֹמַיָּא, אֲרֵי תַעְבְּדוּן יָת דְּבִישׁ קֳדָם יְיָ, לְאַרְגָּזָא קֳדָמוֹהִי בְּעוֹבָדֵי יְדֵיכוֹן: ל וּמַלֵּיל מֹשֶׁה, קֳדָם כָּל קְהָלָא דְיִשְׂרָאֵל, יָת פִּתְגָּמֵי תֻשְׁבַּחְתָּא הָדָא, עַד דִּשְׁלִימוּ:

Parashat Haazinu

32 1 "Listen, heavens, I will speak; / let the earth hear the words of my

רש״י

לב א הַאֲזִינוּ הַשָּׁמַיִם. שֶׁאֲנִי מַתְרֶה בָּהֶם בְּיִשְׂרָאֵל, וְתִהְיוּ עֵדִים
בַּדָּבָר, שֶׁכָּךְ אָמַרְתִּי לָהֶם שֶׁאַתֶּם תִּהְיוּ עֵדִים, וְכֵן "וְתִשְׁמַע הָאָרֶץ".
וְלָמָּה הֵעִיד בָּהֶם שָׁמַיִם וָאָרֶץ? אָמַר מֹשֶׁה: אֲנִי בָּשָׂר וָדָם, לְמָחָר אֲנִי
מֵת, אִם יֹאמְרוּ יִשְׂרָאֵל לֹא קִבַּלְנוּ עָלֵינוּ הַבְּרִית, מִי בָּא וּמַכְחִישָׁם?
לְפִיכָךְ הֵעִיד בָּהֶם שָׁמַיִם וָאָרֶץ, עֵדִים שֶׁהֵם קַיָּמִים לְעוֹלָם. וְעוֹד,
שֶׁאִם יִזְכּוּ יָבוֹאוּ הָעֵדִים וְיִתְּנוּ שְׂכָרָם, "הַגֶּפֶן תִּתֵּן פִּרְיָהּ וְהָאָרֶץ תִּתֵּן
אֶת יְבוּלָהּ וְהַשָּׁמַיִם יִתְּנוּ טַלָּם" (זכריה ח, יב), וְאִם יִתְחַיְּבוּ תִּהְיֶה בָּהֶם יַד
הָעֵדִים תְּחִלָּה, "וְעָצַר אֶת הַשָּׁמַיִם וְלֹא יִהְיֶה מָטָר וְהָאֲדָמָה לֹא תִתֵּן
אֶת יְבוּלָהּ", וְאַחַר כָּךְ: "וַאֲבַדְתֶּם מְהֵרָה" (לעיל יא, יז) עַל יְדֵי הָאֻמּוֹת:

at Sinai, renewed on the banks of the Jordan, and renewed again at significant moments of Jewish history (see note on Deut. 31:13). It is the written record of the agreement, just as a *ketuba* is a written record of the obligations undertaken by a husband toward his wife.

We now also understand the place of Deuteronomy in Tanakh as a whole. Had the generation that left Egypt had the faith and courage to enter the Promised Land, all Jewish history would turn on the revelation at Sinai. In fact, though, the episode of the spies showed that that generation lacked the spirit to do so. Therefore the critical moment came for the next generation, when Moshe at the end of his life renewed the covenant with them as the condition of their inheritance of the land. The four previous books of the Torah lead up to this moment, and all the other books of Tanakh are a commentary on it – an account of how it worked out in the course of time. Deuteronomy is the book of the covenant, the center point of Jewish theology.

Moshe's Song

For a month, Moshe has taught the people. He has told them their history and destiny, and the laws that will make theirs a unique society of people bound in covenant with one another and with God. He has renewed the covenant and then handed the leadership on to his successor and disciple Yehoshua. His final act will be blessing the people, tribe by tribe. But before that, there is one more thing he must do. He must sum up his prophetic message in a way the people will always remember and be inspired by. He knows that the best way of doing so is in music. So the last thing Moshe does before giving the people his deathbed blessing is to teach them a song.

Jewish history is not so much read as sung. Every day, in Judaism, we preface our morning prayers with *Pesukei DeZimra*, the "Verses of Song," with their magnificent crescendo, Psalm 150, in which instruments and the human voice combine to sing God's praises. Mystics go further and speak of the song of the universe, what Pythagoras called "the music of the spheres." This is what Psalm 19 means when it says, "The heavens tell of God's glory.... There is no speech; there are no words; their voice is not heard, yet their music carries across the land, their words to the end of the earth" (Ps. 19:2–5). Beneath the silence, audible only to the inner ear, creation sings to its Creator.

Who hears this song? The priest thinks in terms of universal rules that are eternally valid. The prophet is attuned to the particularities of a given situation and the relationships between those involved. *The prophet has emotional intelligence.* He or she hears the silent cry of the oppressed, and the incipient anger of Heaven. The vehicle of biblical prophecy is not prose, but poetry – language that engages the senses and the unconscious memory through its music. This is what Rabbi Joseph B. Soloveitchik described as "the Torah of his mother." From his mother, he said:

> I learned that Judaism expresses itself not only in formal compliance with the law but also in a living experience. She taught me that there is a flavor, a scent and warmth to mitzvot. I learned from her the most important thing in

פרשת האזינו

לב א הַאֲזִינוּ הַשָּׁמַיִם וַאֲדַבֵּרָה | וְתִשְׁמַע הָאָרֶץ אִמְרֵי־פִי׃ כו

אונקלוס

לב א אַצִיתוּ שְׁמַיָּא וַאֲמַלֵּיל, וְתִשְׁמַע אַרְעָא מֵימְרֵי פּוּמִי:

HAAZINU

Parashat Haazinu consists of the song sung by Moshe as his last lesson to the Israelites before blessing them and ascending Mount Nevo to die. It expresses in poetic form the relationship between the God of righteousness and His often recalcitrant people. The idea behind the song belongs to the logic of covenant, in which one of the parties can bring a case against the other for non-fulfillment of duties agreed to in the covenant itself. This kind of lawsuit (known in Biblical Hebrew as a *riv*) is referred to often by the later prophets, usually an accusation by God against the Israelites but occasionally the opposite.

THE END OF THE COVENANT DOCUMENT

More perhaps than any other book in the Torah, Deuteronomy is a highly structured work, blending together genres in a meticulous composite form. A number of archaeological discoveries have thrown new light on this form. They are the engraved records of ancient treaties between neighboring powers. Among them are the Stele of the Vultures commemorating the victory of Eannatum, ruler of Lagash in southern Mesopotamia, over the people of Umma, and the Stele of Naram-Sin, king of Kish and Akkad, a treaty with the ruler of Elam. Both date from the third millennium BCE, before the time of Avraham.

What the treaties show is the precise form of ancient covenants – closely reflected in the book of Deuteronomy thus far. They had six parts:

1. They began with a *preamble*, establishing the identity of the person or power initiating the covenant – in Deuteronomy: 1:1–1:5.
2. This was followed by a *historical prologue*, reviewing the history of the relationship between the two parties to the covenant: 1:6–4:49.
3. Then came the provisions of the covenant itself, the *stipulations*, which were often stated in two forms: (a) general principles: 5:1–11:32; and (b) detailed provisions: 12:1–26:19.
4. There then followed a provision for the covenant to be *deposited* in a sacred place and *read on a regular basis*: 27:1–26, 31:1–30.
5. Next came the *sanctions* associated with the covenant: the blessings that would follow if it was adhered to, and the curses that would occur if it was broken: 28:1–69.
6. Lastly there was a statement of the *witnesses* to the agreement – usually the gods of the nations involved – in Deuteronomy: "heaven and earth": 30:19–32:1.

The entire book until now is, in fact, structured as a covenant on a monumental scale.

We now see the extraordinary nature of the book. It has taken an ancient political formula and used it for an entirely new purpose. It follows precisely the structure of an ancient suzerainty treaty between a strong power, God, and a weak one, the Israelites. Politically, such treaties were well known in the ancient world, but religiously this is unique. For it means that God has taken an entire nation to be His "partners in the work of creation" by showing all humanity what it is to construct a society that honors each individual as the image of God.

We now understand the meaning of the traditional name for Deuteronomy, *Mishneh Torah*. It means that this book is a "copy" of the covenant between God and the people, made

2 mouth. / May my teaching pour down like rain, / let my speech fall
like the dew; / like gentle rain on tender plants, / like showers upon
3 the grasses. / As I call out the name of the LORD – / come, praise
4 the greatness of our God. / The Rock, His work is whole, / and all
His ways are justice. / A God of faith who does no wrong, / just

רש״י

ב יַעֲרֹף כַּמָּטָר לִקְחִי. זוֹ הִיא הָעֵדוּת שֶׁתָּעִידוּ, שֶׁאֲנִי אוֹמֵר בִּפְנֵיכֶם: תּוֹרָה שֶׁנָּתַתִּי לְיִשְׂרָאֵל שֶׁהִיא חַיִּים לָעוֹלָם, כַּמָּטָר הַזֶּה שֶׁהוּא חַיִּים לָעוֹלָם, כַּאֲשֶׁר יַעַרְפוּ הַשָּׁמַיִם טַל וּמָטָר: יַעֲרֹף. לְשׁוֹן יַטִּיף, וְכֵן: ״יַעַרְפוּ טָל״ (להלן לג, כח), ״יִרְעֲפוּן דָּשֶׁן״ (תהלים סה, יב): תִּזַּל כַּטַּל. שֶׁהַכֹּל שְׂמֵחִים בּוֹ, לְפִי שֶׁהַמָּטָר יֵשׁ בּוֹ עֲגָבִים, כְּגוֹן הוֹלְכֵי דְרָכִים וּמִי שֶׁהָיָה בּוֹרוֹ מָלֵא יַיִן: כִּשְׂעִירִם. לְשׁוֹן ״רוּחַ סְעָרָה״, כְּתַרְגּוּמוֹ: ״כְּרוּחֵי מִטְרָא״, מָה הָרוּחוֹת הַלָּלוּ מְחַזְּקִין אֶת הָעֲשָׂבִים וּמְגַדְּלִין אוֹתָם, אַף דִּבְרֵי תוֹרָה מְחַזְּקִין אֶת לוֹמְדֵיהֶן וּמְגַדְּלִין אוֹתָן: וְכִרְבִיבִים. טִפֵּי מָטָר, וְנִרְאֶה לִי, עַל שֵׁם שֶׁיּוֹרֶה כַּחֵץ נִקְרָא ׳רְבִיב׳, כְּמָה דְאַתְּ אָמַר: ״רֹבֶה קַשָּׁת״ (בראשית כא, כ): דֶשֶׁא. אַרְבְּרִי״ן, עֲטִיפַת הָאָרֶץ מְכֻסָּה בְּיֶרֶק: עֵשֶׂב. קֶלַח אֶחָד קָרוּי ׳עֵשֶׂב׳, וְכָל מִין וּמִין לְעַצְמוֹ קָרוּי ׳עֵשֶׂב׳:

ג כִּי שֵׁם ה׳ אֶקְרָא. הֲרֵי ׳כִּי׳ מְשַׁמֵּשׁ בִּלְשׁוֹן ׳כַּאֲשֶׁר׳, כְּמוֹ: ״כִּי תָבֹאוּ אֶל הָאָרֶץ״, כְּשֶׁאֶקְרָא וְאַזְכִּיר שֵׁם ה׳, אַתֶּם ״הָבוּ גֹדֶל לֵאלֹהֵינוּ״ וּבָרְכוּ שְׁמוֹ. מִכָּאן שֶׁעוֹנִין: ״בָּרוּךְ שֵׁם כְּבוֹד מַלְכוּתוֹ״ אַחַר בְּרָכָה שֶׁבַּמִּקְדָּשׁ:

ד הַצּוּר תָּמִים פָּעֳלוֹ. אַף עַל פִּי שֶׁהוּא חָזָק, כְּשֶׁמֵּבִיא פֻּרְעָנוּת עַל עוֹבְרֵי רְצוֹנוֹ, לֹא בְּשֶׁטֶף הוּא מֵבִיא כִּי אִם בְּדִין, כִּי ״תָּמִים פָּעֳלוֹ״: אֵל אֱמוּנָה. לְשַׁלֵּם לַצַּדִּיקִים צִדְקָתָם לָעוֹלָם הַבָּא, וְאַף עַל פִּי שֶׁמְּאַחֵר אֶת תַּגְמוּלָם, סוֹפוֹ לְאַמֵּן אֶת דְּבָרָיו: וְאֵין עָוֶל. אַף לָרְשָׁעִים מְשַׁלֵּם שְׂכַר צִדְקָתָם בָּעוֹלָם הַזֶּה: צַדִּיק וְיָשָׁר הוּא. הַכֹּל מַצְדִּיקִים עֲלֵיהֶם אֶת דִּינוֹ, וְכָךְ רָאוּי וְיָשָׁר לָהֶם. ״צַדִּיק״ מִפִּי הַבְּרִיּוֹת ״וְיָשָׁר הוּא״, וְרָאוּי לְהַצְדִּיקוֹ:

the very small ones, each according to their power [of understanding]. Yet God said to Israel, "Do not believe that there are many gods in heaven because you heard many voices. Know that I alone am the LORD your God" (Shemot Rabba 29:1).

Judaism, in short, says: "Out of the One, many." The miracle of creation is that unity in heaven produces diversity on earth. Torah is the rain that feeds this diversity, allowing each of us to become what only we can be.

GOD OF FAITH

The Rabbis of the first centuries of the Common Era communicated profound truths in a deceptively simple way. Commenting on the phrase "a God of faith" (simply understood to mean that He is faithful to His promises), they said, "This means the God who had *faith in the world He was about to create*" (Sifrei 307). In that sentence lies an extraordinary suggestion of the risk God took when He made mankind.

Biblical faith, with its emphasis on free will and responsibility, constantly holds before us the paradox of human history. There are times when we scale the heights of goodness. But there are others when we descend to the depths of evil. Modern thought has focused on the wrong question. It has asked how God could have created nature. The Rabbis posed a question altogether more profound. How could God have created man? It is one thing to believe that God in His goodness made the universe. It is another to believe that God in His goodness made a form of life, *Homo sapiens*, capable of inflicting untold cruelty and suffering on its own members. The Torah says that before the flood, contemplating the violence that filled the world, God "regretted that He had made man on earth and His heart was touched with sorrow" (Gen. 6:6). After Auschwitz, that verse echoes with almost unbearable pathos.

The Rabbis gave a remarkable answer. Creation testifies not merely to God's power but also, as it were, to His belief in mankind. At the heart of religion is not just the faith we have in God. No less significant is *the faith God has in us*. That faith is surely often tested. It is tested when we turn our back on God. It is tested no less when we commit evil in His name. Yet He does not lose faith that one day we will learn this: that God, "lover of peoples" (Deut. 33:3), has given us many universes of faith but only one world in which to live together.

ב יַעֲרֹ֤ף כַּמָּטָר֙ לִקְחִ֔י תִּזַּ֥ל כַּטַּ֖ל אִמְרָתִ֑י
כִּשְׂעִירִ֣ם עֲלֵי־דֶ֔שֶׁא וְכִרְבִיבִ֖ים עֲלֵי־עֵֽשֶׂב׃
ג כִּ֛י שֵׁ֥ם יהוה אֶקְרָ֑א הָב֥וּ גֹ֖דֶל לֵאלֹהֵֽינוּ׃
ד הַצּוּר֙ תָּמִ֣ים פָּעֳל֔וֹ כִּ֥י כָל־דְּרָכָ֖יו מִשְׁפָּ֑ט
אֵ֤ל אֱמוּנָה֙ וְאֵ֣ין עָ֔וֶל צַדִּ֥יק וְיָשָׁ֖ר הֽוּא׃

אונקלוס

ב יִבְסַם כְּמִטְרָא אֻלְפָנִי, יִתְקַבַּל כְּטַלָּא מֵימְרִי, כְּרוּחֵי מִטְרָא דְּנָשְׁבִין עַל דִּתְאָה, וְכִרְסִיסֵי מַלְקוֹשָׁא דְּעַל עִסְבָּא: ג אֲרֵי, בִּשְׁמָא דַּייָ אֲנָא מְצַלֵּי, הַבוּ רְבוּתָא קֳדָם אֱלָהַנָא: ד תַּקִּיפָא דְּשַׁלְמִין עוֹבָדוֹהִי, אֲרֵי כָל אוֹרְחָתֵיהּ דִּינָא, אֱלָהָא מְהֵימְנָא דְּמִן קֳדָמוֹהִי עַוְלָא לָא נָפֵיק, מִן קֳדָם דְּזַכַּאי וְקַשִּׁיט הוּא:

life – to feel the presence of the Almighty and the gentle pressure of His hand resting upon my frail shoulders. Without her teachings, which quite often were transmitted to me in silence, I would have grown up a soulless being, dry and insensitive. ("A Tribute to the Rebbetzin of Talne")

At the very end of his life, the greatest of all the prophets turns to emotional intelligence, to the spirituality of song, knowing that unless he does so, his teachings might enter the minds of the Israelites but not their hearts, their passions, their emotive DNA. It is feelings that move us to act, give us the energy to aspire, and fuel our ability to hand on our commitments to those who come after us. As Robert Frost said, "Poetry is what is lost in translation." And faith is poetry, not prose.

32:2 יַעֲרֹף כַּמָּטָר לִקְחִי *May my teaching pour down like rain* – We are invited to think of the Torah as being like the rain that waters the ground so that it brings forth produce. Sifrei puts it thus:

> "May my teaching pour down like rain": Just as the rain is one thing, yet it falls on trees, enabling each to produce tasty fruit according to the kind of tree it is – the vine in its way, the olive tree in its way, and the date palm in its way – so the Torah is one, yet its words yield Scripture, Mishna, laws, and lore.
>
> "Like showers upon the grasses": Just as showers fall upon plants and make them grow, some green, some red, some black, some white, so the words of Torah produce teachers, worthy individuals, sages, the righteous, and the pious." (Haazinu 306)

There is only one Torah, yet it has multiple effects. It gives rise to different kinds of teaching, different sorts of virtue. Torah is sometimes seen by its critics as overly prescriptive, as if it sought to make everyone the same. The Midrash argues otherwise. The Torah is compared to rain precisely to emphasize that its most important effect is to make each of us grow into what we could become. As the Mishna puts it: "When a human being makes many coins from the same mint, they are all the same. God makes everyone in the same image – His image – yet none is the same as another" (Yerushalmi, Sanhedrin 4:5). There is no single role model of the religious hero or heroine in Tanakh. The patriarchs and matriarchs each had their own unmistakable character. Kings, priests, and prophets had different roles to play. Even among the prophets, "no two prophesy in the same style," said the Sages (Sanhedrin 89a). Eliyahu was zealous, Elisha gentle. Hoshea speaks of love; Amos speaks of justice. Yeshayahu's visions are less opaque than those of Yeḥezkel.

The same applies to the revelation at Sinai itself. Each individual heard, in the same words, a different inflection:

> "The Lord's voice rings with power" (Ps. 29:4): that is, according to the power of each individual, young, old,

5 is He and upright. / Did He act ruinously? No, with His children lies the
6 fault, / a warped and twisted generation. / Is this how you repay the
LORD, / you foolish, unwise people? / Is not He your Father, your
7 Maker, / who formed you and set you on your feet? / Remember SHENI
the days of old, / consider the years of ages past; / ask your father,
8 and he will tell you; / your elders, and they will speak. / When the
Highest gave nations their heritage, / when He divided humankind, /
He fixed the boundaries of peoples / by the number of Israel's sons. /
9 The LORD's own share is His people, / Yaakov His allotted place. /

רש״י

ה **שִׁחֵת לוֹ וְגוֹ׳.** כְּתַרְגּוּמוֹ: "חַבִּילוּ לְהוֹן לָא לֵיהּ": **בָּנָיו מוּמָם.** בָּנָיו הָיוּ, וְהַשְׁחָתָה שֶׁהִשְׁחִיתוּ הִיא מוּמָם: **בָּנָיו מוּמָם.** מוּמָם שֶׁל בָּנָיו הָיָה וְלֹא מוּמוֹ: **דּוֹר עִקֵּשׁ.** עָקוֹם וּמְעֻקָּל, כְּמוֹ: "וְאֵת כָּל הַיְשָׁרָה יְעַקֵּשׁוּ" (מיכה ג, ט), וּבִלְשׁוֹן מִשְׁנָה: "חֻלְדָּה שֶׁשִּׁנֶּיהָ עֲקוּמוֹת וַעֲקוּשׁוֹת" (ראה חולין נו ע״א): **וּפְתַלְתֹּל.** אנטורטליי״ן, כַּפְּתִיל הַזֶּה שֶׁגּוֹדְלִין אוֹתוֹ וּמַקִּיפִין אוֹתוֹ סְבִיבוֹת הַגְּדִיל: **פְּתַלְתֹּל.** מִן הַתֵּיבוֹת הַכְּפוּלוֹת כְּמוֹ 'יְרַקְרַק' (ויקרא יג, מט), 'אֲדַמְדָּם' (שם), 'סְחַרְחַר' (תהלים לח, יא), 'סְגַלְגַּל' (תרגום, מלכים א׳ ז, כג):

ו **הַלַה׳ תִּגְמְלוּ זֹאת.** לְשׁוֹן תֵּמַהּ, וְכִי לְפָנָיו אַתֶּם מַעֲצִיבִין, שֶׁיֵּשׁ בְּיָדוֹ לְפָּרַע מִכֶּם וְשֶׁהֵיטִיב לָכֶם בְּכָל הַטּוֹבוֹת?: **עַם נָבָל.** שֶׁשָּׁכְחוּ אֶת הֶעָשׂוּי לָהֶם: **וְלֹא חָכָם.** לְהָבִין אֶת הַנּוֹלָדוֹת שֶׁיֵּשׁ בְּיָדוֹ לְהֵיטִיב וּלְהָרַע: **הֲלוֹא הוּא אָבִיךָ קָּנֶךָ.** שֶׁקְּנָאֲךָ, שֶׁקִּנֶּנְךָ בְּקַן הַסְּלָעִים וּבְאֶרֶץ חֲזָקָה, שֶׁתִּקֶּנְךָ בְּכָל מִינֵי תַּקָּנָה: **הוּא עָשְׂךָ.** אֻמָּה בָּאֻמּוֹת: **וַיְכֹנְנֶךָ.** אַחֲרֵי כֵן בְּכָל מִינֵי בָּסִיס וְכַן, מִכֶּם כֹּהֲנִים מִכֶּם נְבִיאִים וּמִכֶּם מְלָכִים, כְּרַךְ שֶׁהַכֹּל תָּלוּי בּוֹ:

ז **זְכֹר יְמוֹת עוֹלָם.** מֶה עָשָׂה בָּרִאשׁוֹנִים שֶׁהִכְעִיסוּ לְפָנָיו: **בִּינוּ שְׁנוֹת דֹּר וָדֹר.** דּוֹר אֱנוֹשׁ שֶׁהֵצִיף עֲלֵיהֶם מֵי אוֹקְיָנוֹס, וְדוֹר הַמַּבּוּל שֶׁשְּׁטָפָם. דָּבָר אַחֵר, לֹא נְתַתֶּם לִבְּכֶם עַל שֶׁעָבַר, "בִּינוּ שְׁנוֹת דֹּר וָדֹר" לְהַכִּיר לְהַבָּא, שֶׁיֵּשׁ בְּיָדוֹ לְהֵיטִיב לָכֶם וּלְהַנְחִיל לָכֶם יְמוֹת הַמָּשִׁיחַ וְהָעוֹלָם הַבָּא: **שְׁאַל אָבִיךָ.** אֵלּוּ הַנְּבִיאִים שֶׁנִּקְרְאוּ אָבוֹת, כְּמוֹ שֶׁנֶּאֱמַר בֶּאֱלִיָּהוּ: "אָבִי אָבִי רֶכֶב יִשְׂרָאֵל" (מלכים ב׳ ב, יב): **זְקֵנֶיךָ.** אֵלּוּ הַחֲכָמִים: **וְיֹאמְרוּ לָךְ.** הָרִאשׁוֹנוֹת:

ח **בְּהַנְחֵל עֶלְיוֹן גּוֹיִם.** כְּשֶׁהִנְחִיל הַקָּדוֹשׁ בָּרוּךְ הוּא לְמַכְעִיסָיו אֶת חֵלֶק נַחֲלָתָן, הֱצִיפָם וּשְׁטָפָם: **בְּהַפְרִידוֹ בְּנֵי אָדָם.** כְּשֶׁהֵפִיץ דּוֹר הַפַּלָּגָה הָיָה בְּיָדוֹ לְהַעֲבִירָם מִן הָעוֹלָם, וְלֹא עָשָׂה כֵן, אֶלָּא "יַצֵּב גְּבֻלֹת עַמִּים", קִיְּמָם וְלֹא אִבְּדָם: **לְמִסְפַּר בְּנֵי יִשְׂרָאֵל.** בִּשְׁבִיל מִסְפַּר בְּנֵי יִשְׂרָאֵל שֶׁעֲתִידִין לָצֵאת מִבְּנֵי שֵׁם, וּלְמִסְפַּר שִׁבְעִים נֶפֶשׁ שֶׁל בְּנֵי יִשְׂרָאֵל שֶׁיָּרְדוּ לְמִצְרַיִם הִצִּיב "גְּבֻלֹת עַמִּים" שִׁבְעִים לָשׁוֹן:

ט **כִּי חֵלֶק ה׳ עַמּוֹ.** לָמָּה כָּל זֹאת? לְפִי שֶׁהָיָה חֶלְקוֹ כָּבוּשׁ בֵּינֵיהֶם וְעָתִיד לָצֵאת. וּמִי הוּא חֶלְקוֹ? "עַמּוֹ". וּמִי הוּא עַמּוֹ? "יַעֲקֹב חֶבֶל נַחֲלָתוֹ", וְהוּא הַשְּׁלִישִׁי בָּאָבוֹת, הַמְשֻׁלָּשׁ בְּשָׁלֹשׁ זְכֻיּוֹת, זְכוּת אֲבִי אָבִיו וּזְכוּת אָבִיו וּזְכוּתוֹ, הֲרֵי שָׁלֹשׁ, כַּחֶבֶל הַזֶּה שֶׁהוּא עָשׂוּי בִּשְׁלֹשָׁה גְּדִילִים; וְהוּא וּבָנָיו הָיוּ לוֹ לְנַחֲלָה, וְלֹא יִשְׁמָעֵאל בֶּן אַבְרָהָם וְלֹא עֵשָׂו בְּנוֹ שֶׁל יִצְחָק:

comes from the same root as *novelet*, which means "unripe fruit" or "the incomplete or lesser substitute for something else." Therefore, the phrase in this verse could be read as "the people who, though they received the Torah, remained unwise." This, says Netziv, foreshadowed the situation during the last days of the Second Temple. We have no problem in understanding why the people of the First Temple suffered defeat. They were far removed from the Torah, guilty of cardinal sins. However, the men of the late Second Temple "studied and labored in the Torah, which prepares us to be righteous and upright." Yet they "remained unwise and were not careful to avoid bad conduct." The tragedy of the Second Temple period is that "some of the worst behavior came from those who were outstanding Torah scholars (*ba hakilkul al yedei gedolei Torah*)." The patriarchs of Genesis were generous in their behavior even to idolaters. The Torah scholars of the Second Temple – at least some of them – were vicious in their conduct even toward other religious Jews if they acted in any way differently from them, treating them as if they were heretics or sectarians.

That, suggests Netziv, is why we must return time and again to Tanakh, especially to Genesis, for though it contains narrative rather than law, it teaches something that cannot be taught by law alone, namely, how to behave uprightly in one's dealings with others.

ה שִׁחֵת לוֹ לֹא בָּנָיו מוּמָם דּוֹר עִקֵּשׁ וּפְתַלְתֹּל:
ו הַ לַיהוה תִּגְמְלוּ־זֹאת עַם נָבָל וְלֹא חָכָם
הֲלוֹא־הוּא אָבִיךָ קָּנֶךָ הוּא עָשְׂךָ וַיְכֹנְנֶךָ:
ז זְכֹר יְמוֹת עוֹלָם בִּינוּ שְׁנוֹת דֹּר־וָדֹר שני
שְׁאַל אָבִיךָ וְיַגֵּדְךָ זְקֵנֶיךָ וְיֹאמְרוּ לָךְ:
ח בְּהַנְחֵל עֶלְיוֹן גּוֹיִם בְּהַפְרִידוֹ בְּנֵי אָדָם
יַצֵּב גְּבֻלֹת עַמִּים לְמִסְפַּר בְּנֵי יִשְׂרָאֵל:
ט כִּי חֵלֶק יהוה עַמּוֹ יַעֲקֹב חֶבֶל נַחֲלָתוֹ:

אונקלוס

ה חַבִּילוּ לְהוֹן, לָא לֵיהּ בְּנַיָּא דִּפְלַחוּ לְטַעֲוָתָא, דָּרָא דְּאַשְׁנִי עוֹבָדוֹהִי וְאִשְׁתַּנִּיו: ו הָא קֳדָם יי אַתּוּן גָּמְלִין דָּא, עַמָּא דְּקַבִּילוּ אוֹרָיְתָא וְלָא חַכִּימוּ, הֲלָא הוּא אֲבוּךְ אַתְּ דִּילֵיהּ, הוּא עַבְדָךְ וְאַתְקְנָךְ: ז אִדְּכַר יוֹמִין דְּמִן עָלְמָא, אִסְתַּכַּל בִּשְׁנֵי דָּר וְדָר, שְׁאַל אֲבוּךְ וִיחַוֵּי לָךְ, סָבָךְ וְיֵימְרוּן לָךְ: ח בְּאַחְסָנָא עִלָּאָה עַמְמַיָּא, בְּפָרָשׁוּתֵיהּ בְּנֵי אֱנָשָׁא, קַיֵּים תְּחוּמֵי עַמְמַיָּא, לְמִנְיַן בְּנֵי יִשְׂרָאֵל: ט אֲרֵי, חוּלָקָא דַּיי עַמֵּיהּ, יַעֲקֹב עֲדַב אַחְסָנְתֵיהּ:

The grant of freedom to humanity was an immense act of self-limitation on the part of God – what the exponents of Lurianic Kabbala called *tzimtzum*. God has faith in man. That faith is often abused, not to say betrayed. Yet God has infinite patience – "in your white-haired years I shall still bear you" (Is. 46:4). Though human beings inflict suffering on one another, God does not give up on His creation. However corrupt we are, He does not relinquish the faith that we will change. However lost, He does not cease to believe that one day we will find our way back to Him. *More than we search for God, God searches for us*, asking us, as He did to Adam, "Where are you?" Sifrei's comment is profound. Creation, even God's creation, when it involves endowing a creature with the capacity to act in freedom, involves risk and therefore faith. "God of faith" means "He who had *faith in the universe* and created it." I know of no lovelier account of the (often unlovely) human condition.

32:5 **לֹא בָּנָיו מוּמָם** *No, with His children lies the fault* – In this verse, we sense the closing of a drama that began in the beginning with Adam and Ḥava in the Garden of Eden. When they sinned, Adam blamed the woman, the woman blamed the serpent. So it was in the beginning and so it still is in the twenty-first century. The story of humanity has been, for the most part, a flight from responsibility. The culprits change. Only the sense of victimhood remains. It wasn't us. It was the politicians. Or the media, or our parents, or the system – be it capitalism, communism, or anything in between. Most of all, it is the fault of the others, the ones not like us, infidels, sons of Satan, children of darkness, the unredeemed. The perpetrators of the greatest crime against humanity in all of history were convinced it wasn't them. They were "only obeying orders." When all else fails, blame God. And if you do not believe in God, blame the people who do. To be human is to seek to escape from responsibility. The first humans lost paradise when they sought to hide from responsibility. We will only ever regain it if we accept responsibility.

32:6 **עַם נָבָל וְלֹא חָכָם** *Foolish, unwise people* – Netziv (1816–93) cites the Targum, which paraphrases the words *am naval* not as "a foolish people" but as "the people who received the Torah." Netziv explains that the word *naval*

10 He found him in a desert land, / in a barren, howling waste; / He
encircled him, watched over him, / guarded him close like the apple of
11 His eye. / As an eagle stirs up its nest, / and hovers over its young; / as it
spreads its plumes and takes them, / bearing them aloft on its wings, /
12 13 just so, the Lord alone led him – / no strange god at His side – / He SHELISHI
set him astride the heights of the earth, / and fed him the bounty of
meadows; / He nursed him with honey from the crag, / and oil from
14 flinty rock; / with curds from the herd, milk from the flock, / and
the fat of lambs and goats, / choice rams of Bashan, / and the
fattest buds of wheat – / you drank fine wine from blood-red grapes.
15 / Yeshurun grew fat, and kicked; / you grew fat, grew gross, grew coarse.
/ They abandoned God who made them, / rejected the Rock of their

רש״י

י **ימצאהו בארץ מדבר.** אותם מצא לו נאמנים בארץ המדבר, שקבלו תורתו ומלכותו ועלו, מה שלא עשו ישמעאל ועשו, שנאמר: "וזרח משעיר למו הופיע מהר פארן" (להלן לג, ב): **ובתהו ילל ישמן.** ארץ ציה ושממה, מקום יללת תנים ובנות יענה, אף שם נמשכו אחר האמונה, ולא אמרו למשה היאך נצא למדברות מקום ציה ושממון, כענין שנאמר: "לכתך אחרי במדבר" (ירמיה ב, ב): **יסבבנהו.** שם סבבם והקיפם בעננים, וסבבם בדגלים לארבע רוחות, וסבבן בתחתית ההר שכפאו עליהם כגיגית: **יבוננהו.** שם בתורה ובינה: **יצרנהו.** מנחש שרף ועקרב ומן האמות: **כאישון עינו.** הוא השחור שבעין שהמאור יוצא הימנו. ואונקלוס תרגם: "ימצאהו" – יספיקהו כל צרכו במדבר, כמו: "ומצא להם" (במדבר יא, כב), "לא ימצא לנו ההר" (יהושע יז, טז). "יסבבנהו" – "אשרינון סחור סחור לשכינתיה", אהל מועד באמצע וארבעה דגלים לארבע רוחות:

יא **כנשר יעיר קנו.** נהגם ברחמים ובחמלה כנשר הזה רחמני על בניו, ואינו נכנס לקנו פתאום עד שהוא מקשקש ומטרף על בניו בכנפיו בין אילן לאילן בין שוכה לחברתה, כדי שיעורו בניו ויהא בהן כח לקבלו: **יעיר קנו.** יעורר בניו: **על גוזליו ירחף.** אינו מכביד עצמו עליהם אלא מחופף, נוגע ואינו נוגע, אף הקדוש ברוך הוא "שדי לא מצאנהו שגיא כח" (איוב לז, כג), כשבא לתן תורה לא נגלה עליהם מרוח אחת אלא מארבע רוחות, שנאמר: "ה' מסיני בא וזרח משעיר למו, הופיע מהר פארן" (להלן לג, ב), "אלוה מתימן יבוא" (חבקוק ג, ג) זו רוח רביעית: **יפרש כנפיו יקחהו.** כשבא לטלן ממקום למקום אינו נוטלן ברגליו כשאר עופות, לפי שאר עופות יראים מן הנשר שהוא מגביה לעוף ופורח עליהם, לפיכך נושאן ברגליו מפני הנשר, אבל הנשר אינו ירא אלא מן החץ, לפיכך נושאן על כנפיו, אומר: מוטב שיכנס החץ בי ולא יכנס בבני. אף הקדוש ברוך הוא, "ואשא אתכם על כנפי נשרים" (שמות יט, ד), כשנסעו מצרים אחריהם והשיגום על הים היו זורקים בהם חצים ואבני בלסטראות, מיד – "ויסע מלאך האלהים וגו' ויבא בין מחנה מצרים" וגו' (שם יד, יט-כ):

יב **ה' בדד ינחנו.** ה' בדד ובטח נהגם במדבר: **ואין עמו אל נכר.** לא היה כח באחד מכל אלהי הגוים להראות כחו ולהלחם עמהם. ורבותינו דרשוהו על העתיד, וכן תרגם אונקלוס. ואני אומר, דברי תוכחה הם להעיד השמים והארץ שתהא השירה לעד שסופן לבגד, ולא יזכרו הראשונות שעשה להם ולא הנולדות שהוא עתיד לעשות להם. לפיכך צריך ליַשב הדבר לכאן ולכאן, וכל הענין מוסב על "זכר ימות עולם בינו שנות דר ודר" (לעיל פסוק ז), כן עשה להם וכן עתיד לעשות, כל זה היה להם לזכר:

יג-יד **ירכבהו על במתי ארץ.** כל המקרא כתרגומו: **ירכבהו.** על שם שארץ ישראל גבוהה מכל הארצות: **ויאכל תנובת שדי.** אלו פרות ארץ ישראל שקלים לנוב ולהתבשל מכל פרות הארצות: **וינקהו דבש מסלע.** מעשה באחד שאמר לבנו בסיכני: הבא לי קציעות מן החבית, הלך ומצא הדבש צף על פיה, אמר לו: זו של דבש היא, אמר לו: השקע ידך לתוכה ואתה מעלה קציעות מתוכה: **ושמן מחלמיש צור.** אלו זיתים של גוש חלב: **חמאת בקר וחלב צאן.** זה היה בימי שלמה, שנאמר: "עשרה בקר בראים ועשרים בקר רעי ומאה צאן" (מלכים א' ה, ג): **עם חלב כרים.** זה היה בימי עשרת השבטים, שנאמר: "ואכלים כרים מצאן" (עמוס ו, ד): **עם חלב כליות חטה.** זה היה בימי שלמה, שנאמר: "ויהי לחם שלמה" וגו' (מלכים א' ה, ב): **ודם ענב תשתה חמר.** בימי עשרת השבטים, "השתים במזרקי יין" (עמוס ו, ו): **במתי ארץ.** לשון גבה: **שדי.** לשון שדה: **חלמיש צור.** תקפו וחזקו של סלע. כשאינו דבוק לתבה שלאחריו נקוד 'חלמיש' (לעיל ח, טו) וכשהוא דבוק

י יִמְצָאֵהוּ בְּאֶרֶץ מִדְבָּר וּבְתֹהוּ יְלֵל יְשִׁמֹן
יְסֹבְבֶנְהוּ יְבוֹנְנֵהוּ יִצְּרֶנְהוּ כְּאִישׁוֹן עֵינוֹ:
יא כְּנֶשֶׁר יָעִיר קִנּוֹ עַל־גּוֹזָלָיו יְרַחֵף
יִפְרֹשׂ כְּנָפָיו יִקָּחֵהוּ יִשָּׂאֵהוּ עַל־אֶבְרָתוֹ:
יב יְהוָה בָּדָד יַנְחֶנּוּ וְאֵין עִמּוֹ אֵל נֵכָר:
יג יַרְכִּבֵהוּ עַל־בָּמוֹתֵי אָרֶץ וַיֹּאכַל תְּנוּבֹת שָׂדָי בָּמֳתֵי שלישי
וַיֵּנִקֵהוּ דְבַשׁ מִסֶּלַע וְשֶׁמֶן מֵחַלְמִישׁ צוּר:
יד חֶמְאַת בָּקָר וַחֲלֵב צֹאן עִם־חֵלֶב כָּרִים
וְאֵילִים בְּנֵי־בָשָׁן וְעַתּוּדִים עִם־חֵלֶב כִּלְיוֹת חִטָּה
טו וְדַם־עֵנָב תִּשְׁתֶּה־חָמֶר: וַיִּשְׁמַן יְשֻׁרוּן וַיִּבְעָט
שָׁמַנְתָּ עָבִיתָ כָּשִׂיתָ וַיִּטֹּשׁ אֱלוֹהַ עָשָׂהוּ

אונקלוס

י סוֹפֵיק צָרְכֵיהוֹן בַּאֲרַע מַדְבְּרָא, וּבֵית צַהֲוָנָא אֲתַר דְּלֵית מַיָּא,
אַשְׁרִינוּן סְחוֹר סְחוֹר לִשְׁכִינְתֵיהּ אַלֵּיפִנּוּן פִּתְגָּמֵי אוֹרָיְתֵיהּ, נְטַרִנּוּן
כְּבָבַת עֵינְהוֹן: יא כְּנִשְׁרָא דִּמְחִישׁ לְקִנֵּיהּ, עַל בְּנוֹהִי מִתְחַפַּף, פָּרֵיס
גַּדְפּוֹהִי מְקַבֵּילְהוֹן, מְנַטֵּילְהוֹן עַל תְּקוֹף אֶבְרוֹהִי: יב יי בִּלְחוֹדֵיהוֹן
עֲתִיד לְאַשְׁרָיוּתְהוֹן בְּעָלְמָא דְּהוּא עֲתִיד לְחַדָּתָא, וְלָא יִתְקַיַּם
קֳדָמוֹהִי פְּלְחַן טָעֲוָן: יג אַשְׁרִינוּן עַל תָּקְפֵי אַרְעָא, אוֹכֵילִנּוּן בִּזַּת
סָנְאֵיהוֹן, יְהַב לְהוֹן בִּזַּת שַׁלִּיטֵי קִרְוִין, וְנִכְסֵי יָתְבֵי כְּרַכִּין תַּקִּיפִין:
יד יְהַב לְהוֹן בִּזַּת מַלְכֵיהוֹן וְשַׁלִּיטֵיהוֹן, עִם עוֹתַר רַבְרְבֵיהוֹן וְתַקִּיפֵיהוֹן,
עַמָּא דַּאֲרַעְהוֹן אַחֲסָנַתְהוֹן, עִם בִּזַּת חֵילֵיהוֹן וּמַשְׁרְיָתְהוֹן, וְדַם
גִּבָּרֵיהוֹן אִתְאֲשַׁד כְּמַיָּא: טו עֲתַר יִשְׂרָאֵל וּבְעַט, אַצְלַח תְּקוֹף קְנָא
נִכְסִין, שְׁבַק פְּלְחַן אֱלָהָא דַּעֲבְדֵיהּ, אַרְגֵּיז קֳדָם תַּקִּיפָא פָּרְקֵיהּ:

רש״י

נָקוּד 'חַלְמִיס': חֶמְאַת בָּקָר. הוּא שֻׁמָּן הַנִּלְקָט עַל גַּבֵּי חָלָב: וַחֲלֵב צֹאן.
חָלָב שֶׁל צֹאן, וּכְשֶׁהוּא דָּבוּק נָקוּד 'חֲלֵב', כְּמוֹ: "כַּחֲלֵב חִמּוֹ" (לעיל יד, כח):
כָּרִים. כְּבָשִׂים: וְאֵילִים. כְּמַשְׁמָעוֹ: בְּנֵי בָשָׁן. שְׁמֵנִים הָיוּ: כִּלְיוֹת חִטָּה.
חִטִּים שְׁמֵנִים כְּחֵלֶב כְּלָיוֹת וְגַסִּין כְּכוּלְיָא: וְדַם עֵנָב. הָיִיתָ שׁוֹתֶה טוֹב
וְטוֹעֵם יַיִן חָשׁוּב: חָמֶר. יַיִן בִּלְשׁוֹן אֲרַמִּי: חֲמַר. אֵין זֶה שֵׁם דָּבָר אֶלָּא
לְשׁוֹן מְשֻׁבָּח בְּטַעַם, ווינו״ש בְּלַעַז. וְעוֹד יֵשׁ לְפָרֵשׁ שְׁנֵי מִקְרָאוֹת הַלָּלוּ
אַחַר תַּרְגּוּם שֶׁל אוּנְקְלוֹס: "אַשְׁרִינוּן עַל תָּקְפֵי אַרְעָא" וְגוֹ':
טו עָבִיתָ. לְשׁוֹן עֹבִי: כָּשִׂיתָ. כְּמוֹ 'כָּסִיתָ', לְשׁוֹן: "כִּי כִסָּה פָנָיו בְחֶלְבּוֹ"
(איוב טו, כז), כְּאָדָם שֶׁשֻּׁמָּן מִבִּפְנִים וּכְסָלָיו נִכְפָּלִים מִבַּחוּץ, וְכֵן הוּא
אוֹמֵר: "וַיַּעַשׂ פִּימָה עֲלֵי כָסֶל" (שם): כָּשִׂיתָ. יֵשׁ לְשׁוֹן קַל בִּלְשׁוֹן כִּסּוּי,

32:15 וַיִּשְׁמַן יְשֻׁרוּן וַיִּבְעָט *Yeshurun grew fat, and kicked* – One of the first historians to give a cyclical account of history, Giambattista Vico, argued that all civilizations were subject to a law of rise and decline. They are born in austerity. They rise to affluence and power. Then they become decadent and eventually decline.

People first sense what is necessary, then consider what is useful, next attend to comfort, later delight in pleasures, soon grow dissolute in luxury, and finally go mad squandering their estates." The only antidote to this, he argued, was religion, which motivates people to act with virtue and concern for the common good. Spiritual systems

16 rescue. / They provoked Him with strange gods, / and angered Him
17 with abominations. / They sacrificed to demons, no-gods, / to deities
they never knew, / new ones, lately arisen, / whom your forebears
18 never feared. / You deserted the Rock that bore you; / you forgot the
19 God who gave you birth. / The LORD saw this and He in turn rejected / REVI'I
20 the sons and daughters who angered Him so. / He said: I will hide
My face from them, / and see what their end will be; / for they are a
21 perverse generation, / children with no faithfulness. / They incensed
Me with a no-god, / they angered Me with their vanities; / I will incense
22 them with a no-people, / enrage them with a fool nation. / For a fire
My anger has kindled, / it burns to the depths of Sheol, / will devour
23 the land and its harvests, / and set fire to the hills' foundations. / I will
24 heap evils upon them, / exhaust My arrows on them: / consuming

רש״י

כְּמוֹ: ״וְכֹסֶה קָלוֹן עָרוּם״ (משלי יב, טז), וְאִם כָּתַב ׳כַּשִּׂיתָ׳ דָּגוּשׁ, הָיָה נִשְׁמָע כִּסִּיתָ אֶת הָאֲחֵרִים: וַיְנַבֵּל צוּר יְשֻׁעָתוֹ. גִּנָּהוּ וּבִזָּהוּ, כְּמוֹ שֶׁנֶּאֱמַר: ״אֲחֹרֵיהֶם אֶל הֵיכַל ה׳״ וְגוֹ׳ (יחזקאל ח, טז), אֵין לְךָ נִבּוּל גָּדוֹל מִזֶּה:

טז יַקְנִאֻהוּ. הִבְעִירוּ חֲמָתוֹ וְקִנְאָתוֹ: בְּתוֹעֵבֹת. בְּמַעֲשִׂים תְּעוּבִים, כְּגוֹן מִשְׁכַּב זָכוּר וּכְשָׁפִים שֶׁנֶּאֱמַר בָּהֶם ׳תּוֹעֵבָה׳:

יז לֹא אֱלֹהַּ. כְּתַרְגּוּמוֹ: ״דְּלֵית בְּהוֹן צְרוֹךְ״, אִלּוּ הָיָה בָּהֶם צֹרֶךְ לֹא הָיְתָה קִנְאָה כְּפוּלָה כְּמוֹ עַכְשָׁיו: חֲדָשִׁים מִקָּרֹב בָּאוּ. אֲפִלּוּ הָאֻמּוֹת לֹא הָיוּ רְגִילִים בָּהֶם, גּוֹי שֶׁהָיָה רוֹאֶה אוֹתָם הָיָה אוֹמֵר: זֶה צֶלֶם יְהוּדִי: לֹא שְׂעָרוּם אֲבֹתֵיכֶם. לֹא יָרְאוּ מֵהֶם, לֹא עָמְדָה שַׂעֲרָתָם מִפְּנֵיהֶם, דֶּרֶךְ שַׂעֲרוֹת הָאָדָם לַעֲמֹד מֵחֲמַת יִרְאָה. כָּךְ נִדְרָשׁ בְּסִפְרֵי. וְיֵשׁ לְפָרֵשׁ עוֹד, ״שְׂעָרוּם״ לְשׁוֹן: ״וּשְׂעִירִים יְרַקְּדוּ שָׁם״ (ישעיה יג, כא), שְׂעִירִים הֵם שֵׁדִים, לֹא עָשׂוּ אֲבוֹתֵיכֶם שְׂעִירִים הַלָּלוּ:

יח תֶּשִׁי. תִּשְׁכַּח. וְרַבּוֹתֵינוּ אָמְרוּ, כְּשֶׁבָּא לְהֵיטִיב לָכֶם אַתֶּם מַכְעִיסִין לְפָנָיו וּמַתִּישִׁים כֹּחוֹ מִלְּהֵיטִיב לָכֶם: אֵל מְחֹלְלֶךָ. מוֹצִיאֲךָ מֵרֶחֶם, לְשׁוֹן: ״חֹלֵל אַיָּלוֹת״ (איוב לט, א), ״חִיל כַּיּוֹלֵדָה״ (ירמיה ו, כד):

כ מָה אַחֲרִיתָם. מַה תַּעֲלֶה בָּהֶם בְּסוֹפָם: כִּי דוֹר תַּהְפֻּכֹת הֵמָּה. מְהַפְּכִין רְצוֹנִי לְכַעַס: לֹא אֵמֻן בָּם. אֵין גִּדּוּלַי נִכָּרִים בָּהֶם, כִּי הוֹרֵיתִים דֶּרֶךְ טוֹבָה וְסָרוּ מִמֶּנָּה: אֵמֻן. לְשׁוֹן: ״וַיְהִי אֹמֵן״ (אסתר ב, ז), נורטור״א בְּלַעַז. דָּבָר אַחֵר, ״אֵמֻן״, לְשׁוֹן אֱמוּנָה, כְּתַרְגּוּמוֹ, אָמְרוּ בְּסִינַי: ״נַעֲשֶׂה וְנִשְׁמָע״ (שמות כד, ז), וְלְשָׁעָה קַלָּה בִּטְּלוּ הַבְטָחָתָם וְעָשׂוּ הָעֵגֶל:

כא קִנְאוּנִי. הִבְעִירוּ חֲמָתִי: בְלֹא אֵל. בְּדָבָר שֶׁאֵינוֹ אֱלוֹהַּ: בְּלֹא עָם. בְּאֻמָּה שֶׁאֵין לָהּ שֵׁם, שֶׁנֶּאֱמַר: ״הֵן אֶרֶץ כַּשְׂדִּים זֶה הָעָם לֹא הָיָה״ (ישעיה כג, יג); בְּעֵשָׂו הוּא אוֹמֵר: ״בָּזוּי אַתָּה מְאֹד״ (עובדיה א, ב): בְּגוֹי נָבָל אַכְעִיסֵם. אֵלּוּ הַמִּינִין, וְכֵן הוּא אוֹמֵר: ״אָמַר נָבָל בְּלִבּוֹ אֵין אֱלֹהִים״ (תהלים יד, א):

כב קָדְחָה. בָּעֲרָה: וַתִּיקַד. בָּכֶם עַד הַיְסוֹד: וַתֹּאכַל. אַרְצְכֶם וִיבוּלָהּ: וַתְּלַהֵט. אֶת יְרוּשָׁלַיִם הַמְיֻסֶּדֶת עַל הֶהָרִים, שֶׁנֶּאֱמַר: ״יְרוּשָׁלַיִם הָרִים סָבִיב לָהּ״ (תהלים קכה, ב):

כג אַסְפֶּה עָלֵימוֹ רָעוֹת. אַחְבִּיר רָעָה עַל רָעָה, לְשׁוֹן: ״סְפוּ שָׁנָה עַל שָׁנָה״ (ישעיה כט, א), ״סְפוֹת הָרָוָה״ (לעיל כט, יח), ״עֹלוֹתֵיכֶם סְפוּ עַל זִבְחֵיכֶם״ (ירמיה ז, כא). דָּבָר אַחֵר, ״אַסְפֶּה״, אֲכַלֶּה, כְּמוֹ: ״פֶּן תִּסָּפֶה״ (בראשית יט, טו): חִצַּי אֲכַלֶּה בָּם. כָּל חִצַּי אַשְׁלִים בָּהֶם, וּקְלָלָה זוֹ לְפִי הַפֻּרְעָנוּת לִבְרָכָה הִיא, חִצַּי כָּלִים וְהֵם אֵינָם כָּלִים:

כד מְזֵי רָעָב. אוּנְקְלוֹס תִּרְגֵּם: ״נְפִיחֵי כְפַן״ וְאֵין לִי עֵד מוֹכִיחַ עָלָיו. וּמִשְּׁמוֹ שֶׁל רַבִּי יְהוּדָה הַדַּרְשָׁן מִטּוּלוּזָא שָׁמַעְתִּי, שְׂעִירֵי רָעָב, אָדָם כָּחוּשׁ מְגַדֵּל שֵׂעָר עַל בְּשָׂרוֹ. ׳מְזֵי׳ לְשׁוֹן אֲרַמִּי שֵׂעָר, מַזְיָא, ״דַּהֲוָה מְהַפֵּךְ בְּמַזְיֵהּ״ (מגילה דף יח ע״א): וּלְחֻמֵי רֶשֶׁף. הַשֵּׁדִים נִלְחֲמוּ בָּהֶם,

it has led us to say: if bad things have happened, let us blame no one but ourselves, and let us labor to make them better. It was this that led Jews, time and again, to emerge from tragedy, shaken, scarred, limping like Yaakov after his encounter with the angel, yet resolved to begin again, to rededicate themselves to their mission and faith.

טז וַיְנַבֵּ֖ל צ֥וּר יְשֻׁעָתֽוֹ׃ יַקְנִאֻ֖הוּ בְּזָרִ֑ים
יז בְּתוֹעֵבֹ֖ת יַכְעִיסֻֽהוּ׃ יִזְבְּח֗וּ לַשֵּׁדִים֙ לֹ֣א אֱלֹ֔הַ
אֱלֹהִ֖ים לֹ֣א יְדָע֑וּם חֲדָשִׁים֙ מִקָּרֹ֣ב בָּ֔אוּ
יח לֹ֥א שְׂעָר֖וּם אֲבֹתֵיכֶֽם׃ צ֥וּר יְלָדְךָ֖ תֶּ֑שִׁי
יט וַתִּשְׁכַּ֖ח אֵ֥ל מְחֹלְלֶֽךָ׃ וַיַּ֥רְא יְהוָ֖ה וַיִּנְאָ֑ץ רביעי
כ מִכַּ֥עַס בָּנָ֖יו וּבְנֹתָֽיו׃ וַיֹּ֗אמֶר אַסְתִּ֤ירָה פָנַי֙ מֵהֶ֔ם
אֶרְאֶ֖ה מָ֣ה אַחֲרִיתָ֑ם כִּ֣י ד֤וֹר תַּהְפֻּכֹת֙ הֵ֔מָּה
כא בָּנִ֖ים לֹא־אֵ֥מֻן בָּֽם׃ הֵ֚ם קִנְא֣וּנִי בְלֹא־אֵ֔ל
כִּעֲס֖וּנִי בְּהַבְלֵיהֶ֑ם וַאֲנִי֙ אַקְנִיאֵ֣ם בְּלֹא־עָ֔ם
כב בְּג֥וֹי נָבָ֖ל אַכְעִיסֵֽם׃ כִּי־אֵשׁ֙ קָדְחָ֣ה בְאַפִּ֔י
וַתִּיקַ֖ד עַד־שְׁא֣וֹל תַּחְתִּ֑ית וַתֹּ֤אכַל אֶ֙רֶץ֙ וִֽיבֻלָ֔הּ
כג וַתְּלַהֵ֖ט מוֹסְדֵ֥י הָרִֽים׃ אַסְפֶּ֥ה עָלֵ֖ימוֹ רָע֑וֹת
כד חִצַּ֖י אֲכַלֶּה־בָּֽם׃ מְזֵ֥י רָעָ֛ב וּלְחֻ֥מֵי רֶ֖שֶׁף

אונקלוס

טז אַקְנִיאוּ קֳדָמוֹהִי בְּפָלְחַן טַעֲוָן, בְּתוֹעֵיבָתָא אַרְגִּיזוּ קֳדָמוֹהִי: יז דַּבַּחוּ, לְשֵׁידִין דְּלֵית בְּהוֹן צְרוֹךְ, דַּחְלָן דְּלָא יְדַעוּנִין, חַדְתָּן דְּמִקְּרִיב אִתְעֲבִידָא, דְּלָא אִתְעַסַּקוּ בְּהוֹן אֲבָהָתְכוֹן: יח דַּחְלַת תַּקִּיפָא דִּי בְרָאָךְ אִתְנְשֵׁיתָא, שְׁבַקְתָּא פָּלְחַן אֱלָהָא דַּעֲבְדָךְ: יט וּגְלֵי קֳדָם יי וּתְקֵיף רֻגְזֵיהּ, מִדְּאַרְגִּיזוּ קֳדָמוֹהִי בְּנִין וּבְנָן: כ וַאֲמַר, אֲסַלֵּיק שְׁכִינְתִּי מִנְּהוֹן, גְּלֵי קֳדָמַי מָא יְהֵי בְּסוֹפְהוֹן, אֲרֵי דָרָא דְּאַשְׁנִי אִנּוּן, בְּנַיָּא דְּלֵית בְּהוֹן הֵימָנוּ: כא אִנּוּן אַקְנִיאוּ קֳדָמַי בְּלָא דַחְלָא, אַרְגִּיזוּ קֳדָמַי בְּטָעֲוָתְהוֹן, וַאֲנָא אַקְנֵינוּן בְּלָא עַם, בְּעַמָּא טַפְשָׁא אַרְגֵּיזִנּוּן: כב אֲרֵי קִדּוֹם תַּקִּיף כְּאֶשָּׁא נְפַק מִן קֳדָמַי בִּרְגַז, שֵׁיצִי עַד שְׁאוֹל אַרְעִיתָא, אֱסֵיף אַרְעָא וַעֲלַלְתַּהּ, שֵׁיצִי עַד סְיָפֵי טוּרַיָּא: כג אֱסֵיף עֲלֵיהוֹן בִּישָׁן, מַכְתְּשַׁי אֲגָרֵי בְּהוֹן: כד נְפִיחֵי כְפַן,

have the capacity to defeat the law of entropy that governs the life of nations.

Here, the first use of the name Yeshurun in the Torah – from the root *y-sh-r*, "upright" – seems deliberately ironic. Israel once knew what it was to be upright, but it will be led astray by a combination of affluence, security, and assimilation to the ways of its neighbors. It will betray the terms of the covenant, and when that happens the people will find that God is no longer with them. Separated from the source of their strength, they will be overpowered by enemies. All that the nation once enjoyed will be lost.

It is a stark and terrifying message. Yet it contains a kernel of hope. Moshe insists that when trouble and tragedy appear, we should search for the cause within ourselves. God is upright and just. The defect is in us, His children. It is a difficult belief, this commitment to seeing justice in history under the sovereignty of God. Yet, throughout history

famine, flaming fever, bitter plague, / and fanged beasts will I send
25 against them, / and venomous vipers crawling in the dust. / Sword
outside and terror within / will claim young men and women, /
26 nursing infants, and the gray-haired old. / I thought I would scatter
27 them, / erasing their memory from man, / were it not for fear of the
enemy's taunts, / lest their adversaries misunderstand / and say, 'Our
28 hand has triumphed; / it was not the LORD who did all this.' / They
29 are a nation devoid of sense; / they have no understanding. / If they HAMISHI
were wise, they would contemplate this, / and know what their end would
30 be. / How could one man pursue a thousand, / and two put ten
thousand to flight, / unless their Rock had sold them, / the LORD
31 had handed them over? / For their rock is not like our Rock; /
32 even in our enemies' judgment. / Their vine is from Sedom, / from
the vineyards of Amora; / their grapes are grapes of poison, /
33 their clusters bitter; / their wine is serpents' venom, / cruel poison
34 of the viper. / Is this not kept in My reserve, / sealed away in My

רש״י

שֶׁנֶּאֱמַר: ״וּבְנֵי רֶשֶׁף יַגְבִּיהוּ עוּף״ (איוב ה, ז), וְהֵם שֵׁדִים: **וְקֶטֶב מְרִירִי.** וּכְרִיתוּת שֵׁד שֶׁשְּׁמוֹ מְרִירִי: **קֶטֶב.** כְּרִיתָה, כְּמוֹ: ״אֱהִי קָטָבְךָ שְׁאוֹל״ (הושע יג, יד): **וְשֶׁן בְּהֵמֹת.** מַעֲשֶׂה הָיָה וְהָיוּ הָרְחֵלוֹת נוֹשְׁכוֹת וּמְמִיתוֹת: **חֲמַת זֹחֲלֵי עָפָר.** אֶרֶס נְחָשִׁים הַמְהַלְּכִים בִּגְחוֹנָם עַל הֶעָפָר כַּמַּיִם הַזּוֹחֲלִים עַל הָאָרֶץ. ׳זְחִילָה׳ לְשׁוֹן מְרוּצַת הַמַּיִם עַל הֶעָפָר, וְכֵן כָּל מְרוּצַת דָּבָר הַמְשַׁפְשֵׁף עַל הֶעָפָר וְהוֹלֵךְ:

כה **מִחוּץ תְּשַׁכֶּל חֶרֶב.** מִחוּץ לָעִיר תְּשַׁכְּלֵם חֶרֶב גְּיָסוֹת: **וּמֵחֲדָרִים אֵימָה.** כְּשֶׁבּוֹרֵחַ וְנִמְלָט מִן הַחֶרֶב חַדְרֵי לִבּוֹ נְקוּפִים עָלָיו מֵאֵימָה וְהוּא מֵת וְהוֹלֵךְ בָּהּ. דָּבָר אַחֵר, ״וּמֵחֲדָרִים אֵימָה״, בַּבַּיִת תִּהְיֶה אֵימַת דֶּבֶר, כְּמָה שֶׁנֶּאֱמַר: ״כִּי עָלָה מָוֶת בְּחַלּוֹנֵינוּ״ (ירמיה ט, כ), וְכֵן תִּרְגֵּם אוּנְקְלוֹס. דָּבָר אַחֵר, ״מִחוּץ תְּשַׁכֶּל חֶרֶב״ עַל מַה שֶּׁעָשׂוּ בַּחוּצוֹת, שֶׁנֶּאֱמַר: ״וּמִסְפַּר חֻצוֹת יְרוּשָׁלַיִם שַׂמְתֶּם מִזְבְּחוֹת לַבֹּשֶׁת״ (שם יא, יג). ״וּמֵחֲדָרִים אֵימָה״ עַל מַה שֶּׁעָשׂוּ בְּחַדְרֵי חֲדָרִים, שֶׁנֶּאֱמַר: ״אֲשֶׁר זִקְנֵי בֵית יִשְׂרָאֵל עֹשִׂים בַּחֹשֶׁךְ אִישׁ בְּחַדְרֵי מַשְׂכִּיתוֹ״ (יחזקאל ח, יב):

כו **אָמַרְתִּי אַפְאֵיהֶם.** אָמַרְתִּי בְּלִבִּי אַפְאֶה אוֹתָם. וְיֵשׁ לְפָרֵשׁ ״אַפְאֵיהֶם״ אֲשִׂיתֵם פֵּאָה, לְהַשְׁלִיכָם מֵעָלַי הֶפְקֵר, וְדֻגְמָתוֹ מָצִינוּ בְּעֶזְרָא: ״וַתִּתֵּן לָהֶם מַמְלָכוֹת וַעֲמָמִים וַתַּחְלְקֵם לְפֵאָה״ (נחמיה ט, כב), לְהֶפְקֵר, וְכֵן חִבְּרוֹ מְנַחֵם. וְיֵשׁ פּוֹתְרִים אוֹתוֹ כְּתַרְגּוּמוֹ: ״יְחוּל רָגְזִי עֲלֵיהוֹן״, וְלֹא יִתָּכֵן, שֶׁאִם כֵּן הָיָה לוֹ לִכְתֹּב ׳אַאַפְאֵיהֶם׳, אַחַת לְשִׁמּוּשׁ וְאַחַת לִיסוֹד, כְּמוֹ: ״אַאַזֶּרְךָ״ (ישעיה מה, ה) ״אַאַמִּצְכֶם בְּמוֹ פִי״ (איוב טז, ה), וְהָאָלֶ״ף הַתִּיכוֹנָה אֵינָהּ רְאוּיָה בּוֹ כְּלָל. וְאוּנְקְלוֹס תִּרְגֵּם אַחַר לְשׁוֹן הַבָּרַיְתָא הַשְּׁנוּיָה

בְּסִפְרֵי (שכב) הַחוֹלֶקֶת תֵּבָה זוֹ לְשָׁלֹשׁ תֵּבוֹת: ׳אָמַרְתִּי אַף אֵי הֵם׳, אָמַרְתִּי בְּאַפִּי אֶתְּנֵם כְּאִלּוּ אֵינָם, שֶׁיֹּאמְרוּ רוֹאֵיהֶם עֲלֵיהֶם אַיֵּה הֵם:

כז-כט **לוּלֵי כַּעַס אוֹיֵב אָגוּר.** אִם לֹא שֶׁכַּעַס הָאוֹיֵב כָּנוּס עֲלֵיהֶם לְהַשְׁחִית, וְאִם יוּכַל לָהֶם וְיַשְׁחִיתֵם יִתְלֶה הַגְּדֻלָּה בּוֹ וּבֵאלֹהָיו וְלֹא יִתְלֶה הַגְּדֻלָּה בִּי, וְזֶהוּ שֶׁנֶּאֱמַר: ״פֶּן יְנַכְּרוּ צָרֵימוֹ״, יְנַכְּרוּ הַדָּבָר לִתְלוֹת גְּבוּרָתִי בְּנָכְרִי שֶׁאֵין הַגְּדֻלָּה שֶׁלּוֹ, ״פֶּן יֹאמְרוּ יָדֵנוּ רָמָה״ וְגוֹ׳. כִּי אוֹתָן גּוֹי ״אֹבַד עֵצוֹת הֵמָּה וְאֵין בָּהֶם תְּבוּנָה״, שֶׁאִלּוּ הָיוּ חֲכָמִים ״יַשְׂכִּילוּ זֹאת... אֵיכָה יִרְדֹּף״ וְגוֹ׳: **יָבִינוּ לְאַחֲרִיתָם.** יִתְּנוּ לֵב לְהִתְבּוֹנֵן לְסוֹף פֻּרְעָנוּתָם שֶׁל יִשְׂרָאֵל:

ל **אֵיכָה יִרְדֹּף אֶחָד.** מִמֶּנּוּ, אֶלֶף מִיִּשְׂרָאֵל: **אִם לֹא כִּי צוּרָם מְכָרָם וַה׳ הִסְגִּירָם.** מְכָרָם וּמְסָרָם בְּיָדֵנוּ, דליברי״ר בְּלַעַז:

לא **כִּי לֹא כְצוּרֵנוּ צוּרָם.** כָּל זֶה הָיָה לָהֶם לָאוֹיְבִים לְהָבִין שֶׁהַשֵּׁם הִסְגִּירָם וְלֹא לָהֶם וְלֵאלֹהֵיהֶם הַנִּצָּחוֹן, שֶׁהֲרֵי עַד הֵנָּה לֹא יָכְלוּ כְּלוּם אֱלֹהֵיהֶם כְּנֶגֶד צוּרֵנוּ, כִּי לֹא כְּסַלְעֵנוּ סַלְעָם. כָּל ׳צוּר׳ שֶׁבַּמִּקְרָא לְשׁוֹן סֶלַע: **וְאֹיְבֵינוּ פְּלִילִים.** וְעַכְשָׁיו אוֹיְבֵינוּ שׁוֹפְטִים אוֹתָנוּ, הֲרֵי שֶׁצּוּרֵנוּ מְכָרָנוּ לָהֶם:

לב **כִּי מִגֶּפֶן סְדֹם גַּפְנָם.** מוּסָב לְמַעְלָה, אָמַרְתִּי בְּלִבִּי אַפְאֵיהֶם וְאַשְׁבִּית זִכְרָם, לְפִי שֶׁמַּעֲשֵׂיהֶם מַעֲשֵׂה סְדוֹם וַעֲמוֹרָה: **שַׁדְמֹת.** שְׂדֵה תְבוּאָה, כְּמוֹ: ״וּשְׁדֵמוֹת לֹא עָשָׂה אֹכֶל״ (חבקוק ג, יז), ״בְּשַׁדְמוֹת קִדְרוֹן״ (מלכים ב׳ כג, ד): **עִנְּבֵי רוֹשׁ.** עֵשֶׂב מַר: **אַשְׁכְּלֹת מְרֹרֹת לָמוֹ.** מַשְׁקֶה מַר

וְקֶ֣טֶב מְרִירִ֑י   וְשֶׁן־בְּהֵמֹת֙ אֲשַׁלַּח־בָּ֔ם
כה עִם־חֲמַ֖ת זֹחֲלֵ֥י עָפָֽר׃   מִחוּץ֙ תְּשַׁכֶּל־חֶ֔רֶב
וּמֵחֲדָרִ֖ים אֵימָ֑ה   גַּם־בָּחוּר֙ גַּם־בְּתוּלָ֔ה
כו יוֹנֵ֖ק עִם־אִ֥ישׁ שֵׂיבָֽה׃   אָמַ֖רְתִּי אַפְאֵיהֶ֑ם
כז אַשְׁבִּ֥יתָה מֵאֱנ֖וֹשׁ זִכְרָֽם׃   לוּלֵ֗י כַּ֤עַס אוֹיֵב֙ אָג֔וּר
פֶּן־יְנַכְּר֖וּ צָרֵ֑ימוֹ   פֶּן־יֹֽאמְרוּ֙ יָדֵ֣נוּ רָ֔מָה
כח וְלֹ֥א יְהֹוָ֖ה פָּעַ֥ל כָּל־זֹֽאת׃   כִּי־ג֛וֹי אֹבַ֥ד עֵצ֖וֹת הֵ֑מָּה
כט וְאֵ֥ין בָּהֶ֖ם תְּבוּנָֽה׃   ל֥וּ חָכְמ֖וּ יַשְׂכִּ֣ילוּ זֹ֑את   חמישי
ל יָבִ֖ינוּ לְאַחֲרִיתָֽם׃   אֵיכָ֞ה יִרְדֹּ֤ף אֶחָד֙ אֶ֔לֶף
וּשְׁנַ֖יִם יָנִ֣יסוּ רְבָבָ֑ה   אִם־לֹא֙ כִּֽי־צוּרָ֣ם מְכָרָ֔ם
לא וַיהֹוָ֖ה הִסְגִּירָֽם׃   כִּ֛י לֹ֥א כְצוּרֵ֖נוּ צוּרָ֑ם
לב וְאֹיְבֵ֖ינוּ פְּלִילִֽים׃   כִּֽי־מִגֶּ֤פֶן סְדֹם֙ גַּפְנָ֔ם
וּמִשַּׁדְמֹ֖ת עֲמֹרָ֑ה   עֲנָבֵ֙מוֹ֙ עִנְּבֵי־ר֔וֹשׁ
לג אַשְׁכְּלֹ֥ת מְרֹרֹ֖ת לָֽמוֹ׃   חֲמַ֥ת תַּנִּינִ֖ם יֵינָ֑ם
לד וְרֹ֥אשׁ פְּתָנִ֖ים אַכְזָֽר׃   הֲלֹא־ה֖וּא כָּמֻ֣ס עִמָּדִ֑י

אונקלוס

וַאֲכִילֵי עוֹף וּכְתִישֵׁי רוּחִין בִּישִׁין, וְשֵׁן חֵיוַת בָּרָא אֲגָרֵי בְהוֹן, עִם חֲמַת תַּנִּינַיָּא דְּזָחֲלִין בְּעַפְרָא: כה מִבָּרָא תְּתַכֵּיל חַרְבָּא, וּמִתַּוָּנַיָּא חַרְגַּת מוֹתָא, אַף עוּלֵימֵיהוֹן אַף עוּלֵימָתְהוֹן, יָנְקֵיהוֹן עִם סָבֵיהוֹן: כו אֲמָרִית יְחוּל רְגָזִי עֲלֵיהוֹן וַאֲשֵׁיצֵינּוּן, אֲבַטֵּיל מִן בְּנֵי אֲנָשָׁא דָּכְרָנְהוֹן: כז אִלּוּ לָא פּוֹן, רְגָזָא דְּסָנְאָה כְּנִישׁ, דִּלְמָא יִתְרָרַב בְּעֵיל דְּבָבָא, דִּלְמָא יֵימְרוּן יְדַנָא תְּקֵיפַת לַנָא, וְלָא מִן קֳדָם יי הֲוָת כָּל דָּא: כח אֲרֵי עַם, מְאַבְּדֵי עֵיצָא אִנּוּן, וְלֵית בְּהוֹן סֻכְלְתָנוּ:

כט אִלּוּ חֲכִימוּ אִסְתַּכַּלוּ בְּדָא, סַבַּרוּ מָא יְהֵי בְּסוֹפְהוֹן: ל אֵיכְדֵין, יִרְדּוֹף חַד לְאַלְפָא, וּתְרֵין יְעָרְקוּן לְרִבּוֹתָא, אֱלָהֵין תַּקִּיפְהוֹן מְסַרְנוּן, וַיי אַשְׁלֵימִנּוּן: לא אֲרֵי, לָא כְתָקְפַנָא תָּקְפְהוֹן, וּבַעֲלֵי דְבָבָנָא הֲווֹ דַּיָּנָנָא: לב אֲרֵי כְּפֻרְעָנוּת עַמָּא דִסְדוֹם כָּס פֻּרְעָנוּתְהוֹן, וְלָקוּתְהוֹן כְּעַם עֲמוֹרָה, מַחָתְהוֹן בִּישִׁין כְּרֵישֵׁי חִוְיָן, וְתֻשְׁלְמַת עוֹבָדֵיהוֹן כִּמְרָרוּתְהוֹן: לג הָא כִמְרַת תַּנִּינַיָּא כָּס פֻּרְעָנוּתְהוֹן, וּכְרֵישׁ פִּתְנֵי חִוְיָן אַכְזְרָאִין: לד הֲלָא כָּל עוֹבָדֵיהוֹן גְּלַן קֳדָמַי,

רש״י

רָאוּי לָהֶם, לְפִי מַעֲשֵׂיהֶם פֻּרְעָנוּתָם. וְכֵן תִּרְגֵּם אוּנְקְלוֹס: "וְתוּשְׁלְמַת עוֹבָדֵיהוֹן כִּמְרָרוּתְהוֹן".

לג חֲמַת תַּנִּינִם יֵינָם. כְּתַרְגּוּמוֹ: "הָא כִמְרַת תַּנִּינַיָּא כָּס פֻּרְעָנוּתְהוֹן", הִנֵּה כִּמְרִירַת נְחָשִׁים כּוֹס מִשְׁתֵּה פֻּרְעָנוּתָם: וְרֹאשׁ פְּתָנִים אַכְזָר. כּוֹסָם, שֶׁהוּא אַכְזָר לִנְשֹׁךְ – אוֹיֵב אַכְזָרִי יָבֹא וְיִפָּרַע מֵהֶם:

לד הֲלֹא הוּא כָּמֻס עִמָּדִי. כְּתַרְגּוּמוֹ, כִּסְבוּרִים הֵם שֶׁשָּׁכַחְתִּי מַעֲשֵׂיהֶם,

35 treasury? / Vengeance is Mine; I will repay: / in time, their foot will
slip; / their day of disaster is near, / their destiny hastens to meet
36 them. / For the LORD will vindicate His people, / bring solace to His
servants, / when He sees their strength has slipped away, / no one
37 remains, no bond nor free. / He will say: Where are these gods of
38 theirs, / the rock they went to for refuge, / that ate their sacrificial fat /
and drank their wine of libation? / Let those rise up and help you
39 now, / let them be your protection! / See now that I, I alone, am He; /
there is no god apart from Me. / I deal death and I bring life; / I

רש״י

כֻּלָּם גְּנוּזִים וּשְׁמוּרִים לְפָנַי: **הֲלֹא הוּא.** פְּרִי גַּפְנָם וּתְבוּאַת שַׁדְמוֹתָם "כָּמֻס עִמָּדִי":

לה **לִי נָקָם וְשִׁלֵּם.** עִמִּי נָכוֹן וּמְזֻמָּן פֻּרְעָנוּת נָקָם, וִישַׁלֵּם לָהֶם כְּמַעֲשֵׂיהֶם, הַנָּקָם יְשַׁלֵּם לָהֶם גְּמוּלָם. וְיֵשׁ מְפָרְשִׁים "וְשִׁלֵּם" שֵׁם דָּבָר, כְּמוֹ 'וְשִׁלּוּם', וְהוּא מִגִּזְרַת: "וְהַדִּבֵּר אֵין בָּהֶם" (ירמיה ה, יג), כְּמוֹ 'וְהַדִּבּוּר'. וְאֵימָתַי אֲשַׁלֵּם לָהֶם? "לְעֵת תָּמוּט רַגְלָם", כְּשֶׁתִּתֹּם זְכוּת אֲבוֹתָם שֶׁהֵם סְמוּכִים עָלָיו: **כִּי קָרוֹב יוֹם אֵידָם.** מִשֶּׁאֶרְצֶה לְהָבִיא עֲלֵיהֶם יוֹם אֵידָם, קָרוֹב וּמְזֻמָּן לְפָנַי לְהָבִיא עַל יְדֵי שְׁלוּחִים הַרְבֵּה: **וְחָשׁ עֲתִדֹת לָמוֹ.** וּמַהֵר יָבֹאוּ הָעֲתִידוֹת לָהֶם: **וְחָשׁ.** כְּמוֹ "יְמַהֵר יָחִישָׁה" (ישעיה ה, יט).

עַד כָּאן הֵעִיד עֲלֵיהֶם מֹשֶׁה דִּבְרֵי תוֹכָחָה לִהְיוֹת הַשִּׁירָה הַזֹּאת לְעֵד, כְּשֶׁתָּבוֹא עֲלֵיהֶם הַפֻּרְעָנוּת יֵדְעוּ שֶׁאֲנִי הוֹדַעְתִּים מֵרֹאשׁ. מִכָּאן וְאֵילַךְ הֵעִיד עֲלֵיהֶם דִּבְרֵי תַנְחוּמִין שֶׁיָּבֹאוּ עֲלֵיהֶם כִּכְלוֹת הַפֻּרְעָנוּת, כְּכֹל אֲשֶׁר אָמַר לְמַעְלָה: "וְהָיָה כִּי יָבֹאוּ עָלֶיךָ... הַבְּרָכָה וְהַקְּלָלָה וְגוֹ' וְשָׁב ה' אֱלֹהֶיךָ אֶת שְׁבוּתְךָ" וְגוֹ' (לעיל ל, א-ג):

לו **כִּי יָדִין ה' עַמּוֹ.** כְּשֶׁיִּשְׁפֹּט אוֹתָם בְּיִסּוּרִין הַלָּלוּ הָאֲמוּרִים עֲלֵיהֶם, כְּמוֹ: "כִּי בָם יָדִין עַמִּים" (איוב לו, לא), יְיַסֵּר עַמִּים. 'כִּי' זֶה אֵינוֹ מְשַׁמֵּשׁ בִּלְשׁוֹן 'דְּהָא' לָתֵת טַעַם לַדְּבָרִים שֶׁל מַעְלָה, אֶלָּא לְשׁוֹן תְּחִלַּת דִּבּוּר, כְּמוֹ: "כִּי תָבֹאוּ אֶל הָאָרֶץ" (ויקרא כה, ב), כְּשֶׁיָּבֹאוּ עֲלֵיהֶם מִשְׁפָּטִים הַלָּלוּ וְיִתְנַחֵם הַקָּדוֹשׁ בָּרוּךְ הוּא עַל עֲבָדָיו לָשׁוּב וּלְרַחֵם עֲלֵיהֶם: **יִתְנֶחָם.** לְשׁוֹן הֵפֶךְ מַחֲשָׁבָה, לְהֵיטִיב אוֹ לְהָרַע. כְּשֶׁתִּרְאֶה כִּי אָזְלַת יַד הָאוֹיֵב הוֹלֶכֶת וַחֲזָקָה עֲלֵיהֶם, וְ"אֶפֶס" בָּהֶם "עָצוּר וְעָזוּב": **עָצוּר.** נוֹשַׁע עַל יְדֵי עוֹצֵר וּמוֹשֵׁל שֶׁיַּעֲצֹר בָּהֶם: **עָזוּב.** עַל יְדֵי עוֹזֵב. 'עוֹצֵר' הוּא הַמּוֹשֵׁל הָעוֹצֵר בָּעָם שֶׁלֹּא יֵלְכוּ מְפֻזָּרִים בְּצֵאתָם לַצָּבָא עַל הָאוֹיֵב: **עָצוּר.** הוּא הַנּוֹשָׁע בְּמַעֲצוֹר הַמּוֹשֵׁל: **עָזוּב.** מְחֻזָּק, כְּמוֹ: "וַיַּעַזְבוּ יְרוּשָׁלַיִם עַד הַחוֹמָה" (נחמיה ג, ח), "אֵיךְ לֹא עֻזְּבָה עִיר תְּהִלָּת" (ירמיה מט, כה): **עָצוּר.** מייטני"ר: **עָזוּב.** אישפורצא"ר בְּלַעַז:

לז **וְאָמַר.** הַקָּדוֹשׁ בָּרוּךְ הוּא עֲלֵיהֶם: "אֵי אֱלֹהֵימוֹ" עֲבוֹדָה זָרָה שֶׁעָבְדוּ: **צוּר חָסָיוּ בוֹ.** הַסֶּלַע שֶׁהָיוּ מִתְכַּסִּין בּוֹ מִפְּנֵי הַחַמָּה וְהַצִּנָּה, כְּלוֹמַר שֶׁהָיוּ בּוֹטְחִין בּוֹ לְהָגֵן עֲלֵיהֶם מִן הָרָעָה:

לח **אֲשֶׁר חֵלֶב זְבָחֵימוֹ.** הָיוּ אוֹתָן אֱלֹהוּת אוֹכְלִים, שֶׁהָיוּ מַקְרִיבִים לִפְנֵיהֶם, וְשׁוֹתִין "יֵין נְסִיכָם": **יְהִי עֲלֵיכֶם סִתְרָה.** אוֹתוֹ הַצּוּר יִהְיֶה לָכֶם מַחֲסֶה וּמִסְתּוֹר:

לט **רְאוּ עַתָּה.** הָבִינוּ מִן הַפֻּרְעָנוּת שֶׁהֵבֵאתִי עֲלֵיכֶם וְאֵין לָכֶם מוֹשִׁיעַ, וּמִן הַתְּשׁוּעָה שֶׁאוֹשִׁיעֲכֶם וְאֵין מוֹחֶה בְּיָדִי: **אֲנִי אֲנִי הוּא.** אֲנִי לְהַשְׁפִּיל וַאֲנִי לְהָרִים: **וְאֵין אֱלֹהִים עִמָּדִי.** עוֹמֵד כְּנֶגְדִּי לִמְחוֹת: **עִמָּדִי.** דֻּגְמָתִי וְכָמוֹנִי:

name of the God of love. We can still hear their responses: they are recorded for us in many of the lamentations, *kinot*, we say on the Ninth of Av. Yes, they appeal to God's vengeance, which is to say, to God's justice. But Jews did not seek to take vengeance. That is something you leave to God. There is a justice we will not see this side of the end of days. In the meantime, it is sufficient to live, and affirm life, and seek no more than the right to be true to your faith without fear – no more than the right to live and defend that selfsame right for your children. Yes, we seek justice and we fight for justice, but the search for *perfect* justice is not for us, here, now. It is – as Moshe taught the Israelites in the great song he sang at the end of his life – something that faith demands we leave to God, who alone knows the human heart, who alone knows what is just in a world of conflicting claims, and who will establish perfect justice at a time, and in a way, of His choosing, not ours.

לה חָתוּם בְּאוֹצְרֹתָי׃ | לִי נָקָם וְשִׁלֵּם
לְעֵת תָּמוּט רַגְלָם | כִּי קָרוֹב יוֹם אֵידָם
לו וְחָשׁ עֲתִדֹת לָמוֹ׃ | כִּי־יָדִין יהוה עַמּוֹ
וְעַל־עֲבָדָיו יִתְנֶחָם | כִּי יִרְאֶה כִּי־אָזְלַת יָד
לז וְאֶפֶס עָצוּר וְעָזוּב׃ | וְאָמַר אֵי אֱלֹהֵימוֹ
לח צוּר חָסָיוּ בוֹ׃ | אֲשֶׁר חֵלֶב זְבָחֵימוֹ יֹאכֵלוּ
יִשְׁתּוּ יֵין נְסִיכָם | יָקוּמוּ וְיַעְזְרֻכֶם
לט יְהִי עֲלֵיכֶם סִתְרָה׃ | רְאוּ ׀ עַתָּה כִּי אֲנִי אֲנִי הוּא
וְאֵין אֱלֹהִים עִמָּדִי | אֲנִי אָמִית וַאֲחַיֶּה

אונקלוס

גְּנִיזִין לְיוֹם דִּינָא בְּאוֹצְרָי: לה קֳדָמַי פֻּרְעֲנוּתָא וַאֲנָא אֲשַׁלֵּים, בְּעִדָּן
דְּיִגְלוֹן מֵאַרְעֲהוֹן, אֲרֵי קָרִיב יוֹם תְּבָרְהוֹן, וּמַבַע דַּעֲתִיד לְהוֹן: לו אֲרֵי
יְדִין יי דִּינָא דְעַמֵּיהּ, וּפֻרְעֲנוּת עַבְדּוֹהִי צַדִּיקַיָּא יִתְפְּרַע, אֲרֵי גְלֵי
קֳדָמוֹהִי דִּבְעִדָּן דְּתִתְקַף עֲלֵיהוֹן מַחַת סָנְאָה, יְהוֹן מְטַלְטְלִין וּשְׁבִיקִין:
לז וְיֵימַר אָן דַּחֲלַתְהוֹן, תַּקִּיפָא דַּהֲווֹ רְחִיצִין בֵּיהּ: לח דְּתַרְב נִכְסַתְהוֹן הֲווֹ
אָכְלִין, שָׁתַן חֲמַר נִסְכֵּיהוֹן, יְקוּמוּן כְּעַן וְיִסַעֲדוּנְכוֹן, יְהוֹן עֲלֵיכוֹן לְמַגֵּין:
לט חֲזוֹ כְּעַן, אֲרֵי אֲנָא אֲנָא הוּא, וְלֵית אֱלָהּ בַּר מִנִּי, אֲנָא מְמִית וּמְחֵי,

GOD'S VENGEANCE

God forbids revenge (Lev. 19:18). He commands forgiveness, as Yosef forgave his brothers – and as we, on Judaism's holiest day, ask Him to forgive us. To quote Rambam, "As long as one nurses a grievance and keeps it in mind, one may come to take revenge. The Torah therefore emphatically warns us not to bear a grudge, so that the impression of the wrong shall be wholly obliterated and no longer remembered. This is the right principle. It alone makes society and human interaction possible" (*Hilkhot Deot* 7:8). Note that Rambam means this as a general rule for humanity, not limited to Jews.

Yet this *parasha* contains lines such as "He will avenge His servants' blood," which are difficult to reconcile with an ethic of non-revenge. Three thinkers, Jan Assmann, Henri Atlan, and Miroslav Volf, help us to understand this tension. Assmann points out that in the Hebrew Bible anger is "theologized" and thus "transferred…from earth to heaven." Atlan argues likewise that "the best way to rid the world of the violent sacred is to project it onto a transcendence." The "transcendence of violence" results in "its being expelled from the normal horizon of things." In other words, vengeance is removed from human calculation. It is God, not man, who is entitled to exercise it. Volf agrees, adding that "in a world of violence we are faced with an inescapable alternative: either God's violence or human violence." He adds: "Most people who insist on God's 'nonviolence' cannot resist using violence themselves (or tacitly sanctioning its use by others). They deem the talk of God's judgment irreverent, but think nothing of entrusting judgment into human hands…. And so violence thrives, secretly nourished by belief in a God who refuses to wield the sword."

I think of the Jews of the Middle Ages, who saw their fellow Jews accused of killing Christian children to drink their blood, of poisoning wells, of desecrating the host and spreading the plague, and then murdered en masse in the

40 wounded but will heal; / and there is no rescue from My hand. / For SHISHI
41 I lift My hand skyward and swear: / as sure as I live forever, / when I
whet My flashing sword, / and My hand grasps justice; / I will wreak
42 vengeance on My foes, / and repay those who hate Me. / I will make
My arrows drunk with blood, / while My sword devours flesh, / the
blood of the slain and the captives, / leaders of the long-haired foe. /
43 O nations, sing out of His people, / for He will avenge His servants'
blood, / take vengeance upon His foes, / and cleanse His land and
His people."

44 Moshe came and proclaimed all the words of this song in the hearing of the SHEVI'I
45 people, he and Hoshea son of Nun. When Moshe had finished speaking all

רש"י

וְאֵין מִיָּדִי מַצִּיל. הַפּוֹשְׁעִים בִּי:

מ **כִּי אֶשָּׂא אֶל שָׁמַיִם יָדִי.** כִּי בַּחֲרוֹן אַפִּי אֶשָּׂא יָדִי אֶל עַצְמִי בִּשְׁבוּעָה: **וְאָמַרְתִּי חַי אָנֹכִי.** לְשׁוֹן שְׁבוּעָה הוּא, אֲנִי נִשְׁבָּע 'חַי אָנִי':

מא **אִם שַׁנּוֹתִי בְּרַק חַרְבִּי.** אִם אֲשַׁנֵּן אֶת לַהַב חַרְבִּי, כְּמוֹ: "לְמַעַן הֱיוֹת לָהּ בָּרָק", פלאנדו"ר: **וְתֹאחֵז בְּמִשְׁפָּט יָדִי.** לְהַנִּיחַ מִדַּת רַחֲמִים בְּאוֹיְבַי שֶׁהֵרֵעוּ לָכֶם, "אֲשֶׁר אֲנִי קָצַפְתִּי מְעָט וְהֵמָּה עָזְרוּ לְרָעָה" (זכריה א, טו), וְתֹאחֵז יָדִי אֶת מִדַּת הַמִּשְׁפָּט לְהַחֲזִיק בָּהּ וְלִנְקֹם נָקָם: **אָשִׁיב נָקָם וגו'.** לָמְדוּ רַבּוֹתֵינוּ בְּאַגָּדָה מִתּוֹךְ לְשׁוֹן הַמִּקְרָא שֶׁאָמַר: "וְתֹאחֵז בְּמִשְׁפָּט יָדִי" – לֹא כְּמִדַּת בָּשָׂר וָדָם מִדַּת הַקָּדוֹשׁ בָּרוּךְ הוּא, מִדַּת בָּשָׂר וָדָם זוֹרֵק חֵץ וְאֵינוֹ יָכוֹל לַהֲשִׁיבוֹ, וְהַקָּדוֹשׁ בָּרוּךְ הוּא זוֹרֵק חִצָּיו וְיֵשׁ בְּיָדוֹ לַהֲשִׁיבָם כְּאִלּוּ אוֹחֲזָן בְּיָדוֹ, שֶׁהֲרֵי בָּרָק הוּא חִצּוֹ, שֶׁנֶּאֱמַר כָּאן: "בְּרַק חַרְבִּי וְתֹאחֵז בְּמִשְׁפָּט יָדִי", וְהַמִּשְׁפָּט הַזֶּה לְשׁוֹן פֻּרְעָנוּת הוּא, בְּלַעַז יוסטיצי"א:

מב **אַשְׁכִּיר חִצַּי מִדָּם.** הָאוֹיֵב: **וְחַרְבִּי תֹּאכַל.** בְּשָׂרָם: **מִדַּם חָלָל וְשִׁבְיָה.** זֹאת תִּהְיֶה לָהֶם מֵעֲוֹן דַּם חַלְלֵי יִשְׂרָאֵל וְשִׁבְיָה שֶׁשָּׁבוּ מֵהֶם: **מֵרֹאשׁ פַּרְעוֹת אוֹיֵב.** מִפֶּשַׁע תְּחִלַּת פִּרְעוֹת הָאוֹיֵב, כִּי כְּשֶׁהַקָּדוֹשׁ בָּרוּךְ הוּא נִפְרָע מִן הָאֻמּוֹת פּוֹקֵד עֲלֵיהֶם עֲוֹנָם וַעֲוֹנוֹת אֲבוֹתֵיהֶם מֵרֵאשִׁית פִּרְצָה שֶׁפָּרְצוּ בְּיִשְׂרָאֵל:

מג **הַרְנִינוּ גוֹיִם עַמּוֹ.** לְאוֹתוֹ הַזְּמַן יְשַׁבְּחוּ הָאֻמּוֹת אֶת יִשְׂרָאֵל, רְאוּ מַה שִּׁבְחָהּ שֶׁל אֻמָּה זוֹ שֶׁדָּבְקוּ בְּהַקָּדוֹשׁ בָּרוּךְ הוּא בְּכָל הַתְּלָאוֹת שֶׁעָבְרוּ עֲלֵיהֶם וְלֹא עֲזָבוּהוּ, יוֹדְעִים הָיוּ בְּטוּבוֹ וּבְשִׁבְחוֹ: **כִּי דַם עֲבָדָיו יִקּוֹם.** שְׁפִיכוּת דְּמֵיהֶם, כְּמַשְׁמָעוֹ: **וְנָקָם יָשִׁיב לְצָרָיו.** עַל הַגָּזֵל וְעַל הֶחָמָס, כְּעִנְיָן שֶׁנֶּאֱמַר: "מִצְרַיִם לִשְׁמָמָה תִהְיֶה וֶאֱדוֹם לְמִדְבַּר שְׁמָמָה תִּהְיֶה, מֵחֲמַס בְּנֵי יְהוּדָה" (יואל ד, יט), וְאוֹמֵר: "מֵחֲמַס אָחִיךָ יַעֲקֹב" וגו' (עובדיה א, י): **וְכִפֶּר אַדְמָתוֹ עַמּוֹ.** וִיפַיֵּס אַדְמָתוֹ וְעַמּוֹ עַל הַצָּרוֹת שֶׁעָבְרוּ עֲלֵיהֶם וְשֶׁעָשׂוּ לָהֶם הָאוֹיֵב: **וְכִפֶּר.** לְשׁוֹן רִצּוּי וּפִיּוּס, כְּמוֹ: "אֲכַפְּרָה פָנָיו" – "אֲנִיחֵנֵּיהּ לְרָגְזֵיהּ" (בראשית לב, כ; אונקלוס שם): **וְכִפֶּר אַדְמָתוֹ.** וּמָה הִיא אַדְמָתוֹ? – "עַמּוֹ", כְּשֶׁעַמּוֹ מִתְנַחֲמִים אַרְצוֹ מִתְנַחֶמֶת, וְכֵן הוּא אוֹמֵר: "רָצִיתָ ה' אַרְצֶךָ" (תהלים פה, ב), בַּמֶּה רָצִיתָ אַרְצֶךָ? "שַׁבְתָּ שְׁבוּת יַעֲקֹב" (שם).

בְּפָנִים אֲחֵרִים הָיְתָה נִדְרֶשֶׁת בְּסִפְרֵי וְנֶחְלְקוּ בָּהּ רַבִּי יְהוּדָה וְרַבִּי נְחֶמְיָה. רַבִּי יְהוּדָה דּוֹרֵשׁ כֻּלָּהּ כְּנֶגֶד יִשְׂרָאֵל, וְרַבִּי נְחֶמְיָה דּוֹרֵשׁ אֶת כֻּלָּהּ כְּנֶגֶד הָאֻמּוֹת. רַבִּי יְהוּדָה דּוֹרְשָׁהּ כְּלַפֵּי יִשְׂרָאֵל: **אָמַרְתִּי אַפְאֵיהֶם.** (לעיל פסוק כו) כְּמוֹ שֶׁפֵּרַשְׁתִּי, עַד "וְלֹא ה' פָּעַל כָּל זֹאת" (לעיל פסוק כז): **כִּי גוֹי אֹבַד עֵצוֹת הֵמָּה.** (לעיל פסוק כח) אִבְּדוּ תּוֹרָתִי שֶׁהִיא לָהֶם עֵצָה נְכוֹנָה: **וְאֵין בָּהֶם תְּבוּנָה.** לְהִתְבּוֹנֵן "אֵיכָה יִרְדֹּף אֶחָד" מִן הָאֻמּוֹת "אֶלֶף" מֵהֶם, "אִם לֹא כִּי צוּרָם מְכָרָם" (לעיל פסוק ל). "כִּי לֹא כְצוּרֵנוּ צוּרָם" (לעיל פסוק לא), הַכֹּל כְּמוֹ שֶׁפֵּרַשְׁתִּי עַד תַּכְלִית.

וְרַבִּי נְחֶמְיָה דּוֹרְשָׁהּ כְּלַפֵּי הָאֻמּוֹת: כִּי גוֹי אֹבַד עֵצוֹת הֵמָּה. כְּמוֹ שֶׁפֵּרַשְׁתִּי תְּחִלָּה, עַד "וְאֹיְבֵינוּ פְּלִילִים" (לעיל פסוק לא):

לב **כִּי מִגֶּפֶן סְדֹם גַּפְנָם.** שֶׁל אֻמּוֹת: **וּמִשַּׁדְמוֹת עֲמֹרָה וגו'.** וְלֹא יָשִׂימוּ לִבָּם לִתְלוֹת הַגְּדֻלָּה בִּי: **עֲנָבֵמוֹ עִנְּבֵי רוֹשׁ.** הוּא שֶׁאָמַר: "לוּלֵי כַּעַס אוֹיֵב אָגוּר" (לעיל פסוק כז) עַל יִשְׂרָאֵל לְהַרְעִילָם וּלְהַמְרִירָם, לְפִיכָךְ: "אַשְׁכְּלֹת מְרֹרֹת לָמוֹ" לְהַלְעִיט אוֹתָם עַל מַה שֶּׁעָשׂוּ לְבָנַי:

לג **חֲמַת תַּנִּינִם יֵינָם.** מוּכָן לְהַשְׁקוֹתָם עַל מַה שֶּׁעוֹשִׂין לָהֶם:

לד **כָּמֻס עִמָּדִי.** אוֹתוֹ הַכּוֹס, שֶׁנֶּאֱמַר: "כִּי כוֹס בְּיַד ה'" וגו' (תהלים עה, ט):

לה **לְעֵת תָּמוּט רַגְלָם.** כְּעִנְיָן שֶׁנֶּאֱמַר "תִּרְמְסֶנָּה רָגֶל" (ישעיה כו, ו):

לו **כִּי יָדִין ה' עַמּוֹ.** כְּלָשׁוֹן זֶה מְשַׁמֵּשׁ "כִּי יָדִין" בִּלְשׁוֹן 'דְּהָא', וְאֵין "יָדִין" לְשׁוֹן יִסּוּרִין, אֶלָּא כְּמוֹ כִּי יָרִיב אֶת רִיבָם מִיַּד עוֹשְׁקֵיהֶם, "כִּי יִרְאֶה כִּי אָזְלַת יָד" וגו':

מָחַצְתִּי וַאֲנִי אֶרְפָּא   וְאֵין מִיָּדִי מַצִּיל:
מ כִּי־אֶשָּׂא אֶל־שָׁמַיִם יָדִי   וְאָמַרְתִּי חַי אָנֹכִי לְעֹלָם: ששי
מא אִם־שַׁנּוֹתִי בְּרַק חַרְבִּי   וְתֹאחֵז בְּמִשְׁפָּט יָדִי
אָשִׁיב נָקָם לְצָרָי   וְלִמְשַׂנְאַי אֲשַׁלֵּם:
מב אַשְׁכִּיר חִצַּי מִדָּם   וְחַרְבִּי תֹּאכַל בָּשָׂר
מִדַּם חָלָל וְשִׁבְיָה   מֵרֹאשׁ פַּרְעוֹת אוֹיֵב:
מג הַרְנִינוּ גוֹיִם עַמּוֹ   כִּי דַם־עֲבָדָיו יִקּוֹם
וְנָקָם יָשִׁיב לְצָרָיו   וְכִפֶּר אַדְמָתוֹ עַמּוֹ:

מד וַיָּבֹא מֹשֶׁה וַיְדַבֵּר אֶת־כָּל־דִּבְרֵי הַשִּׁירָה־הַזֹּאת בְּאָזְנֵי הָעָם הוּא שביעי
מה וְהוֹשֵׁעַ בִּן־נוּן: וַיְכַל מֹשֶׁה לְדַבֵּר אֶת־כָּל־הַדְּבָרִים הָאֵלֶּה אֶל־כָּל־

אונקלוס

מְחֵינָא וְאַף מַסֵּינָא, וְלֵית מִן יְדִי מְשֵׁיזֵיב: מ אֲרֵי אַתְקֵינִית בִּשְׁמַיָּא בֵּית שְׁכִינְתִּי, וַאֲמַרִית, קַיָּם אֲנָא לְעָלְמִין: מא אִם עַל חַד תְּרֵין כְּחֵיזוּ בַּרְקָא, מִסּוֹף שְׁמַיָּא וְעַד סוֹף שְׁמַיָּא תִּתְגְּלֵי חַרְבִּי, וְתִתַּקַּף בְּדִינָא יְדִי, אֲתִיב פֻּרְעָנוּתָא לְסָנְאַי, וּלְבַעֲלֵי דְבָבִי אֲשַׁלֵּים: מב אַרְוֵי גִּרַּי מִדְּמָא, וְחַרְבִּי תְּקַטֵּיל בְּעַמְמַיָּא, מִדַּם קְטִילִין וּשְׁבַן, לְאַעְדָּאָה כִּתְרִין מֵרֵישׁ סָנְאָה וּבְעֵיל דְּבָבָא: מג שַׁבַּחוּ עַמְמַיָּא עַמֵּיהּ, אֲרֵי פֻּרְעָנוּת עַבְדּוֹהִי צַדִּיקַיָּא יִתְפְּרַע, וּפֻרְעָנוּתָא יָתִיב לְסָנְאוֹהִי, וִיכַפַּר עַל אַרְעֵיהּ וְעַל עַמֵּיהּ: מד וַאֲתָא מֹשֶׁה, וּמַלֵּיל, יָת כָּל פִּתְגָּמֵי תֻּשְׁבַּחְתָּא הָדָא קֳדָם עַמָּא, הוּא וְהוֹשֵׁעַ בַּר נוּן: מה וְשֵׁיצִי מֹשֶׁה, לְמַלָּלָא, יָת כָּל פִּתְגָּמַיָּא הָאִלֵּין עִם כָּל

רש״י

לז וְאָמַר אֵי אֱלֹהֵימוֹ. וְהָאוֹיֵב יֹאמַר: ״אֵי אֱלֹהֵימוֹ״ שֶׁל יִשְׂרָאֵל, כְּמוֹ שֶׁאָמַר טִיטוּס הָרָשָׁע כְּשֶׁגִּדֵּר אֶת הַפָּרֹכֶת, כְּעִנְיָן שֶׁנֶּאֱמַר: ״וְתֵרֶא אֹיַבְתִּי וּתְכַסֶּהָ בוּשָׁה הָאֹמְרָה אֵלַי אַיּוֹ ה׳ אֱלֹהָיִךְ״ (מיכה ז, י):

לט רְאוּ עַתָּה כִּי אֲנִי וְגוֹ׳. אָז יִגָּלֶה הַקָּדוֹשׁ בָּרוּךְ הוּא יְשׁוּעָתוֹ, וְיֹאמַר: ״רְאוּ עַתָּה כִּי אֲנִי אֲנִי הוּא״, מֵאִתִּי בָּאת עֲלֵיהֶם הָרָעָה, וּמֵאִתִּי תָּבֹא עֲלֵיהֶם הַטּוֹבָה: וְאֵין מִיָּדִי מַצִּיל. מִי שֶׁיַּצִּיל אֶתְכֶם מִן הָרָעָה אֲשֶׁר אָבִיא עֲלֵיכֶם:

מ כִּי אֶשָּׂא אֶל שָׁמַיִם יָדִי. כְּמוֹ ׳כִּי נָשָׂאתִי׳, תָּמִיד אֲנִי מַשְׁרֶה מְקוֹם שְׁכִינָתִי בַּשָּׁמַיִם, כְּתַרְגּוּמוֹ. אֲפִלּוּ אָדָם חַלָּשׁ לְמַעְלָה וְגִבּוֹר לְמַטָּה, אֵימַת עֶלְיוֹן עַל הַתַּחְתּוֹן, וְכָל שֶׁכֵּן שֶׁגִּבּוֹר לְמַעְלָה וְחַלָּשׁ מִלְּמַטָּה: יָדִי. מְקוֹם שְׁכִינָתִי, כְּמוֹ: ״אִישׁ עַל יָדוֹ״ (במדבר ב, יז), וְהָיָה בְּיָדִי לְהִפָּרַע מִכֶּם, אֲבָל אָמַרְתִּי שֶׁ״חַי אָנֹכִי לְעֹלָם״, אֵינִי מְמַהֵר לִפָּרַע לְפִי שֶׁיֵּשׁ שָׁהוּת בַּדָּבָר, אֲנִי חַי לְעוֹלָם וּבְדוֹרוֹת אַחֲרוֹנִים אֲנִי נִפְרָע מֵהֶם, וְהַיְכֹלֶת בְּיָדִי לִפָּרַע מִן הַמֵּתִים וּמִן הַחַיִּים. מֶלֶךְ בָּשָׂר וָדָם שֶׁהוּא הוֹלֵךְ לָמוּת, מְמַהֵר נִקְמָתוֹ לִפָּרַע בְּחַיָּיו, כִּי שֶׁמָּא יָמוּת הוּא אוֹ אוֹיְבוֹ וְנִמְצָא שֶׁלֹּא רָאָה נִקְמָתוֹ מִמֶּנּוּ, אֲבָל אֲנִי חַי לְעוֹלָם, וְאִם יָמוּתוּ הֵם וְאֵינִי נִפְרָע בְּחַיֵּיהֶם, אֶפָּרַע בְּמוֹתָם:

מא אִם שַׁנּוֹתִי בְּרַק חַרְבִּי. הַרְבֵּה ׳אִם׳ יֵשׁ שֶׁאֵינָם תְּלוּיִין, כְּשֶׁאֶשְׁנֵן ״בְּרַק חַרְבִּי וְתֹאחֵז בְּמִשְׁפָּט יָדִי״, כְּלוֹ כְּמוֹ שֶׁפֵּרַשְׁתִּי לְמַעְלָה:

מד הוּא וְהוֹשֵׁעַ בִּן נוּן. שַׁבָּת שֶׁל דְּיוֹזְגֵי הָיְתָה, נִטְּלָה רְשׁוּת מִזֶּה וְנִתְּנָה לָזֶה, הֶעֱמִיד לוֹ מֹשֶׁה מְתֻרְגְּמָן לִיהוֹשֻׁעַ שֶׁיְּהֵא דּוֹרֵשׁ בְּחַיָּיו, כְּדֵי שֶׁלֹּא יֹאמְרוּ יִשְׂרָאֵל: בְּחַיֵּי רַבְּךָ לֹא הָיָה לְךָ לְהָרִים רֹאשׁ. וְלָמָּה קוֹרֵהוּ כָּאן ׳הוֹשֵׁעַ׳? לוֹמַר שֶׁלֹּא זָחָה דַּעְתּוֹ עָלָיו, שֶׁאַף עַל פִּי שֶׁנִּתְּנָה לוֹ גְּדֻלָּה, הִשְׁפִּיל עַצְמוֹ כַּאֲשֶׁר מִתְּחִלָּתוֹ:

46 these words to all Israel, he said to them: "Take to heart all the words I testify
to you today, and charge your children with them, so that they may take care
47 to keep all the words of this Law. For these are not idle words for you; they are
your very life. By this word you may live long in the land that you are crossing
over the Jordan to possess."
48 49 On that very day the LORD spoke to Moshe: "Ascend this mountain of Avarim, MAFTIR
Mount Nevo, in the land of Moav, facing Yeriḥo, and gaze upon the land of
50 Canaan, which I am giving to the Israelites as a holding. There, on the mountain
that you ascend, you will die and be gathered to your people, as your brother

רש"י

מו **שִׂימוּ לְבַבְכֶם.** צָרִיךְ אָדָם שֶׁיִּהְיוּ עֵינָיו וְלִבּוֹ וְאָזְנָיו מְכֻוָּנִים לְדִבְרֵי תוֹרָה, וְכֵן הוּא אוֹמֵר: "בֶּן אָדָם רְאֵה בְעֵינֶיךָ וּבְאָזְנֶיךָ שְׁמָע וְשִׂים לִבְּךָ" וְגוֹ' (יחזקאל מ, ד), וַהֲרֵי דְּבָרִים קַל וָחֹמֶר: וּמַה תַּבְנִית הַבַּיִת שֶׁהוּא נִרְאֶה לָעֵינַיִם וְנִמְדָּד בְּקָנֶה, צָרִיךְ אָדָם שֶׁיִּהְיוּ עֵינָיו וְאָזְנָיו וְלִבּוֹ מְכֻוָּנִים לְהָבִין, דִּבְרֵי תוֹרָה שֶׁהֵן כַּהֲרָרִין תְּלוּיִין בְּשַׂעֲרָה, עַל אַחַת כַּמָּה וְכַמָּה:

מז **כִּי לֹא דָבָר רֵק הוּא מִכֶּם.** לֹא לְחִנָּם אַתֶּם יְגֵעִים בָּהּ, כִּי הַרְבֵּה שָׂכָר תָּלוּי בָּהּ, "כִּי הוּא חַיֵּיכֶם". דָּבָר אַחֵר, אֵין לְךָ דָּבָר רֵיקָן בַּתּוֹרָה שֶׁאִם תִּדְרְשֶׁנּוּ שֶׁאֵין בּוֹ מַתַּן שָׂכָר. תֵּדַע לְךָ, שֶׁכֵּן אָמְרוּ חֲכָמִים: "וַאֲחוֹת לוֹטָן תִּמְנָע" (בראשית לו, כב), "וְתִמְנַע הָיְתָה פִילֶגֶשׁ" וְגוֹ' (שם יב), לְפִי שֶׁאָמְרָה: אֵינִי כְדַאי לִהְיוֹת לוֹ אִשָּׁה, הַלְוַאי וְאֶהְיֶה פִּילַגְשׁוֹ, וְכָל כָּךְ לָמָּה? לְהוֹדִיעַ שִׁבְחוֹ שֶׁל אַבְרָהָם, שֶׁהָיוּ שִׁלְטוֹנִים וּמְלָכִים מִתְאַוִּים לִדָּבֵק בְּזַרְעוֹ:

מח **וַיְדַבֵּר ה' אֶל מֹשֶׁה בְּעֶצֶם הַיּוֹם הַזֶּה.** בִּשְׁלֹשָׁה מְקוֹמוֹת נֶאֱמַר "בְּעֶצֶם הַיּוֹם הַזֶּה": נֶאֱמַר בְּנֹחַ: "בְּעֶצֶם הַיּוֹם הַזֶּה בָּא נֹחַ" וְגוֹ' (בראשית ז, יג), בְּמַרְאִית אוֹרוֹ שֶׁל יוֹם; לְפִי שֶׁהָיוּ בְּנֵי דוֹרוֹ אוֹמְרִים, מִכָּךְ וְכָךְ, אִם אָנוּ מַרְגִּישִׁין בּוֹ אֵין אָנוּ מַנִּיחִין אוֹתוֹ לִכָּנֵס בַּתֵּבָה, וְלֹא עוֹד אֶלָּא אָנוּ נוֹטְלִין כַּשִּׁילִין וְקַרְדֻּמּוֹת וּמְבַקְּעִין אֶת הַתֵּבָה. אָמַר הַקָּדוֹשׁ בָּרוּךְ הוּא: הֲרֵינִי מַכְנִיסוֹ בַּחֲצִי הַיּוֹם, וְכָל מִי שֶׁיֵּשׁ בְּיָדוֹ כֹּחַ לִמְחוֹת יָבֹא וְיִמְחֶה. בְּמִצְרַיִם נֶאֱמַר: "בְּעֶצֶם הַיּוֹם הַזֶּה הוֹצִיא ה'" (שמות יב, נא), לְפִי שֶׁהָיוּ מִצְרִיִּים אוֹמְרִים, מִכָּךְ וְכָךְ, אִם אָנוּ מַרְגִּישִׁין בָּהֶם אֵין אָנוּ מַנִּיחִין אוֹתָם לָצֵאת, וְלֹא עוֹד אֶלָּא אָנוּ נוֹטְלִין סַיָּפוֹת וּכְלֵי זַיִן וְהוֹרְגִין בָּהֶם. אָמַר הַקָּדוֹשׁ בָּרוּךְ הוּא: הֲרֵינִי מוֹצִיאָן בַּחֲצִי הַיּוֹם, וְכָל מִי שֶׁיֵּשׁ בּוֹ כֹּחַ לִמְחוֹת יָבֹא וְיִמְחֶה. אַף כָּאן בְּמִיתָתוֹ שֶׁל מֹשֶׁה נֶאֱמַר: "בְּעֶצֶם הַיּוֹם הַזֶּה", לְפִי שֶׁהָיוּ יִשְׂרָאֵל אוֹמְרִים, מִכָּךְ וְכָךְ, אִם אָנוּ מַרְגִּישִׁין בּוֹ אֵין אָנוּ מַנִּיחִין אוֹתוֹ, אָדָם שֶׁהוֹצִיאָנוּ מִמִּצְרַיִם, וְקָרַע לָנוּ אֶת הַיָּם, וְהוֹרִיד לָנוּ אֶת הַמָּן, וְהֵגִיז לָנוּ אֶת הַשְּׂלָו, וְהֶעֱלָה לָנוּ אֶת הַבְּאֵר, וְנָתַן לָנוּ אֶת הַתּוֹרָה, אֵין אָנוּ מַנִּיחִין אוֹתוֹ. אָמַר הַקָּדוֹשׁ בָּרוּךְ הוּא: הֲרֵינִי מַכְנִיסוֹ בַּחֲצִי הַיּוֹם וְכוּ':

נ **כַּאֲשֶׁר מֵת אַהֲרֹן אָחִיךָ.** בְּאוֹתָהּ מִיתָה שֶׁרָאִיתָ וְחָמַדְתָּ אוֹתָהּ, שֶׁהִפְשִׁיט מֹשֶׁה אֶת אַהֲרֹן בֶּגֶד רִאשׁוֹן וְהִלְבִּישׁוֹ לְאֶלְעָזָר, וְכֵן שֵׁנִי, וְכֵן

And so Moshe's death on the far side of the Jordan is a consolation for all of us. None of us should feel guilty or frustrated or angry or defeated that there are things we hoped to achieve but did not. That is what it is to be human.

Nor should we be haunted by our mistakes. That, I believe, is why the Torah tells us, and now reminds us, that Moshe sinned. Did it really have to include the episode of the water, the stick, the rock, and Moshe's anger (Num. 20)? It passes over thirty-eight of the forty years in the wilderness in silence. Why not, then, pass over this too in silence, sparing Moshe's good name? What other religious literature has ever been so candid about the failings of even the greatest of its heroes?

the chance we would light the dark places of the world with the radiance of the faith for which they risked life itself. "For these are not idle words for you; they are your very life."

MOSHE'S FAILING

Humanity at its highest is still human. We are mortal. We are creatures of flesh and blood. We are born, we grow, we learn, we make our way in the world. If we are lucky we find love. If we are blessed, we have children. But we also age. The body grows old even if the spirit stays young. We know that this gift of life does not last forever because in this physical universe, nothing lasts forever, not even planets or stars. We each have a destination we will not reach.

מו יִשְׂרָאֵל׃ וַיֹּאמֶר אֲלֵהֶם שִׂימוּ לְבַבְכֶם לְכָל־הַדְּבָרִים אֲשֶׁר אָנֹכִי מֵעִיד
בָּכֶם הַיּוֹם אֲשֶׁר תְּצַוֻּם אֶת־בְּנֵיכֶם לִשְׁמֹר לַעֲשׂוֹת אֶת־כָּל־דִּבְרֵי
מז הַתּוֹרָה הַזֹּאת׃ כִּי לֹא־דָבָר רֵק הוּא מִכֶּם כִּי־הוּא חַיֵּיכֶם וּבַדָּבָר
הַזֶּה תַּאֲרִיכוּ יָמִים עַל־הָאֲדָמָה אֲשֶׁר אַתֶּם עֹבְרִים אֶת־הַיַּרְדֵּן שָׁמָּה
לְרִשְׁתָּהּ׃
מח מט וַיְדַבֵּר יהוה אֶל־מֹשֶׁה בְּעֶצֶם הַיּוֹם הַזֶּה לֵאמֹר׃ עֲלֵה אֶל־הַר הָעֲבָרִים מפטיר
הַזֶּה הַר־נְבוֹ אֲשֶׁר בְּאֶרֶץ מוֹאָב אֲשֶׁר עַל־פְּנֵי יְרֵחוֹ וּרְאֵה אֶת־אֶרֶץ
נ כְּנַעַן אֲשֶׁר אֲנִי נֹתֵן לִבְנֵי יִשְׂרָאֵל לַאֲחֻזָּה׃ וּמֻת בָּהָר אֲשֶׁר אַתָּה עֹלֶה
שָׁמָּה וְהֵאָסֵף אֶל־עַמֶּיךָ כַּאֲשֶׁר־מֵת אַהֲרֹן אָחִיךָ בְּהֹר הָהָר וַיֵּאָסֶף

אונקלוס

יִשְׂרָאֵל: מו וַאֲמַר לְהוֹן שַׁווֹ לִבְּכוֹן, לְכָל פִּתְגָמַיָּא, דַּאֲנָא, מַסְהֵיד בְּכוֹן יוֹמָא דֵין, דִּתְפַקְּדוּנוּן יָת בְּנֵיכוֹן, לְמִטַּר לְמֶעְבַּד, יָת כָּל פִּתְגָמֵי אוֹרָיְתָא הָדָא: מז אֲרֵי, לָא פִּתְגָם רֵיקָן הוּא מִנְּכוֹן, אֲרֵי הוּא חַיֵּיכוֹן, וּבְפִתְגָמָא הָדֵין, תֵּיְרְכוּן יוֹמִין עַל אַרְעָא, דְּאַתּוּן, עָבְרִין יָת יַרְדְּנָא, לְתַמָּן לְמֵירְתַהּ: מח וּמַלֵּיל יי עִם מֹשֶׁה, בִּכְרַן, יוֹמָא הָדֵין לְמֵימַר: מט סַק, לְטוּרָא דְּעִבְרָאֵי הָדֵין לְטוּרָא דִּנְבוֹ, דִּבְאַרְעָא דְמוֹאָב, דְּעַל אַפֵּי יְרֵחוֹ, וַחְזִי יָת אַרְעָא דִּכְנַעַן, דַּאֲנָא יָהֵיב, לִבְנֵי יִשְׂרָאֵל לְאַחְסָנָא: נ וּמוּת, בְּטוּרָא דְּאַתְּ סָלֵיק לְתַמָּן, וְאִתְכְּנֵישׁ לְעַמָּךְ, כְּמָא דְמִית, אַהֲרֹן אֲחוּךְ בְּהוֹר טוּרָא, וְאִתְכְּנֵישׁ

32:47 **כִּי־הוּא חַיֵּיכֶם** *They are your very life* – The holiest object in Judaism is a *sefer Torah*, a scroll of the law. Still written today as it was thousands of years ago, by hand with a quill on parchment, it symbolizes some of Judaism's deepest beliefs: that God is to be found in words, that these words are to be found in the Torah, and that they form the basis of the covenant – the bond of love – between God and the Jewish people.

I wonder if any people has ever loved a book as we love the Torah. We stand when it passes as if it were a king. We dance with it as if it were a bride. If it is desecrated or destroyed, we bury it as if it were a relative or friend. We study it endlessly as if in it were hidden all the secrets of our being. Heinrich Heine once called the Torah the "portable homeland" of the Jewish people. When we lacked a land, we found our home in words.

"These words" contain the dream that sustained us through twenty centuries of exile. We dreamed of inspiring the world by the simplicity and grace of Judaism as a way of life. We dreamed of creating in the Holy Land a society of justice and compassion, where the dignity of the individual and the sanctity of human life would be maintained, where love of God would translate into love of the neighbor and the stranger, and religion itself would be the prime driver of social justice and inclusion. It was a utopian vision, but the mere act of aspiring to it lifted our ancestors to spiritual, intellectual, and moral heights. Bounded in a nutshell, they counted themselves kings of infinite space.

That is the future that beckons us now. Yes, there is antisemitism, and yes, we have enemies. But we survived them all in the past and we will do so again in the future. We need the courage to be unashamedly ourselves, to educate our children in Judaic literacy, and to create in Israel a society of such moral force and spiritual generosity that it speaks to all those whose minds are open. The time has come to honor the trust our ancestors had in us, that when we had

51 Aharon died on Mount Hor and was gathered to his people; because both of
you broke faith with Me in the midst of the Israelites at the waters of Merivat
Kadesh in the Wilderness of Tzin, failing to affirm My holiness among the
52 Israelites. You will see the land from afar, but you shall not enter it – the land
that I am giving to the people of Israel."

The haftara for Parashat Haazinu in on page 1624.
On the Shabbat between Rosh Hashana and Yom Kippur,
read the haftara for Shabbat Shuva on page 1622.

רש״י

שְׁלִישִׁי, וְרָאָה בְּנוֹ בִּכְבוֹדוֹ. אָמַר לוֹ מֹשֶׁה: אַהֲרֹן אָחִי, עֲלֵה לַמִּטָּה, וְעָלָה. פְּשֹׁט יָדֶיךָ, וּפָשַׁט. פְּשֹׁט רַגְלֶיךָ, וּפָשַׁט. עֲצֹם עֵינֶיךָ, וְעָצַם. קְמֹץ פִּיךָ, וְקָמַץ. וְהָלַךְ לוֹ. אָמַר מֹשֶׁה: אַשְׁרֵי מִי שֶׁמֵּת בְּמִיתָה זוֹ:

נא| **עַל אֲשֶׁר מְרִיתֶם פִּי** (על פי במדבר כ, כד; שם כז, יד) – גְּרַמְתֶּם לַמְרוֹת פִּי: **עַל אֲשֶׁר לֹא קִדַּשְׁתֶּם אוֹתִי.** גְּרַמְתֶּם לִי שֶׁלֹּא אֶתְקַדֵּשׁ. אָמַרְתִּי לָכֶם: ״וְדִבַּרְתֶּם אֶל הַסֶּלַע״ (במדבר כ, ח) וְהֵם הִכּוּהוּ, וְהֻצְרְכוּ לְהַכּוֹתוֹ פַּעֲמַיִם, וְאִלּוּ דִּבְּרוּ עִמּוֹ וְנָתַן מֵימָיו בְּלֹא הַכָּאָה, הָיָה מִתְקַדֵּשׁ שֵׁם שָׁמַיִם, שֶׁהָיוּ יִשְׂרָאֵל אוֹמְרִים: וּמַה הַסֶּלַע הַזֶּה שֶׁאֵינוֹ לְשָׂכָר וְלֹא לְפֻרְעָנוּת, אִם זָכָה אֵין לוֹ מַתַּן שָׂכָר וְאִם חָטָא אֵינוֹ לוֹקֶה, כָּךְ מְקַיֵּם מִצְוַת בּוֹרְאוֹ, אָנוּ לֹא כָּל שֶׁכֵּן?:

נב| **כִּי מִנֶּגֶד.** מֵרָחוֹק: **תִּרְאֶה וְגוֹ׳.** כִּי אִם לֹא תִּרְאֶנָּה עַכְשָׁיו, לֹא תִּרְאֶנָּה עוֹד בְּחַיֶּיךָ: **וְשָׁמָּה לֹא תָבוֹא.** וְיָדַעְתִּי כִּי חֲבִיבָה הִיא לְךָ, עַל כֵּן אֲנִי אוֹמֵר לְךָ: ״עֲלֵה... וּרְאֵה״ (לעיל פסוק מט):

righteous as Moshe or as evil as Yorovam" (*Hilkhot Teshuva* 5:2). That is an astonishing sentence. There only ever was one Moshe. The Torah says so. Yet what Rambam is saying is clear. Prophetically, there was only one Moshe. But morally, the choice lies before us every time we make a decision that will affect the lives of others. That Moshe was mortal, that the greatest leader who ever lived did not see his mission completed, that even he was capable of making a mistake, is the most profound gift God could give each of us.

נא אֶל־עַמָּיו׃ עַל אֲשֶׁר מְעַלְתֶּם בִּי בְּתוֹךְ בְּנֵי יִשְׂרָאֵל בְּמֵי־מְרִיבַת קָדֵשׁ
נב מִדְבַּר־צִן עַל אֲשֶׁר לֹא־קִדַּשְׁתֶּם אוֹתִי בְּתוֹךְ בְּנֵי יִשְׂרָאֵל׃ כִּי מִנֶּגֶד
תִּרְאֶה אֶת־הָאָרֶץ וְשָׁמָּה לֹא תָבוֹא אֶל־הָאָרֶץ אֲשֶׁר־אֲנִי נֹתֵן לִבְנֵי
יִשְׂרָאֵל׃

The הפטרה *for* פרשת האזינו *in on page 1625.*
On the שבת *between* ראש השנה *and* יום כיפור*,*
read the הפטרה *for* שבת שובה *on page 1623.*

אונקלוס

לְעַמֵּיהּ: נא עַל דְּשַׁקַּרְתּוּן בְּמֵימְרִי, בְּגוֹ בְּנֵי יִשְׂרָאֵל, בְּמֵי מַצּוּת רְקַם
מַדְבְּרָא דְצִין, עַל דְּלָא קַדֵּישְׁתּוּן יָתִי, בְּגוֹ בְּנֵי יִשְׂרָאֵל: נב אֲרֵי מִקֳּבֵיל
תִּחְזֵי יָת אַרְעָא, וּלְתַמָּן לָא תֵיעוֹל, לְאַרְעָא, דַּאֲנָא יָהֵיב לִבְנֵי
יִשְׂרָאֵל:

Because that is what it is to be human. Even the greatest human beings make mistakes, fail as often as they succeed, and have moments of black despair. What makes them great is not that they are perfect but that they keep going. They learn from every error, refuse to give up hope, and eventually acquire the great gift that only failure can grant, namely humility. They understand that life is about falling a hundred times and getting up again. It is about never losing your ideals even when you know how hard it is to change the world. It is about getting up every morning and walking one more day toward the Promised Land even though you know you may never get there, but knowing also that you helped others get there.

Rambam writes that every human being can become "as

Parashat Vezot Haberakha

33 1 This is the blessing with which Moshe, man of God, blessed the Israelites before
2 he died. Moshe said: "The Lord came from Sinai, He shone upon them from
Se'ir, He appeared over the crest of Paran and came among myriads of holy ones:
3 at His right hand, darting fire. He is a lover of peoples, all His holy ones are in
4 Your hand; they place themselves at Your feet, upholding Your words. Moshe

רש״י

לג א| **וְזֹאת הַבְּרָכָה. לִפְנֵי מוֹתוֹ.** סָמוּךְ לְמִיתָתוֹ, שֶׁאִם לֹא עַכְשָׁיו אֵימָתַי:

ב| **וַיֹּאמַר ה׳ מִסִּינַי בָּא.** פָּתַח תְּחִלָּה בְּשִׁבְחוֹ שֶׁל מָקוֹם, וְאַחַר כָּךְ פָּתַח בְּצָרְכֵיהֶם שֶׁל יִשְׂרָאֵל, וּבַשֶּׁבַח שֶׁפָּתַח בּוֹ יֵשׁ בּוֹ הַזְכָּרַת זְכוּת לְיִשְׂרָאֵל, וְכָל זֶה דֶּרֶךְ רִצּוּי הוּא, כְּלוֹמַר כְּדַאי הֵם אֵלּוּ שֶׁתָּחוּל עֲלֵיהֶם בְּרָכָה: **מִסִּינַי בָּא.** יָצָא לִקְרָאתָם כְּשֶׁבָּאוּ לְהִתְיַצֵּב בְּתַחְתִּית הָהָר כְּחָתָן הַיּוֹצֵא לְהַקְבִּיל פְּנֵי כַלָּה, שֶׁנֶּאֱמַר: "לִקְרַאת הָאֱלֹהִים" (שמות יט, יז), לָמַדְנוּ שֶׁיָּצָא כְּנֶגְדָּם: **וְזָרַח מִשֵּׂעִיר לָמוֹ.** שֶׁפָּתַח לִבְנֵי עֵשָׂו שֶׁיְּקַבְּלוּ אֶת הַתּוֹרָה וְלֹא רָצוּ: **הוֹפִיעַ.** לָהֶם: **מֵהַר פָּארָן.** שֶׁהָלַךְ שָׁם וּפָתַח לִבְנֵי יִשְׁמָעֵאל שֶׁיְּקַבְּלוּהָ וְלֹא רָצוּ: **וְאָתָה.** לְיִשְׂרָאֵל: **מֵרִבְבֹת קֹדֶשׁ.** וְעִמּוֹ מִקְצָת רִבְבוֹת מַלְאֲכֵי קֹדֶשׁ, וְלֹא כֻלָּם וְלֹא רֻבָּם, וְלֹא כְּדֶרֶךְ בָּשָׂר וָדָם שֶׁמַּרְאֶה כָּל כְּבוֹד עָשְׁרוֹ וְתִפְאַרְתּוֹ בְּיוֹם חֻפָּתוֹ: **אֵשׁ דָּת.** שֶׁהָיְתָה כְתוּבָה מֵאָז לְפָנָיו בְּאֵשׁ שְׁחוֹרָה עַל גַּבֵּי אֵשׁ לְבָנָה, נָתַן לָהֶם בַּלּוּחוֹת כְּתַב יַד יְמִינוֹ. דָּבָר אַחֵר, "אֵשׁ דָּת", כְּתַרְגּוּמוֹ, שֶׁנְּתָנָהּ לָהֶם מִתּוֹךְ הָאֵשׁ:

ג-ד| **אַף חֹבֵב עַמִּים.** גַּם חִבָּה יְתֵרָה חִבֵּב אֶת הַשְּׁבָטִים, כָּל אֶחָד וְאֶחָד קָרוּי 'עַם', שֶׁהֲרֵי בִּנְיָמִין לְבַדּוֹ הָיָה עָתִיד לְהִוָּלֵד כְּשֶׁאָמַר הַקָּדוֹשׁ בָּרוּךְ הוּא לְיַעֲקֹב: "גּוֹי וּקְהַל גּוֹיִם יִהְיֶה מִמֶּךָּ" (בראשית לה, יא): **כָּל קְדֹשָׁיו בְּיָדֶךָ.** נַפְשׁוֹת הַצַּדִּיקִים גְּנוּזוֹת תַּחַת כִּסֵּא הַכָּבוֹד, כְּעִנְיָן שֶׁנֶּאֱמַר: "וְהָיְתָה נֶפֶשׁ אֲדֹנִי צְרוּרָה בִּצְרוֹר הַחַיִּים אֵת ה׳ אֱלֹהֶיךָ" (שמואל א׳ כה, כט): **וְהֵם תֻּכּוּ לְרַגְלֶךָ.** וְהֵם רְאוּיִים לְכָךְ, שֶׁהֲרֵי תִּוְּכוּ עַצְמָם לְתוֹךְ תַּחְתִּית הָהָר לְרַגְלֶיךָ בְּסִינַי. "תֻּכּוּ" לְשׁוֹן פֻּעֲלוּ, הִתְוַכּוּ לְתוֹךְ מַרְגְּלוֹתֶיךָ: **יִשָּׂא מִדַּבְּרֹתֶיךָ.** נָשְׂאוּ עֲלֵיהֶם עֹל תּוֹרָתֶךָ: **מִדַּבְּרֹתֶיךָ.** הַמֵּ"ם בּוֹ קָרוֹב לַיְסוֹד, כְּמוֹ: "וַיִּשְׁמַע אֶת הַקּוֹל מִדַּבֵּר אֵלָיו" (במדבר ז, פט), "וָאֶשְׁמַע אֵת מִדַּבֵּר אֵלָי" (יחזקאל ב, ב), כְּמוֹ: מִתְדַּבֵּר אֵלָי, אַף זֶה "מִדַּבְּרֹתֶיךָ", מַה שֶּׁהָיִיתָ מְדַבֵּר לְהַשְׁמִיעֵנִי לֵאמֹר לָהֶם, טי"ש פורפלידור"ש בְּלַעַז. וְאוּנְקְלוֹס תִּרְגֵּם, שֶׁהָיוּ נוֹסְעִים עַל פִּי דְּבָרֶיךָ, וְהַמֵּ"ם בּוֹ שִׁמּוּשׁ, מְשַׁמֶּשֶׁת לְשׁוֹן 'מִן'. דָּבָר אַחֵר, "אַף חֹבֵב עַמִּים", אַף בְּשָׁעַת חִבָּתָן שֶׁל אֻמּוֹת הָעוֹלָם, שֶׁהֶרְאֵיתָ לָאֻמּוֹת פָּנִים שׂוֹחֲקוֹת וּמָסַרְתָּ אֶת יִשְׂרָאֵל בְּיָדָם, "כָּל קְדֹשָׁיו בְּיָדֶךָ", כָּל צַדִּיקֵיהֶם וְטוֹבֵיהֶם דָּבְקוּ בְךָ וְלֹא מָשׁוּ מֵאַחֲרֶיךָ וְאַתָּה שׁוֹמְרָם: **וְהֵם תֻּכּוּ לְרַגְלֶךָ.** מִתְמַצְּעִים וּמִתְכַּנְּסִים לְתַחַת צִלְּךָ: **יִשָּׂא מִדַּבְּרֹתֶיךָ.** מְקַבְּלִין גְּזֵרוֹתֶיךָ וְדָתוֹתֶיךָ בְּשִׂמְחָה, וְאֵלֶּה דִּבְרֵיהֶם:

covenant with God. Whoever wishes to join and undertake the responsibilities of that covenant may do so. Rashbam is here echoing the sentiment of Rambam's famous letter to Ovadya the Proselyte, written at about the same time, in which he explains that converts are the spiritual children of Avraham, and should not think of themselves as any less so than his biological children.

33:4 **תּוֹרָה צִוָּה־לָנוּ מֹשֶׁה מוֹרָשָׁה קְהִלַּת יַעֲקֹב** *Moshe charged us with the Law, heritage of Yaakov's assembly* – On the one hand, the Torah describes itself as an inheritance: "Moshe charged us with the Law, heritage (*morasha*) of Yaakov's assembly." On the other, the Sages were insistent that Torah is *not* an inheritance: "R. Yosei said: Prepare yourself to learn Torah, for it is not given to you as an inheritance (*yerusha*)" (Avot 2:12; see also Num. 27, "Moshe's Continuity").

The resolution of the contradiction is that there are two kinds of inheritance. Biblical Hebrew contains two different words for what we receive as a legacy: *yerusha*/*morasha* and *naḥala*. *Naḥala* is related to the word *naḥal*, "river." It signifies something passed down automatically across the

פרשת וזאת הברכה

לג א וְזֹ֣את הַבְּרָכָ֗ה אֲשֶׁ֨ר בֵּרַ֥ךְ מֹשֶׁ֛ה אִ֥ישׁ הָאֱלֹהִ֖ים אֶת־בְּנֵ֣י יִשְׂרָאֵ֑ל לִפְנֵ֖י כז
ב מוֹתֽוֹ׃ וַיֹּאמַ֗ר יְהֹוָ֞ה מִסִּינַ֥י בָּא֙ וְזָרַ֤ח מִשֵּׂעִיר֙ לָ֔מוֹ הוֹפִ֙יעַ֙ מֵהַ֣ר פָּארָ֔ן
ג וְאָתָ֖ה מֵרִבְבֹ֣ת קֹ֑דֶשׁ מִֽימִינ֕וֹ אֵשְׁדָּ֖ת לָֽמוֹ׃ אַ֚ף חֹבֵ֣ב עַמִּ֔ים כׇּל־קְדֹשָׁ֖יו אֵ֣שׁ דָּ֖ת
ד בְּיָדֶ֑ךָ וְהֵם֙ תֻּכּ֣וּ לְרַגְלֶ֔ךָ יִשָּׂ֖א מִדַּבְּרֹתֶֽיךָ׃ תּוֹרָ֥ה צִוָּה־לָ֖נוּ מֹשֶׁ֑ה מוֹרָשָׁ֖ה

אונקלוס

לג א וְדָא בִּרְכְתָא, דִּבָרֵיךְ מֹשֶׁה, נְבִיָּא דַּיְיָ יָת בְּנֵי יִשְׂרָאֵל, קֳדָם מוֹתֵיהּ: ב וַאֲמַר, יְיָ, מִסִּינַי אִתְגְּלִי וְזִיהוֹר יְקָרֵיהּ מִשֵּׂעִיר אִתַּחְזִי לָנָא, אִתְגְּלִי בִּגְבוּרְתֵיהּ עַל טוּרָא דְּפָארָן, וְעִמֵּיהּ רִבְוָת קַדִּישִׁין, כְּתַב יְמִינֵיהּ, מִגּוֹ אִישָּׁתָא אוֹרָיְתָא יְהַב לָנָא: ג אַף חַבֵּיבִנּוּן לְשִׁבְטַיָּא, כָּל קַדִּישׁוֹהִי בֵּית יִשְׂרָאֵל בִּגְבוּרָא אַפֵּיקִנּוּן מִמִּצְרַיִם, וְאִנּוּן מְדַבְּרִין תְּחוֹת עֲנָנָךְ, נָטְלִין עַל מֵימְרָךְ: ד אוֹרָיְתָא יְהַב לָנָא מֹשֶׁה, מַסְרַהּ יְרֻתָּא

VEZOT HABERAKHA

The final *parasha* of the Torah consists of Moshe's blessing, delivered in the last day of his life, to the Israelites, tribe by tribe. It concludes poignantly with Moshe's death and his burial, seemingly by the hand of God, in the land of Moav, so that "to this day no one knows his burial place" (Deut. 34:6). The closing verses of the Torah are a tribute to the greatest leader and prophet the Israelites ever had, yet the ultimate accolade the Torah gives him is touching in its simplicity. He was "the man Moshe" (Num. 12:3), "the Lord's own servant" (Deut. 34:5). The Moshe we encounter in the Torah is simply a human being made great by the task he was set and by the humility that made him supremely one through whom the word and power of God flowed. The *parasha*, read not as an ordinary Sabbath portion, but on the festival of Simḥat Torah, is a profound commentary on mortality and the human condition. In one of the most intense convergences in Jewish time, this *parasha* brings together the last day in the life of Israel's greatest leader and the completion of the Torah.

33:1 בֵּרַךְ מֹשֶׁה אִישׁ הָאֱלֹהִים אֶת־בְּנֵי יִשְׂרָאֵל *Moshe, man of God, blessed the Israelites* – The book of Deuteronomy evokes the old Jewish custom that parents write their children *tzavaot*, ethical wills. The custom is based on the idea that the most important legacy we can give our children is not money or possessions, but spiritual ideals. Yaakov blessed his children at the end of his life, and likewise Moshe at the end of his blesses the next generation. Just as he handed on his role to his successor, Yehoshua, with a full heart, so here Moshe blesses them with a full heart, giving each tribe the words that would encourage them to fulfill their destiny. There is a beautiful midrash: "Moshe was not called 'the man of God' until he blessed the Israelites" (Pesikta DeRav Kahana, Vezot Haberakha). You do not need to be godly to criticize. Anyone can do that. Godliness lies with those who praise, defend, and bless.

33:3 אַף חֹבֵב עַמִּים *He is a lover of peoples* – Many commentators understand "peoples" to refer to the tribes of Israel – a natural reading, given that the chapter is about Moshe blessing each of the tribes. Rashbam, however, suggests that it refers to Gentiles who join Israel and become proselytes. Before turning to the tribes, Moshe specifically includes converts – signaling that the children of Israel are not a race or ethnicity but a religious community defined by their

▶

5 charged us with the Law, heritage of Yaakov's assembly. He became king in
Yeshurun, when the heads of the people gathered – the tribes of Israel together.
6 7 May Reuven live, and not die, even though his men are few." And this
he said of Yehuda: "Listen, Lord, to Yehuda's voice, and bring him home to his
people; strengthen his hands, be his support against his foes."
8 And of Levi he said: "Let Your Tumim and Urim be with Your faithful, the SHENI
9 one You tested at Masa, and challenged at the Meriva waters; who said of his
father and mother, 'I do not regard them,' ignored his brothers, and did not
acknowledge his children – instead keeping Your word, and guarding close
10 Your covenant. They shall teach Your laws to Yaakov, and Your instruction to
Israel; they shall place incense before You, and whole offerings on Your altar.

רש"י

תּוֹרָה. אֲשֶׁר "צִוָּה לָנוּ מֹשֶׁה, מוֹרָשָׁה" הִיא לִקְהִלַּת יַעֲקֹב, אֲחַזְנוּהָ וְלֹא נַעַזְבֶנָּה:

ה וַיְהִי. הַקָּדוֹשׁ בָּרוּךְ הוּא: **בִישֻׁרוּן מֶלֶךְ.** תָּמִיד עֹל מַלְכוּתוֹ עֲלֵיהֶם, בְּכָל הִתְאַסֵּף רָאשֵׁי חֶשְׁבּוֹן אֲסִיפָתָם: **רָאשֵׁי.** כְּמוֹ: "כִּי תִשָּׂא אֶת רֹאשׁ" (שמות ל, יב), רְאוּיִין אֵלּוּ שֶׁאֲחַבְּרְכֶם. דָּבָר אַחֵר, "בְּהִתְאַסֵּף", בְּהִתְאַסְּפָם יַחַד בַּאֲגֻדָּה אַחַת וְשָׁלוֹם בֵּינֵיהֶם – הוּא מַלְכָּם, וְלֹא כְּשֶׁיֵּשׁ מַחְלֹקֶת בֵּינֵיהֶם:

ו **יְחִי רְאוּבֵן.** בָּעוֹלָם הַזֶּה: **וְאַל יָמֹת.** לָעוֹלָם הַבָּא, שֶׁלֹּא יִזָּכֵר לוֹ מַעֲשֵׂה בִלְהָה: **וִיהִי מְתָיו מִסְפָּר.** נִמְנִין בְּמִנְיַן שְׁאָר אֶחָיו, דֻּגְמָא הִיא זוֹ, כְּעִנְיָן שֶׁנֶּאֱמַר: "וַיִּשְׁכַּב אֶת בִּלְהָה... וַיִּהְיוּ בְנֵי יַעֲקֹב שְׁנֵים עָשָׂר" (בראשית לה, כב), שֶׁלֹּא יָצָא מִן הַמִּנְיָן:

ז **וְזֹאת לִיהוּדָה.** סָמַךְ יְהוּדָה לִרְאוּבֵן מִפְּנֵי שֶׁשְּׁנֵיהֶם הוֹדוּ עַל קִלְקוּל שֶׁבְּיָדָם, שֶׁנֶּאֱמַר: "אֲשֶׁר חֲכָמִים יַגִּידוּ וְגוֹ' לָהֶם לְבַדָּם נִתְּנָה הָאָרֶץ וְלֹא עָבַר זָר בְּתוֹכָם" (איוב טו, יח-יט). וְעוֹד פֵּרְשׁוּ רַבּוֹתֵינוּ: כָּל אַרְבָּעִים שָׁנָה שֶׁהָיוּ יִשְׂרָאֵל בַּמִּדְבָּר, הָיוּ עַצְמוֹת יְהוּדָה מִתְגַּלְגְּלִין בָּאָרוֹן מִפְּנֵי נִדּוּי שֶׁקִּבֵּל עָלָיו, שֶׁנֶּאֱמַר: "וְחָטָאתִי לְאָבִי כָּל הַיָּמִים" (בראשית מד, לב), אָמַר מֹשֶׁה: מִי גָּרַם לִרְאוּבֵן שֶׁיּוֹדֶה? יְהוּדָה וְכוּ': **שְׁמַע ה' קוֹל יְהוּדָה.** תְּפִלַּת דָּוִד וּשְׁלֹמֹה, וְאָסָא מִפְּנֵי הַכּוּשִׁים, וִיהוֹשָׁפָט מִפְּנֵי הָעַמּוֹנִים, וְחִזְקִיָּה מִפְּנֵי סַנְחֵרִיב: **וְאֶל עַמּוֹ תְּבִיאֶנּוּ.** לְשָׁלוֹם מִפְּנֵי הַמִּלְחָמָה: **יָדָיו רָב לוֹ.** יָרִיבוּ רִיבוֹ וְיִנְקְמוּ נִקְמָתוֹ: **וְעֵזֶר מִצָּרָיו תִּהְיֶה.** עַל יְהוֹשָׁפָט נִתְפַּלֵּל, עַל מִלְחֶמֶת רָמוֹת גִּלְעָד, "וַיִּזְעַק יְהוֹשָׁפָט וַה' עֲזָרוֹ" (דברי הימים ב' יח, לא). דָּבָר אַחֵר, "שְׁמַע ה' קוֹל יְהוּדָה", כָּאן רָמַז בְּרָכָה לְשִׁמְעוֹן מִתּוֹךְ בִּרְכוֹתָיו שֶׁל יְהוּדָה, וְאַף כְּשֶׁחָלְקוּ אֶרֶץ יִשְׂרָאֵל נָטַל שִׁמְעוֹן מִתּוֹךְ גּוֹרָלוֹ שֶׁל יְהוּדָה, שֶׁנֶּאֱמַר: "מֵחֶבֶל בְּנֵי יְהוּדָה נַחֲלַת בְּנֵי שִׁמְעוֹן" (יהושע יט, ט):

ח **וּלְלֵוִי אָמַר.** וְעַל לֵוִי אָמַר: **תֻּמֶּיךָ וְאוּרֶיךָ.** כְּלַפֵּי שְׁכִינָה הוּא מְדַבֵּר: **אֲשֶׁר נִסִּיתוֹ בְּמַסָּה.** שֶׁלֹּא נִתְלוֹנְנוּ עִם שְׁאָר הַמִּתְלוֹנְנִים: **תְּרִיבֵהוּ וְגוֹ'.** כְּתַרְגּוּמוֹ. "תְּרִיבֵהוּ עַל מֵי מְרִיבָה", נִסְתַּקַּפְתָּ לוֹ לָבֹא בַּעֲלִילָה, אִם מֹשֶׁה אָמַר: "שִׁמְעוּ נָא הַמֹּרִים" (במדבר כ, י), אַהֲרֹן וּמִרְיָם מֶה עָשׂוּ?:

ט **הָאֹמֵר לְאָבִיו וּלְאִמּוֹ לֹא רְאִיתִיו.** כְּשֶׁחָטְאוּ בָּעֵגֶל וְאָמַרְתִּי: "מִי לַה' אֵלָי" (שמות לב, כו) נֶאֶסְפוּ אֵלַי כָּל בְּנֵי לֵוִי, וְצִוִּיתִים לַהֲרֹג אֶת אֲבִי אִמּוֹ וְהוּא מִיִּשְׂרָאֵל אוֹ אֶת אָחִיו מֵאִמּוֹ אוֹ בֶּן בִּתּוֹ, וְכֵן עָשׂוּ. וְאִי אֶפְשָׁר לְפָרֵשׁ אָבִיו מַמָּשׁ, וְאָחִיו מֵאָבִיו, וְכֵן בָּנָיו מַמָּשׁ, שֶׁהֲרֵי לְוִיִּם הֵם, וּמִשֵּׁבֶט לֵוִי לֹא חָטָא אֶחָד מֵהֶם, שֶׁנֶּאֱמַר: "כָּל בְּנֵי לֵוִי" (שם): **כִּי שָׁמְרוּ אִמְרָתֶךָ.** "לֹא יִהְיֶה לְךָ אֱלֹהִים אֲחֵרִים" (שמות כ, ג): **וּבְרִיתְךָ יִנְצֹרוּ.** בְּרִית מִילָה, שֶׁאוֹתָם שֶׁנּוֹלְדוּ בַּמִּדְבָּר, שֶׁל יִשְׂרָאֵל לֹא מָלוּ אֶת בְּנֵיהֶם, וְהֵם הָיוּ מוֹלִין וּמָלִין אֶת בְּנֵיהֶם:

י **יוֹרוּ מִשְׁפָּטֶיךָ.** רְאוּיִין אֵלּוּ לְכָךְ: **וְכָלִיל.** עוֹלָה:

the people, as parents: "Teach them to your children" (Deut. 6:7). The Levites are now charged with being the first in a tradition of public teachers.

The Rabbis were therefore drawing on a long tradition when they organized perhaps the first genuinely universal system of education in history. Its evolution in the late Second Temple period is described in the Talmud: "At first, if a child had a father, his father taught him; if he had not a father, he did not learn at all.... Then they introduced an ordinance that teachers of children be appointed in Jerusalem.... Even so, if a child had a father, the father would take him to Jerusalem and have him learn there; but if he had no father, he would

ה קְהִלַּת יַעֲקֹב: וַיְהִי בִישֻׁרוּן מֶלֶךְ בְּהִתְאַסֵּף רָאשֵׁי עָם יַחַד שִׁבְטֵי
ו ז יִשְׂרָאֵל: יְחִי רְאוּבֵן וְאַל־יָמֹת וִיהִי מְתָיו מִסְפָּר: וְזֹאת
לִיהוּדָה וַיֹּאמַר שְׁמַע יהוה קוֹל יְהוּדָה וְאֶל־עַמּוֹ תְּבִיאֶנּוּ יָדָיו רָב לוֹ
וְעֵזֶר מִצָּרָיו תִּהְיֶה:
ח וּלְלֵוִי אָמַר תֻּמֶּיךָ וְאוּרֶיךָ לְאִישׁ חֲסִידֶךָ אֲשֶׁר נִסִּיתוֹ בְּמַסָּה תְּרִיבֵהוּ שני
ט עַל־מֵי מְרִיבָה: הָאֹמֵר לְאָבִיו וּלְאִמּוֹ לֹא רְאִיתִיו וְאֶת־אֶחָיו לֹא
י הִכִּיר וְאֶת־בָּנָו לֹא יָדָע כִּי שָׁמְרוּ אִמְרָתֶךָ וּבְרִיתְךָ יִנְצֹרוּ: יוֹרוּ
מִשְׁפָּטֶיךָ לְיַעֲקֹב וְתוֹרָתְךָ לְיִשְׂרָאֵל יָשִׂימוּ קְטוֹרָה בְּאַפֶּךָ וְכָלִיל

אונקלוס

לִכְנִשַׁת יַעֲקֹב: ה וַהֲוָה בְיִשְׂרָאֵל מַלְכָּא, בְּאִתְכַּנָּשׁוּת רֵישֵׁי עַמָּא, כַּחֲדָא שִׁבְטַיָּא דְיִשְׂרָאֵל: ו יֵיחֵי רְאוּבֵן בְּחַיֵּי עָלְמָא וּמוֹתָא תִנְיָנָא לָא יְמוּת, וִיקַבְּלוּן בְּנוֹהִי אַחְסַנְתְּהוֹן בְּמִנְיָנְהוֹן: ז וְדָא לִיהוּדָה וַאֲמַר, קַבֵּיל יי צְלוֹתֵיהּ דִיהוּדָה בְּמִפְּקֵיהּ לִקְרָבָא, וּלְעַמֵּיהּ תְּתִיבִנֵּיהּ בִּשְׁלָם, יְדוֹהִי יַעְבְּדָן לֵיהּ פֻּרְעֲנוּתָא מִסַּנְאוֹהִי, וְסָעִיד מִבַּעֲלֵי דְבָבָא הֱוֵי לֵיהּ: ח וּלְלֵוִי אֲמַר, תֻּמַּיָּא וְאוּרַיָּא אַלְבֵּישְׁתָּא לִגְבַר דְּאִשְׁתְּכַח חֲסִיד קֳדָמָךְ, דְּנַסִּיתָהִי בְּנִסֵּיתָא וַהֲוָה שְׁלִים, בַּחַנְתָּהִי עַל מֵי מַצּוּתָא וְאִשְׁתְּכַח מְהֵימָן: ט דְּעַל אֲבוּהִי וְעַל אִמֵּיהּ לָא רַחֵים כַּד חָבוּ מִן דִּינָא, וְאַפֵּי אֲחוֹהִי וּבְנוֹהִי לָא נְסֵיב, אֲרֵי נְטַרוּ מַטְּרַת מֵימְרָךְ, וּקְיָמָךְ לָא אַשְׁנִיאוּ: י כַּשְׁרִין אִלֵּין דְּיַלְּפוּן דִּינָךְ לְיַעֲקֹב, וְאוֹרָיְתָךְ לְיִשְׂרָאֵל, יְשַׁווּן קְטוֹרֶת בֻּסְמִין קֳדָמָךְ, וּגְמִיר לְרַעֲוָא

generations, as river water flows downstream. *Yerusha* comes from the root *y-r-sh*, meaning "to *take* possession." It refers to something to which you have legitimate title, but which you need positive action to acquire. The Sages themselves put it more beautifully: "'Moshe charged us with the Law, heritage (*morasha*) of Yaakov's assembly' – read not 'inheritance (*morasha*)' but 'betrothed (*meorasa*)'" (Berakhot 57a). By a simple change in pronunciation – turning a *shin* ("sh") into a *sin* ("s"), "inheritance" into "betrothal" – the Rabbis signaled that, yes, there is an inheritance relationship between Torah and the Jew, but nonetheless, the former has to be loved if it is to be earned.

33:6 יְחִי רְאוּבֵן וְאַל־יָמֹת *May Reuven live, and not die* – The tribe of Reuven has chosen to live east of the Jordan, and will thus be highly exposed to enemy attacks – hence, the need for this blessing. Note the absence of Shimon from these blessings. Yaakov, in his deathbed speech, already predicted that the tribes of Shimon and Levi would be scattered among the other tribes (Gen. 49:7). According to Joshua 19:1–9, Shimon's townships all lay within the territory of Yehuda. Thus their blessing is included in that of the tribe of Yehuda.

33:10 יוֹרוּ מִשְׁפָּטֶיךָ לְיַעֲקֹב *They shall teach Your laws to Yaakov* – The priests and Levites had a special role as educators to the people (see Neh. 8:7–8). The prophet Malakhi says of the ideal priest: "True teaching was in his mouth, no sin from his lips; he walked with Me in peace and uprightness and returned many from iniquity. For a priest's lips should safeguard knowledge, and the people should seek teaching from his mouth, for he is a messenger of the LORD of Hosts" (Mal. 2:6–7).

The Jewish concern with education has its roots in the ancient history of Israel. In the book of Genesis, for example, the sole explanation for the covenant with Avraham is: "For I have chosen him so that he may direct his children and his household after him to keep the way of the LORD by doing what is right and just" (Gen. 18:19). Moshe has already told

11 Bless, O Lord, his vigor, and accept the work of his hands; crush the loins of
12 his foes; let his enemies rise no more." Of Binyamin he said: "Beloved
of the Lord, may he dwell in safety with Him – He protects him all day long as
13 he rests between His shoulders." And of Yosef he said: "Blessed by the SHELISHI
Lord be his land, with the bounty of heaven, with dew, and the deep waters
14 that lie below; with the bounty brought forth by the sun, and the bounteous
15 yield of the moon; with the best from the age-old mountains, and the bounty
16 of the everlasting hills; with the bounty of earth and its fullness, and the will
of Him who dwelt in the bush. May these rest on Yosef's head, on the brow
17 of the prince among brothers. His glory is that of a firstborn bull, his horns
the grand horns of the wild ox; with them he gores the peoples, all, to the
ends of the earth. These are the myriads of Efrayim, these the thousands of
18 Menashe." And of Zevulun he said: "Rejoice, Zevulun, as you set out; REVI'I

רש״י

יא **מְחַץ מָתְנַיִם קָמָיו.** מְחַץ קָמָיו מַכַּת מָתְנַיִם, כְּעִנְיָן שֶׁנֶּאֱמַר: "וּמָתְנֵיהֶם תָּמִיד הַמְעַד" (תהלים סט, כד), וְעַל הַמִּתְקוֹמְמִין עַל הַכְּהֻנָּה אָמַר כֵּן. דָּבָר אַחֵר, רָאָה שֶׁעֲתִידִין חַשְׁמוֹנַאי וּבָנָיו לְהִלָּחֵם עִם הַיְּוָנִים, וְהִתְפַּלֵּל עֲלֵיהֶם לְפִי שֶׁהָיוּ מוּעָטִים, שְׁנֵים עָשָׂר בְּנֵי חַשְׁמוֹנַאי וְאֶלְעָזָר כְּנֶגֶד כַּמָּה רְבָבוֹת, לְכָךְ נֶאֱמַר: "בָּרֵךְ ה' חֵילוֹ וּפֹעַל יָדָיו תִּרְצֶה": **וּמְשַׂנְאָיו מִן יְקוּמוּן.** מְחַץ קָמָיו וּמְשַׂנְאָיו מִהְיוֹת לָהֶם תְּקוּמָה:

יב **לְבִנְיָמִן אָמַר.** לְפִי שֶׁבִּרְכַּת לֵוִי בַּעֲבוֹדַת הַקָּרְבָּנוֹת וְשֶׁל בִּנְיָמִין בְּבִנְיַן בֵּית הַמִּקְדָּשׁ בְּחֶלְקוֹ, סְמָכָן זֶה לָזֶה, וְסָמַךְ יוֹסֵף אַחֲרָיו, שֶׁאַף הוּא מִשְׁכַּן שִׁילֹה הָיָה בָנוּי בְּחֶלְקוֹ, שֶׁנֶּאֱמַר: "וַיִּמְאַס בְּאֹהֶל יוֹסֵף" וְגוֹ' (תהלים עח, סז). וּלְפִי שֶׁבֵּית עוֹלָמִים חָבִיב מִשִּׁילֹה, לְכָךְ הִקְדִּים בִּנְיָמִין לְיוֹסֵף: **חֹפֵף עָלָיו.** מְכַסֶּה אוֹתוֹ וּמֵגֵן עָלָיו: **כָּל הַיּוֹם.** לְעוֹלָם, מִשֶּׁנִּבְחֲרָה יְרוּשָׁלַיִם לֹא שָׁרְתָה שְׁכִינָה בְּמָקוֹם אַחֵר: **וּבֵין כְּתֵפָיו שָׁכֵן.** בְּגָבְהֵ אַרְצוֹ הָיָה בֵּית הַמִּקְדָּשׁ בָּנוּי, אֶלָּא שֶׁנָּמוּךְ עֶשְׂרִים וְשָׁלֹשׁ אַמָּה מֵעֵין עֵיטָם, וְשָׁם הָיָה דַּעְתּוֹ שֶׁל דָּוִד לִבְנוֹתוֹ, כִּדְאִיתָא בִּשְׁחִיטַת קָדָשִׁים (זבחים נד ע"ב): אָמְרֵי נַחֲתֵי בֵּיהּ פּוּרְתָּא מִשּׁוּם דִּכְתִיב: "וּבֵין כְּתֵפָיו שָׁכֵן", אֵין לְךָ נָאֶה בַּשּׁוֹר יוֹתֵר מִכְּתֵפָיו:

יג **מְבֹרֶכֶת ה' אַרְצוֹ.** שֶׁלֹּא הָיְתָה בְּנַחֲלַת הַשְּׁבָטִים אֶרֶץ מְלֵאָה כָּל טוּב כְּאַרְצוֹ שֶׁל יוֹסֵף: **מִמֶּגֶד.** לְשׁוֹן עֲדָנִים וּמֶתֶק: **וּמִתְּהוֹם.** שֶׁהַתְּהוֹם עוֹלֶה וּמְלַחְלֵחַ אוֹתָהּ מִלְּמַטָּה. אַתָּה מוֹצֵא בְּכָל הַשְּׁבָטִים בִּרְכָתוֹ שֶׁל מֹשֶׁה מֵעֵין בִּרְכָתוֹ שֶׁל יַעֲקֹב:

יד **וּמִמֶּגֶד תְּבוּאֹת שָׁמֶשׁ.** שֶׁהָיְתָה אַרְצוֹ פְּתוּחָה לַחַמָּה וּמְמַתֶּקֶת הַפֵּרוֹת: **גֶּרֶשׁ יְרָחִים.** יֵשׁ פֵּרוֹת שֶׁהַלְּבָנָה מְבַשַּׁלְתָּן, וְאֵלּוּ הֵן קִשּׁוּאִין וּדְלוּעִין. דָּבָר אַחֵר, "גֶּרֶשׁ יְרָחִים", שֶׁהָאָרֶץ מְגָרֶשֶׁת וּמוֹצִיאָה מֵחֹדֶשׁ לְחֹדֶשׁ:

טו **וּמֵרֹאשׁ הַרְרֵי קֶדֶם.** וּמְבֹרֶכֶת מֵרֵאשִׁית בִּשּׁוּל הַפֵּרוֹת, שֶׁהֲרָרֶיהָ מַקְדִּימִין לְבַכֵּר בִּשּׁוּל פֵּרוֹתֵיהֶם. דָּבָר אַחֵר, מַגִּיד שֶׁקָּדְמָה בְּרִיאָתָן לִשְׁאָר הָרִים: **גִּבְעוֹת עוֹלָם.** גְּבָעוֹת הָעוֹשׂוֹת פֵּרוֹת לְעוֹלָם וְאֵינָן פּוֹסְקוֹת מֵעֹצֶר הַגְּשָׁמִים:

טז **וּרְצוֹן שֹׁכְנִי סְנֶה.** כְּמוֹ: 'שׁוֹכֵן סְנֶה', וּתְהֵא אַרְצוֹ מְבֹרֶכֶת מֵרְצוֹנוֹ וְנַחַת רוּחוֹ שֶׁל הַקָּדוֹשׁ בָּרוּךְ הוּא הַנִּגְלֶה עָלַי תְּחִלָּה בַּסְּנֶה: **רְצוֹן.** נַחַת רוּחַ וּפִיּוּס, וְכֵן כָּל 'רָצוֹן' שֶׁבַּמִּקְרָא: **תָּבוֹאתָה.** בְּרָכָה זוֹ "לְרֹאשׁ יוֹסֵף": **נְזִיר אֶחָיו.** שֶׁהֻפְרַשׁ מֵאֶחָיו בִּמְכִירָתוֹ:

יז **בְּכוֹר שׁוֹרוֹ.** יֵשׁ בְּכוֹר שֶׁהוּא לְשׁוֹן גְּדֻלָּה וּמַלְכוּת, שֶׁנֶּאֱמַר: "אַף אָנִי בְּכוֹר אֶתְּנֵהוּ" (תהלים פט, כח), וְכֵן: "בְּנִי בְכֹרִי יִשְׂרָאֵל" (שמות ד, כב): **בְּכוֹר.** מֶלֶךְ הַיּוֹצֵא מִמֶּנּוּ, וְהוּא יְהוֹשֻׁעַ: **שׁוֹרוֹ.** שֶׁכֹּחוֹ קָשֶׁה כְּשׁוֹר לִכְבֹּשׁ כַּמָּה מְלָכִים: **הָדָר לוֹ.** נָתוּן לוֹ, שֶׁנֶּאֱמַר: "וְנָתַתָּה מֵהוֹדְךָ עָלָיו" (במדבר כז, כ): **וְקַרְנֵי רְאֵם קַרְנָיו.** שׁוֹר – כֹּחוֹ קָשֶׁה וְאֵין קַרְנָיו נָאוֹת, רְאֵם – קַרְנָיו נָאוֹת וְאֵין כֹּחוֹ קָשֶׁה, נָתַן לִיהוֹשֻׁעַ כֹּחוֹ שֶׁל שׁוֹר וְיֹפִי קַרְנֵי רְאֵם: **אַפְסֵי אָרֶץ.** שְׁלֹשִׁים וְאֶחָד מְלָכִים, אֶפְשָׁר שֶׁכֻּלָּם מֵאֶרֶץ יִשְׂרָאֵל הָיוּ? אֶלָּא אֵין לְךָ כָּל מֶלֶךְ וְשִׁלְטוֹן שֶׁלֹּא קָנָה לוֹ פַּלְטֵרִין וַאֲחֻזָּה בְּאֶרֶץ יִשְׂרָאֵל, שֶׁחֲשׁוּבָה לְכֻלָּם הִיא, שֶׁנֶּאֱמַר: "נַחֲלַת צְבִי צִבְאוֹת גּוֹיִם" (ירמיה ג, יט): **וְהֵם רִבְבוֹת אֶפְרַיִם.** אוֹתָם הַמְנֻגָּחִים הֵם הָרְבָבוֹת שֶׁהָרַג יְהוֹשֻׁעַ שֶׁבָּא מֵאֶפְרַיִם: **וְהֵם אַלְפֵי מְנַשֶּׁה.** הֵם הָאֲלָפִים שֶׁהָרַג גִּדְעוֹן בְּמִדְיָן, שֶׁנֶּאֱמַר: "וְזֶבַח וְצַלְמֻנָּע בַּקַּרְקֹר" וְגוֹ' (שופטים ח, י):

יח-יט **וְלִזְבוּלֻן אָמַר.** אֵלּוּ חֲמִשָּׁה שְׁבָטִים שֶׁבֵּרַךְ בָּאַחֲרוֹנָה: זְבוּלֻן גָּד דָּן

יא עַל־מִזְבְּחֶךָ: בָּרֵךְ יהוה חֵילוֹ וּפֹעַל יָדָיו תִּרְצֶה מְחַץ מָתְנַיִם קָמָיו
יב וּמְשַׂנְאָיו מִן־יְקוּמוּן: לְבִנְיָמִן אָמַר יְדִיד יהוה יִשְׁכֹּן לָבֶטַח
יג עָלָיו חֹפֵף עָלָיו כָּל־הַיּוֹם וּבֵין כְּתֵפָיו שָׁכֵן: וּלְיוֹסֵף שלישי
אָמַר מְבֹרֶכֶת יהוה אַרְצוֹ מִמֶּגֶד שָׁמַיִם מִטָּל וּמִתְּהוֹם רֹבֶצֶת תָּחַת:
יד טו וּמִמֶּגֶד תְּבוּאֹת שָׁמֶשׁ וּמִמֶּגֶד גֶּרֶשׁ יְרָחִים: וּמֵרֹאשׁ הַרְרֵי־קֶדֶם וּמִמֶּגֶד
טז גִּבְעוֹת עוֹלָם: וּמִמֶּגֶד אֶרֶץ וּמְלֹאָהּ וּרְצוֹן שֹׁכְנִי סְנֶה תָּבוֹאתָה לְרֹאשׁ
יז יוֹסֵף וּלְקָדְקֹד נְזִיר אֶחָיו: בְּכוֹר שׁוֹרוֹ הָדָר לוֹ וְקַרְנֵי רְאֵם קַרְנָיו
בָּהֶם עַמִּים יְנַגַּח יַחְדָּו אַפְסֵי־אָרֶץ וְהֵם רִבְבוֹת אֶפְרַיִם וְהֵם אַלְפֵי
יח מְנַשֶּׁה: וְלִזְבוּלֻן אָמַר שְׂמַח זְבוּלֻן בְּצֵאתֶךָ וְיִשָּׂשכָר רביעי

אונקלוס

עַל מַדְבְּחָךְ: יא בָּרֵיךְ יי נִכְסוֹהִי, וְקֻרְבַּן יְדוֹהִי קַבֵּיל בְּרַעֲוָא, תַּבַּר חַרְצָא דְסָנְאוֹהִי, וּדְבַעֲלֵי דְבָבוֹהִי דְּלָא יְקוּמוּן: יב לְבִנְיָמִין אֲמַר, רְחִימָא דַיי, יִשְׁרֵי לְרָחְצָן עֲלוֹהִי, יְהֵי מַגֵּין עֲלוֹהִי כָּל יוֹמָא, וּבְאַרְעֵיהּ תִּשְׁרֵי שְׁכִינְתָא: יג וּלְיוֹסֵף אֲמַר, מְבָרְכָא מִן קֳדָם יי אַרְעֵיהּ, עָבְדָא מַגְדָּנִין מִטַּלָּא דִשְׁמַיָּא מִלְּעֵילָא, וּמִמַּבּוּעֵי עֵינָוָן וּתְהוֹמִין, דְּנָגְדִין מִמַּעֲמַקֵּי אַרְעָא מִלְּרַע: יד עָבְדָא מַגְדָּנִין וַעֲלָלָן מִיבוּל שִׁמְשָׁא, עָבְדָא מַגְדָּנִין מֵרֵישׁ יְרַח בִּירַח: טו וּמֵרֵישׁ טוּרַיָּא בַּכִּירַיָּא, וּמִטּוּב רָמָן דְּלָא פָסְקָן: טז וּמִטּוּב, אַרְעָא וּמְלָאַהּ, רְעֵי לֵיהּ דִּשְׁכִינְתֵיהּ בִּשְׁמַיָּא וְעַל מֹשֶׁה אִתְגְּלִי בְּאַסְנָא, יֵיתְיָן כָּל אִלֵּין לְרֵישָׁא דְיוֹסֵף, גַּבְרָא פְרִישָׁא דַאֲחוֹהִי: יז רַבָּא דִבְנוֹהִי זִיוָא לֵיהּ, וּגְבוּרָן אִתְעֲבִידָא לֵיהּ מִן קֳדָם דְּתֻקְפָּא וְרוּמָא דִּילֵיהּ, בִּגְבוּרְתֵיהּ, עַמְמַיָּא, יְקַטֵּיל כַּחְדָא עַד סְיָפֵי אַרְעָא, וְאִנּוּן רִבְוָתָא דְבֵית אֶפְרַיִם, וְאִנּוּן אַלְפַיָּא דְבֵית מְנַשֶּׁה: יח וְלִזְבוּלוּן אֲמַר, חֲדִי זְבוּלוּן בְּמִפְּקָךְ לְאַגָּחָא קְרָבָא עַל בַּעֲלֵי דְבָבָךְ, וְיִשָּׂשכָר

רש״י

וְנַפְתָּלִי וְחָשֵׁר, כְּפַל שְׁמוֹתֵיהֶם לְחַזְּקָם וּלְהַגְבִּירָם, לְפִי שֶׁהָיוּ חַלָּשִׁים שֶׁבְּכָל הַשְּׁבָטִים, הֵם הֵם שֶׁהוֹלִיךְ יוֹסֵף לִפְנֵי פַרְעֹה, שֶׁנֶּאֱמַר: "וּמִקְצֵה אֶחָיו לָקַח חֲמִשָּׁה אֲנָשִׁים" (בראשית מז, ב), לְפִי שֶׁנִּרְאִים חַלָּשִׁים וְלֹא יָשִׂים אוֹתָם לוֹ שָׂרֵי מִלְחַמְתּוֹ: שְׂמַח זְבוּלֻן בְּצֵאתֶךָ וְיִשָּׂשכָר בְּאֹהָלֶיךָ. זְבוּלוּן וְיִשָּׂשכָר עָשׂוּ שֻׁתָּפוּת, זְבוּלוּן יוֹשֵׁב לְחוֹף יַמִּים וְיוֹצֵא לִפְרַקְמַטְיָא בִּסְפִינוֹת וּמִשְׂתַּכֵּר, וְנוֹתֵן לְתוֹךְ פִּיו שֶׁל יִשָּׂשכָר, וְהֵם יוֹשְׁבִים וְעוֹסְקִים בַּתּוֹרָה. לְפִיכָךְ הִקְדִּים זְבוּלוּן לְיִשָּׂשכָר, שֶׁתּוֹרָתוֹ שֶׁל יִשָּׂשכָר עַל יְדֵי זְבוּלוּן הָיְתָה: שְׂמַח זְבוּלֻן בְּצֵאתֶךָ. הַצְלַח בִּיצִיאָתְךָ לִסְחוֹרָה: וְיִשָּׂשכָר. הַצְלַח בִּישִׁיבַת אֹהָלֶיךָ לַתּוֹרָה, לֵישֵׁב וּלְעַבֵּר שָׁנִים וְלִקְבֹּעַ חֳדָשִׁים, כְּמוֹ שֶׁנֶּאֱמַר: "וּמִבְּנֵי יִשָּׂשכָר יוֹדְעֵי בִינָה לָעִתִּים... רָאשֵׁיהֶם מָאתַיִם" (דברי

not go up there to learn. They therefore ordained that teachers be appointed in each district and that boys enter school at the age of sixteen or seventeen. But because a boy who was punished by his teacher would rebel and leave school, Yehoshua ben Gamla introduced a regulation that teachers of young children be appointed in each district and town, and that children begin their schooling at the age of six or seven" (Bava Batra 21a). This structure was in place by the time of the destruction of the Temple. A rabbinic dictum of the third century states that a town which lacks a school is to be excommunicated, on the grounds that "the world only exists in virtue of the breath of children at school" (Shabbat 119b). Here, Moshe "our teacher" accords to the Levites the blessing, and honor, of teaching others.

19 and Yissakhar, in your tents. They summon peoples to the mountain; there they
offer righteous sacrifice; they will feast on the plenty of oceans and the hidden,
20 buried riches of the sands." And of Gad he said: "Blessed be He who
21 enlarges Gad! He lives like a lion, he tears at arm and scalp. He chose the first
portion for himself, for there the lawgiver's portion is reserved, where the
heads of the people come. He executed the LORD's justice, and His ordinances
22 for Israel." And of Dan he said: "Dan is a lion's whelp springing forth HAMISHI
23 from Bashan." And of Naftali he said: "Naftali, sated with favor, filled with the
24 LORD's blessing, west and south possess." And of Asher he said: "Most
blessed of sons is Asher; may he win his brothers' favor, and bathe his feet in
25 oil. Your bars are iron and bronze; may your strength be equal to your days.

רש"י

הימים א' יב, לג), ראשי סנהדרין היו עוסקים בכך. ועל פי קביעת עתיהם ועבוריהם, "עמים" של שבטי ישראל "הר יקראו" – להר המוריה יאספו. כל אסיפה על ידי קריאה היא, "ושם יזבחו" ברגלים "זבחי צדק": **כי שפע ימים יינקו.** יששכר וזבולון, ויהא להם פנאי לעסק בתורה: **ושפני טמוני חול.** כסויי טמוני חול, טרית וחלזון וזכוכית לבנה היוצאים מן הים ומן החול, ובחלקו של זבולון היה, כמו שאמור במסכת מגלה (דף ו ע"א): "זבלון עם חרף נפשו למות" (שופטים ה, יח) משום ד"נפתלי על מרומי שדה" (שם), היה מתרעם זבולון על חלקו, לאחי נתת שדות וכרמים וכו': **ושפני.** לשון כסוי, כמו שנאמר: "ויספן את הבית" (מלכים א' ו, ט), "וספון בארז" (ירמיה כב, יד), ותרגומו: "ומטלל בכיורי ארזיא". דבר אחר, "עמים הר יקראו", על ידי פרקמטיא של זבולון, תגרי אמות העולם באים אל ארצו, והיא עומדת על הספר, והם אומרים: הואיל ונטרענו עד כאן נלך עד ירושלים ונראה מה יראתה של אמה זו ומה מעשיה, והם רואים כל ישראל עובדים לאלוה אחד ואוכלים מאכל אחד, לפי שהגוים אלהו של זה לא כאלהו של זה ומאכלו של זה לא כמאכלו של זה, והם אומרים: אין אמה כשרה כזו, ומתגירין שם, שנאמר: "שם יזבחו זבחי צדק": **כי שפע ימים יינקו.** זבולון ויששכר, הים נותן להם ממון בשפע:

כ **ברוך מרחיב גד.** מלמד שהיה תחומו של גד מרחיב והולך כלפי מזרח: **כלביא שכן.** לפי שהיה סמוך לספר לפיכך נמשל כאריות, שכל סמוכי ספר צריכים להיות גבורים: **וטרף זרוע אף קדקד.** הרוגיהם היו נכרים, חותכים הראש עם הזרוע במכה אחת:

כא **וירא ראשית לו.** ראה לטל לו חלק בארץ סיחון ועוג שהיא ראשית כבוש הארץ: **כי שם חלקת.** כי ידע אשר שם בנחלתו חלקת שדה קבורת מחוקק, והוא משה: **ספון.** אותה חלקה ספונה וטמונה מכל בריה, שנאמר: "ולא ידע איש את קברתו" (להלן לד, ו): **ויתא.** גד: **ראשי עם.** הם היו הולכים לפני החלוץ בכבוש הארץ לפי שהיו גבורים, וכן הוא אומר: "חלוצים תעברו לפני אחיכם" וגו' (לעיל ג, יח): **צדקת ה' עשה.** שהאמינו דבריהם ושמרו הבטחתם לעבר את הירדן עד שכבשו וחלקו. דבר אחר, "ויתא" משה "ראשי עם". "צדקת ה' עשה" על משה אמור:

כב **דן גור אריה.** אף הוא היה סמוך לספר, לפיכך מושלו באריות: **יזנק מן הבשן.** כתרגומו, שהיה הירדן יוצא מחלקו ממערת פמיאס, והיא לשם שהיא בחלקו של דן, שנאמר: "ויקראו ללשם דן" (יהושע יט, מז), וזנוקו וקלוחו מן הבשן. דבר אחר, מה זנוק זה יוצא ממקום אחד ונחלק לשני מקומות, כך שבטו של דן נטלו חלק בשני מקומות. תחלה נטלו בצפונית מערבית, עקרון וסביבותיה, ולא ספקו להם, ובאו ונלחמו עם לשם שהיא פמיאס, והיא בצפונית מזרחית, שהרי הירדן יוצא ממערת פמיאס והוא במזרחה של ארץ ישראל, ובא מהצפון לדרום, וכלה בקצה ים המלח שהוא במזרח יהודה שנטל בדרומה של ארץ ישראל, כמו שמפרש בספר יהושע, והוא שנאמר: "ויצא גבול בני דן מהם ויעלו בני דן וילחמו עם לשם" וגו' (יהושע שם), יצא גבולם מכל אותה הרוח שהתחילו לנחל בה:

כג **שבע רצון.** שהיתה ארצו שבעה כל רצון יושביה: **ים ודרום ירשה.** ים כנרת נפל בחלקו, ונטל מלא חבל חרם בדרומה לפרש חרמים ומכמרות:

כד **ברוך מבנים אשר.** ראיתי בספרי (שם): אין לך בכל השבטים שנתברך בבנים כאשר. ואיני יודע כיצד: **יהי רצוי אחיו.** שהיה מתרצה לאחיו בשמן אנפיקינון. דבר אחר, "יהי רצוי אחיו", שהיו בנותיו נאות, והוא שנאמר בדברי הימים (א' ז, לא): "הוא אבי ברזית", שהיו בנותיו נשואות לכהנים גדולים ולמלכים הנמשחים בשמן זית: **וטבל בשמן רגלו.** שהיתה ארצו מושכת שמן כמעין. ומעשה שנצטרכו אנשי לודקיא לשמן, מנו להם פולמוסטוס אחד כו' [אמרו לו: לך והבא לנו שמן במאה ריבוא. הלך לירושלים, אמרו לו: לך

יט בְּאֹהָלֶיךָ׃ עַמִּים הַר־יִקְרָאוּ שָׁם יִזְבְּחוּ זִבְחֵי־צֶדֶק כִּי שֶׁפַע יַמִּים
כ יִינָקוּ וּשְׂפֻנֵי טְמוּנֵי חוֹל׃ וּלְגָד אָמַר בָּרוּךְ מַרְחִיב גָּד כְּלָבִיא
כא שָׁכֵן וְטָרַף זְרוֹעַ אַף־קָדְקֹד׃ וַיַּרְא רֵאשִׁית לוֹ כִּי־שָׁם חֶלְקַת מְחֹקֵק סָפוּן
כב וַיֵּתֵא רָאשֵׁי עָם צִדְקַת יהוה עָשָׂה וּמִשְׁפָּטָיו עִם־יִשְׂרָאֵל׃ וּלְדָן חמישי
כג אָמַר דָּן גּוּר אַרְיֵה יְזַנֵּק מִן־הַבָּשָׁן׃ וּלְנַפְתָּלִי אָמַר נַפְתָּלִי שְׂבַע רָצוֹן
כד וּמָלֵא בִּרְכַּת יהוה יָם וְדָרוֹם יְרָשָׁה׃ וּלְאָשֵׁר אָמַר
כה בָּרוּךְ מִבָּנִים אָשֵׁר יְהִי רְצוּי אֶחָיו וְטֹבֵל בַּשֶּׁמֶן רַגְלוֹ׃ בַּרְזֶל וּנְחֹשֶׁת

אונקלוס

בְּמַהֲכָךְ לְמֶעֱבַד זְמַנֵי מוֹעֲדַיָא בִּירוּשְׁלֵם: יט שִׁבְטַיָא דְיִשְׂרָאֵל לְטוּר בֵּית מַקְדְּשָׁא יִתְכַּנְשׁוּן, תַּמָּן יִכְּסוּן נִכְסַת קֻדְשִׁין לְרַעֲוָא, אֲרֵי נִכְסֵי עַמְמַיָא יֵיכְלוּן, וְסִימָן דִּמְטַמְרָן בְּחָלָא מִתְגַּלְיָן לְהוֹן: כ וּלְגָד אֲמַר, בְּרִיךְ דְּאַפְתִּי לְגָד, כְּלֵיתָא שָׁרֵי, וְיִקְטֵיל שִׁלְטוֹנִין עִם מַלְכִין: כא וְאִתְקַבַּל בְּקַדְמֵיתָא דִּילֵיהּ, אֲרֵי תַמָּן, בְּאַחְסָנְתֵיהּ מֹשֶׁה סָפְרָא רַבָּא דְיִשְׂרָאֵל קְבִיר, הוּא נְפַק וְעָאל בְּרֵישׁ עַמָּא, זָכְוָן קֳדָם יי עֲבַד, וְדִינוֹהִי עִם יִשְׂרָאֵל: כב וּלְדָן אֲמַר, דָּן תַּקִּיף כְּגוּר אַרְיָוָן, אַרְעֵיהּ שָׁתְיָא מִן נַחְלַיָא דְּנָגְדִין מִן מַתְנַן: כג וּלְנַפְתָּלִי אֲמַר, נַפְתָּלִי סְבַע רַעֲוָא, וּמְלֵי בִּרְכָן מִן קֳדָם יי, מַעְרַב יַם גִּנֵּיסַר וְדָרוֹמוֹהִי יֵירַת: כד וּלְאָשֵׁר אֲמַר, בְּרִיךְ מִבִּרְכַּת בְּנַיָא אָשֵׁר, יְהֵי רַעֲוָא לַאֲחוֹהִי, וְיִתְרַבֵּא בְּתַפְנוּקֵי מַלְכִין: כה תַּקִּיף כְּבַרְזְלָא וְכִנְחָשָׁא

רש״י

לצור. הלך לצור, אמרו לו: לך לגוש חלב. הלך לגוש חלב, אמרו לו: לך אצל פלוני לשדה הלז, ומצאו שהיה עוזק תחת זיתיו. אמר לו: יש לך שמן במאה ריבוא שאני צריך? אמר לו: המתן לי עד שאסיים מלאכתי. המתין עד שסיים מלאכתו. לאחר שסיים מלאכתו, הפשיל כליו לאחוריו והיה מסקל ובא בדרכו. אמר לו: יש לך שמן במאה ריבוא? כמדומה אני ששחוק שחקו בי היהודים. כיון שהגיע

33:21 חֶלְקַת מְחֹקֵק סָפוּן *The lawgiver's portion is reserved* – This "reserved (literally 'hidden') portion" may refer to Moshe's gravesite in the territory of Gad. The Torah insists (Deut. 34:6) that no one knows exactly where Moshe is buried. His tomb must never become a place of pilgrimage and worship. What a contrast between Moshe and the heroes of other civilizations, whose burial places become monuments, shrines, places of pilgrimage.

An obsession with death ultimately devalues life. Fear of our own mortality led the ancient world to enslave the masses, turning them into giant labor forces to build monumental buildings that would stand as long as time itself. Why fight against the evils and injustices of the world if this life is only a preparation for the World to Come?

That is why in place of a pyramid or a temple such as Ramesses II built at Abu Simbel, all the Israelites had for almost five centuries until the days of Solomon was the *Mishkan*, a portable sanctuary, more like a tent than a temple. That is why, in Judaism, death defiles and why the rite of the red heifer was necessary to purify people from contact with it. That is why the holier you are – if you are a priest, more so if you are the High Priest – the less you can be in contact or under the same roof as a dead person. God is not in death but in life.

We believe that the greatest mistake is to worship human beings as if they were gods. We admire human beings; we do not worship them. Moshe's hidden tomb is an honor to Gad, but not a pilgrimage site. "We do not make monuments for the dead; their words are their memorial" (Yerushalmi, Shekalim 2:5).

26 There is none like the God of Yeshurun, riding the skies to help you, the heavens,
27 in His grandeur. Your refuge the God of time immemorial, you rest in eternal HATAN HATORAH
28 arms. Dispelling every enemy before you, He spoke: 'Destroy!' So Israel dwells
in safety; Yaakov takes refuge alone in a land of grain and wine, where the skies
29 drop their dew. Happy are you, Israel. Who is like you, a people rescued by
the LORD? He is your shield of help, your sword of triumph. Your enemies
34 1 will cower before you, and you shall tread their high places." Then
Moshe went up from the plains of Moav to Mount Nevo, to the summit of
Pisga, facing Yeriḥo. The LORD showed him all the land: from Gilad to Dan,
2 all of Naftali, the land of Efrayim and Menashe, all the land of Yehuda as far

רש״י

לעירו, הוציאה לו שפחתו קומקמוס של חמין ורחץ בו ידיו ורגליו, הוציאה לו ספל של זהב מלאה שמן וטבל בו ידיו ורגליו, לקיים מה שנאמר: "וטבל בשמן רגלו". לאחר שאכלו ושתו, מדד לו שמן במאה ריבוא. אמר לו: כלום אתה צריך ליותר? אמר לו: הן, אלא שאין לי דמים. אמר לו: אם אתה רוצה ליקח קח, ואני אלך עמך ואטול דמיו, מדד לו שמן בשמונה עשר ריבוא. אמרו: לא הניח אותו האיש לא סוס ולא פרד ולא גמל ולא חמור בארץ ישראל שלא שכרו. כיון שהגיע לעירו יצאו אנשי עירו לקלסו, אמר להם: לא לי קלסוני אלא לזה שבא עמי, שמדד לי שמן במאה ריבוא והרי נושה בי בשמונה עשרה ריבוא], כִּדְאִיתָא בִּמְנָחוֹת (דף פה ע״ב):

כה **בַּרְזֶל וּנְחֹשֶׁת מִנְעָלֶךָ.** עַכְשָׁיו הוּא מְדַבֵּר כְּנֶגֶד כָּל יִשְׂרָאֵל, שֶׁהָיוּ גִּבּוֹרֵיהֶם יוֹשְׁבִים בְּעָרֵי הַסְּפָר וְנוֹעֲלִים אוֹתָהּ שֶׁלֹּא יוּכְלוּ הָאוֹיְבִים לִכָּנֵס בָּהּ, כְּאִלּוּ הִיא סְגוּרָה בְּמַנְעוּלִים וּבְרִיחִים שֶׁל בַּרְזֶל וּנְחֹשֶׁת. דָּבָר אַחֵר, "בַּרְזֶל וּנְחֹשֶׁת מִנְעָלֶךָ", אַרְצְכֶם נְעוּלָה בֶּהָרִים שֶׁחוֹצְבִין מֵהֶם בַּרְזֶל וּנְחֹשֶׁת, וְאַרְצוֹ שֶׁל אָשֵׁר הָיְתָה מַנְעוּלָהּ שֶׁל אֶרֶץ יִשְׂרָאֵל: **וּכְיָמֶיךָ דָּבְאֶךָ.** וְכַיָּמִים שֶׁהֵם טוֹבִים לְךָ, שֶׁהֵן יְמֵי תְּחִלָּתְךָ, יְמֵי נְעוּרֶיךָ, כֵּן יִהְיוּ יְמֵי זִקְנוּתְךָ שֶׁהֵם דּוֹאֲבִים זָבִים וּמִתְמוֹטְטִים. דָּבָר אַחֵר, "וּכְיָמֶיךָ דָּבְאֶךָ", כְּמִנְיַן יָמֶיךָ, כָּל הַיָּמִים אֲשֶׁר אַתֶּם עוֹשִׂים רְצוֹנוֹ שֶׁל מָקוֹם, יִהְיוּ "דָּבְאֶךָ", שֶׁכָּל הָאֲרָצוֹת יִהְיוּ דּוֹבְאוֹת כֶּסֶף לְאֶרֶץ יִשְׂרָאֵל, שֶׁתְּהֵא מְבֹרֶכֶת בְּפֵרוֹת וְכָל הָאֲרָצוֹת מִתְפַּרְנְסוֹת הֵימֶנָּה, וּמַמְשִׁיכוֹת לָהּ כַּסְפָּם וּזְהָבָם, אשקורנ״ט, הַכֶּסֶף כָּלֶה מֵהֶם שֶׁהֵן מְזִיבוֹת אוֹתוֹ לְאַרְצְכֶם:

כו-כז **אֵין כָּאֵל יְשֻׁרוּן.** דַּע לְךָ "יְשֻׁרוּן", שֶׁ"אֵין כָּאֵל" בְּכָל אֱלֹהֵי הָעַמִּים, וְלֹא כְּצוּרְךָ צוּרָם: **רֹכֵב שָׁמַיִם.** הוּא אוֹתוֹ אֱלוֹהַּ שֶׁ"בְּעֶזְרֶךָ", "וּבְגַאֲוָתוֹ" הוּא רוֹכֵב "שְׁחָקִים": **מְעֹנָה אֱלֹהֵי קֶדֶם.** לְמָעוֹן הֵם הַשְּׁחָקִים לֵאלֹהֵי קֶדֶם, שֶׁקָּדַם לְכָל אֱלֹהִים, וּבֵרַר לוֹ שְׁחָקִים לְשִׁבְתּוֹ וּמְעוֹנָתוֹ, וּמִתַּחַת מְעוֹנָתוֹ כָּל בַּעֲלֵי זְרוֹעַ שׁוֹכְנִים: **זְרֹעֹת עוֹלָם.** סִיחוֹן וְעוֹג וּמַלְכֵי כְנַעַן שֶׁהָיוּ תָּקְפּוֹ וּגְבוּרָתוֹ שֶׁל עוֹלָם, לְפִיכָךְ עַל כָּרְחָם יֶחֶרְדוּ וְיָזוּעוּ וְכֹחָם חָלַשׁ מִפָּנָיו, כִּי לְעוֹלָם אֵימַת הַגָּבוֹהַּ עַל הַנָּמוּךְ. וְהוּא, שֶׁהַכֹּחַ וְהַגְּבוּרָה שֶׁלּוֹ "בְּעֶזְרֶךָ", "וַיְגָרֶשׁ מִפָּנֶיךָ אוֹיֵב", "וַיֹּאמֶר" לְךָ: "הַשְׁמֵד" אוֹתָם: **מְעֹנָה.** כָּל תֵּבָה שֶׁצְּרִיכָה לָמֶ״ד בִּתְחִלָּתָהּ הֵטִיל לָהּ הֵ״א בְּסוֹפָהּ:

כח **בֶּטַח בָּדָד.** כָּל יָחִיד וְיָחִיד אִישׁ תַּחַת גַּפְנוֹ, מְפֻזָּרִים, וְאֵין צְרִיכִין לְהִתְאַסֵּף וְלֵישֵׁב יַחַד מִפְּנֵי הָאוֹיֵב: **עֵין יַעֲקֹב.** כְּמוֹ: "וְעֵינוֹ כְּעֵין הַבְּדֹלַח" (במדבר יא, ז), כְּעֵין הַבְּרָכָה שֶׁבֵּרְכָם יַעֲקֹב. לֹא כְּ"בָדָד" שֶׁאָמַר יִרְמְיָה: "בָּדָד יָשַׁבְתִּי" (ירמיה טו, יז), אֶלָּא כְּעֵין הַבְטָחָה שֶׁהִבְטִיחָם יַעֲקֹב: "וְהָיָה אֱלֹהִים עִמָּכֶם וְהֵשִׁיב אֶתְכֶם אֶל אֶרֶץ אֲבֹתֵיכֶם" (בראשית מח, כא): **יַעַרְפוּ.** יִטְפוּ: **אַף שָׁמָיו יַעַרְפוּ טָל.** אַף בִּרְכָתוֹ שֶׁל יִצְחָק נוֹסֶפֶת עַל שֶׁל יַעֲקֹב: "וְיִתֶּן לְךָ הָאֱלֹהִים מִטַּל הַשָּׁמַיִם" וְגוֹ' (בראשית כז, כח):

כט **אַשְׁרֶיךָ יִשְׂרָאֵל.** לְאַחַר שֶׁפֵּרַט לָהֶם בְּרָכוֹת, אָמַר לָהֶם: מָה לִי לִפְרֹט לָכֶם? כְּלַל דָּבָר, הַכֹּל שֶׁלָּכֶם: **אַשְׁרֶיךָ יִשְׂרָאֵל מִי כָמוֹךָ.** תְּשׁוּעָתְךָ בַּה' אֲשֶׁר הוּא "מָגֵן עֶזְרֶךָ" וְ"חֶרֶב גַּאֲוָתֶךָ": **וְיִכָּחֲשׁוּ אֹיְבֶיךָ לָךְ.** כְּגוֹן הַגִּבְעוֹנִים, שֶׁאָמְרוּ: "מֵאֶרֶץ רְחוֹקָה... בָּאוּ עֲבָדֶיךָ" וְגוֹ' (יהושע ט, ט): **וְאַתָּה עַל בָּמוֹתֵימוֹ תִדְרֹךְ.** כְּעִנְיָן שֶׁנֶּאֱמַר: "שִׂימוּ אֶת רַגְלֵיכֶם עַל צַוְּארֵי הַמְּלָכִים הָאֵלֶּה" (שם י, כד):

לד א **מֵעַרְבֹת מוֹאָב אֶל הַר נְבוֹ.** כַּמָּה מַעֲלוֹת הָיוּ, וּפְסָעָן מֹשֶׁה בִּפְסִיעָה אַחַת: **אֶת כָּל הָאָרֶץ.** הֶרְאָהוּ אֶת כָּל אֶרֶץ יִשְׂרָאֵל בְּשַׁלְוָתָהּ, וְהַמְּצִיקִין הָעֲתִידִין לִהְיוֹת מְצִיקִין לָהּ: **עַד דָּן.** הֶרְאָהוּ בְּנֵי דָן עוֹבְדֵי עֲבוֹדָה זָרָה, שֶׁנֶּאֱמַר: "וַיָּקִימוּ לָהֶם בְּנֵי דָן אֶת הַפָּסֶל" (שופטים יח, ל), וְהֶרְאָהוּ שִׁמְשׁוֹן שֶׁעָתִיד לָצֵאת מִמֶּנּוּ לְמוֹשִׁיעַ:

ב **וְאֵת כָּל נַפְתָּלִי.** הֶרְאָהוּ אַרְצוֹ בְּשַׁלְוָתָהּ וְחֻרְבָּנָהּ, וְהֶרְאָהוּ דְּבוֹרָה וּבָרָק מִקֶּדֶשׁ נַפְתָּלִי נִלְחָמִים עִם סִיסְרָא וַחֲיָלוֹתָיו: **וְאֶת אֶרֶץ אֶפְרַיִם וּמְנַשֶּׁה.** הֶרְאָהוּ אַרְצָם בְּשַׁלְוָתָהּ וּבְחֻרְבָּנָהּ, וְהֶרְאָהוּ יְהוֹשֻׁעַ נִלְחָם עִם

כו מִנְעָלֶךָ וּכְיָמֶיךָ דׇּבְאֶךָ: אֵין כָּאֵל יְשֻׁרוּן רֹכֵב שָׁמַיִם בְּעֶזְרֶךָ וּבְגַאֲוָתוֹ
כז שְׁחָקִים: מְעֹנָה אֱלֹהֵי קֶדֶם וּמִתַּחַת זְרֹעֹת עוֹלָם וַיְגָרֶשׁ מִפָּנֶיךָ אוֹיֵב חתן התורה
כח וַיֹּאמֶר הַשְׁמֵד: וַיִּשְׁכֹּן יִשְׂרָאֵל בֶּטַח בָּדָד עֵין יַעֲקֹב אֶל־אֶרֶץ דָּגָן
כט וְתִירוֹשׁ אַף־שָׁמָיו יַעַרְפוּ־טָל: אַשְׁרֶיךָ יִשְׂרָאֵל מִי כָמוֹךָ עַם נוֹשַׁע
בַּיהוָה מָגֵן עֶזְרֶךָ וַאֲשֶׁר־חֶרֶב גַּאֲוָתֶךָ וְיִכָּחֲשׁוּ אֹיְבֶיךָ לָךְ וְאַתָּה עַל־
לד א בָּמוֹתֵימוֹ תִדְרֹךְ: וַיַּעַל מֹשֶׁה מֵעַרְבֹת מוֹאָב אֶל־הַר
נְבוֹ רֹאשׁ הַפִּסְגָּה אֲשֶׁר עַל־פְּנֵי יְרֵחוֹ וַיַּרְאֵהוּ יְהוָה אֶת־כׇּל־הָאָרֶץ
ב אֶת־הַגִּלְעָד עַד־דָּן: וְאֵת כׇּל־נַפְתָּלִי וְאֶת־אֶרֶץ אֶפְרַיִם וּמְנַשֶּׁה וְאֵת

אונקלוס

בֵּית מוֹתְבָךְ, וּכְיוֹמֵי עוּלֵימוּתָךְ תְּקָפָךְ: כו לֵית אֱלָהּ אֱלָא אֱלָהָא דְּיִשְׂרָאֵל, דִּשְׁכִינְתֵיהּ בִּשְׁמַיָּא בְּסַעְדָּךְ, וְתֻקְפֵיהּ בִּשְׁמֵי שְׁמַיָּא: כז מְדוֹר אֱלָהָא דְּמִלְּקַדְמִין, דִּבְמֵימְרֵיהּ אִתְעֲבִיד עָלְמָא, וְתָרֵיךְ מִן קֳדָמָךְ, סָנְאָה וַאֲמַר שֵׁיצִי: כח וּשְׁרָא יִשְׂרָאֵל לְרֻחְצָן בִּלְחוֹדֵיהוֹן כְּעֵין בִּרְכְתָא דְּבָרֵיכִנּוּן יַעֲקֹב אֲבוּהוֹן, בַּאֲרַע עָבְדָא עֲבוּר וַחֲמַר, אַף שְׁמַיָּא דְּעִלָּוֵיהוֹן יְשַׁמְּשׁוּנוּן בְּטַלָּא: כט טוּבָךְ יִשְׂרָאֵל לֵית דִּכְוָתָךְ, עַמָּא דִּפְרָקְנֵיהּ מִן קֳדָם יי תְּקוֹף בְּסַעְדָּךְ, וּדְמִן קֳדָמוֹהִי נִצְחָן גְּבָרְוָתָךְ, וְיִתְכַּדְּבוּן סָנְאָךְ לָךְ, וְאַתְּ עַל פְּרִקַת צַוְּרֵי מַלְכֵיהוֹן תִּדְרוֹךְ: לד א וּסְלֵיק מֹשֶׁה, מִמֵּישְׁרַיָּא דְּמוֹאָב לְטוּרָא דִנְבוֹ, רֵישׁ רָמְתָא, דְּעַל אַפֵּי יְרֵיחוֹ, וְאַחְזְיֵהּ יי יָת כׇּל אַרְעָא, יָת גִּלְעָד עַד דָּן: ב וְיָת כׇּל נַפְתָּלִי, וְיָת אֲרַע אֶפְרַיִם וּמְנַשֶּׁה, וְיָת

33:29 מִי כָמוֹךָ עַם נוֹשַׁע בַּיהוה *Who is like you, a people rescued by the Lord* – This verse contains Moshe's last words to the people he has led from slavery to freedom, through the wilderness, to the brink of the Promised Land. His message is moving and clear: If the people stay faithful to God, they will be safe from their enemies, and need have no fear. The real challenge will not be military but spiritual.

I find it moving that in all the centuries when they were considered pariahs by others, Jews were spared from the worst excesses of self-hatred. On the festivals they remembered the past and hoped for the future. On the Sabbath, however poor they were, they sat at the Sabbath table like free men and women, and sang. Though they could be racked by poverty, still they built houses of study and sat learning Talmud and cultivated the life of the mind. And though they were poor they knew there were others poorer than themselves, and they gave them aid, and invited them to their festive meals, and considered themselves bound by a covenant of mutual responsibility.

We are not defined by those who do not like us. This is how we have come through the Holocaust and still believe in life, lived through what Israel has lived through and still strive for peace, experienced the degree of hate poured out against us by some of Europe's greatest minds and remain undefiled. We still hear, every year, Moshe's loving words to us, his children: "Who is like you?" To be a Jew is to be defined by the One who loves us: "a people rescued by the Lord."

3 as the Westward Sea, the Negev, and the plain – the Valley of Yeriḥo, city of
4 palm trees – as far as Tzoar. The LORD said to him, "This is the land I promised
Avraham, Yitzḥak, and Yaakov, saying, 'I will give this to your descendants';
I have let you see it with your eyes, but to that place you will not cross over."
5 Then Moshe, the LORD's own servant, died there in the land of Moav, at the
6 LORD's word. He buried him in Moav, in a valley opposite Beit Peor, and to
7 this day no one knows his burial place. Moshe was a hundred and twenty

רש״י

מַלְכֵי כְנַעַן, שֶׁבָּא מֵאֶפְרַיִם, וְגִדְעוֹן שֶׁבָּא מִמְּנַשֶּׁה נִלְחָם עִם מִדְיָן וַעֲמָלֵק: **וְאֵת כָּל אֶרֶץ יְהוּדָה.** בְּשַׁלְוָתָהּ וּבְחֻרְבָּנָהּ, וְהֶרְאָהוּ מַלְכוּת בֵּית דָּוִד וְנִצְחוֹנָם: **עַד הַיָּם הָאַחֲרוֹן.** אֶרֶץ הַמַּעֲרָב בְּשַׁלְוָתָהּ וּבְחֻרְבָּנָהּ. דָּבָר אַחֵר, אַל תִּקְרֵי "הַיָּם הָאַחֲרוֹן" אֶלָּא 'הַיּוֹם הָאַחֲרוֹן' – כָּל הַמְּאֹרָעוֹת לְיִשְׂרָאֵל עַד שֶׁיִּחְיוּ הַמֵּתִים:

ג **וְאֶת הַנֶּגֶב.** אֶרֶץ הַדָּרוֹם. דָּבָר אַחֵר, מְעָרַת הַמַּכְפֵּלָה, שֶׁנֶּאֱמַר: "וַיַּעֲלוּ בַנֶּגֶב וַיָּבֹא עַד חֶבְרוֹן" (במדבר יג, כב): **וְאֶת הַכִּכָּר.** הֶרְאָהוּ שְׁלֹמֹה יוֹצֵק כְּלֵי בֵּית הַמִּקְדָּשׁ בְּכִכַּר הַיַּרְדֵּן בְּמַעֲבֵה הָאֲדָמָה:

ד **לֵאמֹר לְזַרְעֲךָ אֶתְּנֶנָּה, הֶרְאִיתִיךָ.** כְּדֵי שֶׁתֵּלֵךְ וְתֹאמַר לְאַבְרָהָם לְיִצְחָק וּלְיַעֲקֹב, שְׁבוּעָה שֶׁנִּשְׁבַּע לָכֶם הַקָּדוֹשׁ בָּרוּךְ הוּא – קִיְּמָהּ, וְזֶהוּ "לֵאמֹר", לְכָךְ הֶרְאִיתִיהָ לְךָ, אֲבָל גְּזֵרָה הִיא מִלְּפָנַי שֶׁ"שָּׁמָּה לֹא תַעֲבֹר", שֶׁאִלּוּלֵי כָךְ, הָיִיתִי מְקַיֶּמְךָ עַד שֶׁתִּרְאֶה אוֹתָם נְטוּעִים וּקְבוּעִים בָּהּ וְתֵלֵךְ וְתַגִּיד לָהֶם:

ה **וַיָּמָת שָׁם.** אֶפְשָׁר מֹשֶׁה מֵת, וְכָתַב: "וַיָּמָת שָׁם"? אֶלָּא מִכָּאן וְאֵילָךְ כָּתַב יְהוֹשֻׁעַ. רַבִּי מֵאִיר אוֹמֵר: אֶפְשָׁר סֵפֶר הַתּוֹרָה חָסֵר כְּלוּם, וְהוּא אוֹמֵר: "לָקֹחַ אֵת סֵפֶר הַתּוֹרָה הַזֶּה" (לעיל לא, כו)? אֶלָּא הַקָּדוֹשׁ בָּרוּךְ הוּא אוֹמֵר וּמֹשֶׁה כּוֹתֵב בְּדֶמַע: **עַל פִּי ה׳.** בִּנְשִׁיקָה:

ו **וַיִּקְבֹּר אֹתוֹ.** הַקָּדוֹשׁ בָּרוּךְ הוּא בִּכְבוֹדוֹ. רַבִּי יִשְׁמָעֵאל אוֹמֵר: הוּא קָבַר אֶת עַצְמוֹ, וְזֶה הוּא אֶחָד מִשְּׁלֹשָׁה אֶתִּים שֶׁהָיָה רַבִּי יִשְׁמָעֵאל דּוֹרֵשׁ כֵּן. כַּיּוֹצֵא בוֹ: "בְּיוֹם מְלֹאת יְמֵי נִזְרוֹ יָבִיא אֹתוֹ" (במדבר ו, יג), הוּא מֵבִיא אֶת עַצְמוֹ. כַּיּוֹצֵא בוֹ: "וְהִשִּׂיאוּ אוֹתָם עֲוֹן אַשְׁמָה" (ויקרא כב, טז), וְכִי אֲחֵרִים מַשִּׂיאִים אוֹתָם? אֶלָּא הֵם מַשִּׂיאִים אֶת עַצְמָם: **מוּל בֵּית פְּעוֹר.** קִבְרוֹ מוּכָן שָׁם מִשֵּׁשֶׁת יְמֵי בְרֵאשִׁית לְכַפֵּר עַל מַעֲשֵׂה פְעוֹר, וְזֶה אֶחָד מִן הַדְּבָרִים שֶׁנִּבְרְאוּ בְּעֶרֶב שַׁבָּת בֵּין הַשְּׁמָשׁוֹת (אבות ה, ו):

34:7 **לֹא־כָהֲתָה עֵינוֹ וְלֹא־נָס לֵחֹה** *His eyes had not grown dim, nor his vitality fled* – Moshe did not fade. Somehow, he defied the law of entropy that states that all systems lose energy over time. The law also applies to people, especially leaders. The kind of leadership Moshe undertook, getting people to change, persuading them to cease to think and feel like slaves and instead embrace the responsibilities of freedom – is stressful and exhausting. There were times when Moshe came close to burnout and despair. What then was the secret of the undiminished energy of his last years?

The Torah suggests the answer in the very words in which it describes the phenomenon. I used to think that "his eyes had not grown dim" and "his vitality [had not] fled" were simply two descriptions, until it dawned on me that the first was an explanation of the second. Why had his vitality not fled? Because his eyes had not grown dim. He never lost the vision and high ideals of his youth. Despite the many setbacks he experienced, he did not allow himself to become disillusioned, or to give way to despair. He did not become embittered or sad, though he had sufficient reason to be. His undimmed faith in the God he served, the people he led, and the mission to which he dedicated his life was his energy source. His commitment to justice, compassion, liberty, and responsibility was unyielding. He was as passionate at the end as he was at the beginning. He knew there were things he would not live to achieve, so he taught the next generation how to achieve them. He was never afraid to learn something new. The result was that his vitality did not flee. His body was old, but his mind and soul stayed young.

Without passion you cannot be a transformative leader. Unless you yourself are inspired you cannot inspire others. Moshe never lost the vision of his first encounter with God at the bush that burned but was not consumed. That is how

ג כָּל־אֶרֶץ יְהוּדָה עַד הַיָּם הָאַחֲרוֹן: וְאֶת־הַנֶּגֶב וְאֶת־הַכִּכָּר בִּקְעַת
ד יְרֵחוֹ עִיר הַתְּמָרִים עַד־צֹעַר: וַיֹּאמֶר יְהוָה אֵלָיו זֹאת הָאָרֶץ אֲשֶׁר
נִשְׁבַּעְתִּי לְאַבְרָהָם לְיִצְחָק וּלְיַעֲקֹב לֵאמֹר לְזַרְעֲךָ אֶתְּנֶנָּה הֶרְאִיתִיךָ
ה בְעֵינֶיךָ וְשָׁמָּה לֹא תַעֲבֹר: וַיָּמָת שָׁם מֹשֶׁה עֶבֶד־יְהוָה בְּאֶרֶץ מוֹאָב
ו עַל־פִּי יְהוָה: וַיִּקְבֹּר אֹתוֹ בַגַּי בְּאֶרֶץ מוֹאָב מוּל בֵּית פְּעוֹר וְלֹא־יָדַע
ז אִישׁ אֶת־קְבֻרָתוֹ עַד הַיּוֹם הַזֶּה: וּמֹשֶׁה בֶּן־מֵאָה וְעֶשְׂרִים שָׁנָה בְּמֹתוֹ

אונקלוס

כָּל אֲרַע יְהוּדָה, עַד יַמָּא מַעְרְבָאָה: ג וְיָת דָּרוֹמָא, וְיָת מֵישְׁרָא, בִּקְעַת יְרֵיחוֹ, קִרְיַת דִּקְלַיָּא עַד צוֹעַר: ד וַאֲמַר יי לֵיהּ, דָּא אַרְעָא דְּקַיֵּימִית, לְאַבְרָהָם לְיִצְחָק וּלְיַעֲקֹב לְמֵימַר, לִבְנָךְ אֶתְּנִנַּהּ, אַחֲזִיתָךְ בְּעֵינָךְ, וּלְתַמָּן לָא תִעְבַּר: ה וּמִית תַּמָּן, מֹשֶׁה עַבְדָּא דַּייָ, בְּאַרְעָא דְּמוֹאָב עַל מֵימְרָא דַּייָ: ו וּקְבַר יָתֵיהּ בְּחֵילְתָא בְּאַרְעָא דְּמוֹאָב, לָקֳבֵיל בֵּית פְּעוֹר, וְלָא יְדַע אֱנָשׁ יָת קְבוּרְתֵיהּ, עַד יוֹמָא הָדֵין: ז וּמֹשֶׁה, בַּר מְאָה וְעַשְׂרִין, שְׁנִין כַּד מִית,

34:4 לֹא תַעֲבֹר *You will not cross over* – Franz Kafka gave voice to a compelling truth. Moshe

> is on the track of Canaan all his life; it is incredible that he should see the land only when on the verge of death. This dying vision of it can only be intended to illustrate how incomplete a moment is human life; incomplete because a life like this could last forever and still be nothing but a moment. Moses fails to enter Canaan not because his life was too short but because it is a human life. (Franz Kafka, *Diaries 1914–1923*)

Moshe at the end of his life becomes a symbol both of the possibilities of a human life and of its limits. "It is not for you to complete the task," said R. Tarfon, "but neither are you free to stand aside from it" (Avot 2:21). If we lived forever, life itself would have no shape, no edge, no urgency, no compelling purpose. We would not act. For anything we wished to do, there would always be time in the future. If we lived forever, we would not know love, for the very power of love is tied to the knowledge that its moment is all too brief and that soon it too will perish. Love lives in its vulnerability. It is our deepest longing for timelessness in the midst of time.

If we lived forever, we would not create – for the deepest source of the creative urge is the desire to make something that will live on after us, that will have the immortality we lack. Therefore we choose and plan and act. We become creators of the most consequential work of art we will ever execute – our life itself. We are the co-author and central character of our story – and because it is finite, life is capable of having a storylike structure. A novel that never ends is not a story. The ending itself – happy, tragic, serene, unfulfilled – gives the whole its color and tone.

We are mortal. But we have immortal longings. We live on because the story of which we are a part is itself immortal. The world did not begin with us, nor will it end with our departure. We belong to a larger narrative. From Moshe we learn: We are mortal; therefore make every day count. We are fallible; therefore learn to grow from each mistake. We will not complete the journey; therefore inspire others to continue what we began.

34:6 וַיִּקְבֹּר אֹתוֹ בַגַּי בְּאֶרֶץ מוֹאָב *He buried him in Moav* – The Torah ends as it began, with an act of loving-kindness on the part of God (Sota 14a). Just as at the beginning, He had breathed the breath of life into the first man, so now at the close of the Mosaic books He buries the greatest of men as the breath of life departs from him.

8 years old when he died; his eyes had not grown dim, nor his vitality fled. The
Israelites wept for Moshe in the plains of Moav for thirty days, until the time of
9 weeping and mourning for him was over. Yehoshua son of Nun was filled with
the spirit of wisdom, for Moshe had laid his hands upon him, and the Israelites
10 listened to him, and did as the Lord had commanded Moshe. There has never
11 arisen a prophet in Israel like Moshe, whom the Lord knew face-to-face, in
all the signs and wonders the Lord sent him to perform in Egypt, against
12 Pharaoh, all his officials, and all of his land, and in all the acts of a mighty hand
and of terrifying power that Moshe performed before the eyes of all Israel.

רש"י

ז| **לֹא כָהֲתָה עֵינוֹ.** אַף מִשֶּׁמֵּת: **וְלֹא נָס לֵחֹה.** לַחְלוּחִית שֶׁבּוֹ. לֹא שָׁלַט בּוֹ רִקָּבוֹן וְלֹא נֶהְפַּךְ תֹּאַר פָּנָיו:

ח| **בְּנֵי יִשְׂרָאֵל.** הַזְּכָרִים, אֲבָל בְּאַהֲרֹן מִתּוֹךְ שֶׁהָיָה רוֹדֵף שָׁלוֹם וְנוֹתֵן שָׁלוֹם בֵּין אִישׁ לְרֵעֵהוּ וּבֵין אִשָּׁה לְבַעְלָהּ, נֶאֱמַר: "כֹּל בֵּית יִשְׂרָאֵל" (במדבר כ, כט), זְכָרִים וּנְקֵבוֹת:

י| **אֲשֶׁר יְדָעוֹ ה׳ פָּנִים אֶל פָּנִים.** שֶׁהָיָה לִבּוֹ גַּס בּוֹ וּמְדַבֵּר אֵלָיו בְּכָל עֵת שֶׁרוֹצֶה, כְּעִנְיָן שֶׁנֶּאֱמַר: "וְעַתָּה אֶעֱלֶה אֶל ה׳" (שמות לב, ל), "עִמְדוּ וְאֶשְׁמְעָה מַה יְצַוֶּה ה׳ לָכֶם" (במדבר ט, ח):

יב| **וּלְכֹל הַיָּד הַחֲזָקָה.** שֶׁקִּבֵּל אֶת הַתּוֹרָה בַּלּוּחוֹת בְּיָדָיו: **וּלְכֹל הַמּוֹרָא הַגָּדוֹל.** נִסִּים וּגְבוּרוֹת שֶׁבַּמִּדְבָּר הַגָּדוֹל וְהַנּוֹרָא: **לְעֵינֵי כָּל יִשְׂרָאֵל.** שֶׁנְּשָׂאוֹ לִבּוֹ לִשְׁבֹּר הַלּוּחוֹת לְעֵינֵיהֶם, שֶׁנֶּאֱמַר: "וָאֲשַׁבְּרֵם לְעֵינֵיכֶם" (לעיל ט, יז), וְהִסְכִּימָה דַּעַת הַקָּדוֹשׁ בָּרוּךְ הוּא לְדַעְתּוֹ, שֶׁנֶּאֱמַר: "אֲשֶׁר שִׁבַּרְתָּ" (שמות לד, א) – יִישַׁר כֹּחֲךָ שֶׁשִּׁבַּרְתָּ:

Behold, I will send you Eliya the prophet before the great and terrible day of the Lord. And he will return the hearts of parents back to their children, and the hearts of children back to their parents. (Mal. 3:23–24)

Nevi'im, which includes the great historical as well as prophetic books, thus concludes neither in the present nor the past, but by looking forward to a time not yet reached. Ketuvim (the Writings), the third and final section, ends with King Koresh of Persia granting permission to the Jewish exiles in Babylon to return to their land and rebuild the Temple.

None of these is an ending in the conventional sense. Each leaves us with a sense of a promise not yet fulfilled, a task not yet completed, a future seen from afar but not yet reached. For each of us, likewise, there is a river we will not cross, a promised land we will not enter. Even the greatest life is an unfinished symphony.

Wallace Stevens, in his poem "Thirteen Ways of Looking at a Blackbird," wrote:

I do not know which to prefer,
the beauty of inflections
or the beauty of innuendoes,
the blackbird whistling
or just after.

After the inflections, the innuendoes remain, the hints, the intimations, Eliyahu's "faint sound of silence" (I Kings 19:12), Wordsworth's "sense of something far more deeply interfused." When all the data are in, the great questions still remain. Even when we close the book, the story continues.

Torah is God's book of humanity, and each of us is a chapter in its unfinished story. Every age has added its commentaries, and so must ours. Moshe is buried, but we wind the scroll back to Genesis and begin again. The words form our covenant with Heaven. And as we listen and respond, we add our voice to the unbroken conversation between the Jewish people and its destiny.

ח לֹא־כָהֲתָה עֵינוֹ וְלֹא־נָס לֵחֹה: וַיִּבְכּוּ בְנֵי יִשְׂרָאֵל אֶת־מֹשֶׁה בְּעַרְבֹת
ט מוֹאָב שְׁלֹשִׁים יוֹם וַיִּתְּמוּ יְמֵי בְכִי אֵבֶל מֹשֶׁה: וִיהוֹשֻׁעַ בִּן־נוּן מָלֵא רוּחַ
חָכְמָה כִּי־סָמַךְ מֹשֶׁה אֶת־יָדָיו עָלָיו וַיִּשְׁמְעוּ אֵלָיו בְּנֵי־יִשְׂרָאֵל וַיַּעֲשׂוּ
י כַּאֲשֶׁר צִוָּה יהוה אֶת־מֹשֶׁה: וְלֹא־קָם נָבִיא עוֹד בְּיִשְׂרָאֵל כְּמֹשֶׁה
יא אֲשֶׁר יְדָעוֹ יהוה פָּנִים אֶל־פָּנִים: לְכָל־הָאֹתֹת וְהַמּוֹפְתִים אֲשֶׁר שְׁלָחוֹ
יב יהוה לַעֲשׂוֹת בְּאֶרֶץ מִצְרָיִם לְפַרְעֹה וּלְכָל־עֲבָדָיו וּלְכָל־אַרְצוֹ: וּלְכֹל
הַיָּד הַחֲזָקָה וּלְכֹל הַמּוֹרָא הַגָּדוֹל אֲשֶׁר עָשָׂה מֹשֶׁה לְעֵינֵי כָּל־יִשְׂרָאֵל:

אונקלוס

לָא כְהַת עֵינֵיהּ וְלָא שְׁנָא זִיו יְקָרָא דְאַפּוֹהִי: ח וּבְכוֹ בְנֵי יִשְׂרָאֵל יָת מֹשֶׁה, בְּמֵישְׁרַיָּא דְמוֹאָב תְּלָתִין יוֹמִין, וּשְׁלִימוּ, יוֹמֵי בְכִיתָא אֶבְלָא דְמֹשֶׁה: ט וִיהוֹשֻׁעַ בַּר נוּן, אִתְמְלִי רוּחַ חָכְמְתָא, אֲרֵי סְמַךְ מֹשֶׁה, יָת יְדוֹהִי עֲלוֹהִי, וְקַבִּילוּ מִנֵּיהּ בְּנֵי יִשְׂרָאֵל וַעֲבַדוּ, כְּמָא דְּפַקֵּיד יי יָת מֹשֶׁה: י וְלָא קָם נְבִיָּא עוֹד, בְּיִשְׂרָאֵל כְּמֹשֶׁה, דְּאִתְגְּלִי לֵיהּ יי, אַפִּין בְּאַפִּין: יא לְכָל אָתַיָּא וּמוֹפְתַיָּא, דְּשַׁלְחֵיהּ יי, לְמֶעְבַּד בְּאַרְעָא דְמִצְרַיִם, לְפַרְעֹה וּלְכָל עַבְדוֹהִי וּלְכָל אַרְעֵיהּ: יב וּלְכָל יְדָא תַקִּיפְתָא, וּלְכָל חֶזְוָנָא רַבָּא, דַּעֲבַד מֹשֶׁה, לְעֵינֵי כָּל יִשְׂרָאֵל:

I see Moshe: as the man who burned but was not consumed. So long as that vision stayed with him, as it did until the end of his life, he remained full of energy. You feel that in the sustained power of the book of Deuteronomy, the greatest sequence of speeches in Tanakh. If you want to stay young, never give up on your ideals.

34:8 וַיִּבְכּוּ בְנֵי יִשְׂרָאֵל אֶת־מֹשֶׁה בְּעַרְבֹת מוֹאָב שְׁלֹשִׁים יוֹם *The Israelites wept for Moshe in the plains of Moav for thirty days* – Rashi notes that the mourning for Aharon was more widespread than for Moshe. Of Aharon it says, "The whole House of Israel wept" (Num. 20:29); in the case of Moshe the word "whole" is missing. Perhaps the reason is that Aharon was a man of peace; Moshe was a man of truth. People of truth have enemies as well as friends. Moshe was aflame with a passion for justice, and, unlike Aharon his brother, preferred principle to compromise. Even Moshe, the greatest of men, needed the peace-making skills of Aharon to maintain the balance of his leadership.

34:10 וְלֹא־קָם נָבִיא עוֹד בְּיִשְׂרָאֵל כְּמֹשֶׁה *There has never arisen a prophet in Israel like Moshe* – Moshe's greatness was his humility (Num. 12:3). It was his absence of self that allowed God's spirit to work through him, and his inability to speak (Ex. 4:10) that enabled God to place His words in his mouth. In a manuscript discovered after his death in 1778, Jean-Jacques Rousseau wrote:

> The Jews provide us with an astonishing spectacle: the laws of Numa, Lycurgus, Solon are dead; the very much older laws of Moses are still alive. Athens, Sparta, Rome have perished and no longer have children left on earth; Zion, destroyed, has not lost its children.

There never was another Moshe. There were other prophets but no other lawgiver, no other voice-of-God-for-eternity.

THE END OF THE TORAH

The Jewish story began with a repeated promise to Avraham that he would inherit the land of Canaan. Yet by the time we reach the end of the Torah, the Israelites have still not crossed the Jordan. Nevi'im (the Prophets), the second part of Tanakh, ends with Malakhi foreseeing the distant future, understood by tradition to mean the Messianic age:

הפטרות
HAFTAROT

Haftarat Bereshit

On Erev Rosh Hodesh Marheshvan, read the haftara on page 1637.

42 1 My servant, I uphold him, the one I chose, I wanted. I have placed My spirit over him to draw justice **ISAIAH**
2 3 out to nations; he will not shout nor raise his voice; in the street he will not be heard; not one crushed *Yemenites begin here*
4 reed will break beneath him, no dimming wick be quelled; he will open out judgment to truth, never
himself dimmed or crushed until he has brought the world justice, and all the distant coastlands quake
5 before his teaching. *So says God, the Lord, who created the skies, who stretched them *Ashkenazim and Sepharadim begin here*
across and set down the land and all her children, and gave humanity upon her breath, and spirit to
6 those who walk her. I, the Lord, call you forth in victory, and I will hold your hand; I shall form you
7 and make you a covenant people, make you a light unto nations, to open blinded eyes, to bring prison-
8 ers out of captivity, and those who dwell in darkness from their jail. I am the Lord; this is My name,
9 and I share not My glory with others, My praise with idols. What I said at the beginning: see, it has
come, and I tell you now what will be afresh before it pushes through the earth; you will hear it first
10 from Me. Sing out to the Lord a new song, His praise from the ends of the earth, You who
11 go to sea, and all that fill it, distant coastlands and you who live there. Desert and its towns, raise your
voices, Kedarites in their scattered camps; those who dwell in the rocks must sing out joy from the
12 mountaintops, shout and give the Lord His glory; His praise will be spoken in the distant coastlands.
13 The Lord sets out like a hero, rousing His passion like a man of war; He gives the war cry, bellows the
14 war cry, overthrows His enemies. Always I held still and was silent, held back; I will bellow
15 out like one giving birth, breathing out, breathing in all together, will vanquish hills and mountains
16 and will dry up all the green; I shall turn the rivers into coastlands and desiccate the lakes, and lead the
blind along a way they know not, on paths unknown shall guide them; I shall turn darkness to light *Yemenites end here*
before them, the treacherous road to open highway; these things I will perform, and will not fail.*
17 Those who trust in idols will step back ashamed, those who say to molded statuary, "You – you are our
18 19 gods." All you deaf ones – listen, and you who are blind – now see. Who is blind if not My
servant, who deaf like the messenger I send? Who could be blind like him – who is devoted, blind like
20 21 this, the Lord's servant? Many things seen, but you remember not, with open ears, hear nothing. Yet
the Lord has desired them, that His righteousness be known, to raise aloft His teachings, to confer
22 majesty.** He is with this plundered, this torn-apart people, who are trapped away in pits, hidden in *Sepharadim and Chabad end here*
23 prison, plunder with none to save them, given over to looters with none to cry, "Give back!" Who
24 among you will listen to this, will hear it and heed for the future? Who was it who gave Yaakov up for
looting, Israel for plunder – was it not the Lord? Him against whom we sinned; whose ways they
25 cared not to follow, whose Law they did not heed. He poured out the fire of His rage against them,
His terrible warfare, and flames raged all around them, yet they did not know; they burned but still
43 1 they took it not to heart. And now, Yaakov, so says the Lord, your Creator, the One who
2 formed you, Israel: Do not fear: I redeem you; I name you: you are Mine. Though you pass through
waters – I am with you; through rivers – they will not wash you away. Though you walk right through
3 the fire, you will not be burned, and no flame will take hold of you, for I am the Lord your God,
the Holy One of Israel, your rescuer. I have paid Egypt as your ransom, Kush and Seva in your place.
4 Because you are valued in My eyes, you are honored. I love you enough to give up other men for you,
5 whole nations in your place. Do not fear, for I am with you. I will bring your children from the east, will
6 gather you back from the west. To the north I will say, "Give over"; to the south, "Imprison no more."
7 Bring My sons from far away, My daughters back from the ends of the earth, all the people I called by
8 My name, created for My glory; I formed them, I made them. He brought out a people – blind though

הפטרת בראשית

On ערב ראש חודש מרחשון *some read the* הפטרה *on page 1637.*

ישעיה

מב א ב הֵן עַבְדִּי אֶתְמָךְ־בּוֹ בְּחִירִי רָצְתָה נַפְשִׁי נָתַתִּי רוּחִי עָלָיו מִשְׁפָּט לַגּוֹיִם יוֹצִיא: לֹא יִצְעַק וְלֹא יִשָּׂא וְלֹא־
ג ד יַשְׁמִיעַ בַּחוּץ קוֹלוֹ: קָנֶה רָצוּץ לֹא יִשְׁבּוֹר וּפִשְׁתָּה כֵהָה לֹא יְכַבֶּנָּה לֶאֱמֶת יוֹצִיא מִשְׁפָּט: לֹא יִכְהֶה וְלֹא
ה יָרוּץ עַד־יָשִׂים בָּאָרֶץ מִשְׁפָּט וּלְתוֹרָתוֹ אִיִּים יְיַחֵלוּ: * כֹּה־אָמַר הָאֵל ׀ יהוה בּוֹרֵא הַשָּׁמַיִם
ו וְנוֹטֵיהֶם רֹקַע הָאָרֶץ וְצֶאֱצָאֶיהָ נֹתֵן נְשָׁמָה לָעָם עָלֶיהָ וְרוּחַ לַהֹלְכִים בָּהּ: אֲנִי יְהוָה קְרָאתִיךָ בְצֶדֶק
ז וְאַחְזֵק בְּיָדֶךָ וְאֶצָּרְךָ וְאֶתֶּנְךָ לִבְרִית עָם לְאוֹר גּוֹיִם: לִפְקֹחַ עֵינַיִם עִוְרוֹת לְהוֹצִיא מִמַּסְגֵּר אַסִּיר מִבֵּית
ח ט כֶּלֶא יֹשְׁבֵי חֹשֶׁךְ: אֲנִי יְהוָה הוּא שְׁמִי וּכְבוֹדִי לְאַחֵר לֹא־אֶתֵּן וּתְהִלָּתִי לַפְּסִילִים: הָרִאשֹׁנוֹת הִנֵּה־בָאוּ
י וַחֲדָשׁוֹת אֲנִי מַגִּיד בְּטֶרֶם תִּצְמַחְנָה אַשְׁמִיעַ אֶתְכֶם: שִׁירוּ לַיהוָה שִׁיר חָדָשׁ תְּהִלָּתוֹ מִקְצֵה
יא הָאָרֶץ יוֹרְדֵי הַיָּם וּמְלֹאוֹ אִיִּים וְיֹשְׁבֵיהֶם: יִשְׂאוּ מִדְבָּר וְעָרָיו חֲצֵרִים תֵּשֵׁב קֵדָר יָרֹנּוּ יֹשְׁבֵי סֶלַע מֵרֹאשׁ
יב יג הָרִים יִצְוָחוּ: יָשִׂימוּ לַיהוָה כָּבוֹד וּתְהִלָּתוֹ בָּאִיִּים יַגִּידוּ: יְהוָה כַּגִּבּוֹר יֵצֵא כְּאִישׁ מִלְחָמוֹת יָעִיר קִנְאָה
יד יָרִיעַ אַף־יַצְרִיחַ עַל־אֹיְבָיו יִתְגַּבָּר: הֶחֱשֵׁיתִי מֵעוֹלָם אַחֲרִישׁ אֶתְאַפָּק כַּיּוֹלֵדָה אֶפְעֶה אֶשֹּׁם
טו טז וְאֶשְׁאַף יָחַד: אַחֲרִיב הָרִים וּגְבָעוֹת וְכָל־עֶשְׂבָּם אוֹבִישׁ וְשַׂמְתִּי נְהָרוֹת לָאִיִּים וַאֲגַמִּים אוֹבִישׁ: וְהוֹלַכְתִּי
עִוְרִים בְּדֶרֶךְ לֹא יָדָעוּ בִּנְתִיבוֹת לֹא־יָדְעוּ אַדְרִיכֵם אָשִׂים מַחְשָׁךְ לִפְנֵיהֶם לָאוֹר וּמַעֲקַשִּׁים לְמִישׁוֹר
יז אֵלֶּה הַדְּבָרִים עֲשִׂיתִם וְלֹא עֲזַבְתִּים: * נָסֹגוּ אָחוֹר יֵבֹשׁוּ בֹשֶׁת הַבֹּטְחִים בַּפָּסֶל הָאֹמְרִים לְמַסֵּכָה אַתֶּם
יח יט אֱלֹהֵינוּ: הַחֵרְשִׁים שְׁמָעוּ וְהַעִוְרִים הַבִּיטוּ לִרְאוֹת: מִי עִוֵּר כִּי אִם־עַבְדִּי וְחֵרֵשׁ כְּמַלְאָכִי
כ כא אֶשְׁלָח מִי עִוֵּר כִּמְשֻׁלָּם וְעִוֵּר כְּעֶבֶד יְהוָה: רָאִית רַבּוֹת וְלֹא תִשְׁמֹר פָּקוֹחַ אָזְנַיִם וְלֹא יִשְׁמָע: יְהוָה חָפֵץ
כב לְמַעַן צִדְקוֹ יַגְדִּיל תּוֹרָה וְיַאְדִּיר: * וְהוּא עַם־בָּזוּז וְשָׁסוּי הָפֵחַ בַּחוּרִים כֻּלָּם וּבְבָתֵּי כְלָאִים הָחְבָּאוּ הָיוּ
כג כד לָבַז וְאֵין מַצִּיל מְשִׁסָּה וְאֵין־אֹמֵר הָשַׁב: מִי בָכֶם יַאֲזִין זֹאת יַקְשִׁב וְיִשְׁמַע לְאָחוֹר: מִי־נָתַן לִמְשׁוֹסָה
כה יַעֲקֹב וְיִשְׂרָאֵל לְבֹזְזִים הֲלוֹא יְהוָה זוּ חָטָאנוּ לוֹ וְלֹא־אָבוּ בִדְרָכָיו הָלוֹךְ וְלֹא שָׁמְעוּ בְּתוֹרָתוֹ: וַיִּשְׁפֹּךְ עָלָיו
מג א חֵמָה אַפּוֹ וֶעֱזוּז מִלְחָמָה וַתְּלַהֲטֵהוּ מִסָּבִיב וְלֹא יָדָע וַתִּבְעַר־בּוֹ וְלֹא־יָשִׂים עַל־לֵב: וְעַתָּה
ב כֹּה־אָמַר יְהוָה בֹּרַאֲךָ יַעֲקֹב וְיֹצֶרְךָ יִשְׂרָאֵל אַל־תִּירָא כִּי גְאַלְתִּיךָ קָרָאתִי בְשִׁמְךָ לִי־אָתָּה: כִּי־תַעֲבֹר
ג בַּמַּיִם אִתְּךָ־אָנִי וּבַנְּהָרוֹת לֹא יִשְׁטְפוּךָ כִּי־תֵלֵךְ בְּמוֹ־אֵשׁ לֹא תִכָּוֶה וְלֶהָבָה לֹא תִבְעַר־בָּךְ: כִּי אֲנִי יְהוָה
ד אֱלֹהֶיךָ קְדוֹשׁ יִשְׂרָאֵל מוֹשִׁיעֶךָ נָתַתִּי כָפְרְךָ מִצְרַיִם כּוּשׁ וּסְבָא תַּחְתֶּיךָ: מֵאֲשֶׁר יָקַרְתָּ בְעֵינַי נִכְבַּדְתָּ
ה וַאֲנִי אֲהַבְתִּיךָ וְאֶתֵּן אָדָם תַּחְתֶּיךָ וּלְאֻמִּים תַּחַת נַפְשֶׁךָ: אַל־תִּירָא כִּי אִתְּךָ־אָנִי מִמִּזְרָח אָבִיא זַרְעֶךָ
ו ז וּמִמַּעֲרָב אֲקַבְּצֶךָּ: אֹמַר לַצָּפוֹן תֵּנִי וּלְתֵימָן אַל־תִּכְלָאִי הָבִיאִי בָנַי מֵרָחוֹק וּבְנוֹתַי מִקְצֵה הָאָרֶץ: כֹּל
ח הַנִּקְרָא בִשְׁמִי וְלִכְבוֹדִי בְּרָאתִיו יְצַרְתִּיו אַף־עֲשִׂיתִיו: הוֹצִיא עַם־עִוֵּר וְעֵינַיִם יֵשׁ וְחֵרְשִׁים וְאָזְנַיִם לָמוֹ:

Marginal notes: *Yemenites begin here* (42:2) · *Ashkenazim and Sepharadim begin here* (42:5) · *Yemenites end here* (42:17) · רָאוֹת (42:20) · *Sepharadim and Chabad end here* (42:21) · לִמְשִׁסָּה (42:24)

BERESHIT

During his life, the prophet Yeshayahu had to confront idolatrous worldviews that threatened faith in God, and fight for the place of the nation of Israel in the world. In this prophecy, he contrasts three opposed pairs: (1) God, the creator and ruler of the universe, versus the worthless idols of the nations; (2) Israel, God's eternal people, versus the wicked nations who will be punished; and (3) redemption and a perfected world versus the situation of sin and evil that he saw would bring ruin upon Israel. The theme common to these three contrasts is the emphasis on what is true and enduring as opposed to what is worthless and passing. This insight – that what endures will triumph over what is transient – is the basis for the path the prophet traces from the creation of the world to his vision of the end of days.

9 they have eyes, deaf though they have ears. Were all the nations to gather, the peoples to come into session, who of them could tell of this? Who could speak of this before? Let them bring their witnesses to
10 vindicate them, so that hearers may say, "This is truth." No – you are My witnesses, so says the LORD,
My servants whom I chose, so that you should know, and trust in Me and understand that I am He;
before Me, no god was made, and after Me – no other.

HAFTARAT NOAḤ

On Rosh Ḥodesh Marḥeshvan, read the maftir from Numbers 28:9–15, and the haftara on page 1634.

ISAIAH

54 1 Barren woman, never a mother, rejoice; break out in joyful song though you have not given birth, for the
2 children of the forsaken woman will outnumber those of the wife, so says the LORD. Broaden the site of
your tent; stretch out your canvas home; do not hold back; lengthen your tent cords, and strengthen its
3 pegs: you shall overflow rightward and left, your children possessing nations, and filling forsaken towns
4 with life. Do not fear – you will not be shamed; fear not, for none can disgrace you. You will forget your
5 youthful abjection; the debasement of your widowhood you will call no more to mind, for your husband, He who made you – the LORD of Hosts is His name, and your redeemer, Israel's Holy One – will
6 be named God of all the world, for as a woman abandoned, of sorrowful spirit, the LORD has called to
7 you: Can the young bride ever be rejected? says your God; for one small moment I left you; with infinite
8 care shall I gather you back; in the flash of My fury I hid My face from you for just a moment, and in
9 everlasting love will I care for you now. So speaks the LORD, your redeemer. For these are the
waters of Noaḥ to Me, and I swore that the waters of Noaḥ would never sweep again over the earth. And
10 so did I swear no more to be furious with you, no more to rebuke you. For mountains may move, hills
may crumble away; but My love for you will not be moved, nor My pact of peace crumble. So speaks the
11 LORD, who cares for you. * Oppressed and storm swept, never comforted; behold: I am paving
12 your ground with garnet, lapis lazuli your foundations. I am fitting your windows with rubies, your gates
13 with glowing granite, marking your borders with stones men covet. All your children will be students
14 of the LORD, and great will be your children's peace. On righteousness will you be founded; stay far
15 from oppression; you will not fear, and terror will never come near you. No strife can arise without My
16 assent; who among you fears one who could come upon you? For I create the craftsman who blows the
17 charcoal fire and brings forth the tools of his trade; I create also the destroyer to do harm. No weapon
made to harm you can prevail; any tongue that calls you into judgment, you will prove its fault. This is
55 1 the birthright of the LORD's servants, for their innocence is Mine; so says the LORD. You who
are thirsty, all, come to water; you who have no silver, come, take food and eat; come and take food
2 without silver, wine and milk without cost, for why should you weigh out your silver for no bread, your
labor bringing you no fullness? Listen – listen to Me: let goodness nourish you, and let your souls de-
3 light in plenty. Turn your ear to Me and come; listen, that your souls may live; let Me forge an everlasting
4 covenant with you, like David's faithful promises,* for I make him a witness to nations, a leader, a ruler
5 of nations; for you shall call out, call, to a people you know not, and a people who know you not will
come running out to you for the sake of the LORD your God, the Holy One of Israel, your glory.

Sepharadim and Chabad end here

Yemenites end here

---

number of them were banished from it and a sizable portion of the territory laid waste. These words of encouragement and advice were appropriate for their time, and they remain trenchant today. Jews throughout the exile have taken heart reading this *haftara* every year.

ט כָּל־הַגּוֹיִם נִקְבְּצוּ יַחְדָּו וְיֵאָסְפוּ לְאֻמִּים מִי בָהֶם יַגִּיד זֹאת וְרִאשֹׁנוֹת יַשְׁמִיעֻנוּ יִתְּנוּ עֵדֵיהֶם וְיִצְדָּקוּ
י וְיִשְׁמְעוּ וְיֹאמְרוּ אֱמֶת: אַתֶּם עֵדַי נְאֻם־יְהוָה וְעַבְדִּי אֲשֶׁר בָּחָרְתִּי לְמַעַן תֵּדְעוּ וְתַאֲמִינוּ לִי וְתָבִינוּ
כִּי־אֲנִי הוּא לְפָנַי לֹא־נוֹצַר אֵל וְאַחֲרַי לֹא יִהְיֶה:

הפטרת נח

On ראש חודש מרחשון *read the* מפטיר *from* במדבר כח, ט–טו*, and the* הפטרה *on page 1635.*

נד א ב רָנִּי עֲקָרָה לֹא יָלָדָה פִּצְחִי רִנָּה וְצַהֲלִי לֹא־חָלָה כִּי־רַבִּים בְּנֵי־שׁוֹמֵמָה מִבְּנֵי בְעוּלָה אָמַר יְהוָה: הַרְחִיבִי ׀ ישעיה
ג מְקוֹם אָהֳלֵךְ וִירִיעוֹת מִשְׁכְּנוֹתַיִךְ יַטּוּ אַל־תַּחְשֹׂכִי הַאֲרִיכִי מֵיתָרַיִךְ וִיתֵדֹתַיִךְ חַזֵּקִי: כִּי־יָמִין וּשְׂמֹאול
ד תִּפְרֹצִי וְזַרְעֵךְ גּוֹיִם יִירָשׁ וְעָרִים נְשַׁמּוֹת יוֹשִׁיבוּ: אַל־תִּירְאִי כִּי־לֹא תֵבוֹשִׁי וְאַל־תִּכָּלְמִי כִּי לֹא תַחְפִּירִי
ה כִּי בֹשֶׁת עֲלוּמַיִךְ תִּשְׁכָּחִי וְחֶרְפַּת אַלְמְנוּתַיִךְ לֹא תִזְכְּרִי־עוֹד: כִּי בֹעֲלַיִךְ עֹשַׂיִךְ יְהוָה צְבָאוֹת שְׁמוֹ וְגֹאֲלֵךְ
ו קְדוֹשׁ יִשְׂרָאֵל אֱלֹהֵי כָל־הָאָרֶץ יִקָּרֵא: כִּי־כְאִשָּׁה עֲזוּבָה וַעֲצוּבַת רוּחַ קְרָאָךְ יְהוָה וְאֵשֶׁת נְעוּרִים כִּי
ז ח תִמָּאֵס אָמַר אֱלֹהָיִךְ: בְּרֶגַע קָטֹן עֲזַבְתִּיךְ וּבְרַחֲמִים גְּדֹלִים אֲקַבְּצֵךְ: בְּשֶׁצֶף קֶצֶף הִסְתַּרְתִּי פָנַי רֶגַע
ט מִמֵּךְ וּבְחֶסֶד עוֹלָם רִחַמְתִּיךְ אָמַר גֹּאֲלֵךְ יְהוָה: כִּי־מֵי נֹחַ זֹאת לִי אֲשֶׁר נִשְׁבַּעְתִּי מֵעֲבֹר מֵי־נֹחַ
י עוֹד עַל־הָאָרֶץ כֵּן נִשְׁבַּעְתִּי מִקְּצֹף עָלַיִךְ וּמִגְּעָר־בָּךְ: כִּי הֶהָרִים יָמוּשׁוּ וְהַגְּבָעוֹת תְּמוּטֶינָה וְחַסְדִּי מֵאִתֵּךְ
יא לֹא־יָמוּשׁ וּבְרִית שְׁלוֹמִי לֹא תָמוּט אָמַר מְרַחֲמֵךְ יְהוָה:* עֲנִיָּה סֹעֲרָה לֹא נֻחָמָה הִנֵּה אָנֹכִי *Sepharadim and Chabad end here*
יב מַרְבִּיץ בַּפּוּךְ אֲבָנַיִךְ וִיסַדְתִּיךְ בַּסַּפִּירִים: וְשַׂמְתִּי כַּדְכֹד שִׁמְשֹׁתַיִךְ וּשְׁעָרַיִךְ לְאַבְנֵי אֶקְדָּח וְכָל־גְּבוּלֵךְ
יג יד לְאַבְנֵי־חֵפֶץ: וְכָל־בָּנַיִךְ לִמּוּדֵי יְהוָה וְרַב שְׁלוֹם בָּנָיִךְ: בִּצְדָקָה תִּכּוֹנָנִי רַחֲקִי מֵעֹשֶׁק כִּי־לֹא תִירָאִי וּמִמְּחִתָּה
טו טז כִּי לֹא־תִקְרַב אֵלָיִךְ: הֵן גּוֹר יָגוּר אֶפֶס מֵאוֹתִי מִי־גָר אִתָּךְ עָלַיִךְ יִפּוֹל: הן אָנֹכִי בָּרָאתִי חָרָשׁ נֹפֵחַ בְּאֵשׁ פֶּחָם הִנֵּה
יז וּמוֹצִיא כְלִי לְמַעֲשֵׂהוּ וְאָנֹכִי בָּרָאתִי מַשְׁחִית לְחַבֵּל: כָּל־כְּלִי יוּצַר עָלַיִךְ לֹא יִצְלָח וְכָל־לָשׁוֹן תָּקוּם־אִתָּךְ
נה א לַמִּשְׁפָּט תַּרְשִׁיעִי זֹאת נַחֲלַת עַבְדֵי יְהוָה וְצִדְקָתָם מֵאִתִּי נְאֻם־יְהוָה: הוֹי כָּל־צָמֵא לְכוּ לַמַּיִם
ב וַאֲשֶׁר אֵין־לוֹ כָּסֶף לְכוּ שִׁבְרוּ וֶאֱכֹלוּ וּלְכוּ שִׁבְרוּ בְּלוֹא־כֶסֶף וּבְלוֹא מְחִיר יַיִן וְחָלָב: לָמָּה תִשְׁקְלוּ־כֶסֶף
ג בְּלוֹא־לֶחֶם וִיגִיעֲכֶם בְּלוֹא לְשָׂבְעָה שִׁמְעוּ שָׁמוֹעַ אֵלַי וְאִכְלוּ־טוֹב וְתִתְעַנַּג בַּדֶּשֶׁן נַפְשְׁכֶם: הַטּוּ אָזְנְכֶם וּלְכוּ
ד אֵלַי שִׁמְעוּ וּתְחִי נַפְשְׁכֶם וְאֶכְרְתָה לָכֶם בְּרִית עוֹלָם חַסְדֵי דָוִד הַנֶּאֱמָנִים:* הֵן עֵד לְאוּמִּים נְתַתִּיו *Yemenites end here*
ה נָגִיד וּמְצַוֵּה לְאֻמִּים: הֵן גּוֹי לֹא־תֵדַע תִּקְרָא וְגוֹי לֹא־יְדָעוּךָ אֵלֶיךָ יָרוּצוּ לְמַעַן יְהוָה אֱלֹהֶיךָ וְלִקְדוֹשׁ
יִשְׂרָאֵל כִּי פֵאֲרָךְ:

NOAḤ

The flood, which threw the world back into a state of chaos, came as a punishment for wickedness and oppression. The prophet draws a parallel between it and the destruction and exile of the Israelite kingdoms centuries later, which also came as a result of disobedience to God. He insists that crisis and suffering are not the natural way of things, even if they can seem never-ending. The covenant with God must be founded on the basis of justice and mercy – if we do this, we are promised blessing and light that will banish these difficult times. Then, in place of helplessness and sadness, we will find great mercy and eternal charity, for one good act leads to another. These words of the prophet Yeshayahu were spoken against the background of the exile of the kingdom of Israel, which occurred during his lifetime. For the first time since the people of Israel had arrived in the land, a great

▶

Haftarat Lekh Lekha

ISAIAH
Yemenites begin here

40 25 26 Whom can you compare Me to – so speaks the Holy One – and find them equal? Raise your eyes skyward
27 and see: Who created all these? Who summons their legions by number and calls each man by name?
27 In His great might, His adamantine strength, not one of them is lost. *Why do you say, Yaakov;
28 Israel, why declare, "My way is hidden from the LORD; my God overlooks my claim"? Do you not know
this; have you not heard? The LORD is God eternal, Creator of all horizons; He does not weary, does not
29 tire; no one can plumb His understanding. He gives the weary strength, the helpless, power: more and
30 31 more. Youths will tire, grow weary; young men will falter and fall, but those who wait for the LORD, their
strength will be renewed; they will rise on their wings like eagles, will run and never grow weary, will
41 1 walk on and never grow tired. Hush before Me, coastlands and nations; renew your strength,
2 and then come forward, speak, draw close; let us come into judgment. Who roused the one from the east
and called victory to his feet? Who herded nations before him, laid their kings low, and made his swords
3 numerous as dust, his bowshots like chaff in the wind? He pursued them and came through in peace on
4 paths that his feet never walked. Who was it who acted and did this, who called forth generations long
5 before? I, the LORD, am the first, and I shall be, I, with the last who will be. Coastlands witness this and
6 fear, earth's horizons witness, tremble, draw near, come. *Each man helps his fellow and tells his brother, "Be*
strong." "Strong," says the wright to the goldsmith, the hammerman to him who beats. He says of the glue, "This
7 8 *is good," and firms it up with nails, never to fall.* And you, Israel, My servant, Yaakov whom I chose,
9 children of Avraham who loved Me, whom I lifted and brought from the ends of the earth, calling you
forth from its furthest corners, telling you: You are My servant; You have I chosen, and I will not reject
10 you; do not fear, for I am with you; do not be afraid: I am your God; I strengthen you and help you, up-
11 hold you with My right hand of righteousness. All who rage against you will be shamed, debased; become
12 like nothing, lost, all those who fight you. Look for them then – you will not find them – the men with
13 whom you are wrestling, adversaries in war, like nothing, like no more. For I am the LORD your God,
14 holding your right hand, telling you: Do not fear, for I am here: I help you. Yaakov: worm, men
15 of Israel, do not fear; I will help you, so speaks the LORD, the Holy One of Israel, your redeemer. You shall
see: I have made you a slotted threshing board, new and razor edged; you will thresh mountains, turn
16 them to powder, and hills into chaff. As you winnow, the wind will lift them, and the storm will spread
17 them far; you will rejoice in the LORD and will, through the Holy One of Israel, be praised. The
oppressed, impoverished, beg for water – there is none; their tongues are seared with thirst. I am the
LORD; I will answer them; Israel's God, I will not leave them.

Ashkenazim and Sephardim begin here (*)

Ashkenazim and Sephardim end here

Haftarat Vayera

II KINGS

4 1 A woman – the wife of one of the brotherhood of the prophets – cried out to Elisha, "Your servant,
my husband, is dead! You know that your servant always feared the LORD. Now a creditor has come

---

between God and "the children of Avraham who loved Me," and it gives us strength to overcome our doubts and continue in our battle against the darkness of the world's idols with confidence. This prophecy was not directed at a specific time or context, and it is relevant throughout the long night of our people's struggle against foreign powers and their political and cultural influence.

VAYERA

In this *haftara*, we find two instances of a mother's concern

הפטרת לך לך

ישעיה

Yemenites begin here

מ כה כו וְאֶל־מִי תְדַמְּיוּנִי וְאֶשְׁוֶה יֹאמַר קָדוֹשׁ: שְׂאוּ־מָרוֹם עֵינֵיכֶם וּרְאוּ מִי־בָרָא אֵלֶּה הַמּוֹצִיא בְמִסְפָּר צְבָאָם

Ashkenazim and Sepharadim begin here

כז לְכֻלָּם בְּשֵׁם יִקְרָא מֵרֹב אוֹנִים וְאַמִּיץ כֹּחַ אִישׁ לֹא נֶעְדָּר: *לָמָּה תֹאמַר יַעֲקֹב וּתְדַבֵּר יִשְׂרָאֵל
כח נִסְתְּרָה דַרְכִּי מֵיהוה וּמֵאֱלֹהַי מִשְׁפָּטִי יַעֲבוֹר: הֲלוֹא יָדַעְתָּ אִם־לֹא שָׁמַעְתָּ אֱלֹהֵי עוֹלָם ׀ יהוה בּוֹרֵא
כט ל קְצוֹת הָאָרֶץ לֹא יִיעַף וְלֹא יִיגָע אֵין חֵקֶר לִתְבוּנָתוֹ: נֹתֵן לַיָּעֵף כֹּחַ וּלְאֵין אוֹנִים עָצְמָה יַרְבֶּה: וְיִעֲפוּ
לא נְעָרִים וְיִגָעוּ וּבַחוּרִים כָּשׁוֹל יִכָּשֵׁלוּ: וְקוֹיֵ יהוה יַחֲלִיפוּ כֹחַ יַעֲלוּ אֵבֶר כַּנְּשָׁרִים יָרוּצוּ וְלֹא יִיגָעוּ יֵלְכוּ וְלֹא
מא א ב יִיעָפוּ: הַחֲרִישׁוּ אֵלַי אִיִּים וּלְאֻמִּים יַחֲלִיפוּ כֹחַ יִגְּשׁוּ אָז יְדַבֵּרוּ יַחְדָּו לַמִּשְׁפָּט נִקְרָבָה: מִי
ג הֵעִיר מִמִּזְרָח צֶדֶק יִקְרָאֵהוּ לְרַגְלוֹ יִתֵּן לְפָנָיו גּוֹיִם וּמְלָכִים יַרְדְּ יִתֵּן כֶּעָפָר חַרְבּוֹ כְּקַשׁ נִדָּף קַשְׁתּוֹ: יִרְדְּפֵם
ד יַעֲבוֹר שָׁלוֹם אֹרַח בְּרַגְלָיו לֹא יָבוֹא: מִי־פָעַל וְעָשָׂה קֹרֵא הַדֹּרוֹת מֵרֹאשׁ אֲנִי יהוה רִאשׁוֹן וְאֶת־אַחֲרֹנִים
ה ו אֲנִי־הוּא: רָאוּ אִיִּים וְיִירָאוּ קְצוֹת הָאָרֶץ יֶחֱרָדוּ קָרְבוּ וַיֶּאֱתָיוּן: אִישׁ אֶת־רֵעֵהוּ יַעְזֹרוּ וּלְאָחִיו יֹאמַר
ז חֲזָק: וַיְחַזֵּק חָרָשׁ אֶת־צֹרֵף מַחֲלִיק פַּטִּישׁ אֶת־הוֹלֶם פָּעַם אֹמֵר לַדֶּבֶק טוֹב הוּא וַיְחַזְּקֵהוּ בְמַסְמְרִים
ח ט לֹא יִמּוֹט: וְאַתָּה יִשְׂרָאֵל עַבְדִּי יַעֲקֹב אֲשֶׁר בְּחַרְתִּיךָ זֶרַע אַבְרָהָם אֹהֲבִי: אֲשֶׁר הֶחֱזַקְתִּיךָ
י מִקְצוֹת הָאָרֶץ וּמֵאֲצִילֶיהָ קְרָאתִיךָ וָאֹמַר לְךָ עַבְדִּי־אַתָּה בְּחַרְתִּיךָ וְלֹא מְאַסְתִּיךָ: אַל־תִּירָא כִּי עִמְּךָ־
יא אָנִי אַל־תִּשְׁתָּע כִּי־אֲנִי אֱלֹהֶיךָ אִמַּצְתִּיךָ אַף־עֲזַרְתִּיךָ אַף־תְּמַכְתִּיךָ בִּימִין צִדְקִי: הֵן יֵבֹשׁוּ וְיִכָּלְמוּ כֹּל
יב הַנֶּחֱרִים בָּךְ יִהְיוּ כְאַיִן וְיֹאבְדוּ אַנְשֵׁי רִיבֶךָ: תְּבַקְשֵׁם וְלֹא תִמְצָאֵם אַנְשֵׁי מַצֻּתֶךָ יִהְיוּ כְאַיִן וּכְאֶפֶס אַנְשֵׁי
יג יד מִלְחַמְתֶּךָ: כִּי אֲנִי יהוה אֱלֹהֶיךָ מַחֲזִיק יְמִינֶךָ הָאֹמֵר לְךָ אַל־תִּירָא אֲנִי עֲזַרְתִּיךָ: אַל־
טו תִּירְאִי תּוֹלַעַת יַעֲקֹב מְתֵי יִשְׂרָאֵל אֲנִי עֲזַרְתִּיךְ נְאֻם־יהוה וְגֹאֲלֵךְ קְדוֹשׁ יִשְׂרָאֵל: הִנֵּה שַׂמְתִּיךְ לְמוֹרַג
טז חָרוּץ חָדָשׁ בַּעַל פִּיפִיּוֹת תָּדוּשׁ הָרִים וְתָדֹק וּגְבָעוֹת כַּמֹּץ תָּשִׂים: תִּזְרֵם וְרוּחַ תִּשָּׂאֵם וּסְעָרָה תָּפִיץ
יז אֹתָם וְאַתָּה תָּגִיל בַּיהוה בִּקְדוֹשׁ יִשְׂרָאֵל תִּתְהַלָּל: הָעֲנִיִּים וְהָאֶבְיוֹנִים מְבַקְשִׁים מַיִם

Ashkenazim and Sepharadim end here

וָאַיִן לְשׁוֹנָם בַּצָּמָא נָשָׁתָּה אֲנִי יהוה אֶעֱנֵם אֱלֹהֵי יִשְׂרָאֵל לֹא אֶעֶזְבֵם:

הפטרת וירא

מלכים ב׳

ד א וְאִשָּׁה אַחַת מִנְּשֵׁי בְנֵי־הַנְּבִיאִים צָעֲקָה אֶל־אֱלִישָׁע לֵאמֹר עַבְדְּךָ אִישִׁי מֵת וְאַתָּה יָדַעְתָּ כִּי עַבְדְּךָ
ב הָיָה יָרֵא אֶת־יהוה וְהַנֹּשֶׁה בָּא לָקַחַת אֶת־שְׁנֵי יְלָדַי לוֹ לַעֲבָדִים: וַיֹּאמֶר אֵלֶיהָ אֱלִישָׁע מָה אֶעֱשֶׂה־לָּךְ

LEKH LEKHA

God's choice of Avraham – the first iconoclast – and his descendants put the Jewish people at the forefront of the war against the moral distortions that are the hallmark of idolatry. This bitter struggle throughout human history has often left the "worm of Yaakov" weak and pained, anxious to understand why God appears absent from our world. Against this backdrop, the strong words of consolation from the prophet Yeshayahu repeat over and over the refrain "do not fear." This assurance creates a special sense of closeness

▶

2 to take my two children away to be his slaves." "What can I do for you?" said Elisha. "Tell me, what do
3 you have in the house?" "Your servant has nothing at all at home," she said, "except for a jar of oil." "Go
out and borrow vessels from all your neighbors," he said to her, "empty vessels – as many as you can.
4 When you come back in, close the door behind you and your sons. Then pour away into all those ves-
5 sels, setting them aside when they are full." And so she left him. When she closed the door behind her
6 and her sons, they kept bringing vessels to her while she kept pouring. When the vessels were full, she
said to her son, "Bring me another vessel," and he said to her, "There are no more vessels" – and the oil
7 stopped flowing. She came and told the man of God, and he said, "Go, sell the oil and pay off your debt,
8 and you and your sons can live on the rest." One day, Elisha was passing through Shunem, and
a wealthy woman there urged him to have something to eat. So whenever he passed through, he would
9 stop there for some food. She said to her husband, "Look, I am sure that the man who passes through
10 here regularly is a holy man of God. Let us make him a small enclosed upper chamber and provide him
11 with a bed, table, chair, and lamp there, so that whenever he comes to us, he can turn in there." One
12 day, he came by; he turned in to the upper chamber and lay down there. He said to Geḥazi, his servant,
13 "Call the Shunamite woman." He called her, and she stood before him. He said to him, "Please say to
her, 'You have shown us so much concern. What can we do for you? Shall I speak to the king on your
14 behalf, or to the army commander?'" "I live among my own people," she said. "Then what can be done
15 for her?" he said. "Well, she is childless," said Geḥazi, "and her husband is old." "Call her," he said, and
16 he called her, and she stood in the entrance. "At this time next year," he said, "you will be embracing a
17 son." "No, my lord, man of God," she said. "Do not delude your servant." But the woman did conceive,
18 and she bore a son at that time during the following year, just as Elisha had promised her. The child
19 grew up. One day, he went out to his father, who was with the reapers. "My head! My head!" he said
20 to his father, who said to the servant, "Carry him to his mother." He carried him over and brought him
21 to his mother; he sat on her lap until noon, and then he died. She went up and laid him on the man of
22 God's bed, closed the door behind him, and went out. Then she called to her husband. "Send me one of
the servants and one of the donkeys at once," she said. "I must rush over to the man of God and come
23 right back." "Why are you going to him today?" he said. "It is not the New Moon, nor the Sabbath." "All
24 is well," she said.* She saddled the donkey and said to her servant, "Drive! Be off! Do not stop riding *Sepharadim end here*
25 on my account unless I tell you." She set out and reached the man of God at Mount Carmel. When
the man of God saw her in the distance, he said to Geḥazi, his servant, "Look, there is that Shunamite
26 woman. Run to meet her straightaway and say to her, 'Are you well? Is your husband well? Is your
27 child well?'" "All is well," she said. But she came up to the man of God at the mountain and grasped his
feet. Geḥazi came forward to push her away, but the man of God said, "Leave her be, for she is bitter
28 of spirit, and the Lord has hidden this from me and did not tell me." "Did I ask my lord for a son?"
29 she said. "Did I not say, 'Do not lead me on?'" "Hitch up your tunic," Elisha said to Geḥazi. "Take my
staff in your hand, and set out. If you meet anyone, do not greet them, and if anyone greets you, do not
30 answer them. Place my staff on the boy's face." "As the Lord lives, and by your own life," said the boy's
31 mother, "I will not leave you." So he followed straight behind her. Geḥazi went on ahead of them and
placed the staff on the boy's face, but there was no sound and no response. He went back to meet him
32 and told him, "The boy did not wake." Elisha entered the house, and there was the boy laid out on his
33 34 bed – dead. He entered and closed the door behind the two of them, and he prayed to the Lord. Then

---

the same time, he promoted the idea that the connection between God and His people is strong and innate, like the experience of motherhood and a mother's connection to her children.

ג הַגִּידִי לִי מַה־יֶּשׁ־לָכִי בַּבָּיִת וַתֹּאמֶר אֵין לְשִׁפְחָתְךָ כֹל בַּבַּיִת כִּי אִם־אָסוּךְ שָׁמֶן׃ וַיֹּאמֶר לְכִי שַׁאֲלִי־לכי   לָךְ
ד כֵּלִים מִן־הַחוּץ מֵאֵת כָּל־שכניכי כֵּלִים רֵקִים אַל־תַּמְעִיטִי׃ וּבָאת וְסָגַרְתְּ הַדֶּלֶת בַּעֲדֵךְ וּבְעַד־בָּנַיִךְ   שְׁכֵנָיִךְ
ה וְיָצַקְתְּ עַל כָּל־הַכֵּלִים הָאֵלֶּה וְהַמָּלֵא תַּסִּיעִי׃ וַתֵּלֶךְ מֵאִתּוֹ וַתִּסְגֹּר הַדֶּלֶת בַּעֲדָהּ וּבְעַד בָּנֶיהָ הֵם מַגִּשִׁים
ו אֵלֶיהָ וְהִיא מיצקת׃ וַיְהִי ׀ כִּמְלֹאת הַכֵּלִים וַתֹּאמֶר אֶל־בְּנָהּ הַגִּישָׁה אֵלַי עוֹד כֶּלִי וַיֹּאמֶר אֵלֶיהָ אֵין   מוּצֶקֶת
ז עוֹד כֶּלִי וַיַּעֲמֹד הַשָּׁמֶן׃ וַתָּבֹא וַתַּגֵּד לְאִישׁ הָאֱלֹהִים וַיֹּאמֶר לְכִי מִכְרִי אֶת־הַשֶּׁמֶן וְשַׁלְּמִי אֶת־נשיכי   נִשְׁיֵךְ
ח ואת בניכי תִּחְיִי בַּנּוֹתָר׃ וַיְהִי הַיּוֹם וַיַּעֲבֹר אֱלִישָׁע אֶל־שׁוּנֵם וְשָׁם אִשָּׁה גְדוֹלָה וַתַּחֲזֶק־בּוֹ   וּבָנַיִךְ
ט לֶאֱכָל־לָחֶם וַיְהִי מִדֵּי עָבְרוֹ יָסֻר שָׁמָּה לֶאֱכָל־לָחֶם׃ וַתֹּאמֶר אֶל־אִישָׁהּ הִנֵּה־נָא יָדַעְתִּי כִּי אִישׁ אֱלֹהִים
י קָדוֹשׁ הוּא עֹבֵר עָלֵינוּ תָּמִיד׃ נַעֲשֶׂה־נָּא עֲלִיַּת־קִיר קְטַנָּה וְנָשִׂים לוֹ שָׁם מִטָּה וְשֻׁלְחָן וְכִסֵּא וּמְנוֹרָה
יא יב וְהָיָה בְּבֹאוֹ אֵלֵינוּ יָסוּר שָׁמָּה׃ וַיְהִי הַיּוֹם וַיָּבֹא שָׁמָּה וַיָּסַר אֶל־הָעֲלִיָּה וַיִּשְׁכַּב־שָׁמָּה׃ וַיֹּאמֶר אֶל־
יג גֵּיחֲזִי נַעֲרוֹ קְרָא לַשּׁוּנַמִּית הַזֹּאת וַיִּקְרָא־לָהּ וַתַּעֲמֹד לְפָנָיו׃ וַיֹּאמֶר לוֹ אֱמָר־נָא אֵלֶיהָ הִנֵּה חָרַדְתְּ ׀
אֵלֵינוּ אֶת־כָּל־הַחֲרָדָה הַזֹּאת מֶה לַעֲשׂוֹת לָךְ הֲיֵשׁ לְדַבֶּר־לָךְ אֶל־הַמֶּלֶךְ אוֹ אֶל־שַׂר הַצָּבָא וַתֹּאמֶר
יד טו בְּתוֹךְ עַמִּי אָנֹכִי יֹשָׁבֶת׃ וַיֹּאמֶר וּמֶה לַעֲשׂוֹת לָהּ וַיֹּאמֶר גֵּיחֲזִי אֲבָל בֵּן אֵין־לָהּ וְאִישָׁהּ זָקֵן׃ וַיֹּאמֶר
טז קְרָא־לָהּ וַיִּקְרָא־לָהּ וַתַּעֲמֹד בַּפָּתַח׃ וַיֹּאמֶר לַמּוֹעֵד הַזֶּה כָּעֵת חַיָּה אתי חֹבֶקֶת בֵּן וַתֹּאמֶר אַל־אֲדֹנִי   אַתְּ
יז אִישׁ הָאֱלֹהִים אַל־תְּכַזֵּב בְּשִׁפְחָתֶךָ׃ וַתַּהַר הָאִשָּׁה וַתֵּלֶד בֵּן לַמּוֹעֵד הַזֶּה כָּעֵת חַיָּה אֲשֶׁר־דִּבֶּר אֵלֶיהָ
יח יט אֱלִישָׁע׃ וַיִּגְדַּל הַיָּלֶד וַיְהִי הַיּוֹם וַיֵּצֵא אֶל־אָבִיו אֶל־הַקֹּצְרִים׃ וַיֹּאמֶר אֶל־אָבִיו רֹאשִׁי ׀ רֹאשִׁי וַיֹּאמֶר
כ כא אֶל־הַנַּעַר שָׂאֵהוּ אֶל־אִמּוֹ׃ וַיִּשָּׂאֵהוּ וַיְבִיאֵהוּ אֶל־אִמּוֹ וַיֵּשֶׁב עַל־בִּרְכֶּיהָ עַד־הַצָּהֳרַיִם וַיָּמֹת׃ וַתַּעַל
כב וַתַּשְׁכִּבֵהוּ עַל־מִטַּת אִישׁ הָאֱלֹהִים וַתִּסְגֹּר בַּעֲדוֹ וַתֵּצֵא׃ וַתִּקְרָא אֶל־אִישָׁהּ וַתֹּאמֶר שִׁלְחָה נָא לִי
כג אֶחָד מִן־הַנְּעָרִים וְאַחַת הָאֲתֹנוֹת וְאָרוּצָה עַד־אִישׁ הָאֱלֹהִים וְאָשׁוּבָה׃ וַיֹּאמֶר מַדּוּעַ אתי הלכתי אֵלָיו   אַתְּ הֹלֶכֶת
כד הַיּוֹם לֹא־חֹדֶשׁ וְלֹא שַׁבָּת וַתֹּאמֶר שָׁלוֹם׃* וַתַּחֲבֹשׁ הָאָתוֹן וַתֹּאמֶר אֶל־נַעֲרָהּ נְהַג וָלֵךְ אַל־תַּעֲצָר־לִי   *Sepharadim end here*
כה לִרְכֹּב כִּי אִם־אָמַרְתִּי לָךְ׃ וַתֵּלֶךְ וַתָּבוֹא אֶל־אִישׁ הָאֱלֹהִים אֶל־הַר הַכַּרְמֶל וַיְהִי כִּרְאוֹת אִישׁ־הָאֱלֹהִים
כו אֹתָהּ מִנֶּגֶד וַיֹּאמֶר אֶל־גֵּיחֲזִי נַעֲרוֹ הִנֵּה הַשּׁוּנַמִּית הַלָּז׃ עַתָּה רוּץ־נָא לִקְרָאתָהּ וֶאֱמָר־לָהּ הֲשָׁלוֹם
כז לָךְ הֲשָׁלוֹם לְאִישֵׁךְ הֲשָׁלוֹם לַיָּלֶד וַתֹּאמֶר שָׁלוֹם׃ וַתָּבֹא אֶל־אִישׁ הָאֱלֹהִים אֶל־הָהָר וַתַּחֲזֵק בְּרַגְלָיו
וַיִּגַּשׁ גֵּיחֲזִי לְהָדְפָהּ וַיֹּאמֶר אִישׁ הָאֱלֹהִים הַרְפֵּה־לָהּ כִּי־נַפְשָׁהּ מָרָה־לָהּ וַיהוה הֶעְלִים מִמֶּנִּי וְלֹא הִגִּיד
כח כט לִי׃ וַתֹּאמֶר הֲשָׁאַלְתִּי בֵן מֵאֵת אֲדֹנִי הֲלֹא אָמַרְתִּי לֹא תַשְׁלֶה אֹתִי׃ וַיֹּאמֶר לְגֵיחֲזִי חֲגֹר מָתְנֶיךָ וְקַח
מִשְׁעַנְתִּי בְיָדְךָ וָלֵךְ כִּי־תִמְצָא אִישׁ לֹא תְבָרְכֶנּוּ וְכִי־יְבָרֶכְךָ אִישׁ לֹא תַעֲנֶנּוּ וְשַׂמְתָּ מִשְׁעַנְתִּי עַל־פְּנֵי
ל לא הַנָּעַר׃ וַתֹּאמֶר אֵם הַנַּעַר חַי־יהוה וְחֵי־נַפְשְׁךָ אִם־אֶעֶזְבֶךָּ וַיָּקָם וַיֵּלֶךְ אַחֲרֶיהָ׃ וְגֵחֲזִי עָבַר לִפְנֵיהֶם וַיָּשֶׂם
לב אֶת־הַמִּשְׁעֶנֶת עַל־פְּנֵי הַנַּעַר וְאֵין קוֹל וְאֵין קָשֶׁב וַיָּשָׁב לִקְרָאתוֹ וַיַּגֶּד־לוֹ לֵאמֹר לֹא הֵקִיץ הַנָּעַר׃ וַיָּבֹא
לג אֱלִישָׁע הַבָּיְתָה וְהִנֵּה הַנַּעַר מֵת מֻשְׁכָּב עַל־מִטָּתוֹ׃ וַיָּבֹא וַיִּסְגֹּר הַדֶּלֶת בְּעַד שְׁנֵיהֶם וַיִּתְפַּלֵּל אֶל־יהוה׃
לד וַיַּעַל וַיִּשְׁכַּב עַל־הַיֶּלֶד וַיָּשֶׂם פִּיו עַל־פִּיו וְעֵינָיו עַל־עֵינָיו וְכַפָּיו עַל־כַּפָּו וַיִּגְהַר עָלָיו וַיָּחָם בְּשַׂר הַיָּלֶד׃

for her children. In both, the mother is aided by miracles worked by the prophet Elisha. The desire to have and raise children brings both of these mothers to the point of great sacrifice and commitment to a goal until it is accomplished. At the end of the reign of Aḥav and in the early days of the dynasty of Yehu, Elisha the prophet battled against idol worship. He comforted and supported those loyal to God and emphasized the rewards God gives those who stand by Him. This was his way of inspiring the people to give over Baal worship in favor of devotion to the Almighty. At

he mounted the bed and lay on top of the boy; he placed his mouth on his mouth and his eyes on his
35 eyes and his palms on his palms, and he bent down over him, and the child's body became warm. He
went back down and paced about the house, back and forth, then he climbed up and crouched down
36 over him. And the boy sneezed – seven times – and the boy opened his eyes. He called to Geḥazi and
said to him, "Call the Shunamite woman." He called her, and she came to him. "Pick up your son," he
37 said. And she came and fell at his feet and bowed to the ground. Then she picked up her son and went
out.

Haftarat Ḥayei Sara

I KINGS

1 1 King David was old, advanced in years, and though they covered him with bedclothes, he never
2 felt warm. His servants said to him, "Let a young virgin be sought out for our lord the king, to wait
upon the king and become his companion; when she lies in your embrace, our lord the king will feel
3 warm." They searched throughout Israel's borders for a beautiful girl, found Avishag the Shunamite,
4 and brought her to the king. The girl was most beautiful, and she became the king's companion and
5 served him, but the king was not intimate with her. Meanwhile, Adoniya son of Ḥagit promoted himself, declaring, "I will become king," and he procured a chariot and riders and fifty men to run before
6 him. Now his father had never disciplined him, saying, "Why have you acted like that?" He was born
7 after Avshalom, and he too was devastatingly handsome. He conspired with Yoav son of Tzeruya and
8 Evyatar the priest, and they lent their support to Adoniya. But Tzadok the priest, Benayahu son of Ye-
9 hoyada, Natan the prophet, Shimi and Rei, and David's warriors were not on Adoniyahu's side. Adoniyahu sacrificed sheep, oxen, and fatlings by the Zoḥelet Stone near the Rogel Spring, and he invited
10 all his brothers – the king's sons – and all the men of Yehuda, the king's subjects. But he did not invite
11 the prophet Natan or Benayahu or the warriors, or his brother Shlomo. And Natan said to Batsheva,
Shlomo's mother, "Have you heard? Adoniyahu the son of Ḥagit has become king without our lord
12 David's knowledge. Come now, let me give you advice – to save your own life and the life of your
13 son Shlomo. Go to King David at once and say to him, 'My lord the king, did you not swear to your
handmaid, "Your son Shlomo will rule after me, and he will sit on my throne"? Why, then, has Adoni-
14 yahu become king?' And while you are still speaking there with the king, I will come in after you and
15 confirm your words." So Batsheva went to the king in the inner chamber – the king had aged severely,
16 and Avishag the Shunamite was tending to him – and Batsheva bowed down low in homage to the
17 king. "What is the matter?" asked the king. "My lord," she said to him, "you swore by the Lord your
18 God to your handmaid, 'Your son Shlomo will rule after me, and he will sit on my throne.' But now,
19 look – Adoniya has become king – and you, my lord the king, did not even know! He has sacrificed a
wealth of oxen and fatlings and sheep and invited all the king's sons, the priest Evyatar, and the army
20 commander Yoav, but he did not invite your servant Shlomo. But all the eyes of Israel look to you, my
21 lord the king, to tell them who will succeed my lord the king on his throne. Otherwise, when my lord
22 the king lies with his ancestors, my son Shlomo and I will be considered offenders." And as she was still
23 speaking with the king, Natan the prophet arrived. "Here is Natan the prophet," they announced to the
24 king, and he came before the king and bowed to him with his face to the ground. "My lord the king,"
25 said Natan, "did you yourself say, 'Adoniyahu will be king after me, and he will sit on my throne'? For

---

David about the coup. David commands the two of them to quickly crown Shlomo, exposing Adoniya and his followers and rebels. This action succeeds in preventing a civil war during this fraught time of transition of power – a conflict which might have destroyed the united kingdom that it had taken David decades to build.

לה וַיָּשָׁב וַיֵּלֶךְ בַּבַּיִת אַחַת הֵנָּה וְאַחַת הֵנָּה וַיַּעַל וַיִּגְהַר עָלָיו וַיְזוֹרֵר הַנַּעַר עַד־שֶׁבַע פְּעָמִים וַיִּפְקַח הַנַּעַר
לו אֶת־עֵינָיו׃ וַיִּקְרָא אֶל־גֵּיחֲזִי וַיֹּאמֶר קְרָא אֶל־הַשֻּׁנַמִּית הַזֹּאת וַיִּקְרָאֶהָ וַתָּבֹא אֵלָיו וַיֹּאמֶר שְׂאִי בְנֵךְ׃
לז וַתָּבֹא וַתִּפֹּל עַל־רַגְלָיו וַתִּשְׁתַּחוּ אָרְצָה וַתִּשָּׂא אֶת־בְּנָהּ וַתֵּצֵא׃

הפטרת חיי שרה

מלכים א׳

א א ב וְהַמֶּלֶךְ דָּוִד זָקֵן בָּא בַּיָּמִים וַיְכַסֻּהוּ בַּבְּגָדִים וְלֹא יִחַם לוֹ׃ וַיֹּאמְרוּ לוֹ עֲבָדָיו יְבַקְשׁוּ לַאדֹנִי הַמֶּלֶךְ נַעֲרָה
ג בְתוּלָה וְעָמְדָה לִפְנֵי הַמֶּלֶךְ וּתְהִי־לוֹ סֹכֶנֶת וְשָׁכְבָה בְחֵיקֶךָ וְחַם לַאדֹנִי הַמֶּלֶךְ׃ וַיְבַקְשׁוּ נַעֲרָה יָפָה
ד בְּכֹל גְּבוּל יִשְׂרָאֵל וַיִּמְצְאוּ אֶת־אֲבִישַׁג הַשּׁוּנַמִּית וַיָּבִאוּ אֹתָהּ לַמֶּלֶךְ׃ וְהַנַּעֲרָה יָפָה עַד־מְאֹד וַתְּהִי
ה לַמֶּלֶךְ סֹכֶנֶת וַתְּשָׁרְתֵהוּ וְהַמֶּלֶךְ לֹא יְדָעָהּ׃ וַאֲדֹנִיָּה בֶן־חַגִּית מִתְנַשֵּׂא לֵאמֹר אֲנִי אֶמְלֹךְ וַיַּעַשׂ לוֹ
ו רֶכֶב וּפָרָשִׁים וַחֲמִשִּׁים אִישׁ רָצִים לְפָנָיו׃ וְלֹא־עֲצָבוֹ אָבִיו מִיָּמָיו לֵאמֹר מַדּוּעַ כָּכָה עָשִׂיתָ וְגַם־הוּא
ז טוֹב־תֹּאַר מְאֹד וְאֹתוֹ יָלְדָה אַחֲרֵי אַבְשָׁלוֹם׃ וַיִּהְיוּ דְבָרָיו עִם יוֹאָב בֶּן־צְרוּיָה וְעִם אֶבְיָתָר הַכֹּהֵן
ח וַיַּעְזְרוּ אַחֲרֵי אֲדֹנִיָּה׃ וְצָדוֹק הַכֹּהֵן וּבְנָיָהוּ בֶן־יְהוֹיָדָע וְנָתָן הַנָּבִיא וְשִׁמְעִי וְרֵעִי וְהַגִּבּוֹרִים אֲשֶׁר לְדָוִד
ט לֹא הָיוּ עִם־אֲדֹנִיָּהוּ׃ וַיִּזְבַּח אֲדֹנִיָּהוּ צֹאן וּבָקָר וּמְרִיא עִם אֶבֶן הַזֹּחֶלֶת אֲשֶׁר־אֵצֶל עֵין רֹגֵל וַיִּקְרָא
י אֶת־כָּל־אֶחָיו בְּנֵי הַמֶּלֶךְ וּלְכָל־אַנְשֵׁי יְהוּדָה עַבְדֵי הַמֶּלֶךְ׃ וְאֶת־נָתָן הַנָּבִיא וּבְנָיָהוּ וְאֶת־הַגִּבּוֹרִים
יא וְאֶת־שְׁלֹמֹה אָחִיו לֹא קָרָא׃ וַיֹּאמֶר נָתָן אֶל־בַּת־שֶׁבַע אֵם־שְׁלֹמֹה לֵאמֹר הֲלוֹא שָׁמַעַתְּ כִּי מָלַךְ
יב אֲדֹנִיָּהוּ בֶן־חַגִּית וַאֲדֹנֵינוּ דָוִד לֹא יָדָע׃ וְעַתָּה לְכִי אִיעָצֵךְ נָא עֵצָה וּמַלְּטִי אֶת־נַפְשֵׁךְ וְאֶת־נֶפֶשׁ בְּנֵךְ
יג שְׁלֹמֹה׃ לְכִי וּבֹאִי ׀ אֶל־הַמֶּלֶךְ דָּוִד וְאָמַרְתְּ אֵלָיו הֲלֹא־אַתָּה אֲדֹנִי הַמֶּלֶךְ נִשְׁבַּעְתָּ לַאֲמָתְךָ לֵאמֹר
יד כִּי־שְׁלֹמֹה בְנֵךְ יִמְלֹךְ אַחֲרַי וְהוּא יֵשֵׁב עַל־כִּסְאִי וּמַדּוּעַ מָלַךְ אֲדֹנִיָּהוּ׃ הִנֵּה עוֹדָךְ מְדַבֶּרֶת שָׁם עִם־
טו הַמֶּלֶךְ וַאֲנִי אָבוֹא אַחֲרַיִךְ וּמִלֵּאתִי אֶת־דְּבָרָיִךְ׃ וַתָּבֹא בַת־שֶׁבַע אֶל־הַמֶּלֶךְ הַחַדְרָה וְהַמֶּלֶךְ זָקֵן
טז מְאֹד וַאֲבִישַׁג הַשּׁוּנַמִּית מְשָׁרַת אֶת־הַמֶּלֶךְ׃ וַתִּקֹּד בַּת־שֶׁבַע וַתִּשְׁתַּחוּ לַמֶּלֶךְ וַיֹּאמֶר הַמֶּלֶךְ מַה־לָּךְ׃
יז וַתֹּאמֶר לוֹ אֲדֹנִי אַתָּה נִשְׁבַּעְתָּ בַּיהוָה אֱלֹהֶיךָ לַאֲמָתֶךָ כִּי־שְׁלֹמֹה בְנֵךְ יִמְלֹךְ אַחֲרָי וְהוּא יֵשֵׁב עַל־
יח יט כִּסְאִי׃ וְעַתָּה הִנֵּה אֲדֹנִיָּה מָלָךְ וְעַתָּה אֲדֹנִי הַמֶּלֶךְ לֹא יָדָעְתָּ׃ וַיִּזְבַּח שׁוֹר וּמְרִיא־וְצֹאן לָרֹב וַיִּקְרָא
כ לְכָל־בְּנֵי הַמֶּלֶךְ וּלְאֶבְיָתָר הַכֹּהֵן וּלְיֹאָב שַׂר הַצָּבָא וְלִשְׁלֹמֹה עַבְדְּךָ לֹא קָרָא׃ וְאַתָּה אֲדֹנִי הַמֶּלֶךְ
כא עֵינֵי כָל־יִשְׂרָאֵל עָלֶיךָ לְהַגִּיד לָהֶם מִי יֵשֵׁב עַל־כִּסֵּא אֲדֹנִי־הַמֶּלֶךְ אַחֲרָיו׃ וְהָיָה כִּשְׁכַּב אֲדֹנִי־הַמֶּלֶךְ
כב כג עִם־אֲבֹתָיו וְהָיִיתִי אֲנִי וּבְנִי שְׁלֹמֹה חַטָּאִים׃ וְהִנֵּה עוֹדֶנָּה מְדַבֶּרֶת עִם־הַמֶּלֶךְ וְנָתָן הַנָּבִיא בָּא׃ וַיַּגִּידוּ
כד לַמֶּלֶךְ לֵאמֹר הִנֵּה נָתָן הַנָּבִיא וַיָּבֹא לִפְנֵי הַמֶּלֶךְ וַיִּשְׁתַּחוּ לַמֶּלֶךְ עַל־אַפָּיו אָרְצָה׃ וַיֹּאמֶר נָתָן אֲדֹנִי
כה הַמֶּלֶךְ אַתָּה אָמַרְתָּ אֲדֹנִיָּהוּ יִמְלֹךְ אַחֲרָי וְהוּא יֵשֵׁב עַל־כִּסְאִי׃ כִּי ׀ יָרַד הַיּוֹם וַיִּזְבַּח שׁוֹר וּמְרִיא־

HAYEI SARA

This *haftara* recounts an attempted coup by one of David's sons toward the end of the king's reign. Shlomo, David's intended successor, was still young, and Adoniya, his older brother, ought to have been the next king by right of being the eldest. Adoniya gathers a group of conspirators opposed to Shlomo and tries to seize the throne by putting on a show-coronation meant to imply that David has changed his mind and settled instead on Adoniya as the next king. Natan the prophet, together with Shlomo's mother, Batsheva, informs

he went down today and sacrificed a wealth of oxen, fatlings, and sheep and invited all the king's sons,
the army officers, and Evyatar the priest. And now they are feasting before him and toasting him and
26 declaring, 'Long live King Adoniyahu!' But he did not invite me, your servant, or the priest Tzadok, or
27 Benayahu son of Yehoyada, or your servant Shlomo. Could it be that my lord the king has decided this
28 without informing your servant who will succeed my lord the king on his throne?" "Summon Batsheva
to me," King David said in response, and she came before the king and stood in the king's presence.
29 30 And the king swore an oath. "As the LORD lives," he said, "who has rescued me from every danger, what
I swore to you by the LORD, God of Israel – that Shlomo your son will rule after me, and that he will sit
31 on my throne in my place – I shall fulfill this very day." And Batsheva bowed her face to the ground in
royal homage and said, "May my lord, King David, live forever!"

HAFTARAT TOLEDOT

On Erev Rosh Ḥodesh Kislev, read the haftara on page 1637.

MALACHI

1 1 2 An oracle: the word of the LORD to Israel through Malakhi. The LORD says, "I have loved you." But
you say, "How have You loved us?" Is Esav not a brother to Yaakov? So says the LORD: Yet I loved Yaa-
3 kov and hated Esav, so I made his mountains desolate and gave his inheritance over to desert jackals.
4 Even should Edom say, "We have been destroyed, but we will return and rebuild the ruins," says the
LORD of Hosts, they will build; I will destroy, and they will be called the territory of evil and the na-
5 tion that suffers the LORD's wrath forever. Your eyes will see this, and you will say, "The LORD is great
6 beyond the territory of Israel." A son honors his father, and a slave his master; if I am a Father, where is
My honor, and if I am the Master, where is My reverence? So says the LORD of Hosts to you, the priests
7 who scorn My name. Yet you say, "How have we scorned Your name?" You offer defiled bread on My
8 altar. Yet you say, "How have we defiled You?" In saying the LORD's table is repugnant. When you offer
a blind animal to be sacrificed, is this no evil? And when you offer the lame and the sick, is this no evil?
Offer it if you will to your governor. Would he then accept you – let you lift your face to him? So says
9 the LORD of Hosts. Now, please, beseech God, and let Him be gracious to us. This was in your hands –
10 would He turn His face for any one of you? So says the LORD of Hosts: O, who is there among you who
would close the doors so that you might not light My altar for naught? I have no desire for you, says the
11 LORD of Hosts. I will accept no offering from your hands. For from one end of the earth to the other,
My name is great among the nations. Incense is offered in My name, a pure offering everywhere, for
12 My name is great among the nations, says the LORD of Hosts. Yet you desecrate it by saying that the
13 Lord's table is defiled and its fruit too repugnant to be consumed. You say, "O, how wearisome," and
you snort at it, says the LORD of Hosts. You bring what is stolen, the LORD says, what is lame, what is
14 ill; you bring this offering. Am I to accept it from your hands? Cursed is the knave who has a ram in his
flock but pledges and sacrifices a damaged animal to the Lord. For I am a great King, says the LORD of
2 1 2 Hosts, and My name is revered among the nations. Now, this is your command, priests: If you do not
listen, if you do not take it to heart to honor My name, says the LORD of Hosts, then I will set a curse on
you, and I will curse your blessings – indeed, I have cursed your blessing, for you do not take it to heart.

---

the rest of the people after them toward truthfulness and godliness. This is also the key to advancing the process of the return to Zion and attaining the redemption it holds in store.

וְצֹאן לָרֹב וַיִּקְרָא לְכָל־בְּנֵי הַמֶּלֶךְ וּלְשָׂרֵי הַצָּבָא וּלְאֶבְיָתָר הַכֹּהֵן וְהִנָּם אֹכְלִים וְשֹׁתִים לְפָנָיו וַיֹּאמְרוּ
כו כז יְחִי הַמֶּלֶךְ אֲדֹנִיָּהוּ׃ וְלִי אֲנִי־עַבְדֶּךָ וּלְצָדֹק הַכֹּהֵן וְלִבְנָיָהוּ בֶן־יְהוֹיָדָע וְלִשְׁלֹמֹה עַבְדְּךָ לֹא קָרָא׃ אִם
מֵאֵת אֲדֹנִי הַמֶּלֶךְ נִהְיָה הַדָּבָר הַזֶּה וְלֹא הוֹדַעְתָּ אֶת־עבדיך מִי יֵשֵׁב עַל־כִּסֵּא אֲדֹנִי־הַמֶּלֶךְ אַחֲרָיו׃ עַבְדְּךָ
כח כט וַיַּעַן הַמֶּלֶךְ דָּוִד וַיֹּאמֶר קִרְאוּ־לִי לְבַת־שָׁבַע וַתָּבֹא לִפְנֵי הַמֶּלֶךְ וַתַּעֲמֹד לִפְנֵי הַמֶּלֶךְ׃ וַיִּשָּׁבַע הַמֶּלֶךְ
ל וַיֹּאמַר חַי־יהוה אֲשֶׁר־פָּדָה אֶת־נַפְשִׁי מִכָּל־צָרָה׃ כִּי כַּאֲשֶׁר נִשְׁבַּעְתִּי לָךְ בַּיהוה אֱלֹהֵי יִשְׂרָאֵל לֵאמֹר
לא כִּי־שְׁלֹמֹה בְנֵךְ יִמְלֹךְ אַחֲרַי וְהוּא יֵשֵׁב עַל־כִּסְאִי תַּחְתָּי כִּי כֵּן אֶעֱשֶׂה הַיּוֹם הַזֶּה׃ וַתִּקֹּד בַּת־שֶׁבַע
אַפַּיִם אֶרֶץ וַתִּשְׁתַּחוּ לַמֶּלֶךְ וַתֹּאמֶר יְחִי אֲדֹנִי הַמֶּלֶךְ דָּוִד לְעֹלָם׃

הפטרת תולדת

On ערב ראש חודש כסלו *read the* הפטרה *on page 1637.*

א א ב מַשָּׂא דְבַר־יהוה אֶל־יִשְׂרָאֵל בְּיַד מַלְאָכִי׃ אָהַבְתִּי אֶתְכֶם אָמַר יהוה וַאֲמַרְתֶּם בַּמָּה אֲהַבְתָּנוּ הֲלוֹא־ מלאכי
ג אָח עֵשָׂו לְיַעֲקֹב נְאֻם־יהוה וָאֹהַב אֶת־יַעֲקֹב׃ וְאֶת־עֵשָׂו שָׂנֵאתִי וָאָשִׂים אֶת־הָרָיו שְׁמָמָה וְאֶת־נַחֲלָתוֹ
ד לְתַנּוֹת מִדְבָּר׃ כִּי־תֹאמַר אֱדוֹם רֻשַּׁשְׁנוּ וְנָשׁוּב וְנִבְנֶה חֳרָבוֹת כֹּה אָמַר יהוה צְבָאוֹת הֵמָּה יִבְנוּ וַאֲנִי
ה אֶהֱרוֹס וְקָרְאוּ לָהֶם גְּבוּל רִשְׁעָה וְהָעָם אֲשֶׁר־זָעַם יהוה עַד־עוֹלָם׃ וְעֵינֵיכֶם תִּרְאֶינָה וְאַתֶּם תֹּאמְרוּ
ו יִגְדַּל יהוה מֵעַל לִגְבוּל יִשְׂרָאֵל׃ בֵּן יְכַבֵּד אָב וְעֶבֶד אֲדֹנָיו וְאִם־אָב אָנִי אַיֵּה כְבוֹדִי וְאִם־אֲדוֹנִים אָנִי אַיֵּה
ז מוֹרָאִי אָמַר ׀ יהוה צְבָאוֹת לָכֶם הַכֹּהֲנִים בּוֹזֵי שְׁמִי וַאֲמַרְתֶּם בַּמֶּה בָזִינוּ אֶת־שְׁמֶךָ׃ מַגִּישִׁים עַל־מִזְבְּחִי
ח לֶחֶם מְגֹאָל וַאֲמַרְתֶּם בַּמֶּה גֵאַלְנוּךָ בֶּאֱמָרְכֶם שֻׁלְחַן יהוה נִבְזֶה הוּא׃ וְכִי־תַגִּשׁוּן עִוֵּר לִזְבֹּחַ אֵין רָע
ט וְכִי תַגִּישׁוּ פִּסֵּחַ וְחֹלֶה אֵין רָע הַקְרִיבֵהוּ נָא לְפֶחָתֶךָ הֲיִרְצְךָ אוֹ הֲיִשָּׂא פָנֶיךָ אָמַר יהוה צְבָאוֹת׃ וְעַתָּה
י חַלּוּ־נָא פְנֵי־אֵל וִיחָנֵנוּ מִיֶּדְכֶם הָיְתָה זֹּאת הֲיִשָּׂא מִכֶּם פָּנִים אָמַר יהוה צְבָאוֹת׃ מִי גַם־בָּכֶם וְיִסְגֹּר
יא דְּלָתַיִם וְלֹא־תָאִירוּ מִזְבְּחִי חִנָּם אֵין־לִי חֵפֶץ בָּכֶם אָמַר יהוה צְבָאוֹת וּמִנְחָה לֹא־אֶרְצֶה מִיֶּדְכֶם׃ כִּי
מִמִּזְרַח־שֶׁמֶשׁ וְעַד־מְבוֹאוֹ גָּדוֹל שְׁמִי בַּגּוֹיִם וּבְכָל־מָקוֹם מֻקְטָר מֻגָּשׁ לִשְׁמִי וּמִנְחָה טְהוֹרָה כִּי־גָדוֹל
יב שְׁמִי בַּגּוֹיִם אָמַר יהוה צְבָאוֹת׃ וְאַתֶּם מְחַלְּלִים אוֹתוֹ בֶּאֱמָרְכֶם שֻׁלְחַן אֲדֹנָי מְגֹאָל הוּא וְנִיבוֹ נִבְזֶה
יג אָכְלוֹ׃ וַאֲמַרְתֶּם הִנֵּה מַתְּלָאָה וְהִפַּחְתֶּם אוֹתוֹ אָמַר יהוה צְבָאוֹת וַהֲבֵאתֶם גָּזוּל וְאֶת־הַפִּסֵּחַ וְאֶת־
יד הַחוֹלֶה וַהֲבֵאתֶם אֶת־הַמִּנְחָה הַאֶרְצֶה אוֹתָהּ מִיֶּדְכֶם אָמַר יהוה׃ וְאָרוּר נוֹכֵל וְיֵשׁ בְּעֶדְרוֹ זָכָר וְנֹדֵר וְזֹבֵחַ
ב א מָשְׁחָת לַאדֹנָי כִּי מֶלֶךְ גָּדוֹל אָנִי אָמַר יהוה צְבָאוֹת וּשְׁמִי נוֹרָא בַגּוֹיִם׃ וְעַתָּה אֲלֵיכֶם הַמִּצְוָה הַזֹּאת
ב הַכֹּהֲנִים׃ אִם־לֹא תִשְׁמְעוּ וְאִם־לֹא תָשִׂימוּ עַל־לֵב לָתֵת כָּבוֹד לִשְׁמִי אָמַר יהוה צְבָאוֹת וְשִׁלַּחְתִּי בָכֶם
ג אֶת־הַמְּאֵרָה וְאָרוֹתִי אֶת־בִּרְכוֹתֵיכֶם וְגַם אָרוֹתִיהָ כִּי אֵינְכֶם שָׂמִים עַל־לֵב׃ הִנְנִי גֹעֵר לָכֶם אֶת־הַזֶּרַע

TOLEDOT

Malakhi, the last of the prophets, lived during the beginning of the Second Temple Period. His time was a difficult one in the Persian province of Judea. The Temple was built, but the return of the Jews to Zion was not progressing as it should have. There was a great feeling of impotence, and the Jews had largely forsaken their spiritual lives. The behavior of the people and the priests in the Temple was so disgraceful that the prophet declares: "I have no desire for you…. I will accept no offering from your hands." The key to change lies in the hands of the priests, Malakhi proclaims. If they serve as a model of integrity for the people, they will draw

3 I will drive away the crops because of you, and I will scatter filth in your face, the filth of your holiday
4 sacrifices, and you will be carried away after it. And you will know that I sent you this command so
5 that My covenant may endure with Levi, says the LORD of Hosts. My covenant endures in him – life
6 and peace. I gave them to him so as to be revered. He revered Me and was in awe of My name. True
teaching was in his mouth, no sin from his lips; he walked with Me in peace and uprightness and re-
7 turned many from iniquity. For a priest's lips should safeguard knowledge, and the people should seek
8 teaching from his mouth, for he is a messenger of the LORD of Hosts.* But you have strayed from the
path and caused many to stumble by your teaching. You have destroyed the covenant of Levi, says the
9 LORD of Hosts. So indeed I will make you scorned and degraded before the whole nation because you
10 do not safeguard My ways, and you distort the face of the Torah. Do we not all have one Father? Were
we not all created by one God? Why should a man be faithless to his brother, desecrating the covenant
11 of our fathers? For Yehuda has been faithless, and an abomination has been perpetrated in Israel and
Jerusalem. For Yehuda, whom He loves, has desecrated that which is holy to the LORD and married
12 the daughter of a foreign god. Let the man who does this be cut off by the LORD – kith and kin – from
13 the tents of Yaakov – even one who brings offerings to the LORD of Hosts. And this you also
do: flood the LORD's altar with tears – weeping and sighing because He no longer turns toward the
14 offerings nor accepts favor from your hands. And you say, "Why?" For the LORD is witness between
you and the wife of your youth, to whom you have been faithless, though she is your companion and
15 your covenantal wife. Did He not make them one being? All remaining spirit accords with that. And
what does the One seek? Children of God. So take care of your spirits, and let none of you be faithless
16 to the wife of your youth. If anyone hates and sends her away, says the LORD, God of Israel, corruption covers his wedding clothes, says the LORD of Hosts, and so, take care with your spirit and be not
17 faithless. You have wearied the LORD with your talk. But you say, "How have we wearied
Him?" By saying every evildoer is good in the eyes of the LORD and it is them whom He desires; or,
3 1 "Where is the God of justice?" Behold: I am sending My messenger, and he will clear a path before
Me. Suddenly, the Lord whom you seek will arrive at His Temple. The angel of the covenant whom
2 you desire – behold, he is coming, says the LORD of Hosts. Who can survive the day of His coming,
and who can remain standing when He appears? For He is like the smelter's fire and the washers' lye.
3 And He will sit smelting and purifying silver, and He will purify the sons of Levi and refine them like
4 gold and silver, and they will be the LORD's – bringing offerings in righteousness. Then the offering of
Yehuda and Jerusalem will be pleasing to the LORD as in days of old and years past.

Ashkenazim and Sepharadim end here

HAFTARAT VAYETZE

HOSEA

Sepharadim, Chabad, and Yemenites begin here

11 7 My people waver – whether to turn back to Me, although Israel is summoned upward, they will not
8 praise Him together. How can I relinquish you, Efrayim; hand you over, Israel? How can I make you
like Adma and treat you like Tzevoyim? My heart has turned upon Me; My compassion has been
9 kindled. No, I will not unleash My burning wrath, I will not turn again to destroy Efrayim – for I am
10 God, I am not a man; within you, My holiness dwells; I will not enter the city with hatred. They will

---

called upon the Israelites to abandon their idolatrous ways and return to worship God. The verses of this *haftara* hint at events in Yaakov's life. The thread tying them together is God's providential guardianship over Yaakov in his struggles against Esav and Lavan. This providence was the secret to Yaakov's success in his lifetime, and it extends to all of his

ד וְזֵרִיתִי פֶרֶשׁ עַל־פְּנֵיכֶם פֶּרֶשׁ חַגֵּיכֶם וְנָשָׂא אֶתְכֶם אֵלָיו׃ וִידַעְתֶּם כִּי שִׁלַּחְתִּי אֲלֵיכֶם אֵת הַמִּצְוָה הַזֹּאת
ה לִהְיוֹת בְּרִיתִי אֶת־לֵוִי אָמַר יהוה צְבָאוֹת׃ בְּרִיתִי ׀ הָיְתָה אִתּוֹ הַחַיִּים וְהַשָּׁלוֹם וָאֶתְּנֵם־לוֹ מוֹרָא וַיִּירָאֵנִי
ו וּמִפְּנֵי שְׁמִי נִחַת הוּא׃ תּוֹרַת אֱמֶת הָיְתָה בְּפִיהוּ וְעַוְלָה לֹא־נִמְצָא בִשְׂפָתָיו בְּשָׁלוֹם וּבְמִישׁוֹר הָלַךְ אִתִּי
ז וְרַבִּים הֵשִׁיב מֵעָוֺן׃ כִּי־שִׂפְתֵי כֹהֵן יִשְׁמְרוּ־דַעַת וְתוֹרָה יְבַקְשׁוּ מִפִּיהוּ כִּי מַלְאַךְ יהוה־צְבָאוֹת הוּא׃ ★ *Ashkenazim and Sepharadim end here*
ח ט וְאַתֶּם סַרְתֶּם מִן־הַדֶּרֶךְ הִכְשַׁלְתֶּם רַבִּים בַּתּוֹרָה שִׁחַתֶּם בְּרִית הַלֵּוִי אָמַר יהוה צְבָאוֹת׃ וְגַם־אֲנִי נָתַתִּי
י אֶתְכֶם נִבְזִים וּשְׁפָלִים לְכָל־הָעָם כְּפִי אֲשֶׁר אֵינְכֶם שֹׁמְרִים אֶת־דְּרָכַי וְנֹשְׂאִים פָּנִים בַּתּוֹרָה׃ הֲלוֹא אָב
יא אֶחָד לְכֻלָּנוּ הֲלוֹא אֵל אֶחָד בְּרָאָנוּ מַדּוּעַ נִבְגַּד אִישׁ בְּאָחִיו לְחַלֵּל בְּרִית אֲבֹתֵינוּ׃ בָּגְדָה יְהוּדָה וְתוֹעֵבָה
יב נֶעֶשְׂתָה בְיִשְׂרָאֵל וּבִירוּשָׁלָ͏ִם כִּי ׀ חִלֵּל יְהוּדָה קֹדֶשׁ יהוה אֲשֶׁר אָהֵב וּבָעַל בַּת־אֵל נֵכָר׃ יַכְרֵת יהוה
יג לָאִישׁ אֲשֶׁר יַעֲשֶׂנָּה עֵר וְעֹנֶה מֵאָהֳלֵי יַעֲקֹב וּמַגִּישׁ מִנְחָה לַיהוה צְבָאוֹת׃ וְזֹאת שֵׁנִית
תַּעֲשׂוּ כַּסּוֹת דִּמְעָה אֶת־מִזְבַּח יהוה בְּכִי וַאֲנָקָה מֵאֵין עוֹד פְּנוֹת אֶל־הַמִּנְחָה וְלָקַחַת רָצוֹן מִיֶּדְכֶם׃
יד וַאֲמַרְתֶּם עַל־מָה עַל כִּי־יהוה הֵעִיד בֵּינְךָ וּבֵין ׀ אֵשֶׁת נְעוּרֶיךָ אֲשֶׁר אַתָּה בָּגַדְתָּה בָּהּ וְהִיא חֲבֶרְתְּךָ
טו וְאֵשֶׁת בְּרִיתֶךָ׃ וְלֹא־אֶחָד עָשָׂה וּשְׁאָר רוּחַ לוֹ וּמָה הָאֶחָד מְבַקֵּשׁ זֶרַע אֱלֹהִים וְנִשְׁמַרְתֶּם בְּרוּחֲכֶם
טז וּבְאֵשֶׁת נְעוּרֶיךָ אַל־יִבְגֹּד׃ כִּי־שָׂנֵא שַׁלַּח אָמַר יהוה אֱלֹהֵי יִשְׂרָאֵל וְכִסָּה חָמָס עַל־לְבוּשׁוֹ אָמַר יהוה
יז צְבָאוֹת וְנִשְׁמַרְתֶּם בְּרוּחֲכֶם וְלֹא תִבְגֹּדוּ׃ הוֹגַעְתֶּם יהוה בְּדִבְרֵיכֶם וַאֲמַרְתֶּם בַּמָּה הוֹגָעְנוּ
ג א בֶּאֱמָרְכֶם כָּל־עֹשֵׂה רָע טוֹב ׀ בְּעֵינֵי יהוה וּבָהֶם הוּא חָפֵץ אוֹ אַיֵּה אֱלֹהֵי הַמִּשְׁפָּט׃ הִנְנִי שֹׁלֵחַ מַלְאָכִי
וּפִנָּה־דֶרֶךְ לְפָנָי וּפִתְאֹם יָבוֹא אֶל־הֵיכָלוֹ הָאָדוֹן ׀ אֲשֶׁר־אַתֶּם מְבַקְשִׁים וּמַלְאַךְ הַבְּרִית אֲשֶׁר אַתֶּם
ב חֲפֵצִים הִנֵּה־בָא אָמַר יהוה צְבָאוֹת׃ וּמִי מְכַלְכֵּל אֶת־יוֹם בּוֹאוֹ וּמִי הָעֹמֵד בְּהֵרָאוֹתוֹ כִּי־הוּא כְּאֵשׁ
ג מְצָרֵף וּכְבֹרִית מְכַבְּסִים׃ וְיָשַׁב מְצָרֵף וּמְטַהֵר כֶּסֶף וְטִהַר אֶת־בְּנֵי־לֵוִי וְזִקַּק אֹתָם כַּזָּהָב וְכַכָּסֶף וְהָיוּ
ד לַיהוה מַגִּישֵׁי מִנְחָה בִּצְדָקָה׃ וְעָרְבָה לַיהוה מִנְחַת יְהוּדָה וִירוּשָׁלָ͏ִם כִּימֵי עוֹלָם וּכְשָׁנִים קַדְמֹנִיּוֹת׃

הפטרת ויצא

הושע
Sepharadim, Chabad, and Yemenites begin here

יא ח וְעַמִּי תְלוּאִים לִמְשׁוּבָתִי וְאֶל־עַל יִקְרָאֻהוּ יַחַד לֹא יְרוֹמֵם׃ אֵיךְ אֶתֶּנְךָ אֶפְרַיִם אֲמַגֶּנְךָ יִשְׂרָאֵל אֵיךְ
ט אֶתֶּנְךָ כְאַדְמָה אֲשִׂימְךָ כִּצְבֹאיִם נֶהְפַּךְ עָלַי לִבִּי יַחַד נִכְמְרוּ נִחוּמָי׃ לֹא אֶעֱשֶׂה חֲרוֹן אַפִּי לֹא אָשׁוּב
י לְשַׁחֵת אֶפְרָיִם כִּי אֵל אָנֹכִי וְלֹא־אִישׁ בְּקִרְבְּךָ קָדוֹשׁ וְלֹא אָבוֹא בְּעִיר׃ אַחֲרֵי יהוה יֵלְכוּ כְּאַרְיֵה יִשְׁאָג

VAYETZE

The prophet Hoshea accompanied the kings of Israel at the height of their power, from the reign of Yorovam son of Yoash (the greatest of the kings of the dynasty of Yehu) until the destruction during the reign of Hoshea son of Ela. At that time, the Assyrian Empire conquered the entire Levant. The prophet Hoshea (and others such as Yeshayahu, Amos, and Mikha) tried to prevent the fall of the kingdom of Israel. He

follow after the LORD; He will roar like a lion. When He roars, His children will rush forth from the
11 west. They will be like a frightened bird coming out of Egypt, like a dove leaving the land of Assyria.
12 1 I will bring them to settle safely in their homes. So declares the LORD. Efrayim besieges Me
with lies, the House of Israel with deception, but Yehuda still walks with God and remains faithful to
2 the Holy One. Efrayim shepherds the wind; he chases the east winds. Day and night he increases lies
3 and ruin; he makes pacts with Assyria and to Egypt bears oil. But also with Yehuda the LORD has a dis-
4 pute: He will visit upon Yaakov as he deserves, as befits his deeds – He will repay him. In the womb he
5 grasped his brother by the heel, and with all his strength he struggled with God. He struggled with an
angel and prevailed; he cried and pleaded with him; in Beit El He found him, and there He spoke to us.
6 7 But the LORD, God of Hosts, the LORD is His name. Now you, too, return to your God, uphold com-
8 passion and justice, and long for your God forever more. Still the merchant possesses false scales; he
9 loves to exploit. Efrayim exclaims, "I have become wealthy; I have found fortune from my own labors;
10 in all the fruits of my toil they will find neither sin nor iniquity." I am the LORD your God from the time
11 you were in the land of Egypt; once more I will settle you safely in tents as in days of old. I have spoken
by way of the prophets; I endowed them with many visions, and through images I communicated with
12 the prophets. As Gilad is rampant with iniquity, so too they are empty and vain; in Gilgal they sacrifice *Some end here*
13 oxen, and their altars too will become like rocks piled high in furrows of the fields. *Yaakov fled to the *Ashkenazim begin here*
14 lands of Aram, and Yisrael labored to acquire a bride; for a bride he kept sheep. With a prophet the LORD
15 brought Israel up out of Egypt, and with a prophet He kept watch over us.* Efrayim has provoked bitter *Yemenites and Chabad end here*
anger; the guilt from the blood he shed will remain, and the Lord will turn his scorn back upon him.
13 1 So it was: when Efrayim spoke, they trembled in fear; he was esteemed in Israel, but when found guilty
2 of worshipping Baal, he was as dead. Now their sinning goes on and on; they cast graven images from
their silver, mold idols as they understood, each entirely the craft of men; of them they say, "Men who
3 offer sacrifices must kiss calves." So they will dissolve like morning mist, like dew at daybreak that
4 swiftly fades. They will scatter like chaff from the threshing floor, like smoke from the window. I am the
LORD your God from the land of Egypt; you know no God other than Me; no one can save you except
5 6 for Me. I knew you, cared for you in the desert, in the parched, bereft land.* But when they grazed, they *Sepharadim end here*
7 became sated and satisfied; their hearts became haughty – then they forgot Me. Therefore I will be as a
8 lion to them; as a leopard I will watch, lurking on the path. I will fall upon them like a bear who mourns
her whelps and tear apart their sealed hearts; there I will consume them like a lion; wild beasts will shred
9 10 them to pieces. You have brought ruin upon yourself, Israel, for your help is to be found in Me. I am your
King, then who will save you in all your cities, and what of your judges of whom you said, "Appoint me
11 12 a king and officers"? In My rage I gave you a king, and in My wrath I will take him away. The
13 sinfulness of Efrayim is tied together; his sins are stored away. Pangs of birth will overcome him, but
14 he is not a wise son, for when the moment of birth comes, he will break and not survive. I will rescue
them from Sheol; I will redeem them from the clutches of death. I shall be your plague, O Death; I will
15 be your destruction, O Sheol; any qualms will be concealed from My eyes. For though he will flourish
wildly among the reeds, an east wind will come; a gust from the LORD will rise from the wilderness. His
14 1 fountain will dry up; his spring will parch; his enemy will plunder all of his treasures. Shomron will be
held guilty, for she has rebelled against her God; she will fall by the sword, her young smashed to pieces,
2 her women with child ripped apart. O Israel, return, go back to the LORD your God, for you
3 have stumbled in your own sinfulness. Take words of remorse with you and return to the LORD; say to
Him, "Forgive all of our sins; accept our goodness – instead of calves we offer You our words of prayer.
4 Assyria will not save us; no more will we ride upon horses; never again will we say, 'You are our god'
5 to the work of our hands, for only in You will the orphan find mercy." I will mend their rebellion with

יא כִּי־הוּא יִשְׁאַג וְיֶחֶרְדוּ בָנִים מִיָּם: יֶחֶרְדוּ כְצִפּוֹר מִמִּצְרַיִם וּכְיוֹנָה מֵאֶרֶץ אַשּׁוּר וְהוֹשַׁבְתִּים עַל־בָּתֵּיהֶם

יב א נְאֻם־יהוה: סְבָבֻנִי בְכַחַשׁ אֶפְרַיִם וּבְמִרְמָה בֵּית יִשְׂרָאֵל וִיהוּדָה עֹד רָד עִם־אֵל וְעִם־קְדוֹשִׁים

ב נֶאֱמָן: אֶפְרַיִם רֹעֶה רוּחַ וְרֹדֵף קָדִים כָּל־הַיּוֹם כָּזָב וָשֹׁד יַרְבֶּה וּבְרִית עִם־אַשּׁוּר יִכְרֹתוּ וְשֶׁמֶן לְמִצְרַיִם

ג ד יוּבָל: וְרִיב לַיהוה עִם־יְהוּדָה וְלִפְקֹד עַל־יַעֲקֹב כִּדְרָכָיו כְּמַעֲלָלָיו יָשִׁיב לוֹ: בַּבֶּטֶן עָקַב אֶת־אָחִיו וּבְאוֹנוֹ

ה ו שָׂרָה אֶת־אֱלֹהִים: וַיָּשַׂר אֶל־מַלְאָךְ וַיֻּכָל בָּכָה וַיִּתְחַנֶּן־לוֹ בֵּית־אֵל יִמְצָאֶנּוּ וְשָׁם יְדַבֵּר עִמָּנוּ: וַיהוה אֱלֹהֵי

ז ח הַצְּבָאוֹת יהוה זִכְרוֹ: וְאַתָּה בֵּאלֹהֶיךָ תָשׁוּב חֶסֶד וּמִשְׁפָּט שְׁמֹר וְקַוֵּה אֶל־אֱלֹהֶיךָ תָּמִיד: כְּנַעַן בְּיָדוֹ מֹאזְנֵי

ט מִרְמָה לַעֲשֹׁק אָהֵב: וַיֹּאמֶר אֶפְרַיִם אַךְ עָשַׁרְתִּי מָצָאתִי אוֹן לִי כָּל־יְגִיעַי לֹא יִמְצְאוּ־לִי עָוֺן אֲשֶׁר־חֵטְא:

י יא וְאָנֹכִי יהוה אֱלֹהֶיךָ מֵאֶרֶץ מִצְרָיִם עֹד אוֹשִׁיבְךָ בָאֳהָלִים כִּימֵי מוֹעֵד: וְדִבַּרְתִּי עַל־הַנְּבִיאִים וְאָנֹכִי חָזוֹן

יב הִרְבֵּיתִי וּבְיַד הַנְּבִיאִים אֲדַמֶּה: אִם־גִּלְעָד אָוֶן אַךְ־שָׁוְא הָיוּ בַּגִּלְגָּל שְׁוָרִים זִבֵּחוּ גַּם מִזְבְּחוֹתָם כְּגַלִּים עַל

יג יד תַּלְמֵי שָׂדָי: ★ וַיִּבְרַח יַעֲקֹב שְׂדֵה אֲרָם וַיַּעֲבֹד יִשְׂרָאֵל בְּאִשָּׁה וּבְאִשָּׁה שָׁמָר: ▪ וּבְנָבִיא הֶעֱלָה יהוה אֶת־

טו יִשְׂרָאֵל מִמִּצְרָיִם וּבְנָבִיא נִשְׁמָר: ▴ הִכְעִיס אֶפְרַיִם תַּמְרוּרִים וְדָמָיו עָלָיו יִטּוֹשׁ וְחֶרְפָּתוֹ יָשִׁיב לוֹ אֲדֹנָיו:

יג א ב כְּדַבֵּר אֶפְרַיִם רְתֵת נָשָׂא הוּא בְּיִשְׂרָאֵל וַיֶּאְשַׁם בַּבַּעַל וַיָּמֹת: וְעַתָּה ׀ יוֹסִפוּ לַחֲטֹא וַיַּעֲשׂוּ לָהֶם מַסֵּכָה

ג מִכַּסְפָּם כִּתְבוּנָם עֲצַבִּים מַעֲשֵׂה חָרָשִׁים כֻּלֹּה לָהֶם הֵם אֹמְרִים זֹבְחֵי אָדָם עֲגָלִים יִשָּׁקוּן: לָכֵן יִהְיוּ כַּעֲנַן־

ד בֹּקֶר וְכַטַּל מַשְׁכִּים הֹלֵךְ כְּמֹץ יְסֹעֵר מִגֹּרֶן וּכְעָשָׁן מֵאֲרֻבָּה: וְאָנֹכִי יהוה אֱלֹהֶיךָ מֵאֶרֶץ מִצְרָיִם וֵאלֹהִים

ה ו זוּלָתִי לֹא תֵדָע וּמוֹשִׁיעַ אַיִן בִּלְתִּי: אֲנִי יְדַעְתִּיךָ בַּמִּדְבָּר בְּאֶרֶץ תַּלְאֻבוֹת: * כְּמַרְעִיתָם וַיִּשְׂבָּעוּ שָׂבְעוּ וַיָּרָם

ז ח לִבָּם עַל־כֵּן שְׁכֵחוּנִי: וָאֱהִי לָהֶם כְּמוֹ־שָׁחַל כְּנָמֵר עַל־דֶּרֶךְ אָשׁוּר: אֶפְגְּשֵׁם כְּדֹב שַׁכּוּל וְאֶקְרַע סְגוֹר לִבָּם

ט י וָאֹכְלֵם שָׁם כְּלָבִיא חַיַּת הַשָּׂדֶה תְּבַקְּעֵם: שִׁחֶתְךָ יִשְׂרָאֵל כִּי־בִי בְעֶזְרֶךָ: אֱהִי מַלְכְּךָ אֵפוֹא וְיוֹשִׁיעֲךָ בְּכָל־

יא יב עָרֶיךָ וְשֹׁפְטֶיךָ אֲשֶׁר אָמַרְתָּ תְּנָה־לִּי מֶלֶךְ וְשָׂרִים: אֶתֶּן־לְךָ מֶלֶךְ בְּאַפִּי וְאֶקַּח בְּעֶבְרָתִי: צָרוּר

יג עֲוֺן אֶפְרָיִם צְפוּנָה חַטָּאתוֹ: חֶבְלֵי יוֹלֵדָה יָבֹאוּ לוֹ הוּא־בֵן לֹא חָכָם כִּי־עֵת לֹא־יַעֲמֹד בְּמִשְׁבַּר בָּנִים:

יד טו מִיַּד שְׁאוֹל אֶפְדֵּם מִמָּוֶת אֶגְאָלֵם אֱהִי דְבָרֶיךָ מָוֶת אֱהִי קָטָבְךָ שְׁאוֹל נֹחַם יִסָּתֵר מֵעֵינָי: כִּי הוּא בֵּין

אַחִים יַפְרִיא יָבוֹא קָדִים רוּחַ יהוה מִמִּדְבָּר עֹלֶה וְיֵבוֹשׁ מְקוֹרוֹ וְיֶחֱרַב מַעְיָנוֹ הוּא יִשְׁסֶה אוֹצַר כָּל־כְּלִי

יד א ב חֶמְדָּה: תֶּאְשַׁם שֹׁמְרוֹן כִּי מָרְתָה בֵּאלֹהֶיהָ בַּחֶרֶב יִפֹּלוּ עֹלְלֵיהֶם יְרֻטָּשׁוּ וְהָרִיּוֹתָיו יְבֻקָּעוּ: שׁוּבָה

ג יִשְׂרָאֵל עַד יהוה אֱלֹהֶיךָ כִּי כָשַׁלְתָּ בַּעֲוֺנֶךָ: קְחוּ עִמָּכֶם דְּבָרִים וְשׁוּבוּ אֶל־יהוה אִמְרוּ אֵלָיו כָּל־

ד תִּשָּׂא עָוֺן וְקַח־טוֹב וּנְשַׁלְּמָה פָרִים שְׂפָתֵינוּ: אַשּׁוּר ׀ לֹא יוֹשִׁיעֵנוּ עַל־סוּס לֹא נִרְכָּב וְלֹא־נֹאמַר עוֹד

ה ו אֱלֹהֵינוּ לְמַעֲשֵׂה יָדֵינוּ אֲשֶׁר־בְּךָ יְרֻחַם יָתוֹם: אֶרְפָּא מְשׁוּבָתָם אֹהֲבֵם נְדָבָה כִּי שָׁב אַפִּי מִמֶּנּוּ: אֶהְיֶה

★ *Ashkenazim begin here*
▪ *Some end here*
▴ *Yemenites and Chabad end here*

Sephardim end here

descendants even after his death. Because of this, the Israelites' betrayal of God and adherence to the idolatrous customs of the Assyrians represent ingratitude in the face of God's beneficence. Such ingratitude is distorted and unsustainable. The prophet paints a picture of the fate awaiting those who do not repent: "They will dissolve like morning mist, like dew at daybreak that swiftly fades." Like such fleeting visions that dissipate quickly, so too will the desire for Assyrian culture, at that time so intense and widespread, prove itself a mirage that will evaporate along with its adherents.

6 gracious love, for I have turned My anger away from them. I will be as dew to Israel; he will bloom like
7 a lily and set down roots as deep as the trees of Lebanon. His branches will spread wide; his splendor
8 will be as the olive tree, and his fragrance as the trees of Lebanon. They who return will dwell beneath
his shade; they will revive once again as grain and flower like vines; their acclaim will linger as the scent
9 of the wine of Lebanon. Efrayim will say, "What need do I have of these idols?" And I will answer him; I
10 will look after him. I will be as a cypress tree, lush and leafy; you will find in Me your source of fruit. He
who is wise will fathom these words; the insightful will grasp them, for the ways of the Lord are just,
and the righteous will walk in them, but sinners will stumble over them.

Some add YOEL

2 26 You will eat, eat and be sated, and you will praise the name of the Lord, your God, who has done
27 wonders for you, for My nation will never be ashamed. You will know that I am among Israel, and I am
the Lord, your God; there is no other. My nation will never be ashamed.

Haftarat Vayishlaḥ

OBADIAH *For Ashkenazim, Sephardim, and Yemenites*

1 1 This is Ovadya's vision: So says the Lord God to Edom – we have heard tidings from the Lord: and
2 an envoy has been sent among the nations, "Come, let us rise up in battle against her." Look, I have
3 made you small among nations; you are utterly scorned. The arrogance of your heart deceived you,
you who dwell in the cliff's niches, your lofty abode, saying in your heart, "Who could bring me down
4 to earth?" But even if you rise as high as an eagle, if you make your nest among the stars, I shall bring
5 you down from there, declares the Lord. If thieves come upon you, bandits in the night, do they not
6 take only their fill? If grape gatherers come upon you, do they not leave gleanings? Yet how has Esav
7 been ransacked, his hidden treasures laid bare. Your allies all have forced you to the borders; those with
whom you had made peace all deceived you, defeated you. Those with whom you broke your bread
8 laid a snare for you, bereft of awareness. Behold, on that day, says the Lord, I will purge Edom of wise
9 men, the mountains of Esav of awareness. Your warriors will be frightened, Teiman, for the mountains
10 of Esav will be unmanned by slaughter. For the violence you wrought against your brother Yaakov
11 shame will cover you, and you will be cut off forever. The day you stood aside, the day strangers took
captive his forces, and foreigners entered his gates, casting lots for Jerusalem – you too were like one of
12 them. Do not gloat over the day of your brother's destruction, the day he becomes a stranger. Do not
rejoice over the children of Yehuda on the day of their destruction. Do not open your mouth on the
13 day of trouble. Do not enter My people's gate on the day of their ruin. Do not gloat over its misfortune
14 on the day of its ruin. Do not extend your hands to take its wealth on the day of his ruin. Do not stand
15 at the crossroads to cut down his refugees. Do not surrender his survivors on the day of trouble. For
the day of the Lord draws near for all the nations. What you have done shall be done to you; what you
16 have wrought will return upon your head. What you drank on My holy mountain, all the nations will
17 always drink. They will drink and they will swallow, and they will be as if they never were. There will be
a remnant on Mount Zion, and it will be holy, and the House of Yaakov will possess their inheritance.
18 The House of Yaakov will be fire, the House of Yosef, flame; the House of Esav, straw. They will blaze
among them and consume them, and there will be no survivors of the House of Esav, for the Lord
19 has spoken. They will take possession of the Negev, along with the mountains of Esav, and the Shefela,

---

Esav, and dominion shall be the Lord's." The exact time of Ovadya's life is unknown, but his words accurately reflect the atmosphere during the period of Jerusalem's destruction by the Babylonians.

ז כַטַּל לְיִשְׂרָאֵל יִפְרַח כַּשּׁוֹשַׁנָּה וְיַךְ שָׁרָשָׁיו כַּלְּבָנוֹן: יֵלְכוּ יֹנְקוֹתָיו וִיהִי כַזַּיִת הוֹדוֹ וְרֵיחַ לוֹ כַּלְּבָנוֹן:
ח ט יָשֻׁבוּ יֹשְׁבֵי בְצִלּוֹ יְחַיּוּ דָגָן וְיִפְרְחוּ כַגָּפֶן זִכְרוֹ כְּיֵין לְבָנוֹן: אֶפְרַיִם מַה־לִּי עוֹד לָעֲצַבִּים אֲנִי עָנִיתִי וַאֲשׁוּרֶנּוּ
י אֲנִי כִּבְרוֹשׁ רַעֲנָן מִמֶּנִּי פֶּרְיְךָ נִמְצָא: מִי חָכָם וְיָבֵן אֵלֶּה נָבוֹן וְיֵדָעֵם כִּי־יְשָׁרִים דַּרְכֵי יהוה וְצַדִּקִים יֵלְכוּ
בָם וּפֹשְׁעִים יִכָּשְׁלוּ בָם:

Some add יואל

ב כו וַאֲכַלְתֶּם אָכוֹל וְשָׂבוֹעַ וְהִלַּלְתֶּם אֶת־שֵׁם יהוה אֱלֹהֵיכֶם אֲשֶׁר־עָשָׂה עִמָּכֶם לְהַפְלִיא וְלֹא־יֵבֹשׁוּ עַמִּי
כז לְעוֹלָם: וִידַעְתֶּם כִּי בְקֶרֶב יִשְׂרָאֵל אָנִי וַאֲנִי יהוה אֱלֹהֵיכֶם וְאֵין עוֹד וְלֹא־יֵבֹשׁוּ עַמִּי לְעוֹלָם:

הפטרת וישלח

עובדיה
For Ashkenazim, Sepharadim, and Yemenites

א א חֲזוֹן עֹבַדְיָה כֹּה־אָמַר אֲדֹנָי יֱהוִה לֶאֱדוֹם שְׁמוּעָה שָׁמַעְנוּ מֵאֵת יהוה וְצִיר בַּגּוֹיִם שֻׁלָּח קוּמוּ וְנָקוּמָה
ב ג עָלֶיהָ לַמִּלְחָמָה: הִנֵּה קָטֹן נְתַתִּיךָ בַּגּוֹיִם בָּזוּי אַתָּה מְאֹד: זְדוֹן לִבְּךָ הִשִּׁיאֶךָ שֹׁכְנִי בְחַגְוֵי־סֶלַע מְרוֹם
ד שִׁבְתּוֹ אֹמֵר בְּלִבּוֹ מִי יוֹרִדֵנִי אָרֶץ: אִם־תַּגְבִּיהַּ כַּנֶּשֶׁר וְאִם־בֵּין כּוֹכָבִים שִׂים קִנֶּךָ מִשָּׁם אוֹרִידְךָ נְאֻם־
ה יהוה: אִם־גַּנָּבִים בָּאוּ־לְךָ אִם־שׁוֹדְדֵי לַיְלָה אֵיךְ נִדְמֵיתָה הֲלוֹא יִגְנְבוּ דַּיָּם אִם־בֹּצְרִים בָּאוּ לָךְ הֲלוֹא
ו ז יַשְׁאִירוּ עֹלֵלוֹת: אֵיךְ נֶחְפְּשׂוּ עֵשָׂו נִבְעוּ מַצְפֻּנָיו: עַד־הַגְּבוּל שִׁלְּחוּךָ כֹּל אַנְשֵׁי בְרִיתֶךָ הִשִּׁיאוּךָ יָכְלוּ
ח לְךָ אַנְשֵׁי שְׁלֹמֶךָ לַחְמְךָ יָשִׂימוּ מָזוֹר תַּחְתֶּיךָ אֵין תְּבוּנָה בּוֹ: הֲלוֹא בַּיּוֹם הַהוּא נְאֻם־יהוה וְהַאֲבַדְתִּי
ט י חֲכָמִים מֵאֱדוֹם וּתְבוּנָה מֵהַר עֵשָׂו: וְחַתּוּ גִבּוֹרֶיךָ תֵּימָן לְמַעַן יִכָּרֶת־אִישׁ מֵהַר עֵשָׂו מִקָּטֶל: מֵחֲמַס
יא אָחִיךָ יַעֲקֹב תְּכַסְּךָ בוּשָׁה וְנִכְרַתָּ לְעוֹלָם: בְּיוֹם עֲמָדְךָ מִנֶּגֶד בְּיוֹם שְׁבוֹת זָרִים חֵילוֹ וְנָכְרִים בָּאוּ שְׁעָרָו
יב וְעַל־יְרוּשָׁלִַם יַדּוּ גוֹרָל גַּם־אַתָּה כְּאַחַד מֵהֶם: וְאַל־תֵּרֶא בְיוֹם־אָחִיךָ בְּיוֹם נָכְרוֹ וְאַל־תִּשְׂמַח לִבְנֵי־יְהוּדָה
יג בְּיוֹם אָבְדָם וְאַל־תַּגְדֵּל פִּיךָ בְּיוֹם צָרָה: אַל־תָּבוֹא בְשַׁעַר־עַמִּי בְּיוֹם אֵידָם אַל־תֵּרֶא גַם־אַתָּה בְּרָעָתוֹ
יד בְּיוֹם אֵידוֹ וְאַל־תִּשְׁלַחְנָה בְחֵילוֹ בְּיוֹם אֵידוֹ: וְאַל־תַּעֲמֹד עַל־הַפֶּרֶק לְהַכְרִית אֶת־פְּלִיטָיו וְאַל־תַּסְגֵּר
טו שְׂרִידָיו בְּיוֹם צָרָה: כִּי־קָרוֹב יוֹם־יהוה עַל־כָּל־הַגּוֹיִם כַּאֲשֶׁר עָשִׂיתָ יֵעָשֶׂה לָּךְ גְּמֻלְךָ יָשׁוּב בְּרֹאשֶׁךָ:
טז יז כִּי כַּאֲשֶׁר שְׁתִיתֶם עַל־הַר קָדְשִׁי יִשְׁתּוּ כָל־הַגּוֹיִם תָּמִיד וְשָׁתוּ וְלָעוּ וְהָיוּ כְּלוֹא הָיוּ: וּבְהַר צִיּוֹן
יח תִּהְיֶה פְלֵיטָה וְהָיָה קֹדֶשׁ וְיָרְשׁוּ בֵּית יַעֲקֹב אֵת מוֹרָשֵׁיהֶם: וְהָיָה בֵית־יַעֲקֹב אֵשׁ וּבֵית יוֹסֵף
יט לֶהָבָה וּבֵית עֵשָׂו לְקַשׁ וְדָלְקוּ בָהֶם וַאֲכָלוּם וְלֹא־יִהְיֶה שָׂרִיד לְבֵית עֵשָׂו כִּי יהוה דִּבֵּר: וְיָרְשׁוּ
הַנֶּגֶב אֶת־הַר עֵשָׂו וְהַשְּׁפֵלָה אֶת־פְּלִשְׁתִּים וְיָרְשׁוּ אֶת־שְׂדֵה אֶפְרַיִם וְאֵת שְׂדֵה שֹׁמְרוֹן וּבִנְיָמִן

VAYISHLAḤ

The relationship between Yaakov and Esav has become symbolic of the tension between Israel and the peoples of the world. In this *haftara*, the prophet Ovadya describes the cruelty of the nation Edom (Esav's descendants) to the neighboring people of Yehuda. Edom has allied itself with the enemy besieging Jerusalem, attacked refugees from Yehuda, and taken part in its plunder. This arrogant and willful behavior betrays the natural feelings of brotherhood that cousin peoples should feel for each other. It is no coincidence that Esav has become an enemy to Yaakov, a symbol of baseless hatred of Israel. The eradication of this hatred is part of the process of the world's redemption: "And saviors shall go up to Mount Zion to judge the mountains of

▶

from the Philistines. And they will take possession of the land of Efrayim and the land of Shomron;
20 and Binyamin, along with the Gilad – they, the exiled force of the children of Israel who are among
the Canaanites as far as Tzarfat and the exiled of Jerusalem who are in Sepharad will take possession
21 of the cities of the Negev. And saviors shall go up to Mount Zion to judge the mountains of Esav, and
dominion shall be the LORD's.

HOSEA
For Minhag Anglia

11 7 My people waver – whether to turn back to Me, although Israel is summoned upward, they will not
8 praise Him together. How can I relinquish you, Efrayim; hand you over, Israel? How can I make you
like Adma and treat you like Tzevoyim? My heart has turned upon Me; My compassion has been
9 kindled. No, I will not unleash My burning wrath, I will not turn again to destroy Efrayim – for I am
10 God, I am not a man; within you, My holiness dwells; I will not enter the city with hatred. They will
follow after the LORD; He will roar like a lion. When He roars, His children will rush forth from the
11 west. They will be like a frightened bird coming out of Egypt, like a dove leaving the land of Assyria.
12 1 I will bring them to settle safely in their homes. So declares the LORD. Efrayim besieges Me
with lies, the House of Israel with deception, but Yehuda still walks with God and remains faithful to
2 the Holy One. Efrayim shepherds the wind; he chases the east winds. Day and night he increases lies
3 and ruin; he makes pacts with Assyria and to Egypt bears oil. But also with Yehuda the LORD has a
4 dispute: He will visit upon Yaakov as he deserves, as befits his deeds – He will repay him. In the womb
5 he grasped his brother by the heel, and with all his strength he struggled with God. He struggled with
an angel and prevailed; he cried and pleaded with him; in Beit El He found him, and there He spoke
6 to us. But the LORD, God of Hosts, the LORD is His name. Now you, too, return to your God, uphold
7 8 compassion and justice, and long for your God forever more. Still the merchant possesses false scales;
9 he loves to exploit. Efrayim exclaims, "I have become wealthy; I have found fortune from my own
10 labors; in all the fruits of my toil they will find neither sin nor iniquity." I am the LORD your God from
11 the time you were in the land of Egypt; once more I will settle you safely in tents as in days of old. I have
spoken by way of the prophets; I endowed them with many visions, and through images I communi-
12 cated with the prophets. As Gilad is rampant with iniquity, so too they are empty and vain; in Gilgal
they sacrifice oxen, and their altars too will become like rocks piled high in furrows of the fields.

Haftarat Vayeshev

On Ḥanukka, read the maftir from Numbers chapter 7 (Sepharadim and Yemenites begin at 6:22), and the haftara on *page 1639.*

AMOS

2 6 So says the LORD: On account of Israel's three crimes and on account of the fourth, I will not forgive
7 them. They sold the righteous for silver and the poor for the price of shoes. They are those who trample

---

accomplishing this: We must be courageously introspective, coming to terms with our failures and accepting responsibility for correcting them. Ignoring the distorted and corrupt reality, denying our failures, only perpetuates them and ultimately leads to ruin. The *haftara* ends with a series of seven rhetorical questions. Each of them presents a necessary connection between a cause and an outcome. Anyone who cannot understand the causal connection between the state of society and the way it is run will come to destruction. "A lion roars; who would not fear?"

כ אֶת־הַגִּלְעָד: וְגָלֻת הַחֵל־הַזֶּה לִבְנֵי יִשְׂרָאֵל אֲשֶׁר־כְּנַעֲנִים עַד־צָרְפַת וְגָלֻת יְרוּשָׁלַםִ אֲשֶׁר
כא בִּסְפָרַד יִרְשׁוּ אֵת עָרֵי הַנֶּגֶב: וְעָלוּ מוֹשִׁעִים בְּהַר צִיּוֹן לִשְׁפֹּט אֶת־הַר עֵשָׂו וְהָיְתָה לַיהוָה
הַמְּלוּכָה:

הושע
For Minhag Anglia

יא ח וְעַמִּי תְלוּאִים לִמְשׁוּבָתִי וְאֶל־עַל יִקְרָאֻהוּ יַחַד לֹא יְרוֹמֵם: אֵיךְ אֶתֶּנְךָ אֶפְרַיִם אֲמַגֶּנְךָ יִשְׂרָאֵל אֵיךְ
ט אֶתֶּנְךָ כְאַדְמָה אֲשִׂימְךָ כִּצְבֹאיִם נֶהְפַּךְ עָלַי לִבִּי יַחַד נִכְמְרוּ נִחוּמָי: לֹא אֶעֱשֶׂה חֲרוֹן אַפִּי לֹא אָשׁוּב
י לְשַׁחֵת אֶפְרָיִם כִּי אֵל אָנֹכִי וְלֹא־אִישׁ בְּקִרְבְּךָ קָדוֹשׁ וְלֹא אָבוֹא בְּעִיר: אַחֲרֵי יהוה יֵלְכוּ כְּאַרְיֵה יִשְׁאָג
יא כִּי־הוּא יִשְׁאַג וְיֶחֶרְדוּ בָנִים מִיָּם: יֶחֶרְדוּ כְצִפּוֹר מִמִּצְרַיִם וּכְיוֹנָה מֵאֶרֶץ אַשּׁוּר וְהוֹשַׁבְתִּים עַל־בָּתֵּיהֶם
יב א נְאֻם־יהוה: סְבָבֻנִי בְכַחַשׁ אֶפְרַיִם וּבְמִרְמָה בֵּית יִשְׂרָאֵל וִיהוּדָה עֹד רָד עִם־אֵל וְעִם־
ב קְדוֹשִׁים נֶאֱמָן: אֶפְרַיִם רֹעֶה רוּחַ וְרֹדֵף קָדִים כָּל־הַיּוֹם כָּזָב וָשֹׁד יַרְבֶּה וּבְרִית עִם־אַשּׁוּר יִכְרֹתוּ וְשֶׁמֶן
ג ד לְמִצְרַיִם יוּבָל: וְרִיב לַיהוָה עִם־יְהוּדָה וְלִפְקֹד עַל־יַעֲקֹב כִּדְרָכָיו כְּמַעֲלָלָיו יָשִׁיב לוֹ: בַּבֶּטֶן עָקַב אֶת־
ה אָחִיו וּבְאוֹנוֹ שָׂרָה אֶת־אֱלֹהִים: וַיָּשַׂר אֶל־מַלְאָךְ וַיֻּכָל בָּכָה וַיִּתְחַנֶּן־לוֹ בֵּית־אֵל יִמְצָאֶנּוּ וְשָׁם יְדַבֵּר
ו ז עִמָּנוּ: וַיהוָה אֱלֹהֵי הַצְּבָאוֹת יהוה זִכְרוֹ: וְאַתָּה בֵּאלֹהֶיךָ תָשׁוּב חֶסֶד וּמִשְׁפָּט שְׁמֹר וְקַוֵּה אֶל־אֱלֹהֶיךָ
ח ט תָּמִיד: כְּנַעַן בְּיָדוֹ מֹאזְנֵי מִרְמָה לַעֲשֹׁק אָהֵב: וַיֹּאמֶר אֶפְרַיִם אַךְ עָשַׁרְתִּי מָצָאתִי אוֹן לִי כָּל־יְגִיעַי
י לֹא יִמְצְאוּ־לִי עָוֺן אֲשֶׁר־חֵטְא: וְאָנֹכִי יהוה אֱלֹהֶיךָ מֵאֶרֶץ מִצְרָיִם עֹד אוֹשִׁיבְךָ בְאָהָלִים כִּימֵי מוֹעֵד:
יא יב וְדִבַּרְתִּי עַל־הַנְּבִיאִים וְאָנֹכִי חָזוֹן הִרְבֵּיתִי וּבְיַד הַנְּבִיאִים אֲדַמֶּה: אִם־גִּלְעָד אָוֶן אַךְ־שָׁוְא הָיוּ בַּגִּלְגָּל
שְׁוָרִים זִבֵּחוּ גַּם מִזְבְּחוֹתָם כְּגַלִּים עַל תַּלְמֵי שָׂדָי:

הפטרת וישב

On חנוכה *read the* מפטיר *from* במדבר ז *(Sephardim and Yemenites begin at* ו, כב*),*
and the הפטרה *on page 1639.*

עמוס

ב ו כֹּה אָמַר יהוה עַל־שְׁלֹשָׁה פִּשְׁעֵי יִשְׂרָאֵל וְעַל־אַרְבָּעָה לֹא אֲשִׁיבֶנּוּ עַל־מִכְרָם בַּכֶּסֶף צַדִּיק וְאֶבְיוֹן
ז בַּעֲבוּר נַעֲלָיִם: הַשֹּׁאֲפִים עַל־עֲפַר־אֶרֶץ בְּרֹאשׁ דַּלִּים וְדֶרֶךְ עֲנָוִים יַטּוּ וְאִישׁ וְאָבִיו יֵלְכוּ אֶל־הַנַּעֲרָה

VAYESHEV

Amos prophesied at the height of the Israelite kingdoms' power – the reigns of Uziyahu king of Yehuda and Yorovam ben Yoash king of Israel. Both monarchs ruled for decades. Due to this stability, their commonwealths were strong and wealthy. Amos sounded his call in the kingdom of Israel, warning of the excesses of a lavish society, which lead to social and economic inequality and oppression. Such a society cannot endure.

At times, the reality in which we live can become corrupt. Despite the difficulties, it is possible to overcome this corruption, and there are fundamental conditions for

the dust of the earth atop the heads of the poor; they turn the humble away from the path. A man and
8 his father visit the same girl to desecrate My holy name. They spread confiscated clothing beside every
9 altar and drink wine bought with fines in the house of their gods. But I had destroyed before them the
Amorite, whose height was as tall as cedars and whose strength was like that of oaks. Yet I obliterated their
10 fruit above and their roots below. I brought you up from the land of Egypt and led you in the desert for
11 forty years to inherit Amorite lands. I raised up into prophets some of your sons and into nazirites some
12 of your young men. Is this not so, children of Israel? said the Lord. But you made the nazirites drink
13 wine and ordered the prophets not to prophesy. Behold, I will hold you back in your place, as a wagon
14 loaded with sheaves is held back. The swift will lose the ability to flee; the strong will not gather their
15 strength; the warrior will not escape with his life. The bowman will not stand; the fleet of foot will not
16 escape; the horse rider will not escape with his life. He who considers himself strongest among warriors
3 1 will flee naked on that day, says the Lord. Hear this word, which the Lord has spoken about
2 you, children of Israel: About the whole family I brought up from the land of Egypt, it is only you that I
3 have known from among all the families on earth, so I will visit all your sins upon you. Would two walk
4 together if they had not met? Would a lion roar in the forest if it had not caught prey? Would a young lion
5 raise its voice from its den if it had not seized prey? Would a bird plunge into a trap on the ground if it were
6 not baited? Would the trap spring up from the earth if it had not trapped quarry? Would a warning horn
blow in the city and the people not be afraid? Would disaster come upon the city were it not an act of the
7 Lord? The Lord God does not do anything without revealing His secret to His servants, the prophets.
8 A lion roars; who would not fear?

Haftarat Miketz

On Ḥanukka, read the maftir from Numbers chapter 7, and the haftara on page 1641.

3 15 Then Shlomo awoke – it had all been a dream! When he came to Jerusalem, he stood before the Ark of I KINGS
the Lord's Covenant and offered up burnt offerings and presented peace offerings, and he held a feast
16 17 for all his servants. Then two harlot women came before the king and stood before him. "If
you please, my lord," said the first woman, "this woman and I live in one house, and I gave birth while
18 she was in the house. On the third day after I gave birth, this woman also gave birth. The two of us live
19 together – there was no one else in the house besides us, just the two of us in the house. The son of
20 this woman died in the night, for she lay on him. But she got up during the night and took my own
son from me while your handmaid was sleeping and lay down with him in her embrace, and laid her
21 own dead son in my embrace. I woke up in the morning to nurse my son to find that he was dead! But
22 when I looked at him closely in the morning, why – it wasn't my own son, the one I had borne!" "No!"
said the other woman. "My son is the one who is alive, and your son is the one who died!" "No," she
23 said, "your son is dead, and my son is alive!" and they continued arguing before the king. "This one
says, 'This is my son, who is alive, and your son is dead,'" said the king, "and this one says, 'No, your

---

confronting Shlomo: Courts can only decide cases based on evidence. But here, there was no one to testify who was the true mother of the child. A king, however, has the right to issue rulings based on circumstantial evidence, such as a mother's instinctive psychological reactions. This story teaches us about the wondrous blessing inherent in worthy and wise leadership.

ח למען חלל את־שם קדשי: ועל־בגדים חבלים יטו אצל כל־מזבח ויין ענושים ישתו בית אלהיהם:
ט ואנכי השמדתי את־האמרי מפניהם אשר כגבה ארזים גבהו וחסן הוא כאלונים ואשמיד פריו ממעל
י ושרשיו מתחת: ואנכי העליתי אתכם מארץ מצרים ואולך אתכם במדבר ארבעים שנה לרשת
יא את־ארץ האמרי: ואקים מבניכם לנביאים ומבחוריכם לנזרים האף אין־זאת בני ישראל נאם־יהוה:
יב יג ותשקו את־הנזרים יין ועל־הנביאים צויתם לאמר לא תנבאו: הנה אנכי מעיק תחתיכם כאשר
יד טו תעיק העגלה המלאה לה עמיר: ואבד מנוס מקל וחזק לא־יאמץ כחו וגבור לא־ימלט נפשו: ותפש
טז הקשת לא יעמד וקל ברגליו לא ימלט ורכב הסוס לא ימלט נפשו: ואמיץ לבו בגבורים ערום ינוס
ג א ביום־ההוא נאם־יהוה: שמעו את־הדבר הזה אשר דבר יהוה עליכם בני ישראל על
ב כל־המשפחה אשר העליתי מארץ מצרים לאמר: רק אתכם ידעתי מכל משפחות האדמה על־כן
ג ד אפקד עליכם את כל־עונתיכם: הילכו שנים יחדו בלתי אם־נועדו: הישאג אריה ביער וטרף אין
ה לו היתן כפיר קולו ממענתו בלתי אם־לכד: התפל צפור על־פח הארץ ומוקש אין לה היעלה־פח
ו מן־האדמה ולכוד לא ילכוד: אם־יתקע שופר בעיר ועם לא יחרדו אם־תהיה רעה בעיר ויהוה לא
ז ח עשה: כי לא יעשה אדני יהוה דבר כי אם־גלה סודו אל־עבדיו הנביאים: אריה שאג מי לא יירא
אדני יהוה דבר מי לא ינבא:

הפטרת מקץ

On חנוכה *read the* מפטיר *from* במדבר ז, *and the* הפטרה *on page 1641.*

ג טו ויקץ שלמה והנה חלום ויבוא ירושלם ויעמד | לפני | ארון ברית־אדני ויעל עלות ויעש שלמים ויעש מלכים א׳
טז יז משתה לכל־עבדיו: אז תבאנה שתים נשים זנות אל־המלך ותעמדנה לפניו: ותאמר
יח האשה האחת בי אדני אני והאשה הזאת ישבת בבית אחד ואלד עמה בבית: ויהי ביום השלישי
יט ללדתי ותלד גם־האשה הזאת ואנחנו יחדו אין־זר אתנו בבית זולתי שתים־אנחנו בבית: וימת
כ בן־האשה הזאת לילה אשר שכבה עליו: ותקם בתוך הלילה ותקח את־בני מאצלי ואמתך ישנה
כא ותשכיבהו בחיקה ואת־בנה המת השכיבה בחיקי: ואקם בבקר להיניק את־בני והנה־מת ואתבונן
כב אליו בבקר והנה לא־היה בני אשר ילדתי: ותאמר האשה האחרת לא כי בני החי ובנך המת וזאת
כג אמרת לא כי בנך המת ובני החי ותדברנה לפני המלך: ויאמר המלך זאת אמרת זה־בני החי ובנך
כד המת וזאת אמרת לא כי בנך המת ובני החי: ויאמר המלך קחו לי־חרב ויבאו החרב

MIKETZ

The *haftara* describes a famous event from the beginning of the reign of King Shlomo. Two harlots come to the king, asking him to decide which of them is the true mother of a live child and which of a dead child. Two issues unique to this event emphasize the practical wisdom given to Shlomo by God, as he requested in his dream. Firstly, even women of this low station would come to him for judgment; they knew that they would be given a serious and fair hearing by the king. Secondly, the legal challenge

24 son is dead, and my son is alive.'" And the king said, "Fetch me a sword," and they brought a
25 sword before the king. "Cut the living child into two," the king declared, "and give half to one and half
26 to the other." But the woman whose son was alive spoke up, for she burned with compassion for her
son. "Please, my lord," she said, "give her the living child; do anything but kill him!" while the other
27 one said, "Neither of us will have him – cut him up." And the king spoke up. "Give her the living child,"
28 he said, "and make no move to kill him. She is his mother." When all of Israel heard about the case that
the king had judged, they held the king in awe, for they saw that divine wisdom was within him to do
4 1 justice. King Shlomo was king of all Israel.

Haftarat Vayigash

37 15 16 The word of the Lord came to me, saying: "And you, Man, take a branch and write on it, 'For Yehuda EZEKIEL
and the children of Israel associated with him.' Then take one branch and write on it, 'For Yosef – the
17 branch of Efrayim – and all of the House of Israel associated with him.' Bring them together to make
18 one branch, so that they are one in your hand. When your people say to you, 'Tell us, what do these
19 mean to you?' say to them: So says the Lord God: See, I am going to take the branch of Yosef, which
is in the hand of Efrayim, and the tribes of Israel who are associated with him, and join them with
him, with the branch of Yehuda; I will make them into one branch, and they will be one in My hand.
20 21 Let these branches that you write upon be in your hand before their eyes. Speak to them: So says the
Lord God: See that I am taking the children of Israel from among the nations that they went to; I will
22 gather them from all around, and I will bring them to their land. I will make them into one nation in
the land, in the mountains of Israel; one king will be king for all of them, and they will no longer be two
23 nations; they will no longer be split into two kingdoms. They will no longer be defiled by their idols or
by their detestable things and all their transgressions; I will deliver them from all the dwelling places
24 where they have sinned; I will purify them, and they will be My people, and I will be their God. My
servant David will be king over them; there shall be one shepherd for all, and they will follow My laws,
25 and they will keep My statutes and perform them. They will live on the land that I gave to My servant
Yaakov, where your ancestors lived. They will live upon it, they and their children and their children's
26 children, for eternity, and David My servant will be their prince for eternity. I will make a covenant of
peace with them; it will be an everlasting covenant with them. I will place them securely there, I will
27 make them ever more numerous; I will place My Sanctuary among them for eternity. My presence will
28 be upon them; I will be their God, and they will be My people. And the nations will know that I the
Lord make Israel holy when My Sanctuary is among them for all eternity."

---

tree that bears high-quality fruit, thus creating a hybrid better and stronger than both of the originals. This is the secret of "together," and it is the basis for many other aspects of the future redemption. These words, preached to those banished from their homes in Yehuda on the first occasion of destruction that affected the entire Jewish people (the Temple, the House of David, Jerusalem), breathed hope into the hearts of the people, and gave them the strength to carry on through their time of bitter crisis.

כה לִפְנֵי הַמֶּלֶךְ: וַיֹּאמֶר הַמֶּלֶךְ גִּזְרוּ אֶת־הַיֶּלֶד הַחַי לִשְׁנָיִם וּתְנוּ אֶת־הַחֲצִי לְאַחַת וְאֶת־הַחֲצִי לְאֶחָת:
כו וַתֹּאמֶר הָאִשָּׁה אֲשֶׁר־בְּנָהּ הַחַי אֶל־הַמֶּלֶךְ כִּי־נִכְמְרוּ רַחֲמֶיהָ עַל־בְּנָהּ וַתֹּאמֶר ׀ בִּי אֲדֹנִי תְּנוּ־לָהּ
כז אֶת־הַיָּלוּד הַחַי וְהָמֵת אַל־תְּמִיתֻהוּ וְזֹאת אֹמֶרֶת גַּם־לִי גַם־לָךְ לֹא יִהְיֶה גְּזֹרוּ: וַיַּעַן הַמֶּלֶךְ וַיֹּאמֶר
כח תְּנוּ־לָהּ אֶת־הַיָּלוּד הַחַי וְהָמֵת לֹא תְמִיתֻהוּ הִיא אִמּוֹ: וַיִּשְׁמְעוּ כָל־יִשְׂרָאֵל אֶת־הַמִּשְׁפָּט אֲשֶׁר שָׁפַט
ד א הַמֶּלֶךְ וַיִּרְאוּ מִפְּנֵי הַמֶּלֶךְ כִּי רָאוּ כִּי־חָכְמַת אֱלֹהִים בְּקִרְבּוֹ לַעֲשׂוֹת מִשְׁפָּט: וַיְהִי הַמֶּלֶךְ שְׁלֹמֹה מֶלֶךְ
עַל־כָּל־יִשְׂרָאֵל:

הפטרת ויגש

לז טו טז וַיְהִי דְבַר־יְהוָה אֵלַי לֵאמֹר: וְאַתָּה בֶן־אָדָם קַח־לְךָ עֵץ אֶחָד וּכְתֹב עָלָיו לִיהוּדָה וְלִבְנֵי יִשְׂרָאֵל חֲבֵרָו יחזקאל
יז וּלְקַח עֵץ אֶחָד וּכְתוֹב עָלָיו לְיוֹסֵף עֵץ אֶפְרַיִם וְכָל־בֵּית יִשְׂרָאֵל חֲבֵרָו: וְקָרַב אֹתָם אֶחָד אֶל־אֶחָד לְךָ
יח לְעֵץ אֶחָד וְהָיוּ לַאֲחָדִים בְּיָדֶךָ: וְכַאֲשֶׁר יֹאמְרוּ אֵלֶיךָ בְּנֵי עַמְּךָ לֵאמֹר הֲלוֹא־תַגִּיד לָנוּ מָה־אֵלֶּה לָּךְ:
יט דַּבֵּר אֲלֵהֶם כֹּה־אָמַר אֲדֹנָי יְהוִה הִנֵּה אֲנִי לֹקֵחַ אֶת־עֵץ יוֹסֵף אֲשֶׁר בְּיַד־אֶפְרַיִם וְשִׁבְטֵי יִשְׂרָאֵל חֲבֵרָו
כ וְנָתַתִּי אוֹתָם עָלָיו אֶת־עֵץ יְהוּדָה וַעֲשִׂיתִם לְעֵץ אֶחָד וְהָיוּ אֶחָד בְּיָדִי: וְהָיוּ הָעֵצִים אֲשֶׁר־תִּכְתֹּב
כא עֲלֵיהֶם בְּיָדְךָ לְעֵינֵיהֶם: וְדַבֵּר אֲלֵיהֶם כֹּה־אָמַר אֲדֹנָי יְהוִה הִנֵּה אֲנִי לֹקֵחַ אֶת־בְּנֵי יִשְׂרָאֵל מִבֵּין הַגּוֹיִם
כב אֲשֶׁר הָלְכוּ־שָׁם וְקִבַּצְתִּי אֹתָם מִסָּבִיב וְהֵבֵאתִי אוֹתָם אֶל־אַדְמָתָם: וְעָשִׂיתִי אֹתָם לְגוֹי אֶחָד בָּאָרֶץ
בְּהָרֵי יִשְׂרָאֵל וּמֶלֶךְ אֶחָד יִהְיֶה לְכֻלָּם לְמֶלֶךְ וְלֹא יהיה־עוֹד לִשְׁנֵי גוֹיִם וְלֹא יֵחָצוּ עוֹד לִשְׁתֵּי מַמְלָכוֹת יִהְיוּ־
כג עוֹד: וְלֹא יִטַּמְּאוּ עוֹד בְּגִלּוּלֵיהֶם וּבְשִׁקּוּצֵיהֶם וּבְכֹל פִּשְׁעֵיהֶם וְהוֹשַׁעְתִּי אֹתָם מִכֹּל מוֹשְׁבֹתֵיהֶם אֲשֶׁר
כד חָטְאוּ בָהֶם וְטִהַרְתִּי אוֹתָם וְהָיוּ־לִי לְעָם וַאֲנִי אֶהְיֶה לָהֶם לֵאלֹהִים: וְעַבְדִּי דָוִד מֶלֶךְ עֲלֵיהֶם וְרוֹעֶה
כה אֶחָד יִהְיֶה לְכֻלָּם וּבְמִשְׁפָּטַי יֵלֵכוּ וְחֻקֹּתַי יִשְׁמְרוּ וְעָשׂוּ אוֹתָם: וְיָשְׁבוּ עַל־הָאָרֶץ אֲשֶׁר נָתַתִּי לְעַבְדִּי
לְיַעֲקֹב אֲשֶׁר יָשְׁבוּ־בָהּ אֲבוֹתֵיכֶם וְיָשְׁבוּ עָלֶיהָ הֵמָּה וּבְנֵיהֶם וּבְנֵי בְנֵיהֶם עַד־עוֹלָם וְדָוִד עַבְדִּי נָשִׂיא
כו לָהֶם לְעוֹלָם: וְכָרַתִּי לָהֶם בְּרִית שָׁלוֹם בְּרִית עוֹלָם יִהְיֶה אוֹתָם וּנְתַתִּים וְהִרְבֵּיתִי אוֹתָם וְנָתַתִּי אֶת־
כז כח מִקְדָּשִׁי בְּתוֹכָם לְעוֹלָם: וְהָיָה מִשְׁכָּנִי עֲלֵיהֶם וְהָיִיתִי לָהֶם לֵאלֹהִים וְהֵמָּה יִהְיוּ־לִי לְעָם: וְיָדְעוּ הַגּוֹיִם
כִּי אֲנִי יְהוָה מְקַדֵּשׁ אֶת־יִשְׂרָאֵל בִּהְיוֹת מִקְדָּשִׁי בְּתוֹכָם לְעוֹלָם:

VAYIGASH

In his prophecies of comfort and encouragement, the prophet Yeḥezkel, who accompanied the Jewish exiles to Babylon, paints a picture of the future kingdom in the land of Israel when they return to their land, and describes its characteristics: the ingathering of exiles, the reestablishment of the dynasty of David, spiritual purity and adherence to the Torah and its commandments, and peace. He takes pains to discuss the unity of the nation. Unity, a central pillar of the future order, is described by the symbolic act from the field of agriculture: the grafting of a tree. When grafting, one joins the trunk of a strong, rooted tree with a branch of another

Haftarat Vayeḥi

I KINGS

2 1 2 The time of David's death was drawing near, and he gave instructions to his son Shlomo. "I am going
3 the way of all the earth," he said. "You must be strong and prove yourself a man. You must keep the
charge of the Lord your God, following His ways and keeping His laws and commandments, His
rulings and decrees, as written in the teaching of Moshe. For then you will succeed in whatever you
4 do, wherever you turn. For then, the Lord will fulfill the promise He made to me, saying: If your
sons keep to their path and walk before Me truly, with all their heart and all their soul, then no one
5 of your lineage will be cut off from the throne of Israel. Now you know what Yoav son of Tzeruya did
to me – how he dealt with the two commanders of Israel's forces, Avner son of Ner and Amasa son
of Yeter. By killing them, he shed the blood of war in peacetime and tainted the belt around his waist
6 and the shoes upon his feet with the blood of war. Use your wisdom – do not let his gray-haired head
7 go down to Sheol in peace. As for the sons of Barzilai the Gileadite, show them loyalty and
let them dine at your table, for they befriended me when I was fleeing from Avshalom your brother.
8 Now, look – though Shimi son of Gera the Benjaminite from Baḥurim is with you, he cursed me with a
vehement curse on the day I left Maḥanayim. When he came down to meet me by the Jordan, I swore
9 to him by the Lord that I would not put him to death by sword – but now, do not let him go free. You
are a wise man, and you will know how to deal with him – bring his gray-haired head down in blood to
10 11 Sheol." And David slept with his ancestors and was buried in the City of David. The length
of time that David had reigned over Israel was forty years; he reigned in Ḥevron for seven years, and
12 he reigned in Jerusalem for thirty-three years. Now Shlomo sat on his father David's throne, and his
kingdom was firmly established.

Haftarat Shemot

ISAIAH
For Ashkenazim and Chabad

27 6 In days to come, Yaakov will take root, Israel will put out buds and flower, and all the land on all the
7 earth will be covered with the fruits. Was he beaten as are beaten those who beat him? Was his
8 slaying like the slaying of their slain? With a faithful measure, driving them out You fight them; He blew
9 them away with His blasting spirit on the day of the gale. This, then, is how the iniquity of Israel may be
atoned – and that, all the fruit of removing his sin – by rendering all his altar stones smashed limestone,
10 no sacred trees or incense shrines rising again. The fortress city will sit alone, a shelter left behind,
11 lonely as desert. Calves will graze there, there will they lie, and eat up all their branches. When their
yield dries up they will be broken down. Women will come and use them as firewood, for this is not a
12 wise people; and so its Maker will have no compassion, its Creator will grant it no grace. On
that day, the Lord will beat the branches from the Euphrates's surge to the River of Egypt and gather
13 you up one by one, you children of Israel. It will be, on that day: a great ram's horn will sound,

---

principled adherence to the faith and values outlined at the beginning of his speech to Shlomo.

SHEMOT
Ashkenazim

The distance from success to excess is short. It is easy to be carried away by earthly achievements, and difficult to maintain a mindset of humility having made them. The drunkenness of society's successes causes us to become "wine benumbed." Such a society will fritter away its ability to achieve full redemption. Instead of hearing the call of the herald: "A great ram's horn will sound, and they will come, all those lost in the land of Assyria…and bow low to the Lord on the holy mount in Jerusalem," we will bemoan

הפטרת ויחי

ב מלכים א׳

א ב ויקרבו ימי־דוד למות ויצו את־שלמה בנו לאמר: אנכי הלך בדרך כל־הארץ וחזקת והיית לאיש:
ג ושמרת את־משמרת | יהוה אלהיך ללכת בדרכיו לשמר חקתיו מצותיו ומשפטיו ועדותיו ככתוב
ד בתורת משה למען תשכיל את כל־אשר תעשה ואת כל־אשר תפנה שם: למען יקים יהוה את־דברו
אשר דבר עלי לאמר אם־ישמרו בניך את־דרכם ללכת לפני באמת בכל־לבבם ובכל־נפשם לאמר
ה לא־יכרת לך איש מעל כסא ישראל: וגם אתה ידעת את אשר־עשה לי יואב בן־צרויה אשר עשה
לשני־שרי צבאות ישראל לאבנר בן־נר ולעמשא בן־יתר ויהרגם וישם דמי־מלחמה בשלם ויתן
ו דמי מלחמה בחגרתו אשר במתניו ובנעלו אשר ברגליו: ועשית כחכמתך ולא־תורד שיבתו בשלם
ז שאל: ולבני ברזלי הגלעדי תעשה־חסד והיו באכלי שלחנך כי־כן קרבו אלי בברחי מפני
ח אבשלום אחיך: והנה עמך שמעי בן־גרא בן־הימיני מבחרים והוא קללני קללה נמרצת ביום לכתי
ט מחנים והוא־ירד לקראתי הירדן ואשבע לו ביהוה לאמר אם־אמיתך בחרב: ועתה אל־תנקהו כי
י איש חכם אתה וידעת את אשר תעשה־לו והורדת את־שיבתו בדם שאול: וישכב דוד עם־אבתיו
יא ויקבר בעיר דוד: והימים אשר מלך דוד על־ישראל ארבעים שנה בחברון מלך
יב שבע שנים ובירושלם מלך שלשים ושלש שנים: ושלמה ישב על־כסא דוד אביו ותכן מלכתו מאד:

הפטרת שמות

כז ישעיה

For Ashkenazim and Chabad

ו ז הבאים ישרש יעקב יציץ ופרח ישראל ומלאו פני־תבל תנובה: הכמכת מכהו הכהו
ח ט אם־כהרג הרגיו הרג: בסאסאה בשלחה תריבנה הגה ברוחו הקשה ביום קדים: לכן בזאת יכפר
עון־יעקב וזה כל־פרי הסר חטאתו בשומו | כל־אבני מזבח כאבני־גר מנפצות לא־יקמו אשרים
יא וחמנים: כי עיר בצורה בדד נוה משלח ונעזב כמדבר שם ירעה עגל ושם ירבץ וכלה סעפיה: ביבש
קצירה תשברנה נשים באות מאירות אותה כי לא עם־בינות הוא על־כן לא־ירחמנו עשהו ויצרו
יב לא יחננו: והיה ביום ההוא יחבט יהוה משבלת הנהר עד־נחל מצרים ואתם תלקטו
יג לאחד אחד בני ישראל: והיה | ביום ההוא יתקע בשופר גדול ובאו האבדים בארץ אשור

VAYEḤI

King David conveys his last will and testament to his son Shlomo. In the first part, he emphasizes the importance of adhering to the Torah and its commandments as a condition for success in life and as a ruler. In the second, he prepares his son for the sensitive task of succession to power. Some personalities in the royal court are liable to take advantage of the period of instability to try to seize power. Such a struggle, against the best efforts of the old king to ensure stability by publicly designating Shlomo as his successor, could pose a threat to the safety of the kingdom. In fateful and dangerous times such as this, Shlomo must work quickly and determinedly to forestall irrevocable damage to all his father had worked so hard to build. The Davidic kingdom was at that point a strong and united empire with wealth and standing. David understood this, and he saw it as an outcome of the

and they will come, all those lost in the land of Assyria, and those who are exiled to the land of Egypt,
28 1 and bow low to the LORD on the holy mount in Jerusalem. Woe to the proud garland of
Efrayim's drunkards, for the withered lotus flower that was the glorious supremacy crowning the oiled
2 valley of the wine benumbed. See what comes – something strong and determined of the Lord, like
pelting hail, like a cataclysmic storm, like a river of great waters, flooding waters, heavy-handed, casting
3 4 people down to earth, trampling underfoot the garland pride of Efrayim's drunkards. Like a withered
lotus flower it shall be, its glorious supremacy that crowned the fat valley like the first fig before har-
5 vest; the one that all who saw would swallow up sooner than hold it. On that day the LORD of
6 Hosts will be a garland of splendor, the crown of supremacy, to the remnant of His people, He will be
the spirit of justice in those who preside over justice, and of might in those who drive war back from
7 the gate. For these men too have gone astray with wine, they have lost themselves in ale – priest and
prophet – gone astray with their ale, been swallowed up in wine, got lost by their ale, gone astray in
8 their vision, fallen over in judgment; the tables are soaked, all, in vomit and filth, until there is no space
9 left. Whom would he teach knowledge, whom bring to comprehend his words? Those barely
10 weaned of milk, those just taken from the breast? *Law after law, law after law, line after line, line after line,*
11 12 *a little bit here, a little bit there* – in a babble of words, in a different tongue he speaks to this people. He
13 told them, "This is rest: leave the weary be; this is calm." They would not hear. So the word of the LORD
is to them law after law, law after law, line after line, line after line, a little bit here, a little bit there, for
them to walk and stumble on backward, be broken, be beaten, be caught.

29 22 And so, this is what the LORD has said – Avraham's redeemer – to the House of Yaakov: No more will
23 Yaakov be ashamed, his face no more grow pale, for when he sees his children, the work of My hands,
in his midst, sanctifying My name, it is Yaakov's Holy One they sanctify; it is Israel's God they worship.

JEREMIAH
For Sepharadim

1 1 The words of Yirmeyahu, son of Ḥilkiyahu, one of the priests who were in Anatot in the land of
2 Binyamin, to whom the word of the LORD came in the days of Yoshiyahu son of Amon, king of Ye-
3 huda, in the thirteenth year of his reign, and continued during the days of Yehoyakim son of Yoshiyahu, king of Yehuda, until the end of the eleventh year of Tzidkiyahu son of Yoshiyahu, king of Ye-
4 huda – until the exile of Jerusalem in the fifth month: The word of the LORD came to me:
5 "Before I formed you in the womb I knew you. Before you were born I consecrated you. I placed
6 you as a prophet to the nations." I said, "Please, Lord GOD, I am not capable of speaking, for I am
7 still only a boy." The LORD replied to me, "Do not say, 'I am a boy,' for you shall go to all to whom I send
8 you, and you shall speak as I instruct you. Do not fear them, for I am with you to rescue you, declares the
9 10 LORD." The LORD extended His hand and touched my mouth and the LORD said to me, "Look, I have
placed My words in your mouth. I have appointed you this day against the kingdoms and against the
11 nations to uproot and tear down, to destroy and demolish, to build and to plant." The word of
the LORD came to me: "What do you see, Yirmeyahu?" I replied, "I see the branch of an almond tree."

---

nation. On the other, he was one of the people and loved them. In this context God's words of encouragement to him take on special meaning: "Stand up and speak to them as I will instruct you. Do not break down because of them.... I have made you today a fortress city, an iron column, and walls of bronze.... They will wage battle against you, but they will not prevail." Yirmeyahu's attempts to avoid this terrible role, like Moshe's centuries earlier, testify to this difficulty as well.

כח א וְהַנִּדָּחִים בְּאֶרֶץ מִצְרָיִם וְהִשְׁתַּחֲווּ לַיהוָה בְּהַר הַקֹּדֶשׁ בִּירוּשָׁלָםִ׃ הוֹי עֲטֶרֶת גֵּאוּת שִׁכֹּרֵי
ב אֶפְרַיִם וְצִיץ נֹבֵל צְבִי תִפְאַרְתּוֹ אֲשֶׁר עַל־רֹאשׁ גֵּיא־שְׁמָנִים הֲלוּמֵי יָיִן׃ הִנֵּה חָזָק וְאַמִּץ לַאדֹנָי כְּזֶרֶם
ג בָּרָד שַׂעַר קָטֶב כְּזֶרֶם מַיִם כַּבִּירִים שֹׁטְפִים הִנִּיחַ לָאָרֶץ בְּיָד׃ בְּרַגְלַיִם תֵּרָמַסְנָה עֲטֶרֶת גֵּאוּת שִׁכּוֹרֵי
ד אֶפְרָיִם׃ וְהָיְתָה צִיצַת נֹבֵל צְבִי תִפְאַרְתּוֹ אֲשֶׁר עַל־רֹאשׁ גֵּיא שְׁמָנִים כְּבִכּוּרָהּ בְּטֶרֶם קַיִץ אֲשֶׁר יִרְאֶה
ה הָרֹאֶה אוֹתָהּ בְּעוֹדָהּ בְּכַפּוֹ יִבְלָעֶנָּה׃ בַּיּוֹם הַהוּא יִהְיֶה יהוה צְבָאוֹת לַעֲטֶרֶת צְבִי וְלִצְפִירַת
ו ז תִּפְאָרָה לִשְׁאָר עַמּוֹ׃ וּלְרוּחַ מִשְׁפָּט לַיּוֹשֵׁב עַל־הַמִּשְׁפָּט וְלִגְבוּרָה מְשִׁיבֵי מִלְחָמָה שָׁעְרָה׃ וְגַם־אֵלֶּה
בַּיַּיִן שָׁגוּ וּבַשֵּׁכָר תָּעוּ כֹּהֵן וְנָבִיא שָׁגוּ בַשֵּׁכָר נִבְלְעוּ מִן־הַיַּיִן תָּעוּ מִן־הַשֵּׁכָר שָׁגוּ בָּרֹאֶה פָּקוּ פְּלִילִיָּה׃
ח ט כִּי כָּל־שֻׁלְחָנוֹת מָלְאוּ קִיא צֹאָה בְּלִי מָקוֹם׃ אֶת־מִי יוֹרֶה דֵעָה וְאֶת־מִי יָבִין שְׁמוּעָה גְּמוּלֵי
י יא מֵחָלָב עַתִּיקֵי מִשָּׁדָיִם׃ כִּי צַו לָצָו צַו לָצָו קַו לָקָו קַו לָקָו זְעֵיר שָׁם זְעֵיר שָׁם׃ כִּי בְּלַעֲגֵי שָׂפָה וּבְלָשׁוֹן
יב אַחֶרֶת יְדַבֵּר אֶל־הָעָם הַזֶּה׃ אֲשֶׁר ׀ אָמַר אֲלֵיהֶם זֹאת הַמְּנוּחָה הָנִיחוּ לֶעָיֵף וְזֹאת הַמַּרְגֵּעָה וְלֹא אָבוּא
יג שְׁמוֹעַ׃ וְהָיָה לָהֶם דְּבַר־יהוה צַו לָצָו צַו לָצָו קַו לָקָו קַו לָקָו זְעֵיר שָׁם זְעֵיר שָׁם לְמַעַן יֵלְכוּ וְכָשְׁלוּ אָחוֹר
וְנִשְׁבָּרוּ וְנוֹקְשׁוּ וְנִלְכָּדוּ׃
כט כב לָכֵן כֹּה־אָמַר יהוה אֶל־בֵּית יַעֲקֹב אֲשֶׁר פָּדָה אֶת־אַבְרָהָם לֹא־עַתָּה יֵבוֹשׁ יַעֲקֹב וְלֹא עַתָּה פָּנָיו יֶחֱוָרוּ׃
כג כִּי בִרְאֹתוֹ יְלָדָיו מַעֲשֵׂה יָדַי בְּקִרְבּוֹ יַקְדִּישׁוּ שְׁמִי וְהִקְדִּישׁוּ אֶת־קְדוֹשׁ יַעֲקֹב וְאֶת־אֱלֹהֵי יִשְׂרָאֵל יַעֲרִיצוּ׃

ירמיה
For Sepharadim

א א ב דִּבְרֵי יִרְמְיָהוּ בֶּן־חִלְקִיָּהוּ מִן־הַכֹּהֲנִים אֲשֶׁר בַּעֲנָתוֹת בְּאֶרֶץ בִּנְיָמִן׃ אֲשֶׁר הָיָה דְבַר־יהוה אֵלָיו בִּימֵי
ג יֹאשִׁיָּהוּ בֶן־אָמוֹן מֶלֶךְ יְהוּדָה בִּשְׁלֹשׁ־עֶשְׂרֵה שָׁנָה לְמָלְכוֹ׃ וַיְהִי בִּימֵי יְהוֹיָקִים בֶּן־יֹאשִׁיָּהוּ מֶלֶךְ
יְהוּדָה עַד־תֹּם עַשְׁתֵּי־עֶשְׂרֵה שָׁנָה לְצִדְקִיָּהוּ בֶן־יֹאשִׁיָּהוּ מֶלֶךְ יְהוּדָה עַד־גְּלוֹת יְרוּשָׁלַםִ בַּחֹדֶשׁ
ד ה הַחֲמִישִׁי׃ וַיְהִי דְבַר־יהוה אֵלַי לֵאמֹר׃ בְּטֶרֶם אצורך בַבֶּטֶן יְדַעְתִּיךָ וּבְטֶרֶם תֵּצֵא מֵרֶחֶם אֶצָּרְךָ
ו ז הִקְדַּשְׁתִּיךָ נָבִיא לַגּוֹיִם נְתַתִּיךָ׃ וָאֹמַר אֲהָהּ אֲדֹנָי יֱהוִה הִנֵּה לֹא־יָדַעְתִּי דַּבֵּר כִּי־נַעַר אָנֹכִי׃ וַיֹּאמֶר
ח יהוה אֵלַי אַל־תֹּאמַר נַעַר אָנֹכִי כִּי עַל־כָּל־אֲשֶׁר אֶשְׁלָחֲךָ תֵּלֵךְ וְאֵת כָּל־אֲשֶׁר אֲצַוְּךָ תְּדַבֵּר׃ אַל־תִּירָא
ט מִפְּנֵיהֶם כִּי־אִתְּךָ אֲנִי לְהַצִּלֶךָ נְאֻם־יהוה׃ וַיִּשְׁלַח יהוה אֶת־יָדוֹ וַיַּגַּע עַל־פִּי וַיֹּאמֶר יהוה אֵלַי הִנֵּה נָתַתִּי
י דְבָרַי בְּפִיךָ׃ רְאֵה הִפְקַדְתִּיךָ ׀ הַיּוֹם הַזֶּה עַל־הַגּוֹיִם וְעַל־הַמַּמְלָכוֹת לִנְתוֹשׁ וְלִנְתוֹץ וּלְהַאֲבִיד וְלַהֲרוֹס
יא לִבְנוֹת וְלִנְטוֹעַ׃ וַיְהִי דְבַר־יהוה אֵלַי לֵאמֹר מָה־אַתָּה רֹאֶה יִרְמְיָהוּ וָאֹמַר מַקֵּל שָׁקֵד אֲנִי

the "trampling underfoot the garland pride of Efrayim's drunkards."

Sepharadim

Yirmeyahu prophesied during the reigns of the final kings of Yehuda up till the destruction of Jerusalem and afterward. His call to prophecy emphasizes the harsh daily reality of the prophet. Yirmeyahu's career was especially fraught. He was the first and only prophet that foretold the destruction as it occurred. His challenge stemmed from his complex nature: On the one hand he was a divine messenger, commanded to deliver a message of impending doom to the

12 13 And the LORD said to me: "You have seen well, for I am watchful about keeping My word." The
word of the LORD came to me a second time: "What do you see?" I answered, "I see a boiling cauldron
14 facing the north." And the LORD said to me: "From the north disaster shall burst forth upon all the
15 inhabitants of the land, for I am about to summon all the tribes of the kingdoms of the north," declares
the LORD. "They shall come; each shall set up a throne at the entrance of the gates of Jerusalem against
16 her ramparts roundabout and against all the cities of Yehuda. Thus will I pronounce My judgment upon
them on account of their wickedness: they abandoned Me, sacrificed to other gods, and worshipped the
17 works of their own hands. As for you, be courageous; stand up and speak to them as I will instruct you.
18 Do not break down because of them lest I break you down before them. I have made you today a fortress
city, an iron column, and walls of bronze against the entire land – against the kings of Yehuda, its princes,
19 its priests, and the people of the land. They will wage battle against you, but they will not prevail, for
2 1 2 I am with you," declares the LORD, "to rescue you." The word of the LORD came to me: "Go
and proclaim to the people of Jerusalem: 'This is what the LORD has said: I recall on your behalf the
devotion of your youth, your bridal love, when you followed Me into the wilderness, a land unseeded.
3 Israel is a treasure to the LORD, His choice harvest. All who eat of it will be held to account. Evil will
befall them, declares the LORD.'"

EZEKIEL
For Yemenites

16 1 2 The word of the LORD came to me, saying, "Man, make known to Jerusalem her abominations and say:
3 So says the Lord GOD to Jerusalem: Your ancestry and your birth were in the land of the Canaanites.
4 Your father was Amorite, your mother Hittite and as for your birth, on the day you were born your
cord was not cut, you were not washed clean with water, you were not rubbed with salt, and you were
5 not swaddled. No eye took enough pity on you to do any of these things out of compassion for you.
6 You were thrown out into the open field, loathed, on the day you were born. And when I passed by
you, I saw you floundering in your own blood, and I said to you, 'There in your blood, live'; I said to
7 you, 'In your blood, live!' I made you flourish like the shoots of the field. You grew up, matured, were
8 beautifully adorned – your breasts were firm, your hair grew long – but you were naked and bare. Then
I passed by you and saw that you had reached the age of love, so I spread My cloak out over you and
covered your nakedness. I made My vow to you, entered into a covenant with you, declares the Lord
9 GOD, and you became Mine. I washed you with water, I rinsed your blood off you, and I anointed you
10 with oil. I clothed you in embroidered cloth, I placed on you leather shoes, I wound about your head
11 fine linen, and I covered you with silk. I adorned you with jewelry; I put bracelets upon your arms and
12 a necklace round your neck. I put a nose ring in your nose, earrings in your ears, and a glorious crown
13 upon your head. You were adorned with gold and silver; your clothing was fine linen, silk, and embroidered cloth; you ate fine flour, honey, and oil; and you were exceptionally beautiful, fit to be a queen.
14 You became known among the nations for your beauty for, with the splendor I placed upon you, it was
perfect, declares the Lord GOD."

---

and takes her in, raising her into a mature, beautiful, and strong woman, and then marries her. This story highlights the special providence of God for Israel from the nadir of the yoke of Egypt until the covenant at Sinai. Verses from this prophecy are woven into the Passover Haggada.

The continuation of the prophecy, after the conclusion of the *haftara*, describes the people's betrayal of God, despite all the good He did for them.

יב יג רֹאֶה: וַיֹּאמֶר יהוה אֵלַי הֵיטַבְתָּ לִרְאוֹת כִּי־שֹׁקֵד אֲנִי עַל־דְּבָרִי לַעֲשֹׂתוֹ: וַיְהִי דְבַר־יהוה ׀
יד אֵלַי שֵׁנִית לֵאמֹר מָה אַתָּה רֹאֶה וָאֹמַר סִיר נָפוּחַ אֲנִי רֹאֶה וּפָנָיו מִפְּנֵי צָפוֹנָה: וַיֹּאמֶר יהוה אֵלָי מִצָּפוֹן
טו תִּפָּתַח הָרָעָה עַל כָּל־יֹשְׁבֵי הָאָרֶץ: כִּי ׀ הִנְנִי קֹרֵא לְכָל־מִשְׁפְּחוֹת מַמְלְכוֹת צָפוֹנָה נְאֻם־יהוה וּבָאוּ
טז וְנָתְנוּ אִישׁ כִּסְאוֹ פֶּתַח ׀ שַׁעֲרֵי יְרוּשָׁלִַם וְעַל כָּל־חוֹמֹתֶיהָ סָבִיב וְעַל כָּל־עָרֵי יְהוּדָה: וְדִבַּרְתִּי מִשְׁפָּטַי
יז אוֹתָם עַל כָּל־רָעָתָם אֲשֶׁר עֲזָבוּנִי וַיְקַטְּרוּ לֵאלֹהִים אֲחֵרִים וַיִּשְׁתַּחֲווּ לְמַעֲשֵׂי יְדֵיהֶם: וְאַתָּה תֶּאְזֹר
יח מָתְנֶיךָ וְקַמְתָּ וְדִבַּרְתָּ אֲלֵיהֶם אֵת כָּל־אֲשֶׁר אָנֹכִי אֲצַוֶּךָּ אַל־תֵּחַת מִפְּנֵיהֶם פֶּן־אֲחִתְּךָ לִפְנֵיהֶם: וַאֲנִי
הִנֵּה נְתַתִּיךָ הַיּוֹם לְעִיר מִבְצָר וּלְעַמּוּד בַּרְזֶל וּלְחֹמוֹת נְחֹשֶׁת עַל־כָּל־הָאָרֶץ לְמַלְכֵי יְהוּדָה לְשָׂרֶיהָ
ב יט א לְכֹהֲנֶיהָ וּלְעַם הָאָרֶץ: וְנִלְחֲמוּ אֵלֶיךָ וְלֹא־יוּכְלוּ לָךְ כִּי־אִתְּךָ אֲנִי נְאֻם־יהוה לְהַצִּילֶךָ: וַיְהִי
ב דְבַר־יהוה אֵלַי לֵאמֹר: הָלֹךְ וְקָרָאתָ בְאָזְנֵי יְרוּשָׁלִַם לֵאמֹר כֹּה אָמַר יהוה זָכַרְתִּי לָךְ חֶסֶד נְעוּרַיִךְ
ג אַהֲבַת כְּלוּלֹתָיִךְ לֶכְתֵּךְ אַחֲרַי בַּמִּדְבָּר בְּאֶרֶץ לֹא זְרוּעָה: קֹדֶשׁ יִשְׂרָאֵל לַיהוה רֵאשִׁית תְּבוּאָתֹה כָּל־
אֹכְלָיו יֶאְשָׁמוּ רָעָה תָּבֹא אֲלֵיהֶם נְאֻם־יהוה:

יחזקאל
For Yemenites

טז א ב ג וַיְהִי דְבַר־יהוה אֵלַי לֵאמֹר: בֶּן־אָדָם הוֹדַע אֶת־יְרוּשָׁלִַם אֶת־תּוֹעֲבֹתֶיהָ: וְאָמַרְתָּ כֹּה־אָמַר אֲדֹנָי יֱהֹוִה
ד לִירוּשָׁלִַם מְכֹרֹתַיִךְ וּמֹלְדֹתַיִךְ מֵאֶרֶץ הַכְּנַעֲנִי אָבִיךְ הָאֱמֹרִי וְאִמֵּךְ חִתִּית: וּמוֹלְדוֹתַיִךְ בְּיוֹם הוּלֶּדֶת אוֹתָךְ
ה לֹא־כָרַּת שָׁרֵּךְ וּבְמַיִם לֹא־רֻחַצְתְּ לְמִשְׁעִי וְהָמְלֵחַ לֹא הֻמְלַחַתְּ וְהָחְתֵּל לֹא חֻתָּלְתְּ: לֹא־חָסָה עָלַיִךְ עַיִן
ו לַעֲשׂוֹת לָךְ אַחַת מֵאֵלֶּה לְחֻמְלָה עָלָיִךְ וַתֻּשְׁלְכִי אֶל־פְּנֵי הַשָּׂדֶה בְּגֹעַל נַפְשֵׁךְ בְּיוֹם הֻלֶּדֶת אֹתָךְ: וָאֶעֱבֹר
ז עָלַיִךְ וָאֶרְאֵךְ מִתְבּוֹסֶסֶת בְּדָמָיִךְ וָאֹמַר לָךְ בְּדָמַיִךְ חֲיִי וָאֹמַר לָךְ בְּדָמַיִךְ חֲיִי: רְבָבָה כְּצֶמַח הַשָּׂדֶה
ח נְתַתִּיךְ וַתִּרְבִּי וַתִּגְדְּלִי וַתָּבֹאִי בַּעֲדִי עֲדָיִים שָׁדַיִם נָכֹנוּ וּשְׂעָרֵךְ צִמֵּחַ וְאַתְּ עֵרֹם וְעֶרְיָה: וָאֶעֱבֹר עָלַיִךְ
וָאֶרְאֵךְ וְהִנֵּה עִתֵּךְ עֵת דֹּדִים וָאֶפְרֹשׂ כְּנָפִי עָלַיִךְ וָאֲכַסֶּה עֶרְוָתֵךְ וָאֶשָּׁבַע לָךְ וָאָבוֹא בִבְרִית אֹתָךְ נְאֻם
ט י אֲדֹנָי יֱהֹוִה וַתִּהְיִי־לִי: וָאֶרְחָצֵךְ בַּמַּיִם וָאֶשְׁטֹף דָּמַיִךְ מֵעָלָיִךְ וָאֲסֻכֵךְ בַּשָּׁמֶן: וָאַלְבִּישֵׁךְ רִקְמָה וָאֶנְעֲלֵךְ
יא יב תָּחַשׁ וָאֶחְבְּשֵׁךְ בַּשֵּׁשׁ וַאֲכַסֵּךְ מֶשִׁי: וָאֶעְדֵּךְ עֶדִי וָאֶתְּנָה צְמִידִים עַל־יָדַיִךְ וְרָבִיד עַל־גְּרוֹנֵךְ: וָאֶתֵּן נֶזֶם
יג עַל־אַפֵּךְ וַעֲגִילִים עַל־אָזְנָיִךְ וַעֲטֶרֶת תִּפְאֶרֶת בְּרֹאשֵׁךְ: וַתַּעְדִּי זָהָב וָכֶסֶף וּמַלְבּוּשֵׁךְ ששי וָמֶשִׁי וְרִקְמָה שֵׁשׁ
יד סֹלֶת וּדְבַשׁ וָשֶׁמֶן אכלתי וַתִּיפִי בִּמְאֹד מְאֹד וַתִּצְלְחִי לִמְלוּכָה: וַיֵּצֵא לָךְ שֵׁם בַּגּוֹיִם בְּיָפְיֵךְ כִּי ׀ כָּלִיל אָכָלְתְּ
הוּא בַּהֲדָרִי אֲשֶׁר־שַׂמְתִּי עָלַיִךְ נְאֻם אֲדֹנָי יֱהֹוִה:

Yemenites

Speaking to fellow exiles from Jerusalem, the prophet Yeḥezkel describes the reasons for the impending final destruction of the city. He surveys the relationship between God and Israel from the days of slavery in Egypt onward, using the metaphor of a man who takes in an abandoned child, a baby girl, thrown out into the street on the day she is born. The man, passing by the child, takes pity on her

Haftarat Vaera

On Rosh Ḥodesh Shevat read the maftir from Bemidbar 28:9–15, and the haftara on page 1635.

EZEKIEL
Yemenites begin here
Ashkenazim and Sepharadim begin here

28 24 The House of Israel will no longer suffer stabbing briars, scratching thorns, from those in their sur-
25 roundings who scorn them, and they will know that I am the Lord God. *So says the Lord
God: When I gather the House of Israel in from the peoples where they have been scattered and I
am sanctified through them in the eyes of the nations, when they live on their land that I gave to My
26 servant Yaakov – they will live on it in safety; they will build houses, plant vineyards, live safely; when
I execute judgments over all those from their surroundings who scorn them, they will know that I am
29 1 the Lord, their God." In the tenth year in the tenth month on the twelfth of the month, the
2 word of the Lord came to me: "Man, set your face against Pharaoh, king of Egypt; prophesy against
3 him and against all of Egypt. Speak and say: So says the Lord God: Behold, I am upon you, Pharaoh,
king of Egypt, great crocodile crouching in his Nile streams who says, 'It is mine, this Nile; I made it
4 for myself.' I will fix hooks into your jaw; I will make the fish from your streams stick to your scales; I
5 will drag you up out of your streams, and all the fish from your streams will stick to your scales; I will
abandon you in the desert, you and all the fish of your streams. You will fall in the open field and be
neither collected nor gathered up; to the animals of the land and the birds of the skies I will give you
6 over as food. All the inhabitants of Egypt will know that I am the Lord – for they were a reed staff to
7 the House of Israel: when they grasped hold of you, you crumbled, tearing their shoulders; when they
8 leaned upon you, you broke, buckling their loins. So the Lord God says this: I will bring the
9 sword down upon you, cut off man and beast from you. The land of Egypt will be desolate, ruined, and
10 they will know that I am the Lord. Because he said, 'The Nile is mine; I made it,' for this, I am coming
down upon you and your Nile streams. I will turn the land of Egypt into a waste of desolate ruins from
11 Migdol to Sevene and to the border with Kush. The foot of no man will pass through her; the foot of
12 no animal will pass through her; she will not be inhabited for forty years. For forty years I will make
the land of Egypt desolate among desolate lands, and her cities will lie desolate among ruined cities. I
13 will strew Egypt among the nations, scatter them over the lands. Yet, so says the Lord God,
14 at the end of forty years I will gather Egypt in from the people among whom they were scattered. I
will restore the fortunes of Egypt; I will restore them to the land of Patros, the land of their origin, and
15 there they will be a lowly kingdom. She will be the lowest of the kingdoms and will never again elevate
herself above the nations; I will reduce them to a state where they cannot dominate among the nations.
16 They will no longer be a source of trust for the House of Israel but merely a reminder of Israel's sin in
17 turning to them, and they will know that I am the Lord God." It was in the twenty-seventh
18 year in the first month on the first day of the month that the word of the Lord came to me: "Man:
Nevukhadretzar, king of Babylon, exerted his army to labor hard against Tyre. Every head was rubbed
raw, every shoulder worn down bare, but from Tyre neither he nor his army received pay for the hard
19 work with which they toiled against her. So the Lord God says this: See that to Nevukhadretzar, king of Babylon, I will give the land of Egypt. He will carry off her wealth, ransack her spoils, and
20 seize her loot; she will be the pay for his army. I shall give him the land of Egypt as his payment, for

---

judged we see Egypt. After the plagues that God will inflict upon the Egyptians, "they will know that I am the Lord." Both Egypt and Israel will understand God's role as the orchestrator of history, for they will eventually see the return of Israel to its homeland.

הפטרת וארא

On ראש חודש שבט *read the* מפטיר *from* במדבר כח, ט–טו, *and the* הפטרה *on page 1635.*

כח כד וְלֹא־יִהְיֶה עוֹד לְבֵית יִשְׂרָאֵל סִלּוֹן מַמְאִיר וְקוֹץ מַכְאִב מִכֹּל סְבִיבֹתָם הַשָּׁאטִים אוֹתָם וְיָדְעוּ כִּי יחזקאל
כה אֲנִי אֲדֹנָי יֱהֹוִה: *כֹּה־אָמַר אֲדֹנָי יֱהֹוִה בְּקַבְּצִי ׀ אֶת־בֵּית יִשְׂרָאֵל מִן־הָעַמִּים אֲשֶׁר נָפֹצוּ *Yemenites begin here* / *Ashkenazim and Sephardim begin here*
כו בָם וְנִקְדַּשְׁתִּי בָם לְעֵינֵי הַגּוֹיִם וְיָשְׁבוּ עַל־אַדְמָתָם אֲשֶׁר נָתַתִּי לְעַבְדִּי לְיַעֲקֹב: וְיָשְׁבוּ עָלֶיהָ לָבֶטַח
וּבָנוּ בָתִּים וְנָטְעוּ כְרָמִים וְיָשְׁבוּ לָבֶטַח בַּעֲשׂוֹתִי שְׁפָטִים בְּכֹל הַשָּׁאטִים אֹתָם מִסְּבִיבוֹתָם וְיָדְעוּ כִּי
כט א אֲנִי יְהוָה אֱלֹהֵיהֶם: בַּשָּׁנָה הָעֲשִׂרִית בָּעֲשִׂרִי בִּשְׁנֵים עָשָׂר לַחֹדֶשׁ הָיָה דְבַר־יְהוָה אֵלַי
ב ג לֵאמֹר: בֶּן־אָדָם שִׂים פָּנֶיךָ עַל־פַּרְעֹה מֶלֶךְ מִצְרָיִם וְהִנָּבֵא עָלָיו וְעַל־מִצְרַיִם כֻּלָּהּ: דַּבֵּר וְאָמַרְתָּ כֹּה־
אָמַר ׀ אֲדֹנָי יֱהֹוִה הִנְנִי עָלֶיךָ פַּרְעֹה מֶלֶךְ־מִצְרַיִם הַתַּנִּים הַגָּדוֹל הָרֹבֵץ בְּתוֹךְ יְאֹרָיו אֲשֶׁר אָמַר לִי יְאֹרִי
ד וַאֲנִי עֲשִׂיתִנִי: וְנָתַתִּי חחיים בִלְחָיֶיךָ וְהִדְבַּקְתִּי דְגַת־יְאֹרֶיךָ בְּקַשְׂקְשֹׂתֶיךָ וְהַעֲלִיתִיךָ מִתּוֹךְ יְאֹרֶיךָ וְאֵת חַחִים
ה כָּל־דְּגַת יְאֹרֶיךָ בְּקַשְׂקְשֹׂתֶיךָ תִּדְבָּק: וּנְטַשְׁתִּיךָ הַמִּדְבָּרָה אוֹתְךָ וְאֵת כָּל־דְּגַת יְאֹרֶיךָ עַל־פְּנֵי הַשָּׂדֶה
ו תִּפּוֹל לֹא תֵאָסֵף וְלֹא תִקָּבֵץ לְחַיַּת הָאָרֶץ וּלְעוֹף הַשָּׁמַיִם נְתַתִּיךָ לְאָכְלָה: וְיָדְעוּ כָּל־יֹשְׁבֵי מִצְרַיִם כִּי
ז אֲנִי יְהוָה יַעַן הֱיוֹתָם מִשְׁעֶנֶת קָנֶה לְבֵית יִשְׂרָאֵל: בְּתָפְשָׂם בְּךָ בככפך תֵּרוֹץ וּבָקַעְתָּ לָהֶם כָּל־כָּתֵף בַכַּף
ח וּבְהִשָּׁעֲנָם עָלֶיךָ תִּשָּׁבֵר וְהַעֲמַדְתָּ לָהֶם כָּל־מָתְנָיִם: לָכֵן כֹּה אָמַר אֲדֹנָי יֱהֹוִה הִנְנִי
ט מֵבִיא עָלַיִךְ חָרֶב וְהִכְרַתִּי מִמֵּךְ אָדָם וּבְהֵמָה: וְהָיְתָה אֶרֶץ־מִצְרַיִם לִשְׁמָמָה וְחָרְבָּה וְיָדְעוּ כִּי־אֲנִי
י יְהוָה יַעַן אָמַר יְאֹר לִי וַאֲנִי עָשִׂיתִי: לָכֵן הִנְנִי אֵלֶיךָ וְאֶל־יְאֹרֶיךָ וְנָתַתִּי אֶת־אֶרֶץ מִצְרַיִם לְחָרְבוֹת חֹרֶב
יא שְׁמָמָה מִמִּגְדֹּל סְוֵנֵה וְעַד־גְּבוּל כּוּשׁ: לֹא תַעֲבָר־בָּהּ רֶגֶל אָדָם וְרֶגֶל בְּהֵמָה לֹא תַעֲבָר־בָּהּ וְלֹא תֵשֵׁב
יב אַרְבָּעִים שָׁנָה: וְנָתַתִּי אֶת־אֶרֶץ מִצְרַיִם שְׁמָמָה בְּתוֹךְ ׀ אֲרָצוֹת נְשַׁמּוֹת וְעָרֶיהָ בְּתוֹךְ עָרִים מָחֳרָבוֹת
יג תִּהְיֶיןָ שְׁמָמָה אַרְבָּעִים שָׁנָה וַהֲפִצֹתִי אֶת־מִצְרַיִם בַּגּוֹיִם וְזֵרִיתִים בָּאֲרָצוֹת: כִּי כֹּה אָמַר
יד אֲדֹנָי יֱהֹוִה מִקֵּץ אַרְבָּעִים שָׁנָה אֲקַבֵּץ אֶת־מִצְרַיִם מִן־הָעַמִּים אֲשֶׁר־נָפֹצוּ שָׁמָּה: וְשַׁבְתִּי אֶת־שְׁבוּת
טו מִצְרַיִם וַהֲשִׁבֹתִי אֹתָם אֶרֶץ פַּתְרוֹס עַל־אֶרֶץ מְכוּרָתָם וְהָיוּ שָׁם מַמְלָכָה שְׁפָלָה: מִן־הַמַּמְלָכוֹת תִּהְיֶה
טז שְׁפָלָה וְלֹא־תִתְנַשֵּׂא עוֹד עַל־הַגּוֹיִם וְהִמְעַטְתִּים לְבִלְתִּי רְדוֹת בַּגּוֹיִם: וְלֹא יִהְיֶה־עוֹד לְבֵית יִשְׂרָאֵל
יז לְמִבְטָח מַזְכִּיר עָוֺן בִּפְנוֹתָם אַחֲרֵיהֶם וְיָדְעוּ כִּי אֲנִי אֲדֹנָי יֱהֹוִה: וַיְהִי בְּעֶשְׂרִים וָשֶׁבַע שָׁנָה
יח בָּרִאשׁוֹן בְּאֶחָד לַחֹדֶשׁ הָיָה דְבַר־יְהוָה אֵלַי לֵאמֹר: בֶּן־אָדָם נְבוּכַדְרֶאצַּר מֶלֶךְ־בָּבֶל הֶעֱבִיד אֶת־חֵילוֹ
עֲבֹדָה גְדוֹלָה אֶל־צֹר כָּל־רֹאשׁ מֻקְרָח וְכָל־כָּתֵף מְרוּטָה וְשָׂכָר לֹא־הָיָה לוֹ וּלְחֵילוֹ מִצֹּר עַל־הָעֲבֹדָה
יט אֲשֶׁר־עָבַד עָלֶיהָ: לָכֵן כֹּה אָמַר אֲדֹנָי יֱהֹוִה הִנְנִי נֹתֵן לִנְבוּכַדְרֶאצַּר מֶלֶךְ־בָּבֶל אֶת־אֶרֶץ
כ מִצְרָיִם וְנָשָׂא הֲמֹנָהּ וְשָׁלַל שְׁלָלָהּ וּבָזַז בִּזָּהּ וְהָיְתָה שָׂכָר לְחֵילוֹ: פְּעֻלָּתוֹ אֲשֶׁר־עָבַד בָּהּ נָתַתִּי לוֹ אֶת־

VA'ERA

The middle portion of the book of Ezekiel contains prophecies concerning the nations surrounding Israel. Yeḥezkel pronounced these messages in Babylon to those Jews who had come with him into exile, around the same time as the final Babylonian siege on Jerusalem was progressing. One of the questions being asked at that time was: Why has God given these nations the power to destroy His own Temple, the house of David, and the kingdom of Yehuda? In these chapters of prophecy for the surrounding nations, God clarifies that He will hold each of them accountable for the evil they have committed in lending a hand to the war against His people. There is a Judge, and there will be a reckoning even at the darkest hour. On the list of nations that will be

21 which he has labored, which he has done for Me, declares the Lord God. On that day I will make a
horn of strength grow for the House of Israel, and you – I will let your voice be heard among them, and
they will know that I am the Lord."

Haftarat Bo

JEREMIAH
For Ashkenazim and Sepharadim

46 13 The word that the Lord spoke to Yirmeyahu the prophet – how Nevukhadretzar, king of Babylon,
14 would come to attack the land of Egypt: Tell it in Egypt, let it be heard in Migdol, and let it be heard
in Nof and in Taḥpanḥes! Say, "Stand firm and prepare yourself, for the sword has devoured your sur-
15 roundings." Why have your warriors been swept away? They did not stand because the Lord pushed
16 them down. He made many falter. Each man fell upon his comrade and said, "Get up and let us return
17 to our people and to the land of our birth, away from the sword of the oppressor." There they will
18 taunt: "Pharaoh, king of Egypt, king over a multitude, allowed the appointed time to go by." As I live –
declares the King, Lord of Hosts is His name – just as Tabor is among the mountains, and Carmel is
19 by the sea, so will he come. Make for yourselves baggage for exile, you who dwell securely, daughter
20 Egypt, for Nof will become a desolation, laid waste, with no inhabitant. A very beautiful calf
21 was Egypt, but a murderous enemy attacks her from the north. Even her hired soldiers within her army
are like fattened calves. They too shall turn away, flee together, and not stand firm. Their day of doom
22 has arrived, when they will meet their fate. Her voice will go forth like a snake's, for they will attack
23 her with force and come upon her with axes like woodcutters. They shall cut down her forest, declares
the Lord, although it cannot be fathomed. There are more of them than locusts; they are innumer-
24 25 able. Shamed is daughter Egypt, given over into the hands of the northern people. Said the Lord of
Hosts, the God of Israel, I will inflict punishment upon Amon of No, and upon Pharaoh, and upon
26 Egypt, upon her gods and upon her kings, upon Pharaoh and all who trust in him. I will give them over
into the hands of those who seek their lives and into the hands of Nevukhadretzar, king of Babylon,
and into the hands of his servants. Afterward, she shall be inhabited as in days of old, declares the
27 Lord. As for you, My servant Yaakov, do not fear, and Israel, do not be terrified, for I will deliver you from a distant land and your descendants from their land of captivity. For Yaakov it will again
28 be quiet and tranquil, with none to frighten him. And you, My servant Yaakov, do not fear, declares the
Lord, for I am with you. For I will make an end of all the nations among whom I have scattered you,
but of you I will not make an end. I will discipline you justly, but I will surely not annihilate you.

ISAIAH
For Yemenites

19 1 The burden of Egypt: Behold the Lord, riding upon swift cloud and coming to Egypt. The gods of
2 Egypt all sway before Him; the heart of Egypt will dissolve. I shall make Egypt wrestle with Egypt;
3 brother will fight against brother, friend against friend, city against city, realm against realm. Egypt

---

punished with utter destruction for their cruel and wicked acts in the context of world events. It is God who directs the course of world history, and it is He who will hold wicked states to account. It is He too who will always leave Israel standing on the world stage, even after punishing it for its sins.

For Yemenites

In the prophecy of Yeshayahu, as part of a collection of prophecies directed at various nations, we find one singling out Egypt and describing its future in two stages. At the first stage, there will be internal strife within the Egyptian state that will lead to its conquest by a tyrannical foreign ruler

כא אֶרֶץ מִצְרָיִם אֲשֶׁר עָשׂוּ לִי נְאֻם אֲדֹנָי יֱהֹוִה׃ בַּיּוֹם הַהוּא אַצְמִיחַ קֶרֶן לְבֵית יִשְׂרָאֵל וּלְךָ אֶתֵּן פִּתְחוֹן־פֶּה
בְּתוֹכָם וְיָדְעוּ כִּי־אֲנִי יהוה׃

הפטרת בא

ירמיה
For Ashkenazim and Sepharadim

מו יג הַדָּבָר אֲשֶׁר דִּבֶּר יהוה אֶל־יִרְמְיָהוּ הַנָּבִיא לָבוֹא נְבוּכַדְרֶאצַּר מֶלֶךְ בָּבֶל לְהַכּוֹת אֶת־אֶרֶץ מִצְרָיִם׃
יד הַגִּידוּ בְמִצְרַיִם וְהַשְׁמִיעוּ בְמִגְדּוֹל וְהַשְׁמִיעוּ בְנֹף וּבְתַחְפַּנְחֵס אִמְרוּ הִתְיַצֵּב וְהָכֵן לָךְ כִּי־אָכְלָה חֶרֶב
טו טז סְבִיבֶיךָ׃ מַדּוּעַ נִסְחַף אַבִּירֶיךָ לֹא עָמַד כִּי יהוה הֲדָפוֹ׃ הִרְבָּה כּוֹשֵׁל גַּם־נָפַל אִישׁ אֶל־רֵעֵהוּ וַיֹּאמְרוּ
יז קוּמָה ׀ וְנָשֻׁבָה אֶל־עַמֵּנוּ וְאֶל־אֶרֶץ מוֹלַדְתֵּנוּ מִפְּנֵי חֶרֶב הַיּוֹנָה׃ קָרְאוּ שָׁם פַּרְעֹה מֶלֶךְ־מִצְרַיִם שָׁאוֹן
יח יט הֶעֱבִיר הַמּוֹעֵד׃ חַי־אָנִי נְאֻם־הַמֶּלֶךְ יהוה צְבָאוֹת שְׁמוֹ כִּי כְּתָבוֹר בֶּהָרִים וּכְכַרְמֶל בַּיָּם יָבוֹא׃ כְּלֵי
כ גוֹלָה עֲשִׂי לָךְ יוֹשֶׁבֶת בַּת־מִצְרָיִם כִּי־נֹף לְשַׁמָּה תִהְיֶה וְנִצְּתָה מֵאֵין יוֹשֵׁב׃ עֶגְלָה יְפֵה־פִיָּה
כא מִצְרָיִם קֶרֶץ מִצָּפוֹן בָּא בָא׃ גַּם־שְׂכִרֶיהָ בְקִרְבָּהּ כְּעֶגְלֵי מַרְבֵּק כִּי־גַם־הֵמָּה הִפְנוּ נָסוּ יַחְדָּיו לֹא עָמָדוּ
כב כִּי יוֹם אֵידָם בָּא עֲלֵיהֶם עֵת פְּקֻדָּתָם׃ קוֹלָהּ כַּנָּחָשׁ יֵלֵךְ כִּי־בְחַיִל יֵלֵכוּ וּבְקַרְדֻּמּוֹת בָּאוּ לָהּ כְּחֹטְבֵי
כג כד עֵצִים׃ כָּרְתוּ יַעְרָהּ נְאֻם־יהוה כִּי לֹא יֵחָקֵר כִּי רַבּוּ מֵאַרְבֶּה וְאֵין לָהֶם מִסְפָּר׃ הֹבִישָׁה בַּת־מִצְרָיִם נִתְּנָה
כה בְּיַד עַם־צָפוֹן׃ אָמַר יהוה צְבָאוֹת אֱלֹהֵי יִשְׂרָאֵל הִנְנִי פוֹקֵד אֶל־אָמוֹן מִנֹּא וְעַל־פַּרְעֹה וְעַל־מִצְרַיִם
כו וְעַל־אֱלֹהֶיהָ וְעַל־מְלָכֶיהָ וְעַל־פַּרְעֹה וְעַל הַבֹּטְחִים בּוֹ׃ וּנְתַתִּים בְּיַד מְבַקְשֵׁי נַפְשָׁם וּבְיַד נְבוּכַדְרֶאצַּר
כז מֶלֶךְ־בָּבֶל וּבְיַד עֲבָדָיו וְאַחֲרֵי־כֵן תִּשְׁכֹּן כִּימֵי־קֶדֶם נְאֻם־יהוה׃ וְאַתָּה אַל־תִּירָא עַבְדִּי
יַעֲקֹב וְאַל־תֵּחַת יִשְׂרָאֵל כִּי הִנְנִי מוֹשִׁעֲךָ מֵרָחוֹק וְאֶת־זַרְעֲךָ מֵאֶרֶץ שִׁבְיָם וְשָׁב יַעֲקוֹב וְשָׁקַט וְשַׁאֲנַן
כח וְאֵין מַחֲרִיד׃ אַתָּה אַל־תִּירָא עַבְדִּי יַעֲקֹב נְאֻם־יהוה כִּי אִתְּךָ אָנִי כִּי אֶעֱשֶׂה כָלָה בְּכָל־הַגּוֹיִם ׀ אֲשֶׁר
הִדַּחְתִּיךָ שָׁמָּה וְאֹתְךָ לֹא־אֶעֱשֶׂה כָלָה וְיִסַּרְתִּיךָ לַמִּשְׁפָּט וְנַקֵּה לֹא אֲנַקֶּךָּ׃

ישעיה
For Yemenites

יט א מַשָּׂא מִצְרָיִם הִנֵּה יהוה רֹכֵב עַל־עָב קַל וּבָא מִצְרַיִם וְנָעוּ אֱלִילֵי מִצְרַיִם מִפָּנָיו וּלְבַב מִצְרַיִם יִמַּס בְּקִרְבּוֹ׃
ב ג וְסִכְסַכְתִּי מִצְרַיִם בְּמִצְרַיִם וְנִלְחֲמוּ אִישׁ בְּאָחִיו וְאִישׁ בְּרֵעֵהוּ עִיר בְּעִיר מַמְלָכָה בְּמַמְלָכָה׃ וְנָבְקָה
רוּחַ־מִצְרַיִם בְּקִרְבּוֹ וַעֲצָתוֹ אֲבַלֵּעַ וְדָרְשׁוּ אֶל־הָאֱלִילִים וְאֶל־הָאִטִּים וְאֶל־הָאֹבוֹת וְאֶל־הַיִּדְּעֹנִים׃

BO

For Ashkenazim and Sepharadim

The prophecies that close the book of Jeremiah address the nations of the Levant. They are harbingers of the doom that awaits those peoples who participated in the destruction of Yehuda and Jerusalem. In one, the prophet describes the expedition of Nevukhadnetzar to conquer Egypt, after he has laid waste to Yehuda. In the prophet's eyes, all peoples are transient, and can cease to exist and be replaced once they have served their role in history. As such, they can be

▶

will empty its spirit from within, and I shall confound all its plans. The people will seek after their
4 false gods and mutterers, necromancers, mediums. I shall dam Egypt through a hard-handed master; a
5 mighty king will tyrannize them, so says the Master, LORD of Hosts. The sea will be emptied of water;
6 the river will be scorched dry. Rivers will be forsaken; Egypt's canals will dwindle and dry, and rush
7 and reed wither. Naked land on the Nile bed, naked the bank of the Nile, and all that seeds and grows
8 in the Nile will dry up, disperse, be gone. The fishermen will lament; all who throw hooks to the river
9 will mourn, all who spread nets over water left waste. The many who work combed flax will be shamed
10 with all those who weave fine cotton; Egypt's foundations – crushed, its dam builders mired spirits.
11 The princes of Tzoan are fools; the wisest of Pharaoh's advisors give idiots' counsel. How can you say
12 to Pharaoh, "I am a son of wise men, heir to the ancient kings?" Where, then – where are these wise
men of yours? Surely they would tell you, surely they must know what the LORD of Hosts has planned
13 for Egypt. The princes of Tzoan are fools; the princes of Nof, deceived. They have lead Egypt astray,
14 the very mainstay of its tribes. The LORD has poured into her a spirit of madness, and they have led
15 Egypt awry in all it does, like a drunk man lurching through his vomit. Nothing in Egypt will be done
16 that is done by head or by tail, by palm or by bulrush of them. On that day, Egypt will be like
17 women who quake and fear the LORD of Hosts' raised hand brandished over them; the land of Judah
will be the terror of Egypt. Whoever may mention its name will strike them with fear of the LORD of
18 Hosts' plan – of what He has destined for them. On that day, five cities of Egypt shall speak
the language of Canaan and swear their oaths by the LORD of Hosts. City of Calamity, one shall be
19 named. On that day, in Egypt's heartlands, an altar to the LORD will stand; at her borders a
20 pillar to the LORD. They will be sign and testament in the land of Egypt to the LORD of Hosts, for the
people shall cry out to the LORD because of their oppressors; He will send them a rescuer, a fighter;
21 he will save them. The LORD will be made known to Egypt, and Egypt will know the LORD on that
22 day. And they will serve by sacrifice and offering; they will make the LORD vows and honor them. The
LORD will plague Egypt – plague it and heal. They will come back to the LORD, and He will receive
23 their appeal and heal. On that day a road will run from Egypt to Assyria. Assyria will come to
24 Egypt. Egypt will come to Assyria, and Egypt with Assyria will worship. On that day, Israel
25 will be one with Egypt and Assyria, a blessing on this earth. For the LORD of Hosts has blessed him,
saying: Blessed are My people, Egypt, Assyria, work of My hands, and Israel, My own possession.

HAFTARAT BESHALAḤ

JUDGES *Ashkenazim and Chabad begin here*

4 4 Devora was a prophetess, the wife of Lapidot; she was judging Israel at that time. She sat beneath
5 Devora's palm between Rama and Beit El in the Efrayim hills; the Israelites would go up to her for
6 judgment. One day, she summoned Barak son of Avinoam from Kedesh Naftali and said to him, "The
LORD, God of Israel, has commanded: Go, take ten thousand men of the people of Naftali and Zevu-
7 lun and lead them to Mount Tavor. And at the Kishon Stream I shall lead to you to Sisera, Yavin's

some hold him to be the emperor of Assyria or even Persia. In its second section, the prophecy clearly describes the end of days, the conditions for which have not yet been fulfilled.

BESHALAḤ

The period of the Judges was characterized by a vacuum of centralized power. This reality projected an appearance of weakness within Israelite society and without, causing the

ד ה וסכרתי את־מצרים ביד אדנים קשה ומלך עז ימשל־בם נאם האדון יהוה צבאות: ונשתו־מים מהים
ו ז ונהר יחרב ויבש: והאזניחו נהרות דללו וחרבו יארי מצור קנה וסוף קמלו: ערות על־יאור על־פי
ח יאור וכל מזרע יאור ייבש נדף ואיננו: ואנו הדיגים ואבלו כל־משליכי ביאור חכה ופרשי מכמרת
ט י על־פני־מים אמללו: ובשו עבדי פשתים שריקות וארגים חורי: והיו שתתיה מדכאים כל־עשי שכר
יא אגמי־נפש: אך־אולים שרי צען חכמי יעצי פרעה עצה נבערה איך תאמרו אל־פרעה בן־חכמים
יב יג אני בן־מלכי־קדם: איים אפוא חכמיך ויגידו נא לך וידעו מה־יעץ יהוה צבאות על־מצרים: נואלו
יד שרי צען נשאו שרי נף התעו את־מצרים פנת שבטיה: יהוה מסך בקרבה רוח עועים והתעו את־
טו מצרים בכל־מעשהו כהתעות שכור בקיאו: ולא־יהיה למצרים מעשה אשר יעשה ראש וזנב כפה
טז ואגמון: ביום ההוא יהיה מצרים כנשים וחרד ׀ ופחד מפני תנופת יד־יהוה צבאות
יז אשר־הוא מניף עליו: והיתה אדמת יהודה למצרים לחגא כל אשר יזכיר אתה אליו יפחד מפני
יח עצת יהוה צבאות אשר־הוא יועץ עליו: ביום ההוא יהיו חמש ערים בארץ מצרים
יט מדברות שפת כנען ונשבעות ליהוה צבאות עיר ההרס יאמר לאחת: ביום ההוא יהיה
כ מזבח ליהוה בתוך ארץ מצרים ומצבה אצל־גבולה ליהוה: והיה לאות ולעד ליהוה צבאות בארץ
כא מצרים כי־יצעקו אל־יהוה מפני לחצים וישלח להם מושיע ורב והצילם: ונודע יהוה למצרים וידעו
כב מצרים את־יהוה ביום ההוא ועבדו זבח ומנחה ונדרו־נדר ליהוה ושלמו: ונגף יהוה את־מצרים
כג נגף ורפוא ושבו עד־יהוה ונעתר להם ורפאם: ביום ההוא תהיה מסלה ממצרים אשורה
כד ובא־אשור במצרים ומצרים באשור ועבדו מצרים את־אשור: ביום ההוא יהיה ישראל
כה שלישיה למצרים ולאשור ברכה בקרב הארץ: אשר ברכו יהוה צבאות לאמר ברוך עמי מצרים
ומעשה ידי אשור ונחלתי ישראל:

הפטרת בשלח

שופטים

Ashkenazim and Chabad begin here

ד ד ה ודבורה אשה נביאה אשת לפידות היא שפטה את־ישראל בעת ההיא: והיא יושבת תחת־תמר
ו דבורה בין הרמה ובין בית־אל בהר אפרים ויעלו אליה בני ישראל למשפט: ותשלח ותקרא
לברק בן־אבינעם מקדש נפתלי ותאמר אליו הלא־צוה ׀ יהוה אלהי־ישראל לך ומשכת בהר
ז תבור ולקחת עמך עשרת אלפים איש מבני נפתלי ומבני זבלון: ומשכתי אליך אל־נחל קישון

who will dominate it. All strata of Egyptian society will be humiliated, and the economy of Egypt will be greatly damaged. All this will lead the Egyptians to recognize the sovereignty of God, who directs all these events. This recognition will lead to a change of perspective in Egypt and in Assyria as well, who will ultimately join Israel in worshipping God alone.

Scholars and commentators debate what events or period of time is referred to in this prophecy. Some identify the tyrannical foreign ruler as a king of Ethiopia, and

8 general, along with his chariots and his hordes, and deliver him into your hands." Barak said to her,
9 "If you go with me, I will go; if not, I will not." "Then I shall go with you," she said, "but you will find
no glory on the path you are taking, for the Lord will deliver Sisera into the hands of a woman." So
10 Devora arose and accompanied Barak to Kedesh. Barak mustered Zevulun and Naftali at Kedesh and
11 advanced with ten thousand men behind him, and Devora went up with him. Ḥever the Kenite had
parted ways from the Kenites, who were descended from Ḥovav, Moshe's father-in-law. He had pitched
12 his tent at Elon BeTzaananim, which was by Kedesh. Sisera was informed that Barak son of Avinoam
13 had advanced to Mount Tavor. And Sisera mustered all his chariots – nine hundred iron chariots – and
14 all his warriors from Ḥaroshet HaGoyim to Kishon Stream. "Rise up!" Devora said to Barak. "For on
this day, the Lord will deliver Sisera into your hands – the Lord marches before you!" Barak charged
15 down Mount Tavor with ten thousand men behind him. And the Lord threw Sisera, all his chariots,
and his entire force into panic before Barak's swords. Sisera dismounted from his chariot and fled on
16 foot. Barak chased the chariots and warriors to Ḥaroshet HaGoyim, and all of Sisera's army fell by the
17 sword; not a single man survived. Now Sisera had fled on foot to the tent of Yael, the wife of Ḥever the
18 Kenite, for there was peace between Yavin, king of Ḥatzor, and Ḥever's family. Yael went out to meet
Sisera. "Turn aside, my lord," she said to him, "turn aside to me – do not fear." He turned aside into her
19 tent, and she covered him with a blanket. "Give me a little water, please," he asked her, "for I am thirsty."
20 She opened a skin of milk, gave him some to drink, and covered him once again. "Stand at the entrance
21 to the tent," he told her, "and if anyone comes and asks you if someone is here, say, 'No.'" Then Yael,
wife of Ḥever, picked up a tent peg, grasped a mallet, crept up to him – he had fallen asleep, exhaust-
22 ed – and hammered the tent peg through his temple until it sunk into the ground and he died. Now
Barak was chasing Sisera, and Yael went out to meet him. "Come," she said to him, "I will show you the
man you seek." He came to her, and there was Sisera, sprawled out dead, with the tent peg through his
23 temple. *On that day, God subdued Yavin, king of Canaan, before the Israelites. And the hand of the *Yemenites begin here*
24 Israelites grew harsher and harsher against Yavin, king of Canaan, until they had destroyed him.

5 1 2 *And Devora sang – and Barak son of Avinoam with her – on that day: / When chaos was loosed in *Sepharadim begin here*
3 Israel, / when people offered themselves willingly – / bless the Lord! / Hear, O kings, / give ear, O
4 rulers, / I – to the Lord I will sing, / I will chant to the Lord, God of Israel. / O Lord, when You
left Se'ir, / when You marched from the fields of Edom, / the earth shook, / the heavens poured – /
5 rain poured from the clouds, / the mountains melted before the Lord, / Sinai itself before the Lord,
6 God of Israel! / In the days of Shamgar son of Anat, / in the days of Yael, / there were no caravans; /
7 wayfarers walked roundabout paths. / There were no unwalled cities in Israel, / none – / until you

---

that lived next to them in the valley of Yizre'el. The danger of Canaanite raids on the main roads created a division between the northern and central tribes. Following God's commandment to the prophetess Devora, an army of volunteers came onto the field under the leadership of Barak son of Avinoam to fight the Canaanite armies. Following the Israelites' surprising and dramatic victory over the Canaanites and their chariots, Devora and Barak sang this song of praise to God, just as generations earlier, the nation redeemed from Egypt had sung the Song at the Sea after their miraculous rescue from the Egyptian cavalry.

ח את־סיסרא שר־צבא יבין ואת־רכבו ואת־המונו ונתתיהו בידך: ויאמר אליה ברק אם־תלכי עמי
ט והלכתי ואם־לא תלכי עמי לא אלך: ותאמר הלך אלך עמך אפס כי לא תהיה תפארתך על־הדרך
י אשר אתה הולך כי ביד־אשה ימכר יהוה את־סיסרא ותקם דבורה ותלך עם־ברק קדשה: ויזעק
יא ברק את־זבולן ואת־נפתלי קדשה ויעל ברגליו עשרת אלפי איש ותעל עמו דבורה: וחבר הקיני
יב נפרד מקין מבני חבב חתן משה ויט אהלו עד־אלון בצענים אשר את־קדש: ויגדו לסיסרא כי עלה בצעננים
יג ברק בן־אבינעם הר־תבור: ויזעק סיסרא את־כל־רכבו תשע מאות רכב ברזל ואת־כל־העם אשר
יד אתו מחרשת הגוים אל־נחל קישון: ותאמר דברה אל־ברק קום כי זה היום אשר נתן יהוה את־
טו סיסרא בידך הלא יהוה יצא לפניך וירד ברק מהר תבור ועשרת אלפים איש אחריו: ויהם יהוה
את־סיסרא ואת־כל־הרכב ואת־כל־המחנה לפי־חרב לפני ברק וירד סיסרא מעל המרכבה וינס
טז ברגליו: וברק רדף אחרי הרכב ואחרי המחנה עד חרשת הגוים ויפל כל־מחנה סיסרא לפי־חרב
יז לא נשאר עד־אחד: וסיסרא נס ברגליו אל־אהל יעל אשת חבר הקיני כי שלום בין יבין מלך־חצור
יח ובין בית חבר הקיני: ותצא יעל לקראת סיסרא ותאמר אליו סורה אדני סורה אלי אל־תירא ויסר
יט אליה האהלה ותכסהו בשמיכה: ויאמר אליה השקיני־נא מעט־מים כי צמתי ותפתח את־נאוד
כ החלב ותשקהו ותכסהו: ויאמר אליה עמד פתח האהל והיה אם־איש יבוא ושאלך ואמר היש־
כא פה איש ואמרת אין: ותקח יעל אשת־חבר את־יתד האהל ותשם את־המקבת בידה ותבוא אליו
כב בלאט ותתקע את־היתד ברקתו ותצנח בארץ והוא־נרדם ויעף וימת: והנה ברק רדף את־סיסרא
ותצא יעל לקראתו ותאמר לו לך ואראך את־האיש אשר־אתה מבקש ויבא אליה והנה סיסרא
כג כד נפל מת והיתד ברקתו: *ויכנע אלהים ביום ההוא את יבין מלך־כנען לפני בני ישראל: ותלך יד *Yemenites begin here*
בני־ישראל הלוך וקשה על יבין מלך־כנען עד אשר הכריתו את יבין מלך־כנען:

ה א * ותשר דבורה וברק בן־אבינעם ביום ההוא *Sepharadim begin here*
ב לאמר: בפרע פרעות בישראל בהתנדב
ג עם ברכו יהוה: שמעו מלכים האזינו
רזנים אנכי ליהוה אנכי אשירה אזמר
ד ליהוה אלהי ישראל: יהוה בצאתך
משעיר בצעדך משדה אדום ארץ
רעשה גם־שמים נטפו גם־עבים נטפו
ה מים: הרים נזלו מפני יהוה זה
ו סיני מפני יהוה אלהי ישראל: בימי שמגר בן־
ענת בימי יעל חדלו ארחות והלכי
ז נתיבות ילכו ארחות עקלקלות: חדלו פרזון בישראל
חדלו עד שקמתי דבורה שקמתי

tribes to become ready prey for their aggressive neighbors. Such was the case in the generation of Devora and Barak. The Canaanites relied on iron chariotry for military power, and they disrupted the everyday life of the Israelite tribes

8 arose, Devora, / until you arose, a mother in Israel! / When they chose new gods, / there was war at the
9 gates – / but no shield or spear was seen / amid forty thousand of Israel! / My heart is with Israel's lead-
10 ers, / the people who offer themselves willingly – / bless the LORD! / O riders of white she-donkeys, /
11 mounted on fine saddles, / O wayfarers: / speak out – / louder than the sound of archers / by the
watering places; / there they shall recount the LORD's graces, / how He graced the unwalled cities
12 in Israel; / then, down to the gates / marched the people of the LORD! / Awake, awake, Devora – /
13 awake, awake, burst into song! / Arise, Barak – / seize your captives, son of Avinoam; / then the rem-
14 nant ruled over the mighty people, / the LORD ruled over the warriors for me! / From Efrayim, rooted
in Amalek: / "After you, Binyamin, with your people!" / From Makhir marched down leaders, / from
15 Zevulun, wielders of the scribal staff. / Yissakhar's chiefs were with Devora, / Yissakhar, like Barak,
16 charged into the valley, / while amongst the clans of Reuven / was great soul-searching. / Why did you
linger among the sheepfolds / to hear the whistling for the flocks? / Amongst the clans of Reuven /
17 was great soul-searching. / Gilad stayed put across the Jordan, / and why did Dan stay by the ships? /
18 Asher lingered by the seashore, / staying put by its harbors. / Zevulun, a people who risked their lives
19 for death / with Naftali on the open heights; / then came the kings to do battle, / then Canaan's kings
20 did battle / at Tanakh, by the waters of Megiddo – / but they took no spoil of silver! / From the heavens
21 they fought; / the stars from their courses fought against Sisera! / Kishon Stream swept them away, /
22 the ancient stream, the Kishon Stream – / march on, my soul, with might! / The hooves of horses
23 hammered / with the gallop, the gallop of the steeds! / "Curse Meroz," said the LORD's angel, / "curse
its people harshly, / for they did not come to the aid of the LORD, / to the aid of the LORD amidst the
24 warriors." / Blessed beyond women be Yael, / wife of Ḥever the Kenite, / blessed beyond women in

ח אֵ֥ם בְּיִשְׂרָאֵֽל׃ יִבְחַר֙ אֱלֹהִ֣ים
חֲדָשִׁ֔ים אָ֖ז לָחֶ֣ם שְׁעָרִ֑ים מָגֵ֤ן
אִם־יֵרָאֶה֙ וָרֹ֔מַח בְּאַרְבָּעִ֥ים אֶ֖לֶף
ט בְּיִשְׂרָאֵֽל׃ לִבִּי֙ לְחוֹקְקֵ֣י יִשְׂרָאֵ֔ל הַמִּֽתְנַדְּבִ֖ים
י בָּעָ֑ם בָּרְכ֖וּ יהוה׃ רֹכְבֵי֙ אֲתֹנ֜וֹת
צְחֹר֗וֹת יֹשְׁבֵ֛י עַל־מִדִּ֖ין וְהֹלְכֵ֥י
יא עַל־דֶּ֖רֶךְ שִֽׂיחוּ׃ מִקּ֣וֹל מְחַצְצִ֗ים בֵּ֚ין
מַשְׁאַבִּ֔ים שָׁ֤ם יְתַנּוּ֙ צִדְק֣וֹת יהוה צִדְקֹ֖ת
פִּרְזֹנ֣וֹ בְּיִשְׂרָאֵ֑ל אָ֛ז יָרְד֥וּ לַשְּׁעָרִ֖ים עַם־
יב יהוה׃ ע֤וּרִי ע֙וּרִי֙ דְּבוֹרָ֔ה ע֥וּרִי
ע֖וּרִי דַּבְּרִי־שִׁ֑יר ק֣וּם בָּרָ֗ק וּֽשֲׁבֵ֥ה שֶׁבְיְךָ֖ בֶּן־
יג אֲבִינֹֽעַם׃ אָ֚ז יְרַ֣ד שָׂרִ֔יד לְאַדִּירִ֖ים עָ֑ם יהוה
יד יְרַד־לִ֖י בַּגִּבּוֹרִֽים׃ מִנִּ֣י אֶפְרַ֗יִם שָׁרְשָׁם֙
בַּעֲמָלֵ֔ק אַחֲרֶ֥יךָ בִנְיָמִ֖ין בַּעֲמָמֶ֑יךָ מִנִּ֣י
מָכִ֗יר יָֽרְדוּ֙ מְחֹ֣קְקִ֔ים וּמִ֨זְּבוּלֻ֔ן מֹשְׁכִ֖ים בְּשֵׁ֥בֶט
טו סֹפֵֽר׃ וְשָׂרַ֤י בְּיִשָּׂשכָר֙ עִם־דְּבֹרָ֔ה וְיִשָּׂשכָר֙
כֵּ֣ן בָּרָ֔ק בָּעֵ֖מֶק שֻׁלַּ֣ח
בְּרַגְלָ֑יו בִּפְלַגּ֣וֹת רְאוּבֵ֔ן גְּדֹלִ֖ים
טז חִקְקֵי־לֵֽב׃ לָ֣מָּה יָשַׁ֗בְתָּ בֵּ֚ין
הַֽמִּשְׁפְּתַ֔יִם לִשְׁמֹ֖עַ שְׁרִק֣וֹת עֲדָרִ֑ים לִפְלַגּ֣וֹת
יז רְאוּבֵ֔ן גְּדוֹלִ֖ים חִקְרֵי־לֵֽב׃ גִּלְעָ֞ד בְּעֵ֤בֶר הַיַּרְדֵּן֙
שָׁכֵ֔ן וְדָ֕ן לָ֥מָּה יָג֖וּר אֳנִיּ֑וֹת אָשֵׁ֗ר
יָשַׁב֙ לְח֣וֹף יַמִּ֔ים וְעַ֥ל מִפְרָצָ֖יו
יח יִשְׁכּֽוֹן׃ זְבֻל֗וּן עַ֣ם חֵרֵ֥ף נַפְשׁ֛וֹ לָמ֖וּת וְנַפְתָּלִ֑י
יט עַ֖ל מְר֥וֹמֵי שָׂדֶֽה׃ בָּ֤אוּ מְלָכִים֙
נִלְחָ֔מוּ אָ֤ז נִלְחֲמוּ֙ מַלְכֵ֣י כְנַ֔עַן בְּתַעְנַ֖ךְ
עַל־מֵ֣י מְגִדּ֑וֹ בֶּ֥צַע כֶּ֖סֶף לֹ֥א
כ לָקָֽחוּ׃ מִן־שָׁמַ֖יִם נִלְחָ֑מוּ הַכּֽוֹכָבִים֙
כא מִֽמְּסִלּוֹתָ֔ם נִלְחֲמ֖וּ עִם־סִֽיסְרָֽא׃ נַ֤חַל קִישׁוֹן֙
גְּרָפָ֔ם נַ֥חַל קְדוּמִ֖ים נַ֣חַל קִישׁ֑וֹן תִּדְרְכִ֥י
כב נַפְשִׁ֖י עֹֽז׃ אָ֥ז הָלְמ֖וּ עִקְּבֵי־
כג ס֑וּס מִֽדַּהֲר֖וֹת דַּהֲר֥וֹת אַבִּירָֽיו׃ א֣וֹרוּ
מֵר֗וֹז אָמַר֙ מַלְאַ֣ךְ יהוה אֹ֖רוּ אָר֣וֹר
יֹשְׁבֶ֑יהָ כִּ֤י לֹא־בָ֙אוּ֙ לְעֶזְרַ֣ת יהוה לְעֶזְרַ֥ת
כד יהוה בַּגִּבּוֹרִֽים׃ תְּבֹרַךְ֙ מִנָּשִׁ֔ים

25 26 tents! / Water he asked for, milk she gave; / in a princely bowl she offered cream. / Her hand shot out
for the tent peg, / her right hand for the workman's hammer, / and hammered Sisera / and crushed his
27 head / and smashed and pierced his temple! / Between her legs he lay slumped, sprawled, / between
28 her legs he slumped, sprawled, / where he slumped, there he sprawled, slain! / Through the window
she peered, / Sisera's mother wailed through the lattice, / "Why does his chariot tarry so? / Why so
29 30 late, the clank of his chariots?" / The wisest of her ladies reply – / she even answers herself – / "Why,
they are dividing up the spoil they found, / a womb or two for every man, / a haul of colors for Sisera, /
31 a haul of colors of embroidery, / colored embroidery, two apiece, for the spoilers' throats." / Thus may
all Your enemies perish, O Lord, / and may His friends be like the risen sun! / And the land was quiet
for forty years.

Haftarat Yitro

ISAIAH

6 1 In the year in which King Uziyahu died I saw the Lord sitting on a high, raised throne, the hem of His
2 clothing filling the Sanctuary. There were seraphim standing above Him, each with six wings – with
3 two they covered their faces, with two they covered their feet, and with two they were flying. And they
called out one to another, "Holy, holy, holy – the Lord of Hosts – all the world's fullness His glory."
4 5 The door pillars shook with the voice of him who called – and smoke filled the House. And I said, "This
ache – I am condemned, for my mouth has been defiled, one man among a people with their mouths
6 defiled, and my eyes see the King, the Lord of Hosts." One of the seraphim flew to me, and in his hand
7 was a coal, taken with tongs from the altar top. With this he touched my lips and said, "When this has
8 touched your lips, your iniquity is gone, and all your sin forgiven." I heard the voice of the Lord saying,
9 "Whom shall I send, and who will go for us?" And I said, "I am here. Send me." He said, "Go – tell this
10 people: Hear, you shall hear but understand it not, see it all but know it not. Fatten the heart of this
people; make their ears heavy; coat their eyes with plaster, lest they see with their eyes and hear with

---

He is tasked with confronting the people of Israel and warning them of the coming destruction if they continue in their evil ways. In the vision, God is seen sitting on a great throne in the Temple hall, surrounded by His heavenly retinue, but the door pillars are shaking and the Temple is filled with smoke, signs of an earthquake or volcanic eruption. These impressions of instability mirror the state of the kingdom at the close of Uziyahu's reign, and they are meant to jar the listener to repentance before it is too late.

יָעֵל	אֵשֶׁת חֶבֶר הַקֵּינִי	מִנָּשִׁים
כה בָּאֹהֶל תְּבֹרָךְ:		מַיִם שָׁאַל חָלָב
כו נָתָנָה	בְּסֵפֶל אַדִּירִים הִקְרִיבָה חֶמְאָה:	יָדָהּ
לַיָּתֵד תִּשְׁלַחְנָה		וִימִינָהּ לְהַלְמוּת
עֲמֵלִים	וְהָלְמָה סִיסְרָא מָחֲקָה רֹאשׁוֹ	וּמָחֲצָה
כז וְחָלְפָה רַקָּתוֹ:		בֵּין רַגְלֶיהָ כָּרַע נָפַל
שָׁכָב	בֵּין רַגְלֶיהָ כָּרַע נָפָל	בַּאֲשֶׁר
כח כָּרַע שָׁם נָפַל שָׁדוּד:		בְּעַד הַחַלּוֹן נִשְׁקְפָה
וַתְּיַבֵּב	אֵם סִיסְרָא בְּעַד הָאֶשְׁנָב	מַדּוּעַ
בֹּשֵׁשׁ רִכְבּוֹ לָבוֹא		מַדּוּעַ אֶחֱרוּ פַּעֲמֵי
כט מַרְכְּבוֹתָיו:	חַכְמוֹת שָׂרוֹתֶיהָ תַּעֲנֶינָּה	אַף־
ל הִיא תָּשִׁיב אֲמָרֶיהָ לָהּ:		הֲלֹא יִמְצְאוּ יְחַלְּקוּ
שָׁלָל	רַחַם רַחֲמָתַיִם לְרֹאשׁ גֶּבֶר	שְׁלַל
צְבָעִים לְסִיסְרָא		שְׁלַל צְבָעִים
לא רִקְמָה	צֶבַע רִקְמָתַיִם לְצַוְּארֵי שָׁלָל:	כֵּן
יֹאבְדוּ כָל־אוֹיְבֶיךָ יהוה		וְאֹהֲבָיו כְּצֵאת הַשֶּׁמֶשׁ
בִּגְבֻרָתוֹ	וַתִּשְׁקֹט הָאָרֶץ	אַרְבָּעִים שָׁנָה:

הפטרת יתרו

ישעיה

ו א ב בִּשְׁנַת־מוֹת הַמֶּלֶךְ עֻזִּיָּהוּ וָאֶרְאֶה אֶת־אֲדֹנָי יֹשֵׁב עַל־כִּסֵּא רָם וְנִשָּׂא וְשׁוּלָיו מְלֵאִים אֶת־הַהֵיכָל: שְׂרָפִים
עֹמְדִים ׀ מִמַּעַל לוֹ שֵׁשׁ כְּנָפַיִם שֵׁשׁ כְּנָפַיִם לְאֶחָד בִּשְׁתַּיִם ׀ יְכַסֶּה פָנָיו וּבִשְׁתַּיִם יְכַסֶּה רַגְלָיו וּבִשְׁתַּיִם
ג ד יְעוֹפֵף: וְקָרָא זֶה אֶל־זֶה וְאָמַר קָדוֹשׁ ׀ קָדוֹשׁ קָדוֹשׁ יהוה צְבָאוֹת מְלֹא כָל־הָאָרֶץ כְּבוֹדוֹ: וַיָּנֻעוּ אַמּוֹת
ה הַסִּפִּים מִקּוֹל הַקּוֹרֵא וְהַבַּיִת יִמָּלֵא עָשָׁן: וָאֹמַר אוֹי־לִי כִי־נִדְמֵיתִי כִּי אִישׁ טְמֵא־שְׂפָתַיִם אָנֹכִי וּבְתוֹךְ
ו עַם־טְמֵא שְׂפָתַיִם אָנֹכִי יֹשֵׁב כִּי אֶת־הַמֶּלֶךְ יהוה צְבָאוֹת רָאוּ עֵינָי: וַיָּעָף אֵלַי אֶחָד מִן־הַשְּׂרָפִים וּבְיָדוֹ
ז רִצְפָּה בְּמֶלְקַחַיִם לָקַח מֵעַל הַמִּזְבֵּחַ: וַיַּגַּע עַל־פִּי וַיֹּאמֶר הִנֵּה נָגַע זֶה עַל־שְׂפָתֶיךָ וְסָר עֲוֺנֶךָ וְחַטָּאתְךָ
ח ט תְּכֻפָּר: וָאֶשְׁמַע אֶת־קוֹל אֲדֹנָי אֹמֵר אֶת־מִי אֶשְׁלַח וּמִי יֵלֶךְ־לָנוּ וָאֹמַר הִנְנִי שְׁלָחֵנִי: וַיֹּאמֶר לֵךְ וְאָמַרְתָּ
י לָעָם הַזֶּה שִׁמְעוּ שָׁמוֹעַ וְאַל־תָּבִינוּ וּרְאוּ רָאוֹ וְאַל־תֵּדָעוּ: הַשְׁמֵן לֵב־הָעָם הַזֶּה וְאָזְנָיו הַכְבֵּד וְעֵינָיו

YITRO

The first part of this *haftara* is read by all different Jewish communities; it describes God's revelation to Yeshayahu. This revelation, like other prophetic revelations described in the Tanakh, comprises two aspects: a verbal component – God's words to the prophet – and a visual component – what the prophet sees. These two parts of the revelation complement one another. In this prophecy, which was revealed to Yeshayahu "in the year in which King Uziyahu died," the prophet volunteers for his calling – an unusual phenomenon.

▶

11 their ears, and their hearts understand and they return – and are healed." I said, "My Lord, how long?"
And He said, "Until the towns are stripped of all who live in them, houses left without people, the land
12 13 stripped bare, and the LORD dispatches man far hence, and swaths of land will be forsaken; if a tenth
there will survive, it will return and will be burnt like the terebinth and oak tree that drop their leaves,
7 1 and yet the trunk remains – and the trunk is holy seed."* In the days of Aḥaz son of Yotam
son of Uziyahu, king of Yehuda, Retzin, king of Aram, and Pekaḥ son of Remalyahu, king of Israel,
2 launched an attack on Jerusalem, but they could not conquer it. The House of David was told, "Aram
is allied with Efrayim." And his heart swayed, and the hearts of his people, as trees of the forest will
3 sway with the wind. And the LORD said to Yeshayahu: Go out now to meet Aḥaz, you and
4 She'ar Yashuv your son, to the end of the Upper Pool's conduit, by the road to the Fuller's Field. And
say to him: Be guarded, stay still, do not fear, and let your heart not soften before these smoking tails
5 of firebrands, before the rage of Retzin and Aram and the son of Remalyahu. For Aram has conspired
6 to harm you, along with Efrayim and Remalyahu's son: "We shall go up to Jerusalem, bring about her
end; we shall break her walls open for ourselves and set a new king over her: the son of Taval."

Sepharadim and Chabad end here; Yemenites continue with 9:5

9 5 For a child is born to us, a son is given us; leadership rests on his shoulders, and he shall be called
6 Mighty God Is Planning Wonders, Eternal Father, Prince of Peace. To instill great leadership, peace
without end, on the throne of David, and over his kingdom, founding and supporting it with justice
and with righteousness now and forever; the passion of the LORD of Hosts will bring all this to be.

Haftarat Mishpatim

On Rosh Ḥodesh Adar Rishon, read the maftir from Numbers 28:9–15, and the haftara on page 1635. On Erev Rosh Ḥodesh Adar Rishon, read the haftara on page 1637. On Shabbat Shekalim (even if it coincides with Rosh Ḥodesh or Erev Rosh Ḥodesh) read the maftir from Exodus 30:11–16 and the haftara on page 1643.

JEREMIAH

34 8 The word that came to Yirmeyahu from the LORD after King Tzidkiyahu had made a covenant with all
9 the people of Jerusalem, proclaiming their freedom: Everyone was to set free his Hebrew manservant
10 and his Hebrew maidservant. No one was to enslave his fellow man of Yehuda. All the officials and all
the people who had entered into the covenant obeyed in that each person set free his manservant and
his maidservant, Hebrew males and females, never to enslave them again. They obeyed and set them
11 free. After a time, they regressed. They recovered the manservants and maidservants that they had set
12 free and forced them to be manservants and maidservants. Then the word of the LORD came
13 to Yirmeyahu from the LORD. This is what the LORD, God of Israel, said: "I made a covenant with your
14 ancestors at the time I took them out of the land of Egypt, the house of bondage, saying, 'At the beginning of the seventh year each of you should set free your brother Hebrew who had been sold to you
and who served you for six years – send him forth from you free.' But your ancestors did not heed Me

---

reaction to this affront was swift; Yirmeyahu prophesies here renewed and worse destruction.

Between the lines, we read about the special ceremony customary at that time for establishing a covenant. A covenant is an agreement, a joining, but it is undertaken through an act of severing. In the ceremony, a calf is killed and cut in two. The parties to the covenant pass between the pieces of the calf to symbolize the dependence of the agreement on the two sides: if each side keeps to its own promises, the covenant will endure.

יא הָשַׁע פֶּן־יִרְאֶה בְעֵינָיו וּבְאָזְנָיו יִשְׁמָע וּלְבָבוֹ יָבִין וָשָׁב וְרָפָא לוֹ: וָאֹמַר עַד־מָתַי אֲדֹנָי וַיֹּאמֶר עַד אֲשֶׁר
יב אִם־שָׁאוּ עָרִים מֵאֵין יוֹשֵׁב וּבָתִּים מֵאֵין אָדָם וְהָאֲדָמָה תִּשָּׁאֶה שְׁמָמָה: וְרִחַק יהוה אֶת־הָאָדָם וְרַבָּה
יג הָעֲזוּבָה בְּקֶרֶב הָאָרֶץ: וְעוֹד בָּהּ עֲשִׂרִיָּה וְשָׁבָה וְהָיְתָה לְבָעֵר כָּאֵלָה וְכָאַלּוֹן אֲשֶׁר בְּשַׁלֶּכֶת מַצֶּבֶת
ז א בָּם זֶרַע קֹדֶשׁ מַצַּבְתָּהּ:* וַיְהִי בִּימֵי אָחָז בֶּן־יוֹתָם בֶּן־עֻזִּיָּהוּ מֶלֶךְ יְהוּדָה עָלָה רְצִין מֶלֶךְ־
ב אֲרָם וּפֶקַח בֶּן־רְמַלְיָהוּ מֶלֶךְ־יִשְׂרָאֵל יְרוּשָׁלִַם לַמִּלְחָמָה עָלֶיהָ וְלֹא יָכֹל לְהִלָּחֵם עָלֶיהָ: וַיֻּגַּד לְבֵית דָּוִד
ג לֵאמֹר נָחָה אֲרָם עַל־אֶפְרָיִם וַיָּנַע לְבָבוֹ וּלְבַב עַמּוֹ כְּנוֹעַ עֲצֵי־יַעַר מִפְּנֵי־רוּחַ: וַיֹּאמֶר יהוה
אֶל־יְשַׁעְיָהוּ צֵא־נָא לִקְרַאת אָחָז אַתָּה וּשְׁאָר יָשׁוּב בְּנֶךָ אֶל־קְצֵה תְּעָלַת הַבְּרֵכָה הָעֶלְיוֹנָה אֶל־מְסִלַּת
ד שְׂדֵה כוֹבֵס: וְאָמַרְתָּ אֵלָיו הִשָּׁמֵר וְהַשְׁקֵט אַל־תִּירָא וּלְבָבְךָ אַל־יֵרַךְ מִשְּׁנֵי זַנְבוֹת הָאוּדִים הָעֲשֵׁנִים
ה הָאֵלֶּה בָּחֳרִי־אַף רְצִין וַאֲרָם וּבֶן־רְמַלְיָהוּ: יַעַן כִּי־יָעַץ עָלֶיךָ אֲרָם רָעָה אֶפְרַיִם וּבֶן־רְמַלְיָהוּ לֵאמֹר:
ו נַעֲלֶה בִיהוּדָה וּנְקִיצֶנָּה וְנַבְקִעֶנָּה אֵלֵינוּ וְנַמְלִיךְ מֶלֶךְ בְּתוֹכָהּ אֵת בֶּן־טָבְאַל:

Sepharadim and Chabad end here; Yemenites continue with 9:5

ט ה כִּי־יֶלֶד יֻלַּד־לָנוּ בֵּן נִתַּן־לָנוּ וַתְּהִי הַמִּשְׂרָה עַל־שִׁכְמוֹ וַיִּקְרָא שְׁמוֹ פֶּלֶא יוֹעֵץ אֵל גִּבּוֹר אֲבִי־עַד שַׂר־
ו שָׁלוֹם: לסרבה הַמִּשְׂרָה וּלְשָׁלוֹם אֵין־קֵץ עַל־כִּסֵּא דָוִד וְעַל־מַמְלַכְתּוֹ לְהָכִין אֹתָהּ וּלְסַעֲדָהּ בְּמִשְׁפָּט לְמַרְבֵּה
וּבִצְדָקָה מֵעַתָּה וְעַד־עוֹלָם קִנְאַת יהוה צְבָאוֹת תַּעֲשֶׂה־זֹּאת:

הפטרת משפטים

On ראש חודש אדר א׳ *read the maftir from* במדבר כח, ט–טו*, and the* הפטרה *on page 1635.*
On ערב ראש חודש אדר א׳ *read the* הפטרה *on page 1637.*
On שבת שקלים *(even if it coincides with* ראש חודש *or* ערב ראש חודש*)*
read the מפטיר *from* שמות ל, יא–טו*, and the* הפטרה *on page 1643.*

ירמיה
לד ח הַדָּבָר אֲשֶׁר־הָיָה אֶל־יִרְמְיָהוּ מֵאֵת יהוה אַחֲרֵי כְּרֹת הַמֶּלֶךְ צִדְקִיָּהוּ בְּרִית אֶת־כָּל־הָעָם אֲשֶׁר
ט בִּירוּשָׁלִַם לִקְרֹא לָהֶם דְּרוֹר: לְשַׁלַּח אִישׁ אֶת־עַבְדּוֹ וְאִישׁ אֶת־שִׁפְחָתוֹ הָעִבְרִי וְהָעִבְרִיָּה
י חָפְשִׁים לְבִלְתִּי עֲבָד־בָּם בִּיהוּדִי אָחִיהוּ אִישׁ: וַיִּשְׁמְעוּ כָל־הַשָּׂרִים וְכָל־הָעָם אֲשֶׁר־בָּאוּ בַבְּרִית
לְשַׁלַּח אִישׁ אֶת־עַבְדּוֹ וְאִישׁ אֶת־שִׁפְחָתוֹ חָפְשִׁים לְבִלְתִּי עֲבָד־בָּם עוֹד וַיִּשְׁמְעוּ וַיְשַׁלֵּחוּ:
יא וַיָּשׁוּבוּ אַחֲרֵי־כֵן וַיָּשִׁבוּ אֶת־הָעֲבָדִים וְאֶת־הַשְּׁפָחוֹת אֲשֶׁר שִׁלְּחוּ חָפְשִׁים ויכבישום לַעֲבָדִים וַיִּכְבְּשׁוּם
יב יג וְלִשְׁפָחוֹת: וַיְהִי דְבַר־יהוה אֶל־יִרְמְיָהוּ מֵאֵת יהוה לֵאמֹר: כֹּה־אָמַר יהוה אֱלֹהֵי
יִשְׂרָאֵל אָנֹכִי כָּרַתִּי בְרִית אֶת־אֲבוֹתֵיכֶם בְּיוֹם הוֹצִאִי אוֹתָם מֵאֶרֶץ מִצְרַיִם מִבֵּית עֲבָדִים לֵאמֹר:
יד מִקֵּץ שֶׁבַע שָׁנִים תְּשַׁלְּחוּ אִישׁ אֶת־אָחִיו הָעִבְרִי אֲשֶׁר־יִמָּכֵר לְךָ וַעֲבָדְךָ שֵׁשׁ שָׁנִים וְשִׁלַּחְתּוֹ חָפְשִׁי

MISHPATIM

During the reign of Tzidkiyahu, at the time of the Babylonian siege on Jerusalem, the people staged a ceremony of mass emancipation of slaves. The need for such a dramatic move testifies to the social-economic crisis that gripped the people of Jerusalem in that time. The ceremony was inspired by the words of the prophet Yirmeyahu, spoken to the people as the siege worsened. Afterward, the military situation improved somewhat, and the siege lightened a bit. In response, many of those who had freed their slaves subjugated them again. God's

15 and did not even bend their ears. You repented today and did what was proper in My eyes, proclaiming
freedom, every person for his fellow, and you made a covenant in My presence in the house which is
16 called by My name. But you regressed and profaned My name. Each of you recovered his manservant
and his maidservant, whom you had set free to do as they desire, and you forced them to remain man-
17 servants and maidservants for yourselves." Therefore, this is what the LORD said: "Because
you did not heed Me to proclaim freedom, everyone for his brother and everyone for his fellow, so
will I set free against you," declares the LORD, "the sword, the pestilence, and the famine, and render
18 you an object of shuddering for all the kingdoms of the earth. And I will deliver to all the people who
violated My covenant and did not uphold the words of the covenant that they made in My presence,
19 the calf that they cut in two, the sections of which they passed between – the officials of Yehuda and the
officials of Jerusalem, the courtiers and the priests, and all the folk of the land who passed between the
20 sections of the calf – I will deliver them into the hands of their enemies, the hands of those that seek
their lives, and their corpses shall become fodder for the birds of the skies and the beasts of the earth.
21 I will deliver Tzidkiyahu, king of Yehuda, and his officials into the hands of their enemies and into the
hands of those who seek their lives and into the army of the king of Babylon, which is withdrawing
22 from you. I shall now utter a command," declares the LORD, "and I shall bring them back to this city.
They will attack it, capture it, and burn it down by fire. The cities of Yehuda I shall render desolate,
without an inhabitant."*

Yemenites continue with chapter 35

33 25 This is what the LORD said: Only if I had no covenant with day and night, and if I had not established
26 the laws of heaven and earth, would I reject the offspring of Yaakov and of David My servant, and not
select any of his offspring as rulers over the offspring of Avraham, Yisḥak, and Yaakov – for I will bring
them back from their captivity and have compassion for them.*

Ashkenazim and Sephardim end here

35 1 The word that came to Yirmeyahu from the LORD in the days of Yehoyakim, son of Yoshiyahu, king of
2 Yehuda: "Go to the house of the descendants of Rekhav and speak to them. Bring them to the House
3 of the LORD, to one of the chambers, and give them wine to drink." I took Yaazanya son of Yirmeyahu
son of Ḥavatzinya, his brothers and all his children and the entire house of the descendants of Rekhav,
4 and I brought them to the House of the LORD, to the chamber of the sons of Ḥanan son of Yigdalyahu,
the man of God, that was adjacent to the chamber of the officials and above the chamber of Maaseyahu
5 son of Shalum, the gatekeeper. I placed goblets full of wine and cups before the sons of the house of
6 Rekhav and said to them, "Drink wine." They said, "We will not drink wine because Yonadav son of
7 Rekhav, our ancestor, commanded us: 'Do not drink wine, neither you nor your children, forever! You
are not to build houses, nor sow seed, nor plant vineyards, nor even possess them for yourselves. Instead, you are to live in tents all your lives so that you will thrive for many days upon the land where you
8 will reside.' We heeded the voice of Yehonadav son of Rekhav our forefather in all that he commanded
9 us, never to drink wine, neither ourselves nor our wives, nor our sons and daughters, and not to build
10 houses in which to live, and not to have vineyard, field, or seed. Rather, we live in tents. We heeded
11 Yonadav our ancestor, and we have done all that he commanded us. However, when Nevukhadretzar,
king of Babylon, rose up against the land, we said, 'Come and let us go up to Jerusalem because of the
12 army of the Chaldeans and because of the army of Aram.' And so we live in Jerusalem." Then
13 the word of the LORD came to Yirmeyahu. This is what the LORD of Hosts, God of Israel, said: "Go
and say to the men of Yehuda and to those that dwell in Jerusalem: It would befit you to take instruc-
14 tion to heed My words, declares the LORD. Fulfilled are the words of Yehonadav son of Rekhav, who
commanded his descendants not to drink wine. They have not drunk wine to this very day, for they
heeded the command of their ancestor. But I spoke to you persistently, and yet you did not heed Me.
15 I sent to you My servants, the prophets, again and again, to tell every one of you to turn away from his

טו מֵעִמָּךְ וְלֹא־שָׁמְעוּ אֲבוֹתֵיכֶם אֵלַי וְלֹא הִטּוּ אֶת־אׇזְנָם׃ וַתָּשֻׁבוּ אַתֶּם הַיּוֹם וַתַּעֲשׂוּ אֶת־הַיָּשָׁר בְּעֵינַי
טז לִקְרֹא דְרוֹר אִישׁ לְרֵעֵהוּ וַתִּכְרְתוּ בְרִית לְפָנַי בַּבַּיִת אֲשֶׁר־נִקְרָא שְׁמִי עָלָיו׃ וַתָּשֻׁבוּ וַתְּחַלְּלוּ אֶת־
שְׁמִי וַתָּשִׁבוּ אִישׁ אֶת־עַבְדּוֹ וְאִישׁ אֶת־שִׁפְחָתוֹ אֲשֶׁר־שִׁלַּחְתֶּם חׇפְשִׁים לְנַפְשָׁם וַתִּכְבְּשׁוּ אֹתָם
יז לִהְיוֹת לָכֶם לַעֲבָדִים וְלִשְׁפָחוֹת׃ לָכֵן כֹּה־אָמַר יהוה אַתֶּם לֹא־שְׁמַעְתֶּם אֵלַי לִקְרֹא דְרוֹר
אִישׁ לְאָחִיו וְאִישׁ לְרֵעֵהוּ הִנְנִי קֹרֵא לָכֶם דְּרוֹר נְאֻם־יהוה אֶל־הַחֶרֶב אֶל־הַדֶּבֶר וְאֶל־הָרָעָב וְנָתַתִּי
יח אֶתְכֶם לזועה לְכֹל מַמְלְכוֹת הָאָרֶץ׃ וְנָתַתִּי אֶת־הָאֲנָשִׁים הָעֹבְרִים אֶת־בְּרִתִי אֲשֶׁר לֹא־הֵקִימוּ לְזַעֲוָה
יט אֶת־דִּבְרֵי הַבְּרִית אֲשֶׁר כָּרְתוּ לְפָנָי הָעֵגֶל אֲשֶׁר כָּרְתוּ לִשְׁנַיִם וַיַּעַבְרוּ בֵּין בְּתָרָיו׃ שָׂרֵי יְהוּדָה וְשָׂרֵי
כ יְרוּשָׁלַם הַסָּרִסִים וְהַכֹּהֲנִים וְכֹל עַם הָאָרֶץ הָעֹבְרִים בֵּין בִּתְרֵי הָעֵגֶל׃ וְנָתַתִּי אוֹתָם בְּיַד אֹיְבֵיהֶם
כא וּבְיַד מְבַקְשֵׁי נַפְשָׁם וְהָיְתָה נִבְלָתָם לְמַאֲכָל לְעוֹף הַשָּׁמַיִם וּלְבֶהֱמַת הָאָרֶץ׃ וְאֶת־צִדְקִיָּהוּ מֶלֶךְ־
יְהוּדָה וְאֶת־שָׂרָיו אֶתֵּן בְּיַד אֹיְבֵיהֶם וּבְיַד מְבַקְשֵׁי נַפְשָׁם וּבְיַד חֵיל מֶלֶךְ בָּבֶל הָעֹלִים מֵעֲלֵיכֶם׃
כב הִנְנִי מְצַוֶּה נְאֻם־יהוה וַהֲשִׁבֹתִים אֶל־הָעִיר הַזֹּאת וְנִלְחֲמוּ עָלֶיהָ וּלְכָדוּהָ וּשְׂרָפֻהָ בָאֵשׁ וְאֶת־עָרֵי יְהוּדָה
אֶתֵּן שְׁמָמָה מֵאֵין יֹשֵׁב׃*

Yemenites continue with chapter 35

לג כה כו כֹּה אָמַר יהוה אִם־לֹא בְרִיתִי יוֹמָם וָלָיְלָה חֻקּוֹת שָׁמַיִם וָאָרֶץ לֹא־שָׂמְתִּי׃ גַּם־זֶרַע יַעֲקוֹב וְדָוִד
עַבְדִּי אֶמְאַס מִקַּחַת מִזַּרְעוֹ מֹשְׁלִים אֶל־זֶרַע אַבְרָהָם יִשְׂחָק וְיַעֲקֹב כִּי־אשוב אֶת־שְׁבוּתָם אָשִׁיב
וְרִחַמְתִּים׃*

Ashkenazim and Sepharadim end here

לה א ב הַדָּבָר אֲשֶׁר־הָיָה אֶל־יִרְמְיָהוּ מֵאֵת יהוה בִּימֵי יְהוֹיָקִים בֶּן־יֹאשִׁיָּהוּ מֶלֶךְ יְהוּדָה לֵאמֹר׃ הָלוֹךְ
אֶל־בֵּית הָרֵכָבִים וְדִבַּרְתָּ אוֹתָם וַהֲבִאוֹתָם בֵּית יהוה אֶל־אַחַת הַלְּשָׁכוֹת וְהִשְׁקִיתָ אוֹתָם יָיִן׃
ג וָאֶקַּח אֶת־יַאֲזַנְיָה בֶן־יִרְמְיָהוּ בֶּן־חֲבַצִּנְיָה וְאֶת־אֶחָיו וְאֶת־כׇּל־בָּנָיו וְאֵת כׇּל־בֵּית הָרֵכָבִים׃
ד וָאָבִא אֹתָם בֵּית יהוה אֶל־לִשְׁכַּת בְּנֵי חָנָן בֶּן־יִגְדַּלְיָהוּ אִישׁ הָאֱלֹהִים אֲשֶׁר־אֵצֶל לִשְׁכַּת
ה הַשָּׂרִים אֲשֶׁר מִמַּעַל לְלִשְׁכַּת מַעֲשֵׂיָהוּ בֶן־שַׁלֻּם שֹׁמֵר הַסַּף׃ וָאֶתֵּן לִפְנֵי ׀ בְּנֵי בֵית־הָרֵכָבִים
ו גְּבִעִים מְלֵאִים יַיִן וְכֹסוֹת וָאֹמַר אֲלֵיהֶם שְׁתוּ־יָיִן׃ וַיֹּאמְרוּ לֹא נִשְׁתֶּה־יָּיִן כִּי יוֹנָדָב בֶּן־רֵכָב
ז אָבִינוּ צִוָּה עָלֵינוּ לֵאמֹר לֹא תִשְׁתּוּ־יַיִן אַתֶּם וּבְנֵיכֶם עַד־עוֹלָם׃ וּבַיִת לֹא־תִבְנוּ וְזֶרַע לֹא־
תִזְרָעוּ וְכֶרֶם לֹא־תִטָּעוּ וְלֹא יִהְיֶה לָכֶם כִּי בָּאֳהָלִים תֵּשְׁבוּ כׇּל־יְמֵיכֶם לְמַעַן תִּחְיוּ יָמִים רַבִּים
ח עַל־פְּנֵי הָאֲדָמָה אֲשֶׁר אַתֶּם גָּרִים שָׁם׃ וַנִּשְׁמַע בְּקוֹל יְהוֹנָדָב בֶּן־רֵכָב אָבִינוּ לְכֹל אֲשֶׁר צִוָּנוּ
ט לְבִלְתִּי שְׁתוֹת־יַיִן כׇּל־יָמֵינוּ אֲנַחְנוּ נָשֵׁינוּ בָּנֵינוּ וּבְנֹתֵינוּ׃ וּלְבִלְתִּי בְּנוֹת בָּתִּים לְשִׁבְתֵּנוּ וְכֶרֶם
יא וְשָׂדֶה וָזֶרַע לֹא יִהְיֶה־לָּנוּ׃ וַנֵּשֶׁב בָּאֳהָלִים וַנִּשְׁמַע וַנַּעַשׂ כְּכֹל אֲשֶׁר־צִוָּנוּ יוֹנָדָב אָבִינוּ׃ וַיְהִי
בַּעֲלוֹת נְבוּכַדְרֶאצַּר מֶלֶךְ־בָּבֶל אֶל־הָאָרֶץ וַנֹּאמֶר בֹּאוּ וְנָבוֹא יְרוּשָׁלַם מִפְּנֵי חֵיל הַכַּשְׂדִּים
יב יג וּמִפְּנֵי חֵיל אֲרָם וַנֵּשֶׁב בִּירוּשָׁלָם׃ וַיְהִי דְּבַר־יהוה אֶל־יִרְמְיָהוּ לֵאמֹר׃ כֹּה־אָמַר יהוה
צְבָאוֹת אֱלֹהֵי יִשְׂרָאֵל הָלֹךְ וְאָמַרְתָּ לְאִישׁ יְהוּדָה וּלְיוֹשְׁבֵי יְרוּשָׁלָם הֲלוֹא תִקְחוּ מוּסָר לִשְׁמֹעַ
יד אֶל־דְּבָרַי נְאֻם־יהוה׃ הוּקַם אֶת־דִּבְרֵי יְהוֹנָדָב בֶּן־רֵכָב אֲשֶׁר־צִוָּה אֶת־בָּנָיו לְבִלְתִּי שְׁתוֹת־יַיִן
וְלֹא שָׁתוּ עַד־הַיּוֹם הַזֶּה כִּי שָׁמְעוּ אֵת מִצְוַת אֲבִיהֶם וְאָנֹכִי דִּבַּרְתִּי אֲלֵיכֶם הַשְׁכֵּם וְדַבֵּר וְלֹא
טו שְׁמַעְתֶּם אֵלָי׃ וָאֶשְׁלַח אֲלֵיכֶם אֶת־כׇּל־עֲבָדַי הַנְּבִאִים ׀ הַשְׁכֵּים וְשָׁלֹחַ ׀ לֵאמֹר שֻׁבוּ־נָא אִישׁ
מִדַּרְכּוֹ הָרָעָה וְהֵיטִיבוּ מַעַלְלֵיכֶם וְאַל־תֵּלְכוּ אַחֲרֵי אֱלֹהִים אֲחֵרִים לְעׇבְדָם וּשְׁבוּ אֶל־הָאֲדָמָה

evil path, to correct his actions, and not to follow other gods to worship them. Then you would live
upon the land which I gave you and your ancestors. But you did not bend your ears. You did not listen
16 to Me. For the children of Yehonadav son of Rekhav obeyed their ancestor's command just as he had
17 commanded them, but this people have not obeyed Me. Therefore, this is what the LORD,
God of Hosts, God of Israel, said: Now I will bring upon Yehuda, and upon all who dwell in Jerusalem,
every disaster which I have decreed upon them, for I spoke to them and they did not listen; I called
18 to them and they did not respond." Yirmeyahu said to the house of the Rekhabites, "This is what the
LORD of Hosts, God of Israel, said: Because you listened to the command of Yehonadav your ancestor,
19 and kept all his precepts, and did exactly as he commanded you, this is what the LORD of Hosts, God
of Israel, therefore said: There will never cease to be a descendant of Yonadav son of Rekhav who will
stand before Me, for all time."

HAFTARAT TERUMA

On Rosh Ḥodesh Adar Rishon, read the maftir from Numbers 28:9–15, and the haftara on page 1635. On Shabbat Shekalim (even if it coincides with Rosh Ḥodesh or Erev Rosh Ḥodesh) read the maftir from Exodus 30:11–16, and the haftara on page 1643. On Shabbat Zakhor read the maftir from Deuteronomy 25:17–19, and the haftara on page 1645.

I KINGS

5 26 The LORD had endowed Shlomo with wisdom, as He had promised him. There was peace between
27 Ḥiram and Shlomo, and the two of them formed an alliance. King Shlomo began to levy forced labor
28 upon all of Israel; the levy was thirty thousand men. He had ten thousand men sent to Lebanon every
month, in shifts; they would spend a month in Lebanon and two months at home. Adoniram was in
29 charge of the forced labor. And Shlomo had seventy thousand porters and eight thousand quar-
30 riers in the mountains, besides Shlomo's three thousand and three hundred prefect officers in charge of
31 the labor, who supervised the people who performed the labor. At the king's command, they quarried
enormous blocks of prime stone so that the foundations of the House would be laid with hewn stone.
32 And Shlomo's builders, together with Ḥiram's builders and the Gevalites, carved the wood and the
6 1 stone in preparation for the construction of the House. In the four hundred and eightieth
year after the Israelites left Egypt, in the month of Ziv – the second month – of the fourth year of
2 Shlomo's reign over Israel, he began to build the House for the LORD. The House that King Shlomo
3 built for the LORD was sixty cubits long, twenty cubits wide, and thirty cubits high. The Hall leading up to the Sanctuary of the House was twenty cubits long along the width of the House, and ten
4 5 cubits wide leading up to the House. He made recessed, paned windows for the House. Around the
outer wall of the House – the outer walls around the Sanctuary and Inner Sanctuary – he built a tiered
6 structure and made side chambers all around. The lowest tier was five cubits wide, the middle tier
was six cubits wide, and the third tier was seven cubits wide, as he had designed recesses around the
7 outside of the House to avoid making grooves in the walls of the House. The House was entirely built
of finished stones that had been cut at the quarry; no hammer, ax, or iron tool was heard in the House
8 during its construction. There was an entrance through the central alcove on the southern side of the

used in building the Temple or the altar that stood within it. The *haftara* ends during the main phase of construction, with God's message to Shlomo: The observance of the Torah and the commandments is the true test for whether this structure and the Divine Presence within it will weather the storms of history.

טז אֲשֶׁר־נָתַתִּי לָכֶם וְלַאֲבֹתֵיכֶם וְלֹא הִטִּיתֶם אֶת־אָזְנְכֶם וְלֹא שְׁמַעְתֶּם אֵלָי׃ כִּי הֵקִימוּ בְּנֵי יְהוֹנָדָב
יז בֶּן־רֵכָב אֶת־מִצְוַת אֲבִיהֶם אֲשֶׁר צִוָּם וְהָעָם הַזֶּה לֹא שָׁמְעוּ אֵלָי׃ לָכֵן כֹּה־אָמַר יהוה
אֱלֹהֵי צְבָאוֹת אֱלֹהֵי יִשְׂרָאֵל הִנְנִי מֵבִיא אֶל־יְהוּדָה וְאֶל כָּל־יוֹשְׁבֵי יְרוּשָׁלִַם אֵת כָּל־הָרָעָה
יח אֲשֶׁר דִּבַּרְתִּי עֲלֵיהֶם יַעַן דִּבַּרְתִּי אֲלֵיהֶם וְלֹא שָׁמֵעוּ וָאֶקְרָא לָהֶם וְלֹא עָנוּ׃ וּלְבֵית הָרֵכָבִים
אָמַר יִרְמְיָהוּ כֹּה־אָמַר יהוה צְבָאוֹת אֱלֹהֵי יִשְׂרָאֵל יַעַן אֲשֶׁר שְׁמַעְתֶּם עַל־מִצְוַת יְהוֹנָדָב
יט אֲבִיכֶם וַתִּשְׁמְרוּ אֶת־כָּל־מִצְוֺתָיו וַתַּעֲשׂוּ כְּכֹל אֲשֶׁר־צִוָּה אֶתְכֶם׃ לָכֵן כֹּה אָמַר יהוה צְבָאוֹת
אֱלֹהֵי יִשְׂרָאֵל לֹא־יִכָּרֵת אִישׁ לְיוֹנָדָב בֶּן־רֵכָב עֹמֵד לְפָנַי כָּל־הַיָּמִים׃

הפטרת תרומה

On ראש חודש אדר א׳, *read the* מפטיר *from* במדבר כח, ט–טו *and the* הפטרה *on page 1635.*
On שבת שקלים *(even if it coincides with* ראש חודש *or* ערב ראש חודש*) read the* מפטיר
from שמות ל, יא–טז*, and the* הפטרה *on page 1643. On* שבת זכור *read the* מפטיר
from דברים כה, יז–יט*, and the* הפטרה *on page 1645.*

ה כו וַיהוה נָתַן חָכְמָה לִשְׁלֹמֹה כַּאֲשֶׁר דִּבֶּר־לוֹ וַיְהִי שָׁלֹם בֵּין חִירָם וּבֵין שְׁלֹמֹה וַיִּכְרְתוּ בְרִית שְׁנֵיהֶם׃ מלכים א׳
כז כח וַיַּעַל הַמֶּלֶךְ שְׁלֹמֹה מַס מִכָּל־יִשְׂרָאֵל וַיְהִי הַמַּס שְׁלֹשִׁים אֶלֶף אִישׁ׃ וַיִּשְׁלָחֵם לְבָנוֹנָה עֲשֶׂרֶת אֲלָפִים
כט בַּחֹדֶשׁ חֲלִיפוֹת חֹדֶשׁ יִהְיוּ בַלְּבָנוֹן שְׁנַיִם חֳדָשִׁים בְּבֵיתוֹ וַאֲדֹנִירָם עַל־הַמַּס׃ וַיְהִי לִשְׁלֹמֹה
ל שִׁבְעִים אֶלֶף נֹשֵׂא סַבָּל וּשְׁמֹנִים אֶלֶף חֹצֵב בָּהָר׃ לְבַד מִשָּׂרֵי הַנִּצָּבִים לִשְׁלֹמֹה אֲשֶׁר עַל־הַמְּלָאכָה
לא שְׁלֹשֶׁת אֲלָפִים וּשְׁלֹשׁ מֵאוֹת הָרֹדִים בָּעָם הָעֹשִׂים בַּמְּלָאכָה׃ וַיְצַו הַמֶּלֶךְ וַיַּסִּעוּ אֲבָנִים גְּדֹלוֹת אֲבָנִים
לב יְקָרוֹת לְיַסֵּד הַבָּיִת אַבְנֵי גָזִית׃ וַיִּפְסְלוּ בֹּנֵי שְׁלֹמֹה וּבֹנֵי חִירוֹם וְהַגִּבְלִים וַיָּכִינוּ הָעֵצִים וְהָאֲבָנִים לִבְנוֹת
ו א הַבָּיִת׃ וַיְהִי בִשְׁמוֹנִים שָׁנָה וְאַרְבַּע מֵאוֹת שָׁנָה לְצֵאת בְּנֵי־יִשְׂרָאֵל מֵאֶרֶץ־מִצְרַיִם בַּשָּׁנָה
ב הָרְבִיעִית בְּחֹדֶשׁ זִו הוּא הַחֹדֶשׁ הַשֵּׁנִי לִמְלֹךְ שְׁלֹמֹה עַל־יִשְׂרָאֵל וַיִּבֶן הַבַּיִת לַיהוה׃ וְהַבַּיִת אֲשֶׁר בָּנָה
ג הַמֶּלֶךְ שְׁלֹמֹה לַיהוה שִׁשִּׁים־אַמָּה אָרְכּוֹ וְעֶשְׂרִים רָחְבּוֹ וּשְׁלֹשִׁים אַמָּה קוֹמָתוֹ׃ וְהָאוּלָם עַל־פְּנֵי הֵיכַל
ד הַבַּיִת עֶשְׂרִים אַמָּה אָרְכּוֹ עַל־פְּנֵי רֹחַב הַבָּיִת עֶשֶׂר בָּאַמָּה רָחְבּוֹ עַל־פְּנֵי הַבָּיִת׃ וַיַּעַשׂ לַבָּיִת חַלּוֹנֵי
ה שְׁקֻפִים אֲטֻמִים׃ וַיִּבֶן עַל־קִיר הַבַּיִת יצוע סָבִיב אֶת־קִירוֹת הַבַּיִת סָבִיב לַהֵיכָל וְלַדְּבִיר וַיַּעַשׂ צְלָעוֹת יָצִיעַ
ו סָבִיב׃ היצוע הַתַּחְתֹּנָה חָמֵשׁ בָּאַמָּה רָחְבָּהּ וְהַתִּיכֹנָה שֵׁשׁ בָּאַמָּה רָחְבָּהּ וְהַשְּׁלִישִׁית שֶׁבַע בָּאַמָּה הַיָּצִיעַ
ז רָחְבָּהּ כִּי מִגְרָעוֹת נָתַן לַבַּיִת סָבִיב חוּצָה לְבִלְתִּי אֲחֹז בְּקִירוֹת הַבָּיִת׃ וְהַבַּיִת בְּהִבָּנֹתוֹ אֶבֶן־שְׁלֵמָה
ח מַסָּע נִבְנָה וּמַקָּבוֹת וְהַגַּרְזֶן כָּל־כְּלִי בַרְזֶל לֹא־נִשְׁמַע בַּבַּיִת בְּהִבָּנֹתוֹ׃ פֶּתַח הַצֵּלָע הַתִּיכֹנָה אֶל־כֶּתֶף

TERUMA

This *haftara* describes the building of the Temple during the reign of King Shlomo and the preparations for its opening. This project began during the fourth year of Shlomo's reign, 480 years after the exodus from Egypt. The exodus was the time Israel began to rise from its historical nadir of servitude in Egypt. And now, with the inauguration of the Temple, came the pinnacle of its spiritual existence, as we read in the Song at the Sea, "You will bring them, You will plant them on the mountain…the Sanctuary, LORD, that Your hands established (Ex. 15:17). This Sanctuary was modest in its size, but splendid in its construction. No iron tool was

9 House; a winding staircase led to the middle tier and from the middle tier to the third one. When he
10 finished building the House, he paneled the House with beams and planks of cedar. He built the tiered
structure against the whole house, each story five cubits high, so that the House was encased with ce-
11 12 darwood. And the word of the LORD came to Shlomo: "Concerning this House that you are
building: if you follow My laws and uphold My rulings and keep all My commandments by following
13 them, then I will fulfill My promise through you, the promise that I made to your father David. I will
dwell in the midst of the Israelites, and I will never abandon My people Israel."

HAFTARAT TETZAVEH

On Shabbat Zakhor, read the maftir from Deuteronomy 25:17–19, and the haftara on page 1645.
On Purim Meshulash in Jerusalem, read from Exodus 17:8–16, and the haftara on page 1645.

43 10 You, Man, describe this House to the House of Israel so that they feel ashamed of their sins, and let EZEKIEL
11 them take measure of the plan. And if they do feel shame about all they have done, then make known
to them the design of the House and its architectural plan: its exits and entrances, all of its structures
and all of its rules, all its decorative shapes and all the instructions about it. And write it down in front
of them so that they can preserve everything about its design and its rules so that they can carry them
12 out. This is the teaching of the House: the top of the mountain, all its boundary roundabout, is holy of
13 holies. Behold – this is the teaching of the House: These are the dimensions of the altar in cubits, each
cubit being a five-handbreadth cubit plus a handbreadth. But the base is a smaller cubit, as is the cubit
of its width, and the border at its edge all around is one half-cubit, the same as for the top level of the
14 altar. Now from the base on the ground up to the lower ledge there are two cubits, and its excess width
is one cubit, and from the smaller ledge up to the top of the large ledge there are four cubits, with an
15 excess width of one cubit. Now the Harel hearth is four cubits, and from this Ariel upward, there rise
16 17 four horns. And the Ariel is twelve cubits long by twelve cubits wide, square on its four sides. And the
ledge is fourteen in length by fourteen in width on its four sides, and the border surrounding it is half
18 a small cubit. A cubit of its base extends all around, and its ramp is off-center, shifted eastward." Then
He said to me: "Man, thus says the Lord GOD: These are the statutes pertaining to the altar on the day
19 that it is fashioned, to enable you to bring burnt offerings upon it and to sprinkle blood upon it. You
will pass on to the priests, the Levites who are of the seed of Tzadok who approach Me to serve Me,
20 the word of the Lord GOD: a young bull from the cattle herd shall be a purification offering. Take from
its blood and put some on the four altar horns and four corners of the ledge and upon the border all
21 around: you shall purify it so that it can provide atonement. Then take the bull of the purification of-
22 fering and burn it in its designated place in the bounds of the House, outside the Sanctuary. And from
the second day onward, you shall sacrifice a flawless male goat for a purification offering. They shall
23 purify the altar as they purified it before, by sacrificing the bull. When you have finished the purification process, sacrifice a flawless young bull from among the cattle and a flawless ram from among the
24 sheep. You shall bring them near the LORD, and the priests shall throw salt upon them and offer them
25 up as a burnt offering to the LORD. For seven days you shall bring the goat of a purification offering

---

conveyed at the very hour of Israel's darkest nightmare, prevented the Jews from reaching the depths of despair. This *haftara* deals with the construction of the Temple, the altar, and the reconstitution of the priestly service.

ט הַבַּיִת הַיְמָנִית וּבְלוּלִּים יַעֲלוּ עַל־הַתִּיכֹנָה וּמִן־הַתִּיכֹנָה אֶל־הַשְּׁלִשִׁים׃ וַיִּבֶן אֶת־הַבַּיִת וַיְכַלֵּהוּ וַיִּסְפֹּן
י אֶת־הַבַּיִת גֵּבִים וּשְׂדֵרֹת בָּאֲרָזִים׃ וַיִּבֶן אֶת־היצוע עַל־כָּל־הַבַּיִת חָמֵשׁ אַמּוֹת קוֹמָתוֹ וַיֶּאֱחֹז אֶת־הַבַּיִת הַיָּצִיעַ
יא יב בַּעֲצֵי אֲרָזִים׃ וַיְהִי דְּבַר־יְהוָה אֶל־שְׁלֹמֹה לֵאמֹר׃ הַבַּיִת הַזֶּה אֲשֶׁר־אַתָּה בֹנֶה אִם־תֵּלֵךְ
בְּחֻקֹּתַי וְאֶת־מִשְׁפָּטַי תַּעֲשֶׂה וְשָׁמַרְתָּ אֶת־כָּל־מִצְוֺתַי לָלֶכֶת בָּהֶם וַהֲקִמֹתִי אֶת־דְּבָרִי אִתָּךְ אֲשֶׁר דִּבַּרְתִּי
יג אֶל־דָּוִד אָבִיךָ׃ וְשָׁכַנְתִּי בְּתוֹךְ בְּנֵי יִשְׂרָאֵל וְלֹא אֶעֱזֹב אֶת־עַמִּי יִשְׂרָאֵל׃

הפטרת תצוה

On שבת זכור*, read the* מפטיר *from* דברים כה, יז–יט*, and the* הפטרה *on page 1645.*
On פורים משולש *in Jerusalem, read the* מפטיר *from* שמות יז, ח–טז*, and the* הפטרה *on page 1645.*

מג י יא אַתָּה בֶן־אָדָם הַגֵּד אֶת־בֵּית־יִשְׂרָאֵל אֶת־הַבַּיִת וְיִכָּלְמוּ מֵעֲוֺנוֹתֵיהֶם וּמָדְדוּ אֶת־תָּכְנִית׃ וְאִם־נִכְלְמוּ יחזקאל
מִכֹּל אֲשֶׁר־עָשׂוּ צוּרַת הַבַּיִת וּתְכוּנָתוֹ וּמוֹצָאָיו וּמוֹבָאָיו וְכָל־צוּרֹתָו וְאֵת כָּל־חֻקֹּתָיו וְכָל־צוּרֹתָו
יב וְכָל־תּוֹרֹתָו הוֹדַע אוֹתָם וּכְתֹב לְעֵינֵיהֶם וְיִשְׁמְרוּ אֶת־כָּל־צוּרָתוֹ וְאֶת־כָּל־חֻקֹּתָיו וְעָשׂוּ אוֹתָם׃ זֹאת
יג תּוֹרַת הַבָּיִת עַל־רֹאשׁ הָהָר כָּל־גְּבֻלוֹ סָבִיב ׀ סָבִיב קֹדֶשׁ קָדָשִׁים הִנֵּה־זֹאת תּוֹרַת הַבָּיִת׃ וְאֵלֶּה מִדּוֹת
הַמִּזְבֵּחַ בָּאַמּוֹת אַמָּה אַמָּה וָטֹפַח וְחֵיק הָאַמָּה וְאַמָּה־רֹחַב וּגְבוּלָהּ אֶל־שְׂפָתָהּ סָבִיב זֶרֶת הָאֶחָד וְזֶה
יד גַּב הַמִּזְבֵּחַ׃ וּמֵחֵיק הָאָרֶץ עַד־הָעֲזָרָה הַתַּחְתּוֹנָה שְׁתַּיִם אַמּוֹת וְרֹחַב אַמָּה אֶחָת וּמֵהָעֲזָרָה הַקְּטַנָּה
טו עַד־הָעֲזָרָה הַגְּדוֹלָה אַרְבַּע אַמּוֹת וְרֹחַב הָאַמָּה׃ וְהַהַרְאֵל אַרְבַּע אַמּוֹת וּמֵהָאֲרִאֵיל וּלְמַעְלָה הַקְּרָנוֹת
טז יז אַרְבַּע׃ וְהָאֲרִאֵיל שְׁתֵּים עֶשְׂרֵה אֹרֶךְ בִּשְׁתֵּים עֶשְׂרֵה רֹחַב רָבוּעַ אֶל אַרְבַּעַת רְבָעָיו׃ וְהָעֲזָרָה אַרְבַּע
עֶשְׂרֵה אֹרֶךְ בְּאַרְבַּע עֶשְׂרֵה רֹחַב אֶל אַרְבַּעַת רְבָעֶיהָ וְהַגְּבוּל סָבִיב אוֹתָהּ חֲצִי הָאַמָּה וְהַחֵיק־לָהּ אַמָּה
יח סָבִיב וּמַעֲלֹתֵהוּ פְּנוֹת קָדִים׃ וַיֹּאמֶר אֵלַי בֶּן־אָדָם כֹּה אָמַר אֲדֹנָי יֱהוִה אֵלֶּה חֻקּוֹת הַמִּזְבֵּחַ בְּיוֹם הֵעָשׂוֹתוֹ
יט לְהַעֲלוֹת עָלָיו עוֹלָה וְלִזְרֹק עָלָיו דָּם׃ וְנָתַתָּה אֶל־הַכֹּהֲנִים הַלְוִיִּם אֲשֶׁר הֵם מִזֶּרַע צָדוֹק הַקְּרֹבִים אֵלַי
כ נְאֻם אֲדֹנָי יֱהוִה לְשָׁרְתֵנִי פַּר בֶּן־בָּקָר לְחַטָּאת׃ וְלָקַחְתָּ מִדָּמוֹ וְנָתַתָּה עַל־אַרְבַּע קַרְנֹתָיו וְאֶל־אַרְבַּע
כא פִּנּוֹת הָעֲזָרָה וְאֶל־הַגְּבוּל סָבִיב וְחִטֵּאתָ אוֹתוֹ וְכִפַּרְתָּהוּ׃ וְלָקַחְתָּ אֵת הַפָּר הַחַטָּאת וּשְׂרָפוֹ בְּמִפְקַד
כב הַבַּיִת מִחוּץ לַמִּקְדָּשׁ׃ וּבַיּוֹם הַשֵּׁנִי תַּקְרִיב שְׂעִיר־עִזִּים תָּמִים לְחַטָּאת וְחִטְּאוּ אֶת־הַמִּזְבֵּחַ כַּאֲשֶׁר חִטְּאוּ
כג כד בַּפָּר׃ בְּכַלּוֹתְךָ מֵחַטֵּא תַּקְרִיב פַּר בֶּן־בָּקָר תָּמִים וְאַיִל מִן־הַצֹּאן תָּמִים׃ וְהִקְרַבְתָּם לִפְנֵי יְהוָה וְהִשְׁלִיכוּ
כה הַכֹּהֲנִים עֲלֵיהֶם מֶלַח וְהֶעֱלוּ אוֹתָם עֹלָה לַיהוָה׃ שִׁבְעַת יָמִים תַּעֲשֶׂה שְׂעִיר־חַטָּאת לַיּוֹם וּפַר בֶּן־בָּקָר

TETZAVEH

The final vision recounted in the book of Ezekiel offers a lengthy and detailed description of the future structure of Jerusalem and the Temple within it. This prophecy was relayed to the exiles in Babylon after the destruction of the First Temple, Jerusalem, and the dynasty of the House of David. The series of prophecies of comfort at the end of the book foretells the story of the return of the people of Israel to their land and the rebuilding of everything that that had been destroyed. Nothing is irreversible. This powerful message,

26 daily, as well as a young bull from the cattle and a ram from the sheep; they are all to be flawless. For
27 seven days they shall cleanse the altar and purify it and consecrate it. When these days are over, from
the eighth day onward, the priests may prepare your burnt offerings and your peace offerings on the
altar, and I shall respond favorably to you. So spoke the Lord God.

Haftarat Ki Tisa

On Purim Meshulash in Jerusalem read the maftir from Exodus 17:8–16, and the haftara on page 1645.
On Shabbat Para read the maftir from Numbers 19:1–22, and the haftara on page 1649.

18 1 A long time passed. In the third year, the word of the Lord came to Eliyahu: "Go, present yourself to I KINGS
2 Aḥav, and I will send down rain on the face of the earth." So Eliyahu set out to present himself to Aḥav. *Ashkenazim begin here*
3 By then, famine was raging fiercely in Shomron. Aḥav summoned Ovadyahu, who was in charge of the
4 palace – Ovadyahu had deep reverence for the Lord; when Izevel was annihilating the prophets of the
Lord, Ovadyahu had taken one hundred prophets and hidden them, fifty men to a cave, and provided
5 them with food and water. "Go about the land to every spring and every wadi," Aḥav said to Ovadyahu.
"Perhaps we will find some grass to keep the horses and mules alive so that our animals will not be
6 annihilated." They divided up the land between them for exploration; Aḥav set out alone in one direc-
7 tion, while Ovadyahu set out alone in another. As Ovadyahu was on the road, he was suddenly met
8 by Eliyahu. He recognized him at once and fell on his face. "Is that you, my lord Eliyahu?" he said. "It
9 is I," he said to him. "Go and tell your lord: Eliyahu is here." "How have I offended you, that you hand
10 your servant over to Aḥav to be killed?" he said. "As the Lord your God lives – is there a single nation
or kingdom where my lord has not sent and looked for you? And when they said, 'He is not here,' he
11 had every kingdom and every nation swear that you were nowhere to be found. Now you say, 'Go, tell
12 your lord that Eliyahu is here,' but as soon as I leave you, the spirit of the Lord will carry you off – to
where, I know not – and when I go to tell Aḥav and he does not find you, he will kill me, though I, your
13 servant, have revered the Lord from my youth. Has my lord not been told what I did when Izevel was
killing the Lord's prophets, how I hid one hundred of the Lord's prophets, fifty men to a cave, and
14 provided them with food and water? Now you say, 'Go, tell your lord that Eliyahu is here' – but he will
15 kill me." "As the Lord of Hosts lives, whom I serve," said Eliyahu, "today I will present myself to him."
16 17 So Ovadyahu set out toward Aḥav and told him, and Aḥav went to meet Eliyahu. When Aḥav saw Eli-
18 yahu, Aḥav said to him, "Is that you, O scourge of Israel?" "I have not brought a scourge upon Israel,"
he said, "but you and your father's house have by abandoning the Lord's commandments and by
19 following the Be'alim. Now summon all of Israel to gather to me at Mount Carmel, together with the
four hundred fifty prophets of Baal and the four hundred prophets of Ashera, those who dine at Izevel's
20 21 table."* Aḥav summoned all the Israelites and gathered the prophets to Mount Carmel. And Eliyahu *Sepharadim and Chabad begin here*
drew close to all the people and said, "How long will you sway from one side to another? If the Lord

earlier at Mount Sinai: The war against Baal is reminiscent of Moshe's fight against the worshippers of the golden calf. At both the Carmel and Sinai, much of the people sat on the fence, waiting to see which side would emerge victorious. And in each of these contexts, the prophet resorts both to prayer before God and words of reproof to the nation.

כו כז וְאַיִל מִן־הַצֹּאן תְּמִימִים יַעֲשׂוּ: שִׁבְעַת יָמִים יְכַפְּרוּ אֶת־הַמִּזְבֵּחַ וְטִהֲרוּ אֹתוֹ וּמִלְאוּ יָדוֹ: וִיכַלּוּ אֶת־הַיָּמִים
וְהָיָה בַיּוֹם הַשְּׁמִינִי וָהָלְאָה יַעֲשׂוּ הַכֹּהֲנִים עַל־הַמִּזְבֵּחַ אֶת־עוֹלוֹתֵיכֶם וְאֶת־שַׁלְמֵיכֶם וְרָצָאתִי אֶתְכֶם נְאֻם
אֲדֹנָי יֱהֹוִה:

הפטרת כי תשא

On פורים משולש *in Jerusalem read the* מפטיר *from* שמות יז, ח–טז*, and the* הפטרה *on page 1645.*
On שבת פרה *read the* מפטיר *from* במדבר יט, א–כב*, and the* הפטרה *on page 1649.*

מלכים א׳

Ashkenazim and Yemenites begin here

יח א וַיְהִי יָמִים רַבִּים וּדְבַר־יהוה הָיָה אֶל־אֵלִיָּהוּ בַּשָּׁנָה הַשְּׁלִישִׁית לֵאמֹר לֵךְ הֵרָאֵה אֶל־אַחְאָב וְאֶתְּנָה
ב ג מָטָר עַל־פְּנֵי הָאֲדָמָה: וַיֵּלֶךְ אֵלִיָּהוּ לְהֵרָאוֹת אֶל־אַחְאָב וְהָרָעָב חָזָק בְּשֹׁמְרוֹן: וַיִּקְרָא אַחְאָב אֶל־
ד עֹבַדְיָהוּ אֲשֶׁר עַל־הַבָּיִת וְעֹבַדְיָהוּ הָיָה יָרֵא אֶת־יהוה מְאֹד: וַיְהִי בְּהַכְרִית אִיזֶבֶל אֵת נְבִיאֵי יהוה
ה וַיִּקַּח עֹבַדְיָהוּ מֵאָה נְבִיאִים וַיַּחְבִּיאֵם חֲמִשִּׁים אִישׁ בַּמְּעָרָה וְכִלְכְּלָם לֶחֶם וָמָיִם: וַיֹּאמֶר אַחְאָב אֶל־
עֹבַדְיָהוּ לֵךְ בָּאָרֶץ אֶל־כָּל־מַעְיְנֵי הַמַּיִם וְאֶל כָּל־הַנְּחָלִים אוּלַי ׀ נִמְצָא חָצִיר וּנְחַיֶּה סוּס וָפֶרֶד וְלוֹא
ו נַכְרִית מֵהַבְּהֵמָה: וַיְחַלְּקוּ לָהֶם אֶת־הָאָרֶץ לַעֲבָר־בָּהּ אַחְאָב הָלַךְ בְּדֶרֶךְ אֶחָד לְבַדּוֹ וְעֹבַדְיָהוּ הָלַךְ
ז בְּדֶרֶךְ־אֶחָד לְבַדּוֹ: וַיְהִי עֹבַדְיָהוּ בַּדֶּרֶךְ וְהִנֵּה אֵלִיָּהוּ לִקְרָאתוֹ וַיַּכִּרֵהוּ וַיִּפֹּל עַל־פָּנָיו וַיֹּאמֶר הַאַתָּה זֶה
ח ט אֲדֹנִי אֵלִיָּהוּ: וַיֹּאמֶר לוֹ אָנִי לֵךְ אֱמֹר לַאדֹנֶיךָ הִנֵּה אֵלִיָּהוּ: וַיֹּאמֶר מֶה חָטָאתִי כִּי־אַתָּה נֹתֵן אֶת־עַבְדְּךָ
י בְּיַד־אַחְאָב לַהֲמִיתֵנִי: חַי ׀ יהוה אֱלֹהֶיךָ אִם־יֶשׁ־גּוֹי וּמַמְלָכָה אֲשֶׁר לֹא־שָׁלַח אֲדֹנִי שָׁם לְבַקֶּשְׁךָ
יא וְאָמְרוּ אָיִן וְהִשְׁבִּיעַ אֶת־הַמַּמְלָכָה וְאֶת־הַגּוֹי כִּי לֹא יִמְצָאֶכָּה: וְעַתָּה אַתָּה אֹמֵר לֵךְ אֱמֹר לַאדֹנֶיךָ
יב הִנֵּה אֵלִיָּהוּ: וְהָיָה אֲנִי ׀ אֵלֵךְ מֵאִתָּךְ וְרוּחַ יהוה ׀ יִשָּׂאֲךָ עַל אֲשֶׁר לֹא־אֵדָע וּבָאתִי לְהַגִּיד לְאַחְאָב
יג וְלֹא יִמְצָאֲךָ וַהֲרָגָנִי וְעַבְדְּךָ יָרֵא אֶת־יהוה מִנְּעֻרָי: הֲלֹא־הֻגַּד לַאדֹנִי אֵת אֲשֶׁר־עָשִׂיתִי בַּהֲרֹג אִיזֶבֶל
אֵת נְבִיאֵי יהוה וָאַחְבִּא מִנְּבִיאֵי יהוה מֵאָה אִישׁ חֲמִשִּׁים חֲמִשִּׁים אִישׁ בַּמְּעָרָה וָאֲכַלְכְּלֵם לֶחֶם וָמָיִם:
יד טו וְעַתָּה אַתָּה אֹמֵר לֵךְ אֱמֹר לַאדֹנֶיךָ הִנֵּה אֵלִיָּהוּ וַהֲרָגָנִי: וַיֹּאמֶר אֵלִיָּהוּ חַי יהוה צְבָאוֹת אֲשֶׁר עָמַדְתִּי
טז יז לְפָנָיו כִּי הַיּוֹם אֵרָאֶה אֵלָיו: וַיֵּלֶךְ עֹבַדְיָהוּ לִקְרַאת אַחְאָב וַיַּגֶּד־לוֹ וַיֵּלֶךְ אַחְאָב לִקְרַאת אֵלִיָּהוּ: וַיְהִי
יח כִּרְאוֹת אַחְאָב אֶת־אֵלִיָּהוּ וַיֹּאמֶר אַחְאָב אֵלָיו הַאַתָּה זֶה עֹכֵר יִשְׂרָאֵל: וַיֹּאמֶר לֹא עָכַרְתִּי אֶת־יִשְׂרָאֵל
יט כִּי אִם־אַתָּה וּבֵית אָבִיךָ בַּעֲזָבְכֶם אֶת־מִצְוֺת יהוה וַתֵּלֶךְ אַחֲרֵי הַבְּעָלִים: וְעַתָּה שְׁלַח קְבֹץ אֵלַי אֶת־
כָּל־יִשְׂרָאֵל אֶל־הַר הַכַּרְמֶל וְאֶת־נְבִיאֵי הַבַּעַל אַרְבַּע מֵאוֹת וַחֲמִשִּׁים וּנְבִיאֵי הָאֲשֵׁרָה אַרְבַּע מֵאוֹת

Sepharadim and Chabad begin here

כ כא אֹכְלֵי שֻׁלְחַן אִיזָבֶל: *וַיִּשְׁלַח אַחְאָב בְּכָל־בְּנֵי יִשְׂרָאֵל וַיִּקְבֹּץ אֶת־הַנְּבִיאִים אֶל־הַר הַכַּרְמֶל: וַיִּגַּשׁ
אֵלִיָּהוּ אֶל־כָּל־הָעָם וַיֹּאמֶר עַד־מָתַי אַתֶּם פֹּסְחִים עַל־שְׁתֵּי הַסְּעִפִּים אִם־יהוה הָאֱלֹהִים לְכוּ אַחֲרָיו

KI TISA

The dramatic confrontation between the prophet Eliyahu and the priests of Baal on Mount Carmel, witnessed by all Israel, was the culmination of a titanic struggle that had lasted three years. Eliyahu had battled the idolatrous influence of Queen Izevel and decreed a devastating drought to prove that only God, and not Baal, has the power to give rain. King Aḥav went along with Eliyahu and allowed him to organize a contest after which the drought would break. This contest mirrors in some ways the events that had occurred centuries

22 is God, then follow Him, and if Baal, follow him!" But the people had no reply. "I am the only prophet
left to the LORD," Eliyahu said to the people, "while the prophets of Baal are four hundred fifty men.
23 Let two bulls be given to us; let them choose one bull for themselves, cut it up, and position it on the
wood without setting it alight, while I prepare the other bull and place it on the wood without setting
24 it alight. You will invoke your god by name, while I will invoke the LORD by name, and the God who
25 answers with fire – He is God." And all the people answered, "We accept." "Choose one bull for yourselves, and go first," Eliyahu said to the prophets of Baal, "for you are the majority. Do not set it alight
26 yourselves; invoke your god by name." They took the bull that was given to them and prepared it, then
invoked Baal by name from morning to noon, crying, "O Baal, answer us," but there was no sound and
27 no reply, and they swayed around the altar that had been prepared. At noon, Eliyahu began to mock
them: "Shout louder," he said, "for he is a god – he may be in conversation, or busy, or out traveling;
28 he may be asleep – he might wake!" And they shouted louder and gashed themselves with swords and
29 spears, as was their custom, until blood streamed down them. Noon passed by, and they raved until the
30 time of the grain offering, but there was no sound and no answer and no response. Then Eliyahu said to
all the people, "Draw close to me." All the people drew close, and he began to repair the LORD's ruined
31 altar. Eliyahu took twelve stones, corresponding to the number of the tribes of the sons of Yaakov, who
32 received the word of the LORD: "Yisrael shall be your name." With the stones he built an altar for the
33 name of the LORD and made a trench large enough for two *se'a* of seed all around the altar. He arranged
34 the wood, cut up the bull, and placed it on the wood. "Fill four jugs with water," he said, "and pour it
over the offering and the wood. Now do it a second time," he said, and they did it a second time. "Do it
35 a third time," he said, and they did it a third time. The water flowed around the altar; he even filled the
36 trench with water. At the time of the grain offering, the prophet Eliyahu drew close and said, "O LORD,
God of Avraham, Yitzḥak, and Yisrael, let it be known today that You are the God in Israel and that I
37 am Your servant, and it was by Your word that I have done all these things. Answer me, LORD, answer
me, so that this people will know that You, O LORD, are God; it was You who turned their hearts back-
38 ward." And fire from the LORD flared down and consumed the offering, the wood, the stones, and the
39 dirt, and licked up the water in the trench. And all the people saw, and they fell on their faces and cried,
40 "The LORD – He is God! The LORD – He is God!" *"Seize the prophets of Baal!" Eliyahu said to them.
"Let none of them escape!" They seized them, then Eliyahu led them down to the Kishon Stream and
41 slaughtered them there. "Go up to eat and drink," Eliyahu then said to Aḥav, "for here comes the sound
42 of roaring rain." And Aḥav went up to eat and drink while Eliyahu went up to the top of Mount Carmel.
43 He crouched down on the ground and pressed his face between his knees. "Go up now," he said to his
boy, "and look out to sea." He went up and looked out. "Nothing is there," he said. Seven times he said,
44 "Go back." The seventh time, he said, "A tiny cloud, the size of a man's hand, is rising up from the sea."
"Go up," he said, "and say to Aḥav, 'Harness up and make your way down so that the rain will not hold
45 you back.'" And all the while, the skies grew dark with clouds and wind, and heavy rain began to fall.
Aḥav mounted his chariot and rode out to Yizre'el.

Ashkenazim and Sephardim end here

כב וְאִם־הַבַּעַל לְכוּ אַחֲרָיו וְלֹא־עָנוּ הָעָם אֹתוֹ דָּבָר: וַיֹּאמֶר אֵלִיָּהוּ אֶל־הָעָם אֲנִי נוֹתַרְתִּי נָבִיא לַיהוה לְבַדִּי
כג וּנְבִיאֵי הַבַּעַל אַרְבַּע־מֵאוֹת וַחֲמִשִּׁים אִישׁ: וְיִתְּנוּ־לָנוּ שְׁנַיִם פָּרִים וְיִבְחֲרוּ לָהֶם הַפָּר הָאֶחָד וִינַתְּחֻהוּ
וְיָשִׂימוּ עַל־הָעֵצִים וְאֵשׁ לֹא יָשִׂימוּ וַאֲנִי אֶעֱשֶׂה ׀ אֶת־הַפָּר הָאֶחָד וְנָתַתִּי עַל־הָעֵצִים וְאֵשׁ לֹא אָשִׂים:
כד וּקְרָאתֶם בְּשֵׁם אֱלֹהֵיכֶם וַאֲנִי אֶקְרָא בְשֵׁם־יהוה וְהָיָה הָאֱלֹהִים אֲשֶׁר־יַעֲנֶה בָאֵשׁ הוּא הָאֱלֹהִים וַיַּעַן
כה כׇּל־הָעָם וַיֹּאמְרוּ טוֹב הַדָּבָר: וַיֹּאמֶר אֵלִיָּהוּ לִנְבִיאֵי הַבַּעַל בַּחֲרוּ לָכֶם הַפָּר הָאֶחָד וַעֲשׂוּ רִאשֹׁנָה כִּי
כו אַתֶּם הָרַבִּים וְקִרְאוּ בְּשֵׁם אֱלֹהֵיכֶם וְאֵשׁ לֹא תָשִׂימוּ: וַיִּקְחוּ אֶת־הַפָּר אֲשֶׁר־נָתַן לָהֶם וַיַּעֲשׂוּ וַיִּקְרְאוּ
בְשֵׁם־הַבַּעַל מֵהַבֹּקֶר וְעַד־הַצׇּהֳרַיִם לֵאמֹר הַבַּעַל עֲנֵנוּ וְאֵין קוֹל וְאֵין עֹנֶה וַיְפַסְּחוּ עַל־הַמִּזְבֵּחַ אֲשֶׁר
כז עָשָׂה: וַיְהִי בַצׇּהֳרַיִם וַיְהַתֵּל בָּהֶם אֵלִיָּהוּ וַיֹּאמֶר קִרְאוּ בְקוֹל־גָּדוֹל כִּי־אֱלֹהִים הוּא כִּי־שִׂיחַ וְכִי־שִׂיג
כח לוֹ וְכִי־דֶרֶךְ לוֹ אוּלַי יָשֵׁן הוּא וְיִקָץ: וַיִּקְרְאוּ בְּקוֹל גָּדוֹל וַיִּתְגֹּדְדוּ כְּמִשְׁפָּטָם בַּחֲרָבוֹת וּבָרְמָחִים עַד־
כט שְׁפׇךְ־דָּם עֲלֵיהֶם: וַיְהִי כַּעֲבֹר הַצׇּהֳרַיִם וַיִּתְנַבְּאוּ עַד לַעֲלוֹת הַמִּנְחָה וְאֵין־קוֹל וְאֵין־עֹנֶה וְאֵין קָשֶׁב:
ל לא וַיֹּאמֶר אֵלִיָּהוּ לְכׇל־הָעָם גְּשׁוּ אֵלַי וַיִּגְּשׁוּ כׇל־הָעָם אֵלָיו וַיְרַפֵּא אֶת־מִזְבַּח יהוה הֶהָרוּס: וַיִּקַּח אֵלִיָּהוּ
שְׁתֵּים עֶשְׂרֵה אֲבָנִים כְּמִסְפַּר שִׁבְטֵי בְנֵי־יַעֲקֹב אֲשֶׁר הָיָה דְבַר־יהוה אֵלָיו לֵאמֹר יִשְׂרָאֵל יִהְיֶה שְׁמֶךָ:
לב לג וַיִּבְנֶה אֶת־הָאֲבָנִים מִזְבֵּחַ בְּשֵׁם יהוה וַיַּעַשׂ תְּעָלָה כְּבֵית סָאתַיִם זֶרַע סָבִיב לַמִּזְבֵּחַ: וַיַּעֲרֹךְ אֶת־הָעֵצִים
לד וַיְנַתַּח אֶת־הַפָּר וַיָּשֶׂם עַל־הָעֵצִים: וַיֹּאמֶר מִלְאוּ אַרְבָּעָה כַדִּים מַיִם וְיִצְקוּ עַל־הָעֹלָה וְעַל־הָעֵצִים
לה לו וַיֹּאמֶר שְׁנוּ וַיִּשְׁנוּ וַיֹּאמֶר שַׁלֵּשׁוּ וַיְשַׁלֵּשׁוּ: וַיֵּלְכוּ הַמַּיִם סָבִיב לַמִּזְבֵּחַ וְגַם אֶת־הַתְּעָלָה מִלֵּא־מָיִם: וַיְהִי ׀
בַּעֲלוֹת הַמִּנְחָה וַיִּגַּשׁ אֵלִיָּהוּ הַנָּבִיא וַיֹּאמַר יהוה אֱלֹהֵי אַבְרָהָם יִצְחָק וְיִשְׂרָאֵל הַיּוֹם יִוָּדַע כִּי־אַתָּה
לז אֱלֹהִים בְּיִשְׂרָאֵל וַאֲנִי עַבְדֶּךָ ובדבריך עָשִׂיתִי אֵת כׇּל־הַדְּבָרִים הָאֵלֶּה: עֲנֵנִי יהוה עֲנֵנִי וְיֵדְעוּ הָעָם הַזֶּה וּבִדְבָרְךָ
לח כִּי־אַתָּה יהוה הָאֱלֹהִים וְאַתָּה הֲסִבֹּתָ אֶת־לִבָּם אֲחֹרַנִּית: וַתִּפֹּל אֵשׁ־יהוה וַתֹּאכַל אֶת־הָעֹלָה וְאֶת־
לט הָעֵצִים וְאֶת־הָאֲבָנִים וְאֶת־הֶעָפָר וְאֶת־הַמַּיִם אֲשֶׁר־בַּתְּעָלָה לִחֵכָה: וַיַּרְא כׇּל־הָעָם וַיִּפְּלוּ עַל־פְּנֵיהֶם
מ וַיֹּאמְרוּ יהוה הוּא הָאֱלֹהִים יהוה הוּא הָאֱלֹהִים:* וַיֹּאמֶר אֵלִיָּהוּ לָהֶם תִּפְשׂוּ ׀ אֶת־נְבִיאֵי הַבַּעַל אִישׁ

Ashkenazim and Sepharadim end here

מא אַל־יִמָּלֵט מֵהֶם וַיִּתְפְּשׂוּם וַיּוֹרִדֵם אֵלִיָּהוּ אֶל־נַחַל קִישׁוֹן וַיִּשְׁחָטֵם שָׁם: וַיֹּאמֶר אֵלִיָּהוּ לְאַחְאָב עֲלֵה
מב אֱכֹל וּשְׁתֵה כִּי־קוֹל הֲמוֹן הַגָּשֶׁם: וַיַּעֲלֶה אַחְאָב לֶאֱכֹל וְלִשְׁתּוֹת וְאֵלִיָּהוּ עָלָה אֶל־רֹאשׁ הַכַּרְמֶל וַיִּגְהַר
מג אַרְצָה וַיָּשֶׂם פָּנָיו בֵּין בִּרְכָּו: וַיֹּאמֶר אֶל־נַעֲרוֹ עֲלֵה־נָא הַבֵּט דֶּרֶךְ־יָם וַיַּעַל וַיַּבֵּט וַיֹּאמֶר אֵין מְאוּמָה
מד וַיֹּאמֶר שֻׁב שֶׁבַע פְּעָמִים: וַיְהִי בַּשְּׁבִעִית וַיֹּאמֶר הִנֵּה־עָב קְטַנָּה כְּכַף־אִישׁ עֹלָה מִיָּם וַיֹּאמֶר עֲלֵה אֱמֹר
מה אֶל־אַחְאָב אֱסֹר וָרֵד וְלֹא יַעַצׇרְכָה הַגָּשֶׁם: וַיְהִי ׀ עַד־כֹּה וְעַד־כֹּה וְהַשָּׁמַיִם הִתְקַדְּרוּ עָבִים וְרוּחַ וַיְהִי
גֶּשֶׁם גָּדוֹל וַיִּרְכַּב אַחְאָב וַיֵּלֶךְ יִזְרְעֶאלָה:

Haftarat Vayak'hel

On Shabbat Shekalim, read the maftir from Exodus 30:11–16, and the haftara on page 1643.
On Shabbat Para, read the maftir from Numbers 19:1–22, and the haftara on page 1649.
On Shabbat HaḤodesh, read the maftir from Exodus 12:1–20, and the haftara on page 1651.
When Vayak'hel and Pekudei are read together, read the haftara for Pekudei on page 1557.

I KINGS
For Sepharadim, Chabad, and Yemenites

7 13 14 King Shlomo sent and had Ḥiram fetched from Tyre. He was the son of a widow from the tribe of
Naftali, and his father had been a Tyrian coppersmith. He was brimming with the talent, expertise,
15 and skill to craft any work in bronze; he came to King Shlomo and crafted all his work. He formed
the two pillars of bronze; each pillar was eighteen cubits high, and the circumference of both pillars
16 was twelve cubits. He crafted two capitals, cast in bronze, to place atop the pillars – the height of each
17 capital was five cubits – as well as fronds of meshwork and garlands of chainwork for the capitals atop
18 the pillars, seven for each of the two capitals. He crafted the pillars with two rows around one mesh to
19 cover the capitals that were above the pomegranates, and he did the same with the second capital. The
20 capitals atop the pillars in the Hall were crafted in the form of a lily four cubits high; the capitals atop
both pillars bulged out through the meshwork over the rows of two hundred pomegranates encircling
21 both capitals. He erected the pillars by the Hall of the Sanctuary; he set up the right pillar and named
22 it Yakhin, and he set up the left pillar and named it Boaz. Atop each pillar was the form of a lily; thus
23 the work of the pillars was complete. *He made the Molten Sea, ten cubits across from rim to
24 rim and perfectly round. It was five cubits high and thirty cubits in circumference. There were bulb-
shaped knobs beneath its rim, encircling it all around, clustered around the Sea ten to a cubit; the two
25 rows of bulbs were cast together with it. It stood upon twelve oxen, three facing north, three facing
west, three facing south, and three facing east; the Sea was on top of them, and their haunches were all
26 turned inward. It was a handbreadth thick, and its rim was like the rim of a cup, like the petals of a lily;
its capacity was two thousand *bat*.

Yemenites end here

I KINGS
For Ashkenazim

7 40 Ḥiram crafted the lavers and the shovels and the basins. And so Ḥiram completed all the work for the
41 House of the Lord as commissioned by King Shlomo: two pillars and two globe-shaped capitals for
42 the pillar tops; two pieces of meshwork to cover the two globe-shaped capitals for the pillar tops; four
hundred pomegranates for the two pieces of meshwork – two rows of pomegranates for each piece of
43 meshwork, which covered the two globe-shaped capitals on top of the pillars; ten stands and ten lavers
44 45 for the stands; one Sea with twelve oxen beneath the Sea; pots, shovels, and basins. All these vessels,
46 which Ḥiram crafted for King Shlomo, for the House of the Lord, were of burnished bronze. The
47 king had them cast in clay molds on the Jordan plain between Sukkot and Tzartan. Due to their sheer
abundance, Shlomo left all the vessels out of account; the weight of the bronze was not determined.
48 Shlomo made all the vessels for the House of the Lord: the altar was of gold, and the table for the
49 showbread was of gold. The candelabra – five on the right and five on the left, in front of the Inner

---

the Temple, just as Betzalel had built the Tabernacle in an earlier generation. It details the beauty of the structure and its accoutrements, including the wonderful golden candelabra that gave light to the luxurious Temple. The work of building the Sanctuary was complex and arduous, but after seven years it was completed, and the Temple was dedicated with pomp and festivity.

הפטרת ויקהל

On שבת שקלים, *read the* מפטיר *from* שמות ל, יא–טז, *and the* הפטרה *on page 1643.*
On שבת פרה, *read the* מפטיר *from* במדבר יט, א–כב, *and the* הפטרה *on page 1649.*
On שבת החודש, *read the* מפטיר *from* שמות יב, א–כ, *and the* הפטרה *on page 1651.*
When ויקהל *and* פקודי *are read together, read the* הפטרה *for* פקודי *on page 1557.*

מלכים א׳
For Sepharadim, Chabad, and Yemenites

ז יג יד וַיִּשְׁלַח הַמֶּלֶךְ שְׁלֹמֹה וַיִּקַּח אֶת־חִירָם מִצֹּר: בֶּן־אִשָּׁה אַלְמָנָה הוּא מִמַּטֵּה נַפְתָּלִי וְאָבִיו אִישׁ־צֹרִי חֹרֵשׁ
נְחֹשֶׁת וַיִּמָּלֵא אֶת־הַחָכְמָה וְאֶת־הַתְּבוּנָה וְאֶת־הַדַּעַת לַעֲשׂוֹת כָּל־מְלָאכָה בַּנְּחֹשֶׁת וַיָּבוֹא אֶל־הַמֶּלֶךְ
טו שְׁלֹמֹה וַיַּעַשׂ אֶת־כָּל־מְלַאכְתּוֹ: וַיָּצַר אֶת־שְׁנֵי הָעַמּוּדִים נְחֹשֶׁת שְׁמֹנֶה עֶשְׂרֵה אַמָּה קוֹמַת הָעַמּוּד
טז הָאֶחָד וְחוּט שְׁתֵּים־עֶשְׂרֵה אַמָּה יָסֹב אֶת־הָעַמּוּד הַשֵּׁנִי: וּשְׁתֵּי כֹתָרֹת עָשָׂה לָתֵת עַל־רָאשֵׁי הָעַמּוּדִים
יז מֻצַק נְחֹשֶׁת חָמֵשׁ אַמּוֹת קוֹמַת הַכֹּתֶרֶת הָאֶחָת וְחָמֵשׁ אַמּוֹת קוֹמַת הַכֹּתֶרֶת הַשֵּׁנִית: שְׂבָכִים מַעֲשֵׂה
שְׂבָכָה גְּדִלִים מַעֲשֵׂה שַׁרְשְׁרוֹת לַכֹּתָרֹת אֲשֶׁר עַל־רֹאשׁ הָעַמּוּדִים שִׁבְעָה לַכֹּתֶרֶת הָאֶחָת וְשִׁבְעָה
יח לַכֹּתֶרֶת הַשֵּׁנִית: וַיַּעַשׂ אֶת־הָעַמּוּדִים וּשְׁנֵי טוּרִים סָבִיב עַל־הַשְּׂבָכָה הָאֶחָת לְכַסּוֹת אֶת־הַכֹּתָרֹת אֲשֶׁר
יט עַל־רֹאשׁ הָרִמֹּנִים וְכֵן עָשָׂה לַכֹּתֶרֶת הַשֵּׁנִית: וְכֹתָרֹת אֲשֶׁר עַל־רֹאשׁ הָעַמּוּדִים מַעֲשֵׂה שׁוּשַׁן בָּאוּלָם
כ אַרְבַּע אַמּוֹת: וְכֹתָרֹת עַל־שְׁנֵי הָעַמּוּדִים גַּם־מִמַּעַל מִלְּעֻמַּת הַבֶּטֶן אֲשֶׁר לְעֵבֶר שבכה וְהָרִמּוֹנִים מָאתַיִם הַשְּׂבָכָה
כא טֻרִים סָבִיב עַל הַכֹּתֶרֶת הַשֵּׁנִית: וַיָּקֶם אֶת־הָעַמֻּדִים לְאֻלָם הַהֵיכָל וַיָּקֶם אֶת־הָעַמּוּד הַיְמָנִי וַיִּקְרָא אֶת־
כב שְׁמוֹ יָכִין וַיָּקֶם אֶת־הָעַמּוּד הַשְּׂמָאלִי וַיִּקְרָא אֶת־שְׁמוֹ בֹּעַז: וְעַל רֹאשׁ הָעַמּוּדִים מַעֲשֵׂה שׁוֹשָׁן וַתִּתֹּם
כג מְלֶאכֶת הָעַמּוּדִים:* וַיַּעַשׂ אֶת־הַיָּם מוּצָק עֶשֶׂר בָּאַמָּה מִשְּׂפָתוֹ עַד־שְׂפָתוֹ עָגֹל ׀ סָבִיב וְחָמֵשׁ *Yemenites end here*
כד בָּאַמָּה קוֹמָתוֹ וקוה שְׁלֹשִׁים בָּאַמָּה יָסֹב אֹתוֹ סָבִיב: וּפְקָעִים מִתַּחַת לִשְׂפָתוֹ ׀ סָבִיב סֹבְבִים אֹתוֹ עֶשֶׂר וְקָו
כה בָּאַמָּה מַקִּפִים אֶת־הַיָּם סָבִיב שְׁנֵי טוּרִים הַפְּקָעִים יְצֻקִים בִּיצֻקָתוֹ: עֹמֵד עַל־שְׁנֵי עָשָׂר בָּקָר שְׁלֹשָׁה
פֹּנִים ׀ צָפוֹנָה וּשְׁלֹשָׁה פֹּנִים ׀ יָמָּה וּשְׁלֹשָׁה ׀ פֹּנִים נֶגְבָּה וּשְׁלֹשָׁה פֹּנִים מִזְרָחָה וְהַיָּם עֲלֵיהֶם מִלְמָעְלָה
כו וְכָל־אֲחֹרֵיהֶם בָּיְתָה: וְעָבְיוֹ טֶפַח וּשְׂפָתוֹ כְּמַעֲשֵׂה שְׂפַת־כּוֹס פֶּרַח שׁוֹשָׁן אַלְפַּיִם בַּת יָכִיל:

מלכים א׳
For Ashkenazim

ז מ וַיַּעַשׂ חִירוֹם אֶת־הַכִּיֹּרוֹת וְאֶת־הַיָּעִים וְאֶת־הַמִּזְרָקוֹת וַיְכַל חִירָם לַעֲשׂוֹת אֶת־כָּל־הַמְּלָאכָה
מא אֲשֶׁר עָשָׂה לַמֶּלֶךְ שְׁלֹמֹה בֵּית יְהוָה: עַמֻּדִים שְׁנַיִם וְגֻלֹּת הַכֹּתָרֹת אֲשֶׁר־עַל־רֹאשׁ הָעַמֻּדִים
מב שְׁתָּיִם וְהַשְּׂבָכוֹת שְׁתַּיִם לְכַסּוֹת אֶת־שְׁתֵּי גֻּלּוֹת הַכֹּתָרֹת אֲשֶׁר עַל־רֹאשׁ הָעַמּוּדִים: וְאֶת־
הָרִמֹּנִים אַרְבַּע מֵאוֹת לִשְׁתֵּי הַשְּׂבָכוֹת שְׁנֵי־טוּרִים רִמֹּנִים לַשְּׂבָכָה הָאֶחָת לְכַסּוֹת אֶת־שְׁתֵּי
מג גֻּלּוֹת הַכֹּתָרֹת אֲשֶׁר עַל־פְּנֵי הָעַמּוּדִים: וְאֶת־הַמְּכֹנוֹת עָשֶׂר וְאֶת־הַכִּיֹּרֹת עֲשָׂרָה עַל־הַמְּכֹנוֹת:
מד מה וְאֶת־הַיָּם הָאֶחָד וְאֶת־הַבָּקָר שְׁנֵים־עָשָׂר תַּחַת הַיָּם: וְאֶת־הַסִּירוֹת וְאֶת־הַיָּעִים וְאֶת־הַמִּזְרָקוֹת וְאֵת
מו כָּל־הַכֵּלִים האהל אֲשֶׁר עָשָׂה חִירָם לַמֶּלֶךְ שְׁלֹמֹה בֵּית יְהוָה נְחֹשֶׁת מְמֹרָט: בְּכִכַּר הַיַּרְדֵּן יְצָקָם הַמֶּלֶךְ הָאֵלֶּה
מז בְּמַעֲבֵה הָאֲדָמָה בֵּין סֻכּוֹת וּבֵין צָרְתָן: וַיַּנַּח שְׁלֹמֹה אֶת־כָּל־הַכֵּלִים מֵרֹב מְאֹד מְאֹד לֹא נֶחְקַר מִשְׁקַל
מח הַנְּחֹשֶׁת: וַיַּעַשׂ שְׁלֹמֹה אֵת כָּל־הַכֵּלִים אֲשֶׁר בֵּית יְהוָה אֵת מִזְבַּח הַזָּהָב וְאֶת־הַשֻּׁלְחָן אֲשֶׁר עָלָיו
מט לֶחֶם הַפָּנִים זָהָב: וְאֶת־הַמְּנֹרוֹת חָמֵשׁ מִיָּמִין וְחָמֵשׁ מִשְּׂמֹאול לִפְנֵי הַדְּבִיר זָהָב סָגוּר וְהַפֶּרַח וְהַנֵּרֹת

VAYAK'HEL

The First Temple, built in the reign of King Shlomo, was constructed from the finest materials and using the most advanced methods in existence. The richness of the structure was a testament to God's glory. This *haftara* describes the work of Ḥiram, the architect charged with constructing

50 Sanctuary – were of solid gold; the flowers, the lamps, and the tongs were all of gold. The bowls, shears,
basins, spoons, and firepans were of solid gold. The hinges of the doors to the inner House, to the Holy
of Holies, and of the doors of the House to the Sanctuary, were of gold.

Haftarat Pekudei

When Vayak'hel and Pekudei are read together, read this haftara.
On Shabbat Shekalim read the maftir from Exodus 30:11–16, and the haftara on page 1643.
On Shabbat Para, read the maftir from Numbers 19:1–22, and the haftara on page 1649.
On Shabbat HaḤodesh, read the maftir from Exodus 12:1–20, and the haftara on page 1651.

I KINGS
Sepharadim and Yemenites begin here

7 40 Ḥiram crafted the lavers and the shovels and the basins. And so Ḥiram completed all the work for
41 the House of the Lord as commissioned by King Shlomo: two pillars and two globe-shaped capitals for the pillar tops; two pieces of meshwork to cover the two globe-shaped capitals for the pil-
42 lar tops; four hundred pomegranates for the two pieces of meshwork – two rows of pomegranates
43 for each piece of meshwork, which covered the two globe-shaped capitals on top of the pillars; ten
44 stands and ten lavers for the stands; one Sea with twelve oxen beneath the Sea; pots, shovels, and
45 basins. All these vessels, which Ḥiram crafted for King Shlomo, for the House of the Lord, were of
46 burnished bronze. The king had them cast in clay molds on the Jordan plain between Sukkot and
47 Tzartan. Due to their sheer abundance, Shlomo left all the vessels out of account; the weight of the
48 bronze was not determined. Shlomo made all the vessels for the House of the Lord: the altar was
49 of gold, and the table for the showbread was of gold. The candelabra – five on the right and five on
the left, in front of the Inner Sanctuary – were of solid gold; the flowers, the lamps, and the tongs
50 were all of gold. The bowls, shears, basins, spoons, and firepans were of solid gold. The hinges of the
doors to the inner House, to the Holy of Holies, and of the doors of the House to the Sanctuary,
51 were of gold. *When all the work that King Shlomo did for the House of the Lord was finished, Shlomo brought what David his father had dedicated – the silver, the gold, and the vessels – and
8 1 placed them in the treasury of the House of the Lord. Then Shlomo assembled the elders
of Israel – all the heads of the tribes, the ancestral leaders of the Israelites – before King Shlomo in
2 Jerusalem, to bring up the Ark of the Lord's Covenant from the City of David, Zion. All the men
of Israel assembled before King Shlomo in the month of Etanim, the seventh month, at the festival.
3 When all the elders of Israel had arrived, the priests lifted up the Ark and brought up the Ark of the
4 Lord, the Tent of Meeting, and all the sacred vessels in the Tent. While the priests and the Levites
5 brought them up, King Shlomo and the whole community of Israel, who had met him before the
6 Ark, sacrificed sheep and oxen – far too many to number or count. The priests brought the Ark of the
Lord's Covenant to its place – to the House's Inner Sanctuary, the Holy of Holies, to under the shade
7 of the wings of the cherubim. For the wings of the cherubim were spread over the place of the Ark so
8 that the cherubim sheltered the Ark and its poles from above. The poles extended so that the ends of
the poles were visible from the Holy Place in front of the Inner Sanctuary, but they could not be seen

Sepharadim and Yemenites end here
Ashkenazim and Chabad begin here

time, which contained the tablets of the covenant, from the City of David to the new Temple. From then on, its home would be the Holy of Holies in the structures' Sanctuary building. Second was Shlomo's long prayer of thanksgiving, designating the Temple as a house of prayer for the people of Israel and all humanity.

נ והמלקחים זהב: והספות והמזמרות והמזרקות והכפות והמחתות זהב סגור והפתות לדלתות
הבית הפנימי לקדש הקדשים לדלתי הבית להיכל זהב:

הפטרת פקודי

When ויקהל *and* פקודי *are read together, read this* הפטרה*.*
On שבת שקלים*, read the* מפטיר *from* שמות ל, יא–טז*, and the* הפטרה *on page 1643.*
On שבת פרה*, read the* מפטיר *from* במדבר יט, א–כב*, and the* הפטרה *on page 1649.*
On שבת החודש*, read the* מפטיר *from* שמות יב, א–כ*, and the* הפטרה *on page 1651.*

מלכים א׳

Sepharadim and Yemenites begin here

ז מ ויעש חירום את הכירות ואת היעים ואת המזרקות ויכל חירם לעשות את כל המלאכה
מא אשר עשה למלך שלמה בית יהוה: עמדים שנים וגלת הכתרת אשר על ראש העמודים
מב שתים והשבכות שתים לכסות את שתי גלות הכתרת אשר על ראש העמודים: ואת
הרמנים ארבע מאות לשתי השבכות שני טורים רמנים לשבכה האחת לכסות את שתי
מג גלות הכתרת אשר על פני העמודים: ואת המכנות עשר ואת הכירת עשרה על המכנות:
מד מה ואת הים האחד ואת הבקר שנים עשר תחת הים: ואת הסירות ואת היעים ואת המזרקות ואת
מו כל הכלים האהל אשר עשה חירם למלך שלמה בית יהוה נחשת ממרט: בככר הירדן יצקם המלך האלה
מז במעבה האדמה בין סכות ובין צרתן: וינח שלמה את כל הכלים מרב מאד מאד לא נחקר משקל
מח הנחשת: ויעש שלמה את כל הכלים אשר בית יהוה את מזבח הזהב ואת השלחן אשר עליו
מט לחם הפנים זהב: ואת המנרות חמש מימין וחמש משמאול לפני הדביר זהב סגור והפרח והנרת
נ והמלקחים זהב: והספות והמזמרות והמזרקות והכפות והמחתות זהב סגור והפתות לדלתות
נא הבית הפנימי לקדש הקדשים לדלתי הבית להיכל זהב:* *ותשלם כל המלאכה אשר

Sepharadim and Yemenites end here
Ashkenazim and Chabad begin here

עשה המלך שלמה בית יהוה ויבא שלמה את קדשי | דוד אביו את הכסף ואת הזהב ואת הכלים
ח א נתן באצרות בית יהוה: אז יקהל שלמה את זקני ישראל את כל ראשי המטות נשיאי
האבות לבני ישראל אל המלך שלמה ירושלם להעלות את ארון ברית יהוה מעיר דוד היא ציון:
ב ג ויקהלו אל המלך שלמה כל איש ישראל בירח האתנים בחג הוא החדש השביעי: ויבאו כל זקני
ד ישראל וישאו הכהנים את הארון: ויעלו את ארון יהוה ואת אהל מועד ואת כל כלי הקדש אשר
ה באהל ויעלו אתם הכהנים והלוים: והמלך שלמה וכל עדת ישראל הנועדים עליו אתו לפני הארון
ו מזבחים צאן ובקר אשר לא יספרו ולא ימנו מרב: ויבאו הכהנים את ארון ברית יהוה אל מקומו
ז אל דביר הבית אל קדש הקדשים אל תחת כנפי הכרובים: כי הכרובים פרשים כנפים אל מקום
ח הארון ויסכו הכרבים על הארון ועל בדיו מלמעלה: ויארכו הבדים ויראו ראשי הבדים מן הקדש

PEKUDEI

With the conclusion of the construction of the Temple during the reign of King Shlomo, the people prepare for the dedication ceremony for the new Sanctuary. All Israel arrived for the festivities, celebrating for fourteen days during the month of Tishrei, until Shemini Atzeret. At the center of this celebration were two main events, described here in detail. First was the moving of the Ark built in Moshe's

9 from the outside, and they are there to this day. The Ark contained nothing but the two stone tablets
Moshe placed there at Ḥorev when the Lord made a covenant with the Israelites as they left the land
10 11 of Egypt. And as the priests left the Holy Place, a cloud filled the House of the Lord; the priests
could not stand and serve because of the cloud, for the glory of the Lord had filled the House of the
12 13 Lord. Then Shlomo declared: "The Lord promised that He would dwell in deep mist; I have
14 now built You an exalted House, a permanent place for Your abode." And the king turned his face and
15 blessed the whole assembly of Israel, while the whole assembly of Israel stood. "Blessed is the Lord,
God of Israel," he said, "who made a promise to my father David with His own mouth and has now
16 fulfilled it with His own hand, saying: From the day I brought My people, Israel, out of Egypt, I never
chose a city from among all the tribes of Israel, to build a House where My name would be; but I
17 chose David to be over My people Israel. My father David had his heart set on building a House for
18 the name of the Lord, God of Israel. But the Lord said to my father David: Though you have set
19 your heart on building a House for My name, and though you have set your heart well, you will not
be the one to build the House. But your son, the issue of your own loins – he will be the one to build
20 the House for My name. The Lord has fulfilled the promise He made; I have risen in my father's
stead, and I sit upon Israel's throne, as the Lord promised. I have built the House for the name of the
21 Lord, God of Israel. And there I have set a place for the Ark, which contains the covenant that the
Lord made with our ancestors when He brought them out of the land of Egypt."

Haftarat Vayikra

On Shabbat Zakhor, read the maftir from Deuteronomy 25:17–19, and the haftara on page 1645.
On Shabbat HaḤodesh, read the maftir from Exodus 12:1–20, and the haftara on page 1651.

43 21 22 The people I have formed for Me, who are to tell My praises. It is not Me you call for, Yaakov; Israel, ISAIAH
23 you wearied of Me. You did not bring Me the lamb of your offering; it was not Me your sacrifice hon-
24 ored; I did not enslave you to My gifts or weary you with frankincense. You did not pay silver for
calamus for Me or slake My thirst with fat of the sacrifice, yet you enslaved Me to your iniquity and
25 wearied Me with your sins. I am I, who expunge your offenses for My own sake and will not keep
26 27 your sins in mind. Recall Me now; let us argue this out; tell Me so that you may be vindicated. Your
28 first father sinned, and those who spoke for you rebelled against Me, so I desecrated your Sanctuary's
44 1 ministers and marked you for destruction, Yaakov; Israel, to be denounced. And now listen,
2 Yaakov My servant, Israel whom I chose; so says the Lord who made you, the One who made you in
3 the womb, who helps you: Do not fear, My servant Yaakov, Yeshurun whom I chose. As I pour water
on thirsty earth, water upon parched land, I shall pour forth My spirit upon your children, upon your
4 5 offspring My blessing. They will sprout among the grasses, like willows on streams of water, and a man
will say, "I am the Lord's," while another invokes the name of Yaakov, and a third one will inscribe on
6 his hand, "The Lord's," to name himself Israel. So says the Lord, King of Israel, its rescue,

---

a religious imperative as well as a political one. Israel, as God's people, must respond to the prophet's call in His name: "I am the first and I the last; beside Me is no God." If they internalize this, they will have no need to fear the threat from gods of wood and stone. The prophet mocks these idols, while stressing that in Israel's own religion, the sacrificial service is not an end in itself but a means, and that true closeness to God comes through the perfection of our character.

ט עַל־פְּנֵי הַדְּבִיר וְלֹא יֵרָאוּ הַחוּצָה וַיִּהְיוּ שָׁם עַד הַיּוֹם הַזֶּה׃ אֵין בָּאָרוֹן רַק שְׁנֵי לֻחוֹת הָאֲבָנִים אֲשֶׁר
י הִנִּחַ שָׁם מֹשֶׁה בְּחֹרֵב אֲשֶׁר כָּרַת יהוה עִם־בְּנֵי יִשְׂרָאֵל בְּצֵאתָם מֵאֶרֶץ מִצְרָיִם׃ וַיְהִי בְּצֵאת הַכֹּהֲנִים
יא מִן־הַקֹּדֶשׁ וְהֶעָנָן מָלֵא אֶת־בֵּית יהוה׃ וְלֹא־יָכְלוּ הַכֹּהֲנִים לַעֲמֹד לְשָׁרֵת מִפְּנֵי הֶעָנָן כִּי־מָלֵא כְבוֹד־יהוה
יב יג אֶת־בֵּית יהוה׃ אָז אָמַר שְׁלֹמֹה יהוה אָמַר לִשְׁכֹּן בָּעֲרָפֶל׃ בָּנֹה בָנִיתִי בֵּית זְבֻל לָךְ מָכוֹן
יד טו לְשִׁבְתְּךָ עוֹלָמִים׃ וַיַּסֵּב הַמֶּלֶךְ אֶת־פָּנָיו וַיְבָרֶךְ אֵת כָּל־קְהַל יִשְׂרָאֵל וְכָל־קְהַל יִשְׂרָאֵל עֹמֵד׃ וַיֹּאמֶר
טז בָּרוּךְ יהוה אֱלֹהֵי יִשְׂרָאֵל אֲשֶׁר דִּבֶּר בְּפִיו אֵת דָּוִד אָבִי וּבְיָדוֹ מִלֵּא לֵאמֹר׃ מִן־הַיּוֹם אֲשֶׁר הוֹצֵאתִי
אֶת־עַמִּי אֶת־יִשְׂרָאֵל מִמִּצְרַיִם לֹא־בָחַרְתִּי בְעִיר מִכֹּל שִׁבְטֵי יִשְׂרָאֵל לִבְנוֹת בַּיִת לִהְיוֹת שְׁמִי שָׁם
יז וָאֶבְחַר בְּדָוִד לִהְיוֹת עַל־עַמִּי יִשְׂרָאֵל׃ וַיְהִי עִם־לְבַב דָּוִד אָבִי לִבְנוֹת בַּיִת לְשֵׁם יהוה אֱלֹהֵי יִשְׂרָאֵל׃
יח וַיֹּאמֶר יהוה אֶל־דָּוִד אָבִי יַעַן אֲשֶׁר הָיָה עִם־לְבָבְךָ לִבְנוֹת בַּיִת לִשְׁמִי הֱטִיבֹתָ כִּי הָיָה עִם־לְבָבֶךָ׃
יט כ רַק אַתָּה לֹא תִבְנֶה הַבָּיִת כִּי אִם־בִּנְךָ הַיֹּצֵא מֵחֲלָצֶיךָ הוּא־יִבְנֶה הַבַּיִת לִשְׁמִי׃ וַיָּקֶם יהוה אֶת־דְּבָרוֹ
אֲשֶׁר דִּבֵּר וָאָקֻם תַּחַת דָּוִד אָבִי וָאֵשֵׁב ׀ עַל־כִּסֵּא יִשְׂרָאֵל כַּאֲשֶׁר דִּבֶּר יהוה וָאֶבְנֶה הַבַּיִת לְשֵׁם יהוה
כא אֱלֹהֵי יִשְׂרָאֵל׃ וָאָשִׂם שָׁם מָקוֹם לָאָרוֹן אֲשֶׁר־שָׁם בְּרִית יהוה אֲשֶׁר כָּרַת עִם־אֲבֹתֵינוּ בְּהוֹצִיאוֹ אֹתָם
מֵאֶרֶץ מִצְרָיִם׃

הפטרת ויקרא

On שבת זכור*, read the* מפטיר *from* דברים כה, יז–יט*, and the* הפטרה *on page 1645.*
On שבת החודש*, read the* מפטיר *from* שמות יב, א–כ*, and the* הפטרה *on page 1651.*

מג כא כב כג עַם־זוּ יָצַרְתִּי לִי תְּהִלָּתִי יְסַפֵּרוּ׃ וְלֹא־אֹתִי קָרָאתָ יַעֲקֹב כִּי־יָגַעְתָּ בִּי יִשְׂרָאֵל׃ לֹא־הֵבֵיאתָ לִּי שֵׂה עֹלֹתֶיךָ ישעיה
כד וּזְבָחֶיךָ לֹא כִבַּדְתָּנִי לֹא הֶעֱבַדְתִּיךָ בְּמִנְחָה וְלֹא הוֹגַעְתִּיךָ בִּלְבוֹנָה׃ לֹא־קָנִיתָ לִּי בַכֶּסֶף קָנֶה וְחֵלֶב
כה זְבָחֶיךָ לֹא הִרְוִיתָנִי אַךְ הֶעֱבַדְתַּנִי בְּחַטֹּאותֶיךָ הוֹגַעְתַּנִי בַּעֲוֺנֹתֶיךָ׃ אָנֹכִי אָנֹכִי הוּא מֹחֶה פְשָׁעֶיךָ לְמַעֲנִי
כו כז וְחַטֹּאתֶיךָ לֹא אֶזְכֹּר׃ הַזְכִּירֵנִי נִשָּׁפְטָה יָחַד סַפֵּר אַתָּה לְמַעַן תִּצְדָּק׃ אָבִיךָ הָרִאשׁוֹן חָטָא וּמְלִיצֶיךָ
מד כח א פָּשְׁעוּ בִי׃ וַאֲחַלֵּל שָׂרֵי קֹדֶשׁ וְאֶתְּנָה לַחֵרֶם יַעֲקֹב וְיִשְׂרָאֵל לְגִדּוּפִים׃ וְעַתָּה שְׁמַע יַעֲקֹב עַבְדִּי
ב וְיִשְׂרָאֵל בָּחַרְתִּי בוֹ׃ כֹּה־אָמַר יהוה עֹשֶׂךָ וְיֹצֶרְךָ מִבֶּטֶן יַעְזְרֶךָּ אַל־תִּירָא עַבְדִּי יַעֲקֹב וִישֻׁרוּן בָּחַרְתִּי
ג ד בוֹ׃ כִּי אֶצָּק־מַיִם עַל־צָמֵא וְנֹזְלִים עַל־יַבָּשָׁה אֶצֹּק רוּחִי עַל־זַרְעֶךָ וּבִרְכָתִי עַל־צֶאֱצָאֶיךָ׃ וְצָמְחוּ בְּבֵין
ה חָצִיר כַּעֲרָבִים עַל־יִבְלֵי־מָיִם׃ זֶה יֹאמַר לַיהוה אָנִי וְזֶה יִקְרָא בְשֵׁם־יַעֲקֹב וְזֶה יִכְתֹּב יָדוֹ לַיהוה וּבְשֵׁם
ו יִשְׂרָאֵל יְכַנֶּה׃ כֹּה־אָמַר יהוה מֶלֶךְ־יִשְׂרָאֵל וְגֹאֲלוֹ יהוה צְבָאוֹת אֲנִי רִאשׁוֹן וַאֲנִי אַחֲרוֹן

VAYIKRA

The military conflicts that plagued Israel from their entry into the land until the time of Yeshayahu were on a small scale, and never came close to the destruction and exile that would be the people's fate later. In Yeshayahu's lifetime, however, during the reign of Ḥizkiyahu, the Assyrian superpower destroyed the kingdom of Israel utterly and exiled its people. Yehuda was in acute danger of suffering a similar fate. The confrontation with Assyria was presented by its emissaries as a struggle between deities. Victory for Assyria would be taken as a victory of Assyria's gods over the God of Israel. To save Yehuda from Assyria was therefore

7 the LORD of Hosts: I am the first and I the last; beside Me is no God. Who like Me calls the future *Yemenites end here*
forth and tells it? Let them lay their claim before Me. I have formed an eternal people, so let them bring
8 out signs and tell what is to come. Do not fear, do not lose faith; have I not let you hear this from the
9 start? I told it, and you are My witnesses: Is there any God but Me? There is no rock I do not know. All
those makers of images – all emptiness, their gorgeous objects useless, and all their witnesses see noth-
10 ing and know not and are shamed. Who has made a god and molded an idol to bring him no good?
11 All his company will be shamed; craftsmen – they are human; let them come together, all, and stand
12 and fear and feel their shame together, for the craftsman in iron makes a chisel, works it over the coals
and forms it with hammers, works it with his arms' strength, grows hungry and has no strength, fails
13 to drink water until he grows faint. The carpenter stretches out his line and marks it with a thread; he
forms it with his planes and marks it with a compass. He is making it into the form of a man, a supreme
14 human frame, to sit in a house. He cuts down cedars for his work or chooses a cypress or oak and sees
15 it grow strong in the forest, plants a bay laurel and lets rain nourish it to grow. These become firewood
for a man; he takes them and warms himself, kindles them and bakes bread, and works the rest into a
16 god, and worships a statue and prostrates himself before it. Half of it he burns in the fire; thanks to that
half he eats meat, roasts the roast, feels fullness, warms himself, says, "Ah – I am warmed; I have seen
17 the flames." And with what is left over, he makes a god, a statue to prostrate himself in front of and to
18 worship, pray to, say, "Save me, please: you are my god." They know not; they do not comprehend, for
19 their eyes are smeared over, not to see, not to let understanding into their hearts, so they do not take it
to heart, nor find mind or wisdom to say, "I burned half in the fire; I baked bread on the coals; I roasted
meat and ate it; with the rest should I make this disgusting thing, this slab of wood, and bow down?"
20 He courts ashes; his deceived heart has misled him; he cannot save himself; he cannot say, "This in
21 my right hand – it is a lie." Hold these things in mind, Yaakov, Israel, for you are My servant. I
22 made you – you are My servant; do not forget Me, Israel. I dispelled your offenses like mist, like a cloud
23 all your sins – come back to Me, for I have redeemed you. Sing out, heavens, for the LORD has acted.
Sound the trumpets, lowest depths of earth; hills, break out in song, and forests, all their trees, for the
LORD has redeemed Yaakov; in Israel is He glorified.

HAFTARAT TZAV

On Shabbat Zakhor read the maftir from Deuteronomy 25:17–19, and the haftara on page 1645.
On Purim Meshulash in Jerusalem read the maftir from Exodus 17:8–16, and the haftara on page 1645.
On Shabbat Para read the maftir from Numbers 19:1–22, and the haftara on page 1649.
On Shabbat HaGadol read the haftara on page 1653.

7 21 This is what the LORD of Hosts, the God of Israel, said: Heap your burnt offerings upon your other sac- JEREMIAH
22 rifices and eat the meat. For when I brought your forefathers out of Egypt, I did not speak to them, nor
23 did I command them about matters of burnt offerings and sacrifices. Rather, this is what I commanded
them: Heed My voice so that I will be your God and you will be My people. Walk in all the ways as I

---

institution of the sacrifices is meant to arouse worshippers to correct their ways, to repent, and draw closer to God. The important thing is a person's behavior, not the sacrifices he or she brings. Those who act in a perverse way and come to bring sacrifices in the Temple to atone are carrying out a pointless exercise, only exacerbating God's displeasure. Just as God does charity, kindness, and justice on earth, He commands that we humans act likewise.

ז וּמִבַּלְעָדַי אֵין אֱלֹהִים: וּמִי־כָמוֹנִי יִקְרָא וְיַגִּידֶהָ וְיַעְרְכֶהָ לִי מִשּׂוּמִי עַם־עוֹלָם וְאֹתִיּוֹת וַאֲשֶׁר תָּבֹאנָה *Yemenites end here*
ח יַגִּידוּ לָמוֹ: אַל־תִּפְחֲדוּ וְאַל־תִּרְהוּ הֲלֹא מֵאָז הִשְׁמַעְתִּיךָ וְהִגַּדְתִּי וְאַתֶּם עֵדָי הֲיֵשׁ אֱלוֹהַּ מִבַּלְעָדַי וְאֵין
ט צוּר בַּל־יָדָעְתִּי: יֹצְרֵי־פֶסֶל כֻּלָּם תֹּהוּ וַחֲמוּדֵיהֶם בַּל־יוֹעִילוּ וְעֵדֵיהֶם הֵמָּה בַּל־יִרְאוּ וּבַל־יֵדְעוּ לְמַעַן
י יא יֵבֹשׁוּ: מִי־יָצַר אֵל וּפֶסֶל נָסָךְ לְבִלְתִּי הוֹעִיל: הֵן כָּל־חֲבֵרָיו יֵבֹשׁוּ וְחָרָשִׁים הֵמָּה מֵאָדָם יִתְקַבְּצוּ כֻלָּם
יב יַעַמְדוּ יִפְחֲדוּ יֵבֹשׁוּ יָחַד: חָרַשׁ בַּרְזֶל מַעֲצָד וּפָעַל בַּפֶּחָם וּבַמַּקָּבוֹת יִצְּרֵהוּ וַיִּפְעָלֵהוּ בִּזְרוֹעַ כֹּחוֹ גַּם־רָעֵב
יג וְאֵין כֹּחַ לֹא־שָׁתָה מַיִם וַיִּעָף: חָרַשׁ עֵצִים נָטָה קָו יְתָאֲרֵהוּ בַשֶּׂרֶד יַעֲשֵׂהוּ בַּמַּקְצֻעוֹת וּבַמְּחוּגָה יְתָאֳרֵהוּ
יד וַיַּעֲשֵׂהוּ כְּתַבְנִית אִישׁ כְּתִפְאֶרֶת אָדָם לָשֶׁבֶת בָּיִת: לִכְרָת־לוֹ אֲרָזִים וַיִּקַּח תִּרְזָה וְאַלּוֹן וַיְאַמֶּץ־לוֹ
טו בַּעֲצֵי־יָעַר נָטַע אֹרֶן וְגֶשֶׁם יְגַדֵּל: וְהָיָה לְאָדָם לְבָעֵר וַיִּקַּח מֵהֶם וַיָּחָם אַף־יַשִּׂיק וְאָפָה לָחֶם אַף־יִפְעַל־
טז אֵל וַיִּשְׁתָּחוּ עָשָׂהוּ פֶסֶל וַיִּסְגָּד־לָמוֹ: חֶצְיוֹ שָׂרַף בְּמוֹ־אֵשׁ עַל־חֶצְיוֹ בָּשָׂר יֹאכֵל יִצְלֶה צָלִי וְיִשְׂבָּע אַף־
יז יָחֹם וְיֹאמַר הֶאָח חַמּוֹתִי רָאִיתִי אוּר: וּשְׁאֵרִיתוֹ לְאֵל עָשָׂה לְפִסְלוֹ יסגוד־לוֹ וְיִשְׁתַּחוּ וְיִתְפַּלֵּל אֵלָיו יִסְגָּד־
יח יט וְיֹאמַר הַצִּילֵנִי כִּי אֵלִי אָתָּה: לֹא יָדְעוּ וְלֹא יָבִינוּ כִּי טַח מֵרְאוֹת עֵינֵיהֶם מֵהַשְׂכִּיל לִבֹּתָם: וְלֹא־יָשִׁיב
אֶל־לִבּוֹ וְלֹא דַעַת וְלֹא־תְבוּנָה לֵאמֹר חֶצְיוֹ שָׂרַפְתִּי בְמוֹ־אֵשׁ וְאַף אָפִיתִי עַל־גֶּחָלָיו לֶחֶם אֶצְלֶה בָשָׂר
כ וְאֹכֵל וְיִתְרוֹ לְתוֹעֵבָה אֶעֱשֶׂה לְבוּל עֵץ אֶסְגּוֹד: רֹעֶה אֵפֶר לֵב הוּתַל הִטָּהוּ וְלֹא־יַצִּיל אֶת־נַפְשׁוֹ וְלֹא
כא יֹאמַר הֲלוֹא שֶׁקֶר בִּימִינִי: זְכָר־אֵלֶּה יַעֲקֹב וְיִשְׂרָאֵל כִּי עַבְדִּי־אָתָּה יְצַרְתִּיךָ עֶבֶד־לִי אַתָּה
כב כג יִשְׂרָאֵל לֹא תִנָּשֵׁנִי: מָחִיתִי כָעָב פְּשָׁעֶיךָ וְכֶעָנָן חַטֹּאותֶיךָ שׁוּבָה אֵלַי כִּי גְאַלְתִּיךָ: רָנּוּ שָׁמַיִם כִּי־עָשָׂה
יהוה הָרִיעוּ תַּחְתִּיּוֹת אָרֶץ פִּצְחוּ הָרִים רִנָּה יַעַר וְכָל־עֵץ בּוֹ כִּי־גָאַל יהוה יַעֲקֹב וּבְיִשְׂרָאֵל יִתְפָּאָר:

הפטרת צו

On שבת זכור *read the* מפטיר *from* דברים כה, יז–יט*, and the* הפטרה *on page 1645.*
On פורים משולש *in Jerusalem read the* מפטיר *from* שמות יז, ח–טז*, and the* הפטרה *on page 1645.*
On שבת פרה *read the* מפטיר *from* במדבר יט, א–כב*, and the* הפטרה *on page 1649.*
On שבת הגדול *read the* הפטרה *on page 1653.*

ירמיה ז כא כב כֹּה אָמַר יהוה צְבָאוֹת אֱלֹהֵי יִשְׂרָאֵל עֹלוֹתֵיכֶם סְפוּ עַל־זִבְחֵיכֶם וְאִכְלוּ בָשָׂר: כִּי לֹא־דִבַּרְתִּי אֶת־
כג אֲבוֹתֵיכֶם וְלֹא צִוִּיתִים בְּיוֹם הוֹצִיא אוֹתָם מֵאֶרֶץ מִצְרָיִם עַל־דִּבְרֵי עוֹלָה וָזָבַח: כִּי אִם־אֶת־הַדָּבָר הַזֶּה
צִוִּיתִי אוֹתָם לֵאמֹר שִׁמְעוּ בְקוֹלִי וְהָיִיתִי לָכֶם לֵאלֹהִים וְאַתֶּם תִּהְיוּ־לִי לְעָם וַהֲלַכְתֶּם בְּכָל־הַדֶּרֶךְ אֲשֶׁר

TZAV

During the reign of King Yehoyakim the fate of Jerusalem's destruction was sealed. The cruelty of this ruler, his cultivation of idolatry (including human sacrifice), and his persecution of God's prophets tipped the scales. Yirmeyahu prophesied the bitter decree, which put him in serious danger as well.

In this *haftara*, Yirmeyahu reminds the people that the

24 will command you so that it will be good for you. But they did not listen, nor even bend an ear. They
25 followed their own counsel, their stubborn, wicked hearts. They went backward, not forward. From
the day your forefathers left the land of Egypt until this very day, I sent to them all of My servants, the
26 prophets – early every day, and persistently. But they did not listen to Me, nor even bend an ear. They
27 stiffened their necks. They did worse than their fathers. You will speak all these words to them, but they
28 will not hear you. You will call to them, but they will not answer you. You shall say to them: "This is
the nation that did not obey the voice of the LORD its God and that did not accept correction. Gone
29 is faithfulness, severed from their mouths."* Shear your hair and throw it away. Raise a lament *Yemenites and Chabad continue in chapter 9*
upon the high places, for the LORD has despised and has abandoned the generation that enraged Him.
30 For the children of Yehuda have done evil in My eyes, declares the LORD. They have placed their vile
31 objects in the House which is called by My name, thereby defiling it. They have built the altars of Tofet,
which are in the Valley of Ben Hinom, to burn their sons and daughters in fire, something that I did not
32 command and that never entered My mind. Therefore, days are fast approaching, declares the
LORD, when men will no longer speak of "Tofet" and "Valley of Ben Hinom" but rather of "Valley of
33 Slaughter." They will bury in Tofet for lack of space elsewhere. The carcasses of this people will become
34 food for the birds of the heavens and the beasts of the earth, and none will frighten them away. I will
silence from the cities of Yehuda and the streets of Jerusalem the sound of joy and the sound of hap-
8 1 piness, the voice of the groom and the voice of the bride, for the land shall come to ruin. At that time,
declares the LORD, they will remove the bones of the kings of Yehuda and the bones of its princes,
the bones of the priests, and the bones of the prophets, and the bones of the inhabitants of Jerusalem
2 from their graves. They will spread them beneath the sun, the moon, and all the host of heaven that
they loved, and that they served, after which they followed, and which they sought, and to which they
bowed. They will neither be collected nor reburied but shall remain as dung upon the face of the earth.
3 Death will be preferable to life for all the surviving remnant of this evil clan in all the other places to
which I have expelled them, declares the LORD of Hosts.

9 22 Thus said the LORD: Let not the wise man boast of his wisdom. Let not the mighty man boast of his
23 might. Let not the wealthy boast of his wealth. Someone may boast only of his conscious devotion to
Me, for I the LORD act with loving-kindness, justice, and righteousness in the world. For it is these
things that I desire, declares the LORD.

HAFTARAT SHEMINI

On Shabbat Para read the maftir from Numbers 19:1–22, and the haftara on page 1649.
On Shabbat HaḤodesh, read the maftir from Exodus 12:1–20, and the haftara on page 1651.

6 1 David mustered all of Israel's elite once more, thirty thousand. Then David, along with all the troops II SAMUEL
2 with him, set out from Baalim of Yehuda. From there they brought up the Ark of God, which is called
3 by a name: The Name of the LORD of Hosts Enthroned upon the Cherubim is upon it. They mounted

---

of power and inspiration for his rule. This idea characterizes David's interactions with his wife Michal, daughter of Sha'ul, and the prophet Natan. Standing before the Ark, David feels no different from or superior to any of his subjects, but this does nothing to truly compromise his standing. The honor of a ruler of Israel only grows the more he humbles himself before God.

כד אֲצַוֶּה אֶתְכֶם לְמַעַן יִיטַב לָכֶם׃ וְלֹא שָׁמְעוּ וְלֹא־הִטּוּ אֶת־אָזְנָם וַיֵּלְכוּ בְּמֹעֵצוֹת בִּשְׁרִרוּת לִבָּם הָרָע
כה וַיִּהְיוּ לְאָחוֹר וְלֹא לְפָנִים׃ לְמִן־הַיּוֹם אֲשֶׁר יָצְאוּ אֲבוֹתֵיכֶם מֵאֶרֶץ מִצְרַיִם עַד הַיּוֹם הַזֶּה וָאֶשְׁלַח אֲלֵיכֶם
כו אֶת־כָּל־עֲבָדַי הַנְּבִיאִים יוֹם הַשְׁכֵּם וְשָׁלֹחַ׃ וְלוֹא שָׁמְעוּ אֵלַי וְלֹא הִטּוּ אֶת־אָזְנָם וַיַּקְשׁוּ אֶת־עָרְפָּם הֵרֵעוּ
כז מֵאֲבוֹתָם׃ וְדִבַּרְתָּ אֲלֵיהֶם אֶת־כָּל־הַדְּבָרִים הָאֵלֶּה וְלֹא יִשְׁמְעוּ אֵלֶיךָ וְקָרָאתָ אֲלֵיהֶם וְלֹא יַעֲנוּכָה׃
כח וְאָמַרְתָּ אֲלֵיהֶם זֶה הַגּוֹי אֲשֶׁר לוֹא־שָׁמְעוּ בְּקוֹל יהוה אֱלֹהָיו וְלֹא לָקְחוּ מוּסָר אָבְדָה הָאֱמוּנָה וְנִכְרְתָה
כט מִפִּיהֶם׃* גָּזִּי נִזְרֵךְ וְהַשְׁלִיכִי וּשְׂאִי עַל־שְׁפָיִם קִינָה כִּי מָאַס יהוה וַיִּטֹּשׁ אֶת־דּוֹר עֶבְרָתוֹ׃

Yemenites and Chabad continue in chapter 9

ל/לא כִּי־עָשׂוּ בְנֵי־יְהוּדָה הָרַע בְּעֵינַי נְאֻם־יהוה שָׂמוּ שִׁקּוּצֵיהֶם בַּבַּיִת אֲשֶׁר־נִקְרָא־שְׁמִי עָלָיו לְטַמְּאוֹ׃ וּבָנוּ
בָּמוֹת הַתֹּפֶת אֲשֶׁר בְּגֵיא בֶן־הִנֹּם לִשְׂרֹף אֶת־בְּנֵיהֶם וְאֶת־בְּנֹתֵיהֶם בָּאֵשׁ אֲשֶׁר לֹא צִוִּיתִי וְלֹא עָלְתָה
לב עַל־לִבִּי׃ לָכֵן הִנֵּה־יָמִים בָּאִים נְאֻם־יהוה וְלֹא־יֵאָמֵר עוֹד הַתֹּפֶת וְגֵיא בֶן־הִנֹּם כִּי אִם־גֵּיא
לג הַהֲרֵגָה וְקָבְרוּ בְתֹפֶת מֵאֵין מָקוֹם׃ וְהָיְתָה נִבְלַת הָעָם הַזֶּה לְמַאֲכָל לְעוֹף הַשָּׁמַיִם וּלְבֶהֱמַת הָאָרֶץ
לד וְאֵין מַחֲרִיד׃ וְהִשְׁבַּתִּי ׀ מֵעָרֵי יְהוּדָה וּמֵחֻצוֹת יְרוּשָׁלִַם קוֹל שָׂשׂוֹן וְקוֹל שִׂמְחָה קוֹל חָתָן וְקוֹל כַּלָּה כִּי
ח א לְחָרְבָּה תִּהְיֶה הָאָרֶץ׃ בָּעֵת הַהִיא נְאֻם־יהוה ויוציאו אֶת־עַצְמוֹת מַלְכֵי־יְהוּדָה וְאֶת־עַצְמוֹת שָׂרָיו יוֹצִיאוּ
ב וְאֶת־עַצְמוֹת הַכֹּהֲנִים וְאֵת ׀ עַצְמוֹת הַנְּבִיאִים וְאֵת עַצְמוֹת יוֹשְׁבֵי־יְרוּשָׁלִָם מִקִּבְרֵיהֶם׃ וּשְׁטָחוּם לַשֶּׁמֶשׁ
וְלַיָּרֵחַ וּלְכֹל ׀ צְבָא הַשָּׁמַיִם אֲשֶׁר אֲהֵבוּם וַאֲשֶׁר עֲבָדוּם וַאֲשֶׁר הָלְכוּ אַחֲרֵיהֶם וַאֲשֶׁר דְּרָשׁוּם וַאֲשֶׁר
ג הִשְׁתַּחֲווּ לָהֶם לֹא יֵאָסְפוּ וְלֹא יִקָּבֵרוּ לְדֹמֶן עַל־פְּנֵי הָאֲדָמָה יִהְיוּ׃ וְנִבְחַר מָוֶת מֵחַיִּים לְכֹל הַשְּׁאֵרִית
הַנִּשְׁאָרִים מִן־הַמִּשְׁפָּחָה הָרָעָה הַזֹּאת בְּכָל־הַמְּקֹמוֹת הַנִּשְׁאָרִים אֲשֶׁר הִדַּחְתִּים שָׁם נְאֻם יהוה
צְבָאוֹת׃

ט כב כֹּה ׀ אָמַר יהוה אַל־יִתְהַלֵּל חָכָם בְּחָכְמָתוֹ וְאַל־יִתְהַלֵּל הַגִּבּוֹר בִּגְבוּרָתוֹ אַל־יִתְהַלֵּל עָשִׁיר בְּעָשְׁרוֹ׃
כג כִּי אִם־בְּזֹאת יִתְהַלֵּל הַמִּתְהַלֵּל הַשְׂכֵּל וְיָדֹעַ אוֹתִי כִּי אֲנִי יהוה עֹשֶׂה חֶסֶד מִשְׁפָּט וּצְדָקָה בָּאָרֶץ כִּי־
בְאֵלֶּה חָפַצְתִּי נְאֻם־יהוה׃

הפטרת שמיני

On שבת פרה *read the* מפטיר *from* במדבר יט, א–כב, *and the* הפטרה *on page 1649.*
On שבת החודש, *read the* מפטיר *from* שמות יב, א–כ, *and the* הפטרה *on page 1651.*

ו א/ב וַיֹּסֶף עוֹד דָּוִד אֶת־כָּל־בָּחוּר בְּיִשְׂרָאֵל שְׁלֹשִׁים אָלֶף׃ וַיָּקָם ׀ וַיֵּלֶךְ דָּוִד וְכָל־הָעָם אֲשֶׁר אִתּוֹ מִבַּעֲלֵי שמואל ב׳
ג יְהוּדָה לְהַעֲלוֹת מִשָּׁם אֵת אֲרוֹן הָאֱלֹהִים אֲשֶׁר־נִקְרָא שֵׁם שֵׁם יהוה צְבָאוֹת יֹשֵׁב הַכְּרֻבִים עָלָיו׃ וַיַּרְכִּבוּ

SHEMINI

This *haftara* is one of a set of chapters in II Samuel that recounts the piety of King David's thirty-three-year rule in Jerusalem. Here, we are told of the journey of the Ark to David's new capital. The Ark had previously been taken captive from the Tabernacle by the Philistines and returned, but it had been kept since then at various temporary locations. The symbolic move of reclaiming the Ark and bringing it to be near his palace shows David's devotion to the Almighty and intention of having God's Torah be a source

the Ark of God upon a new cart and conveyed it from the house of Avinadav in Giva, with Uza and
4 Aḥyo, the sons of Avinadav, driving the new cart. They conveyed it from the house of Avinadav in
5 Giva – the Ark of God, Aḥyo walking before the Ark, and David and all the House of Israel revel-
ing before the Lord with all kinds of instruments of cypress wood, lyres, harps, timbrels, sistra, and
6 cymbals. When they reached the threshing floor of Nakhon, Uza reached out toward the Ark of God
7 and grasped hold of it, for the oxen had stumbled. And the Lord's rage flared up against Uza, and
8 God struck him down on the spot for his impudence; he died there with the Ark of God. David was
enraged that the Lord had burst out against Uza, and that place has been called Peretz Uza to this day.
9 10 David feared the Lord on that day, and he said, "How will the Ark of the Lord come to me?" And
David was not willing to have the Ark of the Lord removed to him in the City of David; David had
11 it redirected to the house of Oved Edom, the Gittite. The Ark of the Lord remained at the house of
Oved Edom, the Gittite, for three months, and the Lord blessed Oved Edom and his whole house-
12 hold. When it was reported to King David that the Lord had blessed Oved Edom's household and all
that was his because of the Ark of God, David went and brought up the Ark of God from the house of
13 Oved Edom to the City of David, with joy. When the bearers of the Ark of the Lord had advanced
14 six paces, he sacrificed an ox and a fatling. And David danced with all his might before the Lord;
15 David was clad in a linen ephod. So David and all the House of Israel led the Ark of the Lord up with
16 joyous shouting and the sound of the ram's horn. As the Ark of the Lord entered the City of David,
Mikhal, Sha'ul's daughter, was watching through the window; when she saw David – the king! – leap-
17 ing and dancing before the Lord, she felt a rush of contempt for him. They brought the Ark of the
Lord and set it in its place within the tent David had pitched for it, and David offered burnt offerings
18 and peace offerings before the Lord. When David had finished offering the burnt offering and the
19 peace offerings, he blessed the people in the name of the Lord of Hosts. He then distributed a ring
of bread, a share of meat, and a cake of raisins to all the people – to all the multitudes of Israel, every
20 single man and woman. Then all the people, every one, made their way home.* When David returned *Sepharadim and Chabad end here*
to bless his own household, Mikhal, Sha'ul's daughter, came out to meet him. "How dignified the king
of Israel was today," she said, "exposing himself before all the eyes of his servants' slave girls just as
21 one of the rabble might expose himself!" "It was before the Lord, who chose me instead of your
father and all his household and appointed me as ruler over the Lord's people, Israel," David said
22 to Mikhal. "I danced before the Lord. And I would have lowered myself even further and been hu-
23 miliated in my own eyes – but to the slave girls you speak of, I would still be dignified." And Mikhal,
7 1 Sha'ul's daughter, never had a child – to her dying day. Once the king had settled in his pal-
2 ace, and the Lord had granted him repose from all his surrounding enemies, the king said to the
prophet Natan, "Look now – I am dwelling in a cedarwood palace while the Ark of God is dwell-
3 ing in a tent." "Go – do whatever you have in mind," Natan said to the king, "for the Lord is with
4 5 you."* But that same night, the word of the Lord came to Natan. "Go, and say to *Yemenites end here*
My servant David: Thus says the Lord: Shall you be the one to build a house for Me, for My abode?
6 For I have not dwelt in a house from the day I brought the Israelites out of Egypt to this day; I have
7 roamed in tent and tabernacle. But wherever I roamed, among all the Israelites, have I ever spoken a
word to any of the tribes of Israel whom I charged to shepherd My people Israel, saying, 'Why have
8 you not built Me a cedarwood palace?' Now you shall say so to My servant David: Thus says the
Lord of Hosts: I took you out of the pastures, from following the sheep, to be ruler over My people
9 Israel. I have been with you wherever you went, and I have cut down all your enemies before you.
10 I will make your name great – one of the greatest names on earth. I will set aside a place for My people
Israel and let them take root and settle down within it, and they will be disturbed no longer; violent

אֶת־אֲרוֹן הָאֱלֹהִים אֶל־עֲגָלָה חֲדָשָׁה וַיִּשָּׂאֻהוּ מִבֵּית אֲבִינָדָב אֲשֶׁר בַּגִּבְעָה וְעֻזָּא וְאַחְיוֹ בְּנֵי אֲבִינָדָב
ד נֹהֲגִים אֶת־הָעֲגָלָה חֲדָשָׁה: וַיִּשָּׂאֻהוּ מִבֵּית אֲבִינָדָב אֲשֶׁר בַּגִּבְעָה עִם אֲרוֹן הָאֱלֹהִים וְאַחְיוֹ הֹלֵךְ לִפְנֵי
ה הָאָרוֹן: וְדָוִד | וְכָל־בֵּית יִשְׂרָאֵל מְשַׂחֲקִים לִפְנֵי יהוה בְּכֹל עֲצֵי בְרוֹשִׁים וּבְכִנֹּרוֹת וּבִנְבָלִים וּבְתֻפִּים
ו וּבִמְנַעַנְעִים וּבְצֶלְצֶלִים: וַיָּבֹאוּ עַד־גֹּרֶן נָכוֹן וַיִּשְׁלַח עֻזָּא אֶל־אֲרוֹן הָאֱלֹהִים וַיֹּאחֶז בּוֹ כִּי שָׁמְטוּ הַבָּקָר:
ז ח וַיִּחַר־אַף יהוה בְּעֻזָּה וַיַּכֵּהוּ שָׁם הָאֱלֹהִים עַל־הַשַּׁל וַיָּמָת שָׁם עִם אֲרוֹן הָאֱלֹהִים: וַיִּחַר לְדָוִד עַל
ט אֲשֶׁר פָּרַץ יהוה פֶּרֶץ בְּעֻזָּה וַיִּקְרָא לַמָּקוֹם הַהוּא פֶּרֶץ עֻזָּה עַד הַיּוֹם הַזֶּה: וַיִּרָא דָוִד אֶת־יהוה בַּיּוֹם
י הַהוּא וַיֹּאמֶר אֵיךְ יָבוֹא אֵלַי אֲרוֹן יהוה: וְלֹא־אָבָה דָוִד לְהָסִיר אֵלָיו אֶת־אֲרוֹן יהוה עַל־עִיר דָּוִד
יא וַיַּטֵּהוּ דָוִד בֵּית עֹבֵד־אֱדֹם הַגִּתִּי: וַיֵּשֶׁב אֲרוֹן יהוה בֵּית עֹבֵד אֱדֹם הַגִּתִּי שְׁלֹשָׁה חֳדָשִׁים וַיְבָרֶךְ יהוה
יב אֶת־עֹבֵד אֱדֹם וְאֶת־כָּל־בֵּיתוֹ: וַיֻּגַּד לַמֶּלֶךְ דָּוִד לֵאמֹר בֵּרַךְ יהוה אֶת־בֵּית עֹבֵד אֱדֹם וְאֶת־כָּל־אֲשֶׁר־
לוֹ בַּעֲבוּר אֲרוֹן הָאֱלֹהִים וַיֵּלֶךְ דָּוִד וַיַּעַל אֶת־אֲרוֹן הָאֱלֹהִים מִבֵּית עֹבֵד אֱדֹם עִיר דָּוִד בְּשִׂמְחָה:
יג יד וַיְהִי כִּי צָעֲדוּ נֹשְׂאֵי אֲרוֹן־יהוה שִׁשָּׁה צְעָדִים וַיִּזְבַּח שׁוֹר וּמְרִיא: וְדָוִד מְכַרְכֵּר בְּכָל־עֹז לִפְנֵי יהוה
טו טז וְדָוִד חָגוּר אֵפוֹד בָּד: וְדָוִד וְכָל־בֵּית יִשְׂרָאֵל מַעֲלִים אֶת־אֲרוֹן יהוה בִּתְרוּעָה וּבְקוֹל שׁוֹפָר: וְהָיָה
אֲרוֹן יהוה בָּא עִיר דָּוִד וּמִיכַל בַּת־שָׁאוּל נִשְׁקְפָה | בְּעַד הַחַלּוֹן וַתֵּרֶא אֶת־הַמֶּלֶךְ דָּוִד מְפַזֵּז וּמְכַרְכֵּר
יז לִפְנֵי יהוה וַתִּבֶז לוֹ בְּלִבָּהּ: וַיָּבִאוּ אֶת־אֲרוֹן יהוה וַיַּצִּגוּ אֹתוֹ בִּמְקוֹמוֹ בְּתוֹךְ הָאֹהֶל אֲשֶׁר נָטָה־לוֹ
יח דָּוִד וַיַּעַל דָּוִד עֹלוֹת לִפְנֵי יהוה וּשְׁלָמִים: וַיְכַל דָּוִד מֵהַעֲלוֹת הָעוֹלָה וְהַשְּׁלָמִים וַיְבָרֶךְ אֶת־הָעָם
יט בְּשֵׁם יהוה צְבָאוֹת: וַיְחַלֵּק לְכָל־הָעָם לְכָל־הֲמוֹן יִשְׂרָאֵל לְמֵאִישׁ וְעַד־אִשָּׁה לְאִישׁ חַלַּת לֶחֶם
Sepharadim and Chabad end here
כ אַחַת וְאֶשְׁפָּר אֶחָד וַאֲשִׁישָׁה אֶחָת וַיֵּלֶךְ כָּל־הָעָם אִישׁ לְבֵיתוֹ:* וַיָּשָׁב דָּוִד לְבָרֵךְ אֶת־בֵּיתוֹ וַתֵּצֵא
מִיכַל בַּת־שָׁאוּל לִקְרַאת דָּוִד וַתֹּאמֶר מַה־נִּכְבַּד הַיּוֹם מֶלֶךְ יִשְׂרָאֵל אֲשֶׁר נִגְלָה הַיּוֹם לְעֵינֵי אַמְהוֹת
כא עֲבָדָיו כְּהִגָּלוֹת נִגְלוֹת אַחַד הָרֵקִים: וַיֹּאמֶר דָּוִד אֶל־מִיכַל לִפְנֵי יהוה אֲשֶׁר בָּחַר־בִּי מֵאָבִיךְ וּמִכָּל־
כב בֵּיתוֹ לְצַוֹּת אֹתִי נָגִיד עַל־עַם יהוה עַל־יִשְׂרָאֵל וְשִׂחַקְתִּי לִפְנֵי יהוה: וּנְקַלֹּתִי עוֹד מִזֹּאת וְהָיִיתִי
כג שָׁפָל בְּעֵינָי וְעִם־הָאֲמָהוֹת אֲשֶׁר אָמַרְתְּ עִמָּם אִכָּבֵדָה: וּלְמִיכַל בַּת־שָׁאוּל לֹא־הָיָה לָהּ יֶלֶד עַד
ז א ב יוֹם מוֹתָהּ: וַיְהִי כִּי־יָשַׁב הַמֶּלֶךְ בְּבֵיתוֹ וַיהוה הֵנִיחַ־לוֹ מִסָּבִיב מִכָּל־אֹיְבָיו: וַיֹּאמֶר הַמֶּלֶךְ
ג אֶל־נָתָן הַנָּבִיא רְאֵה נָא אָנֹכִי יוֹשֵׁב בְּבֵית אֲרָזִים וַאֲרוֹן הָאֱלֹהִים יֹשֵׁב בְּתוֹךְ הַיְרִיעָה: וַיֹּאמֶר נָתָן
Yemenites end here
ד אֶל־הַמֶּלֶךְ כֹּל אֲשֶׁר בִּלְבָבְךָ לֵךְ עֲשֵׂה כִּי יהוה עִמָּךְ:* וַיְהִי בַּלַּיְלָה הַהוּא וַיְהִי
ה דְּבַר־יהוה אֶל־נָתָן לֵאמֹר: לֵךְ וְאָמַרְתָּ אֶל־עַבְדִּי אֶל־דָּוִד כֹּה אָמַר יהוה הַאַתָּה תִּבְנֶה־לִּי בַיִת לְשִׁבְתִּי:
ו כִּי לֹא יָשַׁבְתִּי בְּבַיִת לְמִיּוֹם הַעֲלֹתִי אֶת־בְּנֵי יִשְׂרָאֵל מִמִּצְרַיִם וְעַד הַיּוֹם הַזֶּה וָאֶהְיֶה מִתְהַלֵּךְ בְּאֹהֶל
ז וּבְמִשְׁכָּן: בְּכֹל אֲשֶׁר־הִתְהַלַּכְתִּי בְּכָל־בְּנֵי יִשְׂרָאֵל הֲדָבָר דִּבַּרְתִּי אֶת־אַחַד שִׁבְטֵי יִשְׂרָאֵל אֲשֶׁר צִוִּיתִי
ח לִרְעוֹת אֶת־עַמִּי אֶת־יִשְׂרָאֵל לֵאמֹר לָמָּה לֹא־בְנִיתֶם לִי בֵּית אֲרָזִים: וְעַתָּה כֹּה־תֹאמַר לְעַבְדִּי לְדָוִד
ט כֹּה אָמַר יהוה צְבָאוֹת אֲנִי לְקַחְתִּיךָ מִן־הַנָּוֶה מֵאַחַר הַצֹּאן לִהְיוֹת נָגִיד עַל־עַמִּי עַל־יִשְׂרָאֵל: וָאֶהְיֶה
עִמְּךָ בְּכֹל אֲשֶׁר הָלַכְתָּ וָאַכְרִתָה אֶת־כָּל־אֹיְבֶיךָ מִפָּנֶיךָ וְעָשִׂתִי לְךָ שֵׁם גָּדוֹל כְּשֵׁם הַגְּדֹלִים אֲשֶׁר בָּאָרֶץ:
י וְשַׂמְתִּי מָקוֹם לְעַמִּי לְיִשְׂרָאֵל וּנְטַעְתִּיו וְשָׁכַן תַּחְתָּיו וְלֹא יִרְגַּז עוֹד וְלֹא־יֹסִיפוּ בְנֵי־עַוְלָה לְעַנּוֹתוֹ כַּאֲשֶׁר

11 men will no longer oppress them as they once did in the days when I appointed judges over My people
Israel. To you I will grant repose from all your enemies; moreover, the LORD declares that the LORD
12 will establish a house for you. For when your days are done and you lie with your ancestors, I will raise
13 up your own seed after you – the issue of your own loins – and I will establish his kingdom. He will
14 build a house in My name, and I will firmly establish his royal throne forever. I will be a father to him,
and he will be a son to Me; and should he do wrong, I will berate him with the rod of mortals and with
15 human afflictions. But My loyalties shall not move from him, as I removed them from Sha'ul, whom
16 I removed before you. And your house and your kingdom will be ever steadfast before you, and your
17 throne will be secure forever." Natan related all these words and all this vision to David.

Haftarat Tazria

On Shabbat HaḤodesh read the maftir from Exodus 12:1–20, and the haftara on page 1651.
When Tazria and Metzora are read together, read the haftara for Metzora on page 1569.

4 42 A man came from Baal Shalisha and brought the man of God bread made of the first grain: twenty loaves II KINGS
43 of barley bread and some fresh grain in his sack. "Give it to the people and let them eat," he said. "How can
I set this before a hundred people?" asked his attendant. "Give it to the people and let them eat," he said,
44 "for thus says the LORD: They will eat and leave some over." So he set it before them and they ate, and there
5 1 was some left over, fulfilling the word of the LORD. Naaman, the commander of the king of
Aram's army, was highly esteemed by his master and held in favor, for the LORD had granted victory
2 to Aram through him. But this powerful man suffered from an impure blight. Once, when the Arameans were out raiding, they captured a young girl from the land of Israel, and she became a servant of
3 Naaman's wife. She said to her mistress, "If only my master would present himself to the prophet in
4 Shomron, he would cure him of his blight." Naaman then went and told his own master about what the
5 girl from the land of Israel had said. "Prepare to set out," said the king of Aram, "and I will send along
a letter to the king of Israel." He set out, taking ten talents of silver, six thousand pieces of gold, and
6 ten sets of clothing with him. And he brought the letter to the king of Israel, which read: "Now, as this
7 letter reaches you, I have sent my servant Naaman to you, that you may cure him of his blight." When
the king of Israel read the letter, he rent his clothes. "Am I God, dealing death and granting life, that this
one sends me a man to cure his blight?" he said, "Be aware now, look – he must be provoking a quarrel
8 with me." When Elisha, the man of God, heard that the king of Israel had rent his clothes, he sent to the
king, saying, "Why have you rent your clothes? Let him come to me now, and he will know that there is
9 a prophet in Israel." So Naaman came with his horses and chariots and halted at the entrance of Elisha's
10 house. And Elisha sent a messenger to him, saying, "Go and bathe in the Jordan seven times; your skin
11 will be restored to you, and you will be cleansed." Naaman was furious and walked away. "I was certain
he would come out to me," he said, "and stand and invoke the name of the LORD, his God, and wave

---

Elisha's behavior toward Naaman carries a message: It is God who heals; the prophet does nothing by himself – this is why he refuses to accept Naaman's reward. Naaman understands this, and thus learns the difference between a prophet and a magician.

Aram had been the bitter enemy of Israel for two centuries. Naaman, the enemy warlord, converted to worship God, and this had a profound impact on both Aram and Israel. This was another aim of Elisha.

יא בָרִאשׁוֹנָה: וּלְמִן־הַיּוֹם אֲשֶׁר צִוִּיתִי שֹׁפְטִים עַל־עַמִּי יִשְׂרָאֵל וַהֲנִיחֹתִי לְךָ מִכָּל־אֹיְבֶיךָ וְהִגִּיד לְךָ יהוה
יב כִּי־בַיִת יַעֲשֶׂה־לְּךָ יהוה: כִּי ׀ יִמְלְאוּ יָמֶיךָ וְשָׁכַבְתָּ אֶת־אֲבֹתֶיךָ וַהֲקִימֹתִי אֶת־זַרְעֲךָ אַחֲרֶיךָ אֲשֶׁר יֵצֵא
יג יד מִמֵּעֶיךָ וַהֲכִינֹתִי אֶת־מַמְלַכְתּוֹ: הוּא יִבְנֶה־בַּיִת לִשְׁמִי וְכֹנַנְתִּי אֶת־כִּסֵּא מַמְלַכְתּוֹ עַד־עוֹלָם: אֲנִי אֶהְיֶה־
טו לּוֹ לְאָב וְהוּא יִהְיֶה־לִּי לְבֵן אֲשֶׁר בְּהַעֲוֺתוֹ וְהֹכַחְתִּיו בְּשֵׁבֶט אֲנָשִׁים וּבְנִגְעֵי בְּנֵי אָדָם: וְחַסְדִּי לֹא־יָסוּר
טז מִמֶּנּוּ כַּאֲשֶׁר הֲסִרֹתִי מֵעִם שָׁאוּל אֲשֶׁר הֲסִרֹתִי מִלְּפָנֶיךָ: וְנֶאְמַן בֵּיתְךָ וּמַמְלַכְתְּךָ עַד־עוֹלָם לְפָנֶיךָ כִּסְאֲךָ
יז יִהְיֶה נָכוֹן עַד־עוֹלָם: כְּכֹל הַדְּבָרִים הָאֵלֶּה וּכְכֹל הַחִזָּיוֹן הַזֶּה כֵּן דִּבֶּר נָתָן אֶל־דָּוִד:

הפטרת תזריע

On שבת החודש *read the* מפטיר *from* שמות יב, א–כ*, and the* הפטרה *on page 1651.*
When תזריע *and* מצרע *are read together, read the* הפטרה *for* מצרע *on page 1569.*

ד מב וְאִישׁ בָּא מִבַּעַל שָׁלִשָׁה וַיָּבֵא לְאִישׁ הָאֱלֹהִים לֶחֶם בִּכּוּרִים עֶשְׂרִים־לֶחֶם שְׂעֹרִים וְכַרְמֶל בְּצִקְלֹנוֹ מלכים ב׳
מג וַיֹּאמֶר תֵּן לָעָם וְיֹאכֵלוּ: וַיֹּאמֶר מְשָׁרְתוֹ מָה אֶתֵּן זֶה לִפְנֵי מֵאָה אִישׁ וַיֹּאמֶר תֵּן לָעָם וְיֹאכֵלוּ כִּי כֹה
ה מד א אָמַר יהוה אָכֹל וְהוֹתֵר: וַיִּתֵּן לִפְנֵיהֶם וַיֹּאכְלוּ וַיּוֹתִרוּ כִּדְבַר יהוה: וְנַעֲמָן שַׂר־
צְבָא מֶלֶךְ־אֲרָם הָיָה אִישׁ גָּדוֹל לִפְנֵי אֲדֹנָיו וּנְשֻׂא פָנִים כִּי־בוֹ נָתַן־יהוה תְּשׁוּעָה לַאֲרָם וְהָאִישׁ הָיָה
ב גִּבּוֹר חַיִל מְצֹרָע: וַאֲרָם יָצְאוּ גְדוּדִים וַיִּשְׁבּוּ מֵאֶרֶץ יִשְׂרָאֵל נַעֲרָה קְטַנָּה וַתְּהִי לִפְנֵי אֵשֶׁת נַעֲמָן:
ג ד וַתֹּאמֶר אֶל־גְּבִרְתָּהּ אַחֲלֵי אֲדֹנִי לִפְנֵי הַנָּבִיא אֲשֶׁר בְּשֹׁמְרוֹן אָז יֶאֱסֹף אֹתוֹ מִצָּרַעְתּוֹ: וַיָּבֹא וַיַּגֵּד
ה לַאדֹנָיו לֵאמֹר כָּזֹאת וְכָזֹאת דִּבְּרָה הַנַּעֲרָה אֲשֶׁר מֵאֶרֶץ יִשְׂרָאֵל: וַיֹּאמֶר מֶלֶךְ־אֲרָם לֶךְ־בֹּא וְאֶשְׁלְחָה
סֵפֶר אֶל־מֶלֶךְ יִשְׂרָאֵל וַיֵּלֶךְ וַיִּקַּח בְּיָדוֹ עֶשֶׂר כִּכְּרֵי־כֶסֶף וְשֵׁשֶׁת אֲלָפִים זָהָב וְעֶשֶׂר חֲלִיפוֹת בְּגָדִים:
ו וַיָּבֵא הַסֵּפֶר אֶל־מֶלֶךְ יִשְׂרָאֵל לֵאמֹר וְעַתָּה כְּבוֹא הַסֵּפֶר הַזֶּה אֵלֶיךָ הִנֵּה שָׁלַחְתִּי אֵלֶיךָ אֶת־נַעֲמָן
ז עַבְדִּי וַאֲסַפְתּוֹ מִצָּרַעְתּוֹ: וַיְהִי כִּקְרֹא מֶלֶךְ־יִשְׂרָאֵל אֶת־הַסֵּפֶר וַיִּקְרַע בְּגָדָיו וַיֹּאמֶר הַאֱלֹהִים אָנִי
לְהָמִית וּלְהַחֲיוֹת כִּי־זֶה שֹׁלֵחַ אֵלַי לֶאֱסֹף אִישׁ מִצָּרַעְתּוֹ כִּי אַךְ־דְּעוּ־נָא וּרְאוּ כִּי־מִתְאַנֶּה הוּא לִי:
ח וַיְהִי כִּשְׁמֹעַ ׀ אֱלִישָׁע אִישׁ־הָאֱלֹהִים כִּי־קָרַע מֶלֶךְ־יִשְׂרָאֵל אֶת־בְּגָדָיו וַיִּשְׁלַח אֶל־הַמֶּלֶךְ לֵאמֹר לָמָּה
ט קָרַעְתָּ בְּגָדֶיךָ יָבֹא־נָא אֵלַי וְיֵדַע כִּי יֵשׁ נָבִיא בְּיִשְׂרָאֵל: וַיָּבֹא נַעֲמָן בְּסוּסָו וּבְרִכְבּוֹ וַיַּעֲמֹד פֶּתַח־הַבַּיִת
י לֶאֱלִישָׁע: וַיִּשְׁלַח אֵלָיו אֱלִישָׁע מַלְאָךְ לֵאמֹר הָלוֹךְ וְרָחַצְתָּ שֶׁבַע־פְּעָמִים בַּיַּרְדֵּן וְיָשֹׁב בְּשָׂרְךָ לְךָ וּטְהָר:
יא וַיִּקְצֹף נַעֲמָן וַיֵּלַךְ וַיֹּאמֶר הִנֵּה אָמַרְתִּי אֵלַי ׀ יֵצֵא יָצוֹא וְעָמַד וְקָרָא בְּשֵׁם־יהוה אֱלֹהָיו וְהֵנִיף יָדוֹ אֶל־

TAZRIA

This *haftara* describes the miraculous healing of the leprosy of general Naaman, head of the armies of Aram. This miracle is one of several worked by the prophet Elisha as described in the book of Kings. Naaman appears at Elisha's home in Shomron, accompanied by his retinue. He expects the prophet to come out to him and work his magic in order to heal him. Elisha, however, ignores him and instead sends him some simple instructions that will heal him. Naaman becomes angry with Elisha and goes on his way, but when he comes to the Jordan River he carries out Elisha's instructions, and is instantly healed. Shaken, he returns to thank the prophet and declare his faith in the God of Israel. He offers Elisha a rich reward, but the prophet refuses adamantly.

12 his hand toward the affected area and cure my blight. Why, Amana and Parpar, the rivers of Damascus,
are better than all the waters of Israel – if I bathe in them, will I not be cleansed?" And he turned and
13 stormed off in a rage. But his servants approached him and spoke to him. "Father," they said, "had the
prophet given you more difficult instructions, would you not carry them out? All the more so when
14 he has only said to you, 'Bathe and be cleansed.'" So he went down and immersed in the Jordan seven
times, fulfilling the instruction of the man of God, and his skin became like the skin of a young boy,
15 and he was cleansed. He went back to the man of God along with all his company, and he came and
stood before him. "Now I know that there is no God in all the world except in Israel," he said. "Now,
16 please accept your servant's gift." "As the Lord lives, whom I serve," he said, "I will not accept it." He
17 urged him to accept, but he refused. "If not," said Naaman, "may your servant be given two mule loads'
worth of soil, for your servant will no longer offer burnt offering or sacrifice to other gods, but only to
18 the Lord. But may the Lord forgive your servant this: when my master comes to the temple of Rimon
to bow down there, he leans on my hand so that I must bow down in the temple of Rimon. So when I
19 bow down in the temple of Rimon, may the Lord forgive your servant for this." "Go in peace," he said
to him. When he had traveled some distance away from him.

Haftarat Metzora

When Tazria and Metzora are read together, read this haftara.
On Shabbat HaGadol read the haftara on page 1653.
On Rosh Ḥodesh Iyar, read the maftir from Numbers 28:9–15, and the haftara on page 1635. On Erev Rosh Ḥodesh Iyar read the haftara on page 1637.

II KINGS

Yemenites begin here

7 1 And Elisha said, "Hear the word of the Lord. Thus says the Lord: By this time tomorrow, a *se'a* of fine
2 flour will sell for a shekel, and two *se'a* of barley will sell for a shekel at the gate of Shomron." The adjutant upon whose arm the king leaned spoke up and said to the man of God, "Even if the Lord were
to make floodgates in the heavens, how could this possibly come to pass?" "You will see it with your
3 own eyes," he said, "but you will not eat of it." *There were four men, who were lepers, at the
4 entrance to the gate, and they said to one another, "Why should we sit here until we die? If we decide
to enter the city when there is famine in the city, we will die there; and if we stay here, we will die. So let
5 us now defect to the Aramean camp; if they let us live, we will live, and if they kill us, we will die." They
set out at dusk to reach the Aramean camp, but when they reached the edge of the Aramean camp,
6 there was no one there. For the Lord had caused the Aramean camp to hear the sound of chariots,
the sound of horses, the sound of a vast army – and the men had said to one another, "Look, the king
7 of Israel must have hired the Hittite kings and the kings of Egypt against us, to attack us!" They rose
and fled at dusk, leaving their tents, their horses and their donkeys, and the camp as it was, and they
8 ran for their lives. When those lepers reached the edge of the camp, they entered one tent and ate and
drank. Then they carried off silver and gold and garments from there and went and hid them. When
9 they came back, they went into another tent, carried off what was in it, and went and hid it. But then

Ashkenazim and Sephardim begin here

After checking the truthfulness of their claims, the people of Shomron too are able to take part in the victory.

Leprosy is traditionally seen as a divine punishment for slander and gossip. It is interesting to note that in this story, it is specifically lepers who discover that the siege has lifted. In returning to the city, they are the bearers of good news, rather than hurtful stories, and thus serve to correct their ways and bring blessing on their fellows in the city and themselves.

יב הַמָּקוֹם וְאָסַף הַמְּצֹרָע: הֲלֹא טוֹב אבנה וּפַרְפַּר נַהֲרוֹת דַּמֶּשֶׂק מִכֹּל מֵימֵי יִשְׂרָאֵל הֲלֹא־אֶרְחַץ בָּהֶם אֲמָנָה
יג וְטָהָרְתִּי וַיִּפֶן וַיֵּלֶךְ בְּחֵמָה: וַיִּגְּשׁוּ עֲבָדָיו וַיְדַבְּרוּ אֵלָיו וַיֹּאמְרוּ אָבִי דָּבָר גָּדוֹל הַנָּבִיא דִּבֶּר אֵלֶיךָ הֲלוֹא
יד תַעֲשֶׂה וְאַף כִּי־אָמַר אֵלֶיךָ רְחַץ וּטְהָר: וַיֵּרֶד וַיִּטְבֹּל בַּיַּרְדֵּן שֶׁבַע פְּעָמִים כִּדְבַר אִישׁ הָאֱלֹהִים וַיָּשָׁב
טו בְּשָׂרוֹ כִּבְשַׂר נַעַר קָטֹן וַיִּטְהָר: וַיָּשָׁב אֶל־אִישׁ הָאֱלֹהִים הוּא וְכָל־מַחֲנֵהוּ וַיָּבֹא וַיַּעֲמֹד לְפָנָיו וַיֹּאמֶר
טז הִנֵּה־נָא יָדַעְתִּי כִּי אֵין אֱלֹהִים בְּכָל־הָאָרֶץ כִּי אִם־בְּיִשְׂרָאֵל וְעַתָּה קַח־נָא בְרָכָה מֵאֵת עַבְדֶּךָ: וַיֹּאמֶר
יז חַי־יְהוָה אֲשֶׁר־עָמַדְתִּי לְפָנָיו אִם־אֶקָּח וַיִּפְצַר־בּוֹ לָקַחַת וַיְמָאֵן: וַיֹּאמֶר נַעֲמָן וָלֹא יֻתַּן־נָא לְעַבְדְּךָ מַשָּׂא
יח צֶמֶד־פְּרָדִים אֲדָמָה כִּי לוֹא־יַעֲשֶׂה עוֹד עַבְדְּךָ עֹלָה וָזֶבַח לֵאלֹהִים אֲחֵרִים כִּי אִם־לַיהוָה: לַדָּבָר הַזֶּה
יִסְלַח יְהוָה לְעַבְדֶּךָ בְּבוֹא אֲדֹנִי בֵית־רִמּוֹן לְהִשְׁתַּחֲוֺת שָׁמָּה וְהוּא ׀ נִשְׁעָן עַל־יָדִי וְהִשְׁתַּחֲוֵיתִי בֵּית
יט רִמֹּן בְּהִשְׁתַּחֲוָיָתִי בֵּית רִמֹּן יִסְלַח־נא־יְהוָה לְעַבְדְּךָ בַּדָּבָר הַזֶּה: וַיֹּאמֶר לוֹ לֵךְ לְשָׁלוֹם וַיֵּלֶךְ מֵאִתּוֹ נא כתיב ולא קרי
כִּבְרַת אָרֶץ:

הפטרת מצרע

When תזריע *and* מצרע *are read together, read this* הפטרה*.*
On שבת הגדול *read the* הפטרה *on page 1653.*
On ראש חודש אייר *read the* מפטיר *from* במדבר כח, ט–טו *and the* הפטרה *on page 1635.*
On ערב ראש חודש אייר *read the* הפטרה *on page 1637.*

מלכים ב׳
ז א וַיֹּאמֶר אֱלִישָׁע שִׁמְעוּ דְּבַר־יְהוָה כֹּה ׀ אָמַר יְהוָה כָּעֵת ׀ מָחָר סְאָה־סֹלֶת בְּשֶׁקֶל וְסָאתַיִם שְׂעֹרִים בְּשֶׁקֶל *Yemenites begin here*
ב בְּשַׁעַר שֹׁמְרוֹן: וַיַּעַן הַשָּׁלִישׁ אֲשֶׁר־לַמֶּלֶךְ נִשְׁעָן עַל־יָדוֹ אֶת־אִישׁ הָאֱלֹהִים וַיֹּאמַר הִנֵּה יְהוָה עֹשֶׂה
ג אֲרֻבּוֹת בַּשָּׁמַיִם הֲיִהְיֶה הַדָּבָר הַזֶּה וַיֹּאמֶר הִנְּכָה רֹאֶה בְּעֵינֶיךָ וּמִשָּׁם לֹא תֹאכֵל: *וְאַרְבָּעָה *Ashkenazim and Sephardim begin here*
ד אֲנָשִׁים הָיוּ מְצֹרָעִים פֶּתַח הַשָּׁעַר וַיֹּאמְרוּ אִישׁ אֶל־רֵעֵהוּ מָה אֲנַחְנוּ יֹשְׁבִים פֹּה עַד־מָתְנוּ: אִם־אָמַרְנוּ
נָבוֹא הָעִיר וְהָרָעָב בָּעִיר וָמַתְנוּ שָׁם וְאִם־יָשַׁבְנוּ פֹה וָמָתְנוּ וְעַתָּה לְכוּ וְנִפְּלָה אֶל־מַחֲנֵה אֲרָם אִם־יְחַיֻּנוּ
ה נִחְיֶה וְאִם־יְמִיתֻנוּ וָמָתְנוּ: וַיָּקֻמוּ בַנֶּשֶׁף לָבוֹא אֶל־מַחֲנֵה אֲרָם וַיָּבֹאוּ עַד־קְצֵה מַחֲנֵה אֲרָם וְהִנֵּה אֵין־שָׁם
ו אִישׁ: וַאדֹנָי הִשְׁמִיעַ ׀ אֶת־מַחֲנֵה אֲרָם קוֹל רֶכֶב קוֹל סוּס קוֹל חַיִל גָּדוֹל וַיֹּאמְרוּ אִישׁ אֶל־אָחִיו הִנֵּה
ז שָׂכַר־עָלֵינוּ מֶלֶךְ יִשְׂרָאֵל אֶת־מַלְכֵי הַחִתִּים וְאֶת־מַלְכֵי מִצְרַיִם לָבוֹא עָלֵינוּ: וַיָּקוּמוּ וַיָּנוּסוּ בַנֶּשֶׁף וַיַּעַזְבוּ
ח אֶת־אָהֳלֵיהֶם וְאֶת־סוּסֵיהֶם וְאֶת־חֲמֹרֵיהֶם הַמַּחֲנֶה כַּאֲשֶׁר־הִיא וַיָּנֻסוּ אֶל־נַפְשָׁם: וַיָּבֹאוּ הַמְצֹרָעִים הָאֵלֶּה
עַד־קְצֵה הַמַּחֲנֶה וַיָּבֹאוּ אֶל־אֹהֶל אֶחָד וַיֹּאכְלוּ וַיִּשְׁתּוּ וַיִּשְׂאוּ מִשָּׁם כֶּסֶף וְזָהָב וּבְגָדִים וַיֵּלְכוּ וַיַּטְמִנוּ
ט וַיָּשֻׁבוּ וַיָּבֹאוּ אֶל־אֹהֶל אַחֵר וַיִּשְׂאוּ מִשָּׁם וַיֵּלְכוּ וַיַּטְמִנוּ: וַיֹּאמְרוּ אִישׁ אֶל־רֵעֵהוּ לֹא־כֵן ׀ אֲנַחְנוּ עֹשִׂים

METZORA

The Aramean siege on Shomron in the time of the prophet Elisha cut off the Israelite capital from the surrounding country. Outside the city stood four lepers. The harsh famine afflicting the city affected them as well, and they decide to try their luck looking for food with the besieging Aramean army. As they approach the camp, they are shocked to discover that it has been abandoned; the whole army has fled in the middle of the night, leaving large amounts of food and property. The hungry lepers set upon their spoils and eat until they satisfy their hunger. Then they return to the city and inform the inhabitants of what they have seen.

▶

one man said to another, "We are not doing what is right. This is a day of good news, yet we are silent.
If we wait until the light of morning, we will be found guilty. We must go and report to the royal palace
10 right now." When they arrived, they called out to the city gatekeepers and reported to them, "We came
to the Aramean camp, but there was not a man or a human voice there, with the horses still tied up and
11 the donkeys still tied up and the tents just as they were." The gatekeepers called out, and it was reported
12 inside the royal palace. The king rose in the night and said to his servants, "Let me tell you what the
Arameans are doing to us. They know we are starving, so they have left the camp to hide in the field,
13 planning, 'When they leave the city, we will catch them alive and enter the city.'" One of his servants
spoke up. "Let them take five of the remaining horses that are still here," he said. "Look, either they will
be like all the masses of Israelites who remain or like all the masses of Israelites who have perished. Let
14 us send and find out." So they took two chariots with horses, and the king sent them after the Aramean
15 camp, ordering them, "Go and find out." They followed them as far as the Jordan to find that the whole
road was full of garments and vessels that Aram had cast aside in their haste, and the messengers went
16 back and reported to the king. Then the people went out and ransacked the Aramean camp, so that a
se'a of fine flour fetched a shekel, and two *se'a* of barley fetched a shekel, fulfilling the word of the Lord.
17 Meanwhile, the king had stationed the adjutant on whose arm he leaned by the gate, and the people
trampled him to death by the gate – just as the man of God had pronounced when the king came down
18 to him. For when the man of God had told the king, "Two *se'a* of barley will fetch a shekel, and a *se'a* of
19 fine flour will fetch a shekel by this time tomorrow at the gate of Shomron," the adjutant had retorted
to the man of God, "Even if the Lord were to make floodgates in the heavens, how could this possibly
20 come to pass?" "You will see it with your own eyes," he had said, "but you will not eat of it." And that is
exactly what happened to him – the people trampled him to death by the gate.

Yemenites add

13 23 But the Lord was gracious and compassionate toward them; He turned to them for the sake of His
covenant with Avraham, Yitzḥak, and Yaakov, and He was unwilling to destroy them or cast them away
from His presence – for now.

Haftarat Aḥarei Mot

When Aḥarei Mot and Kedoshim are read together, read the haftara for Kedoshim on page 1573. On Shabbat HaGadol read the haftara on page 1653. Chabad: Aharei Mot, Aharei Mot-Kedoshim: Amos 9:7-15; Kedoshim: Ezekiel 20:2-20 (See the haftara for Kedoshim on page 1573).

EZEKIEL

22 1 2 The word of the Lord came to me, saying, "And you, Man, will you accuse – will you accuse the
3 bloody city? Make all her abominations known to her. Say: So says the Lord God: City that spills
4 blood in her own midst, hastening her time and making idols in her to defile her, in spilling your own
blood, you have become guilty; in making your own idols, you have been defiled. You have brought
your days near; you have come to the end of your years, so I give you over as a reproach to the nations, a
5 6 mockery to all the lands. Those near and far will mock you, you of impure name, filled with panic. Here
7 are the leaders of Israel: each used his power to spill blood among you; they have dishonored mother

---

question. He reviews the terrible mistakes that characterized the Israelites' behavior, both among themselves and toward God. This moral rot, which we brought upon ourselves, is the root of our suffering. Understanding the causes of the disaster mitigates the bitterness of defeat and allows for us to move on and mend our ways. This is the path to future redemption.

היום הזה יום־בשרה הוא ואנחנו מחשים וחכינו עד־אור הבקר ומצאנו עוון ועתה לכו ונבאה ונגידה
י בית המלך: ויבאו ויקראו אל־שער העיר ויגידו להם לאמר באנו אל־מחנה ארם והנה אין־שם איש
יא וקול אדם כי אם־הסוס אסור והחמור אסור ואהלים כאשר המה: ויקרא השערים ויגידו בית המלך
יב פנימה: ויקם המלך לילה ויאמר אל־עבדיו אגידה־נא לכם את אשר־עשו לנו ארם ידעו כי־רעבים
יג אנחנו ויצאו מן־המחנה להחבה בהשדה לאמר כי־יצאו מן־העיר ונתפשם חיים ואל־העיר נבא: ויען בשדה
אחד מעבדיו ויאמר ויקחו־נא חמשה מן־הסוסים הנשארים אשר נשארו־בה הנם ככל־ההמון ישראל ההמון
יד אשר נשארו־בה הנם ככל־המון ישראל אשר־תמו ונשלחה ונראה: ויקחו שני רכב סוסים וישלח
טו המלך אחרי מחנה־ארם לאמר לכו וראו: וילכו אחריהם עד־הירדן והנה כל־הדרך מלאה בגדים
טז וכלים אשר־השליכו ארם בהחפזם וישבו המלאכים ויגדו למלך: ויצא העם ויבזו את מחנה ארם בחפזם
יז ויהי סאה־סלת בשקל וסאתים שערים בשקל כדבר יהוה: והמלך הפקיד את־השליש אשר־נשען
על־ידו על־השער וירמסהו העם בשער וימת כאשר דבר איש האלהים אשר דבר ברדת המלך אליו:
יח ויהי כדבר איש האלהים אל־המלך לאמר סאתים שערים בשקל וסאה־סלת בשקל יהיה כעת
יט מחר בשער שמרון: ויען השליש את־איש האלהים ויאמר והנה יהוה עשה ארבות בשמים היהיה
כ כדבר הזה ויאמר הנך ראה בעיניך ומשם לא תאכל: ויהי־לו כן וירמסו אתו העם בשער וימת:

יג כג ויחן יהוה אתם וירחמם ויפן אליהם למען בריתו את־אברהם יצחק ויעקב ולא אבה השחיתם *Yemenites add*
ולא־השליכם מעל־פניו עד־עתה:

הפטרת אחרי מות

When אחרי מות *and* קדשים *are read together, read the* הפטרה *for* קדשים *on page 1573.*
On שבת הגדול *read the* הפטרה *on page 1653. Chabad:* אחרי מות-קדשים, אחרי מות:
עמוס *9:7-15;* קדשים: יחזקאל *20:2-20 (see the* הפטרה *for* קדשים *on page 1573).*

כב א ב ויהי דבר־יהוה אלי לאמר: ואתה בן־אדם התשפט התשפט את־עיר הדמים והודעתה את כל־ יחזקאל
ג תועבותיה: ואמרת כה אמר אדני יהוה עיר שפכת דם בתוכה לבוא עתה ועשתה גלולים עליה
ד לטמאה: בדמך אשר־שפכת אשמת ובגלוליך אשר־עשית טמאת ותקריבי ימיך ותבוא עד־שנותיך
ה על־כן נתתיך חרפה לגוים וקלסה לכל־הארצות: הקרבות והרחקות ממך יתקלסו־בך טמאת השם
ו רבת המהומה: הנה נשיאי ישראל איש לזרעו היו בך למען שפך־דם: אב ואם הקלו בך לגר עשו

AḤAREI MOT

The terrible crisis in the twilight of the kingdom of Yehuda was when, for the first time in history, all the physical symbols of Jewish peoplehood were destroyed. The Temple, Jerusalem, and the dynasty of David were no more, and the human suffering brought by the destruction and exile were so immense as to make everyone ask: "Why could such a thing have been brought upon us?" The prophet Yeḥezkel, who had been exiled a generation previously with King Yehoyakhin, prepares his fellow Jews to deal with this ▶

and father within you; they have oppressed the foreigner in your midst; they have mistreated orphan
8 9 and widow within you. You despised My holy things; you desecrated My Sabbaths. Slanderers have
been among you so as to spill blood; on the mountains they have eaten among you; depravities they
10 have performed in your midst. Their father's nakedness they have uncovered within you; the impure,
11 menstrual woman they have forced within you. One man committed abominations with another's
wife; another has defiled his daughter-in-law with depravity; another in you has forced his sister, the
12 daughter of his father – within you! They have taken bribes within you so as to spill blood; you have
taken both advanced and accrued interest; you have taken advantage of your friend with extortion;
13 and Me you have forgotten, declares the Lord God. See: I clap My hands over the dishonest gain you
14 have taken and over the bloodshed that were in your midst. Will your heart stand firm, will your hands
15 stay strong for the days when I deal with you? I am the Lord; I have spoken and will do it. I will strew
16 you among the nations, scatter you over the lands: I will purge your impurity from you. You will be
17 debased in yourself before the eyes of nations, and you will know that I am the Lord." *

Ashkenazim, Sepharadim, and Yemenites end here

And
18 the word of the Lord came to me, saying, "Man, to Me the House of Israel are dross; they are bronze,
tin, iron, and lead in a crucible; they are the dross of silver.

Minhag Anglia continues

So the Lord God says this: Because
19 you have all become dross, I am gathering you in to Jerusalem.

Haftarat Kedoshim

When Aḥarei Mot and Kedoshim are read together, read this haftara.
On Rosh Ḥodesh Iyar, read the maftir from Numbers 28:9–15, and the haftara on page 1635.

AMOS
For Ashkenazim and Chabad

9 7 Are you not to Me like the children of Kush, O children of Israel? Did I not bring up Israel from the
8 land of Egypt as I brought the Philistines up from Kaftor and Aram from Kir? Yes, the eyes of the Lord
God are upon the sinning kingdom; I will wipe it off the face of the earth, but the House of Yaakov I
9 will never destroy, says the Lord. For I will but command, and I will shake the House of Israel among
10 all the nations as one shakes a sieve; not one pebble will fall to the earth. All the sinners of My nation
11 will be killed by the sword – those who say, "Disaster will not reach, will not advance upon us." On
that day, I will lift up David's fallen tabernacle, repair its breaches, and lift up its ruins, rebuild it as it
12 was in days of yore. And so they will possess the remnants of Edom and all the nations who are called
13 in My name, says the Lord who does this. Behold, days are coming. The Lord has spoken.
The plow man will meet the reaper, and the grape crusher the seed sower; the mountains will drip with
14 sweet wine, and all the hills will dissolve. I will bring back the exiled of My nation, Israel. They will
build ruined cities and settle. They will plant vineyards and drink their wine. They will grow gardens
15 and eat their fruit. I will plant them on their land, and never again will they be uprooted from the land
which I gave to them, says the Lord, your God.

---

that no one can guarantee the continuation of their privileged existence. Only moral behavior and observance of the commandments can preserve what they have gained. This *haftara*, the conclusion of the book of Amos, ends with a note of hope and promise for the future redemption.

ח ט בעשק בתוכך יתום ואלמנה הונו בך: קדשי בזית ואת־שבתתי חללת: אנשי רכיל היו בך למען
יא שפך־דם ואל־ההרים אכלו בך זמה עשו בתוכך: ערות־אב גלה־בך טמאת הנדה ענו־בך: ואיש ׀
יב את־אשת רעהו עשה תועבה ואיש את־כלתו טמא בזמה ואיש את־אחתו בת־אביו ענה־בך: שחד
לקחו־בך למען שפך־דם נשך ותרבית לקחת ותבצעי רעיך בעשק ואתי שכחת נאם אדני יהוה:
יג יד והנה הכיתי כפי אל־בצעך אשר עשית ועל־דמך אשר היו בתוכך: היעמד לבך אם־תחזקנה ידיך
טו לימים אשר אני עשה אותך אני יהוה דברתי ועשיתי: והפיצותי אותך בגוים וזריתיך בארצות

Ashkenazim, Sepharadim, and Yemenites end here
Minhag Anglia continues

טז יז והתמתי טמאתך ממך: ונחלת בך לעיני גוים וידעת כי־אני יהוה:* ויהי דבר־יהוה
יח אלי לאמר: בן־אדם היו־לי בית־ישראל לסוג כלם נחשת ובדיל וברזל ועופרת בתוך כור סיגים לסיג
יט כסף היו: לכן כה אמר אדני יהוה יען היות כלכם לסגים לכן הנני קבץ אתכם אל־
תוך ירושלם:

הפטרת קדשים

When אחרי מות *and* קדשים *are read together, read this* הפטרה.
On ראש חודש אייר *read the* מפטיר *from* במדבר כח, ט–טו *and the* הפטרה *on page 1635.*

עמוס

For Ashkenazim and Chabad

ט ז הלוא כבני כשיים אתם לי בני ישראל נאם־יהוה הלוא את־ישראל העליתי מארץ מצרים ופלשתיים
ח מכפתור וארם מקיר: הנה עיני ׀ אדני יהוה בממלכה החטאה והשמדתי אתה מעל פני האדמה אפס
ט כי לא השמיד אשמיד את־בית יעקב נאם־יהוה: כי־הנה אנכי מצוה והנעותי בכל־הגוים את־בית
י ישראל כאשר ינוע בכברה ולא־יפול צרור ארץ: בחרב ימותו כל חטאי עמי האמרים לא־תגיש
יא ותקדים בעדינו הרעה: ביום ההוא אקים את־סכת דויד הנפלת וגדרתי את־פרציהן והרסתיו אקים
יב ובניתיה כימי עולם: למען יירשו את־שארית אדום וכל־הגוים אשר־נקרא שמי עליהם נאם־יהוה
יג עשה זאת: הנה ימים באים נאם־יהוה ונגש חורש בקצר ודרך ענבים במשך הזרע
יד והטיפו ההרים עסיס וכל־הגבעות תתמוגגנה: ושבתי את־שבות עמי ישראל ובנו ערים נשמות
טו וישבו ונטעו כרמים ושתו את־יינם ועשו גנות ואכלו את־פריהם: ונטעתים על־אדמתם ולא ינתשו
עוד מעל אדמתם אשר נתתי להם אמר יהוה אלהיך:

KEDOSHIM

Ashkenazim

The prophet Amos was active throughout the kingdom of Israel during the era when it and the kingdom of Yehuda were at their strongest, under the reign of Uziyahu king of Yehuda and Yorovam son of Yoash king of Israel. Both monarchs reigned for decades, contributing unprecedented stability and wealth that also led to corruption and oppression among the Israelites. Amos warns against these moral ills that can accompany success and reminds the people

▶

EZEKIEL

Yemenites begin here

Sepharadim and Chabad begin here

20 1 And it was in the seventh year in the fifth month on the tenth day of the month that men from the
2 elders of Israel came and sat before me to consult the LORD. *And the word of the LORD
3 came to me: "Man, speak to the elders of Israel; say to them: So says the Lord GOD: Have you come
4 to seek Me? As I live, I will not be sought by you, declares the Lord GOD. Will you accuse them, Man,
5 will you accuse them? Make known to them their fathers' abominations. Say to them: So says the Lord
GOD: On the day that I chose Israel, raising My hand in promise to the descendants of the House of
Yaakov and making Myself known to them in the land of Egypt, I raised My hand in promise to them,
6 saying: 'I the LORD am your God.' On that day, I raised My hand in promise to them to take them from
the land of Egypt to the land that flows with milk and honey, the most beautiful of all lands, that I had
7 sought out for them. I said to them: 'Throw off, each of you, the detestable things before your eyes; do
8 not defile yourselves with Egyptian idols: I the LORD am your God.' But they defied Me; they were not
prepared to listen to Me; none threw off the detestable things before their eyes; they did not relinquish
their Egyptian idols. And I thought of pouring out My fury, exhausting My anger upon them in the
9 midst of the land of Egypt. But I acted for the sake of My name so that it would not be desecrated in
the eyes of the nations among whom they were – and before whose eyes I had made Myself known in
10 taking them out from the land of Egypt. I took them out from the land of Egypt and brought them into
11 12 the wilderness. I gave them My statutes, made My laws known to them, by which a person shall live. I
even gave them My Sabbaths as a sign between Myself and them so that they should know that I, the
13 LORD, make them holy. But the House of Israel defied me in the wilderness. They did not follow My
statutes; they rejected My laws, by which each person was to live; they wholly desecrated My Sabbaths.
14 I thought of pouring out My fury upon them in the wilderness and destroying them, but I acted for the
sake of My name so that it would not be desecrated in the eyes of the nations before whose eyes I had
15 taken them out. I even raised My hand in promise to them in the desert not to bring them to the land
16 that flows with milk and honey, the most beautiful of all lands, which I had given them,* because they
rejected My laws, did not follow My statutes, desecrated My Sabbaths – for their hearts followed after
17 their idols. But My eye pitied them, and I could not destroy them; I did not bring them to their end
18 in the wilderness. I said to their children in the wilderness: 'Do not follow the statutes of your fathers,
19 do not keep their laws; do not be defiled by their idols. I the LORD am your God: follow My statutes,
20 keep My laws, perform them, make My Sabbaths holy – it will be a sign between Me and you to know
that I the LORD am your God.'"

Yemenites end here

the nations. At the end of this prophecy, Yeḥezkel formulates the historical logic that governs all Israel's special relationship with God. Whatever happens, nothing can break the bond between God and Israel. If Israel breaks the terms of their covenant with God, they will be punished – but they will never be wiped out, and they will never be able to constitute themselves in any other land and govern it. This is what makes the ultimate redemption inevitable, no matter how long it may take.

יחזקאל

Yemenites begin here

Sepharadim and Chabad begin here

כ א וַיְהִי ׀ בַּשָּׁנָה הַשְּׁבִיעִית בַּחֲמִשִׁי בֶּעָשׂוֹר לַחֹדֶשׁ בָּאוּ אֲנָשִׁים מִזִּקְנֵי יִשְׂרָאֵל לִדְרֹשׁ אֶת־יהוה וַיֵּשְׁבוּ
ב ג לְפָנָי: *וַיְהִי דְבַר־יהוה אֵלַי לֵאמֹר: בֶּן־אָדָם דַּבֵּר אֶת־זִקְנֵי יִשְׂרָאֵל וְאָמַרְתָּ אֲלֵהֶם כֹּה
ד אָמַר אֲדֹנָי יֱהֹוִה הֲלִדְרֹשׁ אֹתִי אַתֶּם בָּאִים חַי־אָנִי אִם־אִדָּרֵשׁ לָכֶם נְאֻם אֲדֹנָי יֱהֹוִה: הֲתִשְׁפֹּט אֹתָם
ה הֲתִשְׁפּוֹט בֶּן־אָדָם אֶת־תּוֹעֲבֹת אֲבוֹתָם הוֹדִיעֵם: וְאָמַרְתָּ אֲלֵיהֶם כֹּה־אָמַר אֲדֹנָי יֱהֹוִה בְּיוֹם בָּחֳרִי
בְיִשְׂרָאֵל וָאֶשָּׂא יָדִי לְזֶרַע בֵּית יַעֲקֹב וָאִוָּדַע לָהֶם בְּאֶרֶץ מִצְרָיִם וָאֶשָּׂא יָדִי לָהֶם לֵאמֹר אֲנִי יהוה
ו אֱלֹהֵיכֶם: בַּיּוֹם הַהוּא נָשָׂאתִי יָדִי לָהֶם לְהוֹצִיאָם מֵאֶרֶץ מִצְרָיִם אֶל־אֶרֶץ אֲשֶׁר־תַּרְתִּי לָהֶם זָבַת
ז חָלָב וּדְבַשׁ צְבִי הִיא לְכָל־הָאֲרָצוֹת: וָאֹמַר אֲלֵהֶם אִישׁ שִׁקּוּצֵי עֵינָיו הַשְׁלִיכוּ וּבְגִלּוּלֵי מִצְרַיִם אַל־
ח תִּטַּמָּאוּ אֲנִי יהוה אֱלֹהֵיכֶם: וַיַּמְרוּ־בִי וְלֹא אָבוּ לִשְׁמֹעַ אֵלַי אִישׁ אֶת־שִׁקּוּצֵי עֵינֵיהֶם לֹא הִשְׁלִיכוּ
ט וְאֶת־גִּלּוּלֵי מִצְרַיִם לֹא עָזָבוּ וָאֹמַר לִשְׁפֹּךְ חֲמָתִי עֲלֵיהֶם לְכַלּוֹת אַפִּי בָּהֶם בְּתוֹךְ אֶרֶץ מִצְרָיִם: וָאַעַשׂ
לְמַעַן שְׁמִי לְבִלְתִּי הֵחֵל לְעֵינֵי הַגּוֹיִם אֲשֶׁר־הֵמָּה בְתוֹכָם אֲשֶׁר נוֹדַעְתִּי אֲלֵיהֶם לְעֵינֵיהֶם לְהוֹצִיאָם
י יא מֵאֶרֶץ מִצְרָיִם: וָאוֹצִיאֵם מֵאֶרֶץ מִצְרָיִם וָאֲבִאֵם אֶל־הַמִּדְבָּר: וָאֶתֵּן לָהֶם אֶת־חֻקּוֹתַי וְאֶת־מִשְׁפָּטַי
יב הוֹדַעְתִּי אוֹתָם אֲשֶׁר יַעֲשֶׂה אוֹתָם הָאָדָם וָחַי בָּהֶם: וְגַם אֶת־שַׁבְּתוֹתַי נָתַתִּי לָהֶם לִהְיוֹת לְאוֹת בֵּינִי
יג וּבֵינֵיהֶם לָדַעַת כִּי אֲנִי יהוה מְקַדְּשָׁם: וַיַּמְרוּ־בִי בֵית־יִשְׂרָאֵל בַּמִּדְבָּר בְּחֻקּוֹתַי לֹא־הָלָכוּ וְאֶת־מִשְׁפָּטַי
מָאָסוּ אֲשֶׁר יַעֲשֶׂה אֹתָם הָאָדָם וָחַי בָּהֶם וְאֶת־שַׁבְּתֹתַי חִלְּלוּ מְאֹד וָאֹמַר לִשְׁפֹּךְ חֲמָתִי עֲלֵיהֶם
יד טו בַּמִּדְבָּר לְכַלּוֹתָם: וָאֶעֱשֶׂה לְמַעַן שְׁמִי לְבִלְתִּי הֵחֵל לְעֵינֵי הַגּוֹיִם אֲשֶׁר הוֹצֵאתִים לְעֵינֵיהֶם: וְגַם־אֲנִי
נָשָׂאתִי יָדִי לָהֶם בַּמִּדְבָּר לְבִלְתִּי הָבִיא אוֹתָם אֶל־הָאָרֶץ אֲשֶׁר־נָתַתִּי זָבַת חָלָב וּדְבַשׁ צְבִי הִיא לְכָל־
טז הָאֲרָצוֹת:* יַעַן בְּמִשְׁפָּטַי מָאָסוּ וְאֶת־חֻקּוֹתַי לֹא־הָלְכוּ בָהֶם וְאֶת־שַׁבְּתוֹתַי חִלֵּלוּ כִּי אַחֲרֵי גִלּוּלֵיהֶם
יז יח לִבָּם הֹלֵךְ: וַתָּחָס עֵינִי עֲלֵיהֶם מִשַּׁחֲתָם וְלֹא־עָשִׂיתִי אוֹתָם כָּלָה בַּמִּדְבָּר: וָאֹמַר אֶל־בְּנֵיהֶם בַּמִּדְבָּר
יט בְּחוּקֵּי אֲבוֹתֵיכֶם אַל־תֵּלֵכוּ וְאֶת־מִשְׁפְּטֵיהֶם אַל־תִּשְׁמֹרוּ וּבְגִלּוּלֵיהֶם אַל־תִּטַּמָּאוּ: אֲנִי יהוה אֱלֹהֵיכֶם
כ בְּחֻקּוֹתַי לֵכוּ וְאֶת־מִשְׁפָּטַי שִׁמְרוּ וַעֲשׂוּ אוֹתָם: וְאֶת־שַׁבְּתוֹתַי קַדֵּשׁוּ וְהָיוּ לְאוֹת בֵּינִי וּבֵינֵיכֶם לָדַעַת כִּי
אֲנִי יהוה אֱלֹהֵיכֶם:

Yemenites end here

Sepharadim and Yemenites

After the exile of Yehoyakhin and many residents of Jerusalem to Babylon, but still four years before the final destruction of the city and the Temple, the exiled Jewish elders gather in the home of the prophet Yeḥezkel to hear his explanation for the dramatic events they have witnessed. In addressing them, the prophet reviews the history of the relationship between God and Israel ever since the days of Egyptian servitude, and up until the coming destruction. Yeḥezkel cites historical examples of Israel's wickedness, times when they deserved to be destroyed, but God treated them with mercy out of concern for His own honor among

Haftarat Emor

EZEKIEL

44 15 But the priests who are Levites descended from Tzadok, who protected the preciousness of My Sanctuary
when the children of Israel strayed from Me, they are the ones who may draw near Me in order to serve
16 Me, and they shall stand before Me to offer Me fat and blood: this is the word of the Lord God. They are
the ones who will enter My Sanctuary, and they shall approach My table to serve Me; they shall dutifully
17 protect My precious things. This is how it shall be when they approach the gates of the inner courtyard:
they will wear linen garments, and no wool shall be upon them when they serve at the gates of the inner
18 courtyard and within. There will be linen turbans on their heads and linen trousers on their loins; they
19 shall not gird themselves in a way that causes perspiration. And when they leave to go to the outer courtyard – to the outer courtyard to the people – they shall remove the garments in which they serve, leaving
them in the holy chambers, and put on other clothing, in order not to give the impression, by mingling
20 with them wearing their holy garments, that the people are equal to them in sanctity. They shall not shave
21 their heads nor grow their hair long in disarray; they shall keep their heads carefully trimmed. Nor shall
22 any priest drink wine when they enter the inner courtyard. And they shall not take as a wife a widow
or a divorcée. Rather, they shall take as wives only virgins of the seed of the House of Israel, or a widow
23 who is the widow of a priest. And they shall teach My people the difference between the sacred and the
24 profane and make known to them the difference between impure and pure. When there is controversy,
they shall stand in judgment, adjudicating it according to My laws. And they shall keep My teachings and
25 My statutes at all the times I have appointed, and sanctify My Sabbaths. The priest shall not approach a
human corpse and become impure because of it, though for a father or a mother, for a son or a daughter,
26 for a brother or for a sister who is unmarried, they may become impure. After a priest's purification pro-
27 cess begins, seven days are counted for him. And on the day he comes to the Sanctuary, into the inner
courtyard to minister in the Sanctuary, he is to bring his purification offering – this is the word of the Lord
28 God. And this shall be the priests' inheritance: I am their inheritance. Give them no territory to possess
29 in the land of Israel; I am their possession. They shall eat the grain offering and the purification offering
30 and the guilt offering, and everything consecrated by vow in Israel shall be theirs. The choicest of all first
fruits of every kind and every gift offering out of all your various donations belongs to the priests. And
31 your first kneading you shall give to the priest so that a blessing settles upon your home. Whether it be
bird or beast, the priests may not eat any creature that died on its own or was torn to pieces as prey.

Haftarat Behar

When Behar and Beḥukotai are read together, read the haftara for Beḥukotai on page 1581.

JEREMIAH
For Ashkenazim and Sepharadim

32 6 7 And Yirmeyahu said: The word of the Lord came to me: Ḥanamel, son of your uncle Shalum, shall
come to you and say, "Purchase for yourself my field that is in Anatot, for yours is the right of redemp-
8 tion by purchase." Ḥanamel, my uncle's son, came to me – just as the Lord had said – to the prison

of their own. They do this through the institutions of the tithes and the priestly gifts. This system of support comes directly from the people; it is not collected or managed by the king or government. And in turn, the king has no right to influence the religious and moral content taught by the Levites to the people. "The priests who are Levites," i.e., the educational system, are thus in their own right a separate branch of governance, independent of the executive.

BEHAR

Ashkenazim and Sepharadim

A few months before the destruction of the Temple, at the

הפטרת אמר

יחזקאל

מד טו וְהַכֹּהֲנִים הַלְוִיִּם בְּנֵי צָדוֹק אֲשֶׁר שָׁמְרוּ אֶת־מִשְׁמֶרֶת מִקְדָּשִׁי בִּתְעוֹת בְּנֵי־יִשְׂרָאֵל מֵעָלַי הֵמָּה יִקְרְבוּ
טז אֵלַי לְשָׁרְתֵנִי וְעָמְדוּ לְפָנַי לְהַקְרִיב לִי חֵלֶב וָדָם נְאֻם אֲדֹנָי יֱהֹוִה: הֵמָּה יָבֹאוּ אֶל־מִקְדָּשִׁי וְהֵמָּה יִקְרְבוּ
יז אֶל־שֻׁלְחָנִי לְשָׁרְתֵנִי וְשָׁמְרוּ אֶת־מִשְׁמַרְתִּי: וְהָיָה בְּבוֹאָם אֶל־שַׁעֲרֵי הֶחָצֵר הַפְּנִימִית בִּגְדֵי פִשְׁתִּים יִלְבָּשׁוּ
יח וְלֹא־יַעֲלֶה עֲלֵיהֶם צֶמֶר בְּשָׁרְתָם בְּשַׁעֲרֵי הֶחָצֵר הַפְּנִימִית וָבָיְתָה: פַּאֲרֵי פִשְׁתִּים יִהְיוּ עַל־רֹאשָׁם וּמִכְנְסֵי
יט פִשְׁתִּים יִהְיוּ עַל־מָתְנֵיהֶם לֹא יַחְגְּרוּ בַּיָּזַע: וּבְצֵאתָם אֶל־הֶחָצֵר הַחִיצוֹנָה אֶל־הֶחָצֵר הַחִיצוֹנָה אֶל־הָעָם
יִפְשְׁטוּ אֶת־בִּגְדֵיהֶם אֲשֶׁר־הֵמָּה מְשָׁרְתִם בָּם וְהִנִּיחוּ אוֹתָם בְּלִשְׁכֹת הַקֹּדֶשׁ וְלָבְשׁוּ בְּגָדִים אֲחֵרִים וְלֹא־
כ כא יְקַדְּשׁוּ אֶת־הָעָם בְּבִגְדֵיהֶם: וְרֹאשָׁם לֹא יְגַלֵּחוּ וּפֶרַע לֹא יְשַׁלֵּחוּ כָּסוֹם יִכְסְמוּ אֶת־רָאשֵׁיהֶם: וְיַיִן לֹא־יִשְׁתּוּ
כב כָּל־כֹּהֵן בְּבוֹאָם אֶל־הֶחָצֵר הַפְּנִימִית: וְאַלְמָנָה וּגְרוּשָׁה לֹא־יִקְחוּ לָהֶם לְנָשִׁים כִּי אִם־בְּתוּלֹת מִזֶּרַע בֵּית
כג יִשְׂרָאֵל וְהָאַלְמָנָה אֲשֶׁר תִּהְיֶה אַלְמָנָה מִכֹּהֵן יִקָּחוּ: וְאֶת־עַמִּי יוֹרוּ בֵּין קֹדֶשׁ לְחֹל וּבֵין־טָמֵא לְטָהוֹר
כד יוֹדִעֻם: וְעַל־רִיב הֵמָּה יַעַמְדוּ לשפט בְּמִשְׁפָּטַי ושפטהו וְאֶת־תּוֹרֹתַי וְאֶת־חֻקֹּתַי בְּכָל־מוֹעֲדַי יִשְׁמֹרוּ לְמִשְׁפָּט | יִשְׁפְּטֻהוּ
כה וְאֶת־שַׁבְּתוֹתַי יְקַדֵּשׁוּ: וְאֶל־מֵת אָדָם לֹא יָבוֹא לְטָמְאָה כִּי אִם־לְאָב וּלְאֵם וּלְבֵן וּלְבַת לְאָח וּלְאָחוֹת אֲשֶׁר־
כו לֹא־הָיְתָה לְאִישׁ יִטַּמָּאוּ: וְאַחֲרֵי טָהֳרָתוֹ שִׁבְעַת יָמִים יִסְפְּרוּ־לוֹ: וּבְיוֹם בֹּאוֹ אֶל־הַקֹּדֶשׁ אֶל־
כח הֶחָצֵר הַפְּנִימִית לְשָׁרֵת בַּקֹּדֶשׁ יַקְרִיב חַטָּאתוֹ נְאֻם אֲדֹנָי יֱהֹוִה: וְהָיְתָה לָהֶם לְנַחֲלָה אֲנִי נַחֲלָתָם
כט וַאֲחֻזָּה לֹא־תִתְּנוּ לָהֶם בְּיִשְׂרָאֵל אֲנִי אֲחֻזָּתָם: הַמִּנְחָה וְהַחַטָּאת וְהָאָשָׁם הֵמָּה יֹאכְלוּם וְכָל־חֵרֶם
ל בְּיִשְׂרָאֵל לָהֶם יִהְיֶה: וְרֵאשִׁית כָּל־בִּכּוּרֵי כֹל וְכָל־תְּרוּמַת כֹּל מִכֹּל תְּרוּמוֹתֵיכֶם לַכֹּהֲנִים יִהְיֶה וְרֵאשִׁית
לא עֲרִיסוֹתֵיכֶם תִּתְּנוּ לַכֹּהֵן לְהָנִיחַ בְּרָכָה אֶל־בֵּיתֶךָ: כָּל־נְבֵלָה וּטְרֵפָה מִן־הָעוֹף וּמִן־הַבְּהֵמָה לֹא יֹאכְלוּ
הַכֹּהֲנִים:

הפטרת בהר

When בהר *and* בחקתי *are read together, read the* הפטרה *for* בחקתי *on page 1581.*

ירמיה
For Ashkenazim and Sepharadim

לב ו ז וַיֹּאמֶר יִרְמְיָהוּ הָיָה דְבַר־יהוה אֵלַי לֵאמֹר: הִנֵּה חֲנַמְאֵל בֶּן־שַׁלֻּם דֹּדְךָ בָּא אֵלֶיךָ לֵאמֹר קְנֵה לְךָ אֶת־
ח שָׂדִי אֲשֶׁר בַּעֲנָתוֹת כִּי לְךָ מִשְׁפַּט הַגְּאֻלָּה לִקְנוֹת: וַיָּבֹא אֵלַי חֲנַמְאֵל בֶּן־דֹּדִי כִּדְבַר יהוה אֶל־חֲצַר

EMOR

In Yeḥezkel's prophetic virtual tour of the future reconstructed Temple, communicated twenty-four years after the destruction, the prophet reassures the exiles that the redemption will come one day. The *haftara* opens with the words "the priests who are Levites," evoking the role of the priests as educators and religious guides, mentioned in Moshe's final blessings in the book of Deuteronomy (33:10): "They shall teach Your laws to Yaakov, and Your instruction to Israel."

The people of Israel, whom the tribe of Levi represents before God and on whose behalf they work, bears the responsibility of sustaining the Levites, who have no land

▶

courtyard, and said to me, "Please purchase my field in Anatot, in the territory of Binyamin, for yours
is the right of inheritance, and it is your right to redeem it. Purchase it for yourself." Then I knew that
9 this was the word of the LORD. And so I purchased the field that was in Anatot from my uncle's son
10 Ḥanamel. I weighed out the silver to him: seven shekel and ten silver coins. I wrote it upon a scroll and
11 sealed it, and I had it witnessed; and I weighed out the silver on a scale. I took the deed of purchase,
12 sealed as prescribed by law and custom, along with the unsealed document. And I gave the deed of purchase to Barukh son of Neriya son of Maḥseya in the presence of Ḥanamel my uncle, in the presence
of the witnesses who were listed in the deed of purchase, and in the presence of all the men of Yehuda
13 14 who were sitting in the prison courtyard. In their presence I instructed Barukh, saying, "This is what the
LORD of Hosts, God of Israel, said: Take these scrolls, this deed of purchase, the sealed section and the
15 unsealed section, and place it in a clay vessel, so that it might be preserved for many days." For
this is what the LORD of Hosts, God of Israel, has said: Houses, fields, and vineyards shall once again
16 be purchased in this land. After I gave this deed of purchase to Barukh son of Neriya, I prayed
17 to the LORD, saying, "O Lord GOD! You made the heavens and the earth with Your great strength and
18 with Your arm stretched forth. Nothing is too wonderful for You. You perform loving-kindness to thousands but repay the sins of fathers unto the bosoms of their children after them. The great and mighty
19 God, LORD of Hosts is His name. Great in counsel, mighty in deed, Your eyes are open to all of the
ways of humans, to give each one according to his ways, to each according to the fruits of his actions.
20 You set signs and wonders in the land of Egypt to this day for Israel and for humankind, and You made
21 a name for Yourself as on this day. You brought out Your people Israel from the land of Egypt with
22 signs and wonders, a mighty hand and an arm stretched forth, and with terrifying power. You gave
them this land that You swore to their fathers that You would give them, a land flowing with milk and
23 honey. They came and possessed it, but they neither heeded Your voice nor followed Your teaching.
All that You had commanded them to do they did not do, and so You caused all this disaster to come
24 upon them. The siege ramps have come near the city in order to capture it, and the city is about to be
delivered, because of the sword and the famine and the pestilence, into the hands of the Chaldeans *Chabad end here*
25 who are attacking it. That which you spoke about has happened, and You see it for Yourself. And yet
You say to me, Lord GOD, 'Purchase this field for yourself for silver and have it witnessed, when the
26 city is about to be delivered into the hands of the Chaldeans'?" And the word of the LORD
27 came to Yirmeyahu: "Look, I am the LORD, God of all flesh. Is anything beyond My power?"

16 19 The LORD is my strength and my might, my refuge in a day of trouble. To You the nations will come JEREMIAH
from the ends of the earth, and they will say: "Our ancestors inherited nothing but falsehood, futility, *For Yemenites*
20 21 and things of no use. Can a human make gods for himself when they are not gods?" Therefore, I am
about to make them know; this time I will make them know of My power and My strength, and they
17 1 shall come to know that My name is the LORD. Yehuda's sin is written with an iron pen with a

God's answer clarifies that the punishment of destruction is not irreversible. The symbolic act of purchasing a field right before the kingdom's demise concretizes this idea. The purchase and sale of land evokes the normality of day-to-day life, which will one day return to the hills and cities of Yehuda.

Yemenites

See commentary on Haftarat Behukotai for Ashkenazim and Sepharadim.

הַמַּטָּרָה וַיֹּאמֶר אֵלַי קְנֵה נָא אֶת־שָׂדִי אֲשֶׁר־בַּעֲנָתוֹת אֲשֶׁר ׀ בְּאֶרֶץ בִּנְיָמִין כִּי לְךָ מִשְׁפַּט הַיְרֻשָּׁה וּלְךָ
ט הַגְּאֻלָּה קְנֵה־לָךְ וָאֵדַע כִּי דְבַר־יְהוָה הוּא: וָאֶקְנֶה אֶת־הַשָּׂדֶה מֵאֵת חֲנַמְאֵל בֶּן־דֹּדִי אֲשֶׁר בַּעֲנָתוֹת
י וָאֶשְׁקֲלָה־לּוֹ אֶת־הַכֶּסֶף שִׁבְעָה שְׁקָלִים וַעֲשָׂרָה הַכָּסֶף: וָאֶכְתֹּב בַּסֵּפֶר וָאֶחְתֹּם וָאָעֵד עֵדִים וָאֶשְׁקֹל
יא יב הַכֶּסֶף בְּמֹאזְנָיִם: וָאֶקַּח אֶת־סֵפֶר הַמִּקְנָה אֶת־הֶחָתוּם הַמִּצְוָה וְהַחֻקִּים וְאֶת־הַגָּלוּי: וָאֶתֵּן אֶת־הַסֵּפֶר
הַמִּקְנָה אֶל־בָּרוּךְ בֶּן־נֵרִיָּה בֶּן־מַחְסֵיָה לְעֵינֵי חֲנַמְאֵל דֹּדִי וּלְעֵינֵי הָעֵדִים הַכֹּתְבִים בְּסֵפֶר הַמִּקְנָה לְעֵינֵי
יג יד כָּל־הַיְּהוּדִים הַיֹּשְׁבִים בַּחֲצַר הַמַּטָּרָה: וָאֲצַוֶּה אֶת־בָּרוּךְ לְעֵינֵיהֶם לֵאמֹר: כֹּה־אָמַר יְהוָה צְבָאוֹת אֱלֹהֵי
יִשְׂרָאֵל לָקוֹחַ אֶת־הַסְּפָרִים הָאֵלֶּה אֵת סֵפֶר הַמִּקְנָה הַזֶּה וְאֵת הֶחָתוּם וְאֵת סֵפֶר הַגָּלוּי הַזֶּה וּנְתַתָּם
טו בִּכְלִי־חָרֶשׂ לְמַעַן יַעַמְדוּ יָמִים רַבִּים: כִּי כֹה אָמַר יְהוָה צְבָאוֹת אֱלֹהֵי יִשְׂרָאֵל עוֹד יִקָּנוּ בָתִּים
טז וְשָׂדוֹת וּכְרָמִים בָּאָרֶץ הַזֹּאת: וָאֶתְפַּלֵּל אֶל־יְהוָה אַחֲרֵי תִתִּי אֶת־סֵפֶר הַמִּקְנָה אֶל־בָּרוּךְ
יז בֶּן־נֵרִיָּה לֵאמֹר: אֲהָהּ אֲדֹנָי יֱהוִה הִנֵּה ׀ אַתָּה עָשִׂיתָ אֶת־הַשָּׁמַיִם וְאֶת־הָאָרֶץ בְּכֹחֲךָ הַגָּדוֹל וּבִזְרֹעֲךָ
יח הַנְּטוּיָה לֹא־יִפָּלֵא מִמְּךָ כָּל־דָּבָר: עֹשֶׂה חֶסֶד לַאֲלָפִים וּמְשַׁלֵּם עֲוֺן אָבוֹת אֶל־חֵיק בְּנֵיהֶם אַחֲרֵיהֶם
יט הָאֵל הַגָּדוֹל הַגִּבּוֹר יְהוָה צְבָאוֹת שְׁמוֹ: גְּדֹל הָעֵצָה וְרַב הָעֲלִילִיָּה אֲשֶׁר־עֵינֶיךָ פְקֻחוֹת עַל־כָּל־דַּרְכֵי
כ בְּנֵי אָדָם לָתֵת לְאִישׁ כִּדְרָכָיו וְכִפְרִי מַעֲלָלָיו: אֲשֶׁר שַׂמְתָּ אֹתוֹת וּמֹפְתִים בְּאֶרֶץ מִצְרַיִם עַד־הַיּוֹם הַזֶּה
כא וּבְיִשְׂרָאֵל וּבָאָדָם וַתַּעֲשֶׂה־לְּךָ שֵׁם כַּיּוֹם הַזֶּה: וַתֹּצֵא אֶת־עַמְּךָ אֶת־יִשְׂרָאֵל מֵאֶרֶץ מִצְרָיִם בְּאֹתוֹת
כב וּבְמוֹפְתִים וּבְיָד חֲזָקָה וּבְאֶזְרוֹעַ נְטוּיָה וּבְמוֹרָא גָּדוֹל: וַתִּתֵּן לָהֶם אֶת־הָאָרֶץ הַזֹּאת אֲשֶׁר־נִשְׁבַּעְתָּ
כג לַאֲבוֹתָם לָתֵת לָהֶם אֶרֶץ זָבַת חָלָב וּדְבָשׁ: וַיָּבֹאוּ וַיִּרְשׁוּ אֹתָהּ וְלֹא־שָׁמְעוּ בְקוֹלֶךָ ובתרותך לֹא־הָלָכוּ וּבְתוֹרָתְךָ
כד אֵת כָּל־אֲשֶׁר צִוִּיתָה לָהֶם לַעֲשׂוֹת לֹא עָשׂוּ וַתַּקְרֵא אֹתָם אֵת כָּל־הָרָעָה הַזֹּאת:* הִנֵּה הַסֹּלְלוֹת בָּאוּ *Chabad end here*
הָעִיר לְלָכְדָהּ וְהָעִיר נִתְּנָה בְּיַד הַכַּשְׂדִּים הַנִּלְחָמִים עָלֶיהָ מִפְּנֵי הַחֶרֶב וְהָרָעָב וְהַדָּבֶר וַאֲשֶׁר דִּבַּרְתָּ
כה הָיָה וְהִנְּךָ רֹאֶה: וְאַתָּה אָמַרְתָּ אֵלַי אֲדֹנָי יֱהוִה קְנֵה־לְךָ הַשָּׂדֶה בַּכֶּסֶף וְהָעֵד עֵדִים וְהָעִיר נִתְּנָה בְּיַד
כו כז הַכַּשְׂדִּים: וַיְהִי דְּבַר־יְהוָה אֶל־יִרְמְיָהוּ לֵאמֹר: הִנֵּה אֲנִי יְהוָה אֱלֹהֵי כָּל־בָּשָׂר הֲמִמֶּנִּי יִפָּלֵא
כָּל־דָּבָר:

ירמיה
For Yemenites

טז יט יְהוָה עֻזִּי וּמָעֻזִּי וּמְנוּסִי בְּיוֹם צָרָה אֵלֶיךָ גּוֹיִם יָבֹאוּ מֵאַפְסֵי־אָרֶץ וְיֹאמְרוּ אַךְ־שֶׁקֶר נָחֲלוּ אֲבוֹתֵינוּ הֶבֶל
כ כא וְאֵין־בָּם מוֹעִיל: הֲיַעֲשֶׂה־לּוֹ אָדָם אֱלֹהִים וְהֵמָּה לֹא אֱלֹהִים: לָכֵן הִנְנִי מוֹדִיעָם בַּפַּעַם הַזֹּאת אוֹדִיעֵם
יז א אֶת־יָדִי וְאֶת־גְּבוּרָתִי וְיָדְעוּ כִּי־שְׁמִי יְהוָה: חַטַּאת יְהוּדָה כְּתוּבָה בְּעֵט בַּרְזֶל בְּצִפֹּרֶן שָׁמִיר

darkest hour of the Babylonian siege, Yirmeyahu is imprisoned by King Tzidkiyahu, who fears Yirmeyahu's prophecies of destruction. In his dungeon, Yirmeyahu receives a prophetic command to buy a field from a cousin, who arrives at the prison to visit him. Even though the financial investment in such a purchase by a prisoner during a siege makes no logical sense, Yirmeyahu follows God's command. The purchasing ceremony is carried out following all the customary and legal forms. Afterward, Yirmeyahu turns to God and requests an explanation for the strange mission.

2 diamond point, engraved upon the tablets of their hearts and upon the corners of your altars. As they
yearn for their children, so do they for their altars and their sacred trees beside verdant trees upon the
3 high hills. Mountain dweller – because of the sin of your high places in all your territories, I will turn
4 your wealth and all your treasures into booty upon the field. You will forfeit, by your own fault, the heritage which I have given you. I will make you a slave to your enemies in a land that you never knew, for
5 you kindled a fire in My nostrils which shall blaze forever. This is what the LORD said: Cursed
is he who trusts in man, who makes flesh his strength and who turns his heart away from the LORD.
6 He will be like a shrub in the desert, never witnessing prosperity. He will dwell scorched in the wilder-
7 ness, a salty, uninhabited land. Blessed is the person who trusts in the LORD. The LORD will
8 be his protector. He will be like a tree planted beside the water, its roots spreading along the stream.
It need not be concerned when heat comes, for its leaves will remain verdant. It need not worry in a
9 year of drought, for it will never cease to produce fruit. More devious is the heart than all else, and it is
10 hopelessly sick. Who can know it? I, the LORD, search out the heart and examine inner thoughts so as
11 to treat each person according to his ways, according to the fruits of his actions. Like the bird
that hatches what she did not lay, so is he who accumulated his wealth unjustly. After half of his days,
12 his fortune will leave him, and in the end he will be proven a fool. Like the throne of glory, elevated
13 from the beginning, so is the place of our Temple. The hope of Israel is the LORD. All who forsake You
will be humiliated. Those who stray from Me will be written in the earth, for they have forsaken the
14 source of living waters, declares the LORD. Heal me, LORD, so that I may be healed. Save me
so that I may be saved, for it is You whom I praise.

HAFTARAT BEḤUKOTAI

When Behar and Beḥukotai are read together, read this haftara.

JEREMIAH
For Ashkenazim and Sepharadim

16 19 The LORD is my strength and my might, my refuge in a day of trouble. To You the nations will come
from the ends of the earth, and they will say: "Our ancestors inherited nothing but falsehood, futility,
20 21 and things of no use. Can a human make gods for himself when they are not gods?" Therefore, I am
about to make them know; this time I will make them know of My power and My strength, and they
17 1 shall come to know that My name is the LORD. Yehuda's sin is written with an iron pen with a
2 diamond point, engraved upon the tablets of their hearts and upon the corners of your altars. As they
yearn for their children, so do they for their altars and their sacred trees beside verdant trees upon the
3 high hills. Mountain dweller – because of the sin of your high places in all your territories, I will turn
4 your wealth and all your treasures into booty upon the field. You will forfeit, by your own fault, the heritage which I have given you. I will make you a slave to your enemies in a land that you never knew, for
5 you kindled a fire in My nostrils which shall blaze forever. This is what the LORD said: Cursed

---

the nation could mend its ways, or idolatry could triumph, bringing destruction and exile on the people of Israel. Because Yirmeyahu aided Yoshiyahu in pressuring the people to repent, he met concerted resistance from those who favored the status quo. His relationship with God gave him strength to overcome the hostility directed at him by the people.

ב חרושה על־לוח לבם ולקרנות מזבחותיכם: כזכר בניהם מזבחותם ואשריהם על־עץ רענן על גבעות
ג ד הגבהות: הררי בשדה חילך כל־אוצרותיך לבז אתן במתיך בחטאת בכל־גבוליך: ושמטתה ובך
מנחלתך אשר נתתי לך והעבדתיך את־איביך בארץ אשר לא־ידעת כי־אש קדחתם באפי עד־
ה עולם תוקד: כה | אמר יהוה ארור הגבר אשר יבטח באדם ושם בשר זרעו ומן־יהוה
ו יסור לבו: והיה כערער בערבה ולא יראה כי־יבוא טוב ושכן חררים במדבר ארץ מלחה ולא
ז ח תשב: ברוך הגבר אשר יבטח ביהוה והיה יהוה מבטחו: והיה כעץ | שתול על־מים ועל־
יובל ישלח שרשיו ולא ירא כי־יבא חם והיה עלהו רענן ובשנת בצרת לא ידאג ולא ימיש מעשות
ט פרי: עקב הלב מכל ואנש הוא מי ידענו: אני יהוה חקר לב בחן כליות ולתת לאיש כדרכו כפרי
יא מעלליו: קרא דגר ולא ילד עשה עשר ולא במשפט בחצי ימו יעזבנו ובאחריתו יהיה נבל:
יב יג כסא כבוד מרום מראשון מקום מקדשנו: מקוה ישראל יהוה כל־עזביך יבשו יסורי בארץ יכתבו כי וסורי
יד עזבו מקור מים־חיים את־יהוה: רפאני יהוה וארפא הושיעני ואושעה כי תהלתי אתה:

הפטרת בחקתי

When בהר *and* בחקתי *are read together, read this* הפטרה.

ירמיה
For Ashkenazim and Sepharadim

טז יט יהוה עזי ומעזי ומנוסי ביום צרה אליך גוים יבאו מאפסי־ארץ ויאמרו אך־שקר נחלו אבותינו
כ כא הבל ואין־בם מועיל: היעשה־לו אדם אלהים והמה לא אלהים: לכן הנני מודיעם בפעם הזאת
יז א אודיעם את־ידי ואת־גבורתי וידעו כי־שמי יהוה: חטאת יהודה כתובה בעט ברזל
ב בצפרן שמיר חרושה על־לוח לבם ולקרנות מזבחותיכם: כזכר בניהם מזבחותם ואשריהם על־עץ
ג רענן על גבעות הגבהות: הררי בשדה חילך כל־אוצרותיך לבז אתן במתיך בחטאת בכל־גבוליך:
ד ושמטתה ובך מנחלתך אשר נתתי לך והעבדתיך את־איביך בארץ אשר לא־ידעת כי־אש קדחתם
ה באפי עד־עולם תוקד: כה | אמר יהוה ארור הגבר אשר יבטח באדם ושם בשר זרעו

BEḤUKOTAI

Ashkenazim and Sepharadim

Yirmeyahu prophesied during the final forty years of the kingdom of Yehuda. It seems that the prophecy in this *haftara* was delivered during the reign of King Yoshiyahu. Yoshiyahu worked hard to correct the many evils that were present in the kingdom when he inherited it, and he was helped in this work by Yirmeyahu. The pair saw two options laid out before them:

▶

is he who trusts in man, who makes flesh his strength and who turns his heart away from the LORD.
6 He will be like a shrub in the desert, never witnessing prosperity. He will dwell scorched in the wilder-
7 ness, a salty, uninhabited land. Blessed is the person who trusts in the LORD. The LORD will
8 be his protector. He will be like a tree planted beside the water, its roots spreading along the stream.
It need not be concerned when heat comes, for its leaves will remain verdant. It need not worry in a
9 year of drought, for it will never cease to produce fruit. More devious is the heart than all else, and it is
10 hopelessly sick. Who can know it? I, the LORD, search out the heart and examine inner thoughts so as
11 to treat each person according to his ways, according to the fruits of his actions. Like the bird
that hatches what she did not lay, so is he who accumulated his wealth unjustly. After half of his days,
12 his fortune will leave him, and in the end he will be proven a fool. Like the throne of glory, elevated
13 from the beginning, so is the place of our Temple. The hope of Israel is the LORD. All who forsake You
will be humiliated. Those who stray from Me will be written in the earth, for they have forsaken the
14 source of living waters, declares the LORD. Heal me, LORD, so that I may be healed. Save me
so that I may be saved, for it is You whom I praise.

EZEKIEL
For Yemenites

34 1 2 The word of the LORD came to me: "Man, prophesy against the shepherds of Israel; prophesy and say
to them, to the shepherds: So says the Lord GOD: Woe, shepherds of Israel who have been tending
3 themselves when surely it is the sheep the shepherds should tend. You ate the fat, you wore the wool,
4 and you slaughtered the fattest, but you did not tend the sheep: you did not strengthen the weak, you
did not nurse the sick, you did not bind the broken, you did not recover the stray, and you did not
5 search for the lost; you ruled over them with force and with harshness. They scattered, for they had
6 no shepherd; they became food for every animal of the field and scattered. My sheep are wandering
upon all the mountains, all the high hills; My sheep have scattered over the face of the earth; no one
7 8 searches for them; no one seeks them out. So, shepherds, listen to the word of the LORD: Surely as I
live, declares the Lord GOD, because My sheep were spoils, My sheep became the food of every animal
of the field for want of a shepherd, and because My shepherds did not search for My sheep but tended
9 10 themselves and did not tend My sheep, so, shepherds, listen to the word of the LORD: So says
the Lord GOD: Behold, I am coming down upon the shepherds; I will seek redress for My sheep from
their hands and put an end to their shepherding; no more will the shepherds tend themselves; I will
11 save My sheep from their mouths; it will not be their food. For so says the Lord GOD: Behold,
12 it is I; I will search for My sheep and care for them; just as a shepherd cares for his flock when he is
among his sheep who have dispersed, so will I care for My sheep. I will save them from all the places
13 they have been scattered on a day of heavy cloud, thick fog. I will take them out from the nations; I will
gather them in from the lands and bring them to their soil. I will tend them on the mountains of Israel,
14 in the ravines, in all the settled parts of the land. I will tend them on good grazing-land; the high hills of
Israel will be their pasture; there will they lie down on lush pasture; they will graze on rich grazing-land

---

more refugees fleeing the final destruction of the kingdom of Yehuda. Everyone begins to look toward the future – the return to Zion several decades in the future. To correct the Jews' situation means correcting the mistakes of the past. And one of the most serious of the past problems that must be correct is corrupt leadership. The kings of Yehuda and Israel had oppressed the people rather than helping them, exploiting the resources and funds of the kingdom for their own personal gain. Here, the prophet describes two types of government: that of the past saw only itself and its own good as its goals; that of the future sees its aim as promoting the good of the people. Making this shift is the root of redemption.

ו וּמִן־יְהוָה יָסוּר לִבּוֹ: וְהָיָה כְּעַרְעָר בָּעֲרָבָה וְלֹא יִרְאֶה כִּי־יָבוֹא טוֹב וְשָׁכַן חֲרֵרִים בַּמִּדְבָּר אֶרֶץ מְלֵחָה
ז ח וְלֹא תֵשֵׁב: בָּרוּךְ הַגֶּבֶר אֲשֶׁר יִבְטַח בַּיהוָה וְהָיָה יְהוָה מִבְטַחוֹ: וְהָיָה כְּעֵץ ׀ שָׁתוּל עַל־מַיִם
וְעַל־יוּבַל יְשַׁלַּח שָׁרָשָׁיו וְלֹא יִרְאֶ כִּי־יָבֹא חֹם וְהָיָה עָלֵהוּ רַעֲנָן וּבִשְׁנַת בַּצֹּרֶת לֹא יִדְאָג וְלֹא יָמִישׁ
ט י מֵעֲשׂוֹת פֶּרִי: עָקֹב הַלֵּב מִכֹּל וְאָנֻשׁ הוּא מִי יֵדָעֶנּוּ: אֲנִי יְהוָה חֹקֵר לֵב בֹּחֵן כְּלָיוֹת וְלָתֵת לְאִישׁ כִּדְרָכָו
יא כִּפְרִי מַעֲלָלָיו: קֹרֵא דָגַר וְלֹא יָלָד עֹשֶׂה עֹשֶׁר וְלֹא בְמִשְׁפָּט בַּחֲצִי יָמָו יַעַזְבֶנּוּ וּבְאַחֲרִיתוֹ
יב יג יִהְיֶה נָבָל: כִּסֵּא כָבוֹד מָרוֹם מֵרִאשׁוֹן מְקוֹם מִקְדָּשֵׁנוּ: מִקְוֵה יִשְׂרָאֵל יְהוָה כָּל־עֹזְבֶיךָ יֵבֹשׁוּ יסורי וְסוּרַי
יד בָּאָרֶץ יִכָּתֵבוּ כִּי עָזְבוּ מְקוֹר מַיִם־חַיִּים אֶת־יְהוָה: רְפָאֵנִי יְהוָה וְאֵרָפֵא הוֹשִׁיעֵנִי וְאִוָּשֵׁעָה
כִּי תְהִלָּתִי אָתָּה:

לד א ב וַיְהִי דְבַר־יְהוָה אֵלַי לֵאמֹר: בֶּן־אָדָם הִנָּבֵא עַל־רוֹעֵי יִשְׂרָאֵל הִנָּבֵא וְאָמַרְתָּ אֲלֵיהֶם לָרֹעִים כֹּה־אָמַר ׀ יחזקאל *For Yemenites*
ג אֲדֹנָי יֱהֹוִה הוֹי רֹעֵי־יִשְׂרָאֵל אֲשֶׁר הָיוּ רֹעִים אוֹתָם הֲלוֹא הַצֹּאן יִרְעוּ הָרֹעִים: אֶת־הַחֵלֶב תֹּאכֵלוּ וְאֶת־
ד הַצֶּמֶר תִּלְבָּשׁוּ הַבְּרִיאָה תִּזְבָּחוּ הַצֹּאן לֹא תִרְעוּ: אֶת־הַנַּחְלוֹת לֹא חִזַּקְתֶּם וְאֶת־הַחוֹלָה לֹא־רִפֵּאתֶם
וְלַנִּשְׁבֶּרֶת לֹא חֲבַשְׁתֶּם וְאֶת־הַנִּדַּחַת לֹא הֲשֵׁבֹתֶם וְאֶת־הָאֹבֶדֶת לֹא בִקַּשְׁתֶּם וּבְחָזְקָה רְדִיתֶם אֹתָם
ה ו וּבְפָרֶךְ: וַתְּפוּצֶינָה מִבְּלִי רֹעֶה וַתִּהְיֶינָה לְאָכְלָה לְכָל־חַיַּת הַשָּׂדֶה וַתְּפוּצֶינָה: יִשְׁגּוּ צֹאנִי בְּכָל־הֶהָרִים
ז וְעַל כָּל־גִּבְעָה רָמָה וְעַל כָּל־פְּנֵי הָאָרֶץ נָפֹצוּ צֹאנִי וְאֵין דּוֹרֵשׁ וְאֵין מְבַקֵּשׁ: לָכֵן רֹעִים שִׁמְעוּ אֶת־דְּבַר
ח יְהוָה: חַי־אָנִי נְאֻם ׀ אֲדֹנָי יֱהֹוִה אִם־לֹא יַעַן הֱיוֹת־צֹאנִי ׀ לָבַז וַתִּהְיֶינָה צֹאנִי לְאָכְלָה לְכָל־חַיַּת הַשָּׂדֶה
ט מֵאֵין רֹעֶה וְלֹא־דָרְשׁוּ רֹעַי אֶת־צֹאנִי וַיִּרְעוּ הָרֹעִים אוֹתָם וְאֶת־צֹאנִי לֹא רָעוּ: לָכֵן הָרֹעִים שִׁמְעוּ דְּבַר־
י יְהוָה: כֹּה־אָמַר אֲדֹנָי יֱהֹוִה הִנְנִי אֶל־הָרֹעִים וְדָרַשְׁתִּי אֶת־צֹאנִי מִיָּדָם וְהִשְׁבַּתִּים מֵרְעוֹת צֹאן
יא וְלֹא־יִרְעוּ עוֹד הָרֹעִים אוֹתָם וְהִצַּלְתִּי צֹאנִי מִפִּיהֶם וְלֹא־תִהְיֶיןָ לָהֶם לְאָכְלָה: כִּי כֹּה אָמַר אֲדֹנָי
יב יֱהֹוִה הִנְנִי־אָנִי וְדָרַשְׁתִּי אֶת־צֹאנִי וּבִקַּרְתִּים: כְּבַקָּרַת רֹעֶה עֶדְרוֹ בְּיוֹם־הֱיוֹתוֹ בְתוֹךְ־צֹאנוֹ נִפְרָשׁוֹת כֵּן
יג אֲבַקֵּר אֶת־צֹאנִי וְהִצַּלְתִּי אֶתְהֶם מִכָּל־הַמְּקוֹמֹת אֲשֶׁר נָפֹצוּ שָׁם בְּיוֹם עָנָן וַעֲרָפֶל: וְהוֹצֵאתִים מִן־הָעַמִּים
וְקִבַּצְתִּים מִן־הָאֲרָצוֹת וַהֲבִיאוֹתִים אֶל־אַדְמָתָם וּרְעִיתִים אֶל־הָרֵי יִשְׂרָאֵל בָּאֲפִיקִים וּבְכֹל מוֹשְׁבֵי
יד הָאָרֶץ: בְּמִרְעֶה־טּוֹב אֶרְעֶה אֹתָם וּבְהָרֵי מְרוֹם־יִשְׂרָאֵל יִהְיֶה נְוֵהֶם שָׁם תִּרְבַּצְנָה בְּנָוֶה טּוֹב וּמִרְעֶה

The word "land" (*eretz*) appears in this *haftara* with four different senses. It means the whole earth, a specific country, the ground from which plants grow, and a low place that is trodden on. To summarize the *haftara*: The people of Israel are located in the "land" of Israel. All the peoples of the "land" (i.e., of the earth) are supposed to learn from us the proper and pious way to behave. If Israel does not set a proper example, the "land" will become barren, the people will go into exile, and its honor will be brought down to the "land" (i.e., to the ground).

Yemenites

After news of the destruction of Jerusalem and the Temple reaches the exiles in Babylon, in the twelfth year after the exile of Yehoyakhin, Yeḥezkel begins to issue prophecies of comfort and reassurance. The exiles present in Babylon are joined by

15 in the hills of Israel. I Myself will tend My sheep: I will lay them down, declares the Lord God; I will
16 seek the lost, I will recover the stray, I will bind the broken, I will strengthen the sick, but the robust,
17 the strong, I will destroy; I will tend them with justice. As for you, My sheep, so says the Lord God:
18 Behold that I will judge between one sheep and another, rams and he-goats. Is it not enough for you
to graze on good grazing-land; must your feet trample the rest of your grazing-land? And when you
19 drink clear waters, must you muddy the rest with your feet? My sheep graze on what has been trampled
20 by your feet and drink from what has been muddied by your feet. So the Lord God says this
21 to them: Behold, it is I – I will judge between the fat sheep and the thin sheep. Because you pushed
22 with flank and shoulder and rammed all the weak with your horns until you scattered them, I will save
23 My sheep; they will no longer be spoils; I will judge between one sheep and another. I will establish
over them one single shepherd who will tend them; My servant, David, he will tend them; he will be a
24 shepherd to them; I, the Lord, will be their God, and My servant David will be prince among them;
25 I, the Lord, have spoken. I will make a covenant of peace with them, I will rid the land of wild ani-
26 mals, and even in the wilderness they will live securely and sleep in the forests. I will make them and
27 all around My hill a blessing; I will make rain fall at its right time – they will be blessed rains; the trees
of the field will bear their fruit, and the land will yield its produce. They will be secure upon their soil,
and they will know that I am the Lord when I break the bars of their yoke and save them from those
who enslave them.

Haftarat Bemidbar

On Erev Rosh Ḥodesh Sivan read the haftara on page 1637.

HOSEA

2 1 Yet the children of Israel will number like the sands of the sea, not measurable or countable, and rather
2 than being told, "You are Not My People," they will be told, "You are the sons of the living God." Then
the children of Yehuda and the children of Israel will gather together; they will designate one leader
3 and escape from the land, for the day of Yizre'el will be a great one. Say then to your brothers "People,"
4 and to your sisters "Loved." Berate your mother, for she is not my wife, nor I her husband. Let her
5 remove her prostitute's rouge from her face, her adulterous acts from between her breasts, lest I strip
her naked as the day she was born and make her as a desert wilderness. I will make her into parched
6 wasteland and let her die from thirst. As for her sons, I will have no mercy, for they are the sons of a
7 harlot, for their mother has whored; she has conceived them in shame. She said, "I will follow after
8 my lovers; it is they who give me bread and water, keep me in wools and linens, lotions and wines," so
I will obstruct her path with prickly shrubs; I will fence her in with walls; her way will be lost to her.
9 She will pursue her lovers but not catch them; she will search them out but never find them. Then she
10 will say, "I will go and return to my first husband, for I fared better then than now." But she did not care
to know that it was I who furnished her with grain, wine, and oil, I who lavished silver upon her and
11 gold which they used for Baal. Hence I will take back My grain as it ripens in its season, My wine as

erstwhile lovers are revealed in fact to hate her, not lifting a finger to help her in her time of trouble. This was the situation of the Israelites at the time of the destruction, when all the peoples they thought to be allies turned upon them in their moment of need. Despite all this, God allows His wife to return to Him, renews His covenant with her, and restores her fortunes as of old.

טו טז שְׁמֵן תִּרְעֶינָה אֶל־הָרֵי יִשְׂרָאֵל׃ אֲנִי אֶרְעֶה צֹאנִי וַאֲנִי אַרְבִּיצֵם נְאֻם אֲדֹנָי יֱהֹוִה׃ אֶת־הָאֹבֶדֶת אֲבַקֵּשׁ
וְאֶת־הַנִּדַּחַת אָשִׁיב וְלַנִּשְׁבֶּרֶת אֶחֱבֹשׁ וְאֶת־הַחוֹלָה אֲחַזֵּק וְאֶת־הַשְּׁמֵנָה וְאֶת־הַחֲזָקָה אַשְׁמִיד אֶרְעֶנָּה
יז יח בְמִשְׁפָּט׃ וְאַתֵּנָה צֹאנִי כֹּה אָמַר אֲדֹנָי יֱהֹוִה הִנְנִי שֹׁפֵט בֵּין־שֶׂה לָשֶׂה לָאֵילִים וְלָעַתּוּדִים׃ הַמְעַט מִכֶּם
הַמִּרְעֶה הַטּוֹב תִּרְעוּ וְיֶתֶר מִרְעֵיכֶם תִּרְמְסוּ בְּרַגְלֵיכֶם וּמִשְׁקַע־מַיִם תִּשְׁתּוּ וְאֵת הַנּוֹתָרִים בְּרַגְלֵיכֶם
יט כ תִּרְפֹּשׂוּן׃ וְצֹאנִי מִרְמַס רַגְלֵיכֶם תִּרְעֶינָה וּמִרְפַּשׂ רַגְלֵיכֶם תִּשְׁתֶּינָה׃ לָכֵן כֹּה אָמַר אֲדֹנָי יֱהֹוִה
כא אֲלֵיהֶם הִנְנִי־אָנִי וְשָׁפַטְתִּי בֵּין־שֶׂה בִרְיָה וּבֵין שֶׂה רָזָה׃ יַעַן בְּצַד וּבְכָתֵף תֶּהְדֹּפוּ וּבְקַרְנֵיכֶם תְּנַגְּחוּ כָּל־
כב הַנַּחְלוֹת עַד אֲשֶׁר הֲפִיצוֹתֶם אוֹתָנָה אֶל־הַחוּצָה׃ וְהוֹשַׁעְתִּי לְצֹאנִי וְלֹא־תִהְיֶינָה עוֹד לָבַז וְשָׁפַטְתִּי בֵּין
כג שֶׂה לָשֶׂה׃ וַהֲקִמֹתִי עֲלֵיהֶם רֹעֶה אֶחָד וְרָעָה אֶתְהֶן אֵת עַבְדִּי דָוִיד הוּא יִרְעֶה אֹתָם וְהוּא יִהְיֶה לָהֶן
כד כה לְרֹעֶה׃ וַאֲנִי יְהוָה אֶהְיֶה לָהֶם לֵאלֹהִים וְעַבְדִּי דָוִד נָשִׂיא בְתוֹכָם אֲנִי יְהוָה דִּבַּרְתִּי׃ וְכָרַתִּי לָהֶם בְּרִית
כו שָׁלוֹם וְהִשְׁבַּתִּי חַיָּה־רָעָה מִן־הָאָרֶץ וְיָשְׁבוּ בַמִּדְבָּר לָבֶטַח וְיָשְׁנוּ ביעורים׃ וְנָתַתִּי אוֹתָם וּסְבִיבוֹת בַּיְּעָרִים
כז גִּבְעָתִי בְּרָכָה וְהוֹרַדְתִּי הַגֶּשֶׁם בְּעִתּוֹ גִּשְׁמֵי בְרָכָה יִהְיוּ׃ וְנָתַן עֵץ הַשָּׂדֶה אֶת־פִּרְיוֹ וְהָאָרֶץ תִּתֵּן יְבוּלָהּ
וְהָיוּ עַל־אַדְמָתָם לָבֶטַח וְיָדְעוּ כִּי־אֲנִי יְהוָה בְּשִׁבְרִי אֶת־מֹטוֹת עֻלָּם וְהִצַּלְתִּים מִיַּד הָעֹבְדִים בָּהֶם׃

הפטרת במדבר

On ערב ראש חודש סיון *read the* הפטרה *on page 1637.*

ב א וְהָיָה מִסְפַּר בְּנֵי־יִשְׂרָאֵל כְּחוֹל הַיָּם אֲשֶׁר לֹא־יִמַּד וְלֹא יִסָּפֵר וְהָיָה בִּמְקוֹם אֲשֶׁר־יֵאָמֵר לָהֶם לֹא־ הושע
ב עַמִּי אַתֶּם יֵאָמֵר לָהֶם בְּנֵי אֵל־חָי׃ וְנִקְבְּצוּ בְּנֵי־יְהוּדָה וּבְנֵי־יִשְׂרָאֵל יַחְדָּו וְשָׂמוּ לָהֶם רֹאשׁ אֶחָד
ג ד וְעָלוּ מִן־הָאָרֶץ כִּי גָדוֹל יוֹם יִזְרְעֶאל׃ אִמְרוּ לַאֲחֵיכֶם עַמִּי וְלַאֲחוֹתֵיכֶם רֻחָמָה׃ רִיבוּ בְאִמְּכֶם
ה רִיבוּ כִּי־הִיא לֹא אִשְׁתִּי וְאָנֹכִי לֹא אִישָׁהּ וְתָסֵר זְנוּנֶיהָ מִפָּנֶיהָ וְנַאֲפוּפֶיהָ מִבֵּין שָׁדֶיהָ׃ פֶּן־
אַפְשִׁיטֶנָּה עֲרֻמָּה וְהִצַּגְתִּיהָ כְּיוֹם הִוָּלְדָהּ וְשַׂמְתִּיהָ כַמִּדְבָּר וְשַׁתִּהָ כְּאֶרֶץ צִיָּה וַהֲמִתִּיהָ בַּצָּמָא׃
ו ז וְאֶת־בָּנֶיהָ לֹא אֲרַחֵם כִּי־בְנֵי זְנוּנִים הֵמָּה׃ כִּי זָנְתָה אִמָּם הֹבִישָׁה הוֹרָתָם כִּי אָמְרָה אֵלְכָה אַחֲרֵי
ח מְאַהֲבַי נֹתְנֵי לַחְמִי וּמֵימַי צַמְרִי וּפִשְׁתִּי שַׁמְנִי וְשִׁקּוּיָי׃ לָכֵן הִנְנִי־שָׂךְ אֶת־דַּרְכֵּךְ בַּסִּירִים וְגָדַרְתִּי
ט אֶת־גְּדֵרָהּ וּנְתִיבוֹתֶיהָ לֹא תִמְצָא׃ וְרִדְּפָה אֶת־מְאַהֲבֶיהָ וְלֹא־תַשִּׂיג אֹתָם וּבִקְשָׁתַם וְלֹא תִמְצָא
י וְאָמְרָה אֵלְכָה וְאָשׁוּבָה אֶל־אִישִׁי הָרִאשׁוֹן כִּי טוֹב לִי אָז מֵעָתָּה׃ וְהִיא לֹא יָדְעָה כִּי אָנֹכִי נָתַתִּי
יא לָהּ הַדָּגָן וְהַתִּירוֹשׁ וְהַיִּצְהָר וְכֶסֶף הִרְבֵּיתִי לָהּ וְזָהָב עָשׂוּ לַבָּעַל׃ לָכֵן אָשׁוּב וְלָקַחְתִּי דְגָנִי בְּעִתּוֹ

BEMIDBAR

The prophet Hoshea was active from the height of the reign of Yorovam son of Yoash king of Israel until the destruction of the northern kingdom during the reign of Hoshea son of Ela.

The relationship between God and Israel is described in this *haftara* in terms of the connection between a husband and wife. At first, the couple is in love, and they lead a charmed existence together. After a time, however, the wife betrays the husband – her adulterous affairs symbolize the Israelites' dalliance with foreign nations and gods. This betrayal leads ultimately to disaster, and all the wife's

12 it ages; I will seize My wools and My linens meant to cover her nakedness. And now I will expose her
13 indecency for her lovers to see, and there will be no one to rescue her from My hand. I will put an end
14 to all her joyous occasions – her holidays, her New Moons, her Sabbaths, and all her festive seasons. I
will ravage her vines and fig trees, of which she once said, "These are my harlot's favors, given to me by
15 my lovers." I will make them into abandoned woodlands, and wild animals will feed on them. I will re-
visit upon her the days of the Be'alim, for whom she burned incense and adorned herself with earrings
16 and jewels, how she followed after her lovers and forgot Me. So declares the Lord. Behold,
17 now I will coax her, I will lead her back to the open desert, and I will speak to her heart. Then and
there I will give her vineyards to her, and the Valley of the Scourge will be a doorway to hope; she will
return to Me in song as in the first days of her youth, as on the day when she came up out of the land of
18 Egypt. It will be on that day, says the Lord: you will call Me "my Husband"; no longer will
19 you call Me "my Master." I will eradicate the names of the Be'alim from her mouth; no more will they
20 be mentioned by name. On that day I will make a covenant with them: with the beasts of the fields,
and the birds of heaven, and the crawling creatures of the ground. I will break the bow and the sword; I
21 will crush conflict out from the land, and you will rest in safety. I will betroth you to Me forever; I will
22 betroth you to Me in righteousness and justice, in kindness and compassion. I will betroth you to Me
in faithfulness, and you will know the Lord.

Haftarat Naso

13 2 There was a man of Tzora whose name was Manoaḥ, from the family of Dan. His wife was barren and JUDGES
3 had never given birth. An angel of the Lord appeared to the woman and said to her: "Look! Though
4 you have been barren and have never given birth, you shall conceive and bear a son. Take care: drink
5 neither wine nor strong drink, and eat nothing unclean. For indeed, you shall be with child; you shall
bear a son. Let no razor touch his head, for the boy shall be a nazirite to God from the womb. He will
6 begin to save Israel from the hands of the Philistines." The woman went and told her husband, "A man
of God came to me; he looked like an angel of God – dazzling, awe-inspiring. I did not ask him where
7 he was from, and he did not tell me his name. He said to me, 'You shall be with child, and you shall bear
a son; drink neither wine nor strong drink and eat nothing unclean, for the boy will be a nazirite to the
Lord from the womb until his dying day.'"
8 Then Manoaḥ appealed to the Lord. "Please, my Lord," he said, "let the man of God whom You sent
9 come to us again and teach us what to do with the boy who will be born." God heard Manoaḥ's voice,
and God's angel came to the woman once more. She was sitting in the field, her husband Manoaḥ not
10 with her. The woman rushed to tell her husband. "Look!" she said to him. "The man who came to
11 visit me that day has appeared!" Manoaḥ rose and followed his wife. When he reached the man, he
12 said to him, "Are you the man who spoke to this woman?" "I am," he said. "Now," said Manoaḥ, "may

---

and deliberation. Therefore, even before Shimshon was born, when he was in his mother's womb, she was commanded to take on the ascetic restrictions of a nazirite. Shimshon himself would grow up as a nazirite and would be subject to the restrictions of that status all his life, in order to constantly be reminded of the source and purpose of his great strength. When his long hair, the symbol of his dedication, is removed, his strength will also dissipate. A nazirite, therefore, is one who takes concrete steps to dedicate his or her powers to a higher purpose.

יב וְתִירוֹשִׁי בְּמוֹעֲדוֹ וְהִצַּלְתִּי צַמְרִי וּפִשְׁתִּי לְכַסּוֹת אֶת־עֶרְוָתָהּ: וְעַתָּה אֲגַלֶּה אֶת־נַבְלֻתָהּ לְעֵינֵי
יג מְאַהֲבֶיהָ וְאִישׁ לֹא־יַצִּילֶנָּה מִיָּדִי: וְהִשְׁבַּתִּי כָּל־מְשׂוֹשָׂהּ חַגָּהּ חָדְשָׁהּ וְשַׁבַּתָּהּ וְכֹל מוֹעֲדָהּ:
יד וַהֲשִׁמֹּתִי גַּפְנָהּ וּתְאֵנָתָהּ אֲשֶׁר אָמְרָה אֶתְנָה הֵמָּה לִי אֲשֶׁר נָתְנוּ־לִי מְאַהֲבָי וְשַׂמְתִּים לְיַעַר וַאֲכָלָתַם
טו חַיַּת הַשָּׂדֶה: וּפָקַדְתִּי עָלֶיהָ אֶת־יְמֵי הַבְּעָלִים אֲשֶׁר תַּקְטִיר לָהֶם וַתַּעַד נִזְמָהּ וְחֶלְיָתָהּ וַתֵּלֶךְ אַחֲרֵי
טז מְאַהֲבֶיהָ וְאֹתִי שָׁכְחָה נְאֻם־יהוה: לָכֵן הִנֵּה אָנֹכִי מְפַתֶּיהָ וְהֹלַכְתִּיהָ הַמִּדְבָּר וְדִבַּרְתִּי עַל־
יז לִבָּהּ: וְנָתַתִּי לָהּ אֶת־כְּרָמֶיהָ מִשָּׁם וְאֶת־עֵמֶק עָכוֹר לְפֶתַח תִּקְוָה וְעָנְתָה שָּׁמָּה כִּימֵי נְעוּרֶיהָ וּכְיוֹם
יח עֲלוֹתָהּ מֵאֶרֶץ־מִצְרָיִם: וְהָיָה בַיּוֹם־הַהוּא נְאֻם־יהוה תִּקְרְאִי אִישִׁי וְלֹא־תִקְרְאִי־לִי עוֹד
יט כ בַּעְלִי: וַהֲסִרֹתִי אֶת־שְׁמוֹת הַבְּעָלִים מִפִּיהָ וְלֹא־יִזָּכְרוּ עוֹד בִּשְׁמָם: וְכָרַתִּי לָהֶם בְּרִית בַּיּוֹם הַהוּא עִם־
חַיַּת הַשָּׂדֶה וְעִם־עוֹף הַשָּׁמַיִם וְרֶמֶשׂ הָאֲדָמָה וְקֶשֶׁת וְחֶרֶב וּמִלְחָמָה אֶשְׁבּוֹר מִן־הָאָרֶץ וְהִשְׁכַּבְתִּים
כא כב לָבֶטַח: וְאֵרַשְׂתִּיךְ לִי לְעוֹלָם וְאֵרַשְׂתִּיךְ לִי בְּצֶדֶק וּבְמִשְׁפָּט וּבְחֶסֶד וּבְרַחֲמִים: וְאֵרַשְׂתִּיךְ לִי בֶּאֱמוּנָה
וְיָדַעַתְּ אֶת־יהוה:

הפטרת נשא

שופטים

יג ב ג וַיְהִי אִישׁ אֶחָד מִצָּרְעָה מִמִּשְׁפַּחַת הַדָּנִי וּשְׁמוֹ מָנוֹחַ וְאִשְׁתּוֹ עֲקָרָה וְלֹא יָלָדָה: וַיֵּרָא מַלְאַךְ־יהוה אֶל־
ד הָאִשָּׁה וַיֹּאמֶר אֵלֶיהָ הִנֵּה־נָא אַתְּ־עֲקָרָה וְלֹא יָלַדְתְּ וְהָרִית וְיָלַדְתְּ בֵּן: וְעַתָּה הִשָּׁמְרִי נָא וְאַל־תִּשְׁתִּי
ה יַיִן וְשֵׁכָר וְאַל־תֹּאכְלִי כָּל־טָמֵא: כִּי הִנָּךְ הָרָה וְיֹלַדְתְּ בֵּן וּמוֹרָה לֹא־יַעֲלֶה עַל־רֹאשׁוֹ כִּי־נְזִיר אֱלֹהִים
ו יִהְיֶה הַנַּעַר מִן־הַבָּטֶן וְהוּא יָחֵל לְהוֹשִׁיעַ אֶת־יִשְׂרָאֵל מִיַּד פְּלִשְׁתִּים: וַתָּבֹא הָאִשָּׁה וַתֹּאמֶר לְאִישָׁהּ
לֵאמֹר אִישׁ הָאֱלֹהִים בָּא אֵלַי וּמַרְאֵהוּ כְּמַרְאֵה מַלְאַךְ הָאֱלֹהִים נוֹרָא מְאֹד וְלֹא שְׁאִלְתִּיהוּ אֵי־מִזֶּה
ז הוּא וְאֶת־שְׁמוֹ לֹא־הִגִּיד לִי: וַיֹּאמֶר לִי הִנָּךְ הָרָה וְיֹלַדְתְּ בֵּן וְעַתָּה אַל־תִּשְׁתִּי ׀ יַיִן וְשֵׁכָר וְאַל־תֹּאכְלִי
כָּל־טֻמְאָה כִּי־נְזִיר אֱלֹהִים יִהְיֶה הַנַּעַר מִן־הַבֶּטֶן עַד־יוֹם מוֹתוֹ:
ח וַיֶּעְתַּר מָנוֹחַ אֶל־יהוה וַיֹּאמַר בִּי אֲדוֹנָי אִישׁ הָאֱלֹהִים אֲשֶׁר שָׁלַחְתָּ יָבוֹא־נָא עוֹד אֵלֵינוּ וְיוֹרֵנוּ
ט מַה־נַּעֲשֶׂה לַנַּעַר הַיּוּלָּד: וַיִּשְׁמַע הָאֱלֹהִים בְּקוֹל מָנוֹחַ וַיָּבֹא מַלְאַךְ הָאֱלֹהִים עוֹד אֶל־הָאִשָּׁה וְהִיא
י יוֹשֶׁבֶת בַּשָּׂדֶה וּמָנוֹחַ אִישָׁהּ אֵין עִמָּהּ: וַתְּמַהֵר הָאִשָּׁה וַתָּרָץ וַתַּגֵּד לְאִישָׁהּ וַתֹּאמֶר אֵלָיו הִנֵּה
יא נִרְאָה אֵלַי הָאִישׁ אֲשֶׁר־בָּא בַיּוֹם אֵלָי: וַיָּקָם וַיֵּלֶךְ מָנוֹחַ אַחֲרֵי אִשְׁתּוֹ וַיָּבֹא אֶל־הָאִישׁ וַיֹּאמֶר לוֹ
יב הַאַתָּה הָאִישׁ אֲשֶׁר־דִּבַּרְתָּ אֶל־הָאִשָּׁה וַיֹּאמֶר אָנִי: וַיֹּאמֶר מָנוֹחַ עַתָּה יָבֹא דְבָרֶיךָ מַה־יִּהְיֶה מִשְׁפַּט־

NASO

This *haftara* describes the events leading up to the birth of the judge Shimshon. Shimshon's mother was barren, and at that point in time the Israelites were dominated by the Philistines. Everything changes when one day an angel appears to Shimshon's parents, heralding to them the birth of a son who will in the future save Israel from their Philistine oppressors. Shimshon will be blessed with unnatural strength that will aid him in overcoming the enemy. But one given so much power must also act with supreme caution

13 your words come to pass. How should the boy be properly dealt with?" The LORD's angel replied to
14 Manoaḥ, "The woman must be kept from all that I said to her. She must eat nothing derived from
the grapevine, drink neither wine nor strong drink, and eat nothing unclean; she must follow all my
15 instructions." Manoaḥ said to the LORD's angel, "Please let us detain you, and we will prepare a young
16 goat for you." "Even if you detain me, I will not eat your food," the LORD's angel said to Manoaḥ, "but
if you prepare a burnt offering, offer it to the LORD." For Manoaḥ did not realize that he was an angel
17 of the LORD. "What is your name," Manoaḥ asked the LORD's angel, "so that when your words come
18 to pass, we may honor you?" "Why should you ask my name?" the LORD's angel replied to him. "For
19 it is wondrous." Manoaḥ took the young goat and the grain offering and offered them up on the rock
20 to the LORD. As Manoaḥ and his wife were watching, He performed wonders: as the flames flared up
from the altar to the heavens, the LORD's angel ascended in the altar's flames while Manoaḥ and his
21 wife were watching. They threw themselves down with their faces to the ground. When the LORD's
angel did not appear again to Manoaḥ and his wife, Manoaḥ realized that he had been an angel of the
22 LORD. "We will surely die," Manoaḥ said to his wife, "for it was God we saw!" "Had the LORD wanted
23 to kill us," his wife said to him, "He would not have accepted burnt offerings or grain offerings from us.
24 And He would not have shown us all that we saw or made this announcement." The woman bore a son
25 and named him Shimshon. The boy grew up and the LORD blessed him.* The spirit of the LORD first *Yemenites end here*
stirred him in the Dan encampment between Tzora and Eshtaol.

HAFTARAT BEHAALOTEKHA

2 14 Shout out and be joyful, daughter Zion, for I am coming, and I will dwell in your midst – the LORD ZECHARIAH
15 has spoken. Many nations will join themselves to the LORD on that day, and they will be My people.
16 I will dwell in your midst, and you will know that the LORD of Hosts sent me to you. The LORD will
take possession of Yehuda as His portion of holy ground, and He will choose Jerusalem once again.
3 17 1 Hush, all flesh, before the LORD, for He has stirred from His holy abode. Then He showed
me Yehoshua the High Priest standing before an angel of the LORD with the Adversary on his right to
2 oppose him. The LORD said to the Adversary: The LORD drives you away, Adversary. The LORD, who
3 has chosen Jerusalem, drives you away. Yes, this is a firebrand saved from the fire. And Yehoshua, wear-
4 ing filthy clothing, was standing before the angel, who spoke and said to those standing before him,
"Take those filthy clothes off him." Then the angel said to him, "See, I have removed your guilt from
5 you and dressed you in finery." I said, "Place a pure turban on his head," and they placed a pure turban
6 on his head. They dressed him in clothing. The angel of the LORD remained standing. Then that angel
7 of the LORD testified regarding Yehoshua: "So says the LORD of Hosts: If you walk in My ways, if you
keep My watch, if you judge My House, and guard My courtyards, then I will give you walkers among
8 these who are standing. Listen, Yehoshua the High Priest, you and your friends who sit before you, for
9 they are men of wonders: Behold, I am bringing My servant Tzemaḥ. Upon the stone that I set before

---

preaching God's message, put life into the long-stymied project. The prophet described to them the many obstacles on the path to redemption, and to this end he describes his famous vision of the candelabrum. The candelabrum – the source of light – has become a quintessential Jewish symbol, and it traces the path from the Tabernacle to Shlomo's Temple, to the new structure that was to be built.

יג יד הַנַּעַר וּמַעֲשֵׂהוּ׃ וַיֹּאמֶר מַלְאַךְ יְהוָה אֶל־מָנוֹחַ מִכֹּל אֲשֶׁר־אָמַרְתִּי אֶל־הָאִשָּׁה תִּשָּׁמֵר׃ מִכֹּל אֲשֶׁר־
יֵצֵא מִגֶּפֶן הַיַּיִן לֹא תֹאכַל וְיַיִן וְשֵׁכָר אַל־תֵּשְׁתְּ וְכָל־טֻמְאָה אַל־תֹּאכַל כֹּל אֲשֶׁר־צִוִּיתִיהָ תִּשְׁמֹר׃
טו טז וַיֹּאמֶר מָנוֹחַ אֶל־מַלְאַךְ יְהוָה נַעְצְרָה־נָּא אוֹתָךְ וְנַעֲשֶׂה לְפָנֶיךָ גְּדִי עִזִּים׃ וַיֹּאמֶר מַלְאַךְ יְהוָה אֶל־מָנוֹחַ
אִם־תַּעְצְרֵנִי לֹא־אֹכַל בְּלַחְמֶךָ וְאִם־תַּעֲשֶׂה עֹלָה לַיהוָה תַּעֲלֶנָּה כִּי לֹא־יָדַע מָנוֹחַ כִּי־מַלְאַךְ יְהוָה
יז יח הוּא׃ וַיֹּאמֶר מָנוֹחַ אֶל־מַלְאַךְ יְהוָה מִי שְׁמֶךָ כִּי־יָבֹא דבריך וְכִבַּדְנוּךָ׃ וַיֹּאמֶר לוֹ מַלְאַךְ יְהוָה לָמָּה זֶּה דְבָרְךָ
יט תִּשְׁאַל לִשְׁמִי וְהוּא־פֶלִאי׃ וַיִּקַּח מָנוֹחַ אֶת־גְּדִי הָעִזִּים וְאֶת־הַמִּנְחָה וַיַּעַל עַל־הַצּוּר לַיהוָה וּמַפְלִא
כ לַעֲשׂוֹת וּמָנוֹחַ וְאִשְׁתּוֹ רֹאִים׃ וַיְהִי בַעֲלוֹת הַלַּהַב מֵעַל הַמִּזְבֵּחַ הַשָּׁמַיְמָה וַיַּעַל מַלְאַךְ־יְהוָה בְּלַהַב
כא הַמִּזְבֵּחַ וּמָנוֹחַ וְאִשְׁתּוֹ רֹאִים וַיִּפְּלוּ עַל־פְּנֵיהֶם אָרְצָה׃ וְלֹא־יָסַף עוֹד מַלְאַךְ יְהוָה לְהֵרָאֹה אֶל־מָנוֹחַ
כב וְאֶל־אִשְׁתּוֹ אָז יָדַע מָנוֹחַ כִּי־מַלְאַךְ יְהוָה הוּא׃ וַיֹּאמֶר מָנוֹחַ אֶל־אִשְׁתּוֹ מוֹת נָמוּת כִּי אֱלֹהִים רָאִינוּ׃
כג וַתֹּאמֶר לוֹ אִשְׁתּוֹ לוּ חָפֵץ יְהוָה לַהֲמִיתֵנוּ לֹא־לָקַח מִיָּדֵנוּ עֹלָה וּמִנְחָה וְלֹא הֶרְאָנוּ אֶת־כָּל־אֵלֶּה וְכָעֵת
כד כה לֹא הִשְׁמִיעָנוּ כָּזֹאת׃ וַתֵּלֶד הָאִשָּׁה בֵּן וַתִּקְרָא אֶת־שְׁמוֹ שִׁמְשׁוֹן וַיִּגְדַּל הַנַּעַר וַיְבָרְכֵהוּ יְהוָה׃* וַתָּחֶל *Yemenites end here*
רוּחַ יְהוָה לְפַעֲמוֹ בְּמַחֲנֵה־דָן בֵּין צָרְעָה וּבֵין אֶשְׁתָּאֹל׃

הפטרת בהעלתך

ב יד טו רָנִּי וְשִׂמְחִי בַּת־צִיּוֹן כִּי הִנְנִי־בָא וְשָׁכַנְתִּי בְתוֹכֵךְ נְאֻם־יְהוָה׃ וְנִלְווּ גוֹיִם רַבִּים אֶל־יְהוָה בַּיּוֹם הַהוּא זכריה
טז וְהָיוּ לִי לְעָם וְשָׁכַנְתִּי בְתוֹכֵךְ וְיָדַעַתְּ כִּי־יְהוָה צְבָאוֹת שְׁלָחַנִי אֵלָיִךְ׃ וְנָחַל יְהוָה אֶת־יְהוּדָה חֶלְקוֹ עַל
ג יז א אַדְמַת הַקֹּדֶשׁ וּבָחַר עוֹד בִּירוּשָׁלִָם׃ הַס כָּל־בָּשָׂר מִפְּנֵי יְהוָה כִּי נֵעוֹר מִמְּעוֹן קָדְשׁוֹ׃ וַיַּרְאֵנִי
ב אֶת־יְהוֹשֻׁעַ הַכֹּהֵן הַגָּדוֹל עֹמֵד לִפְנֵי מַלְאַךְ יְהוָה וְהַשָּׂטָן עֹמֵד עַל־יְמִינוֹ לְשִׂטְנוֹ׃ וַיֹּאמֶר יְהוָה אֶל־
ג הַשָּׂטָן יִגְעַר יְהוָה בְּךָ הַשָּׂטָן וְיִגְעַר יְהוָה בְּךָ הַבֹּחֵר בִּירוּשָׁלִָם הֲלוֹא זֶה אוּד מֻצָּל מֵאֵשׁ׃ וִיהוֹשֻׁעַ
ד הָיָה לָבֻשׁ בְּגָדִים צוֹאִים וְעֹמֵד לִפְנֵי הַמַּלְאָךְ׃ וַיַּעַן וַיֹּאמֶר אֶל־הָעֹמְדִים לְפָנָיו לֵאמֹר הָסִירוּ הַבְּגָדִים
ה הַצֹּאִים מֵעָלָיו וַיֹּאמֶר אֵלָיו רְאֵה הֶעֱבַרְתִּי מֵעָלֶיךָ עֲוֺנֶךָ וְהַלְבֵּשׁ אֹתְךָ מַחֲלָצוֹת׃ וָאֹמַר יָשִׂימוּ צָנִיף
ו טָהוֹר עַל־רֹאשׁוֹ וַיָּשִׂימוּ הַצָּנִיף הַטָּהוֹר עַל־רֹאשׁוֹ וַיַּלְבִּשֻׁהוּ בְּגָדִים וּמַלְאַךְ יְהוָה עֹמֵד׃ וַיָּעַד מַלְאַךְ
ז יְהוָה בִּיהוֹשֻׁעַ לֵאמֹר׃ כֹּה־אָמַר יְהוָה צְבָאוֹת אִם־בִּדְרָכַי תֵּלֵךְ וְאִם אֶת־מִשְׁמַרְתִּי תִשְׁמֹר וְגַם־אַתָּה
ח תָּדִין אֶת־בֵּיתִי וְגַם תִּשְׁמֹר אֶת־חֲצֵרָי וְנָתַתִּי לְךָ מַהְלְכִים בֵּין הָעֹמְדִים הָאֵלֶּה׃ שְׁמַע־נָא יְהוֹשֻׁעַ ׀ הַכֹּהֵן
ט הַגָּדוֹל אַתָּה וְרֵעֶיךָ הַיֹּשְׁבִים לְפָנֶיךָ כִּי־אַנְשֵׁי מוֹפֵת הֵמָּה כִּי־הִנְנִי מֵבִיא אֶת־עַבְדִּי צֶמַח׃ כִּי ׀ הִנֵּה הָאֶבֶן
אֲשֶׁר נָתַתִּי לִפְנֵי יְהוֹשֻׁעַ עַל־אֶבֶן אַחַת שִׁבְעָה עֵינָיִם הִנְנִי מְפַתֵּחַ פִּתֻּחָהּ נְאֻם יְהוָה צְבָאוֹת וּמַשְׁתִּי

BEHAALOTEKHA

The prophet Zekharya was active in Jerusalem in the second year of the reign of Daryavesh, king of Persia. He gave strength and encouragement to the returnees to Zion after the Babylonian exile, urging them to rebuild the Temple. The construction, which was expressly authorized by the decree of the emperor Koresh, was frozen by the Persian government soon after the cornerstone had been laid, due to lobbying by the enemy nations bordering the Jews in the province of Judea. Zekharya's tireless involvement,

Yehoshua, one stone with seven eyes, I will engrave its inscription, and I will wipe away the guilt of
10 this land in one day. On that day – the LORD of Hosts has spoken – you will call one to another: Come
4 1 under the shade of the vine; come under the shade of the fig." Then the angel with whom I
2 had spoken returned and roused me like a man stirring from his sleep. He said to me, "What do you
see?" I said, "I see a candelabrum of pure gold, its bowl at the top. It has seven lamps – seven – and
3 seven indentations for the lamps, which are at the top. Next to it are two olive trees, one to the right
4 of the bowl and one to its left." I spoke and said to the angel with whom I spoke, "What are these, my
5 lord?" And the angel with whom I spoke replied and said, "You know what these are." I said, "No, my
6 lord." Then he spoke and said to me, "This is the word of the LORD to Zerubavel: Not with valor and
7 not with strength, but with My spirit, says the LORD of Hosts. Who are you, great mountain before
Zerubavel? Surely it will become a level plain. He will remove the re-foundation stone with clamor:
8 9 Favor, favor to her!" *Then the word of the Lord came to me: "Zerubavel's hands founded *Yemenites add*
this House, and his hands will complete it.

Haftarat Shelaḥ

2 1 Yehoshua son of Nun had sent two men as spies from Shitim, in secret: "Go forth and survey the land JOSHUA
and the region of Yeriḥo." So the men had set out, arriving at the house of a harlot named Raḥav, where
2 they lay down for the night. And word reached the king of Yeriḥo: "Listen, people have come here
3 tonight – Israelites – to probe the land." The king of Yeriḥo sent word to Raḥav: "Bring out those men
4 who came to you, who arrived at your house, for they have come to probe the land." Now, the woman
had taken the two men and hidden them, and she replied, "Yes, men came to me, but I did not know
5 where they were from. Just as the gate was being closed at nightfall, the men left, and I do not know
6 where they went. Go after them quickly, for you can overtake them." She had taken the spies up to the
7 roof and hidden them amongst the stalks of flax she had laid out on the roof. The king's men ran after
them toward the Jordan route, over the river fords; and the moment the pursuers left, the gate was
8 9 closed behind them. They were not yet asleep when she went up to them on the roof. "I know that the
LORD has given you the land," she said to the men, "and that dread of you has fallen upon us; for all
10 the inhabitants of the land quake before you. For we have heard that the LORD dried up the waters of
the Sea of Reeds before you when you left Egypt, and we have heard what you did to the two Amorite
11 kings across the Jordan – how you utterly destroyed Siḥon and Og. We heard it and our hearts dissolved; no one has the spirit to face you, for the LORD your God is God of heaven above and earth be-
12 low. Now, please swear to me by the LORD – for I have shown you loyalty – that you, too, will be loyal
13 to my father's house. Give me a true sign that you will spare my father and mother and my brothers
14 and sisters and all that is theirs. Please, save our souls from death!" The men replied to her, "We pledge
to die in your place, if you speak no word of this, and when the LORD gives us the land, we will show

Jordan moved to the front of the battle lines, and Yehoshua sent two spies to study the environs of Yeriḥo. This third tactic is the subject of our *haftara*.

The collection of intelligence must follow specific guidelines. Only the political-military leader (Yehoshua) can be the one to send spies, and the information must go back to him alone. Competent intelligence gatherers must operate in absolute secrecy. Yehoshua's spies were well trained and mission focused, and so even after their expedition encountered difficulties they were able to complete it successfully.

י אֶת־עֲוֺן הָאָרֶץ־הַהִיא בְּיוֹם אֶחָד׃ בַּיּוֹם הַהוּא נְאֻם יְהוָה צְבָאוֹת תִּקְרְאוּ אִישׁ לְרֵעֵהוּ אֶל־תַּחַת גֶּפֶן
ד א ב וְאֶל־תַּחַת תְּאֵנָה׃ וַיָּשָׁב הַמַּלְאָךְ הַדֹּבֵר בִּי וַיְעִירֵנִי כְּאִישׁ אֲשֶׁר־יֵעוֹר מִשְּׁנָתוֹ׃ וַיֹּאמֶר אֵלַי
מָה אַתָּה רֹאֶה ויאמר רָאִיתִי וְהִנֵּה מְנוֹרַת זָהָב כֻּלָּהּ וְגֻלָּהּ עַל־רֹאשָׁהּ וְשִׁבְעָה נֵרֹתֶיהָ עָלֶיהָ שִׁבְעָה וָאֹמַר
ג וְשִׁבְעָה מוּצָקוֹת לַנֵּרוֹת אֲשֶׁר עַל־רֹאשָׁהּ׃ וּשְׁנַיִם זֵיתִים עָלֶיהָ אֶחָד מִימִין הַגֻּלָּה וְאֶחָד עַל־שְׂמֹאלָהּ׃
ד ה וָאַעַן וָאֹמַר אֶל־הַמַּלְאָךְ הַדֹּבֵר בִּי לֵאמֹר מָה־אֵלֶּה אֲדֹנִי׃ וַיַּעַן הַמַּלְאָךְ הַדֹּבֵר בִּי וַיֹּאמֶר אֵלַי הֲלוֹא
ו יָדַעְתָּ מָה־הֵמָּה אֵלֶּה וָאֹמַר לֹא אֲדֹנִי׃ וַיַּעַן וַיֹּאמֶר אֵלַי לֵאמֹר זֶה דְּבַר־יְהוָה אֶל־זְרֻבָּבֶל לֵאמֹר לֹא
ז בְחַיִל וְלֹא בְכֹחַ כִּי אִם־בְּרוּחִי אָמַר יְהוָה צְבָאוֹת׃ מִי־אַתָּה הַר־הַגָּדוֹל לִפְנֵי זְרֻבָּבֶל לְמִישֹׁר וְהוֹצִיא
ח ט אֶת־הָאֶבֶן הָרֹאשָׁה תְּשֻׁאוֹת חֵן ׀ חֵן לָהּ׃ *וַיְהִי דְבַר־יְהוָה אֵלַי לֵאמֹר׃ יְדֵי זְרֻבָּבֶל יִסְּדוּ הַבַּיִת *Yemenites add*
הַזֶּה וְיָדָיו תְּבַצַּעְנָה וְיָדַעְתָּ כִּי־יְהוָה צְבָאוֹת שְׁלָחַנִי אֲלֵיכֶם׃

הפטרת שלח

ב א וַיִּשְׁלַח יְהוֹשֻׁעַ בִּן־נוּן מִן־הַשִּׁטִּים שְׁנַיִם אֲנָשִׁים מְרַגְּלִים חֶרֶשׁ לֵאמֹר לְכוּ רְאוּ אֶת־הָאָרֶץ וְאֶת־ יהושע
ב יְרִיחוֹ וַיֵּלְכוּ וַיָּבֹאוּ בֵּית אִשָּׁה זוֹנָה וּשְׁמָהּ רָחָב וַיִּשְׁכְּבוּ־שָׁמָּה׃ וַיֵּאָמַר לְמֶלֶךְ יְרִיחוֹ לֵאמֹר הִנֵּה
ג אֲנָשִׁים בָּאוּ הֵנָּה הַלַּיְלָה מִבְּנֵי יִשְׂרָאֵל לַחְפֹּר אֶת־הָאָרֶץ׃ וַיִּשְׁלַח מֶלֶךְ יְרִיחוֹ אֶל־רָחָב לֵאמֹר הוֹצִיאִי
ד הָאֲנָשִׁים הַבָּאִים אֵלַיִךְ אֲשֶׁר־בָּאוּ לְבֵיתֵךְ כִּי לַחְפֹּר אֶת־כָּל־הָאָרֶץ בָּאוּ׃ וַתִּקַּח הָאִשָּׁה אֶת־שְׁנֵי
ה הָאֲנָשִׁים וַתִּצְפְּנוֹ וַתֹּאמֶר כֵּן בָּאוּ אֵלַי הָאֲנָשִׁים וְלֹא יָדַעְתִּי מֵאַיִן הֵמָּה׃ וַיְהִי הַשַּׁעַר לִסְגּוֹר בַּחֹשֶׁךְ
ו וְהָאֲנָשִׁים יָצָאוּ לֹא יָדַעְתִּי אָנָה הָלְכוּ הָאֲנָשִׁים רִדְפוּ מַהֵר אַחֲרֵיהֶם כִּי תַשִּׂיגוּם׃ וְהִיא הֶעֱלָתַם הַגָּגָה
ז וַתִּטְמְנֵם בְּפִשְׁתֵּי הָעֵץ הָעֲרֻכוֹת לָהּ עַל־הַגָּג׃ וְהָאֲנָשִׁים רָדְפוּ אַחֲרֵיהֶם דֶּרֶךְ הַיַּרְדֵּן עַל הַמַּעְבְּרוֹת
ח וְהַשַּׁעַר סָגָרוּ אַחֲרֵי כַּאֲשֶׁר יָצְאוּ הָרֹדְפִים אַחֲרֵיהֶם׃ וְהֵמָּה טֶרֶם יִשְׁכָּבוּן וְהִיא עָלְתָה עֲלֵיהֶם עַל־
ט הַגָּג׃ וַתֹּאמֶר אֶל־הָאֲנָשִׁים יָדַעְתִּי כִּי־נָתַן יְהוָה לָכֶם אֶת־הָאָרֶץ וְכִי־נָפְלָה אֵימַתְכֶם עָלֵינוּ וְכִי נָמֹגוּ
י כָּל־יֹשְׁבֵי הָאָרֶץ מִפְּנֵיכֶם׃ כִּי שָׁמַעְנוּ אֵת אֲשֶׁר־הוֹבִישׁ יְהוָה אֶת־מֵי יַם־סוּף מִפְּנֵיכֶם בְּצֵאתְכֶם
מִמִּצְרָיִם וַאֲשֶׁר עֲשִׂיתֶם לִשְׁנֵי מַלְכֵי הָאֱמֹרִי אֲשֶׁר בְּעֵבֶר הַיַּרְדֵּן לְסִיחֹן וּלְעוֹג אֲשֶׁר הַחֲרַמְתֶּם אוֹתָם׃
יא וַנִּשְׁמַע וַיִּמַּס לְבָבֵנוּ וְלֹא־קָמָה עוֹד רוּחַ בְּאִישׁ מִפְּנֵיכֶם כִּי יְהוָה אֱלֹהֵיכֶם הוּא אֱלֹהִים בַּשָּׁמַיִם מִמַּעַל
יב וְעַל־הָאָרֶץ מִתָּחַת׃ וְעַתָּה הִשָּׁבְעוּ־נָא לִי בַּיהוָה כִּי־עָשִׂיתִי עִמָּכֶם חָסֶד וַעֲשִׂיתֶם גַּם־אַתֶּם עִם־בֵּית
יג אָבִי חֶסֶד וּנְתַתֶּם לִי אוֹת אֱמֶת׃ וְהַחֲיִתֶם אֶת־אָבִי וְאֶת־אִמִּי וְאֶת־אַחַי וְאֶת־אחותי וְאֵת כָּל־אֲשֶׁר לָהֶם אַחְיוֹתַי
יד וְהִצַּלְתֶּם אֶת־נַפְשֹׁתֵינוּ מִמָּוֶת׃ וַיֹּאמְרוּ לָהּ הָאֲנָשִׁים נַפְשֵׁנוּ תַחְתֵּיכֶם לָמוּת אִם לֹא תַגִּידוּ אֶת־דְּבָרֵנוּ

SHELAḤ
The events of this *haftara* took place between the seventh and the tenth of Nisan in the fortieth year after the exodus from Egypt, after the mourning period for Moshe had ended. At this point, the nation was occupying the plains of Moav, on the eastern side of the Jordan River, opposite Yeriḥo. God's instructions to Yehoshua to prepare for crossing into the land of Israel were followed on three planes: the nation as a whole prepared for the crossing; the vanguard troops from the tribes that would settle the east bank of the

15 you true loyalty." She let them down by a rope through the window, for her house was built into the
16 city wall; she lived inside the wall. "Flee toward the hills," she said to them, "lest the pursuers run into
17 you. Hide there for three days until the pursuers have returned; only then be on your way." They said to
18 her, "We will be free of this oath you have sworn us to unless, when we come back to the land, you tie
this scarlet thread in the window you let us down from. Bring your father, your mother, your siblings,
19 and all your father's household into your home. If anyone ventures outside the doors of your house,
his blood will be upon his own head – we will be free of blame – while if a hand is laid on anyone who
20 remains in the house with you, his blood shall be upon ours. But if you speak a word of this, we shall
21 be free of the oath we swore to you." "As you say, so be it," she said, and she sent them away. They left,
22 and she tied the scarlet thread in the window. They set out and arrived at the hills. They stayed there for
three days until the pursuers turned back, for the pursuers had searched the entire route but failed to
23 find them. The two men then went back, descended the hills, and crossed over. They came to Yehoshua
24 son of Nun and reported all that had befallen them. "The LORD has delivered the whole land into our
hands," they said to Yehoshua, "and what is more, all the people of the land quake before us."

HAFTARAT KORAḤ

On Rosh Ḥodesh Tamuz read the maftir from Numbers 28:9–15, and the haftara on page 1635.

11 14 And Shmuel said to the people, "Come, let us go to Gilgal, and we will renew the kingship there." I SAMUEL
15 All the people went to Gilgal, and they crowned Sha'ul king there at Gilgal before the LORD. They
sacrificed peace offerings before the LORD, and Sha'ul rejoiced greatly along with all the men of
12 1 Israel. Then Shmuel addressed all of Israel. "Now, I have heeded your voices in all you said to
2 me, and I have crowned a king over you – and now, here is the king, walking before you. I have grown
old and gray, but my sons are here with you; I have been walking before you from my youth until this
3 day. Here I am – testify against me in front of the LORD and in front of His anointed – whose ox have I
seized, and whose donkey have I seized? Whom have I cheated, and whom have I oppressed, and from
4 whose hand have I taken a bribe and averted my eyes from him? Let me repay you." And they said,
5 "You have not cheated us, nor oppressed us, nor taken anything from anyone." "The LORD is witness
against you," he said to them, "and His anointed is witness on this day, that you have found nothing in
6 my possession." And it was declared, "The witness is… the LORD," Shmuel said to the people,
7 "who appointed Moshe and Aharon and brought your ancestors out of the land of Egypt. Now take
your stand, and I will plead my case with you before the LORD: all the LORD's acts of loyalty that He
8 has done for you and your ancestors. When Yaakov arrived in Egypt and your ancestors cried out to
the LORD, the LORD sent Moshe and Aharon to take them out of Egypt, and they settled them in this
9 place. But they forgot the LORD their God, and He sold them into the hands of Sisera, the general of
Ḥatzor, and into the hands of the Philistines, and into the hands of the king of Moav, who attacked
10 them. Then they cried out to the LORD. 'We have sinned,' they said, 'for we left the LORD and served

---

Shmuel stood before the people and asked: "Whose ox have I seized, and whose donkey have I seized? Whom have I cheated, and whom have I oppressed?" A leader must be able, when he retires, to stand before his subjects and say truthfully that he has not abused his position for personal gain. He must be able to say that everything he has done has been for the sake of Heaven and the community.

טו זה והיה בתת־יהוה לנו את־הארץ ועשינו עמך חסד ואמת: ותורדם בחבל בעד החלון כי ביתה
טז בקיר החומה ובחומה היא יושבת: ותאמר להם ההרה לכו פן־יפגעו בכם הרדפים ונחבתם שמה
יז שלשת ימים עד שוב הרדפים ואחר תלכו לדרככם: ויאמרו אליה האנשים נקים אנחנו משבעתך
יח הזה אשר השבעתנו: הנה אנחנו באים בארץ את־תקות חוט השני הזה תקשרי בחלון אשר
יט הורדתנו בו ואת־אביך ואת־אמך ואת־אחיך ואת כל־בית אביך תאספי אליך הביתה: והיה כל
אשר־יצא מדלתי ביתך | החוצה דמו בראשו ואנחנו נקים וכל אשר יהיה אתך בבית דמו בראשנו
כ כא אם־יד תהיה־בו: ואם־תגידי את־דברנו זה והיינו נקים משבעתך אשר השבעתנו: ותאמר כדבריכם
כב כן־הוא ותשלחם וילכו ותקשר את־תקות השני בחלון: וילכו ויבאו ההרה וישבו שם שלשת ימים
כג עד־שבו הרדפים ויבקשו הרדפים בכל־הדרך ולא מצאו: וישבו שני האנשים וירדו מההר ויעברו
כד ויבאו אל־יהושע בן־נון ויספרו־לו את כל־המצאות אותם: ויאמרו אל־יהושע כי־נתן יהוה בידנו
את־כל־הארץ וגם־נמגו כל־ישבי הארץ מפנינו:

הפטרת קרח

On ראש חודש תמוז *read the* מפטיר *from* במדבר כח, ט–טו*, and the* הפטרה *on page 1635.*

יא יד טו ויאמר שמואל אל־העם לכו ונלכה הגלגל ונחדש שם המלוכה: וילכו כל־העם הגלגל וימלכו שם שמואל א׳
את־שאול לפני יהוה בגלגל ויזבחו־שם זבחים שלמים לפני יהוה וישמח שם שאול וכל־אנשי ישראל
יב א עד־מאד: ויאמר שמואל אל־כל־ישראל הנה שמעתי בקלכם לכל אשר־אמרתם לי
ב ואמליך עליכם מלך: ועתה הנה המלך | מתהלך לפניכם ואני זקנתי ושבתי ובני הנם אתכם ואני
ג התהלכתי לפניכם מנערי עד־היום הזה: הנני ענו בי נגד יהוה ונגד משיחו את־שור | מי לקחתי
וחמור מי לקחתי ואת־מי עשקתי את־מי רצותי ומיד־מי לקחתי כפר ואעלים עיני בו ואשיב לכם:
ד ה ויאמרו לא עשקתנו ולא רצותנו ולא־לקחת מיד־איש מאומה: ויאמר אליהם עד יהוה בכם ועד
ו משיחו היום הזה כי לא מצאתם בידי מאומה ויאמר עד: ויאמר שמואל אל־העם יהוה
ז אשר עשה את־משה ואת־אהרן ואשר העלה את־אבותיכם מארץ מצרים: ועתה התיצבו ואשפטה
ח אתכם לפני יהוה את כל־צדקות יהוה אשר־עשה אתכם ואת־אבותיכם: כאשר־בא יעקב מצרים
ויזעקו אבתיכם אל־יהוה וישלח יהוה את־משה ואת־אהרן ויוציאו את־אבותיכם ממצרים וישבום
ט במקום הזה: וישכחו את־יהוה אלהיהם וימכר אתם ביד סיסרא שר־צבא חצור וביד־פלשתים
י וביד מלך מואב וילחמו בם: ויזעקו אל־יהוה ויאמר חטאנו כי עזבנו את־יהוה ונעבד את־הבעלים

KORAḤ

The prophet Shmuel founded the Israelite monarchy after 350 years of leadership by judges. The prospect of choosing a king led to a heated discussion between Shmuel and the people.

The institution of a king brings with it both advantages and dangers. The leaders of the people saw the benefits, but were unclear about the downsides, and it fell to Shmuel to explain these to them. This *haftara* is the conclusion of this discussion, wherein Shmuel passes the reins of political and military leadership to Sha'ul. Shmuel, in his summation of the events, talks about the institution of monarchy. A ruler who has amassed status and power can become intoxicated from it, endangering himself and the people in his charge.

the Be'alim and the Ashterot – oh, save us from the hands of our enemies, and we will serve You.'
11 So the LORD sent Yerubaal and Bedan and Yiftaḥ and Shmuel and saved you from the hands of the
12 enemies around you, and you dwelled in safety. But when you saw that King Naḥash of the Amonites
came upon you, you told me, 'No, we must have a king to reign over us,' though the LORD your God
13 is your King. And now, here is the king that you yourselves have chosen – that you yourselves de-
14 manded – here, the LORD has set a king over you! If you fear the LORD, then serve Him and heed His
voice, and do not spurn the word of GOD; both you and the king who reigns over you must follow the
15 LORD your God. But if you do not heed the LORD's voice and rebel against the LORD's word, then the
16 LORD's hand shall bear down against you and your ancestral houses. And now, stand by and see what
17 a tremendous feat the LORD is about to perform before your very eyes: Is it not the wheat harvest
today? I will call out to the LORD, and He will unleash thunder and rain. Then you will know, and
then you will see, how great an evil you have committed in the eyes of the LORD by asking for a king
18 for yourselves." Then Shmuel called out to the LORD, and the LORD unleashed thunder and
19 rain on that day. All the people were struck with terror of the LORD, and of Shmuel as well. And all the
people said to Shmuel, "Pray on your servants' behalf to the LORD your God so that we will not die;
20 for we have added yet another evil to all our offenses by asking for a king for ourselves." "Do
not fear, though you have done all this evil," Shmuel said to the people, "so long as you do not turn
21 away from the LORD; serve the LORD with all your heart. But do not turn away to follow futilities that
22 neither help nor save, for they are futile. For the LORD will not desert His people for the sake of His
great name, because the LORD has undertaken to make you His people.

Haftarat Ḥukat

On Rosh Ḥodesh Tamuz read the maftir from Numbers 28:9–15, and the haftara on page 1635.
When Ḥukat and Balak are read together, read the haftara on page 1599.

JUDGES

11 1 Yiftaḥ the Gileadite was a valiant warrior. He was the son of a harlot; Gilad sired Yiftaḥ, but Gilad's
2 wife bore him sons as well. When the wife's sons grew up, they drove Yiftaḥ away, telling him, "You
3 shall have no share in our father's estate, for you are the son of another woman." So Yiftaḥ fled from his
brothers; he settled in the land of Tov. Worthless men were drawn to him and went out raiding with
4 him. Time passed, and the Amonites waged war upon Israel. When the Amonites attacked
5
6 Israel, the elders of Gilad set out to bring Yiftaḥ back from the land of Tov. "Come with us," they said
7 to Yiftaḥ, "and be our commander, so that we can fight against the Amonites." "But you despised me,"
Yiftaḥ said to the elders of Gilad, "and drove me away from my father's house. Why do you come to me
8 now, when you are in trouble?" "For that reason we ourselves have come back to you now," the elders
of Gilad said to Yiftaḥ. "You shall march out with us and fight the Amonites, and you shall be the leader
9 of all the people of Gilad." "If you bring me back to fight against the Amonites," Yiftaḥ replied to the

---

knowledge of the historical circumstances of the Israelites' arrival in Canaan generations earlier and their rights to the Gilad. He had this erudition despite having been banished from his home at a young age due to a family conflict. When all efforts to arrive at a peaceful accommodation have failed, Yiftaḥ leads the Gileadites in a preemptive strike that defeats the army of Amon.

יא וְאֶת־הָעַשְׁתָּרוֹת וְעַתָּה הַצִּילֵנוּ מִיַּד אֹיְבֵינוּ וְנַעַבְדֶךָּ׃ וַיִּשְׁלַח יהוה אֶת־יְרֻבַּעַל וְאֶת־בְּדָן וְאֶת־יִפְתָּח
יב וְאֶת־שְׁמוּאֵל וַיַּצֵּל אֶתְכֶם מִיַּד אֹיְבֵיכֶם מִסָּבִיב וַתֵּשְׁבוּ בֶּטַח׃ וַתִּרְאוּ כִּי נָחָשׁ מֶלֶךְ בְּנֵי־עַמּוֹן בָּא עֲלֵיכֶם
יג וַתֹּאמְרוּ לִי לֹא כִּי־מֶלֶךְ יִמְלֹךְ עָלֵינוּ וַיהוה אֱלֹהֵיכֶם מַלְכְּכֶם׃ וְעַתָּה הִנֵּה הַמֶּלֶךְ אֲשֶׁר בְּחַרְתֶּם אֲשֶׁר
יד שְׁאֶלְתֶּם וְהִנֵּה נָתַן יהוה עֲלֵיכֶם מֶלֶךְ׃ אִם־תִּירְאוּ אֶת־יהוה וַעֲבַדְתֶּם אֹתוֹ וּשְׁמַעְתֶּם בְּקֹלוֹ וְלֹא תַמְרוּ
טו אֶת־פִּי יהוה וִהְיִתֶם גַּם־אַתֶּם וְגַם־הַמֶּלֶךְ אֲשֶׁר מָלַךְ עֲלֵיכֶם אַחַר יהוה אֱלֹהֵיכֶם׃ וְאִם־לֹא תִשְׁמְעוּ
טז בְּקוֹל יהוה וּמְרִיתֶם אֶת־פִּי יהוה וְהָיְתָה יַד־יהוה בָּכֶם וּבַאֲבֹתֵיכֶם׃ גַּם־עַתָּה הִתְיַצְּבוּ וּרְאוּ אֶת־הַדָּבָר
יז הַגָּדוֹל הַזֶּה אֲשֶׁר יהוה עֹשֶׂה לְעֵינֵיכֶם׃ הֲלוֹא קְצִיר־חִטִּים הַיּוֹם אֶקְרָא אֶל־יהוה וְיִתֵּן קֹלוֹת וּמָטָר
יח וּדְעוּ וּרְאוּ כִּי־רָעַתְכֶם רַבָּה אֲשֶׁר עֲשִׂיתֶם בְּעֵינֵי יהוה לִשְׁאוֹל לָכֶם מֶלֶךְ׃ וַיִּקְרָא שְׁמוּאֵל
יט אֶל־יהוה וַיִּתֵּן יהוה קֹלֹת וּמָטָר בַּיּוֹם הַהוּא וַיִּירָא כָל־הָעָם מְאֹד אֶת־יהוה וְאֶת־שְׁמוּאֵל׃ וַיֹּאמְרוּ
כָל־הָעָם אֶל־שְׁמוּאֵל הִתְפַּלֵּל בְּעַד־עֲבָדֶיךָ אֶל־יהוה אֱלֹהֶיךָ וְאַל־נָמוּת כִּי־יָסַפְנוּ עַל־כָּל־חַטֹּאתֵינוּ
כ רָעָה לִשְׁאֹל לָנוּ מֶלֶךְ׃ וַיֹּאמֶר שְׁמוּאֵל אֶל־הָעָם אַל־תִּירָאוּ אַתֶּם עֲשִׂיתֶם אֵת כָּל־הָרָעָה
כא הַזֹּאת אַךְ אַל־תָּסוּרוּ מֵאַחֲרֵי יהוה וַעֲבַדְתֶּם אֶת־יהוה בְּכָל־לְבַבְכֶם׃ וְלֹא תָּסוּרוּ כִּי ׀ אַחֲרֵי הַתֹּהוּ
כב אֲשֶׁר לֹא־יוֹעִילוּ וְלֹא יַצִּילוּ כִּי־תֹהוּ הֵמָּה׃ כִּי לֹא־יִטֹּשׁ יהוה אֶת־עַמּוֹ בַּעֲבוּר שְׁמוֹ הַגָּדוֹל כִּי הוֹאִיל
יהוה לַעֲשׂוֹת אֶתְכֶם לוֹ לְעָם׃

הפטרת חקת

On ראש חודש תמוז *read the* מפטיר *from* במדבר כח, ט–טו, *and the* הפטרה *on page 1635.*
When חקת *and* בלק *are read together, read the* הפטרה *on page 1599.*

יא א ב וְיִפְתָּח הַגִּלְעָדִי הָיָה גִּבּוֹר חַיִל וְהוּא בֶּן־אִשָּׁה זוֹנָה וַיּוֹלֶד גִּלְעָד אֶת־יִפְתָּח׃ וַתֵּלֶד אֵשֶׁת־גִּלְעָד לוֹ בָּנִים שופטים
ג וַיִּגְדְּלוּ בְנֵי־הָאִשָּׁה וַיְגָרְשׁוּ אֶת־יִפְתָּח וַיֹּאמְרוּ לוֹ לֹא־תִנְחַל בְּבֵית־אָבִינוּ כִּי בֶּן־אִשָּׁה אַחֶרֶת אָתָּה׃ וַיִּבְרַח
ד יִפְתָּח מִפְּנֵי אֶחָיו וַיֵּשֶׁב בְּאֶרֶץ טוֹב וַיִּתְלַקְּטוּ אֶל־יִפְתָּח אֲנָשִׁים רֵיקִים וַיֵּצְאוּ עִמּוֹ׃ וַיְהִי מִיָּמִים
ה וַיִּלָּחֲמוּ בְנֵי־עַמּוֹן עִם־יִשְׂרָאֵל׃ וַיְהִי כַּאֲשֶׁר־נִלְחֲמוּ בְנֵי־עַמּוֹן עִם־יִשְׂרָאֵל וַיֵּלְכוּ זִקְנֵי גִלְעָד לָקַחַת אֶת־
ו ז יִפְתָּח מֵאֶרֶץ טוֹב׃ וַיֹּאמְרוּ לְיִפְתָּח לְכָה וְהָיִיתָה לָּנוּ לְקָצִין וְנִלָּחֲמָה בִּבְנֵי עַמּוֹן׃ וַיֹּאמֶר יִפְתָּח לְזִקְנֵי גִלְעָד
ח הֲלֹא אַתֶּם שְׂנֵאתֶם אוֹתִי וַתְּגָרְשׁוּנִי מִבֵּית אָבִי וּמַדּוּעַ בָּאתֶם אֵלַי עַתָּה כַּאֲשֶׁר צַר לָכֶם׃ וַיֹּאמְרוּ זִקְנֵי גִלְעָד
אֶל־יִפְתָּח לָכֵן עַתָּה שַׁבְנוּ אֵלֶיךָ וְהָלַכְתָּ עִמָּנוּ וְנִלְחַמְתָּ בִּבְנֵי עַמּוֹן וְהָיִיתָ לָּנוּ לְרֹאשׁ לְכֹל יֹשְׁבֵי גִלְעָד׃
ט וַיֹּאמֶר יִפְתָּח אֶל־זִקְנֵי גִלְעָד אִם־מְשִׁיבִים אַתֶּם אוֹתִי לְהִלָּחֵם בִּבְנֵי עַמּוֹן וְנָתַן יהוה אוֹתָם לְפָנָי אָנֹכִי

ḤUKAT

During the later years of the period of the judges, the tribes of Gilad, on the eastern side of the Jordan, suffered from the aggression of the Amonites. With no central government, the tribes sought a leader with military experience that could lead them in defending themselves. Yiftaḥ had the necessary experience, and after negotiations with the tribal elders he accepts the position. He begins a parley with the kingdom of Amon, to try to convince them to leave off without bloodshed. In his arguments, we can see his thorough

10 elders of Gilad, "and the Lord delivers them to me, then I shall be your leader." The elders of Gilad said
11 to Yiftaḥ, "The Lord shall bear witness between us if we do not comply with your words." So Yiftaḥ went
with the elders of Gilad, and the people made him their head and commander. Yiftaḥ repeated all his
12 terms before the Lord at Mitzpa. Yiftaḥ sent messengers to the king of the Amonites: "What do
13 you have against us, that you came to attack our land?" The king of the Amonites replied to Yiftaḥ's messengers, "Israel seized my lands when they came out of Egypt – from the Arnon to the Yabok and up to the
14 Jordan. Now hand them back peacefully." Once again Yiftaḥ sent messengers to the king of the Amonites.
15 16 "Thus says Yiftaḥ," they said. "Israel did not seize the land of Moav nor the land of the Amonites. For
when they came out of Egypt, Israel trekked through the wilderness to the Sea of Reeds, then they ar-
17 rived at Kadesh. And Israel sent messengers to the king of Edom, saying, 'Please let us pass through your
land,' but the king of Edom would not listen; they also reached out to the king of Moav, but he would not
18 comply. So Israel remained in Kadesh. They trekked through the wilderness, making their way around
the land of Edom and the land of Moav until they reached the eastern side of the land of Moav, where
they encamped across the Arnon. They did not enter Moabite territory, for the Arnon is the Moabite bor-
19 der. Then Israel sent messengers to Siḥon, king of the Amorites, the king of Ḥeshbon. Israel said to him,
20 'Please, let us pass through your land to our own place.' But Siḥon did not trust Israel to pass through his
21 territory. And Siḥon assembled all his troops, encamped at Yahtza, and attacked Israel. The Lord, God
of Israel, delivered Siḥon and all of his people into Israel's hands; they defeated them, and the Israelites
22 took possession of the entire land of the Amorites, who lived in that land. They took possession of all the
23 Amorite territory from Arnon to the Yabok, and from the wilderness to the Jordan. Now, the Lord, God
24 of Israel, dispossessed the Amorites before His people, Israel – why should you possess it? You take possession of what Kemosh, your god, grants you, and we will take possession of everything the Lord, our
25 God, grants us. Now, are you any better than Balak son of Tzipor, king of Moav? Did he pick a quarrel with
26 Israel? Did he wage war against them? Israel has been dwelling in Ḥeshbon and its boroughs, Aroer and
its boroughs, and in all the towns near Arnon, for three hundred years – why have you not reclaimed them
27 all this time? I have never offended you, yet you do me wrong by fighting against me. May the Lord, who
28 judges, judge between the Israelites and the Amonites today." But the king of the Amonites did not listen
29 to the words Yiftaḥ delivered to him. The spirit of the Lord settled upon Yiftaḥ, and he crossed
through Gilad and Menashe; he crossed Mitzpeh Gilad; and from Mitzpeh Gilad he crossed over to the
30 Amonites. Then Yiftaḥ swore a vow to the Lord. He said, "If You deliver the Amonites into my hand,
31 then whatever comes out of the doors of my home to meet me when I return safely from the Amonites
shall be for the Lord, and I shall offer it up as a burnt offering."
32 Yiftaḥ crossed over to the Amonites and attacked them, and the Lord delivered them into his hand.
33 He defeated them from Aroer to Minit, twenty towns, all the way to Avel Keramim – a crushing de-
34 feat – and the Amonites were conquered by the Israelites. *Yiftaḥ arrived home in Mitz- *Yemenites add*
pa – and there was his daughter, coming out to meet him, drumming and dancing! She was his one
35 and only – he had no son or daughter besides her. When he saw her, he rent his clothes. "O, O, my
daughter," he said, "you have brought me down low – you have become my scourge! I have gone and
36 opened up my mouth to the Lord, and I cannot go back." "O, Father," she said to him, "If you opened
your mouth up to the Lord, do to me whatever it was that came out of your mouth – after what the
37 Lord has done for you, defeating your enemies the Amonites. Only grant me this one thing," she said
to her father. "Let me go for two months so that I may roam the hills and weep for my maidenhood,
38 my friends and I." "Go," he said to her, and sent her off for two months; she and her friends went and
39 wept for her maidenhood upon the hills. At the end of two months, she returned to her father. He did
40 to her what he had vowed to do. She never knew a man. It became a custom in Israel: every year, the
daughters of Israel would go and lament the daughter of Yiftaḥ the Gileadite for four days a year.

י אֶהְיֶה לָכֶם לְרֹאשׁ: וַיֹּאמְרוּ זִקְנֵי־גִלְעָד אֶל־יִפְתָּח יהוה יִהְיֶה שֹׁמֵעַ בֵּינוֹתֵינוּ אִם־לֹא כִדְבָרְךָ כֵּן נַעֲשֶׂה:
יא וַיֵּלֶךְ יִפְתָּח עִם־זִקְנֵי גִלְעָד וַיָּשִׂימוּ הָעָם אוֹתוֹ עֲלֵיהֶם לְרֹאשׁ וּלְקָצִין וַיְדַבֵּר יִפְתָּח אֶת־כָּל־דְּבָרָיו לִפְנֵי
יב יהוה בַּמִּצְפָּה: וַיִּשְׁלַח יִפְתָּח מַלְאָכִים אֶל־מֶלֶךְ בְּנֵי־עַמּוֹן לֵאמֹר מַה־לִּי וָלָךְ כִּי־בָאתָ אֵלַי
יג לְהִלָּחֵם בְּאַרְצִי: וַיֹּאמֶר מֶלֶךְ בְּנֵי־עַמּוֹן אֶל־מַלְאֲכֵי יִפְתָּח כִּי־לָקַח יִשְׂרָאֵל אֶת־אַרְצִי בַּעֲלוֹתוֹ מִמִּצְרַיִם
יד מֵאַרְנוֹן וְעַד־הַיַּבֹּק וְעַד־הַיַּרְדֵּן וְעַתָּה הָשִׁיבָה אֶתְהֶן בְּשָׁלוֹם: וַיּוֹסֶף עוֹד יִפְתָּח וַיִּשְׁלַח מַלְאָכִים אֶל־
טו טז מֶלֶךְ בְּנֵי עַמּוֹן: וַיֹּאמֶר לוֹ כֹּה אָמַר יִפְתָּח לֹא־לָקַח יִשְׂרָאֵל אֶת־אֶרֶץ מוֹאָב וְאֶת־אֶרֶץ בְּנֵי עַמּוֹן: כִּי
יז בַּעֲלוֹתָם מִמִּצְרָיִם וַיֵּלֶךְ יִשְׂרָאֵל בַּמִּדְבָּר עַד־יַם־סוּף וַיָּבֹא קָדֵשָׁה: וַיִּשְׁלַח יִשְׂרָאֵל מַלְאָכִים ׀ אֶל־מֶלֶךְ
אֱדוֹם לֵאמֹר אֶעְבְּרָה־נָּא בְאַרְצֶךָ וְלֹא שָׁמַע מֶלֶךְ אֱדוֹם וְגַם אֶל־מֶלֶךְ מוֹאָב שָׁלַח וְלֹא אָבָה וַיֵּשֶׁב
יח יִשְׂרָאֵל בְּקָדֵשׁ: וַיֵּלֶךְ בַּמִּדְבָּר וַיָּסָב אֶת־אֶרֶץ אֱדוֹם וְאֶת־אֶרֶץ מוֹאָב וַיָּבֹא מִמִּזְרַח־שֶׁמֶשׁ לְאֶרֶץ מוֹאָב
יט וַיַּחֲנוּן בְּעֵבֶר אַרְנוֹן וְלֹא־בָאוּ בִּגְבוּל מוֹאָב כִּי אַרְנוֹן גְּבוּל מוֹאָב: וַיִּשְׁלַח יִשְׂרָאֵל מַלְאָכִים אֶל־סִיחוֹן
כ מֶלֶךְ־הָאֱמֹרִי מֶלֶךְ חֶשְׁבּוֹן וַיֹּאמֶר לוֹ יִשְׂרָאֵל נַעְבְּרָה־נָּא בְאַרְצְךָ עַד־מְקוֹמִי: וְלֹא־הֶאֱמִין סִיחוֹן אֶת־
כא יִשְׂרָאֵל עֲבֹר בִּגְבֻלוֹ וַיֶּאֱסֹף סִיחוֹן אֶת־כָּל־עַמּוֹ וַיַּחֲנוּ בְּיָהְצָה וַיִּלָּחֶם עִם־יִשְׂרָאֵל: וַיִּתֵּן יהוה אֱלֹהֵי־
יִשְׂרָאֵל אֶת־סִיחוֹן וְאֶת־כָּל־עַמּוֹ בְּיַד יִשְׂרָאֵל וַיַּכּוּם וַיִּירַשׁ יִשְׂרָאֵל אֵת כָּל־אֶרֶץ הָאֱמֹרִי יוֹשֵׁב הָאָרֶץ
כב כג הַהִיא: וַיִּירְשׁוּ אֵת כָּל־גְּבוּל הָאֱמֹרִי מֵאַרְנוֹן וְעַד־הַיַּבֹּק וּמִן־הַמִּדְבָּר וְעַד־הַיַּרְדֵּן: וְעַתָּה יהוה ׀ אֱלֹהֵי
כד יִשְׂרָאֵל הוֹרִישׁ אֶת־הָאֱמֹרִי מִפְּנֵי עַמּוֹ יִשְׂרָאֵל וְאַתָּה תִּירָשֶׁנּוּ: הֲלֹא אֵת אֲשֶׁר יוֹרִישְׁךָ כְּמוֹשׁ אֱלֹהֶיךָ
כה אוֹתוֹ תִירָשׁ וְאֵת כָּל־אֲשֶׁר הוֹרִישׁ יהוה אֱלֹהֵינוּ מִפָּנֵינוּ אוֹתוֹ נִירָשׁ: וְעַתָּה הֲטוֹב טוֹב אַתָּה מִבָּלָק
כו בֶּן־צִפּוֹר מֶלֶךְ מוֹאָב הֲרוֹב רָב עִם־יִשְׂרָאֵל אִם־נִלְחֹם נִלְחַם בָּם: בְּשֶׁבֶת יִשְׂרָאֵל בְּחֶשְׁבּוֹן וּבִבְנוֹתֶיהָ
וּבְעַרְעוֹר וּבִבְנוֹתֶיהָ וּבְכָל־הֶעָרִים אֲשֶׁר עַל־יְדֵי אַרְנוֹן שְׁלֹשׁ מֵאוֹת שָׁנָה וּמַדּוּעַ לֹא־הִצַּלְתֶּם בָּעֵת
כז הַהִיא: וְאָנֹכִי לֹא־חָטָאתִי לָךְ וְאַתָּה עֹשֶׂה אִתִּי רָעָה לְהִלָּחֶם בִּי יִשְׁפֹּט יהוה הַשֹּׁפֵט הַיּוֹם בֵּין בְּנֵי
כח כט יִשְׂרָאֵל וּבֵין בְּנֵי עַמּוֹן: וְלֹא שָׁמַע מֶלֶךְ בְּנֵי עַמּוֹן אֶל־דִּבְרֵי יִפְתָּח אֲשֶׁר שָׁלַח אֵלָיו: וַתְּהִי
עַל־יִפְתָּח רוּחַ יהוה וַיַּעֲבֹר אֶת־הַגִּלְעָד וְאֶת־מְנַשֶּׁה וַיַּעֲבֹר אֶת־מִצְפֵּה גִלְעָד וּמִמִּצְפֵּה גִלְעָד עָבַר בְּנֵי
ל לא עַמּוֹן: וַיִּדַּר יִפְתָּח נֶדֶר לַיהוה וַיֹּאמַר אִם־נָתוֹן תִּתֵּן אֶת־בְּנֵי עַמּוֹן בְּיָדִי: וְהָיָה הַיּוֹצֵא אֲשֶׁר יֵצֵא מִדַּלְתֵי
בֵיתִי לִקְרָאתִי בְּשׁוּבִי בְשָׁלוֹם מִבְּנֵי עַמּוֹן וְהָיָה לַיהוה וְהַעֲלִיתִהוּ עוֹלָה:
לב לג וַיַּעֲבֹר יִפְתָּח אֶל־בְּנֵי עַמּוֹן לְהִלָּחֶם בָּם וַיִּתְּנֵם יהוה בְּיָדוֹ: וַיַּכֵּם מֵעֲרוֹעֵר וְעַד־בּוֹאֲךָ מִנִּית עֶשְׂרִים עִיר
לד וְעַד אָבֵל כְּרָמִים מַכָּה גְּדוֹלָה מְאֹד וַיִּכָּנְעוּ בְּנֵי עַמּוֹן מִפְּנֵי בְּנֵי יִשְׂרָאֵל: *וַיָּבֹא יִפְתָּח הַמִּצְפָּה *Yemenites add*
לה אֶל־בֵּיתוֹ וְהִנֵּה בִתּוֹ יֹצֵאת לִקְרָאתוֹ בְּתֻפִּים וּבִמְחֹלוֹת וְרַק הִיא יְחִידָה אֵין־לוֹ מִמֶּנּוּ בֵּן אוֹ־בַת: וַיְהִי
כִרְאוֹתוֹ אוֹתָהּ וַיִּקְרַע אֶת־בְּגָדָיו וַיֹּאמֶר אֲהָהּ בִּתִּי הַכְרֵעַ הִכְרַעְתִּנִי וְאַתְּ הָיִית בְּעֹכְרָי וְאָנֹכִי פָּצִיתִי
לו פִי אֶל־יהוה וְלֹא אוּכַל לָשׁוּב: וַתֹּאמֶר אֵלָיו אָבִי פָּצִיתָה אֶת־פִּיךָ אֶל־יהוה עֲשֵׂה לִי כַּאֲשֶׁר יָצָא מִפִּיךָ
לז אַחֲרֵי אֲשֶׁר עָשָׂה לְךָ יהוה נְקָמוֹת מֵאֹיְבֶיךָ מִבְּנֵי עַמּוֹן: וַתֹּאמֶר אֶל־אָבִיהָ יֵעָשֶׂה לִּי הַדָּבָר הַזֶּה הַרְפֵּה
לח מִמֶּנִּי שְׁנַיִם חֳדָשִׁים וְאֵלְכָה וְיָרַדְתִּי עַל־הֶהָרִים וְאֶבְכֶּה עַל־בְּתוּלַי אָנֹכִי ורעיתי: וַיֹּאמֶר לֵכִי וַיִּשְׁלַח וְרֵעוֹתָי
לט אוֹתָהּ שְׁנֵי חֳדָשִׁים וַתֵּלֶךְ הִיא וְרֵעוֹתֶיהָ וַתֵּבְךְּ עַל־בְּתוּלֶיהָ עַל־הֶהָרִים: וַיְהִי מִקֵּץ ׀ שְׁנַיִם חֳדָשִׁים וַתָּשָׁב
מ אֶל־אָבִיהָ וַיַּעַשׂ לָהּ אֶת־נִדְרוֹ אֲשֶׁר נָדָר וְהִיא לֹא־יָדְעָה אִישׁ וַתְּהִי־חֹק בְּיִשְׂרָאֵל: מִיָּמִים ׀ יָמִימָה
תֵּלַכְנָה בְּנוֹת יִשְׂרָאֵל לְתַנּוֹת לְבַת־יִפְתָּח הַגִּלְעָדִי אַרְבַּעַת יָמִים בַּשָּׁנָה:

Haftarat Balak

When Ḥukat and Balak are read together, read this haftara.

5 6 And the remnant of Yaakov will be found amid countless peoples as dew brought down from the MICAH
Lord, as ample rains shower upon grass; they will not look to any man, nor place their hopes in
7 humankind. The remnant of Yaakov will be among nations, amid countless peoples, like a lion among
wild beasts of the forest, like a young lion among flocks of sheep whom, as they pass, he tramples and
8 rips to pieces; there is no one to save them. Your hand shall be raised over your foes; your enemies
9 will be cut down. On that day, so says the Lord: I will cut out the horses from among you,
10 I will destroy your chariots, and I will cut down the fortified cities of your land and demolish all your
11 fortresses. I will cut out all practice of witchcraft, and there will be no more fortune tellers among you.
12 I will cut down your idols, the worship pillars from your midst; no longer will you bow down to the
13 craft of your hands. I will rip out the Ashera from your midst, and I will destroy your cities. I will lash
14 out with My anger and wrath in vengeance against nations who did not heed My words. Hear
6 1 now what the Lord says: Arise; argue your case before the mountains; let the hills hear your plea.
2 Hear, O mountains, the Lord's dispute – you, earth's everlasting foundations. For the Lord has a
3 dispute with His people; He will contend with Israel: My people! How have I wronged you? How have
4 I worn you down? Bear witness against Me, for I brought you up from the land of Egypt; I redeemed
5 you from the house of slavery; I sent Moshe, Aharon, and Miriam to lead you. My people, remember
now how Balak, king of Moav, schemed, and how Bilam son of Beor responded; remember from Shi-
6 tim to Gilgal so that you may come to realize the righteous ways of the Lord. What then can I offer
the Lord when I bow low to the God Most High? Should I come before Him with burnt offerings,
7 with year-old calves? Would the Lord want a thousand rams, untold rivulets of oil? Should I offer
8 my firstborn as payment for my crimes, the fruit of my womb for the sins of my being? Man, God has
told you what is good and what the Lord seeks from you: only to do justice, love goodness, and walk
modestly with your God.

Haftarat Pinḥas

Read this haftara if Shabbat Parashat Pinḥas falls before the Seventeenth of Tamuz.
If it falls afterward, read the haftara on page 1601.

18 46 The hand of the Lord settled on Eliyahu, and he hitched up his tunic and ran before Aḥav until he I KINGS
19 1 reached Yizre'el. When Aḥav told Izevel all that Eliyahu had done and how he had put all the prophets
2 to the sword, Izevel sent a messenger to Eliyahu: "So may the gods do to me and more if by this time
3 tomorrow, I have not treated your life like one of theirs." Frightened, he understood and fled for his

Israel's central mission in the world: modeling the ideal way of serving the Almighty. To put the sacrificial service at the center of our religious consciousness, while forgetting about the demands of charity and justice that the Torah places on us, turns a means into an end. When we do so, we are serving only ourselves and our own conceptions, rather than God.

PINḤAS

When the wicked Queen Izevel hears of Eliyahu's victory over the priests of Baal in the contest on Mount Carmel, she declares war on Eliyahu. Eliyahu realizes that despite the outcome of the contest, he remains alone in the battle against Izevel. Disappointed and desperate, he flees to

הפטרת בלק

When חקת *and* בלק *are read together, read this* הפטרה.

ה ו וְהָיָה ׀ שְׁאֵרִית יַעֲקֹב בְּקֶרֶב עַמִּים רַבִּים כְּטַל מֵאֵת יהוה כִּרְבִיבִים עֲלֵי־עֵשֶׂב אֲשֶׁר לֹא־יְקַוֶּה לְאִישׁ וְלֹא מיכה
ז יְיַחֵל לִבְנֵי אָדָם: וְהָיָה שְׁאֵרִית יַעֲקֹב בַּגּוֹיִם בְּקֶרֶב עַמִּים רַבִּים כְּאַרְיֵה בְּבַהֲמוֹת יַעַר כִּכְפִיר בְּעֶדְרֵי־
ח ט צֹאן אֲשֶׁר אִם עָבַר וְרָמַס וְטָרַף וְאֵין מַצִּיל: תָּרֹם יָדְךָ עַל־צָרֶיךָ וְכָל־אֹיְבֶיךָ יִכָּרֵתוּ: וְהָיָה
י בַיּוֹם־הַהוּא נְאֻם־יהוה וְהִכְרַתִּי סוּסֶיךָ מִקִּרְבֶּךָ וְהַאֲבַדְתִּי מַרְכְּבֹתֶיךָ: וְהִכְרַתִּי עָרֵי אַרְצֶךָ וְהָרַסְתִּי
יא יב כָּל־מִבְצָרֶיךָ: וְהִכְרַתִּי כְשָׁפִים מִיָּדֶךָ וּמְעוֹנְנִים לֹא יִהְיוּ־לָךְ: וְהִכְרַתִּי פְסִילֶיךָ וּמַצֵּבוֹתֶיךָ מִקִּרְבֶּךָ וְלֹא־
יג יד תִשְׁתַּחֲוֶה עוֹד לְמַעֲשֵׂה יָדֶיךָ: וְנָתַשְׁתִּי אֲשֵׁירֶיךָ מִקִּרְבֶּךָ וְהִשְׁמַדְתִּי עָרֶיךָ: וְעָשִׂיתִי בְּאַף וּבְחֵמָה נָקָם
ו א אֶת־הַגּוֹיִם אֲשֶׁר לֹא שָׁמֵעוּ: שִׁמְעוּ־נָא אֵת אֲשֶׁר־יהוה אֹמֵר קוּם רִיב אֶת־הֶהָרִים וְתִשְׁמַעְנָה
ב הַגְּבָעוֹת קוֹלֶךָ: שִׁמְעוּ הָרִים אֶת־רִיב יהוה וְהָאֵתָנִים מֹסְדֵי אָרֶץ כִּי רִיב לַיהוה עִם־עַמּוֹ וְעִם־יִשְׂרָאֵל
ג ד יִתְוַכָּח: עַמִּי מֶה־עָשִׂיתִי לְךָ וּמָה הֶלְאֵתִיךָ עֲנֵה בִי: כִּי הֶעֱלִתִיךָ מֵאֶרֶץ מִצְרַיִם וּמִבֵּית עֲבָדִים פְּדִיתִיךָ
ה וָאֶשְׁלַח לְפָנֶיךָ אֶת־מֹשֶׁה אַהֲרֹן וּמִרְיָם: עַמִּי זְכָר־נָא מַה־יָּעַץ בָּלָק מֶלֶךְ מוֹאָב וּמֶה־עָנָה אֹתוֹ בִּלְעָם
ו בֶּן־בְּעוֹר מִן־הַשִּׁטִּים עַד־הַגִּלְגָּל לְמַעַן דַּעַת צִדְקוֹת יהוה: בַּמָּה אֲקַדֵּם יהוה אִכַּף לֵאלֹהֵי מָרוֹם
ז הַאֲקַדְּמֶנּוּ בְעוֹלוֹת בַּעֲגָלִים בְּנֵי שָׁנָה: הֲיִרְצֶה יהוה בְּאַלְפֵי אֵילִים בְּרִבְבוֹת נַחֲלֵי־שָׁמֶן הַאֶתֵּן בְּכוֹרִי
ח פִּשְׁעִי פְּרִי בִטְנִי חַטַּאת נַפְשִׁי: הִגִּיד לְךָ אָדָם מַה־טּוֹב וּמָה־יהוה דּוֹרֵשׁ מִמְּךָ כִּי אִם־עֲשׂוֹת מִשְׁפָּט
וְאַהֲבַת חֶסֶד וְהַצְנֵעַ לֶכֶת עִם־אֱלֹהֶיךָ:

הפטרת פינחס

Read this הפטרה *if* שבת פרשת פנחס *falls before* שבעה עשר בתמוז.
If it falls afterward, read the הפטרה *on page 1601.*

יח מו / יט א וְיַד־יהוה הָיְתָה אֶל־אֵלִיָּהוּ וַיְשַׁנֵּס מָתְנָיו וַיָּרָץ לִפְנֵי אַחְאָב עַד־בֹּאֲכָה יִזְרְעֶאלָה: וַיַּגֵּד אַחְאָב לְאִיזֶבֶל מלכים א׳
ב אֵת כָּל־אֲשֶׁר עָשָׂה אֵלִיָּהוּ וְאֵת כָּל־אֲשֶׁר הָרַג אֶת־כָּל־הַנְּבִיאִים בֶּחָרֶב: וַתִּשְׁלַח אִיזֶבֶל מַלְאָךְ אֶל־
ג אֵלִיָּהוּ לֵאמֹר כֹּה־יַעֲשׂוּן אֱלֹהִים וְכֹה יוֹסִפוּן כִּי־כָעֵת מָחָר אָשִׂים אֶת־נַפְשְׁךָ כְּנֶפֶשׁ אַחַד מֵהֶם: וַיַּרְא

BALAK

The prophet Mikha was active in the kingdom of Yehuda at the same time as his teacher, the prophet Yeshayahu. At this time, the Assyrian Empire was on the ascent, and the northern kingdom of Israel had now been destroyed. The confrontation with this formidable enemy brought into focus questions of Israel's special status as God's chosen people and of the proper way of worshipping God. The fact that Assyria could destroy the northern kingdom and exile its inhabitants while the southern kingdom of Yehuda survived was difficult for the people to understand.

In this *haftara*, the prophet preaches a message of reassurance to the people. At the same time, he points out the difference between means and ends in serving God. He points out

4 life at once, and he reached Be'er Sheva of Yehuda and left his servant boy there. But he continued a day's
journey into the wilderness, then came and sat under a certain broom tree and prayed that he might die.
5 "Enough!" he said. "O Lord, take my life now, for I am no better than my ancestors." Then he lay down
and fell asleep beneath that broom tree. Suddenly, an angel was touching him, urging him, "Get up; eat."
6 He looked up and there, at his head, was a stone-baked cake and a flask of water. He ate and drank and
7 lay back down. The angel of the Lord came back a second time and touched him. "Get up; eat," it said,
8 "or the long journey will prove too much for you." He got up and ate and drank, and by the strength of
9 that food, he walked forty days and forty nights to the mountain of God, Ḥorev. There he reached a cave,
and there he spent the night. Suddenly, the word of the Lord came to him and said to him, "Why are
10 you here, Eliyahu?" "I acted out of fervor, out of passion for the Lord, God of Hosts," he said, "for the
Israelites have abandoned Your covenant, destroyed Your altars, and put Your prophets to the sword. I am
11 the only one left, and they seek to take my life." "Go out and stand on the mountain before the Lord," He
said, "for the Lord is about to pass by." And a great, powerful wind split mountains and shattered rocks
before the Lord – but the Lord was not in the wind. And after the wind, an earthquake – but the Lord
12 was not in the earthquake. And after the earthquake, fire – but the Lord was not in the fire. And after
13 the fire – a faint sound of silence. And when Eliyahu heard, he wrapped his face in his cloak and went out
and stood by the entrance of the cave. And suddenly a voice came to him and said, "Why are you here,
14 Eliyahu?" "I acted out of fervor, out of passion for the Lord, God of Hosts," he said, "for the Israelites
have abandoned Your covenant, destroyed Your altars, and put Your prophets to the sword. I am the only
15 one left, and they seek to take my life." And the Lord answered him, "Set back out on your way
16 to the Wilderness of Damascus. When you arrive, anoint Ḥazael as king over Aram. As for Yehu son of
Nimshi, anoint him as king over Israel; and as for Elisha son of Shafat of Avel Meḥola, anoint him as a
17 prophet in your place. Whoever escapes the sword of Ḥazael will be killed by Yehu, and whoever escapes
18 the sword of Yehu will be killed by Elisha. I will leave but seven thousand of Israel: every knee that has not
19 bowed to Baal and every mouth that has not kissed him." He set out from there and found Elisha son of
Shafat. He was plowing with twelve pairs of oxen before him, and he was with the twelfth. When Eliyahu
20 reached him, he tossed his cloak over him. He left the oxen and went running after Eliyahu. "Let me just
kiss my father and mother," he said, "and I will follow you." "Go back, then," he said to him. "What have
21 I done to you?" He turned back from him and took the pair of oxen; he slaughtered them, and, using the
oxen gear, he boiled their meat and gave it out to the people to eat. Then he set out and followed Eliyahu
and became his attendant.

Haftarat Pinḥas or Matot

Read this haftara on the Shabbat following the Seventeenth of Tamuz.

JEREMIAH

1 1 The words of Yirmeyahu, son of Ḥilkiyahu, one of the priests who were in Anatot in the land
2 of Binyamin, to whom the word of the Lord came in the days of Yoshiyahu son of Amon, king
3 of Yehuda, in the thirteenth year of his reign, and continued during the days of Yehoyakim son of

---

Eliyahu, nevertheless, is not willing to change his methods, and his answers to God's repeated questions do not change. Ultimately, God commands him to appoint Elisha as prophet in his stead.

MATOT

Yirmeyahu prophesied during the reigns of the final kings of Yehuda up till the destruction of Jerusalem and afterward. His call to prophecy emphasizes the harsh daily reality of the

ד ויקם וילך אל־נפשו ויבא באר שבע אשר ליהודה וינח את־נערו שם: והוא־הלך במדבר דרך יום
ויבא וישב תחת רתם אחת וישאל את־נפשו למות ויאמר ׀ רב עתה יהוה קח נפשי כי לא־טוב אחד
ה אנכי מאבתי: וישכב ויישן תחת רתם אחד והנה־זה מלאך נגע בו ויאמר לו קום אכול: ויבט והנה
ו מראשתיו עגת רצפים וצפחת מים ויאכל וישת וישב וישכב: וישב מלאך יהוה ׀ שנית ויגע־בו ויאמר
ח קום אכל כי רב ממך הדרך: ויקם ויאכל וישתה וילך בכח ׀ האכילה ההיא ארבעים יום וארבעים
ט לילה עד הר האלהים חרב: ויבא־שם אל־המערה וילן שם והנה דבר־יהוה אליו ויאמר לו מה־לך
י פה אליהו: ויאמר קנא קנאתי ליהוה ׀ אלהי צבאות כי־עזבו בריתך בני ישראל את־מזבחתיך
יא הרסו ואת־נביאיך הרגו בחרב ואותר אני לבדי ויבקשו את־נפשי לקחתה: ויאמר צא ועמדת בהר
לפני יהוה והנה יהוה עבר ורוח גדולה וחזק מפרק הרים ומשבר סלעים לפני יהוה לא ברוח יהוה
יב ואחר הרוח רעש לא ברעש יהוה: ואחר הרעש אש לא באש יהוה ואחר האש קול דממה דקה:
יג ויהי ׀ כשמע אליהו וילט פניו באדרתו ויצא ויעמד פתח המערה והנה אליו קול ויאמר מה־לך פה
יד אליהו: ויאמר קנא קנאתי ליהוה ׀ אלהי צבאות כי־עזבו בריתך בני ישראל את־מזבחתיך הרסו
טו ואת־נביאיך הרגו בחרב ואותר אני לבדי ויבקשו את־נפשי לקחתה: ויאמר יהוה אליו לך
טז שוב לדרכך מדברה דמשק ובאת ומשחת את־חזאל למלך על־ארם: ואת יהוא בן־נמשי תמשח
יז למלך על־ישראל ואת־אלישע בן־שפט מאבל מחולה תמשח לנביא תחתיך: והיה הנמלט מחרב
יח חזאל ימית יהוא והנמלט מחרב יהוא ימית אלישע: והשארתי בישראל שבעת אלפים כל־הברכים
יט אשר לא־כרעו לבעל וכל־הפה אשר לא־נשק לו: וילך משם וימצא את־אלישע בן־שפט והוא
כ חרש שנים־עשר צמדים לפניו והוא בשנים העשר ויעבר אליהו אליו וישלך אדרתו אליו: ויעזב
את־הבקר וירץ אחרי אליהו ויאמר אשקה־נא לאבי ולאמי ואלכה אחריך ויאמר לו לך שוב כי
כא מה־עשיתי לך: וישב מאחריו ויקח את־צמד הבקר ויזבחהו ובכלי הבקר בשלם הבשר ויתן לעם
ויאכלו ויקם וילך אחרי אליהו וישרתהו:

הפטרת פינחס או מטות

Read this הפטרה *on the* שבת *following* שבעה עשר בתמוז.

א א ב דברי ירמיהו בן־חלקיהו מן־הכהנים אשר בענתות בארץ בנימן: אשר היה דבר־יהוה אליו בימי ירמיה
ג יאשיהו בן־אמון מלך יהודה בשלש־עשרה שנה למלכו: ויהי בימי יהויקים בן־יאשיהו מלך

Mount Sinai and there has an encounter with God. Speaking to God, Eliyahu requests to end his mission as a prophet. God understands that the terrible drought afflicting Israel has run its course, and it has not been enough to induce the people to mend their ways. Fire from heaven is impressive and has the power to shock people out of their torpor, but its effect is short. Only repentance that answers a "faint sound of silence" can withstand the passage of time.

Yoshiyahu, king of Yehuda, until the end of the eleventh year of Tzidkiyahu son of Yoshiyahu, king
4 of Yehuda – until the exile of Jerusalem in the fifth month: The word of the LORD came to
5 me: "Before I formed you in the womb I knew you. Before you were born I consecrated you. I placed
6 you as a prophet to the nations." I said, "Please, Lord GOD, I am not capable of speaking, for I am
7 still only a boy." The LORD replied to me, "Do not say, 'I am a boy,' for you shall go to all to whom I send
8 you, and you shall speak as I instruct you. Do not fear them, for I am with you to rescue you, declares the
9 LORD." The LORD extended His hand and touched my mouth and the LORD said to me, "Look, I have
10 placed My words in your mouth. I have appointed you this day against the kingdoms and against the
11 nations to uproot and tear down, to destroy and demolish, to build and to plant." The word of
the LORD came to me: "What do you see, Yirmeyahu?" I replied, "I see the branch of an almond tree."
12 And the LORD said to me: "You have seen well, for I am watchful about keeping My word." The
13 word of the LORD came to me a second time: "What do you see?" I answered, "I see a boiling cauldron
14 facing the north." And the LORD said to me: "From the north disaster shall burst forth upon all the
15 inhabitants of the land, for I am about to summon all the tribes of the kingdoms of the north," declares
the LORD. "They shall come; each shall set up a throne at the entrance of the gates of Jerusalem against
16 her ramparts roundabout and against all the cities of Yehuda. Thus will I pronounce My judgment upon
them on account of their wickedness: they abandoned Me, sacrificed to other gods, and worshipped the
17 works of their own hands. As for you, be courageous; stand up and speak to them as I will instruct you.
18 Do not break down because of them lest I break you down before them. I have made you today a fortress
city, an iron column, and walls of bronze against the entire land – against the kings of Yehuda, its princes,
19 its priests, and the people of the land. They will wage battle against you, but they will not prevail, for
2 1 I am with you," declares the LORD, "to rescue you." The word of the LORD came to me: "Go
2 and proclaim to the people of Jerusalem: 'This is what the LORD has said: I recall on your behalf the
devotion of your youth, your bridal love, when you followed Me into the wilderness, a land unseeded.
3 Israel is a treasure to the LORD, His choice harvest. All who eat of it will be held to account. Evil will
befall them, declares the LORD.'"

HAFTARAT MASEI

When Matot and Masei are read together, read this haftara, even on Rosh Ḥodesh Av.

JEREMIAH
For Ashkenazim and Sepharadim

2 4 Listen to the word of the LORD, House of Yaakov and all the tribes of the House of Israel. This is what
5 the LORD said: What fault did your forefathers find with Me that they distanced themselves from Me?
6 They followed nothingness and became nothing. They did not say, "Where is the LORD who lifted us
up from the land of Egypt, who guided us in the wilderness, a land of deserts and pits, an arid land,

---

MASEI
Ashkenazim and Sepharadim

The first prophecy of Yirmeyahu, pronounced during the reign of Yoshiyahu, deals with two topics: (1) abandoning idolatry and returning to God, and (2) retreating from overinvolvement in international politics, since alliances with powerful foreign nations invariably lead to negative foreign influences. To concretize these ideas, the prophet uses metaphors having to do with water. "Flowing water," i.e., clean water found in springs, is cold, and its movement gives it the appearance of life – this symbolizes God's life-giving words and commands. One who has access to such a source of water would be foolish to give it up in exchange for other, inferior sources. If he does so, he loses the important

יְהוּדָה עַד־תֹּם עַשְׁתֵּי־עֶשְׂרֵה שָׁנָה לְצִדְקִיָּהוּ בֶן־יֹאשִׁיָּהוּ מֶלֶךְ יְהוּדָה עַד־גְּלוֹת יְרוּשָׁלַ‍ִם בַּחֹדֶשׁ
ד ה הַחֲמִישִׁי: וַיְהִי דְבַר־יהוה אֵלַי לֵאמֹר: בְּטֶרֶם אצורך בַבֶּטֶן יְדַעְתִּיךָ וּבְטֶרֶם תֵּצֵא מֵרֶחֶם אֶצָּרְךָ
ו ז הִקְדַּשְׁתִּיךָ נָבִיא לַגּוֹיִם נְתַתִּיךָ: וָאֹמַר אֲהָהּ אֲדֹנָי יֱהֹוִה הִנֵּה לֹא־יָדַעְתִּי דַּבֵּר כִּי־נַעַר אָנֹכִי: וַיֹּאמֶר
ח יהוה אֵלַי אַל־תֹּאמַר נַעַר אָנֹכִי כִּי עַל־כָּל־אֲשֶׁר אֶשְׁלָחֲךָ תֵּלֵךְ וְאֵת כָּל־אֲשֶׁר אֲצַוְּךָ תְּדַבֵּר: אַל־תִּירָא
ט מִפְּנֵיהֶם כִּי־אִתְּךָ אֲנִי לְהַצִּלֶךָ נְאֻם־יהוה: וַיִּשְׁלַח יהוה אֶת־יָדוֹ וַיַּגַּע עַל־פִּי וַיֹּאמֶר יהוה אֵלַי הִנֵּה נָתַתִּי
י דְבָרַי בְּפִיךָ: רְאֵה הִפְקַדְתִּיךָ ׀ הַיּוֹם הַזֶּה עַל־הַגּוֹיִם וְעַל־הַמַּמְלָכוֹת לִנְתוֹשׁ וְלִנְתוֹץ וּלְהַאֲבִיד וְלַהֲרוֹס
יא לִבְנוֹת וְלִנְטוֹעַ: וַיְהִי דְבַר־יהוה אֵלַי לֵאמֹר מָה־אַתָּה רֹאֶה יִרְמְיָהוּ וָאֹמַר מַקֵּל שָׁקֵד אֲנִי
יב יג רֹאֶה: וַיֹּאמֶר יהוה אֵלַי הֵיטַבְתָּ לִרְאוֹת כִּי־שֹׁקֵד אֲנִי עַל־דְּבָרִי לַעֲשֹׂתוֹ: וַיְהִי דְבַר־יהוה ׀
יד אֵלַי שֵׁנִית לֵאמֹר מָה אַתָּה רֹאֶה וָאֹמַר סִיר נָפוּחַ אֲנִי רֹאֶה וּפָנָיו מִפְּנֵי צָפוֹנָה: וַיֹּאמֶר יהוה אֵלָי מִצָּפוֹן
טו תִּפָּתַח הָרָעָה עַל כָּל־יֹשְׁבֵי הָאָרֶץ: כִּי ׀ הִנְנִי קֹרֵא לְכָל־מִשְׁפְּחוֹת מַמְלְכוֹת צָפוֹנָה נְאֻם־יהוה וּבָאוּ
טז וְנָתְנוּ אִישׁ כִּסְאוֹ פֶּתַח ׀ שַׁעֲרֵי יְרוּשָׁלַ‍ִם וְעַל כָּל־חוֹמֹתֶיהָ סָבִיב וְעַל כָּל־עָרֵי יְהוּדָה: וְדִבַּרְתִּי מִשְׁפָּטַי
יז אוֹתָם עַל כָּל־רָעָתָם אֲשֶׁר עֲזָבוּנִי וַיְקַטְּרוּ לֵאלֹהִים אֲחֵרִים וַיִּשְׁתַּחֲווּ לְמַעֲשֵׂי יְדֵיהֶם: וְאַתָּה תֶּאְזֹר
יח מָתְנֶיךָ וְקַמְתָּ וְדִבַּרְתָּ אֲלֵיהֶם אֵת כָּל־אֲשֶׁר אָנֹכִי אֲצַוֶּךָּ אַל־תֵּחַת מִפְּנֵיהֶם פֶּן־אֲחִתְּךָ לִפְנֵיהֶם: וַאֲנִי
הִנֵּה נְתַתִּיךָ הַיּוֹם לְעִיר מִבְצָר וּלְעַמּוּד בַּרְזֶל וּלְחֹמוֹת נְחֹשֶׁת עַל־כָּל־הָאָרֶץ לְמַלְכֵי יְהוּדָה לְשָׂרֶיהָ
ב יט א לְכֹהֲנֶיהָ וּלְעַם הָאָרֶץ: וְנִלְחֲמוּ אֵלֶיךָ וְלֹא־יוּכְלוּ לָךְ כִּי־אִתְּךָ אֲנִי נְאֻם־יהוה לְהַצִּילֶךָ: וַיְהִי
ב דְבַר־יהוה אֵלַי לֵאמֹר: הָלֹךְ וְקָרָאתָ בְאָזְנֵי יְרוּשָׁלַ‍ִם לֵאמֹר כֹּה אָמַר יהוה זָכַרְתִּי לָךְ חֶסֶד נְעוּרַיִךְ
ג אַהֲבַת כְּלוּלֹתָיִךְ לֶכְתֵּךְ אַחֲרַי בַּמִּדְבָּר בְּאֶרֶץ לֹא זְרוּעָה: קֹדֶשׁ יִשְׂרָאֵל לַיהוה רֵאשִׁית תְּבוּאָתֹה כָּל־
אֹכְלָיו יֶאְשָׁמוּ רָעָה תָּבֹא אֲלֵיהֶם נְאֻם־יהוה:

הפטרת מסעי

When מטות *and* מסעי *are read together, read this* הפטרה*, even on* ראש חודש אב.

ירמיה

For Ashkenazim and Sephardim

ב ד ה שִׁמְעוּ דְבַר־יהוה בֵּית יַעֲקֹב וְכָל־מִשְׁפְּחוֹת בֵּית יִשְׂרָאֵל: כֹּה ׀ אָמַר יהוה מַה־מָּצְאוּ אֲבוֹתֵיכֶם בִּי עָוֶל
ו כִּי רָחֲקוּ מֵעָלָי וַיֵּלְכוּ אַחֲרֵי הַהֶבֶל וַיֶּהְבָּלוּ: וְלֹא אָמְרוּ אַיֵּה יהוה הַמַּעֲלֶה אֹתָנוּ מֵאֶרֶץ מִצְרָיִם הַמּוֹלִיךְ
אֹתָנוּ בַּמִּדְבָּר בְּאֶרֶץ עֲרָבָה וְשׁוּחָה בְּאֶרֶץ צִיָּה וְצַלְמָוֶת בְּאֶרֶץ לֹא־עָבַר בָּהּ אִישׁ וְלֹא־יָשַׁב אָדָם שָׁם:

prophet. Yirmeyahu's career was especially fraught. He was the first and only prophet who foretold the destruction as it occurred. His challenge stemmed from his complex nature: On the one hand he was a divine messenger, commanded to deliver a message of impending doom to the nation. On the other, he was one of the people and loved them. In this context God's words of encouragement to him take on special meaning: "Stand up and speak to them as I will instruct you. Do not break down because of them.... I have made you today a fortress city, an iron column, and walls of bronze.... They will wage battle against you, but they will not prevail." Yirmeyahu's attempts to avoid this terrible role, like Moshe's centuries earlier, testify to this difficulty as well.

7 deathly dark, a land never traversed by man, where no one ever dwelt?" I brought you to a fertile land, to
8 eat its fruits and bounty, but you came and defiled My land, and made My heritage an abomination. The
priests did not say, "Where is the LORD?" The teachers of the Torah did not know Me. The shepherds be-
9 trayed Me. The prophets prophesied in the name of Baal. They pursued that which was useless. Therefore,
I will continue to contend with them, declares the LORD. I will contend with their children's children.
10 Cross over to the islands of the Kittites and observe. Send emissaries to Kedar and ponder well. See if
11 anything like this ever happened before. Has a people ever exchanged its gods, and they are non-gods? Yet
12 my nation exchanged its glory for something useless. Heavens, be astounded by this. Storm and become
13 utterly desolate, declares the LORD. For My nation has performed two wrongs: they have forsaken Me,
14 the source of living waters, to dig wells, broken wells that cannot hold water. Is Israel a slave? Is he born to
15 a maidservant? Why has he become an object of plunder? Young lions roar at him. They voiced their cries.
16 They laid waste to his land. His cities have been set afire, with no inhabitants. Even the men of Nof and
17 Taḥpanḥes crush your skull. This has been done to you because you deserted the LORD your God during
18 the time He guided you upon the journey. Now of what use is it to you to approach Egypt to drink the
19 waters of Shiḥor? Of what use is it to you to approach Assyria to drink the waters of the river? Your own
evil will discipline you; your own waywardness will rebuke you. Know and see that your abandonment of
the LORD your God has been bad and bitter. There is no fear of Me in you, says the Almighty, LORD of
20 Hosts. I broke your yoke long ago. I tore your restraints asunder. You said, "I will never again transgress!"
21 Yet on every high hilltop and under every leafy tree you recline like a harlot. I planted you as a choice
grape: perfect and genuine seed. How did you change on Me into a weed? Rotten grapes of a strange
22 vine! Although you scrub yourself with natron and heap soap on yourselves, your guilt is stained before
23 Me, declares the Lord GOD. How can you say that you were never defiled? That you never followed the
Be'alim? Look back upon your path in the valley. Recognize what you did, like a young she-camel clinging
24 to her wild ways. Like a wild ass accustomed to the wilderness; inhaling wind as she pleases, her wailing
25 cannot be silenced. Yet those who seek her need not be weary. In her month they will find her. Spare your
foot from becoming bare and your throat from suffering thirst! But you said, "Never mind. No. I have
26 loved strangers; it is them whom I will follow." Like the shame of a thief when he is found out, so will the
27 House of Israel be shamed: They, their kings, their noblemen, their priests, and their prophets. They say
to the tree, "You are my father!" And to the stone, "You gave birth to me!" They have turned their backs
28 to Me, not their faces but in their time of trouble they say, "Arise and save us!" Where are the gods that
you have crafted for yourself? Let them rise if they can save you in your time of trouble. For your gods,
Yehuda, are as numerous as your cities.

3 4 By now, you should have called Me: "Father! You were my childhood companion!" *Ashkenazim and Minhag Anglia add*

4 1 If you, Israel, return to Me, declares the LORD, I will welcome your return. If you remove your abomi- *Sephardim, Chabad, and Minhag Anglia add*
2 nations from My presence, you shall not suffer exile. You will utter oaths – exclaiming "as the LORD
lives" truthfully, justly, and righteously – so that other nations will bless themselves by Him and come
to take pride in Him.

---

be swept away when he tries to drink from the raging river (symbolizing the strong but unreliable river-valley empires of Assyria and Egypt). If Israel gives up on its political and religious independence, it will become empty and worthless, a dead limb appended to the world.

ז וָאָבִיא אֶתְכֶם אֶל־אֶרֶץ הַכַּרְמֶל לֶאֱכֹל פִּרְיָהּ וְטוּבָהּ וַתָּבֹאוּ וַתְּטַמְּאוּ אֶת־אַרְצִי וְנַחֲלָתִי שַׂמְתֶּם לְתוֹעֵבָה:
ח הַכֹּהֲנִים לֹא אָמְרוּ אַיֵּה יהוה וְתֹפְשֵׂי הַתּוֹרָה לֹא יְדָעוּנִי וְהָרֹעִים פָּשְׁעוּ בִי וְהַנְּבִיאִים נִבְּאוּ בַבַּעַל וְאַחֲרֵי
ט י לֹא־יוֹעִלוּ הָלָכוּ: לָכֵן עֹד אָרִיב אִתְּכֶם נְאֻם־יהוה וְאֶת־בְּנֵי בְנֵיכֶם אָרִיב: כִּי עִבְרוּ אִיֵּי כִתִּיִּים וּרְאוּ וְקֵדָר
יא שִׁלְחוּ וְהִתְבּוֹנְנוּ מְאֹד וּרְאוּ הֵן הָיְתָה כָּזֹאת: הַהֵימִיר גּוֹי אֱלֹהִים וְהֵמָּה לֹא אֱלֹהִים וְעַמִּי הֵמִיר כְּבוֹדוֹ
יב יג בְּלוֹא יוֹעִיל: שֹׁמּוּ שָׁמַיִם עַל־זֹאת וְשַׂעֲרוּ חָרְבוּ מְאֹד נְאֻם־יהוה: כִּי־שְׁתַּיִם רָעוֹת עָשָׂה עַמִּי אֹתִי עָזְבוּ
יד מְקוֹר ׀ מַיִם חַיִּים לַחְצֹב לָהֶם בֹּארוֹת בֹּארֹת נִשְׁבָּרִים אֲשֶׁר לֹא־יָכִלוּ הַמָּיִם: הַעֶבֶד יִשְׂרָאֵל אִם־יְלִיד
טו בַּיִת הוּא מַדּוּעַ הָיָה לָבַז: עָלָיו יִשְׁאֲגוּ כְפִרִים נָתְנוּ קוֹלָם וַיָּשִׁיתוּ אַרְצוֹ לְשַׁמָּה עָרָיו נצתה מִבְּלִי יֹשֵׁב: נִצְּתוּ
טז יז גַּם־בְּנֵי־נֹף ותחפנס יִרְעוּךְ קָדְקֹד: הֲלוֹא־זֹאת תַּעֲשֶׂה־לָּךְ עָזְבֵךְ אֶת־יהוה אֱלֹהַיִךְ בְּעֵת מוֹלִכֵךְ בַּדָּרֶךְ: וְתַחְפַּנְחֵס
יח יט וְעַתָּה מַה־לָּךְ לְדֶרֶךְ מִצְרַיִם לִשְׁתּוֹת מֵי שִׁחוֹר וּמַה־לָּךְ לְדֶרֶךְ אַשּׁוּר לִשְׁתּוֹת מֵי נָהָר: תְּיַסְּרֵךְ רָעָתֵךְ
וּמְשֻׁבוֹתַיִךְ תּוֹכִחֻךְ וּדְעִי וּרְאִי כִּי־רַע וָמָר עָזְבֵךְ אֶת־יהוה אֱלֹהָיִךְ וְלֹא פַחְדָּתִי אֵלַיִךְ נְאֻם־אֲדֹנָי יֱהוִה
כ צְבָאוֹת: כִּי מֵעוֹלָם שָׁבַרְתִּי עֻלֵּךְ נִתַּקְתִּי מוֹסְרוֹתַיִךְ וַתֹּאמְרִי לֹא אעבוד כִּי עַל־כָּל־גִּבְעָה גְּבֹהָה וְתַחַת אֶעֱבוֹר
כא כָּל־עֵץ רַעֲנָן אַתְּ צֹעָה זֹנָה: וְאָנֹכִי נְטַעְתִּיךְ שׂוֹרֵק כֻּלֹּה זֶרַע אֱמֶת וְאֵיךְ נֶהְפַּכְתְּ לִי סוּרֵי הַגֶּפֶן נָכְרִיָּה:
כב כג כִּי אִם־תְּכַבְּסִי בַּנֶּתֶר וְתַרְבִּי־לָךְ בֹּרִית נִכְתָּם עֲוֹנֵךְ לְפָנַי נְאֻם אֲדֹנָי יֱהוִה: אֵיךְ תֹּאמְרִי לֹא נִטְמֵאתִי
כד אַחֲרֵי הַבְּעָלִים לֹא הָלַכְתִּי רְאִי דַרְכֵּךְ בַּגַּיְא דְּעִי מֶה עָשִׂית בִּכְרָה קַלָּה מְשָׂרֶכֶת דְּרָכֶיהָ: פֶּרֶה ׀ לִמֻּד
כה מִדְבָּר בְּאַוַּת נפשו שָׁאֲפָה רוּחַ תַּאֲנָתָהּ מִי יְשִׁיבֶנָּה כָּל־מְבַקְשֶׁיהָ לֹא יִיעָפוּ בְּחָדְשָׁהּ יִמְצָאוּנְהָ: מִנְעִי נַפְשָׁהּ
כו רַגְלֵךְ מִיָּחֵף וגורנך מִצִּמְאָה וַתֹּאמְרִי נוֹאָשׁ לוֹא כִּי־אָהַבְתִּי זָרִים וְאַחֲרֵיהֶם אֵלֵךְ: כְּבֹשֶׁת גַּנָּב כִּי יִמָּצֵא וּגְרוֹנֵךְ
כז כֵּן הֹבִישׁוּ בֵּית יִשְׂרָאֵל הֵמָּה מַלְכֵיהֶם שָׂרֵיהֶם וְכֹהֲנֵיהֶם וּנְבִיאֵיהֶם: אֹמְרִים לָעֵץ אָבִי אַתָּה וְלָאֶבֶן אַתְּ
כח ילדתני כִּי־פָנוּ אֵלַי עֹרֶף וְלֹא פָנִים וּבְעֵת רָעָתָם יֹאמְרוּ קוּמָה וְהוֹשִׁיעֵנוּ: וְאַיֵּה אֱלֹהֶיךָ אֲשֶׁר עָשִׂיתָ יְלִדְתָּנוּ
לָּךְ יָקוּמוּ אִם־יוֹשִׁיעוּךָ בְּעֵת רָעָתֶךָ כִּי מִסְפַּר עָרֶיךָ הָיוּ אֱלֹהֶיךָ יְהוּדָה:

Ashkenazim and Minhag Anglia add

ג ד הֲלוֹא מֵעַתָּה קראתי לִי אָבִי אַלּוּף נְעֻרַי אָתָּה: קָרָאת

Sepharadim, Chabad, and Minhag Anglia add

ד א ב אִם־תָּשׁוּב יִשְׂרָאֵל ׀ נְאֻם־יהוה אֵלַי תָּשׁוּב וְאִם־תָּסִיר שִׁקּוּצֶיךָ מִפָּנַי וְלֹא תָנוּד: וְנִשְׁבַּעְתָּ חַי־יהוה
בֶּאֱמֶת בְּמִשְׁפָּט וּבִצְדָקָה וְהִתְבָּרְכוּ בוֹ גוֹיִם וּבוֹ יִתְהַלָּלוּ:

benefits he has received and endangers himself. He will either find himself without water after making himself dependent on cracked cisterns that do not hold water (a metaphor for the empty idolatrous religions), or he will

ISAIAH
For Yemenites

1 1 The vision of Yeshayahu son of Amotz, which he saw regarding Yehuda and Jerusalem in the days of
2 Uziyahu, Yotam, Aḥaz, and Ḥizkiyahu, kings of Yehuda: Listen, heavens, hear, O earth: the Lord has
3 spoken: I brought up children, raised them; they rebelled against Me. Even an ox knows its owner, an
4 ass its master's trough. Israel does not know; My people does not try to understand. Woe to the sinning nation, a people weighed down with iniquity, seed of the wicked, vicious children, they forsook
5 the Lord, defamed the Holy One of Israel, fell away. Why should you suffer more beatings? Yet you
6 spawn more defiance, your head sickened, all, your whole heart ailing. From sole to crown – nothing
7 is sound; laceration, bruise, and open wound never squeezed or bandaged; never eased with oil: your
land is laid waste, your towns burned up in fire; your own land – before your eyes strangers consume
8 it – laid waste: a vision of strangers' overturning. Only daughter Zion stands like the watchman's shack
9 in a vineyard, like the hut in a cucumber field – a town besieged. *Were it not for the Lord of Hosts, who*
10 *left of us a bare remnant, we would have been like Sedom, like Amora – gone.* Listen to the Lord's
11 word, you officers of Sedom; hear the teaching of our God, you townsmen of Amora. Why, says the
Lord, would I want all these offerings? I am sated with burnt offerings, with rams and fleshy creatures'
12 fat, the blood of bulls and sheep and goats – I do not want them. You come, appear before Me. Who
13 asked all this of you, who asked you for all this: trampling My courtyards? Bring no more your empty
gifts – they are foul incense to Me; New Moon and Sabbath, the feast days you proclaim – I cannot
14 endure these sins and assemblies. Your New Moons and festivals, how I hate them; they have become a
15 burden to Me; I am weary, I cannot bear them. When you spread your hands out skyward, I must turn
My eyes away; when you pray with such verbosity, I am not listening. Your hands, they are covered in
16 blood. Wash them, be clean now, remove your terrible deeds from My sight; stop bringing about such
17 evils. Learn to do good. Seek justice. Correct what is cruel. Rule justice for orphans. Fight the widows'
18 cause. Come, let us argue this out; so says the Lord. Though your sins may be like scarlet,
they will grow whiter than snow. Though they redden you more than dye worms, they will be clean
19 20 wool again. If you will it and listen, the best of this earth is yours to eat, but if you refuse and rebel
against Me, the sword will devour you; the Lord has spoken.

Haftarat Devarim

ISAIAH
Ashkenazim and Sepharadim begin here

1 1 The vision of Yeshayahu son of Amotz, which he saw regarding Yehuda and Jerusalem in the days of
2 Uziyahu, Yotam, Aḥaz, and Ḥizkiyahu, kings of Yehuda: Listen, heavens, hear, O earth: the Lord has
3 spoken: I brought up children, raised them; they rebelled against Me. Even an ox knows its owner, an
4 ass its master's trough. Israel does not know; My people does not try to understand. Woe to the sinning nation, a people weighed down with iniquity, seed of the wicked, vicious children, they forsook
5 the Lord, defamed the Holy One of Israel, fell away. Why should you suffer more beatings? Yet you

---

DEVARIM

Yeshayahu prophesied in the kingdom of Yehuda and Jerusalem for decades, during the reigns of Uziyahu, Yotam, Aḥaz, and Ḥizkiyahu. During this period, Yehuda went through spiritual, political-military, and social turmoil. In this *haftara*, Yeshayahu mentions the city of Sedom twice, both for the terrible punishment meted out on it and for the extreme wickedness with which it was saturated. Leaders have a crucial role to play in shaping the communal atmosphere of a place, for good and for bad. The prophet describes a corrupt leadership, which takes advantage of its power for its own purposes and oppresses the weakest members of society,

ישעיה
For Yemenites

א א חֲזוֹן יְשַׁעְיָהוּ בֶן־אָמוֹץ אֲשֶׁר חָזָה עַל־יְהוּדָה וִירוּשָׁלָ͏ִם בִּימֵי עֻזִּיָּהוּ יוֹתָם אָחָז יְחִזְקִיָּהוּ מַלְכֵי יְהוּדָה׃
ב ג שִׁמְעוּ שָׁמַיִם וְהַאֲזִינִי אֶרֶץ כִּי יְהוָה דִּבֵּר בָּנִים גִּדַּלְתִּי וְרוֹמַמְתִּי וְהֵם פָּשְׁעוּ בִי׃ יָדַע שׁוֹר קֹנֵהוּ וַחֲמוֹר
ד אֵבוּס בְּעָלָיו יִשְׂרָאֵל לֹא יָדַע עַמִּי לֹא הִתְבּוֹנָן׃ הוֹי ׀ גּוֹי חֹטֵא עַם כֶּבֶד עָוֺן זֶרַע מְרֵעִים בָּנִים מַשְׁחִיתִים
ה עָזְבוּ אֶת־יְהוָה נִאֲצוּ אֶת־קְדוֹשׁ יִשְׂרָאֵל נָזֹרוּ אָחוֹר׃ עַל מֶה תֻכּוּ עוֹד תּוֹסִיפוּ סָרָה כָּל־רֹאשׁ לָחֳלִי וְכָל־
ו לֵבָב דַּוָּי׃ מִכַּף־רֶגֶל וְעַד־רֹאשׁ אֵין־בּוֹ מְתֹם פֶּצַע וְחַבּוּרָה וּמַכָּה טְרִיָּה לֹא־זֹרוּ וְלֹא חֻבָּשׁוּ וְלֹא רֻכְּכָה
ז בַּשָּׁמֶן׃ אַרְצְכֶם שְׁמָמָה עָרֵיכֶם שְׂרֻפוֹת אֵשׁ אַדְמַתְכֶם לְנֶגְדְּכֶם זָרִים אֹכְלִים אֹתָהּ וּשְׁמָמָה כְּמַהְפֵּכַת
ח ט זָרִים׃ וְנוֹתְרָה בַת־צִיּוֹן כְּסֻכָּה בְכָרֶם כִּמְלוּנָה בְמִקְשָׁה כְּעִיר נְצוּרָה׃ לוּלֵי יְהוָה צְבָאוֹת הוֹתִיר לָנוּ שָׂרִיד
י כִּמְעָט כִּסְדֹם הָיִינוּ לַעֲמֹרָה דָּמִינוּ׃ שִׁמְעוּ דְבַר־יְהוָה קְצִינֵי סְדֹם הַאֲזִינוּ תּוֹרַת אֱלֹהֵינוּ עַם
יא עֲמֹרָה׃ לָמָּה לִּי רֹב־זִבְחֵיכֶם יֹאמַר יְהוָה שָׂבַעְתִּי עֹלוֹת אֵילִים וְחֵלֶב מְרִיאִים וְדַם פָּרִים וּכְבָשִׂים וְעַתּוּדִים
יב יג לֹא חָפָצְתִּי׃ כִּי תָבֹאוּ לֵרָאוֹת פָּנָי מִי־בִקֵּשׁ זֹאת מִיֶּדְכֶם רְמֹס חֲצֵרָי׃ לֹא תוֹסִיפוּ הָבִיא מִנְחַת־שָׁוְא
יד קְטֹרֶת תּוֹעֵבָה הִיא לִי חֹדֶשׁ וְשַׁבָּת קְרֹא מִקְרָא לֹא־אוּכַל אָוֶן וַעֲצָרָה׃ חָדְשֵׁיכֶם וּמוֹעֲדֵיכֶם שָׂנְאָה
טו נַפְשִׁי הָיוּ עָלַי לָטֹרַח נִלְאֵיתִי נְשֹׂא׃ וּבְפָרִשְׂכֶם כַּפֵּיכֶם אַעְלִים עֵינַי מִכֶּם גַּם כִּי־תַרְבּוּ תְפִלָּה אֵינֶנִּי
טז יז שֹׁמֵעַ יְדֵיכֶם דָּמִים מָלֵאוּ׃ רַחֲצוּ הִזַּכּוּ הָסִירוּ רֹעַ מַעַלְלֵיכֶם מִנֶּגֶד עֵינָי חִדְלוּ הָרֵעַ׃ לִמְדוּ הֵיטֵב דִּרְשׁוּ
יח מִשְׁפָּט אַשְּׁרוּ חָמוֹץ שִׁפְטוּ יָתוֹם רִיבוּ אַלְמָנָה׃ לְכוּ־נָא וְנִוָּכְחָה יֹאמַר יְהוָה אִם־יִהְיוּ חֲטָאֵיכֶם
יט כ כַּשָּׁנִים כַּשֶּׁלֶג יַלְבִּינוּ אִם־יַאְדִּימוּ כַתּוֹלָע כַּצֶּמֶר יִהְיוּ׃ אִם־תֹּאבוּ וּשְׁמַעְתֶּם טוּב הָאָרֶץ תֹּאכֵלוּ׃ וְאִם־
תְּמָאֲנוּ וּמְרִיתֶם חֶרֶב תְּאֻכְּלוּ כִּי פִּי יְהוָה דִּבֵּר׃

הפטרת דברים

ישעיה
Ashkenazim and Sepharadim begin here

א א חֲזוֹן יְשַׁעְיָהוּ בֶן־אָמוֹץ אֲשֶׁר חָזָה עַל־יְהוּדָה וִירוּשָׁלָ͏ִם בִּימֵי עֻזִּיָּהוּ יוֹתָם אָחָז יְחִזְקִיָּהוּ מַלְכֵי יְהוּדָה׃
ב ג שִׁמְעוּ שָׁמַיִם וְהַאֲזִינִי אֶרֶץ כִּי יְהוָה דִּבֵּר בָּנִים גִּדַּלְתִּי וְרוֹמַמְתִּי וְהֵם פָּשְׁעוּ בִי׃ יָדַע שׁוֹר קֹנֵהוּ וַחֲמוֹר
ד אֵבוּס בְּעָלָיו יִשְׂרָאֵל לֹא יָדַע עַמִּי לֹא הִתְבּוֹנָן׃ הוֹי ׀ גּוֹי חֹטֵא עַם כֶּבֶד עָוֺן זֶרַע מְרֵעִים בָּנִים מַשְׁחִיתִים
ה עָזְבוּ אֶת־יְהוָה נִאֲצוּ אֶת־קְדוֹשׁ יִשְׂרָאֵל נָזֹרוּ אָחוֹר׃ עַל מֶה תֻכּוּ עוֹד תּוֹסִיפוּ סָרָה כָּל־רֹאשׁ לָחֳלִי וְכָל־

Yemenites

When we look at the words of reproach with which the prophet Yeshayahu berated the people, two lines of thought in particular stand out. First, God is disappointed with the people's disloyal behavior after all He has done for them. Second, God cares nothing about the sacrificial service in the Temple if the worshipper at the same time leads a wicked life. The destruction of many parts of the land of Israel by enemies should have given the Israelites pause to consider the error of their ways, but even these misfortunes could not convince them to repent. The prophet calls on the people to mend their behavior before the final hammer falls.

6 spawn more defiance, your head sickened, all, your whole heart ailing. From sole to crown – nothing is
7 sound; laceration, bruise, and open wound never squeezed or bandaged; never eased with oil: your land
is laid waste, your towns burned up in fire; your own land – before your eyes strangers consume it – laid
8 waste: a vision of strangers' overturning. Only daughter Zion stands like the watchman's shack in a vine-
9 yard, like the hut in a cucumber field – a town besieged. *Were it not for the LORD of Hosts, who left of us a*
10 *bare remnant, we would have been like Sedom, like Amora – gone.* Listen to the LORD's word, you
11 officers of Sedom; hear the teaching of our God, you townsmen of Amora. Why, says the LORD, would
I want all these offerings? I am sated with burnt offerings, with rams and fleshy creatures' fat, the blood
12 of bulls and sheep and goats – I do not want them. You come, appear before Me. Who asked all this of
13 you, who asked you for all this: trampling My courtyards? Bring no more your empty gifts – they are foul
incense to Me; New Moon and Sabbath, the feast days you proclaim – I cannot endure these sins and
14 assemblies. Your New Moons and festivals, how I hate them; they have become a burden to Me; I am
15 weary, I cannot bear them. When you spread your hands out skyward, I must turn My eyes away; when
16 you pray with such verbosity, I am not listening. Your hands, they are covered in blood. Wash them, be
17 clean now, remove your terrible deeds from My sight; stop bringing about such evils. Learn to do good.
18 Seek justice. Correct what is cruel. Rule justice for orphans. Fight the widows' cause. Come,
let us argue this out; so says the LORD. Though your sins may be like scarlet, they will grow whiter than
19 snow. Though they redden you more than dye worms, they will be clean wool again. If you will it and
20 listen, the best of this earth is yours to eat, but if you refuse and rebel against Me, the sword will devour
21 you; the LORD has spoken. *How like a whore is she now, the faithful metropolis. How full she *Yemenites begin here*
22 was of justice once; righteousness lodged with her, now murderers. Your silver has turned into dross,
23 your wine is watered down, your ministers are wayward, friends to thieves, loving corruption, all of
them, chasing bribes. They do not judge an orphan's case; a widow's claim does not even come before
24 them. And so, says the Master, the LORD of Hosts, the Mighty One of Israel: This woe! – I shall
25 seek consolation, crush My foes, wreak vengeance on My enemies. I shall set My hand against you again,
26 as if smelting, refining away your dross; all your lead will I remove. I shall set up your judges again as first
they were, your counselors as long ago. And then you shall be called Righteous City, Faithful Metropolis.
27 Zion will be redeemed by justice, by righteousness – those who return to her;* rebels and sinners will all *Ashkenazim and*
28
29 be broken, those who forsook the LORD all gone. How ashamed you will be of the oaks that you longed *Sepharadim end here*
30 for, how mortified over the gardens you chose. For you will be like an oak with withered leaves, like a
31 garden that sees no water. That mighty oak will become flax fibers and the one who once carved them the
spark; the two will burn together, and no one will be there to quench the fire. *Yemenites end here*

HAFTARAT VAETḤANAN

40 1 Comfort, comfort, My people – these are your God's words – speak to Jerusalem's heart and call out ISAIAH
2 to her that her term is served, her guilt appeased, that she has received at the LORD's hand twice over

VAETḤANAN

The central idea of this *haftara* is the smallness of human beings when compared to the eternal God. The attempts by the nations of the world to erect idolatrous alternatives to the true God are futile. Human beings and their creations are transient. God, who created and controls the world through His providence, determines the course of history. The nation of Israel is in exile not because of the

ו לֵבָב דַּוָּי׃ מִכַּף־רֶגֶל וְעַד־רֹאשׁ אֵין־בּוֹ מְתֹם פֶּצַע וְחַבּוּרָה וּמַכָּה טְרִיָּה לֹא־זֹרוּ וְלֹא חֻבָּשׁוּ וְלֹא רֻכְּכָה
ז בַּשָּׁמֶן׃ אַרְצְכֶם שְׁמָמָה עָרֵיכֶם שְׂרֻפוֹת אֵשׁ אַדְמַתְכֶם לְנֶגְדְּכֶם זָרִים אֹכְלִים אֹתָהּ וּשְׁמָמָה כְּמַהְפֵּכַת
ח ט זָרִים׃ וְנוֹתְרָה בַת־צִיּוֹן כְּסֻכָּה בְכָרֶם כִּמְלוּנָה בְמִקְשָׁה כְּעִיר נְצוּרָה׃ לוּלֵי יהוה צְבָאוֹת הוֹתִיר לָנוּ
י שָׂרִיד כִּמְעָט כִּסְדֹם הָיִינוּ לַעֲמֹרָה דָּמִינוּ׃ שִׁמְעוּ דְבַר־יהוה קְצִינֵי סְדֹם הַאֲזִינוּ תּוֹרַת
יא אֱלֹהֵינוּ עַם עֲמֹרָה׃ לָמָּה־לִּי רֹב־זִבְחֵיכֶם יֹאמַר יהוה שָׂבַעְתִּי עֹלוֹת אֵילִים וְחֵלֶב מְרִיאִים וְדַם פָּרִים
יב יג וּכְבָשִׂים וְעַתּוּדִים לֹא חָפָצְתִּי׃ כִּי תָבֹאוּ לֵרָאוֹת פָּנָי מִי־בִקֵּשׁ זֹאת מִיֶּדְכֶם רְמֹס חֲצֵרָי׃ לֹא תוֹסִיפוּ
יד הָבִיא מִנְחַת־שָׁוְא קְטֹרֶת תּוֹעֵבָה הִיא לִי חֹדֶשׁ וְשַׁבָּת קְרֹא מִקְרָא לֹא־אוּכַל אָוֶן וַעֲצָרָה׃ חָדְשֵׁיכֶם
טו וּמוֹעֲדֵיכֶם שָׂנְאָה נַפְשִׁי הָיוּ עָלַי לָטֹרַח נִלְאֵיתִי נְשֹׂא׃ וּבְפָרִשְׂכֶם כַּפֵּיכֶם אַעְלִים עֵינַי מִכֶּם גַּם כִּי־תַרְבּוּ
טז יז תְפִלָּה אֵינֶנִּי שֹׁמֵעַ יְדֵיכֶם דָּמִים מָלֵאוּ׃ רַחֲצוּ הִזַּכּוּ הָסִירוּ רֹעַ מַעַלְלֵיכֶם מִנֶּגֶד עֵינָי חִדְלוּ הָרֵעַ׃ לִמְדוּ
יח הֵיטֵב דִּרְשׁוּ מִשְׁפָּט אַשְּׁרוּ חָמוֹץ שִׁפְטוּ יָתוֹם רִיבוּ אַלְמָנָה׃ לְכוּ־נָא וְנִוָּכְחָה יֹאמַר יהוה
יט אִם־יִהְיוּ חֲטָאֵיכֶם כַּשָּׁנִים כַּשֶּׁלֶג יַלְבִּינוּ אִם־יַאְדִּימוּ כַתּוֹלָע כַּצֶּמֶר יִהְיוּ׃ אִם־תֹּאבוּ וּשְׁמַעְתֶּם טוּב

Yemenites begin here

כ כא הָאָרֶץ תֹּאכֵלוּ׃ וְאִם־תְּמָאֲנוּ וּמְרִיתֶם חֶרֶב תְּאֻכְּלוּ כִּי פִּי יהוה דִּבֵּר׃ *אֵיכָה הָיְתָה לְזוֹנָה
כב קִרְיָה נֶאֱמָנָה מְלֵאֲתִי מִשְׁפָּט צֶדֶק יָלִין בָּהּ וְעַתָּה מְרַצְּחִים׃ כַּסְפֵּךְ הָיָה לְסִיגִים סָבְאֵךְ מָהוּל בַּמָּיִם׃
כג שָׂרַיִךְ סוֹרְרִים וְחַבְרֵי גַּנָּבִים כֻּלּוֹ אֹהֵב שֹׁחַד וְרֹדֵף שַׁלְמֹנִים יָתוֹם לֹא יִשְׁפֹּטוּ וְרִיב אַלְמָנָה לֹא־יָבוֹא
כד אֲלֵיהֶם׃ לָכֵן נְאֻם הָאָדוֹן יהוה צְבָאוֹת אֲבִיר יִשְׂרָאֵל הוֹי אֶנָּחֵם מִצָּרַי וְאִנָּקְמָה מֵאוֹיְבָי׃
כה כו וְאָשִׁיבָה יָדִי עָלַיִךְ וְאֶצְרֹף כַּבֹּר סִיגָיִךְ וְאָסִירָה כָּל־בְּדִילָיִךְ׃ וְאָשִׁיבָה שֹׁפְטַיִךְ כְּבָרִאשֹׁנָה וְיֹעֲצַיִךְ כְּבַתְּחִלָּה

Ashkenazim and Sephardim end here

כז כח אַחֲרֵי־כֵן יִקָּרֵא לָךְ עִיר הַצֶּדֶק קִרְיָה נֶאֱמָנָה׃ צִיּוֹן בְּמִשְׁפָּט תִּפָּדֶה וְשָׁבֶיהָ בִּצְדָקָה׃* וְשֶׁבֶר פֹּשְׁעִים
כט ל וְחַטָּאִים יַחְדָּו וְעֹזְבֵי יהוה יִכְלוּ׃ כִּי יֵבֹשׁוּ מֵאֵילִים אֲשֶׁר חֲמַדְתֶּם וְתַחְפְּרוּ מֵהַגַּנּוֹת אֲשֶׁר בְּחַרְתֶּם׃ כִּי
לא תִהְיוּ כְּאֵלָה נֹבֶלֶת עָלֶהָ וּכְגַנָּה אֲשֶׁר־מַיִם אֵין לָהּ׃ וְהָיָה הֶחָסֹן לִנְעֹרֶת וּפֹעֲלוֹ לְנִיצוֹץ וּבָעֲרוּ שְׁנֵיהֶם יַחְדָּו
וְאֵין מְכַבֶּה׃

Yemenites end here

הפטרת ואתחנן

ישעיה

מ א ב נַחֲמוּ נַחֲמוּ עַמִּי יֹאמַר אֱלֹהֵיכֶם׃ דַּבְּרוּ עַל־לֵב יְרוּשָׁלִַם וְקִרְאוּ אֵלֶיהָ כִּי מָלְאָה צְבָאָהּ כִּי נִרְצָה עֲוֺנָהּ
ג כִּי לָקְחָה מִיַּד יהוה כִּפְלַיִם בְּכָל־חַטֹּאתֶיהָ׃ קוֹל קוֹרֵא בַּמִּדְבָּר פַּנּוּ דֶּרֶךְ יהוה יַשְּׁרוּ בָּעֲרָבָה

and whose dishonesty filters down into the streets and shops of ordinary citizens. Fake goods are marketed as authentic, and what had once been a city of justice is filled with murderers. Israel can only succeed in correcting these evils if the corrupt leadership is replaced. This is a vision (*ḥazon*) that we must all take to heart on the Shabbat before the Ninth of Av, Shabbat Ḥazon.

3 for all her sins. A voice calls out: "Clear the LORD's way in the desert: smooth across the
4 arid plain a road for our God." Every valley will be raised, each hill and mountain leveled; the twisted
5 road will be made straight; the mountain ranges, open land, to let the LORD's glory be revealed, and all
6 flesh see as one – the voice of the LORD has spoken. A voice speaks: "Call out!" I say, "What
7 shall I call?" All life is nothing more than grass, and all its love, green shoots upon the land. And grass
dries up; shoots wither, when the LORD's breath blows over them and yes – this people is but grass.
8 Grass dries up, and shoots will wither, but the word of our God stands firm; always. O lady,
9 ascend the high mountain, you who bear tidings to Zion; raise your voice in strength, with tidings to
10 Jerusalem. Raise it – do not fear – call out loud to the cities of Yehuda: "Behold: your God." Behold:
the LORD your God coming in all His strength, His mighty arm ruling. Behold: with Him, His prize;
11 His reward walks before Him; like a shepherd He pastures His flock, gathering the lambs into His
12 arms, bearing them in His embrace, guiding His young. Who was it who measured out the
waters in His palm and gauged the skies by His handspan? Who measured in His fingers all the dust
13 of earth; who weighed out the hills on His balance and the mountains upon a hand scale? Who could
14 survey the wind? The LORD. Who is the confidant He would tell? To gain His insight, with whom did
He hold counsel; who taught Him the path of justice? Who ever taught Him awareness; who showed
15 Him the way of insight? Whole nations are like the drop left in His bucket, as inconsequential as dust
16 on the balance. He sweeps up the distant isles like powder. All Lebanon has not wood enough, or
17 animals, for the burnt offering. All the nations are as nothing before Him, less than absence,
18 than emptiness, to Him. And what will you liken to God; what image will you draw of Him? A smith
19
20 molds a statue; the jeweler plates it with gold and fashions chains of silver for it. Mulberry wood his
offering, he chooses a tree that will not rot; he chooses a skilled craftsman to build a statue that can-
21 not fall. Do you not know it, have you not heard, was it not told to you long before? Have you paid no
22 attention to the world's foundations? He sits over the dome of the sky, its dwellers like grasshoppers
23 below; He spreads out the skies like a canvas and pulls them taut like a tent to dwell in. He turns great
24 rulers to nothing, the judges of this earth to emptiness, as if they were not planted, were not sown, as
if their stem had no root within the earth. He breathes on them and they dry up to nothing; the storm
25 will sweep them all away like straw. Whom can you compare Me to – so speaks the Holy
26 One – and find them equal? Raise your eyes skyward and see: Who created all these? Who summons
their legions by number and calls each man by name? In His great might, His adamantine strength, not
one of them is lost.* Why do you say, Yaakov; Israel, why declare, "My way is hidden from the *Ashkenazim and Sepharadim end here*
LORD; my God overlooks my claim"?

41 17 The oppressed, impoverished, beg for water – there is none; their tongues are seared with thirst. I am
the LORD; I will answer them; Israel's God, I will not leave them.

in the sixth year of the reign of Ḥizkiyahu king of Yehuda. Still, the themes here remain relevant to all subsequent exiles, and they echo in our synagogues every year on the first Shabbat after the Ninth of Av.

ד ה מסלה לאלהינו: כל־גיא ינשא וכל־הר וגבעה ישפלו והיה העקב למישור והרכסים לבקעה: ונגלה
ו כבוד יהוה וראו כל־בשר יחדו כי פי יהוה דבר: קול אמר קרא ואמר מה אקרא כל־הבשר
ז ח חציר וכל־חסדו כציץ השדה: יבש חציר נבל ציץ כי רוח יהוה נשבה בו אכן חציר העם: יבש חציר
ט נבל ציץ ודבר אלהינו יקום לעולם: על הר־גבה עלי־לך מבשרת ציון הרימי בכח קולך
י מבשרת ירושלם הרימי אל־תיראי אמרי לערי יהודה הנה אלהיכם: הנה אדני יהוה בחזק יבוא
יא וזרעו משלה לו הנה שכרו אתו ופעלתו לפניו: כרעה עדרו ירעה בזרעו יקבץ טלאים ובחיקו ישא
יב עלות ינהל: מי־מדד בשעלו מים ושמים בזרת תכן וכל בשלש עפר הארץ ושקל בפלס
יג יד הרים וגבעות במאזנים: מי־תכן את־רוח יהוה ואיש עצתו יודיענו: את־מי נועץ ויבינהו וילמדהו
טו בארח משפט וילמדהו דעת ודרך תבונות יודיענו: הן גוים כמר מדלי וכשחק מאזנים נחשבו
טז יז הן איים כדק יטול: ולבנון אין די בער וחיתו אין די עולה: כל־הגוים כאין נגדו מאפס
יח יט ותהו נחשבו־לו: ואל־מי תדמיון אל ומה־דמות תערכו־לו: הפסל נסך חרש וצרף בזהב ירקענו
כ ורתקות כסף צורף: המסכן תרומה עץ לא־ירקב יבחר חרש חכם יבקש־לו להכין פסל לא ימוט:
כא כב הלוא תדעו הלוא תשמעו הלוא הגד מראש לכם הלוא הבינותם מוסדות הארץ: הישב על־חוג
כג הארץ וישביה כחגבים הנוטה כדק שמים וימתחם כאהל לשבת: הנותן רוזנים לאין שפטי ארץ
כד כתהו עשה: אף בל־נטעו אף בל־זרעו אף בל־שרש בארץ גזעם וגם נשף בהם ויבשו וסערה כקש
כה כו תשאם: ואל־מי תדמיוני ואשוה יאמר קדוש: שאו־מרום עיניכם וראו מי־ברא אלה
Ashkenazim and Sepharadim end here המוציא במספר צבאם לכלם בשם יקרא מרב אונים ואמיץ כח איש לא נעדר:* למה תאמר
יעקב ותדבר ישראל נסתרה דרכי מיהוה ומאלהי משפטי יעבור:
מא יז העניים והאביונים מבקשים מים ואין לשונם בצמא נשתה אני יהוה אענם אלהי ישראל לא אעזבם:

victory of foreign gods but because of the abandonment of its own.

God's call to comfort His people is true, and the redemption is inevitable. This first prophecy of reassurance after the destruction was perhaps issued by Yeshayahu after the destruction of the northern kingdom of Israel by Assyria

Haftarat Ekev

49 14 15 Zion speaks: "The LORD has forsaken me; my Lord, He has forgotten me." Can a mother forget her own ISAIAH
16 baby; can she fail to care for the child of her womb? These too may yet forget, but I will not forget you. I
17 have etched you on My palms; your walls are before My eyes always. Your children will run to you; your
18 destroyers, your demolishers, will all be gone from you. Raise your eyes; look around and see: the children all gathered and coming back to you. As I live, so says the LORD, you will wear them all as jewels,
19 which you will bind on like a bride. For your ruins, for your wastelands, for the land of your destruction,
for you will be too narrow for your dwellers, while those who would destroy you will be far away from
20 you. You will yet hear the children say, of whom you were bereaved, "The place is too tight for me; make
21 space for me to sit," while you say in your heart, "Who bore these children, mine, to me, bereft and left
alone, exiled and expelled; these children – who has raised them? I was left all alone, and these – who
22 can they be?" So says the Lord GOD: Behold: I shall raise My hands to nations, lift My banner
toward peoples; they will bring your sons back in the folds of their robes, bearing your daughters upon
23 their shoulders; kings will be your caregivers, their princesses your nursemaids. They will bow to the
ground before you and kiss the dust you tread upon, and you will know: I am the LORD, and those who
24 wait for Me will not be shamed. Can a mighty warrior be plundered; can a victor's captives flee?
25 For so says the LORD: The mighty man's captives may yet be taken, the tyrant's plunder flee, but I shall
26 fight against those who fight you, I will save your children. To those who wrong you, I will feed their own
flesh; their blood will intoxicate them like wine, and all flesh will know then that I am the LORD, your
50 1 rescue, your redeemer, Mighty One of Yaakov. So says the LORD: Where is your mother's bill
of divorce with which I banished her? Which one of My creditors have I, then, sold you to? No, it was for
2 your sins that you were sold; for your faithlessness your mother was sent hence. Why is it that I came,
and no man was here; I cried out, and no one answered? Does My arm fall short to redeem you; have
I not strength to rescue? No – at My rebuke I dry the sea; I turn whole rivers to desert land. Their fish
3 will stink for lack of water, dead of thirst. I will dress the skies in darkness and make mourning sack their
4 covering. The LORD my God made me a learning tongue to sustain the weary with words;
5 morning, early morning, He wakens my ears, He wakes them, like students, to hear. The LORD my God
6 opened my ears, and I did not reject Him; I never shrank back; I gave up my back to beating, my cheeks
7 to those who scratched them. I never hid my face from humiliations, spittle, but the LORD my God will
8 help me, and so no humiliation; I set my face as flint and know I will not be ashamed. He is near who
shows me righteous. Who, then, will contend with me? Let us stand up opposing one another. Who has
9 a claim against me? Let him come to me, for the Lord GOD, He will help me; who then can condemn
10 me? They will wear out like an old cloak; moths will eat them. Who of you reveres the LORD,
and listens to His servant's voice? Let one who walked in darkness, nothing shining for him, trust in the
11 LORD's name, and lean on his God. You – you light your fire and gird yourselves with torchlight. Walk
by the light of your own fire, by torches that you burn. From My hand, all this came to you; you will lie
51 1 2 down in pain. You who chase righteousness, listen to Me, you who seek the LORD: Look to
the rock you are hewed from, the quarry from which you were carved; look to your father, Avraham, to
3 Sara who gave you birth, for I called him, one alone, and blessed him, made him many. And the LORD has
comforted Zion, brought comfort to all her ruins; He has made her desert like Eden, her arid land like the
LORD's garden; celebration, joy are found in her, and thanks, and sounds of song.

---

bring about the ingathering of the exiles and the reconstitution of the people of Israel in their land, belying the exile and destruction that Yeshayahu's listeners saw before their eyes.

הפטרת עקב

ישעיה

מט יד טו ותאמר ציון עזבני יהוה ואדני שכחני: התשכח אשה עולה מרחם בן־בטנה גם־אלה תשכחנה ואנכי
טז לא אשכחך: הן על־כפים חקתיך חומתיך נגדי תמיד: מהרו בניך מהרסיך ומחריביך ממך יצאו:
יח שאי־סביב עיניך וראי כלם נקבצו באו־לך חי־אני נאם־יהוה כי כלם כעדי תלבשי ותקשרים ככלה:
יט כ כי חרבתיך ושממתיך וארץ הרסתך כי עתה תצרי מיושב ורחקו מבלעיך: עוד יאמרו באזניך בני
כא שכליך צר־לי המקום גשה־לי ואשבה: ואמרת בלבבך מי ילד־לי את־אלה ואני שכולה וגלמודה גלה ׀
כב וסורה ואלה מי גדל הן אני נשארתי לבדי אלה איפה הם: כה־אמר אדני יהוה הנה אשא
כג אל־גוים ידי ואל־עמים ארים נסי והביאו בניך בחצן ובנתיך על־כתף תנשאנה: והיו מלכים אמניך
ושרותיהם מיניקתיך אפים ארץ ישתחוו לך ועפר רגליך ילחכו וידעת כי־אני יהוה אשר לא־יבשו
כד כה קוי: היקח מגבור מלקוח ואם־שבי צדיק ימלט: כי־כה ׀ אמר יהוה גם־שבי גבור יקח
כו ומלקוח עריץ ימלט ואת־יריבך אנכי אריב ואת־בניך אנכי אושיע: והאכלתי את־מוניך את־בשרם
נ א וכעסיס דמם ישכרון וידעו כל־בשר כי אני יהוה מושיעך וגאלך אביר יעקב: כה ׀ אמר
יהוה אי זה ספר כריתות אמכם אשר שלחתיה או מי מנושי אשר־מכרתי אתכם לו הן בעונתיכם
ב נמכרתם ובפשעיכם שלחה אמכם: מדוע באתי ואין איש קראתי ואין עונה הקצור קצרה ידי
מפדות ואם־אין־בי כח להציל הן בגערתי אחריב ים אשים נהרות מדבר תבאש דגתם מאין מים
ג ד ותמת בצמא: אלביש שמים קדרות ושק אשים כסותם: אדני יהוה נתן לי לשון למודים
ה לדעת לעות את־יעף דבר יעיר ׀ בבקר בבקר יעיר לי אזן לשמע כלמודים: אדני יהוה פתח־לי אזן
ו ואנכי לא מריתי אחור לא נסוגתי: גוי נתתי למכים ולחיי למרטים פני לא הסתרתי מכלמות ורק:
ז ח ואדני יהוה יעזר־לי על־כן לא נכלמתי על־כן שמתי פני כחלמיש ואדע כי־לא אבוש: קרוב מצדיקי
ט מי־יריב אתי נעמדה יחד מי־בעל משפטי יגש אלי: הן אדני יהוה יעזר־לי מי־הוא ירשיעני הן כלם
י כבגד יבלו עש יאכלם: מי בכם ירא יהוה שמע בקול עבדו אשר ׀ הלך חשכים ואין נגה
יא לו יבטח בשם יהוה וישען באלהיו: הן כלכם קדחי אש מאזרי זיקות לכו ׀ באור אשכם ובזיקות
נא א בערתם מידי היתה־זאת לכם למעצבה תשכבון: שמעו אלי רדפי צדק מבקשי יהוה
ב הביטו אל־צור חצבתם ואל־מקבת בור נקרתם: הביטו אל־אברהם אביכם ואל־שרה תחוללכם
ג כי־אחד קראתיו ואברכהו וארבהו: כי־נחם יהוה ציון נחם כל־חרבתיה וישם מדברה כעדן וערבתה
כגן־יהוה ששון ושמחה ימצא בה תודה וקול זמרה:

EKEV

Two central topics feature in this *haftara*: the ingathering of the exiles and the rebuilding of the land of Israel. Without the return of the Israelites to their land, and without the building of the infrastructure there by them, redemption of the people of Israel cannot occur and none of its other aspects can come to fruition. In the lifetime of Yeshayahu, ten of the tribes of Israel were forced from the northern kingdom into exile, and Shomron, the capital of Israel, was laid waste, and this gave Yeshayahu's prophecies of redemption an air of relevance. At the heart of the process of redemption lies the unbreakable connection between God and His people, and to illustrate this connection Yeshayahu uses two metaphors: that of a woman and her child, and that of a husband and wife. These human connections are natural, powerful, and deep. But the prophet pledges in God's name that the link between Him and the people of Israel is even deeper and more powerful than these. It is this link that will

Haftarat Re'eh

On Rosh Ḥodesh Elul, read the maftir from Numbers 28:9–15. Sepharadim read this haftara even if Shabbat coincides with Erev Rosh Ḥodesh or Rosh Ḥodesh. They conclude the haftara by reading the first and last verses of the haftarot for those days. Ashkenazim read this haftara even if Shabbat coincides with Erev Rosh Ḥodesh; however, on Rosh Ḥodesh Elul, they read the haftara on page 1635. Yemenites read the haftara for Rosh Ḥodesh on page 1635. On Erev Rosh Ḥodesh, some read this haftara, while others read the haftara on page 1637.

54 11 Oppressed and storm swept, never comforted; behold: I am paving your ground with garnet, lapis ISAIAH
12 lazuli your foundations. I am fitting your windows with carnelians, your gates with glowing granite,
13 marking your borders with stones men covet. All your children will be students of the LORD, and great
14 will be your children's peace. On righteousness will you be founded; stay far from oppression; you will
15 not fear, and terror will never come near you. No strife can arise without My assent; who among you
16 fears one who could come upon you? For I create the craftsman who blows the charcoal fire and brings
17 forth the tools of his trade; I create also the destroyer to do harm. No weapon made to harm you can
prevail; any tongue that calls you into judgment, you will prove its fault. This is the birthright of the
55 1 LORD's servants, for their innocence is Mine; so says the LORD. You who are thirsty, all, come
to water; you who have no silver, come, take food and eat; come and take food without silver, wine and
2 milk without cost, for why should you weigh out your silver for no bread, your labor bringing you no
3 fullness? Listen – listen to Me: let goodness nourish you, and let your souls delight in plenty. Turn your
ear to Me and come; listen, that your souls may live; let Me forge an everlasting covenant with you, like
4 5 David's faithful promises, for I make him a witness to nations, a leader, a ruler of nations; for you shall
call out, call, to a people you know not, and a people who know you not will come running out to you
for the sake of the LORD your God, the Holy One of Israel, your glory.

Haftarat Shofetim

51 12 13 It is I, I who comfort you. Who are you to fear mortal man, humanity, that ends like grass, forgetting ISAIAH
the LORD who made you, who stretches out the skies, lays down the earth? All day you fear the oppres-
14 sor's rage as he makes his schemes of violence, yet where is the oppressor's rage? The man bent under
15 his burden – how fast will he be freed; he will not die into the pit, nor will his bread be lacking. I am the
16 LORD your God. I trouble the ocean; its waves roar; the LORD of Hosts is My name. I have placed My
words in your mouth and covered you in My hand's shade, planting the skies, laying down the earth,
17 and saying to Zion: "You are My people." Rouse, rouse yourself and rise, Jerusalem, you who
18 have drunk from the LORD's hand His full cup of rage, the poisoned goblet, drunk and drained it. No
one will guide her back, of all the children she has borne; of all the sons she raised there is none to
19 hold her hand. Two things came to you, but who is moved for you? Massacre and breaking, hunger and
20 the sword; through whom may I comfort you? Your children fainted, fallen at every street corner, like

---

SHOFETIM

The prophecy in this *haftara* features four sets of doubled words: *anokhi anokhi* ("I, I"), *hitoreri hitoreri* ("rouse, rouse"), *uri uri* ("rise, rise"), and *suru suru* ("turn, turn aside"). These phrases emphasize the active role of the people, the prophet's listeners, in the process of redemption. The destruction and exile will create a tremendous rupture in the people's spirit. To help overcome this crisis, God pledges His own active involvement: "It is I, I who comfort you." God the omnipotent calls to us to return from exile; the feeling of powerlessness dissipates and is replaced by the joy of redemption.

הפטרת ראה

On ראש חודש אלול*, read the* מפטיר *from* במדבר ט, טו–כח*. Sepharadim read this* הפטרה *even if* שבת *coincides with* ראש חודש *or* ערב ראש חודש*. They conclude the* הפטרה *by reading the first and last verses of the* הפטרות *for those days. Ashkenazim read this* הפטרה *even if* שבת *coincides with* ערב ראש חודש*; however, on* ראש חודש אלול*, they read the* הפטרה *on page 1635. Yemenites read the* הפטרה *for* ראש חודש *on page page 1635. On* ערב ראש חודש*, some read this* הפטרה*, while others read the* הפטרה *on page 1637.*

נד יא יב עֲנִיָּה סֹעֲרָה לֹא נֻחָמָה הִנֵּה אָנֹכִי מַרְבִּיץ בַּפּוּךְ אֲבָנַיִךְ וִיסַדְתִּיךְ בַּסַּפִּירִים׃ וְשַׂמְתִּי כַּדְכֹד שִׁמְשֹׁתַיִךְ ישעיה
יג יד וּשְׁעָרַיִךְ לְאַבְנֵי אֶקְדָּח וְכָל־גְּבוּלֵךְ לְאַבְנֵי־חֵפֶץ׃ וְכָל־בָּנַיִךְ לִמּוּדֵי יהוה וְרַב שְׁלוֹם בָּנָיִךְ׃ בִּצְדָקָה תִּכּוֹנָנִי
טו רַחֲקִי מֵעֹשֶׁק כִּי־לֹא תִירָאִי וּמִמְּחִתָּה כִּי לֹא־תִקְרַב אֵלָיִךְ׃ הֵן גּוֹר יָגוּר אֶפֶס מֵאוֹתִי מִי־גָר אִתָּךְ עָלַיִךְ
טז יז יִפּוֹל׃ הֵן אָנֹכִי בָּרָאתִי חָרָשׁ נֹפֵחַ בְּאֵשׁ פֶּחָם וּמוֹצִיא כְלִי לְמַעֲשֵׂהוּ וְאָנֹכִי בָּרָאתִי מַשְׁחִית לְחַבֵּל׃ כָּל־ הִנֵּה
כְּלִי יוּצַר עָלַיִךְ לֹא יִצְלָח וְכָל־לָשׁוֹן תָּקוּם־אִתָּךְ לַמִּשְׁפָּט תַּרְשִׁיעִי זֹאת נַחֲלַת עַבְדֵי יהוה וְצִדְקָתָם
נה א מֵאִתִּי נְאֻם־יהוה׃ הוֹי כָּל־צָמֵא לְכוּ לַמַּיִם וַאֲשֶׁר אֵין־לוֹ כָּסֶף לְכוּ שִׁבְרוּ וֶאֱכֹלוּ וּלְכוּ שִׁבְרוּ
ב בְּלוֹא־כֶסֶף וּבְלוֹא מְחִיר יַיִן וְחָלָב׃ לָמָּה תִשְׁקְלוּ־כֶסֶף בְּלוֹא־לֶחֶם וִיגִיעֲכֶם בְּלוֹא לְשָׂבְעָה שִׁמְעוּ שָׁמוֹעַ
ג אֵלַי וְאִכְלוּ־טוֹב וְתִתְעַנַּג בַּדֶּשֶׁן נַפְשְׁכֶם׃ הַטּוּ אָזְנְכֶם וּלְכוּ אֵלַי שִׁמְעוּ וּתְחִי נַפְשְׁכֶם וְאֶכְרְתָה לָכֶם
ד ה בְּרִית עוֹלָם חַסְדֵי דָוִד הַנֶּאֱמָנִים׃ הֵן עֵד לְאוּמִּים נְתַתִּיו נָגִיד וּמְצַוֵּה לְאֻמִּים׃ הֵן גּוֹי לֹא־תֵדַע תִּקְרָא
וְגוֹי לֹא־יְדָעוּךָ אֵלֶיךָ יָרוּצוּ לְמַעַן יהוה אֱלֹהֶיךָ וְלִקְדוֹשׁ יִשְׂרָאֵל כִּי פֵאֲרָךְ׃

הפטרת שפטים

נא יב יג אָנֹכִי אָנֹכִי הוּא מְנַחֶמְכֶם מִי־אַתְּ וַתִּירְאִי מֵאֱנוֹשׁ יָמוּת וּמִבֶּן־אָדָם חָצִיר יִנָּתֵן׃ וַתִּשְׁכַּח יהוה עֹשֶׂךָ ישעיה
נוֹטֶה שָׁמַיִם וְיֹסֵד אָרֶץ וַתְּפַחֵד תָּמִיד כָּל־הַיּוֹם מִפְּנֵי חֲמַת הַמֵּצִיק כַּאֲשֶׁר כּוֹנֵן לְהַשְׁחִית וְאַיֵּה חֲמַת
יד טו הַמֵּצִיק׃ מִהַר צֹעֶה לְהִפָּתֵחַ וְלֹא־יָמוּת לַשַּׁחַת וְלֹא יֶחְסַר לַחְמוֹ׃ וְאָנֹכִי יהוה אֱלֹהֶיךָ רֹגַע הַיָּם וַיֶּהֱמוּ
טז גַּלָּיו יהוה צְבָאוֹת שְׁמוֹ׃ וָאָשִׂם דְּבָרַי בְּפִיךָ וּבְצֵל יָדִי כִּסִּיתִיךָ לִנְטֹעַ שָׁמַיִם וְלִיסֹד אָרֶץ וְלֵאמֹר לְצִיּוֹן
יז עַמִּי־אָתָּה׃ הִתְעוֹרְרִי הִתְעוֹרְרִי קוּמִי יְרוּשָׁלִַם אֲשֶׁר שָׁתִית מִיַּד יהוה אֶת־כּוֹס חֲמָתוֹ אֶת־
יח קֻבַּעַת כּוֹס הַתַּרְעֵלָה שָׁתִית מָצִית׃ אֵין־מְנַהֵל לָהּ מִכָּל־בָּנִים יָלָדָה וְאֵין מַחֲזִיק בְּיָדָהּ מִכָּל־בָּנִים גִּדֵּלָה׃
יט כ שְׁתַּיִם הֵנָּה קֹרְאֹתַיִךְ מִי יָנוּד לָךְ הַשֹּׁד וְהַשֶּׁבֶר וְהָרָעָב וְהַחֶרֶב מִי אֲנַחֲמֵךְ׃ בָּנַיִךְ עֻלְּפוּ שָׁכְבוּ בְּרֹאשׁ

RE'EH

The connection between God and Israel is a central theme throughout the Tanakh and history. The mission of the Jewish people is to bring God's word to humanity. But this mission brings us into conflict with other cultures. If Israel remains loyal to God's Torah and serves as a model of morality and justice for the peoples of the world, God promises that we will not be harmed in this spiritual struggle against foreign influences. The success of Israel in its mission to perfect the world and reveal God's sovereignty in it is a main stage in the process of redemption.

21 netted wild oxen, full of the LORD's rage, your God's rebuke. So listen, woman oppressed and drunk
22 but not with wine. So says the LORD, your Lord; so your God fights His people's cause: Behold: I have taken the poisoned cup from your hand, the goblet of My rage; you will drink from it no
23 more. I shall place it in the hands of those who torment you, who have said to your face, "Bow down
52 1 to let us pass." You made your back like earth, like the road to be walked over. Rise, rise, Zion,
and don your dress of might; wear your garb of glory, Jerusalem, holy town, for no more will uncir-
2 cumcised, impure ones enter you. Shake yourself free of the dust; rise up to take your place, Jerusalem.
3 Break free of the chains around your neck, captive daughter Jerusalem. For so says the
4 LORD: You were sold away for nothing, and it is not for silver that you will be redeemed. For
so says the Lord GOD: My people went down long ago to Egypt, to live there for a time; for nothing,
5 Assyria oppressed them, and now, what is there here for Me? So says the LORD: For nothing My
people is taken captive, its rulers baying. So says the LORD: Unceasingly, all day, My name is defamed,
6 and so – My people will know My name, and so – on that day – they will know that it is I who spoke,
7 that I am here. How lovely upon the mountains: the steps of the bringer of tidings, resounding with peace, tidings of good, resounding of rescue, saying to Zion: "Your God has ascended the
8 throne." The voice of your watchmen, their voices rise as one, singing, for they will see with their own
9 eyes the LORD's return to Zion. Break out in song; sing out together, ruins of Jerusalem, for the LORD
10 has comforted His people, redeemed His Jerusalem. The LORD has uncovered His holy arm before
11 the eyes of all nations, and all ends of this earth will see rescue from our God. Turn, turn
aside – leave that place without touching the defiled. Go out from there; cleanse yourselves, you who
12 bear the LORD's vessels; this time you will not leave in haste, you will not leave in flight. The LORD will
go before you, the God of Israel your rear guard behind.

HAFTARAT KI TETZEH

The custom of the Ashkenazim is that if the haftara for Parashat Re'eh was not read due to it coinciding with Rosh Ḥodesh Elul, that haftara is read after this haftara.

54 1 Barren woman, never a mother, rejoice; break out in joyful song though you have not given birth, ISAIAH
2 for the children of the forsaken woman will outnumber those of the wife, so says the LORD. Broaden
the site of your tent; stretch out your canvas home; do not hold back; lengthen your tent cords, and
3 strengthen its pegs: you shall overflow rightward and left, your children possessing nations, and filling
4 forsaken towns with life. Do not fear – you will not be shamed; fear not, for none can disgrace you.
You will forget your youthful abjection; the debasement of your widowhood you will call no more
5 to mind, for your husband, He who made you – the LORD of Hosts is His name, and your redeemer,
6 Israel's Holy One – will be named God of all the world, for as a woman abandoned, of sorrowful spirit,
7 the LORD has called to you: Can the young bride ever be rejected? says your God; for one small mo-
8 ment I left you; with infinite care shall I gather you back; in the flash of My fury I hid My face from
you for just a moment, and in everlasting love will I care for you now. So speaks the LORD, your

---

be founded on the basis of justice and mercy – *if* we do this, we are promised blessing and light that will banish these difficult times. Then, in place of helplessness and sadness, we will find great mercy and eternal charity, for one good act leads to another.

כא כָּל־חוּצוֹת כְּתוֹא מִכְמָר הַמְלֵאִים חֲמַת־יְהוָה גַּעֲרַת אֱלֹהָיִךְ׃ לָכֵן שִׁמְעִי־נָא זֹאת עֲנִיָּה וּשְׁכֻרַת וְלֹא
כב מִיָּיִן׃ כֹּה־אָמַר אֲדֹנַיִךְ יְהוָה וֵאלֹהַיִךְ יָרִיב עַמּוֹ הִנֵּה לָקַחְתִּי מִיָּדֵךְ אֶת־כּוֹס הַתַּרְעֵלָה אֶת־
כג קֻבַּעַת כּוֹס חֲמָתִי לֹא־תוֹסִיפִי לִשְׁתּוֹתָהּ עוֹד׃ וְשַׂמְתִּיהָ בְּיַד־מוֹגַיִךְ אֲשֶׁר־אָמְרוּ לְנַפְשֵׁךְ שְׁחִי וְנַעֲבֹרָה
נב א וַתָּשִׂימִי כָאָרֶץ גֵּוֵךְ וְכַחוּץ לַעֹבְרִים׃ עוּרִי עוּרִי לִבְשִׁי עֻזֵּךְ צִיּוֹן לִבְשִׁי ׀ בִּגְדֵי תִפְאַרְתֵּךְ יְרוּשָׁלִַם
ב עִיר הַקֹּדֶשׁ כִּי לֹא יוֹסִיף יָבֹא־בָךְ עוֹד עָרֵל וְטָמֵא׃ הִתְנַעֲרִי מֵעָפָר קוּמִי שְּׁבִי יְרוּשָׁלִָם התפתחו מוֹסְרֵי הִתְפַּתְּחִי
ג ד צַוָּארֵךְ שְׁבִיָּה בַּת־צִיּוֹן׃ כִּי־כֹה אָמַר יְהוָה חִנָּם נִמְכַּרְתֶּם וְלֹא בְכֶסֶף תִּגָּאֵלוּ׃ כִּי כֹה
ה אָמַר אֲדֹנָי יֱהֹוִה מִצְרַיִם יָרַד־עַמִּי בָרִאשֹׁנָה לָגוּר שָׁם וְאַשּׁוּר בְּאֶפֶס עֲשָׁקוֹ׃ וְעַתָּה מַה־לִּי־פֹה נְאֻם־
ו יְהוָה כִּי־לֻקַּח עַמִּי חִנָּם מֹשְׁלָו יְהֵילִילוּ נְאֻם־יְהוָה וְתָמִיד כָּל־הַיּוֹם שְׁמִי מִנֹּאָץ׃ לָכֵן יֵדַע עַמִּי שְׁמִי לָכֵן
ז בַּיּוֹם הַהוּא כִּי־אֲנִי־הוּא הַמְדַבֵּר הִנֵּנִי׃ מַה־נָּאווּ עַל־הֶהָרִים רַגְלֵי מְבַשֵּׂר מַשְׁמִיעַ שָׁלוֹם
ח מְבַשֵּׂר טוֹב מַשְׁמִיעַ יְשׁוּעָה אֹמֵר לְצִיּוֹן מָלַךְ אֱלֹהָיִךְ׃ קוֹל צֹפַיִךְ נָשְׂאוּ קוֹל יַחְדָּו יְרַנֵּנוּ כִּי עַיִן בְּעַיִן
ט י יִרְאוּ בְּשׁוּב יְהוָה צִיּוֹן׃ פִּצְחוּ רַנְּנוּ יַחְדָּו חָרְבוֹת יְרוּשָׁלִָם כִּי־נִחַם יְהוָה עַמּוֹ גָּאַל יְרוּשָׁלִָם׃ חָשַׂף יְהוָה
יא אֶת־זְרוֹעַ קָדְשׁוֹ לְעֵינֵי כָּל־הַגּוֹיִם וְרָאוּ כָּל־אַפְסֵי־אָרֶץ אֵת יְשׁוּעַת אֱלֹהֵינוּ׃ סוּרוּ סוּרוּ צְאוּ
יב מִשָּׁם טָמֵא אַל־תִּגָּעוּ צְאוּ מִתּוֹכָהּ הִבָּרוּ נֹשְׂאֵי כְּלֵי יְהוָה׃ כִּי לֹא בְחִפָּזוֹן תֵּצֵאוּ וּבִמְנוּסָה לֹא תֵלֵכוּן
כִּי־הֹלֵךְ לִפְנֵיכֶם יְהוָה וּמְאַסִּפְכֶם אֱלֹהֵי יִשְׂרָאֵל׃

הפטרת כי תצא

The custom of the Ashkenazim is that if the הפטרה *for* פרשת ראה *was not read due to it coinciding with* ראש חודש אלול*, that* הפטרה *is read after this* הפטרה.

נד א ב רָנִּי עֲקָרָה לֹא יָלָדָה פִּצְחִי רִנָּה וְצַהֲלִי לֹא־חָלָה כִּי־רַבִּים בְּנֵי־שׁוֹמֵמָה מִבְּנֵי בְעוּלָה אָמַר יְהוָה׃ הַרְחִיבִי ׀ ישעיה
ג מְקוֹם אָהֳלֵךְ וִירִיעוֹת מִשְׁכְּנוֹתַיִךְ יַטּוּ אַל־תַּחְשֹׂכִי הַאֲרִיכִי מֵיתָרַיִךְ וִיתֵדֹתַיִךְ חַזֵּקִי׃ כִּי־יָמִין וּשְׂמֹאול
ד תִּפְרֹצִי וְזַרְעֵךְ גּוֹיִם יִירָשׁ וְעָרִים נְשַׁמּוֹת יוֹשִׁיבוּ׃ אַל־תִּירְאִי כִּי־לֹא תֵבוֹשִׁי וְאַל־תִּכָּלְמִי כִּי לֹא תַחְפִּירִי
ה כִּי בֹשֶׁת עֲלוּמַיִךְ תִּשְׁכָּחִי וְחֶרְפַּת אַלְמְנוּתַיִךְ לֹא תִזְכְּרִי־עוֹד׃ כִּי בֹעֲלַיִךְ עֹשַׂיִךְ יְהוָה צְבָאוֹת שְׁמוֹ וְגֹאֲלֵךְ
ו קְדוֹשׁ יִשְׂרָאֵל אֱלֹהֵי כָל־הָאָרֶץ יִקָּרֵא׃ כִּי־כְאִשָּׁה עֲזוּבָה וַעֲצוּבַת רוּחַ קְרָאָךְ יְהוָה וְאֵשֶׁת נְעוּרִים כִּי
ז ח תִמָּאֵס אָמַר אֱלֹהָיִךְ׃ בְּרֶגַע קָטֹן עֲזַבְתִּיךְ וּבְרַחֲמִים גְּדֹלִים אֲקַבְּצֵךְ׃ בְּשֶׁצֶף קֶצֶף הִסְתַּרְתִּי פָנַי רֶגַע

KI TETZEH

The flood, which threw the world back into a state of chaos, came as a punishment for wickedness and oppression. The prophet draws a parallel between it and the destruction and exile of the Israelite kingdoms centuries later, which also came as a result of disobedience to God. He insists that crisis and suffering are not the natural way of things, even if they can seem never-ending. The covenant with God must

9 redeemer. For these are the waters of Noaḥ to Me, and I swore that the waters of Noaḥ would
never sweep again over the earth. And so did I swear no more to be furious with you, no more to re-
10 buke you. For mountains may move, hills may crumble away; but My love for you will not be moved,
nor My pact of peace crumble. So speaks the LORD, who cares for you.

Haftarat Ki Tavo

ISAIAH

60 1 2 Rise, give light, for your light has come: the glory of the LORD shines over you, for darkness may cover
the earth, and clouds shroud nations, but over you, the LORD will be shining, His glory manifest over
3 4 you; nations will walk toward your light, and kings into the brilliance you shine forth. Raise your eyes;
look around and see: all of them gathered in, and come to you; your sons have come from far away, your
5 daughters as if clinging to nursemaids' hips. Then you will see and shine; your heart will fill with awe and
6 open wide, for the ocean's abundance will turn to you; the wealth of nations will come to you; herds of
camels will cover your land, young camels from Midyan and Eifa, all having come to you from Sheba,
7 carrying gold and frankincense and tidings of the LORD's praise. All the flocks of Kedar will be gathered
in to you; the rams of Nevayot will be in your service. Offered on My altar, they will be desired; I shall
8 glorify the House of My glory. Who are these sailing like clouds, like doves come back to their roosting
9 cote? It is Me the distant islands wait for; ships of Tarshish come the first, to bring your children from far
away, their silver and gold with them, for the name of the LORD your God, the Holy One of Israel: He
10 has glorified you. The children of strangers will build your walls; their kings will be in your service, for in
11 My fury I beat you, but, desiring you now, I show you mercy, and your gates will be always open, day and
12 night, never closed, as the wealth of nations is brought in to you, their kings led to you, for the nations
13 and kingdoms that do not serve you will be lost, nations desolate, destroyed. Lebanon's glory will come
to you: junipers, cypress trees, and pencil pines together, to lend the place of My Sanctuary splendor; I
14 shall glorify the place of My footstool. The children of those who once oppressed you will come before
you prostrate, bowing themselves to the soles of your feet; all who once denounced you, they will call
15 you The LORD's City, Zion of Israel's Holy One. Where once you were forsaken, hated, never even passed
16 through, I have made you everlasting majesty, the joy of generations. You shall suckle the milk of nations,
suckle at kings' breasts, and know that I am the LORD, your rescue, your redeemer, the Mighty One of
17 Yaakov. Where once there was bronze, I shall bring gold, and where there was iron, silver. Where once
there was wood, I shall bring bronze, and where there was stone, now iron. I shall make peace your com-
18 mander, your ruling class: righteousness. No more will violence be heard of in your land, nor plunder or
19 destruction in your borders. You shall name your walls Rescue, and your gates, Praise. No more, by day,
will the sun be your light, nor the moon's radiance shine for you, for the LORD will be your light forever;
20 your God will be your glory. Your sun will set no longer, nor your moon be gathered in, for the LORD is
21 your light forever; the days of your mourning are done. Your people, all of them righteous, will inherit
22 the land forever, the shoots of My planting, works of My hands, spreading branches in glory. The little
son will become a thousand strong, the youngest child a mighty nation; I am the LORD: when the time
is right, in a flash I will bring it all to be.

---

have committed against Israel and will make amends. Having repented, the peoples of the world will recognize God's sovereignty and Israel's chosenness, and they will become full partners in the redeemed world.

ט מִמֵּךְ וּבְחֶסֶד עוֹלָם רִחַמְתִּיךְ אָמַר גֹּאֲלֵךְ יהוה׃ כִּי־מֵי נֹחַ זֹאת לִי אֲשֶׁר נִשְׁבַּעְתִּי מֵעֲבֹר מֵי־
י נֹחַ עוֹד עַל־הָאָרֶץ כֵּן נִשְׁבַּעְתִּי מִקְּצֹף עָלַיִךְ וּמִגְּעָר־בָּךְ׃ כִּי הֶהָרִים יָמוּשׁוּ וְהַגְּבָעוֹת תְּמוּטֶינָה וְחַסְדִּי
מֵאִתֵּךְ לֹא־יָמוּשׁ וּבְרִית שְׁלוֹמִי לֹא תָמוּט אָמַר מְרַחֲמֵךְ יהוה׃

הפטרת כי תבוא

ס א ב קוּמִי אוֹרִי כִּי בָא אוֹרֵךְ וּכְבוֹד יהוה עָלַיִךְ זָרָח׃ כִּי־הִנֵּה הַחֹשֶׁךְ יְכַסֶּה־אֶרֶץ וַעֲרָפֶל לְאֻמִּים וְעָלַיִךְ יִזְרַח ישעיה
ג ד יהוה וּכְבוֹדוֹ עָלַיִךְ יֵרָאֶה׃ וְהָלְכוּ גוֹיִם לְאוֹרֵךְ וּמְלָכִים לְנֹגַהּ זַרְחֵךְ׃ שְׂאִי־סָבִיב עֵינַיִךְ וּרְאִי כֻּלָּם נִקְבְּצוּ
ה בָאוּ־לָךְ בָּנַיִךְ מֵרָחוֹק יָבֹאוּ וּבְנֹתַיִךְ עַל־צַד תֵּאָמַנָה׃ אָז תִּרְאִי וְנָהַרְתְּ וּפָחַד וְרָחַב לְבָבֵךְ כִּי־יֵהָפֵךְ עָלַיִךְ
ו הֲמוֹן יָם חֵיל גּוֹיִם יָבֹאוּ לָךְ׃ שִׁפְעַת גְּמַלִּים תְּכַסֵּךְ בִּכְרֵי מִדְיָן וְעֵיפָה כֻּלָּם מִשְּׁבָא יָבֹאוּ זָהָב וּלְבוֹנָה
ז יִשָּׂאוּ וּתְהִלֹּת יהוה יְבַשֵּׂרוּ׃ כָּל־צֹאן קֵדָר יִקָּבְצוּ לָךְ אֵילֵי נְבָיוֹת יְשָׁרְתוּנֶךְ יַעֲלוּ עַל־רָצוֹן מִזְבְּחִי וּבֵית
ח ט תִּפְאַרְתִּי אֲפָאֵר׃ מִי־אֵלֶּה כָּעָב תְּעוּפֶינָה וְכַיּוֹנִים אֶל־אֲרֻבֹּתֵיהֶם׃ כִּי־לִי ׀ אִיִּים יְקַוּוּ וָאֳנִיּוֹת תַּרְשִׁישׁ
י בָּרִאשֹׁנָה לְהָבִיא בָנַיִךְ מֵרָחוֹק כַּסְפָּם וּזְהָבָם אִתָּם לְשֵׁם יהוה אֱלֹהַיִךְ וְלִקְדוֹשׁ יִשְׂרָאֵל כִּי פֵאֲרָךְ׃ וּבָנוּ
יא בְנֵי־נֵכָר חֹמֹתַיִךְ וּמַלְכֵיהֶם יְשָׁרְתוּנֶךְ כִּי בְקִצְפִּי הִכִּיתִיךְ וּבִרְצוֹנִי רִחַמְתִּיךְ׃ וּפִתְּחוּ שְׁעָרַיִךְ תָּמִיד יוֹמָם
יב וָלַיְלָה לֹא יִסָּגֵרוּ לְהָבִיא אֵלַיִךְ חֵיל גּוֹיִם וּמַלְכֵיהֶם נְהוּגִים׃ כִּי־הַגּוֹי וְהַמַּמְלָכָה אֲשֶׁר לֹא־יַעַבְדוּךְ יֹאבֵדוּ
יג וְהַגּוֹיִם חָרֹב יֶחֱרָבוּ׃ כְּבוֹד הַלְּבָנוֹן אֵלַיִךְ יָבוֹא בְּרוֹשׁ תִּדְהָר וּתְאַשּׁוּר יַחְדָּו לְפָאֵר מְקוֹם מִקְדָּשִׁי וּמְקוֹם
יד רַגְלַי אֲכַבֵּד׃ וְהָלְכוּ אֵלַיִךְ שְׁחוֹחַ בְּנֵי מְעַנַּיִךְ וְהִשְׁתַּחֲווּ עַל־כַּפּוֹת רַגְלַיִךְ כָּל־מְנַאֲצָיִךְ וְקָרְאוּ לָךְ עִיר יהוה
טו צִיּוֹן קְדוֹשׁ יִשְׂרָאֵל׃ תַּחַת הֱיוֹתֵךְ עֲזוּבָה וּשְׂנוּאָה וְאֵין עוֹבֵר וְשַׂמְתִּיךְ לִגְאוֹן עוֹלָם מְשׂוֹשׂ דּוֹר וָדוֹר׃
טז יז וְיָנַקְתְּ חֲלֵב גּוֹיִם וְשֹׁד מְלָכִים תִּינָקִי וְיָדַעַתְּ כִּי אֲנִי יהוה מוֹשִׁיעֵךְ וְגֹאֲלֵךְ אֲבִיר יַעֲקֹב׃ תַּחַת הַנְּחֹשֶׁת
אָבִיא זָהָב וְתַחַת הַבַּרְזֶל אָבִיא כֶסֶף וְתַחַת הָעֵצִים נְחֹשֶׁת וְתַחַת הָאֲבָנִים בַּרְזֶל וְשַׂמְתִּי פְקֻדָּתֵךְ שָׁלוֹם
יח וְנֹגְשַׂיִךְ צְדָקָה׃ לֹא־יִשָּׁמַע עוֹד חָמָס בְּאַרְצֵךְ שֹׁד וָשֶׁבֶר בִּגְבוּלָיִךְ וְקָרָאת יְשׁוּעָה חוֹמֹתַיִךְ וּשְׁעָרַיִךְ
יט תְּהִלָּה׃ לֹא־יִהְיֶה־לָּךְ עוֹד הַשֶּׁמֶשׁ לְאוֹר יוֹמָם וּלְנֹגַהּ הַיָּרֵחַ לֹא־יָאִיר לָךְ וְהָיָה־לָךְ יהוה לְאוֹר עוֹלָם
כ וֵאלֹהַיִךְ לְתִפְאַרְתֵּךְ׃ לֹא־יָבוֹא עוֹד שִׁמְשֵׁךְ וִירֵחֵךְ לֹא יֵאָסֵף כִּי יהוה יִהְיֶה־לָּךְ לְאוֹר עוֹלָם וְשָׁלְמוּ יְמֵי
כא כב אֶבְלֵךְ׃ וְעַמֵּךְ כֻּלָּם צַדִּיקִים לְעוֹלָם יִירְשׁוּ אָרֶץ נֵצֶר מטעו מַעֲשֵׂה יָדַי לְהִתְפָּאֵר׃ הַקָּטֹן יִהְיֶה לָאֶלֶף מַטָּעַי
וְהַצָּעִיר לְגוֹי עָצוּם אֲנִי יהוה בְּעִתָּהּ אֲחִישֶׁנָּה׃

KI TAVO

The phrase that concludes this *haftara*, "When the time is right, in a flash I will bring it to be," expresses two dynamics of redemption. On the one hand, God will hasten the process so that it will seem to happen in an instant. On the other hand, redemption must wait its turn, coming about at the pace of the natural order of things. How will these two opposed dynamics express themselves? Will the divine light shine through us to illuminate the world for all the nations in a flash? Or will we be unable to project such influence, in which case the perfection of the world will drag on for numerous generations? When we think of the relationship between Israel and the nations, we must place emphasis on the idea that justice must be done. The nations will ultimately recognize the injustices they

HAFTARAT NITZAVIM

When Nitzavim and Vayelekh are read together, read this haftara.

61 9 Their children will be known among the nations, their offspring among peoples, for all those who see ISAIAH
10 them will know who they are: children of the LORD's own blessing. * I shall rejoice, rejoice *Yemenites begin here*
in the LORD; my soul exults in my God; He has wrapped me in garb of rescue, on my shoulders the *Ashkenazim and Sepharadim begin here*
11 mantle of righteousness, as a bridegroom attends in splendor, and a bride puts on her jewels; just as
the land brings forth green life, having all that is planted in her flower like a garden, so will the Lord
62 1 GOD bring forth righteousness and glory before all the nations. For Zion's sake I cannot be silent, for
2 Jerusalem's I cannot be still until righteousness bursts forth shining, and rescue burns like a brand, and
all nations see your righteousness, all the kings your glory. They will call you by a new name spoken
3 from the LORD's own mouth. You will be a crown of glory in the LORD's hand, a kingly diadem in
4 your God's palms. No more will they say of you, "Abandoned," "Desolate" of your land, for you shall
be called "My Desire," your land renamed "Embraced," for it is you the LORD desires, and your land
5 shall be embraced; as a young man embraces a maid, so will your children embrace you, while the joy
6 of a bridegroom over his bride is the joy your God will take in you. Over your walls, Jerusalem, I have
appointed watchmen, all day, all night long, always, and they will not keep silence; you who call the
7 LORD by name, none of you be quiet, and do not give Him quiet until He has established, until He
8 has raised Jerusalem to be the glory of this earth. The LORD has sworn by His right hand and by His
mighty arm: never again to give away your grain as your foes' food, never to let strangers drink the
9 wine that you have labored for. No – the ones who harvest it will eat and sing out the LORD's praise,
10 and those He has gathered in will drink within My sacred courtyards. Pass, pass through the
gates, and make way for the people. Mark, mark a road here; clear the stones; raise a banner above all
11 peoples. Behold: the LORD resounding to the earth's ends; tell daughter Zion, your rescue is come,
12 and with Him, His prize: His work walking before Him. They will call them a holy people, redeemed
ones of the LORD. And you – you shall be called the One Sought After, the City That Will Never Be
63 1 Abandoned. "Who is this, coming from Edom, from Botzra, in reddened clothes? Who, His
2 clothing glorious, striding forth in might?" It is I who speak with rectitude, powerful to rescue. "And
3 why is Your clothing red, your garments, as if You trod the winepress?" I have trodden the vat alone;
no man of any nation was there with Me; I trod them in My fury, trampling them in rage, until their
4 lifeblood steeped My clothes, befouling all My garments, for today in My heart is a day of vengeance;
5 My year of redemption is come. I look, and no one is there to help; with dismay I see – no aid; so My
6 arm will bear My rescue; My rage is My support. My fury will tread peoples low; in My rage I shall
7 make them drunk and pour down their lifeblood to earth. Let me speak the LORD's acts of
kindness, praises of the LORD for all the LORD has done for us, for His great goodness to Israel, per-
8 formed in all compassion, in all His loving-kindness. He said: They, they are My people, My children
9 who would not lie to Me – and He was their rescue. Wherever they suffered, He too suffered, and His
presence, its emissary rescued them; in His love, in His mercy He redeemed them and took them up
and bore them through all those long-past days.

---

of the exile begins with the destruction of Jerusalem. As long as the heart beats, the body can live. But with the silencing of Jerusalem, the heart of the Jewish people, the exile began in earnest. The rebuilding of Jerusalem thus signals the end of the exile, for Jerusalem is no ordinary city; it is the seat of God on earth.

הפטרת נצבים

When נצבים *and* וילך *are read together, read this* הפטרה.

ישעיה

Yemenites begin here

Ashkenazim and Sepharadim begin here

סא ט י וְנוֹדַע בַּגּוֹיִם זַרְעָם וְצֶאֱצָאֵיהֶם בְּתוֹךְ הָעַמִּים כָּל־רֹאֵיהֶם יַכִּירוּם כִּי הֵם זֶרַע בֵּרַךְ יהוה: * שׂוֹשׂ
אָשִׂישׂ בַּיהוה תָּגֵל נַפְשִׁי בֵּאלֹהַי כִּי הִלְבִּישַׁנִי בִּגְדֵי־יֶשַׁע מְעִיל צְדָקָה יְעָטָנִי כֶּחָתָן יְכַהֵן פְּאֵר וְכַכַּלָּה
יא תַּעְדֶּה כֵלֶיהָ: כִּי כָאָרֶץ תּוֹצִיא צִמְחָהּ וּכְגַנָּה זֵרוּעֶיהָ תַצְמִיחַ כֵּן ׀ אֲדֹנָי יֱהוִה יַצְמִיחַ צְדָקָה וּתְהִלָּה נֶגֶד
סב א כָּל־הַגּוֹיִם: לְמַעַן צִיּוֹן לֹא אֶחֱשֶׁה וּלְמַעַן יְרוּשָׁלִַם לֹא אֶשְׁקוֹט עַד־יֵצֵא כַנֹּגַהּ צִדְקָהּ וִישׁוּעָתָהּ כְּלַפִּיד
ב ג יִבְעָר: וְרָאוּ גוֹיִם צִדְקֵךְ וְכָל־מְלָכִים כְּבוֹדֵךְ וְקֹרָא לָךְ שֵׁם חָדָשׁ אֲשֶׁר פִּי יהוה יִקֳּבֶנּוּ: וְהָיִית עֲטֶרֶת
ד תִּפְאֶרֶת בְּיַד־יהוה וּצְנוֹף מְלוּכָה בְּכַף־אֱלֹהָיִךְ: לֹא־יֵאָמֵר לָךְ עוֹד עֲזוּבָה וּלְאַרְצֵךְ לֹא־יֵאָמֵר עוֹד שְׁמָמָה וּצְנִיף
ה כִּי לָךְ יִקָּרֵא חֶפְצִי־בָהּ וּלְאַרְצֵךְ בְּעוּלָה כִּי־חָפֵץ יהוה בָּךְ וְאַרְצֵךְ תִּבָּעֵל: כִּי־יִבְעַל בָּחוּר בְּתוּלָה יִבְעָלוּךְ
ו בָּנָיִךְ וּמְשׂוֹשׂ חָתָן עַל־כַּלָּה יָשִׂישׂ עָלַיִךְ אֱלֹהָיִךְ: עַל־חוֹמֹתַיִךְ יְרוּשָׁלִַם הִפְקַדְתִּי שֹׁמְרִים כָּל־הַיּוֹם וְכָל־
ז הַלַּיְלָה תָּמִיד לֹא יֶחֱשׁוּ הַמַּזְכִּירִים אֶת־יהוה אַל־דֳּמִי לָכֶם: וְאַל־תִּתְּנוּ דֳמִי לוֹ עַד־יְכוֹנֵן וְעַד־יָשִׂים
ח אֶת־יְרוּשָׁלִַם תְּהִלָּה בָּאָרֶץ: נִשְׁבַּע יהוה בִּימִינוֹ וּבִזְרוֹעַ עֻזּוֹ אִם־אֶתֵּן אֶת־דְּגָנֵךְ עוֹד מַאֲכָל לְאֹיְבַיִךְ
ט וְאִם־יִשְׁתּוּ בְנֵי־נֵכָר תִּירוֹשֵׁךְ אֲשֶׁר יָגַעַתְּ בּוֹ: כִּי מְאַסְפָיו יֹאכְלֻהוּ וְהִלְלוּ אֶת־יהוה וּמְקַבְּצָיו יִשְׁתֻּהוּ
י בְּחַצְרוֹת קָדְשִׁי: עִבְרוּ עִבְרוּ בַּשְּׁעָרִים פַּנּוּ דֶּרֶךְ הָעָם סֹלּוּ סֹלּוּ הַמְסִלָּה סַקְּלוּ מֵאֶבֶן הָרִימוּ נֵס
יא עַל־הָעַמִּים: הִנֵּה יהוה הִשְׁמִיעַ אֶל־קְצֵה הָאָרֶץ אִמְרוּ לְבַת־צִיּוֹן הִנֵּה יִשְׁעֵךְ בָּא הִנֵּה שְׂכָרוֹ אִתּוֹ וּפְעֻלָּתוֹ
סג יב א לְפָנָיו: וְקָרְאוּ לָהֶם עַם־הַקֹּדֶשׁ גְּאוּלֵי יהוה וְלָךְ יִקָּרֵא דְרוּשָׁה עִיר לֹא נֶעֱזָבָה: מִי־זֶה ׀ בָּא
ב מֵאֱדוֹם חֲמוּץ בְּגָדִים מִבָּצְרָה זֶה הָדוּר בִּלְבוּשׁוֹ צֹעֶה בְּרֹב כֹּחוֹ אֲנִי מְדַבֵּר בִּצְדָקָה רַב לְהוֹשִׁיעַ: מַדּוּעַ
ג אָדֹם לִלְבוּשֶׁךָ וּבְגָדֶיךָ כְּדֹרֵךְ בְּגַת: פּוּרָה ׀ דָּרַכְתִּי לְבַדִּי וּמֵעַמִּים אֵין־אִישׁ אִתִּי וְאֶדְרְכֵם בְּאַפִּי וְאֶרְמְסֵם
ד ה בַּחֲמָתִי וְיֵז נִצְחָם עַל־בְּגָדַי וְכָל־מַלְבּוּשַׁי אֶגְאָלְתִּי: כִּי יוֹם נָקָם בְּלִבִּי וּשְׁנַת גְּאוּלַי בָּאָה: וְאַבִּיט וְאֵין
ו עֹזֵר וְאֶשְׁתּוֹמֵם וְאֵין סוֹמֵךְ וַתּוֹשַׁע לִי זְרֹעִי וַחֲמָתִי הִיא סְמָכָתְנִי: וְאָבוּס עַמִּים בְּאַפִּי וַאֲשַׁכְּרֵם בַּחֲמָתִי
ז וְאוֹרִיד לָאָרֶץ נִצְחָם: חַסְדֵי יהוה ׀ אַזְכִּיר תְּהִלֹּת יהוה כְּעַל כֹּל אֲשֶׁר־גְּמָלָנוּ יהוה וְרַב־טוּב
ח לְבֵית יִשְׂרָאֵל אֲשֶׁר־גְּמָלָם כְּרַחֲמָיו וּכְרֹב חֲסָדָיו: וַיֹּאמֶר אַךְ־עַמִּי הֵמָּה בָּנִים לֹא יְשַׁקֵּרוּ וַיְהִי לָהֶם
ט לְמוֹשִׁיעַ: בְּכָל־צָרָתָם ׀ לֹא צָר וּמַלְאַךְ פָּנָיו הוֹשִׁיעָם בְּאַהֲבָתוֹ וּבְחֶמְלָתוֹ הוּא גְאָלָם וַיְנַטְּלֵם וַיְנַשְּׂאֵם כָּל־ לוֹ
יְמֵי עוֹלָם:

NITZAVIM

From the time Jerusalem became the capital of the kingdom of Israel in the time of King David, it has been the heart of the Jewish people and the place to which all nations turn in prayer. It has also turned into a site of conflict as different nations battle for control of the holy city. The consciousness ▶

Haftara for Shabbat Shuva

This haftara is read on the Shabbat between Rosh HaShana and Yom Kippur, no matter which parasha is read (Vayelekh or Haazinu).

14 2 3 O Israel, return, go back to the LORD your God, for you have stumbled in your own sinfulness. Take HOSEA
words of remorse with you and return to the LORD; say to Him, "Forgive all of our sins; accept our
4 goodness – instead of calves we offer You our words of prayer. Assyria will not save us; no more will we
ride upon horses; never again will we say, 'You are our god' to the work of our hands, for only in You
5 will the orphan find mercy." I will mend their rebellion with gracious love, for I have turned My anger
6 away from them. I will be as dew to Israel; he will bloom like a lily and set down roots as deep as the
7 trees of Lebanon. His branches will spread wide; his splendor will be as the olive tree, and his fragrance
8 as the trees of Lebanon. They who return will dwell beneath his shade; they will revive once again as
9 grain and flower like vines; their acclaim will linger as the scent of the wine of Lebanon. Efrayim will
say, "What need do I have of these idols?" And I will answer him; I will look after him. I will be as a
10 cypress tree, lush and leafy; you will find in Me your source of fruit. He who is wise will fathom these
words; the insightful will grasp them, for the ways of the LORD are just, and the righteous will walk in
them, but sinners will stumble over them.*

Yemenites end here

2 11 Then the LORD raises His voice before His troops – for His camp is vast, and mighty are the ones JOEL
who carry out His words. For great and terrifying is the day of the LORD – who could withstand it? *Some*
12 13 Even now, so says the LORD, return to Me wholeheartedly, with fasting, weeping, and grief. Rend your *Ashkenazim continue*
hearts, not your clothing, and come back to the LORD your God. For He is gracious and compassion- *from here*
14 ate, slow to anger and abounding in kindness; He may well relent and forswear the evil. Who knows?
Maybe He will reconsider and relent and leave behind blessings; offer grain offerings and libations to
15 the LORD, your God. *Blow a ram's horn in Zion, sanctify a fast day, convene an assembly, *Most*
16 gather the people, sanctify the masses, convene the old, and gather the children and infants. Let the *Ashkenazim continue*
17 groom come from his room and the bride from her wedding chamber. Let the priests, attendants of *from here*
the LORD, weep between the hallway and the altar. Let them say: "Have compassion, O LORD, upon
Your people, and do not allow Your possession to become a reproach – ruled by nations." Why should
18 it be said among the peoples, "Where is their God?" Then the LORD will be fiercely zealous toward
19 His land, and He will have mercy upon His nation. He will reply and say to His nation: So I will send
to you grain, and sweet wine, and young oil. You will be sated with it. I will no longer allow you to be-
20 come a reproach among the nations. I will drive the northerner away from you – I will banish them to
a dry and desolate land; their vanguard to the east sea, their rearguard to the west sea. Their foul smell
21 will ascend, their stench will rise, for they have done terrible things. Fear not, earth. Rejoice! Be glad!
22 For the LORD has done great things. Fear not, animals of My fields, for the desert pasture is green with
23 grass; the tree has borne fruit: the fig and vine have blossomed. Rejoice and be glad in the LORD, your
God, children of Zion. For He has given you the first rain out of generosity. He will rain down for you
24 the first and last rain as it was in the beginning. The granaries will fill with grain, and the press will over-
25 flow with sweet wine and young oil. I will repay you for all the seasons consumed by the locusts, the
springing-locusts, the finisher-locusts, and the chewer-locusts – My great army, which I sent among
26 you. You will eat, eat and be sated, and you will praise the name of the LORD, your God, who has done
27 wonders for you, for My nation will never be ashamed. You will know that I am among Israel, and I am
the LORD, your God; there is no other. My nation will never be ashamed.

הפטרה לשבת שובה

This הפטרה *is read on the* שבת *between* ראש השנה *and* יום כיפור*,*
no matter which פרשה *is read (*האזינו *or* וילך*).*

הושע

יד ב ג שׁוּבָה יִשְׂרָאֵל עַד יְהוָה אֱלֹהֶיךָ כִּי כָשַׁלְתָּ בַּעֲוֺנֶךָ: קְחוּ עִמָּכֶם דְּבָרִים וְשׁוּבוּ אֶל־יְהוָה אִמְרוּ אֵלָיו כׇּל־
ד תִּשָּׂא עָוֺן וְקַח־טוֹב וּנְשַׁלְּמָה פָרִים שְׂפָתֵינוּ: אַשּׁוּר ׀ לֹא יוֹשִׁיעֵנוּ עַל־סוּס לֹא נִרְכָּב וְלֹא־נֹאמַר עוֹד
ה ו אֱלֹהֵינוּ לְמַעֲשֵׂה יָדֵינוּ אֲשֶׁר־בְּךָ יְרֻחַם יָתוֹם: אֶרְפָּא מְשׁוּבָתָם אֹהֲבֵם נְדָבָה כִּי שָׁב אַפִּי מִמֶּנּוּ: אֶהְיֶה
ז ח כַטַּל לְיִשְׂרָאֵל יִפְרַח כַּשּׁוֹשַׁנָּה וְיַךְ שׇׁרָשָׁיו כַּלְּבָנוֹן: יֵלְכוּ יֹנְקוֹתָיו וִיהִי כַזַּיִת הוֹדוֹ וְרֵיחַ לוֹ כַּלְּבָנוֹן: יָשֻׁבוּ
ט יֹשְׁבֵי בְצִלּוֹ יְחַיּוּ דָגָן וְיִפְרְחוּ כַגָּפֶן זִכְרוֹ כְּיֵין לְבָנוֹן: אֶפְרַיִם מַה־לִּי עוֹד לָעֲצַבִּים אֲנִי עָנִיתִי וַאֲשׁוּרֶנּוּ אֲנִי
י כִּבְרוֹשׁ רַעֲנָן מִמֶּנִּי פֶּרְיְךָ נִמְצָא: מִי חָכָם וְיָבֵן אֵלֶּה נָבוֹן וְיֵדָעֵם כִּי־יְשָׁרִים דַּרְכֵי יְהוָה וְצַדִּקִים יֵלְכוּ בָם
וּפֹשְׁעִים יִכָּשְׁלוּ בָם:*

Yemenites end here

יואל

Some Ashkenazim continue from here

Most Ashkenazim continue from here

ב יא וַיהוָה נָתַן קוֹלוֹ לִפְנֵי חֵילוֹ כִּי רַב מְאֹד מַחֲנֵהוּ כִּי עָצוּם עֹשֵׂה דְבָרוֹ כִּי־גָדוֹל יוֹם־יְהוָה וְנוֹרָא מְאֹד וּמִי
יב יג יְכִילֶנּוּ: וְגַם־עַתָּה נְאֻם־יְהוָה שֻׁבוּ עָדַי בְּכׇל־לְבַבְכֶם וּבְצוֹם וּבִבְכִי וּבְמִסְפֵּד: וְקִרְעוּ לְבַבְכֶם וְאַל־בִּגְדֵיכֶם
יד וְשׁוּבוּ אֶל־יְהוָה אֱלֹהֵיכֶם כִּי־חַנּוּן וְרַחוּם הוּא אֶרֶךְ אַפַּיִם וְרַב־חֶסֶד וְנִחָם עַל־הָרָעָה: מִי יוֹדֵעַ יָשׁוּב
טו וְנִחָם וְהִשְׁאִיר אַחֲרָיו בְּרָכָה מִנְחָה וָנֶסֶךְ לַיהוָה אֱלֹהֵיכֶם: *תִּקְעוּ שׁוֹפָר בְּצִיּוֹן קַדְּשׁוּ־צוֹם
טז קִרְאוּ עֲצָרָה: אִסְפוּ־עָם קַדְּשׁוּ קָהָל קִבְצוּ זְקֵנִים אִסְפוּ עוֹלָלִים וְיֹנְקֵי שָׁדָיִם יֵצֵא חָתָן מֵחֶדְרוֹ וְכַלָּה
יז מֵחֻפָּתָהּ: בֵּין הָאוּלָם וְלַמִּזְבֵּחַ יִבְכּוּ הַכֹּהֲנִים מְשָׁרְתֵי יְהוָה וְיֹאמְרוּ חוּסָה יְהוָה עַל־עַמֶּךָ וְאַל־תִּתֵּן
יח נַחֲלָתְךָ לְחֶרְפָּה לִמְשׇׁל־בָּם גּוֹיִם לָמָּה יֹאמְרוּ בָעַמִּים אַיֵּה אֱלֹהֵיהֶם: וַיְקַנֵּא יְהוָה לְאַרְצוֹ וַיַּחְמֹל עַל־
יט עַמּוֹ: וַיַּעַן יְהוָה וַיֹּאמֶר לְעַמּוֹ הִנְנִי שֹׁלֵחַ לָכֶם אֶת־הַדָּגָן וְהַתִּירוֹשׁ וְהַיִּצְהָר וּשְׂבַעְתֶּם אֹתוֹ וְלֹא־אֶתֵּן
כ אֶתְכֶם עוֹד חֶרְפָּה בַּגּוֹיִם: וְאֶת־הַצְּפוֹנִי אַרְחִיק מֵעֲלֵיכֶם וְהִדַּחְתִּיו אֶל־אֶרֶץ צִיָּה וּשְׁמָמָה אֶת־פָּנָיו אֶל־
כא הַיָּם הַקַּדְמֹנִי וְסֹפוֹ אֶל־הַיָּם הָאַחֲרוֹן וְעָלָה בׇאְשׁוֹ וְתַעַל צַחֲנָתוֹ כִּי הִגְדִּיל לַעֲשׂוֹת: אַל־תִּירְאִי אֲדָמָה
כב גִּילִי וּשְׂמָחִי כִּי־הִגְדִּיל יְהוָה לַעֲשׂוֹת: אַל־תִּירְאוּ בַּהֲמוֹת שָׂדַי כִּי דָשְׁאוּ נְאוֹת מִדְבָּר כִּי־עֵץ נָשָׂא פִרְיוֹ
כג תְּאֵנָה וָגֶפֶן נָתְנוּ חֵילָם: וּבְנֵי צִיּוֹן גִּילוּ וְשִׂמְחוּ בַּיהוָה אֱלֹהֵיכֶם כִּי־נָתַן לָכֶם אֶת־הַמּוֹרֶה לִצְדָקָה וַיּוֹרֶד
כד כה לָכֶם גֶּשֶׁם מוֹרֶה וּמַלְקוֹשׁ בָּרִאשׁוֹן: וּמָלְאוּ הַגֳּרָנוֹת בָּר וְהֵשִׁיקוּ הַיְקָבִים תִּירוֹשׁ וְיִצְהָר: וְשִׁלַּמְתִּי לָכֶם
כו אֶת־הַשָּׁנִים אֲשֶׁר אָכַל הָאַרְבֶּה הַיֶּלֶק וְהֶחָסִיל וְהַגָּזָם חֵילִי הַגָּדוֹל אֲשֶׁר שִׁלַּחְתִּי בָּכֶם: וַאֲכַלְתֶּם אָכוֹל
כז וְשָׂבוֹעַ וְהִלַּלְתֶּם אֶת־שֵׁם יְהוָה אֱלֹהֵיכֶם אֲשֶׁר־עָשָׂה עִמָּכֶם לְהַפְלִיא וְלֹא־יֵבֹשׁוּ עַמִּי לְעוֹלָם: וִידַעְתֶּם
כִּי בְקֶרֶב יִשְׂרָאֵל אָנִי וַאֲנִי יְהוָה אֱלֹהֵיכֶם וְאֵין עוֹד וְלֹא־יֵבֹשׁוּ עַמִּי לְעוֹלָם:

HAFTARA FOR SHABBAT SHUVA

In Tanakh, the horse represents military power. The Assyrians, who possessed a large force of chariots (drawn by horses) and mounted cavalry, were considered the most powerful empire of the age. The prophet Hoshea calls on Israel not to pin their hopes on Assyria. The key to a good life is the understanding of the place of human beings in comparison to God. If one fails to comprehend this, they begin to attribute God-like characteristics to human beings, and this is the root of idolatry and the basis of moral degeneration. Centering human beings and their desires, while at the same time fetishizing military power, is sure to result in the corruption of the divine image in us. The prophet urges his listeners to return to God; repentance will bring the people to a better, more worthy state of existence.

MICAH
Sepharadim and some Ashkenazim add

7 18 Is there any God like You who forgives iniquities, who looks beyond the sins of the remnant of His own
19 people, who does not hold onto His wrath forever because He desires kindness? He will again have
20 compassion for us; He will subdue our iniquities and hurl all of our sins into the deepest of seas. You
will show truth to Yaakov, kindness to Avraham, as You swore to our fathers in the earliest days.

Haftarat Haazinu

This haftara is read on the Shabbat between Yom Kippur and Sukkot. If Shabbat Parashat Haazinu falls between Rosh HaShana and Yom Kippur, read the haftara on page 1623.

II SAMUEL
For Ashkenazim and Sepharadim

22 1 David uttered these words of song to the LORD on the day that the LORD saved him from the hands of
2 all his enemies and from the hand of Sha'ul. He said: The LORD is my Rock and my fortress, my own
3 rescuer; // my God is the Rock of my refuge / my shield, the horn of my salvation, my haven, / my ref-
4 uge, my savior who delivers me from violence. // Praise! When I call on the LORD, / I am saved from
5 6 my enemies. // For when waves of death assailed me, / deadly torrents engulfed me, the cords of Sheol
7 entangled me, / snares of death confronted me, // in my distress I called on the LORD; / I called out to
8 my God; / He heard my voice from His Temple, / and my cry rang in His ears. // Then the earth shook
9 and shuddered; / the foundations of heaven trembled; / they shuddered from His wrath. // Smoke
issued from His nostrils; / devouring flames flared from His mouth; / from Him gleaming coals blazed
10 11 forth. // He bent the heavens and descended, / dense cloud beneath His feet; / He mounted a cherub
12 and flew, / appearing on wings of wind. // He surrounded Himself with a shelter of darkness, / of
13 heavy storm clouds dense with rain. // From the brilliant glow of His presence / blazed fiery coals. //
14 15 The LORD thundered from the heavens; / the Most High raised His voice; / He shot arrows to scatter
16 them, / lightning bolts to rout them. // The ocean bed was exposed, / the foundations of the world
17 laid bare / by the onslaught of the LORD, / by the blast of His breath. // From on high He reached
18 down and took me; / He drew me out of the mighty waters. // He saved me from my fierce enemy, /
19 20 from foes too strong for me. // They confronted me on my direst day, / but the LORD was my support. //

HAAZINU
Ashkenazim and Sepharadim

This *haftara* is from the closing chapters of the book of Samuel, which summarize the reign of King David. David was an unparalleled military leader. He survived numerous and prolonged wars and built the kingdom of Israel into a regional empire. Throughout, he always understood that the source of his strength, wisdom, and dedication was God. This song is a song of praise to the Almighty for his achievements. Reading it, we are reminded to always act with the knowledge that our successes are not solely our own.

ז יח מִי־אֵל כָּמוֹךָ נֹשֵׂא עָוֺן וְעֹבֵר עַל־פֶּשַׁע לִשְׁאֵרִית נַחֲלָתוֹ לֹא־הֶחֱזִיק לָעַד אַפּוֹ כִּי־חָפֵץ חֶסֶד הוּא: מיכה
יט כ יָשׁוּב יְרַחֲמֵנוּ יִכְבֹּשׁ עֲוֺנֹתֵינוּ וְתַשְׁלִיךְ בִּמְצֻלוֹת יָם כָּל־חַטֹּאתָם: תִּתֵּן אֱמֶת לְיַעֲקֹב חֶסֶד לְאַבְרָהָם
אֲשֶׁר־נִשְׁבַּעְתָּ לַאֲבֹתֵינוּ מִימֵי קֶדֶם:

Sepharadim and some Ashkenazim add

הפטרת האזינו

This הפטרה *is read on the* שבת *between* יום כיפור *and* סוכות. *If* שבת פרשת האזינו *falls between* ראש השנה *and* יום כיפור, *read the* הפטרה *on page 1623.*

שמואל ב׳
For Ashkenazim and Sepharadim

כב א וַיְדַבֵּר דָּוִד לַיהוָה אֶת־דִּבְרֵי הַשִּׁירָה הַזֹּאת בְּיוֹם הִצִּיל יהוה אֹתוֹ מִכַּף כָּל־אֹיְבָיו וּמִכַּף שָׁאוּל:
ב ג וַיֹּאמַר   יהוה סַלְעִי וּמְצֻדָתִי וּמְפַלְטִי־לִי: אֱלֹהֵי
צוּרִי אֶחֱסֶה־בּוֹ   מָגִנִּי וְקֶרֶן יִשְׁעִי מִשְׂגַּבִּי
ד וּמְנוּסִי   מֹשִׁעִי מֵחָמָס תֹּשִׁעֵנִי: מְהֻלָּל
ה אֶקְרָא יהוה וּמֵאֹיְבַי אִוָּשֵׁעַ:   כִּי אֲפָפֻנִי מִשְׁבְּרֵי־
ו מָוֶת   נַחֲלֵי בְלִיַּעַל יְבַעֲתֻנִי: חֶבְלֵי
שְׁאוֹל סַבֻּנִי   קִדְּמֻנִי מֹקְשֵׁי־
ז מָוֶת: בַּצַּר־לִי אֶקְרָא יהוה   וְאֶל־
אֱלֹהַי אֶקְרָא   וַיִּשְׁמַע מֵהֵיכָלוֹ
ח קוֹלִי   וְשַׁוְעָתִי בְּאָזְנָיו: ותגעש   וַיִּתְגָּעַשׁ
וַתִּרְעַשׁ הָאָרֶץ   מוֹסְדוֹת הַשָּׁמַיִם
ט יִרְגָּזוּ   וַיִּתְגָּעֲשׁוּ כִּי־חָרָה לוֹ:   עָלָה
עָשָׁן בְּאַפּוֹ   וְאֵשׁ מִפִּיו
י תֹּאכֵל   גֶּחָלִים בָּעֲרוּ מִמֶּנּוּ:   וַיֵּט
שָׁמַיִם וַיֵּרַד   וַעֲרָפֶל תַּחַת
יא רַגְלָיו: וַיִּרְכַּב עַל־כְּרוּב וַיָּעֹף   וַיֵּרָא
יב עַל־כַּנְפֵי־רוּחַ:   וַיָּשֶׁת חֹשֶׁךְ סְבִיבֹתָיו
יג סֻכּוֹת   חַשְׁרַת־מַיִם עָבֵי שְׁחָקִים: מִנֹּגַהּ
יד נֶגְדּוֹ בָּעֲרוּ גַּחֲלֵי־אֵשׁ:   יַרְעֵם מִן־שָׁמַיִם
טו יהוה   וְעֶלְיוֹן יִתֵּן קוֹלוֹ:   וַיִּשְׁלַח
טז חִצִּים וַיְפִיצֵם בָּרָק ויהמם: וַיֵּרָאוּ אֲפִקֵי   וַיָּהֹם
יָם   יִגָּלוּ מֹסְדוֹת תֵּבֵל   בְּגַעֲרַת
יז יהוה מִנִּשְׁמַת רוּחַ אַפּוֹ:   יִשְׁלַח מִמָּרוֹם
יח יִקָּחֵנִי   יַמְשֵׁנִי מִמַּיִם רַבִּים: יַצִּילֵנִי
מֵאֹיְבִי עָז   מִשֹּׂנְאַי כִּי אָמְצוּ
יט מִמֶּנִּי: יְקַדְּמֻנִי בְּיוֹם אֵידִי   וַיְהִי
כ יהוה מִשְׁעָן לִי: וַיֹּצֵא לַמֶּרְחָב

21 He brought me out to freedom; / He rescued me because He delighted in me. // The LORD reward-
22 ed me as I deserved; / as my hands were clean, He repaid me, / for I kept the ways of the LORD /
23 and did not betray my God, / for all His laws are before me; / I will not turn away from His statutes. /
24 25 I am blameless to Him / and keep myself from sin. / So the LORD repaid me as I deserved / as I was
26 pure in His sight. // You deal loyally with those who are loyal, / to the blameless warrior You show
27 Yourself blameless; / You are pure with those who are pure, / but with the crooked, You are shrewd. /
28 29 You bring salvation to a humble people; / You cast Your eyes down on the haughty. // For You are my
30 lamp, LORD; / the LORD lights up my darkness. / With You I can rush a ridge; / with my God I can
31 leap over a wall. // God's ways are blameless; / the LORD's words are pure; / He is a shield to all who
32 33 take refuge in Him. // For who is a god besides the LORD; / who is a Rock besides our God? / God is
34 my powerful stronghold; / He frees my way so it is sound. / He makes my legs like a deer's / and stands
35 me on the heights. / He trains my hands for battle / so that my arms can bend a bow of bronze. //
36 37 You gave me the shield of Your victory; / Your battle cry stirred me with power. / You made my steps
38 broad and firm; / my feet never faltered. / I pursued my enemy to destroy them, / never turning back
39 until they perished. / I cut them down and crushed them, and they did not rise; / they fell beneath my
40 41 feet. / You girded me with power for battle / and sunk my adversaries far beneath me; / You made my
42 enemies turn tail before me; / my foes, too, I destroyed. / They looked wildly about, but there was no
43 savior – / called out to the LORD, but He did not answer them – // while I ground them up like dust
44 of the earth; / I crushed and pounded them like street-mud. // You rescued me from civil strife; / You
45 kept me as the head of nations; / peoples I never knew of serve me. / Foreign peoples come cring-
46 ing before me; / they merely hear me and obey; / foreign peoples lose heart / and come trembling
47 out of their forts. // The LORD lives! / Blessed is my Rock; / exalted is God, Rock of my rescue! /

כא	אֹתִ֑י	יְחַלְּצֵ֖נִי כִּֽי־חָ֥פֵֽץ בִּֽי׃	יִגְמְלֵ֥נִי
	יְהוָ֖ה כְּצִדְקָתִ֑י		כְּבֹ֥ר יָדַ֖י יָשִׁ֥יב
כב	לִֽי׃	כִּֽי שָׁמַ֖רְתִּי דַּ֣רְכֵי יְהוָ֑ה	וְלֹ֥א
כג	רָשַׁ֖עְתִּי מֵאֱלֹהָֽי׃		כִּ֥י כָל־מִשְׁפָּטָ֖ו
כד	לְנֶגְדִּ֑י	וְחֻקֹּתָ֖יו לֹא־אָס֥וּר מִמֶּֽנָּה׃	וָאֶהְיֶ֥ה
כה	תָמִ֖ים ל֑וֹ וָאֶשְׁתַּמְּרָ֖ה מֵעֲוֺנִֽי׃		וַיָּ֧שֶׁב יְהוָ֛ה לִ֖י
כו	כְּצִדְקָתִ֑י	כְּבֹרִ֖י לְנֶ֥גֶד עֵינָֽיו׃	עִם־
	חָסִ֖יד תִּתְחַסָּ֑ד		עִם־גִּבּ֥וֹר תָּמִ֖ים
כז	תִּתַּמָּֽם׃	עִם־נָבָ֖ר תִּתָּבָ֑ר	וְעִם־
כח	עִקֵּ֖שׁ תִּתַּפָּֽל׃		וְאֶת־עַ֥ם עָנִ֖י
כט	תּוֹשִׁ֑יעַ	וְעֵינֶ֖יךָ עַל־רָמִ֥ים תַּשְׁפִּֽיל׃	כִּֽי־
	אַתָּ֥ה נֵירִ֖י יְהוָ֑ה		וַיהוָ֖ה יַגִּ֥יהַּ
ל	חָשְׁכִּֽי׃	כִּ֥י בְכָ֖ה אָר֣וּץ גְּד֑וּד	בֵּאלֹהַ֖י
לא	אֲדַלֶּג־שֽׁוּר׃		הָאֵ֖ל תָּמִ֣ים
	דַּרְכּ֑וֹ	אִמְרַ֤ת יְהוָה֙ צְרוּפָ֔ה	מָגֵ֣ן
לב	ה֔וּא לְכֹ֖ל הַחֹסִ֥ים בּֽוֹ׃		כִּ֥י מִי־אֵ֖ל מִבַּלְעֲדֵ֣י
לג	יְהוָ֑ה	וּמִ֥י צ֖וּר מִבַּלְעֲדֵ֥י אֱלֹהֵֽינוּ׃	הָאֵ֖ל
	מָעוּזִּ֣י חָ֑יִל		וַיַּתֵּ֥ר תָּמִ֖ים
לד	דרכֽוֹ׃	מְשַׁוֶּ֥ה רגלָ֖יו כָּֽאַיָּל֑וֹת	וְעַל־ (דַּרְכִּ֥י | רַגְלַ֖י)
לה	בָּמוֹתַ֖י יַעֲמִידֵֽנִי׃		מְלַמֵּ֥ד יָדַ֖י
לו	לַמִּלְחָמָ֑ה	וְנִחַ֥ת קֶֽשֶׁת־נְחוּשָׁ֖ה זְרֹעֹתָֽי׃	וַתִּתֶּן־
לז	לִ֖י מָגֵ֣ן יִשְׁעֶ֑ךָ וַעֲנֹתְךָ֖ תַּרְבֵּֽנִי׃		תַּרְחִ֥יב צַעֲדִ֖י
לח	תַּחְתֵּ֑נִי	וְלֹ֥א מָעֲד֖וּ קַרְסֻלָּֽי׃	אֶרְדְּפָ֥ה
	אֹיְבַ֖י וָאַשְׁמִידֵ֑ם		וְלֹ֥א אָשׁ֖וּב עַד־
לט	כַּלּוֹתָֽם׃	וָאֲכַלֵּ֥ם וָאֶמְחָצֵ֖ם וְלֹ֣א יְקוּמ֑וּן	וַֽיִּפְּל֖וּ
מ	תַּ֥חַת רַגְלָֽי׃		וַתַּזְרֵ֥נִי חַ֖יִל
מא	לַמִּלְחָמָ֑ה	תַּכְרִ֥יעַ קָמַ֖י תַּחְתֵּֽנִי׃	וְאֹ֣יְבַ֔י
מב	תַּ֥תָּה לִּ֖י עֹ֑רֶף		מְשַׂנְאַ֖י וָאַצְמִיתֵֽם׃ יִשְׁע֖וּ וְאֵ֣ין
מג	מֹשִׁ֑יעַ	אֶל־יְהוָ֖ה וְלֹ֥א עָנָֽם׃	וְאֶשְׁחָקֵ֖ם
	כַּעֲפַר־אָ֑רֶץ		כְּטִיט־חוּצ֥וֹת אֲדִקֵּ֖ם
מד	אֶרְקָעֵֽם׃	וַתְּפַלְּטֵ֔נִי מֵרִיבֵ֖י עַמִּ֑י	תִּשְׁמְרֵ֙נִי֙
	לְרֹ֣אשׁ גּוֹיִ֔ם		עַ֥ם לֹא־יָדַ֖עְתִּי
מה	יַעַבְדֻֽנִי׃	בְּנֵ֥י נֵכָ֖ר יִֽתְכַּחֲשׁוּ־לִ֑י	לִשְׁמ֥וֹעַ
מו	אֹ֖זֶן יִשָּׁ֥מְעוּ לִֽי׃		בְּנֵ֥י נֵכָ֖ר יִבֹּ֑לוּ וְיַחְגְּר֖וּ
מז	מִמִּסְגְּרוֹתָֽם׃	חַי־יְהוָ֖ה וּבָר֣וּךְ צוּרִ֑י	וְיָרֻ֕ם

48 49 God who grants vengeance to me, / who subjugates people under me, / my redeemer from my en-
50 emies, / You raise me above those who rise against me; / You save me from violent men. // So I praise
51 You, Lord, among the nations, / and sing to Your name. // He is a tower of victory for His king / and
shows loyalty to His anointed, / to David and his seed forever.

EZEKIEL
For Yemenites

17 22 "So says the Lord God: I will take from the soaring crown of the cedar and place it, I will pluck from
23 the topmost, tender stalks, and I will plant it upon a high and lofty mountain; in the mountainous
height of Israel I will plant it. It will bear branches, grow fruit; it will become a majestic cedar, and
24 every bird of every type will settle beneath it; in the shade of its arms they will dwell. And all the trees
of the field will know that I, the Lord, have brought down the high tree and raised the lowly tree; I
have withered the green tree and made the withered tree bloom; I, the Lord, have spoken and will do
18 1 2 it." And the word of the Lord came to me, saying: "What are you doing, using this proverb
3 on the soil of Israel: 'Fathers eat sour grapes, but the teeth of the children are set on edge'? As I live,
4 declares the Lord God, you will no longer use this proverb in Israel. Behold: all lives are Mine; the
5 life of father and son alike are Mine; that person who sins will die. The person who is righ-
6 teous, who acts in a way that is just and right – he does not eat on the mountains or look up to the
7 idols of the House of Israel, he does not defile another's wife or approach a menstruating woman, he
mistreats no one, he returns his debtor's pledge to him, he commits no robbery, he gives his bread to
8 the hungry, he covers the naked with clothes, he does not lend with advanced interest or take accrued
9 interest, he resists doing wrong, he judges between man and man with true justice, he follows My
10 statutes, keeps My laws, acts with truth – he is righteous; he will live, declares the Lord God. If he
11 bears a violent son, a bloodshedder, who commits any one of these – although he himself committed
12 none of these – who eats on the mountains, who defiles another's wife, who mistreats the poor and
needy, commits robbery, does not return his debtor's pledge, who looks up to the idols, who commits
13 abominable things, who lends with advanced interest and takes accrued interest, will he live? He will
14 not live; he has committed all these abominable acts; he will die – his blood is on his own head. And
if he bears a son, who sees all the sins that his father has committed, who considers them but does not
15 act similarly – he does not eat on the mountains, he does not look up to the idols of the House of Israel,
16 he does not defile another's wife, he mistreats no one, he does not retain his debtor's pledge, he does
17 not commit robbery, he gives his bread to the hungry, he covers the naked with clothes, he refrains
from harming the poor, he takes neither advanced nor accrued interest, he keeps My laws, follows My
18 statutes – he will not die for the iniquity of his father; he will live. Because his father practiced extortion, robbed his own brother, acted in a way that was no good among his people, behold: he will die in
19 his iniquity. And you say: Why does the son not bear the iniquity of the father? The son has acted in a

sins, since we always have the chance to repent. And so, while the fate of destruction for Jerusalem is final, the people have the opportunity to repair the damage done by the willful behavior that the prophets had identified as its cause. The people of Israel can make themselves a foundation for building a better future. The destruction can be undone, but despair will only exacerbate it. Yeḥezkel, at God's behest, was fighting against despair.

מח אֱלֹהֵי צוּר יִשְׁעִי: הָאֵל הַנֹּתֵן נְקָמֹת
מט לִי וּמֹרִיד עַמִּים תַּחְתֵּנִי: וּמוֹצִיאִי
מֵאֹיְבָי וּמִקָּמַי תְּרוֹמְמֵנִי מֵאִישׁ חֲמָסִים
נ תַּצִּילֵנִי: עַל־כֵּן אוֹדְךָ יְהֹוָה בַּגּוֹיִם וּלְשִׁמְךָ
נא אֲזַמֵּר: מגדיל יְשׁוּעוֹת מִגְדּוֹל
מַלְכּוֹ וְעֹשֶׂה־חֶסֶד לִמְשִׁיחוֹ
לְדָוִד וּלְזַרְעוֹ עַד־עוֹלָם:

יחזקאל

For Yemenites

יז כב כֹּה אָמַר אֲדֹנָי יֱהֹוִה וְלָקַחְתִּי אָנִי מִצַּמֶּרֶת הָאֶרֶז הָרָמָה וְנָתָתִּי מֵרֹאשׁ יֹנְקוֹתָיו רַךְ אֶקְטֹף וְשָׁתַלְתִּי אָנִי
כג עַל הַר־גָּבֹהַּ וְתָלוּל: בְּהַר מְרוֹם יִשְׂרָאֵל אֶשְׁתֳּלֶנּוּ וְנָשָׂא עָנָף וְעָשָׂה פֶרִי וְהָיָה לְאֶרֶז אַדִּיר וְשָׁכְנוּ תַחְתָּיו
כד כֹּל צִפּוֹר כָּל־כָּנָף בְּצֵל דָּלִיּוֹתָיו תִּשְׁכֹּנָּה: וְיָדְעוּ כָּל־עֲצֵי הַשָּׂדֶה כִּי אֲנִי יְהֹוָה הִשְׁפַּלְתִּי ׀ עֵץ גָּבֹהַּ הִגְבַּהְתִּי
יח א עֵץ שָׁפָל הוֹבַשְׁתִּי עֵץ לָח וְהִפְרַחְתִּי עֵץ יָבֵשׁ אֲנִי יְהֹוָה דִּבַּרְתִּי וְעָשִׂיתִי: וַיְהִי דְבַר־יְהֹוָה אֵלַי
ב לֵאמֹר: מַה־לָּכֶם אַתֶּם מֹשְׁלִים אֶת־הַמָּשָׁל הַזֶּה עַל־אַדְמַת יִשְׂרָאֵל לֵאמֹר אָבוֹת יֹאכְלוּ בֹסֶר וְשִׁנֵּי הַבָּנִים
ג ד תִּקְהֶינָה: חַי־אָנִי נְאֻם אֲדֹנָי יֱהֹוִה אִם־יִהְיֶה לָכֶם עוֹד מְשֹׁל הַמָּשָׁל הַזֶּה בְּיִשְׂרָאֵל: הֵן כָּל־הַנְּפָשׁוֹת לִי
ה הֵנָּה כְּנֶפֶשׁ הָאָב וּכְנֶפֶשׁ הַבֵּן לִי־הֵנָּה הַנֶּפֶשׁ הַחֹטֵאת הִיא תָמוּת: וְאִישׁ כִּי־יִהְיֶה צַדִּיק
ו וְעָשָׂה מִשְׁפָּט וּצְדָקָה: אֶל־הֶהָרִים לֹא אָכָל וְעֵינָיו לֹא נָשָׂא אֶל־גִּלּוּלֵי בֵּית יִשְׂרָאֵל וְאֶת־אֵשֶׁת רֵעֵהוּ
ז לֹא טִמֵּא וְאֶל־אִשָּׁה נִדָּה לֹא יִקְרָב: וְאִישׁ לֹא יוֹנֶה חֲבֹלָתוֹ חוֹב יָשִׁיב גְּזֵלָה לֹא יִגְזֹל לַחְמוֹ לְרָעֵב יִתֵּן
ח וְעֵירֹם יְכַסֶּה־בָּגֶד: בַּנֶּשֶׁךְ לֹא־יִתֵּן וְתַרְבִּית לֹא יִקָּח מֵעָוֶל יָשִׁיב יָדוֹ מִשְׁפַּט אֱמֶת יַעֲשֶׂה בֵּין אִישׁ לְאִישׁ:
ט י בְּחֻקּוֹתַי יְהַלֵּךְ וּמִשְׁפָּטַי שָׁמַר לַעֲשׂוֹת אֱמֶת צַדִּיק הוּא חָיֹה יִחְיֶה נְאֻם אֲדֹנָי יֱהֹוִה: וְהוֹלִיד בֵּן־פָּרִיץ
יא שֹׁפֵךְ דָּם וְעָשָׂה אָח מֵאַחַד מֵאֵלֶּה: וְהוּא אֶת־כָּל־אֵלֶּה לֹא עָשָׂה כִּי גַם אֶל־הֶהָרִים אָכַל וְאֶת־אֵשֶׁת
יב יג רֵעֵהוּ טִמֵּא: עָנִי וְאֶבְיוֹן הוֹנָה גְּזֵלוֹת גָּזָל חֲבֹל לֹא יָשִׁיב וְאֶל־הַגִּלּוּלִים נָשָׂא עֵינָיו תּוֹעֵבָה עָשָׂה: בַּנֶּשֶׁךְ
יד נָתַן וְתַרְבִּית לָקַח וָחָי לֹא יִחְיֶה אֵת כָּל־הַתּוֹעֵבוֹת הָאֵלֶּה עָשָׂה מוֹת יוּמָת דָּמָיו בּוֹ יִהְיֶה: וְהִנֵּה הוֹלִיד
טו בֵּן וַיַּרְא אֶת־כָּל־חַטֹּאת אָבִיו אֲשֶׁר עָשָׂה וַיִּרְאֶה וְלֹא יַעֲשֶׂה כָּהֵן: עַל־הֶהָרִים לֹא אָכָל וְעֵינָיו לֹא נָשָׂא
טז אֶל־גִּלּוּלֵי בֵּית יִשְׂרָאֵל אֶת־אֵשֶׁת רֵעֵהוּ לֹא טִמֵּא: וְאִישׁ לֹא הוֹנָה חֲבֹל לֹא חָבָל וּגְזֵלָה לֹא גָזָל לַחְמוֹ
יז לְרָעֵב נָתָן וְעֵרוֹם כִּסָּה־בָגֶד: מֵעָנִי הֵשִׁיב יָדוֹ נֶשֶׁךְ וְתַרְבִּית לֹא לָקָח מִשְׁפָּטַי עָשָׂה בְּחֻקּוֹתַי הָלָךְ הוּא
יח לֹא יָמוּת בַּעֲוֺן אָבִיו חָיֹה יִחְיֶה: אָבִיו כִּי־עָשַׁק עֹשֶׁק גָּזַל גֵּזֶל אָח וַאֲשֶׁר לֹא־טוֹב עָשָׂה בְּתוֹךְ עַמָּיו
יט וְהִנֵּה־מֵת בַּעֲוֺנוֹ: וַאֲמַרְתֶּם מַדֻּעַ לֹא־נָשָׂא הַבֵּן בַּעֲוֺן הָאָב וְהַבֵּן מִשְׁפָּט וּצְדָקָה עָשָׂה אֵת כָּל־חֻקּוֹתַי

Yemenites

The prophet Yeḥezkel faces those exiled with him to Babylonia during the reign of Yehoyakhin. "Fathers eat sour grapes, but the teeth of the children are set on edge" – this was the mistaken lesson that the exiles took away from their harrowing experience – our ancestors sinned, and we are bearing their punishments. Such thinking brought about despair among the people, and contributed to an air of passivity and resignation. Yeḥezkel imparts God's word to the people, taking issue with their dejected attitude of futility, as a matter both of principle and of practice. First of all, God's justice in the world works on an individual level: "That person who sins will die; the son will not bear the iniquity of the father." No one is forced to bear the punishment for their forebears'

▶

20 way that is just and right, has kept all My statutes, has performed them – he will live. That person who
sins will die; the son will not bear the iniquity of the father, and the father will not bear the iniquity
of the son; the righteous one's righteousness will be on him, and the wicked one's wickedness will be
21 on him. The wicked one who turns back from all the sins he committed and keeps all My
22 statutes and acts in a way that is just and right – he will live; he will not die. All the transgressions he
committed will not be remembered against him; through the righteousness he has performed he will
23 live. Do I desire the death of the wicked, declares the Lord God, not that he should turn from his ways
24 and live? And the righteous one who turns from his righteousness and does wrong
similar to all the abominable acts the wicked one committed, shall he live? None of the righteous deeds
he has done will be remembered; his betrayal and the sins that he has sinned – because of these he will
25 die. You say, 'The way of the Lord is not fair.' Listen, House of Israel: Is My way not fair? Surely, your
26 ways are not fair. When the righteous one turns from his righteousness and does wrong and dies for it,
27 he dies for that which he has done wrong. And when the wicked one turns from the wicked-
28 ness that he has done and acts in a way that is just and right, he preserves his life. When he considers
29 them and turns from all the transgressions he has committed, he will live; he will not die. And the
House of Israel says, 'The way of the Lord is not fair.' Are My ways not fair, House of Israel? It is your
ways that are not fair. So I will judge you, House of Israel, each man according to his ways, declares the
Lord God; return – turn back from all your transgressions so that they will not be the obstacle that is
31 sin for you. Throw off all the transgressions you have committed; make yourselves a new heart, a new
32 spirit. Why should you die, House of Israel? For I do not desire the death of those who die, declares
the Lord God; turn back and live!

Haftarat Vezot Haberakha

JOSHUA

1 1 After the death of Moshe, the Lord's servant, the Lord said to Moshe's disciple, Yehoshua son of
2 Nun: "Moshe, My servant, is dead; now arise, cross the Jordan here – you and all this people – to
3 the land that I am giving to the Israelites. I have given you every place your foot will tread, just as
4 I promised Moshe. Your territory shall stretch from the wilderness and Lebanon here to the Great
5 River, the Euphrates River, and all the land of the Hittites, to the Great Sea where the sun sets. No
one will be able to stand against you for as long as you live; just as I was with Moshe, I will be with
6 you. I will never let you go, and I will never leave you. Be strong and brave, for you will bring this
7 people into possession of the land I swore to their ancestors to give them. But you must be strong
and brave indeed to uphold faithfully all the Torah that Moshe My servant commanded you; do not
8 stray from it – neither right nor left – so that you may triumph wherever you go. This book of Torah
must never leave your lips; contemplate it day and night, so that you will faithfully uphold all that is
9 written within it. For then your course will succeed; then you will triumph. Hear now – I have charged
you to be strong and brave. Do not be frightened or dismayed, for the Lord your God is with you

threefold encouragement from God in advance of the objectives he must set out to attain. Three times God says to him: "Be strong and brave." In answer to his call to the tribes of the eastern side of the Jordan to fulfill their pledge and take the lead in the invasion, Yehoshua receives additional support and affirmation of his leadership. These votes of confidence from God and the people were crucial in this sensitive time.

כ שָׁמַר וַיַּעֲשֶׂה אֹתָם חָיֹה יִחְיֶה: הַנֶּפֶשׁ הַחֹטֵאת הִיא תָמוּת בֵּן לֹא־יִשָּׂא ׀ בַּעֲוֺן הָאָב וְאָב לֹא יִשָּׂא בַּעֲוֺן
כא הַבֵּן צִדְקַת הַצַּדִּיק עָלָיו תִּהְיֶה וְרִשְׁעַת רשע עָלָיו תִּהְיֶה: וְהָרָשָׁע כִּי יָשׁוּב מִכָּל־חַטֹּאתוֹ הָרָשָׁע
כב אֲשֶׁר עָשָׂה וְשָׁמַר אֶת־כָּל־חֻקּוֹתַי וְעָשָׂה מִשְׁפָּט וּצְדָקָה חָיֹה יִחְיֶה לֹא יָמוּת: כָּל־פְּשָׁעָיו אֲשֶׁר עָשָׂה לֹא
כג יִזָּכְרוּ לוֹ בְּצִדְקָתוֹ אֲשֶׁר־עָשָׂה יִחְיֶה: הֶחָפֹץ אֶחְפֹּץ מוֹת רָשָׁע נְאֻם אֲדֹנָי יֱהֹוִה הֲלוֹא בְּשׁוּבוֹ מִדְּרָכָיו
כד וְחָיָה: וּבְשׁוּב צַדִּיק מִצִּדְקָתוֹ וְעָשָׂה עָוֶל כְּכֹל הַתּוֹעֵבוֹת אֲשֶׁר־עָשָׂה הָרָשָׁע יַעֲשֶׂה וָחָי
כה כָּל־צִדְקֹתָו אֲשֶׁר־עָשָׂה לֹא תִזָּכַרְנָה בְּמַעֲלוֹ אֲשֶׁר־מָעַל וּבְחַטָּאתוֹ אֲשֶׁר־חָטָא בָּם יָמוּת: וַאֲמַרְתֶּם
כו לֹא יִתָּכֵן דֶּרֶךְ אֲדֹנָי שִׁמְעוּ־נָא בֵּית יִשְׂרָאֵל הֲדַרְכִּי לֹא יִתָּכֵן הֲלֹא דַרְכֵיכֶם לֹא יִתָּכֵנוּ: בְּשׁוּב־צַדִּיק
כז מִצִּדְקָתוֹ וְעָשָׂה עָוֶל וּמֵת עֲלֵיהֶם בְּעַוְלוֹ אֲשֶׁר־עָשָׂה יָמוּת: וּבְשׁוּב רָשָׁע מֵרִשְׁעָתוֹ אֲשֶׁר
כח עָשָׂה וַיַּעַשׂ מִשְׁפָּט וּצְדָקָה הוּא אֶת־נַפְשׁוֹ יְחַיֶּה: וַיִּרְאֶה וישוב מִכָּל־פְּשָׁעָיו אֲשֶׁר עָשָׂה חָיוֹ יִחְיֶה לֹא וַיָּשָׁב
כט יָמוּת: וְאָמְרוּ בֵּית יִשְׂרָאֵל לֹא יִתָּכֵן דֶּרֶךְ אֲדֹנָי הַדְּרָכַי לֹא יִתָּכְנוּ בֵּית יִשְׂרָאֵל הֲלֹא דַרְכֵיכֶם לֹא יִתָּכֵן:
ל לָכֵן אִישׁ כִּדְרָכָיו אֶשְׁפֹּט אֶתְכֶם בֵּית יִשְׂרָאֵל נְאֻם אֲדֹנָי יֱהֹוִה שׁוּבוּ וְהָשִׁיבוּ מִכָּל־פִּשְׁעֵיכֶם וְלֹא־יִהְיֶה
לא לָכֶם לְמִכְשׁוֹל עָוֺן: הַשְׁלִיכוּ מֵעֲלֵיכֶם אֶת־כָּל־פִּשְׁעֵיכֶם אֲשֶׁר פְּשַׁעְתֶּם בָּם וַעֲשׂוּ לָכֶם לֵב חָדָשׁ וְרוּחַ
לב חֲדָשָׁה וְלָמָּה תָמֻתוּ בֵּית יִשְׂרָאֵל: כִּי לֹא אֶחְפֹּץ בְּמוֹת הַמֵּת נְאֻם אֲדֹנָי יֱהֹוִה וְהָשִׁיבוּ וִחְיוּ:

הפטרת וזאת הברכה

א א ב וַיְהִי אַחֲרֵי מוֹת מֹשֶׁה עֶבֶד יְהוָה וַיֹּאמֶר יְהוָה אֶל־יְהוֹשֻׁעַ בִּן־נוּן מְשָׁרֵת מֹשֶׁה לֵאמֹר: מֹשֶׁה עַבְדִּי מֵת יהושע
וְעַתָּה קוּם עֲבֹר אֶת־הַיַּרְדֵּן הַזֶּה אַתָּה וְכָל־הָעָם הַזֶּה אֶל־הָאָרֶץ אֲשֶׁר אָנֹכִי נֹתֵן לָהֶם לִבְנֵי יִשְׂרָאֵל:
ג ד כָּל־מָקוֹם אֲשֶׁר תִּדְרֹךְ כַּף־רַגְלְכֶם בּוֹ לָכֶם נְתַתִּיו כַּאֲשֶׁר דִּבַּרְתִּי אֶל־מֹשֶׁה: מֵהַמִּדְבָּר וְהַלְּבָנוֹן הַזֶּה
ה וְעַד־הַנָּהָר הַגָּדוֹל נְהַר־פְּרָת כֹּל אֶרֶץ הַחִתִּים וְעַד־הַיָּם הַגָּדוֹל מְבוֹא הַשָּׁמֶשׁ יִהְיֶה גְּבוּלְכֶם: לֹא־יִתְיַצֵּב
ו אִישׁ לְפָנֶיךָ כֹּל יְמֵי חַיֶּיךָ כַּאֲשֶׁר הָיִיתִי עִם־מֹשֶׁה אֶהְיֶה עִמָּךְ לֹא אַרְפְּךָ וְלֹא אֶעֶזְבֶךָּ: חֲזַק וֶאֱמָץ כִּי אַתָּה
ז תַּנְחִיל אֶת־הָעָם הַזֶּה אֶת־הָאָרֶץ אֲשֶׁר־נִשְׁבַּעְתִּי לַאֲבוֹתָם לָתֵת לָהֶם: רַק חֲזַק וֶאֱמַץ מְאֹד לִשְׁמֹר
לַעֲשׂוֹת כְּכָל־הַתּוֹרָה אֲשֶׁר צִוְּךָ מֹשֶׁה עַבְדִּי אַל־תָּסוּר מִמֶּנּוּ יָמִין וּשְׂמֹאול לְמַעַן תַּשְׂכִּיל בְּכֹל אֲשֶׁר
ח תֵּלֵךְ: לֹא־יָמוּשׁ סֵפֶר הַתּוֹרָה הַזֶּה מִפִּיךָ וְהָגִיתָ בּוֹ יוֹמָם וָלַיְלָה לְמַעַן תִּשְׁמֹר לַעֲשׂוֹת כְּכָל־הַכָּתוּב בּוֹ
ט כִּי־אָז תַּצְלִיחַ אֶת־דְּרָכֶךָ וְאָז תַּשְׂכִּיל: הֲלוֹא צִוִּיתִיךָ חֲזַק וֶאֱמָץ אַל־תַּעֲרֹץ וְאַל־תֵּחָת כִּי עִמְּךָ יְהוָה

VEZOT HABERAKHA

This *haftara* is the direct continuation of the end of the events described in the book of Deuteronomy. Moshe's death, and the assumption of the mantle of responsibility by the prophet Yehoshua, were events that created challenges for all the people set to enter the land of Israel, especially Yehoshua. Moshe, who had led the people for forty years, left enormous shoes to fill. The difficulties posed in crossing the Jordan and waging war against the peoples of Canaan were formidable. In his first prophecy, Yehoshua receives

10 11 wherever you go.” Yehoshua commanded the officers of the people: “Cross through the camp
and instruct the people: ‘Prepare provisions for yourselves, for in three days’ time you are to cross the
Jordan here, to come and take possession of the land that the LORD your God is giving you as your
12 13 own.’” Yehoshua then told the Reubenites, the Gadites, and half the tribe of Menashe: “Remember what Moshe, the LORD’s servant, commanded you: The LORD your God has granted you rest
14 and given you this land. Your wives and little ones and your cattle shall dwell in the land that Moshe
gave you across the Jordan, but all your warriors shall cross over armed to join your brothers and assist
15 them, until the LORD grants rest like yours to your brothers and they too take possession of the land
that the LORD your God is giving them. Then you shall return to your own land, which Moshe, the
16 LORD’s servant, gave you on the eastern side of the Jordan – and you shall take possession of it.” They
17 answered Yehoshua, “As we obeyed Moshe, so we will obey you as long as the LORD your God is with
18 you, as He was with Moshe. Whoever rebels against your word or disobeys anything you command
shall be put to death; only be strong and brave.”

Sepharadim end here
Yemenites skip to Joshua 6:27

Ashkenazim end here

6 27 The LORD was with Yehoshua, and his fame rang out across the land.

עשרת הדיברות שבפרשת יתרו
בטעם העליון

אָנֹכִי יְהוָה אֱלֹהֶיךָ אֲשֶׁר הוֹצֵאתִיךָ
מֵאֶרֶץ מִצְרַיִם מִבֵּית עֲבָדִים לֹא יִהְיֶה לְךָ אֱלֹהִים אֲחֵרִים עַל־פָּנַי לֹא תַעֲשֶׂה־לְךָ
פֶּסֶל ׀ וְכָל־תְּמוּנָה אֲשֶׁר בַּשָּׁמַיִם ׀ מִמַּעַל וַאֲשֶׁר בָּאָרֶץ מִתַּחַת וַאֲשֶׁר בַּמַּיִם ׀
מִתַּחַת לָאָרֶץ לֹא־תִשְׁתַּחֲוֶה לָהֶם וְלֹא תָעָבְדֵם כִּי אָנֹכִי יְהוָה אֱלֹהֶיךָ אֵל קַנָּא
פֹּקֵד עֲוֺן אָבֹת עַל־בָּנִים עַל־שִׁלֵּשִׁים וְעַל־רִבֵּעִים לְשֹׂנְאָי וְעֹשֶׂה חֶסֶד לַאֲלָפִים
לְאֹהֲבַי וּלְשֹׁמְרֵי מִצְוֺתָי׃ לֹא תִשָּׂא אֶת־שֵׁם־יְהוָה אֱלֹהֶיךָ לַשָּׁוְא כִּי
לֹא יְנַקֶּה יְהוָה אֵת אֲשֶׁר־יִשָּׂא אֶת־שְׁמוֹ לַשָּׁוְא׃

The *taam elyon* presented here is according to the position of Rabbi Yaakov Emden (Germany, 1696–1776). However, according to Rabbi Wolf Heidenheim (Germany, 1757–1832), the first commandment (until the words מבית עבדים) ought to be read the same in *taam elyon* and *taam taḥton*.

Rabbi Ḥizkiya ben Manoaḥ, author of the commentary *Ḥizkuni*, writes that on the holiday of Shavuot, the Ten Commandments should be read in the synagogue using *taam elyon*, while when read as part of the weekly *parasha*, *taam taḥton* should be used. This is the custom of most Ashkenazic congregations. However, Rabbi Menaḥem de Lonzano (Middle East, sixteenth century) in his book *Or Torah* writes that *taam elyon* should always be used when reading publicly in the synagogue, and only individuals reading to themselves should use *taam taḥton*. This is the custom of Sephardic congregations. In the communities of Yemen, only *taam elyon* was extant, since the Yemenite customs largely mirror the traditions of the Babylonian Jews.

Sepharadim end here
Yemenites skip to Joshua 6:27

י יא אֱלֹהֶיךָ בְּכֹל אֲשֶׁר תֵּלֵךְ׃* וַיְצַו יְהוֹשֻׁעַ אֶת־שֹׁטְרֵי הָעָם לֵאמֹר׃ עִבְרוּ ׀ בְּקֶרֶב הַמַּחֲנֶה וְצַוּוּ
אֶת־הָעָם לֵאמֹר הָכִינוּ לָכֶם צֵידָה כִּי בְּעוֹד ׀ שְׁלֹשֶׁת יָמִים אַתֶּם עֹבְרִים אֶת־הַיַּרְדֵּן הַזֶּה לָבוֹא לָרֶשֶׁת
יב אֶת־הָאָרֶץ אֲשֶׁר יְהוָה אֱלֹהֵיכֶם נֹתֵן לָכֶם לְרִשְׁתָּהּ׃ וְלָרְאוּבֵנִי וְלַגָּדִי וְלַחֲצִי שֵׁבֶט הַמְנַשֶּׁה
יג אָמַר יְהוֹשֻׁעַ לֵאמֹר׃ זָכוֹר אֶת־הַדָּבָר אֲשֶׁר צִוָּה אֶתְכֶם מֹשֶׁה עֶבֶד־יְהוָה לֵאמֹר יְהוָה אֱלֹהֵיכֶם מֵנִיחַ
יד לָכֶם וְנָתַן לָכֶם אֶת־הָאָרֶץ הַזֹּאת׃ נְשֵׁיכֶם טַפְּכֶם וּמִקְנֵיכֶם יֵשְׁבוּ בָּאָרֶץ אֲשֶׁר נָתַן לָכֶם מֹשֶׁה בְּעֵבֶר
טו הַיַּרְדֵּן וְאַתֶּם תַּעַבְרוּ חֲמֻשִׁים לִפְנֵי אֲחֵיכֶם כֹּל גִּבּוֹרֵי הַחַיִל וַעֲזַרְתֶּם אוֹתָם׃ עַד אֲשֶׁר־יָנִיחַ יְהוָה ׀
לַאֲחֵיכֶם כָּכֶם וְיָרְשׁוּ גַם־הֵמָּה אֶת־הָאָרֶץ אֲשֶׁר־יְהוָה אֱלֹהֵיכֶם נֹתֵן לָהֶם וְשַׁבְתֶּם לְאֶרֶץ יְרֻשַּׁתְכֶם
טז וִירִשְׁתֶּם אוֹתָהּ אֲשֶׁר ׀ נָתַן לָכֶם מֹשֶׁה עֶבֶד יְהוָה בְּעֵבֶר הַיַּרְדֵּן מִזְרַח הַשָּׁמֶשׁ׃ וַיַּעֲנוּ אֶת־יְהוֹשֻׁעַ לֵאמֹר
יז כֹּל אֲשֶׁר־צִוִּיתָנוּ נַעֲשֶׂה וְאֶל־כָּל־אֲשֶׁר תִּשְׁלָחֵנוּ נֵלֵךְ׃ כְּכֹל אֲשֶׁר־שָׁמַעְנוּ אֶל־מֹשֶׁה כֵּן נִשְׁמַע אֵלֶיךָ רַק
יח יִהְיֶה יְהוָה אֱלֹהֶיךָ עִמָּךְ כַּאֲשֶׁר הָיָה עִם־מֹשֶׁה׃ כָּל־אִישׁ אֲשֶׁר־יַמְרֶה אֶת־פִּיךָ וְלֹא־יִשְׁמַע אֶת־דְּבָרֶיךָ
לְכֹל אֲשֶׁר־תְּצַוֶּנּוּ יוּמָת רַק חֲזַק וֶאֱמָץ׃*

Ashkenazim end here

ו כז וַיְהִי יְהוָה אֶת־יְהוֹשֻׁעַ וַיְהִי שָׁמְעוֹ בְּכָל־הָאָרֶץ׃

עשרת הדיברות שבפרשת ואתחנן
בטעם העליון

אָנֹכִי יְהוָה אֱלֹהֶיךָ
אֲשֶׁר הוֹצֵאתִיךָ מֵאֶרֶץ מִצְרַיִם מִבֵּית עֲבָדִים לֹא־יִהְיֶה לְךָ אֱלֹהִים אֲחֵרִים
עַל־פָּנַי לֹא תַעֲשֶׂה־לְךָ פֶסֶל ׀ כָּל־תְּמוּנָה אֲשֶׁר בַּשָּׁמַיִם ׀ מִמַּעַל וַאֲשֶׁר בָּאָרֶץ
מִתַּחַת וַאֲשֶׁר בַּמַּיִם מִתַּחַת לָאָרֶץ לֹא־תִשְׁתַּחֲוֶה לָהֶם וְלֹא תָעָבְדֵם כִּי אָנֹכִי
יְהוָה אֱלֹהֶיךָ אֵל קַנָּא פֹּקֵד עֲוֺן אָבוֹת עַל־בָּנִים וְעַל־שִׁלֵּשִׁים וְעַל־רִבֵּעִים לְשֹׂנְאָי
וְעֹשֶׂה חֶסֶד לַאֲלָפִים לְאֹהֲבַי וּלְשֹׁמְרֵי מצותו׃ לֹא תִשָּׂא אֶת־שֵׁם־יְהוָה מִצְוֺתָי
אֱלֹהֶיךָ לַשָּׁוְא כִּי לֹא יְנַקֶּה יְהוָה אֵת אֲשֶׁר־יִשָּׂא אֶת־שְׁמוֹ לַשָּׁוְא׃ שָׁמוֹר

THE TEN COMMANDMENTS IN TAAM ELYON

There are two traditional sets of *taamim* (cantillation marks) for the Ten Commandments. One is called *taam elyon*, and the other *taam taḥton*. In *taam elyon*, each commandment (except for perhaps the first; see below) comprises one and only one verse. This results in some verses that are very long, with a wealth of elaborate *taamim* such as *pazer* and *telisha*. This gives the reading a dignified and festive air. The difference between *taam elyon* and *taam taḥton* can also result in slight differences in the vocalization of the words – *nikkud*.

It seems that the original division of the verses customary in the land of Israel was *taam taḥton*, while the *taam elyon* has roots in the Babylonian Jewish tradition. Nevertheless, even the oldest extant manuscripts include both systems, though the most ancient ones superimposed them on the same quoted text. This superimposition led to much confusion and disagreement, particularly with regard to the first verse.

זָכוֹר אֶת־יוֹם הַשַּׁבָּת לְקַדְּשׁוֹ שֵׁשֶׁת יָמִים תַּעֲבֹד וְעָשִׂיתָ כָל־מְלַאכְתֶּךָ וְיוֹם
הַשְּׁבִיעִי שַׁבָּת ׀ לַיהוָה אֱלֹהֶיךָ לֹא תַעֲשֶׂה כָל־מְלָאכָה אַתָּה וּבִנְךָ וּבִתֶּךָ
עַבְדְּךָ וַאֲמָתְךָ וּבְהֶמְתֶּךָ וְגֵרְךָ אֲשֶׁר בִּשְׁעָרֶיךָ כִּי שֵׁשֶׁת־יָמִים עָשָׂה יְהוָה
אֶת־הַשָּׁמַיִם וְאֶת־הָאָרֶץ אֶת־הַיָּם וְאֶת־כָּל־אֲשֶׁר־בָּם וַיָּנַח בַּיּוֹם הַשְּׁבִיעִי
עַל־כֵּן בֵּרַךְ יְהוָה אֶת־יוֹם הַשַּׁבָּת וַיְקַדְּשֵׁהוּ׃ כַּבֵּד אֶת־
אָבִיךָ וְאֶת־אִמֶּךָ לְמַעַן יַאֲרִכוּן יָמֶיךָ עַל הָאֲדָמָה אֲשֶׁר־יְהוָה אֱלֹהֶיךָ
נֹתֵן לָךְ׃ לֹא תִרְצָח׃ לֹא
תִנְאָף׃ לֹא תִגְנֹב׃ לֹא־
תַעֲנֶה בְרֵעֲךָ עֵד שָׁקֶר׃ לֹא
תַחְמֹד בֵּית רֵעֶךָ לֹא־
תַחְמֹד אֵשֶׁת רֵעֶךָ וְעַבְדּוֹ וַאֲמָתוֹ וְשׁוֹרוֹ וַחֲמֹרוֹ וְכֹל אֲשֶׁר לְרֵעֶךָ׃

HAFTARA FOR SHABBAT ROSH ḤODESH

The maftir for Shabbat Rosh Ḥodesh is read from Numbers 28:9–15.
If Rosh Ḥodesh is on Shabbat and Sunday, Sepharadim and Chabad conclude this haftara by reading the first and last verses of the haftara for Erev Rosh Ḥodesh, on page 1637.

66 1 Thus speaks the LORD: The heavens are My throne; the world, My footstool. What house, then, would ISAIAH
2 You build for Me, where could I rest? All this – My own hands made, all these are Mine, so says the
LORD. And these are the ones I look toward: the poor, of humbled spirit, who tremble at My words.
3 While he, killing his ox is like a murderer of men, the one who offers up a lamb might so well behead
a dog; the offering brought may just as well be pigs' blood; and his remembrance incense is a blessing
4 of iniquity. These men, they choose their paths, their souls desire their disgusting things, and so I too
will choose – will choose their torments, and bring to them what they most fear. I called out – no one
answered; I spoke, but none was listening. They did what was evil in My sight, and chose what I never
5 desired. You who tremble to hear His word, listen to the LORD's word: Your brothers said,
the ones who hated you, who cast you out, "Because of my name, the LORD is honored." We will see
6 your joy, and they will be shamefaced. A voice roaring out from the city, a voice, out of the Sanctuary,
7 a voice – it is the LORD's, as He repays His enemies. Before she had writhed in labor she gave birth;

---

of Yehuda the Messiah." This chance was never realized because Ḥizkiyahu neglected to write a song of praise for God as his ancestor David had done, and hence expressed insufficient gratitude for his salvation from the Assyrians. In the future redemption, however, all the peoples of the world will give praise to God for His providence, and the song will thus be completed.

אֶת־יוֹם הַשַּׁבָּת לְקַדְּשׁוֹ כַּאֲשֶׁר צִוְּךָ ׀ יְהוָה אֱלֹהֶיךָ שֵׁשֶׁת יָמִים תַּעֲבֹד וְעָשִׂיתָ
כָּל־מְלַאכְתֶּךָ וְיוֹם הַשְּׁבִיעִי שַׁבָּת ׀ לַיהוָה אֱלֹהֶיךָ לֹא־תַעֲשֶׂה כָל־מְלָאכָה אַתָּה
וּבִנְךָ־וּבִתֶּךָ וְעַבְדְּךָ־וַאֲמָתֶךָ וְשׁוֹרְךָ וַחֲמֹרְךָ וְכָל־בְּהֶמְתֶּךָ וְגֵרְךָ אֲשֶׁר בִּשְׁעָרֶיךָ
לְמַעַן יָנוּחַ עַבְדְּךָ וַאֲמָתְךָ כָּמוֹךָ וְזָכַרְתָּ כִּי־עֶבֶד הָיִיתָ ׀ בְּאֶרֶץ מִצְרַיִם וַיֹּצִאֲךָ
יְהוָה אֱלֹהֶיךָ מִשָּׁם בְּיָד חֲזָקָה וּבִזְרֹעַ נְטוּיָה עַל־כֵּן צִוְּךָ יְהוָה אֱלֹהֶיךָ לַעֲשׂוֹת
אֶת־יוֹם הַשַּׁבָּת׃ כַּבֵּד אֶת־אָבִיךָ וְאֶת־אִמֶּךָ כַּאֲשֶׁר צִוְּךָ יְהוָה
אֱלֹהֶיךָ לְמַעַן ׀ יַאֲרִיכֻן יָמֶיךָ וּלְמַעַן יִיטַב לָךְ עַל הָאֲדָמָה אֲשֶׁר־יְהוָה אֱלֹהֶיךָ נֹתֵן
לָךְ׃ לֹא תִרְצָח׃ וְלֹא
תִנְאָף׃ וְלֹא תִגְנֹב׃ וְלֹא־
תַעֲנֶה בְרֵעֲךָ עֵד שָׁוְא׃ וְלֹא
תַחְמֹד אֵשֶׁת רֵעֶךָ וְלֹא
תִתְאַוֶּה בֵּית רֵעֶךָ שָׂדֵהוּ וְעַבְדּוֹ וַאֲמָתוֹ שׁוֹרוֹ וַחֲמֹרוֹ וְכֹל אֲשֶׁר לְרֵעֶךָ׃

הפטרת שבת ראש חודש

The מפטיר *for* שבת ראש חודש *is read from* במדבר כח, ט–טו.
If ראש חודש *is on* שבת *and Sunday, Sepharadim and Chabad conclude this* הפטרה *by reading the first and last verses of the* הפטרה *for* ערב ראש חודש, *on page 1637.*

סו א ב כֹּה אָמַר יְהוָה הַשָּׁמַיִם כִּסְאִי וְהָאָרֶץ הֲדֹם רַגְלָי אֵי־זֶה בַיִת אֲשֶׁר תִּבְנוּ־לִי וְאֵי־זֶה מָקוֹם מְנוּחָתִי׃ וְאֶת־ ישעיה
ג כָּל־אֵלֶּה יָדִי עָשָׂתָה וַיִּהְיוּ כָל־אֵלֶּה נְאֻם־יְהוָה וְאֶל־זֶה אַבִּיט אֶל־עָנִי וּנְכֵה־רוּחַ וְחָרֵד עַל־דְּבָרִי׃ שׁוֹחֵט
הַשּׁוֹר מַכֵּה־אִישׁ זוֹבֵחַ הַשֶּׂה עֹרֵף כֶּלֶב מַעֲלֵה מִנְחָה דַּם־חֲזִיר מַזְכִּיר לְבֹנָה מְבָרֵךְ אָוֶן גַּם־הֵמָּה בָּחֲרוּ
ד בְּדַרְכֵיהֶם וּבְשִׁקּוּצֵיהֶם נַפְשָׁם חָפֵצָה׃ גַּם־אֲנִי אֶבְחַר בְּתַעֲלֻלֵיהֶם וּמְגוּרֹתָם אָבִיא לָהֶם יַעַן קָרָאתִי
ה וְאֵין עוֹנֶה דִּבַּרְתִּי וְלֹא שָׁמֵעוּ וַיַּעֲשׂוּ הָרַע בְּעֵינַי וּבַאֲשֶׁר לֹא־חָפַצְתִּי בָּחָרוּ׃ שִׁמְעוּ דְּבַר־יְהוָה
הַחֲרֵדִים אֶל־דְּבָרוֹ אָמְרוּ אֲחֵיכֶם שֹׂנְאֵיכֶם מְנַדֵּיכֶם לְמַעַן שְׁמִי יִכְבַּד יְהוָה וְנִרְאֶה בְשִׂמְחַתְכֶם וְהֵם
ו ז יֵבֹשׁוּ׃ קוֹל שָׁאוֹן מֵעִיר קוֹל מֵהֵיכָל קוֹל יְהוָה מְשַׁלֵּם גְּמוּל לְאֹיְבָיו׃ בְּטֶרֶם תָּחִיל יָלָדָה בְּטֶרֶם יָבוֹא

HAFTARA FOR SHABBAT ROSH ḤODESH

The conclusion of this *haftara*, which is also the close of the book of Isaiah, describes a vision of the future in which all humanity will come to the Temple to offer homage to God. In it, we see emphasis on the tension between the fallen present and the redeemed future. The transition from reality to vision is a central theme in all the book of Isaiah. The prophet Yeshayahu preached during the first exile – that of the northern kingdom of Israel – while at the same time, in the southern kingdom, there was an opportunity for full redemption, as the Talmud (Sanhedrin 94a) teaches: "The Holy One, blessed be He, sought to make Ḥizkiyahu king

8 before the agonies took her she was delivered of a boy. Who ever heard of anything like this? Who ever
saw such happenings as these? Can the land give birth in a day? Can a nation be born at a single step?
9 Yet Zion has labored, and has birthed her children. Would I bring on the labor and not deliver? So the
10 LORD speaks: Would I who fathered close the womb? So your God speaks. Bring Jerusalem
11 joy, exult in her, all of you who love her; celebrate her joy with her, all of you who mourned her. That
you may suck your fill from the bosom of her comforting; may suckle, take delight in the brilliance of
12 her glory. For thus says the LORD: See Me make peace flow to her like a river, and the substance of nations – like a rushing brook – and you shall suckle. You will be borne upon hips, playing
13 upon loving laps; as a man is consoled by his mother, just so shall I comfort you, and in Jerusalem, you
14 shall be consoled. You shall look on, your heart rejoicing, while your bones grow vigorous, like grass,
15 and the hand of the LORD becomes known to His servants, and His rage known to all His foes. For see:
the LORD is coming in fire, His chariots a storm wind, to slake His fury in rage, His rebuke in flames
16 of fire. For in fire, the LORD comes to judgment, and by the sword, to all flesh, and many are those the
17 LORD will execute. Those in the gardens, sanctifying and cleansing themselves, one after the other in
the midst of it, while eating the flesh of pigs and pests and mice, they will all be gathered in together:
18 so the LORD has spoken. For I – I know their works, their thoughts; and time will come, to gather all
19 nations and tongues, and they will come, and look upon My glory. I shall place a sign among them,
send out survivors from them to all nations, to Tarshish, Pul, and Lud, to the great archers, Tuval,
Yavan, to the distant coastlands where none ever heard tell of Me or saw My glory, and they will tell
20 of My glory to the nations. And they will bring back all your brothers from among all other nations,
an offering to the LORD, on horseback and on chariot, on camels, mules, dromedaries, to My holy
mount, Jerusalem – so says the LORD – just as the children of Israel would bring up their offerings in
21 pure vessels, to the LORD's House, and from among them also I shall take priests and Levites, so says
22 the LORD. For just as the new heavens, the new earth that I am now forming, will stand forever before
23 Me, so says the LORD, so will stand your children, your name. And it will be – every New Moon, every
24 Sabbath – all flesh will come to worship Me, so says the LORD. Going out, they will see bodies of those
people who sinned against Me, for the worms will not die nor the fire be quenched, and they will be
repugnant to all flesh.

And it will be – every New Moon, every Sabbath –
all flesh will come to worship Me, so says the LORD.

HAFTARA FOR SHABBAT EREV ROSH ḤODESH

I SAMUEL

20 18 Yehonatan then said to David, "Tomorrow is the New Month, and you shall be missed, for your
19 seat will be empty. Now wait three days, then on the day people go back to work, make your way
20 swiftly down to your hiding place, and stay close to the Ezel Stone. As for me – I will shoot three
21 arrows to its side, as though aiming at a target. Now, when I send the boy off to find the arrows, if

---

must flee from Sha'ul, but first he wants to check if all other recourses are exhausted. He designs a test together with his friend, Sha'ul's son Yonatan, to see how Sha'ul will respond to his absence from the customary Rosh Ḥodesh festivities in the palace. Sha'ul's reaction is extreme, and Yonatan confirms to David in his hiding place that they must separate. The two hold a touching final meeting.

ח חָבְלָ֖הּ וְהִמְלִ֥יטָה זָכָֽר׃ מִֽי־שָׁמַ֣ע כָּזֹ֗את מִ֤י רָאָה֙ כָּאֵ֔לֶּה הֲי֤וּחַל אֶ֙רֶץ֙ בְּי֣וֹם אֶחָ֔ד אִם־יִוָּ֥לֵד גּ֖וֹי פַּ֣עַם אֶחָ֑ת
ט כִּי־חָ֛לָה גַּם־יָלְדָ֥ה צִיּ֖וֹן אֶת־בָּנֶֽיהָ׃ הַאֲנִ֥י אַשְׁבִּ֛יר וְלֹ֥א אוֹלִ֖יד יֹאמַ֣ר יְהוָ֑ה אִם־אֲנִ֧י הַמּוֹלִ֛יד וְעָצַ֖רְתִּי אָמַ֥ר
י אֱלֹהָֽיִךְ׃ שִׂמְח֧וּ אֶת־יְרוּשָׁלַ֛͏ִם וְגִ֥ילוּ בָ֖הּ כָּל־אֹהֲבֶ֑יהָ שִׂ֤ישׂוּ אִתָּהּ֙ מָשׂ֔וֹשׂ כָּל־הַמִּֽתְאַבְּלִ֖ים
יא יב עָלֶֽיהָ׃ לְמַ֤עַן תִּֽינְקוּ֙ וּשְׂבַעְתֶּ֔ם מִשֹּׁ֖ד תַּנְחֻמֶ֑יהָ לְמַ֧עַן תָּמֹ֛צּוּ וְהִתְעַנַּגְתֶּ֖ם מִזִּ֥יז כְּבוֹדָֽהּ׃ כִּי־כֹ֣ה ׀
אָמַ֣ר יְהוָ֗ה הִנְנִ֣י נֹטֶֽה־אֵ֠לֶיהָ כְּנָהָ֨ר שָׁל֜וֹם וּכְנַ֧חַל שׁוֹטֵ֛ף כְּב֥וֹד גּוֹיִ֖ם וִינַקְתֶּ֑ם עַל־צַד֙ תִּנָּשֵׂ֔אוּ וְעַל־בִּרְכַּ֖יִם
יג יד תְּשָׁעֳשָֽׁעוּ׃ כְּאִ֕ישׁ אֲשֶׁ֥ר אִמּ֖וֹ תְּנַחֲמֶ֑נּוּ כֵּ֤ן אָֽנֹכִי֙ אֲנַ֣חֶמְכֶ֔ם וּבִירוּשָׁלַ֖͏ִם תְּנֻחָֽמוּ׃ וּרְאִיתֶם֙ וְשָׂ֣שׂ לִבְּכֶ֔ם
טו וְעַצְמוֹתֵיכֶ֖ם כַּדֶּ֣שֶׁא תִפְרַ֑חְנָה וְנוֹדְעָ֤ה יַד־יְהוָה֙ אֶת־עֲבָדָ֔יו וְזָעַ֖ם אֶת־אֹיְבָֽיו׃ כִּֽי־הִנֵּ֤ה יְהוָה֙ בָּאֵ֣שׁ יָב֔וֹא
טז וְכַסּוּפָ֖ה מַרְכְּבֹתָ֑יו לְהָשִׁ֤יב בְּחֵמָה֙ אַפּ֔וֹ וְגַעֲרָת֖וֹ בְּלַהֲבֵי־אֵֽשׁ׃ כִּ֤י בָאֵשׁ֙ יְהוָ֣ה נִשְׁפָּ֔ט וּבְחַרְבּ֖וֹ אֶת־כָּל־בָּשָׂ֑ר
יז וְרַבּ֖וּ חַלְלֵ֥י יְהוָֽה׃ הַמִּתְקַדְּשִׁ֨ים וְהַמִּֽטַּהֲרִ֜ים אֶל־הַגַּנּ֗וֹת אַחַ֤ר אחד֙ בַּתָּ֔וֶךְ אֹֽכְלֵי֙ בְּשַׂ֣ר הַחֲזִ֔יר וְהַשֶּׁ֖קֶץ אַחַת֙
יח וְהָעַכְבָּ֑ר יַחְדָּ֥ו יָסֻ֖פוּ נְאֻם־יְהוָֽה׃ וְאָנֹכִ֗י מַעֲשֵׂיהֶם֙ וּמַחְשְׁבֹ֣תֵיהֶ֔ם בָּאָ֕ה לְקַבֵּ֥ץ אֶת־כָּל־הַגּוֹיִ֖ם וְהַלְּשֹׁנ֑וֹת וּבָ֖אוּ
יט וְרָא֥וּ אֶת־כְּבוֹדִֽי׃ וְשַׂמְתִּ֨י בָהֶ֜ם א֗וֹת וְשִׁלַּחְתִּ֣י מֵהֶ֣ם ׀ פְּלֵיטִ֡ים אֶל־הַגּוֹיִם֩ תַּרְשִׁ֨ישׁ פּ֥וּל וְל֛וּד מֹ֥שְׁכֵי קֶ֖שֶׁת
תֻּבַ֣ל וְיָוָ֑ן הָאִיִּ֣ים הָרְחֹקִ֗ים אֲשֶׁ֨ר לֹא־שָׁמְע֤וּ אֶת־שִׁמְעִי֙ וְלֹא־רָא֣וּ אֶת־כְּבוֹדִ֔י וְהִגִּ֥ידוּ אֶת־כְּבוֹדִ֖י בַּגּוֹיִֽם׃
כ וְהֵבִ֣יאוּ אֶת־כָּל־אֲחֵיכֶ֣ם ׀ מִכָּל־הַגּוֹיִ֣ם ׀ מִנְחָ֣ה ׀ לַיהוָ֡ה בַּסּוּסִ֡ים וּ֠בָרֶכֶב וּבַצַּבִּ֨ים וּבַפְּרָדִ֜ים וּבַכִּרְכָּר֗וֹת עַ֣ל
כא הַ֥ר קָדְשִׁ֛י יְרוּשָׁלַ֖͏ִם אָמַ֣ר יְהוָ֑ה כַּאֲשֶׁ֣ר יָבִיאוּ֩ בְנֵ֨י יִשְׂרָאֵ֧ל אֶת־הַמִּנְחָ֛ה בִּכְלִ֥י טָה֖וֹר בֵּ֥ית יְהוָֽה׃ וְגַם־מֵהֶ֥ם
כב אֶקַּ֛ח לַכֹּהֲנִ֥ים לַלְוִיִּ֖ם אָמַ֥ר יְהוָֽה׃ כִּ֣י כַאֲשֶׁ֣ר הַשָּׁמַ֣יִם הַ֠חֲדָשִׁים וְהָאָ֨רֶץ הַחֲדָשָׁ֜ה אֲשֶׁ֨ר אֲנִ֥י עֹשֶׂ֛ה עֹמְדִ֥ים
כג לְפָנַ֖י נְאֻם־יְהוָ֑ה כֵּ֛ן יַעֲמֹ֥ד זַרְעֲכֶ֖ם וְשִׁמְכֶֽם׃ וְהָיָ֗ה מִֽדֵּי־חֹ֙דֶשׁ֙ בְּחָדְשׁ֔וֹ וּמִדֵּ֥י שַׁבָּ֖ת בְּשַׁבַּתּ֑וֹ יָב֧וֹא כָל־בָּשָׂ֛ר
כד לְהִשְׁתַּחֲוֺ֥ת לְפָנַ֖י אָמַ֥ר יְהוָֽה׃ וְיָצְא֣וּ וְרָא֔וּ בְּפִגְרֵי֙ הָאֲנָשִׁ֔ים הַפֹּשְׁעִ֖ים בִּ֑י כִּ֣י תוֹלַעְתָּ֞ם לֹ֣א תָמ֗וּת וְאִשָּׁם֙
לֹ֣א תִכְבֶּ֔ה וְהָי֥וּ דֵרָא֖וֹן לְכָל־בָּשָֽׂר׃

והיה מדי חדש בחדשו ומדי שבת בשבתו
יבוא כל בשר להשתחות לפני אמר יהוה

הפטרת שבת ערב ראש חודש

כ יח יט וַיֹּאמֶר־ל֥וֹ יְהוֹנָתָ֖ן מָחָ֣ר חֹ֑דֶשׁ וְנִפְקַ֕דְתָּ כִּ֥י יִפָּקֵ֖ד מוֹשָׁבֶֽךָ׃ וְשִׁלַּשְׁתָּ֙ תֵּרֵ֣ד מְאֹ֔ד וּבָאתָ֙ אֶל־הַמָּק֔וֹם אֲשֶׁר־ שמואל א׳
כ נִסְתַּ֥רְתָּ שָּׁ֖ם בְּי֣וֹם הַֽמַּעֲשֶׂ֑ה וְיָ֣שַׁבְתָּ֔ אֵ֖צֶל הָאֶ֥בֶן הָאָֽזֶל׃ וַאֲנִ֕י שְׁלֹ֥שֶׁת הַחִצִּ֖ים צִדָּ֣ה אוֹרֶ֑ה לְשַֽׁלַּֽח־לִ֖י
כא לְמַטָּרָֽה׃ וְהִנֵּה֙ אֶשְׁלַ֣ח אֶת־הַנַּ֔עַר לֵ֖ךְ מְצָ֣א אֶת־הַחִצִּ֑ים אִם־אָמֹ֨ר אֹמַ֜ר לַנַּ֗עַר הִנֵּ֧ה הַחִצִּ֣ים ׀ מִמְּךָ֣ וָהֵ֗נָּה

HAFTARA FOR SHABBAT EREV ROSH ḤODESH

The events described in this *haftara* occur over the space of four days, from the day before Rosh Ḥodesh until the day after the second day of Rosh Ḥodesh. During this period, the tension between King Sha'ul and David reaches its peak. Sha'ul understands that David will be the next ruler, and he makes the decision to kill him. Once Sha'ul has twice threatened to skewer David with his spear, David realizes that he

I say to him, 'Look, the arrows are just past you, come take them,' then come, for all is well with you,
22 and there is nothing wrong – as the LORD lives. But if I say to the boy, 'Look, the arrows are far past
23 you,' then go, for the LORD has sent you away. As for the matter we spoke of, you and I – the LORD
24 is between me and you forever." David hid out in the field. The New Month came around,
25 and the king sat down at the feast to eat. When the king sat in his usual seat by the wall, Yehonatan rose,
26 and Avner sat by Sha'ul's side while David's seat remained empty. Sha'ul did not mention anything that
27 day. "It must be by chance that he is not clean," he thought; "he must be unclean." But the next
day, on the second day of the New Month, David's seat was still empty, and Sha'ul asked Yehonatan,
28 his son, "Why did the son of Yishai fail to come to the feast – both yesterday and today?" "David ur-
29 gently asked me for leave to Beit Leḥem," Yehonatan answered Sha'ul. "He said, 'Please let me go, for
we have a family feast in the city, and my brother has bid me – so now, if I have gained your favor, please
30 let me get away to see my brothers.' That is why he has not come to the king's table." Sha'ul
burst into a rage at Yehonatan. "Son of a perverse, wayward woman!" he said. "Oh, I knew you would
31 side with the son of Yishai – to your own disgrace and the disgrace of your mother's nakedness! But
as long as the son of Yishai lives on this earth, you and your kingship will not endure – so bring him
32 to me now, for he is a dead man!" But Yehonatan answered Sha'ul, his father. "Why should
33 he be killed?" he said to him. "What has he done?" And Sha'ul hurled the spear toward him to strike
34 him down, and Yehonatan realized that his father was determined to kill David. Furious, Yehonatan rose up from the table; he ate no food on the second day of the New Month out of anguish
35 for David, for his father had humiliated him. In the morning, Yehonatan went out to the field
36 for the rendezvous with David, a young boy with him. He said to his boy, "Now, run and find the arrows
37 I am about to shoot." The boy ran off, and he shot the arrows past him. When the boy reached the place
where Yehonatan's arrows had fallen, Yehonatan called out after the boy, "Oh – the arrows are far past
38 you." Then Yehonatan called out after the boy, "Quick – hurry, do not linger." When Yehonatan's boy
39 gathered up the arrows and came back to his master – the boy knew nothing; only Yehonatan and David
40 knew about the arrangement – Yehonatan gave his gear to his boy and said to him, "Go – bring these back
41 to town." When the boy had left, David emerged from the southern side of the stone, flung his face to the
ground, and bowed three times. And they kissed each other and wept with each other until David's sobs
42 reached a crescendo. "Go in peace," Yehonatan said to David, "for the two of us have sworn in the name
of the LORD, 'May the Lord be between me and you, and between my seed and your seed, forever.'"

HAFTARA FOR THE FIRST SHABBAT OF ḤANUKKA

On the first day of Ḥanukka, Sepharadim and Yemenites read the maftir from Numbers 6:22–7:17. Ashkenazim begin the maftir at Numbers 7:1.

On subsequent days of Ḥanukka, read the maftir for the appropriate day from Numbers chapter 7.

When the Shabbat of Ḥanukka coincides with Rosh Ḥodesh, three Torah scrolls are removed from the ark. The first six aliyot are read from Parashat Miketz. The seventh consists of the addition for Rosh Ḥodesh, Numbers 28:9–15. Afterward, half-Kaddish is recited, and the maftir is read for the sixth day of Ḥanukka.

2 14 Shout out and be joyful, daughter Zion, for I am coming, and I will dwell in your midst – the LORD ZECHARIAH
15 has spoken. Many nations will join themselves to the LORD on that day, and they will be My people.

---

the Babylonian exile, urging them to rebuild the Temple. The construction, which was expressly authorized by the decree of the emperor Koresh, was frozen by the Persian government soon after the cornerstone had been laid, due

כב קְחֶנּוּ וָבֹאָה כִּי־שָׁלוֹם לְךָ וְאֵין דָּבָר חַי־יהוה׃ וְאִם־כֹּה אֹמַר לָעֶלֶם הִנֵּה הַחִצִּים מִמְּךָ וָהָלְאָה לֵךְ כִּי
כג כד שִׁלַּחֲךָ יהוה׃ וְהַדָּבָר אֲשֶׁר דִּבַּרְנוּ אֲנִי וָאָתָּה הִנֵּה יהוה בֵּינִי וּבֵינְךָ עַד־עוֹלָם׃ וַיִּסָּתֵר דָּוִד
כה בַּשָּׂדֶה וַיְהִי הַחֹדֶשׁ וַיֵּשֶׁב הַמֶּלֶךְ עַל־הַלֶּחֶם לֶאֱכוֹל׃ וַיֵּשֶׁב הַמֶּלֶךְ עַל־מוֹשָׁבוֹ כְּפַעַם ׀ בְּפַעַם אֶל־מוֹשַׁב אֶל־
כו הַקִּיר וַיָּקָם יְהוֹנָתָן וַיֵּשֶׁב אַבְנֵר מִצַּד שָׁאוּל וַיִּפָּקֵד מְקוֹם דָּוִד׃ וְלֹא־דִבֶּר שָׁאוּל מְאוּמָה בַּיּוֹם הַהוּא כִּי
כז אָמַר מִקְרֶה הוּא בִּלְתִּי טָהוֹר הוּא כִּי־לֹא טָהוֹר׃ וַיְהִי מִמָּחֳרַת הַחֹדֶשׁ הַשֵּׁנִי וַיִּפָּקֵד מְקוֹם
כח דָּוִד וַיֹּאמֶר שָׁאוּל אֶל־יְהוֹנָתָן בְּנוֹ מַדּוּעַ לֹא־בָא בֶן־יִשַׁי גַּם־תְּמוֹל גַּם־הַיּוֹם אֶל־הַלָּחֶם׃ וַיַּעַן יְהוֹנָתָן
כט אֶת־שָׁאוּל נִשְׁאֹל נִשְׁאַל דָּוִד מֵעִמָּדִי עַד־בֵּית לָחֶם׃ וַיֹּאמֶר שַׁלְּחֵנִי נָא כִּי זֶבַח מִשְׁפָּחָה לָנוּ בָּעִיר וְהוּא
צִוָּה־לִי אָחִי וְעַתָּה אִם־מָצָאתִי חֵן בְּעֵינֶיךָ אִמָּלְטָה נָּא וְאֶרְאֶה אֶת־אֶחָי עַל־כֵּן לֹא־בָא אֶל־שֻׁלְחַן
ל הַמֶּלֶךְ׃ וַיִּחַר־אַף שָׁאוּל בִּיהוֹנָתָן וַיֹּאמֶר לוֹ בֶּן־נַעֲוַת הַמַּרְדּוּת הֲלוֹא יָדַעְתִּי כִּי־בֹחֵר אַתָּה
לא לְבֶן־יִשַׁי לְבָשְׁתְּךָ וּלְבֹשֶׁת עֶרְוַת אִמֶּךָ׃ כִּי כָל־הַיָּמִים אֲשֶׁר בֶּן־יִשַׁי חַי עַל־הָאֲדָמָה לֹא תִכּוֹן אַתָּה
לב וּמַלְכוּתֶךָ וְעַתָּה שְׁלַח וְקַח אֹתוֹ אֵלַי כִּי בֶן־מָוֶת הוּא׃ וַיַּעַן יְהוֹנָתָן אֶת־שָׁאוּל אָבִיו וַיֹּאמֶר
לג אֵלָיו לָמָּה יוּמַת מֶה עָשָׂה׃ וַיָּטֶל שָׁאוּל אֶת־הַחֲנִית עָלָיו לְהַכֹּתוֹ וַיֵּדַע יְהוֹנָתָן כִּי־כָלָה הִיא מֵעִם אָבִיו
לד לְהָמִית אֶת־דָּוִד׃ וַיָּקָם יְהוֹנָתָן מֵעִם הַשֻּׁלְחָן בָּחֳרִי־אָף וְלֹא־אָכַל בְּיוֹם־הַחֹדֶשׁ הַשֵּׁנִי לֶחֶם
לה כִּי נֶעְצַב אֶל־דָּוִד כִּי הִכְלִמוֹ אָבִיו׃ וַיְהִי בַבֹּקֶר וַיֵּצֵא יְהוֹנָתָן הַשָּׂדֶה לְמוֹעֵד דָּוִד וְנַעַר קָטֹן
לו עִמּוֹ׃ וַיֹּאמֶר לְנַעֲרוֹ רֻץ מְצָא־נָא אֶת־הַחִצִּים אֲשֶׁר אָנֹכִי מוֹרֶה הַנַּעַר רָץ וְהוּא־יָרָה הַחֵצִי לְהַעֲבִרוֹ׃
לז וַיָּבֹא הַנַּעַר עַד־מְקוֹם הַחֵצִי אֲשֶׁר יָרָה יְהוֹנָתָן וַיִּקְרָא יְהוֹנָתָן אַחֲרֵי הַנַּעַר וַיֹּאמֶר הֲלוֹא הַחֵצִי מִמְּךָ
לח וָהָלְאָה׃ וַיִּקְרָא יְהוֹנָתָן אַחֲרֵי הַנַּעַר מְהֵרָה חוּשָׁה אַל־תַּעֲמֹד וַיְלַקֵּט נַעַר יְהוֹנָתָן אֶת־החצי וַיָּבֹא הַחִצִּים
לט מ אֶל־אֲדֹנָיו׃ וְהַנַּעַר לֹא־יָדַע מְאוּמָה אַךְ יְהוֹנָתָן וְדָוִד יָדְעוּ אֶת־הַדָּבָר׃ וַיִּתֵּן יְהוֹנָתָן אֶת־כֵּלָיו אֶל־הַנַּעַר
מא אֲשֶׁר־לוֹ וַיֹּאמֶר לוֹ לֵךְ הָבֵיא הָעִיר׃ הַנַּעַר בָּא וְדָוִד קָם מֵאֵצֶל הַנֶּגֶב וַיִּפֹּל לְאַפָּיו אַרְצָה וַיִּשְׁתַּחוּ שָׁלֹשׁ
מב פְּעָמִים וַיִּשְּׁקוּ ׀ אִישׁ אֶת־רֵעֵהוּ וַיִּבְכּוּ אִישׁ אֶת־רֵעֵהוּ עַד־דָּוִד הִגְדִּיל׃ וַיֹּאמֶר יְהוֹנָתָן לְדָוִד לֵךְ לְשָׁלוֹם
אֲשֶׁר נִשְׁבַּעְנוּ שְׁנֵינוּ אֲנַחְנוּ בְּשֵׁם יהוה לֵאמֹר יהוה יִהְיֶה ׀ בֵּינִי וּבֵינֶךָ וּבֵין זַרְעִי וּבֵין זַרְעֲךָ עַד־עוֹלָם׃

הפטרה לשבת ראשונה של חנוכה

On the first day of חנוכה*, Sepharadim and Yemenites read the* מפטיר *from* במדבר ו, כב – ז, יז*. Ashkenazim begin the* מפטיר *at* במדבר ז, א*.*

On subsequent days of חנוכה*, read the* מפטיר *for the appropriate day from* במדבר ז*.*

When the שבת *of* חנוכה *coincides with* ראש חודש*, three Torah scrolls are removed from the ark. The first six* עליות *are read from* פרשת מקץ*. The seventh consists of the addition for* ראש חודש*,* במדבר כח, ט–טו*. Afterward,* חצי קדיש *is recited, and the* מפטיר *is read for the sixth day of* חנוכה*.*

ב יד טו רָנִּי וְשִׂמְחִי בַּת־צִיּוֹן כִּי הִנְנִי־בָא וְשָׁכַנְתִּי בְתוֹכֵךְ נְאֻם־יהוה׃ וְנִלְווּ גוֹיִם רַבִּים אֶל־יהוה בַּיּוֹם הַהוּא וְהָיוּ זכריה

HAFTARA FOR THE FIRST SHABBAT OF ḤANUKKA

The prophet Zekharya was active in Jerusalem in the second year of the reign of Daryavesh, king of Persia. He gave strength and encouragement to the returnees to Zion after

▶

16 I will dwell in your midst, and you will know that the LORD of Hosts sent me to you. The LORD will
take possession of Yehuda as His portion of holy ground, and He will choose Jerusalem once again.
3 17 Hush, all flesh, before the LORD, for He has stirred from His holy abode. 1 Then He showed
me Yehoshua the High Priest standing before an angel of the LORD with the Adversary on his right to
2 oppose him. The LORD said to the Adversary: The LORD drives you away, Adversary. The LORD, who
3 has chosen Jerusalem, drives you away. Yes, this is a firebrand saved from the fire. And Yehoshua, wear-
4 ing filthy clothing, was standing before the angel, who spoke and said to those standing before him,
"Take those filthy clothes off him." Then the angel said to him, "See, I have removed your guilt from
5 you and dressed you in finery." I said, "Place a pure turban on his head," and they placed a pure turban
6 on his head. They dressed him in clothing. The angel of the LORD remained standing. Then that angel
7 of the LORD testified regarding Yehoshua: "So says the LORD of Hosts: If you walk in My ways, if you
keep My watch, if you judge My House, and guard My courtyards, then I will give you walkers among
8 these who are standing. Listen, Yehoshua the High Priest, you and your friends who sit before you, for
9 they are men of wonders: Behold, I am bringing My servant Tzemaḥ. Upon the stone that I set before
Yehoshua, one stone with seven eyes, I will engrave its inscription, and I will wipe away the guilt of this
10 land in one day. On that day – the LORD of Hosts has spoken – you will call one to another: Come un-
4 1 der the shade of the vine; come under the shade of the fig." Then the angel with whom I had
2 spoken returned and roused me like a man stirring from his sleep. He said to me, "What do you see?"
I said, "I see a candelabrum of pure gold, its bowl at the top. It has seven lamps – seven – and seven
3 indentations for the lamps, which are at the top. Next to it are two olive trees, one to the right of the
4 bowl and one to its left." I spoke and said to the angel with whom I spoke, "What are these, my lord?"
5 And the angel with whom I spoke replied and said, "You know what these are." I said, "No, my lord."
6 Then he spoke and said to me, "This is the word of the LORD to Zerubavel: Not with valor and not with
7 strength, but with My spirit, says the LORD of Hosts. Who are you, great mountain before Zerubavel?
Surely it will become a level plain. He will remove the re-foundation stone with clamor: Favor, favor to
8 her!"* 9 Then the word of the LORD came to me: "Zerubavel's hands founded this House, and
his hands will complete it. You will know that the LORD of Hosts sent me to you."

Ashkenazim and Sepharadim end here

HAFTARA FOR THE SECOND SHABBAT OF ḤANUKKA

The maftir for the second Shabbat of Ḥanukka is read from Numbers 7:54–8:4.

I KINGS

7 40 Ḥiram crafted the lavers and the shovels and the basins. And so Ḥiram completed all the work for the
41 House of the LORD as commissioned by King Shlomo: two pillars and two globe-shaped capitals for
42 the pillar tops; two pieces of meshwork to cover the two globe-shaped capitals for the pillar tops; four
hundred pomegranates for the two pieces of meshwork – two rows of pomegranates for each piece of

---

constructed from the finest materials and most advanced methods in existence. The richness of the structure was a testament to God's glory. This *haftara* describes the work of Ḥiram, the architect charged with constructing the Temple just as Betzalel had built the Tabernacle in an earlier generation. It details the beauty of the structure and its accoutrements, including the wonderful golden candelabra that gave light to the luxurious Temple. The work of building the Sanctuary was complex and arduous, but after seven years it was completed, and the Temple was dedicated with pomp and festivity.

טז לִי לְעָם וְשָׁכַנְתִּי בְתוֹכֵךְ וְיָדַעַתְּ כִּי־יהוה צְבָאוֹת שְׁלָחַנִי אֵלָיִךְ: וְנָחַל יהוה אֶת־יְהוּדָה חֶלְקוֹ עַל אַדְמַת
ג יז א הַקֹּדֶשׁ וּבָחַר עוֹד בִּירוּשָׁלָםִ: הַס כָּל־בָּשָׂר מִפְּנֵי יהוה כִּי נֵעוֹר מִמְּעוֹן קָדְשׁוֹ: וַיַּרְאֵנִי אֶת־יְהוֹשֻׁעַ
ב הַכֹּהֵן הַגָּדוֹל עֹמֵד לִפְנֵי מַלְאַךְ יהוה וְהַשָּׂטָן עֹמֵד עַל־יְמִינוֹ לְשִׂטְנוֹ: וַיֹּאמֶר יהוה אֶל־הַשָּׂטָן יִגְעַר יהוה
ג בְּךָ הַשָּׂטָן וְיִגְעַר יהוה בְּךָ הַבֹּחֵר בִּירוּשָׁלָםִ הֲלוֹא זֶה אוּד מֻצָּל מֵאֵשׁ: וִיהוֹשֻׁעַ הָיָה לָבֻשׁ בְּגָדִים צוֹאִים
ד וְעֹמֵד לִפְנֵי הַמַּלְאָךְ: וַיַּעַן וַיֹּאמֶר אֶל־הָעֹמְדִים לְפָנָיו לֵאמֹר הָסִירוּ הַבְּגָדִים הַצֹּאִים מֵעָלָיו וַיֹּאמֶר אֵלָיו
ה רְאֵה הֶעֱבַרְתִּי מֵעָלֶיךָ עֲוֺנֶךָ וְהַלְבֵּשׁ אֹתְךָ מַחֲלָצוֹת: וָאֹמַר יָשִׂימוּ צָנִיף טָהוֹר עַל־רֹאשׁוֹ וַיָּשִׂימוּ הַצָּנִיף
ו ז הַטָּהוֹר עַל־רֹאשׁוֹ וַיַּלְבִּשֻׁהוּ בְּגָדִים וּמַלְאַךְ יהוה עֹמֵד: וַיָּעַד מַלְאַךְ יהוה בִּיהוֹשֻׁעַ לֵאמֹר: כֹּה־אָמַר
יהוה צְבָאוֹת אִם־בִּדְרָכַי תֵּלֵךְ וְאִם אֶת־מִשְׁמַרְתִּי תִשְׁמֹר וְגַם־אַתָּה תָּדִין אֶת־בֵּיתִי וְגַם תִּשְׁמֹר אֶת־חֲצֵרָי
ח וְנָתַתִּי לְךָ מַהְלְכִים בֵּין הָעֹמְדִים הָאֵלֶּה: שְׁמַע־נָא יְהוֹשֻׁעַ ׀ הַכֹּהֵן הַגָּדוֹל אַתָּה וְרֵעֶיךָ הַיֹּשְׁבִים לְפָנֶיךָ
ט כִּי־אַנְשֵׁי מוֹפֵת הֵמָּה כִּי־הִנְנִי מֵבִיא אֶת־עַבְדִּי צֶמַח: כִּי ׀ הִנֵּה הָאֶבֶן אֲשֶׁר נָתַתִּי לִפְנֵי יְהוֹשֻׁעַ עַל־אֶבֶן
י אַחַת שִׁבְעָה עֵינָיִם הִנְנִי מְפַתֵּחַ פִּתֻּחָהּ נְאֻם יהוה צְבָאוֹת וּמַשְׁתִּי אֶת־עֲוֺן הָאָרֶץ־הַהִיא בְּיוֹם אֶחָד: בַּיּוֹם
ד א הַהוּא נְאֻם יהוה צְבָאוֹת תִּקְרְאוּ אִישׁ לְרֵעֵהוּ אֶל־תַּחַת גֶּפֶן וְאֶל־תַּחַת תְּאֵנָה: וַיָּשָׁב
ב הַמַּלְאָךְ הַדֹּבֵר בִּי וַיְעִירֵנִי כְּאִישׁ אֲשֶׁר־יֵעוֹר מִשְּׁנָתוֹ: וַיֹּאמֶר אֵלַי מָה אַתָּה רֹאֶה ויאמר רָאִיתִי וְהִנֵּה וָאֹמַר
מְנוֹרַת זָהָב כֻּלָּהּ וְגֻלָּהּ עַל־רֹאשָׁהּ וְשִׁבְעָה נֵרֹתֶיהָ עָלֶיהָ שִׁבְעָה וְשִׁבְעָה מוּצָקוֹת לַנֵּרוֹת אֲשֶׁר עַל־
ג ד רֹאשָׁהּ: וּשְׁנַיִם זֵיתִים עָלֶיהָ אֶחָד מִימִין הַגֻּלָּה וְאֶחָד עַל־שְׂמֹאלָהּ: וָאַעַן וָאֹמַר אֶל־הַמַּלְאָךְ הַדֹּבֵר
ה בִּי לֵאמֹר מָה־אֵלֶּה אֲדֹנִי: וַיַּעַן הַמַּלְאָךְ הַדֹּבֵר בִּי וַיֹּאמֶר אֵלַי הֲלוֹא יָדַעְתָּ מָה־הֵמָּה אֵלֶּה וָאֹמַר לֹא
ו אֲדֹנִי: וַיַּעַן וַיֹּאמֶר אֵלַי לֵאמֹר זֶה דְּבַר־יהוה אֶל־זְרֻבָּבֶל לֵאמֹר לֹא בְחַיִל וְלֹא בְכֹחַ כִּי אִם־בְּרוּחִי אָמַר
ז יהוה צְבָאוֹת: מִי־אַתָּה הַר־הַגָּדוֹל לִפְנֵי זְרֻבָּבֶל לְמִישֹׁר וְהוֹצִיא אֶת־הָאֶבֶן הָרֹאשָׁה תְּשֻׁאוֹת חֵן ׀ חֵן
ח ט לָהּ:* וַיְהִי דְבַר־יהוה אֵלַי לֵאמֹר: יְדֵי זְרֻבָּבֶל יִסְּדוּ הַבַּיִת הַזֶּה וְיָדָיו תְּבַצַּעְנָה וְיָדַעְתָּ
כִּי־יהוה צְבָאוֹת שְׁלָחַנִי אֲלֵיכֶם:

Ashkenazim and Sepharadim end here

הפטרה לשבת שנייה של חנוכה

The מפטיר *for the second* שבת *of* חנוכה *is read from* במדבר ז, נד – ח, ד.

מלכים א׳

ז מ וַיַּעַשׂ חִירוֹם אֶת־הַכִּיֹּרוֹת וְאֶת־הַיָּעִים וְאֶת־הַמִּזְרָקוֹת וַיְכַל חִירָם לַעֲשׂוֹת אֶת־כָּל־הַמְּלָאכָה אֲשֶׁר
מא עָשָׂה לַמֶּלֶךְ שְׁלֹמֹה בֵּית יהוה: עַמֻּדִים שְׁנַיִם וְגֻלֹּת הַכֹּתָרֹת אֲשֶׁר־עַל־רֹאשׁ הָעַמֻּדִים שְׁתָּיִם
מב וְהַשְּׂבָכוֹת שְׁתַּיִם לְכַסּוֹת אֶת־שְׁתֵּי גֻּלֹּת הַכֹּתָרֹת אֲשֶׁר עַל־רֹאשׁ הָעַמּוּדִים: וְאֶת־הָרִמֹּנִים אַרְבַּע
מֵאוֹת לִשְׁתֵּי הַשְּׂבָכוֹת שְׁנֵי־טוּרִים רִמֹּנִים לַשְּׂבָכָה הָאֶחָת לְכַסּוֹת אֶת־שְׁתֵּי גֻּלֹּת הַכֹּתָרֹת אֲשֶׁר

to lobbying by the enemy nations bordering the Jews in the province of Judea. Zekharya's tireless involvement, preaching God's message, put life into the long-stymied project. The prophet described to them the many obstacles on the path to redemption, and to this end he describes his famous vision of the candelabrum. The candelabrum – the source of light – has become a quintessential Jewish symbol, and it traces the path from the Tabernacle to Shlomo's Temple, the new structure that was to be built.

HAFTARA FOR THE SECOND SHABBAT OF ḤANUKKA

The First Temple, built in the reign of King Shlomo, was

43 meshwork, which covered the two globe-shaped capitals on top of the pillars; ten stands and ten lavers
44 for the stands; one Sea with twelve oxen beneath the Sea; pots, shovels, and basins. All these vessels,
45 46 which Ḥiram crafted for King Shlomo, for the House of the Lord, were of burnished bronze. The
47 king had them cast in clay molds on the Jordan plain between Sukkot and Tzartan. Due to their sheer
abundance, Shlomo left all the vessels out of account; the weight of the bronze was not determined.
48 Shlomo made all the vessels for the House of the Lord: the altar was of gold, and the table for the
49 showbread was of gold. The candelabra – five on the right and five on the left, in front of the Inner
50 Sanctuary – were of solid gold; the flowers, the lamps, and the tongs were all of gold. The bowls, shears,
basins, spoons, and firepans were of solid gold. The hinges of the doors to the inner House, to the Holy
of Holies, and of the doors of the House to the Sanctuary, were of gold.

Haftarat Parashat Shekalim

The maftir of Parashat Shekalim is read from Exodus 30:11–16.

When Shabbat Shekalim coincides with Rosh Ḥodesh Adar, three Torah scrolls are removed from the ark. The first six aliyot are read from the weekly parasha. The seventh consists of the addition for Rosh Ḥodesh, Numbers 28:9–15. Afterward, half-Kaddish is recited, and the maftir is read from Parashat Shekalim.

11 17 Then Yehoyada reinstated the covenant between the Lord, the king, and the people, to be the II KINGS
18 Lord's people; and between the king and the people. All the people of the land came to the temple *Sepharadim, Chabad,*
of Baal and tore it down and shattered its altars and images through and through, and killed Matan, *and Minhag Anglia begin here*
19 the priest of Baal, in front of the altars. The priest set watchmen over the House of the Lord, and
he had the officers of the hundreds, the Keretites, the sentry, and all the people of the land escort
the king down from the House of the Lord. They came in through the sentry gate of the royal pal-
20 ace, and he took his seat upon the royal throne. All the people of the land rejoiced, and calm settled
12 1 over the city. As for Atalya, they had put her to death by sword in the royal palace. *Yehoash *Ashkenazim and*
2 was seven years old when he became king; Yehoash became king in the seventh year of Yehu, and *Yemenites begin here*
3 for forty years, he reigned in Jerusalem. His mother's name was Tzivya, of Be'er Sheva. Yehoash did
4 what was right in the eyes of the Lord all his days, as the priest Yehoyada had taught him. Yet the
5 high shrines were not removed; the people still offered sacrifices and incense at the high shrines. Yehoash said to the priests, "All the dedicated money brought to the House of the Lord – the money
from the census, the money equivalent to a person's worth, or any money that a person is moved to
6 bring to the House of the Lord – let the priests accept it, each from his donor, and they will see to
7 the repair of the House wherever damage may be found." But by the twenty-third year of
8 King Yehoash, the priests had not seen to the repair of the House, and King Yehoash summoned the
priest Yehoyada and the priests. "Why have you not kept the House in repair?" he said to them. "From
now on, do not take any money from your donors; rather, you must donate it toward the repair of
9 the House." The priests agreed that they would neither take money from the people nor see to the

---

military power, a process that began at the end of the rule of Aḥav king of Israel and Yehoshafat king of Yehuda. The state required many reforms to correct its principal ills, and Yehoyada, who acted as regent until Yoash came of age, knew that he must turn over a new leaf in his kingdom's history. He worked hard to collect the money necessary to renovate the Temple, and to that purpose he made use of the annual collection of silver shekels mentioned in the Torah.

מג מד עַל־פְּנֵי הָעַמּוּדִים: וְאֶת־הַמְּכֹנוֹת עֶשֶׂר וְאֶת־הַכִּיֹּרֹת עֲשָׂרָה עַל־הַמְּכֹנוֹת: וְאֶת־הַיָּם הָאֶחָד וְאֶת־
מה הַבָּקָר שְׁנֵים־עָשָׂר תַּחַת הַיָּם: וְאֶת־הַסִּירוֹת וְאֶת־הַיָּעִים וְאֶת־הַמִּזְרָקוֹת וְאֵת כָּל־הַכֵּלִים האהל הָאֵלֶּה
מו אֲשֶׁר עָשָׂה חִירָם לַמֶּלֶךְ שְׁלֹמֹה בֵּית יהוה נְחֹשֶׁת מְמֹרָט: בְּכִכַּר הַיַּרְדֵּן יְצָקָם הַמֶּלֶךְ בְּמַעֲבֵה הָאֲדָמָה
מז מח בֵּין סֻכּוֹת וּבֵין צָרְתָן: וַיַּנַּח שְׁלֹמֹה אֶת־כָּל־הַכֵּלִים מֵרֹב מְאֹד מְאֹד לֹא נֶחְקַר מִשְׁקַל הַנְּחֹשֶׁת: וַיַּעַשׂ
שְׁלֹמֹה אֵת כָּל־הַכֵּלִים אֲשֶׁר בֵּית יהוה אֵת מִזְבַּח הַזָּהָב וְאֶת־הַשֻּׁלְחָן אֲשֶׁר עָלָיו לֶחֶם הַפָּנִים זָהָב:
מט וְאֶת־הַמְּנֹרוֹת חָמֵשׁ מִיָּמִין וְחָמֵשׁ מִשְּׂמֹאול לִפְנֵי הַדְּבִיר זָהָב סָגוּר וְהַפֶּרַח וְהַנֵּרֹת וְהַמֶּלְקָחַיִם זָהָב:
נ וְהַסִּפּוֹת וְהַמְזַמְּרוֹת וְהַמִּזְרָקוֹת וְהַכַּפּוֹת וְהַמַּחְתּוֹת זָהָב סָגוּר וְהַפֹּתוֹת לְדַלְתוֹת הַבַּיִת הַפְּנִימִי לְקֹדֶשׁ
הַקֳּדָשִׁים לְדַלְתֵי הַבַּיִת לְהֵיכָל זָהָב:

הפטרת פרשת שקלים

The מפטיר *of* פרשת שקלים *is read from* שמות ל, יא–טז.
When שבת שקלים *coincides with* ראש חודש אדר, *three Torah scrolls are removed from the ark.*
The first six עליות *are read from the weekly* פרשה.
The seventh consists of the addition for ראש חודש, במדבר כח, ט–טו.
Afterward, חצי קדיש *is recited, and the* מפטיר *is read from* פרשת שקלים.

יא יז וַיִּכְרֹת יְהוֹיָדָע אֶת־הַבְּרִית בֵּין יהוה וּבֵין הַמֶּלֶךְ וּבֵין הָעָם לִהְיוֹת לְעָם לַיהוה וּבֵין הַמֶּלֶךְ וּבֵין הָעָם: מלכים ב׳
יח וַיָּבֹאוּ כָל־עַם הָאָרֶץ בֵּית־הַבַּעַל וַיִּתְּצֻהוּ אֶת־מִזְבְּחֹתָו וְאֶת־צְלָמָיו שִׁבְּרוּ הֵיטֵב וְאֵת מַתָּן כֹּהֵן הַבַּעַל *Sepharadim, Chabad, and Minhag Anglia begin here*
יט הָרְגוּ לִפְנֵי הַמִּזְבְּחוֹת וַיָּשֶׂם הַכֹּהֵן פְּקֻדֹּת עַל־בֵּית יהוה: וַיִּקַּח אֶת־שָׂרֵי הַמֵּאוֹת וְאֶת־הַכָּרִי וְאֶת־
הָרָצִים וְאֵת ׀ כָּל־עַם הָאָרֶץ וַיֹּרִידוּ אֶת־הַמֶּלֶךְ מִבֵּית יהוה וַיָּבוֹאוּ דֶּרֶךְ־שַׁעַר הָרָצִים בֵּית הַמֶּלֶךְ
כ וַיֵּשֶׁב עַל־כִּסֵּא הַמְּלָכִים: וַיִּשְׂמַח כָּל־עַם־הָאָרֶץ וְהָעִיר שָׁקָטָה וְאֶת־עֲתַלְיָהוּ הֵמִיתוּ בַחֶרֶב בֵּית
יב א ב מלך: *בֶּן־שֶׁבַע שָׁנִים יְהוֹאָשׁ בְּמָלְכוֹ: בִּשְׁנַת־שֶׁבַע לְיֵהוּא מָלַךְ יְהוֹאָשׁ וְאַרְבָּעִים שָׁנָה הַמֶּלֶךְ *Ashkenazim and Yemenites begin here*
ג מָלַךְ בִּירוּשָׁלָ‍ִם וְשֵׁם אִמּוֹ צִבְיָה מִבְּאֵר שָׁבַע: וַיַּעַשׂ יְהוֹאָשׁ הַיָּשָׁר בְּעֵינֵי יהוה כָּל־יָמָיו אֲשֶׁר הוֹרָהוּ
ד ה יְהוֹיָדָע הַכֹּהֵן: רַק הַבָּמוֹת לֹא־סָרוּ עוֹד הָעָם מְזַבְּחִים וּמְקַטְּרִים בַּבָּמוֹת: וַיֹּאמֶר יְהוֹאָשׁ אֶל־הַכֹּהֲנִים
כֹּל כֶּסֶף הַקֳּדָשִׁים אֲשֶׁר יוּבָא בֵית־יהוה כֶּסֶף עוֹבֵר אִישׁ כֶּסֶף נַפְשׁוֹת עֶרְכּוֹ כָּל־כֶּסֶף אֲשֶׁר יַעֲלֶה עַל
ו לֶב־אִישׁ לְהָבִיא בֵּית יהוה: יִקְחוּ לָהֶם הַכֹּהֲנִים אִישׁ מֵאֵת מַכָּרוֹ וְהֵם יְחַזְּקוּ אֶת־בֶּדֶק הַבַּיִת לְכֹל
ז אֲשֶׁר־יִמָּצֵא שָׁם בָּדֶק: וַיְהִי בִּשְׁנַת עֶשְׂרִים וְשָׁלֹשׁ שָׁנָה לַמֶּלֶךְ יְהוֹאָשׁ לֹא־חִזְּקוּ הַכֹּהֲנִים
ח אֶת־בֶּדֶק הַבָּיִת: וַיִּקְרָא הַמֶּלֶךְ יְהוֹאָשׁ לִיהוֹיָדָע הַכֹּהֵן וְלַכֹּהֲנִים וַיֹּאמֶר אֲלֵהֶם מַדּוּעַ אֵינְכֶם מְחַזְּקִים
ט אֶת־בֶּדֶק הַבָּיִת וְעַתָּה אַל־תִּקְחוּ־כֶסֶף מֵאֵת מַכָּרֵיכֶם כִּי־לְבֶדֶק הַבַּיִת תִּתְּנֻהוּ: וַיֵּאֹתוּ הַכֹּהֲנִים לְבִלְתִּי

HAFTARAT PARASHAT SHEKALIM

The events of this *haftara* transpire during the reign of Yoash king of Yehuda and Yehoyada the High Priest, his uncle. Before Yoash was crowned, the kingdom had been ruled for six years by the wicked Queen Atalya from the family of King Aḥav of Israel. Atalya had despised and neglected the Temple in Jerusalem, and her tyrannical rule was ended by a revolution in which she was killed.

Spiritual and political crises plagued the kingdom of Yehuda: the revolt of Yehu to the north, in which Aḥazya, Yoash's father, was killed, the regime of Atalya, the introduction of idolatry into the Temple, and waning political and

10 House's repair. So the priest Yehoyada took a chest, made a hole in its lid, and placed it to the right of
the altar, where people entered the House of the LORD. There, the priestly guardians of the thresh-
11 old placed all the money that was brought to the House of the LORD. Whenever they saw that there
was a considerable amount of money in the chest, the royal scribe and the High Priest would come
12 up, tie it into a bundle, and count the money found in the House of the LORD. They then gave the
weighed-out money to the foremen in charge of the House of the LORD, who would use it to pay the
13 carpenters and the builders who worked in the House of the LORD, and the masons and stonecutters,
and to purchase timber and quarry stones to keep the House of the LORD in repair, and for any other
14 expenses for maintenance of the House. However, no silver bowls, shears, basins, or trumpets – or any
15 golden or silver vessels – were made from the money that was brought to the House of the LORD, as
16 it was given to the overseers, who used it to keep the House of the LORD in repair. They did not need
to keep track of the men who received the money to pay out to the workers, for they dealt honestly.
17 Money from guilt offerings and money from purification offerings was not brought to the House of the
LORD; it belonged to the priests.

HAFTARAT PARASHAT ZAKHOR

The maftir of Parashat Zakhor is read from Deuteronomy 25:17–19.
The maftir of Purim Meshulash is read from Exodus 17:8–16.

14 52 There was fierce war against the Philistines all the days of Sha'ul, and whenever Sha'ul saw any strong — I SAMUEL *Yemenites begin here*
15 1 man or valiant warrior, he would recruit him. *Shmuel said to Sha'ul, "It was I — *Sepharadim and*
whom the LORD sent to anoint you as king over His people, over Israel; now, heed the words of the — *Minhag Anglia begin here*
2 LORD. *Thus says the LORD of Hosts: I have taken note of what Amalek did to Israel; how — *Ashkenazim and Chabad begin here*
3 they set upon them on the way as they came out of Egypt. Now, go and strike down Amalek; you must
utterly destroy all that is theirs – spare nothing. You must slay man and woman; child and infant; ox
4 and sheep; camel and donkey." Sha'ul summoned the men and mustered them at Telaim; two
5 hundred thousand infantrymen and ten thousand men from Yehuda. Sha'ul reached the city of Amalek
6 and lay in wait in the wadi. And Sha'ul said to the Kenites, "Leave; turn and withdraw from among the
Amalekites lest I destroy you together with them; you dealt loyally with all the Israelites when they left
7 Egypt," and the Kenites departed from Amalek. Then Sha'ul struck down Amalek from Ḥavila up to
8 Shur, which is east of Egypt. He captured King Agag of Amalek alive and utterly destroyed the entire
9 people by the sword. But Sha'ul and the men spared Agag and the best of the sheep, cattle, fat calves,
and lambs – the very best of everything; they were not willing to destroy them. As for all the spurned,
10 worthless property – that, they utterly destroyed. Then the word of the LORD reached Shm-
11 uel: "I regret that I crowned Sha'ul as king, for he has turned away from following Me and he has failed

---

children. Just like the ancient city of Sedom, the symbol of a society of organized and systematic evil, Amalek had turned into an incarnation of pure wickedness, which had to be pulled out from the root. In Sha'ul's time, circumstances came about that allowed for a protracted military campaign against this ancient and ruthless foe. And only one who could mount a relentless fight to the death against this evil could be considered worthy to rule Israel.

When we read Parashat Zakhor, the Jewish people raise the standard of good against evil in the world, in all its forms.

י קַחַת־כֶּסֶף מֵאֵת הָעָם וּלְבִלְתִּי חַזֵּק אֶת־בֶּדֶק הַבָּיִת׃ וַיִּקַּח יְהוֹיָדָע הַכֹּהֵן אֲרוֹן אֶחָד וַיִּקֹּב חֹר בְּדַלְתּוֹ
וַיִּתֵּן אֹתוֹ אֵצֶל הַמִּזְבֵּחַ בימין בְּבוֹא־אִישׁ בֵּית יהוה וְנָתְנוּ־שָׁמָּה הַכֹּהֲנִים שֹׁמְרֵי הַסַּף אֶת־כָּל־הַכֶּסֶף מִיָּמִין
יא הַמּוּבָא בֵית־יְהוָה׃ וַיְהִי כִּרְאוֹתָם כִּי־רַב הַכֶּסֶף בָּאָרוֹן וַיַּעַל סֹפֵר הַמֶּלֶךְ וְהַכֹּהֵן הַגָּדוֹל וַיָּצֻרוּ וַיִּמְנוּ
יב אֶת־הַכֶּסֶף הַנִּמְצָא בֵית־יְהוָה׃ וְנָתְנוּ אֶת־הַכֶּסֶף הַמְתֻכָּן עַל־יַד עֹשֵׂי הַמְּלָאכָה הפקדים בֵּית יְהוָה הַמֻּפְקָדִים
יג וַיּוֹצִיאֻהוּ לְחָרָשֵׁי הָעֵץ וְלַבֹּנִים הָעֹשִׂים בֵּית יהוה׃ וְלַגֹּדְרִים וּלְחֹצְבֵי הָאֶבֶן וְלִקְנוֹת עֵצִים וְאַבְנֵי מַחְצֵב
יד לְחַזֵּק אֶת־בֶּדֶק בֵּית־יְהוָה וּלְכֹל אֲשֶׁר־יֵצֵא עַל־הַבַּיִת לְחָזְקָה׃ אַךְ לֹא יֵעָשֶׂה בֵּית יהוה סִפּוֹת כֶּסֶף
טו מְזַמְּרוֹת מִזְרָקוֹת חֲצֹצְרוֹת כָּל־כְּלִי זָהָב וּכְלִי־כֶסֶף מִן־הַכֶּסֶף הַמּוּבָא בֵית־יְהוָה׃ כִּי־לְעֹשֵׂי הַמְּלָאכָה
טז יִתְּנֻהוּ וְחִזְּקוּ־בוֹ אֶת־בֵּית יְהוָה׃ וְלֹא יְחַשְּׁבוּ אֶת־הָאֲנָשִׁים אֲשֶׁר יִתְּנוּ אֶת־הַכֶּסֶף עַל־יָדָם לָתֵת לְעֹשֵׂי
יז הַמְּלָאכָה כִּי בֶאֱמֻנָה הֵם עֹשִׂים׃ כֶּסֶף אָשָׁם וְכֶסֶף חַטָּאוֹת לֹא יוּבָא בֵּית יהוה לַכֹּהֲנִים יִהְיוּ׃

הפטרת פרשת זכור

The מפטיר *of* פרשת זכור *is read from* דברים כה, יז–יט.
The מפטיר *of* פורים משולש *is read from* שמות יז, ח–טז.

שמואל א׳

Yemenites begin here

יד נב וַתְּהִי הַמִּלְחָמָה חֲזָקָה עַל־פְּלִשְׁתִּים כֹּל יְמֵי שָׁאוּל וְרָאָה שָׁאוּל כָּל־אִישׁ גִּבּוֹר וְכָל־בֶּן־חַיִל וַיַּאַסְפֵהוּ

Sepharadim and Minhag Anglia begin here

טו א אֵלָיו׃ *וַיֹּאמֶר שְׁמוּאֵל אֶל־שָׁאוּל אֹתִי שָׁלַח יהוה לִמְשָׁחֲךָ לְמֶלֶךְ עַל־עַמּוֹ עַל־יִשְׂרָאֵל

Ashkenazim and Chabad begin here

ב וְעַתָּה שְׁמַע לְקוֹל דִּבְרֵי יְהוָה׃ *כֹּה אָמַר יְהוָה צְבָאוֹת פָּקַדְתִּי אֵת אֲשֶׁר־עָשָׂה עֲמָלֵק
ג לְיִשְׂרָאֵל אֲשֶׁר־שָׂם לוֹ בַּדֶּרֶךְ בַּעֲלֹתוֹ מִמִּצְרָיִם׃ עַתָּה לֵךְ וְהִכִּיתָה אֶת־עֲמָלֵק וְהַחֲרַמְתֶּם אֶת־כָּל־
אֲשֶׁר־לוֹ וְלֹא תַחְמֹל עָלָיו וְהֵמַתָּה מֵאִישׁ עַד־אִשָּׁה מֵעֹלֵל וְעַד־יוֹנֵק מִשּׁוֹר וְעַד־שֶׂה מִגָּמָל וְעַד־
ד חֲמוֹר׃ וַיְשַׁמַּע שָׁאוּל אֶת־הָעָם וַיִּפְקְדֵם בַּטְּלָאִים מָאתַיִם אֶלֶף רַגְלִי וַעֲשֶׂרֶת אֲלָפִים
ה ו אֶת־אִישׁ יְהוּדָה׃ וַיָּבֹא שָׁאוּל עַד־עִיר עֲמָלֵק וַיָּרֶב בַּנָּחַל׃ וַיֹּאמֶר שָׁאוּל אֶל־הַקֵּינִי לְכוּ סֻּרוּ רְדוּ
מִתּוֹךְ עֲמָלֵקִי פֶּן־אֹסִפְךָ עִמּוֹ וְאַתָּה עָשִׂיתָה חֶסֶד עִם־כָּל־בְּנֵי יִשְׂרָאֵל בַּעֲלוֹתָם מִמִּצְרָיִם וַיָּסַר קֵינִי מִתּוֹךְ
ז ח עֲמָלֵק׃ וַיַּךְ שָׁאוּל אֶת־עֲמָלֵק מֵחֲוִילָה בּוֹאֲךָ שׁוּר אֲשֶׁר עַל־פְּנֵי מִצְרָיִם׃ וַיִּתְפֹּשׂ אֶת־אֲגַג מֶלֶךְ־עֲמָלֵק
ט חָי וְאֶת־כָּל־הָעָם הֶחֱרִים לְפִי־חָרֶב׃ וַיַּחְמֹל שָׁאוּל וְהָעָם עַל־אֲגָג וְעַל־מֵיטַב הַצֹּאן וְהַבָּקָר וְהַמִּשְׁנִים
י וְעַל־הַכָּרִים וְעַל־כָּל־הַטּוֹב וְלֹא אָבוּ הַחֲרִימָם וְכָל־הַמְּלָאכָה נְמִבְזָה וְנָמֵס אֹתָהּ הֶחֱרִימוּ׃ וַיְהִי
יא דְּבַר יְהוָה אֶל־שְׁמוּאֵל לֵאמֹר׃ נִחַמְתִּי כִּי־הִמְלַכְתִּי אֶת־שָׁאוּל לְמֶלֶךְ כִּי־שָׁב מֵאַחֲרַי וְאֶת־דְּבָרַי לֹא

HAFTARAT PARASHAT ZAKHOR

Sha'ul was the first king in Israel after 350 years of decentralized leadership by the judges. The enemies of Israel during this time had sensed their weakness and attacked them again and again. The judges were charged with warding off the marauding neighboring armies, and then they would return to their normal daily lives. One of the enemies long involved in hostilities with Israel was Amalek. These attacks were characterized by great wickedness and cruelty, like that which that same nation had brought to bear against the Israelites when they left Egypt centuries earlier. So it was late in Sha'ul's reign: the Amalekites would attack their neighbors, Israelites, Philistines, or Egyptians, unprovoked, for the sake of plunder and human trafficking, including of women and

12 to fulfill My words." This enraged Shmuel, and he cried out to the LORD all night long. And Shmuel set
out early in the morning toward Sha'ul, and Shmuel was told, "Sha'ul has gone to Carmel, where he set up
13 a monument for himself; then he turned off and made his way down to Gilgal." When Shmuel reached
14 Sha'ul, Sha'ul said to him, "Blessed are you to the LORD! I have fulfilled the LORD's word." "Then what
15 is this bleating of sheep in my ears," said Shmuel, "and the lowing of cattle that I hear?" "They brought
them from the Amalekites," said Sha'ul, "for the men spared the best of the sheep and cattle for sacri-
16 ficing to the LORD, your God – but we utterly destroyed the rest." "Stop," said Shmuel, "and
17 let me tell you what the LORD told me last night." "Speak," he said to him. And Shmuel said,
"Though you may seem small in your own eyes, you are the head of the tribes of Israel, and the LORD
18 anointed you as king over Israel. The LORD sent you on a mission, bidding, 'Go and utterly destroy
19 the offenders – Amalek – and fight them until you have destroyed them.' But why did you fail to heed
20 the voice of the LORD, pouncing on the spoil and doing evil in the eyes of the LORD?" "But
I did heed the voice of the LORD," Sha'ul said to Shmuel. "I set out on the mission the LORD as-
21 signed me, and I brought Agag, king of Amalek, and utterly destroyed Amalek. And the men took
of the spoil – the choicest sheep and cattle from what was banned – to sacrifice to the LORD, your
22 God, at Gilgal." And Shmuel said, "Does the LORD delight in burnt offerings and sacrifices as
much as obedience to the LORD's voice? Behold – obedience is better than sacrifice, and compliance
23 than the fat of rams. For rebellion is as bad as the sin of divination, and presumption as corruption and
24 idolatry. Because you rejected the word of the LORD, He has rejected you as king." "I have
sinned," Sha'ul said to Shmuel, "for I violated the LORD's command and your word, because I feared
25 the people and heeded their voice. But now, please forgive my sin and return with me, so I may worship
26 before the LORD." "I will not return with you," Shmuel said to Sha'ul, "for you have rejected the word
27 of the LORD – and the LORD has rejected you from being king over Israel." And Shmuel turned to go,
28 but Sha'ul grabbed the corner of his robe, and it tore. "The LORD has torn the kingship of Israel away
29 from you today," Shmuel said to him, "and has granted it to your peer, who is better than you. What is
30 more, Israel's Eternal will not betray or waver, for He is not a mere wavering human." "I have sinned,"
he said. "Now please honor me in front of the elders of my people and in front of Israel; return with
31 me and I will worship the LORD your God." So Shmuel followed Sha'ul back, and Sha'ul worshipped
32 the LORD. Shmuel then gave the order, "Bring Agag, king of Amalek, to me." Agag walked up
33 to him with stately steps. "So," said Agag, "the bitterness of death is upon me." And Shmuel said, "As
your sword has made women childless, so your mother shall be childless among women!" And Shmuel
34 hacked Agag to pieces before the LORD at Gilgal.* Then Shmuel went to Rama while Sha'ul *Yemenites end here*
made his way up to his home in Givat Sha'ul.

יב הֵקִים וַיִּחַר לִשְׁמוּאֵל וַיִּזְעַק אֶל־יהוה כָּל־הַלָּיְלָה: וַיַּשְׁכֵּם שְׁמוּאֵל לִקְרַאת שָׁאוּל בַּבֹּקֶר וַיֻּגַּד לִשְׁמוּאֵל
יג לֵאמֹר בָּא־שָׁאוּל הַכַּרְמֶלָה וְהִנֵּה מַצִּיב לוֹ יָד וַיִּסֹּב וַיַּעֲבֹר וַיֵּרֶד הַגִּלְגָּל: וַיָּבֹא שְׁמוּאֵל אֶל־שָׁאוּל וַיֹּאמֶר
יד לוֹ שָׁאוּל בָּרוּךְ אַתָּה לַיהוה הֲקִימֹתִי אֶת־דְּבַר יהוה: וַיֹּאמֶר שְׁמוּאֵל וּמֶה קוֹל־הַצֹּאן הַזֶּה בְּאָזְנָי וְקוֹל
טו הַבָּקָר אֲשֶׁר אָנֹכִי שֹׁמֵעַ: וַיֹּאמֶר שָׁאוּל מֵעֲמָלֵקִי הֱבִיאוּם אֲשֶׁר חָמַל הָעָם עַל־מֵיטַב הַצֹּאן וְהַבָּקָר
טז לְמַעַן זְבֹחַ לַיהוה אֱלֹהֶיךָ וְאֶת־הַיּוֹתֵר הֶחֱרַמְנוּ: וַיֹּאמֶר שְׁמוּאֵל אֶל־שָׁאוּל הֶרֶף וְאַגִּידָה
יז לְךָ אֵת אֲשֶׁר דִּבֶּר יהוה אֵלַי הַלָּיְלָה ויאמרו לוֹ דַּבֵּר: וַיֹּאמֶר שְׁמוּאֵל הֲלוֹא אִם־קָטֹן אַתָּה וַיֹּאמֶר
יח בְּעֵינֶיךָ רֹאשׁ שִׁבְטֵי יִשְׂרָאֵל אָתָּה וַיִּמְשָׁחֲךָ יהוה לְמֶלֶךְ עַל־יִשְׂרָאֵל: וַיִּשְׁלָחֲךָ יהוה בְּדָרֶךְ וַיֹּאמֶר לֵךְ
יט וְהַחֲרַמְתָּה אֶת־הַחַטָּאִים אֶת־עֲמָלֵק וְנִלְחַמְתָּ בוֹ עַד־כַּלּוֹתָם אֹתָם: וְלָמָּה לֹא־שָׁמַעְתָּ בְּקוֹל יהוה
כ וַתַּעַט אֶל־הַשָּׁלָל וַתַּעַשׂ הָרַע בְּעֵינֵי יהוה: וַיֹּאמֶר שָׁאוּל אֶל־שְׁמוּאֵל אֲשֶׁר שָׁמַעְתִּי בְּקוֹל
כא יהוה וָאֵלֵךְ בַּדֶּרֶךְ אֲשֶׁר־שְׁלָחַנִי יהוה וָאָבִיא אֶת־אֲגַג מֶלֶךְ עֲמָלֵק וְאֶת־עֲמָלֵק הֶחֱרַמְתִּי: וַיִּקַּח הָעָם
כב מֵהַשָּׁלָל צֹאן וּבָקָר רֵאשִׁית הַחֵרֶם לִזְבֹּחַ לַיהוה אֱלֹהֶיךָ בַּגִּלְגָּל: וַיֹּאמֶר שְׁמוּאֵל הַחֵפֶץ
כג לַיהוה בְּעֹלוֹת וּזְבָחִים כִּשְׁמֹעַ בְּקוֹל יהוה הִנֵּה שְׁמֹעַ מִזֶּבַח טוֹב לְהַקְשִׁיב מֵחֵלֶב אֵילִים: כִּי חַטַּאת־
כד קֶסֶם מֶרִי וְאָוֶן וּתְרָפִים הַפְצַר יַעַן מָאַסְתָּ אֶת־דְּבַר יהוה וַיִּמְאָסְךָ מִמֶּלֶךְ: וַיֹּאמֶר שָׁאוּל אֶל־
כה שְׁמוּאֵל חָטָאתִי כִּי־עָבַרְתִּי אֶת־פִּי־יהוה וְאֶת־דְּבָרֶיךָ כִּי יָרֵאתִי אֶת־הָעָם וָאֶשְׁמַע בְּקוֹלָם: וְעַתָּה שָׂא
כו נָא אֶת־חַטָּאתִי וְשׁוּב עִמִּי וְאֶשְׁתַּחֲוֶה לַיהוה: וַיֹּאמֶר שְׁמוּאֵל אֶל־שָׁאוּל לֹא אָשׁוּב עִמָּךְ כִּי מָאַסְתָּה
כז אֶת־דְּבַר יהוה וַיִּמְאָסְךָ יהוה מִהְיוֹת מֶלֶךְ עַל־יִשְׂרָאֵל: וַיִּסֹּב שְׁמוּאֵל לָלֶכֶת וַיַּחֲזֵק בִּכְנַף־מְעִילוֹ וַיִּקָּרַע:
כח כט וַיֹּאמֶר אֵלָיו שְׁמוּאֵל קָרַע יהוה אֶת־מַמְלְכוּת יִשְׂרָאֵל מֵעָלֶיךָ הַיּוֹם וּנְתָנָהּ לְרֵעֲךָ הַטּוֹב מִמֶּךָּ: וְגַם
ל נֵצַח יִשְׂרָאֵל לֹא יְשַׁקֵּר וְלֹא יִנָּחֵם כִּי לֹא אָדָם הוּא לְהִנָּחֵם: וַיֹּאמֶר חָטָאתִי עַתָּה כַּבְּדֵנִי נָא נֶגֶד זִקְנֵי־
לא עַמִּי וְנֶגֶד יִשְׂרָאֵל וְשׁוּב עִמִּי וְהִשְׁתַּחֲוֵיתִי לַיהוה אֱלֹהֶיךָ: וַיָּשָׁב שְׁמוּאֵל אַחֲרֵי שָׁאוּל וַיִּשְׁתַּחוּ שָׁאוּל
לב לַיהוה: וַיֹּאמֶר שְׁמוּאֵל הַגִּישׁוּ אֵלַי אֶת־אֲגַג מֶלֶךְ עֲמָלֵק וַיֵּלֶךְ אֵלָיו אֲגַג מַעֲדַנֹּת וַיֹּאמֶר אֲגַג
לג אָכֵן סָר מַר־הַמָּוֶת: וַיֹּאמֶר שְׁמוּאֵל כַּאֲשֶׁר שִׁכְּלָה נָשִׁים חַרְבֶּךָ כֵּן־תִּשְׁכַּל מִנָּשִׁים אִמֶּךָ וַיְשַׁסֵּף שְׁמוּאֵל
לד אֶת־אֲגַג לִפְנֵי יהוה בַּגִּלְגָּל:* וַיֵּלֶךְ שְׁמוּאֵל הָרָמָתָה וְשָׁאוּל עָלָה אֶל־בֵּיתוֹ גִּבְעַת שָׁאוּל: *Yemenites end here*

Haftarat Parashat Para

The maftir of Parashat Para is read from Numbers 19:1–22.

EZEKIEL

36 16 The word of the LORD came to me: "Man, the House of Israel dwelled upon their soil and defiled
17 it with their ways and their deeds – their ways were like the impurity of the menstrual woman be-
18 fore Me. I poured out My fury upon them for the blood they spilled upon the land and the idols
19 they defiled her with. I scattered them among the nations – they were strewn across the countries –
20 and I punished them according to their ways and their deeds. There, in whichever nations they came
to, they desecrated My holy name because it was said of them, 'These are the LORD's people, and
21 they have left His land.' And I am concerned for My holy name, which the House of Israel has des-
22 ecrated among the nations to which they have come. So, say to the House of Israel: So says
the Lord GOD: It is not for your sake that I do this, House of Israel, but for My holy name that you
23 desecrated among the nations to which you came. I will sanctify My great name that has been desecrated among the nations – that you desecrated among them. The nations will know that I am the
24 LORD, declares the Lord GOD, when I am sanctified through you before their eyes. I will take you
25 from the nations; I will gather you from all the countries and bring you to your land. I will sprinkle
over you purifying waters, and you will be cleansed; I will cleanse you of all your impurities and all
26 your idols. I will give you a new heart and put a new spirit into you; I will remove the heart of stone
27 from your flesh and give you a heart of flesh; I will put My spirit into you; make sure that you follow
28 My decrees and that you keep My laws and fulfill them. You will live in the land that I gave to your
29 fathers; you will be My people, and I will be your God. I will deliver you from all your impurities; I
30 will summon the grain, make it plentiful; I will not bring famine upon you. I will make the fruit of the
trees and the produce of the fields plentiful so that you will no longer have to endure the reproach of
31 famine among the nations. You will remember your evil ways and your actions that were no good;
32 you will loathe yourselves for your iniquities and your abominations. Not for your sake do I act, declares the Lord GOD; let that be known to you; be ashamed, disgraced by your own ways, House of
Israel.
33 So says the Lord GOD: On the day when I cleanse you of all your iniquities, I will reinhabit the cities;
34 the ruins will be rebuilt. The desolate land will be tilled there, where she was desolate in the sight of
35 every passerby. They will say, 'This land that was desolate has become like the garden of Eden; its towns
36 that were ruined, devastated, and destroyed have been fortified and inhabited.' And the nations that
remain around you will know that I, the LORD, have rebuilt what was destroyed, have sown what was
37 desolated; I the LORD have spoken and will do it.* So says the Lord GOD: This, too – I will
respond to the House of Israel's request to do this for them: I will multiply their people like a flock of
38 sheep, like the flocks for sacred offerings, like the flocks of Jerusalem during her holy times; this is how
the ruined cities will be, filled with flocks of people, and they will know that I am the LORD."

Sepharadim, Chabad, and Yemenites end here

---

their land will be a sanctification of God's name. The ingathering of exiles is a crucial stage of the process of redemption. When the people return to their land, they must purge themselves of their impurity in order to raise themselves to a state of piety and observance. A lyrical description of the softening of the people's "stone heart" and its replacement by a "heart of flesh" expresses this idea.

Earthly expressions of redemption will be material abundance and thriving, flourishing settlements. What had been a wasteland will become a paradise.

הפטרת פרשת פרה

The מפטיר of פרשת פרה is read from במדבר יט, א–כב.

לו טז יז וַיְהִי דְבַר־יהוה אֵלַי לֵאמֹר: בֶּן־אָדָם בֵּית יִשְׂרָאֵל יֹשְׁבִים עַל־אַדְמָתָם וַיְטַמְּאוּ אוֹתָהּ בְּדַרְכָּם יחזקאל
יח וּבַעֲלִילוֹתָם כְּטֻמְאַת הַנִּדָּה הָיְתָה דַרְכָּם לְפָנָי: וָאֶשְׁפֹּךְ חֲמָתִי עֲלֵיהֶם עַל־הַדָּם אֲשֶׁר־שָׁפְכוּ עַל־
יט כ הָאָרֶץ וּבְגִלּוּלֵיהֶם טִמְּאוּהָ: וָאָפִיץ אֹתָם בַּגּוֹיִם וַיִּזָּרוּ בָּאֲרָצוֹת כְּדַרְכָּם וְכַעֲלִילוֹתָם שְׁפַטְתִּים: וַיָּבוֹא
כא אֶל־הַגּוֹיִם אֲשֶׁר־בָּאוּ שָׁם וַיְחַלְּלוּ אֶת־שֵׁם קָדְשִׁי בֶּאֱמֹר לָהֶם עַם־יהוה אֵלֶּה וּמֵאַרְצוֹ יָצָאוּ: וָאֶחְמֹל
כב עַל־שֵׁם קָדְשִׁי אֲשֶׁר חִלְּלֻהוּ בֵּית יִשְׂרָאֵל בַּגּוֹיִם אֲשֶׁר־בָּאוּ שָׁמָּה: לָכֵן אֱמֹר לְבֵית־יִשְׂרָאֵל
כֹּה אָמַר אֲדֹנָי יֱהֹוִה לֹא לְמַעַנְכֶם אֲנִי עֹשֶׂה בֵּית יִשְׂרָאֵל כִּי אִם־לְשֵׁם־קָדְשִׁי אֲשֶׁר חִלַּלְתֶּם בַּגּוֹיִם
כג אֲשֶׁר־בָּאתֶם שָׁם: וְקִדַּשְׁתִּי אֶת־שְׁמִי הַגָּדוֹל הַמְחֻלָּל בַּגּוֹיִם אֲשֶׁר חִלַּלְתֶּם בְּתוֹכָם וְיָדְעוּ הַגּוֹיִם כִּי־
כד אֲנִי יהוה נְאֻם אֲדֹנָי יֱהֹוִה בְּהִקָּדְשִׁי בָכֶם לְעֵינֵיהֶם: וְלָקַחְתִּי אֶתְכֶם מִן־הַגּוֹיִם וְקִבַּצְתִּי אֶתְכֶם מִכָּל־
כה הָאֲרָצוֹת וְהֵבֵאתִי אֶתְכֶם אֶל־אַדְמַתְכֶם: וְזָרַקְתִּי עֲלֵיכֶם מַיִם טְהוֹרִים וּטְהַרְתֶּם מִכֹּל טֻמְאוֹתֵיכֶם
כו וּמִכָּל־גִּלּוּלֵיכֶם אֲטַהֵר אֶתְכֶם: וְנָתַתִּי לָכֶם לֵב חָדָשׁ וְרוּחַ חֲדָשָׁה אֶתֵּן בְּקִרְבְּכֶם וַהֲסִרֹתִי אֶת־לֵב
כז הָאֶבֶן מִבְּשַׂרְכֶם וְנָתַתִּי לָכֶם לֵב בָּשָׂר: וְאֶת־רוּחִי אֶתֵּן בְּקִרְבְּכֶם וְעָשִׂיתִי אֵת אֲשֶׁר־בְּחֻקַּי תֵּלֵכוּ וּמִשְׁפָּטַי
כח תִּשְׁמְרוּ וַעֲשִׂיתֶם: וִישַׁבְתֶּם בָּאָרֶץ אֲשֶׁר נָתַתִּי לַאֲבֹתֵיכֶם וִהְיִיתֶם לִי לְעָם וְאָנֹכִי אֶהְיֶה לָכֶם לֵאלֹהִים:
כט ל וְהוֹשַׁעְתִּי אֶתְכֶם מִכֹּל טֻמְאוֹתֵיכֶם וְקָרָאתִי אֶל־הַדָּגָן וְהִרְבֵּיתִי אֹתוֹ וְלֹא־אֶתֵּן עֲלֵיכֶם רָעָב: וְהִרְבֵּיתִי
לא אֶת־פְּרִי הָעֵץ וּתְנוּבַת הַשָּׂדֶה לְמַעַן אֲשֶׁר לֹא תִקְחוּ עוֹד חֶרְפַּת רָעָב בַּגּוֹיִם: וּזְכַרְתֶּם אֶת־דַּרְכֵיכֶם
לב הָרָעִים וּמַעַלְלֵיכֶם אֲשֶׁר לֹא־טוֹבִים וּנְקֹטֹתֶם בִּפְנֵיכֶם עַל עֲוֹנֹתֵיכֶם וְעַל תּוֹעֲבוֹתֵיכֶם: לֹא לְמַעַנְכֶם
אֲנִי־עֹשֶׂה נְאֻם אֲדֹנָי יֱהֹוִה יִוָּדַע לָכֶם בּוֹשׁוּ וְהִכָּלְמוּ מִדַּרְכֵיכֶם בֵּית יִשְׂרָאֵל:
לג לד כֹּה אָמַר אֲדֹנָי יֱהֹוִה בְּיוֹם טַהֲרִי אֶתְכֶם מִכֹּל עֲוֹנוֹתֵיכֶם וְהוֹשַׁבְתִּי אֶת־הֶעָרִים וְנִבְנוּ הֶחֳרָבוֹת: וְהָאָרֶץ
לה הַנְּשַׁמָּה תֵּעָבֵד תַּחַת אֲשֶׁר הָיְתָה שְׁמָמָה לְעֵינֵי כָּל־עוֹבֵר: וְאָמְרוּ הָאָרֶץ הַלֵּזוּ הַנְּשַׁמָּה הָיְתָה כְּגַן־
לו עֵדֶן וְהֶעָרִים הֶחֳרֵבוֹת וְהַנְשַׁמּוֹת וְהַנֶּהֱרָסוֹת בְּצוּרוֹת יָשָׁבוּ: וְיָדְעוּ הַגּוֹיִם אֲשֶׁר יִשָּׁאֲרוּ סְבִיבוֹתֵיכֶם כִּי ׀
לז אֲנִי יהוה בָּנִיתִי הַנֶּהֱרָסוֹת נָטַעְתִּי הַנְּשַׁמָּה אֲנִי יהוה דִּבַּרְתִּי וְעָשִׂיתִי:* כֹּה אָמַר אֲדֹנָי יֱהֹוִה *Sepharadim, Chabad, and Yemenites end here*
לח עוֹד זֹאת אִדָּרֵשׁ לְבֵית־יִשְׂרָאֵל לַעֲשׂוֹת לָהֶם אַרְבֶּה אֹתָם כַּצֹּאן אָדָם: כְּצֹאן קָדָשִׁים כְּצֹאן יְרוּשָׁלִַם
בְּמוֹעֲדֶיהָ כֵּן תִּהְיֶינָה הֶעָרִים הֶחֳרֵבוֹת מְלֵאוֹת צֹאן אָדָם וְיָדְעוּ כִּי־אֲנִי יהוה:

HAFTARAT PARASHAT PARA

The prophet Yeḥezkel accompanied the people into exile in Babylon during the reign of Yehoyakhin king of Yehuda, eleven years before the destruction of Jerusalem, the Temple, and the House of David. He prepared them mentally and spiritually for the coming blow. When the news of the destruction arrived, the prophet shifted to messages of comfort and reassurance, and prepared them for the coming redemption. This *haftara* is one of these prophecies.

It is natural for a people to be settled in their own land. It is their sins which cause them to be exiled. For Israel to be in exile is a desecration of God's name, and their return to

Haftarat Parashat HaḤodesh

The maftir of Parashat HaḤodesh is read from Exodus 12:1–20.
When Shabbat HaḤodesh coincides with Rosh Ḥodesh Nisan, three Torah scrolls are removed from the ark.
The first six aliyot are read from the weekly parasha. The seventh consists of the addition for Rosh Ḥodesh,
Numbers 28:9–15. Afterward, half-Kaddish is recited, and the maftir is read from Parashat HaḤodesh.

45 9 "Thus says the Lord God: You have gone far enough, O princes of Israel! Stop your violence and EZEKIEL
robbery, do what is just and right! Remove from My people your exacting taxes that evict them from *Yemenites begin here*
10 their land, says the Lord God. You shall have honest scales and honest measures of the ephah and the
11 *bat*. The ephah and the *bat* contain the same amount, so the *bat* contains one-tenth of a homer, and
12 one-tenth of a homer is also an ephah: their measure is relative to the homer. Now the shekel is twenty
13 gerah. Twenty shekel, twenty-five shekel, fifteen shekel together shall be your maneh. This is the contribution that you shall offer up: one-sixth of an ephah per homer of wheat and one-sixth of an ephah
14 per homer of barley. The rule regarding oil: the *bat* is the measure of oil; you shall offer one-tenth of
15 a *bat* out of the *kor*, which is a homer of ten *bat*, for ten *bat* make up a homer. And you shall offer one
lamb out of two hundred from your flock in the well-watered pastureland of Israel. These shall serve
as the grain offering and as the burnt offering and as the peace offering to atone for them, says the
16 Lord God. *All the people of the land shall give this contribution to the prince of *Ashkenazim begin here*
17 Israel. And it shall be the prince's duty to provide burnt offerings and grain offerings and libations on
festivals, New Moons, and Sabbaths; at all the times appointed for the House of Israel, he shall prepare the purification offering and the grain offering and the burnt offering and the peace offering to
18 provide atonement for the House of Israel. Thus says the Lord God: In the first month, on *Sepharadim and Chabad begin here*
19 the first day of the month, you shall take a young bull with no blemish to purify the Sanctuary. And the
priest shall take from the blood of this purification offering and put it on the doorposts of the House,
on the four corners of the ledge of the altar, and on the doorpost of the gate of the inner courtyard.
20 And so shall you do on the seventh day of the month for anyone who has sinned by mistake or due
21 to ignorance: thus you shall provide atonement for the House. In the first month, on the fourteenth
day of the month, you shall bring the Passover sacrifice, for a festival of seven days, unleavened bread
22 shall be eaten. On that day the prince shall prepare a bull as a purification offering for himself and for
23 all the people of the land. And on every one of the seven days of the festival he shall prepare a burnt
offering to the Lord: seven bulls and seven rams with no blemish every day for seven days, and a
24 daily purification offering consisting of one male goat. And he shall prepare a grain offering consisting
25 of one ephah for each bull and one ephah for each ram and a hin of oil for each ephah. In the seventh
month, on the fifteenth day of the month, during the festival, he shall prepare offerings just like those
on the seven days: a similar purification offering, a similar burnt offering, and a similar grain offering,
46 1 and a like amount of oil. Thus says the Lord God: The gate of the inner courtyard that faces
eastward shall be closed during the six days of labor, but on the Sabbath it shall be opened, and on the
2 day of the New Moon it shall be opened. The prince shall enter from outside by way of the entrance
hall of the gate and shall stand by the doorpost of the gate. The priests shall prepare his burnt offering
and his peace offering, and he shall bow down at the threshold of the gate and then leave, but the gate
3 shall not be closed until the evening so that the ordinary people can also bow down before the Lord

---

commoner. The service of the king in the Temple will be "for all the people," i.e., on behalf of a nation that stands before God. "When they enter, he enters, and when they leave, they leave together."

הפטרת פרשת החודש

The מפטיר *of* פרשת החודש *is read from* שמות יב, א–כ.

When שבת החודש *coincides with* ראש חודש ניסן, *three Torah scrolls are removed from the ark. The first six* עליות *are read from the weekly* פרשה. *The seventh consists of the addition for* ראש חודש, במדבר כח, ט–טו. *Afterward,* חצי קדיש *is recited, and the* מפטיר *is read from* פרשת החודש.

מה ט כֹּה־אָמַר אֲדֹנָי יֱהוִה רַב־לָכֶם נְשִׂיאֵי יִשְׂרָאֵל חָמָס וָשֹׁד הָסִירוּ וּמִשְׁפָּט וּצְדָקָה עֲשׂוּ הָרִימוּ גְרֻשֹׁתֵיכֶם יחזקאל
י יא מֵעַל עַמִּי נְאֻם אֲדֹנָי יֱהוִה׃ מֹאזְנֵי־צֶדֶק וְאֵיפַת־צֶדֶק וּבַת־צֶדֶק יְהִי לָכֶם׃ הָאֵיפָה וְהַבַּת תֹּכֶן אֶחָד יִהְיֶה *Yemenites begin here*
יב לָשֵׂאת מַעְשַׂר הַחֹמֶר הַבָּת וַעֲשִׂירִת הַחֹמֶר הָאֵיפָה אֶל־הַחֹמֶר יִהְיֶה מַתְכֻּנְתּוֹ׃ וְהַשֶּׁקֶל עֶשְׂרִים גֵּרָה
יג עֶשְׂרִים שְׁקָלִים חֲמִשָּׁה וְעֶשְׂרִים שְׁקָלִים עֲשָׂרָה וַחֲמִשָּׁה שֶׁקֶל הַמָּנֶה יִהְיֶה לָכֶם׃ זֹאת הַתְּרוּמָה אֲשֶׁר
יד תָּרִימוּ שִׁשִּׁית הָאֵיפָה מֵחֹמֶר הַחִטִּים וְשִׁשִּׁיתֶם הָאֵיפָה מֵחֹמֶר הַשְּׂעֹרִים׃ וְחֹק הַשֶּׁמֶן הַבַּת הַשֶּׁמֶן מַעְשַׂר
טו הַבַּת מִן־הַכֹּר עֲשֶׂרֶת הַבַּתִּים חֹמֶר כִּי־עֲשֶׂרֶת הַבַּתִּים חֹמֶר׃ וְשֶׂה־אַחַת מִן־הַצֹּאן מִן־הַמָּאתַיִם מִמַּשְׁקֵה
טז יִשְׂרָאֵל לְמִנְחָה וּלְעוֹלָה וְלִשְׁלָמִים לְכַפֵּר עֲלֵיהֶם נְאֻם אֲדֹנָי יֱהוִה׃ *כֹּל הָעָם הָאָרֶץ יִהְיוּ *Ashkenazim begin here*
יז אֶל־הַתְּרוּמָה הַזֹּאת לַנָּשִׂיא בְּיִשְׂרָאֵל׃ וְעַל־הַנָּשִׂיא יִהְיֶה הָעוֹלוֹת וְהַמִּנְחָה וְהַנֵּסֶךְ בַּחַגִּים וּבֶחֳדָשִׁים
וּבַשַּׁבָּתוֹת בְּכָל־מוֹעֲדֵי בֵּית יִשְׂרָאֵל הוּא־יַעֲשֶׂה אֶת־הַחַטָּאת וְאֶת־הַמִּנְחָה וְאֶת־הָעוֹלָה וְאֶת־הַשְּׁלָמִים
יח לְכַפֵּר בְּעַד בֵּית־יִשְׂרָאֵל׃ *כֹּה־אָמַר אֲדֹנָי יֱהוִה בָּרִאשׁוֹן בְּאֶחָד לַחֹדֶשׁ תִּקַּח פַּר־ *Sepharadim and Chabad begin here*
יט בֶּן־בָּקָר תָּמִים וְחִטֵּאתָ אֶת־הַמִּקְדָּשׁ׃ וְלָקַח הַכֹּהֵן מִדַּם הַחַטָּאת וְנָתַן אֶל־מְזוּזַת הַבַּיִת וְאֶל־אַרְבַּע
כ פִּנּוֹת הָעֲזָרָה לַמִּזְבֵּחַ וְעַל־מְזוּזַת שַׁעַר הֶחָצֵר הַפְּנִימִית׃ וְכֵן תַּעֲשֶׂה בְּשִׁבְעָה בַחֹדֶשׁ מֵאִישׁ שֹׁגֶה וּמִפֶּתִי
כא וְכִפַּרְתֶּם אֶת־הַבָּיִת׃ בָּרִאשׁוֹן בְּאַרְבָּעָה עָשָׂר יוֹם לַחֹדֶשׁ יִהְיֶה לָכֶם הַפָּסַח חָג שְׁבֻעוֹת יָמִים מַצּוֹת
כב כג יֵאָכֵל׃ וְעָשָׂה הַנָּשִׂיא בַּיּוֹם הַהוּא בַּעֲדוֹ וּבְעַד כָּל־עַם הָאָרֶץ פַּר חַטָּאת׃ וְשִׁבְעַת יְמֵי־הֶחָג יַעֲשֶׂה עוֹלָה
כד לַיהוָה שִׁבְעַת פָּרִים וְשִׁבְעַת אֵילִים תְּמִימִם לַיּוֹם שִׁבְעַת הַיָּמִים וְחַטָּאת שְׂעִיר עִזִּים לַיּוֹם׃ וּמִנְחָה
כה אֵיפָה לַפָּר וְאֵיפָה לָאַיִל יַעֲשֶׂה וְשֶׁמֶן הִין לָאֵיפָה׃ בַּשְּׁבִיעִי בַּחֲמִשָּׁה עָשָׂר יוֹם לַחֹדֶשׁ בֶּחָג יַעֲשֶׂה כָאֵלֶּה
מו א שִׁבְעַת הַיָּמִים כַּחַטָּאת כָּעֹלָה וְכַמִּנְחָה וְכַשָּׁמֶן׃ כֹּה־אָמַר אֲדֹנָי יֱהוִה שַׁעַר הֶחָצֵר הַפְּנִימִית
ב הַפֹּנֶה קָדִים יִהְיֶה סָגוּר שֵׁשֶׁת יְמֵי הַמַּעֲשֶׂה וּבְיוֹם הַשַּׁבָּת יִפָּתֵחַ וּבְיוֹם הַחֹדֶשׁ יִפָּתֵחַ׃ וּבָא הַנָּשִׂיא דֶּרֶךְ
אוּלָם הַשַּׁעַר מִחוּץ וְעָמַד עַל־מְזוּזַת הַשַּׁעַר וְעָשׂוּ הַכֹּהֲנִים אֶת־עוֹלָתוֹ וְאֶת־שְׁלָמָיו וְהִשְׁתַּחֲוָה עַל־
ג מִפְתַּן הַשַּׁעַר וְיָצָא וְהַשַּׁעַר לֹא־יִסָּגֵר עַד־הָעָרֶב׃ וְהִשְׁתַּחֲווּ עַם־הָאָרֶץ פֶּתַח הַשַּׁעַר הַהוּא בַּשַּׁבָּתוֹת

HAFTARAT PARASHAT HAḤODESH

The prophecy that appears in this week's *haftara* was communicated by Yeḥezkel to the exiles in Babylon fourteen years after the destruction of Jerusalem. In a prophetic virtual tour of the future rebuilt Jerusalem, we are informed about the daily rituals in the Temple, including the Passover sacrifice. The "prince" (*nasi*), i.e., the king, is the representative of the people in the Temple and works alongside the priests. A *nasi* in Hebrew can be a prince, but the word also means "cloud." Both stand above others: a leader of the people is held up over his charges, while a cloud hovers above the ground. However, this lofty status is not for their own sake. The prince receives his power from the people in order to improve their condition, just like a cloud, sent up over the fields, is charged with watering them and helping them grow. When a cloud is emptied of its life-giving waters, it dissipates and is gone.

In a redeemed world, all the classes of people will be present in the Temple, from the king to the lowest

4 at the threshold of that gate on Sabbaths and New Moons. The burnt offering that the prince shall offer
to the LORD on every Sabbath day consists of six lambs with no blemish and a ram with no blemish.
5 And his accompanying grain offering shall be one ephah for the ram; as for the lambs, his grain offering
6 shall be whatever he chooses to give as well as a hin of oil for each ephah of grain. And on the day of
the New Moon his offering shall consist of a young bull with no blemish as well as six lambs and a ram,
7 all without blemish. He shall prepare a grain offering of one ephah for the bull and one ephah for the
ram; as for the lambs, his grain offering shall be whatever he chooses to give as well as a hin of oil for
8 each ephah of grain. And when the prince comes, he shall enter by way of the entrance hall of the gate –
9 and by way of it shall he exit. But when the people come before the LORD on festivals, a person who
enters by way of the northern gate in order to bow down shall exit by the southern gate, and a person
who enters by way of the southern gate shall exit by way of the northern gate. He shall not return by
10 way of the gate through which he entered but shall exit through the one across from it. And the prince
shall be among the people on those days: when they enter, he enters, and when they leave, they leave
11 together. And on the festivals and at the appointed times the grain offering shall be an ephah for the
bull, an ephah for the ram, and as for the lambs, whatever he chooses to give as well as a hin of oil for
12 each ephah of grain.* Now, should the prince make a voluntary offering, a burnt offering *Yemenites end here*
or peace offering, voluntarily offered to the LORD on a weekday, the gate facing eastward shall be open
for him, and he shall prepare his burnt offering or peace offering just as he would do on the Sabbath,
13 but when he leaves, the gate will be closed after his exit. And you shall prepare a daily burnt offering to
14 the LORD consisting of a lamb in its first year without blemish; you shall prepare it every morning. And
you shall prepare a grain offering for it every morning: one-sixth of an ephah and one-third of a hin of
oil to moisten the finely ground flour as a grain offering to the LORD: a perpetual, everlasting decree.
15 Thus shall they prepare the lamb and the grain offering with the oil every morning as a regular burnt
16 offering.* Thus says the Lord GOD: Should the prince give a gift to one of his sons, it is his *Sepharadim and Chabad end here*
17 estate that will belong to his sons; it is their possession by inheritance. But should he give a gift from his
estate to one of his servants, the servant owns it until the year of freedom, when it returns to the prince,
18 for his heritors are his sons: it belongs to them. This is so that the prince does not take anything from
the people's inheritance, throwing them wrongfully out of their landholding. He shall pass his own landholding onto his sons so that My people will not be scattered, each ousted from his landholding."

HAFTARAT SHABBAT HAGADOL

According to Minhag Chabad this Haftara is only read when Pesaḥ falls on Motzei Shabbat.

3 4 Then the offering of Yehuda and Jerusalem will be pleasing to the LORD as in days of old and years past. MALACHI
5 I will draw close to you in judgment, and I will be a swift witness against the sorcerers and adulterers
and those who falsely swear; against those who withhold payment from the worker or the widow or the
6 orphan; against those who turn away the stranger. They do not fear Me, says the LORD of Hosts. For I
7 am the LORD. I have not changed. And you, children of Yaakov, you have not perished. Ever since the

to their children and the hearts of children back to their parents." The process of return is reciprocal. The people (the children) must return to God (their Father), and vice versa. The past (symbolized by the parents) must make its peace with the future (the children), and vice versa. On the night of the Seder, all the family sits together. The parents speak to the children about the exodus from Egypt, and these founding values are the basis for the Jewish people's future, which continues to climb higher and higher.

ד וּבֶחֳדָשִׁים לִפְנֵי יהוה: וְהָעֹלָה אֲשֶׁר־יַקְרִב הַנָּשִׂיא לַיהוה בְּיוֹם הַשַּׁבָּת שִׁשָּׁה כְבָשִׂים תְּמִימִם וְאַיִל
ה ו תָּמִים: וּמִנְחָה אֵיפָה לָאַיִל וְלַכְּבָשִׂים מִנְחָה מַתַּת יָדוֹ וְשֶׁמֶן הִין לָאֵיפָה: וּבְיוֹם הַחֹדֶשׁ פַּר בֶּן־בָּקָר
ז תְּמִימִם וְשֵׁשֶׁת כְּבָשִׂים וָאַיִל תְּמִימִם יִהְיוּ: וְאֵיפָה לַפָּר וְאֵיפָה לָאַיִל יַעֲשֶׂה מִנְחָה וְלַכְּבָשִׂים כַּאֲשֶׁר
ח ט תַּשִּׂיג יָדוֹ וְשֶׁמֶן הִין לָאֵיפָה: וּבְבוֹא הַנָּשִׂיא דֶּרֶךְ אוּלָם הַשַּׁעַר יָבוֹא וּבְדַרְכּוֹ יֵצֵא: וּבְבוֹא עַם־הָאָרֶץ
לִפְנֵי יהוה בַּמּוֹעֲדִים הַבָּא דֶּרֶךְ שַׁעַר צָפוֹן לְהִשְׁתַּחֲוֹת יֵצֵא דֶּרֶךְ־שַׁעַר נֶגֶב וְהַבָּא דֶּרֶךְ־שַׁעַר נֶגֶב יֵצֵא
י דֶּרֶךְ־שַׁעַר צָפוֹנָה לֹא יָשׁוּב דֶּרֶךְ הַשַּׁעַר אֲשֶׁר־בָּא בוֹ כִּי נִכְחוֹ יצאו: וְהַנָּשִׂיא בְּתוֹכָם בְּבוֹאָם יָבוֹא יֵצֵא
יא וּבְצֵאתָם יֵצֵאוּ: וּבַחַגִּים וּבַמּוֹעֲדִים תִּהְיֶה הַמִּנְחָה אֵיפָה לַפָּר וְאֵיפָה לָאַיִל וְלַכְּבָשִׂים מַתַּת יָדוֹ וְשֶׁמֶן
יב הִין לָאֵיפָה:* וְכִי־יַעֲשֶׂה הַנָּשִׂיא נְדָבָה עוֹלָה אוֹ־שְׁלָמִים נְדָבָה לַיהוה וּפָתַח לוֹ אֶת־הַשַּׁעַר *Yemenites end here*
הַפֹּנֶה קָדִים וְעָשָׂה אֶת־עֹלָתוֹ וְאֶת־שְׁלָמָיו כַּאֲשֶׁר יַעֲשֶׂה בְּיוֹם הַשַּׁבָּת וְיָצָא וְסָגַר אֶת־הַשַּׁעַר אַחֲרֵי
יג יד צֵאתוֹ: וְכֶבֶשׂ בֶּן־שְׁנָתוֹ תָּמִים תַּעֲשֶׂה עוֹלָה לַיּוֹם לַיהוה בַּבֹּקֶר בַּבֹּקֶר תַּעֲשֶׂה אֹתוֹ: וּמִנְחָה תַעֲשֶׂה
עָלָיו בַּבֹּקֶר בַּבֹּקֶר שִׁשִּׁית הָאֵיפָה וְשֶׁמֶן שְׁלִישִׁית הַהִין לָרֹס אֶת־הַסֹּלֶת מִנְחָה לַיהוה חֻקּוֹת עוֹלָם
טו טז תָּמִיד: ועשו אֶת־הַכֶּבֶשׂ וְאֶת־הַמִּנְחָה וְאֶת־הַשֶּׁמֶן בַּבֹּקֶר בַּבֹּקֶר עוֹלַת תָּמִיד:* כֹּה־אָמַר יַעֲשׂוּ *Sepharadim and Chabad end here*
יז אֲדֹנָי יֱהֹוִה כִּי־יִתֵּן הַנָּשִׂיא מַתָּנָה לְאִישׁ מִבָּנָיו נַחֲלָתוֹ הִיא לְבָנָיו תִּהְיֶה אֲחֻזָּתָם הִיא בְּנַחֲלָה: וְכִי־יִתֵּן
מַתָּנָה מִנַּחֲלָתוֹ לְאַחַד מֵעֲבָדָיו וְהָיְתָה לּוֹ עַד־שְׁנַת הַדְּרוֹר וְשָׁבַת לַנָּשִׂיא אַךְ נַחֲלָתוֹ בָּנָיו לָהֶם תִּהְיֶה:
יח וְלֹא־יִקַּח הַנָּשִׂיא מִנַּחֲלַת הָעָם לְהוֹנֹתָם מֵאֲחֻזָּתָם מֵאֲחֻזָּתוֹ יַנְחִל אֶת־בָּנָיו לְמַעַן אֲשֶׁר לֹא־יָפֻצוּ עַמִּי
אִישׁ מֵאֲחֻזָּתוֹ:

הפטרת שבת הגדול

According to Minhag Chabad this הפטרה *is only read when* פסח *falls on* מוצאי שבת.

ג ד ה וְעָרְבָה לַיהוה מִנְחַת יְהוּדָה וִירוּשָׁלָם כִּימֵי עוֹלָם וּכְשָׁנִים קַדְמֹנִיּוֹת: וְקָרַבְתִּי אֲלֵיכֶם לַמִּשְׁפָּט וְהָיִיתִי ׀ מלאכי
עֵד מְמַהֵר בַּמְכַשְּׁפִים וּבַמְנָאֲפִים וּבַנִּשְׁבָּעִים לַשָּׁקֶר וּבְעֹשְׁקֵי שְׂכַר־שָׂכִיר אַלְמָנָה וְיָתוֹם וּמַטֵּי־גֵר וְלֹא
ו ז יְרֵאוּנִי אָמַר יהוה צְבָאוֹת: כִּי אֲנִי יהוה לֹא שָׁנִיתִי וְאַתֶּם בְּנֵי־יַעֲקֹב לֹא כְלִיתֶם: לְמִימֵי אֲבֹתֵיכֶם סַרְתֶּם

HAFTARAT SHABBAT HAGADOL

Malakhi was the last of the prophets, living around the time of Neḥemya. At that time, the Jews newly returned to the land of Israel were in distress. An economic crisis and complicated social and spiritual situation sowed confusion and despair among the populace. To break out of such a situation required a communal conversation about the values on which their new reality would be founded. The discourse between the prophet and the people was meant to start such a conversation.

The prophet declares: "Come back to Me, and I will come back to you," and "Return the hearts of parents back

days of your forefathers you have strayed from My statutes, and you did not keep them. Come back to
8 Me, and I will come back to you, says the LORD of Hosts. But you say, "How shall we come back?" Can
a person steal from God? Yet you steal from Me. But you say, "What have we stolen from You?" The
9 tithes and donations. You are being cursed with the curse because you steal from Me – the whole nation.
10 Bring the entire tithe to the treasury, and it will be food for My House, and put Me to the test, please,
in this, says the LORD of Hosts. See if I do not open up the floodgates of heaven for you and pour out
11 blessings upon you endlessly. I will drive away for you that which devours. Your produce will not be
12 destroyed, and your vines in the field will not be barren, says the LORD of Hosts. All the nations will
13 call you happy, for you, yours will be a desired land, says the LORD of Hosts. The LORD says,
14 "You have spoken harshly against Me." Yet you say, "What have we said of You?" You say, "It is useless
to serve God, and what do we gain in keeping His watch, or by walking in dark sorrow before the
15 LORD of Hosts? Now we call the arrogant happy; evildoers have built themselves up; they have tested
16 God and escaped." Then those who fear the LORD spoke one to another, and the LORD listened and
He heard, and it was written – a book of remembrance before Him for those who fear the LORD and
17 keep His name in mind. And they shall be Mine, says the LORD of Hosts, on the day on which I choose
My cherished possession, and I will take pity on them as a man takes pity on his son who serves him.
18 And you will once again distinguish between the righteous and the wicked, between one who serves
19 God and one who does not serve Him. For behold, the day is coming, burning like an oven;
the arrogant and the evildoers will be straw, and the coming day will consume them, says the LORD
20 of Hosts, so that neither root nor branch will remain of them. But for you, fearers of My name, a sun
of righteousness will shine with healing under its wings, and you will go out and frolic like stall-fatted
21 calves. You will trample evildoers – for they will be ashes under the soles of your feet on the day on
22 which I act, says the LORD of Hosts. Remember the Teaching of Moshe My servant, which
23 I commanded to him at Ḥorev, statutes and laws for all of Israel. Behold, I will send you Eliya the
24 prophet before the great and terrible day of the LORD. And he will return the hearts of parents back to
their children and the hearts of children back to their parents, lest I come and lay the earth waste.

Behold, I will send you Eliya the prophet
before the great and terrible day of the LORD.

HAFTARA FOR THE FIRST DAY OF PESAḤ

The maftir of the first day of Pesaḥ is read from Numbers 28:16–25.

JOSHUA
Some begin here

3 5 And Yehoshua told the people, "Sanctify yourselves, for tomorrow the LORD will perform wonders in
6 your midst." "Raise up the Ark of the Covenant," said Yehoshua to the priests, "and cross before the peo-
7 ple." So they raised up the Ark of the Covenant and advanced to the front of the people. And
the LORD said to Yehoshua, "Today I shall begin to exalt you in the eyes of all Israel so that they may
know that I shall be with you as I was with Moshe.

---

festival as free men and women, confident that God's promise to give them the land of Israel as an inheritance will soon be realized. This promise is emphasized by the discontinuance of the manna, signaling that the era of the exodus has ended and the time to settle the land has arrived. The *haftara* ends with Yehoshua encountering the angelic general of God's army, presaging the miraculous conquest of Canaan that will soon follow.

ח מֵחֻקַּי וְלֹא שְׁמַרְתֶּם שׁוּבוּ אֵלַי וְאָשׁוּבָה אֲלֵיכֶם אָמַר יהוה צְבָאוֹת וַאֲמַרְתֶּם בַּמֶּה נָשׁוּב: הֲיִקְבַּע אָדָם
ט אֱלֹהִים כִּי אַתֶּם קֹבְעִים אֹתִי וַאֲמַרְתֶּם בַּמֶּה קְבַעֲנוּךָ הַמַּעֲשֵׂר וְהַתְּרוּמָה: בַּמְּאֵרָה אַתֶּם נֵאָרִים וְאֹתִי
י אַתֶּם קֹבְעִים הַגּוֹי כֻּלּוֹ: הָבִיאוּ אֶת־כָּל־הַמַּעֲשֵׂר אֶל־בֵּית הָאוֹצָר וִיהִי טֶרֶף בְּבֵיתִי וּבְחָנוּנִי נָא בָּזֹאת
יא אָמַר יהוה צְבָאוֹת אִם־לֹא אֶפְתַּח לָכֶם אֵת אֲרֻבּוֹת הַשָּׁמַיִם וַהֲרִיקֹתִי לָכֶם בְּרָכָה עַד־בְּלִי־דָי: וְגָעַרְתִּי
יב לָכֶם בָּאֹכֵל וְלֹא־יַשְׁחִת לָכֶם אֶת־פְּרִי הָאֲדָמָה וְלֹא־תְשַׁכֵּל לָכֶם הַגֶּפֶן בַּשָּׂדֶה אָמַר יהוה צְבָאוֹת: וְאִשְּׁרוּ
יג אֶתְכֶם כָּל־הַגּוֹיִם כִּי־תִהְיוּ אַתֶּם אֶרֶץ חֵפֶץ אָמַר יהוה צְבָאוֹת: חָזְקוּ עָלַי דִּבְרֵיכֶם אָמַר
יד יהוה וַאֲמַרְתֶּם מַה־נִּדְבַּרְנוּ עָלֶיךָ: אֲמַרְתֶּם שָׁוְא עֲבֹד אֱלֹהִים וּמַה־בֶּצַע כִּי שָׁמַרְנוּ מִשְׁמַרְתּוֹ וְכִי הָלַכְנוּ
טו קְדֹרַנִּית מִפְּנֵי יהוה צְבָאוֹת: וְעַתָּה אֲנַחְנוּ מְאַשְּׁרִים זֵדִים גַּם־נִבְנוּ עֹשֵׂי רִשְׁעָה גַּם בָּחֲנוּ אֱלֹהִים וַיִּמָּלֵטוּ:
טז אָז נִדְבְּרוּ יִרְאֵי יהוה אִישׁ אֶל־רֵעֵהוּ וַיַּקְשֵׁב יהוה וַיִּשְׁמָע וַיִּכָּתֵב סֵפֶר זִכָּרוֹן לְפָנָיו לְיִרְאֵי יהוה וּלְחֹשְׁבֵי
יז שְׁמוֹ: וְהָיוּ לִי אָמַר יהוה צְבָאוֹת לַיּוֹם אֲשֶׁר אֲנִי עֹשֶׂה סְגֻלָּה וְחָמַלְתִּי עֲלֵיהֶם כַּאֲשֶׁר יַחְמֹל אִישׁ עַל־בְּנוֹ
יח יט הָעֹבֵד אֹתוֹ: וְשַׁבְתֶּם וּרְאִיתֶם בֵּין צַדִּיק לְרָשָׁע בֵּין עֹבֵד אֱלֹהִים לַאֲשֶׁר לֹא עֲבָדוֹ: כִּי־הִנֵּה
הַיּוֹם בָּא בֹּעֵר כַּתַּנּוּר וְהָיוּ כָל־זֵדִים וְכָל־עֹשֵׂה רִשְׁעָה קַשׁ וְלִהַט אֹתָם הַיּוֹם הַבָּא אָמַר יהוה צְבָאוֹת
כ אֲשֶׁר לֹא־יַעֲזֹב לָהֶם שֹׁרֶשׁ וְעָנָף: וְזָרְחָה לָכֶם יִרְאֵי שְׁמִי שֶׁמֶשׁ צְדָקָה וּמַרְפֵּא בִּכְנָפֶיהָ וִיצָאתֶם וּפִשְׁתֶּם
כא כְּעֶגְלֵי מַרְבֵּק: וְעַסּוֹתֶם רְשָׁעִים כִּי־יִהְיוּ אֵפֶר תַּחַת כַּפּוֹת רַגְלֵיכֶם בַּיּוֹם אֲשֶׁר אֲנִי עֹשֶׂה אָמַר יהוה
כב צְבָאוֹת: זִכְרוּ תּוֹרַת מֹשֶׁה עַבְדִּי אֲשֶׁר צִוִּיתִי אוֹתוֹ בְחֹרֵב עַל־כָּל־יִשְׂרָאֵל חֻקִּים וּמִשְׁפָּטִים:
כג כד הִנֵּה אָנֹכִי שֹׁלֵחַ לָכֶם אֵת אֵלִיָּה הַנָּבִיא לִפְנֵי בּוֹא יוֹם יהוה הַגָּדוֹל וְהַנּוֹרָא: וְהֵשִׁיב לֵב־אָבוֹת עַל־בָּנִים
וְלֵב בָּנִים עַל־אֲבוֹתָם פֶּן־אָבוֹא וְהִכֵּיתִי אֶת־הָאָרֶץ חֵרֶם:

הנה אנכי שלח לכם את אליה הנביא
לפני בוא יום יהוה הגדול והנורא

הפטרת יום ראשון של פסח

The מפטיר *of* יום ראשון של פסח *is read from* במדבר כח, טז–כה.

יהושע
Some begin here

ג ה ו וַיֹּאמֶר יְהוֹשֻׁעַ אֶל־הָעָם הִתְקַדָּשׁוּ כִּי מָחָר יַעֲשֶׂה יהוה בְּקִרְבְּכֶם נִפְלָאוֹת: וַיֹּאמֶר יְהוֹשֻׁעַ אֶל־
הַכֹּהֲנִים לֵאמֹר שְׂאוּ אֶת־אֲרוֹן הַבְּרִית וְעִבְרוּ לִפְנֵי הָעָם וַיִּשְׂאוּ אֶת־אֲרוֹן הַבְּרִית וַיֵּלְכוּ לִפְנֵי
ז הָעָם: וַיֹּאמֶר יהוה אֶל־יְהוֹשֻׁעַ הַיּוֹם הַזֶּה אָחֵל גַּדֶּלְךָ בְּעֵינֵי כָּל־יִשְׂרָאֵל אֲשֶׁר יֵדְעוּן כִּי
כַּאֲשֶׁר הָיִיתִי עִם־מֹשֶׁה אֶהְיֶה עִמָּךְ:

FIRST DAY OF PESAḤ

The Torah reading for the first day of Pesaḥ describes the first Paschal sacrifice offered by the people of Israel, in the land of Egypt. The *haftara*, read from the book of Joshua, describes the first paschal sacrifice offered in the land of Israel. Having just crossed the Jordan river, Yehoshua orders the people first to circumcise themselves, in keeping with God's commandment (Ex. 12:48): "No uncircumcised man may eat of it." The leader then assures the people that by doing so, they have rid themselves of the "shame of Egypt," and can celebrate the

5 2 At that time, the LORD said to Yehoshua, "Make yourselves knives of flint and circumcise the Israelites *Most begin here*
3 a second time." So Yehoshua made knives of flint and circumcised the Israelites at the Hill of Foreskins.
4 This is why Yehoshua circumcised them: all the men who left Egypt – all the males fit for battle – had
5 died in the wilderness during the journey, as they came away from Egypt. And while all the men who
left there had been circumcised, all those who were born in the wilderness during the journey away
6 from Egypt had not been circumcised. For forty years the Israelites had wandered in the wilderness
until those among the nation who had left Egypt fit for battle had perished. They disobeyed the voice
of the LORD, and the LORD swore not to show them the land He had sworn to our ancestors that He
7 would give us – a land flowing with milk and honey. Yehoshua circumcised those children that He
raised in their stead, for they still had their foreskins, not having been circumcised during the journey.
8 When the whole nation's circumcision was over, they remained in place in the camp until they recov-
9 ered. The LORD said to Yehoshua, "Today, I have rolled the shame of Egypt away from you." He
10 has named that place Gilgal, as it is known to this day. The Israelites encamped at Gilgal and performed
11 the Passover sacrifice on the fourteenth day of the month at dusk on the plains of Yeriḥo. On the day
after the Passover sacrifice, they ate of the yield of the land – unleavened bread and roasted grain – that
12 very day. The manna stopped falling the day after they had eaten from the yield of the land. The Israelites
13 never had manna again; from that year on they ate from the crops of the land of Canaan. When
Yehoshua was near Yeriḥo, he looked up and suddenly saw a man standing opposite him, drawn sword
14 in hand. Yehoshua approached him and asked, "Are you for us or for our enemies?" He said, "No, for I
am the commander of the LORD's hosts. Now I have come!" Yehoshua flung his face to the ground and
15 prostrated himself, asking him, "What does my lord bid his servant?" The commander of the LORD's
hosts said to Yehoshua, "Remove the shoes from your feet, for the place where you stand is holy." And
6 1 Yehoshua did so. Yeriḥo was barred and bolted against the Israelites; no one came out, and no one
went in.
27 The LORD was with Yehoshua, and his fame rang out across the land.

HAFTARA FOR THE SECOND DAY OF PESAḤ IN THE DIASPORA

The maftir of the second day of Pesaḥ in the Diaspora is read from Numbers 28:16–25.

22 1 Yoshiyahu was eight years old when he became king, and for thirty-one years he reigned in Jerusalem. II KINGS
2 His mother's name was Yedida daughter of Adaya, from Botzkat. He did what was right in the eyes *Yemenites begin here*
3 of the LORD and followed in all the ways of his ancestor David, straying neither right nor left. In the
eighteenth year of King Yoshiyahu, the king sent the scribe Shafan son of Atzalyahu son of Meshulam
4 to the House of the LORD with this message: "Go up to Ḥilkiyahu the High Priest and have him calculate
the silver that has been brought to the House of the LORD, which the guardians of the threshold have col-
5 lected from the people. Have them give it to the foremen in charge of the House of the LORD, and they

---

the reigns of his father and grandfather. Inspired by its words, Yoshiyahu calls a gathering of all the leaders of the people to renew the covenant with God and forswear idolatry in all its forms. Yoshiyahu's enactments culminate in the grand and festive celebration of the Paschal offering. "No such Passover sacrifice had been made since the days of the judges who ruled Israel, nor throughout all the time of the kings of Israel or the kings of Yehuda."

Most begin here

ה ב ג בָּעֵת הַהִיא אָמַר יְהוָה אֶל־יְהוֹשֻׁעַ עֲשֵׂה לְךָ חַרְבוֹת צֻרִים וְשׁוּב מֹל אֶת־בְּנֵי־יִשְׂרָאֵל שֵׁנִית: וַיַּעַשׂ־לוֹ
ד יְהוֹשֻׁעַ חַרְבוֹת צֻרִים וַיָּמָל אֶת־בְּנֵי יִשְׂרָאֵל אֶל־גִּבְעַת הָעֲרָלוֹת: וְזֶה הַדָּבָר אֲשֶׁר־מָל יְהוֹשֻׁעַ כָּל־הָעָם
ה הַיֹּצֵא מִמִּצְרַיִם הַזְּכָרִים כֹּל | אַנְשֵׁי הַמִּלְחָמָה מֵתוּ בַמִּדְבָּר בַּדֶּרֶךְ בְּצֵאתָם מִמִּצְרָיִם: כִּי־מֻלִים הָיוּ כָּל־
ו הָעָם הַיֹּצְאִים וְכָל־הָעָם הַיִּלֹּדִים בַּמִּדְבָּר בַּדֶּרֶךְ בְּצֵאתָם מִמִּצְרַיִם לֹא־מָלוּ: כִּי | אַרְבָּעִים שָׁנָה הָלְכוּ
בְנֵי־יִשְׂרָאֵל בַּמִּדְבָּר עַד־תֹּם כָּל־הַגּוֹי אַנְשֵׁי הַמִּלְחָמָה הַיֹּצְאִים מִמִּצְרַיִם אֲשֶׁר לֹא־שָׁמְעוּ בְּקוֹל יְהוָה
אֲשֶׁר נִשְׁבַּע יְהוָה לָהֶם לְבִלְתִּי הַרְאוֹתָם אֶת־הָאָרֶץ אֲשֶׁר נִשְׁבַּע יְהוָה לַאֲבוֹתָם לָתֶת לָנוּ אֶרֶץ זָבַת חָלָב
ז ח וּדְבָשׁ: וְאֶת־בְּנֵיהֶם הֵקִים תַּחְתָּם אֹתָם מָל יְהוֹשֻׁעַ כִּי־עֲרֵלִים הָיוּ כִּי לֹא־מָלוּ אוֹתָם בַּדָּרֶךְ: וַיְהִי כַּאֲשֶׁר־
ט תַּמּוּ כָל־הַגּוֹי לְהִמּוֹל וַיֵּשְׁבוּ תַחְתָּם בַּמַּחֲנֶה עַד חֲיוֹתָם: וַיֹּאמֶר יְהוָה אֶל־יְהוֹשֻׁעַ הַיּוֹם גַּלּוֹתִי
י אֶת־חֶרְפַּת מִצְרַיִם מֵעֲלֵיכֶם וַיִּקְרָא שֵׁם הַמָּקוֹם הַהוּא גִּלְגָּל עַד הַיּוֹם הַזֶּה: וַיַּחֲנוּ בְנֵי־יִשְׂרָאֵל בַּגִּלְגָּל
יא וַיַּעֲשׂוּ אֶת־הַפֶּסַח בְּאַרְבָּעָה עָשָׂר יוֹם לַחֹדֶשׁ בָּעֶרֶב בְּעַרְבוֹת יְרִיחוֹ: וַיֹּאכְלוּ מֵעֲבוּר הָאָרֶץ מִמָּחֳרַת
יב הַפֶּסַח מַצּוֹת וְקָלוּי בְּעֶצֶם הַיּוֹם הַזֶּה: וַיִּשְׁבֹּת הַמָּן מִמָּחֳרָת בְּאָכְלָם מֵעֲבוּר הָאָרֶץ וְלֹא־הָיָה עוֹד לִבְנֵי
יג יִשְׂרָאֵל מָן וַיֹּאכְלוּ מִתְּבוּאַת אֶרֶץ כְּנַעַן בַּשָּׁנָה הַהִיא: וַיְהִי בִּהְיוֹת יְהוֹשֻׁעַ בִּירִיחוֹ וַיִּשָּׂא
עֵינָיו וַיַּרְא וְהִנֵּה־אִישׁ עֹמֵד לְנֶגְדּוֹ וְחַרְבּוֹ שְׁלוּפָה בְּיָדוֹ וַיֵּלֶךְ יְהוֹשֻׁעַ אֵלָיו וַיֹּאמֶר לוֹ הֲלָנוּ אַתָּה אִם־
יד לְצָרֵינוּ: וַיֹּאמֶר | לֹא כִּי אֲנִי שַׂר־צְבָא־יְהוָה עַתָּה בָאתִי וַיִּפֹּל יְהוֹשֻׁעַ אֶל־פָּנָיו אַרְצָה וַיִּשְׁתָּחוּ וַיֹּאמֶר
טו לוֹ מָה אֲדֹנִי מְדַבֵּר אֶל־עַבְדּוֹ: וַיֹּאמֶר שַׂר־צְבָא יְהוָה אֶל־יְהוֹשֻׁעַ שַׁל־נַעַלְךָ מֵעַל רַגְלֶךָ כִּי הַמָּקוֹם
ו א אֲשֶׁר אַתָּה עֹמֵד עָלָיו קֹדֶשׁ הוּא וַיַּעַשׂ יְהוֹשֻׁעַ כֵּן: וִירִיחוֹ סֹגֶרֶת וּמְסֻגֶּרֶת מִפְּנֵי בְּנֵי יִשְׂרָאֵל אֵין יוֹצֵא
וְאֵין בָּא:
כז וַיְהִי יְהוָה אֶת־יְהוֹשֻׁעַ וַיְהִי שָׁמְעוֹ בְּכָל־הָאָרֶץ:

הפטרת יום שני של פסח בחוץ לארץ

The מפטיר *of* יום שני של פסח בחוץ לארץ *is read from* במדבר כח, טו–כה.

מלכים ב

Yemenites begin here

כב א בֶּן־שְׁמֹנֶה שָׁנָה יֹאשִׁיָּהוּ בְמָלְכוֹ וּשְׁלֹשִׁים וְאַחַת שָׁנָה מָלַךְ בִּירוּשָׁלָםִ וְשֵׁם אִמּוֹ יְדִידָה בַת־
ב ג עֲדָיָה מִבָּצְקַת: וַיַּעַשׂ הַיָּשָׁר בְּעֵינֵי יְהוָה וַיֵּלֶךְ בְּכָל־דֶּרֶךְ דָּוִד אָבִיו וְלֹא־סָר יָמִין וּשְׂמֹאול: וַיְהִי
בִּשְׁמֹנֶה עֶשְׂרֵה שָׁנָה לַמֶּלֶךְ יֹאשִׁיָּהוּ שָׁלַח הַמֶּלֶךְ אֶת־שָׁפָן בֶּן־אֲצַלְיָהוּ בֶן־מְשֻׁלָּם הַסֹּפֵר
ד בֵּית יְהוָה לֵאמֹר: עֲלֵה אֶל־חִלְקִיָּהוּ הַכֹּהֵן הַגָּדוֹל וְיַתֵּם אֶת־הַכֶּסֶף הַמּוּבָא בֵּית יְהוָה אֲשֶׁר
ה אָסְפוּ שֹׁמְרֵי הַסַּף מֵאֵת הָעָם: וְיִתְּנֻה עַל־יַד עֹשֵׂי הַמְּלָאכָה הַמֻּפְקָדִים בבֵית יְהוָה וְיִתְּנוּ אֹתוֹ בֵּית

SECOND DAY OF PESAḤ IN THE DIASPORA

In this *haftara* we read of the far-reaching reforms of King Yoshiyahu of Yehuda. The rule of his grandfather, Menashe, had been catastrophic, normalizing idolatry throughout the kingdom and converting the Temple of Jerusalem into a house of worship for Ashera. After the short rule and violent death of his father, Amon, Yoshiyahu sought to make amends, in consultation with the High Priest Ḥilkiyahu. He renovated the Temple, removing the idols there, and rediscovered a copy of the Torah, which had been forgotten under

6 will pay it out to the workers in the House of the LORD to keep the House in repair – to the carpenters,
7 builders, and masons – and to purchase wood and quarry stones to repair the House. But there is no need
to keep track of the silver entrusted to them, for they deal honestly."
23 1 The king summoned all the elders of Yehuda and Jerusalem, who gathered to him. And the king went *Ashkenazim and Sepharadim begin here*
2 up to the House of the LORD, along with all the men of Yehuda and all the inhabitants of Jerusalem, *Yemenites skip this*
the priests and the prophets and all the people, from the smallest to the greatest. And he read out to
3 them all the words of the scroll of the covenant that had been found in the House of the LORD. The
king stood on the platform and reinstated the covenant before the LORD: to follow the LORD and to
keep His commandments, decrees, and laws with all their heart and all their soul; to fulfill the words of
4 this covenant as written in this book. And all the people pledged themselves to the covenant. The king
then commanded Ḥilkiyahu, the High Priest, the deputy priests, and the guardians of the threshold
to remove from the LORD's Sanctuary all the vessels that had been made for Baal, Ashera, and all the
heavenly hosts. He burned them outside of Jerusalem in the fields of Kidron and removed their ashes
5 to Beit El. He shut down the idolatrous priests whom the kings of Yehuda had appointed to offer sacrifices at the high shrines in the towns of Yehuda and the area around Jerusalem as well as those who
6 offered sacrifices to Baal, to the sun and moon and stars, and to all the heavenly hosts. He brought out
the Ashera from the House of the LORD to the Kidron Valley outside of Jerusalem, and he burned it
in the Kidron Valley and ground it to dust, then he scattered the dust over the common burial ground.
7 He tore down the booths of the male ritual prostitutes in the House of the LORD, where the women
8 would weave coverings for Ashera. He brought in all the priests from the towns of Yehuda and defiled
the high shrines where the priests had offered sacrifices from Geva to Be'er Sheva. And he tore down
the high shrines by the gates, those by the entrance to the gate of Joshua, the city governor; they were
9 on a person's left at the city gate. Though the shrine priests could not go up to the Altar of the LORD in
Jerusalem, they did eat of the unleavened bread along with their kin.
21 The king then commanded all the people: "Make the Passover sacrifice to the LORD your God, as it is *Yemenites continue here*
22 written in this book of the covenant." Now no such Passover sacrifice had been made since the days of the
23 judges who ruled Israel, nor throughout all the time of the kings of Israel or the kings of Yehuda. But in the
24 eighteenth year of King Yoshiyahu, such a Passover sacrifice was made to the LORD in Jerusalem. As for
the necromancers, mediums, household gods, idols, and all the detestable things that had appeared in the
land of Yehuda and Jerusalem, Yoshiyahu stamped them out in order to uphold the words of the teaching
25 written in the book that Ḥilkiyahu the priest had found in the House of the LORD. There was none like
him before him – a king who returned to the LORD with all his heart, all his soul, and all his might, following all the teaching of Moshe, and none like him ever arose after him.

Haftarat Shabbat Ḥol HaMoed Pesaḥ

The maftir of Shabbat Ḥol HaMoed Pesaḥ in the Diaspora is read from Numbers 28:19–25.

36 37 So says the Lord GOD: This, too – I will respond to the House of Israel's request to do this for them: *Yemenites begin here*
38 I will multiply their people like a flock of sheep, like the flocks for sacred offerings, like the flocks of
Jerusalem during her holy times; this is how the ruined cities will be, filled with flocks of people, and
they will know that I am the LORD."

consciousness as a powerfully moving allegory for salvation and deliverance. The image of God opening up the graves of the people of Israel, resurrecting them, clothing them in flesh and sinew, and breathing the spirit of life back into

ו לְעֹשֵׂי הַמְּלָאכָה אֲשֶׁר בְּבֵית יהוה לְחַזֵּק בֶּדֶק הַבָּיִת: לֶחָרָשִׁים וְלַבֹּנִים וְלַגֹּדְרִים וְלִקְנוֹת עֵצִים
ז וְאַבְנֵי מַחְצֵב לְחַזֵּק אֶת־הַבָּיִת: אַךְ לֹא־יֵחָשֵׁב אִתָּם הַכֶּסֶף הַנִּתָּן עַל־יָדָם כִּי בֶאֱמוּנָה הֵם
עֹשִׂים:

Ashkenazim and Sepharadim begin here
Yemenites skip this

כג א ב וַיִּשְׁלַח הַמֶּלֶךְ וַיַּאַסְפוּ אֵלָיו כָּל־זִקְנֵי יְהוּדָה וִירוּשָׁלִָם: וַיַּעַל הַמֶּלֶךְ בֵּית־יהוה וְכָל־אִישׁ יְהוּדָה
וְכָל־יֹשְׁבֵי יְרוּשָׁלִַם אִתּוֹ וְהַכֹּהֲנִים וְהַנְּבִיאִים וְכָל־הָעָם לְמִקָּטֹן וְעַד־גָּדוֹל וַיִּקְרָא בְאָזְנֵיהֶם אֶת־כָּל־
ג דִּבְרֵי סֵפֶר הַבְּרִית הַנִּמְצָא בְּבֵית יהוה: וַיַּעֲמֹד הַמֶּלֶךְ עַל־הָעַמּוּד וַיִּכְרֹת אֶת־הַבְּרִית ׀ לִפְנֵי יהוה
לָלֶכֶת אַחַר יהוה וְלִשְׁמֹר מִצְוֺתָיו וְאֶת־עֵדְוֺתָיו וְאֶת־חֻקֹּתָיו בְּכָל־לֵב וּבְכָל־נֶפֶשׁ לְהָקִים אֶת־דִּבְרֵי
ד הַבְּרִית הַזֹּאת הַכְּתֻבִים עַל־הַסֵּפֶר הַזֶּה וַיַּעֲמֹד כָּל־הָעָם בַּבְּרִית: וַיְצַו הַמֶּלֶךְ אֶת־חִלְקִיָּהוּ הַכֹּהֵן
הַגָּדוֹל וְאֶת־כֹּהֲנֵי הַמִּשְׁנֶה וְאֶת־שֹׁמְרֵי הַסַּף לְהוֹצִיא מֵהֵיכַל יהוה אֵת כָּל־הַכֵּלִים הָעֲשׂוּיִם לַבַּעַל
וְלָאֲשֵׁרָה וּלְכֹל צְבָא הַשָּׁמָיִם וַיִּשְׂרְפֵם מִחוּץ לִירוּשָׁלִַם בְּשַׁדְמוֹת קִדְרוֹן וְנָשָׂא אֶת עֲפָרָם בֵּית־אֵל:
ה וְהִשְׁבִּית אֶת־הַכְּמָרִים אֲשֶׁר נָתְנוּ מַלְכֵי יְהוּדָה וַיְקַטֵּר בַּבָּמוֹת בְּעָרֵי יְהוּדָה וּמְסִבֵּי יְרוּשָׁלִָם וְאֶת־
ו הַמְקַטְּרִים לַבַּעַל לַשֶּׁמֶשׁ וְלַיָּרֵחַ וְלַמַּזָּלוֹת וּלְכֹל צְבָא הַשָּׁמָיִם: וַיֹּצֵא אֶת־הָאֲשֵׁרָה מִבֵּית יהוה מִחוּץ
לִירוּשָׁלִַם אֶל־נַחַל קִדְרוֹן וַיִּשְׂרֹף אֹתָהּ בְּנַחַל קִדְרוֹן וַיָּדֶק לְעָפָר וַיַּשְׁלֵךְ אֶת־עֲפָרָהּ עַל־קֶבֶר בְּנֵי הָעָם:
ז ח וַיִּתֹּץ אֶת־בָּתֵּי הַקְּדֵשִׁים אֲשֶׁר בְּבֵית יהוה אֲשֶׁר הַנָּשִׁים אֹרְגוֹת שָׁם בָּתִּים לָאֲשֵׁרָה: וַיָּבֵא אֶת־כָּל־
הַכֹּהֲנִים מֵעָרֵי יְהוּדָה וַיְטַמֵּא אֶת־הַבָּמוֹת אֲשֶׁר קִטְּרוּ־שָׁמָּה הַכֹּהֲנִים מִגֶּבַע עַד־בְּאֵר שָׁבַע וְנָתַץ
ט אֶת־בָּמוֹת הַשְּׁעָרִים אֲשֶׁר־פֶּתַח שַׁעַר יְהוֹשֻׁעַ שַׂר־הָעִיר אֲשֶׁר־עַל־שְׂמֹאול אִישׁ בְּשַׁעַר הָעִיר: אַךְ
לֹא יַעֲלוּ כֹּהֲנֵי הַבָּמוֹת אֶל־מִזְבַּח יהוה בִּירוּשָׁלִָם כִּי אִם־אָכְלוּ מַצּוֹת בְּתוֹךְ אֲחֵיהֶם:

Yemenites continue here

כא כב וַיְצַו הַמֶּלֶךְ אֶת־כָּל־הָעָם לֵאמֹר עֲשׂוּ פֶסַח לַיהוה אֱלֹהֵיכֶם כַּכָּתוּב עַל סֵפֶר הַבְּרִית הַזֶּה: כִּי לֹא
כג נַעֲשָׂה כַּפֶּסַח הַזֶּה מִימֵי הַשֹּׁפְטִים אֲשֶׁר שָׁפְטוּ אֶת־יִשְׂרָאֵל וְכֹל יְמֵי מַלְכֵי יִשְׂרָאֵל וּמַלְכֵי יְהוּדָה: כִּי
כד אִם־בִּשְׁמֹנֶה עֶשְׂרֵה שָׁנָה לַמֶּלֶךְ יֹאשִׁיָּהוּ נַעֲשָׂה הַפֶּסַח הַזֶּה לַיהוה בִּירוּשָׁלִָם: וְגַם אֶת־הָאֹבוֹת וְאֶת־
הַיִּדְּעֹנִים וְאֶת־הַתְּרָפִים וְאֶת־הַגִּלֻּלִים וְאֵת כָּל־הַשִּׁקֻּצִים אֲשֶׁר נִרְאוּ בְּאֶרֶץ יְהוּדָה וּבִירוּשָׁלִַם בִּעֵר
יֹאשִׁיָּהוּ לְמַעַן הָקִים אֶת־דִּבְרֵי הַתּוֹרָה הַכְּתֻבִים עַל־הַסֵּפֶר אֲשֶׁר מָצָא חִלְקִיָּהוּ הַכֹּהֵן בֵּית יהוה:
כה וְכָמֹהוּ לֹא־הָיָה לְפָנָיו מֶלֶךְ אֲשֶׁר־שָׁב אֶל־יהוה בְּכָל־לְבָבוֹ וּבְכָל־נַפְשׁוֹ וּבְכָל־מְאֹדוֹ כְּכֹל תּוֹרַת מֹשֶׁה
וְאַחֲרָיו לֹא־קָם כָּמֹהוּ:

הפטרת שבת חול המועד פסח

The מפטיר *of* שבת חול המועד פסח *is read from* במדבר כח, יט–כה.

יחזקאל

Yemenites begin here

לו לז לח כֹּה אָמַר אֲדֹנָי יֱהֹוִה עוֹד זֹאת אִדָּרֵשׁ לְבֵית־יִשְׂרָאֵל לַעֲשׂוֹת לָהֶם אַרְבֶּה אֹתָם כַּצֹּאן אָדָם: כְּצֹאן
קָדָשִׁים כְּצֹאן יְרוּשָׁלִַם בְּמוֹעֲדֶיהָ כֵּן תִּהְיֶינָה הֶעָרִים הֶחֳרֵבוֹת מְלֵאוֹת צֹאן אָדָם וְיָדְעוּ כִּי־אֲנִי יהוה:

SHABBAT ḤOL HAMOED PESAḤ

The famous vision of the dry bones, shown by God to Yeḥezkel in the aftermath of the destruction of Jerusalem, has earned a place of prominence in the popular ▶

Ashkenazim and Sepharadim begin here

37 1 And the hand of the LORD came upon me. He brought me out by the spirit of the LORD and set me
2 down in the valley. It was full of bones. He led me around through them all; there were so very many
3 of them out upon the valley, and they were utterly dry. And He said to me, "Man, can they come to life,
4 these bones?" And I said, "My Lord GOD, You know." He said to me: "Prophesy to these bones; say
5 to them: Dry bones – hear the word of the LORD! So says the Lord GOD to these bones: See – I will
6 bring breath into you, and you will come to life. I will give you sinews, I will make flesh grow on you,
I will spread skin over you, I will put breath into you, you will come to life, and you will know that I
7 am the LORD." I prophesied as I had been commanded. There was a noise as I was prophesying, and
8 then a rattling, and the bones moved together, each bone to its bone. And I saw there on them sinews,
9 flesh forming, and skin spreading a cover over them – but there was no breath in them. And He said to
me: "Prophesy to the breath; Man, prophesy and say to the breath: So says the Lord GOD: From the
10 four winds, come; breath, breathe into these slain so that they come to life." I prophesied as He had
commanded me, and the breath entered them, and they came to life; they stood upon their feet, a vast
11 army. And He said to me: "Man, these bones are the whole House of Israel. See, they say, 'Our bones
12 are dried out, our hope is lost, and we are completely cut off.' So, prophesy; say to them: So says the
Lord GOD: See, I am opening up your graves; I will lift you out of your graves, My people, and I will
13 bring you to the soil of Israel. You will know that I am the LORD when I open up your graves, when I
14 lift you out of your graves, My people. I will put My breath into you, and you will come to life; I will
set you upon your soil, and you will know that I am the LORD; I have spoken, and I will do it, declares
the LORD."

HAFTARA FOR THE SEVENTH DAY OF PESAḤ

The maftir of the seventh day of Pesaḥ is read from Numbers 28:19–25.

II SAMUEL

22 1 David uttered these words of song to the LORD on the day that the LORD saved him from the hands
2 of all his enemies and from the hand of Sha'ul. He said: The LORD is my Rock and my fortress, my
3 own rescuer; // my God is the Rock of my refuge / my shield, the horn of my salvation, my haven, /
4 my refuge, my savior who delivers me from violence. // Praise! When I call on the LORD, / I am saved
5 6 from my enemies. // For when waves of death assailed me, / deadly torrents engulfed me, the cords of
7 Sheol entangled me, / snares of death confronted me, // in my distress I called on the LORD; / I called
8 out to my God; / He heard my voice from His temple, / and my cry rang in His ears. // Then the earth

SEVENTH DAY OF PESAḤ

Having just read the triumphant Song of the Sea in the wake of God's rescue of Israel from Pharaoh's armies, we now turn to a parallel song in the words of the prophets. King David began his life subdued, oppressed, and persecuted, like the Israelites in Egypt generations before. Overshadowed at first by his brothers, his rise to prominence was frustrated by the jealousy of King Sha'ul, and he was forced to spend years in hiding. Even after Sha'ul's death, the early days of David's reign were fraught with dangers from Sha'ul's loyalists and foreign kings and warlords bent on quashing his kingdom before it could grow. David's constant loyalty to God, however, was repaid in full by a series of miraculous and improbable victories over all who sought to stymie him. At every stage, David recognized that triumph and salvation comes not through our own strength or talents, but by God's favor. Now, finally victorious over all his enemies, David offers a paean of thanks to the Almighty for his deliverance, no less stirring than that of his ancient ancestors.

Ashkenazim and Sepharadim begin here

לז א ב הָיְתָה עָלַי יַד־יהוה וַיּוֹצִאֵנִי בְרוּחַ יהוה וַיְנִיחֵנִי בְּתוֹךְ הַבִּקְעָה וְהִיא מְלֵאָה עֲצָמוֹת: וְהֶעֱבִירַנִי עֲלֵיהֶם
ג סָבִיב | סָבִיב וְהִנֵּה רַבּוֹת מְאֹד עַל־פְּנֵי הַבִּקְעָה וְהִנֵּה יְבֵשׁוֹת מְאֹד: וַיֹּאמֶר אֵלַי בֶּן־אָדָם הֲתִחְיֶינָה
ד הָעֲצָמוֹת הָאֵלֶּה וָאֹמַר אֲדֹנָי יֱהוִה אַתָּה יָדָעְתָּ: וַיֹּאמֶר אֵלַי הִנָּבֵא עַל־הָעֲצָמוֹת הָאֵלֶּה וְאָמַרְתָּ
ה אֲלֵיהֶם הָעֲצָמוֹת הַיְבֵשׁוֹת שִׁמְעוּ דְּבַר־יהוה: כֹּה אָמַר אֲדֹנָי יֱהוִה לָעֲצָמוֹת הָאֵלֶּה הִנֵּה אֲנִי מֵבִיא
ו בָכֶם רוּחַ וִחְיִיתֶם: וְנָתַתִּי עֲלֵיכֶם גִּידִים וְהַעֲלֵתִי עֲלֵיכֶם בָּשָׂר וְקָרַמְתִּי עֲלֵיכֶם עוֹר וְנָתַתִּי בָכֶם רוּחַ
ז וִחְיִיתֶם וִידַעְתֶּם כִּי־אֲנִי יהוה: וְנִבֵּאתִי כַּאֲשֶׁר צֻוֵּיתִי וַיְהִי־קוֹל כְּהִנָּבְאִי וְהִנֵּה־רַעַשׁ וַתִּקְרְבוּ עֲצָמוֹת
ח עֶצֶם אֶל־עַצְמוֹ: וְרָאִיתִי וְהִנֵּה־עֲלֵיהֶם גִּדִים וּבָשָׂר עָלָה וַיִּקְרַם עֲלֵיהֶם עוֹר מִלְמָעְלָה וְרוּחַ אֵין בָּהֶם:
ט וַיֹּאמֶר אֵלַי הִנָּבֵא אֶל־הָרוּחַ הִנָּבֵא בֶן־אָדָם וְאָמַרְתָּ אֶל־הָרוּחַ כֹּה־אָמַר | אֲדֹנָי יֱהוִה מֵאַרְבַּע רוּחוֹת
י בֹּאִי הָרוּחַ וּפְחִי בַּהֲרוּגִים הָאֵלֶּה וְיִחְיוּ: וְהִנַּבֵּאתִי כַּאֲשֶׁר צִוָּנִי וַתָּבוֹא בָהֶם הָרוּחַ וַיִּחְיוּ וַיַּעַמְדוּ עַל־
יא רַגְלֵיהֶם חַיִל גָּדוֹל מְאֹד מְאֹד: וַיֹּאמֶר אֵלַי בֶּן־אָדָם הָעֲצָמוֹת הָאֵלֶּה כָּל־בֵּית יִשְׂרָאֵל הֵמָּה הִנֵּה אֹמְרִים
יב יָבְשׁוּ עַצְמוֹתֵינוּ וְאָבְדָה תִקְוָתֵנוּ נִגְזַרְנוּ לָנוּ: לָכֵן הִנָּבֵא וְאָמַרְתָּ אֲלֵיהֶם כֹּה־אָמַר אֲדֹנָי יֱהוִה הִנֵּה אֲנִי
יג פֹתֵחַ אֶת־קִבְרוֹתֵיכֶם וְהַעֲלֵיתִי אֶתְכֶם מִקִּבְרוֹתֵיכֶם עַמִּי וְהֵבֵאתִי אֶתְכֶם אֶל־אַדְמַת יִשְׂרָאֵל: וִידַעְתֶּם
יד כִּי־אֲנִי יהוה בְּפִתְחִי אֶת־קִבְרוֹתֵיכֶם וּבְהַעֲלוֹתִי אֶתְכֶם מִקִּבְרוֹתֵיכֶם עַמִּי: וְנָתַתִּי רוּחִי בָכֶם וִחְיִיתֶם
וְהִנַּחְתִּי אֶתְכֶם עַל־אַדְמַתְכֶם וִידַעְתֶּם כִּי אֲנִי יהוה דִּבַּרְתִּי וְעָשִׂיתִי נְאֻם־יהוה:

הפטרת יום שביעי של פסח

The מפטיר *of* יום שביעי של פסח *is read from* במדבר כח, יט–כה.

כב א וַיְדַבֵּר דָּוִד לַיהוה אֶת־דִּבְרֵי הַשִּׁירָה הַזֹּאת בְּיוֹם הִצִּיל יהוה אֹתוֹ מִכַּף כָּל־אֹיְבָיו וּמִכַּף שָׁאוּל: שמואל ב
ב ג וַיֹּאמַר   יהוה סַלְעִי וּמְצֻדָתִי וּמְפַלְטִי־לִי: אֱלֹהֵי
צוּרִי אֶחֱסֶה־בּוֹ   מָגִנִּי וְקֶרֶן יִשְׁעִי מִשְׂגַּבִּי
ד וּמְנוּסִי   מֹשִׁעִי מֵחָמָס תֹּשִׁעֵנִי: מְהֻלָּל
ה אֶקְרָא יהוה וּמֵאֹיְבַי אִוָּשֵׁעַ:   כִּי אֲפָפֻנִי מִשְׁבְּרֵי־
ו מָוֶת   נַחֲלֵי בְלִיַּעַל יְבַעֲתֻנִי: חֶבְלֵי
שְׁאוֹל סַבֻּנִי   קִדְּמֻנִי מֹקְשֵׁי־
ז מָוֶת: בַּצַּר־לִי אֶקְרָא יהוה   וְאֶל־
אֱלֹהַי אֶקְרָא   וַיִּשְׁמַע מֵהֵיכָלוֹ
ח קוֹלִי   וְשַׁוְעָתִי בְּאָזְנָיו: ותגעש וַיִּתְגָּעַשׁ

them echoes the themes of hope and redemption that are the primary focus of the holiday of Pesaḥ. The culmination of the vision – a divine promise to bring the great, resurrected host and replant them on the soil of Israel – inspires us today with hope for a future end to the exile and complete restoration, just as the Israelites were saved from Egypt and brought to the promised land so many years ago.

shook and shuddered; / the foundations of heaven trembled; / they shuddered from His wrath. //
9 Smoke issued from His nostrils; / devouring flames flared from His mouth; / from Him gleaming
10 11 coals blazed forth. // He bent the heavens and descended, / dense cloud beneath His feet; / He
12 mounted a cherub and flew, / appearing on wings of wind. // He surrounded Himself with a shelter
13 of darkness, / of heavy storm clouds dense with rain. // From the brilliant glow of His presence /
14 blazed fiery coals. // The LORD thundered from the heavens; / the Most High raised His voice; /
15 16 He shot arrows to scatter them, / lightning bolts to rout them. // The ocean bed was exposed, / the
foundations of the world laid bare / by the onslaught of the LORD, / by the blast of His breath. //
17 18 From on high He reached down and took me; / He drew me out of the mighty waters. // He saved
19 me from my fierce enemy, / from foes too strong for me. // They confronted me on my direst day, /
20 but the LORD was my support. // He brought me out to freedom; / He rescued me because He de-
21 lighted in me. // The LORD rewarded me as I deserved; / as my hands were clean, He repaid me, /
22 23 for I kept the ways of the LORD / and did not betray my God, / for all His laws are before me; / I will
24 25 not turn away from His statutes. / I am blameless to Him / and keep myself from sin. / So the LORD
26 repaid me as I deserved / as I was pure in His sight. // You deal loyally with those who are loyal, /
27 to the blameless warrior You show Yourself blameless; / You are pure with those who are pure, / but
28 with the crooked, You are shrewd. / You bring salvation to a humble people; / You cast Your eyes
29 30 down on the haughty. // For You are my lamp, LORD; / the LORD lights up my darkness. / With You
31 I can rush a ridge; / with my God I can leap over a wall. // God's ways are blameless; / the LORD's
32 words are pure; / He is a shield to all who take refuge in Him. // For who is a god besides the LORD; /
33 who is a Rock besides our God? / God is my powerful stronghold; / He frees my way so it is sound. /

וַתִּרְעַשׁ הָאָרֶץ   מוֹסְדוֹת הַשָּׁמַיִם
ט יִרְגָּזוּ   וַיִּתְגָּעֲשׁוּ כִּי־חָרָה לוֹ׃   עָלָה
עָשָׁן בְּאַפּוֹ   וְאֵשׁ מִפִּיו
י תֹּאכֵל   גֶּחָלִים בָּעֲרוּ מִמֶּנּוּ׃   וַיֵּט
שָׁמַיִם וַיֵּרַד   וַעֲרָפֶל תַּחַת
יא רַגְלָיו׃   וַיִּרְכַּב עַל־כְּרוּב וַיָּעֹף   וַיֵּרָא
יב עַל־כַּנְפֵי־רוּחַ׃   וַיָּשֶׁת חֹשֶׁךְ סְבִיבֹתָיו
יג סֻכּוֹת   חַשְׁרַת־מַיִם עָבֵי שְׁחָקִים׃   מִנֹּגַהּ
יד נֶגְדּוֹ בָּעֲרוּ גַּחֲלֵי־אֵשׁ׃   יַרְעֵם מִן־שָׁמַיִם
טו יְהוָה   וְעֶלְיוֹן יִתֵּן קוֹלוֹ׃   וַיִּשְׁלַח
טז חִצִּים וַיְפִיצֵם בָּרָק ויהמם׃   וַיֵּרָאוּ אֲפִקֵי   וַיָּהֹם
יָם   יִגָּלוּ מֹסְדוֹת תֵּבֵל   בְּגַעֲרַת
יז יְהוָה מִנִּשְׁמַת רוּחַ אַפּוֹ׃   יִשְׁלַח מִמָּרוֹם
יח יִקָּחֵנִי   יַמְשֵׁנִי מִמַּיִם רַבִּים׃   יַצִּילֵנִי
מֵאֹיְבִי עָז   מִשֹּׂנְאַי כִּי אָמְצוּ
יט מִמֶּנִּי׃   יְקַדְּמֻנִי בְּיוֹם אֵידִי   וַיְהִי
כ יְהוָה מִשְׁעָן לִי׃   וַיֹּצֵא לַמֶּרְחָב
כא אֹתִי   יְחַלְּצֵנִי כִּי־חָפֵץ בִּי׃   יִגְמְלֵנִי
יְהוָה כְּצִדְקָתִי   כְּבֹר יָדַי יָשִׁיב
כב לִי׃   כִּי שָׁמַרְתִּי דַּרְכֵי יְהוָה   וְלֹא
כג רָשַׁעְתִּי מֵאֱלֹהָי׃   כִּי כָל־מִשְׁפָּטָו
כד לְנֶגְדִּי   וְחֻקֹּתָיו לֹא־אָסוּר מִמֶּנָּה׃   וָאֶהְיֶה
כה תָמִים לוֹ וָאֶשְׁתַּמְּרָה מֵעֲוֺנִי׃   וַיָּשֶׁב יְהוָה לִי
כו כְּצִדְקָתִי   כְּבֹרִי לְנֶגֶד עֵינָיו׃   עִם־
חָסִיד תִּתְחַסָּד   עִם־גְּבוֹר תָּמִים
כז תִּתַּמָּם׃   עִם־נָבָר תִּתָּבָר   וְעִם־
כח עִקֵּשׁ תִּתַּפָּל׃   וְאֶת־עַם עָנִי
כט תּוֹשִׁיעַ   וְעֵינֶיךָ עַל־רָמִים תַּשְׁפִּיל׃   כִּי־
אַתָּה נֵירִי יְהוָה   וַיהוָה יַגִּיהַּ
ל חָשְׁכִּי׃   כִּי בְכָה אָרוּץ גְּדוּד   בֵּאלֹהַי
לא אֲדַלֶּג־שׁוּר׃   הָאֵל תָּמִים
דַּרְכּוֹ   אִמְרַת יְהוָה צְרוּפָה   מָגֵן
לב הוּא לְכֹל הַחֹסִים בּוֹ׃   כִּי מִי־אֵל מִבַּלְעֲדֵי
לג יְהוָה   וּמִי צוּר מִבַּלְעֲדֵי אֱלֹהֵינוּ׃   הָאֵל
מָעוּזִּי חָיִל   וַיַּתֵּר תָּמִים

34 35 He makes my legs like a deer's / and stands me on the heights. / He trains my hands for battle / so that
36 my arms can bend a bow of bronze. // You gave me the shield of Your victory; / Your battle cry stirred
37 38 me with power. / You made my steps broad and firm; / my feet never faltered. / I pursued my enemy
39 to destroy them, / never turning back until they perished. / I cut them down and crushed them, and
40 they did not rise; / they fell beneath my feet. / You girded me with power for battle / and sunk my
41 adversaries far beneath me; / You made my enemies turn tail before me; / my foes, too, I destroyed. /
42 They looked wildly about, but there was no savior – / called out to the LORD, but He did not answer
43 them – // while I ground them up like dust of the earth; / I crushed and pounded them like street-
44 mud. // You rescued me from civil strife; / you kept me as the head of nations; / peoples I never knew
45 46 of serve me. / Foreign peoples come cringing before me; / they merely hear me and obey; / foreign
47 peoples lose heart / and come trembling out of their forts. // The LORD lives! / Blessed is my Rock; /
48 exalted is God, Rock of my rescue! / God who grants vengeance to me, / who subjugates people under
49 me, / my redeemer from my enemies, / You raise me above those who rise against me; / You save me
50 51 from violent men. // So I praise You, LORD, among the nations, / and sing to Your name. // He is a
tower of victory for His king / and shows loyalty to His anointed, / to David and his seed forever.

HAFTARA FOR THE EIGHTH DAY OF PESAḤ IN THE DIASPORA

The maftir for the eighth day of Pesaḥ in the Diaspora is read from Numbers 28:19–25.

10 32 This very day, he stands at Nov, waving his hand toward the mount of daughter Zion, Jerusalem's ISAIAH
33 hill. Behold the Master, the LORD of Hosts, stirring dread, shearing off branches. Those who
34 held their heads high are brought down; the exalted will be laid low. He fells the forest groves with
11 1 iron, Lebanon falls to the blows of majesty. A new shoot will grow from the stem of Yishai;
2 from his roots a branch will bud. And the spirit of the LORD will rest upon him – a spirit of wisdom,

the Messiah and his personality, the image of the "lion lying down with the lamb," and the ingathering of the exiles from all the lands – including Egypt – where they will have been held captive for so long. This includes an oblique allusion

לד דַּרְכּוֹ: מְשַׁוֶּה רגליו כָּאַיָּלוֹת וְעַל־ דַּרְכִּי | רַגְלָי
לה בָּמוֹתַי יַעֲמִידֵנִי: מְלַמֵּד יָדַי
לו לַמִּלְחָמָה וְנִחַת קֶשֶׁת־נְחוּשָׁה זְרֹעֹתָי: וַתִּתֶּן־
לו לִי מָגֵן יִשְׁעֶךָ וַעֲנֹתְךָ תַּרְבֵּנִי: תַּרְחִיב צַעֲדִי
לח תַּחְתֵּנִי וְלֹא מָעֲדוּ קַרְסֻלָּי: אֶרְדְּפָה
אֹיְבַי וָאַשְׁמִידֵם וְלֹא אָשׁוּב עַד־
לט כַּלּוֹתָם: וָאֲכַלֵּם וָאֶמְחָצֵם וְלֹא יְקוּמוּן וַיִּפְּלוּ
מ תַּחַת רַגְלָי: וַתַּזְרֵנִי חַיִל
מא לַמִּלְחָמָה תַּכְרִיעַ קָמַי תַּחְתֵּנִי: וְאֹיְבַי
מב תַּתָּה לִּי עֹרֶף מְשַׂנְאַי וָאַצְמִיתֵם: יִשְׁעוּ וְאֵין
מג מֹשִׁיעַ אֶל־יהוה וְלֹא עָנָם: וְאֶשְׁחָקֵם
כַּעֲפַר־אָרֶץ כְּטִיט־חוּצוֹת אֲדִקֵּם
מד אֶרְקָעֵם: וַתְּפַלְּטֵנִי מֵרִיבֵי עַמִּי תִּשְׁמְרֵנִי
לְרֹאשׁ גּוֹיִם עַם לֹא־יָדַעְתִּי
מה יַעַבְדֻנִי: בְּנֵי נֵכָר יִתְכַּחֲשׁוּ־לִי לִשְׁמוֹעַ
מו אֹזֶן יִשָּׁמְעוּ לִי: בְּנֵי נֵכָר יִבֹּלוּ וְיַחְגְּרוּ
מז מִמִּסְגְּרוֹתָם: חַי־יהוה וּבָרוּךְ צוּרִי וְיָרֻם
מח אֱלֹהֵי צוּר יִשְׁעִי: הָאֵל הַנֹּתֵן נְקָמֹת
מט לִי וּמוֹרִיד עַמִּים תַּחְתֵּנִי: וּמוֹצִיאִי
מֵאֹיְבָי וּמִקָּמַי תְּרוֹמְמֵנִי מֵאִישׁ חֲמָסִים
נ תַּצִּילֵנִי: עַל־כֵּן אוֹדְךָ יהוה בַּגּוֹיִם וּלְשִׁמְךָ
נא אֲזַמֵּר: מגדיל יְשׁוּעוֹת מִגְדּוֹל
מַלְכּוֹ וְעֹשֶׂה־חֶסֶד לִמְשִׁיחוֹ
לְדָוִד וּלְזַרְעוֹ עַד־עוֹלָם:

הפטרת יום שמיני של פסח בחוץ לארץ

The מפטיר *of* יום שביעי של פסח *is read from* במדבר כח, יט–כה.

ישעיהו

י לב לג עוֹד הַיּוֹם בְּנֹב לַעֲמֹד יְנֹפֵף יָדוֹ הַר בית־צִיּוֹן גִּבְעַת יְרוּשָׁלִָם: הִנֵּה הָאָדוֹן יהוה צְבָאוֹת בַּת־
לד מְסָעֵף פֻּארָה בְּמַעֲרָצָה וְרָמֵי הַקּוֹמָה גְּדֻעִים וְהַגְּבֹהִים יִשְׁפָּלוּ: וְנִקַּף סִבְכֵי הַיַּעַר בַּבַּרְזֶל וְהַלְּבָנוֹן בְּאַדִּיר
יא א ב יִפּוֹל: וְיָצָא חֹטֶר מִגֵּזַע יִשָׁי וְנֵצֶר מִשָּׁרָשָׁיו יִפְרֶה: וְנָחָה עָלָיו רוּחַ יהוה רוּחַ חָכְמָה וּבִינָה רוּחַ

EIGHTH DAY OF PESAḤ IN THE DIASPORA

Having read throughout the holiday of Pesaḥ of God's numerous deliverances of the Jewish people over history, we now, on the last day, turn to Isaiah's famous vision of the future redemption. This account includes some of the most well-known descriptions of that future time, an account of

▶

3 of knowing, a spirit of guidance and might, a spirit of insight and awe of the Lord. With awe of the
Lord infusing his senses, he will not judge by his eyes' perception, nor rule by what his ears can
4 grasp; he will judge poor people justly, render judgment rightly for oppressed ones in the land; he
will strike the land with the staff of his speech, and the spirit that crosses his lips will execute those
5 6 who do evil. He will gird his loins with righteousness: his battle dress is truth. Wolf will lie down
beside lamb, the leopard will lie beside the young goat; calf, lion cub, fatted lamb together – a little
7 child will tend them. The cow and the bear will graze with their young lying down together, and lion,
8 like ox, will feed upon straw. A baby will play at the cobra's hole, and an infant's hand will explore
9 the viper's nest. There will be no wrong or violence on all My holy mountain, for knowledge of the
10 Lord will fill the earth as waters cover the ocean. On that day, that offshoot of Yishai that
stands as a banner to all the peoples, nations will come to seek him, and his resting place will be glo-
11 rious. On that day this will be: The Lord will stretch forth His hand again to take back the
remnant of His people, those who remain, from Assyria and Egypt, from Patros and from Kush, from
12 Eilam and from Shinar, Ḥamat and the islands of the sea. He will lift up a banner to nations and gather
in the banished ones of Israel; He will gather in the scattered ones of Israel from all four edges of
13 the world. Efrayim's jealousy will fall away, the enemies in Yehuda will be cut down, Efrayim will no
14 more be jealous of Yehuda; Yehuda will bear toward Efrayim no more enmity. They will fly west to
the Philistines, shoulder to shoulder; together they will sack the people of the East; they will thrust
15 their hand against Edom and Moav, and the people of Amon will obey them. The Lord will destroy
the Egyptian Sea gulf and wave His hand over the River through His fearsome wind; He will beat
16 it into seven separate streams that people may cross in their shoes. A path will be there for the remnant of His people, those who remain, from Assyria, as there was for the people of Israel on the day
12 1 they came up from the land of Egypt. And you will say on that day: *I thank You, Lord for You raged*
2 *against me, but You turned back Your rage, and now You console me. Behold the God of my salvation; I*
3 *trust and will not fear, for God, the Lord, is my strength and song, and now my salvation.* With joy you
4 will draw water from the flowing springs of rescue. And you will say upon that day: *Give thanks to the*
5 *Lord; call on His name; proclaim His acts among the peoples; recount: His name is transcendent. Sing*
6 *out to the Lord: He has performed grandeur; all across the world this thing is known. Cry out, sing out*
joy, all you who dwell in Zion; for great in your midst is the Holy One of Israel.

Haftara for the First Day of Shavuot

The maftir of the first day of Shavuot is read from Numbers 28:26–31.

1 1 It was in the thirtieth year in the fourth month on the fifth day of the month. I was in the exile, by the EZEKIEL
2 Kevar River; the heavens opened up, and I saw Godly visions. On the fifth day of the month, the fifth
3 year of the exile of King Yoyakhin, so it was: the word of the Lord came to Yeḥezkel son of Buzi the

fitting continuation of this theme by describing the incredible revelation of God's majesty to the prophet Yeḥezkel, in exile in Babylon. The symbolism of the strange vision of God's chariot and the creatures bearing it has long been the subject of intense debate, and the Sages taught that speculation about it should be reserved for only those with advanced wisdom and knowledge. But the wonder and amazement it inspires is nonetheless fitting for the sacred day, along with its reminder that even through the mist of God's incomprehensibility and strangeness, we can discern how we were created in His image.

ג עצה וגבורה רוח דעת ויראת יהוה: והריחו ביראת יהוה ולא־למראה עיניו ישפוט ולא־למשמע
ד אזניו יוכיח: ושפט בצדק דלים והוכיח במישור לענוי־ארץ והכה־ארץ בשבט פיו וברוח שפתיו
ה ו ימית רשע: והיה צדק אזור מתניו והאמונה אזור חלציו: וגר זאב עם־כבש ונמר עם־גדי ירבץ ועגל
ז וכפיר ומריא יחדו ונער קטן נהג בם: ופרה ודב תרעינה יחדו ירבצו ילדיהן ואריה כבקר יאכל־תבן:
ח ט ושעשע יונק על־חר פתן ועל מאורת צפעוני גמול ידו הדה: לא־ירעו ולא־ישחיתו בכל־הר קדשי
י כי־מלאה הארץ דעה את־יהוה כמים לים מכסים: והיה ביום ההוא שרש ישי אשר
יא עמד לנס עמים אליו גוים ידרשו והיתה מנחתו כבוד: והיה ׀ ביום ההוא יוסיף אדני ׀
שנית ידו לקנות את־שאר עמו אשר ישאר מאשור וממצרים ומפתרוס ומכוש ומעילם ומשנער
יב ומחמת ומאיי הים: ונשא נס לגוים ואסף נדחי ישראל ונפצות יהודה יקבץ מארבע כנפות הארץ:
יג וסרה קנאת אפרים וצררי יהודה יכרתו אפרים לא־יקנא את־יהודה ויהודה לא־יצר את־אפרים:
יד ועפו בכתף פלשתים ימה יחדו יבזו את־בני־קדם אדום ומואב משלוח ידם ובני עמון משמעתם:
טו והחרים יהוה את לשון ים־מצרים והניף ידו על־הנהר בעים רוחו והכהו לשבעה נחלים והדריך
טז בנעלים: והיתה מסלה לשאר עמו אשר ישאר מאשור כאשר היתה לישראל ביום עלתו מארץ
יב א ב מצרים: ואמרת ביום ההוא אודך יהוה כי אנפת בי ישב אפך ותנחמני: הנה אל ישועתי אבטח ולא
ג ד אפחד כי־עזי וזמרת יה יהוה ויהי־לי לישועה: ושאבתם־מים בששון ממעיני הישועה: ואמרתם
ה ביום ההוא הודו ליהוה קראו בשמו הודיעו בעמים עלילתיו הזכירו כי נשגב שמו: זמרו יהוה כי
ו גאות עשה מידעת זאת בכל־הארץ: צהלי ורני יושבת ציון כי־גדול בקרבך קדוש ישראל: מודעת

הפטרת יום ראשון של שבועות

The מפטיר *of* יום ראשון של שבועות *is read from* במדבר כח, כו–לא.

א א ויהי ׀ בשלשים שנה ברביעי בחמשה לחדש ואני בתוך־הגולה על־נהר־כבר נפתחו השמים ואראה יחזקאל
ב ג מראות אלהים: בחמשה לחדש היא השנה החמישית לגלות המלך יויכין: היה היה דבר־יהוה אל־

to the splitting of the Sea of Reeds, commemorated on the last day of Pesaḥ: "The Lord will destroy the Egyptian Sea gulf and wave His hand over the River through His fearsome wind; He will beat it into seven separate streams that people may cross in their shoes. A path will be there for the remnant of His people, those who remain, from Assyria, as there was for the people of Israel on the day they came up from the land of Egypt."

FIRST DAY OF SHAVUOT

The holiday of Shavuot celebrates God's miraculous and awe-inspiring revelation at Mount Sinai. This *haftara* offers a

4 priest, in the land of the Chaldeans by the Kevar River; there the hand of the LORD was upon him. And
I looked: Behold, a storm wind came from the north, a great cloud and a flaring fire with a radiance
5 around it, and inside it, within the fire, the look of something luminous, and within that was the form
6 of four living beings. This was their appearance: they had the form of a man; each one had four faces,
7 and each one of them had four wings; their legs were straight-standing, and their feet were like a calf's
8 hoof, gleaming with a look of burnished bronze; they had man's hands beneath their wings on their
9 four sides, and the four of them had faces and wings. Their wings were joined to each other; they did
10 not turn when they moved but moved in the direction of one of the faces. Their faces were in the form
of the face of a man with the face of a lion on the right of the four, the face of an ox on the left of the four,
11 and the face of an eagle on all four of them. Their faces and their wings were separated above: each one
12 had two joining it to the others and two covering its body; each moved in the direction of one of the
13 faces – wherever the spirit would move, they moved – they did not turn when they moved. The form of
the living beings, their appearance, was like coals burning, like the appearance of torch flames; it passed
14 among the living beings; the fire had a radiance, lightning flashed out from the fire, and the living be-
15 ings ran forward and back with the appearance of darting flames. I looked at the living beings, and
16 there, a wheel was on the ground beside each of the living beings with the four faces. The appearance
of the wheels and their design had the look of an aquamarine gem, all four of them with the same form;
17 their appearance and their design were as though one wheel were inside the other. When they moved,
18 they moved on any of their four sides; they did not turn as they moved. Their rims, towering, inspired
19 fear; and the rims of all four of them were covered, all around, with eyes. When the living beings moved,
the wheels moved beside them, and when the living beings rose above the ground, the wheels also rose;
20 wherever the spirit would move, they moved; there where the spirit moved, the wheels rose with them,
21 for the spirit of the living being was also in the wheels: when they moved, they too moved, and when
they stood still, they too stood still, and when they rose from the ground, the wheels too rose with them
22 because the spirit of the living being was in the wheels. Above the head of the living being was the form
23 of an expanse with a look of ice, its overawing glare, suspended over their heads from above, and beneath the expanse, their wings reached out toward each other. Each had a pair covering them; each had
24 a pair covering their bodies. I heard the sound of their wings when they moved; it was like the sound
of great rushing waters, like the voice of Shaddai, a clamor like the noise of a gathered army. Standing
25 still, they lowered their wings; a voice came from upon the expanse which was over their heads –
26 standing still, they lowered their wings. Above the film which was over their heads, with the appearance of a sapphire, was the form of a throne; and upon the form of the throne – upon it, above – was a
27 form with the appearance of a man. And I saw: something that looked luminous, the appearance of fire
encasing it from what appeared to be his waist and above; and from what appeared to be his waist and
28 below, I saw an appearance like fire with a radiance around it; it was like the appearance of a rainbow in
the clouds on a rainy day; the radiance around it had that appearance. This was the appearance of the
2 1 form of the glory of the LORD. I saw it and I fell upon my face, and I heard a voice speak. He
2 said to me: "Man, stand on your feet, and I will speak to you." As He spoke to me, a spirit came into me
and set me on my feet, and I heard him speaking to me.

Ashkenazim and Sephardim skip these verses

3 12 A spirit then lifted me up, and I heard a great, thunderous noise behind me: "Blessed is the LORD's
glory from its place!"

Ashkenazim and Sephardim continue here

ד יְחֶזְקֵאל בֶּן־בּוּזִי הַכֹּהֵן בְּאֶרֶץ כַּשְׂדִּים עַל־נְהַר־כְּבָר וַתְּהִי עָלָיו שָׁם יַד־יהוה: וָאֵרֶא וְהִנֵּה רוּחַ סְעָרָה
ה בָּאָה מִן־הַצָּפוֹן עָנָן גָּדוֹל וְאֵשׁ מִתְלַקַּחַת וְנֹגַהּ לוֹ סָבִיב וּמִתּוֹכָהּ כְּעֵין הַחַשְׁמַל מִתּוֹךְ הָאֵשׁ: וּמִתּוֹכָהּ
ו דְּמוּת אַרְבַּע חַיּוֹת וְזֶה מַרְאֵיהֶן דְּמוּת אָדָם לָהֵנָּה: וְאַרְבָּעָה פָנִים לְאֶחָת וְאַרְבַּע כְּנָפַיִם לְאַחַת לָהֶם:
ז ח וְרַגְלֵיהֶם רֶגֶל יְשָׁרָה וְכַף רַגְלֵיהֶם כְּכַף רֶגֶל עֵגֶל וְנֹצְצִים כְּעֵין נְחֹשֶׁת קָלָל: וידו אָדָם מִתַּחַת כַּנְפֵיהֶם וִידֵי
ט עַל אַרְבַּעַת רִבְעֵיהֶם וּפְנֵיהֶם וְכַנְפֵיהֶם לְאַרְבַּעְתָּם: חֹבְרֹת אִשָּׁה אֶל־אֲחוֹתָהּ כַּנְפֵיהֶם לֹא־יִסַּבּוּ בְלֶכְתָּן
י אִישׁ אֶל־עֵבֶר פָּנָיו יֵלֵכוּ: וּדְמוּת פְּנֵיהֶם פְּנֵי אָדָם וּפְנֵי אַרְיֵה אֶל־הַיָּמִין לְאַרְבַּעְתָּם וּפְנֵי־שׁוֹר מֵהַשְּׂמֹאול
יא לְאַרְבַּעְתָּן וּפְנֵי־נֶשֶׁר לְאַרְבַּעְתָּן: וּפְנֵיהֶם וְכַנְפֵיהֶם פְּרֻדוֹת מִלְמָעְלָה לְאִישׁ שְׁתַּיִם חֹבְרוֹת אִישׁ וּשְׁתַּיִם
יב מְכַסּוֹת אֵת גְּוִיֹּתֵיהֶנָה: וְאִישׁ אֶל־עֵבֶר פָּנָיו יֵלֵכוּ אֶל אֲשֶׁר יִהְיֶה־שָּׁמָּה הָרוּחַ לָלֶכֶת יֵלֵכוּ לֹא יִסַּבּוּ
יג בְּלֶכְתָּן: וּדְמוּת הַחַיּוֹת מַרְאֵיהֶם כְּגַחֲלֵי־אֵשׁ בֹּעֲרוֹת כְּמַרְאֵה הַלַּפִּדִים הִיא מִתְהַלֶּכֶת בֵּין הַחַיּוֹת
יד טו וְנֹגַהּ לָאֵשׁ וּמִן־הָאֵשׁ יוֹצֵא בָרָק: וְהַחַיּוֹת רָצוֹא וָשׁוֹב כְּמַרְאֵה הַבָּזָק: וָאֵרֶא הַחַיּוֹת וְהִנֵּה אוֹפַן אֶחָד
טז בָּאָרֶץ אֵצֶל הַחַיּוֹת לְאַרְבַּעַת פָּנָיו: מַרְאֵה הָאוֹפַנִּים וּמַעֲשֵׂיהֶם כְּעֵין תַּרְשִׁישׁ וּדְמוּת אֶחָד לְאַרְבַּעְתָּן
יז וּמַרְאֵיהֶם וּמַעֲשֵׂיהֶם כַּאֲשֶׁר יִהְיֶה הָאוֹפַן בְּתוֹךְ הָאוֹפָן: עַל־אַרְבַּעַת רִבְעֵיהֶן בְּלֶכְתָּם יֵלֵכוּ לֹא יִסַּבּוּ
יח יט בְּלֶכְתָּן: וְגַבֵּיהֶן וְגֹבַהּ לָהֶם וְיִרְאָה לָהֶם וְגַבֹּתָם מְלֵאֹת עֵינַיִם סָבִיב לְאַרְבַּעְתָּן: וּבְלֶכֶת הַחַיּוֹת יֵלְכוּ
כ הָאוֹפַנִּים אֶצְלָם וּבְהִנָּשֵׂא הַחַיּוֹת מֵעַל הָאָרֶץ יִנָּשְׂאוּ הָאוֹפַנִּים: עַל אֲשֶׁר יִהְיֶה־שָּׁם הָרוּחַ לָלֶכֶת יֵלֵכוּ
כא שָׁמָּה הָרוּחַ לָלֶכֶת וְהָאוֹפַנִּים יִנָּשְׂאוּ לְעֻמָּתָם כִּי רוּחַ הַחַיָּה בָּאוֹפַנִּים: בְּלֶכְתָּם יֵלֵכוּ וּבְעָמְדָם יַעֲמֹדוּ
כב וּבְהִנָּשְׂאָם מֵעַל הָאָרֶץ יִנָּשְׂאוּ הָאוֹפַנִּים לְעֻמָּתָם כִּי רוּחַ הַחַיָּה בָּאוֹפַנִּים: וּדְמוּת עַל־רָאשֵׁי הַחַיָּה רָקִיעַ
כג כְּעֵין הַקֶּרַח הַנּוֹרָא נָטוּי עַל־רָאשֵׁיהֶם מִלְמָעְלָה: וְתַחַת הָרָקִיעַ כַּנְפֵיהֶם יְשָׁרוֹת אִשָּׁה אֶל־אֲחוֹתָהּ
כד לְאִישׁ שְׁתַּיִם מְכַסּוֹת לָהֵנָּה וּלְאִישׁ שְׁתַּיִם מְכַסּוֹת לָהֵנָּה אֵת גְּוִיֹּתֵיהֶם: וָאֶשְׁמַע אֶת־קוֹל כַּנְפֵיהֶם כְּקוֹל
כה מַיִם רַבִּים כְּקוֹל־שַׁדַּי בְּלֶכְתָּם קוֹל הֲמֻלָּה כְּקוֹל מַחֲנֶה בְּעָמְדָם תְּרַפֶּינָה כַנְפֵיהֶן: וַיְהִי־קוֹל מֵעַל לָרָקִיעַ
כו אֲשֶׁר עַל־רֹאשָׁם בְּעָמְדָם תְּרַפֶּינָה כַנְפֵיהֶן: וּמִמַּעַל לָרָקִיעַ אֲשֶׁר עַל־רֹאשָׁם כְּמַרְאֵה אֶבֶן־סַפִּיר דְּמוּת
כז כִּסֵּא וְעַל דְּמוּת הַכִּסֵּא דְּמוּת כְּמַרְאֵה אָדָם עָלָיו מִלְמָעְלָה: וָאֵרֶא | כְּעֵין חַשְׁמַל כְּמַרְאֵה־אֵשׁ בֵּית־לָהּ
כח סָבִיב מִמַּרְאֵה מָתְנָיו וּלְמָעְלָה וּמִמַּרְאֵה מָתְנָיו וּלְמַטָּה רָאִיתִי כְּמַרְאֵה־אֵשׁ וְנֹגַהּ לוֹ סָבִיב: כְּמַרְאֵה
הַקֶּשֶׁת אֲשֶׁר יִהְיֶה בֶעָנָן בְּיוֹם הַגֶּשֶׁם כֵּן מַרְאֵה הַנֹּגַהּ סָבִיב הוּא מַרְאֵה דְּמוּת כְּבוֹד־יהוה וָאֶרְאֶה
א וָאֶפֹּל עַל־פָּנַי וָאֶשְׁמַע קוֹל מְדַבֵּר: וַיֹּאמֶר אֵלַי בֶּן־אָדָם עֲמֹד עַל־רַגְלֶיךָ וַאֲדַבֵּר אֹתָךְ: ב
ב וַתָּבֹא בִי רוּחַ כַּאֲשֶׁר דִּבֶּר אֵלַי וַתַּעֲמִדֵנִי עַל־רַגְלָי וָאֶשְׁמַע אֵת מִדַּבֵּר אֵלָי:
יב וַתִּשָּׂאֵנִי רוּחַ וָאֶשְׁמַע אַחֲרַי קוֹל רַעַשׁ גָּדוֹל בָּרוּךְ כְּבוֹד־יהוה מִמְּקוֹמוֹ: ג

Ashkenazim and Sepharadim skip these verses

Ashkenazim and Sepharadim continue here

Haftara for the Second Day of Shavuot in the Diaspora

The maftir of the second day of Shavuot in the Diaspora is read from Numbers 28:26–31.

HABAKKUK

2 20 1 But the LORD is in His heavenly dwelling. All the earth, be silent before Him. *A prayer Ḥavakuk
3 2 the prophet sung with *shiggayon*: LORD, I have heard accounts of You and am afraid. O LORD, in the
coming years renew Your deeds; in the coming years, make Yourself known; in wrath, remember mercy.
3 God appears from Teiman, the Holy One from Mount Paran. Selah His splendor covers the heavens;
4 the earth is filled with His glory. His radiance illuminates like light; rays emanate from His every side;
5 6 therein lies His hidden strength. Before Him will come plague, fiery blight at His feet. He stands and
the earth shakes; He looks and nations tremble; age-old mountains shatter; everlasting hills bow low;
7 all the world's ways are His. I saw Kushan's tents afflicted for sinning, the curtains in the land of Midy-
8 an quiver. Is the LORD angry at the rivers; is it against the rivers that You rage? Is Your fury
9 against the ocean so that You ride upon Your horses of war, Your chariots of deliverance? Your bow is un-
10 sheathed; You keep Your word, Your oath to the tribes, Selah, and split the earth open with rivers. When
the mountains see You they shiver; streams of water flow through; the deep sounds with thunder, lifting
11 its hands up high. The sun, the moon stand still in their spheres; by the light of Your bolts the world will
12 13 march, by the glow of Your flashing spear. In rage, You tread the earth; in wrath, You trample nations. You
emerge to liberate Your people, to liberate Your king. You crush the head of the house of evil, stripping
14 it from the core up to its neck, Selah. You pierce heads of cities with their own spears,
15 they who come in a storm to shatter me, rejoicing as though secretly devouring the needy. You trample
16 the ocean floor with Your steeds, stirring mighty seas. I hear this, and my gut churns; my lips tremble at
the sound. Rot eats at my bones; I shudder in my place. Could I rest on the day of terror, the day God rises
17 up for His nation? Though the fig tree will not flower, nor will fruit fill the vines, olives will grow gaunt
and grain fields yield no produce, sheep will be removed from their pens, and cattle will not be found
18 19 in the sheds, yet I will delight in the LORD; I will rejoice in the God who will save me. GOD, my Lord,
my strength, He makes my legs like a deer's and guides me to stride to the heights. This song is for the
conductor; to Him I offer my melodies.

Haftara for the First Day of Sukkot

The maftir of the first day of Sukkot is read from Numbers 29:12–16.

ZECHARIAH

Yemenites begin here

13 9 I will pass that third through fire and refine them as one refines silver, and test them as one tests gold.
He will call in My name, and I will answer him. I will say, "He is My nation," and he will say, "The
14 1 LORD is my God." *Behold, a day of the LORD is coming; your spoil will be divided up in
2 your midst. I will gather all the nations to Jerusalem in war: the city will be taken, the houses will be
plundered, and the women will be raped; half of the city will go into exile, but the remainder of the

Ashkenazim and Sepharadim begin here

---

that on these days that God decides the fate of all peoples – for war or peace, plenty or hunger, rain or drought. As an expression of this idea, we read as today's *haftara* Zekharya's chilling account of God's future judgment of the nations. After a violent and ruthless conquest of Jerusalem by foreign armies, it will seem that all is lost. But God Himself will appear to fight on behalf of Israel, punishing those nations that oppressed her with fire and plague. Afterward, all people will know that God alone rules the earth, and they will show their newfound loyalty by appearing in Jerusalem every year for the Sukkot festival.

הפטרת יום שני של שבועות בחוץ לארץ

The מפטיר *of* יום שני של שבועות בחוץ לארץ *is read from* במדבר כח, כו–לא.

ב ג כ א ב וַיהוָה בְּהֵיכַל קָדְשׁוֹ הַס מִפָּנָיו כָּל־הָאָרֶץ: *תְּפִלָּה לַחֲבַקּוּק הַנָּבִיא עַל שִׁגְיֹנוֹת: יְהוָה חבקוק
ג שָׁמַעְתִּי שִׁמְעֲךָ יָרֵאתִי יְהוָה פָּעָלְךָ בְּקֶרֶב שָׁנִים חַיֵּיהוּ בְּקֶרֶב שָׁנִים תּוֹדִיעַ בְּרֹגֶז רַחֵם תִּזְכּוֹר: אֱלוֹהַּ
ד מִתֵּימָן יָבוֹא וְקָדוֹשׁ מֵהַר־פָּארָן סֶלָה כִּסָּה שָׁמַיִם הוֹדוֹ וּתְהִלָּתוֹ מָלְאָה הָאָרֶץ: וְנֹגַהּ כָּאוֹר תִּהְיֶה
ה ו קַרְנַיִם מִיָּדוֹ לוֹ וְשָׁם חֶבְיוֹן עֻזֹּה: לְפָנָיו יֵלֶךְ דָּבֶר וְיֵצֵא רֶשֶׁף לְרַגְלָיו: עָמַד | וַיְמֹדֶד אֶרֶץ רָאָה וַיַּתֵּר
ז גּוֹיִם וַיִּתְפֹּצְצוּ הַרְרֵי־עַד שַׁחוּ גִּבְעוֹת עוֹלָם הֲלִיכוֹת עוֹלָם לוֹ: תַּחַת אָוֶן רָאִיתִי אָהֳלֵי כוּשָׁן יִרְגְּזוּן
ח יְרִיעוֹת אֶרֶץ מִדְיָן: הֲבִנְהָרִים חָרָה יְהוָה אִם בַּנְּהָרִים אַפֶּךָ אִם־בַּיָּם עֶבְרָתֶךָ כִּי תִרְכַּב
ט עַל־סוּסֶיךָ מַרְכְּבֹתֶיךָ יְשׁוּעָה: עֶרְיָה תֵעוֹר קַשְׁתֶּךָ שְׁבֻעוֹת מַטּוֹת אֹמֶר סֶלָה נְהָרוֹת תְּבַקַּע־אָרֶץ:
י יא רָאוּךָ יָחִילוּ הָרִים זֶרֶם מַיִם עָבָר נָתַן תְּהוֹם קוֹלוֹ רוֹם יָדֵיהוּ נָשָׂא: שֶׁמֶשׁ יָרֵחַ עָמַד זְבֻלָה לְאוֹר חִצֶּיךָ
יב יג יְהַלֵּכוּ לְנֹגַהּ בְּרַק חֲנִיתֶךָ: בְּזַעַם תִּצְעַד־אָרֶץ בְּאַף תָּדוּשׁ גּוֹיִם: יָצָאתָ לְיֵשַׁע עַמֶּךָ לְיֵשַׁע אֶת־מְשִׁיחֶךָ
יד מָחַצְתָּ רֹּאשׁ מִבֵּית רָשָׁע עָרוֹת יְסוֹד עַד־צַוָּאר סֶלָה: נָקַבְתָּ בְמַטָּיו רֹאשׁ פְּרָזָו יִסְעֲרוּ
טו טז לַהֲפִיצֵנִי עֲלִיצֻתָם כְּמוֹ־לֶאֱכֹל עָנִי בַּמִּסְתָּר: דָּרַכְתָּ בַיָּם סוּסֶיךָ חֹמֶר מַיִם רַבִּים: שָׁמַעְתִּי | וַתִּרְגַּז בִּטְנִי
יז לְקוֹל צָלְלוּ שְׂפָתַי יָבוֹא רָקָב בַּעֲצָמַי וְתַחְתַּי אֶרְגָּז אֲשֶׁר אָנוּחַ לְיוֹם צָרָה לַעֲלוֹת לְעַם יְגוּדֶנּוּ: כִּי־תְאֵנָה
לֹא־תִפְרָח וְאֵין יְבוּל בַּגְּפָנִים כִּחֵשׁ מַעֲשֵׂה־זַיִת וּשְׁדֵמוֹת לֹא־עָשָׂה אֹכֶל גָּזַר מִמִּכְלָה צֹאן וְאֵין בָּקָר
יח יט בָּרְפָתִים: וַאֲנִי בַּיהוָה אֶעְלוֹזָה אָגִילָה בֵּאלֹהֵי יִשְׁעִי: יְהוִה אֲדֹנָי חֵילִי וַיָּשֶׂם רַגְלַי כָּאַיָּלוֹת וְעַל־בָּמוֹתַי
יַדְרִכֵנִי לַמְנַצֵּחַ בִּנְגִינוֹתָי:

הפטרת יום ראשון של סוכות

The מפטיר *of* יום ראשון של סוכות *is read from* במדבר כט, יב–טו.

ט וְהֵבֵאתִי אֶת־הַשְּׁלִשִׁית בָּאֵשׁ וּצְרַפְתִּים כִּצְרֹף אֶת־הַכֶּסֶף וּבְחַנְתִּים כִּבְחֹן אֶת־הַזָּהָב הוּא | יִקְרָא בִשְׁמִי זכריה *Yemenites begin here*
יד א וַאֲנִי אֶעֱנֶה אֹתוֹ אָמַרְתִּי עַמִּי הוּא וְהוּא יֹאמַר יְהוָה אֱלֹהָי: *הִנֵּה יוֹם־בָּא לַיהוָה וְחֻלַּק *Ashkenazim and Sepharadim begin here*
ב שְׁלָלֵךְ בְּקִרְבֵּךְ: וְאָסַפְתִּי אֶת־כָּל־הַגּוֹיִם | אֶל־יְרוּשָׁלִַם לַמִּלְחָמָה וְנִלְכְּדָה הָעִיר וְנָשַׁסּוּ הַבָּתִּים וְהַנָּשִׁים

SECOND DAY OF SHAVUOT IN THE DIASPORA

Like the *haftara* of the first day of Shavuot, that of the second day provides an image of God's majestic figure as revealed to the prophet, this time in His "heavenly dwelling" [*heikhal kodsho*] – which can also be seen as a reference to the holy Temple on earth. The prophet describes God's tremendous might, moving mountains and oceans. The natural world melds to His will as He performs wonders mirroring the thunder and fire of the revelation at Sinai.

FIRST DAY OF SUKKOT

According to the Sages, Sukkot is a holiday of judgment for the entire world. The seventy sacrificial bulls brought in the Temple signified the seventy nations of the earth, teaching

3 people will not be cut off from the city. The LORD will go out, and He will fight against these nations as
4 He has fought on days of battle. On that day His feet will stand upon the Mount of Olives which faces
Jerusalem on the east, and the Mount of Olives will split through its middle – into a great valley – from
5 east to west. Half the mountain will shift northward and half southward. And you will flee from this
Valley of the Mountains, for the Valley of the Mountains will reach as far as Atzal; you will flee as you
fled from the earthquake in the days of Uziya, the king of Yehuda, and the LORD will come – my God,
6 and all the holy ones with You. This is what will be: on that day there will be neither bright light nor
7 thick darkness. This is what will be: there will be a day known to the LORD; it will be neither day nor
8 night, but at evening time there will be light. This is what will be: on that day living waters will flow out
from Jerusalem, half to the eastern sea and half to the western sea; in summer and winter it will be so.
9 Then the LORD shall be King over all the earth; on that day the LORD shall be One and His name One.
10 Then the land will be smoothed out like a plain from Geva to Rimon, until the area south of Jerusalem,
and Jerusalem will be lifted up in her place. From the Gate of Binyamin to the site of the First Gate and
11 to the Corner Gate, from the Tower of Ḥananel to the king's winery, they will inhabit her. There will be
12 no more devastation, and Jerusalem will live in safety. This will be the plague that the LORD
will bring upon all the peoples who fought against Jerusalem: their flesh will rot away as they stand on
13 their feet, their eyes will rot in their sockets, and their tongues will rot in their mouths. This is what will
be: on that day the turmoil the LORD brings on them will be great, and each man will seize another
14 by the arm and raise his fist against his neighbor's fist. And Yehuda too will fight in Jerusalem, and the
wealth of all the surrounding nations, great quantities of gold, silver, and clothing, will be gathered
15 in. There will be a plague just like this plague on the horses, the mules, the camels, and the donkeys,
16 and on every animal in those camps. This is what will be: all those remaining from all the nations who
came up against Jerusalem will go up year after year to bow down to the King, LORD of Hosts, and to
17 celebrate the Festival of Tabernacles. This is what will be: the families of the land who do not go up
18 to Jerusalem and bow down to the King, LORD of Hosts, rain shall not fall for them. If the family of
Egypt does not go up, does not come, it shall not be upon them. This will be the plague that the LORD
19 will bring upon the nations who do not go up to celebrate the Festival of Tabernacles. Such will be the
punishment of Egypt and the punishment of all the nations who do not come up to celebrate the Festi-
20 val of Tabernacles. On that day even the bells of the horses will be inscribed "sacred to the LORD," and
21 the pots in the House of the LORD will be like basins before the Altar. This is what will be: every pot
in Jerusalem and in Yehuda will be sacred to the LORD of Hosts, and all those who come to sacrifice
will take them and will cook in them. On that day, there will be no more need for traders in the House
of the LORD of Hosts.

HAFTARA FOR THE SECOND DAY OF SUKKOT IN THE DIASPORA

The maftir of the second day of Sukkot in the Diaspora is read from Numbers 29:12–16.

I KINGS

Yemenites begin here

7 51 When all the work that King Shlomo did for the House of the LORD was finished, Shlomo brought
what David his father had dedicated – the silver, the gold, and the vessels – and placed them in the
8 1 treasury of the House of the LORD. Then Shlomo assembled the elders of Israel – all the heads
of the tribes, the ancestral leaders of the Israelites – before King Shlomo in Jerusalem, to bring up the

Israel convene in Jerusalem, and the priests bring the holy Ark into the new Sanctuary to begin its service. King Shlomo opens the ceremony with a long address, the conclusion of which will be read as the *haftara* of Shemini Atzeret, calling

ג תשגלנה וְיָצָא חֲצִי הָעִיר בַּגּוֹלָה וְיֶתֶר הָעָם לֹא יִכָּרֵת מִן־הָעִיר׃ וְיָצָא יהוה וְנִלְחַם בַּגּוֹיִם הָהֵם כְּיוֹם תִּשָּׁכַבְנָה
ד הִלָּחֲמוֹ בְּיוֹם קְרָב׃ וְעָמְדוּ רַגְלָיו בַּיּוֹם־הַהוּא עַל־הַר הַזֵּתִים אֲשֶׁר עַל־פְּנֵי יְרוּשָׁלִַם מִקֶּדֶם וְנִבְקַע הַר
ה הַזֵּיתִים מֵחֶצְיוֹ מִזְרָחָה וָיָמָּה גֵּיא גְּדוֹלָה מְאֹד וּמָשׁ חֲצִי הָהָר צָפוֹנָה וְחֶצְיוֹ נֶגְבָּה׃ וְנַסְתֶּם גֵּיא־הָרַי
כִּי־יַגִּיעַ גֵּי־הָרִים אֶל־אָצַל וְנַסְתֶּם כַּאֲשֶׁר נַסְתֶּם מִפְּנֵי הָרַעַשׁ בִּימֵי עֻזִּיָּה מֶלֶךְ־יְהוּדָה וּבָא יהוה אֱלֹהַי
ו ז כָּל־קְדֹשִׁים עִמָּךְ׃ וְהָיָה בַּיּוֹם הַהוּא לֹא־יִהְיֶה אוֹר יְקָרוֹת יקפאון׃ וְהָיָה יוֹם־אֶחָד הוּא יִוָּדַע לַיהוה וְקִפָּאוֹן
ח לֹא־יוֹם וְלֹא־לָיְלָה וְהָיָה לְעֵת־עֶרֶב יִהְיֶה־אוֹר׃ וְהָיָה | בַּיּוֹם הַהוּא יֵצְאוּ מַיִם־חַיִּים מִירוּשָׁלִַם חֶצְיָם
ט אֶל־הַיָּם הַקַּדְמוֹנִי וְחֶצְיָם אֶל־הַיָּם הָאַחֲרוֹן בַּקַּיִץ וּבָחֹרֶף יִהְיֶה׃ וְהָיָה יהוה לְמֶלֶךְ עַל־כָּל־הָאָרֶץ בַּיּוֹם
י הַהוּא יִהְיֶה יהוה אֶחָד וּשְׁמוֹ אֶחָד׃ יִסּוֹב כָּל־הָאָרֶץ כָּעֲרָבָה מִגֶּבַע לְרִמּוֹן נֶגֶב יְרוּשָׁלִָם וְרָאֲמָה וְיָשְׁבָה
תַחְתֶּיהָ לְמִשַּׁעַר בִּנְיָמִן עַד־מְקוֹם שַׁעַר הָרִאשׁוֹן עַד־שַׁעַר הַפִּנִּים וּמִגְדַּל חֲנַנְאֵל עַד יִקְבֵי הַמֶּלֶךְ׃
יא יב וְיָשְׁבוּ בָהּ וְחֵרֶם לֹא יִהְיֶה־עוֹד וְיָשְׁבָה יְרוּשָׁלִַם לָבֶטַח׃ וְזֹאת | תִּהְיֶה הַמַּגֵּפָה אֲשֶׁר
יִגֹּף יהוה אֶת־כָּל־הָעַמִּים אֲשֶׁר צָבְאוּ עַל־יְרוּשָׁלִָם הָמֵק | בְּשָׂרוֹ וְהוּא עֹמֵד עַל־רַגְלָיו וְעֵינָיו תִּמַּקְנָה
יג בְחֹרֵיהֶן וּלְשׁוֹנוֹ תִּמַּק בְּפִיהֶם׃ וְהָיָה בַּיּוֹם הַהוּא תִּהְיֶה מְהוּמַת־יהוה רַבָּה בָּהֶם וְהֶחֱזִיקוּ אִישׁ יַד רֵעֵהוּ
יד וְעָלְתָה יָדוֹ עַל־יַד רֵעֵהוּ׃ וְגַם־יְהוּדָה תִּלָּחֵם בִּירוּשָׁלִָם וְאֻסַּף חֵיל כָּל־הַגּוֹיִם סָבִיב זָהָב וָכֶסֶף וּבְגָדִים
טו לָרֹב מְאֹד׃ וְכֵן תִּהְיֶה מַגֵּפַת הַסּוּס הַפֶּרֶד הַגָּמָל וְהַחֲמוֹר וְכָל־הַבְּהֵמָה אֲשֶׁר יִהְיֶה בַּמַּחֲנוֹת הָהֵמָּה
טז כַּמַּגֵּפָה הַזֹּאת׃ וְהָיָה כָּל־הַנּוֹתָר מִכָּל־הַגּוֹיִם הַבָּאִים עַל־יְרוּשָׁלִָם וְעָלוּ מִדֵּי שָׁנָה בְשָׁנָה לְהִשְׁתַּחֲוֺת
יז לְמֶלֶךְ יהוה צְבָאוֹת וְלָחֹג אֶת־חַג הַסֻּכּוֹת׃ וְהָיָה אֲשֶׁר לֹא־יַעֲלֶה מֵאֵת מִשְׁפְּחוֹת הָאָרֶץ אֶל־יְרוּשָׁלִַם
יח לְהִשְׁתַּחֲוֺת לְמֶלֶךְ יהוה צְבָאוֹת וְלֹא עֲלֵיהֶם יִהְיֶה הַגָּשֶׁם׃ וְאִם־מִשְׁפַּחַת מִצְרַיִם לֹא־תַעֲלֶה וְלֹא בָאָה
יט וְלֹא עֲלֵיהֶם תִּהְיֶה הַמַּגֵּפָה אֲשֶׁר יִגֹּף יהוה אֶת־הַגּוֹיִם אֲשֶׁר לֹא יַעֲלוּ לָחֹג אֶת־חַג הַסֻּכּוֹת׃ זֹאת תִּהְיֶה
כ חַטַּאת מִצְרָיִם וְחַטַּאת כָּל־הַגּוֹיִם אֲשֶׁר לֹא יַעֲלוּ לָחֹג אֶת־חַג הַסֻּכּוֹת׃ בַּיּוֹם הַהוּא יִהְיֶה עַל־מְצִלּוֹת
כא הַסּוּס קֹדֶשׁ לַיהוה וְהָיָה הַסִּירוֹת בְּבֵית יהוה כַּמִּזְרָקִים לִפְנֵי הַמִּזְבֵּחַ׃ וְהָיָה כָּל־סִיר בִּירוּשָׁלִַם וּבִיהוּדָה
קֹדֶשׁ לַיהוה צְבָאוֹת וּבָאוּ כָּל־הַזֹּבְחִים וְלָקְחוּ מֵהֶם וּבִשְּׁלוּ בָהֶם וְלֹא־יִהְיֶה כְנַעֲנִי עוֹד בְּבֵית־יהוה
צְבָאוֹת בַּיּוֹם הַהוּא׃

הפטרת יום שני של סוכות בחוץ לארץ

The מפטיר of יום שני של סוכות בחוץ לארץ is read from במדבר כט, יב–טז.

ז נא וַתִּשְׁלַם כָּל־הַמְּלָאכָה אֲשֶׁר עָשָׂה הַמֶּלֶךְ שְׁלֹמֹה בֵּית יהוה וַיָּבֵא שְׁלֹמֹה אֶת־קָדְשֵׁי | דָּוִד אָבִיו אֶת־ מלכים א
ח א הַכֶּסֶף וְאֶת־הַזָּהָב וְאֶת־הַכֵּלִים נָתַן בְּאֹצְרוֹת בֵּית יהוה׃ אָז יַקְהֵל שְׁלֹמֹה אֶת־זִקְנֵי יִשְׂרָאֵל

Yemenites begin here

SECOND DAY OF SUKKOT IN THE DIASPORA

The *haftara* recounts the most important event of Jewish history to have occurred on Sukkot: the inauguration of King Shlomo's Temple. With pomp and fanfare, all the people of ▶

2 Ark of the Lord's Covenant from the City of David, Zion. *All the men of Israel assembled before King
3 Shlomo in the month of Etanim, the seventh month, at the festival. When all the elders of Israel had
4 arrived, the priests lifted up the Ark and brought up the Ark of the LORD, the Tent of Meeting, and all
5 the sacred vessels in the Tent. While the priests and the Levites brought them up, King Shlomo and
the whole community of Israel, who had met him before the Ark, sacrificed sheep and oxen – far too
6 many to number or count. The priests brought the Ark of the Lord's Covenant to its place – to the
7 House's Inner Sanctuary, the Holy of Holies, to under the shade of the wings of the cherubim. For the
wings of the cherubim were spread over the place of the Ark so that the cherubim sheltered the Ark
8 and its poles from above. The poles extended so that the ends of the poles were visible from the Holy
Place in front of the Inner Sanctuary, but they could not be seen from the outside, and they are there
9 to this day. The Ark contained nothing but the two stone tablets Moshe placed there at Ḥorev when
10 the LORD made a covenant with the Israelites as they left the land of Egypt. And as the priests left the
11 Holy Place, a cloud filled the House of the LORD; the priests could not stand and serve because of the
12 cloud, for the glory of the LORD had filled the House of the LORD. Then Shlomo declared:
13 "The LORD promised that He would dwell in deep mist; I have now built You an exalted House, a per-
14 manent place for Your abode." And the king turned his face and blessed the whole assembly of Israel,
15 while the whole assembly of Israel stood. "Blessed is the LORD, God of Israel," he said, "who made a
promise to my father David with His own mouth and has now fulfilled it with His own hand, saying:
16 From the day I brought My people, Israel, out of Egypt, I never chose a city from among all the tribes
of Israel, to build a House where My name would be; but I chose David to be over My people Israel.
17 18 My father David had his heart set on building a House for the name of the LORD, God of Israel. But
the LORD said to my father David: Though you have set your heart on building a House for My name,
19 and though you have set your heart well, you will not be the one to build the House. But your son, the
20 issue of your own loins – he will be the one to build the House for My name. The LORD has fulfilled
the promise He made; I have risen in my father's stead, and I sit upon Israel's throne, as the LORD
21 promised. I have built the House for the name of the LORD, God of Israel. And there I have set a place
for the Ark, which contains the covenant that the LORD made with our ancestors when He brought
them out of the land of Egypt."

Ashkenazim and Sepharadim begin here

Haftarat Shabbat Ḥol HaMoed Sukkot

The maftir of Shabbat Ḥol HaMoed Sukkot is read the offering for the respective day (in the Diaspora adding the offering for the previous day).

EZEKIEL

Yemenites begin here

38 1 2 The word of the LORD came to me: "Man, set your face toward Gog of the land of Magog, the chief prince
3 of Meshekh and Tuval. Prophesy against him; say: So says the Lord GOD: Behold – I am against you,
4 Gog, chief prince of Meshekh and Tuval. I will turn you around, fix hooks into your jaw, and bring you
out with all your troops, horses, and cavalry in complete regalia, a great horde with shields and bucklers,
5 6 all wielding swords. And with them Persia, Kush, and Put, all with shields and helmets; Gomer and all her

SHABBAT ḤOL HAMOED SUKKOT

The fitting counterpart to Zekharya's apocalyptic prophecy, read on the first day of Sukkot, is Yeḥezkel's premonition of the war of Gog and Magog, read on Shabbat of Ḥol HaMoed. Here too we witness a titanic assault against Israel by the surrounding nations in the end of days. And here too, it

אֶת־כׇּל־רָאשֵׁי הַמַּטּוֹת נְשִׂיאֵי הָאָבוֹת לִבְנֵי יִשְׂרָאֵל אֶל־הַמֶּלֶךְ שְׁלֹמֹה יְרוּשָׁלָ͏ִם לְהַעֲלוֹת אֶת־אֲרוֹן
ב בְּרִית־יְהֹוָה מֵעִיר דָּוִד הִיא צִיּוֹן׃* וַיִּקָּהֲלוּ אֶל־הַמֶּלֶךְ שְׁלֹמֹה כׇּל־אִישׁ יִשְׂרָאֵל בְּיֶרַח הָאֵתָנִים בֶּחָג הוּא *Ashkenazim and Sepharadim begin here*
ג ד הַחֹדֶשׁ הַשְּׁבִיעִי׃ וַיָּבֹאוּ כֹּל זִקְנֵי יִשְׂרָאֵל וַיִּשְׂאוּ הַכֹּהֲנִים אֶת־הָאָרוֹן׃ וַיַּעֲלוּ אֶת־אֲרוֹן יְהֹוָה וְאֶת־אֹהֶל
ה מוֹעֵד וְאֶת־כׇּל־כְּלֵי הַקֹּדֶשׁ אֲשֶׁר בָּאֹהֶל וַיַּעֲלוּ אֹתָם הַכֹּהֲנִים וְהַלְוִיִּם׃ וְהַמֶּלֶךְ שְׁלֹמֹה וְכׇל־עֲדַת יִשְׂרָאֵל
ו הַנּוֹעָדִים עָלָיו אִתּוֹ לִפְנֵי הָאָרוֹן מְזַבְּחִים צֹאן וּבָקָר אֲשֶׁר לֹא־יִסָּפְרוּ וְלֹא יִמָּנוּ מֵרֹב׃ וַיָּבִאוּ הַכֹּהֲנִים
ז אֶת־אֲרוֹן בְּרִית־יְהֹוָה אֶל־מְקוֹמוֹ אֶל־דְּבִיר הַבַּיִת אֶל־קֹדֶשׁ הַקֳּדָשִׁים אֶל־תַּחַת כַּנְפֵי הַכְּרוּבִים׃ כִּי
ח הַכְּרוּבִים פֹּרְשִׂים כְּנָפַיִם אֶל־מְקוֹם הָאָרוֹן וַיָּסֹכּוּ הַכְּרֻבִים עַל־הָאָרוֹן וְעַל־בַּדָּיו מִלְמָעְלָה׃ וַיַּאֲרִכוּ
ט הַבַּדִּים וַיֵּרָאוּ רָאשֵׁי הַבַּדִּים מִן־הַקֹּדֶשׁ עַל־פְּנֵי הַדְּבִיר וְלֹא יֵרָאוּ הַחוּצָה וַיִּהְיוּ שָׁם עַד הַיּוֹם הַזֶּה׃ אֵין
בָּאָרוֹן רַק שְׁנֵי לֻחוֹת הָאֲבָנִים אֲשֶׁר הִנִּחַ שָׁם מֹשֶׁה בְּחֹרֵב אֲשֶׁר כָּרַת יְהֹוָה עִם־בְּנֵי יִשְׂרָאֵל בְּצֵאתָם
י יא מֵאֶרֶץ מִצְרָיִם׃ וַיְהִי בְּצֵאת הַכֹּהֲנִים מִן־הַקֹּדֶשׁ וְהֶעָנָן מָלֵא אֶת־בֵּית יְהֹוָה׃ וְלֹא־יָכְלוּ הַכֹּהֲנִים לַעֲמֹד
יב לְשָׁרֵת מִפְּנֵי הֶעָנָן כִּי־מָלֵא כְבוֹד־יְהֹוָה אֶת־בֵּית יְהֹוָה׃ אָז אָמַר שְׁלֹמֹה יְהֹוָה אָמַר לִשְׁכֹּן
יג יד בָּעֲרָפֶל׃ בָּנֹה בָנִיתִי בֵּית זְבֻל לָךְ מָכוֹן לְשִׁבְתְּךָ עוֹלָמִים׃ וַיַּסֵּב הַמֶּלֶךְ אֶת־פָּנָיו וַיְבָרֶךְ אֵת כׇּל־קְהַל
טו יִשְׂרָאֵל וְכׇל־קְהַל יִשְׂרָאֵל עֹמֵד׃ וַיֹּאמֶר בָּרוּךְ יְהֹוָה אֱלֹהֵי יִשְׂרָאֵל אֲשֶׁר דִּבֶּר בְּפִיו אֵת דָּוִד אָבִי וּבְיָדוֹ
טז מִלֵּא לֵאמֹר׃ מִן־הַיּוֹם אֲשֶׁר הוֹצֵאתִי אֶת־עַמִּי אֶת־יִשְׂרָאֵל מִמִּצְרַיִם לֹא־בָחַרְתִּי בְעִיר מִכֹּל שִׁבְטֵי
יז יִשְׂרָאֵל לִבְנוֹת בַּיִת לִהְיוֹת שְׁמִי שָׁם וָאֶבְחַר בְּדָוִד לִהְיוֹת עַל־עַמִּי יִשְׂרָאֵל׃ וַיְהִי עִם־לְבַב דָּוִד אָבִי
יח לִבְנוֹת בַּיִת לְשֵׁם יְהֹוָה אֱלֹהֵי יִשְׂרָאֵל׃ וַיֹּאמֶר יְהֹוָה אֶל־דָּוִד אָבִי יַעַן אֲשֶׁר הָיָה עִם־לְבָבְךָ לִבְנוֹת בַּיִת
יט לִשְׁמִי הֱטִיבֹתָ כִּי הָיָה עִם־לְבָבֶךָ׃ רַק אַתָּה לֹא תִבְנֶה הַבָּיִת כִּי אִם־בִּנְךָ הַיֹּצֵא מֵחֲלָצֶיךָ הוּא־יִבְנֶה
כ הַבַּיִת לִשְׁמִי׃ וַיָּקֶם יְהֹוָה אֶת־דְּבָרוֹ אֲשֶׁר דִּבֵּר וָאָקֻם תַּחַת דָּוִד אָבִי וָאֵשֵׁב ׀ עַל־כִּסֵּא יִשְׂרָאֵל כַּאֲשֶׁר
כא דִּבֶּר יְהֹוָה וָאֶבְנֶה הַבַּיִת לְשֵׁם יְהֹוָה אֱלֹהֵי יִשְׂרָאֵל׃ וָאָשִׂם שָׁם מָקוֹם לָאָרוֹן אֲשֶׁר־שָׁם בְּרִית יְהֹוָה
אֲשֶׁר כָּרַת עִם־אֲבֹתֵינוּ בְּהוֹצִיאוֹ אֹתָם מֵאֶרֶץ מִצְרָיִם׃

הפטרת שבת חול המועד סוכות

The מפטיר *of* שבת חול המועד סוכות *is read from the offering for the respective day (in the Diaspora adding the offering for the previous day).*

לח א ב וַיְהִי דְבַר־יְהֹוָה אֵלַי לֵאמֹר׃ בֶּן־אָדָם שִׂים פָּנֶיךָ אֶל־גּוֹג אֶרֶץ הַמָּגוֹג נְשִׂיא רֹאשׁ מֶשֶׁךְ וְתֻבָל וְהִנָּבֵא יחזקאל *Yemenites begin here*
ג ד עָלָיו׃ וְאָמַרְתָּ כֹּה אָמַר אֲדֹנָי יֱהֹוִה הִנְנִי אֵלֶיךָ גּוֹג נְשִׂיא רֹאשׁ מֶשֶׁךְ וְתֻבָל׃ וְשׁוֹבַבְתִּיךָ וְנָתַתִּי חַחִים
בִּלְחָיֶיךָ וְהוֹצֵאתִי אוֹתְךָ וְאֶת־כׇּל־חֵילֶךָ סוּסִים וּפָרָשִׁים לְבֻשֵׁי מִכְלוֹל כֻּלָּם קָהָל רָב צִנָּה וּמָגֵן תֹּפְשֵׂי

on God to answer the prayers of His people. The role of the Temple as an address of prayer and supplication echoes the themes of prayers for rain and deliverance that characterize Sukkot's special *hoshanot* petitions. During these *hoshanot,* we march around the synagogue *bima,* in remembrance of those prayers that took place on that holiday in that ancient Temple, around its enormous altar.

7 forces; Beit Togarma from the far edges of the north and all her forces – many peoples with you. Prepare,
8 ready yourself, you and all of the hordes assembled around you; you are their guarding commander. After
many days you will be summoned; at the end of years, you will come against the land which has been
restored after the sword, which has been gathered back from many nations upon the mountains of Israel
that long lay in ruins – she who will have been brought out from the nations, a people who all now live se-
9 curely. You will advance, you will come like a devastating storm, and you will be like a cloud covering the
10 land – you, all your forces, and the many peoples with you. So says the Lord GOD: On
11 that day, certain thoughts will occur to you; you will devise an evil scheme. You will say, 'I will advance
against the land of open villages; I will come upon those who are tranquil, living securely, all of whom live
12 in unwalled towns and without bars or gates,' to ransack spoils and seize loot, to turn your hand against
reinhabited ruins and a people gathered in from the nations who have built up livestock and possessions,
13 who live at the center of the land. Sheba, Dedan, and the merchants of Tarshish and all her young warriors will say to you, 'Have you come to ransack spoils? Have you assembled your hordes to seize loot – to
14 carry off silver and gold, to take livestock and possessions, to ransack great spoils?' So, prophesy,
Man; say to Gog: So says the Lord GOD: Surely, on the day that My people Israel lives securely, you will
15 know it, and you will come from your place, from the far edges of the north, you and many peoples with
16 you, all of them on horseback, with a great horde and a mighty army. You will advance against My people
Israel like a cloud covering the land. This is what will be in the end of days, and I will bring you to My land
17 so that the nations will know Me when I am sanctified through you before their eyes, Gog. So
says the Lord GOD: It is you whom I spoke of in former days through My servants the prophets of Israel,
18 who in those days, for years, prophesied that I would bring you against them. *And it shall be, *Ashkenazim and Sepharadim begin here*
19 on that day, on the day that Gog comes onto the soil of Israel, says the Lord GOD: My fury will blaze; in
My passionate anger, in the fire of My rage I have spoken: Surely on that day there will be a great quaking
20 upon the soil of Israel; they will quake before Me: the fish of the seas and the birds of the sky, the animals
of the field, every creeping thing that crawls upon the earth, and every man on the face of the earth; the
21 mountains will be demolished, the terraces will collapse, and every wall shall fall to the ground. I will call
the sword down against him across My mountains, says the Lord GOD; each man's sword will be turned
22 against his brother. I will execute judgment on him with pestilence and blood; I will pour down torrential
rain and crystal hailstone, fire and sulfur over him and his troops, and over the many peoples who are with
23 him. I will be magnified, I will be sanctified, and I will make Myself known in the eyes of many nations –
39 1 and they will know that I am the LORD.* And you, Man, prophesy against Gog and say: So *Yemenites end here*
2 says the Lord GOD: Behold – I am against you, Gog, chief prince of Meshekh and Tuval. I will turn you
around; I will drive you forward; I will make you advance from the far edges of the north and bring you
3 to the mountains of Israel. I will strike your bow from your left hand; I will make the arrows fall from your
4 right; upon the mountains of Israel you will fall – you, all your troops, and the peoples who are with you.
5 I will give you up to birds of prey of every kind and to the animals of the field as food; upon the open field
6 you will fall, for I have spoken, says the Lord GOD. I will set loose fire on Magog and on those living se-
7 curely in the coastlands, and they will know that I am the LORD. I will make My holy name known among
My people Israel; I will no longer allow My holy name to be desecrated, and the nations will know that
8 I am the LORD, holy in Israel. Behold: it is coming, it will be, says the Lord GOD: This is the day I have
spoken of. The inhabitants of the cities of Israel will come out, and they will kindle and burn the weapons,
9 the shields and bucklers, the bows and arrows, and the clubs and spears; they will burn them as fuel for
10 fire for seven years. They will not take wood from the fields or chop down trees from the forests, for they
will fuel their fires with weapons. They will ransack those who despoiled them and loot those who looted
11 them, says the Lord GOD. And it will happen on that day: I will grant Gog a burial place there in

ה ו חֲרָבוֹת כֻּלָּם: פָּרַס כּוּשׁ וּפוּט אִתָּם כֻּלָּם מָגֵן וְכוֹבָע: גֹּמֶר וְכָל־אֲגַפֶּיהָ בֵּית תּוֹגַרְמָה יַרְכְּתֵי צָפוֹן וְאֶת־
ז כָּל־אֲגַפָּיו עַמִּים רַבִּים אִתָּךְ: הִכֹּן וְהָכֵן לְךָ אַתָּה וְכָל־קְהָלֶךָ הַנִּקְהָלִים עָלֶיךָ וְהָיִיתָ לָהֶם לְמִשְׁמָר:
ח מִיָּמִים רַבִּים תִּפָּקֵד בְּאַחֲרִית הַשָּׁנִים תָּבוֹא | אֶל־אֶרֶץ | מְשׁוֹבֶבֶת מֵחֶרֶב מְקֻבֶּצֶת מֵעַמִּים רַבִּים עַל
ט הָרֵי יִשְׂרָאֵל אֲשֶׁר־הָיוּ לְחָרְבָּה תָּמִיד וְהִיא מֵעַמִּים הוּצָאָה וְיָשְׁבוּ לָבֶטַח כֻּלָּם: וְעָלִיתָ כַּשֹּׁאָה תָבוֹא
י כֶּעָנָן לְכַסּוֹת הָאָרֶץ תִּהְיֶה אַתָּה וְכָל־אֲגַפֶּיךָ וְעַמִּים רַבִּים אוֹתָךְ: כֹּה אָמַר אֲדֹנָי יֱהֹוִה
יא וְהָיָה | בַּיּוֹם הַהוּא יַעֲלוּ דְבָרִים עַל־לְבָבֶךָ וְחָשַׁבְתָּ מַחֲשֶׁבֶת רָעָה: וְאָמַרְתָּ אֶעֱלֶה עַל־אֶרֶץ פְּרָזוֹת
יב אָבוֹא הַשֹּׁקְטִים יֹשְׁבֵי לָבֶטַח כֻּלָּם יֹשְׁבִים בְּאֵין חוֹמָה וּבְרִיחַ וּדְלָתַיִם אֵין לָהֶם: לִשְׁלֹל שָׁלָל וְלָבֹז בַּז
יג לְהָשִׁיב יָדְךָ עַל־חֳרָבוֹת נוֹשָׁבֹת וְאֶל־עַם מְאֻסָּף מִגּוֹיִם עֹשֶׂה מִקְנֶה וְקִנְיָן יֹשְׁבֵי עַל־טַבּוּר הָאָרֶץ: שְׁבָא
וּדְדָן וְסֹחֲרֵי תַרְשִׁישׁ וְכָל־כְּפִרֶיהָ יֹאמְרוּ לְךָ הֲלִשְׁלֹל שָׁלָל אַתָּה בָא הֲלָבֹז בַּז הִקְהַלְתָּ קְהָלֶךָ לָשֵׂאת |
יד כֶּסֶף וְזָהָב לָקַחַת מִקְנֶה וְקִנְיָן לִשְׁלֹל שָׁלָל גָּדוֹל: לָכֵן הִנָּבֵא בֶן־אָדָם וְאָמַרְתָּ לְגוֹג כֹּה
טו אָמַר אֲדֹנָי יֱהֹוִה הֲלוֹא | בַּיּוֹם הַהוּא בְּשֶׁבֶת עַמִּי יִשְׂרָאֵל לָבֶטַח תֵּדָע: וּבָאתָ מִמְּקוֹמְךָ מִיַּרְכְּתֵי צָפוֹן
טז אַתָּה וְעַמִּים רַבִּים אִתָּךְ רֹכְבֵי סוּסִים כֻּלָּם קָהָל גָּדוֹל וְחַיִל רָב: וְעָלִיתָ עַל־עַמִּי יִשְׂרָאֵל כֶּעָנָן לְכַסּוֹת
הָאָרֶץ בְּאַחֲרִית הַיָּמִים תִּהְיֶה וַהֲבִאוֹתִיךָ עַל־אַרְצִי לְמַעַן דַּעַת הַגּוֹיִם אֹתִי בְּהִקָּדְשִׁי בְךָ לְעֵינֵיהֶם
יז גּוֹג: כֹּה־אָמַר אֲדֹנָי יֱהֹוִה הַאַתָּה־הוּא אֲשֶׁר־דִּבַּרְתִּי בְּיָמִים קַדְמוֹנִים בְּיַד עֲבָדַי נְבִיאֵי יִשְׂרָאֵל
Ashkenazim and Sepharadim begin here
יח הַנִּבְּאִים בַּיָּמִים הָהֵם שָׁנִים לְהָבִיא אֹתְךָ עֲלֵיהֶם: *וְהָיָה | בַּיּוֹם הַהוּא בְּיוֹם בּוֹא גוֹג עַל־
יט אַדְמַת יִשְׂרָאֵל נְאֻם אֲדֹנָי יֱהֹוִה תַּעֲלֶה חֲמָתִי בְּאַפִּי: וּבְקִנְאָתִי בְאֵשׁ־עֶבְרָתִי דִּבַּרְתִּי אִם־לֹא | בַּיּוֹם
כ הַהוּא יִהְיֶה רַעַשׁ גָּדוֹל עַל אַדְמַת יִשְׂרָאֵל: וְרָעֲשׁוּ מִפָּנַי דְּגֵי הַיָּם וְעוֹף הַשָּׁמַיִם וְחַיַּת הַשָּׂדֶה וְכָל־הָרֶמֶשׂ
הָרֹמֵשׂ עַל־הָאֲדָמָה וְכֹל הָאָדָם אֲשֶׁר עַל־פְּנֵי הָאֲדָמָה וְנֶהֶרְסוּ הֶהָרִים וְנָפְלוּ הַמַּדְרֵגוֹת וְכָל־חוֹמָה
כא כב לָאָרֶץ תִּפּוֹל: וְקָרָאתִי עָלָיו לְכָל־הָרַי חֶרֶב נְאֻם אֲדֹנָי יֱהֹוִה חֶרֶב אִישׁ בְּאָחִיו תִּהְיֶה: וְנִשְׁפַּטְתִּי אִתּוֹ
בְּדֶבֶר וּבְדָם וְגֶשֶׁם שׁוֹטֵף וְאַבְנֵי אֶלְגָּבִישׁ אֵשׁ וְגָפְרִית אַמְטִיר עָלָיו וְעַל־אֲגַפָּיו וְעַל־עַמִּים רַבִּים אֲשֶׁר
Yemenites end here
כג א אִתּוֹ: וְהִתְגַּדִּלְתִּי וְהִתְקַדִּשְׁתִּי וְנוֹדַעְתִּי לְעֵינֵי גּוֹיִם רַבִּים וְיָדְעוּ כִּי־אֲנִי יְהוָה:* וְאַתָּה לט
ב בֶן־אָדָם הִנָּבֵא עַל־גּוֹג וְאָמַרְתָּ כֹּה אָמַר אֲדֹנָי יֱהֹוִה הִנְנִי אֵלֶיךָ גּוֹג נְשִׂיא רֹאשׁ מֶשֶׁךְ וְתֻבָל: וְשֹׁבַבְתִּיךָ
ג וְשִׁשֵּׁאתִיךָ וְהַעֲלִיתִיךָ מִיַּרְכְּתֵי צָפוֹן וַהֲבִאוֹתִךָ עַל־הָרֵי יִשְׂרָאֵל: וְהִכֵּיתִי קַשְׁתְּךָ מִיַּד שְׂמֹאולְךָ וְחִצֶּיךָ
ד מִיַּד יְמִינְךָ אַפִּיל: עַל־הָרֵי יִשְׂרָאֵל תִּפּוֹל אַתָּה וְכָל־אֲגַפֶּיךָ וְעַמִּים אֲשֶׁר אִתָּךְ לְעֵיט צִפּוֹר כָּל־כָּנָף וְחַיַּת
ה ו הַשָּׂדֶה נְתַתִּיךָ לְאָכְלָה: עַל־פְּנֵי הַשָּׂדֶה תִּפּוֹל כִּי אֲנִי דִבַּרְתִּי נְאֻם אֲדֹנָי יֱהֹוִה: וְשִׁלַּחְתִּי־אֵשׁ בְּמָגוֹג
ז וּבְיֹשְׁבֵי הָאִיִּים לָבֶטַח וְיָדְעוּ כִּי־אֲנִי יְהוָה: וְאֶת־שֵׁם קָדְשִׁי אוֹדִיעַ בְּתוֹךְ עַמִּי יִשְׂרָאֵל וְלֹא־אַחֵל אֶת־
ח שֵׁם־קָדְשִׁי עוֹד וְיָדְעוּ הַגּוֹיִם כִּי־אֲנִי יְהוָה קָדוֹשׁ בְּיִשְׂרָאֵל: הִנֵּה בָאָה וְנִהְיָתָה נְאֻם אֲדֹנָי יֱהֹוִה הוּא
ט הַיּוֹם אֲשֶׁר דִּבַּרְתִּי: וְיָצְאוּ יֹשְׁבֵי | עָרֵי יִשְׂרָאֵל וּבִעֲרוּ וְהִשִּׂיקוּ בְּנֶשֶׁק וּמָגֵן וְצִנָּה בְּקֶשֶׁת וּבְחִצִּים וּבְמַקֵּל
י יָד וּבְרֹמַח וּבִעֲרוּ בָהֶם אֵשׁ שֶׁבַע שָׁנִים: וְלֹא־יִשְׂאוּ עֵצִים מִן־הַשָּׂדֶה וְלֹא יַחְטְבוּ מִן־הַיְּעָרִים כִּי בַנֶּשֶׁק

is God who will save Israel, fighting by Himself against the besieging nations and devastating them with supernatural wonders and plagues. As a result, God promises, "I will be magnified, I will be sanctified, and I will make Myself known in the eyes of many nations – and they will know that I am the Lord." This recognition by all peoples that God alone is sovereign in the world is the universalist vision of the holiday of Sukkot.

Israel, the Valley of the Travelers, east of the sea, and it will block the travelers. Here they will bury Gog
12 and his horde; they will call it the Valley of the Horde of Gog. For seven months the House of Israel will
13 bury them to purify the land. All the people in the land shall bury them, and it will make them renowned
14 on the day of My glory, says the Lord God. They shall select men to cross the land constantly, burying the
invaders' remains that lie upon the ground – to purify it. They will search for a period of seven months.
15 Whenever these men assigned to cross the land see a human bone, they shall place a sign next to it until
16 the buriers have buried it in the Valley of the Horde of Gog. There will also be a city named Horde. Thus
they shall purify the land.

Haftarat Shemini Atzeret in the Diaspora

The maftir of Shemini Atzeret in the Diaspora is read from Numbers 29:35–30:1.

8 54 When Shlomo had finished offering the whole of this prayer and plea to the Lord, he rose from before
the Altar of the Lord, where he had been kneeling on his knees with his palms raised heavenward.
55 56 And he stood and blessed the whole assembly of Israel in a loud voice: "Blessed is the Lord, who has
granted rest to His people Israel, fulfilling all His promises," he said. "Not one thing is unfulfilled from
57 all the good promises He made through Moshe, His servant. May the Lord our God be with us as He
58 was with our ancestors; may He never leave us or abandon us. May He sway our hearts toward Him so
that we follow in all His ways and keep His commandments, laws and rulings that He commanded our
59 ancestors. May these words of mine, which I have pleaded before the Lord, stay close to the Lord our
God day and night, to uphold the cause of His servant and the cause of His people Israel as each day's
60 needs arise – so that all the peoples of the land will know that the Lord is God, and there is no other.
61 May your hearts be fully with the Lord our God, following His laws and keeping His command-
62 63 ments, as today." And the king, together with all of Israel, offered sacrifices before the Lord; Shlomo
sacrificed the peace sacrifices he offered to the Lord – twenty-two thousand cattle and one hundred
64 twenty thousand sheep – and thus the king and all of Israel dedicated the House of the Lord. On that
day, the king consecrated the center of the courtyard in front of the House of the Lord, for it was there
that he prepared the burnt offering, the grain offering, and the fats of the peace offerings. The bronze
altar before the Lord was too small to contain the burnt offering, the grain offering, and the fats of the
65 peace offerings. At that same time, Shlomo celebrated the festival together with all of Israel; they were
a great assembly, from Levo Ḥamat to the Wadi of Egypt, before the Lord our God for seven days and
66 seven days more – fourteen days in all. On the eighth day he sent the people off, and they blessed the
king; they went back to their homes joyful and glad at heart for all the goodness the Lord had shown
9 1 to David, His servant, and Israel, His people. * When Shlomo had finished building the House
of the Lord and the king's own house, and fulfilled every desire he wished to fulfill.

Yemenites, Chabad, and Minhag Anglia end here

Lord is God, and there is no other." The desire to see God recognized and worshipped by "all peoples of the land" is a central theme of Sukkot, expressed in the other *haftarot* read on the days leading up to Shemini Atzeret. His prayer and blessing ended, Shlomo turns to the service of the Sukkot holiday, which they celebrate for seven days. On the eighth day, Shemini Atzeret, he releases the people to their homes, but the Sages teach that they chose to remain to feast and rejoice for this last day of Shemini Atzeret, and returned home only afterward.

יא יְבַעֲרוּ־אֵשׁ וְשָׁלְלוּ אֶת־שֹׁלְלֵיהֶם וּבָזְזוּ אֶת־בֹּזְזֵיהֶם נְאֻם אֲדֹנָי יֱהֹוִה׃ וְהָיָה בַיּוֹם הַהוּא
אֶתֵּן לְגוֹג ׀ מְקוֹם־שָׁם קֶבֶר בְּיִשְׂרָאֵל גֵּי הָעֹבְרִים קִדְמַת הַיָּם וְחֹסֶמֶת הִיא אֶת־הָעֹבְרִים וְקָבְרוּ שָׁם
יב אֶת־גּוֹג וְאֶת־כָּל־הֲמוֹנֹה וְקָרְאוּ גֵּיא הֲמוֹן גּוֹג׃ וּקְבָרוּם בֵּית יִשְׂרָאֵל לְמַעַן טַהֵר אֶת־הָאָרֶץ שִׁבְעָה
יג יד חֳדָשִׁים׃ וְקָבְרוּ כָּל־עַם הָאָרֶץ וְהָיָה לָהֶם לְשֵׁם יוֹם הִכָּבְדִי נְאֻם אֲדֹנָי יֱהֹוִה׃ וְאַנְשֵׁי תָמִיד יַבְדִּילוּ עֹבְרִים
בָּאָרֶץ מְקַבְּרִים אֶת־הָעֹבְרִים אֶת־הַנּוֹתָרִים עַל־פְּנֵי הָאָרֶץ לְטַהֲרָהּ מִקְצֵה שִׁבְעָה־חֳדָשִׁים יַחְקֹרוּ׃
טו וְעָבְרוּ הָעֹבְרִים בָּאָרֶץ וְרָאָה עֶצֶם אָדָם וּבָנָה אֶצְלוֹ צִיּוּן עַד קָבְרוּ אֹתוֹ הַמְקַבְּרִים אֶל־גֵּיא הֲמוֹן גּוֹג׃
טז וְגַם שֶׁם־עִיר הֲמוֹנָה וְטִהֲרוּ הָאָרֶץ׃

הפטרת שמיני עצרת בחוץ לארץ

The מפטיר *of* שמיני עצרת בחוץ לארץ *is read from* במדבר כט, לה – ל, א.

מלכים א

ח נד וַיְהִי ׀ כְּכַלּוֹת שְׁלֹמֹה לְהִתְפַּלֵּל אֶל־יהוה אֵת כָּל־הַתְּפִלָּה וְהַתְּחִנָּה הַזֹּאת קָם מִלִּפְנֵי מִזְבַּח יהוה מִכְּרֹעַ
נה נו עַל־בִּרְכָּיו וְכַפָּיו פְּרֻשׂוֹת הַשָּׁמָיִם׃ וַיַּעֲמֹד וַיְבָרֶךְ אֵת כָּל־קְהַל יִשְׂרָאֵל קוֹל גָּדוֹל לֵאמֹר׃ בָּרוּךְ יהוה
אֲשֶׁר נָתַן מְנוּחָה לְעַמּוֹ יִשְׂרָאֵל כְּכֹל אֲשֶׁר דִּבֵּר לֹא־נָפַל דָּבָר אֶחָד מִכֹּל דְּבָרוֹ הַטּוֹב אֲשֶׁר דִּבֶּר בְּיַד
נז נח מֹשֶׁה עַבְדּוֹ׃ יְהִי יהוה אֱלֹהֵינוּ עִמָּנוּ כַּאֲשֶׁר הָיָה עִם־אֲבֹתֵינוּ אַל־יַעַזְבֵנוּ וְאַל־יִטְּשֵׁנוּ׃ לְהַטּוֹת לְבָבֵנוּ
נט אֵלָיו לָלֶכֶת בְּכָל־דְּרָכָיו וְלִשְׁמֹר מִצְוֺתָיו וְחֻקָּיו וּמִשְׁפָּטָיו אֲשֶׁר צִוָּה אֶת־אֲבֹתֵינוּ׃ וְיִהְיוּ דְבָרַי אֵלֶּה
אֲשֶׁר הִתְחַנַּנְתִּי לִפְנֵי יהוה קְרֹבִים אֶל־יהוה אֱלֹהֵינוּ יוֹמָם וָלָיְלָה לַעֲשׂוֹת ׀ מִשְׁפַּט עַבְדּוֹ וּמִשְׁפַּט עַמּוֹ
ס סא יִשְׂרָאֵל דְּבַר־יוֹם בְּיוֹמוֹ׃ לְמַעַן דַּעַת כָּל־עַמֵּי הָאָרֶץ כִּי יהוה הוּא הָאֱלֹהִים אֵין עוֹד׃ וְהָיָה לְבַבְכֶם
סב שָׁלֵם עִם יהוה אֱלֹהֵינוּ לָלֶכֶת בְּחֻקָּיו וְלִשְׁמֹר מִצְוֺתָיו כַּיּוֹם הַזֶּה׃ וְהַמֶּלֶךְ וְכָל־יִשְׂרָאֵל עִמּוֹ זֹבְחִים זֶבַח
סג לִפְנֵי יהוה׃ וַיִּזְבַּח שְׁלֹמֹה אֵת זֶבַח הַשְּׁלָמִים אֲשֶׁר זָבַח לַיהוה בָּקָר עֶשְׂרִים וּשְׁנַיִם אֶלֶף וְצֹאן מֵאָה
סד וְעֶשְׂרִים אָלֶף וַיַּחְנְכוּ אֶת־בֵּית יהוה הַמֶּלֶךְ וְכָל־בְּנֵי יִשְׂרָאֵל׃ בַּיּוֹם הַהוּא קִדַּשׁ הַמֶּלֶךְ אֶת־תּוֹךְ הֶחָצֵר
אֲשֶׁר לִפְנֵי בֵית־יהוה כִּי־עָשָׂה שָׁם אֶת־הָעֹלָה וְאֶת־הַמִּנְחָה וְאֵת חֶלְבֵי הַשְּׁלָמִים כִּי־מִזְבַּח הַנְּחֹשֶׁת
סה אֲשֶׁר לִפְנֵי יהוה קָטֹן מֵהָכִיל אֶת־הָעֹלָה וְאֶת־הַמִּנְחָה וְאֵת חֶלְבֵי הַשְּׁלָמִים׃ וַיַּעַשׂ שְׁלֹמֹה בָעֵת־הַהִיא ׀
אֶת־הֶחָג וְכָל־יִשְׂרָאֵל עִמּוֹ קָהָל גָּדוֹל מִלְּבוֹא חֲמָת ׀ עַד־נַחַל מִצְרַיִם לִפְנֵי יהוה אֱלֹהֵינוּ שִׁבְעַת יָמִים
סו וְשִׁבְעַת יָמִים אַרְבָּעָה עָשָׂר יוֹם׃ בַּיּוֹם הַשְּׁמִינִי שִׁלַּח אֶת־הָעָם וַיְבָרֲכוּ אֶת־הַמֶּלֶךְ וַיֵּלְכוּ לְאָהֳלֵיהֶם
ט א שְׂמֵחִים וְטוֹבֵי לֵב עַל כָּל־הַטּוֹבָה אֲשֶׁר עָשָׂה יהוה לְדָוִד עַבְדּוֹ וּלְיִשְׂרָאֵל עַמּוֹ׃* וַיְהִי
כְּכַלּוֹת שְׁלֹמֹה לִבְנוֹת אֶת־בֵּית־יהוה וְאֶת־בֵּית הַמֶּלֶךְ וְאֵת כָּל־חֵשֶׁק שְׁלֹמֹה אֲשֶׁר חָפֵץ לַעֲשׂוֹת׃

Yemenites, Chabad, and Minhag Anglia end here

SHEMINI ATZERET IN THE DIASPORA

This *haftara* concludes the great prayer of King Shlomo at the inauguration of the Temple, the beginning of which was read as the *haftara* for the second day of Sukkot. The petition ends with the memorable plea, recited at the end of each of the Sukkot *hoshana* prayers, that "these words of mine, which I have pleaded before the LORD, stay close to the LORD our God day and night, to uphold the cause of His servant and the cause of His people Israel as each day's needs arise – so that all the peoples of the land will know that the

Haftarat Simḥat Torah

The maftir of Simḥat Torah is read from Numbers 29:35–30:01.

1 1 After the death of Moshe, the Lord's servant, the Lord said to Moshe's disciple, Yehoshua son of
2 Nun: "Moshe, My servant, is dead; now arise, cross the Jordan here – you and all this people – to the
3 land that I am giving to the Israelites. I have given you every place your foot will tread, just as I prom-
4 ised Moshe. Your territory shall stretch from the wilderness and Lebanon here to the Great River, the
5 Euphrates River, and all the land of the Hittites, to the Great Sea where the sun sets. No one will be able
to stand against you for as long as you live; just as I was with Moshe, I will be with you. I will never let
6 you go, and I will never leave you. Be strong and brave, for you will bring this people into possession
7 of the land I swore to their ancestors to give them. But you must be strong and brave indeed to uphold
faithfully all the Torah that Moshe My servant commanded you; do not stray from it – neither right
8 nor left – so that you may triumph wherever you go. This book of Torah must never leave your lips;
contemplate it day and night, so that you will faithfully uphold all that is written within it. For then
9 your course will succeed; then you will triumph. Hear now – I have charged you to be strong and brave.
10 Do not be frightened or dismayed, for the Lord your God is with you wherever you go."* Ye- *Sepharadim end here*
11 hoshua commanded the officers of the people: "Cross through the camp and instruct the people: 'Pre- *Yemenites skip ahead*
pare provisions for yourselves, for in three days' time you are to cross the Jordan here, to come and take
12 possession of the land that the Lord your God is giving you as your own.'" Yehoshua then
13 told the Reubenites, the Gadites, and half the tribe of Menashe: "Remember what Moshe, the Lord's
14 servant, commanded you: The Lord your God has granted you rest and given you this land. Your
wives and little ones and your cattle shall dwell in the land that Moshe gave you across the Jordan, but
15 all your warriors shall cross over armed to join your brothers and assist them, until the Lord grants
rest like yours to your brothers and they too take possession of the land that the Lord your God is
giving them. Then you shall return to your own land, which Moshe, the Lord's servant, gave you on
16 the eastern side of the Jordan – and you shall take possession of it." They answered Yehoshua, saying,
17 "Whatever you have commanded us we shall do; wherever you send us we shall go. As we obeyed
18 Moshe, so we will obey you as long as the Lord your God is with you, as He was with Moshe. Whoever
rebels against your word or disobeys anything you command shall be put to death; only be strong and
brave."
6 27 The Lord was with Yehoshua, and his fame rang out across the land. *Yemenites add*

---

to actualize Moshe's vision of settling the land of Israel and establishing there an Israelite society committed to the covenant with God. By implication, this same story, and that same work, continues with us today. We must therefore take to our own hearts God's repeated word of encouragement to Yehoshua, also shouted as a refrain upon the completion of every book of the Torah: *Ḥazak* – "Be strong!"

הפטרת שמחת תורה

The מפטיר *of* שמחת תורה *is read from* במדבר כט, לה – ל, א.

א א ב ויהי אחרי מות משה עבד יהוה ויאמר יהוה אל־יהושע בן־נון משרת משה לאמר: משה עבדי מת יהושע
ועתה קום עבר את־הירדן הזה אתה וכל־העם הזה אל־הארץ אשר אנכי נתן להם לבני ישראל:
ג ד כל־מקום אשר תדרך כף־רגלכם בו לכם נתתיו כאשר דברתי אל־משה: מהמדבר והלבנון הזה
ה ועד־הנהר הגדול נהר־פרת כל ארץ החתים ועד־הים הגדול מבוא השמש יהיה גבולכם: לא־יתיצב
ו איש לפניך כל ימי חייך כאשר הייתי עם־משה אהיה עמך לא ארפך ולא אעזבך: חזק ואמץ כי אתה
ז תנחיל את־העם הזה את־הארץ אשר־נשבעתי לאבותם לתת להם: רק חזק ואמץ מאד לשמר
לעשות ככל־התורה אשר צוך משה עבדי אל־תסור ממנו ימין ושמאול למען תשכיל בכל אשר
ח תלך: לא־ימוש ספר התורה הזה מפיך והגית בו יומם ולילה למען תשמר לעשות ככל־הכתוב בו
ט כי־אז תצליח את־דרכך ואז תשכיל: הלוא צויתיך חזק ואמץ אל־תערץ ואל־תחת כי עמך יהוה
י יא אלהיך בכל אשר תלך:* ויצו יהושע את־שטרי העם לאמר: עברו | בקרב המחנה וצוו *Sepharadim end here* *Yemenites skip ahead*
את־העם לאמר הכינו לכם צדה כי בעוד | שלשת ימים אתם עברים את־הירדן הזה לבוא לרשת
יב את־הארץ אשר יהוה אלהיכם נתן לכם לרשתה: ולראובני ולגדי ולחצי שבט המנשה
יג אמר יהושע לאמר: זכור את־הדבר אשר צוה אתכם משה עבד־יהוה לאמר יהוה אלהיכם מניח
יד לכם ונתן לכם את־הארץ הזאת: נשיכם טפכם ומקניכם ישבו בארץ אשר נתן לכם משה בעבר
טו הירדן ואתם תעברו חמשים לפני אחיכם כל גבורי החיל ועזרתם אותם: עד אשר־יניח יהוה |
לאחיכם ככם וירשו גם־המה את־הארץ אשר־יהוה אלהיכם נתן להם ושבתם לארץ ירשתכם
טז וירשתם אותה אשר | נתן לכם משה עבד יהוה בעבר הירדן מזרח השמש: ויענו את־יהושע לאמר
יז כל אשר־צויתנו נעשה ואל־כל־אשר תשלחנו נלך: ככל אשר־שמענו אל־משה כן נשמע אליך רק
יח יהיה יהוה אלהיך עמך כאשר היה עם־משה: כל־איש אשר־ימרה את־פיך ולא־ישמע את־דבריך
לכל אשר־תצונו יומת רק חזק ואמץ:

Yemenites add
ו כז ויהי יהוה את־יהושע ויהי שמעו בכל־הארץ:

SIMḤAT TORAH

Simḥat Torah marks the close, and the opening, of the yearly cycle of Torah reading. No sooner do we read the Torah's final story, Moshe's death, than we begin again with the creation of the world, showing with our actions that there can be no beginning or ending to the Torah's wisdom or to our devotion to studying. The *haftara* continues this idea, reminding us that the story of the Jewish people and its relationship to God did not end with the death of Moshe. Rather, it continued on through his successor Yehoshua, who would work

FOR FURTHER READING

SEFER BERESHIT

The Ḥumash commentary was compiled with great care from Rabbi Sacks' vast array of books, articles, commentaries, and lectures. The following section is not intended as a comprehensive bibliography for each comment in the commentary; rather, it points the reader toward Rabbi Sacks' works containing similar ideas for further reading and insights.

Due to the various editions of Rabbi Sacks' books in print, we have noted chapter numbers rather than specific page numbers, for relevance across all editions.

For liturgical sources, we used the Ashkenaz editions of siddurim and *maḥzorim* (the most widely used editions at the time of printing).

Abbreviations for *Covenant & Conversation* (C&C) volumes:

LL – Lessons in Leadership

SS – Studies in Spirituality

EE – Essays on Ethics

JLCI – Judaism's Life-Changing Ideas

Bereshit

THE BOOK OF GENESIS: Genesis: An Introduction (C&C Genesis).

BERESHIT: Introduction to Bereshit (C&C Genesis).

1:1 When God began: Bereshit: The Book of Teaching (C&C Genesis).

1:1 Heaven and earth: Rabbi Sacks Torah and *Ḥokhma* lecture; Bereshit: The Book of Teaching (C&C Genesis); *The Great Partnership*, ch. 3; *Radical Then, Radical Now*, ch. 7; *Faith in the Future*, ch. 12.

LET THERE BE…: Bereshit: Three Stages of Creation (C&C Genesis).

1:4 It was good: Bereshit: The Genesis of Justice (C&C EE).

1:4 God separated the light from the darkness: Rabbi Sacks Lecture at Kings: "Confronting Violence in the Name of God"; Haazinu: The Arc of the Moral Universe (C&C EE).

1:6 Let it separate: Kedoshim: The Priestly Moral Imagination (C&C Leviticus).

1:12 Each of its kind: Humanitas Lecture 1; Leviticus: The Democratization of Holiness (C&C Leviticus).

1:14 To serve for signs and seasons: *The Great Partnership*, ch. 3.

1:21 The great sea serpents: *The Great Partnership*, ch. 3; *Radical Then, Radical Now*, ch. 6; Video: "Rabbi Sacks on *The Great Partnership*."

1:21 All the kinds of crawling, living things: *The Great Partnership*, ch. 11.

1:22 God blessed them: *Faith in the Future*, ch. 29.

MAN IN GOD'S IMAGE: Bereshit: The Genesis of Justice (C&C EE); *Faith in the Future*, ch. 29.

1:26 Let us make humankind: *Faith in the Future*, ch. 29.

1:28 Be fertile and multiply: *Tradition in an Untraditional Age*, ch. 1.

1:28 Fill the earth and subdue it: *Faith in the Future*, ch. 30.

1:31 Very good: Kedoshim: The Priestly Moral Imagination (C&C Leviticus).

THE SEVENTH DAY: *Faith in the Future*, ch. 20.

2:3 That God had created and done: *The Great Partnership*, ch. 11.

THE SECOND STORY OF CREATION: *Radical Then, Radical Now*, ch. 7; Shofetim: The Ecological Imperative (C&C Deuteronomy).

2:7 The man became a living being: Bereshit: Three Stages of Creation (C&C Genesis).

2:15 To work it and safeguard it: Video: "The Stewardship Paradigm – A Thought for Tu BiShvat."

THE TREE OF KNOWLEDGE OF GOOD AND EVIL: Bereshit: The Art of Listening (C&C SS); *Morality*, ch. 15.

2:17 You may not eat: Shemini: The Eighth Day (C&C Leviticus).

2:18 It is not good: *Radical Then, Radical Now*, ch. 7.

2:18 For man to be alone: Bereshit: The Genesis of Love (C&C Rabbi Sacks Website).

2:19 To see what he would call them: Article: "It's Good to Talk – Perhaps Even Holy Too," *The Times*, June 2011; *Morality*, ch. 20.

2:23 For from man was this one taken: *Radical Then, Radical Now*, ch. 7; *Future Tense*, ch. 9.

2:24 And cleaves to his wife: *Morality*, ch. 4.

3:6 Enticing to the eyes… insight: Bereshit: Taking Responsibility (C&C LL).

3:9 Where are you? Bereshit: Taking Responsibility (C&C LL).

3:12 The woman You put here: Bereshit: Taking Responsibility (C&C LL); *Celebrating Life*, ch. 30.

3:15 Between your children and hers: *The Great Partnership*, ch. 11.

3:16 You will long… but he will rule over you: *The Koren Sacks Pesaḥ Maḥzor*, pp. 964–65.

3:19 By the sweat of your brow: *Faith in the Future*, ch. 28.

3:19 You are dust, and you will return to dust: Bereshit: Garments of Light (C&C Genesis).

3:21 God made garments of skins for Adam and his wife and clothed them: Bereshit: Garments of Light (C&C Genesis).

3:22 He must not be allowed to… live forever: Ḥukat: The Consolations of Mortality (C&C Rabbi Sacks Website).

3:23 To work the land: Shemini: The Eighth Day (C&C Leviticus).

4:1 The man knew: *The Great Partnership*, ch. 3; Video: "Rabbi Sacks in Conversation with Professor Fania Oz-Salzberger, Hosted by Makom."

4:1 With the Lord's help I have made a man: Bereshit: Garments of Light (C&C Genesis); Bereshit: The Genesis of Love (C&C Rabbi Sacks Website); *The Great Partnership*, ch. 3.

4:2 Hevel: Article: "Happiness Is to Be Found in Being, Not in Having," *The Times*, October 2008.

4:5 Kayin became very angry: Bereshit: Violence in the Name of God (C&C Genesis).

4:7 But you must rule over it: *The Great Partnership*, ch. 6; Beḥukkotai: The Politics of Responsibility (C&C EE).

4:8 Kayin said to his brother Hevel: *Future Tense*, ch. 9.

THE FIRST MURDER: *The Home We Build Together*, ch. 5; *Not in God's Name*, ch. 1.

4:19 Lemekh: *The Great Partnership*, ch. 11.

4:24 Lemekh, seventy-seven: *Not in God's Name*, ch. 4.

5:3 In his own likeness and image: Bereshit: The Essence of Man (C&C Genesis); *The Koren Sacks Yom Kippur Maḥzor*, introduction.

5:29 This one will bring us comfort: *To Heal a Fractured World*, ch. 10.

6:6 The Lord regretted: *Not in God's Name*, ch. 1.

Noaḥ

NOAḤ: Noaḥ: Drama in Four Acts (C&C Genesis).

THE FLOOD AND THE TOWER: Noaḥ: Individual and Collective Responsibility (C&C Rabbi Sacks Website).

6:9 Righteous… in his generation: *To Heal a Fractured World*, ch. 10.

6:9 Noaḥ walked with God: Noaḥ: Righteousness Is Not Leadership (C&C LL); Noaḥ: Beyond Obedience (C&C Genesis).

6:11 Corrupt… full of violence: Noaḥ: Individual and Collective Responsibility (C&C Rabbi Sacks Website).

6:14 Make yourself an ark of cypress wood: *To Heal a Fractured World*, ch. 10.

6:16 Make a window: Noaḥ: The Light in the Ark (C&C Rabbi Sacks Website); *Future Tense*, ch. 10.

7:1 I have seen you alone to be righteous: Noaḥ: Righteousness Is Not Leadership (C&C LL).

7:5 Noaḥ did all that the Lord commanded him: *A Judaism Engaged with the World*, p. 18; Noaḥ: Righteousness Is Not Leadership (C&C LL).

8:16 Leave the ark: Noaḥ: Hero or Zero? (C&C Rabbi Sacks Website).

THE NOAHIDE COVENANT: Noaḥ: Trace of God (C&C JLCI); Humanitas Lecture 3; *To Heal a Fractured World*, ch. 5.

8:21 The devisings of the human heart: Noaḥ: Beyond Nature (C&C EE).

8:21 Evil from its youth: *Not in God's Name*, ch. 9.

8:22 As long as earth and time endure: Bereshit: The Faith of God (C&C JLCI).

THE NOAHIDE COVENANT: "OBJECTIVE" MORALITY: Lecture: "Markets, Governments and Virtues – The Mais Lectures"; Noaḥ: The Objectivity of Morality (C&C Genesis).

9:3 I allow them all to you: Tzav: Violence and the Sacred (C&C EE).

9:6 By man shall his blood be shed: *Koren Shalem Siddur,* pp. xxxix–xxx.

9:6 In God's image: *Not in God's Name,* ch. 11.

9:10 Every living creature on earth: *To Heal a Fractured World,* ch. 9.

9:13 The sign of the covenant: Lecture: "Faith and Fate: The Lambeth Conference Address"; *Future Tense,* ch. 4.

9:17 The covenant that I have established: Noaḥ: The Trace of God (C&C JLCI).

9:23 The nakedness of their father: Noaḥ: Beyond Obedience (C&C Genesis).

THE TOWER OF BAVEL: *To Heal a Fractured World,* ch. 10.

11:1 The whole world spoke… the same words: *Not in God's Name,* ch. 11; Humanitas Lecture 1; *Future Tense,* ch. 4.

11:3 Let us bake them thoroughly: *The Dignity of Difference,* ch. 3.

11:4 A city and a tower: Noaḥ: Babel: A Story of Heaven and Earth (C&C Genesis).

11:4 Otherwise we will be scattered: Humanitas Lecture 1; Noaḥ: A Tale of Four Cities (Rabbi Sacks Website); Naso: What Counts? (C&C Numbers).

11:4 Across the face of the earth: Humanitas Lecture 1.

11:5 The LORD came down: Noaḥ: Babel: A Story of Heaven and Earth (C&C Genesis).

11:7 Confuse their language: Humanitas Lecture 1; Noaḥ: Babel: A Story of Heaven and Earth (C&C Genesis).

11:9 From there the LORD scattered them: *Not in God's Name,* ch. 11.

11:31 Teraḥ took his son Avram: Lekh Lekha: Fathers and Sons (C&C Genesis).

Lekh Lekha

LEKH LEKHA: Introduction to Lekh Lekha (C&C Genesis); *To Heal a Fractured World,* ch. 10; Lekh Lekha: The Long Walk to Freedom (C&C Genesis).

AVRAHAM'S CALL: *Radical Then, Radical Now,* ch. 5.

12:1 Go: Lekh Lekha: The Heroism of Ordinary Life (C&C Rabbi Sacks Website).

12:1 Go – from your land: Lekh Lekha: The Heroism of Ordinary Life (C&C Rabbi Sacks Website).

12:1 From your land, your birthplace, and your father's house: *To Heal a Fractured World,* ch. 10.

12:1 To the land that I will show you: Lekh Lekha: Four Dimensions of the Journey (C&C Genesis).

12:2 You will become a blessing: Lekh Lekha: A New Kind of Hero (C&C Genesis).

12:3 All the families of the earth will be blessed: *Faith in the Future,* ch. 27.

12:4 As the LORD had told him: Lekh Lekha: The Long Walk to Freedom (C&C Genesis).

12:10 Avram went down to Egypt: Lekh Lekha: How Perfect Were the Patriarchs and Matriarchs? (C&C EE).

13:10 Lot raised his eyes: Lekh Lekha: Promise and Fulfillment (C&C Genesis).

14:14 He marshaled: Lekh Lekha: The Courage Not to Conform (C&C LL).

14:14 He… went in pursuit: *Not in God's Name,* ch. 11; Vayeshev: What is the Theme of the Stories of Genesis? (C&C Rabbi Sacks Website).

14:18 Malki Tzedek, king of Shalem: *Future Tense,* ch. 4.

15:1 Do not be afraid, Avram: Video: "In the Room with Jonathan Sacks."

THE PROMISE OF CHILDREN: *The Koren Sacks Rosh HaShana Maḥzor,* pp. 736–41.

15:2 Eliezer of Damascus: Lekh Lekha: Promise and Fulfillment (C&C Genesis).

15:6 Avram put his trust in the LORD: *Community of Faith,* ch. 9.

15:14 Afterward they will go free: *Faith in the Future,* introduction.

15:14 Afterward… with great wealth: *The Jonathan Sacks Haggada,* pp. 59–61.

HAGAR: *Not in God's Name,* ch. 6.

16:6 Sarai treated her harshly: *Not in God's Name,* ch. 6.

16:12 A wild donkey of a man: Lekh Lekha: How Perfect Were the Patriarchs and Matriarchs? (C&C EE).

17:7 *An eternal covenant:* *Will We Have Jewish Grandchildren?*, ch. 1.

17:10 *Every male among you shall be circumcised:* *Radical Then, Radical Now*, ch. 7.

17:20 *Twelve princes:* *Not in God's Name*, ch. 6.

17:21 *I will establish My covenant with Yitzḥak:* Lekh Lekha: Promise and Fulfillment (C&C Genesis).

Vayera

VAYERA: Lekh Lekha: The Long Walk to Freedom (C&C Genesis); Introduction to Vayera (C&C Genesis).

THE THREE VISITORS: Vayera: God and Strangers (C&C Genesis).

18:1 *The Lord appeared to him… in the heat of the day:* Vayera: God and Strangers (C&C Genesis).

18:4 *Rest under the tree:* *The Koren Sacks Sukkot Maḥzor*, pp. 180–83.

18:8 *Standing by them:* Vayera: God and Strangers (C&C Genesis).

AVRAHAM INTERCEDES FOR SEDOM: Vayera: Challenging God (C&C Genesis).

18:19 *By doing what is right and just:* *The Great Partnership*, epilogue; *Will We Have Jewish Grandchildren?*, ch. 1.

18:24 *Righteous people in the city:* *Will We Have Jewish Grandchildren?*, ch. 7.

18:25 *Shall the judge of all the earth not do justice?* *Faith in the Future*, ch. 7.

LOT IN SEDOM: Vayera: The Ambivalent Jew (C&C Genesis).

19:3 *Unleavened bread:* *The Jonathan Sacks Haggada*: "The First Pesaḥ," p. 159.

19:16 *He hesitated:* Vayera: The Music of Ambivalence (C&C Rabbi Sacks Website).

19:26 *Lot's wife looked back:* Article: "Thoughts for Elul: The Future of the Past," September 2014.

19:29 *The overthrow that overturned the cities:* *The Home We Build Together*, ch. 11.

20:11 *They will kill me because of my wife:* Vayeshev: What Is the Theme of the Stories of Genesis? (C&C Rabbi Sacks Website).

21:3 *Yitzḥak:* *The Koren Sacks Rosh Hashana Maḥzor*, pp. 466–67.

21:9 *Mocking:* *Not in God's Name*, ch. 6.

21:13 *Because he is your child:* *Not in God's Name*, ch. 6.

THE BANISHMENT OF YISHMAEL: *Not in God's Name*, ch. 6.

21:17 *God has heard the boy's cry:* *Tradition in an Untraditional Age*, ch. 11.

21:17 *There, where he is:* *Tradition in an Untraditional Age*, ch. 11.

AKEDAT YITZḤAK: Vayera: The Binding of Isaac: A New Interpretation (C&C EE).

22:2 *Go:* Vayera: The Space Between Us (C&C JLCI).

22:8 *God will see to… my son:* Vayera: Negative Capability (C&C Rabbi Sacks Website).

22:23 *Rivka:* Toledot: Isaac and Esau (C&C Rabbi Sacks Website).

Ḥayei Sara

ḤAYEI SARA: Introduction to Ḥayei Sara (C&C Genesis); Ḥayei Sara: Land and Children (C&C Genesis).

THE YEARS OF SARA'S LIFE: Ḥayei Sara: To Have a Why (C&C Rabbi Sacks Website).

23:3 *Then Avraham rose:* Ḥayei Sara: A Call from the Future (C&C Rabbi Sacks Website).

23:4 *A migrant and a visitor:* *Not in God's Name*, ch. 10.

23:4 *Sell me a burial site:* Ḥayei Sara: Land and Children (C&C Genesis).

23:6 *You are a prince of God in our midst:* *A Judaism Engaged with the World*, pp.18–19.

THE SERVANT'S TEST: Ḥayei Sara: The Kindness of Strangers (C&C EE).

24:12 *He said:* Vayera: The Music of Ambivalence (C&C Rabbi Sacks Website).

24:19 *I will draw water for your camels, too:* *To Heal a Fractured World*, ch. 1.

24:20 *And ran back:* Video: "On Leadership"; *Morality*, ch. 17; Article: "Marriage Is a Song for Two Voices in Harmony," *The Times*, June 2000.

24:34 *I am Avraham's servant:* Ḥayei Sara: Parental

Authority and the Choice of a Marriage Partner (C&C Genesis).
24:55 Let the young woman stay… or ten months: Ḥayei Sara: Hopes and Fears (C&C Rabbi Sacks Website).
24:58 I will: *Celebrating Life*, ch. 26.
24:60 They blessed Rivka: *The Koren Shalem Siddur*, p. 1035.
24:63 Toward evening: Ḥayei Sara: Prayer and Conversation (C&C Genesis).
24:63 To meditate: Ḥayei Sara: Prayer and Conversation (C&C Genesis).
24:64 Rivka too looked up – and saw Yitzḥak: Ḥayei Sara: Isaac and Prayer (C&C Rabbi Sacks Website).
25:1 Ketura: Ḥayei Sara: On Judaism and Islam (C&C Genesis).
AVRAHAM'S DEATH: Ḥayei Sara: A Journey of a Thousand Miles (C&C Rabbi Sacks Website).
25:9 His sons, Yitzḥak and Yishmael: Ḥayei Sara: On Judaism and Islam (C&C Genesis).

Toledot

TOLEDOT: Introduction to Toledot (C&C Genesis); *Not in God's Name*, ch. 5.
YAAKOV AND ESAV: *Not in God's Name*, chs. 5, 7.
25:19 Avraham was Yitzḥak's father: Toledot: On Clones and Identity (C&C Genesis).
25:22 So she went to inquire of the Lord: Toledot: The Price of Silence (C&C LL).
25:23 Two nations are inside your womb: Toledot: The Future of the Past (C&C Genesis); *Not in God's Name*, ch. 7.
25:23 The greater will the younger serve: Toledot: The Future of the Past (C&C Genesis).
25:28 Yitzḥak loved Esav: Toledot: A Father's Love (C&C SS).
25:34 Esav disdained his birthright: *Not in God's Name*, ch. 7.
26:6 So Yitzḥak now settled in Gerar: Toledot: The Courage of Persistence (C&C Genesis).
STOPPING UP THE WELLS: Toledot: The Courage of Persistence (C&C Genesis).
26:18 The same names his father had given them: Toledot: The Courage of Persistence (C&C Genesis).
26:22 Reḥovot: Toledot: The Courage of Persistence (C&C Genesis).
27:4 Prepared in the way that I love: Toledot: A Father's Love (C&C SS).
27:10 So that he may give you his blessing: Toledot: Was Jacob Right to Take Esau's Blessing? (C&C EE).
27:22 But the hands are the hands of Esav: *Not in God's Name*, ch. 7.
27:38 Have you only one blessing, father? Toledot: The Other Face of Esau (C&C Genesis).
"BLESS ME TOO": Toledot: Isaac and Esau (C&C Rabbi Sacks Website).
27:39 Of the cream of the land: *Not in God's Name*, ch. 7.
27:40 But when you break loose: Toledot: The Future of the Past (C&C Genesis).
27:44 Stay with him a while: Article: "The Family Is Where We Find Passion, Affection and Companionship," *The Times*, May 2004.
28:4 Avraham's blessing: Toledot: Was Jacob Right to Take Esau's Blessing? (C&C EE).
28:4 The land where… you live as a stranger: *Faith in the Future*, ch. 27.
28:8 Esav realized: Toledot: The Price of Silence (C&C LL).

Vayetze

VAYETZE: Introduction to Vayetze (C&C Genesis); Vayetze: Out of the Depths (C&C JLCI).
THE VISION OF THE LADDER: Vayetze: The Ladder of Prayer (C&C Genesis).
28:11 He chanced upon a certain place: Vayetze: How the Light Gets In (C&C SS); Vayetze: Encountering God (C&C Genesis).
28:12 And he dreamed: Vayetze: Encountering God (C&C Genesis).

VAYISHLAḤ

DINA AND SHEKHEM: Vayishlaḥ: The Parable of the Tribes (C&C EE).

34:3 He became deeply drawn to Dina: Vayishlaḥ: The Parable of the Tribes (C&C EE).

34:13 They spoke deceptively: Vayishlaḥ: The Parable of the Tribes (C&C EE).

34:31 Should our sister be treated like a whore? Vayishlaḥ: The Parable of the Tribes (C&C EE).

35:8 Oak of Weeping: Hukkat: Healing the Trauma of Loss (C&C SS).

35:10 Thus He named him Yisrael: Vayishlaḥ: No Longer Shall You Be Called Jacob (C&C Rabbi Sacks Website); Vayishlaḥ: Be Thyself (C&C LL).

35:18 But his father called him Binyamin: *To Heal a Fractured World,* ch. 16.

35:22 Lay with… Bilha: Vayeshev: Reuben: The Might-Have-Been (C&C Rabbi Sacks Website).

THE CHILDREN OF ISRAEL: Vayishlaḥ: The Jewish Journey (C&C Rabbi Sacks Website); Jacob's Destiny, Israel's Name (C&C Genesis).

36:31 Who reigned… before any king reigned over the Israelites: *Not in God's Name,* ch. 7.

Vayeshev

VAYESHEV: Introduction to Vayeshev (C&C Genesis).

37:1 Yaakov settled: *Not in God's Name,* ch. 8.

37:4 They hated him: *Not in God's Name,* ch. 8.

37:4 Could not say a peaceful word to him: Article: "It's Good to Talk – Perhaps Even Holy Too," *The Times,* June 2011.

37:15 A man found him wandering: Vayeshev: The Angel Who Did Not Know He Was an Angel (C&C Rabbi Sacks Website).

37:18 In the distance: Vayigash: The Space Between (C&C Rabbi Sacks Website).

37:20 What will come of his dreams: *Not in God's Name,* ch. 8.

REUVEN'S GOOD INTENTIONS: Vayeshev: Reuben: The Might-Have-Been (C&C Rabbi Sacks Website).

37:25 They saw a caravan of Ishmaelites: *The Great Partnership,* ch. 11.

37:26 What do we gain by killing our brother? *Ceremony & Celebration,* Shavuot: The Greatest Gift.

37:28 And they sold him: Miketz: Man proposes, God disposes (C&C Genesis).

37:35 He refused to be comforted: *The Great Partnership,* ch. 12.

TAMAR: Vayeshev: A Tale of Two Women (C&C Genesis).

38:25 To whom this seal and cord and staff belong: Vayeshev: The Heroism of Tamar (C&C EE).

38:26 She is more righteous than I: Vayeshev: The Heroism of Tamar (C&C EE).

39:8 But he refused: Vayera: The Ambivalent Jew (C&C Genesis).

40:8 Tell me your dreams: Vayeshev: How to Change the World (C&C SS).

40:23 He forgot him: Vayeshev: Improbable Endings and the Defeat of Despair (C&C JLCI).

Miketz

MIKETZ: Introduction to Miketz (C&C Genesis).

"TWO YEARS PASSED": Miketz: To Wait Without Despair (C&C SS).

41:16 Not I: Miketz: The Author of Our Lives (C&C Rabbi Sacks Website).

41:27 Seven years of famine: Miketz: The Power of Dreams (C&C LL).

41:32 He is soon to bring it about: Miketz: Between Freedom and Providence (C&C Genesis); Miketz: Man Proposes, God Disposes (C&C Genesis).

41:37 The plan seemed good: Miketz: The Power of Dreams (C&C LL).

PHARAOH, YOSEF, AND *ELOKIM*: Miketz: Faith, Universal and Particular (C&C Rabbi Sacks Website).

41:49 It was beyond measure: Miketz: Jews and Economics (C&C JLCI).

41:52 Fruitful in the land of my affliction: "On Creative Minorities," Erasmus Lecture, October 2013.

YOSEF AND HIS BROTHERS MEET AGAIN: *Not in God's Name,* ch. 8.

42:7 Yosef recognized: *Not in God's Name,* ch. 8.

Vayigash

Vayeḥi

SEFER SHEMOT

A number of the comments in the parashot that follow are taken directly from Rabbi Sacks' own commentary drafts. These have not been referenced for further reading because they are unpublished works, but many of the ideas they contain are reflected in his other writings on the book of Exodus.

Shemot

THE BOOK OF EXODUS: Exodus: The Birth of a Nation (C&C Exodus); Lecture: "A New Concept of Freedom," a *shiur* at UCL for Passover, March 2018.

SHEMOT: Introduction to Shemot (C&C Exodus).

1:1 And these: *Future Tense,* ch. 11.

1:1 The names: Rabbi Sacks draft commentary.

THE PEOPLE OF ISRAEL: Exodus: The Birth of a Nation (C&C Exodus).

1:8 A new king: Ki Tetzeh: Two Types of Hate (C&C Rabbi Sacks Website).

1:8 Who had not known Yosef: Shemot: Turning Curses into Blessings (C&C SS).

1:9 The Israelite people: *Will We Have Jewish Grandchildren?,* introduction.

1:9 More powerful than we: Vayetzeh: The Birth of the World's Oldest Hate (C&C Rabbi Sacks Website).

1:10 Deal wisely with them: *The Jonathan Sacks Haggada,* pp. 54–57.

1:10 They may join our enemies: *The Jonathan Sacks Haggada,* pp. 14–15.

1:11 Pitom and Ramesses: Rabbi Sacks draft commentary.

1:14 Embittering their lives: *The Jonathan Sacks Haggada,* p. 57.

MIDWIVES TO THE HEBREWS : *The Jonathan Sacks Haggada,* pp. 123–124; Shemot: Civil Disobedience (C&C Exodus).

1:21 He granted them households: Shemot: Civil Disobedience (C&C Exodus).

1:22 Then Pharaoh commanded his entire people: Shemot: Civil Disobedience (C&C Exodus).

2:1 A man of the house of Levi went and married a daughter of Levi: *Crisis and Covenant,* ch. 2.

2:2 She saw what a fine child he was: Rabbi Sacks draft commentary.

2:2 She kept him hidden: Numbers: Then and Now (C&C Numbers).

2:3 Placed it among the reeds by the bank of the Nile: *The Jonathan Sacks Haggada,* pp. 117–18.

PHARAOH'S DAUGHTER: Shemot: The Light at the Heart of Darkness (C&C Exodus).

2:6 The boy was crying: *The Jonathan Sacks Haggada,* p. 59.

2:7 Then his sister asked Pharaoh's daughter: Shemot: The Light at the Heart of Darkness (C&C Exodus).

2:10 She named him Moshe: *The Koren Sacks Pesaḥ Maḥzor,* pp. xxxiv–xxxv.

2:11 Went out to his people: Rabbi Sacks draft commentary.

2:17 Moshe stood up to defend them: Article: "Seven Principles of Jewish Leadership," *Jewish Chronicle,* June 2021.

2:22 I have been a stranger in an alien land: Massei: Miles to Go Before I Sleep (C&C JLCI).

2:24 And God heard: *The Jonathan Sacks Haggada,* pp. 58–59.

2:25 And God knew: *The Jonathan Sacks Haggada,* pp. 60–61.

THE BURNING BUSH: *Faith in the Future,* ch. 6.

3:2 From the midst of a bush: Rabbi Sacks draft commentary.

3:4 Here I am: *The Koren Sacks Yom Kippur Maḥzor,* pp. 770–71.

3:5 Remove the shoes from your feet: Rabbi Sacks draft commentary.

3:11 Who am I: Vayishlaḥ: Feeling the Fear (C&C SS).

I WILL BE WHAT I WILL BE: Shemot: Faith in the Future (C&C Rabbi Sacks Website); *The Great Partnership,* ch. 3.

3:15 The LORD God of your fathers: Ki Tavo: We Are What We Remember (C&C Deuteronomy).

4:1 They will not believe me: Shemot: The Belief of a Leader (C&C Exodus).

4:6 White as snow: Shemot: Leadership and the People (C&C Rabbi Sacks Website).

4:10 I am not a man of words: Shemini: When Weakness Becomes Strength (C&C JLCI).

4:13 Send someone else: Article: "Strength from Faith Is God's Faith in Us," *The Times*, October 2012.

4:14 His heart will rejoice: Tetzaveh: Brothers: A Drama in Five Acts (C&C Exodus); *Not in God's Name*, ch. 9.

THE ENCOUNTER ON THE WAY TO EGYPT: Vayishlaḥ: Feeling the Fear (C&C SS).

4:20 Moshe took his wife and sons: Rabbi Sacks draft commentary.

4:22 Israel is My son, My firstborn: *The Jonathan Sacks Haggada*, p. 125.

4:25 Tzipora took a flint knife: Exodus: The Birth of a Nation (C&C Exodus).

5:1 Send My people forth: Rabbi Sacks draft commentary.

5:2 I do not know the Lord: Video: "The Home of the Book for the People of the Book."

5:21 May the Lord look on you and judge: Vaera: Overcoming Setbacks (C&C LL).

5:22 Why, Lord, have You brought harm to this people?: *The Koren Sacks Rosh Hashana Maḥzor*, pp. 580–82.

Vaera

VAERA: Introduction to Vaera (C&C Exodus).

I AM THE LORD: Vaera: The God Who Acts in History (C&C Exodus).

6:2 I am the Lord: Rabbi Sacks draft commentary.

6:3 But by My name the Lord I did not make Myself known: Rabbi Sacks draft commentary.

6:6 I will free you from the forced labor of the Egyptians: Vaera: The God Who Acts in History (C&C Exodus).

6:8 I will bring you: Vaera: The Cup of Hope (C&C Exodus).

6:9 They did not listen to him: Vaera: Spirits in a Material World (C&C SS).

6:12 How then will Pharaoh listen?: Rabbi Sacks draft commentary.

6:12 Uncircumcised lips: Rabbi Sacks draft commentary.

6:14 These were the heads: Rabbi Sacks draft commentary.

6:20 Amram married Yokheved, his father's sister: Rabbi Sacks draft commentary.

6:26 Aharon and Moshe: Rabbi Sacks draft commentary.

7:1 Like a god to Pharaoh: Rabbi Sacks draft commentary.

THE HARDENING OF PHARAOH'S HEART: Rabbi Sacks draft commentary.

7:9 A serpent: Rabbi Sacks draft commentary.

THE PLAGUES: Bo: Heart of Darkness (C&C Exodus).

7:17 It will become blood: Rabbi Sacks draft commentary.

7:22 But the Egyptian magicians did the same thing by their sorcery: Rabbi Sacks draft commentary.

7:27 I will scourge your land with frogs: Rabbi Sacks draft commentary.

8:4 Pray to the Lord: Rabbi Sacks draft commentary.

8:4 And I will send your people forth: Rabbi Sacks draft commentary.

8:5 Gloat over me: Rabbi Sacks draft commentary.

8:6 Then you will know: Rabbi Sacks draft commentary.

8:10 They gathered them up: Rabbi Sacks draft commentary.

8:10 The stench filled the whole land: Rabbi Sacks draft commentary.

THE FINGER OF GOD: Vaera: A Handful of Dust (C&C Exodus).

8:16 Send My people forth, so that they may serve Me: Rabbi Sacks draft commentary.

8:17 Swarms of insects: Rabbi Sacks draft commentary.

8:18 That I am the Lord, here on earth: Rabbi Sacks draft commentary.

8:19 I will mark out a separation: Rabbi Sacks draft commentary.

8:21 Pharaoh called for Moshe and Aharon: Rabbi Sacks draft commentary.

8:22 An abomination to the Egyptian: Rabbi Sacks draft commentary.

MOSHE'S REQUEST: Vaera: Freedom and Truth (C&C Rabbi Sacks Website).

9:3 The Lord's hand: Rabbi Sacks draft commentary.

9:3 A deadly epidemic: Rabbi Sacks draft commentary.

9:7 Pharaoh investigated the matter: Rabbi Sacks draft commentary.

9:8 A handful of soot: Rabbi Sacks draft commentary.

9:12 But the Lord strengthened Pharaoh's heart: Rabbi Sacks draft commentary.

9:14 I will set the full force of My plagues upon you: Rabbi Sacks draft commentary.

9:16 My name known throughout the land: Exodus: The Birth of a Nation (C&C Exodus).

9:22 Reach your hand out: Rabbi Sacks draft commentary.
9:24 The hail, with fire blazing inside it: Rabbi Sacks draft commentary.
9:27 This time I have sinned: Rabbi Sacks draft commentary.
9:29 As I leave the city: *The Great Partnership*, chs. 3, 7, 14.

Bo

BO: Bo: The Story We Tell (C&C JLCI).
10:1 His heart and his officials': Rabbi Sacks draft commentary.
10:3 How much longer will you refuse to submit to Me?: Rabbi Sacks draft commentary.
10:2 And so that you may tell your children and grandchildren: Rabbi Sacks draft commentary.
10:4 Locusts: Rabbi Sacks draft commentary.
10:6 Your parents and grandparents: Rabbi Sacks draft commentary.
10:6 Then Moshe turned: Vaera: The Hardened Heart (C&C Exodus).
10:9 With our youths and our elderly folk: Rabbi Sacks draft commentary.
10:10 Evil is staring you in the face: Rabbi Sacks draft commentary.
10:13 The Lord caused an east wind: Rabbi Sacks draft commentary.
10:17 Forgive my sin: Rabbi Sacks draft commentary.
THE PLAGUE OF DARKNESS: Bo: Heart of Darkness (C&C Exodus).
10:21 Darkness so deep it can be felt: Bo: Heart of Darkness (C&C Exodus).
11:3 The Lord granted the people favor in the eyes of the Egyptians: Rabbi Sacks draft commentary.
11:3 The man Moshe: Rabbi Sacks draft commentary.
11:8 Blazing with anger: Article: "Seven Principles of Jewish Leadership," *Jewish Chronicle* and *Jerusalem Post*, June 2012.
"THIS MONTH SHALL BE TO YOU…": Article: "To Master Time Is to Be Truly Free," *The Times*, April 2012; *The Jonathan Sacks Haggada*, p. 15.
12:2 To you: Emor: The Duality of Jewish Time (C&C Rabbi Sacks Website).
12:2 The beginning of months: Rabbi Sacks draft commentary.
12:3 Community of Israel: *Future Tense*, ch. 2.
12:4 Let him and a close neighbor take a lamb together: *The Jonathan Sacks Haggada*, pp. 21–23.
12:7 Two sides and top of the doorframes: Rabbi Sacks draft commentary.
12:8 Unleavened bread: *The Jonathan Sacks Haggada*, p. 23.
12:8 Bitter herbs: Video: "Inspiration for Shabbat HaGadol and Pesach 2020."
12:11 Passover: *The Jonathan Sacks Haggada*, "Matza," p. 87.
12:14 This day… a memorial for you: *Future Tense*, ch. 11.
12:15 You shall have removed leaven from your houses: *The Koren Sacks Pesaḥ Maḥzor*, pp. 2–3.
EDUCATION: Bo: The Spiritual Child (C&C SS).
12:32 But bless me too: *The Koren Sacks Pesaḥ Maḥzor*, pp. 456–547.
12:35 Items of silver and gold: Ki Tetzeh: Letting Go of Hate (C&C Rabbi Sacks Website).
12:38 A great variety of other people: *The Home We Build Together*, ch. 8; Humanitas Lecture 1.
12:39 They… could not delay: *The Koren Sacks Pesaḥ Maḥzor*, p. 548.
12:49 The stranger who lives among you: *The Koren Sacks Pesaḥ Maḥzor*, pp. 550–51.
13:2 Consecrate every firstborn: *The Koren Shalem Siddur*, pp. 1026–27.
13:8 You must tell your child: Rabbi Sacks draft commentary.
13:9 It shall be a sign: *Community of Faith*, ch. 10.
13:14 What is this?: Bo: The Spiritual Child (C&C SS).
13:14 You shall answer: Bo: Schools of Freedom (C&C Exodus).

Beshalaḥ

BESHALAḤ: Beshalaḥ: The Turning Point (C&C Exodus).
THE JOURNEY BEGINS: Beshalaḥ: Time and Social Transformation (C&C Exodus).

Yitro

A KINGDOM OF PRIESTS AND A HOLY NATION: Yitro: A Nation of Leaders (C&C LL).
19:6 A holy nation: Yitro: A Holy Nation (C&C Exodus).
19:8 And the people answered as one: *The Koren Sacks Shavuot Maḥzor*, pp. 406–7; *Future Tense*, ch. 8.
19:20 And the LORD descended: *The Koren Sacks Shavuot Maḥzor*, p. 96.
THE TEN COMMANDMENTS: Yitro: The Structure of the Good Society (C&C EE).
20:2 I am the LORD your God: *Celebrating Life*, ch. 23; Ten Paths to God: Faith Study Guide.
20:5 To the third and fourth generation: *The Koren Sacks Shavuot Maḥzor*, p. 410; *Will We Have Jewish Grandchildren?*, ch. 3.
20:7 Do not speak the name… in vain: *The Persistence of Faith*, Lecture 5; *Morality*, introduction; *Not in God's Name*, ch. 1.
20:10 You, nor your son or daughter...servant...livestock... migrant: *The Koren Sacks Shavuot Maḥzor*, pp. 412–13; *Faith in the Future*, ch. 19.
20:10 Made it holy: Leviticus: The Democratisation of Holiness (C&C Leviticus); Yitro: A Holy Nation (C&C Exodus); Lecture: "Markets and Morals – The 1998 Hayek Lecture."
20:12 Honor your father and mother: *The Koren Sacks Shavuot Maḥzor*, p. 412; Yitro: The Structure of the Good Society (C&C EE).
20:13 Do not commit adultery: *The Politics of Hope*, ch. 16.
20:13 Do not steal: Yitro: The Structure of the Good Society (C&C EE); *The Dignity of Difference*, ch. 5.
20:13 Do not bear false witness: Yitro: The Structure of the Good Society (C&C EE).
20:14 Do not crave: Yitro: To Thank Before We Think (C&C SS).
20:22 In wielding a sword upon it, you profane it: *Not in God's Name*, ch. 12.

Mishpatim

MISHPATIM: (C&C Exodus); Mishpatim: God Is in the Details (C&C Exodus).
21:1 And these are the laws: Mishpatim: God Is in the Details (C&C Exodus).
SLAVERY: Mishpatim: The Slow End of Slavery (C&C Rabbi Sacks Website).
21:6 Pierce his ear with an awl: Yitro: Justice or Peace? (C&C Exodus); Mishpatim: God's Nudge (C&C Rabbi Sacks Website).
21:7 If a man sells his daughter as a maidservant: *Faith in the Future*, ch. 28.
TEXT AND INTERPRETATION: THE CASE OF ACCIDENTAL MISCARRIAGE: Mishpatim: Text and Interpretation: The Case of Abortion (C&C Exodus).
21:29 Its owner was warned: *The Dignity of Difference*, ch. 6.
22:1 If a burglar is caught tunneling in: Vayishlaḥ: Physical Fear, Moral Distress (C&C Genesis).
22:20 For you yourselves were strangers in the land of Egypt: Mishpatim: Loving the Stranger (C&C Exodus).
22:24 If you lend money to one of My people who is poor: *The Koren Sacks Pesaḥ Maḥzor*, p. 814; *Morality*, introduction.
22:26 I will be listening: Va'etḥanan; Listening Is an Art (C&C Deuteronomy); Video: "Rabbi Sacks on Connecting to God" (J Insider).
22:26 I am gracious: Mishpatim: God Is in the Details (C&C Exodus).
23:2 Do not pervert justice: Mishpatim: God Is in the Details (C&C Exodus).
23:2 Siding with the crowd: *The Koren Sacks Pesaḥ Maḥzor*, p. 816.
23:3 Do not show favoritism even to a poor man: Mishpatim; God Is in the Details (C&C Exodus); *The Koren Sacks Pesaḥ Maḥzor*, p. 816.
23:4 Your enemy's ox: Mishpatim: Helping an Enemy (C&C Exodus).
23:7 The innocent and righteous: *The Koren Sacks Pesaḥ Maḥzor*, p. 819.
23:9 For you yourselves were strangers in the land of Egypt: Mishpatim: Loving the Stranger (C&C Exodus); *Not in God's Name*, ch. 10; *To Heal a Fractured World*, ch. 8.
SHEMITTA AND THE SABBATH: Shofetim: Environmental Responsibility (C&C EE); Behar: Eminent Domain (C&C Leviticus).
23:18 Do not boil a kid in the milk of its mother: *The Koren Sacks Pesaḥ Maḥzor*, p. 821; Shemini: Food for Thought (C&C Rabbi Sacks Website).

23:20 ***I am sending a messenger:*** *The Jonathan Sacks Haggada,*, pp. 62–65.
24:7 ***We shall do:*** Mishpatim: Doing and Hearing (C&C SS); Mishpatim: We Will Do and We Will Hear (C&C Rabbi Sacks Website).
WE SHALL DO AND WE SHALL HEED: Mishpatim: Doing and Hearing (C&C SS).
24:8 ***Regarding all these words:*** Mishpatim: Vision and Detail (C&C LL).
24:10 ***They saw a vision:*** *To Heal a Fractured World,* ch. 10.

Teruma

TERUMA: Introduction to Teruma (C&C Exodus); *Community of Faith,* ch. 2.
CALLING FOR CONTRIBUTIONS: *The Home We Build Together,* ch. 12.
25:2 ***All whose heart moves them to give:*** Teruma: Voluntary Contribution (C&C Exodus).
25:3 ***The offerings you shall receive from them:*** Teruma: The Gift of Giving (C&C SS).
25:8 ***In their midst:*** Teruma: A Portable Home (C&C Exodus).
THE DETAILS OF THE TABERNACLE: Teruma: The Architecture of Holiness (C&C Rabbi Sacks Website); *The Home We Build Together,* ch. 12.
25:10 ***Make an Ark of acacia wood:*** Teruma: The Making of an Ark (C&C Exodus).
25:20 ***They should face one another:*** *The Koren Sacks Rosh Hashana Maḥzor,* pp. 634–37; *To Heal a Fractured World,* ch. 4.
25:22 ***There, from above the cover:*** *To Heal a Fractured World,* ch. 5; Pekudei: Making Space (C&C JLCI).
25:31 ***A candelabrum of pure gold:*** Vayak'hel: God's Shadow (C&C Rabbi Sacks Website); Vayak'hel: The Beauty of Holiness or the Holiness of Beauty (C&C Family Edition); Article: "The Festival of Lights Signifies an Inextinguishable Faith," *The Times,* December 2012.
A TENT: *The Home We Build Together,* ch. 12.
27:1 ***Make the altar:*** Tzav: Understanding Sacrifice (C&C SS).

Tetzaveh

TETZAVEH: Introduction to Tetzaveh (C&C Exodus); Tetzaveh: The Ethic of Holiness (C&C EE).
27:20 ***To kindle the lamp, every night:*** Tetzaveh: Crushed for the Light (C&C JLCI).
27:21 ***Aharon and his sons:*** Tetzaveh: Priests and Prophets (C&C Exodus).
28:1 ***To serve Me as priests:*** Tetzaveh: Priests and Prophets (C&C Exodus).
PRIESTLY VESTMENTS: Tetzaveh: Dressing to Impress (C&C Rabbi Sacks Website).
28:3 ***Speak:*** Tetzaveh: Leadership Means Making Space (C&C Rabbi Sacks Website).
THE AESTHETIC IN JUDAISM: Tetzaveh: The Aesthetic in Judaism (C&C Rabbi Sacks Website).
28:15 ***Make a breast piece:*** *The Koren Sacks Yom Kippur Maḥzor,* p. 404; Tetzaveh: The Aesthetic in Judaism (C&C Rabbi Sacks Website).
28:21 ***Yisrael's sons.… the twelve tribes:*** Vayeshev: A Tale of Two Women (C&C Genesis); *The Dignity of Difference,* ch. 6.
PROPHETIC AND PRIESTLY PRAYER: Tetzaveh: Whose Footsteps Do We Follow When We Pray? (C&C Exodus); Ki Tisa: Between Truth and Peace (C&C Rabbi Sacks Website); Ḥayei Sara: Prayer and Conversation (C&C Genesis).
28:35 ***So that he will not die:*** Tetzaveh: The Ethic of Holiness (C&C EE).
28:43 ***A law for Aharon and his descendants for all time:*** Tetzaveh: Who Is Honored? (C&C Rabbi Sacks Website).
29:24 ***A wave offering before the LORD:*** *The Great Partnership,* introduction; *Celebrating Life,* ch. 50.
29:33 ***Through which atonement will be made:*** *Radical Then, Radical Now,* ch. 11.
THE REGULAR BURNT OFFERING: Tetzaveh: Inspiration and Perspiration (C&C SS).

Ki Tisa

KI TISA: Introduction to Ki Tisa (C&C Exodus); Ki Tisa: A Stiff-Necked People (C&C Exodus).

THE CENSUS: *From Renewal to Responsibility*; Ki Tisa: Counting Jews (C&C Exodus).

30:13 Half a shekel: *To Heal a Fractured World*, ch. 20.

31:2 Betzalel: *Faith in the Future*, ch. 20.

31:17 And on the seventh day He ceased and was revived: *Faith in the Future*, ch. 20.

THE GOLDEN CALF: Leviticus: The Democratisation of Holiness (C&C Leviticus).

32:2 Bring them to me: Ki Tisa: Between Truth and Peace (C&C Rabbi Sacks Website).

32:3 Brought them to Aharon: *Will We Have Jewish Grandchildren?*, ch. 5.

32:11 Moshe implored: Ki Tisa: Moses Annuls a Vow (C&C Rabbi Sacks Website).

32:16 Engraved on the tablets: Ki Tisa: The Birth of a New Freedom (C&C Rabbi Sacks Website).

32:24 They gave it to me: Ki Tisa: How Leaders Fail (C&C LL).

32:32 The book You have written: *The Koren Sacks Rosh Hashana Maḥzor* p. 68.

33:8 When Moshe went out: Ki Tisa: The Closeness of God (C&C SS).

33:13 Please show me Your ways: Ki Tisa: The Closeness of God (C&C SS).

33:18 Show me, please, Your glory: Ki Tisa: The Closeness of God (C&C SS).

33:19 Will show mercy to whom I decide to show mercy: Ki Tisa: The Closeness of God (C&C SS).

34:1 Carve two tablets of stone like the first: Ki Tisa: Awakening from Above, Awakening from Below (C&C Exodus).

THE THIRTEEN ATTRIBUTES OF MERCY: *The Koren Sacks Yom Kippur Maḥzor*, pp. 134–36; Ki Tisa: Can There Be Compassion Without Justice? (C&C EE).

34:7 Who does not acquit the guilty: Ki Tisa: Can There Be Compassion Without Justice? (C&C EE).

34:9 Though this is a stiff-necked people: Ki Tisa: A Stiff-Necked People (C&C Exodus).

34:21 On the seventh day you shall rest: Ki Tisa: Shabbat and the Golden Calf: Reflections on the Great Crash of 2008 (C&C Exodus).

34:26 Do not cook a kid in the milk of its mother: *The Koren Sacks Sukkot Maḥzor*, p. 868.

34:29 The skin of his face shone with light: Ki Tisa: Two Types of Religious Encounter (C&C Rabbi Sacks Website).

Vayak'hel

VAYAK'HEL: Introduction to Vayak'hel (C&C Exodus).

THE SABBATH AND THE SANCTUARY: Video: "Vayak'hel-Pekudei in the Time of the Coronavirus Pandemic."

35:3 On the Sabbath day: Vayak'hel: The Sabbath: First Day or the Last? (C&C Exodus).

35:29 All the men and women whose hearts moved them to bring anything… as a freewill offering to the LORD: Vayak'hel: Three Kinds of Community (C&C Exodus).

35:33 Working in every other craft: Vayak'hel: The Beauty of Holiness or the Holiness of Beauty (C&C Exodus).

36:35 With a design of cherubim worked into it: Vayak'hel: God's Shadow (C&C Exodus); *The Dignity of Difference*, ch. 5; *Future Tense*, ch. 10.

37:29 With the skill of a perfumer… the fragrant incense: Video: "Understanding Prayer – Framing Beliefs."

WOMEN AND THE MAKING OF THE TABERNACLE: Vayak'hel: Mirrors of Love (C&C Rabbi Sacks Website).

THE COMPLETION OF THE BUILDING WORK: Vayak'hel: Three Kinds of Community (C&C Exodus); Teruma: The Home We Build Together (C&C LL); *The Home We Build Together*, ch. 20; Vayak'hel: Nation-Building: Ancient Answer, Contemporary Problem (C&C Exodus).

Pekudei

PEKUDEI: Introduction to Pekudei (C&C Exodus); Pekudei: Encampments and Journeys (C&C Exodus).

THE ACCOUNTS OF THE TABERNACLE: Pekudei: Integrity in Public Life (C&C EE).

SEFER VAYIKRA

Vayikra

Tzav

8:23 It was slaughtered: Tzav: On Not Trying to Be What You Are Not (C&C LL).

JUSTICE AND OBEDIENCE: Vayikra: The Prophetic View of Sacrifice (C&C Rabbi Sacks Website).

Shemini

SHEMINI: Shemini: Fire: Holy and Unholy (C&C Leviticus); Shemini: Spontaneity: Good or Bad? (C&C Leviticus); Shemini: The Integrity of Nature (C&C Leviticus).

THE EIGHTH DAY: Shemini: The Eighth Day (C&C Leviticus).

9:7 Approach the altar: Shemini: Reticence vs. Impetuosity (C&C LL).

NADAV AND AVIHU: Shemini: Fire: Holy and Unholy (C&C Leviticus).

10:2 And fire came forth: Shemini: Fire: Holy and Unholy (C&C Leviticus).

10:2 They died before the LORD: *The Koren Sacks Yom Kippur Maḥzor*, introduction; Shemini: Spontaneity: Good or Bad? (C&C Leviticus).

10:3 Aharon was silent: Shemini: Between Hope and Humanity (C&C Leviticus).

10:9 Wine or strong drink: Shemini: Reticence vs. Impetuosity (C&C LL); Shemini: The Dangers of Enthusiasm (C&C SS).

10:10 Between impure and pure: Metzora: The Laws of Purity (C&C Leviticus); Shemini: The Eighth Day (C&C Leviticus).

10:20 Moshe listened; and it was right in his eyes: Shemini: Between Hope and Humanity (C&C Leviticus).

THE DIETARY LAWS: Shemini: The Integrity of Nature (C&C Leviticus); Shemini: The Eighth Day (C&C Leviticus).

11:19 The stork: *Faith in the Future*, ch. 12.

11:44 Be holy, for I am holy: Shemini: The Integrity of Nature (C&C Leviticus).

11:46 This is the law concerning… all creatures: *Future Tense*, ch. 10.

Tazria

TAZRIA: Introduction to Tazria (C&C Leviticus).

CIRCUMCISION: Tazria: Circumcision, Sex, and Violence (C&C Leviticus); Tazria: The Sign of the Covenant (Rabbi Sacks C&C Website); Tazria: The Circumcision of Desire (C&C Leviticus).

12:3 The child's foreskin shall be circumcised: Tazria: Circumcision, Sex, and Violence (C&C Leviticus); Tazria: The Sign of the Covenant (C&C Rabbi Sacks Website); Tazria: The Circumcision of Desire (C&C Leviticus).

OFFERINGS AFTER CHILDBIRTH: Tazria: The Sacrifices of Childbirth (C&C Leviticus); Leviticus: The Democratisation of Holiness (C&C Leviticus).

12:6 When the days of her purification are complete: Tazria: Holiness and Childbirth (C&C Leviticus).

12:7 The law for a woman who bears a child: Tetzaveh: The Ethic of Holiness (C&C EE); Tazria: Holiness and Childbirth (C&C Leviticus); *The Koren Shalem Siddur*, p. 1031.

12:8 One for the burnt offering: Tazria: The Sacrifices of Childbirth (C&C Leviticus).

TZARAAT: THE IMPURE BLIGHT : Tazria: Of Skin Disease, Mildew, and Evil Speech (C&C Leviticus); Leviticus: The Democratisation of Holiness (C&C Leviticus).

13:10 The priest shall look: Tazria: Of Skin Disease, Mildew, and Evil Speech (C&C Leviticus); *To Heal a Fractured World*, ch. 20.

13:21 Shall quarantine the patient for seven days: Tazria: The Power of Bad (C&C JLIC); The Price of Free Speech (C&C LL); The Plague of Evil Speech (C&C Rabbi Sacks Website); Metzora: The Power of Praise (C&C JLIC).

ILLNESS AND OSTRACIZATION: Metzora: The Power of Shame (C&C EE); *Faith in the Future*, ch. 30.

Metzora

METZORA: Introduction to Metzora (C&C Leviticus).

REINTEGRATION: Tazria: The Power of Bad (C&C JLCI);

Aḥarei Mot

Kedoshim

the Elderly Adds Life to Their Years" (BBC Radio 4's *Thought for the Day*, May 2013).

19:34 Love him as your own self: Mishpatim: Loving the Stranger (C&C Exodus).

19:36 Honest scales: *Faith in the Future*, ch. 28; Lecture: "Markets and Morals – The 1998 Hayek Lecture," June 1998.

20:18 He has laid her hidden source bare: *The Politics of Hope*, ch. 16; Video: "A Life Worth Living."

20:26 I have set you apart: Kedoshim: Made with Love (C&C Rabbi Sacks Website).

Emor

EMOR: Introduction to Emor (C&C Leviticus).

21:1 No one of you shall render himself impure: Emor: Eternity and Mortality (C&C Rabbi Sacks Website).

A PRIEST WITH A PHYSICAL BLEMISH: Emor: Eternity and Mortality (C&C Rabbi Sacks Website); *Faith in the Future*, ch. 18.

21:11 But if a priest acquires a slave: *The Home We Build Together*, ch. 11; Behar: Evolution or Revolution? (C&C Leviticus); Article: "Giving and Belonging: The Lesson Jews Can Offer New Immigrants," *The Times*, October 2005.

21:32 Do not profane My holy name: Emor: On Not Being Afraid of Greatness (C&C LL).

21:32 In the midst of the Israelites: *Community of Faith*, ch. 10.

21:32 I am the LORD, who makes you holy: *To Heal a Fractured World*, ch. 5.

THE JEWISH CALENDAR: Emor: Holy Times (C&C SS).

23:3 Sabbath of complete rest: Emor: Three Versions of Shabbat (C&C Leviticus).

23:5 Passover: *The Jonathan Sacks Haggada*, p. 87.

COUNTING THE OMER: Emor: Counting Time (C&C Rabbi Sacks Website).

23:34 Festival of Tabernacles: Emor: Sukkot: The Dual Festival (C&C Leviticus).

23:43 I brought them out of the land of Egypt: Article: "In Memory of Yoni Jesner," *Jewish Telegraph*, September 2002.

23:44 The LORD's appointed times to the Israelites: Emor: In the Diary (C&C JLCI).

THE EXECUTION OF THE BLASPHEMER: Emor: The Blasphemer (C&C Leviticus).

24:20 An eye for an eye: Emor: The Blasphemer (C&C Leviticus); Ekev: The Morality of Love (C&C Deuteronomy).

24:22 There shall be one law: Emor: The Blasphemer (C&C Leviticus); Video: "Just Punishment and the Holocaust."

Behar

BEHAR: Introduction to Behar (C&C Leviticus).

25:1 On Mount Sinai: Leviticus: The Democratisation of Holiness (C&C Leviticus).

25:4 To the land a Sabbath: *The Koren Sacks Shalem Siddur*, introduction; Behar: The Chronological Imagination (C&C Leviticus); *The Jonathan Sacks Haggada*, pp. 32–33.

25:8 And you shall count: Behar: Think Long (C&C LL).

THE JUBILEE YEAR: Emor: Real Responsibilities (C&C Rabbi Sacks Website); Lecture: "Markets and Morals – The 1998 Hayek Lecture," June 1998.

25:14 [His] Brother: Behar: Family Feeling (C&C SS).

25:14 Brother must not cheat brother: *Faith in the Future*, ch. 28.

25:23 The land is Mine: Behar: Eminent Domain (C&C Leviticus).

REDEMPTION: Behar: The Concept of Redemption (C&C Leviticus).

25:29 The period of redemption: Emor: New Light on an Old Controversy (C&C Leviticus); *The Dignity of Difference*, ch. 5.

THE RIGHTS OF STRANGERS: Behar: Minority Rights (C&C Leviticus).

25:35 That he may live among you: *To Heal a Fractured World*, ch. 3; *Tradition in an Untraditional Age*, ch. 10.

25:44 Acquire a male or female slave: Behar: Evolution or Revolution? (C&C Leviticus).

Beḥukotai

SEFER BEMIDBAR

Bemidbar

Naso

Peace (C&C Numbers); *The Dignity of Difference,* ch. 3; *To Heal a Fractured World,* ch. 8.

5:23 Wash them off into the bitter water: Naso: Pursuing Peace (C&C Numbers); *To Heal a Fractured World,* ch. 8.

THE NAZIRITE: Naso: Sages and Saints (C&C Numbers).

6:4 Anything that comes from the grapevine: Naso: Sages and Saints (C&C Numbers).

THE PRIESTLY BLESSING: Naso: The Blessing of Love (C&C SS); Naso: The Priestly Blessings (C&C Numbers).

6:24 May the Lord bless you and watch over you: Naso: The Priestly Blessings (C&C Numbers).

6:25 May the Lord make His face shine upon you and be gracious to you: Naso: The Priestly Blessings (C&C Numbers).

6:26 May the Lord raise His face toward you and grant you peace: Naso: The Priestly Blessings (C&C Numbers).

6:27 I will bless them: Naso: The Priestly Blessings (C&C Numbers).

THE OFFERINGS OF THE PRINCES: Naso: Tribes (C&C Numbers).

7:18 On the second day: Naso: Pursuing Peace (C&C Numbers).

A LITANY OF GIFTS: Video: "On Living a Responsible Life," *J Insider* (March 2010); *Celebrating Life,* ch. 14; Video: "On Love as Deed" *J Insider* (March 2010).

7:89 When Moshe entered: Naso: The Politics of Envy (C&C LL); Naso: Pursuing Peace (C&C Numbers).

Behaalotekha

BEHAALOTEKHA: Numbers: Then and Now (C&C Numbers); Introduction to Behaalotekha (C&C Numbers).

LIGHTING THE CANDELABRUM: Video: "The Light of Judaism" (Rabbi Sacks Website).

8:3 Aharon did so: Behaalotekha: The Book Between the Books (C&C Numbers).

9:1 The first month of the second year: Video: "An Unforgiving Age" (Midnight Selichot 5779).

CONGREGATION AND CAMP: Behaalotekha: Camp and Congregation (C&C Numbers).

10:30 I will not come: Behaalotekha: Seventy Elders (C&C Numbers).

A BOOK BETWEEN THE BOOKS: Behaalotekha: The Book Between the Books (C&C Numbers).

10:35 When the Ark set out: Behaalotekha: The Book Between the Books (C&C Numbers).

11:1 The people began to rail bitterly: Behaalotekha: Miriam's Error (C&C Numbers).

11:6 Nothing at all but this manna: Behaalotekha: From Despair to Hope (C&C SS); *The Jonathan Sacks Haggada,* pp. 76–77.

11:12 As a nursemaid carries a baby: Behaalotekha: Is a Leader a Nursing Father? (C&C Numbers).

THE SEVENTY ELDERS: Behaalotekha: The Seventy Elders (C&C Numbers).

11:17 You will not have to bear it alone: Behaalotekha: Faith and Friendship (C&C JLCI).

11:29 The Lord would put His spirit upon them all: Behaalotekha: Power or Influence? (C&C LL).

11:30 Together with the elders of Israel: Behaalotekha: From Despair to Hope (C&C SS).

MIRIAM AND AHARON SPEAK ABOUT MOSHE: Behaalotekha: The Book Between the Books (C&C Numbers).

12:1 Because of his Kushite wife: Ki Tetzeh: Against Hate (C&C LL).

12:3 Now the man Moshe was very humble: Behaalotekha: From Pain to Humility (C&C EE).

12:7 Not so with Moshe: *Tradition in an Untraditional Age,* ch. 15.

12:13 Heal her now: Behaalotekha: Miriam's Error (C&C Numbers); *To Heal a Fractured World,* ch. 4.

Shelaḥ

SHELAḤ: Introduction to Shelaḥ (C&C Numbers).

THE SENDING OF THE SPIES: Shelaḥ: Confidence (C&C LL); *Tradition in an Untraditional Age,* ch. 12; *Future Tense,* ch. 10.

13:2 Men: Pinḥas: The Lost Masterpiece (C&C JLCI).

13:16 And Moshe named Hoshe'a... Yehoshua: Shelaḥ: What Made Yehoshua and Kalev Different? (C&C Numbers); Shelaḥ: Confidence (C&C LL).

13:28 The cities are fortified: Shelaḥ: Without Walls (C&C Numbers).

13:33 And so we were in theirs: Shelaḥ: Law and Narrative: Believing and Seeing (C&C Numbers); Shelaḥ: Confidence (C&C LL).

THE SPIES' REPORT: Shelaḥ: What Is Going On? (C&C Rabbi Sacks Website).

14:17 The LORD is slow to anger: *The Koren Sacks Yom Kippur Maḥzor*, pp. 122–123.

14:35 In this wilderness they shall come to their end: Shelaḥ: Time as a Factor in Politics (C&C Numbers).

14:41 It will not work: Shelaḥ: Freedom Needs Patience (C&C Rabbi Sacks Website).

15:15 You and the migrant shall be the same before the LORD: *The Jonathan Sacks Haggada*, p. 32.

15:26 Because all the people acted in error: *The Koren Sacks Yom Kippur Maḥzor*, pp. 74–75.

15:32 A man gathering wood on the Sabbath: *Tradition in an Untraditional Age*, ch. 10; Shelaḥ: Assembling Reminders (C&C EE).

TZITZIT: Shelaḥ: Law and Narrative: Believing and Seeing (C&C Numbers); *The Koren Sacks Rosh Hashana Maḥzor*, pp. 58–63.

15:38 Throughout the generations: Shelaḥ: Fringe Phenomena (C&C Numbers).

15:39 You shall remember: Shelaḥ: Assembling Reminders (C&C EE).

15:39 Your heart or of your eyes: Shelaḥ: Seeing What Isn't There (C&C JLCI).

Koraḥ

KORAḤ: Introduction to Koraḥ (C&C Numbers).

THE KORAḤ REBELLION: Koraḥ: Argument for the Sake of Heaven (C&C Numbers); Koraḥ: The First Populist (C&C JLCI); *Morality* , ch. 13; *Future Tense*, ch. 9.

16:1 Son of Kehat son of Levi: Koraḥ: Servant Leadership (C&C Numbers).

16:1 Descendants of Reuven: Koraḥ: Servant Leadership (C&C Numbers); Koraḥ: A Lesson in Conflict Resolution (C&C Rabbi Sacks Website).

16:1 Took: Koraḥ: A Cloak Entirely Blue (C&C Numbers).

16:3 All the community is holy, every one of them: Koraḥ: The Egalitarian Impulse in Judaism (C&C Numbers).

16:4 He fell upon his face: Koraḥ: Not Taking It Personally (C&C Numbers).

16:5 In the morning: Koraḥ: Not Taking It Personally (C&C Numbers).

16:10 Yet you seek the priesthood also: Koraḥ: Not Taking It Personally (C&C Numbers).

16:13 Out of a land flowing with milk and with honey: *Morality*, ch. 13.

16:15 Pay no attention to their offering: Koraḥ: Not Taking It Personally (C&C Numbers).

16:15 I have not taken a single donkey from them: Koraḥ: Not Taking It Personally (C&C Numbers).

THE NATURE OF THE ARGUMENT: Koraḥ: Argument for the Sake of Heaven (C&C Numbers); *Morality*, ch. 13; Koraḥ: The First Populist (C&C JLCI).

16:32 The earth opened its mouth: *The Koren Shalem Siddur*, pp. 668–71.

17:6 You have killed the LORD's people: Koraḥ: Argument for the Sake of Heaven (C&C Numbers).

17:11 Go quickly.... the plague has begun: *Faith in the Future*, ch. 31; *The Koren Shalem Siddur*, p. 153.

THE SIGN OF THE STAFFS: Koraḥ: A Lesson in Conflict Resolution (C&C Rabbi Sacks Website).

17:23 Bearing almonds: Koraḥ: Argument for the Sake of Heaven (C&C Numbers); Koraḥ: Not Taking It Personally (C&C Numbers).

18:6 I have singled out your brothers: Koraḥ: The Egalitarian Impulse in Judaism (C&C Numbers).

18:20 I am your share, your inheritance: *To Heal a Fractured World*, ch. 19.

Ḥukat

ḤUKAT: Introduction to Ḥukat (C&C Numbers).

THE DECREE OF THE LAW: Ḥukat: Kohelet, Tolstoy, and the Red Heifer (C&C JLCI).

THE RED HEIFER: Ḥukat: Kohelet, Tolstoy, and the Red Heifer (C&C JLCI); Ḥukat: The Consolations of Mortality (C&C Rabbi Sacks Website).

19:11 *Seven Days:* Ḥukat: Kohelet, Tolstoy, and the Red Heifer (C&C JLCI).

19:17 *Living water:* Ḥukat: Law and Narrative (C&C Rabbi Sacks Website).

MOSHE AND MIRIAM: Ḥukat: Miriam, Moshe's Friend (C&C LL); Healing the Trauma of Loss (C&C SS).

20:10 *Listen now, rebels:* Ḥukat: Anger Management (C&C EE).

MOSHE'S PUNISHMENT: Ḥukat: Why was Moses Not Destined to Enter the Land (C&C Rabbi Sacks Website); *Future Tense*, introduction.

20:29 *The whole House of Israel wept for Aharon for thirty days:* Ḥukat: Statute and Story (C&C Numbers).

THE BOOK OF THE WARS OF THE LORD: Ḥukat: Love in the End (C&C Numbers).

21:17 *Then the Israelites sang this song:* Haazinu, The Spirituality of Song (C&C Deuteronomy); Vayikra: Why do we sacrifice? (C&C Rabbi Sacks Website).

THE FIRST CONQUEST OF LAND: *Not in God's Name*, ch. 12.

Balak

BALAK: Introduction to Balak (C&C Numbers); Balak: The Hardest Word to Hear (C&C Numbers); Balak: The Man Without Loyalties (C&C Numbers).

BILAM THE PROPHET: Balak: The Man Without Loyalties (C&C Numbers).

22:5 *Bilam son of Beor who was at Petor near the River in his native land:* Balak: The Hardest Word to Hear (C&C Numbers).

22:6 *Stronger than I:* Balak: The Hardest Word to Hear (C&C Numbers).

22:20 *You may… go with them:* Balak: The Hardest Word to Hear (C&C Numbers).

22:33 *The donkey saw me:* Balak: What Makes God Laugh (C&C SS).

BILAM'S BLESSINGS: Balak: The Hidden Meaning of the Bilam Story (C&C Rabbi Sacks Website).

23:9 *A people that dwells alone:* Balak: The Curse of Loneliness (C&C Rabbi Sacks Website); *Future Tense*, ch. 1.

23:9 *Not reckoning itself among nations:* Balak: A People That Dwells Alone (C&C JLCI); Balak: The Curse of Loneliness (C&C Rabbi Sacks Website).

23:21 *He has seen no sin in Israel:* Balak: Let Someone Else Praise You (C&C Numbers).

24:2 *Bilam raised his eyes and saw:* *The Great Partnership*, ch. 10.

24:5 *Your homes, O Israel:* *Community of Faith*, ch. 2.

25:1 *To consort with Moabite women:* Balak: The Hidden Meaning of the Bilam Story (C&C Rabbi Sacks Website); Balak: Tragic Irony (C&C Numbers).

25:7 *He rose from the midst of the community:* Pinḥas: The Zealot (C&C Numbers); Balak: Tragic Irony (C&C Numbers).

THE END OF THE BAAL PEOR AFFAIR: Balak: Tragic Irony (C&C Numbers).

Pinḥas

PINḤAS: Introduction to Pinḥas (C&C Numbers).

PINḤAS THE ZEALOT: Pinḥas: The Zealot (C&C Numbers).

25:12 *My covenant of peace:* Pinḥas: Acts and Consequences (C&C Numbers); Pinḥas: Moral vs. Political Decisions (C&C Rabbi Sacks Website).

PREFACE TO THE SECOND CENSUS: *Will We Have Jewish Grandchildren?*, ch. 2; The Torah You Learn from Life: Introduction to Leadership (C&C Rabbi Sacks Website); Pinḥas: When Words Fail (C&C Numbers).

26:21 *Peretz's descendants:* *The Koren Sacks Shavuot Maḥzor*, introduction.

THE DAUGHTERS OF TZELOFḤAD: Pinḥas: The Lost Masterpiece (C&C JLCI); Video: "Questions Answered, Part 2"; Video: "Bridging the Divides: A Conversation with Yair Lapid."

27:12 *Ascend this mountain:* *Future Tense*, ch. 1.

MOSHE'S CONTINUITY: Pinḥas: Moshe's Disappointment (C&C SS); Pinḥas: The Crown All Can Wear (C&C Numbers).

27:16 God of the spirit of all flesh: Pinḥas: Lessons of a Leader (C&C LL).

27:16 Appoint a man: Pinḥas: Lessons of a Leader (C&C LL).

27:17 Who will lead them out and bring them home: Pinḥas: Leadership and the Art of Pacing (C&C Numbers).

27:18 Take Yehoshua son of Nun: Pinḥas: Lessons of a Leader (C&C LL).

27:19 Give him this charge: Pinḥas: Lessons of a Leader (C&C LL).

THE SACRIFICIAL YEAR: Leviticus: The Democratisation of Holiness (C&C Leviticus); *The Jonathan Sacks Haggada*, p. 17.

28:11 On your New Moons: *The Koren Shalem Siddur*, pp. 744–47.

28:26 The day of the first produce: *The Koren Sacks Shavuot Maḥzor*, introduction.

29:1 A day of the horn's sounding: *The Koren Sacks Rosh Hashana Maḥzor*, introduction

29:13 Thirteen young bulls: Emor: Sukkot, the Dual Festival (C&C Leviticus); *The Koren Sacks Sukkot Maḥzor*, introduction.

29:35 You shall hold an assembly: *The Koren Sacks Sukkot Maḥzor*, introduction.

Matot

MATOT: Matot: Priorities (C&C Numbers).

VOWS AND OATHS: Matot: The World We Make with Words (C&C Numbers).

30:3 Or takes an oath: Matot: Subject/Object (C&C JLCI).

30:3 Vow… oath… obligation: Matot: Oaths and Vows (C&C Rabbi Sacks Website); *Faith in the Future*, ch. 25.

30:6 If her father restrains her: *Faith in the Future*, introduction; *The Koren Sacks Sukkot Maḥzor*, pp. 826–27.

A WAR OF RETRIBUTION: *Not in God's Name*, ch. 1.

31:16 On Bilam's advice: Bereshit: Taking Responsibility (C&C LL); Balak: Tragic Irony (C&C Numbers).

31:23 Pass through the fire and it will be purified: *Future Tense*, ch. 9; Vayehi: Transforming the Story (C&C Rabbi Sacks Website).

THE NEGOTIATION: Matot: Priorities (C&C Numbers); Matot: Conflict Resolution (C&C LL).

32:6 Are your brothers to go… while you stay here?: Matot: Conflict Resolution (C&C LL).

32:16 Then they set forward: Matot: Priorities (C&C Numbers); Matot: Conflict Resolution (C&C LL)

32:20 If you do this: Matot: Conflict Resolution (C&C LL).

32:22 Be clear before the LORD and before Israel: Matot: Above Suspicion (C&C Numbers).

32:24 Towns for your children and pens for your flocks: Matot: Priorities (C&C Numbers).

Masei

MASEI: Introduction to Masei (C&C Numbers).

THESE WERE THE JOURNEYS: Masei: The Long Walk to Freedom (C&C Numbers); Numbers: Then and Now (C&C Numbers); *Faith in the Future*, introduction.

33:2 Every journey at the LORD's command: Masei: Miles to Go Before I Sleep (C&C JLCI).

33:5 Sukkot: *Faith in the Future*, ch. 23.

33:16 Kivrot HaTaava: Bemidbar: Law as Love (C&C EE).

33:48 They set out…. And camped: Masei: Miles to Go Before I Sleep (C&C JLCI).

THE LAND OF ISRAEL: Masei: The Religious Significance of Israel (C&C Numbers).

CITIES OF REFUGE: Masei: Retribution and Revenge (C&C EE).

34:11 Refuge cities: Mattot: My Teacher: In Memoriam (C&C Rabbi Sacks Website).

34:12 Ending at the Dead Sea: *To Heal a Fractured World*, ch. 3.

35:25 Until the death of the High Priest: Masei: The Death of the High Priest (C&C Numbers).

35:33 Blood pollutes the land: Masei: Individual and Community (C&C Numbers).

THE DAUGHTERS OF TZELOFḤAD – EPILOGUE: Masei: The Complexity of Human Rights (C&C Numbers).

NUMBERS: THE NARRATIVE STRUCTURE: Numbers: Then and Now (C&C Numbers); Bemidbar: The Ever-Repeated Story (C&C Rabbi Sacks Website).

SEFER DEVARIM

Devarim

THE BOOK OF DEUTERONOMY: Devarim: Words (C&C Rabbi Sacks Website).

DEVARIM: Devarim: The World We Make with Words (C&C Deuteronomy).

"THESE ARE THE WORDS": Devarim: Words (C&C Rabbi Sacks Website); Vaethanan: The First Commandment (C&C Rabbi Sacks Website).

1:1 All Israel: Devarim: The Birth of a Nation (C&C Rabbi Sacks Website).

1:1 Di Zahav: Devarim: Counsel for the Defence (C&C Deuteronomy).

1:5 Moshe began to expound this Law: Devarim: The Teacher as Hero (C&C Deuteronomy).

1:12 How can I bear alone: The Birth of a Nation (C&C Rabbi Sacks Website).

1:16 Judge fairly: Devarim: Why Are There So Many Jewish Lawyers? (C&C EE).

1:17 Do not show partiality in judgment: *The Koren Sacks Shavuot Maḥzor*, p. ixx; *Ceremony & Celebration*, p. 315.

1:17 Judgment belongs to God: Devarim: *Tzedek*: Justice Tempered by Compassion (C&C Deuteronomy).

RETELLING THE STORY OF THE SPIES: Devarim: The First Follower (C&C Rabbi Sacks Website).

1:37 The LORD was enraged even with me: Devarim: The First Follower (C&C Rabbi Sacks Website).

2:10 As tall as the Anakites: *The Jonathan Sacks Haggada*, pp. 38–39.

2:26 I sent messengers… to Siḥon, king of Ḥeshbon, with an offer of peace: *Not in God's Name*, ch. 12.

2:29 Just as the descendants of Esav living in Se'ir… did for us: Toledot: The Other Face of Esau (C&C Rabbi Sacks Website).

3:12 I gave to the Reubenites and Gadites the territory: Mattot: Conflict Resolution (C&C LL).

3:21 I charged Yehoshua: Devarim: The Leader as Teacher (C&C LL).

Vaetḥanan

VAETḤANAN: Introduction to Vaetḥanan (C&C Deuteronomy); Vaetḥanan: The Power of Why (C&C SS).

3:26 And would not listen to me: *Letters to the Next Generation*, Letter 12.

IN THE EYES OF THE PEOPLES: *Future Tense*, ch. 4; Vaetḥanan: In the Eyes of the Nations (C&C Deuteronomy).

4:6 A wise and understanding people: *Future Tense*, ch. 10.

4:12 There was only a voice: Vaetḥanan: Listening Is an Art (C&C Deuteronomy).

4:32 Has anything… happened before: *The Jonathan Sacks Haggada*, pp. 36–37.

4:32 Has anyone heard of anything like this?: *Will We Have Jewish Grandchildren?*, ch. 1.

THE TEN COMMANDMENTS: Vaetḥanan: Philosophy or Prophecy? (C&C Rabbi Sacks Website).

5:6 Out of the house of slaves: Vaetḥanan: Philosophy or Prophecy? (C&C Rabbi Sacks Website).

5:14 Do no work at all: Deuteronomy: Covenant Society (C&C Deuteronomy).

5:19 And He added no more: *The Koren Sacks Shavuot Maḥzor*, p. xxxix; *Ceremony & Celebration*, p. 283; Video: "Conversation with Daniel Taub – Not in God's Name: Confronting Religious Violence."

LISTEN: Vaetḥanan: The Meanings of *Shema* (C&C Deuteronomy); *The Koren Shalem Siddur*, pp. 470–71.

6:4 The LORD is one: *The Koren Sacks Yom Kippur Maḥzor*, p. 1196.

LOVE: Vaetḥanan: Making Love Last (C&C JLCI).

6:5 With all your heart: *The Jonathan Sacks Haggada*, p. 40.

6:6 Impressed upon your heart: *The Home We Build Together*, ch. 9.

*6:7 **Teach them to your children:*** Devarim: The Teacher as Hero (C&C Deuteronomy); *Will We Have Jewish Grandchildren?*, ch. 9.

*6:8 **Bind them as a sign:*** *The Koren Shalem Siddur*, pp. 14–15.

*6:16 **Do not test the Lord your God:*** *The Great Partnership*, ch. 4.

THE RIGHT AND THE GOOD: Vaetḥanan: The Right and the Good (C&C EE).

*7:7 **You are the smallest of all peoples:*** Vaetḥanan: Why Is the Jewish People So Small? (C&C Deuteronomy).

*7:9 **Keeps His covenant and the love:*** Video: "A Life of Vertical and Horizontal Responsibility: Shavuot During the Coronavirus Pandemic," May 2020.

Ekev

EKEV: Introduction to Ekev (C&C Deuteronomy)

GOD OF LOVE: Ekev: The Morality of Love (C&C Deuteronomy).

*7:17 **These nations are more numerous:*** Vaetḥanan: The Fewest of All Peoples (C&C LIL); *Letters to the Next Generation*, Letter 2.

*7:18 **Remember well:*** Ekev: The Politics of Memory (C&C Deuteronomy).

*8:10 **You shall bless the Lord your God:*** *The Jonathan Sacks Haggada*, pp. 102–5.

*8:17 **My power, the strength of my own hand:*** Ekev: The Power of Gratitude (C&C EE).

*8:18 **It is He who gives you the power:*** Ekev: The Politics of Memory (C&C Deuteronomy).

*9:4 **Because of their own wickedness:*** *Not in God's Name*, ch. 11.

*9:5 **Not for your righteousness:*** *Not in God's Name*, ch. 11.

*9:6 **You are a stiff-necked people:*** *Future Tense*, ch. 9.

*9:7 **You have always been rebellious against the Lord:*** Devarim: The Effective Critic (C&C JLCI).

*9:20 **I prayed for Aharon also at that time:*** Ki Tisa: How Leaders Fail (C&C LIL).

MOSHE'S PRAYER: *The Koren Sacks Shalem Siddur*, pp. 142–45.

LOVE WITH JUSTICE: Ekev: The Morality of Love (C&C Deuteronomy).

*10:19 **You too must love the stranger:*** Ekev: Greatness and Humility (C&C Deuteronomy).

THE CONDITIONAL PROSPERITY OF THE LAND: *Future Tense*, ch. 7.

*11:13 **If you heed:*** Ekev: Listen, Really Listen (C&C JLCI).

*11:19 **Teach them:*** *To Heal a Fractured World*, ch. 2.

*11:19 **To your children:*** Ekev: A Nation of Educators (C&C Deuteronomy).

*11:22 **Holding fast to Him:*** *Tradition in an Untraditional Age*, ch. 11.

*11:23 **Larger and mightier than you:*** *The Dignity of Difference*, ch. 4.

Re'eh

RE'EH: Introduction to Re'eh (C&C Deuteronomy).

*11:26 **See this:*** Re'eh: Seeing and Hearing (C&C Rabbi Sacks Website).

THE CHOICE: Re'eh: The Politics of Freedom (C&C Deuteronomy).

*11:32 **To keep all the decrees and laws:*** Re'eh: Defining Reality (C&C LIL).

*12:7 **Rejoicing:*** Re'eh: The Deep Power of Joy (C&C SIS); Re'eh: Defining Reality (C&C LIL).

*12:8 **Right in his own eyes:*** *Faith in the Future*, chs.2, 7.

*12:11 **Choice gifts that you commit by vow to the Lord:*** Re'eh: The Second Tithe and the Making of a Strong Society (C&C EE); *The Koren Sacks Sukkot Maḥzor*, p. 1092.

CENTRALIZED SACRIFICE, "SECULAR" SLAUGHTER: *To Heal a Fractured World*, ch. 18.

*12:18 **Along with your sons and daughters, your male and female servants:*** Re'eh: Collective Joy (C&C Deuteronomy).

*13:4 **Do not listen to the words of that prophet:*** Nitzavim: Not in Heaven (C&C Deuteronomy); Shofetim: The Sage Is Greater than the Prophet (C&C Rabbi Sacks Website).

13:15 Seek the truth, investigate, and inquire thoroughly: Video: "Post-Truth and the Erosion of Trust," June 2017.

13:17 It shall be an eternal ruin: *Not in God's Name,* ch. 12; Shofetim: Environmental Responsibility (C&C EE).

PROHIBITED MOURNING RITES: Re'eh: The Limits of Grief (C&C Rabbi Sacks Website).

14:1 You are children of the LORD your God: *The Koren Sacks Rosh Hashana Maḥzor,* pp. 718–19.

KOSHER AND NON-KOSHER ANIMALS: Shemini: The Integrity of Nature (C&C Leviticus).

14:21 In the milk of its mother: *The Dignity of Difference,* ch. 9.

14:23 You may learn to hold the LORD your God in awe always: Re'eh: The Second Tithe and the Making of a Strong Society (C&C EE).

15:1 A remission of debts: *The Koren Sacks Sukkot Maḥzor,* pp. 1094–95; Behar: The Chronological Imagination (C&C Leviticus).

15:4 The land that the LORD your God is giving you to possess: *The Dignity of Difference,* ch. 9.

LAWS OF *TZEDAKA*: Re'eh: The Untranslatable Virtue (C&C Deuteronomy); *To Heal a Fractured World,* ch. 3.

15:8 To answer all his needs: Re'eh: The Psychology of Dignity (C&C Deuteronomy); Re'eh: The Untranslatable Virtue (C&C Deuteronomy).

15:9 You will be held guilty: *Wealth and Poverty,* pp. 6–7.

THE THREE PILGRIMAGE FESTIVALS: Emor: Holy Times (C&C SIS); *The Koren Sacks Sukkot Maḥzor,* pp. 1092–93.

16:15 You shall be wholly joyful: Re'eh: Insecurity and Joy (C&C Deuteronomy).

Shofetim

SHOFETIM: Introduction to Shofetim (C&C Deuteronomy).

16:18 Appoint judges: Vayishlaḥ: Collective Responsibility (C&C Rabbi Sacks Website).

"PURSUE JUSTICE": *Faith in the Future,* ch. 1; Devarim: *Tzedek*: Justice and Compassion (C&C Rabbi Sacks Website); *To Heal a Fractured World,* ch. 2.

17:3 By going off to serve: *To Heal a Fractured World,* ch. 19.

17:9 Inquire of them: *Faith in the Future,* ch. 6; *The Great Partnership,* epilogue.

SELECTING A MONARCH: *The Dignity of Difference,* ch. 5; Shofetim: To Lead Is to Serve (C&C JLCI).

17:17 Nor should he amass large amounts of silver and gold: Shofetim: Greatness Is Humility (C&C Rabbi Sacks Website).

17:19 He shall read from it all the days of his life: Shofetim: Learning and Leadership (C&C LIL).

17:20 Not considering himself superior to his people: Shofetim: The Greatness of Humility (C&C SIS).

17:20 Then he and his descendants will reign long: *The Dignity of Difference,* ch. 10; Shofetim: The Three Crowns (C&C Deuteronomy).

18:10 Let no one be found among you... who casts spells: Vaera: Of Lice and Men (C&C Rabbi Sacks Website).

18:21 How can we recognize a message that the LORD has not spoken? Shofetim: True and False Prophets (C&C Deuteronomy).

19:5 That man may flee to one of these cities and live: Masei: Individual and Community (C&C Numbers).

19:11 If one person hates his fellow: *Future Tense,* ch. 9.

19:19 You must purge the evil from your midst: *Morality,* ch. 11.

THE PROHIBITION OF DESTROYING FRUIT TREES: Shofetim: The Ecological Imperative (C&C Deuteronomy); *Faith in the Future,* ch. 29.

20:19 You must not cut them down: Shofetim: The Ecological Imperative (C&C Deuteronomy).

20:19 Are trees of the field human beings: *Faith in the Future,* ch. 29.

21:7 Our hands did not shed this blood: "We Have to Ask the Wider Question of Moral Responsibility" (BBC Radio 4's *Thought for the Day,* August 2015); Vayishlaḥ: Collective Responsibility (C&C Rabbi Sacks Website).

Ki Tetzeh

KI TETZEH: Ki Tetzeh: Animal Welfare (C&C Deuteronomy).

21:10 When you wage war: *Not in God's Name*, ch. 12; *Faith in the Future*, ch. 14.

21:11 A beautiful woman among the captives: Ki Tetzeh: Love Is Not Enough (C&C Deuteronomy).

LAW AND LOVE: Ki Tetzeh: Love Is Not Enough (C&C Deuteronomy).

21:15 Loves one but not the other: Ḥayei Sara: Parental Authority and the Choice of a Marriage Partner (C&C Genesis); "Marriage as a Metaphor for our Relationship with God," *The Times*, April 2003.

THE WAYWARD AND REBELLIOUS SON: Ki Tetzeh: Stubborn and Rebellious Sons (C&C Deuteronomy); *Tradition in an Untraditional Age*, ch. 10.

22:4 Help him to lift it: Ki Tetzeh: Social Capital and Fallen Donkeys (C&C JLCI).

LAWS OF A BIRD'S NEST: Ki Tetzeh: Animal Welfare (C&C Deuteronomy).

22:9 A second kind of seed: *Faith in the Future*, ch. 29.

23:4 Even to the tenth generation: *The Koren Sacks Shavuot Maḥzor*. p. lxvi; *Ceremony and Celebration*, p. 310; *Not in God's Name*, ch. 12.

23:8 Do not despise an Edomite: Ki Tetzeh: Against Hate (C&C LIL).

23:8 Do not despise an Egyptian, for you lived as a stranger in his land: *Not in God's Name*, ch. 14; Ki Tetzeh: Letting Go (C&C Deuteronomy).

23:9 In the third generation: *The Dignity of Difference*, ch. 10.

23:13 Designate an area outside the camp: *Faith in the Future*, ch. 29.

23:16 Do not hand him back: *To Heal a Fractured World*, ch. 3.

23:20 Do not charge interest on loans to your kinsmen: *The Dignity of Difference*, ch. 8; *Faith in the Future*, ch. 28.

24:5 Bring happiness to the woman he has married: Tazria: The Circumcision of Desire (C&C EE); *The Home We Build Together*, ch. 18; *Radical Then, Radical Now*, ch. 7.

24:14 Poor and destitute laborer: *The Jonathan Sacks Haggada*, pp. 31–32.

24:16 A person shall be put to death only for his own sin: Ki Tetzeh: To the Third and Fourth Generations (C&C EE).

24:18 Remember that you were a slave: *The Koren Sacks Pesaḥ Maḥzor*, pp. xxii–xxvi; *Faith in the Future*, ch. 13.

24:19 Leave it for the migrant, the orphan, and the widow: *To Heal a Fractured World*, ch. 8; Video: "The Challenge to Faith in the Twenty-First Century," lecture at the University of Dallas, 2014.

25:3 Your kinsman will be degraded in your eyes: Ki Tetzeh: Rehabilitation of Offenders (C&C Deuteronomy).

25:4 Do not muzzle an ox while it is treading out the grain: Ki Tetzeh: Animal Welfare (C&C Deuteronomy).

THE LAST OF THE ETHICAL COMMANDMENTS: *To Heal a Fractured World*, ch. 8.

AMALEK: Ki Tetzeh: Hate: Curable and Incurable (C&C Deuteronomy).

Ki Tavo

KI TAVO: Introduction to Ki Tavo (C&C Deuteronomy).

THE CEREMONY OF THE FIRST FRUITS: Ki Tavo: History and Memory (C&C Deuteronomy).

26:2 Some of every first fruit of the soil: Ki Tavo: The Greatest Challenge (C&C Deuteronomy); Ki Tavo: A Sense of History (C&C Rabbi Sacks Website).

26:5 My ancestor was a wandering Aramean: *The Jonathan Sacks Haggada*, pp. 46–49.

26:5 There he became a nation: *The Jonathan Sacks Haggada*, pp. 50–53.

26:11 Then you, with the Levites and the migrants… shall rejoice: Re'eh: Collective Joy (C&C Deuteronomy).

26:17 You have proclaimed: Ki Tavo: Covenant and Conversation (C&C Deuteronomy).

27:3 And write on them: *The Home We Build Together*, ch. 14; Ki Tavo: A Nation of Storytellers (C&C LIL).

27:8 Very clearly: *Not in God's Name*, ch. 12.

27:9 Be still and listen: Ki Tavo: Listening and Moral Growth (C&C Deuteronomy).

CURSES AND BLESSINGS: Deuteronomy: Covenant Society (C&C introduction), p. 12; *Morality*, ch. 21.

28:5 Your basket and your kneading pan: *The Dignity of Difference,* ch. 5; Ki Tavo: The Pursuit of Joy (C&C EE).

28:9 Walk in His ways: Kedoshim: Being Holy (C&C Leviticus); *To Heal a Fractured World,* ch. 2.

THE *TOKHEḤA*: Ki Tavo: Judaism's Greatest Challenge (C&C Rabbi Sacks Website); Ki Tavo: The Blessing and the Curse (C&C Deuteronomy).

28:33 A people… will eat the fruit… of your labor: *To Heal a Fractured World,* chs. 3, 16.

28:47 Because you did not serve the LORD your God with joy: Ki Tavo: The Pursuit of Joy (C&C EE); Ki Tavo: Judaism's Greatest Challenge (C&C Rabbi Sacks Website).

28:48 The enemies whom the LORD will send against you: Ki Tavo: The Blessing and the Curse (C&C Deuteronomy).

28:54 Will begrudge food: *The Jonathan Sacks Haggada,* pp. 24–25.

28:65 No resting place: *To Heal a Fractured World,* ch. 2.

28:69 The covenant that He had made with them: Ki Tavo: The Blessing and the Curse (C&C Deuteronomy).

Nitzavim

NITZAVIM: Introduction to Nitzavim (C&C Deuteronomy).

29:9 All of you: Community of Faith, ch. 9.

A CHOICE FOR THE GENERATIONS: Nitzavim: Why Judaism? (C&C EE); *Radical Then, Radical Now,* ch. 1.

29:17 Let there be among you no root: *Future Tense,* ch. 8.

29:28 Hidden things belong to the LORD: *Future Tense,* ch. 11.

RETURN: Nitzavim: Two Concepts of *Teshuva* (C&C Deuteronomy).

NOT IN HEAVEN: *To Heal a Fractured World,* ch. 2; *The Great Partnership,* ch. 10.

30:12 Not in heaven: Nitzavim: Not in Heaven (C&C Deuteronomy).

GOD IS CLOSE: Nitzavim: Not Beyond the Sea (C&C Deuteronomy).

30:16 Survive and thrive: *From Renewal to Responsibility,* "An Open Letter to British Jewry."

30:19 Choose life: Nitzavim: The Fourteenth Principle of Faith (C&C Deuteronomy); Nitzavim: Why Judaism? (C&C EE).

Vayelekh

VAYELEKH: Introduction to Vayelekh (C&C Deuteronomy).

COMMAND AND CONSENSUS: Vayelekh: Leadership: Consensus or Command? (C&C Deuteronomy).

THE *HAK'HEL* CEREMONY: Vayelekh: How to Renew a Nation (C&C Rabbi Sacks Website); Vayelekh: Covenantal Politics (C&C Rabbi Sacks Website).

31:12 Assemble the people: Vayelekh: How to Renew a Nation (C&C Rabbi Sacks Website).

31:12 Men, women, and children… migrants: Video: "The Home of the Book for the People of the Book," May 2014.

31:13 Their children, who do not know it: *Future Tense,* ch. 8; Vayelekh: To Renew Our Days (C&C Deuteronomy); Vayelekh: Covenantal Politics (C&C Rabbi Sacks Website).

THE HIDING OF GOD'S FACE: *Faith in the Future,* chs. 14, 33.

31:18 At that time: *Crisis and Covenant,* ch. 2.

"WRITE THIS SONG": Vayelekh: The Singers and the Song (C&C Rabbi Sacks Website); Vayelekh: The Torah as God's Song (C&C Deuteronomy).

Haazinu

HAAZINU: Introduction to Haazinu (C&C Deuteronomy).

THE END OF THE COVENANT DOCUMENT: Deuteronomy: Covenant Society (C&C Deuteronomy).

MOSHE'S SONG: Haazinu: The Spirituality of Song (C&C Deuteronomy); Haazinu: Emotional Intelligence (C&C JLCI); Humanitas Lecture 2 (2012).

Vezot Haberakha

NUMBER OF VERSES PER PARASHA

BERESHIT/GENESIS

Bereshit	146 pesukim	Vayetze	148 pesukim
Noaḥ	153 pesukim	Vayishlaḥ	153 pesukim
Lekh Lekha	126 pesukim	Vayeshev	112 pesukim
Vayera	147 pesukim	Miketz	146 pesukim
Ḥayei Sara	105 pesukim	Vayigash	106 pesukim
Toledot	106 pesukim	Vayeḥi	85 pesukim

SHEMOT/EXODUS

Shemot	124 pesukim	Teruma	96 pesukim
Vaera	121 pesukim	Tetzaveh	101 pesukim
Bo	106 pesukim	Ki Tisa	139 pesukim
Beshalaḥ	116 pesukim	Vayak'hel	122 pesukim
Yitro	75 pesukim	Pekudei	92 pesukim
Mishpatim	118 pesukim		

VAYIKRA/LEVITICUS

Vayikra	111 pesukim	Aḥarei Mot	80 pesukim
Tzav	97 pesukim	Kedoshim	64 pesukim
Shemini	91 pesukim	Emor	124 pesukim
Tazria	67 pesukim	Behar	57 pesukim
Metzora	90 pesukim	Beḥukotai	78 pesukim

BEMIDBAR/NUMBERS

Bemidbar	159 pesukim	Ḥukat	87 pesukim
Naso	176 pesukim	Balak	104 pesukim
Behaalotekha	136 pesukim	Pinḥas	168 pesukim
Shelaḥ	119 pesukim	Matot	112 pesukim
Koraḥ	95 pesukim	Masei	132 pesukim

DEVARIM/DEUTERONOMY

Devarim	105 pesukim	Ki Tavo	122 pesukim
Vaetḥanan	122 pesukim	Nitzavim	40 pesukim
Ekev	111 pesukim	Vayelekh	30 pesukim
Re'eh	126 pesukim	Haazinu	52 pesukim
Shofetim	97 pesukim	Vezot Haberakha	41 pesukim
Ki Tetzeh	110 pesukim		

KOREN